IN LOVING MEMORY OF

Dr. William R. Bright

1921-2003

"We can trace

all of our human problems

to our view of God."

DR. BILL BRIGHT

Presented to

---

by

---

on the occasion of

---

date

Welcome to the Discover God Study Bible

Dear Friends,

My husband, Bill Bright, believed that there is nothing more important in life than discovering who God really is. That is why he has repeatedly said over the years, "The most important thing we can teach another believer is who God is."

Therefore, it is with a sense of deep joy and reverential awe that I introduce you to the *Discover God Study Bible.*

Everything about our lives—our attitudes, motives, desires, actions, and even our words—is influenced by our view of God. Our behavior reflects our beliefs about the One who created us.

Do you really trust God? It depends a lot on how you view God. Do you really believe He is good? Are you convinced He loves you unconditionally? Do you honestly believe He is worthy of your trust?

The Bible is the place we mere humans meet the living God. It is God's book written to us. Bill said that when he began to study the Bible, he discovered for the first time the real, living God—and what he discovered filled his heart with awe.

No one meets the God of the Bible and is unchanged. Both Bill and I want as many people as possible to truly discover who God really is through His Word and reflect His character in their lives.

To help people in the discovery process, we commissioned a team of Bible teachers and scholars to organize Scripture into ten core teachings of the Bible in a convenient TopicGuide (starting on page A7).

But the greatest distinctive of this Bible is that the lessons Bill learned during 50 years of ministry are clearly incorporated throughout—lessons that enabled him to live supernaturally, empowered by the Spirit of God. The result was Campus Crusade for Christ (in over 191 countries), *The Jesus Film* (viewed by over 5 billion people) and *The Four Spiritual Laws* (2.5 billion copies distributed), a great marriage (of which I was the primary beneficiary), but most importantly, an intimate and powerful relationship with the living God.

I pray this physical result of Bill's life-long vision to know and serve God will bear fruit in your life—just as it has touched my life in a deep way.

Lovingly,

Vonette Bright

THE TOPICGUIDE™

YOUR ESSENTIAL GUIDE TO THE BIBLE'S 10 KEY THEMES

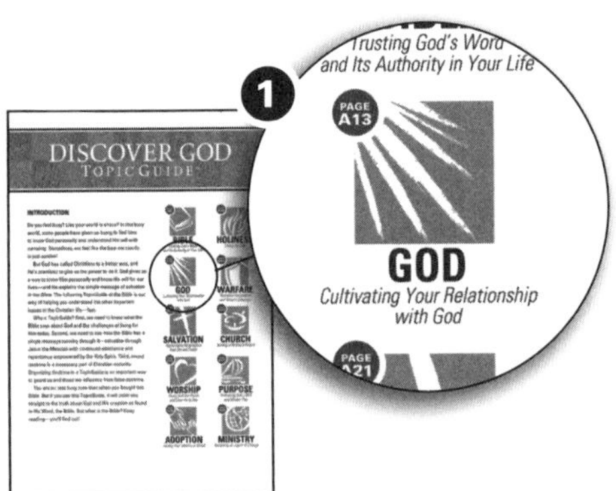

Begin with the TopicGuide (page A7) and select one of ten themes. In this example, we will study the theme of **GOD.**

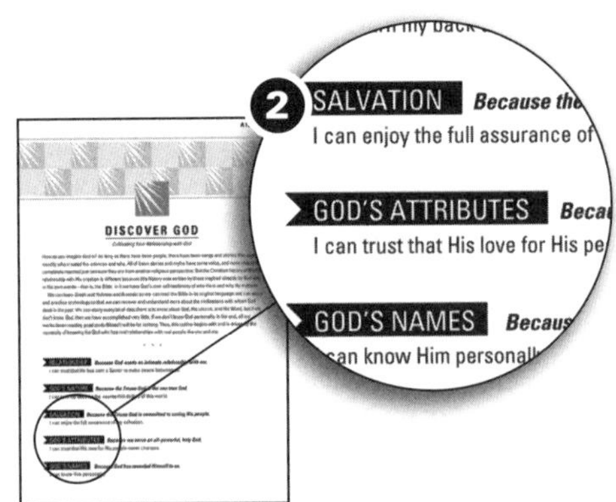

To read the overview of your selected theme, turn to page A13. Select a topic. In this example, we have selected **GOD'S ATTRIBUTES.**

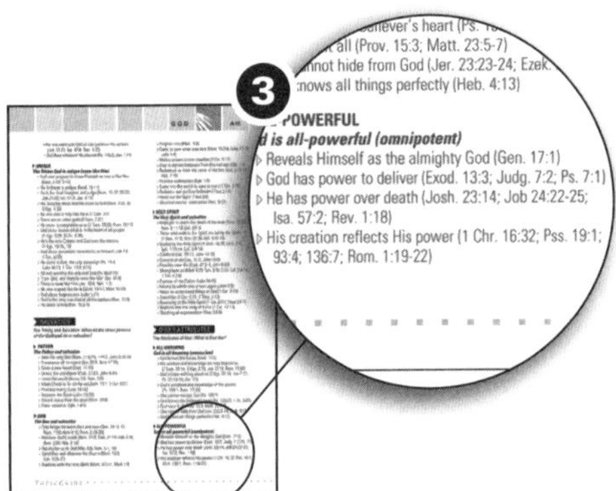

Identify a key topic and subtopic. Read and study each passage to gain a comprehensive understanding of God's Word. In this example, under **God's Attributes,** we are looking up the subtopic called **"All-Powerful"** and are interested in "His creation reflects His power" (Psalm 19:1-4).

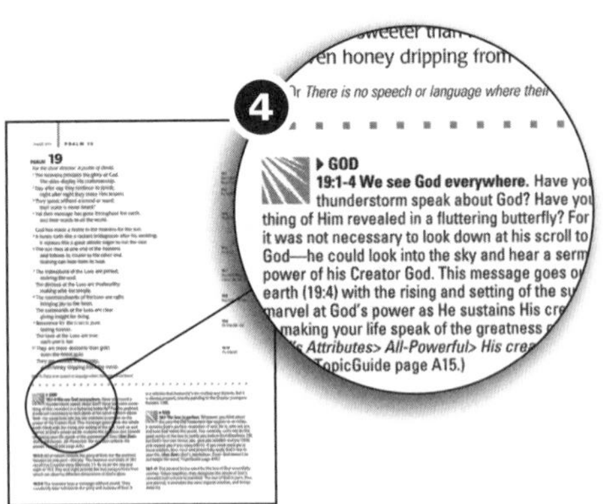

To gain understanding of the subtopic and your theme, read the related verses and study notes. Then refer turn back to the TopicGuide to locate the next related passage.

THE TOPICLINK™ SYSTEM

HOW TO FIND MORE ABOUT A THEME WHILE READING THROUGH THE BIBLE

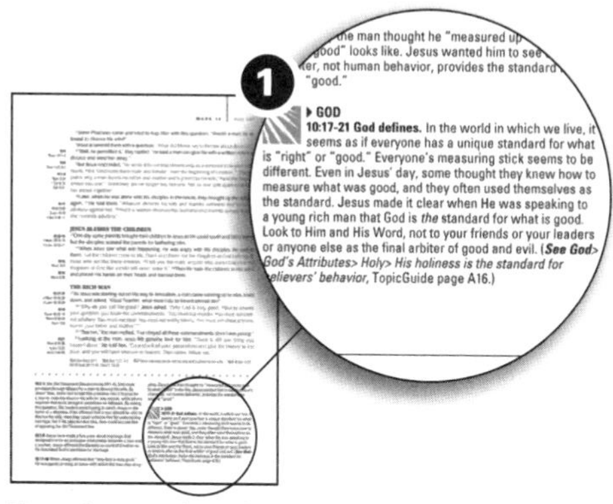

To study more about the theme of God when you are reading Mark 10, simply look at the last sentence of the note, which will refer you back to the TopicGuide.

Once in the TopicGuide, you'll see numerous passages pertaining to the overall theme.

Using both the TopicGuide and the TopicLink study tools, you will gain a more complete understanding of God's Word. As you understand these themes and your knowledge of God grows, your life can't help but be changed.

No one meets the God of the Bible and goes unchanged!

DISCOVER GOD TOPIC GUIDE™

INTRODUCTION

Do you feel busy? Like your world is chaos? In this busy world, some people have given up trying to find time to know God personally and understand His will with certainty. Sometimes, we feel like the best we can do is just survive!

But God has called Christians to a better way, and He's promised to give us the power to do it. God gives us a way to know Him personally and know His will for our lives—and He explains the simple message of salvation in the Bible. The following TopicGuide of the Bible is our way of helping you understand the other important issues in the Christian life—fast.

Why a TopicGuide? First, we need to know what the Bible says about God and the challenges of living for Him today. Second, we need to see how the Bible has a single message running through it—salvation through Jesus the Messiah with continued obedience and repentance empowered by the Holy Spirit. Third, sound doctrine is a necessary part of Christian maturity. Organizing doctrine in a TopicGuide is an important way to guard us and those we influence from false doctrine.

You are no less busy now than when you bought this Bible. But if you use this TopicGuide, it will point you straight to the truth about God and His creation as found in His Word, the Bible. But what is the Bible? Keep reading—you'll find out!

DISCOVER THE BIBLE

Trusting God's Word and Its Authority in Your Life

People have markedly different opinions about the Bible. It's hard not to have an opinion about the most popular book of all time, with between 6 and 7 billion copies printed so far.

In this section of the outline, you will learn what the Bible teaches about itself. This sets it apart from every other book—that throughout its pages, you never read a word of doubt about its divine origin or absolute trustworthiness. On the contrary, it persistently asserts both—and much, much more.

Many well-intended people have argued with the Bible's claims and promises. Entire organizations have been formed to discover and publicize the contradictions in the Bible. But after almost two thousand years of attacks, the Bible stands firm—in fact, the more it is tried, the more it shows itself as superior to any other work of literature.

As you study this outline of what the Bible teaches about itself, you will realize that if the Bible is trustworthy, then we must take seriously its claim that it is *more than trustworthy*—it is the very Word of God, to you, to the church, and for the world.

■ ■ ■

UNIQUENESS ***Because the Bible is unique—flawless, authoritative, and inspired by God—***
I can trust it as the perfect guide for faith and obedience.

UNITY ***Because the Bible contains one unified message,***
I will find God's one message for humanity in its pages.

POWER ***Because the Bible is life-changing and powerful,***
I can depend on it to equip me for life in the real world.

UNIQUENESS

The Uniqueness of the Bible: *What makes the Bible a supernatural Book, different from all other books?*

▶ AUTHORITATIVE

The Bible is authoritative (trustworthy)

- ▷ Demands heart obedience (Num. 15:22; 1 Sam. 3:1; Matt. 5:27-28)
- ▷ Demands repentance (2 Sam. 3:12; Isa. 55:7; Matt. 4:17)
- ▷ Demonstrates credibility (1 Kgs. 16:5; 1 Chr. 4:22; Ezek. 12:22; Dan. 9:2; Luke 16:29-31; 2 Cor. 7:15)
- ▷ All-sufficient (1 Chr. 20:1; Matt. 4:4, 7, 10; Luke 16:19-31)
- ▷ Demands exclusive allegiance (Jer. 48:7; Matt. 4:10; Acts 19:13-20)

▶ FLAWLESS

The Bible is flawless (inerrant)

- ▷ God's Word leaves some puzzles (Exod. 12:37)
- ▷ Scripture is sure and convincing (Prov. 30:5; Jer. 27:14; 43:2-3; 2 Pet. 1:19)
- ▷ God's Word abides forever (Isa. 40:8; 1 Jn. 2:24-25)
- ▷ Scripture is indestructible (John 10:35)
- ▷ God cannot lie (Heb. 6:18)

▶ INSPIRED

The Bible is inspired by God (breathed out)

- ▷ Written by God's finger (Exod. 31:18)
- ▷ A record of God's own words (Lev. 1:1; Num. 33:2; Deut. 1:1; Matt. 22:29)
- ▷ Internally consistent (Num. 1:44; Ps. 119:105)
- ▷ His promises never fail (Deut. 7:7-8; 28:1; 2 Sam. 7:29; 2 Chr. 36:17; Ps. 146:6; Acts 27:44; Phil. 3:12; 1 Pet. 1:4)
- ▷ Divinely inspired (Zech. 7:12; 2 Tim. 3:16)

UNITY

The Unity of Scripture: *The Bible is one book rather than sixty-six books.*

▶ AUTHORS

The message is uniform despite multiple authors (Deut. 2:12)

- ▷ The fullness of salvation revealed to Old Testament prophets (Isa. 53:1; 1 Pet. 1:10-12)
- ▷ Old Testament prophets predict Christ's sufferings (Luke 24:25-26)
- ▷ Jesus affirmed the unity of Scripture (John 5:46)

▶ CHRIST

Unity of Scripture in the theme of Christ

- ▷ Christ in the promise to Abraham (Gen. 22:11-12; 2 Sam. 5:12; Matt. 1:1-16; Gal. 3:6-9)
- ▷ Christ in the body of Jacob (Gen. 32:26)
- ▷ Christ in Moses the deliverer (Exod. 3:10)
- ▷ Christ in Samson's self-sacrificing victory (Judg. 13:3; 16:28-31)
- ▷ Christ is "mercy" (1 Sam. 9:16; 1 Kgs. 1:51; John 3:16)
- ▷ Christ is the "LORD of Heaven's Armies" (1 Sam. 17:37; Hag. 1:2)
- ▷ Christ in the wisdom of Solomon (1 Kgs. 3:24; Prov. 4:7; 9:10)
- ▷ Christ in Elijah's judgment (1 Kgs. 18)
- ▷ Christ is the "LORD God of Heaven's Armies" (2 Kgs. 3:17; Amos 3:13)
- ▷ Christ is the "suffering servant" (Isa. 53:10; Mark 10:46-52)
- ▷ Christ is "redemption" (Hos. 13:14)
- ▷ Christ is the "day of the LORD" (Joel 2:11)
- ▷ Christ is the "LORD" (Obad. 1:1; Mic. 6:1; John 13:13)
- ▷ Christ is our "strong refuge" (Nah. 1:7)
- ▷ Christ is "salvation" (Hab. 3:8)
- ▷ Christ is the "God of Israel" (Zeph. 2:9; Phil. 2:8-9)
- ▷ Christ is the "Branch" (Ezek. 17:22-24; Zech. 3:8-9)
- ▷ Christ is the "messenger" (Mal. 3:1)
- ▷ Christ is the "descendant of David" (Matt. 1:1)

▶ COVENANTS

Unity of Scripture in the theme of covenants

- ▷ Adamic covenant (Gen. 2:15-17)
- ▷ Universal covenant [with nature] (Gen. 9:1-6)
- ▷ Covenant of grace (Gen. 17:1-2, 7)
- ▷ Sinaitic covenant (Exod. 19:5-6)
- ▷ New Covenant (New Testament)

▶ CREATION

Unity of Scripture in Creation (Rom. 1:19-22)

- ▷ The beginning (Gen. 1:1-27)
- ▷ Creation and marriage (Song 4:12; Jer. 44:15-19; 1 Cor. 6:14-20; Eph. 5:24-25, 31-32)
- ▷ Creation's link to redemption (Eph. 1:4, 7)
- ▷ Creation shall be destroyed (2 Pet. 3:4-7)

▶ DOCTRINES

Unity of the Scripture in doctrines

- ▷ Doctrine of natural revelation (Gen. 1; Eccl. 12:2; Rom. 1:20)
- ▷ Doctrine of Creation (Gen. 1:1-31; Acts 17:24)
- ▷ Doctrine of the Word (Gen. 1:3; John 1:1)
- ▷ Doctrine of the Cultural Mandate (Gen. 1:28; 1 Cor. 10:31)
- ▷ Principle of life (Gen. 2:7; John 10:10)
- ▷ Doctrine of covenant (Gen. 2:15-17; New Testament)
- ▷ Principle of death (Gen. 2:17; Eccl. 5:15; Rom. 6:23)
- ▷ Principles of marriage (Gen. 2:18-25; Num. 5:30; Deut. 24:1; Prov. 5:18; 12:4; Song 2:16; 3:11; 6:3; 7:12; Mal. 2:16; Matt. 19:8; Col. 3:18-19)
- ▷ Principle of temptation (Gen. 3:1; Eph. 6:10-18)
- ▷ Doctrine of sin (Gen. 3:6-7; Rom. 3:23)
- ▷ Principle of judgment (Gen. 3:8-24; Rev. 20:11-15)
- ▷ Doctrine of redemption (Gen. 3:15; Rom. 16:20)
- ▷ Principle of worship (Gen. 4:26; Rev. 19:1-10)

▶ GOD'S MESSAGE

Unity of Scripture in the message of God—his will and ways for mankind

- ▷ Separation from the world (Exod. 19:6, 10-15; Lev. 11:2; 2 Cor. 6:14-18)
- ▷ Children to be obedient (Exod. 20:12; Eph. 6:1)

▷ Disobedience brings death (Num. 4:20; 1 Kgs. 20:36; Rom. 6:23)
▷ Devotion to God (Num. 22:20; Ps. 131:2; Prov. 3:9; Dan. 6:6; 1 Cor. 6:20; 7:32-38)
▷ Call to consecration (1 Sam. 1:11; Rom. 12:1-2)
▷ Teaching on sin and righteousness (Ps. 53; Rom. 3)

▸ KINGDOM OF GOD
Unity of Scripture in the theme of the Kingdom of God
(***See also Worship****> NT> Christ's kingship*)
▷ Kingdom is associated with forgiveness of sins (Lev. 24:20; 2 Kgs. 20:1-6; Matt. 18:21-35)
▷ Repentance and faith embodies the Kingdom (1 Kgs. 15:5; Jer. 8:14; 19:5, 9; Matt. 4:17)
▷ Seeking the Kingdom is highest priority (1 Chr. 28:9; Matt. 25:34; Luke 10:38-42)
▷ Kingdom is within (Jer. 24:7; Luke 17:21)
▷ Kingdom is a mystery (Zech. 3:1; Mark 4:11; Rev. 10:4)
▷ Prophets foretold the Kingdom (Zech. 9:9)
▷ Righteous living typifies the Kingdom (Matt. 5:3; 5:17-20)
▷ Present aspect of the Kingdom (Matt. 6:10)
▷ Kingdom is the content of preaching (Matt. 13:44)
▷ God's Kingdom brings judgment (Matt. 13:47-50)
▷ Future aspect of the Kingdom (Matt. 16:28)
▷ New birth supplies entrance to the Kingdom (John 3:5)
▷ Kingdom to glorify God (Rom. 14:17)

▸ SALVATION
Unity of Scripture in the message of salvation
▷ Old Testament and New Testament teach salvation by faith (Gen. 17:10-11; Eccl. 7:24; Hab. 2:4; Rom. 4)
▷ Redemption accomplished by God's power and grace (Deut. 7:8; Rom. 3:24-25)
▷ Old Testament sacrificial system cannot save (Ps. 50:13; Heb. 10)
▷ God's everlasting love (Ps. 86:15; John 3:16; 10:10)
▷ Fulfilled in the Messiah (Isa. 59:16-17; Luke 1:69, 77)
▷ Salvation completed by God (Jer. 33:31; Phil. 1:6)
▷ Conditioned by regeneration (Ezek. 36:26; John 3:3-8)

▸ OT POINTS TO NT
The Old Testament points to the New Testament
▷ Fulfillment of Old Testament prophecy in the New Testament (Hos. 11:1; Luke 1:26, 28; Gal. 4:4; 2 Pet. 1:19)
▷ Christ in the Old Testament revealed in the New Testament (Luke 24:24-26, 44-46; Rom. 5:12; Heb. 9:4)

▸ OT TYPES
The New Testament reveals types/shadows of Christ in the Old Testament
▷ Lamb (Gen. 4:4; Num. 28:9; John 1:29)
▷ Adam (Gen. 5:1; Rom. 5:12)
▷ Noah's ark (Gen. 6:14; Heb. 11:7)
▷ Melchizedek (Gen. 14:18; Heb. 5:5-6)
▷ Isaac (Gen. 22:9; Phil. 2:5-8)
▷ Ram (Gen. 22:9; Heb. 10:5-10)
▷ Joseph (Gen. 37:20; 45:7; Mark 15:10; 1 Jn. 4:9)
▷ Onan (Gen. 38:8-10)
▷ Moses (Exod. 1:15; 3:1; 34:28; Deut. 34:10-11; 2 Cor. 1:10)
▷ Passover (Exod. 12:11; 1 Pet. 1:18-19)
▷ Manna (Exod. 16:15, 35; John 6:49-51)
▷ Water from the rock (Exod. 17:5-6; Num. 20:8; 1 Cor. 10:4)
▷ Tabernacle (Exod. 25:9; Heb. 9:4)
▷ The torn curtain (Exod. 26:31-33; Matt. 27:51)
▷ Aaron (Exod. 28:38; Heb. 7:1-28; 9:1-28)
▷ Burnt Offering (Lev. 1:3; Heb. 9:11-14)
▷ Peace Offering (Lev. 3:1; Eph. 2:17)
▷ Sin Offering (Lev. 4:3; 2 Cor. 5:21)
▷ High Priest (Lev. 8:12; Heb. 1:9)
▷ Bronze Serpent (Num. 21:9; John 3:14-15)
▷ Joshua (Josh. 1:1; John 1:17)
▷ Kinsman Redeemer (Ruth 2:1; Luke 21:28)
▷ Samuel (1 Sam. 2:26; 3:19-21; Luke 2:52)
▷ Ark of the Covenant (1 Chr. 15:2; Heb. 5:1-10; 7:15-25)
▷ Jonah (Jon. 1:17; Matt. 12:39-40)

POWER

The Power of Scripture: *What makes the Bible life-changing?*

▸ CONVICT
The Bible's power to convict
▷ Cuts through deception (Prov. 10:17; Matt. 24:4-6; 2 Tim. 2:15; Heb. 4:12)
▷ Compared to fire and a hammer (Prov. 17:3; Jer. 23:29)
▷ Endures the ages (Isa. 40:6-8)
▷ Condemns the hypocrite (Rom. 2:17-29)

▸ EQUIP
The Bible's power to equip
▷ Sustains our lives (Exod. 16:19-20; Matt. 4:4; Luke 6:46-49)
▷ Delivers from bondage (2 Chr. 34:16-28; Ps. 107:20-21)
▷ To be hidden in the heart (Ps. 119:11)
▷ Lightens the heart (Prov. 12:25)
▷ Provides insight (Ezek. 10:20)
▷ Sword of the Spirit (Mal. 3:1-5; Eph. 6:17)
▷ Catalyst for faith (Matt. 17:6; Rom. 10:17)
▷ Gives God's spirit and life (John 6:63)
▷ Cleans our hearts and minds (John 15:3; 17:7)
▷ Foundation for defending truth (Rom. 10:2; 1 Pet. 3:15)
▷ Provides everything for life and godliness (2 Tim. 3:16-17)

▸ WISDOM
The Bible's power to provide wisdom
▷ Administer civil justice (Exod. 21:12; Deut. 19:21; Judg. 20:13; 1 Kgs. 3:28; 2 Chr. 19:7)
▷ Guidance for life (Num. 10:11; Pss. 119:105; 121:1; 1 Cor. 10:11)
▷ Instruction through God's Word (Deut. 26:16; 1 Sam. 19:2; 2 Sam. 6:13; 1 Kgs. 12:6-11; 1 Chr. 13:1; Neh. 8:1; Ps. 78:1; Jer. 20:8; Hag. 2:4-5)
▷ Instruction leads to wisdom (2 Sam. 16:10; Job 28:12; Prov. 1:2, 7; Hos. 4:5-9; Luke 8:18)
▷ Solomon's wisdom (1 Kgs. 3:7-9)
▷ The beginning of wisdom is obedience to Scripture (Ps. 111:10; Jer. 39:4; Jas. 3:13-17)
▷ His Word forever settled (Ps. 119:89)
▷ Gives light to the simple (Ps. 119:130)
▷ Supplies God's insights in trials (Jas. 1:5-8)

▸ WORLDVIEW

The Bible's power to provide a world and life view

- ▹ Offers God's perspective on issues (1 Sam. 21:2; 2 Cor. 4:16-18; 10:5; Heb. 12:1)
- ▹ Eternal truth (Neh. 8:12; Luke 21:33)
- ▹ Discernment against worldly philosophy (Dan. 1:3-7; Col. 2:8)
- ▹ A light to the world (Matt. 5:14)
- ▹ Means to know all truth (John 8:31-32; Heb. 2:1)
- ▹ In all our endeavors (1 Cor. 10:31)

DISCOVER GOD

Cultivating Your Relationship with God

How do you imagine God is? As long as there have been people, there have been songs and stories that explore exactly who created the universe and why. All of these stories and myths have some value, and none should be completely rejected just because they are from another religious perspective. But the Christian history of God's relationship with His creation is different because this history was written by those inspired directly by God and in His own words—that is, the Bible. In it we have God's own self-testimony of who He is and why He matters.

We can learn Greek and Hebrew and Aramaic so we can read the Bible in its original language; we can study and practice archeology so that we can recover and understand more about the civilizations with whom God dealt in the past. We can study every bit of data there is to know about God, His church, and His Word, but if we don't know *God*, then we have accomplished very little. If we don't know God personally, in the end, all our works (even reading good study Bibles!) will be for nothing. Thus, this outline begins with and is driven by the necessity of knowing the God who has real relationships with real people like you and me.

■ ■ ■

RELATIONSHIP ***Because God wants an intimate relationship with me,***
I can trust that He has sent a Savior to make peace between us.

GOD'S NATURE ***Because the Triune God is the one true God,***
I can turn my back on the counterfeit deities of this world.

SALVATION ***Because the Triune God is committed to saving His people,***
I can enjoy the full assurance of my salvation.

GOD'S ATTRIBUTES ***Because we serve an all-powerful, holy God,***
I can trust that His love for His people never changes.

GOD'S NAMES ***Because God has revealed Himself to us,***
I can know Him personally.

RELATIONSHIP

Relationship with God: *What does God want with me?*

▶ GOD'S DESIRE
God's desire for a relationship with us (Matt. 23:37)
- ▷ God does not leave His people without hope (Exod. 2:23)
- ▷ God pursues a relationship (1 Kgs. 18:37; Hos. 1:2; 3:1; Joel 2:27; Matt. 16:8-11; 18:12-14; John 15:16, 19)
- ▷ God loves and wants to be loved (Isa. 1:3; John 3:16-18; Rev. 2:4)
- ▷ God's Covenants
  God covenants with people
  - ▽Adamic covenant (Gen. 2:15-17)
  - ▽Universal covenant [with nature] (Gen. 9:1-4)
  - ▽Covenant of grace (Gen. 17:1-2, 7-8; Jude 1:4)
  - ▽Sinaitic covenant (Exod. 19:5-6)
  - ▽New Covenant (New Testament)

▶ GOD ENABLES
God enables a relationship through Christ
- ▷ Relationship with God requires sacrificial living (Gen. 12:1; 22:3; Mark 8:34-38)
- ▷ Relationship with God requires purity (Lev. 2:1; 15:31; 18:22; Num. 19:17; Ps. 24:4; 1 Thes. 4:3-5)
- ▷ Relationship with God requires a right heart (Lev. 12:8; Ps. 4:4; Isa. 1:16; Ezek. 11:19; Dan. 7:28; Mic. 6:6-8; Rev. 22:20)
- ▷ Relationship with God requires obedience (Lev. 19:2; 2 Chr. 34:32; Job 41:11; 1 Pet. 1:13-16)
- ▷ Relationship with God requires worship (2 Sam. 6:5; Pss. 105:4; 147:1; John 4:24)
- ▷ God accepts us through Christ (Ps. 62:9; Matt. 26:69-75; John 14:6; Rom. 5:1-2; Heb. 8:1-13)
- ▷ God interacts with people (Mark 5:25-34; Phil. 4:6)
- ▷ God provides for maintenance of our relationship with Him (Rom. 8:12-15)

▶ BARRIERS
Barriers to a relationship with God
- ▷ Disobedience (Gen. 3:1-13; 1 Sam. 7:2; Jer. 11:15)
- ▷ Pride (Deut. 9:5; Judg. 8:22; 2 Sam. 18:9; 2 Chr. 26:16; Job 35:12; Prov. 13:10; 16:18; Isa. 39:6; Ezek. 30:18; Dan. 4:30, 35; Luke 18:9-14; John 5:31-47; Jas. 4:6)
- ▷ Unconfessed transgressions (1 Sam. 15:15; Pss. 60:1; 66:18; Isa. 30:18; Luke 5:31-32)
- ▷ Demonic influence (1 Sam. 28:14; Acts 10:38)
- ▷ Refusing to honor God as God (Ps. 20:7; Rom. 1:21)
- ▷ Sin (Hab. 1:13)
- ▷ Unforgiving heart (Matt. 6:12-15)
- ▷ Hardened heart (Mark 6:52)
- ▷ Deep-seated grudge against another (Eph. 4:26-27)

GOD'S NATURE

The Nature of the Trinity: *How is the triune God different from false gods?*

▶ ALIVE
The Triune God is alive
- ▷ God lives, false gods don't (Exod. 3:14; 1 Sam. 5:4)
- ▷ God lives; idols don't (Judg. 18:24; Jer. 10:6-11; 44:18)
- ▷ The Living One endures forever (Dan. 6:26)
- ▷ The Living One is the source of all life (John 5:25-26)
- ▷ The Living God dwells in believers (2 Cor. 6:16)
- ▷ Conversion is turning to the Living God (1 Thes. 1:9)

▶ DIVINE
The Triune God has a divine nature
- ▷ Three persons (Father, Son, Holy Spirit) (Gen. 1:26; Matt. 28:19)
- ▷ One being (Deut. 6:4-5)
- ▷ God is Spirit (John 4:24)
- ▷ One essence (John 10:30; 14:9)

▶ ETERNAL
The Triune God is eternally existent (***See God****> God's Attributes> Self-existent*)
- ▷ Assumed throughout Scripture (Gen. 1:1; Exod. 3:15; Ps. 41:13; Eccl. 3:11; Isa. 9:6; 40:28, 57:15; Jer. 10:10; Rom. 1:20; 1 Jn. 1:2; 5:20; Rev. 1:8)
- ▷ God's eternity expressed in His name (Exod. 3:6; 13-15)
- ▷ He precedes all else that exists (Ps. 41:13; Rom. 4:17; Rev. 4:11)

▶ PERSONALITY
The Triune God has a personality
- ▷ Emotion
  God's Emotion
  - ▽God is compassionate and loving (Gen. 34:30; Exod. 34:6; Lev. 13:3; 2 Kgs. 4:2; Ps. 56:8; Isa. 17:10; Jer. 30:16-17; 42:10; Lam. 2:20; Mark 8:1-9)
  - ▽God jealously desires exclusive worship (Exod. 34:14; Deut. 4:24; Hos. 2:6-8; 1 Cor. 10:21-22)
  - ▽Rebellion rightly angers God (Num. 20:10-17; Deut. 1:37; 1 Sam. 6:6; Ezek. 20:7-8; Amos 1:8)
  - ▽God executes vengeance on all disobedient nations (Judg. 16:28; Mic. 5:15)
  - ▽God can be moved to grief (1 Sam. 15:10-11; Isa. 15:5; John 11:35)
  - ▽God loves the whole world (Isa. 66:18; John 3:16)
  - ▽The disobedient will ultimately fall under wrath (Rev. 6:15-17)
- ▷ Intellect
  God's Intellect
  - ▽God knows everything there is to know (Ps. 61:2; Col. 2:3)
  - ▽God needs no teachers (Isa. 40:14)
  - ▽God's thoughts surpass people's (Isa. 55:8-9)
- ▷ Relationships
  God's Relationships
  - ▽God has always dialogued with people (Gen. 3:8ff)
  - ▽God wants a relationship with His people (Gen. 17:7-8; Rev. 21:7)
  - ▽He wants to be known (Ruth 1:16; 1 Sam. 6:13; Ezek. 34:30; 39:28)
  - ▽God walks and lives with His people (Ps. 63:8; 2 Cor. 6:16)
- ▷ Will
  God's Will
  - ▽He accomplishes His purposes and good pleasure (2 Chr. 10:15; Eccl. 3:11; Isa. 46:5-11)

▿No one obstructs God or can question His actions (Job 12:23; Isa. 47:8; Dan. 4:35)
▿God does whatever He pleases (Ps. 115:3; Jon. 1:14)

▶ UNIQUE
The Triune God is unique (none like Him)
- ▹ God sent plagues to show Pharaoh no one is like Him (Exod. 8:10; 9:14)
- ▹ His holiness is unique (Exod. 15:11)
- ▹ He is the final lawgiver and judge (Num. 15:32; 35:33; Job 21:22; Isa. 51:7; Jas. 4:12)
- ▹ His miracles show that He alone is God (Deut. 4:32-35; 2 Kgs. 4:36)
- ▹ No one else is holy like He is (1 Sam. 2:2)
- ▹ There are no other gods (2 Sam. 7:22)
- ▹ He alone is completely wise (2 Sam. 20:22; Rom. 16:17)
- ▹ God alone knows what is in the heart of all people (1 Kgs. 8:39; 2 Chr. 6:30)
- ▹ He's the only Creator and God over the nations (1 Kgs. 19:15, 19)
- ▹ God alone possesses immortality in Himself (Job 7:6; 1 Tim. 6:16)
- ▹ He alone is God, the only sovereign (Ps. 11:4; Luke 16:13; 1 Tim. 1:17; 6:15)
- ▹ All will worship the only real God (Ps. 86:8-10)
- ▹ "I am God, and there is none like Me" (Isa. 46:9)
- ▹ There is none like Him (Jer. 10:6; Nah. 1:2)
- ▹ No one is good like He is (Matt. 19:17; Mark 10:18)
- ▹ God alone forgives sins (Luke 5:21)
- ▹ God is the only true God of all the nations (Rom. 3:29)
- ▹ He alone is holy (Rev. 15:3-4)

SALVATION

The Trinity and Salvation: *What do the three persons of the Godhead do in salvation?*

▶ FATHER
The Father and salvation
- ▹ Sent His only Son (Num. 11:8; Ps. 144:3; John 3:16-18)
- ▹ Commands all to repent (Isa. 20:6; Acts 17:30)
- ▹ Gives a new heart (Ezek. 11:19)
- ▹ Draws the unbeliever (Ezek. 37:23; John 6:44)
- ▹ Loves the world (Amos 1:8; Rom. 5:8)
- ▹ Made Christ to be sin for us (Zech. 13:7; 2 Cor. 5:21)
- ▹ Provides mercy (Luke 18:13)
- ▹ Bestows the Spirit (John 15:26)
- ▹ Raised Jesus from the dead (Rom. 10:9)
- ▹ Plans salvation (Eph. 1:4-5)

▶ SON
The Son and salvation
- ▹ Only bridge between God and man (Gen. 28:12-13; Num. 7:89; Acts 4:12; Rom. 2:28-29)
- ▹ Removes God's wrath (Num. 21:8; Ezek. 21:14; Hab. 2:16; Rom. 3:25; Heb. 2:16)
- ▹ Reconciles us to God (Mic. 5:5; Rom. 5:1, 10)
- ▹ Sanctifies and cleanses the church (Zech. 13:2; Eph. 5:25-27)
- ▹ Baptizes with the Holy Spirit (Matt. 3:3-11; Mark 1:8)
- ▹ Forgives sins (Matt. 9:2)
- ▹ Came to save what was lost (Matt. 11:2-6; Luke 19:10; John 4:4)
- ▹ Makes sinners a new creation (2 Cor. 5:17)
- ▹ Died to deliver believers from this evil age (Gal. 1:4)
- ▹ Redeemed us from the curse of the law (Gal. 3:13-14; Heb. 7:19)
- ▹ Provides redemption (Eph. 1:7)
- ▹ Came into the world to save sinners (1 Tim. 1:15)
- ▹ Redeems and purifies believers (Titus 2:14)
- ▹ Pours out the Spirit (Titus 3:6)
- ▹ Obtained eternal redemption (Heb. 9:12)

▶ HOLY SPIRIT
The Holy Spirit and salvation
- ▹ Helps put to death the deeds of the body (Deut. 22:13-25; Rom. 8:11-13; Col. 3:5-9)
- ▹ Those who walk in the Spirit are led by the Spirit (1 Sam. 11:6; Acts 22:30; Gal. 5:16-18)
- ▹ Sealed by the Holy Spirit (1 Sam. 16:14; Ezek. 9:4; Eph. 1:13-14; Col. 3:8-14)
- ▹ Comforts (Jer. 29:11; John 14:16)
- ▹ Convicts of sin (Jer. 47:7; John 16:8)
- ▹ Provides new life (Ezek. 47:2-9; John 6:63)
- ▹ Strengthens us (Mark 9:29; Eph. 3:16; 3:20; Col. 3:8-14; 1 Tim. 4:7-8)
- ▹ Promise of the Father (Luke 24:49)
- ▹ Means by which one is born again (John 3:5)
- ▹ Helps us understand things of God (1 Cor. 2:12)
- ▹ Sanctifies (1 Cor. 6:11; 2 Thes. 2:13)
- ▹ Renewing of the Holy Spirit (1 Cor. 6:11; Titus 3:5-7)
- ▹ Baptizes into the body of Christ (1 Cor. 12:13)
- ▹ Washing of regeneration (Titus 3:5-6)

GOD'S ATTRIBUTES

The Attributes of God: *What is God like?*

▶ ALL-KNOWING
God is all-knowing (omniscient)
- ▹ God knows the future (Exod. 11:1)
- ▹ His wisdom and knowledge are way beyond us (2 Sam. 17:14; 2 Kgs. 2:10; Job 12:13; Rom. 11:33)
- ▹ God misses nothing about us (2 Kgs. 20:19; Job 7:17; Ps. 33:13-15; Jer. 1:5)
- ▹ God's unfathomable knowledge of His people (Ps. 139:1; Rom. 11:33)
- ▹ One cannot escape God (Ps. 139:7)
- ▹ God knows the believer's heart (Ps. 139:23; 1 Jn. 3:20)
- ▹ God sees it all (Prov. 15:3; Matt. 23:5-7)
- ▹ One cannot hide from God (Jer. 23:23-24; Ezek. 8:12)
- ▹ God knows all things perfectly (Heb. 4:13)

▶ ALL-POWERFUL
God is all-powerful (omnipotent)
- ▹ Reveals Himself as the almighty God (Gen. 17:1)
- ▹ God has power to deliver (Exod. 13:3; Judg. 7:2; Ps. 7:1)
- ▹ He has power over death (Josh. 23:14; Job 24:22-25; Isa. 57:2; Rev. 1:18)
- ▹ His creation reflects His power (1 Chr. 16:32; Pss. 19:1; 93:4; 136:7; Rom. 1:19-22)

- ▷ God has the power to create anything from nothing (Job 26:14; Ps. 33:6-9)
- ▷ God's creative power is beyond our comprehension (Job 38:4; Ps. 96:12)
- ▷ No one can challenge what God does (Job 40:4; Isa. 37:5-6; Dan. 4:35)
- ▷ God speaks and things happen (Ps. 29:3-9; Rev. 9:1-5)
- ▷ His resurrection power is immeasurably great (Dan. 6:17; Matt. 28:5, 10; Eph. 1:19-20)
- ▷ His powerful word sustains everything (Heb. 1:3)

▶ ALL-PRESENT

God is all-present (omnipresent)

- ▷ God can always hear us (Exod. 33:11)
- ▷ All creation is dependent upon His presence (1 Sam. 4:22; Col. 1:17)
- ▷ God is everywhere (1 Kgs 13:2; Job 3:3; 31:4; Ps. 139:7-12)
- ▷ God's continual presence brings contentment (2 Kgs. 2:14; Job 10:15; Eccl. 6:9; Lam. 3:22-23; Heb. 13:5)
- ▷ One cannot hide from God (Jer. 23:23-24)
- ▷ No task is too large or too difficult for Him (Jer. 32:17, 27)

▶ ETERNAL

God is eternal

- ▷ God is eternal (Gen. 21:33; Eccl. 3:11)
- ▷ The eternal God is the believer's source of security (Deut. 33:27; Ps. 125:1; Prov. 14:26; Isa. 25:1; Rom. 8:38-39)
- ▷ God is timeless (Job 4:20; Ps. 90:2)
- ▷ God has no end of days (Ps. 102:27)
- ▷ The Son's reign will have no end (Ps. 132:11; Isa. 16:5; Luke 1:32-33; Rev. 11:15-17)
- ▷ The Living One endures forever (Dan. 6:26)
- ▷ God alone possesses immortality in Himself (1 Tim. 6:16)
- ▷ God always existed and always will (Rev. 1:8)
- ▷ He lives and will be worshiped forever (Rev. 4:9-10)

▶ FAITHFUL

God is faithful

- ▷ God is gracious (Gen. 43:29)
- ▷ God is faithful to fulfill His promises (Lev. 26:42; 1 Sam. 4:11; Ps. 12:6; Heb. 10:23)
- ▷ God is faithful to the faithful (Deut. 7:7-11)
- ▷ God deserves thanks for His constant faithfulness (Judg. 16:17; 1 Sam. 15:12; Pss. 92:2; 100:5; 138:1; Isa. 38:16; Luke 1:68-79)
- ▷ God faithfully matures believers (2 Sam. 21:15; Ps. 66:10; Rom. 4:18-25; 1 Thes. 5:24)
- ▷ His faithfulness endures (1 Chr. 28:20; Pss. 48:14; 119:90; Jer. 2:3-8; 51:5)
- ▷ God forgives the repentant (2 Chr. 6:24; Lam. 2:17; 1 Jn. 1:9)
- ▷ God is faithful through calamity (Job 3:25; Ps. 44:26; Jer. 20:11-18; Lam. 3:22-23)
- ▷ His faithfulness is immeasurable (Ps. 36:5)

▶ FORGIVING

God is forgiving

- ▷ God's forgiveness clears one's record (Lev. 4:2; 5:18; Ps. 130:3; Jer. 50:20)
- ▷ God's forgiveness leads believers to forgive others (Lev. 14:23-34; 1 Sam. 24:10; Col. 3:13)
- ▷ God is ready to forgive (Num. 14:5; Ps. 86:5; Mic. 7:18-20; Heb. 8:12)
- ▷ God forgives His people when they repent (Deut. 30:1-3; 2 Chr. 7:14)
- ▷ God forgives those who repent (2 Sam. 12:13; Ps. 85:2; Jon. 3:5-10; Rom. 1:26-27; 1 Jn. 1:9)
- ▷ Jesus has authority to forgive sins (Luke 5:17-26)
- ▷ Those forgiven much will love much (Luke 7:36-50)

▶ GOOD

God is good

- ▷ God provides for our needs (Exod. 16:12)
- ▷ God creates only good things (Deut. 2:30; 1 Tim. 4:4)
- ▷ All are invited to experience the goodness of God (Ps. 34:8)
- ▷ God is good to His covenant people (Ps. 73:1; Jer. 32:40)
- ▷ God deserves thanks for His goodness (Pss. 79:13; 100:5)
- ▷ All good comes from God (Ps. 112:5-7; Ezek. 27:3; Jas. 1:17)
- ▷ God is good to all (Ps. 145:9)
- ▷ No one is good except God (Mark 10:18; Luke 18:19)

▶ HOLY

God is holy

- ▷ His holiness is unique (Exod. 15:11)
- ▷ His holiness is the standard for believers' behavior (Lev. 11:45; 19:2; Mark 10:17-21; 1 Pet. 1:15-16)
- ▷ His holiness demands exclusive worship (Josh. 24:19; Ezek. 43:12; Acts 9:31)
- ▷ No one else is holy like He is (1 Sam. 2:2)
- ▷ The Most Holy One deserves constant honor (2 Kgs. 16:18; Rev. 4:8)
- ▷ His holy presence rejects impurity (Isa. 6:3-5)
- ▷ God guards His holy reputation (Ezek. 35:11; 36:21-23)
- ▷ He disciplines believers to impart His holiness to them (Heb. 12:10)

▶ INFINITE

God is infinite

- ▷ He has no limits, boundaries, or end (1 Sam. 4:12; Isa. 40:12-14)
- ▷ Even heaven cannot limit God (1 Kgs. 8:27)
- ▷ God, who exists before and after time, deserves honor (2 Kgs. 20:11; Jude 1:25)
- ▷ Heaven and earth cannot contain Him (2 Chr. 6:18; Ps. 76:4)
- ▷ He is not limited by time (Ps. 90:2)
- ▷ He is at the beginning and the end of all things (Rev. 22:13)

▶ JUST

God is just

- ▷ He exercises justice toward all humanity (Gen. 18:25)
- ▷ God's justice often requires punishment (Exod. 12:29)
- ▷ God judges all people with justice (Exod. 21:24; Job 18:8; Ps. 9:8; Prov. 21:15; Ezek. 30:3; Rom. 2:3)
- ▷ God's law and judgments are completely righteous (Lev. 17:4; 2 Sam. 6:8; Ps. 19:7-9)
- ▷ All God's ways are righteous and deserve praise (Deut. 8:19; Ps. 148:1; Rev. 15:3)
- ▷ He is just in all His ways (Deut. 32:4)

- ▹ Jesus, our righteous defender before the Father (Judg. 3:31; Job 17:3; 1 Jn. 2:1)
- ▹ God rightly judges heart, mind, and deeds (Ruth 4:13; 1 Sam. 12:19; Eccl. 8:13; Jer. 7:14; 17:10)
- ▹ All sin is ultimately against a righteous God (Ps. 51:4)
- ▹ The Messiah will judge all with complete justice (Ps. 58:1; Isa. 11:4-5)
- ▹ God alone is the judge (Isa. 10:1; Jas. 4:12)
- ▹ The righteous Messiah will establish a righteous people (Jer. 33:16)
- ▹ The righteous God justifies those who believe in Jesus (Mic. 6:10-12; Rom. 3:25-26)
- ▹ A day is fixed for His righteous judgment of the world (Mal. 4:1-3; Acts 17:31)

▶ LOVING
God is loving
- ▹ To love enemies and the wicked is to be like God (Exod. 23:5; Job 31:29; Ezek. 32:18; Luke 6:35)
- ▹ God loves His people, even when they are faithless (Num. 13:33; Hos. 3:1; Mark 16:7)
- ▹ God loves and preserves His godly people (Ps. 37:28)
- ▹ God deserves thanks because of His perpetual love (Pss. 42:4; 100:5)
- ▹ Nothing can separate the believer from His love (Ps. 136:1; Rom. 8:38-39)
- ▹ As a father, God corrects His beloved children (Prov. 3:12)
- ▹ Eternal plans are motivated by His love (Jer. 31:3-4; Eph. 1:4-5)
- ▹ Believers should imitate God's universal love (Matt. 5:44-45)
- ▹ God loved the world enough to send His Son to die (Luke 23:33-49; John 3:16)
- ▹ God loves those who love His Son (and obey Him) (John 2:7; 14:21)
- ▹ His love is poured into believers' hearts (Rom. 5:5)
- ▹ God is love, and those who know God love others (1 Jn. 4:7-8, 9-10, 20-21)

▶ MERCIFUL
God is merciful
- ▹ God reveals Himself (Exod. 6:3)
- ▹ God is merciful according to His own purposes (Exod. 7:14; 33:19; 1 Kgs. 14:13; Rom. 9:15)
- ▹ God is merciful to sinners (Judg. 15:18; Zeph. 1:12; John 8:1-11)
- ▹ God gives mercy to those who are merciful (1 Sam. 11:13; 24:4; 2 Kgs. 6:22; Matt. 5:7)
- ▹ God's mercy endures through trials (1 Kgs. 19:4; Job 16:17; Lam. 3:22)
- ▹ God is merciful (2 Chr. 28:9; Ps. 86:15)
- ▹ Salvation and new life come through His mercy (Isa. 24:16; Titus 3:5)
- ▹ In Christ God kept His promise of mercy to His people (Luke 1:54-55)
- ▹ God's rich mercy gives believers new life in Christ (Eph. 2:4)
- ▹ He causes believers to be born again by His mercy (1 Pet. 1:3)

▶ PATIENT
God is patient
- ▹ God is slow to anger (Exod. 15:24-25; 34:6; 1 Sam. 18:29)
- ▹ God patiently awaits repentance (2 Sam. 12:1-7; Jon. 4:2)
- ▹ Believers can appeal to their patient God (Ps. 86:15; Zech. 1:12)
- ▹ God delays punishment as he awaits repentance (Jer. 16:10-13; 2 Pet. 3:9, 15)
- ▹ God is patient—but he will not wait forever (Joel 2:12-17)

▶ RIGHTEOUS
God is righteous
- ▹ People must declare humbly that God alone is righteous (Exod. 9:27; 2 Chr. 12:6)
- ▹ His righteousness demands punishment (Exod. 34:7)
- ▹ His righteousness is absolute (Ps. 71:19)
- ▹ He rules out of righteousness (Ps. 97:2)
- ▹ He is righteous in everything He does (Ps. 145:17)
- ▹ He delights in demonstrating righteousness (Jer. 9:24)
- ▹ The Lord's name: "The LORD Is Our Righteousness" (Jer. 23:6; 33:16)
- ▹ In the end, the righteous Judge will judge righteously (2 Tim. 4:8)

▶ SELF-EXISTENT
God is self-existent (independent and uncreated)
- ▹ God exists; false gods don't (Exod. 3:14)
- ▹ We have nothing materially that God needs or wants (Ps. 50:12; Luke 21:1-4)
- ▹ The King is before and after everything (Isa. 6:1-4; Rev. 21:6)
- ▹ The Creator is completely independent (Isa. 40:12-31)
- ▹ The living God is the source of life (John 5:26)

▶ SELF-SUFFICIENT
God is self-sufficient (has no needs)
- ▹ God supplies all things their life and breath (2 Chr. 23:21; Job 14:2, 5; 34:14-15; Acts 17:25)
- ▹ The One Creator originates and controls His creation (Job 9:9; Eccl. 12:1; Jer. 10:6-14)
- ▹ We need the Creator, but He's entirely independent (Isa. 40:12-31)
- ▹ God has no equal (Isa. 40:25)
- ▹ He does things simply because He wants to (Dan. 4:34-35)
- ▹ The Source of all life needs no one to give Him life (John 5:25-26)

▶ SOVEREIGN
God is sovereign
- ▹ God powerfully delivered His people from Egypt (Exod. 12:29-32; 13:13-31)
- ▹ He raises and removes rulers (Deut. 2:33; Eccl. 4:1; Isa. 45:11-13; Jer. 25:9; Dan. 2:21)
- ▹ He is the only Sovereign (Deut. 4:32; Ezek. 29:6-7; 1 Tim. 1:17; 6:15)
- ▹ He has a plan for His people and will carry it out (Judg. 14:4; Ps. 138:8; Joel 3:16; Eph. 1:5, 11)
- ▹ God is in control of all things (2 Sam. 24:1; 2 Chr. 18:21, 33)
- ▹ God has dominion over the affairs of people (1 Kgs. 19:13; Job 12:16; Eccl. 9:11; Isa. 41:26; Amos 1:4-5; Acts 23:10-11)
- ▹ The Creator looks after His creation (Ezra 5:5; Ps. 104:9)
- ▹ God controls nature for His purposes (Job 37:2-13; Isa. 10:15; Matt. 8:23-27)

- ▷ God controls time and seasons (Job 38:33; Ps. 148:8; Dan. 2:21; Zeph. 1:5)
- ▷ The powerful Creator reduces human rulers to nothing (Isa. 40:24)
- ▷ God chose His people to become like Christ (Rom. 8:28-30; Phil. 2:5-11)
- ▷ God chose His people before He made the world (Eph. 1:4)
- ▷ God's eternal purpose is to make His wisdom known (Eph. 3:10-11)
- ▷ He chose His people to save and purify them (2 Thes. 2:13)

▶ TRUE
God is true/truthful
- ▷ His Spirit guides believers into all truth (Lev. 5:1; 2 Chr. 35:19; John 16:13)
- ▷ God follows through on His promises (Lev. 5:4; Num. 11:22-23, 31-34; Ps. 65:5; 2 Cor. 5:6-8)
- ▷ God doesn't lie but keeps His word (Num. 23:19; 2 Sam. 1:10; Pss. 3:5; 19:7; 21:2, 5; 22:1, 18; 23:1, 4; 27:4, 10; 37:25)
- ▷ God's words are faithful and true (Job 29:23; Ezek. 2:8–3:4; Rev. 21:5; 22:6)
- ▷ God's words are true and completely righteous (Ps. 19:9; Matt. 15:12-14)
- ▷ He is "the God of truth" (Ps. 31:5; Isa. 65:16)
- ▷ God's truth is everlasting (Ps. 117:2; Jer. 40:2)
- ▷ God's truth can be suppressed to our peril (Prov. 9:10; Rom. 1:18ff)
- ▷ He is full of grace and truth (John 1:14)
- ▷ Believers know that God is true (John 3:33)
- ▷ True freedom comes from abiding in God's truth (John 8:31-32; Gal. 5:13-15)
- ▷ God is the Truth (John 14:6)
- ▷ The Holy Spirit is characterized by truth in every way (John 14:17; 15:26; 1 Jn. 5:10-11)
- ▷ Eternal life is knowing the only true God (John 17:3)
- ▷ God's word is truth (John 17:17)
- ▷ Even if all humanity lies, God remains true (Rom. 3:4)

▶ UNCHANGING
God is unchanging
- ▷ He doesn't lie and is true to His word (Num. 23:19)
- ▷ God is consistent throughout all time (Num. 23:27; Heb. 13:8)
- ▷ Though the universe will change, God never will (Ps. 102:25; Heb. 1:10-12)
- ▷ His love is never-ending (Song 5:1; Lam. 3:22-23; Mal. 3:6)
- ▷ God never changes (Jer. 26:17-19; Mal. 3:6)
- ▷ God is good—all the time (Jas. 1:17)

GOD'S NAMES

The Names and Nature of God: *Who is God?*

▶ GOD
God has many names and roles in Scripture
- ▷ God (*El/Elohim*) (Gen. 1:1; 35:1)
- ▷ LORD God (*YHWH Elohim;* the one existing God of power) (Gen. 2:4)
- ▷ LORD (*YHWH;* the one true God who exists) (Gen. 12:1)
- ▷ God Most High (*El Elyon*) (Gen. 14:20; Ps. 78:35)
- ▷ Sovereign LORD (*Adonai YHWH;* the Lord of all) (Gen. 15:2)
- ▷ God Almighty (*El Shaddai;* properly, the Almighty God) (Gen. 17:1)
- ▷ Lord (*Adonai;* Ruler or owner of all creation) (Gen. 18:26-27)
- ▷ The Eternal God (*El Olam*) (Gen. 21:33)
- ▷ The LORD, the provider (*YHWH Jireh*) (Gen. 22:14; Song 1:7)
- ▷ Shepherd (Gen. 48:15; Song 1:7; Ezek. 34:12)
- ▷ Helper (Gen. 49:25; Ps. 22:19; Isa. 41:14)
- ▷ The LORD, the healer (*YHWH Rapha*) (Exod. 15:26; Isa. 38:3)
- ▷ The LORD, the banner of his people (*YHWH Nissi*) (Exod. 17:15)
- ▷ The LORD is peace (*YHWH Shalom*) (Lev. 3:1; Judg. 6:23-24; Isa. 9:6; Matt. 5:9)
- ▷ Lawgiver (Josh. 2:4; Isa. 33:22; Jas. 4:12)
- ▷ LORD of Heaven's Armies (*YHWH Sabaoth;* the warrior God) (Josh. 5:13-15; Isa. 6:3; 26:21; 44:6; Nah. 2:13)
- ▷ Holy One of Israel (2 Kgs. 19:22; Isa. 41:14; Ezek. 39:7)
- ▷ King (Ezra 1:1; Ps. 47:2; Isa. 6:5; 33:22; 44:6; Jer. 23:5-6)
- ▷ Redeemer (Job 19:25; Isa. 41:14; 63:16)
- ▷ Refuge (Pss. 16:1-11; 46:1; 61:3)
- ▷ Rock (Pss. 18:2; 19:14; 89:26; 92:15)
- ▷ Fortress (Pss. 18:2; 31:3; 59:16)
- ▷ The LORD, the Shepherd (*YHWH Ra-ah*) (Ps. 23:1)
- ▷ Tower (Ps. 61:3; Prov. 18:10)
- ▷ Deliverer/Savior (Ps. 79:9; Isa. 11:1; 43:3, 11; Dan. 3:29)
- ▷ Judge (Isa. 3:13; 33:22)
- ▷ LORD GOD (*YH YHWH;* the one true God who exists) (Isa. 12:2; 26:4)
- ▷ Husband (Isa. 54:5; Ezek. 16:32)
- ▷ The LORD, the righteousness of His people (*YHWH Tsidkenu*) (Jer. 23:6)
- ▷ The LORD who is there (*YHWH Shammah*) (Ezek. 48:35)
- ▷ Just One (Rom. 3:26)
- ▷ Justifier (Rom. 3:26)

▶ FATHER
The Father has many names and roles in Scripture: Who is God the Father?
- ▷ Creates (Gen. 1:1; 2:25; Job 10:11)
- ▷ Shepherd (Gen. 48:15)
- ▷ "I AM" (Exod. 3:14)
- ▷ Father (2 Sam. 7:14; Ps. 89:26)
- ▷ Gardener (Vinedresser) (Ps. 80:14; John 15:1)
- ▷ Heavenly Father (Matt. 6:26)
- ▷ Sends the Holy Spirit (John 14:26)
- ▷ Sender of Christ (John 16:5)
- ▷ Holy Father (John 17:11)
- ▷ Righteous Father (John 17:25)
- ▷ Abba Father (Rom. 8:15)
- ▷ Predestines (Rom. 8:28-30; Eph. 1:3-6)
- ▷ Father of Compassion (2 Cor. 1:3)
- ▷ Father of Christ (Eph. 1:3)
- ▷ Glorious Father (Eph. 1:17)

▶ SON
The Son has many names and roles in Scripture: Who is God the Son?
- ▷ Friend of sinners (Gen. 26:30; Ps. 25:14; Prov. 20:6; Ezek. 5:13; Matt. 11:19; Luke 7:34)

- ▷ King (Josh. 13:1; Zech. 9:9; Col. 1:13; Heb. 1:8)
- ▷ Redeemer (Job 19:25; 1 Cor. 1:30; Gal. 4:5; Titus 2:14)
- ▷ The Way (Job 22:15; John 14:6)
- ▷ Advocate/Intercessor (Pss. 43:1; 110:4; Heb. 7:25; 1 Jn. 2:2)
- ▷ Immanuel (Isa. 7:14; Matt. 1:23)
- ▷ The Life (Zech. 14:8; John 11:25; 14:6)
- ▷ Virgin birth (Matt. 1:18-25)
- ▷ Jesus (Matt. 1:21)
- ▷ Baptism (Matt. 3:13-17)
- ▷ Temptation (Matt. 4:1-11)
- ▷ Healer (Matt. 4:23-24; Luke 5:17-26)
- ▷ Son of Man (Matt. 9:6; Luke 19:10)
- ▷ Son of God (Matt. 14:33; Mark 15:37-39; John 5:21-22, 26; 7:12)
- ▷ Messiah/Christ (note: In the New Testament, one word is translated two ways according to two audiences: Jewish audience/Greco-Roman audience, respectively) (Matt. 16:16, 21; Luke 7:21-23; John 1:41)
- ▷ Ransom (Matt. 20:28)
- ▷ Judge (Matt. 25:31ff; Rev. 19:15)
- ▷ Annunciation (Luke 1:26-38)
- ▷ Incarnation (Luke 2:1-20; Phil. 2:5-11)
- ▷ Forgiver of sins (Luke 5:20)
- ▷ Crucifixion (Luke 23:33-49)
- ▷ Resurrection (historical) (Luke 24:1-12)
- ▷ The Word (John 1:1; Rev. 19:13)
- ▷ God (John 1:1, 18; Titus 2:13)
- ▷ Died for the sins of the world (John 3:16)
- ▷ Bread of Life (John 6:35)
- ▷ Bread of Heaven (John 6:41)
- ▷ "I AM" (John 8:58)
- ▷ Light of the world (John 9:5)
- ▷ Door (John 10:7, 9)
- ▷ Good Shepherd (John 10:11, 14)
- ▷ The Resurrection (John 11:25)
- ▷ Teacher (John 13:13)
- ▷ Lord (John 13:13; Rom. 1:4)
- ▷ The Truth (John 14:6)
- ▷ True Vine (John 15:1, 5)
- ▷ Revealer (John 15:15)
- ▷ Sends the Holy Spirit (John 15:26)
- ▷ Glorification (through the Crucifixion and Resurrection) (John 17:5; Eph. 1:20-22; Rev. 1:5-6)
- ▷ Trial (John 18:28-40)
- ▷ Ascension (Acts 1:9)
- ▷ Emptied Himself (Phil. 2:5-11)
- ▷ Wholly God/Wholly Man (Phil. 2:5-11; Col. 2:9)
- ▷ Savior (Jesus) (Titus 2:13)
- ▷ Creator (Col. 1:16; Heb. 1:8-10)
- ▷ Brother to His own (Heb. 2:11-12)
- ▷ Tempted/without sin (Heb. 4:15)
- ▷ Sinless (1 Jn. 3:5)
- ▷ Alpha and Omega (Rev. 22:13)

▶ HOLY SPIRIT

The Holy Spirit has many names and roles in Scripture: Who is God the Holy Spirit?

- ▷ Empowers (Gen. 41:38; Exod. 31:2-5; Num. 27:16-18; Judg. 14:6; 1 Sam. 10:16; Zech. 4:14; Eph. 3:16)
- ▷ Being filled (Exod. 31:3; 35:31)
- ▷ Clothing (Judg. 6:34; 1 Chr. 12:18; 2 Chr. 24:20)
- ▷ Overpowering (Judg. 14:6, 19; 15:14; 1 Sam. 10:10; 11:6)
- ▷ Produces spiritual fruit (Judg. 17:13; Gal. 5:22-23)
- ▷ Guide/Counselor (2 Sam. 13:51; 2 Kgs. 13:14; Esth. 1:21; Ps. 57:2; John 14:26; 15:26; 16:13)
- ▷ Enables true worship (2 Chr. 8:14; Phil. 3:3)
- ▷ Gives life (Ps. 104:30; Rom. 8:11)
- ▷ Entering into (Ezek. 2:2; 3:24)
- ▷ Gives gifts (Dan. 1:17-20; 1 Cor. 12:7ff; 1 Tim. 4:14-15)
- ▷ Revealer (Hab. 3:19; Luke 2:26; Eph. 3:5; Heb. 9:8)
- ▷ Holy (Matt. 1:18-20; Rom. 14:17)
- ▷ Spirit of God (Matt. 3:16; Rom. 8:9; 1 Cor. 3:16)
- ▷ Fills (Luke 1:15, 67; Eph. 5:18)
- ▷ Speaks (Luke 2:26-35; Acts 13:2; Rev. 2:7; 14:13)
- ▷ Regenerates (John 3:5)
- ▷ Indwells Christians (John 7:38-39; 1 Jn. 2:27; 3:24)
- ▷ Comforter (John 14:16, 26; 15:25; 16:7)
- ▷ Sent by the Father and the Son (John 14:26; 15:26; Acts 2:33)
- ▷ Teacher (John 14:26; 1 Cor. 2:10)
- ▷ Spirit of Truth (John 15:26; 16:13; 1 Jn. 5:6)
- ▷ Convicts (John 16:8-11)
- ▷ Glorifies Christ (John 16:14)
- ▷ God (Acts 5:3-4; 2 Cor. 3:16-18)
- ▷ Leads (Acts 13:2; 16:6-7; Rom. 8:14; Rev. 2:7, 11, 17, 29)
- ▷ Spirit of Christ/Jesus (Acts 16:7; Rom. 8:9; 1 Jn. 4:2)
- ▷ Frees from sin (Rom. 8:2)
- ▷ Applies salvation (Rom. 8:9)
- ▷ Raises the dead (Rom. 8:11)
- ▷ Confirms salvation (Rom. 8:15-16; Gal. 4:6)
- ▷ Helper (Rom. 8:26; 2 Tim. 1:14)
- ▷ Advocate/Intercessor (Rom. 8:26-27)
- ▷ Fills with hope (Rom. 15:13; Titus 2:12-13)
- ▷ Sanctifies (1 Cor. 6:11; 2 Cor. 3:17-18; 1 Pet. 1:2)
- ▷ Unifies (1 Cor. 12:12-13; Eph. 4:3-4)
- ▷ Baptizes (1 Cor. 12:13)
- ▷ Frees (2 Cor. 3:17)
- ▷ Opposes the flesh (Gal. 5:16-17)
- ▷ Guarantee of salvation (Eph. 1:13; 2 Cor. 1:22; 5:5)
- ▷ Gives grace (Heb. 10:29)
- ▷ Inspires the Scriptures (2 Pet. 1:21)
- ▷ **Comes Upon**

  Comes upon people (Ezek. 11:5)
  - ▽Is blasphemed (Matt. 12:31-32)
  - ▽Is resisted (Acts 7:51)
  - ▽Is grieved (Eph. 4:30)
  - ▽Is quenched (1 Thes. 5:19)
  - ▽Is insulted (Heb. 10:29)
- ▷ **Lives In**

  Lives in believers
  - ▽Joseph (Gen. 41:38)
  - ▽Joshua (Num. 27:18)
  - ▽David (1 Sam. 16:12-13; Ps. 51:11)
  - ▽Daniel (Dan. 4:8; 5:11-14; 6:3)
  - ▽John the Baptist (Luke 1:15)
  - ▽All believers (John 7:37-39; 14:16; Rom. 8:9; Eph. 1:13)

DISCOVER GOD'S SALVATION

Appreciating Redemption from Sin and Death

A Christian educator walked down a busy city street, enjoying a breath of fresh air before his next lecture. As he turned the corner, a tract-wielding, zealous young Christian confronted him. "Are you saved, brother?" the young woman asked. "Saved from what?" That response seemed to confuse the young woman, but it started a good conversation.

The Bible doesn't start with the question "Are you saved?" but instead with the statement "In the beginning God created the heavens and the earth" (Gen. 1:1). What follows is the story of how this perfect creation was marred by angelic and human rebellion, but how God had a plan to save His people from the consequences of their rebellion. How this would work was prefigured in the sacrificial system of Old Testament Judaism, but was made real in the predicted sacrifice of the God-Man, Jesus Christ.

So, "Saved from what?" This section of the outline focuses on the human need for rescue from sin and ourselves and the explicit instructions from the Bible on how we can turn to God and, by faith alone, experience the best gift anyone could ever want—Jesus Christ—and access to all His promised blessings.

■ ■ ■

OUR NEED ***Because I am a weak and helpless sinner,***
I must rely on the merit of Christ alone for salvation.

JESUS' WORK ***Because Jesus Christ lived and died to save sinners,***
I can live boldly and die at peace knowing His sacrifice saves all who believe.

RECEIVING ***Because all who genuinely call upon God for salvation will be saved,***
I can joyfully share the gospel with everyone I know.

OUR NEED

Human Need for Salvation: *Why should I accept Jesus?*

SINFUL

Appreciating our sinful condition

- Influence of father (Gen. 26:7; 1 Chr. 22:5; Jer. 6:11-12)
- Rejecting God's rule (Gen. 37:10)
- Dead in sin (first and second deaths) (Gen. 38:7; Ezek. 18:20; Jon. 2:9; Rom. 6:23; Rev. 20:14-15)
- Enslaved to sin (2 Sam. 11:1-2; John 8:34; Rom. 6:17; Titus 3:3)
- Cut off from God (Isa. 29:2; Gal. 5:4)
- Inability to save oneself (Isa. 64:6; Luke 18:24-27; Eph. 2:8-9; Heb. 1:3)
- Depraved (Ezek. 23:3; Dan. 5:2-4; Mark 7:14-23; Rom. 3:10-16; 1 Cor. 2:14; Eph. 2:1)
- Guilty before God/condemned (Rom. 5:16, 18; Gal. 3:19)

CORRUPT

Acknowledging our corrupt lifestyle

- Bondage of the will in life's decisions (Jer. 52:33; Rom. 8:7)
- Tendency toward sinfulness (sinful nature) (Hos. 10:1-2; Eph. 2:3; 4:17)
- Lives under the wrath/anger of God (Nah. 1:2-6; Rom. 1:18; Eph. 2:3)
- Under Satan's influence in all areas (Eph. 2:2)

JESUS' WORK

The Redemptive Work of Jesus: *What did Jesus do to redeem me?*

SINLESS LIFE

Christ's sinless life

- Knew no sin (2 Cor. 5:21)
- Was tempted, yet without sin (Heb. 4:15)
- Committed no sin (1 Pet. 2:21-22)

CRUCIFIXION

Christ's crucifixion/atonement

- Propitiation for sin (Lev. 1:17; Rom. 3:25-26)
- Jesus bore our sins (Lev. 4:28; Hos. 4:18-19; Heb. 9:28)
- Gave His life as a ransom (Lev. 17:11; Matt. 20:28)
- Assumed our iniquity at the cross (Isa. 53:5-6)
- One sacrifice good for all time (Matt. 26:26-28; 1 Pet. 3:18)
- Died for us (Mark 14:22-25; 1 Cor. 15:3)
- The Word dwelt among us (John 1:14)
- Substitutionary atonement (Rom. 5:8)
- Condemned sin in the flesh (Rom. 8:3)
- Jesus came to save sinners (1 Tim. 1:15)
- Christ made purification for sins (Heb. 1:3)

BURIAL

The burial of Christ

- Prepared for burial (Matt. 26:12)
- Buried according to Jewish custom (John 19:40)
- Laid in a tomb (John 19:42)
- Buried according to the Scriptures (1 Cor. 15:4)
- Believer buried in baptism (Col. 2:12)

RESURRECTION

Christ's resurrection

- Symbolized in feast of firstfruits (Lev. 23:10-11)
- Rose according to the Scriptures (Lev. 23:10-11; 1 Cor. 15:1-7)
- Old Testament points to resurrection (Ps. 6:5; Isa. 53:11; Dan. 12:2)
- Appeared to Peter and the twelve (Mark 16:14; Luke 24:34; John 20:19; 1 Cor. 15:5)
- Appearance on road to Emmaus (Luke 24:13-35)
- Appeared to apostles (Luke 24:1-12; Acts 1:2-3)
- Appeared to Paul (Acts 9:3-8; 1 Cor. 15:8)
- Paul's view (Acts 26:8; Rom. 4:17; Eph. 4:9)
- Link to believers (Rom. 8:11; 1 Cor. 15:22-23, 44-49; Phil. 3:10, 21; 1 Pet. 1:3)
- Appeared to over 500 people (1 Cor. 15:6)
- Appeared to James (1 Cor. 15:7)

RECEIVING

Receiving Redemption: *How do I receive Jesus?*

HOW

How salvation is obtained

- Submit to God's grace/special favor (Exod. 24:3; 1 Sam. 17:55; 2 Sam. 9:13; 2 Kgs. 8:6; Rom. 6:14; Eph. 2:5, 8-9; Titus 3:7; Heb. 4:16; Rev. 17:14)
- Repent of/turn from sin (Lev. 13:46; 1 Kgs. 14:3; Job 18:11; Ezek. 33:20; Matt. 4:17; Luke 5:32; 20:17-18; 24:47; Acts 2:38; 11:18; 2 Tim. 2:25; 2 Pet. 3:9; Rev. 20:10)
- Faith in Christ (Matt. 9:2; Mark 7:24-30; Luke 7:1-10; 18:17; John 1:12; Rom. 3:27-28, 30; 4:4-5, 9; Gal. 3:9; Eph. 2:8-9; Phil. 3:7-9; Heb. 4:2; 1 Pet. 1:21)
- Respond to God's call/invitation to salvation (Matt. 11:25-26; Mark 4:1-11; Luke 3:21-22; Acts 2:39; 15:17; Rom. 8:28-30, 33; Eph. 1:4-6; 1 Tim. 4:10; Titus 1:1; 2 Pet. 1:3; 2:10; 1 Jn. 2:2)
- Receive Christ (John 1:12)
- Role of the Spirit (John 16:7-11; 1 Cor. 12:3; Eph. 1:13; Titus 3:5)
- Call upon the Lord (Acts 2:21; Rom. 10:9)

WHEN

When we receive Christ

- New creation/new life (Gen. 15:6; Rom. 6:13; 2 Cor. 5:17; Col. 2:12; 3:1)
- Heirs of God and Christ (Gen. 27:11; Rom. 8:17)
- Set apart for God (positional aspect) (Exod. 28:1; Acts 26:18; 1 Cor. 6:11)
- Justified/declared innocent (Josh. 3:5; Gal. 2:16; 3:24; 5:16; 1 Cor. 6:11; Titus 3:7)
- Delivered or rescued (Judg. 6:6; 2 Chr. 7:14; Neh. 6:13; Rom. 5:10; Gal. 1:3-5; Col. 1:13; 1 Thes. 1:10)
- Born to a living hope (Job 9:29; 1 Pet. 1:3)
- Heir and citizen of heaven (Ps. 137:4; Phil. 1:27; 3:20; Rev. 3:12)
- Redeemed/rescued/ransomed (Zech. 10:8-10; Matt. 20:28; Rom. 3:24; Gal. 3:13; Eph. 1:7; 1 Pet. 1:18)
- New master (Matt. 6:24; Rom. 6:18)

- ▷ Member of God's family (Luke 6:35-36; Rom. 8:15; Eph. 1:5; 2:19; 1 Tim. 5:1-2; 1 Jn. 3:9)
- ▷ Given the gift of the Holy Spirit (Luke 24:49; Acts 2:38; 5:32)
- ▷ Expiation/removal of sins (John 1:29; Col. 2:13-14)
- ▷ Born again (John 3:3)
- ▷ Born of the Spirit (John 3:6)
- ▷ Eternal life (John 3:16, 36; 5:24; 6:47; 11:26; Acts 11:18; 13:48; Rom. 6:23; 2 Tim. 1:12; 1 Jn. 3:14; 5:13)
- ▷ Forgiven (Acts 10:43; Rom. 3:25; Eph. 1:7; Col. 1:14; 1 Jn. 2:12)
- ▷ Accepted (Rom. 3:30; 5:16; 14:3; Gal. 4:31)
- ▷ Adopted (Rom. 8:15; Gal. 4:5; Eph. 1:5)
- ▷ Glorified (Rom. 8:30; Rev. 21:5-11)
- ▷ Indwelt by the Godhead (1 Cor. 6:19; Gal. 2:20; Eph. 1:23; 3:19)
- ▷ Baptized in the Spirit (1 Cor. 12:13)
- ▷ Sealed with identification marker (the Holy Spirit) (2 Cor. 1:22; Eph. 1:13; 4:30)
- ▷ Belonging "to Christ" (2 Cor. 5:17; Eph. 1:3-4; 2:13)
- ▷ Reconciled (2 Cor. 5:19-21; 1 Tim. 2:5)
- ▷ Declared righteous (Eph. 4:24; Phil. 3:9; Rev. 7:14-15)
- ▷ Regenerated/given new life (Titus 3:5)
- ▷ Member of a holy and royal priesthood (1 Pet. 2:5, 9; Rev. 1:6; 20:6)

▶ RESULTS

Salvation's results

- ▷ Gratitude (Gen. 40:23)
- ▷ New life (Lev. 8:35; Acts 19:17-20; Rom. 6:8)
- ▷ Sanctification (progressive aspect) (Deut. 7:6; Lam. 5:21; John 17:17; Rom. 8:29; Col. 3:5-11; 1 Pet. 1:2)
- ▷ Perseverance (Ps. 42:2; John 10:27-29; Rom. 8:31-39)
- ▷ Bear fruit of the Spirit (Hos. 8:1-2; Gal. 5:22-23; Col. 1:6)
- ▷ Expressed in obedience to Great Commission (Mark 16:15; Acts 25:14)
- ▷ Bear spiritual fruit (John 15:8)
- ▷ Slaves of Christ (Rom. 1:1; 8:15; Eph. 6:6)
- ▷ Assurance (2 Cor. 13:5; 1 Jn. 2:3; 3:14; 3:24; 5:11-12)
- ▷ Life of faith (Gal. 5:22-26)
- ▷ Works

Good works

- ▽Expression of gratitude (Lev. 7:12; Ps. 95:10; John 14:15, 23; 20:1; Gal. 5:6)
- ▽Defined by God's Word (Deut. 12:32; Gal. 5:14; 1 Tim. 5:21)
- ▽Scripture helps us do good works (Deut. 12:32; 2 Tim. 3:16-17; Jas. 1:25)
- ▽Bring God's blessing (1 Chr. 4:9; Esth. 6:1, 6; Jas. 1:25)
- ▽Have the glory and praise of God as their object (Ezra 7:28; Phil. 1:11)
- ▽God remembers them (Neh. 13:14; Esth. 7:1; Lam. 5:1; Amos 8:7; Heb. 6:9-10)
- ▽Produced in us by God (Esth. 2:7; Isa. 26:12; Phil. 2:13)
- ▽Spring from a believing heart (Jer. 5:31; Rom. 10:9-10; Eph. 2:10; Jas. 2:18-22)
- ▽Evidence of faith at final judgment (Matt. 25:34-40; Jas. 2:14-20)
- ▽To be done in Jesus' name (John 14:13; Col. 3:17)
- ▽Produced by abiding in Christ (John 15:4-5)
- ▽Redeemed from curse of the law (Gal. 4:5; Rev. 6:16-17)
- ▽Saints created for them (Eph. 2:10)
- ▽Saints should be established in them (Eph. 2:10)
- ▽Result of God's good pleasure (Phil. 2:13)
- ▽Redeemed from Satan (Col. 1:13-14)
- ▽Ministers should exhort us to do them (1 Tim. 6:17-18)
- ▽Saints should provoke each other to them (Phil. 1:6; Heb. 10:24)

DISCOVER WORSHIP

Giving God the Praise and Glory He Is Due

When discussing the topic of God, some people throw up their hands in despair. However, the Bible says we should throw up our hands in praise, lift up our voice in song, and rejoice in God's mercy to us all.

We don't approach Him demanding our needs be met. We don't come to God offering up our obedience, as if He needed our help with anything. True worship, and this outline, begins with awestruck reverence for who God is and what He has done for us. This positive, holy fear of our grand God is (and always has been) the foundation for proper worship.

God didn't have to reveal Himself to us, you know. He could have left us in the dark, groping around for the right things to be, say, and do to please Him. But He gave clear instructions in the Bible for how He did (and didn't!) want to be worshiped. This section of the outline lays out God's preferences for how He wants us to show our love for Him.

■ ■ ■

OT ***Because God revealed Himself to the ancients as worthy of worship,***
God's people showed their faith by offering the sacrifices God required.

NT ***Because Jesus initiated a better covenant between God and man,***
You can always approach God through Christ, in the power of the Holy Spirit.

OT

Worship in the Old Testament: *How did people worship God in Old Testament times?*

▸ FASTING AND PRAYER

Fasting and prayer in Old Testament worship (corporate, personal)

- ▹ Fasting
  - ▿ Occasions
    Occasions for fasting
    - The Day of Atonement (Lev. 16:29-31; 23:26-32; Num. 29:7)
    - Fasting as a means to afflict or humble the soul (Lev. 23:26-32; Ps. 35:13)
    - Fasting while seeking forgiveness (Deut. 9:15-18; 1 Kgs. 21:17-29; Dan. 9:3-5; Jon. 3:4-10)
    - Fasting in war or at the threat of it (Deut. 20:1-4; Judg. 20:26; 1 Sam. 7:6)
    - Fasting when a leader dies (1 Sam. 31:13; 1 Chr. 10:12)
    - David and the people fasted for Saul and Jonathan (2 Sam. 1:12)
    - Fasting when a loved one was sick (2 Sam. 12:16-23)
    - Fasting when facing impending danger (2 Chr. 20:3)
    - Return from exile (Ezra 8:21)
    - Fasting as a means to receive God's favor (Ezra 8:23; Isa. 57:15; 66:1-2)
    - Nehemiah fasted when he heard of the state of Jerusalem (Neh. 1:4)
    - General fast at the communal reading of the Law by Ezra (Neh. 9:1)
    - The Jews fasted when they heard of the king's decree (Esth. 4:3)
    - Esther and Mordecai fasted before she went before the king (Esth. 4:16)
    - Fasting for enemies (Pss. 35:11-13; 109:24)
    - Afflicting one's soul was understood to refer to fasting (Ps. 69:10)
    - Tragedies
      Fasting to commemorate tragedies
      - Beginning of the siege of Jerusalem (2 Kgs. 25:1)
      - Fall of Jerusalem (2 Kgs. 25:3-4)
      - Murder of Gedaliah (2 Kgs. 25:23-95)
      - Burning of the Temple (Jer. 52:12-13)
  - ▿ Length
    Length of fasts
    - Forty days (Exod. 34:28; Deut. 9:9; 1 Kgs. 19:8)
    - One day (sunrise to sunset) (Judg. 20:26; 1 Sam. 14:24; 2 Sam. 1:12; 3:35)
    - Seven days (1 Sam. 31:13; 2 Sam. 12:16-18; 1 Chr. 10:12)
    - Day and night (Esth. 4:16)
    - Three days (Esth. 4:15-16)
    - One night (Dan. 6:18)
    - Three weeks (Dan. 10:2-3)
- ▹ Prayer
  - ▿ God does not always say yes (Exod. 32:30-35; Job 11:5; Lam. 3:57)
  - ▿ God vows to answer according to His will (2 Sam. 24:25; Ps. 91:15; Jer. 33:3)
  - ▿ Bear with one another (Job 4:4)
  - ▿ Devote yourselves to prayer (Job 27:8-10; Ps. 116:1)
  - ▿ Prophets pray unceasingly (Ps. 116:18; Isa. 6; Dan. 9:20ff; Hab. 2:1-3)
  - ▿ Prayer for those in authority (Prov. 14:34)
  - ▿ Jeremiah is commanded not to intercede (Jer. 7:16; 11:14; 14:11-18)
  - ▿ At others' request (Jer. 37:2-3)
  - ▿ Individual
    Prayer of individuals
    - Of Moses (Exod. 32:11-13, 31-32; 33:12-16; Num. 11:11-15; 14:13-19; Deut. 9:18-21)
    - Of Aaron (Num. 6:22-27)
    - Of Samuel (1 Sam. 7:5-13; 12:23)
    - Of Solomon (1 Kgs. 8:22-53)
    - Of Hezekiah (2 Kgs. 19:14-19)
  - ▿ Psalms
    Psalms of prayer
    - Wisdom poems (Pss. 1; 37; 73; 112)
    - Royal psalms (also prayers) (Pss. 2; 18; 20; 21)
    - Laments of the individual Israelite (Pss. 3; 5–7; 13)
    - Liturgies (Pss. 15; 24; 60; 75)
    - Thanksgiving of the individual Israelite (Pss. 30; 32; 138)
    - Communal prayers (Pss. 33; 145–150)
    - Communal laments (Pss. 44; 74; 79)
    - Thanksgiving of the community (Pss. 67; 124)
    - Songs for pilgrimage (Pss. 84; 122)

▸ FESTIVALS

Feasts and sacred days in Old Testament worship

- ▹ Sabbath (Gen. 2:2-3; Exod. 20:8-11; 31:13; 35:2; Lev. 23:3; Deut. 5:12-15; Neh. 13:22; Isa. 56:2; Jer. 17:21-27)
- ▹ Passover (Exod. 12:1-14; Lev. 23:5-6; Num. 9:1-14; Ezra 6:22)
- ▹ Unleavened Bread (Exod. 12:15-20; 13:3-10; 23:15; 34:18; Num. 28:17-25)
- ▹ Sabbath Year (Exod. 23:10-11; Lev. 25:1-7)
- ▹ Harvest (Exod. 23:16; 34:22; Lev. 23:33-36, 39-43; Deut. 16:13-15; Zech. 14:16-19)
- ▹ Final Harvest (Pentecost) (Exod. 23:16a; 34:22a; Deut. 16:9-12)
- ▹ Day of Atonement (Lev. 16; 23:26-32; Num. 29:7-11)
- ▹ Firstfruits (Lev. 23:9-14)
- ▹ Trumpets (Lev. 23:23-25; Num. 29:1-6)
- ▹ Year of Jubilee (Lev. 25:8-55; Num. 36:4)
- ▹ Holy Assembly (Num. 29:35-38)
- ▹ Purim (Esth. 9:19)

▸ GOD'S SUPREMACY

The supremacy of God in Old Testament worship

- ▹ The Spirit was worshiped (Gen. 1:2; Job 33:4; Ps. 139:7-10)
- ▹ Required obedience in daily life and affairs (Exod. 20:1-17; Deut. 27:10; 1 Sam. 5:22; Job 23:10; Isa. 50:4; Jer. 10:2; Amos 5:23-24; Mic. 2:1)
- ▹ God alone was to be worshiped—no one else (Exod. 20:2-3; Deut. 5:7-9; 6:14; Ps. 83:18; Amos 5:4-6; Matt. 4:10)

- ▷ Required personal and ritual holiness (Lev. 11:44; 12:2; Deut. 7:6)
- ▷ Required personal and ritual cleanliness (Lev. 12:2; 13:28; Num. 8:21; 19:9; Pss. 51:10; 81:7; Ezek. 36:25)
- ▷ Was God-centered (not worshiper-centered) (Deut. 12:4; Pss. 2:11; 34:3; 71:7; 99:9; 108:2; Isa. 2:8; 44:15; Ezek. 8:16; Dan. 2:18-23; 3:18; Mic. 5:13)
- ▷ Required a proper heart attitude (Deut. 30:15-18; Isa. 58:2; Jer. 7:21-23; Hos. 13:1-3; Mic. 6:8)
- ▷ Putting God first (Ezra 3:6)
- ▷ God delivered/saved in order to be worshiped and served (Esth. 8:17; Pss. 18:2-3; 119:170; Prov. 19:17)
- ▷ The Son was worshiped (Pss. 2; 45; 72; 110)
- ▷ Glorified and blessed God (Pss. 29:10; 103:1; Eccl. 11:9)

▶ MUSIC

Sacred music in Old Testament worship

- ▷ Song of Moses commemorates victory (Exod. 15; Deut. 32:1-43)
- ▷ Deborah and Barak give a war chant (Judg. 5)
- ▷ Hannah sings her prayer at the dedication of Samuel (1 Sam. 2:1-10)
- ▷ David mourns Saul and Jonathan through song (2 Sam. 1:8)
- ▷ **Psalms (2 Sam. 5:1-3)**
  Worship through Psalms
  - ▽**Lament**
    Lament psalms
    - Repentance (2 Chr. 30:22; Pss. 6; 38; 51; 102; 130; 143)
    - Retaliation (Pss. 35; 69; 83; 88; 109; 137; 140)
    - Individual (Pss. 3; 4; 5; 7; 9–10; 13; 14; 17; 22; 25; 26; 27; 28; 30; 36; 39; 40:12-17; 41; 42–43; 49; 52; 53; 54; 55; 56; 57; 59; 61; 64; 70; 71; 77; 86; 89; 120; 139; 141; 142)
    - Community (Pss. 12; 44; 58; 60; 74; 79; 80; 83; 85; 89; 90; 94; 123; 126; 129)
  - ▽**Liturgy**
    Psalms for public worship (liturgy)
    - Royal (Pss. 2; 18; 20; 21; 29; 45; 47; 72; 93; 95; 96; 97; 98; 99; 101; 110; 144)
    - Temple Liturgy (Pss. 15; 24; 68; 82; 115; 134)
    - Songs of Zion (Pss. 46; 48; 76; 84; 87; 122)
    - Covenant (Pss. 50; 78; 81; 89; 132)
  - ▽**Praise**
    Praise psalms (Pss. 8; 19:1-6; 33; 57; 66:1-12; 67; 95; 100; 103; 104; 111; 113; 114; 117; 145; 146; 147; 148; 149; 150)
  - ▽**Thanksgiving**
    Thanksgiving psalms
    - Reliance (Neh. 12:8, 27; Pss. 11; 16; 23; 27; 62; 63; 91; 121; 125; 131)
    - Rescue (Pss. 8; 105–106; 135; 136)
    - Individual (Pss. 18; 21; 30; 32; 34; 40:3; 66:13-20; 92; 108; 116; 118; 138)
    - Community (Pss. 65; 67; 75; 107; 124; 136)
  - ▽**Special**
    Specialized themes in liturgical psalms
    - Law (Pss. 1; 19:7-14; 119)
    - Wisdom (Pss. 1; 36; 37; 49; 73; 112; 127; 128; 133)

▶ OFFERINGS

Sacrifices/offerings in Old Testament worship

- ▷ **Blood Sacrifices**
  Four blood sacrifices of the Old Testament
  - ▽Burnt Offering (Lev. 1; 6:8-13; 8:18-21; 16:24; Ezek. 42:13)
  - ▽Sin Offering (Lev. 1:4; 4:1–5:13; 6:24-30; 8:14-17; 16:3-22)
  - ▽Guilt Offering (Lev. 5:14–6:7; 7:1-6)
  - ▽Peace Offering (Lev. 3:9-10; 7:12-16)
- ▷ **Other Sacrifices**
  Additional sacrifices
  - ▽Grain offerings (Lev. 2:1-16; 6:14-18)
  - ▽Freewill offerings (Lev. 7:16)
  - ▽Drink offerings (Num. 6:17; 15:1-12)
  - ▽Vows (Judg. 11:30-31; 1 Sam. 14:24-46; 2 Sam. 9:1; Eccl. 5:1-7)
  - ▽**Tithing (Ezek. 46:12)**
    Finances given to support the state and Temple
    - A tithe as a fee paid to the temple for every firstborn male (Exod. 13; 22:29; Num. 3)
    - A tithe as a fixed temple tax on every male over 20 (Exod. 30)
    - A tithe as a thank-offering for farming in Israel (Lev. 27; Num. 18:20-32; Mal. 3:8-12)
    - A tithe to pay for the journey to and celebration in Jerusalem (Deut. 14:22)
    - A tithe on the third year of the seven-year harvest cycle for poverty relief (Deut. 26:1-19)
    - A tithe should be used properly (Job 36:18)

▶ PLACE

A sacred space for Old Testament worship: Tabernacle, Temple

- ▷ **Tabernacle (Exod. 25:8; 31:6)**
  - ▽The Old Testament Tabernacle points to Christ (Exod. 25–27; 31:6; Heb. 10:10)
  - ▽Bread of the Presence (Exod. 25:23-30; Lev. 24:2-9; John 6:32-35, 50-51)
  - ▽Lamp (Exod. 25:31-40; 27:20-21; John 8:12)
  - ▽Bronze Altar (Exod. 29:36-37; Heb. 13:10-16)
  - ▽Altar of Incense (Exod. 30:1-8; Rev. 8:3-4)
  - ▽Washbasin (Exod. 30:18-21; Eph. 5:25-27)
  - ▽Glory of the Lord filled the house (Exod. 33:23; 40:35)
  - ▽How the Tabernacle was set up and sanctified (Exod. 40)
  - ▽Christ is the final High Priest (Lev. 16:15, 22; Heb. 4:14; 5:6; 9:6-14)
  - ▽The veil rent at Christ's death (Lev. 16:34; Matt. 27:50-51)
  - ▽Christ fulfills the Old Testament sacrificial system (Ezek. 40:38-43; Heb. 9:15-23)
  - ▽Ark of the Covenant (Heb. 9:4-7)
- ▷ **Temple (Ezek. 41:4)**
  - ▽God's promise to build the Temple through Solomon (2 Sam. 7:12-13; 2 Chr. 2:1-10; Ps. 132:5)
  - ▽Building of the Temple (1 Kgs. 6:37-38; 2 Chr. 3:1-2)
  - ▽Dimensions of God's house (1 Kgs. 7:1-12; 2 Chr. 3:3-17)
  - ▽Furnishings of God's house (1 Kgs. 7:13-51; 2 Chr. 4:1-22)

- ▿Glory of the Lord filled the house (1 Kgs. 8:10-11; 2 Chr. 5:11-14)
- ▿Housed the Ark (1 Kgs. 8:20-21; 2 Chr. 5:1-10)
- ▿Dedication of the Temple (1 Kgs. 8:22-66; 2 Chr. 6)
- ▿Temple cannot contain God (1 Kgs. 8:27; 2 Chr. 2:6)
- ▿The Lord's glory comes down (2 Chr. 7:1-3; Hab. 3:16)
- ▿Restoring the Temple (2 Chr. 24:13)
- ▿Set apart from sin (Ezek. 7:22)

▸ POSTURE

Varieties of posture in Old Testament worship

- ▹ Bowing (Gen. 42:6)
- ▹ Sitting (2 Sam. 7:18)
- ▹ Hands uplifted (1 Kgs. 8:22; Pss. 28:1; 134:2)
- ▹ Kneeling (1 Kgs. 8:54; Ezra 9:5; Job 42:8; Ps. 95:6; Dan. 6:10; Acts 20:36)
- ▹ Standing (Jer. 18:20)
- ▹ **Dancing (Exod. 15:1, 20)**

  Sacred dance in Old Testament worship
  - ▿Miriam danced (Exod. 15:20)
  - ▿Women dancers (Exod. 15:20; Judg. 21:19; 1 Sam. 18:6; Ps. 68:25)
  - ▿Singers and dancers celebrate the glory of Zion (Deut. 16:11; Ps. 87:7)
  - ▿Military victories call forth dance (Judg. 11:34; 1 Sam. 18:16)
  - ▿David danced before the Lord (2 Sam. 6:12-15, 20; 1 Chr. 15:29)
  - ▿Even the wicked rejoice with dance (Job 21:11)
  - ▿Dance in corporate worship (Ps. 149:3)
  - ▿Praise Him with timbrel and dance (Ps. 150:2)
  - ▿There is a time to dance (Eccl. 3:4)
  - ▿Dancing as a response to God's rebuilding the land (Jer. 31:4)
  - ▿Redemption of Israel celebrated (Jer. 31:13)
  - ▿Mourning turned to dancing (Jer. 45:3; Lam. 5:15)

▸ PRIESTHOOD

The high priest and priesthood in Old Testament worship

- ▹ **Duties (1 Sam. 1:14)**

  Duties of the high priest
  - ▿Officiating in the Holy Place (Exod. 30:7-10)
  - ▿Offering the sacrifices (Lev. 9)
  - ▿Teaching of the Law (Lev. 10:11)
  - ▿Inspecting ceremonially unclean persons (Lev. 13–14; Num. 5:3; Deut. 14:3)
  - ▿Physical blemishes disqualified (Lev. 21:17-23)
  - ▿Only Aaron and his descendants could serve as priests (Num. 3:10; 18:1-7; 16:40; Ezek. 44:7)
  - ▿Special arrangements (Num. 9:7)
  - ▿Maintaining the Tabernacle and the Temple (Num. 18:3)
  - ▿Functioned as tax collectors (Num. 18:21, 26; Heb. 7:5)
  - ▿Adjudicated disputes (Deut. 17:8-13)
- ▹ **Garments (Exod. 39:1)**

  Garments of the high priest
  - ▿The ephod (Exod. 28:5-14; 39:2-7)
  - ▿The shoulder stones (Exod. 28:9-12)
  - ▿The breastplate (Exod. 28:15-30)
  - ▿The robe (Exod. 28:31-35)
  - ▿The turban and the crown (Exod. 28:36-38)
- ▹ **Lineage**

  Lineage of the priests (Exod. 28:29; 40:12-16; 29:1-9; Num. 16:5; 18:1, 8)

▸ PROHIBITIONS

Prohibitions in Old Testament worship

- ▹ **Wrong Objects**

  Wrong objects of worship
  - ▿Other gods (Exod. 32:5; 34:14; Lev. 20:27; Num. 24:1)
  - ▿Heavenly host (Deut. 17:3)
  - ▿Images (Ezek. 41:18-19; Dan. 3:5-18)
- ▹ **Wrong Forms**

  Wrong forms of worship
  - ▿Plant offering instead of animal (Gen. 4:3-5)
  - ▿Pagan forms of worship (Exod. 20:24)
  - ▿Strange fire and incense (Lev. 10:1-2; Num. 3:4)
  - ▿Person not qualified (1 Sam. 13:8-13; 2 Chr. 26:16-18)
- ▹ **Wrong Preparation**

  Wrong preparation for worship
  - ▿Not holy due to ceremonial uncleanness (Lev. 5:2; 7:19-21; Num. 9:10)
  - ▿Not holy due to breaking the Sabbath (Lev. 23:3)
  - ▿Not holy due to attitude (1 Sam. 13:8-10; 2 Chr. 26:26)
  - ▿Not holy due to unrepentant idolatry (2 Chr. 15:16; Ezek. 20:39; 43:7)
  - ▿Not holy due to unrepentant immorality (Ps. 15)

▸ PROPHETS

Prophets proclaimed God's character and deeds in Old Testament worship

- ▹ Prophets are God's spokesmen (Exod. 4:15-16; 7:1; 1 Kgs. 13:21; 1 Chr. 17:3)
- ▹ Moses, the standard of Old Testament prophets (Num. 12:1; Deut. 34:10)
- ▹ God spoke directly to Moses (Num. 12:1-8)
- ▹ Israel to listen to and obey God's prophets (Deut. 18:15-18; 1 Chr. 21:1; Isa. 34:1)
- ▹ Prophetic office of divine origin (Deut. 18:15-18; Jer. 23:31-40)
- ▹ Test of the prophet (Deut. 18:20-22; Dan. 2:1-3)
- ▹ Prophets spoke to their times (Isa. 7:3; 21:5)
- ▹ Old Testament prophets witnessed to the future salvation in Christ (Isa. 65:1; Dan. 11:31; Heb. 3:1-6)
- ▹ Moses, a type of Christ (Heb. 3:1-6)

▸ REVERENCE

Reverence, awe, and fear in Old Testament worship

- ▹ Abraham's fear contrasted with the world (Gen. 20:1-18)
- ▹ Put away idols (Gen. 35:2; Deut. 4:16; 7:26; Josh. 24:14-15; 1 Sam. 7:3; 1 Kgs.15:13; 2 Chr. 31:1; Isa. 2:8; 16:12)
- ▹ God requires us to fear Him (Gen. 42:18; Exod. 19:9, 16; Deut. 6:13; 10:12-13, 20; 1 Chr. 13:12; Job 13:11; Ps. 56:4)
- ▹ Giving God the credit He deserves (Exod. 14:26)
- ▹ Awe of God means obeying His commandments (Exod. 20:19; Deut. 1:22, 26; 8:6; 1 Sam. 19:23; 2 Kgs. 17:26; Neh. 10:29; Ps. 111:10; Jon. 3:8-9)

- ▷ The fear of the Lord to be upon us (Deut. 6:13; 2 Chr. 19:7)
- ▷ God shows mercy to those who fear Him (Deut. 17:6; Ps. 103:13; Joel 2:12-13; Hab. 2:9)
- ▷ Fear Him because of what he has done (1 Sam. 6:19; 12:24; Isa. 13:6)
- ▷ Let the earth fear God (1 Sam. 17:11; Job 25:5; Ps. 33:8; Ezek. 1:28; Mal. 1:6)
- ▷ For those who came before (1 Sam. 31:12; 2 Chr. 29:2; Rom. 9:5)
- ▷ God helps those who fear Him (2 Sam. 4:1; Pss. 34:9; 124:8)
- ▷ Taught and modeled by Solomon (1 Kgs. 2:46; Prov. 1:1; 4:26; Eccl. 8:12-13; 12:13-14)
- ▷ Compared to treasure (2 Chr. 5:10; Isa. 33:6)
- ▷ Flee from evil (Job 28:28)
- ▷ Kiss the Son (Ps. 2:12)
- ▷ Revere God because His judgments are true (Ps. 19:9)
- ▷ God delivers those who fear Him (Pss. 33:18; 34:7; Ezek. 2:9; Amos 1:2; Hab. 1:2)
- ▷ Revere God in the assembly (Ps. 89:7; Mic. 1:8)
- ▷ He blesses those who revere Him (Pss. 115:13; 128:3)
- ▷ The beginning of knowledge (Prov. 1:2, 7; 2:20; 1 Cor. 8:1-3)
- ▷ The beginning of wisdom (Prov. 2:6; 9:10)
- ▷ Leads to humility (Prov. 15:33; Jer. 36:23; Amos 2:6)
- ▷ Our duty (Eccl. 12:6, 13)
- ▷ The sanctity of physical love (Song 1:15; 3:6)

▸ REPENTANCE

Repentance and covenant renewal in Old Testament worship

- ▷ Nature

  The nature of repentance and renewal
  - ▿Mosaic covenant is renewed by repentance (Exod. 34:10-28)
  - ▿Obedience guarantees success in the land of Canaan (Lev. 18:28; Num. 13:18; Deut. 3:18-22; 29:2-15)
  - ▿Obedience leads to blessing, failure to repent leads to curses (Lev. 26:3-4; Deut. 11:26-28; 30:15-18; 1 Sam. 2:5; 13:12; 2 Kgs. 21:13; Lam. 1:8; Zech. 8:3-23)
  - ▿Contriteness before the Law ensures God's blessings (Num. 6:24; Deut. 4:1-2, 5-8; Ezra 10:1)
  - ▿Results in change of behavior (Num. 14:40)
  - ▿Keeping God's commands leads to life (Deut. 4:1; 30:15; 2 Kgs. 21:13)
  - ▿To obey is better than sacrifice (1 Sam. 15:22; 2 Kgs. 18:4; Ps. 51:16-17)
  - ▿Repentance is characterized as turning from idols to the living God (2 Kgs. 17:13; 18:4; Isa. 19:22; Jer. 3:12, 14, 22; Ezek. 14:3; Jon. 3:10)
- ▷ Examples

  Examples of repentance and renewal
  - ▿Joshua sets up memorial stones at Gilgal (Josh. 4)
  - ▿Covenant ceremonies resumed at Gilgal (Josh. 5:9)
  - ▿Josiah discovers the Law and repents (1 Kgs. 23)
  - ▿Jews called to repent in order to partake in the Passover (2 Chr. 30:6-8)
  - ▿Ezra intercedes for the exiles (Ezra 9:15)
  - ▿Exiles called to covenant renewal (Neh. 7:72–10:40; Ezek. 18:2)
  - ▿Job repents in dust and ashes (Job 42:6)
  - ▿Judah refuses to repent (Jer. 5:3)

▸ SACRAMENTS

The sacraments of Old Testament worship

- ▷ Circumcision (Gen. 17:9-10; Lev. 12:3; John 7:22; Rom. 4:11)
- ▷ Passover (Exod. 12; Num. 9; 2 Kgs. 23:20-24; Luke 22)

▸ TEACHING AND PREACHING

Teaching and Preaching in Old Testament Worship

- ▷ First great teacher was Moses (Deut. 6:1)
- ▷ Primary religious responsibility of the family to their children was education (Deut. 6:7-8; Joel 1:3)
- ▷ Learning to trust God (Job 6:10)
- ▷ Teaching ideally flowed from the Temple (Isa. 2:3; Mic. 4:2; Matt. 21:23)
- ▷ John the Baptist was the last and greatest prophet and teacher under the Old Covenant (Matt. 11:11; John 3:26)
- ▷ Teaching became the exclusive property of religious professionals (Mark 9:11; 12:35)

Worship in the New Testament: *How should people worship God today?*

▸ TRINITARIAN

Worship is Trinitarian: Worship is given to God, through Christ, by the power of the Holy Spirit

- ▷ The Spirit is jointly worshiped and glorified with the Father and the Son (Matt. 28:19; 1 Cor. 12:4-6; 2 Cor. 13:14)
- ▷ The Son and the Father are to be worshiped and glorified together (John 17:4)
- ▷ Salvation is accomplished by the Trinity (Eph. 1:3-13)

▸ TO THE FATHER

Worship is given to the Father

- ▷ God is to receive all praise and glory (2 Chr. 7:3; Rom. 12:1-2; 2 Cor. 4:7-10)
- ▷ Worship of the Father combats temptation (Matt. 4:10; Heb. 2:18)
- ▷ Jesus taught all to worship the Father (John 4:21-23)
- ▷ Fruit of the Christian life glorifies the Father (John 15:8)
- ▷ God saves people in order to be worshiped and glorified (John 17:4; Rev. 4:6-11)

▸ CHRIST'S SUPREMACY

Christ is the center of New Testament worship

- ▷ His sacrifice provides eternal rest (Judg. 8:4; Matt. 11:28)
- ▷ His sacrifice provides true cleansing from sin (1 Sam. 15:24; Rom. 12:1-2; Heb. 10:10, 14)
- ▷ Jesus is God with us (Matt. 1:23; 2:1-11)
- ▷ Jesus' disciples worship Him (Matt. 14:32-33; 28:9, 17)
- ▷ Christ willingly provided a sacrifice (Matt. 27:34; John 6:38; Heb. 10:7-9; Rev. 5:9-14)
- ▷ Jesus, a ransom for many (Mark 10:45)
- ▷ Jesus is worshiped by the blind man (John 9:37-38)

- ▷ Christ's name commands reverence (John 18:40; Acts 4:12; Phil. 2:9-11)
- ▷ Thomas worships Jesus alone as God (John 20:28)
- ▷ God's plan for salvation is Christ-centered (Eph. 1:9)
- ▷ Jesus' sacrifice gives a clear conscience (Col. 2:14-17; Heb. 9:9)
- ▷ Jesus came to save sinners (1 Tim. 1:15)
- ▷ Proven by His sitting at God's right hand (Heb. 1:3; 8:1)
- ▷ Worshiped by the angels (Heb. 1:6)
- ▷ Christ demonstrates superior priesthood (Heb. 4:16–8:6)
- ▷ One sacrifice based in a new covenant (Heb. 8:7-13)
- ▷ One sacrifice based in a lasting sanctuary (Heb. 9:1-28)
- ▷ Christ's sacrifice makes Him the mediator of a new covenant (Heb. 9:15)
- ▷ God provided a lasting sacrifice in a human body (Heb. 10:5; 1 Jn. 4:10)
- ▷ One sacrifice good for all times (Heb. 10:12-13)
- ▷ Provides true remission from sin (Heb. 10:15-17)
- ▷ No need for more sacrifices (Heb. 10:18)

▶ CHRIST'S KINGSHIP
Christ's kingship in New Testament worship

- ▷ Jesus shall return as king and judge (Judg. 2:8; Matt. 24:30-31; Mark 14:62; 1 Thes. 5:2)
- ▷ Jesus' kingship shall last forever (Luke 1:32-33)
- ▷ Kingdom of God

  The Kingdom of God is Jesus' central teaching theme (Matt. 4:17; Mark 1:15)
  - ▽The two foundations (Matt. 7:24-29; Luke 6:47-49)
  - ▽New cloth and old garment (Matt. 9:16; Mark 2:21-22; Luke 5:36)
  - ▽New wine in old bottles (Matt. 9:17; Mark 2:22; Luke 5:37-39)
  - ▽The sower and soils (Matt. 13:3-9, 18-23; Mark 4:1-9, 14-20; Luke 8:4-8, 11-15; Heb. 6:7-8)
  - ▽The weeds among the wheat (Matt. 13:24-30, 36-43)
  - ▽The mustard seed (Matt. 13:31-32; Mark 4:30-34; Luke 13:18-19)
  - ▽The householder on a journey (Matt. 13:32-37)
  - ▽The yeast (Matt. 13:33-35; Luke 13:13-21)
  - ▽The hidden treasure (Matt. 13:44)
  - ▽The costly pearl (Matt. 13:45-46)
  - ▽The dragnet (Matt. 13:47-52)
  - ▽The lost sheep (Matt. 18:12-14; Luke 15:4-7)
  - ▽The unmerciful servant (Matt. 18:23-35)
  - ▽The laborers in the vineyard (Matt. 20:1-16)
  - ▽The two sons (Matt. 21:28-32)
  - ▽The wicked farmer (Matt. 21:33-40; Mark 12:1-12; Luke 20:9-18)
  - ▽The fig tree (Matt. 24:32-33; Mark 13:28-29; Luke 21:29-31)
  - ▽The marriage feast (Matt. 22:1-14)
  - ▽The ten bridesmaids (Matt. 25:1-13)
  - ▽The ten talents (Matt. 25:14-30)
  - ▽The sheep and goats (Matt. 25:31-33)
  - ▽The two debtors (Luke 7:41-47)
  - ▽The Good Samaritan (Luke 10:30-37)
  - ▽The friend at midnight (Luke 11:5-8)
  - ▽The rich fool (Luke 12:16-21)
  - ▽The wedding feast (Luke 12:35-38)
  - ▽The wise steward (Luke 12:41-48)
  - ▽The barren fig tree (Luke 13:6-9)
  - ▽The dinner (Luke 14:16-24)
  - ▽The lost coin (Luke 15:8-10)
  - ▽The prodigal son (Luke 15:11-32)
  - ▽The unjust steward (Luke 16:1-8)
  - ▽The rich man and Lazarus (Luke 16:19-31)
  - ▽The unprofitable servants (Luke 17:7-10)
  - ▽The unjust judge (Luke 18:1-8)
  - ▽The Pharisee and publican (Luke 18:9-14)
  - ▽The ten slaves (Luke 19:11-27)

▶ CHURCH GOVERNMENT
Local assemblies and organized government in New Testament worship

- ▷ Peter gives charge to elders (Lev. 21:1; 1 Pet. 5:1-6)
- ▷ Qualifications for elders (Judg. 18:20; 1 Tim. 3:1-7; Titus 1:5-9)
- ▷ Local church (2 Chr. 11:16; 1 Cor. 1:2; Phil. 1:2; Col. 1:2)
- ▷ Jesus, the "cornerstone" of the church (Jer. 49:1-2; Eph. 2:20)
- ▷ "Ruler" of synagogue is historical precedent for New Testament elder (Matt. 15:2; Luke 8:41; John 3:1; 7:26)
- ▷ Christ shall build His church (Matt. 16:18)
- ▷ Qualifications for original apostles (Acts 1:21-22)
- ▷ Early house churches (Acts 2:46; 12:12; 20:7-12, 20)
- ▷ First appointment of deacons (Acts 6:1-6)
- ▷ Apostles ordained elders to lead local churches (Acts 14:23; Titus 1:5)
- ▷ First general council of church officers (Acts 15:2)
- ▷ Paul calls elders for meeting (Acts 20:17)
- ▷ Elders also called "overseers" or "bishops" (Acts 20:28; Phil. 1:1)
- ▷ Jesus Christ is "head" of the Church (Eph. 1:20-23; 4:15)
- ▷ Church's foundation built upon apostles and prophets (Eph. 2:20)
- ▷ Five-fold office (Eph. 4:11-13)
- ▷ Qualifications for deacons (1 Tim. 3:8-13)
- ▷ Elders comprise a presbytery (1 Tim. 4:14)
- ▷ Believers to assemble on the Lord's Day (Heb. 10:25)
- ▷ Obedience to officers of the Church (Heb. 13:17; 1 Pet. 5:5)

▶ CLEANSING
God's Cleansing in New Testament worship

- ▷ God requires repentance from known sin (Lev. 6:4; Deut. 30:11; John 7:37-39; 1 Jn. 1:8-10; 2:29–3:1)
- ▷ Drinking from Christ produces living water (John 7:37-38)
- ▷ Believers are cleansed by God's Word (John 17:17)
- ▷ Our hearts are cleansed by faith (Acts 15:8-9; 26:18)
- ▷ The Christian life is a crucified life (Gal. 2:20)
- ▷ The church to have no spot or wrinkle (Eph. 5:27)
- ▷ Work out your salvation (Phil. 2:12-13)
- ▷ God will sanctify wholly (1 Thes. 5:23)
- ▷ Sanctified by the Spirit and truth (2 Thes. 2:13)
- ▷ We are cleansed by Christ's death (Heb. 10:10-14)
- ▷ Believers are partakers of the divine nature (2 Pet. 1:3-4)

▶ FELLOWSHIP
Fellowship in New Testament worship

- ▷ Nature

  The nature of fellowship in New Testament worship
  - ▽Tell the unvarnished truth to each other (Josh. 2:12; 6:22; 1 Sam. 16:2; 1 Kgs. 18:27; Matt. 23:16-22; Jas. 5:12)

- ▽Fellowship based on one faith, one body (Ezra 3:12; 1 Cor. 1:10; Eph. 4:5)
- ▽God lives in us as we love each other (John 5:10; 1 Jn. 4:12)
- ▽First Christian fellowship (Acts 2:44-47)
- ▽Basis of fellowship is acceptance by Christ (Rom. 15:7)
- ▽Community based in fellowship with Christ (1 Cor. 1:9)
- ▽Christ's body, one bread (1 Cor. 10:16)
- ▽Fellowship with Him, not darkness (2 Cor. 10:16; 1 Jn. 1:6)
- ▽Fellowship in the Holy Spirit (2 Cor. 13:14)
- ▽No fellowship with works of darkness (Eph. 5:11)
- ▽Fellowship in the gospel (Phil. 1:5)
- ▽Fellowship in the Spirit (Phil. 2:1)
- ▽Do not forsake gathering together (Heb. 10:25)
- ▽Walking in the light produces fellowship (1 Jn. 1:7)

▷ Preserving

Preserving fellowship in New Testament worship

- ▽Honor one another (Num. 27:1-11; 1 Sam. 30:24-25; Ezra 3:10; Rom. 12:10)
- ▽Be like-minded and accepting (Deut. 23:1-4; Rom. 15:5-7)
- ▽Teach one another (Judg. 2:10; Col. 3:16)
- ▽Look to the interests of one another (Ruth 2:23; Phil. 2:4)
- ▽Love one another (1 Sam. 20:41; John 13:35)
- ▽Encourage one another (Ezra 7:7; Heb. 3:13)
- ▽Serve one another (Esth. 10:3; John 13:3-5; Gal. 5:13)
- ▽Forgive one another (Matt. 18:23-35; Eph. 4:2, 32; Col. 3:13)
- ▽Be devoted to one another (Rom. 12:10)
- ▽Live in harmony (Rom. 12:16)
- ▽Build up one another (Rom. 14:19; 1 Thes. 5:11)
- ▽Admonish one another (Rom. 15:14; 1 Cor. 5:9-13; Col. 3:16)
- ▽Be caring (1 Cor. 12:25)
- ▽Comfort one another (2 Cor. 1:3-7; 1 Thes. 4:18)
- ▽Consider others more important (2 Cor. 13:9; Phil. 2:3)
- ▽Bear one another's burdens (Gal. 6:2)
- ▽Be patient with one another (Eph. 4:2; Col. 3:13)
- ▽Be kind and compassionate (Eph. 4:32)
- ▽Submit to one another (Eph. 5:21; 1 Pet. 5:5)
- ▽Bear with one another (Col. 3:13)
- ▽Stir up to love and good deeds (Heb. 10:24)
- ▽Confess our faults to one another (Jas. 5:16)
- ▽Pray for one another (Jas. 5:16)
- ▽Show hospitality (1 Pet. 4:9)

▶ HOLY SPIRIT

The Holy Spirit energizes New Testament worship

- ▷ The Church is one body with many members (Lev. 8:3; Rom. 15:20-21; 1 Cor. 12:14-27)
- ▷ Do not blaspheme the Spirit (Matt. 12:31)
- ▷ The Spirit reveals God's will in worship (Acts 13:2)
- ▷ We are called to discern our gifts in humility (Rom. 12:3)
- ▷ We are to exercise our gifts properly (Rom. 12:6-21; 1 Cor. 12:7-10)
- ▷ The Spirit gives gifts to use in personal and public worship (1 Cor. 12; 14)
- ▷ There is one God but a variety of gifts (1 Cor. 12:4-6)
- ▷ Spirit distributes gifts (1 Cor. 12:11)
- ▷ Desire the greater gifts (1 Cor. 12:28-31)
- ▷ Pursue love, yet desire spiritual gifts (1 Cor. 14:1)
- ▷ Prophecy is superior to tongues (1 Cor. 14:2-5)
- ▷ Tongues are to be interpreted (1 Cor. 14:13, 27)
- ▷ Tongues are to be interpreted and are limited to three within a meeting (1 Cor. 14:27)
- ▷ All gifts are to be used for edification (1 Cor. 14:26-28)
- ▷ Prophecies are to be judged (1 Cor. 14:29; 1 Thes. 5:20-21)
- ▷ Prophecy is to be done one at a time (1 Cor. 14:31)
- ▷ In public worship, the Spirit works for unity, not confusion (1 Cor. 14:33, 40)
- ▷ Do not forbid tongues (1 Cor. 14:39)
- ▷ God's plan of salvation is through the Spirit (Eph. 1:12-14)
- ▷ Worship is by the Spirit (Phil. 3:3)
- ▷ Each should employ his or her special gift (1 Pet. 4:10)
- ▷ Worship is in the Spirit (Rev. 1:10)

▶ MUSIC

Music in New Testament worship

- ▷ Hymns of praise (Mark 14:26; Acts 16:25; Heb. 2:12)
- ▷ Newly composed songs for worship (1 Cor. 14:26)
- ▷ Paul's "doxology" of praise (Eph. 1:3-14)
- ▷ Early Christian hymns in Scripture (Eph. 5:14; Phil. 2:6-11; Col. 1:15-20; 1 Tim. 3:16)
- ▷ Believers urged to sing psalms, hymns, and spiritual songs (Eph. 5:19; Col. 3:16)
- ▷ Book of Revelation depicts heavenly singing (Rev. 5:9; 14:3)

▶ OFFERINGS

Tithes, offerings, and giving in New Testament worship

- ▷ Widow's offering (Lev. 5:11; Mark 12:41-44; Luke 19:8)
- ▷ Contributions for the poor (Deut. 24:19; Isa. 11:4; Rom. 15:25-28; 1 Cor. 16:1-4; 2 Cor. 8–9)
- ▷ Be faithful with riches (Deut. 26:12; 1 Chr. 26:27; Isa. 23:3; Luke 16:11; Jas. 5:1-6)
- ▷ God loves a cheerful giver (Neh. 10:35; Jer. 9:25-26; 2 Cor. 9:6-7)
- ▷ Give in secret (Matt. 6:1-4; 19:21)
- ▷ Lay up treasures in heaven (Matt. 6:19; 19:21)
- ▷ Tithing and the heart (Matt. 23:23; Luke 11:42; 2 Cor. 8:3-5)
- ▷ Faithful stewards (Matt. 25:14-30; 1 Cor. 4:2)
- ▷ Give and it will be given to you (Luke 6:38)
- ▷ Churches of Macedonia give liberally (2 Cor. 8:1-3)
- ▷ Christ's example of generosity (2 Cor. 8:9; Phlm. 1:6)
- ▷ Support full-time workers (Gal. 6:6-7)
- ▷ Paul thankful for generous offering (Phil. 4:13-19)

▶ OUR ROLE

Our role in New Testament worship

▷ Attitude

Attitude of the heart in New Testament worship

- ▽Trusting in the midst of trials (Judg. 7:7; Ruth 1:20; 2 Chr. 16:10; Esth. 8:10; Isa. 30:2; Rom. 8:28; Gal. 1:9)
- ▽Cooperative with other believers (Judg. 15:12; 2 Sam. 15:37; 1 Cor. 10:32; 1 Cor. 14:12; Heb. 2:12)
- ▽Submissive before authority (2 Sam. 15:6; 1 Chr. 11:3; Heb. 13:17; 1 Pet. 2:13-15)

- ▽Willing to repent of bad attitude (2 Chr. 16:10; Acts 8:22)
- ▽Self-effacing when successful (Prov. 16:18; Jas. 4:6, 10)
- ▽Conciliatory in the face of misunderstanding (Matt. 5:9; Phil. 2:14; Col. 3:13)
- ▽Biblical response to sin (Matt. 18:8-9; Gal. 6:1)
- ▽Compassionate to the lost (Matt. 18:11-14; 2 Cor. 5:18; 2 Pet. 3:9)
- ▽Reverent and submissive before God (Mark 12:30; John 14:15; Jas. 4:7)
- ▽Focused and persevering in our work (Luke 16:10; 1 Cor. 4:2)
- ▽Patient when wronged (Luke 18:7; Rom. 12:19)
- ▽Loving and encouraging to others (Rom. 12:10; 1 Cor. 13:4-8; Heb. 3:13; 1 Thes. 5:11)
- ▽Willing to submit thoughts and attitude to God (2 Cor. 10:5)
- ▽Show impartiality (Eph. 4:2; Jas. 2:9)
- ▽Kindness to others (Eph. 4:32)
- ▽Attitude improved by dwelling on things above (Phil. 4:8)

▷ Holiness

Personal holiness in New Testament worship

- ▽Christian life means being transformed (Lev. 10:9-10; 1 Cor. 3:1-4, 18)
- ▽Flee immorality (Lev. 18:4; 2 Chr. 20:35; 1 Cor. 6:12-20)
- ▽Sin not to reign in our bodies (2 Sam. 11:11; Rom. 6:12-14)
- ▽Two great commandments (Ezek. 44:7; Matt. 20:36-40)
- ▽Worship confronts temptation (Matt. 4:10)
- ▽Believers are to consider themselves dead to sin (Rom. 6:9)
- ▽Believers are slaves of righteousness (Rom. 6:15-18)
- ▽Unrighteous will not inherit the Kingdom of God (1 Cor. 6:9-11)
- ▽Called to be separate from the world (2 Cor. 6:16-17)
- ▽God will not approve evil (Phil. 2:12)
- ▽Salvation worked out through obedience (Phil. 2:12)
- ▽Our hearts to be established in holiness (1 Thes. 3:12-13; Jas. 4:1-2)
- ▽God will sanctify us entirely (1 Thes. 5:23-25)
- ▽Failure to obey can lead to punishment (2 Thes. 1:9)
- ▽Jesus, the model of holiness (Heb. 4:15)
- ▽You shall be holy (Heb. 10:10, 14; 1 Pet. 1:15-16)
- ▽No one will see God without holiness (Heb. 12:14)

▷ Mind and Heart

New Testament believers worship with mind and heart

- ▽We offer our bodies as a living sacrifice (Lev. 22:20; Rom. 12:1-2)
- ▽Worship in spirit and in truth because God is Spirit (Num. 3:4; John 4:23-24; 1 Cor. 14:14-16)
- ▽Worship decently and in order (Judg. 10:1-2; 1 Cor. 14:40)
- ▽Must be in respect and holy fear (2 Kgs. 5:17; Heb. 12:28-29)
- ▽We are to have heaven's wisdom (Isa. 37:1; Jer. 42:3; Eph. 5:17)
- ▽Lord's Supper to be taken in a worthy manner (Jer. 25:15; 1 Cor. 11:27-29)
- ▽Heart-felt worship (Matt. 15:8; Mark 7:6-13)
- ▽Fervent in Spirit (Matt. 26:6-13; Mark 14:3-9; John 2:17; Rom. 12:11)
- ▽God's truth central, not the precepts of men (Mark 7:7)
- ▽The truth shall make you free (John 8:32)
- ▽Worship through Jesus only (John 14:6)
- ▽Worship not directed to God results in ignorance (Acts 17:23)
- ▽Glorify God in worship and all we do (1 Cor. 6:20; 2 Cor. 11:30)
- ▽Pray and sing with understanding (1 Cor. 14:15)
- ▽Our thinking is to be mature (1 Cor. 14:20)
- ▽God is not a God of confusion (1 Cor. 14:33)
- ▽Filled with the Spirit (Eph. 5:18)
- ▽Filled with the Word (Col. 3:18)

▷ Obedience

Obedience in New Testament worship

- ▽To believe Jesus is to obey Him (Lev. 20:2; John 3:16-21)
- ▽Obedient to masters (employers) (Job 31:15; Eph. 6:4; Col. 3:22; Titus 2:9; 1 Pet. 2:18)
- ▽Believer not to be conformed to the world (Isa. 8:11; Rom. 12:1-2)
- ▽Show faith by our works (Jer. 14:12; Jas. 2:18)
- ▽Called to keep a Sabbath (Luke 6:1-5; Acts 9:2; 17:2; 18:4)
- ▽Loving Jesus means keeping His commands (John 14:15; 1 Jn. 1:3-4)
- ▽Do not neglect doing good (John 19:27; Heb. 13:15-16)
- ▽Loving God means keeping His commandments (Acts 23:1; 1 Jn. 5:3)
- ▽Not to live for ourselves, but for Christ (2 Cor. 5:14-15)
- ▽Obedient to husbands (Eph. 5:21-22, 24; Col. 3:18; Titus 2:5; 1 Pet. 3:1, 5-6)
- ▽Obedient to parents (Eph. 6:1; Col. 3:20)
- ▽Jesus, the supreme example of obedience (Phil. 2:8)
- ▽Faith without works is dead (Jas. 2:15-17)
- ▽Called to be obedient children (1 Pet. 1:4)

▶ REVERENCE

Reverence, awe, and fear in New Testament worship

- ▷ We fear God because He has power over life and death (1 Sam. 2:12; 1 Chr. 10:13; Luke 12:5)
- ▷ Jesus is our eternal Master (1 Sam. 29:8; Rev. 19:5)
- ▷ Fear/awe of God is characteristic of faith (2 Kgs. 7:19; Heb. 11:7)
- ▷ We fear Jesus, eternal creator and judge of mankind (Jer. 51:15; Rev. 14:7)
- ▷ God demands our undivided reverence (Matt. 6:24; 28:17)
- ▷ Fear/awe was a mark of the early church (Acts 9:31)
- ▷ God is Lord of heaven and earth (Acts 17:24)
- ▷ Called to work out our salvation with fear (Phil. 2:12)
- ▷ We fear God because He judges all men impartially (1 Pet. 1:17)
- ▷ Apostolic command to fear God (1 Pet. 2:17)
- ▷ God is worthy of reverent worship (Rev. 4:8-11)
- ▷ God alone is holy (Rev. 15:4)

▶ POSTURE

Varieties of posture in New Testament worship

- ▷ Pray by laying on hands (Matt. 19:13-14; Mark 10:16; Acts 6:6; 28:8)

- ▷ Sitting (Matt. 26:20; Acts 13:14)
- ▷ Bowing prostrate (Matt. 26:39; Mark 14:35; Luke 22:41)
- ▷ Raised hands (1 Tim. 2:8)

▶ PRAYER

Corporate and personal prayer in New Testament worship

- ▷ Instructions
  Instructions about prayer in the New Testament
  - ▽Draw near with confidence (Lev. 5:18; Heb. 4:16; 10:19-22)
  - ▽Pray with fasting (Num. 6:2; Matt. 17:21; Luke 2:37-38; 5:33; Acts 13:3; 14:23)
  - ▽Widows to pray (Judg. 12:13; 1 Tim. 5:5)
  - ▽Pray for enemies (1 Sam. 10:1; Obad. 1:14; Matt. 5:43-45)
  - ▽Pray for wisdom (1 Kgs. 3:7-9; Jas. 1:5-8)
  - ▽Pray for those in authority (Deut. 23:1-4; Isa. 3:8; 1 Tim. 2:1-2)
  - ▽Pray in secret (Matt. 6:6)
  - ▽Prayer promises (Matt. 7:7-11; Luke 11:9-13; John 14:13-14; 15:7, 16; 16:23-24, 26-27; Phil. 4:6-9)
  - ▽Devote yourselves to prayer (Matt. 7:7-11; Luke 18:1-8; Col. 4:2-4)
  - ▽Pray for workers (Matt. 9:37-39; Luke 10:2)
  - ▽Prayer before meals (Matt. 14:19; 15:35-36; John 6:11)
  - ▽Prayer certainty (Matt. 18:18-20; Mark 11:21-24)
  - ▽The church is called a house of prayer (Matt. 21:13)
  - ▽Pray with humility (Matt. 21:21-22; Luke 18:10-14)
  - ▽Pray believing (Matt. 21:22; Mark 9:2-8; 11:24; Luke 18:40-42)
  - ▽Pray concerning the end times (Matt. 24:20; Mark 13:18)
  - ▽Pray to avoid temptation (Matt. 26:41; Mark 14:38; Luke 22:40-46)
  - ▽Pray without ceasing (Mark 1:35; 1 Thes. 5:16-18)
  - ▽Sanctify all things with prayer (Luke 10:2; 1 Tim. 4:4-5)
  - ▽Persevere in prayer (Luke 11:5-13; 18:1-8)
  - ▽Christ intercedes for us (Luke 22:39-40; John 17:9-10)
  - ▽The Holy Spirit in prayer (John 14:12-17)
  - ▽Pray in decision-making (Acts 1:24-26)
  - ▽The Holy Spirit helps us pray (Rom. 8:26-27)
  - ▽Pray for Israel (Rom. 9:3-5; 10:1)
  - ▽Couples may abstain for prayer (1 Cor. 7:4-5)
  - ▽Be anxious for nothing (Phil. 4:6-7; Rev. 8:3-4)
  - ▽Prayers are heard due to piety (Heb. 5:7)
  - ▽Pray for one another (Jas. 5:13-15)
  - ▽Pray earnestly (Jas. 4:3-8; 5:17-18)
  - ▽Pray soberly (1 Pet. 4:7)
  - ▽Pray for one who commits sin not leading to death (1 Jn. 5:16)
  - ▽Believers' prayers are an offering to God (Rev. 5:8; 8:3-4)
- ▷ Examples
  Examples of prayer in the New Testament
  - ▽Jesus
    - The Lord's Prayer (Matt. 6:9-13; Luke 11:2-4)
    - Christ prayed as a regular practice (Matt. 14:23; Mark 1:35; Luke 3:21; 5:16; 6:12; 9:29-30; John 6:11)
    - Christ's prayer in the Garden of Gethsemane (Matt. 26:36; Mark 14:32; Luke 22:41-42; John 17:20)
    - Christ's prayer of thanks during the Last Supper (John 6:11)
    - Prayer for unity (John 17:20-26)
  - ▽Paul
    - For Himself
      Paul's prayers for himself
      - For confidence (Acts 4:29-30)
      - For acceptable service (Rom. 15:30-32)
      - For deliverance (2 Cor. 1:10b-11)
      - For other saints and for boldness (Eph. 6:18-20)
      - For clarity and open doors (Col. 4:2-4)
    - For Others
      Paul's prayers for others
      - To grow in spiritual maturity (2 Cor. 13:7, 9; Eph. 4:11-16; Heb. 5:12)
      - For their participation in the gospel (Phil. 1:3)
      - To grow in a spirit of wisdom and revelation (Eph. 1:15-19)
      - To be filled up to all the fullness of God (Eph. 3:14-21)
      - To experience abounding love (Phil. 1:9-11)
      - For continuing faith (Col. 1:3)
      - To bear much spiritual fruit (Col. 1:9-12)
      - For a complete faith (1 Thes. 3:9-10)
      - To fulfill their calling (2 Thes. 1:11-12)
      - For Timothy (2 Tim. 1:3)
      - Philemon to grow in love and faith (Phlm. 1:6)
  - ▽Others
    - Anna in the Temple (Luke 2:37-38)
    - The disciples pray in an upper room (Acts 2:4)
    - The first disciples devote themselves to prayer (Acts 2:42; 6:4; 21:5)
    - The disciples pray in the Temple (Acts 3:1; 22:17)
    - The apostles pray for the filling of the Spirit (Acts 8:14-17)
    - Simon the sorcerer's prayer for forgiveness (Acts 8:22-24)
    - Peter's prayer and vision (Acts 11:5)
    - Believers pray for Peter in prison (Acts 12:5)
    - Paul and Silas pray in prison (Acts 16:25)
    - Epaphras's prayer for the saints (Col. 4:12)
    - John prays for good health of believers (3 Jn. 1:2)

▶ PROHIBITIONS

Prohibitions in New Testament worship

- ▷ Wrong Forms
  Wrong forms of worship
  - ▽Ignorant (John 4:22)
  - ▽Lacking submission (1 Cor. 11:2-16)
  - ▽Unworthy (1 Cor. 11:27)
  - ▽Confused (1 Cor. 14:33, 40)
- ▷ Wrong Objects
  Wrong objects of worship
  - ▽Money (1 Chr. 29:14; Eph. 5:5; 1 Tim. 6:6-10, 17-19; Heb. 13:4-5)
  - ▽Religious leaders (2 Chr. 2:11; 1 Cor. 1:10-17)
  - ▽Political leaders (2 Chr. 2:11; Acts 12:23)
  - ▽Idols (Acts 17:23; Rom. 1:23; 1 Cor. 10:14)
  - ▽State-established gods (Acts 19:27)
  - ▽The anti-Christ (2 Thes. 2:4)
  - ▽Angels (Rev. 22:8)

▷ Wrong Preparation
Wrong preparation for worship
▽Bitterness (Acts 8:20-23)
▽Not repentant (1 Cor. 5:1-5)
▽Spiritual pride (1 Cor. 5:6)
▽Hungry (1 Cor. 11:20-22)

▶ SACRAMENTS
The sacraments in New Testament worship
▷ Lord's Supper
▽Institution of the Lord's Supper (Exod. 12:1; Matt. 26:26-28)
▽Early Church devoted to the Lord's Supper (Acts 2:42)
▽Paul's instruction regarding the breaking of bread (1 Cor. 11:23-34)
▷ Baptism
▽Baptism identifies the believer with community of faith (Lev. 12:3; Col. 2:11-12)
▽Jesus' baptism (Matt. 3:13-17; Mark 1:9-11)
▽Baptism is part of Great Commission (Matt. 28:19)
▽Relationship of water baptism to the baptism of the Holy Spirit (Acts 1:5)
▽First believers are baptized as individuals, groups, and families (Acts 2:38; 8–9; 16)
▽John the Baptist's baptism functioned as a sign of repentance, readiness for the Messiah (Acts 19:4)
▽Baptism is a sign, pointing to the reality of God's work in all who believe (Rom. 6:3-4; Titus 3:5-6)
▽Paul's description of baptism (Rom. 6:3-5; Col. 2:12)
▽Parting of the Red Sea, a type of baptism (1 Cor. 10:1-2)
▽Baptism symbolizes unity with one another (1 Cor. 12:13; Eph. 4:4-5)
▽Baptism is a seal, ratifying God's promise of salvation to all who believe (2 Cor. 1:21-22; Eph. 1:13-14; 4:30)
▽Washing symbolizes inner cleansing (Heb. 10:22)
▽Baptism as a symbol of salvation (1 Pet. 3:21)

▶ SACRIFICIAL LIVING
Sacrificial living in New Testament worship
▷ The rich called to sacrifice for kingdom of heaven (Judg. 10:3-4; Matt. 19:21-22; 1 Tim. 6:17-19)
▷ Sacrificial living is pleasing to God (Ezra 1:6; Phil. 4:18)
▷ Planning and budgeting part of sacrificial living (Ezra 2:68; Matt. 13:22)
▷ Enables us to help meet others' needs (Jer. 22:15-16; Matt. 14:16-19; 25:31-46; Acts 4:34-37; 2 Cor. 8:12-14)
▷ Sacrificial living means laying up treasure in heaven (Matt. 6:19-20; Luke 18:22-34)
▷ Sacrifice for Jesus may lead to maltreatment (Matt. 19:29; Mark 1:16-20; Luke 5:11, 27-28)
▷ More blessed to give than to receive (Mark 12:41-44; Acts 20:34-35; 2 Cor. 9:11)
▷ Counting the cost of following Jesus (Mark 8:34-38; Luke 9:57-62; 14:27-32)
▷ Jesus' example (Luke 9:57-58; 2 Cor. 8:9)
▷ Quality of spiritual worship (Rom. 12:1)
▷ Sacrificial giving helps to support full-time workers (1 Cor. 9:10-12; Phil. 4:10-19)
▷ Paul's example (2 Cor. 11:23-33; 12:15)
▷ Sacrificial living joined with contentment (1 Tim. 6:8)
▷ Sacrifice for Jesus may mean loss of property (Heb. 10:34)

▶ TEACHING AND PREACHING
Biblical teaching and preaching in New Testament worship
▷ Persecution for preaching the Word (2 Chr. 30:10-12; John 16:2; Acts 13:50; 17:5-9; 17:13; 21:28; Heb. 10:33-34)
▷ Telling stories (Jer. 28:13)
▷ Gospel to be preached to the nations (Mark 13:10)
▷ Early pattern of expositional preaching (Luke 4:11-19; 24:27)
▷ Peter's sermon (Acts 2:14-36)
▷ Steven's defense (Acts 7)
▷ Philip expounds on the Word to an Ethiopian (Acts 8:26-35)
▷ All Jerusalem hears the Word (Acts 13:44)
▷ Paul turns his preaching to the Gentiles (Acts 13:46)
▷ Preaching central in missionary journeys (Acts 14:7, 25, 36; 16:10)
▷ Paul teaches in the synagogue (Acts 17:2)
▷ Paul's Sermon on Mars Hill (Acts 17:22-31)
▷ Paul's ministry of the Word in Corinth (Acts 18:5)
▷ Paul speaks boldly in Ephesus (Acts 19:8)
▷ Word of the Lord prevails in Ephesus (Acts 19:20)
▷ Paul exhorts people in Macedonia (Acts 20:2)
▷ Paul did not shrink back from declaring the Word (Acts 20:20, 27)
▷ Paul's last days spent preaching and teaching (Acts 28:23)
▷ Paul longed to preach (Rom. 1:15)
▷ Law has a place in New Testament teaching (Rom. 2:13; 3:31; 7:7, 22; 8:3; Heb. 8:10)
▷ Preacher's message is beautiful (Rom. 10:15)
▷ Exhortation to study Scripture (Col. 3:16; 1 Tim. 4:13)
▷ Preach the word in season and out (1 Thes. 1:5; 2 Tim. 4:2)
▷ Believers born again through the Word's being preached (1 Pet. 1:23)

DISCOVER GOD'S ADOPTION

Finding Your Identity in Christ

The God who created the heavens and the earth with just a thought—how big must God be to do something like that? Not only that, but every moment, God sustains the universe, continuing its existence by the power of His will. With all that, what must He think of us? Are we like insects to Him?

If God did not value us, He would not have sent His beloved Son to die for us. If God did not value us, He would not then call us His children, placing us in His beloved family with His Son, Jesus.

Our parents may die, or they may live but reject us. Our entire family may turn against us, but Christians can never be orphans. In this section of the outline, we can see how God makes cursed rebels into blessed children of God by adopting us into His family and linking all believers to Christ and one another forever.

■ ■ ■

WITHOUT CHRIST ***Because we are separated from God the Father,***
Only the work of His only Son can establish an eternal relationship with Him.

WITH CHRIST ***Because I am united with Christ by faith,***
I can rejoice that I am a treasured child in God's family.

IN HEAVEN ***Because I am a member of the family of God,***
I will dwell in His house with all God's people forever.

WITHOUT CHRIST

Life without Christ: *What is our spiritual condition apart from Christ?*

SEPARATED FROM GOD
Spiritual separation from God

- Spiritually dead (Gen. 2:17; 3:17; Ezek. 18:4, 20; 1 Kgs. 2:42; Rom. 3:23)
- Facing physical death (Gen. 3:3; Ps. 88:3; Eccl. 12:7; Rom. 5:14)
- Banished from God's fellowship (Gen. 3:23-24)
- Bad spiritual heart (Gen. 8:21; Exod. 8:15; Ps. 14:1; Prov. 12:20; Ezek. 44:7; Matt. 15:18; Mark 7:20-23; Acts 7:51; Rom. 2:4-5)
- Facing judgment (Deut. 3:6; Job 38:3; Ps. 76:7; 2 Thes. 1:9; Heb. 9:27)
- Sold into sin (1 Kgs. 21:20, 25; 2 Kgs. 17:17; Rom. 7:14; Gal. 4:3)
- A world of lost sinners (Pss. 14:1-3; 53:2; Rom. 5:12)
- Worship through lip service only (Isa. 29:13; Jer. 38:16; Mark 7:6-8)
- Unrighteous (Isa. 55:7; Jer. 22:13; Rom. 2:10-18; 1 Cor. 6:9)
- No fellowship with God (Isa. 59:1-2; 1 Tim. 5:6)
- Facing second death (Hos. 13:14; 2 Thes. 1:9; Rev. 20:14-15; 21:8; 22:15)
- Enslaved to sin (John 8:34; Rom. 6:17; Titus 3:3)
- Aligned with Satan (John 8:44; 2 Cor. 4:4; 1 Jn. 3:8)
- Under sin (Rom. 3:9)
- Killed by the law (Rom. 7:9-11)
- Aligned with the world's system (1 Jn. 2:15-17)

CONNECTED TO GOD
Connections to God in spite of spiritual condition

- Human Nature
  - Created in the image of God (Gen. 1:26-27; 5:1; 9:5-6; Lev. 24:21; 1 Cor. 11:7; Jas. 3:9)
  - Created with a sense of eternity (Eccl. 3:11)
  - Created with the law in our hearts (Rom. 2:14-15)
- Human Experience
  - Reason as God does to one another (Isa. 1:18; 1 Pet. 3:15)
  - Walk the same earth as Jesus did (John 1:14-16)
  - Share a love of humanity (John 3:16)

WITH CHRIST

Life with Christ: *What is our spiritual condition in Christ?*

CHILDREN OF GOD
We are children of God

- God disciplines His children (Lev. 26:33; Num. 14:28; Deut. 8:15; Prov. 3:11; Isa. 27:7-9; 2 Cor. 7:8-10; Heb. 12:10)
- Protected by God (Num. 22:6)
- Children share suffering and glory (Judg. 2:22-23; Acts 14:22; Rom. 8:17; 1 Thes. 3:3; Rev. 16:6)
- Loved by the Father (Luke 15:11-32; 1 Jn. 3:1)
- God gives good things to His children (Luke 18:15-17; John 14:13-14; 1 Jn. 5:14-15)
- Children of God raised to new life (Luke 20:36)
- Children of God by receiving Christ (John 1:12)
- Spirit tells us we are children (Rom. 8:15-17)
- Children through faith (Gal. 3:26)
- God's own children (Gal. 4:6-7; Eph. 2:19)
- As God's children we have His Spirit (Gal. 4:6)
- Children chosen of God (Eph. 1:4; 1 Pet. 4:16)
- Adopted children of God (Eph. 1:4-5)
- Imitate God as children (Eph. 5:1)
- Children of light (Eph. 5:8)

HEIRS OF GOD
We are heirs of God in Christ

- Receive inheritance through faith and patience (Gen. 25:33; 27:11; Deut. 6:10; Heb. 6:12)
- Our inheritance includes sharing His glory (Lev. 9:6; Rom. 8:29-30)
- Protected by God (Num. 22:6)
- Spiritual blessing of wisdom (1 Kgs. 4:1; 1 Cor. 3:18; Eph. 1:7-8)
- Inheritance reserved in heaven (Neh. 11:20; Matt. 22:1-14; 1 Pet. 1:4)
- Receive inheritance through suffering (Jer. 15:15; Rom. 8:17)
- Inheritance shared by Jews and Gentiles alike (Jer. 39:16-17; Ezek. 16:61; 47:22-23; Eph. 3:6)
- We shall reign with Him (Ezek. 46:16-18; Luke 22:29-30)
- Treasure in heaven (Matt. 6:19-21)
- Endowed with eternal life (John 3:16; 5:24; 17:3; Titus 3:7)
- Our inheritance includes glorified bodies (1 Cor. 15:42-43)
- Heirs as God's children (Gal. 4:7)
- Every spiritual blessing (Eph. 1:3)
- Spirit is guarantee of inheritance (Eph. 1:14)
- God loves His children unconditionally (1 Jn. 3:1)

NEW NATURE
We are saints with a new nature

- Light of the world (Matt. 5:14)
- Born of the Spirit (John 3:5, 8; Titus 3:5)
- Born again (John 3:7; 1 Pet. 1:3; 1 Jn. 3:9; 5:18)
- Holy Spirit-controlled mind (Rom. 8:6)
- We have the mind of Christ (1 Cor. 2:16)
- Made right with God (1 Cor. 6:11)
- One in Christ (Gal. 3:28; Eph. 2:14, 17-18)
- God's masterpiece (Eph. 2:10; 4:22-24)
- Called saints by name (Phil. 1:1; Col. 1:2)
- Completely righteous in Christ (Phil. 3:8-9)
- Freed from kingdom of darkness (Col. 1:13)
- Alive with Christ (Col. 2:13-14)
- Imparts righteousness into spirit, soul, and body (1 Thes. 5:23-24)
- Kingdom of priests (1 Pet. 2:9)

REDEMPTION
We experience redemption and assurance in Christ

- Every spiritual blessing in the heavenlies (Lev. 9:22; Eph. 1:3ff)
- Citizen of Christ's kingdom/heaven (Lev. 20:23; Eph. 2:19; Phil. 3:20)

- ▷ Freedom from meaninglessness and despair (Job 30:16; Eccl. 1:2; John 10:10)
- ▷ Sheep of His pasture (Ps. 23:1; John 1:14)
- ▷ Promise of rescue from trouble (Pss. 34:17-19; 54:1; Mark 5:35-43)
- ▷ Freedom from oppressive guilt (Isa. 61:10)
- ▷ Forgiveness of sins (Zech. 5:9; Eph. 1:7)
- ▷ Humble self-estimation (Luke 14:7-11; Rom. 12:3, 16; 2 Cor. 10:17-18; Titus 3:1-2)
- ▷ Branch of the Vine (John 15:1, 5)
- ▷ Friend of Christ (John 15:15)
- ▷ No condemnation (Rom. 8:1)
- ▷ Heir of God and co-heir with Christ (Rom. 8:17)
- ▷ Freedom from dependency and lust (Rom. 13:14; Gal. 5:16-18)
- ▷ Indwelt by the Spirit (1 Cor. 3:16; 6:19)
- ▷ God's special possession (1 Cor. 6:19-20; 1 Pet. 2:9)
- ▷ Reconciled to God (2 Cor. 5:18)
- ▷ Sonship (Gal. 4:6-7)
- ▷ Living stones in God's spiritual house (1 Pet. 2:4-5; see also 1 Cor. 3:16)
- ▷ Partakers of the divine nature (2 Pet. 1:4)
- ▷ Certainty of salvation (1 Jn. 5:11-13)

▶ SERVANTS

We are servants of Christ

- ▷ Chosen to be holy (Lev. 8:23; Col. 3:12; 1 Pet. 1:14-16)
- ▷ Ambassadors for Christ (Lev. 22:33; Matt. 28:18-20; 2 Cor. 5:20)
- ▷ Slaves of righteousness (Deut. 15:17; Rom. 6:17)
- ▷ Provided spiritual weapons (2 Kgs. 10:16; 2 Cor. 10:3-5)
- ▷ Unified community of believers (Neh. 3:5; 1 Cor. 12:25; Eph. 4:1-3)
- ▷ Witness for Christ (Ps. 26:12; Isa. 12:5; 22:4; 52:7; Ezek. 33:7; Matt. 28:18-20; Acts 24:14)
- ▷ Created to do good works (Prov. 6:6; Matt. 20:26-27; Eph. 2:10; Jas. 2:14-26; Titus 3:8, 14)
- ▷ Appointed to bear fruit (Prov. 11:30; Matt. 12:33-37; John 15:16)
- ▷ Salt of the earth (Matt. 5:13)
- ▷ Light of the world (Matt. 5:14)
- ▷ Entrusted keys to the kingdom (Matt. 16:19; 18:18)
- ▷ Temple of the Holy Spirit (1 Cor. 6:19)
- ▷ God's workmanship/masterpiece (Eph. 2:10)
- ▷ Children of light, not darkness (1 Thes. 5:5)
- ▷ Have a heavenly calling (Heb. 3:1)
- ▷ Aliens living in this world (1 Pet. 2:11)
- ▷ Devil's enemy (1 Pet. 5:8)
- ▷ Defeated the evil world (1 Jn. 5:4-5; Rev. 18:2)

▶ SUPERNATURAL

We experience a supernatural life in Christ

- ▷ An abundant life (Gen. 25:8; John 10:10; Rom. 6:6-11; 7:24-25; Rev. 3:20)
- ▷ Speak godly words (Exod. 5:19-23; Num. 22:22; 1 Sam. 22:9; 1 Kgs. 12:10; 1 Chr. 12:14; Esth. 2:22; Job 32:18; Pss. 64:3; 141:3; Prov. 15:28; 16:24)
- ▷ Freedom from envy and coveting (Exod. 20:17; 1 Sam. 18:9; Heb. 13:5)
- ▷ All things are new (Lev. 14:4; Matt. 12:13; 2 Cor. 5:17)
- ▷ A life of liberating freedom (Lev. 25:10; John 8:32; Rom. 6:19; 1 Cor. 8:9-13; Gal. 5:1)
- ▷ A life of everlasting peace (Judg. 14:17; 2 Chr. 13:12; Ps. 120:6; Isa. 48:22; John 14:27; Rom. 5:1; Phil. 4:6-7)
- ▷ Freedom from rejection (2 Sam. 17:23; Rom. 8:31)
- ▷ All things accomplished through Christ (2 Sam. 22:1; Rom. 15:18)
- ▷ Victory over Satan (1 Kgs. 18:24; Ps. 60:12; Acts 25:2; 2 Thes. 3:3)
- ▷ A life of supernatural power (2 Chr. 16:9; Acts 1:8; Phil. 3:10; 4:11-13; 2 Tim. 1:7)
- ▷ Quick to listen (Job 21:2; Ps. 85:8; Prov. 18:13; Ezek. 3:10-11; Luke 8:43-48)
- ▷ A life of immeasurable riches (Job 27:18; Rom. 5:1-2)
- ▷ Controlled by Christ (Job 34:31; Prov. 5:12-13; Rom. 8:9, 14)
- ▷ A life of infinite joy (Ps. 58:11; Isa. 61:7; Jer. 41:13; Matt. 13:44; Luke 22:14-30; Rom. 14:17; Phil. 1:21)
- ▷ No foolish talk (Eccl. 5:2; Eph. 4:29-31; 5:1)
- ▷ Raised from the dead (Ezek. 37:12; Eph. 2:4-6)
- ▷ Freedom from worry (Zeph. 3:17; Luke 12:22-23; Rom. 8:15; 1 Pet. 5:7)
- ▷ Freedom from selfishness (Mark 8:34-35; Luke 10:30-37; Phil. 2:3-4)
- ▷ Christ lives through believers (Mark 16:15-20; Gal. 2:20)
- ▷ Buried and raised with Christ (Rom. 6:4)
- ▷ Dead to sin but alive to God (Rom. 6:6-14, 22)
- ▷ More than conquerors (Rom. 8:35-37; 2 Cor. 10:3-5)
- ▷ The source for extraordinary living (1 Cor. 16:1-2; Col. 1:15-17)
- ▷ A life of triumph over adversity (2 Cor. 2:14)
- ▷ A life of faith (Gal. 3:11-14; Heb. 11:6)
- ▷ Do the will of God as a slave of Christ (Eph. 6:6)
- ▷ Our lives hidden with Christ (Col. 3:3)

▶ UNITED WITH CHRIST

We are connected to Christ and His people

- ▷ Slave of righteousness (Gen. 15:6; Rom. 6:18)
- ▷ New heart (Deut. 30:6; Jer. 24:7; 31:33; 32:40; Ezek. 11:19-20; 36:26)
- ▷ Loved by God (Ps. 52:8; Isa. 49:15; Rom. 5:8-9; 1 Thes. 5:4)
- ▷ Enslaved to God (Ps. 123:2; Rom. 6:22)
- ▷ Spiritually alive (John 10:28; 11:25)
- ▷ United to Christ (Rom. 7:4; Col. 2:6, 13)
- ▷ New creation in Christ (1 Cor. 6:9-11; 2 Cor. 5:17; Eph. 2:10)
- ▷ One in/with Christ (1 Cor. 6:17; Gal. 3:28; Eph. 2:14-18)
- ▷ Member of the body of Christ (1 Cor. 12:27)
- ▷ Crucified with Christ (Gal. 2:19-20)
- ▷ The exchanged life (Rom. 6:3; Gal. 2:20)
- ▷ Saint/holy one (Eph. 1:1; 1 Cor. 1:2; Phil. 1:1; Col. 1:2)
- ▷ Provides blessings (Eph. 1:3)
- ▷ Seated in heavenly places (Eph. 2:6; Col. 3:1-3)
- ▷ Righteous (Eph. 4:24)
- ▷ Sanctified positionally (Col. 3:1ff)
- ▷ Hidden with Christ in God (Col. 3:3)
- ▷ Members of a holy priesthood (1 Pet. 2:9)

IN HEAVEN

Life in Heaven: ***What is our condition in heaven?***

- ▷ Living water (Lev. 23:34; Ps. 63:1; Ezek. 47:1-10; Zech. 14:8; Rev. 7:17)
- ▷ Rewarded saints (Job 16:19; Matt. 5:12; 25:14-30; Luke 12:41-48; 1 Cor. 3:12; 2 Cor. 5:10; 2 Tim. 4:7-8)
- ▷ Eternally with Christ (Job 19:26; 1 Cor. 13:12; 1 Jn. 3:2)
- ▷ Bodily resurrection (Ps. 16; 1 Cor. 15:20; 1 Thes. 4:13-18)
- ▷ Married to Christ (Ps. 45:13; Matt. 22:30)
- ▷ Immortal (Ps. 73:24; 2 Tim. 1:10)
- ▷ Future full of spiritual riches (Ps. 146:2; Zeph. 2:7; Eph. 1:18)
- ▷ Complete in knowledge (Eccl. 1:14; 1 Cor. 13:9-12)
- ▷ No tears or death (Isa. 25:8; Rev. 21:4)
- ▷ No hunger, thirst, or scorching heat (Isa. 49:10)
- ▷ God dwells with His people forever (Ezek. 43:7, 9; Joel 3:17; Zech. 2:10-13)
- ▷ Enjoying heavenly treasure (Matt. 6:19-20; Luke 12:33; 18:22; Jas. 5:3)
- ▷ Abiding in our eternal home (John 14:2-3; 1 Cor. 15:43-53; Col. 3:4)
- ▷ Marriage dissolved by death (1 Cor. 7:39)
- ▷ Glorified state (2 Cor. 5:1-4; Phil. 3:21)
- ▷ We shall reign with Him (2 Tim. 2:10-12)
- ▷ Restful (Heb. 4:9; Rev. 7:16-17; 14:13)
- ▷ Possess full inheritance (1 Pet. 1:4)
- ▷ Fully saved (1 Pet. 1:5; Rev. 19:1)
- ▷ Workers (Rev. 1:6; 7:15; 22:3)
- ▷ Access to the tree of life (Rev. 2:7; 22:2, 14, 19)
- ▷ We shall judge with Him (Rev. 2:26-28)
- ▷ Worshiping throughout eternity (Rev. 5:11-14; 11:16; 15:2-4; 19:4)
- ▷ United with the saints of all ages (Rev. 7:9)
- ▷ White robes (Rev. 7:9; 19:7-8)
- ▷ Name found in the Book of Life at the great white throne (Rev. 13:8; 20:12)
- ▷ No pain (Rev. 21:4)
- ▷ At home in the New Jerusalem (Rev. 21:10)
- ▷ No defilement of evil (Rev. 21:27)
- ▷ Dwelling in light (Rev. 21:23-25)
- ▷ No curse (Rev. 22:3)

DISCOVER HOLINESS

Living for God

What is personal holiness? Some seem to say that it's a dark, depressed, dismal life devoid of all joy—but nothing could be further from the truth. Personal holiness is a joyful life, regulated by God's truth as found in a plain reading of the Bible.

A commitment to personal holiness means that after God changes us from rebels to friends, we now have a new mission—obedience. God has given direct orders to us in His Word and requires that we obey Him perfectly, without arguing or complaining. Anything less is treason against our Commander and detrimental to those serving around us.

In this section of the outline, we will see that as we delight in God, we will also rejoice in repentance from sin. As we walk through the Christian life, delighting in God and rejoicing in repentance are our right and left feet. Keep walking!

▪ ▪ ▪

SET APART ***Because God has set me apart as His special possession,*** I can live a transformed life of holy service.

MATURING ***Because God has commanded me to grow in grace and obedience,*** I will look to Christ's perfect example as my standard for holiness.

SUBMISSION ***Because God expects me to have an active role in my spiritual growth,*** I will delight to submit to His Spirit and His Word.

CHANGED BY GOD ***Because the Triune God is fully committed to enabling His people to live a new life,*** *I can trust that no detour can keep me from completing my spiritual journey.*

LAW AND GRACE ***Because God has always commanded obedience to His law by the power of His grace,*** *I will reject neither God's law nor God's grace as the means to my holiness.*

DISCIPLINES ***Because God calls us to thoughtful, intentional living,*** I will regularly practice spiritual disciplines.

GOD'S BLESSING ***Because God promises to reward those who obey Him,*** I will love God boldly and expect a life producing spiritual fruit.

SET APART

Being Set Apart: *What does it mean to be holy?*

▶ BLESSING

Blessing those in the community

- ▷ People of Israel (Deut. 26:15; Isa. 12:6; Ezek. 37:28)
- ▷ Spouses and children (1 Cor. 7:14)

▶ RELIGIOUS SERVICE

Set apart for religious service (consecration)

- ▷ The Tabernacle (Exod. 40:9; Heb. 9:2)
- ▷ Priests and Levites (Num. 8:12-16; Judg. 19:25; 1 Sam. 8:1; Ezra 8:24-28)
- ▷ The Temple and its articles (1 Kgs. 9:3-7; 2 Chr. 7; Ezra 8:28)
- ▷ The nation of Israel (Jer. 2:3; Ezek. 20:40)

▶ TRANSFORMING

Transforming soul and life (sanctification)

- ▷ In the older covenants (Ps. 51; Ezek. 18:30-32; 1 Pet. 3:5)
- ▷ In the New Covenant (2 Sam. 23:1-5; Matt. 3:11; Acts 2:38-40; Rom. 12:1-2; Jas. 2:21-24)

MATURING

Maturing as a Christian: *What are the standards of personal holiness?*

▶ AVOIDING BARRIERS

Avoiding barriers to holy living (***See Spiritual Warfare****> Resisting Sin and Evil*)

▶ CONFORMITY TO CHRIST

- ▷ Following the Royal Law of love (Lev. 19:18; 27:34; Josh. 23:7; 2 Kgs. 23:2; Luke 10:27; 1 Cor. 16:22; Jas. 2:8)
- ▷ Christ's behavior (Matt. 12:1-2; Phil. 2:19-30; 3 Jn. 1:11)
- ▷ Christ's teachings (Luke 9:23-26; 1 Pet. 1:2; 2 Jn. 1:6)
- ▷ Christ's likeness (Rom. 8:29; 2 Cor. 3:18; 1 Pet. 1:15-16; 1 Jn. 3:2; 4:17)

▶ IMITATING GOD

Imitating God's character

- ▷ His law (Exod. 20:1-17; Deut. 17:14-15)
- ▷ His mercy (Deut. 15:1; 2 Kgs. 4:2)
- ▷ His faithfulness (1 Kgs. 9:10)
- ▷ His commands (Jer. 7:23; Dan. 3:5-12)
- ▷ His likeness (Matt. 5:44-48; Eph. 5:1; 1 Tim. 2:9-10; Jas. 3:7-12)

▶ OBEYING GOD'S WORD

Obedience to God's Word

- ▷ Justice is essential to obedience (Exod. 21:2)
- ▷ Obedience to God's Word is empowered by and demonstrates love (Job 31:15; 2 Jn. 1:6)
- ▷ Faithfulness is critical to obeying God's Word (Rom. 1:5; 14:23; 2 Pet. 1:5-9)
- ▷ Jesus learned to obey God's Word through His suffering (Heb. 5:8)
- ▷ Obedience to God's Word encourages our assurance of salvation (2 Pet. 3:11; 1 Jn. 2:5)

SUBMISSION

Submitting to God: *What is our role in holiness?*

▶ DELIGHTING IN GOD

Delighting in God rather than sin

- ▷ Rejoicing in repentance (Exod. 9:27; Job 22:26; 32:5; Ps. 51:8; Isa. 23:17; Heb. 9:14)
- ▷ Gladness in God (Deut. 28:27; Job 21:16; Pss. 70:4; 149:4; Isa. 61:10; Zeph. 3:16-17)
- ▷ Joy in Discovering God (Pss. 62:1; 66:1; 144:15; Isa. 35:1-2; Matt. 13:34; Acts 16:34; Heb. 12:2)

▶ IDENTIFYING WITH CHRIST

Identifying ourselves with Christ's life and work

- ▷ Suffering with Him (Exod. 8:24; Isa. 53:3; Dan. 12:10; Joel 1:19; Matt. 16:25; John 19:3; Rom. 8:17; 2 Cor. 1:5-7; 6:8-10; Phil. 1:29; 3:10)
- ▷ Rescuing others from sin (Num. 20:24; 1 Thes. 1:10; Jas. 5:19-20)
- ▷ Living as an adopted son (2 Chr. 23:13; Matt. 5:43; Gal. 3:26–4:7; Eph. 1:5; Heb. 12:7)
- ▷ Living a gospel-centered life (Luke 14:25-27; Rom. 1:16-17; Gal. 2:11–3:5; 2 Tim. 2:8-10; 1 Pet. 4:17-19)
- ▷ Abiding in Christ (John 15:5-8; 1 Cor. 1:10-17; 1 Jn. 2:24-27)

▶ LEARNING GOD'S WORD

Educating ourselves and our family with God's truth

- ▷ Teaching your children (Gen. 24:6; Exod. 2:2-3; 10:2; 13:8; Deut. 4:9-10; 6:7; Josh. 4:9; 2 Sam. 14:14, 33; 1 Kgs. 1:6; 2:2; 2 Chr. 17:1; Ezra 2:3; Ps. 101:2; Matt. 11:25; Acts 16:34)
- ▷ Public teaching (Deut. 5:1; Josh. 8:35; Ezra 7:10; Isa. 61:1; Eph. 3:8; 2 Tim. 4:2)
- ▷ Glorifying God with the mind (2 Chr. 15:13; Ezra 2:3; Luke 10:27-28)
- ▷ Makes us aware of worldly ideas to beware of their sin (Prov. 26:11; 2 Cor. 10:5; Col. 2:8)
- ▷ Central to the mission of the church (John 13:14-15; 2 Tim. 1:11)
- ▷ Renewing the mind (Rom. 12:1-2; 8:6-7; 1 Cor. 1:10; 4:2-4)

▶ TRUSTING GOD

Trusting God while facing temptation

- ▷ Overcoming (Gen. 32:28; 39:9; Judg. 6:15; 2 Kgs. 7:6; Job 5:8; Ps. 143:7; Isa. 4:5-6; 36:4; Jer. 1:19; Matt. 16:18; Jas. 1:5-8; 1 Jn. 5:3-5; ***see also Spiritual Warfare****> Resisting Sin and Evil*)
- ▷ Obedience (Num. 9:17; 1 Kgs. 19:19; Job 15:20; Isa. 29:16; Jer. 35:13; 37:17; Mark 3:1-5; 6:6-13; ***see also Worship****> NT> Our role> Obedience;* ***Holiness****> Maturing> Obeying God's Word*)
- ▷ Love (Deut. 6:5; 1 Jn. 4:19-20; ***see also God****> God's Attributes> Loving*)
- ▷ True happiness (Ps. 84:12)

- ▷ Trust in God, not humans (Exod. 1:17; Isa. 2:22)
- ▷ Faithfulness (Hos. 4:1; Matt. 15:21-28; 23:23; 25:14-30; Mark 14:66-72; Luke 8:49-56; Gal. 5:22; Phil. 3:12-14; Heb. 11:6; 3 Jn. 1:3)
- ▷ Light to the world (Matt. 5:14-16; Acts 13:47; 1 Thes. 5:5)

▶ YIELDING TO SPIRIT
Yielding to the Spirit
- ▷ Resist the world's influence (Gen. 34:9; Deut. 21:1; Prov. 31:10; Ezek. 20:26)
- ▷ The Spirit yields growth (Exod. 14:11)
- ▷ Guidance from the Spirit (Exod. 14:22)
- ▷ Do not attempt to stop the Spirit's work (Num. 10:9; Jon. 4:4; Eph. 4:30)
- ▷ Power of the Spirit is for all (Num. 11:29; Judg. 6:34; Luke 13:22-27; Acts 2:17-18; Eph. 3:16-19; 5:15-18)
- ▷ Present yourselves holy (Deut. 6:5; Mal. 2:12; Rom. 12:1-2)
- ▷ Surrender your heart (Josh. 24:23; 1 Sam. 1:18; 2 Kgs. 19:7; Ps. 142:5; Ezek. 5:13; Matt. 3:9; 23:25-26; Mark 8:34-35; Luke 13:22-27; Heb. 3:12-13)
- ▷ Resist fleshly empowerment (Judg. 9:2-5; Mic. 3:2; Zech. 4:6)
- ▷ Accept the unexpected (1 Sam. 10:6-11; Luke 1:38)
- ▷ Depend upon the Spirit's intercession (Rom. 8:26)

CHANGED BY GOD

Being Changed by God: *What is God's role in sanctification?*

▶ GOD PROVIDES
God sovereignly provides for us
- ▷ Extending grace to us (Gen. 13:9; 2 Kgs. 25:27; Jer. 10:23; Ezek. 16:5; Matt. 20:15; Acts 20:32; 2 Thes. 2:16; Jas. 4:6-10)
- ▷ By providence (Gen. 50:20; Judg. 7:21; Dan. 4:34-35; Acts 2:22-24)
- ▷ Death (Lev. 10:1-3; Acts 5:1-11)
- ▷ Temporal misery (Lev. 26:14-39; Job 2:5; Eccl. 7:14; Ezek. 28:26; 1 Cor. 11:30-32)
- ▷ Restricting our choices (Num. 22:22-33; 1 Sam. 29:1-11; Ps. 39:1)
- ▷ Conviction of sin (2 Sam. 12; 1 Chr. 19:19; Ps. 32:3; Hos. 7:14-16; Heb. 4:12-13; 12:10)
- ▷ Empowering us (Neh. 11:2; Acts 2; 3:12; 2 Cor. 3:4-5; 2 Tim. 3:1-5; 2 Pet. 1:3)
- ▷ Directing us (Ps. 48:14; Isa. 48:17; Jon. 4:10; Zech. 10:1-3)
- ▷ By His Word (Ps. 119; Luke 10:21-22; 2 Tim. 3:16)
- ▷ Rewarding us (Ps. 126:5; Matt. 6:19-21; 2 Cor. 5:9-10; 1 Jn. 2:28)
- ▷ Provides words to say (Matt. 10:17-20; Luke 12:11-12)
- ▷ Chastening us (Luke 4:1-14; Heb. 6:12; 12:4-17)
- ▷ By the Holy Spirit (Rom. 8:14; Gal. 5:18)
- ▷ Praying for us (Rom. 8:26, 34)
- ▷ Glorifying us (Rom. 8:30; 1 Jn. 3:2-3)

▶ THE FATHER FOREORDAINS
The Father foreordains us for His glory
- ▷ Follows allegiance to God (1 Sam. 20:13; Rom. 6:22; ***see also Holiness***> *Submission*)
- ▷ Flows from God to us (Isa. 6:1-8; 2 Cor. 1:12)
- ▷ Is God's perfect will (Rom. 8:30; Eph. 1:4; 1 Thes. 4:3)
- ▷ Follows regeneration (1 Jn. 2:29; 3:9-14; 5:4-18)

▶ THE SON PURCHASES
The Son purchases us by His stripes
- ▷ Jesus' peacemaking with God (Judg. 11:1-27; Ezek. 34:25-31; Col. 1:21-22)
- ▷ Jesus' priestly work (John 17:17; Heb. 4:14-16)
- ▷ Jesus' active obedience (John 17:19)
- ▷ Jesus' love (Eph. 5:25-26)
- ▷ Jesus' redemption (Titus 2:14)
- ▷ Jesus bore our sins (1 Pet. 2:24)

▶ THE SPIRIT ENABLES
The Spirit enables our obedience
- ▷ Seals believers (2 Sam. 7:10; Eph. 1:13; 4:30)
- ▷ Indwells believers (Ezra 8:28; Ps. 51:11; Hos. 5:4; Rom. 8:9; Eph. 2:22)
- ▷ Regenerates believers (Ezek. 36:26-27; Hos. 5:4; John 3:3-18; 2 Cor. 5:17; 1 Pet. 1:22-23)
- ▷ Baptizes believers (Acts 1:5; 11:16; 1 Cor. 12:13)

LAW AND GRACE

The Graciousness of the Law: *How do grace and law work in the Christian life?*

▶ LAW
We do not reject the law
- ▷ Marriage (Gen. 2:19-25; 20:3; Exod. 21:10; Lev. 20:14–22:12; Deut. 7:3; Judg. 12:8-10; Song 7:1)
- ▷ Old Covenant laws of ceremonial cleanness (Gen. 7:2; Lev. 13–15; Acts 10:9-15)
- ▷ A picture of God and His character (Exod. 3:15-16; Lev. 22:2; Isa. 33:22; Rom. 7:2-9, 12; Gal. 3:19)
- ▷ Property rights (Exod. 21:36; 22:8-11; Lev. 6:3-4; 25:10-46; Luke 16:12)
- ▷ Old Testament laws relating to ancient Israel (Exod. 32:27; 34:13-17; Deut. 18:1)
- ▷ Old Covenant sacrificial system (Lev. 1:1–7:38; Heb. 10:1-26)
- ▷ Leaders and followers (Lev. 10:20; Num. 27:20; Deut. 17:14-20; 28:25-36; 31:29; Josh. 1:18; Judg. 19:1; 1 Sam. 2:29; 8:5-22; 1 Kgs. 1:5; 12:27; 2 Kgs. 13:10; 1 Chr. 18:14; 2 Chr. 1:11; 22:9; 31:3-5; Neh. 7:2; Esth. 3:15; Isa. 36:18; Jer. 43:6)
- ▷ Parents and children (Lev. 20:2-4; Num. 3:49; Deut. 6:7; 11:16-21; Judg. 17:2; 2 Sam. 18:5; 2 Kgs. 3:27; Prov. 17:6; 29:15)
- ▷ Adore God (Deut. 6:5; 11:1-22; 30:16; Josh. 23:11; Mark 12:30; 1 Cor. 16:22)
- ▷ The moral law of God (Deut. 27:15; Pss. 112:1; 119:18; Jer. 6:27-30; John 4:34)
- ▷ God's Law is good (Judg. 12:11; Ps. 1:2; Rom. 7:22-25; 1 Tim. 1:8)
- ▷ A mirror to view ourselves (1 Kgs. 9:4-9; Ps. 51:4; Prov. 27:2; Matt. 5:17-19; Rom. 3:19-20)
- ▷ Exalt goodness (2 Chr. 6:41; Neh. 9:25-26; Amos 5:15; Gal. 5:22)

- ▷ Hate evil (Pss. 52:3; 97:10; Prov. 8:13; 9:13; Amos 5:15; ***see also Holiness****> Maturing*)
- ▷ A window to view the world (Prov. 3:31; Isa. 51:4; Mic. 4:2)

▶ GRACE

We do not reject grace

- ▷ The gift of grace (Gen. 33:11; Matt. 19:26; Rom. 5:17; 6:14-15; 12:6; 2 Cor. 9:8; Gal. 2:21; Titus 2:11-14; Heb. 10:19-25)
- ▷ Self-reliance (2 Chr. 14:11; Isa. 31:1; 1 Jn. 4:15-16)
- ▷ True teachings (Hab. 1:13; 2 Cor. 11:4; Heb. 13:9; Titus 2:11-15)
- ▷ Christ is the end of the law (Matt. 5:17-18; Rom. 8:1-4; 10:4; Gal. 4:3-5; 5:4; Eph. 2:14-15; Col. 2:8, 13-14, 20; Heb. 8:13)
- ▷ Jesus Christ (John 1:14-18; Heb. 4:16; 2 Pet. 1:18; 2 Jn. 1:3)
- ▷ The true gospel (Rom. 1:16-17; Gal. 1:6; 2:14; Titus 3:4-7)
- ▷ Not an opportunity for the flesh (1 Cor. 5:1-2; Jude 1:4)
- ▷ Obliged to keep the whole law (Gal. 5:3)

DISCIPLINES

The Disciplines of the Faith: *What spiritual disciplines do God's people practice?*

▶ OF ABSTINENCE

Spiritual disciplines of abstinence

- ▷ Chastity (Exod. 19:15; 1 Kgs. 11:1; 1 Cor. 7:5)
- ▷ Stewardship (Num. 1:2-3; Deut. 22:8; 2 Kgs. 5:26; Job 39:9; Prov. 22:26; Amos 6:4-6; Matt. 12:41-43; 25:14-30; Luke 12:13-24; Rom. 15:26-29; 2 Cor. 9:7-8)
- ▷ Fasting (Num. 6:2; Judg. 20:26; Acts 13:2-3; 14:23)
- ▷ Resisting sinful urges (Num. 14:4; Job 5:3; 20:14; Prov. 24:12; Song 8:4; Ezek. 15:8; Rom. 7:17-18; 15:16; Eph. 4:30; 2 Thes. 2:13)
- ▷ Secrecy (Judg. 16:5-15; Isa. 45:3; Jer. 13:17; Matt. 6:4-6, 18; 1 Cor. 4:1)
- ▷ Resisting worldly influences (Neh. 5:12; Job 30:13; Prov.7:27; Ezek. 13:18-19; Mic. 3:8; Zech. 4:6; Acts 5:3-11; 1 Pet. 3:3-4; 2 Pet. 2:19)
- ▷ Resisting Satan's schemes (Nah. 2:4; Mark 12:26; Eph. 3:14-19; Jas. 4:4-10)
- ▷ Silence/Solitude (Matt. 14:23; Luke 22:39-45)

▶ OF ENGAGEMENT

Spiritual disciplines of engagement

- ▷ Confession (Lev. 5:5; 6:2; Neh. 9:3; Rom. 10:9-10; Jas. 5:16)
- ▷ Honesty (Deut. 25:13; 2 Sam. 16:4; 2 Cor. 1:18-22)
- ▷ Endurance (1 Kgs. 11:42)
- ▷ Fellowship (Ps. 133; Acts 2:42; 2 Cor. 6:14; 1 Jn. 1:3-7)
- ▷ Call to study (Prov. 1:8; 23:12, 23; Isa. 50:7; Jer. 36:4)
- ▷ Value of study (Jer. 8:8; Luke 10:38-42; Col. 2:8)
- ▷ Service (Matt. 5:2-11; Mark 10:41-45; John 4:34; Acts 6:1-6; 1 Pet. 2:16; 4:10-11)
- ▷ What to study (Phil. 4:8-9; Col. 3:1-17)
- ▷ Source of truth (2 Tim. 3:16-17; Heb. 4:11-13; Jas. 1:5)

GOD'S BLESSING

Receiving God's Blessing: *What are the consequences of obedience?*

- ▷ Obedience leads to hardship and persecution (Gen. 40:15; Jer. 26:8; 29:26; Mark 13:9-13; Acts 11:19; 14:22; 1 Cor. 4:8-14; Heb. 10:33)
- ▷ Obedience gives greater assurance of salvation (Deut. 29:18-19; Isa. 24:2; Heb. 10:19-22; 2 Pet. 1:10)
- ▷ Obedience brings God's favor (2 Chr. 27:6)
- ▷ Obedience improves our relationship with God (Ps. 34:20; Mark 13:9-13; John 14:15-24; 1 Jn. 5:3)
- ▷ Obedience bears spiritual fruit (Isa. 28:29; Jer. 17:5-10; 24:8-10; John 15:2-4; Rom. 7:4)
- ▷ Obedience honors God (Jer. 33:9; 1 Cor. 6:20; 1 Pet. 2:12; Rev. 16:9)
- ▷ Obedience leads to true joy (Rom. 16:19; Heb. 13:17)

DISCOVER SPIRITUAL WARFARE

Resisting Temptation and Satan's Schemes

It's true that the Christian life is a joyful life. But that happiness does not come with laziness. It comes to those who have the courage to recognize the darkness in ourselves and in our world and commit to fight against it.

When Jesus changes us from rebels to relatives and from enemies to friends, He calls us to something—and it's not a perpetual vacation. We do not become holy while we sleep. We do not change the world into a better place as we watch our television.

In this section of the outline, you will discover why a Christian life in this world is not an armchair but an arena. You will discover that the devil is not resting quietly, waiting for his final defeat, but is raging and active and seeking to tear down every government, every church, and every person who dares name Christ as master.

Will you stand by and let yourself and everyone around you be ravaged by sin and Satan, or will you take a stand and defend God's people with prayer, faith, and His Word? Read ahead and see what it means to be a joyful, courageous soldier of God.

■ ■ ■

ORIGIN OF SIN ***Because Satan sinned and then tempted humanity to join him,***
I will tell everyone I know that God can free him or her from evil's snares.

ORIGINATOR OF SIN ***Because Satan is a liar who opposes my best and God's glory,***
I will reject him and recognize his strategies for ruining my life.

GOD AND SIN ***Because God allowed sin and calamity into His perfect world,***
I can trust that God even uses sin to glorify Himself.

RESISTING SIN AND EVIL ***Because God has warned us of the dangers of this world,***
I will walk by faith, resist temptation, and follow my commander, Jesus Christ.

ORIGIN OF SIN

The Origin and Effects of Sin and Evil: *How did sin change the created order?*

▸ SATAN'S FALL

Satan's fall destroyed his standing with God

- ▹ Satan's honor reduced (Gen. 3:14-15)
- ▹ Satan's power reduced (Luke 10:18; Jude 1:6)
- ▹ Satan's freedom reduced (2 Pet. 2:4; Rev. 20:1-3)

▸ HUMANITY'S FALL

Humanity's fall destroyed our standing with God

- ▹ Historical situation (Gen. 3; 1 Cor. 11:3, 8-11)
- ▹ Spiritual
  Spiritual significance (Rom. 5:12-19)
  - ▿Sinful from birth (Ps. 51:5; John 3:6; 1 Tim. 1:15)
  - ▿Spiritually blind (Isa. 5:21; Jer. 4:22; 13:20; Luke 3:34; 1 Jn. 2:9-11)
  - ▿Subjugated to Satan (Isa. 61:1; Heb. 2:14-15)
  - ▿Separated from God (Ezek. 28:2; Eph. 4:18)
- ▹ Physical
  Physical significance (Gen. 3)
  - ▿Exposed and naked (Gen. 2:25; 2 Sam. 10:4; Ezek. 16:39; Rev. 16:15)
  - ▿Extreme labor necessary to survive (Gen. 3:16, 19)
  - ▿Excluded from God's manifest presence (Gen. 3:24)
  - ▿End of perpetual physical life (Ps. 90:3; 1 Cor. 15:22)

▸ CREATION IN BONDAGE

Humanity's fall subjected creation to bondage

- ▹ God Created
  God created all things for His glory (Job 37:14; Pss. 19:1; 50:6; 74:16; Rom. 1:19-20)
- ▹ God Curses
  God curses creation (Gen. 3:16-19; Isa. 11:6; Rom. 8:18-22)
  - ▿Cosmos
    God curses the cosmos
    - •Conflict between good and evil (Gen. 3:14-15)
    - •Searing heat (2 Kgs. 4:18-20; Isa. 49:10; John 4:8)
    - •Decay (Rom. 8:20-21)
    - •Solution in heaven (Rev. 21:23)
  - ▿Vegetation
    Vegetation was also cursed
    - •Growth of weeds and thorns was accelerated (Gen. 2:17-18)
    - •Decline in production illustrative of spiritual condition (John 15:2-6)
    - •Healing from heaven's fruit (Rev. 22:1-5)
  - ▿Humanity humbled (***See Spiritual Warfare***> *Origin of Sin> Humanity's fall*)
- ▹ God Sustains
  God sustains the cursed creation (Gen. 8:21-22; Pss. 65:9; 89:9; 104; 135:7; 145:16; 147:8; Dan. 2:21a; Col. 1:15-17; Heb. 1:1-3, 8-12)

ORIGINATOR OF SIN

The Originator of Sin and Evil: *Who is Satan and what does he do?*

▸ SATAN'S TITLES

- ▹ Serpent (Gen. 3:1-4; Rev. 12–13; 20:2)
- ▹ Father of lies (Prov. 10:18; John 8:44)
- ▹ Beelzebub (prince of demons) (Matt. 12:24)
- ▹ Evil one (Matt. 13:19)
- ▹ Satan (adversary) (Luke 10:18)
- ▹ Ruler of the world (John 14:30)
- ▹ God of this world (2 Cor. 4:4)
- ▹ Beliar/Belial (wicked one) (2 Cor. 6:15)
- ▹ Commander of the power of the air (Eph. 2:2)
- ▹ Abaddon (angel of the pit) (Rev. 9:11)
- ▹ Apollyon (destroyer) (Rev. 9:11)
- ▹ Accuser (Rev. 12:10)

▸ SATAN'S CHARACTER

- ▹ Crafty (Gen. 3:1; 2 Cor. 11:3)
- ▹ Slanderous (Josh. 22:16-30; Job 1:6)
- ▹ Deceitful (Jer. 41:6; John 8:44; Rev. 12:9)
- ▹ Vicious (Luke 8:29)
- ▹ Murderous (John 8:44; 1 Pet. 5:8)
- ▹ Devious (2 Cor. 11:14)
- ▹ Mighty (Eph. 2:2)
- ▹ Conceited (1 Tim. 3:6)
- ▹ Cowardly (Jas. 4:7)
- ▹ Malevolent (1 Jn. 2:13)

▸ SATAN'S POWER

Satan's power over his followers

- ▹ He possesses them (Luke 22:3)
- ▹ He commands them (John 8:44)
- ▹ He blinds them (2 Cor. 4:4)
- ▹ He misleads them (Rev. 20:7-8)

▸ SATAN'S INFLUENCE

Satan's influence over God's people

- ▹ He tempts them (1 Chr. 21:1)
- ▹ He distresses them (Job 2:7; Luke 13:16)
- ▹ He indicts them (Zech. 3:1)
- ▹ He harasses them (Luke 22:31)
- ▹ He deceives them (2 Cor. 11:3)

▸ SATAN'S LIMITS

Satan's power has limits

- ▹ God sets boundaries on him (Job 1:9-12)
- ▹ Christians overcome him (Matt. 16:18-19; 1 Pet. 5:8-9; 1 Jn. 2:13)
- ▹ Christians watch for him (2 Cor. 2:11)
- ▹ Christians fight him (Eph. 6:11-16)
- ▹ Christians resist him (Jas. 4:7; 1 Pet. 5:9)

▸ SATAN'S DOMAIN

Satan rules the kingdom of darkness

- ▹ Receives false worship (Deut. 32:17; Ps. 106:36; 1 Cor. 10:20)
- ▹ Believers can aid it (Isa. 48:1-11)
- ▹ Doomed to destruction (Jer. 52:2-3; Lam. 1:22; Ezek. 38:16; Dan. 4:3; Zech. 11:17; Matt. 12:28; 25:41; Mark 3:23-27; Luke 11:17-22; John 12:36; 16:11; Rom. 16:20; 1 Jn. 4:4; Rev. 11:15)
- ▹ In opposition to the Kingdom of Light (Eph. 1:21; Rev. 12–13)

- ▷ Satan is its prince (Eph. 2:2)
- ▷ Unbelievers are citizens of it (Col. 1:13; Rev. 16:10)
- ▷ Synonymous with the world's system (Rev. 16:14)

▶ SATAN'S GOALS

- ▷ Tempt men to curse God's name (Job 2:4-5; Jer. 34:16)
- ▷ Keep men from faith in God (Matt. 13:19; Mark 4:15; Rev. 12:3-11)
- ▷ Betray Christ (John 13:2, 27)
- ▷ Receive worship (2 Thes. 2:3-4)

▶ SATAN'S STRATEGIES

Satan's strategies for victory

- ▷ Lie (Gen. 3:1; Judg. 1:28)
- ▷ Disguise himself (Isa. 44:20; 2 Cor. 2:11; 11:14)
- ▷ Misuse Scripture (Matt. 4:6)
- ▷ Extend suffering (Luke 13:16)
- ▷ Demons

  Demons serve in the kingdom of darkness
  - ▽Fallen angels oppose God (Gen. 3:12; Ezek. 28:12; Luke 4:3; John 8:44; 2 Cor. 11:14; 1 Jn. 3:8)
  - ▽Demons sow false doctrine (Deut. 13:3; Ezek. 11:2; 1 Tim. 4:1; 2 Pet. 2:13-14)
  - ▽Demons bring emotional suffering (1 Sam. 16:14)
  - ▽Demons cause loss (Job 2)
  - ▽Demons trouble believers and unbelievers (Matt. 5:16-18; 8:16, 28, 33; 12:22-28)
  - ▽Demons are beings, not forces (Matt. 8:31)
  - ▽Demons bring destruction (Matt. 8:32)
  - ▽Demons are servants of Satan (Matt. 12:24-30)
  - ▽Demons have an evil nature (Luke 10:17-18)
  - ▽Demons are limited in their power (***See Spiritual Warfare****>* *Originator of Sin*)
  - ▽Demons are doomed for destruction (***See Spiritual Warfare****>* *Originator of Sin*)
- ▷ Idolatry

  Demons are associated with false gods and idols (Rev. 9:20)
  - ▽Worship of demons is idolatry (Deut. 32:17; Ps. 106:36-37; 1 Cor. 10:20)
  - ▽Demons are behind false miracles or signs (1 Cor. 10:19-20)
  - ▽Worshipers of demons will not enter the kingdom of heaven (Gal. 5:20-21)

GOD AND SIN

God and Sin and Evil: *What is God's role in sin and evil?*

▶ SIN'S ORIGIN

God does not create sin

- ▷ God passively permits sin for His glory (Gen. 50:19-20; Isa. 10:5-7; Rom. 4:15; 11:36; Rev. 17:17)
- ▷ God is perfect (Deut. 32:4)
- ▷ The wise understand evil's source (1 Sam. 24:20; Job 34:10; Prov. 13:20; 26:24)
- ▷ Temptation not from God (2 Sam. 12:11; Jas. 1:13-14)
- ▷ Source of evil created by God (Isa. 54:16; John 1:3)
- ▷ Evil is from the world (1 Jn. 2:16)

▶ NATURAL DISASTER'S ORIGIN

God causes natural evil and disasters

- ▷ God stops calamity (Exod. 14:30; 1 Sam. 24:16; 2 Chr. 32:22; John 6)
- ▷ God brings calamity (1 Kgs. 17:1; Jer. 14:16; 32:42; Amos 3:6)
- ▷ God uses calamity to glorify Himself (Ezek. 35:5-8; Luke 13:1-3)

RESISTING SIN AND EVIL

Resisting Sin and Evil: *How do we stand firm in spiritual warfare?*

▶ RESISTING TEMPTATION

Resisting temptation by the power of the Holy Spirit

- ▷ What to Resist
  - ▽We are to resist sinful urges (Gen. 39:7-12; 2 Sam. 1:26; Esth. 5:9; Ps. 101:3-4; Jon. 1:3; Rom. 8:2, 13; 1 Cor. 6:18; 10:13; 15:31; 2 Cor. 10:5; Gal. 5:16; 2 Tim. 2:22; Heb. 4:15; Jas. 1:13-15; 1 Pet. 2:23)
  - ▽We are to resist worldly influences (Num. 25:3; Deut. 18:9; 1 Kgs. 7:1-2; 2 Chr. 8:11; Isa. 28:1; Matt. 4:10; 6:24; 1 Cor. 1:28; 2 Cor. 2:14; Eph. 5:8; Phil. 3:8; Col. 3:1; Jas. 4:4; 1 Jn. 2:15-17)
  - ▽We are to resist Satan's schemes (Matt. 4:1-11; Eph. 4:7; 2 Cor. 2:11; 10:3-6; Jas. 4:7; 1 Pet. 5:8-9)
- ▷ How to Resist
  - ▽By the help of our spouse (1 Sam. 25:11-35; 1 Cor. 7:14)
  - ▽By the help of our friends (2 Sam. 19:6; Prov. 27:17; Acts 21:19; Jas. 5:19-20)
  - ▽By the help of God (Job 17:12; Luke 22:39-40; Rom. 8:2; Gal. 5:16; 1 Thes. 2:18; Jas. 1:13-15)
  - ▽By the help of angels (Dan. 10:12-14)
  - ▽By Scripture (Matt. 4:1-17)
  - ▽By the help of the church (1 Cor. 5:5)
  - ▽By wearing the armor of God (Eph. 6:10-18)
- ▷ Examples

  Examples of temptation
  - ▽Satan's Schemes
    - •Against David (1 Chr. 21:1)
    - •Against Job (Job 1:9; 2:2)
    - •Against Jeshua (Zech. 3:1-5)
    - •Against Jesus (Luke 4:1-13; Heb. 4:15)
    - •Against Peter (Luke 22:31)
    - •Against families (1 Cor. 7:5)
  - ▽Worldly Influences
    - •On the poor (Ps. 10:2; Prov. 30:8-9)
    - •On the affluent (Prov. 28:22; 1 Tim. 6:9)
    - •On the religious professional (Mark 11:15-18)
    - •On Ananias and Sapphira (Acts 5:1-11)

▶ EMBRACING CHRIST

- ▷ Entrust yourself to God's care (Neh. 6:9; Pss. 9:10; 28:7; 49:7; Isa. 32:2; Matt. 8:5-13; Mark 4:35-41; 8:34-35; Rom. 16:18-25)
- ▷ Clothed in Christ's righteousness (Job 17:9; Isa. 61:10; Luke 15:22; Rev. 3:18; 21:2)
- ▷ Obey His Word (Ps. 119; Acts 5:29; 1 Pet. 2:22)

- ▹ Repent of your sin (Isa. 22:12; Acts 11:18; Rom. 2:4; 2 Cor. 7:9-10)
- ▹ Believe the Good News (Mark 1:14-15; Acts 2:14-41; Gal. 1:6-9)

▸ STANDING FIRM

Standing firm through the power of the Holy Spirit

- ▹ Empowered to obey (Lev. 20:7-8; 2 Kgs. 9:22; 10:31; Neh. 4:2; Rom. 7:6; Gal. 5:16-18; Eph. 2:2; 1 Pet. 1:2)
- ▹ Empowered to help others see their sin (2 Chr. 14:14; Mic. 4:8)
- ▹ Empowered to do spiritual warfare (Ezek. 42:1; Luke 4:36; Acts 1:8; Rev. 20:10; ***see also God****> Salvation> Holy Spirit;* ***God****> God's Names> Holy Spirit;* ***Holiness****> Changed by God> The Spirit enables*)
- ▹ Empowered to hope (Rom. 15:13)

▸ TRUSTING GOD

Trusting God as our commander

- ▹ Faithful Soldiers
  Trusting that God wants faithful soldiers
  - ▿ Give glory to the Commander (Judg. 4:17-21; 2 Tim. 4:18)
  - ▿ Be alert (2 Kgs. 11:18; 1 Cor. 16:13)
  - ▿ Hold firmly to the truth (Neh. 7:5; Titus 1:9)
  - ▿ Endure hardship (Hos. 5:15; 2 Tim. 2:3-10)
  - ▿ Deny self (1 Cor. 9:23; 13:4-7; Phil. 2:29-30)
  - ▿ Avoid entanglements (2 Cor. 6:14; 2 Tim. 2:4)
  - ▿ Control yourself (2 Cor. 12:6; 1 Thes. 5:6)
  - ▿ Fight as a team (Phil. 1:2)
- ▹ God as Warrior
  Trusting that God is the great Warrior (Exod. 15:3-5; Josh. 5:13-15; 8:4)
  - ▿ God's fight against the enemies of Israel (Exod. 15:2-3; Num. 21:1; Ps. 59:1; Isa. 17:13)
  - ▿ God's fight against disobedient Israel (Deut. 28:25-26; Rev. 2:16)
  - ▿ God's fight to final victory (Judg. 3:15-30; 1 Sam. 7:10; Dan. 7:13; Rev. 13:8-10; 19:11-21)
  - ▿ Be content with your victory (2 Kgs. 14:10)
  - ▿ God confuses our enemies (2 Chr. 20:22)
  - ▿ God's fight against Satan (Matt. 3:10-12; Col. 2:14-15)
- ▹ God's Wisdom
  Trusting that God is a merciful and wise Commander (Exod. 34:6; Hos. 11:8-9)
- ▹ Obeying God
  Trusting that God is not to be disobeyed (Num. 20:21; Deut. 20:10-18; Josh. 9:14; Ps. 127:1; Jer. 9:11)

▸ PUTTING ON AND OFF

Putting on the right things and taking off bad things through the power of God

- ▹ Putting On
  What we are to put on
  - ▿ The weapons of righteousness (Josh. 10:8; 2 Cor. 5:21)
  - ▿ The whole armor of God (Neh. 4:23; Rom. 13:12; Eph. 6:15-18; 1 Thes. 5:8)
  - ▿ The easy yoke of Jesus (Matt. 11:29)
  - ▿ Power from on high (Luke 24:49)
  - ▿ Christ (Gal. 3:26)
  - ▿ The new self (Eph. 4:24; Col. 3:10)
- ▹ Taking Off
  What we are to take off
  - ▿ The filthy clothes of guiltiness (Zech. 3:4)
  - ▿ The yoke of legalism (Acts 15:10; Rom. 8:1; Gal. 5:1; Heb. 9:10)
  - ▿ The mask of deception (1 Thes. 2:5)

▸ CONSEQUENCES

The consequences of obedience and disobedience

- ▹ Of Obedience
  Consequences of obedience
  - ▿ A sweet aroma to God (Lev. 3:16)
  - ▿ Joy (Deut. 4:40; Pss. 32:11; 51:12)
  - ▿ Pleases God (Deut. 12:28; Matt. 21:1-3; Gal. 1:10; Phil. 2:13; 1 Jn. 3:22)
  - ▿ Assurance of salvation (Deut. 33:27; Col. 1:23-27; 1 Jn. 2:3)
  - ▿ Persecution (1 Kgs. 17:18; Dan. 11:35; 2 Tim. 3:11-12; Rev. 14:12)
  - ▿ Potential for a more peaceable life (2 Chr. 9:5; Job 33:28; Prov. 6:14; Jer. 35:15; 1 Pet. 1:2)
  - ▿ Rewards from God (Ps. 111:10; Jer. 17:10; 1 Cor. 3:13-15; Heb. 11:6)
  - ▿ Bearing of spiritual fruit (John 15:2; Gal. 5:22-23)
  - ▿ Fellowship with other believers (Acts 2:42; 1 Cor. 5:2; 2 Cor. 6:14–7:1)
  - ▿ Glorifying God (Isa. 26:8; Rom. 1:5; 2 Cor. 9:13)
- ▹ Of Disobedience
  Consequences of disobedience
  - ▿ Tempt others to sin (Gen. 12:10-20)
  - ▿ Death (Lev. 10:2; Judg. 1:7; 2 Sam. 1:16; 4:11; 2 Kgs. 10:27; Lam. 4:9; Acts 5:1-11; 1 Cor. 11:30)
  - ▿ Falling under discipline (Num. 21:5; Deut. 8:5; 2 Kgs. 22:19; 2 Chr. 24:18; Ps. 94:12; Jer. 3:13-14; 15:6; 21:13-14)
  - ▿ God may allow consequences to run their course (Deut. 19:16-20; Josh. 7:25; 2 Kgs. 9:39; 16:7-8; 2 Chr. 12:8; 25:20; Esth. 7:6; Ezek. 23:46-48; 44:12; Gal. 6:8)
  - ▿ Further disobedience (2 Sam. 11:15)
  - ▿ God is not mocked (1 Kgs. 9:9; 2 Kgs. 2:23; 17:7)
  - ▿ Displeases God (1 Chr. 21:7; Ezek. 18:23; 19:14)
  - ▿ Guilt (Pss. 5:10; 32:5; Heb. 10:1-18; 1 Jn. 3:21)
  - ▿ Conviction of the Spirit/lack of joy (Pss. 38:18; 51:12; 119:93; Lam. 5:21)
  - ▿ Broken relationships (Prov. 11:9; Mal. 2:16; Matt. 5:31-32; Gal. 2:12-13; 2 Tim. 3:4)
  - ▿ Banishment from community of faith (Matt. 18:15-20; 1 Cor. 5:9-13)

DISCOVER CHURCH

Joining with God's People

The Bible does not speak of a solitary "Jesus and Me" version of Christianity. When God brings us into His family, He spiritually connects us with other believers. The physical manifestation of that connection is the church—a group gathered by God to honor Him through community, obedience, and praise.

In the Bible, the idea of the church develops gradually, beginning in the Old Testament in the Garden of Eden, growing during the ministry of Moses, maturing with the building of the Temple by Solomon, and then taking its final form on the Day of Pentecost in Acts 2. But the final unveiling of everything that the church will be is found in Revelation, as the Spotless Bride is finally fully united to her Husband, Jesus (Rev. 19:7), the Ruler and King of the church.

As you'll see in this section, it's natural for our understanding of the place of the church in our lives to develop slowly—that's the way it developed in the Bible. Take your time and look at how God has grown His church, and ask yourself how you fit into your local congregation. By doing so, you'll be placing yourself in the very center of where God is at work.

■ ■ ■

WHAT ***Because God has set aside a holy people to glorify Him together,***
I must regularly participate in a biblical and God-centered church.

WHO ***Because God is no discriminator against persons,***
He has called His holy people from every place and every age.

MISSION ***Because God has called His gathered people to change the world,***
I will give my time and resources to accomplish the holy goals of my church.

ROLE ***Because God's Word reveals the role of a healthy church in my life,***
I will celebrate the blessings and responsibilities of membership in a local church.

WHAT

What is the Church?

▶ SUPERNATURAL BODY

The church is a supernatural body

- ▷ Care given to the weakest (yet most necessary) parts (Dan. 8:27; Rom. 14:1; 1 Cor. 12:12-31)
- ▷ Under Christ (Matt. 16:15-18; Eph. 1:22-23; 4:15-16)
- ▷ Unified and harmonious (1 Cor. 12:16-17)
- ▷ Respect given to the heavenly head (Eph. 4:15; Col. 1:18)
- ▷ Power given to those who are in the body (Col. 2:19)
- ▷ Relationship
  Supernatural relationship of Christ to His church
  - ▽Treasured by Christ (Matt. 10:28-30; Eph. 5:25)
  - ▽Built by Christ (Matt. 16:18)
  - ▽Abides in Christ (John 15:1-11)
  - ▽Bought by Christ (Acts 20:28)
  - ▽Owned by Christ (Rom. 7:4; Heb. 5:9)
  - ▽Established on Christ (Eph. 2:19-20)
  - ▽Purified by Christ (Eph. 5:26-27)

▶ MANY TITLES

The church is a body with many titles

- ▷ People of God (Exod. 19:3; 32:11; 1 Pet. 2:10)
- ▷ Branches (Ps. 80:14; Isa. 5:7; John 15:1-8)
- ▷ Crown in God's hand (Isa. 62:3)
- ▷ Cornerstone/holy temple (Ezek. 43:2-5; Eph. 2:20-21; 1 Pet. 2:4-8)
- ▷ Building (Matt. 16:18; 1 Cor. 3:9)
- ▷ Field of God (1 Cor. 3:9)
- ▷ Last Adam/new creation (Rom. 5:12-21; Gal. 6:15)
- ▷ Olive tree (Rom. 11:17-24)
- ▷ Dwelling place of God (Eph. 2:22)
- ▷ Place of Glory (Eph. 3:21)
- ▷ The city of God (Jer. 22:8; Heb. 12:22)
- ▷ Flock (Acts 20:28; 1 Pet. 5:2)
  - ▽A place to honor one another (Rom. 16:4-16)
  - ▽A place for Christians (1 Cor. 1:2)
  - ▽A place to honor God through obedience (1 Tim. 3:15)
  - ▽A place for God's family (Heb. 12:23; 3 Jn. 1:5-6)
- ▷ Kingdom (Heb. 12:28; Col. 1:13)
- ▷ Bride
  Bride (Ruth 3:4; Rev. 21:2, 9)
  - ▽Who joyfully awaits the wedding day (2 Chr. 10:5; Song 2:8; Matt. 25:1-13; Rev. 19:7)
  - ▽Who rejoices and fasts (Song 8:13; Matt. 9:15)
  - ▽Who submits to her husband (Eph. 5:22-33)
- ▷ Priests
  Kingdom of priests
  - ▽Our high privilege is to be in covenant with God (Ezek. 20:37; Heb. 8:6)
  - ▽Our high priest is Jesus (Heb. 5:5-10; 6:20; 7:26; 9:11)
  - ▽Our high calling is to be God's priestly nation (1 Pet. 2:9-10)
- ▷ Servants
  - ▽Servants must be prepared to work (Josh. 17:14-18; 2 Chr. 32:5-8; Ezra 4:5; Eccl. 11:5; 2 Tim. 2:21)
  - ▽Servants must be helpful (Col. 1:7)
  - ▽Servants are also masters (Col. 4:1, 7)
  - ▽Servants do not undermine the Master (Jude 1:4)
- ▷ Sheep
  Sheep (John 10:14)
  - ▽The sheep trust the protection of the shepherd (2 Kgs. 6:16; Ps. 77:20; Jer. 1:19; Ezek. 34:10-12; Matt. 14:28-31; John 10:11, 14; 1 Pet. 2:24-25)
  - ▽The sheep trust the rewards of the shepherd (Jer. 23:1; 1 Pet. 5:4)
  - ▽The sheep trust the final destination of the shepherd (Rev. 7:17)

WHO

Who and where is the church?

▶ FROM EVERY PLACE AND AGE

The church is called from every place and age

- ▷ Believers in the Old Testament (Gen. 4:26; 15:6; Judg. 20:2; Acts 7:38)
- ▷ Universal church (Jer. 4:2; Matt. 16:18; Eph. 3:20)
- ▷ Local church (Amos 9:12; 1 Cor. 1:2; Phil. 2; 1 Thes. 1:1; Rev. 2–3)
- ▷ Church in the future (Zech. 2:11; John 14:1-2; Rev. 3:12; 21:2)
- ▷ Church in the New Testament (Matt. 16:18; Acts 2; 15; 1 Cor. 14; Eph. 5)

▶ FROM EVERY PEOPLE

The church is called from among every people

- ▷ Pre-Jewish believers in the church (Gen. 4:26)
- ▷ Children are included in the older covenants (Gen. 9:9-17; 12:1-3; 17:7; Exod. 20:5; Deut. 29:10-13; 1 Sam. 2:1; Ezek. 26:2)
- ▷ Children are blessed by inclusion in covenant community (2 Sam. 12:22; 1 Kgs. 14:31; 1 Cor. 7:14)
- ▷ Those who have persevered until the end (2 Chr. 25:14; Heb. 6:4-6; Rev. 3:10)
- ▷ Those who are tempted to apostasy by suffering (2 Chr. 28:21; Lam. 4:22; Heb. 10:36; 12:1; Jas. 1:12)
- ▷ The community of the saved (Neh. 1:2; Eph. 5:25)
- ▷ Those who know much of God (Matt. 7:21-23; Mark 1:16-18; 1 Tim. 4:16; Heb. 6:4-8)
- ▷ Those not under discipline (Matt. 18:15-17; 1 Cor. 5:1-5, 9-13; 2 Cor. 2:5-11)
- ▷ Gentile converts (Matt. 21:28-31; John 3; Heb. 11:31)
- ▷ The "least of these" (Matt. 25:31-46; Luke 17:11-19; 1 Cor. 1:26-29)
- ▷ Children are included in the New Covenant (Luke 10:21; 18:16; Acts 2:38-39; 16:33)
- ▷ Together in unity (Acts 14:1-5; Rom. 3:29; 9:24-29; Eph. 5:21-33)
- ▷ Children in the church need to trust Christ (Rom. 3:22-23; 10:9-10)

MISSION

The mission of the church

▶ ESTABLISH

To establish the Kingdom of God

- ▷ The Old Testament speaks about the Kingdom (Isa. 9:6-7; Dan. 4:34-35)

- ▷ The gospel of Christ is Kingdom-oriented (Matt. 3:2; 4:23; 24:14; 20:25)
- ▷ The church inherits the Kingdom (Matt. 25:34; Col. 1:12-14)
- ▷ The Head of the Church is the Head of the Kingdom (Matt. 28:18; Col. 1:13)
- ▷ The Kingdom is both now and not yet (Luke 11:20; 16:16; 17:20-37; 22:16-30)
- ▷ The church manifests Christ's Kingdom rule (Acts 1:3; 28:23-31)

▶ EVANGELIZE

To tell others the good news of Jesus Christ (***See Ministry***> *Great Commission> Witness*)

▶ NURTURE

To nurture believers (***See Worship***> *Our role> Holiness*)

- ▷ Fostering community (Gen. 28:3; Ps. 133; Prov. 31:9; Hag. 1:2; Acts 2:42-47; Rom. 15:1-7; Heb. 10:25; 11:40)
- ▷ True teaching (Exod. 18:20; Deut. 6:1; Prov. 25:18; Jer. 5:4; Matt. 28:19-20; 1 Tim. 4:11; 2 Tim. 2:24-26)
- ▷ Developing maturity (Prov. 22:15; 1 Cor. 11:23-26; Gal. 6:1; Eph. 4:12-13; Col. 1:28)

ROLE

The role of the church

▶ CHURCH COMMUNITY

The church as a community of faithful followers

- ▷ Encouraging one another (1 Kgs. 16:30; Neh. 4:20; Ezek. 26:2; Acts 14:22; 20:1; Rom. 12:8; Eph. 4:29; 1 Thes. 2:12)
- ▷ Using their gifts to build up the body (1 Chr. 6:32; Rom. 12:6-8; 1 Cor. 12–14; 12:7)
- ▷ Living as family (Ezra 2:3; Esth. 2:11; Matt. 12:48-50; 1 Pet. 4:17; 1 Jn. 2:9-14)
- ▷ Submitting to one another (1 Cor. 16:15-16; Eph. 5:21; Heb. 13:17)
- ▷ Loving one another (Gal. 5:13; Jas. 2:2-9; 1 Pet. 1:22; 1 Jn. 4:7-18; 2 Jn. 1:5)

▶ CHURCH GOVERNMENT

- ▷ Local
  Authority in the local church
  - ▽To spiritually lead (2 Kgs. 15:4; Ezek. 22:2; Rom. 12:8)
  - ▽To pronounce forgiveness or judgment (Matt. 16:19; 18:17-18; John 20:21-23; 1 Cor. 5:12–6:3; 2 Cor. 2:6-8; 1 Tim. 1:20)
- ▷ Universal
  Authority in the church universal
  - ▽Judgment against Paul appealed to a church court in Jerusalem (Acts 15)
  - ▽Judgments over various churches by Paul (1 Cor. 1; Gal. 1)
  - ▽Judgments over various churches by Christ (Rev. 2–3)
- ▷ Society
  Authority of the church in society
  - ▽Government should honor the spiritual authority of the church (Exod. 1:18; 1 Chr. 14:17; Matt. 17:25-27; Acts 16:37)
  - ▽Church influences governments (Judg. 9:56-57; Matt. 5:14-16; Acts 19:24-40)
  - ▽Church honors authority of government (2 Kgs. 15:19; Matt. 22:21; Rom. 13:1-7; 1 Pet. 2:17)
  - ▽Christ is the ruler of all (Rev. 1:5; 17:14)

▶ CHURCH OFFICES

- ▷ Pastor-Teachers (Ezek. 22:30; 34:2; Eph. 4:11; 1 Tim. 5:17-18; also called elders/overseers [Acts 20:28-31; 1 Tim. 3:1-7; Titus 1:5-9; 1 Pet. 5:1-4])
- ▷ Apostles (Eph. 2:20; 4:11)
- ▷ Prophets (Eph. 2:20; 4:11)
- ▷ Evangelists (Eph. 4:11)
- ▷ Deacons (Phil. 1:1; 1 Tim. 3:8-13)

▶ CONFLICT

Resolving conflict in the church

- ▷ Peacemaking (2 Sam. 2:4; Eph. 4:32; 5:21; Jas. 3:18)
- ▷ Restoration (2 Sam. 2:26; Matt. 18:15-18; 2 Cor. 2:5-11)
- ▷ Formal discipline (Matt. 18:15-17; Acts 5:9-11; 1 Cor. 5:12-13)
- ▷ Preventative teaching (John 13:35; 18:10; Gal. 5:13-15; 1 Pet. 3:8; 1 Jn. 3:11)
- ▷ General counsel
  - ▽Overlook another's faults (Deut. 9:27; Prov. 19:11; Acts 17:30)
  - ▽Go to your elders for counsel (Esth. 5:14; Acts 15:1-2)
  - ▽Forgive each other (Matt. 6:15; 2 Cor. 2:10-11; Eph. 4:31-32)
  - ▽Go to your brother who has sinned (Matt. 18:15-17)
  - ▽Part from each other (Acts 15:36-39)

▶ GLORIFY GOD

- ▷ As a community (Ezra 6:16; Rom. 15:5-6)
- ▷ As a motive toward obedience (Dan. 5:17; 2 Cor. 9:13)
- ▷ As a final prayer (Rom. 16:27)
- ▷ As the result of his work in us (Eph. 3:20-21)
- ▷ As a response to his everlasting reign (1 Tim. 1:17)

▶ PREACH

Exhort, reprove, and teach from God's inspired Word

- ▷ Examples
  Biblical examples of preachers
  - ▽Noah (2 Pet. 2:5)
  - ▽Moses (Exod. 4:10-12; Deut. 31:22)
  - ▽Solomon (Eccl. 1:1, 12)
  - ▽Ezra (Ezra 7:12)
  - ▽John the Baptist (Matt. 3:2; Mark 1:4, 15)
  - ▽Jesus (Matt. 8:19)
  - ▽Apollos (Acts 18:24)
  - ▽Paul (1 Cor. 9:18; 1 Tim. 2:7)
  - ▽Titus (2 Cor. 8:18)
- ▷ Instructions
  Instructions to preachers
  - ▽Train in godly behavior and thinking (2 Chr. 18:1; Eccl. 5:7; 1 Tim. 5:1-16; ***see also Church***> *Mission> Nurture*)
  - ▽Reach the nations (Matt. 28:18-20)
  - ▽Be dedicated to the task (Acts 2:42; 6:4)

- ▿Equip the saints for the work of ministry (Eph. 4:11-16; 2 Tim. 4:11)
- ▿Prevent doctrinal error (Eph. 4:14-15; 1 Tim. 6:3-5; Titus 1:5, 9-11, 13-14; 2:1; 2 Jn. 1:7-9)
- ▿Tell the whole truth (Hos. 9:7; Col. 1:25)
- ▿Submit to God (1 Tim. 3:1-7; 4:9-11)
- ▿Be ready to do the work at any moment (2 Tim. 4:2)
- ▿**Use Caution**
  Take care around gray areas
  - Submission to government and other authorities (Exod. 2:15; Deut. 16:18; Matt. 17:24-27; Rom. 13)
  - Various differences of opinion (Rom. 14:1–15:13)
  - Conscience differences in eating and drinking (Jer. 35:5; 1 Cor. 8:1–11:1)

▹ **Topics**
Preaching topics
- ▿Proper use of spiritual gifts (Exod. 35:35; Rom. 12:3-8; 1 Cor. 12–14; 14:26; 1 Pet. 4:10-11)
- ▿Consolation and comfort (Job 16:5; Isa. 40:1; 1 Cor. 14:3; 1 Thes. 2:12)
- ▿Repentance (Matt. 4:17; Luke 3:3)
- ▿**Disciple**
  Disciple believers (Matt. 28:18-20; 2 Pet. 3:18)
  - Encourage the saints to love and good deeds (Job 29:11; Titus 1:16; Heb. 10:24-25)
  - Discipline believers (Matt. 18:17ff; 1 Cor. 5:3; 2 Cor. 2:6; 1 Tim. 5:19-20)
  - Edify (1 Cor. 14:3-5, 12, 26; Eph. 4:11-13, 29)
- ▿The Kingdom of God (Luke 8:1)
- ▿The sacrificial death and resurrection of Christ (Acts 2:38; 17:3)
- ▿The cross of Christ (1 Cor. 1:23)
- ▿**Exhortations**
  Exhortations (1 Cor. 14:3; 2 Tim. 4:2)
  - Pray corporately (Acts 2:42; 6:4; 1 Tim. 2:1-4, 8)
  - Provide fellowship (Acts 2:42; 1 Jn. 1:3-7)
  - Regulate abuse of spiritual gifts (1 Cor. 14)
  - Regulate worship gatherings (1 Cor. 14:26-40; 16:2-3; Heb. 10:25)
- ▿**Godly Lives**
  Live godly lives before the world
  - Kindness to neighbors (Lev. 19:18; Ruth 2:10; Job 6:21; 7:1; Prov. 3:27)
  - Live quietly and work hard (Judg. 3:9; Eccl. 5:7; Isa. 30:15; Amos 5:13; 1 Thes. 4:11)
  - Care for their poor, widows, and orphans (Job 24:3; Ps. 82:3; Rom. 15:26; Gal. 2:10; 1 Tim. 5:3-16; Jas. 1:27)
  - Make the most of opportunities for kindness (Ps. 41:1; Col. 4:5-6)
  - Caring for the injured (Luke 10:25-37)
  - First to believers, then the world (Gal. 6:10)
  - Pray for authorities everywhere (1 Tim. 2:1-4)
- ▿**Collect Resources**
  - For salaries of ministers (Exod. 29:26; Deut. 25:4; 2 Kgs. 12:7; Neh. 13:10; 1 Tim. 5:17-18)
  - For food and mercy ministries (Acts 6:1-7)
  - For missions (1 Cor. 16:2-3; 2 Cor. 8–9)
- ▿**Evangelize**
  Evangelize the lost
  - Around the world (Exod. 12:38; 1 Kgs. 8:60; Ps. 67:2; Mark 16:15; Acts 13:32; 15:7-12; 2 Cor. 10:16)
  - As a normal part of pastoral ministry (2 Tim. 4:5)

▸ SACRAMENTS
Celebrate the sacraments
- ▹ As a covenant-renewal ceremony (2 Chr. 15:12; Luke 22:19-20; 1 Cor. 11:25)
- ▹ As Christ has instructed us (Matt. 26:26-28)
- ▹ As a command to be obeyed (Matt. 28:19-20)
- ▹ As an entrance to the visible church (Acts 2:38, 41; 8:36-38; 16:15, 33)
- ▹ As a regular part of the Christian experience (Acts 2:38, 41-42)
- ▹ As a celebration of the resurrection (1 Cor. 11:23-26)

▸ WORSHIP
Worship (see Worship)
- ▹ Lifestyle (public and private) worship (Rom. 12:1-2; Eph. 1:12)
- ▹ Liturgical (corporate and public) worship (1 Cor. 11:17-34; 14:1-40; Col. 1:16)

DISCOVER GOD'S PURPOSE

Embracing God's Will and Master Plan

We face difficult decisions in this sinful, mixed-up world. "What is God's will for my life? " the young man asked, crying. "Should I leave my wife, who won't go to church with me, or should I stay with her and be spiritually dragged down by her? " He ignores the advice of his pastor and leaves his wife, saying, "I've never felt such a peace!"

People often make decisions about God's will based on feeling rather than fact. While feelings are important, it is the facts found in the Bible, not our feelings, that need to be the final arbiter of important decisions in our life.

As you read this section of the outline, you'll see that God makes His will known to humanity through His Word—He either speaks directly to people or instructs them by His appointed messengers. In either case, neither conflicts with a commonsense reading of the Bible.

Dr. Bill Bright said in the first of his *Four Spiritual Laws* that God offers a wonderful plan for your life. This plan is found as we trust a sovereign God to empower us to play a part in His master plan to rescue the world from the power of sin. Will you do your part to be His agent of positive change in a negative world?

■ ■ ■

GOD'S PURPOSE ***Because the goal of God's creation is to discover and reflect His greatness,*** I will seek a progressively higher view of God's character and person.

GOD'S MEANS ***Because God's master plan for this universe is perfect,*** I can best participate in God's mission by submitting my will to His.

GOD'S DEEDS ***Because God's actions are not limited by time and space,*** I will pray for His miraculous intervention in impossible situations.

GOD'S PURPOSE

God's purpose for creating the universe is for all creation to discover His greatness

- ▷ The heavens tell of his greatness (Ps. 19:1; Isa. 45:18)
- ▷ Evil and sickness tell of his greatness (John 11:4)
- ▷ Obedience proclaims the glory of God (Rom. 6:10-11)
- ▷ Every action is to be motivated by our desire for God's renown (1 Cor. 10:31)
- ▷ Every tongue will confess God's greatness (Phil. 2:11)
- ▷ God will accomplish his plan when His magnificence will fill the new heaven and new earth (Rev. 21:11)

GOD'S MEANS

God's means of accomplishing his plan

▶ GOD'S SOVEREIGNTY

God's sovereignty in his master plan

- ▷ God sustains His creation (Gen. 8:21-22; Lev. 25:4; Pss. 89:9; 104; 135:7; 145:16; 147:8; Dan. 2:21a; Col. 1:17; Heb. 1:1-3, 8-12)
- ▷ God is King over every nation (Deut. 2:26-37; Judg. 21:7; Isa. 40:15; 66:18; Mal. 1:14; Luke 20:20-26; 2 Thes. 2:7)
- ▷ God knows all (Deut. 7:7-8; 1 Chr. 17:18; 2 Chr. 32:31; Isa. 18:4; 45:3; Jer. 1:5; Matt. 7:22-23; Acts 2:23; 1 Pet. 1:2)
- ▷ God chooses some and leaves others in their rebellion (1 Sam. 2:25; 2 Sam. 17:14; Isa. 6:9-10; Matt. 11:25; 24:22; Mark 13:22; Luke 18:7; John 5:21; 6:37-40, 44; 10:27-28; Rom. 8:33; 9:6-13, 15-18, 21-24; 2 Cor. 2:15-16)
- ▷ God has always had a plan (1 Sam. 23:28; Job 30:26; Eccl. 3:1; Isa. 41:26; 46:10; 64:1; Dan. 4:35; Rom. 8:28; 9:11; Eph. 1:11)
- ▷ God decrees all (1 Kgs. 11:26-27; Ezra 4:6; Ps. 135:6; Isa. 45:3; 46:11; Jer. 12:14; 50:1; Dan. 2:22; Rom. 8:29-30; Acts 4:28; Eph. 1:4-6, 11; 1 Cor. 1:26-31; 2 Tim. 1:9; 1 Pet. 1:3; 2 Pet. 1:10)
- ▷ God's people are chosen for service (1 Chr. 29:11; Esth. 1:3; Dan. 2:21b; John 6:70; 1 Cor. 1:26; 15:58; Eph. 2:10)

▶ HUMAN CHOICE

Human choice in God's master plan

- ▷ Human view (Gen. 19:22; Deut. 30:19; Josh. 24:15; 1 Kgs. 18:21; Prov. 28:4; Phil. 2:12)
- ▷ Bringing our wills in subjection to God's will (Deut. 3:27; 29:29; Josh. 3:16; 18:10; 1 Sam. 9:21; 23:9; 1 Kgs. 3:5; Neh. 2:8; Ps. 50:23; Prov. 23:2-8; Jer. 28:8-9; 49:20; 1 Cor. 9:27; 11:31; Col. 3:5; Jas. 1:26)
- ▷ God's view (Ezra 6:22; Prov. 21:1; Isa. 45:1-3; Dan. 4:32, 35; Hos. 14:9; Matt. 10:30)

GOD'S DEEDS

What does God do to accomplish His master plan?

▶ SPECIAL ACTS

Special acts in God's master plan (Exod. 3:1; Deut. 11:7)

- ▷ Creation (Gen. 1:1, 21; 2:3-4; 5:2; Deut. 4:32; Pss. 8; 74:16-17; 89:11-12, 47; 104:5, 24; 139:13; 146:6; 148:5; Isa. 40:26; 42:5; 43:7-8; 45:12, 18; Matt. 19:14; Eph. 3:9; Col. 1:16; 1 Tim. 2:13; Heb. 1:2; Rev. 10:6)
- ▷ Guidance (Gen. 24:12; Jas. 1:5; 3:13-17)
- ▷ Saving acts/deliverance (Gen. 45:7; 49:18; Exod. 3:1, 8; Josh. 6:20; Judg. 4:7; 15:18; 1 Sam. 7:3; 1 Chr. 11:14; Neh. 9:27; Job 5:19; Pss. 3:8; 32:7; 68:20; Isa. 59:17; Hos. 6:1-2; Joel 2:32; Jon. 2:9; Luke 4:18; Rev. 7:10)
- ▷ Judgment (Exod. 9:6)
- ▷ Miracles

  Miracles/signs/wonders (Exod. 4:8; 34:10; Num. 14:22; Deut. 6:22; Josh. 3:5; Ps. 72:18; John 2:11; Rom. 15:19; Gal. 3:5; Heb. 2:4)

  - ▽OT

    Old Testament miracles

    - The Flood (Gen. 7)
    - Confusion of tongues (Gen. 11:7)
    - Destruction of Sodom and Gomorrah (Gen. 19:24)
    - Lot's wife turned to a pillar of salt (Gen. 19:26)
    - Burning bush (Exod. 3:2)
    - Aaron's rod becomes a serpent (Exod. 7:8-13)
    - Water turned to blood (Exod. 7:14-25)
    - Frogs invade the land (Exod. 8:1-15)
    - Plague of insects (Exod. 8:16-32)
    - Plague of boils (Exod. 9:8-17)
    - Cattle die (Exod. 9:17)
    - Plague of hail (Exod. 9:18-35)
    - Plague of locusts (Exod. 10:1-20)
    - Darkness over the land (Exod. 10:21-29)
    - Firstborn killed (Exod. 11:1)
    - Red Sea divided (Exod. 14:21-31; Ps. 114:7)
    - Waters turned sweet at Marah (Exod. 15:23-25)
    - Provision of manna (Exod. 16:14-35; Num. 11:8)
    - Water from rock at Rephidim (Exod. 17:5-7)
    - A plague for idol worship (Exod. 32:35)
    - Nadab and Abihu judged (Lev. 10:1-2)
    - Judgment on portion of Israel (Num. 11:1-3)
    - Korah's rebellion (Num. 16:2, 32-35)
    - Aaron's rod budding (Num. 17:1-13)
    - Waters at Meribah (Num. 20:7-11)
    - The bronze snake (Num. 21:8-9)
    - Donkey speaks (Num. 22:21-33)
    - Jordan River stopped (Josh. 3:14-17)
    - Walls of Jericho fall (Josh. 6:6-20)
    - Sun and moon stayed (Josh. 10:11-14)
    - Water pours from the hollow place (Judg. 15:19)
    - Dagon falls (1 Sam. 5:1-12)
    - Men of Beth-shemesh smitten (1 Sam. 6:19)
    - Thunderstorm creates panic among Philistines (1 Sam. 7:10-12)
    - Sound in the poplar trees (2 Sam. 5:23-25)
    - Uzzah struck dead (2 Sam. 6:7)
    - Jeroboam's hand withered (1 Kgs. 13:4-6)
    - Widow of Zarephath's meal and oil increased by Elijah (1 Kgs. 17:14-16)
    - Drought, fire from heaven, and Elijah prays for rain (1 Kgs. 18:17-46)
    - Wall of the Aphek falls, destroying Syrians (1 Kgs. 20:30)

- Ahaziah's captains and men consumed by fire (2 Kgs. 1:10-14)
- Jordan River divided by prophets (2 Kgs. 2:7-8, 14)
- Elijah translated to heaven (2 Kgs. 2:11)
- Waters of Jericho (2 Kgs. 2:21-22)
- Elisha purifies spring (2 Kgs. 2:24)
- Water for Jehoshaphat and the allied army (2 Kgs. 3:16-20)
- Increase of oil (1 Kgs. 17:15; 2 Kgs. 4:2-7)
- Shunammite's son raised (2 Kgs. 4:14-37)
- Deadly stew (2 Kgs. 4:38-41)
- Feeding of the hundred (2 Kgs. 4:42-44)
- Naaman cured (2 Kgs. 5:10-27)
- Syrian army blinded and cured (2 Kgs. 6:18-20)
- Elisha's bones resurrect the dead (2 Kgs. 13:21)
- Sennacherib's army destroyed by an angel (2 Kgs. 19:35)
- Shadow of the sun turned back ten degrees (2 Kgs. 20:9-11)
- Uzziah struck with leprosy (2 Chr. 26:16-21)
- Recollection of deliverance (Ps. 78:44)
- Fiery furnace (Dan. 3:19-27)
- Daniel preserved (Dan. 6:16-23)
- Jonah in a great fish's belly (Jon. 2:1-10)
- Jonah delivered (Jon. 2:1-10)

▽Jesus

Jesus' miracles

- Leper cleansed (Matt. 8:2-4; Mark 1:40-45; Luke 5:12-16)
- Centurion's servant healed (Matt. 8:5-13; Luke 7:1-10)
- Peter's mother-in-law healed (Matt. 8:14-15; Mark 1:29-31; Luke 4:38-39)
- Jesus stills the storm (Matt. 8:18, 23-27; Mark 4:35-41; Luke 8:22-25)
- Gadarene demoniacs delivered (Matt. 8:28-34; Mark 5:1-20; Luke 8:26-39)
- Paralytic healed (Matt. 9:2-8; Mark 2:3-12; Luke 5:18-26)
- Jairus's daughter raised (Matt. 9:18-19, 23-26; Mark 5:22-24, 35-43; Luke 8:41-42, 49-56)
- Healing the woman with an issue of blood (Matt. 9:20-22; Mark 5:25-34; Luke 8:43-48; see also Lev. 15:25)
- Two blind men healed (Matt. 9:27-30)
- A mute demon delivered (Matt. 9:32-33)
- Healing of a man with a shriveled hand (Matt. 12:9-13; Mark 3:1-5; Luke 6:6-10)
- Blind and mute demoniac delivered (Matt. 12:22; Luke 11:14)
- Feeding the 5,000 (Matt. 14:14-21; Mark 6:30-44; Luke 9:10-17; John 6:5-13)
- Walking on the water (Matt. 14:24-33; Mark 6:45-52; John 6:16-21)
- Syrophoenician's daughter healed (Matt. 15:21-28; Mark 7:24-30)
- Feeding of the 4,000 (Matt. 15:32-39; Mark 8:1-9)
- Demon-possessed boy delivered (Matt. 17:14; Mark 9:14-29; Luke 9:38-42)
- Tax money provided (Matt. 17:24-27)
- Blind Bartimaeus healed (Matt. 20:29-34; Mark 10:46-52; Luke 18:35-43)
- Withering of the fig tree (Matt. 21:18-19; Mark 11:12-14)
- Delivering a demoniac (Mark 1:23-28; Luke 4:31-36)
- Healing a deaf mute in Decapolis (Mark 7:31-37)
- Blind man at Bethsaida healed (Mark 8:22-26)
- First miraculous catch of fish (Luke 5:1-11)
- Raising a widow's son (Luke 7:11-15)
- Healing a crippled woman on the Sabbath (Luke 13:10-17)
- Healing a man with dropsy (Luke 14:2-4)
- Ten lepers cleansed (Luke 17:11-19)
- Malchus's ear restored (Luke 22:49-51; John 18:10)
- Turning water into wine (John 2:1-11)
- Healing a nobleman's son at Cana (John 4:46-54)
- Healing a lame man at the pool of Bethesda (John 5:1-9)
- Man born blind healed (John 9:1-7)
- Lazarus raised (John 11:17-44)
- Second miraculous catch of fish (John 21:1-11)

▽Others

Miracles of Others

- By seventy disciples (Luke 10:17-20)
- By Peter and John (Acts 3:2-11)
- By the apostles (Acts 3:6, 12-13, 16; 4:10, 30; 9:34-35; 16:18)
- By Peter (Acts 5:5, 10, 15-16)
- By Paul (Acts 13:11; 14:10; 28)
- By evil beings (Rev. 13:3, 13-14; 16:14)

▶ JUDGMENT

Acts of judgment in God's master plan (Ezek. 24:14)

- ▷ Judgment upon the whole race, as a consequence of the fall (Gen. 3:14-24)
- ▷ Great Flood (Gen. 6:5; 7:16)
- ▷ Confusion of tongues (Gen. 11:1-9)
- ▷ Famine (Gen. 12:10; 26:1; 41:1; Ruth 1:1; 2 Sam. 21:1; 1 Kgs. 18:1; 2 Kgs. 4:38; 6:24; 7:3; 8:1; 25:2; 1 Chr. 21:1; Neh. 5:3; Ps. 37:18; Isa. 14:30; Jer. 11:22; 52:6; Acts 11:27)
- ▷ The destruction of Sodom and Gommorah (Gen. 18:20)
- ▷ The plagues of Egypt (Exod. 6:6; 12:12)
- ▷ Plague upon Israel's enemies (Exod. 7–12; 1 Sam. 6:32; Isa. 19:22; 29:6; Ezek. 32:15)
- ▷ Amalekites destroyed (Exod. 17:12)
- ▷ God sends hornets (Exod. 23:27)
- ▷ Calf brings judgment (Exod. 32:34)
- ▷ Korah and followers swallowed by earthquake (Num. 16:32-35)
- ▷ Sin of Peor (Num. 25:1)
- ▷ God promises judgment (Num. 31:2; Deut. 28:15; 32:23; Isa. 13:13; Ezek. 5:11; 6:9; 7:14; 12:15; 14:12; 25:12; 26:7; 28:20; Joel 2:1; Zech. 14:1)
- ▷ Jericho falls (Josh. 6:20)
- ▷ Community suffers due to individual's sin (Josh. 7:1; 22:16)
- ▷ Mountains quake/earthquake (Judg. 5:4; 1 Sam. 4:5; 2 Sam. 22:7; 1 Kgs. 19:11; Pss. 18:7; 46:2; 75:3; 77:18;

Ezek. 38:19; Amos 1:1; 4:12-13; Zech. 14:5; Matt. 27:53; Acts 16:25)
- ▷ Call to repentance (1 Kgs. 22:15; 2 Chr. 7:12; 33:17)
- ▷ 70,000 die in Israel due to plague (1 Chr. 21:14)
- ▷ Deliverance from judgment (2 Chr. 20:9; Pss. 91:2; 105:15; 106:28; Jer. 18:7-10; Jon. 2:6)
- ▷ God sends delivering angel (2 Chr. 32:21)
- ▷ God sends hail (Job 38:22)
- ▷ God will destroy with famine, sword, and plague (Jer. 14:11; 16:3; 21:5; 24:9; 44:11)
- ▷ And the evil that came upon other oppressors of Israel (Ezek. 25:11; 28:22)
- ▷ Signs of last days (Matt. 24:6; Mark 13:5; Luke 21:10)
- ▷ Ananias and Sapphira (Acts 5:1)
- ▷ Seven seals judgment (Rev. 5–7)
- ▷ The trumpet judgments (Rev. 8–9)
- ▷ Seven last plagues (Rev. 15:1)
- ▷ Bowls of wrath (Rev. 16)
- ▷ Babylon destroyed (Rev. 18:1; see also Zech. 6:8)
- ▷ Great white throne judgment (Rev. 20:11)

▶ MANIFESTATIONS
Divine manifestations in God's master plan
- ▷ Use of angelic agents (Gen. 16:7; 18:2; 19:1; 1 Kgs. 19:5-7; Ps. 91:11; Isa. 6:6; Ezek. 9:1-8; Dan. 10:13; 12:1; Matt. 4:11; Luke 1:1, 19; 2:13-15; 15:6-7; John 1:51; Acts 12:23; 1 Thes. 4:16-17; Heb. 13:2; Rev. 4:6-11; 5:6-14; 6:1, 3, 5, 7; 7:1, 11-12; 12:7; 14:3, 17; 15:7; 19:4-5)
- ▷ Appearances of God (Gen. 17:1; 18:1; Exod. 6:2-3; 24:9-11; 33:11; Num. 12:6-8)

▶ COMMON GRACE
Common grace in God's master plan
- ▷ Restrains sin (Gen. 6:3; Ps. 81:11-12; Acts 7:42; Rom. 1:24-28; 2 Thes. 2:6-7)
- ▷ Helps unbelievers do good without earning salvation (Num. 21:14; 1 Kgs. 5:5-7; 2 Kgs. 10:29-30; 12:2; 14:3; Luke 6:33; Rom. 2:14)
- ▷ On creation (Ps. 145:9; Matt. 6:26-30; 10:29; Luke 12:6; Rom. 8:20)
- ▷ On individuals (Isa. 42:5; Ezek. 18:23; 33:1; Matt. 5:44-45; Luke 6:35-36; Acts 14:14-18; 17:28; Rom. 2:4; 1 Tim. 4:10)

▶ COVENANTS
Covenants in God's master plan
- ▷ Covenant with Adam (Gen. 2:15-17)
- ▷ Covenant of grace (Gen. 3:15; 17:1-2, 7)
- ▷ Covenant with Noah (Gen. 9:1-6)
- ▷ Covenant at Sinai (Exod. 19:5-6; Deut. 10:4)
- ▷ Covenant with David (2 Sam. 7)
- ▷ New Covenant predicted and accomplished (Jer. 31:31; Heb. 8:7-13)
- ▷ Our part in God's masterplan (see topics ***Holiness*** and ***Ministry***)

DISCOVER MINISTRY

Becoming an Agent of Change

Have you ever been friends with a minister? If you know a Christian, then you have. We are all called to be ministers, representatives of Christ to our friends and in our world. We might not be paid by the church, but we are all called by God to be ministers wherever we are—in the home, on the job, or in our churches.

Many of us do important jobs. We may be leaders, or we may be followers, but all of us have tools we use to get our work done. Usually, we work on a schedule, and if it's not done on time, someone gets in trouble or even fired.

God's greatest tool to accomplish His will on earth is His church. But the church uses the preaching of the Word, the sacraments, evangelism, prayer, fasting—all of these are required by God at various times, but none of them have an instant effect. God has a plan, and He has the right tools, but He waits for the perfect moment to change our hearts and minds. To be an agent of change in God's kingdom, you must be patient, for God has His own sense of timing that may be far different from our own.

Do you see yourself as a minister? Consider yourself ordained by God to be a minister—first to your family, then to the world. Let your entire life be a sermon that teaches the world about your God.

■ ■ ■

GREAT COMMISSION ***Because God has given us the good news of salvation,***
I will encourage my family, friends, and the world to know and act on His gospel.

TRANSFORMATION ***Because God has made me to transform His world,***
I will risk everything to see His kingdom come and His will be done.

GREAT COMMISSION

Being a Witness of Christ to the World: *How can we help fulfill the Great Commission?*

▸ WITNESS

Being a witness

- ▹ Witness in the power of the Holy Spirit (Josh. 5:1; Pss. 69:6; 96:2; Luke 4:14, 18; 24:46-49; John 4:4; 14:26; 15:26; 16:7-8, 13-15; Acts 1:5; 2:4; 7:2; 20:23; Rom. 8:16; 1 Thes. 1:5; 2 Tim. 1:6; Heb. 10:15)
- ▹ Turn others from Satan to God (Josh. 24:2-3; Ps. 107:2; Isa. 61:1; 63:7; Acts 10:38; 26:17-18; Rom. 2:19; Col. 1:13; 1 Thes. 5:5; 1 Tim. 3:7; 2 Tim. 2:26; Heb. 2:14; 1 Pet. 2:9; 2 Pet. 3:15; 1 Jn. 3:8-10)
- ▹ Having a bold witness (Ezra 3:3; Luke 3:7; Acts 18:8)
- ▹ Locally, regionally, worldwide (Job 37:24; Prov. 29:27; Jer. 46:26; Acts 1:8)
- ▹ Christ issues the call of the gospel (Ps. 20:5; Matt. 4:19; 9:9, 13, 37-38; Mark 1:16-20; 2:3-17; 3:13-14; Luke 5:10; 5:27, 32; 6:13; John 1:35-51; 5:16; Acts 1:24; 9:15; 22:21; 26:16; 2 Tim. 1:11)
- ▹ Witness in word and deed (Luke 9:1-6; 10:3-12)
- ▹ Barriers

  Barriers to evangelism
  - ▿God deludes some people (Isa. 6:10; Rom. 9:13; 2 Thes. 2:10)
  - ▿People don't want to hear the truth (Ezek. 2:4-7; Matt. 27:43, 63; Rom. 1:18)
  - ▿No one to preach the gospel (Rom. 10:14-16)
  - ▿Satan blinds people (2 Cor. 4:3-4)

▸ MAKE DISCIPLES

Making disciples of all nations

- ▹ Disciples enjoy God's presence (Gen. 39:2-3, 21; Exod. 3:12; Josh. 1:5; Ps. 140:13; Isa. 7:14; 9:6; Ezek. 48:35; Matt. 1:22-23; 28:20; Acts 18:9-10; 2 Tim. 4:16-17)
- ▹ Disciples are obligated to share Christ with others (Exod. 21:6; Ezra 5:11; Luke 12:37; 17:10; Rom. 1:1, 14-17; 6:16-18; 2 Cor. 5:14-15; Gal. 1:10; 6:10; Phil. 1:1; Col. 1:7; 3:23; 2 Tim. 2:2; 4:7; Jas. 1:1; 1 Pet. 1:1; 1 Jn. 2:6; 4:19)
- ▹ Disciples strategically use material wealth (Deut. 6:10-12; 8:18; 1 Sam. 2:7; Job 8:15; 20:21; Matt. 6:19-21; 19:16; Mark 10:17; Luke 12:15; 18:18; 1 Tim. 6:17-18; 1 Jn. 3:17)
- ▹ Disciples strategically use knowledge, skills, and abilities (1 Sam. 27:10; 2 Chr. 29:34; Neh. 4:15; Prov. 3:21; 15:22; 18:1; Eccl. 12:9; Matt. 4:18-22; Rom. 12:1-3; 1 Pet. 4:10-11)
- ▹ Disciples are team-players (Neh. 3:8; 4:6; 1 Cor. 12:18; Eph. 4:15-16; Gal. 5:26; 1 Pet. 2:4-5)
- ▹ Disciples are not just followers, but also witnesses (Ezek. 44:19-25; Matt. 10:24-39; Mark 8:34; 10:21; Luke 9:23, 57-62; 14:26-27; John 1:43; 12:10; 14:12-13; 1 Pet. 2:9)
- ▹ Disciples function under God's authority (Ezek. 45:8-9; Matt. 28:18; Luke 10:19-20; Acts 19:13-16; Heb. 1:1-4; 1 Pet. 3:22)
- ▹ Disciples pray (Amos 7:2; Luke 10:2; John 17; 2 Cor. 4:4)
- ▹ Disciple by baptizing (Matt. 3:13, 16; 28:19; Mark 16:15-16; Acts 8:35-39; 9:18; 19:5; 22:16; Rom. 6:3-8; Eph. 4:5; Col. 2:12-13)
- ▹ Disciple by teaching (Matt. 4:23; 9:35; 21:23; 26:55; 28:20; Mark 6:6; 14:49; Luke 5:17; 13:10, 22; 21:37; 23:5; Acts 2:42; 5:25; 15:35; 18:11; 28:31; Rom. 12:7; 1 Cor. 13:10; Col. 1:28; 3:16; 1 Thes. 4:2ff)
- ▹ Disciples take advantage of open doors (1 Cor. 14:27; 16:9; 2 Cor. 2:12; Col. 4:3)
- ▹ Prayers

  Prayers for unbelievers
  - ▿That they would seek God (Deut. 4:29)
  - ▿That God would reveal Himself (Judg. 7:14; Luke 10:21-22)
  - ▿That they would confess Christ as Lord (2 Kgs. 17:41; Rom. 10:9-10)
  - ▿That they would believe in Christ as Savior (2 Chr. 11:15; John 1:12; 5:24)
  - ▿That Satan would not blind them (Matt. 13:19; 2 Cor. 4:4)
  - ▿That God would draw them (John 6:44)
  - ▿That the Holy Spirit works in them (John 16:8-13)
  - ▿That they might turn from their sin (Acts 3:19; 17:30-31)
  - ▿That they would believe God's Word (Rom. 10:14-17; 1 Thes. 2:13)
  - ▿That they would start with a solid root (Col. 2:6-7)

▸ RISK

Change requires risk

- ▹ Stepping outside of your "comfort zone" (Neh. 1:10; Esth. 3:2; Ezek. 4:10-17; Matt. 6:33; 8:18-22; 10:5-15, 22, 37-39; 16:24-28; 19:29-30; 20:16; Mark 10:29-31; Luke 9:57-62; 14:27; 18:29-30; Acts 9:15; Jas. 1:8)
- ▹ Opposition and ill-treatment (Ps. 118:6; Matt. 5:10-12; Luke 6:22-23; 22:28; Rom. 6:5; 8:17; 2 Cor. 1:5; 4:8-12, 17; Phil. 3:10; Col. 1:24; 1:29–2:1; 2 Tim. 3:12; 1 Pet. 3:13-21; 4:12-16)

▸ RECONCILE

Sharing a ministry of reconciliation

- ▹ Necessary because there is enmity between God and humanity (Isa. 59:2-8)
- ▹ All believers have this ministry (2 Cor. 5:18–6:2)
- ▹ Believers are ambassadors for Christ (2 Cor. 5:20)

▸ DESCRIPTION

Describing a ministry of reconciliation

- ▹ People are invited to Christ (Matt. 9:35-38; Mark 2:13-17; John 1:45-46; 1 Pet. 3:15-16)
- ▹ Good news for bad people (Luke 4:18-19)
- ▹ Reconciliation makes us holy, blameless, and irreproachable in His sight (Rom. 4:6-8; 2 Cor. 5:19)
- ▹ The cross bridges the gap between God and humanity (Rom. 5:10; Col. 1:21-22)
- ▹ People hear of Christ through preaching (Rom. 10:14-15)
- ▹ Jesus gives us His perfect relationship with God (2 Cor. 5:21)
- ▹ It is made possible through Christ (Col. 1:19-20)
- ▹ God offers sacrifice (1 Jn. 2:1-2; 4:10)

TRANSFORMATION

Impacting the World for Christ: *How can we help transform society and culture?*

▸ FILL AND SUBDUE

Filling the earth and subduing it

- ▹ Caretakers of the earth's resources (Gen. 1:26-28; 2:15; Deut. 20:19; Ps. 8; Dan. 7:27; Heb. 2:5-8)
- ▹ Tearing down spiritual strongholds (Josh. 6; 1 Sam. 22:5; Matt. 12:29; Mark 3:27; Luke 10:17; 2 Cor. 10:3-6; Eph. 6:12; 1 Pet. 2:11-12)
- ▹ Being salt and light in the world (1 Kgs. 4:29; 2 Kgs. 5:8; Prov. 25:21; Isa. 21:4; 58:8; 60:1-3; Mic. 4:5; Matt. 5:13-16; 10:42; 25:40-46; Mark 9:41, 50; Luke 2:32; 14:14; John 1:9; 8:12; 2 Cor. 2:14-16; 4:4; Eph. 2:10; 5:8-9, 13; Phil. 2:14-16; 1 Pet. 2:9-12; 5:1-4; Jude 1:20-23)
- ▹ Influencing every sphere of life (2 Chr. 3:5; Neh. 2:4; 10:31; Ps. 113:3; Prov. 24:17; Eccl. 2:25; Mark 1:15; John 1:3; Eph. 1:10, 21-32; Col. 1:16-17, 20)

▸ VOCATIONS

Vocations that were used by God to transform His world

- ▹ Keeper of flocks (Gen. 4:2)
- ▹ Metal forger (Gen. 4:22)
- ▹ Hunter (Gen. 10:9)
- ▹ Brickmaker (Gen. 11:3)
- ▹ Shepherd/Herdsman (Gen. 13:7; 1 Sam. 21:7)
- ▹ King (Gen. 14:1; 1 Sam. 8:5; 12:15)
- ▹ Priest (Gen. 14:18)
- ▹ Servant (Gen. 15:3; Exod. 20:10)
- ▹ Prophet (Gen. 20:7)
- ▹ Archer (Gen. 21:20)
- ▹ Midwife (Gen. 35:17)
- ▹ Baker (Gen. 40:1)
- ▹ Cupbearer (Gen. 40:1)
- ▹ Steward (Gen. 43:16)
- ▹ Slave (Gen. 44:10)
- ▹ Judge (Exod. 2:14)
- ▹ Moneylender (Exod. 22:25)
- ▹ Engraver (Exod. 28:11)
- ▹ Jeweler (Exod. 28:11)
- ▹ Designer (Exod. 35:35)
- ▹ Embroiderer (Exod. 35:35)
- ▹ Weaver (Exod. 35:35)
- ▹ Creditor (Deut. 15:2)
- ▹ Maidservant (Deut. 15:17)
- ▹ Water carrier (Josh. 9:21)
- ▹ Woodcutter (Josh. 9:21)
- ▹ Commander (Judg. 4:4)
- ▹ Armor bearer (Judg. 9:54)
- ▹ Warrior (Judg. 11:1)
- ▹ Silversmith (Judg. 17:4)
- ▹ Cook (1 Sam. 8:13)
- ▹ Perfumer (1 Sam. 8:13)
- ▹ Seer (1 Sam. 9:9)
- ▹ Blacksmith (1 Sam. 13:19)
- ▹ Guard (1 Sam. 22:17)
- ▹ Messenger (1 Sam. 23:27)
- ▹ Bodyguard (1 Sam. 28:2)
- ▹ Stonemason (2 Sam. 5:11)
- ▹ Sheepshearer (2 Sam. 13:23)
- ▹ Watchman (2 Sam. 13:34)
- ▹ Counselor (2 Sam. 15:12)
- ▹ Gatekeeper (2 Sam. 18:26)
- ▹ Queen (1 Kgs. 10:1)
- ▹ Chariot driver (1 Kgs. 22:34)
- ▹ Swordsman (2 Kgs. 3:26)
- ▹ Harvester (2 Kgs. 4:18; Jas. 5:4)
- ▹ Horseman (2 Kgs. 9:17)
- ▹ Trumpeter (2 Kgs. 11:14)
- ▹ Builder (2 Kgs. 12:11)
- ▹ Mason (2 Kgs. 12:12)
- ▹ Stonecutter (2 Kgs. 12:12)
- ▹ Doorkeeper (2 Kgs. 22:4)
- ▹ Governor (2 Kgs. 23:8)
- ▹ Charioteer (1 Chr. 19:18)
- ▹ Scribe (1 Chr. 24:6)
- ▹ Teacher (1 Chr. 25:8; Prov. 5:13)
- ▹ Officer (1 Chr. 26:24)
- ▹ Woodsman (2 Chr. 2:10)
- ▹ Courier (2 Chr. 30:6)
- ▹ Treasurer (Ezra 1:8)
- ▹ Writer (Ps. 45:1)
- ▹ Musician (Ps. 68:25)
- ▹ Grinder (Eccl. 12:3)
- ▹ Poet (Song 4:1; Acts 17:28)
- ▹ Fisherman (Isa. 19:8)
- ▹ Bowmen (Isa. 21:17)
- ▹ Potter (Isa. 29:16)
- ▹ Goldsmith (Isa. 40:19)
- ▹ Astronomer (Isa. 47:13)
- ▹ Minister (Isa. 61:6)
- ▹ Physician (Jer. 8:22; Col. 4:14)
- ▹ Grape picker (Jer. 49:9)
- ▹ Oarsmen (Ezek. 27:8)
- ▹ Vine grower (Joel 1:11)
- ▹ Planter (Amos 9:13)
- ▹ Plowman (Amos 9:13)
- ▹ Refiner (Mal. 3:3)
- ▹ Tax collector (Matt. 10:3)
- ▹ Merchant (Matt. 13:45)
- ▹ Landowner (Matt. 20:1)
- ▹ Butcher (Matt. 22:4)
- ▹ Rabbi (Matt. 23:7)
- ▹ Banker (Matt. 25:27)
- ▹ Carpenter (Mark 6:3)
- ▹ Executioner (Mark 6:27)
- ▹ Innkeeper (Luke 10:35)
- ▹ Magistrate (Luke 12:58)
- ▹ Soldier (John 19:23)
- ▹ Gardener (John 20:15)
- ▹ Proconsul (Acts 13:7)
- ▹ Jailer (Acts 16:23)
- ▹ Tentmaker (Acts 18:3)
- ▹ Overseer (Acts 20:28)
- ▹ Lawyer (Acts 24:1)
- ▹ Emperor (Acts 25:25)
- ▹ Athlete (2 Tim. 2:5)
- ▹ Farmer (2 Tim. 2:6)
- ▹ Preacher (2 Pet. 2:5)
- ▹ Harpist (Rev. 14:2)

ALL-POWERFUL • EVER-PRESENT • ALL-KNOWING • SOVEREIGN
CREATOR
GOD
is . . .
SAVIOR
JUDGE
LOVE • MERCIFUL • FAITHFUL • UNCHANGING
HOLY • TRUTH • RIGHTEOUS • JUST
PERSONAL

THE ATTRIBUTES OF GOD

My father, Bill Bright, said, "We can trace all our human problems to our view of God." What we believe to be true about God's character affects every aspect of our lives. All of our actions are driven by our view of God. Therefore, nothing in life could be more important than knowing who God really is.

It is no simple task to understand who God really is. In fact, it is a lifelong adventure. Too often, we let experiences influence how we view God, rather than letting the reality of who God is shape how we view those experiences.

Our view of God is the foundation of who we are. If the foundation is strong we can become strong. But if the foundation is weak we will always remain weak–lacking in joy, hope and faith. The degree to which your view of God is flawed will be the same degree to which you lack power to experience real transformation.

In light of this, the *Discover God Study Bible* is designed to do two things. First, it will help you build a strong foundation–a more accurate view of God. Second, it will help you build on that foundation, teaching you how to follow God.

As you look at the diagram on the left, you will see twelve attributes of God. They are divided into three categories to help you better grasp how His attributes interrelate. Finally, they are all wrapped in the context that He is personal–that He can be intimately known by anyone who seeks Him. Although God has many additional attributes, these are some of the most basic.

Not long before he went home to be with the Lord, my father wrote the book *Discover God* and then commissioned the *Discover God Study Bible.* He passionately desired to help others discover who God really is, resulting in life transformation. We hope you find this Bible to be a tremendous resource to you in that process. For additional information and other helpful resources, please go to our Web site: www.DiscoverGod.com. We pray that you may more deeply discover God for who He really is.

Yours for Making GOD the Issue,

Brad Bright

National Director, *DISCOVER GOD*

President & CEO, Bright Media Foundation

BECAUSE GOD IS HOLY

I will devote myself to Him in purity, worship and service.

Genesis 2:3 .... page 9
Exodus 15:11 .... page 136
Leviticus 20:7 .... page 222
1 Samuel 2:2 .... page 485
1 Samuel 6:20 .... page 493
Psalm 72:19 .... page 1042
Proverbs 9:10 .... page 1160
Ezekiel 14:6 .... page 1516
1 Peter 1:15 .... page 2237
1 John 4:12 .... page 2260
1 John 5:21 .... page 2262
Revelation 4:8 .... page 2287

BECAUSE GOD IS A PERSONAL SPIRIT

I will seek intimate fellowship with Him.

2 Chronicles 16:9 .... page 785
Psalm 84:2 .... page 1059

BECAUSE GOD IS ALL-POWERFUL

He can help me with anything.

Philippians 4:13 .... page 2141

BECAUSE GOD IS EVER-PRESENT

He is always with me.

Deuteronomy 31:8 .... page 368
Joshua 1:9 .... page 381
Job 31:4 .... page 932
Matthew 28:20 .... page 1802
1 Corinthians 3:16 .... page 2062
Hebrews 13:5 .... page 2220

BECAUSE GOD KNOWS EVERYTHING

I will go to Him with all my questions and concerns.

Ezekiel 11:5 .... page 1512
Daniel 2:21 .... page 1585
Matthew 10:30 .... page 1762
Romans 11:33 .... page 2044
1 John 3:20 .... page 2258

BECAUSE GOD IS ABSOLUTE TRUTH

I will believe what He says and live accordingly.

BECAUSE GOD IS RIGHTEOUS

I will live by His standards.

BECAUSE GOD IS JUST

He will always treat me fairly.

BECAUSE GOD IS LOVE

He is unconditionally committed to my well-being.

BECAUSE GOD IS MERCIFUL

He forgives me of my sins when I sincerely confess them.

BECAUSE GOD IS SOVEREIGN

I will joyfully submit to His will.

BECAUSE GOD IS FAITHFUL

I will trust Him to always keep His promises.

BECAUSE GOD NEVER CHANGES

My future is secure and eternal.

DISCOVER GOD STUDY BIBLE

New Living Translation®

SECOND EDITION

Tyndale House Publishers, Inc. • Carol Stream, Illinois

Library of Congress Cataloging-in-Publication Data

Bible. English. New Living Translation. 2007.
Discover God study Bible.
p. cm.
Includes indexes.
ISBN-13: 978-0-8423-6918-3 (hc)
ISBN-10: 0-8423-6918-X (hc)
ISBN-13: 978-0-8423-6919-0 (black bonded leather)
ISBN-10: 0-8423-6919-8 (black bonded leather)
[etc.]
I. Tyndale House Publishers. II. Title.
BS195.N394 2007
220.5'20834—dc22 2007002323

ISBN-13: 978-0-8423-6918-3 – ISBN-10: 0-8423-6918-X Hardcover
ISBN-13: 978-0-8423-6923-7 – ISBN-10: 0-8423-6923-6 Chestnut/Brown LeatherLike
ISBN-13: 978-0-8423-6919-0 – ISBN-10: 0-8423-6919-8 Bonded Leather Black

Printed in the United States of America

13 12 11 10 09 08 07

7 6 5 4 3 2 1

Tyndale House Publishers and Wycliffe Bible Translators share the vision for an understandable, accurate translation of the Bible for every person in the world. Each sale of the *Holy Bible,* New Living Translation, benefits Wycliffe Bible Translators. Wycliffe is working with partners around the world to accomplish Vision 2025—an initiative to start a Bible translation program in every language group that needs it by the year 2025.

TABLE OF CONTENTS

ACKNOWLEDGMENTS

During his lifetime, my dear husband, Bill Bright, eagerly awaited the release of new study Bibles and felt honored to endorse many of them. It was not until the later years of his ministry that he considered incorporating the timeless truths that God had blessed in our ministry with Campus Crusade for Christ into a study Bible. Our dear friend Ken Taylor was a precious encouragement to Bill, and it was a touching moment to observe the two men in what proved to be the last years of their lives commit to the Discover God Study Bible project.

Both Ken Taylor and Bill Bright knew that a proper understanding of who God is leads to a life of blessing now and for generations to follow—a life of victory, power, joy and fruitfulness.

My sons, Zac and Brad, join me in expressing our gratitude to the many people who have dedicated several years to see this project through to completion. The folks at Tyndale House Publishers have made a major investment of financial and human resources and we are very grateful for their commitment to excellence. Mark Taylor, Ron Beers and Jon Farrar have stayed the course with us and their professional guidance has proved very valuable.

John Nill has directed the Bible project from its earliest days. His experience and expertise have been invaluable.

Robert Barnes worked faithfully leading the editorial team of biblical scholars and was tireless in ensuring theological accuracy from start to finish.

As stylistic editor, Brenda Josee read every word in the manuscript multiple times to ensure that the lessons God taught Bill Bright over a lifetime of ministry were reflected in every note. Her efforts have contributed greatly to the Bible you now hold in your hands.

Thank you to so many of our Campus Crusade for Christ staff family who graciously contributed their time and energies along the way, particularly Keith Davies and his team.

We are grateful for the financial contributions to the Bill Bright Memorial Fund from so many friends around the world which helped fund the development of this study Bible. I know Bill would be very pleased and grateful to each of you.

Thank you to each person who has had a part in making this Bible possible. I trust you are pleased with the results of your combined contributions in making this Bible a reality.

May the combined efforts of each contributor prove to be a blessing to every reader.

THE DISCOVER GOD STUDY BIBLE CONTRIBUTORS:

Project Director: John Nill
Managing Editor: Rev. Robert F. Barnes, MDiv
Project Editor: David P. Barrett, MA
Stylistic Editor: Brenda Josee
Assistant Editor: Leanne Roberts
Greg Bailey, MDiv
Michael Beates, DMin
Valerie Anne Bost, MDiv
Stephen Carlson, PhD
Chuck Donet, MDiv
Darren Edington, MDiv
Felix Fernandez, MDiv
Bill Fullilove, MDiv
William Kruidenier, MDiv
Ra McLaughlin, MDiv
Brian Onken, MDiv
Mike Sacasas, MDiv
Cary Smith, MDiv
Melanie Webb, MDiv
Joette Whims, MDiv

Greg Bailey, ThM
Michael Beates, DMin
Valerie Anne Bost, MDiv
Stephen Carlson, MA
Chuck Dorey, MDiv
Darren Ellington, MDiv
Felix Fernandez, MA
Bill Hillgrove, MDiv

Mike Sneeden, MDiv
Gary Smith, MDiv
Melanie Webb, MDiv
Jeanie Whitis, MDiv

Note to Readers

The *Holy Bible,* New Living Translation, was first published in 1996. It quickly became one of the most popular Bible translations in the English-speaking world. While the NLT's influence was rapidly growing, the Bible Translation Committee determined that an additional investment in scholarly review and text refinement could make it even better. So shortly after its initial publication, the committee began an eight-year process with the purpose of increasing the level of the NLT's precision without sacrificing its easy-to-understand quality. This second-generation text was completed in 2004 and is reflected in this edition of the New Living Translation.

The goal of any Bible translation is to convey the meaning and content of the ancient Hebrew, Aramaic, and Greek texts as accurately as possible to contemporary readers. The challenge for our translators was to create a text that would communicate as clearly and powerfully to today's readers as the original texts did to readers and listeners in the ancient biblical world. The resulting translation is easy to read and understand, while also accurately communicating the meaning and content of the original biblical texts. The NLT is a general-purpose text especially good for study, devotional reading, and reading aloud in worship services.

We believe that the New Living Translation–which combines the latest biblical scholarship with a clear, dynamic writing style–will communicate God's word powerfully to all who read it. We publish it with the prayer that God will use it to speak his timeless truth to the church and the world in a fresh, new way.

The Publishers
July 2004

INTRODUCTION TO THE NEW LIVING TRANSLATION

TRANSLATION PHILOSOPHY AND METHODOLOGY

English Bible translations tend to be governed by one of two general translation theories. The first theory has been called "formal-equivalence," "literal," or "word-for-word" translation. According to this theory, the translator attempts to render each word of the original language into English and seeks to preserve the original syntax and sentence structure as much as possible in translation. The second theory has been called "dynamic-equivalence," "functional-equivalence," or "thought-for-thought" translation. The goal of this translation theory is to produce in English the closest natural equivalent of the message expressed by the original-language text, both in meaning and in style.

Both of these translation theories have their strengths. A formal-equivalence translation preserves aspects of the original text—including ancient idioms, term consistency, and original-language syntax—that are valuable for scholars and professional study. It allows a reader to trace formal elements of the original-language text through the English translation. A dynamic-equivalence translation, on the other hand, focuses on translating the message of the original-language text. It ensures that the meaning of the text is readily apparent to the contemporary reader. This allows the message to come through with immediacy, without requiring the reader to struggle with foreign idioms and awkward syntax. It also facilitates serious study of the text's message and clarity in both devotional and public reading.

The pure application of either of these translation philosophies would create translations at opposite ends of the translation spectrum. But in reality, all translations contain a mixture of these two philosophies. A purely formal-equivalence translation would be unintelligible in English, and a purely dynamic-equivalence translation would risk being unfaithful to the original. That is why translations shaped by dynamic-equivalence theory are usually quite literal when the original text is relatively clear, and the translations shaped by formal-equivalence theory are sometimes quite dynamic when the original text is obscure.

The translators of the New Living Translation set out to render the message of the original texts of Scripture into clear, contemporary English. As they did so, they kept the concerns of both formal-equivalence and dynamic-equivalence in mind. On the one hand, they translated as simply and literally as possible when that approach yielded an accurate, clear, and natural English text. Many words and phrases were rendered literally and consistently into English, preserving essential literary and rhetorical devices, ancient metaphors, and word choices that give structure to the text and provide echoes of meaning from one passage to the next.

On the other hand, the translators rendered the message more dynamically when the literal rendering was hard to understand, was misleading, or yielded archaic or foreign wording. They clarified difficult metaphors and terms to aid in the reader's understanding. The translators first struggled with the meaning of the words and phrases in the ancient context; then they rendered the message into clear, natural English. Their goal was to be both faithful to the ancient texts and eminently readable. The result is a translation that is both exegetically accurate and idiomatically powerful.

TRANSLATION PROCESS AND TEAM

To produce an accurate translation of the Bible into contemporary English, the translation team needed the skills necessary to enter into the thought patterns of the ancient authors and then to render their ideas, connotations, and effects into clear, contemporary English. To begin this process, qualified biblical scholars were needed to interpret the meaning of the original text and to check it against our base English translation. In order to guard against personal and theological biases, the scholars needed to represent a diverse group of evangelicals who would employ the best exegetical tools. Then to work alongside the scholars, skilled English stylists were needed to shape the text into clear, contemporary English.

With these concerns in mind, the Bible Translation Committee recruited teams of scholars that represented a broad spectrum of denominations, theological perspectives, and backgrounds within the worldwide evangelical community. (These scholars are listed at the end of this introduction.) Each book of the Bible was assigned to three different scholars with proven expertise in the book or group of books to be reviewed. Each of these scholars made a thorough review of a base translation and submitted suggested revisions to the appropriate Senior Translator. The Senior Translator then reviewed and summarized these suggestions and proposed a first-draft revision of the base text. This draft served as the basis for several additional phases of exegetical and stylistic committee review. Then the Bible Translation Committee jointly reviewed and approved every verse of the final translation.

Throughout the translation and editing process, the Senior Translators and their scholar teams were given a chance to review the editing done by the team of stylists. This ensured that exegetical errors would not be introduced late in the process and that the entire Bible Translation Committee was happy with the final result. By choosing a team of qualified scholars and skilled stylists and by setting up a process that allowed their interaction throughout the process, the New Living Translation has been refined to preserve the essential formal elements of the original biblical texts, while also creating a clear, understandable English text.

The New Living Translation was first published in 1996. Shortly after its initial publication, the Bible Translation Committee began a process of further committee review and translation refinement. The purpose of this continued revision was to increase the level of precision without sacrificing the text's easy-to-understand quality. This second-edition text was completed in 2004, and this printing of the New Living Translation reflects the updated text.

WRITTEN TO BE READ ALOUD

It is evident in Scripture that the biblical documents were written to be read aloud, often in public worship (see Nehemiah 8; Luke 4:16-20; 1 Timothy 4:13; Revelation 1:3). It is still the case today that more people will hear the Bible read aloud in church than are likely to read it for themselves. Therefore, a new translation must communicate with clarity and power when it is read publicly. Clarity was a primary goal for the NLT translators, not only to facilitate private reading and understanding, but also to ensure that it would be excellent for public reading and make an immediate and powerful impact on any listener.

THE TEXTS BEHIND THE NEW LIVING TRANSLATION

The Old Testament translators used the Masoretic Text of the Hebrew Bible as represented in *Biblia Hebraica Stuttgartensia* (1977), with its extensive system of textual notes; this is an update of Rudolf Kittel's *Biblia Hebraica* (Stuttgart, 1937). The translators also further compared the Dead Sea Scrolls, the Septuagint and other Greek manuscripts, the Samaritan Pentateuch, the Syriac Peshitta, the Latin Vulgate, and any other versions or manuscripts that shed light on the meaning of difficult passages.

The New Testament translators used the two standard editions of the Greek New Testament: the *Greek New Testament,* published by the United Bible Societies (UBS, fourth revised edition, 1993), and *Novum Testamentum Graece,* edited by Nestle and Aland (NA, twenty-seventh edition, 1993). These two editions, which have the same text but differ in punctuation and textual notes, represent, for the most part, the best in modern textual scholarship. However, in cases where strong textual or other scholarly evidence supported the decision, the translators sometimes chose to differ from the UBS and NA Greek texts and followed variant readings found in other ancient witnesses. Significant textual variants of this sort are always noted in the textual notes of the New Living Translation.

TRANSLATION ISSUES

The translators have made a conscious effort to provide a text that can be easily understood by the typical reader of modern English. To this end, we sought to use only vocabulary and language structures in common use today. We avoided using language likely to become quickly dated or that reflects only a narrow sub-dialect of English, with the goal of making the New Living Translation as broadly useful and timeless as possible.

But our concern for readability goes beyond the concerns of vocabulary and sentence structure. We are also concerned about historical and cultural barriers to understanding the Bible, and we have sought to translate terms shrouded in history and culture in ways that can be immediately understood. To this end:

- We have converted ancient weights and measures (for example, "ephah" [a unit of dry volume] or "cubit" [a unit of length]) to modern English (American) equivalents, since the ancient measures are not generally meaningful to today's readers. Then in the textual footnotes we offer the literal Hebrew, Aramaic, or Greek measures, along with modern metric equivalents.
- Instead of translating ancient currency values literally, we have expressed them in common terms that communicate the message. For example, in the Old Testament, "ten shekels of silver" becomes "ten pieces of silver" to convey the intended message. In the New Testament, we have often translated the "denarius" as "the normal daily wage" to facilitate understanding. Then a footnote offers: "Greek *a denarius,* the payment for a full day's wage." In general, we give a clear English rendering and then state the literal Hebrew, Aramaic, or Greek in a textual footnote.
- Since the names of Hebrew months are unknown to most contemporary readers, and since the Hebrew lunar calendar fluctuates from year to year in relation to the solar calendar used today, we have looked for clear ways to communicate the time of year the Hebrew months (such as Abib) refer to. When an expanded or interpretive rendering is given in the text, a textual note gives the literal rendering. Where it is possible to define a specific ancient date in terms of our modern calendar, we use modern dates in the text. A textual footnote then gives the literal Hebrew date and states the rationale for our rendering. For example, Ezra 6:15 pinpoints the date when the post-exilic Temple was completed in Jerusalem: "the third day of the month Adar." This was during the sixth year of King Darius's reign (that is, 515 B.C.). We have translated that date as March 12, with a footnote giving the Hebrew and identifying the year as 515 B.C.
- Since ancient references to the time of day differ from our modern methods of denoting time, we have used renderings that are instantly understandable to the

modern reader. Accordingly, we have rendered specific times of day by using approximate equivalents in terms of our common "o'clock" system. On occasion, translations such as "at dawn the next morning" or "as the sun was setting" have been used when the biblical reference is more general.

- When the meaning of a proper name (or a wordplay inherent in a proper name) is relevant to the message of the text, its meaning is often illuminated with a textual footnote. For example, in Exodus 2:10 the text reads: "The princess named him Moses, for she explained, 'I lifted him out of the water.'" The accompanying footnote reads: "*Moses* sounds like a Hebrew term that means 'to lift out.'"

  Sometimes, when the actual meaning of a name is clear, that meaning is included in parentheses within the text itself. For example, the text at Genesis 16:11 reads: "You are to name him Ishmael *(which means 'God hears'),* for the LORD has heard your cry of distress." Since the original hearers and readers would have instantly understood the meaning of the name "Ishmael," we have provided modern readers with the same information so they can experience the text in a similar way.
- Many words and phrases carry a great deal of cultural meaning that was obvious to the original readers but needs explanation in our own culture. For example, the phrase "they beat their breasts" (Luke 23:48) in ancient times meant that people were very upset, often in mourning. In our translation we chose to translate this phrase dynamically for clarity: "They went home *in deep sorrow.*" Then we included a footnote with the literal Greek, which reads: "Greek *went home beating their breasts.*" In other similar cases, however, we have sometimes chosen to illuminate the existing literal expression to make it immediately understandable. For example, here we might have expanded the literal phrase to read: "They went home beating their breasts *in sorrow.*" If we had done this, we would not have included a textual footnote, since the literal Greek clearly appears in translation.
- Metaphorical language is sometimes difficult for contemporary readers to understand, so at times we have chosen to translate or illuminate the meaning of a metaphor. For example, the ancient poet writes, "Your neck is *like* the tower of David" (Song of Songs 4:4). We have rendered it "Your neck is *as beautiful as* the tower of David" to clarify the intended positive meaning of the simile. Another example comes in Ecclesiastes 12:3, which can be literally rendered: "Remember him . . . when the grinding women cease because they are few, and the women who look through the windows see dimly." We have rendered it: "Remember him before your teeth—your few remaining servants—stop grinding; and before your eyes—the women looking through the windows—see dimly." We clarified such metaphors only when we believed a typical reader might be confused by the literal text.
- When the content of the original language text is poetic in character, we have rendered it in English poetic form. We sought to break lines in ways that clarify and highlight the relationships between phrases of the text. Hebrew poetry often uses parallelism, a literary form where a second phrase (or in some instances a third or fourth) echoes the initial phrase in some way. In Hebrew parallelism, the subsequent parallel phrases continue, while also furthering and sharpening, the thought expressed in the initial line or phrase. Whenever possible, we sought to represent these parallel phrases in natural poetic English.
- The Greek term *hoi Ioudaioi* is literally translated "the Jews" in many English translations. In the Gospel of John, however, this term doesn't always refer to the Jewish people generally. In some contexts, it refers more particularly to the Jewish

religious leaders. We have attempted to capture the meaning in these different contexts by using terms such as "the people" (with a footnote: Greek *the Jewish people*) or "the religious leaders," where appropriate.

- One challenge we faced was how to translate accurately the ancient biblical text that was originally written in a context where male-oriented terms were used to refer to humanity generally. We needed to respect the nature of the ancient context while also trying to make the translation clear to a modern audience that tends to read male-oriented language as applying only to males. Often the original text, though using masculine nouns and pronouns, clearly intends that the message be applied to both men and women. A typical example is found in the New Testament letters, where the believers are called "brothers" (*adelphoi*). Yet it is clear from the content of these letters that they were addressed to all the believers–male and female. Thus, we have usually translated this Greek word as "brothers and sisters" in order to represent the historical situation more accurately.

  We have also been sensitive to passages where the text applies generally to human beings or to the human condition. In some instances we have used plural pronouns (they, them) in place of the masculine singular (he, him). For example, a traditional rendering of Proverbs 22:6 is: "Train up a child in the way he should go, and when he is old he will not turn from it." We have rendered it: "Direct your children onto the right path, and when they are older, they will not leave it." At times, we have also replaced third person pronouns with the second person to ensure clarity. A traditional rendering of Proverbs 26:27 is: "He who digs a pit will fall into it, and he who rolls a stone, it will come back on him." We have rendered it: "If you set a trap for others, you will get caught in it yourself. If you roll a boulder down on others, it will crush you instead."

- We should emphasize, however, that all masculine nouns and pronouns used to represent God (for example, "Father") have been maintained without exception. All decisions of this kind have been driven by the concern to reflect accurately the intended meaning of the original texts of Scripture.

LEXICAL CONSISTENCY IN TERMINOLOGY

For the sake of clarity, we have translated certain original-language terms consistently, especially within synoptic passages and for commonly repeated rhetorical phrases, and within certain word categories such as divine names and non-theological technical terminology (e.g., liturgical, legal, cultural, zoological, and botanical terms). For theological terms, we have allowed a greater semantic range of acceptable English words or phrases for a single Hebrew or Greek word. We have avoided some theological terms that are not readily understood by many modern readers. For example, we avoided using words such as "justification" and "sanctification," which are carryovers from Latin translations. In place of these words, we have provided renderings such as "made right with God" and "made holy."

THE SPELLING OF PROPER NAMES

Many individuals in the Bible, especially the Old Testament, are known by more than one name (e.g., Uzziah/Azariah). For the sake of clarity, we have tried to use a single spelling for any one individual, footnoting the literal spelling whenever we differ from it. This is especially helpful in delineating the kings of Israel and Judah. King Joash/Jehoash of Israel has been consistently called Jehoash, while King Joash/Jehoash of Judah is called Joash. A similar distinction has been used to distinguish between Joram/Jehoram of Israel and Joram/Jehoram of Judah. All such decisions were made with the goal of clarifying the text for the reader. When the ancient biblical writers clearly had a theological purpose in their choice of a variant name (e.g., Esh-baal/ Ishbosheth), the different names have been maintained with an explanatory footnote.

For the names Jacob and Israel, which are used interchangeably for both the individual patriarch and the nation, we generally render it "Israel" when it refers to the nation and "Jacob" when it refers to the individual. When our rendering of the name differs from the underlying Hebrew text, we provide a textual footnote, which includes this explanation: "The names 'Jacob' and 'Israel' are often interchanged throughout the Old Testament, referring sometimes to the individual patriarch and sometimes to the nation."

THE RENDERING OF DIVINE NAMES

All appearances of *'el, 'elohim,* or *'eloah* have been translated "God," except where the context demands the translation "god(s)." We have generally rendered the tetragrammaton (*YHWH*) consistently as "the LORD," utilizing a form with small capitals that is common among English translations. This will distinguish it from the name *'adonai,* which we render "Lord." When *'adonai* and *YHWH* appear together, we have rendered it "Sovereign LORD." This also distinguishes *'adonai YHWH* from cases where *YHWH* appears with *'elohim,* which is rendered "LORD God." When *YH* (the short form of *YHWH*) and *YHWH* appear together, we have rendered it "LORD GOD." When *YHWH* appears with the term *tseba'oth,* we have rendered it "LORD of Heaven's Armies" to translate the meaning of the name. In a few cases, we have utilized the transliteration, *Yahweh,* when the personal character of the name is being invoked in contrast to another divine name or the name of some other god (for example, see Exod 3:15; 6:2-3).

In the New Testament, the Greek word *christos* has been translated as "Messiah" when the context assumes a Jewish audience. When a Gentile audience can be assumed, *christos* has been translated as "Christ." The Greek word *kurios* is consistently translated "Lord," except that it is translated "LORD" wherever the New Testament text explicitly quotes from the Old Testament, and the text there has it in small capitals.

TEXTUAL FOOTNOTES

The New Living Translation provides several kinds of textual footnotes, all designated in the text with an asterisk:

- When for the sake of clarity the NLT renders a difficult or potentially confusing phrase dynamically, we generally give the literal rendering in a textual footnote. This allows the reader to see the literal source of our dynamic rendering and how our translation relates to other more literal translations. These notes are prefaced with "Hebrew," "Aramaic," or "Greek," identifying the language of the underlying source text. For example, in Acts 2:42 we translated the literal "breaking of bread" (from the Greek) as "the Lord's Supper" to clarify that this verse refers to the ceremonial practice of the church rather than just an ordinary meal. Then we attached a footnote to "the Lord's Supper," which reads: "Greek *the breaking of bread.*"
- Textual footnotes are also used to show alternative renderings, prefaced with the word "Or." These normally occur for passages where an aspect of the meaning is debated. On occasion, we also provide notes on words or phrases that represent a departure from long-standing tradition. These notes are prefaced with "Traditionally rendered." For example, the footnote to the translation "serious skin disease" at Leviticus 13:2 says: "Traditionally rendered *leprosy.* The Hebrew word used throughout this passage is used to describe various skin diseases."

- When our translators follow a textual variant that differs significantly from our standard Hebrew or Greek texts (listed earlier), we document that difference with a footnote. We also footnote cases when the NLT excludes a passage that is included in the Greek text known as the *Textus Receptus* (and familiar to readers through its translation in the King James Version). In such cases, we offer a translation of the excluded text in a footnote, even though it is generally recognized as a later addition to the Greek text and not part of the original Greek New Testament.
- All Old Testament passages that are quoted in the New Testament are identified by a textual footnote at the New Testament location. When the New Testament clearly quotes from the Greek translation of the Old Testament, and when it differs significantly in wording from the Hebrew text, we also place a textual footnote at the Old Testament location. This note includes a rendering of the Greek version, along with a cross-reference to the New Testament passage(s) where it is cited (for example, see notes on Proverbs 3:12; Psalms 8:2; 53:3).
- Some textual footnotes provide cultural and historical information on places, things, and people in the Bible that are probably obscure to modern readers. Such notes should aid the reader in understanding the message of the text. For example, in Acts 12:1, "King Herod" is named in this translation as "King Herod Agrippa" and is identified in a footnote as being "the nephew of Herod Antipas and a grandson of Herod the Great."
- When the meaning of a proper name (or a wordplay inherent in a proper name) is relevant to the meaning of the text, it is either illuminated with a textual footnote or included within parentheses in the text itself. For example, the footnote concerning the name "Eve" at Genesis 3:20 reads: "Eve sounds like a Hebrew term that means 'to give life.'" This wordplay in the Hebrew illuminates the meaning of the text, which goes on to say that Eve "would be the mother of all who live."

AS WE SUBMIT this translation for publication, we recognize that any translation of the Scriptures is subject to limitations and imperfections. Anyone who has attempted to communicate the richness of God's Word into another language will realize it is impossible to make a perfect translation. Recognizing these limitations, we sought God's guidance and wisdom throughout this project. Now we pray that he will accept our efforts and use this translation for the benefit of the church and of all people.

We pray that the New Living Translation will overcome some of the barriers of history, culture, and language that have kept people from reading and understanding God's Word. We hope that readers unfamiliar with the Bible will find the words clear and easy to understand and that readers well versed in the Scriptures will gain a fresh perspective. We pray that readers will gain insight and wisdom for living, but most of all that they will meet the God of the Bible and be forever changed by knowing him.

The Bible Translation Committee
July 2004

When our translation follows a textual variant that differs significantly from our standard Hebrew or Greek texts (listed earlier), we document that difference with a footnote. We also footnote cases when the NLT excludes a passage that is included in the Greek text known as the *Textus Receptus* (and familiar to readers through its translation in the King James Version). In such cases, we offer a translation of the excluded text in a footnote, even though it is generally recognized as a later addition to the Greek text and not part of the original Greek New Testament.

All Old Testament passages that are quoted in the New Testament are identified by a textual footnote at the New Testament location. When the New Testament clearly quotes from the Greek translation of the Old Testament, and when it differs significantly in wording from the Hebrew text, we also place a textual footnote at the Old Testament location. This note includes a rendering of the Greek version, along with a cross-reference to the New Testament passage(s) where it is cited (for example, see notes on Proverbs 3:12; Psalms 8:2; 53:3).

Some textual footnotes provide cultural and historical information on places, things, and people in the Bible that are probably obscure to modern readers. Such notes should aid the reader in understanding the message of the text. For example, in Acts 12:1, "King Herod" is named in this translation as "King Herod Agrippa" and is identified in a footnote as being "the nephew of Herod Antipas and a grandson of Herod the Great."

When the meaning of a proper name (or a wordplay inherent in a proper name) is relevant to the meaning of the text, it is either illuminated with a textual footnote or included within parentheses in the text itself. For example, the footnote concerning the name "Eve" at Genesis 3:20 reads: "*Eve* sounds like a Hebrew term that means 'to give life.'" This wordplay in the Hebrew illuminates the meaning of the text, which goes on to say that Eve "would be the mother of all who live."

As we submit this translation for publication, we recognize that any translation of the Scriptures is subject to limitations and imperfections. Anyone who has attempted to communicate the richness of God's Word into another language will realize it is impossible to make a perfect translation. Recognizing these limitations, we sought God's guidance and wisdom throughout this project. Now we pray that he will accept our efforts and use this translation for the benefit of the church and of all people.

We pray that the New Living Translation will overcome some of the barriers of history, culture, and language that have kept people from reading and understanding God's Word. We hope that readers unfamiliar with the Bible will find the words clear and easy to understand and that readers well versed in the Scriptures will gain a fresh perspective. We pray that readers will gain insight and wisdom for living, but most of all that they will meet the God of the Bible and be forever changed by knowing him.

The Bible Translation Committee
July 2004

Bible Translation Team

HOLY BIBLE, NEW LIVING TRANSLATION

PENTATEUCH
Daniel I. Block, Senior Translator
Wheaton College

GENESIS
Allen Ross, Beeson Divinity School, Samford University
Gordon Wenham, *University of Gloucester*

EXODUS
Robert Bergen, *Hannibal-LaGrange College*
Daniel I. Block, *Wheaton College*
Eugene Carpenter, *Bethel College, Mishawaka, Indiana*

LEVITICUS
David Baker, *Ashland Theological Seminary*
Victor Hamilton, *Asbury College*
Kenneth Mathews, *Beeson Divinity School, Samford University*

NUMBERS
Dale A. Brueggemann, *Assemblies of God Division of Foreign Missions*
R. K. Harrison (deceased), *Wycliffe College*
Paul R. House, *Wheaton College*
Gerald L. Mattingly, *Johnson Bible College*

DEUTERONOMY
J. Gordon McConville, *University of Gloucester*
Eugene H. Merrill, *Dallas Theological Seminary*
John A. Thompson (deceased), *University of Melbourne*

HISTORICAL BOOKS
Barry J. Beitzel, Senior Translator
Trinity Evangelical Divinity School

JOSHUA, JUDGES
Carl E. Armerding, *Schloss Mittersill Study Centre*
Barry J. Beitzel, *Trinity Evangelical Divinity School*
Lawson Stone, *Asbury Theological Seminary*

1 & 2 SAMUEL
Robert Gordon, *Cambridge University*
V. Philips Long, *Regent College*
J. Robert Vannoy, *Biblical Theological Seminary*

1 & 2 KINGS
Bill T. Arnold, *Asbury Theological Seminary*
William H. Barnes, *North Central University*
Frederic W. Bush, *Fuller Theological Seminary*

1 & 2 CHRONICLES
Raymond B. Dillard (deceased), *Westminster Theological Seminary*
David A. Dorsey, *Evangelical School of Theology*
Terry Eves, *Erskine College*

RUTH, EZRA–ESTHER
William C. Williams, *Vanguard University*
H. G. M. Williamson, *Oxford University*

WISDOM BOOKS
Tremper Longman III, Senior Translator
Westmont College

JOB
August Konkel, *Providence Theological Seminary*
Tremper Longman III, *Westmont College*
Al Wolters, *Redeemer College*

PSALMS 1–75
Mark D. Futato, *Reformed Theological Seminary*
Douglas Green, *Westminster Theological Seminary*
Richard Pratt, *Reformed Theological Seminary*

PSALMS 76–150
David M. Howard Jr., *Bethel Theological Seminary*
Raymond C. Ortlund Jr., *Trinity Evangelical Divinity School*
Willem VanGemeren, *Trinity Evangelical Divinity School*

PROVERBS
Ted Hildebrandt, *Gordon College*
Richard Schultz, *Wheaton College*
Raymond C. Van Leeuwen, *Eastern College*

ECCLESIASTES, SONG OF SONGS
Daniel C. Fredericks, *Belhaven College*
David Hubbard (deceased), *Fuller Theological Seminary*
Tremper Longman III, *Westmont College*

PROPHETS
John N. Oswalt, Senior Translator
Wesley Biblical Seminary

ISAIAH
John N. Oswalt, *Wesley Biblical Seminary*
Gary Smith, *Midwestern Baptist Theological Seminary*
John Walton, *Wheaton College*

JEREMIAH, LAMENTATIONS
G. Herbert Livingston, *Asbury Theological Seminary*
Elmer A. Martens, *Mennonite Brethren Biblical Seminary*

EZEKIEL
Daniel I. Block, *Wheaton College*
David H. Engelhard, *Calvin Theological Seminary*
David Thompson, *Asbury Theological Seminary*

DANIEL, HAGGAI–MALACHI
Joyce Baldwin Caine (deceased), *Trinity College, Bristol*
Douglas Gropp, *Catholic University of America*
Roy Hayden, *Oral Roberts School of Theology*
Andrew Hill, *Wheaton College*
Tremper Longman III, *Westmont College*

HOSEA–ZEPHANIAH
Joseph Coleson, *Nazarene Theological Seminary*
Roy Hayden, *Oral Roberts School of Theology*
Andrew Hill, *Wheaton College*
Richard Patterson, *Liberty University*

GOSPELS AND ACTS

Grant R. Osborne, Senior Translator
Trinity Evangelical Divinity School

MATTHEW
Craig Blomberg, *Denver Seminary*
Donald A. Hagner, *Fuller Theological Seminary*
David Turner, *Grand Rapids Baptist Seminary*

MARK
Robert Guelich (deceased), *Fuller Theological Seminary*
George Guthrie, *Union University*
Grant R. Osborne, *Trinity Evangelical Divinity School*

LUKE
Darrell Bock, *Dallas Theological Seminary*
Scot McKnight, *North Park University*
Robert Stein, *The Southern Baptist Theological Seminary*

JOHN
Gary M. Burge, *Wheaton College*
Philip W. Comfort, *Coastal Carolina University*
Marianne Meye Thompson, *Fuller Theological Seminary*

ACTS
D. A. Carson, *Trinity Evangelical Divinity School*
William J. Larkin, *Columbia International University*
Roger Mohrlang, *Whitworth University*

LETTERS AND REVELATION

Norman R. Ericson, Senior Translator
Wheaton College

ROMANS, GALATIANS
Gerald Borchert, *Northern Baptist Theological Seminary*
Douglas J. Moo, *Wheaton College*
Thomas R. Schreiner, *The Southern Baptist Theological Seminary*

1 & 2 CORINTHIANS
Joseph Alexanian, *Trinity International University*
Linda Belleville, *Bethel College, Mishawaka, Indiana*
Douglas A. Oss, *Central Bible College*
Robert Sloan, *Baylor University*

EPHESIANS–PHILEMON
Harold W. Hoehner, *Dallas Theological Seminary*
Moises Silva, *Gordon-Conwell Theological Seminary*
Klyne Snodgrass, *North Park Theological Seminary*

HEBREWS, JAMES, 1 & 2 PETER, JUDE
Peter Davids, *Schloss Mittersill Study Centre*
Norman R. Ericson, *Wheaton College*
William Lane (deceased), *Seattle Pacific University*
J. Ramsey Michaels, *S. W. Missouri State University*

1–3 JOHN, REVELATION
Greg Beale, *Wheaton College*
Robert Mounce, *Whitworth University*
M. Robert Mulholland Jr., *Asbury Theological Seminary*

SPECIAL REVIEWERS

F. F. Bruce (deceased), *University of Manchester*
Kenneth N. Taylor (deceased), *Translator,* The Living Bible

COORDINATING TEAM

Mark D. Taylor, *Director and Chief Stylist*
Ronald A. Beers, *Executive Director and Stylist*
Mark R. Norton, *Managing Editor and O.T. Coordinating Editor*
Philip W. Comfort, *N.T. Coordinating Editor*
Daniel W. Taylor, *Bethel University, Senior Stylist*

OLD TESTAMENT

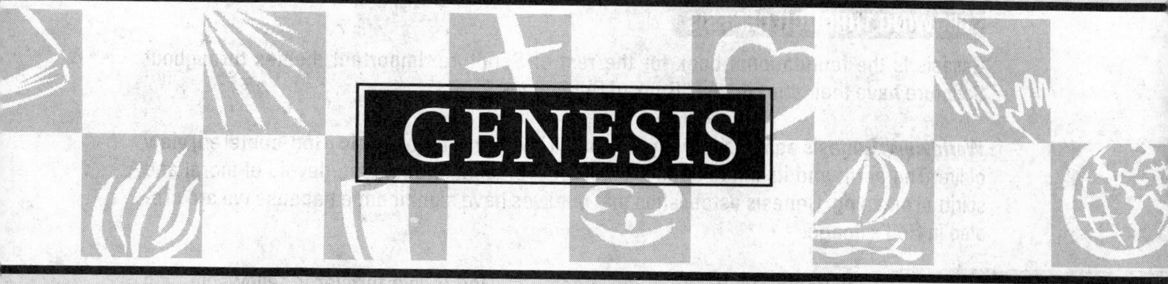

GENESIS

PURPOSE

To teach the new nation of Israel about God's purpose for their journey to Canaan through a review of God's purpose in human history.

"In the beginning God created the heavens and the earth." These majestic words, the first ones in the Bible's first book, Genesis, tell us that everything and everyone had a beginning—except God. He has existed from eternity, and it is He who, by the word of His power, caused all things to be.

Because Genesis tells the story of God's creative work, it is sometimes called "The Book of Beginnings." But Genesis tells of more than the origin of the universe, of our world, of plants and animals, and of human beings. It also tells the story of the beginning of God's relationship with man. In Genesis we see a God who goes to extraordinary lengths to have a relationship with His created beings, even when they rebel against Him.

Genesis tells us the beginning of God's great work of redemption, of how He began to set apart a special people for Himself and set in motion the process that would culminate in the coming of Jesus Christ at the crux of history.

DISCOVER GOD IN GENESIS

The following aspects of God's character stand out in Genesis:

Power: God's power is unlimited. This is demonstrated in His creation of the universe. His power is manifested through His words: "Then God said, 'Let there be light,' and there was light" (Genesis 1:3). Through the prophet Isaiah, God said that His Word always accomplishes the purpose for which it is uttered (Isaiah 55:11). The fact that God's power is sufficient to bring order out of chaos and to create the world out of nothing (Genesis 1:1–2:3) should give us confidence that He is able to effect change in our lives.

Sovereignty: Because God created everything, the earth and all its inhabitants belong to Him. God in His sovereignty rules over them. His purposes are carried out both on a global basis (Creation, the Flood) and individually (the choosing of Abraham, Isaac, Jacob, and their descendants). In Genesis, we see God working behind the scenes to bring good out of evil (Genesis 50:20). God is powerful, yet personal, as He carries out His ultimate desires. When the unexplainable and unwanted intrude into our lives, we can find comfort in God's sovereign control over all things.

GROWING THROUGH GENESIS

Genesis is the foundational book for the rest of Scripture. Important themes throughout Scripture have their start in this "Book of Beginnings."

Worldview: Genesis establishes why we should live with a theocentric (God-centered) view of life. The earth and its inhabitants are not an evolutionary accident, devoid of moral and spiritual meaning. Genesis establishes that our lives have significance because we are created in God's image.

DISCOVERY VERSES

"And I will cause hostility between you and the woman, and between your offspring and her Offspring. He will strike your head, and you will strike His heel." (GENESIS 3:15)

In the beginning God created the heavens and the earth. (GENESIS 1:1)

"I will bless those who bless you and curse those who treat you with contempt. All the families on earth will be blessed through you." (GENESIS 12:3)

And Abram believed the LORD, and the LORD counted him as righteous because of his faith. (GENESIS 15:6)

Redemption: People were created by God to live forever in fellowship with Him. The chaos and troubles of our world are explained by the human choice to rebel against God. Genesis records the first redemptive acts by which God set in motion a plan to save our fallen race: His forgiveness and clothing of Adam and Eve in the Garden of Eden; His rescue of Noah and his family in the ark; His calling of Abram out of a life of idolatry. Faith is established in Genesis as an attitude of trust, manifested in obedience, which results in salvation.

Providence: As much as any book in the Bible, Genesis shows God's guiding hand behind the affairs of nations and individuals. Reading Genesis helps us trust that God is active in our lives, even when we can't understand what is happening around us.

Consistency: Though times and people change throughout the Bible, God is consistent. The God we meet in Genesis—and the basis of relating to Him by faith—does not change. Because God is the same yesterday, today, and forever, everything we learn about Him in Genesis we can apply to our lives today.

GENESIS FACTS

Author: Scripture frequently refers to Moses as the author of Genesis and the four books following it. Jesus affirms this in Mark 7:10 and 12:26. The Apostles confess it in Acts 3:22. The author of Hebrews attributes the Law (the first five books of the Bible) to Moses (Hebrews 3:5; 7:14; 12:21).

Written to: The nation of Israel.

Date of writing: Moses led the Israelites out of Egypt around 1446 BC and up to the borders of the Promised Land forty years later. Moses likely wrote Genesis during that forty-year period.

Setting: There are three distinct locations in Genesis: Chapters 1–11 are set in Mesopotamia (modern Iraq); chapters 12–36 are set in the land of Canaan (modern Israel); and chapters 37–50 are set in Egypt, where the Hebrews lived as slaves for four hundred years.

OUTLINE

- **GENESIS 1–2**—A history of God's creation of all things for himself.
- **GENESIS 3:1–11:9**—A history of God's creation of a people for himself.
- **GENESIS 11:10–50:26**—A history of God's work among his people.

THE ACCOUNT OF CREATION

1:1 Pss 89:11; 102:25; Isa 42:5; 48:13; John 1:1-2
1:2 Ps 104:30; Isa 45:18
1:3 Pss 33:9; 104:2; Isa 45:7; 2 Cor 4:6

1 In the beginning God created the heavens and the earth.* 2The earth was formless
and empty, and darkness covered the deep waters. And the Spirit of God was hover-
ing over the surface of the waters.
3Then God said, "Let there be light," and there was light. 4And God saw that the light
was good. Then He separated the light from the darkness. 5God called the light "day"
and the darkness "night."
And evening passed and morning came, marking the first day.

1:1 Or *In the beginning when God created the heavens and the earth, . . .* Or *When God began to create the heavens and the earth, . . .*

1:1 God existed before the creation of all things. In fact, He has always existed. In our ever-changing world, He alone is eternal. Because we are creatures of time and space, it is difficult for us to grasp the concept of eternity. We have created many ways to measure time, but none of them is adequate to express time without end. However, God's eternal existence gives us confidence in His dependability.

▸ BIBLE
1:1-31 Doctrine of creation. Scripture affirms that "God created the heavens and the earth." The universe did not begin through evolution or any other "natural" means. Only a being who is external to the natural universe could have created it—and that being is God (Isaiah 45:11-12). The supernatural nature of God is evidenced in *how* He created the universe. When we *create* a work of art, we begin with a material and craft it into a new form. But God created the heavens and the earth out of nothing. Because God is the Creator, we can depend on Him (Psalm 24:1). (***See Bible*****>** *Unity> Doctrines,* TopicGuide page A10.)

1:1-31 There has been much debate about how God created. It is important to focus on the basics and not digress into disputes about literal days or the length of each day. We know that God created all that is from nothing; how He did it is something we will understand better when we stand before Him and see life from His perspective instead of our limited vantage point. The fact that we do not have all the answers about the process of creation should not limit our faith in the Creator.

1:2 God is a spirit and does not have a physical body like men and women. The Gospel writer John quoted Jesus as stating this very fact: "For God is Spirit, so those who worship Him must worship in spirit and in truth" (John 4:24). The Spirit of God, hovering over the formless mass of earth, indicates the protective, creative power of God.

▸ BIBLE
1:3 Doctrine of the Word. The fact that God said "Let there be light" in order to create light amid the primordial darkness demonstrates the creative power of God's Word. Throughout the Bible, God's Word is presented as having many of the same attributes that belong to God Himself. His words are eternal (Isaiah 40:8; see also John 10:35), always true (Psalm 119:160), and completely trustworthy (Psalm 119:105). As God's people, we can rely wholly on God's Word, its revelation of who God is, and its promises for us. God has given us His word. (***See Bible*****>** *Unity> Doctrines,* TopicGuide page A10.)

DAYS OF CREATION

The days of Creation represent two sets of three days each. In the first set of days, God created the different spheres within Creation. In the second set of days, he filled these spheres with inhabitants. The days of creating the spheres and the days of filling the spheres follow the same order.

Day One (Genesis 1:2-5)	God created the spheres of day and night.	God created the sun to fill the day, and He created the stars and moon to fill the night.	Day Four (Genesis 1:14-19)
Day Two (Genesis 1:6-8)	God created the spheres of sky and sea.	God created the birds to fill the sky, and He created the fish to fill the sea.	Day Five (Genesis 1:20-23)
Day Three (Genesis 1:9-13)	God created the dry ground and prepared it to support life.	God created land animals and human beings to fill the dry land.	Day Six (Genesis 1:24-31)

KEY PLACES IN GENESIS

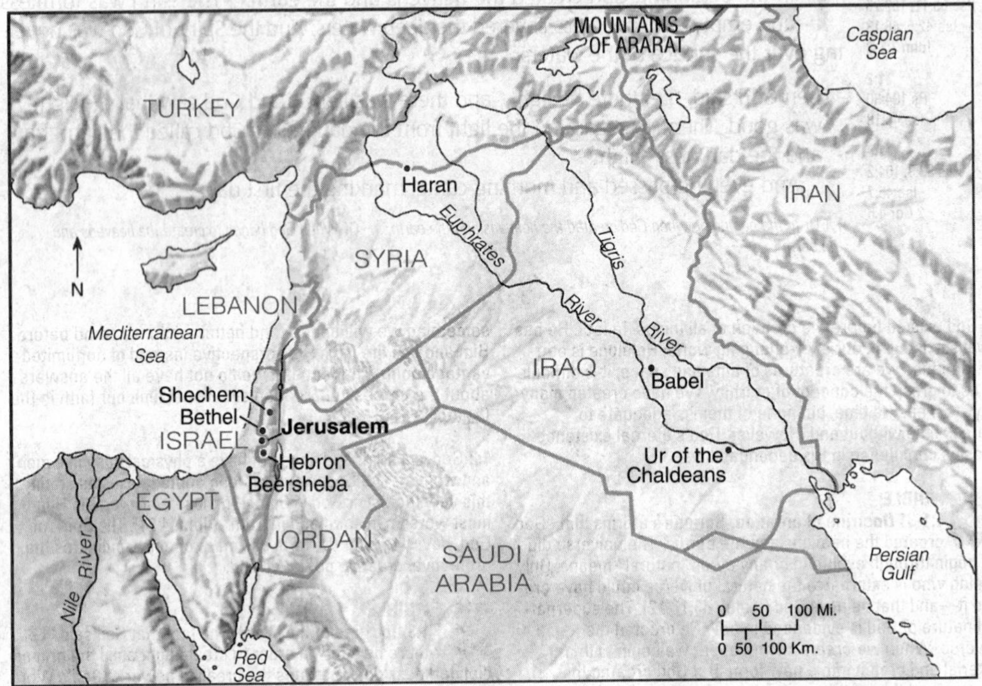

Modern names and boundaries are shown in gray.

God created the universe and the earth. Then He made man and woman, giving them a home in a beautiful garden. Unfortunately, Adam and Eve disobeyed God and were banished from the garden (3:23).

1 Mountains of Ararat Adam and Eve's sin brought sin into the human race. Years later, sin had run rampant, and God decided to destroy the earth with a great flood. But Noah, his family, and two of each animal were safe in a boat. When the floods receded, the boat rested on the mountains of Ararat (8:4).

2 Babel People never learn. Again sin abounded, and the pride of the people led them to build a huge tower as a monument to their own greatness —obviously they had no thought of God. As punishment, God scattered the people by giving them different languages (11:8, 9).

3 Ur of the Chaldeans Abram, a descendant of Shem and father of the Hebrew nation, was born in this great city (11:27, 28).

4 Haran Terah, Abram, Lot, and Sarai left Ur and, following the fertile crescent of the Euphrates River, headed toward the land of Canaan. Along the way, they settled in the village of Haran for a while (11:31).

5 Shechem God urged Abram to leave Haran and go to a place where he would become the father of a great nation (12:1, 2). So Abram, Lot, and Sarai traveled to the land of Canaan and settled near a city called Shechem (12:6).

6 Hebron Abraham moved on to Hebron where he put down his deepest roots (13:18). Abraham, Isaac, and Jacob all lived and were buried here.

7 Beersheba The well at Beersheba was a source of conflict between Abraham and King Abimelech and later became a sign of the oath that they swore there (21:31). Years later, as Isaac was moving from place to place, God appeared to him here and passed on to him the covenant he had made with his father, Abraham (26:23-25).

8 Bethel After deceiving his brother, Jacob left Beersheba and fled to Haran. Along the way, God revealed Himself to Jacob in a dream and passed on the covenant He had made with Abraham and Isaac (28:10-22). Jacob lived in Haran, worked for Laban, and married Leah and Rachel (29:15-30). After a tense meeting with his brother, Esau, Jacob returned to Bethel (35:1).

9 Egypt Jacob had 12 sons, including Joseph, Jacob's favorite. Joseph's 10 older brothers grew jealous, until one day the brothers sold him to Ishmaelite traders going to Egypt. Eventually, Joseph rose from Egyptian slave to Pharaoh's "right-hand man," saving Egypt from famine. His entire family moved from Canaan to Egypt and settled there (46:3-7).

6Then God said, "Let there be a space between the waters, to separate the waters of the
heavens from the waters of the earth." 7And that is what happened. God made this
space to separate the waters of the earth from the waters of the heavens. 8God called
the space "sky."
And evening passed and morning came, marking the second day.

9Then God said, "Let the waters beneath the sky flow together into one place, so dry
ground may appear." And that is what happened. 10God called the dry ground "land"
and the waters "seas." And God saw that it was good. 11Then God said, "Let the land
sprout with vegetation—every sort of seed-bearing plant, and trees that grow seed-
bearing fruit. These seeds will then produce the kinds of plants and trees from which
they came." And that is what happened. 12The land produced vegetation—all sorts of
seed-bearing plants, and trees with seed-bearing fruit. Their seeds produced plants
and trees of the same kind. And God saw that it was good.
13And evening passed and morning came, marking the third day.

14Then God said, "Let lights appear in the sky to separate the day from the night.
Let them mark off the seasons, days, and years. 15Let these lights in the sky shine
down on the earth." And that is what happened. 16God made two great lights—
the larger one to govern the day, and the smaller one to govern the night. He also
made the stars. 17God set these lights in the sky to light the earth, 18to govern the
day and night, and to separate the light from the darkness. And God saw that it was
good.
19And evening passed and morning came, marking the fourth day.

20Then God said, "Let the waters swarm with fish and other life. Let the skies be filled
with birds of every kind." 21So God created great sea creatures and every living thing
that scurries and swarms in the water, and every sort of bird—each producing offspring
of the same kind. And God saw that it was good. 22Then God blessed them, saying, "Be
fruitful and multiply. Let the fish fill the seas, and let the birds multiply on the earth."
23And evening passed and morning came, marking the fifth day.

24Then God said, "Let the earth produce every sort of animal, each producing offspring
of the same kind—livestock, small animals that scurry along the ground, and wild ani-
mals." And that is what happened. 25God made all sorts of wild animals, livestock, and
small animals, each able to produce offspring of the same kind. And God saw that it
was good.
26Then God said, "Let Us make human beings* in Our image, to be like Us. They
will reign over the fish in the sea, the birds in the sky, the livestock, all the wild ani-
mals on the earth, and the small animals that scurry along the ground."

1:26 Or *man;* Hebrew reads *adam.*

1:6 Job 26:10; Ps 136:5-6; Isa 40:22; Jer 10:12
1:7 Job 38:8-11; Ps 148:4; Prov 8:28
1:8 Gen 1:5
1:9 Job 26:7; Ps 95:5; Prov 8:29; Jer 5:22; 2 Pet 3:5
1:10 Pss 33:7; 95:5
1:11 Gen 2:9; Ps 104:14; Matt 6:30
1:14 Pss 74:16; 104:19
1:15 Gen 1:5
1:16 Pss 8:3; 19:1-6; 136:8-9; 1 Cor 15:41
1:18 Jer 33:20, 25
1:20 Gen 2:19; Ps 146:6
1:21 Ps 104:25-28
1:24 Gen 2:19
1:26 Gen 5:1; 9:6; Ps 8:6-8; Acts 17:28-29

1:25 Our world bears the effects of generations of human sinfulness. But when God created the world and everything in it, He pronounced it good. The word *good* didn't have a special meaning; it meant just what it said. The heavenly bodies, the animals, the people, the soil, and all that grew in it were good things, things to be protected and honored. When we see God's original evaluation of His creation, we gain a better understanding of our responsibility to care for it.

1:26 God refers to Himself in the plural, saying, "Let *Us.*" Throughout history, God has revealed Himself as God the Father, God the Son (Jesus Christ), and God the Holy Spirit. God has always existed as these three persons. The New Testament writer Paul the apostle confirmed this truth: "For through [Christ] God created everything in the heavenly realms and on earth. . . . Everything was created through Him and for Him" (Colossians 1:16). In describing Jesus, John the disciple wrote: "He existed in the beginning with God. God created everything through Him, and nothing was created except through Him" (John 1:2-3).

1:26 God created humanity in His image. This does not mean that we look like God, for God is a Spirit and does not have a physical form as we do. However, we are like Him in numerous ways. We have wills. We have souls. We are creative. We are relational beings. In creating us this way, God intended that we should mirror His character.

27 So God created human beings* in His own image.
In the image of God He created them;
male and female He created them.

28Then God blessed them and said, "Be fruitful and multiply. Fill the earth and
govern it. Reign over the fish in the sea, the birds in the sky, and all the animals that
scurry along the ground."
29Then God said, "Look! I have given you every seed-bearing plant throughout the
earth and all the fruit trees for your food. 30And I have given every green plant as
food for all the wild animals, the birds in the sky, and the small animals that scurry
along the ground—everything that has life." And that is what happened.
31 Then God looked over all He had made, and He saw that it was very good!
And evening passed and morning came, marking the sixth day.

1:27 *Matt 19:4 *Mark 10:6
1:29 Gen 9:3 Pss 104:13; 136:25
1:30 Pss 104:14; 145:15
1:31 Ps 104:24

2 So the creation of the heavens and the earth and everything in them was com-
pleted. 2On the seventh day God had finished His work of creation, so He rested*

2:1 Deut 4:19; 17:3 Ps 104:2 Isa 45:12
2:2 Exod 20:11; 31:17 *Heb 4:4

1:27 Or *the man;* Hebrew reads *ha-adam.* 2:2 Or *ceased;* also in 2:3.

▶ BIBLE
1:28 Doctrine of the Cultural Mandate. God's charge to Adam and Eve to be masters over the created order is often called the Cultural Mandate or Dominion Mandate. Initially, the first couple's responsibilities were limited to exercising dominion over the land and animal life. However, this stewardship over the earth eventually led Adam and Eve and their descendants from their humble agrarian beginnings to develop all the earth's resources for the advancement of worldwide civilizations. Therefore, it is from this command that the church derives its responsibility to shape every area of culture according to God's will, including politics, the fine arts, science, law, medical ethics, and more. This is what we, as God's people, should seek to do every day. (***See Bible***> *Unity> Doctrines,* TopicGuide page A10.)

▶ WORSHIP
2:2-3 God rested from all His work. God did not rest because He was tired. He rested because His work was complete. The fourth of the Ten Commandments instructs us to follow God's example: "Remember to observe the Sabbath day" (Exodus 20:8). However, there is a truer, deeper rest than merely ceasing from physical labor. The author of Hebrews writes, "For all who have entered into God's rest have rested from their labors, just as God did after creating the world. So let us do our best to enter that rest" (Hebrews 4:10-11). This rest, this final salvation, comes through faith in God's completed work of redemption. Therein lies our true Sabbath. (***See Worship***> *OT> Festivals> Sabbath,* TopicGuide page A26.)

MY RESPONSE TO GOD

Seeking God through His Word

GENESIS 1–2

We cannot advance our knowledge of God beyond a rough character sketch through our own human abilities. But God, in His love and mercy, has taken steps to make Himself known to us in many ways. His primary vehicle for revealing Himself to those who hunger and thirst to know Him is His holy Word, the Bible.

In Genesis 1–2, God reveals Himself as our great Creator, unveiling His mighty works, unlimited power, and eternal knowledge. We learn immediately that our Creator-God knows no limitations.

The remainder of the Old Testament shows how God builds a nation of people dedicated to Him, and how He leads and blesses those people. God gives Israel laws and promises that establish His character as the perfect Judge.

In the New Testament, God reveals Himself most fully as our gracious Savior. The life, death, and resurrection of Jesus prove God's mercy and faithfulness. Through Jesus, we find that our Creator and Judge is also our loving Father.

2:3 Isa 58:13
2:4 Gen 5:1; 6:9; 10:1; Job 38:4-11
2:7 Job 33:4; Ps 103:14; Ezek 37:5; John 20:22; *1 Cor 15:45
2:8 Gen 3:23; 13:10; Isa 51:3; Ezek 28:13; Joel 2:3
2:9 Prov 3:18; 11:30; Ezek 47:12; Rev 2:7; 22:2, 14
2:10 Rev 22:1, 17
2:14 Gen 15:18; Dan 10:4
2:16 Gen 3:1-3
2:17 Gen 3:1, 16-17; Deut 30:15, 19-20; Rom 6:23; Jas 1:15

from all His work. 3And God blessed the seventh day and declared it holy, because it
was the day when He rested from all His work of creation.

4This is the account of the creation of the heavens and the earth.

THE MAN AND WOMAN IN EDEN

When the LORD God made the earth and the heavens, 5neither wild plants nor grains were
growing on the earth. For the LORD God had not yet sent rain to water the earth, and there
were no people to cultivate the soil. 6Instead, springs* came up from the ground and wa-
tered all the land. 7Then the LORD God formed the man from the dust of the ground. He
breathed the breath of life into the man's nostrils, and the man became a living person.
8Then the LORD God planted a garden in Eden in the east, and there He placed the man
He had made. 9The LORD God made all sorts of trees grow up from the ground—trees that
were beautiful and that produced delicious fruit. In the middle of the garden He placed the
tree of life and the tree of the knowledge of good and evil.
10A river flowed from the land of Eden, watering the garden and then dividing into four
branches. 11The first branch, called the Pishon, flowed around the entire land of Havilah,
where gold is found. 12The gold of that land is exceptionally pure; aromatic resin and onyx
stone are also found there. 13The second branch, called the Gihon, flowed around the en-
tire land of Cush. 14The third branch, called the Tigris, flowed east of the land of Asshur.
The fourth branch is called the Euphrates.
15The LORD God placed the man in the Garden of Eden to tend and watch over it. 16But
the LORD God warned him, "You may freely eat the fruit of every tree in the garden—
17except the tree of the knowledge of good and evil. If you eat its fruit, you are sure to die."
18Then the LORD God said, "It is not good for the man to be alone. I will make a helper
who is just right for him." 19So the LORD God formed from the ground all the wild ani-
mals and all the birds of the sky. He brought them to the man* to see what he would call

2:6 Or *mist.* 2:19 Or *Adam,* and so throughout the chapter.

2:7 God made the first human being from the dust of the ground. He then breathed into Adam the breath of life. From the most basic elements of the planet on which we live, God formed a body and combined it with a soul to create an eternal being. God then made a woman from the man, the next generation of creation. When we die, God's process of creation is reversed. Our souls return to the One who breathed us into being in the first place. Our bodies also return to the state from which they began. The psalmist says, "For He knows how weak we are; He remembers we are only dust. But the love of the LORD remains forever with those who fear Him" (Psalm 103:14, 17).

2:9 God, who is holy, created a world He deemed good, so it is perplexing that evil came to exist in it, especially since the knowledge of good and evil was the one taboo in the original paradise. We have no definitive record of the origin of evil, but we know that as soon as God created the world, evil was in place to put it at risk. Tradition holds that Satan, the embodiment of evil, is actually a fallen angel. To support this idea, some scholars interpret Isaiah 14:12-15, a passage about the king of Babylon, as describing Satan's fall. But for all that we don't know about the origin of evil, we do know that God is greater and redemption from evil is possible through faith in God's Son, Jesus Christ.

2:10-14 Two of the rivers mentioned here, the Tigris and the Euphrates, are still flowing today. In some places, they flow so closely together that canals have been dug between them. The Garden of Eden was probably at the place where these two rivers, along with the Pishon and Gihon, found their source. The Pishon and Gihon have disappeared since these ancient days, and we have no record of their location. From the description given here, the Garden was probably in southern Mesopotamia, later known as Babylonia. Today this would be in southeast Iraq.

▸ ADOPTION

2:17 Spiritually dead. God's prohibition against eating of the "tree of the knowledge of good and evil" was not motivated by fear that human knowledge might become equal to His own. It was aimed at frustrating any attempt on the part of the man and woman to pursue their own way in life. God's warning was clear: Sin would bring severe spiritual consequences. Although Adam and Eve did not die on the spot when they violated this command, they did suffer immediate spiritual death that later led to physical death. From their story, believers can know that although our eternal relationship with God is forever secure, sin affects our fellowship with the Father and can lead to far greater consequences unless we repent. (***See Adoption> Without Christ> Separated from God,*** TopicGuide page A36.)

2:18-24 God Himself declared that it was not good for the man to be alone, but none of the animals could provide the kind of companionship Adam needed. So God created another human being—not another man but a woman. He did so by taking a rib from Adam and using it to fashion Eve. By creating her in this way, God showed that man and woman are to come together in the physical and spiritual unity of marriage. While the Bible does include examples of polygamy, these always represent exceptions to God's original instructions for one man and one woman to marry for life.

them, and the man chose a name for each one. 20 He gave names to all the livestock, all the birds of the sky, and all the wild animals. But still there was no helper just right for him.

21 So the LORD God caused the man to fall into a deep sleep. While the man slept, the LORD God took out one of the man's ribs* and closed up the opening. 22 Then the LORD God made a woman from the rib, and He brought her to the man.

23 "At last!" the man exclaimed.

"This one is bone from my bone,
  and flesh from my flesh!
She will be called 'woman,'
  because she was taken from 'man.'"

24 This explains why a man leaves his father and mother and is joined to his wife, and the two are united into one.

25 Now the man and his wife were both naked, but they felt no shame.

THE MAN AND WOMAN SIN

3 The serpent was the shrewdest of all the wild animals the LORD God had made. One day he asked the woman, "Did God really say you must not eat the fruit from any of the trees in the garden?"

2 "Of course we may eat fruit from the trees in the garden," the woman replied. 3 "It's only the fruit from the tree in the middle of the garden that we are not allowed to eat. God said, 'You must not eat it or even touch it; if you do, you will die.'"

4 "You won't die!" the serpent replied to the woman. 5 "God knows that your eyes will be opened as soon as you eat it, and you will be like God, knowing both good and evil."

6 The woman was convinced. She saw that the tree was beautiful and its fruit looked delicious, and she wanted the wisdom it would give her. So she took some of the fruit and ate it. Then she gave some to her husband, who was with her, and he ate it, too. 7 At that

2:18 Gen 3:12; Prov 18:22
2:19 Gen 1:20-25
2:22 1 Cor 11:8-9; 1 Tim 2:13
2:23 Gen 29:14; Eph 5:28-30
2:24 *Matt 19:5; *1 Cor 6:16; Eph 5:31
2:25 Gen 3:7, 10-11
3:1 2 Cor 11:3; Rev 12:9; 20:2
3:2 Gen 2:16
3:4 John 8:44; 2 Cor 11:3
3:5 Gen 2:17; 3:22; Isa 14:14; Ezek 28:2
3:6 2 Cor 11:3; 1 Tim 2:14; Jas 1:14-15; 1 Jn 2:16

2:21 Or *took a part of the man's side.*

▸ BIBLE
3:1 Principle of temptation. As a crafty serpent, Satan convinced Eve to doubt God's goodness and believe that she would be happier by disobeying Him. In the same way, this seductive tempter suggests that we will experience greater satisfaction, fulfillment, and happiness if we live contrary to God's will. He entices us with worldly pleasures to make us distrust and ignore God's Word, doubt His character, and question His motives. As we do, we lower our shield and expose ourselves to Satan's deception. But when we hold fast to our faith in God and join forces with fellow believers, we are kept safe. The spiritual shield that Christ has provided for us protects us against Satan's assaults. (***See Bible> Unity> Doctrines,*** TopicGuide page A10.)

3:1 Satan came to Eve in the form of a serpent to persuade her to ignore God's instructions. As punishment for tempting the woman, the serpent was cursed to crawl on its belly, which is the present form of snakes. Before this judgment, the snake may have had legs. Throughout the Bible, the image of the serpent is used to denote deception and wickedness. For instance, the serpent image is used to describe the speech of evil people (Psalm 140:3) and hypocritical Pharisees (Matthew 3:7). One of the most notable uses is Revelation 12:9, which describes the "ancient serpent called the devil, or Satan, the one deceiving the whole world."

3:1-2 Would humanity have stayed true to God if Satan had not been allowed access to Eden? The truth is that Adam and Eve, who had been created in God's image, had the ability to choose. Whether Satan's influence or the first couple's ability to choose evil was the cause of humanity's fall into sin, God allowed this choice to be made. However, He also provided a way for redemption.

3:3-6 The serpent's argument was cunning. He said that, by eating the fruit, Eve somehow would increase in her knowledge of good and evil, but she would not die, as God had said. But those arguments should not have been the basis of Eve's decision. What was at stake was not just getting more knowledge, but Eve's relationship with her Maker. The same is at stake for each of us. No matter what the serpent argues, spiritual death and physical death have always been the consequences of disobedience.

3:7 Before Adam and Eve acquired the knowledge of good and evil, they felt no shame. They experienced the world in pure innocence. With their new knowledge came a new embarrassment about their nakedness. They were so ashamed, in fact, that they created clothing from leaves and tried to hide from God, who had created them naked and innocent. Sin has the same effect today. The guilt we feel because of it drives us to hide from God, from each other, and even from ourselves. Sin feeds the irrational belief that we can somehow control God's perception of us, and thus His love and acceptance.

moment their eyes were opened, and they suddenly felt shame at their nakedness. So
3:8 they sewed fig leaves together to cover themselves.
Lev 26:12 Deut 23:14 [8]When the cool evening breezes were blowing, the man* and his wife heard the LORD
Job 31:33 God walking about in the garden. So they hid from the LORD God among the trees. [9]Then
3:9 the LORD God called to the man, "Where are you?"
Gen 4:9; 18:9 [10]He replied, "I heard You walking in the garden, so I hid. I was afraid because I was
3:10 Deut 5:5 naked."
[11]"Who told you that you were naked?" the LORD God asked. "Have you eaten from the
3:12 Prov 28:13 tree whose fruit I commanded you not to eat?"
3:13 [12]The man replied, "It was the woman You gave me who gave me the fruit, and I
2 Cor 11:3 ate it."
1 Tim 2:14 [13]Then the LORD God asked the woman, "What have you done?"
3:14 Deut 28:15 "The serpent deceived me," she replied. "That's why I ate it."
Isa 65:25 [14]Then the LORD God said to the serpent,

"Because you have done this, you are cursed
more than all animals, domestic and wild.
You will crawl on your belly,
3:15 groveling in the dust as long as you live.
John 8:44 Rom 16:20 [15] And I will cause hostility between you and the woman,
Heb 2:14 and between your offspring and her Offspring.
He will strike* your head,
and you will strike His heel."

3:8 Or *Adam,* and so throughout the chapter. 3:15 Or *bruise;* also in 3:15b.

3:8-9 The fellowship between God and His creation in the Garden was unique. During the time of Moses, God appeared in glory so powerful that He was dangerous to those who encountered him (Exodus 19:21-22). But the picture of God's presence here is of a friend walking through the woods and calling our name. It is akin to Jesus' presence among His disciples. The crushing effect of the Fall was that this sweet fellowship was broken. While it wasn't broken irreparably, the restoration of fellowship with God required ultimate sacrifice (Hebrews 9:14) and ultimate faith (John 14:23-24).

3:15 Part of God's curse on Satan was the inauguration of a state of permanent enmity between his followers and God's followers. Unbelievers hate God and, by extension, those who belong to Him and seek to follow His ways. But this word of curse contained a hint of ultimate blessing. God declared that the conflict between Satan's followers and God's would come to a head one day when one of Eve's offspring would crush the head of the serpent at the cost of a wound to His heel. Christians throughout the ages have seen this verse as a prophecy of the work of Christ. His suffering and death were wrenching for Him, but death could not hold Him; He rose again on the third day. For Satan, however, the cross brought about complete and total defeat.

BECAUSE GOD IS HOLY

I will devote myself to him in purity, worship and service.

And God blessed the seventh day and declared it holy.

GENESIS 2:3

FOR THE NEXT *GOD IS HOLY* FEATURE SEE PAGE 136.

16 Then He said to the woman,

"I will sharpen the pain of your pregnancy,
and in pain you will give birth.
And you will desire to control your husband,
but he will rule over you.*"

17 And to the man He said,

"Since you listened to your wife and ate from the tree
whose fruit I commanded you not to eat,
the ground is cursed because of you.
All your life you will struggle to scratch a living from it.
18 It will grow thorns and thistles for you,
though you will eat of its grains.
19 By the sweat of your brow
will you have food to eat
until you return to the ground
from which you were made.
For you were made from dust,
and to dust you will return."

PARADISE LOST: GOD'S JUDGMENT

20 Then the man—Adam—named his wife Eve, because she would be the mother of all
who live.* 21 And the LORD God made clothing from animal skins for Adam and his wife.
22 Then the LORD God said, "Look, the human beings* have become like Us, knowing
both good and evil. What if they reach out, take fruit from the tree of life, and eat it?
Then they will live forever!" 23 So the LORD God banished them from the Garden of Eden,
and He sent Adam out to cultivate the ground from which he had been made. 24 After
sending them out, the LORD God stationed mighty cherubim to the east of the Garden of
Eden. And He placed a flaming sword that flashed back and forth to guard the way to the
tree of life.

3:16 1 Cor 11:3; Eph 5:22; 1 Tim 2:15
3:17 Job 5:7; Eccl 1:3; Rom 8:20-22
3:18 Job 31:40; Heb 6:8
3:19 Gen 2:7; Pss 90:3; 104:29; Eccl 12:7; 1 Cor 15:47
3:20 2 Cor 11:3; 1 Tim 2:13
3:21 2 Cor 5:2-3
3:22 Gen 1:26
3:24 Ezek 10:1; Rev 2:7; 22:2, 14

3:16 Or *And though you will have desire for your husband, / he will rule over you.* 3:20 *Eve* sounds like a Hebrew term that means "to give life." 3:22 Or *the man;* Hebrew reads *ha-adam.*

▸ SPIRITUAL WARFARE

3:16-19 The Fall subjected creation to bondage. The first couple's disobedience incurred a divine curse by which God doomed the woman to intense pain and suffering in childbirth and placed a curse on the ground that made man's work difficult. Clearly God disciplines the disobedient. This is because God's standard is nothing short of sinlessness. However, only one person, our Lord Jesus Christ, has achieved that standard; we sin daily in manifold ways. Our goal and inner desire should be to please God through obedience. When we succumb to temptation, if we are truly repentant, God forgives our sin. However, as in the case of Adam and Eve, He may let us live with the consequences of our disobedience as a reminder to obey Him in the future. (***See Spiritual Warfare**> Origin of Sin> Creation in bondage> God curses creation,* TopicGuide page A44.)

3:21 In a gesture that revealed the depth of His grace and compassion for His people, God made clothing for Adam and Eve from animal skins. Their attempt to cover their nakedness with leaves was pathetically inadequate, but God's clothing was durable and effective. In this simple gesture, we see another foreshadowing of what Christ accomplished for His people much later. By obeying God's law in every point, Christ compiled a record of perfect righteousness that God transfers to those He calls to Himself. This "clothing" of righteousness covers all the shame of those who are soiled by sin.

3:22-23 The Genesis account identifies two significant trees in the Garden: the tree of the knowledge of good and evil, and the tree of life. From these verses, we can assume that with access to the tree of life, Adam and Eve could have lived forever in their sinful state. Thus, barring Adam and Eve from access to this tree was an act of mercy on God's part. The tree of life reappears at the end of the scriptural record as the book of Revelation describes the new heaven and new earth that God has waiting for us. In that new world there is another paradise, with two trees of life-bearing fruit waiting for everyone who believes (Revelation 22:2). It is a full-circle journey to the life God has offered all along.

CAIN AND ABEL

4:2 Luke 11:50-51
4:3 Lev 2:1-2; Num 18:12
4:4 Exod 13:12; Heb 11:4
4:6 Jon 4:4
4:7 Rom 6:12, 16; Jas 1:15
4:8 Matt 23:35; 1 Jn 3:12

4 Now Adam* had sexual relations with his wife, Eve, and she became pregnant. When
she gave birth to Cain, she said, "With the LORD's help, I have produced* a man!"
2Later she gave birth to his brother and named him Abel.
When they grew up, Abel became a shepherd, while Cain cultivated the ground. 3When
it was time for the harvest, Cain presented some of his crops as a gift to the LORD. 4Abel
also brought a gift—the best of the firstborn lambs from his flock. The LORD accepted Abel
and his gift, 5but He did not accept Cain and his gift. This made Cain very angry, and he
looked dejected.
6"Why are you so angry?" the LORD asked Cain. "Why do you look so dejected? 7You will
be accepted if you do what is right. But if you refuse to do what is right, then watch out! Sin is
crouching at the door, eager to control you. But you must subdue it and be its master."
8One day Cain suggested to his brother, "Let's go out into the fields."* And while they
were in the field, Cain attacked his brother, Abel, and killed him.

4:1a Or *the man;* also in 4:25. 4:1b Or *I have acquired. Cain* sounds like a Hebrew term that can mean "produce" or "acquire." 4:8 As in Samaritan Pentateuch, Greek and Syriac versions, and Latin Vulgate; Masoretic Text lacks *"Let's go out into the fields."*

4:2 Adam and Eve's sons had occupations. Cain was a farmer and Abel was a shepherd. When God explained the consequences of sin to Adam in Genesis 3:17-19, He made it clear that the earth no longer would provide free bounty. Instead, life would be a struggle—people would have to "scratch a living" for themselves. Still, it could be done. Since human beings were created in God's image, they, too, could create. When Cain was driven out after killing Abel, he was unable even to raise crops. But within a few generations, his family produced herdsmen, musicians, and metalsmiths.

4:3-5 These verses give no clear reason as to why God didn't accept Cain's offering. But Hebrews 11:4 sheds more light, telling us that Abel's faith made his offering more acceptable. The brothers not only came with different offerings but with different attitudes. Abel brought his very best; Cain did not. Cain's reaction revealed his inner spirit: jealousy, violence, and self-centeredness. Even when God banished him, his first concern was his safety rather than any kind of remorse. It wasn't necessarily that sheep were a better sacrifice than produce. It was that a pure heart was more acceptable to a righteous God.

4:6-7 God's answer to Cain was clear: "You will be accepted if you do what is right." As we look back through history, we sometimes think that God asked for a different kind of faith in the Old Testament, but God's response to Cain reveals that His requirements for us have never changed. Cain's attitude alienated him from God. On the other hand, Romans 4:3 says that God declared Abraham righteous because of his faith. From those early times to the present, God has always wanted a relationship with His people based on trust and love.

4:8-10 It took only one generation for the sin unleashed in the Garden to lead to the first act of violence. And Cain didn't just give his brother a bloody nose; he took his life. By the time Noah came on the scene several generations later, the world was filled with violence (Genesis 6:11). This is a hallmark of human history; it has never been easy to find nonviolent options for settling disagreements. Prophets like Isaiah called violence a trademark of evil (Isaiah 59:6) and Solomon wrote proverbs warning against violence (Proverbs 13:2). Yet we continue to struggle against the violence unleashed at the beginning of the world.

BECAUSE GOD IS MERCIFUL

He forgives me of my sins when I sincerely confess them.

And the LORD God made clothing . . . for Adam and his wife.

GENESIS 3:21

FOR THE NEXT *GOD IS MERCIFUL* FEATURE SEE PAGE 268.

[9]Afterward the LORD asked Cain, "Where is your brother? Where is Abel?"
"I don't know," Cain responded. "Am I my brother's guardian?"
[10]But the LORD said, "What have you done? Listen! Your brother's blood cries out to
Me from the ground! [11]Now you are cursed and banished from the ground, which has
swallowed your brother's blood. [12]No longer will the ground yield good crops for you,
no matter how hard you work! From now on you will be a homeless wanderer on the
earth."
[13]Cain replied to the LORD, "My punishment* is too great for me to bear! [14]You have ban-
ished me from the land and from Your presence; You have made me a homeless wan-
derer. Anyone who finds me will kill me!"
[15]The LORD replied, "No, for I will give a sevenfold punishment to anyone who kills you."
Then the LORD put a mark on Cain to warn anyone who might try to kill him. [16]So Cain left
the LORD's presence and settled in the land of Nod,* east of Eden.

4:9 Gen 3:9
4:10 Num 35:33; Deut 21:1; Heb 12:24
4:11 Deut 27:15-26
4:12 Deut 28:15-24
4:14 Gen 9:6; Job 15:22

THE DESCENDANTS OF CAIN

[17]Cain had sexual relations with his wife, and she became pregnant and gave birth to
Enoch. Then Cain founded a city, which he named Enoch, after his son. [18]Enoch had a son
named Irad. Irad became the father of* Mehujael. Mehujael became the father of Methu-
shael. Methushael became the father of Lamech.
[19]Lamech married two women. The first was named Adah, and the second was Zillah.
[20]Adah gave birth to Jabal, who was the first of those who raise livestock and live in tents.
[21]His brother's name was Jubal, the first of all who play the harp and flute. [22]Lamech's
other wife, Zillah, gave birth to a son named Tubal-cain. He became an expert in forging
tools of bronze and iron. Tubal-cain had a sister named Naamah. [23]One day Lamech said
to his wives,

4:17 Ps 49:11
4:23 Lev 19:18; Deut 32:35

4:13 Or *My sin.* 4:16 *Nod* means "wandering." 4:18 Or *the ancestor of,* and so throughout the verse.

4:9 Cain's response to God is well known. The King James Bible famously renders it: "Am I my brother's keeper?" Rather than confess or repent in response to God's question, Cain lied and became defensive. Adam had a similar response when God confronted his disobedience. While he was honest about eating the taboo fruit, Adam immediately cast the blame on Eve. Eve then followed suit by blaming the serpent (Genesis 3:12-13). As humans, we avoid the twin truths that there is no hiding from God and that there is no one else but ourselves to blame for our actions.

4:12-13 God banished Cain from his farmland and declared that it no longer would yield crops for him. This punishment hit Cain hard, for he was a man of the land who had offered God produce he had raised himself. His descendants became a nomadic people with nowhere to settle, a family of fugitives. By his own admission, Cain also lost access to God's presence. But God had promised Cain earlier (Genesis 4:7) that if he responded with the right attitude, he would be accepted. It was Cain's choice, then, to be a self-made man with nowhere to call home.

4:15 Cain was afraid other people would hurt him. We don't know who these other people were—probably descendants of Adam and Eve's other children. We also don't know the exact nature of Cain's "mark" or how anyone else was to recognize and understand it. But since Cain's punishment was worse than he could imagine, he must have felt some reassurance in knowing that an even more terrible retribution awaited any enemies he encountered. While Cain failed to submit to God's leadership, he accepted God's power to dole out his punishment.

4:17 Cain's wife was likely a sister or a niece. Today, such a marriage would be a forbidden act. It is not healthy for people to procreate with close family members, which is why we have laws against it. But in Cain's time, the world was new and the gene pool was clean. No chromosomal and genetic abnormalities existed to be passed down. Soon, however, these kinds of relationships would be subjected to guidelines (Leviticus 18:11-18).

4:17 When Cain first left the Garden, he was in the land of Nod. *Nod* means "wandering." Soon, however, Cain established a city and named it for his son, Enoch. Little is known about this city, but the fact that Cain named it shows that the inhabitants of the earth were organizing themselves very quickly. The birth of Enoch also represented the establishment of a bloodline from Cain, but that bloodline was lost in the Flood in which only Noah's family survived. Noah was descended from Seth, Adam and Eve's third son.

4:20-22 Imagine the discoveries of the tradesmen listed in this verse. How did Jabal react when he conceived new ways to manage larger herds? What must Jubal have thought when he was able to produce his first clear tone? What did Tubal-cain feel when he discovered methods for shaping metal to make his day-to-day work easier? After only five generations, people were living in tents, playing music, and working with metals. They were doing more than surviving—they were enjoying God's creation, employing it within their lives, and creating things. Perhaps without even understanding it, they were expressing God's image by creating and building a life.

"Adah and Zillah, hear my voice;
listen to me, you wives of Lamech.
I have killed a man who attacked me,
a young man who wounded me.
24 If someone who kills Cain is punished seven times,
then the one who kills me will be punished seventy-seven times!"

4:25 Gen 4:8; 5:3 · 1 Chr 1:1 · Luke 3:38

THE BIRTH OF SETH

4:26 Gen 12:8 · 1 Kgs 18:24 · Joel 2:32 · Zeph 3:9 · Acts 2:21

25 Adam had sexual relations with his wife again, and she gave birth to another son. She
named him Seth,* for she said, "God has granted me another son in place of Abel, whom
Cain killed." 26 When Seth grew up, he had a son and named him Enosh. At that time peo-
ple first began to worship the LORD by name.

THE DESCENDANTS OF ADAM

5:1 Gen 1:26; 6:9 · 1 Chr 1:1
5:2 Gen 1:27 · *Matt 19:4 · *Mark 10:6
5:3 Gen 1:26; 4:25 · 1 Cor 15:49
5:5 Gen 2:17 · Heb 9:27
5:6 Luke 3:38
5:9 1 Chr 1:2 · Luke 3:37
5:12 1 Chr 1:2 · Luke 3:37
5:15 1 Chr 1:2 · Luke 3:37

5 This is the written account of the descendants of Adam. When God created human
beings,* He made them to be like Himself. 2 He created them male and female, and
He blessed them and called them "human."

3 When Adam was 130 years old, he became the father of a son who was just like
him—in his very image. He named his son Seth. 4 After the birth of Seth, Adam lived
another 800 years, and he had other sons and daughters. 5 Adam lived 930 years,
and then he died.
6 When Seth was 105 years old, he became the father of* Enosh. 7 After the birth of*
Enosh, Seth lived another 807 years, and he had other sons and daughters. 8 Seth
lived 912 years, and then he died.
9 When Enosh was 90 years old, he became the father of Kenan. 10 After the birth of Ke-
nan, Enosh lived another 815 years, and he had other sons and daughters. 11 Enosh
lived 905 years, and then he died.
12 When Kenan was 70 years old, he became the father of Mahalalel. 13 After the birth
of Mahalalel, Kenan lived another 840 years, and he had other sons and daughters.
14 Kenan lived 910 years, and then he died.
15 When Mahalalel was 65 years old, he became the father of Jared. 16 After the birth
of Jared, Mahalalel lived another 830 years, and he had other sons and daughters.
17 Mahalalel lived 895 years, and then he died.

4:25 *Seth* probably means "granted"; the name may also mean "appointed." 5:1 Or *man;* Hebrew reads *adam;* similarly in 5:2. 5:6 Or *the ancestor of;* also in 5:9, 12, 15, 18, 21, 25. 5:7 Or *the birth of this ancestor of;* also in 5:10, 13, 16, 19, 22, 26.

4:23-24 If Lamech and his family demonstrate progress in fulfillment of the Cultural Mandate, they also display a gross regression in terms of godly living. Lamech married two women in violation of God's design. He also boasted of having killed a man for only wounding him. And he arrogantly swore that anyone who took vengeance on him would pay a far worse price than the penalty set by God for killing Cain. These ungodly descendants of Cain display a hardening of their hearts, a deepening of their rebellion against God. By contrast, the godly line descending from Adam and Eve through Seth worships and follows God.

▶ CHURCH

4:26 The church worships in every age and place. This is the first instance Scripture records of God's people coming together to worship Him. The name *Enosh,* like *Adam,* means "man." However, some scholars believe that *Enosh* carries the further meaning of "frail man," which would better highlight the humble God-worship of the line of Seth (in contrast with the self-worship of the line of Cain, represented by Lamech). The image of Enosh as a "frail" man of humble reliance on God must not be lost. Self-reliance always leads to worship of self, while meekness before God has always been essential to biblical worship. (***See Church*> *Who*> *From every place and age*> *Believers in the Old Testament,*** TopicGuide page A48.)

5:3-32 While they seem like dry reading today, genealogies were incredibly important in the ancient world. There were no courthouse records or even a common written language. The only way to keep track of many things was by oral tradition. Genealogies were a form of that tradition. In this way, ancient peoples kept track not only of the family or clan to which they belonged but of the land to which they had access. Land was the ultimate possession. As time passed and God set apart His people, the descendants of Israel, family histories became even more essential. They delineated both the land assigned to the tribe and, in some cases, the tasks given to them.

18When Jared was 162 years old, he became the father of Enoch. 19After the birth of
Enoch, Jared lived another 800 years, and he had other sons and daughters. 20Ja-
red lived 962 years, and then he died.
21When Enoch was 65 years old, he became the father of Methuselah. 22After the
birth of Methuselah, Enoch lived in close fellowship with God for another
300 years, and he had other sons and daughters. 23Enoch lived 365 years,
24walking in close fellowship with God. Then one day he disappeared, because
God took him.
25When Methuselah was 187 years old, he became the father of Lamech. 26After the
birth of Lamech, Methuselah lived another 782 years, and he had other sons and
daughters. 27Methuselah lived 969 years, and then he died.
28When Lamech was 182 years old, he became the father of a son. 29Lamech
named his son Noah, for he said, "May he bring us relief* from our work and
the painful labor of farming this ground that the LORD has cursed." 30After the
birth of Noah, Lamech lived another 595 years, and he had other sons and
daughters. 31Lamech lived 777 years, and then he died.
32By the time Noah was 500 years old, he was the father of Shem, Ham, and
Japheth.

5:18 1 Chr 1:3; Luke 3:37; Jude 1:14
5:21 1 Chr 1:3; Luke 3:37
5:22 Gen 6:9; 48:15
5:24 2 Kgs 2:1, 11; Ps 73:24; Heb 11:5
5:25 1 Chr 1:3; Luke 3:36
5:29 Gen 3:17; 1 Chr 1:3; Luke 3:36; Rom 8:20
5:32 Gen 7:6; 9:18

A WORLD GONE WRONG

6 Then the people began to multiply on the earth, and daughters were born to them.
2The sons of God saw the beautiful women* and took any they wanted as their
wives. 3Then the LORD said, "My Spirit will not put up with* humans for such a long time,
for they are only mortal flesh. In the future, their normal lifespan will be no more than
120 years."

6:1 Gen 1:28
6:3 Ps 78:39; 1 Pet 3:20

5:29 *Noah* sounds like a Hebrew term that can mean "relief" or "comfort." 6:2 Hebrew *daughters of men;* also in 6:4. 6:3 Greek version reads *will not remain in.*

5:24 Enoch is set apart in history much like the prophet Elijah. According to the Bible, neither man died. Instead, both were taken directly to heaven while still alive. According to Hebrews 11:5, "It was by faith that Enoch was taken up to heaven without dying." Enoch also shares a distinction with Noah. Only of Enoch and Noah does the Bible say, he walked "in close fellowship with God." This implies an intimacy of fellowship that stands out in all of Scripture's historical records. In both cases, this close walk with God was made possible by the same element that led to Enoch's translation to heaven—faith.

5:29-30 Did ancient people actually live such fantastically long lives as described in this chapter? Some scholars believe that the ages listed here do correspond to our modern understanding. Indeed, the lifespans described in ancient historical and cultural records other than Scripture are also longer than we experience today. However, some of the historical records list years between main characters in a family line as opposed to actual birth and death dates. Whether the ages here were counted as we do today or whether the calendar was evolving and with it the concept of years and age, it is clear that human lifespans diminished after the Flood. By the time of Moses, a typical lifespan was similar to modern expectations. In Psalm 90:10, Moses says, "Seventy years are given to us!"

6:1-2 Some believe that the "sons of God" in this verse were angels or fallen angels who became involved with mortal women. However, the fantastic nature of this theory argues against it, as does the context of these verses. In chapters 4 and 5, Moses outlined two groups of descendants from Adam and Eve: a godly line and an ungodly line. One possible theory is that these verses describe an intermingling of the two lines, with male descendants of Seth taking wives for themselves from female descendants of Cain. Their poor spousal choices represented a decline in the godliness of Seth's line. Their sin also may have involved taking more than one wife per man, taking "any that they wanted," a violation of God's design for the marriage relationship.

▸ PURPOSE
6:3 Common grace restrains sin. God said His Spirit would "not put up with humans for such a long time." Still, the Spirit continued (and continues) to put up with people for many years. Many theologians see the patience of God's Spirit described here as referring to God's *common grace,* which is granted to and experienced by all people. One action of common grace is the restraining of sin in the world so that people, including non-Christians, can do good for others. This good is not related to salvation, but has to do principally with the performance of civic responsibilities. Without the Holy Spirit restraining the wickedness of men so that they can do good, the world would quickly degenerate into anarchy. The order that common grace provides also gives Christians time to spread the gospel before the end of the present age. (***See Purpose*> *God's Deeds*> *Common grace*, TopicGuide page A54.)

4 In those days, and for some time after, giant Nephilites lived on the earth, for whenever
the sons of God had intercourse with women, they gave birth to children who became the
heroes and famous warriors of ancient times.
5 The LORD observed the extent of human wickedness on the earth, and He saw that
everything they thought or imagined was consistently and totally evil. 6 So the LORD was
sorry He had ever made them and put them on the earth. It broke His heart. 7 And the
LORD said, "I will wipe this human race I have created from the face of the earth. Yes, and I
will destroy every living thing—all the people, the large animals, the small animals that
scurry along the ground, and even the birds of the sky. I am sorry I ever made them." 8 But
Noah found favor with the LORD.

THE STORY OF NOAH

9 This is the account of Noah and his family. Noah was a righteous man, the only blame-
less person living on earth at the time, and he walked in close fellowship with God. 10 Noah
was the father of three sons: Shem, Ham, and Japheth.
11 Now God saw that the earth had become corrupt and was filled with violence. 12 God
observed all this corruption in the world, for everyone on earth was corrupt. 13 So God said
to Noah, "I have decided to destroy all living creatures, for they have filled the earth with
violence. Yes, I will wipe them all out along with the earth!
14 "Build a large boat* from cypress wood* and waterproof it with tar, inside and out.
Then construct decks and stalls throughout its interior. 15 Make the boat 450 feet long,
75 feet wide, and 45 feet high.* 16 Leave an 18-inch opening* below the roof all the way

6:4 Num 13:33
6:5 Ps 14:1-3
6:6 Exod 32:14; Num 23:19; 1 Sam 15:11, 35; 2 Sam 24:16
6:7 Deut 29:20
6:8 Exod 33:17
6:9 Job 1:1; Ezek 14:14
6:11 Deut 31:29; Judg 2:19; Ezek 8:17
6:12 Ps 14:1-3
6:13 Isa 34:1-4; Ezek 7:2-3
6:14 Exod 2:3; 1 Pet 3:20

6:14a Traditionally rendered *an ark.* 6:14b Or *gopher wood.* 6:15 Hebrew *300 cubits* [138 meters] *long, 50 cubits* [23 meters] *wide, and 30 cubits* [13.8 meters] *high.* 6:16 Hebrew *an opening of 1 cubit* [46 centimeters].

6:4 The words translated as "giant Nephilites" here appears in other translations as *Nephilim,* a race of very large people. While some of the ancient words used to describe giants can also mean "mighty" or "warrior," it seems clear that there were early races that were of unusual size. When the Hebrew spies did reconnaissance in the Promised Land, they saw the Nephilim there and came back too scared to launch an invasion. The spies said they felt like grasshoppers compared to these men (Numbers 13:33). Another race of large people was called the Rephaim. King Og of Bashan was a Rephaite. His bed was thirteen feet long and six feet wide (Deuteronomy 3:11). Goliath, the Philistine, was also a giant, perhaps descended from a race of large people called the Anakim (1 Samuel 17:4-7).

6:5-13 Jesus later described this era on earth. He said that right up until the time Noah entered the ark, "people were enjoying banquets and parties and weddings" (Matthew 24:38). Jesus' words may make the people sound more oblivious than sinful. But when we read the description here, we find that violence and depravity were commonplace. People lived to satisfy themselves rather than honor their Creator. The Bible goes so far as to say that God was sorry He had made them. He was so grieved by human sin that He sent a flood to cover the earth. Jesus' statement shows the unexpected suddenness of that judgment.

6:9 Moses describes Noah as "a righteous man" and "the only blameless person living on earth at the time." He represents a new flowering of the godly line of Seth, which had become largely indistinguishable from the ungodly descendants of Cain. However, these descriptions of Noah do not mean that he was sinless. In fact, after the Flood, he sinned by getting drunk with wine (Genesis 9:20). But Noah sought to obey God and to walk with him by faith as no one else on earth did. Still, Noah was chosen by God to be saved from the Flood not because of the way he lived but because he "found favor with the LORD" (Genesis 6:8). Other translations render this passage this way: "Noah found grace in the eyes of the LORD." Noah walked with Him by faith and was saved from judgment because God willed it to be so. It is the same for all believers everywhere.

▸BIBLE

6:14 Types and shadows of Christ. God commanded Noah to build a boat (an "ark"), which is a *type,* or picture, of the salvation provided by Christ alone. Jesus is the ark of our salvation. He alone is the One who can spare us from God's just wrath. While God's covenant promise to Noah provided salvation only for his family and for a select group of animals, Peter uses the Flood to remind us to seek salvation in Christ in light of God's final judgment (2 Peter 3:6-10). (***See Bible****> Unity> OT types> Noah's Ark,* TopicGuide page A11.)

6:15-16 God gave detailed instructions for Noah's boat. According to this description, it seems that the boat would have been box-like, with ventilation all the way around the roof. God's instructions were specific, even down to His reminder in verse 21 to bring enough food. There are other times in Scripture whe n God gave instructions this specific. In Exodus, He presented very detailed directions for setting up the Tent of Meeting. In fact, in Exodus 30:22-26, God even provided Moses a recipe for making anointing oil. Likewise, the book of Leviticus is full of guidelines for the priests and Levites who managed the worship center of the people.

around the boat. Put the door on the side, and build three decks inside the boat—lower,
middle, and upper.
17"Look! I am about to cover the earth with a flood that will destroy every living thing
that breathes. Everything on earth will die. 18But I will confirm My covenant with you. So
enter the boat—you and your wife and your sons and their wives. 19Bring a pair of every
kind of animal—a male and a female—into the boat with you to keep them alive during
the flood. 20Pairs of every kind of bird, and every kind of animal, and every kind of small
animal that scurries along the ground, will come to you to be kept alive. 21And be sure to
take on board enough food for your family and for all the animals."
22So Noah did everything exactly as God had commanded him.

THE FLOOD COVERS THE EARTH

7 When everything was ready, the LORD said to Noah, "Go into the boat with all your
family, for among all the people of the earth, I can see that you alone are righteous.
2Take with you seven pairs—male and female—of each animal I have approved for eating
and for sacrifice,* and take one pair of each of the others. 3Also take seven pairs of every
kind of bird. There must be a male and a female in each pair to ensure that all life will sur-
vive on the earth after the flood. 4Seven days from now I will make the rains pour down on
the earth. And it will rain for forty days and forty nights, until I have wiped from the earth
all the living things I have created."
5So Noah did everything as the LORD commanded him.
6Noah was 600 years old when the flood covered the earth. 7He went on board the boat
to escape the flood—he and his wife and his sons and their wives. 8With them were all the
various kinds of animals—those approved for eating and for sacrifice and those that were
not—along with all the birds and the small animals that scurry along the ground. 9They en-
tered the boat in pairs, male and female, just as God had commanded Noah. 10After seven
days, the waters of the flood came and covered the earth.
11When Noah was 600 years old, on the seventeenth day of the second month, all the
underground waters erupted from the earth, and the rain fell in mighty torrents from the
sky. 12The rain continued to fall for forty days and forty nights.
13That very day Noah had gone into the boat with his wife and his sons—Shem, Ham,
and Japheth—and their wives. 14With them in the boat were pairs of every kind of ani-
mal—domestic and wild, large and small—along with birds of every kind. 15Two by two
they came into the boat, representing every living thing that breathes. 16A male and fe-
male of each kind entered, just as God had commanded Noah. Then the LORD closed the
door behind them.

6:17 Ps 29:10; 2 Pet 2:5
6:18 Gen 9:9-16; 17:7; 19:12
6:20 Gen 7:3
6:21 Gen 1:29
6:22 Gen 7:5; Exod 40:16
7:1 Gen 6:18; Matt 24:38; Luke 17:26-27; Heb 11:7; 1 Pet 3:20
7:2 Lev 11:1-47; Deut 14:3-20; Ezek 44:23
7:4 Gen 6:7, 13
7:6 Gen 5:32
7:7 Gen 6:18
7:9 Gen 6:22
7:11 Ps 78:23; Ezek 26:19; Mal 3:10
7:13 1 Pet 3:20; 2 Pet 2:5
7:15 Gen 6:19; 7:9

7:2 Hebrew *of each clean animal;* similarly in 7:8.

▶ HOLINESS
7:2 Old Covenant laws of ceremonial cleanness. The directive to "take with you seven pairs . . . of each animal" that were clean but only "one pair of each of the others" is explained by the fact that Noah needed more ceremonially clean animals to sacrifice to the Lord (see Genesis 8:20) and to eat. This command points to the spiritual truth that only those who are clean in God's eyes are acceptable to Him. God makes us clean when He forgives our sins and welcomes us into His family (see Titus 3:5). (***See Holiness**> Law and Grace> Law*, TopicGuide page A41.)

7:2 The assumption in this command is that Noah knew which animals were good to eat and acceptable for sacrifice. Clearly, God already had communicated these guidelines in some way. He would formalize them much later, in the days of Moses. Leviticus, in particular, laid out standards for which animals were clean for eating.

▶ PURPOSE
7:16 Acts of judgment: great flood. One of the more sobering facts about the last minutes before the earth was covered by floodwaters is that God "closed the door behind them." Imagine scores of people clawing at the door of the ark in a last-gasp effort to escape the raging waters. Yet it was not Noah who sealed the doors of the ark; it was God. Condemnation for sin comes from the hand of God. Someday we will stand before God to give an account for our deeds in the flesh (Hebrews 9:27). Are you prepared for that day? (***See Purpose**> God's Deeds> Judgment*, TopicGuide page A53.)

17 For forty days the floodwaters grew deeper, covering the ground and lifting the boat
high above the earth. 18 As the waters rose higher and higher above the ground, the boat
floated safely on the surface. 19 Finally, the water covered even the highest mountains on
the earth, 20 rising more than twenty-two feet* above the highest peaks. 21 All the living
things on earth died—birds, domestic animals, wild animals, small animals that scurry
along the ground, and all the people. 22 Everything that breathed and lived on dry land
died. 23 God wiped out every living thing on the earth—people, livestock, small animals
that scurry along the ground, and the birds of the sky. All were destroyed. The only peo-
ple who survived were Noah and those with him in the boat. 24 And the floodwaters cov-
ered the earth for 150 days.

7:19 Ps 104:6
7:20 2 Pet 3:6
7:23 Matt 24:38-39; Luke 17:26-27; 1 Pet 3:20; 2 Pet 2:5
7:24 Gen 8:3

THE FLOOD RECEDES

8 But God remembered Noah and all the wild animals and livestock with him in the
boat. He sent a wind to blow across the earth, and the floodwaters began to re-
cede. 2 The underground waters stopped flowing, and the torrential rains from the sky
were stopped. 3 So the floodwaters gradually receded from the earth. After 150 days,
4 exactly five months from the time the flood began,* the boat came to rest on the
mountains of Ararat. 5 Two and a half months later,* as the waters continued to go
down, other mountain peaks became visible.

6 After another forty days, Noah opened the window he had made in the boat 7 and re-
leased a raven. The bird flew back and forth until the floodwaters on the earth had dried
up. 8 He also released a dove to see if the water had receded and it could find dry ground.
9 But the dove could find no place to land because the water still covered the ground. So it
returned to the boat, and Noah held out his hand and drew the dove back inside. 10 After
waiting another seven days, Noah released the dove again. 11 This time the dove re-
turned to him in the evening with a fresh olive leaf in its beak. Then Noah knew that the
floodwaters were almost gone. 12 He waited another seven days and then released the
dove again. This time it did not come back.

13 Noah was now 601 years old. On the first day of the new year, ten and a half months
after the flood began,* the floodwaters had almost dried up from the earth. Noah lifted

8:1 Gen 19:29; 30:22; Exod 2:24; 14:21; Job 12:15; Isa 44:27
8:2 Gen 7:4, 12
8:4 Gen 7:20
8:7 Lev 11:15; Deut 14:14; 1 Kgs 17:4; Luke 12:24
8:8 Isa 60:8; Hos 11:11; Matt 10:16
8:13 Gen 5:32

7:20 Hebrew *15 cubits* [6.9 meters]. 8:4 Hebrew *on the seventeenth day of the seventh month;* see 7:11. 8:5 Hebrew *On the first day of the tenth month;* see 7:11 and note on 8:4. 8:13 Hebrew *On the first day of the first month;* see 7:11.

7:17-20 Many passages in the Bible refer to Noah and to the Flood. Historical documents from many cultures also confirm the reality of a great Flood. The question most debated by scholars, however, is whether the Flood covered the entire earth. The human population at that time lived in Mesopotamia. Thus, a flood of Mesopotamia would have destroyed all human life. Other scholars contend that in order for the waters to rise above the highest mountains of Ararat, they would have had to cover more than just Mesopotamia. The Flood was most likely universal.

7:21-23 From a modern perspective, it seems unnecessary for animals to have been destroyed in the Flood. After all, the people were sinful, not the animals. On this point, we, like Job, have to defer to God's wisdom as being above our own (Job 38:1-7). God could have chosen any way that He liked to destroy rebellious humanity. But His choice emphasizes the new beginning that God offers all who experience His miraculous rescue.

8:4 The mountains of Ararat are a range that includes an extinct volcano. The range is in modern-day Turkey and northern Iran. Many people have searched there for evidence of Noah's boat. In fact, one peak is known locally as the Mount of Noah. Thus far, though, no conclusive evidence of the ark or artifacts from it has been found. Although there have been hailed sightings and even an excavation of a wooden artifact, the exact landing point of Noah's ark remains a mystery.

8:13-14 Twelve and a half months on a houseboat full of animals—how did Noah's family do it? It has been determined that the dimensions of the ark would have made it seaworthy by modern boat-making standards. The floor space would have totaled more than 100,000 square feet, enough to fit nearly 600 railroad boxcars. Keeping in mind that the animals represented species and not breeds (dogs, not collies, spaniels, and hounds), and assuming that seafaring creatures could have survived outside, some have estimated that the ark housed less than 8,000 individual animals. If the animals were young, they may have averaged the size of a large goat, which means about 350 boxcars could have held them. That would have left plenty of space for Noah's family and some storage.

back the covering of the boat and saw that the surface of the ground was drying. 14 Two more months went by,* and at last the earth was dry!

15 Then God said to Noah, 16 "Leave the boat, all of you—you and your wife, and your sons and their wives. 17 Release all the animals—the birds, the livestock, and the small animals that scurry along the ground—so they can be fruitful and multiply throughout the earth."

18 So Noah, his wife, and his sons and their wives left the boat. 19 And all of the large and small animals and birds came out of the boat, pair by pair.

20 Then Noah built an altar to the LORD, and there he sacrificed as burnt offerings the animals and birds that had been approved for that purpose.* 21 And the LORD was pleased with the aroma of the sacrifice and said to Himself, "I will never again curse the ground because of the human race, even though everything they think or imagine is bent toward evil from childhood. I will never again destroy all living things. 22 As long as the earth remains, there will be planting and harvest, cold and heat, summer and winter, day and night."

GOD CONFIRMS HIS COVENANT

9 Then God blessed Noah and his sons and told them, "Be fruitful and multiply. Fill the earth. 2 All the animals of the earth, all the birds of the sky, all the small animals that scurry along the ground, and all the fish in the sea will look on you with fear and terror. I have placed them in your power. 3 I have given them to you for food, just as I have given you grain and vegetables. 4 But you must never eat any meat that still has the lifeblood in it.

5 "And I will require the blood of anyone who takes another person's life. If a wild animal kills a person, it must die. And anyone who murders a fellow human must die. 6 If anyone takes a human life, that person's life will also be taken by human hands. For God made human beings* in His own image. 7 Now be fruitful and multiply, and repopulate the earth."

8:16 Gen 7:13
8:17 Gen 1:22
8:20 Gen 4:4; 12:7; 13:18; 22:2
8:21 Gen 3:17; Exod 29:18, 25; Lev 1:9, 13; Isa 54:9
8:22 Ps 74:17
9:1 Gen 1:22
9:2 Gen 1:26-29; Ps 8:6-8
9:3 Ps 104:14
9:4 Lev 3:17; 7:26; 17:10; Deut 12:16; Acts 15:20, 29
9:5 Exod 21:28-32
9:6 Exod 20:13; 21:12; Num 35:33

8:14 Hebrew *The twenty-seventh day of the second month arrived;* see note on 8:13. 8:20 Hebrew *every clean animal and every clean bird.* 9:6 Or *man;* Hebrew reads *ha-adam.*

8:20 In Noah's time, building an altar and offering a sacrifice was a way to commemorate a great event, particularly an act of God's providence. Noah's sacrifice apparently involved the burning of the animals. Later, when God codified the sacrificial system for His people, He designated the burnt offering as an atoning sacrifice (Leviticus 1:4). *Atone* literally means "to cover over." Thus, each time the Israelites sacrificed an animal, they were reminded that the blood of another was necessary to cover their sins—a powerful depiction of what Christ would accomplish in God's time.

▸ PURPOSE

8:21-22 God keeps His promises. On his way to church one Sunday morning, a preacher was met by one of the deacons. "What a bitterly cold morning," the deacon remarked. "I am sorry the weather is so wintry." Smiling, the minister replied, "I was just thanking God for keeping His Word." "What do you mean?" the deacon asked with a puzzled look. "Well," the preacher said, "more than three thousand years ago, God promised that cold and heat should not cease, so I am strengthened by this weather that emphasizes the sureness of His promises." Let the seasons remind you that we serve a God who providentially keeps His promises. (***See Purpose***> *God's Means> God's sovereignty> God sustains His creation,* TopicGuide page A52.)

9:1-7 God gave Noah dominion over the earth and commanded him and his family to multiply and fill the world with people again. These were the same responsibilities God conferred upon Adam. Interestingly, He now granted the living creatures to humanity for food, whereas earlier He had dictated that the diet of Adam and Eve and their children should consist of fruit and vegetables only (Genesis 1:29). The only requirement was that they should not eat animals with the lifeblood in them. Leviticus gives two reasons for this strange requirement. First, refraining from eating blood shows respect for the sanctity of life. Second, it is by blood that atonement for sin must be made.

▸ ADOPTION

9:5-6 The value of human life. God clearly states that murder is forbidden. To break this law deserves capital punishment. Why? Because human beings are created in the very image of God. Thus, to take the life of another human being is to attack the Creator God. Imagine that someone destroyed something you had made and cherished. Would you not feel as though you had been personally attacked? This simple analogy, however, does not capture the seriousness of murder. God values life, and humans are the pinnacle of His creation. There is no clearer way to assault the Creator than to destroy a living person—His finest creation. (***See Adoption***> *Without Christ> Connected to God> Created in the image of God,* TopicGuide page A36.)

8 Then God told Noah and his sons, 9 "I hereby confirm My covenant with you and your
descendants, 10 and with all the animals that were on the boat with you—the birds, the live-
9:11 stock, and all the wild animals—every living creature on earth. 11 Yes, I am confirming My
Isa 24:5 covenant with you. Never again will floodwaters kill all living creatures; never again will a
9:12 flood destroy the earth."
Gen 17:11 12 Then God said, "I am giving you a sign of My covenant with you and with all living
9:13 creatures, for all generations to come. 13 I have placed My rainbow in the clouds. It is the
Ezek 1:28 sign of My covenant with you and with all the earth. 14 When I send clouds over the earth,
9:15 the rainbow will appear in the clouds, 15 and I will remember My covenant with you and
Deut 7:9 with all living creatures. Never again will the floodwaters destroy all life. 16 When I see the
rainbow in the clouds, I will remember the eternal covenant between God and every living
creature on earth." 17 Then God said to Noah, "Yes, this rainbow is the sign of the covenant
I am confirming with all the creatures on earth."

NOAH'S SONS

18 The sons of Noah who came out of the boat with their father were Shem, Ham, and Ja-
pheth. (Ham is the father of Canaan.) 19 From these three sons of Noah came all the people
9:21 who now populate the earth.
Gen 19:35 20 After the flood, Noah began to cultivate the ground, and he planted a vineyard. 21 One
9:22 day he drank some wine he had made, and he became drunk and lay naked inside his
Hab 2:15 tent. 22 Ham, the father of Canaan, saw that his father was naked and went outside and

9:8-11 Throughout history, God has called people into a relationship with Himself, a relationship based on covenants under which He promised great blessings and required trust and fidelity. God promised life to Adam and his descendants if he would refrain from eating from one tree. Then He made a covenant with Noah in which He promised deliverance from the Flood. This covenant was expanded in these verses with the promise that the earth would never be destroyed again by a flood; all of Noah's descendants were safe. Years later, God made a covenant with Abraham, promising to give his descendants a land, to make them a great nation, and to bless all peoples through them. In Jesus Christ, God ushered in a new covenant, promising that anyone who trusts in Jesus' sacrificial death may be saved (2 Corinthians 3:9, 12).

9:12-16 What did the rainbow mean? The Flood may have represented the first occurrence of rain on the earth. If so, the rainbow God placed in the sky was likely the first one ever seen by human beings. Perhaps the rainbow was a symbol of beauty made from what had been destructive. More than a natural phenomenon, however, it stood as a sign between God and all living creatures. Since the Hebrew word for rainbow can also be used to refer to a *bow*—as in a bow used to shoot arrows—some have said that the rainbow was an image of God hanging up His bow in the sky, declaring no more destruction of humanity. Finally, following the archery analogy, it could represent God pointing a war-bow at Himself, forever reminding us that He would sooner perish than break His promises to us.

FOR THE NEXT *GOD NEVER CHANGES* FEATURE SEE PAGE 1738.

BECAUSE GOD NEVER CHANGES

My future is secure and eternal.

When I see the rainbow in the clouds, I will remember the eternal covenant between God and every living creature on earth.

GENESIS 9:16

told his brothers. 23 Then Shem and Japheth took a robe, held it over their shoulders, and
backed into the tent to cover their father. As they did this, they looked the other way so
they would not see him naked.
24 When Noah woke up from his stupor, he learned what Ham, his youngest son, had
done. 25 Then he cursed Canaan, the son of Ham:

> "May Canaan be cursed!
> May he be the lowest of servants to his relatives."

9:25 Deut 27:16

26 Then Noah said,

> "May the LORD, the God of Shem, be blessed,
> and may Canaan be his servant!
> 27 May God expand the territory of Japheth!
> May Japheth share the prosperity of Shem,*
> and may Canaan be his servant."

9:26 Gen 14:20

9:27 Gen 10:2-5; Isa 66:19

28 Noah lived another 350 years after the great flood. 29 He lived 950 years, and then he died.

9:29 Gen 2:17

10 This is the account of the families of Shem, Ham, and Japheth, the three sons of
Noah. Many children were born to them after the great flood.

10:1 Gen 9:18; 1 Chr 1:4

DESCENDANTS OF JAPHETH

2 The descendants of Japheth were Gomer, Magog, Madai, Javan, Tubal, Meshech, and
Tiras.
3 The descendants of Gomer were Ashkenaz, Riphath, and Togarmah.
4 The descendants of Javan were Elishah, Tarshish, Kittim, and Rodanim.* 5 Their descen-
dants became the seafaring peoples that spread out to various lands, each identified
by its own language, clan, and national identity.

10:2 1 Chr 1:5-7; Isa 66:19; Ezek 27:13; 38:2-3, 6

10:3 Jer 51:27; Ezek 27:14

10:4 1 Chr 1:6-7

DESCENDANTS OF HAM

6 The descendants of Ham were Cush, Mizraim, Put, and Canaan.
7 The descendants of Cush were Seba, Havilah, Sabtah, Raamah, and Sabteca. The
descendants of Raamah were Sheba and Dedan.

10:6 1 Chr 1:8-10

10:7 Isa 43:3; Ezek 27:15, 20, 22

9:27 Hebrew *May he live in the tents of Shem.* 10:4 As in some Hebrew manuscripts and Greek version (see also 1 Chr 1:7); most Hebrew manuscripts read *Dodanim.*

9:22 Many questions have been asked and conclusions drawn about Ham's misdeed. The simplest explanation is that Ham was disrespectful of his father, so Noah cursed all of Ham's descendants through his son Canaan. Some are troubled by the reference to Ham as Noah's youngest son, because Ham has always been listed as the middle son. This may be a clue that it was Canaan, not Ham, who actually committed the misdeed.

9:22-25 The Canaanites settled in the land east of Egypt, an area that eventually became known by the name of their forefather. By the time Abraham settled there, people other than those who were of the lineage of Canaan (the man) may have become known as Canaanites by virtue of living in the land. These ungodly peoples opposed Israel's conquest of the land, and God used Israel to fulfill the curse Noah uttered in these verses.

10:1 Because the Flood destroyed most of the earth's population, all of humanity can be traced back to the sons of Noah. This chapter outlines the nations that formed from these three family lines and identifies the regions where these nations lived. While differences became evident as each nation expanded, separated, and grew distinct, it is important to remember that all humans originally came from the same family, from three brothers who survived a catastrophe in a boat.

10:2-5 Japheth was the oldest of Noah's sons, though Shem is often listed first. Japheth had seven sons. His descendants became the northern people of southeastern Europe, including the Greeks, who were also called Hellenes or Gentiles. Many believe that Noah's reference to Japheth sharing the prosperity of Shem came to pass during the Greek occupation of Palestine shortly before the time of Jesus. The Greek descendants of Japheth strongly influenced the culture in which the first-century church blossomed, and one of the greatest conflicts of the early church was whether Gentiles (descendants of Japheth) had to become Jews (descendants of Shem) in order to be followers of Christ (Acts 11; 15-21).

10:6-19 Ham's descendants included the Egyptians (*Mizraim* is Hebrew for "Egypt"), as well as some Africans and Arabs. The Bible gives us the most information about the descendants of

8 Cush was also the ancestor of Nimrod, who was the first heroic warrior on earth.
9 Since he was the greatest hunter in the world,* his name became proverbial. People
10:10 would say, "This man is like Nimrod, the greatest hunter in the world." 10 He built his
Gen 11:9 kingdom in the land of Babylonia,* with the cities of Babylon, Erech, Akkad, and Cal-
10:11 Mic 5:6 neh. 11 From there he expanded his territory to Assyria,* building the cities of Nine-
10:13 veh, Rehoboth-ir, Calah, 12 and Resen (the great city located between Nineveh and
Jer 46:9 Calah).
10:14 13 Mizraim was the ancestor of the Ludites, Anamites, Lehabites, Naphtuhites,
1 Chr 1:12 14 Pathrusites, Casluhites, and the Caphtorites, from whom the Philistines
10:15 came.*
Gen 15:20; 23:3 1 Chr 1:13 15 Canaan's oldest son was Sidon, the ancestor of the Sidonians. Canaan was also
Jer 47:4 the ancestor of the Hittites, 16 Jebusites, Amorites, Girgashites, 17 Hivites, Arkites,
10:16 Sinites, 18 Arvadites, Zemarites, and Hamathites. The Canaanite clans eventually
Gen 15:18-21 spread out, 19 and the territory of Canaan extended from Sidon in the north to
10:19 Gerar and Gaza in the south, and east as far as Sodom, Gomorrah, Admah, and
Gen 14:2 Zeboiim, near Lasha.
20 These were the descendants of Ham, identified by clan, language, territory, and national
identity.

DESCENDANTS OF SHEM

21 Sons were also born to Shem, the older brother of Japheth.* Shem was the ancestor
of all the descendants of Eber.
10:22 22 The descendants of Shem were Elam, Asshur, Arphaxad, Lud, and Aram.
2 Kgs 15:29 Isa 66:19 23 The descendants of Aram were Uz, Hul, Gether, and Mash.
10:23 24 Arphaxad was the father of Shelah,* and Shelah was the father of Eber.
Job 1:1 25 Eber had two sons. The first was named Peleg (which means "division"), for during his
10:24 lifetime the people of the world were divided into different language groups. His
Luke 3:35 brother's name was Joktan.
26 Joktan was the ancestor of Almodad, Sheleph, Hazarmaveth, Jerah, 27 Hadoram, Uzal,
Diklah, 28 Obal, Abimael, Sheba, 29 Ophir, Havilah, and Jobab. All these were descen-
dants of Joktan. 30 The territory they occupied extended from Mesha all the way to
Sephar in the eastern mountains.
31 These were the descendants of Shem, identified by clan, language, territory, and na-
tional identity.

CONCLUSION

10:32 32 These are the clans that descended from Noah's sons, arranged by nation according to
Gen 9:19; 10:1 their lines of descent. All the nations of the earth descended from these clans after the
great flood.

10:9 Hebrew *a great hunter before the LORD;* also in 10:9b. **10:10** Hebrew *Shinar.* **10:11** Or *From that land Assyria went out.* **10:14** Hebrew *Casluhites, from whom the Philistines came, and Caphtorites.* Compare Jer 47:4; Amos 9:7. **10:21** Or *Shem, whose older brother was Japheth.* **10:24** Greek version reads *Arphaxad was the father of Cainan, Cainan was the father of Shelah.* Compare Luke 3:36.

Canaan, the Canaanites, who were cursed by God. The curse included the subjugation of Canaan's descendants to the descendants of Shem (Semitic peoples) and Japheth (Indo-Europeans). While the Canaanites did inhabit the Promised Land and influence the Israelites as they resettled that land, by the time of the New Testament they had ceased to exist as a unified people group.

10:21-31 Shem's descendants included the Lydians (Lud) in Asia Minor, the Elamites (Elam) east of the Tigris River, the Arameans (Aram) or Syrians in Syria and Mesopotamia, and the Assyrians (Asshur). The Assyrians actually had origins in the family of Ham as well as that of Shem. It is from the name *Shem* that we get the term *Semitic*. Judaism, Christianity, and Islam all have roots in the lineage of Shem, and it was through the line of Shem that Abraham, King David, and Jesus were born.

THE TOWER OF BABEL

11 At one time all the people of the world spoke the same language and used the
same words. 2As the people migrated to the east, they found a plain in the land of
Babylonia* and settled there.
3They began saying to each other, "Let's make bricks and harden them with fire." (In this
region bricks were used instead of stone, and tar was used for mortar.) 4Then they said,
"Come, let's build a great city for ourselves with a tower that reaches into the sky. This will
make us famous and keep us from being scattered all over the world."
5But the LORD came down to look at the city and the tower the people were building.
6"Look!" He said. "The people are united, and they all speak the same language. After
this, nothing they set out to do will be impossible for them! 7Come, let's go down and
confuse the people with different languages. Then they won't be able to understand each
other."
8In that way, the LORD scattered them all over the world, and they stopped building
the city. 9That is why the city was called Babel,* because that is where the LORD con-
fused the people with different languages. In this way He scattered them all over the
world.

THE LINE OF DESCENT FROM SHEM TO ABRAM

10This is the account of Shem's family.

Two years after the great flood, when Shem was 100 years old, he became the father
of* Arphaxad. 11After the birth of* Arphaxad, Shem lived another 500 years and had
other sons and daughters.
12When Arphaxad was 35 years old, he became the father of Shelah. 13After the
birth of Shelah, Arphaxad lived another 403 years and had other sons and
daughters.*
14When Shelah was 30 years old, he became the father of Eber. 15After the birth of
Eber, Shelah lived another 403 years and had other sons and daughters.
16When Eber was 34 years old, he became the father of Peleg. 17After the birth of
Peleg, Eber lived another 430 years and had other sons and daughters.

11:2 Gen 10:10; 14:1; Isa 11:11
11:3 Gen 14:10
11:4 2 Sam 8:13
11:5 Gen 18:21; Exod 19:11
11:6 Gen 9:19; 11:1
11:7 Gen 1:26
11:8 Gen 9:19
11:9 Gen 10:10
11:10 Gen 10:22-25; Luke 3:36
11:12 Luke 3:36
11:13 1 Chr 1:17
11:14 Luke 3:35
11:16 Luke 3:35

11:2 Hebrew *Shinar.* 11:9 Or *Babylon. Babel* sounds like a Hebrew term that means "confusion." 11:10 Or *the ancestor of;* also in 11:12, 14, 16, 18, 20, 22, 24. 11:11 Or *the birth of this ancestor of;* also in 11:13, 15, 17, 19, 21, 23, 25. 11:12-13 Greek version reads [12]*When Arphaxad was 135 years old, he became the father of Cainan.* [13]*After the birth of Cainan, Arphaxad lived another 430 years and had other sons and daughters, and then he died. When Cainan was 130 years old, he became the father of Shelah. After the birth of Shelah, Cainan lived another 330 years and had other sons and daughters, and then he died.* Compare Luke 3:35-36.

11:1-4 As the descendants of Noah's three sons repopulated the earth, people naturally moved outward in search of resources, slowly filling the earth as God intended. As they went, they took their common language with them. Eventually, they came into the fertile plains of the land of Babylonia to the east of the land that eventually became Canaan. This seemed to be a place where many people could live together, halting the migrations that were separating them from one another and creating cultural differences. They hoped a city and a tower would unite them and celebrate what they saw as their greatness.

11:6 In this verse, God almost sounds fearful of what people might accomplish. But since that goes against everything the Bible teaches about God, we need to understand His words in their context. At this point in history, God had watched the human race fail time and time again. Adam and Eve had disobeyed. Then the culture had become so depraved and violent that God had destroyed everyone except Noah's family. As the human population grew again, it would have been only a matter of time until the downward spiral of morality resumed. While God had no reason to fear for Himself, He had reason to protect His creatures. The builders of Babel were prideful to the point of separation from God. Scattering humanity was a step toward saving people from themselves.

▶ PURPOSE

11:7 Confusion of tongues. The people's desire to "build a great city" using their common language was in direct violation of God's desire for the earth to be populated by many peoples. Left unchecked, this desire would transform Babylonia into a seat of idolatry. The people obviously had not learned one of the key lessons of the Flood—that God hates and judges all pride and idolatry. So God stepped in to confuse their language and stop the building of this great city—a sign of their pride. Correction and discipline is God's way to teach us and show us His love (see Hebrews 12:5-6). To return to our selfish ways reveals the hardness of our heart. Moreover, a pattern of disobedience grieves the heart of God, who loves us and wants us to experience the abundant life He has in store for us. (***See Purpose**> God's Deeds> Special acts> Miracles> OT,* TopicGuide page A52.)

11:20 Luke 3:35 18When Peleg was 30 years old, he became the father of Reu. 19After the birth of Reu,
11:22 Peleg lived another 209 years and had other sons and daughters.
Luke 3:34 20When Reu was 32 years old, he became the father of Serug. 21After the birth of
11:24 Serug, Reu lived another 207 years and had other sons and daughters.
Josh 24:2 22When Serug was 30 years old, he became the father of Nahor. 23After the birth of
Luke 3:34 Nahor, Serug lived another 200 years and had other sons and daughters.
11:26 Gen 22:20 24When Nahor was 29 years old, he became the father of Terah. 25After the birth of
1 Chr 1:26-27 Terah, Nahor lived another 119 years and had other sons and daughters.
Luke 3:34 26When Terah was 70 years old, he had become the father of Abram, Nahor, and
Haran.

THE FAMILY OF TERAH

11:29 27This is the account of Terah's family. Terah was the father of Abram, Nahor, and Haran;
Gen 17:15; 20:11-12; and Haran was the father of Lot. 28But Haran died in Ur of the Chaldeans, the land of his
22:20 birth, while his father, Terah, was still living. 29Meanwhile, Abram and Nahor both married.
11:30 Gen 16:1; 18:11; The name of Abram's wife was Sarai, and the name of Nahor's wife was Milcah. (Milcah
25:21 and her sister Iscah were daughters of Nahor's brother Haran.) 30But Sarai was unable to
1 Sam 1:5 Luke 1:7 become pregnant and had no children.
31One day Terah took his son Abram, his daughter-in-law Sarai (his son Abram's
11:31 Gen 27:43 wife), and his grandson Lot (his son Haran's child) and moved away from Ur of the
Josh 24:2 Chaldeans. He was headed for the land of Canaan, but they stopped at Haran and set-
Acts 7:4 tled there. 32Terah lived for 205 years* and died while still in Haran.

THE CALL OF ABRAM

12:1 Gen 15:7 **12** The LORD had said to Abram, "Leave your native country, your relatives, and
*Acts 7:3 your father's family, and go to the land that I will show you. 2I will make you
Heb 11:8 into a great nation. I will bless you and make you famous, and you will be a blessing to

11:32 Some ancient versions read *145 years;* compare 11:26 and 12:4.

11:27-28 Abram's hometown was known as Ur of the Chaldeans. It was possibly located in southern Mesopotamia, in the area where Nebuchadnezzar's great city of Babylon was later located. Ur was an educational center. Students there learned to read, write, and do sophisticated mathematics, including square roots. Wool was manufactured in Ur, though much of the income of the city revolved around religion. The main deity worshiped in Ur was a moon god named Nannar. Ur contained both a ziggurat (a pyramid-like tower) and a temple dedicated to the worship of Nannar and his moon goddess. It was out of this polytheistic culture that God called Abram.

11:27-32 Abram's family lived in tents that were probably much like the Bedouins of today. Some were large enough to be divided into rooms, with curtains as walls. Mats or rugs often covered the floor, and the sides could be raised for ventilation or lowered for protection from the elements. Although buildings and sheds could be built at that time, portable homes were more suitable for Abram and his relatives, for they were nomadic herdsman who moved from place to place to keep their animals fed and watered. At times, the number of tents a person owned was a sign of wealth. When Abram and Lot settled together, for instance, Lot was described as a man with many tents (Genesis 13:5).

11:31 Genesis tells us that Abram's father, Terah, initiated the move from Ur of the Chaldeans to Canaan. Terah set out with Abram and Abram's wife, Sarai, and with his grandson, Lot. They traveled northwestward, following the Euphrates River. However, when they came to Haran, near the headwaters of the Euphrates, Terah halted. It was only later, after the death of Terah in Haran, that Abram moved on to Canaan. However, in his great sermon just before his martyrdom, Stephen declared that Abram heard God's call to go to Canaan while still in Ur (Acts 7:2-4). But no matter when the call came, Abram showed great trust in leaving his ancestral home and relatives to travel to an unknown, unidentified land.

▸GOD

12:1 God's names: the LORD. God is identified here by the name *Yahweh.* Here translated "LORD," Yahweh is also translated "I AM" (Exodus 3:14-15). The name reveals that God is self-existent and is not dependent on anyone. When Jesus used God's personal name, I AM, to describe Himself (John 8:58), the Jewish leaders picked up stones to kill Him, angry that He was claiming to be the self-existent God. Because of the significance of God's personal name, it is used with many of the titles we find precious, such as "I AM the Healer" and "I AM the Lord who Provides." As you read the Yahweh names of God in the Bible, note the promises they contain for you and praise God for His wonderful character. (***See God***> *God's Names*> *God,* TopicGuide page A18.)

others. 3I will bless those who bless you and curse those who treat you with contempt. All
the families on earth will be blessed through you."
4So Abram departed as the LORD had instructed, and Lot went with him. Abram was
seventy-five years old when he left Haran. 5He took his wife, Sarai, his nephew Lot, and all
his wealth—his livestock and all the people he had taken into his household at Haran—and
headed for the land of Canaan. When they arrived in Canaan, 6Abram traveled through
the land as far as Shechem. There he set up camp beside the oak of Moreh. At that time,
the area was inhabited by Canaanites.
7Then the LORD appeared to Abram and said, "I will give this land to your descen-
dants.*" And Abram built an altar there and dedicated it to the LORD, who had appeared
to him. 8After that, Abram traveled south and set up camp in the hill country, with Bethel
to the west and Ai to the east. There he built another altar and dedicated it to the LORD,

12:3 Gen 22:18; 26:4 Exod 23:22 Acts 3:25 *Gal 3:8

12:4 Gen 11:26, 31

12:6 Gen 33:18; 35:4 Deut 11:30

12:7 Gen 13:15 *Gal 3:16

12:8 Gen 4:26; 8:20; 22:9

12:7 Hebrew *seed.*

12:1-3 God made a covenant with Abram (who was later called Abraham). A covenant is part promise, part contract. God promised blessings to Abraham and asked something of him. What did God promise? He promised to give Abram many descendants and much influence. What did God ask? He asked that Abram go to a certain land and live a certain way. This covenant between Abram and God is the foundation for much of the rest of the Bible. It was upon this agreement that the nation of Israel was established and the Messiah, Jesus, was foretold. It was by Jesus, a descendant of Abraham, that Abraham would be a blessing to "all the families on earth." Through Abram, God displayed the relationship that He desires to have with His creation through faith.

12:4-6 Abraham was willing to leave his extended family and set out for an unknown destination. Taking his wife, his nephew, all his livestock, and his many servants, he went south. He was able to do so because he had faith in God's promise to lead him and watch over him. The Scriptures laud this attitude of trust in Abraham, characterizing him as the father of the faithful (Romans 4:16).

12:6 The first Canaanites were descendants of Noah's grandson Canaan, son of Ham. Canaan's descendants comprised eleven groups that lived in Syria and Palestine. In time, however, the term *Canaanites* came to be attached to all the people inhabiting the land between Egypt and Asia Minor. God promised part of this land to Abram. Later, when the Israelites began to inhabit this land, God commanded them to completely destroy the Canaanites and their false religious practices and idols. Because they failed to do so, the Israelites were continually led away from God by the Canaanites, consistently neglecting the purity of worship that God asked of them.

12:7 This was the first of several altars that Abram built. This altar commemorated an important visit from God, during which God revealed that Abram had reached his destination, a land that God was planning to give to him. Abram's next altar, at Bethel, was solely for worship (12:8). He built another altar in Hebron (13:18). Abram built his last altar on Mount Moriah out of obedience, when God asked him to sacrifice his only son (22:9-14). Altars were a universal component of ancient worship. They were always raised and were most often used for animal sacrifices or to commemorate an act of God. Moses built an altar after his victory over the army of Amalek in Exodus 17:10-16. There were also altars in the Tabernacle and later the Temple, the Israelite centers of worship.

12:7-9 This was the first time God appeared to Abram, but not the last. God appeared to him again when he was 99 years old, changing Abram's name to Abraham and promising him a son (Genesis 17:1-19). God appeared once more to Abraham at noon in an oak grove, announcing the coming of Abraham's son in just a year's time (Genesis 18:1-12). Two others, possibly angels, accompanied God on this visit. God, or His messengers, appeared to many people throughout Old Testament history.

BECAUSE GOD IS FAITHFUL

I will trust Him to always keep His promises.

I will bless you . . . and you will be a blessing to others.

GENESIS 12:1-2

FOR THE NEXT *GOD IS FAITHFUL* FEATURE SEE PAGE 330.

12:9 and he worshiped the LORD. [9]Then Abram continued traveling south by stages toward the
Gen 13:1; 20:1 Negev.

ABRAM AND SARAI IN EGYPT

12:10 [10]At that time a severe famine struck the land of Canaan, forcing Abram to go down to
Gen 26:1; 42:5 Egypt, where he lived as a foreigner. [11]As he was approaching the border of Egypt, Abram
12:11 Gen 29:17 said to his wife, Sarai, "Look, you are a very beautiful woman. [12]When the Egyptians see
12:12 you, they will say, 'This is his wife. Let's kill him; then we can have her!' [13]So please tell
Gen 20:11 them you are my sister. Then they will spare my life and treat me well because of their in-
terest in you."
[14]And sure enough, when Abram arrived in Egypt, everyone spoke of Sarai's beauty.
[15]When the palace officials saw her, they sang her praises to Pharaoh, their king, and
12:16 Sarai was taken into his palace. [16]Then Pharaoh gave Abram many gifts because of
Gen 20:14; 24:35 her—sheep, goats, cattle, male and female donkeys, male and female servants, and
camels.
12:17 [17]But the LORD sent terrible plagues upon Pharaoh and his household because of Sarai,
1 Chr 16:21 Abram's wife. [18]So Pharaoh summoned Abram and accused him sharply. "What have
Ps 105:14 you done to me?" he demanded. "Why didn't you tell me she was your wife? [19]Why did
12:18 Gen 20:9-10 you say, 'She is my sister,' and allow me to take her as my wife? Now then, here is your
12:19 wife. Take her and get out of here!" [20]Pharaoh ordered some of his men to escort them,
Gen 20:5; 26:9 and he sent Abram out of the country, along with his wife and all his possessions.

ABRAM AND LOT SEPARATE

13:1 Gen 12:9 **13** So Abram left Egypt and traveled north into the Negev, along with his wife and
13:2 Lot and all that they owned. [2](Abram was very rich in livestock, silver, and
Gen 12:5 gold.) [3]From the Negev, they continued traveling by stages toward Bethel, and they
13:3 Gen 12:8-9 pitched their tents between Bethel and Ai, where they had camped before. [4]This was
the same place where Abram had built the altar, and there he worshiped the LORD
13:5 Gen 12:5 again.
[5]Lot, who was traveling with Abram, had also become very wealthy with flocks of sheep
13:6 Gen 12:5; 36:7 and goats, herds of cattle, and many tents. [6]But the land could not support both Abram

12:10-16 Did Sarai have any choice in the matter? Her husband told her to pretend she was his sister. Then the king took her into his harem. It seems clear that Sarai didn't have as much freedom as women do today. Women in the ancient world were often considered the property of their husbands; their worth was defined by their relationships with the men in their lives, as well as by their ability to work and bear children. While women today seek equal pay and equal rights, in the ancient world they were often treated more like servants than full members of a household.

▶ SPIRITUAL WARFARE

12:10-20 Consequences of disobedience. Abram's foolish plan for Sarai to present herself to the Egyptians as his sister was based on a false fear of persecution. Moreover, Abram's action tempted both his wife and Pharaoh to sin. Fear and disbelief not only lead to a multitude of problems in our life but can also drag down others. When the Lord is our trust, we can say with the psalmist: "The LORD is for me, so I will have no fear. What can mere people do to me?" (Psalm 118:6). (***See Spiritual Warfare****> Resisting Sin and Evil> Consequences> Of Disobedience> Tempt others to sin,* TopicGuide page A46.)

12:17 God stepped in to clean up the mess Abram had made for himself and others. Interestingly, God chose to exercise His sovereignty by sending a plague upon the Egyptians, prompting Pharaoh to expel Abram, Sarai, and their household. Moses clearly included this episode in Genesis so that his readers, the people of Israel, would see that just as God had brought them out of Egypt amid plagues, He had done the same centuries earlier for their great forefather. Then, of course, God took Abram back to Canaan—and the people of Israel could rest assured that God would do the same for them, just as He had promised.

13:1-2 Both Abram and Lot were wealthy men. They lived at a time when the concept of currency was still in its infancy; the few universal standards included gold, silver, and cattle. Hence, Abram's wealth could be understood wherever he traveled. In the Old Testament, wealth was also seen as a sign of God's favor. Rich men such as King David, King Solomon, and Job were held in honor. In the New Testament, however, Jesus portrayed wealth as a potential obstacle to faith instead of a byproduct of it. Jesus warned the rich that their money could keep them from the Kingdom of Heaven (Matthew 19:23).

and Lot with all their flocks and herds living so close together. 7So disputes broke out be-
tween the herdsmen of Abram and Lot. (At that time Canaanites and Perizzites were also
living in the land.)
8Finally Abram said to Lot, "Let's not allow this conflict to come between us or our herds-
men. After all, we are close relatives! 9The whole countryside is open to you. Take your
choice of any section of the land you want, and we will separate. If you want the land to
the left, then I'll take the land on the right. If you prefer the land on the right, then I'll go to
the left."
10Lot took a long look at the fertile plains of the Jordan Valley in the direction of Zoar.
The whole area was well watered everywhere, like the garden of the LORD or the beautiful
land of Egypt. (This was before the LORD destroyed Sodom and Gomorrah.) 11Lot chose for
himself the whole Jordan Valley to the east of them. He went there with his flocks and ser-
vants and parted company with his uncle Abram. 12So Abram settled in the land of Ca-
naan, and Lot moved his tents to a place near Sodom and settled among the cities of the
plain. 13But the people of this area were extremely wicked and constantly sinned against
the LORD.
14After Lot had gone, the LORD said to Abram, "Look as far as you can see in every direc-
tion—north and south, east and west. 15I am giving all this land, as far as you can see, to
you and your descendants* as a permanent possession. 16And I will give you so many de-
scendants that, like the dust of the earth, they cannot be counted! 17Go and walk through
the land in every direction, for I am giving it to you."
18So Abram moved his camp to Hebron and settled near the oak grove belonging to
Mamre. There he built another altar to the LORD.

ABRAM RESCUES LOT

14 About this time war broke out in the region. King Amraphel of Babylonia,* King
Arioch of Ellasar, King Kedorlaomer of Elam, and King Tidal of Goiim 2fought
against King Bera of Sodom, King Birsha of Gomorrah, King Shinab of Admah, King Shem-
eber of Zeboiim, and the king of Bela (also called Zoar).

13:15 Hebrew *seed;* also in 13:16. 14:1 Hebrew *Shinar;* also in 14:9.

13:7 Gen 12:6; 26:20
13:8 Prov 15:18; 20:3
13:9 Gen 20:15
13:10 Gen 2:8-10
13:13 Gen 18:20; Num 32:23; Isa 1:10; 3:9; 2 Pet 2:8
13:14 Gen 28:14; Deut 3:27; 34:1-4
13:15 *Gal 3:16; Gen 12:2, 7; 15:18; 17:7-8
13:16 Num 23:10
13:17 Num 13:17-25
13:18 Gen 14:13; 18:1
14:1 Gen 10:10; 11:2
14:2 Gen 10:19; 13:10; Deut 29:23

▸ HOLINESS
13:9 God provides by extending grace to us. Abram's offer to let Lot take any section of the land demonstrated Abram's giving character. Paul reminds us that God, too, has a giving character: "Since He did not spare even His own Son but gave Him up for us all, won't He also give us everything else?" (Romans 8:32). What are you facing today? If God has given us Christ, then certainly He will "give us everything else" pertaining to life and godliness. Like Lot, who accepted Abram's offer, you must take hold of God's promises. (***See Holiness****> Changed by God> God provides,* TopicGuide page A41.)

13:13 This description is reminiscent of the people on earth just before the Flood. Genesis 6:5 says that "the LORD observed the extent of human wickedness on the earth, and He saw that everything they thought or imagined was consistently and totally evil." We don't know how many years it took after the Flood for people to repopulate the earth and return to corruption, but we know that throughout human history, people have gone through times of turning away from and then turning back to God. The Israelites followed a consistent cycle of living in disobedience until they began to self-destruct, then turning back to God, then falling into disobedience again. The Old Testament displays this cycle from the time of Noah to the time of the Israelite exile.

13:14-15 It was for this promise that Abram first left his homeland and all his relatives (12:1-7). The land became the greatest possession and hope of Abram's descendants. Abram settled in it, as did his son Isaac and Isaac's son, Israel. However, Israel left the land because of famine, and about 400 years passed before God brought the nation of Israel back to reclaim it. God's promise to Abram laid the foundation for many hopes and many conflicts over the land of Israel even to this day.

13:16 When God first promised descendants to Abram, it may have seemed like an impossible dream because Abram and his wife were both beyond normal childbearing years. Their childlessness was probably a source of shame for Abram, for an inheritance—a child to carry on his legacy—was of the utmost importance to every man of the ancient Near East. But even though it seemed impossible, Abram believed God, and God fulfilled His promise. When the family of Abram's grandson Israel (Jacob) entered Egypt during the famine, they numbered only 70. When they returned from Egypt to reclaim their land, they numbered more than 2 million. God's promise to Abram had been fulfilled.

14:3 Num 34:3, 12; Deut 3:17; Josh 3:16
14:5 Gen 15:20; Deut 2:10, 20; 3:11; Josh 13:19
14:7 Gen 16:14; 20:1; Num 13:26; Deut 1:4; 2 Chr 20:2
14:12 Gen 11:27
14:13 Gen 10:16; 13:18; 39:14
14:14 Gen 12:5; Deut 34:1
14:15 Gen 15:2
14:17 2 Sam 18:18
14:18 Pss 76:2; 110:4; Heb 5:6, 10; 7:1
14:19 Gen 27:25; 48:9; Mark 10:16

3This second group of kings joined forces in Siddim Valley (that is, the valley of the
Dead Sea*). 4For twelve years they had been subject to King Kedorlaomer, but in the
thirteenth year they rebelled against him.
5One year later Kedorlaomer and his allies arrived and defeated the Rephaites at
Ashteroth-karnaim, the Zuzites at Ham, the Emites at Shaveh-kiriathaim, 6and the
Horites at Mount Seir, as far as El-paran at the edge of the wilderness. 7Then they
turned back and came to En-mishpat (now called Kadesh) and conquered all the
territory of the Amalekites, and also the Amorites living in Hazazon-tamar.
8Then the rebel kings of Sodom, Gomorrah, Admah, Zeboiim, and Bela (also
called Zoar) prepared for battle in the valley of the Dead Sea.* 9They fought
against King Kedorlaomer of Elam, King Tidal of Goiim, King Amraphel of Babylo-
nia, and King Arioch of Ellasar—four kings against five. 10As it happened, the val-
ley of the Dead Sea was filled with tar pits. And as the army of the kings of Sodom
and Gomorrah fled, some fell into the tar pits, while the rest escaped into the
mountains. 11The victorious invaders then plundered Sodom and Gomorrah and
headed for home, taking with them all the spoils of war and the food supplies.
12They also captured Lot—Abram's nephew who lived in Sodom—and carried off
everything he owned.
13But one of Lot's men escaped and reported everything to Abram the Hebrew, who
was living near the oak grove belonging to Mamre the Amorite. Mamre and his relatives,
Eshcol and Aner, were Abram's allies.
14When Abram heard that his nephew Lot had been captured, he mobilized the
318 trained men who had been born into his household. Then he pursued Kedorlao-
mer's army until he caught up with them at Dan. 15There he divided his men and at-
tacked during the night. Kedorlaomer's army fled, but Abram chased them as far as
Hobah, north of Damascus. 16Abram recovered all the goods that had been taken, and
he brought back his nephew Lot with his possessions and all the women and other
captives.

MELCHIZEDEK BLESSES ABRAM

17After Abram returned from his victory over Kedorlaomer and all his allies, the king of
Sodom went out to meet him in the valley of Shaveh (that is, the King's Valley).
18And Melchizedek, the king of Salem and a priest of God Most High,* brought Abram
some bread and wine. 19Melchizedek blessed Abram with this blessing:

14:3 Hebrew *Salt Sea.* 14:8 Hebrew *Siddim Valley* (see 14:3); also in 14:10. 14:18 Hebrew *El-Elyon;* also in 14:19, 20, 22.

14:13 This is the first time the Bible uses the term *Hebrew.* The term may derive from the name *Eber,* one of Noah's grandsons (Genesis 10:21). It may also be a corruption of the Egyptian word *shazu* or wanderer. Later, God changed the name of Abram's grandson Jacob to *Israel,* and Israel's descendants came to be called *Israelites,* or the nation of Israel (Genesis 46:8). Still later, after the nation had split into the kingdoms of Israel and Judah and both were sent into exile, the people began to be known as *Jews,* short for Judeans (Ezra 4:12). Today, these three terms—*Hebrews, Israelites,* and *Jews*—are used almost interchangeably to refer to the descendants of Abraham and Israel.

14:13-16 Abram heard of Lot's capture while he was camped near Hebron in southern Canaan. Abram gathered 318 of his own men to pursue the invaders, and Aner, Eshcol, and Mamre, all brothers, helped him as allies in the conflict. Abram showed prowess as a military leader by attacking at night and from different directions. His good standing in the community and his ability to build relationships with his neighbors also contributed to the victory. But the most important factor was the assistance of God, who enabled Abraham and his small band of amateur soldiers to overcome a powerful king and his mighty army.

14:18 Melchizedek was the king of Salem, the city that many believe became Jerusalem, and "a priest of God Most High." Abram recognized Melchizedek as his spiritual superior by accepting his blessing. Little is known about Melchizedek; in fact, he is mentioned in only three places in the Bible. In Psalm 110:4, David compares the coming Christ to the ancient priest-king. The writer of the book of Hebrews describes Christ as superior to the first high priest, Aaron, just as Melchizedek was superior to Abraham. Some believe that Melchizedek was a rare pre-Incarnation appearance of Jesus Christ.

"Blessed be Abram by God Most High,
Creator of heaven and earth.
20 And blessed be God Most High,
who has defeated your enemies for you."

Then Abram gave Melchizedek a tenth of all the goods he had recovered.
21 The king of Sodom said to Abram, "Give back my people who were captured. But
you may keep for yourself all the goods you have recovered."
22 Abram replied to the king of Sodom, "I solemnly swear to the LORD, God Most High,
Creator of heaven and earth, 23 that I will not take so much as a single thread or sandal
thong from what belongs to you. Otherwise you might say, 'I am the one who made
Abram rich.' 24 I will accept only what my young warriors have already eaten, and I
request that you give a fair share of the goods to my allies—Aner, Eshcol, and
Mamre."

14:20 Gen 9:26; 24:27 *Heb 7:1-2
14:22 Gen 1:1
14:23 2 Kgs 5:16
14:24 Gen 14:13

14:19-20 Melchizedek had come to faith in God in the midst of a culture that worshiped many gods. That faith may have come from a direct encounter with God such as Abram experienced in Genesis 12:1-4 or Moses experienced in Exodus 3:2-4. On the other hand, Melchizedek may have been taught about God through oral tradition passed down from Noah. However he arrived at his belief system, Melchizedek clearly believed that there was one true, living God who had nothing to do with the system of idolatry that was rampant in Canaan. Melchizedek blessed this one true God and invoked a blessing from Him for Abram.

▸ **GOD**
14:20 God's names: God Most High. This is the first appearance in the Bible of the name *God Most High* (*El-Elyon*). It signifies God's kingship over the cosmos. The Bible shows that throughout history, God Most High reduces kings and raises them up again. He demonstrates absolute power over all earthly authorities. Clearly, God Most High can do as He pleases in your life. Acknowledge God Most High and praise Him for His supreme power. (***See God***> *God's Names*> *God,* TopicGuide page A18.)

14:20 This is the first record of a payment of a tithe (tenth). However, the concept of tithing already was widespread. A tenth was often considered the appropriate amount to pay as tribute to a ruler or to give for a religious obligation. Ancient Babylon, Persia, Arabia, Egypt, Rome, and China all practiced this custom. Once the nation of Israel was established, God gave guidelines to Moses for the combination of tithes and offerings to support their state and religious affairs (Deuteronomy 14:22-29). The obligation of God's people to obey God's financial laws was such that the prophet Malachi could declare that failure to tithe was the equivalent of robbing God (Malachi 3:8-10).

14:21-24 The king of Sodom offered to let Abram keep *all* of the plunder that Kederlaomer and his army had taken from Sodom. But Abram refused to take *any* of it, except for the provisions his men had already eaten (though he did ask that his Canaanite allies be given a share). Abram said he had sworn an oath to take none of the plunder because he did not wish for the king of the wicked city of Sodom to be able to say he had contributed to Abram's prosperity. Abram's desire to dissociate himself from the wickedness of the Canaanites stands in strong contrast to Lot's willingness to live near and even in Sodom.

BECAUSE GOD IS SOVEREIGN

I will joyfully submit to His will.

Blessed be Abram by God Most High, Creator of heaven and earth.

GENESIS 14:19

FOR THE NEXT *GOD IS SOVEREIGN* FEATURE SEE PAGE 321.

GOD IS ALL-POWERFUL

WITH A SINGLE UTTERANCE, God spoke the universe into being—a universe that astronomers estimate contains more than 100 billion galaxies. But all of the power contained within this universe—the combined energy of every star, storm, wind, ocean wave, and atom—does not equal even a fraction of God's almighty power. He is not restrained or inhibited by any of His created beings. People and nations are powerless when confronted by His might.

For some people, the idea that God is all-powerful is little comfort, because they are skeptical about His willingness to get intimately involved in their affairs. They assume we must live by luck or by good breaks produced by our own hard work and cleverness.

However, when we look at the universe, we see order and design. Everything has its place, its purpose. God's Word confirms that He has a design for this world and for every person in it: "I have a plan for the whole earth, a hand of judgment upon all the nations" (Isaiah 14:26).

Such unlimited power would be terrifying if God were a tyrant who meted out His power indiscriminately. Fortunately, the Bible says God acts out of love and righteousness. Simply put, God cares for us. No matter what you might be facing, God can help you. Nothing is too hard for Him. There is no need too great for Him to meet. There is no problem too complicated for Him to solve. There is no foe too strong for Him to conquer. There is no prayer too difficult for Him to answer.

Some of us may question why God does not answer our prayers when and in the way that we ask. But God is not a genie or Santa Claus; He does not give us everything we want just the way we want it. We must remember that, in addition to His power, God has perfect knowledge. He alone knows everything, so He knows what we need far better than we do.

No matter what happens anywhere in the world at any moment, God is in control. This is a comforting truth. Would you like to live in a world where everyone could do whatever he or she wanted? Can you imagine the chaos? While it might seem at times that this world is chaotic and out of control, God knows what is in the future. He is not the author of evil and suffering, and neither is He responsible for the consequences of humankind's sins.

God is seeking faithful servants to be channels of His incredible power. The Bible is full of instances in which God did extraordinary miracles through His servants. Although we feel weak at times, through the power of the name of Jesus Christ and through faith in our almighty and powerful God, we can stand firm and say no to temptation. We can quit any habit or addiction. We can speak up to tell the truth at any time.

If we really believe that God is all-powerful, we will no longer walk in fear and unbelief. Like Abram, we will place our faith in God—not necessarily *great faith* in God, but faith in a *great God,* who is omnipotent. In turn, He will lead us into a life full of adventure and purpose. There is no better way to live!

THE LORD'S COVENANT PROMISE TO ABRAM

15 Some time later, the LORD spoke to Abram in a vision and said to him, "Do not be
afraid, Abram, for I will protect you, and your reward will be great."
2But Abram replied, "O Sovereign LORD, what good are all Your blessings when I don't
even have a son? Since You've given me no children, Eliezer of Damascus, a servant in my
household, will inherit all my wealth. 3You have given me no descendants of my own, so
one of my servants will be my heir."
4Then the LORD said to him, "No, your servant will not be your heir, for you will have a
son of your own who will be your heir." 5Then the LORD took Abram outside and said to
him, "Look up into the sky and count the stars if you can. That's how many descendants
you will have!"
6And Abram believed the LORD, and the LORD counted him as righteous because of his
faith.
7Then the LORD told him, "I am the LORD who brought you out of Ur of the Chaldeans to
give you this land as your possession."
8But Abram replied, "O Sovereign LORD, how can I be sure that I will actually possess it?"

15:1 Gen 21:17; 26:24 Num 12:6 Deut 33:29 Ps 3:3

15:4 *Gal 4:28

15:5 Gen 12:2; 22:17; 32:13 *Rom 4:18

15:6 Ps 106:31 *Rom 4:3, 9, 22 *Gal 3:6

15:7 Gen 12:1; 13:17 Acts 7:2-4

15:8 Luke 1:18

▸GOD

15:2 God's names: Sovereign LORD. Abram cries, "O Sovereign LORD" (*Adonai Yahweh*), thus recognizing his submission to God's will in his life. Are you fully submitted to God's sovereign will? Jesus said: "If any of you wants to be My follower, you must turn from your selfish ways, take up your cross, and follow Me" (Mark 8:34). Do not place personal desire ahead of God's will. Like Abram, submit your life to God, and He will bless you beyond your greatest hopes. (***See God****> God's Names> God,* TopicGuide page A18.)

15:2-3 God's promise of blessing could not dispel a painful problem that was troubling Abram: He had no family to whom he could leave God's blessings. There were many ancient customs and laws regarding inheritance. A man's children and land were his wealth. Usually the firstborn son received the birthright, a double share of the inheritance. The rest was divided among the other sons, or, in their absence, the daughters. To be childless was a desolate condition, because there was no way to keep land in the family. Since Abram had no children, he could only leave his inheritance to a servant.

15:4-8 God assured Abram that he need not worry—he would father a son before he died. And from that one child would come a nation of people who would be like the stars of the sky in number, too numerous to court. This was an awesome promise, yet Abram was able to trust God to do as He said. But then God reminded Abram that He had brought him out of Ur in order to give him the land of Canaan. Believing God for this promise may have been an even greater challenge for Abram, for the land was large and filled with Canaanites. So Abram asked for a sign to bolster his faith, a sign God was pleased to give.

▸SALVATION

15:6 New creation. Righteousness is sometimes defined as "right standing with God." God considers you right with Him on the basis of faith. Abram was an Old Testament illustration of this exciting truth, which was not fully revealed until Jesus came some 2,000 years later. Consequently, the principles of salvation are the same throughout the Old and New Testaments. You are made right in God's sight when God's righteousness is freely given to you in response to your faith in God's only Son, Jesus Christ (see Romans 3:27-28 and Hebrews 11:7). (***See Salvation****> Receiving> When,* TopicGuide page A22.)

BECAUSE GOD IS RIGHTEOUS

I will live by His standards.

And Abram believed the LORD, and the LORD counted him as righteous because of his faith.

GENESIS 15:6

FOR THE NEXT *GOD IS RIGHTEOUS* FEATURE SEE PAGE 373.

COVENANTS

Covenants may be described either as events, such as a ceremony in which a covenant is sworn between two parties, or as relationships, such as the ongoing relationship between God and His people. Many different covenants punctuate Old Testament history. These covenants generally follow the pattern of Ancient Near-Eastern treaties between great empires and their servant nations. They were typically made between God as the Great King and an individual human leader who represented the servant nation. Covenants bound both parties to certain behaviors. The Great King promised blessings and benevolence in return for the obedience of the servant nation, and threatened punishment should the servant nation rebel. In the New Testament, Jesus became the Servant King over the nation of Israel.

Covenant	Requirements	Blessings & Curses
Covenant with Adam as the head of humanity (Genesis 1:28-30; 2:15-17)	Work and keep the Garden of Eden, minister to the Lord therein, and refrain from eating of the Tree of the Knowledge of Good and Evil. Multiply and take dominion over the earth.	Obedience would bring humanity's rule over the earth as God's vice-regents. Disobedience would result in the death of the entire human race.
Covenant with Noah as the head of humanity (Genesis 6:18-22; 9:1-17)	Observe and maintain God's moral requirements, including multiplying and taking dominion over the earth.	Blessing of global stability so that life and multiplication could continue. Disobedience would result in death.
Covenant with Abraham as the head of Israel (Genesis 15:9-21; 17:1-27)	Serve God faithfully and blamelessly, and maintain the practice of circumcision in order to multiply and take dominion over the earth.	Obedience would bring blessings to all nations through Abraham's many descendants and inheritance of the Promised Land. The disobedient would fall under God's judgment.
Covenant with Israel through the mediation of Moses (Exodus 19–24)	Keep the whole Mosaic Law, including the command to inhabit the Promised Land and extend God's kingdom to the ends of the earth.	Obedience would be blessed with long, prosperous life in the Promised Land. Disobedience would bring many curses, culminating in exile.
Covenant with David as the head of Israel (2 Samuel 7; Psalms 89; 132)	The nation and its Davidic kings were to keep the whole Mosaic Law. The kings were to be especially faithful to God.	Obedience would provide godly leadership to the nation, resulting in prosperity and the expansion of the kingdom to the whole earth. Disobedience would bring exile.
New Covenant, made with Jesus as the head of Israel (Isaiah 54:10; Jeremiah 31:31-34; Ezekiel 34:25; 37:26; Hebrews 8:6-13)	Perfect obedience to God's law, and the perfect fulfillment of all His prior requirements. Attainable only through the obedience of Christ.	The obedience of Christ results in eternal life of dominion over the new earth for the faithful. Disobedience of unbelievers is punished by eternal condemnation in hell.

[9]The LORD told him, "Bring Me a three-year-old heifer, a three-year-old female
goat, a three-year-old ram, a turtledove, and a young pigeon." [10]So Abram presented
all these to Him and killed them. Then he cut each animal down the middle and laid
the halves side by side; he did not, however, cut the birds in half. [11]Some vultures
swooped down to eat the carcasses, but Abram chased them away.

[12]As the sun was going down, Abram fell into a deep sleep, and a terrifying darkness
came down over him. [13]Then the LORD said to Abram, "You can be sure that your descen-
dants will be strangers in a foreign land, where they will be oppressed as slaves for
400 years. [14]But I will punish the nation that enslaves them, and in the end they will come
away with great wealth. [15](As for you, you will die in peace and be buried at a ripe old
age.) [16]After four generations your descendants will return here to this land, for the sins of
the Amorites do not yet warrant their destruction."

[17]After the sun went down and darkness fell, Abram saw a smoking firepot and a flam-
ing torch pass between the halves of the carcasses. [18]So the LORD made a covenant with
Abram that day and said, "I have given this land to your descendants, all the way from
the border of Egypt* to the great Euphrates River—[19]the land now occupied by the Ke-
nites, Kenizzites, Kadmonites, [20]Hittites, Perizzites, Rephaites, [21]Amorites, Canaanites,
Girgashites, and Jebusites."

15:9 Lev 1:14
15:10 Lev 1:17
15:12 Gen 2:21; 28:11
15:13 Exod 12:40; *Acts 7:6; Gal 3:17
15:14 Exod 6:5
15:15 Gen 25:8
15:16 Exod 12:40
15:17 Jer 34:18-19
15:18 Num 34:1-15; Deut 1:7-8
15:19 Num 24:21
15:21 Gen 10:15-16

THE BIRTH OF ISHMAEL

16 Now Sarai, Abram's wife, had not been able to bear children for him. But she had
an Egyptian servant named Hagar. [2]So Sarai said to Abram, "The LORD has pre-
vented me from having children. Go and sleep with my servant. Perhaps I can have chil-
dren through her." And Abram agreed with Sarai's proposal. [3]So Sarai, Abram's wife, took
Hagar the Egyptian servant and gave her to Abram as a wife. (This happened ten years af-
ter Abram had settled in the land of Canaan.)

[4]So Abram had sexual relations with Hagar, and she became pregnant. But when
Hagar knew she was pregnant, she began to treat her mistress, Sarai, with contempt.
[5]Then Sarai said to Abram, "This is all your fault! I put my servant into your arms, but now
that she's pregnant she treats me with contempt. The LORD will show who's wrong—you
or me!"

16:1 Gen 11:30; Gal 4:24-25
16:2 Gen 30:3
16:3 Gen 12:4-5
16:4 Gen 16:15
16:5 Gen 31:53

15:18 Hebrew *the river of Egypt,* referring either to an eastern branch of the Nile River or to the Brook of Egypt in the Sinai (see Num 34:5).

15:9-11, 17 Abram's vision was filled with powerful images—sacrificed animals, a torch, a firepot or oven. In the ancient world, these were meaningful symbols that revealed God's power to cleanse and to judge. They were also symbols of the sacred nature of God's covenant with Abram. While we cannot fully understand every nuance of the vision, we know that similar ceremonies in the Ancient Near East communicated the intent of participants to be torn apart (as the animals were) if they did not keep their covenant obligations. This part of the vision increased Abram's belief that God would do what He had promised, since God would sooner die than break His word.

15:13-16 God's words to Abram did become reality. The families of his son, Isaac, and his grandson, Israel, settled in the land that God had promised. But because of a famine, Israel's family moved to Egypt, where they grew into a nation of people (Genesis 37–41). They grew so mighty in number that the king of Egypt became afraid of them and enslaved them. After 400 years in Egypt, God used Moses to lead His people, the nation of Israel, back again to the land that God had promised their ancestor Abram (Exodus 6–12).

16:1-3 In Genesis 15:1-7, God promised Abram an heir and descendants more numerous than the stars in the sky. Abram believed God. Because of that early faith, it is disappointing that Abram was willing to take part in Sarai's scheme to make God's promise come true in her own way. Not only did Sarai's plan bring tension to the family, it confused the issue of God's provision and initiated a family rivalry that has affected Abram's descendants throughout their history. The New Testament writer, Paul, wrote about Sarai's (Sarah's) mistake in Galatians 4:21-29.

16:2 Fertility was of major importance in the ancient world. In agrarian cultures, it was a great shame and practical hardship for a woman to be unable to bear children, particularly sons. Because of this, it was an accepted practice for a woman to have her maidservant sleep with her husband. Any child conceived by such a liaison was considered an heir of the husband and wife. But while this form of adoption was a common practice, it was also an act of distrust and impatience in this case. God had promised a son through Sarai and Abram. In the end, He delivered that son just as He had said He would.

6 Abram replied, "Look, she is your servant, so deal with her as you see fit." Then Sarai
treated Hagar so harshly that she finally ran away.
7 The angel of the LORD found Hagar beside a spring of water in the wilderness, along
the road to Shur. 8 The angel said to her, "Hagar, Sarai's servant, where have you come
from, and where are you going?"
"I'm running away from my mistress, Sarai," she replied.
9 The angel of the LORD said to her, "Return to your mistress, and submit to her author-
ity." 10 Then he added, "I will give you more descendants than you can count."
11 And the angel also said, "You are now pregnant and will give birth to a son. You are
to name him Ishmael (which means 'God hears'), for the LORD has heard your cry of dis-
tress. 12 This son of yours will be a wild man, as untamed as a wild donkey! He will raise
his fist against everyone, and everyone will be against him. Yes, he will live in open hos-
tility against all his relatives."
13 Thereafter, Hagar used another name to refer to the LORD, who had spoken
to her. She said, "You are the God who sees me."* She also said, "Have I truly seen
the One who sees me?" 14 So that well was named Beer-lahai-roi (which means
"well of the Living One who sees me"). It can still be found between Kadesh and
Bered.
15 So Hagar gave Abram a son, and Abram named him Ishmael. 16 Abram was eighty-six
years old when Ishmael was born.

ABRAM IS NAMED ABRAHAM

17 When Abram was ninety-nine years old, the LORD appeared to him and said,
"I am El-Shaddai—'God Almighty.' Serve Me faithfully and live a blameless life.
2 I will make a covenant with you, by which I will guarantee to give you countless descen-
dants."
3 At this, Abram fell face down on the ground. Then God said to him, 4 "This is My

16:7 Gen 21:17; 22:11, 15
16:8 Gen 3:9; 4:9
16:9 Gen 21:12; Eph 6:5; Titus 2:9
16:10 Gen 17:20
16:11 Gen 16:15; Exod 3:7-8
16:12 Job 39:5-8
16:13 Gen 32:30
16:14 Gen 14:7
16:15 Gen 21:9; 25:12
16:16 Gen 12:4; 16:3
17:1 Gen 12:7; 28:3; 35:11; 48:3; Deut 18:13; Matt 5:48
17:2 Gen 12:2; 15:18

16:13 Hebrew *El-roi.*

▸PURPOSE

16:7 Use of angelic agents. The angel found Hagar beside a desert spring. Sarai's mistreatment of Hagar caused the maidservant to try to flee to her home in Egypt. But God pursued and comforted Hagar. The spring is a sign of life in the wilderness and symbolizes hope in the midst of suffering. Regardless of any injustice we may experience, God's comforting hand is with us. His presence in the midst of trouble is like a spring in a dry, barren desert. We may run away from our problems, but we can never run away from God. (***See Purpose**> God's Deeds> Manifestations,* TopicGuide page A54.)

16:10-12 The angel's promise to Hagar was very similar to the promise God had made to Abram—many descendants. Descendants were often considered the true wealth of a person. The angel's promise came true in the life of Ishmael—he had 12 sons, just as Isaac did. Although Ishmael lived a nomadic life, he remained connected with Abram's family and took part in Abram's burial. Arab nations of today claim roots in Ishmael. While Ishmael was not the child God had promised to Abram, God did not forsake him.

16:14 Hagar's story is a description of God's compassion. Both the name that the angel gave to the child—Ishmael, or "God hears"—and the name that Hagar gave to the spring— "well of the Living One who sees me"—are suggestive of a redeeming experience with God in a time of need. Hagar's encounter with God reminds us that He honors His promises even when His people make messes of their lives. Her story shows that although God was focused on His relationship with Abram and his descendants, His compassion was big enough to encompass others as well.

▸GOD

17:1 God's names: God Almighty. God appeared to Abram, revealing Himself as *El Shaddai*, which is translated "Almighty God" or "God Almighty." This name of God is associated with His covenant promises relating to offspring, as seen in the lives of Abram and Sarai. Abram was 99 and Sarai was 90 when God renewed this promise of numerous descendants; it had been 24 years since God called Abram from Ur and promised to make him the father of nations. Now he and Sarai were 24 years further past their childbearing years. Nothing short of a miracle would allow them to produce a child at this point. Abram actually laughed at the thought of such an old couple having children (Genesis 17:17), but God proved Himself faithful to His promise. No matter how impossible your situation may appear, God is able to provide for your needs. Cling to the God who keeps His promises, and He will bring them to pass. (***See God**> God's Names> God,* TopicGuide page A18.)

covenant with you: I will make you the father of a multitude of nations! 5What's more, I
am changing your name. It will no longer be Abram. Instead, you will be called Abraham,*
for you will be the father of many nations. 6I will make you extremely fruitful. Your de-
scendants will become many nations, and kings will be among them!
7"I will confirm My covenant with you and your descendants* after you, from genera-
tion to generation. This is the everlasting covenant: I will always be your God and the God
of your descendants after you. 8And I will give the entire land of Canaan, where you now
live as a foreigner, to you and your descendants. It will be their possession forever, and I
will be their God."

17:5 Neh 9:7 *Rom 4:17
17:6 Gen 35:11
17:7 Gen 15:18 Lev 11:45; 26:12 Ps 105:8-11 *Gal 3:16
17:9 Exod 19:5
17:10 John 7:22 Acts 7:8
17:11 Exod 12:48 Deut 10:16 Josh 5:2
17:12 Gen 21:4 Lev 12:3 Luke 1:59; 2:21
17:14 Exod 30:33 Lev 7:20

THE MARK OF THE COVENANT

9Then God said to Abraham, "Your responsibility is to obey the terms of the covenant.
You and all your descendants have this continual responsibility. 10This is the covenant
that you and your descendants must keep: Each male among you must be circum-
cised. 11You must cut off the flesh of your foreskin as a sign of the covenant between
Me and you. 12From generation to generation, every male child must be circumcised
on the eighth day after his birth. This applies not only to members of your family but
also to the servants born in your household and the foreign-born servants whom you
have purchased. 13All must be circumcised. Your bodies will bear the mark of My ever-
lasting covenant. 14Any male who fails to be circumcised will be cut off from the cov-
enant family for breaking the covenant."

17:5 *Abram* means "exalted father"; *Abraham* sounds like a Hebrew term that means "father of many." 17:7 Hebrew *seed;* also in 17:7b, 8, 9, 10, 19.

17:2-8 God first revealed Himself to Abram in Genesis 12, promising to bless him with countless descendants, even though Abram was already an old man. Then, in Genesis 15, God repeated His promises and formalized His relationship with Abram by making a covenant. Here, God reiterated His promises and reaffirmed His covenant with Abram, changing his name to *Abraham* as a sign. The covenant included God's promise of family, security, and heritage, and Abraham's responsibility of faith, obedience, and purity.

17:4, 6 God's promise to Abraham was fulfilled through his grandson, Jacob, who became the father of the nation of Israel. But the promise was also fulfilled in a spiritual sense. Christians are the spiritual descendants of Abraham. Just as Abraham was declared righteous through his faith in God's promises, so also God declares us righteous on the basis of faith in Jesus Christ. Thus, the people of God are not just those who are of Abraham's bloodline. Everyone who comes to God through faith is a child of Abraham and a fulfillment of God's promise to him.

17:5 Names held great significance in the ancient Hebrew culture. God changed the name *Abram,* which means "exalted father," to *Abraham,* or "father of many," to reflect His promise to Abraham. Likewise, He changed Abraham's wife's name from *Sarai* to *Sarah,* which means "princess." While more subtle, this name change also reflected God's promise to enlarge the couple's legacy. When Abraham and Sarah had a son, they named him *Isaac,* or "he laughs," commemorating Abraham's and Sarah's responses to God's promise (Genesis 17:17; 18:12).

▸GOD

17:7-8 God's covenant of grace. God's relationship with you is everlasting because He is faithful to His Word and never changes. This language stems from legal language in ancient Israel, which guaranteed that at the death of a landowner the land would be passed down to the next generation. Likewise, at the heart of the New Covenant is God's guarantee to provide you, and your believing children after you, eternal life in Christ as it is received by faith (John 3:16; 10:10). God is not a God of the past but is a God of the future, committed to seeing future generations rejoice in Him. (***See God****> Relationship> God's desire> God's covenants,* TopicGuide page A14.)

▸BIBLE

17:10-11 Message of salvation. God's covenant with Abraham required each male to undergo circumcision, which was God's appointed sign that signified a person's absolute commitment to the Lord. Today, believers are no longer required to keep the ceremonial laws of ancient Israel. However, the New Testament teaches that all God's people are to have circumcised *hearts.* What is a circumcised heart? It is "faith expressing itself in love" (Galatians 5:6). You evidence a circumcised heart when you practice faith in God and love for your neighbor. These activities are enhanced when you consistently pray and study God's Word. (***See Bible****> Unity> Salvation,* TopicGuide page A11.)

17:10-14 Circumcision was practiced by other ancient cultures besides the Hebrews. What set Hebrew circumcision apart was the fact that it was done to infants as the mark of inclusion in God's everlasting covenant. While other cultures practiced circumcision as a rite of passage at puberty, the Israelites used it to identify themselves as God's chosen people.

SARAI IS NAMED SARAH

17:15 Gen 17:5 15Then God said to Abraham, "Regarding Sarai, your wife—her name will no longer be Sa-
17:16 Gen 18:10 rai. From now on her name will be Sarah.* 16And I will bless her and give you a son from
her! Yes, I will bless her richly, and she will become the mother of many nations. Kings of
nations will be among her descendants."
17:17 Gen 17:3; 18:11-13 17Then Abraham bowed down to the ground, but he laughed to himself in disbelief.
"How could I become a father at the age of 100?" he thought. "And how can Sarah have a
baby when she is ninety years old?" 18So Abraham said to God, "May Ishmael live under
Your special blessing!"
17:19 Gen 21:2; 26:2-5 19But God replied, "No—Sarah, your wife, will give birth to a son for you. You will name
him Isaac,* and I will confirm My covenant with him and his descendants as an everlasting
17:20 Gen 25:12-16 covenant. 20As for Ishmael, I will bless him also, just as you have asked. I will make him
17:21 Gen 18:10, 14 extremely fruitful and multiply his descendants. He will become the father of twelve
princes, and I will make him a great nation. 21But My covenant will be confirmed with
17:22 Gen 18:33; 35:13 Isaac, who will be born to you and Sarah about this time next year." 22When God had fin-
ished speaking, he left Abraham.
17:23 Gen 14:14 23On that very day Abraham took his son, Ishmael, and every male in his household, in-
17:24 Rom 4:11 cluding those born there and those he had bought. Then he circumcised them, cutting off
their foreskins, just as God had told him. 24Abraham was ninety-nine years old when he
17:25 Gen 16:16 was circumcised, 25and Ishmael, his son, was thirteen. 26Both Abraham and his son, Ish-
mael, were circumcised on that same day, 27along with all the other men and boys of the
household, whether they were born there or bought as servants. All were circumcised with
him.

A SON IS PROMISED TO SARAH

18:1 Gen 12:7; 13:18 **18** The LORD appeared again to Abraham near the oak grove belonging to Mamre.
One day Abraham was sitting at the entrance to his tent during the hottest part of
18:2 Gen 32:24 Josh 5:13 Judg 13:6-11 the day. 2He looked up and noticed three men standing nearby. When he saw them, he
ran to meet them and welcomed them, bowing low to the ground.
3"My lord," he said, "if it pleases You, stop here for a while. 4Rest in the shade of this tree
18:4 Gen 19:2; 24:32 while water is brought to wash Your feet. 5And since You've honored Your servant with
18:5 Judg 6:18-19; 13:15-16 this visit, let me prepare some food to refresh You before You continue on Your journey."
"All right," they said. "Do as you have said."
6So Abraham ran back to the tent and said to Sarah, "Hurry! Get three large measures*
of your best flour, knead it into dough, and bake some bread." 7Then Abraham ran out to

17:15 *Sarai* and *Sarah* both mean "princess." 17:19 *Isaac* means "he laughs." 18:6 Hebrew *3 seahs,* about 15 quarts or 18 liters.

17:20 Ishmael received a blessing, even though Isaac was the son of God's promise. Ishmael's blessing paralleled Isaac's; 12 princes were among his descendants, just as Isaac's 12 grandsons became the 12 tribes of Israel. The Ishmaelites, as Ishmael's descendants were called, settled in the deserts of northern Arabia. They were nomadic, famous for their skill with the bow. Eventually, the term *Ishmaelite* became a description for all of the nomadic people in the area. When Joseph's brothers sold him into slavery, it was Ishmaelite traders who carried him to Egypt.

▸ PURPOSE
18:1 Appearances of God. The Lord appeared again to Abraham, and Abraham responded in worship. In the Old Testament, God sometimes appeared visibly to people. Today, He is most fully present in the hearts of His people. Paul writes, "And this is the secret: Christ lives in you. This gives you assurance of sharing his glory" (Colossians 1:27). Because God lives within you, every day of your life should be an act of heartfelt devotion. The secret to a happy, fulfilled Christian walk is to keep Christ on the throne of your life by worshiping Him with all of your heart, soul, mind, and strength. (***See Purpose****> God's Deeds> Manifestations,* TopicGuide page A54.)

18:2-5 Abraham's hospitality was typical of the time. In fact, our modern wariness toward strangers would have been considered rude in the ancient Middle East. In that culture, if strangers came needing food or drink, a host was obliged to meet their need. But God's visit to Abraham was no imposition of obligation. Rather, it was a precious act of intimacy, as He allowed Abraham to serve Him and show Him kindness. God shared a meal with Abraham instead of appearing to him in a vision or speaking to him through a prophet.

the herd and chose a tender calf and gave it to his servant, who quickly prepared it. 8When the food was ready, Abraham took some yogurt and milk and the roasted meat, and he served it to the men. As they ate, Abraham waited on them in the shade of the trees.

9"Where is Sarah, your wife?" the visitors asked.

"She's inside the tent," Abraham replied.

10Then one of them said, "I will return to you about this time next year, and your wife, Sarah, will have a son!"

Sarah was listening to this conversation from the tent. 11Abraham and Sarah were both very old by this time, and Sarah was long past the age of having children. 12So she laughed silently to herself and said, "How could a worn-out woman like me enjoy such pleasure, especially when my master—my husband—is also so old?"

13Then the LORD said to Abraham, "Why did Sarah laugh? Why did she say, 'Can an old woman like me have a baby?' 14Is anything too hard for the LORD? I will return about this time next year, and Sarah will have a son."

15Sarah was afraid, so she denied it, saying, "I didn't laugh."

But the LORD said, "No, you did laugh."

ABRAHAM INTERCEDES FOR SODOM

16Then the men got up from their meal and looked out toward Sodom. As they left, Abraham went with them to send them on their way.

17"Should I hide My plan from Abraham?" the LORD asked. 18"For Abraham will certainly become a great and mighty nation, and all the nations of the earth will be blessed through him. 19I have singled him out so that he will direct his sons and their families to keep the way of the LORD by doing what is right and just. Then I will do for Abraham all that I have promised."

20So the LORD told Abraham, "I have heard a great outcry from Sodom and Gomorrah, because their sin is so flagrant. 21I am going down to see if their actions are as wicked as I have heard. If not, I want to know."

22The other men turned and headed toward Sodom, but the LORD remained with Abraham. 23Abraham approached Him and said, "Will You sweep away both the righteous and the wicked? 24Suppose You find fifty righteous people living there in the city—will You still sweep it away and not spare it for their sakes? 25Surely You wouldn't do such a

18:10 *Rom 9:9
18:11 Gen 17:17
18:12 1 Pet 3:6
18:14 Gen 18:10; Jer 32:17, 27; *Rom 9:9
18:16 Gen 18:22; 19:1
18:17 Gen 19:24
18:18 Gen 12:2-3; *Gal 3:18
18:19 Neh 9:7
18:20 Gen 19:13
18:21 Gen 11:5; Exod 3:8
18:22 Gen 18:16; 19:1
18:23 Exod 23:7
18:25 Deut 1:16-17; 32:4; Ps 58:11

18:12-14 Like Abraham (17:17), Sarah could not restrain laughter at the thought of bearing a child at her advanced age. Confronted by the daily realities of her physical condition, she found it impossible to believe God's promise. But though she muffled her laughter and denied it when confronted, God knew of it. His rhetorical question—"Is anything too hard for the LORD"—was the ultimate rebuke of Sarah's unbelief and of our own. The God who gave a child to aged Abraham and Sarah, the God who later caused a virgin to conceive, can do whatsoever He pleases.

18:17-19 Moses, the author of Genesis through the inspiration of God's Spirit, here presents a glimpse of the thoughts of God. These thoughts reveal God's concern for His children and His willingness to be patient with them, as He explained Himself to Abraham the way a father might explain something to a child.

18:20-21 God's interactions with people in the ancient world may seem out of place to us today. For instance, if God knows everything, why did He go down to earth to check the validity of a report about Sodom and Gomorrah? It is true that the ancient writers interpreted God's actions through their own perspectives, just as we do today. But the fundamental truth is that God chose to interact with people in this way. He often made appearances or allowed His angels to appear to people. In doing so, He purposefully took opportunities to interact with and redeem His creation.

▸GOD

18:25 God is just. God's choice to destroy the innocent with the guilty seemed unfair to Abraham. But we must remember that there are really no "innocent" people, for all have sinned and are subject to God's judgment. Rather than allowing the world's standards of right and wrong to frame your thinking about how God should act, let God's actions revealed in Scripture shape your heart and mind. His attributes assure you of justice. He is all-knowing and present everywhere at once. You can rest assured that His decisions are just. (***See God*** *> God's Attributes> Just> He exercises justice toward all humanity,* TopicGuide page A16.)

thing, destroying the righteous along with the wicked. Why, You would be treating the
righteous and the wicked exactly the same! Surely You wouldn't do that! Should not the
Judge of all the earth do what is right?"
26And the LORD replied, "If I find fifty righteous people in Sodom, I will spare the entire
city for their sake."
18:27 Gen 2:7 Job 30:19; 42:6
27Then Abraham spoke again. "Since I have begun, let me speak further to my Lord,
even though I am but dust and ashes. 28Suppose there are only forty-five righteous people
rather than fifty? Will You destroy the whole city for lack of five?"
And the LORD said, "I will not destroy it if I find forty-five righteous people there."
29Then Abraham pressed his request further. "Suppose there are only forty?"
And the LORD replied, "I will not destroy it for the sake of the forty."
18:30 Exod 32:32
30"Please don't be angry, my Lord," Abraham pleaded. "Let me speak—suppose only
thirty righteous people are found?"
And the LORD replied, "I will not destroy it if I find thirty."
31Then Abraham said, "Since I have dared to speak to the Lord, let me continue—sup-
pose there are only twenty?"
And the LORD replied, "Then I will not destroy it for the sake of the twenty."
32Finally, Abraham said, "Lord, please don't be angry with me if I speak one more time.
Suppose only ten are found there?"
And the LORD replied, "Then I will not destroy it for the sake of the ten."
18:33 Gen 17:22; 35:13
33When the LORD had finished His conversation with Abraham, He went on His way, and
Abraham returned to his tent.

SODOM AND GOMORRAH DESTROYED

19:1 Gen 18:2
19 That evening the two angels came to the entrance of the city of Sodom. Lot
was sitting there, and when he saw them, he stood up to meet them. Then he

▸ **GOD**
18:26-27 God's names: Lord. "Lord" is the English translation of *Adonai*, which means "Ruler of all creation." In his dealings with this great Ruler, Abraham saw himself as "dust and ashes." Seeing yourself in this way does not mean that you are meaningless in God's eyes. On the contrary, genuinely yielding your life to God is a means to obtaining all the supernatural resources of the Holy Spirit. This is the key to the abundant Christian life! Let your Lord's supremacy over the universe inspire you to live before Him in humility and holy awe. (***See God***> *God's Names*> *God*, TopicGuide page A18.)

19:1 Scholars believe Sodom and Gomorrah were among five cities located at the southern tip of the Dead Sea. Due to geological shifts throughout the centuries, it is possible that these cities have been covered by the sea. This portion of the sea is only 12 to 15 feet deep, unlike the northern part of the sea, which can reach up to 1,300 feet. Interestingly, five streams continue to feed into the southern part of the Dead Sea even today.

BECAUSE GOD IS JUST

He will always treat me fairly.

I will do for Abraham all that I have promised.

GENESIS 18:19

FOR THE NEXT *GOD IS JUST* FEATURE SEE PAGE 370.

welcomed them and bowed with his face to the ground. 2“My lords,” he said, “come **19:2**
to my home to wash your feet, and be my guests for the night. You may then get up Gen 18:4
early in the morning and be on your way again.”
“Oh no,” they replied. “We’ll just spend the night out here in the city square.”
3But Lot insisted, so at last they went home with him. Lot prepared a feast for them, **19:3**
complete with fresh bread made without yeast, and they ate. 4But before they retired for Gen 18:6-8
the night, all the men of Sodom, young and old, came from all over the city and sur- **19:4**
rounded the house. 5They shouted to Lot, “Where are the men who came to spend the Gen 13:13; 18:20
night with you? Bring them out to us so we can have sex with them!” **19:5** Lev 18:22
6So Lot stepped outside to talk to them, shutting the door behind him. 7“Please, my Judg 19:22
brothers,” he begged, “don’t do such a wicked thing. 8Look, I have two virgin daughters. **19:8**
Let me bring them out to you, and you can do with them as you wish. But please, leave Deut 23:17
these men alone, for they are my guests and are under my protection.”
9“Stand back!” they shouted. “This fellow came to town as an outsider, and now he’s **19:9**
acting like our judge! We’ll treat you far worse than those other men!” And they lunged to- Exod 2:14
ward Lot to break down the door. **19:10**
10But the two angels* reached out, pulled Lot into the house, and bolted the door. Gen 19:1
11Then they blinded all the men, young and old, who were at the door of the house, so **19:11**
they gave up trying to get inside. Deut 28:28-29 2 Kgs 6:18
12Meanwhile, the angels questioned Lot. “Do you have any other relatives here in the Acts 13:11
city?” they asked. “Get them out of this place—your sons-in-law, sons, daughters, or any-
one else. 13For we are about to destroy this city completely. The outcry against this place is **19:13**
so great it has reached the LORD, and He has sent us to destroy it.” Gen 18:20
14So Lot rushed out to tell his daughters’ fiancés, “Quick, get out of the city! The LORD is 1 Chr 21:15
about to destroy it.” But the young men thought he was only joking. Jude 1:7
15At dawn the next morning the angels became insistent. “Hurry,” they said to Lot. **19:14** Exod 9:21
“Take your wife and your two daughters who are here. Get out right now, or you will be Jer 5:12; 43:1-2
swept away in the destruction of the city!”
16When Lot still hesitated, the angels seized his hand and the hands of his wife and two
daughters and rushed them to safety outside the city, for the LORD was merciful. 17When
they were safely out of the city, one of the angels ordered, “Run for your lives! And don’t
look back or stop anywhere in the valley! Escape to the mountains, or you will be swept **19:17**
away!” Gen 13:10; 19:26 Jer 48:6
18“Oh no, my lord!” Lot begged. 19“You have been so gracious to me and saved my life,
and you have shown such great kindness. But I cannot go to the mountains. Disaster
would catch up to me there, and I would soon die. 20See, there is a small village nearby.
Please let me go there instead; don’t you see how small it is? Then my life will be saved.”

19:10 Hebrew *men;* also in 19:12, 16.

19:4-5 God told Abraham in Genesis 18 that He planned to destroy Sodom and Gomorrah for their wickedness. Abraham bargained with God to preserve the cities if a mere ten innocent people could be found in them, but this chapter reveals that there weren’t even ten. The culture of Sodom had become marked by a bottomless appetite for sin. The people’s sensitivities were so dulled that when two angels of God visited, the men of the city wanted only to have sexual relations with them. Depravity had overrun the city to the point where the presence of God Himself went unrecognized.

19:6-8 Lot’s repulsive response to the mob reflected a warped morality. Evidently he had grown accustomed to the corruption in Sodom. But while his offer to sacrifice his daughters to the mob was abhorrent, his only other option was to sacrifice two men whom he believed to be messengers from God. Given Lot’s situation and the lowly position of women in this culture, perhaps it wasn’t surprising that Lot offered his daughters. And given the depravity of Sodom, it was less surprising when the men refused to accept Lot’s offer—sin-crazed people are not interested in making deals.

19:11 We don’t know what kind of blindness the angels inflicted on the men who sought to attack Lot. While it might have been a permanent blindness, it also could have been a temporary state. Either way, the purpose was to keep the men from finding Lot’s doorway. In 2 Kings 6:18, the same Hebrew word for “blindness” was used when Elisha prayed for a temporary blindness upon the Aramean army. In both cases, blindness was used to confound people who were working against God’s purposes.

19:22 Gen 13:10
19:24 Luke 17:29 Jude 1:7
19:25 Deut 29:23 Isa 13:19 Lam 4:6 2 Pet 2:6
19:26 Gen 19:17 Luke 17:32
19:27 Gen 18:22
19:28 Rev 9:2
19:29 Deut 7:8; 9:5 2 Pet 2:7-8
19:30 Gen 13:10
19:33 Gen 9:21
19:37 Gen 36:35 Exod 15:15 Num 21:29 Deut 2:9 Ruth 1:1
19:38 Num 21:24 Deut 2:19

21 “All right,” the angel said, “I will grant your request. I will not destroy the little village.
22 But hurry! Escape to it, for I can do nothing until you arrive there.” (This explains why
that village was known as Zoar, which means “little place.”)
23 Lot reached the village just as the sun was rising over the horizon. 24 Then the LORD
rained down fire and burning sulfur from the sky on Sodom and Gomorrah. 25 He utterly
destroyed them, along with the other cities and villages of the plain, wiping out all the
people and every bit of vegetation. 26 But Lot’s wife looked back as she was following be-
hind him, and she turned into a pillar of salt.
27 Abraham got up early that morning and hurried out to the place where he had stood in
the LORD’s presence. 28 He looked out across the plain toward Sodom and Gomorrah and
watched as columns of smoke rose from the cities like smoke from a furnace.
29 But God had listened to Abraham’s request and kept Lot safe, removing him from the
disaster that engulfed the cities on the plain.

LOT AND HIS DAUGHTERS

30 Afterward Lot left Zoar because he was afraid of the people there, and he went to live in
a cave in the mountains with his two daughters. 31 One day the older daughter said to her
sister, “There are no men left anywhere in this entire area, so we can’t get married like
everyone else. And our father will soon be too old to have children. 32 Come, let’s get him
drunk with wine, and then we will have sex with him. That way we will preserve our family
line through our father.”
33 So that night they got him drunk with wine, and the older daughter went in and had
intercourse with her father. He was unaware of her lying down or getting up again.
34 The next morning the older daughter said to her younger sister, “I had sex with
our father last night. Let’s get him drunk with wine again tonight, and you go in and
have sex with him. That way we will preserve our family line through our father.” 35 So
that night they got him drunk with wine again, and the younger daughter went in and
had intercourse with him. As before, he was unaware of her lying down or getting up
again.
36 As a result, both of Lot’s daughters became pregnant by their own father. 37 When the
older daughter gave birth to a son, she named him Moab.* He became the ancestor of the
nation now known as the Moabites. 38 When the younger daughter gave birth to a son,
she named him Ben-ammi.* He became the ancestor of the nation now known as the Am-
monites.

19:37 *Moab* sounds like a Hebrew term that means “from father.” 19:38 *Ben-ammi* means “son of my kinsman.”

▶ PURPOSE

19:22 God uses human choice. The angel’s admission that he could do nothing until Lot arrived at Zoar underscores the important role of human choice in God’s sovereign plan. Each day, we are confronted with many choices. We can let unbelief, jealousy, anger, and powerlessness rule our life, or we can be empowered by God’s Holy Spirit and live a fruitful, exciting, and happy Christian life. Some people expect God to bless them with abundant life even if they do not choose God’s best. But God’s blessings come to you in response to faith (see Hebrews 11:6). (***See Purpose***> *God’s Means*> *Human choice*> *Human view,* TopicGuide page A52.)

▶ PURPOSE

19:26 Lot’s wife turned into a pillar of salt. Lot’s wife looked back, and God turned her into a pillar of salt. To “look back” means to long for the sin from which God has delivered you. The analogy deepens when you understand that, in biblical times, land was strewn with salt in order to make it barren. Returning to a pattern of sin makes barren your spiritual walk with the Lord. Confession, forgiveness, and restitution restore your fellowship with God and open the door once again for the Holy Spirit to empower you (see 1 John 1:8-10). (***See Purpose***> *God’s Deeds*> *Special acts*> *Miracles*> *OT,* TopicGuide page A52.)

19:30-38 Lot’s daughters had no way of understanding the far-reaching ramifications of their incest. Each daughter gave birth to a son who fathered a nation. These nations, the Moabites and Ammonites, plagued Israel throughout its history. The Ammonite king Sihon refused to give the Israelites permission to pass through his land as they approached the Promised Land (Numbers 21:21-24). The Moabite king Balak called for the prophet Balaam to curse the Israelites (Numbers 22–24). During the time of the judges, the Moabites and Ammonites were also among the nations that tempted Israel to be spiritually unfaithful to God (Judges 10:6-8). By the reign of King Jehoshaphat, the Ammonites and Moabites had joined together to war against Israel (2 Chronicles 20:1-12).

ABRAHAM DECEIVES ABIMELECH

20 Abraham moved south to the Negev and lived for a while between Kadesh and
Shur, and then he moved on to Gerar. While living there as a foreigner, 2Abra-
ham introduced his wife, Sarah, by saying, "She is my sister." So King Abimelech of Gerar
sent for Sarah and had her brought to him at his palace.
3But that night God came to Abimelech in a dream and told him, "You are a dead man,
for that woman you have taken is already married!"
4But Abimelech had not slept with her yet, so he said, "Lord, will You destroy an inno-
cent nation? 5Didn't Abraham tell me, 'She is my sister'? And she herself said, 'Yes, he is
my brother.' I acted in complete innocence! My hands are clean."
6In the dream God responded, "Yes, I know you are innocent. That's why I kept you
from sinning against Me, and why I did not let you touch her. 7Now return the woman to
her husband, and he will pray for you, for he is a prophet. Then you will live. But if you
don't return her to him, you can be sure that you and all your people will die."
8Abimelech got up early the next morning and quickly called all his servants together.
When he told them what had happened, his men were terrified. 9Then Abimelech called
for Abraham. "What have you done to us?" he demanded. "What crime have I commit-
ted that deserves treatment like this, making me and my kingdom guilty of this great sin?
No one should ever do what you have done! 10Whatever possessed you to do such a
thing?"
11Abraham replied, "I thought, 'This is a godless place. They will want my wife and will
kill me to get her.' 12And she really is my sister, for we both have the same father, but dif-
ferent mothers. And I married her. 13When God called me to leave my father's home and
to travel from place to place, I told her, 'Do me a favor. Wherever we go, tell the people
that I am your brother.'"
14Then Abimelech took some of his sheep and goats, cattle, and male and female ser-
vants, and he presented them to Abraham. He also returned his wife, Sarah, to him.
15Then Abimelech said, "Look over my land and choose any place where you would

20:1 Gen 14:7; 18:1; 26:1
20:2 Gen 12:13
20:3 Gen 28:12; 31:24; 37:5
20:4 Gen 18:23-25
20:5 Gen 12:19; 1 Kgs 9:4; Pss 7:8; 26:6
20:7 1 Sam 7:5; Job 42:8
20:9 Gen 12:18
20:11 Gen 12:12; 42:18
20:13 Gen 12:1
20:14 Gen 12:16

▸ WORSHIP

20:1-18 Abraham's fear. Once again, Abraham presented Sarah as his sister (see Genesis 12:10-20; 26:7), which was an act of cowardice and fear. Jesus differs from Abraham in an important respect. Whereas Abraham was willing to give his wife to Abimelech, Jesus is the husband who never abandons His bride (Isaiah 62:5; Revelation 21:2-3). You can be confident that the intimate presence of Jesus will always be near you and will never forsake you. You can live with purpose and power, knowing that Jesus is your faithful companion. The life of Jesus within you is the key to a joyful and radiant Christian life. (***See Worship***> *OT> Reverence,* TopicGuide page A28.)

20:3 In Scripture, God sometimes spoke to people through dreams. Here He gave important information to King Abimelech. God also communicated through dreams to Jacob, the father of the Israelite nation (Genesis 28:10-15), and his son Joseph (Genesis 37:5-11). Joseph later interpreted dreams for the king of Egypt (Genesis 41), as did Daniel for the king of Babylon (Daniel 2). These dreams revealed that God reaches out to people of all stations of life, all faiths, and all levels of spiritual development.

▸ HOLINESS

20:3 The law of marriage. God came to Abimelech in a dream to warn him that Sarah was a married woman, so he would not commit adultery. God established marriage as a part of the created order (see Genesis 1:27; 2:23-25; Ephesians 5:31). Adultery divides husband and wife, damaging both. As an illustration of this, glue two pieces of paper together. These pieces represent two married people who have become one flesh. Then pull the two pieces of paper apart. What happens? Both pieces rip. No matter how much care is taken in separating them, both are damaged. This is a vivid picture of the consequences of adultery, which we should make every effort to avoid. (***See Holiness***> *Law and Grace> Law,* TopicGuide page A41.)

20:4-5 Sarah was a half-sister to Abraham, with the same father but a different mother. Their marriage would be unacceptable in most cultures today. However, in Abraham's time, God had not yet laid down His laws against such unions. Eventually, in the time of Israel's formulation as a nation, God would give prohibitions against marrying within family clans.

20:11-13 No matter how Abraham rationalized his lie, the fact remained that he had covered the truth to save his skin. Of course, looking out for one's survival is a natural tendency. However, God had called Abraham into a special relationship of faith with Him. God had promised to create a great nation out of Abraham's descendants; surely He wouldn't allow a

20:16 like to live." [16]And he said to Sarah, "Look, I am giving your 'brother' 1,000 pieces of
Gen 23:15 silver* in the presence of all these witnesses. This is to compensate you for any wrong
I may have done to you. This will settle any claim against me, and your reputation is
20:17 cleared."
Num 12:13; 21:7 [17]Then Abraham prayed to God, and God healed Abimelech, his wife, and his female
20:18 servants, so they could have children. [18]For the LORD had caused all the women to be infer-
Gen 12:17 tile because of what happened with Abraham's wife, Sarah.

21:1 THE BIRTH OF ISAAC

Gen 17:16, 21 **21** The LORD kept His word and did for Sarah exactly what He had promised.
21:2 Gen 18:10 Gal 4:22 [2]She became pregnant, and she gave birth to a son for Abraham in his old age.
Heb 11:11 This happened at just the time God had said it would. [3]And Abraham named their son
21:3 Isaac. [4]Eight days after Isaac was born, Abraham circumcised him as God had com-
Gen 17:19 manded. [5]Abraham was 100 years old when Isaac was born.
21:4 [6]And Sarah declared, "God has brought me laughter.* All who hear about this will laugh
Gen 17:10, 12 with me. [7]Who would have said to Abraham that Sarah would nurse a baby? Yet I have
21:5 Gen 12:4 Heb 6:15 given Abraham a son in his old age!"

21:7 HAGAR AND ISHMAEL ARE SENT AWAY

Gen 18:13 [8]When Isaac grew up and was about to be weaned, Abraham prepared a huge feast
21:8 to celebrate the occasion. [9]But Sarah saw Ishmael—the son of Abraham and her Egyptian
1 Sam 1:23 servant Hagar—making fun of her son, Isaac.* [10]So she turned to Abraham and demanded,
21:9 "Get rid of that slave woman and her son. He is not going to share the inheritance with my
Gal 4:29 son, Isaac. I won't have it!"
21:10 *Gal 4:30 [11]This upset Abraham very much because Ishmael was his son. [12]But God told Abra-
21:12 ham, "Do not be upset over the boy and your servant. Do whatever Sarah tells you, for
*Rom 9:7 Isaac is the son through whom your descendants will be counted. [13]But I will also make a
*Heb 11:18 nation of the descendants of Hagar's son because he is your son, too."
21:13 [14]So Abraham got up early the next morning, prepared food and a container of water,
Gen 16:10; 21:18; 25:12-18 and strapped them on Hagar's shoulders. Then he sent her away with their son, and she
21:14 wandered aimlessly in the wilderness of Beersheba.
Gen 16:1 [15]When the water was gone, she put the boy in the shade of a bush. [16]Then she went
21:16 and sat down by herself about a hundred yards* away. "I don't want to watch the boy die,"
Jer 6:26 she said, as she burst into tears.

20:16 Hebrew *1,000 shekels of silver,* about 25 pounds or 11.4 kilograms in weight. 21:6 The name *Isaac* means "he laughs." 21:9 As in Greek version and Latin Vulgate; Hebrew omits *of her son, Isaac.* 21:16 Hebrew *a bowshot.*

lecherous king to kill Abraham. Yet Abraham struggled to trust God. Faith in God had not yet seeped into every part of his life. This passage reveals a man learning to trust God but not yet living that faith out completely.

21:1-7 Both Abraham and Sarah laughed when God promised to give them a son in their old age. At that time, they laughed at the seeming impossibility of the promise. But when God did as he had said He would and caused a son to be born to them when Abraham was 100 years old and Sarah was 90, they laughed not for incredulity but for joy. Sarah even predicted that all who heard about the miracle would laugh with her. As a reminder of their joy—and perhaps of their lack of faith, too—the couple named their son Isaac, which means "he laughs."

21:8-12 There are two conflicts in this brief story, the first being the conflict between Ishmael and Isaac. Sarah rightly understood the minor conflict between Ishmael and Isaac would escalate, and with God's approval, the threat to their covenant child (see Genesis 21:1-7) was sent away (Genesis 21:12).

21:8-21 Sarah's attitude toward Ishmael changed once she had her own son. Seeing Ishmael making fun of Isaac, as boys will do, Sarah became upset and demanded that Abraham "get rid" of Ishmael and his mother, Hagar. This upset Abraham, for though Ishmael was not the son of promise, he was a son of Abraham's body. Furthermore, God had told Abraham that both Isaac and Ishmael would produce great nations. Abraham reluctantly agreed to Sarah's demand, but God intervened to save Hagar and Ishmael. God also revealed to Hagar in her distress what He had already promised to Abraham concerning Ishmael's legacy. God had mercy on Hagar, a broken-hearted mother, even though her child was a result of Sarah's faithlessness. God's compassion for all people in all situations is evidenced here.

17 But God heard the boy crying, and the angel of God called to Hagar from heaven,
"Hagar, what's wrong? Do not be afraid! God has heard the boy crying as he lies there.
18 Go to him and comfort him, for I will make a great nation from his descendants."
19 Then God opened Hagar's eyes, and she saw a well full of water. She quickly filled her
water container and gave the boy a drink.
20 And God was with the boy as he grew up in the wilderness. He became a skillful ar-
cher, 21 and he settled in the wilderness of Paran. His mother arranged for him to marry a
woman from the land of Egypt.

ABRAHAM'S COVENANT WITH ABIMELECH

22 About this time, Abimelech came with Phicol, his army commander, to visit Abraham.
"God is obviously with you, helping you in everything you do," Abimelech said. 23 "Swear
to me in God's name that you will never deceive me, my children, or any of my descen-
dants. I have been loyal to you, so now swear that you will be loyal to me and to this coun-
try where you are living as a foreigner."
24 Abraham replied, "Yes, I swear to it!" 25 Then Abraham complained to Abimelech
about a well that Abimelech's servants had taken by force from Abraham's servants.
26 "This is the first I've heard of it," Abimelech answered. "I have no idea who is responsi-
ble. You have never complained about this before."
27 Abraham then gave some of his sheep, goats, and cattle to Abimelech, and they
made a treaty. 28 But Abraham also took seven additional female lambs and set them
off by themselves. 29 Abimelech asked, "Why have you set these seven apart from the
others?"
30 Abraham replied, "Please accept these seven lambs to show your agreement that I
dug this well." 31 Then he named the place Beersheba (which means "well of the oath"), be-
cause that was where they had sworn the oath.
32 After making their covenant at Beersheba, Abimelech left with Phicol, the com-
mander of his army, and they returned home to the land of the Philistines. 33 Then Abra-
ham planted a tamarisk tree at Beersheba, and there he worshiped the LORD, the Eternal
God.* 34 And Abraham lived as a foreigner in Philistine country for a long time.

21:17 Exod 3:7; Deut 26:7; Ps 6:8
21:18 Gen 26:24
21:20 Gen 28:15
21:21 Gen 25:18
21:22 Gen 26:26
21:23 Gen 24:3
21:25 Gen 26:15
21:27 Gen 26:31
21:30 Gen 31:44
21:31 Gen 21:14; 26:33
21:33 1 Sam 22:6; 31:13; Ps 90:2; Isa 9:6; 40:28

21:33 Hebrew *El-Olam.*

21:13-21 The second conflict in this section is that when Hagar and Ishmael were sent into the desert wilderness, they soon came to the point of perishing. But as before (Genesis 21:12-13), God spoke and showed a way out of the danger (Genesis 21:19).

21:22-23 Abimelech, one of the lords of the Philistines, came to Abraham to seek something resembling a nonaggression treaty. Not many years before, Abraham spent time in Abimelech's land and, because he feared the Philistine king, asked Sarah to say that she was his sister. But now Abimelech seeks a negotiated peace. How had Abraham become so great and formidable as to engender this respect? The answer is that it had nothing to do with Abraham. Abimelech said it was clear that God was helping Abraham in everything. The Philistine respected the power of Abraham's God. Perhaps he had heard how God had caused a son to be born in Abraham's old age, which was a powerful miracle indicating great divine favor.

21:24, 30 In Abraham's time, an oath was a serious matter, more binding than a simple promise. When people took an oath, they swore by something larger than themselves. They might say: "The Lord is witness between you and me forever that I will . . ." The third commandment had something to do with oaths—not taking God's name in vain meant not swearing by His name to do something and then disregarding your oath. To break an oath was far more than a change of mind; it was a sign of disrespect for God. A confirmation, such as Abraham's ewe lambs, functioned to seal an agreement.

▸ GOD

21:33 God's names: the Eternal God. Abraham worshiped "the Eternal God" (*El Olam*), who existed before time began and who will live on when this present age has ended. The verlasting arms of the Eternal God always protect you from danger, discouragement, and defeat. He is the source of everlasting comfort, never-ending love, and eternal life. People may abandon you and the world may snub you, but your Eternal God will be with you always. (***See God*****>** *God's Names> God,* TopicGuide page A18.)

ABRAHAM'S FAITH TESTED

22:1 **22** Some time later, God tested Abraham's faith. "Abraham!" God called.
Exod 15:25; 16:4 Deut 8:2, 16 "Yes," he replied. "Here I am."
22:2 2"Take your son, your only son—yes, Isaac, whom you love so much—and go to the
2 Chr 3:1 John 3:16 land of Moriah. Go and sacrifice him as a burnt offering on one of the mountains, which I
will show you."
3The next morning Abraham got up early. He saddled his donkey and took two of his
servants with him, along with his son, Isaac. Then he chopped wood for a fire for a burnt
offering and set out for the place God had told him about. 4On the third day of their jour-
ney, Abraham looked up and saw the place in the distance. 5"Stay here with the donkey,"
Abraham told the servants. "The boy and I will travel a little farther. We will worship there,
and then we will come right back."
22:6 John 19:17 6So Abraham placed the wood for the burnt offering on Isaac's shoulders, while he him-
self carried the fire and the knife. As the two of them walked on together, 7Isaac turned to
22:7 Gen 8:20 Abraham and said, "Father?"
Exod 29:38-42 "Yes, my son?" Abraham replied.
John 1:29, 36 Rev 13:8 "We have the fire and the wood," the boy said, "but where is the sheep for the burnt
offering?"
8"God will provide a sheep for the burnt offering, my son," Abraham answered. And
they both walked on together.
22:9 9When they arrived at the place where God had told him to go, Abraham built an altar
Heb 11:17-19 and arranged the wood on it. Then he tied his son, Isaac, and laid him on the altar on top
Jas 2:21 of the wood. 10And Abraham picked up the knife to kill his son as a sacrifice. 11At that mo-
22:11 ment the angel of the LORD called to him from heaven, "Abraham! Abraham!"
Gen 16:7; 21:17 "Yes," Abraham replied. "Here I am!"
22:12 12"Don't lay a hand on the boy!" the angel said. "Do not hurt him in any way, for now
Heb 11:17 I know that you truly fear God. You have not withheld from Me even your son, your
only son."

22:1 God tested Abraham's faith. Testing can be considered the other side of the coin of temptation. In the New Testament, Jesus was both tested and tempted in the wilderness (Matthew 4). In the New Testament book that bears his name, James wrote that God does not tempt His children with evil. However, God tests His children, primarily that they may know their level of faith. Satan, on the other hand, tempts with evil in order to destroy. So God did not tempt Abraham toward sin. Rather, He tested him to clarify the intent and hope of Abraham's heart.

22:1-2 To Abraham, losing his son could well have seemed like losing God's promise to him. But the key to that promise lay in Abraham's relationship with God, not in the life of Isaac. This relationship was the crux of Abraham's solemn journey to Moriah. Was Abraham's faith still resting in God's promise? According to Hebrews 11:18-19, Abraham trusted that God had a plan in mind to save his son. When Abraham and Isaac reached the mountain God had designated for the sacrifice, Abraham spoke to the servants who had come with them. He did not say, "*I* will come right back," but, "*we* will come right back" (Genesis 22:5).

▸ GOD

22:3 Relationship with God requires sacrificial living. The morning after receiving God's devastating command, Abraham got up early and set out to sacrifice his son Isaac. Abraham is called the "father of the faithful" due to his bold, uncompromising faith in God. As a servant of Jesus, you are not called to an easy faith, but to a faith that is willing to sacrifice anything and everything God requires. He may call you to forfeit a personal goal, a relationship, or a job that does not represent His best for you. Being a Christian means being prepared to lay everything on the worship altar to God. (***See God****> Relationship> God enables,* TopicGuide page A14.)

22:7 Isaac's question was a reasonable one. Lambs and goats were often used for sacrifices. Abel brought "the best of the firstborn lambs from his flock" to offer to God (Genesis 4:4). Later, once the Hebrew system of sacrifices had been established, the priests offered two lambs every day, one in the morning and one in the evening, and four lambs on the Sabbath. We know Abraham built altars on occasion, so sacrifices may have been a regular part of his and Isaac's lives.

▸ GOD

22:8 God's names: the LORD, the provider. Abraham expressed faith that God would provide a lamb for the sacrifice. When God sent a ram, Abraham named the place "The LORD will provide" (*Yahweh Yireh*). God will provide for us just as He provided for Abraham (v. 14). He will provide for our needs, but we, like Abraham, must be willing to place our life completely into His hands, trusting that He is faithful. What is your need? Stop right now and praise God for His marvelous provision. Trust Him to care supernaturally for your every need. He will never fail you. (***See God****> God's Names> God,* TopicGuide page A18.)

13 Then Abraham looked up and saw a ram caught by its horns in a thicket. So he
took the ram and sacrificed it as a burnt offering in place of his son. 14 Abraham named
the place Yahweh-Yireh (which means "the LORD will provide"). To this day, people still
use that name as a proverb: "On the mountain of the LORD it will be provided."
15 Then the angel of the LORD called again to Abraham from heaven. 16 "This is what
the LORD says: Because you have obeyed Me and have not withheld even your son,
your only son, I swear by My own name that 17 I will certainly bless you. I will multiply
your descendants* beyond number, like the stars in the sky and the sand on the sea-
shore. Your descendants will conquer the cities of their enemies. 18 And through your
descendants all the nations of the earth will be blessed—all because you have obeyed
Me."
19 Then they returned to the servants and traveled back to Beersheba, where Abraham
continued to live.
20 Soon after this, Abraham heard that Milcah, his brother Nahor's wife, had borne Na-
hor eight sons. 21 The oldest was named Uz, the next oldest was Buz, followed by Kemuel
(the ancestor of the Arameans), 22 Kesed, Hazo, Pildash, Jidlaph, and Bethuel. 23 (Bethuel
became the father of Rebekah.) In addition to these eight sons from Milcah, 24 Nahor had
four other children from his concubine Reumah. Their names were Tebah, Gaham, Ta-
hash, and Maacah.

THE BURIAL OF SARAH

23 When Sarah was 127 years old, 2 she died at Kiriath-arba (now called Hebron) in
the land of Canaan. There Abraham mourned and wept for her.
3 Then, leaving her body, he said to the Hittite elders, 4 "Here I am, a stranger and a
foreigner among you. Please sell me a piece of land so I can give my wife a proper
burial."
5 The Hittites replied to Abraham, 6 "Listen, my lord, you are an honored prince among
us. Choose the finest of our tombs and bury her there. No one here will refuse to help you
in this way."
7 Then Abraham bowed low before the Hittites and said, 8 "Since you are willing to help
me in this way, be so kind as to ask Ephron son of Zohar 9 to let me buy his cave at Mach-
pelah, down at the end of his field. I will pay the full price in the presence of witnesses, so I
will have a permanent burial place for my family."

22:13 Gen 8:20
22:14 Gen 22:7-8
22:16 *Heb 6:13-14
22:17 Gen 12:2; 15:5; 26:4; *Heb 6:14
22:18 *Acts 3:25; *Gal 3:8, 16
22:19 Gen 21:14
22:20 Gen 11:29
22:23 Gen 24:15
23:2 Josh 14:15
23:3 Gen 10:15
23:4 Lev 25:23; 1 Chr 29:15; Ps 39:12; Heb 11:9
23:6 Gen 14:14-16
23:8-9 Gen 25:9

22:17 Hebrew *seed;* also in 22:17b, 18.

22:13 The substitution of a ram as the sacrifice in place of Isaac foreshadowed the eventual sacrifice of Jesus Christ, God's only Son, as the substitute for sinners. Another Old Testament image of Christ can be found in the Passover lambs that the Hebrews sacrificed before God led them out of Egypt. When Jesus approached John the Baptist, John said, "Look! The Lamb of God who takes away the sin of the world!" (John 1:29). Later, Paul wrote to the church at Corinth, "Christ, our Passover Lamb, has been sacrificed for us" (1 Corinthians 5:7).

22:17 God again repeated His promise to Abraham. In Genesis 13:14-16, God showed Abraham the Promised Land and told him that his descendants would outnumber the dust. In Genesis 15:5, God took Abraham out under the night sky and promised him as many descendants as the stars. In Genesis 17:5, God changed his name from Abram to Abraham, meaning "father of many nations." Each time, God reassured Abraham, His faithful follower, that what He had promised from the beginning would come to pass.

23:3 The Hittites descended from Canaan, the son of Noah's son Ham. Ham's impropriety brought God's curse on Canaan (Genesis 9:20-25). The Hittite nation descended specifically from Canaan's son Heth and settled in what is now central Turkey. Although the Hittite elders treated Abraham kindly here, the Hittites would become one of the Israelites' three main enemies when they returned to conquer the Promised Land.

23:5-15 The conversation between Abraham and Ephron reveals the subtleties of ancient bargaining. As with modern negotiations, there were several levels of communication. By reading between the lines, we can see that Ephron wasn't interested in letting the cave go without the field. When Abraham mentioned the cave, Ephron responded by speaking of the cave and the field, for the land was what had value. Although Ephron offered to give Abraham the field, he also mentioned the field's price, thereby letting Abraham know how much he wanted to be paid. In this way, the men graciously let their expectations be known.

23:10 Ruth 4:1, 11
23:15 Exod 30:13
23:16 Jer 32:9
23:17-18 Gen 25:9; 49:29-30; 50:13

10 Ephron was sitting there among the others, and he answered Abraham as the others
listened, speaking publicly before all the Hittite elders of the town. 11 "No, my lord," he said
to Abraham, "please listen to me. I will give you the field and the cave. Here in the pres-
ence of my people, I give it to you. Go and bury your dead."

12 Abraham again bowed low before the citizens of the land, 13 and he replied to Ephron
as everyone listened. "No, listen to me. I will buy it from you. Let me pay the full price for
the field so I can bury my dead there."

14 Ephron answered Abraham, 15 "My lord, please listen to me. The land is worth
400 pieces* of silver, but what is that between friends? Go ahead and bury your dead."

16 So Abraham agreed to Ephron's price and paid the amount he had suggested—
400 pieces of silver, weighed according to the market standard. The Hittite elders wit-
nessed the transaction.

17 So Abraham bought the plot of land belonging to Ephron at Machpelah, near Mamre.
This included the field itself, the cave that was in it, and all the surrounding trees. 18 It was
transferred to Abraham as his permanent possession in the presence of the Hittite elders
at the city gate. 19 Then Abraham buried his wife, Sarah, there in Canaan, in the cave of
Machpelah, near Mamre (also called Hebron). 20 So the field and the cave were trans-
ferred from the Hittites to Abraham for use as a permanent burial place.

A WIFE FOR ISAAC

24:1 Gen 12:2; 24:35
24:2 Gen 47:29
24:3 Gen 14:19
24:4 Gen 12:1
24:5 Gen 24:39
24:7 Gen 12:1, 7; 16:7; 22:11 Rom 4:13 *Gal 3:16

24 Abraham was now a very old man, and the LORD had blessed him in every way.
2 One day Abraham said to his oldest servant, the man in charge of his house-
hold, "Take an oath by putting your hand under my thigh. 3 Swear by the LORD, the God of
heaven and earth, that you will not allow my son to marry one of these local Canaanite
women. 4 Go instead to my homeland, to my relatives, and find a wife there for my son
Isaac."

5 The servant asked, "But what if I can't find a young woman who is willing to travel so
far from home? Should I then take Isaac there to live among your relatives in the land you
came from?"

6 "No!" Abraham responded. "Be careful never to take my son there. 7 For the LORD, the
God of heaven, who took me from my father's house and my native land, solemnly prom-
ised to give this land to my descendants.* He will send His angel ahead of you, and He will
see to it that you find a wife there for my son. 8 If she is unwilling to come back with you,

23:15 Hebrew *400 shekels,* about 10 pounds or 4.6 kilograms in weight; also in 23:16. 24:7 Hebrew *seed;* also in 24:60.

23:12-20 Abraham got much more from the deal than a tomb. In that time, families were buried in their native land. Although Abraham's homeland was in Mesopotamia, he bought this small portion of land in Canaan, the land God had promised to him, as a burial plot. By purchasing the field and the tomb, Abraham made a claim to God's promise and a statement to his family that there was no going back. Canaan would become Abraham's homeland. Eventually, Abraham was also buried in the tomb, as were Isaac and Jacob (Abraham's son and grandson) and their wives Rebekah and Leah.

24:2-4 Abraham most likely wanted to find a wife for Isaac from among his relatives because the Canaanites were not worshipers of God. Throughout their history, God warned the Israelites against marrying people from cultures with other religious practices. Whenever the Israelites disregarded God's warning, they inevitably were led away from faith in God. Solomon made this mistake and ended up disillusioned, unsure of what he believed. After the Jews had lost their kingdom and been taken into exile, they returned home to face this issue of intermarriage once again (Nehemiah 13:26-27).

▸ HOLINESS

24:6 Teaching your children. Abraham's warning, "Be careful never to take my son there," demonstrates his faithfulness to God's call to abandon his homeland and live in the land God had promised. Now Abraham seeks to make sure that his son remains faithful as well. How important it is that parents disciple their children as faithful followers of the Lord! Proverbs states: "Direct your children onto the right path, and when they are older, they will not leave it" (Proverbs 22:6). Your children are the next generation. What hope is there for the future of the nation and the world unless you provide them with solid biblical instruction? (***See Holiness***> *Submission*> *Learning God's Word,* TopicGuide page A40.)

then you are free from this oath of mine. But under no circumstances are you to take my
son there.”
9 So the servant took an oath by putting his hand under the thigh of his master, Abra-
ham. He swore to follow Abraham’s instructions. 10 Then he loaded ten of Abraham’s cam- **24:10**
els with all kinds of expensive gifts from his master, and he traveled to distant Aram- Gen 11:29 Deut 23:4
naharaim. There he went to the town where Abraham’s brother Nahor had settled. 11 He
made the camels kneel beside a well just outside the town. It was evening, and the **24:11** Gen 24:42
women were coming out to draw water.
12 “O LORD, God of my master, Abraham,” he prayed. “Please give me success today, **24:12**
and show unfailing love to my master, Abraham. 13 See, I am standing here beside this Gen 24:27, 48
spring, and the young women of the town are coming out to draw water. 14 This is my re- **24:14**
quest. I will ask one of them, ‘Please give me a drink from your jug.’ If she says, ‘Yes, have Judg 6:17 1 Sam 14:10
a drink, and I will water your camels, too!’—let her be the one you have selected as Isaac’s
wife. This is how I will know that you have shown unfailing love to my master.”
15 Before he had finished praying, he saw a young woman named Rebekah coming out **24:15** Gen 22:20-24
with her water jug on her shoulder. She was the daughter of Bethuel, who was the son of
Abraham’s brother Nahor and his wife, Milcah. 16 Rebekah was very beautiful and old **24:16**
enough to be married, but she was still a virgin. She went down to the spring, filled her jug, Gen 12:11; 29:17
and came up again. 17 Running over to her, the servant said, “Please give me a little drink **24:17**
of water from your jug.” 1 Kgs 17:10 John 4:7
18 “Yes, my lord,” she answered, “have a drink.” And she quickly lowered her jug from
her shoulder and gave him a drink. 19 When she had given him a drink, she said, “I’ll draw **24:19**
water for your camels, too, until they have had enough to drink.” 20 So she quickly emp- Gen 24:14
tied her jug into the watering trough and ran back to the well to draw water for all his
camels.
21 The servant watched her in silence, wondering whether or not the LORD had given him
success in his mission. 22 Then at last, when the camels had finished drinking, he took out **24:22**
a gold ring for her nose and two large gold bracelets* for her wrists. Gen 24:47
23 “Whose daughter are you?” he asked. “And please tell me, would your father have
any room to put us up for the night?” **24:24**
24 “I am the daughter of Bethuel,” she replied. “My grandparents are Nahor and Milcah. Gen 24:15
25 Yes, we have plenty of straw and feed for the camels, and we have room for guests.” **24:26**
26 The man bowed low and worshiped the LORD. 27 “Praise the LORD, the God of my mas- Exod 4:31
ter, Abraham,” he said. “The LORD has shown unfailing love and faithfulness to my master, **24:27** Gen 14:20; 24:12, 48
for he has led me straight to my master’s relatives.” **24:28**
28 The young woman ran home to tell her family everything that had happened. Gen 29:12

24:22 Hebrew *a gold nose-ring weighing a half shekel* [0.2 ounces or 6 grams] *and two gold bracelets weighing 10 shekels* [4 ounces or 114 grams].

▸ PURPOSE

24:12 Prayer for guidance. God’s people often have no idea how to pray. God knows this, for He freely offers us wisdom (James 1:5; 3:13-17). But the servant asks for more than this—he requests a miracle to accomplish his oath to Abraham (v. 9). The servant had no right to ask for such a revelation from God, and God was certainly not obliged to answer such a prayer, but God was determined to fulfill His promises to Abraham (Genesis 12:1-3). God sees fit to work in, with, through, and even against our prayers to accomplish His goals. (***See Purpose***> *God’s Deeds> Special acts> Guidance,* TopicGuide page A52.)

24:12 Abraham’s servant addressed God indirectly as the “God of my master.” Because God had forged a unique relationship with Abraham amidst a people who worshiped many gods, this title held special meaning. The servant wasn’t praying to just any god, but to the God who had led his master for many years, performing miracles on his behalf along the way. The servant’s prayer sounds similar to the statement Ruth made many years later to Naomi: “Your people will be my people, and your God will be my God” (Ruth 1:16). God proved Himself through the lives of His people. In a land that touted many gods, it made sense to identify God by those who believed in Him.

24:28-32 Laban’s long interaction with Abraham’s family began here (Genesis 24:48). Laban’s sister married Isaac, and then, years later, when Isaac’s son Jacob had to run for his life, he came to Laban for help. While there, Jacob fell in love with Laban’s daughter Rachel. Laban tricked Jacob into marrying his older daughter Leah first, then Rachel, and from these two marriages came the nation of Israel. Leah and Rachel’s sons, Laban’s grandchildren, became the 12 tribes of Israel.

24:29 29 Now Rebekah had a brother named Laban, who ran out to meet the man at the spring.
Gen 25:20; 29:5 30 He had seen the nose-ring and the bracelets on his sister's wrists, and had heard Rebek-
24:30 Gen 24:10 ah tell what the man had said. So he rushed out to the spring, where the man was still
24:31 Gen 26:29 standing beside his camels. Laban said to him, 31 "Come and stay with us, you who are
blessed by the Lord! Why are you standing here outside the town when I have a room
all ready for you and a place prepared for the camels?"

32 So the man went home with Laban, and Laban unloaded the camels, gave him straw
for their bedding, fed them, and provided water for the man and the camel drivers to wash
their feet. 33 Then food was served. But Abraham's servant said, "I don't want to eat until I
have told you why I have come."

"All right," Laban said, "tell us."

24:34 Gen 24:1 34 "I am Abraham's servant," he explained. 35 "And the Lord has greatly blessed my mas-
24:35 Gen 12:2 ter; he has become a wealthy man. The Lord has given him flocks of sheep and goats,
herds of cattle, a fortune in silver and gold, and many male and female servants and cam-
24:36 Gen 21:1-7; 25:5 els and donkeys.

36 "When Sarah, my master's wife, was very old, she gave birth to my master's son,
24:37 Gen 24:2-4 and my master has given him everything he owns. 37 And my master made me take
an oath. He said, 'Do not allow my son to marry one of these local Canaanite
women. 38 Go instead to my father's house, to my relatives, and find a wife there for
my son.'

24:40 Gen 24:7 39 "But I said to my master, 'What if I can't find a young woman who is willing to go back
with me?' 40 He responded, 'The Lord, in whose presence I have lived, will send His angel
with you and will make your mission successful. Yes, you must find a wife for my son from
among my relatives, from my father's family. 41 Then you will have fulfilled your obliga-
tion. But if you go to my relatives and they refuse to let her go with you, you will be free
from my oath.'

42 "So today when I came to the spring, I prayed this prayer: 'O Lord, God of my master,
Abraham, please give me success on this mission. 43 See, I am standing here beside this
spring. This is my request. When a young woman comes to draw water, I will say to her,
"Please give me a little drink of water from your jug." 44 If she says, "Yes, have a drink, and I
will draw water for your camels, too," let her be the one You have selected to be the wife of
my master's son.'

24:45 1 Sam 1:13 45 "Before I had finished praying in my heart, I saw Rebekah coming out with her water
jug on her shoulder. She went down to the spring and drew water. So I said to her, 'Please
give me a drink.' 46 She quickly lowered her jug from her shoulder and said, 'Yes, have a
drink, and I will water your camels, too!' So I drank, and then she watered the camels.

24:47 Gen 24:23-24 47 "Then I asked, 'Whose daughter are you?' She replied, 'I am the daughter of Bethuel,
and my grandparents are Nahor and Milcah.' So I put the ring on her nose, and the brace-
lets on her wrists.

48 "Then I bowed low and worshiped the Lord. I praised the Lord, the God of my master,
24:49 Gen 47:29 Abraham, because He had led me straight to my master's niece to be his son's wife. 49 So
tell me—will you or won't you show unfailing love and faithfulness to my master? Please
tell me yes or no, and then I'll know what to do next."

24:50 Ps 118:23 50 Then Laban and Bethuel replied, "The Lord has obviously brought you here, so there
is nothing we can say. 51 Here is Rebekah; take her and go. Yes, let her be the wife of your
master's son, as the Lord has directed."

24:52 Gen 24:26 52 When Abraham's servant heard their answer, he bowed down to the ground and
worshiped the Lord. 53 Then he brought out silver and gold jewelry and clothing
and presented them to Rebekah. He also gave expensive presents to her brother and
24:54 Gen 30:25 mother. 54 Then they ate their meal, and the servant and the men with him stayed there
overnight.

But early the next morning, Abraham's servant said, "Send me back to my master."

55 "But we want Rebekah to stay with us at least ten days," her brother and mother said. "Then she can go."

56 But he said, "Don't delay me. The LORD has made my mission successful; now send me back so I can return to my master."

57 "Well," they said, "we'll call Rebekah and ask her what she thinks." 58 So they called Rebekah. "Are you willing to go with this man?" they asked her.

And she replied, "Yes, I will go."

59 So they said good-bye to Rebekah and sent her away with Abraham's servant and his men. The woman who had been Rebekah's childhood nurse went along with her. 60 They gave her this blessing as she parted:

"Our sister, may you become
  the mother of many millions!
May your descendants be strong
  and conquer the cities of their enemies."

61 Then Rebekah and her servant girls mounted the camels and followed the man. So Abraham's servant took Rebekah and went on his way.

62 Meanwhile, Isaac, whose home was in the Negev, had returned from Beer-lahai-roi. 63 One evening as he was walking and meditating in the fields, he looked up and saw the camels coming. 64 When Rebekah looked up and saw Isaac, she quickly dismounted from her camel. 65 "Who is that man walking through the fields to meet us?" she asked the servant.

And he replied, "It is my master." So Rebekah covered her face with her veil. 66 Then the servant told Isaac everything he had done.

67 And Isaac brought Rebekah into his mother Sarah's tent, and she became his wife. He loved her deeply, and she was a special comfort to him after the death of his mother.

THE DEATH OF ABRAHAM

25 Abraham married another wife, whose name was Keturah. 2 She gave birth to Zimran, Jokshan, Medan, Midian, Ishbak, and Shuah. 3 Jokshan was the father of Sheba and Dedan. Dedan's descendants were the Asshurites, Letushites, and Leummites. 4 Midian's sons were Ephah, Epher, Hanoch, Abida, and Eldaah. These were all descendants of Abraham through Keturah.

5 Abraham gave everything he owned to his son Isaac. 6 But before he died, he gave gifts to the sons of his concubines and sent them off to a land in the east, away from Isaac.

7 Abraham lived for 175 years, 8 and he died at a ripe old age, having lived a long and satisfying life. He breathed his last and joined his ancestors in death. 9 His sons Isaac and Ishmael buried him in the cave of Machpelah, near Mamre, in the field of Ephron son of

24:55 Judg 19:4
24:59 Gen 35:8
24:60 Gen 17:16; 22:17
24:62 Gen 16:14
24:63 Ps 119:15, 27, 48
24:67 Gen 23:1-2; 25:20; 29:18
25:1-4 //1 Chr 1:32-33
25:5 Gen 24:35-36
25:7 Gen 12:4
25:8 Gen 15:15; 25:17; 35:29; 49:29, 33
25:9-10 Gen 23:17-18; 49:29; 50:13

24:64-67 Rebekah's journey to Isaac's home must have been one of anticipation and intrigue. An arranged marriage would have been a significant transition even if it hadn't involved moving to an unknown land. Rebekah may have traveled casually, because she didn't stop to put on her veil—the sign of an unmarried woman—until she saw Isaac coming her way. Although Rebekah and Isaac grew to have affection for one other, Rebekah proved to be a conniver in the marriage, conspiring with their son Jacob to steal Isaac's blessing from their oldest son, Esau (Genesis 27).

25:1 Even though the word *wife* is used to describe Keturah, she may have been a concubine. A concubine was a sexual partner for a man, but did not have the status of a wife. Also, dowries were not required for concubines, so taking a concubine was an economical choice. Men sometimes took concubines if their wives were unable to bear children. While taking concubines was an accepted custom of the day, as were harems and polygamy, it was never God's ideal. In Abraham's case, the consequences of this choice, through the descendants of Keturah, were far-reaching.

Zohar the Hittite. [10]This was the field Abraham had purchased from the Hittites and where
25:11 he had buried his wife Sarah. [11]After Abraham's death, God blessed his son Isaac, who set-
Gen 12:2; 24:62 tled near Beer-lahai-roi in the Negev.

ISHMAEL'S DESCENDANTS

[12]This is the account of the family of Ishmael, the son of Abraham through Hagar, Sar-
ah's Egyptian servant. [13]Here is a list, by their names and clans, of Ishmael's descendants:
The oldest was Nebaioth, followed by Kedar, Adbeel, Mibsam, [14]Mishma, Dumah, Massa,
25:12-16 [15]Hadad, Tema, Jetur, Naphish, and Kedemah. [16]These twelve sons of Ishmael became
//1 Chr 1:29-31 the founders of twelve tribes named after them, listed according to the places they settled
25:17 and camped. [17]Ishmael lived for 137 years. Then he breathed his last and joined his an-
Gen 25:8 cestors in death. [18]Ishmael's descendants occupied the region from Havilah to Shur,
25:18 which is east of Egypt in the direction of Asshur. There they lived in open hostility toward
Gen 16:12; 20:1 all their relatives.*

THE BIRTHS OF ESAU AND JACOB

[19]This is the account of the family of Isaac, the son of Abraham. [20]When Isaac was forty
years old, he married Rebekah, the daughter of Bethuel the Aramean from Paddan-aram
25:21 and the sister of Laban the Aramean.
Gen 21:2 [21]Isaac pleaded with the LORD on behalf of his wife, because she was unable to have
children. The LORD answered Isaac's prayer, and Rebekah became pregnant with twins.
[22]But the two children struggled with each other in her womb. So she went to ask the LORD
25:23 about it. "Why is this happening to me?" she asked.
Gen 17:2-4; 27:29; [23]And the LORD told her, "The sons in your womb will become two nations. From the
48:19 Num 20:14 very beginning, the two nations will be rivals. One nation will be stronger than the other;
Deut 2:4, 8 and your older son will serve your younger son."
*Rom 9:11-12 [24]And when the time came to give birth, Rebekah discovered that she did indeed
25:25 have twins! [25]The first one was very red at birth and covered with thick hair like a fur
Gen 27:11 coat. So they named him Esau.* [26]Then the other twin was born with his hand grasping
25:26 Hos 12:3 Esau's heel. So they named him Jacob.* Isaac was sixty years old when the twins were
born.

25:18 The meaning of the Hebrew is uncertain. 25:25 *Esau* sounds like a Hebrew term that means "hair." 25:26 *Jacob* sounds like the Hebrew words for "heel" and "deceiver."

▸ ADOPTION

25:8 An abundant life. Abraham died at a "ripe old age," a fulfillment of God's promise to give him a long and abundant life (Genesis 15:15). Just as he blessed Abraham, God loves you and offers a wonderful plan for your life. Christ said, "My purpose is to give them a rich and satisfying life" (John 10:10). Many people, however, do not know the full, abundant life that Christ offers because they live a self-directed life. They sit on the thrones of their lives. If you are on the throne of your life, repent of your selfishness and yield the throne to Christ. Only then can you live a Christ-directed life. (***See Adoption**> With Christ> Supernatural,* TopicGuide page A37.)

25:11 God's blessings on Isaac were a continuation of His promise to Abraham. While Abraham had other children, Isaac was the son of God's covenant with Abraham (Galatians 4:22-23). God promised Abraham that his descendants would be as numerous as the stars and the sand. It was through Isaac, not his half-brother Ishmael, that God's promise was to be fulfilled (Genesis 21:9-13). God protected that promise by keeping Isaac safe and providing a large inheritance for him to pass on to his son Jacob, through whom God's covenant promise continued (Genesis 25–27).

25:23 God's revelation to Rebekah was fulfilled literally. The boys were in conflict even before their births. Jacob's descendants, the Israelites, experienced ongoing conflict with Esau's descendants, the Edomites. Under King David and King Solomon, Israel took control of Edom, but only for a time. Generations later, when the Jews were in exile in Babylon, Edomites began to infiltrate their land. The Old Testament book of Obadiah was a prophecy against Edom, and many other Old Testament prophets spoke judgment upon Edom as well, including Isaiah, Ezekiel, Joel, Amos, and Malachi.

ESAU SELLS HIS BIRTHRIGHT

27 As the boys grew up, Esau became a skillful hunter. He was an outdoorsman, but Ja-
cob had a quiet temperament, preferring to stay at home. 28 Isaac loved Esau because
he enjoyed eating the wild game Esau brought home, but Rebekah loved Jacob.
29 One day when Jacob was cooking some stew, Esau arrived home from the wil-
derness exhausted and hungry. 30 Esau said to Jacob, "I'm starved! Give me some **25:30**
of that red stew!" (This is how Esau got his other name, Edom, which means "red.") Gen 36:1, 8
31 "All right," Jacob replied, "but trade me your rights as the firstborn son." **25:31**
32 "Look, I'm dying of starvation!" said Esau. "What good is my birthright to me now?" Deut 21:16-17
33 But Jacob said, "First you must swear that your birthright is mine." So Esau swore an 1 Chr 5:1-2
oath, thereby selling all his rights as the firstborn to his brother, Jacob. **25:33**
34 Then Jacob gave Esau some bread and lentil stew. Esau ate the meal, then got up and Gen 27:36
left. He showed contempt for his rights as the firstborn. Heb 12:16

ISAAC DECEIVES ABIMELECH

26 A severe famine now struck the land, as had happened before in Abraham's **26:1**
time. So Isaac moved to Gerar, where Abimelech, king of the Philistines, lived. Gen 12:10; 20:1-2
2 The LORD appeared to Isaac and said, "Do not go down to Egypt, but do as I tell you.
3 Live here as a foreigner in this land, and I will be with you and bless you. I hereby con- **26:2** Gen 12:1, 7
firm that I will give all these lands to you and your descendants,* just as I solemnly prom- **26:3**
ised Abraham, your father. 4 I will cause your descendants to become as numerous as the Gen 12:7; 15:15, 18
stars of the sky, and I will give them all these lands. And through your descendants all the **26:4**
nations of the earth will be blessed. 5 I will do this because Abraham listened to Me and Gen 15:5; 22:17
obeyed all My requirements, commands, decrees, and instructions." 6 So Isaac stayed in Exod 32:13 *Acts 3:25
Gerar. *Gal 3:8

26:3 Hebrew *seed;* also in 26:4, 24.

25:31 In the ancient Hebrew world, all children typically received an inheritance, but only the eldest son received a birthright. The birthright included privilege as well as responsibility. With the birthright came a double portion of the father's inheritance, as well as the responsibility of family leadership, which included caring for any sisters who remained unmarried. When the father had more than one wife, the birthright usually went to the firstborn of the first wife, even if the husband had older sons with a second wife or concubine. The birthright could be traded among family members, as it was with Jacob and Esau, but it was seldom traded away from the children of the first wife.

▸ ADOPTION

25:33 Heirs of God. When Jacob insisted that Esau swear over his birthright, which included Esau's double share of the inheritance, he demonstrated an ungodly concern for instant gratification. But God is not always interested in our immediate satisfaction. He wants us to grow into Christ-centered people. This means that our focus should not be on earthly things but on our kingdom inheritance. When our priorities are right, God meets our daily needs. Jesus said, "Your heavenly Father already knows all your needs. Seek the Kingdom of God above all else, and live righteously, and he will give you everything you need" (Matthew 6:32-33). (***See Adoption**> With Christ> Heirs of God> Receive inheritance through faith and patience,* TopicGuide page A36.)

26:1 Gerar was in Philistia, a region to the south and west of Israel along the Mediterranean Sea. Its inhabitants were called Philistines. The word *Palestine* actually comes from the word *Philistine.* They were more advanced in their technology than the Hebrews. While they are merely mentioned in the days of Abraham, by the eras of the judges and the kings, the Philistines had become major enemies of the Hebrews. Abraham also spent time in Gerar and had dealings with a king named Abimelech (Genesis 20–21), but the Abimelech in this passage was probably a later king of the same name.

26:2 It is important to remember that these people did not have access to the Scriptures, so God's instructions sometimes came in very direct ways. Genesis records several instances in which the Lord appeared to people, just as He did to Isaac here. God walked in the Garden with Adam and Eve (Genesis 3:8-10). He conversed with Cain (Genesis 4:6-16). He appeared to Isaac's father Abraham on several occasions (Genesis 13:14-17; 15:1-21; 17:1-21). Later, God would appear to Isaac's son Jacob in a dream at Bethel (Genesis 28:10-15), promising him the same land that had been promised to his grandfather Abraham and his father Isaac.

26:3-5 God here made with Isaac the same covenant He made with Isaac's father, Abraham, giving Isaac the same promises (see Genesis 12:1-3; 13:14-17; 15:13-16). In the outworking of these promises, God gave Isaac's son Jacob 12 sons, and these sons became the ancestors of the 12 tribes of Israel. During the next 400 years, Isaac's descendants grew from a family of around 70 to a nation of more than two million people. Then God delivered them from slavery in Egypt and led them back to take possession of the very land where Isaac was given the promise. Finally, through Isaac's great descendant, Jesus Christ, people of all the nations of the earth were blessed.

26:7 Gen 12:11-13; 7When the men who lived there asked Isaac about his wife, Rebekah, he said, "She is
20:2, 12 my sister." He was afraid to say, "She is my wife." He thought, "They will kill me to get her,
because she is so beautiful." 8But some time later, Abimelech, king of the Philistines,
looked out his window and saw Isaac caressing Rebekah.
9Immediately, Abimelech called for Isaac and exclaimed, "She is obviously your wife!
Why did you say, 'She is my sister'?"
"Because I was afraid someone would kill me to get her from me," Isaac replied.
26:10 10"How could you do this to us?" Abimelech exclaimed. "One of my people might
Gen 20:7-10 easily have taken your wife and slept with her, and you would have made us guilty of
great sin."
11Then Abimelech issued a public proclamation: "Anyone who touches this man or his
wife will be put to death!"

CONFLICT OVER WATER RIGHTS

26:12 12When Isaac planted his crops that year, he harvested a hundred times more grain than
Gen 26:3 he planted, for the LORD blessed him. 13He became a very rich man, and his wealth con-
26:13 tinued to grow. 14He acquired so many flocks of sheep and goats, herds of cattle, and
Gen 24:35; 25:5 servants that the Philistines became jealous of him. 15So the Philistines filled up all of
26:15 Gen 21:25 Isaac's wells with dirt. These were the wells that had been dug by the servants of his fa-
ther, Abraham.
26:16 16Finally, Abimelech ordered Isaac to leave the country. "Go somewhere else," he said,
Exod 1:9 "for you have become too powerful for us."
17So Isaac moved away to the Gerar Valley, where he set up their tents and settled
down. 18He reopened the wells his father had dug, which the Philistines had filled in after
Abraham's death. Isaac also restored the names Abraham had given them.
26:19 19Isaac's servants also dug in the Gerar Valley and discovered a well of fresh water.
John 4:10-11 20But then the shepherds from Gerar came and claimed the spring. "This is our water,"
they said, and they argued over it with Isaac's herdsmen. So Isaac named the well Esek
(which means "argument"). 21Isaac's men then dug another well, but again there was a
26:22 dispute over it. So Isaac named it Sitnah (which means "hostility"). 22Abandoning that
Pss 4:1; 18:19 one, Isaac moved on and dug another well. This time there was no dispute over it, so
Isa 54:2 Isaac named the place Rehoboth (which means "open space"), for he said, "At last the
LORD has created enough space for us to prosper in this land."

26:6-11 Isaac was repeating his father's mistake. Twice when Abraham traveled with his wife, Sarah, he introduced her as his sister (Genesis 12:10-20; 20:1-18). This was technically true—she was his half-sister—but it was not right for him to neglect revealing that she was also his wife. Abraham did this so that the men of the town he was visiting wouldn't kill him in order to get her. In both cases, Abraham's choice was foolish and ended badly, though God intervened to minimize the damage. In a similar situation, Isaac copied his father's lie for the same reason, even though Rebekah was actually a cousin. (Her father was Bethuel and her grandfather was Nahor. Nahor was Abraham's brother, and thus Isaac's uncle.)

▸ SALVATION

26:7 Appreciating sin. "She is my sister" is a familiar statement in Genesis (see Genesis 12:10-20; 20:1-18). How could Isaac commit such a grievous sin on the heels of an intimate encounter with God (Genesis 26:1-5)? His sin was due to two things: 1) the frailty of his own flesh and 2) the bad example of his father, Abraham. Today you may be living a life of total surrender to Christ. But be watchful. Heed the warning of 1 Corinthians 10:12: "If you think you are standing strong, be careful not to fall." (***See Salvation****> Our Need> Sinful> Influence of father,* TopicGuide page A22.)

26:12-15 In verse 3, God told Isaac to stay in Gerar instead of traveling to Egypt as his father, Abraham, had done in the midst of a famine. God was promising Isaac that if he stayed in the land that had been promised to his ancestors, blessings would come his way. That is exactly what happened. Here we learn about those blessings. Isaac acquired great wealth to the point that the locals, who were Philistines, tried to force him out of the land by harassing him. Abraham had faced a similar situation when his livestock grew so numerous that he and his nephew Lot had to move apart just to have enough pastureland (Genesis 13:1-10). Eventually, the superabundant blessings of God so impressed Gerar's king, Abimelech, that he sought a peace treaty with Isaac, just as an earlier Abimelech did with Abraham (Genesis 21:22-34).

23From there Isaac moved to Beersheba, 24where the LORD appeared to him on the night of his arrival. "I am the God of your father, Abraham," He said. "Do not be afraid, for I am with you and will bless you. I will multiply your descendants, and they will become a great nation. I will do this because of My promise to Abraham, My servant." 25Then Isaac built an altar there and worshiped the LORD. He set up his camp at that place, and his servants dug another well.

ISAAC'S COVENANT WITH ABIMELECH

26One day King Abimelech came from Gerar with his adviser, Ahuzzath, and also Phicol, his army commander. 27"Why have you come here?" Isaac asked. "You obviously hate me, since you kicked me off your land."

28They replied, "We can plainly see that the LORD is with you. So we want to enter into a sworn treaty with you. Let's make a covenant. 29Swear that you will not harm us, just as we have never troubled you. We have always treated you well, and we sent you away from us in peace. And now look how the LORD has blessed you!"

30So Isaac prepared a covenant feast to celebrate the treaty, and they ate and drank together. 31Early the next morning, they each took a solemn oath not to interfere with each other. Then Isaac sent them home again, and they left him in peace.

32That very day Isaac's servants came and told him about a new well they had dug. "We've found water!" they exclaimed. 33So Isaac named the well Shibah (which means "oath"). And to this day the town that grew up there is called Beersheba (which means "well of the oath").

34At the age of forty, Esau married two Hittite wives: Judith, the daughter of Beeri, and Basemath, the daughter of Elon. 35But Esau's wives made life miserable for Isaac and Rebekah.

JACOB STEALS ESAU'S BLESSING

27 One day when Isaac was old and turning blind, he called for Esau, his older son, and said, "My son."

"Yes, Father?" Esau replied.

2"I am an old man now," Isaac said, "and I don't know when I may die. 3Take your bow and a quiver full of arrows, and go out into the open country to hunt some wild game for me. 4Prepare my favorite dish, and bring it here for me to eat. Then I will pronounce the blessing that belongs to you, my firstborn son, before I die."

5But Rebekah overheard what Isaac had said to his son Esau. So when Esau left to hunt for the wild game, 6she said to her son Jacob, "Listen. I overheard your father say to Esau,

26:23 Gen 22:19
26:24 Gen 17:7; 22:17 Exod 3:6
26:25 Gen 12:7-8; 13:4
26:26 Gen 21:22
26:27 Gen 26:16
26:28 Gen 21:22-23
26:30 Gen 31:54
26:31 Gen 21:31
26:33 Gen 21:31
26:34 Gen 28:8
26:35 Gen 27:46
27:1 Gen 25:25; 48:10
27:2 Gen 47:29
27:3 Gen 25:27
27:4 Gen 24:60; 27:19; 48:9
27:5-6 Gen 25:27-28

▸ **GOD**

26:30 Names and roles of the Son: Friend of sinners. Isaac prepared a great feast because a covenant typically was sealed with a meal. The meal demonstrated shared friendship and mutual commitment (see Exodus 24:11; 1 Corinthians 11:23-34). This idea of shared friendship is echoed by Jesus, who says, "You are My friends if you do what I command" (John 15:14). Jesus is a friend to sinners, but having Jesus as your close friend requires you to be His committed friend in return. You can have no greater friend than Jesus. Give Him your wholehearted commitment today. (***See God> God's Names> Son***, TopicGuide page A18.)

27:4 In the ancient world, the firstborn son usually received the family birthright (leadership responsibilities as well as a double portion of the inheritance) and a blessing (which was more of a legal transfer of property and authority than merely kind words and good wishes). Generally, the birthright and the blessing went hand in hand. Esau had already sold his birthright to his younger twin, Jacob, for a bowl of stew (Genesis 25:27-34). Now Isaac was preparing to bestow the blessing on Esau, but Jacob, with Rebekah's help, cheated him out of it. This fulfilled God's promise that the younger son would be the family leader (Genesis 25:23).

27:5-29 This story leaves the impression that Rebekah was a manipulative, conniving wife and mother. Only one bit of information in the Scriptures justifies her actions. Before the boys were born, God told Rebekah that there were two nations in her womb. He also told her that the older boy would serve the younger (Genesis 25:22-23). Rebekah held that prophecy in her memory for more than 40 years. When it came time for the authority to be established between the boys, she believed that Jacob must have Isaac's blessing. So she did the same thing that Sarah, her mother-in-law, had done (Genesis 16:1-5). Instead of leaving the situation to God, she took matters into her own hands, causing such hatred between her sons that Jacob had to run for his life. She would never see Jacob again.

7'Bring me some wild game and prepare me a delicious meal. Then I will bless you in the
27:8 LORD's presence before I die.' 8Now, my son, listen to me. Do exactly as I tell you. 9Go out
Gen 27:13, 43 to the flocks, and bring me two fine young goats. I'll use them to prepare your father's fa-
vorite dish. 10Then take the food to your father so he can eat it and bless you before he
dies."

27:11 11"But look," Jacob replied to Rebekah, "my brother, Esau, is a hairy man, and my skin is
Gen 25:25 smooth. **27:12** 12What if my father touches me? He'll see that I'm trying to trick him, and then
Gen 9:25; 27:21-22 he'll curse me instead of blessing me."

13But his mother replied, "Then let the curse fall on me, my son! Just do what I tell you.
27:13 Gen 27:8 Go out and get the goats for me!"

14So Jacob went out and got the young goats for his mother. Rebekah took them and
prepared a delicious meal, just the way Isaac liked it. 15Then she took Esau's favorite
27:15 Gen 27:27 clothes, which were there in the house, and gave them to her younger son, Jacob. 16She
covered his arms and the smooth part of his neck with the skin of the young goats. 17Then
she gave Jacob the delicious meal, including freshly baked bread.

18So Jacob took the food to his father. "My father?" he said.

"Yes, my son," Isaac answered. "Who are you—Esau or Jacob?"

27:19 19Jacob replied, "It's Esau, your firstborn son. I've done as you told me. Here is the wild
Gen 27:31 game. Now sit up and eat it so you can give me your blessing."

20Isaac asked, "How did you find it so quickly, my son?"

"The LORD your God put it in my path!" Jacob replied.

27:21 21Then Isaac said to Jacob, "Come closer so I can touch you and make sure that you
Gen 27:12 really are Esau." 22So Jacob went closer to his father, and Isaac touched him. "The voice is
27:23 Jacob's, but the hands are Esau's," Isaac said. 23But he did not recognize Jacob, because Ja-
Gen 27:16 cob's hands felt hairy just like Esau's. So Isaac prepared to bless Jacob. 24"But are you real-
ly my son Esau?" he asked.

"Yes, I am," Jacob replied.

27:25 25Then Isaac said, "Now, my son, bring me the wild game. Let me eat it, and then I will
Gen 27:4 give you my blessing." So Jacob took the food to his father, and Isaac ate it. He also drank
the wine that Jacob served him. Then Isaac said to Jacob, 26"Please come a little closer and
kiss me, my son."

27:27 Ps 65:10 27So Jacob went over and kissed him. And when Isaac caught the smell of his clothes, he
Heb 11:20 was finally convinced, and he blessed his son. He said, "Ah! The smell of my son is like the
smell of the outdoors, which the LORD has blessed!

27:28 Deut 7:13; 33:13, 28 28 "From the dew of heaven
Zech 8:12 and the richness of the earth,
may God always give you abundant harvests of grain
and bountiful new wine.

27:29 29 May many nations become your servants,
Gen 9:25-27; 12:3 Isa 45:14 and may they bow down to you.
May you be the master over your brothers,
and may your mother's sons bow down to you.
All who curse you will be cursed,
and all who bless you will be blessed."

SALVATION

27:11 Heirs of God. The name *Jacob* in Hebrew means "he will grab the heel" or "he will trick." Jacob was an individual who sought to take by trickery what God would have given him had he been willing to wait. Impatience with God's plan is a problem for most Christians. Yet the prophet Isaiah declares, "Those who trust in the LORD will find new strength. They will soar high on wings like eagles. They will run and not grow weary. They will walk and not faint" (Isaiah 40:31). Waiting on God's promises is hard. But it is in those times of waiting, and sometimes suffering, that God matures us and makes us more like Christ (see 1 Peter 4:12-13). (***See Salvation**> Receiving> When> Heirs of God,* TopicGuide page A22.)

30As soon as Isaac had finished blessing Jacob, and almost before Jacob had left his fa-
ther, Esau returned from his hunt. 31Esau prepared a delicious meal and brought it to his 27:31
father. Then he said, "Sit up, my father, and eat my wild game so you can give me your Gen 27:4
blessing."
32But Isaac asked him, "Who are you?" 27:32 Gen 27:18
Esau replied, "It's your son, your firstborn son, Esau."
33Isaac began to tremble uncontrollably and said, "Then who just served me wild 27:33
game? I have already eaten it, and I blessed him just before you came. And yes, that bless- Gen 27:35
ing must stand!"
34When Esau heard his father's words, he let out a loud and bitter cry. "Oh my father, 27:34
what about me? Bless me, too!" he begged. Heb 12:17
35But Isaac said, "Your brother was here, and he tricked me. He has taken away your 27:35
blessing." Gen 27:19
36Esau exclaimed, "No wonder his name is Jacob, for now he has cheated me twice.* 27:36
First he took my rights as the firstborn, and now he has stolen my blessing. Oh, haven't Gen 25:26
you saved even one blessing for me?"
37Isaac said to Esau, "I have made Jacob your master and have declared that all his 27:37
brothers will be his servants. I have guaranteed him an abundance of grain and wine— Gen 27:28-29
what is left for me to give you, my son?"
38Esau pleaded, "But do you have only one blessing? Oh my father, bless me, too!" Then 27:38
Esau broke down and wept. Heb 12:17
39Finally, his father, Isaac, said to him, 27:39 Heb 11:20

"You will live away from the richness of the earth,
and away from the dew of the heaven above.
40 You will live by your sword, 27:40 2 Kgs 8:20-22
and you will serve your brother.
But when you decide to break free,
you will shake his yoke from your neck."

JACOB FLEES TO PADDAN-ARAM

41From that time on, Esau hated Jacob because their father had given Jacob the blessing. 27:41 Gen 32:3-11; 37:4
And Esau began to scheme: "I will soon be mourning my father's death. Then I will kill my
brother, Jacob."
42But Rebekah heard about Esau's plans. So she sent for Jacob and told him, "Lis-

27:36 *Jacob* sounds like the Hebrew words for "heel" and "deceiver."

27:33-39 It is inconceivable to our modern way of thinking that Isaac couldn't just call his family together and correct the mistake. In this time, however, paperwork wasn't the binding factor in a legal agreement. A verbal blessing carried the same weight as a legal transaction. Jacob had received the rights to the family leadership and a large part of the family fortune. That would forever change his legacy, as well as Esau's.

27:37 Genesis displays a pattern of a younger son taking power over an older son. For example, Abraham's first son was Ishmael, but Isaac was the son of Abraham's first wife and the son of God's promise (Genesis 21:9-13). Isaac then had twin sons; Esau was born before Jacob, but as an adult, Jacob got both the birthright and the blessing (Genesis 25:29-34; 27:5-30). Jacob then passed the birthright on to his favorite son, Joseph, his older son by his most beloved wife. This bypassed Reuben, who was actually Jacob's oldest son (Genesis 49:3-4). Finally, of Joseph's sons, Manasseh was older than Ephraim, but when Joseph asked his father to bless them, Jacob gave the greater blessing to the younger son (Genesis 48:13-20).

27:39-40 In response to Esau's anguished plea for a blessing, any blessing, from his father, Isaac said, "You will live away from the richness of the earth, and away from the dew of the heaven above." The Hebrew text of this passage actually indicates that Isaac, speaking prophetically, was saying that Esau would live away from the fertile lands that Jacob would occupy. This prophecy found fulfillment as Esau's descendants, the Edomites, settled in desert lands south of the Dead Sea. Isaac also said that Esau's family would live by the sword and that, after a time of serving Jacob's descendants, would break free from their domination. These prophecies also were fulfilled in the following centuries.

27:43 ten, Esau is consoling himself by plotting to kill you. 43So listen carefully, my son. Get
Gen 27:8 ready and flee to my brother, Laban, in Haran. 44Stay there with him until your
27:44 brother cools off. 45When he calms down and forgets what you have done to him, I
Gen 31:41 will send for you to come back. Why should I lose both of you in one day?"
46Then Rebekah said to Isaac, "I'm sick and tired of these local Hittite women! I would
27:46 Gen 26:34-35 rather die than see Jacob marry one of them."

28 So Isaac called for Jacob, blessed him, and said, "You must not marry any of
28:1 these Canaanite women. 2Instead, go at once to Paddan-aram, to the house of
Gen 24:3 your grandfather Bethuel, and marry one of your uncle Laban's daughters. 3May God Al-
28:2 mighty* bless you and give you many children. And may your descendants multiply and
Gen 25:20 become many nations! 4May God pass on to you and your descendants* the blessings
28:3 Gen 17:16; 35:11 He promised to Abraham. May you own this land where you are now living as a for-
28:4 eigner, for God gave this land to Abraham."
Gen 12:1-3; 15:7; 5So Isaac sent Jacob away, and he went to Paddan-aram to stay with his uncle Laban,
35:11 his mother's brother, the son of Bethuel the Aramean.
6Esau knew that his father, Isaac, had blessed Jacob and sent him to Paddan-
28:6 Gen 28:1 aram to find a wife, and that he had warned Jacob, "You must not marry a Canaan-
ite woman." 7He also knew that Jacob had obeyed his parents and gone to Paddan-
aram. 8It was now very clear to Esau that his father did not like the local Canaanite
28:8 women. 9So Esau visited his uncle Ishmael's family and married one of Ishmael's
Gen 26:35 daughters, in addition to the wives he already had. His new wife's name was Maha-
28:9 Gen 36:2 lath. She was the sister of Nebaioth and the daughter of Ishmael, Abraham's son.

JACOB'S DREAM AT BETHEL

10Meanwhile, Jacob left Beersheba and traveled toward Haran. 11At sundown he arrived at
28:10 a good place to set up camp and stopped there for the night. Jacob found a stone to rest
Gen 26:23 his head against and lay down to sleep. 12As he slept, he dreamed of a stairway that

28:3 Hebrew *El-Shaddai*. 28:4 Hebrew *seed;* also in 28:13, 14.

27:43 Jacob's uncle Laban entered the story when Jacob's grandfather, Abraham, sent his servant to Haran to find a bride for Isaac, Jacob's father (Genesis 24:1-4). In Haran, the servant met Rebekah, Laban's sister. Rebekah and Laban were grandchildren of Abraham's brother Nahor. Thus, Rebekah was Isaac's cousin, but that was not a taboo relationship at that time. Now, after many years, Rebekah sent Jacob back to her brother and her homeland so Jacob could escape death at Esau's hand.

28:1-4 When Isaac sent Jacob away, he did so with his blessing. He was not angry or vengeful toward Rebekah and Jacob. In fact, in his blessing, he passed on to Jacob the same promises that God had given to Abraham (Genesis 17:4-8) and to him (Genesis 26:3-4). Why was Isaac so benevolent? Esau had already taken two wives, both Canaanite. That means they were local women who probably worshiped Canaanite gods. These wives "made life miserable for Isaac and Rebekah" (Genesis 26:34-35). Isaac may have realized that if Esau had received the birthright, God's promised nation would have begun with divided interests in worship.

▶ CHURCH

28:3 The church's mission. Isaac's blessing foresaw that Jacob would have children from "many nations" (Genesis 17:5; see also Genesis 12:3). When we apply this vision for Israel to the local church, we learn that we must be willing to foster a community of people comprised of every nation, tribe, and tongue. Jesus said, "Therefore, go and make disciples of *all* the nations, baptizing them in the name of the Father and the Son and the Holy Spirit" (Matthew 28:19, italics added). The most important thing you can do is to be part of God's exciting plan to fulfill this command of Jesus, which is known as the Great Commission. This includes discipling people into an ethnically diverse community of believers. (***See Church***> *Mission*> *Nurture*> *Fostering community,* TopicGuide page A49.)

28:6-9 Hearing that Jacob had obeyed Isaac and Rebekah and had gone to Paddan-aram to seek a wife among his mother's relatives, Esau made a pathetic attempt to please his parents. He took one of the daughters of Ishmael as a wife. Ishmael was a son of Abraham and a half-brother of Isaac, and Esau apparently thought these family connections would make his new wife acceptable to Isaac and Rebekah. He did not understand that Isaac, not Ishmael, was the son of God's promise, the family line chosen for God's blessing. In the same way, Jacob had been chosen over Esau to receive the promises.

reached from the earth up to heaven. And he saw the angels of God going up and down
the stairway.
13 At the top of the stairway stood the LORD, and He said, "I am the LORD, the God of your
grandfather Abraham, and the God of your father, Isaac. The ground you are lying on be-
longs to you. I am giving it to you and your descendants. 14 Your descendants will be as
numerous as the dust of the earth! They will spread out in all directions—to the west and
the east, to the north and the south. And all the families of the earth will be blessed
through you and your descendants. 15 What's more, I am with you, and I will protect you
wherever you go. One day I will bring you back to this land. I will not leave you until I
have finished giving you everything I have promised you."
16 Then Jacob awoke from his sleep and said, "Surely the LORD is in this place, and I
wasn't even aware of it!" 17 But he was also afraid and said, "What an awesome place this
is! It is none other than the house of God, the very gateway to heaven!"
18 The next morning Jacob got up very early. He took the stone he had rested his head
against, and he set it upright as a memorial pillar. Then he poured olive oil over it. 19 He
named that place Bethel (which means "house of God"), although the name of the nearby
village was Luz.
20 Then Jacob made this vow: "If God will indeed be with me and protect me on this jour-
ney, and if He will provide me with food and clothing, 21 and if I return safely to my father's
home, then the LORD will certainly be my God. 22 And this memorial pillar I have set up will
become a place for worshiping God, and I will present to God a tenth of everything He
gives me."

28:12 Gen 20:3; Num 12:6; *John 1:51
28:14 Gen 12:2; 13:14; 22:17
28:15 Gen 48:21; Deut 7:9; 31:6, 8
28:17 Exod 3:5; Ps 68:35
28:18 Gen 35:14
28:19 Gen 12:8; 35:6; 48:3
28:21 Exod 15:2
28:22 Gen 14:20; 35:7; Deut 14:22

JACOB ARRIVES AT PADDAN-ARAM

29 Then Jacob hurried on, finally arriving in the land of the east. 2 He saw a well in
the distance. Three flocks of sheep and goats lay in an open field beside it, wait-
ing to be watered. But a heavy stone covered the mouth of the well.
3 It was the custom there to wait for all the flocks to arrive before removing the stone
and watering the animals. Afterward the stone would be placed back over the mouth of
the well. 4 Jacob went over to the shepherds and asked, "Where are you from, my
friends?"

29:1 Judg 6:3, 33
29:2 Gen 24:10-11
29:4 Gen 28:10

▸ **GOD**

28:12-13 Jesus' work. Jacob dreamed of a "stairway that reached from the earth up to heaven." Often called "Jacob's ladder," the image was more like a flight of stairs that accommodated angels ascending and descending between heaven and earth. This is one of many Old Testament images that foreshadow Christ. Jesus said, "I tell you the truth, you will all see heaven open and the angels of God going up and down on the Son of Man, the one who is the stairway between heaven and earth" (John 1:51). Jesus is the bridge between heaven and earth, the only Mediator between God and people (see 1 Timothy 2:5). If you have not received Him, do so today, for "There is salvation in no one else! God has given no other name under heaven by which we must be saved" (Acts 4:12). (***See God*> *Salvation*> *Son*> *Only bridge between God and man*, TopicGuide page A15.)**

28:13 God identified Himself according to Jacob's family legacy. Jacob had surely been taught the old family stories of God's promises to make Abraham's descendants a great nation. In a world that honored many gods, Jacob would trust the same God who had led his ancestors.

28:13-15 The promise that God announced in Jacob's dream was the same promise that God had first made to Abraham, Jacob's grandfather, and later had confirmed to Isaac, Jacob's father (see Genesis 13:14-17; 15:1-21; 26:4, 24). God promised to give the land of Canaan to Jacob and his descendants, to make Jacob's descendants into a vast nation, and to bless people from all over the earth through them. Moreover, God gave Jacob a very personal promise: God said that He would go with Jacob as he temporarily left the land, that He would protect him, and that He would bring him back to Canaan someday.

28:20-22 This was a turning point in Jacob's life and in the legacy he passed on to his descendants. Much of Jacob's life to this point had been filled with deception and selfishness. He had taken advantage of his brother and deceived his father. Now he was fleeing in part because of his brother's anger toward him (Genesis 27:34-41). But despite this sinful life, God came to Jacob and showered him with gracious promises. Jacob still wasn't willing to step out in faith, as his grandfather Abraham did—he wanted to see God keep His promises before committing to Him. But God now had his attention.

"We are from Haran," they answered.
29:5 5 "Do you know a man there named Laban, the grandson of Nahor?" he asked.
Gen 11:29 "Yes, we do," they replied.
29:6 6 "Is he doing well?" Jacob asked.
Exod 2:16 "Yes, he's well," they answered. "Look, here comes his daughter Rachel with the flock
now."
7 Jacob said, "Look, it's still broad daylight—too early to round up the animals. Why don't
you water the sheep and goats so they can get back out to pasture?"
8 "We can't water the animals until all the flocks have arrived," they replied. "Then the
shepherds move the stone from the mouth of the well, and we water all the sheep and
goats."
9 Jacob was still talking with them when Rachel arrived with her father's flock, for she
29:10 was a shepherd. 10 And because Rachel was his cousin—the daughter of Laban, his
Exod 2:17 mother's brother—and because the sheep and goats belonged to his uncle Laban, Jacob
went over to the well and moved the stone from its mouth and watered his uncle's flock.
11 Then Jacob kissed Rachel, and he wept aloud. 12 He explained to Rachel that he was her
29:11 Gen 33:4 cousin on her father's side—the son of her aunt Rebekah. So Rachel quickly ran and told
29:12 her father, Laban.
Gen 28:5 13 As soon as Laban heard that his nephew Jacob had arrived, he ran out to meet him.
29:14 He embraced and kissed him and brought him home. When Jacob had told him his story,
Judg 9:2 14 Laban exclaimed, "You really are my own flesh and blood!"
2 Sam 5:1

JACOB MARRIES LEAH AND RACHEL

After Jacob had stayed with Laban for about a month, 15 Laban said to him, "You shouldn't
29:15 Gen 30:28; 31:7, 41 work for me without pay just because we are relatives. Tell me how much your wages
should be."
16 Now Laban had two daughters. The older daughter was named Leah, and the youn-
29:16 ger one was Rachel. 17 There was no sparkle in Leah's eyes,* but Rachel had a beautiful
Gen 29:25-26 29:17 figure and a lovely face. 18 Since Jacob was in love with Rachel, he told her father, "I'll
Gen 12:11 work for you for seven years if you'll give me Rachel, your younger daughter, as my
29:18 wife."
Gen 24:67 Hos 12:12 19 "Agreed!" Laban replied. "I'd rather give her to you than to anyone else. Stay and work

29:17 Or *Leah had dull eyes,* or *Leah had soft eyes.* The meaning of the Hebrew is uncertain.

29:7-8 Jacob was basically "talking shop." His family had been herders for generations. Jacob's grandfather, Abraham, had been rich in livestock. In fact, at one point Abraham had parted ways with his nephew Lot because their livestock had become too abundant for the available pastureland (Genesis 13:1-10). Jacob's father, Isaac, had become so rich in grain, sheep, goats, and cattle that the Philistines tried to harass him out of the land (Genesis 26:12-22). So the care and feeding of livestock were topics that Jacob could easily make conversation about. He eventually spent twenty years working livestock with Laban, Rachel's father. Through selective breeding, Jacob built a large herd to take with him when he traveled back to the land God had promised him.

29:11 Jacob had been sent on this journey to find a wife from his own people. His family lived among the Canaanites. His brother, Esau, had married Canaanite women, which had made Jacob and Esau's parents miserable (Genesis 26:34-35). Jacob was looking for the family of Laban so that he could find a wife who came from the same heritage that he did. It was from this family that his mother, Rebekah, had come. In fact, Laban was Rebekah's brother, which meant that Rachel was Jacob's cousin. In that time such close family ties were no barrier to marriage.

29:19 Large, extended families were extremely important in this time. Many felt it was safer to marry within a familiar community, so marriage between half-siblings and cousins was acceptable. Abraham's wife, Sarah, was also his half-sister, and Isaac's wife, Rebekah, was his cousin (Genesis 20:11-13; 24:15). Therefore, Laban was thrilled to have his daughter (and eventually both his daughters) marry a cousin like Jacob. As people spread out and populated the earth, marriage between close relatives became taboo.

with me." 20 So Jacob worked seven years to pay for Rachel. But his love for her was so strong that it seemed to him but a few days.

21 Finally, the time came for him to marry her. "I have fulfilled my agreement," Jacob said to Laban. "Now give me my wife so I can marry her."

22 So Laban invited everyone in the neighborhood and prepared a wedding feast. 23 But that night, when it was dark, Laban took Leah to Jacob, and he slept with her. 24 (Laban had given Leah a servant, Zilpah, to be her maid.)

25 But when Jacob woke up in the morning—it was Leah! "What have you done to me?" Jacob raged at Laban. "I worked seven years for Rachel! Why have you tricked me?"

26 "It's not our custom here to marry off a younger daughter ahead of the firstborn," Laban replied. 27 "But wait until the bridal week is over, then we'll give you Rachel, too—provided you promise to work another seven years for me."

28 So Jacob agreed to work seven more years. A week after Jacob had married Leah, Laban gave him Rachel, too. 29 (Laban gave Rachel a servant, Bilhah, to be her maid.) 30 So Jacob slept with Rachel, too, and he loved her much more than Leah. He then stayed and worked for Laban the additional seven years.

JACOB'S MANY CHILDREN

31 When the LORD saw that Leah was unloved, He enabled her to have children, but Rachel could not conceive. 32 So Leah became pregnant and gave birth to a son. She named him Reuben,* for she said, "The LORD has noticed my misery, and now my husband will love me."

33 She soon became pregnant again and gave birth to another son. She named him Simeon,* for she said, "The LORD heard that I was unloved and has given me another son."

34 Then she became pregnant a third time and gave birth to another son. She named him Levi,* for she said, "Surely this time my husband will feel affection for me, since I have given him three sons!"

35 Once again Leah became pregnant and gave birth to another son. She named him Judah,* for she said, "Now I will praise the LORD!" And then she stopped having children.

30 When Rachel saw that she wasn't having any children for Jacob, she became jealous of her sister. She pleaded with Jacob, "Give me children, or I'll die!"

2 Then Jacob became furious with Rachel. "Am I God?" he asked. "He's the One who has kept you from having children!"

3 Then Rachel told him, "Take my maid, Bilhah, and sleep with her. She will bear children for me,* and through her I can have a family, too." 4 So Rachel gave her servant, Bil-

29:20 Song 8:7
29:22 Judg 14:10
29:23 Gen 24:65; 38:14
29:24 Gen 30:9
29:25 Gen 12:18
29:27 Judg 14:12
29:29 Gen 30:3
29:30 Gen 29:16
29:31 Deut 21:15-17
29:32 Gen 30:23; 37:21; 46:8
29:33 Deut 21:15
29:34 Gen 49:5
29:35 Gen 49:8 Matt 1:2-3
30:1 1 Sam 1:5-6
30:2 Gen 20:18; 29:31
30:3-4 Gen 16:2-4

29:32 *Reuben* means "Look, a son!" It also sounds like the Hebrew for "He has seen my misery." 29:33 *Simeon* probably means "one who hears." 29:34 *Levi* sounds like a Hebrew term that means "being attached" or "feeling affection for." 29:35 *Judah* sounds like the Hebrew term for "praise." 30:3 Hebrew *bear children on my knees.*

29:23-25 Jacob's name in Hebrew meant "he will grab the heel" or "he will trick." It was an apt name, for Jacob lived much of his early life by cunning and deception. But now Jacob found himself deceived, and he wasn't very happy about it. God would use Laban to teach Jacob to rely on Him, not on his own wits.

29:31 In this time, a woman's worth was largely defined by her ability to bear children for her husband—particularly sons. If she did not accomplish this, the husband's legacy ended with his death. That was seen as a shameful fate. Both Jacob's mother, Rebekah, and his grandmother, Sarah, had struggled to have children. Later, a great Israelite leader, Samuel, was born out of his mother's prayer that God would end her infertility and give her a son (1 Samuel 1:1-20). The lesson of these stories is that it is God who gives—or withholds—the fruit of the womb for His own purposes. Jacob recognized this truth (Genesis 30:2), as did Solomon, who called children "a gift from the LORD" (Psalm 127:3).

30:3 It was not unusual for Rachel to offer her servant to Jacob as a way to get children. In fact, Abraham's wife, Sarah, had done the same thing with her servant, Hagar (Genesis 16:1-5). Most often when a woman's servant became pregnant by the husband, the child was still considered an heir of the husband and wife. The wife often came to the birth and laid the child on her knee to define her role as mother (Genesis 16:1-3). In this way, the servant functioned as a surrogate for the family. In the cases of both Sarah and Rachel, desperation was unnecessary. Both eventually bore sons for their husbands.

30:6 hah, to Jacob as a wife, and he slept with her. [5]Bilhah became pregnant and presented
Gen 30:23 him with a son. [6]Rachel named him Dan,* for she said, "God has vindicated me! He has
heard my request and given me a son." [7]Then Bilhah became pregnant again and gave Ja-
30:8 cob a second son. [8]Rachel named him Naphtali,* for she said, "I have struggled hard with
Gen 32:28 my sister, and I'm winning!"
[9]Meanwhile, Leah realized that she wasn't getting pregnant anymore, so she took her
servant, Zilpah, and gave her to Jacob as a wife. [10]Soon Zilpah presented him with a son.
30:11 [11]Leah named him Gad,* for she said, "How fortunate I am!" [12]Then Zilpah gave Jacob a
Gen 35:26; 46:16; 49:19 second son. [13]And Leah named him Asher,* for she said, "What joy is mine! Now the other
women will celebrate with me."
30:14 [14]One day during the wheat harvest, Reuben found some mandrakes growing in a field
Song 7:13 and brought them to his mother, Leah. Rachel begged Leah, "Please give me some of your
son's mandrakes."
[15]But Leah angrily replied, "Wasn't it enough that you stole my husband? Now will you
steal my son's mandrakes, too?"
Rachel answered, "I will let Jacob sleep with you tonight if you give me some of the
mandrakes."
[16]So that evening, as Jacob was coming home from the fields, Leah went out to meet
him. "You must come and sleep with me tonight!" she said. "I have paid for you with some
30:17 mandrakes that my son found." So that night he slept with Leah. [17]And God answered
Gen 25:21 Leah's prayers. She became pregnant again and gave birth to a fifth son for Jacob. [18]She
30:18 named him Issachar,* for she said, "God has rewarded me for giving my servant to my
Gen 49:14 husband as a wife." [19]Then Leah became pregnant again and gave birth to a sixth son for
Jacob. [20]She named him Zebulun,* for she said, "God has given me a good reward. Now
my husband will treat me with respect, for I have given him six sons." [21]Later she gave
30:22 birth to a daughter and named her Dinah.
1 Sam 1:19-20 [22]Then God remembered Rachel's plight and answered her prayers by enabling her to
30:23 have children. [23]She became pregnant and gave birth to a son. "God has removed my dis-
Luke 1:25 grace," she said. [24]And she named him Joseph,* for she said, "May the LORD add yet an-
30:24 other son to my family."
Gen 35:17

JACOB'S WEALTH INCREASES

30:26 [25]Soon after Rachel had given birth to Joseph, Jacob said to Laban, "Please release me so I
Gen 29:18 can go home to my own country. [26]Let me take my wives and children, for I have earned
Hos 12:12 them by serving you, and let me be on my way. You certainly know how hard I have
30:27 worked for you."
Gen 18:3; 39:2-5 [27]"Please listen to me," Laban replied. "I have become wealthy, for* the LORD has blessed
30:28 me because of you. [28]Tell me how much I owe you. Whatever it is, I'll pay it."
Gen 29:15; 31:7

30:6 *Dan* means "he judged" or "he vindicated." 30:8 *Naphtali* means "my struggle." 30:11 *Gad* means "good fortune." 30:13 *Asher* means "happy." 30:18 *Issachar* sounds like a Hebrew term that means "reward." 30:20 *Zebulun* probably means "honor." 30:24 *Joseph* means "may he add." 30:27 Or *I have learned by divination that.*

30:3-13, 18-20, 24 These sons, as well as Leah's first four (Genesis 29:31-35) and Benjamin, who was born later, became the patriarchs of the 12 "tribes" of Israel. The entire nation of Israel was organized around a tribal structure. When the Israelites returned to the Promised Land from Egypt, each tribe was allotted a region of land. Joseph was the one exception. His sons, Ephraim and Manasseh, were each given land. In this way, Joseph was not skipped over, but rather given a double portion. His family received twice the inheritance—in essence, the birthright was passed on to him, even though he was not Jacob's oldest son. The number of tribes still remained at 12, however, because instead of an allotment of land, the tribe of Levi was given religious leadership among the people.

30:25 Jacob had worked for Laban for 14 years in order to marry Laban's daughters. During those 14 years, Jacob saw God begin to fulfill His promise of innumerable descendants, and he had to have been constantly aware of God's promise to give his people the land of Canaan. When his obligation to Laban was fulfilled, Jacob decided to move his family back home. This journey would be risky because, when Jacob had left Canaan, his brother Esau had threatened to kill him (Genesis 27:41). It seems Jacob was finally ready to act on the basis of faith in God.

29 Jacob replied, "You know how hard I've worked for you, and how your flocks and herds have grown under my care. 30 You had little indeed before I came, but your wealth has increased enormously. The LORD has blessed you through everything I've done. But now, what about me? When can I start providing for my own family?"

31 "What wages do you want?" Laban asked again.

Jacob replied, "Don't give me anything. Just do this one thing, and I'll continue to tend and watch over your flocks. 32 Let me inspect your flocks today and remove all the sheep and goats that are speckled or spotted, along with all the black sheep. Give these to me as my wages. 33 In the future, when you check on the animals you have given me as my wages, you'll see that I have been honest. If you find in my flock any goats without speckles or spots, or any sheep that are not black, you will know that I have stolen them from you."

30:32 Gen 31:8, 12

34 "All right," Laban replied. "It will be as you say." 35 But that very day Laban went out and removed the male goats that were streaked and spotted, all the female goats that were speckled and spotted or had white patches, and all the black sheep. He placed them in the care of his own sons, 36 who took them a three-days' journey from where Jacob was. Meanwhile, Jacob stayed and cared for the rest of Laban's flock.

37 Then Jacob took some fresh branches from poplar, almond, and plane trees and peeled off strips of bark, making white streaks on them. 38 Then he placed these peeled branches in the watering troughs where the flocks came to drink, for that was where they mated. 39 And when they mated in front of the white-streaked branches, they gave birth to young that were streaked, speckled, and spotted. 40 Jacob separated those lambs from Laban's flock. And at mating time he turned the flock to face Laban's animals that were streaked or black. This is how he built his own flock instead of increasing Laban's.

41 Whenever the stronger females were ready to mate, Jacob would place the peeled branches in the watering troughs in front of them. Then they would mate in front of the branches. 42 But he didn't do this with the weaker ones, so the weaker lambs belonged to Laban, and the stronger ones were Jacob's. 43 As a result, Jacob became very wealthy, with large flocks of sheep and goats, male and female servants, and many camels and donkeys.

30:43 Gen 13:2; 24:35; 26:13

JACOB FLEES FROM LABAN

31 But Jacob soon learned that Laban's sons were grumbling about him. "Jacob has robbed our father of everything!" they said. "He has gained all his wealth at our father's expense." 2 And Jacob began to notice a change in Laban's attitude toward him.

3 Then the LORD said to Jacob, "Return to the land of your father and grandfather and to your relatives there, and I will be with you."

31:3 Gen 28:15; 32:9

4 So Jacob called Rachel and Leah out to the field where he was watching his flock.

30:37-43 Jacob's strategy for increasing his herds was a combination of superstition and selective breeding. No scientific evidence says that having cattle look at something streaked before they mate will cause them to produce streaked offspring, but Jacob followed the superstition of the day. He also urged his spotted females toward the spotted males, thus producing the desired offspring. More important, however, Jacob acknowledged that God was looking out for him (Genesis 31:7). Even though Laban was less than honorable, God blessed Jacob's efforts. By the time Jacob left Laban, his own wealth had increased tremendously.

31:1-3 Laban previously understood that God had blessed him because Jacob was living with him (Genesis 30:27). But when Jacob's herds and flocks began to increase, Laban's sons began to grumble, and their discontent apparently affected Laban. It was at this time, just as things were becoming uncomfortable for Jacob, that God spoke to him and told him to return to Canaan.

31:4-9 Jacob noticed Laban's cooler attitude toward him and spoke of it to his wives. He complained that Laban had treated him unfairly and admitted that he had engaged in selective breeding to build his flocks. But Jacob also acknowledged that he didn't have ultimate control over whether the animals mated as he desired. God had that control, and Jacob believed that God had caused it to happen to increase his flocks. He was now aware that God had both the power and the inclination to intervene on his behalf.

5He said to them, "I have noticed that your father's attitude toward me has changed.
31:6 Gen 30:29 But the God of my father has been with me. 6You know how hard I have worked for your
father, 7but he has cheated me, changing my wages ten times. But God has not al-
31:7 Gen 29:25; 31:41 lowed him to do me any harm. 8For if he said, 'The speckled animals will be your
31:8 Gen 30:32 wages,' the whole flock began to produce speckled young. And when he changed
his mind and said, 'The striped animals will be your wages,' then the whole flock pro-
duced striped young. 9In this way, God has taken your father's animals and given
them to me.

10"One time during the mating season, I had a dream and saw that the male goats mat-
31:11 Gen 16:7-11; 22:11, 15 ing with the females were streaked, speckled, and spotted. 11Then in my dream, the angel
of God said to me, 'Jacob!' And I replied, 'Yes, here I am.'

12"The angel said, 'Look up, and you will see that only the streaked, speckled, and spot-
31:12 Gen 30:32 Exod 3:7 ted males are mating with the females of your flock. For I have seen how Laban has
treated you. 13I am the God who appeared to you at Bethel,* the place where you anointed
31:13 Gen 28:10-22 the pillar of stone and made your vow to Me. Now get ready and leave this country and re-
turn to the land of your birth.'"

14Rachel and Leah responded, "That's fine with us! We won't inherit any of our father's
31:15 Gen 29:20, 27 wealth anyway. 15He has reduced our rights to those of foreign women. And after he sold
us, he wasted the money you paid him for us. 16All the wealth God has given you from our
father legally belongs to us and our children. So go ahead and do whatever God has told
you."

31:18 Gen 25:20 17So Jacob put his wives and children on camels, 18and he drove all his livestock in front
of him. He packed all the belongings he had acquired in Paddan-aram and set out for the
31:19 Judg 17:5 land of Canaan, where his father, Isaac, lived. 19At the time they left, Laban was some dis-
tance away, shearing his sheep. Rachel stole her father's household idols and took them
31:20 Gen 31:27 with her. 20Jacob outwitted Laban the Aramean, for they set out secretly and never told La-
31:21 Gen 37:25 Num 32:1 ban they were leaving. 21So Jacob took all his possessions with him and crossed the Eu-
phrates River,* heading for the hill country of Gilead.

LABAN PURSUES JACOB

22Three days later, Laban was told that Jacob had fled. 23So he gathered a group of his rel-
atives and set out in hot pursuit. He caught up with Jacob seven days later in the hill coun-
31:22 Gen 30:36 try of Gilead. 24But the previous night God had appeared to Laban the Aramean in a
31:24 Gen 25:20 dream and told him, "I'm warning you—leave Jacob alone!"

25Laban caught up with Jacob as he was camped in the hill country of Gilead,
and he set up his camp not far from Jacob's. 26"What do you mean by stealing
away like this?" Laban demanded. "How dare you drag my daughters away like
prisoners of war? 27Why did you slip away secretly? Why did you steal away? And

31:13 As in Greek version and an Aramaic Targum; Hebrew reads *the God of Bethel.* 31:21 Hebrew *the river.*

31:19 The fact that Rachel stole household gods from her father reveals that she had been raised in a home influenced by idol worship. These idols were so important to Laban that he chased after Jacob's family to retrieve them. When he couldn't find them, he established a treaty with Jacob so that Jacob could do him no harm (Genesis 31:43-55). As for Rachel, the theft reveals a less-than-shining character and raises troubling questions about why she would take Laban's household gods.

31:24 When Laban learned that Jacob had left to return to Canaan, he pursued him with a group of his relatives. It is possible that he was prepared to engage in violence to reclaim his household gods and the flocks he regarded as stolen. But God was faithful to His promise to be with Jacob. The night before Laban overtook Jacob, God appeared to him in a dream and warned him to be very careful in what he said to Jacob. Laban wisely heeded this warning. When Laban told Jacob of God's appearance to him, Jacob regarded it as divine vindication (v. 42).

why didn't you say you wanted to leave? I would have given you a farewell feast, with
singing and music, accompanied by tambourines and harps. 28Why didn't you let me 31:28
kiss my daughters and grandchildren and tell them good-bye? You have acted very fool- Gen 31:55
ishly! 29I could destroy you, but the God of your father appeared to me last night
and warned me, 'Leave Jacob alone!' 30I can understand your feeling that you
must go, and your intense longing for your father's home. But why have you sto-
len my gods?"

31"I rushed away because I was afraid," Jacob answered. "I thought you would take 31:31
your daughters from me by force. 32But as for your gods, see if you can find them, and Gen 20:11
let the person who has taken them die! And if you find anything else that belongs to you, 31:32
identify it before all these relatives of ours, and I will give it back!" But Jacob did not Gen 44:9
know that Rachel had stolen the household idols.

33Laban went first into Jacob's tent to search there, then into Leah's, and then the
tents of the two servant wives—but he found nothing. Finally, he went into Rachel's tent.
34But Rachel had taken the household idols and hidden them in her camel saddle, and
now she was sitting on them. When Laban had thoroughly searched her tent without
finding them, 35she said to her father, "Please, sir, forgive me if I don't get up for you.
I'm having my monthly period." So Laban continued his search, but he could not find
the household idols.

36Then Jacob became very angry, and he challenged Laban. "What's my crime?" he de-
manded. "What have I done wrong to make you chase after me as though I were a crimi-
nal? 37You have rummaged through everything I own. Now show me what you found that 31:37
belongs to you! Set it out here in front of us, before our relatives, for all to see. Let them Gen 31:33
judge between us!

38"For twenty years I have been with you, caring for your flocks. In all that time your 31:38
sheep and goats never miscarried. In all those years I never used a single ram of yours Gen 27:44
for food. 39If any were attacked and killed by wild animals, I never showed you the car- 31:39
cass and asked you to reduce the count of your flock. No, I took the loss myself! You Exod 22:10-13
made me pay for every stolen animal, whether it was taken in broad daylight or in the
dark of night.

40"I worked for you through the scorching heat of the day and through cold and
sleepless nights. 41Yes, for twenty years I slaved in your house! I worked for four- 31:41 Gen 29:30
teen years earning your two daughters, and then six more years for your flock. And
you changed my wages ten times! 42In fact, if the God of my father had not been on 31:42
my side—the God of Abraham and the fearsome God of Isaac*—you would have sent Gen 29:32
me away empty-handed. But God has seen your abuse and my hard work. That is
why He appeared to you last night and rebuked you!"

JACOB'S TREATY WITH LABAN

43Then Laban replied to Jacob, "These women are my daughters, these children are my
grandchildren, and these flocks are my flocks—in fact, everything you see is mine. But
what can I do now about my daughters and their children? 44So come, let's make a cov- 31:44
enant, you and I, and it will be a witness to our commitment." Gen 21:27, 30

45So Jacob took a stone and set it up as a monument. 46Then he told his family mem- 31:45
bers, "Gather some stones." So they gathered stones and piled them in a heap. Then Ja- Gen 28:18
cob and Laban sat down beside the pile of stones to eat a covenant meal. 47To Josh 24:26-27
commemorate the event, Laban called the place Jegar-sahadutha (which means "wit-
ness pile" in Aramaic), and Jacob called it Galeed (which means "witness pile" in He-
brew).

48Then Laban declared, "This pile of stones will stand as a witness to remind us of 31:48
the covenant we have made today." This explains why it was called Galeed—"Wit- Gen 21:30

31:42 Or *and the Fear of Isaac.*

31:49 ness Pile." 49But it was also called Mizpah (which means "watchtower"), for Laban
Judg 10:17; 11:29 said, "May the LORD keep watch between us to make sure that we keep this covenant
when we are out of each other's sight. 50If you mistreat my daughters or if you marry
31:50 Judg 11:10 other wives, God will see it even if no one else does. He is a witness to this covenant
1 Sam 12:5 between us.
Jer 29:23; 42:5 51"See this pile of stones," Laban continued, "and see this monument I have set between
31:52 us. 52They stand between us as witnesses of our vows. I will never pass this pile of stones
Gen 31:29, 42 to harm you, and you must never pass these stones or this monument to harm me. 53I call
31:53 Gen 24:12 on the God of our ancestors—the God of your grandfather Abraham and the God of my
grandfather Nahor—to serve as a judge between us."
So Jacob took an oath before the fearsome God of his father, Isaac,* to respect the
31:54 boundary line. 54Then Jacob offered a sacrifice to God there on the mountain and invited
Exod 18:12 everyone to a covenant feast. After they had eaten, they spent the night on the mountain.
31:55 Gen 31:28 55*Laban got up early the next morning, and he kissed his grandchildren and his daugh-
ters and blessed them. Then he left and returned home.

32:1 **32** 1*As Jacob started on his way again, angels of God came to meet him. 2When
Gen 16:11 2 Kgs 6:16-17 Jacob saw them, he exclaimed, "This is God's camp!" So he named the place
32:2 Mahanaim.*
Josh 13:26; 21:38 2 Sam 2:8

JACOB SENDS GIFTS TO ESAU

32:3 3Then Jacob sent messengers ahead to his brother, Esau, who was living in the region of
Gen 27:41-42 Seir in the land of Edom. 4He told them, "Give this message to my master Esau: 'Humble
32:4 Gen 31:41 greetings from your servant Jacob. Until now I have been living with Uncle Laban, 5and
now I own cattle, donkeys, flocks of sheep and goats, and many servants, both men and
women. I have sent these messengers to inform my lord of my coming, hoping that you
will be friendly to me.'"
6After delivering the message, the messengers returned to Jacob and reported, "We met
your brother, Esau, and he is already on his way to meet you—with an army of 400 men!"
32:7 Gen 33:1 7Jacob was terrified at the news. He divided his household, along with the flocks and
herds and camels, into two groups. 8He thought, "If Esau meets one group and attacks it,
32:9 perhaps the other group can escape."
Gen 28:13-15; 31:13 9Then Jacob prayed, "O God of my grandfather Abraham, and God of my father,

31:53 Or *the Fear of his father, Isaac.* 31:55 Verse 31:55 is numbered 32:1 in Hebrew text. 32:1 Verses 32:1-32 are numbered 32:2-33 in Hebrew text. 32:2 *Mahanaim* means "two camps."

31:48 Monuments of various kinds were often used to mark agreements or great events. For example, Noah built an altar when he left the ark (Genesis 8:20). Later in Israel's history, the people set up stones to commemorate God's miracles on their behalf (Deuteronomy 27:1-8). The monument functioned as a reminder. In this case, the act of creating a monument served to solidify the agreement between Jacob and Laban. It was to be a physical reminder of the commitment being made.

32:1 Jacob's family's history, as well as his own, involved conversations with angelic beings and even God Himself. God had appeared to Jacob's grandfather, Abraham (Genesis 13:14-17; 15:1-21; 17:1-21) and to his father, Isaac (Genesis 26;1-4). God also had appeared to Jacob himself in a dream at Bethel as he was leaving Canaan (Genesis 28:10-19). That dream also featured angels ascending and descending on a stairway between heaven and earth. Now, as Jacob returned to Canaan, angels came to him once more, perhaps signifying God's protection.

32:6 Twenty years had passed since Jacob had run away from his brother's rage. Jacob had convinced Esau to swap his family birthright for a bowl of stew. Then Jacob had conspired with their mother to trick their father into giving Jacob the blessing instead of Esau. Esau was so enraged that he planned to kill Jacob after their father's death (Genesis 27:36-41). Now the brothers were to face each other once again. The news that Esau was coming with an army of 400 men terrified Jacob—with good reason.

32:9-12 This is the first prayer of Jacob recorded for us in Scripture. Both the fact that he prayed and the words that he uttered in this hour of fear and need revealed that great changes had taken place in his heart. He left Canaan promising to serve God *if* He would protect him and supply his needs (Genesis 28:20-21). In other words, God had to prove Himself. But Jacob returned readily acknowledging that God had blessed him abundantly and that he deserved none of those blessings. In his fear, he fell back on the covenant promises of God to treat him kindly and to multiply his descendants.

Isaac—O LORD, You told me, 'Return to your own land and to your relatives.' And You
promised me, 'I will treat you kindly.' 10I am not worthy of all the unfailing love and faith- 32:10
fulness You have shown to me, Your servant. When I left home and crossed the Jordan Gen 24:27
River, I owned nothing except a walking stick. Now my household fills two large camps!
11O LORD, please rescue me from the hand of my brother, Esau. I am afraid that he is 32:11
coming to attack me, along with my wives and children. 12But You promised me, 'I will Gen 27:41
surely treat you kindly, and I will multiply your descendants until they become as nu- 32:12
merous as the sands along the seashore—too many to count.'" Gen 28:14

13Jacob stayed where he was for the night. Then he selected these gifts from his posses-
sions to present to his brother, Esau: 14200 female goats, 20 male goats, 200 ewes,
20 rams, 1530 female camels with their young, 40 cows, 10 bulls, 20 female donkeys, and
10 male donkeys. 16He divided these animals into herds and assigned each to different
servants. Then he told his servants, "Go ahead of me with the animals, but keep some dis-
tance between the herds."

17He gave these instructions to the men leading the first group: "When my brother,
Esau, meets you, he will ask, 'Whose servants are you? Where are you going? Who
owns these animals?' 18You must reply, 'They belong to your servant Jacob, but they 32:18
are a gift for his master Esau. Look, he is coming right behind us.'" Gen 32:13

19Jacob gave the same instructions to the second and third herdsmen and to all who fol-
lowed behind the herds: "You must say the same thing to Esau when you meet him. 20And 32:20
be sure to say, 'Look, your servant Jacob is right behind us.'" 1 Sam 25:19

Jacob thought, "I will try to appease him by sending gifts ahead of me. When I see him
in person, perhaps he will be friendly to me." 21So the gifts were sent on ahead, while Ja-
cob himself spent that night in the camp.

JACOB WRESTLES WITH GOD

22During the night Jacob got up and took his two wives, his two servant wives, and his
eleven sons and crossed the Jabbok River with them. 23After taking them to the other side, 32:22 Deut 3:16
he sent over all his possessions. Josh 12:2

24This left Jacob all alone in the camp, and a Man came and wrestled with him until the 32:24
dawn began to break. 25When the Man saw that He would not win the match, He touched Gen 18:2
Jacob's hip and wrenched it out of its socket. 26Then the Man said, "Let Me go, for the 32:26
dawn is breaking!" Hos 12:3-4

But Jacob said, "I will not let You go unless You bless me."

27"What is your name?" the Man asked.

He replied, "Jacob."

28"Your name will no longer be Jacob," the Man told him. "From now on you will be 32:28 Gen 35:10
called Israel,* because you have fought with God and with men and have won." 1 Kgs 18:31

32:28 *Jacob* sounds like the Hebrew words for "heel" and "deceiver." *Israel* means "God fights."

32:24-26 A "man" came and wrestled with Jacob all night, but Jacob regarded the Man as God Himself in human form (v. 30). God certainly could have defeated Jacob in an instant's time, but He accommodated His strength to Jacob's. In that situation, Jacob wrestled tenaciously, for he wanted God's blessing. Nevertheless, as dawn approached, the Man knocked Jacob's hip out of joint with a mere touch, reminding Jacob of the supernatural strength of the God with whom he was dealing. This all-night struggle was symbolic of Jacob's lifelong struggle to submit to God.

▸ BIBLE

32:26 Christ and Jacob. Did you know that Jacob had a lot in common with Jesus? Both had a birthright that should have belonged to someone else (Esau, the older brother, traded his birthright; Adam, the first man, forfeited his birthright through his sin). Further, as Jacob labored many years for his bride, Rachel, so Jesus became a servant to labor for His bride, the church. As God worked with Jacob—wrestled with him, in fact—so He works with us to make us more and more like Christ. "And I am certain that God, who began the good work within you, will continue His work until it is finally finished on the day when Christ Jesus returns" (Philippians 1:6). What part of your life still needs work? (***See Bible***> *Unity*> *Christ*> *Christ in the body of Jacob*, TopicGuide page A10.)

32:29 29"Please tell me Your name," Jacob said.
Exod 3:13 Judg 13:17 "Why do you want to know My name?" the Man replied. Then He blessed Jacob
32:30 there.
Gen 16:13 30Jacob named the place Peniel (which means "face of God"), for he said, "I have seen
Exod 24:10; 33:20 Num 12:8 God face to face, yet my life has been spared." 31The sun was rising as Jacob left Peniel,*
Deut 5:24; 34:10 and he was limping because of the injury to his hip. 32(Even today the people of Israel
Judg 6:22 don't eat the tendon near the hip socket because of what happened that night when the
John 1:18 Man strained the tendon of Jacob's hip.)

JACOB AND ESAU MAKE PEACE

33:1 Gen 32:6-7 **33** Then Jacob looked up and saw Esau coming with his 400 men. So he divided the
children among Leah, Rachel, and his two servant wives. 2He put the servant
wives and their children at the front, Leah and her children next, and Rachel and Joseph
33:3 Gen 18:2; 42:6 last. 3Then Jacob went on ahead. As he approached his brother, he bowed to the ground
seven times before him. 4Then Esau ran to meet him and embraced him, threw his arms
33:4 Gen 45:14-15 around his neck, and kissed him. And they both wept.
33:5 5Then Esau looked at the women and children and asked, "Who are these people with
Gen 48:9 you?"
"These are the children God has graciously given to me, your servant," Jacob replied.
6Then the servant wives came forward with their children and bowed before him. 7Next
came Leah with her children, and they bowed before him. Finally, Joseph and Rachel
came forward and bowed before him.
33:8 8"And what were all the flocks and herds I met as I came?" Esau asked.
Gen 32:14-16 Jacob replied, "They are a gift, my lord, to ensure your friendship."
33:9 9"My brother, I have plenty," Esau answered. "Keep what you have for yourself."
Gen 27:39 10But Jacob insisted, "No, if I have found favor with you, please accept this gift from me.
And what a relief to see your friendly smile. It is like seeing the face of God! 11Please take
this gift I have brought you, for God has been very gracious to me. I have more than
enough." And because Jacob insisted, Esau finally accepted the gift.

32:31 Hebrew *Penuel,* a variant spelling of Peniel.

32:28 The name *Israel* means "one who struggles with God." Jacob's name was changed because *Israel* reflected the reality of his life. He had indeed struggled with God. Names carried more significance in this ancient culture than they do in modern Western culture. For instance, both Sarah and Abraham were given new names by God to reflect what He was doing in their lives (Genesis 17:5, 15). And Esau, Jacob's twin, received a new name, Edom, at a key point in his life when he sold his own birthright for a bowl of stew (Genesis 25:30).

▸ HOLINESS

32:28 Trust God in temptation. God changed Jacob's name to *Israel* (see Genesis 35:9-12). Likewise, God changes us, giving us the name *Christian* when we receive Jesus into our hearts. As new creations in Christ, we are called to struggle against sin, just as Jacob struggled. This means that being a Christian involves the pursuit of holiness. Holiness is not an option for Christians; it is a command. The fruitful Christian life is lived daily in surrender to the lordship of Christ. It is then that you appropriate the fullness of the Holy Spirit and live in power. (***See Holiness****> Submission> Trusting God> Overcoming,* TopicGuide page A40.)

33:1-4 Jacob approached Esau with great fear. He lined up his family in order, putting his concubines and their children first, then Leah and her children, and finally Rachel and Joseph bringing up the rear. He hoped that if Esau was less than happy to see his family, Rachel would have some warning and some time to run away with Joseph. To Jacob's credit he himself walked at the front of the line. To Esau's credit, he bore no ill will toward his brother or his brother's family. Instead, he came forward and embraced Jacob warmly.

▸ HOLINESS

33:11 God's grace. Jacob's claim that "God has been very gracious to me" was in contrast to his earlier life of striving after God's blessing (see Genesis 27:11-12). Jacob's assertion is one that every believer can make. God gave you eternal life in Jesus, He loves you with an everlasting love, and He promises to protect you from all harm. It has been said that the Christian life is totally the product of God's grace. Contemplate all that God has done for you and you will agree with Jacob that God has indeed been very gracious to you! (***See Holiness****> Law and Grace> Grace> The gift of grace,* TopicGuide page A42.)

12"Well," Esau said, "let's be going. I will lead the way."
13But Jacob replied, "You can see, my lord, that some of the children are very young,
and the flocks and herds have their young, too. If they are driven too hard, even for one
day, all the animals could die. 14Please, my lord, go ahead of your servant. We will fol-
low slowly, at a pace that is comfortable for the livestock and the children. I will meet
you at Seir."
15"All right," Esau said, "but at least let me assign some of my men to guide and protect
you."
Jacob responded, "That's not necessary. It's enough that you've received me warmly,
my lord!"
16So Esau turned around and started back to Seir that same day. 17Jacob, on the other
hand, traveled on to Succoth. There he built himself a house and made shelters for his
livestock. That is why the place was named Succoth (which means "shelters").
18Later, having traveled all the way from Paddan-aram, Jacob arrived safely at the
town of Shechem, in the land of Canaan. There he set up camp outside the town. 19Ja-
cob bought the plot of land where he camped from the family of Hamor, the father of
Shechem, for 100 pieces of silver.* 20And there he built an altar and named it El-Elohe-
Israel.*

33:14 Gen 32:3
33:17 Judg 8:5, 14; Ps 60:6
33:18 Gen 12:6; 25:20
33:19 Josh 24:32; John 4:5

REVENGE AGAINST SHECHEM

34 One day Dinah, the daughter of Jacob and Leah, went to visit some of the young
women who lived in the area. 2But when the local prince, Shechem son of Hamor
the Hivite, saw Dinah, he seized her and raped her. 3But then he fell in love with her, and
he tried to win her affection with tender words. 4He said to his father, Hamor, "Get me this
young girl. I want to marry her."
5Soon Jacob heard that Shechem had defiled his daughter, Dinah. But since his sons
were out in the fields herding his livestock, he said nothing until they returned. 6Hamor,
Shechem's father, came to discuss the matter with Jacob. 7Meanwhile, Jacob's sons had
come in from the field as soon as they heard what had happened. They were shocked and
furious that their sister had been raped. Shechem had done a disgraceful thing against Ja-
cob's family,* something that should never be done.
8Hamor tried to speak with Jacob and his sons. "My son Shechem is truly in love with

34:1 Gen 30:21
34:2 Deut 21:14; 2 Sam 13:14
34:4 Gen 21:21
34:7 2 Sam 13:12

33:19 Hebrew *100 kesitahs;* the value or weight of the kesitah is no longer known. 33:20 *El-Elohe-Israel* means "God, the God of Israel." 34:7 Hebrew *a disgraceful thing in Israel.*

33:18 The place called Shechem was a part of Hebrew history from the time of Abraham. Shechem was Abraham's first campsite in the land and the place where he built his first altar (Genesis 12:6-8). Here we see that Jacob also settled in Shechem. Years later, Joseph went to Shechem to look for his brothers and ended up sold into slavery (Genesis 37:14). Still later in Israel's history, Shechem became one of the cities of refuge that belonged to the priests.

33:19-20 Years before, Abraham stopped in this area and built an altar to commemorate a visit from God (Genesis 12:7). In much the same way, Jacob built an altar, perhaps to commemorate his return from Paddan-aram. He gave the altar a name meaning "God, the God of Israel." At this point, Israel was Jacob, not the nation that would come from him, so this name is a personal testimony. Jacob is giving God the glory for bringing him back to the land God had promised him.

34:1-4 While women were given far less status in this ancient world than they are today, rape was still taken seriously. At the very least, it was seen as a violation of another man's property—if not the property of the woman's husband, then of her father and brothers. Later in Israel's history, when the laws of the nation were formalized, God declared that a man who raped a non-engaged woman must pay damages to her father, marry the woman, and never divorce her. A man who raped a woman engaged to another man was killed.

34:7 In Jacob's time, families were often communities unto themselves. Thus, in a sense, when Shechem took Dinah forcibly, he violated not only her but her whole family. In this situation, it is puzzling that Jacob did nothing. Perhaps his inaction was due to the fact that Dinah was the daughter of Leah rather than Rachel, Jacob's most beloved wife. Unfortunately, his lack of action meant that his sons took matters into their own hands.

your daughter," he said. "Please let him marry her. 9In fact, let's arrange other marriages,
too. You give us your daughters for our sons, and we will give you our daughters for your
34:10 sons. 10And you may live among us; the land is open to you! Settle here and trade with us.
Gen 33:19 And feel free to buy property in the area."
11Then Shechem himself spoke to Dinah's father and brothers. "Please be kind to me,
34:12 and let me marry her," he begged. "I will give you whatever you ask. 12No matter what
Exod 22:16 dowry or gift you demand, I will gladly pay it—just give me the girl as my wife."
34:13 13But since Shechem had defiled their sister, Dinah, Jacob's sons responded deceitfully
Gen 27:36 to Shechem and his father, Hamor. 14They said to them, "We couldn't possibly allow this,
34:14 because you're not circumcised. It would be a disgrace for our sister to marry a man like
Gen 17:14 you! 15But here is a solution. If every man among you will be circumcised like we are,
16then we will give you our daughters, and we'll take your daughters for ourselves. We
will live among you and become one people. 17But if you don't agree to be circumcised,
we will take her and be on our way."
34:19 18Hamor and his son Shechem agreed to their proposal. 19Shechem wasted no time in
Gen 29:20 acting on this request, for he wanted Jacob's daughter desperately. Shechem was a highly
34:20 respected member of his family, 20and he went with his father, Hamor, to present this pro-
Gen 18:1 posal to the leaders at the town gate.
21"These men are our friends," they said. "Let's invite them to live here among us and
trade freely. Look, the land is large enough to hold them. We can take their daughters as
34:22 wives and let them marry ours. 22But they will consider staying here and becoming one
Gen 34:15 people with us only if all of our men are circumcised, just as they are. 23But if we do this, all
their livestock and possessions will eventually be ours. Come, let's agree to their terms
and let them settle here among us."
34:24 Gen 28:15 24So all the men in the town council agreed with Hamor and Shechem, and every male
34:25 in the town was circumcised. 25But three days later, when their wounds were still sore, two
Gen 49:5-7 of Jacob's sons, Simeon and Levi, who were Dinah's full brothers, took their swords and
Josh 5:8 entered the town without opposition. Then they slaughtered every male there, 26including
Hamor and his son Shechem. They killed them with their swords, then took Dinah from
Shechem's house and returned to their camp.
27Meanwhile, the rest of Jacob's sons arrived. Finding the men slaughtered, they plun-
34:28 dered the town because their sister had been defiled there. 28They seized all the flocks
Gen 43:18 and herds and donkeys—everything they could lay their hands on, both inside the town
and outside in the fields. 29They looted all their wealth and plundered their houses.
They also took all their little children and wives and led them away as captives.

HOLINESS

34:9 Resist the world's influence. Shechem's invitation to Jacob to "give us your daughters for our sons, and we will give you your daughters for your sons" would have violated the law of God (that the original audience of Genesis would have already heard) forbidding intermarriage with unbelievers (see Deuteronomy 7:3). This prohibition was designed to keep Israel from becoming absorbed by the surrounding culture. Today's worldly culture tempts you to violate your commitment to Christ. This inducement is seen in movies, books, entertainment, and many other areas that celebrate immorality and human independence from God. What is vying for your heart and mind this day? Be careful of the world's seductive lure, while being certain to yield your heart and mind wholly to Christ. (***See Holiness**> Submission> Yielding to Spirit,* TopicGuide page A41.)

34:13-17 God's covenant with Abraham included the rite of circumcision (Genesis 17:9-14). While men underwent circumcision in some other cultures of the day, Israel's circumcision was unique because it was not a rite of fertility but an external sign of their unique covenant with God. For this reason, it was not surprising that Dinah's brothers requested that Shechem's family be circumcised. However, their request was not based on a desire to observe a command of God. Rather, it was a subterfuge for vengeance.

34:24-29 Shechem and his father persuaded all the local men to undergo circumcision. Three days later, when the men were still incapacitated by their pain, two of Jacob's sons, Simeon and Levi, came upon them and slaughtered them all. Then Simeon, Levi, and their nine brothers plundered the town. Why did only Simeon and Levi do the actual killing? Years later, on his deathbed, Jacob declared that "their weapons are instruments of violence" (Genesis 49:5). For that, Jacob prophesied that the descendants of Simeon and Levi would be scattered among the other tribes of Israel.

[30]Afterward Jacob said to Simeon and Levi, "You have ruined me! You've made me
stink among all the people of this land—among all the Canaanites and Perizzites. We are
so few that they will join forces and crush us. I will be ruined, and my entire household will
be wiped out!"
[31]"But why should we let him treat our sister like a prostitute?" they retorted angrily.

34:30 Gen 13:7; 49:5-7 Exod 5:21 2 Sam 10:6 1 Chr 16:19

JACOB'S RETURN TO BETHEL

35 Then God said to Jacob, "Get ready and move to Bethel and settle there. Build an altar there to the God who appeared to you when you fled from your brother, Esau."

35:1 Gen 12:8; 28:19

▸ GOD

34:30 God's caring personality. Jacob's claim that Levi and Simeon "made me stink" before the Canaanites shows that he was less concerned about Dinah's harsh treatment than about his own reputation. Put differently, Jacob's response was tactical, not ethical. Concern over personal reputation is a false god in many people's lives. Living for Jesus means thinking less of one's self and more highly of others (see Philippians 2:3-4). Place your focus on the needs and well-being of others, for this reflects God's compassionate and caring heart. (***See God****> God's Nature> Personality> Emotion> God is compassionate and loving,* TopicGuide page A14.)

35:1 God explained to Jacob that he now must worship Him alone. He told Jacob to return to Bethel and build an altar. In case Jacob had any questions about who this God was, God reminded him of their previous encounter at Bethel. While Jacob had been fleeing from Esau, he had laid down to rest and had a dream of a great stairway going to heaven—with God standing at the top. In that vision, God repeated to Jacob the covenant He had given to Abraham and Isaac (Genesis 28:10-15).

▸ GOD

35:1 God's names: God. The word for *God* in the original Hebrew language is *El*. Typically used in conjunction with other terms (for instance, *El Elyon or El Shaddai*), by itself the name means "God" or "mighty one." The Mighty One of Israel is not removed from His people, but delivers them in the midst of trouble. Jacob notes this truth, stating, "God . . . answered my prayers when I was in distress. He has been with me wherever I have gone" (Genesis 35:3). The mighty God of Israel is ready to meet you in your distress and to answer your prayers. He is with you wherever you go and in your darkest hour. Worship God as Jacob did and praise Him for His intimate presence in your life. (***See God****> God's Names> God,* TopicGuide page A18.)

MY RESPONSE TO GOD

Resisting Temptation

GENESIS 34:2

God's Word teaches that every Christian should be prepared for battles with sin. There will never be a time in this life when you will be free from temptation. Satan is a real foe, and we must be prepared for both his subtle, cunning ways and his obvious attempts to defeat and destroy us.

There is a difference, however, between temptation and sin. Temptation is the initial impression to do something contrary to God's will. Even Jesus was not immune to temptation. But temptation becomes sin when you meditate on the impression and develop an unholy desire, which is an emotional sin that may be followed by a mental or physical act of disobedience.

So, how do you avoid temptation? First, surrender yourself to the control of the Holy Spirit, trusting Him to direct and empower you (Ephesians 5:18). Do not fight against the Spirit (Ephesians 4:30), but submit. Second, and more practically speaking, you simply recognize your weakness whenever you are tempted and ask the Lord to lead you away from temptation (Matthew 6:13). Like Joseph, you can also seek to avoid compromising situations. Ask God to cleanse your mind and thoughts with His blood, and to control and empower you with the Holy Spirit so you will not yield to any temptation.

35:2 2 So Jacob told everyone in his household, "Get rid of all your pagan idols, purify your-
Gen 31:19 selves, and put on clean clothing. 3 We are now going to Bethel, where I will build an altar
35:3 Gen 28:15-22 to the God who answered my prayers when I was in distress. He has been with me wher-
35:4 ever I have gone."
Exod 32:3 4 So they gave Jacob all their pagan idols and earrings, and he buried them under the
Judg 8:24 great tree near Shechem. 5 As they set out, a terror from God spread over the people in all
Hos 2:13 35:5 the towns of that area, so no one attacked Jacob's family.
Exod 15:16 6 Eventually, Jacob and his household arrived at Luz (also called Bethel) in Canaan.
35:6 7 Jacob built an altar there and named the place El-bethel (which means "God of Beth-
Gen 28:19 el"), because God had appeared to him there when he was fleeing from his brother,
35:7 Esau.
Gen 28:19 8 Soon after this, Rebekah's old nurse, Deborah, died. She was buried beneath the oak
35:8 tree in the valley below Bethel. Ever since, the tree has been called Allon-bacuth (which
Gen 24:59 means "oak of weeping").
9 Now that Jacob had returned from Paddan-aram, God appeared to him again at Bethel.
35:9 Gen 28:13 God blessed him, 10 saying, "Your name is Jacob, but you will not be called Jacob any lon-
35:10 ger. From now on your name will be Israel."* So God renamed him Israel.
Gen 32:28 11 Then God said, "I am El-Shaddai—'God Almighty.' Be fruitful and multiply. You will
become a great nation, even many nations. Kings will be among your descendants!
35:11 12 And I will give you the land I once gave to Abraham and Isaac. Yes, I will give it to you
Gen 12:2; 17:1, 6 and your descendants after you." 13 Then God went up from the place where He had spo-
35:12 ken to Jacob.
Gen 13:15; 28:13 14 Jacob set up a stone pillar to mark the place where God had spoken to him. Then he
35:13 poured wine over it as an offering to God and anointed the pillar with olive oil. 15 And Ja-
Judg 6:21; 13:20 cob named the place Bethel (which means "house of God"), because God had spoken to
35:14 Gen 28:18-19 him there.

THE DEATHS OF RACHEL AND ISAAC

35:16 16 Leaving Bethel, Jacob and his clan moved on toward Ephrath. But Rachel went into la-
Ruth 4:11 bor while they were still some distance away. Her labor pains were intense. 17 After a
35:17 Gen 30:22-24 very hard delivery, the midwife finally exclaimed, "Don't be afraid—you have another
35:18 son!" 18 Rachel was about to die, but with her last breath she named the baby Ben-oni
Gen 49:27 (which means "son of my sorrow"). The baby's father, however, called him Benjamin
35:19 (which means "son of my right hand"). 19 So Rachel died and was buried on the way to
Gen 48:7 35:22 Ephrath (that is, Bethlehem). 20 Jacob set up a stone monument over Rachel's grave, and
Gen 49:4 it can be seen there to this day.
Lev 18:8 21 Then Jacob* traveled on and camped beyond Migdal-eder. 22 While he was living
1 Chr 5:1

35:10 *Jacob* sounds like the Hebrew words for "heel" and "deceiver." *Israel* means "God fights." 35:21 Hebrew *Israel;* also in 35:22a. The names "Jacob" and "Israel" are often interchanged throughout the Old Testament, referring sometimes to the individual patriarch and sometimes to the nation.

▶ WORSHIP

35:2 Fear of God. Jacob's charge to destroy the idols signifies his household's renewed commitment to God. Repentance of sin always involves two things: 1) turning *to* the Lord; 2) turning *from* personal idols. A personal idol can be a person, work, sex, sports, a hobby—anything you allow to absorb your life and thus keep you from making Christ your number-one priority. Is unconfessed sin hindering your walk with Christ? Present every area of your life to Christ, for only then will you know the fruitful life He offers. (***See Worship***> *OT> Reverence> Put away idols,* TopicGuide page A28.)

35:9-14 God again appeared to Jacob and repeated the covenant to him. When God had departed from him, Jacob set up a stone as a memorial of God's appearance. He then poured wine and very valuable olive oil on the stone, thereby indicating the great value he placed on Bethel and his encounters with God there.

there, Reuben had intercourse with Bilhah, his father's concubine, and Jacob soon heard about it.

These are the names of the twelve sons of Jacob:

23 The sons of Leah were Reuben (Jacob's oldest son), Simeon, Levi, Judah, Issachar, and Zebulun.
24 The sons of Rachel were Joseph and Benjamin.
25 The sons of Bilhah, Rachel's servant, were Dan and Naphtali.
26 The sons of Zilpah, Leah's servant, were Gad and Asher.
These are the names of the sons who were born to Jacob at Paddan-aram.

27 So Jacob returned to his father, Isaac, in Mamre, which is near Kiriath-arba (now called Hebron), where Abraham and Isaac had both lived as foreigners. 28 Isaac lived for 180 years. 29 Then he breathed his last and died at a ripe old age, joining his ancestors in death. And his sons, Esau and Jacob, buried him.

DESCENDANTS OF ESAU

36 This is the account of the descendants of Esau (also known as Edom). 2 Esau married two young women from Canaan: Adah, the daughter of Elon the Hittite; and Oholibamah, the daughter of Anah and granddaughter of Zibeon the Hivite. 3 He also married his cousin Basemath, who was the daughter of Ishmael and the sister of Nebaioth. 4 Adah gave birth to a son named Eliphaz for Esau. Basemath gave birth to a son named Reuel. 5 Oholibamah gave birth to sons named Jeush, Jalam, and Korah. All these sons were born to Esau in the land of Canaan.

6 Esau took his wives, his children, and his entire household, along with his livestock and cattle—all the wealth he had acquired in the land of Canaan—and moved away from his brother, Jacob. 7 There was not enough land to support them both because of all the livestock and possessions they had acquired. 8 So Esau (also known as Edom) settled in the hill country of Seir.

9 This is the account of Esau's descendants, the Edomites, who lived in the hill country of Seir.

10 These are the names of Esau's sons: Eliphaz, the son of Esau's wife Adah; and Reuel, the son of Esau's wife Basemath.
11 The descendants of Eliphaz were Teman, Omar, Zepho, Gatam, and Kenaz. 12 Timna, the concubine of Esau's son Eliphaz, gave birth to a son named Amalek. These are the descendants of Esau's wife Adah.

35:23-26 //1 Chr 2:1-2
35:23 Gen 29:31-35; 30:18-20
35:24 Gen 30:24
35:25 Gen 30:5-8
35:26 Gen 30:10-13
35:27 Gen 13:18; 23:2
35:28 Gen 25:7-8, 20
36:1 Gen 25:30
36:2 Gen 26:34; 1 Chr 1:40
36:3 Gen 25:13
36:4 1 Chr 1:35
36:5 Gen 36:18
36:7 Gen 13:6
36:8 Gen 14:6; 25:30
36:9 Gen 36:43
36:10-14 //1 Chr 1:35-37

35:22 A concubine was like a second-class wife, so Reuben's act was incestuous, as well as disrespectful of his father (Deuteronomy 22:30). In Genesis 49, when Jacob was pronouncing blessings and curses on his sons, he referred to Reuben's foolishness and described him as "unruly as a flood." Reuben should have been the son in line for the birthright, which included family leadership and a double portion of the inheritance. But Jacob did not convey that blessing to Reuben, the firstborn of Leah. Instead, Jacob gave the birthright to Joseph, the firstborn of Rachel.

35:27-29 When Jacob returned to Canaan with his wives and servants, Esau welcomed him and eventually moved out of the area. Esau and Jacob came together once again to bury their father, just as before them Isaac and Ishmael had come together to bury Abraham (Genesis 25:7-9).

36:1 Before shifting the focus of the Genesis narrative to Jacob's sons, Moses recounted the history of Esau's family. Through various means, Jacob gained the birthright and blessing that should have gone to Esau. Nevertheless, God blessed Esau with a large family. His descendants, the Edomites, developed a tribal structure, just as the Israelites did, but the Edomites crowned a king long before Saul was anointed to rule over Israel (v. 31).

36:6-8 In an echo of the parting of Abraham and Lot (Genesis 13), Esau left Canaan to Jacob because there was not enough pastureland for all of their flocks. It was necessary for Jacob to live in Canaan, for God had promised the land to Abraham's descendants, then to Isaac's, and then to Jacob's. Esau moved south to Seir, which was later called Edom. While the animosity between the brothers seems to have lifted, their descendants did not maintain friendly relations. When the Israelites (Jacob's descendants) later made their way from Egypt back to Canaan, the Edomites refused to let them pass through their territory (Numbers 20:14-18). The prophet Obadiah spoke against the Edomites because they rejoiced to see Jerusalem destroyed and the Israelites taken into captivity (see the book of Obadiah).

13 The descendants of Reuel were Nahath, Zerah, Shammah, and Mizzah. These are the
descendants of Esau's wife Basemath.
14 Esau also had sons through Oholibamah, the daughter of Anah and granddaughter of
Zibeon. Their names were Jeush, Jalam, and Korah.

15 These are the descendants of Esau who became the leaders of various clans:

The descendants of Esau's oldest son, Eliphaz, became the leaders of the clans of Te-
man, Omar, Zepho, Kenaz, 16 Korah, Gatam, and Amalek. These are the clan leaders
in the land of Edom who descended from Eliphaz. All these were descendants of
Esau's wife Adah.
17 The descendants of Esau's son Reuel became the leaders of the clans of Nahath,
Zerah, Shammah, and Mizzah. These are the clan leaders in the land of Edom
who descended from Reuel. All these were descendants of Esau's wife
Basemath.
18 The descendants of Esau and his wife Oholibamah became the leaders of the clans of
Jeush, Jalam, and Korah. These are the clan leaders who descended from Esau's wife
Oholibamah, the daughter of Anah.

36:19 1 Chr 1:35
19 These are the clans descended from Esau (also known as Edom), identified by their clan
leaders.

ORIGINAL PEOPLES OF EDOM

36:20-28 //1 Chr 1:38-42
20 These are the names of the tribes that descended from Seir the Horite. They lived in the
36:20 Gen 14:6 Deut 2:12, 22
land of Edom: Lotan, Shobal, Zibeon, Anah, 21 Dishon, Ezer, and Dishan. These were the
Horite clan leaders, the descendants of Seir, who lived in the land of Edom.

22 The descendants of Lotan were Hori and Heman. Lotan also had a sister named
Timna.
23 The descendants of Shobal were Alvan, Manahath, Ebal, Shepho, and Onam.
24 The descendants of Zibeon were Aiah and Anah. (This is the Anah who discovered
the hot springs in the wilderness while he was grazing his father's donkeys.)
36:25 Gen 36:2, 5, 14, 18 1 Chr 1:41
25 The descendants of Anah were his son, Dishon, and his daughter, Oholibamah.
26 The descendants of Dishon* were Hemdan, Eshban, Ithran, and Keran.
36:27 1 Chr 1:38, 42
27 The descendants of Ezer were Bilhan, Zaavan, and Akan.
28 The descendants of Dishan were Uz and Aran.
36:29-30 Gen 36:20
29 So these were the leaders of the Horite clans: Lotan, Shobal, Zibeon, Anah, 30 Dishon,
Ezer, and Dishan. The Horite clans are named after their clan leaders, who lived in the land
of Seir.

RULERS OF EDOM

36:31-43 //1 Chr 1:43-54
31 These are the kings who ruled in the land of Edom before any king ruled over the
Israelites*:

32 Bela son of Beor, who ruled in Edom from the city of Dinhabah.
33 After Bela died, Jobab son of Zerah from Bozrah became king in his place.
34 After Jobab died, Husham from the land of the Temanites became king in his
place.
35 After Husham died, Hadad son of Bedad became king in his place and ruled from the
city of Avith. He was the one who defeated the Midianites in the land of Moab.
36 After Hadad died, Samlah from the city of Masrekah became king in his place.
37 After Samlah died, Shaul from the city of Rehoboth-on-the-River became king in his
place.

36:26 Hebrew *Dishan,* a variant spelling of Dishon; compare 36:21, 28. **36:31** Or *before an Israelite king ruled over them.*

38After Shaul died, Baal-hanan son of Acbor became king in his place.
39After Baal-hanan son of Acbor died, Hadad* became king in his place and ruled from
the city of Pau. Hadad's wife was Mehetabel, the daughter of Matred and grand-
daughter of Me-zahab.

40These are the names of the leaders of the clans descended from Esau, who lived in
the places named for them: Timna, Alvah, Jetheth, 41Oholibamah, Elah, Pinon, 42Kenaz,
Teman, Mibzar, 43Magdiel, and Iram. These are the leaders of the clans of Edom, listed
according to their settlements in the land they occupied. They all descended from Esau,
the ancestor of the Edomites.

JOSEPH'S DREAMS

37 So Jacob settled again in the land of Canaan, where his father had lived as a for- **37:1**
eigner. Gen 17:8; 28:4
2This is the account of Jacob and his family. When Joseph was seventeen years old, he **37:2**
often tended his father's flocks. He worked for his half brothers, the sons of his father's Gen 35:22-26; 41:46
wives Bilhah and Zilpah. But Joseph reported to his father some of the bad things his
brothers were doing.
3Jacob* loved Joseph more than any of his other children because Joseph had been **37:3**
born to him in his old age. So one day Jacob had a special gift made for Joseph—a beauti- Gen 37:23, 32; 44:20
ful robe.* 4But his brothers hated Joseph because their father loved him more than the rest **37:4**
of them. They couldn't say a kind word to him. Gen 27:41
5One night Joseph had a dream, and when he told his brothers about it, they hated him **37:5**
more than ever. 6"Listen to this dream," he said. 7"We were out in the field, tying up bun- Gen 28:12 Num 12:6
dles of grain. Suddenly my bundle stood up, and your bundles all gathered around and Dan 2:1
bowed low before mine!" **37:7**
8His brothers responded, "So you think you will be our king, do you? Do you actually Gen 42:6, 9; 43:26
think you will reign over us?" And they hated him all the more because of his dreams and **37:8**
the way he talked about them. Deut 33:16
9Soon Joseph had another dream, and again he told his brothers about it. "Listen, I have
had another dream," he said. "The sun, moon, and eleven stars bowed low before me!"
10This time he told the dream to his father as well as to his brothers, but his father
scolded him. "What kind of dream is that?" he asked. "Will your mother and I and your **37:10**
brothers actually come and bow to the ground before you?" 11But while his brothers were Gen 27:29
jealous of Joseph, his father wondered what the dreams meant. **37:11**
12Soon after this, Joseph's brothers went to pasture their father's flocks at Shechem. Luke 2:19, 51
13When they had been gone for some time, Jacob said to Joseph, "Your brothers are pas- Acts 7:9
turing the sheep at Shechem. Get ready, and I will send you to them." **37:13**
"I'm ready to go," Joseph replied. Gen 33:19

36:39 As in some Hebrew manuscripts, Samaritan Pentateuch, and Syriac version (see also 1 Chr 1:50); most Hebrew manuscripts read *Hadar.* **37:3a** Hebrew *Israel;* also in 37:13. See note on 35:21. **37:3b** Traditionally rendered *a coat of many colors.* The exact meaning of the Hebrew is uncertain.

37:3 Joseph not only was born to Jacob in his old age, Joseph was the firstborn of Rachel, the woman Jacob loved most. Rachel had only two children, Joseph and Benjamin, and she died during Benjamin's birth. For these reasons, Jacob showed a measure of favoritism toward Joseph, giving him a beautiful robe. This parental favoritism was obvious to Joseph's older brothers, and it caused them to hate Joseph.

▸ SALVATION

37:10 Rejecting God's rule. Joseph told his dream to his father and his brothers. His father scolded him, indignant at even the suggestion that Joseph might rule over the family. This critical spirit is seen in the carnally minded who scoff at the mere thought of living under the rule of Christ. Refusing to bend the knee in worship before God, they choose to keep themselves on the thrones of their lives. Who is in control of your life? Sincerely desiring to be directed and empowered by Christ is a non-negotiable element in a life that genuinely honors God. (***See Salvation***> *Our Need> Sinful,* TopicGuide page A22.)

37:14 14 "Go and see how your brothers and the flocks are getting along," Jacob said. "Then
Gen 35:27 come back and bring me a report." So Jacob sent him on his way, and Joseph traveled to
Shechem from their home in the valley of Hebron.
15 When he arrived there, a man from the area noticed him wandering around the
countryside. "What are you looking for?" he asked.
16 "I'm looking for my brothers," Joseph replied. "Do you know where they are pasturing
their sheep?"
37:17 17 "Yes," the man told him. "They have moved on from here, but I heard them say, 'Let's
2 Kgs 6:13 go on to Dothan.'" So Joseph followed his brothers to Dothan and found them there.

JOSEPH SOLD INTO SLAVERY

18 When Joseph's brothers saw him coming, they recognized him in the distance.
As he approached, they made plans to kill him. 19 "Here comes the dreamer!" they
said. 20 "Come on, let's kill him and throw him into one of these cisterns. We can
37:20 tell our father, 'A wild animal has eaten him.' Then we'll see what becomes of his
Gen 37:33 dreams!"
21 But when Reuben heard of their scheme, he came to Joseph's rescue. "Let's not kill
37:21 Gen 42:22 him," he said. 22 "Why should we shed any blood? Let's just throw him into this empty cis-
37:22 tern here in the wilderness. Then he'll die without our laying a hand on him." Reuben was
Gen 37:29 secretly planning to rescue Joseph and return him to his father.
37:23 23 So when Joseph arrived, his brothers ripped off the beautiful robe he was wearing.
Gen 37:3 24 Then they grabbed him and threw him into the cistern. Now the cistern was empty;
37:24 Jer 38:6; 41:7 there was no water in it. 25 Then, just as they were sitting down to eat, they looked up and
saw a caravan of camels in the distance coming toward them. It was a group of Ishmaelite
37:25 Gen 31:21; 37:28 traders taking a load of gum, balm, and aromatic resin from Gilead down to Egypt.
Jer 8:22; 46:11 26 Judah said to his brothers, "What will we gain by killing our brother? His blood would
37:28 just give us a guilty conscience. 27 Instead of hurting him, let's sell him to those Ishmaelite
Gen 39:1; 45:4-5 Lev 27:5 traders. After all, he is our brother—our own flesh and blood!" And his brothers agreed.
Judg 8:22-24 28 So when the Ishmaelites, who were Midianite traders, came by, Joseph's brothers pulled
Acts 7:9 him out of the cistern and sold him to them for twenty pieces* of silver. And the traders
37:29 took him to Egypt.
Gen 37:34; 44:13 29 Some time later, Reuben returned to get Joseph out of the cistern. When he discov-
Num 14:6 ered that Joseph was missing, he tore his clothes in grief. 30 Then he went back to his broth-
37:30 Gen 42:13, 36 ers and lamented, "The boy is gone! What will I do now?"
31 Then the brothers killed a young goat and dipped Joseph's robe in its blood. 32 They
37:32 Luke 15:30 sent the beautiful robe to their father with this message: "Look at what we found. Doesn't
37:33 this robe belong to your son?"
Gen 37:20; 44:28 33 Their father recognized it immediately. "Yes," he said, "it is my son's robe. A wild

37:28 Hebrew *20 shekels,* about 8 ounces or 228 grams in weight.

▶ BIBLE
37:20 Types and shadows of Christ. Exclaiming "Come on, let's kill him," Joseph's brothers demonstrated the same malevolence the murderous crowds showed toward Jesus of Nazareth (see Matthew 27:22). Joseph's brothers stripped him of his beautiful robe (Genesis 37:23). Likewise, the soldiers stripped Jesus of his clothes and divided them among themselves (see John 19:23-24). What is your reaction to the fact that the Father allowed His only Son to be brutally persecuted for your sins? Serving Jesus should be the greatest privilege of your life. Respond to Him by offering your life in service to His kingdom. (***See Bible***> *Unity> OT types> Joseph,* TopicGuide page A11.)

37:25 Ishmaelites were descendants of Ishmael, the half-brother of Isaac. Both were sons of Abraham. God had promised a son to Abraham and Sarah when they were very old, but Sarah took it upon herself to help God fulfill His promise by allowing her maidservant, Hagar, to bear Abraham a son. That son was Ishmael.

animal must have eaten him. Joseph has clearly been torn to pieces!" 34Then Jacob tore
his clothes and dressed himself in burlap. He mourned deeply for his son for a long time.
35His family all tried to comfort him, but he refused to be comforted. "I will go to my
grave* mourning for my son," he would say, and then he would weep.
36Meanwhile, the Midianite traders* arrived in Egypt, where they sold Joseph to Pot-
iphar, an officer of Pharaoh, the king of Egypt. Potiphar was captain of the palace
guard.

JUDAH AND TAMAR

38 About this time, Judah left home and moved to Adullam, where he stayed
with a man named Hirah. 2There he saw a Canaanite woman, the daughter
of Shua, and he married her. When he slept with her, 3she became pregnant and
gave birth to a son, and he named the boy Er. 4Then she became pregnant again
and gave birth to another son, and she named him Onan. 5And when she gave birth
to a third son, she named him Shelah. At the time of Shelah's birth, they were living
at Kezib.
6In the course of time, Judah arranged for his firstborn son, Er, to marry a young
woman named Tamar. 7But Er was a wicked man in the LORD's sight, so the LORD took
his life. 8Then Judah said to Er's brother Onan, "Go and marry Tamar, as our law requires
of the brother of a man who has died. You must produce an heir for your brother."
9But Onan was not willing to have a child who would not be his own heir. So when-
ever he had intercourse with his brother's wife, he spilled the semen on the ground.
This prevented her from having a child who would belong to his brother. 10But the
LORD considered it evil for Onan to deny a child to his dead brother. So the LORD took
Onan's life, too.
11Then Judah said to Tamar, his daughter-in-law, "Go back to your parents' home and
remain a widow until my son Shelah is old enough to marry you." (But Judah didn't really
intend to do this because he was afraid Shelah would also die, like his two brothers.) So
Tamar went back to live in her father's home.
12Some years later Judah's wife died. After the time of mourning was over, Judah and

37:34 Gen 37:29
37:35 Gen 44:29; 2 Sam 12:17; Ps 77:2
37:36 Gen 39:1; 40:3
38:1 Josh 15:35; 1 Sam 22:1
38:2 Gen 24:3; 34:2; 38:12
38:3 Gen 46:12; Num 26:19
38:6 Matt 1:3
38:7 Gen 6:5; 13:13; 19:13; 38:10; 1 Chr 2:3
38:8 Lev 18:15; Num 36:8; Deut 25:5-10; *Matt 22:24; *Mark 12:19
38:11 Ruth 1:13
38:12 Gen 31:19; Josh 15:10, 57

37:35 Hebrew *go down to Sheol.* 37:36 Hebrew *the Medanites.* The relationship between the Midianites and Medanites is unclear; compare 37:28. See also 25:2.

37:34-35 Jacob jumped to the conclusion his sons hoped he would—that Joseph had been killed by an animal. That sent him into a period of deep mourning. Genesis tells us that "his family"—including the 10 brothers who knew the truth—tried to comfort him, but he would not be consoled. The brothers' hatred for Joseph and their resentment over their father's favoritism was so strong that even his great grief could not induce them to tell the truth and relieve their father's sorrow.

▸SALVATION
38:7 Dead in sin. Er was a wicked man, so the Lord took his life. The fact that God ended Er's life is a vivid reminder that sin has consequences (see Romans 6:23). The concept of *sin* is not popular today. But if you look into your heart, you must admit that you have lied, looked at a man or a woman lustfully, coveted someone else's property, or done something else that God says is sin. While most people do not want to admit their sinfulness, the Bible says that such people only fool themselves (see 1 John 1:8). Take a lesson from Er—sin is a great offense to the holy character of God and must be punished. Thankfully, a Christian can suffer the temporal consequences of sin but will never suffer its eternal condemnation. (***See Salvation***> *Our Need*> *Sinful,* TopicGuide page A22.)

38:8 To have an heir was a priority in this time. If a man died without an heir, his closest male relative often married his widow. The child they produced was then considered the heir of the deceased. In this way, a man's legacy could continue. The relative who took in the widow was referred to as the "family redeemer" because he redeemed the inheritance.

▸BIBLE
38:8-10 Types and shadows of Christ. Onan was willing to have relations with Tamar, but not to impregnate her, thus failing in his responsibility as a family redeemer. Jesus, however, is the Redeemer who never fails. Not only did He pay the complete penalty for your sins on the cross, He continues to work in your life to make you just like Him. Rejoice in His unfailing love! (***See Bible***> *Unity*> *OT types*> *Onan,* TopicGuide page A11.)

his friend Hirah the Adullamite went up to Timnah to supervise the shearing of his sheep.
13 Someone told Tamar, "Look, your father-in-law is going up to Timnah to shear his
sheep."
38:14 14 Tamar was aware that Shelah had grown up, but no arrangements had been made for
Josh 15:34 her to come and marry him. So she changed out of her widow's clothing and covered herself
with a veil to disguise herself. Then she sat beside the road at the entrance to the village of
Enaim, which is on the road to Timnah. 15 Judah noticed her and thought she was a prosti-
38:16 tute, since she had covered her face. 16 So he stopped and propositioned her. "Let me have
2 Sam 13:11 sex with you," he said, not realizing that she was his own daughter-in-law.
"How much will you pay to have sex with me?" Tamar asked.
38:17 17 "I'll send you a young goat from my flock," Judah promised.
Gen 38:20 "But what will you give me to guarantee that you will send the goat?" she asked.
18 "What kind of guarantee do you want?" he replied.
38:18 Gen 41:42 She answered, "Leave me your identification seal and its cord and the walking stick you
Hos 4:11 are carrying." So Judah gave them to her. Then he had intercourse with her, and she be-
came pregnant. 19 Afterward she went back home, took off her veil, and put on her
widow's clothing as usual.
20 Later Judah asked his friend Hirah the Adullamite to take the young goat to the
woman and to pick up the things he had given her as his guarantee. But Hirah couldn't
find her. 21 So he asked the men who lived there, "Where can I find the shrine prostitute
who was sitting beside the road at the entrance to Enaim?"
"We've never had a shrine prostitute here," they replied.
22 So Hirah returned to Judah and told him, "I couldn't find her anywhere, and the men
of the village claim they've never had a shrine prostitute there."
23 "Then let her keep the things I gave her," Judah said. "I sent the young goat as we
agreed, but you couldn't find her. We'd be the laughingstock of the village if we went back
again to look for her."
38:24 24 About three months later, Judah was told, "Tamar, your daughter-in-law, has acted
Lev 20:10; 21:9 like a prostitute. And now, because of this, she's pregnant."
"Bring her out, and let her be burned!" Judah demanded.
25 But as they were taking her out to kill her, she sent this message to her father-in-law:
"The man who owns these things made me pregnant. Look closely. Whose seal and cord
and walking stick are these?"
38:26 26 Judah recognized them immediately and said, "She is more righteous than I am, be-
1 Sam 24:17 cause I didn't arrange for her to marry my son Shelah." And Judah never slept with Tamar
38:27 Gen 25:24 again.
38:29 27 When the time came for Tamar to give birth, it was discovered that she was carrying
Gen 46:12 twins. 28 While she was in labor, one of the babies reached out his hand. The midwife grabbed
Num 26:20-21 it and tied a scarlet string around the child's wrist, announcing, "This one came out first." 29 But
Ruth 4:12 1 Chr 2:4 then he pulled back his hand, and out came his brother! "What!" the midwife exclaimed. "How
Matt 1:3 did you break out first?" So he was named Perez.* 30 Then the baby with the scarlet string on
Luke 3:33 his wrist was born, and he was named Zerah.*

38:29 *Perez* means "breaking out." 38:30 *Zerah* means "scarlet" or "brightness."

38:18 The objects Tamar requested were the ancient equivalent of a form of identification with a signature on it. The seal had Judah's name or sign on it. It probably hung around his neck by a cord, and he used it to mark documents. The walking stick also may have borne his insignia. These were items that would identify a man without question. That, of course, was why Tamar requested them. When she later presented them to Judah, he could not deny her right as the mother of his unborn child (Genesis 38:25).

38:24 It seems absurd that Judah would judge Tamar for playing the role of a prostitute yet not judge himself for going to a prostitute. However, double standards existed just as surely in the ancient world as they do today. Once Judah was faced with evidence of his own deed, he admitted that he had done wrong by Tamar and did not carry through with her punishment.

JOSEPH IN POTIPHAR'S HOUSE

39 When Joseph was taken to Egypt by the Ishmaelite traders, he was purchased by 39:1
Potiphar, an Egyptian officer. Potiphar was captain of the guard for Pharaoh, the Gen 37:25
king of Egypt.
2The LORD was with Joseph, so he succeeded in everything he did as he served in 39:2
the home of his Egyptian master. 3Potiphar noticed this and realized that the LORD was Acts 7:9
with Joseph, giving him success in everything he did. 4This pleased Potiphar, so he 39:4
soon made Joseph his personal attendant. He put him in charge of his entire house- Gen 40:4 Prov 22:29
hold and everything he owned. 5From the day Joseph was put in charge of his mas- 39:5
ter's household and property, the LORD began to bless Potiphar's household for Deut 28:3-4, 11
Joseph's sake. All his household affairs ran smoothly, and his crops and livestock
flourished. 6So Potiphar gave Joseph complete administrative responsibility over 39:6
everything he owned. With Joseph there, he didn't worry about a thing—except what 1 Sam 16:12, 18 Acts 7:20
kind of food to eat!
Joseph was a very handsome and well-built young man, 7and Potiphar's wife soon be- 39:7
gan to look at him lustfully. "Come and sleep with me," she demanded. Prov 7:15-20
8But Joseph refused. "Look," he told her, "my master trusts me with everything in his en- 39:8
tire household. 9No one here has more authority than I do. He has held back nothing from Gen 39:4-5 Prov 6:23-24
me except you, because you are his wife. How could I do such a wicked thing? It would be
a great sin against God."
10She kept putting pressure on Joseph day after day, but he refused to sleep with her, 39:10 1 Thes 5:22
and he kept out of her way as much as possible. 11One day, however, no one else was
around when he went in to do his work. 12She came and grabbed him by his cloak, de- 39:12 Prov 7:13
manding, "Come on, sleep with me!" Joseph tore himself away, but he left his cloak in her 2 Tim 2:22
hand as he ran from the house.
13When she saw that she was holding his cloak and he had fled, 14she called out to her
servants. Soon all the men came running. "Look!" she said. "My husband has brought this
Hebrew slave here to make fools of us! He came into my room to rape me, but I screamed.
15When he heard me scream, he ran outside and got away, but he left his cloak behind
with me."
16She kept the cloak with her until her husband came home. 17Then she told him her 39:17 Exod 20:16; 23:1
story. "That Hebrew slave you've brought into our house tried to come in and fool Ps 55:3

39:1 Because of its proximity to the Promised Land, Egypt played a significant role in much of Israel's history. Abraham went there during a famine, for the rich land of the Nile Delta sometimes provided food at times when other areas were suffering. Joseph's presence there, along with another famine in Canaan, would bring Jacob's entire family to Egypt. Over the next 400 years, the family would grow into the nation of Israel. Later in Israel's history, Egypt would sometimes be an ally and sometimes an enemy.

▸ MINISTRY

39:2-3 Disciples enjoy God's presence. Just as the Lord was with Joseph, He promises to be with us as we carry out the Great Commission (see Matthew 28:18-20). Christ's presence, however, is not assured without our faithful obedience. Notice that Joseph demonstrated complete trust in God despite the temptations of Egypt. You can discover the same success in life and in ministry if, like Joseph, your heart is totally committed to God. However, God's definitions of success are not necessarily the same as ours—even the most faithful of saints may labor with relatively little fruit (compare Jeremiah 1 and Isaiah 6:9-12). The Lord's supernatural presence in your life does ensure that your labor for Him will honor His name and accomplish His purposes. (*See **Ministry**> Great Commission> Make disciples,* TopicGuide page A56.)

▸ HOLINESS

39:9 Overcoming temptation. Joseph is clear that adultery is a sin against God. Refusing the seductive lure of Potiphar's wife, Joseph demonstrated faith in God. As a believer, you are to flee anything that stimulates ungodly passion. The promise found in 1 Corinthians 10:13 can be a great help: "And God is faithful. He will not allow the temptation to be more than you can stand. When you are tempted, He will show you a way out so that you can endure." Claim the promises of Scripture, and God will not allow the temptation to be more than you can stand. (*See **Holiness**> Submission> Trusting God> Overcoming,* TopicGuide page A40.)

around with me," she said. 18 "But when I screamed, he ran outside, leaving his cloak
with me!"

JOSEPH PUT IN PRISON

39:20 Gen 40:1-3, 15; 41:10; Ps 105:18
39:21 Ps 105:19; Acts 7:9
39:22 Gen 39:4
39:23 Gen 39:3

19 Potiphar was furious when he heard his wife's story about how Joseph had treated
her. 20 So he took Joseph and threw him into the prison where the king's prisoners were
held, and there he remained. 21 But the LORD was with Joseph in the prison and showed
him His faithful love. And the LORD made Joseph a favorite with the prison warden.
22 Before long, the warden put Joseph in charge of all the other prisoners and over
everything that happened in the prison. 23 The warden had no more worries, because
Joseph took care of everything. The LORD was with him and caused everything he did
to succeed.

JOSEPH INTERPRETS TWO DREAMS

40:1 Neh 1:11
40:4 Gen 37:36; 39:4
40:5 Gen 20:3; 41:11
40:8 Gen 41:15-16; Dan 2:27-28
40:12 Gen 41:12
40:13 Gen 40:19-20
40:14 1 Sam 20:14
40:15 Gen 37:26-28; 39:20

40 Some time later, Pharaoh's chief cup-bearer and chief baker offended their royal
master. 2 Pharaoh became angry with these two officials, 3 and he put them in the
prison where Joseph was, in the palace of the captain of the guard. 4 They remained in
prison for quite some time, and the captain of the guard assigned them to Joseph, who
looked after them.
5 While they were in prison, Pharaoh's cup-bearer and baker each had a dream one
night, and each dream had its own meaning. 6 When Joseph saw them the next morning,
he noticed that they both looked upset. 7 "Why do you look so worried today?" he asked
them.
8 And they replied, "We both had dreams last night, but no one can tell us what they
mean."
"Interpreting dreams is God's business," Joseph replied. "Go ahead and tell me your
dreams."
9 So the chief cup-bearer told Joseph his dream first. "In my dream," he said, "I saw a
grapevine in front of me. 10 The vine had three branches that began to bud and blossom,
and soon it produced clusters of ripe grapes. 11 I was holding Pharaoh's wine cup in my
hand, so I took a cluster of grapes and squeezed the juice into the cup. Then I placed the
cup in Pharaoh's hand."
12 "This is what the dream means," Joseph said. "The three branches represent three
days. 13 Within three days Pharaoh will lift you up and restore you to your position as his
chief cup-bearer. 14 And please remember me and do me a favor when things go well for
you. Mention me to Pharaoh, so he might let me out of this place. 15 For I was kidnapped

---

39:19-23 Wherever Joseph landed, he seemed to find success. First he successfully managed Potiphar's household. After being falsely accused of rape, he went to prison, but then rose to leadership there. While in prison, he made contacts that eventually led to a leadership position in Egypt's national government. Joseph's success was a direct result of God's presence with him to bless him (v. 21).

40:1-4 The king of Egypt was called the *Pharaoh*, which literally means "great house." Pharaohs were considered to be earthly representatives of gods. Because of this, they wielded much power among their people, both spiritually and politically. The fact that Joseph was put in proximity to servants of Pharaoh proved to be significant in his life. Through that connection, Joseph, a Hebrew shepherd, received access to the greatest religious and civil leader of one of the mightiest kingdoms of the time. About 400 years later, the same thing happened when Moses was adopted by a pharaoh's daughter (Exodus 2:5-10) and grew up in the palace.

40:8 Joseph began examining his dreams at an early age. As a young man, his dreams caused family conflict. Joseph once described a dream in which he and his brothers were gathering grain, and his brothers' bundles of grain bowed down to his. This did not sit well with his brothers, who all (except Benjamin) were older than he was. Even Joseph's father, Jacob, was upset by Joseph's second dream, in which the moon, sun, and eleven stars bowed down to one star. It wasn't difficult to understand that as a picture of Joseph's parents and his 11 brothers bowing down to him (Genesis 37:5-11). While his family resented the implications at the time, the dreams eventually came true (Genesis 43:26-28).

from my homeland, the land of the Hebrews, and now I'm here in prison, but I did nothing
to deserve it."
16When the chief baker saw that Joseph had given the first dream such a positive inter-
pretation, he said to Joseph, "I had a dream, too. In my dream there were three baskets of
white pastries stacked on my head. 17The top basket contained all kinds of pastries for
Pharaoh, but the birds came and ate them from the basket on my head."
18"This is what the dream means," Joseph told him. "The three baskets also represent **40:18**
three days. 19Three days from now Pharaoh will lift you up and impale your body on a Gen 40:12
pole. Then birds will come and peck away at your flesh." **40:19**
20Pharaoh's birthday came three days later, and he prepared a banquet for all his offi- Deut 21:22-23
cials and staff. He summoned* his chief cup-bearer and chief baker to join the other offi-
cials. 21He then restored the chief cup-bearer to his former position, so he could again
hand Pharaoh his cup. 22But Pharaoh impaled the chief baker, just as Joseph had pre- **40:22**
dicted when he interpreted his dream. 23Pharaoh's chief cup-bearer, however, forgot all Gen 40:19
about Joseph, never giving him another thought. **40:23** Gen 40:14

PHARAOH'S DREAMS

41 Two full years later, Pharaoh dreamed that he was standing on the bank of the **41:2**
Nile River. 2In his dream he saw seven fat, healthy cows come up out of the river Isa 19:6-7
and begin grazing in the marsh grass. 3Then he saw seven more cows come up behind
them from the Nile, but these were scrawny and thin. These cows stood beside the fat
cows on the riverbank. 4Then the scrawny, thin cows ate the seven healthy, fat cows! At
this point in the dream, Pharaoh woke up.
5But he fell asleep again and had a second dream. This time he saw seven heads of **41:5**
grain, plump and beautiful, growing on a single stalk. 6Then seven more heads of grain 2 Kgs 4:42 **41:6**
appeared, but these were shriveled and withered by the east wind. 7And these thin heads Ezek 19:12
swallowed up the seven plump, well-formed heads! Then Pharaoh woke up again and re-
alized it was a dream.
8The next morning Pharaoh was very disturbed by the dreams. So he called for all the **41:8** Exod 7:11-12
magicians and wise men of Egypt. When Pharaoh told them his dreams, not one of them Dan 2:1-3; 4:5-7
could tell him what they meant.

40:20 Hebrew *He lifted up the head of.*

▸ HOLINESS

40:15 Obedience in persecution. Joseph told the cupbearer that he was in prison even though he had done "nothing to deserve it." Joseph's life embodied a fundamental truth: God's children are often called to suffer without cause. People may slander you, friends may abandon you, and even family members may disown you—all because you are a Christian. But Jesus offers comfort. Jesus said that when you suffer for the sake of being His follower, God blesses you (see Matthew 5:11-12). Entrust yourself to God in the midst of suffering, and He will reward you richly. (***See Holiness***> *God's Blessing> Obedience leads to hardship and persecution,* TopicGuide page A42.)

▸ SALVATION

40:23 Salvation results in gratitude. The cupbearer forgot about Joseph. Despite the fact that Joseph had given him comfort and hope, the cupbearer proved himself to be an unfaithful friend. You must not be like the cupbearer. Christ's selfless sacrifice has released you from the consequences of sin. How wrong would it be for you to walk away from Jesus and to forget all about Him? The proper response is to serve Him all the days of your life out of a heart filled with gratitude for what He has done for you. (***See Salvation***> *Receiving> Results,* TopicGuide page A23.)

41:1-7 Throughout the Bible, God spoke through dreams to many different people. When Abraham lied about Sarah being his wife, God warned King Abimelech in a dream not to marry her (Genesis 20:3-7). Joseph's father, Jacob, heard God's promises through a dream at a place he named Bethel (Genesis 28:10-19). Joseph himself interpreted dreams for Pharaoh's servants before he did so for Pharaoh himself (Genesis 40:8-19). God spoke to King Solomon through a dream (1 Kings 3:5-15). Later, in the days of Israel's exile, Daniel was a dream interpreter for King Nebuchadnezzar of Babylon. In the New Testament, God instructed Joseph through dreams (Matthew 1:20; 2:13, 19), as He did the wise men (Matthew 2:12).

41:8 In ancient Egypt, magicians, wise men, and astrologers were part of the priesthood. Such men had a place in civilizations from the earliest culture of the Persians. The group grew larger, darker, and more esoteric as societies progressed.

41:9 Gen 40:14 9Finally, the king's chief cup-bearer spoke up. "Today I have been reminded of my
failure," he told Pharaoh. 10"Some time ago, you were angry with the chief baker
41:10 Gen 40:2 and me, and you imprisoned us in the palace of the captain of the guard. 11One
41:11 night the chief baker and I each had a dream, and each dream had its own meaning.
Gen 40:5 12There was a young Hebrew man with us in the prison who was a slave of the cap-
41:12 Gen 40:12 tain of the guard. We told him our dreams, and he told us what each of our dreams
meant. 13And everything happened just as he had predicted. I was restored to my
41:13 Gen 40:22 position as cup-bearer, and the chief baker was executed and impaled on a pole."
41:14 Ps 105:20 14Pharaoh sent for Joseph at once, and he was quickly brought from the prison. After he
shaved and changed his clothes, he went in and stood before Pharaoh. 15Then Pharaoh
41:15 Dan 2:25 said to Joseph, "I had a dream last night, and no one here can tell me what it means. But I
have heard that when you hear about a dream you can interpret it."
16"It is beyond my power to do this," Joseph replied. "But God can tell you what it means
41:16 Gen 40:8 and set you at ease."
41:17 17So Pharaoh told Joseph his dream. "In my dream," he said, "I was standing on the
Gen 41:1 2 Kgs 8:1 bank of the Nile River, 18and I saw seven fat, healthy cows come up out of the river
and begin grazing in the marsh grass. 19But then I saw seven sick-looking cows,
scrawny and thin, come up after them. I've never seen such sorry-looking animals in
all the land of Egypt. 20These thin, scrawny cows ate the seven fat cows. 21But after-
ward you wouldn't have known it, for they were still as thin and scrawny as before!
Then I woke up.
22"Then I fell asleep again, and I had another dream. This time I saw seven heads of
grain, full and beautiful, growing on a single stalk. 23Then seven more heads of grain ap-
peared, but these were blighted, shriveled, and withered by the east wind. 24And the shriv-
eled heads swallowed the seven healthy heads. I told these dreams to the magicians, but
no one could tell me what they mean."
25Joseph responded, "Both of Pharaoh's dreams mean the same thing. God is telling
Pharaoh in advance what He is about to do. 26The seven healthy cows and the seven
healthy heads of grain both represent seven years of prosperity. 27The seven thin,
scrawny cows that came up later and the seven thin heads of grain, withered by the east
wind, represent seven years of famine.
28"This will happen just as I have described it, for God has revealed to Pharaoh in ad-
41:29 Gen 41:47 vance what He is about to do. 29The next seven years will be a period of great prosperity
throughout the land of Egypt. 30But afterward there will be seven years of famine so great
41:30 Gen 47:13 that all the prosperity will be forgotten in Egypt. Famine will destroy the land. 31This fam-
ine will be so severe that even the memory of the good years will be erased. 32As for hav-
ing two similar dreams, it means that these events have been decreed by God, and He will
soon make them happen.
41:33 Gen 41:39 33"Therefore, Pharaoh should find an intelligent and wise man and put him in charge of
the entire land of Egypt. 34Then Pharaoh should appoint supervisors over the land and let
them collect one-fifth of all the crops during the seven good years. 35Have them gather all
the food produced in the good years that are just ahead and bring it to Pharaoh's store-
41:36 Gen 47:14 houses. Store it away, and guard it so there will be food in the cities. 36That way there will
be enough to eat when the seven years of famine come to the land of Egypt. Otherwise
this famine will destroy the land."

41:16, 25 When Joseph interpreted the dreams of Pharaoh's servants, he told them the same thing he told Pharaoh here: What God tells you in dreams is His business. Joseph was very clear that he was not to receive credit; he was just the one who listened to God and let Him guide and explain. Joseph's awareness of God's sovereignty would later give him perspective on his brothers' mistreatment of him. At the end of Genesis, when his brothers finally asked forgiveness, Joseph's response was, "You intended to harm me, but God intended it all for good" (Genesis 50:20). Joseph knew that God was in control.

JOSEPH MADE RULER OF EGYPT

37 Joseph's suggestions were well received by Pharaoh and his officials. 38 So Pharaoh 41:38 Dan 4:8, 18; 5:11, 14
asked his officials, "Can we find anyone else like this man so obviously filled with the spirit
of God?" 39 Then Pharaoh said to Joseph, "Since God has revealed the meaning of the 41:39 Gen 41:33
dreams to you, clearly no one else is as intelligent or wise as you are. 40 You will be in 41:40
charge of my court, and all my people will take orders from you. Only I, sitting on my Gen 39:9 Ps 105:21
throne, will have a rank higher than yours." Acts 7:10
41 Pharaoh said to Joseph, "I hereby put you in charge of the entire land of Egypt." 41:41
42 Then Pharaoh removed his signet ring from his hand and placed it on Joseph's finger. Esth 8:2
He dressed him in fine linen clothing and hung a gold chain around his neck. 43 Then he Dan 6:3
had Joseph ride in the chariot reserved for his second-in-command. And wherever Joseph 41:42
went, the command was shouted, "Kneel down!" So Pharaoh put Joseph in charge of all Esth 3:10; 6:8
Egypt. 44 And Pharaoh said to him, "I am Pharaoh, but no one will lift a hand or foot in the 41:44 Gen 45:8
entire land of Egypt without your approval." Ps 105:22

▸ GOD

41:38 Holy Spirit's power. Pharaoh could see that Joseph was filled with the spirit of God. How do you demonstrate that you are filled with the Spirit? All Christians are filled with the same Spirit (1 Corinthians 12:12-13) just as all are justified, united with Christ, and are being sanctified. But surrounding that sanctification or purification process, there is also a continued replenishing of the Spirit's power that God says we should ask for (Ephesians 5:15-18) and that is connected to our joy (Acts 13:52). If prayer was involved in your conversion experience, it was not the actual means by which you received Christ; rather, it served as a verbal expression of the faith God was giving you. Likewise, when you ask God to fill you with His Spirit, remember that it is by faith, not by prayer, that you are filled with the Spirit (Romans 15:13). (***See God> God's Names> Holy Spirit> Empowers,*** TopicGuide page A19.)

MY RESPONSE TO GOD

Embracing God's Will and Master Plan

GENESIS 41:37-57

As members of a democratic society rife with individualism, Americans have difficulty understanding God as an absolute Ruler. We tend to argue and debate our points of view with everyone, even our leaders, to get our agendas accepted. Compromise, even on moral issues, is considered a virtue.

Yet Joseph demonstrated none of these characteristics. God's agenda for him included years spent as a slave and a prisoner. Through it all, Joseph remained morally pure and faithful to God. He accepted God's plan for his life—a plan that eventually led him to the highest reaches of power in ancient Egypt.

We cannot argue, debate, or negotiate with God, the King of the universe. If He is the Lord of our lives and we are His true disciples, we must say, "Yes, Lord!" Saying "No, Lord" is a contradiction of terms.

Don't be fooled by the teaching of some who say that if you have enough faith in God, repeat the name of Jesus, or quote a formula of phrases or Scripture verses, then you will get everything you want. We cannot force God to do things our way. Neither can we understand fully what He is doing in our lives. Sometimes, in His wisdom and sovereign plan, His answer to our prayers is "No" or "Wait." Like Joseph, our response must be to trust, believe, and obey, not to demand. In the end, God's plan for us will always reveal His love and faithfulness.

41:45 45Then Pharaoh gave Joseph a new Egyptian name, Zaphenath-paneah.* He also gave
Ezek 30:17 him a wife, whose name was Asenath. She was the daughter of Potiphera, the priest of
41:46 On.* So Joseph took charge of the entire land of Egypt. 46He was thirty years old when he
Gen 37:2 began serving in the court of Pharaoh, the king of Egypt. And when Joseph left Pharaoh's
presence, he inspected the entire land of Egypt.
47As predicted, for seven years the land produced bumper crops. 48During those years,
Joseph gathered all the crops grown in Egypt and stored the grain from the surrounding
fields in the cities. 49He piled up huge amounts of grain like sand on the seashore. Finally,
he stopped keeping records because there was too much to measure.
50During this time, before the first of the famine years, two sons were born to Joseph
41:51 Gen 48:1 and his wife, Asenath, the daughter of Potiphera, the priest of On. 51Joseph named his
Deut 33:17 older son Manasseh,* for he said, "God has made me forget all my troubles and everyone
41:52 in my father's family." 52Joseph named his second son Ephraim,* for he said, "God has
Gen 17:6 made me fruitful in this land of my grief."
53At last the seven years of bumper crops throughout the land of Egypt came to an end.
41:54 54Then the seven years of famine began, just as Joseph had predicted. The famine also
Gen 41:30 struck all the surrounding countries, but throughout Egypt there was plenty of food.
Ps 105:16 55Eventually, however, the famine spread throughout the land of Egypt as well. And when
Acts 7:11 the people cried out to Pharaoh for food, he told them, "Go to Joseph, and do whatever he
41:55 tells you." 56So with severe famine everywhere, Joseph opened up the storehouses and
Gen 41:41 distributed grain to the Egyptians, for the famine was severe throughout the land of Egypt.
41:57 57And people from all around came to Egypt to buy grain from Joseph because the famine
Gen 42:5; 47:15 Ps 105:16 was severe throughout the world.

JOSEPH'S BROTHERS GO TO EGYPT

42:1 Acts 7:12 **42** When Jacob heard that grain was available in Egypt, he said to his sons, "Why are
you standing around looking at one another? 2I have heard there is grain in
42:2 Gen 43:2, 4 Egypt. Go down there, and buy enough grain to keep us alive. Otherwise we'll die."
3So Joseph's ten older brothers went down to Egypt to buy grain. 4But Jacob wouldn't let
42:4 Gen 35:24 Joseph's younger brother, Benjamin, go with them, for fear some harm might come to
42:5 him. 5So Jacob's* sons arrived in Egypt along with others to buy food, for the famine was
Gen 41:57 in Canaan as well.
Acts 7:11 6Since Joseph was governor of all Egypt and in charge of selling grain to all the people,
42:6 Ps 105:16-21 it was to him that his brothers came. When they arrived, they bowed before him with their

41:45a *Zaphenath-paneah* probably means "God speaks and lives." 41:45b Greek version reads *of Heliopolis;* also in 41:50. 41:51 *Manasseh* sounds like a Hebrew term that means "causing to forget." 41:52 *Ephraim* sounds like a Hebrew term that means "fruitful." 42:5 Hebrew *Israel's.* See note on 35:21.

41:45 Joseph's sudden promotion to second in command to Pharaoh was nothing short of miraculous. Pharaoh granted Joseph a new life, a new name, and a new wife. Around 400 years later, a similar miracle happened to another Hebrew. Moses was adopted by the daughter of the Pharaoh of his day. He was given a new home and a new name—Moses (Exodus 2:1-10). These two men were placed and used by God. Joseph brought the family of Jacob to Egypt to flourish and grow. Moses led them back out to resettle their land and fulfill God's promise to their ancestor Abraham (Genesis 12:1-3).

42:4, 38 Jacob was unwilling to risk losing Benjamin. Rachel, Jacob's first love and favorite wife, had borne him two sons, Joseph and Benjamin. Unfortunately, she had died giving birth to Benjamin. Jacob was devastated when he lost Joseph, presumably to death (Genesis 37:33-35). He could not bear the thought of losing the only other son of his beloved Rachel.

▸ WORSHIP

42:6 Old Testament worship: bowing. Joseph's brothers bowed low before him. By assuming a position of humble submission, the brothers unsuspectingly fulfilled Joseph's dream (see Genesis 37:5-11; 43:26). The picture of men bowing before a ruler whom they once sought to kill is also found in the New Testament. Paul teaches that the day will come when "every tongue confess that Jesus Christ is Lord" (Philippians 2:11). At the final judgment, not only heartfelt worshipers but also hostile nonbelievers will bow before Jesus as Lord and Savior. Don't be like those who someday will acknowledge the Lord of glory unwillingly; worship Him today from a heart of love and gratitude for His marvelous goodness toward you. (***See Worship***> *OT*> *Posture,* TopicGuide page A28.)

faces to the ground. 7 Joseph recognized his brothers instantly, but he pretended to be a
stranger and spoke harshly to them. "Where are you from?" he demanded.
"From the land of Canaan," they replied. "We have come to buy food."
8 Although Joseph recognized his brothers, they didn't recognize him. 9 And he remem-
bered the dreams he'd had about them many years before. He said to them, "You are
spies! You have come to see how vulnerable our land has become."
10 "No, my lord!" they exclaimed. "Your servants have simply come to buy food. 11 We
are all brothers—members of the same family. We are honest men, sir! We are not spies!"
12 "Yes, you are!" Joseph insisted. "You have come to see how vulnerable our land has
become."
13 "Sir," they said, "there are actually twelve of us. We, your servants, are all brothers,
sons of a man living in the land of Canaan. Our youngest brother is back there with our fa-
ther right now, and one of our brothers is no longer with us."
14 But Joseph insisted, "As I said, you are spies! 15 This is how I will test your story. I
swear by the life of Pharaoh that you will never leave Egypt unless your youngest
brother comes here! 16 One of you must go and get your brother. I'll keep the rest of you
here in prison. Then we'll find out whether or not your story is true. By the life of Pha-
raoh, if it turns out that you don't have a younger brother, then I'll know you are spies."
17 So Joseph put them all in prison for three days. 18 On the third day Joseph said to
them, "I am a God-fearing man. If you do as I say, you will live. 19 If you really are honest
men, choose one of your brothers to remain in prison. The rest of you may go home
with grain for your starving families. 20 But you must bring your youngest brother back
to me. This will prove that you are telling the truth, and you will not die." To this they
agreed.
21 Speaking among themselves, they said, "Clearly we are being punished because of
what we did to Joseph long ago. We saw his anguish when he pleaded for his life, but we
wouldn't listen. That's why we're in this trouble."
22 "Didn't I tell you not to sin against the boy?" Reuben asked. "But you wouldn't listen.
And now we have to answer for his blood!"
23 Of course, they didn't know that Joseph understood them, for he had been speaking
to them through an interpreter. 24 Now he turned away from them and began to weep.
When he regained his composure, he spoke to them again. Then he chose Simeon from
among them and had him tied up right before their eyes.
25 Joseph then ordered his servants to fill the men's sacks with grain, but he also gave
secret instructions to return each brother's payment at the top of his sack. He also gave
them supplies for their journey home. 26 So the brothers loaded their donkeys with the
grain and headed for home.
27 But when they stopped for the night and one of them opened his sack to get grain for
his donkey, he found his money in the top of his sack. 28 "Look!" he exclaimed to his broth-

42:7 Gen 42:30
42:8 Gen 37:2
42:9 Gen 42:16, 30-34
42:10 Gen 37:6-9
42:11 Gen 42:19, 31-34
42:13 Gen 37:30-33; 44:20; 46:31
42:14 Gen 42:9
42:17 Gen 40:4
42:18 Gen 20:11 Lev 25:43
42:20 Gen 42:34; 43:15
42:21 Gen 37:23-28; 45:3-5
42:22 Gen 9:5-6; 37:21-22
42:24 Gen 43:14, 23
42:25 Gen 44:1
42:28 Gen 43:23

▸ WORSHIP

42:18 Fear of God. Joseph told his brothers that he was a "God-fearing man." Because Joseph feared God, his brothers could follow his instructions with confidence and live. We, too, are to be God-fearing in all we do and think. Fearing God begins with a deep respect for His authority in your life (see Proverbs 1:7). He demonstrated His authority, as well as His awesome power, when He fashioned the heavens and the earth from nothing, gave the Ten Commandments to the nation of Israel, and raised Jesus from the dead. Today you may be facing a need for direction in your life. Begin by checking to see if you are living before God in holy reverence, willing to heed His voice. (*See Worship> OT> Reverence> God requires us to fear him,* TopicGuide page A28.)

42:21-22 Joseph concealed his identity from his brothers to determine whether they had repented of the wrongs they had done to him. Here Joseph got the first hint that their attitudes had changed. They saw what was happening to them as the providential judgment of God. Implicit in their statements is recognition that what they did to Joseph was wrong. God was working in their hearts to bring them to repentance.

ers. "My money has been returned; it's here in my sack!" Then their hearts sank. Trem-
bling, they said to each other, "What has God done to us?"
42:30 Gen 42:7 [29]When the brothers came to their father, Jacob, in the land of Canaan, they told him
everything that had happened to them. [30]"The man who is governor of the land spoke
42:31 Gen 42:11 very harshly to us," they told him. "He accused us of being spies scouting the land. [31]But
42:32 Gen 42:13 we said, 'We are honest men, not spies. [32]We are twelve brothers, sons of one father.
One brother is no longer with us, and the youngest is at home with our father in the land
of Canaan.'
[33]"Then the man who is governor of the land told us, 'This is how I will find out if you
42:34 Gen 34:10 are honest men. Leave one of your brothers here with me, and take grain for your starving
families and go on home. [34]But you must bring your youngest brother back to me. Then I
will know you are honest men and not spies. Then I will give you back your brother, and
42:35 Gen 43:12, 15, 18 you may trade freely in the land.' "
[35]As they emptied out their sacks, there in each man's sack was the bag of money he
42:36 Gen 43:14; 44:20-22 had paid for the grain! The brothers and their father were terrified when they saw the
bags of money. [36]Jacob exclaimed, "You are robbing me of my children! Joseph is
gone! Simeon is gone! And now you want to take Benjamin, too. Everything is going
42:37 Gen 43:9; 44:32 against me!"
[37]Then Reuben said to his father, "You may kill my two sons if I don't bring Benjamin
42:38 Gen 37:35; 44:29, 34 back to you. I'll be responsible for him, and I promise to bring him back."
[38]But Jacob replied, "My son will not go down with you. His brother Joseph is dead, and
he is all I have left. If anything should happen to him on your journey, you would send this
grieving, white-haired man to his grave.*"

43:1 Gen 41:56-57

THE BROTHERS RETURN TO EGYPT

43 But the famine continued to ravage the land of Canaan. [2]When the grain they
43:2 Gen 42:25 had brought from Egypt was almost gone, Jacob said to his sons, "Go back and
43:3 Gen 42:15; 44:23 buy us a little more food."
[3]But Judah said, "The man was serious when he warned us, 'You won't see my face
again unless your brother is with you.' [4]If you send Benjamin with us, we will go down and
buy more food. [5]But if you don't let Benjamin go, we won't go either. Remember, the man
said, 'You won't see my face again unless your brother is with you.' "
[6]"Why were you so cruel to me?" Jacob* moaned. "Why did you tell him you had an-
43:7 Gen 42:13; 43:27 other brother?"
[7]"The man kept asking us questions about our family," they replied. "He asked, 'Is your
father still alive? Do you have another brother?' So we answered his questions. How could
43:8 Gen 42:2 we know he would say, 'Bring your brother down here'?"
[8]Judah said to his father, "Send the boy with me, and we will be on our way. Otherwise
43:9 Gen 42:37 we will all die of starvation—and not only we, but you and our little ones. [9]I personally
Phlm 1:18-19 guarantee his safety. You may hold me responsible if I don't bring him back to you. Then
43:11 Gen 32:13; 37:25 let me bear the blame forever. [10]If we hadn't wasted all this time, we could have gone and
returned twice by now."
43:12 Gen 42:25, 35 [11]So their father, Jacob, finally said to them, "If it can't be avoided, then at least do this.
Pack your bags with the best products of this land. Take them down to the man as gifts—
balm, honey, gum, aromatic resin, pistachio nuts, and almonds. [12]Also take double the

42:38 Hebrew *to Sheol.* 43:6 Hebrew *Israel;* also in 43:11. See note on 35:21.

43:11 These products were typical for Canaan—a narrow strip of land between the Mediterranean Sea and the Jordan River. Part of the land was green and fertile, with almond, fig, olive, and pomegranate trees, as well as grape vines of all varieties. Many other plants were used for medicinal purposes and flavoring, such as aloe, balm, cumin, dill, myrrh, and mustard.

money that was put back in your sacks, as it was probably someone's mistake. 13 Then 43:13
take your brother, and go back to the man. 14 May God Almighty* give you mercy as you Gen 43:3
go before the man, so that he will release Simeon and let Benjamin return. But if I must 43:14
lose my children, so be it." Gen 42:24 Ps 106:46
15 So the men packed Jacob's gifts and double the money and headed off with Ben-
jamin. They finally arrived in Egypt and presented themselves to Joseph. 16 When Jo- 43:16
seph saw Benjamin with them, he said to the manager of his household, "These men Gen 44:1
will eat with me this noon. Take them inside the palace. Then go slaughter an animal,
and prepare a big feast." 17 So the man did as Joseph told him and took them into Jo-
seph's palace.
18 The brothers were terrified when they saw that they were being taken into Joseph's 43:18 Gen 42:28, 35
house. "It's because of the money someone put in our sacks last time we were here," they
said. "He plans to pretend that we stole it. Then he will seize us, make us slaves, and take
our donkeys."

A FEAST AT JOSEPH'S PALACE

19 The brothers approached the manager of Joseph's household and spoke to him
at the entrance to the palace. 20 "Sir," they said, "we came to Egypt once before to
buy food. 21 But as we were returning home, we stopped for the night and opened 43:21
our sacks. Then we discovered that each man's money—the exact amount paid— Gen 42:25, 35; 43:12
was in the top of his sack! Here it is; we have brought it back with us. 22 We also
have additional money to buy more food. We have no idea who put our money in 43:22
our sacks." Gen 42:28
23 "Relax. Don't be afraid," the household manager told them. "Your God, the God of 43:23 Gen 42:24
your father, must have put this treasure into your sacks. I know I received your payment."
Then he released Simeon and brought him out to them.
24 The manager then led the men into Joseph's palace. He gave them water to wash 43:24
their feet and provided food for their donkeys. 25 They were told they would be eating Gen 18:4; 24:32
there, so they prepared their gifts for Joseph's arrival at noon. 43:27
26 When Joseph came home, they gave him the gifts they had brought him, then bowed Gen 43:7; 45:3
low to the ground before him. 27 After greeting them, he asked, "How is your father, the old 43:28
man you spoke about? Is he still alive?" Exod 18:7
28 "Yes," they replied. "Our father, your servant, is alive and well." And they bowed low 43:29
again. Num 6:25 Ps 67:1
29 Then Joseph looked at his brother Benjamin, the son of his own mother. "Is this your 43:30
youngest brother, the one you told me about?" Joseph asked. "May God be gracious to Gen 42:24; 45:2, 14-
you, my son." 30 Then Joseph hurried from the room because he was overcome with emo- 15; 46:29
tion for his brother. He went into his private room, where he broke down and wept. 31 After 43:31
washing his face, he came back out, keeping himself under control. Then he ordered, Gen 45:1
"Bring out the food!" 43:32 Gen 46:34
32 The waiters served Joseph at his own table, and his brothers were served at a sep- Exod 8:26

43:14 Hebrew *El-Shaddai.*

▸ **GOD**

43:29 God is gracious. "May God be gracious to you" is a precursor to the Aaronic benediction (see Numbers 6:22-27). What is God's grace? The Hebrew word translated *gracious* is more broadly used to define God's faithfulness and forbearance needed to make the covenant relationship continue, despite incidents of backsliding. Joseph set a powerful example of mercy and forgiveness. We need to see that we are just as undeserving of grace as Joseph's brothers were. God's grace becomes practical for you when you acknowledge your total unworthiness of His love and your total dependence on God for all things. (***See God***> *God's Attributes*> *Faithful,* TopicGuide page A16.)

43:33 arate table. The Egyptians who ate with Joseph sat at their own table, because Egyptians
Gen 44:12 despise Hebrews and refuse to eat with them. 33Joseph told each of his brothers where
to sit, and to their amazement, he seated them according to age, from oldest to youn-
gest. 34And Joseph filled their plates with food from his own table, giving Benjamin
five times as much as he gave the others. So they feasted and drank freely with him.

JOSEPH'S SILVER CUP

44:1 **44** When his brothers were ready to leave, Joseph gave these instructions to his pal-
Gen 42:25; 43:16 ace manager: "Fill each of their sacks with as much grain as they can carry, and
put each man's money back into his sack. 2Then put my personal silver cup at the top of
the youngest brother's sack, along with the money for his grain." So the manager did as
Joseph instructed him.
3The brothers were up at dawn and were sent on their journey with their loaded don-
44:4 keys. 4But when they had gone only a short distance and were barely out of the city, Jo-
Prov 17:13 seph said to his palace manager, "Chase after them and stop them. When you catch up
44:5 with them, ask them, 'Why have you repaid my kindness with such evil? 5Why have you
Gen 30:27 stolen my master's silver cup,* which he uses to predict the future? What a wicked thing
Deut 18:10-14 you have done!'"
6When the palace manager caught up with the men, he spoke to them as he had been
instructed.
7"What are you talking about?" the brothers responded. "We are your servants and
44:8 Gen 43:21 would never do such a thing! 8Didn't we return the money we found in our sacks? We
44:9 brought it back all the way from the land of Canaan. Why would we steal silver or gold
Gen 31:32 from your master's house? 9If you find his cup with any one of us, let that man die. And all
the rest of us, my lord, will be your slaves."
10"That's fair," the man replied. "But only the one who stole the cup will be my slave.
The rest of you may go free."
11They all quickly took their sacks from the backs of their donkeys and opened them.
44:12 Gen 44:2 12The palace manager searched the brothers' sacks, from the oldest to the youngest. And
44:13 the cup was found in Benjamin's sack! 13When the brothers saw this, they tore their cloth-
Gen 37:29, 34 ing in despair. Then they loaded their donkeys again and returned to the city.
14Joseph was still in his palace when Judah and his brothers arrived, and they fell to the
44:15 ground before him. 15"What have you done?" Joseph demanded. "Don't you know that a
Gen 44:5 man like me can predict the future?"
44:16 16Judah answered, "Oh, my lord, what can we say to you? How can we explain this?
Gen 42:11; 43:18 How can we prove our innocence? God is punishing us for our sins. My lord, we have all
returned to be your slaves—all of us, not just our brother who had your cup in his sack."
17"No," Joseph said. "I would never do such a thing! Only the man who stole the cup will
be my slave. The rest of you may go back to your father in peace."

JUDAH SPEAKS FOR HIS BROTHERS

44:18 18Then Judah stepped forward and said, "Please, my lord, let your servant say just one
Gen 37:7-8; 41:40-44 word to you. Please, do not be angry with me, even though you are as powerful as Pha-
raoh himself.

44:5 As in Greek version; Hebrew lacks this phrase.

44:13 The action of the brothers in tearing their clothes seems dramatic in a modern world that keeps emotions at bay. In the ancient world, however, grief and trouble had very specific responses. Tearing one's clothes, wearing rough sackcloth (burlap), and putting ashes on one's head were all signs of grief or despair. In revealing their distress, these men also made a statement about their innocence. Given the brothers' promise to their father that they would bring Benjamin home from Egypt, they had much at stake. Finding the cup in Benjamin's bag was the worst possible scenario for them.

19“My lord, previously you asked us, your servants, ‘Do you have a father or a brother?’
20And we responded, ‘Yes, my lord, we have a father who is an old man, and his youngest
son is a child of his old age. His full brother is dead, and he alone is left of his mother’s chil-
dren, and his father loves him very much.’

21“And you said to us, ‘Bring him here so I can see him with my own eyes.’ 22But we
said to you, ‘My lord, the boy cannot leave his father, for his father would die.’ 23But you
told us, ‘Unless your youngest brother comes with you, you will never see my face
again.’

24“So we returned to your servant, our father, and told him what you had said. 25Later,
when he said, ‘Go back again and buy us more food,’ 26we replied, ‘We can’t go unless
you let our youngest brother go with us. We’ll never get to see the man’s face unless our
youngest brother is with us.’

27“Then my father said to us, ‘As you know, my wife had two sons, 28and one of them
went away and never returned. Doubtless he was torn to pieces by some wild animal. I
have never seen him since. 29Now if you take his brother away from me, and any harm
comes to him, you will send this grieving, white-haired man to his grave.*’

30“And now, my lord, I cannot go back to my father without the boy. Our father’s life is
bound up in the boy’s life. 31If he sees that the boy is not with us, our father will die. We,
your servants, will indeed be responsible for sending that grieving, white-haired man to
his grave. 32My lord, I guaranteed to my father that I would take care of the boy. I told him,
‘If I don’t bring him back to you, I will bear the blame forever.’

33“So please, my lord, let me stay here as a slave instead of the boy, and let the boy re-
turn with his brothers. 34For how can I return to my father if the boy is not with me? I
couldn’t bear to see the anguish this would cause my father!”

JOSEPH REVEALS HIS IDENTITY

45 Joseph could stand it no longer. There were many people in the room, and he
said to his attendants, “Out, all of you!” So he was alone with his brothers when
he told them who he was. 2Then he broke down and wept. He wept so loudly the Egyp-
tians could hear him, and word of it quickly carried to Pharaoh’s palace.

3“I am Joseph!” he said to his brothers. “Is my father still alive?” But his brothers were
speechless! They were stunned to realize that Joseph was standing there in front of
them. 4“Please, come closer,” he said to them. So they came closer. And he said again,
“I am Joseph, your brother, whom you sold into slavery in Egypt. 5But don’t be upset,
and don’t be angry with yourselves for selling me to this place. It was God who sent me
here ahead of you to preserve your lives. 6This famine that has ravaged the land for
two years will last five more years, and there will be neither plowing nor harvesting.
7God has sent me ahead of you to keep you and your families alive and to preserve
many survivors.* 8So it was God who sent me here, not you! And He is the One who

44:19 Gen 42:11; 43:7
44:21 Gen 42:11, 15
44:23 Gen 43:3
44:24 Gen 42:29-34
44:25 Gen 42:2
44:26 Gen 43:5
44:27 Gen 46:19
44:28 Gen 37:33
44:29 Gen 42:38
44:30 1 Sam 18:1
44:32 Gen 43:9
45:1 Gen 43:31
45:3 Gen 43:7
45:4 Gen 37:28
45:5 Gen 50:20
45:6 Gen 41:30
45:8 Gen 41:41 Judg 17:10

44:29 Hebrew *to Sheol;* also in 44:31. 45:7 Or *and to save you with an extraordinary rescue.* The meaning of the Hebrew is uncertain.

44:33 Judah was the brother who suggested selling Joseph into slavery, seeing more profit in that than killing him (Genesis 36:26-27). He was quite callous about how Joseph’s disappearance would affect his father. But Judah had seen the sorrow his idea had caused Jacob, and he knew Jacob would be even more devastated to lose Benjamin. He honorably chose to make his father’s interests a priority by offering himself as a substitute for Benjamin. Here, at last, was solid proof of the change of heart Joseph was looking for.

▸ PURPOSE

45:7 God’s saving acts. Joseph told his brothers that God sent him to Egypt to “keep you and your families alive.” God providentially used the brothers’ evil intent against Joseph as a means to bless him, and also to preserve his brothers and their families during a severe famine. Let the story of Joseph remind you that though your circumstances may appear to be spiraling out of control, God is able not only to rescue you, but also to use you as a blessing to others. Rejoice that God is always in control! (***See Purpose*** > *God’s Deeds* > *Special acts* > *Saving acts/ deliverance,* TopicGuide page A52.)

made me an adviser* to Pharaoh—the manager of his entire palace and the governor of
all Egypt.
45:9 9“Now hurry back to my father and tell him, ‘This is what your son Joseph says: God has
Acts 7:14 made me master over all the land of Egypt. So come down to me immediately! 10You can
45:10 Gen 46:28, 34 live in the region of Goshen, where you can be near me with all your children and grand-
45:11 children, your flocks and herds, and everything you own. 11I will take care of you there, for
Gen 47:12 there are still five years of famine ahead of us. Otherwise you, your household, and all
your animals will starve.’ ”
12Then Joseph added, “Look! You can see for yourselves, and so can my brother Benja-
45:13 min, that I really am Joseph! 13Go tell my father of my honored position here in Egypt. De-
Acts 7:14 scribe for him everything you have seen, and then bring my father here quickly.”
45:14 14Weeping with joy, he embraced Benjamin, and Benjamin did the same. 15Then Joseph
Gen 45:2 kissed each of his brothers and wept over them, and after that they began talking freely
with him.

PHARAOH INVITES JACOB TO EGYPT

45:16 Acts 7:13 16The news soon reached Pharaoh’s palace: “Joseph’s brothers have arrived!” Pharaoh
and his officials were all delighted to hear this.
45:17 17Pharaoh said to Joseph, “Tell your brothers, ‘This is what you must do: Load your
Gen 42:26 pack animals, and hurry back to the land of Canaan. 18Then get your father and all of your
45:18 families, and return here to me. I will give you the very best land in Egypt, and you will eat
Gen 27:28 from the best that the land produces.’ ”
45:19 Gen 45:27; 46:5 19Then Pharaoh said to Joseph, “Tell your brothers, ‘Take wagons from the land of
45:20 Egypt to carry your little children and your wives, and bring your father here. 20Don’t
Gen 46:6 worry about your personal belongings, for the best of all the land of Egypt is yours.’ ”
21So the sons of Jacob* did as they were told. Joseph provided them with wagons, as
45:22 Gen 24:53 Pharaoh had commanded, and he gave them supplies for the journey. 22And he gave
2 Kgs 5:5 each of them new clothes—but to Benjamin he gave five changes of clothes and
45:23 300 pieces* of silver. 23He also sent his father ten male donkeys loaded with the finest
Gen 43:11 products of Egypt, and ten female donkeys loaded with grain and bread and other sup-
plies he would need on his journey.
45:24 Gen 42:21-22 24So Joseph sent his brothers off, and as they left, he called after them, “Don’t quarrel
about all this along the way!” 25And they left Egypt and returned to their father, Jacob, in
45:26 the land of Canaan.
Gen 37:31-35 26“Joseph is still alive!” they told him. “And he is governor of all the land of Egypt!” Jacob

45:8 Hebrew *a father.* 45:21 Hebrew *Israel;* also in 45:28. See note on 35:21. 45:22 Hebrew *300 shekels,* about 7.5 pounds or 3.4 kilograms in weight.

45:10 For his family, Joseph picked the land of Goshen, an area of about 900 square miles in the northeastern part of the Nile Delta. It was excellent land for raising livestock, which had been the family business for generations. Some considered this land to be the richest in Egypt.

45:16-20 Joseph obviously enjoyed great favor with Pharaoh. After all, had it not been for Joseph’s interpretation of Pharaoh’s dream years earlier, Egypt would have been suffering through the famine as much as the surrounding nations. Pharaoh honored Joseph by allowing his family to have the best land in Egypt. In this way, Pharaoh saved the lives of Joseph’s family, much as Joseph had saved the lives of the Egyptians by instituting a plan that would carry the nation through the seven-year famine (Genesis 41:25-36).

45:25 The roads between Egypt and Israel were well-used. Abraham traveled to Egypt in a time of famine with his wife, Sarah (Genesis 12:10-11). Joseph arrived there with Ishmaelite traders (Genesis 37:28). Joseph’s brothers traveled back and forth several times, before their father Jacob gathered together his whole household with his belongings and flocks and traveled to Egypt to live. They probably followed a route roughly parallel to the Mediterranean Sea that long had been used by caravans moving between North Africa through Canaan and on to points north and east, or another called the Way to Shur, which was further inland.

45:26 After Joseph’s brothers sold him into slavery, they soaked Joseph’s robe in goat’s blood and took it to their father. They then let Jacob come to his own conclusion that a wild animal must have killed Joseph. There is no record of Joseph or his brothers telling Jacob what really happened. However, after Jacob died, the brothers told Joseph that Jacob had instructed them to ask for his forgiveness (Genesis 50:14-18). Whether that was true or whether they were simply trying to save their own skins, Joseph chose to trust God’s providence rather than punish his brothers’ for their hate-driven actions.

was stunned at the news—he couldn't believe it. 27But when they repeated to Jacob every-
thing Joseph had told them, and when he saw the wagons Joseph had sent to carry him,
their father's spirits revived.
28Then Jacob exclaimed, "It must be true! My son Joseph is alive! I must go and see him
before I die."

JACOB'S JOURNEY TO EGYPT

46 So Jacob* set out for Egypt with all his possessions. And when he came to Beer-
sheba, he offered sacrifices to the God of his father, Isaac. 2During the night God
spoke to him in a vision. "Jacob! Jacob!" he called.
"Here I am," Jacob replied.
3"I am God,* the God of your father," the voice said. "Do not be afraid to go down to
Egypt, for there I will make your family into a great nation. 4I will go with you down
to Egypt, and I will bring you back again. But you will die in Egypt with Joseph attending to
you."
5So Jacob left Beersheba, and his sons took him to Egypt. They carried him and their lit-
tle ones and their wives in the wagons Pharaoh had provided for them. 6They also took all
their livestock and all the personal belongings they had acquired in the land of Canaan. So
Jacob and his entire family went to Egypt—7sons and grandsons, daughters and grand-
daughters—all his descendants.
8These are the names of the descendants of Israel—the sons of Jacob—who went to
Egypt:
Reuben was Jacob's oldest son. 9The sons of Reuben were Hanoch, Pallu, Hezron, and
Carmi.
10The sons of Simeon were Jemuel, Jamin, Ohad, Jakin, Zohar, and Shaul. (Shaul's
mother was a Canaanite woman.)

45:27 Gen 45:19
45:28 Gen 44:28
46:1 Gen 21:14; 26:24; 28:13; 31:42
46:2 Gen 22:11; 31:11 Num 12:6
46:3 Gen 17:1; 26:2
46:4 Gen 28:13 Exod 3:8
46:5 Gen 45:19
46:6 Num 20:15 Deut 26:5 Acts 7:15
46:8 Gen 29:32; 35:26
46:9 1 Chr 5:3
46:10 1 Chr 4:24

46:1 Hebrew *Israel;* also in 46:29, 30. See note on 35:21. **46:3** Hebrew *I am El.*

JACOB MOVES TO EGYPT
After hearing the joyful news that Joseph was alive, Jacob packed up and moved his family to Egypt. Stopping first in Beersheba, Jacob offered sacrifices and received assurance from God that Egypt was where he should go. Jacob and his family settled in the region of Goshen, in the northeastern part of Egypt.

46:1 Beersheba was the southernmost town of the territory God had promised to Abraham, Isaac, Jacob, and their descendants. In fact, the phrase used to describe the whole of Israel, from north to south, was "from Dan to Beersheba." Beersheba had longstanding significance for Jacob's family. Abraham, Jacob's grandfather, lived there for some time (Genesis 21–22). It was there that Jacob's Uncle Ishmael would have died had God not intervened (Genesis 21:14-16). It was there that Abraham made a treaty with Abimelech and established a place of worship (Genesis 21:22-34). It was also in Beersheba that Isaac, Jacob's father, built an altar (Genesis 26:23-25) on his way to live in Canaan. Here Jacob was traveling through Beersheba on his way to Egypt to be reunited with his son Joseph.

46:3-4 It would have been important to Jacob to know that this journey to Egypt was part of God's plan. He had been raised with the knowledge that God made a promise to his grandfather, Abraham, that his descendants would become a great nation. That promise then fell on Isaac, Abraham's son and Jacob's father. Jacob knew his line was the one through which God would uphold his promise to Abraham. He probably was concerned that if he traveled to Egypt, his people might not return to Canaan. God's gracious assurances were enough, so Jacob traveled on to Egypt with his family. About 400 years later, more than 2 million of his descendants would return to resettle the Promised Land.

11 The sons of Levi were Gershon, Kohath, and Merari.
12 The sons of Judah were Er, Onan, Shelah, Perez, and Zerah (though Er and Onan had
died in the land of Canaan). The sons of Perez were Hezron and Hamul.
13 The sons of Issachar were Tola, Puah,* Jashub,* and Shimron.
14 The sons of Zebulun were Sered, Elon, and Jahleel.
15 These were the sons of Leah and Jacob who were born in Paddan-aram, in addition to
their daughter, Dinah. The number of Jacob's descendants (male and female) through
Leah was thirty-three.

16 The sons of Gad were Zephon,* Haggi, Shuni, Ezbon, Eri, Arodi, and Areli.
17 The sons of Asher were Imnah, Ishvah, Ishvi, and Beriah. Their sister was Serah. Beri-
ah's sons were Heber and Malkiel.
18 These were the sons of Zilpah, the servant given to Leah by her father, Laban. The num-
ber of Jacob's descendants through Zilpah was sixteen.
19 The sons of Jacob's wife Rachel were Joseph and Benjamin.
20 Joseph's sons, born in the land of Egypt, were Manasseh and Ephraim. Their mother
was Asenath, daughter of Potiphera, the priest of On.*
21 Benjamin's sons were Bela, Beker, Ashbel, Gera, Naaman, Ehi, Rosh, Muppim,
Huppim, and Ard.
22 These were the sons of Rachel and Jacob. The number of Jacob's descendants through
Rachel was fourteen.

23 The son of Dan was Hushim.
24 The sons of Naphtali were Jahzeel, Guni, Jezer, and Shillem.
25 These were the sons of Bilhah, the servant given to Rachel by her father, Laban. The
number of Jacob's descendants through Bilhah was seven.

26 The total number of Jacob's direct descendants who went with him to Egypt, not count-
ing his sons' wives, was sixty-six. 27 In addition, Joseph had two sons* who were born in
Egypt. So altogether, there were seventy* members of Jacob's family in the land of Egypt.

46:11 1 Chr 6:16
46:12 1 Chr 2:3
46:13 1 Chr 7:1
46:14 Gen 30:20
46:15 Gen 30:21
46:16 Gen 30:11; Num 26:15
46:17 Gen 30:13
46:19 Gen 44:27
46:20 Gen 41:45, 50-52
46:21 Num 26:38-41; 1 Chr 7:6-12
46:22 Gen 35:24
46:23 Gen 30:6; Num 26:42
46:24 Gen 30:8
46:25 Gen 35:25
46:27 Exod 1:5; Deut 10:22; Acts 7:14

JACOB'S FAMILY ARRIVES IN GOSHEN

28 As they neared their destination, Jacob sent Judah ahead to meet Joseph and get di-
rections to the region of Goshen. And when they finally arrived there, 29 Joseph pre-
pared his chariot and traveled to Goshen to meet his father, Jacob. When Joseph
arrived, he embraced his father and wept, holding him for a long time. 30 Finally, Jacob
said to Joseph, "Now I am ready to die, since I have seen your face again and know you
are still alive."
31 And Joseph said to his brothers and to his father's entire family, "I will go to Pharaoh
and tell him, 'My brothers and my father's entire family have come to me from the land of
Canaan. 32 These men are shepherds, and they raise livestock. They have brought with
them their flocks and herds and everything they own.' "

46:28 Gen 43:3; 45:10
46:29 Gen 45:14-15
46:30 Gen 44:28
46:31 Gen 47:1
46:32 Gen 37:2; 47:3

46:13a As in Syriac version and Samaritan Pentateuch (see also 1 Chr 7:1); Hebrew reads *Puvah.* **46:13b** As in some Greek manuscripts and Samaritan Pentateuch (see also Num 26:24; 1 Chr 7:1); Hebrew reads *Iob.* **46:16** As in Greek version and Samaritan Pentateuch (see also Num 26:15); Hebrew reads *Ziphion.* **46:20** Greek version reads *of Heliopolis.* **46:27a** Greek version reads *nine sons,* probably including Joseph's grandsons through Ephraim and Manasseh (see 1 Chr 7:14-20). **46:27b** Greek version reads *seventy-five;* see note on Exod 1:5.

46:26 We can assume that the wives of Jacob's sons went with Jacob's family to Egypt, but since they were not blood relatives of Jacob, they were not included in the count. In other places in Scripture, numbers are given only for the men in a group, even though women and children were present as well. Astonishingly, this family entered Egypt with fewer than 100 travelers and later returned as a nation of millions, just as God had promised (Genesis 13:16).

33 Then he said, "When Pharaoh calls for you and asks you about your occupation, 46:33
34 you must tell him, 'We, your servants, have raised livestock all our lives, as our ances- Gen 47:3
tors have always done.' When you tell him this, he will let you live here in the region of 46:34
Goshen, for the Egyptians despise shepherds." Gen 13:7; 26:20; 37:2

JACOB BLESSES PHARAOH

47 Then Joseph went to see Pharaoh and told him, "My father and my brothers have 47:1
arrived from the land of Canaan. They have come with all their flocks and herds Gen 46:31
and possessions, and they are now in the region of Goshen."
2 Joseph took five of his brothers with him and presented them to Pharaoh. 3 And Pha- 47:2
raoh asked the brothers, "What is your occupation?" Gen 43:15
They replied, "We, your servants, are shepherds, just like our ancestors. 4 We have 47:3 Gen 46:32-33
come to live here in Egypt for a while, for there is no pasture for our flocks in Canaan. The 47:4
famine is very severe there. So please, we request permission to live in the region of Gen 46:34
Goshen."
5 Then Pharaoh said to Joseph, "Now that your father and brothers have joined you 47:6
here, 6 choose any place in the entire land of Egypt for them to live. Give them the best Gen 45:18
land of Egypt. Let them live in the region of Goshen. And if any of them have special skills, Exod 18:21, 25
put them in charge of my livestock, too."
7 Then Joseph brought in his father, Jacob, and presented him to Pharaoh. And Jacob 47:7
blessed Pharaoh. Gen 47:10
8 "How old are you?" Pharaoh asked him. 2 Sam 14:22 1 Kgs 8:66
9 Jacob replied, "I have traveled this earth for 130 hard years. But my life has been short
compared to the lives of my ancestors." 10 Then Jacob blessed Pharaoh again before leav- 47:10
ing his court. Gen 14:19
11 So Joseph assigned the best land of Egypt—the region of Rameses—to his father and 47:11 Exod 1:11; 12:37
his brothers, and he settled them there, just as Pharaoh had commanded. 12 And Joseph
provided food for his father and his brothers in amounts appropriate to the number of 47:12 Gen 45:11; 47:24
their dependents, including the smallest children.

JOSEPH'S LEADERSHIP IN THE FAMINE

13 Meanwhile, the famine became so severe that all the food was used up, and people 47:13
were starving throughout the lands of Egypt and Canaan. 14 By selling grain to the people, Gen 41:30 Acts 7:11
Joseph eventually collected all the money in Egypt and Canaan, and he put the money in
Pharaoh's treasury. 15 When the people of Egypt and Canaan ran out of money, all the 47:14 Gen 41:56
Egyptians came to Joseph. "Our money is gone!" they cried. "But please give us food, or
we will die before your very eyes!" 47:15 Gen 47:18-19
16 Joseph replied, "Since your money is gone, bring me your livestock. I will give you
food in exchange for your livestock." 17 So they brought their livestock to Joseph in ex- 47:17 Exod 14:9
change for food. In exchange for their horses, flocks of sheep and goats, herds of cattle,
and donkeys, Joseph provided them with food for another year.

46:34 The Egyptians did not have a high regard for Hebrew people or for shepherds. Joseph's family was both. However, God providentially used this attitude of the Egyptians. Joseph was able to settle his family on some of the best land in Egypt because it was far enough away from the Egyptian population centers that the Egyptians did not have to mingle with the Hebrews. Also, the separation served as a safeguard for the people of Israel, keeping them away from the Egyptians' pagan practices.

47:7, 10 Today, "blessing" someone is usually taken to mean wishing him well or doing something nice for him. In Jacob's day, it meant conferring God's favor. Jacob walked in as a foreigner, yet he blessed the powerful king of Egypt. Jacob was acting by faith. In the historical perspective, Jacob himself was the head of a great nation that would be saved by this very move to Egypt. The greatest power that Jacob had ever known was the power of God to provide and direct. To speak that power over Pharaoh was the greatest gift Jacob could offer. It was the only gift that was appropriate in light of the grand kindnesses that Pharaoh was giving Joseph's family.

18But that year ended, and the next year they came again and said, "We cannot hide
the truth from you, my lord. Our money is gone, and all our livestock and cattle are yours.
47:19 We have nothing left to give but our bodies and our land. 19Why should we die before
Neh 5:2 Job 2:4 your very eyes? Buy us and our land in exchange for food; we offer our land and our-
Lam 1:11 selves as slaves for Pharaoh. Just give us grain so we may live and not die, and so the
land does not become empty and desolate."
20So Joseph bought all the land of Egypt for Pharaoh. All the Egyptians sold him their
fields because the famine was so severe, and soon all the land belonged to Pharaoh. 21As
47:22 for the people, he made them all slaves,* from one end of Egypt to the other. 22The only
Deut 14:28-29 land he did not buy was the land belonging to the priests. They received an allotment of
food directly from Pharaoh, so they didn't need to sell their land.
23Then Joseph said to the people, "Look, today I have bought you and your land for
47:24 Pharaoh. I will provide you with seed so you can plant the fields. 24Then when you har-
Gen 41:34 vest it, one-fifth of your crop will belong to Pharaoh. You may keep the remaining four-
fifths as seed for your fields and as food for you, your households, and your little ones."
25"You have saved our lives!" they exclaimed. "May it please you, my lord, to let us be
47:25 Gen 32:5 Pharaoh's servants." 26Joseph then issued a decree still in effect in the land of Egypt, that
47:26 Pharaoh should receive one-fifth of all the crops grown on his land. Only the land belong-
Gen 47:22 ing to the priests was not given to Pharaoh.
27Meanwhile, the people of Israel settled in the region of Goshen in Egypt. There they
47:27 acquired property, and they were fruitful, and their population grew rapidly. 28Jacob lived
Exod 1:7 for seventeen years after his arrival in Egypt, so he lived 147 years in all.
47:29 Gen 24:2; 50:24-25 29As the time of his death drew near, Jacob* called for his son Joseph and said to him,
47:30 "Please do me this favor. Put your hand under my thigh and swear that you will treat me
Gen 23:17-20; 25:9; with unfailing love by honoring this last request: Do not bury me in Egypt. 30When I die,
49:29 please take my body out of Egypt and bury me with my ancestors."
Acts 7:15-16 So Joseph promised, "I will do as you ask."

47:21 As in Greek version and Samaritan Pentateuch; Hebrew reads *he moved them all into the towns.* **47:29** Hebrew *Israel;* also in 47:31b. See note on 35:21.

47:22 The priests mentioned here were Egyptians. In Egypt, as in early Israel, government and religion were closely connected. In fact, Egyptians saw their Pharaoh as the embodiment of the gods. Pharaoh provided for the priests in a way that he did not for his people. Under God's direction, Moses would later structure Israel similarly. The Israelite priests did not own land, but they got their food from the offerings the people made at the Tabernacle and later the Temple. Guidelines for Israel's priests can be found in the book of Leviticus.

47:26 The book of Genesis was not written when it happened. Instead, it was written later, in the time of Moses. That likely explains why Moses wrote that a certain law "is still the law." At the time Moses recorded these events that law was already in place. Most scholars assume that Moses wrote the book of Genesis around 1400 BC. The events he described here may have happened as early as 1800 BC. Moses was well-prepared to write down this history because he was raised by both Hebrews and Egyptians. He not only had God's supernatural revelation but had been privy to history as remembered and recorded by both nations, and he was guided by the Holy Spirit in using such sources accurately.

47:27 As long as Joseph was a remembered and honored part of Egyptian history, the Israelites were treated well and allowed to control their own lives. It was not until a Pharaoh arose who did not honor Joseph's memory that Egypt became a place of oppression for the Israelites (Exodus 1:8-10).

47:29 Jacob was asking for an oath from Joseph. In some versions of the Bible, the phrase "swear [most solemnly]" is translated as a request by Jacob for Joseph to put his hand under Jacob's thigh, near his genitals. This was a gesture of generational commitment in the ancient world. First, it meant that the oath spanned generations. Second, it meant that if the oath were broken, the children of these men would take vengeance on the covenant-breakers. Thus, a person who took such an oath was betting his family's lives on his commitment to keep his word. Also note that Abraham used this form of oath when he asked his servant to find a wife for Isaac (Genesis 24:1-9), underlining the seriousness of his request.

47:29-30 Jacob's whole life had been based on God's promise to Abraham, Jacob's grandfather, that Canaan would be his family's homeland. When Abraham's wife, Sarah, died, Abraham bought a field and cave in Canaan to use as a family tomb. Purchasing this plot of land was Abraham's way of claiming God's promise, for people wanted to be buried in their native land. Even though God had told Jacob that he would die in Egypt (Genesis 46:3-4), Jacob wanted to be buried in the family tomb. Also buried there were Abraham, Isaac, Rebekah, and Leah.

[31]"Swear that you will do it," Jacob insisted. So Joseph gave his oath, and Jacob bowed 47:31
humbly at the head of his bed.* Heb 11:21

JACOB BLESSES MANASSEH AND EPHRAIM

48 One day not long after this, word came to Joseph, "Your father is failing rapidly." 48:1
So Joseph went to visit his father, and he took with him his two sons, Manasseh Gen 41:51-52 Heb 11:21
and Ephraim.
[2]When Joseph arrived, Jacob was told, "Your son Joseph has come to see you." So Ja-
cob* gathered his strength and sat up in his bed.
[3]Jacob said to Joseph, "God Almighty* appeared to me at Luz in the land of Canaan and 48:3
blessed me. [4]He said to me, 'I will make you fruitful, and I will multiply your descendants. I Gen 28:13-19;
will make you a multitude of nations. And I will give this land of Canaan to your descen- 35:9-12
dants* after you as an everlasting possession.'
[5]"Now I am claiming as my own sons these two boys of yours, Ephraim and Manas- 48:5
seh, who were born here in the land of Egypt before I arrived. They will be my sons, Gen 29:32-33
just as Reuben and Simeon are. [6]But any children born to you in the future will be
your own, and they will inherit land within the territories of their brothers Ephraim
and Manasseh.
[7]"Long ago, as I was returning from Paddan-aram, Rachel died in the land of Canaan. 48:7
We were still on the way, some distance from Ephrath (that is, Bethlehem). So with great Gen 35:19
sorrow I buried her there beside the road to Ephrath."
[8]Then Jacob looked over at the two boys. "Are these your sons?" he asked.
[9]"Yes," Joseph told him, "these are the sons God has given me here in Egypt." 48:9
And Jacob said, "Bring them closer to me, so I can bless them." Gen 33:5
[10]Jacob was half blind because of his age and could hardly see. So Joseph brought the 48:10
boys close to him, and Jacob kissed and embraced them. [11]Then Jacob said to Joseph, "I Gen 27:1
never thought I would see your face again, but now God has let me see your children, too!" 48:11
[12]Joseph moved the boys, who were at their grandfather's knees, and he bowed with his Gen 44:28
face to the ground. [13]Then he positioned the boys in front of Jacob. With his right hand he di- 48:12 Gen 33:3; 42:6
rected Ephraim toward Jacob's left hand, and with his left hand he put Manasseh at Jacob's 48:14
right hand. [14]But Jacob crossed his arms as he reached out to lay his hands on the boys' Gen 41:51-52
heads. He put his right hand on the head of Ephraim, though he was the younger boy, and his

47:31 Greek version reads *and Israel bowed in worship as he leaned on his staff.* Compare Heb 11:21. 48:2 Hebrew *Israel;* also in 48:8, 10, 11, 13, 14, 21. See note on 35:21. 48:3 Hebrew *El-Shaddai.* 48:4 Hebrew *seed;* also in 48:19.

48:5-6 When Jacob adopted Manasseh and Ephraim, he was ensuring that each of his grandsons would receive the same inheritance as Joseph's other brothers. In this way, Joseph received the double portion of the inheritance that was given to the son who received the birthright. Typically, the firstborn son would receive this honor, but Jacob's eldest son, Reuben, had disappointed his father. Also, Joseph was the firstborn son of Jacob's most beloved wife, Rachel. Jacob would have been particularly sensitive to the power of the birthright, as well as the paternal blessing, because he had gone to great lengths as a young man to receive these from his father, Isaac (Genesis 25–27).

48:6 Jacob's adoption of Joseph's sons ensured that the Promised Land would be divided among 12 tribes. Jacob had 12 sons. One of them, Levi, would become the ancestor of the tribe set apart to help God's people worship Him. Those descending from Aaron served as priests, while the other Levites served as Temple assistants. Levites were not given an inheritance of land because their focus was to be on the spiritual life of the nation. Their food came from the offerings of other tribes. By Jacob's adoption, Manasseh and Ephraim were made tribal patriarchs, taking the places of Levi and Joseph, and restoring the number of tribes inheriting land to 12.

48:10-14 The birthright and paternal blessing typically went to the firstborn son. Since the right hand was considered the favored hand, Joseph positioned his sons so that Jacob's right hand would be on his older son. Against Joseph's wishes, however, Jacob switched hands so that Ephraim, the younger son, received the greater blessing. This paralleled Jacob's own experience. He had been born the younger twin to Esau. Jacob went through a great amount of effort to be sure that he, rather than his older brother, received the birthright and his father's blessing (Genesis 25; 27). He could have saved himself the trouble, however, for it had been God's plan from the beginning to bless Jacob (Genesis 25:23). In this case, God was also leading Jacob to prophetically bless the younger boy over the older.

48:15 Gen 17:1; 49:24 left hand on the head of Manasseh, though he was the firstborn. 15 Then he blessed Joseph
and said,

"May the God before whom my grandfather Abraham
 and my father, Isaac, walked—
the God who has been my shepherd
 all my life, to this very day,
48:16 Gen 22:11; 28:13-15; 31:11 *Heb 11:21 16 the Angel who has redeemed me from all harm—
 may He bless these boys.
May they preserve my name
 and the names of Abraham and Isaac.
And may their descendants multiply greatly
 throughout the earth."

17 But Joseph was upset when he saw that his father placed his right hand on Ephraim's
head. So Joseph lifted it to move it from Ephraim's head to Manasseh's head. 18 "No, my fa-
ther," he said. "This one is the firstborn. Put your right hand on his head."
19 But his father refused. "I know, my son; I know," he replied. "Manasseh will also become a
48:19 Gen 28:14; 46:3 great people, but his younger brother will become even greater. And his descendants will be-
come a multitude of nations."
48:20 Ruth 4:11 20 So Jacob blessed the boys that day with this blessing: "The people of Israel will use
your names when they give a blessing. They will say, 'May God make you as prosperous
as Ephraim and Manasseh.' " In this way, Jacob put Ephraim ahead of Manasseh.
48:21 Gen 28:15; 46:4; 50:24 21 Then Jacob said to Joseph, "Look, I am about to die, but God will be with you and will
take you back to Canaan, the land of your ancestors. 22 And beyond what I have given
48:22 Josh 24:32 John 4:5 your brothers, I am giving you an extra portion of the land* that I took from the Amorites
with my sword and bow."

JACOB'S LAST WORDS TO HIS SONS

49:1 Num 24:14 **49** Then Jacob called together all his sons and said, "Gather around me, and I will
tell you what will happen to each of you in the days to come.

2 "Come and listen, you sons of Jacob;
 listen to Israel, your father.

49:3 Num 26:5 Deut 21:17 Pss 78:51; 105:36 3 "Reuben, you are my firstborn, my strength,
 the child of my vigorous youth.
 You are first in rank and first in power.

48:22 Or *an extra ridge of land.* The meaning of the Hebrew is uncertain.

▶ **GOD**

48:15 God's names: Shepherd. Jacob said that God had been his shepherd, which, after King David's time, became a royal metaphor underscoring God's protection and provision (see Psalm 23:1). Do you recognize God's special shepherding in your life? Just as a shepherd loves and protects his sheep, God loves you with an everlasting love and protects your soul from harm. He seeks you when you wander from His care and works to restore you to active fellowship with Him. God is indeed your heavenly Shepherd-King. (***See God****> God's Names> Father> Shepherd,* TopicGuide page A18.)

48:19-20 The descendants of both Ephraim and Manasseh received prime land when the Israelites resettled in Canaan. However, Ephraim's land was the most productive of the 12 tribal regions (Deuteronomy 33:14-17). Joshua, who led Israel in the resettlement, was from the tribe of Ephraim. For a time, the Israelite worship center was located at Shiloh, a city in Ephraim's territory.

49:3-4 Reuben had slept with his father's concubine (Genesis 35:22). Although a concubine didn't have full rights as a wife, she was connected specifically to one man, so Reuben's act was gravely disrespectful. Later, when Hebrew society was organized under the leadership of Moses, laws were written that prohibited Reuben's actions (Deuteronomy 22:30), making them punishable by death. Reuben's act cost him the birthright and blessing that should have been his as Jacob's firstborn son.

4 But you are as unruly as a flood,
and you will be first no longer.
For you went to bed with my wife;
you defiled my marriage couch.

49:4 Gen 35:22 Deut 27:20

5 "Simeon and Levi are two of a kind;
their weapons are instruments of violence.
6 May I never join in their meetings;
may I never be a party to their plans.
For in their anger they murdered men,
and they crippled oxen just for sport.
7 A curse on their anger, for it is fierce;
a curse on their wrath, for it is cruel.
I will scatter them among the descendants of Jacob;
I will disperse them throughout Israel.

49:5 Gen 29:33-34; 34:25-30
49:6 Gen 34:26
49:7 Josh 19:1, 9; 21:1-42

8 "Judah, your brothers will praise you.
You will grasp your enemies by the neck.
All your relatives will bow before you.
9 Judah, my son, is a young lion
that has finished eating its prey.
Like a lion he crouches and lies down;
like a lioness—who dares to rouse him?
10 The scepter will not depart from Judah,
nor the ruler's staff from his descendants,*
until the coming of the One to whom it belongs,*
the One whom all nations will honor.
11 He ties his foal to a grapevine,
the colt of his donkey to a choice vine.
He washes his clothes in wine,
his robes in the blood of grapes.
12 His eyes are darker than wine,
and his teeth are whiter than milk.

49:8 1 Chr 5:2 Heb 7:14
49:9 Num 24:9 Mic 5:8
49:10 Num 24:17 Pss 2:6-9; 60:7
49:11 Deut 8:7-8 2 Kgs 18:32

13 "Zebulun will settle by the seashore
and will be a harbor for ships;
his borders will extend to Sidon.

49:13 Deut 33:18-19

49:10a Hebrew *from between his feet.* **49:10b** Or *until tribute is brought to him and the peoples obey;* traditionally rendered *until Shiloh comes.*

49:5-7 Simeon and Levi were responsible for the deaths of all the men in a whole town (Genesis 34). A young Canaanite prince named Shechem had raped their sister, Dinah. In bloodthirsty vengeance, Simeon and Levi's families killed all the men of Shechem. This terrible crime explains why Joseph, not Simeon or Levi, his older brothers, was chosen by God as the covenant leader.

49:8-12 Judah, Jacob's fourth son, received the most significant blessing. He was given the promise that his family would always rule. King David, the great king of Israel, was of the tribe of Judah. Jesus was later born in the region of Judea, and he, too, was of the tribe of Judah. Since Jesus' reign will never end, Judah's reign lasts forever.

49:10 While this prophecy certainly came true in part during the reign of King David, it was fulfilled more completely through Jesus, the Messiah of Israel. Because this verse mentions a scepter and a ruler's staff, the people over time began to hope that God's deliverance would come in the form of a great warrior Savior who would restore their nation. Instead God sent a *servant* Savior who restored God's kingdom on earth through the faith of His followers.

49:13 The tribe of Zebulun eventually received land in northern Canaan, not far from the Mediterranean Sea, from which it drew great prosperity. The region of Zebulun contained the city of Jesus' boyhood, Nazareth, and His ministry brought "glory" to the people of that area (see Isaiah 9:1-2).

49:14 Judg 5:16 Ps 68:13

14 "Issachar is a sturdy donkey,
resting between two saddlepacks.*

49:15 Josh 19:17-23

15 When he sees how good the countryside is
and how pleasant the land,
he will bend his shoulder to the load
and submit himself to hard labor.

49:16 Deut 33:22 Judg 18:26-27

16 "Dan will govern his people,
like any other tribe in Israel.
17 Dan will be a snake beside the road,
a poisonous viper along the path
that bites the horse's hooves
so its rider is thrown off.
18 I trust in You for salvation, O LORD!

49:19 Deut 33:20

19 "Gad will be attacked by marauding bands,
but he will attack them when they retreat.

49:20 Deut 33:24-25

20 "Asher will dine on rich foods
and produce food fit for kings.

49:21 Deut 33:23

21 "Naphtali is a doe set free
that bears beautiful fawns.

49:22 Deut 33:13-17

22 "Joseph is the foal of a wild donkey,
the foal of a wild donkey at a spring—
one of the wild donkeys on the ridge.*

49:14 Or *sheepfolds,* or *hearths.* 49:22 Or *Joseph is a fruitful tree, / a fruitful tree beside a spring. / His branches reach over the wall.* The meaning of the Hebrew is uncertain.

49:14-15 The people of Issachar received a good territory west of the Jordan River and south of the Sea of Galilee. Jacob's prophecy about the tribe is difficult to interpret, but it may refer to the subjugation of the Israelites by the Canaanite king Jabin during the time of the judges. The people of Issachar joined with Deborah and Barak to defeat Jabin's army (see Judges 5:15).

49:16-17 The tribe of Dan settled along the Mediterranean Sea, where they came into frequent conflict with Canaanites. Though the tribe was small, its warriors were fierce (like a serpent). Samson was a Danite who almost single-handedly liberated the Israelites from Philistine oppression.

▶ PURPOSE

49:18 God's saving acts. "I trust in You for salvation!" Jacob exclaimed. The patriarch inserted this statement between a series of blessings, in anticipation of fierce antagonism against the tribes of Israel. Just because you have been granted the blessing of eternal life does not mean that you will never face earthly battles. Satan, the old sinful nature, and all conceivable worldly forces stand opposed to the follower of Christ who seeks to live in full surrender to the gospel. But Jesus says to "take heart, because I have overcome the world" (John 16:33). Trust in Jesus not only for eternal salvation but also for protection from every earthly trial and sorrow. (***See Purpose***> *God's Deeds*> *Special acts*> *Saving acts/deliverance,* TopicGuide page A52.)

49:19 The name *Gad* actually means "attack," so this prophecy was a play on words. Generations later, when the Israelites resettled the Promised Land, some of the tribes stayed on the east side of the Jordan River so that their flocks would have plenty of pastureland. Gad was one of those tribes, as well as Reuben and part of Manasseh. These tribes were particularly susceptible to attack from the east. They were border countries and had no natural defenses, such as rivers or mountains. The Assyrians eventually carried the Gadites away as captives, and the Ammonites took over their land.

49:20 Asher's tribe eventually settled along the northern border of Canaan, a land rich for farming. Unfortunately, the tribe did not fully take over its land. Eventually, the Asherites ceased to exist as a separate people, it's distinctness worn away by the surrounding nations.

49:21 Naphtali's tribe inherited a mountain region. The people of Naphtali lived northwest of the Sea of Galilee, so they really did live like deer in the high country. The tribe of Naphtali was eventually deported in an Assyrian attack. Gentiles then settled the territory. Jesus traveled to this area in His itinerant ministry.

49:22-24 Joseph's legacy lived on in his two sons, Ephraim and Manasseh. Joseph's descendants included several great leaders. Joshua, who succeeded Moses as leader of the Israelites, was a descendant of Joseph through Ephraim. Deborah, a female judge, was probably of the tribe of Ephraim as well. Another judge of Israel, Gideon, was of the tribe of Manasseh.

23 Archers attacked him savagely;
they shot at him and harassed him.
24 But his bow remained taut,
and his arms were strengthened
by the hands of the Mighty One of Jacob,
by the Shepherd, the Rock of Israel.
25 May the God of your father help you;
May the Almighty bless you
with the blessings of the heavens above,
and blessings of the watery depths below,
and blessings of the breasts and womb.
26 May the blessings of your father
surpass the blessings of the ancient mountains,*
reaching to the heights of the eternal hills.
May these blessings rest on the head of Joseph,
who is a prince among his brothers.

27 "Benjamin is a ravenous wolf,
devouring his enemies in the morning
and dividing his plunder in the evening."

28 These are the twelve tribes of Israel, and this is what their father said as he told his
sons good-bye. He blessed each one with an appropriate message.

49:23 Gen 37:24
49:24 Ps 132:2, 5; Isa 41:10; 49:26
49:25 Gen 28:13
49:26 Deut 33:15-16
49:27 Deut 33:12
49:29 Gen 23:16-20; 25:8-9

JACOB'S DEATH AND BURIAL

29 Then Jacob instructed them, "Soon I will die and join my ancestors. Bury me with my
father and grandfather in the cave in the field of Ephron the Hittite. 30 This is the cave
in the field of Machpelah, near Mamre in Canaan, that Abraham bought from Ephron
the Hittite as a permanent burial site. 31 There Abraham and his wife Sarah are buried.
There Isaac and his wife, Rebekah, are buried. And there I buried Leah. 32 It is the plot
of land and the cave that my grandfather Abraham bought from the Hittites."
33 When Jacob had finished this charge to his sons, he drew his feet into the bed,
breathed his last, and joined his ancestors in death.

49:31 Gen 23:19; 25:9; 35:29
49:33 Gen 25:8; Acts 7:15

49:26 Or *of my ancestors.*

49:24 These names of God held great meaning for the people of Israel. Identifying God with the name of Jacob gave the people a common unity. They were all descendants of Jacob, and their faith was part of the blessing of their inheritance. They were also people who understood the role of a shepherd caring for his sheep. Understanding God in this way gave them a sense of security. Finally, they all knew the safety of hiding behind a large rock, something that couldn't be moved by human hands. God's protection of His people was akin to that safety.

▸ GOD
49:25 God's names: Helper. Jacob called on "the God of your father" to bless Joseph in terms of both land and body. The dual emphasis harkened back to the creation account and the Cultural Mandate (see Genesis 1:28), when God gave Adam and Eve dominion over the earth and told them to be fruitful and multiply. Like Joseph and the first couple, you need God's rich blessing on your work and on your family. While today's relativistic culture rejects God's standards, true success in life is achieved only when you acknowledge God in all things. Having God's blessing is the key to a prosperous and successful life. (***See God*>** *God's Names> God,* TopicGuide page A18.)

49:27 True to Jacob's prophecy, Benjamin's descendants were at times a violent people. Judges 20:1-7 tells the gruesome story of a woman raped until she was dead by men of the tribe of Benjamin, an act that sparked a civil war. Ehud, a man from Benjamin, killed the Moabite king Eglon with a dagger (Judges 3:15-30). Saul, the first king of Israel, was of the tribe of Benjamin; he was a mighty warrior but a tortured man who lost his kingdom to David. On a more positive note, the apostle Paul of the New Testament was also of the tribe of Benjamin.

49:32 This cave and the surrounding field constituted the only property Abraham ever owned in the land promised to him by God. He purchased the land in order to bury his wife, Sarah. It was the custom to bury a person in his or her homeland, so when Abraham purchased the field, he was responding to God's promise and claiming Canaan as his and Sarah's native land.

50:1 **50** Joseph threw himself on his father and wept over him and kissed him. [2]Then Jo-
Gen 46:4 seph told the physicians who served him to embalm his father's body; so Jacob*
50:2 was embalmed. [3]The embalming process took the usual forty days. And the Egyptians
Gen 50:26 mourned his death for seventy days.
50:3 Num 20:29 [4]When the period of mourning was over, Joseph approached Pharaoh's advisers
Deut 34:8 and said, "Please do me this favor and speak to Pharaoh on my behalf. [5]Tell him
50:5 that my father made me swear an oath. He said to me, 'Listen, I am about to die.
Gen 47:29-31 Take my body back to the land of Canaan, and bury me in the tomb I prepared for
myself.' So please allow me to go and bury my father. After his burial, I will return
without delay."
[6]Pharaoh agreed to Joseph's request. "Go and bury your father, as he made you prom-
ise," he said. [7]So Joseph went up to bury his father. He was accompanied by all of Pha-
raoh's officials, all the senior members of Pharaoh's household, and all the senior officers
50:8 of Egypt. [8]Joseph also took his entire household and his brothers and their households.
Gen 45:10 But they left their little children and flocks and herds in the land of Goshen. [9]A great num-
ber of chariots and charioteers accompanied Joseph.
50:9 Gen 41:43 [10]When they arrived at the threshing floor of Atad, near the Jordan River, they held a very
great and solemn memorial service, with a seven-day period of mourning for Joseph's father.
[11]The local residents, the Canaanites, watched them mourning at the threshing floor of Atad.
Then they renamed that place (which is near the Jordan) Abel-mizraim,* for they said, "This is
a place of deep mourning for these Egyptians."
50:12 Gen 49:29 [12]So Jacob's sons did as he had commanded them. [13]They carried his body to the
50:13 land of Canaan and buried him in the cave in the field of Machpelah, near Mamre.
Gen 23:16-18 This is the cave that Abraham had bought as a permanent burial site from Ephron the
Hittite.

50:15

JOSEPH REASSURES HIS BROTHERS

Gen 42:21-22 [14]After burying Jacob, Joseph returned to Egypt with his brothers and all who had accom-
50:16 panied him to his father's burial. [15]But now that their father was dead, Joseph's brothers
Gen 49:29 became fearful. "Now Joseph will show his anger and pay us back for all the wrong we did
50:17 Gen 45:5, 7 to him," they said.
Matt 6:14 Luke 6:27 [16]So they sent this message to Joseph: "Before your father died, he instructed us [17]to
Rom 12:19 say to you: 'Please forgive your brothers for the great wrong they did to you—for their sin
in treating you so cruelly.' So we, the servants of the God of your father, beg you to forgive

50:2 Hebrew *Israel.* See note on 35:21. 50:11 *Abel-mizraim* means "mourning of the Egyptians."

50:2-5 Joseph had lived in Egypt for most of his life, so it is not surprising that he had Jacob buried according to Egyptian customs. Embalming was a distinctively Egyptian burial technique at that time. The time spent in mourning was significant as well. In Egypt, 40 days were typical for mourning, since the embalming process took that long. But in the case of a king, the typical mourning period was 72 days. For Jacob, the people mourned 70 days. This showed the extreme respect the people had for Joseph and his family. Joseph still traveled home to Canaan to bury Jacob in the family burial ground.

50:17 Joseph's brothers had reason to be afraid. Their cruelty toward Joseph in selling him into slavery had landed him in Egypt. Now that their father was dead, Joseph might have felt free to retaliate. He certainly had the power to do so. So the brothers sent Joseph a message that purported to convey Jacob's wish that Joseph would forgive his brothers. It is unclear whether Jacob really made this request, but the important thing is that the brothers also included their own plea for forgiveness. Now their repentance for their evil deed was complete.

50:17 This was not the first time Joseph had displayed such emotion. When his brothers first traveled to Egypt to get relief from the famine, they did not recognize Joseph, although he knew them immediately. Without giving away his identity, Joseph made them bring Benjamin, his closest brother, back to Egypt. When Joseph saw Benjamin, he was overwhelmed, leaving the room and weeping (Genesis 43:29-31). Later, when Joseph revealed himself to his brothers, the Bible says that he "broke down and wept. He wept so loudly the Egyptians could hear him" (Genesis 45:2). While Joseph had risen to power within a foreign culture, he evidently had stayed tender toward his family.

our sin." When Joseph received the message, he broke down and wept. [18]Then his broth-
ers came and threw themselves down before Joseph. "Look, we are your slaves!" they 50:18 Gen 37:7-10
said.
[19]But Joseph replied, "Don't be afraid of me. Am I God, that I can punish you? [20]You in- 50:19 Gen 30:2
tended to harm me, but God intended it all for good. He brought me to this position so I 50:20
could save the lives of many people. [21]No, don't be afraid. I will continue to take care of Gen 37:26-27
you and your children." So he reassured them by speaking kindly to them. 50:21 Gen 45:11

THE DEATH OF JOSEPH

[22]So Joseph and his brothers and their families continued to live in Egypt. Joseph lived to
the age of 110. [23]He lived to see three generations of descendants of his son Ephraim, and
he lived to see the birth of the children of Manasseh's son Makir, whom he claimed as his
own.* 50:24 Gen 13:15; 28:13
[24]"Soon I will die," Joseph told his brothers, "but God will surely come to help you and

50:23 Hebrew *who were born on Joseph's knees.*

50:18 Early in Joseph's life, he shared two dreams with his family. In the first, Joseph and his brothers were gathering grain. Joseph's bundle of grain stood up while the bundles of his brothers bowed down. The second dream involved the moon, sun, and 11 stars (symbolic of Joseph's father, mother, and brothers) bowing down before Joseph (Genesis 37:4-11). These dreams eventually turned into reality.

▸ HOLINESS
50:20 God's provision. God turned into good what Joseph's brothers had meant for evil. The sovereign God used the animosity of a group of men toward their brother to achieve His long-range goal of sparing the lives of many people during a time of severe famine. Many years later, God used the hatred of men toward another Israelite, Jesus of Nazareth, to save countless people from the consequences of their sin. What trial are you facing today? Know that the God who channeled the course of history in ages past to achieve His saving purposes is the same God who is at work in your life today. Trust Him with unqualified faith, and He will turn into good what Satan means for evil. (***See Holiness****> Changed by God> God provides> By providence,* TopicGuide page A41.)

50:23 Other versions of this verse describe Joseph as placing his grandchildren and great-grandchildren on his knees. In this ancient culture, that was a form of adoption, so this verse aptly says that Jacob cared for these children, "whom he claimed as his own." This practice was similar to that of infertile women who allowed their maidservants to bear children for their husbands.

50:24 Joseph's prophecy came to pass, but not for more than 400 years. After Joseph's death, his family stayed in Egypt and increased in number. Finally, an Egyptian pharaoh who had not known Joseph enslaved the Israelites so that they would not rise up and take too much control. Eventually, another young man came out of the Israelites' ranks and, miraculously, grew up in Pharaoh's palace. This young man was Moses. The book of Exodus tells how Moses grew up in Egypt, was forced into exile, and then was called by God to lead his people out of Egypt and back to the Promised Land.

BECAUSE GOD IS ABSOLUTE TRUTH

I will believe what He says and live accordingly.

He [God] will bring you back to the land He solemnly promised . . . to Abraham.

GENESIS 50:24

FOR THE NEXT *GOD IS ABSOLUTE TRUTH* FEATURE SEE PAGE 288.

50:25 lead you out of this land of Egypt. He will bring you back to the land He solemnly prom-
Exod 13:19 Josh 24:32 ised to give to Abraham, to Isaac, and to Jacob."
Heb 11:22 25Then Joseph made the sons of Israel swear an oath, and he said, "When God comes to
50:26 help you and lead you back, you must take my bones with you." 26So Joseph died at the
Exod 1:6 age of 110. The Egyptians embalmed him, and his body was placed in a coffin in Egypt.

50:25 Joseph requested that he eventually be buried in the land God had promised to his family. Even though the journey back home came 400 years and many generations later, when the Israelites left Egypt, they carried Joseph's bones with them (Exodus 13:19). Joseph was buried in land that his father, Jacob, had purchased from a man named Hamor (Genesis 33:19). This land was in the region allotted to Joseph's sons, Ephraim and Manasseh (Joshua 24:32).

KEY PLACES IN EXODUS

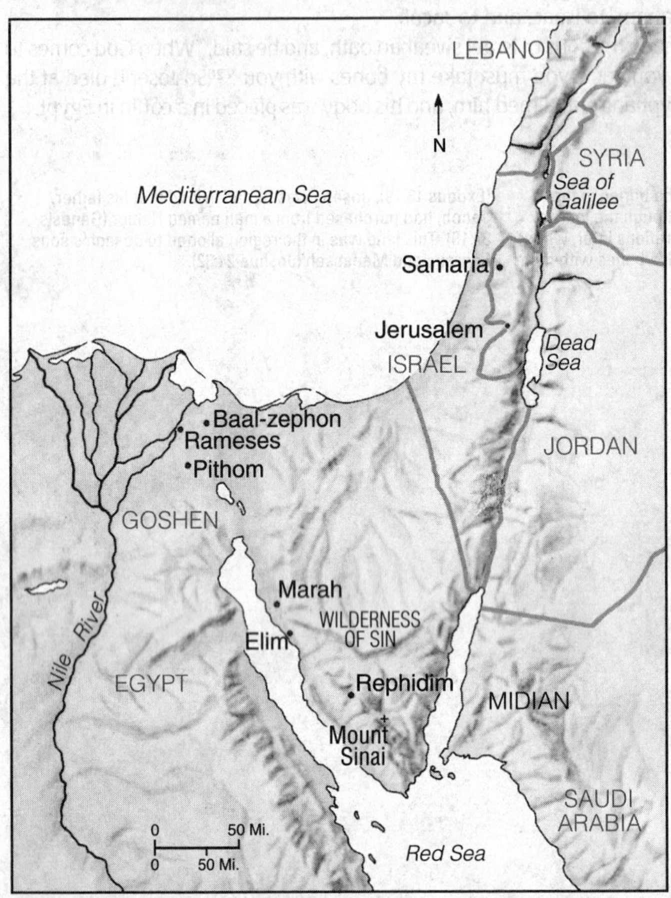

Modern names and boundaries are shown in gray.

1 Goshen This area was given to Jacob and his family when they moved to Egypt (Genesis 47:5, 6). It became the Hebrews' homeland for 400 years and remained separate from the main Egyptian centers, since Egyptian culture looked down upon shepherds and nomads. As the years passed, Jacob's family grew into a large nation (1:7).

2, 3 Pithom and Rameses During the Israelites' stay in the land of Egypt, a pharaoh came to the throne who had no respect for these descendants of Joseph and feared their large numbers. He forced them into slavery in order to oppress and subdue them. Out of their slave labor, the supply cities of Pithom and Rameses were built (1:11).

4 Midian Moses, an Egyptian prince who was born a Hebrew, killed an Egyptian and fled for his life to Midian. Here he became a shepherd and married a woman named Zipporah. It was while he was here that God commissioned him for the job of leading the Hebrew people out of Egypt (2:15–4:31).

5 Baal-zephon Slavery was not to last because God planned to deliver his people. After choosing Moses and Aaron to be his spokesmen to Pharaoh, God worked a series of dramatic miracles in the land of Egypt to convince Pharaoh to let the Hebrews go (5:1–12:33). When finally freed, the entire nation set out with the riches of Egypt (12:34-36). One of their first stops was at Baal-zephon (14:2), where Pharaoh, who had changed his mind, chased the Hebrews and trapped them against the sea. But God parted the waters and led the people through the sea on dry land. When Pharaoh's army tried to pursue, the waters collapsed around them, and they drowned (14:5-31).

6 Marah Moses now led the people southward. The long trek across the desert brought hot tempers and parched throats for this mass of people. At Marah, the water they found was bitter, but God sweetened it (15:22-25).

7 Elim As they continued their journey, the Hebrews (now called Israelites) came to Elim, an oasis with 12 springs (15:27).

8 Wilderness of Sin Leaving Elim, the people headed into the Wilderness of Sin. Here the people became hungry, so God provided them with manna that came from heaven and covered the ground each morning (16:1, 13-15). The people ate this manna until they entered the Promised Land.

9 Rephidim Moses led the people to Rephidim, where they found no water. But God miraculously provided water from a rock (17:1, 5, 6). Here the Israelites encountered their first test in battle: The Amalekites attacked and were defeated (17:9-13). Moses' father-in-law, Jethro, then arrived on the scene with some sound advice on delegating responsibilities (18).

10 Mount Sinai God had previously appeared to Moses on this mountain and commissioned him to lead Israel (3:1-10). Now Moses returned with the people God had asked him to lead. For almost a year the people camped at the foot of Mount Sinai. During this time God gave them His Ten Commandments as well as other laws for right living. He also provided the blueprint for building the Tabernacle (19–40). God was forging a holy nation, prepared to live for and serve Him alone.

EXODUS

PURPOSE

To demonstrate Moses' authority as God's chosen leader and to encourage Israel to remain faithful to God's covenant with them.

What's the greatest danger you've ever been in? How were you rescued from it?

Exodus relates the story of one of God's greatest rescues: Israel's escape from slavery in Egypt. Under the leadership of Moses, Israel followed the Lord's command to leave Egypt and travel toward the Promised Land. Along the way, God confirmed His covenant with His people and delivered to them His written Law, including the Ten Commandments and instructions for building His sacred Tabernacle. Exodus records that Israel faithfully built the Tabernacle according to God's instructions. In response, God manifested His presence there in a special way.

Exodus establishes patterns for worship and behavior that Israel was to follow from generation to generation. In Exodus, God encouraged Israel to follow His Law by demonstrating the blessings that come to His people when they obey Him, as well as the curses that fall upon them when they disobey.

DISCOVER GOD IN EXODUS

Exodus reveals two contrasting yet complementary aspects of God's character:

Judgment: Throughout Exodus, God's judgment falls upon those who oppose Him, whether they are the false gods (idols) of Egypt (Exodus 12:12), the evil Egyptians themselves (Exodus 14:28-31), or God's own people (32:25-28). By demonstrating His power over the so-called gods of Egypt, the Lord revealed Himself afresh as the only true and sovereign Ruler of the world. By cursing the Egyptians, God showed His intention to defend His people and to take vengeance on their behalf. And by striking down His own sinful people, God demonstrated that He requires holiness and fidelity from His followers. His covenant is a two-edged sword, blessing the obedient and cursing the wicked.

Blessing: Exodus presents many blessings to those who love God and obey His commandments. In delivering Israel from slavery, God showed His eagerness to bless those who are in covenant with Him (Exodus 34:6-7) and His special love for the families of faithful believers (Exodus 2:24-25; 32:13-14). By sustaining Israel in the wilderness (Exodus 16:4-31), God demonstrated His desire to meet not only the spiritual needs of His people, but also their physical needs. By forgiving Israel's sin (Exodus 34:7), God indicated His eagerness to restore believers to a right relationship with Himself. By giving Israel His codified Law, the Lord privileged

His people more than any other nation in the world. Only they knew Him intimately enough to be shown His heart, and to learn clearly how to obtain all His blessings (Deuteronomy 30:16; James 1:25). And by dwelling in the midst of His people, God granted to them the greatest imaginable honor, security, peace, and provision.

GROWING THROUGH EXODUS

Exodus establishes the terms of God's covenant Law, which is the basis on which God metes out blessings and curses under the Old Covenant.

A God Who Promises: When people first sinned, God made a promise to redeem them (Genesis 3:15). He confirmed and expanded these promised blessings in his pact with Noah (Genesis 6; 9) and in his agreement with Abraham (Genesis 15; 17). God's covenant promises included not only blessings for these men, but also for their descendants. In Moses' day, God remembered His promises to these great patriarchs and came to Israel's rescue. In the same way, the Lord keeps His covenant promises to Christians, who are in covenant with God through His Son Jesus Christ. These promises secure eternal life and forgiveness of sins for those who keep the terms of the covenant, but they guarantee eternal destruction in hell for those who do not. Although no one has the natural ability to keep this covenant, Jesus has kept it on behalf of all those who trust in Him. By trusting in Him alone for salvation, believers will eventually receive all the covenant blessings. Those who do not receive Christ will die in their sins and fall under God's promised judgment.

A God Who Reveals: God wants His people to know Him, to love Him, and to obey Him. To this end, He has inspired holy men who have written and delivered the Scriptures to His people. Just as Israel was blessed to receive the Ten Commandments and the Book of the Covenant after leaving Egypt, and just as their children received the entire book of Exodus, modern Christians have received both the Old and the New Testaments through which we can learn about God's character and covenant.

A God Who Commands: Believers in the Old Testament were saved by the blood of Christ, just as modern believers are. Nevertheless, God still required them to obey His Law. When they did not, He disciplined them according to the terms of His covenant (Exodus 34:7; Deuteronomy 8:5-6; Hebrews 12:5-11). In the same way, modern Christians must obey God's Law (Matthew 5:17-19; John 14:15) in order to receive His blessings in both this life and the life to come (Psalm 1:1-3; Matthew 6:31-33; 19:21; 1 Timothy 6:18-19).

DISCOVERY VERSES

"Now if you will obey Me and keep My covenant, you will be My own special treasure from among all the peoples on earth; for all the earth belongs to Me. And you will be My kingdom of priests, My holy nation."

(EXODUS 19:5-6)

The LORD passed in front of Moses, calling out, "Yahweh! The LORD! The God of compassion and mercy! I am slow to anger and filled with unfailing love and faithfulness. I lavish unfailing love to a thousand generations. I forgive iniquity, rebellion, and sin. But I do not excuse the guilty. I lay the sins of the parents upon their children and grandchildren; the entire family is affected—even children in the third and fourth generations."

(EXODUS 34:6-7)

EXODUS FACTS

Author: According to the Scriptures, Moses authored the book of Exodus (Joshua 8:30-32; Malachi 4:4; Mark 7:10; 12:26; Romans 10:5). Some portions, however, were written by the hand of God Himself (Exodus 31:18).

Written to: Exodus was written for the nation of Israel. While some portions of it were clearly written for the generation that participated in the Exodus (Exodus 24:3-7), the completed book was delivered to the children and grandchildren of that generation (Exodus 16:35).

Date of writing: Portions were written immediately after the Exodus (Exodus 24:3-7), which probably took place in 1446 BC. The book was not completed until the nation reached the Promised Land around 1406 BC (Exodus 16:35).

Setting: The events in Exodus took place in three locations: Egypt, where the descendants of Jacob were enslaved for over four hundred years; Mount Sinai, where Moses received the Law; and the wilderness surrounding Sinai, where Israel camped while building the Tabernacle.

OUTLINE

- **EXODUS 1–18**—Through Moses, God delivered Israel from slavery in Egypt
  - ***EXODUS 1–2****—Moses' background and early life*
  - ***EXODUS 3:1–15:21****—Moses delivers Israel*
  - ***EXODUS 15:22–18:27****—Moses leads Israel toward Sinai*
- **EXODUS 19–24**—Through Moses, God confirmed his covenant with Israel at Sinai
  - ***EXODUS 19****—Preparation for confirming the covenant*
  - ***EXODUS 20–23****—The codified terms of the covenant*
  - ***EXODUS 24****—Confirmation and ratification of the covenant*
- **EXODUS 25–40**—Through Moses, God established proper worship in Israel
  - ***EXODUS 25–31****—Instructions for building the tabernacle*
  - ***EXODUS 32–34****—Israel's sin and restoration*
  - ***EXODUS 35–40****—Building the tabernacle*

THE ISRAELITES IN EGYPT

1 These are the names of the sons of Israel (that is, Jacob) who moved to Egypt with their father, each with his family: 2Reuben, Simeon, Levi, Judah, 3Issachar, Zebulun, Benjamin, 4Dan, Naphtali, Gad, and Asher. 5In all, Jacob had seventy* descendants in Egypt, including Joseph, who was already there.

6In time, Joseph and all of his brothers died, ending that entire generation. 7But their descendants, the Israelites, had many children and grandchildren. In fact, they multiplied so greatly that they became extremely powerful and filled the land.

8Eventually, a new king came to power in Egypt who knew nothing about Joseph or what he had done. 9He said to his people, "Look, the people of Israel now outnumber us and are stronger than we are. 10We must make a plan to keep them from growing even more. If we don't, and if war breaks out, they will join our enemies and fight against us. Then they will escape from the country.*"

11So the Egyptians made the Israelites their slaves. They appointed brutal slave drivers

1:1 Gen 46:8-27
1:5 Gen 46:26
1:6 Gen 50:26; Acts 7:15-16
1:7 Gen 12:2; 35:11; 46:3; 47:27; 48:4; *Acts 7:17
1:8 Acts 7:18-19
1:9 Ps 105:25
1:10 Ps 105:24-25; Acts 7:17-19

1:5 Dead Sea Scrolls and Greek version read *seventy-five;* see notes on Gen 46:27. 1:10 Or *will take the country.*

1:1-5 The nation of Israel descended from Jacob. God originally offered to make a great nation of Abraham (Genesis 12:1-4), who was aged and childless at the time. In fulfillment of God's promise, Abraham and his wife Sarah miraculously had a son, whom they named Isaac. Isaac later had twin sons, Esau and Jacob. Jacob inherited both the family leadership and God's promise. God later changed Jacob's name to *Israel,* and Israel's 12 sons became the progenitors of the 12 tribes of Israel. Jacob's family moved from the Promised Land to Egypt in order to find sustenance during a famine (Genesis 47).

1:6 Joseph died in approximately 1805 BC. The history of Joseph and the rest of Jacob's family in Egypt is recorded in Genesis 37–50.

1:8-14 The Hebrews were enslaved for approximately 400 years (Genesis 15:13). Because the Exodus took place around 1446 BC, Jacob's family must have been enslaved shortly after Joseph's death in 1805 BC. Slavery was a typical covenant curse (Genesis 9:25-27; Deuteronomy 28:32, 68). Israel's slavery in Egypt was also a basis for the Sabbath (Deuteronomy 5:15) and a motivation to treat servants well (Deuteronomy 15:15).

1:11 Rameses is believed to be Pirameses, the capital city of Pharaoh Ramses II (1290–1224 BC). Ancient records attribute the building of this city to Ramses II. Because the Exodus took place around 1446 BC, it is likely that Ramses II simply renamed and perhaps renovated the city that the Hebrews had built at least 150 years earlier. It was most likely located in the northeastern Nile Delta. Rameses was the site from which the Exodus began (Exodus 12:37). Pithom was probably located in the Wadi Tumilat, between the Nile Delta and Lake Timsah.

over them, hoping to wear them down with crushing labor. They forced them to build the
cities of Pithom and Rameses as supply centers for the king. [12]But the more the Egyptians
oppressed them, the more the Israelites multiplied and spread, and the more alarmed the 1:14
Egyptians became. [13]So the Egyptians worked the people of Israel without mercy. [14]They Exod 2:23
made their lives bitter, forcing them to mix mortar and make bricks and do all the work in
the fields. They were ruthless in all their demands.
[15]Then Pharaoh, the king of Egypt, gave this order to the Hebrew midwives, Shiphrah 1:16
and Puah: [16]"When you help the Hebrew women as they give birth, watch as they de- Acts 7:19
liver.* If the baby is a boy, kill him; if it is a girl, let her live." [17]But because the midwives
feared God, they refused to obey the king's orders. They allowed the boys to live, too.
[18]So the king of Egypt called for the midwives. "Why have you done this?" he de- 1:19
manded. "Why have you allowed the boys to live?" Josh 2:4-6
[19]"The Hebrew women are not like the Egyptian women," the midwives replied. "They 2 Sam 17:20
are more vigorous and have their babies so quickly that we cannot get there in time." 1:20
[20]So God was good to the midwives, and the Israelites continued to multiply, growing Exod 1:12
more and more powerful. [21]And because the midwives feared God, He gave them families 1:22
of their own. Acts 7:19
[22]Then Pharaoh gave this order to all his people: "Throw every newborn Hebrew boy
into the Nile River. But you may let the girls live."

THE BIRTH OF MOSES 2:1

2 About this time, a man and woman from the tribe of Levi got married. [2]The woman Exod 6:20 Num 26:59
became pregnant and gave birth to a son. She saw that he was a special baby and 2:2
kept him hidden for three months. [3]But when she could no longer hide him, she got a Acts 7:20 Heb 11:23

1:16 Hebrew *look upon the two stones;* perhaps the reference is to a birthstool.

1:15 There were certainly more than two midwives for the Hebrews. Shiphrah and Puah may have been leaders among the midwives, or they may have been mentioned because they disobeyed Pharaoh. Their names are Semitic, and the women both feared God (Exodus 1:17, 21), so they were probably Hebrews rather than Egyptians.

▸ BIBLE
1:15 Discovering Jesus in the birth of Moses. One way we learn about God is by seeing Jesus' life reflected in the lives of those who preceded Him. Like Jesus, Moses was the child of a commoner, but Moses grew up the son of royalty. Moses was threatened with death as an infant (Exodus 1:15-16), surviving only by his parents' disobedience to the king, just like Jesus' near escape (Matthew 2:13-16). Both Jesus and Moses were born while their nation groaned in bondage, and both spent their childhoods in Egypt (Exodus 2:1-10; Matthew 2:13-15). (***See Bible****> Unity> OT Types> Moses,* TopicGuide page A11.)

1:17-20 This section contains several ethically puzzling stories showing the Hebrews deceiving the Egyptians. The goal is not to teach that it is normally permitted to lie (which would contradict Exodus 20:16), but that the mighty Egyptians, the most educated and powerful people in the world at that time, were easily overcome by the God-fearing guile of simple Hebrew slaves. For more on the ethics of truth telling, compare this section to 1 Kings 22:14-23.

▸ HOLINESS
1:17 Caught in a bind. In this confusing world, things can get complicated. You may be caught between two warring parties, both demanding your allegiance. What do you do when there seems to be no right answer, no clear path? God's people have faced these challenges before—you are not alone. We must trust God and His Word, believing that faithfulness to Him is the answer to any ethical challenge. (***See Holiness****> Submission> Trusting God> Trust in God, not humans,* TopicGuide page A41.)

▸ CHURCH
1:18 Christians and the government. Christians are commanded to obey all legitimate authority (Romans 13), but government authority ends where God's instructions begin (Acts 5:29). When any government commands what the Scriptures forbid, or forbids what the Scriptures command, then Christians must prayerfully and respectfully disobey. (***See Church****> Role> Church Government> Society> Government should honor the spiritual authority of the church,* TopicGuide page A49.)

▸ HOLINESS
2:2 Teaching your children to love others. It took no special message from God—no dream or vision—to motivate Moses' parents to protect him from harm. Their deep love was expressed in a rather risky adoption strategy that God blessed with success, and the outcome was more than they could have imagined. Moses would grow up in his parents' home and learn of God's love for him, yet also be educated and protected from harm as a prince in the Egyptian court. When we raise our children to love God, we can know that God has His hand on them, even when that is not immediately obvious. (***See Holiness****> Submission> Learning God's Word,* TopicGuide page A40.)

2:2 The theme that the mighty Egyptians were easily overcome by God's people continues. Moses' parents engaged in deception in order to protect their child, and as with the midwives (Exodus 1:17-20), God blessed their efforts.

2:3 basket made of papyrus reeds and waterproofed it with tar and pitch. She put the baby in
Gen 6:14 Isa 18:2 the basket and laid it among the reeds along the bank of the Nile River. 4The baby's sis-
ter then stood at a distance, watching to see what would happen to him.
2:4 Exod 15:20 5Soon Pharaoh's daughter came down to bathe in the river, and her attendants walked
Num 26:59 along the riverbank. When the princess saw the basket among the reeds, she sent her
2:5 maid to get it for her. 6When the princess opened it, she saw the baby. The little boy was
Exod 7:15; 8:20 Acts 7:21 crying, and she felt sorry for him. "This must be one of the Hebrew children," she said.
7Then the baby's sister approached the princess. "Should I go and find one of the He-
brew women to nurse the baby for you?" she asked.
8"Yes, do!" the princess replied. So the girl went and called the baby's mother.
9"Take this baby and nurse him for me," the princess told the baby's mother. "I will pay
you for your help." So the woman took her baby home and nursed him.
2:10 10Later, when the boy was older, his mother brought him back to Pharaoh's daughter,
1 Sam 1:20 who adopted him as her own son. The princess named him Moses,* for she explained, "I
2 Sam 22:17 lifted him out of the water."

MOSES ESCAPES TO MIDIAN

11Many years later, when Moses had grown up, he went out to visit his own people, the
2:11 Acts 7:23-24 Hebrews, and he saw how hard they were forced to work. During his visit, he saw an
Heb 11:24-26 Egyptian beating one of his fellow Hebrews. 12After looking in all directions to make sure
2:12 no one was watching, Moses killed the Egyptian and hid the body in the sand.
Acts 7:24 13The next day, when Moses went out to visit his people again, he saw two Hebrew men
2:13 fighting. "Why are you beating up your friend?" Moses said to the one who had started the fight.
Acts 7:26-28 14The man replied, "Who appointed you to be our prince and judge? Are you going to
2:14 kill me as you killed that Egyptian yesterday?"
*Acts 7:27, 35 Then Moses was afraid, thinking, "Everyone knows what I did." 15And sure enough, Pha-
raoh heard what had happened, and he tried to kill Moses. But Moses fled from Pharaoh
2:15 and went to live in the land of Midian.
Acts 7:29 When Moses arrived in Midian, he sat down beside a well. 16Now the priest of Midian
2:16 Gen 24:11 had seven daughters who came as usual to draw water and fill the water troughs for their
Exod 3:1; 18:1

2:10 *Moses* sounds like a Hebrew term that means "to lift out."

2:3-5 The Hebrew word for *basket* here is the same word consistently used to describe Noah's boat. In the Old Testament, the word appears only in these two accounts. This implies that Moses is to be seen as filling a role similar to Noah's. God established covenants through both men (Genesis 9:9-17; Exodus 19–24).

2:5-9 Pharaoh's own daughter disobeyed his command to kill all the Hebrew baby boys (Exodus 1:22). This demonstrates God's powerful providential protection of Moses. It may also imply that Pharaoh's command was commonly understood to be unreasonable.

2:10 The name *Moses* sounds like both the Hebrew word for *draw out* and the Egyptian name meaning *son.* While the princess evidently intended the Hebrew association, the implication for the Egyptians would have been that Moses was a son of the pharaoh. God demonstrated His power and protection by causing Moses to be adopted into the family of the pharaoh who had ordered Moses' death as an infant.

2:11-12 In order to defend an Israelite slave, Moses killed an Egyptian. At his martyrdom, Stephen indicated that Moses had done this because God had chosen him to rescue Israel (Acts 7:23-25). Moses' action was not malicious; it was a righteous act of divine deliverance.

2:13-14 As Exodus 3–4 makes clear, God appointed Moses to be Israel's deliverer. By rejecting Moses' leadership and deliverance at this time, Israel chose to remain in slavery.

2:15 Midian lay east of Egypt across the Sinai Peninsula. The Israelites descended from Isaac, the son of promise born to Abraham and Sarah (Genesis 17:19-21). The Midianites were the Israelites' cousins, descending from Abraham through his second wife, Keturah.

▸ CHURCH
2:15 Should I disobey authority? Moses disobeyed authority in order to protect God's people. While Moses had the right motive, his decision to flee punishment was likely wrong. As God's people, if we must disobey authority, we must also be willing to accept the consequences of such behavior (Romans 13:4). If you must stand up for what is right, you should also receive the consequences with courage. (***See Church****> Role> Preach> Instructions> Use Caution> Submission to government and other authorities,* TopicGuide page A50.)

2:16-21 Reuel was a priest of Midian who served the God of Israel (compare Exodus 18:1-12). *Reuel* was also called *Jethro* (compare Exodus 18:2).

father's flocks. [17]But some other shepherds came and chased them away. So Moses jumped up and rescued the girls from the shepherds. Then he drew water for their flocks.

[18]When the girls returned to Reuel, their father, he asked, "Why are you back so soon today?"

[19]"An Egyptian rescued us from the shepherds," they answered. "And then he drew water for us and watered our flocks."

[20]"Then where is he?" their father asked. "Why did you leave him there? Invite him to come and eat with us."

[21]Moses accepted the invitation, and he settled there with him. In time, Reuel gave Moses his daughter Zipporah to be his wife. [22]Later she gave birth to a son, and Moses named him Gershom,* for he explained, "I have been a foreigner in a foreign land."

[23]Years passed, and the king of Egypt died. But the Israelites continued to groan under their burden of slavery. They cried out for help, and their cry rose up to God. [24]God heard their groaning, and He remembered His covenant promise to Abraham, Isaac, and Jacob. [25]He looked down on the people of Israel and knew it was time to act.*

2:17 Gen 29:10
2:18 Num 10:29
2:20 Gen 18:5
2:21 Exod 4:25; 18:2 Acts 7:29
2:22 Gen 23:4 Heb 11:13
2:23 Exod 6:5, 9 Acts 7:34
2:24 Gen 22:16-18; 26:2-3; 28:13 Ps 105:10, 42

MOSES AND THE BURNING BUSH

3 One day Moses was tending the flock of his father-in-law, Jethro,* the priest of Midian. He led the flock far into the wilderness and came to Sinai,* the mountain of God.

2:22 *Gershom* sounds like a Hebrew term that means "a foreigner there." 2:25 Or *and acknowledged His obligation to help them.* 3:1a Moses' father-in-law went by two names, Jethro and Reuel. 3:1b Hebrew *Horeb,* another name for Sinai.

2:20 Hospitality to strangers was a common cultural and religious practice in Old Testament times (Genesis 18:2-8; 19:1-3; 24:15-61; Leviticus 25:35). When it came to food, water, or shelter, there was an understood obligation to care even for strangers.

▸ GOD
2:23 God does not leave His people without hope. The Israelites felt the same despair we sometimes feel—"Help! God has abandoned me!" The promise (or covenant) God made with Abraham (Genesis 15 and 17) appeared to be in danger of failing as the Egyptians enslaved and then attempted to destroy God's people. Though the Hebrews could not see it, God was still at work, arranging a way to rescue His people from hopelessness. (***See God****> Relationship> God's Desire> God does not leave His people without hope,* TopicGuide page A14.)

2:24 God's covenants with people groups always included three main elements: divine benevolence, requirements of human obedience, and consequences. God's covenant with Abraham formed the core of the Hebrew identity. In this covenant, God had promised to reward Abraham's obedience with land, descendants, and honor (Genesis 15; 17). God confirmed Abraham's covenant with Abraham's son Isaac, and with Isaac's son Jacob (whom God later renamed Israel). Through Jacob, the covenant extended to the 12 patriarchs of Israel, and to their descendants. In accordance with His covenant benevolence, God responded to Israel's cries for help.

MOSES FLEES TO MIDIAN
After murdering an Egyptian, Moses escaped into Midian. There he married Zipporah and became a shepherd.

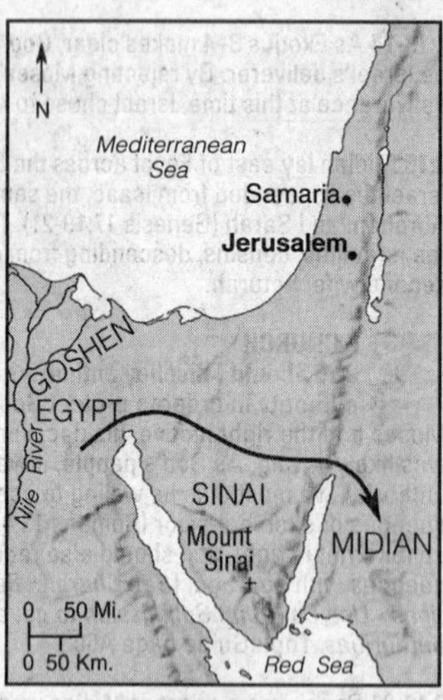

▸ BIBLE
3:1 Discovering Jesus in the life of Moses. The life and ministry of Jesus is reflected in the life and ministry of Moses, showing us that Jesus' ministry was not an accident—it was completely in line with the way God had been doing things for thousands of years. Just like Moses, Jesus identified with those who rejected Him (John 1:11). Moses shepherded God's people (Numbers 27:15-17), just as Jesus still does as He cares for the flock of His chosen people (John 10:11-16). Both Moses and Jesus worked miracles. Each was a prophet (Deuteronomy 18:18; John 7:16) and a priest (Psalm 99:6; Hebrews 9:11). Many scholars recognize more than 60 further examples of parallels between Jesus and Moses. (***See Bible****> Unity> OT Types> Moses,* TopicGuide page A11.)

▸ PURPOSE
3:1 God is active in our world. God is not silent or uninvolved; He is at all times accomplishing His master plan. One way He does this is by delivering His people from sin and danger. In Exodus 3, God showed His intention to redeem His people from slavery through Moses. How can you be God's "Moses" to the hurting people in your world? (***See Purpose****> God's Deeds> Special acts in God's master plan,* TopicGuide page A52.)

3:2 *Acts 7:30
3:3 *Acts 7:31
3:5 Gen 28:17; Josh 5:15; *Acts 7:33
3:6 *Matt 22:32; *Mark 12:26; *Luke 20:37; *Acts 3:13; 7:32
3:7 *Acts 7:34
3:8 Gen 15:18-19; 46:4; 50:24; Exod 3:17; Deut 6:3; 8:7-9; 11:9; 26:9
3:10 *Acts 7:34
3:11 Exod 4:10; 6:12
3:12 Exod 4:12; 19:2; *Acts 7:7
3:13 Exod 15:3

2 There the angel of the LORD appeared to him in a blazing fire from the middle of a bush.
Moses stared in amazement. Though the bush was engulfed in flames, it didn't burn up.
3 "This is amazing," Moses said to himself. "Why isn't that bush burning up? I must go see it."
4 When the LORD saw Moses coming to take a closer look, God called to him from the
middle of the bush, "Moses! Moses!"
"Here I am!" Moses replied.
5 "Do not come any closer," the LORD warned. "Take off your sandals, for you are stand-
ing on holy ground. 6 I am the God of your father*—the God of Abraham, the God of Isaac,
and the God of Jacob." When Moses heard this, he covered his face because he was afraid
to look at God.
7 Then the LORD told him, "I have certainly seen the oppression of My people in Egypt. I
have heard their cries of distress because of their harsh slave drivers. Yes, I am aware of
their suffering. 8 So I have come down to rescue them from the power of the Egyptians and
lead them out of Egypt into their own fertile and spacious land. It is a land flowing with
milk and honey—the land where the Canaanites, Hittites, Amorites, Perizzites, Hivites, and
Jebusites now live. 9 Look! The cry of the people of Israel has reached Me, and I have seen
how harshly the Egyptians abuse them. 10 Now go, for I am sending you to Pharaoh. You
must lead My people Israel out of Egypt."
11 But Moses protested to God, "Who am I to appear before Pharaoh? Who am I to lead
the people of Israel out of Egypt?"
12 God answered, "I will be with you. And this is your sign that I am the One who has sent
you: When you have brought the people out of Egypt, you will worship God at this very
mountain."
13 But Moses protested, "If I go to the people of Israel and tell them, 'The God of your

3:6 Greek version reads *your fathers.*

3:2 The angel of the Lord was God's authoritative messenger and representative. The Bible commonly does not distinguish clearly between the angel of the Lord and the Lord Himself (compare Exodus 3:6). For this reason, many believe that the angel of the Lord was the pre-incarnate Christ, the Son of God. The presence of the angel of the Lord indicates that God Himself was taking an active hand in directing the course of history and in communicating His will to His people.

3:5 The story of the burning bush continues Moses' theme of how to approach a holy God. The removal of sandals (made from the skin of dead animals) was an ancient custom for ensuring that holy places were not defiled. In this case, the spot was made sacred by God's presence (see Exodus 19:23; 24:2). In Moses' writings, this theme reaches its climax in the cleansing of the Holy Land and the settling of God's people (and God's presence, via the Tabernacle), but modern readers can see it continuing far past Moses' time, into the New Testament and the ministry of Jesus, who made peace between unclean, rebellious humanity and a holy God (Romans 5:1).

3:6 The angel of the Lord (Exodus 3:2) speaks as if he is God Himself. This either means that the angel was a physical manifestation of the invisible God (Colossians 1:15) or was an ambassador of God that represented Him to such a degree that he could speak using the first person pronoun. Regardless, Moses clearly believed the angel should be addressed as God.

3:7 Throughout Genesis, the covenant people of God had been identified as those descending from Abraham, through his son Isaac, and through Isaac's son Jacob (Exodus 3:6, 15). Because Israel descended from Jacob, they were in covenant with God. This did not mean they had eternal life, but that they lived under the law of God, with certain responsibilities and promised blessings. Unsaved children who live in a Christian home are in a similar situation today (Romans 11:16; 1 Corinthians 7:14).

3:8 The land identified here had been promised to Abraham as a perpetual inheritance (Genesis 15:18-21). It was commonly known as Canaan and in Scripture is often referred to as the Promised Land. The people groups mentioned here were descendants of early Canaanites.

3:12 The evidence God offered to counter Moses' doubt was that He would be faithful to do the impossible—lead the slave-nation of Israel back to this site. God's faithfulness and power were manifested as the Hebrews worshiped at Sinai in Exodus 19–24.

3:13-16 God's covenant with Abraham, Isaac, and Jacob involved turning their small clan into a great nation. God told Abraham that his descendants would be slaves for 400 years, but that God would free His people from this slavery (Genesis 15:13-14). By identifying Himself as the God of these three men, the Lord assured Moses that the time of their slavery was coming to an end, and that the one who had made them into a nation would also free them to serve Him.

3:13 Moses negotiated with God, and God honored Moses' objection. Throughout the Bible godly men frequently objected to God's stated intentions, and God often responded by accommodating them (compare Genesis 18:16-33; 19; Exodus 4:1-17).

ancestors has sent me to you,' they will ask me, 'What is His name?' Then what should I
tell them?"
14 God replied to Moses, "I AM WHO I AM.* Say this to the people of Israel: I AM has sent
me to you." 15 God also said to Moses, "Say this to the people of Israel: Yahweh,* the God of
your ancestors—the God of Abraham, the God of Isaac, and the God of Jacob—has sent me
to you.

This is My eternal name,
  My name to remember for all generations.

16 "Now go and call together all the elders of Israel. Tell them, 'The LORD, the God of your
ancestors—the God of Abraham, Isaac, and Jacob—has appeared to me. He told me, "I
have been watching closely, and I see how the Egyptians are treating you. 17 I have prom-
ised to rescue you from your oppression in Egypt. I will lead you to a land flowing with
milk and honey—the land where the Canaanites, Hittites, Amorites, Perizzites, Hivites, and
Jebusites now live."'
18 "The elders of Israel will accept your message. Then you and the elders must go to the
king of Egypt and tell him, 'The LORD, the God of the Hebrews, has met with us. So please let
us take a three-day journey into the wilderness to offer sacrifices to the LORD, our God.'
19 "But I know that the king of Egypt will not let you go unless a mighty hand forces him.*
20 So I will raise My hand and strike the Egyptians, performing all kinds of miracles among
them. Then at last he will let you go. 21 And I will cause the Egyptians to look favorably on
you. They will give you gifts when you go so you will not leave empty-handed. 22 Every Is-
raelite woman will ask for articles of silver and gold and fine clothing from her Egyptian
neighbors and from the foreign women in their houses. You will dress your sons and
daughters with these, stripping the Egyptians of their wealth."

3:14 Exod 6:3; John 8:58; Rev 1:8; 4:8
3:15 Pss 72:17; 102:12; 135:13; *Acts 3:13
3:16 Exod 4:29
3:17 Exod 3:8; Josh 24:11
3:18 Exod 4:23; 5:1, 3; Num 23:4, 16
3:19 Exod 5:2; 6:1; 7:4
3:20 Exod 11:1; 12:31-33; Neh 9:10; Acts 7:36
3:21 Exod 11:2-3
3:22 Exod 11:2; 12:35

SIGNS OF THE LORD'S POWER

4 But Moses protested again, "What if they won't believe me or listen to me? What if
they say, 'The LORD never appeared to you'?"
2 Then the LORD asked him, "What is that in your hand?"
"A shepherd's staff," Moses replied.

4:1 Exod 3:15-16, 18

3:14 Or *I WILL BE WHAT I WILL BE.* 3:15 *Yahweh* is a transliteration of the proper name *YHWH* that is sometimes rendered "Jehovah"; in this translation it is usually rendered "the LORD" (note the use of small capitals). 3:19 As in Greek and Latin versions; Hebrew reads *will not let you go, not by a mighty hand.*

3:14-15 God's special covenant name indicates that God is consistently the same God throughout history. Because His character does not change, He always remains faithful to His covenant. For this reason, Moses and the Israelites could have confidence that God would fight for them just as He had fought for their ancestors Abraham, Isaac, and Jacob (compare Malachi 3:6).

▸ GOD
3:14 Who is God—now? When people want you to know them, they tell you their name. God wants His people to know Him, so He's told us His name—*I AM.* This name can also be translated *I HAVE BEEN* or *I WILL BE.* This name points to God as the foundation of all that is. It also shows that knowing God means experiencing a personal relationship with Him, for if He always has been and always will be, then He certainly is where you are! Your relationship with God can only partially be aided by past experience; for your spiritual life to grow, you must experience God in the here and now. (***See God***> *God's Nature> Alive> God lives, false gods don't,* TopicGuide page A14; ***God***> *God's Attributes> Self-existent,* TopicGuide page A17; ***God***> *God's Names> God,* TopicGuide page A18.)

3:17 God repeats his promise to rescue Abraham's descendants from slavery (Genesis 15:13-16) and bring them into a blessed land. The image of "a land flowing with milk and honey" is used fifteen times in Moses' writings to speak of the fertility of Israel (Exodus 13:5; 33:3; Numbers 13:27; Deuteronomy 11:9; 31:20).

3:18 Moses' request likely intended to fulfill the sign of returning to Sinai to worship (Exodus 3:12). If the people worshiped at Sinai, it would prove that God was going to liberate them from Egypt.

3:21-22 God had promised to rescue Abraham's descendants in a way that made them wealthy (Genesis 15:14). That the Egyptians would give their wealth to Israel strongly implied to the Hebrews that a permanent release rather than a three-day journey was in their future.

4:1, 10, 13 Like many godly men in the Bible, Moses objected to things God had said. God graciously accommodated Moses by assuring Moses that He would empower him and by assigning Moses' brother Aaron to speak on Moses' behalf.

NAMES OF GOD

Name of God	Meaning	Reference	Significance
Elohim	God	Genesis 1:1; Numbers 23:19; Psalm 19:1	Refers to God's power and might. He is the only supreme and true God.
Yahweh	The LORD	Genesis 2:4 Exodus 6:2-3	The proper name of the divine Person.
El Elyon	God Most High	Genesis 14:17-20; Numbers 24:16; Psalm 7:17; Isaiah 14:13-14	He is above all gods; nothing in life is more sacred.
El Roi	God Who Sees	Genesis 16:13	God oversees all of creation and the affairs of people.
El Shaddai	God Almighty	Genesis 17:1; Psalm 91:1	God is all-powerful.
Yahweh Yireh	The LORD Will Provide	Genesis 22:14	God will provide our real needs.
Yahweh Nissi	The LORD Is My Banner	Exodus 17:15	We should remember God for helping us.
Adonai	Lord	Deuteronomy 6:4	God alone is the head over all.
Yahweh Elohe Yisrael	LORD God of Israel	Judges 5:3; Psalm 59:5; Isaiah 17:6; Zephaniah 2:9	He is the God of the nation.
Yahweh Shalom	The LORD Is Peace.	Judges 6:24	God gives us peace so we need not fear.
Qedosh Yisrael	Holy One of Israel	Isaiah 1:4	God is morally perfect.
Yahweh Sabaoth	LORD of Heaven's Armies	1 Samuel 1:3; Isaiah 6:1-3	God is our Savior and Protector. (Heaven's Armies, sometimes rendered Hosts, refers also to all the heavenly powers.)
El Olam	The Everlasting God	Isaiah 40:28-31	God is eternal. He will never die.
Yahweh Tsidkenu	The LORD Is Our Righteousness	Jeremiah 23:6; 33:16	God is our standard for good behavior. He alone can make us righteous.
Yahweh Shammah	The LORD Is There	Ezekiel 48:35	God is always present with us.
Attiq Yomin	Ancient of Days	Daniel 7:9, 13	God is the ultimate authority. He will one day judge all the nations.

3“Throw it down on the ground,” the LORD told him. So Moses threw down the staff, and
it turned into a snake! Moses jumped back.
4Then the LORD told him, “Reach out and grab its tail.” So Moses reached out and
grabbed it, and it turned back into a shepherd’s staff in his hand.
5“Perform this sign,” the LORD told him. “Then they will believe that the LORD, the God of
their ancestors—the God of Abraham, the God of Isaac, and the God of Jacob—really has
appeared to you.”
6Then the LORD said to Moses, “Now put your hand inside your cloak.” So Moses put his
hand inside his cloak, and when he took it out again, his hand was white as snow with a
severe skin disease.* 7“Now put your hand back into your cloak,” the LORD said. So Moses
put his hand back in, and when he took it out again, it was as healthy as the rest of his
body.
8The LORD said to Moses, “If they do not believe you and are not convinced by the first
miraculous sign, they will be convinced by the second sign. 9And if they don’t believe you
or listen to you even after these two signs, then take some water from the Nile River and
pour it out on the dry ground. When you do, the water from the Nile will turn to blood on
the ground.”
10But Moses pleaded with the LORD, “O Lord, I’m not very good with words. I never have
been, and I’m not now, even though You have spoken to me. I get tongue-tied, and my
words get tangled.”
11Then the LORD asked Moses, “Who makes a person’s mouth? Who decides whether
people speak or do not speak, hear or do not hear, see or do not see? Is it not I, the LORD?
12Now go! I will be with you as you speak, and I will instruct you in what to say.”
13But Moses again pleaded, “Lord, please! Send anyone else.”
14Then the LORD became angry with Moses. “All right,” He said. “What about your
brother, Aaron the Levite? I know he speaks well. And look! He is on his way to meet you
now. He will be delighted to see you. 15Talk to him, and put the words in his mouth. I will
be with both of you as you speak, and I will instruct you both in what to do. 16Aaron will be
your spokesman to the people. He will be your mouthpiece, and you will stand in the
place of God for him, telling him what to say. 17And take your shepherd’s staff with you,
and use it to perform the miraculous signs I have shown you.”

4:3 Exod 7:8-12, 15
4:5 Exod 4:31; 19:9
4:6 Num 12:10; 2 Kgs 5:27
4:7 2 Kgs 5:14; Matt 8:3; Luke 17:12-14
4:9 Exod 7:17-21
4:10 Exod 3:11; Jer 1:6
4:11 Ps 94:9; Matt 11:5
4:12 Deut 18:15, 18; Matt 10:19-20; Mark 13:11
4:14 Exod 4:27
4:15 Isa 51:16; Jer 1:9
4:16 Exod 7:1; 18:19-20
4:17 Exod 14:16; 17:9

4:6 Or *with leprosy.* The Hebrew word used here can describe various skin diseases.

4:5 Abraham, Isaac, and Jacob were the forefathers of the nation of Israel. God’s covenant with them (Exodus 2:24) was a promise that God would rescue the Israelites from 400 years of slavery and would make them into a great nation (Genesis 15:13-16). By identifying Himself as the God of these men, the Lord assured Moses and the Israelites that He was planning to keep this covenant promise by freeing them.

4:6 This condition that afflicted Moses in this passage may or may not have been Hansen’s disease, the modern illness often referred to as *leprosy.* Hansen’s disease and biblical leprosy both affected the skin, but the symptoms listed in Leviticus 13–14 do not match those of Hansen’s disease. The biblical word for *leprosy* probably referred to a variety of skin diseases and disorders, some of which were curable (Leviticus 13–14).

▸ PURPOSE

4:8 Signs and wonders. God used miracles to confirm Moses’ ministry, specifically showing that Moses’ words came directly from God (see Exodus 4:30-31). God also caused these types of signs to accompany the teaching ministries of Elijah, Elisha, and other prophets of the Old Covenant. During the ministry of Christ and His disciples, signs sent by God showed that their words were His words and were to be trusted and preserved for coming generations. (***See Purpose***> *God’s Deeds> Special Acts> Miracles,* TopicGuide page A52.)

4:10 Moses’ self-description may imply a weak voice, a speech impediment, a lack of fluency in the official language of the Egyptian court, or another verbal inability or ineptitude.

4:13-16 With no excuses left, Moses tried to simply decline God’s offer. But God was not interested in Moses’ opinion. He summoned Aaron to be Moses’ mouthpiece, and with no further discussion, Moses’ ministry began.

4:16 Aaron would speak according to Moses’ instruction, just as Moses spoke according to God’s instruction. This illumines the role of the prophet in the Bible, as the prophet is to God what Aaron was to Moses (See also 6:30; 7:1).

4:17, 20 Moses’ and Aaron’s staffs were used as the means through which they performed many miracles (compare Exodus 7:9-12, 15-20; 8:5, 16; 9:23; 10:13; 14:16; 17:5-6, 9-13). Aaron’s staff was last used by Moses in Numbers 20:9-11 and was then placed back inside the Ark of the Covenant (Hebrews 9:4).

WE TEND TO PUT CONDITIONS on our relationships. "If you look good, I will love you." "If you have lots of money, you can be part of my inner circle." "If you do this for me, I'll do that for you."

God's faithfulness, however, is unconditional. We can sometimes see that quality reflected in the godly examples of faithfulness among His people. Consider the example of Dr. J. Robertson McQuilkin. He was the well-loved president of the highly respected Columbia International University. After his wife began to show symptoms of Alzheimer's disease, McQuilkin resigned his distinguished position to care for her.

When we hear of someone who is faithful to another, as McQuilkin was to his wife, our spirit is lifted, because this kind of sacrifice is so rare. We realize that actions like these are not normal. They must originate from a higher source.

God's faithfulness is so much a part of who He is that He cannot become unfaithful to anyone. He even remains faithful to ungrateful believers and to skeptics who deny His existence. As Paul assures us, "If we are unfaithful, He remains faithful, for He cannot deny who He is" (2 Timothy 2:13). Sadly, for those who are unfaithful to God, He remains faithful to them by holding them accountable to His Law, and by disciplining them accordingly. But God is faithful to believers in a very loving way, even when we feel we have no faith left. On the night of His arrest, Jesus told Peter that he would deny Him three times. Then he added these words of encouragement, "Simon, Simon, Satan has asked to sift each of you like wheat. But I have pleaded in prayer for you, Simon, that your faith should not fail. So when you have repented and turned to Me again, strengthen your brothers" (Luke 22:31-32). Even when our hold on God is weak, His hold on us is strong.

By the time God spoke to Moses from the burning bush (Exodus 3), many Israelites must have begun to doubt God's faithfulness. They had been slaves for many years. God's promise of their own land—a promise repeated to Abraham, Isaac, and Jacob—must have seemed a distant dream. Yet God had not forgotten them. He revealed His special name, I AM, to the Israelites to remind them of His unchanging faithfulness.

God always keeps His promises or covenants—without fail. The psalmist declares, "He always stands by His covenant—the commitment He made to a thousand generations" (Psalm 105:8). That is why we can completely trust God's Word. The writer to the Hebrews encourages us: "Let us hold tightly without wavering to the hope we affirm, for God can be trusted to keep His promise" (Hebrews 10:23).

It is God's plan for his people to become holy and to advance His kingdom, and He is faithful to bring this to pass. He helps us through hard times, delivers us from temptation, forgives us when we are unfaithful, and gives us gifts to serve Him. He will leave nothing undone to bring us to a point of maturity in our Christian growth and faith. Paul declared to the Philippians, "And I am certain that God, who began the good work within you, will continue His work until it is finally finished on the day when Christ Jesus returns" (Philippians 1:6).

MOSES RETURNS TO EGYPT

18So Moses went back home to Jethro, his father-in-law. "Please let me return to my rela-
tives in Egypt," Moses said. "I don't even know if they are still alive."
"Go in peace," Jethro replied.
19Before Moses left Midian, the LORD said to him, "Return to Egypt, for all those who
wanted to kill you have died."
20So Moses took his wife and sons, put them on a donkey, and headed back to the land
of Egypt. In his hand he carried the staff of God.
21And the LORD told Moses, "When you arrive back in Egypt, go to Pharaoh and perform
all the miracles I have empowered you to do. But I will harden his heart so he will refuse to
let the people go. 22Then you will tell him, 'This is what the LORD says: Israel is My firstborn
son. 23I commanded you, "Let My son go, so he can worship Me." But since you have re-
fused, I will now kill your firstborn son!' "
24On the way to Egypt, at a place where Moses and his family had stopped for the night,
the LORD confronted him and was about to kill him. 25But Moses' wife, Zipporah, took a
flint knife and circumcised her son. She touched his feet* with the foreskin and said, "Now
you are a bridegroom of blood to me." 26(When she said "a bridegroom of blood," she was
referring to the circumcision.) After that, the LORD left him alone.
27Now the LORD had said to Aaron, "Go out into the wilderness to meet Moses." So Aaron
went and met Moses at the mountain of God, and he embraced him. 28Moses then told
Aaron everything the LORD had commanded him to say. And he told him about the mirac-
ulous signs the LORD had commanded him to perform.
29Then Moses and Aaron returned to Egypt and called all the elders of Israel together.
30Aaron told them everything the LORD had told Moses, and Moses performed the miracu-
lous signs as they watched. 31Then the people of Israel were convinced that the LORD had
sent Moses and Aaron. When they heard that the LORD was concerned about them and
had seen their misery, they bowed down and worshiped.

4:19 Exod 2:15, 23
4:20 Exod 18:3; Acts 7:29
4:21 Exod 7:3, 13; 9:12; Deut 2:30; John 12:40
4:22 Isa 63:16; 64:8; Jer 31:9; Hos 11:1; Rom 9:4
4:23 Exod 5:1; 6:11; 7:16
4:24 Num 22:22; 1 Chr 21:16
4:25-26 Josh 5:2-3
4:27 Exod 4:14
4:28 Exod 4:16
4:29 Exod 3:16
4:30 Exod 4:15
4:31 Exod 3:18; 12:27

MOSES AND AARON SPEAK TO PHARAOH

5 After this presentation to Israel's leaders, Moses and Aaron went and spoke to Pha-
raoh. They told him, "This is what the LORD, the God of Israel, says: Let My people go
so they may hold a festival in My honor in the wilderness."
2"Is that so?" retorted Pharaoh. "And who is the LORD? Why should I listen to Him and let
Israel go? I don't know the LORD, and I will not let Israel go."
3But Aaron and Moses persisted. "The God of the Hebrews has met with us," they de-
clared. "So let us take a three-day journey into the wilderness so we can offer sacrifices to
the LORD our God. If we don't, He will kill us with a plague or with the sword."
4Pharaoh replied, "Moses and Aaron, why are you distracting the people from their
tasks? Get back to work! 5Look, there are many of your people in the land, and you are
stopping them from their work."

5:1 Exod 3:18; 4:23
5:2 Exod 3:19; Job 21:15
5:3 Exod 3:18; Deut 28:21
5:4-5 Exod 1:11

4:25 The Hebrew word for "feet" may refer here to the male sex organ.

4:22-23 The firstborn, particularly the firstborn male, held a special status in ancient culture. This was true for both animals and people. The firstborn son received a double inheritance and assumed leadership of the family when his father died. The death of a firstborn was one of the greatest losses a family could experience.

4:24-26 Moses' lack of participation in the Abrahamic Covenant (Genesis 12:1-3; 15; 17:10-14) was a grave sin. Even God threatening to kill Moses' firstborn wasn't enough to move him to obedience, so Zipporah hastily intervened with a flint knife. Her angry "bridegroom of blood" (v. 26) retort was likely some sort of ironic or sarcastic comment to shame Moses for his lack of obedience.

4:25 Circumcision played a significant role in Abraham's covenant with God (Genesis 17:10-14). Other cultures also practiced circumcision (such as Egypt), but many of Israel's enemies, most notably the Philistines, did not. Moses disobeyed God in not enforcing the rite of circumcision during his leadership. Joshua immediately reinstituted it when he became the leader of Israel (Joshua 5:2-8).

5:2 Pharaoh's question concerning God's identity will be answered by the upcoming plagues that judge him, his nation, and Egypt's many deities.

MAKING BRICKS WITHOUT STRAW

5:6 Exod 3:7; 5:10, 14 [6]That same day Pharaoh sent this order to the Egyptian slave drivers and the Israelite fore-
men: [7]"Do not supply any more straw for making bricks. Make the people get it them-
5:7 Gen 11:13 selves! [8]But still require them to make the same number of bricks as before. Don't reduce
the quota. They are lazy. That's why they are crying out, 'Let us go and offer sacrifices to
our God.' [9]Load them down with more work. Make them sweat! That will teach them to lis-
ten to lies!"

[10]So the slave drivers and foremen went out and told the people: "This is what Pharaoh
says: I will not provide any more straw for you. [11]Go and get it yourselves. Find it wherever
you can. But you must produce just as many bricks as before!" [12]So the people scattered
throughout the land of Egypt in search of stubble to use as straw.

[13]Meanwhile, the Egyptian slave drivers continued to push hard. "Meet your daily quota
5:14 Isa 10:24 of bricks, just as you did when we provided you with straw!" they demanded. [14]Then they
whipped the Israelite foremen they had put in charge of the work crews. "Why haven't you
met your quotas either yesterday or today?" they demanded.

[15]So the Israelite foremen went to Pharaoh and pleaded with him. "Please don't treat
your servants like this," they begged. [16]"We are given no straw, but the slave drivers still
demand, 'Make bricks!' We are being beaten, but it isn't our fault! Your own people are to
blame!"

5:17 Exod 5:8 [17]But Pharaoh shouted, "You're just lazy! Lazy! That's why you're saying, 'Let us go and
offer sacrifices to the LORD.' [18]Now get back to work! No straw will be given to you, but you
must still produce the full quota of bricks."

[19]The Israelite foremen could see that they were in serious trouble when they were
5:21 Gen 16:5; 34:30 told, "You must not reduce the number of bricks you make each day." [20]As they left Pha-
raoh's court, they confronted Moses and Aaron, who were waiting outside for them.
5:22 Num 11:11 Jer 4:10 [21]The foremen said to them, "May the LORD judge and punish you for making us stink
before Pharaoh and his officials. You have put a sword into their hands, an excuse to kill
5:23 Exod 3:8 us!"

[22]Then Moses went back to the LORD and protested, "Why have You brought all this
trouble on Your own people, Lord? Why did You send me? [23]Ever since I came to Pharaoh
as Your spokesman, he has been even more brutal to Your people. And You have done
nothing to rescue them!"

PROMISES OF DELIVERANCE

6:1 Exod 3:19-20; 11:1; 12:31 **6** Then the LORD told Moses, "Now you will see what I will do to Pharaoh. When he feels
the force of My strong hand, he will let the people go. In fact, he will force them to
leave his land!"

5:7-9 Bricks made from the mud of the Nile required straw to achieve maximum strength. The ruins of Pithom, an Egyptian city built around the time of Hebrew enslavement (Exodus 1:11), has at its lowest layers bricks made with straw. Above these, archeologists found layers made with stubble while the highest levels include bricks made with no straw (*Tyndale Bible Dictionary*, p. 1045).

▸ ADOPTION

5:19-23 Complaining and its consequences. What's the harm of telling those around us how awful things are? The people complained to Moses and Aaron about their circumstances, leading Moses to doubt God's goodness ("Why have You brought all this trouble on Your own people, Lord?") and to question God's call on his life ("Why did You send me?"). The people's refusal to trust in God's deliverance from Egypt led to paralyzing discouragement (Exodus 6:9). Instead of complaining, God's people should speak to one another with words seasoned by grace and faith in God's promises (Ephesians 4:29; Colossians 3:16-17; 4:6). (***See Adoption**> With Christ> Supernatural> Speak godly words,* TopicGuide page A37.)

5:22-23 Throughout the Bible God's people came to him with questions similar to Moses' protests. Moses' successor Joshua questioned God on behalf of His people as they faced battles in settling the land (Joshua 7:7). The great prophet Elijah questioned God (1 Kings 17:20). On the cross, even Jesus asked God, "Why have You abandoned Me?" (Matthew 27:46). Sometimes these questions and protestations are part of God's plan to change His revealed course of action (compare Genesis 18:25-33; Numbers 11:11-23; Amos 7:2, 5).

2And God said to Moses, "I am Yahweh—'the LORD.'* 3I appeared to Abraham, to Isaac,
and to Jacob as El-Shaddai—'God Almighty'*—but I did not reveal My name, Yahweh, to
them. 4And I reaffirmed My covenant with them. Under its terms, I promised to give them
the land of Canaan, where they were living as foreigners. 5You can be sure that I have
heard the groans of the people of Israel, who are now slaves to the Egyptians. And I am
well aware of My covenant with them.
6"Therefore, say to the people of Israel: 'I am the LORD. I will free you from your oppres-
sion and will rescue you from your slavery in Egypt. I will redeem you with a powerful arm
and great acts of judgment. 7I will claim you as My own people, and I will be your God.
Then you will know that I am the LORD your God who has freed you from your oppression
in Egypt. 8I will bring you into the land I swore to give to Abraham, Isaac, and Jacob. I will
give it to you as your very own possession. I am the LORD!'"
9So Moses told the people of Israel what the LORD had said, but they refused to listen
anymore. They had become too discouraged by the brutality of their slavery.
10Then the LORD said to Moses, 11"Go back to Pharaoh, the king of Egypt, and tell him to
let the people of Israel leave his country."
12"But LORD!" Moses objected. "My own people won't listen to me anymore. How can I
expect Pharaoh to listen? I'm such a clumsy speaker!*"
13But the LORD spoke to Moses and Aaron and gave them orders for the Israelites and for
Pharaoh, the king of Egypt. The LORD commanded Moses and Aaron to lead the people of
Israel out of Egypt.

THE ANCESTORS OF MOSES AND AARON

14These are the ancestors of some of the clans of Israel:

The sons of Reuben, Israel's oldest son, were Hanoch, Pallu, Hezron, and Carmi. Their
descendants became the clans of Reuben.
15The sons of Simeon were Jemuel, Jamin, Ohad, Jakin, Zohar, and Shaul. (Shaul's
mother was a Canaanite woman.) Their descendants became the clans of Simeon.
16These are the descendants of Levi, as listed in their family records: The sons of Levi
were Gershon, Kohath, and Merari. (Levi lived to be 137 years old.)

6:2 Exod 3:14-15
6:3 Gen 17:1; Ps 83:18; Isa 52:6
6:4 Gen 15:18
6:5 Exod 2:23-24
6:6 Exod 3:17; 13:3, 14; Deut 6:12; 26:8
6:7 Exod 16:12; Deut 4:20; Isa 60:16
6:8 Num 14:30; Josh 24:13
6:11 Exod 5:1; 7:2
6:12 Exod 4:10; 6:30
6:14 Gen 46:9; Num 26:5-11
6:15 Gen 46:10
6:16 Gen 46:11; Num 3:17; 1 Chr 6:1, 16-19

6:2 *Yahweh* is a transliteration of the proper name *YHWH* that is sometimes rendered "Jehovah"; in this translation it is usually rendered "the LORD" (note the use of small capitals). 6:3 *El-Shaddai,* which means "God Almighty," is the name for God used in Gen 17:1; 28:3; 35:11; 43:14; 48:3. 6:12 Hebrew *I have uncircumcised lips;* also in 6:30.

6:3 God revealed Himself to Abraham, Isaac, and Jacob primarily as *God Almighty* (Genesis 17:1; 28:3; 35:11; 48:3). Abraham, Isaac, and Jacob knew God's special covenant name *Yahweh,* usually translated *LORD* (Genesis 15:2, 8; 21:33; 22:14), but evidently God did not reveal the full form or meaning of that name to them as He revealed it to Moses (Exodus 3:14).

▸ GOD
6:3 God reveals Himself. When we talk about learning a great deal in a brief period of time, we say it's like *drinking water through a fire hydrant.* We may feel frustrated that God reveals Himself only a little at a time, but He knows that we would be overwhelmed otherwise. Abraham, Isaac, and Jacob may never have had as complete a revelation of God as Moses did. Nevertheless, their partial view of God was accurate and sufficient for salvation. Make it your goal to take whatever you know about God and, by His grace, apply it to your life. (***See God> God's Attributes> Merciful,*** TopicGuide page A17.)

6:4 In Moses' day, the land of Canaan had roughly the same borders as the modern nation of Israel and was initially settled by the descendants of Noah's grandson Canaan (Genesis 10:15-19). Abraham moved to Canaan at the Lord's direction (Genesis 12:1-9). Apart from a brief stay in Egypt (Genesis 12:10–13:1), Abraham and his descendants lived there until they relocated to Egypt during the time of Joseph (Genesis 47:11).

6:5-8 The Lord was faithful to redeem Israel from slavery because of the covenant He had made with Abraham (Genesis 15:13-16) and confirmed with Isaac (Genesis 26:24-25) and Jacob (Genesis 28:13-15).

6:12 Despite the fact that the Lord had not yet redeemed Israel as Moses had expected, He still required Moses to obey Him faithfully. The Lord did not rebuke Moses' discouragement but offered renewed encouragement (Exodus 7:1-5).

6:14-30 This record provides the genealogy for Aaron and Moses in order to establish them as legitimate leaders within Israel. Levi's descendants are also mentioned in order to establish a historical record of the legitimate priestly families (Exodus 28:1). Genealogies typically listed sons from oldest to youngest. The genealogy begins with Reuben and Simeon because they were older than Levi (Genesis 35:23).

6:17 Num 3:18-20 17The descendants of Gershon included Libni and Shimei, each of whom became
1 Chr 6:17 the ancestor of a clan.
6:18 18The descendants of Kohath included Amram, Izhar, Hebron, and Uzziel. (Kohath
Num 3:25-30 lived to be 133 years old.)
1 Chr 6:2, 18 19The descendants of Merari included Mahli and Mushi.
6:19 1 Chr 6:19 These are the clans of the Levites, as listed in their family records.

6:20 Exod 2:1-2 20Amram married his father's sister Jochebed, and she gave birth to his sons, Aaron and
Num 26:59 Moses. (Amram lived to be 137 years old.)
6:21 21The sons of Izhar were Korah, Nepheg, and Zicri.
Num 16:1 22The sons of Uzziel were Mishael, Elzaphan, and Sithri.
6:22 Lev 10:4 23Aaron married Elisheba, the daughter of Amminadab and sister of Nahshon, and she
gave birth to his sons, Nadab, Abihu, Eleazar, and Ithamar.
6:23 Ruth 4:19-20 24The sons of Korah were Assir, Elkanah, and Abiasaph. Their descendants became the
clans of Korah.
6:24 1 Chr 6:22-23, 37 25Eleazar son of Aaron married one of the daughters of Putiel, and she gave birth to his
son, Phinehas.
6:25 Num 25:7, 11 Josh 24:33 These are the ancestors of the Levite families, listed according to their clans.

26The Aaron and Moses named in this list are the same ones to whom the LORD said,
6:26 Exod 6:13 "Lead the people of Israel out of the land of Egypt like an army." 27It was Moses and Aaron
6:29 who spoke to Pharaoh, the king of Egypt, about leading the people of Israel out of Egypt.
Exod 6:2, 6, 8; 7:2 28When the LORD spoke to Moses in the land of Egypt, 29He said to him, "I am the
6:30 Exod 4:10; 6:12 LORD! Tell Pharaoh, the king of Egypt, everything I am telling you." 30But Moses argued
with the LORD, saying, "I can't do it! I'm such a clumsy speaker! Why should Pharaoh lis-
ten to me?"

AARON'S STAFF BECOMES A SERPENT

7:1 **7** Then the LORD said to Moses, "Pay close attention to this. I will make you seem like
Exod 4:16 God to Pharaoh, and your brother, Aaron, will be your prophet. 2Tell Aaron every-
thing I command you, and Aaron must command Pharaoh to let the people of Israel leave
7:3 Exod 4:21 his country. 3But I will make Pharaoh's heart stubborn so I can multiply My miraculous
7:4 signs and wonders in the land of Egypt. 4Even then Pharaoh will refuse to listen to you. So I
Exod 11:9 will bring down My fist on Egypt. Then I will rescue My forces—My people, the Israelites—
7:5 from the land of Egypt with great acts of judgment. 5When I raise My powerful hand and
Exod 8:19 bring out the Israelites, the Egyptians will know that I am the LORD."
7:7 6So Moses and Aaron did just as the LORD had commanded them. 7Moses was eighty
Deut 34:7 Acts 7:23, 30 years old, and Aaron was eighty-three when they made their demands to Pharaoh.
7:9 8Then the LORD said to Moses and Aaron, 9"Pharaoh will demand, 'Show me a miracle.'
Exod 4:3 When he does this, say to Aaron, 'Take your staff and throw it down in front of Pharaoh,
Isa 7:11 and it will become a serpent.*'"

7:9 Hebrew *tannin,* which elsewhere refers to a sea monster. Greek version translates it "dragon."

7:1 Moses would seem like God because of the miracles he would accomplish (Exodus 7:3-4). God's prophets were His authoritative representatives who spoke in His stead. Aaron would resemble a prophet in that he would speak in Moses' stead.

7:3-5 According to God's covenant with Abraham, the Egyptians deserved God's severe judgment because they had oppressed and enslaved Abraham's descendants (Genesis 15:13-14). God chose to make an example of the Egyptians in order that Egypt and all other nations would recognize and fear God's power, and thereby treat His people well (compare Leviticus 26:45; Numbers 24:8-9; Joshua 2:9-11).

7:7 Moses had spent 40 years in Midian (Acts 7:30) before God called him back to Egypt. Therefore, he had been about 40 years old when he had fled Egypt, since he is said to be 80 years old at the time of his confrontation with Pharaoh. After the Exodus from Egypt, Moses led the Israelites for 40 years in the wilderness (Deuteronomy 8:2), so that he was 120 years old when the people were allowed to enter the Promised Land (Deuteronomy 31:1-3).

10So Moses and Aaron went to Pharaoh and did what the LORD had commanded
them. Aaron threw down his staff before Pharaoh and his officials, and it became a
serpent! 11Then Pharaoh called in his own wise men and sorcerers, and these Egyp-
tian magicians did the same thing with their magic. 12They threw down their staffs,
which also became serpents! But then Aaron's staff swallowed up their staffs. 13Pha-
raoh's heart, however, remained hard. He still refused to listen, just as the LORD had
predicted.

7:11 Gen 41:8; Exod 8:7, 18; 2 Tim 3:8-9
7:13 Exod 4:21

A PLAGUE OF BLOOD

14Then the LORD said to Moses, "Pharaoh's heart is stubborn,* and he still refuses to let the
people go. 15So go to Pharaoh in the morning as he goes down to the river. Stand on the
bank of the Nile and meet him there. Be sure to take along the staff that turned into a
snake. 16Then announce to him, 'The LORD, the God of the Hebrews, has sent me to tell
you, "Let My people go, so they can worship Me in the wilderness." Until now, you have
refused to listen to Him. 17So this is what the LORD says: "I will show you that I am the
LORD." Look! I will strike the water of the Nile with this staff in my hand, and the river will
turn to blood. 18The fish in it will die, and the river will stink. The Egyptians will not be able
to drink any water from the Nile.'"
19Then the LORD said to Moses: "Tell Aaron, 'Take your staff and raise your hand over
the waters of Egypt—all its rivers, canals, ponds, and all the reservoirs. Turn all the water to
blood. Everywhere in Egypt the water will turn to blood, even the water stored in wooden
bowls and stone pots.'"
20So Moses and Aaron did just as the LORD commanded them. As Pharaoh and all of his
officials watched, Aaron raised his staff and struck the water of the Nile. Suddenly, the
whole river turned to blood! 21The fish in the river died, and the water became so foul that
the Egyptians couldn't drink it. There was blood everywhere throughout the land of Egypt.
22But again the magicians of Egypt used their magic, and they, too, turned water into
blood. So Pharaoh's heart remained hard. He refused to listen to Moses and Aaron, just as
the LORD had predicted. 23Pharaoh returned to his palace and put the whole thing out of
his mind. 24Then all the Egyptians dug along the riverbank to find drinking water, for they
couldn't drink the water from the Nile.
25Seven days passed from the time the LORD struck the Nile.

7:14 Exod 8:15
7:15 Exod 2:5; 8:20
7:16 Exod 4:23
7:17 Rev 11:6; 16:4
7:19 Exod 14:21
7:20 Pss 78:44; 105:29
7:22 Exod 8:7

7:14 Hebrew *heavy*.

7:10-12 Ancient kings often sought advice from wise men or magicians. Here, Pharaoh's own wise men and magicians used sorcery to duplicate the Lord's miracle. The Lord demonstrated his superiority by causing Aaron's staff to devour those of Pharaoh's counselors. This special staff was instrumental in many miracles (compare Exodus 4:17; 7:15-20; 8:5, 16; 9:23; 10:13; 14:16; 17:5-6, 9-13).

▸ GOD
7:14 Killing and kindness. Does God make good things come from bad circumstances? When the Egyptians sinned against God's command, they exposed themselves to the punishment God had been mercifully withholding. By changing the Nile, a symbol of life, into a symbol of death, God established that the Egyptians should trust in Him alone for salvation. God's judgment or discipline often forms the basis for God's mercy. Look at the serious consequences in your life and in those around you and ask, "How is God showing mercy through this?" You will be surprised. (***See God**> God's Attributes> Merciful> God is merciful according to His own purposes,* TopicGuide page A17.)

7:18 Any threat against the Nile River, which sustained human existence in northeast Africa, was taken seriously. When the Nile flooded each year, the water softened the ground and washed rich silt onto its surface. It also provided drinking water for the region.

7:19-21 The first plague destroyed all the water in Egypt, not just the Nile. Even water in drinking vessels within homes was corrupted (v. 19). But the water was probably not turned entirely to blood, but rather was corrupted by blood, since Exodus 7:24 suggests that the water of the Nile could be filtered through the earth in order to purify it sufficiently for human consumption.

7:22 Again, the magicians counterfeited God's miracle (compare Exodus 7:12; 8:7). However, they were still defeated because they were not able to reverse the plague by creating clean water. Their efforts only compounded the problem.

THE PLAGUES ON EGYPT

Reference	Plague	What Happened	Result
7:14-24	Blood	Fish die, the river smells, the people are without water	Pharaoh's magicians duplicate the miracle by "their magic," and Pharaoh is unmoved
8:1-15	Frogs	Frogs come up from the water and completely cover the land	Again, Pharaoh's magicians duplicate the miracle by sorcery, and Pharaoh is unmoved
8:16-19	Gnats	All the dust of Egypt becomes a massive swarm of gnats	Magicians are unable to duplicate this; they say it is the "finger of God," but Pharaoh's heart remains hard
8:20-32	Flies	Swarms of flies cover the land	Pharaoh promises to let the Hebrews go but then hardens his heart and refuses
9:1-7	Livestock	All the Egyptian livestock die—but none of Israel's is even sick	Pharaoh still refuses to let the people go
9:8-12	Boils	Horrible boils break out on everyone in Egypt	Magicians cannot respond because they are struck down with boils as well—Pharaoh refuses to listen
9:13-35	Hail	Hailstorms kill all the slaves and animals left out or unprotected and strip or destroy almost every plant	Pharaoh admits his sin but then changes his mind and refuses to let Israel go
10:1-20	Locusts	Locusts cover Egypt and eat everything left after the hail	Everyone advises Pharaoh to let the Hebrews go, but God hardens Pharaoh's heart and he refuses
10:21-29	Darkness	Total darkness covers Egypt for three days so no one can even move—except the Hebrews, who have light as usual	Pharaoh again promises to let Israel go but again changes his mind
11:1–12:33	Death of Firstborn	The firstborn of all the people and cattle of Egypt die—but Israel is spared	Pharaoh and the Egyptians urge Israel to leave quickly; after they are gone, Pharaoh again changes his mind and chases after them

A PLAGUE OF FROGS

8:1 Exod 5:1 **8** 1*Then the LORD said to Moses, "Go back to Pharaoh and announce to him, 'This is
what the LORD says: Let My people go, so they can worship Me. 2If you refuse to let
8:2 Ps 105:30 them go, I will send a plague of frogs across your entire land. 3The Nile River will swarm
with frogs. They will come up out of the river and into your palace, even into your bed-
room and onto your bed! They will enter the houses of your officials and your people.

8:1 Verses 8:1-4 are numbered 7:26-29 in Hebrew text.

8:2-6 In Egypt, frogs were a symbol of life and birth; Heqet, the Egyptian goddess of birth, was depicted with a frog's head. Under the Lord's influence, their pagan symbol became an instrument of judgment. Moses and Aaron's special staff continued to be featured prominently (compare Exodus 4:17; 7:9-12, 15-20; 8:16; 9:23; 10:13; 14:16; 17:5-6, 9-13).

They will even jump into your ovens and your kneading bowls. 4Frogs will jump on you, your people, and all your officials.' "

5*Then the LORD said to Moses, "Tell Aaron, 'Raise the staff in your hand over all the rivers, canals, and ponds of Egypt, and bring up frogs over all the land.' " 6So Aaron raised his hand over the waters of Egypt, and frogs came up and covered the whole land! 7But the magicians were able to do the same thing with their magic. They, too, caused frogs to come up on the land of Egypt.

8Then Pharaoh summoned Moses and Aaron and begged, "Plead with the LORD to take the frogs away from me and my people. I will let your people go, so they can offer sacrifices to the LORD."

9"You set the time!" Moses replied. "Tell me when you want me to pray for you, your officials, and your people. Then you and your houses will be rid of the frogs. They will remain only in the Nile River."

10"Do it tomorrow," Pharaoh said.

"All right," Moses replied, "it will be as you have said. Then you will know that there is no one like the LORD our God. 11The frogs will leave you and your houses, your officials, and your people. They will remain only in the Nile River."

12So Moses and Aaron left Pharaoh's palace, and Moses cried out to the LORD about the frogs He had inflicted on Pharaoh. 13And the LORD did just what Moses had predicted. The frogs in the houses, the courtyards, and the fields all died. 14The Egyptians piled them into great heaps, and a terrible stench filled the land. 15But when Pharaoh saw that relief had come, he became stubborn.* He refused to listen to Moses and Aaron, just as the LORD had predicted.

A PLAGUE OF GNATS

16So the LORD said to Moses, "Tell Aaron, 'Raise your staff and strike the ground. The dust will turn into swarms of gnats throughout the land of Egypt.' " 17So Moses and Aaron did just as the LORD had commanded them. When Aaron raised his hand and struck the ground with his staff, gnats infested the entire land, covering the Egyptians and their animals. All the dust in the land of Egypt turned into gnats. 18Pharaoh's magicians tried to do the same thing with their secret arts, but this time they failed. And the gnats covered everyone, people and animals alike.

8:5 Exod 7:9-20
8:6 Pss 78:45; 105:30
8:7 Exod 7:11
8:10 Exod 9:14; 15:11 Deut 4:35 Isa 46:9
8:12 Exod 8:30; 9:33; 10:18
8:15 Exod 7:14 Eccl 8:11
8:16 Exod 4:2
8:17 Ps 105:31
8:18 Exod 7:11; 9:11

8:5 Verses 8:5-32 are numbered 8:1-28 in Hebrew text. **8:15** Hebrew *made his heart heavy;* also in 8:32.

8:7 As with the snakes and the blood, the magicians duplicated Moses' efforts (compare Exodus 7:12, 22). Again, however, they only succeeded in worsening Egypt's condition.

8:8 For the first time, Pharaoh recognized that even though his magicians could duplicate the curse, the true source of the plague was the Lord.

8:9-15 Moses allowed Pharaoh to designate his own sign from God. The sign was given as requested, increasing Pharaoh's obligation to repent and to obey God. Nevertheless, Pharaoh did not relent.

▸ ADOPTION
8:15 Hardening of the heart. In the account of the plagues, Pharaoh is described as hardening his own heart (NLT "became stubborn"; see also Exodus 8:15, 32) and as having his heart hardened by God (Exodus 9:12; 10:20). In both cases, the result was a stubborn hatred toward God and His people. Perhaps these were two separate processes, but they may also be two different perspectives on the same event. It may well be that the first perspective represents a human viewpoint, and the second, God's. But whether these texts speak of one or two processes, it is still true that Pharaoh freely chose to disobey God, while God withdrew His protective grace from Pharaoh, exposing him to the soul-shattering consequences of his rebellion. We all face choices in life; Pharaoh clearly chose a path of doom. You must choose to keep your heart open to God and to fill your heart with love for God and others (Deuteronomy 6:5; 15:7-11). (***See Adoption***> *Without Christ*> *Separated from God*> *Bad spiritual heart,* TopicGuide page A36.)

8:16 Gnats were any of a variety of small insects. Some translations call these insects *lice*, but lice don't travel in swarms that would rise out of the dust. More than likely, these gnats were small flies or even the smallest members of the mosquito family. The sand fly is a likely candidate because its bite is painful, it swarms quietly, and only the finest netting can deter it.

8:18-19 For the first time, the magicians were not able to duplicate the miracle. They rightly interpreted their failure as proof that the God of the Israelites had caused the plague. It is unclear whether or not Pharaoh believed, as did the magicians, that the Lord was responsible for the plague.

8:19 Exod 7:5 19 "This is the finger of God!" the magicians exclaimed to Pharaoh. But Pharaoh's heart
1 Sam 6:9 remained hard. He wouldn't listen to them, just as the LORD had predicted.

A PLAGUE OF FLIES

8:20 Exod 7:15 20 Then the LORD told Moses, "Get up early in the morning and stand in Pharaoh's way
as he goes down to the river. Say to him, 'This is what the LORD says: Let My people go,
so they can worship Me. 21 If you refuse, then I will send swarms of flies on you, your
officials, your people, and all the houses. The Egyptian homes will be filled with flies,
8:22 and the ground will be covered with them. 22 But this time I will spare the region of
Exod 9:4; 10:23 Goshen, where My people live. No flies will be found there. Then you will know that I
am the LORD and that I am present even in the heart of your land. 23 I will make a clear
distinction between* My people and your people. This miraculous sign will happen
tomorrow.'"

8:24 24 And the LORD did just as He had said. A thick swarm of flies filled Pharaoh's palace
Pss 78:45; 105:31 and the houses of his officials. The whole land of Egypt was thrown into chaos by the
flies.

8:25 25 Pharaoh called for Moses and Aaron. "All right! Go ahead and offer sacrifices to your
Exod 8:8; 10:8 God," he said. "But do it here in this land."

26 But Moses replied, "That wouldn't be right. The Egyptians detest the sacrifices that we
offer to the LORD our God. Look, if we offer our sacrifices here where the Egyptians can see
8:27 Exod 3:18 us, they will stone us. 27 We must take a three-day trip into the wilderness to offer sacrifices
to the LORD our God, just as He has commanded us."

8:28 28 "All right, go ahead," Pharaoh replied. "I will let you go into the wilderness to offer sac-
Exod 8:8 rifices to the LORD your God. But don't go too far away. Now hurry and pray for me."

29 Moses answered, "As soon as I leave you, I will pray to the LORD, and tomorrow the
swarms of flies will disappear from you and your officials and all your people. But I am
warning you, Pharaoh, don't lie to us again and refuse to let the people go to sacrifice to
the LORD."

8:30 30 So Moses left Pharaoh's palace and pleaded with the LORD to remove all the flies.
Exod 8:12 31 And the LORD did as Moses asked and caused the swarms of flies to disappear from Pha-
8:32 Exod 8:8, 15 raoh, his officials, and his people. Not a single fly remained. 32 But Pharaoh again became
stubborn and refused to let the people go.

8:23 As in Greek and Latin versions; Hebrew reads *I will set redemption between.*

8:21 The Hebrew word translated here as *flies* is a generic term for many kinds of winged insects from houseflies to butterflies, mosquitoes, and dragonflies. The area around Palestine was inhabited by houseflies, horseflies, botflies (which infect livestock), and tsetse flies. These insects were both a nuisance and a source of infection and disease.

8:22-23 When Joseph's family came to live in Egypt, Joseph obtained permission for them to settle in Goshen in northern Egypt (Genesis 47:1-11). It was green, fertile land, excellent for raising herds. Several plagues that affected Egypt did not affect the Israelites in Goshen: flies, diseased livestock, hail, and darkness. The death of the firstborn did not affect the Israelites that placed blood on their doorposts (Exodus 12:13). By exempting the Israelites from the plagues, the Lord demonstrated that their God was sending the curses.

▸ HOLINESS

8:24 Divinely appointed suffering. Has suffering ever motivated you to cling to God and to love Him more deeply than you did before? God sometimes allows suffering to direct us to repent of our sins and to turn to Him for comfort. In these passages, God was directing the Egyptians to abandon their faith in false gods and to cease their brutal enslavement of His chosen people. What is the sharpest point of suffering in your life? Are you going to God for comfort? (***See Holiness*****>** *Submission***>** *Identifying with Christ***>** *Suffering with Him,* TopicGuide page A40.)

8:25-32 Apparently, Pharaoh rightly recognized that Moses' God was sending the curses, and that God would listen to Moses' petition to withdraw the curse. He probably did not, however, rightly measure the Lord's power, as he reneged on his agreement to permit the Israelites' worship.

8:26 The Israelite form of sacrificial worship involved slaying cattle, sheep, and in some cases smaller animals such as birds. The specific practice that might have offended the Egyptians is unknown, although it may have been related to the Egyptians' disgust for shepherds (Genesis 46:34).

8:32 Pharaoh may have changed his mind about the Lord's involvement in the plagues. He also may have believed that the Lord's power was insufficient to do further or long-term damage. More likely, he simply acted out of defiance.

A PLAGUE AGAINST LIVESTOCK

9 "Go back to Pharaoh," the LORD commanded Moses. "Tell him, 'This is what the
LORD, the God of the Hebrews, says: Let My people go, so they can worship Me. 2If
you continue to hold them and refuse to let them go, 3the hand of the LORD will strike all
your livestock—your horses, donkeys, camels, cattle, sheep, and goats—with a deadly
plague. 4But the LORD will again make a distinction between the livestock of the Israelites
and that of the Egyptians. Not a single one of Israel's animals will die! 5The LORD has al-
ready set the time for the plague to begin. He has declared that He will strike the land to-
morrow.'"
6And the LORD did just as He had said. The next morning all the livestock of the
Egyptians died, but the Israelites didn't lose a single animal. 7Pharaoh sent his offi-
cials to investigate, and they discovered that the Israelites had not lost a single ani-
mal! But even so, Pharaoh's heart remained stubborn,* and he still refused to let the
people go.

A PLAGUE OF FESTERING BOILS

8Then the LORD said to Moses and Aaron, "Take handfuls of soot from a brick kiln, and
have Moses toss it into the air while Pharaoh watches. 9The ashes will spread like fine dust
over the whole land of Egypt, causing festering boils to break out on people and animals
throughout the land."
10So they took soot from a brick kiln and went and stood before Pharaoh. As Pharaoh
watched, Moses threw the soot into the air, and boils broke out on people and animals
alike. 11Even the magicians were unable to stand before Moses, because the boils had
broken out on them and all the Egyptians. 12But the LORD hardened Pharaoh's heart, and
just as the LORD had predicted to Moses, Pharaoh refused to listen.

A PLAGUE OF HAIL

13Then the LORD said to Moses, "Get up early in the morning and stand before Pharaoh.
Tell him, 'This is what the LORD, the God of the Hebrews, says: Let My people go, so they
can worship Me. 14If you don't, I will send more plagues on you* and your officials and
your people. Then you will know that there is no one like Me in all the earth. 15By now I
could have lifted My hand and struck you and your people with a plague to wipe you off
the face of the earth. 16But I have spared you for a purpose—to show you My power* and
to spread My fame throughout the earth. 17But you still lord it over My people and re-
fuse to let them go. 18So tomorrow at this time I will send a hailstorm more devastating

9:1 Exod 8:1; 10:3
9:3 Exod 7:4
9:4 Exod 8:23; 9:26
9:7 Exod 7:14; 8:32
9:9 Lev 13:18; Rev 16:2
9:11 Exod 8:18
9:12 Exod 4:21
9:13 Exod 8:20
9:14 Exod 8:10; 15:11
9:16 Exod 14:4, 17; *Rom 9:17
9:18 Exod 9:23-24

9:7 Hebrew *heavy.* 9:14 Hebrew *on your heart.* 9:16 Greek version reads *to display My power in you;* compare Rom 9:17.

9:2 The plagues on Egypt were contingent upon Pharaoh's continued disobedience. Pharaoh always retained the opportunity to repent and to submit to God's demands. Had he submitted, the plagues would have ended. However, this was contrary to God's plan (Exodus 4:21; 9:16), and so the Lord hardened Pharaoh against compliance with Moses' demands (Exodus 4:21; 9:12; 10:27; 11:10).

9:4-6 By keeping the Israelites safe from this plague, the Lord demonstrated that he was the force behind the curses, and that Egypt would continue to suffer as long as Israel was oppressed.

▸ PURPOSE
9:6 God's judgments are perfect. God is a good judge. He will neither allow those who are rebellious against Him to go unpunished, nor will He punish those who do not deserve it. Sometimes we obtain protection in the midst of His wrath through completely passive means, as in the plague against the livestock. At other times, God ordains that we actively avoid danger, as in Exodus 9:19 when God gave a clear warning to the people to avoid disaster. Stay clear of the areas of sin that bring about natural consequences and God's judgment. (***See Purpose***> *God's Deeds*> *Judgment,* TopicGuide page A53.)

9:10-12 *Boils* is a broad term encompassing a variety of skin conditions. Since both people and animals were affected, it may have been similar to anthrax or smallpox/cowpox.

9:18-19 The judgment of the hailstorm was contingent upon the people's reaction to Moses (compare Exodus 9:2-3). Those who believed and respected God avoided the curse. Those who did not suffered great loss.

than any in all the history of Egypt. [19]Quick! Order your livestock and servants to come
in from the fields to find shelter. Any person or animal left outside will die when the hail
falls.' "
9:20 [20]Some of Pharaoh's officials were afraid because of what the LORD had said. They
Prov 13:13 quickly brought their servants and livestock in from the fields. [21]But those who paid no at-
9:22 tention to the word of the LORD left theirs out in the open.
Rev 16:21 [22]Then the LORD said to Moses, "Lift your hand toward the sky so hail may fall on the
people, the livestock, and all the plants throughout the land of Egypt."
9:23 Gen 19:24 [23]So Moses lifted his staff toward the sky, and the LORD sent thunder and hail, and light-
Josh 10:11 ning flashed toward the earth. The LORD sent a tremendous hailstorm against all the land
Ps 78:47 Rev 8:7; 16:21 of Egypt. [24]Never in all the history of Egypt had there been a storm like that, with such dev-
9:25 astating hail and continuous lightning. [25]It left all of Egypt in ruins. The hail struck down
Ps 105:32 everything in the open field—people, animals, and plants alike. Even the trees were de-
9:26 stroyed. [26]The only place without hail was the region of Goshen, where the people of Isra-
Exod 8:22; 10:23 el lived.
9:27 [27]Then Pharaoh quickly summoned Moses and Aaron. "This time I have sinned," he
2 Chr 12:6 confessed. "The LORD is the righteous One, and my people and I are wrong. [28]Please beg
Ps 129:4 the LORD to end this terrifying thunder and hail. We've had enough. I will let you go; you
9:28 don't need to stay any longer."
Exod 8:8; 10:16-17 [29]"All right," Moses replied. "As soon as I leave the city, I will lift my hands and pray
9:29 Ps 24:1 to the LORD. Then the thunder and hail will stop, and you will know that the earth be-
1 Cor 10:26 longs to the LORD. [30]But I know that you and your officials still do not fear the LORD
9:30 God."
Exod 8:29 [31](All the flax and barley were ruined by the hail, because the barley had formed heads
and the flax was budding. [32]But the wheat and the emmer wheat were spared, because
they had not yet sprouted from the ground.)
[33]So Moses left Pharaoh's court and went out of the city. When he lifted his hands to the

9:26 The Israelites were exempt from several plagues: flies, diseased livestock, hail, darkness, and the death of the firstborn. This exemption demonstrated that the plagues were not random; God sent them as punishments against those who oppressed His people.

▸ HOLINESS
9:27-35 False repentance. Do we see a little bit of ourselves in Pharaoh in this passage? Pharaoh was convinced that his country would be left in ruins if he did not do something, so he repented of his sin—or did he? Moses sensed that the leaders feared God to some degree, but still not as they should have. As soon as the storm ended, Pharaoh again refused to obey God's direct order. The opportunity to repent and avoid true disaster was missed by the leaders of Egypt, but God offers the opportunity for repentance for all who will listen today. (***See Holiness> Submission> Delighting in God> Rejoicing in repentance,*** TopicGuide page A40.)

9:27-28 Pharaoh's first admission of guilt sounds authentic. It was apparently inspired by the realization that he is no match for God's superior might. As demonstrated by his refusal to honor God (Exodus 9:34-35), Pharaoh's motive was self-preservation, not genuine repentance.

9:31-33 Details such as the ripeness of barley and blooming of flax place the events in January, or perhaps as late as February. Egyptian history also records January–February as the season for hailstorms.

RAIN SEASON	EGYPTIAN MONTHS	JULIAN MONTHS
Akhet **"inundation"**	Thoth	July
	Phaophi	August
	Aythyr	September
	Choiak	October
Peret **"emergence"**	Tybi	November
	Mechyr	December
	Phamenoth	January
	Pharmuthi	February
Shemu **"low water"**	Pachons	March
	Payni	April
	Epiphi	May
	Mesore	June

MASTERS OF TIME
Around 3200 BC, the Egyptians understood that a year was 365.25636 days long, whereas the Romans in 48 BC miscalculated a year to be 365.25 days. This inaccuracy accounts for the 13-day variation in the religious calendars of the Orthodox churches (who follow the Egyptian calendar) and non-Orthodox churches (who follow the Roman/Julian calendar).

THE PLAGUES AS JUDGMENT ON EGYPT'S DEITIES

Plagues from God	Judgment on Deities
1. The plague of blood Exodus 7:14	Khnum, Sati, Hapi, Osiris, Neith, Sobek Apepi
2. The plague of frogs 8:1	Heka
3. The plague of lice 8:16	Seth, Geb
4. The plague of flies 8:20	Vatchit, Beelzebub
5. The plague of cattle disease 9:1	Ptah, Apis, Hathor
6. The plague of boils 9:8	Sekhmet, Imhotep, Serapis
7. The plague of hail 9:13	Geb, Nut, Amun-Ra, Osiris
8. The plague of locusts 10:1	Sobek, Ra, Shu, Geb, and Osiris
9. The plague of darkness 10:21	Nut, Hathor, Amun-Ra
10. Death of firstborn 11:1	Pharaoh, Isis, Heka, Min, Horus, Bes, Seker

LORD, the thunder and hail stopped, and the downpour ceased. 34 But when Pharaoh saw
that the rain, hail, and thunder had stopped, he and his officials sinned again, and Pha-
raoh again became stubborn.* 35 Because his heart was hard, Pharaoh refused to let the
people leave, just as the LORD had predicted through Moses.

9:35 Exod 4:21

A PLAGUE OF LOCUSTS

10 Then the LORD said to Moses, "Return to Pharaoh and make your demands again. I
have made him and his officials stubborn* so I can display My miraculous signs
among them. 2 I've also done it so you can tell your children and grandchildren about how
I made a mockery of the Egyptians and about the signs I displayed among them—and so
you will know that I am the LORD."
3 So Moses and Aaron went to Pharaoh and said, "This is what the LORD, the God of the

10:1 Exod 4:21; 7:14
10:2 Exod 13:8, 14 Deut 4:9 Ps 44:1
10:3 Exod 4:23

9:34 Hebrew *made his heart heavy.* 10:1 Hebrew *have made his heart and his officials' hearts heavy.*

9:34 As he had before (Exodus 8:32; 9:7), Pharaoh stubbornly refused to fulfill his arrangement with Moses. His motives are unclear, though by this time it stretches credibility to imagine that he did not understand that Moses' God was causing the disasters. His stubbornness may imply that he willingly chose to rebel against God's obviously superior force or that he was still trusting in his gods to rescue him from the God of the Hebrews.

10:1, 20, 27 We know that God did not force Pharaoh and his officials to sin because the Scriptures say that God does not tempt anyone (James 1:13). Because they were unbelievers, they already lacked the ability to act righteously (Genesis 6:5; Isaiah 64:6; Romans 8:7-8). Had they complied with Moses' demands, they would have done so for evil reasons. In an act of judgment against their unbelief, God left them without the ability to choose the particular evil of falsely complying. This was in order to make an example of them before the rest of the world.

▸ HOLINESS

10:2 Telling your children about God. How do you tell kids about God? God encouraged the Israelites to tell their children stories of how God rescued His people from danger and how God was active in their lives. By hearing about a loving, powerful God who protects His people, children are readied to hear the good news of the gospel—and so are we! (***See Holiness***> *Submission> Learning God's Word> Teaching your children,* TopicGuide page A40.)

10:2 God's plan was not simply to compel Pharaoh to release His people, but to accomplish their release in a dramatic way that would prove even to future generations that the God of Israel is the true God. The events of the Exodus from Egypt were the content of the most precious stories of Israel and are regularly mentioned as the greatest acts of God's redemption. Not until Christ's ministry was the Exodus eclipsed by an even greater revelation of God's power and salvation (compare Jeremiah 16:14-15; 23:7-8; 2 Corinthians 3:5-11).

Hebrews, says: How long will you refuse to submit to Me? Let My people go, so they can
10:4 Rev 9:3 worship Me. 4 If you refuse, watch out! For tomorrow I will bring a swarm of locusts on your
country. 5 They will cover the land so that you won't be able to see the ground. They will
10:5 Exod 9:32 devour what little is left of your crops after the hailstorm, including all the trees growing in
Joel 1:4; 2:25 the fields. 6 They will overrun your palaces and the homes of your officials and all the
houses in Egypt. Never in the history of Egypt have your ancestors seen a plague like this
one!" And with that, Moses turned and left Pharaoh.
10:7 Exod 7:5 7 Pharaoh's officials now came to Pharaoh and appealed to him. "How long will you let
this man hold us hostage? Let the men go to worship the LORD their God! Don't you realize
that Egypt lies in ruins?"
10:8 Exod 8:8, 25 8 So Moses and Aaron were brought back to Pharaoh. "All right," he told them, "go and
worship the LORD your God. But who exactly will be going with you?"
10:9 9 Moses replied, "We will all go—young and old, our sons and daughters, and our flocks
Exod 12:37 and herds. We must all join together in celebrating a festival to the LORD."
10:10 Gen 50:8 10 Pharaoh retorted, "The LORD will certainly need to be with you if I let you take your lit-
Exod 12:31 tle ones! I can see through your evil plan. 11 Never! Only the men may go and worship the
10:11 LORD, since that is what you requested." And Pharaoh threw them out of the palace.
Exod 10:28 12 Then the LORD said to Moses, "Raise your hand over the land of Egypt to bring on the
10:12 locusts. Let them cover the land and devour every plant that survived the hailstorm."
Exod 7:19 13 So Moses raised his staff over Egypt, and the LORD caused an east wind to blow over
10:13 the land all that day and through the night. When morning arrived, the east wind had
Pss 78:46; 105:34 brought the locusts. 14 And the locusts swarmed over the whole land of Egypt, settling in
10:14 Joel 1:4, 7; 2:1-11 dense swarms from one end of the country to the other. It was the worst locust plague in
Egyptian history, and there has never been another one like it. 15 For the locusts covered
10:15 Exod 10:5 the whole country and darkened the land. They devoured every plant in the fields and all
Ps 105:35 the fruit on the trees that had survived the hailstorm. Not a single leaf was left on the trees
10:16 and plants throughout the land of Egypt.
Exod 8:8; 9:27 16 Pharaoh quickly summoned Moses and Aaron. "I have sinned against the LORD your
10:17 Exod 8:8, 29 God and against you," he confessed. 17 "Forgive my sin, just this once, and plead with the
1 Sam 15:25 LORD your God to take away this death from me."
10:18 18 So Moses left Pharaoh's court and pleaded with the LORD. 19 The LORD responded by
Exod 8:30 shifting the wind, and the strong west wind blew the locusts into the Red Sea.* Not a single
10:20 locust remained in all the land of Egypt. 20 But the LORD hardened Pharaoh's heart again, so
Exod 4:21; 11:10 he refused to let the people go.

10:21 Deut 28:29

A PLAGUE OF DARKNESS

10:22 21 Then the LORD said to Moses, "Lift your hand toward heaven, and the land of Egypt will
Ps 105:28 be covered with a darkness so thick you can feel it." 22 So Moses lifted his hand to the sky,
10:23 Exod 8:22 and a deep darkness covered the entire land of Egypt for three days. 23 During all that time

10:19 Hebrew *sea of reeds.*

10:4, 14-15 Grasshoppers occasionally travel in swarms so tightly packed that they literally block out the sun. When traveling en masse, these grasshoppers are called *locusts.* The swarms eat vegetation voraciously, at times devouring entire fields. The only weapon against them in ancient times was fire.

10:7 Presumably, Pharaoh's refusal to release the Israelites was based on his desire to benefit from their work (Exodus 5:4-5). By this time, Egypt lay in ruins and the damage God had done to Egypt outweighed the benefits the Egyptians received from their Israelite slaves. It was evident, at least to Pharaoh's court officials, that Pharaoh was not acting in the best interests of Egypt.

10:8-11 Pharaoh imagined that the three-day worship pilgrimage was a ruse and that Moses intended to lead the nation in a clandestine escape. But God intended to free Israel openly and powerfully in order to show His power (Exodus 9:16; 10:1).

10:16-17 Pharaoh's second show of repentance was no more genuine than his first (compare Exodus 9:27-35).

10:22-23 As with the prior plagues of flies, diseased livestock, hail, and the coming death of the firstborn, the Hebrews were not subjected to God's curse. However, to avoid harm, the Hebrews had to stay clear of the cursed areas of Egypt (Exodus 8:22) or follow God's explicit instructions (Exodus 12:23).

the people could not see each other, and no one moved. But there was light as usual
where the people of Israel lived.
24Finally, Pharaoh called for Moses. "Go and worship the LORD," he said. "But leave your
flocks and herds here. You may even take your little ones with you."
25"No," Moses said, "you must provide us with animals for sacrifices and burnt offerings
to the LORD our God. 26All our livestock must go with us, too; not a hoof can be left behind.
We must choose our sacrifices for the LORD our God from among these animals. And we
won't know how we are to worship the LORD until we get there."
27But the LORD hardened Pharaoh's heart once more, and he would not let them go.
28"Get out of here!" Pharaoh shouted at Moses. "I'm warning you. Never come back to see
me again! The day you see my face, you will die!"
29"Very well," Moses replied. "I will never see your face again."

DEATH FOR EGYPT'S FIRSTBORN

11 Then the LORD said to Moses, "I will strike Pharaoh and the land of Egypt with one
more blow. After that, Pharaoh will let you leave this country. In fact, he will be so ea-
ger to get rid of you that he will force you all to leave. 2Tell all the Israelite men and women to
ask their Egyptian neighbors for articles of silver and gold." 3(Now the LORD had caused the
Egyptians to look favorably on the people of Israel. And Moses was considered a very great
man in the land of Egypt, respected by Pharaoh's officials and the Egyptian people alike.)
4Moses had announced to Pharaoh, "This is what the LORD says: At midnight tonight I
will pass through the heart of Egypt. 5All the firstborn sons will die in every family in Egypt,
from the oldest son of Pharaoh, who sits on his throne, to the oldest son of his lowliest ser-
vant girl who grinds the flour. Even the firstborn of all the livestock will die. 6Then a loud
wail will rise throughout the land of Egypt, a wail like no one has heard before or will ever
hear again. 7But among the Israelites it will be so peaceful that not even a dog will bark.
Then you will know that the LORD makes a distinction between the Egyptians and the Isra-
elites. 8All the officials of Egypt will run to me and fall to the ground before me. 'Please
leave!' they will beg. 'Hurry! And take all your followers with you.' Only then will I go!"
Then, burning with anger, Moses left Pharaoh.
9Now the LORD had told Moses earlier, "Pharaoh will not listen to you, but then I will do
even more mighty miracles in the land of Egypt." 10Moses and Aaron performed these mir-
acles in Pharaoh's presence, but the LORD hardened Pharaoh's heart, and he wouldn't let
the Israelites leave the country.

10:24 Exod 8:8, 10
10:26 Exod 10:9
10:27 Exod 4:21; 14:4
10:28 Exod 10:11
10:29 Heb 11:27
11:1 Exod 12:31, 33, 39
11:2 Exod 3:22; 12:35-36
11:3 Exod 3:21; 12:36 Deut 34:10-12
11:4 Exod 12:29
11:5 Exod 12:12, 29 Pss 78:51; 105:36; 135:8; 136:10
11:6 Exod 12:30 Amos 5:17
11:7 Exod 8:22
11:8 Exod 12:31-33 Heb 11:27
11:9 Exod 7:3-4
11:10 Exod 4:21 Rom 2:5; 9:17

▸ GOD
11:1 Who knows the future? Every step along the way, God kept Moses informed. This time, God told Moses exactly what would happen next and how the Egyptians would respond. God is not only fully knowledgeable of the end, but He also oversees the means to that end. Thus, God is never surprised by what His enemies do. For this reason, we can rely on Him to prepare us for future conflicts with the world and the devil. We can also rely on Him to bring about His good end through these conflicts. (***See God****> God's Attributes> All-knowing> God knows the future,* TopicGuide page A15.)

11:1 No doubt the Israelites grew impatient at the continual delays of their freedom. God assured them that His purposes in sending the curses on Egypt were nearly fulfilled and that their redemption was at hand. This assurance confirmed God's prior statement that Pharaoh would not release the people until this specific disaster had fallen upon Egypt (Exodus 4:23).

11:5 By refusing to release the Israelites, Pharaoh risked losing his successor, the next ruler of Egypt. This curse demonstrated that God favored Israel as His own son (Exodus 4:22).

11:7 The plagues on Egypt were intended, in part, to demonstrate that the only true God in the universe favored the Israelites. Those who opposed God's favored people would be cursed (compare Genesis 12:3).

11:9 God orchestrated every event, including Pharaoh's refusals to release Israel, to lead up to this climactic curse and Israel's release (Exodus 9:16; 10:27; 11:10; Romans 9:17-18).

11:10 God did not force Pharaoh to sin (James 1:13) by hardening him. Pharaoh was unable to act righteously because he was an unbeliever (Isaiah 64:6; Romans 8:7-8). Even if he had released the Israelites, Pharaoh would still have been sinning because he would not have done it with a faithful, loving heart toward God (Matthew 22:36-40; John 15:5; Hebrews 11:6). God hardened Pharaoh's heart by withholding undeserved moral grace from him in judgment against his wickedness.

THE FIRST PASSOVER

12 While the Israelites were still in the land of Egypt, the LORD gave the following in-
structions to Moses and Aaron: 2“From now on, this month will be the first month
of the year for you. 3Announce to the whole community of Israel that on the tenth day of
this month each family must choose a lamb or a young goat for a sacrifice, one animal for
each household. 4If a family is too small to eat a whole animal, let them share with an-
other family in the neighborhood. Divide the animal according to the size of each family
and how much they can eat. 5The animal you select must be a one-year-old male, either a
sheep or a goat, with no defects.
6“Take special care of this chosen animal until the evening of the fourteenth day of this
first month. Then the whole assembly of the community of Israel must slaughter their
lamb or young goat at twilight. 7They are to take some of the blood and smear it on the
sides and top of the doorframes of the houses where they eat the animal. 8That same
night they must roast the meat over a fire and eat it along with bitter salad greens and
bread made without yeast. 9Do not eat any of the meat raw or boiled in water. The whole
animal—including the head, legs, and internal organs—must be roasted over a fire. 10Do
not leave any of it until the next morning. Burn whatever is not eaten before morning.
11“These are your instructions for eating this meal: Be fully dressed,* wear your sandals,
and carry your walking stick in your hand. Eat the meal with urgency, for this is the LORD's
Passover. 12On that night I will pass through the land of Egypt and strike down every first-
born son and firstborn male animal in the land of Egypt. I will execute judgment against all
the gods of Egypt, for I am the LORD! 13But the blood on your doorposts will serve as a sign,
marking the houses where you are staying. When I see the blood, I will pass over you. This
plague of death will not touch you when I strike the land of Egypt.
14“This is a day to remember. Each year, from generation to generation, you must celebrate

12:11 Hebrew *Bind up your loins.*

12:2 Exod 13:4; 23:15; 34:18 Deut 16:1
12:3 Mark 14:12 1 Cor 5:7
12:5 Lev 22:18-20 Heb 9:14
12:6 Lev 23:5 Num 9:3 Deut 16:4, 6
12:7 Exod 12:22
12:8 Exod 34:25 Num 9:11-12 Deut 16:7
12:10 Exod 23:18; 34:25
12:11 Num 28:16
12:12 Exod 11:4-5 Num 33:4
12:13 Heb 11:28
12:14-20 //Lev 23:4-8 //Num 28:16-25 //Deut 16:1-8

▸WORSHIP

12:1 Do we still eat the Passover meal? The Passover is a symbolic meal celebrating God's rescue of His people from Egypt. During the celebration of a Passover meal with His disciples, Jesus instituted the sacrament of the Lord's Supper as a reminder that He Himself fulfills the Passover symbolism (1 Corinthians 5:7). So, in observing the Lord's Supper, we follow the New Testament version of the Passover (Acts 2:42-46; 20:7; 1 Corinthians 11:20-33). God calls all Christians to regularly celebrate God's salvation of His people through partaking of the Lord's Supper (Exodus 12:24). (***See Worship****> OT> Sacraments> Passover*, TopicGuide page A29.)

12:2 This probably marks the institution of a new religious calendar for the Israelites. The first Passover took place in the month *Abib*, the name of which relates to the progression of the barley harvest. Following the Babylonian exile, God's people also used the Babylonian name *Nisan* for this month. Abib corresponds to late March and early April on modern calendars. Each year was to begin with a celebration of God's deliverance of Israel from slavery.

12:6 The Hebrews reckoned days from sunset to sunset. The lamb was to be slaughtered at sunset (Deuteronomy 16:6), marking the beginning of the new day.

12:8, 15-20, 34, 39 Bread making was an important skill to master in the ancient world. The process begins with harvesting various grains, which are then crushed (Proverbs 27:22). A mixture of this crushed grain (flour), water, salt, leaven, and occasionally oil is then allowed to rise. After the bread has expanded, it is placed in an oven and baked. Leaving out the leaven (a bit of unsalted, yeast-infused dough) produced a tough, flat loaf that could be cooked more quickly and was used for travel food due to its shape. It is for these reasons that leaven was originally left out of the bread. Leaven later came to symbolize sin (1 Corinthians 5:8) and false teachers (Matthew 16:6, 12; Galatians 5:8-9).

12:12 The conflict between Moses and Egypt began as a request to offer worship to God (Exodus 5:3), and was intended partly to demonstrate to Egypt that the God of the Israelites was the true God (Exodus 7:5, 17; 8:22; 10:2). The death of the firstborn punished all those who were not in houses marked by the blood of lambs that had been sacrificed to God (compare Exodus 12:7, 13). In essence, it punished all those who did not worship the true God. By striking against the unbelieving Egyptians in this manner, God proved that their gods were no match for him; the Egyptians' false gods could not prevent the Lord from slaughtering the people of Egypt.

12:13 Blood represented the life within a creature (Leviticus 17:11). The lamb whose blood marked the doorway was counted as a substitute for the firstborn of the household (compare Exodus 13:12-15).

12:14-20 These instructions on future worship interrupt the narrative in order to teach Moses' readers to maintain proper worship throughout all generations. The details provided generations after Moses with both a method and a purpose for maintaining God's worship as it had been established under Moses.

THE HEBREW CALENDAR

A Hebrew month began in the middle of a month on our calendar today. Crops are planted in November and December and harvested in March and April.

Month	Today's Calendar	Bible Reference	Israel's Holidays
1 Abib (Nisan)	March–April	Exodus 13:4; 23:15; 34:18; Deuteronomy 16:1	Passover (Leviticus 23:5) Unleavened Bread (Leviticus 23:6) First Harvest (Leviticus 23:10)
2 Ziv (Iyyar)	April–May	1 Kings 6:1, 37	Second Passover (Numbers 9:10, 11)
3 Sivan	May–June		Harvest (Pentecost) (Leviticus 23:16)
4 Tammuz	June–July		
5 Ab	July–August		
6 Elul	August–September		
7 Ethanaim (Tishri)	September–October	1 Kings 8:2	Trumpets (Numbers 29:1; Leviticus 23:24) Day of Atonement (Leviticus 23:27) Shelters (Leviticus 23:34)
8 Bul (Marchesh van)	October–November	1 Kings 6:38	
9 Kislev	November–December	Nehemiah 1:1	Dedication (Hanukkah) (John 10:22)
10 Tebeth	December–January		
11 Shebat	January–February		
12 Adar	February–March		Purim (Esther 9:24-32)

12:15 Exod 23:15; 34:18 Lev 23:5-6 Deut 16:3
12:16 Lev 23:7-8
12:17 Exod 13:3
12:18 Lev 23:5-8 Num 28:16-25
12:19 Exod 12:15
12:21 Mark 14:12-16 Heb 11:28
12:22 Lev 14:4, 6 Num 19:18 Ps 51:7 Heb 11:28
12:23 Exod 12:12 Isa 37:36
12:24 Exod 13:4-5, 10
12:25 Exod 3:17
12:26 Exod 10:2; 13:14-15
12:27 Exod 4:31
12:29 Exod 4:23; 11:4 Pss 78:51; 105:36

it as a special festival to the LORD. This is a law for all time. 15 For seven days the bread you eat
must be made without yeast. On the first day of the festival, remove every trace of yeast from
your homes. Anyone who eats bread made with yeast during the seven days of the festival
will be cut off from the community of Israel. 16 On the first day of the festival and again on the
seventh day, all the people must observe an official day for holy assembly. No work of any
kind may be done on these days except in the preparation of food.
17 "Celebrate this Festival of Unleavened Bread, for it will remind you that I brought your
forces out of the land of Egypt on this very day. This festival will be a permanent law for
you; celebrate this day from generation to generation. 18 The bread you eat must be made
without yeast from the evening of the fourteenth day of the first month until the evening
of the twenty-first day of that month. 19 During those seven days, there must be no trace of
yeast in your homes. Anyone who eats anything made with yeast during this week will be
cut off from the community of Israel. These regulations apply both to the foreigners living
among you and to the native-born Israelites. 20 During those days you must not eat any-
thing made with yeast. Wherever you live, eat only bread made without yeast."
21 Then Moses called all the elders of Israel together and said to them, "Go, pick out a lamb or
young goat for each of your families, and slaughter the Passover animal. 22 Drain the blood into
a basin. Then take a bundle of hyssop branches and dip it into the blood. Brush the hyssop
across the top and sides of the doorframes of your houses. And no one may go out through the
door until morning. 23 For the LORD will pass through the land to strike down the Egyptians. But
when He sees the blood on the top and sides of the doorframe, the LORD will pass over your
home. He will not permit His death angel to enter your house and strike you down.
24 "Remember, these instructions are a permanent law that you and your descendants must
observe forever. 25 When you enter the land the LORD has promised to give you, you will con-
tinue to observe this ceremony. 26 Then your children will ask, 'What does this ceremony
mean?' 27 And you will reply, 'It is the Passover sacrifice to the LORD, for He passed over the
houses of the Israelites in Egypt. And though He struck the Egyptians, He spared our families.'"
When Moses had finished speaking, all the people bowed down to the ground and worshiped.
28 So the people of Israel did just as the LORD had commanded through Moses and
Aaron. 29 And that night at midnight, the LORD struck down all the firstborn sons in the land

---

12:15 Being exiled from the people of God is a grave matter; it meant either death by exposure, death by surrounding enemies, or the possibility of joining with Israel's enemies. This was an extreme curse against those who had broken God's covenant (compare Genesis 17:14). Those who failed to keep the Passover were counted as rejecting God's redemption of His people from Egypt. We see a similar event in 1 Corinthians 5:12-13.

12:19 At every stage in Israel's history there were foreigners who worshiped God and lived among the nation. This was part of the fulfillment of God's promise to Abraham that all nations would be blessed through Abraham's descendants (Genesis 18:18). Gentiles in Israel were bound to keep all the laws of the nation, including the religious laws.

12:22 Hyssop is a species of marjoram with leaves and branches sufficient to trap liquids (compare Numbers 19:18). The blood in the hyssop was a sign that a substitute had been killed in place of the firstborn of the household (Exodus 13:12-15).

12:24 God provided no hint that his people might eventually cease to observe Passover (compare Deuteronomy 29:29; Psalm 119:160; Matthew 5:17-19). Nevertheless, the Bible consistently demonstrates that God's laws must be applied differently in different stages of history. With regard to Passover, first note that the Lord's Supper is a version of the holy Passover meal, distilled to the essential components—wine and bread. Second, Christ's one sacrifice satisfies or fulfills the Passover command for all time (1 Corinthians 5:7), so that all believers are always celebrating Christ's sacrificial rescue.

12:25 The land spoken of here is the property given by God to Abraham as the permanent dwelling place of his descendants (Genesis 15:18-21; Exodus 3:8).

▸ GOD

12:29 God's justice often requires punishment. You may hear people say, "God never does anything that hurts anyone." But here we see God doing something that seems wrong and harmful—killing the firstborn children of the Egyptians. How was this right? First, God warned the Egyptians that they could escape the judgment by repenting of their enslavement of the Hebrews. They also could have escaped judgment by following the instructions that God gave His people (Exodus 12:21-23). Second, this judgment was right because the Egyptians had previously ordered the murder of newborn males of the Hebrews (see Exodus 1), an edict possibly lasting for over 80 years. God's love for the victims could certainly allow Him to follow through with a punishment matching the crimes against His people. It was also allowable for God to mercifully end Egyptian lives, limiting the degree of their eternal punishment (Luke 12:47-48). You may not like it, but the Bible teaches that God brings death and suffering into our lives for our best and His glory. (***See God***> *God's Attributes*> *Just,* TopicGuide page A16.)

of Egypt, from the firstborn son of Pharaoh, who sat on his throne, to the firstborn son of
the prisoner in the dungeon. Even the firstborn of their livestock were killed. 30Pharaoh
and all his officials and all the people of Egypt woke up during the night, and loud wailing
was heard throughout the land of Egypt. There was not a single house where someone
had not died.

ISRAEL'S EXODUS FROM EGYPT

31Pharaoh sent for Moses and Aaron during the night. "Get out!" he ordered. "Leave my
people—and take the rest of the Israelites with you! Go and worship the LORD as you have
requested. 32Take your flocks and herds, as you said, and be gone. Go, but bless me as
you leave." 33All the Egyptians urged the people of Israel to get out of the land as quickly
as possible, for they thought, "We will all die!"

34The Israelites took their bread dough before yeast was added. They wrapped their
kneading boards in their cloaks and carried them on their shoulders. 35And the people of
Israel did as Moses had instructed; they asked the Egyptians for clothing and articles of
silver and gold. 36The LORD caused the Egyptians to look favorably on the Israelites, and
they gave the Israelites whatever they asked for. So they stripped the Egyptians of their
wealth!

37That night the people of Israel left Rameses and started for Succoth. There were about
600,000 men,* plus all the women and children. 38A rabble of non-Israelites went with
them, along with great flocks and herds of livestock. 39For bread they baked flat cakes
from the dough without yeast they had brought from Egypt. It was made without yeast be-
cause the people were driven out of Egypt in such a hurry that they had no time to prepare
the bread or other food.

40The people of Israel had lived in Egypt* for 430 years. 41In fact, it was on the last
day of the 430th year that all the LORD's forces left the land. 42On this night the LORD
kept His promise to bring His people out of the land of Egypt. So this night belongs to
Him, and it must be commemorated every year by all the Israelites, from generation to
generation.

12:30 Exod 11:6
12:31 Exod 8:8, 25
12:33 Exod 10:7; 11:1
12:35 Exod 3:22
12:36 Exod 3:22
12:37 Exod 38:26; Num 1:46
12:38 Num 11:4
12:39 Exod 11:1
12:40-41 Gen 15:13, 16; Acts 7:6; Gal 3:17
12:42 Exod 3:10; Deut 16:1

12:37 Or *fighting men;* Hebrew reads *men on foot.* 12:40 Samaritan Pentateuch reads *in Canaan and Egypt;* Greek version reads *in Egypt and Canaan.*

12:36 Israel's escape from Egypt's army is presented as a military victory because their warrior God fought and defeated the Egyptians on their behalf (compare Exodus 14:14). As the Lord had promised Abraham (Genesis 15:14) and reminded Moses (Exodus 3:21-22), God's people plundered their captors, receiving restitution for their years of slavery.

▸ BIBLE

12:37 How many left Egypt? The Hebrew word for *thousand* could also be translated *families* or *clans.* While it is certainly possible that four centuries of slavery could have produced a nation of 600,000 males, the Hebrew language leaves room for the number only having been 600 families. However, the conquering of the land of Canaan with only 600 families—and only a few thousand men of fighting age—would be as great a miracle as the provision of food and water for up to two million people journeying through the desert. Regardless of which number is correct, God worked great miracles to enable His people to have a great victory. We can trust His Word, regardless of the occasional puzzles it presents to modern readers. (***See Bible****> Uniqueness> Flawless> God's Word leaves some puzzles,* TopicGuide page A10.)

▸ CHURCH

12:38 God's family grows. God had worked in the hearts of many people in Egypt so that they preferred to leave their homes and travel with God's people rather than stay behind in a nation cursed by God (see also Exodus 12:48-49). This is a testimony not only to God's power, but to the Hebrews' witness to their captors. From the beginning, God's people included both natural descendants of Abraham, Isaac, and Jacob, and foreigners who were faithful to God (compare Genesis 18:18; 22:18; Isaiah 56:3). This reflected God's plan that people from every nation would someday worship Him together (Revelation 7:9-10). (***See Church****> Role> Preach> Topics> Evangelize> Around the world,* TopicGuide page A50.)

12:39 Unleavened bread was to be used perpetually during Passover and the Festival of Unleavened Bread (Exodus 12:15-20) as a symbol of the haste with which the Israelites left Egypt.

12:42 Moses interrupted the story of the Exodus in order to emphasize the importance of establishing and maintaining proper worship in Israel. These instructions contain principles that may be applied to modern worship because Christians are still called to remember the Lord's deliverance.

INSTRUCTIONS FOR THE PASSOVER

12:43 Num 9:14 43 Then the LORD said to Moses and Aaron, "These are the instructions for the festival of
12:44 Passover. No outsiders are allowed to eat the Passover meal. 44 But any slave who has
Gen 17:12-13 been purchased may eat it if he has been circumcised. 45 Temporary residents and hired
Lev 22:11 servants may not eat it. 46 Each Passover lamb must be eaten in one house. Do not carry
12:46 Num 9:12 any of its meat outside, and do not break any of its bones. 47 The whole community of Isra-
John 19:33, 36 el must celebrate this Passover festival.
12:48 48 "If there are foreigners living among you who want to celebrate the LORD's Passover,
Num 9:13-14 let all their males be circumcised. Only then may they celebrate the Passover with you like
Gal 3:28 any native-born Israelite. But no uncircumcised male may ever eat the Passover meal.
12:49 Lev 24:22 49 This instruction applies to everyone, whether a native-born Israelite or a foreigner living
Num 15:15-16 among you."
12:50 50 So all the people of Israel followed all the LORD's commands to Moses and Aaron.
Exod 12:28 51 On that very day the LORD brought the people of Israel out of the land of Egypt like an
army.

13:2 Exod 13:12-13;

DEDICATION OF THE FIRSTBORN

22:29; 34:20 **13** Then the LORD said to Moses, 2 "Dedicate to Me every firstborn among the Israel-
Lev 27:26 Num 3:13 ites. The first offspring to be born, of both humans and animals, belongs to Me."
Deut 15:19 3 So Moses said to the people, "This is a day to remember forever—the day you left
*Luke 2:23 Egypt, the place of your slavery. Today the LORD has brought you out by the power of His
13:3 Exod 3:20; 6:1 mighty hand. (Remember, eat no food containing yeast.) 4 On this day in early spring, in
13:4 the month of Abib,* you have been set free. 5 You must celebrate this event in this month
Exod 12:2 each year after the LORD brings you into the land of the Canaanites, Hittites, Amorites, Hi-
13:5 vites, and Jebusites. (He swore to your ancestors that He would give you this land—a land
Exod 3:8, 17; 12:25-26 flowing with milk and honey.) 6 For seven days the bread you eat must be made without
13:6 Exod 12:15-20 yeast. Then on the seventh day, celebrate a feast to the LORD. 7 Eat bread without yeast

13:4 Hebrew *On this day in the month of Abib.* This first month of the ancient Hebrew lunar calendar usually occurs within the months of March and April.

12:43-49 Many laws and provisions in the books of Moses (Genesis through Deuteronomy) pertain to foreigners within the nation of Israel. God gave these foreigners many rights, but they did not share all the rights afforded to those who were the physical descendants of Abraham, Isaac, and Jacob. Those foreigners who received Israelite circumcision demonstrated that they willingly subjected themselves to the Lord by joining the community of His covenant people (compare Genesis 17:10-14).

12:46 The Passover lamb was an image of Christ (1 Corinthians 5:7). That the lamb's bones were not to be broken fore-shadowed a detail of Christ's crucifixion (John 19:31-36).

12:50-51 Moses recorded that God's rescue of Israel took place when the nation obeyed Moses and Aaron. This emphasis on the leadership of Moses and Aaron as God's representatives can be found throughout Exodus. Moses recorded these details because he wanted later generations to know that blessings would come to them only if they observed the regulations and patterns of worship established under him and Aaron.

13:1 The instructions for future worship in this chapter are prefaced by a reminder that Moses received these instructions from the Lord. Future generations were to observe the practices of their ancestors because these practices had been commanded by God, not invented by Moses.

13:2 Persons and things were dedicated to the Lord either by the process of consecration (compare Exodus 29:1) or by being sacrificed.

13:3-16 Moses instructed the Israelites regarding future in the Promised Land. The preceding record of the Exodus provides the basis for the practices that future generations of Israelites were to follow.

13:3 The annual celebration of Passover (Exodus 12:11) and of the Festival of Unleavened Bread (Exodus 12:17) was intended to be a constant reminder of God's great power and mercy in rescuing the Israelites from Egypt.

13:3-7 The hastily made flat bread was made without leaven in order to allow the Israelites to depart quickly. Leaven and yeast would come to have other symbolic meanings (see Exodus 12:8 and note).

13:5 According to Genesis 10:15-17, all of these people groups descended from Noah's grandson Canaan. The Canaanites were dispersed throughout the Promised Land in Moses' day. The Hittites were inhabitants of a powerful empire centered north of the Promised Land. The Amorites probably migrated from the north, while the Hivites inhabited parts of the mountains of Lebanon and Mount Hermon. Jebusites probably lived in the area that was later renamed Jerusalem (2 Samuel 5:6).

during those seven days. In fact, there must be no yeast bread or any yeast at all found
within the borders of your land during this time.
8 "On the seventh day you must explain to your children, 'I am celebrating what the LORD
did for me when I left Egypt.' 9 This annual festival will be a visible sign to you, like a mark
branded on your hand or your forehead. Let it remind you always to recite this teaching of
the LORD: 'With a strong hand, the LORD rescued you from Egypt.'* 10 So observe the decree
of this festival at the appointed time each year.
11 "This is what you must do when the LORD fulfills the promise He swore to you and to
your ancestors. When He gives you the land where the Canaanites now live, 12 you must
present all firstborn sons and firstborn male animals to the LORD, for they belong to Him.
13 A firstborn donkey may be bought back from the LORD by presenting a lamb or young
goat in its place. But if you do not buy it back, you must break its neck. However, you must
buy back every firstborn son.
14 "And in the future, your children will ask you, 'What does all this mean?' Then you will
tell them, 'With the power of His mighty hand, the LORD brought us out of Egypt, the place
of our slavery. 15 Pharaoh stubbornly refused to let us go, so the LORD killed all the firstborn
males throughout the land of Egypt, both people and animals. That is why I now sacrifice
all the firstborn males to the LORD—except that the firstborn sons are always bought back.'
16 This ceremony will be like a mark branded on your hand or your forehead. It is a reminder that the power of the LORD's mighty hand brought us out of Egypt."

ISRAEL'S WILDERNESS DETOUR

17 When Pharaoh finally let the people go, God did not lead them along the main road that
runs through Philistine territory, even though that was the shortest route to the Promised
Land. God said, "If the people are faced with a battle, they might change their minds and

13:9 Exod 12:14; Deut 6:8
13:10 Exod 12:24-25
13:12 Exod 13:2; 22:29; Num 3:13; *Luke 2:23
13:13 Exod 34:20; Num 18:15-16
13:14 Exod 12:26-27; Deut 6:20-23
13:15 Exod 12:29
13:16 Exod 13:9; Deut 6:8
13:17 Exod 14:11; Num 14:1-4; Deut 17:16

13:9 Or *Let it remind you always to keep the instructions of the LORD on the tip of your tongue, because with a strong hand, the LORD rescued you from Egypt.*

▸ HOLINESS

13:8 Religious traditions. Many of the religious traditions of ancient Israel were integrated with the family. Thus, God commanded the leaders of the households to explain the meaning of these traditions whenever they occurred (Exodus 13:14). We should take time on each Sabbath and at every religious holiday to explain its meaning to our children so that the biblical traditions we cherish can be passed on to the next generation. (***See Holiness****> Submission> Learning God's Word> Teaching your children,* TopicGuide page A40)

THE EXODUS The Israelites left Succoth and camped first at Etham before going toward Baal-zephon to camp by the sea (14:2). God miraculously brought them across the sea, into the Desert of Shur (15:22). After stopping at the oasis of Elim, the people moved into the Wilderness of Sin (16:1).

13:9, 16 The metaphor "like a mark branded" indicates that the ceremonies were to be obvious and unforgettable reminders of God's grace toward them. One of the greatest sins against God is to forget Him and His great mercy (Deuteronomy 32:18; Judges 3:7; 2 Peter 1:9).

13:12 All who were firstborn were seen as belonging to God (Exodus 13:2, 12-13), so a price was paid to "redeem" or keep them. This was different from the practice of dedicating a person, animal, or home to God (Leviticus 27). But both involved bringing a substitutionary offering to the Aaronic priest. This offering helped support the religious activities surrounding the Tabernacle and, later, the Temple.

13:15 Sacrificing the firstborn animals to the Lord reenacted the death of the firstborn during the Exodus and thus honored God's power in destroying Israel's captor Egypt. Likewise, redeeming firstborn sons honored God's mercy and love by reenacting His preservation of firstborn Israelites.

13:17 Even the escape route of the Hebrews was carefully planned by God. While God is all-powerful, He chose to display His power by utterly defeating the awesome Egyptians rather than the relatively minor, yet fierce, Philistines who dwelt along the coast of the Mediterranean.

13:18 Josh 1:14; 4:13 return to Egypt." 18So God led them in a roundabout way through the wilderness toward
the Red Sea.* Thus the Israelites left Egypt like an army ready for battle.*
13:19 Gen 50:24-25 19Moses took the bones of Joseph with him, for Joseph had made the sons of Israel
Josh 24:32 swear to do this. He said, "God will certainly come to help you. When He does, you must
Acts 7:16 take my bones with you from this place."
13:20 Exod 12:37 20The Israelites left Succoth and camped at Etham on the edge of the wilderness. 21The
Num 33:6-8 LORD went ahead of them. He guided them during the day with a pillar of cloud, and He
13:21 provided light at night with a pillar of fire. This allowed them to travel by day or by night.
Exod 14:19, 24; 33:9-10 22And the LORD did not remove the pillar of cloud or pillar of fire from its place in front of
Ps 105:39 1 Cor 10:1 the people.

14:2 Num 33:7-8 **14** Then the LORD gave these instructions to Moses: 2"Order the Israelites to turn back
Jer 44:1 and camp by Pi-hahiroth between Migdol and the sea. Camp there along the
14:4 shore, across from Baal-zephon. 3Then Pharaoh will think, 'The Israelites are confused.
Exod 4:21; 7:5 Rom 9:17, 22-23 They are trapped in the wilderness!' 4And once again I will harden Pharaoh's heart, and he
will chase after you.* I have planned this in order to display My glory through Pharaoh and
his whole army. After this the Egyptians will know that I am the LORD!" So the Israelites
camped there as they were told.

14:5 Ps 105:25

THE EGYPTIANS PURSUE ISRAEL

5When word reached the king of Egypt that the Israelites had fled, Pharaoh and his offi-
14:7 Exod 15:4 cials changed their minds. "What have we done, letting all those Israelite slaves get
14:8 away?" they asked. 6So Pharaoh harnessed his chariot and called up his troops. 7He took
Num 33:3 with him 600 of Egypt's best chariots, along with the rest of the chariots of Egypt, each
Acts 13:17 with its commander. 8The LORD hardened the heart of Pharaoh, the king of Egypt, so he
14:9 chased after the people of Israel, who had left with fists raised in defiance. 9The Egyptians
Exod 14:2; 15:9 chased after them with all the forces in Pharaoh's army—all his horses and chariots, his
Josh 24:6 14:10 charioteers, and his troops. The Egyptians caught up with the people of Israel as they were
Josh 24:7 camped beside the shore near Pi-hahiroth, across from Baal-zephon.
Neh 9:9 10As Pharaoh approached, the people of Israel looked up and panicked when they saw
14:11 the Egyptians overtaking them. They cried out to the LORD, 11and they said to Moses, "Why
Exod 5:21; 15:24 did you bring us out here to die in the wilderness? Weren't there enough graves for us in
Ps 106:7-8 Egypt? What have you done to us? Why did you make us leave Egypt? 12Didn't we tell you
this would happen while we were still in Egypt? We said, 'Leave us alone! Let us be slaves
to the Egyptians. It's better to be a slave in Egypt than a corpse in the wilderness!'"

13:18a Hebrew *sea of reeds.* 13:18b Greek version reads *left Egypt in the fifth generation.* 14:4 Hebrew *after them.*

13:19 Jacob's son Joseph had risen to great power in Egypt (Genesis 37–50). During a famine, Jacob's entire family moved to Goshen in Egypt to obtain safety and sustenance. Prior to his death, Joseph had prophesied that the Israelites would return to the Promised Land, and the Israelites had promised to bring Joseph's body with them when this return took place (Genesis 50:24-25).

13:21-22 Typical physical manifestations of God (Exodus 33:9-10; 40:34-38; Numbers 9:15-22; 11:25) were fire and smoke. God's visible presence assured the Israelites that just as He had protected them and fought for them in Egypt, He would continue to do so throughout their travels.

14:2-4 The Lord instructed the Israelites to lead the Egyptian army into a trap. God had not merely planned an escape for Israel; He had planned a devastating military victory that would crush the power of Egypt.

14:5-9 In light of the horrible curses that had fallen on Egypt in response to their enslavement of the Israelites, it seems incredible that the Egyptians would have wanted the Israelites to return. But God hardened Pharaoh's heart (Exodus 14:4, 8) in order that the Egyptians would commit themselves to this foolish course of action.

▸ HOLINESS

14:11 The Spirit yields growth. As before, the people complained to Moses (Exodus 5:19-21). But the Lord had strengthened Moses (Exodus 14:13-14), so this time he was not so distraught. He responded with words of confidence in God. God strengthens us, too, so that we don't always react as we have in the past. The Holy Spirit stimulates the spiritual growth of those whom He indwells (Philippians 1:6). (***See Holiness****> Submission> Yielding to Spirit,* TopicGuide page A41.)

13 But Moses told the people, "Don't be afraid. Just stand still and watch the LORD rescue
you today. The Egyptians you see today will never be seen again. 14 The LORD Himself will
fight for you. Just stay calm."

ESCAPE THROUGH THE RED SEA

15 Then the LORD said to Moses, "Why are you crying out to Me? Tell the people to get
moving! 16 Pick up your staff and raise your hand over the sea. Divide the water so the Isra-
elites can walk through the middle of the sea on dry ground. 17 And I will harden the hearts
of the Egyptians, and they will charge in after the Israelites. My great glory will be dis-
played through Pharaoh and his troops, his chariots, and his charioteers. 18 When My glory
is displayed through them, all Egypt will see My glory and know that I am the LORD!"
19 Then the angel of God, who had been leading the people of Israel, moved to the rear
of the camp. The pillar of cloud also moved from the front and stood behind them. 20 The
cloud settled between the Egyptian and Israelite camps. As darkness fell, the cloud turned
to fire, lighting up the night. But the Egyptians and Israelites did not approach each other
all night.
21 Then Moses raised his hand over the sea, and the LORD opened up a path through the
water with a strong east wind. The wind blew all that night, turning the seabed into dry
land. 22 So the people of Israel walked through the middle of the sea on dry ground, with
walls of water on each side!
23 Then the Egyptians—all of Pharaoh's horses, chariots, and charioteers—chased them
into the middle of the sea. 24 But just before dawn the LORD looked down on the Egyptian
army from the pillar of fire and cloud, and He threw their forces into total confusion. 25 He
twisted* their chariot wheels, making their chariots difficult to drive. "Let's get out of here—
away from these Israelites!" the Egyptians shouted. "The LORD is fighting for them against
Egypt!"
26 When all the Israelites had reached the other side, the LORD said to Moses, "Raise your
hand over the sea again. Then the waters will rush back and cover the Egyptians and their

14:13 Gen 15:1; Exod 14:30; 15:2
14:14 Exod 15:3; Deut 1:30; 3:22; Isa 30:15
14:15 Josh 7:10
14:16 Exod 4:17, 20; Num 20:8-9, 11
14:18 Exod 14:25
14:19 Exod 13:21-22
14:21 Exod 7:19; Pss 106:9; 114:3, 5; Isa 63:12-13
14:22 Exod 15:19; Neh 9:11; Pss 66:6; 78:13; Heb 11:29
14:24 Exod 13:21
14:26 Exod 14:16

14:25 As in Greek version, Samaritan Pentateuch, and Syriac version; Hebrew reads *He removed.*

14:14 God's people continue to identify God as their Holy Warrior (1 Samuel 17:45; Revelation 12:7; 17:14). In the ancient world, war was a sacred undertaking in which the honor of the opposing deities was at stake. Similarly, Moses presented God as the Divine Warrior who would continue to fight on behalf of His people (compare Exodus 14:25; 15:3; Isaiah 42:13).

14:17 God's purpose in devastating Egypt was not only to rescue Israel and punish Egypt, but also to spread His own fame in the form of praise from His people and fear from His enemies.

14:18 Here, as in many other places in the Bible, to "know" the Lord is not about faith, but to have a true understanding of His power. Unbelieving Egypt would come to realize God's power and to fear Him, but not in a way that would lead to their salvation.

14:19 In many passages of Scripture, the angel of the Lord or the angel of God is hard to distinguish from God Himself (see Exodus 3:2). For this reason, many interpreters believe that the angel is a pre-incarnate appearance of Christ. Here, the angel of God is distinct from the cloud.

▸ HOLINESS

14:22 Guidance from the Spirit. Though the Israelites had shown a remarkable lack of faith up to this point, when the waters parted they demonstrated trust in God and marched along the bottom of the sea. God is not usually so obvious in showing us where to go—but when we do recognize God's voice and will, we must march forward in obedience to Him. (***See Holiness***> *Submission*> *Yielding to Spirit,* TopicGuide page A41.)

14:23 It is nearly unfathomable that any reasonable person would have pursued the Israelites in the face of such an obvious demonstration of God's power as the parting of the sea. To overcome this natural hesitation, God intervened by hardening the Egyptians' hearts (Exodus 14:17).

▸ WORSHIP

14:26 Giving God the credit He deserves. Was it Moses or God who opened and closed the Red Sea? Moses, the author of Exodus, made it clear in Exodus 14:31—it was done by the power of God. In response to God's display of might, the people feared and put their faith in God and then followed His servant Moses. Have you ever been tempted to claim credit for something that God did? Pray that God will give you the grace to let Him work through you. Remember to give Him the credit when He does. (***See Worship***> *OT*> *Reverence,* TopicGuide page A28.)

14:26-27 As he had in many of the curses on Egypt (Exodus 6–12), God chose to work through Moses in order to demonstrate that Moses was His chosen, authoritative representative. The emphasis on Moses throughout these accounts indicated to later generations of Israelites that they should follow the laws and worship regulations that Moses had established, such as those listed in Exodus 20–40.

14:27 Exod 15:1, 7 Deut 11:4 Heb 11:29
14:28 Exod 15:19 Neh 9:11 Pss 78:53; 106:11
14:29 Ps 66:6 Isa 11:15
14:30 Ps 106:8 Isa 63:8, 11
14:31 Exod 4:31; 19:9 Ps 106:12
15:1 Ps 106:12 Isa 12:5; 42:10-12 Jer 51:21 Rev 15:3
15:2 Exod 3:15-16 Deut 10:21 2 Sam 22:47 Ps 18:1 Isa 12:2
15:3 Exod 14:14 Pss 24:8; 83:18
15:4 Exod 14:6-7, 17, 28
15:5 Exod 14:28 Neh 9:11
15:6 Exod 3:20 Ps 118:15-16

chariots and charioteers." 27 So as the sun began to rise, Moses raised his hand over the
sea, and the water rushed back into its usual place. The Egyptians tried to escape, but the
LORD swept them into the sea. 28 Then the waters returned and covered all the chariots and
charioteers—the entire army of Pharaoh. Of all the Egyptians who had chased the Israelites
into the sea, not a single one survived.

29 But the people of Israel had walked through the middle of the sea on dry ground, as
the water stood up like a wall on both sides. 30 That is how the LORD rescued Israel from the
hand of the Egyptians that day. And the Israelites saw the bodies of the Egyptians washed
up on the seashore. 31 When the people of Israel saw the mighty power that the LORD had
unleashed against the Egyptians, they were filled with awe before Him. They put their
faith in the LORD and in His servant Moses.

A SONG OF DELIVERANCE

15 Then Moses and the people of Israel sang this song to the LORD:

"I will sing to the LORD,
for He has triumphed gloriously;
He has hurled both horse and rider
into the sea.
2 The LORD is my strength and my song;
He has given me victory.
This is my God, and I will praise Him—
my father's God, and I will exalt Him!
3 The LORD is a warrior;
Yahweh* is His name!
4 Pharaoh's chariots and army
He has hurled into the sea.
The finest of Pharaoh's officers
are drowned in the Red Sea.*
5 The deep waters gushed over them;
they sank to the bottom like a stone.

6 "Your right hand, O LORD,
is glorious in power.
Your right hand, O LORD,
smashes the enemy.

15:3 *Yahweh* is a transliteration of the proper name *YHWH* that is sometimes rendered "Jehovah"; in this translation it is usually rendered "the LORD" (note the use of small capitals). 15:4 Hebrew *sea of reeds;* also in 15:22.

14:29 The Israelites' crossing of the sea on dry land is one of the best-known stories of the Bible. This miracle performed at the beginning of their journey was paralleled by a similar miracle when the people later entered the Promised Land (Joshua 3).

14:31 God's power was frightening and terrible, and Israel rightly feared what He might do to them if they displeased Him as the Egyptians had. Nevertheless, their fear inspired confidence that God could and would follow through with His plan to bring them to the Promised Land.

▸ WORSHIP

15:1 Praise through song and dance. God's people were free! Their natural response was worship—they immediately composed a song for the occasion. Miriam, a prophet and the sister of Moses and Aaron, led the women in a dance to accompany the song. Turn your talents toward God in worship and find creative ways to thank Him for setting you free from sin. (***See Worship****> OT> Posture> Dancing,* TopicGuide page A28.)

15:2 This is an acknowledgement of the faithfulness of God throughout the generations from Abraham, Isaac, and Jacob to the days of Moses (compare Exodus 2:24; 3:6, 15-16; 4:5; 6:3-8).

15:3 God is often portrayed as a warrior who fights on behalf of His people and who unfailingly defeats His enemies. This was a great assurance to the Israelites whom Moses was about to lead into the Promised Land, a land inhabited by many different peoples who would oppose the Israelites with strong military force (compare Exodus 14:14, 25; Isaiah 42:13).

7 In the greatness of Your majesty,
You overthrow those who rise against You.
You unleash Your blazing fury;
it consumes them like straw.
8 At the blast of Your breath,
the waters piled up!
The surging waters stood straight like a wall;
in the heart of the sea the deep waters became hard.

9 "The enemy boasted, 'I will chase them
and catch up with them.
I will plunder them
and consume them.
I will flash my sword;
my powerful hand will destroy them.'
10 But You blew with Your breath,
and the sea covered them.
They sank like lead
in the mighty waters.

11 "Who is like You among the gods, O LORD—
glorious in holiness,
awesome in splendor,
performing great wonders?
12 You raised Your right hand,
and the earth swallowed our enemies.

13 "With Your unfailing love You lead
the people You have redeemed.
In Your might, You guide them
to Your sacred home.

15:7 Exod 9:16; 14:24 Ps 78:49-50

15:8 Exod 14:22, 29 Ps 78:13

15:9 Exod 14:5-9

15:10 Exod 14:27-28

15:11 Exod 8:10 Deut 3:24 1 Sam 2:2 2 Sam 7:22 Pss 22:23; 72:18 Isa 6:3 Rev 4:8

15:12 Exod 15:6

15:13 Neh 9:12 Ps 77:15, 20

15:7 By opposing and oppressing God's people, and by ignoring His authoritative representative Moses, the Egyptians opposed God Himself.

15:11 The conflict between Egypt and Israel was not merely human. It also involved a supernatural conflict between the gods of Egypt and the God of Israel (Exodus 12:12). Each of Egypt's gods was either a figment of human imagination or a demon (Isaiah 44:14-17; Jeremiah 2:27-28; 1 Corinthians 8:5-7; 10:19-20). Only the God of Israel is truly God.

BECAUSE GOD IS HOLY

I will devote myself to him in purity, worship and service.

Who is like You among the gods, O LORD—glorious in holiness, awesome in splendor, performing great wonders?

EXODUS 15:11

FOR THE NEXT *GOD IS HOLY* FEATURE SEE PAGE 222.

14 The peoples hear and tremble;
anguish grips those who live in Philistia.
15 The leaders of Edom are terrified;
the nobles of Moab tremble.
All who live in Canaan melt away;
16 terror and dread fall upon them.
The power of Your arm
makes them lifeless as stone
until Your people pass by, O LORD,
until the people You purchased pass by.
17 You will bring them in and plant them on Your own mountain—
the place, O LORD, reserved for Your own dwelling,
the sanctuary, O Lord, that Your hands have established.
18 The LORD will reign forever and ever!"

19 When Pharaoh's horses, chariots, and charioteers rushed into the sea, the LORD
brought the water crashing down on them. But the people of Israel had walked through
the middle of the sea on dry ground!
20 Then Miriam the prophet, Aaron's sister, took a tambourine and led all the women as
they played their tambourines and danced. 21 And Miriam sang this song:

"Sing to the LORD,
for He has triumphed gloriously;
He has hurled both horse and rider
into the sea."

BITTER WATER AT MARAH

22 Then Moses led the people of Israel away from the Red Sea, and they moved out into
the desert of Shur. They traveled in this desert for three days without finding any water.
23 When they came to the oasis of Marah, the water was too bitter to drink. So they called
the place Marah (which means "bitter").
24 Then the people complained and turned against Moses. "What are we going to
drink?" they demanded. 25 So Moses cried out to the LORD for help, and the LORD showed
him a piece of wood. Moses threw it into the water, and this made the water good to drink.
It was there at Marah that the LORD set before them the following decree as a standard to
test their faithfulness to Him. 26 He said, "If you will listen carefully to the voice of the LORD
your God and do what is right in His sight, obeying His commands and keeping all His de-
crees, then I will not make you suffer any of the diseases I sent on the Egyptians; for I am
the LORD who heals you."

15:14 Deut 2:25; Hab 3:7
15:15 Num 22:3; Deut 2:4; Josh 2:11; 5:1
15:17 Exod 23:20; 32:34; Pss 2:6; 78:54, 68; Isa 5:2; Jer 2:21
15:18 Pss 10:16; 29:10; Isa 57:15
15:19 Exod 14:22, 28
15:20 Exod 2:4; Num 26:59; 1 Sam 18:6; Pss 30:11; 150:4
15:21 Exod 15:1
15:22 Num 33:8; Pss 77:20; 78:52
15:23 Num 33:8; Ruth 1:20
15:24 Exod 14:11; Ps 106:13
15:25 Exod 14:10; 16:4
15:26 Exod 19:5-6; Deut 7:15; Ps 103:3

15:14-16 Although the Egyptians did not live to tell of God's exploits (Exodus 14:28), God's fame still spread to many nations (Numbers 14:13-16; Joshua 2:8-11; 1 Samuel 4:8-9). Through this, Israel's enemies trembled in fear of their approach (Joshua 2:8-9), and some followed the mighty God of Israel (Jethro in Exodus 18; Ruth in Ruth 1:16; Rahab in Joshua 2).

▶ GOD
15:24-25 Failing the test. With God leading the way, the multitude traveled deep into the desert. They began to grow weak from lack of water, and when they discovered that their water supply was fouled, they rebelled. As God had planned, Moses made the water sweet and pure so that the people would not die of thirst. But their continued health and safety were contingent upon listening carefully to God and obeying Him. Be careful that you do not fail the tests of faith that come your way. Failing to heed God's voice and keep His commands always has consequences. (***See God****> God's Attributes> Patient> God is slow to anger,* TopicGuide page A17.)

▶ GOD
15:26 God's names: the LORD, the Healer. Have you ever wondered if God can really heal people? Here, God revealed Himself to the newly freed Israelites as *Yahweh-Rapha*—"The LORD who Heals." His promise to keep the Israelites free from disease was conditioned upon their continued repentance and obedience. Deuteronomy 29:5-6 makes it clear that God kept His word and preserved them during their journey. And the ministry of Jesus and the apostles continued to demonstrate that God has profound power over human suffering. Trust that even today God has the power to heal you of sickness—but He may also extend His power to enable you to suffer for His glory. (***See God****> God's names> God,* TopicGuide page A18.)

27After leaving Marah, the Israelites traveled on to the oasis of Elim, where they found 15:27
twelve springs and seventy palm trees. They camped there beside the water. Num 33:9

MANNA AND QUAIL FROM HEAVEN

16 Then the whole community of Israel set out from Elim and journeyed into the wil- 16:1
derness of Sin,* between Elim and Mount Sinai. They arrived there on the fifteenth Exod 17:1 Num 33:11-12
day of the second month, one month after leaving the land of Egypt.* 2There, too, the 16:2
whole community of Israel complained about Moses and Aaron. Exod 14:11
3"If only the LORD had killed us back in Egypt," they moaned. "There we sat around pots 1 Cor 10:10
filled with meat and ate all the bread we wanted. But now you have brought us into this
wilderness to starve us all to death."
4Then the LORD said to Moses, "Look, I'm going to rain down food from heaven for you. 16:4
Each day the people can go out and pick up as much food as they need for that day. I will Deut 8:2-3, 16 Pss 78:24; 105:40
test them in this to see whether or not they will follow My instructions. 5On the sixth day John 6:31
they will gather food, and when they prepare it, there will be twice as much as usual." 1 Cor 10:3
6So Moses and Aaron said to all the people of Israel, "By evening you will realize it was 16:5
the LORD who brought you out of the land of Egypt. 7In the morning you will see the glory Exod 16:22
of the LORD, because He has heard your complaints, which are against Him, not against us. 16:6
What have we done that you should complain about us?" 8Then Moses added, "The LORD Exod 6:6
will give you meat to eat in the evening and bread to satisfy you in the morning, for He 16:7 Exod 16:12
has heard all your complaints against Him. What have we done? Yes, your complaints are Num 14:27; 16:11
against the LORD, not against us." 16:10
9Then Moses said to Aaron, "Announce this to the entire community of Israel: 'Present Num 16:19
yourselves before the LORD, for He has heard your complaining.'" 10And as Aaron spoke to 16:12
the whole community of Israel, they looked out toward the wilderness. There they could Exod 16:7
see the awesome glory of the LORD in the cloud. 16:13 Num 11:31
11Then the LORD said to Moses, 12"I have heard the Israelites' complaints. Now tell them, Pss 78:27-28; 105:40
'In the evening you will have meat to eat, and in the morning you will have all the bread 16:14
you want. Then you will know that I am the LORD your God.'" Num 11:7-9 Deut 8:3
13That evening vast numbers of quail flew in and covered the camp. And the next morn- 16:15
ing the area around the camp was wet with dew. 14When the dew evaporated, a flaky sub- Exod 16:31 Neh 9:5
stance as fine as frost blanketed the ground. 15The Israelites were puzzled when they saw John 6:31
it. "What is it?" they asked each other. They had no idea what it was. 1 Cor 10:3

16:1a The geographical name *Sin* is related to *Sinai* and should not be confused with the English word *sin*. 16:1b The Exodus had occurred on the fifteenth day of the first month (see Num 33:3).

16:1 The precise locations of these sites—Elim, the wilderness of Sin, and Mount Sinai—are unknown. The traditional locations, chosen during medieval times, are in the Sinai Peninsula, between the modern gulfs of Suez and Aqaba.

▸ GOD

16:12 Quail and manna. Most of us have never gone hungry because of poverty, war, or another tragic circumstance. But historically, God's people have not always been rich and powerful. In fact, many have not even had access to food and water. Nevertheless, God provides for His people when they are faithful to Him (Matthew 6:25-34). God cares about basic human needs, and He calls us to give generously on His behalf to those who are truly needy (James 2:15-17). (***See God****> God's Attributes> Good> God provides for our needs,* TopicGuide page A16.)

16:14-31 The description of the food or *manna* that God provided here does not precisely match the description of the *manna* in Numbers 11:7-8. In Exodus, it is described as white and flaky, and its taste is compared to honey. In Numbers, it is pale yellow and shaped like coriander seeds, which are round, and it is said to taste like olive oil. It is possible that both passages describe the same substance from somewhat different perspectives. It is also possible that God varied the manna He provided. The description in Exodus resembles a secretion of insects that live in tamarisks. This secretion solidifies in the cold of the night, but melts in the heat of the day.

▸ BIBLE

16:15 Discovering God in the manna. How is Jesus Christ like the mysterious bread that God gave to ancient Israel? Jesus claimed to be the "bread from heaven" that gives eternal life (John 6:50-51). Unlike those who ate and died in the wilderness, anyone who partakes of the "true bread that came down from heaven" (John 6:58) will never die. The provision of manna (Exodus 16:31) to fill the physical hunger of ancient Israel prefigures the provision of Christ to fill the spiritual hunger of God's people for all time. (***See Bible****> Unity> OT Types> Manna,* TopicGuide page A11.)

16:16 And Moses told them, "It is the food the LORD has given you to eat. [16]These are the
Exod 16:33, 36 LORD's instructions: Each household should gather as much as it needs. Pick up two quarts*
for each person in your tent."
[17]So the people of Israel did as they were told. Some gathered a lot, some only a little.
16:18 [18]But when they measured it out,* everyone had just enough. Those who gathered a lot had
*2 Cor 8:15 nothing left over, and those who gathered only a little had enough. Each family had just
what it needed.
16:19 [19]Then Moses told them, "Do not keep any of it until morning." [20]But some of them
Exod 12:10; 23:18 didn't listen and kept some of it until morning. But by then it was full of maggots and had a
terrible smell. Moses was very angry with them.
[21]After this the people gathered the food morning by morning, each family according
to its need. And as the sun became hot, the flakes they had not picked up melted and
16:22 disappeared. [22]On the sixth day, they gathered twice as much as usual—four quarts* for
Exod 16:5; 34:31 each person instead of two. Then all the leaders of the community came and asked
16:23 Moses for an explanation. [23]He told them, "This is what the LORD commanded: Tomor-
Gen 2:3 Exod 20:8; 23:12 row will be a day of complete rest, a holy Sabbath day set apart for the LORD. So bake or
Neh 9:14 boil as much as you want today, and set aside what is left for tomorrow."
16:24 [24]So they put some aside until morning, just as Moses had commanded. And in the
Exod 16:20 morning the leftover food was wholesome and good, without maggots or odor. [25]Moses
said, "Eat this food today, for today is a Sabbath day dedicated to the LORD. There will be
no food on the ground today. [26]You may gather the food for six days, but the seventh day
is the Sabbath. There will be no food on the ground that day."
16:28 [27]Some of the people went out anyway on the seventh day, but they found no food.
Ps 78:10 [28]The LORD asked Moses, "How long will these people refuse to obey My commands and
instructions? [29]They must realize that the Sabbath is the LORD's gift to you. That is why He
gives you a two-day supply on the sixth day, so there will be enough for two days. On the
Sabbath day you must each stay in your place. Do not go out to pick up food on the sev-
enth day." [30]So the people did not gather any food on the seventh day.
16:31 [31]The Israelites called the food manna.* It was white like coriander seed, and it tasted
Num 11:7-9 Deut 8:3, 16 like honey wafers.
16:33 [32]Then Moses said, "This is what the LORD has commanded: Fill a two-quart container
Heb 9:4 with manna to preserve it for your descendants. Then later generations will be able to see
Rev 2:17 the food I gave you in the wilderness when I set you free from Egypt."
16:34 [33]Moses said to Aaron, "Get a jar and fill it with two quarts of manna. Then put it in a sa-
Exod 25:16, 21 Num 1:50 cred place before the LORD to preserve it for all future generations." [34]Aaron did just as the
16:35 LORD had commanded Moses. He eventually placed it in the Ark of the Covenant—in
Josh 5:12 Neh 9:20-21 front of the stone tablets inscribed with the terms of the covenant.* [35]So the people of Israel

16:16 Hebrew *1 omer* [2 liters]; also in 16:32, 33. 16:18 Hebrew *measured it with an omer.* 16:22 Hebrew *2 omers* [4 liters]. 16:31 *Manna* means "What is it?" See 16:15. 16:34 Hebrew *He placed it in front of the Testimony;* see note on 25:16.

▶ BIBLE
16:19-20 God's sustaining Word. Just as the Hebrews couldn't live on yesterday's provision of manna, we cannot sustain our spiritual lives on the Bible study or prayer or worship services of the distant past. We must feed on God's truths and live in God's presence on a regular basis. We cannot be faithful if we are not "faith-full." (***See Bible*** *> Power> Equip> Sustains our lives,* TopicGuide page A11.)

16:22-30 The Jewish Sabbath was confirmed in the Law provided to Moses on Mount Sinai (Exodus 20:8-11). The Sabbath was a day of rest, so that no manna could be gathered on this day. For six days of the week God provided manna, but on the seventh day of the cycle of manna, He provided none.

16:24 In contrast to the other days of the cycle on which leftover food spoiled (Exodus 16:20), God miraculously provided for the Sabbath by preserving food that naturally would have spoiled.

16:32-33 Moses again emphasized one of his primary concerns in composing the book of Exodus: motivating future generations of Israelites to maintain the laws and worship established by God through Moses.

16:34 The Ark of the Covenant was essentially a wooden chest made to strict specifications. God had not yet instructed Moses to make the Ark (compare Exodus 25:10-22). The eventual craftsman of the Ark was a man named Bezalel (Exodus 37:1-9).

ate manna for forty years until they arrived at the land where they would settle. They ate manna until they came to the border of the land of Canaan.

36The container used to measure the manna was an omer, which was one tenth of an ephah; it held about two quarts.*

WATER FROM THE ROCK

17 At the LORD's command, the whole community of Israel left the wilderness of Sin* and moved from place to place. Eventually they camped at Rephidim, but there was no water there for the people to drink. 2So once more the people complained against Moses. "Give us water to drink!" they demanded.

"Quiet!" Moses replied. "Why are you complaining against me? And why are you testing the LORD?"

3But tormented by thirst, they continued to argue with Moses. "Why did you bring us out of Egypt? Are you trying to kill us, our children, and our livestock with thirst?"

4Then Moses cried out to the LORD, "What should I do with these people? They are ready to stone me!"

5The LORD said to Moses, "Walk out in front of the people. Take your staff, the one you used when you struck the water of the Nile, and call some of the elders of Israel to join you. 6I will stand before you on the rock at Mount Sinai.* Strike the rock, and water will come gushing out. Then the people will be able to drink." So Moses struck the rock as he was told, and water gushed out as the elders looked on.

7Moses named the place Massah (which means "test") and Meribah (which means "arguing") because the people of Israel argued with Moses and tested the LORD by saying, "Is the LORD here with us or not?"

ISRAEL DEFEATS THE AMALEKITES

8While the people of Israel were still at Rephidim, the warriors of Amalek attacked them. 9Moses commanded Joshua, "Choose some men to go out and fight the army of Amalek for us. Tomorrow, I will stand at the top of the hill, holding the staff of God in my hand."

10So Joshua did what Moses had commanded and fought the army of Amalek. Meanwhile, Moses, Aaron, and Hur climbed to the top of a nearby hill. 11As long as Moses held up the staff in his hand, the Israelites had the advantage. But whenever he dropped his hand, the Amalekites gained the advantage. 12Moses' arms soon became so tired he

17:1 Exod 16:1; 19:2 Num 33:15
17:2 Exod 14:11-12 Num 20:3 Deut 6:16 1 Cor 10:10
17:3 Exod 16:2-3
17:4 Num 14:10; 16:19
17:5 Exod 7:20; 14:16
17:6 Num 20:8-10 Pss 78:15-16; 105:41 1 Cor 10:4
17:7 Deut 6:16; 9:22 Pss 81:7; 95:8
17:8 Gen 36:12, 16 Num 24:20 Deut 25:17-19
17:9 Exod 24:13 Num 11:28
17:10 Exod 24:14; 31:2
17:12 Isa 35:3

16:36 Hebrew *An omer is one tenth of an ephah.* 17:1 The geographical name *Sin* is related to *Sinai* and should not be confused with the English word *sin.* 17:6 Hebrew *Horeb,* another name for Sinai.

16:35 In Canaan God continued to provide food for His people; He caused crops to grow with little effort on the part of the people (Deuteronomy 11:10-15).

▸ BIBLE
17:5-6 Discovering God in the water from the rock. How is Jesus like a battered, water-spurting rock? The apostle Paul notes that in the same way that the rock provided life-giving water in Moses' day, Jesus Christ produces life-giving salvation for all who believe (1 Corinthians 10:3-5). (***See Bible****> Unity> OT Types> Water from the rock,* TopicGuide page A11.)

17:6 God promises to be present with Moses "on the rock." God is described as a rock in the Song of Moses (Deuteronomy 32:4, 15, 18, 31) and in the psalms that speak of this historical event (Psalm 78:15, 20, 35; 95:1). Moses' action of striking or digging into the rock is a solemn matter, as Moses later hit the rock without God's permission and sinned grievously (Numbers 20:9-12).

17:8-16 The Amalekites descended from Esau's grandson Amalek. While the feud between Jacob and Esau seemed to have been settled during their lifetime (Genesis 32–33), the Amalekites remained enemies of the Israelites.

17:9-14 Joshua, first mentioned here, played a prominent future role in Israel's history, succeeding Moses as Israel's leader (Joshua 1:1-2). The book of Joshua records much of what Joshua accomplished as Israel's leader, including bringing the Israelites into the Promised Land.

17:10-13 Joshua's success in battle depended on Moses' leadership. This is symbolically reflected in the fact that Joshua prevailed only when Moses held aloft his staff. This detail instructed the Israelites who followed Joshua into the Promised Land (Joshua 1) that Joshua was to be trusted and followed because he obeyed Moses.

17:12 Even great men like Moses grew exhausted in service. Today, our leaders need our help. They are not only tired, they are also specially targeted by Satan's temptations. Can you support civil and religious leaders by prayer, encouragement, or financial support?

could no longer hold them up. So Aaron and Hur found a stone for him to sit on. Then they
stood on each side of Moses, holding up his hands. So his hands held steady until sunset.
13 As a result, Joshua overwhelmed the army of Amalek in battle.
17:14 Exod 24:4; 34:27 Num 33:2 14 After the victory, the LORD instructed Moses, "Write this down on a scroll as a perma-
nent reminder, and read it aloud to Joshua: I will erase the memory of Amalek from under
heaven." 15 Moses built an altar there and named it Yahweh-nissi (which means "the LORD
17:15 Gen 22:14 is my banner"). 16 He said, "They have raised their fist against the LORD's throne, so now*
the LORD will be at war with Amalek generation after generation."

JETHRO'S VISIT TO MOSES

18:1 Exod 2:16, 18; 3:1 **18** Moses' father-in-law, Jethro, the priest of Midian, heard about everything God had
done for Moses and His people, the Israelites. He heard especially about how the
LORD had rescued them from Egypt.
18:2 Exod 2:21; 4:25 2 Earlier, Moses had sent his wife, Zipporah, and his two sons back to Jethro, who had
taken them in. 3 (Moses' first son was named Gershom,* for Moses had said when the boy
18:3 Exod 2:22 Acts 7:29 was born, "I have been a foreigner in a foreign land." 4 His second son was named Eliezer,*
for Moses had said, "The God of my ancestors was my helper; He rescued me from the
sword of Pharaoh.") 5 Jethro, Moses' father-in-law, now came to visit Moses in the wilder-
18:4 Gen 49:25 ness. He brought Moses' wife and two sons with him, and they arrived while Moses and
18:5 Exod 3:1 the people were camped near the mountain of God. 6 Jethro had sent a message to Moses,
saying, "I, Jethro, your father-in-law, am coming to see you with your wife and your two
sons."
18:7 Gen 43:28 7 So Moses went out to meet his father-in-law. He bowed low and kissed him. They
asked about each other's welfare and then went into Moses' tent. 8 Moses told his father-
18:8 Exod 15:6, 16 Num 20:14 in-law everything the LORD had done to Pharaoh and Egypt on behalf of Israel. He also told
about all the hardships they had experienced along the way and how the LORD had res-
18:9 Isa 63:7-14 cued His people from all their troubles. 9 Jethro was delighted when he heard about all the
good things the LORD had done for Israel as He rescued them from the hand of the Egyp-
18:10 1 Kgs 8:56 Ps 68:19-20 tians.
10 "Praise the LORD," Jethro said, "for He has rescued you from the Egyptians and from
Pharaoh. Yes, He has rescued Israel from the powerful hand of Egypt! 11 I know now that
18:11 Exod 12:12; 15:11 the LORD is greater than all other gods, because He rescued His people from the oppres-
18:12 Gen 31:54 Exod 24:5 sion of the proud Egyptians."
12 Then Jethro, Moses' father-in-law, brought a burnt offering and sacrifices to God.

17:16 Or *Hands have been lifted up to the LORD's throne, and now.* 18:3 *Gershom* sounds like a Hebrew term that means "a foreigner there." 18:4 *Eliezer* means "God is my helper."

17:14 This instruction emphasized Joshua's future importance in leading Israel. The next generation of Israelites was to follow him as he succeeded Moses (Joshua 1) because God had chosen him and because he had obeyed Moses. The Lord largely fulfilled this curse of destroying Amalek through Saul in 1 Samuel 15, but Saul's sin prevented the Amalekites' total destruction. They were finally eliminated by Hezekiah (1 Chronicles 4:43).

▸ GOD

17:15 God's names: the LORD, the banner of His people. How do you celebrate special events? To commemorate extraordinary occasions, the Hebrews would often erect a pile of stones, either as an altar or a monument. The name given to this altar celebrated an aspect of God's character by revealing a new name for God, *Yahweh-Nissi,* or "The LORD Is My Banner." Today we honor this revelation of God by proudly bearing the name of Christ, even when it may bring persecution (Matthew 5:11-12). (***See God***> *God's Names*> *God,* TopicGuide page A18.)

18:1-7 When Moses fled from Egypt (Exodus 2:13-15) he traveled to Midian. There he met his future wife Zipporah and her father, Jethro (also called Reuel) (Exodus 2:18, 21). Jethro was a Midianite, descending from Abraham through Abraham's second wife Keturah (Genesis 25:1-2). Moses was also a descendant of Abraham, but through Abraham's first wife, Sarah.

18:5 Mount Sinai is also called Mount Horeb. Its designation as the "mountain of God" marks it as a royal sanctuary of the Lord.

18:11 As an early priest of God, Jethro might not have known that other gods were false gods, being figments of human imagination and/or demons (Isaiah 44:14-17; Jeremiah 2:27-28; 1 Corinthians 8:5-7; 10:19-20). His affirmation here emphasized God's power over all other supernatural forces, both real and imagined.

Aaron and all the elders of Israel came out and joined him in a sacrificial meal in God's
presence.

JETHRO'S WISE ADVICE

13 The next day, Moses took his seat to hear the people's disputes against each other. They
waited before him from morning till evening.
14 When Moses' father-in-law saw all that Moses was doing for the people, he asked,
"What are you really accomplishing here? Why are you trying to do all this alone while
everyone stands around you from morning till evening?"
15 Moses replied, "Because the people come to me to get a ruling from God. 16 When a
dispute arises, they come to me, and I am the one who settles the case between the quar-
reling parties. I inform the people of God's decrees and give them His instructions."
17 "This is not good!" Moses' father-in-law exclaimed. 18 "You're going to wear yourself
out—and the people, too. This job is too heavy a burden for you to handle all by yourself.
19 Now listen to me, and let me give you a word of advice, and may God be with you. You
should continue to be the people's representative before God, bringing their disputes to
Him. 20 Teach them God's decrees, and give them His instructions. Show them how to con-
duct their lives. 21 But select from all the people some capable, honest men who fear God
and hate bribes. Appoint them as leaders over groups of one thousand, one hundred, fifty,
and ten. 22 They should always be available to solve the people's common disputes, but
have them bring the major cases to you. Let the leaders decide the smaller matters them-
selves. They will help you carry the load, making the task easier for you. 23 If you follow
this advice, and if God commands you to do so, then you will be able to endure the pres-
sures, and all these people will go home in peace."
24 Moses listened to his father-in-law's advice and followed his suggestions. 25 He chose
capable men from all over Israel and appointed them as leaders over the people. He put
them in charge of groups of one thousand, one hundred, fifty, and ten. 26 These men were
always available to solve the people's common disputes. They brought the major cases to
Moses, but they took care of the smaller matters themselves.
27 Soon after this, Moses said good-bye to his father-in-law, who returned to his own land.

THE LORD REVEALS HIMSELF AT SINAI

19 Exactly two months after the Israelites left Egypt,* they arrived in the wilderness of
Sinai. 2 After breaking camp at Rephidim, they came to the wilderness of Sinai and
set up camp there at the base of Mount Sinai.

18:15 Num 9:8; Deut 17:8-13
18:16 Exod 24:14
18:18 Num 11:14, 17; Deut 1:9
18:19-20 Deut 1:18
18:21 Deut 1:13, 15; Ps 15:1-5
18:22 Num 11:17; Deut 1:17-18
18:25 Deut 1:15; 16:18
18:26 Deut 16:18
18:27 Num 10:29-30
19:1 Exod 12:51; 16:1
19:2 Exod 17:1; 18:5

19:1 Hebrew *In the third month after the Israelites left Egypt, on the very day,* i.e., two lunar months to the day after leaving Egypt. Compare Num 33:3.

18:13-26 Prior to Jethro's advice, Moses himself judged all of Israel's disputes that could not be easily settled. Jethro recommended a system whereby Moses would appoint lower courts to hear the official cases. Cases would reach Moses only when the lower courts failed to reach a decision. In Acts 15, the church used a similar system of graded courts to decide how Gentiles were to be integrated into the church.

18:19 We all need someone who can tell us when it is time to slow down. In this case, Jethro saw that Moses was becoming burdened with the judicial tasks of leading the new nation. Jethro suggested a system of graded courts in which lesser judges reported to Moses (Exodus 18:26; compare Deuteronomy 17:8-12). Moses saw the wisdom of this suggestion and did everything that Jethro said (Exodus 18:24). Do you feel alone in your responsibilities, or do you have someone in your life who can give you wise counsel? Build relationships with godly, mature people who can offer you advice.

18:26 Even Moses did not always know the answers to hard cases. He appealed to the Lord for guidance on more than one occasion (compare Numbers 15:32-35; 27:1-7), indicating that the Lord Himself was the supreme judge of Israel (compare 2 Chronicles 19:6).

19:2 Mount Sinai is traditionally located on the Sinai Peninsula in a wilderness area between the modern gulfs of Suez and Aqaba. Alternately, it may have been located in or near Midian on the eastern side of the Gulf of Aqaba. The alternate location better corresponds with Jethro's home being in Midian. Moses was tending Jethro's flock when he first met the Lord at Sinai (Exodus 3:1). Traditional sites were often chosen for their ease of accessibility for ancient religious pilgrims.

3 Then Moses climbed the mountain to appear before God. The LORD called to him from
the mountain and said, "Give these instructions to the family of Jacob; announce it to the
descendants of Israel: 4 'You have seen what I did to the Egyptians. You know how I carried
you on eagles' wings and brought you to Myself. 5 Now if you will obey Me and keep My
covenant, you will be My own special treasure from among all the peoples on earth; for all
the earth belongs to Me. 6 And you will be My kingdom of priests, My holy nation.' This is
the message you must give to the people of Israel."
7 So Moses returned from the mountain and called together the elders of the people and
told them everything the LORD had commanded him. 8 And all the people responded to-
gether, "We will do everything the LORD has commanded." So Moses brought the people's
answer back to the LORD.
9 Then the LORD said to Moses, "I will come to you in a thick cloud, Moses, so the people
themselves can hear Me when I speak with you. Then they will always trust you."
Moses told the LORD what the people had said. 10 Then the LORD told Moses, "Go down
and prepare the people for My arrival. Consecrate them today and tomorrow, and have
them wash their clothing. 11 Be sure they are ready on the third day, for on that day the
LORD will come down on Mount Sinai as all the people watch. 12 Mark off a boundary all
around the mountain. Warn the people, 'Be careful! Do not go up on the mountain or even
touch its boundaries. Anyone who touches the mountain will certainly be put to death.
13 No hand may touch the person or animal that crosses the boundary; instead, stone them
or shoot them with arrows. They must be put to death.' However, when the ram's horn
sounds a long blast, then the people may go up on the mountain.*"
14 So Moses went down to the people. He consecrated them for worship, and they
washed their clothes. 15 He told them, "Get ready for the third day, and until then abstain
from having sexual intercourse."
16 On the morning of the third day, thunder roared and lightning flashed, and a dense
cloud came down on the mountain. There was a long, loud blast from a ram's horn, and all

19:3 Acts 7:38
19:4 Deut 29:2; Isa 40:31; 63:9; Rev 12:14
19:5 Exod 15:26; Deut 10:14
19:6 Lev 11:44-45; Deut 33:3; *1 Pet 2:5, 9; Rev 1:6; 5:10
19:7 Exod 4:29-30; 24:9
19:8 Exod 24:3, 7; Deut 5:27; 26:17
19:9 Deut 4:11; Ps 99:7
19:10 Gen 35:2; Lev 11:44-45; Num 8:7; 19:19; Heb 10:22; Rev 22:14
19:13 *Heb 12:20
19:15 1 Sam 21:4; 1 Cor 7:5
19:16 Heb 12:18-19

19:13 Or *up to the mountain.*

19:5-6 God had promised to bless Abraham's descendants. These blessings included belonging to God as His people. But Abraham's descendants could not receive these blessings unless they faithfully obeyed God (Genesis 17:8-9).

19:6 In the ancient world, lesser kings and nations often served more powerful kings or emperors. Each person in Israel was to be both priest and king by honoring and worshiping God, by keeping His covenant, by spreading His Word throughout the world, by bringing the Lord's blessings to all peoples (Genesis 18:18; 22:18), and ultimately by living as His vice-regents wherever they went (Genesis 1:26-28). This dual king/priest obligation is taught in the New Testament (1 Peter 2:9; Revelation 1:6) and is fulfilled through obedience to the Great Commission (Matthew 28:18-20).

19:7-8 The leaders or elders of the people represented the entire nation. Their consent was counted as the consent of the entire nation and obligated the entire nation to keep the covenant the leaders had confirmed with God.

19:9 Through Moses' unique access to Himself, God demonstrated to all Israel that Moses was His authoritative representative and that Israel was to obey and follow Moses faithfully.

▸ WORSHIP

19:9, 16 Discovering God at Mount Sinai. Dark clouds, thunder, lightning, fire, mountains with invisible boundaries—it's not a new sci-fi movie but a description of God's presence! The people of Israel were about to find out that God was awesomely frightening not only to His enemies but to His friends, too. We are commanded to fear God, for He is awesome and untamed. (***See Worship****> OT> Reverence> God requires us to fear Him,* TopicGuide page A28.)

▸ BIBLE

19:10-15 Ritual cleansing. The preparation in this verse is not a command to dress up when you are going to be in God's presence; it is a symbolic gesture about the importance of being pure before a holy God. Notice that there is even a command to abstain from sex in Exodus 19:15 (compare Leviticus 15:16-18). It's not that God thinks sex is dirty or that soiled clothes are an insult to Him. But as with many ceremonial commands regarding purification and cleanness in the Old Testament, these instructions communicate His utter holiness, and separateness or otherness (compare Leviticus 11:44-45). What can you do to further your understanding of God's holiness in your life? (***See Bible****> Unity> God's Message> Separation from the world,* TopicGuide page A10.)

19:15 Except in specific temporary situations, Scripture does not encourage married couples to abstain from sexual relations (1 Corinthians 7:3-5). Abstinence in this case was needed for the ritual purification of the nation before they met with God (compare Leviticus 15:16-18). In marriage, each partner belongs to the other so fully that Paul can call the withholding of sex an act of theft or defrauding (1 Corinthians 7:5).

the people trembled. 17 Moses led them out from the camp to meet with God, and they
stood at the foot of the mountain. 18 All of Mount Sinai was covered with smoke because
the LORD had descended on it in the form of fire. The smoke billowed into the sky like
smoke from a brick kiln, and the whole mountain shook violently. 19 As the blast of the
ram's horn grew louder and louder, Moses spoke, and God thundered His reply. 20 The
LORD came down on the top of Mount Sinai and called Moses to the top of the mountain.
So Moses climbed the mountain.

21 Then the LORD told Moses, "Go back down and warn the people not to break through
the boundaries to see the LORD, or they will die. 22 Even the priests who regularly come near
to the LORD must purify themselves so that the LORD does not break out and destroy them."

23 "But LORD," Moses protested, "the people cannot come up to Mount Sinai. You already
warned us. You told me, 'Mark off a boundary all around the mountain to set it apart as holy.'"

24 But the LORD said, "Go down and bring Aaron back up with you. In the meantime, do
not let the priests or the people break through to approach the LORD, or He will break out
and destroy them."

25 So Moses went down to the people and told them what the LORD had said.

TEN COMMANDMENTS FOR THE COVENANT COMMUNITY

20 Then God gave the people all these instructions*:

2 "I am the LORD your God, who rescued you from the land of Egypt, the place of
your slavery.

3 "You must not have any other god but Me.

4 "You must not make for yourself an idol of any kind or an image of anything in the
heavens or on the earth or in the sea. 5 You must not bow down to them or worship
them, for I, the LORD your God, am a jealous God who will not tolerate your affec-
tion for any other gods. I lay the sins of the parents upon their children; the entire
family is affected—even children in the third and fourth generations of those who

19:17 Deut 4:11
19:18 Exod 24:17; Deut 5:4; Pss 68:7-8; 104:32
19:19 Ps 81:7
19:20 Exod 24:12; Neh 9:13
19:21 Exod 3:5
19:22 Lev 10:3; 21:6-8
19:24 Exod 24:1, 9
20:1-17 //Deut 5:6-21
20:3 Exod 15:11; 20:23; Deut 5:7; 6:14
20:4 Lev 26:1; Deut 4:15-19
20:5 Exod 23:13, 24; 34:14; Num 14:18; Deut 4:24

20:1 Hebrew *all these words.*

19:22-24 The Aaronic priesthood had yet to be installed (see Exodus 28). Some priests before Aaron, like Jethro (also called Reuel [Exodus 2:16-18; 3:1; 18:1]), and Melchizedek before him (Genesis 14:18-20), appear to have held their priesthoods perpetually. Others were temporarily consecrated for special service (compare Exodus 24:5).

▸ HOLINESS

20:1 Giving of the law. The Ten Commandments. Doesn't the New Testament say we no longer live "under the requirements of the law," but "under the freedom of God's grace" (Romans 6:14)? Yes, but that doesn't mean the Old Testament law is not good for us (Romans 7:10-16). It doesn't even mean that we are free to disobey relevant Old Testament laws (Matthew 5:17-19). While being "in Christ" takes us out from under the jurisdiction of the law that condemns us (Romans 7:4), the law remains God's authoritative revelation and standard of right and wrong. How can God's law help you to know God better? To be more like Him? (***See Holiness****> Maturing> Imitating God> His law,* TopicGuide page A40.)

20:1-17 Exodus 34:28 refers to these commands as the Ten Commandments. Different traditions reckon these statements in different ways. Some count verse 2 as the first commandment or word, and verses 3-6 as the second commandment. Others treat verses 3-6 as the first commandment, and divide verse 17 into two different commandments. The most common division in Protestantism is to count verse 3 as the first commandment, verses 4-6 as the second commandment, and the entirety of verse 17 as the tenth commandment.

20:3 This literally means *before my face*, or *in my presence.* The commandment most specifically forbids the presence of false gods in the Lord's sanctuaries, such as Mount Sinai (Exodus 3; 19) and the Tabernacle (Exodus 26), and later the Temple. Traditionally, the commandment has also been understood to forbid all worship of any gods other than the Lord. There is some overlap in this regard between the first commandment (Exodus 20:3) and the second (Exodus 20:4-6).

20:4 In the Old Testament world, idols were worshiped in temples and shrines, and also used like good-luck charms. Many homes had private idols (Genesis 31:19-34; Isaiah 44:16-17). Idols were often made of wood or clay. They could be poles, animals, people, or objects from nature such as mountains or the sun. Traditionally this commandment has also been understood to forbid making and/or worshiping images that represent God Himself.

20:5-6 God stated in general terms some of the blessings of His covenant (Exodus 19:5; 24:7) that would come to those who were faithful to Him, and some of the curses that would fall on those who broke the terms of His covenant. God covenanted to curse many subsequent generations of those who broke His covenant, and to bless all those generations that obeyed Him. In the Mosaic Covenant, blessings and curses were contingent upon each generation's obedience or disobedience.

20:5 God expressly forbade all worship of other gods. He is to be the one and only recipient of our worship.

ABUNDANT, JOYFUL LIFE IN CHRIST does not happen automatically. You have a part to play—obedience. The fact is that absolutely no one can know the abundant life Christ offers without living in obedience to God's commands. That is why the Ten Commandments play such a critical role in your life. There is no escaping this irrefutable truth: When a person lives in obedience to God and His law, that person experiences the blessings of God. In these laws and the others God gave to Israel, you will find many commands and promises that you can apply to your personal life, church, community, and country. The Holy Spirit is waiting to help you!

The psalmist poured out his love for God's law in the Psalm 119, the longest chapter in the Bible. He writes, "I pant with expectation, longing for your commands" (119:131). But perhaps you are thinking, *This is too hard to do. I can never obtain the perfection that the Ten Commandments demand. Why would I want to meditate on commands that I so frequently fail to obey?*

That's a good question. The Ten Commandments, simple and profound as they are, are impossible for any of us to keep. We are imperfect humans who regularly fail to live up to God's standards (Romans 7:14-25).

Is the answer to ignore them? That is a recipe for disaster. For example, some people avoid going to the doctor so they will not hear bad news about their health. They feel that if they ignore the symptoms, their illness will go away. At times, we treat the Ten Commandments in a similar way—we feel that knowing what God expects of us threatens our way of life; thus we turn our backs on God's rules.

There is a better way. You can use the Ten Commandments in the way God intended—as:

- a gauge of our love for Him
- a guide for our life in Him
- a gift of grace to our world

The law of God is a gauge of our love for Him because as we are challenged to obey, we are reminded of how far we have to go to perfectly love God (commandments 1–4) and our neighbors (5–10). The law not only guides our behavior, it also functions as a gift of grace to the world as it reveals God's ideal pattern for human behavior.

Above all, the law of God is a picture of God. As we read God's law, we see His character, His heart, and His mind revealed. Nothing else compares to the joy of knowing God.

reject Me. [6]But I lavish unfailing love for a thousand generations on those* who
love Me and obey My commands.
[7]"You must not misuse the name of the LORD your God. The LORD will not let you go
unpunished if you misuse His name.
[8]"Remember to observe the Sabbath day by keeping it holy. [9]You have six days each
week for your ordinary work, [10]but the seventh day is a Sabbath day of rest dedicated
to the LORD your God. On that day no one in your household may do any work. This
includes you, your sons and daughters, your male and female servants, your livestock,
and any foreigners living among you. [11]For in six days the LORD made the heavens, the
earth, the sea, and everything in them; but on the seventh day He rested. That is why
the LORD blessed the Sabbath day and set it apart as holy.
[12]"Honor your father and mother. Then you will live a long, full life in the land the LORD
your God is giving you.
[13]"You must not murder.
[14]"You must not commit adultery.
[15]"You must not steal.
[16]"You must not testify falsely against your neighbor.
[17]"You must not covet your neighbor's house. You must not covet your neighbor's wife,
male or female servant, ox or donkey, or anything else that belongs to your neighbor."

[18]When the people heard the thunder and the loud blast of the ram's horn, and when
they saw the flashes of lightning and the smoke billowing from the mountain, they stood
at a distance, trembling with fear.
[19]And they said to Moses, "You speak to us, and we will listen. But don't let God speak
directly to us, or we will die!"

20:6 Hebrew *for thousands of those.*

20:6 Deut 7:9
20:7 Lev 19:12; Deut 6:13
20:8 Deut 5:12
20:11 Ps 146:6; *Acts 4:24
20:12 Deut 5:16, 33; *Matt 15:4; *Eph 6:2
20:13 Gen 4:8-12; 9:5; *Matt 5:21; 19:18; *Rom 13:9; *Jas 2:11
20:14 Lev 18:10; 20:10; *Matt 5:27
20:15 *Matt 19:18; *Rom 13:9
20:16 Matt 19:18
20:17 *Rom 7:7
20:18 Heb 12:18
20:19 Deut 5:23-27

20:7 People in the ancient world often invoked the name of deities in their oaths, calling their gods as official witnesses who would hold them accountable to these vows. To break such an oath was one of the primary ways that one might misuse the name of a god. In this context, the third commandment primarily regulates the uses of God's name in oaths, such as in marriage ceremonies, ordination into religious service, or legal testimony.

20:8 The Sabbath day here meant a time of rest from employment and normal labor. It was not a restriction against all exertion, but a holy day, consecrated to God. By refraining from work, the Sabbath-keeper acknowledges that God, not his work, sustains him and his family.

20:11 The Sabbath commandment is based on a creation ordinance. By resting after creating the world (Genesis 2:1-3), God indicated that every seventh day was holy to Him. Many theologians have understood from this fact that the Sabbath is still binding today (compare Matthew 5:17-19), though it is to be observed somewhat differently now that Christ has come and fulfilled the Old Covenant ceremonial aspects of the Sabbath (Colossians 2:16).

20:12 In Ephesians 6:2-3 Paul noted that this commandment to honor parents was the first one that had a specific promise attached to it, although promises of general blessing are also present in Exodus 20:6. Dishonoring or cursing one's parents could be punished by death (Exodus 21:17), but there is no record in Scripture of this ultimate punishment being applied.

20:13 The commandment is rightly translated "murder" because the Old Testament applications of this law permitted many types of killing, such as the sacrifice of animals, killing people in holy war, and carrying out death sentences. Murder (unlawful and premeditated killing of a human being) is consistently condemned (Numbers 35). Jesus applied this principle to all forms of unrighteous conflict (Matthew 5:21-22).

20:14 Jesus applied this principle of faithful sexual relations quite broadly to include not only acts but also thoughts (Matthew 5:27-28). Broadly speaking, the commandment summarizes prohibitions against all forms of sexual immorality, including fornication, adultery, and bestiality (compare Leviticus 18; 20).

20:16 This is a specific reference to testimony in court. The commandment broadly prohibits the perversion of justice; it is not limited to the specific instance of lying in court (compare Leviticus 5:1).

20:17 Coveting is a discontented desire for that which cannot morally be obtained. Positively, this is a command to be satisfied with what we have (1 Timothy 6:6).

20:18–23:33 This section of Scripture is commonly referred to as the Book of the Covenant (compare Exodus 24:7).

▸ WORSHIP
20:19 Hearing God. Were the people of Israel so frightened of the voice of God that they couldn't stand to hear it? Were they being respectful of God, saying, "We're not worthy! Just speaking to Moses will be enough for us!" Or were they afraid that God would kill them if they transgressed His holy standard? Whatever their fear, Moses wanted it to keep them from sin (Exodus 20:20). How does the fear of God help you in your daily battle against sin? (***See Worship***> *OT> Reverence> Awe of God means obeying His commandments,* TopicGuide page A28.)

20“Don’t be afraid,” Moses answered them, “for God has come in this way to test you,
and so that your fear of Him will keep you from sinning!”
21As the people stood in the distance, Moses approached the dark cloud where God
was.

PROPER USE OF ALTARS

22And the LORD said to Moses, “Say this to the people of Israel: You saw for yourselves that
I spoke to you from heaven. 23Remember, you must not make any idols of silver or gold to
rival Me.
24“Build for Me an altar made of earth, and offer your sacrifices to Me—your burnt offer-
ings and peace offerings, your sheep and goats, and your cattle. Build My altar wherever I
cause My name to be remembered, and I will come to you and bless you. 25If you use
stones to build My altar, use only natural, uncut stones. Do not shape the stones with a tool,
for that would make the altar unfit for holy use. 26And do not approach My altar by going up
steps. If you do, someone might look up under your clothing and see your nakedness.

FAIR TREATMENT OF SLAVES

21 “These are the regulations you must present to Israel.
2“If you buy a Hebrew slave, he may serve for no more than six years. Set him
free in the seventh year, and he will owe you nothing for his freedom. 3If he was single
when he became your slave, he shall leave single. But if he was married before he became
a slave, then his wife must be freed with him.
4“If his master gave him a wife while he was a slave and they had sons or daughters,
then only the man will be free in the seventh year, but his wife and children will still be-
long to his master. 5But the slave may declare, ‘I love my master, my wife, and my chil-
dren. I don’t want to go free.’ 6If he does this, his master must present him before God.*
Then his master must take him to the door or doorpost and publicly pierce his ear with an
awl. After that, the slave will serve his master for life.
7“When a man sells his daughter as a slave, she will not be freed at the end of six years

20:21 Deut 5:22; Ps 97:2
20:23 Exod 32:4; Deut 29:17-18
20:24 Exod 10:25; 18:12; 24:5; Lev 1:2; Deut 12:5
20:25 Deut 27:5-6; Josh 8:31
20:26 Exod 28:42
21:1 Deut 4:14
21:2-6 Lev 25:39-41; //Deut 15:12-18
21:2 Jer 34:14
21:5 Deut 15:16
21:6 Exod 22:8-9
21:7 Neh 5:5

21:6 Or *before the judges.*

20:20 Moses encouraged the Israelites to respect God’s awesome holiness and power and to understand the consequences of breaking God’s covenant. Moses wanted the Israelites to understand that as their covenant Lord, God wanted to be gracious toward the nation, not capricious or impatient (compare Exodus 34:6; Matthew 23:37). Nevertheless, He would not fail to destroy those who were unfaithful to Him.

▸ WORSHIP
20:24 Avoiding pagan forms of worship. The moral commands of God are often straightforward and commonsensical. For instance, most of us intuitively know what the Bible means when it says, “You must not murder” and “You must not steal.” But some ceremonial commands of God sound arbitrary and odd to modern ears. In Exodus 20:22-26, God stated several divine preferences for how He was to be worshiped. It was not that God was against masonry or stairs or nakedness. Rather, in each case, He was ensuring that Israel’s worship would be distinct from the pagan ceremonies they had seen in Egypt and would see in Canaan. Are you careful to ensure that your worship is based on biblical principles rather than on things you like in the world? (***See Worship****> OT> Prohibitions> Wrong forms,* TopicGuide page A28.)

▸ HOLINESS
21:2 Fair treatment of slaves. The Israelites were allowed to own slaves, but they were to treat their slaves well—especially since they themselves had been slaves for 400 years. God regulated the contracts surrounding slavery very carefully, knowing how easily a system of slavery could be abused (see also Ephesians 6:5-9). As history shows, when a master’s rights are not limited and the slave’s interests are not protected, great harm usually comes to those involved. We should treat those who serve us in any capacity with great kindness, knowing that God has freed us from the bondage of sin to be His servants (Romans 6:22). (***See Holiness****> Maturing> Obeying God’s Word> Justice is essential to obedience,* TopicGuide page A40.)

21:2 Israelite slaves retained their full rights, even being able to conduct business and own property. Ideally, they were to be treated as hired workers (Leviticus 25:39-40). Male Israelite slaves were to serve for a maximum of six years, after which time they became free. If a Jubilee occurred before six years, slaves were to be freed at Jubilee (Leviticus 25:40). They could not be willed to heirs but were to be freed upon their master’s death. Israelite slaves retained the right of redemption; they or a relative could purchase their freedom at any time. Israelite slavery was designed primarily as a form of debt management (Leviticus 25:39).

21:6 The “for life” aspect of this contract indicates that this contract was not subject to the normal time limitations. Such a slave could still be redeemed.

as the men are. 8 If she does not satisfy her owner, he must allow her to be bought back again. But he is not allowed to sell her to foreigners, since he is the one who broke the contract with her. 9 But if the slave's owner arranges for her to marry his son, he may no longer treat her as a slave but as a daughter.

10 "If a man who has married a slave wife takes another wife for himself, he must not neglect the rights of the first wife to food, clothing, and sexual intimacy. 11 If he fails in any of these three obligations, she may leave as a free woman without making any payment.

CASES OF PERSONAL INJURY

12 "Anyone who assaults and kills another person must be put to death. 13 But if it was simply an accident permitted by God, I will appoint a place of refuge where the slayer can run for safety. 14 However, if someone deliberately kills another person, then the slayer must be dragged even from My altar and be put to death.

15 "Anyone who strikes father or mother must be put to death.

16 "Kidnappers must be put to death, whether they are caught in possession of their victims or have already sold them as slaves.

17 "Anyone who dishonors* father or mother must be put to death.

18 "Now suppose two men quarrel, and one hits the other with a stone or fist, and the injured person does not die but is confined to bed. 19 If he is later able to walk outside again, even with a crutch, the assailant will not be punished but must compensate his victim for lost wages and provide for his full recovery.

20 "If a man beats his male or female slave with a club and the slave dies as a result, the owner must be punished. 21 But if the slave recovers within a day or two, then the owner shall not be punished, since the slave is his property.

21:10 1 Cor 7:3, 5
21:12 Gen 9:6 Lev 24:21
21:13 Num 35:22 Deut 19:4-5 Josh 20:9
21:14 Num 35:30-31 1 Kgs 2:28-34
21:16 Deut 24:7
21:17 Lev 20:9 Deut 5:16 *Matt 15:4 *Mark 7:10
21:21 Lev 25:44-46

21:17 Greek version reads *Anyone who speaks disrespectfully of.* Compare Matt 15:4; Mark 7:10.

21:8 The purchasing of a bride was carefully legislated in ancient cultures. If a man chose not to marry her after purchase, he acted deceitfully and unfairly toward her (compare Deuteronomy 21:14).

21:10 Many women felt shame for being unable to bear children. This is one of the reasons a wife had authority over her husband's body, so that he could not refuse to sleep with her, even if she had entered the marriage through a slave contract (compare 1 Corinthians 7:3).

21:11 An Israelite man who purchased a female slave was required to marry her perpetually (Exodus 21:8), give her to his son in marriage and treat her well (Exodus 21:9), or continue to fulfill her marriage rights if he ever married another woman (Exodus 21:10). If he failed on any of these three counts, the husband violated the contract he entered when purchasing the woman, and she was therefore given her freedom immediately.

▸ BIBLE
21:12 Put him to death. Our western legal system is clogged with both just and frivolous personal injury lawsuits. In ancient Israel, there was no distinction between criminal and civil litigation—there was one set of legal codes and a set of suggested maximum punishments for common crimes. God placed a premium on resolving disputes immediately, mediating disputes in a simple manner, and discouraging future acts of mayhem upon the innocent. If you have a legal dispute, seek a solution that mirrors God's priorities (1 Corinthians 6:1-7). (***See Bible****> Power> Wisdom> Administer civil justice*, TopicGuide page A11.)

21:12-32 These laws seem to communicate maximum penalties rather than mandatory penalties—"must be" may be better translated "is liable up to." It was up to the judges to ensure that the punishment was commensurate with the crime. This explains how God's people could receive leniency on a national level (Deuteronomy 30:3) and a personal level (Psalm 41:4). The legal system He created appears to have the same flexibility in practice as modern systems.

21:13 Those guilty of involuntary manslaughter could run from the kinsman avenger of the deceased (Numbers 35:9-28) to a city of safety, where he would receive a judgment.

21:14 The explicit qualification that the slayer is to be dragged from the altar indicates two things: First, that in this specific instance the death penalty is mandatory. Second, that justice should never be so hasty as to break God's holiness commands. In this case, killing a human on or around the altar of God would defile the altar (Leviticus 21:11). An example of the guilty fleeing to an altar is found in 1 Kings 1:51.

21:18-19 As throughout the legal code, what was lost determined what should be repaid. Punishment and compensation were to be commensurate with the offense. The offender's intentions in this matter lessen his or her crime.

21:20-21 These verses are not referring to random or inappropriate beatings; slaves were to be treated well (Leviticus 25:43). But because the slave was under the family headship of the owner, the owner was responsible to act as judge with regard to the slave in certain matters. The laws contained in these verses prohibited owners from punishing their slaves excessively.

22“Now suppose two men are fighting, and in the process they accidentally strike a
pregnant woman so she gives birth prematurely.* If no further injury results, the man who
struck the woman must pay the amount of compensation the woman’s husband demands
21:23 and the judges approve. 23But if there is further injury, the punishment must match the in-
Lev 24:19 jury: a life for a life, 24an eye for an eye, a tooth for a tooth, a hand for a hand, a foot for a
21:24 Lev 24:20 foot, 25a burn for a burn, a wound for a wound, a bruise for a bruise.
*Matt 5:38 26“If a man hits his male or female slave in the eye and the eye is blinded, he must let
21:26 the slave go free to compensate for the eye. 27And if a man knocks out the tooth of his
Job 31:13 male or female slave, he must let the slave go free to compensate for the tooth.
21:28 Gen 9:5 28“If an ox* gores a man or woman to death, the ox must be stoned, and its flesh may
not be eaten. In such a case, however, the owner will not be held liable. 29But suppose
the ox had a reputation for goring, and the owner had been informed but failed to keep
it under control. If the ox then kills someone, it must be stoned, and the owner must also
be put to death. 30However, the dead person’s relatives may accept payment to compen-
sate for the loss of life. The owner of the ox may redeem his life by paying whatever is
demanded.
21:32 Gen 37:28 31“The same regulation applies if the ox gores a boy or a girl. 32But if the ox gores a
Zech 11:12-13 slave, either male or female, the animal’s owner must pay the slave’s owner thirty silver
Matt 26:15; 27:3, 9 coins,* and the ox must be stoned.
21:33 Luke 14:5 33“Suppose someone digs or uncovers a pit and fails to cover it, and then an ox or a
donkey falls into it. 34The owner of the pit must pay full compensation to the owner of the
animal, but then he gets to keep the dead animal.
35“If someone’s ox injures a neighbor’s ox and the injured ox dies, then the two owners
must sell the live ox and divide the price equally between them. They must also divide the
dead animal. 36But if the ox had a reputation for goring, yet its owner failed to keep it
under control, he must pay full compensation—a live ox for the dead one—but he may
keep the dead ox.

21:22 Or *so she has a miscarriage;* Hebrew reads *so her children come out.* 21:28 Or *bull,* or *cow;* also in 21:29-36.
21:32 Hebrew *30 shekels of silver,* about 12 ounces or 342 grams in weight.

21:22 The entire law assumes that judges will decide cases and that the judges will ensure that the punishment fits the crime. Because the Hebrew justice system was based on the decision of the judge, and not a jury, there are many warnings of the dangers of unfair or immoral judges (Exodus 18:21; Psalm 82:2).

21:22-23 The text does not specify whether it is the mother or the child who is harmed. However, the context implies that harm to the child is primarily in view. The offender is liable for death in this case, indicating that the unborn child is treated as fully human.

▸ GOD

21:24 Punishing crimes. Jesus addressed this specific Scripture of “punishment fits the crime” in Matthew 5:38-42, where He taught us to “offer the other cheek” when treated unfairly. Moses was explaining just sentencing and punishment that was to take place in public courts. Jesus, on the other hand, was attacking unloving, vengeful applications of these verses. At the same time that He corrected perversions of the justice Moses described, Jesus also insisted that all of Moses’ law applies to us in the New Testament age (Matthew 5:17-19). Christians can support a state that matches severe crimes with severe sentences (Romans 13) and may defend their property and families (Exodus 22:2) with appropriate force. (***See God****> God’s Attributes> Just> God judges all people with justice,* TopicGuide page A16.)

21:26-27 Rather than taking an eye for an eye in the case of a slave, the owner was punished by relinquishing all rights to the slave. This also improved the slave’s condition by releasing the slave of financial debt and allowing him to return to his family.

21:28-36 One who failed to take proper precautions to protect others, such as by restricting a dangerous animal or failing to cover a pit, was negligent. In the case of negligence, the offender was liable for greater punishment and obligated to make greater restitution than an offender in an accident not involving negligence. See David’s application of this principle in 2 Samuel 12:6.

▸ HOLINESS

21:36 Paying restitution. Has your dog ever bitten someone? Or have you been in a car accident that was your fault? The Bible teaches that if we injure someone or damage their property, and if there is no negligence on our part, then the loss is shared by both parties. But if we harm someone in an irresponsible fashion, the vast majority of the loss is borne by us. Be generous to anyone who has suffered loss on account of your actions or inactions. (***See Holiness****> Law and Grace> Law> Property rights,* TopicGuide page A41.)

PROTECTION OF PROPERTY

22 1*"If someone steals an ox* or sheep and then kills or sells it, the thief must pay 22:1 Lev 6:1-7
back five oxen for each ox stolen, and four sheep for each sheep stolen. 2 Sam 12:6
2*"If a thief is caught in the act of breaking into a house and is struck and killed in the Prov 6:31 Luke 19:8
process, the person who killed the thief is not guilty of murder. 3But if it happens in day-
light, the one who killed the thief is guilty of murder. 22:2 Num 35:26-27
"A thief who is caught must pay in full for everything he stole. If he cannot pay, he must 22:3
be sold as a slave to pay for his theft. 4If someone steals an ox or a donkey or a sheep and it Exod 21:2
is found in the thief's possession, then the thief must pay double the value of the stolen 22:4
animal. Prov 6:31 Jer 2:26
5"If an animal is grazing in a field or vineyard and the owner lets it stray into someone John 12:6
else's field to graze, then the animal's owner must pay compensation from the best of his 22:5
own grain or grapes. Exod 21:34
6"If you are burning thornbushes and the fire gets out of control and spreads into an-
other person's field, destroying the sheaves or the uncut grain or the whole crop, the one
who started the fire must pay for the lost crop.
7"Suppose someone leaves money or goods with a neighbor for safekeeping, and they 22:7 Lev 6:1-7
are stolen from the neighbor's house. If the thief is caught, the compensation is double the
value of what was stolen. 8But if the thief is not caught, the neighbor must appear before 22:8 Exod 21:6
God,* who will determine if he stole the property. Deut 17:8-9; 19:17
9"Suppose there is a dispute between two people who both claim to own a particular ox, 22:9
donkey, sheep, article of clothing, or any lost property. Both parties must come before God, Deut 25:1
and the person whom God declares* guilty must pay double compensation to the other.
10"Now suppose someone leaves a donkey, ox, sheep, or any other animal with a
neighbor for safekeeping, but it dies or is injured or gets away, and no one sees what hap-
pened. 11The neighbor must then take an oath in the presence of the LORD. If the LORD con-
firms that the neighbor did not steal the property, the owner must accept the verdict, and
no payment will be required. 12But if the animal was indeed stolen, the guilty person must
pay compensation to the owner. 13If it was torn to pieces by a wild animal, the remains of 22:13 Gen 31:39
the carcass must be shown as evidence, and no compensation will be required.
14"If someone borrows an animal from a neighbor and it is injured or dies when the
owner is absent, the person who borrowed it must pay full compensation. 15But if the owner
was present, no compensation is required. And no compensation is required if the animal
was rented, for this loss is covered by the rental fee.

SOCIAL RESPONSIBILITY

16"If a man seduces a virgin who is not engaged to anyone and has sex with her, he must 22:16-17
pay the customary bride price and marry her. 17But if her father refuses to let him marry Deut 22:28-29
her, the man must still pay him an amount equal to the bride price of a virgin.

22:1a Verse 22:1 is numbered 21:37 in Hebrew text. 22:1b Or *bull*, or *cow;* also in 22:4, 9, 10. 22:2 Verses 22:2-31 are numbered 22:1-30 in Hebrew text. 22:8 Or *before the judges.* 22:9 Or *before the judges, and the person whom the judges declare.*

22:1, 4 Restitution in the case of theft exceeded that in the case of an accident (compare Exodus 21:35-36). Punitive damages were added to the standard compensation.

22:2-3 In the light of day it could be seen that a thief was not a threat to life or limb, and therefore self-defense was not warranted. In the darkness, however, it was not possible to verify the type of threat the thief posed, and it was appropriate to presume the worst of him.

22:8-9 God gets involved in resolving injustice. In this ancient culture, for example, the accused swore an oath before God to declare innocence (compare Exodus 22:11), and people often cast lots to allow God to indicate the guilty party (compare Joshua 18:6-10). This demonstrates just how concerned God is that the guilty be found and punished.

22:16-31 If you could create a society, what sort of government would you create? What sort of social practices would be taboo? What would be permitted? Exodus 22:16-31 helps us to see, in an ancient culture, a list of socially responsible behaviors designed to create a "holy people" (Exodus 22:31). What would God have you do (or not do!) in your modern social situations to promote holiness?

18 “You must not allow a sorceress to live.

19 “Anyone who has sexual relations with an animal must certainly be put to death.

20 “Anyone who sacrifices to any god other than the LORD must be destroyed.*

21 “You must not mistreat or oppress foreigners in any way. Remember, you yourselves were once foreigners in the land of Egypt.

22 “You must not exploit a widow or an orphan. 23 If you exploit them in any way and they cry out to Me, then I will certainly hear their cry. 24 My anger will blaze against you, and I will kill you with the sword. Then your wives will be widows and your children fatherless.

25 “If you lend money to any of My people who are in need, do not charge interest as a money lender would. 26 If you take your neighbor’s cloak as security for a loan, you must return it before sunset. 27 This coat may be the only blanket your neighbor has. How can a person sleep without it? If you do not return it and your neighbor cries out to Me for help, then I will hear, for I am merciful.

28 “You must not dishonor God or curse any of your rulers.

29 “You must not hold anything back when you give Me offerings from your crops and your wine.

“You must give Me your firstborn sons.

30 “You must also give Me the firstborn of your cattle, sheep, and goats. But leave the newborn animal with its mother for seven days; then give it to Me on the eighth day.

31 “You must be My holy people. Therefore, do not eat any animal that has been torn up and killed by wild animals. Throw it to the dogs.

A CALL FOR JUSTICE

23 “You must not pass along false rumors. You must not cooperate with evil people by lying on the witness stand.

2 “You must not follow the crowd in doing wrong. When you are called to testify in a dispute, do not be swayed by the crowd to twist justice. 3 And do not slant your testimony in favor of a person just because that person is poor.

4 “If you come upon your enemy’s ox or donkey that has strayed away, take it back to its

22:18 Lev 20:27; Deut 18:10
22:19 Lev 18:23; 20:15
22:20 Exod 32:8; 34:15
22:21 Lev 19:33
22:22 Deut 24:17-18
22:25 Lev 25:35-37; Deut 23:19-20
22:26 Deut 24:6, 10-13
22:28 Lev 24:15-16; Acts 23:5
22:29 Exod 13:2; 23:16, 19; 34:20; Deut 26:2
22:30 Gen 17:12; Lev 12:3; 22:27
22:31 Exod 19:6; Lev 7:24; 17:15; 22:8
23:1 Exod 20:16; Ps 35:11
23:2 Deut 1:17; 16:19
23:4-5 Deut 22:1-4

22:20 The Hebrew term used here refers to the complete consecration of things or people to the LORD, either by destroying them or by giving them as an offering.

22:18 A sorceress practices a variety of occult practices, including divining the future, summoning spirits, and casting spells and charms, all with a special emphasis on the use of hallucinogenic herbs. Whether known to or admitted by the practitioners or not, such magic was not empowered by plants, but by demonic forces (Acts 16:16-19).

22:19 Bestiality was common among Canaanites, as evidenced by the sexual perversions illustrated in the art of this region.

22:22-24 Widows and orphans had no family advocate in the public courts. As such, they were more vulnerable to mistreatment than others were. So, God Himself served as their family defender. He protected them in part by placing a much higher penalty on those who oppressed them.

22:25-27 Israelites were to treat each other as family, not seeking to profit from those in need (compare Leviticus 25:35-37).

22:28 To curse a ruler in Israel was to curse the Lord’s appointed representative, and thus to curse God Himself.

22:31 Animals killed by wild animals might be edible, but were considered unclean because the blood had not been adequately drained (Leviticus 17:15).

23:1-3, 6-8 This is an exposition of the ninth commandment. Testimony in court was not to be manipulative; it was to be true in order that justice might prevail. Both judges and witnesses were to pursue justice. A blatant abuse of this commandment in the Bible was the story of Naboth (1 Kings 21:1-16). Naboth refused to sell a vineyard to the king. The queen, therefore, planned a ceremony ostensibly in Naboth’s honor, and then brought in liars to bear false witness; this resulted in Naboth’s death and the transfer of the vineyard to King Ahab. False witnesses were also a part of the proceedings of Jesus’ trial, though they were evidently so unprepared that their stories contradict each other (Mark 14:55-59).

23:4-5 God’s Law has always required God’s people to love their enemies (compare to Matthew 5:17-19, 43-48 and Romans 12:9). We show love for our enemies by praying for them and showing mercy toward them where possible, so that they may possibly be converted and repent of their evil (1 Peter 2:12). Passages such as Psalm 139:22, which speak of King David’s hatred of the enemies of God, are not expressions of personal revenge, but demonstrate his desires that the enemies of God would be struck down. David may have “hated” God’s enemies, but he demonstrated remarkable mercy and kindness toward them in practice (1 Samuel 24:17-22).

owner. 5If you see that the donkey of someone who hates you has collapsed under its
load, do not walk by. Instead, stop and help.
6"In a lawsuit, you must not deny justice to the poor.
7"Be sure never to charge anyone falsely with evil. Never sentence an innocent or
blameless person to death, for I never declare a guilty person to be innocent.
8"Take no bribes, for a bribe makes you ignore something that you clearly see. A bribe
makes even a righteous person twist the truth.
9"You must not oppress foreigners. You know what it's like to be a foreigner, for you
yourselves were once foreigners in the land of Egypt.
10"Plant and harvest your crops for six years, 11but let the land be renewed and lie un-
cultivated during the seventh year. Then let the poor among you harvest whatever grows
on its own. Leave the rest for wild animals to eat. The same applies to your vineyards and
olive groves.
12"You have six days each week for your ordinary work, but on the seventh day you
must stop working. This gives your ox and your donkey a chance to rest. It also allows
your slaves and the foreigners living among you to be refreshed.
13"Pay close attention to all My instructions. You must not call on the name of any other
gods. Do not even speak their names.

THREE ANNUAL FESTIVALS

14"Each year you must celebrate three festivals in My honor. 15First, celebrate the Festival
of Unleavened Bread. For seven days the bread you eat must be made without yeast, just
as I commanded you. Celebrate this festival annually at the appointed time in early spring,
in the month of Abib,* for that is the anniversary of your departure from Egypt. No one
may appear before Me without an offering.
16"Second, celebrate the Festival of Harvest,* when you bring Me the first crops of your
harvest.

23:6 Exod 23:2-3
23:7 Exod 20:13, 16; Deut 27:25
23:8 Deut 16:19
23:9 Exod 22:21; Lev 19:33-34
23:10 Lev 25:3
23:11 Lev 25:1-7
23:12 Exod 20:8-11
23:13 Deut 4:9, 23
23:14 Exod 34:23-24; Deut 16:16
23:15 Exod 12:15; 13:4; Lev 23:5
23:16 Exod 34:22; Lev 23:34; Deut 16:13

23:15 Hebrew *appointed time in the month of Abib.* This first month of the ancient Hebrew lunar calendar usually occurs within the months of March and April. 23:16a Or *Festival of Weeks.* This was later called the Festival of Pentecost (see Acts 2:1). It is celebrated today as Shavuat (or Shabuoth).

▸ GOD

23:5 Who's important? There are people in life who do not like you, and frankly, you don't care much for them either. What would you do if you saw their car broken down on the side of the road? Would you chuckle and speed past them? Or would you stop and help? God's pattern for His people is to pay special attention to those we would normally pass by—those opposed by the majority, those who hate us, the poor, and foreigners (Exodus 23:2-6, 9). Even neutral parties, like nature, are to be cared for (Exodus 23:10-12). Ignore those things that may command great attention in our culture (Exodus 23:13) and seek to pay attention to the priorities of God. (***See God****> God's Attributes> Loving> To love enemies and the wicked is to be like God*, TopicGuide page A17.)

23:7 The warning not to put the innocent to death stands in contrast to the practice of abortion and euthanasia in many parts of the ancient and modern world.

23:9 Like widows and orphans, foreigners lacked advocates in Israel's courts (compare Exodus 22:22-24). God requires that His people act and rule justly in every instance, so that even those without advocates are treated fairly.

23:11 The poor did not have the means to store up goods for the Sabbath year. As a result, they were exempted from the Sabbath year's prohibition against agricultural labor. The Sabbath commandments have always exempted those who labor of necessity or mercy (compare Matthew 12:11-12).

23:11-12 God's concern for His creation extends to the animals over which man rules (compare Genesis 1:28), and He provides benefits to them.

23:15 When the ancient Israelites made bread, it was normally made with *leaven*, or yeast, which caused the bread to rise. Leaven was added to the bread dough by mixing in a small portion of dough that had been saved from a previous batch of bread. The Israelites were permitted to leaven their bread throughout the year, but at Passover (see Exodus 12) they were to throw out their leaven (the portion of dough that was saved for later batches) and create a fresh batch of dough (compare Genesis 19:3; 1 Corinthians 5:7-8). The *Festival of Unleavened Bread* began the day after Passover.

23:16 The *Festival of the Final Harvest* got its name from its arrival at the end of the agricultural season. The Festival of Final Harvest was a one-day feast celebrated exactly 50 days after the closing ceremonies of the Feast of Unleavened Bread. It marked the transition from the barley harvest to the wheat harvest. In the New Testament this feast was associated with the coming of the Holy Spirit (Acts 2).

"Finally, celebrate the Festival of the Final Harvest* at the end of the harvest season, when you have harvested all the crops from your fields. 17 At these three times each year, every man in Israel must appear before the Sovereign, the LORD.

18 "You must not offer the blood of My sacrificial offerings together with any baked goods containing yeast. And do not leave the fat from the festival offerings until the next morning.

19 "As you harvest your crops, bring the very best of the first harvest to the house of the LORD your God.

"You must not cook a young goat in its mother's milk.

A PROMISE OF THE LORD'S PRESENCE

20 "See, I am sending an angel before you to protect you on your journey and lead you safely to the place I have prepared for you. 21 Pay close attention to him, and obey his instructions. Do not rebel against him, for he is My representative, and he will not forgive your rebellion. 22 But if you are careful to obey him, following all My instructions, then I will be an enemy to your enemies, and I will oppose those who oppose you. 23 For My angel will go before you and bring you into the land of the Amorites, Hittites, Perizzites, Canaanites, Hivites, and Jebusites, so you may live there. And I will destroy them completely. 24 You must not worship the gods of these nations or serve them in any way or imitate their evil practices. Instead, you must utterly destroy them and smash their sacred pillars.

25 "You must serve only the LORD your God. If you do, I* will bless you with food and water, and I will protect you from illness. 26 There will be no miscarriages or infertility in your land, and I will give you long, full lives.

27 "I will send My terror ahead of you and create panic among all the people whose lands you invade. I will make all your enemies turn and run. 28 I will send terror* ahead of you to drive out the Hivites, Canaanites, and Hittites. 29 But I will not drive them out in a single year, because the land would become desolate and the wild animals would multiply and threaten you. 30 I will drive them out a little at a time until your population has increased enough to take possession of the land. 31 And I will fix your boundaries from the Red Sea to the Mediterranean Sea,* and from the eastern wilderness to the Euphrates River.* I will hand over to you the people now living in the land, and you will drive them out ahead of you.

23:17 Deut 16:16
23:18 Exod 12:8; 34:25 Lev 2:11
23:19 Exod 22:29 Deut 14:21
23:20 Exod 32:34
23:21 Exod 3:14; 34:5 Num 14:10-11
23:22 Num 24:9 Deut 30:7
23:23 Josh 24:8, 11
23:24 Exod 20:5; 34:13
23:25 Exod 15:26 Lev 26:3-13 Deut 7:12-15; 28:1-14
23:27 Gen 35:5 Exod 15:14 Deut 7:23
23:28 Deut 7:20
23:29-30 Deut 7:22
23:31 Gen 15:18 Josh 21:44; 24:12, 18

23:16b Or *Festival of Ingathering.* This was later called the Festival of Shelters or Festival of Tabernacles (see Lev 23:33-36). It is celebrated today as Sukkot (or Succoth). **23:25** As in Greek and Latin versions; Hebrew reads *he.* **23:28** Often rendered *the hornet.* The meaning of the Hebrew is uncertain. **23:31a** Hebrew *from the sea of reeds to the sea of the Philistines.* **23:31b** Hebrew *from the wilderness to the river.*

23:17 Through the representation of adult males or "every man," the entire nation was considered to have attended and observed the festivals. When they appeared at the Tabernacle preceding the building of the first Temple in Jerusalem, and at the Temple thereafter, they considered themselves as "before the Sovereign, the LORD," in the revealed presence of God.

23:20-23 The Bible commonly speaks of the angel of the Lord and of the Lord Himself in ways that blur the distinction between them (compare Exodus 3:6). For example, the angel appears to have the authority to refuse to forgive sins, and his instructions are said to be the Lord's. Because of this, many believe the angel to be Christ. That the angel was present shows that God was actively ruling history and intervening on behalf of His people.

23:21 This angel bore God's name, asserting that the angel carries God's delegated authority. This explains why those who praised Jesus during His triumphal entry into Jerusalem during Passover cried out "Blessings on the One who comes in the name of the LORD! Hail to the King of Israel!" (John 12:13).

23:22-31 Some of God's blessings are conditional upon our obedience. This is a mark of the arrangement God had with Israel (Deuteronomy 6:18). Today, some of God's blessings continue to be conditional upon our obedience (1 Corinthians 3:12-15), but the greatest blessings of eternal life are, even as under the Old Covenant, conditional only upon the obedience and sacrifice of Christ, whose righteousness is applied to us.

23:24 Israel never fully obeyed this command to purify the land God had given them.

23:25-30 Before God ratified His covenant with Israel in Exodus 24, He listed all the benefits that Israel would receive by becoming a covenant partner.

23:31 These borders encompassed the Promised Land. The Red Sea was to the south. The Mediterranean was the western coast. The Euphrates River ran to the northeast. The Arabian Desert was the southwest border from the Red Sea to the Euphrates. The Israelites did not consistently maintain control over all this land. Their kingdom was largest during the reign of King Solomon, son of King David (1 Kings 4:21, 24).

32"Make no treaties with them or their gods. 33They must not live in your land, or they
will cause you to sin against Me. If you serve their gods, you will be caught in the trap of
idolatry."

ISRAEL ACCEPTS THE LORD'S COVENANT

24 Then the LORD instructed Moses: "Come up here to Me, and bring along Aaron,
Nadab, Abihu, and seventy of Israel's elders. All of you must worship from a dis-
tance. 2Only Moses is allowed to come near to the LORD. The others must not come near,
and none of the other people are allowed to climb up the mountain with him."
3Then Moses went down to the people and repeated all the instructions and regulations
the LORD had given him. All the people answered with one voice, "We will do everything
the LORD has commanded."
4Then Moses carefully wrote down all the LORD's instructions. Early the next morning
Moses got up and built an altar at the foot of the mountain. He also set up twelve pillars,
one for each of the twelve tribes of Israel. 5Then he sent some of the young Israelite men
to present burnt offerings and to sacrifice bulls as peace offerings to the LORD. 6Moses
drained half the blood from these animals into basins. The other half he splattered against
the altar.
7Then he took the Book of the Covenant and read it aloud to the people. Again they all
responded, "We will do everything the LORD has commanded. We will obey."
8Then Moses took the blood from the basins and splattered it over the people, declar-
ing, "Look, this blood confirms the covenant the LORD has made with you in giving you
these instructions."
9Then Moses, Aaron, Nadab, Abihu, and the seventy elders of Israel climbed up the
mountain. 10There they saw the God of Israel. Under His feet there seemed to be a surface
of brilliant blue lapis lazuli, as clear as the sky itself. 11And though these nobles of Israel
gazed upon God, He did not destroy them. In fact, they ate a covenant meal, eating and
drinking in His presence!
12Then the LORD said to Moses, "Come up to Me on the mountain. Stay there, and I will
give you the tablets of stone on which I have inscribed the instructions and commands so
you can teach the people." 13So Moses and his assistant Joshua set out, and Moses
climbed up the mountain of God.

23:32 Deut 7:2
23:33 Deut 7:1-5, 16
24:1 Exod 6:23; 19:24
24:2 Num 12:6-8
24:3 Exod 19:8; 24:7 Deut 5:27; 11:1
24:4 Deut 31:9
24:5 Exod 18:12
24:6 Heb 9:18
24:7 Exod 19:8; 24:3 Heb 9:19
24:8 Zech 9:11 Matt 26:28 1 Cor 11:25 *Heb 9:20 1 Pet 1:2
24:10 Exod 33:20 Num 12:8 Isa 6:5 Ezek 1:26
24:12 Exod 31:18; 32:15-16 Jer 31:33 2 Cor 3:3
24:13 Exod 17:9-14; 33:11

23:33 Israel's well-being was strongly linked to their spiritual fidelity. The more they allowed themselves to be influenced by idol worship, the more God would withdraw His blessings and mete out His curses on them.

24:1 Moses had been the Israelites' leader since their freedom from Egypt. Aaron was Moses' brother. He later became the nation's high priest (Exodus 29:29-30). Nadab and Abihu were Aaron's sons (Exodus 28:1). They would later become priests. These two men did not stay in leadership, for Leviticus 10:1-3 records that they were burned to death by a fire from God, the result of disobeying God's guidelines for the offerings.

24:2 Moses is singled out in order to demonstrate his special relationship with God and his special authority.

▸ SALVATION
24:3 Submission to God. The people's agreement here is exactly the sort of humble submission required of believers today (Romans 12:1-2). While becoming a Christian is a joyful, freeing experience, surrendering to God also means surrendering to His rules (Matthew 5:17-19; John 14:15, 21). Those rules of loving God and loving our neighbor are summarized in Luke 10:26-28. (***See Salvation**> Receiving> How> Submit to God's grace/special favor*, TopicGuide page A22.)

24:4 The Israelites were organized into 12 tribes, according to the 12 sons of Jacob (Genesis 49:2-27). The two exceptions were Levi and Joseph. The Levites were religious workers who didn't own land. This left only 11 tribes to fill the land of Canaan, but the allotment that would have belonged to Joseph was doubled and allotted to his sons, Manasseh and Ephraim.

24:10-11 In what sense did the elders see God? The emphasis placed on the safety of the elders indicates that this was not a viewing of God's typical manifestation as cloud or fire (Exodus 13:21-22). A viewing of God in his glory is more likely indicated, though not a full view (Exodus 33:18-20; John 1:18). This passage looks forward to the day when all Christians may partake of the Lord's Supper, a holy meal in the sacred presence of God.

24:13 At Moses' death, Joshua took over the leadership of the people, leading them into the Promised Land (Joshua 1). The Lord allowed Joshua to ascend the mountain with Moses in order to demonstrate the special grace and calling given to Joshua. This record indicated to the next generation that Joshua had been chosen and gifted by God to lead them after Moses.

24:16 Exod 16:10 Num 14:10 — 14 Moses told the elders, "Stay here and wait for us until we come back. Aaron and Hur
are here with you. If anyone has a dispute while I am gone, consult with them."
24:17 Exod 3:2 Deut 4:24, 36 Heb 12:18, 29 — 15 Then Moses climbed up the mountain, and the cloud covered it. 16 And the glory of
the LORD settled down on Mount Sinai, and the cloud covered it for six days. On the sev-
enth day the LORD called to Moses from inside the cloud. 17 To the Israelites at the foot of
24:18 Exod 34:28 Deut 9:9; 10:10 1 Kgs 19:8 — the mountain, the glory of the LORD appeared at the summit like a consuming fire. 18 Then
Moses disappeared into the cloud as he climbed higher up the mountain. He remained on
the mountain forty days and forty nights.

OFFERINGS FOR THE TABERNACLE

25:1-7 //Exod 35:4-9 — **25** The LORD said to Moses, 2 "Tell the people of Israel to bring Me their sacred offer-
25:2 1 Chr 29:2-5 Ezra 2:68 Neh 7:70-72 2 Cor 8:11-12; 9:7 — ings. Accept the contributions from all whose hearts are moved to offer them.
3 Here is a list of sacred offerings you may accept from them:

gold, silver, and bronze;
4 blue, purple, and scarlet thread;
25:6 Exod 27:20; 30:23, 34 — fine linen and goat hair for cloth;
5 tanned ram skins and fine goatskin leather;
25:8 Exod 29:45; 36:1-5 Deut 12:11 Rev 21:3 — acacia wood;
6 olive oil for the lamps;
spices for the anointing oil and the fragrant incense;
25:9 Acts 7:44 Heb 8:5 — 7 onyx stones, and other gemstones to be set in the ephod and the priest's chestpiece.

8 "Have the people of Israel build Me a holy sanctuary so I can live among them. 9 You must
build this Tabernacle and its furnishings exactly according to the pattern I will show you.

PLANS FOR THE ARK OF THE COVENANT

25:10-20 //Exod 37:1-9 — 10 "Have the people make an Ark of acacia wood—a sacred chest 45 inches long,
27 inches wide, and 27 inches high.* 11 Overlay it inside and outside with pure gold, and

25:10 Hebrew *2.5 cubits* [115 centimeters] *long, 1.5 cubits* [69 centimeters] *wide, and 1.5 cubits high.*

24:15-18 Cloud and fire were familiar forms in which God manifested His presence (compare Exodus 13:21-22; 33:9-10; 40:34-38; Numbers 9:15-22; 11:25). God's visible presence assured the Israelites that God was meeting with Moses, revealing to Moses the instructions that Moses would later deliver to the people. This compelled the Israelites to receive Moses' instructions as the authoritative Word of the Lord.

25:1 Here begin the instructions Moses received during his forty-day stay on the mountain with God (Exodus 24:16-18). The Israelites were to recognize that Moses had received this revelation from God, and therefore the worship patterns Moses established were binding on future generations.

25:2-7 The Israelites were invited to bring freewill offerings as building materials for the Tabernacle (Exodus 25:8-9). Although the Israelites had been slaves in Egypt, and thus had not acquired vast wealth of their own, the Lord had caused the Egyptians to bestow great gifts upon the Israelites during the Exodus (Exodus 12:36).

▸WORSHIP

25:8 A sacred residence. "Where is God?" asks the Children's Catechism. "God is everywhere!" is the answer. However, in ancient Israel, God manifested His presence and glory in a special way in the Tabernacle that He directed Moses to build. In this tent were a variety of items such as a gold-laden box called the Ark, a gold-rimmed table, and a golden lampstand. These items were lost following the destruction of Solomon's Temple in 586 BC. This loss foreshadowed Jesus' words that God would no longer limit His manifestations to certain holy places (John 4:21-24) but would be among believers wherever two or more gathered (Matthew 18:20). (***See Worship****> OT> Place> Tabernacle,* TopicGuide page A27.)

25:9 The Tabernacle was a lavish portable tent that functioned as a sanctuary. There was a general area in which the people could gather; a smaller Holy Place accessible only to the religious leadership; and the Most Holy Place, a chamber only accessed by the high priest in the most sacred of ceremonies. God manifested his glory in the Most Holy Place and spoke directly with the high priest from there (Exodus 25:22). The Tabernacle was God's primary sanctuary until King Solomon built the Temple in Jerusalem. Exodus 25–31 describes how the Tabernacle was to be built, detailing everything: the altars, the utensils, the oils and incense, and the dedication of the priests. Exodus 35–40 describes how the Israelites built the Tabernacle precisely according to God's instructions.

25:10 The Ark of the Covenant was spoken of as God's footstool (1 Chronicles 28:2). Its presence in the Most Holy Place (Exodus 26:33-34) of the Tabernacle demonstrated that the Tabernacle was God's throne room on earth and made it clear that the Lord was Israel's king (1 Samuel 8:7-8). God manifested His presence and communicated His will from His throne above the Ark (Exodus 25:22; Leviticus 16:2; 1 Samuel 4:4). Sacred relics from the journey of the Israelites were stored in this chest: Aaron's staff, the stone tablets upon which were written the Ten Commandments, and a jar of manna.

run a molding of gold all around it. 12Cast four gold rings and attach them to its four feet,
two rings on each side. 13Make poles from acacia wood, and overlay them with gold.
14Insert the poles into the rings at the sides of the Ark to carry it. 15These carrying poles
must stay inside the rings; never remove them. 16When the Ark is finished, place inside it
the stone tablets inscribed with the terms of the covenant,* which I will give to you.

17"Then make the Ark's cover—the place of atonement—from pure gold. It must be
45 inches long and 27 inches wide.* 18Then make two cherubim from hammered gold,
and place them on the two ends of the atonement cover. 19Mold the cherubim on each
end of the atonement cover, making it all of one piece of gold. 20The cherubim will face
each other and look down on the atonement cover. With their wings spread above it, they
will protect it. 21Place inside the Ark the stone tablets inscribed with the terms of the cov-
enant, which I will give to you. Then put the atonement cover on top of the Ark. 22I will
meet with you there and talk to you from above the atonement cover between the gold
cherubim that hover over the Ark of the Covenant.* From there I will give you My com-
mands for the people of Israel.

25:12 Exod 26:29; 27:7; 37:5; 38:7
25:13 Exod 30:5; 37:4; 40:20
25:15 1 Kgs 8:8
25:16 Exod 16:34 Heb 9:4
25:17 Exod 37:6 Lev 16:13 Rom 3:25 Heb 9:5
25:20 1 Kgs 8:7 Heb 9:5
25:21 Exod 26:34
25:22 Exod 30:6, 36 Lev 1:1

PLANS FOR THE TABLE

23"Then make a table of acacia wood, 36 inches long, 18 inches wide, and 27 inches
high.* 24Overlay it with pure gold and run a gold molding around the edge. 25Decorate it
with a 3-inch border* all around, and run a gold molding along the border. 26Make four
gold rings for the table and attach them at the four corners next to the four legs. 27Attach
the rings near the border to hold the poles that are used to carry the table. 28Make these
poles from acacia wood, and overlay them with gold. 29Make special containers of pure
gold for the table—bowls, pans, pitchers, and jars—to be used in pouring out liquid offer-
ings. 30Place the Bread of the Presence on the table to remain before Me at all times.

25:23-29 //Exod 37:10-16
25:29 Exod 37:16 Num 4:7
25:30 Exod 39:36; 40:23 Lev 24:5-9 Num 4:7

PLANS FOR THE LAMPSTAND

31"Make a lampstand of pure, hammered gold. Make the entire lampstand and its decora-
tions of one piece—the base, center stem, lamp cups, buds, and petals. 32Make it with six
branches going out from the center stem, three on each side. 33Each of the six branches
will have three lamp cups shaped like almond blossoms, complete with buds and petals.
34Craft the center stem of the lampstand with four lamp cups shaped like almond blos-
soms, complete with buds and petals. 35There will also be an almond bud beneath each

25:31-39 //Exod 37:17-24
25:31 Exod 37:17 1 Kgs 7:49 Heb 9:2 Rev 1:12

25:16 Hebrew *Place inside the Ark the Testimony;* similarly in 25:21. The Hebrew word for "testimony" refers to the terms of the LORD's covenant with Israel as written on stone tablets, and also to the covenant itself. 25:17 Hebrew *2.5 cubits* [115 centimeters] *long and 1.5 cubits* [69 centimeters] *wide.* 25:22 Or *Ark of the Testimony.* 25:23 Hebrew *2 cubits* [92 centimeters] *long, 1 cubit* [46 centimeters] *wide, and 1.5 cubits* [69 centimeters] *high.* 25:25 Hebrew *a border of a handbreadth* [8 centimeters].

25:15 The Ark was so sacred that no one was to touch it directly when it was carried (see 2 Samuel 6:1-8).

25:17 Blood was sprinkled on the "place of atonement" (some translations read "mercy seat") annually on the Day of Atonement to make atonement for the sins of the people (Leviticus 16:15).

25:18-20 Cherubim are angels who served as guards for God's throne room (see Genesis 3:24). They are also identified as bearers of God's chariot throne (see Ezekiel 10). Images of cherubim were abundant in the Tabernacle and later in the Temple. God's prohibition against worshiping images (Exodus 20:4-5) did not preclude the use of images like these in places of worship so long as those images were not venerated and used only according to His command.

25:22 God would meet with and speak to Moses and other leaders of Israel from His throne above the place of atonement (2 Kings 19:15; Psalm 80:1). That God spoke from His throne indicates that His words were royal dictates from Israel's divine King.

25:23-30 A table was constructed to hold the Bread of the Presence, which was baked and set before the Lord each Sabbath as an offering from the nation of Israel (Leviticus 24:5-9).

25:31-39 Oil lamps were usually saucer-shaped cups made of pottery or metal with a pinched lip or spout on one side that held the wick, which was commonly a piece of flax. The lampstand with its lamps resembled an almond tree. The image of the fruitful tree coupled with the cherubim (Exodus 25:18-22) may have been intended to reflect the Garden of Eden (Genesis 3:24).

pair of branches where the six branches extend from the center stem. 36 The almond buds
25:37 and branches must all be of one piece with the center stem, and they must be hammered
Exod 27:21 from pure gold. 37 Then make the seven lamps for the lampstand, and set them so they re-
Zech 4:2 Rev 1:4, 12, 20; 4:5 flect their light forward. 38 The lamp snuffers and trays must also be made of pure gold.
25:40 39 You will need seventy-five pounds* of pure gold for the lampstand and its accessories.
Acts 7:44 40 "Be sure that you make everything according to the pattern I have shown you here on
*Heb 8:5 the mountain.

PLANS FOR THE TABERNACLE

26:1-37 //Exod 36:8-38 **26** "Make the Tabernacle from ten curtains of finely woven linen. Decorate the cur-
tains with blue, purple, and scarlet thread and with skillfully embroidered cheru-
bim. 2 These ten curtains must all be exactly the same size—42 feet long and 6 feet wide.*
26:3 3 Join five of these curtains together to make one long curtain, then join the other five into
Exod 36:10 a second long curtain. 4 Put loops of blue yarn along the edge of the last curtain in each set.
26:5 5 The fifty loops along the edge of one curtain are to match the fifty loops along the edge
Exod 36:12 of the other curtain. 6 Then make fifty gold clasps and fasten the long curtains together
with the clasps. In this way, the Tabernacle will be made of one continuous piece.
26:7 7 "Make eleven curtains of goat-hair cloth to serve as a tent covering for the Tabernacle.
Exod 36:14 8 These eleven curtains must all be exactly the same size—45 feet long and 6 feet wide.*
9 Join five of these curtains together to make one long curtain, and join the other six into a
second long curtain. Allow 3 feet of material from the second set of curtains to hang over
26:11 the front* of the sacred tent. 10 Make fifty loops for one edge of each large curtain. 11 Then
Exod 36:18 make fifty bronze clasps, and fasten the loops of the long curtains with the clasps. In this
way, the tent covering will be made of one continuous piece. 12 The remaining 3 feet* of
this tent covering will be left to hang over the back of the Tabernacle. 13 Allow 18 inches*
of remaining material to hang down over each side, so the Tabernacle is completely cov-
26:14 ered. 14 Complete the tent covering with a protective layer of tanned ram skins and a layer
Exod 36:19 of fine goatskin leather.
26:15 15 "For the framework of the Tabernacle, construct frames of acacia wood. 16 Each frame
Exod 36:20-34 must be 15 feet high and 27 inches wide,* 17 with two pegs under each frame. Make all the
frames identical. 18 Make twenty of these frames to support the curtains on the south side
of the Tabernacle. 19 Also make forty silver bases—two bases under each frame, with the
26:20 pegs fitting securely into the bases. 20 For the north side of the Tabernacle, make another
Exod 36:23 twenty frames, 21 with their forty silver bases, two bases under each frame. 22 Make six

25:39 Hebrew *1 talent* [34 kilograms]. **26:2** Hebrew *28 cubits* [12.9 meters] *long and 4 cubits* [1.8 meters] *wide.* **26:8** Hebrew *30 cubits* [13.8 meters] *long and 4 cubits* [1.8 meters] *wide.* **26:9** Hebrew *Double over the sixth sheet at the front.* **26:12** Hebrew *The half sheet that is left over.* **26:13** Hebrew *1 cubit* [46 centimeters]. **26:16** Hebrew *10 cubits* [4.6 meters] *high and 1.5 cubits* [69 centimeters] *wide.*

26:1 The Tabernacle was a portable tent that served as God's sanctuary. It was constructed of a framework covered by four layers of material.

26:1, 31-36 Blue, purple, and scarlet were the richest and most desirable colors of the day. Purple was obtained from mollusks and was the most valued color. It was associated with royalty. Blue was often made from mollusks as well, so it may have had a slight purple hue. Scarlet, sometimes called *crimson,* was manufactured from the dried bodies of the female cochineal, an insect.

26:1-6 The innermost layer of the Tabernacle was expensive and luxurious. Its sides stopped 18 inches above the ground.

26:7-13 A heavy layer of cloth was sandwiched above the fine linen (Exodus 26:1-6) and the outer protective layers (Exodus 26:14). Its sides reached the ground.

26:11, 37 Bronze is an alloy of copper and tin. It was the hardest metal available during this time.

26:14 Scholars are not completely sure of the type of animal skin that is called *goatskin* here. It has also been translated "badger skins," "porpoise skins," or "sea cow (manatee) skins" in other contexts.

26:15, 26, 32, 37 The acacia is a member of the mimosa family, abundant in ancient Palestine. Acacia wood had an orange tint that grew darker with age. It is hard, strong, and durable. In many cases, the wood was covered with gold or bronze to strengthen and beautify it.

frames for the rear—the west side of the Tabernacle—23 along with two additional frames
to reinforce the rear corners of the Tabernacle. 24 These corner frames will be matched at
the bottom and firmly attached at the top with a single ring, forming a single corner unit.
Make both of these corner units the same way. 25 So there will be eight frames at the rear
of the Tabernacle, set in sixteen silver bases—two bases under each frame.

26 "Make crossbars of acacia wood to link the frames, five crossbars for the north side of
the Tabernacle 27 and five for the south side. Also make five crossbars for the rear of the
Tabernacle, which will face west. 28 The middle crossbar, attached halfway up the frames,
will run all the way from one end of the Tabernacle to the other. 29 Overlay the frames with
gold, and make gold rings to hold the crossbars. Overlay the crossbars with gold as well.

30 "Set up this Tabernacle according to the pattern you were shown on the mountain.

31 "For the inside of the Tabernacle, make a special curtain of finely woven linen. Deco-
rate it with blue, purple, and scarlet thread and with skillfully embroidered cherubim.
32 Hang this curtain on gold hooks attached to four posts of acacia wood. Overlay the posts
with gold, and set them in four silver bases. 33 Hang the inner curtain from clasps, and put
the Ark of the Covenant* in the room behind it. This curtain will separate the Holy Place
from the Most Holy Place.

34 "Then put the Ark's cover—the place of atonement—on top of the Ark of the Covenant
inside the Most Holy Place. 35 Place the table outside the inner curtain on the north side of
the Tabernacle, and place the lampstand across the room on the south side.

36 "Make another curtain for the entrance to the sacred tent. Make it of finely woven
linen and embroider it with exquisite designs, using blue, purple, and scarlet thread.
37 Craft five posts from acacia wood. Overlay them with gold, and hang the curtain from
them with gold hooks. Cast five bronze bases for the posts.

PLANS FOR THE ALTAR OF BURNT OFFERING

27 "Using acacia wood, construct a square altar 7½ feet wide, 7½ feet long, and
4½ feet high.* 2 Make horns for each of its four corners so that the horns and altar
are all one piece. Overlay the altar with bronze. 3 Make ash buckets, shovels, basins, meat
forks, and firepans, all of bronze. 4 Make a bronze grating for it, and attach four bronze
rings at its four corners. 5 Install the grating halfway down the side of the altar, under the
ledge. 6 For carrying the altar, make poles from acacia wood, and overlay them with
bronze. 7 Insert the poles through the rings on the two sides of the altar. 8 The altar must be
hollow, made from planks. Build it just as you were shown on the mountain.

PLANS FOR THE COURTYARD

9 "Then make the courtyard for the Tabernacle, enclosed with curtains made of finely
woven linen. On the south side, make the curtains 150 feet long.* 10 They will be held up

26:25 Exod 36:30
26:30 Exod 25:9, 40; Acts 7:44; *Heb 8:5
26:31 Exod 36:35; 2 Chr 3:14; Matt 27:51; Heb 9:3
26:33 Exod 25:16; 40:21; Heb 9:2-3
26:34 Exod 25:21; 37:6; Heb 9:5
26:36 Exod 40:28
26:37 Exod 36:38
27:1-8 //Exod 38:1-7
27:1 Ezek 43:13
27:2 Exod 29:12; Lev 4:7
27:3 Num 4:14
27:6 Exod 25:13
27:8 Exod 25:40; 26:30
27:9-19 //Exod 38:9-20
27:10 Exod 38:17

26:33 Or *Ark of the Testimony;* also in 26:34. 27:1 Hebrew *5 cubits* [2.3 meters] *wide, 5 cubits long, a square, and 3 cubits* [1.4 meters] *high.* 27:9 Hebrew *100 cubits* [46 meters]; also in 27:11.

▶ BIBLE
26:31-33 The torn curtain. This special curtain separated the Most Holy Place from the rest of the Tabernacle. When Jesus died, it is likely that this is the thick curtain that was torn apart (Luke 23:44-46). What did that mean? It symbolized several things—first, the tearing of the curtain, and hence the exposure of the inner sanctuary of God, symbolized the free access to God's throne that we now have through Jesus Christ. Second, that Jesus' holy suffering, the tearing of His flesh, made peace between humanity and God. When you trust in the merit of Jesus' sacrifice, you are able to approach God directly, and you have peace with God because of what Jesus Christ our Lord has done (Romans 5:1). (***See Bible***> *Unity*> *OT Types,* TopicGuide page A11.)

27:1-8 The altar was placed in the courtyard outside the Tabernacle. It was covered in bronze to protect it from the fire that consumed the sacrifices.

27:2-6, 10-11, 17-19 Bronze is an alloy of copper and a small amount of tin. Lead was also added to the alloy to increase malleability.

27:9-18 Much of the service related to the Tabernacle was performed in the courtyard, such as performing ritual washings, slaughtering animals, and presenting burnt offerings. Like the Tabernacle, the walls of the courtyard were constructed of strong, luxurious materials (compare Exodus 26).

by twenty posts set securely in twenty bronze bases. Hang the curtains with silver hooks
and rings. 11 Make the curtains the same on the north side—150 feet of curtains held up
by twenty posts set securely in bronze bases. Hang the curtains with silver hooks and
rings. 12 The curtains on the west end of the courtyard will be 75 feet long,* supported by
27:14 ten posts set into ten bases. 13 The east end of the courtyard, the front, will also be
Exod 38:15 75 feet long. 14 The courtyard entrance will be on the east end, flanked by two curtains.
The curtain on the right side will be 22½ feet long,* supported by three posts set into
three bases. 15 The curtain on the left side will also be 22½ feet long, supported by three
posts set into three bases.

27:16 Exod 36:37 16 "For the entrance to the courtyard, make a curtain that is 30 feet long.* Make it from
finely woven linen, and decorate it with beautiful embroidery in blue, purple, and scarlet
thread. Support it with four posts, each securely set in its own base. 17 All the posts around
the courtyard must have silver rings and hooks and bronze bases. 18 So the entire court-
yard will be 150 feet long and 75 feet wide, with curtain walls 7½ feet high,* made from
finely woven linen. The bases for the posts will be made of bronze.

19 "All the articles used in the rituals of the Tabernacle, including all the tent pegs used to
support the Tabernacle and the courtyard curtains, must be made of bronze.

LIGHT FOR THE TABERNACLE

27:20-21 //Lev 24:1-3 20 "Command the people of Israel to bring you pure oil of pressed olives for the light, to
Zech 4:11-12 keep the lamps burning continually. 21 The lampstand will stand in the Tabernacle, in front
27:21 of the inner curtain that shields the Ark of the Covenant.* Aaron and his sons must keep
Exod 25:22 the lamps burning in the LORD's presence all night. This is a permanent law for the people
Lev 3:17; 16:34 of Israel, and it must be observed from generation to generation.

CLOTHING FOR THE PRIESTS

28:1 Exod 24:1, 9 **28** "Call for your brother, Aaron, and his sons, Nadab, Abihu, Eleazar, and Ithamar.
Num 18:7 Set them apart from the rest of the people of Israel so they may minister to Me
Ps 99:6 and be My priests. 2 Make sacred garments for Aaron that are glorious and beautiful.
Heb 5:1, 4 3 Instruct all the skilled craftsmen whom I have filled with the spirit of wisdom. Have them
28:2 Exod 29:5, 9; 31:10 make garments for Aaron that will distinguish him as a priest set apart for My service.
Lev 8:7, 30 4 These are the garments they are to make: a chestpiece, an ephod, a robe, a patterned tu-
Num 20:26 nic, a turban, and a sash. They are to make these sacred garments for your brother, Aaron,
28:5 and his sons to wear when they serve Me as priests. 5 So give them fine linen cloth, gold
Exod 25:3-4 thread, and blue, purple, and scarlet thread.

27:12 Hebrew *50 cubits* [23 meters]; also in 27:13. 27:14 Hebrew *15 cubits* [6.9 meters]; also in 27:15. 27:16 Hebrew *20 cubits* [9.2 meters]. 27:18 Hebrew *100 cubits* [46 meters] *long and 50 cubits* [23 meters] *wide and 5 cubits* [2.3 meters] *high.* 27:21 Hebrew *in the Tent of Meeting, outside the inner curtain that is in front of the Testimony.* See note on 25:16.

27:20 What percentage of your income do you set aside for helping the needy, or supporting missionaries, or paying your pastor? From the beginning, God's people contributed their finest to the upkeep of the church. We can freely give of our best for the upkeep of the church and faithful ministries today.

27:20-21 This lampstand probably is the same one mentioned in Exodus 25:31-39 (see Leviticus 24:1-4).

▸ SALVATION

28:1 Ministers and me. For whom do ministers work? For the church? For the congregation? For their denomination? From earliest times, God wanted those in full-time ministry to focus on pleasing Him above anyone else. Paul explained his holy chain-of-command in this way: "So look at Apollos and me as mere servants of Christ who have been put in charge of explaining God's mysteries" (1 Corinthians 4:1). Ministers and congregations must recognize that both must ultimately submit to God. (***See Salvation***> *Receiving*> *When*> *Set apart for God*, TopicGuide page A22.)

28:1 Although true priests of God existed before Aaron, the formal Israelite priesthood began with Aaron and his sons. The Levites (descendants of Levi) were all set apart for special service and Tabernacle service, but within the Levites only Aaron and his descendants were to be ordained as priests.

DESIGN OF THE EPHOD

6"The craftsmen must make the ephod of finely woven linen and skillfully embroider it 28:6-14 //Exod 39:2-7
with gold and with blue, purple, and scarlet thread. 7It will consist of two pieces, front and
back, joined at the shoulders with two shoulder-pieces. 8The decorative sash will be made
of the same materials: finely woven linen embroidered with gold and with blue, purple,
and scarlet thread.

9"Take two onyx stones, and engrave on them the names of the tribes of Israel. 10Six
names will be on each stone, arranged in the order of the births of the original sons of
Israel. 11Engrave these names on the two stones in the same way a jeweler engraves a
seal. Then mount the stones in settings of gold filigree. 12Fasten the two stones on the 28:12 Exod 39:7
shoulder-pieces of the ephod as a reminder that Aaron represents the people of Israel.
Aaron will carry these names on his shoulders as a constant reminder whenever he goes
before the LORD. 13Make the settings of gold filigree, 14then braid two cords of pure gold
and attach them to the filigree settings on the shoulders of the ephod.

DESIGN OF THE CHESTPIECE

15"Then, with great skill and care, make a chestpiece to be worn for seeking a decision 28:15-28
from God.* Make it to match the ephod, using finely woven linen embroidered with gold //Exod 39:8-21
and with blue, purple, and scarlet thread. 16Make the chestpiece of a single piece of cloth
folded to form a pouch nine inches* square. 17Mount four rows of gemstones* on it. The 28:17
first row will contain a red carnelian, a pale-green peridot, and an emerald. 18The second Exod 39:10
row will contain a turquoise, a blue lapis lazuli, and a white moonstone. 19The third row
will contain an orange jacinth, an agate, and a purple amethyst. 20The fourth row will con-
tain a blue-green beryl, an onyx, and a green jasper. All these stones will be set in gold fili-
gree. 21Each stone will represent one of the twelve sons of Israel, and the name of that 28:21
tribe will be engraved on it like a seal. Exod 39:14

22"To attach the chestpiece to the ephod, make braided cords of pure gold thread.
23Then make two gold rings and attach them to the top corners of the chestpiece. 24Tie the 28:24
two gold cords to the two rings on the chestpiece. 25Tie the other ends of the cords to the Exod 39:17
gold settings on the shoulder-pieces of the ephod. 26Then make two more gold rings and 28:26
attach them to the inside edges of the chestpiece next to the ephod. 27And make two more Exod 39:17
gold rings and attach them to the front of the ephod, below the shoulder-pieces, just
above the knot where the decorative sash is fastened to the ephod. 28Then attach the bot-
tom rings of the chestpiece to the rings on the ephod with blue cords. This will hold the
chestpiece securely to the ephod above the decorative sash.

29"In this way, Aaron will carry the names of the tribes of Israel on the sacred chestpiece* 28:29
over his heart when he goes into the Holy Place. This will be a continual reminder that he Exod 28:12
represents the people when he comes before the LORD. 30Insert the Urim and Thummim 28:30
into the sacred chestpiece so they will be carried over Aaron's heart when he goes into the Lev 8:8 Num 27:21
LORD's presence. In this way, Aaron will always carry over his heart the objects used to de-
termine the LORD's will for His people whenever he goes in before the LORD.

28:15 Hebrew *a chestpiece for decision.* **28:16** Hebrew *1 span* [23 centimeters]. **28:17** The identification of some of these gemstones is uncertain. **28:29** Hebrew *the chestpiece for decision;* also in 28:30. See 28:15.

28:29 Like other books, the Bible ascribes human attributes to non-human entities, such as God (Genesis 4:10; Jeremiah 12:4; Revelation 16:19). This is not a weakness or contradiction, but simply a literary device; it is not intended to be interpreted outside of Scripture's general teaching on God's nature. In this case, Aaron "reminded" an all-knowing God (1 John 3:20) by calling His attention to the covenant He had made with the nation of Israel.

28:30 The *Urim and Thummim* can also be translated "sacred lots," literally "lights and perfections." *Urim* begins with the first letter of the Hebrew alphabet, and *Thummim* with the last. It is not known what these items were or how they functioned. Many have speculated that they were stones. In any case, they were used to obtain oracles from God (Numbers 27:21; 1 Samuel 28:6). By the time of the New Testament, this practice seems to have ended, initially being replaced by casting lots (Proverbs 18:18; Acts 1:26). Later, the Bible, accompanied by illumination of the Spirit of God upon the community and its leaders (John 16:13), became the only physical object associated with knowing God's will.

ADDITIONAL CLOTHING FOR THE PRIESTS

31“Make the robe that is worn with the ephod from a single piece of blue cloth, 32with an
opening for Aaron’s head in the middle of it. Reinforce the opening with a woven collar* so
it will not tear. 33Make pomegranates out of blue, purple, and scarlet yarn, and attach
them to the hem of the robe, with gold bells between them. 34The gold bells and pome-
granates are to alternate all around the hem. 35Aaron will wear this robe whenever he
ministers before the LORD, and the bells will tinkle as he goes in and out of the LORD’s pres-
ence in the Holy Place. If he wears it, he will not die.
36“Next make a medallion of pure gold, and engrave it like a seal with these words:
HOLY TO THE LORD. 37Attach the medallion with a blue cord to the front of Aaron’s turban,
where it must remain. 38Aaron must wear it on his forehead so he may take on himself
any guilt of the people of Israel when they consecrate their sacred offerings. He must al-
ways wear it on his forehead so the LORD will accept the people.
39“Weave Aaron’s patterned tunic from fine linen cloth. Fashion the turban from this
linen as well. Also make a sash, and decorate it with colorful embroidery.
40“For Aaron’s sons, make tunics, sashes, and special head coverings that are glorious
and beautiful. 41Clothe your brother, Aaron, and his sons with these garments, and then
anoint and ordain them. Consecrate them so they can serve as My priests. 42Also make
linen undergarments for them, to be worn next to their bodies, reaching from their hips to
their thighs. 43These must be worn whenever Aaron and his sons enter the Tabernacle* or
approach the altar in the Holy Place to perform their priestly duties. Then they will not in-
cur guilt and die. This is a permanent law for Aaron and all his descendants after him.

28:31-43 //Exod 39:22-31
28:36 Exod 39:30-31; Lev 8:9
28:38 Lev 10:17; 22:16; Num 18:1; Heb 9:28; 1 Pet 2:24
28:40 Exod 39:27-29; Lev 8:13
28:41 Exod 29:7-9; Lev 8:1-36; Heb 7:28
28:42 Lev 6:10; 16:4; Ezek 44:18
28:43 Exod 20:26; 27:21

DEDICATION OF THE PRIESTS

29 “This is the ceremony you must follow when you consecrate Aaron and his sons
to serve Me as priests: Take a young bull and two rams with no defects. 2Then,
using choice wheat flour and no yeast, make loaves of bread, thin cakes mixed with olive
oil, and wafers spread with oil. 3Place them all in a single basket, and present them at the
entrance of the Tabernacle, along with the young bull and the two rams.
4“Present Aaron and his sons at the entrance of the Tabernacle,* and wash them with

29:1-37 //Lev 8:1-36
29:2 Lev 6:19-23
29:4 Exod 40:12; Heb 10:22

28:32 The meaning of the Hebrew is uncertain. 28:43 Hebrew *Tent of Meeting.* 29:4 Hebrew *Tent of Meeting;* also in 29:10, 11, 30, 32, 42, 44.

28:35 Ministering before the Lord was both a comfort and a risk. The bells on the hem of the priest’s garment marked his going in and out of the Holy Place. As he entered there on behalf of his people, the sound of the bells might have comforted them. Jewish tradition holds that when the priest entered the holy place, a cord was tied to him so that, should he be struck dead, the people could pull him out of the area without risking their own lives by entering the chamber themselves.

28:36 The phrase on the medallion *“HOLY TO THE LORD”* refers to Aaron. He was consecrated to God as the high priest of Israel. As such, he was permitted to enter the Most Holy Place to meet with God and to make atonement for the people there (Exodus 25:17; 26:34).

28:38 Aaron wore a medallion that symbolized God’s call to Aaron to make atonement for the people. By faith, God’s people were accepted as righteous as they offered the sacrifices God required. Jesus’ future sacrifice (Hebrews 10:4-14) is the perfect sacrifice to which all other sacrifices point, but the faithful use of the blood of animals was the means by which it was applied to the people under the Old Covenant.

▸ BIBLE
28:38 Discovering Jesus in the work of the high priest. It’s hard to take the blame for something you didn’t do. But this was Aaron’s job—to take responsibility for the ceremonial errors of God’s people. The book of Hebrews says that Jesus is our great High Priest (Hebrews 4:14-16, 5:5-6; 9:6-14), who bore our guilt and continues to pray and to intercede for us in heaven. Knowing that Jesus’ prayers to the Father will be answered, what do you want Jesus to be praying for you today? (***See Bible***> *Unity*> *OT Types*> *Aaron,* TopicGuide page A11, and ***Worship***> *OT*> *Priesthood,* TopicGuide page A28.)

28:43 Only Aaron’s direct descendants were to serve as priests and high priests. This ordinance was to be kept and honored by all future generations of Israelites. Christ’s priesthood has marked similarities and differences to the Aaronic line of priests (see Hebrews 7).

29:1-46 Aaron’s ordination began an entire order of priests within Israel. This order only needed to be established once; the dedication and ordination ceremonies were never to be repeated. Exodus was written after Aaron’s ordination (Exodus 40:12-16), and the Aaronic priesthood was both exclusive and perpetual, so the details included here did not instruct the nation how to commence future orders of priests. Rather, the details provide the background for many practices that were continued throughout Israel’s generations.

water. 5Dress Aaron in his priestly garments—the tunic, the robe worn with the ephod, the
ephod itself, and the chestpiece. Then wrap the decorative sash of the ephod around him.
6Place the turban on his head, and fasten the sacred medallion to the turban. 7Then anoint
him by pouring the anointing oil over his head. 8Next present his sons, and dress them in
their tunics. 9Wrap the sashes around the waists of Aaron and his sons, and put their spe-
cial head coverings on them. Then the right to the priesthood will be theirs by law forever.
In this way, you will ordain Aaron and his sons.

10"Bring the young bull to the entrance of the Tabernacle, where Aaron and his sons will
lay their hands on its head. 11Then slaughter the bull in the LORD's presence at the en-
trance of the Tabernacle. 12Put some of its blood on the horns of the altar with your finger,
and pour out the rest at the base of the altar. 13Take all the fat around the internal organs,
the long lobe of the liver, and the two kidneys and the fat around them, and burn it all on
the altar. 14Then take the rest of the bull, including its hide, meat, and dung, and burn it
outside the camp as a sin offering.

15"Next Aaron and his sons must lay their hands on the head of one of the rams. 16Then
slaughter the ram, and splatter its blood against all sides of the altar. 17Cut the ram into
pieces, and wash off the internal organs and the legs. Set them alongside the head and the
other pieces of the body, 18then burn the entire animal on the altar. This is a burnt offering
to the LORD; it is a pleasing aroma, a special gift presented to the LORD.

19"Now take the other ram, and have Aaron and his sons lay their hands on its head.
20Then slaughter it, and apply some of its blood to the right earlobes of Aaron and his
sons. Also put it on the thumbs of their right hands and the big toes of their right feet.
Splatter the rest of the blood against all sides of the altar. 21Then take some of the blood
from the altar and some of the anointing oil, and sprinkle it on Aaron and his sons and on
their garments. In this way, they and their garments will be set apart as holy.

22"Since this is the ram for the ordination of Aaron and his sons, take the fat of the ram,
including the fat of the broad tail, the fat around the internal organs, the long lobe of the
liver, and the two kidneys and the fat around them, along with the right thigh. 23Then take
one round loaf of bread, one thin cake mixed with olive oil, and one wafer from the basket
of bread without yeast that was placed in the LORD's presence. 24Put all these in the hands
of Aaron and his sons to be lifted up as a special offering to the LORD. 25Afterward take the
various breads from their hands, and burn them on the altar along with the burnt offering.
It is a pleasing aroma to the LORD, a special gift for Him. 26Then take the breast of Aaron's
ordination ram, and lift it up in the LORD's presence as a special offering to Him. Then keep
it as your own portion.

27"Set aside the portions of the ordination ram that belong to Aaron and his sons. This
includes the breast and the thigh that were lifted up before the LORD as a special offering.

29:5 Exod 28:2, 5
29:6 Exod 28:36
29:7 Exod 28:41; Lev 8:12-13; Ps 133:2
29:9 Exod 40:15; Num 3:10; 18:7; 25:13; Deut 18:5
29:10 Lev 1:4; 8:14
29:12 Exod 27:2; Lev 8:15
29:13 Lev 3:3-5
29:14 Lev 4:11-12, 21; Heb 13:11
29:15 Exod 29:10
29:18 Gen 8:21
29:21 Exod 30:25, 31; Heb 9:22
29:23 Lev 8:26
29:24 Lev 7:30
29:26 Lev 7:31, 34; 8:29
29:27 Lev 7:31, 34; Num 18:11-12; Deut 18:3

29:7 Anointing demonstrated that the priest held a special office as God's representative, similar to that of kings. Anointed offices were to be respected even when those who held the offices were wicked (compare 1 Samuel 24:5-6; Acts 23:2-5).

29:9 While priests were mentioned as early as Abraham's encounter with Melchizedek (Genesis 14:18-20), this is the establishment of Israel's first national order of priests.

29:13 The custom of reserving the fat for God preceded the Exodus (compare Genesis 4:4). In the ancient world, fat represented flavor, opulence, and lavishness; it was the best part of the animal.

29:15-18 This was a consecration offering which purified the worshiper. It was a prerequisite for fellowship or communal offerings such as those in Exodus 29:19. Aaron and his sons' actions presented a model for all consecration offerings thereafter.

29:21 This very clothing would be important to future generations, who would inherit and wear these special vestments (Exodus 29:29-30).

▸ CHURCH

29:26 Fair pay for faithful ministers. "Poor as a preacher" is a common saying in some cultures because churches often fail to pay ministers a living wage. God made provisions in the earliest forms of worship for His ministers to receive adequate recompense for their labors. Are you generous to those who work in your church (1 Timothy 5:17-18)? Encourage godly, faithful ministers by giving them fair compensation. (***See Church****> Role> Preach> Topics> Collect Resources> For salaries of ministers,* TopicGuide page A50.)

29:27-28 The Lord established the practice of allowing the priests to keep as food specific portions of animals offered in sacrifice to enable them to feed their families.

28In the future, whenever the people of Israel lift up a peace offering, a portion of it must
be set aside for Aaron and his descendants. This is their permanent right, and it is a sacred
offering from the Israelites to the LORD.
29"Aaron's sacred garments must be preserved for his descendants who succeed him,
and they will wear them when they are anointed and ordained. 30The descendant who
succeeds him as high priest will wear these clothes for seven days as he ministers in the
Tabernacle and the Holy Place.
31"Take the ram used in the ordination ceremony, and boil its meat in a sacred place.
32Then Aaron and his sons will eat this meat, along with the bread in the basket, at the
Tabernacle entrance. 33They alone may eat the meat and bread used for their purification*
in the ordination ceremony. No one else may eat them, for these things are set apart and
holy. 34If any of the ordination meat or bread remains until the morning, it must be
burned. It may not be eaten, for it is holy.
35"This is how you will ordain Aaron and his sons to their offices, just as I have com-
manded you. The ordination ceremony will go on for seven days. 36Each day you must
sacrifice a young bull as a sin offering to purify them, making them right with the LORD.*
Afterward, cleanse the altar by purifying it*; make it holy by anointing it with oil. 37Purify
the altar, and consecrate it every day for seven days. After that, the altar will be absolutely
holy, and whatever touches it will become holy.
38"These are the sacrifices you are to offer regularly on the altar. Each day, offer two
lambs that are a year old, 39one in the morning and the other in the evening. 40With one
of them, offer two quarts of choice flour mixed with one quart of pure oil of pressed olives;
also, offer one quart of wine* as a liquid offering. 41Offer the other lamb in the evening,
along with the same offerings of flour and wine as in the morning. It will be a pleasing
aroma, a special gift presented to the LORD.
42"These burnt offerings are to be made each day from generation to generation. Offer
them in the LORD's presence at the Tabernacle entrance; there I will meet with you and
speak with you. 43I will meet the people of Israel there, in the place made holy by My glori-
ous presence. 44Yes, I will consecrate the Tabernacle and the altar, and I will consecrate
Aaron and his sons to serve Me as priests. 45Then I will live among the people of Israel and
be their God, 46and they will know that I am the LORD their God. I am the One who brought
them out of the land of Egypt so that I could live among them. I am the LORD their God.

29:29 Num 20:26, 28
29:30 Lev 8:35
29:33 Lev 22:10, 13
29:34-35 Lev 8:32-33
29:36 Exod 40:10; Heb 10:11
29:37 Exod 40:10; Matt 23:19
29:38 Num 28:3-31; 29:6-38; 1 Chr 16:40; Dan 12:11
29:41 2 Kgs 16:15; Ezra 9:4-5; Ps 141:2
29:42 Exod 30:8
29:43 1 Kgs 8:11
29:45 Exod 25:8; Lev 26:12; Num 5:3; Deut 12:11; Ps 68:18; Zech 2:10; 2 Cor 6:16; Rev 21:3
29:46 Exod 20:2

PLANS FOR THE INCENSE ALTAR

30:1-5 //Exod 37:25-28; 1 Kgs 6:20; Rev 8:3

30 "Then make another altar of acacia wood for burning incense. 2Make it 18 inches
square and 36 inches high,* with horns at the corners carved from the same
piece of wood as the altar itself. 3Overlay the top, sides, and horns of the altar with pure

29:33 Or *their atonement.* 29:36a Or *to make atonement.* 29:36b Or *by making atonement for it;* similarly in 29:37. 29:40 Hebrew *1/10 of an ephah* [2.2 liters] *of choice flour . . . 1/4 of a hin* [1 liter] *of pure oil . . . 1/4 of a hin of wine.* 30:2 Hebrew *1 cubit* [46 centimeters] *long and 1 cubit wide, a square, and 2 cubits* [92 centimeters] *high.*

29:28 Peace and thanksgiving offerings were given spontaneously by the people. Those who were already at peace with God (through a consecration offering) offered peace and thanksgiving offerings in order to show love and appreciation.

29:29-30 Details about Aaron's clothes were included for the instruction of the nation in future generations. The priesthood was to preserve, hand down, and wear these special holy clothes throughout Israel's history.

29:37 As part of the ordination of Aaron and his sons, the altar itself was sanctified. It was important for future generations to know how and why their altar was holy, and for them to preserve and protect its purity.

29:38-42 Aaron's ordination ceremony established the basis for the perpetual morning and evening offerings at the Tabernacle and later at the Temple.

29:45 The Aaronic priesthood established and maintained the rituals that resulted in God dwelling with His people. Future generations were to respect and support these efforts in order that God would continue to bless them with His presence and power.

30:1-8 Aaron's example was to be maintained throughout all Israel's generations on a daily basis.

gold, and run a gold molding around the entire altar. 4 Make two gold rings, and attach
them on opposite sides of the altar below the gold molding to hold the carrying poles.
5 Make the poles of acacia wood and overlay them with gold. 6 Place the incense altar just **30:6**
outside the inner curtain that shields the Ark of the Covenant,* in front of the Ark's cover— Exod 25:21-22
the place of atonement—that covers the tablets inscribed with the terms of the covenant.*
I will meet with you there.

7 "Every morning when Aaron maintains the lamps, he must burn fragrant incense **30:7**
on the altar. 8 And each evening when he lights the lamps, he must again burn incense Exod 27:21; 30:34-35 1 Sam 2:28
in the LORD's presence. This must be done from generation to generation. 9 Do not offer Luke 1:9
any unholy incense on this altar, or any burnt offerings, grain offerings, or liquid
offerings.

10 "Once a year Aaron must purify* the altar by smearing its horns with blood from the **30:10** Lev 16:8
offering made to purify the people from their sin. This will be a regular, annual event from
generation to generation, for this is the LORD's most holy altar."

MONEY FOR THE TABERNACLE

11 Then the LORD said to Moses, 12 "Whenever you take a census of the people of Israel, **30:12** Exod 38:25-26
each man who is counted must pay a ransom for himself to the LORD. Then no plague will Num 1:2; 26:2
strike the people as you count them. 13 Each person who is counted must give a small 2 Sam 24:1 Matt 20:28
piece of silver as a sacred offering to the LORD. (This payment is half a shekel,* based on
the sanctuary shekel, which equals twenty gerahs.) 14 All who have reached their twenti- **30:13** Matt 17:24
eth birthday must give this sacred offering to the LORD. 15 When this offering is given to **30:15**
the LORD to purify your lives, making you right with Him,* the rich must not give more Prov 22:2
than the specified amount, and the poor must not give less. 16 Receive this ransom money
from the Israelites, and use it for the care of the Tabernacle.* It will bring the Israelites to
the LORD's attention, and it will purify your lives."

PLANS FOR THE WASHBASIN

17 Then the LORD said to Moses, 18 "Make a bronze washbasin with a bronze stand. Place it **30:18**
between the Tabernacle and the altar, and fill it with water. 19 Aaron and his sons will wash Exod 38:8; 40:7, 30
their hands and feet there. 20 They must wash with water whenever they go into the Taber- **30:19** Exod 40:31-32
nacle to appear before the LORD and when they approach the altar to burn up their special

30:6a Or *Ark of the Testimony;* also in 30:26. 30:6b Hebrew *that covers the Testimony;* see note on 25:16. 30:10 Or *make atonement for;* also in 30:10b. 30:13 Or *0.2 ounces,* or *6 grams.* 30:15 Or *to make atonement for your lives;* similarly in 30:16. 30:16 Hebrew *Tent of Meeting;* also in 30:18, 20, 26, 36.

30:9-10 Unholy incense was any incense not made according to the recipe in Exodus 30:34-38. God is profoundly unlike His creatures in His power and perfections, and His superiority is to be recognized and honored at every point. By treating God's holy altar with disdain or lack of respect, one implied the same disdain for the altar's Lord (compare Leviticus 10:1-3).

30:13 The ransom payment was one-fifth of an ounce of silver, but was later reduced to an eighth of an ounce due to hardship (see Exodus 10:32). This demonstrates that God's approach to giving includes both situational flexibility and clear standards.

30:15 Because the life of each man was worth the same amount regardless of his wealth, all men were to pay the same amount (Exodus 30:12).

30:16 This doesn't sound right—if the blood of sacrificial animals couldn't make things right with God (Hebrews 10:4, 11), how could silver do it? In all Old Testament sacrifices, the basis for forgiveness and atonement was the work of Jesus Christ (Hebrews 10:1-12), even though the means by which forgiveness was applied to faithful believers was the Mosaic sacrificial system. The word *atonement* refers to the *ransom* paid as a substitute for one's life (compare Exodus 22:29; 30:12). This fee reminded the people that they belonged to God as His firstborn (Exodus 4:22) and were free from the curses of Egypt through His mercy and power.

30:16 This ransom payment is one of the few mentions of atonement being made without the shedding of blood (compare Leviticus 5:11).

30:18-21 The details of Aaron's practice established a perpetual rule for all generations that followed. Any priest who ministered in the Tabernacle had to purify himself in the same manner as Aaron.

30:21 gifts to the LORD—or they will die! 21 They must always wash their hands and feet, or they
Exod 28:43 will die. This is a permanent law for Aaron and his descendants, to be observed from gen-
eration to generation."

THE ANOINTING OIL

22 Then the LORD said to Moses, 23 "Collect choice spices—12½ pounds of pure myrrh,
6¼ pounds of fragrant cinnamon, 6¼ pounds of fragrant calamus,* 24 and 12½ pounds of
30:25 Exod 37:29; 40:9 cassia*—as measured by the weight of the sanctuary shekel. Also get one gallon of olive
30:26 oil.* 25 Like a skilled incense maker, blend these ingredients to make a holy anointing oil.
Lev 8:10 26 Use this sacred oil to anoint the Tabernacle, the Ark of the Covenant, 27 the table and all
Num 7:1 its utensils, the lampstand and all its accessories, the incense altar, 28 the altar of burnt of-
30:29 fering and all its utensils, and the washbasin with its stand. 29 Consecrate them to make
Exod 29:37 them absolutely holy. After this, whatever touches them will also become holy.
30:30 30 "Anoint Aaron and his sons also, consecrating them to serve Me as priests. 31 And say
Lev 8:2, 12, 30 to the people of Israel, 'This holy anointing oil is reserved for Me from generation to gen-
30:33 Gen 17:14 eration. 32 It must never be used to anoint anyone else, and you must never make any
Exod 12:15 blend like it for yourselves. It is holy, and you must treat it as holy. 33 Anyone who makes a
Lev 7:20-21 blend like it or anoints someone other than a priest will be cut off from the community.'"

THE INCENSE

34 Then the LORD said to Moses, "Gather fragrant spices—resin droplets, mollusk shell, and
galbanum—and mix these fragrant spices with pure frankincense, weighed out in equal
30:36 amounts. 35 Using the usual techniques of the incense maker, blend the spices together
Lev 2:3 and sprinkle them with salt to produce a pure and holy incense. 36 Grind some of the mix-
ture into a very fine powder and put it in front of the Ark of the Covenant,* where I will
meet with you in the Tabernacle. You must treat this incense as most holy. 37 Never use
this formula to make this incense for yourselves. It is reserved for the LORD, and you must
treat it as holy. 38 Anyone who makes incense like this for personal use will be cut off from
the community."

CRAFTSMEN: BEZALEL AND OHOLIAB

31:2-6 //Exod 35:30–36:1 **31** Then the LORD said to Moses, 2 "Look, I have specifically chosen Bezalel son of Uri,
1 Chr 2:20 grandson of Hur, of the tribe of Judah. 3 I have filled him with the Spirit of God, giv-
31:3 ing him great wisdom, ability, and expertise in all kinds of crafts. 4 He is a master crafts-
1 Kgs 7:14 man, expert in working with gold, silver, and bronze. 5 He is skilled in engraving and
mounting gemstones and in carving wood. He is a master at every craft!

30:23 Hebrew *500 shekels* [5.7 kilograms] *of pure myrrh, 250 shekels* [2.9 kilograms] *of fragrant cinnamon, 250 shekels of fragrant calamus.* 30:24a Hebrew *500 shekels* [5.7 kilograms] *of cassia.* 30:24b Hebrew *1 hin* [3.8 liters] *of olive oil.* 30:36 Hebrew *in front of the Testimony;* see note on 25:16.

30:22-25 Spices were a valued commodity in the ancient world. They were a major trade item throughout the world. Myrrh was made from gum resin in shrub-like trees. Cinnamon came from an evergreen tree. Sweet cane was likely sugar cane, and cassia was related to cinnamon and made of bark. The buds of the cassia tree were used in the place of cloves when they were not available.

30:31-33 Fidelity to the worship established under Moses and Aaron was critical to Israel's life and blessedness. Departure from proper worship could result in the extreme curse of exile from the community.

30:34 Resin droplets probably came from the storax tree. Galbanum was a bitter gum extracted from a member of the carrot or parsley family. It was not pleasantly aromatic, but it caused the incense's aroma to last longer. Frankincense was a resin from a type of balsam tree.

30:37-38 Aaron's practice was to be handed down to all priests, who themselves were to remain faithful to the worship established under Aaron and Moses.

31:1-6 Craftsmen like Bezalel and his assistant Oholiab were revered in their ancient community (compare 2 Chronicles 2:13-14). They were most often men who worked with materials such as fabric, wood, and metal. God specially gifted them with technical skill in order that they would be able to fulfill what He had commanded through Moses.

6"And I have personally appointed Oholiab son of Ahisamach, of the tribe of Dan, to be his assistant. Moreover, I have given special skill to all the gifted craftsmen so they can make all the things I have commanded you to make: 31:6 Exod 35:31-34; 36:1

7 the Tabernacle;* 31:7 Exod 37:1-9
the Ark of the Covenant;*
the Ark's cover—the place of atonement;
all the furnishings of the Tabernacle;
8 the table and its utensils; 31:8 Exod 37:10-16 Lev 24:4
the pure gold lampstand with all its accessories;
the incense altar;
9 the altar of burnt offering with all its utensils;
the washbasin with its stand;
10 the beautifully stitched garments—the sacred garments for Aaron the priest, and the garments for his sons to wear as they minister as priests;

31:7a Hebrew *the Tent of Meeting.* 31:7b Hebrew *the Ark of the Testimony.*

▸ WORSHIP
31:6 Artists blessed by God. The Tabernacle and its contents were an art exhibit of the highest caliber, declaring both God's beauty and God's love of beauty. God gave eternal honor to the profession of craftsmanship by placing His Spirit on Bezalel to create beautiful objects. This also reminds us that for art to reach its pinnacle, the artist must be filled with the Spirit of God. (***See Worship***> *OT*> *Place*> *Tabernacle,* TopicGuide page A27.)

MY RESPONSE TO GOD

Written by God or Man?

EXODUS 31

When the devil confronted Jesus and tried to tempt Him to sin, how did Jesus respond? He rebuked the devil with the Word of God. Jesus said to Satan, "No! The Scriptures say, 'People do not live by bread alone, but by every word that comes from the mouth of God'" (Matthew 4:4).

The church echoes the teaching of Jesus by agreeing that the Bible is the Word of God. But this doesn't mean that the Bible was ordinarily written by God's own divine hand (Exodus 31:18) or that God controlled people like robots to create it. The Bible testifies repeatedly to its human authors, both explicitly (Luke 1:1-2) and implicitly through the many styles of writing, unique vocabularies, different perspectives, and so forth.

So why is the Bible called the Word of God if it has the voices of human beings all throughout it? Christians have historically accepted the Bible's testimony about itself—that it is not the mere religious opinions of men, but that God inspired their words. Although the Bible came from God (2 Timothy 3:16), it came through human beings. So the prophets could legitimately preface their words with "Thus says the Lord" and yet speak the next phrase from their own lips. God guided the human authors of Scripture so that their original writings were freely composed but free from all types of error. So we can trust God's Word, even though it came through people just like us.

31:11 11 the anointing oil;
Exod 30:23-32 the fragrant incense for the Holy Place.
The craftsmen must make everything as I have commanded you."

INSTRUCTIONS FOR THE SABBATH

31:13 12 The LORD then gave these instructions to Moses: 13 "Tell the people of Israel: 'Be careful
Lev 19:3, 30; Ezek 20:12-13 to keep My Sabbath day, for the Sabbath is a sign of the covenant between Me and you
31:14 from generation to generation. It is given so you may know that I am the LORD, who makes
Exod 16:23; 35:2 you holy. 14 You must keep the Sabbath day, for it is a holy day for you. Anyone who dese-
John 7:23 crates it must be put to death; anyone who works on that day will be cut off from the com-
munity. 15 You have six days each week for your ordinary work, but the seventh day must
31:16 be a Sabbath day of complete rest, a holy day dedicated to the LORD. Anyone who works
Exod 20:8 on the Sabbath must be put to death. 16 The people of Israel must keep the Sabbath day by
31:17 observing it from generation to generation. This is a covenant obligation for all time. 17 It is
Gen 2:2-3; Exod 20:11 a permanent sign of My covenant with the people of Israel. For in six days the LORD made
31:18 heaven and earth, but on the seventh day He stopped working and was refreshed.' "
Exod 24:12; 32:15- 18 When the LORD finished speaking with Moses on Mount Sinai, He gave him the two
16; 34:1, 28 stone tablets inscribed with the terms of the covenant,* written by the finger of God.

THE GOLD CALF

32:1 **32** When the people saw how long it was taking Moses to come back down the
Exod 24:18 mountain, they gathered around Aaron. "Come on," they said, "make us some
Deut 9:9-12; *Acts 7:40 gods who can lead us. We don't know what happened to this fellow Moses, who brought
32:2 us here from the land of Egypt."
Exod 35:22 2 So Aaron said, "Take the gold rings from the ears of your wives and sons and daugh-
32:4 ters, and bring them to me."
Exod 20:23; Deut 9:16 3 All the people took the gold rings from their ears and brought them to Aaron. 4 Then
Ps 106:19; Acts 7:41 Aaron took the gold, melted it down, and molded it into the shape of a calf. When the

31:18 Hebrew *the two tablets of the Testimony;* see note on 25:16.

31:11 Several times in Exodus, God threatened the Israelites with death if they disdained the purity of His worship (Exodus 28:35, 43; 30:20; 35:2). God is patient with those who err in worship when they do so with a good heart (2 Chronicles 30:18-20), but His threats still indicate that worship is a very serious matter.

▸WORSHIP
31:13 Keep my Sabbath day. Most of us take a day off from work and errands when we are exhausted or schedules permit. But God has a different slant on rest. God wanted His people to continue celebrating the Sabbath so that "you may know that I am the LORD, who makes you holy." Are you allowing God to make you holy, or are you trusting in your own strenuous efforts—striving when you should be resting? Take one day each week to remember the Lord, and focus on the One who can make you holy. (***See Worship****> OT> Festivals> Sabbath*, TopicGuide page A26.)

31:14-15 "Must be" might be better translated "will be liable unto." Hebrew legal language typically speaks in terms of maximum penalties rather than mandatory penalties. Judges were to determine the extent of the violation, and to find an appropriate punishment. When a man was found violating this law, his death was not a foregone conclusion (Numbers 15:32-35).

31:16-17 Under the Old Covenant, to disregard God's Sabbath was to reject His covenant and risk falling under the covenant's curses. The Sabbath commandment is a perpetual law (Matthew 5:17-19), although its celebration under the New Covenant is more flexible than in Moses' day (Colossians 2:16) since the New Covenant is "better" (Hebrews 7:22; 8:6).

31:18 The Ten Commandments were inscribed twice. This first time, God Himself carved the words in stone (see also Exodus 32:15-16). Moses destroyed these tablets when the Israelites committed idolatry (Exodus 32:19). Later, God asked Moses to come to the mountain again, and Moses spent forty days and nights there while God wrote the Ten Commandments again, inscribing the commandments with his own hand (Exodus 34:1, 27-28). These second tablets were then placed in the Ark of the Covenant, the sacred chest that sat in the innermost chamber of the Tabernacle. If the practice was as most in the Ancient Near East, there were two copies—one for Israel and one for God. The commandments are listed in Exodus 20 and Deuteronomy 5.

32:2 Both men and women wore earrings in ancient Israel. The instruction to take them off is more literally rendered "tear off" or "break off." Some of these earrings were permanent (Exodus 21:6).

32:4 In violation of the very law Moses was receiving at the time (Exodus 20:4), and in witness against Aaron's lie (Exodus 32:24), the idol was molded and tooled.

people saw it, they exclaimed, "O Israel, these are the gods who brought you out of the
land of Egypt!"
5 Aaron saw how excited the people were, so he built an altar in front of the calf. Then he
announced, "Tomorrow will be a festival to the LORD!"
6 The people got up early the next morning to sacrifice burnt offerings and peace offer-
ings. After this, they celebrated with feasting and drinking, and they indulged in pagan rev-
elry.
7 The LORD told Moses, "Quick! Go down the mountain! Your people whom you brought
from the land of Egypt have corrupted themselves. 8 How quickly they have turned away
from the way I commanded them to live! They have melted down gold and made a calf,
and they have bowed down and sacrificed to it. They are saying, 'These are your gods,
O Israel, who brought you out of the land of Egypt.'"
9 Then the LORD said, "I have seen how stubborn and rebellious these people are. 10 Now
leave Me alone so My fierce anger can blaze against them, and I will destroy them. Then I
will make you, Moses, into a great nation."
11 But Moses tried to pacify the LORD his God. "O LORD!" he said. "Why are You so angry
with Your own people whom You brought from the land of Egypt with such great power
and such a strong hand? 12 Why let the Egyptians say, 'Their God rescued them with the
evil intention of slaughtering them in the mountains and wiping them from the face of the
earth'? Turn away from Your fierce anger. Change Your mind about this terrible disaster
You have threatened against Your people! 13 Remember Your servants Abraham, Isaac,
and Jacob.* You bound Yourself with an oath to them, saying, 'I will make your descen-
dants as numerous as the stars of heaven. And I will give them all of this land that I have
promised to your descendants, and they will possess it forever.'"
14 So the LORD changed His mind about the terrible disaster He had threatened to bring
on His people.
15 Then Moses turned and went down the mountain. He held in his hands the two stone
tablets inscribed with the terms of the covenant.* They were inscribed on both sides, front and
back. 16 These tablets were God's work; the words on them were written by God Himself.
17 When Joshua heard the boisterous noise of the people shouting below them, he ex-
claimed to Moses, "It sounds like war in the camp!"
18 But Moses replied, "No, it's not a shout of victory nor the wailing of defeat. I hear the
sound of a celebration."

32:6 Num 25:2; Acts 7:41; *1 Cor 10:7
32:7 Exod 19:24; 33:1; Deut 9:12
32:8 Exod 22:20; 34:15; Deut 32:17
32:9 Exod 33:5; Num 14:11; Acts 7:51
32:10 Num 14:12; Deut 9:14
32:11 Deut 9:18, 26; Ps 106:23
32:12 Num 14:13-16; Deut 9:28
32:13 Gen 15:5; 22:16-18; Heb 6:13
32:14 2 Sam 24:16; Ps 106:45
32:15 Exod 24:18; Deut 9:15
32:16 Exod 31:18

32:13 Hebrew *Israel.* The names "Jacob" and "Israel" are often interchanged throughout the Old Testament, referring sometimes to the individual patriarch and sometimes to the nation. 32:15 Hebrew *the two tablets of the Testimony;* see note on 25:16.

▸ WORSHIP

32:5 Destructive worship. Not everything that touches our emotions is good for us, including religious fervor. Aaron and the people were going away from God's strict instructions concerning idol worship. Regardless of how it made them feel, they were in disobedience. Pledge to evaluate everything in your life, including your worship, by the standard of God's Word. (***See Worship> OT> Prohibitions> Wrong Objects> Other gods,*** TopicGuide page A28.)

32:5 Aaron might have been trying to worship God through pagan means, but he might also have been trying to subvert the people's intentions by turning their idolatry into more proper worship. He was mistaken in both his understanding of what was proper (Exodus 20:4) and in his ability to change the people's hearts (Exodus 32:8-9).

32:6 The "pagan revelry" mentioned here probably involved sexual immorality, which was very common among Ancient Near Eastern religions.

32:8 The people of Israel had turned away from the proper modes of worship detailed in the laws God had just delivered to Moses (Exodus 25–31).

32:11-13 Moses' intercessions on behalf of Israel appealed to God's stated purposes in freeing Israel from slavery in Egypt: spreading news of His power throughout the world (Exodus 9:15-16), and honoring His covenant with Abraham, Isaac, and Jacob (Genesis 17:15-18; 26:23-25; 28:12-15), the patriarchs of the nation of Israel.

32:14 God commonly changes his mind with regard to offered blessings and threatened curses (Jeremiah 18:1-10). The only time He is guaranteed not to change His mind is when He has promised a particular course of action (Malachi 3:6).

32:19 19 When they came near the camp, Moses saw the calf and the dancing, and he burned
Exod 32:6 with anger. He threw the stone tablets to the ground, smashing them at the foot of the
Deut 9:16-17 32:20 mountain. 20 He took the calf they had made and burned it. Then he ground it into powder,
Deut 9:21 threw it into the water, and forced the people to drink it.
21 Finally, he turned to Aaron and demanded, "What did these people do to you to make
you bring such terrible sin upon them?"
32:22 22 "Don't get so upset, my lord," Aaron replied. "You yourself know how evil these peo-
Deut 9:24 ple are. 23 They said to me, 'Make us gods who will lead us. We don't know what hap-
32:23 Exod 32:1 pened to this fellow Moses, who brought us here from the land of Egypt.' 24 So I told them,
'Whoever has gold jewelry, take it off.' When they brought it to me, I simply threw it into
the fire—and out came this calf!"
32:25 1 Kgs 12:28-30 25 Moses saw that Aaron had let the people get completely out of control, much to the
32:26 amusement of their enemies.* 26 So he stood at the entrance to the camp and shouted, "All
2 Sam 20:11 of you who are on the LORD's side, come here and join me." And all the Levites gathered
around him.
32:27 Num 25:5 27 Moses told them, "This is what the LORD, the God of Israel, says: Each of you, take your
Deut 33:9 swords and go back and forth from one end of the camp to the other. Kill everyone—even
your brothers, friends, and neighbors." 28 The Levites obeyed Moses' command, and about
32:28 3,000 people died that day.
Num 16:32; 25:9 29 Then Moses told the Levites, "Today you have ordained yourselves* for the service of
32:29 Deut 13:6; 33:9 the LORD, for you obeyed Him even though it meant killing your own sons and brothers.
Today you have earned a blessing."

MOSES INTERCEDES FOR ISRAEL

32:31 Exod 20:23 30 The next day Moses said to the people, "You have committed a terrible sin, but I will go
32:32 back up to the LORD on the mountain. Perhaps I will be able to obtain forgiveness* for your
Ps 69:28 sin."
Isa 4:3 Dan 12:1 31 So Moses returned to the LORD and said, "Oh, what a terrible sin these people have
Mal 3:16-17 committed. They have made gods of gold for themselves. 32 But now, if You will only for-
Phil 4:3 Rev 3:5; 21:27 give their sin—but if not, erase my name from the record You have written!"
32:33 33 But the LORD replied to Moses, "No, I will erase the name of everyone who has sinned
Deut 29:20 against Me. 34 Now go, lead the people to the place I told you about. Look! My angel will
Ps 9:5 Rev 3:5 lead the way before you. And when I come to call the people to account, I will certainly
hold them responsible for their sins."
32:34 Exod 3:17; 23:20 35 Then the LORD sent a great plague upon the people because they had worshiped the
Ps 99:8 calf Aaron had made.

32:25 Or *out of control, and they mocked anyone who opposed them.* The meaning of the Hebrew is unclear.
32:29 As in Greek and Latin versions; Hebrew reads *Today ordain yourselves.* 32:30 Or *to make atonement.*

32:19 God later replaced the broken tablets (Exodus 34:27-28).

32:24 Aaron's lie was an attempt to hide his guilt (compare Exodus 32:4), but his story was as foolish as his behavior.

32:25 The enemies mentioned in this verse were probably the Amalekites (Exodus 17) and the Egyptians (Exodus 14), but other small nomadic groups could have observed Israel's folly.

32:27-29 God punished false worship by death. The language here is reminiscent of that used to describe holy war (Deuteronomy 32:43) against Israel's enemies.

32:32-35 Moses' offer to be a substitute for the people reflected the principles of substitutionary atonement embodied in the law God had just given him (compare Exodus 13:13). God's rejection of Moses' offer might be explained in at least two ways: Moses was not a sufficient sacrifice, and the people had not repented of their sin.

▸ PURPOSE

32:35 A plague upon the people. Israel broke their covenant with God, and just as He promised, God allowed a plague like the ones in Egypt to fall on them (Exodus 23:24-25; Amos 4:10). Today, when breaking contracts is just another negotiation tactic, it is good to know that God takes His promises seriously. We can always trust God to keep His Word. (***See Purpose***> *God's Deeds*> *Special Acts*> *Miracles*> *OT,* TopicGuide page A52.)

33 The LORD said to Moses, "Get going, you and the people you brought up from the
land of Egypt. Go up to the land I swore to give to Abraham, Isaac, and Jacob. I
told them, 'I will give this land to your descendants.' 2And I will send an angel before you
to drive out the Canaanites, Amorites, Hittites, Perizzites, Hivites, and Jebusites. 3Go up to
this land that flows with milk and honey. But I will not travel among you, for you are a
stubborn and rebellious people. If I did, I would surely destroy you along the way."
4When the people heard these stern words, they went into mourning and stopped wear-
ing their jewelry and fine clothes. 5For the LORD had told Moses to tell them, "You are a
stubborn and rebellious people. If I were to travel with you for even a moment, I would de-
stroy you. Remove your jewelry and fine clothes while I decide what to do with you." 6So
from the time they left Mount Sinai,* the Israelites wore no more jewelry or fine clothes.
7It was Moses' practice to take the Tent of Meeting* and set it up some distance from the
camp. Everyone who wanted to make a request of the LORD would go to the Tent of Meet-
ing outside the camp.
8Whenever Moses went out to the Tent of Meeting, all the people would get up and
stand in the entrances of their own tents. They would all watch Moses until he disap-
peared inside. 9As he went into the tent, the pillar of cloud would come down and hover at
its entrance while the LORD spoke with Moses. 10When the people saw the cloud standing
at the entrance of the tent, they would stand and bow down in front of their own tents.
11Inside the Tent of Meeting, the LORD would speak to Moses face to face, as one speaks to
a friend. Afterward Moses would return to the camp, but the young man who assisted him,
Joshua son of Nun, would remain behind in the Tent of Meeting.

MOSES SEES THE LORD'S GLORY

12One day Moses said to the LORD, "You have been telling me, 'Take these people up to
the Promised Land.' But You haven't told me whom You will send with me. You have told
me, 'I know you by name, and I look favorably on you.' 13If it is true that You look favor-
ably on me, let me know Your ways so I may understand You more fully and continue to
enjoy Your favor. And remember that this nation is Your very own people."
14The LORD replied, "I will personally go with you, Moses, and I will give you rest—every-
thing will be fine for you."
15Then Moses said, "If You don't personally go with us, don't make us leave this place.
16How will anyone know that You look favorably on me—on me and on Your people—if

33:1 Gen 12:7; Exod 32:7, 13
33:2 Exod 23:27-31
33:3 Exod 3:8, 17; 32:9-10
33:4 Num 14:1, 39
33:5 Exod 33:3
33:7 Exod 29:42-43
33:8 Num 16:27
33:9 Exod 13:21; 19:9; 25:22; Ps 99:7
33:11 Num 12:8; Deut 34:10
33:12 Exod 3:10; 32:34; John 10:14-15; 2 Tim 2:19
33:13 Exod 34:9; Pss 25:4; 27:11
33:14 Exod 13:21; Josh 22:4; Isa 63:9
33:15 Ps 80:3, 7, 19
33:16 Exod 34:10; Lev 20:24, 26; Num 14:14

33:6 Hebrew *Horeb*, another name for Sinai. 33:7 This "Tent of Meeting" is different from the Tabernacle described in chapters 26 and 36.

33:1-3 God Himself had led the people (Exodus 13:21-22); Moses had not acted alone. But here God's language dissociated Him from His covenant people. Rather than remain their advocate, He had become their adversary.

33:2 Here God clearly distinguishes Himself from His angel (compare Exodus 3:2-6).

33:11 The phrase translated "face to face" is a figure of speech suggesting directness and intimacy. Moses did not actually see God's face (compare Exodus 33:20), for God is a spirit and has no body as we do (Hebrews 11:27).

▶ GOD
33:11 Inside the Tent of Meeting. Wouldn't it be nice to have a certain place to go to meet with God, a place where you knew He would be present? Here's the good news—you are already there! God is with us everywhere. And if we live in the light of God's presence, we will enjoy the benefit of fellowship with others and freedom from our sins (1 John 1:7). (***See God**> God's Attributes> All-Present> God can always hear*, TopicGuide page A16.)

33:12 Moses had not forgotten about the angel (Exodus 33:2). Rather, he was petitioning God for mercy, asking God to fulfill His offer to live among the people of Israel (Exodus 29:45) despite their sin.

33:13 Moses responded directly to God's reference to Israel as "the people you brought" (Exodus 33:1) as opposed to "My people." As in the prior verse, Moses asked for God's gracious fulfillment of His offer in Exodus 29:45.

33:14 This was not a promise, but a conditional offer of blessing that would be fulfilled if Israel obeyed (compare Jeremiah 18:1-10).

33:15-16 Moses suspected that Israel would not fulfill God's condition of obedience and that God might not accompany them. Moses asked God to accompany them on the basis of His grace, rather than on the basis of their merit.

33:17 you don't go with us? For Your presence among us sets Your people and me apart from all
Exod 33:12 other people on the earth."
33:18 17 The LORD replied to Moses, "I will indeed do what you have asked, for I look favorably
Exod 33:20, 23 on you, and I know you by name."
33:19 *Rom 9:15 18 Moses responded, "Then show me Your glorious presence."
33:20 19 The LORD replied, "I will make all My goodness pass before you, and I will call out My
Isa 6:5 name, Yahweh,* before you. For I will show mercy to anyone I choose, and I will show
John 1:18 compassion to anyone I choose. 20 But you may not look directly at My face, for no one
1 Tim 6:16 may see Me and live." 21 The LORD continued, "Look, stand near Me on this rock. 22 As My
33:22 Ps 91:1, 4 glorious presence passes by, I will hide you in the crevice of the rock and cover you with
Isa 49:2; 51:16 My hand until I have passed by. 23 Then I will remove My hand and let you see Me from
33:23 behind. But My face will not be seen."
John 1:18

A NEW COPY OF THE COVENANT

34:1 **34** Then the LORD told Moses, "Chisel out two stone tablets like the first ones. I will
Exod 24:12; 32:19 write on them the same words that were on the tablets you smashed. 2 Be ready
Deut 10:2, 4 in the morning to climb up Mount Sinai and present yourself to Me on the top of the
mountain. 3 No one else may come with you. In fact, no one is to appear anywhere on the
34:3 mountain. Do not even let the flocks or herds graze near the mountain."
Exod 19:12-13
4 So Moses chiseled out two tablets of stone like the first ones. Early in the morning he
climbed Mount Sinai as the LORD had commanded him, and he carried the two stone tablets
in his hands.
34:5 5 Then the LORD came down in a cloud and stood there with him; and He called out His
Exod 33:19 own name, Yahweh.* 6 The LORD passed in front of Moses, calling out,

34:6 "Yahweh!* The LORD!
Num 14:18 Neh 9:17 The God of compassion and mercy!
Pss 86:15; 103:8 I am slow to anger
34:7 Exod 20:6-7 and filled with unfailing love and faithfulness.
Deut 5:10 7 I lavish unfailing love to a thousand generations.*
Nah 1:3 I forgive iniquity, rebellion, and sin.

33:19 *Yahweh* is a transliteration of the proper name *YHWH* that is sometimes rendered "Jehovah"; in this translation it is usually rendered "the LORD" (note the use of small capitals). 34:5 *Yahweh* is a transliteration of the proper name *YHWH* that is sometimes rendered "Jehovah"; in this translation it is usually rendered "the LORD" (note the use of small capitals). 34:6 See note on 34:5. 34:7 Hebrew *for thousands.*

33:20-23 Not even Moses was permitted to see God in all His unveiled glory. The Bible does not explicitly state why such a revelation would have killed Moses, but seeing God as He is has an effect on humans (compare Exodus 34:29-35 and 1 John 3:2).

▶ WORSHIP
33:23 The face of God. How do you see the invisible? God is an invisible spirit and has no physical body (John 4:24; Colossians 1:15; Hebrews 11:27). In this case, God's "face" is symbolic. We cannot comprehend God's full presence or glory. The apostle John wrote that our greatest privilege in heaven will be seeing God, and in that seeing, we will be changed (1 John 3:2). This will be just one of the many exciting mysteries that heaven reveals. What do you most look forward to? (***See Worship****> OT> Place> Tabernacle> Glory of the Lord filled the house*, TopicGuide page A27.)

34:1-4 God wrote the first tablets by His own hand (Exodus 31:18; 32:16), but Moses destroyed them when the people sinned. Replacing the tablets was an act of renewing the covenant with God that the people had broken.

34:3 When the covenant was first made, many priests and elders had been present on the mountain as Israel's representatives. This time Israel's only representative was to be Moses. This circumstance greatly emphasized Moses' importance as Israel's leader, mediator, and advocate. In this sense, Moses shows us something about the future ministry of Jesus as our Leader, Mediator, and Advocate (1 John 2:1; 5:15).

34:6-7 In the renewal of the covenant, God confirmed His benevolence toward Israel, but also reminded His people that they had an obligation to obey Him, and that the covenant blessings were conditioned upon their obedience.

▶ GOD
34:7 Consequences of sin. God has never punished the innocent for the sins of the wicked (Genesis 18:25; Deuteronomy 24:16; Ezekiel 18), but sometimes His punishment of the wicked has repercussions that affect entire families. For example, God might allow a husband and father to lose his job as a result of sin, and this punishment would certainly impact his wife and children. How might God's discipline of your own sins affect the ones you love? (***See God****> God's Attributes> Righteous> His righteousness demands punishment*, TopicGuide page A17.)

But I do not excuse the guilty.
I lay the sins of the parents upon their children and grandchildren;
the entire family is affected—
even children in the third and fourth generations."

8Moses immediately threw himself to the ground and worshiped. 9And he said, "O Lord,
if it is true that I have found favor with You, then please travel with us. Yes, this is a stub-
born and rebellious people, but please forgive our iniquity and our sins. Claim us as Your
own special possession."
10The LORD replied, "Listen, I am making a covenant with you in the presence of all your
people. I will perform miracles that have never been performed anywhere in all the earth
or in any nation. And all the people around you will see the power of the LORD—the awe-
some power I will display for you. 11But listen carefully to everything I command you to-
day. Then I will go ahead of you and drive out the Amorites, Canaanites, Hittites,
Perizzites, Hivites, and Jebusites.
12"Be very careful never to make a treaty with the people who live in the land where
you are going. If you do, you will follow their evil ways and be trapped. 13Instead, you
must break down their pagan altars, smash their sacred pillars, and cut down their Ashe-
rah poles. 14You must worship no other gods, for the LORD, whose very name is Jealous, is
a God who is jealous about His relationship with you.
15"You must not make a treaty of any kind with the people living in the land. They lust
after their gods, offering sacrifices to them. They will invite you to join them in their sacrifi-
cial meals, and you will go with them. 16Then you will accept their daughters, who sacri-
fice to other gods, as wives for your sons. And they will seduce your sons to commit
adultery against Me by worshiping other gods. 17You must not make any gods of molten
metal for yourselves.
18"You must celebrate the Festival of Unleavened Bread. For seven days the bread you
eat must be made without yeast, just as I commanded you. Celebrate this festival annually
at the appointed time in early spring, in the month of Abib,* for that is the anniversary of
your departure from Egypt.
19"The firstborn of every animal belongs to Me, including the firstborn males from your
herds of cattle and your flocks of sheep and goats. 20A firstborn donkey may be bought
back from the LORD by presenting a lamb or young goat in its place. But if you do not buy it
back, you must break its neck. However, you must buy back every firstborn son.
"No one may appear before Me without an offering.

34:9 Num 14:19; Deut 4:20; 32:9; Ps 25:11
34:10 Deut 5:2-3; Pss 72:18; 136:4
34:11 Exod 33:2; Deut 6:3
34:12 Exod 23:32-33
34:13 Exod 23:24; Deut 7:5; 12:3; 16:21; 2 Chr 34:3-4
34:14 Exod 20:3; Deut 4:24
34:15 Judg 2:17; Num 25:2
34:16 Deut 7:3; Josh 23:12
34:17 Exod 20:4, 23
34:18 Exod 12:2, 15-17
34:19 Exod 13:2; 22:29
34:20 Exod 13:13, 15; Num 3:45

34:18 Hebrew *appointed time in the month of Abib.* This first month of the ancient Hebrew lunar calendar usually occurs within the months of March and April.

34:9 In this covenant renewal, Moses echoed his earlier request for confirmation of God's intentions (Exodus 33:18), asking God to make Israel His own.

34:11 God's covenant blessings have always been conditioned upon the obedience of His people (compare Genesis 17:1-2; 2 Chronicles 6:16; Romans 2:26). Jesus made it clear that obedience is the way we show our love for God (John 14:15, 21). James states that faith without the good works to support it is not valid faith (James 2:20). Because all human beings are sinful, they may be counted as obedient only by God's grace through faith in Him for salvation, and on the basis of the obedience of Christ (2 Corinthians 5:21).

34:12-17 Israel was to avoid both treaties and intermarriage with other nations in Canaan, for such alliances would lead to idolatry. Throughout Israel's history, foreign wives were permitted when they converted to worship the true God (Deuteronomy 21:11-12; Ruth 4). Alliances with foreign peoples were permitted when those foreigners were faithful to the Lord (Genesis 12:3; 18:18; Exodus 12:48-49).

▸ GOD

34:14 A God who is passionate. It's hard to believe—God *wants* a relationship with His people. And He isn't interested in waiting until heaven—God desires a relationship with you today! Though your emotions and faith may waver, God always desires to know you and to be known by you. In your wildest dreams, it would be difficult to imagine that the God who created the universe wants to know you and be known by you, but that is precisely what the Bible teaches. (***See God*> *God's Nature*> *Personality*> *Emotion*> *God jealously desires exclusive worship,* TopicGuide page A14.)

34:18-26 This section summarizes a number of laws in a section of Scripture called the "Book of the Covenant" (Exodus 20:22–23:19).

34:21 Exod 31:15; 35:2 21 "You have six days each week for your ordinary work, but on the seventh day you
must stop working, even during the seasons of plowing and harvest.
34:22 Exod 23:16 22 "You must celebrate the Festival of Harvest* with the first crop of the wheat harvest, and cel-
34:23 ebrate the Festival of the Final Harvest* at the end of the harvest season. 23 Three times each
Exod 23:14-17 year every man in Israel must appear before the Sovereign, the LORD, the God of Israel. 24 I will
Deut 16:16 drive out the other nations ahead of you and expand your territory, so no one will covet and
34:24 conquer your land while you appear before the LORD your God three times each year.
Exod 33:2 Josh 11:23 25 "You must not offer the blood of My sacrificial offerings together with any baked
34:25 goods containing yeast. And none of the meat of the Passover sacrifice may be kept over
Exod 12:10; 23:18 until the next morning.
34:26 26 "As you harvest your crops, bring the very best of the first harvest to the house of the
Exod 23:19 LORD your God.
Deut 26:2 "You must not cook a young goat in its mother's milk."
34:27 27 Then the LORD said to Moses, "Write down all these instructions, for they represent the
Exod 17:14; 24:4 terms of the covenant I am making with you and with Israel."
34:28 Exod 24:18 28 Moses remained there on the mountain with the LORD forty days and forty nights. In
Deut 4:13; 10:4 all that time he ate no bread and drank no water. And the LORD* wrote the terms of the cov-
enant—the Ten Commandments*—on the stone tablets.
34:29 Exod 32:15 29 When Moses came down Mount Sinai carrying the two stone tablets inscribed with
Matt 17:2 the terms of the covenant,* he wasn't aware that his face had become radiant because he
2 Cor 3:7, 13 had spoken to the LORD. 30 So when Aaron and the people of Israel saw the radiance of
Moses' face, they were afraid to come near him.
31 But Moses called out to them and asked Aaron and all the leaders of the community to
come over, and he talked with them. 32 Then all the people of Israel approached him, and
34:33 2 Cor 3:13 Moses gave them all the instructions the LORD had given him on Mount Sinai. 33 When
34:34 Moses finished speaking with them, he covered his face with a veil. 34 But whenever he went
2 Cor 3:16 into the Tent of Meeting to speak with the LORD, he would remove the veil until he came out
34:35 again. Then he would give the people whatever instructions the LORD had given him, 35 and
2 Cor 3:13 the people of Israel would see the radiant glow of his face. So he would put the veil over his
face until he returned to speak with the LORD.

INSTRUCTIONS FOR THE SABBATH

35:2 Exod 20:9-10; 23:12; **35** Then Moses called together the whole community of Israel and told them,
31:15; 34:21 Num 15:32-36 "These are the instructions the LORD has commanded you to follow. 2 You have
Deut 5:13-14 six days each week for your ordinary work, but the seventh day must be a Sabbath day

34:22a Hebrew *Festival of Weeks;* compare 23:16. This was later called the Festival of Pentecost. It is celebrated today as Shavuat (or Shabuoth). 34:22b Or *Festival of Ingathering.* This was later called the Festival of Shelters or Festival of Tabernacles (see Lev 23:33-36). It is celebrated today as Sukkot (or Succoth). 34:28a Hebrew *He.* 34:28b Hebrew *the ten words.* 34:29 Hebrew *the two tablets of the Testimony;* see note on 25:16.

▸ BIBLE

34:28 Discovering Jesus in the life of Moses. Just as Moses' ministry was confirmed by this miraculous fast, God demonstrated His approval of His Son by sustaining Jesus for 40 days during His temptation (Matthew 4:1-2). Of the many similarities between these two events, there was one difference: Jesus was not only communing with God, He was defeating Satan (Matthew 4:11). Moses was great, but we as God's people need more than a holy man to save us—we need a Champion! Worship the victorious Jesus Christ! (***See Bible***> *Unity> OT Types> Moses,* TopicGuide page A11.)

34:29-35 As a side effect of being in close proximity to a physical manifestation of God's glory, Moses' face emanated light. The Bible does not explain this phenomenon, but the effect of this glow was to identify Moses as a man with special access to God—and as such, his word should be trusted.

35:1-3 Exodus 35–40 details the construction of the Tabernacle. Moses began by reasserting the Sabbath commandment (compare Exodus 16:23-30; 31:13-17) so that the nation would remember not to violate it as they worked to build the Tabernacle.

▸ WORSHIP

35:2 A day of total rest. If the Sabbath is supposed to be a day of rest, then why do I always seem to need a nap by two o'clock? While the Sabbath is a day of resting from our ordinary labors, enthusiastic worship is also appropriate on this day (Leviticus 23:3). Doing this (and making sure the rest of the family does it too!) may not always be physically restful, but it is spiritually and emotionally refreshing. (***See Worship***> *OT> Festivals> Sabbath,* TopicGuide page A26.)

of complete rest, a holy day dedicated to the LORD. Anyone who works on that day must 35:3
be put to death. 3 You must not even light a fire in any of your homes on the Sabbath." Exod 16:23

OFFERINGS FOR THE TABERNACLE

4 Then Moses said to the whole community of Israel, "This is what the LORD has com- 35:4-9
manded: 5 Take a sacred offering for the LORD. Let those with generous hearts present the //Exod 25:1-9
following gifts to the LORD:

KEY TABERNACLE PIECES

Name	Function and Significance
Ark of the Covenant	• A golden rectangular box that contained the Ten Commandments • Symbolized God's covenant with Israel's people • Located in the Most Holy Place
Atonement Cover	• The lid to the Ark of the Covenant • Symbolized the presence of God among his people
Curtain	• The curtain that divided the two sacred rooms of the Tabernacle—the Holy Place and the Most Holy Place • Symbolized how the people were separated from God because of sin
Table	• A wooden table located in the Holy Place of the Tabernacle; the Bread of the Presence and various utensils were kept on this table
Bread of the Presence	• Twelve loaves of baked bread, one for each tribe of Israel • Symbolized the spiritual nourishment God offers his people
Lampstands and Lamps	• A golden lampstand located in the Holy Place, which held seven burning oil lamps • The lampstand lit the Holy Place for the priests
Incense Altar	• An altar in the Holy Place in front of the curtain • Used for burning God's special incense and symbolic of acceptable prayer
Anointing Oil	• A special oil used to anoint the priests and all the pieces in the Tabernacle • A sign of being set apart for God
Altar of Burnt Offering	• The bronze altar outside the Tabernacle used for the sacrifices • Symbolized how sacrifice restored one's relationship with God
Washbasin	• A large washbasin outside the Tabernacle used by the priests to cleanse themselves before performing their duties • Symbolized the need for spiritual cleansing

35:5-9 The record of the actual building of the Tabernacle begins with instructions for freewill offerings of building materials. This parallels the beginning of the record of the building instructions (Exodus 25:2-7).

gold, silver, and bronze;
6 blue, purple, and scarlet thread;
fine linen and goat hair for cloth;
7 tanned ram skins and fine goatskin leather;
acacia wood;
8 olive oil for the lamps;
spices for the anointing oil and the fragrant incense;
9 onyx stones, and other gemstones to be set in the ephod and the priest's chestpiece.

35:10-19 //Exod 39:32-41

10 "Come, all of you who are gifted craftsmen. Construct everything that the LORD has commanded:

11 the Tabernacle and its sacred tent, its covering, clasps, frames, crossbars, posts, and bases;
12 the Ark and its carrying poles;
the Ark's cover—the place of atonement;
the inner curtain to shield the Ark;
13 the table, its carrying poles, and all its utensils;
the Bread of the Presence;
14 for light, the lampstand, its accessories, the lamp cups, and the olive oil for lighting;
15 the incense altar and its carrying poles;
the anointing oil and fragrant incense;
the curtain for the entrance of the Tabernacle;
16 the altar of burnt offering;
the bronze grating of the altar and its carrying poles and utensils;
the washbasin with its stand;
17 the curtains for the walls of the courtyard;
the posts and their bases;
the curtain for the entrance to the courtyard;
18 the tent pegs of the Tabernacle and courtyard and their ropes;
19 the beautifully stitched garments for the priests to wear while ministering in the Holy Place—the sacred garments for Aaron the priest, and the garments for his sons to wear as they minister as priests."

35:21 Exod 25:2; 35:5

20 So the whole community of Israel left Moses and returned to their tents. 21 All whose
hearts were stirred and whose spirits were moved came and brought their sacred offer-
ings to the LORD. They brought all the materials needed for the Tabernacle,* for the per-
formance of its rituals, and for the sacred garments. 22 Both men and women came, all
whose hearts were willing. They brought to the LORD their offerings of gold—brooches,
earrings, rings from their fingers, and necklaces. They presented gold objects of every
kind as a special offering to the LORD. 23 All those who owned the following items will-
ingly brought them: blue, purple, and scarlet thread; fine linen and goat hair for cloth;
and tanned ram skins and fine goatskin leather. 24 And all who had silver and bronze ob-
jects gave them as a sacred offering to the LORD. And those who had acacia wood
brought it for use in the project.

35:23 Exod 39:1

35:25 Exod 28:3

25 All the women who were skilled in sewing and spinning prepared blue, purple, and
scarlet thread, and fine linen cloth. 26 All the women who were willing used their skills to

35:21 Hebrew *Tent of Meeting.*

35:10-19 Moses calls for all the talented workers in Israel to help to build the Tabernacle. The call summarizes the instructions for the Tabernacle and its accoutrements (compare Exodus 25–31), perhaps in order to indicate which types of workers were needed. The Tabernacle was a large tent that served as a portable sanctuary. It was the place of God's residence with the Israelites.

spin the goat hair into yarn. 27The leaders brought onyx stones and the special gemstones 35:27
to be set in the ephod and the priest's chestpiece. 28They also brought spices and olive oil 1 Chr 29:6
for the light, the anointing oil, and the fragrant incense. 29So the people of Israel—every Ezra 2:68 35:29
man and woman who was eager to help in the work the LORD had given them through 1 Chr 29:9
Moses—brought their gifts and gave them freely to the LORD.
30Then Moses told the people of Israel, "The LORD has specifically chosen Bezalel son of 35:30-35
Uri, grandson of Hur, of the tribe of Judah. 31The LORD has filled Bezalel with the Spirit of //Exod 31:2-6
God, giving him great wisdom, ability, and expertise in all kinds of crafts. 32He is a master
craftsman, expert in working with gold, silver, and bronze. 33He is skilled in engraving and
mounting gemstones and in carving wood. He is a master at every craft. 34And the LORD 35:34
has given both him and Oholiab son of Ahisamach, of the tribe of Dan, the ability to teach Exod 31:6
their skills to others. 35The LORD has given them special skills as engravers, designers, 35:35 Exod 31:3, 6; 35:31
embroiderers in blue, purple, and scarlet thread on fine linen cloth, and weavers. They ex- 1 Kgs 7:14
cel as craftsmen and as designers.

36 "The LORD has gifted Bezalel, Oholiab, and the other skilled craftsmen with wis- 36:1
dom and ability to perform any task involved in building the sanctuary. Let them Exod 25:8
construct and furnish the Tabernacle, just as the LORD has commanded."
2So Moses summoned Bezalel and Oholiab and all the others who were specially 36:2 Exod 35:21, 26
gifted by the LORD and were eager to get to work. 3Moses gave them the materials do- 1 Chr 29:5
nated by the people of Israel as sacred offerings for the completion of the sanctuary. But
the people continued to bring additional gifts each morning. 4Finally the craftsmen who
were working on the sanctuary left their work. 5They went to Moses and reported, "The 36:5
people have given more than enough materials to complete the job the LORD has com- 2 Chr 24:14; 31:6-10
manded us to do!" 2 Cor 8:2-3
6So Moses gave the command, and this message was sent throughout the camp: "Men
and women, don't prepare any more gifts for the sanctuary. We have enough!" So the
people stopped bringing their sacred offerings. 7Their contributions were more than 36:7
enough to complete the whole project. 1 Kgs 8:64

BUILDING THE TABERNACLE

8The skilled craftsmen made ten curtains of finely woven linen for the Tabernacle. Then 36:8-38 //Exod 26:1-37
Bezalel* decorated the curtains with blue, purple, and scarlet thread and with skillfully em-
broidered cherubim. 9All ten curtains were exactly the same size—42 feet long and 6 feet
wide.* 10Five of these curtains were joined together to make one long curtain, and the

36:8 Hebrew *he;* also in 36:16, 20, 35. See 37:1. 36:9 Hebrew *28 cubits* [12.9 meters] *long and 4 cubits* [1.8 meters] *wide.*

35:20-29; 36:3-7 Israel enthusiastically complies with the request for freewill offerings (compare Exodus 25:2-7; 35:5-9). This wealth came from the Egyptians, who bestowed gifts upon the Israelites during the Exodus (Exodus 12:36).

35:30-35 Craftsmen such as Bezalel and his assistant Oholiab were highly regarded in the ancient world. For this building project, their natural abilities were enhanced (Exodus 36:1).

▸ CHURCH
35:35 Special skills. What does it mean to be a Christian artist? These artists made all sorts of decorations for the Tabernacle, many of which were seen only by the high priest and God Himself. Has God given you special artistic skills? Whatever it is, whatever you do, do it for God. What would it look like for you to make something special—just for God? (***See Church****> Role> Preach> Topics> Proper use of spiritual gifts*, TopicGuide page A50.)

36:8-38 The Tabernacle was a tent built to serve as a sanctuary. It included a general area in which the people could gather; a smaller area, the Holy Place, accessed by the religious leadership; and the Most Holy Place, a chamber accessed only by the high priest in the most sacred of ceremonies. The Most Holy Place was the site of God's throne, including the Ark of the Covenant, which was his footstool (1 Chronicles 28:2). The Tabernacle was used, in one form or another, by the Israelite people until King Solomon built the Temple. The Tabernacle was built in strict compliance to God's instructions (Exodus 26).

36:8 The embroidered cherubim surrounded the Tabernacle, symbolizing the heavenly host that surround God's earthly and heavenly throne (2 Kings 19:15; Revelation 5:11). The commandment against worshiping images (Exodus 20:4-5) did not preclude the use of images like these in places of worship, so long as those images were ordained by God.

other five were joined to make a second long curtain. 11 He made fifty loops of blue yarn
and put them along the edge of the last curtain in each set. 12 The fifty loops along the
edge of one curtain matched the fifty loops along the edge of the other curtain. 13 Then he
made fifty gold clasps and fastened the long curtains together with the clasps. In this way,
the Tabernacle was made of one continuous piece.

36:14 14 He made eleven curtains of goat-hair cloth to serve as a tent covering for the Taber-
Exod 26:7 nacle. 15 These eleven curtains were all exactly the same size—45 feet long and 6 feet
wide.* 16 Bezalel joined five of these curtains together to make one long curtain, and the
other six were joined to make a second long curtain. 17 He made fifty loops for the edge
of each large curtain. 18 He also made fifty bronze clasps to fasten the long curtains to-
gether. In this way, the tent covering was made of one continuous piece. 19 He com-
pleted the tent covering with a layer of tanned ram skins and a layer of fine goatskin
leather.

36:20-34 20 For the framework of the Tabernacle, Bezalel constructed frames of acacia wood.
Exod 26:15-29; 21 Each frame was 15 feet high and 27 inches wide,* 22 with two pegs under each frame. All
40:18-19 the frames were identical. 23 He made twenty of these frames to support the curtains on
the south side of the Tabernacle. 24 He also made forty silver bases—two bases under each
frame, with the pegs fitting securely into the bases. 25 For the north side of the Tabernacle,
he made another twenty frames, 26 with their forty silver bases, two bases under each
frame. 27 He made six frames for the rear—the west side of the Tabernacle—28 along with
two additional frames to reinforce the rear corners of the Tabernacle. 29 These corner
frames were matched at the bottom and firmly attached at the top with a single ring, form-
ing a single corner unit. Both of these corner units were made the same way. 30 So there
were eight frames at the rear of the Tabernacle, set in sixteen silver bases—two bases
under each frame.

31 Then he made crossbars of acacia wood to link the frames, five crossbars for the north
side of the Tabernacle 32 and five for the south side. He also made five crossbars for the
rear of the Tabernacle, which faced west. 33 He made the middle crossbar to attach halfway
up the frames; it ran all the way from one end of the Tabernacle to the other. 34 He overlaid
the frames with gold and made gold rings to hold the crossbars. Then he overlaid the
crossbars with gold as well.

36:35-38 35 For the inside of the Tabernacle, Bezalel made a special curtain of finely woven linen.
Exod 26:31-37 He decorated it with blue, purple, and scarlet thread and with skillfully embroidered cher-
ubim. 36 For the curtain, he made four posts of acacia wood and four gold hooks. He over-
laid the posts with gold and set them in four silver bases.

37 Then he made another curtain for the entrance to the sacred tent. He made it of finely
woven linen and embroidered it with exquisite designs using blue, purple, and scarlet
thread. 38 This curtain was hung on gold hooks attached to five posts. The posts with their
decorated tops and hooks were overlaid with gold, and the five bases were cast from
bronze.

36:15 Hebrew *30 cubits* [13.8 meters] *long and 4 cubits* [1.8 meters] *wide.* 36:21 Hebrew *10 cubits* [4.6 meters] *high and 1.5 cubits* [69 centimeters] *wide.*

36:8-10 The innermost layer of the Tabernacle was luxurious. Its sides stopped 18 inches above the ground (compare Exodus 36:15).

36:14-16 Actually, this "tent covering" was a middle layer. Two more layers covered this one (Exodus 36:19). This second layer of the Tabernacle reached the ground.

36:18, 38 Bronze is an alloy of copper and tin, and it was the hardest metal available during this time.

36:19 Translators differ on the precise type of leather described here as "fine goatskin."

36:20, 31, 36; 37:1, 4, 10, 15, 25, 28 The acacia is a tree of the mimosa family, abundant in ancient Palestine. Acacia wood had an orange tint that grew darker with age. It was hard, strong, and durable.

BUILDING THE ARK OF THE COVENANT

37 Next Bezalel made the Ark of acacia wood—a sacred chest 45 inches long, 37:1-9
27 inches wide, and 27 inches high.* 2He overlaid it inside and outside with pure //Exod 25:10-20
gold, and he ran a molding of gold all around it. 3He cast four gold rings and attached 37:1
them to its four feet, two rings on each side. 4Then he made poles from acacia wood and Deut 10:3
overlaid them with gold. 5He inserted the poles into the rings at the sides of the Ark to
carry it.

6Then he made the Ark's cover—the place of atonement—from pure gold. It was
45 inches long and 27 inches wide.* 7He made two cherubim from hammered gold and
placed them on the two ends of the atonement cover. 8He molded the cherubim on each
end of the atonement cover, making it all of one piece of gold. 9The cherubim faced each
other and looked down on the atonement cover. With their wings spread above it, they
protected it.

BUILDING THE TABLE

10Then Bezalel* made the table of acacia wood, 36 inches long, 18 inches wide, and 37:10-16
27 inches high.* 11He overlaid it with pure gold and ran a gold molding around the edge. //Exod 25:23-29;
12He decorated it with a 3-inch border* all around, and he ran a gold molding along the 40:22
border. 13Then he cast four gold rings for the table and attached them at the four corners
next to the four legs. 14The rings were attached near the border to hold the poles that
were used to carry the table. 15He made these poles from acacia wood and overlaid them
with gold. 16Then he made special containers of pure gold for the table—bowls, pans, jars,
and pitchers—to be used in pouring out liquid offerings.

BUILDING THE LAMPSTAND

37:17-24
17Then Bezalel made the lampstand of pure, hammered gold. He made the entire lamp- //Exod 25:31-39;
stand and its decorations of one piece—the base, center stem, lamp cups, buds, and petals. 40:24
18The lampstand had six branches going out from the center stem, three on each side. 37:17 Heb 9:2
19Each of the six branches had three lamp cups shaped like almond blossoms, complete Rev 1:12

37:1 Hebrew *2.5 cubits* [115 centimeters] *long, 1.5 cubits* [69 centimeters] *wide, and 1.5 cubits high.* 37:6 Hebrew *2.5 cubits* [115 centimeters] *long and 1.5 cubits* [69 centimeters] *wide.* 37:10a Hebrew *he;* also in 37:17, 25. 37:10b Hebrew *2 cubits* [92 centimeters] *long, 1 cubit* [46 centimeters] *wide, and 1.5 cubits* [69 centimeters] *high.* 37:12 Hebrew *a border of a handbreadth* [8 centimeters].

37:1-3 The Ark of the Covenant was a chest that served as God's footstool (1 Chronicles 28:2). Its presence in the Most Holy Place (Exodus 26:33-34) of the Tabernacle demonstrated that the Tabernacle was God's throne room on earth and made it clear that the Lord was Israel's king (1 Samuel 8:7-8). God manifested His presence and spoke from His throne above the Ark (Exodus 25:22; Leviticus 16:2; 1 Samuel 4:4).

37:1 Have you ever looked at a picture or read a poem and wondered what, if anything, it meant? There is certainly symbolism attached to many of the decorative features of the Ark, the Tabernacle, and their contents. But we must be careful not to speculate too much as we attempt to understand them. It is a mistake to attempt to develop doctrines based on a subjective interpretation of these objects. We would be unwise to look for meaning in these symbols beyond that which is taught more clearly in other passages of Scripture.

37:4-5 The Ark was so sacred that it was not to be touched directly when it was carried (compare 2 Samuel 6:1-8).

37:6 The *place of atonement* is called "mercy seat" in other translations. Blood was sprinkled here on the annual Day of Atonement to represent atonement for the sins of the people (Leviticus 16:15).

37:7, 9 Cherubim were angelic guards in God's throne room (compare Genesis 3:24) and bearers of God's chariot throne (see Ezekiel 10).

37:10-16 A table was constructed to hold the Bread of the Presence (compare Exodus 25:23-30) and had rings attached to it to hold the poles used to carry it. Like the Ark, it remained untouched by human hands except on rare occasions.

37:17-24 The lampstand resembled an almond tree (compare Exodus 25:31-39). The image of the fruitful tree coupled with the cherubim throughout the Tabernacle (Exodus 36:8, 35; 37:7-9) may have been intended to reflect the Garden of Eden (Genesis 3:24), but Christians today also see it as an image of the future city of God (Revelation 21:1–22:6).

with buds and petals. 20 The center stem of the lampstand was crafted with four lamp cups shaped like almond blossoms, complete with buds and petals. 21 There was an almond bud beneath each pair of branches where the six branches extended from the center stem, all made of one piece. 22 The almond buds and branches were all of one piece with the center stem, and they were hammered from pure gold.

23 He also made seven lamps for the lampstand, lamp snuffers, and trays, all of pure gold. 24 The entire lampstand, along with its accessories, was made from seventy-five pounds* of pure gold.

BUILDING THE INCENSE ALTAR

37:25-28 //Exod 30:1-5
37:25 Heb 9:4; Rev 8:3

25 Then Bezalel made the incense altar of acacia wood. It was 18 inches square and 36 inches high,* with horns at the corners carved from the same piece of wood as the altar itself. 26 He overlaid the top, sides, and horns of the altar with pure gold, and he ran a gold molding around the entire altar. 27 He made two gold rings and attached them on opposite sides of the altar below the gold molding to hold the carrying poles. 28 He made the poles of acacia wood and overlaid them with gold.

37:29 Exod 30:22-23; 40:9; Lev 8:10

29 Then he made the sacred anointing oil and the fragrant incense, using the techniques of a skilled incense maker.

BUILDING THE ALTAR OF BURNT OFFERING

38:1-7 //Exod 27:1-8; 40:10, 29

38 Next Bezalel* used acacia wood to construct the square altar of burnt offering. It was 7½ feet wide, 7½ feet long, and 4½ feet high.* 2 He made horns for each of its four corners so that the horns and altar were all one piece. He overlaid the altar with bronze. 3 Then he made all the altar utensils of bronze—the ash buckets, shovels, basins, meat forks, and firepans. 4 Next he made a bronze grating and installed it halfway down the side of the altar, under the ledge. 5 He cast four rings and attached them to the corners of the bronze grating to hold the carrying poles. 6 He made the poles from acacia wood and overlaid them with bronze. 7 He inserted the poles through the rings on the sides of the altar. The altar was hollow and was made from planks.

BUILDING THE WASHBASIN

38:8 Exod 30:18
38:9-20 //Exod 27:9-19; 40:8

8 Bezalel made the bronze washbasin and its bronze stand from bronze mirrors donated by the women who served at the entrance of the Tabernacle.*

BUILDING THE COURTYARD

9 Then Bezalel made the courtyard, which was enclosed with curtains made of finely woven linen. On the south side the curtains were 150 feet long.* 10 They were held up by twenty posts set securely in twenty bronze bases. He hung the curtains with silver hooks and rings. 11 He made a similar set of curtains for the north side—150 feet of curtains held

37:24 Hebrew *1 talent* [34 kilograms]. **37:25** Hebrew *1 cubit* [46 centimeters] *long and 1 cubit wide, a square, and 2 cubits* [92 centimeters] *high.* **38:1a** Hebrew *he;* also in 38:8, 9. **38:1b** Hebrew *5 cubits* [2.3 meters] *wide, 5 cubits long, a square, and 3 cubits* [1.4 meters] *high.* **38:8** Hebrew *Tent of Meeting;* also in 38:30. **38:9** Hebrew *100 cubits* [46 meters]; also in 38:11.

37:25-28 The incense altar was constructed according to the instructions in Exodus 30:1-6.

37:29 The oil and incense was made according to the special recipe in Exodus 30:23-25, 34-35.

38:1-7 The altar was built according to the specifications in Exodus 27:1-8. In contrast to the incense altar inside the Tabernacle (Exodus 37:25-28), this large altar for burning animal sacrifices was in the courtyard outside the Tabernacle. Its bronze covering protected it from the fire that consumed the sacrifices.

38:9-20 The courtyard was constructed according to the instructions in Exodus 27:9-18. Much of the service related to the Tabernacle was performed in the courtyard, such as performing ritual washings, slaughtering animals, and presenting burnt offerings. Like the Tabernacle, the courtyard was constructed of strong, luxurious materials (compare Exodus 26), though they only covered the sides.

up by twenty posts set securely in bronze bases. He hung the curtains with silver hooks
and rings. 12The curtains on the west end of the courtyard were 75 feet long,* hung with
silver hooks and rings and supported by ten posts set into ten bases. 13The east end, the
front, was also 75 feet long.

14The courtyard entrance was on the east end, flanked by two curtains. The curtain on
the right side was 22½ feet long* and was supported by three posts set into three bases.
15The curtain on the left side was also 22½ feet long and was supported by three posts set
into three bases. 16All the curtains used in the courtyard were made of finely woven linen.
17Each post had a bronze base, and all the hooks and rings were silver. The tops of the
posts of the courtyard were overlaid with silver, and the rings to hold up the curtains were
made of silver.

18He made the curtain for the entrance to the courtyard of finely woven linen, and
he decorated it with beautiful embroidery in blue, purple, and scarlet thread. It was 30
feet long, and its height was 7½ feet,* just like the curtains of the courtyard walls. 19It was
supported by four posts, each set securely in its own bronze base. The tops of the posts
were overlaid with silver, and the hooks and rings were also made of silver.

20All the tent pegs used in the Tabernacle and courtyard were made of bronze.

INVENTORY OF MATERIALS

21This is an inventory of the materials used in building the Tabernacle of the Covenant.*
The Levites compiled the figures, as Moses directed, and Ithamar son of Aaron the priest
served as recorder. 22Bezalel son of Uri, grandson of Hur, of the tribe of Judah, made
everything just as the LORD had commanded Moses. 23He was assisted by Oholiab son of
Ahisamach, of the tribe of Dan, a craftsman expert at engraving, designing, and embroi-
dering with blue, purple, and scarlet thread on fine linen cloth.

24The people brought special offerings of gold totaling 2,193 pounds,* as mea-
sured by the weight of the sanctuary shekel. This gold was used throughout the Tab-
ernacle.

25The whole community of Israel gave 7,545 pounds* of silver, as measured by the **38:25-26**
weight of the sanctuary shekel. 26This silver came from the tax collected from each man Exod 12:37; 30:11-16
registered in the census. (The tax is one beka, which is half a shekel,* based on the sanctu- Num 1:46; 26:51
ary shekel.) The tax was collected from 603,550 men who had reached their twentieth
birthday. 27The hundred bases for the frames of the sanctuary walls and for the posts sup-
porting the inner curtain required 7,500 pounds of silver, about 75 pounds for each base.*
28The remaining 45 pounds* of silver was used to make the hooks and rings and to over-
lay the tops of the posts.

29The people also brought as special offerings 5,310 pounds* of bronze, 30which was
used for casting the bases for the posts at the entrance to the Tabernacle, and for the
bronze altar with its bronze grating and all the altar utensils. 31Bronze was also used to
make the bases for the posts that supported the curtains around the courtyard, the bases
for the curtain at the entrance of the courtyard, and all the tent pegs for the Tabernacle
and the courtyard.

38:12 Hebrew *50 cubits* [23 meters]; also in 38:13. **38:14** Hebrew *15 cubits* [6.9 meters]; also in 38:15. **38:18** Hebrew *20 cubits* [9.2 meters] *long and 5 cubits* [2.3 meters] *high.* **38:21** Hebrew *the Tabernacle, the Tabernacle of the Testimony.* **38:24** Hebrew *29 talents and 730 shekels* [994 kilograms]. Each shekel weighed about 0.4 ounces. **38:25** Hebrew *100 talents and 1,775 shekels* [3,420 kilograms]. **38:26** Or *0.2 ounces,* or *6 grams.* **38:27** Hebrew *100 talents* [3,400 kilograms] *of silver, 1 talent* [34 kilograms] *for each base.* **38:28** Hebrew *1,775 shekels* [20.2 kilograms]. **38:29** Hebrew *70 talents and 2,400 shekels* [2,407 kilograms].

38:22-23 Bezalel and Oholiab were craftsmen endowed by the Holy Spirit with special talents for conducting tasks and for training other craftsmen who served under them (Exodus 35:30-35).

CLOTHING FOR THE PRIESTS

39:1 Exod 35:23 **39** The craftsmen made beautiful sacred garments of blue, purple, and scarlet
cloth—clothing for Aaron to wear while ministering in the Holy Place, just as the
LORD had commanded Moses.

MAKING THE EPHOD

39:2-7 //Exod 28:6-14 2Bezalel* made the ephod of finely woven linen and embroidered it with gold and with
blue, purple, and scarlet thread. 3He made gold thread by hammering out thin sheets of
gold and cutting it into fine strands. With great skill and care, he worked it into the fine
linen with the blue, purple, and scarlet thread.
4The ephod consisted of two pieces, front and back, joined at the shoulders with two
shoulder-pieces. 5The decorative sash was made of the same materials: finely woven
linen embroidered with gold and with blue, purple, and scarlet thread, just as the LORD had
commanded Moses. 6They mounted the two onyx stones in settings of gold filigree. The
stones were engraved with the names of the tribes of Israel, just as a seal is engraved. 7He
fastened these stones on the shoulder-pieces of the ephod as a reminder that the priest
represents the people of Israel. All this was done just as the LORD had commanded Moses.

MAKING THE CHESTPIECE

39:8-21 //Exod 28:15-28 8Bezalel made the chestpiece with great skill and care. He made it to match the ephod, us-
ing finely woven linen embroidered with gold and with blue, purple, and scarlet thread.
9He made the chestpiece of a single piece of cloth folded to form a pouch nine inches*
square. 10They mounted four rows of gemstones* on it. The first row contained a red car-
nelian, a pale-green peridot, and an emerald. 11The second row contained a turquoise, a
blue lapis lazuli, and a white moonstone. 12The third row contained an orange jacinth, an
agate, and a purple amethyst. 13The fourth row contained a blue-green beryl, an onyx,
39:14 Rev 21:12 and a green jasper. All these stones were set in gold filigree. 14Each stone represented one
of the twelve sons of Israel, and the name of that tribe was engraved on it like a seal.
15To attach the chestpiece to the ephod, they made braided cords of pure gold thread.
16They also made two settings of gold filigree and two gold rings and attached them to the
top corners of the chestpiece. 17They tied the two gold cords to the rings on the chest-
piece. 18They tied the other ends of the cords to the gold settings on the shoulder-pieces of
the ephod. 19Then they made two more gold rings and attached them to the inside edges
of the chestpiece next to the ephod. 20Then they made two more gold rings and attached
them to the front of the ephod, below the shoulder-pieces, just above the knot where
the decorative sash was fastened to the ephod. 21They attached the bottom rings of the
chestpiece to the rings on the ephod with blue cords. In this way, the chestpiece was held

39:2 Hebrew *He;* also in 39:8, 22. **39:9** Hebrew *1 span* [23 centimeters]. **39:10** The identification of some of these gemstones is uncertain.

▸ WORSHIP

39:1 Holy clothing. How do you dress when you go to church? We are not required to wear special clothes to church, but God clothes us in "clothing of salvation" (Isaiah 61:10; Colossians 3:9-10). We also are told to put on the armor of God (Ephesians 6:11). As believers, we wear these garments always, for we are continually involved in dangerous, holy ministry. You may not always need to wear your best to church, but you always need to wear God's best—the armor of God. (***See Worship****> OT> Priesthood> Garments*, TopicGuide page A28.)

39:1-3 These garments were made according to the instructions in Exodus 28:6-42.

39:6-14 Israel was organized into 12 tribes, according to the 12 sons of Jacob (Genesis 49:2-27). The names on his clothing demonstrated the fact that as high priest for the nation, Aaron represented every person in every tribe.

39:7 The memorial stones functioned as a "reminder" in the same sense that pictures of our loved ones remind us of our love and commitment to them. The memorial stones did not function as a means to help God remember Israel, for God never forgets His people (Isaiah 49:14-16) or anything else. God knows all about us (Psalm 139:1-4), knows all outcomes (Matthew 11:21), knows all facts (1 John 3:20), and even knows what is in the deepest recesses of our mind (Psalm 44:21).

securely to the ephod above the decorative sash. All this was done just as the LORD had
commanded Moses.

ADDITIONAL CLOTHING FOR THE PRIESTS

22 Bezalel made the robe that is worn with the ephod from a single piece of blue woven 39:22-31
cloth, 23 with an opening for Aaron's head in the middle of it. The opening was reinforced //Exod 28:31-43
with a woven collar* so it would not tear. 24 They made pomegranates of blue, purple,
and scarlet yarn, and attached them to the hem of the robe. 25 They also made bells of
pure gold and placed them between the pomegranates along the hem of the robe,
26 with bells and pomegranates alternating all around the hem. This robe was to be worn
whenever the priest ministered before the LORD, just as the LORD had commanded
Moses.

27 They made tunics for Aaron and his sons from fine linen cloth. 28 The turban and the 39:27
special head coverings were made of fine linen, and the undergarments were also made Exod 28:39-40, 42
of finely woven linen. 29 The sashes were made of finely woven linen and embroidered
with blue, purple, and scarlet thread, just as the LORD had commanded Moses.

30 Finally, they made the sacred medallion—the badge of holiness—of pure gold. They 39:30
engraved it like a seal with these words: HOLY TO THE LORD. 31 They attached the medallion Exod 28:36-37
with a blue cord to Aaron's turban, just as the LORD had commanded Moses.

MOSES INSPECTS THE WORK

32 And so at last the Tabernacle* was finished. The Israelites had done everything just as 39:32-41
the LORD had commanded Moses. 33 And they brought the entire Tabernacle to Moses: //Exod 35:10-19

the sacred tent with all its furnishings, clasps, frames, crossbars, posts, and bases;
34 the tent coverings of tanned ram skins and fine goatskin leather;
the inner curtain to shield the Ark;
35 the Ark of the Covenant* and its carrying poles;
the Ark's cover—the place of atonement;
36 the table and all its utensils;
the Bread of the Presence;
37 the pure gold lampstand with its symmetrical lamp cups, all its accessories, and the
olive oil for lighting;
38 the gold altar;
the anointing oil and fragrant incense;
the curtain for the entrance of the sacred tent;
39 the bronze altar;
the bronze grating and its carrying poles and utensils;
the washbasin with its stand;
40 the curtains for the walls of the courtyard;
the posts and their bases;
the curtain for the entrance to the courtyard;
the ropes and tent pegs;
all the furnishings to be used in worship at the Tabernacle;
41 the beautifully stitched garments for the priests to wear while ministering in the Holy

39:23 The meaning of the Hebrew is uncertain. 39:32 Hebrew *the Tabernacle, the Tent of Meeting;* also in 39:40.
39:35 Or *Ark of the Testimony.*

39:30 *HOLY TO THE LORD* **refers to Aaron. He was consecrated to God as the high priest of Israel. He alone was permitted to enter the Most Holy Place to meet with God where he demonstrated his faith by bringing the sacrifices God required to make atonement for their sins (Exodus 25:17; 26:34).**

39:32-43 **Exodus 25–31 provided instructions for building the Tabernacle. Moses verified that the Israelites had followed these instructions well in building the components. Exodus 35–39 details the construction of the various items listed here.**

Place—the sacred garments for Aaron the priest, and the garments for his sons to wear as they minister as priests.

39:43 Lev 9:22-23; Num 6:23-26; 1 Kgs 8:14; 2 Chr 30:27

42 So the people of Israel followed all of the LORD's instructions to Moses. 43 Then Moses inspected all their work. When he found it had been done just as the LORD had commanded him, he blessed them.

THE TABERNACLE COMPLETED

40:2 Exod 12:2; 19:1; 40:17; Num 1:1
40:3 Exod 26:33; 40:21-30; Num 4:5
40:4 Exod 25:30
40:7 Exod 30:18
40:9 Exod 30:26

40 Then the LORD said to Moses, 2 "Set up the Tabernacle* on the first day of the new year.* 3 Place the Ark of the Covenant* inside, and install the inner curtain to enclose the Ark within the Most Holy Place. 4 Then bring in the table, and arrange the utensils on it. And bring in the lampstand, and set up the lamps.

5 "Place the gold incense altar in front of the Ark of the Covenant. Then hang the curtain at the entrance of the Tabernacle. 6 Place the altar of burnt offering in front of the Tabernacle entrance. 7 Set the washbasin between the Tabernacle* and the altar, and fill it with water. 8 Then set up the courtyard around the outside of the tent, and hang the curtain for the courtyard entrance.

9 "Take the anointing oil and anoint the Tabernacle and all its furnishings to consecrate them and make them holy. 10 Anoint the altar of burnt offering and its utensils to consecrate them. Then the altar will become absolutely holy. 11 Next anoint the washbasin and its stand to consecrate them.

40:12 Lev 8:1-13
40:15 Exod 29:9; Num 25:13
40:17 Exod 40:2; Num 7:1
40:20 Exod 25:16; Deut 10:5; 1 Kgs 8:9; 2 Chr 5:10; Heb 9:4

12 "Present Aaron and his sons at the entrance of the Tabernacle, and wash them with water. 13 Dress Aaron with the sacred garments and anoint him, consecrating him to serve Me as a priest. 14 Then present his sons and dress them in their tunics. 15 Anoint them as you did their father, so they may also serve Me as priests. With their anointing, Aaron's descendants are set apart for the priesthood forever, from generation to generation."

16 Moses proceeded to do everything just as the LORD had commanded him. 17 So the Tabernacle was set up on the first day of the first month of the second year. 18 Moses erected the Tabernacle by setting down its bases, inserting the frames, attaching the crossbars, and setting up the posts. 19 Then he spread the coverings over the Tabernacle framework and put on the protective layers, just as the LORD had commanded him.

20 He took the stone tablets inscribed with the terms of the covenant and placed them*

40:2a Hebrew *the Tabernacle, the Tent of Meeting;* also in 40:6, 29. **40:2b** Hebrew *the first day of the first month.* This day of the ancient Hebrew lunar calendar occurred in March or April. **40:3** Or *Ark of the Testimony;* also in 40:5, 21. **40:7** Hebrew *Tent of Meeting;* also in 40:12, 22, 24, 26, 30, 32, 34, 35. **40:20** Hebrew *He placed the Testimony;* see note on 25:16.

40:2, 17 The religious calendar began in the month of Abib, which began in late March. The Tabernacle was completed two weeks before the Passover Festival (Exodus 12:6).

40:3 This Ark or box carries royal connotations (1 Chronicles 28:2) because God functioned as Israel's king (1 Samuel 8:7-8). God manifested Himself and communicated from His throne above the Ark (Exodus 25:22; Leviticus 16:2; 1 Samuel 4:4).

40:4 The details for the creation of these objects are repeated in Exodus 25.

40:5 Incense burned on this altar twice daily throughout Israel's generations (Exodus 30:1-10). This accompanied the tending of the lamps in the inner sanctuary (Exodus 30:7-8). The smoke from the incense and the light of the lamp likely reminded Israel of the smoke and fire that God used to guide them out of the captivity of Egypt (Exodus 13:21; Isaiah 4:5). Once a year, on the Day of Atonement, a special animal sacrifice was offered there (Exodus 30:10).

40:6 The altar of burnt offering was constructed and placed according to the instructions in Exodus 27:1-8.

40:9-11 The special oil was made according to the recipe in Exodus 30:23-25. Things and people anointed with this oil became ceremonially clean (Exodus 28:41; 29:21, 36; 30:30).

40:12-15 The priests were anointed and installed according to the Lord's instructions in Exodus 29. Repeating these and other instructions insured that no copying errors occurred in either version. The book of Leviticus contains the same sort of intentional repetition.

40:16-33 Moses had received directly from the Lord the instructions for constructing and servicing the Tabernacle, and for Israel's continual worship. He complied with God's instructions without flaw. Therefore, all future generations of Israel were required to adhere to the worship practices and forms established under Moses.

inside the Ark. Then he attached the carrying poles to the Ark, and he set the Ark's cover—
the place of atonement—on top of it. 21 Then he brought the Ark of the Covenant into the
Tabernacle and hung the inner curtain to shield it from view, just as the LORD had commanded him.

22Next Moses placed the table in the Tabernacle, along the north side of the Holy Place,
just outside the inner curtain. 23And he arranged the Bread of the Presence on the table
before the LORD, just as the LORD had commanded him.

24He set the lampstand in the Tabernacle across from the table on the south side of the
Holy Place. 25Then he lit the lamps in the LORD's presence, just as the LORD had commanded him.
26He also placed the gold incense altar in the Tabernacle, in the Holy Place
in front of the inner curtain. 27On it he burned the fragrant incense, just as the LORD had
commanded him.

28He hung the curtain at the entrance of the Tabernacle, 29and he placed the altar of
burnt offering near the Tabernacle entrance. On it he offered a burnt offering and a grain
offering, just as the LORD had commanded him.

30Next Moses placed the washbasin between the Tabernacle and the altar. He filled it
with water so the priests could wash themselves. 31 Moses and Aaron and Aaron's sons
used water from it to wash their hands and feet. 32Whenever they approached the altar
and entered the Tabernacle, they washed themselves, just as the LORD had commanded
Moses.

33Then he hung the curtains forming the courtyard around the Tabernacle and the altar.
And he set up the curtain at the entrance of the courtyard. So at last Moses finished the
work.

40:23 Exod 25:30; Lev 24:5-8
40:31 Exod 30:19-21

THE LORD'S GLORY FILLS THE TABERNACLE

34Then the cloud covered the Tabernacle, and the glory of the LORD filled the Tabernacle.
35Moses could no longer enter the Tabernacle because the cloud had settled down over it,
and the glory of the LORD filled the Tabernacle.

36Now whenever the cloud lifted from the Tabernacle, the people of Israel would set out
on their journey, following it. 37But if the cloud did not rise, they remained where they
were until it lifted. 38The cloud of the LORD hovered over the Tabernacle during the day,
and at night fire glowed inside the cloud so the whole family of Israel could see it. This
continued throughout all their journeys.

40:34 Num 9:15-23; 1 Kgs 8:11
40:35 1 Kgs 8:10-11
40:36 Num 9:17; 10:11
40:37 Num 9:19-22
40:38 1 Cor 10:1

40:23 The Bread of the Presence was the 12 large loaves of bread sprinkled with frankincense, arranged on a table just outside of the innermost chamber of the Tabernacle. They were baked and set before the Lord each Sabbath as an offering from the nation of Israel (Leviticus 24:5-9).

40:34-38 These verses demonstrate that Moses' program for constructing the Tabernacle, for consecrating the Aaronic priesthood, and for worship had truly come from God. When the people obeyed Moses, God blessed them with His special presence. This established the basis for all future generations remaining faithful to Moses' program for worship and Tabernacle service and to the Aaronic priesthood.

▸ WORSHIP

40:35 The glory of the Lord. The word *glory* means different things depending on the context. In Exodus 40:35 it refers to a manifestation of God's presence that was in the form of fire and smoke. When Jesus raised Lazarus from the dead, He reminded His disciples that they were seeing "God's glory" (John 11:40). This meant that Lazarus' resurrection was a sign demonstrating that Jesus is God. Jesus Himself was the greatest manifestation of God's glory (2 Corinthians 4:6). (***See Worship****> OT> Place> Tabernacle> Glory of the Lord filled the house*, TopicGuide page A27.)

LEVITICUS

PURPOSE

To establish proper worship for God's people.

Some have likened Leviticus to a cookbook—the pots and pans section of the Bible. Why such a strange comparison? Because in Leviticus we have the "recipes" for how Israel was to worship God in their newly constructed Tabernacle. In Exodus, God delivered through Moses the instructions for building the Tabernacle. It was to be a place where God would dwell in the midst of His people, to enjoy intimacy and fellowship with them. And in Leviticus, directions were given for how the worship of God was to be carried out.

The name *Leviticus* means "pertaining to the Levites," the tribe of Israelites from whom the priests in Israel were to be appointed. Because God is a holy God, those who worship Him must be holy. The Levitical priests were to teach the people how to establish and maintain their purity before God. Israel was a promised people in Genesis, a purchased people in Exodus, and now in Leviticus they would become a perfect (holy) people unto the Lord their God.

For these reasons, Leviticus undoubtedly presents the greatest challenge to the modern reader. But by keeping the purpose and outline of Leviticus in mind, the reader can learn eternal principles relating to the need for personal holiness and the necessity of a New Covenant that would deal with humanity's sin-problem once and for all (Hebrews 9:15, 10:11).

DISCOVER GOD IN LEVITICUS

There is one principle attribute of God that dominates the book of Leviticus:

Holiness: After Moses and the Israelites crossed safely through the Red Sea, Moses led the throng in a victory song that asked, "Who is like You among the gods, O Lord—glorious in holiness, awesome in splendor, performing great wonders?" (Exodus 15:11). Those questions reflect the very heart of holiness, the essence of who God is: separateness, or "set-apartness." Because there is no person, thing, or being like God, He is holy, separate from all others. In the Old Testament, for example, mundane objects could be declared holy—like the ground (Exodus 3:5), crops and grain (Leviticus 23:20), places (Leviticus 4:6), and utensils used by priests (Leviticus 8:11). Because they were set apart from the profane and mundane, they were made holy and kept holy by their continued use for their unique purpose. So it is with the Godhead—Father, Son, and Holy Spirit are holy because They are set apart in their purity, perfection, and deity.

GROWING THROUGH LEVITICUS

The primary attribute of God in Leviticus—holiness—leads to the primary theme of the book for Christians: personal holiness.

Personal Holiness: The content of the book of Leviticus was given by God to teach Israel about God's holiness—but it didn't stop there: "For I am the LORD your God. You must be consecrate yourselves and be holy, because I am holy" (Leviticus 11:44). If the Israelites were to become the people of a holy God, they themselves must be holy. If their God was righteous, they must be righteous. If their God was set apart, they must be set apart. If their God was unique in all the earth, they must be unique as well. Had they thought about it, this would not have been a totally new concept for the Israelites—God had, after all, set them apart in the land of Goshen for four centuries (Genesis 43:32; 46:33-34; Exodus 9:26). But now they were about to move into the broader world—the land of Canaan—into the midst of pagan peoples. The Israelites needed to learn how to live *apart* while living *among*. They needed to know how to be *in* the world but not *of* the world. They needed to learn how to be holy in an unholy world, and this call now extends to us (Ephesians 2:19).

Position versus Practice: Holiness, the primary theme of Leviticus, is a double-sided coin in this book and in the rest of Scripture. By offering a sacrifice, the people of God were *made holy* in God's sight—a legal declaration. But by sanctification, the people of God were *kept holy* in God's sight—a practical application. To accomplish the former, God gave laws for the priests regarding blood sacrifice, the most important being the annual Day of Atonement (*Yom Kippur*; Leviticus 23:28). On that day, sins were forgiven and the people were made holy. And to accomplish the latter, laws of sanctification were given regarding the conduct of daily life—how holy people should live in the midst of pagan cultures (Leviticus 18–27). The same tension exists in the New Testament. The people of God are declared to be holy (Colossians 1:2; translated "saints" in some versions), but are also exhorted how to live as holy people (Colossians 3:12).

Worship as Lifestyle: First, proper worship established a path *to* God (by encouraging repentance and obedience, focusing on obedience to the ceremonial law). Second, it established a path *with* God (by encouraging holiness and growth in their sanctification). Third, the sacrificial offerings illustrated the covering of the Israelites' sins and, by faith in the truth behind that illustration, they gained access *to* God. Fellowship and thanksgiving offerings maintained and deepened their relationship *with* God, as they honored His holiness and remembered His faithfulness.

LEVITICUS FACTS

Author: Moses (see Genesis Introduction, Author). Leviticus 1:1 establishes this fact: God spoke to Moses and Moses then spoke to the people, a pattern that occurs more than fifty times in the book of Leviticus and many more times throughout the Pentateuch (Deuteronomy 31:9). New Testament references to Moses as the author of the first five books of the Bible confirm Mosaic authorship (Acts 13:39; 15:5; 28:23; 1 Corinthians 9:9).

Written to: The new nation of Israel, specifically the Levites and Aaronic priests who had just been released from 430 years of slavery.

Date of writing: Shortly after the Exodus (1446 BC), as Moses received it from God at Mount Sinai. It was probably compiled with the other four books of the Pentateuch (Genesis, Exodus, Numbers, and Deuteronomy) during the nearly-forty-year period of wilderness wanderings (see Numbers).

Setting: Mount Sinai in the Sinai Desert (modern eastern Egypt) where the Israelites camped almost a year after leaving (northern) Egypt.

OUTLINE

- **LEVITICUS 1:1–7:38**—Sacrificial Laws
- **LEVITICUS 8:1–10:20**—Aaronic priesthood established
- **LEVITICUS 11:1–16:34**—Social and ceremonial uncleanness
- **LEVITICUS 17:1–27:34**—Habits of the Holy

PROCEDURES FOR THE BURNT OFFERING

1:2 Lev 6:9-13; 17:1-8; 22:19-25 **1** The LORD called to Moses from the Tabernacle* and said to him, 2“Give the following
1:3 instructions to the people of Israel. When you present an animal as an offering to the
Heb 9:14 LORD, you may take it from your herd of cattle or your flock of sheep and goats.
1:4 3“If the animal you present as a burnt offering is from the herd, it must be a male with
Exod 29:10, 15, 19 Lev 4:13-35 no defects. Bring it to the entrance of the Tabernacle so you* may be accepted by the LORD.
Num 8:10-12; 15:25 4Lay your hand on the animal’s head, and the LORD will accept its death in your place to
2 Chr 29:23-24 purify you, making you right with Him.* 5Then slaughter the young bull in the LORD’s pres-
1:5 ence, and Aaron’s sons, the priests, will present the animal’s blood by splattering it against
Lev 1:11; 3:8 Heb 12:24 all sides of the altar that stands at the entrance to the Tabernacle. 6Then skin the animal
1:6 and cut it into pieces. 7The sons of Aaron the priest will build a wood fire on the altar.
Lev 7:8 8They will arrange the pieces of the offering, including the head and fat, on the wood

1:1 Hebrew *Tent of Meeting;* also in 1:3, 5. 1:3 Or *it.* 1:4 Or *to make atonement for you.*

BIBLE

1:1 Through Moses, from God. Throughout the Old Testament, God often revealed Himself audibly and plainly to His prophets, who were His authoritative representatives (Amos 3:7). Frequently, these prophets wrote down what God had said to them, and these writings became the books of the Old Testament itself. In the New Testament, the Lord continued to speak authoritatively through certain prophets, especially through those whom He appointed as apostles (Ephesians 2:20), and these men wrote or approved the books of the New Testament. Today, we hear the clear voice of the Lord primarily through the writings of the Old and New Testament prophets, but also through nature, the inner promptings of the Holy Spirit, and godly counselors. (***See Bible****> Uniqueness> Inspired> A record of God’s own words,* TopicGuide page A10.)

1:1 The Tabernacle was a portable sanctuary constructed of heavy curtains and poles. The innermost chamber was the Most Holy Place, where God’s presence resided. God regularly issued instructions to Moses within the Most Holy Place (Exodus 25:22; 30:6, 36).

1:2 This instruction specifies that offered animals had to come from one’s own flock. Wild animals, which cost the worshiper nothing, could not be offered (compare 2 Samuel 24:24).

1:3, 10 In order for an offering to be acceptable to the Lord, the worshiper had to show his or her faith by making the right kind of offering, in the right place and in the right manner. Only the best animals could be offered (compare Genesis 4:4; Malachi 1:7-14) and, at this point in Israel’s history, offerings could only be made at the Tabernacle.

WORSHIP

1:4 Doing away with sin. It sounds very odd to us that the spilling of animal blood improved the Israelites’ relationship with God. But the goal of the sacrificial system was atonement—the satisfaction of God’s just requirement that sin be punished by death. The blood of animals flowed to remind the Israelites that although they deserved to perish for their sins, God had made a way of salvation through faith in Him. Even in Old Testament times, believers knew that these sacrifices themselves were not enough to please God (Genesis 15:6; Psalm 51:16-19). They looked forward in hope. We look back in faith to the perfect Lamb of God, who came to atone permanently for our sins (John 1:29; Hebrews 10:1-20; 1 Peter 1:19). (***See Worship****> OT> Offerings> Blood Sacrifices> Sin offering,* TopicGuide page A27.)

1:4 By laying his hand on the head of the offering, the worshiper identified himself with the animal. By this identification the animal became the worshiper’s substitute, so that its death symbolized the worshiper’s death.

1:5 Only men descended from Moses’ brother Aaron were called to be priests (Exodus 29).

1:5, 7, 9, 11-13, 15-17 The altar for burnt offerings stood in the courtyard outside the Tabernacle (Exodus 40:6).

1:5, 11, 15 God chose the perfect symbol—blood—to represent life. Blood sacrifice continued to be a major part of the way God atoned for human sin (Leviticus 17:11; Hebrews 9:22).

THE OFFERINGS

Listed here are the five key offerings the Israelites made to God. They made these offerings in order to have their sins forgiven and to restore their fellowship with God. The death of Jesus Christ made these sacrifices unnecessary. Because of His death, our sins were completely forgiven, and fellowship with God has been restored.

Offering	Purpose	Significance	Christ, the Perfect Offering
Burnt Offering (Leviticus 1—voluntary)	To make payment for sins in general	Showed a person's devotion to God	Christ's death was the perfect offering
Grain Offering (Leviticus 2—voluntary)	To show honor and respect to God in worship	Acknowledged that all we have belongs to God	Christ was the perfect Man, who gave all of Himself to God and others
Peace Offering (Leviticus 3—voluntary)	To express gratitude to God	Symbolized peace and fellowship with God	Christ is the only way to fellowship with God
Sin Offering (Leviticus 4—required)	To make payment for unintentional sins of uncleanness, neglect, or thoughtlessness	Restored the sinner to fellowship with God; showed seriousness of sin	Christ's death restores our fellowship with God
Guilt Offering (Leviticus 5—required)	To make payment for sins against God and others. A sacrifice was made to God, and the injured person was repaid or compensated.	Provided compensation for injured parties	Christ's death takes away the deadly consequences of sin

burning on the altar. 9But the internal organs and the legs must first be washed with water. 1:9
Then the priest will burn the entire sacrifice on the altar as a burnt offering. It is a special Gen 8:21
gift, a pleasing aroma to the LORD. Exod 29:17 Eph 5:2
10"If the animal you present as a burnt offering is from the flock, it may be either a sheep
or a goat, but it must be a male with no defects. 11Slaughter the animal on the north side of
the altar in the LORD's presence, and Aaron's sons, the priests, will splatter its blood against
all sides of the altar. 12Then cut the animal in pieces, and the priests will arrange the pieces
of the offering, including the head and fat, on the wood burning on the altar. 13But the in-
ternal organs and the legs must first be washed with water. Then the priest will burn the en-
tire sacrifice on the altar as a burnt offering. It is a special gift, a pleasing aroma to the LORD. 1:14
14"If you present a bird as a burnt offering to the LORD, choose either a turtledove or a Gen 15:9 Lev 12:8
young pigeon. 15The priest will take the bird to the altar, wring off its head, and burn it on 1:15
the altar. But first he must drain its blood against the side of the altar. 16The priest must Lev 5:8-9

1:10 Male animals were generally valued more highly than female animals, and thus were preferred sacrifices. For certain sacrifices other than burnt offerings, female animals were permitted (Leviticus 3:6) or even required (Leviticus 4:28, 32; 5:6; 14:10).

also remove the crop and the feathers* and throw them in the ashes on the east side of the
altar. 17 Then, grasping the bird by its wings, the priest will tear the bird open, but without
tearing it apart. Then he will burn it as a burnt offering on the wood burning on the altar. It
is a special gift, a pleasing aroma to the LORD.

PROCEDURES FOR THE GRAIN OFFERING

2 "When you present grain as an offering to the LORD, the offering must consist of choice
flour. You are to pour olive oil on it, sprinkle it with frankincense, 2 and bring it to Aaron's
sons, the priests. The priest will scoop out a handful of the flour moistened with oil, together with
all the frankincense, and burn this representative portion on the altar. It is a special gift, a pleas-
ing aroma to the LORD. 3 The rest of the grain offering will then be given to Aaron and his sons.
This offering will be considered a most holy part of the special gifts presented to the LORD.
4 "If your offering is a grain offering baked in an oven, it must be made of choice flour,
but without any yeast. It may be presented in the form of thin cakes mixed with olive oil or
wafers spread with olive oil. 5 If your grain offering is cooked on a griddle, it must be made
of choice flour mixed with olive oil but without any yeast. 6 Break it in pieces and pour ol-
ive oil on it; it is a grain offering. 7 If your grain offering is prepared in a pan, it must be
made of choice flour and olive oil.
8 "No matter how a grain offering for the LORD has been prepared, bring it to the priest,
who will present it at the altar. 9 The priest will take a representative portion of the grain of-
fering and burn it on the altar. It is a special gift, a pleasing aroma to the LORD. 10 The rest of
the grain offering will then be given to Aaron and his sons as their food. This offering will
be considered a most holy part of the special gifts presented to the LORD.
11 "Do not use yeast in preparing any of the grain offerings you present to the LORD, because
no yeast or honey may be burned as a special gift presented to the LORD. 12 You may add
yeast and honey to an offering of the first crops of your harvest, but these must never be of-
fered on the altar as a pleasing aroma to the LORD. 13 Season all your grain offerings with salt
to remind you of God's eternal covenant. Never forget to add salt to your grain offerings.
14 "If you present a grain offering to the LORD from the first portion of your harvest, bring

2:1 Exod 29:2; Lev 6:14-18; 24:7; Num 15:4-21
2:2 Lev 5:12-13; 6:15-18
2:3 Lev 10:12-13
2:4 Exod 29:2; Lev 7:12
2:9 Gen 8:21; Lev 2:2; 6:15
2:10 Lev 2:3
2:11 Lev 6:16-17
2:12 Lev 7:13; 23:9-14
2:13 Num 18:19; 2 Chr 13:5; Ezek 43:24; Mark 9:49
2:14 Lev 23:9-14; 2 Kgs 4:42

1:16 Or *the crop and its contents.* The meaning of the Hebrew is uncertain.

▸ SALVATION

1:17 Pleasing to the Lord. What does it say about God that He was pleased with the dismembering and burning of a bird? Some say this couldn't be the Christian God of love and forgiveness, but these people forget that in the New Testament God was pleased by the slaughter of His own Son. The Old Testament sacrifices reveal two things about God. First, He is holy and offended by sin. Second, He loves us enough to provide a substitute to die in our place. As the God-Man, Jesus knew both these things, so He offered Himself as the sacrifice we needed (1 John 2:2). There is no need for morbid depression over sin or for self-atonement schemes—Jesus has done everything God requires to atone for our sins. (***See Salvation****> Jesus' Work> Crucifixion> Propitiation for sin,* TopicGuide page A22.)

▸ GOD

2:1 Food as a symbol. All of the sacrifices and offerings of Leviticus represented spiritual truths for the Israelites. For example, they were not to bring just any flour as a grain offering, but "choice" flour. Why the distinction? Pure flour with no yeast (Exodus 23:18; Leviticus 2:4-5) or sweetener (Leviticus 2:11) was to be offered as a picture of the worshiper's heart. Only pure hearts can produce pure offerings of gratitude to God. (***See God****> Relationship> God Enables> Relationship with God requires purity,* TopicGuide page A14.)

2:1-2 Frankincense was resin from a type of balsam tree. In addition to being used as a spice, it was frequently burned as incense.

2:3, 10 The portions of the sacrifices that were not burned were given to the priests for food. This was an important part of the priests' income (compare Numbers 18:8-32).

2:5, 11-12 Literally, the grain offerings were to be free of any leaven, or any catalyst that would cause baked goods to rise. This meant using clean bowls and utensils with no leftover dough from previous batches.

2:13 Salt was also directly associated with God's covenants with Aaron and David (see Numbers 18:19 and 2 Chronicles 13:5, where the Hebrew word translated *covenant* literally means a "covenant of salt"). As a preservative it symbolized permanence.

▸ WORSHIP

2:14 The first portion. When you sit down to pay your monthly bills, which check do you write first? That can be a subtle indication of our priorities. After all, what we can least afford to do without usually gets paid first. The Israelites faced that same decision every fall at the annual harvest—what to do with the first mature grain. A sign of their thankfulness to God was to offer the first portion of the harvest to Him (Proverbs 3:9). Giving to God first, then and now, is a way to say "thank you" for all His provision. (***See Worship****> OT> Offerings> Other Sacrifices> Grain offerings,* TopicGuide page A27.)

fresh grain that is coarsely ground and roasted on a fire. 15 Put olive oil on this grain offer-
ing, and sprinkle it with frankincense. 16 The priest will take a representative portion of the 2:16 Lev 2:1-2
grain moistened with oil, together with all the frankincense, and burn it as a special gift
presented to the LORD.

PROCEDURES FOR THE PEACE OFFERING

3 "If you present an animal from the herd as a peace offering to the LORD, it may be a 3:1
male or a female, but it must have no defects. 2 Lay your hand on the animal's head, Lev 1:3; 7:11-21
and slaughter it at the entrance of the Tabernacle.* Then Aaron's sons, the priests, will splat- 3:2 Exod 29:11
ter its blood against all sides of the altar. 3 The priest must present part of this peace offering Lev 1:4; 7:14
as a special gift to the LORD. This includes all the fat around the internal organs, 4 the two kid- 3:3
neys and the fat around them near the loins, and the long lobe of the liver. These must be Exod 29:13, 22
removed with the kidneys, 5 and Aaron's sons will burn them on top of the burnt offering on Lev 3:9-11
the wood burning on the altar. It is a special gift, a pleasing aroma to the LORD. 3:5
6 "If you present an animal from the flock as a peace offering to the LORD, it may be a Num 15:8-10
male or a female, but it must have no defects. 7 If you present a sheep as your offering, 3:6
bring it to the LORD, 8 lay your hand on its head, and slaughter it in front of the Tabernacle. Lev 3:1
Aaron's sons will then splatter the sheep's blood against all sides of the altar. 9 The priest
must present the fat of this peace offering as a special gift to the LORD. This includes the fat
of the broad tail cut off near the backbone, all the fat around the internal organs, 10 the two
kidneys and the fat around them near the loins, and the long lobe of the liver. These must
be removed with the kidneys, 11 and the priest will burn them on the altar. It is a special gift
of food presented to the LORD.
12 "If you present a goat as your offering, bring it to the LORD, 13 lay your hand on its 3:13
head, and slaughter it in front of the Tabernacle. Aaron's sons will then splatter the goat's Lev 1:5
blood against all sides of the altar. 14 The priest must present part of this offering as a spe- 3:15-16
cial gift to the LORD. This includes all the fat around the internal organs, 15 the two kidneys Lev 4:26; 7:23-25
and the fat around them near the loins, and the long lobe of the liver. These must be re-

3:2 Hebrew *Tent of Meeting;* also in 3:8, 13.

▸ GOD

3:1 Peace offering. A quick glance at the daily newspaper or television news will reveal the absence of peace somewhere in our world. But as much as we would love to live in a world in which all people are at peace with each other, what we need most is peace with God. It is no wonder that when the Israelites discovered they could have this kind of peace, they celebrated regularly! They brought fellowship or peace offerings from the flock or herd, and had a celebratory meal (the name for the offering is related to *shalom,* the Hebrew word for "peace"). They ate these sacrifices, just as we celebrate peace with God by memorializing the body and blood of Christ at the Communion table (Romans 5:1; 1 Corinthians 11:24-25). (***See God****> God's Names> God> The LORD is peace,* TopicGuide page A18.)

3:1, 3, 6, 9 Peace offerings were voluntary, usually given to show gratitude or to petition the Lord for a blessing. Portions of the sacrifices were to be burned on the altar, and others given to the priests, but the majority was to be eaten by the worshiper's family (Leviticus 7:11-35).

3:1, 6 Only the best animals were to be offered. It was disrespectful to offer blind, crippled, diseased, or otherwise defective animals (compare Genesis 4:3-7; Malachi 1:7-14).

3:2, 8, 13 Worshipers identified themselves with their offerings by laying their hands on the animal's head. This marked the animal as the worshiper's substitute, so that the animal's death served in place of the worshiper.

3:3-4, 9-10, 14-16 The fat of the animals represented wealth and lavishness (compare Genesis 45:18). Only the specified portions of the fat were reserved for God and forbidden to the people. The rest of the fat throughout the animals could be eaten.

▸ WORSHIP

3:9-10 Two kidneys with the fat. What seems like a gory task to us—cutting out an animal's fat, kidneys, and liver and burning these on the altar to the Lord—probably suggested something specific to the Israelites. In ancient cultures, the internal organs were thought to be the seat of the will and emotions (in Psalm 16:7, David's reference to the *heart* is actually the Hebrew word for *kidneys*). When we become a living sacrifice to God, we offer mind, will, and emotions to Him (Romans 12:1). Inside and out, we belong to God. (***See Worship****> OT> Offerings> Blood Sacrifices> Peace offering,* TopicGuide page A27.)

3:11, 16 The portions burned on the altar were counted as God's food. The sacrifices were not intended to sustain Him, nor did the Israelites imagine that God actually ate the food. The sacrifice was referred to as food probably as a metaphor that indicated God's pleasure, just as other sacrifices were said to smell good to God (Leviticus 3:5, 16 refers to the sacrifices as a "pleasing aroma"). It may also have been intended to symbolize table fellowship between God and the worshiper (compare Exodus 24:11).

moved with the kidneys, 16and the priest will burn them on the altar. It is a special gift of
3:17 food, a pleasing aroma to the LORD. All the fat belongs to the LORD.
Lev 7:25-26; 17:10 17"You must never eat any fat or blood. This is a permanent law for you, and it must be
Deut 12:16 Acts 15:20 observed from generation to generation, wherever you live."

PROCEDURES FOR THE SIN OFFERING

4:2 Lev 4:22; 22:14 **4** Then the LORD said to Moses, 2"Give the following instructions to the people of Israel.
Num 15:22-29 This is how you are to deal with those who sin unintentionally by doing anything that
violates one of the LORD's commands.
4:3 3"If the high priest* sins, bringing guilt upon the entire community, he must give a sin of-
Lev 4:14; 9:2 Ezek 43:19 fering for the sin he has committed. He must present to the LORD a young bull with no de-
fects. 4He must bring the bull to the LORD at the entrance of the Tabernacle,* lay his hand
4:5 on the bull's head, and slaughter it before the LORD. 5The high priest will then take some of
Lev 4:16; 16:14 the bull's blood into the Tabernacle, 6dip his finger in the blood, and sprinkle it seven
4:7 times before the LORD in front of the inner curtain of the sanctuary. 7The priest will then put
Lev 8:15 some of the blood on the horns of the altar for fragrant incense that stands in the LORD's
presence inside the Tabernacle. He will pour out the rest of the bull's blood at the base of
4:8 the altar for burnt offerings at the entrance of the Tabernacle. 8Then the priest must re-
Lev 3:3 move all the fat of the bull to be offered as a sin offering. This includes all the fat around
the internal organs, 9the two kidneys and the fat around them near the loins, and the long
lobe of the liver. He must remove these along with the kidneys, 10just as he does with cat-
tle offered as a peace offering, and burn them on the altar of burnt offerings. 11But he
4:11 Num 19:5 must take whatever is left of the bull—its hide, meat, head, legs, internal organs, and
Heb 13:11 dung—12and carry it away to a place outside the camp that is ceremonially clean, the
place where the ashes are dumped. There, on the ash heap, he will burn it on a wood fire.
4:13 Num 15:23-26 13"If the entire Israelite community sins by violating one of the LORD's commands, but the

4:3 Hebrew *the anointed priest;* also in 4:5, 16. 4:4 Hebrew *Tent of Meeting;* also in 4:5, 7, 14, 16, 18.

▸ SPIRITUAL WARFARE

3:16 A sweet aroma to God. This verse describes the offering as pleasing God through its aroma. Of course, God didn't take pleasure in the literal scent of burning organs, but in what the scent represented: the faithful obedience of the Israelites and their desire to fellowship with Him. The New Testament tells us there are other sacrifices we can perform that likewise bring great pleasure to God, such as doing good and sharing what we have with the poor (see Hebrews 13:16). (***See Spiritual Warfare**> Resisting Sin and Evil> Consequences> Of obedience,* TopicGuide page A46.)

▸ GOD

4:2 Unintentional sin. Leviticus 4 outlines four categories of individuals who might sin without realizing that what they have done violates God's law. There are at least two implications in these instructions. First, even when we do not have evil motives, we may still sin. We sin not only when our intentions are not pure but also when our actions do not conform to God's law. If we are to perform righteous acts, we must do the right thing for the right reason. Second, the one who has sinned must take the responsibility of asking for forgiveness and cleansing (1 John 1:9). The issue in this life is not whether or not we will sin—we will. The issue is whether or not we turn to God for His forgiveness. (***See God**> God's Attributes> Forgiving> God's forgiveness clears one's record,* TopicGuide page A16.)

4:3 The high priest was the religious leader of the nation and a descendant of Aaron (Leviticus 16:32), the first high priest (Exodus 29:30). Because he was the representative head of the nation in religious matters, his sin was also counted as their sin.

4:3, 23, 28, 32 God's people were expected to offer God their best gifts. The animals were to have no physical defects, such as blindness, lameness, or disease (compare Genesis 4:4; Malachi 1:7-14).

4:4, 15, 24, 29, 33 By the laying on of hands, the worshiper identified with the animal, marking it as the worshiper's substitute. By this identification, the animal's death took the place of the worshiper's.

4:5-7 Blood was sprinkled on the accoutrements of the Tabernacle not to obtain forgiveness for the high priest, but to cleanse him from defilement. The high priest's office was so high and so holy that the Tabernacle and its furnishings were corrupted by his presence when he sinned.

4:7, 18 The incense altar was God's supremely holy altar (Exodus 30:1-10). It was used daily in the Tabernacle ritual. The altar of burnt offerings stood in the courtyard just outside the Tabernacle (Exodus 40:6).

4:13 Community or corporate sin might be committed in a number of ways. If the representatives of the people sinned, the entire community sometimes incurred guilt (Leviticus 4:3; 10:6). If a large number of people within the community sinned, the entire community might share the blame (Exodus 32). Even the sin of a single individual who was not a leader sometimes brought blame on the entire nation (Joshua 7:1). Every person in the nation often suffered covenant curses for corporate sin, even though some or even many individuals had not personally sinned.

people don't realize it, they are still guilty. 14When they become aware of their sin, the peo- 4:14
ple must bring a young bull as an offering for their sin and present it before the Tabernacle. Lev 4:3
15The elders of the community must then lay their hands on the bull's head and slaughter it 4:15
before the LORD. 16The high priest will then take some of the bull's blood into the Tabernacle, Lev 8:14 Num 8:10-12
17dip his finger in the blood, and sprinkle it seven times before the LORD in front of the inner 4:17
curtain. 18He will then put some of the blood on the horns of the altar for fragrant incense that Lev 4:6
stands in the LORD's presence inside the Tabernacle. He will pour out the rest of the blood at
the base of the altar for burnt offerings at the entrance of the Tabernacle. 19Then the priest 4:19
must remove all the animal's fat and burn it on the altar, 20just as he does with the bull offered Lev 4:8
as a sin offering for the high priest. Through this process, the priest will purify the people, mak- 4:20
ing them right with the LORD,* and they will be forgiven. 21Then the priest must take what is Num 15:25 4:21
left of the bull and carry it outside the camp and burn it there, just as is done with the sin offer- Lev 4:12
ing for the high priest. This offering is for the sin of the entire congregation of Israel.

22"If one of Israel's leaders sins by violating one of the commands of the LORD his God but 4:22
doesn't realize it, he is still guilty. 23When he becomes aware of his sin, he must bring as his offer- Lev 4:2, 13
ing a male goat with no defects. 24He must lay his hand on the goat's head and slaughter it at the 4:24
place where burnt offerings are slaughtered before the LORD. This is an offering for his sin. 25Then Lev 6:25
the priest will dip his finger in the blood of the sin offering and put it on the horns of the altar for 4:25 Lev 4:7
burnt offerings. He will pour out the rest of the blood at the base of the altar. 26Then he must burn 4:26
all the goat's fat on the altar, just as he does with the peace offering. Through this process, the Lev 4:19-20
priest will purify the leader from his sin, making him right with the LORD, and he will be forgiven.

27"If any of the common people sin by violating one of the LORD's commands, but they 4:27
don't realize it, they are still guilty. 28When they become aware of their sin, they must bring Lev 4:2
as an offering for their sin a female goat with no defects. 29They must lay a hand on the 4:28
head of the sin offering and slaughter it at the place where burnt offerings are slaughtered. Lev 4:23
30Then the priest will dip his finger in the blood and put it on the horns of the altar for burnt 4:30
offerings. He will pour out the rest of the blood at the base of the altar. 31Then he must re- Lev 4:7
move all the goat's fat, just as he does with the fat of the peace offering. He will burn the fat 4:31 Gen 8:21
on the altar, and it will be a pleasing aroma to the LORD. Through this process, the priest will Exod 29:18
purify the people, making them right with the LORD, and they will be forgiven. Lev 2:2; 4:8; 6:15

4:20 Or *will make atonement for the people;* similarly in 4:26, 31, 35.

4:14-15 Just as community guilt could be incurred through the actions of the nation's leaders, community forgiveness could be obtained through their representation.

4:14–5:13 In conjunction with confession, sin offerings were the required means of obtaining forgiveness when certain unintentional sins or defilement occurred.

4:16-18 As with the high priest's sin (Leviticus 4:5-7), the seriousness of national sin corrupted the Tabernacle so that it had to be cleansed with blood.

4:20, 26, 31, 35 God's justice requires that sin be punished by death. Animals atoned for the sins of human beings by serving as their substitutes. Because these sacrifices were not absolutely perfect, being products of a fallen world, and because they were not as valuable as a human life, they were insufficient to satisfy God's wrath. Nevertheless, they pointed to the then-future sacrifice of Christ, which was the true basis for forgiveness even in the Old Testament (Matthew 11:13; Luke 24:25-27). When these offerings were performed in faith, God reckoned that faith as righteousness (Genesis 15:6; Psalm 51:16-19) on the basis of Christ's merit (John 1:29; 1 Peter 1:19; Hebrews 10:1-20).

4:22-25 A leader's sin was not as serious as the high priest's or the nation's. It required a lesser sacrifice (a goat rather than a bull), and the repentance of only the leader who sinned. It did not require that any place or furnishings inside the Tabernacle be cleansed (compare Leviticus 4:6-7, 17-18).

4:27-31 Although certainly not trivial, the sin of a common individual was less serious than that of a leader, the nation, or the high priest. As such, it required the least valuable of the four possible sacrifices for unintentional sins: a female goat (females were less valuable than males, and goats were less valuable than bulls). It also did not require the cleansing of the Tabernacle or its furnishings.

▸ SALVATION

4:28 No free forgiveness. Whether it was a priest, a leader, the whole community, or an individual who had sinned, one thing was clear: there was no free forgiveness. They all had to bring an offering from their own possessions as a sacrifice (a prized animal without defect; see 4:3, 23, 28, 32). The point was to communicate the deadly seriousness of sin—whether major or minor, every sin is a sin that must be atoned for. This Old Testament practice was wonderfully fulfilled in the New Testament with the death of Christ (Hebrews 9:11-22). When we, by faith, bring the atoning sacrifice of Christ to God and ask for forgiveness, it is granted. (***See Salvation**> Jesus' Work> Crucifixion> Jesus bore our sins,* TopicGuide page A22.)

4:32 32“If the people bring a sheep as their sin offering, it must be a female with no defects.
Lev 4:28 33They must lay a hand on the head of the sin offering and slaughter it at the place
where burnt offerings are slaughtered. 34Then the priest will dip his finger in the blood of
the sin offering and put it on the horns of the altar for burnt offerings. He will pour out
4:35 the rest of the blood at the base of the altar. 35Then he must remove all the sheep’s fat,
Lev 3:5 just as he does with the fat of a sheep presented as a peace offering. He will burn the fat
on the altar on top of the special gifts presented to the LORD. Through this process, the
priest will purify the people from their sin, making them right with the LORD, and they will
be forgiven.

SINS REQUIRING A SIN OFFERING

5:1 **5** “If you are called to testify about something you have seen or that you know about, it
Prov 29:24 is sinful to refuse to testify, and you will be punished for your sin.
5:2 2“Or suppose you unknowingly touch something that is ceremonially unclean, such as
Lev 11:4-11, 24-39 the carcass of an unclean animal. When you realize what you have done, you must admit
Num 19:11-16 Deut 14:3-21 your defilement and your guilt. This is true whether it is a wild animal, a domestic animal,
or an animal that scurries along the ground.
5:4 3“Or suppose you unknowingly touch something that makes a person unclean. When
Num 30:6-8 you realize what you have done, you must admit your guilt.
5:5 Lev 16:21 4“Or suppose you make a foolish vow of any kind, whether its purpose is for good or for
Num 5:7 bad. When you realize its foolishness, you must admit your guilt.
Josh 7:19 5“When you become aware of your guilt in any of these ways, you must confess your
5:6 sin. 6Then you must bring to the LORD as the penalty for your sin a female from the flock,
Lev 4:28, 32 either a sheep or a goat. This is a sin offering with which the priest will purify you from
5:7 Lev 12:8 your sin, making you right with the LORD.*
Luke 2:24 7“But if you cannot afford to bring a sheep, you may bring to the LORD two

5:6 Or *will make atonement for you;* similarly in 5:10, 13, 16, 18.

▸ **GOD**
5:1 Telling the truth. Sometimes we hear of people who stand by while a crime is being committed, or refuse to testify when called as a witness. “I don’t want to get involved,” they often say. Moses told the Israelites that noninvolvement was sinful because it hampered justice. Because silence prevents the truth from coming to light, it might even be called a form of lying. For this reason those who refused to testify were held liable. In the Bible both Israel in the Old Testament and the church in the New Testament are presented as living, unified organisms. Refusing to protect the purity of this organism contributes to the pollution of all its members. According to God, to testify for the sake of justice is to speak the truth in love (Ephesians 4:15). (***See God****> God’s Attributes> True> His Spirit guides believers into all truth,* TopicGuide page A18.)

5:2-3 In order to understand and respect God’s holiness, the Israelites were obligated to follow practices that separated them from defilement and from neighboring nations. Much of their understanding of holiness paralleled basic cleanliness. As a result, these regulations probably helped preserve the people’s health. The main purpose of the regulations, however, was to lay a foundation for understanding moral purity and God’s character. God’s requirement of outward cleanliness implied an even greater requirement of purity of the heart. In the cases mentioned here, ceremonial uncleanness was accompanied by actual guilt, and therefore required atonement.

▸ **GOD**
5:4 A poor promise. Everyone has had the embarrassing experience of promising something and then failing to follow through: “I promise to pray for you”; “No matter what, I’ll exercise with you every day until you lose the weight”; “We’ll play ball together as soon as I get home from work—I promise!” Promises made to God or to others are serious commitments that say a lot about who we are. When we fail to keep our promises, we act hypocritically. God always keeps His promises (Titus 1:2; Hebrews 6:16-18), and He requires us to do the same. It’s better not to vow than to vow and not pay (Ecclesiastes 5:4-7). For this reason, if we are not committed to following through, we ought not to promise anything. (***See God****> God’s Attributes> True> God follows through on His promises,* TopicGuide page A18.)

5:4 Vows were often made in the hopes of gaining a blessing from God, and generally involved a promised offering in return. If God provided the blessing, the one who made the vow would fulfill his or her reciprocal obligation. Vows also involved explicit or implicit curses on the one who made the promise, should the vow be broken.

5:6, 10, 13, 16, 18 Animals were offered as substitutes to atone for human beings who sinned. They were not equal substitutes, however, because human beings are more valuable than animals. Nevertheless, they pointed forward to Christ’s sacrifice as the ultimate basis for forgiveness (Matthew 11:13; Luke 24:25-27). When these sacrifices were offered in faith, God forgave the worshipers on the basis of Christ’s merit (John 1:29; 1 Peter 1:19; Hebrews 10:1-20).

5:6-15 Sin offerings were mandatory for certain unintentional sins and defilement. They accompanied confession and served as means of obtaining forgiveness.

turtledoves or two young pigeons as the penalty for your sin. One of the birds will be for
a sin offering, and the other for a burnt offering. 8You must bring them to the priest, who 5:8
will present the first bird as the sin offering. He will wring its neck but without severing its Lev 1:15, 17
head from the body. 9Then he will sprinkle some of the blood of the sin offering 5:9
against the sides of the altar, and the rest of the blood will be drained out at the base of Lev 4:7; 7:2
the altar. This is an offering for sin. 10The priest will then prepare the second bird as a 5:10
burnt offering, following all the procedures that have been prescribed. Through this Lev 1:14-17
process the priest will purify you from your sin, making you right with the LORD, and
you will be forgiven.

11"If you cannot afford to bring two turtledoves or two young pigeons, you may bring 5:11
two quarts* of choice flour for your sin offering. Since it is an offering for sin, you must not Lev 14:21
moisten it with olive oil or put any frankincense on it. 12Take the flour to the priest, who *Luke 2:24
will scoop out a handful as a representative portion. He will burn it on the altar on top of
the special gifts presented to the LORD. It is an offering for sin. 13Through this process, the
priest will purify those who are guilty of any of these sins, making them right with the
LORD, and they will be forgiven. The rest of the flour will belong to the priest, just as with
the grain offering."

PROCEDURES FOR THE GUILT OFFERING

14Then the LORD said to Moses, 15"If one of you commits a sin by unintentionally defiling 5:15
the LORD's sacred property, you must bring a guilt offering to the LORD. The offering must Exod 30:13
be your own ram with no defects, or you may buy one of equal value with silver, as mea- Lev 6:6; 7:1-10; 22:14
sured by the weight of the sanctuary shekel.* 16You must make restitution for the sacred 5:16
property you have harmed by paying for the loss, plus an additional 20 percent. When Lev 6:5; 22:14
you give the payment to the priest, he will purify you with the ram sacrificed as a guilt of-
fering, making you right with the LORD, and you will be forgiven.

17"Suppose you sin by violating one of the LORD's commands. Even if you are unaware 5:17
of what you have done, you are guilty and will be punished for your sin. 18For a guilt offer- Lev 5:15
ing, you must bring to the priest your own ram with no defects, or you may buy one of
equal value. Through this process the priest will purify you from your unintentional sin,
making you right with the LORD, and you will be forgiven. 19This is a guilt offering, for you
have been guilty of an offense against the LORD."

5:11 Hebrew *1/10 of an ephah* [2.2 liters]. 5:15 Each shekel was about 0.4 ounces or 11 grams in weight.

▸ WORSHIP

5:11 Too little money for God? Sometimes people stay away from church because they feel as if they don't have enough money to contribute to the offering plate. There is no one too poor for God, but Moses faced a similar situation as he set forth instructions about those who came to be purified from sin. The normal sacrificial offering for purification was a female lamb or goat (Leviticus 5:6). But if the person couldn't afford a lamb or goat, two doves or pigeons (5:7) could be substituted. If the person was too poor to afford the pigeons, two quarts of flour would suffice (5:11). The point here is the same one made in the New Testament: Gifts to God are based on what we have, not on what we don't have (2 Corinthians 8:12). Access to God is based on the price He paid, not on the price we can pay. (***See Worship***> *NT> Offerings> Widow's offering,* TopicGuide page A31.)

5:11 Blood was a standard element in most sacrifices that resulted in forgiveness of sins. However, the poor were allowed to bring bloodless offerings for this purpose in a number of cases (compare Hebrews 9:22).

5:15-19 The guilt offering applied to offenses in which restitution had to be made, as well as to ceremonial defilement. Restitution generally involved replacement of costs plus an additional penalty.

▸ GOD

5:18 Guilt and forgiveness. Guilt is a common human emotion—and sometimes it is rightly deserved. If we haven't asked forgiveness from the person we've offended, then we shouldn't feel forgiven. But when we *are* forgiven, we should take that to heart by feeling and *acting* forgiven. The essence of the Bible's message is that God has provided a way for us to receive forgiveness. In the Old Testament, forgiveness was obtained by means of faithful confession and sacrifice; in the New Testament, it is obtained by means of confession alone. But in both Testaments, forgiveness comes only on the basis of the sacrifice of Christ (Hebrews 10:1-20). If you are a Christian, you are forgiven! Don't let feelings of guilt rob you of the gift God gives (Romans 8:1). (***See God***> *God's Attributes> Forgiving> God's forgiveness clears one's record,* TopicGuide page A16; ***Worship***> *NT> Prayer> Instructions> Draw near with confidence,* TopicGuide page A33.)

SINS REQUIRING A GUILT OFFERING

6:2 Exod 22:7-15; Num 5:6; Col 3:9
6:3 Deut 22:1-3
6:5-6 Lev 5:15-16; Num 5:8

6 1*Then the LORD said to Moses, 2"Suppose one of you sins against your associate and
is unfaithful to the LORD. Suppose you cheat in a deal involving a security deposit, or
you steal or commit fraud, 3or you find lost property and lie about it, or you lie while
swearing to tell the truth, or you commit any other such sin. 4If you have sinned in any of
these ways, you are guilty. You must give back whatever you stole, or the money you took
by extortion, or the security deposit, or the lost property you found, 5or anything obtained
by swearing falsely. You must make restitution by paying the full price plus an additional
20 percent to the person you have harmed. On the same day you must present a guilt of-
fering. 6As a guilt offering to the LORD, you must bring to the priest your own ram with no
defects, or you may buy one of equal value. 7Through this process, the priest will purify
you before the LORD, making you right with Him,* and you will be forgiven for any of these
sins you have committed."

FURTHER INSTRUCTIONS FOR THE BURNT OFFERING

6:9 Exod 29:38-42; Lev 6:12-13; Num 28:1-25
6:10 Exod 28:39-43
6:12 Lev 3:5

8*Then the LORD said to Moses, 9"Give Aaron and his sons the following instructions re-
garding the burnt offering. The burnt offering must be left on top of the altar until the next
morning, and the fire on the altar must be kept burning all night. 10In the morning, after
the priest on duty has put on his official linen clothing and linen undergarments, he must
clean out the ashes of the burnt offering and put them beside the altar. 11Then he must
take off these garments, change back into his regular clothes, and carry the ashes outside
the camp to a place that is ceremonially clean. 12Meanwhile, the fire on the altar must be
kept burning; it must never go out. Each morning the priest will add fresh wood to the fire
and arrange the burnt offering on it. He will then burn the fat of the peace offerings on it.
13Remember, the fire must be kept burning on the altar at all times. It must never go out.

6:1 Verses 6:1-7 are numbered 5:20-26 in Hebrew text. **6:7** *Or will make atonement for you before the LORD.*
6:8 Verses 6:8-30 are numbered 6:1-23 in Hebrew text.

▸ HOLINESS
6:2 Sin against two? If you asked a person on the street what constitutes a sin against God, the answer would probably be things like taking the Lord's name in vain or not going to church. A more religious person might go further—loving material things more than God, for instance. But Moses says we sin against God even when we defraud our neighbor. What is a sin against another person is also a sin against God, the One who made that person. Every sin is a sin against God (Psalm 51:4). That means sin usually requires asking forgiveness twice—once from your neighbor and once from your God. Don't leave either party out when making amends for interpersonal sin. (***See Holiness****> Disciplines> Of Engagement> Confession,* TopicGuide page A42.)

▸ WORSHIP
6:4 Payback. In ancient Israel, as in many modern cultures, when a person was found guilty of defrauding another, the sinner was to pay not only for the actual damages to the victim, but also punitive damages as a fine. The value of the goods stolen had to be paid back, plus a surcharge of 20 percent for good measure. In addition to this, the guilty Israelite had to present a guilt offering to God. Being sorry was not sufficient. Reparation gave evidence of true repentance leading to restoration (2 Corinthians 7:9-11) and eased the suffering of the victim. (***See Worship****> NT> Cleansing> God requires repentance from known sin,* TopicGuide page A30.)

6:6 Guilt offerings were required for offenses in which restitution had to be made, as well as for ceremonial defilement (compare Leviticus 5:15-19).

6:7, 30 Though animals were offered to atone for human sinners, they were not equal substitutes, nor were they the basis for forgiveness. They pointed forward to and received meaning from Jesus' sacrifice on the cross (Matthew 11:13; Luke 24:25-27). God forgave faithful worshipers on the basis of Christ's merit (John 1:29; 1 Peter 1:19; Hebrews 10:1-20).

6:8–7:36 This section specifically addresses Aaron and his sons. While God referred to the whole nation of Israel as a "kingdom of priests" (Exodus 19:5-6), He set apart the Levites to do the special work of caring for the Tabernacle (Numbers 1:50-51). Within the tribe of Levi, God set apart Aaron and his descendants to function as priests (Exodus 29–30). The priests had housekeeping-type chores, such as tending the lamps in the Tabernacle, but they also mediated between God and His people. Later, Jesus became the one and only High Priest (Hebrews 9:11; 10:21) and mediator (1 Timothy 2:5).

6:9-13 The perpetual fire was probably intended as a reminder of the people's constant need for forgiveness.

6:10-11 The clothing for the priest was not suited to the task so much as suited to the holy place where he ministered and to the God he honored (Exodus 28:4-5). He was to wear his holy clothing while cleaning out the ashes, but he was to wear his common clothes when he left the holy grounds of the Tabernacle to dispose of the ashes.

FURTHER INSTRUCTIONS FOR THE GRAIN OFFERING

14 "These are the instructions regarding the grain offering. Aaron's sons must present this of-
fering to the LORD in front of the altar. 15 The priest on duty will take from the grain offering a
handful of the choice flour moistened with olive oil, together with all the frankincense. He will
burn this representative portion on the altar as a pleasing aroma to the LORD. 16 Aaron and his
sons may eat the rest of the flour, but it must be baked without yeast and eaten in a sacred
place within the courtyard of the Tabernacle.* 17 Remember, it must never be prepared with
yeast. I have given it to the priests as their share of the special gifts presented to Me. Like the
sin offering and the guilt offering, it is most holy. 18 Any of Aaron's male descendants may eat
from the special gifts presented to the LORD. This is their permanent right from generation to
generation. Anyone or anything that touches these offerings will become holy."

6:14 Lev 2:1
6:15 Lev 2:1-2, 9
6:16 Lev 10:12-15; Num 18:10
6:17 Lev 2:11; 6:29; 10:17
6:18 Lev 6:29; Num 18:10; 1 Cor 9:13

PROCEDURES FOR THE ORDINATION OFFERING

19 Then the LORD said to Moses, 20 "On the day Aaron and his sons are anointed, they must
present to the LORD a grain offering of two quarts* of choice flour, half to be offered in the
morning and half to be offered in the evening. 21 It must be carefully mixed with olive oil
and cooked on a griddle. Then slice* this grain offering and present it as a pleasing aroma to
the LORD. 22 In each generation, the high priest* who succeeds Aaron must prepare this same
offering. It belongs to the LORD and must be burned up completely. This is a permanent law.
23 All such grain offerings of a priest must be burned up entirely. None of it may be eaten."

6:21 Lev 2:5, 8; 7:9
6:22-23 Exod 29:30

FURTHER INSTRUCTIONS FOR THE SIN OFFERING

24 Then the LORD said to Moses, 25 "Give Aaron and his sons the following instructions regard-
ing the sin offering. The animal given as an offering for sin is a most holy offering, and it must
be slaughtered in the LORD's presence at the place where the burnt offerings are slaughtered.
26 The priest who offers the sacrifice as a sin offering must eat his portion in a sacred place
within the courtyard of the Tabernacle. 27 Anyone or anything that touches the sacrificial meat
will become holy. If any of the sacrificial blood spatters on a person's clothing, the soiled gar-
ment must be washed in a sacred place. 28 If a clay pot is used to boil the sacrificial meat, it
must then be broken. If a bronze pot is used, it must be scoured and thoroughly rinsed with
water. 29 Any male from a priest's family may eat from this offering; it is most holy. 30 But the
offering for sin may not be eaten if its blood was brought into the Tabernacle as an offering for
purification* in the Holy Place. It must be completely burned with fire.

6:25 Lev 4:24, 29
6:27 Exod 29:37
6:28 Lev 11:33; 15:12
6:29 Lev 6:18
6:30 Lev 4:1, 18

FURTHER INSTRUCTIONS FOR THE GUILT OFFERING

7 "These are the instructions for the guilt offering. It is most holy. 2 The animal sacri-
ficed as a guilt offering must be slaughtered at the place where the burnt offerings
are slaughtered, and its blood must be splattered against all sides of the altar. 3 The priest

7:1 Lev 5:14–6:7
7:2 Lev 1:11
7:3 Lev 3:3, 9

6:16 Hebrew *Tent of Meeting*; also in 6:26, 30. 6:20 Hebrew *1/10 of an ephah* [2.2 liters]. 6:21 The meaning of this Hebrew term is uncertain. 6:22 Hebrew *the anointed priest.* 6:30 Or *an offering to make atonement.*

6:14-23 Besides those mentioned here, grain offerings were often offered in voluntary worship to express thankfulness or devotion (compare Leviticus 2).

6:18, 27 Just as physical contact with defiled objects or people spread ritual uncleanness, contact with holy things spread holiness. That which became holy was thereby set apart for God's special use.

6:25-30 Sin offerings, coupled with faithful confession, were the required means of obtaining forgiveness in cases of certain unintentional sins or defilement. They also served as part of the priests' income. Because this food was holy, it had to be eaten on the holy ground of the Tabernacle courtyard.

6:28 The typical utensils for the Tabernacle—ash buckets, shovels, basins, meat hooks, fire pans—were made of bronze, which was nonporous and could be scoured, boiled, and scraped. Clay pots, on the other hand, were porous and could not be sufficiently cleaned.

7:1-7 Guilt offerings were presented for sins that required restitution, and for ceremonial defilement (compare Leviticus 5:15-19). The animals were slaughtered in the courtyard on the north side of the altar of burnt offerings (Leviticus 1:11). Portions of the sacrifice served as income for the priests, but because this food was holy it had to be eaten within the holy grounds of the Tabernacle courtyard.

will then offer all its fat on the altar, including the fat of the broad tail, the fat around the in-
ternal organs, 4the two kidneys and the fat around them near the loins, and the long lobe
of the liver. These are to be removed with the kidneys, 5and the priests will burn them on
7:6 the altar as a special gift presented to the LORD. This is the guilt offering. 6Any male from a
Lev 6:18, 29 Num 18:10 priest's family may eat the meat. It must be eaten in a sacred place, for it is most holy.
7:7 7"The same instructions apply to both the guilt offering and the sin offering. Both belong to
Lev 14:13 the priest who uses them to purify someone, making that person right with the LORD.* 8In the
7:9 case of the burnt offering, the priest may keep the hide of the sacrificed animal. 9Any grain of-
Lev 2:5, 8 fering that has been baked in an oven, prepared in a pan, or cooked on a griddle belongs to
the priest who presents it. 10All other grain offerings, whether made of dry flour or flour moist-
ened with olive oil, are to be shared equally among all the priests, the descendants of Aaron.

FURTHER INSTRUCTIONS FOR THE PEACE OFFERING

7:11 11"These are the instructions regarding the different kinds of peace offerings that may be
Lev 3:1-17 presented to the LORD. 12If you present your peace offering as an expression of thanks-
7:12 giving, the usual animal sacrifice must be accompanied by various kinds of bread made
Lev 2:4 Num 6:15 without yeast—thin cakes mixed with olive oil, wafers spread with oil, and cakes made of
7:13 choice flour mixed with olive oil. 13This peace offering of thanksgiving must also be ac-
Lev 2:12; 23:17 companied by loaves of bread made with yeast. 14One of each kind of bread must be pre-
sented as a gift to the LORD. It will then belong to the priest who splatters the blood of the
7:15 peace offering against the altar. 15The meat of the peace offering of thanksgiving must be
Lev 22:29-30 eaten on the same day it is offered. None of it may be saved for the next morning.
7:16 Lev 19:6-8 16"If you bring an offering to fulfill a vow or as a voluntary offering, the meat must be
eaten on the same day the sacrifice is offered, but whatever is left over may be eaten on
7:17 Exod 12:10 the second day. 17Any meat left over until the third day must be completely burned up. 18If
any of the meat from the peace offering is eaten on the third day, the person who pre-
7:19 sented it will not be accepted by the LORD. You will receive no credit for offering it. By then
Lev 11:47 the meat will be contaminated; if you eat it, you will be punished for your sin.
7:20 Gen 17:14 19"Meat that touches anything ceremonially unclean may not be eaten; it must be com-
Lev 22:3-7 pletely burned up. The rest of the meat may be eaten, but only by people who are ceremo-
Num 19:13 nially clean. 20If you are ceremonially unclean and you eat meat from a peace offering

7:7 Or *to make atonement.*

7:11 While some of the sacrifices were required at specific places and times, the peace and thanksgiving offerings were offered spontaneously. These offerings were given to show love and appreciation. They were categorized as "fellowship offerings." The priests did receive part of these offerings, but rather than being required to eat the food at the Tabernacle, the priests could share the offering with their families.

7:12-36 The nature of the peace offering revealed that the ancient Israelites knew that they needed God's help to live in harmony with Him. Being an Israelite or being good people wasn't enough to gain true peace with God. This system of sacrifice symbolizes the atonement all people need to break down the barriers between God and man (Leviticus 3:1; Ephesians 2:17; Romans 5:1).

▸ SALVATION

7:12 As a thanksgiving offering. The psalmist later wrote: "I will fulfill my vows to You, O God, and will offer a sacrifice of thanks for Your help" (Psalm 56:12). In addition to the animal sacrifice, the worshiper was to bring cakes and wafers made with various mixtures of flour, oil, and yeast. This generous offering, along with the meat of the sacrifice, was to be shared with the priest and people, rich and poor. God's goodness became a cause for celebration, and generosity became evidence of gratitude. (***See Salvation****> Receiving> Results> Works> Expression of gratitude,* TopicGuide page A23.)

▸ WORSHIP

7:16 Freewill offering. The occasion for the freewill offering was, well, just because! In other words, there was not a specific reason, such as gratitude for something specific God had done, or the completion of a vow made to God (verse 16). It was an offering that flowed from a grateful heart for no other reason than just being thankful for knowing God. When was the last time you offered a word, an act, or a gift of thanksgiving to God just because you loved Him? Just being a recipient of His love and salvation is reason enough for worship (Hebrews 13:15). (***See Worship****> OT> Offerings> Other sacrifices,* TopicGuide page A27.)

7:19-21 Every day, ancient Israelites were busy determining what was clean and unclean. God required practices that communicated the need to be a holy people; as such, they might better understand their holy God. A practical outworking of the holiness codes included basic cleanliness. God established strict regulations about what the people could touch, eat, and drink. Ceremonially unclean things included dead bodies, dead animals, menstruating or postpartum women, and animals considered unclean to eat, such as pigs or catfish.

that was presented to the LORD, you will be cut off from the community. 21 If you touch any-
thing that is unclean (whether it is human defilement or an unclean animal or any other
unclean, detestable thing) and then eat meat from a peace offering presented to the LORD,
you will be cut off from the community."

7:21 Lev 5:2-3

THE FORBIDDEN BLOOD AND FAT

22 Then the LORD said to Moses, 23 "Give the following instructions to the people of Israel. You
must never eat fat, whether from cattle, sheep, or goats. 24 The fat of an animal found dead or
torn to pieces by wild animals must never be eaten, though it may be used for any other pur-
pose. 25 Anyone who eats fat from an animal presented as a special gift to the LORD will be cut
off from the community. 26 No matter where you live, you must never consume the blood of
any bird or animal. 27 Anyone who consumes blood will be cut off from the community."

7:23 Lev 17:3
7:24 Exod 22:31; Lev 17:15
7:26 Gen 9:4; Lev 17:10-14; Acts 15:20, 29

A PORTION FOR THE PRIESTS

28 Then the LORD said to Moses, 29 "Give the following instructions to the people of Israel. When
you present a peace offering to the LORD, bring part of it as a gift to the LORD. 30 Present it to the
LORD with your own hands as a special gift to the LORD. Bring the fat of the animal, together with
the breast, and lift up the breast as a special offering to the LORD. 31 Then the priest will burn the
fat on the altar, but the breast will belong to Aaron and his descendants. 32 Give the right thigh
of your peace offering to the priest as a gift. 33 The right thigh must always be given to the priest
who offers the blood and the fat of the peace offering. 34 For I have reserved the breast of the
special offering and the right thigh of the sacred offering for the priests. It is the permanent right
of Aaron and his descendants to share in the peace offerings brought by the people of Israel.
35 This is their rightful share. The special gifts presented to the LORD have been reserved for
Aaron and his descendants from the time they were set apart to serve the LORD as priests. 36 On
the day they were anointed, the LORD commanded the Israelites to give these portions to the
priests as their permanent share from generation to generation."

37 These are the instructions for the burnt offering, the grain offering, the sin offering,
and the guilt offering, as well as the ordination offering and the peace offering. 38 The LORD
gave these instructions to Moses on Mount Sinai when He commanded the Israelites to
present their offerings to the LORD in the wilderness of Sinai.

7:29 Lev 3:1
7:30 Exod 29:26-27; Lev 8:29; Num 6:20
7:31 Lev 7:34; Num 18:11
7:32 Num 18:18
7:34 Exod 29:22; Lev 10:15
7:36 Exod 29:22-34; 40:13-15
7:38 Lev 26:46

ORDINATION OF THE PRIESTS

8
Then the LORD said to Moses, 2 "Bring Aaron and his sons, along with their sacred gar-
ments, the anointing oil, the bull for the sin offering, the two rams, and the basket of
bread made without yeast, 3 and call the entire community of Israel together at the en-
trance of the Tabernacle.*"

8:2 Exod 28:1

8:3 Hebrew *Tent of Meeting;* also in 8:4, 31, 33, 35.

7:31 The priesthood was a professional group in the sense that their living was made by their service. They received their food from the sacrifices—not only the portions of meat listed here, but also portions of the grain and wine offerings (Numbers 6:19-20). This practice helps establish the precedent for paying those in ministry today.

7:37-38 These verses provide the postscript for the section on various sacrifices.

7:38 Mount Sinai was the preeminent sacred geographic space for the Israelite nation prior to the completion of the Temple in Jerusalem in 960 BC. The traditional location of the Sinai Peninsula called *Jebel Musa* was chosen in the fourth century for a variety of reasons, mostly to facilitate easy access for pilgrims. The location of Sinai is still in dispute, but evidence points towards either Har Karkom, a mountain in the Negev desert, located between Kadesh-barnea and Petra, or a site on the other side of the Gulf of Aqaba in modern Saudi Arabia.

▸ WORSHIP

8:3 Public accountability. Have you ever wondered why we invite friends and relatives to weddings? Or why we baptize new members of the faith in front of the whole church? Or why pastors, elders, and other leaders are ordained in the presence of the whole congregation? It's not just to share the joy of the occasion—it's because witnesses are important! When Moses ordained priests for Israel, he had all the people witness the event, agreeing by their presence that Aaron and his sons would be their new spiritual leaders. We need witnesses to provide the accountability and support it takes to live a joyful, productive Christian life. (***See Worship***> *NT*> *Holy Spirit*> *The church is one body with many members,* TopicGuide page A31.)

4 So Moses followed the LORD's instructions, and the whole community assembled at the
Tabernacle entrance. 5 Moses announced to them, "This is what the LORD has commanded
us to do!" 6 Then he presented Aaron and his sons and washed them with water. 7 He put
the official tunic on Aaron and tied the sash around his waist. He dressed him in the robe,
placed the ephod on him, and attached the ephod securely with its decorative sash. 8 Then
Moses placed the chestpiece on Aaron and put the Urim and the Thummim inside it. 9 He
placed the turban on Aaron's head and attached the gold medallion—the badge of holi-
ness—to the front of the turban, just as the LORD had commanded him.

10 Then Moses took the anointing oil and anointed the Tabernacle and everything in it,
making them holy. 11 He sprinkled the oil on the altar seven times, anointing it and all its
utensils, as well as the washbasin and its stand, making them holy. 12 Then he poured
some of the anointing oil on Aaron's head, anointing him and making him holy for his
work. 13 Next Moses presented Aaron's sons. He clothed them in their tunics, tied their
sashes around them, and put their special head coverings on them, just as the LORD had
commanded him.

14 Then Moses presented the bull for the sin offering. Aaron and his sons laid their hands
on the bull's head, 15 and Moses slaughtered it. Moses took some of the blood, and with
his finger he put it on the four horns of the altar to purify it. He poured out the rest of the
blood at the base of the altar. Through this process, he made the altar holy by purifying it.*
16 Then Moses took all the fat around the internal organs, the long lobe of the liver, and the
two kidneys and the fat around them, and he burned it all on the altar. 17 He took the rest
of the bull, including its hide, meat, and dung, and burned it on a fire outside the camp,
just as the LORD had commanded him.

18 Then Moses presented the ram for the burnt offering. Aaron and his sons laid their
hands on the ram's head, 19 and Moses slaughtered it. Then Moses took the ram's blood
and splattered it against all sides of the altar. 20 Then he cut the ram into pieces, and he
burned the head, some of its pieces, and the fat on the altar. 21 After washing the internal
organs and the legs with water, Moses burned the entire ram on the altar as a burnt offer-
ing. It was a pleasing aroma, a special gift presented to the LORD, just as the LORD had com-
manded him.

22 Then Moses presented the other ram, which was the ram of ordination. Aaron and his
sons laid their hands on the ram's head, 23 and Moses slaughtered it. Then Moses took some
of its blood and applied it to the lobe of Aaron's right ear, the thumb of his right hand, and
the big toe of his right foot. 24 Next Moses presented Aaron's sons and applied some of the

8:6 Exod 29:3-4
8:8 Exod 28:30-31; Ezra 2:63
8:9 Exod 28:4, 36-38
8:10 Exod 30:26-33
8:11 Exod 29:37; Lev 16:14
8:12 Exod 28:41; 30:30; Lev 21:10-12
8:13 Exod 28:4, 39
8:14 Exod 29:10-14; Lev 4:4
8:15 Lev 4:7
8:17 Lev 4:11
8:18 Exod 29:15-19
8:22 Exod 29:31
8:23 Exod 29:20-21

8:15 Or *by making atonement for it;* or *that offerings for purification might be made on it.*

8:8 The mysterious *Urim* and *Thummim* slid into the priest's breastplate. They were used to make yes or no decisions, functioning a bit like tossing dice or flipping a coin. Among other civilizations, casting lots was a common practice for making decisions. In the story of Jonah, the crew of the ship he was on used lots to determine who was responsible for the storm (Jonah 1:7). New Testament Roman soldiers used lots ("throwing dice") to gamble for Jesus' garments (Matthew 27:35). And the apostles used lots to choose a new apostle to take Judas' place (Acts 1:23-26).

8:10, 30 Anointing oil was olive oil spiced with myrrh, cinnamon, cassia, and sweet cane. These spices were valued in the ancient world. Myrrh was made from gum resin in shrub trees. Cinnamon came from an evergreen tree. At that time it was a rare commodity. Cassia, related to cinnamon, was made of bark. The buds of the same tree were used like cloves. Sweet cane may have been sugar cane, which was not used to make sugar at that time, but was used to sweeten food and drinks. Mixed with oil, these ingredients would have been quite fragrant.

▸ ADOPTION

8:23 Ear, hand, toe. The ordination of Aaron and his sons as the new priests of Israel included the sacrifice of a bull and two rams. The second ram was sacrificed specifically for Aaron and his sons and included the application of the blood of the ram to the lobe of their right ears, the thumb of their right hands, and the big toe of their right feet. This was a sign of consecration to the Lord—that what they heard, what they touched, and where they went would be holy to the Lord. Christians are priests of the Lord (1 Peter 2:9) whose hearts have been made pure by the blood of our sacrificial Lamb, Jesus Christ (Hebrews 9:14). (***See Adoption***> *With Christ*> *Servants*> *Chosen to be holy,* TopicGuide page A37.)

8:23 The Scripture is very specific here about where the blood was placed on Aaron's body and the bodies of his sons. For many of the sacrifices, blood was also poured around the altar, sprinkled in front of the Most Holy Place, and put on the horns of the altars (prongs that were built onto the frame of the main altar and the incense altar).

blood to the lobes of their right ears, the thumbs of their right hands, and the big toes of their
right feet. He then splattered the rest of the blood against all sides of the altar.
25Next Moses took the fat, including the fat of the broad tail, the fat around the internal 8:25
organs, the long lobe of the liver, and the two kidneys and the fat around them, along with Exod 29:22
the right thigh. 26On top of these he placed a thin cake of bread made without yeast, a 8:26
cake of bread mixed with olive oil, and a wafer spread with olive oil. All these were taken Exod 29:23
from the basket of bread made without yeast that was placed in the LORD's presence. 27He 8:27
put all these in the hands of Aaron and his sons, and he lifted them up as a special offering Exod 29:24
to the LORD. 28Moses then took all the offerings back from them and burned them on the 8:28
altar on top of the burnt offering. This was the ordination offering. It was a pleasing aroma, Exod 29:25
a special gift presented to the LORD. 29Then Moses took the breast and lifted it up as a spe- 8:29
cial offering to the LORD. This was Moses' portion of the ram of ordination, just as the LORD Exod 29:26 Lev 7:31-34
had commanded him.
30Next Moses took some of the anointing oil and some of the blood that was on the al- 8:30
tar, and he sprinkled them on Aaron and his garments and on his sons and their garments. Exod 29:21
In this way, he made Aaron and his sons and their garments holy. 8:31
31Then Moses said to Aaron and his sons, "Boil the remaining meat of the offerings at Exod 29:31-32
the Tabernacle entrance, and eat it there, along with the bread that is in the basket of of- 8:32 Exod 29:34
ferings for the ordination, just as I commanded when I said, 'Aaron and his sons will eat it.' 8:33
32Any meat or bread that is left over must then be burned up. 33You must not leave the Exod 29:35
Tabernacle entrance for seven days, for that is when the ordination ceremony will be com- 8:34
pleted. 34Everything we have done today was commanded by the LORD in order to purify Heb 7:16
you, making you right with Him.* 35Now stay at the entrance of the Tabernacle day and 8:35
night for seven days, and do everything the LORD requires. If you fail to do this, you will Num 3:7; 9:19
die, for this is what the LORD has commanded." 36So Aaron and his sons did everything the Deut 11:1 1 Kgs 2:3
LORD had commanded through Moses. Ezek 48:11

THE PRIESTS BEGIN THEIR WORK

9 After the ordination ceremony, on the eighth day, Moses called together Aaron and
his sons and the elders of Israel. 2He said to Aaron, "Take a young bull for a sin offer-
ing and a ram for a burnt offering, both without defects, and present them to the LORD.
3Then tell the Israelites, 'Take a male goat for a sin offering, and take a calf and a lamb, 9:3
both a year old and without defects, for a burnt offering. 4Also take a bull* and a ram for a Lev 4:3
peace offering and flour moistened with olive oil for a grain offering. Present all these of- 9:4
ferings to the LORD because the LORD will appear to you today.'" Exod 29:43
5So the people presented all these things at the entrance of the Tabernacle,* just as
Moses had commanded. Then the whole community came forward and stood before the
LORD. 6And Moses said, "This is what the LORD has commanded you to do so that the glory 9:6
of the LORD may appear to you." Lev 9:23

8:34 Or *to make atonement for you.* 9:4 Or *cow;* also in 9:18, 19. 9:5 Hebrew *Tent of Meeting;* also in 9:23.

▸ SALVATION

8:35 Seven days to change. Psychologists tell us it takes 30 days of alternate behavior to break a bad habit. Just as the passage of time is an important element in developing a new lifestyle, so it was important in Aaron and his sons' transition to being priests. Their lives would never be the same after their ordination; to immerse them in their new realities, God had them perform their ordination sacrifices for seven straight days. The priesthood was not a job; it was a lifestyle. Similarly, when we become a Christian, we must do more than adopt a new set of behaviors: we must transition to a new way of life—a new way of thinking, feeling, and behaving (Colossians 2:10). (***See Salvation****> Receiving> Results> New life,* TopicGuide page A23.)

▸ ADOPTION

9:6 The presence of the Lord. Part of Israel's religious ritual was to appear before the Lord on a regular basis (Exodus 23:17). Sacrifices and worship were to be offered, and then the glorious presence of the Lord would appear to the people (Psalm 63:2). Often, the presence of the Lord was manifested in the form of fire, representing the consuming nature of God's power and holiness (Leviticus 9:24). In the New Testament, God's glory was primarily and preeminently revealed in the person of Jesus Christ, "and we have seen his glory, the glory of the Father's one and only Son" (John 1:14). (***See Adoption****> With Christ> Heirs of God> Our inheritance includes sharing His glory,* TopicGuide page A36.)

9:7 [7]Then Moses said to Aaron, "Come to the altar and sacrifice your sin offering and your
Heb 5:1-3; 7:27 burnt offering to purify yourself and the people. Then present the offerings of the people
9:9 to purify them, making them right with the LORD,* just as He has commanded."
Lev 4:6-7 [8]So Aaron went to the altar and slaughtered the calf as a sin offering for himself. [9]His
sons brought him the blood, and he dipped his finger in it and put it on the horns of the al-
tar. He poured out the rest of the blood at the base of the altar. [10]Then he burned on the al-
tar the fat, the kidneys, and the long lobe of the liver from the sin offering, just as the LORD
had commanded Moses. [11]The meat and the hide, however, he burned outside the camp.
[12]Next Aaron slaughtered the animal for the burnt offering. His sons brought him the
blood, and he splattered it against all sides of the altar. [13]Then they handed him each
piece of the burnt offering, including the head, and he burned them on the altar. [14]Then
he washed the internal organs and the legs and burned them on the altar along with the
rest of the burnt offering.
9:15 [15]Next Aaron presented the offerings of the people. He slaughtered the people's goat
Lev 4:27-31; 9:3 and presented it as an offering for their sin, just as he had first done with the offering for
9:16 Lev 1:3, 10 his own sin. [16]Then he presented the burnt offering and sacrificed it in the prescribed way.
9:17 [17]He also presented the grain offering, burning a handful of the flour mixture on the altar,
Lev 2:1-3; 3:5 in addition to the regular burnt offering for the morning.
9:18 [18]Then Aaron slaughtered the bull and the ram for the people's peace offering. His sons
Lev 3:1-11 brought him the blood, and he splattered it against all sides of the altar. [19]Then he took the
9:19 fat of the bull and the ram—the fat of the broad tail and from around the internal organs—
Lev 3:9 9:21 along with the kidneys and the long lobes of the livers. [20]He placed these fat portions on top
Lev 7:30, 32 of the breasts of these animals and burned them on the altar. [21]Aaron then lifted up the
breasts and right thighs as a special offering to the LORD, just as Moses had commanded.
9:22 [22]After that, Aaron raised his hands toward the people and blessed them. Then, after pre-
Num 6:24-26 senting the sin offering, the burnt offering, and the peace offering, he stepped down from
9:23 the altar. [23]Then Moses and Aaron went into the Tabernacle, and when they came back out,
Num 16:19, 42 they blessed the people again, and the glory of the LORD appeared to the whole community.
9:24 [24]Fire blazed forth from the LORD's presence and consumed the burnt offering and the fat on
1 Kgs 18:38 the altar. When the people saw this, they shouted with joy and fell face down on the ground.

THE SIN OF NADAB AND ABIHU

10:1 Exod 6:23 **10** Aaron's sons Nadab and Abihu put coals of fire in their incense burners and sprin-
Num 3:2 kled incense over them. In this way, they disobeyed the LORD by burning before

9:7 Or *to make atonement for them.*

▸ ADOPTION
9:22 Tangible blessings. Sometimes we close our letters or e-mails with "Blessings." Or we say "God bless you" when parting from a friend. What does it mean to bless another? The root idea is to enrich or endow another; to gift them with something. When we say "God bless you," we are expressing a hope or prayer that God will enrich that person's life. But when Aaron blessed the people, he was speaking, as high priest, for God. He probably spoke the blessing recorded in Numbers 6:24-26, which assured covenant keepers of God's protection, grace, favor, and peace. The New Testament tells us that Christians have received all those provisions as well—and more (Ephesians 1:3). (***See Adoption***> *With Christ> Redemption> Every spiritual blessing in the heavenlies,* TopicGuide page A36.)

9:23-24 This was not the first or the last time God's presence was accompanied by fire. God first called Moses to leadership from a burning bush (Exodus 3:2-4). Later when Solomon completed the Temple, the permanent settling place for the Tabernacle, a fire appeared and burned up the offerings and sacrifices (2 Chronicles 7:1-3). In the New Testament when the Holy Spirit came in special power upon the believers, something like flames appeared and settled on each of them. Now all believers could enjoy the same power of the Holy Spirit that was previously reserved for only a few (Acts 2:17-18; Joel 2:28-29).

10:1 Incense played an important role in the Tabernacle (and later the Temple). Each morning the priest would burn the special incense, which represented the prayers of God's people (Psalm 141:2; Revelation 5:8). The incense used was a specific recipe and was to be used only in liturgical worship.

10:1 We don't know exactly what Nadab and Abihu did wrong in offering their incense. Very specific guidelines had been given as to where the coals should come from (Leviticus 16:12), when the incense should be burned (Exodus 30:7-9), and how the priest should serve (Leviticus 10:9). These two young priests may have broken any of these guidelines. Many believe they may have been drunk, since the admonition for sobriety comes on the heels of this account. Whatever they did or did not do, they dishonored God in a way that required immediate punishment.

Him the wrong kind of fire, different than He had commanded. 2 So fire blazed forth from 10:2 Num 26:61
the LORD's presence and burned them up, and they died there before the LORD.
3 Then Moses said to Aaron, "This is what the LORD meant when He said, 10:3 Exod 19:22 Ezek 38:16

'I will display My holiness
through those who come near Me.
I will display My glory
before all the people.'"

And Aaron was silent.
4 Then Moses called for Mishael and Elzaphan, Aaron's cousins, the sons of Aaron's uncle 10:4 Exod 6:18
Uzziel. He said to them, "Come forward and carry away the bodies of your relatives from in
front of the sanctuary to a place outside the camp." 5 So they came forward and picked them
up by their garments and carried them out of the camp, just as Moses had commanded.
6 Then Moses said to Aaron and his sons Eleazar and Ithamar, "Do not show grief by 10:6 Lev 21:1-15
leaving your hair uncombed* or by tearing your clothes. If you do, you will die, and the Num 1:53; 16:22
LORD's anger will strike the whole community of Israel. However, the rest of the Israelites, Josh 7:1
your relatives, may mourn because of the LORD's fiery destruction of Nadab and Abihu.
7 But you must not leave the entrance of the Tabernacle* or you will die, for you have been 10:7 Lev 21:12
anointed with the LORD's anointing oil." So they did as Moses commanded.

INSTRUCTIONS FOR PRIESTLY CONDUCT

8 Then the LORD said to Aaron, 9 "You and your descendants must never drink wine or any other 10:9 Ezek 44:21
alcoholic drink before going into the Tabernacle. If you do, you will die. This is a permanent law 10:10
for you, and it must be observed from generation to generation. 10 You must distinguish between Lev 11:47
what is sacred and what is common, between what is ceremonially unclean and what is clean. Ezek 22:26
11 And you must teach the Israelites all the decrees that the LORD has given them through Moses." 10:11 Deut 33:10
12 Then Moses said to Aaron and his remaining sons, Eleazar and Ithamar, "Take what is 10:12
left of the grain offering after a portion has been presented as a special gift to the LORD, Lev 21:22
and eat it beside the altar. Make sure it contains no yeast, for it is most holy. 13 You must Num 3:2
eat it in a sacred place, for it has been given to you and your descendants as your portion
of the special gifts presented to the LORD. These are the commands I have been given. 10:14
14 But the breast and thigh that were lifted up as a special offering may be eaten in any Lev 7:28-36
place that is ceremonially clean. These parts have been given to you and your descen- 10:15
dants as your portion of the peace offerings presented by the people of Israel. 15 You must Lev 7:30-34

10:6 Or *by uncovering your heads.* 10:7 Hebrew *Tent of Meeting;* also in 10:9.

▶ SPIRITUAL WARFARE

10:2 Worship is serious business. Earlier, the glory of the Lord was revealed in a way the people could clearly appreciate at the conclusion of the priestly ordination: Fire came out from the presence of the Lord and consumed the sacrifices (Leviticus 9:24). Here, the glory of the Lord was again revealed by fire, but this time in judgment. Taking the lives of two of Aaron's sons was a way for God to reaffirm His holiness—and to reaffirm that perfect obedience was expected. But it also served as a reminder of the destructive power of sin. The consequences of sin, even a single one, are more destructive than any natural disaster or illness or sorrow we can imagine. Christians must learn obedience and avoid sin (Colossians 2:6). (***See Spiritual Warfare****> Resisting Sin and Evil> Consequences> Of Disobedience> Death,* TopicGuide page A46.)

10:2 See 2 Samuel 6:3-8 for another example of God's wrath revealed through immediate punishment for sin.

▶ WORSHIP

10:9-10 Holy and ordinary. Aaron and his sons were not allowed to drink alcoholic beverages before serving in their official capacity in the Tabernacle. This was not because alcohol was evil, for wine was offered to God and given to the priests on a regular basis (Leviticus 23:13). Going regularly into the presence of God's holiness meant the priests had to be sober and aware of every detail. Because Christians live in the presence of God at all times, we must learn to be sober and careful in our worship, only performing that which God has requested, allowed, or required. (***See Worship****> NT> Our Role> Holiness> Christian life means being transformed,* TopicGuide page A32.)

10:10 Many similarities exist between the ancient Israelites and people today; we all live, die, eat, dream, struggle in our relationships, and so forth. But a unique aspect of their lives was the constant struggle for ceremonial cleanliness. We do not have a sense of wondering if a certain item has touched a dead person, or if a certain object has mold on it (Leviticus 13). This required an intense, watchful attitude. The closest contemporary equivalent is our vigilant attitude toward the devil and his schemes (2 Thessalonians 3:3).

PURE AS SUGAR

CHILDREN WILL DO the strangest things.

While his family was out for a picnic, a little boy noticed the small, pink, plastic container sitting on the table. Jason stuck his finger into the container and held it up. It was coated with grains of sugar. Yum! He licked off the white crumbs. As children will do, he impulsively took the container, crawled off the bench, and ducked under the table. There he poured handfuls of soft dirt into the sugar.

After a while, he stuck his finger into the sugar for another taste, but this time, his finger came out stuck with sugar and dirt. It tasted horrible! Crying, he brought the container to his mother. "Mama, take the dirt out!"

But there was nothing to do but pour it out. The sugar was ruined.

Long ago, God created perfect human beings. But because of our unbelief, we sinned. We are now filled with sin, every part of us contaminated by it, and therefore unable to be used for the purpose God originally created us for. Does He simply pour us out? No, for He has a way to clean us up.

The first step to holy living is to confess every sin to God. Only He can cleanse us (1 John 1:9). Ask Him to search your heart and reveal those corners of your life that displease Him. Second, commit yourself to fleeing from temptation whenever and wherever it arises. Finally, turn away from self-centered living and devote yourself to Him in worship and service. Fulfilling His holy purpose for your life will bring joy and satisfaction, and one day you'll have the privilege of standing before God, pure and holy, never to sin again (Revelation 21:4).

lift up the thigh and breast as a special offering to the LORD, along with the fat of the special
gifts. These parts will belong to you and your descendants as your permanent right, just as
the LORD has commanded."

16 Moses then asked them what had happened to the goat of the sin offering. When he dis- 10:16
covered it had been burned up, he became very angry with Eleazar and Ithamar, Aaron's re- Lev 9:3
maining sons. 17 "Why didn't you eat the sin offering in the sacred area?" he demanded. "It is a 10:17
holy offering! The LORD has given it to you to remove the guilt of the community and to purify Lev 6:24-30
the people, making them right with the LORD.* 18 Since the animal's blood was not brought into 10:18 Lev 6:26, 30
the Holy Place, you should have eaten the meat in the sacred area as I ordered you."

19 Then Aaron answered Moses, "Today my sons presented both their sin offering and 10:19
their burnt offering to the LORD. And yet this tragedy has happened to me. If I had eaten Lev 9:8, 12
the people's sin offering on such a tragic day as this, would the LORD have been pleased?"
20 And when Moses heard this, he was satisfied.

CEREMONIALLY CLEAN AND UNCLEAN ANIMALS

11 Then the LORD said to Moses and Aaron, 2 "Give the following instructions to the 11:1-23
people of Israel. //Deut 14:3-20

"Of all the land animals, these are the ones you may use for food. 3 You may eat any an-
imal that has completely split hooves and chews the cud. 4 You may not, however, eat the 11:4
following animals* that have split hooves or that chew the cud, but not both. The camel Acts 10:14
chews the cud but does not have split hooves, so it is ceremonially unclean for you. 5 The
hyrax* chews the cud but does not have split hooves, so it is unclean. 6 The hare chews the
cud but does not have split hooves, so it is unclean. 7 The pig has evenly split hooves but 11:7
does not chew the cud, so it is unclean. 8 You may not eat the meat of these animals or Isa 65:4; 66:3, 17
even touch their carcasses. They are ceremonially unclean for you. 11:8

9 "Of all the marine animals, these are ones you may use for food. You may eat anything Heb 9:10
from the water if it has both fins and scales, whether taken from salt water or from 11:9-10
streams. 10 But you must never eat animals from the sea or from rivers that do not have Deut 14:9-10
both fins and scales. They are detestable to you. This applies both to little creatures that
live in shallow water and to all creatures that live in deep water. 11 They will always be de-
testable to you. You must never eat their meat or even touch their dead bodies. 12 Any ma-
rine animal that does not have both fins and scales is detestable to you.

13 "These are the birds that are detestable to you. You must never eat them: the griffon 11:13
vulture, the bearded vulture, the black vulture, 14 the kite, falcons of all kinds, 15 ravens of Deut 14:12-19

10:17 Or *to make atonement for the people before the LORD.* **11:4** The identification of some of the animals, birds, and insects in this chapter is uncertain. **11:5** Or *coney,* or *rock badger.*

▶ HOLINESS

10:20 Patient leadership. Leaders should manifest many positive character traits, not the least of which are patience and understanding. Moses was a great leader and a spiritual giant. Both qualities were demonstrated when Aaron's two remaining sons failed to carry out a particular part of the sacrifice correctly. Moses became angry, but after receiving an explanation from Aaron, he relented. There was no rebellion or deceit involved—it appeared to be an honest mistake (verse 19). Not just leaders, but all Christians are filled with the Holy Spirit (Acts 6:3), the result of which is patience (Galatians 5:22-23). Whoever you lead, from children to employees, make sure you lead patiently. (***See Holiness**> Law and Grace> Law> Leaders and followers,* TopicGuide page A41.)

▶ BIBLE

11:2 Mixed company. When God rescued the Hebrews from slavery in Egypt, He purposed that they should be a separate people from the surrounding nations. Because they were going to live among unholy (unclean) nations, certain regulations were established to help them keep their distance from foreigners. Among other health benefits, food laws kept the Israelites from sitting down in a fellowship setting over a meal and becoming intimate with those who did not worship God. Food laws were for ancient Israel—we are free to follow them if we wish, but they are not required today (Acts 10:9-22). More importantly, watch the relationships you have with unbelievers. Make sure you do not stray into the kind of intimacy that will lead you into sin. (***See Bible**> Unity> God's Message> Separation from the world,* TopicGuide page A10.)

11:13-19 The birds, or flying animals, in this list are mostly carnivorous, and some are scavengers. They either feed on dead animals or, as with the hoopoe, they forage for insects in the ground. Eating the meat of these birds would be only one step removed from eating unclean bugs or animals that were already dead, both strict prohibitions among the Israelites (Leviticus 11:20-27). It makes sense, then, that they would be forbidden. While this prohibition aided in the Israelites' health and sanitation, their obedience to the command aided in their sanctification.

all kinds, [16]the eagle owl, the short-eared owl, the seagull, hawks of all kinds, [17]the little
owl, the cormorant, the great owl, [18]the barn owl, the desert owl, the Egyptian vulture,
[19]the stork, herons of all kinds, the hoopoe, and the bat.
[20]"You must not eat winged insects that walk along the ground; they are detestable to
you. [21]You may, however, eat winged insects that walk along the ground and have
11:22 jointed legs so they can jump. [22]The insects you are permitted to eat include all kinds of
Matt 3:4 locusts, bald locusts, crickets, and grasshoppers. [23]All other winged insects that walk along
Mark 1:6 the ground are detestable to you.
[24]"The following creatures will make you ceremonially unclean. If any of you touch
11:25 their carcasses, you will be defiled until evening. [25]If you pick up their carcasses, you must
Lev 11:28, 40 wash your clothes, and you will remain defiled until evening.
Num 19:11-13 [26]"Any animal that has split hooves that are not evenly divided or that does not chew the
cud is unclean for you. If you touch the carcass of such an animal, you will be defiled. [27]Of the
animals that walk on all fours, those that have paws are unclean. If you touch the carcass of
such an animal, you will be defiled until evening. [28]If you pick up its carcass, you must wash
your clothes, and you will remain defiled until evening. These animals are unclean for you.
[29]"Of the small animals that scurry along the ground, these are unclean for you: the mole
rat, the rat, large lizards of all kinds, [30]the gecko, the monitor lizard, the common lizard, the
sand lizard, and the chameleon. [31]All these small animals are unclean for you. If any of you
11:32 touch the dead body of such an animal, you will be defiled until evening. [32]If such an animal
Lev 15:12 dies and falls on something, that object will be unclean. This is true whether the object is
made of wood, cloth, leather, or burlap. Whatever its use, you must dip it in water, and it will
remain defiled until evening. After that, it will be ceremonially clean and may be used again.
11:33 [33]"If such an animal falls into a clay pot, everything in the pot will be defiled, and the pot
Lev 6:28 must be smashed. [34]If the water from such a container spills on any food, the food will be
defiled. And any beverage in such a container will be defiled. [35]Any object on which the
carcass of such an animal falls will be defiled. If it is an oven or hearth, it must be de-
stroyed, for it is defiled, and you must treat it accordingly.
[36]"However, if the carcass of such an animal falls into a spring or a cistern, the water will
still be clean. But anyone who touches the carcass will be defiled. [37]If the carcass falls on
seed grain to be planted in the field, the seed will still be considered clean. [38]But if the
seed is wet when the carcass falls on it, the seed will be defiled.
[39]"If an animal you are permitted to eat dies and you touch its carcass, you will be de-
11:40 filed until evening. [40]If you eat any of its meat or carry away its carcass, you must wash
Lev 11:25; 17:15 Deut 14:21 your clothes, and you will remain defiled until evening.
Ezek 4:14; 44:31 [41]"All small animals that scurry along the ground are detestable, and you must never eat
11:41 them. [42]This includes all animals that slither along on their bellies, as well as those with four
Lev 11:29 legs and those with many feet. All such animals that scurry along the ground are detestable,
11:44-45 and you must never eat them. [43]Do not defile yourselves by touching them. You must not
Exod 6:7; 19:6 Lev 19:2 make yourselves ceremonially unclean because of them. [44]For I am the LORD your God. You
1 Thes 4:7 must consecrate yourselves and be holy, because I am holy. So do not defile yourselves
*1 Pet 1:16 with any of these small animals that scurry along the ground. [45]For I, the LORD, am the One

11:21-22 The four varieties of grasshoppers listed here—locusts, crickets, bald locusts (katydids), and grasshoppers—were primarily vegetarian. Because of the damage a swarm could impose on crops, locusts were often used as symbols of destruction in the Old Testament. The prophet Joel used the image of locusts to predict the attack of a great army. Nevertheless, these insects were a part of the ancient Middle Eastern diet. Most notably, John the Baptist had the distinction of subsisting on locusts and wild honey (Mark 1:6). The insects were (and sometimes still are) eaten raw or roasted. Sometimes they were ground into powder to make a kind of flour or paste mixed with honey.

▸ GOD

11:45 God is holy. God's reason for the food regulations in Leviticus 11 comes at the end of the chapter: "Therefore, you must be holy because I am holy" (11:45). The word *holy* means "set apart" or "separate." Because God was set apart and different from the gods of the nations surrounding Israel, His people needed to be set apart (holy) as well. They were to be a reflection of the God they served. This is true for Christians today. In the same ways that Jesus stood out in His world, we need to stand out in ours and spread His holy fragrance (2 Corinthians 2:15). (***See God****> God's Attributes> Holy> His holiness is the standard for believers' behavior,* TopicGuide page A16.)

who brought you up from the land of Egypt, that I might be your God. Therefore, you must
be holy because I am holy.
46"These are the instructions regarding land animals, birds, marine creatures, and ani-
mals that scurry along the ground. 47By these instructions you will know what is unclean 11:47 Lev 10:10
and clean, and which animals may be eaten and which may not be eaten." Ezek 22:26; 44:23

PURIFICATION AFTER CHILDBIRTH

12 The LORD said to Moses, "Give the following instructions to the people of Isra-
el. 2If a woman becomes pregnant and gives birth to a son, she will be cere- 12:2
monially unclean for seven days, just as she is unclean during her menstrual period. Lev 15:19; 18:19
3On the eighth day the boy's foreskin must be circumcised. 4After waiting thirty-three 12:3
days, she will be purified from the bleeding of childbirth. During this time of purifica- Gen 17:12-14
tion, she must not touch anything that is set apart as holy. And she must not enter the
sanctuary until her time of purification is over. 5If a woman gives birth to a daughter,
she will be ceremonially unclean for two weeks, just as she is unclean during her
menstrual period. After waiting sixty-six days, she will be purified from the bleeding
of childbirth.
6"When the time of purification is completed for either a son or a daughter, the woman 12:6
must bring a one-year-old lamb for a burnt offering and a young pigeon or turtledove for a Luke 2:22
purification offering. She must bring her offerings to the priest at the entrance of the Tab-
ernacle.* 7The priest will then present them to the LORD to purify her.* Then she will be cer-
emonially clean again after her bleeding at childbirth. These are the instructions for a
woman after the birth of a son or a daughter.
8"If a woman cannot afford to bring a lamb, she must bring two turtledoves or two 12:8
young pigeons. One will be for the burnt offering and the other for the purification offer- Lev 5:7
ing. The priest will sacrifice them to purify her, and she will be ceremonially clean." Luke 2:24

12:6 Hebrew *Tent of Meeting.* 12:7 Or *to make atonement for her;* also in 12:8.

▸ WORSHIP
12:2 Naturally unclean. Some women are troubled by the idea of being described as unclean by God following childbirth. After all, wasn't it God who commanded married couples to be fruitful and multiply (Genesis 1:28)? Understanding the meaning of "unclean" is critical. The term doesn't mean dirty or unworthy. It simply meant that a woman's normal lifestyle had been interrupted by the very physical act of childbirth. Until her body resumed its normal state, she was not to enter the sanctuary. Men, too, were forbidden to participate in liturgical worship due to some natural body functions (Deuteronomy 23:10). The need for ceremonial cleanness before entering God's presence reminds us that in our natural state we remain cut off from God, both unclean and cursed (Romans 3:23). (***See Worship****> OT> God's Supremacy> Required personal and ritual cleanliness,* TopicGuide page A27.)

12:2 The prohibitions regarding blood—in this case from childbirth or menstruation—functioned on several levels. From the perspective of health, care with body fluids mattered. Blood was also considered the essence of life (Leviticus 17:11). On a spiritual level this set up the significance of the sacrifice of Christ—His life covers us, fills us, and raises us from spiritual death.

▸ WORSHIP
12:3 Circumcision and baptism. How do you define church membership? In the Old Testament, membership to the community was defined by whether you were in a covenant family. The leaders of the family were marked with circumcision as a sign that he and his family were members of God's covenant with Abraham (Genesis 17:12-13). In the New Covenant, men, women and children can bear the mark of membership in the covenant community—baptism. If you love Christ and have never been baptized, find a Bible-believing church and request the sign of baptism. Baptism does not save, but it does mark us as united to Christ and set apart from the world. (***See Worship****> NT> Sacraments> Baptism> Baptism identifies the believer with the community of faith,* TopicGuide page A34; ***Worship****> OT> Sacraments> Circumcision,* TopicGuide page A29.)

12:8 Before Moses communed with God on Mount Sinai, the people abstained from sexual relations and washed their clothes (Exodus 19:14-15). This taught them that people can't simply saunter into God's presence; we must prepare ourselves, fundamentally through faith in Christ's final sacrifice for sin (Romans 5:1).

▸ GOD
12:8 Offerings large and small. If a woman was unable to afford a lamb for the burnt offering, she could substitute a pigeon or a dove. After Jesus' birth, Mary and Joseph brought birds instead of a lamb for the offering (Luke 2:22-24). God was (and is) not as concerned about the size of our offerings as much as the motivation of the heart. God accepts and honors even our smallest acts of obedience when done with the right motive. (***See God****> Relationship> God Enables> Relationship with God requires a right heart,* TopicGuide page A14.)

SERIOUS SKIN DISEASES

13:2-3 **13** The LORD said to Moses and Aaron, 2"If anyone has a swelling or a rash or discol-
Lev 14:56 Deut 24:8 ored skin that might develop into a serious skin disease,* that person must be
brought to Aaron the priest or to one of his sons.* 3The priest will examine the affected
area of the skin. If the hair in the affected area has turned white and the problem appears
to be more than skin-deep, it is a serious skin disease, and the priest who examines it must
pronounce the person ceremonially unclean.
4"But if the affected area of the skin is only a white discoloration and does not appear to
be more than skin-deep, and if the hair on the spot has not turned white, the priest will
quarantine the person for seven days. 5On the seventh day the priest will make another
examination. If he finds the affected area has not changed and the problem has not
spread on the skin, the priest will quarantine the person for seven more days. 6On the sev-
enth day the priest will make another examination. If he finds the affected area has faded
and has not spread, the priest will pronounce the person ceremonially clean. It was only a
rash. The person's clothing must be washed, and the person will be ceremonially clean.
7But if the rash continues to spread after the person has been examined by the priest and
13:6 has been pronounced clean, the infected person must return to be examined again. 8If the
Lev 11:25 priest finds that the rash has spread, he must pronounce the person ceremonially unclean,
for it is indeed a skin disease.
9"Anyone who develops a serious skin disease must go to the priest for an examination.
13:10 10If the priest finds a white swelling on the skin, and some hair on the spot has turned
Num 12:10 white, and there is an open sore in the affected area, 11it is a chronic skin disease, and the
2 Kgs 5:27 priest must pronounce the person ceremonially unclean. In such cases the person need
not be quarantined, for it is obvious that the skin is defiled by the disease.
12"Now suppose the disease has spread all over the person's skin, covering the body
from head to foot. 13When the priest examines the infected person and finds that the dis-
ease covers the entire body, he will pronounce the person ceremonially clean. Since the
skin has turned completely white, the person is clean. 14But if any open sores appear, the
infected person will be pronounced ceremonially unclean. 15The priest must make this
pronouncement as soon as he sees an open sore, since open sores indicate the presence
13:16 of a skin disease. 16However, if the open sores heal and turn white like the rest of the skin,
Luke 5:12-14 the person must return to the priest 17for another examination. If the affected areas have
indeed turned white, the priest will then pronounce the person ceremonially clean by de-
claring, 'You are clean!'
13:18 18"If anyone has a boil on the skin that has started to heal, 19but a white swelling or a
Exod 9:9 reddish white spot develops in its place, that person must go to the priest to be examined.
20If the priest examines it and finds it to be more than skin-deep, and if the hair in the

13:2a Traditionally rendered *leprosy.* The Hebrew word used throughout this passage is used to describe various skin diseases. 13:2b Or *one of his descendants.*

13:1-9 The priests were the clearinghouses for much of Israelite culture, addressing the community's spiritual, civil, and medicinal needs. Before this formalization of the role of the priests, the heads of Israel's households likely handled many of these duties. The newly anointed Hebrew priests diagnosed disease, prescribed treatment, and then verified healing. While the Levites all tended to religious tasks, it was only those descended from Aaron that fulfilled the role of the priest.

13:2 Some translations render all skin conditions as leprosy, but the underlying term is broad, referring to a variety of skin disorders. The priests discerned how serious these were and then enforced health codes to protect the population. They did not heal the people of their diseases so much as recognize and measure the healing that took place.

▸ GOD

13:3 Sick and unclean. When reading these parts of Leviticus, it is tempting to question God's compassion—how could He call sick people unclean? God is communicating to His people that we are naturally "infected" with the fallen state of this world. Disease is another manifestation of the fallen state of the creation, with the earth itself groaning to be set free from the curse of sin (Romans 8:18-23). God's perspective on sickness is seen in Jesus, who had mercy on the sick. His example is what we must follow—mercy to those who are sick, even if it means making sure they know how sick they really are. (***See God**> God's Nature> Personality> Emotion> God is compassionate and loving,* TopicGuide page A14.)

affected area has turned white, the priest must pronounce the person ceremonially un-
clean. The boil has become a serious skin disease. 21 But if the priest finds no white hair on
the affected area and the problem appears to be no more than skin-deep and has faded,
the priest must quarantine the person for seven days. 22 If during that time the affected
area spreads on the skin, the priest must pronounce the person ceremonially unclean, be-
cause it is a serious disease. 23 But if the area grows no larger and does not spread, it is
merely the scar from the boil, and the priest will pronounce the person ceremonially clean.

24 "If anyone has suffered a burn on the skin and the burned area changes color, becom-
ing either reddish white or shiny white, 25 the priest must examine it. If he finds that the
hair in the affected area has turned white and the problem appears to be more than skin-
deep, a skin disease has broken out in the burn. The priest must then pronounce the per-
son ceremonially unclean, for it is clearly a serious skin disease. 26 But if the priest finds no
white hair on the affected area and the problem appears to be no more than skin-deep
and has faded, the priest must quarantine the infected person for seven days. 27 On the 13:27
seventh day the priest must examine the person again. If the affected area has spread on Lev 13:5
the skin, the priest must pronounce that person ceremonially unclean, for it is clearly a se-
rious skin disease. 28 But if the affected area has not changed or spread on the skin and has
faded, it is simply a swelling from the burn. The priest will then pronounce the person cer-
emonially clean, for it is only the scar from the burn.

29 "If anyone, either a man or woman, has a sore on the head or chin, 30 the priest must
examine it. If he finds it is more than skin-deep and has fine yellow hair on it, the priest
must pronounce the person ceremonially unclean. It is a scabby sore of the head or chin.
31 If the priest examines the scabby sore and finds that it is only skin-deep but there is no
black hair on it, he must quarantine the person for seven days. 32 On the seventh day the
priest must examine the sore again. If he finds that the scabby sore has not spread, and
there is no yellow hair on it, and it appears to be only skin-deep, 33 the person must shave 13:33
off all hair except the hair on the affected area. Then the priest must quarantine the person Lev 14:9
for another seven days. 34 On the seventh day he will examine the sore again. If it has not 13:34 Lev 14:8
spread and appears to be no more than skin-deep, the priest will pronounce the person
ceremonially clean. The person's clothing must be washed, and the person will be cere-
monially clean. 35 But if the scabby sore begins to spread after the person is pronounced
clean, 36 the priest must do another examination. If he finds that the sore has spread, the
priest does not need to look for yellow hair. The infected person is ceremonially unclean.
37 But if the color of the scabby sore does not change and black hair has grown on it, it has
healed. The priest will then pronounce the person ceremonially clean.

38 "If anyone, either a man or woman, has shiny white patches on the skin, 39 the priest
must examine the affected area. If he finds that the shiny patches are only pale white, this
is a harmless skin rash, and the person is ceremonially clean.

40 "If a man loses his hair and his head becomes bald, he is still ceremonially clean. 13:40
41 And if he loses hair on his forehead, he simply has a bald forehead; he is still clean. 2 Kgs 2:23 Isa 15:2
42 However, if a reddish white sore appears on the bald area at the top or back of his head, Ezek 29:18
this is a skin disease. 43 The priest must examine him, and if he finds swelling around the Amos 8:10
reddish white sore anywhere on the man's head and it looks like a skin disease, 44 the man
is indeed infected with a skin disease and is unclean. The priest must pronounce him cere- 13:45
monially unclean because of the sore on his head. Lam 4:15

45 "Those who suffer from a serious skin disease must tear their clothing and leave their Ezek 24:17, 22 Mic 3:7

13:45 Even into the first century, entire families lived and slept in a single room. This made contagious diseases very dangerous. Certain contagious diseases were so dangerous that the ill were removed from the general population. The description here—torn clothes, uncombed hair—was similar to the signs of mourning, for the sick had lost their place in their society. Unless they were healed, they were outcasts. In the New Testament, Jesus came upon ten lepers who recognized Him and, rather than cry out a warning cried out for mercy (Luke 17:11-14). Jesus commanded them to go to the priest (Leviticus 14:2), and as they obeyed Jesus, they were healed.

13:46 Num 5:1-4; 12:14 hair uncombed.* They must cover their mouth and call out, 'Unclean! Unclean!' 46As long
2 Kgs 7:3; 15:5 as the serious disease lasts, they will be ceremonially unclean. They must live in isolation
Luke 17:12 in their place outside the camp.

TREATMENT OF CONTAMINATED CLOTHING

47"Now suppose mildew* contaminates some woolen or linen clothing, 48woolen or linen
fabric, the hide of an animal, or anything made of leather. 49If the contaminated area in
the clothing, the animal hide, the fabric, or the leather article has turned greenish or red-
dish, it is contaminated with mildew and must be shown to the priest. 50After examining
13:51 the affected spot, the priest will put the article in quarantine for seven days. 51On the sev-
Lev 14:44 enth day the priest must inspect it again. If the contaminated area has spread, the clothing
or fabric or leather is clearly contaminated by a serious mildew and is ceremonially un-
clean. 52The priest must burn the item—the clothing, the woolen or linen fabric, or piece of
leather—for it has been contaminated by a serious mildew. It must be completely de-
stroyed by fire.

53"But if the priest examines it and finds that the contaminated area has not spread in
the clothing, the fabric, or the leather, 54the priest will order the object to be washed and
then quarantined for seven more days. 55Then the priest must examine the object again. If
he finds that the contaminated area has not changed color after being washed, even if it
did not spread, the object is defiled. It must be completely burned up, whether the con-
taminated spot* is on the inside or outside. 56But if the priest examines it and finds that the
contaminated area has faded after being washed, he must cut the spot from the clothing,
the fabric, or the leather. 57If the spot later reappears on the clothing, the fabric, or the
leather article, the mildew is clearly spreading, and the contaminated object must be
burned up. 58But if the spot disappears from the clothing, the fabric, or the leather article
after it has been washed, it must be washed again; then it will be ceremonially clean.

59"These are the instructions for dealing with mildew that contaminates woolen or linen
clothing or fabric or anything made of leather. This is how the priest will determine
whether these items are ceremonially clean or unclean."

CLEANSING FROM SKIN DISEASES

14:2 Matt 8:4 **14** And the LORD said to Moses, 2"The following instructions are for those seeking
Mark 1:40-45 ceremonial purification from a skin disease.* Those who have been healed must
Luke 5:12-14; 17:12-14 be brought to the priest, 3who will examine them at a place outside the camp. If the priest
14:3 Lev 13:46

13:45 Or *and uncover their heads.* 13:47 Traditionally rendered *leprosy.* The Hebrew term used throughout this passage is the same term used for the various skin diseases described in 13:1-46. 13:55 The meaning of the Hebrew is uncertain. 14:2 Traditionally rendered *leprosy;* see note on 13:2a.

▸ SALVATION

13:46 Outside the camp. Because skin infections (for example, leprosy) are contagious, Israel's law required infected persons to separate themselves from the congregation—to be quarantined to arrest the spread of the disease. Not only was it a medical safeguard, but there was a spiritual lesson as well: Anything unclean must be put away so as not to morally or spiritually infect others. The apostle Paul used this same strategy to protect the church at Corinth. He demanded that an unrepentant believer be expelled from the church so that his sin would not spread like yeast and infect the whole body (1 Corinthians 5:1-13). Sin is best dealt with immediately in our families and in the church. (***See Salvation***> *Receiving> How> Repent of/turn from sin,* TopicGuide page A22.)

13:47-48 In a modern world full of disinfectant and bleach, this much attention to mildew can seem to be overkill. Consider, though, that these people were a traveling nation. They were not living in brick homes, but tents made of hemp fabric and natural hides. Just as skin diseases could be easily spread and difficult to contain, so could a growing organism like mildew. Also, in keeping with the overall message of Leviticus, these laws trained the minds of the people to discern between clean and unclean, pure and impure, and thus holy and unholy.

14:2-7 The idea of purity was often on the mind of the ancient Israelite. Purification took several forms. Here, a rather elaborate ceremony was performed, sacrificing one bird and setting another free. At other times purification required a waiting period. Sometimes this period was just until sundown, such as when a person touched a dead animal (Leviticus 11:24). In other scenarios it was days or even weeks. Purification could also require washing the clothes or the person (Leviticus 15:1-6). Sometimes fire or special substances were required to complete the process (Numbers 31:23).

finds that someone has been healed of a serious skin disease, 4 he will perform a purification ceremony, using two live birds that are ceremonially clean, a stick of cedar,* some scarlet yarn, and a hyssop branch. 5 The priest will order that one bird be slaughtered over a clay pot filled with fresh water. 6 He will take the live bird, the cedar stick, the scarlet yarn, and the hyssop branch, and dip them into the blood of the bird that was slaughtered over the fresh water. 7 The priest will then sprinkle the blood of the dead bird seven times on the person being purified of the skin disease. When the priest has purified the person, he will release the live bird in the open field to fly away.

8 "The persons being purified must then wash their clothes, shave off all their hair, and bathe themselves in water. Then they will be ceremonially clean and may return to the camp. However, they must remain outside their tents for seven days. 9 On the seventh day they must again shave all the hair from their heads, including the hair of the beard and eyebrows. They must also wash their clothes and bathe themselves in water. Then they will be ceremonially clean.

10 "On the eighth day each person being purified must bring two male lambs and a one-year-old female lamb, all with no defects, along with a grain offering of six quarts* of choice flour moistened with olive oil, and a cup* of olive oil. 11 Then the officiating priest will present that person for purification, along with the offerings, before the LORD at the entrance of the Tabernacle.* 12 The priest will take one of the male lambs and the olive oil and present them as a guilt offering, lifting them up as a special offering before the LORD. 13 He will then slaughter the male lamb in the sacred area where sin offerings and burnt offerings are slaughtered. As with the sin offering, the guilt offering belongs to the priest. It is a most holy offering. 14 The priest will then take some of the blood of the guilt offering and apply it to the lobe of the right ear, the thumb of the right hand, and the big toe of the right foot of the person being purified.

15 "Then the priest will pour some of the olive oil into the palm of his own left hand. 16 He will dip his right finger into the oil in his palm and sprinkle some of it with his finger seven times before the LORD. 17 The priest will then apply some of the oil in his palm over the blood from the guilt offering that is on the lobe of the right ear, the thumb of the right hand, and the big toe of the right foot of the person being purified. 18 The priest will apply the oil remaining in his hand to the head of the person being purified. Through this process, the priest will purify* the person before the LORD.

19 "Then the priest must present the sin offering to purify the person who was cured of the skin disease. After that, the priest will slaughter the burnt offering 20 and offer it on the altar along with the grain offering. Through this process, the priest will purify the person who was healed, and the person will be ceremonially clean.

21 "But anyone who is too poor and cannot afford these offerings may bring one male lamb for a guilt offering, to be lifted up as a special offering for purification. The person must also bring two quarts* of choice flour moistened with olive oil for the grain offering

14:4 Lev 14:6, 49-52; Num 19:6
14:6 Ps 51:7
14:8 Lev 14:9; Num 8:7
14:9 Lev 13:33; 14:8; Num 6:9
14:10 Lev 23:12-13; Num 6:10; Matt 8:4; Mark 1:44; Luke 5:14
14:12 Exod 29:24
14:13 Lev 1:11-13; 6:24–7:10
14:14 Exod 29:20; Lev 8:23-24
14:20 Lev 14:8
14:21 Lev 5:7, 11; 12:8

14:4 Or *juniper;* also in 14:6, 49, 51. 14:10a Hebrew *3/10 of an ephah* [6.6 liters]. 14:10b Hebrew *1 log* [0.3 liters]; also in 14:21. 14:11 Hebrew *Tent of Meeting;* also in 14:23. 14:18 Or *will make atonement for;* similarly in 14:19, 20, 21, 29, 31, 53. 14:21 Hebrew *1/10 of an ephah* [2.2 liters].

▸ ADOPTION

14:4 Wild birds. While Leviticus 13 dealt with the separation of the unclean sick person from the community, chapter 14 deals with his restoration after healing. As part of the ceremony of restoration, two live birds were brought. The priest killed one as a symbol of life apart from God: Death is the natural outcome of disease and separation. The second bird was dipped in the blood of the first and set free—a picture of the new life restored to the now-clean person. The New Testament says we were dead in our sins without Christ (Ephesians 2:5), but that in Him we have new life (Colossians 2:12). "The old life is gone; a new life has begun!" (2 Corinthians 5:17). (*See* ***Adoption****> With Christ> Supernatural> All things are new,* TopicGuide page A37.)

14:14, 17 The people healed of a skin disease received the same anointing that Aaron and his sons had when they were ordained—the ear, the hand, and the foot (see Leviticus 8). This could symbolize a consecration of what they heard, what they did, and where they went. James the brother of Jesus wrote about using oil to anoint a believer in preparation for healing (James 5:14-15).

14:22 Lev 5:7 and a cup of olive oil. 22The offering must also include two turtledoves or two young pi-
geons, whichever the person can afford. One of the pair must be used for the sin offering
14:23 Lev 14:11 and the other for a burnt offering. 23On the eighth day of the purification ceremony, the
person being purified must bring the offerings to the priest in the LORD's presence at the
entrance of the Tabernacle. 24The priest will take the lamb for the guilt offering, along with
14:25 Lev 14:14 the olive oil, and lift them up as a special offering to the LORD. 25Then the priest will slaugh-
ter the lamb for the guilt offering. He will take some of its blood and apply it to the lobe of
the right ear, the thumb of the right hand, and the big toe of the right foot of the person be-
ing purified.

26"The priest will also pour some of the olive oil into the palm of his own left hand. 27He
will dip his right finger into the oil in his palm and sprinkle some of it seven times before
the LORD. 28The priest will then apply some of the oil in his palm over the blood from the
guilt offering that is on the lobe of the right ear, the thumb of the right hand, and the big
toe of the right foot of the person being purified. 29The priest will apply the oil remaining
in his hand to the head of the person being purified. Through this process, the priest will
purify the person before the LORD.

30"Then the priest will offer the two turtledoves or the two young pigeons, whichever
the person can afford. 31One of them is for a sin offering and the other for a burnt offering,
to be presented along with the grain offering. Through this process, the priest will purify
the person before the LORD. 32These are the instructions for purification for those who
have recovered from a serious skin disease but who cannot afford to bring the offerings
normally required for the ceremony of purification."

TREATMENT OF CONTAMINATED HOUSES

14:34 Gen 17:8 Num 32:22 Deut 7:1 33Then the LORD said to Moses and Aaron, 34"When you arrive in Canaan, the land I am
giving you as your own possession, I may contaminate some of the houses in your land
with mildew.* 35The owner of such a house must then go to the priest and say, 'It appears
14:35 Ps 91:10 that my house has some kind of mildew.' 36Before the priest goes in to inspect the house,
he must have the house emptied so nothing inside will be pronounced ceremonially un-
clean. 37Then the priest will go in and examine the mildew on the walls. If he finds green-
ish or reddish streaks and the contamination appears to go deeper than the wall's surface,
38the priest will step outside the door and put the house in quarantine for seven days.
39On the seventh day the priest must return for another inspection. If he finds that the mil-
14:39 Lev 13:5 dew on the walls of the house has spread, 40the priest must order that the stones from
those areas be removed. The contaminated material will then be taken outside the town
to an area designated as ceremonially unclean. 41Next the inside walls of the entire house
must be scraped thoroughly and the scrapings dumped in the unclean place outside the
town. 42Other stones will be brought in to replace the ones that were removed, and the
walls will be replastered.

43"But if the mildew reappears after all the stones have been replaced and the house

14:34 Traditionally rendered *leprosy;* see note on 13:47.

▸ GOD

14:23-34 Tabernacle entrance. Restoration of a diseased person to the community took eight days: the first seven days' rituals were outside the camp (14:3-9), and on the eighth day, offerings were made inside the camp at the entrance to the Tabernacle (14:10-20). Whether cleansing from physical disease or the disease of sin, the goal in both cases is restoration to holiness and fellowship. In 1 Corinthians 5 the apostle Paul ordered the removal of an unrepentant believer from the church at Corinth. He later directed the believer's forgiveness and restoration (2 Corinthians 2:5-11). Cleansing from sin is only complete when restoration follows repentance. (***See God*** *> God's Attributes> Forgiving> God's forgiveness leads believers to forgive others,* TopicGuide page A16.)

14:34 Canaan was the land that God promised to Abraham and his descendants, roughly equivalent to the united kingdom of Israel under Solomon. The area was originally named for the descendants of Canaan, Noah's grandson. By the time the Hebrews resettled their land, anyone who had come to live there was considered a Canaanite.

has been scraped and replastered, 44the priest must return and inspect the house again. If he finds that the mildew has spread, the walls are clearly contaminated with a serious mildew, and the house is defiled. 45It must be torn down, and all its stones, timbers, and plaster must be carried out of town to the place designated as ceremonially unclean. 46Those who enter the house during the period of quarantine will be ceremonially unclean until evening, 47and all who sleep or eat in the house must wash their clothing.

14:45 Lev 14:41-45

48"But if the priest returns for his inspection and finds that the mildew has not reappeared in the house after the fresh plastering, he will pronounce it clean because the mildew is clearly gone. 49To purify the house the priest must take two birds, a stick of cedar, some scarlet yarn, and a hyssop branch. 50He will slaughter one of the birds over a clay pot filled with fresh water. 51He will take the cedar stick, the hyssop branch, the scarlet yarn, and the live bird, and dip them into the blood of the slaughtered bird and into the fresh water. Then he will sprinkle the house seven times. 52When the priest has purified the house in exactly this way, 53he will release the live bird in the open fields outside the town. Through this process, the priest will purify the house, and it will be ceremonially clean.

14:49 Lev 14:4; Num 19:6

54"These are the instructions for dealing with serious skin diseases,* including scabby sores; 55and mildew,* whether on clothing or in a house; 56and a swelling on the skin, a rash, or discolored skin. 57This procedure will determine whether a person or object is ceremonially clean or unclean.

14:56 Lev 13:2

"These are the instructions regarding skin diseases and mildew."

BODILY DISCHARGES

15 The LORD said to Moses and Aaron, 2"Give the following instructions to the people of Israel.

15:2 Lev 22:4; Num 5:2

"Any man who has a bodily discharge is ceremonially unclean. 3This defilement is caused by his discharge, whether the discharge continues or stops. In either case the man is unclean. 4Any bed on which the man with the discharge lies and anything on which he sits will be ceremonially unclean. 5So if you touch the man's bed, you must wash your clothes and bathe yourself in water, and you will remain unclean until evening. 6If you sit where the man with the discharge has sat, you must wash your clothes and bathe yourself in water, and you will remain unclean until evening. 7If you touch the man with the discharge, you must wash your clothes and bathe yourself in water, and you will remain unclean until evening. 8If the man spits on you, you must wash your clothes and bathe yourself in water, and you will remain unclean until evening. 9Any saddle blanket on which the man rides will be ceremonially unclean. 10If you touch anything that was under the man, you will be unclean until evening. You must wash your clothes and bathe yourself in water, and you will remain unclean until evening. 11If the man touches you without first rinsing his hands, you must wash your clothes and bathe yourself in water, and you will remain unclean until evening. 12Any clay pot the man touches must be broken, and any wooden utensil he touches must be rinsed with water.

15:12 Lev 6:28; 11:32-33

13"When the man with the discharge is healed, he must count off seven days for the period of purification. Then he must wash his clothes and bathe himself in fresh water, and he will be ceremonially clean. 14On the eighth day he must get two turtledoves or two young pigeons and come before the LORD at the entrance of the Tabernacle* and give his offerings to the priest. 15The priest will offer one bird for a sin offering and the other for a

15:13 Lev 15:28

15:15 Lev 14:30-31

14:54 Traditionally rendered *leprosy;* see note on 13:2a. 14:55 Traditionally rendered *leprosy;* see note on 13:47.
15:14 Hebrew *Tent of Meeting;* also in 15:29.

15:2 This discharge may very well be a description of gonorrhea or a similar condition. While to the modern mind this kind of condition would be more dangerous than a skin condition, it was treated here with less severity. Also, to the modern mind, these commands may seem to concern only hygiene, but for the Israelites they were religious guidelines as well. The people were learning about the holiness of God by way of the cleanliness of their community.

burnt offering. Through this process, the priest will purify* the man before the LORD for his
discharge.
15:16 16“Whenever a man has an emission of semen, he must bathe his entire body in water,
Lev 22:4 Deut 23:10-11 and he will remain ceremonially unclean until the next evening.* 17Any clothing or leather
with semen on it must be washed in water, and it will remain unclean until evening.
15:18 18After a man and a woman have sexual intercourse, they must each bathe in water, and
1 Sam 21:4 they will remain unclean until the next evening.
15:19 19“Whenever a woman has her menstrual period, she will be ceremonially unclean for
Lev 12:2 seven days. Anyone who touches her during that time will be unclean until evening.
20Anything on which the woman lies or sits during the time of her period will be unclean.
21If any of you touch her bed, you must wash your clothes and bathe yourself in water,
and you will remain unclean until evening. 22If you touch any object she has sat on, you
must wash your clothes and bathe yourself in water, and you will remain unclean until
15:24 evening. 23This includes her bed or any other object she has sat on; you will be unclean
Lev 18:19; 20:18 until evening if you touch it. 24If a man has sexual intercourse with her and her blood
Ezek 18:6 touches him, her menstrual impurity will be transmitted to him. He will remain unclean for
seven days, and any bed on which he lies will be unclean.
15:25 Matt 9:20 25“If a woman has a flow of blood for many days that is unrelated to her menstrual pe-
Mark 5:25 riod, or if the blood continues beyond the normal period, she is ceremonially unclean. As
Luke 8:43-44 during her menstrual period, the woman will be unclean as long as the discharge contin-
ues. 26Any bed she lies on and any object she sits on during that time will be unclean, just
as during her normal menstrual period. 27If any of you touch these things, you will be cer-
emonially unclean. You must wash your clothes and bathe yourself in water, and you will
remain unclean until evening.
28“When the woman’s bleeding stops, she must count off seven days. Then she will
be ceremonially clean. 29On the eighth day she must bring two turtledoves or two young
15:30 pigeons and present them to the priest at the entrance of the Tabernacle. 30The priest
Lev 5:7; 14:22 will offer one for a sin offering and the other for a burnt offering. Through this process,
the priest will purify her before the LORD for the ceremonial impurity caused by her
bleeding.
15:31 31“This is how you will guard the people of Israel from ceremonial uncleanness. Other-
Num 5:3; 19:13, 20 wise they would die, for their impurity would defile My Tabernacle that stands among
them. 32These are the instructions for dealing with anyone who has a bodily discharge—a
man who is unclean because of an emission of semen 33or a woman during her menstrual
period. It applies to any man or woman who has a bodily discharge, and to a man who has
sexual intercourse with a woman who is ceremonially unclean.”

15:15 Or *will make atonement for;* also in 15:30. 15:16 Hebrew *until evening;* also in 15:18.

15:19 Even before these laws were instituted, there were concessions made for a menstruating woman. Genesis 31:28-35 records an account when Rachel’s tent was searched and she remained seated on her camel saddle with the excuse, “Please, sir, forgive me if I don’t get up for you. I’m having my monthly period.” Her father did not require her to move.

▶ PURPOSE

15:25 Discharges of blood. Temporary and chronic discharges of blood or bodily fluids from men and women rendered them ceremonially unclean. As with the earlier regulations regarding postpartum uncleanness, God is not condemning that which is normal and unavoidable. Rather, again He compares that which is earthy and physical with that which is pure and spiritual, teaching the Israelites that His presence requires the latter. A woman with a chronic discharge of blood touched Jesus’ robe, and she was made clean by faith in Him. (Matthew 9:20-27) (***See Purpose****> God’s Deeds> Special Acts> Miracles> Jesus> Healing the woman with an issue of blood,* TopicGuide page A53.)

▶ GOD

15:31 Goodness revealed by the worst. Can bad art teach us about beauty? Can darkness reveal the brightness of light? The Old Covenant laws of uncleanness used human physical defects and processes as a contrast with God’s spiritual perfection (Hebrews 13:4). God doesn’t reject people with handicaps or illness, but their predicament is an illustration of how outside of a life of repentance and belief, moral failings cut us off from God (Ephesians 2:1-2). Seek God’s healing touch for your body and soul today. (***See God****> Relationship> God Enables> Relationship with God requires purity,* TopicGuide page A14.)

THE DAY OF ATONEMENT

16 The LORD spoke to Moses after the death of Aaron's two sons, who died after they
entered the LORD's presence and burned the wrong kind of fire before Him. 2 The
LORD said to Moses, "Warn your brother, Aaron, not to enter the Most Holy Place behind the
inner curtain whenever he chooses; if he does, he will die. For the Ark's cover—the place of
atonement—is there, and I Myself am present in the cloud above the atonement cover.
3 "When Aaron enters the sanctuary area, he must follow these instructions fully. He
must bring a young bull for a sin offering and a ram for a burnt offering. 4 He must put on
his linen tunic and the linen undergarments worn next to his body. He must tie the linen
sash around his waist and put the linen turban on his head. These are sacred garments, so
he must bathe himself in water before he puts them on. 5 Aaron must take from the com-
munity of Israel two male goats for a sin offering and a ram for a burnt offering.
6 "Aaron will present his own bull as a sin offering to purify himself and his family, mak-
ing them right with the LORD.* 7 Then he must take the two male goats and present them to
the LORD at the entrance of the Tabernacle.* 8 He is to cast sacred lots to determine which
goat will be reserved as an offering to the LORD and which will carry the sins of the people
to the wilderness of Azazel. 9 Aaron will then present as a sin offering the goat chosen by
lot for the LORD. 10 The other goat, the scapegoat chosen by lot to be sent away, will be kept
alive, standing before the LORD. When it is sent away to Azazel in the wilderness, the peo-
ple will be purified and made right with the LORD.*
11 "Aaron will present his own bull as a sin offering to purify himself and his family, mak-
ing them right with the LORD. After he has slaughtered the bull as a sin offering, 12 he will fill
an incense burner with burning coals from the altar that stands before the LORD. Then he
will take two handfuls of fragrant powdered incense and will carry the burner and the in-
cense behind the inner curtain. 13 There in the LORD's presence he will put the incense on
the burning coals so that a cloud of incense will rise over the Ark's cover—the place of
atonement—that rests on the Ark of the Covenant.* If he follows these instructions, he will
not die. 14 Then he must take some of the blood of the bull, dip his finger in it, and sprinkle
it on the east side of the atonement cover. He must sprinkle blood seven times with his fin-
ger in front of the atonement cover.

16:1 Lev 10:1-2
16:2 Exod 25:21-22; 30:10; Heb 9:25
16:3 Lev 16:6-7
16:4 Exod 28:39-43; 39:27-29; Ezek 44:17-18
16:6 Lev 9:7; Heb 5:1-3; 7:27-28; 9:7
16:10 Isa 53:4-10
16:11 Heb 9:7
16:12 Exod 30:34-38; Num 16:18, 46
16:13 Exod 25:22; Lev 22:9
16:14 Lev 4:17

16:6 Or *to make atonement for himself and his family;* similarly in 16:11, 17b, 24, 34. 16:7 Hebrew *Tent of Meeting;* also in 16:16, 17, 20, 23, 33. 16:10 Or *wilderness, it will make atonement for the people.* 16:13 Hebrew *that is above the Testimony.* The Hebrew word for "testimony" refers to the terms of the LORD's covenant with Israel as written on stone tablets, which were kept in the Ark, and also to the covenant itself.

16:1 Leviticus 10 gives an account of Aaron's sons Nadab and Abihu. They were described as burning "the wrong kind of fire" before God, and they experienced immediate death. We don't know exactly what Nadab and Abihu did wrong in offering their incense. Very specific guidelines had been given, such as where the coals should come from (Leviticus 16:12), when the incense should be burned (Exodus 30:7-9), and how the priests should conduct themselves (Exodus 30:19-20). These two young priests may have broken any of these guidelines. Many believe they may have been drunk, since the admonition for sobriety follows the account (Leviticus 10:9).

16:2 The resting place of this chest was in the most holy inner chamber of the portable Tabernacle, then later in the Temple in Jerusalem. This Most Holy Place represented God's residence with the Israelites. Stored inside the Ark were sacred relics—manna, Aaron's rod, the Ten Commandments—that served as holy souvenirs of God's miraculous provision.

16:2 The high priest was only allowed to enter the Most Holy Place once a year on the Day of Atonement. At the time of Christ's death, a curtain that served as the doorway to this chamber was ripped in two, pointing to the beginning of the New Covenant and the new intimacy available to God's people. All believers can be in the Most Holy Place, where God's presence is revealed.

16:8 The closest thing today to which we can compare casting lots is tossing dice or flipping a coin. In the case of the Israelite priests on the Day of Atonement, they trusted God to guide the lots to decide upon the scapegoat. Casting lots was also a common practice among other early civilizations. Haman of Persia cast lots to determine when to exterminate the Jews there (Esther 3:7). In the story of Jonah, the crew of the ship he was on used lots to determine who was responsible for the storm (Jonah 1:7). New Testament Roman soldiers used lots ("throwing dice") to gamble for Jesus' garments (Matthew 27:35). The last apostle was chosen in a similar manner (Acts 1:26).

16:12-13 Incense played an important role in Old Testament worship. In this case, it appears as if the rising smoke concealed the Ark's cover, the precise place where God's glory most manifested itself. The penalty for failing to follow these precautions was death (v. 13).

[15]"Then Aaron must slaughter the first goat as a sin offering for the people and carry its
blood behind the inner curtain. There he will sprinkle the goat's blood over the atonement
cover and in front of it, just as he did with the bull's blood. [16]Through this process, he will
purify* the Most Holy Place, and he will do the same for the entire Tabernacle, because of
the defiling sin and rebellion of the Israelites. [17]No one else is allowed inside the Taberna-
cle when Aaron enters it for the purification ceremony in the Most Holy Place. No one may
enter until he comes out again after purifying himself, his family, and all the congregation
of Israel, making them right with the LORD.

[18]"Then Aaron will come out to purify the altar that stands before the LORD. He will do
this by taking some of the blood from the bull and the goat and putting it on each of the
horns of the altar. [19]Then he must sprinkle the blood with his finger seven times over the
altar. In this way, he will cleanse it from Israel's defilement and make it holy.

[20]"When Aaron has finished purifying the Most Holy Place and the Tabernacle and the
altar, he must present the live goat. [21]He will lay both of his hands on the goat's head and
confess over it all the wickedness, rebellion, and sins of the people of Israel. In this way, he
will transfer the people's sins to the head of the goat. Then a man specially chosen for the
task will drive the goat into the wilderness. [22]As the goat goes into the wilderness, it will
carry all the people's sins upon itself into a desolate land.

[23]"When Aaron goes back into the Tabernacle, he must take off the linen garments he
was wearing when he entered the Most Holy Place, and he must leave the garments there.
[24]Then he must bathe himself with water in a sacred place, put on his regular garments,
and go out to sacrifice a burnt offering for himself and a burnt offering for the people.
Through this process, he will purify himself and the people, making them right with the
LORD. [25]He must then burn all the fat of the sin offering on the altar.

[26]"The man chosen to drive the scapegoat into the wilderness of Azazel must wash his
clothes and bathe himself in water. Then he may return to the camp.

[27]"The bull and the goat presented as sin offerings, whose blood Aaron takes into the
Most Holy Place for the purification ceremony, will be carried outside the camp. The ani-
mals' hides, internal organs, and dung are all to be burned. [28]The man who burns them
must wash his clothes and bathe himself in water before returning to the camp.

[29]"On the tenth day of the appointed month in early autumn,* you must deny your-
selves.* Neither native-born Israelites nor foreigners living among you may do any kind
of work. This is a permanent law for you. [30]On that day offerings of purification will be
made for you,* and you will be purified in the LORD's presence from all your sins. [31]It will

16:15 Heb 6:19; 9:3, 7, 12
16:16 Exod 29:36; 30:10; Heb 2:17
16:18 Lev 4:7, 25; Ezek 43:20
16:19 Lev 4:6; 16:14
16:21 Lev 5:5
16:22 Isa 53:12
16:23 Exod 28:42; Lev 16:4
16:24 Exod 29:4-9
16:27 Lev 4:11-12; 6:30
16:28 Num 19:8, 10
16:29 Lev 23:26-32; Num 29:7
16:31 Lev 23:32; Ezra 8:21

16:16 Or *make atonement for;* similarly in 16:17a, 18, 20, 27, 33. **16:29a** Hebrew *On the tenth day of the seventh month.* This day in the ancient Hebrew lunar calendar occurred in September or October. **16:29b** Or *must fast;* also in 16:31. **16:30** Or *atonement will be made for you, to purify you.*

▶ WORSHIP

16:15 Sin offering for the people. God made full accommodations for the sins of the Israelites through various sacrifices and offerings. But once a year a sacrifice was made on *Yom Kippur*, the Day of Atonement, for all the sins of all the people (16:34). The blood of the sacrifice covered every sin. However, that covering was only temporary—there were always more sins for the next year. But Christ's death and once-and-for-all blood sacrifice was good for all sins, not just a year's worth (Hebrews 9:12). No Christian should ever wonder if all his or her sins are forgiven forever. Christ's secured our redemption forever. (***See Worship****> OT> Place> Tabernacle> Christ is the final High Priest,* TopicGuide page A27.)

▶ WORSHIP

16:22 Carry all the people's sins. The Day of Atonement consisted of two events: blood sacrifice for the sins of the high priest and all the people, and the symbolic removal from the community of the sins by the scapegoat. Two goats were involved. One became a blood sacrifice, the other a scapegoat—banished from the community into the wilderness carrying away the sins of the people. So, both by decree and by illustration, every Israelite knew that every sin of the previous year was gone. Christ fulfilled the role of both goats at once. He shed His blood for our sins and also "personally carried our sins in His body on the cross" (1 Peter 2:24). (***See Worship****> OT> Place> Tabernacle> Christ is the final High Priest,* TopicGuide page A27.)

16:29-31 The most holy day in the Israelite year was *Yom Kippur,* or the Day of Atonement (Leviticus 23:26-32). On that day, the High Priest entered the innermost chamber of the Tabernacle (and later, the Temple). The ceremony involved two goats; one sacrificed as a burnt offering, and one released as a "scapegoat." All this pointed to the death of Christ, in which He made Himself a final, perfect sacrifice so that we could be released from our guilt and sin and made right with God.

be a Sabbath day of complete rest for you, and you must deny yourselves. This is a per-
manent law for you. 32In future generations, the purification* ceremony will be per-
formed by the priest who has been anointed and ordained to serve as high priest in
place of his ancestor Aaron. He will put on the holy linen garments 33and purify the Most
Holy Place, the Tabernacle, the altar, the priests, and the entire congregation. 34This is a **16:34**
permanent law for you, to purify the people of Israel from their sins, making them right Lev 23:14, 21, 30-31
with the LORD once each year." Heb 9:7
Moses followed all these instructions exactly as the LORD had commanded him.

PROHIBITIONS AGAINST EATING BLOOD

17 Then the LORD said to Moses, 2"Give the following instructions to Aaron and his
sons and all the people of Israel. This is what the LORD has commanded.
3"If any native Israelite sacrifices a bull* or a lamb or a goat anywhere inside or out-
side the camp 4instead of bringing it to the entrance of the Tabernacle* to present it as **17:4**
an offering to the LORD, that person will be as guilty as a murderer.* Such a person has Deut 12:5-21
shed blood and will be cut off from the community. 5The purpose of this rule is to stop **17:5** Lev 3:1
the Israelites from sacrificing animals in the open fields. It will ensure that they bring Deut 12:4-7
their sacrifices to the priest at the entrance of the Tabernacle, so he can present them **17:6**
to the LORD as peace offerings. 6Then the priest will be able to splatter the blood Exod 29:18
against the LORD's altar at the entrance of the Tabernacle, and he will burn the fat as a Num 18:17
pleasing aroma to the LORD. 7The people must no longer be unfaithful to the LORD by **17:7** Exod 22:20; 32:8
offering sacrifices to the goat idols.* This is a permanent law for them, to be observed Deut 32:17
from generation to generation. 2 Chr 11:15; 1 Cor 10:20
8"Give them this command as well. If any native Israelite or foreigner living among you
offers a burnt offering or a sacrifice 9but does not bring it to the entrance of the Tabernacle **17:9** Lev 17:4
to offer it to the LORD, that person will be cut off from the community. **17:10**
10"And if any native Israelite or foreigner living among you eats or drinks blood in Lev 3:17
any form, I will turn against that person and cut him off from the community of your peo- Deut 12:16, 23-25

16:32 Or *atonement.* 17:3 Or *cow.* 17:4a Hebrew *Tent of Meeting;* also in 17:5, 6, 9. 17:4b Hebrew *will be guilty of blood.* 17:7 Or *goat demons.*

▸ WORSHIP

16:34 Make atonement for the Israelites. The high priest entered the Most Holy Place (some translations call it the "Holy of Holies") only once each year on the Day of Atonement. Access was blocked the rest of the year by a thick curtain that separated the Most Holy Place from the outer Holy Place in the Tabernacle (and later the Temple in Jerusalem). But on the day Christ died sacrificially for the sins of the world, that curtain was ripped in two (Luke 23:45). We may enter boldly at any time into the holy presence of God every moment of every day of the year—thanks to the sacrifice of Christ (Hebrews 4:16). (***See Worship***> *OT*> *Place*> *Tabernacle*> *The veil rent at Christ's death,* TopicGuide page A27.)

17:3-7 Several concerns underlie these commandments to restrict the slaughter of animals. First, God wanted the people's sustenance to come from manna and quail—not from their own hunting and gathering. Also, if a person slaughtered or sacrificed animals away from the Tabernacle, there were no priests to insure that the blood was drained properly (v. 10-16). Finally, one of the idols worshiped by surrounding cultures was shaped like a goat. These laws would have hindered Israelites from secretly engaging in false worship to this god under the ruse of offering their own private sacrifice or preparing their meals.

▸ GOD

17:4 Cut off from the community. Some sins are worse than others. To violate some laws meant drastic measures: banishment, execution, or some other form of divine judgment. Disrespectful worship fell into that category, along with dishonoring a parent, blasphemy, Sabbath breaking, witchcraft, and other forbidden acts. Israel was a theocracy ruled by God; to break His laws was to rebel directly against Him. Because the church today is not a theocracy—a political nation ruled by God—He does not mete out capital civil sentences as a rule (though see 1 Corinthians 11:29-30). God does still discipline His children, however (Hebrews 12:5-9), and warns us to judge ourselves lest we be judged by Him (1 Corinthians 11:31). Repent, and keep repenting, and you are in no danger of judgment. (***See God***> *God's Attributes*> *Just*> *God's law and judgments are completely righteous,* TopicGuide page A16.)

17:10-12 That blood held significance in Israelite culture may sound odd to our ears. After the Flood, God instructed Noah that people could eat the animals for food, but they were not to eat the animals that had not been drained of their blood (Genesis 9:1-4). To this day, the dietary practices referred to as "kosher" involve, in part, specific practices for draining blood from the animals.

ple, 11for the life of the body is in its blood. I have given you the blood on the altar to purify
you, making you right with the LORD.* It is the blood, given in exchange for a life, that
makes purification possible. 12That is why I have said to the people of Israel, 'You must
never eat or drink blood—neither you nor the foreigners living among you.'
13"And if any native Israelite or foreigner living among you goes hunting and kills an
animal or bird that is approved for eating, he must drain its blood and cover it with earth.
14The life of every creature is in its blood. That is why I have said to the people of Israel,
'You must never eat or drink blood, for the life of any creature is in its blood.' So whoever
consumes blood will be cut off from the community.
15"And if any native-born Israelites or foreigners eat the meat of an animal that died nat-
urally or was torn up by wild animals, they must wash their clothes and bathe themselves
in water. They will remain ceremonially unclean until evening, but then they will be clean.
16But if they do not wash their clothes and bathe themselves, they will be punished for
their sin."

FORBIDDEN SEXUAL PRACTICES

18 Then the LORD said to Moses, 2"Give the following instructions to the people of Is-
rael. I am the LORD your God. 3So do not act like the people in Egypt, where you
used to live, or like the people of Canaan, where I am taking you. You must not imitate
their way of life. 4You must obey all My regulations and be careful to obey My decrees, for
I am the LORD your God. 5If you obey My decrees and My regulations, you will find life
through them. I am the LORD.
6"You must never have sexual relations with a close relative, for I am the LORD.
7"Do not violate your father by having sexual relations with your mother. She is your
mother; you must not have sexual relations with her.
8"Do not have sexual relations with any of your father's wives, for this would violate
your father.
9"Do not have sexual relations with your sister or half sister, whether she is your father's
daughter or your mother's daughter, whether she was born into your household or some-
one else's.
10"Do not have sexual relations with your granddaughter, whether she is your son's
daughter or your daughter's daughter, for this would violate yourself.
11"Do not have sexual relations with your stepsister, the daughter of any of your father's
wives, for she is your sister.
12"Do not have sexual relations with your father's sister, for she is your father's close
relative.

17:11 Gen 9:4; Lev 17:14; Heb 9:22
17:13 Deut 12:16; Ezek 24:7
17:14 Gen 9:4; Lev 17:11
17:15 Exod 22:31; Lev 7:24; Deut 14:21
18:2 Exod 6:7; Lev 11:44
18:3 Exod 23:24; Lev 20:23
18:4 Deut 4:1
18:5 Ezek 20:11; Luke 10:28; *Rom 10:5; *Gal 3:12
18:7 Lev 20:11
18:8 Gen 35:22; Lev 20:11; Deut 27:20
18:9 Lev 20:17
18:12 Lev 20:19

17:11 Or *to make atonement for you.*

▸ SALVATION
17:11 Life in the blood. To deal with sin, God provided a system of sacrifices whereby the life of an innocent animal was taken by the shedding of its blood (Hebrews 9:22). Blood was sacred because from one perspective, life is in the blood. Israelites were prohibited from consuming blood, offering it as a sacrifice to idols, or treating it disrespectfully in the field when hunting. Why? Because blood is a synonym of *life* in God's vocabulary. Romans 3:25 explains how Leviticus 17:11 finds its fulfillment in the New Testament for the benefit of disciples of Jesus: "Jesus sacrificed His life, shedding His blood." (***See Salvation****> Jesus' Work> Crucifixion> Gave His life a ransom,* TopicGuide page A22.)

▸ WORSHIP
18:4 You must obey. The chief theological concept underlying God's relationship with Israel was loyalty—theirs was a relationship based on trust, intimacy, and fidelity. In Leviticus 18 God warns Israel about reverting to the pagan sexual practices of Egypt and the perversions they would encounter in Canaan, the Promised Land. It is impossible to maintain spiritual loyalty to God while being sexually immoral. Christians should read these warnings regarding cultural sexual temptations as if they were written to them. Paul summarizes these warnings concisely when he says, "Run from sexual sin!" (1 Corinthians 6:18). (***See Worship****> NT> Our Role> Holiness> Flee immorality,* TopicGuide page A32.)

18:6-17 These commands follow on the heels of God's directive to shun sexually charged worship practices (Deuteronomy 23:17; 1 Kings 14:24).

13 "Do not have sexual relations with your mother's sister, for she is your mother's close relative.

14 "Do not violate your uncle, your father's brother, by having sexual relations with his wife, for she is your aunt.

15 "Do not have sexual relations with your daughter-in-law; she is your son's wife, so you must not have sexual relations with her.

16 "Do not have sexual relations with your brother's wife, for this would violate your brother.

17 "Do not have sexual relations with both a woman and her daughter. And do not take* her granddaughter, whether her son's daughter or her daughter's daughter, and have sexual relations with her. They are close relatives, and this would be a wicked act.

18 "While your wife is living, do not marry her sister and have sexual relations with her, for they would be rivals.

19 "Do not have sexual relations with a woman during her period of menstrual impurity.

20 "Do not defile yourself by having sexual intercourse with your neighbor's wife.

21 "Do not permit any of your children to be offered as a sacrifice to Molech, for you must not bring shame on the name of your God. I am the LORD.

22 "Do not practice homosexuality, having sex with another man as with a woman. It is a detestable sin.

23 "A man must not defile himself by having sex with an animal. And a woman must not offer herself to a male animal to have intercourse with it. This is a perverse act.

24 "Do not defile yourselves in any of these ways, for the people I am driving out before
you have defiled themselves in all these ways. 25 Because the entire land has become
defiled, I am punishing the people who live there. I will cause the land to vomit them out.
26 You must obey all My decrees and regulations. You must not commit any of these detestable sins. This applies both to native-born Israelites and to the foreigners living among you.

27 "All these detestable activities are practiced by the people of the land where I am tak-

18:17 Or *do not marry.*

18:14 Lev 20:20
18:15 Lev 20:12; Ezek 22:11
18:16 Lev 20:21
18:17 Lev 20:14
18:19 Lev 15:24; 20:18
18:20 Exod 20:14; Lev 20:10; Matt 5:27-28; 1 Cor 6:9
18:21 Lev 19:12; 20:1-5; 21:6; Deut 12:31; 2 Kgs 23:10; Mal 1:12
18:22 Gen 19:5; Lev 20:13; Rom 1:27
18:23 Exod 22:19; Lev 20:15-16; Deut 27:21
18:24 Lev 18:3
18:25 Lev 20:22-23; Deut 9:5
18:26 Lev 18:2-3

18:18 Jacob's wives, Rachel and Leah, illustrate the truth of this Scripture. Jacob fell in love with Rachel, but the father of the girls tricked him into marrying Leah (the older sister) first. These two wives competed constantly for Jacob's attention. They also competed to bear him sons. In doing so, they offered their handmaidens to him in marriage, which was a custom of the day. In the end Leah gave Jacob his firstborn and the majority of his 12 sons. Rachel, though, was the beloved wife. The two sons she bore, Joseph and Benjamin, were Jacob's favorites. Rachel died after giving birth to Benjamin.

18:19 While this Scripture forbids sexual contact with a woman during menstruation, Leviticus 15:19-24 made provision for this type of contact, perhaps as an allowance for unintended violation. A woman's menstruation was troublesome because it involved blood, which represented life and was treated as sacred. A woman who was bleeding either from a hemorrhage (Leviticus 20:18) or from her regular cycle was required to follow specific guidelines.

18:21 Molech was a god particularly associated with the Ammonites. God repeatedly forbade His people to have any part in the sexually charged worship of this god. Years later, King Solomon allowed the worship of Molech in Israel, and it took place in the valley of *Gehenna* (as transliterated from the Hebrew). The fires that lit the area during sacrifices to Molech were later replaced by a garbage heap's constantly smoldering fires. Both images combined to create a metaphor for hell used 11 times in the New Testament.

18:22 In Hebrew this verse literally reads, "And with a male you shall not lay in the way a woman lies." The original Hebrew only prohibits men from acting on homosexual urges, but Romans 1:24-28, written by the Old Testament scholar Paul, makes it clear that God never intended women to act out their sexual urges towards one another either.

▶ GOD

18:22 Do not practice homosexuality. Homosexuality was practiced among the Canaanites, and must have been a temptation to Israelites as well, since God made it clear that it was to be avoided. Because homosexuality violated God's original design (see Genesis 2–3) and God's purpose for procreation within the marital union, it was prohibited along with incest, bestiality, and other perversions of God's plan for sexual freedom and happiness. For a follower of Christ, prohibitions against same-sex relations stood 1,500 years later (1 Corinthians 6:9; 1 Timothy 1:10) and still do today. God knows homosexuality is a temptation to many today, but He has provided the dual graces of the Holy Spirit and repentance to enable us to live free from this destructive sin. (***See God****> Relationship> God Enables> Relationship with God requires purity,* TopicGuide page A14.)

ing you, and this is how the land has become defiled. 28 So do not defile the land and give
it a reason to vomit you out, as it will vomit out the people who live there now. 29 Whoever
commits any of these detestable sins will be cut off from the community of Israel. 30 So
obey My instructions, and do not defile yourselves by committing any of these detestable
practices that were committed by the people who lived in the land before you. I am the
LORD your God."

HOLINESS IN PERSONAL CONDUCT

19 The LORD also said to Moses, 2 "Give the following instructions to the entire com-
munity of Israel. You must be holy because I, the LORD your God, am holy.
3 "Each of you must show great respect for your mother and father, and you must always
observe My Sabbath days of rest. I am the LORD your God.
4 "Do not put your trust in idols or make metal images of gods for yourselves. I am the
LORD your God.
5 "When you sacrifice a peace offering to the LORD, offer it properly so you* will be ac-
cepted by God. 6 The sacrifice must be eaten on the same day you offer it or on the next
day. Whatever is left over until the third day must be completely burned up. 7 If any of the
sacrifice is eaten on the third day, it will be contaminated, and I will not accept it. 8 Anyone
who eats it on the third day will be punished for defiling what is holy to the LORD and will
be cut off from the community.
9 "When you harvest the crops of your land, do not harvest the grain along the edges of
your fields, and do not pick up what the harvesters drop. 10 It is the same with your grape
crop—do not strip every last bunch of grapes from the vines, and do not pick up the grapes
that fall to the ground. Leave them for the poor and the foreigners living among you. I am
the LORD your God.
11 "Do not steal.
"Do not deceive or cheat one another.
12 "Do not bring shame on the name of your God by using it to swear falsely. I am the
LORD.
13 "Do not defraud or rob your neighbor.

19:5 Or *it.*

19:2 Exod 19:6 Lev 11:44 *1 Pet 1:16
19:3 Exod 20:8, 12 Lev 11:44
19:4 Exod 20:23 Lev 26:1
19:6-7 Lev 7:16-18
19:9 Lev 23:22 Deut 24:19-22
19:11 Exod 20:15-16
19:13 Exod 22:7-15, 21-27; 23:4-9 Deut 24:14-15 Mal 3:5 Jas 5:4

▶ WORSHIP
18:28 Cleaning out the land. God said the land of Canaan was about to expel its inhabitants because of their vile and immoral practices—which occurred by means of the Israelite invasion (see 18:25). God warned Israel not to give the land a reason to vomit *them* out as well. In time Israel adopted the perverted practices of Canaan, and they were taken from their land to Assyria and Babylon as captives. God's warnings about immorality have national implications—you and your family's choices help determine your nation's character. Live in such a way as to preserve and purify your culture (Matthew 5:13; Romans 1:24-32). (***See Worship****> OT> Repentance> Nature> Obedience guarantees success in the land of Canaan,* TopicGuide page A29.)

▶ GOD
19:2 Acting like God. At first glance, Leviticus 19 appears to be a catchall of unrelated rules and regulations. They are indeed varied, but all are tied together under the prevailing theme of covenant life in Israel: "You must be holy because I, the LORD your God, am holy." That is, these laws are as varied and illustrative as the situations Israelites would face in their daily lives. In all those situations, holiness (acting like God would act) was the standard. Keeping God's commandments then was an expression of loving God with all one's being (Deuteronomy 6:4-9)—and it still is today (Matthew 22:36-38). Jesus asked His disciples, "Why do you keep calling Me 'Lord, Lord!' when you don't do what I say?" (Luke 6:46). He asks us the same question. (***See God****> Relationship> God Enables> Relationship with God requires obedience,* TopicGuide page A14.)

19:5-6 While some of the sacrifices were required at specific places and times, the people gave peace and thanksgiving offerings spontaneously. While burnt offerings and sin offerings were given to *make peace* with God, those who were *already at peace* with God gave the peace offerings. These offerings were given to show love and appreciation. They were categorized as "fellowship offerings." The priests did receive part of these offerings, but rather than being required to eat the food at the Tabernacle (or later the Temple), the priests could share the offering with their families.

19:9-10 This provision for the disenfranchised can be seen in practical application in the Old Testament story of Ruth. Ruth and her mother-in-law Naomi had returned to Bethlehem as penniless widows. In order to have food to eat, Ruth went to the field of a man named Boaz to walk behind the men gathering crops and pick up any barley that they may have dropped or failed to harvest. In this case, Boaz noticed Ruth and actually instructed his men to leave extra behind for the young widow, thus initiating a romance (Ruth 2).

"Do not make your hired workers wait until the next day to receive their pay.
14 "Do not insult the deaf or cause the blind to stumble. You must fear your God; I am the
LORD.
15 "Do not twist justice in legal matters by favoring the poor or being partial to the rich
and powerful. Always judge people fairly.
16 "Do not spread slanderous gossip among your people.*
"Do not stand idly by when your neighbor's life is threatened. I am the LORD.
17 "Do not nurse hatred in your heart for any of your relatives.* Confront people directly
so you will not be held guilty for their sin.
18 "Do not seek revenge or bear a grudge against a fellow Israelite, but love your neigh-
bor as yourself. I am the LORD.
19 "You must obey all My decrees.
"Do not mate two different kinds of animals. Do not plant your field with two different
kinds of seed. Do not wear clothing woven from two different kinds of thread.
20 "If a man has sex with a slave girl whose freedom has never been purchased but who
is committed to become another man's wife, he must pay full compensation to her master.
But since she is not a free woman, neither the man nor the woman will be put to death.
21 The man, however, must bring a ram as a guilt offering and present it to the LORD at the
entrance of the Tabernacle.* 22 The priest will then purify him* before the LORD with the
ram of the guilt offering, and the man's sin will be forgiven.
23 "When you enter the land and plant fruit trees, leave the fruit unharvested for the first
three years and consider it forbidden.* Do not eat it. 24 In the fourth year the entire crop must
be consecrated to the LORD as a celebration of praise. 25 Finally, in the fifth year you may eat
the fruit. If you follow this pattern, your harvest will increase. I am the LORD your God.
26 "Do not eat meat that has not been drained of its blood.
"Do not practice fortune-telling or witchcraft.
27 "Do not trim off the hair on your temples or trim your beards.
28 "Do not cut your bodies for the dead, and do not mark your skin with tattoos. I am the
LORD.

19:14 Deut 27:18
19:15 Exod 23:2-3, 6; Deut 1:17; Prov 24:23; Jas 2:1-4
19:16 Exod 23:1, 7; Ezek 22:9
19:17 Matt 18:15-17; 1 Jn 2:9, 11; 3:15
19:18 Ps 103:9; *Matt 19:19; 22:39; *Mark 12:31; *Luke 10:27; *Rom 13:9; *Gal 5:14; *Heb 2:8; *Jas 2:8
19:19 Deut 22:9-11
19:20 Deut 22:23-27
19:21 Lev 5:15
19:26 Deut 18:10-12
19:27 Lev 21:5
19:28 Lev 21:5; Deut 14:1; Jer 16:6; 41:5

19:16 Hebrew *Do not act as a merchant toward your own people.* 19:17 Hebrew *for your brother.* 19:21 Hebrew *Tent of Meeting.* 19:22 Or *make atonement for him.* 19:23 Hebrew *consider it uncircumcised.*

▸ CHURCH

19:18 Love your neighbor. When Jesus said the command to love God was the most important law in Israel, He quoted from Deuteronomy 6:5. But when He said the second most important law was to love your neighbor as yourself (Matthew 22:39), He quoted this verse in Leviticus. In summary, He said loving God and loving one's neighbor was the essence of all the laws. Reading this verse makes us ask, "And who is my neighbor?" Jesus told a story to answer that question: Your neighbor is anyone with a need that you can meet (Luke 10:25-37). Disciples of Jesus should live daily with that answer in mind. (***See Church***> *Role> Preach> Topics> Godly Lives> Kindness to neighbors,* TopicGuide page A50.)

19:26-29 Application of these texts to modern times can be challenging. The prohibition concerning the eating of meat with blood in it is reaffirmed in the New Testament, but only because it made some observant Jews stumble (Acts 15:19-20). Sorcery is condemned in the New Testament as well (Acts 13:8-10; Revelation 22:15). But the guidelines on hairstyles and body piercing and tattoos are generalized in the New Testament, with the basic idea that women should dress modestly and men should look masculine (1 Corinthians 11:13-16), but even this is noted as being expressed through both creation and universal practice in the church (1 Corinthians 11:16). So in reference to the choice of some Christians to have longer or shorter hair or tattoos or body piercing, recognize that while it may have been sinful in ancient Israel, it may not be sinful today given our different cultural situation. All our choices about personal appearance should be influenced by a desire to obey God, an understanding of the universal practice of the church, and a love for those who may stumble spiritually because of our appearance.

19:27 The physical requirements listed here—not cutting the hair on the temples or clipping the edges of the beard—referred to the religious practices of surrounding cultures. Leviticus 21:5 lists both these same requirements and a ban on self-mutilation. An underlying theme of God's relationship with the Israelites was their religious separation or distinction from the people around them. Obviously, their worship was restricted to God, thus their worship practices were distinguished from the surrounding religions.

19:28 Self-mutilation was a part of the pagan worship of the ancient world. One of the most famous biblical examples was in the days of the prophet Elijah. Elijah faced off with the prophets of a god named Baal. In the process of pleading with their god, the prophets of Baal "cut themselves with knives and swords until the blood gushed out" (1 Kings 18:26-29).

29 "Do not defile your daughter by making her a prostitute, or the land will be filled with
prostitution and wickedness.
30 "Keep My Sabbath days of rest, and show reverence toward My sanctuary. I am the
LORD.
31 "Do not defile yourselves by turning to mediums or to those who consult the spirits of
the dead. I am the LORD your God.
32 "Stand up in the presence of the elderly, and show respect for the aged. Fear your
God. I am the LORD.
33 "Do not take advantage of foreigners who live among you in your land. 34 Treat them
like native-born Israelites, and love them as you love yourself. Remember that you were
once foreigners living in the land of Egypt. I am the LORD your God.
35 "Do not use dishonest standards when measuring length, weight, or volume. 36 Your
scales and weights must be accurate. Your containers for measuring dry materials or liq-
uids must be accurate.* I am the LORD your God who brought you out of the land of Egypt.
37 "You must be careful to keep all of My decrees and regulations by putting them into
practice. I am the LORD."

PUNISHMENTS FOR DISOBEDIENCE

20 The LORD said to Moses, 2 "Give the people of Israel these instructions, which ap-
ply both to native Israelites and to the foreigners living in Israel.
"If any of them offer their children as a sacrifice to Molech, they must be put to death.
The people of the community must stone them to death. 3 I Myself will turn against them
and cut them off from the community, because they have defiled My sanctuary and
brought shame on My holy name by offering their children to Molech. 4 And if the people
of the community ignore those who offer their children to Molech and refuse to execute
them, 5 I Myself will turn against them and their families and will cut them off from the
community. This will happen to all who commit spiritual prostitution by worshiping
Molech.
6 "I will also turn against those who commit spiritual prostitution by putting their trust in
mediums or in those who consult the spirits of the dead. I will cut them off from the com-
munity. 7 So set yourselves apart to be holy, for I am the LORD your God. 8 Keep all My de-
crees by putting them into practice, for I am the LORD who makes you holy.
9 "Anyone who dishonors* father or mother must be put to death. Such a person is guilty
of a capital offense.

19:29 Lev 21:9; Deut 23:17-18
19:30 Exod 20:8-11; Lev 26:2
19:31 Lev 20:6
19:32 1 Tim 5:1-2
19:34 Lev 19:18
19:35 Deut 25:13-16
19:36 Deut 25:13-15; Prov 20:10
20:2 Lev 18:21; 24:14-23
20:3 Lev 18:21; Num 19:20; Ezek 5:11
20:6 Lev 19:26, 31
20:7 Lev 11:44-45; *1 Pet 1:16
20:9 Exod 21:17; Deut 27:16; *Matt 15:4

19:36 Hebrew *Use an honest ephah* [a dry measure] *and an honest hin* [a liquid measure]. 20:9 Greek version reads *Anyone who speaks disrespectfully of.* Compare Matt 15:4; Mark 7:10.

▸ WORSHIP

20:2 Setting limits. Molech was a pagan god worshiped by those living in and around Canaan, Israel's Promised Land. The worship of Molech was gruesome, involving the sacrifice of children. Prohibition against Molech worship was central in Levitical statutes because of the many ramifications, not the least being that if a father would sacrifice his children, what would he *not* do? Unfortunately, Israel eventually did worship Molech—and even worshiped both Molech and God in the Temple on the same day, leading to their destruction (Ezekiel 23:37-39). If you truly believe in God, you will demonstrate it by your actions. Your behavior reveals what you truly value. (***See Worship***> *NT> Our Role> Obedience> To believe Jesus is to obey Him,* TopicGuide page A32.)

▸ SPIRITUAL WARFARE

20:7-8 Set yourself apart. Is there a contradiction here? In verse 7, God tells Israel to set themselves apart to be holy, and in verse 8, He says He is the one who makes them holy. The word *holy* in the Old Testament means "set apart" for a purpose. Indeed, God made the descendants of Abraham a set-apart people, but at the same time Israel had to walk in that "set-apartness" by keeping God's commands. So it's "both-and," not "either-or." In the New Testament, Paul tells us to put into action God's saving work, bearing in mind that it is God who is at work in us to that end (Philippians 2:12-13). God's part is giving us grace to obey; our part is to submit to His grace (Ephesians 4:30). (***See Spiritual Warfare***> *Resisting Sin and Evil> Standing Firm> Empowered to obey,* TopicGuide page A46.)

20:9 The ancient world took the act of cursing one's parents seriously (Proverbs 20:20). It's interesting to note that the fifth commandment—"Honor your father and mother"—is the only commandment that attaches the promise of a long, full life.

10 "If a man commits adultery with his neighbor's wife, both the man and the woman 20:10
who have committed adultery must be put to death. Exod 20:14 Deut 22:22
11 "If a man violates his father by having sex with one of his father's wives, both the man 20:11
and the woman must be put to death, for they are guilty of a capital offense. Lev 18:7-8
12 "If a man has sex with his daughter-in-law, both must be put to death. They have com- Deut 27:20
mitted a perverse act and are guilty of a capital offense. 20:12
13 "If a man practices homosexuality, having sex with another man as with a woman, Lev 18:15
both men have committed a detestable act. They must both be put to death, for they are 20:13 Lev 18:22
guilty of a capital offense.
14 "If a man marries both a woman and her mother, he has committed a wicked act. 20:14
The man and both women must be burned to death to wipe out such wickedness from Lev 18:17 Deut 27:23
among you.
15 "If a man has sex with an animal, he must be put to death, and the animal must be 20:15
killed. Lev 18:23 Deut 27:21
16 "If a woman presents herself to a male animal to have intercourse with it, she and
the animal must both be put to death. You must kill both, for they are guilty of a capital
offense.
17 "If a man marries his sister, the daughter of either his father or his mother, and they 20:17
have sexual relations, it is a shameful disgrace. They must be publicly cut off from the Lev 18:9
community. Since the man has violated his sister, he will be punished for his sin.
18 "If a man has sexual relations with a woman during her menstrual period, both of 20:18
them must be cut off from the community, for together they have exposed the source of Lev 15:24; 18:19
her blood flow.
19 "Do not have sexual relations with your aunt, whether your mother's sister or your fa- 20:19
ther's sister. This would dishonor a close relative. Both parties are guilty and will be pun- Lev 18:12-13
ished for their sin.
20 "If a man has sex with his uncle's wife, he has violated his uncle. Both the man and 20:20 Lev 18:14
woman will be punished for their sin, and they will die childless. 20:21
21 "If a man marries his brother's wife, it is an act of impurity. He has violated his brother, Lev 18:16
and the guilty couple will remain childless. 20:22
22 "You must keep all My decrees and regulations by putting them into practice; other- Lev 18:28

20:22-24 The land of Canaan, the Promised Land, covered much of the region in which Israel is located today. According to Genesis 10:15-19, Canaan was a son of Ham, one of Noah's three sons, and we assume that Canaan's occupants descended from the man of the same name. By the time Moses headed toward Canaan with the Israelites, the Canaanites included several people groups with different religions, all opposed to ancient Judaism. There was little sign of God-worship in that land.

BECAUSE GOD IS HOLY

I will devote myself to him in purity, worship and service.

So set yourselves apart to be holy.

LEVITICUS 20:7

FOR THE NEXT *GOD IS HOLY* FEATURE SEE PAGE 485.

20:23 wise the land to which I am bringing you as your new home will vomit you out. 23 Do not
Lev 18:1-3, 24-30 live according to the customs of the people I am driving out before you. It is because they
20:24 do these shameful things that I detest them. 24 But I have promised you, 'You will possess
Exod 13:5; 33:1-3, 16 their land because I will give it to you as your possession—a land flowing with milk and
honey.' I am the LORD your God, who has set you apart from all other people.
20:25 25 "You must therefore make a distinction between ceremonially clean and unclean ani-
Lev 11:1-47 Deut 14:3-5 mals, and between clean and unclean birds. You must not defile yourselves by eating any
unclean animal or bird or creature that scurries along the ground. I have identified them
20:26 as being unclean for you. 26 You must be holy because I, the LORD, am holy. I have set you
Lev 20:24 apart from all other people to be My very own.
20:27 27 "Men and women among you who act as mediums or who consult the spirits of the
Lev 19:31 dead must be put to death by stoning. They are guilty of a capital offense."

INSTRUCTIONS FOR THE PRIESTS

21:1 Lev 19:28 **21** The LORD said to Moses, "Give the following instructions to the priests, the descen-
Ezek 44:25 dants of Aaron.
"A priest must not make himself ceremonially unclean by touching the dead body of a
21:2 relative. 2 The only exceptions are his closest relatives—his mother or father, son or daugh-
Lev 21:11 ter, brother, 3 or his virgin sister who depends on him because she has no husband. 4 But a
priest must not defile himself and make himself unclean for someone who is related to
21:5 Lev 19:27-28 him only by marriage.
Deut 14:1 Jer 16:6 5 "The priests must not shave their heads or trim their beards or cut their bodies. 6 They
must be set apart as holy to their God and must never bring shame on the name of God.
21:6 Lev 10:3 They must be holy, for they are the ones who present the special gifts to the LORD, gifts of
food for their God.
21:7 Lev 21:14 7 "Priests may not marry a woman defiled by prostitution, and they may not marry a
Ezek 44:22 woman who is divorced from her husband, for the priests are set apart as holy to their
21:8 Lev 11:44 God. 8 You must treat them as holy because they offer up food to your God. You must con-
sider them holy because I, the LORD, am holy, and I make you holy.
21:9 Lev 19:29 9 "If a priest's daughter defiles herself by becoming a prostitute, she also defiles her fa-
ther's holiness, and she must be burned to death.
21:10 Lev 10:6-7 10 "The high priest has the highest rank of all the priests. The anointing oil has been

---

▸ ADOPTION

20:23 Customs of the people. One of the most well-known passages in the New Testament is Romans 12:2: "Don't copy the behavior and customs of this world, but let God transform you into a new person by changing the way you think." Perhaps Paul was thinking of Leviticus 20:23 when he wrote that exhortation. God's chief desire for Israel was that they not succumb to the lifestyles of the culture they were moving into. Today, as then, He wants a holy culture—a kingdom culture, a Christ culture—to be established. In every nation, it is God's desire to see His kingdom come and His will be done on earth, as it is in heaven. Don't be squeezed into this world's mold, but conform yourself and your surroundings to reflect God's ideals. (***See Adoption***> *With Christ> Redemption> Citizen of Christ's kingdom/heaven,* TopicGuide page A37.)

▸ WORSHIP

20:27 Mediums or psychics. A number of capital offenses are noted in this chapter of Leviticus, including: worshiping Molech, cursing parents, incest, homosexuality, bestiality, and consulting or being a medium or psychic. Today we live in an age rife with false spirituality and "New Age" doctrines. The follower of Christ must be careful and trust God alone with the past, present, and future. Otherwise, we are gambling with our spiritual lives. (***See Worship***> *OT> Prohibitions> Wrong Objects> Other gods,* TopicGuide page A28.)

▸ WORSHIP

21:1 Tell the priests. The nation of Israel was designated by God to be a "kingdom of priests," God's "holy nation" (Exodus 19:5-6). That meant every Israelite was to be holy, not that every Israelite officiated as a priest in worship. The Levites were the tribe from whom God had designated the officiating priests in Israel, and they were held to an even higher standard of holiness because of their close proximity to God's presence in the Tabernacle. The principle of high standards for leaders applies in the church as well (1 Timothy 3:1-13; Titus 1:5-9). It is good to aspire to leadership, but the aspiration to holiness must come first. (***See Worship***> *NT> Church Government> Peter gives charge to elders,* TopicGuide page A30.)

21:10-15 Why were there strict requirements for the high priest? This man was the spiritual leader of Israel, and in a theocracy there was no higher leader than a spiritual one. For this reason, the high priest was held to a higher standard. This principle translated over to the New Testament church. James, the brother of Jesus, wrote in his letter that teachers in the church would be judged with a greater strictness because of their position (James 3:1).

poured on his head, and he has been ordained to wear the priestly garments. He must
never leave his hair uncombed* or tear his clothing. [11]He must not defile himself by going
near a dead body. He may not make himself ceremonially unclean even for his father or
mother. [12]He must not defile the sanctuary of his God by leaving it to attend to a dead per-
son, for he has been made holy by the anointing oil of his God. I am the LORD.

[13]"The high priest may marry only a virgin. [14]He may not marry a widow, a woman who
is divorced, or a woman who has defiled herself by prostitution. She must be a virgin from
his own clan, [15]so that he will not dishonor his descendants among his clan, for I am the
LORD who makes him holy."

[16]Then the LORD said to Moses, [17]"Give the following instructions to Aaron: In all future
generations, none of your descendants who has any defect will qualify to offer food to his
God. [18]No one who has a defect qualifies, whether he is blind, lame, disfigured, deformed,
[19]or has a broken foot or arm, [20]or is hunchbacked or dwarfed, or has a defective eye, or
skin sores or scabs, or damaged testicles. [21]No descendant of Aaron who has a defect may
approach the altar to present special gifts to the LORD. Since he has a defect, he may not
approach the altar to offer food to his God. [22]However, he may eat from the food offered
to God, including the holy offerings and the most holy offerings. [23]Yet because of his
physical defect, he may not enter the room behind the inner curtain or approach the altar,
for this would defile My holy places. I am the LORD who makes them holy."

[24]So Moses gave these instructions to Aaron and his sons and to all the Israelites.

22 The LORD said to Moses, [2]"Tell Aaron and his sons to be very careful with the sa-
cred gifts that the Israelites set apart for Me, so they do not bring shame on My
holy name. I am the LORD. [3]Give them the following instructions.

"In all future generations, if any of your descendants is ceremonially unclean when he
approaches the sacred offerings that the people of Israel consecrate to the LORD, he must
be cut off from My presence. I am the LORD.

[4]"If any of Aaron's descendants has a skin disease* or any kind of discharge that makes
him ceremonially unclean, he may not eat from the sacred offerings until he has been pro-
nounced clean. He also becomes unclean by touching a corpse, or by having an emission
of semen, [5]or by touching a small animal that is unclean, or by touching someone who is
ceremonially unclean for any reason. [6]The man who is defiled in any of these ways will re-
main unclean until evening. He may not eat from the sacred offerings until he has bathed
himself in water. [7]When the sun goes down, he will be ceremonially clean again and may
eat from the sacred offerings, for this is his food. [8]He may not eat an animal that has died a
natural death or has been torn apart by wild animals, for this would defile him. I am the
LORD.

[9]"The priests must follow My instructions carefully. Otherwise they will be punished for
their sin and will die for violating My instructions. I am the LORD who makes them holy.

[10]"No one outside a priest's family may eat the sacred offerings. Even guests and hired
workers in a priest's home are not allowed to eat them. [11]However, if the priest buys a
slave for himself, the slave may eat from the sacred offerings. And if his slaves have chil-
dren, they also may share his food. [12]If a priest's daughter marries someone outside the

21:11 Lev 19:28
21:12 Lev 10:7; Num 19:11-13
21:13 Ezek 44:22
21:14 Lev 21:7, 13
21:17 Lev 21:6
21:21 Lev 21:17-21
21:22 1 Cor 9:13
21:23 Lev 21:12
22:3 Lev 7:20-21; Num 19:13
22:4 Lev 11:24, 28, 31, 39-40; 14:1-32
22:5 Lev 11:24-25, 41-44
22:8 Exod 22:31; Lev 17:15
22:9 Exod 28:43; Lev 18:30; Num 18:1-7
22:10 Exod 29:31-34; Lev 22:13
22:11 Gen 17:13; Exod 12:44

21:10 Or *never uncover his head.* 22:4 Traditionally rendered *leprosy;* see note on 13:2a.

▸ HOLINESS

22:2 Bring shame on My holy name. Priests were to be holy. To be otherwise would profane (bring disrespect upon) the name of the Lord. Just as it is possible to misuse the Lord's name (Exodus 20:7), so it is possible to bring disrespect upon Him by our actions. If an unclean priest entered into the holy presence of God in worship, it would create the appearance that such was acceptable to God, thus debasing His character. How do you profane God's name? Is it with foul language, or by living in public sin before people who know you are a Christian, or something else? Do not shame God's name, but increase God's reputation by your actions and words. (***See Holiness***> *Law and Grace*> *Law*> *A picture of God and His character,* TopicGuide page A41.)

22:13 priestly family, she may no longer eat the sacred offerings. 13But if she becomes a widow
Lev 22:10 or is divorced and has no children to support her, and she returns to live in her father's
home as in her youth, she may eat her father's food again. Otherwise, no one outside a
priest's family may eat the sacred offerings.
22:14 14"Any such person who eats the sacred offerings without realizing it must pay the priest
Lev 5:15-16 for the amount eaten, plus an additional 20 percent. 15The priests must not let the Israel-
22:15 Lev 19:8 ites defile the sacred offerings brought to the LORD 16by allowing unauthorized people to
22:16 eat them. This would bring guilt upon them and require them to pay compensation. I am
Lev 22:9 the LORD who makes them holy."

WORTHY AND UNWORTHY OFFERINGS

17And the LORD said to Moses, 18"Give Aaron and his sons and all the Israelites these in-
structions, which apply both to native Israelites and to the foreigners living among you.
"If you present a gift as a burnt offering to the LORD, whether it is to fulfill a vow or is a
22:19 Lev 1:3 voluntary offering, 19you* will be accepted only if your offering is a male animal with no
22:20 defects. It may be a bull, a ram, or a male goat. 20Do not present an animal with defects,
Lev 1:3 because the LORD will not accept it on your behalf.
Deut 15:21 Heb 9:14 21"If you present a peace offering to the LORD from the herd or the flock, whether it is to
1 Pet 1:19 fulfill a vow or is a voluntary offering, you must offer a perfect animal. It may have no de-
fect of any kind. 22You must not offer an animal that is blind, crippled, or injured, or that
has a wart, a skin sore, or scabs. Such animals must never be offered on the altar as special
gifts to the LORD. 23If a bull* or lamb has a leg that is too long or too short, it may be offered
as a voluntary offering, but it may not be offered to fulfill a vow. 24If an animal has dam-
aged testicles or is castrated, you may not offer it to the LORD. You must never do this in
22:25 your own land, 25and you must not accept such an animal from foreigners and then offer
Lev 21:6, 17 it as a sacrifice to your God. Such animals will not be accepted on your behalf, for they are
mutilated or defective."
26And the LORD said to Moses, 27"When a calf or lamb or goat is born, it must be left
with its mother for seven days. From the eighth day on, it will be acceptable as a spe-
22:28 Deut 22:6 cial gift to the LORD. 28But you must not slaughter a mother animal and her offspring on
the same day, whether from the herd or the flock. 29When you bring a thanksgiving of-
22:29 Lev 7:12 fering to the LORD, sacrifice it properly so you will be accepted. 30Eat the entire sacrifi-
22:30 cial animal on the day it is presented. Do not leave any of it until the next morning. I
Lev 7:15 am the LORD.
22:31 31"You must faithfully keep all My commands by putting them into practice, for I am the
Lev 19:37 LORD. 32Do not bring shame on My holy name, for I will display My holiness among the

22:19 Or *it.* 22:23 Or *cow.*

22:17-20 The offerings described here were voluntary. Unlike the sin offerings, which were required of the Israelites, the peace offerings (which included offerings to fulfill a vow or express gratitude) were initiated by the worshiper. It would have been an easy leap of logic to think that, because the offerings were voluntary, the requirements could be more lax. For a sin offering, the animal had to be without blemish—the very best you had! Here God is clarifying that no matter the reason for the sacrifice offered, the standard of that sacrifice should reflect God's nature, not the nature of the giver or the occasion of the gift.

▸ WORSHIP

22:20 Won't be accepted. In the Old Testament some sacrifices and offerings were acceptable to the Lord and some were not. Priests were prohibited from bringing a sacrificial animal that was defective; they were to offer a sacrifice without blemish to a God who Himself is without blemish. Such was reasonable, acceptable, and logical. Paul uses the same thinking when he describes an acceptable sacrifice as "a living and holy sacrifice" (Romans 12:1). We are to live lives that are holy, and then present ourselves wholly to the Lord as living sacrifices. (***See Worship****> NT> Our Role> Mind and Heart> We offer our bodies as a living sacrifice,* TopicGuide page A32.)

22:32 Names, in general, were far more significant in Old Testament culture than in modern times. When God first appeared to Moses, Moses posed this question: "They will ask me, 'What is his name?' Then what should I tell them?" God revealed Himself by the name "I AM" (Exodus 3:13-14). The third commandment specifically addressed the use of God's name. Here, God commands that His name be honored in a specific way— by using His special name (Yahweh) only in worship of Him.

people of Israel. I am the LORD who makes you holy. [33]It was I who rescued you from the 22:33 Lev 11:45
land of Egypt, that I might be your God. I am the LORD."

THE APPOINTED FESTIVALS

23 The LORD said to Moses, [2]"Give the following instructions to the people of Israel. 23:2 Lev 23:21
These are the LORD's appointed festivals, which you are to proclaim as official Num 29:39
days for holy assembly. 23:3
[3]"You have six days each week for your ordinary work, but the seventh day is a Sab- Exod 20:8-11; 23:12;
bath day of complete rest, an official day for holy assembly. It is the LORD's Sabbath day, 31:15
and it must be observed wherever you live. Deut 5:13-14
[4]"In addition to the Sabbath, these are the LORD's appointed festivals, the official days for
holy assembly that are to be celebrated at their proper times each year.

PASSOVER AND THE FESTIVAL OF UNLEAVENED BREAD

[5]"The LORD's Passover begins at sundown on the fourteenth day of the first month.* 23:5 Exod 12:3-20
[6]On the next day, the fifteenth day of the month, you must begin celebrating the Festi- Deut 16:1-8
val of Unleavened Bread. This festival to the LORD continues for seven days, and during 23:6
that time the bread you eat must be made without yeast. [7]On the first day of the festi- Exod 12:14-20
val, all the people must stop their ordinary work and observe an official day for holy
assembly. [8]For seven days you must present special gifts to the LORD. On the seventh
day the people must again stop all their ordinary work to observe an official day for
holy assembly."

23:5 This day in the ancient Hebrew lunar calendar occurred in late March, April, or early May.

▸ADOPTION
22:33 Your very own God. Purpose statements in the Bible may often be identified as beginning with "so that" or "that." Here, God states His purpose for rescuing the Hebrew slaves from Egypt: "that I might be your God." God wanted a people group to know Him as God so that those people could reveal Him to the rest of the human race. Israel was to be an intermediary between God and the unsaved world. The New Testament presents a similar purpose statement for Christians. We are saved "so we can do the good things [God] planned for us long ago" (Ephesians 2:10). Christians are now God's intermediaries, or ambassadors (2 Corinthians 5:20), in the world. Revealing Him as holy requires us to be holy as well. (***See Adoption***> *With Christ> Servants> Ambassadors for Christ,* TopicGuide page A37.)

▸WORSHIP
23:3 The Lord's Sabbath. The original "Sabbath" was the seventh day in the creation cycle when God "rested" (ceased) from His creation work. In the sinless Garden of Eden, that day of rest was a day set aside for special communion between Creator and creature. In the new nation of Israel, the Sabbath was reinstituted as a temporary sign of being in covenant with God in anticipation of an eternal, heavenly rest when perfect communion would be restored. Today, the person who accepts Jesus' gospel invitation can enjoy complete spiritual rest in Him until God's eternal Sabbath rest begins in heaven. And it remains the responsibility and joy of every believer to set aside a special, weekly time to simply enjoy God and fellowship with other believers. (***See Worship***> *OT> Festivals> Sabbath,* TopicGuide page A26.)

23:5 There were two calendars in Israel: the civil and the religious. The Passover Feast was so significant that God ordained it as the New Year feast for the Israelite religious calendar as well. The Passover took place in March, the seventh month of the civil calendar (which began in September/October). Each new religious year would begin with a celebration of freedom and identity as the people remembered how God had delivered them.

▸WORSHIP
23:5-6 Unleavened bread. Passover, a one-day feast, was followed immediately by the Festival of Unleavened Bread, a one-week celebration. Passover commemorated God's protection of the Israelites from the angel of death in Egypt (Exodus 12:21-30; Hebrews 11:28), and Unleavened Bread commemorated the Exodus from Egypt. All the Israelite feasts were later fulfilled in Christ, including these two. "Christ, our Passover Lamb, has been sacrificed for us. So let us celebrate the festival [of Unleavened Bread], not with the old bread of wickedness and evil, but with the new bread of sincerity and truth" (1 Corinthians 5:7-8). Fill your mind with truth and celebrate God's rescue of His people from sin. (***See Worship***> *OT> Festivals> Passover,* TopicGuide page A26.)

23:6 It was natural for the Festival of Unleavened Bread to follow the Passover. Bread made without yeast had been a specific component of the Israelites' flight from Egypt. Since the flat bread did not need time to rise, it was the necessary traveling food for their hasty exit from Egypt. During the feast described here, the people commemorated this time of flight by eating only unleavened bread. As the history of Israel progressed, leaven or yeast came to be used as a metaphor for sin or evil. In the New Testament, Jesus used the image of leavening (yeast) to warn the people about the false teachings of the religious leaders of His day (Matthew 16:11-12).

THE FESTIVALS

Besides enjoying one Sabbath day of rest each week, the Israelites also enjoyed nineteen days when national holidays were celebrated.

Festival	What It Celebrated	Its Importance
Passover–One day (Leviticus 23:5)	When God spared the lives of Israel's firstborn children in Egypt and freed the Hebrews from slavery	Reminded the people of God's deliverance
Unleavened Bread–Seven days (Leviticus 23:6-8)	The Exodus from Egypt	Reminded the people they were leaving the old life behind and entering a new way of living
First Harvest–One day (Leviticus 23:9-14)	The first crops of the barley harvest	Reminded the people how God provided for them
Harvest (Pentecost)–One day (Leviticus 23:15-22)	The end of the barley harvest and beginning of the wheat harvest	Showed joy and thanksgiving over the bountiful harvest
Trumpets–One day (Leviticus 23:23-25)	The beginning of the seventh month (civil new year)	Expressed joy and thanksgiving to God
Day of Atonement–One day (Leviticus 23:26-32)	The removal of sin from the people and the nation	Restored fellowship with God
Shelters–Seven days (Leviticus 23:33-43)	God's protection and guidance in the wilderness	Renewed Israel's commitment to God and trust in his guidance and protection

CELEBRATION OF FIRST HARVEST

23:10 [9]Then the LORD said to Moses, [10]"Give the following instructions to the people of Israel.
Exod 23:19; 34:26 When you enter the land I am giving you and you harvest its first crops, bring the priest a
bundle of grain from the first cutting of your grain harvest. [11]On the day after the Sabbath,
the priest will lift it up before the LORD so it may be accepted on your behalf. [12]On that same
23:13 day you must sacrifice a one-year-old male lamb with no defects as a burnt offering to the
Lev 6:20 LORD. [13]With it you must present a grain offering consisting of four quarts* of choice flour

23:13a Hebrew $^2/_{10}$ *of an ephah* [4.4 liters]; also in 23:17.

▸ SALVATION
23:10 From the first portion. The Festival of Firstfruits was celebrated as part of the Festival of Unleavened Bread. In the spring of the year, when the barley ripened, the first sheaves of the harvest were offered before the Lord. The celebration commemorated God's bounty in the Promised Land and celebrated the rest of the harvest that was yet to be brought in. Christ fulfilled this feast of new life by being the first in a long line of the faithful to be resurrected from the dead and enter into eternal life (1 Corinthians 15:20-23). Join all God's people by celebrating Christ's resurrection—and your future one! (***See Salvation****> Jesus' Work> Resurrection> Rose according to the Scriptures,* TopicGuide page A22.)

23:10 Throughout history it has been customary to bring God the first and very best of what we have, as here He is offered the first portion of grain harvest. This is sometimes referred to as the first crops or first fruits (Numbers 18:13). This was true of the first of all crops as well as the first males born to a herd or flock. It was also true of the first son born to a family. The grain offered here as a first fruit was probably barley, because the barley harvest took place around that time of year (March/April). Some see this as a separate festival from the others listed, but it was probably joined together with the Passover and Feast of Unleavened Bread.

moistened with olive oil. It will be a special gift, a pleasing aroma to the LORD. You must
also offer one quart* of wine as a liquid offering. 14 Do not eat any bread or roasted grain or
fresh kernels on that day until you bring this offering to your God. This is a permanent law
for you, and it must be observed from generation to generation wherever you live.

THE FESTIVAL OF HARVEST

15 "From the day after the Sabbath—the day you bring the bundle of grain to be lifted up as 23:15
a special offering—count off seven full weeks. 16 Keep counting until the day after the sev- Num 28:26-31
enth Sabbath, fifty days later. Then present an offering of new grain to the LORD. 17 From Deut 16:9-12
wherever you live, bring two loaves of bread to be lifted up before the LORD as a special of-
fering. Make these loaves from four quarts of choice flour, and bake them with yeast. They
will be an offering to the LORD from the first of your crops. 18 Along with the bread, present
seven one-year-old male lambs with no defects, one young bull, and two rams as burnt of-
ferings to the LORD. These burnt offerings, together with the grain offerings and liquid of-
ferings, will be a special gift, a pleasing aroma to the LORD. 19 Then you must offer one 23:19
male goat as a sin offering and two one-year-old male lambs as a peace offering. Lev 3:1 Num 28:30
20 "The priest will lift up the two lambs as a special offering to the LORD, together with the 23:20
loaves representing the first of your crops. These offerings, which are holy to the LORD, be- Exod 29:24
long to the priests. 21 That same day will be proclaimed an official day for holy assembly, a
day on which you do no ordinary work. This is a permanent law for you, and it must be ob-
served from generation to generation wherever you live.*
22 "When you harvest the crops of your land, do not harvest the grain along the edges of 23:22
your fields, and do not pick up what the harvesters drop. Leave it for the poor and the for- Lev 19:9-10
eigners living among you. I am the LORD your God." Deut 24:19-21

THE FESTIVAL OF TRUMPETS

23 The LORD said to Moses, 24 "Give the following instructions to the people of Israel. On the first 23:24 Num 10:9-10; 29:1
day of the appointed month in early autumn,* you are to observe a day of complete rest. It will
be an official day for holy assembly, a day commemorated with loud blasts of a trumpet. 25 You 23:25
must do no ordinary work on that day. Instead, you are to present special gifts to the LORD." Lev 23:7

THE DAY OF ATONEMENT

26 Then the LORD said to Moses, 27 "Be careful to celebrate the Day of Atonement on the 23:27
tenth day of that same month—nine days after the Festival of Trumpets.* You must ob- Lev 16:29-30

23:13b Hebrew *¼ of a hin* [1 liter]. **23:21** This celebration, called the Festival of Harvest or the Festival of Weeks, was later called the Festival of Pentecost (see Acts 2:1). It is celebrated today as Shavuat (or Shabuoth). **23:24** Hebrew *On the first day of the seventh month.* This day in the ancient Hebrew lunar calendar occurred in September or October. This festival is celebrated today as Rosh Hashanah, the Jewish new year. **23:27a** Hebrew *on the tenth day of the seventh month;* see 23:24 and the note there. This day in the ancient Hebrew lunar calendar occurred in September or October. It is celebrated today as Yom Kippur.

23:16 The Festival of Harvest (also known as the Festival of Weeks or Pentecost) was one of three feasts where all adult males were required to gather in Jerusalem (Passover/Unleavened Bread and Shelters/Final Harvest being the other two. See Exodus 23:14-17). The Festival of Harvest occurred seven weeks (fifty days) after Passover and was a festival of joyous celebration for the Lord's blessing in the spring harvests. This joyous celebration was the occasion described in Acts 2 when Jews from all over the Mediterranean world witnessed the giving of the Holy Spirit to the church. Disciples of Jesus can continually celebrate their new life that is a source of "joy in the Holy Spirit" (Romans 14:17).

23:24 The Festival of Trumpets, also called *Rosh Hashanah,* had a special connection with God's covenant made with the Israelites at Mount Sinai (Exodus 19–24). The day was both solemn and celebratory, marked by the sounding of trumpets. It was commemorated on the new moon of the month Tishri (October). The Day of Atonement also occurred during Tishri. The Festival of Trumpets marked the civil New Year, while the Passover marked the religious New Year.

23:26-32 The Day of Atonement, also called *Yom Kippur,* was first described in Leviticus 16. It was a high holy day in the Israelite year. It was the one and only day when the high priest entered the innermost chamber of the Tabernacle, seen as God's special dwelling place. It was on this day that two goats were offered. One was burned as a sacrifice. The other was the scapegoat, released into the wild. All this pointed to the work of Christ, who was our atoning sacrifice so that we could be released and made right with God.

serve it as an official day for holy assembly, a day to deny yourselves* and present special
gifts to the LORD. 28 Do no work during that entire day because it is the Day of Atonement,
when offerings of purification are made for you, making you right with* the LORD your
God. 29 All who do not deny themselves that day will be cut off from God's people. 30 And I
will destroy anyone among you who does any work on that day. 31 You must not do any
work at all! This is a permanent law for you, and it must be observed from generation to
generation wherever you live. 32 This will be a Sabbath day of complete rest for you, and
on that day you must deny yourselves. This day of rest will begin at sundown on the ninth
day of the month and extend until sundown on the tenth day."

THE FESTIVAL OF SHELTERS

33 And the LORD said to Moses, 34 "Give the following instructions to the people of Israel. Be-
gin celebrating the Festival of Shelters* on the fifteenth day of the appointed month—five
days after the Day of Atonement.* This festival to the LORD will last for seven days. 35 On
the first day of the festival you must proclaim an official day for holy assembly, when you
do no ordinary work. 36 For seven days you must present special gifts to the LORD. The
eighth day is another holy day on which you present your special gifts to the LORD. This
will be a solemn occasion, and no ordinary work may be done that day.

37 ("These are the LORD's appointed festivals. Celebrate them each year as official days
for holy assembly by presenting special gifts to the LORD—burnt offerings, grain offerings,
sacrifices, and liquid offerings—each on its proper day. 38 These festivals must be observed
in addition to the LORD's regular Sabbath days, and the offerings are in addition to your
personal gifts, the offerings you give to fulfill your vows, and the voluntary offerings you
present to the LORD.)

39 "Remember that this seven-day festival to the LORD—the Festival of Shelters—begins
on the fifteenth day of the appointed month,* after you have harvested all the produce of
the land. The first day and the eighth day of the festival will be days of complete rest. 40 On
the first day gather branches from magnificent trees*—palm fronds, boughs from leafy
trees, and willows that grow by the streams. Then celebrate with joy before the LORD your
God for seven days. 41 You must observe this festival to the LORD for seven days every
year. This is a permanent law for you, and it must be observed in the appointed month*
from generation to generation. 42 For seven days you must live outside in little shelters. All
native-born Israelites must live in shelters. 43 This will remind each new generation of Isra-
elites that I made their ancestors live in shelters when I rescued them from the land of
Egypt. I am the LORD your God."

44 So Moses gave the Israelites these instructions regarding the annual festivals of the
LORD.

23:28 Lev 23:7
23:29 Gen 17:14
23:32 Lev 16:31
23:33-34 Num 29:12-39; Deut 16:13-16; Ezra 3:4; Neh 8:14; Zech 14:16; John 7:2
23:35 Lev 23:7
23:36 Num 29:12-38
23:37 Lev 23:2
23:38 Num 29:39
23:40 Neh 8:15
23:43 Deut 16:13-15; Ps 78:1-8
23:44 Lev 23:37

23:27b Or *to fast;* similarly in 23:29, 32. 23:28 Or *when atonement is made for you before.* 23:34a Or *Festival of Booths,* or *Festival of Tabernacles.* This was earlier called the Festival of the Final Harvest or Festival of Ingathering (see Exod 23:16b). It is celebrated today as Sukkot (or Succoth). 23:34b Hebrew *on the fifteenth day of the seventh month;* see 23:27a and the note there. 23:39 Hebrew *on the fifteenth day of the seventh month.* 23:40 Or *gather fruit from majestic trees.* 23:41 Hebrew *the seventh month.*

▸ ADOPTION

23:34 Festival of Shelters. This third major annual festival (also known as Final Harvest, Booths, or Ingathering) was a weeklong celebration of the harvest, which commemorated the trip through the wilderness to the Promised Land when the Israelites lived in "booths" (makeshift shelters or tents). In Jesus' day, this feast included a daily drawing of water from a pool in Jerusalem in remembrance of the lack of water in the wilderness. On the last day of that feast, Jesus stood and cried out, "Anyone who is thirsty may come to Me!" (John 7:37-39), presenting Himself as the living water for all who thirst. Like the woman in Samaria (John 4:10), all who come to Jesus will never thirst for righteousness again. (***See Adoption***> *In Heaven*> *Living water,* TopicGuide page A38.)

23:34 The Festival of Shelters was also called the Festival (Feast) of Booths, Tabernacles, or Ingathering. Branches were gathered early in the festival. Then those branches were made into shelters (imagine tents or lean-tos). In this way the people orally passed on their history and remembered God's provision. While there are accounts of this festival being celebrated throughout Israel's history in the Old Testament, there were years that lapsed with no celebration.

PURE OIL AND HOLY BREAD

24 The LORD said to Moses, 2"Command the people of Israel to bring you pure oil of
pressed olives for the light, to keep the lamps burning continually. 3This is the
lampstand that stands in the Tabernacle, in front of the inner curtain that shields the Ark of
the Covenant.* Aaron must keep the lamps burning in the LORD's presence all night. This is
a permanent law for you, and it must be observed from generation to generation. 4Aaron
and the priests must tend the lamps on the pure gold lampstand continually in the LORD's
presence.

5"You must bake twelve loaves of bread from choice flour, using four quarts* of flour
for each loaf. 6Place the bread before the LORD on the pure gold table, and arrange the
loaves in two rows, with six loaves in each row. 7Put some pure frankincense near each
row to serve as a representative offering, a special gift presented to the LORD. 8Every Sab-
bath day this bread must be laid out before the LORD. The bread is to be received from
the people of Israel as a requirement of the eternal covenant. 9The loaves of bread will
belong to Aaron and his descendants, who must eat them in a sacred place, for they are
most holy. It is the permanent right of the priests to claim this portion of the special gifts
presented to the LORD."

AN EXAMPLE OF JUST PUNISHMENT

10One day a man who had an Israelite mother and an Egyptian father came out of his
tent and got into a fight with one of the Israelite men. 11During the fight, this son of an Is-
raelite woman blasphemed the Name of the LORD* with a curse. So the man was brought
to Moses for judgment. His mother was Shelomith, the daughter of Dibri of the tribe of
Dan. 12They kept the man in custody until the LORD's will in the matter should become
clear to them.

13Then the LORD said to Moses, 14"Take the blasphemer outside the camp, and tell all
those who heard the curse to lay their hands on his head. Then let the entire community
stone him to death. 15Say to the people of Israel: Those who curse their God will be pun-
ished for their sin. 16Anyone who blasphemes the Name of the LORD must be stoned to
death by the whole community of Israel. Any native-born Israelite or foreigner among you
who blasphemes the Name of the LORD must be put to death.

17"Anyone who takes another person's life must be put to death.

18"Anyone who kills another person's animal must pay for it in full—a live animal for the
animal that was killed.

24:2 Exod 27:20-21
24:4 Exod 25:31
24:5 Exod 25:30; 40:23; Lev 23:13; Heb 9:2
24:9 Lev 6:16-17; Matt 12:4
24:11 Exod 22:28; Job 1:11; 2:5; Isa 8:21
24:14 Lev 20:2, 27; Deut 13:9; 17:7; 21:21
24:15 Exod 22:28
24:17 Gen 9:5-6; Exod 21:12, 14; Num 35:30-31; Deut 19:11-12
24:18 Lev 24:21

24:3 Hebrew *in the Tent of Meeting, outside the inner curtain of the Testimony;* see note on 16:13. 24:5 Hebrew *2/10 of an ephah* [4.4 liters]. 24:11 Hebrew *the Name;* also in 24:16b.

▸ WORSHIP

24:2, 5 Olive oil . . . loaves of bread. Israelites provided oil and bread for the priests. Olive oil kept the lamps in the Tabernacle burning all night, and the loaves of bread were food for the priests, representing God's continual provision. Oil was also used in diverse religious tasks such as anointing the sick (Mark 6:13), marking people and objects as holy (Exodus 29:36), and designating people as empowered by God for ministry (1 Samuel 16:1; 2 Samuel 1:21). Oil also came to symbolize the Holy Spirit (Acts 10:38). Christ fulfilled the image of bread by becoming the "bread of life" (John 6:35). Old Testament believers enjoyed the presence of God by bringing bread and oil, while Christ and the Spirit bring New Testament disciples into God's presence. (***See Worship****> OT> Place> Tabernacle> Bread of the Presence*, TopicGuide page A27.)

24:5-9 The bread described here was not placed in the Most Holy Place, but it was still called the Bread of the Presence and was considered to be in God's presence. Another term for these loaves was *showbread,* or *shewbread.* Over two bushels of flour were required to make these loaves each week. Later in Israel's history, David was searching for food for his men and was offered the loaves in the Tabernacle by the priest Ahimelech (1 Samuel 21:1-6). Jesus referred to this event and to this part of the Temple when he taught that people were more important than even sacred rules and regulations (Luke 6:1-5).

24:10-16 We see in this instance that a man, in the presence of many witnesses, "blasphemed," which was some form of insulting God. After consulting with Moses, these witnesses lay their hands on his head, presumably to swear an oath that they were telling the truth in their testimony, and then commenced to carry out the proper punishment. For a nation in which their special relationship with God meant everything, insulting God was a capital offense.

19 "Anyone who injures another person must be dealt with according to the injury in-
24:20 Exod 21:24-25 flicted—20 a fracture for a fracture, an eye for an eye, a tooth for a tooth. Whatever anyone
Deut 19:21 does to injure another person must be paid back in kind.
Matt 5:38 21 "Whoever kills an animal must pay for it in full, but whoever kills another person must
24:21 be put to death.
Lev 24:17-18 22 "This same standard applies both to native-born Israelites and to the foreigners living
24:22 Exod 12:49 among you. I am the LORD your God."
Num 15:15-16, 29 23 After Moses gave all these instructions to the Israelites, they took the blasphemer outside
the camp and stoned him to death. The Israelites did just as the LORD had commanded Moses.

THE SABBATH YEAR

25:2 Exod 23:11 **25** While Moses was on Mount Sinai, the LORD said to him, 2 "Give the following in-
25:3 structions to the people of Israel. When you have entered the land I am giving
Exod 23:10 you, the land itself must observe a Sabbath rest before the LORD every seventh year. 3 For
25:4 six years you may plant your fields and prune your vineyards and harvest your crops, 4 but
Lev 25:1, 20-23 during the seventh year the land must have a Sabbath year of complete rest. It is the
25:5 LORD's Sabbath. Do not plant your fields or prune your vineyards during that year. 5 And
2 Kgs 19:29 don't store away the crops that grow on their own or gather the grapes from your un-
25:6 Lev 25:20-21 pruned vines. The land must have a year of complete rest. 6 But you may eat whatever the
land produces on its own during its Sabbath. This applies to you, your male and female
servants, your hired workers, and the temporary residents who live with you. 7 Your live-
stock and the wild animals in your land will also be allowed to eat what the land produces.

THE YEAR OF JUBILEE

25:9 8 "In addition, you must count off seven Sabbath years, seven sets of seven years, adding
Num 10:10 up to forty-nine years in all. 9 Then on the Day of Atonement in the fiftieth year,* blow the

25:9 Hebrew *on the tenth day of the seventh month, on the Day of Atonement;* see 23:27a and the note there.

24:19-21 Jesus referred to this principle in Matthew 5:38-39—an eye for an eye, a tooth for a tooth. While the reasoning can seem barbaric to a modern mind, the fundamental principle that the punishment should fit the crime is foundational to modern systems of justice. Jesus introduced the "turn the other cheek" principle to demonstrate that we may have the right to do justice "eye for an eye," but God also allows for a judicious use of mercy.

▶ BIBLE

24:20 Paid back. Is there any more well known, or more misapplied, tenet of Scripture than "eye for eye, tooth for tooth"? Moses' point was not to give permission to exact vengeance but to protect the guilty party: The punishment had to fit the crime, and no more. Jesus brought a kingdom interpretation to this stipulation by suggesting that punishment or retribution was not always necessary. Through forgiveness, the person who has harmed you can be set free from the penalty he or she deserves (Matthew 5:38-42). Followers of Christ are those who are quick to forgive when they have suffered loss. (***See Bible****> Unity> Kingdom of God> Kingdom is associated with forgiveness of sins,* TopicGuide page A11.)

▶ ADOPTION

24:21 Murder in society. Here we have contrasting punishments stipulated in the case of the death of an animal and of a human being. The difference in sentences is instructive: If a person kills an animal, he must make full restitution for the value of the animal. But if a person kills another person, the guilty party must be put to death. In modern society, there are some who seek to equate animals with humans, but in God's economy they have different values: Human beings bear the image of God (Genesis 1:26-27); animals do not. The unnecessary death or suffering of an animal, while regretful and to be avoided, is not the same kind of loss as the death of a human being. Disciples of Jesus must navigate their way through sentimentality and cultural confusion on issues such as these with biblical discernment and reliance on the Holy Spirit. (***See Adoption****> Without Christ> Connected to God> Created in the image of God,* TopicGuide page A36.)

▶ PURPOSE

25:4 A Sabbath year. God stipulated that every seventh year should be a Sabbath year for the land—a time for the land to rest. The people were to live off their stored food and whatever grew naturally during that year; no cultivation was allowed. For nearly 500 years Israel failed to give the land her Sabbath rests, so God removed Israel from the land for 70 years in captivity in Babylon to let the land have its due (Leviticus 26:34, 43; 2 Chronicles 36:21; Jeremiah 25:11-12). How do you fulfill your responsibility to be a good steward of the earth? (Romans 8:19-22). (***See Purpose****> God's Means> God's Sovereignty> God sustains His creation,* TopicGuide page A52.)

25:8-10 The custom of the Jubilee year reminded the people that while they may have used terms like "my land" or "our land," the earth really belonged to the Lord. They were (as we are) merely tenants (Leviticus 25:23). Paul reminded his New Testament readers of a similar truth—that they were citizens of heaven rather than earth (Philippians 3:20-21). Because of the Sabbath year celebrations and then the great Year of Jubilee, the Israelites had a calendar reminder throughout their entire lives that God was the One who supplied their needs, even to the most basic level of land for crops and cattle.

ram's horn loud and long throughout the land. 10 Set this year apart as holy, a time to pro-
claim freedom throughout the land for all who live there. It will be a jubilee year for you,
when each of you may return to the land that belonged to your ancestors and return to
your own clan. 11 This fiftieth year will be a jubilee for you. During that year you must not
plant your fields or store away any of the crops that grow on their own, and don't gather
the grapes from your unpruned vines. 12 It will be a jubilee year for you, and you must
keep it holy. But you may eat whatever the land produces on its own. 13 In the Year of Jubi-
lee each of you may return to the land that belonged to your ancestors.

25:10 Lev 25:8-16, 28-54 Isa 61:1 Jer 34:8, 15, 17 Luke 4:19

25:13 Lev 25:10, 24-31

14 "When you make an agreement with your neighbor to buy or sell property, you
must not take advantage of each other. 15 When you buy land from your neighbor, the
price you pay must be based on the number of years since the last jubilee. The seller
must set the price by taking into account the number of years remaining until the next
Year of Jubilee. 16 The more years until the next jubilee, the higher the price; the fewer
years, the lower the price. After all, the person selling the land is actually selling you a
certain number of harvests. 17 Show your fear of God by not taking advantage of each
other. I am the LORD your God.

25:14 Lev 25:17

18 "If you want to live securely in the land, follow My decrees and obey My regulations.
19 Then the land will yield large crops, and you will eat your fill and live securely in it. 20 But
you might ask, 'What will we eat during the seventh year, since we are not allowed to
plant or harvest crops that year?' 21 Be assured that I will send My blessing for you in the
sixth year, so the land will produce a crop large enough for three years. 22 When you plant
your fields in the eighth year, you will still be eating from the large crop of the sixth year.
In fact, you will still be eating from that large crop when the new crop is harvested in the
ninth year.

REDEMPTION OF PROPERTY

23 "The land must never be sold on a permanent basis, for the land belongs to Me. You are
only foreigners and tenant farmers working for Me.

25:23 Exod 19:5 1 Chr 29:15

24 "With every purchase of land you must grant the seller the right to buy it back. 25 If one
of your fellow Israelites falls into poverty and is forced to sell some family land, then a
close relative should buy it back for him. 26 If there is no close relative to buy the land, but
the person who sold it gets enough money to buy it back, 27 he then has the right to re-
deem it from the one who bought it. The price of the land will be discounted according to
the number of years until the next Year of Jubilee. In this way the original owner can then
return to the land. 28 But if the original owner cannot afford to buy back the land, it will re-
main with the new owner until the next Year of Jubilee. In the jubilee year, the land must
be returned to the original owners so they can return to their family land.

25:25 Ruth 2:20; 4:4, 6 Jer 32:7

25:27 Lev 25:50-52

25:28 Lev 25:10, 13

29 "Anyone who sells a house inside a walled town has the right to buy it back for a full
year after its sale. During that year, the seller retains the right to buy it back. 30 But if it is
not bought back within a year, the sale of the house within the walled town cannot be re-

▸ ADOPTION

25:10 A jubilee year. Every fiftieth year in Israel was set apart to remind Israel that everything they "owned" really belonged to God: money, slaves, land—everything. It was an equalizing year, a year of restoration and new beginnings. Debts were forgiven, slaves were freed, land was returned to families. It was a holy year, a time to give and to receive in honor of God's ownership of everything. Sadly, we have no records of Israel keeping this command from God. Thus, one of the first things Jesus did when He began His ministry was to proclaim a jubilee era—even better than a year! With His coming came release for those oppressed and held captive by sin (Luke 4:16-21). We live today in a spiritual freedom because Christ has set us free. Rejoice! (***See Adoption***> *With Christ*> *Supernatural*> *A life of liberating freedom,* TopicGuide page A37.)

25:24-25 The land that the tribes of Israel received was their inheritance, not only from their immediate family but also through the promises that God made with Abraham, their ancestor. The land was divided according to tribe. These tribes were organized by the descendants of the 12 sons of Jacob (whose name was later changed to Israel, see Genesis 32:28). This familial and covenantal attachment to land explains many of the land regulations in the law.

versed. It will become the permanent property of the buyer. It will not be returned to the
original owner in the Year of Jubilee. 31 But a house in a village—a settlement without forti-
fied walls—will be treated like property in the countryside. Such a house may be bought
back at any time, and it must be returned to the original owner in the Year of Jubilee.
32 "The Levites always have the right to buy back a house they have sold within the
towns allotted to them. 33 And any property that is sold by the Levites—all houses
within the Levitical towns—must be returned in the Year of Jubilee. After all, the houses
25:34 in the towns reserved for the Levites are the only property they own in all Israel. 34 The
Num 35:2-5 open pastureland around the Levitical towns may never be sold. It is their permanent
possession.

REDEMPTION OF THE POOR AND ENSLAVED

25:35 35 "If one of your fellow Israelites falls into poverty and cannot support himself, support
Deut 15:7-11 him as you would a foreigner or a temporary resident and allow him to live with you. 36 Do
Prov 21:26 not charge interest or make a profit at his expense. Instead, show your fear of God by let-
25:36 Exod 22:25 ting him live with you as your relative. 37 Remember, do not charge interest on money you
Deut 23:19-20 lend him or make a profit on food you sell him. 38 I am the LORD your God, who brought
25:38 you out of the land of Egypt to give you the land of Canaan and to be your God.
Lev 11:45 39 "If one of your fellow Israelites falls into poverty and is forced to sell himself to you, do
25:39 not treat him as a slave. 40 Treat him instead as a hired worker or as a temporary resident
Exod 21:2-11 Deut 15:12-18 who lives with you, and he will serve you only until the Year of Jubilee. 41 At that time he
25:40 and his children will no longer be obligated to you, and they will return to their clans and
Lev 25:53 go back to the land originally allotted to their ancestors. 42 The people of Israel are My ser-
vants, whom I brought out of the land of Egypt, so they must never be sold as slaves.
25:43 43 Show your fear of God by not treating them harshly.
Col 4:1 44 "However, you may purchase male and female slaves from among the nations
around you. 45 You may also purchase the children of temporary residents who live
25:46 Lev 25:40, 53 among you, including those who have been born in your land. You may treat them as
your property, 46 passing them on to your children as a permanent inheritance. You may
treat them as slaves, but you must never treat your fellow Israelites this way.
47 "Suppose a foreigner or temporary resident becomes rich while living among you. If
any of your fellow Israelites fall into poverty and are forced to sell themselves to such a
foreigner or to a member of his family, 48 they still retain the right to be bought back, even
25:48 Neh 5:5 after they have been purchased. They may be bought back by a brother, 49 an uncle, or a
25:49 cousin. In fact, anyone from the extended family may buy them back. They may also re-
Lev 25:26 deem themselves if they have prospered. 50 They will negotiate the price of their freedom
25:50 with the person who bought them. The price will be based on the number of years from
Job 7:1 the time they were sold until the next Year of Jubilee—whatever it would cost to hire a
worker for that period of time. 51 If many years still remain until the jubilee, they will repay
the proper proportion of what they received when they sold themselves. 52 If only a few
years remain until the Year of Jubilee, they will repay a small amount for their redemption.
53 The foreigner must treat them as workers hired on a yearly basis. You must not allow a
25:53 Lev 25:40, 46 foreigner to treat any of your fellow Israelites harshly. 54 If any Israelites have not been
25:54 bought back by the time the Year of Jubilee arrives, they and their children must be set
Lev 25:10, 13, 28 free at that time. 55 For the people of Israel belong to Me. They are My servants, whom I
brought out of the land of Egypt. I am the LORD your God.

25:32-34 Later, when the Israelites took possession of the Promised Land, 48 cities were set aside as Levitical cities. This scattered the Levites throughout the 12 tribes. The Levites were not the only residents of these cities, but they did serve in them. Six of the Levitical cities were also named cities of refuge. Those who committed certain capital crimes could run to these refuge cities and be kept safe until trial (Numbers 35:11). Of the 48 cities, 13 were allotted to the priests, the Levitical descendants of Aaron. The rest were for the non-Aaronic descendants of Levi.

BLESSINGS FOR OBEDIENCE

26 "Do not make idols or set up carved images, or sacred pillars, or sculptured
stones in your land so you may worship them. I am the LORD your God. 2 You
must keep My Sabbath days of rest and show reverence for My sanctuary. I am the LORD.
3 "If you follow My decrees and are careful to obey My commands, 4 I will send you the
seasonal rains. The land will then yield its crops, and the trees of the field will produce
their fruit. 5 Your threshing season will overlap with the grape harvest, and your grape har-
vest will overlap with the season of planting grain. You will eat your fill and live securely in
your own land.
6 "I will give you peace in the land, and you will be able to sleep with no cause for fear. I
will rid the land of wild animals and keep your enemies out of your land. 7 In fact, you will
chase down your enemies and slaughter them with your swords. 8 Five of you will chase a
hundred, and a hundred of you will chase ten thousand! All your enemies will fall beneath
your sword.

26:1 Exod 20:4; 34:17 Lev 19:4 Num 33:52
26:2 Exod 20:8-11
26:4 Lev 25:19 Deut 11:14-15
26:6 Ps 29:11
26:8 Deut 28:7; 32:30

26:1-2 Faith, expressed through worship and obedience, is what God has always desired from His people. The first two commandments were dedicated to this: Don't worship other gods or make idols (Exodus 20:1-4). Faith must have the proper object—we must have faith in God alone. After the monarchy divided into two kingdoms (1 Kings 12), the political well-being of those kingdoms rose and fell with the faith of the people in God alone. Most of the warnings of the Old Testament prophets centered around the people's unwillingness to worship God alone.

▸ WORSHIP
26:3-4 Covenant with God. The "if . . . then" language found in the Old Testament is characteristic of ancient covenant treaties. God promised, "If you obey My commands, then I will bless you" (verses 1-13). Conversely, "If you don't obey, then I won't bless you" (verses 14-40). Conditions for blessing are found under the New Covenant as well. For example, Jesus told the disciples, "If you remain in Me and My words remain in you, [then] you may ask for anything you want, and it will be granted!" (John 15:7). Do you wonder why your prayers are often answered no? Intimacy with and obedience to Jesus are conditions for answered prayer. (***See Worship***> *OT*> *Repentance*> *Nature*> *Obedience leads to blessing, failure to repent leads to curses,* TopicGuide page A29.)

MY RESPONSE TO GOD

God Lives with People

LEVITICUS 26

God created people so that He could have a relationship with them, and they can delight in Him. He told the Israelites to make a tent (sanctuary, Tabernacle) so that He could live with them (Exodus 25:8). He wanted to be in their midst. In Leviticus 26:11-12, God said He would live among His people and walk with them. Throughout history, God has continually sought to have fellowship with humanity. So much did He want to be reconciled with His people—to have them live with Him eternally—that He was willing to send His Son to dwell with them on earth. John 1:14 says that "the Word [Jesus] became human and made His home among us." Through the person of Jesus, God took on a physical, human body and came to walk among people.

What a loving God we have! He is not a distant deity whose back is turned to us, whose voice is never heard, or whose will is impossible to know. God wants to walk with us today, and live in us as the center of our affections and the goal of our energies. God loves us and, though He doesn't need it, finds our fellowship delightful, so much so that His plan to rescue fallen creation includes restoring our relationship with Him. And one day God's people will see Him as He is, and that one look will change us forever (1 John 3:2).

[9]"I will look favorably upon you, making you fertile and multiplying your people. And I
will fulfill My covenant with you. [10]You will have such a surplus of crops that you will need
to clear out the old grain to make room for the new harvest! [11]I will live among you, and I
will not despise you. [12]I will walk among you; I will be your God, and you will be My peo-
ple. [13]I am the LORD your God, who brought you out of the land of Egypt so you would no
longer be their slaves. I broke the yoke of slavery from your neck so you can walk with
your heads held high.

PUNISHMENTS FOR DISOBEDIENCE

[14]"However, if you do not listen to Me or obey all these commands, [15]and if you break My
covenant by rejecting My decrees, treating My regulations with contempt, and refusing to
obey My commands, [16]I will punish you. I will bring sudden terrors upon you—wasting dis-
eases and burning fevers that will cause your eyes to fail and your life to ebb away. You
will plant your crops in vain because your enemies will eat them. [17]I will turn against you,
and you will be defeated by your enemies. Those who hate you will rule over you, and
you will run even when no one is chasing you!

[18]"And if, in spite of all this, you still disobey Me, I will punish you seven times over for
your sins. [19]I will break your proud spirit by making the skies as unyielding as iron and the
earth as hard as bronze. [20]All your work will be for nothing, for your land will yield no
crops, and your trees will bear no fruit.

[21]"If even then you remain hostile toward Me and refuse to obey Me, I will inflict disas-
ter on you seven times over for your sins. [22]I will send wild animals that will rob you of
your children and destroy your livestock. Your numbers will dwindle, and your roads will
be deserted.

[23]"And if you fail to learn the lesson and continue your hostility toward Me, [24]then I My-
self will be hostile toward you. I will personally strike you with calamity seven times over
for your sins. [25]I will send armies against you to carry out the curse of the covenant you
have broken. When you run to your towns for safety, I will send a plague to destroy you
there, and you will be handed over to your enemies. [26]I will destroy your food supply, so
that ten women will need only one oven to bake bread for their families. They will ration
your food by weight, and though you have food to eat, you will not be satisfied.

[27]"If in spite of all this you still refuse to listen and still remain hostile toward Me, [28]then
I will give full vent to My hostility. I Myself will punish you seven times over for your sins.
[29]Then you will eat the flesh of your own sons and daughters. [30]I will destroy your pagan
shrines and knock down your places of worship. I will leave your lifeless corpses piled on
top of your lifeless idols,* and I will despise you. [31]I will make your cities desolate and de-
stroy your places of pagan worship. I will take no pleasure in your offerings that should be
a pleasing aroma to Me. [32]Yes, I Myself will devastate your land, and your enemies who
come to occupy it will be appalled at what they see. [33]I will scatter you among the nations
and bring out My sword against you. Your land will become desolate, and your cities will
lie in ruins. [34]Then at last the land will enjoy its neglected Sabbath years as it lies desolate
while you are in exile in the land of your enemies. Then the land will finally rest and enjoy

26:9 Gen 17:6-7
26:10 Lev 25:22
26:11 Exod 29:45-46
26:12 Exod 6:7; *2 Cor 6:16
26:16 Deut 28:22, 33, 65-67; 32:23-25
26:17 Lev 26:36-37; Deut 28:25; Ps 106:41; Prov 28:1
26:18 Lev 26:21, 24, 28
26:19 Deut 28:23; Isa 25:11; 26:5
26:20 Ps 127:1
26:21 Lev 26:18
26:22 Deut 32:24
26:23 Jer 2:30; 5:3
26:25 Deut 28:21-22, 27-29; 32:35
26:26 Isa 3:1; 9:19-20; Ezek 4:16
26:29 Deut 28:53-57; 2 Kgs 6:26-30
26:30 1 Kgs 13:2; Isa 27:9
26:31 Ps 74:3; Isa 63:18
26:32 Jer 12:11; 18:16
26:33 Deut 28:64-68
26:34 Lev 26:43; 2 Chr 36:21

26:30 The Hebrew term (literally *round things*) probably alludes to dung.

▸ ADOPTION

26:33 I will scatter you. God rescued the Hebrew people from Egyptian slavery in order to make them a nation. He gave them laws and land on the condition that they obey Him fully. When they failed to do that, He said that they would be scattered. So first, 10 of the 12 tribes of Israel were captured and taken to Assyria in 722 BC. The two remaining tribes were captured and taken to Babylon in 586 BC. God always keeps His word. God's discipline may take different forms in the New Testament than in the Old Testament (Hebrews 12:1-13), but His expectations are the same: obedience and holiness for all God's people (John 15:10; 1 Peter 1:15). (***See Adoption*****> *With Christ*> *Children of God*> *God disciplines His children,* TopicGuide page A36.)

the Sabbaths it missed. 35As long as the land lies in ruins, it will enjoy the rest you never allowed it to take every seventh year while you lived in it.

36"And for those of you who survive, I will demoralize you in the land of your enemies. You will live in such fear that the sound of a leaf driven by the wind will send you fleeing. You will run as though fleeing from a sword, and you will fall even when no one pursues you. 37Though no one is chasing you, you will stumble over each other as though fleeing from a sword. You will have no power to stand up against your enemies. 38You will die among the foreign nations and be devoured in the land of your enemies. 39Those of you who survive will waste away in your enemies' lands because of their sins and the sins of their ancestors.

40"But at last My people will confess their sins and the sins of their ancestors for betraying Me and being hostile toward Me. 41When I have turned their hostility back on them and brought them to the land of their enemies, then at last their stubborn hearts will be humbled, and they will pay for their sins. 42Then I will remember My covenant with Jacob and My covenant with Isaac and My covenant with Abraham, and I will remember the land. 43For the land must be abandoned to enjoy its years of Sabbath rest as it lies deserted. At last the people will pay for their sins, for they have continually rejected My regulations and despised My decrees.

44"But despite all this, I will not utterly reject or despise them while they are in exile in the land of their enemies. I will not cancel My covenant with them by wiping them out, for I am the LORD their God. 45For their sakes I will remember My ancient covenant with their ancestors, whom I brought out of the land of Egypt in the sight of all the nations, that I might be their God. I am the LORD."

46These are the decrees, regulations, and instructions that the LORD gave through Moses on Mount Sinai as evidence of the relationship between Himself and the Israelites.

26:36 Ezek 21:7
26:38 Deut 4:25-27
26:39 Ezek 33:10
26:40 Jer 3:12-15; Luke 15:18; 1 Jn 1:9
26:42 Gen 12:1-3; 15:1-4, 13-16; 26:2-5; 28:13-15
26:43 Lev 26:34
26:44 Deut 4:29-31; Rom 11:2
26:45 Gen 17:7; Exod 6:6-8
26:46 Lev 27:34

REDEMPTION OF GIFTS OFFERED TO THE LORD

27 The LORD said to Moses, 2"Give the following instructions to the people of Israel. If anyone makes a special vow to dedicate someone to the LORD by paying the value of that person, 3here is the scale of values to be used. A man between the ages of twenty and sixty is valued at fifty shekels* of silver, as measured by the sanctuary shekel. 4A woman of that age is valued at thirty shekels* of silver. 5A boy between the ages of five and twenty is valued at twenty shekels of silver; a girl of that age is valued at ten shekels* of silver. 6A boy between the ages of one month and five years is valued at five shekels of silver; a girl of that age is valued at three shekels* of silver. 7A man older than sixty is valued at fif-

27:3 Exod 30:13; Lev 5:15; 27:25
27:6 Num 3:46-48; 18:14-16

27:3 Or *20 ounces* [570 grams]. 27:4 Or *12 ounces* [342 grams]. 27:5 Or *A boy . . . 8 ounces* [228 grams] *of silver; a girl . . . 4 ounces* [114 grams]. 27:6 Or *A boy . . . 2 ounces* [57 grams] *of silver; a girl . . . 1.2 ounces* [34 grams].

▸ GOD
26:42 I will remember My covenant. Even though Israel would be humbled and removed from the land because of sin, God would bring the nation back because of His promise to Abraham. And that happened when the Jews returned to the Promised Land from exile in Babylon (see Ezra and Nehemiah). Even when we are faithless, God is faithful to keep His promises (2 Timothy 2:13). (***See God****> God's Attributes> Faithful> God is faithful to fulfill His promises,* TopicGuide page A16.)

26:44-45 God's covenant with Abraham, Isaac, and Jacob was the core of the Hebrew identity. In a world in which other cultures often worshiped many gods and idols, the unique series of promises God made with Israel's ancestors was significant (Genesis 12; 15; 17). Abraham passed down this covenant to his son Isaac, and Isaac to his son Jacob, then on to the descendants of Jacob's 12 sons in this text. God once again reminded the people of their role in keeping their family's promises to God.

27:1-8 The vows made to dedicate a person or thing were taken very seriously. In some cases, the gifts listed represented as much as four years' worth of wages. There were cases in the Old Testament in which a person was dedicated to God's service rather than money given on their behalf, such as in 1 Samuel 1, the dedication of young Samuel.

27:2 Vow making was common in the ancient world. The price of making a vow was simple—whatever it took to keep it was the cost. God insisted that promises be kept in Israel, especially those made to Him. Jesus recommended not making vows at all, saying we ought to wisely say "Yes, I will" or "No, I won't" and let our word be our bond (Matthew 5:33-37).

27:8 teen shekels of silver; a woman of that age is valued at ten shekels* of silver. 8If you desire
Lev 14:21-22 to make such a vow but cannot afford to pay the required amount, take the person to the
priest. He will determine the amount for you to pay based on what you can afford.
9"If your vow involves giving an animal that is acceptable as an offering to the LORD, any
27:10 gift to the LORD will be considered holy. 10You may not exchange or substitute it for an-
Lev 27:14-33 other animal—neither a good animal for a bad one nor a bad animal for a good one. But if
you do exchange one animal for another, then both the original animal and its substitute
will be considered holy. 11If your vow involves an unclean animal—one that is not accept-
able as an offering to the LORD—then you must bring the animal to the priest. 12He will as-
sess its value, and his assessment will be final, whether high or low. 13If you want to buy
back the animal, you must pay the value set by the priest, plus 20 percent.
14"If someone dedicates a house to the LORD, the priest will come to assess its value. The
priest's assessment will be final, whether high or low. 15If the person who dedicated the
house wants to buy it back, he must pay the value set by the priest, plus 20 percent. Then
the house will again be his.
16"If someone dedicates to the LORD a piece of his family property, its value will be as-
sessed according to the amount of seed required to plant it—fifty shekels of silver for a
field planted with five bushels of barley seed.* 17If the field is dedicated to the LORD in the
27:18 Year of Jubilee, then the entire assessment will apply. 18But if the field is dedicated after
Lev 25:14-16 the Year of Jubilee, the priest will assess the land's value in proportion to the number of
years left until the next Year of Jubilee. Its assessed value is reduced each year. 19If the
person who dedicated the field wants to buy it back, he must pay the value set by the
priest, plus 20 percent. Then the field will again be legally his. 20But if he does not want to
27:21 buy it back, and it is sold to someone else, the field can no longer be bought back. 21When
Lev 25:8-54 Num 18:14 the field is released in the Year of Jubilee, it will be holy, a field specially set apart* for the
Ezek 44:29 LORD. It will become the property of the priests.
22"If someone dedicates to the LORD a field he has purchased but which is not part of
his family property, 23the priest will assess its value based on the number of years left
until the next Year of Jubilee. On that day he must give the assessed value of the land as
27:24 a sacred donation to the LORD. 24In the Year of Jubilee the field must be returned to the
Lev 25:28 person from whom he purchased it, the one who inherited it as family property. 25(All
27:25 Exod 30:13 the payments must be measured by the weight of the sanctuary shekel,* which equals
Num 3:47; 18:16 twenty gerahs.)
Ezek 45:12 26"You may not dedicate a firstborn animal to the LORD, for the firstborn of your cattle,
27:26 sheep, and goats already belong to Him. 27However, you may buy back the firstborn of a
Exod 13:2, 12 ceremonially unclean animal by paying the priest's assessment of its worth, plus 20 per-
27:28 Josh 6:17-19 cent. If you do not buy it back, the priest will sell it at its assessed value.
27:30 28"However, anything specially set apart for the LORD—whether a person, an animal, or
Gen 28:22 family property—must never be sold or bought back. Anything devoted in this way has
Num 18:26 been set apart as holy, and it belongs to the LORD. 29No person specially set apart for de-
2 Chr 31:5-6 Neh 3:12 struction may be bought back. Such a person must be put to death.
Mal 3:8 30"One tenth of the produce of the land, whether grain from the fields or fruit from the

27:7 Or *A man . . . 6 ounces* [171 grams] *of silver; a woman . . . 4 ounces* [114 grams]. **27:16** Hebrew *50 shekels* [20 ounces, or 570 grams] *of silver for a homer* [182 liters] *of barley seed.* **27:21** The Hebrew term used here refers to the complete consecration of things or people to the LORD, either by destroying them or by giving them as an offering; also in 27:28, 29. **27:25** Each shekel was about 0.4 ounces [11 grams] in weight.

27:30-33 Long before this law was given to farmers, a tenth was seen as the appropriate gift to offer a deity, a monarch, or a person of honor. As early as Abraham's first days in Canaan, he offered the priest Melchizedek a tenth of the goods he recovered in a military victory (Genesis 14:17-20). Abraham's grandson Jacob made a commitment to God at Bethel that included a tenth of everything God blessed him with (Genesis 28:20-22). Samuel gave evidence to national tithes (taxes) later in Israel's history when he warned the people that a king would require tithes of their harvests (1 Samuel 8:10-21). But it should be noted that none of these tithes were a tenth of the total income of the general population.

trees, belongs to the LORD and must be set apart to Him as holy. 31 If you want to buy
back the LORD's tenth of the grain or fruit, you must pay its value, plus 20 percent.
32Count off every tenth animal from your herds and flocks and set them apart for the
LORD as holy. 33 You may not pick and choose between good and bad animals, and you
may not substitute one for another. But if you do exchange one animal for another,
then both the original animal and its substitute will be considered holy and cannot be
bought back."

34These are the commands that the LORD gave through Moses on Mount Sinai for the
Israelites.

27:33 Lev 27:10

27:34 Lev 26:46

▸ HOLINESS

27:34 The Lord gave the law. Three things characterize a nation: land, people, and law. God created a people for Himself through the descendants of Abraham. Their land was Canaan, and Leviticus constituted the bulk of their law, given through Moses. The church of Jesus Christ is not a nation, but we have a "land" (heaven), people (followers of Jesus), and law (1 John 2:7; 2 John 1:5). By loving God and loving our neighbor, we fulfill all the commands of the law of God (Matthew 22:37-40). (***See Holiness***> *Maturing> Conformity to Christ> Following the Royal Law of love,* TopicGuide page A40.)

PURPOSE

To restate God's command to take the Promised Land by citing the example of the previous generation's rebellion against God.

School principals often tell their teachers at the beginning of the school year to establish the rules early. "Don't be afraid to let the students know who is in charge. They may not like you initially, but they will ultimately respect you." God used a similar approach with the nation of Israel when they left Mount Sinai and headed for the Promised Land of Canaan.

God's establishment of His authority can be illustrated by noting the key events in Numbers. Twice God commanded Moses to count all the people in the twelve tribes of Israel (1:1–4:49; 26:1–27:23). It is from these numberings that the book of Numbers takes its name.

Was this redundant? Technically, the process was duplicated—just later with different results, with the events separated by more than thirty-eight years. During the first census, Moses counted the generation of Israelites who left Egypt in the Exodus. But when this generation rebelled against God, they were sentenced to wander in the wilderness until they all died. Thus, the second census was of the new generation of Israelites who grew to adulthood during the wilderness wanderings (chapter 26). Its results showed that God had been faithful to the promises that He made to Abraham (Genesis 12:1-3) in spite of Israel's rebellion. This new generation would inherit the Promised Land.

DISCOVER GOD IN NUMBERS

Two attributes of God shine through the ups and downs of the history of Israel in Numbers:

Holy: In Numbers, God prepared the new nation of Israel for habitation of the land of promise by calling them to a level of holiness befitting His people. Twenty-two times God instructed Israel in the measures they were to take to establish themselves as holy. God explained to Moses that the sin that kept him from entering the Promised Land was this: "you did not trust Me enough to demonstrate My holiness to the people of Israel" (Numbers 20:12). The holiness God wished to see manifested in His people was not arbitrary, but was based on His character—it was "My holiness" that God required Moses to display before the people. Even today God doesn't require His people to simply be morally superior to the surrounding world; this would be rather simple for most. God commands the impossible, humanly speaking—He commands us to receive and manifest His holy character in everything we do (1 Peter 1:15-16).

Savior: After the first generation of Israelites died in the wilderness, the new generation quickly forgot the lessons of their fathers' failures—they, too, began to grumble and complain against Moses' leadership. As a means of driving His people to repentance, God sent poisonous snakes into the camp, and many people died (Numbers 21:4-9). As the people repented of their sin, God directed Moses to make a bronze serpent and lift it high up on a pole in the middle of the camp. Anyone who looked upon the serpent would be saved from the poisonous snakes. Jesus Christ used this incident as an illustration of how He would be lifted up on a cross, and that all who looked upon Him (believed in Him) would be saved from their sin (John 3:14-15). It is part of God's nature to provide a way of salvation.

GROWING THROUGH NUMBERS

The apostle Paul in the New Testament epistles used Israel's experience in the desert from Numbers to highlight spiritual themes for the Christian life (1 Corinthians 10:8-11): purity, trust, and submission.

Purity: When the new generation of Israelites approached Moab, many engaged in sexual immorality with the prostitutes of the pagan religion of Baal (Numbers 25). More than twenty thousand of them were killed in a judgment from God. Faithfulness to God is displayed by purity and practical holiness in our lives.

Trust: When the people did not like the direction Moses took them on one occasion, they rebelled. The poisonous snakes that entered the camp were a direct result of their sin (Numbers 21). Trusting God's direction is both a sign of spiritual maturity and a doorway to greater adventures in God's kingdom.

Submission: When God brought severe judgment upon Korah and his family for their rebellion against Moses, the whole community grumbled—and 14,700 more died (Numbers 16). God establishes all earthly authorities (such as Moses), and submission to God means living in appropriate subordination to those in authority, such as our parents (Exodus 20:12), the church (Hebrews 13:17), and the government (Romans 13:1-7).

NUMBERS FACTS

Author: Numbers names Moses over eighty times as the one to whom God spoke. God directed Moses to write passages such as 33:2, where Moses wrote down the details of the Israelites' journey from Egypt to Canaan.

Written to: After the first generation of Hebrews turned away from the Promised Land, Moses wrote to the second generation of Israelites to encourage them to obey by noting the severe consequences of rebelling against God.

Date of writing: Moses compiled the Numbers material during the more than thirty-eight years of desert wanderings following the Exodus (c. 1444–1405 BC). He compiled the material in the first five books of the Bible during the thirty-eight years of wandering, completing his work just before his death while the nation was camped on the plains of Moab, ready to enter the Promised Land (see Introduction to Deuteronomy).

Setting: Numbers 1:1–10:10 takes place at Mount Sinai (twenty days). Chapters 10:11–25:18 take place in the wilderness just south of Canaan (more than thirty-eight years). Chapters 26:1–36:13 are set on the east bank of the Jordan River in the plains of Moab (about five months). There Moses transfers leadership of the nation to Joshua, who prepares to lead Israel into Canaan to inherit the land promised by God to Abraham (Genesis 15:18-19).

DISCOVERY VERSES

"May the LORD bless you and protect you. May the LORD smile on you and be gracious to you. May the LORD show you His favor and give you His peace."

(NUMBERS 6:24-26)

"When you arrive in your own land and go to war against your enemies who attack you, sound the alarm with the trumpets. Then the LORD your God will remember you and rescue you from your enemies."

(NUMBERS 10:9)

And whenever the Ark set out, Moses would shout, "Arise, O LORD, and let Your enemies be scattered! Let them flee before You!"

(NUMBERS 10:35)

"God is not a man, so He does not lie. He is not human, so He does not change His mind. Has He ever spoken and failed to act? Has He ever promised and not carried it through?"

(NUMBERS 23:19)

OUTLINE

▸ **NUMBERS 1:1–25:18**—The first generation fails to take the land
- ***NUMBERS 1:1–4:49****—Preparation to take the land*
- ***NUMBERS 5:1–9:14****—Preparation for holiness*
- ***NUMBERS 9:15–25:18****—Failure to take the land and its consequences*

▸ **NUMBERS 26:1–36:13**—The second generation takes the land
- ***NUMBERS 26:1–27:11****—Preparation to take the land*
- ***NUMBERS 27:12–23****—Joshua is appointed*
- ***NUMBERS 28:1–31:54****—Preparation for holiness*
- ***NUMBERS 32:1–36:13****—Instructions on successfully taking the land*

REGISTRATION OF ISRAEL'S TROOPS

1:1 **1** A year after Israel's departure from Egypt, the LORD spoke to Moses in the Tabernacle*
Exod 40:2, 17 in the wilderness of Sinai. On the first day of the second month* of that year He said,
1:2 Exod 38:25-26 2"From the whole community of Israel, record the names of all the warriors by their clans
Num 26:2 and families. List all the men 3twenty years old or older who are able to go to war. You
1:4 and Aaron must register the troops, 4and you will be assisted by one family leader from
Exod 18:21 Num 34:18 each tribe.
1:5 Gen 29:32 Rev 7:5 5"These are the tribes and the names of the leaders who will assist you:

Tribe	*Leader*
Reuben	Elizur son of Shedeur

1:1a Hebrew *the Tent of Meeting.* 1:1b This day in the ancient Hebrew lunar calendar occurred in April or May.

1:1 The Israelites had been on their journey to the Promised Land for a little over a year. This midspring day was the first day of the second month of the second year after the Israelites came out of Egypt. During that first year the Israelites made their miraculous escape from Egypt, crossed the Red Sea, traveled to Sinai, and received the Ten Commandments and the plans for the Tabernacle. As Numbers begins, the Tabernacle has been set up and the first Passover Feast celebrated.

1:1 Mount Sinai was a sacred mountain in the history of the Israelite nation. Many believe it was on the peninsula between Egypt and Israel. When Moses fled Egypt after murdering an Egyptian (Exodus 2:11-15), he traveled through this area. Near here God spoke to Moses out of the burning bush, giving Moses his first orders. Later, the whole nation camped at Sinai. Moses received additional instructions from God there, including the Ten Commandments. The life of practicing religious Jews is based on these instructions to this day. But for Christians, God's law is written on our hearts and in our minds.

1:1 The phrases "the LORD spoke to Moses" and "[the LORD] said" are reminders that Moses did not merely lay down laws on his own initiative. Instead, he was inspired by God to establish these guidelines among His people. In his New Testament letter, Peter wrote, "No prophecy in Scripture ever came from the prophet's own understanding. . . . No, those prophets were moved by the Holy Spirit, and they spoke from God" (2 Peter 1:20-21). At this time Israel did not have a formalized government. Religion was united to politics.

▸ HOLINESS

1:2 Take a census. The two surveys (here and at Numbers 26) of the tribes occur to explain which tribes should get the most productive plots of land in Canaan. There is nothing wrong with taking a census—in fact, God ordered Moses to do so. Later in Israel's history, King David would sin greatly in taking one not ordered by God (1 Chronicles 21:8). As you count your possessions, give glory to God for everything He's given you. (***See Holiness****> Disciplines> Of Abstinence> Stewardship,* TopicGuide page A42.)

1:2-3 It is significant that God told Moses to take the census. While the census highlighted those men who were of the age to be soldiers, it accounted for more than the strength of the army. The most ancient ancestor of the Israelites, Abraham, had been given a promise that his descendants would become a great nation (Genesis 12:2; 22:15-19). This census confirmed the fulfillment of that promise.

1:5 Jacob, the son of Isaac, was renamed *Israel* and his 12 sons became the progenitors of the Israelite nation.

1:6-15 The tribes of Israel and their leaders are listed in order according to their mothers. They were all born to Jacob (later renamed Israel): Reuben, Simeon, Judah, Issachar, and Zebulun all by Jacob's first wife, Leah; Joseph (in the two tribes of Ephraim, and Manasseh) and Benjamin by Rachel, his second wife; Dan, Asher, Gad and Naphtali by the two handmaidens, Bilhah and Zilpah. Levi was excluded from the census since the tribe neither received land nor served in the army.

KEY PLACES IN NUMBERS

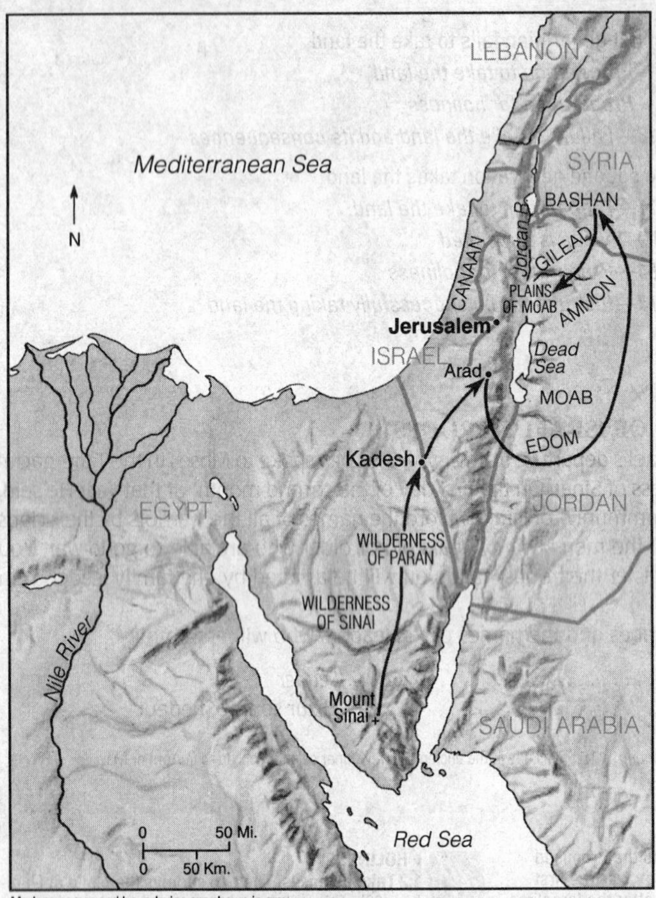

Modern names and boundaries are shown in gray.

1 Mount Sinai Numbers begins at Mount Sinai in the wilderness of Sinai with Moses taking a census of the men eligible for battle. As the battle preparations began, the people also prepared for the spiritual warfare they would face. The Promised Land was full of wicked people who would try to entice the Israelites to sin. God, therefore, taught Moses and the Israelites how to live right (1:1–12:15).

2 Wilderness of Paran After a full year at Mount Sinai, the Israelites broke camp and began their march toward the Promised Land by moving into the wilderness of Paran. From there, one leader from each tribe was sent to spy out the new land. After 40 days they returned, and all but Joshua and Caleb were too afraid to enter. Because of their lack of faith, the Israelites were made to wander in the wilderness for 40 years (12:16–19:22).

3 Kadesh With the years of wandering nearing an end, the Israelites set their sights once again on the Promised Land. Kadesh was the oasis where they spent most of their desert years. Miriam died here. And it was here that Moses angrily struck the rock, which kept him from entering the Promised Land (20).

4 Arad When the king there heard that Israel was on the move, he attacked, but he was soundly defeated. Moses then led the people southward and eastward around the Dead Sea (21:1-3).

5 Edom The Israelites wanted to travel through Edom, but the king of Edom refused them passage (20:14-22). So they traveled around Edom and became very discouraged. The people complained, and God sent poisonous snakes to punish them. Only by looking at a bronze snake on a pole could those bitten be healed (21:4-9).

6 Ammon Next, King Sihon of the Amorites refused Israel passage. When he attacked, Israel defeated his army and conquered the territory as far as the border of Ammon (21:21-32).

7 Bashan Moses sent spies to Bashan. King Og attacked, but he was also defeated (21:33-35).

8 Plains of Moab The people camped on the plains of Moab, east of the Jordan River across from Jericho. They were on the verge of entering the Promised Land (22:1).

9 Moab King Balak of Moab, terrified of the Israelites, called upon Balaam, a famous sorcerer, to curse Israel from the mountains above where the Israelites camped. But the Lord caused Balaam to bless them instead (22:2–24:25).

10 Gilead The tribes of Reuben and Gad decided to settle in the fertile country of Gilead east of the Jordan River because it was a good land for their sheep. But first they promised to help the other tribes conquer the land west of the Jordan River (32).

1:7 6 Simeon .... Shelumiel son of Zurishaddai
Ruth 4:20 7 Judah .... Nahshon son of Amminadab
1 Chr 2:10 8 Issachar .... Nethanel son of Zuar
9 Zebulun .... Eliab son of Helon
10 Ephraim son of Joseph .... Elishama son of Ammihud
Manasseh son of Joseph .... Gamaliel son of Pedahzur
11 Benjamin .... Abidan son of Gideoni
1:14 Num 2:14 12 Dan .... Ahiezer son of Ammishaddai
1:16 13 Asher .... Pagiel son of Ocran
Num 7:2; 16:2; 26:9 14 Gad .... Eliasaph son of Deuel
1:18 15 Naphtali .... Ahira son of Enan

Num 1:1
Ezra 2:59 16These are the chosen leaders of the community, the leaders of their ancestral tribes, the
1:20 heads of the clans of Israel."
Num 26:5-11 17So Moses and Aaron called together these chosen leaders, 18and they assembled the
1:22 whole community of Israel on that very day.* All the people were registered according to
Num 26:12-14 their ancestry by their clans and families. The men of Israel who were twenty years old or
1:24 Num 26:15-18 older were listed one by one, 19just as the LORD had commanded Moses. So Moses re-
1:26 corded their names in the wilderness of Sinai.
Num 26:19-22 20-21This is the number of men twenty years old or older who were able to go to war, as
1:28 their names were listed in the records of their clans and families*:

Num 26:23-25 *Tribe* .... *Number*
1:30 Num 26:26-27 Reuben (Jacob's* oldest son) 46,500
1:32 22-23 Simeon 59,300
Num 26:35-37 24-25 Gad 45,650
1:34 26-27 Judah 74,600
Num 26:28-34 28-29 Issachar 54,400
1:36 30-31 Zebulun 57,400
Num 26:38-41 32-33 Ephraim son of Joseph 40,500
1:38 Num 26:42-43 34-35 Manasseh son of Joseph 32,200
36-37 Benjamin 35,400
1:40 Num 26:44-47 38-39 Dan 62,700
1:42 40-41 Asher 41,500
Num 26:48-50 42-43 Naphtali 53,400

1:44 Num 26:64 44These were the men registered by Moses and Aaron and the twelve leaders of Israel, all
1:46 listed according to their ancestral descent. 45They were registered by families—all the men
Num 2:32; 26:51 of Israel who were twenty years old or older and able to go to war. 46The total number was
603,550.

1:18 Hebrew *on the first day of the second month;* see 1:1. 1:20-21a In the Hebrew text, this phrase (*This is the number of men twenty years old or older who were able to go to war, as their names were listed in the records of their clans and families*) is repeated in 1:22, 24, 26, 28, 30, 32, 34, 36, 38, 40, 42. 1:20-21b Hebrew *Israel's.* The names "Jacob" and "Israel" are often interchanged throughout the Old Testament, referring sometimes to the individual patriarch and sometimes to the nation.

▸ BIBLE

1:44 How large are the numbers? The Bible is God's holy Word, and there were no errors delivered from God to the original authors. But these large figures in Numbers are quite puzzling. If Israel had this many fighting men, then they would have had the largest army in the world and could have easily defeated the small armies of 3,000 to 6,000 sprinkled around Canaan. Yet God made it clear that they feared defeat because the other nations were too large (Deuteronomy 7:7, 17-18). Four explanations have been offered for these large numbers: (1) The numbers are correct. (2) The numbers were originally correct, but were accidentally confused by an early copyist. (3) The Hebrew word for *thousand* may be a technical term for units of men less than 1,000. (4) The numbers are hyperboles, intended exaggerations to highlight the grace God had shown to Israel. In any case, God's grace and power sustained Israel from start to finish, and once again human might is not a challenge for God. (***See Bible***> *Uniqueness> Inspired> Internally consistent,* TopicGuide page A10.)

47 But this total did not include the Levites. 48 For the LORD had said to Moses, 49 "Do not 1:47
include the tribe of Levi in the registration; do not count them with the rest of the Israel- Num 2:33; 26:57
ites. 50 Put the Levites in charge of the Tabernacle of the Covenant,* along with all its fur- 1:50
nishings and equipment. They must carry the Tabernacle and all its furnishings as you Num 3:25-37
travel, and they must take care of it and camp around it. 51 Whenever it is time for the 1:51 Num 4:1-33
Tabernacle to move, the Levites will take it down. And when it is time to stop, they will
set it up again. But any unauthorized person who goes too near the Tabernacle must be
put to death. 52 Each tribe of Israel will camp in a designated area with its own family ban- 1:52
ner. 53 But the Levites will camp around the Tabernacle of the Covenant to protect the Num 2:2
community of Israel from the LORD's anger. The Levites are responsible to stand guard 1:53 Num 1:50
around the Tabernacle."
54 So the Israelites did everything just as the LORD had commanded Moses.

ORGANIZATION FOR ISRAEL'S CAMP

2 Then the LORD gave these instructions to Moses and Aaron: 2 "When the Israelites set 2:2
up camp, each tribe will be assigned its own area. The tribal divisions will camp be- Num 1:52
neath their family banners on all four sides of the Tabernacle,* but at some distance from it.
3-4 "The divisions of Judah, Issachar, and Zebulun are to camp toward the sunrise on the 2:3
east side of the Tabernacle, beneath their family banners. These are the names of the Num 10:14
tribes, their leaders, and the numbers of their registered troops:

	Tribe	*Leader*	*Number*	
	Judah	Nahshon son of Amminadab	74,600	
5-6	Issachar	Nethanel son of Zuar	54,400	2:5 Num 1:8
7-8	Zebulun	Eliab son of Helon	57,400	

9 So the total of all the troops on Judah's side of the camp is 186,400. These three tribes 2:9
are to lead the way whenever the Israelites travel to a new campsite. Num 10:14
10-11 "The divisions of Reuben, Simeon, and Gad are to camp on the south side of the 2:10
Tabernacle, beneath their family banners. These are the names of the tribes, their leaders, Num 1:5
and the numbers of their registered troops:

1:50 Or *Tabernacle of the Testimony;* also in 1:53. 2:2 Hebrew *the Tent of Meeting;* also in 2:17.

1:47-49 Levi's tribe was not part of the census since they were set apart by God to serve in and care for the Tabernacle. Moses and his brother Aaron were of the tribe of Levi. Aaron's descendants became the priests, the religious leaders; the nation was their congregation. They looked after the ceremonial utensils and supervised the sacrifices. The rest of the Levites served in the Tabernacle (and later the Temple) in one capacity or another—groundskeepers, teachers, medics, etc. The high priest, the religious leader of the nation, was always supposed to be a descendant of Aaron.

1:50, 53 The Tabernacle was, in essence, a portable temple. It was a simple structure made from poles and curtains, but the later Temple was based on this structure. It included a general area in which the people could gather; a smaller area, the Holy Place, accessed by the religious leadership; and the Most Holy Place, a chamber only accessed by the high priest in the most sacred of ceremonies. The Most Holy Place represented God's residence with the people. Kept there was the Ark of the Covenant, a chest of sacred relics from the history of the Israelites. The Tabernacle was used, in one form or another, by the Israelite people until King Solomon built the Temple.

2:2 Throughout the Old Testament the Israelites were organized according to the 12 tribes. The tribes were descendants of Jacob's 12 sons. When the Israelites settled the land, each tribe was given an allotment of land. The two exceptions were Levi and Joseph. The Levites were religious workers and did not own land. Joseph's allotment was doubled and awarded to his sons, Manasseh and Ephraim. In this way the tradition of 12 tribes was maintained in 12 regions of land.

2:2 Israel's very identity and structure was established around the 12 tribes. The camp was divided that way; they traveled that way; tasks were assigned that way. When they eventually settled the land, the property was divided among the tribes. To be under the tribal banner was to be identified with—to belong to—that tribe.

2:3-4 Today our maps are oriented in such a way that north is at the top of the page, east to the right, and so forth. Ancient Near Eastern people, however, looked to the sunrise in the east to get their bearings; their maps illustrated this orientation by placing east on the top of the page, south to the right, north to the left, and west at the bottom.

2:5-30 The tribes of Jacob (Israel) were ordered to surround the Tabernacle on all four sides as they traveled and camped. Evidence of such practical protection has been found also in ancient Egyptian and Assyrian artifacts. It was an effective arrangement, allowing both order and defense.

ARRANGEMENT OF TRIBES AROUND THE TABERNACLE WHILE IN THE WILDERNESS

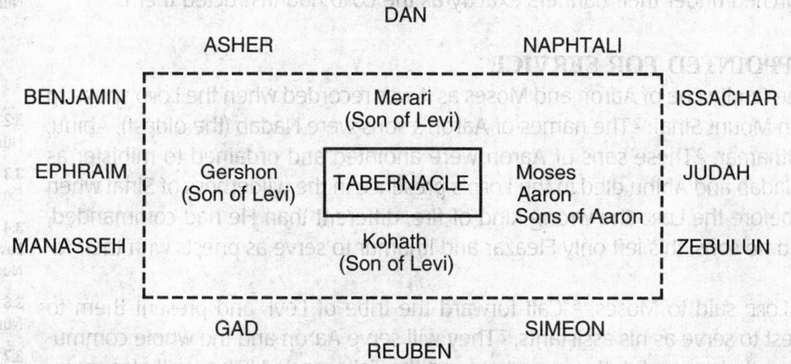

Margin	Verse	*Tribe*	*Leader*	*Number*
		Reuben	Elizur son of Shedeur	46,500
2:12 Num 1:6	12-13	Simeon	Shelumiel son of Zurishaddai	59,300
2:14 Num 1:14	14-15	Gad	Eliasaph son of Deuel*	45,650

16 So the total of all the troops on Reuben's side of the camp is 151,450. These three tribes will be second in line whenever the Israelites travel.

2:17 Num 1:53 17 "Then the Tabernacle, carried by the Levites, will set out from the middle of the camp. All the tribes are to travel in the same order that they camp, each in position under the appropriate family banner.

18-19 "The divisions of Ephraim, Manasseh, and Benjamin are to camp on the west side of the Tabernacle, beneath thei family banners. These are the names of the tribes, their leaders, and the numbers of their registered troops:

Margin	Verse	*Tribe*	*Leader*	*Number*
		Ephraim	Elishama son of Ammihud	40,500
2:20 Num 1:10	20-21	Manasseh	Gamaliel son of Pedahzur	32,200
	22-23	Benjamin	Abidan son of Gideoni	35,400

2:24 Num 10:22 24 So the total of all the troops on Ephraim's side of the camp is 108,100. These three tribes will be third in line whenever the Israelites travel.

2:25 Num 1:12 25-26 "The divisions of Dan, Asher, and Naphtali are to camp on the north side of the Tabernacle, beneath their family banners. These are the names of the tribes, their leaders, and the numbers of their registered troops:

Margin	Verse	*Tribe*	*Leader*	*Number*
		Dan	Ahiezer son of Ammishaddai	62,700
2:27 Num 1:13	27-28	Asher	Pagiel son of Ocran	41,500
	29-30	Naphtali	Ahira son of Enan.	53,400

2:31 Num 10:25 31 So the total of all the troops on Dan's side of the camp is 157,600. These three tribes will be last, marching under their banners whenever the Israelites travel."

2:14-15 As in many Hebrew manuscripts, Samaritan Pentateuch, and Latin Vulgate (see also 1:14); most Hebrew manuscripts read *son of Reuel.*

2:17 The tribe of Levi was in the center with the Tabernacle. Their numbering comes in the next chapter.

32In summary, the troops of Israel listed by their families totaled 603,550. 33But as the LORD had commanded, the Levites were not included in this registration. 34So the people of Israel did everything as the LORD had commanded Moses. Each clan and family set up camp and marched under their banners exactly as the LORD had instructed them.

2:32 Exod 38:26 Num 1:45-46
2:33 Num 1:47

LEVITES APPOINTED FOR SERVICE

3 This is the family line of Aaron and Moses as it was recorded when the LORD spoke to Moses on Mount Sinai: 2The names of Aaron's sons were Nadab (the oldest), Abihu, Eleazar, and Ithamar. 3These sons of Aaron were anointed and ordained to minister as priests. 4But Nadab and Abihu died in the LORD's presence in the wilderness of Sinai when they burned before the LORD the wrong kind of fire, different than He had commanded. Since they had no sons, this left only Eleazar and Ithamar to serve as priests with their father, Aaron.

5Then the LORD said to Moses, 6"Call forward the tribe of Levi, and present them to Aaron the priest to serve as his assistants. 7They will serve Aaron and the whole community, performing their sacred duties in and around the Tabernacle.* 8They will also maintain all the furnishings of the sacred tent,* serving in the Tabernacle on behalf of all the Israelites. 9Assign the Levites to Aaron and his sons. They have been given from among all the people of Israel to serve as their assistants. 10Appoint Aaron and his sons to carry out the duties of the priesthood. But any unauthorized person who goes too near the sanctuary must be put to death."

11And the LORD said to Moses, 12"Look, I have chosen the Levites from among the Israelites to serve as substitutes for all the firstborn sons of the people of Israel. The Levites belong to Me, 13for all the firstborn males are Mine. On the day I struck down all the firstborn sons of the Egyptians, I set apart for Myself all the firstborn in Israel, both of people and of animals. They are Mine; I am the LORD."

3:2 Num 26:60
3:3 Exod 28:41
3:4 Lev 10:1-2 Num 26:61
3:6 Num 8:6-22; 18:2-6
3:7 Num 3:41; 8:16-18
3:10 Num 1:51
3:12 Num 3:41
3:13 Exod 13:2, 12, 15 Num 8:17

REGISTRATION OF THE LEVITES

14The LORD spoke again to Moses in the wilderness of Sinai. He said, 15"Record the names of the members of the tribe of Levi by their families and clans. List every male who is one month old or older." 16So Moses listed them, just as the LORD had commanded.

17Levi had three sons, whose names were Gershon, Kohath, and Merari.
18The clans descended from Gershon were named after two of his descendants, Libni and Shimei.
19The clans descended from Kohath were named after four of his descendants, Amram, Izhar, Hebron, and Uzziel.

3:15 Num 1:47

3:7 Hebrew *around the Tent of Meeting, doing service at the Tabernacle.* 3:8 Hebrew *the Tent of Meeting;* also in 3:25.

WORSHIP

3:4 Nadab and Abihu died. Someone once said, "Nepotism is best kept in the family." Only Aaron and his descendants could be high priests, but that didn't mean they were morally better than other families. Aaron's sons died for their decision to alter the worship instructions that God had given. Today, you can worship God as He has directed if you do so "in spirit and in truth" (John 4:23-24). (***See Worship***> *NT> Our Role> Mind and Heart> Worship in spirit and in truth because God is Spirit,* TopicGuide page A32; ***Worship***> *OT> Prohibitions> Wrong Forms> Strange fire and incense,* TopicGuide page A28.)

3:7 While God referred to the whole nation of Israel as a "kingdom of priests" (Exodus 19:5-6), he set apart the Levites for special work—to care for the Tabernacle. Within the Levites, he set aside Aaron and his descendants to function as priests. Their functions included everything from tending the lamps in the Tabernacle to mediating between God and His people. Later, Jesus Christ became the final, perfect High Priest who stands in our stead before God (Hebrews 3:1-3; 10:19-22).

3:17 Each of Levi's three family lines, Gershon, Kohath, and Merari, were given specific Tabernacle tasks outlined in the next chapter. The Kohathites would carry the furniture that had been prepared by Aaron's priests. The Gershonites cared for the curtains and cloths that made up the walls of the Tabernacle. The descendants of Merari took care of the frame that made up the structure of the Tabernacle.

20 The clans descended from Merari were named after two of his descendants, Mahli
and Mushi.
These were the Levite clans, listed according to their family groups.

21 The descendants of Gershon were composed of the clans descended from Libni and
Shimei. 22 There were 7,500 males one month old or older among these Gershonite clans.
23 They were assigned the area to the west of the Tabernacle for their camp. 24 The leader
3:25 of the Gershonite clans was Eliasaph son of Lael. 25 These two clans were responsible to
Num 4:24-26 care for the Tabernacle, including the sacred tent with its layers of coverings, the curtain at
its entrance, 26 the curtains of the courtyard that surrounded the Tabernacle and altar, the
curtain at the courtyard entrance, the ropes, and all the equipment related to their use.

3:27 Exod 6:18 27 The descendants of Kohath were composed of the clans descended from Amram,
1 Chr 26:23 Izhar, Hebron, and Uzziel. 28 There were 8,600* males one month old or older among
these Kohathite clans. They were responsible for the care of the sanctuary, 29 and they
were assigned the area south of the Tabernacle for their camp. 30 The leader of the Kohath-
ite clans was Elizaphan son of Uzziel. 31 These four clans were responsible for the care of
the Ark, the table, the lampstand, the altars, the various articles used in the sanctuary, the
inner curtain, and all the equipment related to their use. 32 Eleazar, son of Aaron the priest,
was the chief administrator over all the Levites, with special responsibility for the oversight
of the sanctuary.

3:33 33 The descendants of Merari were composed of the clans descended from Mahli and
Exod 6:19 Mushi. 34 There were 6,200 males one month old or older among these Merarite clans.
35 They were assigned the area north of the Tabernacle for their camp. The leader of the
Merarite clans was Zuriel son of Abihail. 36 These two clans were responsible for the care of
the frames supporting the Tabernacle, the crossbars, the pillars, the bases, and all the
equipment related to their use. 37 They were also responsible for the posts of the courtyard
and all their bases, pegs, and ropes.

3:38 38 The area in front of the Tabernacle, in the east toward the sunrise,* was reserved for
Num 1:51; 3:10 the tents of Moses and of Aaron and his sons, who had the final responsibility for the sanc-
tuary on behalf of the people of Israel. Anyone other than a priest or Levite who went too
near the sanctuary was to be put to death.

3:39 39 When Moses and Aaron counted the Levite clans at the LORD's command, the total
Num 26:62 number was 22,000 males one month old or older.

REDEEMING THE FIRSTBORN SONS

40 Then the LORD said to Moses, "Now count all the firstborn sons in Israel who are one
3:41 month old or older, and make a list of their names. 41 The Levites must be reserved for Me
Num 3:12, 45 as substitutes for the firstborn sons of Israel; I am the LORD. And the Levites' livestock must
3:43 Num 3:39 be reserved for Me as substitutes for the firstborn livestock of the whole nation of Israel."

42 So Moses counted the firstborn sons of the people of Israel, just as the LORD had com-
3:45 Lev 11:44 manded. 43 The number of firstborn sons who were one month old or older was 22,273.

3:46 44 Then the LORD said to Moses, 45 "Take the Levites as substitutes for the firstborn sons
Exod 13:13, 15 of the people of Israel. And take the livestock of the Levites as substitutes for the firstborn
Num 18:14-16 livestock of the people of Israel. The Levites belong to Me; I am the LORD. 46 There are

3:28 Some Greek manuscripts read *8,300;* see total in 3:39. 3:38 Hebrew *toward the sunrise, in front of the Tent of Meeting.*

3:32 Though Aaron and Moses were descendants of Kohath, only Aaron's direct line were priests (see also verse 38).

3:40-48 The firstborn, particularly the firstborn male, had unique standing in ancient Israelite culture. This was true of flocks and herds as well as children.

3:43 Compared to census figures in chapter 1, this figure of 22,273 firstborn sons seems unusually small. Some scholars propose this numbering may reflect only males born after the Exodus because redemption of the other firstborn occurred at the first Passover (see Exodus 12:22-23).

273 more firstborn sons of Israel than there are Levites. To redeem these extra firstborn sons, 47 collect five pieces of silver* for each of them (each piece weighing the same as the sanctuary shekel, which equals twenty gerahs). 48 Give the silver to Aaron and his sons as the redemption price for the extra firstborn sons."

3:47 Exod 30:13 Lev 27:1-8

49 So Moses collected the silver for redeeming the firstborn sons of Israel who exceeded the number of Levites. 50 He collected 1,365 pieces of silver* on behalf of these firstborn sons of Israel (each piece weighing the same as the sanctuary shekel). 51 And Moses gave the silver for the redemption to Aaron and his sons, just as the LORD had commanded.

3:50 Num 3:46-48

DUTIES OF THE KOHATHITE CLAN

4 Then the LORD said to Moses and Aaron, 2 "Record the names of the members of the clans and families of the Kohathite division of the tribe of Levi. 3 List all the men between the ages of thirty and fifty who are eligible to serve in the Tabernacle.*

4:3 Num 4:23; 8:24-25

4 "The duties of the Kohathites at the Tabernacle will relate to the most sacred objects. 5 When the camp moves, Aaron and his sons must enter the Tabernacle first to take down the inner curtain and cover the Ark of the Covenant* with it. 6 Then they must cover the inner curtain with fine goatskin leather and spread over that a single piece of blue cloth. Finally, they must put the carrying poles of the Ark in place.

4:6 Num 4:25

7 "Next they must spread a blue cloth over the table where the Bread of the Presence is displayed, and on the cloth they will place the bowls, pans, jars, pitchers, and the special bread. 8 They must spread a scarlet cloth over all of this, and finally a covering of fine goatskin leather on top of the scarlet cloth. Then they must insert the carrying poles into the table.

4:7 Exod 37:10-16 Lev 24:5-8

9 "Next they must cover the lampstand with a blue cloth, along with its lamps, lamp snuffers, trays, and special jars of olive oil. 10 Then they must cover the lampstand and its accessories with fine goatskin leather and place the bundle on a carrying frame.

4:9 Exod 25:37-38

11 "Next they must spread a blue cloth over the gold incense altar and cover this cloth with fine goatskin leather. Then they must attach the carrying poles to the altar. 12 They must take all the remaining furnishings of the sanctuary and wrap them in a blue cloth, cover them with fine goatskin leather, and place them on the carrying frame.

13 "They must remove the ashes from the altar for sacrifices and cover the altar with a purple cloth. 14 All the altar utensils—the firepans, meat forks, shovels, basins, and all the containers—must be placed on the cloth, and a covering of fine goatskin leather must be spread over them. Finally, they must put the carrying poles in place. 15 The camp will be ready to move when Aaron and his sons have finished covering the sanctuary and all the sacred articles. The Kohathites will come and carry these things to the next destination. But they must not touch the sacred objects, or they will die. So these are the things from the Tabernacle that the Kohathites must carry.

4:15 Num 4:19-20

3:47 Hebrew *5 shekels* [2 ounces or 57 grams]. 3:50 Hebrew *1,365 shekels* [34 pounds or 15.5 kilograms].
4:3 Hebrew *the Tent of Meeting;* also in 4:4, 15, 23, 25, 28, 30, 31, 33, 35, 37, 39, 41, 43, 47. 4:5 Or *Ark of the Testimony.*

3:47-49 The "shekel" was a standard unit of weight throughout the Ancient Near East (though throughout history, it would change in weight and value). During this time, 5 sanctuary shekels per person weighed about 2 ounces. Thus, when added together, they gathered approximately 34 pounds of silver.

▸ HOLINESS
3:49 Redemption money. Everything you see belongs to God. Even our next generation, our children, belong to the Lord; we are merely their caretakers. To remind Israel of this reality, God asked them to symbolically redeem, or purchase back from Him, their firstborn sons. Have you given your children to God? How can you demonstrate this to Him? (***See Holiness****> Law and Grace> Law> Parents and Children,* TopicGuide page A41.)

4:4 The duties of the Kohathites included carrying the sacred objects after those objects had been prepared for transport by the priests of Aaron. Later, when the Tabernacle came to a permanent resting place, these duties may have no longer been necessary.

4:15 The instructions for carrying the Ark and the prohibition against touching the holy articles were warnings to all Kohathites (as also in verses 17-20). But in 2 Samuel 6, when improperly transporting the Ark, Uzzah the Kohathite died after touching it. Later, in 1 Chronicles 15:14-15, the instructions were carefully followed.

4:16 Exod 25:1-7; 30:22-34 16"Eleazar son of Aaron the priest will be responsible for the oil of the lampstand, the fra-
grant incense, the daily grain offering, and the anointing oil. In fact, Eleazar will be responsible
for the entire Tabernacle and everything in it, including the sanctuary and its furnishings."
17Then the LORD said to Moses and Aaron, 18"Do not let the Kohathite clans be de-
stroyed from among the Levites! 19This is what you must do so they will live and not die
when they approach the most sacred objects. Aaron and his sons must always go in with
them and assign a specific duty or load to each person. 20The Kohathites must never enter
the sanctuary to look at the sacred objects for even a moment, or they will die."

DUTIES OF THE GERSHONITE CLAN

21And the LORD said to Moses, 22"Record the names of the members of the clans and fami-
4:23 Num 4:3 lies of the Gershonite division of the tribe of Levi. 23List all the men between the ages of
thirty and fifty who are eligible to serve in the Tabernacle.
24"These Gershonite clans will be responsible for general service and carrying loads.
4:25 Num 3:25-26 25They must carry the curtains of the Tabernacle, the Tabernacle itself with its coverings,
the outer covering of fine goatskin leather, and the curtain for the Tabernacle entrance.
26They are also to carry the curtains for the courtyard walls that surround the Tabernacle
and altar, the curtain across the courtyard entrance, the ropes, and all the equipment re-
lated to their use. The Gershonites are responsible for all these items. 27Aaron and his sons
will direct the Gershonites regarding all their duties, whether it involves moving the equip-
ment or doing other work. They must assign the Gershonites responsibility for the loads
they are to carry. 28So these are the duties assigned to the Gershonite clans at the Taber-
nacle. They will be directly responsible to Ithamar son of Aaron the priest.

DUTIES OF THE MERARITE CLAN

29"Now record the names of the members of the clans and families of the Merarite division
4:30 Num 4:3 of the tribe of Levi. 30List all the men between the ages of thirty and fifty who are eligible to
serve in the Tabernacle.
31"Their only duty at the Tabernacle will be to carry loads. They will carry the frames of the
Tabernacle, the crossbars, the posts, and the bases; 32also the posts for the courtyard walls
with their bases, pegs, and ropes; and all the accessories and everything else related to their
use. Assign the various loads to each man by name. 33So these are the duties of the Merarite
clans at the Tabernacle. They are directly responsible to Ithamar son of Aaron the priest."

SUMMARY OF THE REGISTRATION

34So Moses, Aaron, and the other leaders of the community listed the members of the Ko-
hathite division by their clans and families. 35The list included all the men between thirty
and fifty years of age who were eligible for service in the Tabernacle, 36and the total num-
ber came to 2,750. 37So this was the total of all those from the Kohathite clans who were
eligible to serve at the Tabernacle. Moses and Aaron listed them, just as the LORD had com-
manded through Moses.

▸ BIBLE

4:20 God makes things sacred. These were the same objects made by the skilled craftsmen—obviously, the non-priests had looked at these objects while making them, so the objects did not automatically cause death. But God's presence had made them holy, special, and not to be trifled with. God's presence makes people holy, and we should tremble to insult or harm another person who has been made sacred by the indwelling Spirit of God. (***See Bible****> Unity> God's Message> Disobedience brings death,* TopicGuide page A11.)

4:24 The duties of the Gershonites included carrying the tents, curtains, and cloths that made up the divisions and walls of the Tabernacle. When the Tabernacle no longer needed to be moved, these duties were also unnecessary. Centuries later, King David reorganized the tasks of the Levites in preparation for the construction of the Temple. He named Asaph, a Gershonite, to music leadership (see Psalms 50; 73–83). David also appointed Gershonites to manage the Temple treasury.

4:29-33 Though the Merarite duties (carrying poles, crossbars, bases, pegs, etc.) seems mundane, these too were essential and holy tasks for the people of Israel.

38The Gershonite division was also listed by its clans and families. 39The list included all
the men between thirty and fifty years of age who were eligible for service in the Taberna-
cle, 40and the total number came to 2,630. 41So this was the total of all those from the
Gershonite clans who were eligible to serve at the Tabernacle. Moses and Aaron listed
them, just as the LORD had commanded.
42The Merarite division was also listed by its clans and families. 43The list included all
the men between thirty and fifty years of age who were eligible for service in the Taberna-
cle, 44and the total number came to 3,200. 45So this was the total of all those from the Me-
rarite clans who were eligible for service. Moses and Aaron listed them, just as the LORD
had commanded through Moses.
46So Moses, Aaron, and the leaders of Israel listed all the Levites by their clans and fami- **4:46**
lies. 47All the men between thirty and fifty years of age who were eligible for service in the Num 1:19
Tabernacle and for its transportation 48numbered 8,580. 49When their names were re- **4:49**
corded, as the LORD had commanded through Moses, each man was assigned his task and Num 1:47-49
told what to carry.
And so the registration was completed, just as the LORD had commanded Moses.

PURITY IN ISRAEL'S CAMP

5 The LORD gave these instructions to Moses: 2"Command the people of Israel to remove **5:2**
from the camp anyone who has a skin disease* or a discharge, or who has become cer- Lev 13:3, 46; 15:2
emonially unclean by touching a dead person. 3This command applies to men and women **5:3** Lev 26:12
alike. Remove them so they will not defile the camp in which I live among them." 4So the Is- 2 Cor 6:16
raelites did as the LORD had commanded Moses and removed such people from the camp.
5Then the LORD said to Moses, 6"Give the following instructions to the people of Israel: If
any of the people—men or women—betray the LORD by doing wrong to another person,
they are guilty. 7They must confess their sin and make full restitution for what they have **5:7**
done, adding an additional 20 percent and returning it to the person who was wronged. Lev 5:5, 16; 6:4-5
8But if the person who was wronged is dead, and there are no near relatives to whom resti-
tution can be made, the payment belongs to the LORD and must be given to the priest.
Those who are guilty must also bring a ram as a sacrifice, and they will be purified and
made right with the LORD.* 9All the sacred offerings that the Israelites bring to a priest will **5:9**
belong to him. 10Each priest may keep all the sacred donations that he receives." Lev 6:17

PROTECTING MARITAL FAITHFULNESS

11And the LORD said to Moses, 12"Give the following instructions to the people of Israel. **5:12**
"Suppose a man's wife goes astray, and she is unfaithful to her husband 13and has sex Num 5:19-21, 29

5:2 Traditionally rendered *leprosy.* The Hebrew word used here describes various skin diseases. 5:8 Or *bring a ram for atonement, which will make atonement for them.*

5:1–10:10 Having completed the census, Moses devotes the next several chapters of Numbers to commands for holiness in Israel. Uncleanness was seen as the opposite of holiness. Specific forms of uncleanness are described, and all forms led to separation from the camp. Though this instruction was critical for the community, more importantly it reminded Israel of God's holiness and perfection.

▶ WORSHIP
5:3 God's health program. God loves and cares for the weak and ill; the healing ministry of Jesus shows that. This purity law is concerned with reducing infectious diseases and with ceremonial cleanness. Showing no concern for spreading infectious disease or ceremonial uncleanness that would harm others physically and spiritually was sin, just as if they had purposely injured someone (Numbers 5:6-10). (***See Worship****> OT> Priesthood> Duties> Inspecting ceremonially unclean persons,* TopicGuide page A28; ***Worship****> NT> Cleansing,* TopicGuide page A30.)

5:5-10 Personal sin is the focus here. For resolution to occur, there must be confession, restitution, and forgiveness. A sin against an individual was also sin against the Lord.

5:11-31 This ritual, though perhaps appearing mystical and barbaric to modern people, focuses on resolving jealousy and suspicion. For a woman to become infertile in ancient Israel was the worst of fates. The prospect of drinking and taking an oath whose penalty was infertility would test her honesty to the core. This ritual also would have guarded women against a jealous husband who might otherwise have divorced or mistreated his wife based on mere suspicion.

with another man, but neither her husband nor anyone else knows about it. She has de-
filed herself, even though there was no witness and she was not caught in the act. 14 If her
husband becomes jealous and is suspicious of his wife and needs to know whether or not
5:15 Ezek 29:16 she has defiled herself, 15 the husband must bring his wife to the priest. He must also bring
an offering of two quarts* of barley flour to be presented on her behalf. Do not mix it with
olive oil or frankincense, for it is a jealousy offering—an offering to prove whether or not
she is guilty.

16 "The priest will then present her to stand trial before the LORD. 17 He must take some
holy water in a clay jar and pour into it dust he has taken from the Tabernacle floor.
18 When the priest has presented the woman before the LORD, he must unbind her hair and
place in her hands the offering of proof—the jealousy offering to determine whether her
husband's suspicions are justified. The priest will stand before her, holding the jar of bitter
water that brings a curse to those who are guilty. 19 The priest will then put the woman
under oath and say to her, 'If no other man has had sex with you, and you have not gone
astray and defiled yourself while under your husband's authority, may you be immune
from the effects of this bitter water that brings on the curse. 20 But if you have gone astray
by being unfaithful to your husband, and have defiled yourself by having sex with another
man—'

5:21 21 "At this point the priest must put the woman under oath by saying, 'May the people
Josh 6:26; 1 Sam 4:24 know that the LORD's curse is upon you when He makes you infertile, causing your womb
Neh 10:29 to shrivel* and your abdomen to swell. 22 Now may this water that brings the curse enter
your body and cause your abdomen to swell and your womb to shrivel.*' And the woman
will be required to say, 'Yes, let it be so.' 23 And the priest will write these curses on a piece
of leather and wash them off into the bitter water. 24 He will make the woman drink the bit-
ter water that brings on the curse. When the water enters her body, it will cause bitter suf-
fering if she is guilty.

25 "The priest will take the jealousy offering from the woman's hand, lift it up before the
5:26 Lev 2:2 LORD, and carry it to the altar. 26 He will take a handful of the flour as a token portion and
5:27 burn it on the altar, and he will require the woman to drink the water. 27 If she has defiled
Jer 29:18; 42:18 herself by being unfaithful to her husband, the water that brings on the curse will cause
bitter suffering. Her abdomen will swell and her womb will shrink,* and her name will be-
come a curse among her people. 28 But if she has not defiled herself and is pure, then she
will be unharmed and will still be able to have children.

5:29 29 "This is the ritual law for dealing with suspicion. If a woman goes astray and defiles
Num 5:11 herself while under her husband's authority, 30 or if a man becomes jealous and is suspi-
cious that his wife has been unfaithful, the husband must present his wife before the LORD,
and the priest will apply this entire ritual law to her. 31 The husband will be innocent of any
guilt in this matter, but his wife will be held accountable for her sin."

5:15 Hebrew 1/10 of an ephah [2.2 liters]. 5:21 Hebrew *when He causes your thigh to waste away.* 5:22 Hebrew *and your thigh to waste away.* 5:27 Hebrew *and her thigh will waste away.*

5:21 The ritual prescribed here is not magic. The Lord is the one who would bring the curse upon any unfaithful woman.

5:27 Part of a woman's self-worth in Israel was defined by her ability to bear children for her husband—particularly sons. If she did not accomplish this, then the family's legacy ended with her husband's death. This was considered a tragedy. Rachel, Jacob's beloved wife, struggled with infertility. Jacob's mother, Rebekah, and his grandmother, Sarah, had similar struggles. Later in Israel's history, a great Israelite leader, Samuel, was born after his mother's prayer that God would break through her infertility and give her a son (1 Samuel 1:1-20).

▶ BIBLE

5:30 The priest will apply this entire ritual law to her. Wouldn't it be nice if God gave us a foolproof way to know if people were being honest with us? God mercifully offered Israel a supernatural test to determine marital unfaithfulness. Take a moment to examine yourself. Is there anything you need to tell your spouse? Remember, Jesus defines unfaithfulness as a sin of the mind and heart as well as the flesh (Matthew 5:27-30). (***See Bible***> *Unity*> *Doctrines*> *Principles of marriage,* TopicGuide page A10.)

NAZIRITE LAWS

6 Then the LORD said to Moses, "Give the following instructions to the people of Israel. 2 "If any of the people, either men or women, take the special vow of a Nazirite, setting themselves apart to the LORD in a special way, 3 they must give up wine and other alcoholic drinks. They must not use vinegar made from wine or from other alcoholic drinks, they must not drink fresh grape juice, and they must not eat grapes or raisins. 4 As long as they are bound by their Nazirite vow, they are not allowed to eat or drink anything that comes from a grapevine—not even the grape seeds or skins.

5 "They must never cut their hair throughout the time of their vow, for they are holy and set apart to the LORD. Until the time of their vow has been fulfilled, they must let their hair grow long. 6 And they must not go near a dead body during the entire period of their vow to the LORD. 7 Even if the dead person is their own father, mother, brother, or sister, they must not defile themselves, for the hair on their head is the symbol of their separation to God. 8 This requirement applies as long as they are set apart to the LORD.

9 "If someone falls dead beside them, the hair they have dedicated will be defiled. They must wait for seven days and then shave their heads. Then they will be cleansed from their defilement. 10 On the eighth day they must bring two turtledoves or two young pigeons to the priest at the entrance of the Tabernacle.* 11 The priest will offer one of the birds for a sin offering and the other for a burnt offering. In this way, he will purify them* from the guilt they incurred through contact with the dead body. Then they must reaffirm their commitment and let their hair begin to grow again. 12 The days of their vow that were completed before their defilement no longer count. They must rededicate themselves to the LORD as a Nazirite for the full term of their vow, and each must bring a one-year-old male lamb for a guilt offering.

13 "This is the ritual law for Nazirites. At the conclusion of their time of separation as Nazirites, they must each go to the entrance of the Tabernacle 14 and offer their sacrifices to the LORD: a one-year-old male lamb without defect for a burnt offering, a one-year-old female lamb without defect for a sin offering, a ram without defect for a peace offering, 15 a basket of bread made without yeast—cakes of choice flour mixed with olive oil and wafers spread with olive oil—along with their prescribed grain offerings and liquid offerings. 16 The priest will present these offerings before the LORD: first the sin offering and the burnt offering;

6:2 Judg 13:4-5; 16:17; Amos 2:11-12
6:3 Luke 1:15
6:5 1 Sam 1:11
6:6 Lev 21:1-3; Num 19:11-22
6:9 Num 6:18
6:11 Lev 5:7; 12:6-8
6:12 Lev 5:6
6:14 Lev 14:10
6:15 Num 15:1-7
6:18 Num 6:9

6:10 Hebrew *the Tent of Meeting;* also in 6:13, 18. 6:11 Or *make atonement for them.*

6:1-5 The Nazirite vow was a voluntary commitment for special service or sanctification before God that could last for a season (as little as 30 days) or a lifetime, but the most famous Nazirites of the Bible were Nazirites for life. Samson, a judge of Israel known for his long hair, was a Nazirite (Judges 13). Samuel, who came between the judges and kings of Israel, was also a Nazirite (1 Samuel 1:11). Note that Jesus was referred to as a *Nazarene* because he was from Nazareth. While the words *Nazarene* and *Nazirite* sound similar, they have entirely different meanings.

▶ WORSHIP
6:2 The special vow of the Nazirite. In response to a special blessing from God or as a regular part of their devotion to God, men and women in ancient Israelite society could take a Nazirite vow. It included fasting from alcoholic drinks and grape products, remaining ceremonially clean, and leaving hair untrimmed (but the vows could have other custom components; see Paul's vows in Acts 18:18 and 21:26, which appear to be Nazirite vows). God still encourages special times of fasting and prayer for believers today. (***See Worship***> *NT> Prayer> Instructions> Pray with fasting,* TopicGuide page A33; ***Holiness***> *Disciplines> Of Abstinence> Fasting,* TopicGuide page A42.)

6:5 A parallel to the Nazirite vow exists in Leviticus 25:11; this verse contains a prohibition against pruning fruit-bearing trees and vines upon entering the Promised Land (and during the Year of Jubilee). Only after several years passed could the fruit be eaten, and then only to God's glory. The Nazirite's unpruned life was to demonstrate similar maturity over time to God's glory.

6:5-8 Samson is probably the most well-known example of the Nazirite guidelines regarding a person's hair (see Judges 13).

6:6 The Nazirite kept himself from contact with dead bodies at all costs. This command held a lesson about the nature of God. God was (and is) the source of all life. Sin, humanity's broken relationship with God, was (and is) the source of death. The Nazirite, as a person specially set apart for God's service, had to stay away from any dead body because death was a form of decay and destruction—the opposite of who God is.

17 then the ram for a peace offering, along with the basket of bread made without yeast. The
priest must also present the prescribed grain offering and liquid offering to the LORD.
18 "Then the Nazirites will shave their heads at the entrance of the Tabernacle. They will
take the hair that had been dedicated and place it on the fire beneath the peace-offering
sacrifice. 19 After the Nazirite's head has been shaved, the priest will take for each of them
the boiled shoulder of the ram, and he will take from the basket a cake and a wafer made
6:20 without yeast. He will put them all into the Nazirite's hands. 20 Then the priest will lift them
Lev 7:28-34 up as a special offering before the LORD. These are holy portions for the priest, along with
the breast of the special offering and the thigh of the sacred offering that are lifted up be-
fore the LORD. After this ceremony the Nazirites may again drink wine.
21 "This is the ritual law of the Nazirites, who vow to bring these offerings to the LORD.
They may also bring additional offerings if they can afford it. And they must be careful to
do whatever they vowed when they set themselves apart as Nazirites."

THE PRIESTLY BLESSING

6:23 Deut 21:5 22 Then the LORD said to Moses, 23 "Tell Aaron and his sons to bless the people of Israel with
1 Chr 23:13 this special blessing:

24 'May the LORD bless you
6:24 Deut 28:3-6 and protect you.
6:25 25 May the LORD smile on you
Ps 80:3, 7, 19 and be gracious to you.
6:26 26 May the LORD show you His favor
Pss 4:6; 29:11; 44:3 and give you His peace.'

27 Whenever Aaron and his sons bless the people of Israel in My name, I Myself will bless
them."

OFFERINGS OF DEDICATION

7:1 **7** On the day Moses set up the Tabernacle, he anointed it and set it apart as holy. He
Exod 40:9-11 also anointed and set apart all its furnishings and the altar with its utensils. 2 Then the
7:2 leaders of Israel—the tribal leaders who had registered the troops—came and brought their
Num 1:2-16 offerings. 3 Together they brought six large wagons and twelve oxen. There was a wagon

6:17 Grain offerings (sometimes called cereal offerings) accompanied both the required burnt offerings and the voluntary fellowship offerings. They could take the form of fine flour, baked loaves, cakes, or wafers. The priests kept some grain offerings for their own cupboards. In some cases, the worshipers took home a portion after making the offering. Still other grain offerings were burned up entirely for the Lord.

6:21 God did not command people to make vows, nor was it wrong to refrain from entering into such vows. But once taken, vows had to be fulfilled. Vows in Israel were far more solemn than the modern sense of making a promise to a friend. Often the person making a vow hoped to gain something from God. Vows also could be made out of gratitude for blessing. At times vows could be intentionally vetoed or redeemed back with a monetary offering, but they could not simply be forgotten.

6:22-27 In this most beautiful of ancient blessings, each of the three lines is longer that the one before and each builds upon and adds to the blessings of the previous line.

▸ WORSHIP
6:24 Grace from God. With all these rules, it might have been easy for some in Israel to have mistakenly thought that through mechanistic obedience, they could guarantee God's blessing on Israel. But God knew His people would fail to obey Him. This blessing given by the priests clarified that God's approval comes from Him alone and is given by His grace alone, not as a result of our good works. Praise God for His blessings, rich and free! (***See Worship****> OT> Repentance> Nature> Contriteness before the Law ensures God's blessing,* TopicGuide page A29.)

6:26 Peace (*shalom*) in this case is not necessarily the absence of conflict, but the presence of wholeness, well-being, and satisfaction.

7:2 The Israelites were organized according to their family lines. Their original great ancestors were Abraham, Isaac, and Jacob. Abraham was the man to whom the original promise of a nation had been given. His story of being childless and aged before God miraculously gave him his son Isaac is one of the most important stories to this culture's identity. Isaac then carried that promise and passed it on to his son Jacob, who was later renamed Israel. After Jacob, the lineage was restructured in that Jacob's 12 sons became the progenitors of the Israelite nation. Hence you hear the phrase "the twelve tribes of Israel." This census was organized according to those 12 tribes.

for every two leaders and an ox for each leader. They presented these to the LORD in front
of the Tabernacle.
4 Then the LORD said to Moses, 5 "Receive their gifts, and use these oxen and wagons for
transporting the Tabernacle.* Distribute them among the Levites according to the work
they have to do." 6 So Moses took the wagons and oxen and presented them to the Levites.
7 He gave two wagons and four oxen to the Gershonite division for their work, 8 and he
gave four wagons and eight oxen to the Merarite division for their work. All their work was 7:7
done under the leadership of Ithamar son of Aaron the priest. 9 But he gave none of the Num 4:26
wagons or oxen to the Kohathite division, since they were required to carry the sacred ob- 7:8
jects of the Tabernacle on their shoulders. Num 4:33
10 The leaders also presented dedication gifts for the altar at the time it was anointed. 7:9 Num 4:5-15
They each placed their gifts before the altar. 11 The LORD said to Moses, "Let one leader
bring his gift each day for the dedication of the altar."

12 On the first day Nahshon son of Amminadab, leader of the tribe of Judah, presented his
offering.
13 His offering consisted of a silver platter weighing 3¼ pounds and a silver basin
weighing 1¾ pounds* (as measured by the weight of the sanctuary shekel). These
were both filled with grain offerings of choice flour moistened with olive oil. 14 He
also brought a gold container weighing four ounces,* which was filled with incense. 7:14
15 He brought a young bull, a ram, and a one-year-old male lamb for a burnt offering, Exod 30:34
16 and a male goat for a sin offering. 17 For a peace offering he brought two bulls, five 7:16
rams, five male goats, and five one-year-old male lambs. This was the offering Lev 4:3
brought by Nahshon son of Amminadab. 7:17 Lev 3:1

18 On the second day Nethanel son of Zuar, leader of the tribe of Issachar, presented his
offering. 7:18
19 His offering consisted of a silver platter weighing 3¼ pounds and a silver basin Num 1:8
weighing 1¾ pounds (as measured by the weight of the sanctuary shekel). These
were both filled with grain offerings of choice flour moistened with olive oil. 20 He
also brought a gold container weighing four ounces, which was filled with incense.
21 He brought a young bull, a ram, and a one-year-old male lamb for a burnt offering,
22 and a male goat for a sin offering. 23 For a peace offering he brought two bulls, five
rams, five male goats, and five one-year-old male lambs. This was the offering
brought by Nethanel son of Zuar.

7:5 Hebrew *the Tent of Meeting;* also in 7:89. 7:13 Hebrew *silver platter weighing 130 shekels* [1.5 kilograms] *and a silver basin weighing 70 shekels* [800 grams]; also in 7:19, 25, 31, 37, 43, 49, 55, 61, 67, 73, 79, 85. 7:14 Hebrew *10 shekels* [114 grams]; also in 7:20, 26, 32, 38, 44, 50, 56, 62, 68, 74, 80, 86.

7:7-9 The Levite tribe was organized according to the Levi's three sons: Gershon, Kohath, and Merari. Each family line had specific tasks (see Numbers 4). Aaron and Moses were descendants of Kohath, but only Aaron's direct descendants could be priests. Other Levite duties focused on care for and movement of the Tabernacle. The Kohathites cared for and carried the furniture that had been prepared by Aaron's priests. The Gershonites cared for the curtains and cloths that made up the walls of the Tabernacle. The descendants of Merari took care of the framing structures that made up the Tabernacle.

7:11 The command to have only one tribal leader per day make his offering may have been logistical. The sheer amount of time and work necessary to make the sacrifices would have been significant. Numbers 7:15-17 delineates the animal sacrifices of the tribe of Judah. The similar offerings of the other tribes follow through the rest of the chapter. In total there were over 250 animals offered. Some were burned completely; the rest had fat and certain organs burned. Spreading this work over 12 days made it both practical and perhaps more meaningful for each individual tribe.

7:12-83 The gifts given by each tribal leader were identical. Despite the different sizes of the tribes, all had the same standing and responsibility before the LORD. The gifts were also costly. By today's standards the silver platter would cost over $250 (at around $5 per ounce). The silver basin would be worth almost $150 by the same measure. The golden incense container could be almost $2,000 worth of gold (at around $450 per ounce). The total gifts were listed in Numbers 7:84-88, and these amounts don't reflect the choice flour and oil that were included with them. The people gave generously to the Tabernacle.

24 On the third day Eliab son of Helon, leader of the tribe of Zebulun, presented his offering.
25 His offering consisted of a silver platter weighing 3¼ pounds and a silver basin
weighing 1¾ pounds (as measured by the weight of the sanctuary shekel). These
were both filled with grain offerings of choice flour moistened with olive oil. 26 He
also brought a gold container weighing four ounces, which was filled with incense.
27 He brought a young bull, a ram, and a one-year-old male lamb for a burnt offering,
7:29 28 and a male goat for a sin offering. 29 For a peace offering he brought two bulls, five
Lev 7:32 rams, five male goats, and five one-year-old male lambs. This was the offering
brought by Eliab son of Helon.

7:30 30 On the fourth day Elizur son of Shedeur, leader of the tribe of Reuben, presented his of-
Num 1:5 fering.
31 His offering consisted of a silver platter weighing 3¼ pounds and a silver basin
weighing 1¾ pounds (as measured by the weight of the sanctuary shekel). These
were both filled with grain offerings of choice flour moistened with olive oil. 32 He
also brought a gold container weighing four ounces, which was filled with incense.
33 He brought a young bull, a ram, and a one-year-old male lamb for a burnt offering,
7:34 34 and a male goat for a sin offering. 35 For a peace offering he brought two bulls, five
Heb 10:4 rams, five male goats, and five one-year-old male lambs. This was the offering
brought by Elizur son of Shedeur.

7:36 36 On the fifth day Shelumiel son of Zurishaddai, leader of the tribe of Simeon, presented
Num 1:6 his offering.
37 His offering consisted of a silver platter weighing 3¼ pounds and a silver basin
weighing 1¾ pounds (as measured by the weight of the sanctuary shekel). These
were both filled with grain offerings of choice flour moistened with olive oil. 38 He
also brought a gold container weighing four ounces, which was filled with incense.
39 He brought a young bull, a ram, and a one-year-old male lamb for a burnt offering,
40 and a male goat for a sin offering. 41 For a peace offering he brought two bulls, five
rams, five male goats, and five one-year-old male lambs. This was the offering
brought by Shelumiel son of Zurishaddai.

7:42 42 On the sixth day Eliasaph son of Deuel, leader of the tribe of Gad, presented his offering.
Num 1:14 43 His offering consisted of a silver platter weighing 3¼ pounds and a silver basin
weighing 1¾ pounds (as measured by the weight of the sanctuary shekel). These
were both filled with grain offerings of choice flour moistened with olive oil. 44 He
also brought a gold container weighing four ounces, which was filled with incense.
45 He brought a young bull, a ram, and a one-year-old male lamb for a burnt offering,
46 and a male goat for a sin offering. 47 For a peace offering he brought two bulls, five
rams, five male goats, and five one-year-old male lambs. This was the offering
brought by Eliasaph son of Deuel.

7:48 48 On the seventh day Elishama son of Ammihud, leader of the tribe of Ephraim, presented
Num 1:10 his offering.
49 His offering consisted of a silver platter weighing 3¼ pounds and a silver basin
weighing 1¾ pounds (as measured by the weight of the sanctuary shekel). These
were both filled with grain offerings of choice flour moistened with olive oil. 50 He
also brought a gold container weighing four ounces, which was filled with incense.

7:48, 54 Any time the nation of Israel was organized, it was in the order of the 12 sons of Jacob. Here, the whole camp is organized that way for the campsite as well as for these offerings. While there are 12 tribes, they didn't correlate exactly with the 12 sons. The exceptions were Levi and Joseph. The Levites were religious workers who served the people. They were set apart, not counted among the 12 with respect to land and military service. There were still twelve tribes, because the allotment to Joseph was doubled and given to his two sons, Manasseh and Ephraim.

51He brought a young bull, a ram, and a one-year-old male lamb for a burnt offering,
52and a male goat for a sin offering. 53For a peace offering he brought two bulls, five 7:52
rams, five male goats, and five one-year-old male lambs. This was the offering Heb 10:4
brought by Elishama son of Ammihud.

54On the eighth day Gamaliel son of Pedahzur, leader of the tribe of Manasseh, presented
his offering.

55His offering consisted of a silver platter weighing 3¼ pounds and a silver basin
weighing 1¾ pounds (as measured by the weight of the sanctuary shekel). These
were both filled with grain offerings of choice flour moistened with olive oil. 56He
also brought a gold container weighing four ounces, which was filled with incense.
57He brought a young bull, a ram, and a one-year-old male lamb for a burnt offering,
58and a male goat for a sin offering. 59For a peace offering he brought two bulls, five
rams, five male goats, and five one-year-old male lambs. This was the offering
brought by Gamaliel son of Pedahzur.

60On the ninth day Abidan son of Gideoni, leader of the tribe of Benjamin, presented his 7:60
offering. Num 1:11

61His offering consisted of a silver platter weighing 3¼ pounds and a silver basin
weighing 1¾ pounds (as measured by the weight of the sanctuary shekel). These
were both filled with grain offerings of choice flour moistened with olive oil. 62He
also brought a gold container weighing four ounces, which was filled with incense.
63He brought a young bull, a ram, and a one-year-old male lamb for a burnt offering,
64and a male goat for a sin offering. 65For a peace offering he brought two bulls, five
rams, five male goats, and five one-year-old male lambs. This was the offering
brought by Abidan son of Gideoni.

66On the tenth day Ahiezer son of Ammishaddai, leader of the tribe of Dan, presented his 7:66
offering. Num 1:12

67His offering consisted of a silver platter weighing 3¼ pounds and a silver basin
weighing 1¾ pounds (as measured by the weight of the sanctuary shekel). These
were both filled with grain offerings of choice flour moistened with olive oil. 68He
also brought a gold container weighing four ounces, which was filled with incense.
69He brought a young bull, a ram, and a one-year-old male lamb for a burnt offering,
70and a male goat for a sin offering. 71For a peace offering he brought two bulls, five 7:70
rams, five male goats, and five one-year-old male lambs. This was the offering Heb 10:4
brought by Ahiezer son of Ammishaddai.

72On the eleventh day Pagiel son of Ocran, leader of the tribe of Asher, presented his offer-
ing.

73His offering consisted of a silver platter weighing 3¼ pounds and a silver basin
weighing 1¾ pounds (as measured by the weight of the sanctuary shekel). These
were both filled with grain offerings of choice flour moistened with olive oil. 74He
also brought a gold container weighing four ounces, which was filled with incense.
75He brought a young bull, a ram, and a one-year-old male lamb for a burnt offering,
76and a male goat for a sin offering. 77For a peace offering he brought two bulls, five
rams, five male goats, and five one-year-old male lambs. This was the offering
brought by Pagiel son of Ocran.

78On the twelfth day Ahira son of Enan, leader of the tribe of Naphtali, presented his offer- 7:78
ing. Num 1:15

79His offering consisted of a silver platter weighing 3¼ pounds and a silver basin
weighing 1¾ pounds (as measured by the weight of the sanctuary shekel). These
were both filled with grain offerings of choice flour moistened with olive oil. 80He

also brought a gold container weighing four ounces, which was filled with incense.
[81]He brought a young bull, a ram, and a one-year-old male lamb for a burnt offering,
[82]and a male goat for a sin offering. [83]For a peace offering he brought two bulls, five
rams, five male goats, and five one-year-old male lambs. This was the offering
brought by Ahira son of Enan.

7:84 [84]So this was the dedication offering brought by the leaders of Israel at the time the altar
Num 7:10 was anointed: twelve silver platters, twelve silver basins, and twelve gold incense contain-
ers. [85]Each silver platter weighed 3¼ pounds, and each silver basin weighed 1¾ pounds.
The total weight of the silver was 60 pounds* (as measured by the weight of the sanctuary
shekel). [86]Each of the twelve gold containers that was filled with incense weighed four
ounces (as measured by the weight of the sanctuary shekel). The total weight of the gold
was three pounds.* [87]Twelve young bulls, twelve rams, and twelve one-year-old male
lambs were donated for the burnt offerings, along with their prescribed grain offerings.
7:88 Twelve male goats were brought for the sin offerings. [88]Twenty-four bulls, sixty rams, sixty
Num 7:1, 10 male goats, and sixty one-year-old male lambs were donated for the peace offerings. This
7:89 was the dedication offering for the altar after it was anointed.
Exod 25:21-22; 33:9-11 [89]Whenever Moses went into the Tabernacle to speak with the LORD, he heard the voice
Pss 80:1; 99:1 speaking to him from between the two cherubim above the Ark's cover—the place of
atonement—that rests on the Ark of the Covenant.* The LORD spoke to him from there.

PREPARING THE LAMPS

8:2 Exod 25:37 **8** The LORD said to Moses, [2]"Give Aaron the following instructions: When you set up the
seven lamps in the lampstand, place them so their light shines forward in front of the
lampstand." [3]So Aaron did this. He set up the seven lamps so they reflected their light for-
8:4 ward, just as the LORD had commanded Moses. [4]The entire lampstand, from its base to its
Exod 25:18, 31-36, 40 decorative blossoms, was made of beaten gold. It was built according to the exact design
the LORD had shown Moses.

THE LEVITES DEDICATED

8:7
Lev 14:8-9 [5]Then the LORD said to Moses, [6]"Now set the Levites apart from the rest of the people of Is-
Num 19:9, 17-18 rael and make them ceremonially clean. [7]Do this by sprinkling them with the water of pu-
8:8 rification, and have them shave their entire body and wash their clothing. Then they will
Num 15:3-12 be ceremonially clean. [8]Have them bring a young bull and a grain offering of choice flour

7:85 Hebrew *2,400 shekels* [27.6 kilograms]. 7:86 Hebrew *120 shekels* [1.4 kilograms]. 7:89 Or *Ark of the Testimony.*

7:89 Though this verse may seem out of place with what has occurred in chapter 7, it is a necessary transition to what is about to occur in the next chapter.

▸ GOD

7:89 Through Christ's blood. This process symbolizes what is so evident today—you have access to a relationship with God through the atoning work of Jesus Christ. Our relationship with Christ allows communication to God and from God. We have the privilege to approach God through Christ. (Galatians 5:4). (***See God****> Salvation> Son> Only bridge between God and man,* TopicGuide page A15.)

8:1-26 Chapter 8 can be understood in three sections: lighting the lamps (verses 1-4), separating the Levites (verses 5-22), and terms of service for the Levites (verses 23-26).

8:2 The lamp design, including the accessories (described in Exodus 25:31-40), required 75 pounds of gold. This seven-branch candelabra (Hebrew *menorah*) has become a symbol of Judaism. The original menorah burned olive oil rather than candles. Oil lamps usually consisted of a pottery or metal cup. Each cup had a narrowed lip on one side in which the wick lay so that it was in the oil, but not submerged.

8:3 Leviticus 24:3 says that Aaron had responsibility for the arrangement of the lamps. It was a daily task of the priests to maintain the lamps and the lampstand.

8:5-7 Instruction concerning ceremonial cleanliness was meant to teach people the difference between ordinary and holy. This in turn taught them about God's holiness and His worthiness of worship. This ceremonial cleanliness is different from the requirement for the priests of Aaron, who received new clothes (not simply washed garments) and who were anointed and made holy (Leviticus 8:12), not just ceremonially cleansed.

moistened with olive oil, along with a second young bull for a sin offering. 9Then assem-
ble the whole community of Israel, and present the Levites at the entrance of the Taberna-
cle.* 10When you present the Levites before the LORD, the people of Israel must lay their 8:10 Lev 3:2
hands on them. 11Raising his hands, Aaron must then present the Levites to the LORD as a
special offering from the people of Israel, thus dedicating them to the LORD's service.

12"Next the Levites will lay their hands on the heads of the young bulls. Present one as a 8:12 Exod 29:10-14
sin offering and the other as a burnt offering to the LORD, to purify the Levites and make
them right with the LORD.* 13Then have the Levites stand in front of Aaron and his sons,
and raise your hands and present them as a special offering to the LORD. 14In this way, you 8:14 Num 3:12
will set the Levites apart from the rest of the people of Israel, and the Levites will belong to
Me. 15After this, they may go into the Tabernacle to do their work, because you have puri-
fied them and presented them as a special offering.

16"Of all the people of Israel, the Levites are reserved for Me. I have claimed them for 8:16 Num 3:13
Myself in place of all the firstborn sons of the Israelites; I have taken the Levites as their
substitutes. 17For all the firstborn males among the people of Israel are Mine, both of peo- 8:17 Exod 13:12-13
ple and of animals. I set them apart for Myself on the day I struck down all the firstborn
sons of the Egyptians. 18Yes, I have claimed the Levites in place of all the firstborn sons of
Israel. 19And of all the Israelites, I have assigned the Levites to Aaron and his sons. They 8:19 Num 1:53
will serve in the Tabernacle on behalf of the Israelites and make sacrifices to purify* the
people so no plague will strike them when they approach the sanctuary."

20So Moses, Aaron, and the whole community of Israel dedicated the Levites, carefully
following all the LORD's instructions to Moses. 21The Levites purified themselves from sin
and washed their clothes, and Aaron lifted them up and presented them to the LORD as a
special offering. He then offered a sacrifice to purify them and make them right with the
LORD.* 22After that the Levites went into the Tabernacle to perform their duties, assisting
Aaron and his sons. So they carried out all the commands that the LORD gave Moses con-
cerning the Levites.

23The LORD also instructed Moses, 24"This is the rule the Levites must follow: They must 8:24 Num 4:3
begin serving in the Tabernacle at the age of twenty-five, 25and they must retire at the age
of fifty. 26After retirement they may assist their fellow Levites by serving as guards at the
Tabernacle, but they may not officiate in the service. This is how you must assign duties to
the Levites."

THE SECOND PASSOVER

9 A year after Israel's departure from Egypt, the LORD spoke to Moses in the wilder- 9:2 Exod 12:1-6
ness of Sinai. In the first month* of that year He said, 2"Tell the Israelites to cele-

8:9 Hebrew *the Tent of Meeting;* also in 8:15, 19, 22, 24, 26. 8:12 Or *to make atonement for the Levites.* 8:19 Or *make atonement for.* 8:21 Or *then made atonement for them to purify them.* 9:1 The first month of the ancient Hebrew lunar calendar usually occurs within the months of March and April.

8:9-11 The laying on of hands has great significance. When the people or the Levites made an offering, they placed their hands on the head of the animal sacrificed. In this way, they accepted that animal's substitution for them. Here the people lay hands on the Levites, dedicating them for service to the Lord and Israel. The New Testament describes this same practice of laying hands on people to set them apart for service (for one example, see 1 Timothy 4:14).

8:16-18 The firstborn, and particularly the firstborn male, had unique standing in Israel. They belonged to God, just as the firstfruits of crops belonged to God. This was true of the firstborn among the flocks, herds, and children. Firstborn sons carried responsibility for family leadership and received a larger inheritance. Levites become representatives for all firstborn sons in Israel. This had special significance, referring to the final plague before Israel left Egypt. At the Passover, any home without the blood of a lamb on its doorpost experienced the death of the firstborn, including sons, flocks, and herds.

9:2 God instituted the Passover Feast as a feast to begin the Israelite religious calendar. The Passover actually took place in March, the seventh month of the civil calendar (which began in September/October). In this way, each new religious year would begin with a celebration as the people remembered through a feast of rituals God's act of redeeming them from bondage in Egypt. The early name of the month was *Abib,* a word that related to the progression of the barley harvest. Later it was changed to *Nisan.*

brate the Passover at the prescribed time, 3at twilight on the fourteenth day of the first
month.* Be sure to follow all My decrees and regulations concerning this celebra-
tion.”
9:5 4So Moses told the people to celebrate the Passover 5in the wilderness of Sinai as twi-
Josh 5:10 light fell on the fourteenth day of the month. And they celebrated the festival there, just
9:6 Num 19:11-22 as the LORD had commanded Moses. 6But some of the men had been ceremonially de-
filed by touching a dead body, so they could not celebrate the Passover that day. They
came to Moses and Aaron that day 7and said, “We have become ceremonially unclean
by touching a dead body. But why should we be prevented from presenting the LORD’s
offering at the proper time with the rest of the Israelites?”
9:8 8Moses answered, “Wait here until I have received instructions for you from the LORD.”
Exod 18:15 9This was the LORD’s reply to Moses. 10“Give the following instructions to the people of
Israel: If any of the people now or in future generations are ceremonially unclean at Pass-
over time because of touching a dead body, or if they are on a journey and cannot be
9:11 present at the ceremony, they may still celebrate the LORD’s Passover. 11They must offer
Exod 12:8 the Passover sacrifice one month later, at twilight on the fourteenth day of the second
month.* They must eat the Passover lamb at that time with bitter salad greens and bread
9:12 made without yeast. 12They must not leave any of the lamb until the next morning, and
Exod 12:10, 43, 46 *John 19:36 they must not break any of its bones. They must follow all the normal regulations concern-
ing the Passover.
9:13 13“But those who neglect to celebrate the Passover at the regular time, even
Exod 12:15 though they are ceremonially clean and not away on a trip, will be cut off from the
Num 15:30-31 community of Israel. If they fail to present the LORD’s offering at the proper time, they
9:14 will suffer the consequences of their guilt. 14And if foreigners living among you want
Exod 12:48-49 to celebrate the Passover to the LORD, they must follow these same decrees and regu-
lations. The same laws apply both to native-born Israelites and to the foreigners liv-
ing among you.”

9:15

THE FIERY CLOUD

Exod 13:21-22; 40:2, 17, 34 15On the day the Tabernacle was set up, the cloud covered it.* But from evening until
Neh 9:12, 19 morning the cloud over the Tabernacle looked like a pillar of fire. 16This was the regular
Ps 78:14 pattern—at night the cloud that covered the Tabernacle had the appearance of fire.

9:3 This day in the ancient Hebrew lunar calendar occurred in late March, April, or early May. 9:11 This day in the ancient Hebrew lunar calendar occurred in late April, May, or early June. 9:15 Hebrew *covered the Tabernacle, the Tent of the Testimony.*

9:5 Based on the earliest verses in Genesis, the Israelites (and Jews today) consider sunset or twilight as the end of one day and the beginning of the next. Therefore, religious holy day observances begins at twilight.

▸ WORSHIP

9:7 Ceremonially unclean. Have you ever seen or touched a dead person? In ancient times, there were no professional funeral services, so families were obliged to care for the bodies of their loved ones. God knew that these men were bringing a legitimate excuse, so He made provision for such incidents in the future. In a system that emphasized perfection, God recognized the sincere hearts of these men and provided grace to help them in their times of need (Hebrews 4:16). (***See Worship****> OT> Priesthood> Duties> Special arrangements,* TopicGuide page A28.)

9:9-13 These verses display both the flexibility and the rigidity of the law of Moses. Since it was more important for the people to celebrate the Passover than to celebrate at a certain time, provision was made for an alternate date of celebration. But, when it became obvious that the Passover (thus obedience to God) was unimportant to the people, then the law showed no flexibility.

9:14 Many places in the law make provisions for foreigners in Israel. Even in the first Passover, foreigners, such as hired servants and guests, were mentioned (Exodus 12:48-49). Later, the foreigners included whole tribes (the Gibeonites in Joshua 9) or individuals (Rahab in Joshua 2). They were expected to observe most of the Israelite laws, such as keeping the Sabbath and abstaining from eating blood. On the other hand, they were allowed to eat animals that had died a natural death, while the Israelites could not (Deuteronomy 14:21).

9:15 This was not the first appearance of the cloud and the pillar. These signs had led the Israelites since they first left Egypt. The cloud by day served to conceal God's resplendent majesty while the fire by night represented God's ever-present protection.

[17]Whenever the cloud lifted from over the sacred tent, the people of Israel would break
camp and follow it. And wherever the cloud settled, the people of Israel would set up
camp. [18]In this way, they traveled and camped at the LORD's command wherever He told
them to go. Then they remained in their camp as long as the cloud stayed over the Tab-
ernacle. [19]If the cloud remained over the Tabernacle for a long time, the Israelites stayed
and performed their duty to the LORD. [20]Sometimes the cloud would stay over the Taber-
nacle for only a few days, so the people would stay for only a few days, as the LORD com-
manded. Then at the LORD's command they would break camp and move on.
[21]Sometimes the cloud stayed only overnight and lifted the next morning. But day or
night, when the cloud lifted, the people broke camp and moved on. [22]Whether the cloud
stayed above the Tabernacle for two days, a month, or a year, the people of Israel stayed
in camp and did not move on. But as soon as it lifted, they broke camp and moved on.
[23]So they camped or traveled at the LORD's command, and they did whatever the LORD
told them through Moses.

9:17 Exod 40:36-38; Num 10:11, 33-34
9:18 1 Cor 10:1
9:22 Exod 40:36-37

THE SILVER TRUMPETS

10 Now the LORD said to Moses, [2]"Make two trumpets of hammered silver for call-
ing the community to assemble and for signaling the breaking of camp.

▶ **HOLINESS**
9:17 Following God. The Christian life is a journey, and the people of Israel provide an excellent example of going where God told them to go, when God told them to go. In addition, they didn't go where God said not to go. Where is God leading you? Should you settle down and stay where you are, or prepare to move? Be prepared to follow God wherever He may lead. (***See Holiness***> *Submission*> *Trusting God*> *Obedience*, TopicGuide page A40.)

9:17-23 Though these verses seem repetitious, they are notable in that this is one of very few times in Israel's history that the people scrupulously obeyed the leading of the LORD. The repetition serves to emphasize this careful adherence to God's direction.

10:1-2 Archaeologists have discovered numerous evidences of ancient smelting furnaces in the Ancient Near East predating the time of the Exodus. Silver trumpets similar to the ones described here were found in the tomb of King Tutankhamun in Egypt. They date around 1400 BC.

MY RESPONSE TO GOD

A Cloud to Follow

NUMBERS 9:15-23

The Israelites first built the Tabernacle in the middle of a vast wilderness, many miles from the Promised Land. Egypt, the land of their slavery, lay behind them; unknown enemies and dangers lurked ahead. How lost and alone they must have felt! Yet God provided them with a vivid reminder of His presence. Every day He led them by a cloud through the wilderness. At night, the cloud became a pillar of fire and rested above the Tabernacle. As long as the people stayed near God's fiery cloud, they knew He would guide and protect them.

God still leads His people today. Whatever wilderness we find ourselves in, however lost or overwhelmed we become, God is never far from us. In the midst of our struggles, He has promised to be like a voice in our ear, saying, "This is the way you should go" (Isaiah 30:21). God doesn't intend to remove all difficulties from our lives, but He has pledged His presence to guide us through them. Sadly, the Israelites stopped following God at the border of the Promised Land, afraid of the enemies they would face. Avoid their mistake and remember that the safest—and most rewarding—path is always the one within the sound of God's voice.

10:3 [3]When both trumpets are blown, everyone must gather before you at the entrance of
Jer 4:5 the Tabernacle.* [4]But if only one trumpet is blown, then only the leaders—the heads of
the clans of Israel—must present themselves to you.
10:5 [5]"When you sound the signal to move on, the tribes camped on the east side of the Tab-
Num 10:14 ernacle must break camp and move forward. [6]When you sound the signal a second time,
10:7 the tribes camped on the south will follow. You must sound short blasts as the signal for
Joel 2:1 moving on. [7]But when you call the people to an assembly, blow the trumpets with a differ-
10:8 Num 31:6 ent signal. [8]Only the priests, Aaron's descendants, are allowed to blow the trumpets. This
Josh 6:3-9 is a permanent law for you, to be observed from generation to generation.
2 Chr 5:11-12 [9]"When you arrive in your own land and go to war against your enemies who attack
10:9 you, sound the alarm with the trumpets. Then the LORD your God will remember you and
Judg 2:18 Ps 106:4 rescue you from your enemies. [10]Blow the trumpets in times of gladness, too, sounding
10:10 them at your annual festivals and at the beginning of each month. And blow the trumpets
Lev 23:24 over your burnt offerings and peace offerings. The trumpets will remind the LORD your
Num 29:1 Ps 81:3-5 God of His covenant with you. I am the LORD your God."

10:11
THE ISRAELITES LEAVE SINAI

Exod 40:17 [11]In the second year after Israel's departure from Egypt—on the twentieth day of the sec-
10:12 ond month*—the cloud lifted from the Tabernacle of the Covenant.* [12]So the Israelites set
Gen 21:20-21 Num 12:16 out from the wilderness of Sinai and traveled on from place to place until the cloud
10:13 stopped in the wilderness of Paran.
Deut 1:6 [13]When the people set out for the first time, following the instructions the LORD had
10:14 given through Moses, [14]Judah's troops led the way. They marched behind their banner,
Num 2:3-31 and their leader was Nahshon son of Amminadab. [15]They were joined by the troops of the

10:3 Hebrew *Tent of Meeting.* 10:11a This day in the ancient Hebrew lunar calendar occurred in late April, May, or early June. 10:11b Or *Tabernacle of the Testimony.*

10:3-10 The trumpets had different functions, which helped to organize life in Israel. They summoned leaders, sounded alarms for war (summoning God's help), and served as instruments of rejoicing.

▸ HOLINESS
10:9 Stop stopping God! Many of God's blessings are unmerited but are nevertheless conditional. In this case, God graciously offered to aid the Israelites in battle, but one stipulation remained: Blow the horns! Is there anything you are doing or not doing that is stopping God's blessings upon your life? Search your heart for any areas of sin or neglect in your life that are hindering the work of God's Spirit in you. (***See Holiness***> *Submission*> *Yielding to Spirit*> *Do not attempt to stop the Spirit's work,* TopicGuide page A41.)

ISRAEL'S DEPARTURE FROM SINAI
It has been two years since Israel left Egypt. Having received God's travel instructions through Moses, Israel set out from Mount Sinai into the wilderness of Paran on their way toward the Promised Land.

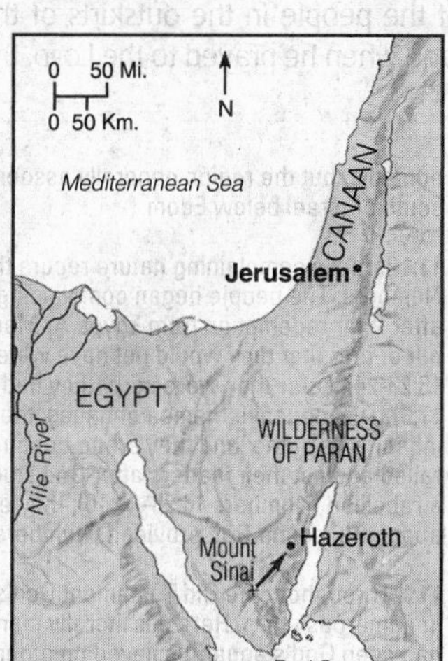

10:10 The sentence "I am the LORD your God" serves to conclude the first major section of Numbers. It reminded Israel that the LORD alone was their God and He alone is supreme.

▸ BIBLE
10:11 The journey of life. What would a snapshot of your life look like? One big blur in a minivan, whipping in and out of parking lots? God shows us a picture of how Israel traveled, noting that it was He who gave Moses the orders to march (Numbers 10:13). Moses was insightful enough to know that God might not always give detailed orders about where to camp, so he recruited his wife's brother to be their guide through the desert. However, Moses still maintained his primary theme: God marked every step of their journey (Numbers 10:34-36). Does your life's journey show signs of God's guidance? (***See Bible***> *Power*> *Wisdom*> *Guidance for Life,* TopicGuide page A11.)

10:12 Paran was an arid, rocky region on the eastern side of the Sinai Peninsula. Abraham's son, Ishmael (by Sarah's handmaiden Hagar), was raised in Paran (Genesis 21:20-21), so the Israelites actually could have had distant relatives in the area.

tribe of Issachar, led by Nethanel son of Zuar, 16 and the troops of the tribe of Zebulun, led
by Eliab son of Helon.
17 Then the Tabernacle was taken down, and the Gershonite and Merarite divisions of **10:17**
the Levites were next in the line of march, carrying the Tabernacle with them. 18 Reuben's Num 4:21-23
troops went next, marching behind their banner. Their leader was Elizur son of Shedeur. **10:18**
19 They were joined by the troops of the tribe of Simeon, led by Shelumiel son of Zurishad- Num 2:10-16
dai, 20 and the troops of the tribe of Gad, led by Eliasaph son of Deuel.
21 Next came the Kohathite division of the Levites, carrying the sacred objects from the **10:21**
Tabernacle. Before they arrived at the next camp, the Tabernacle would already be set up Num 4:1-20
at its new location. 22 Ephraim's troops went next, marching behind their banner. Their **10:22**
leader was Elishama son of Ammihud. 23 They were joined by the troops of the tribe of Ma- Num 2:3-31
nasseh, led by Gamaliel son of Pedahzur, 24 and the troops of the tribe of Benjamin, led by
Abidan son of Gideoni.
25 Dan's troops went last, marching behind their banner and serving as the rear guard
for all the tribal camps. Their leader was Ahiezer son of Ammishaddai. 26 They were joined
by the troops of the tribe of Asher, led by Pagiel son of Ocran, 27 and the troops of the tribe
of Naphtali, led by Ahira son of Enan.
28 This was the order in which the Israelites marched, division by division.
29 One day Moses said to his brother-in-law, Hobab son of Reuel the Midianite, "We are **10:29**
on our way to the place the LORD promised us, for He said, 'I will give it to you.' Come with Exod 2:18-21; 3:1
us and we will treat you well, for the LORD has promised wonderful blessings for Israel!" Judg 4:11
30 But Hobab replied, "No, I will not go. I must return to my own land and family."
31 "Please don't leave us," Moses pleaded. "You know the places in the wilderness where **10:32**
we should camp. Come, be our guide. 32 If you do, we'll share with you all the blessings the Ps 22:27-31
LORD gives us." **10:33**
33 They marched for three days after leaving the mountain of the LORD, with the Ark of Deut 1:33
the LORD's Covenant moving ahead of them to show them where to stop and rest. 34 As **10:34**
they moved on each day, the cloud of the LORD hovered over them. 35 And whenever the Num 9:15-23 **10:35**
Ark set out, Moses would shout, "Arise, O LORD, and let Your enemies be scattered! Let Ps 68:1-2
them flee before You!" 36 And when the Ark was set down, he would say, "Return, O LORD, **10:36**
to the countless thousands of Israel!" Deut 1:10-11

THE PEOPLE COMPLAIN TO MOSES

11 Soon the people began to complain about their hardship, and the LORD heard **11:1**
everything they said. Then the LORD's anger blazed against them, and He sent a Lev 10:1-2
fire to rage among them, and He destroyed some of the people in the outskirts of the Num 14:2; 16:35;
camp. 2 Then the people screamed to Moses for help, and when he prayed to the LORD, the 17:5

10:29 As an adult, Moses had fled from Egypt and ended up in Midian, where he lived with the family of Jethro (or Reuel), a Midianite. Jethro was an advisor to Moses (Exodus 18), and Moses married his daughter, Zipporah. Hobab, then, was probably Zipporah's brother. While it's not made clear here, Hobab probably did stay with Moses because later his descendants are listed as living among the Israelites (Judges 1:16).

10:29 Midian was an area to the east of Egypt across the Sinai Peninsula. The Midianites, like the Israelites, were a people descended from Abraham. Abraham and Sarah had only one child, Isaac. After Sarah's death Abraham married a woman named Keturah. She had six sons with Abraham, and Midian was the fourth. Keturah's sons were half-brothers to Isaac and thus were extended family to Moses. The Midianites were nomadic, but the region generally associated with them is south of Israel below Edom.

11:1 Israel's complaining nature recurs throughout the rest of Numbers. The people began complaining against God soon after their redemption from Egypt. At Marah they complained out of fear that they would not have water to drink (Exodus 15:23-24). Later they were sorry they had left Egypt (Exodus 17:3). This negative theme continues: the people fear the inhabitants of the land they are to conquer (Numbers 14); they railed against their leaders after God stuck down instigators of a rebellion (Numbers 16:28–17:10); they even complained about the manna God provided (Numbers 21:5).

11:1 Throughout the Old Testament God's anger is described in numerous ways. Here it is literally manifested as fire. Israel had seen God's anger displayed on other occasions, but still they seemed prone to stubbornness.

11:3 fire stopped. 3After that, the area was known as Taberah (which means "the place of burn-
Deut 9:22 ing"), because fire from the LORD had burned among them there.
11:4 Exod 12:38 4Then the foreign rabble who were traveling with the Israelites began to crave the good
Lev 24:10-11 Ps 78:18 things of Egypt. And the people of Israel also began to complain. "Oh, for some meat!"
1 Cor 10:6 they exclaimed. 5"We remember the fish we used to eat for free in Egypt. And we had all
11:6 the cucumbers, melons, leeks, onions, and garlic we wanted. 6But now our appetites are
Num 21:5 gone. All we ever see is this manna!"
11:7 7The manna looked like small coriander seeds, and it was pale yellow like gum resin.
Exod 16:14, 31 8The people would go out and gather it from the ground. They made flour by grinding it
11:9 with hand mills or pounding it in mortars. Then they boiled it in a pot and made it into flat
Exod 16:13 cakes. These cakes tasted like pastries baked with olive oil. 9The manna came down on
11:10 Ps 78:21 the camp with the dew during the night.
10Moses heard all the families standing in the doorways of their tents whining, and the
11:11 Exod 5:22 LORD became extremely angry. Moses was also very aggravated. 11And Moses said to the
11:12 LORD, "Why are You treating me, Your servant, so harshly? Have mercy on me! What did I
Gen 26:3 do to deserve the burden of all these people? 12Did I give birth to them? Did I bring them
Exod 13:4-5 Isa 49:23 into the world? Why did You tell me to carry them in my arms like a mother carries a nurs-
11:14 ing baby? How can I carry them to the land You swore to give their ancestors? 13Where am I
Exod 18:18 supposed to get meat for all these people? They keep whining to me, saying, 'Give us meat
Deut 1:12 to eat!' 14I can't carry all these people by myself! The load is far too heavy! 15If this is how
11:15 Exod 32:32 You intend to treat me, just go ahead and kill me. Do me a favor and spare me this misery!"

MOSES CHOOSES SEVENTY LEADERS

11:16 16Then the LORD said to Moses, "Gather before Me seventy men who are recognized as el-
Exod 24:1, 9 ders and leaders of Israel. Bring them to the Tabernacle* to stand there with you. 17I will
11:17 come down and talk to you there. I will take some of the Spirit that is upon you, and I will
Exod 34:5-6 Num 11:25; 12:5 put the Spirit upon them also. They will bear the burden of the people along with you, so
you will not have to carry it alone.
11:18 18"And say to the people, 'Purify yourselves, for tomorrow you will have meat to eat.
Exod 19:10, 14-15 You were whining, and the LORD heard you when you cried, "Oh, for some meat! We were
better off in Egypt!" Now the LORD will give you meat, and you will have to eat it. 19And it
won't be for just a day or two, or for five or ten or even twenty. 20You will eat it for a whole
month until you gag and are sick of it. For you have rejected the LORD, who is here among
you, and you have whined to Him, saying, "Why did we ever leave Egypt?"'"
11:21 21But Moses responded to the LORD, "There are 600,000 foot soldiers here with me, and
Exod 12:37 yet You say, 'I will give them meat for a whole month!' 22Even if we butchered all our

11:16 Hebrew *the Tent of Meeting.*

11:4-5 The Israelites had a four-hundred-year history in Egypt. Even after being forced into slavery, the people had enjoyed some of the good food of Egypt, and they began to miss this food in the desert.

11:6 The term *manna* literally means, "What is it?" Exodus 16 instructed Israel regarding the gathering of manna. Though we do not know its exact nature, manna solved Israel's food dilemma. Later, the people were instructed to put some manna into the Ark of the Covenant along with other highly sacred religious relics. But at this time the people became tired of manna and were ungrateful for the wonderful gift of food spread across the ground each morning.

▸ PURPOSE

11:8 Discovering God in His provision of manna. What is the most astounding way God has provided for your needs? When the people of Israel were thirsty, God sent water to them (Exodus 17:6). When they were hungry, God sent food in the form of manna. Jesus used both miraculous provisions to explain who He was, telling a woman at a well that He was the "living water" (John 4:10) and a crowd in Galilee that He was the "true bread that came down from heaven" (John 6:58). God can still meet your most intense needs through the provision of His Son, Jesus Christ. (***See Purpose****> God's Deeds> Special Acts> Miracles> OT> Provision of manna,* TopicGuide page A52; ***God****> Salvation> Father> Sent His only Son,* TopicGuide page A15.)

11:19-20 God knows what is best for His children. In this case, He teaches Israel a lesson by giving them exactly what they want, allowing them to see how childishly selfish and ungrateful they have been.

11:21-23 The extent of the Lord's promised provision was beyond Moses' belief. He saw the magnitude of the need and questioned how it could happen. God's declaration of omnipotent power is awesome!

flocks and herds, would that satisfy them? Even if we caught all the fish in the sea, would
that be enough?"
[23]Then the LORD said to Moses, "Has My arm lost its power? Now you will see whether or 11:23
not My word comes true!" Isa 50:2
[24]So Moses went out and reported the LORD's words to the people. He gathered the seventy
elders and stationed them around the Tabernacle.* [25]And the LORD came down in the cloud 11:25
and spoke to Moses. Then He gave the seventy elders the same Spirit that was upon Moses. Num 11:16-17
And when the Spirit rested upon them, they prophesied. But this never happened again.
[26]Two men, Eldad and Medad, had stayed behind in the camp. They were listed among
the elders, but they had not gone out to the Tabernacle. Yet the Spirit rested upon them as
well, so they prophesied there in the camp. [27]A young man ran and reported to Moses, "El-
dad and Medad are prophesying in the camp!"
[28]Joshua son of Nun, who had been Moses' assistant since his youth, protested, "Moses, 11:28
my master, make them stop!" Josh 1:1 Mark 9:38-40
[29]But Moses replied, "Are you jealous for my sake? I wish that all the LORD's people were
prophets and that the LORD would put His Spirit upon them all!" [30]Then Moses returned to
the camp with the elders of Israel.

THE LORD SENDS QUAIL

[31]Now the LORD sent a wind that brought quail from the sea and let them fall all around the 11:31
camp. For miles in every direction there were quail flying about three feet above the ground.* Exod 16:13
[32]So the people went out and caught quail all that day and throughout the night and all the Pss 78:26-33; 105:40
next day, too. No one gathered less than fifty bushels*! They spread the quail all around the
camp to dry. [33]But while they were gorging themselves on the meat—while it was still in their 11:33
mouths—the anger of the LORD blazed against the people, and He struck them with a severe Num 11:10
plague. [34]So that place was called Kibroth-hattaavah (which means "graves of gluttony") be- 11:34
cause there they buried the people who had craved meat from Egypt. [35]From Kibroth- Deut 9:22
hattaavah the Israelites traveled to Hazeroth, where they stayed for some time. 11:35 Num 33:17

THE COMPLAINTS OF MIRIAM AND AARON

12 While they were at Hazeroth, Miriam and Aaron criticized Moses because he 12:1 Exod 2:21; 15:20
had married a Cushite woman. [2]They said, "Has the LORD spoken only through 12:2 Num 16:3

11:24 Hebrew *the tent;* also in 11:26. 11:31 Or *there were quail 3 feet* [2 cubits or 92 centimeters] *deep on the ground.* 11:32 Hebrew *10 homers* [1.8 kiloliters].

▶ HOLINESS

11:29 The Holy Spirit's power. Moses might not have known it, but his longing for all God's people to receive a greater gift of God's Spirit would come true. Joel prophesied that this new "spirit-indwelling" would occur in all believers, regardless of class or distinction (Joel 2:28-29). At Pentecost (Acts 2), these prophecies came true as the Holy Spirit came, delivering power to God's people, resting not only upon the apostles, but upon everyone who believed. Do you need more power for living the Christian life? It is available for all who believe through the power of the indwelling Holy Spirit! (***See Holiness****> Submission>Yielding to Spirit> Power of the Spirit is for all,* TopicGuide page A41.)

11:31 God had earlier supplied quail for His people on the eve of the arrival of the first manna (Exodus 16). With that provision came instructions to take only what was necessary for each day. That restraint was missing on this occasion, as the people gathered many bushels of quail. Their lack of trust in God to supply for their needs was clear.

▶ WORSHIP

12:1 Criticical error. Leaders are not above rebuke. But there is a right way and a wrong way to rebuke them, and this was the wrong way. Moses had married a Cushite, or Ethiopian, woman, who may have been his second wife. We don't know any other details, but something about this caused some of Moses' closest family to doubt his right to continue leading. God reaffirms Moses' unique position as leader of Israel and reminds us all that when bringing charges against our leaders, we must not be hasty and must inquire of the Lord first. (***See Worship****> OT> Prophets> Moses, the standard of Old Testament prophets,* TopicGuide page A28.)

12:1 Though Miriam is not identified by name until she was an adult prophetess, she may have played a significant role early in Moses' early life. Jochebed, Moses' mother, saved her newborn son's life by hiding him in a basket at the edge of the Nile River. Moses' sister, possibly Miriam, was sent to watch out for him. An Egyptian princess found Moses floating on the Nile. With ingenuity and quick thought, Moses' sister offered her own mother's services to care for Moses. While this chapter reveals conflict between Miriam and her brother, she did exhibit a life of service.

12:3 Moses? Hasn't He spoken through us, too?" But the LORD heard them. 3(Now Moses was
Matt 11:29 very humble—more humble than any other person on earth.)
4So immediately the LORD called to Moses, Aaron, and Miriam and said, "Go out to the
12:5 Tabernacle,* all three of you!" So the three of them went to the Tabernacle. 5Then the LORD
Num 11:25 descended in the pillar of cloud and stood at the entrance of the Tabernacle.* "Aaron and
12:6 Miriam!" He called, and they stepped forward. 6And the LORD said to them, "Now listen to
Gen 15:1; 31:10-11; what I say:
46:2
1 Kgs 3:5

"If there were prophets among you,
I, the LORD, would reveal Myself in visions.
12:7 I would speak to them in dreams.
Ps 105:26 7 But not with My servant Moses.
Heb 3:2, 5 Of all My house, he is the one I trust.
12:8
Exod 33:11, 19 8 I speak to him face to face,
Deut 34:10 clearly, and not in riddles!
He sees the LORD as He is.
So why were you not afraid
to criticize My servant Moses?"

12:10
Deut 24:9 9The LORD was very angry with them, and He departed. 10As the cloud moved from
12:11 above the Tabernacle, there stood Miriam, her skin as white as snow from leprosy.* When
2 Sam 19:19 Aaron saw what had happened to her, 11he cried out to Moses, "Oh, my master! Please
don't punish us for this sin we have so foolishly committed. 12Don't let her be like a still-
born baby, already decayed at birth."
13So Moses cried out to the LORD, "O God, I beg You, please heal her!"
12:14
Lev 13:46 14But the LORD said to Moses, "If her father had done nothing more than spit in her face,
Num 5:1-3 wouldn't she be defiled for seven days? So keep her outside the camp for seven days, and
Deut 25:9 after that she may be accepted back."
15So Miriam was kept outside the camp for seven days, and the people waited until she
was brought back before they traveled again. 16Then they left Hazeroth and camped in
the wilderness of Paran.

TWELVE SCOUTS EXPLORE CANAAN

13:2
Deut 1:22-25 13 The LORD now said to Moses, 2"Send out men to explore the land of Canaan, the
Josh 1:3 land I am giving to the Israelites. Send one leader from each of the twelve ances-
tral tribes." 3So Moses did as the LORD commanded him. He sent out twelve men, all tribal
leaders of Israel, from their camp in the wilderness of Paran. 4These were the tribes and
the names of their leaders:

12:4 Hebrew *the Tent of Meeting.* 12:5 Hebrew *the tent;* also in 12:10. 12:10 Or *with a skin disease.* The Hebrew word used here can describe various skin diseases.

12:3 Had Moses written in such a manner of his own humility, it would have been a self-defeating act of vain pride. This is an indication that while Moses wrote nearly all the Bible's first five books, there seem to be certain details added for clarification (perhaps by Joshua) after Moses' death.

12:10 Leprosy was a horrible fate in the Ancient Near East. The description of leprosy in Moses' writings (Leviticus 13–14) could include various skin conditions. Leprosy was often permanent and fatal and demanded separation from others. Miriam's condition may have been leprosy or one of the other skin conditions subsumed under that class such as psoriasis or leucoderma. Miriam's recovery is one of numerous biblical accounts of miraculous healings from skin afflictions (see Elisha's healing of Naaman in 2 Kings 5; Jesus' healing of ten lepers in Luke 17:12-19).

12:16 The wilderness of Paran (see note at 10:12) is in the Sinai Peninsula, between Egypt and Canaan.

13:2 Canaan, the land God promised to Abraham and his descendants, comprised roughly the area between the Mediterranean Sea and the Dead Sea (west to east) and between the Sinai desert (the Negev) and the Sea of Galilee (south to north). Throughout these early books of the Bible, this land was also referred to as "the Promised Land," and then "Israel."

Tribe	*Leader*
Reuben	Shammua son of Zaccur
5 Simeon	Shaphat son of Hori
6 Judah	Caleb son of Jephunneh
7 Issachar	Igal son of Joseph
8 Ephraim	Hoshea son of Nun
9 Benjamin	Palti son of Raphu
10 Zebulun	Gaddiel son of Sodi
11 Manasseh son of Joseph	Gaddi son of Susi
12 Dan	Ammiel son of Gemalli
13 Asher	Sethur son of Michael
14 Naphtali	Nahbi son of Vophsi
15 Gad	Geuel son of Maki

16These are the names of the men Moses sent out to explore the land. (Moses called Ho-
shea son of Nun by the name Joshua.)

17Moses gave the men these instructions as he sent them out to explore the land: "Go
north through the Negev into the hill country. 18See what the land is like, and find out
whether the people living there are strong or weak, few or many. 19See what kind of land
they live in. Is it good or bad? Do their towns have walls, or are they unprotected like open
camps? 20Is the soil fertile or poor? Are there many trees? Do your best to bring back sam-
ples of the crops you see." (It happened to be the season for harvesting the first ripe grapes.)

21So they went up and explored the land from the wilderness of Zin as far as Rehob,
near Lebo-hamath. 22Going north, they passed through the Negev and arrived at Hebron,
where Ahiman, Sheshai, and Talmai—all descendants of Anak—lived. (The ancient town of
Hebron was founded seven years before the Egyptian city of Zoan.) 23When they came to

13:8 Num 13:16
13:16 Num 13:8
13:17 Gen 12:9; 13:1; Num 13:21
13:20 Deut 1:25
13:21 Num 20:1; 27:14; Josh 19:28; Judg 1:31; Amos 6:14
13:22 Num 13:33; Josh 11:21; 15:14; Judg 1:20
13:23 Num 13:24; 32:9; Deut 1:24-25

13:16 Names often held great meaning in the Ancient Near East, and changing names was significant (Abraham in Genesis 17:5 for instance). *Hoshea,* which means "salvation," was changed to *Joshua,* which means "the LORD is salvation." This change affirmed that Joshua was not Israel's salvation—they were saved only by trusting in the Lord's power.

▸WORSHIP
13:18 A bright future. Did Moses want to see what the land was like, or did he want to see what his men were like? Moses already knew that the land was rich and fertile and that God had commanded them to take it (Exodus 33:3). He knew the people who held the land would be more powerful than Israel, but God would fight for them (Exodus 23:23). Out of the 12 spies, only Joshua and Caleb remembered God's promises. When you see opportunities in your future, remember God's promises and do not fear. (***See Worship****> OT> Repentance> Nature> Obedience guarantees success in the land of Canaan,* TopicGuide page A29.)

13:21 The men explored the whole land south to north. Zin is located on the southern edge of Canaan below Beersheba, and Rehob is at the northern end of the Jordan Valley near Mount Hermon.

13:22 This obscure reference to Zoan helped the first readers place Hebron in history. Zoan, a prominent Egyptian city, was the center of worship for the Egyptian god Seth. According to Psalm 78, Zoan was where Moses met with Pharaoh (Psalm 78:43) concerning the release of the Israelites. Zoan has also been known as Avaris (when conquered by the Hyksos) and Tanis (by the Greeks). Even today, ruins of Zoan survive.

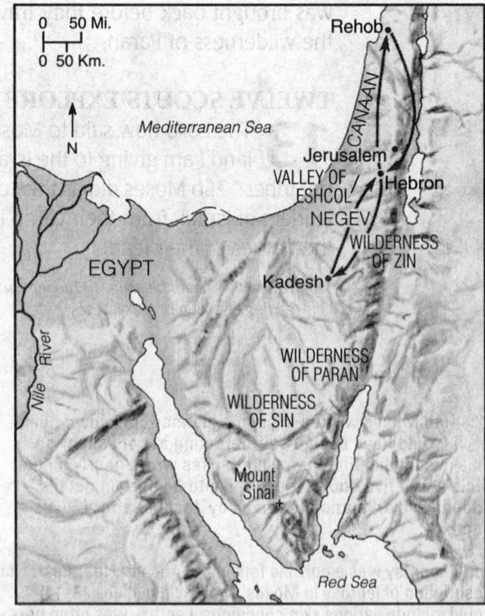

ROUTE OF THE SCOUTS The scouts traveled from Kadesh at the southernmost edge of the wilderness of Zin to Rehob at the northernmost edge and back, a round trip of about 500 miles.

the valley of Eshcol, they cut down a branch with a single cluster of grapes so large that it
took two of them to carry it on a pole between them! They also brought back samples of
the pomegranates and figs. 24 That place was called the valley of Eshcol (which means
"cluster"), because of the cluster of grapes the Israelite men cut there.

THE SCOUTING REPORT

25 After exploring the land for forty days, the men returned 26 to Moses, Aaron, and the
whole community of Israel at Kadesh in the wilderness of Paran. They reported to
the whole community what they had seen and showed them the fruit they had taken from
the land. 27 This was their report to Moses: "We entered the land you sent us to explore,
and it is indeed a bountiful country—a land flowing with milk and honey. Here is the kind
of fruit it produces. 28 But the people living there are powerful, and their towns are large
and fortified. We even saw giants there, the descendants of Anak! 29 The Amalekites live in
the Negev, and the Hittites, Jebusites, and Amorites live in the hill country. The Canaanites
live along the coast of the Mediterranean Sea* and along the Jordan Valley."
30 But Caleb tried to quiet the people as they stood before Moses. "Let's go at once to
take the land," he said. "We can certainly conquer it!"
31 But the other men who had explored the land with him disagreed. "We can't go up
against them! They are stronger than we are!" 32 So they spread this bad report about the land
among the Israelites: "The land we traveled through and explored will devour anyone who
goes to live there. All the people we saw were huge. 33 We even saw giants* there, the descen-
dants of Anak. Next to them we felt like grasshoppers, and that's what they thought, too!"

THE PEOPLE REBEL

14 Then the whole community began weeping aloud, and they cried all night. 2 Their
voices rose in a great chorus of protest against Moses and Aaron. "If only we had
died in Egypt, or even here in the wilderness!" they complained. 3 "Why is the LORD taking
us to this country only to have us die in battle? Our wives and our little ones will be carried
off as plunder! Wouldn't it be better for us to return to Egypt?" 4 Then they plotted among
themselves, "Let's choose a new leader and go back to Egypt!"
5 Then Moses and Aaron fell face down on the ground before the whole community of
Israel. 6 Two of the men who had explored the land, Joshua son of Nun and Caleb son of

13:26 Num 12:16; 13:3; 20:1; 32:8
13:27 Exod 13:5; Deut 1:25
13:28 Num 13:22-23
13:29 Num 14:43
13:30 Num 14:6, 24
13:31 Deut 1:28
13:32 Num 14:36
13:33 Deut 1:28
14:2 Exod 15:24; 16:3; Num 11:1; 16:13; 20:4; 21:5
14:3 Exod 5:21; 16:3; Num 14:31; Deut 1:39
14:5 Num 16:22, 45

13:29 Hebrew *the sea.* 13:33 Hebrew *nephilim.*

13:27 The Promised Land was first described as "flowing with milk and honey" by the Lord to Moses in Exodus 3:8. This description, used another 20 times in the Old Testament, meant that Canaan was a land of fullness and complete satisfaction.

13:30 Caleb was one of two spies (the other being Joshua) who had faith that the people could conquer the land of Canaan. Caleb received the benefits of his faith for years to come. Of all the adults who left Egypt, only Joshua and Caleb actually crossed the border of Canaan to inherit the Promise. He took the city of Hebron and its surrounding area as an inheritance.

▸ GOD

13:33 Giants in the land. The report of the spies is not unlike our own way of dealing with challenges. What started off as "a land flowing with milk and honey" became "We can't go up against them! They are stronger than we are!" and eventually grew to "Next to them we felt like grasshoppers, and that's what they thought, too!" (Apparently they interviewed the giants.) They allowed fear and faithlessness to alter their memories and create a hopeless situation. But with God, there is always hope when we are walking in His will. (***See God***> *God's Attributes*> *Loving*> *God loves His people, even when they are faithless,* TopicGuide page A17.)

▸ HOLINESS

14:4 Planning to doubt. Just as the challenges of Canaan fueled fear in 10 of the spies, the exaggerated bad report from the spies fueled rebellion and wickedness in the hearts of the people in the camp. However, difficult situations do not create unbelief—they only reveal it. What weaknesses in your character does stress reveal? (***See Holiness***> *Disciplines*> *Of Abstinence*> *Resisting sinful urges,* TopicGuide page A42.)

▸ GOD

14:5 Face down. Were Moses and Aaron praying? Or dodging rocks? Or expecting that when God responded to this brewing rebellion, "duck and cover" would be the safest position? Regardless, they knew that they had no resources to deal with this rebellion. Their hearts were in the right place, for when God mused that He should simply destroy Israel and make a nation from Moses, Moses interceded for his people and begged God to forgive them (Numbers 14:19). (***See God***> *God's Attributes*> *Forgiving*> *God is ready to forgive,* TopicGuide page A16.)

Jephunneh, tore their clothing. 7 They said to all the people of Israel, "The land we traveled
through and explored is a wonderful land! 8 And if the LORD is pleased with us, He will bring
us safely into that land and give it to us. It is a rich land flowing with milk and honey. 9 Do
not rebel against the LORD, and don't be afraid of the people of the land. They are only
helpless prey to us! They have no protection, but the LORD is with us! Don't be afraid of
them!"
10 But the whole community began to talk about stoning Joshua and Caleb. Then the
glorious presence of the LORD appeared to all the Israelites at the Tabernacle.* 11 And the
LORD said to Moses, "How long will these people treat Me with contempt? Will they never
believe Me, even after all the miraculous signs I have done among them? 12 I will disown
them and destroy them with a plague. Then I will make you into a nation greater and
mightier than they are!"

MOSES INTERCEDES FOR THE PEOPLE

13 But Moses objected. "What will the Egyptians think when they hear about it?" he asked
the LORD. "They know full well the power You displayed in rescuing Your people from
Egypt. 14 Now if You destroy them, the Egyptians will send a report to the inhabitants of
this land, who have already heard that You live among Your people. They know, LORD,
that You have appeared to Your people face to face and that Your pillar of cloud hovers
over them. They know that You go before them in the pillar of cloud by day and the pillar
of fire by night. 15 Now if You slaughter all these people with a single blow, the nations that
have heard of Your fame will say, 16 'The LORD was not able to bring them into the land He
swore to give them, so He killed them in the wilderness.'
17 "Please, Lord, prove that Your power is as great as You have claimed. For You said,
18 'The LORD is slow to anger and filled with unfailing love, forgiving every kind of sin and
rebellion. But He does not excuse the guilty. He lays the sins of the parents upon their chil-

14:7 Num 13:27; Deut 1:25
14:8 Exod 3:8; Num 13:27
14:9 Deut 1:21, 29; 7:18; 9:7, 23-24
14:10 Exod 16:7, 10; 17:4; 24:16-17; 32:9-13; Lev 9:23
14:12 Exod 32:10; Lev 26:25; Deut 28:21
14:13 Exod 9:28; 32:12
14:14 Exod 13:21; 33:11; Deut 5:4
14:16 Exod 32:12; Deut 9:28; Josh 7:7

14:10 Hebrew *the Tent of Meeting.*

14:10 God's glorious presence represented His majesty, holiness, and power. Such a manifestation was a blessing to the obedient but held the prospect of judgment or a curse for the disobedient.

14:11 God had indeed performed many miraculous signs for the Israelites: plagues in Egypt; the crossing of the Red Sea and the destruction of Pharaoh's army; the provision of quail and manna; the provision of water from the rock (as well as the purification of undrinkable water); and a cloud for guidance by day and a pillar of fire by night. For the people to doubt God's provision after all this was a flagrant disregard for His demonstrated goodness.

14:18-19 God revealed His name to Moses in Exodus 34 using the same phrases found in these verses. This crucial self-description of God and His character is repeated in numerous places throughout the Scriptures.

BECAUSE GOD IS
MERCIFUL

He forgives me of my sins when I sincerely confess them.

The LORD is slow to anger and filled with unfailing love,
forgiving every kind of sin and rebellion.

NUMBERS 14:18

FOR THE NEXT *GOD IS MERCIFUL* FEATURE SEE PAGE 991.

14:19 dren; the entire family is affected—even children in the third and fourth generations.' 19In
Exod 34:9 keeping with Your magnificent, unfailing love, please pardon the sins of this people, just
Ps 106:45 as You have forgiven them ever since they left Egypt."
14:20 20Then the LORD said, "I will pardon them as you have requested. 21But as surely as I
Ps 106:23 live, and as surely as the earth is filled with the LORD's glory, 22not one of these people
Mic 7:18-20 will ever enter that land. They have all seen My glorious presence and the miraculous
signs I performed both in Egypt and in the wilderness, but again and again they have
14:23 tested Me by refusing to listen to My voice. 23They will never even see the land I swore
Num 26:65; 32:11 to give their ancestors. None of those who have treated Me with contempt will ever see
14:24 it. 24But My servant Caleb has a different attitude than the others have. He has remained
Num 32:12 Josh 14:6-15 loyal to Me, so I will bring him into the land he explored. His descendants will possess
14:25 their full share of that land. 25Now turn around, and don't go on toward the land where
Num 13:29 the Amalekites and Canaanites live. Tomorrow you must set out for the wilderness in the
direction of the Red Sea.*"

THE LORD PUNISHES THE ISRAELITES

26Then the LORD said to Moses and Aaron, 27"How long must I put up with this wicked com-
munity and its complaints about Me? Yes, I have heard the complaints the Israelites are
14:28 making against Me. 28Now tell them this: 'As surely as I live, declares the LORD, I will do to
Num 14:21 14:29 you the very things I heard you say. 29You will all drop dead in this wilderness! Because
Num 1:17-19; 26:2 you complained against Me, every one of you who is twenty years old or older and was in-
Heb 3:17 cluded in the registration will die. 30You will not enter and occupy the land I swore to give
14:30 you. The only exceptions will be Caleb son of Jephunneh and Joshua son of Nun.
Num 14:24, 38 31"'You said your children would be carried off as plunder. Well, I will bring them safely
14:31 into the land, and they will enjoy what you have despised. 32But as for you, you will drop
Num 14:3 dead in this wilderness. 33And your children will be like shepherds, wandering in the wil-
14:32 derness for forty years. In this way, they will pay for your faithlessness, until the last of you
Num 26:64-65; 32:13 1 Cor 10:5 lies dead in the wilderness.
14:33 34"'Because your men explored the land for forty days, you must wander in the wilder-
Deut 2:7; 8:2 ness for forty years—a year for each day, suffering the consequences of your sins. Then
you will discover what it is like to have Me for an enemy.' 35I, the LORD, have spoken! I will
certainly do these things to every member of the community who has conspired against
Me. They will be destroyed here in this wilderness, and here they will die!"
36The ten men Moses had sent to explore the land—the ones who incited rebellion
14:36 Num 13:4-16 against the LORD with their bad report—37were struck dead with a plague before the LORD.
38Of the twelve who had explored the land, only Joshua and Caleb remained alive.
14:39 Exod 33:4 39When Moses reported the LORD's words to all the Israelites, the people were filled with
14:40 Deut 1:41-44 grief. 40Then they got up early the next morning and went to the top of the range of hills.

14:25 Hebrew *sea of reeds.*

14:20-25 Though God pardons sin, the consequence of Israel's rebellion is spelled out here with repetition (seven times!) to be sure Israel understood. The consequences are as sure to happen as the fact that God lives and His glory fills the earth—absolutely sure.

▶ ADOPTION

14:28 Known consequences. God is not deaf. He heard every grumble and mumble from His unfaithful people. When their seed of doubt grew into a flower of rebellion, God gave them exactly what they unknowingly foretold would happen—death in the desert. Indeed, "it is a terrible thing to fall into the hands of the living God" (Hebrews 3:16-19; 10:31). Do not flirt with God's discipline or natural consequences by living in sin; He hears and sees all. Instead, repent and find His loving embrace. (***See Adoption****> With Christ> Children of God> God disciplines His children,* TopicGuide page A36.)

▶ WORSHIP

14:40 Too little, too late. How do you know when repentance is just a pretense? One way to discern when you are not truly repentant is when your repentance does not lead you to obedience. God had commanded Israel to return to the desert, but instead they went forward into Canaan, only to be driven back into the wilderness. Repentance means turning from our sin, and toward God—the latter must never be forgotten. (***See Worship****> OT> Repentance> Nature> Results in change of behavior,* TopicGuide page A29.)

"Let's go," they said. "We realize that we have sinned, but now we are ready to enter the
land the LORD has promised us."
41 But Moses said, "Why are you now disobeying the LORD's orders to return to the wil-
derness? It won't work. 42 Do not go up into the land now. You will only be crushed by your
enemies because the LORD is not with you. 43 When you face the Amalekites and Canaan-
ites in battle, you will be slaughtered. The LORD will abandon you because you have aban-
doned the LORD."
44 But the people defiantly pushed ahead toward the hill country, even though neither
Moses nor the Ark of the LORD's Covenant left the camp. 45 Then the Amalekites and the
Canaanites who lived in those hills came down and attacked them and chased them back
as far as Hormah.

14:44 Num 10:33; 31:6
14:45 Num 21:3; Judg 1:17

LAWS CONCERNING OFFERINGS

15 Then the LORD told Moses, 2 "Give the following instructions to the people of Israel.
"When you finally settle in the land I am giving you, 3 you will offer special gifts
as a pleasing aroma to the LORD. These gifts may take the form of a burnt offering, a sacri-
fice to fulfill a vow, a voluntary offering, or an offering at any of your annual festivals, and
they may be taken from your herds of cattle or your flocks of sheep and goats. 4 When you
present these offerings, you must also give the LORD a grain offering of two quarts* of
choice flour mixed with one quart* of olive oil. 5 For each lamb offered as a burnt offering
or a special sacrifice, you must also present one quart of wine as a liquid offering.
6 "If the sacrifice is a ram, give a grain offering of four quarts* of choice flour mixed with
a third of a gallon* of olive oil, 7 and give a third of a gallon of wine as a liquid offering. This
will be a pleasing aroma to the LORD.
8 "When you present a young bull as a burnt offering or as a sacrifice to fulfill a vow or as
a peace offering to the LORD, 9 you must also give a grain offering of six quarts* of choice
flour mixed with two quarts* of olive oil, 10 and give two quarts of wine as a liquid offering.
This will be a special gift, a pleasing aroma to the LORD.
11 "Each sacrifice of a bull, ram, lamb, or young goat should be prepared in this way.
12 Follow these instructions with each offering you present. 13 All of you native-born Israel-
ites must follow these instructions when you offer a special gift as a pleasing aroma to the
LORD. 14 And if any foreigners visit you or live among you and want to present a special gift
as a pleasing aroma to the LORD, they must follow these same procedures. 15 Native-born
Israelites and foreigners are equal before the LORD and are subject to the same decrees.
This is a permanent law for you, to be observed from generation to generation. 16 The
same instructions and regulations will apply both to you and to the foreigners living
among you."

15:3 Lev 1:1; 2:1-16; 22:21; 23:37-38; 27:2
15:5 Num 15:5-10; 28:7
15:8 Lev 3:1; 7:11-18
15:10 Num 28:14
15:15 Num 9:14; 15:29

15:4a Hebrew *1/10 of an ephah* [2.2 liters]. **15:4b** Hebrew *1/4 of a hin* [1 liter]; also in 15:5. **15:6a** Hebrew *2/10 of an ephah* [4.4 liters]. **15:6b** Hebrew *1/3 of a hin* [1.3 liters]; also in 15:7. **15:9a** Hebrew *3/10 of an ephah* [6.6 liters]. **15:9b** Hebrew *1/2 of a hin* [2 liters]; also in 15:10.

14:45 Though the location of Hormah is uncertain (it is also mentioned in ancient Egyptian texts), it is related to the word meaning "destruction."

15:1 The Lord had given careful instructions regarding sacrificial offerings in Leviticus 1–7. While the regulations may seem complex, all the offerings are a pattern for how we approach God. First, offerings of atonement (sin and guilt offerings) allow us to approach God in repentance. Second, offerings of commitment or "consecration" (burnt, grain, and drink offerings) express devotion following repentance. Finally, fellowship offerings (peace, wave, freewill, and others) are voluntary offerings expressing further devotion. Verses 1-21 give further instruction regarding the second class of offerings.

15:4 Grain offerings (or cereal offerings) could take the form of fine flour, baked loaves, cakes, or wafers. The amount of flour used for the baked goods was determined by the size of the accompanying burnt offering.

15:5-7 Drink offerings accompanied other sacrifices. The wine was poured over the meat as it was burned.

15:8 Israelites took vows voluntarily. They considered the vows sacred and gave fellowship offerings upon taking the vow.

17Then the LORD said to Moses, 18"Give the following instructions to the people of Israel.
15:19 "When you arrive in the land where I am taking you, 19and you eat the crops that grow
Josh 5:11-12 there, you must set some aside as a sacred offering to the LORD. 20Present a cake from the
first of the flour you grind, and set it aside as a sacred offering, as you do with the first
grain from the threshing floor. 21Throughout the generations to come, you are to present
a sacred offering to the LORD each year from the first of your ground flour.
15:22 Lev 4:2 22"But suppose you unintentionally fail to carry out all these commands that the LORD
has given you through Moses. 23And suppose your descendants in the future fail to do
everything the LORD has commanded through Moses. 24If the mistake was made uninten-
tionally, and the community was unaware of it, the whole community must present a
young bull for a burnt offering as a pleasing aroma to the LORD. It must be offered along
with its prescribed grain offering and liquid offering and with one male goat for a sin offer-
15:25 Lev 4:20 ing. 25With it the priest will purify the whole community of Israel, making them right with
the LORD,* and they will be forgiven. For it was an unintentional sin, and they have cor-
rected it with their offerings to the LORD—the special gift and the sin offering. 26The whole
community of Israel will be forgiven, including the foreigners living among you, for all the
people were involved in the sin.
27"If one individual commits an unintentional sin, the guilty person must bring a one-
year-old female goat for a sin offering. 28The priest will sacrifice it to purify* the guilty per-
15:29 son before the LORD, and that person will be forgiven. 29These same instructions apply
Num 15:15 both to native-born Israelites and to the foreigners living among you.
15:30 30"But those who brazenly violate the LORD's will, whether native-born Israelites or
Num 14:40-44 Deut 1:43; 17:13 foreigners, have blasphemed the LORD, and they must be cut off from the community.
15:32 31Since they have treated the LORD's word with contempt and deliberately disobeyed
Exod 31:14-15; His command, they must be completely cut off and suffer the punishment for their
35:2-3 guilt."

PENALTY FOR BREAKING THE SABBATH

32One day while the people of Israel were in the wilderness, they discovered a man gath-
ering wood on the Sabbath day. 33The people who found him doing this took him before
Moses, Aaron, and the rest of the community. 34They held him in custody because they
15:35 Lev 24:14, 23 did not know what to do with him. 35Then the LORD said to Moses, "The man must be put
Deut 21:21 to death! The whole community must stone him outside the camp." 36So the whole com-
munity took the man outside the camp and stoned him to death, just as the LORD had com-
manded Moses.

15:25 Or *will make atonement for the whole community of Israel.* 15:28 Or *to make atonement for.*

▶ BIBLE
15:22 Incidents and accidents. God is interested in our motives. Externals are not unimportant, but the heart is what God is most concerned about (1 Samuel 16:7). The complexity of the rituals that God prescribed was daunting, so God looked at people's intentions and provided a way to atone for unintentional failures. With our spouses, friends, children—even ourselves—look at the heart motive when making a judgment about someone's behavior. (***See Bible****> Uniqueness> Authoritative> Demands heart obedience,* TopicGuide page A10.)

15:31 To be cut off from the community was similar to banishment or excommunication. An example occurs as early as the story of Creation; as a result of their sin, Adam and Eve were banished from the garden that had been their home. In the case of the Mosaic law, those punished in this way were cut off from the community in a social and religious sense. A wide variety of infractions could result in a person or family being cut off; examples include failure to circumcise a child (Genesis 17:14), eating blood (Leviticus 17:10), and, as in this case, deliberate sin.

▶ GOD
15:32 Working on the Sabbath. The recent lesson (Numbers 15:22-31) on carefully judging those who break the law needed immediate application. A man was found breaking the Sabbath by gathering wood. Rather than immediately passing the maximum sentence against him (Exodus 31:15), the people brought him to Moses, who took the matter before God Himself to judge. Likewise, bring every moral question to God's Word and seek His counsel before passing judgment on anyone else. (***See God****> God's Nature> Unique> He is the final lawgiver and judge,* TopicGuide page A15.)

15:36 This is the second time Israel used stoning as punishment (see also Leviticus 24:10-23). Reserved for flagrant violations of God's law, stoning was necessary to reinforce God's requirement of holiness and obedience.

TASSELS ON CLOTHING

37 Then the LORD said to Moses, 38 "Give the following instructions to the people of Israel:
Throughout the generations to come you must make tassels for the hems of your clothing
and attach them with a blue cord. 39 When you see the tassels, you will remember and
obey all the commands of the LORD instead of following your own desires and defiling
yourselves, as you are prone to do. 40 The tassels will help you remember that you must
obey all My commands and be holy to your God. 41 I am the LORD your God who brought
you out of the land of Egypt that I might be your God. I am the LORD your God!"

KORAH'S REBELLION

16 One day Korah son of Izhar, a descendant of Kohath son of Levi, conspired with
Dathan and Abiram, the sons of Eliab, and On son of Peleth, from the tribe of Reu-
ben. 2 They incited a rebellion against Moses, along with 250 other leaders of the commu-
nity, all prominent members of the assembly. 3 They united against Moses and Aaron and
said, "You have gone too far! The whole community of Israel has been set apart by the
LORD, and He is with all of us. What right do you have to act as though you are greater than
the rest of the LORD's people?"

4 When Moses heard what they were saying, he fell face down on the ground. 5 Then he
said to Korah and his followers, "Tomorrow morning the LORD will show us who belongs to
Him* and who is holy. The LORD will allow only those whom He selects to enter His own
presence. 6 Korah, you and all your followers must prepare your incense burners. 7 Light
fires in them tomorrow, and burn incense before the LORD. Then we will see whom the
LORD chooses as His holy one. You Levites are the ones who have gone too far!"

8 Then Moses spoke again to Korah: "Now listen, you Levites! 9 Does it seem insignificant
to you that the God of Israel has chosen you from among all the community of Israel to be
near Him so you can serve in the LORD's Tabernacle and stand before the people to minis-
ter to them? 10 Korah, He has already given this special ministry to you and your fellow Le-
vites. Are you now demanding the priesthood as well? 11 The LORD is the One you and
your followers are really revolting against! For who is Aaron that you are complaining
about him?"

12 Then Moses summoned Dathan and Abiram, the sons of Eliab, but they replied, "We

15:38 Lev 3:17; Num 10:8; Deut 22:12; Matt 23:5
15:39 Deut 4:23; 6:12; 8:11, 14
15:40 Lev 11:44; Rom 12:1; Col 1:22; 1 Pet 1:15-16
15:41 Exod 20:2
16:1 Exod 6:21; Num 26:9; Deut 11:6; Jude 1:11
16:2 Num 1:16
16:3 Exod 19:6; Num 16:7; 35:34
16:4 Num 14:5
16:5 Lev 10:3; Num 17:5, 8; Ps 65:4
16:7 Num 16:3
16:10 Num 3:6-10
16:11 Exod 16:7; 1 Cor 10:10

16:5 Greek version reads *God has visited and knows those who are His.* Compare 2 Tim 2:19.

15:37-41 Tassels became an external way to remember and recite the law. The tradition has passed down to this day, with many in Judaism wearing shawls containing tassels with 628 knots—one for each law in the Torah. In Jesus' day, the Pharisees enlarged these tassels to make notice of their strict observance of the Law. In Matthew 23:5, Jesus condemns external religiosity as inadequate when it is not accompanied by heart belief.

16:1-2 Korah was a descendant of Kohath, a son of Levi. The descendants of Levi were set apart for special service, but only Aaron's sons could be priests. This meant that Korah and other descendants of Kohath did not share the priesthood. His rebellion was primarily against God, not Moses as he was attempting to rewrite God's law.

▸ PURPOSE
16:2 Handling rebellion. Korah the Levite incited the people against Moses and Aaron. God's leaders could have responded in several ways. They could have made the fight a political one, using their influence to crush Korah; or they could have made it a physical one, threatening or harming Korah and his family. Instead, Moses and Aaron continually gave God every opportunity to act in a mighty way and resolve the conflict in any way He saw fit—in other words, they learned to wait on God. Not every conflict in life should be handled with this holy passivity, but can you think of at least one? (***See Purpose****> God's Deeds> Special Acts> Miracles> OT> Korah's rebellion,* TopicGuide page A52.)

16:3 Korah was right to say God had "set apart" everyone in Israel. God told Moses that if the people obeyed God's commands, He would make them a "kingdom of priests, My holy nation" (Exodus 19:6). But God had also instituted within this kingdom of priests a leadership structure. Korah was challenging this structure. Korah's rebellion was similar to the conflict Moses had with Miriam and Aaron (Numbers 12). Both questioned if the Lord spoke only through Moses. And in both, the ensuing afflictions were God's confirmations of Moses' special position.

16:6 Burning incense was important in the Tabernacle (and later the Temple). The priests burned incense every morning. The incense used was a specific recipe, and only those instructed to use it, the priests, could bring incense in worship.

16:13 refuse to come before you! 13Isn't it enough that you brought us out of Egypt, a land flow-
Num 11:5; 14:2-3; 20:3-4 ing with milk and honey, to kill us here in this wilderness, and that you now treat us like
16:14 your subjects? 14What's more, you haven't brought us into another land flowing with milk
Exod 22:5 and honey. You haven't given us a new homeland with fields and vineyards. Are you try-
Num 20:5 ing to fool these men?* We will not come."
16:15 15Then Moses became very angry and said to the LORD, "Do not accept their grain offer-
Gen 4:4 ings! I have not taken so much as a donkey from them, and I have never hurt a single one
1 Sam 12:3 of them." 16And Moses said to Korah, "You and all your followers must come here tomor-
row and present yourselves before the LORD. Aaron will also be here. 17You and each of
your 250 followers must prepare an incense burner and put incense on it, so you can all
present them before the LORD. Aaron will also bring his incense burner."
18So each of these men prepared an incense burner, lit the fire, and placed incense on it.
16:19 Then they all stood at the entrance of the Tabernacle* with Moses and Aaron. 19Mean-
Lev 9:6 Num 14:10; 16:42; 20:6 while, Korah had stirred up the entire community against Moses and Aaron, and they all
gathered at the Tabernacle entrance. Then the glorious presence of the LORD appeared to
16:21 the whole community, 20and the LORD said to Moses and Aaron, 21"Get away from all
Exod 32:10 these people so that I may instantly destroy them!"
16:22 22But Moses and Aaron fell face down on the ground. "O God," they pleaded, "You are
Gen 18:23-32 the God who gives breath to all creatures. Must You be angry with all the people when
only one man sins?"
16:24 23And the LORD said to Moses, 24"Then tell all the people to get away from the tents of
Num 16:45 Korah, Dathan, and Abiram."
25So Moses got up and rushed over to the tents of Dathan and Abiram, followed by the
16:26 elders of Israel. 26"Quick!" he told the people. "Get away from the tents of these wicked
Gen 19:12-17 men, and don't touch anything that belongs to them. If you do, you will be destroyed for
their sins." 27So all the people stood back from the tents of Korah, Dathan, and Abiram.
Then Dathan and Abiram came out and stood at the entrances of their tents, together with
their wives and children and little ones.
16:28 Exod 3:12; 4:1-9; 7:9 28And Moses said, "This is how you will know that the LORD has sent me to do all these
things that I have done—for I have not done them on my own. 29If these men die a natural
death, or if nothing unusual happens, then the LORD has not sent me. 30But if the LORD does
something entirely new and the ground opens its mouth and swallows them and all their
belongings, and they go down alive into the grave,* then you will know that these men
have shown contempt for the LORD."
31He had hardly finished speaking the words when the ground suddenly split open be-
16:32 neath them. 32The earth opened its mouth and swallowed the men, along with their
Num 16:30; 26:10 households and all their followers who were standing with them, and everything they
owned. 33So they went down alive into the grave, along with all their belongings. The
earth closed over them, and they all vanished from among the people of Israel. 34All the
people around them fled when they heard their screams. "The earth will swallow us, too!"
16:35 Lev 10:2 they cried. 35Then fire blazed forth from the LORD and burned up the 250 men who were
Num 11:1-3; 26:10 offering incense.

16:14 Hebrew *Are you trying to put out the eyes of these men?* 16:18 Hebrew *the Tent of Meeting;* also in 16:19, 42, 43, 50.
16:30 Hebrew *into Sheol;* also in 16:33.

16:13 The rebels went so far now as to use "a land flowing with milk and honey" to describe, not the land of the promise, but Egypt, the land of slavery and oppression. This explains Moses' anger in the following verses.

16:22 On numerous occasions, Moses complained to God about the people's stubbornness and unwillingness to listen (Exodus 6:12; 17:4). But Moses also pleaded with God to forgive His people and spare them from judgment (for example, Exodus 32). Here, during Korah's rebellion, Moses pleaded with God not to destroy all the people because of one man.

16:33 The "grave" here is the Hebrew word *sheol.* This word sometimes refers to an Ancient Near Eastern concept of a nether world, but in this case it is best understood as simply the physical location of the body after death, usually in a cave owned by the family.

36*And the LORD said to Moses, 37"Tell Eleazar son of Aaron the priest to pull all the incense
burners from the fire, for they are holy. Also tell him to scatter the burning coals. 38Take the in-
cense burners of these men who have sinned at the cost of their lives, and hammer the metal
into a thin sheet to overlay the altar. Since these burners were used in the LORD's presence,
they have become holy. Let them serve as a warning to the people of Israel."
39So Eleazar the priest collected the 250 bronze incense burners that had been used by
the men who died in the fire, and he hammered them into a thin sheet to overlay the altar.
40This would warn the Israelites that no unauthorized person—no one who was not a de- 16:40
scendant of Aaron—should ever enter the LORD's presence to burn incense. If anyone did, Num 1:51; 3:10, 38
the same thing would happen to him as happened to Korah and his followers. So the
LORD's instructions to Moses were carried out.
41But the very next morning the whole community of Israel began muttering again 16:41
against Moses and Aaron, saying, "You have killed the LORD's people!" 42As the commu- Num 16:3
nity gathered to protest against Moses and Aaron, they turned toward the Tabernacle and 16:42 Exod 40:34
saw that the cloud had covered it, and the glorious presence of the LORD appeared. Num 14:10; 16:19
43Moses and Aaron came and stood in front of the Tabernacle, 44and the LORD said to
Moses, 45"Get away from all these people so that I can instantly destroy them!" But Moses 16:45
and Aaron fell face down on the ground. Num 16:21, 24
46And Moses said to Aaron, "Quick, take an incense burner and place burning coals on it 16:46
from the altar. Lay incense on it, and carry it out among the people to purify them and Lev 10:1, 6
make them right with the LORD.* The LORD's anger is blazing against them—the plague has Num 8:19; 18:5;
already begun." 25:13 Deut 9:22
47Aaron did as Moses told him and ran out among the people. The plague had already 16:47
begun to strike down the people, but Aaron burned the incense and purified* the people. Num 25:7-8, 13
48He stood between the dead and the living, and the plague stopped. 49But 14,700 peo- 16:49
ple died in that plague, in addition to those who had died in the affair involving Korah. Num 16:32-35; 25:9
50Then because the plague had stopped, Aaron returned to Moses at the entrance of the
Tabernacle.

THE BUDDING OF AARON'S STAFF

17 1*Then the LORD said to Moses, 2"Tell the people of Israel to bring you twelve
wooden staffs, one from each leader of Israel's ancestral tribes, and inscribe each
leader's name on his staff. 3Inscribe Aaron's name on the staff of the tribe of Levi, for there
must be one staff for the leader of each ancestral tribe. 4Place these staffs in the Taberna- 17:4 Exod 25:22
cle in front of the Ark containing the tablets of the Covenant,* where I meet with you. Num 17:10
5Buds will sprout on the staff belonging to the man I choose. Then I will finally put an end 17:5
to the people's murmuring and complaining against you." Num 16:5; 17:8
6So Moses gave the instructions to the people of Israel, and each of the twelve tribal 17:7
leaders, including Aaron, brought Moses a staff. 7Moses placed the staffs in the LORD's Num 18:2

16:36 Verses 16:36-50 are numbered 17:1-15 in Hebrew text. 16:46 Or *to make atonement for them.* 16:47 Or *and made atonement for.* 17:1 Verses 17:1-13 are numbered 17:16-28 in Hebrew text. 17:4 Hebrew *in the Tent of Meeting before the Testimony.* The Hebrew word for "testimony" refers to the terms of the LORD's covenant with Israel as written on stone tablets, which were kept in the Ark, and also to the covenant itself.

16:39-40 Leviticus 10 records the account of Nadab and Abihu, Aaron's own sons, who were judged for misusing incense in worship. These men were priests who, unlike Korah, were authorized to offer the incense. Yet their act led to God immediately striking them dead. If God judged even priests severely for desecrating this ritual, how much more would He judge men who were not designated to offer the incense? Their incense burners were reformed and used at the altar as a permanent example and warning to Israel.

16:49 It is uncertain if the plague mentioned here is the same as that which struck other rebels in Numbers 14:37. Though the number of casualties seems high, it is less than three percent of the number of fighting men totaled in Numbers 1:46.

17:2 The Hebrew word for "staff" is a wordplay with the word for "tribe." A staff became a symbol of office when inscribed with the owner's name—in this case, the tribal leader.

17:8 presence in the Tabernacle of the Covenant.* [8]When he went into the Tabernacle of the
Num 17:5 Covenant the next day, he found that Aaron's staff, representing the tribe of Levi, had
Heb 9:4 sprouted, budded, blossomed, and produced ripe almonds!
[9]When Moses brought all the staffs out from the LORD's presence, he showed them to
17:10 the people. Each man claimed his own staff. [10]And the LORD said to Moses: "Place Aaron's
Num 17:4 Deut 9:7, 24 staff permanently before the Ark of the Covenant* to serve as a warning to rebels. This
should put an end to their complaints against Me and prevent any further deaths." [11]So
Moses did as the LORD commanded him.
17:12 [12]Then the people of Israel said to Moses, "Look, we are doomed! We are dead! We are
Isa 6:5 17:13 ruined! [13]Everyone who even comes close to the Tabernacle of the LORD dies. Are we all
Num 1:51-53 doomed to die?"

DUTIES OF PRIESTS AND LEVITES

18:1 **18** Then the LORD said to Aaron: "You, your sons, and your relatives from the tribe of
Exod 28:38 Levi will be held responsible for any offenses related to the sanctuary. But you
and your sons alone will be held responsible for violations connected with the priesthood.
18:2 [2]"Bring your relatives of the tribe of Levi—your ancestral tribe—to assist you and your
Num 3:5-10 sons as you perform the sacred duties in front of the Tabernacle of the Covenant.* [3]But as
the Levites go about all their assigned duties at the Tabernacle, they must be careful not to
go near any of the sacred objects or the altar. If they do, both you and they will die. [4]The
Levites must join you in fulfilling their responsibilities for the care and maintenance of the
Tabernacle,* but no unauthorized person may assist you.
18:5 [5]"You yourselves must perform the sacred duties inside the sanctuary and at the altar. If you
Num 16:46 follow these instructions, the LORD's anger will never again blaze against the people of Israel. [6]I
18:6 Num 3:9, 12 Myself have chosen your fellow Levites from among the Israelites to be your special assistants.
They are a gift to you, dedicated to the LORD for service in the Tabernacle. [7]But you and your
18:7 Exod 29:9 sons, the priests, must personally handle all the priestly rituals associated with the altar and with
Num 1:51; 3:10 everything behind the inner curtain. I am giving you the priesthood as your special privilege of
service. Any unauthorized person who comes too near the sanctuary will be put to death."

SUPPORT FOR THE PRIESTS AND LEVITES

18:8 [8]The LORD gave these further instructions to Aaron: "I Myself have put you in charge of all
Lev 7:28-34 Deut 12:6 the holy offerings that are brought to Me by the people of Israel. I have given all these con-
18:9 secrated offerings to you and your sons as your permanent share. [9]You are allotted the
Lev 2:1-16; 6:25-30

17:7 Or *Tabernacle of the Testimony;* also in 17:8. 17:10 Hebrew *before the Testimony;* see note on 17:4.
18:2 Or *Tabernacle of the Testimony.* 18:4 Hebrew *the Tent of Meeting;* also in 18:6, 21, 22, 23, 31.

17:8 The staff of Aaron blossomed and bore fruit in a matter of hours, a miracle of time similar to Jesus' changing water to wine. This confirmed Aaron and his line as God's chosen priesthood. The almond blossom is particularly beautiful, images of which were placed on other instruments in the Tabernacle (see Exodus 25:33).

17:10 We learn in Hebrews 9:4 that this blossoming staff was eventually placed in the Ark of the Covenant along with other sacred articles. While this test *should* have put an end to the rebellion of the people, it didn't. The people continued to exhibit stubbornness and shifted the blame to Moses, their leader.

18:1-7 Following the rebellion in chapter 16 and God's reaffirmation of Aaron's priesthood in chapter 17, this section states in strong language the order of authority in God's service. In fact, God affirms Aaron's status by addressing him directly in these passages. Aaron's descendants were priests; the rest of the Levite tribe was to assist in the work of the Tabernacle, but there were clear lines of authority. In the same way, the New Testament affirms a priesthood of all believers (1 Peter 2:5) but also recognizes the calling and spiritual authority of pastors and teachers (Ephesians 4:11-12).

18:7 The call to service among God's people was seen as a gift from God; it was not deserved or earned.

18:9-11 This section describes the distribution of offerings among God's servants. The whole burnt offerings were completely incinerated on the altar. Priests received no portion of these. Sin and guilt offerings were only burned in part and priests received portions to be eaten only at the Tabernacle with other priests. Fellowship offerings, which were voluntary, had less restrictive guidelines for use. The priests could actually take their portions of this offering home to share with their family. In this way, the Israelite priesthood was actually supported by the worship of the community much as professional ministers are today.

portion of the most holy offerings that is not burned on the fire. This portion of all the most
holy offerings—including the grain offerings, sin offerings, and guilt offerings—will be
most holy, and it belongs to you and your sons. [10]You must eat it as a most holy offering.
All the males may eat of it, and you must treat it as most holy.
[11]"All the sacred offerings and special offerings presented to Me when the Israelites lift
them up before the altar also belong to you. I have given them to you and to your sons
and daughters as your permanent share. Any member of your family who is ceremonially
clean may eat of these offerings.
[12]"I also give you the harvest gifts brought by the people as offerings to the LORD—the
best of the olive oil, new wine, and grain. [13]All the first crops of their land that the people
present to the LORD belong to you. Any member of your family who is ceremonially clean
may eat this food.
[14]"Everything in Israel that is specially set apart for the LORD* also belongs to you.
[15]"The firstborn of every mother, whether human or animal, that is offered to the LORD
will be yours. But you must always redeem your firstborn sons and the firstborn of cere-
monially unclean animals. [16]Redeem them when they are one month old. The redemp-
tion price is five pieces of silver* (as measured by the weight of the sanctuary shekel,
which equals twenty gerahs).
[17]"However, you may not redeem the firstborn of cattle, sheep, or goats. They are holy
and have been set apart for the LORD. Sprinkle their blood on the altar, and burn their fat as
a special gift, a pleasing aroma to the LORD. [18]The meat of these animals will be yours, just
like the breast and right thigh that are presented by lifting them up as a special offering be-
fore the altar. [19]Yes, I am giving you all these holy offerings that the people of Israel bring
to the LORD. They are for you and your sons and daughters, to be eaten as your permanent
share. This is an eternal and unbreakable covenant* between the LORD and you, and it also
applies to your descendants."
[20]And the LORD said to Aaron, "You priests will receive no allotment of land or share of
property among the people of Israel. I am your share and your allotment. [21]As for the tribe
of Levi, your relatives, I will compensate them for their service in the Tabernacle. Instead
of an allotment of land, I will give them the tithes from the entire land of Israel.
[22]"From now on, no Israelites except priests or Levites may approach the Tabernacle. If
they come too near, they will be judged guilty and will die. [23]Only the Levites may serve at
the Tabernacle, and they will be held responsible for any offenses against it. This is a per-
manent law for you, to be observed from generation to generation. The Levites will re-
ceive no allotment of land among the Israelites, [24]because I have given them the
Israelites' tithes, which have been presented as sacred offerings to the LORD. This will be
the Levites' share. That is why I said they would receive no allotment of land among the
Israelites."

18:11 Lev 22:2-3, 11-13
18:12 Exod 23:19; Deut 18:4
18:14 Lev 27:28
18:19 2 Chr 13:5
18:20 Deut 10:9; 18:2; Josh 13:33; Ezek 44:28
18:21 Lev 27:30-33
18:23 Num 18:1, 20

18:14 The Hebrew term used here refers to the complete consecration of things or people to the LORD, either by destroying them or by giving them as an offering. 18:16 Hebrew *5 shekels* [2 ounces or 57 grams] *of silver.* 18:19 Hebrew *a covenant of salt.*

18:15 Firstborn, particularly firstborn males, held unique standing in this culture. This was true of animals and humans. The firstborn son carried the responsibility of family leadership, which included a larger inheritance. An Israelite could offer a firstborn in several different ways. He could literally bring that firstborn to the Tabernacle, or he could redeem it. In essence, he would be offering the firstborn, then buying it back. There was a set price for each kind of firstborn. This routinely happened with firstborn sons.

18:20 Land represented security and strength. The Levites' exemption from receiving land could have been considered a great loss. But the Levites, being set apart for God's service, were given the gift of depending on the Lord for security.

18:21 The people's tithes to the Tabernacle supported the Levites. Even before formal Mosaic law, giving a tenth or a tithe was considered an appropriate gift to offer a deity, a monarch, or a person of honor. Evidence of tithes is found in ancient China, Persia, Babylon, and Egypt. Biblical examples include Abraham, who offered the priest Melchizedek a tenth of the goods he recovered in a military victory (Genesis 14:19-20), and Abraham's grandson, Jacob, who made a commitment to God at Bethel that included a tenth of everything God gave him (Genesis 28:20-22).

18:26 25The LORD also told Moses, 26"Give these instructions to the Levites: When you receive
Num 18:28 from the people of Israel the tithes I have assigned as your allotment, give a tenth of the
Neh 10:38 tithes you receive—a tithe of the tithe—to the LORD as a sacred offering. 27The LORD will
consider this offering to be your harvest offering, as though it were the first grain from
18:28 your own threshing floor or wine from your own winepress. 28You must present one-tenth
Num 18:21 of the tithe received from the Israelites as a sacred offering to the LORD. This is the LORD's
sacred portion, and you must present it to Aaron the priest. 29Be sure to give to the LORD
the best portions of the gifts given to you.

30"Also, give these instructions to the Levites: When you present the best part as your
18:31 Matt 10:10 offering, it will be considered as though it came from your own threshing floor or wine-
Luke 10:7 press. 31You Levites and your families may eat this food anywhere you wish, for it is your
1 Cor 9:13 1 Tim 5:18 compensation for serving in the Tabernacle. 32You will not be considered guilty for accept-
ing the LORD's tithes if you give the best portion to the priests. But be careful not to treat the
18:32 Lev 22:2, 15-16 holy gifts of the people of Israel as though they were common. If you do, you will die."

THE WATER OF PURIFICATION

19:2 Lev 22:20-25 **19** The LORD said to Moses and Aaron, 2"Here is another legal requirement com-
Deut 21:3 manded by the LORD: Tell the people of Israel to bring you a red heifer, a perfect
animal that has no defects and has never been yoked to a plow. 3Give it to Eleazar the
19:4 priest, and it will be taken outside the camp and slaughtered in his presence. 4Eleazar will
Lev 4:6, 17; 16:14 take some of its blood on his finger and sprinkle it seven times toward the front of the Tab-
ernacle.* 5As Eleazar watches, the heifer must be burned—its hide, meat, blood, and dung.
19:6 6Eleazar the priest must then take a stick of cedar,* a hyssop branch, and some scarlet yarn
Lev 14:4, 6, 49 and throw them into the fire where the heifer is burning.

19:7 7"Then the priest must wash his clothes and bathe himself in water. Afterward he may
Lev 11:25; 16:26-28 return to the camp, though he will remain ceremonially unclean until evening. 8The man
who burns the animal must also wash his clothes and bathe himself in water, and he,
19:9 too, will remain unclean until evening. 9Then someone who is ceremonially clean will
Num 8:7; 19:13, 20-21 gather up the ashes of the heifer and deposit them in a purified place outside the camp.
They will be kept there for the community of Israel to use in the water for the purification
19:10 ceremony. This ceremony is performed for the removal of sin. 10The man who gathers
Num 19:7-8, 19 up the ashes of the heifer must also wash his clothes, and he will remain ceremonially
unclean until evening. This is a permanent law for the people of Israel and any foreign-
ers who live among them.

19:4 Hebrew *the Tent of Meeting*. 19:6 Or *juniper*.

18:29 God stipulates that people offer Him not only the first portion, but also the best. Such an offering reminds us first that the earth and all that is in it belongs to God anyway. Second, it reminds us that nothing we may own or produce is more important than God; therefore we give Him the best portion.

18:32 That which is holy is set apart by God. These verses give a strong admonition against taking the holy things of God for granted.

19:1-22 The concerns of the priesthood had been settled, and so chapter 19 moved on to deal with purification rituals for the people as a whole in order to guard the purity of the Tabernacle. While there is some mystery here as to symbolism, this instruction is similar to that seen in Leviticus 12–15.

19:3 Eleazar, Aaron's third son, had special responsibilities at the Tabernacle (Numbers 3:32; 4:16). His two older brothers, the priests Nadab and Abihu, had been killed when they offered inappropriate incense (Leviticus 10). Eleazar and his younger brother Ithamar were the remaining priests in Aaron's bloodline. It was Eleazar who gathered the incense burners after Korah's rebellion (Numbers 16).

19:6 The significance of cedar, hyssop, and scarlet thread are uncertain. Cedar may have been used for its aroma or for its resistance to decay. In ancient times the cedars of Lebanon were renowned throughout the region. Hyssop, when bunched together, held liquid well and may have been used for sprinkling or spraying when shaken. (For example, the Israelites were instructed to use hyssop to paint lamb's blood on their doorposts prior to the Passover).

19:6 Scarlet, a deep shade of red, was a valued commodity in the ancient world and was highlighted in many biblical events. Some of the high priest's clothes were scarlet, as were the curtains of the Tabernacle (Exodus 26; 39). The Old Testament prophet Isaiah described sin in terms of a stain "like scarlet" (or *crimson* in some translations) that could be washed "as white as snow" (Isaiah 1:18).

11"All those who touch a dead human body will be ceremonially unclean for seven days. 12They must purify themselves on the third and seventh days with the water of purification; then they will be purified. But if they do not do this on the third and seventh days, they will continue to be unclean even after the seventh day. 13All those who touch a dead body and do not purify themselves in the proper way defile the LORD's Tabernacle, and they will be cut off from the community of Israel. Since the water of purification was not sprinkled on them, their defilement continues.

14"This is the ritual law that applies when someone dies inside a tent: All those who enter that tent and those who were inside when the death occurred will be ceremonially unclean for seven days. 15Any open container in the tent that was not covered with a lid is also defiled. 16And if someone in an open field touches the corpse of someone who was killed with a sword or who died a natural death, or if someone touches a human bone or a grave, that person will be defiled for seven days.

17"To remove the defilement, put some of the ashes from the burnt purification offering in a jar, and pour fresh water over them. 18Then someone who is ceremonially clean must take a hyssop branch and dip it into the water. That person must sprinkle the water on the tent, on all the furnishings in the tent, and on the people who were in the tent; also on the person who touched a human bone, or touched someone who was killed or who died naturally, or touched a grave. 19On the third and seventh days the person who is ceremonially clean must sprinkle the water on those who are defiled. Then on the seventh day the people being cleansed must wash their clothes and bathe themselves, and that evening they will be cleansed of their defilement.

20"But those who become defiled and do not purify themselves will be cut off from the community, for they have defiled the sanctuary of the LORD. Since the water of purification has not been sprinkled on them, they remain defiled. 21This is a permanent law for the people. Those who sprinkle the water of purification must afterward wash their clothes, and anyone who then touches the water used for purification will remain defiled until evening. 22Anything and anyone that a defiled person touches will be ceremonially unclean until evening."

19:11 Lev 21:1
19:12 Num 19:17-19
19:13 Lev 7:20-21; 15:31; 20:3; 22:3
19:16 Num 19:11; 31:19
19:17 Num 19:9
19:19 Ezek 36:25-27 Heb 10:22
19:20 Num 19:13
19:21 Lev 11:25, 40; 16:26-28 Num 19:7
19:22 Lev 5:2-3; 7:21

MOSES STRIKES THE ROCK

20 In the first month of the year,* the whole community of Israel arrived in the wilderness of Zin and camped at Kadesh. While they were there, Miriam died and was buried.

2There was no water for the people to drink at that place, so they rebelled against Moses and Aaron. 3The people blamed Moses and said, "If only we had died in the LORD's presence with our brothers! 4Why have you brought the congregation of the LORD's people

20:1 Num 13:21
20:2 Exod 17:1
20:3 Exod 17:2 Num 14:2-3; 16:31-35

20:1 The first month of the ancient Hebrew lunar calendar usually occurs within the months of March and April. The number of years since leaving Egypt is not specified.

19:11-22 This ceremony and the idea of the uncleanness of death highlighted the distinction between life and death. God instructed His people toward life, not death and destruction. Encounters with death required a deliberate and careful purification ritual. Looking back to this event through the knowledge of Jesus' sacrifice in the New Testament, we can see a beautiful picture here. Death clung to the person who had touched it, much as death through sin clings to us. People could be purified by being washed in water that was filled with the ashes of a sacrifice. In the same way, Jesus' sacrifice for us cleanses us from the death that results from sin.

▸ GOD

19:17 Pure in heart. If you think it was hard to remain ceremonially pure in ancient Israel, think about how hard it is to be morally pure! Even the best of deeds are mixed with ever-present sinful attitudes such as selfishness or pride. The difficulties of ceremonial purity were just a symbol of how holy God is and how people may be made acceptable to Him only through God's grace. Once and for all, Jesus Christ has died so that all who trust in Him may stand in God's presence without shame. (***See God**> Relationship> God Enables> Relationship with God requires purity,* TopicGuide page A14.)

20:2-5 Once again, these verses show a deep stubbornness in Israel. The people rebelled, blamed Moses and Aaron, and then outrageously complained, wishing they had died with other rebels or that they were still in bondage in Egypt—all for lack of water.

20:5 into this wilderness to die, along with all our livestock? 5 Why did you make us leave Egypt
Num 16:14 and bring us here to this terrible place? This land has no grain, no figs, no grapes, no
pomegranates, and no water to drink!"
6 Moses and Aaron turned away from the people and went to the entrance of the Taber-
nacle,* where they fell face down on the ground. Then the glorious presence of the LORD
20:8 appeared to them, 7 and the LORD said to Moses, 8 "You and Aaron must take the staff and
Exod 4:17, 20 assemble the entire community. As the people watch, speak to the rock over there, and it
will pour out its water. You will provide enough water from the rock to satisfy the whole
community and their livestock."
9 So Moses did as he was told. He took the staff from the place where it was kept before
the LORD. 10 Then he and Aaron summoned the people to come and gather at the rock. "Lis-
20:11 Ps 78:16 ten, you rebels!" he shouted. "Must we bring you water from this rock?" 11 Then Moses
Isa 48:21 raised his hand and struck the rock twice with the staff, and water gushed out. So the en-
1 Cor 10:4 tire community and their livestock drank their fill.
20:12 Lev 10:3 12 But the LORD said to Moses and Aaron, "Because you did not trust Me enough to dem-
Num 20:24 onstrate My holiness to the people of Israel, you will not lead them into the land I am giv-
20:13 ing them!" 13 This place was known as the waters of Meribah (which means "arguing")
Exod 17:7 because there the people of Israel argued with the LORD, and there He demonstrated His
Ps 95:8 holiness among them.

EDOM REFUSES ISRAEL PASSAGE

20:14 14 While Moses was at Kadesh, he sent ambassadors to the king of Edom with this message:
Gen 36:31-39
Josh 2:10; 9:9 "This is what your relatives, the people of Israel, say: You know all the hardships we
have been through. 15 Our ancestors went down to Egypt, and we lived there a long
20:16 time, and we and our ancestors were brutally mistreated by the Egyptians. 16 But
Exod 3:2-6; 14:19 when we cried out to the LORD, He heard us and sent an angel who brought us out of
Egypt. Now we are camped at Kadesh, a town on the border of your land. 17 Please
let us travel through your land. We will be careful not to go through your fields and
vineyards. We won't even drink water from your wells. We will stay on the king's
road and never leave it until we have passed through your territory."

20:6 Hebrew *the Tent of Meeting.*

▸ BIBLE
20:8 Discovering God in the water from the rock. How is Jesus like a battered, water-spurting rock? The apostle Paul noted that in the same way that the rock, which Moses struck, provided life-giving water, Jesus Christ produces life-giving salvation for all who believe (1 Corinthians 10:3-5). (***See Bible****> Unity> OT Types> Water from the rock,* TopicGuide page A11.)

20:8-12 In Exodus 17, God told Moses to strike the rock to produce water so that Israel would trust Moses' leadership. In this case, God instructed Moses to speak to the rock so that Israel would know that God provides, and then Israel would trust Him. This was Moses' greatest failure as a leader—one with profound ramifications both for himself and his brother Aaron (see verse 12).

▸ GOD
20:10-11 Lost temper. Have you ever blown up in anger at someone? You've thought carefully about what to say to let them know how you feel, but then you open your mouth and—was that me talking? Moses not only expressed his anger to the people, "Listen, you rebels!" but, in a way, he struck out at God as well by taking God's glory for himself. Because Moses virtually stole God's glory in public, God declared that Moses would not lead God's people into the Promised Land. We have no record of Moses grumbling over this punishment. Perhaps he was secretly glad to hear that he would have to spend less time leading rebellious Israel! Or, perhaps he accepted his punishment as fair and deserved. (***See God****> God's Nature> Personality> Emotion> Rebellion rightly angers God,* TopicGuide page A14.)

20:14 Edom was the nation descended from Esau, the older twin brother of Jacob, the progenitor of the nation of Israel. Though born second, Jacob (later renamed Israel) cheated Esau out of the birthright reserved for the oldest son. This created family tension and hostility. Esau later married Canaanite women and settled his family to the south and east of the Dead Sea in a land that became known as Edom. Years later hostility remained, as seen here when Edom refused the Israelites passage. The prophecy of Obadiah is directed against Edom, and in the New Testament, Herod the Idumean is from this same people.

20:17 The king's road, also called the King's Highway, was an important trade route running north-south on the eastern side of the Dead Sea from the Gulf of Elat in the south to Damascus in the north. Whoever controlled the access to this road controlled much of the trade in the area. In this case, that meant the Edomites, enemies of Israel.

18But the king of Edom said, “Stay out of my land, or I will meet you with an army!”
19The Israelites answered, “We will stay on the main road. If our livestock drink your
water, we will pay for it. Just let us pass through your country. That's all we ask.”
20But the king of Edom replied, “Stay out! You may not pass through our land.” With that
he mobilized his army and marched out against them with an imposing force. 21Because **20:21**
Edom refused to allow Israel to pass through their country, Israel was forced to turn Num 21:4; Deut 2:8
around. Judg 11:18

THE DEATH OF AARON

22The whole community of Israel left Kadesh and arrived at Mount Hor. 23There, on the
border of the land of Edom, the LORD said to Moses and Aaron, 24“The time has come for
Aaron to join his ancestors in death. He will not enter the land I am giving the people of Is-
rael, because the two of you rebelled against My instructions concerning the water at Mer- **20:25**
ibah. 25Now take Aaron and his son Eleazar up Mount Hor. 26There you will remove Num 3:4; 19:3-4
Aaron's priestly garments and put them on Eleazar, his son. Aaron will die there and join **20:26**
his ancestors.” Num 20:24
27So Moses did as the LORD commanded. The three of them went up Mount Hor to-
gether as the whole community watched. 28At the summit, Moses removed the priestly **20:28**
garments from Aaron and put them on Eleazar, Aaron's son. Then Aaron died there on top Num 33:38
of the mountain, and Moses and Eleazar went back down. 29When the people realized
that Aaron had died, all Israel mourned for him thirty days.

VICTORY OVER THE CANAANITES

21 The Canaanite king of Arad, who lived in the Negev, heard that the Israelites were **21:1**
approaching on the road through Atharim. So he attacked the Israelites and took Num 33:40; Josh 12:14
some of them as prisoners. 2Then the people of Israel made this vow to the LORD: “If You will Judg 1:16
hand these people over to us, we will completely destroy* all their towns.” 3The LORD heard **21:3** Num 14:45

21:2 The Hebrew term used here refers to the complete consecration of things or people to the LORD, either by destroying them or by giving them as an offering; also in 21:3.

▸ **SPIRITUAL WARFARE**

20:21 Turning around. Why didn't God tell Israel to destroy Edom's army, take whatever they wanted, and go on their way? Because God had given His people a mission, and that mission was to enter and occupy the land of Canaan, not Edom or any other country. God has not called us to fight everyone who blocks our path. He wants us to stay focused on accomplishing His goals. Be at peace with all people, if possible (Romans 12:18; Colossians 3:15; Titus 3:2), and only fight the battles that God commands. (***See Spiritual Warfare****> Resisting sin and evil> Trusting God> Obeying God,* TopicGuide page A46.)

▸ **HOLINESS**

20:24 Changing minds. Can we really influence other people enough to change their decisions? In this passage, we learn that Aaron, along with Moses, was barred from the Promised Land. Perhaps it was because he sat by and allowed Moses to sin grievously when he could have stopped him. In the New Testament, James writes that “you can be sure that whoever brings the sinner back will save that person from death and bring about the forgiveness of many sins” (James 5:20). Take a risk and get involved in the life of someone who needs to be rescued from bad choices that lead to sin. (***See Holiness****> Submission> Identifying with Christ> Rescuing others from sin,* TopicGuide page A40.)

20:24 Aaron's death was no small thing for Moses, his brother. From Moses' call by God at the burning bush (Exodus 3), Aaron had served as Moses' spokesman and support. After God gave the Law at Sinai (Exodus 20), Aaron became the high priest, serving Israel in a most visible capacity.

20:26 The priestly garments, including the breastplate containing the *Urim* and *Thummim* (mentioned in Exodus 28:30), were outward symbols of the spiritual authority conferred by God upon His high priest. This transfer from father to son must have been painful. It was necessary that the transfer be visible (verse 27) so the congregation of Israel would know who carried the priestly authority after Aaron's death.

▸ **SPIRITUAL WARFARE**

21:1 The right of self-defense. While God dealt passively with the kingdom of Edom, when a group of small Canaanite towns near Arad attacked Israel unprovoked, God allowed Israel to destroy those towns. This is one of many passages that establish the right of self-defense for God's people. While there are times when we are to turn the other cheek (Matthew 5:39), God allows us to, while following the laws of the land, use appropriate force to defend our families (Exodus 22:2-3, 1 Timothy 5:8). (***See Spiritual Warfare****> Resisting Sin and Evil> Trusting God> God as Warrior> God's fight against the enemies of Israel,* TopicGuide page A46.)

21:1 The ancient ruins of Arad can be found in the northern portion of the Negev, just west of the southern end of the Dead Sea. It was a city of notable size for the period. The Negev is an arid, rocky, rugged region with scarce water supplies.

DO YOU EVER WONDER what happened to justice? Why does it seem to be growing increasingly elusive? What has gone wrong with the human-made judicial systems of this world?

Justice is a pillar of any society. It vindicates the innocent and punishes the guilty. All too often, though, this standard is compromised for personal gain. Corrupt judges tilt the scales of justice; unscrupulous lawyers manipulate laws and juries; witnesses lie. Truth is often distorted to benefit the rich, famous, and powerful.

Since our justice system can often be manipulated, we mistakenly believe we can manipulate God's system of justice. We think our excuses fool God. But how wrong we are! God told Jeremiah, "I, the LORD, search all hearts and examine secret motives. I give all people their due rewards, according to what their actions deserve" (Jeremiah 17:10).

In Numbers 21, the people of Israel began to complain against God. They accused Him of bringing them into the desert to die. God punished their childish outburst by sending poisonous snakes throughout the Israelites' camp.

As the holy and righteous Sovereign of the universe, God cannot ignore or overlook any act of sin. His anger at sin should never be underestimated. We cannot thumb our noses at God's righteous principles and expect to not experience the just consequences of our actions—both in this life and the life to come. However, God also tempers His justice with mercy. When the people of Israel confessed their sin of speaking against God, Moses created a bronze snake for them to look at in order to receive God's forgiveness and healing.

The Cross is the ultimate expression of God's justice and mercy. By paying the just penalty for our sins, Jesus opened the way for God to extend mercy to us. Jesus told Nicodemus, "As Moses lifted up the bronze snake on a pole in the wilderness, so the Son of Man must be lifted up, so that everyone who believes in Him will have eternal life" (John 3:14-15).

All believers are saved because God delays His justice. At what age did you discover God's love and forgiveness—at 15? at 30? at 70? Whatever age we received God's promise of eternal life, we had more than enough time to bring God's judgment upon ourselves. How many evil deeds had we committed before that day? How many people had we hurt? How many sins had we excused? None of us deserves even one day of life because of our sinful, depraved nature, so we must be grateful for a just God who delays punishment.

In this life, we occasionally see instant justice. Other times, we must wait. Often, we will not see true justice done until the great day of judgment promised by God (John 12:48; Matthew 25). But we can be assured that God sees it all—and that He cares about the mistreated even more than we do. God's justice will someday right every wrong, and it will reward eternally those who accept His mercy.

the Israelites' request and gave them victory over the Canaanites. The Israelites completely
destroyed them and their towns, and the place has been called Hormah* ever since.

THE BRONZE SNAKE

4 Then the people of Israel set out from Mount Hor, taking the road to the Red Sea* to go
around the land of Edom. But the people grew impatient with the long journey, 5 and they
began to speak against God and Moses. "Why have you brought us out of Egypt to die
here in the wilderness?" they complained. "There is nothing to eat here and nothing to
drink. And we hate this horrible manna!"
6 So the LORD sent poisonous snakes among the people, and many were bitten and died.
7 Then the people came to Moses and cried out, "We have sinned by speaking against the
LORD and against you. Pray that the LORD will take away the snakes." So Moses prayed for
the people.
8 Then the LORD told him, "Make a replica of a poisonous snake and attach it to a pole. All
who are bitten will live if they simply look at it!" 9 So Moses made a snake out of bronze
and attached it to a pole. Then anyone who was bitten by a snake could look at the bronze
snake and be healed!

21:4 Deut 2:8
21:5 Num 11:5-6; 14:2-3 Ps 78:19
21:6 Deut 8:15 1 Cor 10:9
21:7 Ps 78:34
21:8 Isa 14:29 John 3:14-15
21:9 2 Kgs 18:4 John 3:14; 12:32

ISRAEL'S JOURNEY TO MOAB

10 The Israelites traveled next to Oboth and camped there. 11 Then they went on to Iye-
abarim, in the wilderness on the eastern border of Moab. 12 From there they traveled to the
valley of Zered Brook and set up camp. 13 Then they moved out and camped on the far
side of the Arnon River, in the wilderness adjacent to the territory of the Amorites. The
Arnon is the boundary line between the Moabites and the Amorites. 14 For this reason *The*

21:10 Num 33:43

21:3 *Hormah* means "destruction." 21:4 Hebrew *sea of reeds.*

21:4-5 The people had to go around Edom because the Edomites had refused passage through their own territory (Numbers 20:20-21). Had the Edomites allowed the Israelites to travel there, they would have taken a road almost due north to the east of the Dead Sea and the Jordan River. Instead the people had to take a roundabout path. This cost them time and, as is obvious here, tested their morale and spiritual commitment. The path they had to take was actually backtracking toward the Red Sea, which they had crossed to leave Egypt.

▸ SPIRITUAL WARFARE
21:5 Whining brings judgment. Do you know anyone who likes to complain? The people of Israel complained about God, about Moses' leadership, and about the food God provided (calling God's gift of manna "horrible"!). In the midst of this rebellion, God sent a plague of venomous snakes as punishment. Such punishment was later formalized in the covenant curses Israel would suffer if they refused to obey God (Deuteronomy 30:15-20). What consequences of disobedience has God brought into your life to cause you to cry out and look to Him? (***See Spiritual Warfare**> Resisting sin and evil> Consequences> Of Disobedience> Falling under discipline,* TopicGuide page A46.)

21:6 The Middle East has several poisonous snakes, not all deadly. A species of adder and sand viper common to Sinai may fall in this category. More lethal is a species of carpet viper, which is more common in Africa, but is also found in the Sinai.

21:8 The bronze serpent, though intended as an instrument of healing, became an idol later in Israel's history (see 2 Kings 18:4).

▸ GOD
21:8 Discovering God in the bronze snake. In what way was Jesus like a metal snake on a pole? However odd that sounds, it's a comparison that Jesus made (John 3:14-15) as he explained the way God gave His Son so that anyone who believed in Him could be saved (John 3:16). Jesus pointed out that just as those who looked in faith to the serpent on the pole in the wilderness were saved, so anyone who looks in faith to Jesus receives salvation from sin. You can be saved from the righteous wrath of God toward rebellious humans by looking to Christ as your Savior! (***See God**> Salvation> Son> Removes God's wrath,* TopicGuide page A15.)

21:10-20 The path taken by Israel described here is unclear in that some of the settlements, such as Oboth, are unknown to us today. The streams Zered, Arnon, and Jabbok all flow down from the Transjordanian plateau into the Dead Sea Valley. From this knowledge and additional information in Numbers 33, we can assume that the Israelites headed south below Edom, then traveled to the east of the King's Highway. In this way they circumvented any Edomite land. But it was a more difficult and lengthy route.

▸ PURPOSE
21:14 Truth outside the Bible. Why would God allow quotations from other sources in the Bible? In this case, this book may have contained stories, poems, or songs written in honor of the victories of God over Israel's enemies. This is the only time this book is named, but it may also be the source of the quote in verses 14-15, and the poems in verses 17-18 and 27-30. The apostle Paul quoted secular sources (Acts 17:28), and Jude quoted from extra-biblical religious sources (Jude 1:14). We can study and appreciate knowledge from sources other than the Bible, knowing that God's common grace has made wisdom come even from the mouths of sinners. (***See Purpose**> God's Deeds> Common grace> Helps unbelievers do good without earning salvation,* TopicGuide page A54.)

Book of the Wars of the LORD speaks of "the town of Waheb in the area of Suphah, and the
21:15 Num 21:28 ravines of the Arnon River, 15and the ravines that extend as far as the settlement of Ar on
Deut 2:9 the border of Moab."
21:16 16From there the Israelites traveled to Beer,* which is the well where the LORD said to Moses,
Judg 9:21 "Assemble the people, and I will give them water." 17There the Israelites sang this song:

"Spring up, O well!
Yes, sing its praises!
18 Sing of this well,
which princes dug,
which great leaders hollowed out
with their scepters and staffs."

Then the Israelites left the wilderness and proceeded on through Mattanah, 19Nahaliel,
and Bamoth. 20After that they went to the valley in Moab where Pisgah Peak overlooks the
wasteland.*

VICTORY OVER SIHON AND OG

21:21 Deut 2:26-28 21The Israelites sent ambassadors to King Sihon of the Amorites with this message:
Judg 11:19-21 22"Let us travel through your land. We will be careful not to go through your fields
21:22 Num 20:17 and vineyards. We won't even drink water from your wells. We will stay on the king's
road until we have passed through your territory."
21:23 Num 20:21 Deut 2:32 23But King Sihon refused to let them cross his territory. Instead, he mobilized his entire
Judg 11:20 army and attacked Israel in the wilderness, engaging them in battle at Jahaz. 24But the Is-
21:24 raelites slaughtered them with their swords and occupied their land from the Arnon River
Deut 2:19, 31-37 to the Jabbok River. They went only as far as the Ammonite border because the boundary
Josh 12:1-2; 13:10 of the Ammonites was fortified.*
21:25 Amos 2:10 25So Israel captured all the towns of the Amorites and settled in them, including the city
21:26 of Heshbon and its surrounding villages. 26Heshbon had been the capital of King Sihon of
Ps 135:11 the Amorites. He had defeated a former Moabite king and seized all his land as far as the
Arnon River. 27Therefore, the ancient poets wrote this about him:

"Come to Heshbon and let it be rebuilt!
21:28 Deut 2:9, 18 Let the city of Sihon be restored.
Jer 48:45-46 28 A fire flamed forth from Heshbon,
a blaze from the city of Sihon.
21:29 It burned the city of Ar in Moab;
Judg 11:24 it destroyed the rulers of the Arnon heights.
1 Kgs 11:7, 33 29 What sorrow awaits you, O people of Moab!

21:16 *Beer* means "well." 21:20 Or *overlooks Jeshimon.* 21:24 Or *because the terrain of the Ammonite frontier was rugged;* Hebrew reads *because the boundary of the Ammonites was strong.*

21:21 According to Genesis 10:15-16 the Amorites were descended from Canaan. Before the era described here, the Amorites were quite powerful, occupying large parts of Mesopotamia and Syria. They were then driven from this region and settled in Babylonia, until the Hittites defeated them there. They eventually settled throughout Canaan and perhaps even Egypt. They had a reputation as being a wicked people. In fact, in Genesis 15:16 God specifically promises Abraham that his people would return and claim the land after the sin of the Amorites had run its course.

21:21-35 The defeat of King Sihon and King Og was often used as an historical reminder elsewhere in the Old Testament of how God helped His people defeat their enemies (Psalm 135:10-11).

21:29 Chemosh, a central Moabite deity, is mentioned numerous times in the "Moabite Stone." (This important archaeological artifact, discovered in the last century, dates from 850 BC.) The worship of Chemosh was widespread, pervading even King Solomon's reign through a foreign wife who worshiped the god. Solomon's policy of allowing his foreign wives to continue worshiping their gods introduced Israel to the worship of many deities, including Molech and Ashtoreth. Child sacrifice, firmly condemned by God, was part of the worship of Chemosh and Molech.

You are finished, O worshipers of Chemosh!
Chemosh has left his sons as refugees,
his daughters as captives of Sihon, the Amorite king.
30 We have utterly destroyed them,
from Heshbon to Dibon.
We have completely wiped them out
as far away as Nophah and Medeba.*"

31 So the people of Israel occupied the territory of the Amorites. 32 After Moses sent men 21:32 Num 32:1, 35
to explore the Jazer area, they captured all the towns in the region and drove out the Amo- Jer 48:32
rites who lived there. 33 Then they turned and marched up the road to Bashan, but King Og 21:33
of Bashan and all his people attacked them at Edrei. 34 The LORD said to Moses, "Do not be Deut 3:3-4
afraid of him, for I have handed him over to you, along with all his people and his land. Do
the same to him as you did to King Sihon of the Amorites, who ruled in Heshbon." 35 And
Israel killed King Og, his sons, and all his subjects; not a single survivor remained. Then Is-
rael occupied their land.

BALAK SENDS FOR BALAAM

22 Then the people of Israel traveled to the plains of Moab and camped east of the 22:1 Num 33:48-49
Jordan River, across from Jericho. 2 Balak son of Zippor, the Moabite king, had 22:2
seen everything the Israelites did to the Amorites. 3 And when the people of Moab saw Exod 15:15
how many Israelites there were, they were terrified. 4 The king of Moab said to the elders Deut 2:25
of Midian, "This mob will devour everything in sight, like an ox devours grass in the field!" 22:4
So Balak, king of Moab, 5 sent messengers to call Balaam son of Beor, who was living in Num 22:7; 25:16-18
his native land of Pethor* near the Euphrates River.* His message said: 22:5 Num 23:7 Deut 23:4

"Look, a vast horde of people has arrived from Egypt. They cover the face of the
earth and are threatening me. 6 Please come and curse these people for me because
they are too powerful for me. Then perhaps I will be able to conquer them and drive
them from the land. I know that blessings fall on any people you bless, and curses
fall on people you curse."

21:30 Or *until fire spread to Medeba.* The meaning of the Hebrew is uncertain. 22:5a Or *who was at Pethor in the land of the Amavites.* 22:5b Hebrew *the river.*

21:33 Bashan was territory to the east of the Sea of Galilee. It was known for its sheep and oak trees.

22:1 Jericho, located at the north end of the Dead Sea on the western side of the Jordan River, was the first city besieged by the Israelites when they entered the Promised Land under Joshua's leadership (Joshua 6).

22:1 Moab was a kingdom on the Transjordanian plateau to the east of the Dead Sea. The Moabites were descendants of Abraham's nephew Lot (Genesis 19:34-38).

22:2 All that we know of King Balak of Moab we learn in this account. The lessons are important since the story of Balak and Balaam was remembered throughout Israel's history (see Joshua 24; Judges 11; Micah 6; and even God's word to the church at Pergamum in Revelation 2).

22:5 Balaam son of Beor, often remembered for having an argument with a talking donkey, was a prophet and evidently also some kind of magician or diviner (see Joshua 13:22). Jude 1:11 listed him among Cain, the first murderer (Genesis 4), and Korah, the leader of the rebellion against Moses (Numbers 16). Ancient texts found at Deir 'Alla in Jordan mention "Balaam son of Beor," further affirming the historicity of this account.

22:5 Pethor was in Mesopotamia, quite a distance north and east of Moab, on the Euphrates River. In the early twentieth century more than 20,000 ancient cuneiform tablets were discovered near Mari, a town also on the Euphrates. Some of these describe ancient pagan prophets and seers like Balaam.

22:5 The Euphrates River runs from present-day Armenia to the Persian Gulf. It merges with the Tigris River. Mentioned in the Creation account, the Euphrates also is the northern border of the land promised to Abraham (Genesis 15:17-20).

▶ ADOPTION
22:6 Protected by God. As foolish as Balak was, he wisely associated the success of Israel with God's rich blessing. If that blessing could be removed, Balak knew it would be possible to defeat Israel. This passage leaves open the question of whether Balaam actually had the power to curse Israel, but experience shows that if we live our lives separate from God, we miss the riches of God's blessings. As we walk in the fear of the Lord, we will enjoy the comfort and protection of the Holy Spirit (Acts 9:31). (***See Adoption****> With Christ> Heirs of God,* TopicGuide page A36.)

22:7 Num 23:23 7 Balak's messengers, who were elders of Moab and Midian, set out with money to pay
Balaam to place a curse upon Israel.* They went to Balaam and delivered Balak's message
to him. 8 "Stay here overnight," Balaam said. "In the morning I will tell you whatever the
LORD directs me to say." So the officials from Moab stayed there with Balaam.
9 That night God came to Balaam and asked him, "Who are these men visiting you?"
10 Balaam said to God, "Balak son of Zippor, king of Moab, has sent me this message:
11 'Look, a vast horde of people has arrived from Egypt, and they cover the face of the
earth. Come and curse these people for me. Then perhaps I will be able to stand up to
them and drive them from the land.' "

22:12 Num 23:13-15 12 But God told Balaam, "Do not go with them. You are not to curse these people, for
they have been blessed!"

13 The next morning Balaam got up and told Balak's officials, "Go on home! The LORD
will not let me go with you."
14 So the Moabite officials returned to King Balak and reported, "Balaam refused to
come with us." 15 Then Balak tried again. This time he sent a larger number of even more
distinguished officials than those he had sent the first time. 16 They went to Balaam and
delivered this message to him:

> "This is what Balak son of Zippor says: Please don't let anything stop you from
> 22:17 Num 22:6 coming to help me. 17 I will pay you very well and do whatever you tell me. Just
> come and curse these people for me!"

22:18 Num 23:26; 24:13 18 But Balaam responded to Balak's messengers, "Even if Balak were to give me his pal-
ace filled with silver and gold, I would be powerless to do anything against the will of the
LORD my God. 19 But stay here one more night, and I will see if the LORD has anything else
to say to me."
22:20 Num 22:35; 23:12, 26 20 That night God came to Balaam and told him, "Since these men have come for you,
get up and go with them. But do only what I tell you to do."

BALAAM AND HIS DONKEY

22:21 2 Pet 2:15 21 So the next morning Balaam got up, saddled his donkey, and started off with the Moab-
ite officials. 22 But God was angry that Balaam was going, so He sent the angel of the LORD
to stand in the road to block his way. As Balaam and two servants were riding along, 23 Ba-
laam's donkey saw the angel of the LORD standing in the road with a drawn sword in his
hand. The donkey bolted off the road into a field, but Balaam beat it and turned it back
onto the road. 24 Then the angel of the LORD stood at a place where the road narrowed be-
tween two vineyard walls. 25 When the donkey saw the angel of the LORD, it tried to
squeeze by and crushed Balaam's foot against the wall. So Balaam beat the donkey again.
26 Then the angel of the LORD moved farther down the road and stood in a place too

22:7 Hebrew *set out with the money of divination in their hand.*

▸ BIBLE
22:20 Do what God says. God's instructions to Balaam, first to refuse and then to accept the offers of the Moabite officials, were not a contradiction. God's "no" often sounds the same as His "wait." Heed God's voice carefully as you seek to discern His will, and base your every step on His inerrant Word. (***See Bible****> Unity> God's Message> Devotion to God,* TopicGuide page A11.)

▸ ADOPTION
22:22 A God who is angry. Why was God angry? Didn't God just tell Balaam to go? Yes, but evidently Balaam was leaving with the purpose of saying something that God did not intend. After opposing Balaam (through his donkey!), God affirmed again that it was His will for Balaam to go to Balak (Numbers 22:35) and only proclaim what the Lord gave him to say. Let your words be God's today, judging everything you say with the Scriptures and the urgings of the Holy Spirit. (***See Adoption****> With Christ> Supernatural> Speak godly words,* TopicGuide page A37.)

22:22 The angel of the Lord sometimes appeared as a messenger or a warrior. The distinctness of this appearance is in the fact that the angel was both speaking through and appearing to an animal. Only the donkey saw the angel of the Lord until God opened Balaam's eyes.

narrow for the donkey to get by at all. 27 This time when the donkey saw the angel, it lay
down under Balaam. In a fit of rage Balaam beat the animal again with his staff.
28 Then the LORD gave the donkey the ability to speak. "What have I done to you that de- 22:28
serves your beating me three times?" it asked Balaam. 2 Pet 2:16
29 "You have made me look like a fool!" Balaam shouted. "If I had a sword with me, I
would kill you!"
30 "But I am the same donkey you have ridden all your life," the donkey answered. 22:30
"Have I ever done anything like this before?" 2 Pet 2:16
"No," Balaam admitted.
31 Then the LORD opened Balaam's eyes, and he saw the angel of the LORD standing in 22:31
the roadway with a drawn sword in his hand. Balaam bowed his head and fell face down Josh 5:13-15
on the ground before him.
32 "Why did you beat your donkey those three times?" the angel of the LORD demanded.
"Look, I have come to block your way because you are stubbornly resisting me. 33 Three
times the donkey saw me and shied away; otherwise, I would certainly have killed you by
now and spared the donkey."
34 Then Balaam confessed to the angel of the LORD, "I have sinned. I didn't realize you 22:34
were standing in the road to block my way. I will return home if you are against my going." 1 Sam 15:24
35 But the angel of the LORD told Balaam, "Go with these men, but say only what I tell you 22:35
to say." So Balaam went on with Balak's officials. 36 When King Balak heard that Balaam Num 22:20
was on the way, he went out to meet him at a Moabite town on the Arnon River at the far-
thest border of his land.
37 "Didn't I send you an urgent invitation? Why didn't you come right away?" Balak 22:37-38
asked Balaam. "Didn't you believe me when I said I would reward you richly?" Num 22:18
38 Balaam replied, "Look, now I have come, but I have no power to say whatever I want. I will
speak only the message that God puts in my mouth." 39 Then Balaam accompanied Balak
to Kiriath-huzoth, 40 where the king sacrificed cattle and sheep. He sent portions of the meat to
Balaam and the officials who were with him. 41 The next morning Balak took Balaam up to 22:41
Bamoth-baal. From there he could see some of the people of Israel spread out below him. Num 21:28; 23:13

BALAAM BLESSES ISRAEL

23 Then Balaam said to King Balak, "Build me seven altars here, and prepare seven 23:1
young bulls and seven rams for me to sacrifice." 2 Balak followed his instructions, Num 22:40
and the two of them sacrificed a young bull and a ram on each altar.
3 Then Balaam said to Balak, "Stand here by your burnt offerings, and I will go to see if
the LORD will respond to me. Then I will tell you whatever He reveals to me." So Balaam
went alone to the top of a bare hill, 4 and God met him there. Balaam said to Him, "I have
prepared seven altars and have sacrificed a young bull and a ram on each altar."
5 The LORD gave Balaam a message for King Balak. Then He said, "Go back to Balak and 23:5
give him My message." Num 22:20, 35; 23:16
6 So Balaam returned and found the king standing beside his burnt offerings with all the 23:7
officials of Moab. 7 This was the message Balaam delivered: Num 22:6

22:28 For insight into this notable event, compare this passage with John 12:28-30 and Acts 9:3-7.

22:41 The location of Bamoth-baal is unknown, but its meaning is "high place of Baal" indicating the setting probably offered a panoramic view of surrounding areas.

23:1-2 Altars in some form were a common element of religious practice in the Ancient Near East. God had given instructions to the Israelites to make simple altars of earth and uncut stones (Exodus 20:24-25). This was one way God distinguished the Israelites' worship from the idolatry of surrounding nations.

23:5ff Balak was attempting to access God's favor. From this point through chapter 24, he seeks a curse upon Israel. Instead Balaam pronounces three separate blessings on Israel and curses upon numerous peoples around Israel.

23:7 Throughout the Old Testament, particularly in prophecies, the name *Jacob* was used interchangeably with *Israel.*

22 God brought them out of Egypt; 23:22 Num 24:8
for them He is as strong as a wild ox.
23 No curse can touch Jacob; 23:23 Num 22:7
no magic has any power against Israel.
For now it will be said of Jacob,
'What wonders God has done for Israel!'
24 These people rise up like a lioness, 23:24 Gen 49:9
like a majestic lion rousing itself.
They refuse to rest
until they have feasted on prey,
drinking the blood of the slaughtered!"

25 Then Balak said to Balaam, "Fine, but if you won't curse them, at least don't bless them!" 23:26
26 But Balaam replied to Balak, "Didn't I tell you that I can do only what the LORD tells me?" Num 22:38

BALAAM'S THIRD MESSAGE

27 Then King Balak said to Balaam, "Come, I will take you to one more place. Perhaps it will
please God to let you curse them from there."
28 So Balak took Balaam to the top of Mount Peor, overlooking the wasteland.* 29 Balaam again 23:28
told Balak, "Build me seven altars, and prepare seven young bulls and seven rams for me to sacri- Num 31:16
fice." 30 So Balak did as Balaam ordered and offered a young bull and a ram on each altar. Josh 22:17

24 By now Balaam realized that the LORD was determined to bless Israel, so he did 24:2 Num 11:25-26
not resort to divination as before. Instead, he turned and looked out toward the 1 Sam 10:10 2 Chr 15:1

23:28 Or *overlooking Jeshimon.*

▸ GOD
23:27 No means no! In desperation, Balak suggested that a change of scenery would make God change His mind. How often do you hear a clear no from God, but imagine that if you change the situation just a bit, God's no will somehow become a yes? (***See God***> *God's Attributes> Unchanging> God is consistent through all time,* TopicGuide page A18.)

24:1 Divination attempts to acquire knowledge held by unknown or evil supernatural powers. Seeking knowledge from any other source than the God of Israel was an insult to His holy Being. Diviners used many methods to seek such knowledge: divining rods, reading the stars, dreams and more. Sacrificing animals and "reading the entrails" was another practice, perhaps Balaam's method up to this point. Divination was expressly forbidden in Deuteronomy 18:10-11.

▸ WORSHIP
24:1 Making idols. Custom-made religion cannot please God. Balaam appeared to be a man who prayed to God but who also used forbidden means of obtaining spiritual information (Deuteronomy 18:10; Isaiah 2:6). We must be careful to avoid any pagan practices or beliefs in our life. We can stand against the dark spiritual forces in this world through fasting and prayer (Mark 1:34-39; 1 Timothy 4:1). (***See Worship***> *OT> Prohibitions> Wrong objects> Other gods,* TopicGuide page A28.)

BECAUSE GOD IS
ABSOLUTE TRUTH

I will believe what He says and live accordingly.

God is not a man, so He does not lie. He is not human, so He does not change His mind.

NUMBERS 23:19

FOR THE NEXT *GOD IS ABSOLUTE TRUTH* FEATURE SEE PAGE 421.

"Balak summoned me to come from Aram;
the king of Moab brought me from the eastern hills.
'Come,' he said, 'curse Jacob for me!
Come and announce Israel's doom.'
23:8 Num 22:12 — 8 But how can I curse those
whom God has not cursed?
How can I condemn those
whom the LORD has not condemned?
23:9 Num 22:41 — 9 I see them from the cliff tops;
I watch them from the hills.
I see a people who live by themselves,
set apart from other nations.
23:10 Gen 13:16 Ps 37:37 Isa 57:1 — 10 Who can count Jacob's descendants, as numerous as dust?
Who can count even a fourth of Israel's people?
Let me die like the righteous;
let my life end like theirs."

11 Then King Balak demanded of Balaam, "What have you done to me? I brought you to
23:12 Num 22:20, 38 — curse my enemies. Instead, you have blessed them!"
12 But Balaam replied, "I will speak only the message that the LORD puts in my mouth."

BALAAM'S SECOND MESSAGE

13 Then King Balak told him, "Come with me to another place. There you will see another part of the nation of Israel, but not all of them. Curse at least that many!" 14 So Balak took Balaam to the plateau of Zophim on Pisgah Peak. He built seven altars there and offered a young bull and a ram on each altar.

15 Then Balaam said to the king, "Stand here by your burnt offerings while I go over there to meet the LORD."

23:16 Num 22:38 — 16 And the LORD met Balaam and gave him a message. Then He said, "Go back to Balak
and give him My message."

17 So Balaam returned and found the king standing beside his burnt offerings with all the officials of Moab. "What did the LORD say?" Balak asked eagerly.

18 This was the message Balaam delivered:

"Rise up, Balak, and listen!
Hear me, son of Zippor.
23:19 1 Sam 15:29 Isa 40:8; 55:11 — 19 God is not a man, so He does not lie.
He is not human, so He does not change His mind.
Has He ever spoken and failed to act?
Has He ever promised and not carried it through?
23:20 Isa 43:13 — 20 Listen, I received a command to bless;
God has blessed, and I cannot reverse it!
23:21 Exod 3:12 Deut 31:23 — 21 No misfortune is in His plan for Jacob;
no trouble is in store for Israel.
For the LORD their God is with them;
He has been proclaimed their king.

23:14 Though the plateau of Zophim is unknown, Pisgah Peak is close to Mount Nebo.

▸ GOD

23:19 Discovering God in Balaam's prophecy. Some people view God as a befuddled boss, never knowing for certain what will happen next, often having His plans thwarted by human will. However, both Balak and Balaam discovered that there was no hope of God allowing a curse to rest upon Israel (Numbers 23:23) while His covenant with them was still in power. God's mind is made up: He keeps His promises toward His people. (***See God**> God's Attributes> True> God doesn't lie but keeps his word,* TopicGuide page A18.)

25:3 and worshiped the gods of Moab. [3]In this way, Israel joined in the worship of Baal of Peor,
Num 25:5 Deut 4:3 causing the LORD's anger to blaze against His people.
[4]The LORD issued the following command to Moses: "Seize all the ringleaders and exe-
cute them before the LORD in broad daylight, so His fierce anger will turn away from the
people of Israel."
[5]So Moses ordered Israel's judges, "Each of you must put to death the men under your
authority who have joined in worshiping Baal of Peor."
25:6 Num 22:4 [6]Just then one of the Israelite men brought a Midianite woman into his tent, right before
the eyes of Moses and all the people, as everyone was weeping at the entrance of the Taber-
nacle.* [7]When Phinehas son of Eleazar and grandson of Aaron the priest saw this, he jumped
25:7-8 Ps 106:30 up and left the assembly. He took a spear [8]and rushed after the man into his tent. Phinehas
thrust the spear all the way through the man's body and into the woman's stomach. So the
25:9 *1 Cor 10:8 plague against the Israelites was stopped, [9]but not before 24,000 people had died.
[10]Then the LORD said to Moses, [11]"Phinehas son of Eleazar and grandson of Aaron the
priest has turned My anger away from the Israelites by being as zealous among them as I
was. So I stopped destroying all Israel as I had intended to do in My zealous anger. [12]Now
25:12 Ps 106:30-31 tell him that I am making My special covenant of peace with him. [13]In this covenant, I give
Isa 54:10 him and his descendants a permanent right to the priesthood, for in his zeal for Me, his
God, he purified the people of Israel, making them right with Me.*"
[14]The Israelite man killed with the Midianite woman was named Zimri son of Salu, the
25:15 Num 25:18; 31:8 leader of a family from the tribe of Simeon. [15]The woman's name was Cozbi; she was the
Josh 13:21 daughter of Zur, the leader of a Midianite clan.
[16]Then the LORD said to Moses, [17]"Attack the Midianites and destroy them, [18]because
25:17 Num 31:2 they assaulted you with deceit and tricked you into worshiping Baal of Peor, and because
25:18 of Cozbi, the daughter of a Midianite leader, who was killed at the time of the plague be-
Num 23:28 cause of what happened at Peor."

THE SECOND REGISTRATION OF ISRAEL'S TROOPS

26:1 **26** After the plague had ended, the LORD said to Moses and to Eleazar son of
Num 25:6-9 Aaron the priest, [2]"From the whole community of Israel, record the names of
26:2 all the warriors by their families. List all the men twenty years old or older who are able
Num 1:2-15 to go to war."
[3]So there on the plains of Moab beside the Jordan River, across from Jericho, Moses and

25:6 Hebrew *the Tent of Meeting.* 25:13 Or *he made atonement for the people of Israel.*

25:3 This sexual immorality in Baal worship was a fundamental breach of Israel's covenant with the Lord, but it was just a glimpse of the depraved worship Israel would face in Canaan.

▸ SPIRITUAL WARFARE

25:3 Faithful to God. What Moab had not done with the sword (Numbers 22) or with the curse (Numbers 23) they did with their beautiful women—Moab was victorious over Israel (Numbers 25:17-18). In the arms of pagan women, many men betrayed God and worshiped Baal. Sexual sin is one of the ways Satan tempts God's people away from keeping their promises to God and others. God created sex—but it must exist in harmony with the rest of God's creation and His Word. When it does, it stimulates our relationship with God rather than detracts from it. (***See Spiritual Warfare***> *Resisting Sin and Evil*> *Resisting Temptation*> *What to Resist*> *We are to resist worldly influences,* TopicGuide page A45.)

25:6 Even while the congregation showed signs of contrition, an Israelite man brought a Midianite woman into his tent, reflecting shameless immorality.

25:9 We do not know if Moses carried out the Lord's command to execute the leaders of those who sinned, but the number of those who perished in the resulting plague was larger than those who perished in Korah's rebellion (Numbers 16).

25:13 Phinehas defended God's holiness and so was promised a priestly line (which continued until the dissolution of the priesthood in the New Testament era). His execution of the sinful couple served as substitution (making atonement) for the sins of all the people.

26:2 This second census in Numbers repeats the purpose of the first (Numbers 1–4): to count the adult males of military age. The first generation (except for Joshua and Caleb) had died in the wilderness because of rebellion against God's will (Numbers 14:29-32). Another purpose of this census was to gather information about the population of the tribes so that an appropriate amount of land could be allotted to each tribe after they entered Canaan.

Eleazar the priest issued these instructions to the leaders of Israel: 4"List all the men of Isra-
el twenty years old and older, just as the LORD commanded Moses."
This is the record of all the descendants of Israel who came out of Egypt.

THE TRIBE OF REUBEN

5 These were the clans descended from the sons of Reuben, Jacob's* oldest son: 26:5
The Hanochite clan, named after their ancestor Hanoch. Exod 6:14
The Palluite clan, named after their ancestor Pallu.
6 The Hezronite clan, named after their ancestor Hezron.
The Carmite clan, named after their ancestor Carmi.

7 These were the clans of Reuben. Their registered troops numbered 43,730.
8 Pallu was the ancestor of Eliab, 9 and Eliab was the father of Nemuel, Dathan, and Abi- 26:9 Num 16:1
ram. This Dathan and Abiram are the same community leaders who conspired with Ko-
rah against Moses and Aaron, rebelling against the LORD. 10 But the earth opened up its 26:10
mouth and swallowed them with Korah, and fire devoured 250 of their followers. This Num 16:32, 35, 38
served as a warning to the entire nation of Israel. 11 However, the sons of Korah did not
die that day.

THE TRIBE OF SIMEON

12 These were the clans descended from the sons of Simeon: 26:12 1 Chr 4:24-43
The Jemuelite clan, named after their ancestor Jemuel.*
The Jaminite clan, named after their ancestor Jamin.
The Jakinite clan, named after their ancestor Jakin.
13 The Zoharite clan, named after their ancestor Zohar.*
The Shaulite clan, named after their ancestor Shaul.

14 These were the clans of Simeon. Their registered troops numbered 22,200.

THE TRIBE OF GAD

15 These were the clans descended from the sons of Gad:
The Zephonite clan, named after their ancestor Zephon.
The Haggite clan, named after their ancestor Haggi.
The Shunite clan, named after their ancestor Shuni.
16 The Oznite clan, named after their ancestor Ozni.
The Erite clan, named after their ancestor Eri.
17 The Arodite clan, named after their ancestor Arodi.*
The Arelite clan, named after their ancestor Areli.

18 These were the clans of Gad. Their registered troops numbered 40,500.

26:5 Hebrew *Israel's;* see note on 1:20-21b. 26:12 As in Syriac version (see also Gen 46:10; Exod 6:15); Hebrew reads *Nemuelite . . . Nemuel.* 26:13 As in parallel texts at Gen 46:10 and Exod 6:15; Hebrew reads *Zerahite . . . Zerah.* 26:17 As in Samaritan Pentateuch and Greek and Syriac versions (see also Gen 46:16); Hebrew reads *Arod.*

26:5 Reuben, the eldest son of Jacob, is listed first, though he had lost the place of preeminence due his birthright.

26:8-10 Korah's rebellion (Numbers 16) is included as a reminder to the people as they prepared to enter Canaan. Korah led others in challenging Moses' leadership and decision-making power. Their judgment stood as a constant warning through the ages (see 1 Corinthians 10:1-11). Moses' authority and God's power were confirmed through this event.

26:12 Simeon, the tribe from Jacob's second oldest son, had shrunk to about one third its original size, experiencing the greatest decrease in population of any tribe during the generation of wilderness wandering.

26:15 Gad was the seventh son of Jacob. His tribe, decreasing slightly from the first census, had a reputation for being strong warriors. They settled on the east side of the Jordan River, which left them vulnerable to foreign attack.

THE TRIBE OF JUDAH

19 Judah had two sons, Er and Onan, who had died in the land of Canaan. 20 These were the
clans descended from Judah's surviving sons:
The Shelanite clan, named after their ancestor Shelah.
The Perezite clan, named after their ancestor Perez.
The Zerahite clan, named after their ancestor Zerah.

21 These were the subclans descended from the Perezites:
The Hezronites, named after their ancestor Hezron.
The Hamulites, named after their ancestor Hamul.

22 These were the clans of Judah. Their registered troops numbered 76,500.

THE TRIBE OF ISSACHAR

26:23 1 Chr 7:1-5

23 These were the clans descended from the sons of Issachar:
The Tolaite clan, named after their ancestor Tola.
The Puite clan, named after their ancestor Puah.*
24 The Jashubite clan, named after their ancestor Jashub.
The Shimronite clan, named after their ancestor Shimron.

25 These were the clans of Issachar. Their registered troops numbered 64,300.

THE TRIBE OF ZEBULUN

26 These were the clans descended from the sons of Zebulun:
The Seredite clan, named after their ancestor Sered.
The Elonite clan, named after their ancestor Elon.
The Jahleelite clan, named after their ancestor Jahleel.

27 These were the clans of Zebulun. Their registered troops numbered 60,500.

THE TRIBE OF MANASSEH

26:28 Gen 46:19-21

28 Two clans were descended from Joseph through Manasseh and Ephraim.

29 These were the clans descended from Manasseh:
The Makirite clan, named after their ancestor Makir.
The Gileadite clan, named after their ancestor Gilead, Makir's son.

30 These were the subclans descended from the Gileadites:
The Iezerites, named after their ancestor Iezer.
The Helekites, named after their ancestor Helek.
31 The Asrielites, named after their ancestor Asriel.
The Shechemites, named after their ancestor Shechem.

26:23 As in Samaritan Pentateuch, Greek and Syriac versions, and Latin Vulgate (see also 1 Chr 7:1); Hebrew reads *The Punite clan, named after its ancestor Puvah.*

26:19 Judah was Jacob's fourth son. The tribe of Judah numbered largest in both counts and would continue to be a prominent tribe. In fact, eventually the territory of Judah was all that was left of what had been the Israelite kingdom. In the New Testament era it was referred to as Judea. Jerusalem was a part of that territory.

26:23 Issachar was the ninth son of Jacob. This tribe experienced significant growth during the wilderness wanderings.

26:26 Zebulun was Jacob's tenth son. These clans also experienced slight growth between the first and second census.

26:28 Joseph was the first son born to Rachel, Jacob's most beloved wife, and he was Jacob's favorite son. Joseph received the double portion of inheritance, which went to his two sons, who have tribal names instead of Joseph. This also maintains the 12 tribes since the Levites, being Tabernacle assistants and priests, were not numbered for war or given tribal land.

26:29 Manasseh was actually a grandson of Jacob, rather than a son. The tribe descended from Manasseh settled in two groups on each side of the Jordan River. This tribe grew substantially in military strength during the wilderness wanderings.

32 The Shemidaites, named after their ancestor Shemida.
The Hepherites, named after their ancestor Hepher.
33 (One of Hepher's descendants, Zelophehad, had no sons, but his daughters' names were Mahlah, Noah, Hoglah, Milcah, and Tirzah.)

34 These were the clans of Manasseh. Their registered troops numbered 52,700.

THE TRIBE OF EPHRAIM

35 These were the clans descended from the sons of Ephraim: **26:35** 1 Chr 7:20-25
The Shuthelahite clan, named after their ancestor Shuthelah.
The Bekerite clan, named after their ancestor Beker.
The Tahanite clan, named after their ancestor Tahan.

36 This was the subclan descended from the Shuthelahites:
The Eranites, named after their ancestor Eran.

37 These were the clans of Ephraim. Their registered troops numbered 32,500. **26:37** Num 1:32-35

These clans of Manasseh and Ephraim were all descendants of Joseph.

THE TRIBE OF BENJAMIN

38 These were the clans descended from the sons of Benjamin: **26:38** Gen 46:21 1 Chr 8:1
The Belaite clan, named after their ancestor Bela.
The Ashbelite clan, named after their ancestor Ashbel.
The Ahiramite clan, named after their ancestor Ahiram.
39 The Shuphamite clan, named after their ancestor Shupham.*
The Huphamite clan, named after their ancestor Hupham.

40 These were the subclans descended from the Belaites: **26:40** 1 Chr 8:3
The Ardites, named after their ancestor Ard.*
The Naamites, named after their ancestor Naaman.

41 These were the clans of Benjamin. Their registered troops numbered 45,600.

THE TRIBE OF DAN

42 These were the clans descended from the sons of Dan: **26:42** Gen 46:23-25
The Shuhamite clan, named after their ancestor Shuham.

43 These were the Shuhamite clans of Dan. Their registered troops numbered 64,400.

THE TRIBE OF ASHER

44 These were the clans descended from the sons of Asher: **26:44** Gen 46:1-17
The Imnite clan, named after their ancestor Imnah.

26:39 As in some Hebrew manuscripts, Samaritan Pentateuch, Greek and Syriac versions, and Latin Vulgate; most Hebrew manuscripts read *Shephupham*. 26:40 As in Samaritan Pentateuch, some Greek manuscripts, and Latin Vulgate; Hebrew lacks *named after their ancestor Ard.*

26:35 Ephraim, Manasseh's brother, was actually a grandson of Jacob, rather than a son. The tribe that descended from Ephraim had a strong presence to the point that in some Old Testament prophecies the name *Ephraim* is interchangeable with *Israel*. Unlike Manasseh, this tribe reduced considerably in size between the generations.

26:38 Benjamin was Jacob's youngest son, the second from Jacob's most loved wife, Rachel. She died giving birth to Benjamin. His tribe increased by 10,000 by the second census.

26:42 Dan was the fifth son of Jacob. The tribe descending from Dan was unable to conquer the territory they were given. They moved north, changing the name of an existing city to Dan. This city was so far north that it was used to delineate Israel's north-south boundaries in the phrase, "from Dan to Beersheba." They were the second largest tribe in population.

26:44 Asher was the eighth son of Jacob. The tribe increased in size, moving from ninth to fifth largest by this second census.

The Ishvite clan, named after their ancestor Ishvi.
The Beriite clan, named after their ancestor Beriah.

45 These were the subclans descended from the Beriites:
The Heberites, named after their ancestor Heber.
The Malkielites, named after their ancestor Malkiel.

46 Asher also had a daughter named Serah.

47 These were the clans of Asher. Their registered troops numbered 53,400.

THE TRIBE OF NAPHTALI

26:48 48 These were the clans descended from the sons of Naphtali:
1 Chr 7:13 The Jahzeelite clan, named after their ancestor Jahzeel.
The Gunite clan, named after their ancestor Guni.
49 The Jezerite clan, named after their ancestor Jezer.
The Shillemite clan, named after their ancestor Shillem.

50 These were the clans of Naphtali. Their registered troops numbered 45,400.

RESULTS OF THE REGISTRATION

26:51 51 In summary, the registered troops of all Israel numbered 601,730.
Num 1:43-46 52 Then the LORD said to Moses, 53 "Divide the land among the tribes, and distribute the
grants of land in proportion to the tribes' populations, as indicated by the number of
26:54 Num 33:54 names on the list. 54 Give the larger tribes more land and the smaller tribes less land, each
26:55 group receiving a grant in proportion to the size of its population. 55 But you must assign
Num 33:54; 34:13 the land by lot, and give land to each ancestral tribe according to the number of names on
the list. 56 Each grant of land must be assigned by lot among the larger and smaller tribal
groups."

THE TRIBE OF LEVI

26:57 Gen 46:11 57 This is the record of the Levites who were counted according to their clans:
1 Chr 6:1 The Gershonite clan, named after their ancestor Gershon.
The Kohathite clan, named after their ancestor Kohath.
The Merarite clan, named after their ancestor Merari.

26:58 Num 3:16-35 58 The Libnites, the Hebronites, the Mahlites, the Mushites, and the Korahites were all
subclans of the Levites.
Now Kohath was the ancestor of Amram, 59 and Amram's wife was named Jochebed.
She also was a descendant of Levi, born among the Levites in the land of Egypt. Amram
26:60 and Jochebed became the parents of Aaron, Moses, and their sister, Miriam. 60 To Aaron
Num 3:2 were born Nadab, Abihu, Eleazar, and Ithamar. 61 But Nadab and Abihu died when they
26:61 burned before the LORD the wrong kind of fire, different than He had commanded.
Lev 10:1-2 Num 3:4 62 The men from the Levite clans who were one month old or older numbered 23,000.
26:62 But the Levites were not included in the registration of the rest of the people of Israel be-
Num 3:39 cause they were not given an allotment of land when it was divided among the Israelites.
63 So these are the results of the registration of the people of Israel as conducted by

26:48 Naphtali was Jacob's sixth son, born to Bilhah, Rachel's maid. The tribe that descended from Naphtali settled in the highlands of the north of Canaan.

26:57-61 Levi's descendants were organized according to his sons, Gershon, Kohath, and Merari, whose clans performed different tasks related to caring for the Tabernacle. The Levites were given no territory, since their service was their inheritance. They lived off of the offerings of the people.

26:63-65 This summary of the census reminds the reader that the entire generation that left Egypt had died except Caleb and Joshua, whose faithfulness (see Numbers 13) was rewarded.

Moses and Eleazar the priest on the plains of Moab beside the Jordan River, across from
Jericho. [64]Not one person on this list had been among those listed in the previous registra- 26:64
tion taken by Moses and Aaron in the wilderness of Sinai. [65]For the LORD had said of them, Num 14:20-43 Deut 2:14-15
"They will all die in the wilderness." Not one of them survived except Caleb son of Jephun-
neh and Joshua son of Nun.

THE DAUGHTERS OF ZELOPHEHAD

27 One day a petition was presented by the daughters of Zelophehad—Mahlah, 27:1
Noah, Hoglah, Milcah, and Tirzah. Their father, Zelophehad, was a descendant of Num 26:28-37; 36:1-4
Hepher son of Gilead, son of Makir, son of Manasseh, son of Joseph. [2]These women stood
before Moses, Eleazar the priest, the tribal leaders, and the entire community at the en-
trance of the Tabernacle.* [3]"Our father died in the wilderness," they said. "He was not
among Korah's followers, who rebelled against the LORD; he died because of his own sin.
But he had no sons. [4]Why should the name of our father disappear from his clan just be-
cause he had no sons? Give us property along with the rest of our relatives."

[5]So Moses brought their case before the LORD. [6]And the LORD replied to Moses, [7]"The 27:7
claim of the daughters of Zelophehad is legitimate. You must give them a grant of land Num 36:1-4 Josh 17:4
along with their father's relatives. Assign them the property that would have been given to
their father.

[8]"And give the following instructions to the people of Israel: If a man dies and has no
son, then give his inheritance to his daughters. [9]And if he has no daughter either, transfer
his inheritance to his brothers. [10]If he has no brothers, give his inheritance to his father's
brothers. [11]But if his father has no brothers, give his inheritance to the nearest relative in 27:11
his clan. This is a legal requirement for the people of Israel, just as the LORD commanded Num 35:29
Moses."

JOSHUA CHOSEN TO LEAD ISRAEL

27:12 Num 33:47 Deut 32:49

[12]One day the LORD said to Moses, "Climb one of the mountains east of the river,* and look
out over the land I have given the people of Israel. [13]After you have seen it, you will die 27:13 Deut 32:50-51
like your brother, Aaron, [14]for you both rebelled against My instructions in the wilderness 27:14
of Zin. When the people of Israel rebelled, you failed to demonstrate My holiness to them Num 20:9-13
at the waters." (These are the waters of Meribah at Kadesh* in the wilderness of Zin.) Deut 32:48-52

[15]Then Moses said to the LORD, [16]"O LORD, You are the God who gives breath to all crea- 27:17
tures. Please appoint a new man as leader for the community. [17]Give them someone who 1 Kgs 22:17 Ezek 34:1-24
will guide them wherever they go and will lead them into battle, so the community of the Zech 10:2 Matt 9:36
LORD will not be like sheep without a shepherd." *Mark 6:34

[18]The LORD replied, "Take Joshua son of Nun, who has the Spirit in him, and lay your 27:18
hands on him. [19]Present him to Eleazar the priest before the whole community, and pub- Deut 34:9

27:2 Hebrew *the Tent of Meeting*. 27:12 Or *the mountains of Abarim*. 27:14 Hebrew *waters of Meribah-kadesh*.

▸ WORSHIP
27:1-11 Christianity honors women. Many religions stand accused of devaluing women or treating them as possessions. From the beginning, God has honored women and made accommodations for their unique needs. In this case, the daughters of Zelophehad petitioned the court to turn the land inheritance (and all the responsibilities that went with it) over to them rather than to skip them for the nearest male, as was the custom of that time. Honor women by granting them all the responsibilities and privileges that God's Word says they deserve. (***See Worship> NT> Fellowship> Preserving> Honor one another,*** TopicGuide page A31.)

27:14 On two occasions God used Moses to provide water for the people in the wilderness. The first time (Exodus 17:1-7) Moses was told to strike the rock. This established his authority as God's servant before a complaining people. The second time (Numbers 20:1-12) he was told to speak to the rock so that God's power would be revealed. But Moses had disobeyed God's instructions and in anger hit the rock as before. In this way, Moses took some of God's glory. God mercifully brought him to the edge of the Promised Land, but Moses could not enter.

27:18 Joshua is first mentioned in Scripture in Exodus 17:9, leading Israel in battle against the Amalekites. He became a military and spiritual leader and functioned as Moses' assistant, standing guard at the Tent of Meeting. He even traveled with Moses up Mount Sinai.

27:20 licly commission him to lead the people. 20Transfer some of your authority to him so the
Josh 1:16-17 whole community of Israel will obey him. 21When direction from the LORD is needed, Josh-
27:21 ua will stand before Eleazar the priest, who will use the Urim—one of the sacred lots cast
Exod 28:30 1 Sam 28:6 before the LORD—to determine His will. This is how Joshua and the rest of the community
of Israel will determine everything they should do."
22So Moses did as the LORD commanded. He presented Joshua to Eleazar the priest and
the whole community. 23Moses laid his hands on him and commissioned him to lead the
people, just as the LORD had commanded through Moses.

THE DAILY OFFERINGS

28 The LORD said to Moses, 2"Give these instructions to the people of Israel: The offer-
ings you present as special gifts are a pleasing aroma to Me; they are My food. See
to it that they are brought at the appointed times and offered according to My instructions.
28:3 3"Say to the people: This is the special gift you must present to the LORD as your daily
Exod 29:38-41 burnt offering. You must offer two one-year-old male lambs with no defects. 4Sacrifice one
28:4 Lev 6:19-20 lamb in the morning and the other in the evening. 5With each lamb you must offer a grain
28:5 offering of two quarts* of choice flour mixed with one quart* of pure oil of pressed olives.
Num 15:3-12 6This is the regular burnt offering instituted at Mount Sinai as a special gift, a pleasing aroma
28:7 to the LORD. 7Along with it you must present the proper liquid offering of one quart of alco-
Exod 29:42 Lev 23:13 holic drink with each lamb, poured out in the Holy Place as an offering to the LORD. 8Offer
the second lamb in the evening with the same grain offering and liquid offering. It, too, is a
special gift, a pleasing aroma to the LORD.

THE SABBATH OFFERINGS

9"On the Sabbath day, sacrifice two one-year-old male lambs with no defects. They must
be accompanied by a grain offering of four quarts* of choice flour moistened with olive oil,

28:5a Hebrew *1/10 of an ephah* [2.2 liters]; also in 28:13, 21, 29. 28:5b Hebrew *1/4 of a hin* [1 liter]; also in 28:7. 28:9 Hebrew *2/10 of an ephah* [4.4 liters]; also in 28:12, 20, 28.

▶ HOLINESS

27:20 Authority. Absolute power corrupts absolutely—or so the saying goes. But in ancient Israel and the church today, God gives some people authority over others. As Jesus reminded His disciples, they would be given power to lead the church (Matthew 16:19). This power is not inerrant—mistakes occur. But God gives real authority to parents, ministers, and those in government to carry out His will. (***See Holiness****> Law and Grace> Law> Leaders and followers,* TopicGuide page A41.)

27:21 The "sacred lots"—*Urim* and *Thummim*—were part of the priest's breastplate. Though there is considerable mystery about these items, it seems the priest used them to help make decisions. This is not completely unlike tossing dice or flipping a coin, but it was done trusting that God's sovereign control would be exercised for the good of His people (see Proverbs 16:33; 18:18).

27:21 It is noteworthy that although Joshua would assume the leadership of Israel, there is a clear distinction from Moses' leadership. Joshua would approach God through the priest, while Moses spoke with God directly.

28:1–29:40 These chapters reiterate in careful manner instructions for sacrifices and offerings for Israel's daily, weekly, and monthly ritual and for special festivals. These instructions may occur here to assist in the transition of leadership from Moses to Joshua. While similar to Leviticus 23, the focus there was the duties of the layperson. The emphasis in these verses is on the duties of the priest.

28:3 The whole burnt offerings, accompanied by drink and grain offerings, were completely consumed on the altar for the LORD. Sin and guilt offerings were burned only in part. The priests received portions of these to be eaten at the Tabernacle with other priests. The priests could take portions of other voluntary offerings home to share with their families. In this way, the Israelite priesthood was supported by the worship of the community much as ministers are today.

28:9 The Israelite Sabbath began Friday evening and ended Saturday evening. The word *Shabbat* means "cease and desist." By following the Sabbath concept of rest, you honor the example God set in the pattern of creation and the fourth of the Ten Commandments. Part of honoring the Sabbath meant bringing increased offerings as listed here. Honoring God in a special way one day a week—trusting something besides your own efforts to sustain your own life—is a sign of God's trusted presence and provision among His people.

▶ BIBLE

28:9 Without defects. Have you ever given someone a box of candy with some of the candies missing, or with little bites taken out of some of them? Of course not! The gift would be clearly lacking. For that reason, among others, God asked that whatever animals were sacrificed to Him be fit and strong (Numbers 28:11, 19, 31). Although none of their sacrifices or good works was good enough to make up for sin, these burnt sacrifices foreshadowed the perfect, spotless sacrifice of Jesus Christ to rescue helpless sinners from God's righteous wrath. (***See Bible****> Unity> OT Types> Lamb,* TopicGuide page A11.)

and a liquid offering. 10 This is the burnt offering to be presented each Sabbath day, in ad-
dition to the regular burnt offering and its accompanying liquid offering.

THE MONTHLY OFFERINGS

11 "On the first day of each month, present an extra burnt offering to the LORD of two young bulls,
one ram, and seven one-year-old male lambs, all with no defects. 12 These must be accompa-
nied by grain offerings of choice flour moistened with olive oil—six quarts* with each bull, four
quarts with the ram, 13 and two quarts with each lamb. This burnt offering will be a special gift, a
pleasing aroma to the LORD. 14 You must also present a liquid offering with each sacrifice: two
quarts* of wine for each bull, a third of a gallon* for the ram, and one quart* for each lamb. Pre-
sent this monthly burnt offering on the first day of each month throughout the year.
15 "On the first day of each month, you must also offer one male goat for a sin offering to
the LORD. This is in addition to the regular burnt offering and its accompanying liquid offering.

28:11 Num 10:10; 28:19 Ezek 46:6-7
28:12 Num 15:4-12
28:15 Num 28:3

OFFERINGS FOR THE PASSOVER

16 "On the fourteenth day of the first month,* you must celebrate the LORD's Passover. 17 On
the following day—the fifteenth day of the month—a joyous, seven-day festival will begin,
but no bread made with yeast may be eaten. 18 The first day of the festival will be an offi-
cial day for holy assembly, and no ordinary work may be done on that day. 19 As a special
gift you must present a burnt offering to the LORD—two young bulls, one ram, and seven
one-year-old male lambs, all with no defects. 20 These will be accompanied by grain offer-
ings of choice flour moistened with olive oil—six quarts with each bull, four quarts with the
ram, 21 and two quarts with each of the seven lambs. 22 You must also offer a male goat as
a sin offering to purify yourselves and make yourselves right with the LORD.* 23 Present
these offerings in addition to your regular morning burnt offering. 24 On each of the seven
days of the festival, this is how you must prepare the food offering that is presented as a
special gift, a pleasing aroma to the LORD. These will be offered in addition to the regular
burnt offerings and liquid offerings. 25 The seventh day of the festival will be another offi-
cial day for holy assembly, and no ordinary work may be done on that day.

28:16 Exod 12:6, 18 Lev 23:5-14 Deut 16:1-8
28:19 Num 28:11

OFFERINGS FOR THE FESTIVAL OF HARVEST

26 "At the Festival of Harvest,* when you present the first of your new grain to the LORD, you
must call an official day for holy assembly, and you may do no ordinary work on that day.

28:26 Exod 23:16 Lev 23:9-22 Deut 16:9-12

28:12 Hebrew *3/10 of an ephah* [6.6 liters]; also in 28:20, 28. 28:14a Hebrew *1/2 of a hin* [2 liters]. 28:14b Hebrew *1/3 of a hin* [1.3 liters]. 28:14c Hebrew *1/4 of a hin* [1 liter]. 28:16 This day in the ancient Hebrew lunar calendar occurred in late March, April, or early May. 28:22 Or *to make atonement for yourselves;* also in 28:30. 28:26 Hebrew *Festival of Weeks.* This was later called the Festival of Pentecost (see Acts 2:1). It is celebrated today as Shavuat (or Shabuoth).

28:16–29:40 This next section reviews the five most important special festivals or feasts as they occur through the religious calendar year. The Hebrew calendar is based on the phases of the moon rather than the sun. Passover occurs in March or April, the Festival of Harvest (or Pentecost) seven weeks (fifty days) later, the Festival of Trumpets in late September or early October, the Day of Atonement ten days later, and the Festival of Shelters a few days after that. The effect of the lunar calendar shifts the festivals each year when converted to our modern, solar calendar.

28:16 The Lord's Passover, or the Passover Feast, was the most important ritual feast for Israel. Therefore, it began the religious year (Exodus 12:2-20), which occurred in March, although this was the seventh month of the civil calendar. Passover celebrated freedom and reminded the people through ritual that God had delivered them. The early name of the month was *Abib,* a word that related to the progression of the barley harvest. Later it was changed to *Nisan.*

28:17 Bread made without yeast had been a specific component of the Israelites' flight from Egypt. During the Passover feast the people commemorated this time of deliverance by eating only unleavened bread. Over time, leaven (or yeast) became a symbol for sin or impurity. Thus, yeast-free bread also connoted purity and the holiness God required His children to imitate. In the New Testament, Jesus used the image of leaven (yeast) to warn the people about the false teachings of the religious leaders of His day (Matthew 16:11-12).

28:26 The Festival of Harvest (also called Firstfruits, Feast of Weeks, or Pentecost) had specific timing—the one-day feast occurred exactly 50 days after the end of the Feast of Unleavened Bread. This feast marked the transition from the end of the barley harvest to the beginning of the wheat harvest. As part of the feast, the people offered God the first and best of the barley. In the New Testament era (Acts 2), this feast became associated with the coming of the Holy Spirit seven weeks after the resurrection of Jesus.

27Present a special burnt offering on that day as a pleasing aroma to the LORD. It will con-
sist of two young bulls, one ram, and seven one-year-old male lambs. 28These will be ac-
companied by grain offerings of choice flour moistened with olive oil—six quarts with each
bull, four quarts with the ram, 29and two quarts with each of the seven lambs. 30Also, offer
28:31 Num 28:3 one male goat to purify yourselves and make yourselves right with the LORD. 31Prepare
these special burnt offerings, along with their liquid offerings, in addition to the regular
burnt offering and its accompanying grain offering. Be sure that all the animals you sacri-
fice have no defects.

29:1 Lev 23:23-25 Num 28:26

OFFERINGS FOR THE FESTIVAL OF TRUMPETS

29 "Celebrate the Festival of Trumpets each year on the first day of the appointed
month in early autumn.* You must call an official day for holy assembly, and you
may do no ordinary work. 2On that day you must present a burnt offering as a pleasing
aroma to the LORD. It will consist of one young bull, one ram, and seven one-year-old male
lambs, all with no defects. 3These must be accompanied by grain offerings of choice flour
moistened with olive oil—six quarts* with the bull, four quarts* with the ram, 4and two
quarts* with each of the seven lambs. 5In addition, you must sacrifice a male goat as a sin of-
29:6 Num 28:3 fering to purify yourselves and make yourselves right with the LORD.* 6These special sacri-
fices are in addition to your regular monthly and daily burnt offerings, and they must be
given with their prescribed grain offerings and liquid offerings. These offerings are given as
a special gift to the LORD, a pleasing aroma to Him.

29:7 Lev 16:29-34; 23:26-32

OFFERINGS FOR THE DAY OF ATONEMENT

7"Ten days later, on the tenth day of the same month,* you must call another holy assem-
bly. On that day, the Day of Atonement, the people must go without food and must do no
ordinary work. 8You must present a burnt offering as a pleasing aroma to the LORD. It will
consist of one young bull, one ram, and seven one-year-old male lambs, all with no de-
fects. 9These offerings must be accompanied by the prescribed grain offerings of choice
flour moistened with olive oil—six quarts of choice flour with the bull, four quarts of choice
29:11 Lev 16:1-34 flour with the ram, 10and two quarts of choice flour with each of the seven lambs. 11You
must also sacrifice one male goat for a sin offering. This is in addition to the sin offering of
atonement and the regular daily burnt offering with its grain offering, and their accompa-
nying liquid offerings.

29:12 Lev 23:33-43 Deut 16:13-14

OFFERINGS FOR THE FESTIVAL OF SHELTERS

12"Five days later, on the fifteenth day of the same month,* you must call another holy as-
sembly of all the people, and you may do no ordinary work on that day. It is the beginning

29:1 Hebrew *the first day of the seventh month.* This day in the ancient Hebrew lunar calendar occurred in September or October. This festival is celebrated today as Rosh Hashanah, the Jewish new year. 29:3a Hebrew *3/10 of an ephah* [6.6 liters]; also in 29:9, 14. 29:3b Hebrew *2/10 of an ephah* [4.4 liters]; also in 29:9, 14. 29:4 Hebrew *1/10 of an ephah* [2.2 liters]; also in 29:10, 15. 29:5 Or *to make atonement for yourselves.* 29:7 Hebrew *On the tenth day of the seventh month;* see 29:1 and the note there. This day in the ancient Hebrew lunar calendar occurred in September or October. It is celebrated today as Yom Kippur. 29:12a Hebrew *On the fifteenth day of the seventh month;* see 29:1, 7 and the notes there. This day in the ancient Hebrew lunar calendar occurred in late September, October, or early November.

29:1 The Festival of Trumpets, also called Rosh Hashanah (new year), held special importance for Israel, because it began the seventh month in the religious calendar. It was observed on the new moon of Tishri, which is the first month of the Israelite year. The Festival also marked the civil new year.

29:7 The Day of Atonement (Yom Kippur), first described in Leviticus 16, is a high holy day—the most solemn day in the Israelite year. More a fast than a festival, it was the only day the high priest entered the innermost chamber of the Tabernacle, where God's presence resided. On this day two goats were offered—one burned as a sacrifice, the other appointed as the scapegoat, symbolically bearing Israel's sins into the wild. All this pointed toward the final perfect atoning work of Christ.

▸ WORSHIP

29:12 A holy party. Do you like holidays? If you do, you would have loved ancient Israel. They had many annual festivals commemorating God's faithfulness to them. While Jesus in a sense fulfilled these festivals and other ceremonial laws (Romans 10:4; Colossians 2:16-17; Hebrews 9), these passages can encourage us to gather and celebrate God's faithfulness to us. Invite your friends and neighbors—God deserves a party! (***See Worship****> OT> Festivals,* TopicGuide page A26.)

of the Festival of Shelters,* a seven-day festival to the LORD. 13On the first day of the festi-
val, you must present a burnt offering as a special gift, a pleasing aroma to the LORD. It will
consist of thirteen young bulls, two rams, and fourteen one-year-old male lambs, all with
no defects. 14Each of these offerings must be accompanied by a grain offering of choice
flour moistened with olive oil—six quarts for each of the thirteen bulls, four quarts for each of
the two rams, 15and two quarts for each of the fourteen lambs. 16You must also sacrifice a
male goat as a sin offering, in addition to the regular burnt offering with its accompanying
grain offering and liquid offering.

17"On the second day of this seven-day festival, sacrifice twelve young bulls, two rams,
and fourteen one-year-old male lambs, all with no defects. 18Each of these offerings of
bulls, rams, and lambs must be accompanied by its prescribed grain offering and liquid of-
fering. 19You must also sacrifice a male goat as a sin offering, in addition to the regular **29:19**
burnt offering with its accompanying grain offering and liquid offering. Num 28:3, 11, 31

20"On the third day of the festival, sacrifice eleven young bulls, two rams, and fourteen
one-year-old male lambs, all with no defects. 21Each of these offerings of bulls, rams, and
lambs must be accompanied by its prescribed grain offering and liquid offering. 22You **29:22**
must also sacrifice a male goat as a sin offering, in addition to the regular burnt offering Num 28:15
with its accompanying grain offering and liquid offering.

23"On the fourth day of the festival, sacrifice ten young bulls, two rams, and fourteen
one-year-old male lambs, all with no defects. 24Each of these offerings of bulls, rams, and
lambs must be accompanied by its prescribed grain offering and liquid offering. 25You
must also sacrifice a male goat as a sin offering, in addition to the regular burnt offering
with its accompanying grain offering and liquid offering.

26"On the fifth day of the festival, sacrifice nine young bulls, two rams, and fourteen
one-year-old male lambs, all with no defects. 27Each of these offerings of bulls, rams, and
lambs must be accompanied by its prescribed grain offering and liquid offering. 28You
must also sacrifice a male goat as a sin offering, in addition to the regular burnt offering
with its accompanying grain offering and liquid offering.

29"On the sixth day of the festival, sacrifice eight young bulls, two rams, and fourteen
one-year-old male lambs, all with no defects. 30Each of these offerings of bulls, rams, and
lambs must be accompanied by its prescribed grain offering and liquid offering. 31You
must also sacrifice a male goat as a sin offering, in addition to the regular burnt offering
with its accompanying grain offering and liquid offering.

32"On the seventh day of the festival, sacrifice seven young bulls, two rams, and four-
teen one-year-old male lambs, all with no defects. 33Each of these offerings of bulls, rams,
and lambs must be accompanied by its prescribed grain offering and liquid offering. 34You
must also sacrifice one male goat as a sin offering, in addition to the regular burnt offering
with its accompanying grain offering and liquid offering.

35"On the eighth day of the festival, proclaim another holy day. You must do no ordinary **29:35**
work on that day. 36You must present a burnt offering as a special gift, a pleasing aroma to Lev 23:36
the LORD. It will consist of one young bull, one ram, and seven one-year-old male lambs, all
with no defects. 37Each of these offerings must be accompanied by its prescribed grain of-
fering and liquid offering. 38You must also sacrifice one male goat as a sin offering, in addi-
tion to the regular burnt offering with its accompanying grain offering and liquid offering.

39"You must present these offerings to the LORD at your annual festivals. These are in **29:39**
addition to the sacrifices and offerings you present in connection with vows, or as volun- Lev 23:2 2 Chr 31:3
tary offerings, burnt offerings, grain offerings, liquid offerings, or peace offerings." Ezra 3:5

29:12b Or *Festival of Booths,* or *Festival of Tabernacles.* This was earlier called the Festival of the Final Harvest or Festival of Ingathering (see Exod 23:16b). It is celebrated today as Sukkot (or Succoth).

29:39 The periodic sacrifices, special annual festivals, freewill offerings, burnt offerings, grain offerings, drink offerings, and peace offerings, when considered together, constituted considerably more than a mere ten percent "tithe."

40*So Moses gave all of these instructions to the people of Israel as the LORD had commanded him.

LAWS CONCERNING VOWS

30 1*Then Moses summoned the leaders of the tribes of Israel and told them, "This
30:2 is what the LORD has commanded: 2A man who makes a vow to the LORD or
Deut 23:21-25 makes a pledge under oath must never break it. He must do exactly what he said he would do.

3"If a young woman makes a vow to the LORD or a pledge under oath while she is still
living at her father's home, 4and her father hears of the vow or pledge and does not object
to it, then all her vows and pledges will stand. 5But if her father refuses to let her fulfill the vow or pledge on the day he hears of it, then all her vows and pledges will become invalid. The LORD will forgive her because her father would not let her fulfill them.

6"Now suppose a young woman makes a vow or binds herself with an impulsive pledge
and later marries. 7If her husband learns of her vow or pledge and does not object on the
30:8 day he hears of it, her vows and pledges will stand. 8But if her husband refuses to accept
Gen 3:16 her vow or impulsive pledge on the day he hears of it, he nullifies her commitments, and
the LORD will forgive her. 9If, however, a woman is a widow or is divorced, she must fulfill all her vows and pledges.

10"But suppose a woman is married and living in her husband's home when she makes
a vow or binds herself with a pledge. 11If her husband hears of it and does not object to it,
30:12 her vow or pledge will stand. 12But if her husband refuses to accept it on the day he hears
Eph 5:22 of it, her vow or pledge will be nullified, and the LORD will forgive her. 13So her husband
Col 3:18 may either confirm or nullify any vows or pledges she makes to deny herself. 14But if he
does not object on the day he hears of it, then he is agreeing to all her vows and pledges.
15If he waits more than a day and then tries to nullify a vow or pledge, he will be punished for her guilt."

16These are the regulations the LORD gave Moses concerning relationships between a man and his wife, and between a father and a young daughter who still lives at home.

CONQUEST OF THE MIDIANITES

31:2 **31** Then the LORD said to Moses, 2"On behalf of the people of Israel, take revenge on
Num 25:16-17 the Midianites for leading them into idolatry. After that, you will die and join your ancestors."

3So Moses said to the people, "Choose some men, and arm them to fight the LORD's war
of revenge against Midian. 4From each tribe of Israel, send 1,000 men into battle." 5So
they chose 1,000 men from each tribe of Israel, a total of 12,000 men armed for battle.

29:40 Verse 29:40 is numbered 30:1 in Hebrew text. 30:1 Verses 30:1-16 are numbered 30:2-17 in Hebrew text.

30:2 Vows in the biblical era were far more solemn than the modern sense of a promise made to a friend. Ancient vows were made to God as acts of service or as a commitment to abstain from something. If pronounced out loud and publicly, such vows were considered sacred.

30:3-16 The focus on women and vows in this passage may be related to the teaching on sacred festivals since vows were often taken on such occasions. In the cases mentioned here, vows could be vetoed by one in authority over another.

▸ PURPOSE

31:2 Take vengeance. If God is a God of love, how could He order something like this? God had mercifully withheld his perfect justice against those who had tempted His people into sin (see Numbers 25:17). Then at just the right time, God took vengeance on those who had attacked His covenant people. You can withhold your own attempts at revenge because you can trust that God will one day punish all those who have harmed His people (Romans 12:19; Revelation 6:9-11; 19:15-21). (***See Purpose****> God's Deeds> Judgment> God promises judgment,* TopicGuide page A53.)

31:2 The Moabites and the Midianites had already plotted together against the Israelites (Numbers 22:4-6), even hiring the prophet Balaam from Mesopotamia to curse the Israelites. When this failed, the Moabite and Midianite women seduced Israel into idol worship. God's wrath poured out at this obvious breach of the first commandment (purity of worship) and sixth commandment (adultery). This chapter applies the command Moses had received to destroy the Midianites (Numbers 25:16-18).

6 Then Moses sent them out, 1,000 men from each tribe, and Phinehas son of Eleazar the 31:6
priest led them into battle. They carried along the holy objects of the sanctuary and the Num 10:8-9
trumpets for sounding the charge. 7 They attacked Midian as the LORD had commanded
Moses, and they killed all the men. 8 All five of the Midianite kings—Evi, Rekem, Zur, Hur, 31:8
and Reba—died in the battle. They also killed Balaam son of Beor with the sword. Josh 13:21-22
9 Then the Israelite army captured the Midianite women and children and seized their
cattle and flocks and all their wealth as plunder. 10 They burned all the towns and villages
where the Midianites had lived. 11 After they had gathered the plunder and captives, both
people and animals, 12 they brought them all to Moses and Eleazar the priest, and to the
whole community of Israel, which was camped on the plains of Moab beside the Jordan
River, across from Jericho. 13 Moses, Eleazar the priest, and all the leaders of the commu-
nity went to meet them outside the camp. 14 But Moses was furious with all the generals
and captains* who had returned from the battle.
15 "Why have you let all the women live?" he demanded. 16 "These are the very ones 31:16
who followed Balaam's advice and caused the people of Israel to rebel against the LORD at Num 25:1-18; 2 Pet 2:15-16
Mount Peor. They are the ones who caused the plague to strike the LORD's people. 17 So kill 31:17
all the boys and all the women who have had intercourse with a man. 18 Only the young Judg 21:10-12
girls who are virgins may live; you may keep them for yourselves. 19 And all of you who Deut 7:2; 20:16-18
have killed anyone or touched a dead body must stay outside the camp for seven days.
You must purify yourselves and your captives on the third and seventh days. 20 Purify all
your clothing, too, and everything made of leather, goat hair, or wood."
21 Then Eleazar the priest said to the men who were in the battle, "The LORD has given
Moses this legal requirement: 22 Anything made of gold, silver, bronze, iron, tin, or lead—
23 that is, all metals that do not burn—must be passed through fire in order to be made cer-
emonially pure. These metal objects must then be further purified with the water of purifi-
cation. But everything that burns must be purified by the water alone. 24 On the seventh 31:24
day you must wash your clothes and be purified. Then you may return to the camp." Lev 11:25; 14:9

DIVISION OF THE PLUNDER

25 And the LORD said to Moses, 26 "You and Eleazar the priest and the family leaders of each
tribe are to make a list of all the plunder taken in the battle, including the people and ani-
mals. 27 Then divide the plunder into two parts, and give half to the men who fought the 31:27
battle and half to the rest of the people. 28 From the army's portion, first give the LORD His Josh 22:8
share of the plunder—one of every 500 of the prisoners and of the cattle, donkeys, sheep, 31:28 Num 18:21
and goats. 29 Give this share of the army's half to Eleazar the priest as an offering to the 31:29
LORD. 30 From the half that belongs to the people of Israel, take one of every fifty of the pris- Num 18:25-26
oners and of the cattle, donkeys, sheep, goats, and other animals. Give this share to the
Levites, who are in charge of maintaining the LORD's Tabernacle." 31 So Moses and Eleazar
the priest did as the LORD commanded Moses.

31:14 Hebrew *the commanders of thousands, and the commanders of hundreds;* also in 31:48, 52, 54.

31:6 Since battles in this era were usually considered holy wars between gods with the different people representing them, it was not unusual for the priest and holy objects to accompany the army. Israel's success depended on the Lord being their commander and providing victory. When God was taken for granted and the holy objects used as good luck charms (as in 1 Samuel 4), Israel experienced defeat.

31:16 Balaam knew God had blessed Israel so he could not curse them. But he apparently knew Israel could still be hurt; he accomplished this by polluting their community through sexual sin.

31:17 Many Christians question the love of God from passages such as this. But we must remember several things: First, these pagan people were by no means innocent; second, a death sentence would end any further impact they could have on Israel; and third, the punishment would remind Israel of the cost of sin and rebellion against the Lord.

31:25-30 In this passage, the plunder of war was divided; half of the plunder was given to the warriors, and half went to the rest of the Israelites. Moses then instructed the warriors to give one-fifth of one percent of their plunder to God, and the rest of the people to offer two percent of their portion. Those who bore the brunt of the fighting were thus rewarded with a greater percentage of the plunder.

32 The plunder remaining from everything the fighting men had taken totaled 675,000
sheep and goats, 33 72,000 cattle, 34 61,000 donkeys, 35 and 32,000 virgin girls.
36 Half of the plunder was given to the fighting men. It totaled 337,500 sheep and goats,
37 of which 675 were the LORD's share; 38 36,000 cattle, of which 72 were the LORD's share;
39 30,500 donkeys, of which 61 were the LORD's share; 40 and 16,000 virgin girls, of whom
32 were the LORD's share. 41 Moses gave all the LORD's share to Eleazar the priest, just as
the LORD had directed him.

42 Half of the plunder belonged to the people of Israel, and Moses separated it from the
half belonging to the fighting men. 43 It totaled 337,500 sheep and goats, 44 36,000 cattle,
45 30,500 donkeys, 46 and 16,000 virgin girls. 47 From the half-share given to the people,
Moses took one of every fifty prisoners and animals and gave them to the Levites, who
maintained the LORD's Tabernacle. All this was done as the LORD had commanded Moses.
31:49 48 Then all the generals and captains came to Moses 49 and said, "We, your servants,
Num 1:19 have accounted for all the men who went out to battle under our command; not one of us
is missing! 50 So we are presenting the items of gold we captured as an offering to the LORD
from our share of the plunder—armbands, bracelets, rings, earrings, and necklaces. This
will purify our lives before the LORD and make us right with Him.*"

51 So Moses and Eleazar the priest received the gold from all the military commanders—
all kinds of jewelry and crafted objects. 52 In all, the gold that the generals and captains
31:53 presented as a gift to the LORD weighed about 420 pounds.* 53 All the fighting men had
Deut 20:14 taken some of the plunder for themselves. 54 So Moses and Eleazar the priest accepted the
gifts from the generals and captains and brought the gold to the Tabernacle* as a re-
minder to the LORD that the people of Israel belong to Him.

THE TRIBES EAST OF THE JORDAN

32:1 **32** The tribes of Reuben and Gad owned vast numbers of livestock. So when they
Num 21:32 saw that the lands of Jazer and Gilead were ideally suited for their flocks and
herds, 2 they came to Moses, Eleazar the priest, and the other leaders of the commu-
32:3 nity. They said, 3 "Notice the towns of Ataroth, Dibon, Jazer, Nimrah, Heshbon, Elealeh,
Num 32:33-42 Sibmah,* Nebo, and Beon. 4 The LORD has conquered this whole area for the community
Josh 13:17 Isa 15:4; 16:9 of Israel, and it is ideally suited for all our livestock. 5 If we have found favor with you,
please let us have this land as our property instead of giving us land across the Jordan
River."

32:8 6 "Do you intend to stay here while your brothers go across and do all the fighting?"
Num 13:2-26 Moses asked the men of Gad and Reuben. 7 "Why do you want to discourage the rest of
Deut 1:19-21 the people of Israel from going across to the land the LORD has given them? 8 Your ances-
32:9 Num 13:23-24 tors did the same thing when I sent them from Kadesh-barnea to explore the land. 9 After
32:10 they went up to the valley of Eshcol and explored the land, they discouraged the people of
Num 14:28-30 Israel from entering the land the LORD was giving them. 10 Then the LORD was very angry
Deut 1:34 with them, and He vowed, 11 'Of all those I rescued from Egypt, no one who is twenty years
old or older will ever see the land I swore to give to Abraham, Isaac, and Jacob, for they

31:50 Or *will make atonement for our lives before the LORD.* 31:52 Hebrew *16,750 shekels* [191 kilograms]. 31:54 Hebrew *the Tent of Meeting.* 32:3 As in Samaritan Pentateuch and Greek version (see also 32:38); Hebrew reads *Sebam.*

32:1 Gilead was part of the Transjordanian plateau east of the Jordan River. This area, just conquered by Israel, encompassed fertile uplands about 2,000 feet above sea level. With the recent acquisition of the plunder of war, it is no wonder the tribes had many grazing animals!

32:6-15 When tribal leaders asked for land east of the Jordan River, Moses feared they were displaying lack of faith like the previous generation. This explains his harsh and lengthy response.

32:11 God's covenant with Abraham, Isaac, and Jacob (later renamed Israel) was the core of Israel's identity as a people. God promised Abraham land, many descendants, and a position of eternal significance. Every covenant agreement expected certain responses in return. God expected Abraham to move by faith to the land. He also expected His people to worship one God wholeheartedly. In a time when cultures worshiped many gods, this requirement was significant. God renewed this covenant with Abraham's son Isaac, with Isaac's son Jacob, and with the descendants of Jacob's 12 sons.

have not obeyed Me wholeheartedly. 12The only exceptions are Caleb son of Jephunneh
the Kenizzite and Joshua son of Nun, for they have wholeheartedly followed the LORD.'
13"The LORD was angry with Israel and made them wander in the wilderness for forty
years until the entire generation that sinned in the LORD's sight had died. 14But here you
are, a brood of sinners, doing exactly the same thing! You are making the LORD even an-
grier with Israel. 15If you turn away from Him like this and He abandons them again in the
wilderness, you will be responsible for destroying this entire nation!"

16But they approached Moses and said, "We simply want to build pens for our live-
stock and fortified towns for our wives and children. 17Then we will arm ourselves and
lead our fellow Israelites into battle until we have brought them safely to their land.
Meanwhile, our families will stay in the fortified towns we build here, so they will be safe
from any attacks by the local people. 18We will not return to our homes until all the peo-
ple of Israel have received their portions of land. 19But we do not claim any of the land
on the other side of the Jordan. We would rather live here on the east side and accept
this as our grant of land."

20Then Moses said, "If you keep your word and arm yourselves for the LORD's battles,
21and if your troops cross the Jordan and keep fighting until the LORD has driven out His
enemies, 22then you may return when the LORD has conquered the land. You will have ful-
filled your duty to the LORD and to the rest of the people of Israel. And the land on the east
side of the Jordan will be your property from the LORD. 23But if you fail to keep your word,
then you will have sinned against the LORD, and you may be sure that your sin will find
you out. 24Go ahead and build towns for your families and pens for your flocks, but do
everything you have promised."

25Then the men of Gad and Reuben replied, "We, your servants, will follow your instruc-
tions exactly. 26Our children, wives, flocks, and cattle will stay here in the towns of Gilead.
27But all who are able to bear arms will cross over to fight for the LORD, just as you have
said."

28So Moses gave orders to Eleazar the priest, Joshua son of Nun, and the leaders of
the clans of Israel. 29He said, "The men of Gad and Reuben who are armed for battle
must cross the Jordan with you to fight for the LORD. If they do, give them the land of
Gilead as their property when the land is conquered. 30But if they refuse to arm them-
selves and cross over with you, then they must accept land with the rest of you in the
land of Canaan."

31The tribes of Gad and Reuben said again, "We are your servants, and we will do as the
LORD has commanded! 32We will cross the Jordan into Canaan fully armed to fight for the
LORD, but our property will be here on this side of the Jordan."

33So Moses assigned land to the tribes of Gad, Reuben, and half the tribe of Manasseh
son of Joseph. He gave them the territory of King Sihon of the Amorites and the land of
King Og of Bashan—the whole land with its cities and surrounding lands.

34The descendants of Gad built the towns of Dibon, Ataroth, Aroer, 35Atroth-shophan,
Jazer, Jogbehah, 36Beth-nimrah, and Beth-haran. These were all fortified towns with pens
for their flocks.

32:12 Num 14:6, 24, 30; Deut 1:36; Josh 14:8-9
32:13 Num 14:31-39
32:15 Deut 30:17-18
32:17 Josh 4:12-13
32:18-19 Josh 13:8; 22:4
32:20 Deut 3:18
32:22 Deut 3:20; Josh 22:4
32:24 Num 30:2
32:33 Num 21:23-26; 34:14; Deut 3:8-17; Josh 12:1-6

32:16-19 The tribes of Reuben, Gad, and half of Manasseh stressed to Moses that their plan was neither to break from Israel nor to be unfaithful to God's promise.

32:23 Moses made sure the people understood that not keeping their promise to the other tribes would be first and foremost a sin against God Himself. And though they might escape punishment from Israel, there would be no escape from God's wrath.

32:28-30 When Moses used the "if . . . then" clauses in these verses, the agreement took on the force and severity of a covenant.

32:33 King Sihon of the Amorites was often used as a historical reminder elsewhere in the Old Testament of God's faithfulness to help His people defeat their enemies (Psalm 135:10-11).

32:33 Bashan was an area to the east of the Sea of Galilee (near the modern-day Golan Heights). It was a fertile land, known for sheep and oak trees. Og was the last king of Bashan, and he lost his land to the Israelites much as Sihon, the Amorite king, had done. Og was often mentioned with Sihon in later examples from Israel's history.

37 The descendants of Reuben built the towns of Heshbon, Elealeh, Kiriathaim, 38 Nebo,
Baal-meon, and Sibmah. They changed the names of some of the towns they conquered
and rebuilt.
39 Then the descendants of Makir of the tribe of Manasseh went to Gilead and con-
quered it, and they drove out the Amorites living there. 40 So Moses gave Gilead to the
32:41 Makirites, descendants of Manasseh, and they settled there. 41 The people of Jair, an-
Deut 3:14 other clan of the tribe of Manasseh, captured many of the towns in Gilead and changed
Josh 13:30 1 Chr 2:23 the name of that region to the Towns of Jair.* 42 Meanwhile, a man named Nobah cap-
tured the town of Kenath and its surrounding villages, and he renamed that area No-
bah after himself.

REMEMBERING ISRAEL'S JOURNEY

33 This is the route the Israelites followed as they marched out of Egypt under the
leadership of Moses and Aaron. 2 At the LORD's direction, Moses kept a written rec-
ord of their progress. These are the stages of their march, identified by the different places
where they stopped along the way.
33:3 3 They set out from the city of Rameses in early spring—on the fifteenth day of the first
Exod 12:33-37 month*—on the morning after the first Passover celebration. The people of Israel left defi-
antly, in full view of all the Egyptians. 4 Meanwhile, the Egyptians were burying all their
firstborn sons, whom the LORD had killed the night before. The LORD had defeated the gods
of Egypt that night with great acts of judgment!

33:5 5 After leaving Rameses, the Israelites set up camp at Succoth.
Exod 13:20 6 Then they left Succoth and camped at Etham on the edge of the wilderness.
33:7 7 They left Etham and turned back toward Pi-hahiroth, opposite Baal-zephon, and
Exod 14:2, 9 camped near Migdol.
33:8 8 They left Pi-hahiroth and crossed the Red Sea* into the wilderness beyond. Then they
Exod 14:21-22 traveled for three days into the Etham wilderness and camped at Marah.

32:41 Hebrew *Havvoth-jair.* 33:3 This day in the ancient Hebrew lunar calendar occurred in late March, April, or early May.
33:8 Hebrew *the sea.*

▶ BIBLE

33:2 A written record. One of the greatest sins Israel committed against God was unusual—they *forgot* (Deuteronomy 32:18; Isaiah 51:13; Jeremiah 13:25). They refused to remember the way God had faithfully blessed them, and they forgot the covenant promises they had made to God as a part of His covenant with them. Do you keep a journal? Do you make it a practice to rehearse your spiritual victories and defeats and remember God's faithfulness? Follow Moses' example and keep a record of your spiritual journey. (***See Bible****> Uniqueness> Inspired> A record of God's own words,* TopicGuide page A10.)

33:2 What follows is a travel log with seemingly little detail more than a list of obscure place names. However, it is notable that the record lists 40 stops during the wilderness wanderings, which, according to the accepted length of a generation, took 40 years. The names of many places recount more than geography alone—they often served to remind Israel of instances of their disobedience and/or displays of God's faithfulness.

33:4 The Egyptians were burying their firstborns because of God's final display of power—the Passover. At midnight on an appointed day every firstborn died—unless the blood of a lamb was painted on the doorpost (Exodus 12). There wasn't an unpainted house where someone didn't die. But just as important as God's deliverance of Israel was the Lord's victory over the pagan gods of Egypt. It was a spiritual battle of the highest order.

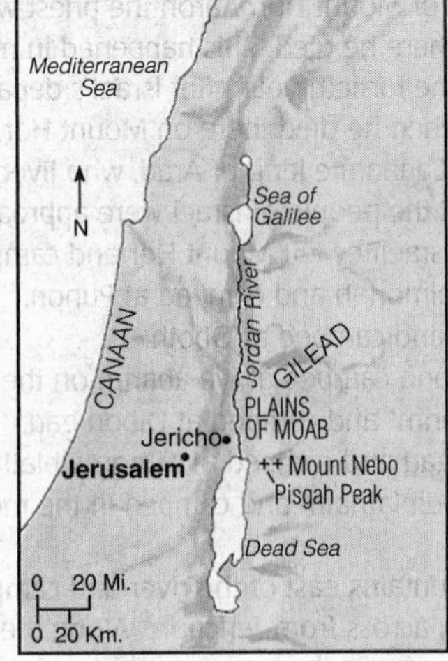

PREPARING TO ENTER THE PROMISED LAND
The Israelites had been camped in the plains of Moab, across from Jericho. From this position, they were ready to enter the Promised Land.

9 They left Marah and camped at Elim, where there were twelve springs of water and 33:9
seventy palm trees. Exod 15:27; 16:1
10 They left Elim and camped beside the Red Sea.*
11 They left the Red Sea and camped in the wilderness of Sin.* 33:11
12 They left the wilderness of Sin and camped at Dophkah. Exod 16:1; 17:1
13 They left Dophkah and camped at Alush.
14 They left Alush and camped at Rephidim, where there was no water for the people to 33:14
drink. Exod 17:1-8
15 They left Rephidim and camped in the wilderness of Sinai. 33:15
16 They left the wilderness of Sinai and camped at Kibroth-hattaavah. Exod 19:1
17 They left Kibroth-hattaavah and camped at Hazeroth. 33:16-17
18 They left Hazeroth and camped at Rithmah. Num 11:34-35
19 They left Rithmah and camped at Rimmon-perez.
20 They left Rimmon-perez and camped at Libnah.
21 They left Libnah and camped at Rissah.
22 They left Rissah and camped at Kehelathah.
23 They left Kehelathah and camped at Mount Shepher.
24 They left Mount Shepher and camped at Haradah.
25 They left Haradah and camped at Makheloth.
26 They left Makheloth and camped at Tahath.
27 They left Tahath and camped at Terah.
28 They left Terah and camped at Mithcah.
29 They left Mithcah and camped at Hashmonah.
30 They left Hashmonah and camped at Moseroth. 33:30
31 They left Moseroth and camped at Bene-jaakan. Deut 10:6
32 They left Bene-jaakan and camped at Hor-haggidgad.
33 They left Hor-haggidgad and camped at Jotbathah. 33:33
34 They left Jotbathah and camped at Abronah. Deut 10:7
35 They left Abronah and camped at Ezion-geber.
36 They left Ezion-geber and camped at Kadesh in the wilderness of Zin.
37 They left Kadesh and camped at Mount Hor, at the border of Edom. 38 While they 33:36 Num 20:1
were at the foot of Mount Hor, Aaron the priest was directed by the LORD to go up the 33:38
mountain, and there he died. This happened in midsummer, on the first day of the Num 20:25-28
fifth month* of the fortieth year after Israel's departure from Egypt. 39 Aaron was
123 years old when he died there on Mount Hor.
40 At that time the Canaanite king of Arad, who lived in the Negev in the land of Ca- 33:40
naan, heard that the people of Israel were approaching his land. Num 21:1
41 Meanwhile, the Israelites left Mount Hor and camped at Zalmonah.
42 Then they left Zalmonah and camped at Punon.
43 They left Punon and camped at Oboth. 33:43
44 They left Oboth and camped at Iye-abarim on the border of Moab. Num 21:10-11
45 They left Iye-abarim* and camped at Dibon-gad.
46 They left Dibon-gad and camped at Almon-diblathaim.
47 They left Almon-diblathaim and camped in the mountains east of the river,* near 33:47
Mount Nebo. Num 27:12
48 They left the mountains east of the river and camped on the plains of Moab beside 33:48 Num 22:1
the Jordan River, across from Jericho. 49 Along the Jordan River they camped from 33:49
Beth-jeshimoth as far as the meadows of Acacia* on the plains of Moab. Num 25:1

33:10 Hebrew *sea of reeds;* also in 33:11. 33:11 The geographical name *Sin* is related to *Sinai* and should not be confused with the English word *sin.* 33:38 This day in the ancient Hebrew lunar calendar occurred in July or August. 33:45 As in 33:44; Hebrew reads *Iyim,* another name for Iye-abarim. 33:47 Or *the mountains of Abarim;* also in 33:48. 33:49 Hebrew *as far as Abel-shittim.*

DIRECTIONS TO WHERE?

RUDY GIULIANI, mayor of New York City during the September 11, 2001, terrorist bombings that destroyed the World Trade Center, tells the story of how people from all over the United States converged on New York City to help in the aftermath of the disaster. Soon after 9-11, the mayor was riding in downtown Manhattan when he noticed a policeman directing traffic in an intersection. Mr. Giuliani got out of his car and greeted the officer, who happened to be from Chicago, 785 miles away.

As the mayor got back into his car, he thought of how wonderful it was for Mayor Daley of Chicago to send a willing police officer to help in New York's time of crisis. But then a thought hit Giuliani—the policeman was directing vehicles in all directions in a professional manner, but did a Chicago native truly know where he was sending the traffic? Where would people end up?

We chuckle at the thought of someone from Chicago directing traffic on one of the busiest streets in New York. But have you ever gotten wrong directions from someone and ended up lost? Even more dangerous is listening to life's directions from people who don't know where they're going. How many people take marriage advice from Hollywood stars who have been divorced several times? How about students who follow the teachings of atheistic college professors who have no faith in God's creation of the universe, no love for God, and no hope for the future?

There is only one person who can direct our lives perfectly. Of course, that person is God. He even uses "bad" things for our good. Romans 8:28—"We know that God causes everything to work together for the good of those who love God and are called according to His purpose for them." He overrules the worst intentions of bad people. The obvious example of this is Christ's death on the cross: God used the indifference of Pilate, the politics of Herod, and the blind hatred of religious rulers to accomplish our salvation.

God is truly in charge of everything; therefore we can submit to His will with all assurance. He will direct us to reach our full potential and His full glory when we obey Him.

[50]While they were camped near the Jordan River on the plains of Moab opposite Jeri-
cho, the LORD said to Moses, [51]"Give the following instructions to the people of Israel:
When you cross the Jordan River into the land of Canaan, [52]you must drive out all the **33:52**
people living there. You must destroy all their carved and molten images and demolish Exod 23:24; 34:13
all their pagan shrines. [53]Take possession of the land and settle in it, because I have Deut 7:2-5, 25-26
given it to you to occupy. [54]You must distribute the land among the clans by sacred lot **33:54**
and in proportion to their size. A larger portion of land will be allotted to each of the Num 26:53-56
larger clans, and a smaller portion will be allotted to each of the smaller clans. The deci-
sion of the sacred lot is final. In this way, the portions of land will be divided among your
ancestral tribes. [55]But if you fail to drive out the people who live in the land, those who **33:55**
remain will be like splinters in your eyes and thorns in your sides. They will harass you in Josh 23:13
the land where you live. [56]And I will do to you what I had planned to do to them." Ps 106:34-36

BOUNDARIES OF THE LAND

34 Then the LORD said to Moses, [2]"Give these instructions to the Israelites: When you **34:2** Gen 17:8
come into the land of Canaan, which I am giving you as your special possession, Deut 1:7-8
these will be the boundaries. [3]The southern portion of your country will extend from the Ezek 47:15
wilderness of Zin, along the edge of Edom. The southern boundary will begin on the east **34:3**
at the Dead Sea.* [4]It will then run south past Scorpion Pass* in the direction of Zin. Its Josh 15:1-4
southernmost point will be Kadesh-barnea, from which it will go to Hazar-addar, and on to **34:4**
Azmon. [5]From Azmon the boundary will turn toward the Brook of Egypt and end at the Num 32:8
Mediterranean Sea.*

[6]"Your western boundary will be the coastline of the Mediterranean Sea. **34:6**

[7]"Your northern boundary will begin at the Mediterranean Sea and run east to Mount Josh 15:4
Hor, [8]then to Lebo-hamath, and on through Zedad [9]and Ziphron to Hazar-enan. This will **34:7** Ezek 47:15-17
be your northern boundary.

[10]"The eastern boundary will start at Hazar-enan and run south to Shepham, [11]then **34:10** Josh 15:5
down to Riblah on the east side of Ain. From there the boundary will run down along the **34:11**
eastern edge of the Sea of Galilee,* [12]and then along the Jordan River to the Dead Sea. 2 Kgs 23:33; 25:6
These are the boundaries of your land." Jer 52:9

34:3 Hebrew *Salt Sea;* also in 34:12. 34:4 Or *the ascent of Akrabbim.* 34:5 Hebrew *the sea;* also in 34:6, 7.
34:11 Hebrew *Sea of Kinnereth.*

33:50-56 The travelogue ends, and the chapter concludes with instructions concerning the conquest of Canaan. Each tribe had to drive out the Canaanites or other inhabitants in their assigned territory. Some tribes did just that. Other tribes dominated their territory while allowing some Canaanites to remain. Still other tribes merely assimilated themselves into the existing culture. All three methods existed in the land, but the ramifications for their worship of God and their relationship with Him differed greatly. The blessings of pure faith did not rest on people who failed to uphold the first commandment of worshiping God alone.

34:3-12 The whole book of Numbers has anticipated Israel entering and conquering the Promised Land. It is fitting, as the book concludes, that the extent of the land should be spelled out clearly. The description of these four borders includes some well-known and attested sites, but others are obscure and unknown locations to us, although not to the original audience.

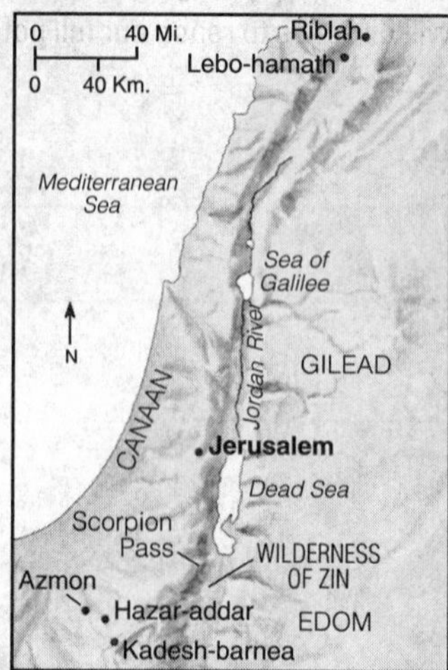

THE BORDERS OF THE PROMISED LAND The borders of the Promised Land stretched from the wilderness of Zin and Kadesh-barnea in the south to Lebo-hamath and Riblah in the north, and from the Mediterranean seacoast on the west to the Jordan River on the east. The land of Gilead was also included.

34:13 13 Then Moses told the Israelites, "This territory is the homeland you are to divide
Josh 14:1-2 among yourselves by sacred lot. The LORD has commanded that the land be divided
34:14 among the nine and a half remaining tribes. 14 The families of the tribes of Reuben, Gad,
Num 32:33 and half the tribe of Manasseh have already received their grants of land 15 on the east
side of the Jordan River, across from Jericho toward the sunrise."

LEADERS TO DIVIDE THE LAND

16 And the LORD said to Moses, 17 "Eleazar the priest and Joshua son of Nun are the men
34:18 designated to divide the grants of land among the people. 18 Enlist one leader from each
Num 1:4, 16 tribe to help them with the task. 19 These are the tribes and the names of the leaders:

Tribe	*Leader*
Judah	Caleb son of Jephunneh
20 Simeon	Shemuel son of Ammihud
21 Benjamin	Elidad son of Kislon
22 Dan	Bukki son of Jogli
23 Manasseh son of Joseph	Hanniel son of Ephod
24 Ephraim son of Joseph	Kemuel son of Shiphtan
25 Zebulun	Elizaphan son of Parnach
26 Issachar	Paltiel son of Azzan
27 Asher	Ahihud son of Shelomi
28 Naphtali	Pedahel son of Ammihud

29 These are the men the LORD has appointed to divide the grants of land in Canaan among
the Israelites."

TOWNS FOR THE LEVITES

35 While Israel was camped beside the Jordan on the plains of Moab across from Jeri-
35:2 cho, the LORD said to Moses, 2 "Command the people of Israel to give to the Levites
Lev 25:32-34 Josh 14:3-4 from their property certain towns to live in, along with the surrounding pasturelands. 3 These
towns will be for the Levites to live in, and the surrounding lands will provide pasture for
their cattle, flocks, and other livestock. 4 The pastureland assigned to the Levites around
these towns will extend 1,500 feet* from the town walls in every direction. 5 Measure off
3,000 feet* outside the town walls in every direction—east, south, west, north—with the
town at the center. This area will serve as the larger pastureland for the towns.
35:6 6 "Six of the towns you give the Levites will be cities of refuge, where a person who has
Josh 20:2-9; 21:3, 13, 21-38 accidentally killed someone can flee for safety. In addition, give them forty-two other
35:7 towns. 7 In all, forty-eight towns with the surrounding pastureland will be given to the Le-
Josh 21:3-42 vites. 8 These towns will come from the property of the people of Israel. The larger tribes
35:8 will give more towns to the Levites, while the smaller tribes will give fewer. Each tribe will
Num 26:54 give property in proportion to the size of its land."

CITIES OF REFUGE

35:11 9 The LORD said to Moses, 10 "Give the following instructions to the people of Israel.
Num 35:22-25 "When you cross the Jordan into the land of Canaan, 11 designate cities of refuge to

35:4 Hebrew *1,000 cubits* [460 meters]. 35:5 Hebrew *2,000 cubits* [920 meters].

35:2 Jacob, the progenitor of the nation of Israel, had given a final blessing to each of his sons. He predicted that Levi would be scattered among the people. The Levitical cities made this a reality. They also enabled the Levites to reach more people with their ministry.

35:4-5 Though the Levites were not given tribal territory, these cities and the surrounding pasturelands were not insignificant. When added together, the Levites may have been given more than 25 square miles of land.

35:6 Six of the Levitical cities were "cities of refuge." Those who committed manslaughter could run to these settlements and be safe until trial (Numbers 35:11). This better ensured protection from feuds or mob revenge.

which people can flee if they have killed someone accidentally. 12 These cities will be 35:12
places of protection from a dead person's relatives who want to avenge the death. The Josh 20:3
slayer must not be put to death before being tried by the community. 13 Designate six cities
of refuge for yourselves, 14 three on the east side of the Jordan River and three on the west
in the land of Canaan. 15 These cities are for the protection of Israelites, foreigners living
among you, and traveling merchants. Anyone who accidentally kills someone may flee
there for safety.

16 "But if someone strikes and kills another person with a piece of iron, it is murder, and 35:16
the murderer must be executed. 17 Or if someone with a stone in his hand strikes and kills Exod 21:12-14
another person, it is murder, and the murderer must be put to death. 18 Or if someone Lev 24:17
strikes and kills another person with a wooden object, it is murder, and the murderer
must be put to death. 19 The victim's nearest relative is responsible for putting the mur-
derer to death. When they meet, the avenger must put the murderer to death. 20 So if
someone hates another person and pushes him or throws a dangerous object at him and
he dies, it is murder. 21 Or if someone hates another person and hits him with a fist and he
dies, it is murder. In such cases, the avenger must put the murderer to death when they
meet.

22 "But suppose someone pushes another person without having shown previous hostil-
ity, or throws something that unintentionally hits another person, 23 or accidentally drops
a huge stone on someone, though they were not enemies, and the person dies. 24 If this
should happen, the community must follow these regulations in making a judgment be-
tween the slayer and the avenger, the victim's nearest relative: 25 The community must
protect the slayer from the avenger and must escort the slayer back to live in the city of
refuge to which he fled. There he must remain until the death of the high priest, who was
anointed with the sacred oil.

26 "But if the slayer ever leaves the limits of the city of refuge, 27 and the avenger finds
him outside the city and kills him, it will not be considered murder. 28 The slayer should
have stayed inside the city of refuge until the death of the high priest. But after the death
of the high priest, the slayer may return to his own property. 29 These are legal require-
ments for you to observe from generation to generation, wherever you may live.

30 "All murderers must be put to death, but only if evidence is presented by more than 35:30
one witness. No one may be put to death on the testimony of only one witness. 31 Also, Deut 17:6-7; 19:15
you must never accept a ransom payment for the life of someone judged guilty of murder Matt 18:16
and subject to execution; murderers must always be put to death. 32 And never accept a 2 Cor 13:1
ransom payment from someone who has fled to a city of refuge, allowing a slayer to re- Heb 10:28
turn to his property before the death of the high priest. 33 This will ensure that the land
where you live will not be polluted, for murder pollutes the land. And no sacrifice except
the execution of the murderer can purify the land from murder.* 34 You must not defile the 35:34
land where you live, for I live there Myself. I am the LORD, who lives among the people of Lev 18:25
Israel."

35:33 Or *can make atonement for murder.*

▸ **GOD**

35:33 God hates murder. Israel had a system for dealing with homicide that was different from ours, but it highlights how much God hates murder. The murder of unborn children pollutes many nations—is there a way you can help? Can you adopt unwanted children, support unwed or single mothers, or help repentant abortion doctors and nurses to find new jobs? Pray that God would deliver your nation from unrestrained violence toward the helpless. (***See God*** *> God's Nature> Unique> He is the final lawgiver and judge,* TopicGuide page A15.)

35:34 Though seeming strange to us, the reason for the careful legislation of refuge was ultimately to honor God's holiness, since He would be dwelling in their midst. Since man is made in God's image, murder is nothing less than striking out in a vain attempt to kill God. Forgiveness for such heinous sin was found only through sacrifice. This is still true today as the only means of true forgiveness is through trusting in the sacrificial death of Jesus.

WOMEN WHO INHERIT PROPERTY

36:1-2 **36** Then the heads of the clans of Gilead—descendants of Makir, son of Manasseh,
Num 27:1-11 son of Joseph—came to Moses and the family leaders of Israel with a petition.
2 They said, "Sir, the LORD instructed you to divide the land by sacred lot among the people
of Israel. You were told by the LORD to give the grant of land owned by our brother Zelo-
phehad to his daughters. 3 But if they marry men from another tribe, their grants of land
will go with them to the tribe into which they marry. In this way, the total area of our tribal
land will be reduced. 4 Then when the Year of Jubilee comes, their portion of land will be
added to that of the new tribe, causing it to be lost forever to our ancestral tribe."

5 So Moses gave the Israelites this command from the LORD: "The claim of the men of the
tribe of Joseph is legitimate. 6 This is what the LORD commands concerning the daughters
of Zelophehad: Let them marry anyone they like, as long as it is within their own ancestral
tribe. 7 None of the territorial land may pass from tribe to tribe, for all the land given to
36:8 1 Chr 23:22 each tribe must remain within the tribe to which it was first allotted. 8 The daughters
throughout the tribes of Israel who are in line to inherit property must marry within their
tribe, so that all the Israelites will keep their ancestral property. 9 No grant of land may pass
from one tribe to another; each tribe of Israel must keep its allotted portion of land."

36:11 10 The daughters of Zelophehad did as the LORD commanded Moses. 11 Mahlah, Tirzah,
Num 26:33; 27:1 Hoglah, Milcah, and Noah all married cousins on their father's side. 12 They married into
the clans of Manasseh son of Joseph. Thus, their inheritance of land remained within their
ancestral tribe.

36:13 13 These are the commands and regulations that the LORD gave to the people of Israel
Lev 7:38; 27:34 through Moses while they were camped on the plains of Moab beside the Jordan River
across from Jericho.

36:2-6 Zelophehad died with no sons to inherit his land. The custom of the day did not allow women to own land. In Numbers 27, Zelophehad's daughters petitioned Moses to help maintain their father's name in Israel by allowing them to inherit the land. But another custom held that if Zelophehad's daughters married into another tribe, their land would go with them and the tribe of Manasseh would lose territory. Land was the ultimate inheritance and legacy, so it is understandable that leaders of Manasseh were concerned about this potential loss. So Moses instructed the daughters to marry within their tribe.

36:4 The Year of Jubilee (Leviticus 25) reminded the people that while they used terms like "my land" or "our land," the earth really belonged to the Lord. They were (as we are) merely tenants. Paul reminded his New Testament readers of a related truth—that they were citizens of heaven rather than earth (Philippians 3:20-21). Because of Sabbath years (every seventh year), and then the great Year of Jubilee (every fiftieth year after seven Sabbaths), the Israelites had calendar reminders throughout their lives that God was the One who supplied their needs, even to the most basic level of land for crops and cattle.

DEUTERONOMY

PURPOSE

To recount for the new generation of Israelites the past (chapters 1–4), present (chapters 5–26), and future (chapters 27–34) of God's covenant relationship with Israel. Moses tells the new generation what God has done, what God expects of them, and what He will do for Israel in the future.

A universal quality of humanity is the tendency to forget. The book of Deuteronomy is divine evidence that God knows this particular weakness and ordains the use of repetition to overcome it. The entire book of Deuteronomy is the second time the law is explained to the Israelites. *Deuteronomy* is from two Greek words meaning "second [*deutero*] law [*nomos*]," or the second giving of the law.

God gave the law to the Israelites through Moses at Sinai after He brought them out of Egypt. This began with the Ten Commandments in Exodus 20. But the entire generation of adults who received that law perished in the wilderness due to their rebellion and lack of faith in the Lord (Numbers 13–14). Therefore, as the people prepared to enter the Promised Land, the rising generation needed to hear the law. Thus this "second giving of the law" was a reminder to a generation of people who were children at Sinai. But it was also the first formal hearing of the law for a new generation of younger people born in the wilderness.

Deuteronomy consists mainly of Moses' recitation of laws and ordinances to the generation who would cross the Jordan to inherit and possess the land.

DISCOVER GOD IN DEUTERONOMY

Moses wrote the book of Deuteronomy toward the end of his long life, making his time-honed reflections of God's involvement in his life and the history of Israel among the most valuable in the Bible. This is one explanation as to why this book is quoted more times in the New Testament than any other Old Testament book. To discover a grand history of God's work in the life of Moses, look no further than the book of Deuteronomy.

Unique: Deuteronomy 6:4, one of the pivotal verses for ancient and modern Judaism, declares that God is one (see NLT footnote). There is no other God but Yahweh, the LORD. This is the creedal center of the law, issuing forth into the great commandment to love this God whole-heartedly. This belief is carried over into Christianity through numerous affirmations of Jesus and the apostles (Mark 12:29; John 10:30; Ephesians 4:6; James 2:19).

Promise-Keeper: In Genesis 15:18-19, as part of the developing covenant God made with Abraham, land was promised as a home for Abraham's many descendants. Abraham was childless at the time. Hundreds of years later, the children of promise (Jacob's descendants) numbered in the millions. From the top of Mount Nebo, God showed Moses the land He had promised to Abraham (Deuteronomy 34:4). While Moses himself could not cross into the land, the connection with Abraham was made, and Moses knew the promise was fulfilled. God is a promise-keeping God. What He says is as good as done. God gives us His "great and precious promises" by which we live today (2 Peter 1:4). With God, the future is as certain as the past.

Merciful: The heart of the message of Deuteronomy is found in chapters 27–30. In a solemn ceremony, God sealed His covenant with Israel. This presentation included blessings for obedience (28:1-14) and curses for disobedience (28:15-68). While this may sound cut and dried and devoid of compassion, it is actually the essence of mercy. God gave them and gives us whatever we need to know in order to live joyful lives, both now and forever (Psalm 19:1-11; Romans 1:18-20; Hebrews 1:1-2).

DISCOVERY VERSES

"But watch out! Be careful never to forget what you yourself have seen. Do not let these memories escape from your mind as long as you live! And be sure to pass them on to your children and grandchildren." (DEUTERONOMY 4:9)

"Listen, O Israel! The LORD is our God, the LORD alone." (DEUTERONOMY 6:4)

"Today I have given you the choice between life and death, between blessings and curses. Now I call on heaven and earth to witness the choice you make. Oh, that you would choose life, so that you and your descendants might live!" (DEUTERONOMY 30:19)

GROWING THROUGH DEUTERONOMY

Three important themes in Deuteronomy apply to believers of all ages:

Choice: Human beings are made in the image of God. Part of His image that we reflect is the ability to make choices. God chooses, and those made in His image choose as well—and we are accountable for our choices. Deuteronomy sets forth Israel's responsibility to listen to God, to remember and not forget, and then to choose: life or death, obedience or disobedience, blessings or curses (Deuteronomy 30:19). Covenant language always says, "If . . . then" (Deuteronomy 28:1). Even Jesus presented "If . . . then" propositions to His disciples (John 8:31-32; 15:7). Deuteronomy makes us think about the choices we make and their implications.

Obedience: Deuteronomy adopts a treaty pattern commonly used by Ancient Near Eastern kings in establishing relationships with their subjects. In this way God spoke in terms the people could understand. A great king would remind people of what he had done for them (as God does in the early chapters of this book). Then the king would spell out what he required from the people (in this case God's law from chapters 5–26). For the subjects' obedience, the king would provide the promise of blessings, sustenance, and protection. But for disobedience, the king would promise dreadful punishment (chapters 27–28). The words of Jesus bring to mind the message of Deuteronomy: "So why do you keep calling me 'Lord, Lord!' when you don't do what I say?" (Luke 6:46). We will find that when the Hebrew text literally says "hearing the voice of the LORD," it is the same as saying "obeying the LORD." If we love Him, we will do what He commands.

Standards: Deuteronomy reminds us that God is absolute truth and that a blessed life is one lived according to His standards. God is like a loving parent who puts protective parameters around His children's activities, knowing that within those boundaries they will be safe and fulfilled. Life without God's standards not only lacks holiness and wholeness, it becomes the opposite of holiness. It becomes anti-holy, characterized by emptiness and dissatisfaction. Far from being restrictive standards robbing people of pleasure, God's law is the root of all real freedom, satisfaction, and peace.

DEUTERONOMY FACTS

Author: Moses (see Genesis Introduction, Author). Deuteronomy contains approximately forty references to Moses as its author. Numerous New Testament passages also support

Mosaic authorship (for example Matthew 19:7-8; Mark 7:10; Acts 3:22-23; Romans 10:19). However, Moses didn't write the record of his own death (34:5-12). Such things were likely written by Joshua or another leader empowered by God.

Written to: The second generation of Israelite adults after the Exodus, those who were small children (or not yet born) at the first giving of the law at Mount Sinai.

Date of writing: Around 1400 BC, forty years after the nation was freed from slavery in Egypt.

Setting: Just east of the Jordan River on the plains of Moab. Israel camped here approximately one month while learning the law from Moses and preparing to cross over into Canaan.

OUTLINE

- **DEUTERONOMY 1–4**—Review of Israel's covenant history
- **DEUTERONOMY 5–26**—Laws of the covenant
  - ***DEUTERONOMY 5–11***—*The great laws*
  - ***DEUTERONOMY 12–26***—*The supplementary laws*
- **DEUTERONOMY 27–30**—Sealing the covenant
- **DEUTERONOMY 31–34**—Changing leaders of the covenant

INTRODUCTION TO MOSES' FIRST ADDRESS

1:1 Deut 2:8, 24; 3:3; 4:1, 44-46

1 These are the words that Moses spoke to all the people of Israel while they were in the
wilderness east of the Jordan River. They were camped in the Jordan Valley* near
Suph, between Paran on one side and Tophel, Laban, Hazeroth, and Di-zahab on the other.
2Normally it takes only eleven days to travel from Mount Sinai* to Kadesh-barnea, going by
way of Mount Seir. 3But forty years after the Israelites left Egypt, on the first day of the elev-
enth month,* Moses addressed the people of Israel, telling them everything the LORD had
1:4 commanded him to say. 4This took place after he had defeated King Sihon of the Amorites,
Num 21:24, 33 who had ruled in Heshbon, and King Og of Bashan, who had ruled in Ashtaroth and Edrei.
5While the Israelites were in the land of Moab east of the Jordan River, Moses carefully
explained the LORD's instructions as follows.

1:1 Hebrew *the Arabah;* also in 1:7. 1:2 Hebrew *Horeb,* another name for Sinai; also in 1:6, 19. 1:3 Hebrew *In the fortieth year, on the first day of the eleventh month.* This day in the ancient Hebrew lunar calendar occurred in January or February.

BIBLE

1:1 The words of God and Moses. The second generation of God's people is ready to cross the Jordan River. In the first section of Deuteronomy, Moses, God's chosen leader for Israel, recounts the 40-year history of this young nation, beginning at Mount Sinai. The narrative is quite personal, with Moses interjecting commentary and insights in a way unseen so far in Scripture—you don't see Moses giving his personal insights on the Creation story! God's inspiration of Scripture is highly organic; even though these are clearly Moses' recollections and comments, God's special care for His Word and blessing upon it are clear throughout the book. (***See Bible***> *Uniqueness> Inspired> A record of God's own words,* TopicGuide page A10.)

1:1 This opening verse, joined with the closing verse of Numbers, shows the close relationship between these two books. Deuteronomy continues the great story of Numbers.

1:2-3 The Israelites traveled from Egypt to Mount Sinai, where they received the Ten Commandments. From there, the journey to Kadesh-barnea, just south of Canaan, typically took just 11 days by foot. But when the Israelites got there, they feared the fighting men of the land. Because of their lack of faith, God sentenced them to wander for 40 years in the wilderness of the Sinai Peninsula, between Egypt and the Promised Land.

1:5 Moab was a small kingdom east of the Dead Sea. The Moabites were direct descendants of Abraham's nephew Lot (Genesis 19:34-38).

THE COMMAND TO LEAVE SINAI

6"When we were at Mount Sinai, the LORD our God said to us, 'You have stayed at this
mountain long enough. 7It is time to break camp and move on. Go to the hill country of
the Amorites and to all the neighboring regions—the Jordan Valley, the hill country, the
western foothills,* the Negev, and the coastal plain. Go to the land of the Canaanites and
to Lebanon, and all the way to the great Euphrates River. 8Look, I am giving all this land to
you! Go in and occupy it, for it is the land the LORD swore to give to your ancestors Abra-
ham, Isaac, and Jacob, and to all their descendants.' "

1:6 Num 10:11-13
1:7 Gen 15:18-21; Josh 10:5, 40
1:8 Gen 12:7; 26:3; Exod 33:1; Num 32:10-11

MOSES APPOINTS LEADERS FROM EACH TRIBE

9Moses continued, "At that time I told you, 'You are too great a burden for me to carry all
by myself. 10The LORD your God has increased your population, making you as numerous
as the stars! 11And may the LORD, the God of your ancestors, multiply you a thousand
times more and bless you as He promised! 12But you are such a heavy load to carry! How
can I deal with all your problems and bickering? 13Choose some well-respected men from
each tribe who are known for their wisdom and understanding, and I will appoint them as
your leaders.'

14"Then you responded, 'Your plan is a good one.' 15So I took the wise and respected
men you had selected from your tribes and appointed them to serve as judges and offi-
cials over you. Some were responsible for a thousand people, some for a hundred, some
for fifty, and some for ten.

16"At that time I instructed the judges, 'You must hear the cases of your fellow Israelites
and the foreigners living among you. Be perfectly fair in your decisions 17and impartial in
your judgments. Hear the cases of those who are poor as well as those who are rich. Don't
be afraid of anyone's anger, for the decision you make is God's decision. Bring me any
cases that are too difficult for you, and I will handle them.'

18"At that time I gave you instructions about everything you were to do.

1:9 Exod 18:18, 24
1:10 Gen 15:5; 22:17; Deut 10:22; 26:5; 28:62
1:11 Deut 1:8, 10
1:12 Exod 18:13-14
1:13 Exod 18:21-22; Num 11:16-17
1:16 Deut 16:18
1:17 Exod 18:25-26; Deut 10:17; 16:19; 24:17; Prov 24:23; Jas 2:1, 9

SCOUTS EXPLORE THE LAND

19"Then, just as the LORD our God commanded us, we left Mount Sinai and traveled
through the great and terrifying wilderness, as you yourselves remember, and headed to-
ward the hill country of the Amorites. When we arrived at Kadesh-barnea, 20I said to you,

1:19 Deut 1:2; 8:15; 32:10

1:7 Hebrew *the Shephelah.*

1:7 According to Genesis 15:16, the Amorites were a particularly wicked people living in the land.

1:8-10 Abraham, Isaac, and Jacob were profoundly significant to the Israelites. God gave Abraham the promise of becoming a great nation with people as numerous as the stars (Genesis 26:4). Abraham was also promised the land of Canaan as an inheritance. Later, his son Isaac carried that promise and passed it on to his son Jacob (later renamed Israel). Jacob's twelve sons became the progenitors of the Israelite nation; thus you hear Abraham's descendants referred to as "the twelve tribes of Israel."

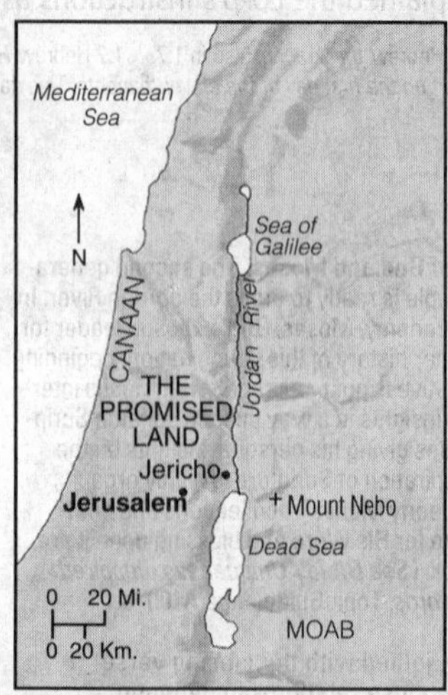

EVENTS IN DEUTERONOMY
The book of Deuteronomy opens with Israel camped east of the Jordan River in the land of Moab. Just before the people crossed the river into the Promised Land, Moses delivered an inspirational speech indicating how they were to live.

'You have now reached the hill country of the Amorites that the LORD our God is giving us.
21 Look! He has placed the land in front of you. Go and occupy it as the LORD, the God of
your ancestors, has promised you. Don't be afraid! Don't be discouraged!'
1:22-23 Num 13:1-3 22 "But you all came to me and said, 'First, let's send out scouts to explore the land for us.
They will advise us on the best route to take and which towns we should enter.'
1:24 Num 13:21-25 23 "This seemed like a good idea to me, so I chose twelve scouts, one from each of your
tribes. 24 They headed for the hill country and came to the valley of Eshcol and explored it.
1:26 25 They picked some of its fruit and brought it back to us. And they reported, 'The land the
Num 14:1-3 LORD our God has given us is indeed a good land.'

1:27

ISRAEL'S REBELLION AGAINST THE LORD

Deut 9:28 Ps 106:25 26 "But you rebelled against the command of the LORD your God and refused to go in.
1:28 27 You complained in your tents and said, 'The LORD must hate us. That's why He has
Num 13:28, 33 brought us here from Egypt—to hand us over to the Amorites to be slaughtered. 28 Where
Deut 9:1-2 can we go? Our brothers have demoralized us with their report. They tell us, "The people
1:30 Exod 14:14 of the land are taller and more powerful than we are, and their towns are large, with walls
Deut 20:4 rising high into the sky! We even saw giants there—the descendants of Anak!"'
1:31 29 "But I said to you, 'Don't be shocked or afraid of them! 30 The LORD your God is going
Deut 32:11 ahead of you. He will fight for you, just as you saw Him do in Egypt. 31 And you saw how
Acts 13:18 the LORD your God cared for you all along the way as you traveled through the wilderness,
1:33 just as a father cares for his child. Now He has brought you to this place.'
Exod 13:21 Num 9:15-23; 10:33-36 32 "But even after all He did, you refused to trust the LORD your God, 33 who goes before
1:34 you looking for the best places to camp, guiding you with a pillar of fire by night and a pil-
Num 14:23; 32:14 lar of cloud by day.
1:36 34 "When the LORD heard your complaining, He became very angry. So He solemnly
Num 14:24 swore, 35 'Not one of you from this wicked generation will live to see the good land I swore
Josh 14:6 to give your ancestors, 36 except Caleb son of Jephunneh. He will see this land because he
1:37 Num 20:12; 27:18 has followed the LORD completely. I will give to him and his descendants some of the very
1:38 land he explored during his scouting mission.'
Num 34:17 Deut 3:28; 31:7 37 "And the LORD was also angry with me because of you. He said to me, 'Moses, not
even you will enter the Promised Land! 38 Instead, your assistant, Joshua son of Nun, will
1:39 Num 14:3, 31 lead the people into the land. Encourage him, for he will lead Israel as they take posses-
sion of it. 39 I will give the land to your little ones—your innocent children. You were afraid

▸ WORSHIP
1:22, 26 Fear and obey. Does the fear of consequences adequately motivate good behavior? Moses is speaking here to the second generation since the Israelites left Egypt, but he refers to them as essentially the same nation that rebelled against God 40 years earlier. Moses knew that these Israelites might rebel just as their forefathers had. These words are a reminder to us of the need for constant faithfulness to the Lord; no past consequence, no matter how horrible, can ensure our current obedience. (***See Worship****> OT> Reverence> Awe of God means obeying His commandments,* TopicGuide page A28.)

1:28 The descendants of Anak were referred to as Anakites or Anakim. They were large people; some translations refer to them as giants. Other people of the ancient world were also considered giants (such as the Emites of Moab in Deuteronomy 2:10-12 and the Zamzummites of Ammon in Deuteronomy 2:20-23). Often these larger peoples were referred to as Nephilites and Rephaites.

1:31-33 God, compared here to a tender, loving father, provided guidance and protection for the Israelites in many ways. He opened the Red Sea, allowing the Israelites to escape from Pharaoh (Exodus 13–14). He miraculously provided quail for meat (Exodus 16; Numbers 11). He provided daily manna for food (Exodus 16) and brought water from a rock (Numbers 20:1-13). He provided a cloud by day and a pillar of fire by night for guidance (Exodus 13:21-22). For these people to doubt God's provision after so many signs and wonders was a flagrant disregard for God's goodness.

▸ GOD
1:37 Regret and repentance. Our memories, particularly of conflict, tend to blur our own mistakes and sharpen the sins of others. Moses summarized the event of his angry striking of the water-bearing rock (Numbers 20:10) in a manner favorable to himself. Was this out of self-protection? No, for Moses was the most humble of men (Numbers 12:3). Moses was seeking to convict the Israelites of their previous rebellion so that they would follow God more faithfully as they entered the Promised Land. Allow memories of your rebellion against God to urge you to deeper faithfulness to God. (***See God****> God's Nature> Personality> Emotion> Rebellion rightly angers God,* TopicGuide page A14.)

they would be captured, but they will be the ones who occupy it. 40As for you, turn around 1:40 Num 14:25
now and go on back through the wilderness toward the Red Sea.*'
41"Then you confessed, 'We have sinned against the LORD! We will go into the land and 1:41 Num 14:40
fight for it, as the LORD our God has commanded us.' So your men strapped on their weap-
ons, thinking it would be easy to attack the hill country.
42"But the LORD told me to tell you, 'Do not attack, for I am not with you. If you go ahead 1:42 Num 14:41-43
on your own, you will be crushed by your enemies.'
43"This is what I told you, but you would not listen. Instead, you again rebelled against 1:43 Num 14:44
the LORD's command and arrogantly went into the hill country to fight. 44But the Amorites 1:44 Num 14:45
who lived there came out against you like a swarm of bees. They chased and battered you
all the way from Seir to Hormah. 45Then you returned and wept before the LORD, but He
refused to listen. 46So you stayed there at Kadesh for a long time.

REMEMBERING ISRAEL'S WANDERINGS

2 "Then we turned around and headed back across the wilderness toward the Red 2:1 Num 21:4
Sea,* just as the LORD had instructed me, and we wandered around in the region of
Mount Seir for a long time.
2"Then at last the LORD said to me, 3'You have been wandering around in this hill coun-
try long enough; turn to the north. 4Give these orders to the people: "You will pass 2:4 Exod 15:15 Num 20:14
through the country belonging to your relatives the Edomites, the descendants of Esau,
who live in Seir. The Edomites will feel threatened, so be careful. 5Do not bother them, for I 2:5 Deut 23:7 Josh 24:4
have given them all the hill country around Mount Seir as their property, and I will not give
you even one square foot of their land. 6If you need food to eat or water to drink, pay
them for it. 7For the LORD your God has blessed you in everything you have done. He has 2:7 Deut 8:2; 29:5
watched your every step through this great wilderness. During these forty years, the LORD
your God has been with you, and you have lacked nothing."' 2:8 Num 20:20
8"So we bypassed the territory of our relatives, the descendants of Esau, who live in Seir.
We avoided the road through the Arabah Valley that comes up from Elath and Ezion-geber. 2:9 Gen 19:37 Deut 2:18, 29
"Then as we turned north along the desert route through Moab, 9the LORD warned us,
'Do not bother the Moabites, the descendants of Lot, or start a war with them. I have given 2:10 Gen 14:5 Num 13:22, 33
them Ar as their property, and I will not give you any of their land.'"
10(A race of giants called the Emites had once lived in the area of Ar. They were as 2:12 Gen 14:6 Num 21:25, 35 Deut 2:22
strong and numerous and tall as the Anakites, another race of giants. 11Both the Emites
and the Anakites are also known as the Rephaites, though the Moabites call them Emites.
12In earlier times the Horites had lived in Seir, but they were driven out and displaced by

1:40 Hebrew *sea of reeds.* 2:1 Hebrew *sea of reeds.*

1:37-38 Moses refers to a time when he stole God's glory and was therefore banned from entering the Promised Land. In Numbers 20:1-12 (see also Psalm 106:32-33) God instructed Moses to speak to a rock and water would come forth. Moses, in anger at the people, hit the rock. Earlier, in a similar situation (Exodus 17:1-17), God told Moses to hit the rock to establish Moses' authority with the people. But in this case, God intended to establish His own authority and glory. It is a flagrant act of pride to attempt to take God's glory for one's self.

2:4-8 Edom was a nation directly descended from Esau, the twin brother of Jacob, the progenitor of the nation of Israel. Though born second, Jacob (later renamed Israel) cheated Esau out of his family birthright. Esau later settled his family south of the Dead Sea. The Edomites were his descendants. Though Jacob and Esau made some peace during their lifetimes, their descendants remained hostile. The prophecy in Obadiah reveals the kind of animosity Edom showed Israel through the centuries.

2:10-11 See note at Deuteronomy 1:28.

▶ BIBLE

2:12 Who really wrote the Bible? Here is quite a puzzler: If, as we claim, Moses wrote Deuteronomy, how could he have composed the material in 2:10-12; 2:20-22; and chapter 34 after Moses had died? These additions to the text were likely clarifying comments by an editor (perhaps Joshua) or a group of editors after the claiming of Canaan. While this raises all sorts of interesting questions, it is not inconsistent with the Bible's self-testimony of being God's inspired Word (2 Timothy 3:16). Even the parenthetical comments of Scripture are God-breathed. (***See Bible***> *Unity*> *Authors,* TopicGuide page A10.)

the descendants of Esau, just as Israel drove out the people of Canaan when the LORD gave
Israel their land.)
13 Moses continued, "Then the LORD said to us, 'Get moving. Cross the Zered Brook.' So
we crossed the brook.
14 "Thirty-eight years passed from the time we first left Kadesh-barnea until we finally
crossed the Zered Brook! By then, all the men old enough to fight in battle had died in the
wilderness, as the LORD had vowed would happen. 15 The LORD struck them down until
they had all been eliminated from the community.
16 "When all the men of fighting age had died, 17 the LORD said to me, 18 'Today you will
cross the border of Moab at Ar 19 and enter the land of the Ammonites, the descendants of
Lot. But do not bother them or start a war with them. I have given the land of Ammon to
them as their property, and I will not give you any of their land.' "
20 (That area was once considered the land of the Rephaites, who had lived there,
though the Ammonites call them Zamzummites. 21 They were also as strong and numer-
ous and tall as the Anakites. But the LORD destroyed them so the Ammonites could occupy
their land. 22 He had done the same for the descendants of Esau who lived in Seir, for He
destroyed the Horites so they could settle there in their place. The descendants of Esau
live there to this day. 23 A similar thing happened when the Caphtorites from Crete* in-
vaded and destroyed the Avvites, who had lived in villages in the area of Gaza.)
24 Moses continued, "Then the LORD said, 'Now get moving! Cross the Arnon Gorge.
Look, I will hand over to you Sihon the Amorite, king of Heshbon, and I will give you his
land. Attack him and begin to occupy the land. 25 Beginning today I will make people
throughout the earth terrified because of you. When they hear reports about you, they will
tremble with dread and fear.' "

VICTORY OVER SIHON OF HESHBON

26 Moses continued, "From the wilderness of Kedemoth I sent ambassadors to King Sihon
of Heshbon with this proposal of peace:

> 27 'Let us travel through your land. We will stay on the main road and won't turn off into
> the fields on either side. 28 Sell us food to eat and water to drink, and we will pay for it. All
> we want is permission to pass through your land. 29 The descendants of Esau who live in
> Seir allowed us to go through their country, and so did the Moabites, who live in Ar. Let
> us pass through until we cross the Jordan into the land the LORD our God is giving us.'

30 "But King Sihon of Heshbon refused to allow us to pass through, because the LORD your
God made Sihon stubborn and defiant so He could help you defeat him, as He has now done.
31 "Then the LORD said to me, 'Look, I have begun to hand King Sihon and his land over
to you. Begin now to conquer and occupy his land.'

2:23 Hebrew *from Caphtor.*

2:14 Num 14:29-35; 26:64-65 Deut 2:7 1 Cor 10:5
2:15 Ps 106:26 Jude 1:5
2:18 Num 21:15 Deut 2:9
2:20 Deut 2:11
2:23 Gen 10:13-14 1 Chr 1:11-12 Jer 47:4 Amos 9:7
2:24 Num 21:13 Judg 11:18
2:25 Exod 15:14-16; 23:27 Deut 11:25 Josh 2:9
2:26 Num 21:21 Deut 20:10 Judg 11:19
2:29 Deut 2:8-9; 23:3
2:30 Exod 4:21 Num 21:23 Josh 11:20

2:15 The two censuses in the book of Numbers mark the passing of the generation described here. When the Israelites turned back from entering the Promised Land the first time (Numbers 13–14), the consequences fell on the adults of those families who had left Egypt. That whole generation passed away before the people prepared to enter the land again. Thus the second census counted adults who had grown into adulthood during the journey and were ready to enter the land.

2:18-19 The Ammonites of Moab described here were descendants of Abraham's nephew, Lot (Genesis 19:34-38).

2:24-25 The battles with Sihon and Og became an important part of the Israelites' legacy (see for instance Nehemiah 9:22; Psalms 135; 136). Foreign peoples (such as the Hivites in Joshua 9) sought treaties with Israel because they knew about Israel's defeat of Og and Sihon. The Israelites referred to these battles to remind themselves of God's provision.

▸GOD
2:30 Removing the restraints. Did the pagan King Sihon need God's help in being stubborn and defiant? No. And neither do we! God made Sihon stubborn simply by removing His gracious moral restraints. This encouraged the king's natural foolish defiance in order to prepare him and his people for the punishment their sins warranted. God allows sin to take place, but He never actively encourages sin nor tempts anyone to sin (James 1:13). Therefore, we should not blame God when evil touches our lives, but, like Job, we should praise God (Job 1:20-22; 2:10) and look to Him to see us through our trial. (***See God*> *God's Attributes*> *Good*> *God creates only good things,* TopicGuide page A16.)

32“Then King Sihon declared war on us and mobilized his forces at Jahaz. 33But the LORD
our God handed him over to us, and we crushed him, his sons, and all his people. 34We
conquered all his towns and completely destroyed* everyone—men, women, and chil-
dren. Not a single person was spared. 35We took all the livestock as plunder for ourselves,
along with anything of value from the towns we ransacked.
36“The LORD our God also helped us conquer Aroer on the edge of the Arnon Gorge,
and the town in the gorge, and the whole area as far as Gilead. No town had walls too
strong for us. 37However, we avoided the land of the Ammonites all along the Jabbok River
and the towns in the hill country—all the places the LORD our God had commanded us to
leave alone.

VICTORY OVER OG OF BASHAN

3 “Next we turned and headed for the land of Bashan, where King Og and his entire
army attacked us at Edrei. 2But the LORD told me, ‘Do not be afraid of him, for I have
given you victory over Og and his entire army, and I will give you all his land. Treat him
just as you treated King Sihon of the Amorites, who ruled in Heshbon.’
3“So the LORD our God handed King Og and all his people over to us, and we killed them
all. Not a single person survived. 4We conquered all sixty of his towns—the entire Argob re-
gion in his kingdom of Bashan. Not a single town escaped our conquest. 5These towns were
all fortified with high walls and barred gates. We also took many unwalled villages at the
same time. 6We completely destroyed* the kingdom of Bashan, just as we had destroyed
King Sihon of Heshbon. We destroyed all the people in every town we conquered—men,
women, and children alike. 7But we kept all the livestock for ourselves and took plunder
from all the towns.
8“So we took the land of the two Amorite kings east of the Jordan River—all the way
from the Arnon Gorge to Mount Hermon. 9(Mount Hermon is called Sirion by the Sidoni-
ans, and the Amorites call it Senir.) 10We had now conquered all the cities on the plateau
and all Gilead and Bashan, as far as the towns of Salecah and Edrei, which were part of
Og’s kingdom in Bashan. 11(King Og of Bashan was the last survivor of the giant Repha-

2:33 Num 21:24-30; Deut 3:6; 29:7
2:35 Deut 3:7, 10
2:36 Ps 44:3
2:37 Deut 3:16
3:1 Num 21:33-35
3:2 Num 21:34
3:3 Josh 9:10
3:4 1 Kgs 4:13
3:6 Deut 2:33-34; 20:16
3:7 Deut 2:35
3:8 Num 32:33-42; Josh 12:1-6; 13:8-13
3:9 Deut 4:48; Josh 11:17; Ps 29:5-6
3:11 Deut 2:11, 20; 2 Sam 11:1; 12:26-27; Jer 49:2

2:34 The Hebrew term used here refers to the complete consecration of things or people to the LORD, either by destroying them or by giving them as an offering. 3:6 The Hebrew term used here refers to the complete consecration of things or people to the LORD, either by destroying them or by giving them as an offering; also in 3:6b.

▸ GOD

2:33 Awesome God. God’s power is not limited to the Bible, to a church, or one special location or event. God’s power extends to every nation, every tribe, every city, and even every person—there is no place or situation in which His power is restricted or excluded. Is your understanding of God’s authority limited? God is sovereign, everywhere and all the time! (***See God****> God’s Attributes> Sovereign> He raises and removes rulers,* TopicGuide page A17.)

2:34 When the people of Israel “completely destroyed everyone,” they were laying claim to the land as holy. Those people who were not holy—not part of God’s covenant community—had to be offered to Him in order to make the land holy. This concept is further developed and clarified in Deuteronomy 7.

3:1 Moses now recounts the battle with Og, the last king of Bashan (Numbers 21:33-35). Israelites often mentioned Og and Sihon when testifying to God’s power, which they recognized as the source of their military victories (as in Psalm 135:10-11).

▸ ADOPTION

3:6 The death penalty. Have you ever wondered if God was wrong to annihilate these towns? There are three key points to understanding the righteousness of God’s actions here. First, God frequently allowed foreign converts to join the nation of Israel. We see people with Egyptian names and Ethiopian names among the Israelites, and God provided laws governing the treatment of foreign converts (Exodus 12:48; Leviticus 19:33-34). Second, the Canaanite culture was extremely wicked (Deuteronomy 9:5). They practiced human sacrifice (even of children), bestiality, religious mutilation, and temple prostitution (Deuteronomy 18:9-14). If allowed to remain, these cultures would have polluted God’s people and perhaps prevented Israel from growing into a suitable people for the preaching of the Good News to the nations. Third, the Canaanites, like all who have rejected God, deserved judgment. God had given them time to repent of their wickedness, but He eventually chose to put a stop to their sin. (***See Adoption****> Without Christ> Separated from God> Facing judgment,* TopicGuide page A36.)

3:11 The reference to a large bed still to be seen in Rabbah reminds us that the original readers could verify the claims of the text by seeing real and existing artifacts. But faith rests not on what is seen but on what is unseen (2 Corinthians 4:18).

ites. His bed was made of iron and was more than thirteen feet long and six feet wide.* It
can still be seen in the Ammonite city of Rabbah.)

LAND DIVISION EAST OF THE JORDAN

3:12 Num 32:33-42 12"When we took possession of this land, I gave to the tribes of Reuben and Gad the terri-
Deut 2:35-36 tory beyond Aroer along the Arnon Gorge, plus half of the hill country of Gilead with its
Josh 13:8-13 towns. 13Then I gave the rest of Gilead and all of Bashan—Og's former kingdom—to the
half-tribe of Manasseh. (This entire Argob region of Bashan used to be known as the land
of the Rephaites. 14Jair, a leader from the tribe of Manasseh, conquered the whole Argob
region in Bashan, all the way to the border of the Geshurites and Maacathites. Jair re-
named this region after himself, calling it the Towns of Jair,* as it is still known today.) 15I
3:15 gave Gilead to the clan of Makir. 16But I also gave part of Gilead to the tribes of Reuben
Num 32:40 and Gad. The area I gave them extended from the middle of the Arnon Gorge in the south
3:17 to the Jabbok River on the Ammonite frontier. 17They also received the Jordan Valley, all
Josh 13:27 the way from the Sea of Galilee down to the Dead Sea,* with the Jordan River serving as
3:18 the western boundary. To the east were the slopes of Pisgah.
Num 32:20 18"At that time I gave this command to the tribes that would live east of the Jordan: 'Al-
Josh 4:12-13 though the LORD your God has given you this land as your property, all your fighting men
must cross the Jordan ahead of your Israelite relatives, armed and ready to assist them.
3:19 Num 32:16 19Your wives, children, and numerous livestock, however, may stay behind in the towns I
Josh 1:14 have given you. 20When the LORD has given security to the rest of the Israelites, as He has
to you, and when they occupy the land the LORD your God is giving them across the Jordan
River, then you may all return here to the land I have given you.'

MOSES FORBIDDEN TO ENTER THE LAND

3:22 21"At that time I gave Joshua this charge: 'You have seen for yourself everything the LORD your
Deut 1:29-30; 20:4 God has done to these two kings. He will do the same to all the kingdoms on the west side of
3:24 the Jordan. 22Do not be afraid of the nations there, for the LORD your God will fight for you.'
Ps 86:8 23"At that time I pleaded with the LORD and said, 24'O Sovereign LORD, You have only

3:11 Hebrew *9 cubits* [4.1 meters] *long and 4 cubits* [1.8 meters] *wide.* 3:14 Hebrew *Havvoth-jair.* 3:17 Hebrew *from Kinnereth to the Sea of the Arabah, the Salt Sea.*

3:12-13 Reuben, Gad, and Manasseh were tribes that chose to live east of the Jordan River. Numbers 32 records the request from the Gadites and Reubenites to keep their herds east of the Jordan where grazing land was plentiful. Moses consented on one condition: The military men of these tribes would still cross the Jordan and help the other tribes conquer and settle the land. These tribes committed to do so, and, under Joshua's leadership, fought alongside the other tribes of Israel.

BECAUSE GOD IS SOVEREIGN

I will joyfully submit to His will.

O Sovereign LORD, You have only begun to show Your greatness and the strength of Your hand to me, Your servant. Is there any god in heaven or on earth who can perform such great and mighty deeds as You do?

DEUTERONOMY 3:24

FOR THE NEXT *GOD IS SOVEREIGN* FEATURE SEE PAGE 556.

begun to show Your greatness and the strength of Your hand to me, Your servant. Is there any god in heaven or on earth who can perform such great and mighty deeds as You do? 25 Please let me cross the Jordan to see the wonderful land on the other side, the beautiful hill country and the Lebanon mountains.'

26 "But the LORD was angry with me because of you, and He would not listen to me. 'That's enough!' He declared. 'Speak of it no more. 27 But go up to Pisgah Peak, and look over the land in every direction. Take a good look, but you may not cross the Jordan River. 28 Instead, commission Joshua and encourage and strengthen him, for he will lead the people across the Jordan. He will give them all the land you now see before you as their possession.' 29 So we stayed in the valley near Beth-peor.

MOSES URGES ISRAEL TO OBEY

4 "And now, Israel, listen carefully to these decrees and regulations that I am about to teach you. Obey them so that you may live, so you may enter and occupy the land that the LORD, the God of your ancestors, is giving you. 2 Do not add to or subtract from these commands I am giving you. Just obey the commands of the LORD your God that I am giving you.

3 "You saw for yourself what the LORD did to you at Baal-peor. There the LORD your God destroyed everyone who had worshiped Baal, the god of Peor. 4 But all of you who were faithful to the LORD your God are still alive today—every one of you.

5 "Look, I now teach you these decrees and regulations just as the LORD my God commanded me, so that you may obey them in the land you are about to enter and occupy. 6 Obey them completely, and you will display your wisdom and intelligence among the surrounding nations. When they hear all these decrees, they will exclaim, 'How wise and prudent are the people of this great nation!' 7 For what great nation has a god as near to them as the LORD our God is near to us whenever we call on Him? 8 And what great nation has decrees and regulations as righteous and fair as this body of instructions that I am giving you today?

9 "But watch out! Be careful never to forget what you yourself have seen. Do not let these memories escape from your mind as long as you live! And be sure to pass them on to your children and grandchildren. 10 Never forget the day when you stood before the

3:26 Deut 1:37; 31:2
3:27 Num 27:12; Deut 1:37
3:28 Num 27:18
4:1 Lev 19:37; Deut 5:32-33; 8:1; 16:20; 30:16; Ezek 20:11; Rom 10:5
4:2 Deut 12:32; Prov 30:6; Matt 5:18; Rev 22:18-19
4:3 Num 25:1-9
4:5 Lev 26:46; 27:34
4:6 Ps 19:7-8; Prov 1:7-9
4:7 Ps 148:14
4:8 Ps 89:14-15
4:10 Exod 19:9, 16

3:24 Moses confesses here that God is a great and powerful being. After all that Moses had seen God do for Israel, he admits that everything so far has been just a hint of the greatness and power of God.

▸ PURPOSE
3:27 Sensing God's will. Have you ever sensed God was forbidding you to do or say something? In this case, God had already commanded Moses not to enter Canaan due to his disobedience; now God commanded Moses not to speak of it again (Deuteronomy 3:26). But God was merciful and allowed Moses to see the land of Canaan from atop Pisgah Peak, the highest point of Mount Nebo, northeast of the Dead Sea. If you believe that God's Spirit is forbidding or encouraging in a certain direction, consult God's Word and the counsel of other wise believers before you act. (***See Purpose****> God's Means> Human Choice> Bringing our wills in subjection to God's will,* TopicGuide page A52.)

▸ WORSHIP
4:1 Listen carefully to the law. How many times do you need to hear something before you understand it? The first generation of Jews had refused to obey and wandered for 40 years in the desert until the second generation grew to adulthood. Moses wanted no misunderstandings with this second generation, so he recited the laws in the form of a treaty. The Israelites were familiar with this general contractual format, and so they likely listened carefully, recognizing the serious manner in which these stipulations were stated. Ask God to give you spiritual ears always willing to listen and a heart ready to obey. (***See Worship****> OT> Repentance> Nature> Keeping God's commands leads to life,* TopicGuide page A29.)

4:3-4 The disaster described here happened just after the king of Moab tried to buy a curse on the Israelites from Balaam the Mesopotamian prophet (see Numbers 22–24). Balaam refused to curse Israel, but disaster came nonetheless when the Israelite men met the Moabite women (Numbers 25). At Acacia Grove many Israelite men became sexually involved with these women, and thus fell into their worship of Baal. At God's command, Moses began to execute the men who had engaged in idol worship. In addition, 24,000 other people were struck down with a plague.

4:6 God not only chose Israel as His own people, but He intended to display His goodness through them to the surrounding nations and to the world.

4:9 This verse is a prime example of the dual emphasis in Deuteronomy to remember what God has said and done and to pass these things down to following generations.

LORD your God at Mount Sinai,* where He told me, 'Summon the people before Me, and I
will personally instruct them. Then they will learn to fear Me as long as they live, and they
will teach their children to fear Me also.'
4:11 Exod 19:18 11"You came near and stood at the foot of the mountain, while flames from the moun-
Heb 12:18 tain shot into the sky. The mountain was shrouded in black clouds and deep darkness.
12And the LORD spoke to you from the heart of the fire. You heard the sound of His words
4:13 but didn't see His form; there was only a voice. 13He proclaimed His covenant—the Ten
Exod 31:18; 34:28 Deut 10:4 Commandments*—which He commanded you to keep, and which He wrote on two stone
tablets. 14It was at that time that the LORD commanded me to teach you His decrees and
regulations so you would obey them in the land you are about to enter and occupy.

4:15 Exod 19:9, 18, 21

A WARNING AGAINST IDOLATRY

15"But be very careful! You did not see the LORD's form on the day He spoke to you from the
4:16 Exod 20:4-5; 32:8 heart of the fire at Mount Sinai. 16So do not corrupt yourselves by making an idol in any
Deut 9:12; 31:29 form—whether of a man or a woman, 17an animal on the ground, a bird in the sky, 18a small
4:19 animal that scurries along the ground, or a fish in the deepest sea. 19And when you look up
2 Kgs 17:16 into the sky and see the sun, moon, and stars—all the forces of heaven—don't be seduced
Acts 7:43 into worshiping them. The LORD your God gave them to all the peoples of the earth.
4:20 1 Kgs 8:51 20Remember that the LORD rescued you from the iron-smelting furnace of Egypt in order to
Jer 11:4 make you His very own people and His special possession, which is what you are today.
4:21 21"But the LORD was angry with me because of you. He vowed that I would not cross the
Num 20:12 Jordan River into the good land the LORD your God is giving you as your special posses-
Deut 1:37 sion. 22You will cross the Jordan to occupy the land, but I will not. Instead, I will die here on
4:23 Exod 20:4-5 the east side of the river. 23So be careful not to break the covenant the LORD your God has
4:24 made with you. Do not make idols of any shape or form, for the LORD your God has forbid-
Exod 24:17; 34:14 den this. 24The LORD your God is a devouring fire; He is a jealous God.
Heb 12:29 25"In the future, when you have children and grandchildren and have lived in the land a
4:25 Deut 4:16; 31:29 long time, do not corrupt yourselves by making idols of any kind. This is evil in the sight of
4:26 the LORD your God and will arouse His anger.
Deut 7:4; 8:19; 31:29 26"Today I call on heaven and earth as witnesses against you. If you break My cov-
4:27 enant, you will quickly disappear from the land you are crossing the Jordan to occupy.
Deut 28:64 You will live there only a short time; then you will be utterly destroyed. 27For the LORD will
4:28 Deut 28:36, 64; 29:17 scatter you among the nations, where only a few of you will survive. 28There, in a foreign
Ps 115:4-8 land, you will worship idols made from wood and stone—gods that neither see nor hear

4:10 Hebrew *Horeb,* another name for Sinai; also in 4:15. 4:13 Hebrew *the ten words.*

4:11-12 Moses' description of Mount Sinai is echoed later in the letter to the Hebrews (12:18-21).

4:15-19 These verses anticipate the commandment against idolatry in the next chapter. The images described here were common idols of the time.

▸ WORSHIP

4:16 Images of God. Does this passage mean you shouldn't have pictures of Jesus in your home or church? While culturally influenced pictures of Jesus can be misleading, they are likely not condemned by this passage. This passage forbids the making and worshiping of an image of *God,* who is the invisible Father (Colossians 1:15; Hebrews 11:27), not the Son, who took on a physical nature in the Incarnation. But while pictures or artistic renderings of Christ are not directly forbidden in Scripture, the use of statues or images in worship is specifically addressed in Leviticus 26:1 and Deuteronomy 27:15. (***See Worship****> OT> Reverence> Put away idols,* TopicGuide page A28.)

▸ GOD

4:24 Is God jealous? For humans, jealousy is a sin because it is self-centered. A jealous person seeks for him or herself the honor, attention, or glory that belongs rightfully to another person. When applied to God, jealousy is not a sin because He truly does deserve all honor and glory. When people give glory to images and other gods, this is the height of idolatry, and God is rightfully jealous for His own glory. So He says in Isaiah 42:8, "I am the LORD; that is My name! I will not give My glory to anyone else, nor share My praise with carved idols." Give God all the praise and honor He deserves. (***See God****> God's Nature> Personality> Emotion> God jealously desires exclusive worship,* TopicGuide page A14.)

4:28 The wording of this verse shows the absolute worthlessness of idols. Lacking sight, hearing, taste, or smell, false gods literally are senseless and figuratively worthless.

nor eat nor smell. 29 But from there you will search again for the LORD your God. And if you search for Him with all your heart and soul, you will find Him.

30 "In the distant future, when you are suffering all these things, you will finally return to the LORD your God and listen to what He tells you. 31 For the LORD your God is a merciful God; He will not abandon you or destroy you or forget the solemn covenant He made with your ancestors.

THERE IS ONLY ONE GOD

32 "Now search all of history, from the time God created people on the earth until now, and search from one end of the heavens to the other. Has anything as great as this ever been seen or heard before? 33 Has any nation ever heard the voice of God* speaking from fire—as you did—and survived? 34 Has any other god dared to take a nation for himself out of another nation by means of trials, miraculous signs, wonders, war, a strong hand, a powerful arm, and terrifying acts? Yet that is what the LORD your God did for you in Egypt, right before your eyes.

35 "He showed you these things so you would know that the LORD is God and there is no other. 36 He let you hear His voice from heaven so He could instruct you. He let you see His great fire here on earth so He could speak to you from it. 37 Because He loved your ancestors, He chose to bless their descendants, and He personally brought you out of Egypt with a great display of power. 38 He drove out nations far greater than you, so He could bring you in and give you their land as your special possession, as it is today.

39 "So remember this and keep it firmly in mind: The LORD is God both in heaven and on earth, and there is no other. 40 If you obey all the decrees and commands I am giving you today, all will be well with you and your children. I am giving you these instructions so you will enjoy a long life in the land the LORD your God is giving you for all time."

EASTERN CITIES OF REFUGE

41 Then Moses set apart three cities of refuge east of the Jordan River. 42 Anyone who killed another person unintentionally, without previous hostility, could flee there to live in safety. 43 These were the cities: Bezer on the wilderness plateau for the tribe of Reuben; Ramoth in Gilead for the tribe of Gad; Golan in Bashan for the tribe of Manasseh.

INTRODUCTION TO MOSES' SECOND ADDRESS

44 This is the body of instruction that Moses presented to the Israelites. 45 These are the laws, decrees, and regulations that Moses gave to the people of Israel when they left Egypt, 46 and as they camped in the valley near Beth-peor east of the Jordan River. (This land was formerly occupied by the Amorites under King Sihon, who ruled from Heshbon. But Moses and the Israelites destroyed him and his people when they came up from Egypt. 47 Israel took possession of his land and that of King Og of Bashan—the two Amorite

4:29 Deut 6:5; 10:12; 30:1-3; 2 Chr 15:4
4:31 Deut 31:6, 8; Josh 1:5; Heb 13:5
4:32 Gen 1:27
4:33 Exod 20:22
4:34 Exod 14:30; Ps 136:12
4:35 Exod 8:10; 9:14; 1 Sam 2:2; Mark 12:29; *Mark 12:32
4:36 Exod 19:9, 19; Neh 9:13
4:38 Num 32:4
4:40 Exod 23:26; Deut 4:2; 5:16, 29, 33; 32:47
4:41 Num 35:6; Deut 19:1-13

4:33 Or *voice of a god.*

▸ **GOD**
4:32 Discovering God through human history. Why did God choose to reveal Himself through human history? For God's covenant people in the Old Testament, it was "so you would know that the LORD is God and there is no other" (Deuteronomy 4:35). All history speaks of God's singular purpose to demonstrate that "The LORD is God both in heaven and on earth, and there is no other" (Deuteronomy 4:39). Is your heart singularly devoted to Him? Or do false gods distract you from Him? (***See God***> *God's Attributes> Sovereign> He is the only Sovereign,* TopicGuide page A17.)

4:34 This single verse contains a sweeping summary of God's providential guidance and protection for Israel. The crossing of the Red Sea (Exodus 13–15), the provision of quail and manna (Exodus 16; Numbers 11), water from the rock (Numbers 20:1-13), and the cloud by day and the pillar of fire by night—all examples of God's care before the Israelite's very eyes.

4:41-43 Forty-eight cities were set aside as Levitical cities. Scattered throughout the 12 tribes and their allotments of land, 13 cities (including the cities of refuge) were allotted to the descendants of Aaron, the priests; the remaining cities were allotted to the other descendants of Levi. Three cities of refuge were located on the east side of the Jordan River.

4:48 Deut 2:35-36 kings east of the Jordan. 48So Israel conquered the entire area from Aroer at the edge of
the Arnon Gorge all the way to Mount Sirion,* also called Mount Hermon. 49And they con-
quered the eastern bank of the Jordan River as far south as the Dead Sea,* below the
slopes of Pisgah.)

TEN COMMANDMENTS FOR THE COVENANT COMMUNITY

5 Moses called all the people of Israel together and said, "Listen carefully, Israel. Hear the
decrees and regulations I am giving you today, so you may learn them and obey them!
5:2 2"The LORD our God made a covenant with us at Mount Sinai.* 3The LORD did not make
Exod 19:5 this covenant with our ancestors, but with all of us who are alive today. 4At the mountain
Mal 4:4 5:4 the LORD spoke to you face to face from the heart of the fire. 5I stood as an intermediary
Num 14:14 between you and the LORD, for you were afraid of the fire and did not want to approach the
5:5 mountain. He spoke to me, and I passed His words on to you. This is what He said:
Exod 19:16, 25 6"I am the LORD your God, who rescued you from the land of Egypt, the place of your
5:6-21 //Exod 20:2-17 slavery.
5:7 7"You must not have any other god but Me.
Exod 20:3 8"You must not make for yourself an idol of any kind, or an image of anything in the
5:8 heavens or on the earth or in the sea. 9You must not bow down to them or worship
Exod 20:4 them, for I, the LORD your God, am a jealous God who will not tolerate your affection
Lev 26:1 Deut 4:16-17 for any other gods. I lay the sins of the parents upon their children; the entire family
5:9 is affected—even children in the third and fourth generations of those who reject Me.
Exod 34:7, 14 10But I lavish unfailing love for a thousand generations on those* who love Me and
obey My commands.
5:11 11"You must not misuse the name of the LORD your God. The LORD will not let you go
Deut 6:13; 10:20 Matt 5:33 unpunished if you misuse His name.
5:12 12"Observe the Sabbath day by keeping it holy, as the LORD your God has commanded
Exod 20:8-11 you. 13You have six days each week for your ordinary work, 14but the seventh day is
a Sabbath day of rest dedicated to the LORD your God. On that day no one in your
household may do any work. This includes you, your sons and daughters, your male
5:15 and female servants, your oxen and donkeys and other livestock, and any foreigners
Exod 20:11 living among you. All your male and female servants must rest as you do. 15Remem-
Deut 15:15; 16:12 ber that you were once slaves in Egypt, but the LORD your God brought you out with

4:48 As in Syriac version (see also 3:9); Hebrew reads *Mount Sion.* **4:49** Hebrew *took the Arabah on the east side of the Jordan as far as the sea of the Arabah.* **5:2** Hebrew *Horeb,* another name for Sinai. **5:10** Hebrew *for thousands of those.*

▸ HOLINESS
5:1 The place of preaching. God uses preaching as one of His main ways of teaching His people. This public declaration of the law was a restatement of the Ten Commandments for the second generation of Israelites. Moses' teaching continues through chapter 26 and includes moral, ceremonial, and civil laws relating to life under the old covenant. For more information, see *Discovering God through His Law* on page 145. (***See Holiness****> Submission> Learning God's Word> Public teaching,* TopicGuide page A40.)

5:2-3 Mount Sinai was a sacred place for Israel. Located on the Sinai Peninsula between Egypt and Israel, God spoke to Moses out of the burning bush in this area. Later, when the whole nation had escaped from Egypt, they camped at Sinai, and Moses received instruction from God there, including the Ten Commandments. The commandments are being restated here.

5:12-14 The Jewish Sabbath begins Friday evening and ends Saturday evening. The word *Sabbath* means, in essence, "cease and desist." Honoring that Sabbath concept of rest was an example God set in the pattern of creation. By Jesus' day, countless extra rules surrounding the Sabbath had been formed. Rather than being "rest" as intended, the Sabbath became a burden to be performed.

▸ WORSHIP
5:12 Observe the Sabbath. Why keep the Sabbath? Not only is it a day commemorating God's satisfied rest after Creation (Genesis 2:2-3), it also reminds us of the freedom from human toil that comes through God's grace. Do you find value only in what your work produces, or do you find your greatest sense of accomplishment in your relationship to God? (***See Worship****> OT> Festivals> Sabbath,* TopicGuide page A26.)

5:15 One difference between the first and second set of Ten Commandments occurs here. In Exodus 20 the basis for the Sabbath was Creation. Here the basis is to remember God's redeeming Israel from bondage. Thus, God's two great acts (Creation and redemption) are both remembered and celebrated in Sabbath.

His strong hand and powerful arm. That is why the LORD your God has commanded
you to rest on the Sabbath day.
16 "Honor your father and mother, as the LORD your God commanded you. Then you
will live a long, full life in the land the LORD your God is giving you.
17 "You must not murder.
18 "You must not commit adultery.
19 "You must not steal.
20 "You must not testify falsely against your neighbor.
21 "You must not covet your neighbor's wife. You must not covet your neighbor's house
or land, male or female servant, ox or donkey, or anything else that belongs to your
neighbor.

22 "The LORD spoke these words to all of you assembled there at the foot of the moun-
tain. He spoke with a loud voice from the heart of the fire, surrounded by clouds and deep
darkness. This was all He said at that time, and He wrote His words on two stone tablets
and gave them to me.

23 "But when you heard the voice from the heart of the darkness, while the mountain
was blazing with fire, all your tribal leaders and elders came to me. 24 They said, 'Look, the
LORD our God has shown us His glory and greatness, and we have heard His voice from
the heart of the fire. Today we have seen that God can speak to us humans, and yet we
live! 25 But now, why should we risk death again? If the LORD our God speaks to us again,
we will certainly die and be consumed by this awesome fire. 26 Can any living thing hear
the voice of the living God from the heart of the fire as we did and yet survive? 27 Go your-
self and listen to what the LORD our God says. Then come and tell us everything He tells
you, and we will listen and obey.'

28 "The LORD heard the request you made to me. And He said, 'I have heard what the
people said to you, and they are right. 29 Oh, that they would always have hearts like this,
that they might fear Me and obey all My commands! If they did, they and their descen-
dants would prosper forever. 30 Go and tell them, "Return to your tents." 31 But you stand
here with Me so I can give you all My commands, decrees, and regulations. You must
teach them to the people so they can obey them in the land I am giving them as their pos-
session.'"

32 So Moses told the people, "You must be careful to obey all the commands of the LORD
your God, following His instructions in every detail. 33 Stay on the path that the LORD your
God has commanded you to follow. Then you will live long and prosperous lives in the
land you are about to enter and occupy.

5:16
Exod 20:12; 21:17
*Matt 15:4; 19:9
*Mark 7:10; 10:9
*Luke 18:20
*Eph 6:2-3
Col 3:20

5:17
Exod 20:13
*Matt 5:21

5:18
Exod 20:14
*Mark 10:19
*Luke 18:20
*Rom 13:9
*Jas 2:11

5:19
Exod 20:15
*Matt 19:19
*Mark 10:19
*Luke 18:20
*Rom 13:9

5:20
*Matt 19:18
*Mark 10:19
*Luke 18:20

5:21
*Rom 7:7; 13:9

5:22
Exod 19:16-19
Deut 4:13

5:25
Exod 20:18-19
Deut 18:16
Heb 12:19

5:26
Exod 24:2

5:29
Deut 5:16, 33
Ps 81:13
Isa 48:18

5:32
Deut 17:20
Josh 1:7; 23:6

5:33
Exod 20:12

A CALL FOR WHOLEHEARTED COMMITMENT

6 "These are the commands, decrees, and regulations that the LORD your God com-
manded me to teach you. You must obey them in the land you are about to enter
and occupy, 2 and you and your children and grandchildren must fear the LORD your God
as long as you live. If you obey all His decrees and commands, you will enjoy a long life.

6:2
Deut 4:9; 10:12

5:22 The Ten Commandments were written twice. Unfortunately, Moses destroyed the first tablets in anger at the Israelites' rebellion. The next time the Commandments were written down, Moses spent another 40 days on Mount Sinai with God. These tablets were then placed in the Ark of the Covenant, the sacred chest that sat in the innermost chamber of the Tabernacle.

5:27 The promise made here was crucial for the Israelite nation: "We will listen and obey." God had promised their great ancestor, Abraham, a land, a people, and a place of honor. It was a covenant agreement in which God expected certain responses. He expected Abraham to move by faith to the land. He also expected him and his descendants to have single-hearted worship of the Lord and a deep commitment to obey Him. Time and again the people failed to exercise this obedience. The less faith and obedience they exhibited, the weaker they became as a nation.

THE NEW TESTAMENT TEACHES that although we receive Christ by faith, the Ten Commandments still play an important role in our lives. Paul, for example, encouraged young Timothy to live by the Old Testament Scriptures, which include the Ten Commandments (see 2 Timothy 3:16-17).

And Jesus said, "I did not come to abolish the law of Moses or the writings of the prophets. No, I came to accomplish their purpose . . . Not even the smallest detail of God's law will disappear until its purpose is achieved" (Matthew 5:17-18).

The New Testament references prove the importance of the Ten Commandments for our lives.

- First commandment—"You must not have any other god but Me": "You must love the LORD your God with all your heart, all your soul, and all your mind" (Matthew 22:37).
- Second commandment—"You must not make for yourself an idol of any kind. . . . You must not bow down to them or worship them": "For we live by believing and not by seeing" (2 Corinthians 5:7).
- Third commandment—"You must not misuse the name of the LORD your God": "What union can there be between God's temple and idols? For we are the temple of the living God" (2 Corinthians 6:16).
- Fourth commandment—"Observe the Sabbath day by keeping it holy": "On the first day of the week, we gathered with the local believers to share in the Lord's Supper" (Acts 20:7).
- Fifth commandment—"Honor your father and mother": "Children, always obey your parents, for this pleases the Lord" (Colossians 3:20).
- Sixth commandment—"You must not murder": "You have heard that our ancestors were told, 'You must not murder. If you commit murder, you are subject to judgment.' But I say, if you are even angry with someone, you are subject to judgment! If you call someone an idiot, you are in danger of being brought before the court. And if you curse someone, you are in danger of the fires of hell" (Matthew 5:21-22).
- Seventh commandment—"You must not commit adultery": "You have heard the commandment that says, 'You must not commit adultery.' But I say, anyone who even looks at a woman with lust has already committed adultery with her in his heart" (Matthew 5:27-28).
- Eighth commandment—"You must not steal": "For the commandments say, 'You must not commit adultery. You must not murder. You must not steal. You must not covet.' These—and other such commandments—are summed up in this one commandment: 'Love your neighbor as yourself'" (Romans 13:9).
- Ninth commandment—"You must not testify falsely against your neighbor": "So stop telling lies. Let us tell our neighbors the truth, for we are all parts of the same body" (Ephesians 4:25).
- Tenth commandment—"You must not covet": "I would never have known that coveting is wrong if the law had not said, 'You must not covet'" (Romans 7:7).

3Listen closely, Israel, and be careful to obey. Then all will go well with you, and you will **6:3**
have many children in the land flowing with milk and honey, just as the LORD, the God of Exod 3:8, 17 Deut 5:33
your ancestors, promised you. **6:4-5**
4"Listen, O Israel! The LORD is our God, the LORD alone.* 5And you must love the LORD Deut 4:35, 39
your God with all your heart, all your soul, and all your strength. 6And you must commit *Matt 22:37 *Mark 12:29-30
yourselves wholeheartedly to these commands that I am giving you today. 7Repeat them Luke 10:27
again and again to your children. Talk about them when you are at home and when you 1 Cor 8:4, 6
are on the road, when you are going to bed and when you are getting up. 8Tie them to **6:7**
your hands and wear them on your forehead as reminders. 9Write them on the doorposts Deut 4:9 Eph 6:4
of your house and on your gates. **6:8**
10"The LORD your God will soon bring you into the land He swore to give you when He Exod 13:9
made a vow to your ancestors Abraham, Isaac, and Jacob. It is a land with large, prosper- **6:9**
ous cities that you did not build. 11The houses will be richly stocked with goods you did Deut 11:20
not produce. You will draw water from cisterns you did not dig, and you will eat from vine- **6:10**
yards and olive trees you did not plant. When you have eaten your fill in this land, 12be Deut 9:1 Josh 24:13
careful not to forget the LORD, who rescued you from slavery in the land of Egypt. 13You **6:13**
must fear the LORD your God and serve Him. When you take an oath, you must use only *Matt 4:10
His name. Luke 4:8
14"You must not worship any of the gods of neighboring nations, 15for the LORD your **6:15**
God, who lives among you, is a jealous God. His anger will flare up against you, and He Deut 4:24; 5:9
will wipe you from the face of the earth. 16You must not test the LORD your God as you did **6:16**
when you complained at Massah. 17You must diligently obey the commands of the LORD Exod 17:7 *Matt 4:7 *Luke 4:12

6:4 Or *The LORD our God is one LORD;* or *The LORD our God, the LORD is one;* or *The LORD is our God, the LORD is one.*

6:4-9 These verses are called the *Shema* ("hear"). They are the fundamental creed of Jewish belief, an essential part of worship at synagogue. Religious Jews repeat these verses three times a day. Jesus referred to the *Shema* in Mark 12:29. A teacher of the law heard Jesus debating with the religious leadership and asked him which law of God was the most important (Mark 12:28-34). Jesus quoted from the *Shema*, then told the man that the second most important command was to "love your neighbor as yourself" (found in Leviticus 19:18).

6:8-9 These commands inspired a Jewish tradition involving Jewish males wearing strips of parchment around their head with Scriptures written on them. Later some portions of Scripture (usually Exodus 13:1-10, 11-16; and Deuteronomy 6:4-9; 11:13-21) were put in small boxes called *phylacteries,* which were strapped to the forehead and arms. Jesus complained that the phylacteries were large just so people would admire the wearer (Matthew 23:5).

▸ADOPTION

6:10 Stealing or reclaiming? In the last chapter, God said, "Do not steal." Yet God invited His people to enter Canaan and take everything from the people who lived there. Does this passage justify stealing? No, for this was the land God promised to their ancestors. Many might see this as an invasion, but God saw it as a claiming of the property that He had given them nearly 500 years earlier (see Genesis 12:1-3). Just as Israel left Egypt with gifts to recompense them for their slavery, Israel would collect bounty from those who had misused their ancestral home for generations. (***See Adoption****> With Christ> Heirs of God> Receive inheritance through faith and patience,* TopicGuide page A36.)

6:12 The Israelites did not enter Egypt as slaves but as an honored family of 70 members. Joseph, the favorite son of Jacob (Israel), had risen to power in Egypt and brought his father's family to settle there when famine struck. Joseph had prepared Egypt for this famine, so plenty of food was in storage. Over several centuries, Jacob's family grew into a nation. Then a king who did not know about or honor Joseph's contribution to Egypt during that famine rose to power. Fearing the sheer numbers of Israelites, the new king forced them into slavery and even attempted to slaughter a generation of baby boys in order to keep them in subjugation (Exodus 1). It was from such slavery that God rescued His people.

▸WORSHIP

6:13 The terror of God. There are different types of fear—a respectful fear of one's parent is not the same as the fear that comes from imminent danger. But the fear of God encouraged in the Scriptures appears to cover a broad spectrum of awe and dread, going painfully beyond what you might perceive to be its limits (Acts 5:11; 9:31). What does it look like to live a happy, healthy, holy life based on a broad fear of God? (***See Worship****> OT> Reverence> The fear of the Lord to be upon us,* TopicGuide page A29.)

▸WORSHIP

6:14 Many masters. How many "false gods" can you name? Consider the devious ones: materialism, technology, acceptance, power, or so many other ideas that command our allegiance. No one can serve two masters—it's hard enough to serve even one. Make it your goal to give your very best to God alone. (***See Worship****> OT> God's Supremacy> God alone was to be worshiped,* TopicGuide page A26.)

6:16 Not long after God rescued the Israelites from Egypt, they came to a place with no water, and they feared they would die in the desert. Rather than appeal to God, who redeemed them, they complained and quarreled. God instructed Moses to strike a rock to produce water. Moses named that place *Massah,* which means "test" (Exodus 17:1-7).

6:17 your God—all the laws and decrees He has given you. 18Do what is right and good in the
Deut 11:22 LORD's sight, so all will go well with you. Then you will enter and occupy the good land that
6:18 the LORD swore to give your ancestors. 19You will drive out all the enemies living in the
Deut 4:40 land, just as the LORD said you would.
6:20 Exod 13:8, 14 20"In the future your children will ask you, 'What is the meaning of these laws, decrees,
and regulations that the LORD our God has commanded us to obey?'
21"Then you must tell them, 'We were Pharaoh's slaves in Egypt, but the LORD brought
us out of Egypt with His strong hand. 22The LORD did miraculous signs and wonders be-
fore our eyes, dealing terrifying blows against Egypt and Pharaoh and all his people.
23He brought us out of Egypt so He could give us this land He had sworn to give our an-
6:24 Deut 6:17; 10:12 cestors. 24And the LORD our God commanded us to obey all these decrees and to fear
Him so He can continue to bless us and preserve our lives, as He has done to this day.
25For we will be counted as righteous when we obey all the commands the LORD our God
has given us.'

THE PRIVILEGE OF HOLINESS

7:1 **7** "When the LORD your God brings you into the land you are about to enter and oc-
Deut 20:17 cupy, He will clear away many nations ahead of you: the Hittites, Girgashites, Amo-
Acts 13:19 rites, Canaanites, Perizzites, Hivites, and Jebusites. These seven nations are greater and
more numerous than you. 2When the LORD your God hands these nations over to you
7:2 Exod 23:32 and you conquer them, you must completely destroy* them. Make no treaties with them
and show them no mercy. 3You must not intermarry with them. Do not let your daugh-
7:3 Josh 23:12 ters and sons marry their sons and daughters, 4for they will lead your children away
from Me to worship other gods. Then the anger of the LORD will burn against you, and He
7:5 Exod 23:24 will quickly destroy you. 5This is what you must do. You must break down their pagan
altars and shatter their sacred pillars. Cut down their Asherah poles and burn their idols.
7:6 Exod 19:5-6 6For you are a holy people, who belong to the LORD your God. Of all the people on earth,
Deut 14:2; 26:18 1 Pet 2:9 the LORD your God has chosen you to be His own special treasure.

7:2 The Hebrew term used here refers to the complete consecration of things or people to the LORD, either by destroying them or by giving them as an offering; also in 7:26.

6:25 Righteousness and obedience are connected. Paul the apostle wrote, "People are counted as righteous, not because of their work, but because of their faith in God who forgives sinners" (Romans 4:5). Yet faith produces obedience that honors God. In fact, obedience can be evidence of faith. The New Testament writer James wrote to the early church about the relationship between faith and obedience, saying, "faith by itself isn't enough. Unless it produces good deeds, it is dead and useless" (James 2:17).

7:2-3 The idea of completely destroying the people is expanded here to show complete separation from that which will defile. As the passage progresses, Israel is told "No treaties, no mercy, no marriage, no use of idols." They were to be separate (holy) for God alone.

▸ HOLINESS

7:3 Intermarriage. Does the Bible teach that races should be kept separate? Many foreigners already made up God's covenant people (Genesis 41:50-51; Exodus 23:9; Numbers 12:1), so this was not a command to pursue racial purity. God wanted them to pursue spiritual purity. In the New Testament, the apostle Paul instructed believers not to "team up with those who are unbelievers" (2 Corinthians 6:14) with the hope of saving God's people much heartache. Nevertheless, God also provides guidance for those who find themselves in spiritually troubled marriages (1 Corinthians 7; Ephesians 5:21-33; Hebrews 13:4). (***See Holiness****> Law and Grace> Law> Marriage,* TopicGuide page A41.)

7:5 Asherah was a feminine Canaanite god, the counterpart to Baal. The worship of Asherah was overtly sexual in nature. Wooden poles or pillars were made in her image. Israel continued to struggle against the worship of Asherah during the time of the judges and the monarchy in Israel (see for example, Judges 6:25-26; 1 Kings 15:9-14). The destruction of these poles was to be complete: "break down . . . shatter . . . cut down . . . and burn their idols."

▸ SALVATION

7:6 Sinful saints. How could God call these sinful people holy? They certainly don't appear to be holy—but, then, neither do we. In this case, the holiness of God's people was less associated with their moral position than with their *covenantal* position—they belonged to God, and that made them special, set apart, and valuable. Believers today are God's precious possessions, too. He cares for us, protects us, and positions us where we can do the good He wants to do through us. (***See Salvation****> Receiving> Results> Sanctification,* TopicGuide page A23.)

7 "The LORD did not set His heart on you and choose you because you were more nu-
merous than other nations, for you were the smallest of all nations! 8 Rather, it was simply
that the LORD loves you, and He was keeping the oath He had sworn to your ancestors.
That is why the LORD rescued you with such a strong hand from your slavery and from the
oppressive hand of Pharaoh, king of Egypt. 9 Understand, therefore, that the LORD your God
is indeed God. He is the faithful God who keeps His covenant for a thousand generations
and lavishes His unfailing love on those who love Him and obey His commands. 10 But He
does not hesitate to punish and destroy those who reject Him. 11 Therefore, you must
obey all these commands, decrees, and regulations I am giving you today.
12 "If you listen to these regulations and faithfully obey them, the LORD your God will
keep His covenant of unfailing love with you, as He promised with an oath to your ances-
tors. 13 He will love you and bless you, and He will give you many children. He will give fer-
tility to your land and your animals. When you arrive in the land He swore to give your
ancestors, you will have large harvests of grain, new wine, and olive oil, and great herds of
cattle, sheep, and goats. 14 You will be blessed above all the nations of the earth. None of
your men or women will be childless, and all your livestock will bear young. 15 And the
LORD will protect you from all sickness. He will not let you suffer from the terrible diseases
you knew in Egypt, but He will inflict them on all your enemies!
16 "You must destroy all the nations the LORD your God hands over to you. Show them
no mercy, and do not worship their gods, or they will trap you. 17 Perhaps you will think to
yourselves, 'How can we ever conquer these nations that are so much more powerful than
we are?' 18 But don't be afraid of them! Just remember what the LORD your God did to Pha-
raoh and to all the land of Egypt. 19 Remember the great terrors the LORD your God sent
against them. You saw it all with your own eyes! And remember the miraculous signs and
wonders, and the strong hand and powerful arm with which He brought you out of Egypt.

7:7 Deut 4:37
7:9 Exod 20:6; Deut 4:39; 5:9-10; 1 Cor 1:9; 1 Thes 5:24; 2 Tim 2:13
7:12 Lev 26:3; Deut 28:1
7:13 Lev 26:9; Deut 28:4; 30:5-6
7:14 Exod 23:26
7:15 Exod 15:26; 23:26
7:16 Exod 23:32; Deut 7:2
7:17 Num 33:53
7:18 Num 14:9; Deut 1:21, 29
7:19 Deut 4:34

▸ BIBLE
7:7-8 Discovering God in His promises to Israel. God had sworn to bring His people into the lovely land promised to their father Abraham. No amount of human sin or weakness could stop God from fulfilling that promise. Yet other promises or covenants God made with Israel were contingent upon obedience (Deuteronomy 28:45-48). God's New Covenant is also contingent upon faith and obedience—of Christ! Because Christ will never fail, we can trust God to never cast us aside, even in our greatest moments of doubt. (*See Bible> Uniqueness> Inspired> His promises never fail,* TopicGuide page A10.)

7:8 The oath God swore was a covenant with Abraham, the progenitor of the Israelites (Genesis 17:5-9). God promised Abraham a land, a people, and a place of honor.

7:9-10 These verses are a restatement of God's self-description of His character first seen in Exodus 34:6-7. Similar wording is used numerous times throughout the Old Testament to describe God's gracious nature and action.

BECAUSE GOD IS FAITHFUL

I will trust Him to always keep His promises.

The LORD your God is indeed God. He is the faithful God who keeps His covenant for a thousand generations.

DEUTERONOMY 7:9

FOR THE NEXT *GOD IS FAITHFUL* FEATURE SEE PAGE 1491.

7:20 The LORD your God will use this same power against all the people you fear. [20]And then
Exod 23:28 the LORD your God will send terror* to drive out the few survivors still hiding from you!
Josh 24:12 [21]"No, do not be afraid of those nations, for the LORD your God is among you, and He is
7:21 Exod 29:45 a great and awesome God. [22]The LORD your God will drive those nations out ahead of you
7:22 little by little. You will not clear them away all at once, otherwise the wild animals would
Exod 23:28-30 multiply too quickly for you. [23]But the LORD your God will hand them over to you. He will
7:24 throw them into complete confusion until they are destroyed. [24]He will put their kings in
Deut 11:25 your power, and you will erase their names from the face of the earth. No one will be able
Josh 1:5; 10:8; 23:9 to stand against you, and you will destroy them all.
7:25 Deut 7:2; 12:3 [25]"You must burn their idols in fire, and you must not covet the silver or gold that covers
Josh 7:1, 21 them. You must not take it or it will become a trap to you, for it is detestable to the LORD
7:26 your God. [26]Do not bring any detestable objects into your home, for then you will be de-
Lev 27:28-29 stroyed, just like them. You must utterly detest such things, for they are set apart for de-
struction.

A CALL TO REMEMBER AND OBEY

8:1 **8** "Be careful to obey all the commands I am giving you today. Then you will live and
Lev 26:3 Deut 4:1; 7:11 multiply, and you will enter and occupy the land the LORD swore to give your ances-
8:2 tors. [2]Remember how the LORD your God led you through the wilderness for these forty
Exod 15:25 years, humbling you and testing you to prove your character, and to find out whether or
2 Chr 32:31 not you would obey His commands. [3]Yes, He humbled you by letting you go hungry and
8:3 Ps 78:24 then feeding you with manna, a food previously unknown to you and your ancestors. He
*Matt 4:4 did it to teach you that people do not live by bread alone; rather, we live by every word
*Luke 4:4 that comes from the mouth of the LORD. [4]For all these forty years your clothes didn't wear
8:4 out, and your feet didn't blister or swell. [5]Think about it: Just as a parent disciplines a child,
Deut 29:5 Neh 9:21 the LORD your God disciplines you for your own good.
8:5 [6]"So obey the commands of the LORD your God by walking in His ways and fearing Him.
Prov 3:11-12 [7]For the LORD your God is bringing you into a good land of flowing streams and pools of
Heb 12:6 water, with fountains and springs that gush out in the valleys and hills. [8]It is a land of
8:7 Deut 11:10-12 wheat and barley; of grapevines, fig trees, and pomegranates; of olive oil and honey. [9]It is
Jer 2:7 a land where food is plentiful and nothing is lacking. It is a land where iron is as common
8:8 as stone, and copper is abundant in the hills. [10]When you have eaten your fill, be sure to
Deut 32:13 praise the LORD your God for the good land He has given you.
8:11 [11]"But that is the time to be careful! Beware that in your plenty you do not forget the
Deut 4:9 LORD your God and disobey His commands, regulations, and decrees that I am giving you

7:20 Often rendered *the hornet*. The meaning of the Hebrew is uncertain.

▸ WORSHIP
7:26 Dangerous possessions. As Israel conquered the land of Canaan, they came across personal possessions that they were generally allowed to keep. But they would also find idols made of gold and silver. They were given clear instructions on how to deal with these valuable idols: burn them. We have decisions to make on what to bring into our homes, too. Do some of your possessions harm you or your family? Make an inventory of the things in your home that might be spiritually harmful and make a plan to get rid of them. (***See Worship***> *OT> Reverence> Put away idols,* TopicGuide page A28.)

▸ ADOPTION
8:5 Disciplined by God. Have you ever had the feeling God was giving you a "smack on the hand"? The writer of Hebrews said, "The LORD disciplines those He loves" (Hebrews 12:6). God's love and God's discipline are connected, for He says, "I am the one who corrects and disciplines everyone I love" (see, for example, Job 5:17-27). Be encouraged—if you sense God is rooting out sin in your life through negative consequences, it is a sign of His passion for your best and for His glory! (***See Adoption***> *With Christ> Children of God> God disciplines His children,* TopicGuide page A36.)

8:7-9 These verses describe well the nature of the land Israel was approaching. Its geography is surprisingly varied, containing a wide variety of natural resources, and land and climate suitable for many different types of crops.

8:9 Archaeological findings have uncovered remnants of copper and bronze smelting works in the general area of Israel, though most metals were produced to the west (in Philistia) and to the south (near Timna). Under David's rule, Edom, with its rich copper and iron deposits, was conquered (2 Samuel 8:13-14). David's military faithfulness was the means that God used to fulfill His promises.

today. [12]For when you have become full and prosperous and have built fine homes to live
in, [13]and when your flocks and herds have become very large and your silver and gold
have multiplied along with everything else, be careful! [14]Do not become proud at that
time and forget the LORD your God, who rescued you from slavery in the land of Egypt.
[15]Do not forget that He led you through the great and terrifying wilderness with its poison-
ous snakes and scorpions, where it was so hot and dry. He gave you water from the rock!
[16]He fed you with manna in the wilderness, a food unknown to your ancestors. He did this
to humble you and test you for your own good. [17]He did all this so you would never say to
yourself, 'I have achieved this wealth with my own strength and energy.' [18]Remember the
LORD your God. He is the One who gives you power to be successful, in order to fulfill the
covenant He confirmed to your ancestors with an oath.
[19]"But I assure you of this: If you ever forget the LORD your God and follow other gods,
worshiping and bowing down to them, you will certainly be destroyed. [20]Just as the LORD
has destroyed other nations in your path, you also will be destroyed if you refuse to obey
the LORD your God.

8:12 Prov 30:9 Hos 13:6
8:15 Exod 17:6 Num 20:11; 21:6 Deut 1:19-21; 32:13 Pss 78:15; 114:8
8:16 Exod 16:15 Deut 8:2 John 6:30-31
8:18 Prov 10:22 Hos 2:8
8:19 Deut 4:26; 30:18
8:20 Ezek 5:15-17

8:15 The mention of poisonous snakes may have caused the people to remember when Israel grumbled and God sent snakes as a judgment against their rebellion (see Numbers 21:4-9).

8:16 This previously unknown food source solved Israel's predicament in the wilderness. Described as pale yellow in color, manna could be ground into flour and made into fried cakes (see Numbers 11). Among Israel's most sacred religious relics kept in the Ark of the Covenant was a container of manna (Hebrews 9:4). The people eventually became tired of the manna and quite ungrateful, but still it was evidence of God's gracious provision and protection.

8:18-19 The covenant promises of God involve blessings of material prosperity. But ironically, God warns that these very blessings can become a source of temptation toward self-reliance and away from spiritual dependence upon God.

▶ **GOD**
8:19 Destroyed by God. One theme of the covenant that God made with Israel was that if Israel broke their part of the covenant, there would be covenant sanctions (Deuteronomy 11:27-28). The entire ministry of the prophets was to announce God's sanctions against unfaithful Israel (see, for example, Isaiah 6; Ezekiel 2; Malachi 1), as well as the great hope offered if they would repent (for example, Isaiah 55 and Ezekiel 37). Today, God warns people that it is not enough merely to go to church or be religious. True Christianity is walking with God by faith in the power of the Holy Spirit. To live any other way is to court disaster (1 Corinthians 10:11-12; Hebrews 6:1-4). (***See God***> *God's Attributes*> *Just*> *All God's ways are righteous and deserve praise,* TopicGuide page A16.)

8:20 The coming centuries of Israel's history testified to the truth of this warning of disaster. After generations of disobedience under various kings, the nation fell and its people were

MY RESPONSE TO GOD

Our Daily Bread

DEUTERONOMY 8:3

How do you feel when you miss a meal? Does your stomach growl? If you go for a long time without eating, you may even start shaking and feel fatigued, your energy drained. However, God says that we do not live on bread alone, but real life comes by feeding on every word that comes from Him (Deuteronomy 8:3; Matthew 4:4).

The Bible is the daily bread we consume to be spiritually energized. Peter challenges us to crave spiritual food, as newborn babies crave milk (1 Peter 2:2). By consuming spiritual food we can grow in our faith. As we grow, we trust more deeply so that we can taste and see that the Lord is good (Psalm 34:8). We don't often skip breakfast, lunch, and dinner, but it is easy to neglect spending time in God's Word because we are busy with other things. When we let such busyness overrun us and we neglect reading God's Word, it is difficult to grow spiritually. So be careful not to starve yourself while you have such rich spiritual food at hand. Keep growing with a steady diet of precious truths from God.

VICTORY BY GOD'S GRACE

9:1 **9** "Listen, O Israel! Today you are about to cross the Jordan River to take over the land
Deut 11:23 belonging to nations much greater and more powerful than you. They live in cities
with walls that reach to the sky! 2The people are strong and tall—descendants of the fa-
9:3 Deut 4:24 mous Anakite giants. You've heard the saying, 'Who can stand up to the Anakites?' 3But
Heb 12:29 recognize today that the LORD your God is the One who will cross over ahead of you like a
devouring fire to destroy them. He will subdue them so that you will quickly conquer them
and drive them out, just as the LORD has promised.
9:4 Lev 18:23-30 4"After the LORD your God has done this for you, don't say in your hearts, 'The LORD has
Deut 7:24; 12:31; given us this land because we are such good people!' No, it is because of the wickedness
18:9-14 of the other nations that He is pushing them out of your way. 5It is not because you are so
good or have such integrity that you are about to occupy their land. The LORD your God
will drive these nations out ahead of you only because of their wickedness, and to fulfill
9:6 the oath He swore to your ancestors Abraham, Isaac, and Jacob. 6You must recognize that
Deut 9:13-14; 10:16; the LORD your God is not giving you this good land because you are good, for you are
31:27 not—you are a stubborn people.

REMEMBERING THE GOLD CALF

9:7 7"Remember and never forget how angry you made the LORD your God out in the
Exod 14:11 Num 14:20-22 wilderness. From the day you left Egypt until now, you have been constantly rebelling
9:8 against Him. 8Even at Mount Sinai* you made the LORD so angry He was ready to destroy
Exod 32:7 you. 9This happened when I was on the mountain receiving the tablets of stone inscribed
Ps 106:19-20 with the words of the covenant that the LORD had made with you. I was there for forty days
9:9 Exod 24:18 and forty nights, and all that time I ate no food and drank no water. 10The LORD gave me
Deut 9:18 the two tablets on which God had written with His own finger all the words He had spoken
to you from the heart of the fire when you were assembled at the mountain.
11"At the end of the forty days and nights, the LORD handed me the two stone tablets in-
9:12 Exod 32:7-8 scribed with the words of the covenant. 12Then the LORD said to me, 'Get up! Go down im-
mediately, for the people you brought out of Egypt have corrupted themselves. How
quickly they have turned away from the way I commanded them to live! They have
melted gold and made an idol for themselves!'
9:13 Exod 32:9 13"The LORD also said to me, 'I have seen how stubborn and rebellious these people are.
14Leave Me alone so I may destroy them and erase their name from under heaven. Then I
will make a mighty nation of your descendants, a nation larger and more powerful than
they are.'
9:15 Exod 32:15 15"So while the mountain was blazing with fire I turned and came down, holding in my
9:16 Exod 32:19 hands the two stone tablets inscribed with the terms of the covenant. 16There below me I

9:8 Hebrew *Horeb*, another name for Sinai.

exiled to foreign lands. Though God never forgot Israel or His covenant with Abraham, Israel spent a significant portion of her history in subjugation to other powers. At the time of Daniel, that power was Babylon, and then Persia, and Greece. At the time of Christ, it was Rome.

9:2-3 The phrase, "You've heard the saying" tells us that the reputation of the Anakites had preceded them, and they were fearsome. The response to this fear is in the phrase "The LORD your God is the one who will cross over ahead of you." The God of Israel was greater than any giant they might meet.

▶ GOD

9:5 Misplaced pride. Pride is a constant temptation for most people. But as we view ourselves from God's perspective, it becomes apparent that our pride is misplaced. All human goodness has its roots in the nature of God, not our own deeds (2 Peter 1:3). Every moral victory comes by God's grace. Remember that any righteousness you may think you have is still insufficient to merit favor with God. (***See God***> *Relationship> Barriers> Pride,* TopicGuide page A14.)

9:6 Note how emphatic this verse is, repeating and driving home the truth that Israel's election by God is not the result of their own spiritual strength—in fact their primary quality seems to be the exact opposite: stubbornness.

could see that you had sinned against the LORD your God. You had melted gold and made
a calf idol for yourselves. How quickly you had turned away from the path the LORD had
commanded you to follow! 17So I took the stone tablets and threw them to the ground,
smashing them before your eyes.
18"Then, as before, I threw myself down before the LORD for forty days and nights. I ate 9:18 Exod 34:8-9, 28
no bread and drank no water because of the great sin you had committed by doing what Deut 9:9; 10:10
the LORD hated, provoking Him to anger. 19I feared that the furious anger of the LORD, 9:19
which turned Him against you, would drive Him to destroy you. But again He listened to Exod 32:10-11
me. 20The LORD was so angry with Aaron that He wanted to destroy him, too. But I prayed *Heb 12:21
for Aaron, and the LORD spared him. 21I took your sin—the calf you had made—and I 9:21 Exod 32:20
melted it down in the fire and ground it into fine dust. Then I threw the dust into the
stream that flows down the mountain.
22"You also made the LORD angry at Taberah,* Massah,* and Kibroth-hattaavah.* 23And 9:22 Exod 17:7
at Kadesh-barnea the LORD sent you out with this command: 'Go up and take over the land Num 11:3, 34
I have given you.' But you rebelled against the command of the LORD your God and re-
fused to put your trust in Him or obey Him. 24Yes, you have been rebelling against the 9:24
LORD as long as I have known you. Exod 32:9 Deut 9:7; 31:27
25"That is why I threw myself down before the LORD for forty days and nights—for the 9:25
LORD said He would destroy you. 26I prayed to the LORD and said, 'O Sovereign LORD, do Deut 9:18
not destroy them. They are Your own people. They are Your special possession, whom 9:26
You redeemed from Egypt by Your mighty power and Your strong hand. 27Please over- Exod 32:11-13
look the stubbornness and the awful sin of these people, and remember instead Your 9:27
servants Abraham, Isaac, and Jacob. 28If You destroy these people, the Egyptians will Exod 32:9
say, "The Israelites died because the LORD wasn't able to bring them to the land He had
promised to give them." Or they might say, "He destroyed them because He hated them;
He deliberately took them into the wilderness to slaughter them." 29But they are Your 9:29
people and Your special possession, whom You brought out of Egypt by Your great Deut 4:34
strength and powerful arm.'

9:22a *Taberah* means "place of burning." See Num 11:1-3. 9:22b *Massah* means "place of testing." See Exod 17:1-7.
9:22c *Kibroth-hattaavah* means "graves of craving." See Num 11:31-34.

▶ WORSHIP

9:18 Sustained by God. How long have you gone without food and water? Fasting is commended in Scripture, but in Moses' case, this seems to be a supernatural fast, enabled by God so Moses would be better able to focus on interceding for Israel. This example helps establish the general rule that God has ordained that fasting can accompany the prayers of God's people. (***See Worship****> OT> Fasting and Prayer> Fasting> Occasions> Fasting while seeking forgiveness,* TopicGuide page A26.)

9:19 Moses pled for the Israelites time and time again. When the people approached the border to the Promised Land but were fearful to enter, Moses begged God to not destroy them (Numbers 14:15-19). When a Levite named Korah challenged the authority of Aaron and Moses, Moses pleaded with God to not destroy the whole nation because of this one man (Numbers 16:22). In this way Moses was an intercessor for his people as Jesus now is for Christians (see Hebrews 7:24-25).

9:20 Moses gives information here not included in the story's original account (Exodus 32). In the Exodus account, while Moses was on the mountain the people talked Aaron into making an idol—the gold calf, related to the gods of Egypt. They then worshiped the idol until they were in a frenzy. When confronted, Aaron blamed the people. Only here do we learn that God was angry with Aaron. This was not Aaron's only error in leadership. Later he and Miriam (Moses' and Aaron's sister) challenged Moses' leadership, resulting in Miriam's leprosy (Numbers 12).

9:22-24 After a short list of several instances of rebelliousness, Moses concludes that rebellion is not just an occasional action of Israel; it seems to be part of the nation's nature.

9:27 Moses appealed not to Israel's goodness or ability to please God, but to God's promise upon which the nation was founded. The nation's whole identity was based on that promise to bring forth from Abraham a nation and to give his descendants a land in which they could settle (Genesis 15). That promise was then passed down to Isaac, to Jacob, and to Israel through Moses. Moses appealed to God's own faithfulness to save His people from their own lack of faith and their stubborn rebellion.

A NEW COPY OF THE COVENANT

10 "At that time the LORD said to me, 'Chisel out two stone tablets like the first ones.
Also make a wooden Ark—a sacred chest to store them in. Come up to Me on the
mountain, 2 and I will write on the tablets the same words that were on the ones you
smashed. Then place the tablets in the Ark.'
3 "So I made an Ark of acacia wood and cut two stone tablets like the first two. Then I
went up the mountain with the tablets in my hand. 4 Once again the LORD wrote the Ten
Commandments* on the tablets and gave them to me. They were the same words the
LORD had spoken to you from the heart of the fire on the day you were assembled at the
foot of the mountain. 5 Then I turned and came down the mountain and placed the tablets
in the Ark of the Covenant, which I had made, just as the LORD commanded me. And the
tablets are still there in the Ark."
6 (The people of Israel set out from the wells of the people of Jaakan* and traveled to
Moserah, where Aaron died and was buried. His son Eleazar ministered as high priest in
his place. 7 Then they journeyed to Gudgodah, and from there to Jotbathah, a land with
many brooks and streams. 8 At that time the LORD set apart the tribe of Levi to carry the Ark
of the LORD's Covenant, and to stand before the LORD as His ministers, and to pronounce
blessings in His name. These are their duties to this day. 9 That is why the Levites have no
share of property or possession of land among the other Israelite tribes. The LORD Himself
is their special possession, as the LORD your God told them.)
10 "As for me, I stayed on the mountain in the LORD's presence for forty days and nights,
as I had done the first time. And once again the LORD listened to my pleas and agreed not
to destroy you. 11 Then the LORD said to me, 'Get up and resume the journey, and lead the
people to the land I swore to give to their ancestors, so they may take possession of it.'

A CALL TO LOVE AND OBEDIENCE

12 "And now, Israel, what does the LORD your God require of you? He requires only that you
fear the LORD your God, and live in a way that pleases Him, and love Him and serve Him
with all your heart and soul. 13 And you must always obey the LORD's commands and de-
crees that I am giving you today for your own good.
14 "Look, the highest heavens and the earth and everything in it all belong to the LORD
your God. 15 Yet the LORD chose your ancestors as the objects of His love. And He chose

10:1 Exod 25:10; 34:1
10:2 Exod 25:16; Deut 4:13
10:3 Exod 34:4; 37:1
10:4 Exod 34:28; Deut 4:13
10:5 Exod 40:20
10:6 Num 20:25-26
10:8 Num 3:6; 18:1; Deut 18:5; 21:5; 31:9
10:9 Num 18:20, 24; Deut 18:2; Ezek 44:28
10:10 Deut 9:18
10:12 Deut 6:5; Mic 6:8
10:14 1 Kgs 8:27; Pss 68:33; 115:16

10:4 Hebrew *the ten words.* **10:6** Or *set out from Beeroth of Bene-jaakan.*

10:1-5 The Ark of the Covenant was a wooden chest made to strict specifications (see Exodus 25:10-22). This chest rested in the most holy chamber of the Tabernacle and later in the Temple in Jerusalem. The special lid of the Ark was called the *atonement cover*, or in other translations, *mercy seat.* It both represents God's throne and points us forward to the sacrifice of Christ that gives us peace with God (Romans 5).

▶ PURPOSE

10:4 Contracts and covenants. Today when a contract is signed, both parties get a copy. In the Ancient Near East, this type of covenant demanded the same administrative action. While many people imagine the first five commandments "written" on one tablet and the next five commandments on the other, more probably each tablet included a complete copy of the terms of the covenant. God has made certain that we have access to His holy Word—the terms of His covenant with us are not hidden. All the blessings and responsibilities of God's people can be found in His Word. Be sure not to neglect your copy. (***See Purpose***> *God's Deeds> Covenants> Covenant at Sinai,* TopicGuide page A54.)

10:6 Eleazar was Aaron's third son. He was "the chief administrator over all the Levites, with special responsibility for the oversight of the sanctuary" (Numbers 3:32). Eleazar's two older brothers, Nadab and Abihu, were killed when they offered incense in an inappropriate manner (Leviticus 10). This incident left Eleazar and his younger brother Ithamar as the remaining priests in Aaron's bloodline.

10:8-9 These two verses give a brief summary of the special place the Levites held in God's order for Israel as a nation. Though Aaron's descendants would minister in the Tabernacle and Temple, other related families held other responsibilities, detailed in Numbers 3.

10:12-16 These verses summarize God's requirements, echoed centuries later by the prophet Micah: "to do what is right, to love mercy, and to walk humbly with your God" (Micah 6:8). Note especially the action verbs in God's requirements: Fear God, live by His will, love Him, worship Him, obey Him. Then later, change your heart and stop being stubborn. Much later, Jesus made it even simpler: Love God wholly and completely, and love others as we love ourselves (Mark 12:18-31).

you, their descendants, above all other nations, as is evident today. [16]Therefore, change
your hearts* and stop being stubborn.
[17]"For the LORD your God is the God of gods and Lord of lords. He is the great God, the
mighty and awesome God, who shows no partiality and cannot be bribed. [18]He ensures
that orphans and widows receive justice. He shows love to the foreigners living among
you and gives them food and clothing. [19]So you, too, must show love to foreigners, for
you yourselves were once foreigners in the land of Egypt. [20]You must fear the LORD your
God and worship Him and cling to Him. Your oaths must be in His name alone. [21]He alone
is your God, the only One who is worthy of your praise, the One who has done these
mighty miracles that you have seen with your own eyes. [22]When your ancestors went
down into Egypt, there were only seventy of them. But now the LORD your God has made
you as numerous as the stars in the sky!

11 "You must love the LORD your God and obey all His requirements, decrees, regula-
tions, and commands. [2]Keep in mind that I am not talking now to your children,
who have never experienced the discipline of the LORD your God or seen His greatness
and His strong hand and powerful arm. [3]They didn't see the miraculous signs and won-
ders He performed in Egypt against Pharaoh and all his land. [4]They didn't see what the
LORD did to the armies of Egypt and to their horses and chariots—how He drowned them in
the Red Sea* as they were chasing you. He destroyed them, and they have not recovered
to this very day!
[5]"Your children didn't see how the LORD cared for you in the wilderness until you ar-
rived here. [6]They didn't see what He did to Dathan and Abiram (the sons of Eliab, a de-
scendant of Reuben) when the earth opened its mouth in the Israelite camp and
swallowed them, along with their households and tents and every living thing that be-
longed to them. [7]But you have seen the LORD perform all these mighty deeds with your
own eyes!

THE BLESSINGS OF OBEDIENCE

[8]"Therefore, be careful to obey every command I am giving you today, so you may have
strength to go in and take over the land you are about to enter. [9]If you obey, you will en-
joy a long life in the land the LORD swore to give to your ancestors and to you, their de-
scendants—a land flowing with milk and honey! [10]For the land you are about to enter and

10:16 Lev 26:41-42; Jer 4:4
10:18 Exod 22:22-24; Pss 68:5; 103:6
10:19 Exod 22:21; Lev 19:34
10:21 Exod 15:2; Ps 109:1
10:22 Gen 46:27; Deut 1:10
11:1 Lev 18:29-30; Deut 6:5-6; 10:12-13
11:2 Deut 5:24
11:4 Exod 14:28; 15:4; Deut 1:40
11:6 Num 16:31; 26:10-11
11:8 Deut 31:6-7, 23; Josh 1:6-7
11:9 Deut 4:40; 5:33; 9:5; Prov 10:27

10:16 Hebrew *circumcise the foreskin of your hearts.* 11:4 Hebrew *sea of reeds.*

10:20 In the ancient world, it was common to invoke the name of deities in oaths. Today we might say, "As God is my witness" or "in the name of God." In the Old Testament world, however, oaths were taken much more seriously than they often are today. A person who made an oath put his life on the line that the oath would be fulfilled. Even more serious was an oath sworn in God's name or on His reputation. To fail to fulfill the oath or take it seriously was an abuse of God's name. How much more offensive to God it would be to take an oath in the name of an idol.

10:22 God used the final phrase of this verse ("as numerous as the stars in the sky") when promising Abraham many heirs to the covenant. At the time, the covenant community was Abraham and Sarah (see Genesis 15:6). Later, Jacob's family went to Egypt with 70 people. Now, several centuries later, Israel has grown into a great nation, fulfilling the exact promise God made to Abraham.

11:2-4 This group would have seen a whole generation of older adults die before coming to the Promised Land. By the time Moses gave this speech, these "children of the Exodus" had grown to become the tribal leaders and soldiers with children of their own, many of whom had not witnessed the earliest miracles.

11:6 Dathan and Abiram had allied with Korah, an angry and jealous Levite, to rebel against Moses' leadership (Numbers 16). Korah wanted a share of Moses' decision-making power. Dathan and Abiram complained that Moses had not done what he promised—they had not entered the Promised Land. In the end, Korah, Dathan, Abiram, and their families and followers were all killed by God's judgment. Moses' authority and God's power were confirmed through this event.

▸ PURPOSE

11:7 God's mighty deeds. Have you ever witnessed God's supernatural power? How did that impact you? It may have been profound, but the blessing of seeing God at work is nothing compared with the blessing of the gift of faith (John 20:29). Rejoice in your changed life and the spiritual blessings God has given you, and look forward to the day when your faith will become sight. (***See Purpose*****> *God's Deeds> Special Acts,* TopicGuide page A52.)

take over is not like the land of Egypt from which you came, where you planted your seed
11:11 and made irrigation ditches with your foot as in a vegetable garden. 11 Rather, the land
Deut 8:7-9 you will soon take over is a land of hills and valleys with plenty of rain—12 a land that the
LORD your God cares for. He watches over it through each season of the year!
11:13 Deut 4:29; 6:17; 13 "If you carefully obey all the commands I am giving you today, and if you love the
10:12 LORD your God and serve Him with all your heart and soul, 14 then He will send the rains in
11:14 their proper seasons—the early and late rains—so you can bring in your harvests of grain,
Lev 26:4-5 Deut 28:12 new wine, and olive oil. 15 He will give you lush pastureland for your livestock, and you
11:15 yourselves will have all you want to eat.
Deut 6:10-12 16 "But be careful. Don't let your heart be deceived so that you turn away from the LORD
11:16 and serve and worship other gods. 17 If you do, the LORD's anger will burn against you. He
Deut 8:19; 29:18 will shut up the sky and hold back the rain, and the ground will fail to produce its harvests.
11:17 Then you will quickly die in that good land the LORD is giving you.
Deut 4:26; 28:24 18 "So commit yourselves wholeheartedly to these words of mine. Tie them to your
11:18 Exod 13:9, 16 hands and wear them on your forehead as reminders. 19 Teach them to your children. Talk
11:19 about them when you are at home and when you are on the road, when you are going to
Deut 4:9; 6:7 bed and when you are getting up. 20 Write them on the doorposts of your house and on
11:22 your gates, 21 so that as long as the sky remains above the earth, you and your children
Deut 6:17; 10:20 may flourish in the land the LORD swore to give your ancestors.
11:23 22 "Be careful to obey all these commands I am giving you. Show love to the LORD your
Deut 4:38; 7:1 God by walking in His ways and holding tightly to Him. 23 Then the LORD will drive out all
11:24 Gen 15:18 the nations ahead of you, though they are much greater and stronger than you, and you
Exod 23:31 will take over their land. 24 Wherever you set foot, that land will be yours. Your frontiers
Deut 1:7-8 will stretch from the wilderness in the south to Lebanon in the north, and from the Euphra-
Josh 1:3 tes River in the east to the Mediterranean Sea in the west.* 25 No one will be able to stand
11:25 Exod 23:27 against you, for the LORD your God will cause the people to fear and dread you, as He
Deut 7:24 promised, wherever you go in the whole land.
11:26 26 "Look, today I am giving you the choice between a blessing and a curse! 27 You will be
Deut 30:1, 15-20 blessed if you obey the commands of the LORD your God that I am giving you today. 28 But
11:29 Deut 27:12-26 you will be cursed if you reject the commands of the LORD your God and turn away from
Josh 8:30-35 Him and worship gods you have not known before.
11:30 29 "When the LORD your God brings you into the land and helps you take possession of
Gen 12:6 it, you must pronounce the blessing at Mount Gerizim and the curse at Mount Ebal.
Josh 4:19 30 (These two mountains are west of the Jordan River in the land of the Canaanites who
11:31 Josh 1:11 live in the Jordan Valley,* near the town of Gilgal, not far from the oaks of Moreh.) 31 For

11:24 Hebrew *to the western sea.* 11:30 Hebrew *the Arabah.*

11:13-16 With all of mankind's abilities to track and predict weather and long-range weather patterns, this passage reminds us that God is the one who sends or holds back rain, who makes the fields and pastures lush and productive. He is sovereign over the daily elements that bring life and prosperity.

11:18-21 These instructions reiterated those Moses gave in Deuteronomy 6:8-9 (see the note there). Jesus addressed an abuse of this command (Matthew 23:5), criticizing people in His day for being guilty of an outward show of spirituality. He reminded people that faith is a matter of the heart, not external acts or ritual. While ritual is not necessarily bad, it is never a substitute for heartfelt faith.

▸ HOLINESS

11:19 Sunday school at home. God established His covenant with an entire nation. But notice how the fate of the nation was tied to the spiritual atmosphere of the home. And today as well, without faithful mothers and fathers teaching the law and the gospel to their children, the spiritual welfare of God's people suffers. Every generation must pass on faith to the next. What can you do to help your family grow spiritually? (***See Holiness>*** *Law and Grace> Law> Parents and children,* TopicGuide page A41.)

11:29-30 The two mountains mentioned here, Gerizim and Ebal, are not particularly large, but they are close together with such a small valley in between that people on one peak could see and hear people on the other. Moreh was significant in Israel's history. Abraham's first stop in the land of Canaan was "beside the oak of Moreh" (Genesis 12:6). Before traveling farther south, Abraham received a promise from God about that land and built an altar there. These sites were near the ancient city of Shechem, which in the New Testament era was in Samaria.

you are about to cross the Jordan River to take over the land the LORD your God is giving
you. When you take that land and are living in it, 32you must be careful to obey all the de-
crees and regulations I am giving you today.

THE LORD'S CHOSEN PLACE FOR WORSHIP

12 "These are the decrees and regulations you must be careful to obey when you 12:1
live in the land that the LORD, the God of your ancestors, is giving you. You must Deut 4:9-10; 6:15
obey them as long as you live.
2"When you drive out the nations that live there, you must destroy all the places where 12:2
they worship their gods—high on the mountains, up on the hills, and under every green 2 Kgs 17:10
tree. 3Break down their altars and smash their sacred pillars. Burn their Asherah poles and
cut down their carved idols. Completely erase the names of their gods!
4"Do not worship the LORD your God in the way these pagan peoples worship their gods.
5Rather, you must seek the LORD your God at the place of worship He Himself will choose 12:5 Exod 20:24
from among all the tribes—the place where His name will be honored. 6There you will bring Deut 26:2
your burnt offerings, your sacrifices, your tithes, your sacred offerings, your offerings to ful- 12:6
fill a vow, your voluntary offerings, and your offerings of the firstborn animals of your herds Deut 14:22
and flocks. 7There you and your families will feast in the presence of the LORD your God, and 12:7
you will rejoice in all you have accomplished because the LORD your God has blessed you. Deut 12:12, 18;
8"Your pattern of worship will change. Today all of you are doing as you please, 9be- 14:26; 15:20
cause you have not yet arrived at the place of rest, the land the LORD your God is giving 12:8
you as your special possession. 10But you will soon cross the Jordan River and live in the Judg 17:6
land the LORD your God is giving you. When He gives you rest from all your enemies and 12:10 Josh 3:17; 11:23
you're living safely in the land, 11you must bring everything I command you—your burnt
offerings, your sacrifices, your tithes, your sacred offerings, and your offerings to fulfill a
vow—to the designated place of worship, the place the LORD your God chooses for His
name to be honored.
12"You must celebrate there in the presence of the LORD your God with your sons and 12:12
daughters and all your servants. And remember to include the Levites who live in your Deut 10:9; 12:7, 18-
towns, for they will receive no allotment of land among you. 13Be careful not to sacrifice 19; 26:11
your burnt offerings just anywhere you like. 14You may do so only at the place the LORD 12:13
will choose within one of your tribal territories. There you must offer your burnt offerings Deut 12:5
and do everything I command you.
15"But you may butcher your animals and eat their meat in any town whenever you 12:15
Deut 12:20-23; 14:3-5

12:1 Chapter 12 begins a large central section of the book continuing through chapter 26. The focus now moves from the primary laws of the covenant to more detailed stipulations for Israel. And, as always, Israel's peace and possession of the land is tied closely to their obedience to these given laws.

12:2-3 As a people set apart (holy) to God, Israel needed to purge the land of pagan shrines, altars, and relics used in false worship. Canaanite religion focused on worship of Asherah, the feminine counterpart to Baal, another Canaanite god. Wooden poles or pillars made in her image continued to be a challenge throughout Israel's history (for example see 1 Kings 12:31; 14:23).

▶ WORSHIP
12:4 Celebrate God. What is the worship service like in your church? The church has a responsibility to make God's Word understandable to God's people (Nehemiah 8:8; Colossians 1:28; 2 Timothy 2:15), but passages such as Deuteronomy 12:4 warn that we can go too far in a desire to be culturally relevant. Corporate worship should primarily celebrate God, not popular culture. (***See Worship***> *OT> God's supremacy> Was God-centered,* TopicGuide page A27.)

12:6 This verse is a short-hand summary and reminder of far more detailed laws contained in Leviticus and Numbers. For more on burnt offerings and sacrifices see Leviticus 1–2; 4–5; for tithes and special and freewill offerings, see Leviticus 3 and Numbers 15; for vows see Leviticus 27 and Numbers 30; and for the significance of the first born offering, see Exodus 13; Numbers 18:14-19.

12:15, 22 The concept of ceremonial cleanness or uncleanness may seem odd to modern sensibilities. But through such distinctions the people could learn about God's holiness being honored in their camp. There were a variety of reasons that a person could have been considered ceremonially unclean. The books of Leviticus and Numbers defined such situations and their remedies. Because Israel is about to disperse and settle throughout the land, some regulations regarding clean and unclean will no longer apply.

want. You may freely eat the animals with which the Lord your God blesses you. All of
you, whether ceremonially clean or unclean, may eat that meat, just as you now eat ga-
12:16 Lev 17:10-12 zelle and deer. 16But you must not eat the blood. You must pour it out on the ground like
Deut 15:23 water.
12:17 17"But you may not eat your offerings in your hometown—neither the tithe of your grain
Deut 12:26; 14:22-23 and new wine and olive oil, nor the firstborn of your flocks and herds, nor any offering to
12:18 fulfill a vow, nor your voluntary offerings, nor your sacred offerings. 18You must eat these
Deut 12:4-5, 26 in the presence of the Lord your God at the place He will choose. Eat them there with your
children, your servants, and the Levites who live in your towns, celebrating in the presence
of the Lord your God in all you do. 19And be very careful never to neglect the Levites as
long as you live in your land.
12:20 Deut 11:24 20"When the Lord your God expands your territory as He has promised, and you
have the urge to eat meat, you may freely eat meat whenever you want. 21It might
happen that the designated place of worship—the place the Lord your God chooses for
His name to be honored—is a long way from your home. If so, you may butcher any of
the cattle, sheep, or goats the Lord has given you, and you may freely eat the meat in
your hometown, as I have commanded you. 22Anyone, whether ceremonially clean or
unclean, may eat that meat, just as you do now with gazelle and deer. 23But never eat
the blood, for the blood is the life, and you must not eat the lifeblood with the meat.
12:25 Deut 4:40 24Instead, pour out the blood on the ground like water. 25Do not eat the blood, so that
all may go well with you and your children after you, because you will be doing what
pleases the Lord.
12:26 26"Take your sacred gifts and your offerings given to fulfill a vow to the place the Lord
Num 5:9-10 Deut 12:17 chooses. 27You must offer the meat and blood of your burnt offerings on the altar of the
Lord your God. The blood of your other sacrifices must be poured out on the altar of the
12:28 Lord your God, but you may eat the meat. 28Be careful to obey all my commands, so that
Deut 4:40 all will go well with you and your children after you, because you will be doing what is
good and pleasing to the Lord your God.
29"When the Lord your God goes ahead of you and destroys the nations and you drive
them out and live in their land, 30do not fall into the trap of following their customs and
worshiping their gods. Do not inquire about their gods, saying, 'How do these nations wor-
12:31 ship their gods? I want to follow their example.' 31You must not worship the Lord your
Lev 18:21 God the way the other nations worship their gods, for they perform for their gods every
Deut 9:5; 18:10 Ps 106:37-38 detestable act that the Lord hates. They even burn their sons and daughters as sacrifices
to their gods.
12:32 32*"So be careful to obey all the commands I give you. You must not add anything to
Deut 4:2 them or subtract anything from them.

12:32 Verse 12:32 is numbered 13:1 in Hebrew text.

12:16, 23 Blood held great significance in Israelite culture. It represented the life within a creature. After the Flood, God permitted Noah to eat animals for food, but only after they had been drained of blood (Genesis 9:1-4). The Jerusalem Council in Acts 15, though freeing Gentiles from many of the Old Testament law's restrictions, still recommended this practice to keep Jewish believers from offense. Modern kosher practices include draining the blood from animals as they are prepared for meals.

12:31 With the strongest language, Israel is reminded that Yahweh "hates" certain idolatrous acts. In the Ancient Near East, including Canaan, some of the worship practices were orgies involving the sacrifice of children. God repeatedly forbade His people to have any part in such "worship." This prohibition reinforces the dignity of all humanity as people made in God's image.

▶ SALVATION

12:32 Subtracting from God. Do you have a custom-made religion, a shrink-to-fit belief system that is wrapped around your own values and personality? God warned Israel of the dangers of assimilating other religions into the one true faith (see Deuteronomy 4:2-4), and He continues to warn believers today. If you add to or subtract from God's Word, then your faith will not multiply. (***See Salvation> Receiving> Results> Works> Scripture helps us do good works,*** TopicGuide page A23.)

A WARNING AGAINST IDOLATRY

13 1*"Suppose there are prophets among you or those who dream dreams about
the future, and they promise you signs or miracles, 2 and the predicted signs or
miracles occur. If they then say, 'Come, let us worship other gods'—gods you have not
known before—3 do not listen to them. The LORD your God is testing you to see if you
truly love Him with all your heart and soul. 4 Serve only the LORD your God and fear Him
alone. Obey His commands, listen to His voice, and cling to Him. 5 The false prophets or
visionaries who try to lead you astray must be put to death, for they encourage rebellion
against the LORD your God, who redeemed you from slavery and brought you out of the
land of Egypt. Since they try to lead you astray from the way the LORD your God com-
manded you to live, you must put them to death. In this way you will purge the evil from
among you.

6 "Suppose someone secretly entices you—even your brother, your son or daughter,
your beloved wife, or your closest friend—and says, 'Let us go worship other gods'—gods
that neither you nor your ancestors have known. 7 They might suggest that you worship
the gods of peoples who live nearby or who come from the ends of the earth. 8 But do not
give in or listen. Have no pity, and do not spare or protect them. 9 You must put them to
death! Strike the first blow yourself, and then all the people must join in. 10 Stone the
guilty ones to death because they have tried to draw you away from the LORD your God,
who rescued you from the land of Egypt, the place of slavery. 11 Then all Israel will hear
about it and be afraid, and no one will act so wickedly again.

12 "When you begin living in the towns the LORD your God is giving you, you may hear
13 that scoundrels among you are leading their fellow citizens astray by saying, 'Let us go
worship other gods'—gods you have not known before. 14 In such cases, you must exam-
ine the facts carefully. If you find that the report is true and such a detestable act has been
committed among you, 15 you must attack that town and completely destroy* all its inhab-
itants, as well as all the livestock. 16 Then you must pile all the plunder in the middle of the
open square and burn it. Burn the entire town as a burnt offering to the LORD your God.
That town must remain a ruin forever; it may never be rebuilt. 17 Keep none of the plunder
that has been set apart for destruction. Then the LORD will turn from His fierce anger and
be merciful to you. He will have compassion on you and make you a large nation, just as
He swore to your ancestors.

18 "The LORD your God will be merciful only if you listen to His voice and keep all His
commands that I am giving you today, doing what pleases Him.

13:1 Matt 24:24; Mark 13:22; 2 Thes 2:9
13:3 Deut 6:5; 8:2, 16
13:4 Deut 10:20
13:5 Deut 13:9; 17:5; 22:21
13:6 Deut 17:2-7; 29:18
13:8 Deut 7:2
13:9 Lev 24:13-14; Deut 13:5; 17:7
13:11 Deut 19:20
13:13 Deut 13:2
13:16 Deut 7:25-26; Josh 6:24
13:17 Exod 32:12; Num 25:4; Deut 7:13; 30:3
13:18 Deut 12:28

13:1 Verses 13:1-18 are numbered 13:2-19 in Hebrew text. 13:15 The Hebrew term used here refers to the complete consecration of things or people to the LORD, either by destroying them or by giving them as an offering; similarly in 13:17.

▶ SPIRITUAL WARFARE

13:3 Prophets and preachers. A good orator can convince people of almost anything. If a smooth-talking but non-biblical minister tries to lead you or your church astray, you should examine the facts carefully (Deuteronomy 13:14), follow the steps of church discipline to remove them (Matthew 18:15-18), and warn them of the judgment that they face (2 Peter 2:1-3). Pray for the leaders in your church, who are to protect you from false teaching. (***See Spiritual Warfare**> Originator of Sin> Satan's Strategies> Demons> Demons sow false doctrine*, TopicGuide page A45.)

13:4 In a chapter warning against drifting from faithfulness toward unbelief, notice the string of verbs in this verse: serve, fear, obey, listen, cling. Every verb has the LORD as the direct or indirect object.

13:6-10 These verses stress intimacy (brother, son or daughter, beloved wife, closest friend). But the main point is covenant loyalty to God. Jesus called for similar loyalty (see Matthew 10:34-37), as did Paul (see 1 Corinthians 5:11-13).

13:10 Stoning was a common capital punishment in this ancient culture. Barbaric as it sounds, stoning was not a mob-instigated event. After a trial the witnesses of the prosecution commonly began the stoning, then spectators joined in. Jesus had the opportunity to participate in a stoning when a guilty woman was brought before him. In this setting He uttered the famous line, "Let the one who has never sinned throw the first stone" (John 8:7). Saul (later Paul the apostle) even stood as an official witness at the stoning of Stephen, an early deacon in Jerusalem (Acts 8:1).

CEREMONIALLY CLEAN AND UNCLEAN ANIMALS

14:1 **14** "Since you are the people of the LORD your God, never cut yourselves or shave the
Lev 19:27-28 Jer 16:6 hair above your foreheads in mourning for the dead. 2 You have been set apart as
14:2 holy to the LORD your God, and He has chosen you from all the nations of the earth to be
Exod 19:5 His own special treasure.
14:3-20 3 "You must not eat any detestable animals that are ceremonially unclean. 4 These are
//Lev 11:1-43 the animals* you may eat: the ox, the sheep, the goat, 5 the deer, the gazelle, the roe deer,
14:3 Ezek 4:14 the wild goat, the addax, the antelope, and the mountain sheep.
6 "You may eat any animal that has completely split hooves and chews the cud, 7 but if
14:4 Acts 10:14 the animal doesn't have both, it may not be eaten. So you may not eat the camel, the hare,
or the hyrax.* They chew the cud but do not have split hooves, so they are ceremonially
unclean for you. 8 And you may not eat the pig. It has split hooves but does not chew the
cud, so it is ceremonially unclean for you. You may not eat the meat of these animals or
even touch their carcasses.
9 "Of all the marine animals, you may eat whatever has both fins and scales. 10 You may
not, however, eat marine animals that do not have both fins and scales. They are ceremo-
nially unclean for you.
14:12 11 "You may eat any bird that is ceremonially clean. 12 These are the birds you may
Lev 11:13 not eat: the griffon vulture, the bearded vulture, the black vulture, 13 the kite, the fal-
con, buzzards of all kinds, 14 ravens of all kinds, 15 the eagle owl, the short-eared owl, the
seagull, hawks of all kinds, 16 the little owl, the great owl, the barn owl, 17 the desert owl,
14:19 the Egyptian vulture, the cormorant, 18 the stork, herons of all kinds, the hoopoe, and the
Lev 11:20 bat.
19 "All winged insects that walk along the ground are ceremonially unclean for you and
14:21 may not be eaten. 20 But you may eat any winged bird or insect that is ceremonially clean.
Exod 23:19; 34:26 Lev 17:15; 22:8 21 "You must not eat anything that has died a natural death. You may give it to a for-
Deut 14:2 eigner living in your town, or you may sell it to a stranger. But do not eat it yourselves, for
Ezek 4:14 you are set apart as holy to the LORD your God.
"You must not cook a young goat in its mother's milk.

14:4 The identification of some of the animals and birds listed in this chapter is uncertain. 14:7 Or *coney*, or *rock badger*.

14:1-2 The language here is emphatic in the Hebrew text: "sons you are, . . . a holy people you are." Israel is reminded of their unique status as God's chosen, and this is the reason they are not to act like the pagan cultures around them. It was common in the Ancient Near East to mutilate the body as part of the mourning process in death. But God's people were to be different.

▸ WORSHIP
14:3 A holy diet. Today we are not forbidden to consume in moderation any of the delightful foods provided in God's creation (Acts 10:10-16). But at earlier times, God banned eating certain foods and certain preparations of common foods in order to protect His people from disease and to teach them about purity. These rules were meant to keep Israel's social structure distinct from their surrounding neighbors, to reduce the possibility of integration with these societies. God wanted to keep His people separate and holy, and the regulation of their diet was one way to accomplish that. Make certain you distinguish yourself from the surrounding culture by partaking wisely of all God's rich blessings. (***See Worship****> OT> Priesthood> Duties> Inspecting ceremonially unclean persons,* TopicGuide page A28.)

14:3-8 Extensive guidelines regarding clean and unclean animals were formalized in Leviticus 11. However, the New Testament church did not retain the practice. Jesus said all foods were acceptable to be eaten (Mark 7:14-19). Later Peter, as a leader of the emerging New Testament church, received a vision of animals, clean and unclean (in Acts 10–11). As a result, from that day on, Peter thought and acted differently regarding what Jewish customs were necessary for this new understanding of faith in Christ.

14:11-18 The birds, or flying animals, in this list are mostly carnivorous and some are scavengers. They either feed on dead animals or they forage for insects in the ground. Eating such birds would be only once removed from eating unclean bugs and dead animals, both strictly prohibited in the law (Leviticus 11:20-27). It made sense, then, that they would also be forbidden. While this prohibition certainly aided the people's health, of greater importance was their obedience to the command, which aided in their sanctification.

14:19-20 There were four varieties of insect listed in Leviticus 11:21-22 as clean—locusts, crickets, bald locusts (katydids) and grasshoppers. These insects were common in Ancient Near Eastern diets. Later, John the Baptist was known to subsist on locusts and wild honey (Mark 1:6). These insects could also be ground into powder, formed into paste, and mixed with honey.

14:21 The injunction against boiling a young goat in its mother's milk has been given twice already (Exodus 23:19; 34:26). Though strange to us today, it likely involved rejecting a Canaanite ritual. This law is the basis of the modern Jewish tradition of separating meat and milk products.

THE GIVING OF TITHES

22"You must set aside a tithe of your crops—one-tenth of all the crops you harvest each 14:22
year. 23Bring this tithe to the designated place of worship—the place the LORD your God Deut 12:6, 17
chooses for His name to be honored—and eat it there in His presence. This applies to your 14:23
tithes of grain, new wine, olive oil, and the firstborn males of your flocks and herds. Doing Deut 4:10; 12:4
this will teach you always to fear the LORD your God.
24"Now when the LORD your God blesses you with a good harvest, the place of worship 14:24
He chooses for His name to be honored might be too far for you to bring the tithe. 25If so, Deut 12:5, 21
you may sell the tithe portion of your crops and herds, put the money in a pouch, and go
to the place the LORD your God has chosen. 26When you arrive, you may use the money 14:26
to buy any kind of food you want—cattle, sheep, goats, wine, or other alcoholic drink. Deut 12:7
Then feast there in the presence of the LORD your God and celebrate with your house- 14:27
hold. 27And do not neglect the Levites in your town, for they will receive no allotment of Num 18:20
land among you. Deut 12:12
28"At the end of every third year, bring the entire tithe of that year's harvest and store 14:28
it in the nearest town. 29Give it to the Levites, who will receive no allotment of land Deut 26:12
among you, as well as to the foreigners living among you, the orphans, and the widows 14:29
in your towns, so they can eat and be satisfied. Then the LORD your God will bless you in Deut 16:11; 24:19
all your work.

RELEASE FOR DEBTORS

15 "At the end of every seventh year you must cancel the debts of everyone who 15:1
owes you money. 2This is how it must be done. Everyone must cancel the loans Deut 31:10-11
they have made to their fellow Israelites. They must not demand payment from their 15:3
neighbors or relatives, for the LORD's time of release has arrived. 3This release from debt, Deut 23:20
however, applies only to your fellow Israelites—not to the foreigners living among you. 15:4 Deut 28:8
4"There should be no poor among you, for the LORD your God will greatly bless you in
the land He is giving you as a special possession. 5You will receive this blessing if you are

▸ WORSHIP

14:22 Our money belongs to God. How are your finances? Could you get along with less—one-third less? The average Israelite was not wealthy by modern standards, but the Law called the farmers to give close to 30 percent of the produce from their work to the upkeep of the church and state. The first tithe was given to the priests and Levites (Numbers 18:22-24). The second tithe was used to cover the expenses of the yearly feasts; this is the one mentioned in this verse. The third tithe was given to care for the poor and others who had fallen on hard times (Deuteronomy 14:28–15:11; 26:12). Regardless of whether you believe the command to give 10 percent of your income to the church still stands, God reveals in the Old Testament that a portion of our income should be set aside for the church, the poor, and mercy ministry. (***See Worship****> OT> Offerings> Other Sacrifices> Tithing> A tithe to pay for the journey to and celebration in Jerusalem,* TopicGuide page A27.)

14:28-29 The Bible contains an undeniable call for God's people to care for the disenfranchised: the poor, foreigners, orphans, and widows. This tithe contributed to that effort. The prophets of Israel often reminded their people to care for the oppressed and poverty-stricken. Later, Jesus pointed out the hypocrisy of the religious leaders by emphasizing the way they treated the widows of their community (Luke 20:45-47). One of the dilemmas of the early church was to establish a structure that would spread the gospel abroad but still care for the unfortunate at home (Acts 6:1). In his early letter to the church, James even called care for orphans and widows a mark of true religion (James 1:27).

▸ HOLINESS

15:1 Canceling all debts. This aspect of the ancient economy of Israel was unique. The forgiveness of debt and release from slavery (Deuteronomy 15:12) was on a seven-year cycle, but the return of all land to its ancestral ownership was on a fifty-year cycle (Leviticus 25:8-13). Sadly, we have no evidence in Scripture that Israel ever obeyed these laws. Despite that, these practices speak to us of God's intent that forgiveness and grace should be manifest in everything we do to people in every level of the community. How can you be more godly in the way you deal with those in debt to you? (***See Holiness****> Maturing> Imitating God> His mercy,* TopicGuide page A40.)

15:4 The idea was a good one—"There should be no poor among you." Unlike the Code of Hammurabi, where slaves and the underclass had less protection under the law, God made provision in His laws for some economic balancing among the people. The Sabbatical year every seven years (described here), and the more elaborate Year of Jubilee every fifty years—a year following the seventh group of seven years (Leviticus 25:8-13)—mandated debt cancellation and the return of land to tribal inheritance. Within God's plan there was room for starting over again, if the society was willing to accept giving up some gain in order to address poverty. As with all law, the key was heart attitude, which is addressed in 15:7-9.

15:6 Deut 28:12-13 careful to obey all the commands of the LORD your God that I am giving you today. 6 The
LORD your God will bless you as He has promised. You will lend money to many nations
but will never need to borrow. You will rule many nations, but they will not rule over you.
15:7 7 "But if there are any poor Israelites in your towns when you arrive in the land the
Deut 15:11 LORD your God is giving you, do not be hard-hearted or tightfisted toward them.
15:9 Exod 22:22-23 8 Instead, be generous and lend them whatever they need. 9 Do not be mean-spirited
Deut 15:1; 24:14-15 and refuse someone a loan because the year for canceling debts is close at hand. If you
Job 34:28 refuse to make the loan and the needy person cries out to the LORD, you will be consid-
15:10 2 Cor 9:5, 7 ered guilty of sin. 10 Give generously to the poor, not grudgingly, for the LORD your God
will bless you in everything you do. 11 There will always be some in the land who are
15:11 poor. That is why I am commanding you to share freely with the poor and with other Is-
John 12:8 raelites in need.

RELEASE FOR HEBREW SLAVES

15:12-18 //Exod 21:2-6 12 "If a fellow Hebrew sells himself or herself to be your servant* and serves you for six
years, in the seventh year you must set that servant free.
15:12 Lev 25:39 13 "When you release a male servant, do not send him away empty-handed. 14 Give him
Jer 34:14 a generous farewell gift from your flock, your threshing floor, and your winepress. Share
15:15 Deut 5:15; 16:12 with him some of the bounty with which the LORD your God has blessed you. 15 Remember
that you were once slaves in the land of Egypt and the LORD your God redeemed you! That
15:16 is why I am giving you this command.
Exod 21:5-6 16 "But suppose your servant says, 'I will not leave you,' because he loves you and your
family, and he has done well with you. 17 In that case, take an awl and push it through his
earlobe into the door. After that, he will be your servant for life. And do the same for your
female servants.
18 "You must not consider it a hardship when you release your servants. Remember that
for six years they have given you services worth double the wages of hired workers, and
the LORD your God will bless you in all you do.

SACRIFICING FIRSTBORN MALE ANIMALS

15:19 Exod 13:2, 12; 34:19 19 "You must set aside for the LORD your God all the firstborn males from your flocks and
herds. Do not use the firstborn of your herds to work your fields, and do not shear the first-
15:20 Deut 12:7 born of your flocks. 20 Instead, you and your family must eat these animals in the presence
of the LORD your God each year at the place He chooses. 21 But if this firstborn animal has
15:21 Lev 22:19 any defect, such as lameness or blindness, or if anything else is wrong with it, you must
Mal 1:8 not sacrifice it to the LORD your God. 22 Instead, use it for food for your family in your home-
15:22 town. Anyone, whether ceremonially clean or unclean, may eat it, just as anyone may eat
Deut 12:15 a gazelle or deer. 23 But you must not eat the blood. You must pour it out on the ground
15:23 Deut 12:16, 23-24 like water.

15:12 Or *If a Hebrew man or woman is sold to you.*

15:15 The basis for all the laws of return is to remind Israel of their own redemption. And the reference in verse 18 to the "hardship" of the command is a reminder in subtle language of the reaction of Pharaoh when he hardened his heart against God.

▶ ADOPTION

15:17 Biblical slavery. Do you have difficulty imagining that you could volunteer for slavery? That is precisely what some did in ancient Israel, due to the many laws protecting the rights of slaves. The apostle Paul used this image for our relationship to God and called himself a "slave of Christ" (1 Corinthians 6:19-20; Philippians 1:1). If you have committed your life to Christ, you have committed your life to humble service. (***See Adoption**> With Christ> Servants> Slaves of righteousness,* TopicGuide page A37.)

15:21 God's people were expected to offer God their best gifts. The animals could have no physical defects. This practice is seen as early as Genesis 4:4 when Abel was described as bringing "the best of the firstborn lambs from his flock." Much later in Israel's history the prophet Malachi reprimanded the people because they were not taking this command seriously. Instead they were bringing their most useless animals to sacrifice. They were giving God their leftovers, which was an act of blatant disrespect (Malachi 1:7-14).

PASSOVER AND THE FESTIVAL OF UNLEAVENED BREAD

16 "In honor of the LORD your God, celebrate the Passover each year in the early
spring, in the month of Abib,* for that was the month in which the LORD your God
brought you out of Egypt by night. 2 Your Passover sacrifice may be from either the flock or
the herd, and it must be sacrificed to the LORD your God at the designated place of wor-
ship—the place He chooses for His name to be honored. 3 Eat it with bread made without
yeast. For seven days the bread you eat must be made without yeast, as when you es-
caped from Egypt in such a hurry. Eat this bread—the bread of suffering—so that as long as
you live you will remember the day you departed from Egypt. 4 Let no yeast be found in
any house throughout your land for those seven days. And when you sacrifice the Pass-
over lamb on the evening of the first day, do not let any of the meat remain until the next
morning.
5 "You may not sacrifice the Passover in just any of the towns that the LORD your God is
giving you. 6 You must offer it only at the designated place of worship—the place the LORD
your God chooses for His name to be honored. Sacrifice it there in the evening as the sun
goes down on the anniversary of your exodus from Egypt. 7 Roast the lamb and eat it in the
place the LORD your God chooses. Then you may go back to your tents the next morning.
8 For the next six days you may not eat any bread made with yeast. On the seventh day
proclaim another holy day in honor of the LORD your God, and no work may be done on
that day.

16:1-8 //Exod 12:14-20 //Lev 23:4-8 //Num 28:16-25
16:1 Exod 12:2 Num 28:16
16:2 Exod 12:5
16:3 Exod 12:8, 15; 34:18
16:4 Exod 13:7; 34:25
16:6 Deut 12:5
16:7 2 Chr 35:13

THE FESTIVAL OF HARVEST

9 "Count off seven weeks from when you first begin to cut the grain at the time of harvest.
10 Then celebrate the Festival of Harvest* to honor the LORD your God. Bring Him a volun-
tary offering in proportion to the blessings you have received from Him. 11 This is a time to
celebrate before the LORD your God at the designated place of worship He will choose for
His name to be honored. Celebrate with your sons and daughters, your male and female
servants, the Levites from your towns, and the foreigners, orphans, and widows who live
among you. 12 Remember that you were once slaves in Egypt, so be careful to obey all
these decrees.

16:9-12 //Lev 23:15-22 //Num 28:26-31
16:9 Exod 23:16; 34:22 Lev 23:15 Num 28:26
16:11 Deut 12:7, 12; 14:29; 24:19
16:12 Deut 15:15

16:1 Hebrew *Observe the month of Abib, and keep the Passover unto the LORD your God.* Abib, the first month of the ancient Hebrew lunar calendar, usually occurs within the months of March and April. 16:10 Hebrew *Festival of Weeks;* also in 16:16. This was later called the Festival of Pentecost (see Acts 2:1). It is celebrated today as Shavuat (or Shabuoth).

16:1 The Passover feast commemorated the last plague in Egypt and was so significant that God made it the new year feast for the Jewish religious calendar. On the first Passover, the angel of death "passed over" Egypt, and the firstborn of every family and flock died during that night—unless the blood of a lamb was painted on the doorpost.

16:3 Bread made without yeast was a specific component of Israel's flight from Egypt. Since the pita-like bread did not need time to rise, it was good traveling food. During the Feast of Unleavened Bread, which always immediately followed Passover, the people commemorated this time of flight by eating only unleavened bread. This yeast-free bread also connoted the purity and holiness that God wanted His people to imitate. In the New Testament, Jesus used the image of leavening (yeast) to warn the people about the false teachings of the religious leaders of His day (Matthew 16:11-12).

16:9-10 The Festival of Harvest was a one-day feast for the offering of new grain. Because it occurred exactly fifty days (or seven weeks) after the previous Feast of Unleavened Bread, it was also called Pentecost or Feast of Weeks. The Festival of Harvest marked the transition from the end of the barley harvest to the beginning of the wheat harvest. In the New Testament, seven weeks after Jesus had been raised from the dead, believers were together on the day of Pentecost when they experienced the coming of the Holy Spirit in miraculous ways (Acts 2).

▶ WORSHIP

16:11 Holy dance. What a party! These times of worship and feasting were multi-racial and multi-generational, from the most respected members of the family to the least of the community. Everyone was invited to partake of the great blessings of God manifested in the many feasts of the Old Testament. Can you imagine sponsoring an event that honors God's work in your town, your neighborhood, and embraces people of all kinds? (***See Worship*** *> OT> Posture> Dancing>* ***Singers and dancers celebrate the glory of Zion,*** TopicGuide page A28.)

THE FESTIVAL OF SHELTERS

16:13-17 //Lev 23:33-43 13 "You must observe the Festival of Shelters* for seven days at the end of the harvest sea-
//Num 29:12-39 son, after the grain has been threshed and the grapes have been pressed. 14 This festival
16:13 will be a happy time of celebrating with your sons and daughters, your male and female
Lev 23:16, 40 servants, and the Levites, foreigners, orphans, and widows from your towns. 15 For seven
days you must celebrate this festival to honor the LORD your God at the place He chooses,
for it is He who blesses you with bountiful harvests and gives you success in all your work.
This festival will be a time of great joy for all.
16:16 Exod 23:14-17; 16 "Each year every man in Israel must celebrate these three festivals: the Festival of Un-
34:20, 22-24 leavened Bread, the Festival of Harvest, and the Festival of Shelters. On each of these oc-
casions, all men must appear before the LORD your God at the place He chooses, but they
must not appear before the LORD without a gift for Him. 17 All must give as they are able, ac-
cording to the blessings given to them by the LORD your God.

JUSTICE FOR THE PEOPLE

16:19 18 "Appoint judges and officials for yourselves from each of your tribes in all the towns the
Exod 23:2-3 LORD your God is giving you. They must judge the people fairly. 19 You must never twist
Lev 19:15 justice or show partiality. Never accept a bribe, for bribes blind the eyes of the wise and
16:21 Exod 34:13 corrupt the decisions of the godly. 20 Let true justice prevail, so you may live and occupy
Deut 7:5 the land that the LORD your God is giving you.
16:22 21 "You must never set up a wooden Asherah pole beside the altar you build for the LORD
Lev 26:1 your God. 22 And never set up sacred pillars for worship, for the LORD your God hates them.

17:1 Deut 15:21 **17** "Never sacrifice sick or defective cattle, sheep, or goats to the LORD your God, for
17:2 He detests such gifts.
Deut 13:6-11 2 "When you begin living in the towns the LORD your God is giving you, a man or
17:4 woman among you might do evil in the sight of the LORD your God and violate the cov-
Deut 13:12-14 enant. 3 For instance, they might serve other gods or worship the sun, the moon, or any of
17:5 the stars—the forces of heaven—which I have strictly forbidden. 4 When you hear about it,
Lev 24:14 investigate the matter thoroughly. If it is true that this detestable thing has been done in
17:6 Israel, 5 then the man or woman who has committed such an evil act must be taken to the
Num 35:30 Deut 19:15 gates of the town and stoned to death. 6 But never put a person to death on the testimony

16:13 Or *Festival of Booths,* or *Festival of Tabernacles;* also in 16:16. This was earlier called the Festival of the Final Harvest or Festival of Ingathering (see Exod 23:16b). It is celebrated today as Sukkot (or Succoth).

16:13 The Festival of Shelters was also called the Feast of Booths, Tabernacles, or Ingathering. It symbolized the journey that the Israelites made after leaving Egypt. Branches were gathered and made into shelters. In this way the people passed on to their children and grandchildren the story of God's provision.

▸ CHURCH
16:18 Appointing wise leaders. It was God's idea to have local systems of judges to establish justice and discipline lawbreakers. God approves of local government. The context shows that true laws sustain true religion, while false worship corrupts whatever laws are present (Deuteronomy 16:21). In a society where false worship flourishes, justice suffers. And the message of the prophets is that in a society where God's people are complicit to injustice, their worship can become offensive to God (Malachi 3:5; Matthew 23:23). (***See Church***> *Role> Preach> Instructions> Use Caution> Submission to government and other authorities,* TopicGuide page A50.)

16:18 From this verse through the end of chapter 18, the focus is on the character of those who will lead Israel: judges, kings, priests, and prophets.

16:21-22 Asherah was a feminine, highly sexualized Canaanite goddess. During the time of the judges and the kings in Israel, righteous leaders and kings who instituted religious reform tore down the Asherah poles throughout the land. See for example Gideon, a hesitant champion of Israel who cut down his own Asherah pole and built an altar to God instead (Judges 6:25-26).

▸ WORSHIP
17:6 Guidelines for testimony. Have you ever been unjustly punished? In ancient Israel it took only one person to make a charge against someone else (Deuteronomy 19:15-16). The death penalty, however, could not be enforced if there was only one witness. There was a range of punishments that depended on certain circumstances rather than a rigid legal code. God's Word encourages careful discernment before punishing those who are accused of criminal activity. Pray for wisdom if you are on a jury or in a position to judge others. (***See Worship***> *OT> Reverence> God shows mercy to those that fear Him,* TopicGuide page A29.)

of only one witness. There must always be two or three witnesses. 7The witnesses must 17:7
throw the first stones, and then all the people may join in. In this way, you will purge the Lev 24:13-14 Deut 13:9
evil from among you. *1 Cor 5:13
8"Suppose a case arises in a local court that is too hard for you to decide—for instance, 17:8
whether someone is guilty of murder or only of manslaughter, or a difficult lawsuit, or a Deut 12:5
case involving different kinds of assault. Take such legal cases to the place the LORD your
God will choose, 9and present them to the Levitical priests or the judge on duty at that
time. They will hear the case and declare the verdict. 10You must carry out the verdict they
announce and the sentence they prescribe at the place the LORD chooses. You must do ex-
actly what they say. 11After they have interpreted the law and declared their verdict, the 17:11
sentence they impose must be fully executed; do not modify it in any way. 12Anyone arro- Deut 25:1
gant enough to reject the verdict of the judge or of the priest who represents the LORD your
God must die. In this way you will purge the evil from Israel. 13Then everyone else will
hear about it and be afraid to act so arrogantly.

GUIDELINES FOR A KING

14"You are about to enter the land the LORD your God is giving you. When you take it over 17:14
and settle there, you may think, 'We should select a king to rule over us like the other na- Deut 11:31
tions around us.' 15If this happens, be sure to select as king the man the LORD your God Josh 21:43
chooses. You must appoint a fellow Israelite; he may not be a foreigner.
16"The king must not build up a large stable of horses for himself or send his people to 17:16
Egypt to buy horses, for the LORD has told you, 'You must never return to Egypt.' 17The 1 Kgs 4:26
king must not take many wives for himself, because they will turn his heart away from Ezek 17:15
the LORD. And he must not accumulate large amounts of wealth in silver and gold for 17:17 2 Sam 5:13
himself. 1 Kgs 11:3-4
18"When he sits on the throne as king, he must copy for himself this body of instruction 17:18
on a scroll in the presence of the Levitical priests. 19He must always keep that copy with Deut 31:9, 24
him and read it daily as long as he lives. That way he will learn to fear the LORD his God by 17:19
obeying all the terms of these instructions and decrees. 20This regular reading will prevent Deut 4:9-10 Josh 1:8
him from becoming proud and acting as if he is above his fellow citizens. It will also pre- 17:20
vent him from turning away from these commands in the smallest way. And it will ensure Deut 5:32
that he and his descendants will reign for many generations in Israel.

17:7 To further prevent false testimony, the witnesses were required to participate in the punishment for capital offenses. Jesus referenced this verse as His legal basis for rescuing the woman caught in adultery in John 8.

17:9 The nation of Israel was a theocracy (under God's divine rule), though one in which Moses, until his death, was the main interpreter of God's will. Hence, the politics and religion of the nation were intertwined. Here the Levitical priests and the judges both had a part in the judicial system. It was up to the priests and the judges to consider the laws Moses had passed down (many written in the book of Leviticus) and interpret the appropriate sentence for the wrongdoings. The priests wielded much greater power than in the modern world, where church and state are usually legally separated.

▸HOLINESS
17:14-15 Plans for a king. Was it God's will that Israel eventually have a king? These verses teach that God's plan allowed for just such rule. Today, leaders should demonstrate a dependence on God (Deuteronomy 17:16), moderation in all things (17:17), and a commitment to justice as defined by God's Word (17:18). God will bless a leader who follows these principles (17:20). In areas where you may have authoritative responsibilities, ask God to give you these qualities and commitments. (***See Holiness****> Maturing> Imitating God> His Law,* TopicGuide page A40.)

17:14-15 While Moses spoke here of Israel eventually seeking a king, the critical instruction was that Israel be sure to select the man God had chosen. After Joshua and a series of judges (of which Samuel was the last) led the nation, the people asked Samuel for a king. Their reason was the very reason listed here: "We should select a king to rule over us like the other nations around us."

17:18 The name of this book (Deuteronomy) is derived from an ancient mistranslation from this verse. Before the time of Jesus, the Greek version of the Old Testament rendered the phrase "copy of these laws" as "this second law" (*deuteronomion*).

17:19-20 With character as the focus in this section, note the primary qualities required of the king: a man who reads the Scripture, fears God, and resists being elevated above God's people.

GIFTS FOR THE PRIESTS AND LEVITES

18:1 Deut 10:9 **18** "Remember that the Levitical priests—that is, the whole of the tribe of Levi—will re-
1 Cor 9:13 ceive no allotment of land among the other tribes in Israel. Instead, the priests
18:2 and Levites will eat from the special gifts given to the LORD, for that is their share. 2They
Num 18:20 will have no land of their own among the Israelites. The LORD Himself is their special pos-
18:4 session, just as He promised them.
Exod 22:29 3"These are the parts the priests may claim as their share from the cattle, sheep, and
18:5 goats that the people bring as offerings: the shoulder, the cheeks, and the stomach. 4You
Exod 28:1 Deut 10:8 must also give to the priests the first share of the grain, the new wine, the olive oil, and the
18:6 wool at shearing time. 5For the LORD your God chose the tribe of Levi out of all your tribes
Num 35:2-3 to minister in the LORD's name forever.
18:8 6"Suppose a Levite chooses to move from his town in Israel, wherever he is living, to the
Lev 27:30 place the LORD chooses for worship. 7He may minister there in the name of the LORD his
Num 18:21 God, just like all his fellow Levites who are serving the LORD there. 8He may eat his share of
the sacrifices and offerings, even if he also receives support from his family.

A CALL TO HOLY LIVING

18:9 Deut 9:5; 12:29-30 9"When you enter the land the LORD your God is giving you, be very careful not to imitate
18:10 the detestable customs of the nations living there. 10For example, never sacrifice your son
Exod 22:18 or daughter as a burnt offering.* And do not let your people practice fortune-telling, or use
Lev 19:26, 31; 20:6 Deut 12:31 sorcery, or interpret omens, or engage in witchcraft, 11or cast spells, or function as medi-
Jer 27:9-10 ums or psychics, or call forth the spirits of the dead. 12Anyone who does these things is de-
18:13 testable to the LORD. It is because the other nations have done these detestable things that
Gen 6:7-10 the LORD your God will drive them out ahead of you. 13But you must be blameless before
Matt 5:48 the LORD your God. 14The nations you are about to displace consult sorcerers and fortune-
tellers, but the LORD your God forbids you to do such things."

TRUE AND FALSE PROPHETS

18:15 Luke 24:19 15Moses continued, "The LORD your God will raise up for you a prophet like me from
John 1:21, 24-25 among your fellow Israelites. You must listen to him. 16For this is what you your-
Acts 3:22; 7:37 selves requested of the LORD your God when you were assembled at Mount Sinai.

18:10 Or *never make your son or daughter pass through the fire.* 18:16 Hebrew *Horeb,* another name for Sinai.

18:1-8 Before he died, Jacob (who was renamed Israel and became the ancestor of the Israelite nation) offered a final blessing to his 12 sons. He announced that Levi's descendants would be scattered throughout the other tribes. This blessing bore itself out in the social organization that the Lord instituted for Israel. The Levites were literally scattered throughout the land in their own cities.

▸ SPIRITUAL WARFARE

18:9 Imitating sinners. Have you ever been accused of being "worldly"? There is a difference between imitating the customs of those who hate God and enjoying the blessings of the culture in which you live, and the difference is sin—nothing less, nothing more. Infanticide (Deuteronomy 18:10) and occultism (18:11-14), both serious sins against humanity and God, are examples Moses gave of the Canaanite cultures. But some other cultural practices are neutral or even positive. What cultural sins against God and others should you and your family avoid? (***See Spiritual Warfare****> Resisting Sin and Evil> Resisting Temptation> What to Resist> We are to resist worldly influences,* TopicGuide page A45.)

18:10 Child sacrifice and other heinous acts were commonly associated with the Ammonite god Molech. Years later, King Solomon allowed the worship of Molech in the land, even building altars for Molech, including one on the famous Mount of Olives. Gehenna, the nearby valley that was used for Molech worship, eventually became a symbol for hell.

18:10-11 Witchcraft and the occult have always held a strange power of curiosity over people of all lands. The Israelite king Saul had outlawed all mediums and psychics from Israel. Yet, at a critical point in his life, he consulted a medium in order to speak with the prophet Samuel, who had died. The witch did this for Saul with great trepidation, particularly once she realized he was the very man who had outlawed her practices. Samuel appeared and told Saul that the battle he faced would be disastrous for him, his family, and his army (1 Samuel 28:7-18).

18:16 When God appeared to the people at Mount Sinai, it was a fearsome sight of fire, smoke, and thunder. The people begged Moses to represent them to God. Moses reviewed this history at the beginning of Deuteronomy. But here he again reminds the people that they had asked for someone to speak for God, so God would speak to them through prophets. But the burden would be on the people to discern whether a prophet was from God.

You said, 'Don't let us hear the voice of the LORD our God anymore or see this blazing fire,
for we will die.'
17"Then the LORD said to me, 'What they have said is right. 18I will raise up a prophet 18:18
like you from among their fellow Israelites. I will put My words in his mouth, and he will *Acts 3:22
tell the people everything I command him. 19I will personally deal with anyone who will 18:19 Deut 17:12
not listen to the messages the prophet proclaims on My behalf. 20But any prophet who *Acts 3:22
falsely claims to speak in My name or who speaks in the name of another god must die.' Heb 12:25
21"But you may wonder, 'How will we know whether or not a prophecy is from the 18:20 Deut 13:1-4
LORD?' 22If the prophet speaks in the LORD's name but his prediction does not happen or
come true, you will know that the LORD did not give that message. That prophet has spo- 18:22 Jer 28:9
ken without My authority and need not be feared.

CITIES OF REFUGE

19 "When the LORD your God destroys the nations whose land He is giving you, you 19:1 Deut 6:10-12
will take over their land and settle in their towns and homes. 2Then you must set 19:2
apart three cities of refuge in the land the LORD your God is giving you. 3Survey the terri- Deut 4:41-42
tory,* and divide the land the LORD your God is giving you into three districts, with one of Josh 20:2
these cities in each district. Then anyone who has killed someone can flee to one of the cit-
ies of refuge for safety.
4"If someone kills another person unintentionally, without previous hostility, the slayer 19:4 Num 35:9-34
may flee to any of these cities to live in safety. 5For example, suppose someone goes into
the forest with a neighbor to cut wood. And suppose one of them swings an ax to chop
down a tree, and the ax head flies off the handle, killing the other person. In such cases,
the slayer may flee to one of the cities of refuge to live in safety.
6"If the distance to the nearest city of refuge is too far, an enraged avenger might be
able to chase down and kill the person who caused the death. Then the slayer would die
unfairly, since he had never shown hostility toward the person who died. 7That is why I
am commanding you to set aside three cities of refuge.
8"And if the LORD your God enlarges your territory, as He swore to your ancestors, and 19:8
gives you all the land He promised them, 9you must designate three additional cities of Deut 11:24
refuge. (He will give you this land if you are careful to obey all the commands I have given 19:9
you—if you always love the LORD your God and walk in His ways.) 10That way you will pre- Deut 6:5; 11:22
vent the death of innocent people in the land the LORD your God is giving you as your spe- 19:10 Num 35:33
cial possession. You will not be held responsible for the death of innocent people. Deut 21:1-9
11"But suppose someone is hostile toward a neighbor and deliberately ambushes and
murders him and then flees to one of the cities of refuge. 12In that case, the elders of the
murderer's hometown must send agents to the city of refuge to bring him back and hand
him over to the dead person's avenger to be put to death. 13Do not feel sorry for that 19:13
murderer! Purge from Israel the guilt of murdering innocent people; then all will go well Deut 7:2
with you.

19:3 Or *Keep the roads in good repair.*

▸ WORSHIP

18:18 Future prophets. Prophets performed two roles in the Old Testament—foretelling future events and "forth-telling" the truth in current situations. Any prophet who led people astray was to be killed. Ironically, Jesus was the great prophet Moses foretold (John 4:15-19), and never prophesied falsely but died for what he believed. In the New Testament, we are instructed to cast unrepentant false teachers out of the church after careful investigation (see 2 Peter 2; 1 John 4; 2 John 1:10-11). Today, it is by God's written Word that our hearts and actions will be judged. Carefully compare whatever anyone else tells you about God against the plain teaching of Scripture. (***See Worship> OT> Prophets> Israel to listen to and obey God's prophets,*** TopicGuide page A28.)

19:1-2 As mentioned in Numbers 35, forty-eight cities were set aside as Levitical cities. This scattered the Levites throughout the tribes. Of the forty-eight cities, thirteen were allotted to the descendants of Aaron, the priests, including the six cities of refuge. These cities served as a deterrent to vigilante justice and feud revenge within and among tribes.

GOD IS ABSOLUTE TRUTH

MANY AROUND THE WORLD have come to an impossible conclusion: "There is no absolute truth." Why is it so impossible? It states an absolute truth about absolute truth while claiming there is no absolute truth! We could follow up with the question, "Is it absolutely true or only relatively true that there is no absolute truth?"

The whole idea that truth is relative contradicts God's nature. In Deuteronomy 18, God instructs the Israelites to disregard a prophet whose words fail to come true. Later, the psalmist sings to God: "The very essence of Your words is truth; all Your just regulations will stand forever" (Psalm 119:160).

If you were asked to describe absolute truth, what would you say? By what standard can we measure truth to determine if it is truth? Following are three qualities of absolute truth.

Absolute truth is internally consistent. Every aspect of a true statement is indisputably true. When we say that our God is absolutely truthful, we mean that above everything else He is internally consistent in His character and being. Proverbs 30:5 states, "Every word of God proves true." In fact, the Hebrew word for *truth* means conformance to a standard—God's standard.

Absolute truth is true for all people in all places at all times. Not everything qualifies as absolute truth. For example, if you said, "Today, the interest rate for home mortgages is 6.5 percent," that may be true for some country at a particular time. But interest rates fluctuate and vary from place to place. They are not set in stone. On the other hand, when you say, "Adultery is wrong," you are stating an absolute truth. Whether you live in Bangladesh, Japan, or the United States, adultery is still wrong. Adultery was just as wrong a thousand years ago as it is today.

Finally, *absolute truth has its source in our holy God.* No human can think up a new truth. Truth has always existed in God's nature, and we must always measure our beliefs by God's Word. Since He is the author of truth and since absolute truth resides in Him, He is the only One who can guide us into absolute truth. It is only through Him that we see and understand truth. Any other guide will only lead us into confusion and deception.

Second Samuel 22:31 says, "God's way is perfect. All the LORD's promises prove true. He is a shield for all who look to Him for protection." God's promises set us free from death, eternal damnation, and bondage to guilt and sin. His Word leads us into lives of peace, freedom, and significance. Solomon writes, "Truthful words stand the test of time, but lies are soon exposed" (Proverbs 12:19). God's truth has endured for thousands of years. Human "truth" has not. And because God's truth lasts for eternity, its power to free us from sin will never diminish.

CONCERN FOR JUSTICE

14 "When you arrive in the land the LORD your God is giving you as your special posses-
sion, you must never steal anyone's land by moving the boundary markers your ancestors
set up to mark their property.
15 "You must not convict anyone of a crime on the testimony of only one witness. The
facts of the case must be established by the testimony of two or three witnesses.
16 "If a malicious witness comes forward and accuses someone of a crime, 17 then both
the accuser and accused must appear before the LORD by coming to the priests and judges
in office at that time. 18 The judges must investigate the case thoroughly. If the accuser has
brought false charges against his fellow Israelite, 19 you must impose on the accuser the
sentence he intended for the other person. In this way, you will purge such evil from
among you. 20 Then the rest of the people will hear about it and be afraid to do such an evil
thing. 21 You must show no pity for the guilty! Your rule should be life for life, eye for eye,
tooth for tooth, hand for hand, foot for foot.

19:14 Deut 27:17; Prov 23:10-11
19:15 Num 35:30; Deut 17:6; *Matt 18:16; *2 Cor 13:1
19:16 Exod 23:1
19:17 Deut 17:9; 21:5
19:19 *1 Cor 5:13; Prov 19:5
19:21 Exod 21:24; Lev 24:20; *Matt 5:38

REGULATIONS CONCERNING WAR

20 "When you go out to fight your enemies and you face horses and chariots and
an army greater than your own, do not be afraid. The LORD your God, who
brought you out of the land of Egypt, is with you! 2 When you prepare for battle, the priest
must come forward to speak to the troops. 3 He will say to them, 'Listen to me, all you men
of Israel! Do not be afraid as you go out to fight your enemies today! Do not lose heart or
panic or tremble before them. 4 For the LORD your God is going with you! He will fight for
you against your enemies, and He will give you victory!'
5 "Then the officers of the army must address the troops and say, 'Has anyone here just
built a new house but not yet dedicated it? If so, you may go home! You might be killed in

20:1 Deut 3:22; 31:6-8
20:2 Num 10:8; 31:6
20:3 Josh 23:10
20:5 Neh 12:27

▸ SPIRITUAL WARFARE
19:16-20 Crying wolf. This is the heart of the ninth commandment against testifying falsely (Exodus 20:16). The punishment was stiff for a lying accuser—the exact punishment that the accused was to suffer. This provided a warning to those who might be considering such a heinous deed against the individual and society. God wants you to consider the consequences of your actions before you sin against those around you. (***See Spiritual Warfare****> Resisting Sin and Evil> Consequences> Of Disobedience> God may allow consequences to run their course,* TopicGuide page A46.)

19:21 This is a restatement of the law given through Moses in Exodus 21:24-25, following just after the Ten Commandments. Jesus also referred to this law when He called His followers to a higher standard. This "eye for eye" standard (often called the *lex talionis* or "law of retaliation") was common in the Ancient Near East, serving to mitigate violence (better a tooth for a tooth than a life for a tooth). It also communicates the serious consequences of sin. It does not yet reflect, however, the forgiveness that marked the New Testament kingdom of God. Jesus called His followers to "turn the other cheek" rather than returning cruelty in kind (Matthew 5:38-42).

▸ BIBLE
19:21 Life for life. Does this sound harsh to you? The Bible recognizes mitigating circumstances when assigning punishment (see Deuteronomy 19:1-13 comparing involuntary manslaughter to murder). A Christian should never retaliate for injuries, and where public peace and safety is not impacted, it is not necessary to press charges (Matthew 5:39). When you must be the judge in a situation, make sure the punishment has a connection to the crime. (***See Bible****> Power> Wisdom> Administer civil justice,* TopicGuide page A11.)

▸ WORSHIP
20:1-4 Do not be afraid. Armies haven't changed very much in 3,500 years. Commanders are still yelling at their troops, still attempting to weed out the weak and buck up the frightened. In this case, fearfulness was a sign of a lack of trust in God's commands. Do you sometimes feel paralyzed and fearful, and blame it on the situation when you should instead blame it on your lack of trusting God? (***See Worship****> OT> Fasting and Prayer> Fasting> Occasions> Fasting in war or at the threat of it,* TopicGuide page A26.)

20:1 Portions of the next several chapters focus on war, but not just any kind of war—holy war. Moses recognized that the battles Israel would face were not merely political and social aggression; first and foremost they would be battles about whose God was true and ruled the earth. When the Israelites went into combat with towns outside of Canaan, God instructed them to allow the enemy an opportunity to surrender (Deuteronomy 20:10). But for towns within the Promised Land (20:16), they were to destroy every living thing associated with the town (see Deuteronomy 3:6 and note).

20:4 Throughout Israel's journey, the people were called to move ahead in God's strength. When the people first approached the border to the Promised Land, they sent scouts to reconnoiter the land. Ten of the scouts scared the people with reports of the warriors in the land. Joshua and Caleb, on the other hand, reminded the people that God was with them and would bring them to victory. Thirty-eight years later, a new generation of Israelites once again faced the border and the battles beyond, and again the advice was the same: Remember that God fights for you.

20:6 Lev 19:23 the battle, and someone else would dedicate your house. [6]Has anyone here just planted a
vineyard but not yet eaten any of its fruit? If so, you may go home! You might die in battle,
20:7 Deut 24:5 and someone else would eat the first fruit. [7]Has anyone here just become engaged to a
woman but not yet married her? Well, you may go home and get married! You might die
in the battle, and someone else would marry her.'
20:8 Judg 7:3 [8]"Then the officers will also say, 'Is anyone here afraid or worried? If you are, you may
go home before you frighten anyone else.' [9]When the officers have finished speaking to
their troops, they will appoint the unit commanders.
20:10 Luke 14:31-32 [10]"As you approach a town to attack it, you must first offer its people terms for peace.
[11]If they accept your terms and open the gates to you, then all the people inside will serve
you in forced labor. [12]But if they refuse to make peace and prepare to fight, you must at-
20:13 Num 31:7 tack the town. [13]When the LORD your God hands the town over to you, use your swords to
kill every man in the town. [14]But you may keep for yourselves all the women, children,
20:14 Josh 8:2 livestock, and other plunder. You may enjoy the plunder from your enemies that the LORD
your God has given you.
[15]"But these instructions apply only to distant towns, not to the towns of the nations in
20:16 Exod 23:31 Deut 7:1-2 the land you will enter. [16]In those towns that the LORD your God is giving you as a special
possession, destroy every living thing. [17]You must completely destroy* the Hittites, Amo-
rites, Canaanites, Perizzites, Hivites, and Jebusites, just as the LORD your God has com-
20:18 Deut 7:4; 9:5; 12:30 manded you. [18]This will prevent the people of the land from teaching you to imitate their
detestable customs in the worship of their gods, which would cause you to sin deeply
against the LORD your God.
[19]"When you are attacking a town and the war drags on, you must not cut down the
trees with your axes. You may eat the fruit, but do not cut down the trees. Are the trees
your enemies, that you should attack them? [20]You may only cut down trees that you
know are not valuable for food. Use them to make the equipment you need to attack the
enemy town until it falls.

CLEANSING FOR UNSOLVED MURDER

21 "When you are in the land the LORD your God is giving you, someone may be
found murdered in a field, and you don't know who committed the murder. [2]In
such a case, your elders and judges must measure the distance from the site of the crime
to the nearby towns. [3]When the nearest town has been determined, that town's elders
must select from the herd a young cow that has never been trained or yoked to a plow.
[4]They must lead it down to a valley that has not been plowed or planted and that has a
stream running through it. There in the valley they must break the young cow's neck.

20:17 The Hebrew term used here refers to the complete consecration of things or people to the LORD, either by destroying them or by giving them as an offering.

20:16-18 Some of the tribes followed the guidelines given here. Some, however, did not rid their territory of *all* the inhabitants. Almost without exception, the Israelites were led astray or afflicted by people who remained in the land. These other peoples were polytheistic, but the Israelites had been called to worship only one God.

▸ MINISTRY

20:19 Save the trees. God was the first environmentalist. He made a perfect world, and His goal is to restore it to its past perfection (2 Peter 3:13; Revelation 21:1). The means to that end include our careful use of the natural resources God has given us (Deuteronomy 22:6-7). Being stewards of the earth is one of the reasons God created human beings (see Genesis 1:26-28 and notes). (***See Ministry*** *Transformation> Fill and Subdue> Caretakers of the earth's resources,* TopicGuide page A56.)

▸ HOLINESS

21:1 Unsolved crimes. Deuteronomy 21 deals with seemingly unrelated laws. But they all deal with sins that bear consequences that spill over into the general population if handled improperly. An unsolved murder must be atoned for by the local citizens (21:2-9); an unjust system of slavery must not be allowed to begin (21:10-14); the social order must not be polluted by familial rebellion (21:18-21); and society must not become numb to death, even the death of a criminal (21:22-23). There are some sins that will pollute an entire society if allowed to continue. Protect your family, your church, and your society from the consequences of your sin by keeping your heart and conduct holy. (***See Holiness****> Submission> Yielding to Spirit> Resist the world's influence,* TopicGuide page A40.)

[5]Then the Levitical priests must step forward, for the LORD your God has chosen them to 21:5 Deut 10:8; 17:9; 19:17
minister before Him and to pronounce blessings in the LORD's name. They are to decide all
legal and criminal cases.
[6]"The elders of the town must wash their hands over the young cow whose neck was 21:6 Matt 27:24
broken. [7]Then they must say, 'Our hands did not shed this person's blood, nor did we see
it happen. [8]O LORD, forgive Your people Israel whom You have redeemed. Do not charge 21:8 Num 35:33-34 Jon 1:14
Your people with the guilt of murdering an innocent person.' Then they will be absolved
of the guilt of this person's blood. [9]By following these instructions, you will do what is right 21:9 Deut 19:13
in the LORD's sight and will cleanse the guilt of murder from your community.

MARRIAGE TO A CAPTIVE WOMAN

[10]"Suppose you go out to war against your enemies and the LORD your God hands them 21:10 Josh 21:44
over to you, and you take some of them as captives. [11]And suppose you see among the
captives a beautiful woman, and you are attracted to her and want to marry her. [12]If this 21:12 Lev 14:8-9 Num 6:9
happens, you may take her to your home, where she must shave her head, cut her nails,
[13]and change the clothes she was wearing when she was captured. She will stay in your 21:13 Ps 45:10
home, but let her mourn for her father and mother for a full month. Then you may marry
her, and you will be her husband and she will be your wife. [14]But if you marry her and she 21:14 Gen 34:2
does not please you, you must let her go free. You may not sell her or treat her as a slave,
for you have humiliated her.

RIGHTS OF THE FIRSTBORN

[15]"Suppose a man has two wives, but he loves one and not the other, and both have given
him sons. And suppose the firstborn son is the son of the wife he does not love. [16]When
the man divides his inheritance, he may not give the larger inheritance to his younger son,
the son of the wife he loves, as if he were the firstborn son. [17]He must recognize the rights 21:17 Gen 49:3
of his oldest son, the son of the wife he does not love, by giving him a double portion. He
is the first son of his father's virility, and the rights of the firstborn belong to him.

DEALING WITH A REBELLIOUS SON

[18]"Suppose a man has a stubborn and rebellious son who will not obey his father or 21:18 Prov 1:8
mother, even though they discipline him. [19]In such a case, the father and mother must
take the son to the elders as they hold court at the town gate. [20]The parents must say to 21:21 Lev 20:2, 27 Num 15:35
the elders, 'This son of ours is stubborn and rebellious and refuses to obey. He is a glutton
and a drunkard.' [21]Then all the men of his town must stone him to death. In this way, you 21:22 Matt 26:65-66 Mark 14:63-64
will purge this evil from among you, and all Israel will hear about it and be afraid.

VARIOUS REGULATIONS

21:23 Josh 8:29 John 19:31 *Gal 3:13

[22]"If someone has committed a crime worthy of death and is executed and hung on a
tree,* [23]the body must not remain hanging from the tree overnight. You must bury the

21:22 Or *impaled on a pole;* similarly in 21:23.

21:15-17 Other Ancient Near Eastern cultures had similar laws protecting the rights of the firstborn son. Though such laws clearly favored the firstborn son in Israel, God routinely chose to circumvent this ideal, lifting up the unexpected lesser child. Joseph is one of many examples (1 Chronicles 5:1-2), which also include Isaac, Gideon, David, and Solomon.

21:18-21 Respect for a person's parents was a serious matter. The fifth commandment was devoted to it. It was, in fact, the only one of the Ten Commandments that had a specific promise attached to it—a long life. In these verses, God treated disrespect in the child-to-parent relationship as a capital offense. Many of the proverbs elaborate on this topic (Proverbs 15:5; 17:21; 28:24). The apostle Paul also stressed the importance of the parent-child relationship in numerous places (for example, Ephesians 6:1-3; 1 Timothy 5:4; 2 Timothy 3:2).

21:22-23 While the normal mode of capital punishment was stoning, in some cases people were executed by hanging and left exposed to public view, if for a brief time, as a warning. The "hanging" most often meant some form of impaling the body. The prohibition against leaving the body exposed overnight was applied to Jesus (Matthew 27:57-58; John 19:31). Paul also used this passage to teach the church that Jesus became a curse in order to remove the curse from sinners (Galatians 3:13; 2 Corinthians 5:21).

body that same day, for anyone who is hung* is cursed in the sight of God. In this way, you will prevent the defilement of the land the LORD your God is giving you as your special possession.

22:1 Exod 23:4 **22** "If you see your neighbor's ox or sheep or goat wandering away, don't ignore
your responsibility.* Take it back to its owner. [2]If its owner does not live nearby or
you don't know who the owner is, take it to your place and keep it until the owner comes
looking for it. Then you must return it. [3]Do the same if you find your neighbor's donkey,
clothing, or anything else your neighbor loses. Don't ignore your responsibility.

[4]"If you see that your neighbor's donkey or ox has collapsed on the road, do not look
the other way. Go and help your neighbor get it back on its feet!

[5]"A woman must not put on men's clothing, and a man must not wear women's cloth-
ing. Anyone who does this is detestable in the sight of the LORD your God.

22:6 [6]"If you happen to find a bird's nest in a tree or on the ground, and there are young ones
Lev 22:28 or eggs in it with the mother sitting in the nest, do not take the mother with the young.
[7]You may take the young, but let the mother go, so that you may prosper and enjoy a
long life.

[8]"When you build a new house, you must build a railing around the edge of its flat roof.
That way you will not be considered guilty of murder if someone falls from the roof.

22:9 [9]"You must not plant any other crop between the rows of your vineyard. If you do, you
Lev 19:19 are forbidden to use either the grapes from the vineyard or the other crop.

22:10 [10]"You must not plow with an ox and a donkey harnessed together.

2 Cor 6:14 [11]"You must not wear clothing made of wool and linen woven together.

22:12 [12]"You must put four tassels on the hem of the cloak with which you cover yourself—on
Num 15:37-39 the front, back, and sides.
Matt 23:5

REGULATIONS FOR SEXUAL PURITY

22:13 [13]"Suppose a man marries a woman, but after sleeping with her, he turns against her [14]and
Deut 24:1 publicly accuses her of shameful conduct, saying, 'When I married this woman, I discovered
she was not a virgin.' [15]Then the woman's father and mother must bring the proof of her vir-
ginity to the elders as they hold court at the town gate. [16]Her father must say to them, 'I gave
my daughter to this man to be his wife, and now he has turned against her. [17]He has ac-
cused her of shameful conduct, saying, "I discovered that your daughter was not a virgin."
But here is the proof of my daughter's virginity.' Then they must spread her bed sheet be-
fore the elders. [18]The elders must then take the man and punish him. [19]They must also fine

21:23 Greek version reads *for everyone who is hung on a tree.* Compare Gal 3:13. 22:1 Hebrew *don't hide yourself;* similarly in 22:3.

22:1-4 Though the familiar commandment to "love your neighbor as yourself" (Leviticus 19:18) is not present in Deuteronomy in this succinct form, these commandments and many others in the book imply such comprehensive love for God and fellow people.

22:5 The language used here (that God detests people who engage in the activity prohibited) suggests that this activity may have been related to Canaanite pagan practices.

▸ HOLINESS
22:8 Applying Old Testament principles. Few people today have flat roofs, and fewer neighbors walk across those roofs, making this biblical command for rooftop guardrails a bit superfluous in our culture. But though we live in a different context than the Old Testament Israelites did, the principle of the passage remains the same—we should take steps to protect those who are on our property. If someone is injured through your negligence, you are held responsible. It honors God when you take appropriate safety precautions with the things He has entrusted to your care. (***See Holiness***> *Disciplines> Of Abstinence> Stewardship,* TopicGuide page A42.)

▸ GOD
22:13-25 Marriage God's way. From God's perspective, sexual sin is so devastating to individuals and the community that He demands a strong penalty against it. This passage deals with sexual sin in a way that may seem harsh to us, but we trust that God knew this punishment made perfect sense for the community of faith He was establishing. Do you take sexual sin as seriously as God does? (See 1 Corinthians 6:12-20 and note.) (***See God***> *Salvation> Holy Spirit> Helps put to death the deeds of the body,* TopicGuide page A15.)

him 100 pieces of silver,* which he must pay to the woman's father because he publicly ac-
cused a virgin of Israel of shameful conduct. The woman will then remain the man's wife,
and he may never divorce her.
20 "But suppose the man's accusations are true, and he can show that she was not a vir-
gin. 21 The woman must be taken to the door of her father's home, and there the men of 22:21
the town must stone her to death, for she has committed a disgraceful crime in Israel by Deut 23:17-18
being promiscuous while living in her parents' home. In this way, you will purge this evil
from among you.
22 "If a man is discovered committing adultery, both he and the woman must die. In this 22:22
way, you will purge Israel of such evil. Lev 20:10 Ezek 16:38
23 "Suppose a man meets a young woman, a virgin who is engaged to be married, and John 8:5
he has sexual intercourse with her. If this happens within a town, 24 you must take both of 22:23
them to the gates of that town and stone them to death. The woman is guilty because she Lev 19:20-22
did not scream for help. The man must die because he violated another man's wife. In this
way, you will purge this evil from among you.
25 "But if the man meets the engaged woman out in the country, and he rapes her, then
only the man must die. 26 Do nothing to the young woman; she has committed no crime
worthy of death. She is as innocent as a murder victim. 27 Since the man raped her out in
the country, it must be assumed that she screamed, but there was no one to rescue her.
28 "Suppose a man has intercourse with a young woman who is a virgin but is not en- 22:28
gaged to be married. If they are discovered, 29 he must pay her father fifty pieces of silver.* Exod 22:16
Then he must marry the young woman because he violated her, and he may never di-
vorce her as long as he lives. 22:30 Lev 18:8; 20:11
30* "A man must not marry his father's former wife, for this would violate his father. Deut 27:20

REGULATIONS CONCERNING WORSHIP

23 1* "If a man's testicles are crushed or his penis is cut off, he may not be admitted 23:1
to the assembly of the LORD. Lev 21:20; 22:24
2 "If a person is illegitimate by birth, neither he nor his descendants for ten generations
may be admitted to the assembly of the LORD.
3 "No Ammonite or Moabite or any of their descendants for ten generations may be ad-
mitted to the assembly of the LORD. 4 These nations did not welcome you with food and 23:3
water when you came out of Egypt. Instead, they hired Balaam son of Beor from Pethor in Neh 13:1-2
distant Aram-naharaim to curse you. 5 But the LORD your God refused to listen to Balaam. 23:4 Num 23:4, 7-10
He turned the intended curse into a blessing because the LORD your God loves you. 6 As 2 Pet 2:15 Jude 1:11

22:19 Hebrew *100 shekels of silver,* about 2.5 pounds or 1.1 kilograms in weight. 22:29 Hebrew *50 shekels of silver,* about 1.25 pounds or 570 grams in weight. 22:30 Verse 22:30 is numbered 23:1 in Hebrew text. 23:1 Verses 23:1-25 are numbered 23:2-26 in Hebrew text.

22:22 Even between consenting adults, the sin of adultery is dangerous and a plague to the entire community. In the New Testament, Paul instructs the church to put unrepentant adulterers out of the church (1 Corinthians 6:9-13). If they repented, they could be received back into the community (2 Corinthians 2:5-11).

▸WORSHIP
23:1-4 The assembly of the Lord. Laws such as this were a way to demonstrate or symbolize the need for spiritual perfection before a holy God. This law restricted some people from the assembly of the Lord or, as translated elsewhere, the "congregation of Israel." King David seems to use this phrase as a reference to a special group in 1 Chronicles 28:8. Perhaps it is a reference to those who were eligible to hold public offices, such as judges, which would make this law similar to the second article of the Constitution of the United States. If this option is correct, it would make sense that those who were considered cursed by most citizens should not serve as judges due to the temptation of bias by the judges. Today, know that all Christians have the same access to God through the Lord Jesus Christ (Galatians 3:28). Do not discriminate unfairly against anyone who wishes to worship God. (***See Worship****> NT> Prayer> Instructions> Pray for those in authority,* TopicGuide page A33.)

23:4 Balaam, son of Beor, was a Mesopotamian prophet hired by Balak, king of Moab, to curse Israel—but God forbade him to do so through the mouth of a talking donkey. He was remembered by the New Testament writer Jude (a brother of Jesus) as a prophet who would do anything for money (Jude 1:11). In fact, Jude listed him with Cain, the first murderer (Genesis 4), and Korah, the leader of the rebellion against Moses (Numbers 16).

long as you live, you must never promote the welfare and prosperity of the Ammonites or Moabites.

23:7 Lev 19:34 Deut 10:19

7 "Do not detest the Edomites or the Egyptians, because the Edomites are your relatives and you lived as foreigners among the Egyptians. 8 The third generation of Edomites and Egyptians may enter the assembly of the LORD.

MISCELLANEOUS REGULATIONS

9 "When you go to war against your enemies, be sure to stay away from anything that is impure.

23:11 Lev 15:16

10 "Any man who becomes ceremonially defiled because of a nocturnal emission must leave the camp and stay away all day. 11 Toward evening he must bathe himself, and at sunset he may return to the camp.

23:14 Lev 26:12

12 "You must have a designated area outside the camp where you can go to relieve yourself. 13 Each of you must have a spade as part of your equipment. Whenever you relieve yourself, dig a hole with the spade and cover the excrement. 14 The camp must be holy, for the LORD your God moves around in your camp to protect you and to defeat your enemies. He must not see any shameful thing among you, or He will turn away from you.

23:15 1 Sam 30:15

15 "If slaves should escape from their masters and take refuge with you, you must not hand them over to their masters. 16 Let them live among you in any town they choose, and do not oppress them.

17 "No Israelite, whether man or woman, may become a temple prostitute. 18 When you are bringing an offering to fulfill a vow, you must not bring to the house of the LORD your God any offering from the earnings of a prostitute, whether a man* or a woman, for both are detestable to the LORD your God.

23:19 Exod 22:25 Lev 25:36
23:20 Deut 28:12

19 "Do not charge interest on the loans you make to a fellow Israelite, whether you loan money, or food, or anything else. 20 You may charge interest to foreigners, but you may not charge interest to Israelites, so that the LORD your God may bless you in everything you do in the land you are about to enter and occupy.

23:21 Num 30:1-2 Eccl 5:4 Matt 5:33

21 "When you make a vow to the LORD your God, be prompt in fulfilling whatever you promised Him. For the LORD your God demands that you promptly fulfill all your vows, or you will be guilty of sin. 22 However, it is not a sin to refrain from making a vow. 23 But once you have voluntarily made a vow, be careful to fulfill your promise to the LORD your God.

23:25 Matt 12:1-2 Mark 2:23 Luke 6:1

24 "When you enter your neighbor's vineyard, you may eat your fill of grapes, but you must not carry any away in a basket. 25 And when you enter your neighbor's field of grain, you may pluck the heads of grain with your hand, but you must not harvest it with a sickle.

23:18 Hebrew *a dog.*

23:6 The Moabites and the Ammonites were descendants of Abraham's nephew Lot. After the burning of Sodom and Gomorrah, Lot's two daughters connived together to conceive babies by their father. From this union, Lot's older daughter had a son named Moab. Lot's younger daughter had a son named Ben-ammi who became the progenitor of the Ammonites (Genesis 19:34-38). The prohibition against aiding these peoples is an example of a commandment that is meant in its strictest sense for the first hearers of this book who had struggled against these peoples.

23:7 The Edomites descended from a man named Esau, the twin brother of Jacob (the progenitor of the Israelites). Though born second, Jacob (who was later renamed Israel) cheated Esau out of his birthright, creating family tension and hostility (Genesis 25:20-34). While the brothers, Jacob and Esau, made peace during their lifetimes, their descendants remained hostile. The prophecy of Obadiah revealed much of the animosity that Edom showed Israel through the centuries.

23:18 The male prostitute in this verse is literally the Hebrew word for *dog*, a particularly contemptuous characterization in the Ancient Near East. This derisive term is also used in the New Testament to characterize other types of people (for example, Matthew 7:6 and Philippians 3:2).

23:21 As mentioned here, God did not command the people to make vows, but He did command them to fulfill the vows they made. Vows taken in ancient Israel were taken far more seriously than a "promise." Vows were made to God, usually committing to an act of service or abstinence from something. In some cases vows could be intentionally vetoed or redeemed back with a monetary offering, but they could never simply be forgotten or disregarded.

24 "Suppose a man marries a woman but she does not please him. Having discovered 24:1 Num 5:12-28
something wrong with her, he writes her a letter of divorce, hands it to her, and sends Deut 22:13-21
her away from his house. 2 When she leaves his house, she is free to marry another man. 3 But if *Matt 5:31; 19:7
the second husband also turns against her and divorces her, or if he dies, 4 the first husband may Mark 10:4-5
not marry her again, for she has been defiled. That would be detestable to the LORD. You must
not bring guilt upon the land the LORD your God is giving you as a special possession.
5 "A newly married man must not be drafted into the army or be given any other official 24:5
responsibilities. He must be free to spend one year at home, bringing happiness to the Deut 20:7
wife he has married.
6 "It is wrong to take a set of millstones, or even just the upper millstone, as security for a
loan, for the owner uses it to make a living.
7 "If anyone kidnaps a fellow Israelite and treats him as a slave or sells him, the kidnap-
per must die. In this way, you will purge the evil from among you.
8 "In all cases involving serious skin diseases,* be careful to follow the instructions of the 24:8 Lev 13:1, 59
Levitical priests; obey all the commands I have given them. 9 Remember what the LORD
your God did to Miriam as you were coming from Egypt. 24:9 Num 12:10
10 "If you lend anything to your neighbor, do not enter his house to pick up the item he is 24:10
giving as security. 11 You must wait outside while he goes in and brings it out to you. 12 If Exod 22:24-26
your neighbor is poor and gives you his cloak as security for a loan, do not keep the cloak
overnight. 13 Return the cloak to its owner by sunset so he can stay warm through the night
and bless you, and the LORD your God will count you as righteous. 24:14
14 "Never take advantage of poor and destitute laborers, whether they are fellow Israel- Lev 19:13 1 Tim 5:18
ites or foreigners living in your towns. 15 You must pay them their wages each day before 24:16
sunset because they are poor and are counting on it. If you don't, they might cry out to the //2 Kgs 14:6
LORD against you, and it would be counted against you as sin. 2 Chr 25:4
16 "Parents must not be put to death for the sins of their children, nor children for the sins Ezek 18:20
of their parents. Those deserving to die must be put to death for their own crimes. 24:17 Exod 22:21-22; 23:2-3
17 "True justice must be given to foreigners living among you and to orphans, and you Deut 1:17; 10:17
must never accept a widow's garment as security for her debt. 18 Always remember that 24:18
you were slaves in Egypt and that the LORD your God redeemed you from your slavery. Deut 5:15
That is why I have given you this command. 24:19
19 "When you are harvesting your crops and forget to bring in a bundle of grain from Lev 19:9-10 Deut 14:28-29

24:8 Traditionally rendered *leprosy*. The Hebrew word used here can describe various skin diseases.

▸ BIBLE

24:1 Divorce in the Old Testament. How many people do you know that have been divorced? Myriad excuses are given for dissolving a marriage. This text discusses only one—when a man discovered that his wife deceived him in some shameful way, likely relating to her virginity. Some have thought that this refers to adultery, but the suggested punishment for adultery was death (Leviticus 20:10), not divorce. Regardless, it established that under the old covenant, misleading one's spouse about one's sexual purity was grounds for divorce. (See Matthew 19:1-11 and note.) (***See Bible****> Unity> Doctrines> Principles of marriage,* TopicGuide page A10.)

24:1 Though divorce is mentioned in other places in the five books of Moses, these verses are the only Old Testament laws giving guidance for the practice.

24:6 The Mosaic laws provided for people's survival without allowing them to take advantage of each other. A miller needed both stones to make a living, so they were not allowed as collateral. Similar laws reflect the compassion of God, which He expects His people to follow (as in Exodus 22:26 and again in Deuteronomy 24:10-13).

24:9 Miriam was the older sister of Moses, perhaps the one used by God to help save Moses in his infancy (Exodus 2:1-10). Later, when Israel was in the wilderness, Miriam confronted Moses' authority and was temporarily stricken with leprosy (Numbers 12).

24:17-18 In these verses we see that true justice is closely tied to the compassion of God to redeem people from slavery. Because God was merciful to Israel when they were foreigners in slavery, Israel was commanded to practice mercy to those in their midst.

▸ WORSHIP

24:19 Mercy ministry. Our attitude towards the disadvantaged in society speaks of our understanding of God's graciousness to us. As in ancient Israel, we should provide for the poor in our midst so that they have the food they need to survive. Whether you are rich or poor by the world's standards, God calls His people to extend kindness and generosity. (See Acts 6:1-7 and note.) (***See Worship****> NT> Offerings> Contributions for the poor,* TopicGuide page A31.)

your field, don't go back to get it. Leave it for the foreigners, orphans, and widows. Then
24:20 Lev 19:10 the LORD your God will bless you in all you do. [20]When you beat the olives from your olive
trees, don't go over the boughs twice. Leave the remaining olives for the foreigners, or-
phans, and widows. [21]When you gather the grapes in your vineyard, don't glean the vines
after they are picked. Leave the remaining grapes for the foreigners, orphans, and widows.
[22]Remember that you were slaves in the land of Egypt. That is why I am giving you this
command.

25:1 **25** "Suppose two people take a dispute to court, and the judges declare that one is
Deut 17:11 right and the other is wrong. [2]If the person in the wrong is sentenced to be
flogged, the judge must command him to lie down and be beaten in his presence with the
25:3 2 Cor 11:24 number of lashes appropriate to the crime. [3]But never give more than forty lashes; more
than forty lashes would publicly humiliate your neighbor.
25:4 [4]"You must not muzzle an ox to keep it from eating as it treads out the grain.
*1 Cor 9:9 *1 Tim 5:18 [5]"If two brothers are living together on the same property and one of them dies without
25:5 a son, his widow may not be married to anyone from outside the family. Instead, her hus-
*Matt 22:24 Mark 12:19 band's brother should marry her and have intercourse with her to fulfill the duties of a
*Luke 20:28 brother-in-law. [6]The first son she bears to him will be considered the son of the dead
brother, so that his name will not be forgotten in Israel.
25:6 [7]"But if the man refuses to marry his brother's widow, she must go to the town gate and
Ruth 4:5 say to the elders assembled there, 'My husband's brother refuses to preserve his brother's
name in Israel—he refuses to fulfill the duties of a brother-in-law by marrying me.' [8]The el-
ders of the town will then summon him and talk with him. If he still refuses and says, 'I
don't want to marry her,' [9]the widow must walk over to him in the presence of the elders,
25:9-10 pull his sandal from his foot, and spit in his face. Then she must declare, 'This is what hap-
Ruth 4:7-8 pens to a man who refuses to provide his brother with children.' [10]Ever afterward in Israel
25:12 Deut 7:2 his family will be referred to as 'the family of the man whose sandal was pulled off'!
25:13 [11]"If two Israelite men get into a fight and the wife of one tries to rescue her husband by
Lev 19:35 grabbing the testicles of the other man, [12]you must cut off her hand. Show her no pity.
Prov 11:1; 16:11 [13]"You must use accurate scales when you weigh out merchandise, [14]and you must use
Ezek 45:10-11 full and honest measures. [15]Yes, always use honest weights and measures, so that you

24:19-22 This provision for the disenfranchised came from the One who ultimately was the landowner—the Lord. A practical application is seen in the story of Ruth and Boaz. In desperation and destitution, Ruth (a Moabite, no less!) went to glean in order that she and her mother-in-law Naomi might survive. That act of gleaning led to the providential meeting with Boaz who would "redeem" Naomi and Ruth.

25:3 While other Ancient Near Eastern cultures had limits of 40 lashes, only Israel's law connected this limit with a concern for the dignity of the person.

▸ CHURCH

25:4 Paying the preacher. How much should you pay your minister? The apostle Paul quoted this passage from Deuteronomy two times (1 Corinthians 9:9 and 1 Timothy 5:18) to argue for the importance of paying a minister for his labor. If we should allow animals to eat as they work, why should we deny preachers that privilege? Make sure your minister and missionaries are paid sufficiently as they labor for the Lord. (***See Church****> Role> Preach> Topics> Collect Resources> For salaries of ministers,* TopicGuide page A50.)

25:4 This verse shows that all creation under God's covenant provisions—even the animals—benefit from His concern for justice.

25:5-10 These verses detail the "levirate" law in Israel. This law, though strange to modern senses, had as a concern the continuity of family lines in Israel as the new nation settled tribal lands. The importance attached to such continuity is seen by the severity of the public demonstration of anger associated with this law (see. 25:9). A much more cordial version of this law is seen played out in Ruth 4 when Boaz and an unnamed relative discuss and decide the future of Naomi and Ruth.

▸ HOLINESS

25:13 Play fair! Are there some people who seem to deserve to be cheated? Just prior to pronouncing a curse upon the Amalekites, Moses made it clear that the Israelites were forbidden to take advantage of someone by using differing measures to weigh out merchandise. However, God chose to deal with the enemies of Israel; they were to be treated honorably in commerce. Are you known as an honest person in your dealings, or as a procrastinator, a time-thief, or someone who cannot keep his or her word? Remember the eighth commandment "You must not steal" applies to every person with whom you have dealings. (***See Holiness****> Disciplines> Of Engagement> Honesty,* TopicGuide page A42.)

may enjoy a long life in the land the LORD your God is giving you. 16All who cheat with dis- 25:16 Prov 11:1
honest weights and measures are detestable to the LORD your God.
17"Never forget what the Amalekites did to you as you came from Egypt. 18They at- 25:17 Exod 17:8-16
tacked you when you were exhausted and weary, and they struck down those who were
straggling behind. They had no fear of God. 19Therefore, when the LORD your God has
given you rest from all your enemies in the land He is giving you as a special possession,
you must destroy the Amalekites and erase their memory from under heaven. Never for-
get this!

HARVEST OFFERINGS AND TITHES

26 "When you enter the land the LORD your God is giving you as a special posses-
sion and you have conquered it and settled there, 2put some of the first produce 26:2 Exod 22:29; 23:16, 19
from each crop you harvest into a basket and bring it to the designated place of worship—
the place the LORD your God chooses for His name to be honored. 3Go to the priest in
charge at that time and say to him, 'With this gift I acknowledge to the LORD your God that
I have entered the land He swore to our ancestors He would give us.' 4The priest will then
take the basket from your hand and set it before the altar of the LORD your God.
5"You must then say in the presence of the LORD your God, 'My ancestor Jacob was a wan- 26:5 Gen 46:27 Deut 1:10; 10:22
dering Aramean who went to live as a foreigner in Egypt. His family arrived few in number,
but in Egypt they became a large and mighty nation. 6When the Egyptians oppressed and 26:6 Exod 1:11-12
humiliated us by making us their slaves, 7we cried out to the LORD, the God of our ancestors.
He heard our cries and saw our hardship, toil, and oppression. 8So the LORD brought us out 26:8 Deut 4:34
of Egypt with a strong hand and powerful arm, with overwhelming terror, and with miracu-
lous signs and wonders. 9He brought us to this place and gave us this land flowing with milk 26:9 Exod 3:8, 17
and honey! 10And now, O LORD, I have brought You the first portion of the harvest You have
given me from the ground.' Then place the produce before the LORD your God, and bow to
the ground in worship before Him. 11Afterward you may go and celebrate because of all the 26:11 Deut 12:7, 12
good things the LORD your God has given to you and your household. Remember to include
the Levites and the foreigners living among you in the celebration.
12"Every third year you must offer a special tithe of your crops. In this year of the special 26:12 Deut 14:28-29 Heb 7:5, 9-10
tithe you must give your tithes to the Levites, foreigners, orphans, and widows, so that
they will have enough to eat in your towns. 13Then you must declare in the presence of
the LORD your God, 'I have taken the sacred gift from my house and have given it to the Le-
vites, foreigners, orphans, and widows, just as You commanded me. I have not violated or
forgotten any of Your commands. 14I have not eaten any of it while in mourning; I have
not handled it while I was ceremonially unclean; and I have not offered any of it to the
dead. I have obeyed the LORD my God and have done everything You commanded me.

25:17 The Amalekites were distant cousins of the Israelites. They were descended from Amalek, the grandson of Jacob's twin brother, Esau. Not only did the Amalekites block Israel's path in their passage out of Egypt, they harassed the Israelites as they traveled. Later, the Amalekites formed alliances against Israel as the nation grew through the era of the judges and into the establishment of the monarchy.

26:5 Jacob grew up in the southern part of Canaan before "wandering" to the northern end of the Mesopotamian valley to find a wife in Haran. He later returned to Canaan, before migrating with his entire clan to Egypt in his old age to be with Joseph. When Jacob died, he was carried back to Canaan and buried there.

26:5-9 These verses are a summary of the first five books of the Old Testament. Remembering what God has done should issue forth in worship and celebration (26:10-11).

▸ WORSHIP

26:12 A special tenth. This is a reference to the "first tithe" (see Deuteronomy 14:22 and note). The tithing system followed a seven-year cycle. After seven cycles with a total of 49 years, the fiftieth year was the Year of Jubilee (Leviticus 25:8-9). Within that larger cycle, there were 16 offerings set aside to pay the ministers and teachers (the priests and Levites), and any extra money went to the poor. Do you set aside money for special gifts to your pastors, missionaries, or the poor? Extend your ministry reach by giving money to those who need it either because of poverty or their singular focus on ministry. (***See Worship****> NT> Offerings> Be faithful with riches,* TopicGuide page A31.)

26:15 15 Now look down from Your holy dwelling place in heaven and bless Your people Israel
Zech 2:13 and the land You swore to our ancestors to give us—a land flowing with milk and honey.'

A CALL TO OBEY THE LORD'S COMMANDS

26:16 16 "Today the LORD your God has commanded you to obey all these decrees and regula-
Deut 4:29 tions. So be careful to obey them wholeheartedly. 17 You have declared today that the
26:17 Ps 48:14 LORD is your God. And you have promised to walk in His ways, and to obey His decrees,
26:18 commands, and regulations, and to do everything He tells you. 18 The LORD has declared
Deut 7:6 today that you are His people, His own special treasure, just as He promised, and that you
26:19 must obey all His commands. 19 And if you do, He will set you high above all the other na-
Deut 28:1 tions He has made. Then you will receive praise, honor, and renown. You will be a nation
that is holy to the LORD your God, just as He promised."

THE ALTAR ON MOUNT EBAL

27 Then Moses and the leaders of Israel gave this charge to the people: "Obey all
27:2 these commands that I am giving you today. 2 When you cross the Jordan River
Josh 8:30-32 and enter the land the LORD your God is giving you, set up some large stones and coat
them with plaster. 3 Write this whole body of instruction on them when you cross the river
to enter the land the LORD your God is giving you—a land flowing with milk and honey, just
as the LORD, the God of your ancestors, promised you. 4 When you cross the Jordan, set up
these stones at Mount Ebal and coat them with plaster, as I am commanding you today.
5 "Then build an altar there to the LORD your God, using natural, uncut stones. You must
not shape the stones with an iron tool. 6 Build the altar of uncut stones, and use it to offer
burnt offerings to the LORD your God. 7 Also sacrifice peace offerings on it, and celebrate by
feasting there before the LORD your God. 8 You must clearly write all these instructions on
the stones coated with plaster."
27:9 9 Then Moses and the Levitical priests addressed all Israel as follows: "O Israel, be quiet
Deut 26:17 and listen! Today you have become the people of the LORD your God. 10 So you must obey
the LORD your God by keeping all these commands and decrees that I am giving you today."

▸ BIBLE
26:16 Cursings unsaid. The Mosaic law is stated here in a nutshell: "God commanded you to obey the law (including the commands to repent of sin and have faith), and you promised to obey. If you keep your promise, He will make you great." Notice that this summary does not include the curses found elsewhere (Deuteronomy 8:19). The lesson: God rarely says everything He has to say about a topic all at once. Even in summary passages, some important points previously mentioned must be remembered. Always read God's Word in context and let the Scriptures help you to understand (interpret) more difficult Scripture. (***See Bible****> Power> Wisdom> Instruction through God's word,* TopicGuide page A11.)

26:16-19 This paragraph sounds a conclusion to the major portion of Deuteronomy focusing on great covenant laws (chapters 5–11) and more detailed stipulations of God's covenant with Israel (chapters 12–26). A consistent phrase used at each place is a reference to the "decrees and regulations" Israel is to follow (see Deuteronomy 5:1; 11:32; 12:1; and here in 26:16).

27:1-26 Having received the law from God through Moses (a second time!), Israel now had to accept their responsibility to uphold this covenant. This chapter contains their ceremony of ratification and acceptance.

27:5 God gave specific instructions for many altars the Israelites would build through the years. Their altars were to be made of uncut stones, as designated here (as well as in Exodus 20:25). This would make their altars distinct from the other religious altars around them. Building altars was not a new practice. Noah built an altar after the Flood (Genesis 8:20). Abraham (at the time called "Abram") built altars at many places where God revealed Himself (Genesis 12:8; 13:4), as did Abraham's son Isaac and grandson Jacob (Genesis 26:25; 33:19-20).

▸ WORSHIP
27:10 Keeping the commands. The previous 21 chapters of holiness code may have seemed a little much, but here Moses makes it clear that all the ceremonial requirements were nothing compared to a holy God's requirement that Israel keep *all* the law—which is the same as saying they were required to be perfect. This underlines the symbolism of the ceremonial law: It reminded Israel of how difficult it was to be holy and acceptable to God and how it was by faith, not personal or communal effort, that they were made righteous and pure in His sight. God still requires perfection from His children (Matthew 5:48), and we are still dependent upon the sacrifice—this time of Jesus, the perfect Lamb of God—to make us able to stand before a holy God. (***See Worship****> OT> God's Supremacy> Required obedience in daily life and affairs,* TopicGuide page A26.)

CURSES FROM MOUNT EBAL

11 That same day Moses also gave this charge to the people: 12 "When you cross the Jor-
dan River, the tribes of Simeon, Levi, Judah, Issachar, Joseph, and Benjamin must stand on
Mount Gerizim to proclaim a blessing over the people. 13 And the tribes of Reuben, Gad,
Asher, Zebulun, Dan, and Naphtali must stand on Mount Ebal to proclaim a curse.
14 "Then the Levites will shout to all the people of Israel:

15 'Cursed is anyone who carves or casts an idol and secretly sets it up. These idols, the work of craftsmen, are detestable to the LORD.'
And all the people will reply, 'Amen.'

16 'Cursed is anyone who dishonors father or mother.'
And all the people will reply, 'Amen.'

17 'Cursed is anyone who steals property from a neighbor by moving a boundary marker.'
And all the people will reply, 'Amen.'

18 'Cursed is anyone who leads a blind person astray on the road.'
And all the people will reply, 'Amen.'

19 'Cursed is anyone who denies justice to foreigners, orphans, or widows.'
And all the people will reply, 'Amen.'

20 'Cursed is anyone who has sexual intercourse with one of his father's wives, for he has violated his father.'
And all the people will reply, 'Amen.'

21 'Cursed is anyone who has sexual intercourse with an animal.'
And all the people will reply, 'Amen.'

22 'Cursed is anyone who has sexual intercourse with his sister, whether she is the daughter of his father or his mother.'
And all the people will reply, 'Amen.'

23 'Cursed is anyone who has sexual intercourse with his mother-in-law.'
And all the people will reply, 'Amen.'

24 'Cursed is anyone who attacks a neighbor in secret.'
And all the people will reply, 'Amen.'

25 'Cursed is anyone who accepts payment to kill an innocent person.'
And all the people will reply, 'Amen.'

26 'Cursed is anyone who does not affirm and obey the terms of these instructions.'
And all the people will reply, 'Amen.'

27:12 Deut 11:26 Josh 8:33-35
27:15 Exod 20:4, 23 Lev 19:4 Deut 4:16; 5:8
27:16 Exod 21:17 Lev 20:9 Ezek 22:7
27:17 Deut 19:14
27:18 Lev 19:14
27:19 Exod 22:21 Lev 19:33 Deut 10:18
27:20 Lev 18:8; 20:11 Deut 22:30
27:21 Exod 22:19 Lev 18:23; 20:15
27:22 Lev 18:9; 20:17
27:23 Lev 18:17; 20:14
27:24 Exod 21:12 Lev 24:17 Num 35:30
27:25 Exod 23:8 Deut 10:17
27:26 Deut 28:15 Gal 3:10

27:12-13 Mount Gerizim and Mount Ebal are opposite each other, with the biblical town Shechem in between (near modern-day Nablus). Moses was only giving instructions at this point, but Joshua 8:30-35 records the actual event when Israel ratified the covenant in the Land of Promise. In the Joshua account, the people stood on both mountains, while the Levites stood in between with the Ark of the Covenant. Joshua then read the curses and blessings.

27:14 Though the preceding verses refer to blessings and curses, only curses are read in the following verses. Israel is accepting the covenant and repeating the blessings (v. 12) and curses.

▶ HOLINESS

27:15 Christ took the curse. We all have our ideas about what things are wrong and what things are *really* wrong. These are based on a variety of factors such as our upbringing, experience, personality, and conscience. But here we get a glimpse of what God thought was truly important in the moral law, and He applied special curses to these activities. These curses seem as if they could still be applied today. However, Christ has taken the "curse" for those who believe in His sacrificial death. We can rejoice in having peace with God through our Lord Jesus Christ! (See Romans 5:1.) (***See Holiness***> *Law and Grace*> *Law*> *The moral law of God,* TopicGuide page A41.)

BLESSINGS FOR OBEDIENCE

28:1 Exod 15:26; 23:22 Lev 26:3 Deut 7:12; 11:13

28 "If you fully obey the LORD your God and carefully keep all His commands that I
am giving you today, the LORD your God will set you high above all the nations of
the world. 2 You will experience all these blessings if you obey the LORD your God:

28:2 Jer 32:24 · 28:3 Ps 144:15 · 28:4 Gen 49:25

3 Your towns and your fields
  will be blessed.
4 Your children and your crops
  will be blessed.
The offspring of your herds and flocks
  will be blessed.
5 Your fruit baskets and breadboards
  will be blessed.

28:6 Ps 121:8

6 Wherever you go and whatever you do,
  you will be blessed.

28:7 Lev 26:8, 17

7 "The LORD will conquer your enemies when they attack you. They will attack you from
one direction, but they will scatter from you in seven!

28:8 Deut 15:4

8 "The LORD will guarantee a blessing on everything you do and will fill your storehouses
with grain. The LORD your God will bless you in the land He is giving you.

28:9 Exod 19:5

9 "If you obey the commands of the LORD your God and walk in His ways, the LORD will es-
tablish you as His holy people as He swore He would do. 10 Then all the nations of the world
will see that you are a people claimed by the LORD, and they will stand in awe of you.

28:11 Deut 28:2-6, 8 · 28:12 Lev 26:4 Deut 11:14; 23:20 · 28:13 Deut 28:1, 44 · 28:14 Deut 5:32-33

11 "The LORD will give you prosperity in the land He swore to your ancestors to give you,
blessing you with many children, numerous livestock, and abundant crops. 12 The LORD
will send rain at the proper time from His rich treasury in the heavens and will bless all the
work you do. You will lend to many nations, but you will never need to borrow from them.
13 If you listen to these commands of the LORD your God that I am giving you today, and if
you carefully obey them, the LORD will make you the head and not the tail, and you will al-
ways be on top and never at the bottom. 14 You must not turn away from any of the com-
mands I am giving you today, nor follow after other gods and worship them.

CURSES FOR DISOBEDIENCE

28:15 Lev 26:14 Josh 23:15-16

15 "But if you refuse to listen to the LORD your God and do not obey all the commands and
decrees I am giving you today, all these curses will come and overwhelm you:

28:1-68 In Ancient Near Eastern treaties, once the covenant was accepted, the sanctions of the covenant were declared. The greater party (in this case the Lord) would promise blessings for obedience and curses for rebellion and disobedience on the part of the lesser party (Israel). To show the seriousness of disobedience, the chapter contains 14 verses of blessing but more than 50 verses of curses.

▸ BIBLE
28:1 Full obedience. Was God misleading Israel by promising them all these rewards that He knew they would never receive because of their disobedience? Of course not! In this case, we see the distinction between God's secret will and His revealed will (see Deuteronomy 29:29 and note). God knew that Israel would ultimately fail, but His revealed will was that they strive for victory. And His rewards for obedience were not inauthentic, no more than telling an overmatched football team that if they win, they will all get a prize. God offers rewards for obedience to His New Testament saints as well (see 1 Corinthians 3:10-14). Obey God's commands, and you will discover the graciousness of God when you succeed and the mercy of God when you fail. (***See Bible****> Uniqueness> Inspired> His promises never fail,* TopicGuide page A10.)

▸ PURPOSE
28:15 Refusing to listen. What was unspoken in Deuteronomy 26:16-19 is declared here in the most explicit language possible. Using the harshest language in the Pentateuch, Moses described the curses and eventual destruction of Israel if they did not obey. But even during the times of the almost complete destruction of Israel that have occurred throughout history, God has protected a faithful remnant. As Paul prayed in Romans 10, we can also pray for the Jews that remain, that they will find their true hope in *Yeshua Ha Meshiach*, Jesus the Messiah (see Romans 11). (***See Purpose****> God's Deeds> Judgment> God promises judgment,* TopicGuide page A53.)

28:15-25 These curses cover a wide spectrum, affecting the person, the family, and the entire nation. Some are short-term and some multi-generational in extent. But consistent throughout is the assertion that the Lord is the agent who acts.

16 Your towns and your fields
will be cursed.
17 Your fruit baskets and breadboards
will be cursed.
18 Your children and your crops
will be cursed.
The offspring of your herds and flocks
will be cursed.
19 Wherever you go and whatever you do,
you will be cursed.

20 "The LORD Himself will send on you curses, confusion, and frustration in everything
you do, until at last you are completely destroyed for doing evil and abandoning Me.
21 The LORD will afflict you with diseases until none of you are left in the land you are about
to enter and occupy. 22 The LORD will strike you with wasting diseases, fever, and inflam-
mation, with scorching heat and drought, and with blight and mildew. These disasters will
pursue you until you die. 23 The skies above will be as unyielding as bronze, and the earth
beneath will be as hard as iron. 24 The LORD will change the rain that falls on your land into
powder, and dust will pour down from the sky until you are destroyed.

25 "The LORD will cause you to be defeated by your enemies. You will attack your ene-
mies from one direction, but you will scatter from them in seven! You will be an object of
horror to all the kingdoms of the earth. 26 Your corpses will be food for all the scavenging
birds and wild animals, and no one will be there to chase them away.

27 "The LORD will afflict you with the boils of Egypt and with tumors, scurvy, and the itch,
from which you cannot be cured. 28 The LORD will strike you with madness, blindness, and
panic. 29 You will grope around in broad daylight like a blind person groping in the dark-
ness, but you will not find your way. You will be oppressed and robbed continually, and
no one will come to save you.

30 "You will be engaged to a woman, but another man will sleep with her. You will build
a house, but someone else will live in it. You will plant a vineyard, but you will never enjoy
its fruit. 31 Your ox will be butchered before your eyes, but you will not eat a single bite of
the meat. Your donkey will be taken from you, never to be returned. Your sheep and goats
will be given to your enemies, and no one will be there to help you. 32 You will watch as
your sons and daughters are taken away as slaves. Your heart will break for them, but you
won't be able to help them. 33 A foreign nation you have never heard about will eat the
crops you worked so hard to grow. You will suffer under constant oppression and harsh
treatment. 34 You will go mad because of all the tragedy you see around you. 35 The LORD
will cover your knees and legs with incurable boils. In fact, you will be covered from head
to foot.

36 "The LORD will exile you and your king to a nation unknown to you and your ances-
tors. There in exile you will worship gods of wood and stone! 37 You will become an object
of horror, ridicule, and mockery among all the nations to which the LORD sends you.

38 "You will plant much but harvest little, for locusts will eat your crops. 39 You will plant
vineyards and care for them, but you will not drink the wine or eat the grapes, for worms
will destroy the vines. 40 You will grow olive trees throughout your land, but you will never
use the olive oil, for the fruit will drop before it ripens. 41 You will have sons and daughters,
but you will lose them, for they will be led away into captivity. 42 Swarms of insects will de-
stroy your trees and crops.

28:20 Deut 8:11; 28:25
28:21 Lev 26:25; Num 14:12; Amos 4:10
28:23 Lev 26:19
28:24 Deut 11:17; 1 Kgs 17:1; Jer 14:1
28:25 2 Chr 29:8; Isa 30:17; Jer 15:4
28:26 Ps 79:2; Jer 7:33; 16:4; 19:7; 34:20
28:27 Exod 9:9; 15:26; Deut 7:15; 1 Sam 5:6, 9, 12
28:29 Exod 10:21; Job 5:14; Isa 59:10
28:30 Deut 20:6-7; Job 31:10; Isa 65:22; Amos 5:11
28:35 Job 2:7
28:36 2 Kgs 17:4, 6; 24:12, 14; 25:7, 11
28:38 Lev 26:20; Isa 5:10; Mic 6:15
28:41 Deut 28:32
28:42 Deut 28:38

28:30-37 This portion of the curses aptly describes the exile Israel would face. Centuries later, as a weakened people, the northern part of Israel was claimed by Assyria, and later Babylon claimed the southern part.

43“The foreigners living among you will become stronger and stronger, while you be-
28:44 Deut 28:12-13 come weaker and weaker. 44They will lend money to you, but you will not lend to them.
They will be the head, and you will be the tail!
45“If you refuse to listen to the LORD your God and to obey the commands and decrees
He has given you, all these curses will pursue and overtake you until you are destroyed.
28:45 Deut 4:25-26 46These horrors will serve as a sign and warning among you and your descendants for-
28:47 ever. 47If you do not serve the LORD your God with joy and enthusiasm for the abundant
Deut 32:15 benefits you have received, 48you will serve your enemies whom the LORD will send
28:49 against you. You will be left hungry, thirsty, naked, and lacking in everything. The LORD
Isa 5:26; 7:18 Jer 5:15 will put an iron yoke on your neck, oppressing you harshly until He has destroyed you.
49“The LORD will bring a distant nation against you from the end of the earth, and it will
swoop down on you like a vulture. It is a nation whose language you do not understand,
50a fierce and heartless nation that shows no respect for the old and no pity for the young.
51Its armies will devour your livestock and crops, and you will be destroyed. They will
leave you no grain, new wine, olive oil, calves, or lambs, and you will starve to death.
28:52 52They will attack your cities until all the fortified walls in your land—the walls you trusted
Jer 10:17-18 Zeph 1:14-15 to protect you—are knocked down. They will attack all the towns in the land the LORD your
God has given you.
28:53 53“The siege and terrible distress of the enemy’s attack will be so severe that you will
Lev 26:29 Jer 19:9 eat the flesh of your own sons and daughters, whom the LORD your God has given you.
Lam 2:20; 4:10 54The most tenderhearted man among you will have no compassion for his own brother,
his beloved wife, and his surviving children. 55He will refuse to share with them the flesh
he is devouring—the flesh of one of his own children—because he has nothing else to eat
during the siege and terrible distress that your enemy will inflict on all your towns. 56The
most tender and delicate woman among you—so delicate she would not so much as touch
the ground with her foot—will be selfish toward the husband she loves and toward her
own son or daughter. 57She will hide from them the afterbirth and the new baby she has
borne, so that she herself can secretly eat them. She will have nothing else to eat during
the siege and terrible distress that your enemy will inflict on all your towns.
58“If you refuse to obey all the words of instruction that are written in this book, and if you
do not fear the glorious and awesome name of the LORD your God, 59then the LORD will over-
whelm you and your children with indescribable plagues. These plagues will be intense and
28:60 Deut 28:21, 27 without relief, making you miserable and unbearably sick. 60He will afflict you with all the
diseases of Egypt that you feared so much, and you will have no relief. 61The LORD will afflict
you with every sickness and plague there is, even those not mentioned in this Book of In-
28:62 struction, until you are destroyed. 62Though you become as numerous as the stars in the
Deut 1:10 sky, few of you will be left because you would not listen to the LORD your God.
28:63 63“Just as the LORD has found great pleasure in causing you to prosper and multiply, the
Jer 45:4 LORD will find pleasure in destroying you. You will be torn from the land you are about to

28:49-57 Around 587 BC Babylon besieged Jerusalem. The city was completely destroyed, much as described here. Exiles were taken, not to return for about 70 years. The Old Testament writings of Ezra and Nehemiah describe this return and the reconstruction of the city, its walls, and the Temple.

28:56-57 The Old Testament prophets either warned about this kind of desolation or they mourned it. Jeremiah’s lamentations described the desperation as so severe that mothers would be tempted to eat their own children to keep from starving (Lamentations 2:20). Zephaniah described the devastation that would come to those who were “complacent in their sins” (Zephaniah 1:12-17). Isaiah described how his people would get “exactly what they deserve” (Isaiah 3:11). Ezekiel referred to the climax of his people’s “wickedness and pride” (Ezekiel 7:10).

28:62 How ironic that Moses quoted the very promise God made to Abraham—that his people would be as numerous as the stars—in announcing their destruction. The legacy and survival of these people depended on their obedience to God’s terms, their completion of the covenant He made with them (Genesis 17:1-14). God’s promises to Abraham included expectations of Abraham’s descendants. God would bless the people, and they in turn would obey and worship only Him. Before the Israelites even entered the land, they were well informed of the consequences they faced if they didn’t uphold their end of the covenant.

enter and occupy. 64For the LORD will scatter you among all the nations from one end of
the earth to the other. There you will worship foreign gods that neither you nor your an-
cestors have known, gods made of wood and stone! 65There among those nations you
will find no peace or place to rest. And the LORD will cause your heart to tremble, your eye-
sight to fail, and your soul to despair. 66Your life will constantly hang in the balance. You
will live night and day in fear, unsure if you will survive. 67In the morning you will say, 'If
only it were night!' And in the evening you will say, 'If only it were morning!' For you will
be terrified by the awful horrors you see around you. 68Then the LORD will send you back
to Egypt in ships, to a destination I promised you would never see again. There you will of-
fer to sell yourselves to your enemies as slaves, but no one will buy you."

29 1*These are the terms of the covenant the LORD commanded Moses to make with
the Israelites while they were in the land of Moab, in addition to the covenant He
had made with them at Mount Sinai.*

MOSES REVIEWS THE COVENANT

2*Moses summoned all the Israelites and said to them, "You have seen with your own
eyes everything the LORD did in the land of Egypt to Pharaoh and to all his servants and to
his whole country—3all the great tests of strength, the miraculous signs, and the amazing
wonders. 4But to this day the LORD has not given you minds that understand, nor eyes that
see, nor ears that hear! 5For forty years I led you through the wilderness, yet your clothes
and sandals did not wear out. 6You ate no bread and drank no wine or other alcoholic
drink, but He gave you food so you would know that He is the LORD your God.

7"When we came here, King Sihon of Heshbon and King Og of Bashan came out to fight
against us, but we defeated them. 8We took their land and gave it to the tribes of Reuben
and Gad and to the half-tribe of Manasseh as their grant of land.

9"Therefore, obey the terms of this covenant so that you will prosper in everything you do.
10All of you—tribal leaders, elders, officers, all the men of Israel—are standing today in the
presence of the LORD your God. 11Your little ones and your wives are with you, as well as the
foreigners living among you who chop your wood and carry your water. 12You are standing

28:64 Lev 26:33; Deut 4:27; 32:17; Neh 1:8
28:65 Lam 1:3
28:66 Heb 10:27
29:1 Lev 27:34; Deut 1:1-5; 5:1
29:2 Exod 19:4
29:4 Isa 6:9-10; Acts 28:26; *Rom 11:8
29:5 Deut 8:2, 4
29:7 Num 21:21; Deut 1:2-5; 2:26
29:8 Num 32:31; Deut 3:12
29:9 Exod 19:5; Deut 4:6; Josh 1:7
29:11 Josh 9:21, 23, 27

29:1a Verse 29:1 is numbered 28:69 in Hebrew text. 29:1b Hebrew *Horeb,* another name for Sinai.
29:2 Verses 29:2-29 are numbered 29:1-28 in Hebrew text.

Chapters 29–30 Now that the law code has been laid out (5–26), the ratification called for (27), and the blessings and curses set forth (27:11–28:68), these two chapters (29–30) provide a final review, a recapitulation of the whole covenant being offered to Israel.

29:2-6 The miraculous signs and amazing wonders Moses referred to included the ten plagues God used to convince the pharaoh in Egypt to let the Israelites go. But God also opened seas, provided water from rocks, brought food from heaven (manna), and even supernaturally provided for clothing and shoes.

29:7 King Sihon of the Amorites and King Og of Bashan made the mistake of opposing and harassing Israel instead of allowing the nation passage through their territories. When the Hivites tricked Joshua into forming a treaty with them, part of the reason they gave for seeking a treaty was their knowledge of the Israelites' defeat of Og and Sihon (Joshua 9).

29:8 The tribes of Reuben, Gad, and the half-tribe of Manasseh settled east of the Jordan River. This was the first land the people saw as they approached the Promised Land. Numbers 32 records the request from the Gadites and Reubenites to keep their herds on the east side of the Jordan in order to have plenty of grazing land. Moses consented, provided that their fighting men would still cross the Jordan and help the other tribes settle their territories. Under the leadership of Joshua, they fought alongside the other Israelites in the conquest of the Promised Land.

▸ CHURCH
29:11 Child-rearing. What difference does it make for a child to be raised in a Christian family? All who lived in an Israelite home enjoyed the benefits and bore the responsibilities of keeping the covenant with the God of Israel. In a similar way, children who live in a Christian home experience blessings under the New Covenant (1 Corinthians 7:14). You have only a brief time to impact the spiritual lives of your children—make the very best of it. (***See Church**> Who> From Every People> Children are included in the older covenants,* TopicGuide page A48.)

29:12 A covenant is like a contractual agreement, a sacred pact. Most such promises hinged on both parties keeping their "part of the bargain." From the beginning of the covenant with Abraham (Genesis 17:1-14) and throughout the history of the Israelites, God laid out requirements of faith and obedience. And much of Deuteronomy consists of reminders that there are consequences for disobedience to God. Yet, here we are reminded that the Lord makes the covenant and the Lord seals the covenant. It is His doing from start to finish.

here today to enter into the covenant of the LORD your God. The LORD is making this cov-
enant, including the curses. 13 By entering into the covenant today, He will establish you as
His people and confirm that He is your God, just as He promised you and as He swore to
your ancestors Abraham, Isaac, and Jacob.
14 "But you are not the only ones with whom I am making this covenant with its curses.
15 I am making this covenant both with you who stand here today in the presence of the
LORD our God, and also with the future generations who are not standing here today.
16 "You remember how we lived in the land of Egypt and how we traveled through the
lands of enemy nations as we left. 17 You have seen their detestable practices and their idols*
made of wood, stone, silver, and gold. 18 I am making this covenant with you so that no one
among you—no man, woman, clan, or tribe—will turn away from the LORD our God to worship
these gods of other nations, and so that no root among you bears bitter and poisonous fruit.
19 "Those who hear the warnings of this curse should not congratulate themselves,
thinking, 'I am safe, even though I am following the desires of my own stubborn heart.'
This would lead to utter ruin! 20 The LORD will never pardon such people. Instead His anger
and jealousy will burn against them. All the curses written in this book will come down on
them, and the LORD will erase their names from under heaven. 21 The LORD will separate
them from all the tribes of Israel, to pour out on them all the curses of the covenant re-
corded in this Book of Instruction.
22 "Then the generations to come, both your own descendants and the foreigners who
come from distant lands, will see the devastation of the land and the diseases the LORD inflicts
on it. 23 They will exclaim, 'The whole land is devastated by sulfur and salt. It is a wasteland
with nothing planted and nothing growing, not even a blade of grass. It is like the cities of Sod-
om and Gomorrah, Admah and Zeboiim, which the LORD destroyed in His intense anger.'
24 "And all the surrounding nations will ask, 'Why has the LORD done this to this land?
Why was He so angry?'
25 "And the answer will be, 'This happened because the people of the land abandoned
the covenant that the LORD, the God of their ancestors, made with them when He brought
them out of the land of Egypt. 26 Instead, they turned away to serve and worship gods they
had not known before, gods that were not from the LORD. 27 That is why the LORD's anger
has burned against this land, bringing down on it every curse recorded in this book. 28 In
great anger and fury the LORD uprooted His people from their land and banished them to
another land, where they still live today!'
29 "The LORD our God has secrets known to no one. We are not accountable for them, but
we and our children are accountable forever for all that He has revealed to us, so that we
may obey all the terms of these instructions.

29:13 Gen 17:7; Exod 6:7
29:14 Jer 31:31; Heb 8:7
29:17 Exod 20:23; Deut 4:28; 28:36
29:18 Deut 13:6; 32:32; Heb 12:15
29:20 Deut 9:14; 2 Kgs 14:27; Pss 74:1; 80:4
29:22 Jer 19:8
29:23 Gen 19:24; Isa 1:7; 34:9; 64:11
29:24 1 Kgs 9:8; Jer 22:8-9
29:25 2 Kgs 17:9; 2 Chr 36:13
29:27 Deut 29:20
29:28 1 Kgs 14:15; Ezek 19:12
29:29 John 5:39; Acts 1:7; 17:11

29:17 The Hebrew term (literally *round things*) probably alludes to dung.

▸ HOLINESS

29:18-19 Drifting away. It is painful to see people drift away from Christ. Do you know people who appeared to be Christians, but, after a while, returned to their old stubborn ways? We should lovingly confront those who walk away from God and gently and humbly help them back to the right path (Galatians 6:1). As James says, "you can be sure that whoever brings the sinner back will save that person from death" (James 5:19-20). Be sure you do not turn from following Christ who has redeemed you! (***See Holiness**> God's Blessing> Obedience gives greater assurance of salvation,* TopicGuide page A42.)

29:23 While Sodom and Gomorrah were the more well known of the "cities of the plain" (Genesis 13:12), Admah and Zeboiim were often mentioned with them, and were joined with them in a military alliance (Genesis 14:3). These cities may have been located in what is now the southern portion of the Dead Sea.

▸ PURPOSE

29:29 The mysteries of God. "What is God's will for my life?" This question often rattles around in our brains. Israel's precise future was hidden in the mind of God, but the things that were revealed plainly to them were their most precious possessions. When you are struggling over what to do next, assess what God has given you, particularly what God has plainly revealed as His will in His Word. God's will for all of us is to live holy lives through the process of *sanctification* (1 Thessalonians 4:7). No matter what vocational, educational, or relational paths we take, we should always walk the way of obedience. And we can live confidently knowing that nothing that happens to us is a surprise to God. (***See Purpose**> God's Means> Human Choice> Bringing our wills in subjection to God's will,* TopicGuide page A52.)

A CALL TO RETURN TO THE LORD

30 "In the future, when you experience all these blessings and curses I have listed
for you, and when you are living among the nations to which the LORD your God
has exiled you, take to heart all these instructions. 2If at that time you and your children
return to the LORD your God, and if you obey with all your heart and all your soul all the
commands I have given you today, 3then the LORD your God will restore your fortunes. He
will have mercy on you and gather you back from all the nations where He has scattered
you. 4Even though you are banished to the ends of the earth, the LORD your God will
gather you from there and bring you back again. 5The LORD your God will return you to
the land that belonged to your ancestors, and you will possess that land again. Then He
will make you even more prosperous and numerous than your ancestors!
6"The LORD your God will change your heart* and the hearts of all your descendants, so
that you will love Him with all your heart and soul and so you may live! 7The LORD your God
will inflict all these curses on your enemies and on those who hate and persecute you.
8Then you will again obey the LORD and keep all His commands that I am giving you today.
9"The LORD your God will then make you successful in everything you do. He will give
you many children and numerous livestock, and He will cause your fields to produce
abundant harvests, for the LORD will again delight in being good to you as He was to your
ancestors. 10The LORD your God will delight in you if you obey His voice and keep the com-
mands and decrees written in this Book of Instruction, and if you turn to the LORD your God
with all your heart and soul.

THE CHOICE OF LIFE OR DEATH

11"This command I am giving you today is not too difficult for you to understand, and it is
not beyond your reach. 12It is not kept in heaven, so distant that you must ask, 'Who will
go up to heaven and bring it down so we can hear it and obey?' 13It is not kept beyond the
sea, so far away that you must ask, 'Who will cross the sea to bring it to us so we can hear
it and obey?' 14No, the message is very close at hand; it is on your lips and in your heart so
that you can obey it.

30:1 Lev 26:40-41; Deut 4:30; 11:26
30:2 Deut 4:29-30; Neh 1:9
30:3 Gen 28:15; Matt 23:37; John 11:51-52
30:4 Isa 43:6
30:5 Deut 13:17; Jer 29:14; 30:3
30:7 Deut 7:15
30:9 Deut 15:10; 29:9
30:10 Deut 4:29
30:11 Isa 45:19
30:12-14 *Rom 10:6-8

30:6 Hebrew *circumcise your heart.*

30:1-20 Chapters 29 and 30 summarize Deuteronomy with a strong admonition to choose obedience and thus life. This is the final call to Israel to embrace the covenant with God. The rest of the book (chapters 31–34) focuses on the transition of leadership from Moses to Joshua.

▸GOD
30:1-3 Repenting of sin. Foreshadowing Israel's up-and-down future, God gives a hypothetical example in which Israel sins against God, but later the people want to return. What would God's response be? God would welcome them, love them, and make them more blessed than they ever could have dreamed! Read Luke 15 and you will find out that God feels the same way about you. Though you sin, if you repent and return, God will receive you and will delight in being as good to you as He would have been if you had lived a perfect life. God loves it when a sinner repents! (***See God****> God's Attributes> Forgiving> God forgives His people when they repent,* TopicGuide page A16.)

▸ADOPTION
30:6 Changing your heart. God's people are in continual need of a changed heart. David prayed that God would give him a clean heart (Psalm 51:10). Jeremiah called on the people of sinful Israel to cleanse their own hearts, a call to repentance that would lead to salvation (Jeremiah 4:14). But in this verse, God pledges to change the hearts of those who approach Him in faith so their love for Him can grow into maturity. Ask God to include your heart in those He cleanses and fills up with His Holy Spirit. (***See Adoption****> With Christ> United with Christ> New heart,* TopicGuide page A37.)

30:6 The Hebrew phrase in this verse literally says God will "circumcise" their hearts. Up until now, physical circumcision was practiced by Israel as an outward sign of cleansing before God. God would practice the circumcision in a way man could not, getting to the root of the problem—the heart.

▸WORSHIP
30:11 Easy commands? After reading all the rules and regulations of the Mosaic law, some might have been tempted to throw up their hands in despair. But God had made a system that includes repentance as an active part of it (Deuteronomy 30:1-10), so when people under the covenant failed, they could approach God and by grace, through faith, find forgiveness for their transgressions. You can live a life that honors God, too. Yes, God requires perfection, for He is a holy God. But He has also provided His only Son who lived for you, died for you, and now intercedes for you. And He has sent the Holy Spirit to live in you, to empower you to obey and, when you fail, to repent. This is the cycle of the Christian life—breathing in the presence and power of the Holy Spirit and breathing out the sin in our lives as we repent by faith. (***See Worship****> NT> Cleansing> God requires repentance from known sin,* TopicGuide page A30.)

30:15 15"Now listen! Today I am giving you a choice between life and death, between prosper-
Deut 11:26 Jer 21:8 ity and disaster. 16For I command you this day to love the LORD your God and to keep His
Matt 7:13-14 commands, decrees, and regulations by walking in His ways. If you do this, you will live
30:16 and multiply, and the LORD your God will bless you and the land you are about to enter
Deut 4:1; 6:5 and occupy.
17"But if your heart turns away and you refuse to listen, and if you are drawn away
30:18 to serve and worship other gods, 18then I warn you now that you will certainly be de-
Deut 4:26 stroyed. You will not live a long, good life in the land you are crossing the Jordan to
occupy.
30:19 19"Today I have given you the choice between life and death, between blessings
Deut 4:26; 30:1 and curses. Now I call on heaven and earth to witness the choice you make. Oh, that
30:20 you would choose life, so that you and your descendants might live! 20You can make
Deut 10:20; 13:4 this choice by loving the LORD your God, obeying Him, and committing yourself
firmly to Him. This* is the key to your life. And if you love and obey the LORD, you will
live long in the land the LORD swore to give your ancestors Abraham, Isaac, and Ja-
cob."

JOSHUA BECOMES ISRAEL'S LEADER

31 When Moses had finished giving these instructions* to all the people of Israel,
31:2 2he said, "I am now 120 years old, and I am no longer able to lead you. The
Deut 34:7 LORD has told me, 'You will not cross the Jordan River.' 3But the LORD your God Himself
31:3 will cross over ahead of you. He will destroy the nations living there, and you will take
Num 27:18 possession of their land. Joshua will lead you across the river, just as the LORD promised.
4"The LORD will destroy the nations living in the land, just as He destroyed Sihon and
Og, the kings of the Amorites. 5The LORD will hand over to you the people who live there,
31:6 and you must deal with them as I have commanded you. 6So be strong and courageous!
Deut 20:1 Do not be afraid and do not panic before them. For the LORD your God will personally go
*Heb 13:5 ahead of you. He will neither fail you nor abandon you."
31:7 7Then Moses called for Joshua, and as all Israel watched, he said to him, "Be strong and
Deut 1:38; 3:28 courageous! For you will lead these people into the land that the LORD swore to their an-
cestors He would give them. You are the one who will divide it among them as their grants
of land. 8Do not be afraid or discouraged, for the LORD will personally go ahead of you. He
will be with you; He will neither fail you nor abandon you."

30:20 Or *He.* 31:1 As in Dead Sea Scrolls and Greek version; Masoretic Text reads *Moses went and spoke.*

▸WORSHIP
30:15 You have a choice. Job learned that sin does not always lead to suffering; neither does righteousness always lead to earthly blessing (Job 1–2). But in the context of the contract God was making with Israel, there was a connection between their personal and corporate righteousness and the blessings they would enjoy. However, especially in the life of Jesus Christ, we see that God sometimes allows suffering even to those who are obedient to Him. Christians are often called to suffer precisely for doing what is right (Matthew 5:11-12). Live a life that runs the risk of suffering for the sake of righteousness. (***See Worship> OT> Repentance> Nature> Keeping God's commands leads to life,*** TopicGuide page A29.)

30:20 Abraham, Isaac, and Jacob were profoundly significant names to the Israelites. Abraham was the man to whom the promises were first given: promises that his people would be as numerous as the stars (Genesis 26:4) and that the land of Canaan would be the inheritance of his people. His son Isaac and his grandson Jacob passed the promises down to the people of Israel. It was fitting to conclude the call to believe by citing these names.

31:1-2 Moses wouldn't enter the Promised Land because of an incident at a place called Meribah (Numbers 20). When Israel arrived at Meribah, they needed water. After another cycle of the people's complaining, God instructed Moses to speak to the rock and water would come forth. Moses did more than merely speak to the rock: He raised his voice, expressed his anger, and struck the rock with his staff. Moses' anger obscured God's great miracle and infringed on His glory. The punishment was that Moses would not enter the Promised Land.

31:4 Sihon of the Amorites and Og of Bashan were defeated by Israel during the tribes' approach to the Promised Land. Og was often listed with Sihon as a testimony to God's power expressed through the victories of the Israelites (Psalm 135:10-11).

PUBLIC READING OF THE BOOK OF INSTRUCTION

9 So Moses wrote this entire body of instruction in a book and gave it to the priests, who
carried the Ark of the LORD's Covenant, and to the elders of Israel. 10 Then Moses gave
them this command: "At the end of every seventh year, the Year of Release, during the
Festival of Shelters, 11 you must read this Book of Instruction to all the people of Israel
when they assemble before the LORD your God at the place He chooses. 12 Call them all to-
gether—men, women, children, and the foreigners living in your towns—so they may hear
this Book of Instruction and learn to fear the LORD your God and carefully obey all the
terms of these instructions. 13 Do this so that your children who have not known these in-
structions will hear them and will learn to fear the LORD your God. Do this as long as you
live in the land you are crossing the Jordan to occupy."

31:9 Num 4:5-6; Deut 10:8
31:10 Deut 15:1
31:12 Deut 4:10

ISRAEL'S DISOBEDIENCE PREDICTED

14 Then the LORD said to Moses, "The time has come for you to die. Call Joshua and present
yourselves at the Tabernacle,* so that I may commission him there." So Moses and Joshua
went and presented themselves at the Tabernacle. 15 And the LORD appeared to them in a
pillar of cloud that stood at the entrance to the sacred tent.
16 The LORD said to Moses, "You are about to die and join your ancestors. After you are
gone, these people will begin to worship foreign gods, the gods of the land where they are
going. They will abandon Me and break My covenant that I have made with them. 17 Then
My anger will blaze forth against them. I will abandon them, hiding My face from them,
and they will be devoured. Terrible trouble will come down on them, and on that day they
will say, 'These disasters have come down on us because God is no longer among us!'

31:14 Num 27:13; Deut 34:5
31:15 Exod 33:9
31:16 Deut 4:25; 32:50; Judg 2:11; 10:6
31:17 Judg 2:12-14

31:14 Hebrew *Tent of Meeting;* also in 31:14b.

31:9 The Ark of the Covenant was a wooden chest made to God's specifications. It rested in the most holy inner chamber of the Tabernacle, then later in the Temple in Jerusalem. This Most Holy Place signified God's residence with the people. The lid of the Ark was called the *atonement cover,* or in other translations *mercy seat.* The Ark contained sacred relics that served as holy reminders of God's miraculous provision: some manna, Aaron's budding rod, and the Ten Commandments.

31:14 During the Exodus and the wilderness journey, Joshua was Moses' administrative assistant. He even climbed Mount Sinai with Moses when Moses met with God. He was one of the two scouts who saw the bounty of the Promised Land and encouraged the Israelites to believe God that they could resettle it. All of this prepared Joshua to take up the role of national leader at Moses' death.

31:14 The Tabernacle was, in essence, a portable temple or shrine. When the Israelites left Egypt, they congregated near Mount Sinai to receive instruction from God. Part of that instruction was the plan for the Tabernacle. It was built as a tent-like structure of heavy curtains and poles. The innermost chamber was the Most Holy Place (or "Holy of Holies"), which represented God's residence with the people. The furniture of the Tabernacle included the altar on which the people made their sacrifices, the Ark of the Covenant, and the seven-pronged lampstand, which is now identified as a menorah.

BECAUSE GOD IS EVER-PRESENT

He is always with me.

Do not be afraid or discouraged, for the LORD will personally go ahead of you. He will be with you; He will neither fail you nor abandon you.

DEUTERONOMY 31:8

FOR THE NEXT *GOD IS EVER-PRESENT* FEATURE SEE PAGE 381.

18 At that time I will hide My face from them on account of all the evil they commit by wor-
shiping other gods.
19 "So write down the words of this song, and teach it to the people of Israel. Help them
31:20 learn it, so it may serve as a witness for Me against them. 20 For I will bring them into the
Deut 6:10-12; 8:19; land I swore to give their ancestors—a land flowing with milk and honey. There they will
11:16-17 become prosperous, eat all the food they want, and become fat. But they will begin to wor-
31:21 ship other gods; they will despise Me and break My covenant. 21 And when great disasters
Lev 26:41 come down on them, this song will stand as evidence against them, for it will never be for-
gotten by their descendants. I know the intentions of these people, even now before they
have entered the land I swore to give them."
22 So that very day Moses wrote down the words of the song and taught it to the Isra-
elites.
23 Then the LORD commissioned Joshua son of Nun with these words: "Be strong and
courageous, for you must bring the people of Israel into the land I swore to give them. I
will be with you."
31:25 24 When Moses had finished writing this entire body of instruction in a book, 25 he gave
Deut 31:9 this command to the Levites who carried the Ark of the LORD's Covenant: 26 "Take this
Book of Instruction and place it beside the Ark of the Covenant of the LORD your God, so it
31:27 may remain there as a witness against the people of Israel. 27 For I know how rebellious
Deut 9:7, 24 and stubborn you are. Even now, while I am still alive and am here with you, you have re-
belled against the LORD. How much more rebellious will you be after my death!
31:28 28 "Now summon all the elders and officials of your tribes, so that I can speak to them di-
Deut 30:19; 32:1 rectly and call heaven and earth to witness against them. 29 I know that after my death you
31:29 Deut 32:5 will become utterly corrupt and will turn from the way I have commanded you to follow. In
the days to come, disaster will come down on you, for you will do what is evil in the LORD's
sight, making Him very angry with your actions."

THE SONG OF MOSES

30 So Moses recited this entire song publicly to the assembly of Israel:

32:1 Deut 4:26 **32** 1 "Listen, O heavens, and I will speak!
Isa 1:2 Hear, O earth, the words that I say!
32:2 2 Let my teaching fall on you like rain;
Ps 72:6 let my speech settle like dew.
Isa 55:10 Let my words fall like rain on tender grass,
like gentle showers on young plants.

▸ HOLINESS
31:29 A sad future. What a heartbreaking, bittersweet time for Moses! On one hand, he was about to die and be with God, to see the Lord in all His glory. On the other, he was turning over command to Joshua, who would likely face the same problems Moses did. Moses was grieved about the people's hardheartedness. Perhaps Moses was even grieved by a belief that he could have been a better leader. Make it your goal not to grieve those who have led you through a spiritual wilderness. Also determine that when you leave a job or position, you leave it better off than when you came. (***See Holiness****> Law and Grace> Law> Leaders and followers,* TopicGuide page A41.)

▸ WORSHIP
32:1 Worship that teaches. Do you sing songs with your children? One of the ways ancient Israel remembered and passed down their history was through songs. On God's command (Deuteronomy 31:19), Moses sang this song to the leaders of Israel so they could pass it down to their families and friends. Make it a goal for your family and church to learn about God together by learning the psalms, hymns, and Scripture songs that carry the truths of the Christian faith. (***See Worship****> OT> Music> Song of Moses commemorates victory,* TopicGuide page A27.)

32:1-43 Just as the book of Deuteronomy as a whole follows a well-known Ancient Near Eastern treaty form, so this song of Moses also seems to be patterned after a common Ancient Near Eastern lawsuit pattern. Witnesses are called (vv. 1-3), the accusation is laid down (vv. 4-9), the goodness of the offended party is declared (vv. 10-14), the broken covenant is affirmed (vv. 15-18), and the punishment is announced (vv. 19-25). In this case, the Lord goes further and adds that He will relent and save His people despite their sin and rebellion (vv. 26-43).

3 I will proclaim the name of the LORD;
how glorious is our God!
4 He is the Rock; His deeds are perfect.
Everything He does is just and fair.
He is a faithful God who does no wrong;
how just and upright He is!
5 "But they have acted corruptly toward Him;
when they act so perversely,
are they really His children?*
They are a deceitful and twisted generation.
6 Is this the way you repay the LORD,
you foolish and senseless people?
Isn't He your Father who created you?
Has He not made you and established you?
7 Remember the days of long ago;
think about the generations past.
Ask your father, and he will inform you.
Inquire of your elders, and they will tell you.
8 When the Most High assigned lands to the nations,
when He divided up the human race,
He established the boundaries of the peoples
according to the number in His heavenly court.*
9 "For the people of Israel belong to the LORD;
Jacob is His special possession.
10 He found them in a desert land,
in an empty, howling wasteland.

32:3 Gen 18:25; Exod 34:5-6; Deut 3:24
32:4 Gen 49:24; Deut 32:18; 2 Sam 22:2
32:5 Deut 4:25; 31:27; Matt 17:17
32:6 Deut 1:31; 32:28
32:7 Deut 7:18-19
32:9 1 Kgs 8:51; Jer 10:16
32:10 Ps 17:8

32:5 The meaning of the Hebrew is uncertain. **32:8** As in Dead Sea Scrolls, which read *the number of the sons of God,* and Greek version, which reads *the number of the angels of God;* Masoretic Text reads *the number of the sons of Israel.*

32:4 The first description of God used in this song calls the Lord "the Rock." Notice that this continues, in fact five times, through the song (see verses 15, 18, 30, 31). Israel understood the image, having spent so many years in the Sinai Peninsula. Their God was big, strong, unbreakable, immoveable, unchangeable, and ever-present. This concept was also a favorite of David and the other psalm writers.

32:9 *Israel* and *Jacob* are commonly used as poetic parallels in biblical literature; Jacob was the father of the 12 tribes and was renamed Israel by God (Genesis 32:22-28).

BECAUSE GOD IS JUST

He will always treat me fairly.

He [God] is the Rock; His deeds are perfect.
Everything He does is just and fair."

DEUTERONOMY 32:4

FOR THE NEXT *GOD IS JUST* FEATURE SEE PAGE 1075.

He surrounded them and watched over them;
He guarded them as He would guard His own eyes.*

32:11 Exod 19:4; Pss 17:8; 18:10-18

11 Like an eagle that rouses her chicks
and hovers over her young,
so He spread His wings to take them up
and carried them safely on His pinions.

32:12 Deut 4:35; Isa 43:12

12 The LORD alone guided them;
they followed no foreign gods.

32:13 Job 29:6; Ps 81:16

13 He let them ride over the highlands
and feast on the crops of the fields.
He nourished them with honey from the rock
and olive oil from the stony ground.

32:14 Ps 147:14

14 He fed them yogurt from the herd
and milk from the flock,
together with the fat of lambs.
He gave them choice rams from Bashan, and goats,
together with the choicest wheat.
You drank the finest wine,
made from the juice of grapes.

32:15 Judg 10:6

15 "But Israel* soon became fat and unruly;
the people grew heavy, plump, and stuffed!
Then they abandoned the God who had made them;
they made light of the Rock of their salvation.

32:16 Pss 78:58; 106:29

16 They stirred up His jealousy by worshiping foreign gods;
they provoked His fury with detestable deeds.

32:17 Lev 17:7; 1 Cor 10:20

17 They offered sacrifices to demons, which are not God,
to gods they had not known before,
to new gods only recently arrived,
to gods their ancestors had never feared.

32:18 Ps 106:21; Deut 8:11; 32:4

18 You neglected the Rock who had fathered you;
you forgot the God who had given you birth.

32:19 Lev 26:30; Ps 106:40

19 "The LORD saw this and drew back,
provoked to anger by His own sons and daughters.

32:20 Deut 32:5

20 He said, 'I will abandon them;
then see what becomes of them.
For they are a twisted generation,
children without integrity.

32:21 1 Kgs 16:13, 26; *Rom 10:19

21 They have roused My jealousy by worshiping things that are not God;
they have provoked My anger with their useless idols.
Now I will rouse their jealousy through people who are not even a people;
I will provoke their anger through the foolish Gentiles.

32:22 Lev 26:20; Ps 18:7-8

22 For My anger blazes forth like fire
and burns to the depths of the grave.*
It devours the earth and all its crops
and ignites the foundations of the mountains.

32:10 Hebrew *as the pupil of His eye.* 32:15 Hebrew *Jeshurun,* a term of endearment for Israel. 32:22 Hebrew *of Sheol.*

32:21 *The nations* (translated "people" here) and *Gentiles* are two terms often used interchangeably in biblical poetry. All non-Jewish peoples—thus all other national groups—were by definition "Gentiles."

23 I will heap disasters upon them
and shoot them down with My arrows.
24 I will weaken them with famine,
burning fever, and deadly disease.
I will send the fangs of wild beasts
and poisonous snakes that glide in the dust.
25 Outside, the sword will bring death,
and inside, terror will strike
both young men and young women,
both infants and the aged.
26 I would have annihilated them,
wiping out even the memory of them.
27 But I feared the taunt of Israel's enemy,
who might misunderstand and say,
"Our own power has triumphed!
The LORD had nothing to do with this!"'

28 "But Israel is a senseless nation;
the people are foolish, without understanding.
29 Oh, that they were wise and could understand this!
Oh, that they might know their fate!
30 How could one person chase a thousand of them,
and two people put ten thousand to flight,
unless their Rock had sold them,
unless the LORD had given them up?
31 But the rock of our enemies is not like our Rock,
as even they recognize.*
32 Their vine grows from the vine of Sodom,
from the vineyards of Gomorrah.
Their grapes are poison,
and their clusters are bitter.
33 Their wine is the venom of serpents,
the deadly poison of cobras.

34 "The LORD says, 'Am I not storing up these things,
sealing them away in My treasury?
35 I will take revenge; I will pay them back.
In due time their feet will slip.
Their day of disaster will arrive,
and their destiny will overtake them.'

36 "Indeed, the LORD will give justice to His people,
and He will change His mind about* His servants,
when He sees their strength is gone
and no one is left, slave or free.
37 Then He will ask, 'Where are their gods,
the rocks they fled to for refuge?
38 Where now are those gods,
who ate the fat of their sacrifices
and drank the wine of their offerings?
Let those gods arise and help you!
Let them provide you with shelter!

32:23 Deut 28:15-19 Ps 85:5
32:24 Deut 28:53 Ps 91:6
32:25 2 Chr 36:17 Lam 1:20; 2:21 Ezek 7:15
32:26 Deut 4:27; 28:64
32:29 Deut 5:29
32:30 Lev 26:7-8 Deut 32:4, 18
32:32 Deut 29:18
32:35 Jer 23:12 Ezek 7:5 *Rom 12:19
32:36 Lev 26:44-45 Deut 30:2-3 *Heb 10:30
32:37 Jer 2:28
32:38 Num 25:1-2 Jer 11:12

32:31 The meaning of the Hebrew is uncertain. Greek version reads *our enemies are fools.* 32:36 Or *will take revenge for.*

32:39 1 Sam 2:6 Ps 50:22 Isa 41:4; 43:10

39 Look now; I Myself am He!
There is no other god but Me!
I am the One who kills and gives life;
I am the One who wounds and heals;
no one can be rescued from My powerful hand!
40 Now I raise My hand to heaven
and declare, "As surely as I live,

32:41 Isa 34:6-8 Jer 12:12; 46:10; 50:28-32

41 when I sharpen My flashing sword
and begin to carry out justice,
I will take revenge on My enemies
and repay those who reject Me.
42 I will make My arrows drunk with blood,
and My sword will devour flesh—
the blood of the slaughtered and the captives,
and the heads of the enemy leaders."'

32:43 *Romans 15:10

43 "Rejoice with Him, you heavens,
and let all of God's angels worship Him.*
Rejoice with His people, you nations,
and let all the angels be strengthened in Him.*
For He will avenge the blood of His servants;
He will take revenge against His enemies.
He will repay those who hate Him*
and cleanse the land for His people."

44So Moses came with Joshua* son of Nun and recited all the words of this song to the
people.

32:46 Deut 4:9 Ezek 40:4; 44:5
32:47 Deut 4:40; 8:3; 30:20

45When Moses had finished reciting all these words to the people of Israel, 46he added:
"Take to heart all the words of warning I have given you today. Pass them on as a com-
mand to your children so they will obey every word of these instructions. 47These instruc-
tions are not empty words—they are your life! By obeying them you will enjoy a long life
in the land you will occupy when you cross the Jordan River."

32:43a As in Dead Sea Scrolls and Greek version; Masoretic Text lacks the first two lines. Compare Heb 1:6. **32:43b** As in Greek version; Hebrew text lacks this line. **32:43c** As in Dead Sea Scrolls and Greek version; Masoretic Text lacks this line. **32:44** Hebrew *Hoshea,* a variant name for Joshua.

BECAUSE GOD IS RIGHTEOUS

I will live by His standards.

Everything He does is just and fair. He is a faithful God who does no wrong; how just and upright He is!

DEUTERONOMY 32:4

FOR THE NEXT *GOD IS RIGHTEOUS* FEATURE SEE PAGE 1966.

MOSES' DEATH FORETOLD

48 That same day the LORD said to Moses, 49 "Go to Moab, to the mountains east of the 32:49 Num 27:12
river,* and climb Mount Nebo, which is across from Jericho. Look out across the land of Ca- Deut 3:27
naan, the land I am giving to the people of Israel as their own special possession. 50 Then 32:50
you will die there on the mountain. You will join your ancestors, just as Aaron, your Gen 25:8
brother, died on Mount Hor and joined his ancestors. 51 For both of you betrayed Me with Num 27:13
the Israelites at the waters of Meribah at Kadesh* in the wilderness of Zin. You failed to 32:51 Num 20:12
demonstrate My holiness to the people of Israel there. 52 So you will see the land from a 32:52
distance, but you may not enter the land I am giving to the people of Israel." Deut 1:37; 3:27

MOSES BLESSES THE PEOPLE

33 This is the blessing that Moses, the man of God, gave to the people of Israel be- 33:1 Josh 14:6
fore his death:

2 "The LORD came from Mount Sinai 33:2 Exod 19:18, 20
and dawned upon us* from Mount Seir; Judg 5:4
He shone forth from Mount Paran Ps 68:8, 17
and came from Meribah-kadesh Dan 7:10 Hab 3:3
with flaming fire at His right hand.* Gal 3:19
3 Indeed, He loves His people;* 33:3 Deut 4:37; 6:1-9; 7:6;
all His holy ones are in His hands. 14:2
They follow in His steps
and accept His teaching.
4 Moses gave us the LORD's instruction, 33:4 Deut 4:2
the special possession of the people of Israel.* Ps 119:111
5 The LORD became king in Israel*— 33:5
when the leaders of the people assembled, Num 23:18-24
when the tribes of Israel gathered as one." Ps 10:16

6 Moses said this about the tribe of Reuben:* 33:6 Gen 49:3

"Let the tribe of Reuben live and not die out,
though they are few in number."

7 Moses said this about the tribe of Judah: 33:7 Gen 49:8-12

"O LORD, hear the cry of Judah
and bring them together as a people.
Give them strength to defend their cause;
help them against their enemies!"

32:49 Hebrew *the mountains of Abarim.* 32:51 Hebrew *waters of Meribath-kadesh.* 33:2a As in Greek and Syriac versions; Hebrew reads *upon them.* 33:2b Or *came from myriads of holy ones, from the south, from His mountain slopes.* The meaning of the Hebrew is uncertain. 33:3 As in Greek version; Hebrew reads *Indeed, lover of the peoples.* 33:4 *Hebrew of Jacob.* The names "Jacob" and "Israel" are often interchanged throughout the Old Testament, referring sometimes to the individual patriarch and sometimes to the nation. 33:5 Hebrew *in Jeshurun,* a term of endearment for Israel. 33:6 Hebrew lacks *Moses said this about the tribe of Reuben.*

32:49 Mount Nebo is on the eastern side of the Great Rift Valley where the Dead Sea is located. It is over 2,600 feet in elevation, and thus gives a view across the valley into the land promised to Israel (as seen in verse 52 below). Jerusalem, on the central ridge in the Promised Land, is virtually the same elevation.

32:51 As seen in the previous chapter (31:1-2), God reminds Moses one more time why His servant would not accompany Israel into the Promised Land.

33:6-25 Moses' final blessings here followed the organizational structure of the Israelites—by tribe. The tribe of Simeon is not mentioned as a fulfillment of Jacob's curse upon Simeon in Genesis 49:5-7, which promised to scatter Simeon's violent ancestors.

33:8 Exod 17:7 Lev 8:8 Num 20:13, 24 Deut 6:16

8Moses said this about the tribe of Levi:

"O LORD, You have given Your Thummim and Urim—the sacred lots—
to Your faithful servants the Levites.*
You put them to the test at Massah
and struggled with them at the waters of Meribah.

33:9 Exod 32:27 Mal 2:5

9 The Levites obeyed Your word
and guarded Your covenant.
They were more loyal to You
than to their own parents.
They ignored their relatives
and did not acknowledge their own children.

33:10 Lev 10:11; 16:12-13 Deut 17:9; 31:9

10 They teach Your regulations to Jacob;
they give Your instructions to Israel.
They present incense before You
and offer whole burnt offerings on the altar.
11 Bless the ministry of the Levites, O LORD,
and accept all the work of their hands.
Hit their enemies where it hurts the most;
strike down their foes so they never rise again."

33:12 Deut 12:10; 32:8

12Moses said this about the tribe of Benjamin:

"The people of Benjamin are loved by the LORD
and live in safety beside Him.
He surrounds them continuously
and preserves them from every harm."

33:13 Gen 27:27-29; 49:22

13Moses said this about the tribes of Joseph:

"May their land be blessed by the LORD
with the precious gift of dew from the heavens
and water from beneath the earth;
14 with the rich fruit that grows in the sun,
and the rich harvest produced each month;
15 with the finest crops of the ancient mountains,
and the abundance from the everlasting hills;

33:16 Exod 3:2

16 with the best gifts of the earth and its bounty,
and the favor of the One who appeared in the burning bush.
May these blessings rest on Joseph's head,
crowning the brow of the prince among his brothers.

33:8 As in Greek version; Hebrew lacks *the Levites.*

33:8 Massah and Meribah were both places where the Israelites received water from a rock. In both cases the people complained and quarreled to the point of Moses' exasperation. At Rephidim, a campsite just before Mount Sinai, God instructed Moses to strike a rock to produce water (Exodus 17:1-7). The people were saved by this miracle. Moses named that place *Massah,* which meant "strife" or "quarreling." At Meribah, God asked Moses to *speak* to the rock, but in Moses' exasperation he again *struck* the rock (Numbers 20:1-13). Because of this disobedience, God allowed Moses to view the Promised Land, but never to enter it.

33:13-17 Rarely do the Scriptures use the phrase "the tribes of Joseph." Joseph was Jacob's favorite son, though not his eldest. He rose to leadership in Egypt—thus the reference to his being a "prince among his brothers." Joseph received the double portion of inheritance usually reserved for the eldest son. This meant there was not a tribe of Joseph, but instead two tribes named for the sons of Joseph—Ephraim and Manasseh (verse 17).

33:16 "The one who appeared in the burning bush" is an unusual but powerful image referring to the Lord when He disclosed Himself to Moses on the far side of the wilderness (Exodus 3:1-10). Joseph also had the favor of this unpredictable and awesome God.

17 Joseph has the majesty of a young bull;
he has the horns of a wild ox.
He will gore distant nations,
driving them to the ends of the earth.
This is my blessing for the multitudes of Ephraim
and the thousands of Manasseh."

18Moses said this about the tribes of Zebulun and Issachar*:

"May the people of Zebulun prosper in their travels.
May the people of Issachar prosper at home in their tents.
19 They summon the people to the mountain
to offer proper sacrifices there.
They benefit from the riches of the sea
and the hidden treasures in the sand."

20Moses said this about the tribe of Gad:

"Blessed is the one who enlarges Gad's territory!
Gad is poised there like a lion
to tear off an arm or a head.
21 The people of Gad took the best land for themselves;
a leader's share was assigned to them.
When the leaders of the people were assembled,
they carried out the LORD's justice
and obeyed His regulations for Israel."

22Moses said this about the tribe of Dan:

"Dan is a lion's cub,
leaping out from Bashan."

23Moses said this about the tribe of Naphtali:

"O Naphtali, you are rich in favor
and full of the LORD's blessings;
may you possess the west and the south."

24Moses said this about the tribe of Asher:

"May Asher be blessed above other sons;
may he be esteemed by his brothers;
may he bathe his feet in olive oil.
25 May the bolts of your gates be of iron and bronze;
may you be secure all your days.

26 "There is no one like the God of Israel.*
He rides across the heavens to help you,
across the skies in majestic splendor.
27 The eternal God is your refuge,
and His everlasting arms are under you.

33:17 Num 23:22; 24:8 1 Kgs 22:11
33:18 Gen 49:13
33:19 Pss 4:5; 51:19
33:20 Gen 49:19
33:21 Num 32:1; 34:14 Josh 4:12; 22:1
33:22 Gen 49:16 Ezek 19:2-3
33:23 Gen 49:21
33:24 Gen 49:20 Job 29:6
33:25 Ps 147:13
33:26 Exod 15:11 Deut 4:35 Ps 68:33
33:27 Gen 49:24 Deut 7:2 Josh 24:18 Ps 90:1

33:18 Hebrew lacks *and Issachar.* 33:26 Hebrew *of Jeshurun,* a term of endearment for Israel.

▸ SPIRITUAL WARFARE

33:27 The refuge of God. Do you sometimes doubt your salvation? Some of the most well-known Christians in history struggled with doubt: Saint Augustine, Martin Luther, Charles Spurgeon, Charles and John Wesley, among many others. But the Scriptures teach that the certainty of our salvation rests not in our own sense of well being, but in God and His pledge to hold us securely in His grasp. Rest in God's promise to hold you in His everlasting arms (see John 6:39; 10:28-29). (***See Spiritual Warfare***> *Resisting Sin and Evil*> *Consequences*> *Of Obedience*> *Assurance of salvation,* TopicGuide page A46.)

He drives out the enemy before you;
He cries out, 'Destroy them!'
28 So Israel will live in safety,
prosperous Jacob in security,
in a land of grain and new wine,
while the heavens drop down dew.
29 How blessed you are, O Israel!
Who else is like you, a people saved by the LORD?
He is your protecting shield
and your triumphant sword!
Your enemies will cringe before you,
and you will stomp on their backs!"

THE DEATH OF MOSES

34 Then Moses went up to Mount Nebo from the plains of Moab and climbed Pisgah
Peak, which is across from Jericho. And the LORD showed him the whole land, from
Gilead as far as Dan; 2 all the land of Naphtali; the land of Ephraim and Manasseh; all the
land of Judah, extending to the Mediterranean Sea*; 3 the Negev; the Jordan Valley with Jeri-
cho—the city of palms—as far as Zoar. 4 Then the LORD said to Moses, "This is the land I prom-
ised on oath to Abraham, Isaac, and Jacob when I said, 'I will give it to your descendants.' I
have now allowed you to see it with your own eyes, but you will not enter the land."
5 So Moses, the servant of the LORD, died there in the land of Moab, just as the LORD had
said. 6 The LORD buried him* in a valley near Beth-peor in Moab, but to this day no one
knows the exact place. 7 Moses was 120 years old when he died, yet his eyesight was
clear, and he was as strong as ever. 8 The people of Israel mourned for Moses on the plains
of Moab for thirty days, until the customary period of mourning was over.
9 Now Joshua son of Nun was full of the spirit of wisdom, for Moses had laid his hands on
him. So the people of Israel obeyed him, doing just as the LORD had commanded Moses.
10 There has never been another prophet in Israel like Moses, whom the LORD knew face
to face. 11 The LORD sent him to perform all the miraculous signs and wonders in the land
of Egypt against Pharaoh, and all his servants, and his entire land. 12 With mighty power,
Moses performed terrifying acts in the sight of all Israel.

33:28 Gen 27:27-29, 37; Deut 33:12-13
33:29 Gen 15:1; Deut 4:32; Pss 66:3; 115:11
34:1 Num 21:20; Deut 32:49, 52
34:2 Exod 23:31; Deut 11:24
34:4 Gen 12:7; 26:3
34:5 Num 12:7-8; Deut 32:50
34:6 Deut 3:29; 4:46; Jude 1:9
34:7 Deut 31:2
34:9 Num 27:18; Isa 11:2
34:10 Num 12:8
34:11-12 Deut 4:34

34:2 Hebrew *the western sea.* 34:6 Hebrew *He buried him;* Samaritan Pentateuch and some Greek manuscripts read *They buried him.*

34:1 Jericho was the first city besieged by the Israelites when they entered the Promised Land under the leadership of Joshua (Joshua 6). This was the famous battle in which the people walked around the city for seven days. When they were finished, the walls crumbled. Jericho was also the home of the prostitute Rahab, who sheltered the Israelite spies, and then was saved along with her family when the walls crumbled. Jericho was located to the west of the Jordan River just north of the Dead Sea. This was the entry route for the people into the Promised Land.

34:1-3 It seems a bit strange that two mountains are listed here. It may be that Nebo refers to a small range of which Mount Pisgah is one particular peak. Pisgah is approximately 2,600 feet in elevation, providing a view across the Jordan Valley into the Promised Land. The land is described moving in a counter-clockwise arc from north to south.

34:3 The Negev was the desert to the south of the territory of Judah, part of the land that the Israelites eventually settled. Even though bounded by the Mediterranean Sea and the Dead Sea, it was an arid region. Later, when the king of Babylon ransacked Jerusalem, many of the city's inhabitants ran to the Negev to find safety.

34:3 When Sodom and Gomorrah were about to be destroyed, angels came to rescue Lot. He asked them to let him run to a nearby town of Zoar, pointing out that it was a town so small that it was not worth destroying. Zoar was known as Bela previous to Lot's inhabiting it. Today, it is probably underwater at the south end of the Dead Sea, as many people believe the cities of Sodom and Gomorrah are.

34:5 Moab, the land where Moses died and was buried, was a small kingdom to the east of the Dead Sea on the Transjordanian Plateau.

▸ BIBLE
34:10 Moses the prophet. Like Christ, Moses functioned as a prophet, priest, and king. But his foremost calling was that of a prophet, and he stood as the standard for all old covenant prophets until the time of Jesus (John 4:15-19). Has there been someone in your life that has impacted you like none other? Has that person always been a positive influence, or mainly negative? Pray that God will bring anointed, influential people into your life that can help you to walk in the Spirit, not in the flesh. (***See Bible***> *Unity*> *OT Types*> *Moses*, TopicGuide page A11.)

KEY PLACES IN JOSHUA

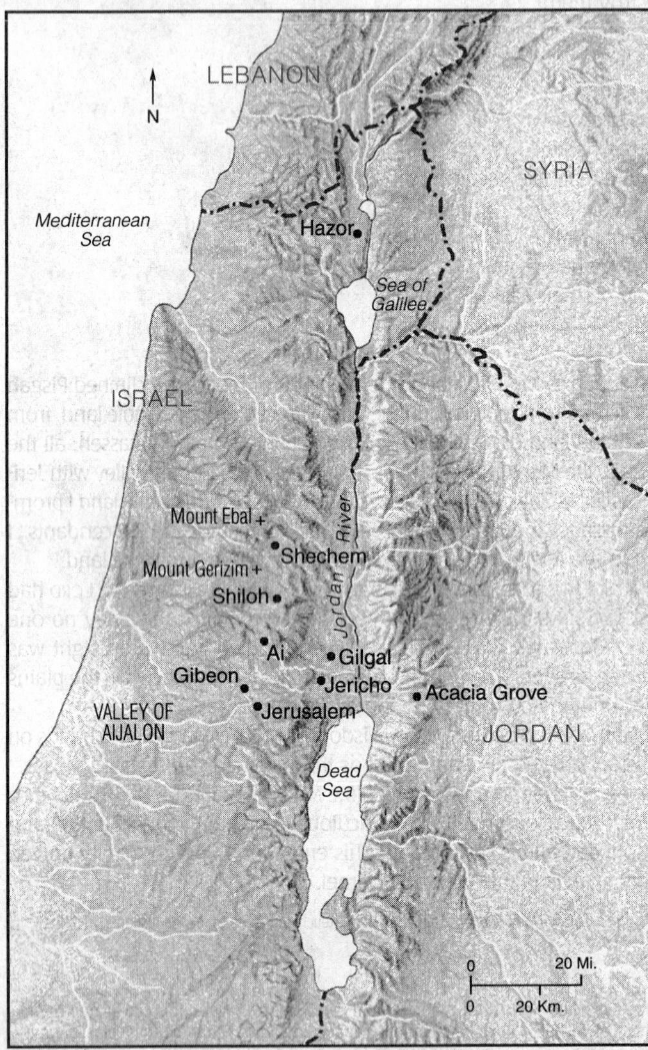

The broken lines (—·—·) indicate modern boundaries.

1 Acacia Grove The story of Joshua begins with the Israelites camping at Acacia Grove. The Israelites under Joshua were ready to enter and conquer Canaan. But before the nation moved out, Joshua received instructions from God (1:1-18).

2 Jordan River The entire nation prepared to cross this river, which was swollen from spring rains. After the spies returned from Jericho with a positive report, Joshua prepared the priests and people for a miracle. As the priests carried the Ark into the Jordan River, the water stopped flowing, and the entire nation crossed on dry ground into the Promised Land (2:1–4:24).

3 Gilgal After crossing the Jordan River, the Israelites camped at Gilgal, where they renewed their commitment to God and celebrated the Passover, the festival commemorating their deliverance from Egypt (see Exodus). As Joshua made plans for the attack on Jericho, an angel appeared to him (5:1-15).

4 Jericho The walled city of Jericho seemed a formidable enemy. But when Joshua followed God's plans, the great walls were no obstacle. The city was conquered with only the obedient marching of the people (6:1-27).

5 Ai Victory could not continue without obedience to God. That is why the disobedience of one man, Achan, brought defeat to the entire nation in the first battle against Ai. But once the sin was recognized and punished, God told Joshua to take heart and try Ai once again. This time the city was taken (7:1–8:29).

6 The Mountains of Ebal and Gerizim After the defeat of Ai, Joshua built an altar at Mount Ebal. Then the people divided themselves, half at the foot of Mount Ebal, half at the foot of Mount Gerizim. The priests stood between the mountains holding the Ark of the Covenant as Joshua read God's law to all the people (8:30-35).

7 Gibeon It was just after the Israelites reaffirmed their covenant with God that their leaders made a major mistake in judgment: They were tricked into making a peace treaty with the city of Gibeon. The Gibeonites pretended that they had traveled a long distance and asked the Israelites for a treaty. The leaders made the agreement without consulting God. The trick was soon discovered, but because the treaty had been made, Israel could not go back on its word. As a result, the Gibeonites saved their own lives, but they were forced to become Israel's slaves (9:1-27).

8 Valley of Aijalon The king of Jerusalem was very angry at Gibeon for making a peace treaty with the Israelites. He gathered armies from four other cities to attack the city. Gibeon summoned Joshua for help. Joshua took immediate action. Leaving Gilgal, he attacked the coalition by surprise. As the battle waged on and moved into the valley of Aijalon, Joshua prayed for the sun to stand still until the enemy could be destroyed (10:1-43).

9 Hazor Up north in Hazor, King Jabin mobilized the kings of the surrounding cities to unite and crush Israel. But God gave Joshua and Israel victory (11:1-23).

10 Shiloh After the armies of Canaan were conquered, Israel gathered at Shiloh to set up the Tabernacle. This movable building had been the nation's center of worship during their years of wandering. The seven tribes who had not received their land were given their allotments (18:1–19:51).

11 Shechem Before Joshua died he called the entire nation together at Shechem to remind them that it was God who had given them their land and that only with God's help could they keep it. The people vowed to follow God. As long as Joshua was alive, the land was at rest from war and trouble (24:1-33).

PURPOSE

To guide later generations of Israelites to listen to God's instructions and live victoriously in the Promised Land.

When traveling from the nation of Jordan to Israel today, one crosses a bridge spanning the Jordan River. In the same way, the book of Joshua serves as a bridge between two epochs in the history of Israel. It was written to be a sequel to the book of Deuteronomy.

The first five books of the Old Testament trace the founding of the nation through whom God intended to bless the whole earth (Genesis 12:1-3). In Genesis, Israel was a promise, but by the end of Deuteronomy, they were a people poised on the eastern bank of the Jordan River, ready to cross over into their homeland. Joshua, the book that describes the conquest of the Promised Land, is appropriately named after the main character who leads the conquest.

DISCOVER GOD IN JOSHUA

In the face of Israel's need to conquer the pagan tribes of Canaan, three aspects of God's character are seen:

God is holy: God commanded Joshua to cleanse the land of Canaan of all its defilement—in other words, Joshua was to kill or drive out all the inhabitants. Despite the violent nature of God's instructions and Israel's obedience, we should not accuse either party of brutality. In reality, God's holiness made such a course of action necessary. Archaeological discoveries have confirmed the perverted and morally bankrupt lifestyles of the Canaanite peoples—sexual immorality, idol worship, and child sacrifice, to name a few. In order for God's people to reflect His holiness, the land where they settled needed to be cleansed and set apart as a place to live.

God is just: Every descendant of Adam and Eve infected with the propensity to sin has violated God's holy standards. Every person, therefore, must be the object of God's justice in some way. When God judges sinners, as He did the Canaanites, He is just. When He "judged" a sheep or goat instead of an Israelite, He was just. And when He judged Jesus Christ for the sins of the world, He was just. God's justice is not always displayed the way it is in Joshua, but it is always a reflection of His holiness.

God is our Divine Warrior: In Joshua, war is an instrument in the service of a holy cause, and God is a Divine Warrior, striking at His enemies. It was God who delivered mighty Jericho into the hands of His people (Joshua 6:2) and God who stopped the sun from setting to enable His people to attain a great victory over the Amorites (Joshua 10:12). The text is clear that success in battle, even against relatively undaunting opponents, is only possible because God causes it to be so (Joshua 7; 8:1).

GROWING THROUGH JOSHUA

Many have seen a parallel between Israel's conquest of Canaan and the Christian's engagement in spiritual warfare:

God's part and our part: Even though "this is the Lord's battle" (1 Samuel 17:47), Joshua and his soldiers still had a part to play: They had to obey the Lord's commands. When they obeyed, they were victorious; when they did not, they were defeated. Our part is to obey; God's part is to give victory.

Weapons of war: Engaging a physical enemy in a physical domain requires physical weapons. Christians have not been commanded to conquer a geographical land, but rather to defeat a spiritual enemy and set his captives free using spiritual weapons of warfare (Luke 4:18-19; Ephesians 6:10-18). By reading about Joshua's exploits, we discover principles that can be applied to spiritual combat.

Discernment: One of Joshua's biggest mistakes during the conquest of Canaan occurred when he met the leaders of a city called Gibeon. The Gibeonites lied about their identity and convinced Joshua to enter into a peace treaty—a treaty that he accepted without seeking the Lord's counsel (Joshua 9:14-15). When Joshua discovered they were Canaanites, the treaty prevented him from driving them out as the Lord had commanded. We should be careful in our contracts with unbelievers (2 Corinthians 6:14-17) lest they become a snare to us in our Christian walk.

DISCOVERY VERSES

Study this Book of Instruction continually. Meditate on it day and night so you will be sure to obey everything written in it. Only then will you prosper and succeed in all you do. This is My command—be strong and courageous! Do not be afraid or discouraged. For the LORD your God is with you wherever you go.
(JOSHUA 1:8-9)

Each one of you will put to flight a thousand of the enemy, for the LORD your God fights for you, just as He has promised.
(JOSHUA 23:10)

If you break the covenant of the LORD your God by worshiping and serving other gods, His anger will burn against you, and you will quickly vanish from the good land He has given you. (JOSHUA 23:16)

JOSHUA FACTS

Author: Joshua is not identified as the author of the book that bears his name, neither in the book itself nor by those quoting it. But Joshua likely contributed to the majority of the details in the book (see Joshua 24:26 for a hint at this) and a number of elements suggest an early date for its completion, perhaps soon after his death. The account of Joshua's death (24:29-33) demonstrates that Joshua could not have been the sole author, and that the book was completed after his death.

Written to: The nation of Israel, who needed to complete the occupation of the Promised Land.

Date of writing: Joshua died around 1390 BC, so the majority of the book must have been written between the beginning of the conquest (1405 BC) and Joshua's death, with the final editing occurring some time soon after his death.

Setting: Joshua takes place in three geographic settings: The Jordan River area as Israel prepares to cross over into Canaan (chapters 1–5); the land of Canaan as Israel divides and conquers (chapters 6:1–13:7); the subdivided land of Canaan inhabited by Israel, plus a portion of the east bank of the Jordan where two and a half tribes settled (chapters 13:8–24:33).

OUTLINE

- **JOSHUA 1–12**—Conquest of the land
- **JOSHUA 13–21**—Distribution of the land
- **JOSHUA 22–24**—Covenant fidelity in the land

THE LORD'S CHARGE TO JOSHUA

1 After the death of Moses the LORD's servant, the LORD spoke to Joshua son of Nun,
Moses' assistant. He said, 2"Moses My servant is dead. Therefore, the time has come
for you to lead these people, the Israelites, across the Jordan River into the land I am giving
them. 3I promise you what I promised Moses: 'Wherever you set foot, you will be on land I
have given you—4from the Negev wilderness in the south to the Lebanon mountains in the
north, from the Euphrates River in the east to the Mediterranean Sea* in the west, including
all the land of the Hittites.' 5No one will be able to stand against you as long as you live. For I
will be with you as I was with Moses. I will not fail you or abandon you.
6"Be strong and courageous, for you are the one who will lead these people to possess
all the land I swore to their ancestors I would give them. 7Be strong and very courageous.
Be careful to obey all the instructions Moses gave you. Do not deviate from them, turning
either to the right or to the left. Then you will be successful in everything you do. 8Study
this Book of Instruction continually. Meditate on it day and night so you will be sure to
obey everything written in it. Only then will you prosper and succeed in all you do. 9This is

1:2 Num 12:7; Deut 34:5
1:3 Deut 11:24
1:5 Deut 7:24; 31:6-8; Heb 13:5
1:7 Deut 5:29, 32; 28:14; 29:9
1:8 Deut 17:8-9; Ps 1:1-3
1:9 Deut 31:6-8

1:4 Hebrew *the Great Sea.*

1:1 Moses led the Israelites out of Egypt and into the Promised Land of Canaan. Moses died just before Israel entered the land, but he passed on his leadership to his faithful aid Joshua before he died.

▸BIBLE

1:1 Hearing from God. How did Joshua know for certain that he was the person God had chosen to lead Israel? After the death of Moses, God began to speak to and through Joshua. This encouraged him to lead the people of Israel with an unmistakable authority that prompted the leaders of Israel to say, "We will do whatever you command us" (1:16, see also 4:14). Joshua prefigured the ministry of Christ, who was the living Word of God (John 1:1). How can you exude confidence? How can you command respect? By heeding God's Word. If you are not a leader, then commit to following those who obey God's Word. (***See Bible****> Unity> OT Types> Joshua,* TopicGuide page A11.)

1:1 Joshua had already played a prominent role in Israel's history. As Moses' administrative assistant during the Exodus and the journey through the wilderness, he was involved in events both great and small. He climbed Mount Sinai with Moses to meet with God. He was one of two scouts who saw the bounty of the Promised Land and believed that God would enable the Israelites to conquer it. All of this prepared Joshua to take up the role of national leader upon Moses' death. The book of Joshua is the account of Joshua's tenure as a spiritual, political, and military leader.

1:4 God's earliest promise regarding the territory that would belong to Israel was made to Abraham. The promised territory was even broader than what would be taken by Israel under Joshua: It would stretch "all the way from the border of Egypt to the great Euphrates River" (Genesis 15:18). Given these boundaries, Israel would have stretched from North Africa eastward across the Sinai Peninsula to the other side of Mesopotamia that bordered ancient Babylon (or modern Iraq), an area of roughly 300,000 square miles, or twice the size of California or Japan. Israel never conquered the land to that extent, and modern Israel is smaller even than the kingdom ruled by David and Solomon—only about the size of New Jersey or Belize (8,800 square miles).

1:4 While little is known about the Hittites, they figured into the history of Israel rather prominently. The original Hittites were probably descendants of Noah's son Ham, specifically of Ham's son Heth. They were listed among the inhabitants of Canaan (the Promised Land) along with the Amorites, the Perizzites, and the Jebusites. Esau, Abraham's grandson, married Hittite women (Genesis 26:34). Bathsheba, the woman with whom King David had an affair and then married, originally was married to Uriah, a Hittite (2 Samuel 11:3). Some of King Solomon's many wives were Hittites (1 Kings 11:1).

BECAUSE GOD IS EVER-PRESENT

He is always with me.

The LORD your God is with you wherever you go.

JOSHUA 1:9

FOR THE NEXT *GOD IS EVER-PRESENT* FEATURE SEE PAGE 932.

My command—be strong and courageous! Do not be afraid or discouraged. For the LORD
your God is with you wherever you go."

JOSHUA'S CHARGE TO THE ISRAELITES

10 Joshua then commanded the officers of Israel, 11 "Go through the camp and tell the peo- **1:10-11** Deut 3:2-4, 15-17
ple to get their provisions ready. In three days you will cross the Jordan River and take
possession of the land the LORD your God is giving you."
12 Then Joshua called together the tribes of Reuben, Gad, and the half-tribe of Manas- **1:12** Num 32:20-22, 33
seh. He told them, 13 "Remember what Moses, the servant of the LORD, commanded you: **1:13**
'The LORD your God is giving you a place of rest. He has given you this land.' 14 Your wives, Deut 3:18-20
children, and livestock may remain here in the land Moses assigned to you on the east
side of the Jordan River. But your strong warriors, fully armed, must lead the other tribes
across the Jordan to help them conquer their territory. Stay with them 15 until the LORD **1:15**
gives them rest, as He has given you rest, and until they, too, possess the land the LORD Josh 22:1-4
your God is giving them. Only then may you return and settle here on the east side of the
Jordan River in the land that Moses, the servant of the LORD, assigned to you."
16 They answered Joshua, "We will do whatever you command us, and we will go wher- **1:16** Num 32:25

1:11 This was not the first time the Israelites had approached the border of Canaan. Not long after leaving Egypt, they arrived at the border but were too afraid to enter the land. Because of that, God caused them to wander for almost 40 years in the desert between Egypt and the Promised Land. During that time, all of those Israelites who had been adults at the Exodus passed away—except Caleb and Joshua, the two scouts who had faith that God would give Israel victory. The new generation received the promise that their parents lacked the faith to receive.

1:12 The Israelite tribes of Reuben, Gad, and the half tribe of Manasseh lived to the east of the Jordan River. Numbers 32 records the request by the Gadites and Reubenites to keep their herds on the east side of the Jordan, where there was plenty of grazing land. Moses consented on one condition: The military men of these tribes would travel across the Jordan and help the other tribes conquer the land. The tribes promised to fulfill Moses' condition once they had built corrals for their animals. Joshua was calling them to keep their promise.

MY RESPONSE TO GOD

Building Intimacy through Spiritual Disciplines

JOSHUA 1

Scripture teaches that we can grow in faith, hope, and love by practicing spiritual disciplines. Spiritual disciplines include private activities such as Bible study, prayer, meditation, and fasting, as well as public activities such as receiving the benefits of biblical preaching and the sacraments by faith.

Some use spiritual disciplines to try to earn God's acceptance. But only what Christ did can make us acceptable to God. When the Father looks at us who are in Christ, He sees all the good works Jesus ever did. And since Jesus was perfect, the Father is perfectly pleased with us. God's saving love can't be gained or lost by our own works (Ephesians 2:1-10).

Others use spiritual disciplines like coins in a vending machine. They put in prayer or Scripture memory and expect automatic blessings, regardless of whether they have faith. But "it is impossible to please God without faith" (Hebrews 11:6). We must trust Him for every blessing.

God has given us spiritual disciplines to help us grow in grace. They are duties, but not just as items on a checklist. God has called us to love Him, and we cannot nurture intimacy in a mechanical way. It must come gradually as we eagerly pursue the delight of intimate contact with God through the means of grace He has given us.

1:17 Josh 1:5, 9 ever you send us. 17We will obey you just as we obeyed Moses. And may the LORD your
God be with you as He was with Moses. 18Anyone who rebels against your orders and
does not obey your words and everything you command will be put to death. So be strong
and courageous!"

RAHAB PROTECTS THE SPIES

2:1 Num 25:1 Heb 11:31 Jas 2:25 **2** Then Joshua secretly sent out two spies from the Israelite camp at Acacia Grove.* He
instructed them, "Scout out the land on the other side of the Jordan River, especially
around Jericho." So the two men set out and came to the house of a prostitute named Ra-
hab and stayed there that night.
2But someone told the king of Jericho, "Some Israelites have come here tonight to spy
out the land." 3So the king of Jericho sent orders to Rahab: "Bring out the men who have
2:4 2 Sam 17:19 come into your house, for they have come here to spy out the whole land."
4Rahab had hidden the two men, but she replied, "Yes, the men were here earlier, but I

2:1 Hebrew *Shittim.*

▸ HOLINESS

1:18 Discerning truth. Policemen can be in only so many places, but members of the general population are almost everywhere. If ordinary people oppose civil immorality, it can be reduced much more effectively than by the passage of a law. The people of Israel showed their support for Joshua's leadership by promising to police themselves against those hostile to his leadership. Do not depend on professional religious leaders alone to discern dangerous people or doctrines. Trust God's Word and the power of the Holy Spirit to reveal spiritual menaces to you. (***See Holiness***> *Law and Grace> Law> Leaders and Followers,* TopicGuide page A41.)

1:18 The men who declared here that rebellion would result in death had eyewitness experience. Dathan and Abiram joined Korah, a disgruntled Levite, and rebelled against Moses' leadership. Korah asked why Moses should have all the decision-making power when God had called all of Israel a "nation of priests." Dathan and Abiram seemed most incensed against Moses because he had not done what he promised—he had not taken Israel into the Promised Land. In the end, Korah, Dathan, Abiram, and their families and followers were killed when God caused a natural disaster. Moses' authority and God's power were confirmed through this event.

2:1 Jericho was located to the west of the Jordan River, just north of the Dead Sea. It was the first city besieged by the Israelites when they entered the Promised Land. Joshua seems to have targeted Jericho as part of a strategy to drive a wedge through the central part of Canaan.

2:1 God prepared an unlikely ally for the Israelite spies—a prostitute named Rahab. She had heard of all that God had done for Israel and had come to believe in God (2:9-11). Her faith led her to hide the spies. Because of that, Rahab and her family were spared when Israel attacked Jericho (Joshua 6). She eventually married an Israelite named Salmon and became an ancestor of Jesus himself. The book of Ruth tells of a romance between a woman named Ruth and a man named Boaz. Boaz was evidently the son of Rahab (Matthew 1:5). Rahab is cited in the New Testament as an example of great faith (Hebrews 11:31) and as a person for whom faith was action, not just words (James 2:25).

▸ GOD

2:4 Discovering God in the deception of Rahab. Can a Christian quarterback fake a handoff? In other words, is there such a thing as a moral lie? Many people believe this makes as much sense as a square circle, but what does the Bible say? To see how God feels about lying is to see His reaction to those who lie on His behalf. Rahab's lie is the best example; she disobeys the ninth commandment by hiding the spies, sending those hunting for them on a false trail, and allowing the spies to escape. But Scripture explicitly praises her actions (Joshua 6:17). In doing so, it establishes that there are exceptions to the ninth commandment, just as there are to the fourth (doing works of mercy on the Sabbath), the sixth (killing in the cases of wartime, self-defense, and capital punishment) and the eighth (taking the property of others in the invasion of the Promised Land). Four principles should be followed to determine when the full truth is not best. First, the lie must be a necessity. It must occur in a situation in which the truth would produce great evil, such as betrayal of your family or nation (Exodus 1:15-21). Second, the motive must be the glory of God, not hatred, malice, or greed (Joshua 7:19). Third, a Christian may never violate his or her conscience (James 4:17)—the Christian must always do what he or she believes to be right. Finally, there may be times when you want to use a lie to avoid suffering, but God would be more glorified by suffering. Should a persecuted Christian lie about his or her love of Christ to avoid suffering and death? No matter how nervous it makes us, it is clear from Scripture that God allows us to lie in certain circumstances. (***See God***> *God's Names> Lawgiver,* TopicGuide page A18.)

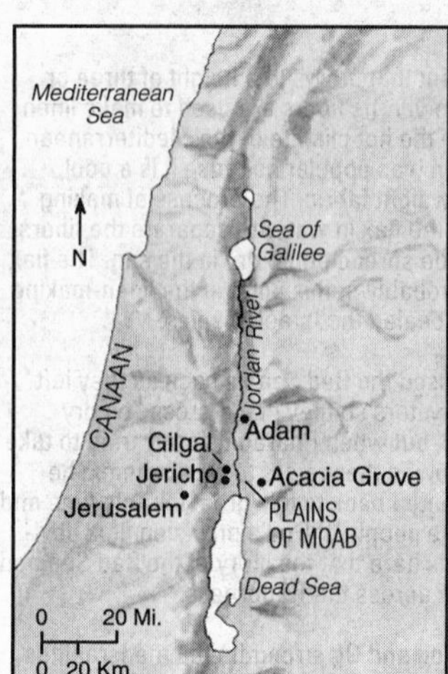

SPY MISSION TO JERICHO
Two spies left the Israelite camp at Acacia Grove, crossed the Jordan River, and slipped into Jericho. The city was built around an oasis in the midst of a hot and desolate valley 840 feet below sea level. Jericho was the first major city the Israelites set out to conquer.

didn't know where they were from. 5 They left the town at dusk, as the gates were about to
close. I don't know where they went. If you hurry, you can probably catch up with them."
6 (Actually, she had taken them up to the roof and hidden them beneath bundles of flax 2:6
she had laid out.) 7 So the king's men went looking for the spies along the road leading to Jas 2:25
the shallow crossings of the Jordan River. And as soon as the king's men had left, the gate
of Jericho was shut.

8 Before the spies went to sleep that night, Rahab went up on the roof to talk with them.
9 "I know the LORD has given you this land," she told them. "We are all afraid of you. Every- 2:9
one in the land is living in terror. 10 For we have heard how the LORD made a dry path for Exod 23:27 Deut 2:25
you through the Red Sea* when you left Egypt. And we know what you did to Sihon and Josh 9:24
Og, the two Amorite kings east of the Jordan River, whose people you completely de- 2:10
stroyed.* 11 No wonder our hearts have melted in fear! No one has the courage to fight af- Exod 14:21 Num 21:21
ter hearing such things. For the LORD your God is the supreme God of the heavens above 2:11
and the earth below. Deut 4:39

12 "Now swear to me by the LORD that you will be kind to me and my family since I have
helped you. Give me some guarantee that 13 when Jericho is conquered, you will let me 2:12
live, along with my father and mother, my brothers and sisters, and all their families." Josh 2:17-18

14 "We offer our own lives as a guarantee for your safety," the men agreed. "If you don't
betray us, we will keep our promise and be kind to you when the LORD gives us the land."

15 Then, since Rahab's house was built into the town wall, she let them down by a rope
through the window. 16 "Escape to the hill country," she told them. "Hide there for three 2:15
days from the men searching for you. Then, when they have returned, you can go on Josh 2:18, 21
your way." 2:16

17 Before they left, the men told her, "We will be bound by the oath we have taken only Jas 2:25
if you follow these instructions. 18 When we come into the land, you must leave this scarlet
rope hanging from the window through which you let us down. And all your family mem-
bers—your father, mother, brothers, and all your relatives—must be here inside the house.
19 If they go out into the street and are killed, it will not be our fault. But if anyone lays a
hand on people inside this house, we will accept the responsibility for their death. 20 If you
betray us, however, we are not bound by this oath in any way."

21 "I accept your terms," she replied. And she sent them on their way, leaving the scarlet
rope hanging from the window.

2:10a Hebrew *sea of reeds.* **2:10b** The Hebrew term used here refers to the complete consecration of things or people to the LORD, either by destroying them or by giving them as an offering.

2:6 Flax is a slender plant that grows to a height of three or four feet, with a blue flower. Its fibers are used to make linen cloth and linseed oil. In the hot climate of the Mediterranean during Bible times, linen was popular because it is a cool, highly absorbent, lightweight fabric. The process of making linen required soaking the flax in water to separate the fibers. The stalks would then be spread out to dry in the sun. The flax on Rahab's roof was probably at this point in the linen-making process when she concealed the Israelite spies.

2:10 The Israelites crossed the Red Sea as soon as they left Egypt. God parted the waters so they could cross "on dry ground" (Exodus 14:29), but when Pharaoh's army tried to take the same path, God allowed the waters to crush them. The Israelite leadership pointed back to this great miracle time and time again to remind the people of God's provision. It is obvious from Rahab's words here that the story of the Red Sea had preceded the Israelites across the wilderness.

2:10 The defeats of Sihon and Og strengthened the Israelites' faith and boosted their reputation as a strong and divinely blessed people. When the Hivites tricked Joshua into forming a treaty with them, one of the reasons they gave for seeking the treaty was their knowledge of the Israelites' defeats of Sihon and Og (Joshua 9). These victories are often listed in Scripture as a testimony to God's power (Psalm 135:10-11).

▶ WORSHIP

2:12 Plan promises. Has anyone ever asked you for something that was not in your power to give? The spies hiding on Rahab's roof found themselves in just such an awkward situation. Rahab wanted them to swear on God's name that she and her family would be saved in the upcoming Israelite invasion. The spies did not have the authority to promise protection to any Canaanites, for God had said they all must die. Thus, they offered their own lives as a guarantee (2:14), so when Jericho was destroyed, only Rahab and her family would be saved (Joshua 6:21-22). Make sure you only promise what you can deliver. (***See Worship***> *NT> Fellowship> Nature> Tell the unvarnished truth to each other,* TopicGuide page A30.)

22 The spies went up into the hill country and stayed there three days. The men who
were chasing them searched everywhere along the road, but they finally returned without
success.
23 Then the two spies came down from the hill country, crossed the Jordan River, and re-
2:24 ported to Joshua all that had happened to them. 24 "The LORD has given us the whole land,"
Josh 2:9; 6:2 they said, "for all the people in the land are terrified of us."

THE ISRAELITES CROSS THE JORDAN

3:1 **3** Early the next morning Joshua and all the Israelites left Acacia Grove* and arrived at
Josh 2:1 3:2 the banks of the Jordan River, where they camped before crossing. 2 Three days later
Josh 1:11 the Israelite officers went through the camp, 3 giving these instructions to the people:
"When you see the Levitical priests carrying the Ark of the Covenant of the LORD your God,
move out from your positions and follow them. 4 Since you have never traveled this way
before, they will guide you. Stay about a half mile* behind them, keeping a clear distance
between you and the Ark. Make sure you don't come any closer."
3:5 5 Then Joshua told the people, "Purify yourselves, for tomorrow the LORD will do great
Exod 19:10 Josh 7:13 wonders among you."
6 In the morning Joshua said to the priests, "Lift up the Ark of the Covenant and lead the
people across the river." And so they started out and went ahead of the people.
3:7 7 The LORD told Joshua, "Today I will begin to make you a great leader in the eyes of all
Josh 4:14 the Israelites. They will know that I am with you, just as I was with Moses. 8 Give this com-
3:8 Josh 3:17 mand to the priests who carry the Ark of the Covenant: 'When you reach the banks of the
Jordan River, take a few steps into the river and stop there.'"
9 So Joshua told the Israelites, "Come and listen to what the LORD your God says.
3:10 10 Today you will know that the living God is among you. He will surely drive out the Ca-
Deut 7:1 naanites, Hittites, Hivites, Perizzites, Girgashites, Amorites, and Jebusites ahead of you.
3:12 Josh 4:2-4 11 Look, the Ark of the Covenant, which belongs to the Lord of the whole earth, will lead
3:13 you across the Jordan River! 12 Now choose twelve men from the tribes of Israel, one from
Exod 15:8 each tribe. 13 The priests will carry the Ark of the LORD, the Lord of all the earth. As soon as

3:1 Hebrew *Shittim.* 3:4 Hebrew *about 2,000 cubits* [920 meters].

3:3-4 The Ark of the Covenant was a wooden chest made to strict specifications. It was kept in the most holy inner chamber of the portable Tabernacle, then later in the Temple in Jerusalem. This most holy place was seen as God's residence. The lid of the Ark was called the atonement cover, or "mercy seat" in some translations; it was regarded as God's throne. Stored inside the Ark were several sacred objects: the stone tablets, on which the Ten Commandments were written; the wooden rod, on which God caused buds to appear as a sign of Moses and Aaron's authority (Numbers 17:1-11); and a jar containing manna, the bread with which God fed the Israelites during their 40-year desert travels (Hebrews 9:4).

3:3 The word *levitical* refers to the descendants of Levi, one of the 12 sons of Jacob. The tribe, or descendants, of Levi was set apart by God to attend to the Tabernacle. Moses and Aaron belonged to this tribe. The Levites were given specific duties, most having to do with the transportation of the Tabernacle (Numbers 3), but Aaron's descendants were designated as priests. The "Levitical priests" mentioned here might have been ordinary Levites carrying out their assigned duties, but it is possible that the priests bore the Ark on this special occasion.

▶ SALVATION
3:5 Purify yourself. If God was coming to visit you tomorrow, what would you do to make yourself more holy? Would you repent of all known sin, brush up on your memory verses, or dress up in your finest clothes? That's all good, but all you really would need to do would be to trust in the final and perfect sacrifice of Christ on your behalf. You must simply believe the gospel and receive the purifying power of the Holy Spirit that alone can make sinners holy and happy. Only then can you stand in God's presence. (***See Salvation****> Receiving> When> Justified/declared innocent,* TopicGuide page A22.)

3:10 The people listed here were those the Israelites would have to defeat in order to inhabit the land God had promised to their ancestor Abraham. The Canaanites, the people of the general region, were descendants of Noah's grandson, Canaan. The Hittites and Amorites probably migrated from the north. The Perizzites possibly lived in northern Palestine. Little is known about the Hivites and Girgashites. The Jebusites probably lived in the area called Jebus—a place that was later renamed Jerusalem and became the religious center for the Israelites.

3:11 The Ark of the Covenant was a symbolic representation of God's presence among His people. At God's command, the Ark was to be carried ahead of the people to signify His leading. After guiding the Israelites through the desert for 40 years, God was about to lead them across the Jordan River and into Canaan.

their feet touch the water, the flow of water will be cut off upstream, and the river will stand up like a wall."

14 So the people left their camp to cross the Jordan, and the priests who were carrying the Ark of the Covenant went ahead of them. 15 It was the harvest season, and the Jordan was overflowing its banks. But as soon as the feet of the priests who were carrying the Ark touched the water at the river's edge, 16 the water above that point began backing up a great distance away at a town called Adam, which is near Zarethan. And the water below that point flowed on to the Dead Sea* until the riverbed was dry. Then all the people crossed over near the town of Jericho.

17 Meanwhile, the priests who were carrying the Ark of the LORD's Covenant stood on dry ground in the middle of the riverbed as the people passed by. They waited there until the whole nation of Israel had crossed the Jordan on dry ground.

3:15 1 Chr 12:15
3:16 Pss 66:6; 74:15; 114:3, 5
3:17 Exod 14:21-22, 29

MEMORIALS TO THE JORDAN CROSSING

4 When all the people had crossed the Jordan, the LORD said to Joshua, 2 "Now choose twelve men, one from each tribe. 3 Tell them, 'Take twelve stones from the very place where the priests are standing in the middle of the Jordan. Carry them out and pile them up at the place where you will camp tonight.'"

4 So Joshua called together the twelve men he had chosen—one from each of the tribes of Israel. 5 He told them, "Go into the middle of the Jordan, in front of the Ark of the LORD your God. Each of you must pick up one stone and carry it out on your shoulder—twelve stones in all, one for each of the twelve tribes of Israel. 6 We will use these stones to build a memorial. In the future your children will ask you, 'What do these stones mean?' 7 Then you can tell them, 'They remind us that the Jordan River stopped flowing when the Ark of the LORD's Covenant went across.' These stones will stand as a memorial among the people of Israel forever."

8 So the men did as Joshua had commanded them. They took twelve stones from the middle of the Jordan River, one for each tribe, just as the LORD had told Joshua. They carried them to the place where they camped for the night and constructed the memorial there.

9 Joshua also set up another pile of twelve stones in the middle of the Jordan, at the place where the priests who carried the Ark of the Covenant were standing. And they are there to this day.

10 The priests who were carrying the Ark stood in the middle of the river until all of the

4:1 Deut 27:2
4:2 Josh 3:12
4:6 Exod 12:26; 13:14
4:8 Josh 4:20
4:9 Gen 28:18

3:16 Hebrew *the sea of the Arabah, the Salt Sea.*

▸ PURPOSE

3:16 Supernatural confirmation. Does this sound familiar? God saved His people by holding back the water at the Red Sea, and in doing so He affirmed the leadership of Moses. In this case, God affirmed the leadership of Joshua and confirmed the mission of taking the Promised Land by supernaturally opening the way to Jericho for the nation of Israel. Have you seen God reveal His will to you in supernatural ways? Have you seen Him open ways for you to pursue a new job, attend a new church, or marry the right person? Praise God today for revealing His will for us. (***See Purpose> God's Means> Human Choice> Bringing our wills in subjection to God's will,*** TopicGuide page A52.)

4:2 Israel was organized into 12 tribes, each of which descended from one of the 12 sons of Jacob, who was renamed Israel. During the wilderness wandering, the people camped with their tribes around the Tabernacle, their center of worship and guidance. Moses organized an administrative plan for dealing with the problems of the people through tribal leaders. The censuses recorded in the book of Numbers were conducted according to tribe (as was the census in which Joseph and Mary participated before Jesus' birth (Luke 2)). An Israelite's identity was completely attached to his heritage, which was defined by the tribe from which he descended.

▸ HOLINESS

4:9 Godly tradition. Not only did Joshua build the memorial that God commanded, but he also built one in the middle of the Jordan. Both of these were done primarily for the sake of the children (4:6, 21), so that future generations would remember the power of God displayed at the Jordan River. God wants us to establish spiritual traditions, take pictures, and create other reminders of God's power manifested in our lives. Leave milestones to help your children understand the faithfulness of God to His covenant people. (***See Holiness> Submission> Learning God's Word> Teaching your children,*** TopicGuide page A40.)

LORD's commands that Moses had given to Joshua were carried out. Meanwhile, the peo-
ple hurried across the riverbed. 11And when everyone was safely on the other side, the
priests crossed over with the Ark of the LORD as the people watched.
4:12 Num 32:17 12The armed warriors from the tribes of Reuben, Gad, and the half-tribe of Manasseh
led the Israelites across the Jordan, just as Moses had directed. 13These armed men—
about 40,000 strong—were ready for battle, and the LORD was with them as they crossed
over to the plains of Jericho.
4:14-15 Josh 3:7-8 14That day the LORD made Joshua a great leader in the eyes of all the Israelites, and for
the rest of his life they revered him as much as they had revered Moses.
15The LORD had said to Joshua, 16"Command the priests carrying the Ark of the Cov-
4:18 Josh 3:15 enant* to come up out of the riverbed." 17So Joshua gave the command. 18As soon as
the priests carrying the Ark of the LORD's Covenant came up out of the riverbed and
their feet were on high ground, the water of the Jordan returned and overflowed its
banks as before.
4:19 Josh 5:9 19The people crossed the Jordan on the tenth day of the first month.* Then they camped
at Gilgal, just east of Jericho. 20It was there at Gilgal that Joshua piled up the twelve stones
taken from the Jordan River.
21Then Joshua said to the Israelites, "In the future your children will ask, 'What do
4:22 Josh 3:17 these stones mean?' 22Then you can tell them, 'This is where the Israelites crossed the
Jordan on dry ground.' 23For the LORD your God dried up the river right before your
eyes, and He kept it dry until you were all across, just as He did at the Red Sea* when
4:24 1 Kgs 8:42-43 Ps 89:13 He dried it up until we had all crossed over. 24He did this so all the nations of the earth
might know that the LORD's hand is powerful, and so you might fear the LORD your God
forever."

5:1 Num 13:29 Josh 2:9-11 **5** When all the Amorite kings west of the Jordan and all the Canaanite kings who lived
along the Mediterranean coast* heard how the LORD had dried up the Jordan River so
the people of Israel could cross, they lost heart and were paralyzed with fear because of
them.

4:16 Hebrew *Ark of the Testimony.* **4:19** This day in the ancient Hebrew lunar calendar occurred in late March, April, or early May. **4:23** Hebrew *sea of reeds.* **5:1** Hebrew *along the sea.*

4:19 The first month mentioned here was the first month of the Jewish religious calendar. When God delivered the Israelites from Egypt, He decreed that the annual commemoration of the Exodus should mark the beginning of the new religious year. The civil new year began in Tishri, which falls in September/October according to the calendar used by the Western world today. The religious new year began in Nisan, which falls in March/April.

5:1 The original Canaanites were descendants of Noah's grandson Canaan. Canaan was the son of Ham, and Noah cursed both because of an indiscretion (Genesis 9:20-25). The land where Canaan's descendants settled eventually came to bear their forefather's name. Later, other peoples settled in Canaan, too, and came to be known as Canaanites simply because of their location. The Canaanites were rank pagans. Among the gods they worshiped were El and his son Baal. From the conquest to the monarchy, the Israelites always faced the temptation to turn from the worship of the Lord to the worship of Baal.

5:1 According to Genesis 10:15-16, the Amorites also were descended from Canaan. It is believed that the Amorites were quite powerful at one time, occupying the larger part of Mesopotamia and Syria. Later, they were driven from that region and settled in Babylonia until the Hittites defeated them there. They then settled throughout Canaan and perhaps even Egypt. Even in the days of Abraham, they had the reputation of being a wicked people. In fact, when God promised Abraham that His people would return and claim the land, He specifically mentioned the sin of the Amorites (Genesis 15:16).

▸ MINISTRY

5:1 Fearing God. God performed the mighty work of holding back the waters of the Jordan not just for the benefit of His people, but also to teach the surrounding nations (some more than 75 miles away) to fear Him. Apparently, the Amorite and Canaanite kings got the message—they recognized that an almighty deity, a God they could not hope to defeat, led and defended the Israelites. When we tell the good news of the gospel and the reality of our personal relationship with God to unbelievers, we are declaring His power to change human hearts. By God's grace, our unbelieving hearers will be converted; but even if they are not, they will at least learn to fear God and will consider His power before they treat Christians harshly. (***See Ministry****> Great Commission> Witness> Witness in the power of the Holy Spirit,* TopicGuide page A56.)

ISRAEL REESTABLISHES COVENANT CEREMONIES

2At that time the LORD told Joshua, "Make flint knives and circumcise this second genera- 5:2-3 Gen 17:9-10, 23
tion of Israelites.*" 3So Joshua made flint knives and circumcised the entire male popula-
tion of Israel at Gibeath-haaraloth.*

4Joshua had to circumcise them because all the men who were old enough to fight in 5:4
battle when they left Egypt had died in the wilderness. 5Those who left Egypt had all been Deut 2:14
circumcised, but none of those born after the Exodus, during the years in the wilderness,
had been circumcised. 6The Israelites had traveled in the wilderness for forty years until all 5:6
the men who were old enough to fight in battle when they left Egypt had died. For they Num 14:29-35; 26:63-65
had disobeyed the LORD, and the LORD vowed He would not let them enter the land He had Deut 2:7
sworn to give us—a land flowing with milk and honey. 7So Joshua circumcised their sons—
those who had grown up to take their fathers' places—for they had not been circumcised
on the way to the Promised Land. 8After all the males had been circumcised, they rested in
the camp until they were healed.

5:2 Or *circumcise the Israelites a second time.* 5:3 *Gibeath-haaraloth* means "hill of foreskins."

5:3-4 The name Gibeath-haaraloth actually means "mountain of foreskins," which is an indication of the enormity of the task Joshua undertook in circumcising "the entire male population of Israel." For the Israelites, circumcision was the divinely ordained sign of inclusion in the covenant God made with Abraham (Genesis 17:10-11). All Israelite males were supposed to be circumcised eight days after birth, but the people had failed to circumcise their sons during their 40 years of traveling in the wilderness. Other cultures practiced circumcision, though usually as a rite of passage into adulthood.

5:6-7 The men and boys Joshua circumcised were those who left Egypt as children or who were born during Israel's time in the wilderness. When Israel first approached the border to Canaan, those who were "old enough to fight in battle" were too afraid to enter. So God told them that every person who had left Egypt as an adult would die before entering the land—every adult except Joshua and Caleb, the two who had faith (Numbers 14:32-35). By the time described in Joshua 5, that generation of adults had died and their children had become tribal leaders and soldiers with children of their own.

MY RESPONSE TO GOD

Bragging about God

JOSHUA 4

Have you ever had something so good happen to you that you had to tell everyone you met? When you understand just how good God is to you, you will naturally share your experience of God's goodness with others.

After the Israelites crossed the Jordan River on dry ground, Joshua, the leader of Israel, asked a man from each tribe to retrieve a stone for a memorial (Joshua 4:1-8). Later, when their children asked what the stones meant, the Israelites could tell of God's miraculous work in bringing them to the Promised Land. King David also beckoned others to share their stories: "Let the whole world know what He has done. . . . Tell everyone about His wonderful deeds" (Psalm 105:1-2).

Jesus gave similar orders to a demon-possessed man who walked among tombs, screaming and hitting himself with stones (Mark 5:5). Jesus cast out the demons, restoring the man to his right mind. When the healed man wanted to accompany the Lord, Jesus told him, "No, go home to your family, and tell them everything the Lord has done for you and how merciful He has been" (Mark 5:19).

Bragging about God is a simple way to serve Him and minister to others. And if you really understand how good He is, it will be the easiest thing you've ever done.

9 Then the LORD said to Joshua, "Today I have rolled away the shame of your slavery in
Egypt." So that place has been called Gilgal* to this day.
5:10 10 While the Israelites were camped at Gilgal on the plains of Jericho, they celebrated
Exod 12:18 Josh 4:19 Passover on the evening of the fourteenth day of the first month.* 11 The very next day
5:12 they began to eat unleavened bread and roasted grain harvested from the land. 12 No
Exod 16:35 manna appeared on the day they first ate from the crops of the land, and it was never seen
again. So from that time on the Israelites ate from the crops of Canaan.

THE LORD'S COMMANDER CONFRONTS JOSHUA

5:13 13 When Joshua was near the town of Jericho, he looked up and saw a Man standing in front
Gen 18:1-2; 32:24 of him with sword in hand. Joshua went up to Him and demanded, "Are You friend or foe?"
Exod 23:23 Num 22:31 14 "Neither one," He replied. "I am the Commander of the LORD's army."
5:14 At this, Joshua fell with his face to the ground in reverence. "I am at Your command,"
Gen 17:3 Joshua said. "What do You want Your servant to do?"
15 The Commander of the LORD's army replied, "Take off your sandals, for the place
where you are standing is holy." And Joshua did as he was told.

THE FALL OF JERICHO

6:2 **6** Now the gates of Jericho were tightly shut because the people were afraid of the Isra-
Deut 7:24 elites. No one was allowed to go out or in. 2 But the LORD said to Joshua, "I have given

5:9 *Gilgal* sounds like the Hebrew word *galal,* meaning "to roll." 5:10 This day in the ancient Hebrew lunar calendar occurred in late March, April, or early May.

▸ WORSHIP

5:9 The shame of the past. Even if you have trusted Christ and been cleansed by His perfect sacrifice on your behalf, you still may feel remorse for past behaviors. But can you imagine feeling shame concerning the behavior of your parents? This generation of Israelites was haunted by the shadow of 400 years of slavery, by the faithlessness of their fathers who turned their backs on the promises of God (Numbers 14), and by the physical reminder of their lack of faithfulness to God's commands. In commanding their circumcision, God took away their shame and signaled a new day for this new nation. Today can be a brand-new day for you—turn from the shame of the past to the joy of walking with God. (***See Worship****> OT> Repentance> Examples> Covenant ceremonies resumed at Gilgal,* TopicGuide page A29.)

5:10 The festival of Passover commemorated the last plague God sent upon the Egyptians. After bringing a series of disasters through Moses, God caused the death of the firstborn male in every household in Egypt. But He warned the Israelites to put the blood of a lamb on the doorpost of each house, and the angel of death "passed over" the households that heeded Him. The death of the firstborn finally broke the will of Pharaoh and induced him to let Israel depart. The Passover mentioned here was Israel's first in the Promised Land.

5:12 Throughout the Israelites' 40 years in the desert, God sent manna (Exodus 16) to feed His people. The fact that no manna appeared marked a transition in God's provision for Israel.

5:13 The city of Jericho remained a part of Israel at the time of Christ. Jesus was leaving Jericho when Bartimaeus, a blind beggar, asked to be healed. Though the crowd discouraged him, Bartimaeus persisted, and Jesus healed him on the spot (Mark 10:46-52). Jesus also used the town of Jericho in His parable of the good Samaritan. According to that story, a Jewish man was traveling from Jerusalem to Jericho when he was attacked (Luke 10:25-42). It was also in Jericho that Jesus met Zacchaeus, the short tax collector who learned about salvation through faith in Christ (Luke 19:1-10).

▸ GOD

5:13-15 Discovering God in the commander of the Lord's army. Why does God's representative (or perhaps God Himself!) take such a neutral position toward Joshua and God's people? After all, God professes His eternal love for His people repeatedly in the Scriptures (Romans 8:35-39). Was God's love for His people different under the older covenants? No, God's love is constant, but that does not prevent His people from making Him their foe. The covenant God made with Israel at Mount Sinai had national implications, and God made it clear that He would destroy the nation of Israel if the people did not keep covenant with Him (see Deuteronomy 8:5-19 and notes). As the angel implied, Joshua and Israel needed to declare allegiance to God, not the other way around. On a personal level, if you live in disobedience, you may find God opposing you. You continue in a life of disobedience at your own risk (Hebrews 6:4-6), for God is not mocked. (***See God****> God's Names> God> LORD of Heaven's Armies,* TopicGuide page A18.)

5:15 Joshua received the same commandment from God that Moses received at the burning bush (Exodus 3). The ground was holy because of God's presence. Moses met with God in the Sinai desert; Joshua met Him on the road to Jericho. The place didn't matter. God's presence made the dust of each place so precious that no man could rightly walk on it with dirty sandals.

6:2 These words of God reassured Joshua that the high, thick walls of Jericho were not insurmountable for Israel. God said He already had given Jericho, its king, and all its warriors into Israel's hands. In other words, God had decreed that Jericho would be defeated, and nothing could prevent His will from coming to pass.

you Jericho, its king, and all its strong warriors. 3You and your fighting men should march
around the town once a day for six days. 4Seven priests will walk ahead of the Ark, each **6:4**
carrying a ram's horn. On the seventh day you are to march around the town seven times, Lev 25:9
with the priests blowing the horns. 5When you hear the priests give one long blast on the
rams' horns, have all the people shout as loud as they can. Then the walls of the town will
collapse, and the people can charge straight into the town."

6So Joshua called together the priests and said, "Take up the Ark of the LORD's Cov-
enant, and assign seven priests to walk in front of it, each carrying a ram's horn." 7Then he **6:7**
gave orders to the people: "March around the town, and the armed men will lead the way Exod 14:15
in front of the Ark of the LORD."

8After Joshua spoke to the people, the seven priests with the rams' horns started marching
in the presence of the LORD, blowing the horns as they marched. And the Ark of the LORD's
Covenant followed behind them. 9Some of the armed men marched in front of the priests **6:9**
with the horns and some behind the Ark, with the priests continually blowing the horns. Isa 52:12
10"Do not shout; do not even talk," Joshua commanded. "Not a single word from any of you
until I tell you to shout. Then shout!" 11So the Ark of the LORD was carried around the town
once that day, and then everyone returned to spend the night in the camp.

12Joshua got up early the next morning, and the priests again carried the Ark of the
LORD. 13The seven priests with the rams' horns marched in front of the Ark of the LORD, **6:13**
blowing their horns. Again the armed men marched both in front of the priests with the Josh 6:4

6:3 God's instructions for Israel's assault on Jericho were exceedingly strange. The army was to march around the city once a day for six days, led by seven priests blowing rams' horns and Levites carrying the Ark of the Covenant. On the seventh day, this strange procession was to make seven trips around the city, after which the priests would sound a final blast on the horns and the people would shout. Then, God promised, the walls of Jericho would collapse. This strange procedure would leave no doubt that God, not Israel, accomplished the conquest of Jericho.

MY RESPONSE TO GOD

The Army of the Lord

JOSHUA 5:13-15

Every day, a battle is waged for your soul and the souls of those around you. As a Christian, you are in the army of the Lord. How can you be a good soldier?

First, know who is in command.

When Joshua began to lead God's people, he likely thought that he was in charge of God's army. But as he approached his first battle at Jericho, he met a powerful man holding a sword. Joshua called out, "'Are You friend or foe?' 'Neither one,' He replied. 'I am the Commander of the LORD'S army'" (Joshua 5:13-14). As this angelic messenger revealed, God was the Commander of the armies of Israel. To succeed, they would need to respect and obey Him.

Second, be ready for a life of suffering and sacrifice.

Paul encourages Timothy to think of the Christian life in these terms: "Endure suffering along with me, as a good soldier of Christ Jesus. Soldiers don't get tied up in the affairs of civilian life, for then they cannot please the officer who enlisted them" (2 Timothy 2:3-4).

Will you be a good soldier, ready to suffer and die for the honor of your cause? It is to this purpose that God has called us, so let us salute Him and go forth into the greatest battle of all time—fighting against our own sin and freeing those held captive by Satan.

horns and behind the Ark of the LORD. All this time the priests were blowing their horns.
[14]On the second day they again marched around the town once and returned to the
camp. They followed this pattern for six days.
[15]On the seventh day the Israelites got up at dawn and marched around the town as
they had done before. But this time they went around the town seven times. [16]The sev-
enth time around, as the priests sounded the long blast on their horns, Joshua com-
6:17 manded the people, "Shout! For the LORD has given you the town! [17]Jericho and
Lev 27:28 everything in it must be completely destroyed* as an offering to the LORD. Only Rahab the
Deut 20:17 prostitute and the others in her house will be spared, for she protected our spies.
6:18 [18]"Do not take any of the things set apart for destruction, or you yourselves will be com-
Deut 20:17 pletely destroyed, and you will bring trouble on the camp of Israel. [19]Everything made from
Josh 7:1, 25 silver, gold, bronze, or iron is sacred to the LORD and must be brought into His treasury."
6:19 Num 31:21-23 [20]When the people heard the sound of the rams' horns, they shouted as loud as they
6:20 could. Suddenly, the walls of Jericho collapsed, and the Israelites charged straight into the
Heb 11:30 town and captured it. [21]They completely destroyed everything in it with their swords—
6:21 men and women, young and old, cattle, sheep, goats, and donkeys.
Deut 20:16 [22]Meanwhile, Joshua said to the two spies, "Keep your promise. Go to the prostitute's
6:22 house and bring her out, along with all her family."
Josh 2:14 Heb 11:31 [23]The men who had been spies went in and brought out Rahab, her father, mother,
brothers, and all the other relatives who were with her. They moved her whole family to a
safe place near the camp of Israel.
[24]Then the Israelites burned the town and everything in it. Only the things made from
6:25 silver, gold, bronze, or iron were kept for the treasury of the LORD's house. [25]So Joshua
Josh 2:6 spared Rahab the prostitute and her relatives who were with her in the house, because she
Heb 11:31 had hidden the spies Joshua sent to Jericho. And she lives among the Israelites to this day.
6:26 1 Kgs 16:34 [26]At that time Joshua invoked this curse:

"May the curse of the LORD fall on anyone
  who tries to rebuild the town of Jericho.

6:17 The Hebrew term used here refers to the complete consecration of things or people to the LORD, either by destroying them or by giving them as an offering; similarly in 6:18, 21.

6:17 God commanded Israel to destroy everyone and everything in Jericho as "an offering to the LORD." There were only two exceptions: Rahab and her family were to be spared, as the spies had promised; and objects of silver, gold, bronze, and iron were to be brought into the Israelite treasury. Though the treasures were not to be destroyed, they were still God's, and no Israelite was to take any of them. God allowed the Israelites to keep some of the plunder they captured in later battles, but He claimed everything in Jericho for Himself. This was fitting since He gave Israel the city by miraculous means.

▸ PURPOSE

6:20 Guided by the Spirit. Have you ever known God's will but tried to accomplish it in an ungodly way? The story of the battle of Jericho is a reminder that knowing God's will is not enough—we must follow His instructions on how to accomplish His will, too. Occasionally, God's directives may not make sense to us. For instance, God tells us that the last shall actually be first, that we become rich through giving away our possessions, and that we find true life by dying. These teachings make little sense outside of faith in God. But the Holy Spirit gives us the ability to walk by faith and believe these truths. Thank Him for His empowering presence. (***See Purpose****> God's Deeds> Special Acts> Saving acts/deliverance,* TopicGuide page A52.)

▸ WORSHIP

6:22 Keep your promises. There's a reason why the Bible counsels us to make few promises—promises can be very difficult to keep (Matthew 5:37). Just as Joshua's promise to the Gibeonites (Joshua 9:15) saved them from destruction, the spies' promise to Rahab (Joshua 2) was honored and she was saved. Even when it is inconvenient, we should always keep our promises—whether they are made to good people or bad. (***See Worship****> NT> Fellowship> Nature>Tell the unvarnished truth to each other,* TopicGuide page A30.)

6:23 Joshua sent the very men who had been protected by Rahab to find her and her family and bring them out of the destruction of Jericho. Following the spies' instructions, Rahab had left hanging from her window the scarlet rope by which the spies had escaped (2:21), thereby marking her house for the Israelites. She had also convinced her extended family to wait there with her. The spies were able to find her house and bring them all to a safe place.

6:26 After Jericho was destroyed, Joshua pronounced a curse. He said anyone who might rebuild the city would lose his oldest and youngest sons. Scripture reveals that the city was resettled within a few years (Joshua 18:21), but the curse was fulfilled much later (1 Kings 16:34). Joshua's intent may have been to discourage anyone from again fortifying the city for war.

At the cost of his firstborn son,
he will lay its foundation.
At the cost of his youngest son,
he will set up its gates."

27So the LORD was with Joshua, and his reputation spread throughout the land.

AI DEFEATS THE ISRAELITES

7 But Israel violated the instructions about the things set apart for the LORD.* A man
named Achan had stolen some of these dedicated things, so the LORD was very angry
with the Israelites. Achan was the son of Carmi, a descendant of Zimri* son of Zerah, of the
tribe of Judah.
2Joshua sent some of his men from Jericho to spy out the town of Ai, east of Bethel, near
Beth-aven. 3When they returned, they told Joshua, "There's no need for all of us to go up
there; it won't take more than two or three thousand men to attack Ai. Since there are so
few of them, don't make all our people struggle to go up there."
4So approximately 3,000 warriors were sent, but they were soundly defeated. The men
of Ai 5chased the Israelites from the town gate as far as the quarries,* and they killed about
thirty-six who were retreating down the slope. The Israelites were paralyzed with fear at
this turn of events, and their courage melted away.
6Joshua and the elders of Israel tore their clothing in dismay, threw dust on their heads,
and bowed face down to the ground before the Ark of the LORD until evening. 7Then Josh-
ua cried out, "Oh, Sovereign LORD, why did you bring us across the Jordan River if you are
going to let the Amorites kill us? If only we had been content to stay on the other side!
8Lord, what can I say now that Israel has fled from its enemies? 9For when the Canaanites
and all the other people living in the land hear about it, they will surround us and wipe our
name off the face of the earth. And then what will happen to the honor of your great
name?"
10But the LORD said to Joshua, "Get up! Why are you lying on your face like this? 11Israel
has sinned and broken My covenant! They have stolen some of the things that I com-
manded must be set apart for Me. And they have not only stolen them but have lied about
it and hidden the things among their own belongings. 12That is why the Israelites are run-
ning from their enemies in defeat. For now Israel itself has been set apart for destruction. I

6:27 Josh 9:1
7:1 Josh 6:18-19; 1 Chr 2:7
7:2 Gen 28:19; Josh 16:2
7:5 Josh 2:11
7:6 Job 2:12; 42:6; Lam 2:10; Rev 18:19
7:7 Exod 5:22
7:9 Exod 32:12; Deut 9:28
7:10 Exod 14:15; 1 Sam 15:24

7:1a The Hebrew term used here refers to the complete consecration of things or people to the LORD, either by destroying them or by giving them as an offering; similarly in 7:11, 12, 13, 15. 7:1b As in Greek version (see also 1 Chr 2:6); Hebrew reads *Zabdi*. Also in 7:17, 18. 7:5 Or *as far as Shebarim*.

▸ PURPOSE

7:1 The power of one sin. Have you ever seen a little fight between two people turn into a huge problem involving many? If two armies are facing each other across a border and one nervous soldier fires a shot, all-out conflict may follow. One rebellious soldier may begin a conflict that can cost many people's lives. Likewise, if the leader of a nation declares war on another country, all the citizens of both countries are a part of the conflict, whether they have animosity toward each other or not. In this case, Achan broke the covenant God had made with Israel, so all Israel suffered, especially the 36 families who lost men in the battle of Ai. This story reminds us that our sin has widespread consequences (7:20). (***See Purpose> God's Deeds> Judgment> Community suffers due to individual's sin,*** TopicGuide page A53.)

7:2 God did not give Joshua detailed instructions for Israel's next move in its conquest of Canaan, so Joshua acted as he thought best, sending men to scout the city of Ai. They reported back that the city was weak and that only a small contingent of Israelite warriors could take it. So Joshua sent 3,000 men, but they were defeated, and 36 men were killed. Was Joshua too self-confident? Did he err by not consulting God in prayer? Perhaps. But we must remember that Israel would have been defeated even if Joshua had sent all his men, for God was punishing His people over Achan's disobedience.

7:6 Joshua and the other leaders of Israel reacted to Israel's defeat with expressions of grief, and Joshua asked God why He had brought the Israelites so far only to let them suffer defeat. To his credit, Joshua recognized God's hand in Israel's defeat, but the possibility that Israel had broken faith with God did not seem to cross his mind. He even suggested that perhaps Israel should have remained outside the Promised Land, echoing the Israelites' frequent complaint that they had it better back in Egypt (Exodus 14:11-12; Numbers 14:2-3). God would soon help Joshua understand what was going on.

will not remain with you any longer unless you destroy the things among you that were
set apart for destruction.
13“Get up! Command the people to purify themselves in preparation for tomorrow. For
this is what the LORD, the God of Israel, says: Hidden among you, O Israel, are things set
apart for the LORD. You will never defeat your enemies until you remove these things from
among you.
14“In the morning you must present yourselves by tribes, and the LORD will point out the
tribe to which the guilty man belongs. That tribe must come forward with its clans, and the
LORD will point out the guilty clan. That clan will then come forward, and the LORD will point
out the guilty family. Finally, each member of the guilty family must come forward one by
one. 15The one who has stolen what was set apart for destruction will himself be burned
with fire, along with everything he has, for he has broken the covenant of the LORD and
has done a horrible thing in Israel.”

ACHAN’S SIN

16Early the next morning Joshua brought the tribes of Israel before the LORD, and the tribe
7:17 of Judah was singled out. 17Then the clans of Judah came forward, and the clan of Zerah
Num 26:20 was singled out. Then the families of Zerah came forward, and the family of Zimri was sin-
gled out. 18Every member of Zimri’s family was brought forward person by person, and
Achan was singled out.
7:19 19Then Joshua said to Achan, “My son, give glory to the LORD, the God of Israel, by tell-
Jer 13:16 John 9:24 ing the truth. Make your confession and tell me what you have done. Don’t hide it from
me.”
20Achan replied, “It is true! I have sinned against the LORD, the God of Israel. 21Among
the plunder I saw a beautiful robe from Babylon,* 200 silver coins,* and a bar of gold
weighing more than a pound.* I wanted them so much that I took them. They are hidden
in the ground beneath my tent, with the silver buried deeper than the rest.”
22So Joshua sent some men to make a search. They ran to the tent and found the stolen
goods hidden there, just as Achan had said, with the silver buried beneath the rest. 23They
took the things from the tent and brought them to Joshua and all the Israelites. Then they
laid them on the ground in the presence of the LORD.
7:24 24Then Joshua and all the Israelites took Achan, the silver, the robe, the bar of gold, his
Josh 15:7 sons, daughters, cattle, donkeys, sheep, goats, tent, and everything he had, and they
7:25 brought them to the valley of Achor. 25Then Joshua said to Achan, “Why have you
Josh 6:18 brought trouble on us? The LORD will now bring trouble on you.” And all the Israelites
stoned Achan and his family and burned their bodies. 26They piled a great heap of stones
7:26 over Achan, which remains to this day. That is why the place has been called the Valley of
Isa 65:10 Hos 2:15 Trouble* ever since. So the LORD was no longer angry.

7:21a Hebrew *Shinar.* 7:21b Hebrew *200 shekels of silver,* about 5 pounds or 2.3 kilograms in weight. 7:21c Hebrew *50 shekels,* about 20 ounces or 570 grams in weight. 7:26 Hebrew *valley of Achor.*

7:14 The Israelites probably used some system of casting lots to find the guilty party. They may have used the high priest’s Urim and Thummim (Exodus 28:30), little-understood devices for determining God’s will. It was understood that God revealed His will by His control of the lot. The lot winnowed the people down, singling out the tribe of Judah, then the clan of Zerah, then the family of Zimri, and finally Achan himself. Identified by God as the offender, Achan confessed his crime and revealed that the stolen goods were concealed under his tent.

▸ SPIRITUAL WARFARE

7:25 Capital punishment. Criminals of all types can find forgiveness through faith in Christ while in prison. But when this happens, are their sentences immediately overturned? Even if they repent and live through years of obedience, they still may spend years in prison or even be executed for the offenses they committed against the state. Achan was certainly guilty of a capital offense, and even though he repented, he still suffered for his crime. The Hebrew text is not entirely clear whether his relatives were executed with him, but if they were, it was because they were complicit in his deception. Remember that your sin always carries consequences, and even if you do repent, one sin carries the destructive power to end life as you know it. Nothing is worse than sin. Avoid it at all costs. (***See Spiritual Warfare> Resisting Sin and Evil> Consequences> Of Disobedience> God may allow consequences to run their course,*** TopicGuide page A46.)

THE ISRAELITES DEFEAT AI

8 Then the LORD said to Joshua, "Do not be afraid or discouraged. Take all your fighting 8:1
men and attack Ai, for I have given you the king of Ai, his people, his town, and his Deut 1:19-21
land. 2You will destroy them as you destroyed Jericho and its king. But this time you may Josh 1:9; 6:2; 10:8
keep the plunder and the livestock for yourselves. Set an ambush behind the town." 8:2 Deut 20:14
3So Joshua and all the fighting men set out to attack Ai. Joshua chose 30,000 of his best Josh 8:27
warriors and sent them out at night 4with these orders: "Hide in ambush close behind the
town and be ready for action. 5When our main army attacks, the men of Ai will come out
to fight as they did before, and we will run away from them. 6We will let them chase us un-
til we have drawn them away from the town. For they will say, 'The Israelites are running
away from us as they did before.' Then, while we are running from them, 7you will jump
up from your ambush and take possession of the town, for the LORD your God will give it to
you. 8Set the town on fire, as the LORD has commanded. You have your orders." 8:8
9So they left and went to the place of ambush between Bethel and the west side of Ai. Judg 20:29-38
But Joshua remained among the people in the camp that night. 10Early the next morning
Joshua roused his men and started toward Ai, accompanied by the elders of Israel. 11All
the fighting men who were with Joshua marched in front of the town and camped on the
north side of Ai, with a valley between them and the town. 12That night Joshua sent 5,000
men to lie in ambush between Bethel and Ai, on the west side of the town. 13So they sta-
tioned the main army north of the town and the ambush west of the town. Joshua himself
spent that night in the valley.
14When the king of Ai saw the Israelites across the valley, he and all his army hurried
out early in the morning and attacked the Israelites at a place overlooking the Jordan Val- 8:14
ley.* But he didn't realize there was an ambush behind the town. 15Joshua and the Israelite Deut 1:1
army fled toward the wilderness as though they were badly beaten. 16Then all the men in Judg 20:34
the town were called out to chase after them. In this way, they were lured away from the
town. 17There was not a man left in Ai or Bethel* who did not chase after the Israelites, and
the town was left wide open.
18Then the LORD said to Joshua, "Point the spear in your hand toward Ai, for I will hand
the town over to you." Joshua did as he was commanded. 19As soon as Joshua gave this 8:18
signal, all the men in ambush jumped up from their position and poured into the town. Exod 14:16; 17:9-13
They quickly captured it and set it on fire. Josh 8:26
20When the men of Ai looked behind them, smoke from the town was filling the sky,
and they had nowhere to go. For the Israelites who had fled in the direction of the wilder-
ness now turned on their pursuers. 21When Joshua and all the other Israelites saw that the
ambush had succeeded and that smoke was rising from the town, they turned and at-
tacked the men of Ai. 22Meanwhile, the Israelites who were inside the town came out and
attacked the enemy from the rear. So the men of Ai were caught in the middle, with Israel-
ite fighters on both sides. Israel attacked them, and not a single person survived or es- 8:22
caped. 23Only the king of Ai was taken alive and brought to Joshua. Deut 7:2
24When the Israelite army finished chasing and killing all the men of Ai in the open fields,

8:14 Hebrew *the Arabah.* 8:17 Some manuscripts lack *or Bethel.*

8:1 After Joshua and the Israelites had dealt with Achan's sin, God graciously reassured Joshua, telling him not to be afraid or discouraged. Furthermore, God told Joshua to attack Ai again and promised that Israel would have victory, just as He had promised before the attack on Jericho. The covenant relationship between God and His people had been restored.

▸ SPIRITUAL WARFARE

8:4 Holy trickery. Though Israel's army outnumbered Ai's, God's battle plan was one of deception, designed not only to defeat Israel's enemies but also to humiliate them. This would arouse fear in the enemies that awaited them in central and northern Canaan. But this plan also continued the odd theme of blessed trickery in the battles of Joshua—the lies of Rahab saved her family, and the surprise attack against the five southern Amorite kings saved the Israelites. This further illustrates that, in wartime situations, deception may be used to defeat your enemy without violation of the ninth commandment. (See Exodus 20 and the *Ten Commandments* article. Also ***see Spiritual Warfare**> Resisting Sin and Evil> Trusting God> God as Warrior,* TopicGuide page A46.)

8:25 they went back and finished off everyone inside. 25 So the entire population of Ai, including
Deut 20:16-18 men and women, was wiped out that day—12,000 in all. 26 For Joshua kept holding out his
8:26 spear until everyone who had lived in Ai was completely destroyed.* 27 Only the livestock
Exod 17:11-12 and the treasures of the town were not destroyed, for the Israelites kept these as plunder for
8:27 Josh 8:2 themselves, as the LORD had commanded Joshua. 28 So Joshua burned the town of Ai,* and it
8:28 became a permanent mound of ruins, desolate to this very day.
Deut 13:16 29 Joshua impaled the king of Ai on a sharpened pole and left him there until evening. At
8:29 sunset the Israelites took down the body, as Joshua commanded, and threw it in front of
Deut 21:22-23 the town gate. They piled a great heap of stones over him that can still be seen today.

THE LORD'S COVENANT RENEWED

8:30 30 Then Joshua built an altar to the LORD, the God of Israel, on Mount Ebal. 31 He followed
Deut 27:2-8 the commands that Moses the LORD's servant had written in the Book of Instruction: "Make
8:31 Exod 20:24-25 Me an altar from stones that are uncut and have not been shaped with iron tools."* Then
Deut 27:5-6 on the altar they presented burnt offerings and peace offerings to the LORD. 32 And as the
Israelites watched, Joshua copied onto the stones of the altar* the instructions Moses had
given them.
8:33 33 Then all the Israelites—foreigners and native-born alike—along with the elders, offi-
Deut 27:12-13 cers, and judges, were divided into two groups. One group stood in front of Mount Geri-
zim, the other in front of Mount Ebal. Each group faced the other, and between them stood
the Levitical priests carrying the Ark of the LORD's Covenant. This was all done according to
the commands that Moses, the servant of the LORD, had previously given for blessing the
people of Israel.
8:34 34 Joshua then read to them all the blessings and curses Moses had written in the Book
Deut 28:61; 31:11 of Instruction. 35 Every word of every command that Moses had ever given was read to the
8:35 entire assembly of Israel, including the women and children and the foreigners who lived
Deut 31:12 among them.

8:26 The Hebrew term used here refers to the complete consecration of things or people to the LORD, either by destroying them or by giving them as an offering. 8:28 *Ai* means "ruin." 8:31 Exod 20:25; Deut 27:5-6. 8:32 Or *onto stones.*

8:29 Israel hung the body of the king of Ai on a tree. Moses had said such a display was a sign of cursedness (Deuteronomy 21:22-23), and in this case it was appropriate, for the king of Ai and all his people (indeed, all of the Canaanites) were under God's curse. But the Israelites were careful to obey Moses' command that no body be left hanging on a tree overnight. In this ritual we see a prefigurement of Christ's suffering on the cross (a tree), which symbolized that God had cursed Him on behalf of His people. Interestingly, the Jewish leaders asked the Romans to break the legs of Jesus and those who were crucified with Him to hasten their deaths and prevent them from hanging on their crosses overnight, but Jesus was already dead (John 19:31-33).

8:30-31 Altars were tools of worship and sacrifice for most ancient religions. But God gave the Israelites very specific instructions regarding their altars. They were to make simple altars of earth and uncut stones (Exodus 20:24-25). God's intent in this command was to distinguish true worship from pagan idolatry and to remind the Israelites that the altar was a thing of God, not a thing of man.

8:31 There were several kinds of sacrifices and offerings in Israelite worship. Whole burnt offerings were completely burned on the altar. Sin and guilt sacrifices were burned only in part, and portions were given to the priests. These offerings were given at designated times and ceremonies. Fellowship offerings, which included peace offerings, were voluntary and could be given spontaneously. Burnt offerings and sin offerings were given to make peace with God, but those who already were at peace with God gave peace offerings to show love and appreciation.

8:33-35 Moses commanded the people to perform this ceremony when they came into the Promised Land (Deuteronomy 27–28). Six of Israel's tribes stood on Mount Gerizim and six stood on Mount Ebal, with the Ark of the Covenant in the valley between them. Joshua then read all the blessings of covenant obedience and curses of covenant disobedience that Moses had spelled out. Finally, Joshua read the entire Mosaic Law. In doing so, he reminded the people of God's expectations of them and of the results of compliance or rebellion.

▸ HOLINESS

8:35 A means of grace. It is unthinkable to have a church without a preaching ministry. The preaching of God's Word has always been central to the education of the covenant community (Mark 16:15; 1 Corinthians 1:21). No one should be kept from God's Word (Romans 10:13-15). Make sure that every person in your family hears Bible-based preaching, for this is the means God has ordained to build up the hearts and minds of His people. If you aren't receiving this kind of preaching, then search for a church that provides this necessary component for your growth. (***See Holiness****> Submission> Learning God's Word> Public teaching,* TopicGuide page A40.)

THE GIBEONITES DECEIVE ISRAEL

9 Now all the kings west of the Jordan River heard about what had happened. These 9:1
were the kings of the Hittites, Amorites, Canaanites, Perizzites, Hivites, and Jebusites, Num 13:17, 29
who lived in the hill country, in the western foothills,* and along the coast of the Mediterra- Josh 3:10; 11:19
nean Sea* as far north as the Lebanon mountains. 2These kings combined their armies to
fight as one against Joshua and the Israelites.
3But when the people of Gibeon heard what Joshua had done to Jericho and Ai, 4they 9:3
resorted to deception to save themselves. They sent ambassadors to Joshua, loading their Josh 10:2; 11:19
donkeys with weathered saddlebags and old, patched wineskins. 5They put on worn-out,
patched sandals and ragged clothes. And the bread they took with them was dry and
moldy. 6When they arrived at the camp of Israel at Gilgal, they told Joshua and the men of
Israel, "We have come from a distant land to ask you to make a peace treaty with us."
7The Israelites replied to these Hivites, "How do we know you don't live nearby? For if 9:7 Exod 23:32
you do, we cannot make a treaty with you." Josh 11:19
8They replied, "We are your servants."
"But who are you?" Joshua demanded. "Where do you come from?"
9They answered, "Your servants have come from a very distant country. We have heard 9:9
of the might of the LORD your God and of all He did in Egypt. 10We have also heard what Josh 9:16-17
He did to the two Amorite kings east of the Jordan River—King Sihon of Heshbon and King 9:10
Og of Bashan (who lived in Ashtaroth). 11So our elders and all our people instructed us, Num 21:24, 33
'Take supplies for a long journey. Go meet with the people of Israel and tell them, "We are
your servants; please make a treaty with us."'
12"This bread was hot from the ovens when we left our homes. But now, as you can see,
it is dry and moldy. 13These wineskins were new when we filled them, but now they are
old and split open. And our clothing and sandals are worn out from our very long jour-
ney."
14So the Israelites examined their food, but they did not consult the LORD. 15Then Josh- 9:14
ua made a peace treaty with them and guaranteed their safety, and the leaders of the Num 27:21
community ratified their agreement with a binding oath.
16Three days after making the treaty, they learned that these people actually lived
nearby! 17The Israelites set out at once to investigate and reached their towns in three 9:17 Josh 18:25-28; 15:9,
days. The names of these towns were Gibeon, Kephirah, Beeroth, and Kiriath-jearim. 18But 60

9:1a Hebrew *the Shephelah*. 9:1b Hebrew *the Great Sea*.

9:1-7 In this passage, the Hivites and the Gibeonites seem to be the same people. The Gibeonites were the inhabitants of Gibeon, a city northwest of Jerusalem, but they are also identified as "these Hivites" (9:7). The Hivites were descendants of Noah's grandson Canaan, the son of Ham, but unlike the Moabites or the Jebusites, who had specific territories, the Hivites were a scattered people. Perhaps the Gibeonites were one clan of the Hivites. The Hivites appeared throughout Israelite history, even in the days of King David and his son Solomon (2 Chronicles 8:7-9).

9:6 From the beginning of their journey, God instructed the Israelites to make no treaties with the people who inhabited the Promised Land. At Mount Sinai, God said to Moses: "I will hand over to you the people now living in the land, and you will drive them out ahead of you. Make no treaties with them or their gods" (Exodus 23:31-32). Had the Hivites been honest about the location of their home, Joshua would not have considered a treaty.

9:9 What had the Hivites heard of all God had done in Egypt? Perhaps they had heard of the miraculous signs God gave Moses to establish his authority, such as turning his staff into a snake and back again. Perhaps they had heard of the ten plagues God inflicted on the Egyptians. Perhaps the Gibeonites also had heard how God parted the Red Sea as Israel left Egypt (Exodus 15).

9:10 The lands of Sihon and Og lay east of the Jordan. Israel had no designs on these territories as they journeyed toward Canaan. But when Moses asked Sihon, king of the Amorites, to let Israel pass peacefully through his territory (a territory he himself had stolen), Sihon refused and launched an unprovoked attack on Israel. However, God gave Israel victory, and Sihon lost his land and his life. Og, the last king of Bashan, also launched an unprovoked attack on Israel and suffered the same fate.

9:14-15 Though he was suspicious of them, Joshua made a peace treaty with the Gibeonites. Unfortunately, he failed to consult God. Only three days later, the Israelites learned the truth—the Gibeonites were actually Canaanites. Joshua and the other leaders chose to honor their commitment to let the Gibeonites live, remembering God's commands about the sanctity of oaths (Numbers 30:2). However, Joshua did force the Gibeonites to cut wood and carry water for the Israelites. The price of their lives was their freedom.

the Israelites did not attack the towns, for the Israelite leaders had made a vow to them in
the name of the LORD, the God of Israel.
The people of Israel grumbled against their leaders because of the treaty. 19But the
leaders replied, "Since we have sworn an oath in the presence of the LORD, the God of Isra-
el, we cannot touch them. 20This is what we must do. We must let them live, for divine an-
9:21 ger would come upon us if we broke our oath. 21Let them live." So they made them
Deut 29:11 woodcutters and water carriers for the entire community, as the Israelite leaders directed.
22Joshua called together the Gibeonites and said, "Why did you lie to us? Why did you
say that you live in a distant land when you live right here among us? 23May you be
cursed! From now on you will always be servants who cut wood and carry water for the
house of my God."
9:24 24They replied, "We did it because we—your servants—were clearly told that the LORD
Deut 7:1-2 your God commanded His servant Moses to give you this entire land and to destroy all the
people living in it. So we feared greatly for our lives because of you. That is why we have
done this. 25Now we are at your mercy—do to us whatever you think is right."
26So Joshua did not allow the people of Israel to kill them. 27But that day he made the Gibe-
9:27 onites the woodcutters and water carriers for the community of Israel and for the altar of the
Deut 12:5 LORD—wherever the LORD would choose to build it. And that is what they do to this day.

ISRAEL DEFEATS THE SOUTHERN ARMIES

10:1 **10** Adoni-zedek, king of Jerusalem, heard that Joshua had captured and completely
Josh 8:22-28; 9:15 destroyed* Ai and killed its king, just as he had destroyed the town of Jericho and
killed its king. He also learned that the Gibeonites had made peace with Israel and were
now their allies. 2He and his people became very afraid when they heard all this because
Gibeon was a large town—as large as the royal cities and larger than Ai. And the Gibeonite
men were strong warriors.
10:3 3So King Adoni-zedek of Jerusalem sent messengers to several other kings: Hoham of
2 Chr 11:9 Hebron, Piram of Jarmuth, Japhia of Lachish, and Debir of Eglon. 4"Come and help me de-
stroy Gibeon," he urged them, "for they have made peace with Joshua and the people of
10:5 Israel." 5So these five Amorite kings combined their armies for a united attack. They
Num 13:29 moved all their troops into place and attacked Gibeon.
Josh 9:2 6The men of Gibeon quickly sent messengers to Joshua at his camp in Gilgal. "Don't

10:1 The Hebrew term used here refers to the complete consecration of things or people to the LORD, either by destroying them or by giving them as an offering; also in 10:28, 35, 37, 39, 40.

9:24 In an age without mass communication, the stories of the Israelites spread person by person. A nation of hundreds of thousands of people was traveling about in a desert area, and curious things kept happening around them. If nothing else, the Israelites were a curiosity, and stories circulated and possibly even grew more spectacular with the telling.

10:1 We often associate Jerusalem with King David because he was the one who made it the capital city of Israel and made plans for the Temple to be built there (2 Chronicles 3:1). But Jerusalem was an important city in the area long before David's reign. For a time it was known as Jebus, so its inhabitants were called Jebusites. The name *Jerusalem* was not original to the Israelites. The original form of the word meant "City of Salem" or "City of Peace." The Bible mentions the city of Salem in the time of Abraham (Genesis 14:18-19).

10:3 Adoni-zedek, the ringleader of this war effort, may have been a descendant of another Jerusalem king, Melchizedek, whom Abraham met on his travels in Canaan. Melchizedek was both a priest and a king, so he blessed Abraham (Genesis 14:17-20). Adoni-zedek was a leader of the wicked Amorite people and did not have the same respect for Israel or Israel's God.

10:3 Nothing is known about Hoham of Hebron beyond this account of his confederation with four other Amorite kings. But there is abundant information about his city, Hebron. Hebron, one of the oldest cities in the world, was located less than 20 miles southwest of Jerusalem. Among other things, Abraham made one of his earliest camps in Canaan near Hebron, and it was there that he bought his first land, a cave in which to bury his wife, Sarah. Later, Hebron was the capital of Israel until David made Jerusalem his seat of government (1 Chronicles 3:4).

10:6 Joshua was wrong to make a treaty with the Gibeonites, but through it God presented the Israelites with an opportunity. Five Amorite kings united against the Gibeonites for making peace with Israel, and the Gibeonites appealed to the Israelites for military aid. Suddenly the Israelites had a chance to make a surprise attack on several enemy armies at one time.

abandon your servants now!" they pleaded. "Come at once! Save us! Help us! For all the
Amorite kings who live in the hill country have joined forces to attack us."
7So Joshua and his entire army, including his best warriors, left Gilgal and set out for
Gibeon. 8"Do not be afraid of them," the LORD said to Joshua, "for I have given you victory **10:8**
over them. Not a single one of them will be able to stand up to you." Josh 1:5, 9
9Joshua traveled all night from Gilgal and took the Amorite armies by surprise. 10The **10:10**
LORD threw them into a panic, and the Israelites slaughtered great numbers of them at Gib- Deut 7:23
eon. Then the Israelites chased the enemy along the road to Beth-horon, killing them all
along the way to Azekah and Makkedah. 11As the Amorites retreated down the road from
Beth-horon, the LORD destroyed them with a terrible hailstorm from heaven that continued
until they reached Azekah. The hail killed more of the enemy than the Israelites killed with
the sword.
12On the day the LORD gave the Israelites victory over the Amorites, Joshua prayed to
the LORD in front of all the people of Israel. He said,

> "Let the sun stand still over Gibeon,
> and the moon over the valley of Aijalon."

13So the sun stood still and the moon stayed in place until the nation of Israel had de- **10:13** 2 Sam 1:18
feated its enemies. Isa 38:8
Is this event not recorded in *The Book of Jashar**? The sun stayed in the middle of the
sky, and it did not set as on a normal day.* 14There has never been a day like this one be- **10:14**
fore or since, when the LORD answered such a prayer. Surely the LORD fought for Israel that Exod 14:14 Deut 1:30
day! **10:15**
15Then Joshua and the Israelite army returned to their camp at Gilgal. Josh 10:6, 43

JOSHUA KILLS THE FIVE SOUTHERN KINGS

16During the battle the five kings escaped and hid in a cave at Makkedah. 17When Joshua **10:16**
heard that they had been found, 18he issued this command: "Cover the opening of the Josh 10:5
cave with large rocks, and place guards at the entrance to keep the kings inside. 19The rest
of you continue chasing the enemy and cut them down from the rear. Don't give them a
chance to get back to their towns, for the LORD your God has given you victory over them."
20So Joshua and the Israelite army continued the slaughter and completely crushed the
enemy. They totally wiped out the five armies except for a tiny remnant that managed to **10:20**
reach their fortified towns. 21Then the Israelites returned safely to Joshua in the camp at Deut 20:16 **10:21**
Makkedah. After that, no one dared to speak even a word against Israel. Josh 10:16

10:13a Or *The Book of the Upright.* **10:13b** Or *did not set for about a whole day.*

▸ SPIRITUAL WARFARE

10:8 Have no fear. Do you feel like the world is against you? Sometimes individuals and the church deserve the ridicule of the world—we appear foolish in how we deal with them at times (1 Peter 3:16-18). But even so, the world opposes the church. The book of Revelation is clear that throughout history, Satan and the rulers of the world have gathered to oppose the church (Revelation 12:7; 13:7). But Christ and all His saints will finally and completely conquer (Revelation 17:14). Stand firm, be patient, and remember that the weapons of our warfare are spiritual, not physical (Ephesians 6:10-18). (***See Spiritual Warfare****> Resisting Sin and Evil> Putting On and Off> Putting On> The weapons of righteousness,* TopicGuide page A46.)

10:12-13 Two sun/time-related events are recorded in the Old Testament. Here, Joshua prayed for the sun and the moon to stand still. In other words, he wanted time to stop so that he could finish his victory over the Amorites, and God allowed it. The book of 2 Kings tells how the prophet Isaiah offered King Hezekiah of Judah a sign from God that he would be healed of a deathly illness. The sign? God would "manually" move the sundial (time) ahead or back, whichever Hezekiah chose. Choosing what he considered the bigger miracle, Hezekiah asked for the sundial to move backward, and God granted his request (2 Kings 20:1-11; Isaiah 38:1-8).

10:13 *The Book of Jashar* was probably a collection of poems or songs about Israelite heroes. Hebrew poetry was not defined by rhyme schemes so much as by writing style, structure, and the use of imagery. Some examples of Hebrew poetry (which some believe may have been a part of *The Book of Jashar* at one time) include Miriam's song (Exodus 15) and Deborah's song (Judges 5). The book of Lamentations is basically a collection of poems or songs by the prophet Jeremiah. Many Hebrew poems were acrostics, or poems in which the first letters of the lines made up the Hebrew alphabet. Examples of acrostics (though in English versions) are Lamentations 1–2 and Proverbs 31:10-31.

10:22 Deut 7:24 22Then Joshua said, “Remove the rocks covering the opening of the cave, and bring the
five kings to me.” 23So they brought the five kings out of the cave—the kings of Jerusalem,
Hebron, Jarmuth, Lachish, and Eglon. 24When they brought them out, Joshua told the
commanders of his army, “Come and put your feet on the kings' necks.” And they did as
they were told.
10:25 Josh 10:8 25“Don't ever be afraid or discouraged,” Joshua told his men. “Be strong and coura-
10:26 Josh 8:29 geous, for the LORD is going to do this to all of your enemies.” 26Then Joshua killed each of
the five kings and impaled them on five sharpened poles, where they hung until evening.
10:27 Deut 21:22-23 27As the sun was going down, Joshua gave instructions for the bodies of the kings to be
taken down from the poles and thrown into the cave where they had been hiding. Then they
covered the opening of the cave with a pile of large rocks, which remains to this very day.

ISRAEL DESTROYS THE SOUTHERN TOWNS

28That same day Joshua captured and destroyed the town of Makkedah. He killed every-
one in it, including the king, leaving no survivors. He destroyed them all, and he killed the
10:29 Num 33:20-21 Josh 15:42 king of Makkedah as he had killed the king of Jericho. 29Then Joshua and the Israelites
went to Libnah and attacked it. 30There, too, the LORD gave them the town and its king. He
killed everyone in it, leaving no survivors. Then Joshua killed the king of Libnah as he had
killed the king of Jericho.
31From Libnah, Joshua and the Israelites went to Lachish and attacked it. 32Here again,
the LORD gave them Lachish. Joshua took it on the second day and killed everyone in it,
just as he had done at Libnah. 33During the attack on Lachish, King Horam of Gezer ar-
rived with his army to help defend the town. But Joshua's men killed him and his army,
leaving no survivors.
34Then Joshua and the Israelite army went on to Eglon and attacked it. 35They captured
it that day and killed everyone in it. He completely destroyed everyone, just as he had
10:36 Josh 14:13; 15:13 done at Lachish. 36From Eglon, Joshua and the Israelite army went up to Hebron and at-
tacked it. 37They captured the town and killed everyone in it, including its king, leaving no
survivors. They did the same thing to all of its surrounding villages. And just as he had
done at Eglon, he completely destroyed the entire population.
38Then Joshua and the Israelites turned back and attacked Debir. 39He captured the
town, its king, and all of its surrounding villages. He completely destroyed everyone in it,
leaving no survivors. He did to Debir and its king just what he had done to Hebron and to
Libnah and its king.
10:40 Deut 1:7; 7:24; 20:16 40So Joshua conquered the whole region—the kings and people of the hill country, the
Negev, the western foothills,* and the mountain slopes. He completely destroyed every-
one in the land, leaving no survivors, just as the LORD, the God of Israel, had commanded.
10:41 Josh 11:16; 15:51 41Joshua slaughtered them from Kadesh-barnea to Gaza and from the region around the
10:42 Josh 10:14 town of Goshen up to Gibeon. 42Joshua conquered all these kings and their land in a sin-
gle campaign, for the LORD, the God of Israel, was fighting for His people.
43Then Joshua and the Israelite army returned to their camp at Gilgal.

10:40 Hebrew *the Shephelah.*

10:26-27 Ancient warfare was exceedingly violent. It was not unusual for a defeated people to be completely wiped out. Neither was it unusual for the leaders of the defeated armies, as described here, to be publicly humiliated or mutilated. Pagan commanders practiced such brutality to build a fearsome reputation. But Israel, of course, was operating as God's instrument of vengeance against the Canaanites during their conquest of the land, and He had instructed them to wipe out their enemies. However, He also had given Israel guidelines for a more merciful form of warfare against non-Canaanites (Deuteronomy 20:1-15).

10:28 Following his victory over the Amorite coalition, Joshua launched a major campaign through southern Canaan. His targets included the cities of three of the five kings he had recently defeated, plus several other cities. Most of these cities fell to Israel almost immediately, and the text makes the reason clear: God gave the Israelites victory. Indeed, “the LORD, the God of Israel, was fighting for His people” (10:42). Wherever God gave Israel victory, Joshua was faithful to carry out God's command to destroy all the inhabitants.

ISRAEL DEFEATS THE NORTHERN ARMIES

11 When King Jabin of Hazor heard what had happened, he sent messages to the fol- **11:1**
lowing kings: King Jobab of Madon; the king of Shimron; the king of Acshaph; 2all Josh 11:10
the kings of the northern hill country; the kings in the Jordan Valley south of Galilee*; the **11:2**
kings in the Galilean foothills*; the kings of Naphoth-dor on the west; 3the kings of Ca- Josh 12:3
naan, both east and west; the kings of the Amorites, the Hittites, the Perizzites, the Jebu-
sites in the hill country, and the Hivites in the towns on the slopes of Mount Hermon in the
land of Mizpah.
4All these kings came out to fight. Their combined armies formed a vast horde. And with **11:4**
all their horses and chariots, they covered the landscape like the sand on the seashore. Judg 7:12
5The kings joined forces and established their camp around the water near Merom to fight
against Israel.
6Then the LORD said to Joshua, "Do not be afraid of them. By this time tomorrow I will **11:6** Josh 10:8
hand all of them over to Israel as dead men. Then you must cripple their horses and burn 2 Sam 8:4
their chariots."
7So Joshua and all his fighting men traveled to the water near Merom and attacked sud-
denly. 8And the LORD gave them victory over their enemies. The Israelites chased them as
far as Greater Sidon and Misrephoth-maim, and eastward into the valley of Mizpah, until
not one enemy warrior was left alive. 9Then Joshua crippled the horses and burned all the
chariots, as the LORD had instructed.
10Joshua then turned back and captured Hazor and killed its king. (Hazor had at one **11:10** Judg 4:2
time been the capital of all these kingdoms.) 11The Israelites completely destroyed* every 1 Sam 12:9
living thing in the city, leaving no survivors. Not a single person was spared. And then 1 Kgs 9:15 2 Kgs 15:29
Joshua burned the city.
12Joshua slaughtered all the other kings and their people, completely destroying them, **11:11** Deut 20:16-17
just as Moses, the servant of the LORD, had commanded. 13But the Israelites did not burn
any of the towns built on mounds except Hazor, which Joshua burned. 14And the Israelites **11:14**
took all the plunder and livestock of the ravaged towns for themselves. But they killed all Num 31:11-12
the people, leaving no survivors. 15As the LORD had commanded His servant Moses, so **11:15**
Moses commanded Joshua. And Joshua did as he was told, carefully obeying all the com- Exod 34:11-12
mands that the LORD had given to Moses.
16So Joshua conquered the entire region—the hill country, the entire Negev, the whole **11:16**
area around the town of Goshen, the western foothills, the Jordan Valley,* the mountains Josh 10:40
of Israel, and the Galilean foothills. 17The Israelite territory now extended all the way from **11:17** Deut 7:24 Josh 12:7

11:2a Hebrew *in the Arabah south of Kinnereth.* 11:2b Hebrew *the Shephelah;* also in 11:16. 11:11 The Hebrew term used here refers to the complete consecration of things or people to the LORD, either by destroying them or by giving them as an offering; also in 11:12, 20, 21. 11:16 Hebrew *the Shephelah, the Arabah.*

11:1 The Hazor that Jabin ruled was in northern Canaan. Another Jabin ruled Hazor during the time of the judges and was defeated by the judge Deborah and her military cohort Barak (Judges 4) in a memorable Israelite victory. During his reign, King Solomon fortified this city (1 Kings 9:15). It was lost to Assyria when the northern kingdom of Israel fell and the people were taken into exile.

11:2 The area called Galilee was to the west of the Sea of Galilee. The Jordan Valley lay to the south of the Sea of Galilee where the Jordan flowed through Israel on its way to the Dead Sea. Jesus' ministry happened all around this area. It was in Cana of Galilee that Jesus performed his first miracle, turning water into wine at a wedding (John 2).

11:15-20 God's instructions to Moses called for Israel to wipe out the Canaanites. This was a holy war—God was using Israel to punish the Canaanites for their great wickedness. The Canaanites should have turned to Israel's God, as Rahab did, and sought peace with God's people. But God had been patient with them for many years, and the time for such repentance had passed. Now God hardened their hearts, causing them to fight Israel instead of asking for peace. Only the Gibeonites, who tricked the Israelites into agreeing to a peace treaty, survived the Israelite assault.

11:16 With these victories, Joshua completed a successful campaign through northern Canaan. He and the Israelite armies first drove a wedge through central Canaan with the capture of Jericho and Ai. Then they defeated a southern coalition and captured the southlands. Finally they made this northern sortie. At this point, most of the land of Canaan was in Israel's hands, but a few pockets of Canaanite resistance remained.

11:19 Josh 9:3-15
11:20 Exod 14:17; Deut 7:16
11:21 Num 13:33; Deut 9:1-2; Josh 14:12; 15:13

Mount Halak, which leads up to Seir in the south, as far north as Baal-gad at the foot of
Mount Hermon in the valley of Lebanon. Joshua killed all the kings of those territories,
18 waging war for a long time to accomplish this. 19 No one in this region made peace with
the Israelites except the Hivites of Gibeon. All the others were defeated. 20 For the LORD
hardened their hearts and caused them to fight the Israelites. So they were completely de-
stroyed without mercy, as the LORD had commanded Moses.

21 During this period Joshua destroyed all the descendants of Anak, who lived in the
hill country of Hebron, Debir, Anab, and the entire hill country of Judah and Israel. He
killed them all and completely destroyed their towns. 22 None of the descendants of
Anak were left in all the land of Israel, though some still remained in Gaza, Gath, and
Ashdod.

11:23 Deut 1:38; 12:9-10; 25:19; Heb 4:8

23 So Joshua took control of the entire land, just as the LORD had instructed Moses. He
gave it to the people of Israel as their special possession, dividing the land among the
tribes. So the land finally had rest from war.

KINGS DEFEATED EAST OF THE JORDAN

12:1 Num 32:33; Deut 3:8; Josh 11:1-3
12:2 Num 21:23; Deut 2:36

12 These are the kings east of the Jordan River who had been killed by the Israelites
and whose land was taken. Their territory extended from the Arnon Gorge to
Mount Hermon and included all the land east of the Jordan Valley.*

2 King Sihon of the Amorites, who lived in Heshbon, was defeated. His kingdom in-
cluded Aroer, on the edge of the Arnon Gorge, and extended from the middle of the
Arnon Gorge to the Jabbok River, which serves as a border for the Ammonites. This terri-
tory included the southern half of the territory of Gilead. 3 Sihon also controlled the Jor-
dan Valley and regions to the east—from as far north as the Sea of Galilee to as far south
as the Dead Sea,* including the road to Beth-jeshimoth and southward to the slopes of
Pisgah.

12:4 Num 21:33; Josh 13:12
12:5 Deut 3:10

4 King Og of Bashan, the last of the Rephaites, lived at Ashtaroth and Edrei. 5 He ruled a
territory stretching from Mount Hermon to Salecah in the north and to all of Bashan in the
east, and westward to the borders of the kingdoms of Geshur and Maacah. This territory
included the northern half of Gilead, as far as the boundary of King Sihon of Heshbon.

6 Moses, the servant of the LORD, and the Israelites had destroyed the people of King Si-
hon and King Og. And Moses gave their land as a possession to the tribes of Reuben, Gad,
and the half-tribe of Manasseh.

KINGS DEFEATED WEST OF THE JORDAN

12:7 Josh 11:17
12:8 Josh 11:16

7 The following is a list of the kings that Joshua and the Israelite armies defeated on the
west side of the Jordan, from Baal-gad in the valley of Lebanon to Mount Halak, which
leads up to Seir. (Joshua gave this land to the tribes of Israel as their possession, 8 includ-
ing the hill country, the western foothills,* the Jordan Valley, the mountain slopes, the
Judean wilderness, and the Negev. The people who lived in this region were the Hittites,

12:1 Hebrew *the Arabah;* also in 12:3, 8. 12:3 Hebrew *from the Sea of Kinnereth to the Sea of the Arabah, which is the Salt Sea.* 12:8 Hebrew *the Shephelah.*

11:21 The descendants of Anak were referred to as Anakites or Anakim. They were large people; some translations refer to them as giants. The Emites of Moab in Deuteronomy 2:10-12 and the Zamzummites of Ammon in Deuteronomy 2:20-23 were also known for their large size. These larger people were known collectively as Nephilites and Rephaites. Some survived Joshua's attacks in Gaza, Gath, and Ashdod, cities of the Philistines. The giant that David later fought, Goliath, was from Philistia and could have been a descendant of these people.

12:1-24 In this chapter, the author of the book of Joshua pauses to review the conquest of Canaan. First, he reviews Israel's victories east of the Jordan—the conquest of King Sihon of the Amorites and King Og of Bashan—as the people were en route to Canaan. Then he turns his attention to the Israelite triumphs in Canaan itself.

12:4 Bashan, the region that Israel captured from King Og, lay east of the Sea of Galilee and the Jordan River. It was known for its sheep (Deuteronomy 32:14) and its oak trees (Zechariah 11:2).

the Amorites, the Canaanites, the Perizzites, the Hivites, and the Jebusites.) These are the kings Israel defeated:

9 The king of Jericho
The king of Ai, near Bethel
10 The king of Jerusalem
The king of Hebron
11 The king of Jarmuth
The king of Lachish
12 The king of Eglon
The king of Gezer
13 The king of Debir
The king of Geder
14 The king of Hormah
The king of Arad

12:9 Josh 6:2; 8:29

12:12 Josh 10:33

12:13 Josh 10:3

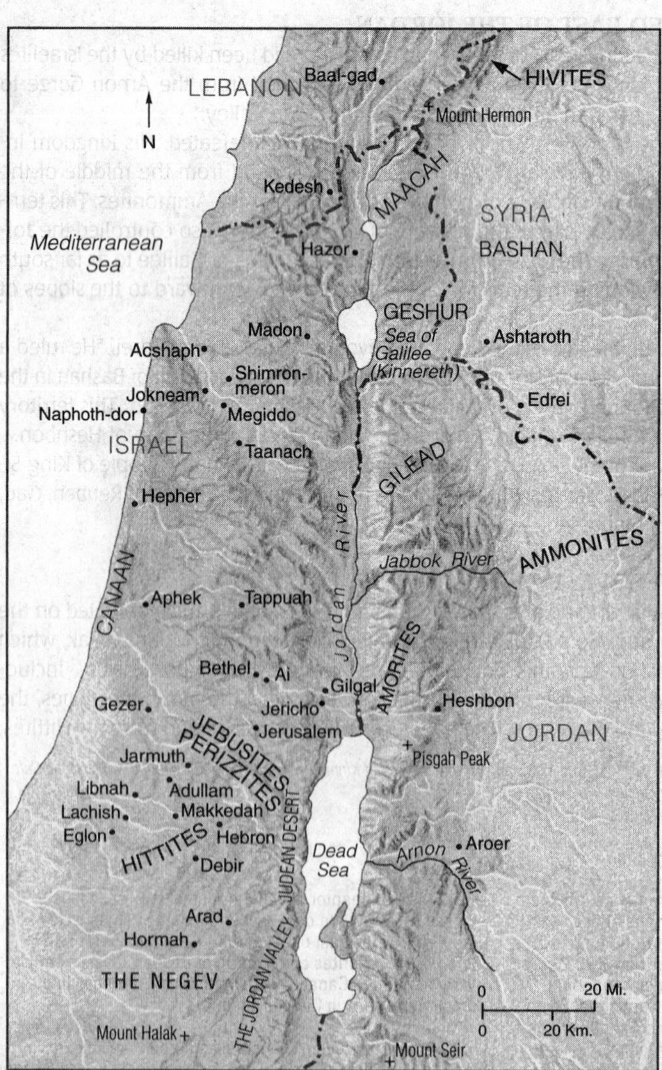

The broken lines (—·—·) indicate modern boundaries.

THE CONQUERED LAND

Joshua displayed brilliant military strategy in the way he went about conquering the land of Canaan. He first captured the well-fortified Jericho to gain a foothold in Canaan and to demonstrate the awesome might of the God of Israel. Then he gained the hill country around Bethel and Gibeon. From there he subdued towns in the lowlands. Then his army conquered important cities in the north, such as Hazor. In all, Israel conquered land both east (12:1–6) and west (12:7–24) of the Jordan River; from Mount Hermon in the north to beyond the Negev to Mount Halak in the south. Thirty-one kings and their cities had been defeated. The Israelites had overpowered the Hittites, the Amorites, the Canaanites, the Perizzites, the Hivites, and the Jebusites. Other peoples living in Canaan were yet to be conquered.

[15] The king of Libnah
The king of Adullam
[16] The king of Makkedah
The king of Bethel
[17] The king of Tappuah
The king of Hepher
[18] The king of Aphek
The king of Lasharon
[19] The king of Madon
The king of Hazor
[20] The king of Shimron-meron
The king of Acshaph
[21] The king of Taanach
The king of Megiddo
[22] The king of Kedesh
The king of Jokneam in Carmel
[23] The king of Dor in the town of Naphoth-dor*
The king of Goyim in Gilgal*
12:24 Deut 7:24 [24] The king of Tirzah.

In all, thirty-one kings were defeated.

THE LAND YET TO BE CONQUERED

13:1 Josh 14:10 **13** When Joshua was an old man, the LORD said to him, "You are growing old, and
much land remains to be conquered. [2] This is the territory that remains: all the re-
13:2 Judg 3:3 gions of the Philistines and the Geshurites, [3] and the larger territory of the Canaanites, ex-
tending from the stream of Shihor on the border of Egypt, northward to the boundary of
Ekron. It includes the territory of the five Philistine rulers of Gaza, Ashdod, Ashkelon, Gath,
and Ekron. The land of the Avvites [4] in the south also remains to be conquered. In the

12:23a Hebrew *Naphath-dor,* a variant spelling of Naphoth-dor. 12:23b Greek version reads *Goyim in Galilee.*

12:24 The Israelites defeated 31 kings in Canaan and destroyed their cities. But that does not mean that Canaan was left desolate. God had promised to give His people cities and houses they had not built, cisterns they had not dug, and vineyards and olive groves they had not planted (Deuteronomy 6:10-11), and these blessings remained to be claimed by the tribes of Israel.

▸ GOD
13:1 Take the land! Joshua had only one thing on his job description: Take the land (Joshua 1:6)! This chapter's negative assessment of Joshua's performance comes as a shock, especially given the list of successes and conquered kings in chapter 12. This failure points to Israel's need for a king who would conquer these territories 400 years later (1 Kings 4:21). Like Israel, we are incomplete without acknowledging our need for the rule of Christ our King (Revelation 11:15). (***See God**> God's Names> Son> King,* TopicGuide page A19.)

13:2 The Philistines were a tribe of people who inhabited a strip of land along the Mediterranean coast in southwestern Canaan. Their advanced metallurgy enabled them to fight effectively against Israel (1 Samuel 13:19-22).

13:2 Two tribes of Geshurites lived in the land. One lived east of the Jordan on the border of Bashan. The other, mentioned here, lived to the south of the Philistines in the western area of Israel. No records exist to tell us whether these two tribes were related. Before David became king, he sought refuge from Saul among the Philistines, and from there he raided the western Geshurites. After he became king, he married Maacah, the daughter of the king of the eastern tribe of Geshurites, forming an alliance with them (2 Samuel 3:3).

13:4 The government of the Philistines consisted of a confederation of five city-states. A lord or overseer controlled each city-state. This type of government was much more akin to the future government of the Romans than that of the ancient Israelites, which was first a theocracy, then a traditional monarchy. An example of how the Philistine lords interacted is found in 1 Samuel 29. David was hiding in the Philistine city of Ziklag with his own troop of warriors. This put him under the Philistine lord of Gath, Achish, who enlisted David to go to war with him against the Israelites. But the other lords didn't trust David and voted him out of the battle.

13:4 Sidon was a principal city of Phoenicia known for trade and craftsmanship, including rich textile dyes and glass blowing. Phoenicia lay along the Mediterranean Sea to the north of Israel, above Tyre and below what is now Beirut. Tyre and Sidon were often mentioned together. When King David gathered supplies for the construction of the Temple, he brought in cedar from Tyre and Sidon (1 Chronicles 22:4). The prophets Joel and Zechariah spoke out against these cities (Joel 3:4; Zechariah 9:1-2). Jesus traveled to the region, where He interacted with a Gentile woman who asked that He help her daughter even though she wasn't a Jew (Matthew 15:21-28).

north, the following area has not yet been conquered: all the land of the Canaanites, including Mearah (which belongs to the Sidonians), stretching northward to Aphek on the border of the Amorites; [5]the land of the Gebalites and all of the Lebanon mountain area to
the east, from Baal-gad below Mount Hermon to Lebo-hamath; [6]and all the hill country 13:6 Josh 11:8
from Lebanon to Misrephoth-maim, including all the land of the Sidonians.

"I Myself will drive these people out of the land ahead of the Israelites. So be sure to give this land to Israel as a special possession, just as I have commanded you. [7]Include all
this territory as Israel's possession when you divide this land among the nine tribes and the half-tribe of Manasseh."

THE LAND DIVIDED EAST OF THE JORDAN

[8]Half the tribe of Manasseh and the tribes of Reuben and Gad had already received their 13:8 Josh 12:1-6
grants of land on the east side of the Jordan, for Moses, the servant of the LORD, had previously assigned this land to them.

[9]Their territory extended from Aroer on the edge of the Arnon Gorge (including the town in the middle of the gorge) to the plain beyond Medeba, as far as 13:9 Num 32:34
Dibon. [10]It also included all the towns of King Sihon of the Amorites, who had reigned in Heshbon, and extended as far as the borders of Ammon. [11]It included
Gilead, the territory of the kingdoms of Geshur and Maacah, all of Mount
Hermon, all of Bashan as far as Salecah, [12]and all the territory of King Og of 13:12 Num 21:33-35
Bashan, who had reigned in Ashtaroth and Edrei. King Og was the last of the Rephaites, for Moses had attacked them and driven them out. [13]But the Israelites
failed to drive out the people of Geshur and Maacah, so they continue to live among the Israelites to this day.

AN ALLOTMENT FOR THE TRIBE OF LEVI

[14]Moses did not assign any allotment of land to the tribe of Levi. Instead, as the LORD had 13:14 Deut 18:1-2
promised them, their allotment came from the offerings burned on the altar to the LORD, the God of Israel.

THE LAND YET TO BE CONQUERED
Canaan was now controlled by the Israelites, although much land and several cities still needed to be conquered. Joshua told the people to include both conquered and unconquered lands in the territorial allotments (13:7). He was certain the people would complete the conquest as God had commanded.

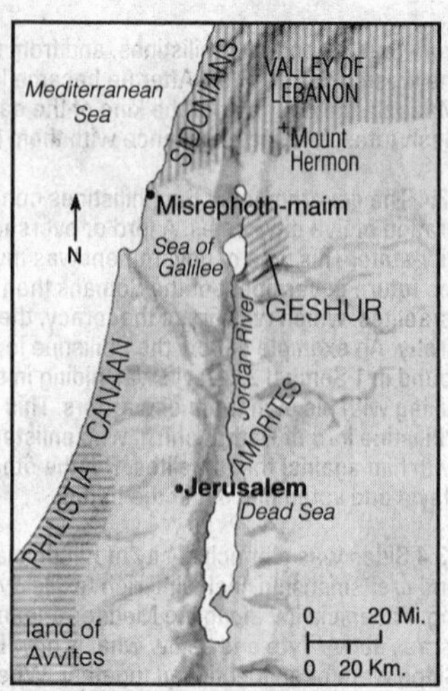

13:7 After giving Joshua an inventory of the portions of the Promised Land that Israel still had not conquered, God promised that He would drive out the Canaanites for His people. He then encouraged Joshua not to fail to include these unconquered regions when he distributed the land to the tribes. What God had promised to His people needed to be assigned to His people, who then would take it by force if necessary.

13:8 The author notes that the tribes of Reuben, Gad, and half of Manasseh already had received their land to the east of the Jordan River. Numbers 32 records the request from the Gadites and Reubenites to keep their herds on the east side of the Jordan to have plenty of grazing land. Moses consented on condition that the military men of these tribes would still travel across the Jordan and help the other tribes take the land, and the tribal leaders agreed. They kept that promise when Joshua led Israel across the Jordan.

13:13 God had commanded Israel to take Canaan and destroy or drive out all who refused to worship Israel's God. But the Israelite tribes east of the Jordan failed to drive out the remaining Canaanites in their territories. This failure was not unique among Israel's tribes. While some tribes dominated their regions, others were unable to overcome the Canaanites and lived in an uneasy peace. The people of the tribe of Dan failed miserably in their attempts to conquer their assigned region, so they moved north to find a region they *could* conquer (Joshua 19:47).

THE LAND GIVEN TO THE TRIBE OF REUBEN

15Moses had assigned the following area to the clans of the tribe of Reuben.

13:16 16Their territory extended from Aroer on the edge of the Arnon Gorge
Josh 12:2 (including the town in the middle of the gorge) to the plain beyond Medeba.
17It included Heshbon and the other towns on the plain—Dibon, Bamoth-baal,
Beth-baal-meon, 18Jahaz, Kedemoth, Mephaath, 19Kiriathaim, Sibmah, Zereth-
shahar on the hill above the valley, 20Beth-peor, the slopes of Pisgah, and Beth-
jeshimoth.

13:21-22 21The land of Reuben also included all the towns of the plain and the entire
Num 31:8 kingdom of Sihon. Sihon was the Amorite king who had reigned in Heshbon and
was killed by Moses along with the leaders of Midian—Evi, Rekem, Zur, Hur, and
Reba—princes living in the region who were allied with Sihon. 22The Israelites had
also killed Balaam son of Beor, who used magic to tell the future. 23The Jordan
River marked the western boundary for the tribe of Reuben. The towns and their
surrounding villages in this area were given as a homeland to the clans of the
tribe of Reuben.

THE LAND GIVEN TO THE TRIBE OF GAD

24Moses had assigned the following area to the clans of the tribe of Gad.

25Their territory included Jazer, all the towns of Gilead, and half of the land of
Ammon, as far as the town of Aroer just west of* Rabbah. 26It extended from
13:27 Heshbon to Ramath-mizpeh and Betonim, and from Mahanaim to Lo-debar.* 27In the
Num 34:11 valley were Beth-haram, Beth-nimrah, Succoth, Zaphon, and the rest of the kingdom
of King Sihon of Heshbon. The western boundary ran along the Jordan River,
extended as far north as the tip of the Sea of Galilee,* and then turned eastward.
28The towns and their surrounding villages in this area were given as a homeland to
the clans of the tribe of Gad.

13:25 Hebrew *in front of.* 13:26 Or *to the territory of Debir.* 13:27 Hebrew *Sea of Kinnereth.*

13:15 Moses gave the tribe of Reuben a region of land to the east of the Jordan River and the Dead Sea. Reuben, the progenitor of this tribe, was the oldest son of Jacob. When Jacob gave his final blessing to his sons, he pronounced Reuben unstable (Genesis 49:3-4), so the birthright and family leadership that customarily would have gone to him were revoked. His most well-known sin was sleeping with his father's concubine, an extremely disrespectful act in this culture (Genesis 35:22). However, as Reuben aged, he seemed to gather some conscience. When his brothers plotted to kill their younger brother Joseph, Rueben objected and even planned an escape for Joseph (Genesis 37:19-30).

13:24 The tribe of Gad was given land east of the Jordan and north of Reuben's allotment. Gad, the seventh son of Jacob, was born to Zilpah, the handmaiden of Jacob's wife Leah. Zilpah functioned as a surrogate for Leah, who had ceased to be fertile. In Jacob's final blessing, he predicted that Gad's family would suffer from foreign invaders ("marauding bands") but would triumph over them (Genesis 49:19). Gad's descendants had a reputation for being strong warriors. Since they lived east of the Jordan, they were more vulnerable to foreign attack than the tribes on the west side of the river.

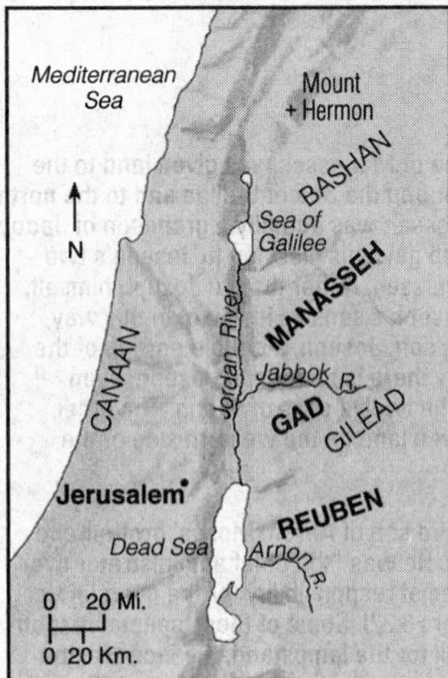

THE TRIBES EAST OF THE JORDAN
Joshua assigned territory to the tribes of Reuben, Gad, and the half-tribe of Manasseh on the east side of the Jordan where they had chosen to remain because of the wonderful livestock country (Numbers 32:1-5).

THE LAND GIVEN TO THE HALF-TRIBE OF MANASSEH

29 Moses had assigned the following area to the clans of the half-tribe of Manasseh.

30 Their territory extended from Mahanaim, including all of Bashan, all the 13:30
former kingdom of King Og, and the sixty towns of Jair in Bashan. 31 It also Num 32:41
included half of Gilead and King Og's royal cities of Ashtaroth and Edrei.
All this was given to the clans of the descendants of Makir, who was
Manasseh's son.

32 These are the allotments Moses had made while he was on the plains of Moab,
across the Jordan River, east of Jericho. 33 But Moses gave no allotment of land to the 13:33
tribe of Levi, for the LORD, the God of Israel, had promised that He Himself would be Num 18:20
their allotment. Josh 13:14

THE LAND DIVIDED WEST OF THE JORDAN

14 The remaining tribes of Israel received land in Canaan as allotted by Eleazar the
priest, Joshua son of Nun, and the tribal leaders. 2 These nine and a half tribes re- 14:1
ceived their grants of land by means of sacred lots, in accordance with the LORD's com- Num 34:16-17
mand through Moses. 3 Moses had already given a grant of land to the two and a half 14:3
tribes on the east side of the Jordan River, but he had given the Levites no such allotment. Num 32:33
4 The descendants of Joseph had become two separate tribes—Manasseh and Ephraim. Josh 13:14
And the Levites were given no land at all, only towns to live in with surrounding pasture-
lands for their livestock and all their possessions. 5 So the land was distributed in strict ac-
cordance with the LORD's commands to Moses.

CALEB REQUESTS HIS LAND

6 A delegation from the tribe of Judah, led by Caleb son of Jephunneh the Kenizzite, 14:6
came to Joshua at Gilgal. Caleb said to Joshua, "Remember what the LORD said to Num 13:30; 14:6,
Moses, the man of God, about you and me when we were at Kadesh-barnea. 7 I was 24, 30
forty years old when Moses, the servant of the LORD, sent me from Kadesh-barnea to
explore the land of Canaan. I returned and gave an honest report, 8 but my brothers
who went with me frightened the people from entering the Promised Land. For my
part, I wholeheartedly followed the LORD my God. 9 So that day Moses solemnly prom- 14:9
ised me, 'The land of Canaan on which you were just walking will be your grant of land Deut 1:36

13:29-31 Part of the tribe of Manasseh was given land to the east of the Jordan River and the Sea of Galilee and to the north of Gad's territory. Manasseh was actually a grandson of Jacob rather than a son. Jacob gave his blessing to Joseph's two sons, Ephraim and Manasseh, rather than to Joseph himself, essentially adopting Joseph's sons as his own. In this way, Jacob gave his favorite son, Joseph, a double portion of the inheritance. That is why there is no tribe of Joseph, even though he was one of the twelve sons of Jacob. The other half of the tribe was given land on the western side of the Jordan River.

14:1 Eleazar was the third son of Aaron, Moses' brother and Israel's first high priest. He was "the chief administrator over all the Levites, with special responsibility for the oversight of the sanctuary" (Numbers 3:32). Some of those special responsibilities included the oil for the lampstand, the incense, the daily grain offering, and the anointing oil (Numbers 4:16). Eleazar's two older brothers, the priests Nadab and Abihu, were killed when they offered incense in an inappropriate way (Leviticus 10). Their deaths left Eleazar and his younger brother Ithamar as the remaining priests in Aaron's bloodline. As high priest, Eleazar would have cast the lots to decide how the land would be allotted.

14:1-2 The author of Joshua now focuses on the division of the land west of the Jordan. Joshua, Eleazar, and the other Israelite leaders portioned out the land by casting lots, just as Moses had instructed them (Numbers 26:55). The lots used were probably the high priest's Urim and Thummim. The land described here was divided among the tribes of Simeon, Ephraim, Judah, Issachar, Zebulun, Benjamin, Dan, Naphtali, Asher, and the other half of Manasseh.

14:4 Joseph's descendants were divided into two groups, the descendants of his sons Ephraim and Manasseh. This was an honor for Joseph—it meant that he received double the inheritance of his brothers. The addition of Ephraim and Manasseh boosted the number of tribes to 13, but the tribe of Levi was dedicated to God and did not receive any land. Therefore, the number of Israel's tribal territories remained 12.

and that of your descendants forever, because you wholeheartedly followed the LORD
my God.’
10 “Now, as you can see, the LORD has kept me alive and well as He promised for all
these forty-five years since Moses made this promise—even while Israel wandered in the
wilderness. Today I am eighty-five years old. 11 I am as strong now as I was when Moses
14:12 sent me on that journey, and I can still travel and fight as well as I could then. 12 So give me
Num 13:33 the hill country that the LORD promised me. You will remember that as scouts we found the
descendants of Anak living there in great, walled towns. But if the LORD is with me, I will
drive them out of the land, just as the LORD said.”
13 So Joshua blessed Caleb son of Jephunneh and gave Hebron to him as his portion of
land. 14 Hebron still belongs to the descendants of Caleb son of Jephunneh the Kenizzite be-
14:15 cause he wholeheartedly followed the LORD, the God of Israel. 15 (Previously Hebron had been
Josh 11:23 called Kiriath-arba. It had been named after Arba, a great hero of the descendants of Anak.)
And the land had rest from war.

THE LAND GIVEN TO THE TRIBE OF JUDAH

15:1 **15** The allotment for the clans of the tribe of Judah reached southward to the border
Num 34:3-4 of Edom, as far south as the wilderness of Zin.
Deut 32:51
15:3-4 2 The southern boundary began at the south bay of the Dead Sea,* 3 ran south of
Num 34:4-5 Scorpion Pass* into the wilderness of Zin, and then went south of Kadesh-barnea to
Hezron. Then it went up to Addar, where it turned toward Karka. 4 From there it
passed to Azmon until it finally reached the Brook of Egypt, which it followed to the
Mediterranean Sea.* This was their* southern boundary.
15:5-6 5 The eastern boundary extended along the Dead Sea to the mouth of the Jordan River.
Josh 18:15-19 The northern boundary began at the bay where the Jordan River empties into the
Dead Sea, 6 went up from there to Beth-hoglah, then proceeded north of Beth-arabah
to the Stone of Bohan. (Bohan was Reuben’s son.) 7 From that point it went through
the valley of Achor to Debir, turning north toward Gilgal, which is across from the
15:8 slopes of Adummim on the south side of the valley. From there the boundary
Josh 15:63 extended to the springs at En-shemesh and on to En-rogel. 8 The boundary then
passed through the valley of Ben-Hinnom, along the southern slopes of the Jebusites,

15:2 Hebrew *the Salt Sea;* also in 15:5. 15:3 Hebrew *Akrabbim.* 15:4a Hebrew *the sea;* also in 15:11. 15:4b Hebrew *your.*

14:10 Caleb was one of two scouts (the other being Joshua) who had faith that the people could conquer the land of Canaan. The ten other scouts who traveled with them gave a fearful report that led the people to want to turn back (Numbers 14). Because Caleb was one of the 12 scouts, we know that he was a leader in his tribe, Judah. According to this verse, 45 years later he still remained a leader at the age of 85. However, he was not ready to retire. On the contrary, he wanted a challenge, so he asked Joshua to give him the portion of Canaan where the scouts had seen the giant Anakites. He had faith that God could enable him to defeat these formidable warriors, and God honored that faith (Joshua 15:14).

15:1 Judah was arguably the most significant tribe of Israel. When Jacob blessed his sons, he declared that the kings of Israel would come from the tribe of his fourth son, Judah (Genesis 49:10). This prophecy was partially fulfilled when David became king. But the prophecy had a deeper meaning, for God promised David that his line would reign for all time (2 Samuel 7:16). This was a promise that the Messiah would be born of the tribe of Judah. This tribe remained faithful to the line of David even as most of the other tribes rebelled and broke away, splitting Israel into two nations. The northern kingdom, which was referred to as Israel, was later conquered by Assyria and assimilated into that and other cultures. The southern kingdom was essentially the tribe of Judah and was known by that name.

15:1 Judah shared a border with distant relatives. Edom was the nation descended from Esau, the twin brother of Jacob, the progenitor of the nation of Israel. Though born second, Jacob (later renamed Israel) cheated Esau out of the family birthright, creating tension and hostility. Esau later married Canaanite women and settled his family to the south of the Dead Sea. The Edomites were his descendants. Though Jacob and Esau made peace during their lifetimes, their descendants remained hostile.

15:2-12 The territory assigned to the tribe of Judah covered most of southern Canaan, from the Dead Sea on the east to the Mediterranean Sea on the west, and stretching south into the wilderness of Zin in the Sinai Peninsula. God made a gracious choice in placing Judah in this location. Judah was the tribe with the greatest population, and hence the greatest military strength. By placing this strong tribe on Israel’s southern flank, God created a natural buffer zone for the other tribes. Enemies such as the Philistines and the Edomites would have had to fight their way through Judah to attack Israel’s heartland.

where the city of Jerusalem is located. Then it went west to the top of the mountain
above the valley of Hinnom, and on up to the northern end of the valley of Rephaim.
9From there the boundary extended from the top of the mountain to the spring at the 15:9
waters of Nephtoah,* and from there to the towns on Mount Ephron. Then it turned Josh 18:15
toward Baalah (that is, Kiriath-jearim). 10The boundary circled west of Baalah to
Mount Seir, passed along to the town of Kesalon on the northern slope of Mount
Jearim, and went down to Beth-shemesh and on to Timnah. 11The boundary then
proceeded to the slope of the hill north of Ekron, where it turned toward Shikkeron
and Mount Baalah. It passed Jabneel and ended at the Mediterranean Sea.
12The western boundary was the shoreline of the Mediterranean Sea.*

These are the boundaries for the clans of the tribe of Judah.

THE LAND GIVEN TO CALEB

13The LORD commanded Joshua to assign some of Judah's territory to Caleb son of Je- 15:13
phunneh. So Caleb was given the town of Kiriath-arba (that is, Hebron), which had been Josh 14:13-15
named after Anak's ancestor. 14Caleb drove out the three groups of Anakites—the descen- 15:14
dants of Sheshai, Ahiman, and Talmai, the sons of Anak. Num 13:33 Deut 9:2
15From there he went to fight against the people living in the town of Debir (formerly Josh 11:21-22
called Kiriath-sepher). 16Caleb said, "I will give my daughter Acsah in marriage to the one
who attacks and captures Kiriath-sepher." 17Othniel, the son of Caleb's brother Kenaz, was 15:17
the one who conquered it, so Acsah became Othniel's wife. Judg 1:12-13; 3:9
18When Acsah married Othniel, she urged him* to ask her father for a field. As she got
down off her donkey, Caleb asked her, "What's the matter?"
19She said, "Give me another gift. You have already given me land in the Negev; now
please give me springs of water, too." So Caleb gave her the upper and lower springs.

THE TOWNS ALLOTTED TO JUDAH

20This was the homeland allocated to the clans of the tribe of Judah.
21The towns of Judah situated along the borders of Edom in the extreme south were 15:21
Kabzeel, Eder, Jagur, 22Kinah, Dimonah, Adadah, 23Kedesh, Hazor, Ithnan, 24Ziph, Gen 35:21
Telem, Bealoth, 25Hazor-hadattah, Kerioth-hezron (that is, Hazor), 26Amam, Shema,
Moladah, 27Hazar-gaddah, Heshmon, Beth-pelet, 28Hazar-shual, Beersheba,
Biziothiah, 29Baalah, Iim, Ezem, 30Eltolad, Kesil, Hormah, 31Ziklag, Madmannah, 15:31
Sansannah, 32Lebaoth, Shilhim, Ain, and Rimmon—twenty-nine towns with their 1 Sam 27:6
surrounding villages.
33The following towns situated in the western foothills* were also given to Judah: 15:33
Eshtaol, Zorah, Ashnah, 34Zanoah, En-gannim, Tappuah, Enam, 35Jarmuth, Adullam, Judg 13:25; 16:31
Socoh, Azekah, 36Shaaraim, Adithaim, Gederah, and Gederothaim—fourteen towns
with their surrounding villages.
37Also included were Zenan, Hadashah, Migdal-gad, 38Dilean, Mizpeh, Joktheel,
39Lachish, Bozkath, Eglon, 40Cabbon, Lahmam, Kitlish, 41Gederoth, Beth-dagon, Naa- 15:39
mah, and Makkedah—sixteen towns with their surrounding villages. Josh 10:3 2 Kgs 14:19
42Besides these, there were Libnah, Ether, Ashan, 43Iphtah, Ashnah, Nezib, 44Keilah,
Aczib, and Mareshah—nine towns with their surrounding villages.
45The territory of the tribe of Judah also included Ekron and its surrounding settle-
ments and villages. 46From Ekron the boundary extended west and included the
towns near Ashdod with their surrounding villages. 47It also included Ashdod with its 15:47
surrounding settlements and villages and Gaza with its settlements and villages, as Num 34:6
far as the Brook of Egypt and along the coast of the Mediterranean Sea.

15:9 Or *the spring at Me-nephtoah.* 15:12 Hebrew *the Great Sea;* also in 15:47. 15:18 Some Greek manuscripts read *he urged her.* 15:33 Hebrew *the Shephelah.*

48 Judah also received the following towns in the hill country: Shamir, Jattir, Socoh,
49 Dannah, Kiriath-sannah (that is, Debir), 50 Anab, Eshtemoh, Anim, 51 Goshen, Holon,
and Giloh—eleven towns with their surrounding villages.
52 Also included were the towns of Arab, Dumah, Eshan, 53 Janim, Beth-tappuah,
Aphekah, 54 Humtah, Kiriath-arba (that is, Hebron), and Zior—nine towns with their
surrounding villages.
55 Besides these, there were Maon, Carmel, Ziph, Juttah, 56 Jezreel, Jokdeam,
Zanoah, 57 Kain, Gibeah, and Timnah—ten towns with their surrounding villages.
58 In addition, there were Halhul, Beth-zur, Gedor, 59 Maarath, Beth-anoth, and
Eltekon—six towns with their surrounding villages.
60 There were also Kiriath-baal (that is, Kiriath-jearim) and Rabbah—two towns with
their surrounding villages.
61 In the wilderness there were the towns of Beth-arabah, Middin, Secacah,
62 Nibshan, the City of Salt, and En-gedi—six towns with their surrounding villages.
15:63 63 But the tribe of Judah could not drive out the Jebusites, who lived in the city of Jerusa-
Judg 1:21 lem, so the Jebusites live there among the people of Judah to this day.
2 Sam 5:6

THE LAND GIVEN TO EPHRAIM AND WEST MANASSEH

16:1
Josh 8:15; 18:12 **16** The allotment for the descendants of Joseph extended from the Jordan River
16:2 near Jericho, east of the springs of Jericho, through the wilderness and into the
Josh 18:13 hill country of Bethel. 2 From Bethel (that is, Luz)* it ran over to Ataroth in the territory
of the Arkites. 3 Then it descended westward to the territory of the Japhletites as far
as Lower Beth-horon, then to Gezer and over to the Mediterranean Sea.*

4 This was the homeland allocated to the families of Joseph's sons, Manasseh and Ephraim.

16:5
THE LAND GIVEN TO EPHRAIM

Josh 18:13 5 The following territory was given to the clans of the tribe of Ephraim.

The boundary of their homeland began at Ataroth-addar in the east. From there it ran
16:6 Josh 17:7 to Upper Beth-horon, 6 then on to the Mediterranean Sea. From Micmethath on the
north, the boundary curved eastward past Taanath-shiloh to the east of Janoah. 7 From
16:8 Janoah it turned southward to Ataroth and Naarah, touched Jericho, and ended at the
Josh 17:8-9 Jordan River. 8 From Tappuah the boundary extended westward, following the Kanah
Ravine to the Mediterranean Sea. This is the homeland allocated to the clans of the
16:10 tribe of Ephraim.
Josh 15:63; 17:12-13 9 In addition, some towns with their surrounding villages in the territory allocated
Judg 1:29 to the half-tribe of Manasseh were set aside for the tribe of Ephraim. 10 They did not
1 Kgs 9:16

16:2 As in Greek version (also see 18:13); Hebrew reads *From Bethel to Luz.* 16:3 Hebrew *the sea;* also in 16:6, 8.

15:63 The city of Jerusalem was actually assigned to the tribe of Benjamin (Joshua 18:28). However, it was quite close to the northern border of Judah's territory, and the men of Judah, in an apparent effort to root out the Jebusites in their territory, went after the Jebusite stronghold of Jerusalem. Sadly, they were unable to take it, and the Jebusites remained in Judah's midst during the time the book of Joshua was written. Later, Judah briefly took the city (Judges 1:8), but it did not become a permanent Israelite possession until it was captured by David centuries later.

16:1 Ephraim and Manasseh received a rich inheritance when Joshua distributed the land of Canaan. Their territories were in the Israelite heartland. Stretching westward from the Jordan, they encompassed the fertile Jordan plain and the rich central hill country.

16:5 Ephraim was the younger of the two sons of Joseph, whom Jacob essentially adopted as his own, giving Joseph a double portion of the inheritance. When Jacob blessed Ephraim and Manasseh, he declared that the descendants of Manasseh would be a great people but that Ephraim's descendants would exceed Manasseh's (Genesis 48:19). The tribe of Ephraim did indeed become so large and influential that in some Old Testament prophecies its name is synonymous with Israel.

drive the Canaanites out of Gezer, however, so the people of Gezer live as slaves among the people of Ephraim to this day.

THE LAND GIVEN TO WEST MANASSEH

17 The next allotment of land was given to the half-tribe of Manasseh, the descen- **17:1**
dants of Joseph's older son. Makir, the firstborn son of Manasseh, was the father Josh 13:8
of Gilead. Because his descendants were experienced soldiers, the regions of Gilead and Bashan on the east side of the Jordan had already been given to them. 2 So the allotment on the west side of the Jordan was for the remaining families within the clans of the tribe of Manasseh: Abiezer, Helek, Asriel, Shechem, Hepher, and Shemida. These clans represent the male descendants of Manasseh son of Joseph.

3 However, Zelophehad, a descendant of Hepher son of Gilead, son of Makir, son of Ma- **17:3**
nasseh, had no sons. He had only daughters, whose names were Mahlah, Noah, Hoglah, Num 26:33; 27:1-7
Milcah, and Tirzah. 4 These women came to Eleazar the priest, Joshua son of Nun, and the Israelite leaders and said, "The LORD commanded Moses to give us a grant of land along with the men of our tribe."

So Joshua gave them a grant of land along with their uncles, as the LORD had commanded. 5 As a result, Manasseh's total allocation came to ten parcels of land, in addition
to the land of Gilead and Bashan across the Jordan River, 6 because the female descen- **17:6**
dants of Manasseh received a grant of land along with the male descendants. (The land of Josh 13:30-31
Gilead was given to the rest of the male descendants of Manasseh.)

7 The boundary of the tribe of Manasseh extended from the border of Asher to Micmethath, near Shechem. Then the boundary went south from Micmethath to the settlement near the spring of Tappuah. 8 The land surrounding Tappuah belonged to Manasseh, but the town of Tappuah itself, on the border of Manasseh's territory, belonged to the tribe of Ephraim. 9 From the spring of Tappuah, the boundary of Manasseh followed the Kanah Ravine to the Mediterranean Sea.* Several towns south of the ravine were inside Manasseh's territory, but they actually belonged to the tribe of Ephraim. 10 In general, however, the land south of the ravine belonged to Ephraim, and the land north of the ravine belonged to Manasseh. Manasseh's boundary ran along the northern side of the ravine and ended at the Mediterranean Sea. North of Manasseh was the territory of Asher, and to the east was the territory of Issachar.

11 The following towns within the territory of Issachar and Asher, however, were **17:11**
given to Manasseh: Beth-shan,* Ibleam, Dor (that is, Naphoth-dor),* Endor, Taanach, 1 Chr 7:29
and Megiddo, each with their surrounding settlements.

17:12
12 But the descendants of Manasseh were unable to occupy these towns. They could not Judg 1:27-28
drive out the Canaanites who continued to live there. 13 Later, however, when the Israelites

17:9 Hebrew *the sea;* also in 17:10. **17:11a** Hebrew *Beth-shean,* a variant spelling of Beth-shan; also in 17:16. **17:11b** The meaning of the Hebrew here is uncertain.

17:1 The tribe of Manasseh received its portion of Canaan after Ephraim, but part of the tribe had already been given land on the east side of the Jordan River, along with the tribes of Reuben and Gad. This verse tells us that it was the descendants of Makir who acquired that eastern land. Makir was a great warrior, and so were his descendants, taking the land they wanted from the Amorites (Numbers 32:39).

17:3-4 One of the descendants of Manasseh had five daughters but no sons. Under traditional inheritance practices, the daughters would not have received any land with the tribe. But they appealed their case to Moses, and Moses appealed on their behalf to God, who accepted their plea and decreed that they should have an inheritance (Numbers 27:7). God even made it a law that daughters could inherit when a man had no sons. This is a striking example of equitable treatment of women in Israelite culture. Here the women reminded Joshua of Moses' promise, and Joshua did as God had decreed.

17:13 The tribes had varying degrees of success in dealing with the Canaanites that remained in their territories. The people of Manasseh were not able to drive out the Canaanites, but they made them slaves, just as the Egyptians had made the Israelites slaves hundreds of years before. From Manasseh's perspective, this may have seemed preferable to letting the Canaanites dwell in their midst as neighbors, but it did not accomplish God's intended purpose—removing the temptation to worship idols. In order to accomplish that, the tribes needed to drive out the Canaanites, destroy them, or convert them.

became strong enough, they forced the Canaanites to work as slaves. But they did not
drive them out of the land.
17:14 [14] The descendants of Joseph came to Joshua and asked, "Why have you given us only
Num 26:28-37 one portion of land as our homeland when the LORD has blessed us with so many people?"
[15] Joshua replied, "If there are so many of you, and if the hill country of Ephraim is not
large enough for you, clear out land for yourselves in the forest where the Perizzites and
Rephaites live."
17:16 [16] The descendants of Joseph responded, "It's true that the hill country is not large
Judg 1:19; 4:3, 13 enough for us. But all the Canaanites in the lowlands have iron chariots, both those in
Beth-shan and its surrounding settlements and those in the valley of Jezreel. They are too
strong for us."
[17] Then Joshua said to the tribes of Ephraim and Manasseh, the descendants of Joseph,
"Since you are so large and strong, you will be given more than one portion. [18] The forests
of the hill country will be yours as well. Clear as much of the land as you wish, and take
possession of its farthest corners. And you will drive out the Canaanites from the valleys,
too, even though they are strong and have iron chariots."

THE ALLOTMENTS OF THE REMAINING LAND

18:1 **18** Now that the land was under Israelite control, the entire community of Israel gath-
Josh 19:51 ered at Shiloh and set up the Tabernacle.* [2] But there remained seven tribes who
Judg 21:19 had not yet been allotted their grants of land.
Jer 7:12 [3] Then Joshua asked them, "How long are you going to wait before taking possession of
18:3 Judg 18:9 the remaining land the LORD, the God of your ancestors, has given to you? [4] Select three
men from each tribe, and I will send them out to explore the land and map it out. They will
then return to me with a written report of their proposed divisions of their new homeland.
18:5 [5] Let them divide the land into seven sections, excluding Judah's territory in the south and
Josh 15:1; 16:1-4 Joseph's territory in the north. [6] And when you record the seven divisions of the land and
bring them to me, I will cast sacred lots in the presence of the LORD our God to assign land
to each tribe.

18:1 Hebrew *Tent of Meeting.*

17:14 No sooner had the tribes of Ephraim and Manasseh received their lands than they came to Joshua with a complaint, saying their territories were not big enough for them. But Joshua saw the truth—parts of their lands were occupied by Canaanites, and the tribes lacked the necessary faith to fight them. They needed to believe and act upon the promise of God (Joshua 13:6).

▶ CHURCH
17:14-18 Working for your wage. Have you ever heard it said that Christians are pushovers? That Christians are weak? Here, the leaders of a powerful tribe came to an aging Joshua and demanded additional land. Rather than take the easiest option and simply redistribute good land from a weaker tribe, Joshua urged the complaining leaders to take more land from the Canaanites. This both made their expansion dependent upon their labor, and furthered the purpose of God entrusted to Joshua to clear the entire land of God's enemies (Joshua 1:6). Do not live with your hand out, expecting blessings with no effort on your part. Give faithful labor to everything you do and pray for the best results. (***See Church> What> Many Titles> Servants> Servants must be prepared to work,*** TopicGuide page A48.)

18:1 The Tabernacle was, in essence, a portable temple. It was a simple structure made from poles and curtains, but the later Temple was based on the same design. It included a general area in which the people could gather; a smaller, enclosed area, the Holy Place, which was accessed only by the religious leadership; and the Most Holy Place, a chamber accessed only by the high priest once a year in the most sacred of ceremonies. The Most Holy Place was seen as God's residence; the Ark of the Covenant was kept there. The Israelites used the Tabernacle, in one form or another, until King Solomon built the Temple.

18:1 Jerusalem is renowned as the center of Israelite religious life, but Shiloh played that role for many years. From this point through the time described in the book of Judges, Shiloh was the place God chose "where His name will be honored" (Deuteronomy 12:5). It was the site of the Tabernacle, making it a place of worship and national decision-making. Shiloh was about 20 miles north of Jerusalem in the territory of Ephraim.

18:2-4 The tribes of Judah, Ephraim, and half of Manasseh had already received land in Canaan, but seven tribes had not. Apparently, they were in no hurry to separate and take on the Canaanites as individual tribes. This was not just sloth but sin, for Israel was neglecting its duty to execute God's wrath on the wicked Canaanites. Therefore, Joshua forced the issue, devising a plan to survey the remaining territory so that God might determine by lot where each tribe would settle.

7 "The Levites, however, will not receive any allotment of land. Their role as priests of 18:7
the LORD is their allotment. And the tribes of Gad, Reuben, and the half-tribe of Manasseh Num 18:7, 20
won't receive any more land, for they have already received their grant of land, which Josh 13:33
Moses, the servant of the LORD, gave them on the east side of the Jordan River."
8 As the men started on their way to map out the land, Joshua commanded them, "Go and 18:8
explore the land and write a description of it. Then return to me, and I will assign the land to Josh 18:1
the tribes by casting sacred lots here in the presence of the LORD at Shiloh." 9 The men did as
they were told and mapped the entire territory into seven sections, listing the towns in each
section. They made a written record and then returned to Joshua in the camp at Shiloh.
10 And there at Shiloh, Joshua cast sacred lots in the presence of the LORD to determine which 18:10
tribe should have each section. Num 34:16-29 Josh 19:51

THE LAND GIVEN TO BENJAMIN

11 The first allotment of land went to the clans of the tribe of Benjamin. It lay between the
territory assigned to the tribes of Judah and Joseph.

12 The northern boundary of Benjamin's land began at the Jordan River, went north
of the slope of Jericho, then west through the hill country and the wilderness of Beth-
aven. 13 From there the boundary went south to Luz (that is, Bethel) and proceeded
down to Ataroth-addar on the hill that lies south of Lower Beth-horon.
14 The boundary then made a turn and swung south along the western edge of the 18:14-15
hill facing Beth-horon, ending at the village of Kiriath-baal (that is, Kiriath-jearim), a Josh 15:5-9
town belonging to the tribe of Judah. This was the western boundary.
15 The southern boundary began at the outskirts of Kiriath-jearim. From that
western point it ran* to the spring at the waters of Nephtoah,* 16 and down to the 18:16
base of the mountain beside the valley of Ben-Hinnom, at the northern end of the 2 Kgs 23:10
valley of Rephaim. From there it went down the valley of Hinnom, crossing south of
the slope where the Jebusites lived, and continued down to En-rogel. 17 From En-rogel 18:17
the boundary proceeded in a northerly direction and came to En-shemesh and on to Josh 15:7-8

18:15a Or *From there it went to Mozah.* The meaning of the Hebrew is uncertain. **18:15b** Or *the spring at Me-nephtoah.*

THE TRIBES WEST OF THE JORDAN

Judah, Ephraim, and the other half-tribe of Manasseh were the first tribes to receive land west of the Jordan because of their past acts of faith. The remaining seven tribes—Benjamin, Zebulun, Issachar, Asher, Naphtali, Simeon, and Dan—were slow to conquer and possess the land allotted to them.

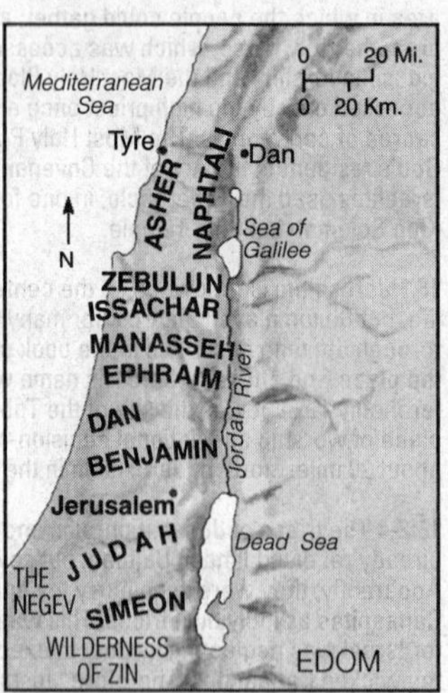

▸ PURPOSE

18:10 Joshua cast sacred lots. From the time of Moses to the time of Ezra and Nehemiah, the Urim and the Thummim (Exodus 28:30) were used in special circumstances to determine God's will (Nehemiah 7:65). Perhaps this is what Joshua used to determine which tribe was responsible for taking which land. In any case, after God gave a negative review of his work (13:1), Joshua immediately went to work to make sure the claiming of the land would be accomplished. This should be your response when you discover you have made an error—seek God's will and endeavor to correct your blunder. (***See Purpose**> God's Means> Human Choice> Bringing our wills in subjection to God's will,* TopicGuide page A52.)

18:11 The tribe of Benjamin received an allotment of land in central Canaan, north of Judah's territory and south of Ephraim and Manasseh's. Benjamin was Jacob's youngest son, one of two boys (the other was Joseph) born to Jacob's most loved wife, Rachel. She died just after Benjamin was born. When Jacob blessed his sons, he recognized Benjamin's warrior abilities (Genesis 49). This reputation was borne out in the tribe that descended from Benjamin. Though it was a small tribe, it made contributions on many levels. It was most notorious for its participation in a highly violent incident with a Levite's concubine. At that time, the other 11 tribes stood against the Benjamites, and the tribe was almost destroyed (Judges 19–21).

Geliloth (which is across from the slopes of Adummim). Then it went down to the
Stone of Bohan. (Bohan was Reuben's son.) 18From there it passed along the north
side of the slope overlooking the Jordan Valley.* The border then went down into the
valley, 19ran past the north slope of Beth-hoglah, and ended at the north bay of the
Dead Sea,* which is the southern end of the Jordan River. This was the southern
boundary.
20The eastern boundary was the Jordan River.

These were the boundaries of the homeland allocated to the clans of the tribe of Benjamin.

THE TOWNS GIVEN TO BENJAMIN

21These were the towns given to the clans of the tribe of Benjamin.

18:24 Jericho, Beth-hoglah, Emek-keziz, 22Beth-arabah, Zemaraim, Bethel, 23Avvim, Parah,
Isa 10:29 Ophrah, 24Kephar-ammoni, Ophni, and Geba—twelve towns with their surrounding
18:28 villages. 25Also Gibeon, Ramah, Beeroth, 26Mizpah, Kephirah, Mozah, 27Rekem, Irpeel,
Josh 15:8 Taralah, 28Zela, Haeleph, Jebus (that is, Jerusalem), Gibeah, and Kiriath-jearim*—
2 Sam 21:14 fourteen towns with their surrounding villages.

This was the homeland allocated to the clans of the tribe of Benjamin.

THE LAND GIVEN TO SIMEON

19 The second allotment of land went to the clans of the tribe of Simeon. Their
homeland was surrounded by Judah's territory.

2Simeon's homeland included Beersheba, Sheba, Moladah, 3Hazar-shual, Balah,
19:5 Ezem, 4Eltolad, Bethul, Hormah, 5Ziklag, Beth-marcaboth, Hazar-susah, 6Beth-lebaoth,
1 Sam 30:1 and Sharuhen—thirteen towns with their surrounding villages. 7It also included Ain,
Rimmon, Ether, and Ashan—four towns with their villages, 8including all the
surrounding villages as far south as Baalath-beer (also known as Ramah of
the Negev).

This was the homeland allocated to the clans of the tribe of Simeon. 9Their allocation
of land came from part of what had been given to Judah because Judah's territory was
too large for them. So the tribe of Simeon received an allocation within the territory of
Judah.

THE LAND GIVEN TO ZEBULUN

10The third allotment of land went to the clans of the tribe of Zebulun.

19:11 The boundary of Zebulun's homeland started at Sarid. 11From there it went
Josh 21:34 west, going past Maralah, touching Dabbesheth, and proceeding to the brook

18:18 Hebrew *overlooking the Arabah,* or *overlooking Beth-arabah.* 18:19 Hebrew *Salt Sea.* 18:28 As in Greek version; Hebrew reads *Kiriath.*

19:1 The tribe of Simeon received land within the southern part of Judah. Simeon, Jacob's second oldest son, is remembered for the violent vengeance he wreaked on the men of Shechem. One of the men had raped Simeon's sister, and then asked to marry her. Simeon and his brothers convinced the men of Shechem to be circumcised, explaining that this had to occur before the marriage could take place. While the men were recovering from the surgeries, Simeon and his brother Levi killed them all (Genesis 34). When Jacob gave his final blessings to his sons, he declared that Simeon's tribe eventually would be absorbed into the other tribes, a grave dishonor. Because of the location of its land, this tribe is often mentioned in conjunction with the tribe of Judah.

19:10 The tribe of Zebulun received a land-locked region north of Manasseh's territory and between the Mediterranean and the Sea of Galilee. Zebulun was Jacob's tenth son, his sixth and last with Leah. In Jacob's final blessing to his sons, he foretold that Zebulun's descendants would be successful in maritime trade (Genesis 49:13). Moses expressed a similar blessing: "May the people of Zebulun prosper in their travels" (Deuteronomy 33:18). While Zebulun's tribe did not actually live in coastal areas, its land bordered regions that did. Jesus' hometown of Nazareth was in the territory of Zebulun.

east of Jokneam. 12In the other direction, the boundary went east from Sarid to the
border of Kisloth-tabor, and from there to Daberath and up to Japhia. 13Then it
continued east to Gath-hepher, Eth-kazin, and Rimmon and turned toward
Neah. 14The northern boundary of Zebulun passed Hannathon and ended at
the valley of Iphtah-el. 15The towns in these areas included Kattath, Nahalal, **19:15**
Shimron, Idalah, and Bethlehem—twelve towns with their surrounding Mic 5:2
villages.

16The homeland allocated to the clans of the tribe of Zebulun included these towns and
their surrounding villages.

THE LAND GIVEN TO ISSACHAR

17The fourth allotment of land went to the clans of the tribe of Issachar.

18Its boundaries included the following towns: Jezreel, Kesulloth, Shunem, **19:18** 1 Sam 28:4
19Hapharaim, Shion, Anaharath, 20Rabbith, Kishion, Ebez, 21Remeth, En-gannim,
En-haddah, and Beth-pazzez. 22The boundary also touched Tabor, Shahazumah,
and Beth-shemesh, ending at the Jordan River—sixteen towns with their surrounding
villages.

23The homeland allocated to the clans of the tribe of Issachar included these towns and
their surrounding villages.

THE LAND GIVEN TO ASHER

24The fifth allotment of land went to the clans of the tribe of Asher.

25Its boundaries included these towns: Helkath, Hali, Beten, Acshaph,
26Allammelech, Amad, and Mishal. The boundary on the west touched Carmel and
Shihor-libnath, 27then it turned east toward Beth-dagon, and ran as far as Zebulun
in the valley of Iphtah-el, going north to Beth-emek and Neiel.It then continued
north to Cabul, 28Abdon,* Rehob, Hammon, Kanah, and as far as Greater Sidon. **19:28** Josh 11:8
29Then the boundary turned toward Ramah and the fortress of Tyre, where
it turned toward Hosah and came to the Mediterranean Sea.* The territory also
included Mehebel, Aczib, 30Ummah, Aphek, and Rehob—twenty-two towns with **19:30**
their surrounding villages. Josh 21:31

31The homeland allocated to the clans of the tribe of Asher included these towns and their
surrounding villages.

19:28 As in some Hebrew manuscripts (see also 21:30); most Hebrew manuscripts read *Ebron*. 19:29 Hebrew *the sea*.

19:17 The tribe of Issachar received land north of Manasseh's territory, south of Zebulun's, and west of the Jordan River. Little is known about Issachar, Jacob's ninth son and his fifth with Leah. When Jacob blessed him, he declared that Issachar was "a sturdy donkey" (Genesis 49:14), but his meaning is unclear. Issachar's tribe supported the Israelite uprising led by Deborah and Barak (Judges 5:15). Later, the tribe's leaders were praised as men who "understood the signs of the times and knew the best course for Israel to take" (1 Chronicles 12:32).

19:24 The tribe of Asher received territory along the Mediterranean coast to the north of Manasseh and Zebulun. Asher was the eighth son of Jacob. His mother was Zilpah, Leah's maid. When Leah, Jacob's first wife, realized she wasn't getting pregnant anymore, she gave her maid to Jacob, as was the custom of the day. In Jacob's final blessing to his sons, he described Asher as a producer of fine foods (Genesis 49:20). The tribe's location on the coast of the Mediterranean ensured a healthy trade. Its territory also was well known for its crops. Sadly, the tribe never fully drove out the Canaanites (Judges 1:31). By the time of King David, Asher wasn't even listed among the tribes.

THE LAND GIVEN TO NAPHTALI

32 The sixth allotment of land went to the clans of the tribe of Naphtali.

33 Its boundary ran from Heleph, from the oak at Zaanannim, and extended across
19:34 to Adami-nekeb, Jabneel, and as far as Lakkum, ending at the Jordan River. 34 The
Deut 33:23 western boundary ran past Aznoth-tabor, then to Hukkok, and touched the border of
Zebulun in the south, the border of Asher on the west, and the Jordan River* on the
east. 35 The fortified towns included in this territory were Ziddim, Zer, Hammath,
Rakkath, Kinnereth, 36 Adamah, Ramah, Hazor, 37 Kedesh, Edrei, En-hazor, 38 Yiron,
Migdal-el, Horem, Beth-anath, and Beth-shemesh—nineteen towns with their
surrounding villages.

39 The homeland allocated to the clans of the tribe of Naphtali included these towns and
their surrounding villages.

THE LAND GIVEN TO DAN

40 The seventh allotment of land went to the clans of the tribe of Dan.

41 The land allocated as their homeland included the following towns: Zorah, Eshtaol,
19:42 Ir-shemesh, 42 Shaalabbin, Aijalon, Ithlah, 43 Elon, Timnah, Ekron, 44 Eltekeh, Gibbethon,
Judg 1:35 Baalath, 45 Jehud, Bene-berak, Gath-rimmon, 46 Me-jarkon, Rakkon, and the territory
across from Joppa.
19:47 47 But the tribe of Dan had trouble taking possession of their land,* so they
Judg 18:27-31 attacked the town of Laish.* They captured it, slaughtered its people, and settled
there. They renamed the town Dan after their ancestor.

48 The homeland allocated to the clans of the tribe of Dan included these towns and their
surrounding villages.

THE LAND GIVEN TO JOSHUA

49 After all the land was divided among the tribes, the Israelites gave a piece of land to
19:50 Joshua as his allocation. 50 For the LORD had said he could have any town he wanted.
Josh 24:30 He chose Timnath-serah in the hill country of Ephraim. He rebuilt the town and lived
there.

51 These are the territories that Eleazar the priest, Joshua son of Nun, and the tribal lead-
19:51 ers allocated as grants of land to the tribes of Israel by casting sacred lots in the presence
Josh 14:1; 18:10 of the LORD at the entrance of the Tabernacle* at Shiloh. So the division of the land was
completed.

19:34 Hebrew *and Judah at the Jordan River.* 19:47a Or *had trouble holding onto their land.* 19:47b Hebrew *Leshem,* a variant spelling of Laish. 19:51 Hebrew *Tent of Meeting.*

19:32 The tribe of Naphtali received land between Asher and the Sea of Galilee, north of Zebulun and Issachar. Naphtali was the second of the two sons borne to Jacob by Bilhah, Rachel's maid. Rachel, who was Jacob's second but more loved wife, had trouble getting pregnant, so she offered her maid to Jacob according to the custom of the day. Bilhah's two sons from that union, Dan and Naphtali, were then considered Rachel's sons. In Jacob's final blessings to his sons, he compared Naphtali to a "doe set free" (Genesis 49:21), a description that fits with Naphtali's territory in the highlands of the north of Canaan. This tribe fought alongside Deborah and Barak against Sisera (Judges 4–5). They also fought with Gideon in his famous battle against the Midianites (Judges 7:23).

19:40 The tribe of Dan was the last to receive its land, a small territory on the Mediterranean coast west of Benjamin, north of Judah, and south of Ephraim and Manasseh. Dan was the fifth son of Jacob and the first of the two sons born to Rachel's maid, Bilhah. In Jacob's final blessing over his sons, he described Dan as a snake beside the road (Genesis 49:17). The tribe was not able to conquer its assigned territory. Because of that, they moved north, changing the name of an existing city to Dan. This city was so far north that it was used to delineate Israel's northern boundary in the phrase "from Dan in the north to Beersheba in the south."

19:49-50 When all of the tribes had been given their land, the Israelites gave Joshua a possession of his own. Apparently they did this in obedience to God's command. Joshua chose the town of Timnath-serah in the territory of Ephraim. Like Caleb (Joshua 14), he did not choose an easy place—Timnath needed rebuilding. But by his willingness to spend his later years actively, Joshua set a strong example of diligence for his fellow Israelites.

THE CITIES OF REFUGE

20 The LORD said to Joshua, 2“Now tell the Israelites to designate the cities of refuge, 20:2
as I instructed Moses. 3Anyone who kills another person accidentally and unin- Num 35:6, 11
tentionally can run to one of these cities; they will be places of refuge from relatives seek- Deut 4:41; 19:2
ing revenge for the person who was killed.
4“Upon reaching one of these cities, the one who caused the death will appear before 20:4
the elders at the city gate and present his case. They must allow him to enter the city and Ruth 4:1-2
give him a place to live among them. 5If the relatives of the victim come to avenge the kill-
ing, the leaders must not release the slayer to them, for he killed the other person uninten-
tionally and without previous hostility. 6But the slayer must stay in that city and be tried by
the local assembly, which will render a judgment. And he must continue to live in that city
until the death of the high priest who was in office at the time of the accident. After that, he
is free to return to his own home in the town from which he fled.”
7The following cities were designated as cities of refuge: Kedesh of Galilee, in the hill 20:7
country of Naphtali; Shechem, in the hill country of Ephraim; and Kiriath-arba (that is, He- Josh 21:11, 32
bron), in the hill country of Judah. 8On the east side of the Jordan River, across from Jeri- 1 Chr 6:76 Luke 1:39
cho, the following cities were designated: Bezer, in the wilderness plain of the tribe of 20:8
Reuben; Ramoth in Gilead, in the territory of the tribe of Gad; and Golan in Bashan, in the Josh 21:27, 36, 38
land of the tribe of Manasseh. 9These cities were set apart for all the Israelites as well as
the foreigners living among them. Anyone who accidentally killed another person could
take refuge in one of these cities. In this way, they could escape being killed in revenge
prior to standing trial before the local assembly.

THE TOWNS GIVEN TO THE LEVITES

21 Then the leaders of the tribe of Levi came to consult with Eleazar the priest, Joshua 21:1
son of Nun, and the leaders of the other tribes of Israel. 2They came to them at Shi- Josh 14:1
loh in the land of Canaan and said, “The LORD commanded Moses to give us towns to live in 21:2
and pasturelands for our livestock.” 3So by the command of the LORD the people of Israel Num 35:2
gave the Levites the following towns and pasturelands out of their own grants of land.
4The descendants of Aaron, who were members of the Kohathite clan within the tribe of 21:4-39
Levi, were allotted thirteen towns that were originally assigned to the tribes of Judah, Sim- //1 Chr 6:54-80

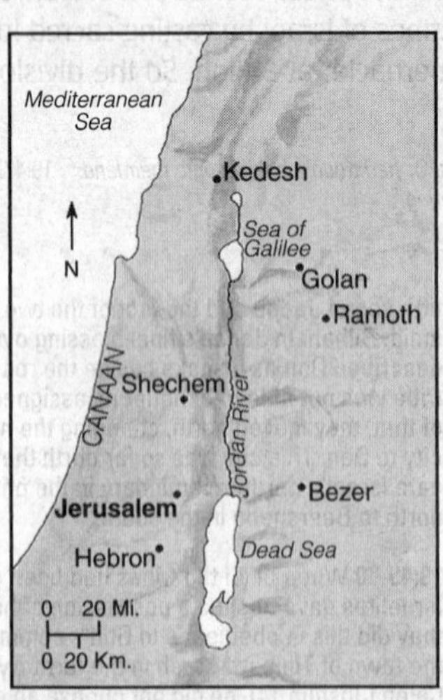

THE CITIES OF REFUGE
A city of refuge was just that—refuge for someone who committed an unintentional murder that would evoke revenge from the victim's friends and relatives. The six cities of refuge were spaced throughout the land so that a person was never too far from one.

20:1-2 Once all the tribes had been given their land allotments, God reminded Joshua to designate “cities of refuge.” God had commanded Moses to do this (Numbers 35). The idea was that if a person killed another unintentionally, then he could flee to one of these cities and be safe from the vengeance of the dead person's family until his case could be judged. In this plan we see God's desire for justice among His people. Joshua responded by designating six cities in all—three to the west of the Jordan and three to the east—as cities of refuge. Scattered throughout the tribes, at least one of these cities was close enough for any Israelite to find refuge quickly.

21:1 The people of the tribe of Levi were not given any territory because they had the privilege of serving God in the Tabernacle (Joshua 18:7). But the Levites needed places to live, and God had told Moses that they were to be given towns and pastureland. Again using sacred lots, the Israelites assigned some 48 towns to the Levites, drawing from the allotted territory of the other tribes. This arrangement fulfilled Jacob's prophetic words about Levi in his final blessing to his sons. Deploring Levi and Simeon's role in the slaughter of the men of Shechem, Jacob said, “I will scatter them among the descendants of Jacob” (Genesis 49:7). But the scattering of the Levites had a positive effect—it put these special servants of God in every corner of the land so that they might serve as examples of obedience to God's law.

eon, and Benjamin. 5The other families of the Kohathite clan were allotted ten towns from
the tribes of Ephraim, Dan, and the half-tribe of Manasseh.
6The clan of Gershon was allotted thirteen towns from the tribes of Issachar, Asher,
Naphtali, and the half-tribe of Manasseh in Bashan.
7The clan of Merari was allotted twelve towns from the tribes of Reuben, Gad, and Zebulun.
8So the Israelites obeyed the LORD's command to Moses and assigned these towns and
pasturelands to the Levites by casting sacred lots.
9The Israelites gave the following towns from the tribes of Judah and Simeon 10to the
21:11 descendants of Aaron, who were members of the Kohathite clan within the tribe of Levi,
Josh 15:13-14 since the sacred lot fell to them first: 11Kiriath-arba (that is, Hebron), in the hill country of
1 Chr 6:57 Judah, along with its surrounding pasturelands. (Arba was an ancestor of Anak.) 12But the
21:13 Josh 15:42, 54; 20:7 open fields beyond the town and the surrounding villages were given to Caleb son of Je-
1 Chr 6:55 phunneh as his possession.
21:15 13The following towns with their pasturelands were given to the descendants of Aaron
Josh 15:49, 51 the priest: Hebron (a city of refuge for those who accidentally killed someone), Libnah,
1 Chr 6:58 14Jattir, Eshtemoa, 15Holon, Debir, 16Ain, Juttah, and Beth-shemesh—nine towns from
21:16 Josh 15:10 these two tribes.
1 Chr 6:59 17From the tribe of Benjamin the priests were given the following towns with their
21:18 pasturelands: Gibeon, Geba, 18Anathoth, and Almon—four towns. 19So in all, thirteen
1 Chr 6:60 towns with their pasturelands were given to the priests, the descendants of Aaron.
20The rest of the Kohathite clan from the tribe of Levi was allotted the following towns
21:21 and pasturelands from the tribe of Ephraim: 21Shechem in the hill country of Ephraim (a
Josh 20:7 city of refuge for those who accidentally killed someone), Gezer, 22Kibzaim, and Beth-
horon—four towns.
23The following towns and pasturelands were allotted to the priests from the tribe of
Dan: Eltekeh, Gibbethon, 24Aijalon, and Gath-rimmon—four towns.
25The half-tribe of Manasseh allotted the following towns with their pasturelands to the
priests: Taanach and Gath-rimmon—two towns. 26So in all, ten towns with their pasture-
lands were given to the rest of the Kohathite clan.
27The descendants of Gershon, another clan within the tribe of Levi, received the follow-
ing towns with their pasturelands from the half-tribe of Manasseh: Golan in Bashan (a city
of refuge for those who accidentally killed someone) and Be-eshterah—two towns.
28From the tribe of Issachar they received the following towns with their pasturelands:
Kishion, Daberath, 29Jarmuth, and En-gannim—four towns.
30From the tribe of Asher they received the following towns with their pasturelands: Mi-
shal, Abdon, 31Helkath, and Rehob—four towns.
21:32 32From the tribe of Naphtali they received the following towns with their pasturelands:
Josh 20:7 Kedesh in Galilee (a city of refuge for those who accidentally killed someone), Hammoth-
dor, and Kartan—three towns. 33So in all, thirteen towns with their pasturelands were allot-
ted to the clan of Gershon.
34The rest of the Levites—the Merari clan—were given the following towns with their
pasturelands from the tribe of Zebulun: Jokneam, Kartah, 35Dimnah, and Nahalal—four
towns.
21:36 36From the tribe of Reuben they received the following towns with their pasturelands:
Josh 20:8 Bezer, Jahaz,* 37Kedemoth, and Mephaath—four towns.
38From the tribe of Gad they received the following towns with their pasturelands: Ra-
moth in Gilead (a city of refuge for those who accidentally killed someone), Mahanaim,
39Heshbon, and Jazer—four towns. 40So in all, twelve towns were allotted to the clan of
Merari.
21:41 41The total number of towns and pasturelands within Israelite territory given to the Le-
Num 35:7 vites came to forty-eight. 42Every one of these towns had pasturelands surrounding it.

21:36 Hebrew *Jahzah,* a variant spelling of Jahaz.

43 So the LORD gave to Israel all the land He had sworn to give their ancestors, and they
took possession of it and settled there. 44 And the LORD gave them rest on every side, just
as He had solemnly promised their ancestors. None of their enemies could stand against
them, for the LORD helped them conquer all their enemies. 45 Not a single one of all the
good promises the LORD had given to the family of Israel was left unfulfilled; everything
He had spoken came true.

THE EASTERN TRIBES RETURN HOME

22 Then Joshua called together the tribes of Reuben, Gad, and the half-tribe of Ma-
nasseh. 2 He told them, "You have done as Moses, the servant of the LORD, com-
manded you, and you have obeyed every order I have given you. 3 During all this time you
have not deserted the other tribes. You have been careful to obey the commands of the
LORD your God right up to the present day. 4 And now the LORD your God has given the
other tribes rest, as He promised them. So go back home to the land that Moses, the ser-
vant of the LORD, gave you as your possession on the east side of the Jordan River. 5 But be
very careful to obey all the commands and the instructions that Moses gave to you. Love
the LORD your God, walk in all His ways, obey His commands, hold firmly to Him, and
serve Him with all your heart and all your soul." 6 So Joshua blessed them and sent them
away, and they went home.
7 Moses had given the land of Bashan, east of the Jordan River, to the half-tribe of Ma-
nasseh. (The other half of the tribe was given land west of the Jordan.) As Joshua sent
them away and blessed them, 8 he said to them, "Go back to your homes with the great
wealth you have taken from your enemies—the vast herds of livestock, the silver, gold,
bronze, and iron, and the large supply of clothing. Share the plunder with your relatives."
9 So the men of Reuben, Gad, and the half-tribe of Manasseh left the rest of Israel at Shi-
loh in the land of Canaan. They started the journey back to their own land of Gilead, the
territory that belonged to them according to the LORD's command through Moses.

THE EASTERN TRIBES BUILD AN ALTAR

10 But while they were still in Canaan, and when they came to a place called Geliloth* near
the Jordan River, the men of Reuben, Gad, and the half-tribe of Manasseh stopped to build
a large and imposing altar.
11 The rest of Israel heard that the people of Reuben, Gad, and the half-tribe of Manas-
seh had built an altar at Geliloth at the edge of the land of Canaan, on the west side of the
Jordan River. 12 So the whole community of Israel gathered at Shiloh and prepared to go to
war against them. 13 First, however, they sent a delegation led by Phinehas son of Eleazar,

21:43 Num 33:53; Deut 11:31; 17:14; 34:4
21:44 Exod 23:31; Deut 7:24
22:2 Num 32:20-22; Josh 1:12-18
22:4 Num 32:18; Deut 3:20
22:5 Deut 5:10; *Mark 12:32
22:7 Num 32:33; Josh 17:1-2
22:9 Deut 32:1, 26, 29
22:11 Deut 12:5
22:13 Num 25:7, 11; 31:6

22:10 Or *to the circle of stones;* similarly in 22:11.

21:43-45 The conclusion of the distribution of the land of Canaan to the tribes of Israel represented a major milestone in God's dealings with His covenant people. God had promised Abraham that his descendants would come to possess the land. Now, after hundreds of years of slavery, a miraculous deliverance from Egypt, 40 years of wandering in the desert, and a war of conquest, that promise was fulfilled in a very tangible way. As this passage says, "Not a single one of all the good promises the LORD had given to the family of Israel was left unfulfilled; everything He had spoken came true." Yes, there were still Canaanites to deal with, but the land essentially belonged to the Israelites. They were free to settle it and enjoy its bounty as long as they were faithful to finish the conquest.

22:1-2 Moses had given land to the tribes of Reuben, Gad, and half of Manasseh on the east side of the Jordan River before Israel ever entered Canaan. But he made these tribes agree that they would help the other tribes conquer Canaan, and Joshua held them to their promise. Afterward, Joshua commended the men of these tribes for keeping their word and released them to return to their own lands and their families to the east. He also allowed them to return home with great riches taken from the conquered Canaanites.

22:10-12 On their way home, the three eastern tribes paused to build a large altar on the west bank of the Jordan. When word of this reached the other tribes, they mobilized for war. Why? God had designated Shiloh as the place for sacrifices and offerings, but now it seemed the eastern tribes were preparing another site for worship. The Israelites had witnessed God's judgment against those who disobeyed Him, and they knew rebellion in the area of worship was particularly perilous. They feared that God might judge the entire nation because of the eastern tribes' error. Therefore, they decided to confront their fellow Israelites over this potential sin.

the priest, to talk with the tribes of Reuben, Gad, and the half-tribe of Manasseh. [14]In this
delegation were ten leaders of Israel, one from each of the ten tribes, and each the head of
his family within the clans of Israel.
[15]When they arrived in the land of Gilead, they said to the tribes of Reuben, Gad, and
the half-tribe of Manasseh, [16]"The whole community of the LORD demands to know why
22:17 you are betraying the God of Israel. How could you turn away from the LORD and build an
Num 25:1-9 altar for yourselves in rebellion against Him? [17]Was our sin at Peor not enough? To this
day we are not fully cleansed of it, even after the plague that struck the entire community
of the LORD. [18]And yet today you are turning away from following the LORD. If you rebel
against the LORD today, He will be angry with all of us tomorrow.
[19]"If you need the altar because the land you possess is defiled, then join us in the
LORD's land, where the Tabernacle of the LORD is situated, and share our land with us. But
22:20 do not rebel against the LORD or against us by building an altar other than the one true al-
Josh 7:1-26 tar of the LORD our God. [20]Didn't divine anger fall on the entire community of Israel when
Achan, a member of the clan of Zerah, sinned by stealing the things set apart for the
LORD*? He was not the only one who died because of his sin."
22:22 [21]Then the people of Reuben, Gad, and the half-tribe of Manasseh answered the heads
Deut 10:17 of the clans of Israel: [22]"The LORD, the Mighty One, is God! The LORD, the Mighty One, is
God! He knows the truth, and may Israel know it, too! We have not built the altar in treach-
erous rebellion against the LORD. If we have done so, do not spare our lives this day. [23]If we
have built an altar for ourselves to turn away from the LORD or to offer burnt offerings or
grain offerings or peace offerings, may the LORD Himself punish us.
[24]"The truth is, we have built this altar because we fear that in the future your descen-
dants will say to ours, 'What right do you have to worship the LORD, the God of Israel?
[25]The LORD has placed the Jordan River as a barrier between our people and you people of
Reuben and Gad. You have no claim to the LORD.' So your descendants may prevent our
22:27 descendants from worshiping the LORD.
Josh 24:27 [26]"So we decided to build the altar, not for burnt offerings or sacrifices, [27]but as a me-
morial. It will remind our descendants and your descendants that we, too, have the right to
worship the LORD at His sanctuary with our burnt offerings, sacrifices, and peace offerings.
Then your descendants will not be able to say to ours, 'You have no claim to the LORD.'
[28]"If they say this, our descendants can reply, 'Look at this copy of the LORD's altar that our
ancestors made. It is not for burnt offerings or sacrifices; it is a reminder of the relationship
22:29 Deut 12:13 both of us have with the LORD.' [29]Far be it from us to rebel against the LORD or turn away from
Him by building our own altar for burnt offerings, grain offerings, or sacrifices. Only the altar
of the LORD our God that stands in front of the Tabernacle may be used for that purpose."

22:20 The Hebrew term used here refers to the complete consecration of things or people to the LORD, either by destroying them or by giving them as an offering.

▶ SPIRITUAL WARFARE

22:16-30 Rush to judgment. Do you know someone who rushes to judgment whenever he or she hears a rumor of trouble in the church? The Israelites living west of the Jordan heard that their brothers on the other side of the river had built a rival altar to the one the Lord had established at Shiloh. What did they do? On one hand, they prepared for war so they could quickly destroy these possibly renegade tribes before they brought God's judgment upon them all, as at Peor (22:17; Numbers 25). But the western tribes also sent representatives to find out whether the rumors were true. They discovered that the altar was a memorial to the Lord and was not for burning sacrifices. We should strive to discover the truth of stories for ourselves before we pass judgment on God's people. (***See Spiritual Warfare***> *Originator of Sin> Satan's Character> Slanderous,* TopicGuide page A44.)

22:24 When asked to explain why they had built a large altar beside the Jordan, the eastern tribes explained that it was not an attempt to set up their own worship center in violation of God's command. Rather, it was to serve as a "memorial" (22:27). It would always remind the eastern tribes that God was to be worshiped in His way, at the place of His choosing. But it also would remind the western tribes that the easterners had a right to come to Shiloh, too. The eastern tribes feared that the distance from their homes to Shiloh would make it difficult for them to attend the yearly feasts. Furthermore, they worried that if they did not attend as frequently, the other tribes in time might conclude that they did not belong at all. They hoped the altar would be a symbol of unity in worship as a nation.

30 When Phinehas the priest and the leaders of the community—the heads of the clans
of Israel—heard this from the tribes of Reuben, Gad, and the half-tribe of Manasseh, they
were satisfied. 31 Phinehas son of Eleazar, the priest, replied to them, "Today we know
the LORD is among us because you have not committed this treachery against the LORD as
we thought. Instead, you have rescued Israel from being destroyed by the hand of the
LORD."
32 Then Phinehas son of Eleazar, the priest, and the other leaders left the tribes of Reu-
ben and Gad in Gilead and returned to the land of Canaan to tell the Israelites what had
happened. 33 And all the Israelites were satisfied and praised God and spoke no more of
war against Reuben and Gad.
34 The people of Reuben and Gad named the altar "Witness,"* for they said, "It is a wit-
ness between us and them that the LORD is our God, too."

JOSHUA'S FINAL WORDS TO ISRAEL

23 The years passed, and the LORD had given the people of Israel rest from all their
enemies. Joshua, who was now very old, 2 called together all the elders, leaders,
judges, and officers of Israel. He said to them, "I am now a very old man. 3 You have seen
everything the LORD your God has done for you during my lifetime. The LORD your God has
fought for you against your enemies. 4 I have allotted to you as your homeland all the land
of the nations yet unconquered, as well as the land of those we have already conquered—
from the Jordan River to the Mediterranean Sea* in the west. 5 This land will be yours, for
the LORD your God will Himself drive out all the people living there now. You will take pos-
session of their land, just as the LORD your God promised you.
6 "So be very careful to follow everything Moses wrote in the Book of Instruction. Do not
deviate from it, turning either to the right or to the left. 7 Make sure you do not associate
with the other people still remaining in the land. Do not even mention the names of their
gods, much less swear by them or serve them or worship them. 8 Rather, cling tightly to the
LORD your God as you have done until now.
9 "For the LORD has driven out great and powerful nations for you, and no one has yet
been able to defeat you. 10 Each one of you will put to flight a thousand of the enemy, for
the LORD your God fights for you, just as He has promised. 11 So be very careful to love the
LORD your God.
12 "But if you turn away from Him and cling to the customs of the survivors of these na-
tions remaining among you, and if you intermarry with them, 13 then know for certain that

22:31 Lev 26:11-12; 2 Chr 15:2
22:34 Gen 31:47-49
23:4 Exod 23:30
23:5 Num 33:53
23:6 Deut 5:32; Josh 1:7
23:7 Exod 20:5; 23:13; Ps 16:4
23:8 Deut 10:20
23:9 Deut 7:24
23:10 Lev 26:8; Deut 28:7
23:12 Deut 7:3-4; Ezra 9:2
23:13 Exod 23:33; 34:12; Deut 7:16

22:34 Some manuscripts lack this word. 23:4 Hebrew *the Great Sea.*

23:1-5 When Joshua was very old and was approaching the end of his life, he called a meeting of the leaders of Israel in order to exhort them on how they should live in the land God had given them. Even in the twilight of his life, Joshua still exhibited the deep faith that made him such a great leader. Though he admitted that some parts of the Promised Land still were not conquered, he declared confidently, "This land will be yours, for the LORD your God will Himself drive out all the people living there now" (23:5). The basis for this confidence was Joshua's faith in God's promise. God had said He would do it, so Joshua was convinced that He would fulfill His promise.

▶ HOLINESS

23:7 Do not associate with foreigners? How many non-Christians do you know? This passage raises the question of how intertwined we should allow our lives to become with nonbelievers. The New Testament updates this command, with two points. First, Jesus said He did not come to take us out of the world. A monk's lifestyle is not a long-term answer to the question of how to live an intentionally separate life (John 17:15). Second, however, not every relationship is allowed. For instance, we should not marry unbelievers (2 Corinthians 6:14-18), and neither should we fellowship with those who are under discipline by a church (1 Corinthians 5:9-13). Still, as the ministry of Jesus illustrates, we may know and love non-Christians for the sake of displaying the love of God to them. Make sure you are close enough to the unbelievers you know so that if God opens an opportunity to share His love, you will be in a position to do so. (*See Holiness*> *Maturing*> *Conformity to Christ*> *Following the Royal Law of love,* TopicGuide page A40.)

23:12-13 The Israelites did not heed Joshua's warning. Through the next few centuries, they did intermingle with the Canaanites. The Canaanites worshiped many gods and even incorporated the Lord into their religious practices. The Israelites found it easy to do the same, but doing so violated the first commandment, the clear divine directive to worship only the Lord. Because of this, the sanction God threatened here—that He would cease to drive out the Canaanites on behalf of His people—became reality.

the LORD your God will no longer drive them out of your land. Instead, they will be a snare
and a trap to you, a whip for your backs and thorny brambles in your eyes, and you will
vanish from this good land the LORD your God has given you.
[14]"Soon I will die, going the way of everything on earth. Deep in your hearts you know
that every promise of the LORD your God has come true. Not a single one has failed! [15]But
as surely as the LORD your God has given you the good things He promised, He will also
bring disaster on you if you disobey Him. He will completely destroy you from this good
land He has given you. [16]If you break the covenant of the LORD your God by worshiping
and serving other gods, His anger will burn against you, and you will quickly vanish from
the good land He has given you."

23:15 Lev 26:14-33; Deut 28:15
23:16 Deut 4:25-26

THE LORD'S COVENANT RENEWED

24 Then Joshua summoned all the tribes of Israel to Shechem, including their elders,
leaders, judges, and officers. So they came and presented themselves to God.
[2]Joshua said to the people, "This is what the LORD, the God of Israel, says: Long ago your
ancestors, including Terah, the father of Abraham and Nahor, lived beyond the Euphrates
River,* and they worshiped other gods. [3]But I took your ancestor Abraham from the land
beyond the Euphrates and led him into the land of Canaan. I gave him many descendants
through his son Isaac. [4]To Isaac I gave Jacob and Esau. To Esau I gave the mountains of
Seir, while Jacob and his children went down into Egypt.

24:1 Josh 23:2
24:2 Gen 11:27-32
24:3 Gen 12:1; 15:5; 21:3; 24:7
24:4 Gen 25:25-26; 46:5-7; Deut 2:5

24:2 Hebrew *the river;* also in 24:3, 14, 15.

▸ GOD

23:14 Death in the Old Testament. What happens after we die? And what did Joshua and other Old Covenant believers understand about the afterlife? Job, who lived during the same time as Abraham (2000 BC), seemed to understand that there was an afterlife and a resurrection (Job 14:7-15). Just as we do today, the faithful of that time patiently waited for the fullest revelation of their future. (***See God****> God's Attributes> All-powerful> He has power over death,* TopicGuide page A15.)

24:1-2 After exhorting the leaders of Israel (chapter 23), Joshua here gathered all the people in a holy assembly. He then spoke to them as a prophet, delivering God's words to them. This was Joshua's farewell address, and he used it to remind the people of God's great works on their behalf and to call them to be faithful to God's covenant.

▸ MINISTRY

24:2-3 Faulty foundations. This review of the history of God's people shows that He can create a holy tree out of unholy roots, for Abraham, the father of the nation of Israel, was an idol worshiper from a family of idolaters. God can bring salvation into modern families who are atheistic, agnostic, or neo-pagan. Don't be afraid to share the gospel with someone just because he or she is under the influence of another religion. (***See Ministry****> Great Commission> Witness> Turn others from Satan to God,* TopicGuide page A56.)

BECAUSE GOD IS ABSOLUTE TRUTH

I will believe what He says and live accordingly.

Deep in your hearts you know that every promise of the LORD your God has come true. Not a single one has failed!

JOSHUA 23:14

FOR THE NEXT *GOD IS ABSOLUTE TRUTH* FEATURE SEE PAGE 975.

5 "Then I sent Moses and Aaron, and I brought terrible plagues on Egypt; and afterward I
brought you out as a free people. 6 But when your ancestors arrived at the Red Sea,* the
Egyptians chased after you with chariots and charioteers. 7 When your ancestors cried out
to the LORD, I put darkness between you and the Egyptians. I brought the sea crashing
down on the Egyptians, drowning them. With your very own eyes you saw what I did.
Then you lived in the wilderness for many years.
8 "Finally, I brought you into the land of the Amorites on the east side of the Jordan.
They fought against you, but I destroyed them before you. I gave you victory over them,
and you took possession of their land. 9 Then Balak son of Zippor, king of Moab, started a
war against Israel. He summoned Balaam son of Beor to curse you, 10 but I would not listen
to him. Instead, I made Balaam bless you, and so I rescued you from Balak.
11 "When you crossed the Jordan River and came to Jericho, the men of Jericho fought
against you, as did the Amorites, the Perizzites, the Canaanites, the Hittites, the Girga-
shites, the Hivites, and the Jebusites. But I gave you victory over them. 12 And I sent terror*
ahead of you to drive out the two kings of the Amorites. It was not your swords or bows
that brought you victory. 13 I gave you land you had not worked on, and I gave you towns
you did not build—the towns where you are now living. I gave you vineyards and olive
groves for food, though you did not plant them.
14 "So fear the LORD and serve Him wholeheartedly. Put away forever the idols your an-
cestors worshiped when they lived beyond the Euphrates River and in Egypt. Serve the
LORD alone. 15 But if you refuse to serve the LORD, then choose today whom you will serve.
Would you prefer the gods your ancestors served beyond the Euphrates? Or will it be the
gods of the Amorites in whose land you now live? But as for me and my family, we will
serve the LORD."
16 The people replied, "We would never abandon the LORD and serve other gods. 17 For the
LORD our God is the One who rescued us and our ancestors from slavery in the land of Egypt.
He performed mighty miracles before our very eyes. As we traveled through the wilderness
among our enemies, He preserved us. 18 It was the LORD who drove out the Amorites and the
other nations living here in the land. So we, too, will serve the LORD, for He alone is our God."
19 Then Joshua warned the people, "You are not able to serve the LORD, for He is a holy
and jealous God. He will not forgive your rebellion and your sins. 20 If you abandon the
LORD and serve other gods, He will turn against you and destroy you, even though He has
been so good to you."

24:5 Exod 3:10; 4:14-17
24:6 Exod 14:2-22
24:7 Exod 14:19-31; Deut 1:46; 2:14
24:8 Num 21:21-31
24:9 Num 22:2-6
24:11 Exod 23:23; Deut 7:1; Josh 3:14-17
24:12 Exod 23:28; Deut 7:20; Ps 44:3, 6
24:13 Deut 6:10-11
24:14 Deut 10:12; 18:13; 1 Sam 12:24
24:15 Ruth 1:15; 1 Kgs 18:21
24:19 Exod 20:5; 23:21; 34:14; Lev 19:2; 20:7, 26
24:20 Deut 4:25-26; Josh 23:15; 1 Chr 28:9; Acts 7:42

24:6 Hebrew *sea of reeds.* 24:12 Often rendered *the hornet.* The meaning of the Hebrew is uncertain.

24:5-7 These verses read like a rehash of Israel's history, but God was actually reminding the people of their unbelief. He worked powerfully on their behalf to free them from slavery by bringing ten plagues on the Egyptians. He then protected them from the pursuing Egyptians, led them through the Red Sea, and finally destroyed the armies of Pharaoh. The Israelites were eyewitnesses of all these great events. And yet, they "lived in the wilderness for many years." Why? Because at their first opportunity to enter the Promised Land, the Israelites failed to trust God's promise to be with them, despite all the evidence of His favor that He had shown them.

24:9-10 Balaam, the son of Beor, is famous for arguing with a talking donkey (Numbers 22). He was a Mesopotamian prophet hired by Balak, the king of Moab, to curse Israel as the people of God were en route to Canaan. God caused Balaam to bless the Israelites rather than curse them, but Balaam was still regarded as an evil man. The New Testament writer Jude (a brother of Jesus) described Balaam as a prophet who would do anything for money (Jude 1:11). In fact, Jude grouped him with Cain, the first murderer (Genesis 4), and Korah, the leader of a rebellion against Moses (Numbers 16).

24:12 There are many stories in the Old Testament involving divinely-caused natural events such as locust attacks and plagues of flies, but there is no record of a war event involving literal hornets. Some believe that the hornets mentioned here are nations that fought and weakened the two kings of the Amorites, Sihon and Og of Bashan, who refused the Israelites passage through their land east of the Jordan River. Their kingdoms were destroyed because of that refusal. Whatever these hornets were, they clearly were instruments of God by which He accomplished the conquest of Canaan on behalf of His people.

24:14-15 Joshua called the people to commit themselves wholeheartedly to God and give up idolatry forever. But Joshua added that if they were unwilling to make such a commitment to God, they should pick another god and commit to him. He was saying they should not treat Israel's God like just another deity, for He demanded total allegiance. Joshua left no doubt that he and his family would serve the LORD.

21 But the people answered Joshua, "No, we will serve the LORD!"
22 "You are a witness to your own decision," Joshua said. "You have chosen to serve the
LORD."
"Yes," they replied, "we are witnesses to what we have said."
23 "All right then," Joshua said, "destroy the idols among you, and turn your hearts to the
LORD, the God of Israel."
24:24 24 The people said to Joshua, "We will serve the LORD our God. We will obey Him alone."
Exod 19:8; 24:3, 7 25 So Joshua made a covenant with the people that day at Shechem, committing them
Deut 5:27 to follow the decrees and regulations of the LORD. 26 Joshua recorded these things in the
24:25 Exod 24:8 Book of God's Instructions. As a reminder of their agreement, he took a huge stone and
rolled it beneath the terebinth tree beside the Tabernacle of the LORD.
24:27 27 Joshua said to all the people, "This stone has heard everything the LORD said to us. It
Josh 22:27 will be a witness to testify against you if you go back on your word to God."
28 Then Joshua sent all the people away to their own homelands.

LEADERS BURIED IN THE PROMISED LAND

24:29 29 After this, Joshua son of Nun, the servant of the LORD, died at the age of 110. 30 They bur-
Judg 2:8 ied him in the land he had been allocated, at Timnath-serah in the hill country of Ephraim,
24:30 north of Mount Gaash.
Josh 19:50 31 The people of Israel served the LORD throughout the lifetime of Joshua and of the el-
ders who outlived him—those who had personally experienced all that the LORD had done
for Israel.
24:32 32 The bones of Joseph, which the Israelites had brought along with them when they left
Gen 50:24-25 Egypt, were buried at Shechem, in the parcel of ground Jacob had bought from the sons of
Exod 13:19 John 4:5 Hamor for 100 pieces of silver.* This land was located in the territory allotted to the de-
Acts 7:16 scendants of Joseph.
24:33 33 Eleazar son of Aaron also died. He was buried in the hill country of Ephraim, in the
Josh 22:13 town of Gibeah, which had been given to his son Phinehas.

24:32 Hebrew *100 kesitahs;* the value or weight of the kesitah is no longer known.

24:25-26 When the Israelites expressed their willingness to commit themselves to God, Joshua took several steps to formalize their commitment. First, he performed a covenant ceremony, by which the people made a solemn oath to be faithful to God. Second, Joshua wrote down the terms of the covenant, almost like a treaty, and placed it with the Book of the Law of God. Third, he set up a large stone as a reminder to the people of the commitment they had made.

24:32 The burial of Joseph's bones brings Israel full circle. Joseph's brothers sold him into slavery, and he was taken from Canaan to Egypt. In time, by the providence of God, the brothers reunited with Joseph and the entire extended family moved to Egypt with him. When Joseph died, he requested that his bones be carried back to Canaan to be buried. Hundreds of years later, when the people left in the Exodus, his bones were taken along. Here the bones were finally buried.

JUDGES

PURPOSE

To establish the need for a king in Israel.

Everyone knows that the hardest part of any difficult job is the last ten percent. We tackle the task with energy, but by the time we near the end we're ready to call it "quits." But it's those final, unfinished parts that ultimately come back to haunt us.

Such was the case with the Israelites in the book of Judges. In stark contrast to their experience in Joshua, where they obeyed and trusted God as they conquered Canaan, Judges recounts their failure to finish the task of expelling the Canaanites from the land. As a result, they ended up living *with* the Canaanites, then living *like* the Canaanites. God would allow them to suffer for a time in their sin; then He would deliver Israel from oppression from pagan attackers. But shortly after they were delivered, they forgot the Lord again, and the cycle began anew.

Rebellion (see 6:1)
Retribution (see 6:2)
Repentance (see 6:7)
Rescue (see 6:14)
Rest (see 8:28)

DISCOVER GOD IN JUDGES

Israel's unfaithfulness during the period of the judges reveals two significant attributes of God:

Patience: The fact that Israel repeats the same cycle of sin-repentance-deliverance seven different times over a period of three and a half centuries reveals that God is patient—or longsuffering, as earlier Bible translations put it. In one of His early encounters with Moses, God called Himself "Yahweh! The LORD! The God of compassion and mercy! I am slow to anger and filled with unfailing love and faithfulness. I lavish unfailing love to a thousand generations. I forgive iniquity, rebellion, and sin" (Exodus 34:6-7a). But He continued with an ominous warning: "But I do not excuse the guilty. I lay the sins of the parents upon their children and grandchildren; the entire family is affected—even children in the third and fourth generations" (34:7b). The seeds of rebellion sown in one generation sprang up generation after generation. God is patient, but that doesn't mean He turns a blind eye to sin.

Forgiveness: Over and over again, Israel "cried out to the LORD" when they were oppressed by their enemies—and He forgave and rescued them (3:9, 15; 4:3; 6:6), even though their oppression was due to their own sin. The attitude of a repentant heart will bring forgiveness from the Lord; He gives repentant sinners forgiveness, even though we will sin again. No one who sins, and sins again, should stop crying out to the Lord for help. It is God's nature to forgive those who confess their sins (1 John 1:9).

GROWING THROUGH JUDGES

The book of Judges is one of the most human books in the Bible; the depravity of man is put on full display. Several themes dominate the book:

Faithlessness vs. faithfulness: The character of man is unfaithful, while the character of God is faithful. The apostle Paul wrote to Timothy words that echo this theme in Judges: "If we are unfaithful, He remains faithful, for He cannot deny who He is" (2 Timothy 2:13).

Godly discipline: When Israel sinned in the period of the judges, God used ungodly nations to discipline His chosen people. The idea of the fatherhood of God—a Father who loves His children too much to allow them to continue unchallenged in their sin—is explored throughout all of Scripture (Hebrews 12:5-13).

DISCOVERY VERSES

After that generation died, another generation grew up who did not acknowledge the LORD or remember the mighty things He had done for Israel. (JUDGES 2:10)

Listen, you kings! Pay attention, you mighty rulers! For I will sing to the LORD. I will make music to the LORD, the God of Israel. (JUDGES 5:3)

In those days Israel had no king; all the people did whatever seemed right in their own eyes. (JUDGES 21:25)

The movement of nations and kings: God uses kings and rulers to accomplish His divine purposes on earth, especially regarding His plan for His people. God used the pagan nations surrounding Israel to accomplish His will in the period of the judges, and He continues to use civil rulers the same way today (Romans 13:1-5; 1 Peter 2:13-17). In a world where it seems kings and rulers make their own decisions, it is reassuring to know that God uses them to accomplish His purposes.

JUDGES FACTS

Author: The author is not named. Most scholars believe the author was the prophet Samuel, or one of his contemporaries, as it shows cultural and linguistic signs of being written around that time.

Written to: The nation of Israel in a leadership crisis.

Date of writing: After the establishment of a king in Israel (Judges 17:6; 18:1) but before David captured Jerusalem (Judges 1:21). Therefore, the time frame may be between 1043 BC (the beginning of the reign of Saul, the first king) and 1004 BC (David's capture of Jerusalem).

Setting: The stories in Judges all take place in the Promised Land of Canaan over a period of approximately 350 years.

OUTLINE

- **JUDGES 1**—The conquest that failed
- **JUDGES 2–16**—The Judges who failed
- **JUDGES 17–21**—The Levites who failed

KEY PLACES IN JUDGES

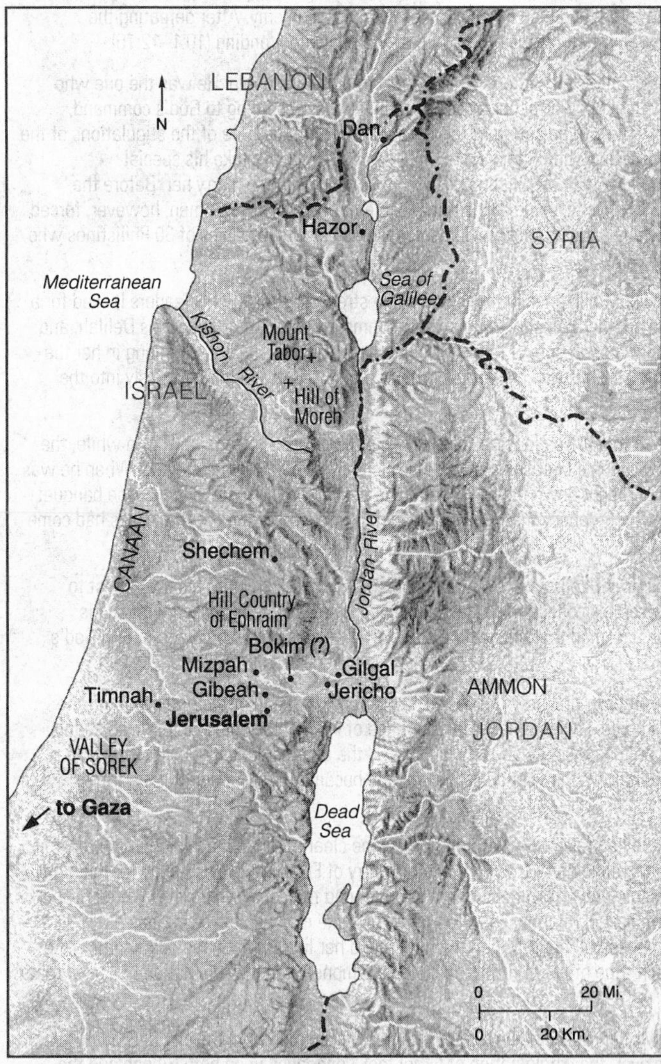

The broken lines (—·—) indicate modern boundaries.

1 Bokim The book of Judges opens with the Israelites continuing their conquest of the Promised Land. Their failure to obey God and destroy all the evil inhabitants soon came back to haunt them in two ways: (1) The enemies reorganized and counterattacked, and (2) Israel turned away from God, adopting the evil and idolatrous practices of the inhabitants of the land. The angel of the Lord appeared at Bokim to inform the Israelites that their sin and disobedience had broken their agreement with God and would result in punishment through oppression (1:1–3:11).

2 Jericho The nation of Moab was one of the first to oppress Israel. Moab's King Eglon conquered much of Israel—including the city of Jericho— and forced the people to pay unreasonable taxes. The messenger chosen to deliver this tax money to King Eglon was named Ehud. But he had more than money to deliver, for he drew his hidden sword and killed the Moabite king. Ehud then escaped, only to return with an army that chased out the Moabites and freed Israel from its oppressors (3:12-31).

3 Hazor After Ehud's death, King Jabin of Hazor conquered Israel and oppressed the people for 20 years. Then Deborah became Israel's leader. She summoned Barak to fight Commander Sisera, the leader of King Jabin's army. Together Deborah and Barak led their army into battle against Jabin's forces in the land between Mount Tabor and the Kishon River and conquered them (4:1–5:31).

4 Hill of Moreh After 40 years of peace, the Midianites began to harass the Israelites by destroying their flocks and crops. When the Israelites finally cried out to God, he chose Gideon, a poor and humble farmer, to be their deliverer. After struggling with doubt and feelings of inferiority, Gideon took courage and knocked down his town's altar to Baal, causing a great uproar among the citizens. Filled with the Spirit of God, he attacked the vast army of Midian, which was camped near the Hill of Moreh. With just a handful of men he sent the enemy running away in confusion (6:1–7:25).

5 Shechem Even great leaders make mistakes. Gideon's relations with a concubine in Shechem resulted in the birth of a son named Abimelech. Abimelech turned out to be treacherous and power hungry—stirring up the people to proclaim him king. To carry out his plan, he went so far as to kill 69 of his 70 half brothers. Eventually some men of Shechem rebelled against Abimelech, but he gathered together an army and defeated them. His lust for power led him to ransack two other cities, but he was killed by a woman who dropped a millstone onto his head (8:28–9:57).

6 Land of Ammon Again Israel turned completely from God; so God turned from them. But when the Ammonites mobilized their army to attack, Israel threw away her idols and called upon God once again. Jephthah, a prostitute's son who had been run out of Israel, was asked to return and lead Israel's forces against the enemy. After defeating the Ammonites, Jephthah became involved in a war with the tribe of Ephraim over a misunderstanding (10:1–12:15).

7 Timnah Israel's next judge, Samson, was a miracle child promised by God to a barren couple. He was the one who would begin to free Israel from their next and most powerful oppressor, the Philistines. According to God's command, Samson was to be a Nazirite—one who took a vow to be set apart for special service to God. One of the stipulations of the vow was that Samson's hair could never be cut. But when Samson grew up, he did not always take his special responsibility to God seriously. He even fell in love with a Philistine girl in Timnah and asked to marry her. Before the wedding, Samson held a party for some men in the city, using a riddle to place a bet with them. The men, however, forced Samson's fiancée into giving the answer. Furious at being tricked, Samson paid his bet with the lives of 30 Philistines who lived in the nearby city of Ashkelon (13:1–14:20).

8 Valley of Sorek Samson killed thousands of Philistines with his incredible strength. The nation's leaders looked for a way to stop him. They got their chance when another Philistine woman stole Samson's heart. Her name was Delilah, and she lived in the valley of Sorek. In exchange for a great sum of money, Delilah deceived Samson into confiding in her the secret of his strength. One night while he slept, Delilah had his hair cut off. As a result, Samson fell helplessly into the hands of the enemy (15:1–16:20).

9 Gaza Samson was blinded and led captive to a prison in Gaza. There his hair began to grow again. After a while, the Philistines held a great festival to celebrate Samson's imprisonment and to humiliate him before the crowds. When he was brought out as the entertainment, he literally brought down the house when he pushed on the main pillars of the banquet hall and killed the thousands trapped inside. The prophecy that he would begin to free Israel from the Philistines had come true (16:21-31).

10 Hill Country of Ephraim In the hill country of Ephraim lived a man named Micah. Micah hired his own priest to perform priestly duties in the shrine that housed his collection of idols. He thought he was pleasing God with all his religiosity! Like many of the Israelites, Micah assumed that his own opinions of what was right would agree with God's (17:1-13).

11 Dan The tribe of Dan migrated north in order to find new territory. They sent spies ahead of them to scout out the land. One night the spies stopped at Micah's home. Looking for some assurance of victory, the spies stole Micah's idols and priest. Rejoining the tribe, they came upon the city of Laish and slaughtered the unarmed and innocent citizens, renaming the conquered city Dan. Micah's idols were then set up in the city and became the focal point of the tribe's worship for many years (18:1-31).

12 Gibeah The extent to which many people had fallen away from God became clear in Gibeah, a village in the territory of Benjamin. A man and his concubine were traveling north toward the hill country of Ephraim. They stopped for the night in Gibeah, thinking they would be safe. But some perverts in the city gathered around the home where they were staying and demanded that the man come out to have sexual relations with them. Instead, the man and his host pushed the concubine out the door. She was raped and abused all night. When the man found her lifeless body the next morning, he cut it into 12 pieces and sent the parts to each tribe of Israel. This tragic event demonstrated that the nation had sunk to its lowest spiritual level (19:1-30).

13 Mizpah The leaders of Israel came to Mizpah to decide how to punish the wicked men from the city of Gibeah. When the city leaders refused to turn the criminals over, the whole nation of Israel took vengeance upon both Gibeah and the tribe of Benjamin where the city was located. When the battle ended, the entire tribe had been destroyed except for a handful of men who took refuge in the hills. Israel had become morally depraved. The stage was now set for the much-needed spiritual renewal that would come under the prophet Samuel (20:1–21:25).

JUDAH AND SIMEON CONQUER THE LAND

1:1 Num 27:21 — 1 After the death of Joshua, the Israelites asked the LORD, "Which tribe should go first to
attack the Canaanites?"
1:2 Gen 49:8 — 2 The LORD answered, "Judah, for I have given them victory over the land."
3 The men of Judah said to their relatives from the tribe of Simeon, "Join with us to fight
1:3 Judg 1:17 — against the Canaanites living in the territory allotted to us. Then we will help you conquer
your territory." So the men of Simeon went with Judah.
1:4 Gen 13:7 — 4 When the men of Judah attacked, the LORD gave them victory over the Canaanites and
1 Sam 11:8 — Perizzites, and they killed 10,000 enemy warriors at the town of Bezek. 5 While at Bezek
they encountered King Adoni-bezek and fought against him, and the Canaanites and Per-
izzites were defeated. 6 Adoni-bezek escaped, but the Israelites soon captured him and cut
off his thumbs and big toes.
7 Adoni-bezek said, "I once had seventy kings with their thumbs and big toes cut off, eat-
ing scraps from under my table. Now God has paid me back for what I did to them." They
took him to Jerusalem, and he died there.
1:8 — 8 The men of Judah attacked Jerusalem and captured it, killing all its people and setting
Josh 15:63 — the city on fire. 9 Then they went down to fight the Canaanites living in the hill country, the
1:10-15 — Negev, and the western foothills.* 10 Judah marched against the Canaanites in Hebron (for-
//Josh 15:13-19 — merly called Kiriath-arba), defeating the forces of Sheshai, Ahiman, and Talmai.
11 From there they went to fight against the people living in the town of Debir (formerly
called Kiriath-sepher). 12 Caleb said, "I will give my daughter Acsah in marriage to the one

1:9 Hebrew *the Shephelah.*

1:1 Joshua was one of two scouts who saw the bounty of the Promised Land and, by faith, believed that God had given it to Israel (Numbers 14). During the Exodus from Egypt and the journey through the wilderness, Joshua had served closely with Moses. This prepared Joshua to assume the role of national leader at Moses' death, but unlike Moses, he had trained no one to take his place when he died.

1:1 Canaan was the region the Hebrews considered the "Promised Land." God had promised it to Abraham, father of the Hebrews. The original Canaanites were descendants of Noah's grandson, Canaan, the son of Ham. Noah cursed both Ham and Canaan because of an indiscretion (Genesis 9:24-25). After the land became associated with Canaan's descendants, others settled there and also came to be known as Canaanites. The Canaanites typically worshiped many gods, including El, his son Baal, and Baal's female counterpart Asherah. From the time of the Israelite conquest and through the periods of the judges and the monarchy, there was conflict between the worshipers of Baal and the worshipers of the Lord.

1:1 The Israelites found their identity in their ancestry. Abraham was considered the father of the Israelite people. God promised to give him a nation of descendants and a land in which to live. God reiterated His promise to Abraham's son Isaac and to Isaac's son Jacob, also known as Israel. Jacob had 12 sons who became the ancestors of the 12 tribes of Israel. Each tribe of Israel had received its own territory to settle.

1:2 The tribe of Judah was the leading tribe of Israel. King David was born into this tribe. When ten of Israel's tribes broke away after the reign of David's son Solomon (1 Kings 12), the tribe of Judah remained loyal to David's descendants, and the southern half of the divided nation took on the name of the tribe.

1:3 Simeon was the second oldest son of Jacob. He disqualified himself from the prominence usually given to the older sons when he and his brother Levi killed all the men in the city of Shechem after their sister was raped (Genesis 34). When Jacob pronounced his final blessings on his sons, he declared that Simeon's tribe eventually would be absorbed into the other tribes—a grave dishonor.

▸ SPIRITUAL WARFARE

1:7 The power of regret. Think back to your past—any qualms about something you did? Do you still carry some sorrow from a past tragedy that was your fault? All people, from pagans to Christians, feel remorse when they truly understand the consequences of their behavior. If you wish to understand the reality of your sin, focus on the terrifying consequences that sin brings to you and everyone else around you. The Bible puts it simply—sin brings death (Romans 5:12-15). No one can deal with the deadly consequences of sin except the One who overcame death—Jesus Christ. Only He can bring hope from regret. (***See Spiritual Warfare*** > *Resisting Sin and Evil> Consequences> Of Disobedience> Death,* TopicGuide page A46.)

1:8 David made Jerusalem the capital city of Israel; it therefore became the political and religious center of the nation (2 Samuel 5; 6). Jerusalem was a religious center prior to this; its more ancient name, Salem, is mentioned as early as the days of Abraham, when it was ruled by the priest-king Melchizedek (Genesis 14:18-19). It remains a religious center for three modern religions—Christianity, Judaism, and Islam.

1:12 When Israel first approached Canaan, Caleb was among 12 tribal leaders who were sent to scout the land. Of the 12, only Caleb and Joshua had faith that God would enable the people to conquer the land. The ten other scouts gave a report that led the people to turn back in fear. As a result, God decreed that the Israelites must wander in the desert for 40 years. Of all the adults who left Egypt in the Exodus, only Joshua and Caleb lived to cross the border into Canaan.

who attacks and captures Kiriath-sepher." 13 Othniel, the son of Caleb's younger brother, 1:13
Kenaz, was the one who conquered it, so Acsah became Othniel's wife. Judg 3:9
14 When Acsah married Othniel, she urged him* to ask her father for a field. As she got
down off her donkey, Caleb asked her, "What's the matter?"
15 She said, "Let me have another gift. You have already given me land in the Negev;
now please give me springs of water, too." So Caleb gave her the upper and lower springs.
16 When the tribe of Judah left Jericho—the city of palms—the Kenites, who were descen- 1:16
dants of Moses' father-in-law, traveled with them into the wilderness of Judah. They set- Deut 34:3
tled among the people there, near the town of Arad in the Negev. Judg 3:13; 4:11
17 Then Judah joined with Simeon to fight against the Canaanites living in Zephath, and
they completely destroyed* the town. So the town was named Hormah.* 18 In addition, Judah 1:17
captured the towns of Gaza, Ashkelon, and Ekron, along with their surrounding territories. Num 21:3

ISRAEL FAILS TO CONQUER THE LAND

19 The LORD was with the people of Judah, and they took possession of the hill country. But 1:19 Josh 17:16
they failed to drive out the people living in the plains, who had iron chariots. 20 The town of Judg 4:3
Hebron was given to Caleb as Moses had promised. And Caleb drove out the people living 1:20
there, who were descendants of the three sons of Anak. Josh 14:6-9; 15:14
21 The tribe of Benjamin, however, failed to drive out the Jebusites, who were living in 1:21
Jerusalem. So to this day the Jebusites live in Jerusalem among the people of Benjamin. Josh 15:63
22 The descendants of Joseph attacked the town of Bethel, and the LORD was with them. 1:22 Gen 28:19
23 They sent men to scout out Bethel (formerly known as Luz). 24 They confronted a man Josh 14:3-4
coming out of the town and said to him, "Show us a way into the town, and we will have 1:24
mercy on you." 25 So he showed them a way in, and they killed everyone in the town ex- Josh 2:12
cept that man and his family. 26 Later the man moved to the land of the Hittites, where he 1:25
built a town. He named it Luz, which is its name to this day. Josh 6:25

1:14 Greek version and Latin Vulgate read *he urged her.* 1:17a The Hebrew term used here refers to the complete consecration of things or people to the LORD, either by destroying them or by giving them as an offering. 1:17b *Hormah* means "destruction."

1:16 The Kenites were a Canaanite tribe mentioned as early as Abraham's time. Evidently Moses' brother-in-law Hobab was a Kenite (Judges 4:11). Their destruction was prophesied (Numbers 24:21-22), but not at the hands of the Israelites. Instead, they would be destroyed by the Assyrians, who eventually destroyed the northern kingdom of Israel as well. Unlike some Canaanite tribes, the Kenites aided Israel on several occasions. By the time of Deborah, a judge and prophet of Israel, Kenites were living in Galilee. Centuries later, before a battle against the Amalekites, Israel's King Saul sent a warning to the Kenites (1 Samuel 15:6), treating them as allies. During the days of David, Kenites were listed as inhabitants of Judah (1 Samuel 27:10).

1:16 The Negev was the desert in the southern portion of the region given to the tribe of Judah. This land was between the Mediterranean Sea and the Dead Sea. Even though waters surrounded it, the region was arid. It did provide pastureland for wandering tribes at certain times of the year, but water supplies were scarce. Arad was a city within the region, just west of the Dead Sea. Later in Israel's history, David went into this area with his men to hide from King Saul. Even later, when the king of Babylon ransacked Jerusalem, many of its inhabitants fled to the Negev for safety.

1:18 Gaza, Ashkelon, and Ekron were three of the five principal cities of the Philistines, who lived in a strip of land along the Mediterranean coast in the southern half of Canaan. The Philistine people were known for their mighty armies. Perhaps the most famous Philistine was Goliath, the great warrior whom young David (yet to be king) felled with a single stone from his sling. The Israelites fought against the Philistines throughout their history, though David sought refuge among them while he was dodging the wrath of King Saul.

1:20 Anak was related to the Anakites or Anakim. They were known as large people; some translations refer to them as giants. The Emim of Moab and the Zamzummim of Ammon were also known for their large size. These tribes of larger people were occasionally referred to as Nephilim.

1:22 The phrase "descendants of Joseph" refers to the tribes of Ephraim and Manasseh. Ephraim and Manasseh were Joseph's sons. Just before he died, Joseph's father, Jacob, symbolically adopted the two boys. Thereafter, the descendants of Ephraim and Manasseh were counted among the "twelve tribes of Israel." The descendants of Jacob's son Levi received no allotment of land and so were not counted among the 12.

1:22 Bethel, a city about ten miles north of Jerusalem, was very significant in Israel's history. Abraham, the father of the Israelites, offered a sacrifice there when he first came to the land, and there he received his promise from God that the land would belong to his descendants (Genesis 12:8). Jacob, Abraham's grandson, also visited Bethel. In fact, he gave the place its name, which means "house of God." In this place, Jacob dreamed of a stairway (some translations called it a ladder) to heaven (Genesis 28:10-20).

1:27 27 The tribe of Manasseh failed to drive out the people living in Beth-shan,* Taanach,
Josh 17:11-13 Dor, Ibleam, Megiddo, and all their surrounding settlements, because the Canaanites were
determined to stay in that region. 28 When the Israelites grew stronger, they forced the Ca-
naanites to work as slaves, but they never did drive them completely out of the land.
1:29 29 The tribe of Ephraim failed to drive out the Canaanites living in Gezer, so the Canaan-
Josh 16:10 ites continued to live there among them.
30 The tribe of Zebulun failed to drive out the residents of Kitron and Nahalol, so the Ca-
naanites continued to live among them. But the Canaanites were forced to work as slaves
for the people of Zebulun.
31 The tribe of Asher failed to drive out the residents of Acco, Sidon, Ahlab, Aczib, Hel-
bah, Aphik, and Rehob. 32 Instead, the people of Asher moved in among the Canaanites,
who controlled the land, for they failed to drive them out.
33 Likewise, the tribe of Naphtali failed to drive out the residents of Beth-shemesh and
Beth-anath. Instead, they moved in among the Canaanites, who controlled the land. Never-
theless, the people of Beth-shemesh and Beth-anath were forced to work as slaves for the
people of Naphtali.
1:34 34 As for the tribe of Dan, the Amorites forced them back into the hill country and would
Judg 18:1 not let them come down into the plains. 35 The Amorites were determined to stay in Mount
Heres, Aijalon, and Shaalbim, but when the descendants of Joseph became stronger, they
1:36 forced the Amorites to work as slaves. 36 The boundary of the Amorites ran from Scorpion
Josh 15:3 Pass* to Sela and continued upward from there.

2:1
THE LORD'S MESSENGER COMES TO BOKIM

Gen 17:7 **2** The Angel of the LORD went up from Gilgal to Bokim and said to the Israelites, "I
Exod 20:2
Judg 6:11 brought you out of Egypt into this land that I swore to give your ancestors, and I said I
2:2 would never break My covenant with you. 2 For your part, you were not to make any cov-
Exod 23:32; 34:12-13 enants with the people living in this land; instead, you were to destroy their altars. But you

1:27 Hebrew *Beth-shean,* a variant spelling of Beth-shan. 1:36 Hebrew *Akrabbim.*

1:27-36 Again and again the refrain is repeated: "The tribe . . . failed" to drive out the Canaanites in its territory. In some cases, the tribe in question enslaved the local Canaanites. In other cases, the tribe could only achieve a state of coexistence with its enemies. In at least one case, that of the tribe of Dan, the Canaanites drove the Israelites off the best portion of their land and into the hills. These failures stemmed more from a lack of willpower than a lack of strength, for God had promised to help the Israelites conquer. The people simply were not committed to obeying God's command to drive the Canaanites out.

▸ SPIRITUAL WARFARE

1:28 The deceit of sin. One of Satan's sneakiest tricks is to get you to settle for the good instead of the best. In spite of God's command to drive out the Canaanites (Joshua 9:24), some of the tribes of Israel were content to live among them and make them into slaves. Perhaps they rationalized that the leisure time they gained thanks to the slaves would give them more time to worship God or teach their children. But no matter how they justified it, it was not best—actually, it was not even good. Be wary of things that appeal to you but fall short of God's best (***See Spiritual Warfare***> *Originator of Sin*> *Satan's Strategies*> *Lie,* TopicGuide page A45.)

2:1 In the Old Testament, the angel of the Lord was sometimes a messenger, sometimes a warrior, and sometimes (it seems) God Himself. When Sarah sent away her handmaiden, Hagar, the angel of the Lord appeared to Hagar with instructions and a promise of survival (Genesis 16). It was the angel of the Lord who shouted to Abraham to stop his sacrifice of Isaac (Genesis 22). The angel of the Lord appeared as a messenger to the prophet Balaam, seen only by a donkey until God opened Balaam's eyes (Numbers 22). In the case of Moses, it was the angel of the Lord who spoke from the burning bush, but Moses addressed the voice as God Himself (Exodus 3).

2:1 The relationship between God and the Israelites was based on a covenant. God had promised the great Israelite ancestor, Abraham, that he would have a land and many descendants, and that his family would be a blessing to all nations. God's covenant required the Israelites to worship Him alone, but they repeatedly and miserably failed to do so. God, however, displayed great patience and mercy toward His rebellious people, disciplining them only after great provocation and always remaining faithful to His promises.

2:2 After they left Egypt, the people of Israel camped at Mount Sinai, where they received the Ten Commandments and other instructions. Through Moses, God said, "I will hand over to you the people now living in the land, and you will drive them out ahead of you. Make no treaties with them or their gods" (Exodus 23:31-32). From the summary in the first chapter of Judges, it is obvious that the people *did* make treaties with the Canaanites, and the angel of the Lord came to rebuke them for their disobedience.

THE JUDGES OF ISRAEL

Judge	Years of Judging	Memorable Act(s)	Reference
OTHNIEL	40	He captured a powerful Canaanite city	Judges 3:7-11
EHUD	80	He killed Eglon and defeated the Moabites	Judges 3:12-30
SHAMGAR	unrecorded	He killed 600 Philistines with an ox goad	Judges 3:31
DEBORAH (w/Barak)	40	She defeated Sisera and the Canaanites and later sang a victory song with Barak	Judges 4; 5
GIDEON	40	He destroyed his family idols, used a fleece to determine God's will, raised an army of 10,000, and defeated 135,000 Midianites with 300 soldiers	Judges 6–8
TOLA	23	He judged Israel for 23 years	Judges 10:1, 2
JAIR	22	He had 30 sons	Judges 10:3-5
JEPHTHAH	6	He made a rash vow, defeated the Ammonites, and later battled jealous Ephraim	Judges 10:6–12:7
IBZAN	7	He had 30 sons and 30 daughters	Judges 12:8-10
ELON	10	Unrecorded	Judges 12:11, 12
ABDON	8	He had 40 sons and 30 grandsons, each of whom had his own donkey	Judges 12:13-15
SAMSON	20	He was a Nazirite, killed a lion with his bare hands, burned the Philistine wheat fields, killed 1,000 Philistines with a donkey's jawbone, tore off an iron gate, was betrayed by Delilah, and destroyed thousands of Philistines in one last mighty act	Judges 13–16
ELI	40	He was a priest who was known for raising Samuel in the Temple	1 Samuel 1:9–4:18
SAMUEL	54	He anointed Israel's first two kings, Saul and David	1 Samuel 7:15–28:3

disobeyed My command. Why did you do this? 3So now I declare that I will no longer 2:3
drive out the people living in your land. They will be thorns in your sides,* and their gods Num 33:55
will be a constant temptation to you."

4When the Angel of the LORD finished speaking to all the Israelites, the people wept
loudly. 5So they called the place Bokim (which means "weeping"), and they offered sacri- 2:5
fices there to the LORD. Josh 7:26

THE DEATH OF JOSHUA

6After Joshua sent the people away, each of the tribes left to take possession of the land allotted 2:6
to them. 7And the Israelites served the LORD throughout the lifetime of Joshua and the leaders Josh 24:28-31
who outlived him—those who had seen all the great things the LORD had done for Israel.

2:3 Hebrew *They will be in your sides;* compare Num 33:55.

2:3 These words of judgment set the stage for all that happens in the book of Judges and even in the historical documents of the monarchy, such as Kings and Chronicles. Because the Israelites had not thoroughly conquered the land and cleared it of other religions, they would have to fight constantly against the other peoples of the land. During the period covered in Judges, the Israelites repeatedly fell away from God, and then were overwhelmed by an enemy. After they had suffered for a time, God graciously raised up a judge, or national champion, who defeated the enemy and called the people back to God. However, once that leader left the picture, the people eventually fell away again.

[8]Joshua son of Nun, the servant of the LORD, died at the age of 110. [9]They buried him in
the land he had been allocated, at Timnath-serah* in the hill country of Ephraim, north of
Mount Gaash.

ISRAEL DISOBEYS THE LORD

2:10 Exod 5:2; 1 Sam 2:12
2:11 Judg 4:1; 6:1; 8:33; 10:6
2:12 Deut 31:16; 32:12; Judg 10:6; Ps 106:40
2:13 Judg 10:6

[10]After that generation died, another generation grew up who did not acknowledge the
LORD or remember the mighty things He had done for Israel.
[11]The Israelites did evil in the LORD's sight and served the images of Baal. [12]They aban-
doned the LORD, the God of their ancestors, who had brought them out of Egypt. They
went after other gods, worshiping the gods of the people around them. And they angered
the LORD. [13]They abandoned the LORD to serve Baal and the images of Ashtoreth. [14]This
made the LORD burn with anger against Israel, so He handed them over to raiders who
stole their possessions. He turned them over to their enemies all around, and they were
no longer able to resist them. [15]Every time Israel went out to battle, the LORD fought
against them, causing them to be defeated, just as He had warned. And the people were in
great distress.

THE LORD RESCUES HIS PEOPLE

2:16 Ps 106:43-45
2:17 Ps 81:11-12

[16]Then the LORD raised up judges to rescue the Israelites from their attackers. [17]Yet Israel
did not listen to the judges but prostituted themselves by worshiping other gods. How
quickly they turned away from the path of their ancestors, who had walked in obedience
to the LORD's commands.
[18]Whenever the LORD raised up a judge over Israel, He was with that judge and rescued
the people from their enemies throughout the judge's lifetime. For the LORD took pity on

2:9 As in parallel text at Josh 24:30; Hebrew reads *Timnath-heres,* a variant spelling of Timnath-serah.

▶ **WORSHIP**

2:8 Learning through repetition. Does God sometimes repeat Himself to you in order to help you learn something? The writer of Judges recounts the end of Joshua's life and gives us a few more important details about his ministry. But the angel of the Lord (2:1) makes clear that even Joshua's fine leadership was not sufficient to keep the nation of Israel in line, and the next 19 chapters demonstrate that the ministry of the judges was also inadequate. What sort of leader could bring Israel to the greatness God had promised? Repeatedly, the author of the book of Judges argues implicitly (and explicitly, see 19:1) that a king of God's choosing was the answer to Israel's leadership problems. (***See Worship****> NT> Christ's Kingship> Jesus shall return as king and judge,* TopicGuide page A30.)

▶ **WORSHIP**

2:10 Godly leaders. A lack of spiritual leadership in the family has consequences. Because of such a lack, the nation of Israel was thrown into 12 cycles of sin, destruction, and repentance—a national chaos that would last for 400 years. Are you a spiritual guide to those around you, leading people to love and obey God? Or do you contribute to the decay of society with your choices (Proverbs 10:7)? God can work through you to build up families, no matter what your circumstances. This is our birthright as Abraham's spiritual children (Genesis 12:2). (***See Worship****> NT> Fellowship> Preserving> Teach one another,* TopicGuide page A31.)

2:11 The worship of Baal always wreaked devastation on the Israelites. During their journey to the Promised Land, just after facing off against Balak, a Moabite king, the Israelite men became involved with Moabite women who worshiped Baal. Before long, a great number of people in the nation were succumbing to the worship of Baal. In judgment against this sin, Moses ordered the ringleaders executed, and God unleashed a plague that killed 24,000 people (Numbers 25:1-9).

2:13 Ashtoreth, also called Asherah, was a Canaanite fertility goddess. She was the female counterpart to Baal, alleged son of another god called El. Wooden poles or pillars were made in her image. The Israelites frequently assimilated the religion of the culture around them, a violation of the first and second of the Ten Commandments. During the time of the judges and the monarchy in Israel, righteous leaders and kings who instituted religious reforms frequently tore down Asherah poles that had been built throughout the land. For example, Gideon, a hesitant judge of Israel, stepped into the national spotlight when he cut down the family Asherah pole and built an altar to God instead (Judges 6:25-26). Likewise, at the beginning of Asa's rule in the southern kingdom of Judah, he cut down the Asherah poles that his grandmother Maacah had built (1 Kings 15:9-14).

2:17 The Bible depicts the relationship between God and believers as a marriage. Therefore, any turning away from God on the part of His people amounts to spiritual prostitution. This theme is found throughout the Bible. The prophet Hosea went so far as to marry and have children with a prostitute. When she proved unfaithful time and time again, he repeatedly took her back. He did this at God's bidding to show the Israelites God's perspective on their spiritual adultery and His own faithful love (Hosea 1). The New Testament church is called the bride of Christ (2 Corinthians 11:2). Jesus spoke of a wedding feast in which He and the church would be united.

His people, who were burdened by oppression and suffering. [19]But when the judge died, 2:19
the people returned to their corrupt ways, behaving worse than those who had lived be- Judg 4:1; 8:33
fore them. They went after other gods, serving and worshiping them. And they refused to
give up their evil practices and stubborn ways.
[20]So the LORD burned with anger against Israel. He said, "Because these people have vi-
olated My covenant, which I made with their ancestors, and have ignored My commands,
[21]I will no longer drive out the nations that Joshua left unconquered when he died. [22]I did 2:21
this to test Israel—to see whether or not they would follow the ways of the LORD as their an- Josh 23:13
cestors did." [23]That is why the LORD left those nations in place. He did not quickly drive
them out or allow Joshua to conquer them all.

THE NATIONS LEFT IN CANAAN

3 These are the nations that the LORD left in the land to test those Israelites who had not 3:1
experienced the wars of Canaan. [2]He did this to teach warfare to generations of Isra- Judg 1:1; 2:21-22
elites who had no experience in battle. [3]These are the nations: the Philistines (those living 3:3
under the five Philistine rulers), all the Canaanites, the Sidonians, and the Hivites living in Josh 13:3
the mountains of Lebanon from Mount Baal-hermon to Lebo-hamath. [4]These people were 3:4
left to test the Israelites—to see whether they would obey the commands the LORD had Deut 8:2
given to their ancestors through Moses. Judg 2:22
[5]So the people of Israel lived among the Canaanites, Hittites, Amorites, Perizzites, Hivites, 3:5 Ps 106:35
and Jebusites, [6]and they intermarried with them. Israelite sons married their daughters, and 3:6
Israelite daughters were given in marriage to their sons. And the Israelites served their gods. Exod 34:16 Deut 7:3-4

OTHNIEL BECOMES ISRAEL'S JUDGE

[7]The Israelites did evil in the LORD's sight. They forgot about the LORD their God, and they
served the images of Baal and the Asherah poles. [8]Then the LORD burned with anger 3:8
against Israel, and He turned them over to King Cushan-rishathaim of Aram-naharaim.* Judg 2:14
And the Israelites served Cushan-rishathaim for eight years.
[9]But when the people of Israel cried out to the LORD for help, the LORD raised up a res- 3:9 Judg 1:13

3:8 *Aram-naharaim* means "Aram of the two rivers," thought to have been located between the Euphrates and Balih Rivers in northwestern Mesopotamia.

2:19 Israel's on-again, off-again spiritual behavior lasted beyond the time of the judges and into the monarchy of Israel. The books of Samuel, Kings, and Chronicles describe the men who ruled Israel. A godly king would clear the land of some, or even all, of the idol worship and the symbols that went with it. Then an ungodly king would take the throne and allow the worship of many gods to resume. To an extent, the strength of Israel rose and fell with its kings. While there was some initial prosperity under a few of the wicked kings, the nation eventually fell under them. All the while, the depravity of the Israelites seemed to grow as each generation behaved more wickedly than the previous one.

▸ ADOPTION
2:22-23 Testing our faith. It is disturbing to some that the Bible speaks of God introducing painful circumstances into our lives. In this case, God gives His reasons, but in others (the events of Job's life, for instance) He is silent. If God had not revealed the wisdom of His plan, the sufferings of Christ would have appeared tragic. Have you seen blessings come from your suffering? Have you experienced the truth that all things happen for the good of those who love God (Romans 8:28)? Look at your suffering through God's eyes and trust that His will is for your best in all things. (***See Adoption****> With Christ> Children of God> Children share suffering and glory,* TopicGuide page A36.)

3:5-6 The actions described here were direct violations of commands Moses had given to his people before he died. In Deuteronomy 7:3-4, Moses warned the people not to let their sons and daughters marry people that did not worship God alone. He warned them that children who intermarried with pagans would be drawn into false worship, as described here.

▸ CHURCH
3:9 Meek and mighty. The first of the 13 men and one woman God sent to guide Israel through this turbulent time was Othniel, a nephew of Caleb (see 1:12-13). He had two problems to solve: Israel was weak both militarily and spiritually. With God's help, Othniel crushed the king who had made the Israelites his subjects (3:10). We are not told anything about Othniel's work to strengthen Israel spiritually, but the 40 years of peace he secured attests to his success in strengthening them militarily. Yet for a rule of 40 years, there is little fanfare. Other than results, he left little mark on history. Do you know anyone who humbly works to make their nation, their church, and their family strong? Can you be the Othniel in your community? (***See Church****> Role> Preach> Topics> Godly Lives> Live quietly and work hard,* TopicGuide page A50.)

3:10 cuer to save them. His name was Othniel, the son of Caleb's younger brother, Kenaz.
Num 11:25-29; 24:2 10The Spirit of the LORD came upon him, and he became Israel's judge. He went to war
Judg 6:34; 11:29 against King Cushan-rishathaim of Aram, and the LORD gave Othniel victory over him. 11So
3:11 Judg 5:31; 8:28 there was peace in the land for forty years. Then Othniel son of Kenaz died.

EHUD BECOMES ISRAEL'S JUDGE

3:12 12Once again the Israelites did evil in the LORD's sight, and the LORD gave King Eglon of
Judg 2:11 Moab control over Israel because of their evil. 13Eglon enlisted the Ammonites and Ama-
3:13 lekites as allies, and then he went out and defeated Israel, taking possession of Jericho,
Judg 1:16 the city of palms. 14And the Israelites served Eglon of Moab for eighteen years.
3:15 Judg 20:16 15But when the people of Israel cried out to the LORD for help, the LORD again raised up a
1 Chr 12:2 rescuer to save them. His name was Ehud son of Gera, a left-handed man of the tribe of
Benjamin. The Israelites sent Ehud to deliver their tribute money to King Eglon of Moab.
16So Ehud made a double-edged dagger that was about a foot* long, and he strapped it to
his right thigh, keeping it hidden under his clothing. 17He brought the tribute money to Eg-
lon, who was very fat.
18After delivering the payment, Ehud started home with those who had helped carry the
tribute. 19But when Ehud reached the stone idols near Gilgal, he turned back. He came to
Eglon and said, "I have a secret message for you."
So the king commanded his servants, "Be quiet!" and he sent them all out of the room.
20Ehud walked over to Eglon, who was sitting alone in a cool upstairs room. And Ehud
said, "I have a message from God for you!" As King Eglon rose from his seat, 21Ehud
reached with his left hand, pulled out the dagger strapped to his right thigh, and plunged it
into the king's belly. 22The dagger went so deep that the handle disappeared beneath the
king's fat. So Ehud did not pull out the dagger, and the king's bowels emptied.* 23Then
Ehud closed and locked the doors of the room and escaped down the latrine.*
3:24 24After Ehud was gone, the king's servants returned and found the doors to the upstairs
1 Sam 24:3 room locked. They thought he might be using the latrine in the room, 25so they waited.
But when the king didn't come out after a long delay, they became concerned and got a
key. And when they opened the doors, they found their master dead on the floor.
26While the servants were waiting, Ehud escaped, passing the stone idols on his way to
Seirah. 27When he arrived in the hill country of Ephraim, Ehud sounded a call to arms.
3:28 Judg 7:24; 12:5 Then he led a band of Israelites down from the hills.
28"Follow me," he said, "for the LORD has given you victory over Moab your enemy." So

3:16 Hebrew *gomed,* the length of which is uncertain. 3:22 Or *and it came out behind.* 3:23 Or *and went out through the porch;* the meaning of the Hebrew is uncertain.

3:12 Moab was a small kingdom to the east of the Dead Sea. The original Moabites were descendants of Abraham's nephew Lot. Lot's wife died when Sodom and Gomorrah were destroyed by God's judgment, but Lot and his two daughters survived. The girls connived together to conceive babies by their father. Lot's older daughter had a son named Moab (Genesis 19:34-38). The Moabites settled in the land that had been occupied by people called the Emites. By the time the Israelites were preparing to invade Canaan, the kingdom of Moab included many peoples besides the original descendants of Lot.

3:12-14 Because of the Israelites' persistent lack of religious purity, God often allowed them to suffer subjugation to neighboring cultures to one degree or another. Here, forces from Moab conquered Israel and occupied the land for 18 years. Later, after the nation divided into the northern kingdom of Israel and the southern kingdom of Judah, the people suffered even greater defeats. Assyria defeated Israel, occupying the land and carrying the people into exile. By doing this, Assyria obliterated the culture of the northern kingdom. The same judgment eventually fell on the southern kingdom of Judah, though some of the people returned home after their exile to Babylon.

▸ SPIRITUAL WARFARE

3:15-30 Crafty and courageous. The second of the 14 judges is the only positive character from the tribe of Benjamin in the book of Judges. This grimly humorous story makes the Moabites appear foolish but leaves Ehud and his band of Israelites looking crafty and pious as they mount attacks upon an enemy that hopelessly outnumbers them. Ehud didn't seem to care about the odds—he only saw the opportunity to receive the victory God had promised him. Let us go forward to receive God's promised victory over sin, never stopping our fight until we stand with Him, finally made whole and holy! (***See Spiritual Warfare***> *Resisting Sin and Evil> Trusting God> God as Warrior> God's fight to final victory,* TopicGuide page A46.)

they followed him. And the Israelites took control of the shallow crossings of the Jordan
River across from Moab, preventing anyone from crossing.
29They attacked the Moabites and killed about 10,000 of their strongest and most able-
bodied warriors. Not one of them escaped. 30So Moab was conquered by Israel that day,
and there was peace in the land for eighty years.

SHAMGAR BECOMES ISRAEL'S JUDGE

31After Ehud, Shamgar son of Anath rescued Israel. He once killed 600 Philistines with an **3:31**
ox goad. Judg 5:6

DEBORAH BECOMES ISRAEL'S JUDGE

4 After Ehud's death, the Israelites again did evil in the LORD's sight. 2So the LORD turned **4:1**
them over to King Jabin of Hazor, a Canaanite king. The commander of his army was Sis- Judg 2:19
era, who lived in Harosheth-haggoyim. 3Sisera, who had 900 iron chariots, ruthlessly op- **4:2** Josh 11:1
pressed the Israelites for twenty years. Then the people of Israel cried out to the LORD for help. Ps 83:9
4Deborah, the wife of Lappidoth, was a prophet who was judging Israel at that time. 5She
would sit under the Palm of Deborah, between Ramah and Bethel in the hill country of **4:6**
Ephraim, and the Israelites would go to her for judgment. 6One day she sent for Barak son 1 Sam 12:11
of Abinoam, who lived in Kedesh in the land of Naphtali. She said to him, "This is what the Heb 11:32
LORD, the God of Israel, commands you: Call out 10,000 warriors from the tribes of Naphtali
and Zebulun at Mount Tabor. 7And I will call out Sisera, commander of Jabin's army, along **4:7**
with his chariots and warriors, to the Kishon River. There I will give you victory over him." Ps 83:9
8Barak told her, "I will go, but only if you go with me."
9"Very well," she replied, "I will go with you. But you will receive no honor in this ven-
ture, for the LORD's victory over Sisera will be at the hands of a woman." So Deborah went
with Barak to Kedesh. 10At Kedesh, Barak called together the tribes of Zebulun and Naph- **4:10**
tali, and 10,000 warriors went up with him. Deborah also went with him. Judg 5:18

▸ GOD
3:31 Mighty man. The judges of Israel fell into four categories: hero, commander, prophet, and priest. Shamgar's brief description speaks of him as a mighty warrior, fighting off attackers with the most primitive of weapons—an ox goad. He was a creative and fierce fighter, unwilling to allow his nation to be further terrorized by foreign armies. We need more people like Shamgar, who refuse to run from trouble and do everything in their power to defend God's people. (***See God***> *God's Attributes*> *Just*> *Jesus, our righteous defender before the Father,* TopicGuide page A17.)

▸ MINISTRY
4:4-24 Wise woman. What do you think of when you hear the word *judge*? In the context of the books of Judges and 1 Samuel, the term *judge* does not typically designate the same function as it does today. Deborah initially gained recognition through her foretelling and forth-telling of God's will—she was a prophet. In the midst of that faithful service, she ascended to the position of judge, one who worked to rescue Israel from bondage through dispensing advice and, if necessary, leading troops into battle (4:9). Ironically, the enemy commander sought to escape Deborah's troops only to be killed by Jael, another brave woman who wasn't afraid to step outside the ordinary roles of women at this time in history. God needs women who will serve Him based on what He, not society, dictates. (***See Ministry***> *Transformation*> *Vocations*> *Commander,* TopicGuide page A57.)

4:6 While there could have been a variety of reasons for Deborah to call out armies specifically from Naphtali and Zebulun, it is easy to understand why she chose the location of Mount Tabor. This mountain was a good rallying point, as it rose up near the borders of Naphtali, Zebulun, and Issachar. Located to the southwest of the Sea of Galilee, Mount Tabor was a flat-topped mountain that was both a popular spot for shrines and a fortified location for battles. Later in the book of Judges, a man named Gideon also fought a battle there (Judges 7). Some believe this was the mountain of Jesus' transfiguration (Mark 9:1-9).

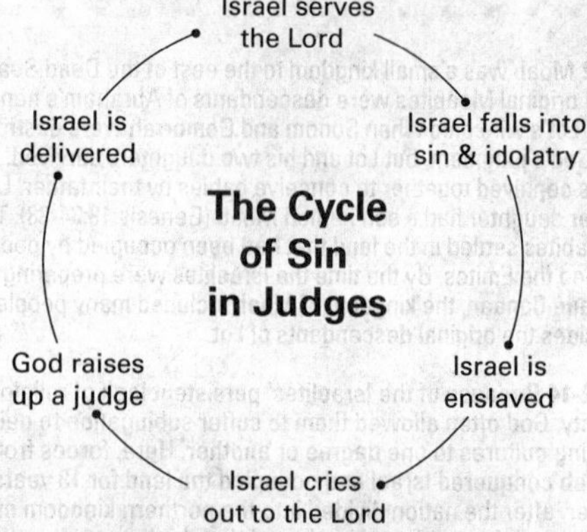

4:11 11 Now Heber the Kenite, a descendant of Moses' brother-in-law* Hobab, had moved
Josh 19:33 Judg 1:16 away from the other members of his tribe and pitched his tent by the oak of Zaanannim
near Kedesh.
12 When Sisera was told that Barak son of Abinoam had gone up to Mount Tabor, 13 he
called for all 900 of his iron chariots and all of his warriors, and they marched from
Harosheth-haggoyim to the Kishon River.
14 Then Deborah said to Barak, "Get ready! This is the day the LORD will give you victory
over Sisera, for the LORD is marching ahead of you." So Barak led his 10,000 warriors
4:15 down the slopes of Mount Tabor into battle. 15 When Barak attacked, the LORD threw Sisera
Josh 10:10 Judg 7:21 and all his chariots and warriors into a panic. Sisera leaped down from his chariot and
4:16 escaped on foot. 16 Then Barak chased the chariots and the enemy army all the way to
Exod 14:28 Harosheth-haggoyim, killing all of Sisera's warriors. Not a single one was left alive.
Ps 83:9 17 Meanwhile, Sisera ran to the tent of Jael, the wife of Heber the Kenite, because He-
ber's family was on friendly terms with King Jabin of Hazor. 18 Jael went out to meet Sisera
and said to him, "Come into my tent, sir. Come in. Don't be afraid." So he went into her
tent, and she covered him with a blanket.
4:19 19 "Please give me some water," he said. "I'm thirsty." So she gave him some milk from a
Judg 5:25 leather bag and covered him again.
20 "Stand at the door of the tent," he told her. "If anybody comes and asks you if there is
anyone here, say no."
21 But when Sisera fell asleep from exhaustion, Jael quietly crept up to him with a ham-
mer and tent peg in her hand. Then she drove the tent peg through his temple and into the
ground, and so he died.
22 When Barak came looking for Sisera, Jael went out to meet him. She said, "Come, and
I will show you the man you are looking for." So he followed her into the tent and found
Sisera lying there dead, with the tent peg through his temple.
23 So on that day Israel saw God defeat Jabin, the Canaanite king. 24 And from that time on
Israel became stronger and stronger against King Jabin until they finally destroyed him.

THE SONG OF DEBORAH

5:1 Exod 15:1 **5** On that day Deborah and Barak son of Abinoam sang this song:

5:2 Ps 110:3 2 "Israel's leaders took charge,
and the people gladly followed.

4:11 Or *father-in-law.*

▶ SPIRITUAL WARFARE

4:17-21 Hostile hostess. Sometimes it's right to be rude. Take Jael, for instance. Jael went against her place in society, her duties as a hostess, and her obligation to maintain her husband's neutrality (4:17) to rescue God's people from the oppression of the northern Canaanites. Deborah had predicted that "the LORD's victory over Sisera would be at the hands of a woman" (4:9), and God was rightly acknowledged as the true victor (4:23). When you succeed where others have failed, give God all the credit. (***See Spiritual Warfare****> Resisting Sin and Evil> Trusting God> Faithful Soldiers> Give glory to the Commander,* TopicGuide page A46.)

▶ WORSHIP

5:1-31 The song of Deborah. It is no wonder that people stood in line to hear Deborah's advice, for she spoke with remarkable authority. In this victory chant, Deborah told the terrible truth—many tribes had let a woman go into battle rather than take up the sword on their own (5:15-17). But others had joined her and Barak, and those tribes deserved honor for their bravery (5:18). She dedicated almost half of her song to Jael's deed, knowing this added to the shame of those who had quaked in fear as God used the women of Israel to drive away their enemies. And finally, she spoke of General Sisera's mother waiting in vain for her son to return with booty from the battle. She understood that the people of northern Canaan would be shocked when their greatest warriors failed to come home, and this would have a great impact on their future dealings with Israel. It seems Deborah would cut friend and foe alike with the Word of God. Tell the unvarnished truth in love to whomever you meet, Christian or non-Christian, and let God worry about the consequences. (***See Worship****> OT> Music> Deborah and Barak give a war chant,* TopicGuide page A27.)

5:1-31 Deborah's song is not the only song of victory recorded in the Scriptures. In addition to the Psalms, Israelite leaders used songs to celebrate triumphs and to record history for generations to come. Miriam, Moses' sister and an Israelite prophet, led the people in a song after Pharaoh's armies were drowned in the waters of the Red Sea (Exodus 15). Before Moses died, he taught his people a song (Deuteronomy 31–32). When King David brought the Ark of the Covenant to Jerusalem, he led the people in a song that became a part of several psalms (1 Chronicles 16:7-36).

Praise the LORD!

3 "Listen, you kings!
Pay attention, you mighty rulers!
For I will sing to the LORD.
I will make music to the LORD, the God of Israel.

4 "LORD, when You set out from Seir
and marched across the fields of Edom,
the earth trembled,
and the cloudy skies poured down rain.
5 The mountains quaked in the presence of the LORD,
the God of Mount Sinai—
in the presence of the LORD,
the God of Israel.

6 "In the days of Shamgar son of Anath,
and in the days of Jael,
people avoided the main roads,
and travelers stayed on winding pathways.
7 There were few people left in the villages of Israel*—
until Deborah arose as a mother for Israel.
8 When Israel chose new gods,
war erupted at the city gates.
Yet not a shield or spear could be seen
among forty thousand warriors in Israel!
9 My heart is with the commanders of Israel,
with those who volunteered for war.
Praise the LORD!

10 "Consider this, you who ride on fine donkeys,
you who sit on fancy saddle blankets,
and you who walk along the road.
11 Listen to the village musicians*
gathered at the watering holes.
They recount the righteous victories of the LORD
and the victories of His villagers in Israel.
Then the people of the LORD
marched down to the city gates.

12 "Wake up, Deborah, wake up!
Wake up, wake up, and sing a song!

5:4 Deut 33:2 Hab 3:6

5:5 Exod 19:18 Pss 97:5; 114:4 Isa 64:3

5:6 Judg 3:31; 4:17

5:8 Deut 32:17

5:10 Judg 10:4; 12:14

5:11 Gen 24:11 1 Sam 12:7

5:7 The meaning of the Hebrew is uncertain. 5:11 The meaning of the Hebrew is uncertain.

5:4 Mount Seir was the territory of the Edomites, a people descended from Esau (whose name was changed to Edom), the twin brother of Jacob (whose name was changed to Israel). Mount Seir was located southeast of the Dead Sea. Deborah speaks of God setting out from Mount Seir and marching across Edomite territory in the context of her battle against the Canaanites. She then tells how the skies poured down rain. It is possible that, during the battle, God caused a great storm to come up from the direction of Edom in order to slow Sisera's chariots.

5:5 Mount Sinai was a sacred mountain in the history of the Israelite nation. It was located somewhere on the Sinai Peninsula between Egypt and Israel. When Moses fled Egypt after murdering an Egyptian (Exodus 2:11-15), he traveled through this area. In fact, it was here that God spoke to Moses from the burning bush and gave him his first marching orders. Later, after God had delivered the Israelites from Egypt, they camped at Sinai. God spoke to them there in thunder so immense that they asked Moses to speak to them for God rather than have God speak directly to them. Moses received additional instructions from God at Sinai, including the Ten Commandments.

Arise, Barak!
Lead your captives away, son of Abinoam!

13 "Down from Tabor marched the few against the nobles.
The people of the LORD marched down against mighty warriors.
14 They came down from Ephraim—
a land that once belonged to the Amalekites;
they followed you, Benjamin, with your troops.
From Makir the commanders marched down;
from Zebulun came those who carry a commander's staff.
15 The princes of Issachar were with Deborah and Barak.
They followed Barak, rushing into the valley.
But in the tribe of Reuben
there was great indecision.
5:16 Num 32:1-2, 24
16 Why did you sit at home among the sheepfolds—
to hear the shepherds whistle for their flocks?
Yes, in the tribe of Reuben
there was great indecision.
5:17 Josh 13:24-28
17 Gilead remained east of the Jordan.
And why did Dan stay home?
Asher sat unmoved at the seashore,
remaining in his harbors.
18 But Zebulun risked his life,
as did Naphtali, on the heights of the battlefield.

5:19 Josh 11:1-5 Judg 1:27
19 "The kings of Canaan came and fought,
at Taanach near Megiddo's springs,
but they carried off no silver treasures.
20 The stars fought from heaven.
The stars in their orbits fought against Sisera.
5:21 Judg 4:7
21 The Kishon River swept them away—
that ancient torrent, the Kishon.
March on with courage, my soul!
5:22 Job 39:19-25
22 Then the horses' hooves hammered the ground,
the galloping, galloping of Sisera's mighty steeds.
23 'Let the people of Meroz be cursed,' said the Angel of the LORD.
'Let them be utterly cursed,
because they did not come to help the LORD—
to help the LORD against the mighty warriors.'

5:14 The Amalekites were distant relatives of the Israelites. They were descended from Amalek, the grandson of Esau, Jacob's twin brother. Jacob tricked Esau out of the family birthright and their father's blessing, and Esau's descendants remained enemies of the Israelites. Not only did the Amalekites block Israel's path from Egypt to Canaan, they harassed the Israelites as they traveled. For this, God declared that Israel should someday wipe out the Amalekites (Deuteronomy 25:17-19).

5:15-18 The battle Deborah described happened around Mount Tabor, southwest of the Sea of Galilee along the borders of the tribes of Naphtali, Zebulun, and Issachar. The warriors of these tribes all helped Deborah and Barak. But other tribes are rebuked here for not helping, though they were not in such close proximity to the battle site. Asher was, perhaps, the closest; its territory bordered Naphtali and Zebulun. The lands of Reuben and Gad were much farther south and on the other side of the Jordan River.

5:21 The Kishon River ran through the Jezreel Valley to the Mediterranean Sea. It was not a long river, but it was important to the water management of the region because it drained many tributaries. The Kishon is mentioned in connection with two major events in the Bible. The first is here, Deborah's battle alongside Barak. The second is in the ministry of the prophet Elijah. Elijah faced the prophets of Baal on Mount Carmel and humiliated them. The prophets then were carried to the valley and executed there (1 Kings 18:40).

24 "Most blessed among women is Jael,
the wife of Heber the Kenite.
May she be blessed above all women who live in tents.
25 Sisera asked for water,
and she gave him milk.
In a bowl fit for nobles,
she brought him yogurt.
26 Then with her left hand she reached for a tent peg,
and with her right hand for the workman's hammer.
She struck Sisera with the hammer, crushing his head.
With a shattering blow, she pierced his temples.
27 He sank, he fell,
he lay still at her feet.
And where he sank,
there he died.

5:24-25 Judg 4:17-19

5:26-27 Judg 4:21-22

28 "From the window Sisera's mother looked out.
Through the window she watched for his return, saying,
'Why is his chariot so long in coming?
Why don't we hear the sound of chariot wheels?'

29 "Her wise women answer,
and she repeats these words to herself:
30 'They must be dividing the captured plunder—
with a woman or two for every man.
There will be colorful robes for Sisera,
and colorful, embroidered robes for me.
Yes, the plunder will include
colorful robes embroidered on both sides.'

5:30 Exod 15:9

31 "LORD, may all Your enemies die like Sisera!
But may those who love You rise like the sun in all its power!"

5:31 Pss 68:1-2; 92:9

Then there was peace in the land for forty years.

GIDEON BECOMES ISRAEL'S JUDGE

6 The Israelites did evil in the LORD's sight. So the LORD handed them over to the Midi-
anites for seven years. 2 The Midianites were so cruel that the Israelites made hiding
places for themselves in the mountains, caves, and strongholds. 3 Whenever the Israel-
ites planted their crops, marauders from Midian, Amalek, and the people of the east
would attack Israel, 4 camping in the land and destroying crops as far away as Gaza.

6:1 Num 22:4; 25:15-18; 31:1-3 Judg 2:11

6:3 Isa 11:14

6:1 Midian was an area to the east of Egypt across the Sinai Peninsula. The Midianites were descended from Abraham just as the Israelites were. Abraham and Sarah had only one child, Isaac. After Sarah's death, Abraham married a woman named Keturah, by whom he had six sons. Midian was the fourth of those sons. The Midianites were nomadic, so their home base fluctuated, but they are generally associated with the region south of Israel below Edom.

6:2 In times of war, the caves of surrounding mountains were places of refuge. In Joshua's famous battle with the five Amorite kings, the leaders ran for a cave in Makkedah (Joshua 10:16). In Saul's losing battle with the Philistines, his men deserted him left and right, hiding in surrounding caves (1 Samuel 13:6). David and his small army hid from Saul's rage in the caves of En-gedi. One story tells of Saul entering the very cave where David and his men were hiding (1 Samuel 24). The prophet Obadiah hid other prophets in caves that they might escape death at the hands of wicked Queen Jezebel (1 Kings 18:4). In a land where deserts were vast and foliage could be scrubby, caves were a welcome shelter.

6:3-4 Gaza was one of the five principal cities of the Philistines, who inhabited a strip of land along the Mediterranean coast on the western edge of Israel's territory. That location is significant. The attackers mentioned here were people "of the east." The fact that they had destroyed crops as far away as Gaza meant they had crossed the entire land of Israel. This widespread looting of crops and livestock had a devastating effect on Israel, leaving the people on the brink of starvation.

They left the Israelites with nothing to eat, taking all the sheep, goats, cattle, and donkeys.
6:5 Judg 7:12 5These enemy hordes, coming with their livestock and tents, were as thick as locusts;
they arrived on droves of camels too numerous to count. And they stayed until the land
6:6 Deut 28:43 was stripped bare. 6So Israel was reduced to starvation by the Midianites. Then the Isra-
elites cried out to the LORD for help.
7When they cried out to the LORD because of Midian, 8the LORD sent a prophet to the Is-
6:8 Exod 18:9 Judg 2:1-2 raelites. He said, "This is what the LORD, the God of Israel, says: I brought you up out of
slavery in Egypt. 9I rescued you from the Egyptians and from all who oppressed you. I
6:10 Josh 24:15 drove out your enemies and gave you their land. 10I told you, 'I am the LORD your God.
You must not worship the gods of the Amorites, in whose land you now live.' But you have
not listened to Me."
6:11 Judg 13:3 Heb 11:32 11Then the Angel of the LORD came and sat beneath the great tree at Ophrah, which be-
longed to Joash of the clan of Abiezer. Gideon son of Joash was threshing wheat at the
bottom of a winepress to hide the grain from the Midianites. 12The Angel of the LORD ap-
peared to him and said, "Mighty hero, the LORD is with you!"
6:13 Deut 31:17 Ps 44:1 13"Sir," Gideon replied, "if the LORD is with us, why has all this happened to us? And
where are all the miracles our ancestors told us about? Didn't they say, 'The LORD brought
us up out of Egypt'? But now the LORD has abandoned us and handed us over to the Midi-
anites."
14Then the LORD turned to him and said, "Go with the strength you have, and rescue Is-
rael from the Midianites. I am sending you!"
6:15 Exod 3:11 15"But Lord," Gideon replied, "how can I rescue Israel? My clan is the weakest in the
whole tribe of Manasseh, and I am the least in my entire family!"
16The LORD said to him, "I will be with you. And you will destroy the Midianites as if you
were fighting against one man."
6:17 Isa 38:7 17Gideon replied, "If You are truly going to help me, show me a sign to prove that it is really
the LORD speaking to me. 18Don't go away until I come back and bring my offering to You."
He answered, "I will stay here until you return."

6:5 The description of these armies as being "as thick as locusts" would have painted a vivid picture for ancient readers. The locusts of Old Testament fame traveled in swarms (at least in one stage of their growth) so tightly packed that they literally could block out the sun. Though these locusts were a type of grasshopper, their group migration set them apart. Like their modern counterparts, they ate vegetation, and they could clean out a whole crop as they passed through an area. Their effect on the environment was so extreme that prophets such as Joel and Amos used them as a symbol of judgment.

▸ SALVATION
6:6 Crying out for help. God did not ignore the pain of His people. However, in each cycle of misery and rescue in Judges, God waited until the perfect moment to save His people. In this case, the adversaries helped save God's people; they caused the rebellious Israelites to cry out to God, and He saved them from their oppressors. Prophets (6:8), angels (6:11), God-empowered leaders (6:12), signs and wonders (6:21)—these are just a few examples of how God releases His grace and power to those who repent. Repent and know that God will rescue you from your sin and sadness. (***See Salvation****> Receiving> When> Delivered or rescued,* TopicGuide page A22.)

6:10 According to Genesis 10:15-16, the Amorites descended from Canaan, the son of Ham, who was one of the three sons of Noah. It is believed that the Amorites were quite powerful at one time, occupying the larger part of Mesopotamia and Syria. They were then driven from that region and settled Babylonia until the Hittites defeated them there. After that, they settled throughout Canaan and perhaps even Egypt. In Genesis 15:16, God specifically mentioned the Amorites' wickedness in His promise of victory to Abraham.

6:13 Gideon asked why so many terrible things had happened to Israel. He concluded that God had abandoned Israel without justification. Gideon did not understand that Israel's sin had provoked God to allow catastrophe to come upon the people, even though God had sent a prophet to them to make it clear. And he did not remember that God had promised never to abandon His covenant people. God was still with the Israelites, but He was disciplining them as a father disciplines a wayward son.

▸ HOLINESS
6:15 How can I do it? Many of God's people have been reluctant heroes. Gideon was the new judge of Israel, but, unlike his predecessors, he shrank from the task, demanding all sorts of signs (6:17, 36-40) before he would believe God's Word. God graciously honored Gideon and turned his doubts into faith. Perhaps you, like Gideon, are unwilling to respond to God's Word without a sign. God wants us to act on His Word by faith, and He can empower you through the indwelling Holy Spirit to accomplish great things for Him. (***See Holiness****> Submission> Trusting God> Overcoming,* TopicGuide page A40.)

19 Gideon hurried home. He cooked a young goat, and with a basket* of flour he 6:19
baked some bread without yeast. Then, carrying the meat in a basket and the broth in Gen 18:6-8
a pot, he brought them out and presented them to the Angel, who was under the great
tree.
20 The Angel of God said to him, "Place the meat and the unleavened bread on this
rock, and pour the broth over it." And Gideon did as he was told. 21 Then the Angel of 6:21
the LORD touched the meat and bread with the tip of the staff in His hand, and fire Lev 9:24
flamed up from the rock and consumed all he had brought. And the Angel of the LORD dis-
appeared.
22 When Gideon realized that it was the Angel of the LORD, he cried out, "Oh, Sovereign 6:22
LORD, I'm doomed! I have seen the Angel of the LORD face to face!" Gen 32:30
23 "It is all right," the LORD replied. "Do not be afraid. You will not die." 24 And Gideon built Exod 33:20
an altar to the LORD there and named it Yahweh-Shalom (which means "the LORD is Judg 13:21-22
peace"). The altar remains in Ophrah in the land of the clan of Abiezer to this day.
25 That night the LORD said to Gideon, "Take the second bull from your father's herd, the 6:25
one that is seven years old. Pull down your father's altar to Baal, and cut down the Ashe- Exod 34:13
rah pole standing beside it. 26 Then build an altar to the LORD your God here on this hilltop Deut 7:5
sanctuary, laying the stones carefully. Sacrifice the bull as a burnt offering on the altar, us-
ing as fuel the wood of the Asherah pole you cut down."
27 So Gideon took ten of his servants and did as the LORD had commanded. But he did it
at night because he was afraid of the other members of his father's household and the
people of the town.
28 Early the next morning, as the people of the town began to stir, someone discovered
that the altar of Baal had been broken down and that the Asherah pole beside it had been
cut down. In their place a new altar had been built, and on it were the remains of the bull
that had been sacrificed. 29 The people said to each other, "Who did this?" And after asking
around and making a careful search, they learned that it was Gideon, the son of Joash.
30 "Bring out your son," the men of the town demanded of Joash. "He must die for de-
stroying the altar of Baal and for cutting down the Asherah pole."
31 But Joash shouted to the mob that confronted him, "Why are you defending Baal?
Will you argue his case? Whoever pleads his case will be put to death by morning! If Baal
truly is a god, let him defend himself and destroy the one who broke down his altar!"

6:19 Hebrew *an ephah* [20 quarts or 22 liters].

6:19 The fact that Gideon cooked his bread without yeast revealed that he saw credibility in his visitor. Yeast, or more generally leaven, had come to symbolize evil, perhaps because of its association with fermentation and its ability to permeate a whole lump of dough. The unleavened bread of the Passover Feast was a symbol of the purity that God expected of His people. Centuries later, Jesus used the image of yeast to describe the corruption of the Pharisees (Matthew 16:11-12), and the apostle Paul used the concept of yeast in dough to warn his readers about evil influences (Galatians 5:9).

▸ GOD

6:24 God is our peace. Why did Gideon declare that the God calling him to war against Israel's enemies was a God of peace? First, Gideon knew that on his own merit, he was not worthy to stand before God or His messenger. When the holy flame consumed the food offering, Gideon knew that if not for God's mercy, that flame could have rightly consumed him. Second, God continued to rescue Gideon by saving him from the violent mob of Baal worshipers (6:30), demonstrating that God could bring peace between Gideon and his fellow Israelites as He had brought it between Himself and Gideon. In this case, Gideon saw peace as an absence of hostility and harm, and God was demonstrating to him that He could keep Gideon safe from anything. In Christ, God has made peace with all His people (Romans 5:1). Thank Him for sending Jesus as our peacemaker. (***See God***> *God's Names*> *God*> *The LORD is peace,* TopicGuide page A18.)

6:26 When God told Gideon to build an altar and lay the stones carefully, Gideon likely knew exactly what He meant. Israel had received specific instructions for building altars. In Exodus, Moses gave the general rule of thumb: Use stones that were uncut, not chipped or shaped. This was a way for the Israelites to make their worship distinct from the Canaanite idol worship around them.

6:27 Gideon's fear revealed that he knew his family and neighbors would not be happy that he was serving God to the exclusion of the Canaanite idols. He knew they would be angry that he had destroyed their idols. This was a testimony to how entrenched idolatry had become in Israel.

32 From then on Gideon was called Jerub-baal, which means "Let Baal defend himself," be-
cause he broke down Baal's altar.

GIDEON ASKS FOR A SIGN

6:33 33 Soon afterward the armies of Midian, Amalek, and the people of the east formed an alli-
Josh 17:16 ance against Israel and crossed the Jordan, camping in the valley of Jezreel. 34 Then the Spirit
6:34 of the LORD took possession of Gideon. He blew a ram's horn as a call to arms, and the men
Judg 3:10 of the clan of Abiezer came to him. 35 He also sent messengers throughout Manasseh, Asher,
6:35 Judg 7:23 Zebulun, and Naphtali, summoning their warriors, and all of them responded.
36 Then Gideon said to God, "If You are truly going to use me to rescue Israel as You
6:36 Judg 6:14 promised, 37 prove it to me in this way. I will put a wool fleece on the threshing floor to-
night. If the fleece is wet with dew in the morning but the ground is dry, then I will know
that You are going to help me rescue Israel as You promised." 38 And that is just what hap-
pened. When Gideon got up early the next morning, he squeezed the fleece and wrung
out a whole bowlful of water.
39 Then Gideon said to God, "Please don't be angry with me, but let me make one more
6:39 Gen 18:32 request. Let me use the fleece for one more test. This time let the fleece remain dry while
the ground around it is wet with dew." 40 So that night God did as Gideon asked. The fleece
was dry in the morning, but the ground was covered with dew.

7:1 Gen 12:6

GIDEON DEFEATS THE MIDIANITES

Deut 11:30 7 So Jerub-baal (that is, Gideon) and his army got up early and went as far as the spring of
Judg 6:32 Harod. The armies of Midian were camped north of them in the valley near the hill of
Moreh. 2 The LORD said to Gideon, "You have too many warriors with you. If I let all of you fight
7:2 Deut 8:17-18 the Midianites, the Israelites will boast to Me that they saved themselves by their own
Isa 10:13 strength. 3 Therefore, tell the people, 'Whoever is timid or afraid may leave this mountain* and
2 Cor 4:7 go home.'" So 22,000 of them went home, leaving only 10,000 who were willing to fight.
7:3 Deut 20:8 4 But the LORD told Gideon, "There are still too many! Bring them down to the spring, and
I will test them to determine who will go with you and who will not." 5 When Gideon took
7:4 1 Sam 14:6 his warriors down to the water, the LORD told him, "Divide the men into two groups. In one
group put all those who cup water in their hands and lap it up with their tongues like dogs.

7:3 Hebrew *may leave Mount Gilead.* The identity of Mount Gilead is uncertain in this context. It is perhaps used here as another name for Mount Gilboa.

6:32 The day after Gideon destroyed the idols, the people of his town confronted his father, demanding Gideon's death. Gideon's father, Joash, pointed out that Baal, if he were real, should be able to defend himself. From then on, Gideon was given the name Jerub-baal, which means "let Baal defend himself." Joash's reasoning and quick thinking saved the life of his son and made an important point to the people who had fallen from pure worship of Jehovah.

▶ HOLINESS
6:34 The power of the Spirit. Have you ever had a sense of the presence of the Holy Spirit? Have you felt God's Spirit move you to humility, mercy, or bravery? In this case, God sent His Spirit to empower Gideon as a commander of Israel's army. This spiritual event obviously didn't make him into God's robot—shortly thereafter he doubted again (6:36). God's special empowering for a certain time or a certain ministry is a glorious gift to all who believe. Today, it is not just God's heroes and kings who receive the power of God—all God's people are Spirit-empowered by Him for ministry (Acts 2). Do not grieve the Holy Spirit by resisting the power He gives to obey (Ephesians 4:30). (***See Holiness****> Submission> Yielding to Spirit> Power of the Spirit is for all,* TopicGuide page A41.)

6:36-40 Despite having been called by the angel of the Lord, hearing the voice of God, and seeing God's protection in his first act of obedience, Gideon was seized by new doubts on the night before the battle. So he asked God to give him just one more sign, a miracle involving a fleece, and God graciously complied. But even that wasn't enough for Gideon. Perhaps thinking that a coincidence had occurred, he asked God to reverse the sign. Once more God displayed His amazing patience and grace as He granted Gideon's request.

▶ GOD
7:2 There are still too many! A spirit of self-sufficiency can be a greater enemy than thousands of troops. How many men, women, and children perish by trusting in themselves rather than God? God knew that if Gideon went into battle with 32,000 men and won, the Israelites would boast that their courage and valor had won the day. So God worked to reduce the number of Gideon's warriors until his force was so small that no one could deny that it was the God of Israel who defeated the army of Midian. When faced with a problem, do you think first of how you can handle the situation, or do you stop and recognize that God can handle anything? (***See God****> God's Attributes> All-Powerful> God has power to deliver,* TopicGuide page A15.)

In the other group put all those who kneel down and drink with their mouths in the
stream." 6 Only 300 of the men drank from their hands. All the others got down on their
knees and drank with their mouths in the stream.

7 The LORD told Gideon, "With these 300 men I will rescue you and give you victory over
the Midianites. Send all the others home." 8 So Gideon collected the provisions and rams'
horns of the other warriors and sent them home. But he kept the 300 men with him.

The Midianite camp was in the valley just below Gideon. 9 That night the LORD said, "Get **7:9**
up! Go down into the Midianite camp, for I have given you victory over them! 10 But if you Josh 2:24; 10:8; 11:6
are afraid to attack, go down to the camp with your servant Purah. 11 Listen to what the Midi-
anites are saying, and you will be greatly encouraged. Then you will be eager to attack."

So Gideon took Purah and went down to the edge of the enemy camp. 12 The armies of **7:12**
Midian, Amalek, and the people of the east had settled in the valley like a swarm of lo- Josh 11:4
custs. Their camels were like grains of sand on the seashore—too many to count! 13 Gideon Judg 6:5; 8:10
crept up just as a man was telling his companion about a dream. The man said, "I had this
dream, and in my dream a loaf of barley bread came tumbling down into the Midianite
camp. It hit a tent, turned it over, and knocked it flat!"

14 His companion answered, "Your dream can mean only one thing—God has given Gid-
eon son of Joash, the Israelite, victory over Midian and all its allies!"

15 When Gideon heard the dream and its interpretation, he bowed in worship before the
LORD.* Then he returned to the Israelite camp and shouted, "Get up! For the LORD has given
you victory over the Midianite hordes!" 16 He divided the 300 men into three groups and
gave each man a ram's horn and a clay jar with a torch in it.

17 Then he said to them, "Keep your eyes on me. When I come to the edge of the camp,
do just as I do. 18 As soon as I and those with me blow the rams' horns, blow your horns,
too, all around the entire camp, and shout, 'For the LORD and for Gideon!'"

19 It was just after midnight,* after the changing of the guard, when Gideon and the
100 men with him reached the edge of the Midianite camp. Suddenly, they blew the rams'
horns and broke their clay jars. 20 Then all three groups blew their horns and broke their
jars. They held the blazing torches in their left hands and the horns in their right hands, **7:21**
and they all shouted, "A sword for the LORD and for Gideon!" 2 Kgs 7:7

21 Each man stood at his position around the camp and watched as all the Midianites

7:15 As in Greek version; Hebrew reads *he bowed.* 7:19 Hebrew *at the beginning of the second watch.*

▸ WORSHIP

7:7 I will rescue you. God whittled down the large force Gideon had summoned until only a few remained. Gideon probably would have preferred to do without this sign of God's power. But God was dealing not only with Gideon's unbelief, but also that of all Israel (7:2). As God works in situations, things don't always go the way we think they should. That is because God's goals are higher than ours. When you are walking with God, open your eyes to His goals and priorities, and you will see that His means of gaining victory are the best. (***See Worship****> NT> Our Role> Attitude> Trusting in the midst of trials,* TopicGuide page A31.)

7:11-15 As the time for battle approached, God provided yet another reassurance for the doubting Gideon. He allowed Gideon to overhear expressions of fear among his enemies because of a dream God had sent. God spoke through dreams throughout the Old Testament. When Abraham lied to a foreign king about Sarah being his wife, God revealed that fact to the king in a dream (Genesis 20:1-3). Joseph had dreams that promised him greatness and won him the disfavor of his brothers. Joseph later interpreted dreams for fellow prisoners and for Pharaoh in Egypt (Genesis 40–41), as Daniel did for the king of Babylon (Daniel 2).

▸ MINISTRY

7:14 God-talk. Does God talk to non-Christians? Does He hear their prayers? Starting with Cain (Genesis 4:10), there were a surprising number of times God supernaturally spoke to people you wouldn't expect. God sent dreams to the pharaoh that Joseph served (Genesis 41) and to the king whom Daniel served (Daniel 4); He also spoke directly to Saul (prior to his conversion and renaming as Paul, see Acts 9:3-5). Pray that God will reveal Himself in surprising ways to the unbelievers in your life. Be ready to share the gospel with them when God creates an opportunity. (***See Ministry****> Great Commission> Make Disciples> Prayers> That God would reveal Himself,* TopicGuide page A56.)

▸ HOLINESS

7:21 God at work. Have you ever prayed that God would do something special—something only He could do—in your life? Watching God at work can be humbling—even frightening. When God intervenes in human affairs, all the forces in the universe are at His command. From the inner emotions (Proverbs 21:1) to the natural world (Psalm 107:29; Luke 8:24), God is supreme—what He wants, He gets! Pray for God's special intervention in the affairs of your life and those around you—but be prepared for Him to do as you ask. (***See Holiness****> Changed by God> God Provides> By providence,* TopicGuide page A41.)

rushed around in a panic, shouting as they ran to escape. 22When the 300 Israelites blew
their rams' horns, the LORD caused the warriors in the camp to fight against each other with
their swords. Those who were not killed fled to places as far away as Beth-shittah near Zer-
erah and to the border of Abel-meholah near Tabbath.
23Then Gideon sent for the warriors of Naphtali, Asher, and Manasseh, who joined in
7:24 chasing the army of Midian. 24Gideon also sent messengers throughout the hill country of
Judg 3:27-28 Ephraim, saying, "Come down to attack the Midianites. Cut them off at the shallow cross-
ings of the Jordan River at Beth-barah."
7:25 So all the men of Ephraim did as they were told. 25They captured Oreb and Zeeb, the
Judg 8:4 Ps 83:11 two Midianite commanders, killing Oreb at the rock of Oreb, and Zeeb at the winepress of
Isa 10:26 Zeeb. And they continued to chase the Midianites. Afterward the Israelites brought the
heads of Oreb and Zeeb to Gideon, who was by the Jordan River.

GIDEON KILLS ZEBAH AND ZALMUNNA

8:1 **8** Then the people of Ephraim asked Gideon, "Why have you treated us this way? Why
Judg 12:1 didn't you send for us when you first went out to fight the Midianites?" And they ar-
gued heatedly with Gideon.
2But Gideon replied, "What have I accomplished compared to you? Aren't even the left-
over grapes of Ephraim's harvest better than the entire crop of my little clan of Abiezer?
3God gave you victory over Oreb and Zeeb, the commanders of the Midianite army. What
have I accomplished compared to that?" When the men of Ephraim heard Gideon's an-
swer, their anger subsided.
8:5 4Gideon then crossed the Jordan River with his 300 men, and though exhausted, they
Gen 33:17 continued to chase the enemy. 5When they reached Succoth, Gideon asked the leaders of
the town, "Please give my warriors some food. They are very tired. I am chasing Zebah
and Zalmunna, the kings of Midian."
6But the officials of Succoth replied, "Catch Zebah and Zalmunna first, and then we will
8:7 feed your army."
Judg 7:15 7So Gideon said, "After the LORD gives me victory over Zebah and Zalmunna, I will return
8:8 and tear your flesh with the thorns and briers from the wilderness."
Gen 32:30 8From there Gideon went up to Peniel* and again asked for food, but he got the same an-
1 Kgs 12:25 swer. 9So he said to the people of Peniel, "After I return in victory, I will tear down this tower."
8:10 10By this time Zebah and Zalmunna were in Karkor with 15,000 warriors—all that re-
Isa 9:4 mained of the allied armies of the east, for 120,000 had already been killed. 11Gideon cir-
8:12 cled around by the caravan route east of Nobah and Jogbehah, taking the Midianite army
Ps 83:11 by surprise. 12Zebah and Zalmunna, the two Midianite kings, fled, but Gideon chased
them down and captured all their warriors.
13After this, Gideon returned from the battle by way of Heres Pass. 14There he captured a

8:8 Hebrew *Penuel,* a variant spelling of Peniel; also in 8:9, 17.

7:25 The treatment of Oreb and Zeeb highlights the fact that ancient warfare was a hands-on, violent event. It was not unusual for a defeated people to be completely destroyed. Neither was it unusual for the strongest of those people to be carried away and assimilated into the conquering culture (as in the scenarios described in the books of Daniel and Esther). It was highly likely that leaders of defeated armies, as described here, would be publicly humiliated or mutilated. The reputation that preceded an army into battle carried much weight. Human nature being what it is, the more dramatic the victory, the more widespread the tales of it.

▸ WORSHIP

8:4 Running on empty. If you ask people how they are doing, you will most likely receive the reply "Tired!" or "Busy!" This has become the way of life in the Western world. But your busy lifestyle does not preclude you from serving God. Likewise, Gideon and his warriors were focused on God's will, and mere exhaustion could not distract them from their prize—they pressed forward in their battle against the enemies of Israel in spite of exhaustion from within and rejection from without (8:6-9).Stay focused on God's purpose for your life; say no to requests on your time and energy that would hinder your pursuit of God's will and heart. On your Sabbath day, celebrate the literal and spiritual rest offered by God, through Christ. (***See Worship****> NT> Christ's Supremacy> His sacrifice provides eternal rest,* TopicGuide page A29.)

young man from Succoth and demanded that he write down the names of all the seventy-
seven officials and elders in the town. 15Gideon then returned to Succoth and said to the 8:15 Judg 8:6
leaders, "Here are Zebah and Zalmunna. When we were here before, you taunted me, say-
ing, 'Catch Zebah and Zalmunna first, and then we will feed your exhausted army.'" 16Then
Gideon took the elders of the town and taught them a lesson, punishing them with thorns
and briers from the wilderness. 17He also tore down the tower of Peniel and killed all the 8:17 Judg 8:8
men in the town.

18Then Gideon asked Zebah and Zalmunna, "The men you killed at Tabor—what were
they like?"

"Like you," they replied. "They all had the look of a king's son."

19"They were my brothers, the sons of my own mother!" Gideon exclaimed. "As surely
as the LORD lives, I wouldn't kill you if you hadn't killed them."

20Turning to Jether, his oldest son, he said, "Kill them!" But Jether did not draw his
sword, for he was only a boy and was afraid.

21Then Zebah and Zalmunna said to Gideon, "Be a man! Kill us yourself!" So Gideon
killed them both and took the royal ornaments from the necks of their camels.

GIDEON'S SACRED EPHOD

22Then the Israelites said to Gideon, "Be our ruler! You and your son and your grandson
will be our rulers, for you have rescued us from Midian."

23But Gideon replied, "I will not rule over you, nor will my son. The LORD will rule over you! 8:23 1 Sam 12:12
24However, I do have one request—that each of you give me an earring from the plunder you
collected from your fallen enemies." (The enemies, being Ishmaelites, all wore gold earrings.)

25"Gladly!" they replied. They spread out a cloak, and each one threw in a gold earring
he had gathered from the plunder. 26The weight of the gold earrings was forty-three
pounds,* not including the royal ornaments and pendants, the purple clothing worn by the
kings of Midian, or the chains around the necks of their camels.

27Gideon made a sacred ephod from the gold and put it in Ophrah, his hometown. But 8:27 Exod 28:6
soon all the Israelites prostituted themselves by worshiping it, and it became a trap for Judg 17:5
Gideon and his family.

28That is the story of how the people of Israel defeated Midian, which never recovered.
Throughout the rest of Gideon's lifetime—about forty years—there was peace in the land.

29Then Gideon* son of Joash returned home. 30He had seventy sons born to him, for he 8:30 Judg 9:2, 5
had many wives. 31He also had a concubine in Shechem, who gave birth to a son, whom 8:31 Judg 9:1

8:26 Hebrew *1,700 shekels* [19.4 kilograms]. 8:29 Hebrew *Jerub-baal;* see 6:32.

▸ GOD

8:22 Pride. When Gideon succeeded, the people began to think he was someone special. Gideon initially corrected them, for he understood that God did not want a king to rule in Israel at that time. But Gideon soon began to "believe his own press." He began to appreciate the applause, and it led to idolatry (8:27) and immorality (8:30-31). He went so far as to name one of his sons Abimelech, meaning "my father is king." You may be walking in the Spirit right now, but do not grow proud. Make sure you do everything you can to avoid both the lust for power and the things that can draw you into idolatry and immorality. (***See God***> *Relationship> Barriers> Pride,* TopicGuide page A14.)

8:27 An ephod was a ceremonial vest. The most famous ephod was the one worn by Israel's high priest. It was highly decorative, with the names of the 12 tribes chiseled on stones. Gideon may have had pure intentions in creating the ephod; after all, he had just refused to rule the people since God was officially their King. Unfortunately, the ephod became an object of worship, just as Moses' bronze snake did generations later during the reign of King Hezekiah (see Numbers 21:9; 2 Kings 18:4).

8:28 Gideon's power and leadership brought 40 years of peace in the land. Othniel, Ehud, and Deborah, judges who influenced the nation before Gideon rose to power, also secured long periods of peace. After Gideon, though, no judges were noted for bringing an extended time of peace to Israel, not even Samson. The decay of the nation, both spiritually and politically, seemed to speed up, with less respite from the consequences of the people's idolatry.

8:31 Concubines were an accepted part of ancient cultures, even those that held up the ideal of monogamous marriage. A concubine, sometimes called a second wife, was a woman who filled the sexual role of a marriage partner without the requirement of a dowry or bride-price. The Law of Moses even made provision for these women (Exodus 21:7-11; Deuteronomy 21:10-14). If a wife was unable to bear children, she often offered her handmaiden to her husband, thus giving him a second wife. But the first wife would adopt any children of that union as members of her family. Sarah did this for Abraham (Genesis 16). Leah and Rachel did it for Jacob (Genesis 30).

he named Abimelech. [32]Gideon died when he was very old, and he was buried in the
grave of his father, Joash, at Ophrah in the land of the clan of Abiezer.
8:33 [33]As soon as Gideon died, the Israelites prostituted themselves by worshiping the im-
Judg 2:11 ages of Baal, making Baal-berith their god. [34]They forgot the LORD their God, who had res-
8:34 Deut 4:9 cued them from all their enemies surrounding them. [35]Nor did they show any loyalty to
Judg 3:7 the family of Jerub-baal (that is, Gideon), despite all the good he had done for Israel.

ABIMELECH RULES OVER SHECHEM

9:1 **9** One day Gideon's* son Abimelech went to Shechem to visit his uncles—his mother's
Judg 8:31 brothers. He said to them and to the rest of his mother's family, [2]"Ask the leading citi-
zens of Shechem whether they want to be ruled by all seventy of Gideon's sons or by one
man. And remember that I am your own flesh and blood!"
[3]So Abimelech's uncles gave his message to all the citizens of Shechem on his behalf.
And after listening to this proposal, the people of Shechem decided in favor of Abimelech
9:4 because he was their relative. [4]They gave him seventy silver coins from the temple of
Judg 8:33 Baal-berith, which he used to hire some reckless troublemakers who agreed to follow him.
9:5 [5]He went to his father's home at Ophrah, and there, on one stone, they killed all seventy of
Judg 6:11; 8:32 his half brothers, the sons of Gideon.* But the youngest brother, Jotham, escaped and hid.
[6]Then all the leading citizens of Shechem and Beth-millo called a meeting under the
oak beside the pillar* at Shechem and made Abimelech their king.

9:7 JOTHAM'S PARABLE

Deut 11:29; 27:12 John 4:20 [7]When Jotham heard about this, he climbed to the top of Mount Gerizim and shouted,

"Listen to me, citizens of Shechem!
Listen to me if you want God to listen to you!
9:8 [8]Once upon a time the trees decided to elect a king.
2 Kgs 14:9 Ezek 17:3 First they said to the olive tree,
Dan 4:10 'Be our king!'

9:1 Hebrew *Jerub-baal's* (see 6:32); also in 9:2, 24. 9:5 Hebrew *Jerub-baal* (see 6:32); also in 9:16, 19, 28, 57. 9:6 The meaning of the Hebrew is uncertain.

9:1 Shechem was a city in the tribal region of west Manasseh. It had a long history among the Israelites. It was Abraham's first campsite upon entering Canaan, the place where he built his first altar (Genesis 12:6-7). But perhaps the most notorious event in the history of Shechem was the rape of Dinah, one of Jacob's daughters. The man who raped her claimed to want to marry her. Dinah's brothers declared that all the men of Shechem would have to be circumcised before the marriage. While those men were recovering from their surgery, Simeon and Levi killed them all (Genesis 34).

▶ HOLINESS
9:2-5 Politics of destruction. Gideon's son Abimelech went to his kin and provided a razor-thin justification for selecting him as their leader—having seventy judges would be too confusing! After hiring some thugs, he attacked his half-brothers and killed all but one of them. And after all that, he was named king. What is the lesson here? Grasping for power is a bloody affair, and there is no justification for a demanding or controlling attitude. Such behavior destroys people and incites God's discipline upon those who do not repent. Flee from the ways of violence and intimidation. (***See Holiness*** > *Submission* > *Yielding to Spirit* > *Resist fleshly empowerment,* TopicGuide page A41.)

9:6 The subject of an Israelite monarchy was in the background for centuries. From the time the people left Egypt until they settled in Canaan, Israel was a theocracy—God was her king. Moses, Joshua, and the judges led Israel under God's direction. And yet, there were hints that God intended for Israel to have a human king someday: Jacob spoke of "the scepter" belonging to the tribe of Judah (Genesis 49:10) and Moses gave guidelines for a monarchy (Deuteronomy 17:14-20). The key was that any human king must be God's choice and must understand that he was under God's authority, serving as God's vice-regent. A problem arose during the time of Samuel when the people decided they wanted a king like those of the pagan nations around them. In effect, they tried to throw off God's authority. The people of Shechem did the same when they named Abimelech as their king.

9:7-15 Jotham told a very pointed parable to the people of Shechem. It made the point that the greatest men are those who have the strongest desire to serve, not to be lifted up. By that standard, Abimelech was a very poor choice as a leader. He was willing to bully his way into leadership at the cost of his brother's lives and his own righteousness—and he was willing to pay such a price even though his kingship was unofficial and small in scope. According to Jotham, this behavior proved that Abimelech was an unworthy leader.

9 But the olive tree refused, saying,
'Should I quit producing the olive oil
that blesses both God and people,
just to wave back and forth over the trees?'
10 "Then they said to the fig tree,
'You be our king!'
11 But the fig tree also refused, saying,
'Should I quit producing my sweet fruit
just to wave back and forth over the trees?'
12 "Then they said to the grapevine,
'You be our king!'
13 But the grapevine also refused, saying,
'Should I quit producing the wine
that cheers both God and people,
just to wave back and forth over the trees?'
14 "Then all the trees finally turned to the thornbush and said,
'Come, you be our king!'
15 And the thornbush replied to the trees,
'If you truly want to make me your king,
come and take shelter in my shade.
If not, let fire come out from me
and devour the cedars of Lebanon.'"

16 Jotham continued, "Now make sure you have acted honorably and in good faith by mak-
ing Abimelech your king, and that you have done right by Gideon and all of his descendants.
Have you treated him with the honor he deserves for all he accomplished? 17 For he fought for
you and risked his life when he rescued you from the Midianites. 18 But today you have revolted 9:18
against my father and his descendants, killing his seventy sons on one stone. And you have Judg 8:31
chosen his slave woman's son, Abimelech, to be your king just because he is your relative.
19 "If you have acted honorably and in good faith toward Gideon and his descendants
today, then may you find joy in Abimelech, and may he find joy in you. 20 But if you have
not acted in good faith, then may fire come out from Abimelech and devour the leading
citizens of Shechem and Beth-millo; and may fire come out from the citizens of Shechem
and Beth-millo and devour Abimelech!"
21 Then Jotham escaped and lived in Beer because he was afraid of his brother Abimelech.

SHECHEM REBELS AGAINST ABIMELECH

22 After Abimelech had ruled over Israel for three years, 23 God sent a spirit that stirred up 9:23 1 Sam 16:14
trouble between Abimelech and the leading citizens of Shechem, and they revolted. 24 God 9:24
was punishing Abimelech for murdering Gideon's seventy sons, and the citizens of She- Num 35:33
chem for supporting him in this treachery of murdering his brothers. 25 The citizens of She- Deut 27:25
chem set an ambush for Abimelech on the hilltops and robbed everyone who passed that
way. But someone warned Abimelech about their plot.
26 One day Gaal son of Ebed moved to Shechem with his brothers and gained the confi-

9:23-24 God chose to enact judgment on His enemy in a more covert fashion than Jotham suggested. Abimelech ruled over the people of Shechem for three years, but we discover that God providentially "stirred up trouble" between the ruler and the ruled in order to punish both Abimelech and the citizens of Shechem for the hideous mass murder of Gideon's sons.

9:26-29 The interaction between the people of Shechem and the followers of Gaal offers a picture of ancient politics. Gaal and his brothers "gained the confidence" of the people of Shechem. They did this by going to a holiday party, getting drunk, listening to the disgruntled, and offering a leadership alternative. There were no polls, no political commercials, and no local media coverage. The people of Shechem engaged in a kind of mob mentality that, true to human nature, considered the grass greener on any other side. They may have been right in desiring a new leader, but the new faction also depended on cruelty and murder. The results (Judges 9:42-54) were not surprising.

9:27 dence of the leading citizens of Shechem. 27During the annual harvest festival at She-
Judg 8:33 chem, held in the temple of the local god, the wine flowed freely, and everyone began
cursing Abimelech. 28"Who is Abimelech?" Gaal shouted. "He's not a true son of She-
chem,* so why should we be his servants? He's merely the son of Gideon, and this Zebul is
merely his deputy. Serve the true sons of Hamor, the founder of Shechem. Why should we
serve Abimelech? 29If I were in charge here, I would get rid of Abimelech. I would say* to
him, 'Get some soldiers, and come out and fight!'"

30But when Zebul, the leader of the city, heard what Gaal was saying, he was furious.
31He sent messengers to Abimelech in Arumah,* telling him, "Gaal son of Ebed and his
brothers have come to live in Shechem, and now they are inciting the city to rebel against
9:33 you. 32Come by night with an army and hide out in the fields. 33In the morning, as soon as
1 Sam 10:7 it is daylight, attack the city. When Gaal and those who are with him come out against you,
you can do with them as you wish."

34So Abimelech and all his men went by night and split into four groups, stationing
themselves around Shechem. 35Gaal was standing at the city gates when Abimelech and
his army came out of hiding. 36When Gaal saw them, he said to Zebul, "Look, there are
people coming down from the hilltops!"

Zebul replied, "It's just the shadows on the hills that look like men."

37But again Gaal said, "No, people are coming down from the hills.* And another group
is coming down the road past the Diviners' Oak.*"

38Then Zebul turned on him and asked, "Now where is that big mouth of yours? Wasn't
it you that said, 'Who is Abimelech, and why should we be his servants?' The men you
mocked are right outside the city! Go out and fight them!"

39So Gaal led the leading citizens of Shechem into battle against Abimelech. 40But
Abimelech chased him, and many of Shechem's men were wounded and fell along the
road as they retreated to the city gate. 41Abimelech returned to Arumah, and Zebul drove
Gaal and his brothers out of Shechem.

42The next day the people of Shechem went out into the fields to battle. When Abime-
lech heard about it, 43he divided his men into three groups and set an ambush in the
fields. When Abimelech saw the people coming out of the city, he and his men jumped up
from their hiding places and attacked them. 44Abimelech and his group stormed the city
gate to keep the men of Shechem from getting back in, while Abimelech's other two
9:45 groups cut them down in the fields. 45The battle went on all day before Abimelech finally
Deut 29:23 captured the city. He killed the people, leveled the city, and scattered salt all over the
ground.

9:46 46When the leading citizens who lived in the tower of Shechem heard what had
Judg 8:33

9:28 Hebrew *Who is Shechem?* 9:29 As in Greek version; Hebrew reads *And he said.* 9:31 Or *in secret;* Hebrew reads *in Tormah;* compare 9:41. 9:37a Or *the center of the land.* 9:37b Hebrew *Elon-meonenim.*

9:27 This festival was not the Israelite festival of the new grain, which marked the transition from the end of the barley harvest to the beginning of the wheat harvest. The barley harvest would have been earlier in the year, so this festival was probably celebrating the grape harvest. This festival was held at the "temple of the local god," a phrase that reveals the state of the nation. The people had done the very thing God had prohibited—they had mingled with the cultures and the religions around them.

9:28 Hamor was an ancient king in the Shechem area. Jacob bought land near Shechem from Hamor. Later, Hamor's son, also named Shechem, abducted and raped Dinah, Jacob's daughter, then asked to marry her. Jacob's sons told Hamor and Shechem that they, and all the men of their town, would have to be circumcised before the marriage could take place. The men of the town agreed to undergo circumcision, but when the men were recovering from surgery, two of Jacob's sons, Levi and Simeon, stole into the camp and killed them all (Genesis 34).

9:45 Scattering salt was a curse on the land, leaving it infertile and useless. In Moses' final words to the Israelites, he said that the land would be "sulfur and salt" (Deuteronomy 29:22-24) if the people followed their own way rather than God's instructions. Jeremiah used the image of salty, unproductive ground in his description of people who trust in human strength: such people live on "salty land" and "have no hope for the future" (Jeremiah 17:5-6).

happened, they ran and hid in the temple of Baal-berith.* 47Someone reported to Abime-
lech that the citizens had gathered in the temple, 48so he led his forces to Mount Zalmon. 9:48
He took an ax and chopped some branches from a tree, then put them on his shoulder. Ps 68:14
"Quick, do as I have done!" he told his men. 49So each of them cut down some branches,
following Abimelech's example. They piled the branches against the walls of the temple
and set them on fire. So all the people who had lived in the tower of Shechem died—about
1,000 men and women.

50Then Abimelech attacked the town of Thebez and captured it. 51But there was a 9:50
strong tower inside the town, and all the men and women—the entire population—fled to 2 Sam 11:21
it. They barricaded themselves in and climbed up to the roof of the tower. 52Abimelech
followed them to attack the tower. But as he prepared to set fire to the entrance, 53a
woman on the roof dropped a millstone that landed on Abimelech's head and crushed 9:53
his skull. 2 Sam 11:21

54He quickly said to his young armor bearer, "Draw your sword and kill me! Don't let it
be said that a woman killed Abimelech!" So the young man ran him through with his
sword, and he died. 55When Abimelech's men saw that he was dead, they disbanded and
returned to their homes.

56In this way, God punished Abimelech for the evil he had done against his father by
murdering his seventy brothers. 57God also punished the men of Shechem for all their
evil. So the curse of Jotham son of Gideon was fulfilled.

TOLA BECOMES ISRAEL'S JUDGE

10 After Abimelech died, Tola son of Puah, son of Dodo, was the next person to res-
cue Israel. He was from the tribe of Issachar but lived in the town of Shamir in the
hill country of Ephraim. 2He judged Israel for twenty-three years. When he died, he was
buried in Shamir.

JAIR BECOMES ISRAEL'S JUDGE

3After Tola died, Jair from Gilead judged Israel for twenty-two years. 4His thirty sons rode 10:4
around on thirty donkeys, and they owned thirty towns in the land of Gilead, which are Num 32:41
still called the Towns of Jair.* 5When Jair died, he was buried in Kamon.

9:46 Hebrew *El-berith,* another name for Baal-berith; compare 9:4. 10:4 Hebrew *Havvoth-jair.*

9:54 It was very important for a soldier to die an honorable death. In Abimelech's twisted mind, dying at the hand of a woman would be a greater humiliation than dying in honorable combat, so he asked his armor bearer to inflict a mortal wound on him. In a similar situation centuries later, King Saul was wounded by the Philistines and asked his armor bearer to kill him so that he would not have to die by the hand of Israel's enemies. Saul's armor bearer had less nerve than Abimelech's—he could not bring himself to kill his master. Saul resorted to suicide by falling on his own sword (1 Samuel 31:4).

▸ CHURCH

9:56-57 Discovering God in the revolt against Abimelech. There may be a separation of church and state, but there's no separation of God and state. God's authority extends to political structures of all types. In this case, God fueled a rebellion against a false judge of Israel in order to punish the ones who had sponsored his rise to power (9:44-45) and to destroy Abimelech (9:52-55). When you cast your vote for a candidate, remember that you are accountable to God for your choice. Pray for both a fair election process and the victory of the best candidate. (***See Church***> *Role> Church Government> Society> Church influences governments,* TopicGuide page A49.)

▸ WORSHIP

10:1-2 No news is good news. Have you ever stepped into a chaotic situation and discovered that it was your job to bring the circumstances into order? Then you know how Tola felt. We know very little about Tola except that his rule passed without incident. Considering the calamity that had preceded his judgeship, this silence is likely a sign of God's favor. If you find yourself in a disordered or confused situation, be God's agent of order. Even if history doesn't record your deeds, God will—and His rewards will be great. (***See Worship***> *NT> Our Role> Mind and Heart> Worship decently and in order,* TopicGuide page A32.)

▸ WORSHIP

10:3-4 Godly use of wealth. Who is the wealthiest person you know? The next judge of Israel, Jair, was a man of considerable wealth—he owned 30 towns! Those who are rich have special responsibilities. How well have you done in using your resources to help God's people? You should have no problem finding someone less prosperous than you are—use the material blessings God gives you to bless others, particularly during times of distress. (***See Worship***> *NT> Sacrificial Living> The rich called to sacrifice for kingdom of heaven,* TopicGuide page A34.)

THE AMMONITES OPPRESS ISRAEL

10:6 6 Again the Israelites did evil in the LORD's sight. They served the images of Baal and Ashto-
Judg 2:11-13 reth, and the gods of Aram, Sidon, Moab, Ammon, and Philistia. They abandoned the LORD
10:7 and no longer served Him at all. 7 So the LORD burned with anger against Israel, and He
1 Sam 12:9 turned them over to the Philistines and the Ammonites, 8 who began to oppress them that
year. For eighteen years they oppressed all the Israelites east of the Jordan River in the
land of the Amorites (that is, in Gilead). 9 The Ammonites also crossed to the west side of
the Jordan and attacked Judah, Benjamin, and Ephraim.

10:10 The Israelites were in great distress. 10 Finally, they cried out to the LORD for help, saying,
Judg 3:9 "We have sinned against You because we have abandoned You as our God and have
served the images of Baal."

10:11 11 The LORD replied, "Did I not rescue you from the Egyptians, the Amorites, the Ammon-
Exod 14:30 ites, the Philistines, 12 the Sidonians, the Amalekites, and the Maonites? When they op-
Judg 3:13 pressed you, you cried out to Me for help, and I rescued you. 13 Yet you have abandoned
10:14 Me and served other gods. So I will not rescue you anymore. 14 Go and cry out to the gods
Deut 32:37 you have chosen! Let them rescue you in your hour of distress!"

10:15 15 But the Israelites pleaded with the LORD and said, "We have sinned. Punish us as You
1 Sam 3:18 see fit, only rescue us today from our enemies." 16 Then the Israelites put aside their for-
10:16 eign gods and served the LORD. And He was grieved by their misery.
Deut 32:36 17 At that time the armies of Ammon had gathered for war and were camped in Gilead, and
Josh 24:23
Jer 18:8 the people of Israel assembled and camped at Mizpah. 18 The leaders of Gilead said to each
other, "Whoever attacks the Ammonites first will become ruler over all the people of Gilead."

JEPHTHAH BECOMES ISRAEL'S JUDGE

11:1 **11** Now Jephthah of Gilead was a great warrior. He was the son of Gilead, but his
1 Sam 12:11 mother was a prostitute. 2 Gilead's wife also had several sons, and when these half
Heb 11:32 brothers grew up, they chased Jephthah off the land. "You will not get any of our father's

---

10:7 The original Ammonites were descendants of Abraham's nephew Lot. Lot's wife died in the destruction of Sodom and Gomorrah, but Lot and his two daughters survived. The girls plotted together to conceive babies by their father. Lot's older daughter had a son named Moab (Genesis 19:34-38), who became the progenitor of the Moabites. Lot's younger daughter had a son named Ben-ammi. He became the progenitor of the Ammonites. Both groups were eventually destroyed because of their sin against God (Ezekiel 25:10).

10:13-15 In light of the later divine deliverances, God's pledge to no longer rescue Israel sounds like an empty threat. But the context of God's words reveals that there is no contradiction. The Israelites were making an essentially empty repentance, confessing their sin in worshiping false gods but taking no concrete action to put those gods away. When God told the people to seek the help of the false gods they had chosen, He was saying that He would not help them *as long as those gods remained a part of their lives.* When the Israelites got rid of their false gods, God "was grieved by their misery" (10:16) and soon sent a deliverer.

10:17 Gilead was an area east of the Jordan River where the tribes of Reuben, Gad, and half the tribe of Manasseh lived. The Israelites saw this land first as they approached Canaan. The abundant grazing land in Gilead prompted the tribes of Reuben and Gad to ask Moses to let them live there (Numbers 32). Moses consented on one condition: that the military men of these tribes would still travel across the Jordan and help the other tribes conquer the land. The men of Reuben and Gad agreed to do so once they had built corrals for their livestock. Under the leadership of Joshua, they fought in some battles to the west of the Jordan and then moved back to Gilead.

▸ HOLINESS

11:1-27 War and peace. Israel was in such disarray that even a great warrior was treated with dishonor for the sake of a larger inheritance. The leaders of Gilead had stood by as Jephthah's inheritance was stolen from him, but as soon as they felt threatened, they rashly gave him authority over the entire region. Jephthah proved that, despite many faults, he was a skilled diplomat (11:14-27). He did not rely on brute force as his only weapon, but used his wisdom to attempt to avert violence. When confronted with a crisis, don't immediately take the most expedient course, but take time to consider the most peaceful solution. Jesus pronounced His blessing upon those who seek the ways of peace (Matthew 5:9). (***See Holiness*** *> Changed by God> The Son Purchases> Jesus' peacemaking with God,* TopicGuide page A41.)

11:1-3 Jephthah is described here in a less than favorable light, as the child of his father's unfaithfulness; yet he is listed in the Hall of Faith in the New Testament book of Hebrews alongside such judges as Gideon, Barak, Samson, and Samuel (Hebrews 11:32). Samuel, the last judge of Israel, also listed Jephthah among Israel's rescuers in the midst of their unfaithfulness (1 Samuel 12:11). Tob, the land to which Jephthah fled, was probably east of Gilead, which was east of the Jordan River. Tob was mentioned during the reign of Israel's King David, but only as the place from which David's enemies hired 12,000 mercenaries to fight against him (2 Samuel 10:6-8).

inheritance," they said, "for you are the son of a prostitute." 3 So Jephthah fled from his broth- **11:3**
ers and lived in the land of Tob. Soon he had a band of worthless rebels following him. Judg 9:4
4 At about this time, the Ammonites began their war against Israel. 5 When the Ammon- 2 Sam 10:6, 8
ites attacked, the elders of Gilead sent for Jephthah in the land of Tob. The elders said, **11:4**
6 "Come and be our commander! Help us fight the Ammonites!" Judg 10:9
7 But Jephthah said to them, "Aren't you the ones who hated me and drove me from my
father's house? Why do you come to me now when you're in trouble?"
8 "Because we need you," the elders replied. "If you lead us in battle against the Ammon-
ites, we will make you ruler over all the people of Gilead."
9 Jephthah said to the elders, "Let me get this straight. If I come with you and if the LORD
gives me victory over the Ammonites, will you really make me ruler over all the people?"
10 "The LORD is our witness," the elders replied. "We promise to do whatever you say." **11:10**
11 So Jephthah went with the elders of Gilead, and the people made him their ruler and Gen 31:50
commander of the army. At Mizpah, in the presence of the LORD, Jephthah repeated what **11:11** Judg 10:17
he had said to the elders.
12 Then Jephthah sent messengers to the king of Ammon, asking, "Why have you come
out to fight against my land?"
13 The king of Ammon answered Jephthah's messengers, "When the Israelites came out **11:13**
of Egypt, they stole my land from the Arnon River to the Jabbok River and all the way to Num 21:24-26
the Jordan. Now then, give back the land peaceably."
14 Jephthah sent this message back to the Ammonite king:

15 "This is what Jephthah says: Israel did not steal any land from Moab or Ammon.
16 When the people of Israel arrived at Kadesh on their journey from Egypt after **11:16**
crossing the Red Sea,* 17 they sent messengers to the king of Edom asking for Num 20:1-21
permission to pass through his land. But their request was denied. Then they asked **11:17** Num 20:14-21
the king of Moab for similar permission, but he wouldn't let them pass through Josh 24:9
either. So the people of Israel stayed in Kadesh.
18 "Finally, they went around Edom and Moab through the wilderness. They traveled **11:18**
along Moab's eastern border and camped on the other side of the Arnon River. But they Num 21:4
never once crossed the Arnon River into Moab, for the Arnon was the border of Moab. Deut 2:1-9, 18-19
19 "Then Israel sent messengers to King Sihon of the Amorites, who ruled from Heshbon,
asking for permission to cross through his land to get to their destination. 20 But King Sihon **11:19** Num 21:21-22
didn't trust Israel to pass through his land. Instead, he mobilized his army at Jahaz and
attacked them. 21 But the LORD, the God of Israel, gave His people victory over King Sihon. **11:21**
So Israel took control of all the land of the Amorites, who lived in that region, 22 from the Deut 2:32-34
Arnon River to the Jabbok River, and from the eastern wilderness to the Jordan.

11:16 Hebrew *sea of reeds.*

11:13 When Jephthah requested an explanation for the Ammonites' attack on Israel, the king of Ammon responded with a bogus claim, saying that the Israelites took his land when they came out of Egypt. In his reply, Jephthah set the record straight. He noted that Israel requested and was denied permission to pass through the territories of Edom and Moab, so Israel went around them. Then Israel sought permission from Sihon, king of the Amorites, to cross his territory. That territory was the same land the Ammonites were now claiming. Unfortunately for the Ammonites, Sihon not only denied permission for the Israelites to pass, he attacked them. When God gave His people victory over Sihon, the land became Israel's.

11:19-20 When King Sihon of the Amorites attacked the Israelites, he lost his life, and his people lost their land. The same thing happened to Og, the last king of Bashan. Sihon and Og's demise were often recounted as a testimony to God's power, which the Israelites recognized as the source of their military victories (Psalm 135:10-11). When the Gibeonites (also called Hivites) tricked Joshua into forming a treaty with them, part of the reason they gave for their ruse was their knowledge of the Israelites' defeats of Sihon and Og (Joshua 9).

11:22 The Arnon and Jabbok rivers were important landmarks in the region of Israel. The Jordan River divided the eastern and western territories of Israel. The Sea of Galilee was at the northern end of the Jordan and the Dead Sea was at the southern end. Several other rivers flowed from the east, resembling the rungs of a ladder when viewed on a map. As you read about the journey of the Israelites, you hear the names of these rivers: the Zered Brook, the Arnon River, and the Jabbok River. The southernmost of these, the Zered Brook, connected to the southern end of the Dead Sea. The Arnon River connected to the Dead Sea. The Jabbok River connected to the Jordan River north of where the Israelites initially crossed into Canaan.

23“So you see, it was the LORD, the God of Israel, who took away the land from the
11:24 Num 21:27-30 Amorites and gave it to Israel. Why, then, should we give it back to you? 24You keep
1 Kgs 11:7 whatever your god Chemosh gives you, and we will keep whatever the LORD our God
11:25 gives us. 25Are you any better than Balak son of Zippor, king of Moab? Did he try to
Num 22:2 make a case against Israel for disputed land? Did he go to war against them?
11:26 26“Israel has been living here for 300 years, inhabiting Heshbon and its surround-
Num 21:25 ing settlements, all the way to Aroer and its settlements, and in all the towns along
the Arnon River. Why have you made no effort to recover it before now? 27Therefore,
I have not sinned against you. Rather, you have wronged me by attacking me. Let
the LORD, who is judge, decide today which of us is right—Israel or Ammon.”
28But the king of Ammon paid no attention to Jephthah's message.

JEPHTHAH'S VOW

11:29 29At that time the Spirit of the LORD came upon Jephthah, and he went throughout the land
Judg 3:10 of Gilead and Manasseh, including Mizpah in Gilead, and from there he led an army
against the Ammonites. 30And Jephthah made a vow to the LORD. He said, “If You give me
victory over the Ammonites, 31I will give to the LORD whatever comes out of my house to
meet me when I return in triumph. I will sacrifice it as a burnt offering.”
32So Jephthah led his army against the Ammonites, and the LORD gave him victory. 33He
crushed the Ammonites, devastating about twenty towns from Aroer to an area near Min-
nith and as far away as Abel-keramim. In this way Israel defeated the Ammonites.
11:34 Exod 15:20 34When Jephthah returned home to Mizpah, his daughter came out to meet him, play-
1 Sam 18:6 ing on a tambourine and dancing for joy. She was his one and only child; he had no other
Jer 31:4 sons or daughters. 35When he saw her, he tore his clothes in anguish. “Oh, my daughter!”
11:35 Num 30:2 he cried out. “You have completely destroyed me! You've brought disaster on me! For I
Eccl 5:2, 4-5 have made a vow to the LORD, and I cannot take it back.”
11:36 36And she said, “Father, if you have made a vow to the LORD, you must do to me what
2 Sam 18:19 you have vowed, for the LORD has given you a great victory over your enemies, the Am-
Luke 1:38 monites. 37But first let me do this one thing: Let me go up and roam in the hills and weep
with my friends for two months, because I will die a virgin.”

11:24 Chemosh was the main god of the Moabites, but the Ammonites worshiped him, too. Solomon, the great Israelite king, allowed the worship of Chemosh among his people because he had married a foreign wife who worshiped the god. (Solomon also allowed worship of the gods Molech and Ashtoreth.) The prophet Ahijah revealed God's offense at Solomon's actions. Later, in an attempt at national renewal, the righteous King Josiah destroyed the shrines Solomon had built (2 Kings 23:12). Child sacrifice was a part of the worship of Chemosh. God firmly condemned this practice.

11:25 Balak, son of Zippor, king of Moab, tried to pay Balaam to curse the Israelites (Numbers 22–24). He was repeatedly unsuccessful. However, the people of Moab succeeded in enticing the Israelites into idolatry (Numbers 25). The story of Balak and Balaam was retold and remembered throughout the history of the Israelites. Joshua reminded the people of God's protection against Balak (Joshua 24:9-10). The prophet Micah reminded his people of King Balak (Micah 6:5). Even the apostle John, in his apocalyptic letter of Revelation, referred to Balaam and Balak in his message to the church at Pergamum (Revelation 2:14).

▸ WORSHIP
11:30-31 Jephthah made a vow to the Lord . . . . “If You give me victory over the Ammonites, I will give to the LORD whatever comes out of my house to meet me when I return in triumph. I will sacrifice it as a burnt offering.” This is a perplexing passage of Scripture, but the intent is clear—those in leadership in Israel, even with the power of the Holy Spirit, could be rash to the point of useless murder. Shamefully, the community let this atrocity happen, only lamenting it much later (11:39, 40). For us, this passage teaches the danger of imprudent promises to God. For instance, this passage shows that while a Christian should not marry a non-Christian (2 Corinthians 6:14-16), he or she is still bound by those marriage vows (1 Corinthians 7:17). Make your promises carefully, and when you make them, keep them. (***See Worship**> OT> Offerings> Other Sacrifices> Vows,* TopicGuide page A27.)

11:30 God did not command the people to make vows, but He did command them to fulfill the vows they made. Vows taken in Jephthah's day were far more solemn than the modern sense of a promise made to a friend. These ancient vows were made to God as an act of service or a commitment to abstain from something. Often the person making the vow (Jephthah in this case), hoped to gain something from God—either His favor in general or a specific response. Vows also could be made out of gratitude when a great blessing came upon a family or person. At times, vows could be vetoed or redeemed with a monetary offering, but they could not be simply forgotten.

38“You may go,” Jephthah said. And he sent her away for two months. She and her
friends went into the hills and wept because she would never have children. 39When she
returned home, her father kept the vow he had made, and she died a virgin.
So it has become a custom in Israel 40for young Israelite women to go away for four
days each year to lament the fate of Jephthah’s daughter.

EPHRAIM FIGHTS WITH JEPHTHAH

12 Then the people of Ephraim mobilized an army and crossed over the Jordan River 12:1
to Zaphon. They sent this message to Jephthah: “Why didn’t you call for us to help Judg 8:1
you fight against the Ammonites? We are going to burn down your house with you in it!”
2Jephthah replied, “I summoned you at the beginning of the dispute, but you refused to
come! You failed to help us in our struggle against Ammon. 3So when I realized you 12:3
weren’t coming, I risked my life and went to battle without you, and the LORD gave me vic- 1 Sam 19:5
tory over the Ammonites. So why have you now come to fight me?” Job 13:14
4The people of Ephraim responded, “You men of Gilead are nothing more than fugitives
from Ephraim and Manasseh.” So Jephthah gathered all the men of Gilead and attacked
the men of Ephraim and defeated them.
5Jephthah captured the shallow crossings of the Jordan River, and whenever a fugitive from 12:5
Ephraim tried to go back across, the men of Gilead would challenge him. “Are you a member Josh 2:7
of the tribe of Ephraim?” they would ask. If the man said, “No, I’m not,” 6they would tell him to Judg 3:28; 7:24
say “Shibboleth.” If he was from Ephraim, he would say “Sibboleth,” because people from
Ephraim cannot pronounce the word correctly. Then they would take him and kill him at the
shallow crossings of the Jordan. In all, 42,000 Ephraimites were killed at that time.
7Jephthah judged Israel for six years. When he died, he was buried in one of the towns 12:7
of Gilead. Heb 11:32

IBZAN BECOMES ISRAEL’S JUDGE

8After Jephthah died, Ibzan from Bethlehem judged Israel. 9He had thirty sons and thirty
daughters. He sent his daughters to marry men outside his clan, and he brought in thirty
young women from outside his clan to marry his sons. Ibzan judged Israel for seven years.
10When he died, he was buried at Bethlehem.

ELON BECOMES ISRAEL’S JUDGE

11After Ibzan died, Elon from the tribe of Zebulun judged Israel for ten years. 12When he
died, he was buried at Aijalon in Zebulun.

12:8-10 Bethlehem, Ibzan’s hometown, was probably not the same city as the Bethlehem where King David and Jesus Christ were born. That Bethlehem, located a few miles south of Jerusalem in the tribal territory of Judah, was sometimes referred to as Ephrath (Genesis 48:7) or Bethlehem-judah to avoid confusion. Ibzan’s hometown was probably located far north of Jerusalem in the tribal territory of Zebulun, near Jesus’ childhood home of Nazareth.

▸ HOLINESS
12:8-10 Prepare for the future. Have you ever known a parent or a leader who focused on the next generation? Ibzan appears to have been that sort of man. He ruled Israel, but he seems to have spent most of his time managing the relationships of his 60 children, making sure his sons and daughters brought “new blood” into his clan by marrying outside the tribe, strengthening his clan’s relationship with the others. We don’t know much about him, but he appears to have focused on making sure the next generation of Israel was better than the one before. Help the children in your family or church understand how holy, vibrant marriages make the church stronger. (***See Holiness****> Law and Grace> Law> Marriage,* TopicGuide page A41.)

12:8-15 The descriptions of Ibzan and Abdon establish them as men of some prestige for this time period. First of all, the more sons a man had, the greater his status. When Ibzan had his sons and daughters marry outside of his clan, he built alliances that, in a practical sense, doubled his status. The fact that each of Abdon’s sons and grandsons had his own donkey signified money and mobility. The situation would be analogous to each son having his own car when automobiles first came on the market in the West.

▸ HOLINESS
12:11 A nation from every race. Elon’s name tells us that Israel was racially diverse. The first mention of the name *Elon* in the Bible is found in Genesis 26:34, a reference to the Hittite father of one of Esau’s wives. Names like this remind us that the people of God were never an isolated race, but had physical and cultural traces from Egypt, the Hittites, the Moabites, and many other surrounding nations. God allowed some of these influences with His blessing but warned His people to reject influences from the religions of other nations. Accept people from other races and cultures into your family, your church, and your life, and rejoice in the diversity of God’s creation. (***See Holiness****> Law and Grace> Law> God’s Law is good,* TopicGuide page A41.)

ABDON BECOMES ISRAEL'S JUDGE

[13]After Elon died, Abdon son of Hillel, from Pirathon, judged Israel. [14]He had forty
12:14 sons and thirty grandsons, who rode on seventy donkeys. He judged Israel for eight
Judg 5:10 years. [15]When he died, he was buried at Pirathon in Ephraim, in the hill country of the
Amalekites.

THE BIRTH OF SAMSON

13:1 **13** Again the Israelites did evil in the LORD's sight, so the LORD handed them over to
Judg 2:11 the Philistines, who oppressed them for forty years.
13:2 [2]In those days a man named Manoah from the tribe of Dan lived in the town of Zorah.
Josh 19:41 His wife was unable to become pregnant, and they had no children. [3]The Angel of the
13:3 Gen 16:7 LORD appeared to Manoah's wife and said, "Even though you have been unable to have
Judg 6:12 children, you will soon become pregnant and give birth to a son. [4]So be careful; you must
13:4-5 not drink wine or any other alcoholic drink nor eat any forbidden food.* [5]You will become
Num 6:1-5 Judg 13:14 pregnant and give birth to a son, and his hair must never be cut. For he will be dedicated to
Luke 1:15 God as a Nazirite from birth. He will begin to rescue Israel from the Philistines."
13:6 [6]The woman ran and told her husband, "A Man of God appeared to me! He looked like
1 Sam 2:27 one of God's angels, terrifying to see. I didn't ask where He was from, and He didn't tell me
His name. [7]But He told me, 'You will become pregnant and give birth to a son. You must
not drink wine or any other alcoholic drink nor eat any forbidden food. For your son will
be dedicated to God as a Nazirite from the moment of his birth until the day of his death.'"
[8]Then Manoah prayed to the LORD, saying, "Lord, please let the Man of God come back
to us again and give us more instructions about this son who is to be born."
[9]God answered Manoah's prayer, and the Angel of God appeared once again to his wife
as she was sitting in the field. But her husband, Manoah, was not with her. [10]So she quickly
ran and told her husband, "The Man who appeared to me the other day is here again!"

13:4 Hebrew *any unclean thing;* also in 13:7, 14.

▸ WORSHIP

12:13 Elderly, but active. How many seniors do you know who are still active? As people live longer, the retirement mentality that many embrace must be compared to the examples we find in the Bible. Abdon was very likely an elderly man, since he had forty sons and thirty grandsons, but he still served as judge for eight years, applying the wisdom of his years to the good of his people. God wants us to be active in serving Him no matter what our age. (***See Worship****> NT> Prayer> Instructions> Widows to pray,* TopicGuide page A33.)

13:1 After Abdon's judgeship, Israel again sinned against God, so He once again allowed them to be oppressed by the Philistines. This oppression lasted for 40 years, stretching beyond the time covered in the book of Judges. The last of the major judges of Israel, Samson, was still to come, but despite his great deeds, Samson never completely freed the Israelites from Philistine oppression. Indeed, Israel remained under the heel of the Philistines or fighting against them until David became king of all Israel.

▸ BIBLE

13:3 Discovering Christ in the life of Samson. It's not hard to imagine finding truths about Jesus reflected in the lives of heroes like Joseph, Moses, or David, but what about the scoundrel Samson? As with Jesus, Samson's birth was announced by an angel (13:6). Samson's office of judge prefigured Jesus' office of King and reminds us that Jesus came to defeat all God's enemies (Psalm 110:1-6; Hebrews 1:13). Finally, Samson's purposeful demise (Judges 16:24-30) reminds us of Jesus' sacrificial death (Romans 5:15-21). Looking at the rampant sin between Samson's birth and death does make us wonder how it's fair to compare him to Jesus in any way. But that's surely no more a wonder than God welcoming us into His presence and saying, "Well done!" at the end of our journey. Live in gratitude that God's grace works through sinners like Samson and even you. (***See Bible****> Unity> Christ> Christ in Samson's self-sacrificing victory,* TopicGuide page A10.)

13:3-5 Most of the instructions the angel gave to Samson's mother pertained to the vow of the Nazirite. In Numbers 6, Moses gave God's guidelines for a person who chose to set himself apart for God in this way. He was to abstain from alcohol, fermented drinks, grapes and raisins; refrain from cutting his hair for the entire time of the vow; and not go near anything dead. If the person found himself near something dead through no fault of his own, he was required to shave his head completely and renew his vow. Samson's mother was prohibited from drinking wine even while she was pregnant so that Samson's vow would be pure from birth.

13:5 The Nazirite vow could last for a season of time (as little as 30 days) or for a lifetime, but the most famous Nazirites of the Bible were Nazirites for life. Samson was a Nazirite from birth. Samuel, who bridged the gap between the judges and the kings of Israel, was also a Nazirite (1 Samuel 1). In the New Testament, John the Baptist was known as a Nazirite from birth (Luke 1:13-15). Keep in mind that Jesus was referred to as a *Nazarene* because he was from Nazareth. While the words have similar spellings, they have entirely different meanings.

11Manoah ran back with his wife and asked, "Are You the Man who spoke to my wife
the other day?"
"Yes," He replied, "I am."
12So Manoah asked him, "When your words come true, what kind of rules should gov-
ern the boy's life and work?"
13The Angel of the LORD replied, "Be sure your wife follows the instructions I gave her.
14She must not eat grapes or raisins, drink wine or any other alcoholic drink, or eat any
forbidden food."
15Then Manoah said to the Angel of the LORD, "Please stay here until we can prepare a 13:15
young goat for You to eat." Judg 6:19
16"I will stay," the Angel of the LORD replied, "but I will not eat anything. However, you
may prepare a burnt offering as a sacrifice to the LORD." (Manoah didn't realize it was the
Angel of the LORD.)
17Then Manoah asked the Angel of the LORD, "What is Your name? For when all this 13:17
comes true, we want to honor You." Gen 32:29
18"Why do you ask My name?" the Angel of the LORD replied. "It is too wonderful for you
to understand."
19Then Manoah took a young goat and a grain offering and offered it on a rock as a 13:19
sacrifice to the LORD. And as Manoah and his wife watched, the LORD did an amazing Judg 6:20-21
thing. 20As the flames from the altar shot up toward the sky, the Angel of the LORD as-
cended in the fire. When Manoah and his wife saw this, they fell with their faces to the
ground. 13:22
21The Angel did not appear again to Manoah and his wife. Manoah finally realized it Gen 32:30
was the Angel of the LORD, 22and he said to his wife, "We will certainly die, for we have Judg 6:22
seen God!"
23But his wife said, "If the LORD were going to kill us, He wouldn't have accepted our
burnt offering and grain offering. He wouldn't have appeared to us and told us this won- 13:24
derful thing and done these miracles." 1 Sam 3:19
Luke 1:80
24When her son was born, she named him Samson. And the LORD blessed him as he Heb 11:32
grew up. 25And the Spirit of the LORD began to stir him while he lived in Mahaneh-dan, 13:25
which is located between the towns of Zorah and Eshtaol. Judg 3:10; 18:11-12; 1 Sam 10:6, 10

SAMSON'S RIDDLE

14 One day when Samson was in Timnah, one of the Philistine women caught his 14:2
eye. 2When he returned home, he told his father and mother, "A young Philistine Gen 21:21
woman in Timnah caught my eye. I want to marry her. Get her for me."
3His father and mother objected. "Isn't there even one woman in our tribe or among all 14:3
the Israelites you could marry?" they asked. "Why must you go to the pagan Philistines to Deut 7:3
find a wife?"
But Samson told his father, "Get her for me! She looks good to me." 4His father and 14:4
mother didn't realize the LORD was at work in this, creating an opportunity to work against Josh 11:20
the Philistines, who ruled over Israel at that time.

14:3 Samson's infatuation with a Philistine woman met with strong initial resistance from his parents. It seems that they remembered what Samson did not—that God had commanded the Israelites not to intermarry with pagans like the Philistines (Deuteronomy 7:3). Plus, the Israelites were under the Philistines' control, meaning Samson desired to consort with the enemy. Unfortunately, Samson's insistence wore down his parents' resolve so that they eventually gave in and helped him make this sinful marriage.

▸ GOD

14:4 Unusual providence. Someone wise once said, "God draws straight lines with crooked sticks." Or, as wise Joseph said to his brothers, "You intended to harm me, but God intended it all for good" (Genesis 50:20). God sovereignly works His purposes out through, and even in spite of, our actions. This truth in no way excuses our sin, but it does give us assurance that when we sin, God's master plan is not set back. Our sin is never bigger than God's plan. (***See God> God's Attributes> Sovereign> He has a plan for His people and will carry it out,*** TopicGuide page A17.)

[5]As Samson and his parents were going down to Timnah, a young lion suddenly at-
14:6 tacked Samson near the vineyards of Timnah. [6]At that moment the Spirit of the LORD came
Judg 13:25 powerfully upon him, and he ripped the lion's jaws apart with his bare hands. He did it as
1 Sam 17:34-36 easily as if it were a young goat. But he didn't tell his father or mother about it. [7]When
Samson arrived in Timnah, he talked with the woman and was very pleased with her.
[8]Later, when he returned to Timnah for the wedding, he turned off the path to look at
the carcass of the lion. And he found that a swarm of bees had made some honey in the
carcass. [9]He scooped some of the honey into his hands and ate it along the way. He also
gave some to his father and mother, and they ate it. But he didn't tell them he had taken
the honey from the carcass of the lion.
[10]As his father was making final arrangements for the marriage, Samson threw a party
at Timnah, as was the custom for elite young men. [11]When the bride's parents* saw him,
they selected thirty young men from the town to be his companions.
14:12 [12]Samson said to them, "Let me tell you a riddle. If you solve my riddle during these
Gen 29:27 seven days of the celebration, I will give you thirty fine linen robes and thirty sets of festive
Ezek 17:2 clothing. [13]But if you can't solve it, then you must give me thirty fine linen robes and thirty
sets of festive clothing."
"All right," they agreed, "let's hear your riddle."
[14]So he said:

"Out of the one who eats came something to eat;
out of the strong came something sweet."

14:15 Three days later they were still trying to figure it out. [15]On the fourth* day they said
Judg 15:6; 16:5 to Samson's wife, "Entice your husband to explain the riddle for us, or we will burn
down your father's house with you in it. Did you invite us to this party just to make us
poor?"
[16]So Samson's wife came to him in tears and said, "You don't love me; you hate me!
You have given my people a riddle, but you haven't told me the answer."
"I haven't even given the answer to my father or mother," he replied. "Why should I tell
you?" [17]So she cried whenever she was with him and kept it up for the rest of the celebra-
tion. At last, on the seventh day he told her the answer because she was tormenting him
with her nagging. Then she explained the riddle to the young men.
[18]So before sunset of the seventh day, the men of the town came to Samson with their
answer:

14:11 Hebrew *they.* 14:15 As in Greek version; Hebrew reads *seventh.*

14:6 Judges speaks of the Spirit of God coming upon several judges, including Othniel (3:10), Gideon (6:34), and Jephthah (11:29). But Samson is the most frequent recipient of the Spirit's visitations (13:25; 14:6, 19; 15:14). In all cases, the Spirit enabled the judges to lead the Israelites against their enemies; but in Samson's case the Spirit always manifested itself in feats of great individual strength.

14:9 The fact that Samson, a Nazirite, took the honey from a carcass was a problem. A Nazirite was to keep himself from contact with dead bodies at all costs (Numbers 6:6). This command, like most of the Bible's commands regarding cleanness and uncleanness, held a lesson about the nature of God: God was (and is) the source of all life, while sin, humanity's broken relationship with God, was (and is) the source of death. As a form of decay and destruction, death is the opposite of who God is.

▶ ADOPTION

14:17 Pestering or peacemaking? What a pair! Samson betrayed his vows to God by courting a pagan woman, while she betrayed her betrothal vows to Samson at the threat of death to her family. We can sympathize with her reasons for breaking her vows, but Samson continued his path of violence with revenge as his only justification. How do you and those you love break promises to each other? Do you enable those around you to be more obedient or less so? Ask God to make you an instrument of His peace and holiness in the lives of those around you. (***See Adoption*** *> With Christ> Supernatural> A life of everlasting peace,* TopicGuide page A37.)

14:19 Ashkelon was one of the five principal cities of Philistia. Samson was in the midst of a wedding celebration with a Philistine bride, yet he killed Philistine men for the clothing to pay off his bet. Many of Samson's dealings were with the Philistines; in the end he was one of the great forces of Israel against the Philistines.

"What is sweeter than honey?
What is stronger than a lion?"

Samson replied, "If you hadn't plowed with my heifer, you wouldn't have solved my
riddle!"

19 Then the Spirit of the LORD came powerfully upon him. He went down to the town of 14:19
Ashkelon, killed thirty men, took their belongings, and gave their clothing to the men who Judg 3:10
had solved his riddle. But Samson was furious about what had happened, and he went
back home to live with his father and mother. 20 So his wife was given in marriage to the 14:20
man who had been Samson's best man at the wedding. John 3:29

SAMSON'S VENGEANCE ON THE PHILISTINES

15 Later on, during the wheat harvest, Samson took a young goat as a present to his
wife. He said, "I'm going into my wife's room to sleep with her," but her father
wouldn't let him in.

2 "I truly thought you must hate her," her father explained, "so I gave her in marriage to 15:2
your best man. But look, her younger sister is even more beautiful than she is. Marry her Judg 14:20
instead."

3 Samson said, "This time I cannot be blamed for everything I am going to do to you
Philistines." 4 Then he went out and caught 300 foxes. He tied their tails together in
pairs, and he fastened a torch to each pair of tails. 5 Then he lit the torches and let the
foxes run through the grain fields of the Philistines. He burned all their grain to the
ground, including the sheaves and the uncut grain. He also destroyed their vineyards and
olive groves.

6 "Who did this?" the Philistines demanded. 15:6

"Samson," was the reply, "because his father-in-law from Timnah gave Samson's wife to Judg 14:15
be married to his best man." So the Philistines went and got the woman and her father and
burned them to death.

7 "Because you did this," Samson vowed, "I won't rest until I take my revenge on you!"
8 So he attacked the Philistines with great fury and killed many of them. Then he went to
live in a cave in the rock of Etam.

9 The Philistines retaliated by setting up camp in Judah and spreading out near the town
of Lehi. 10 The men of Judah asked the Philistines, "Why are you attacking us?"

The Philistines replied, "We've come to capture Samson. We've come to pay him back
for what he did to us."

11 So 3,000 men of Judah went down to get Samson at the cave in the rock of Etam. They 15:11
said to Samson, "Don't you realize the Philistines rule over us? What are you doing to us?" Judg 13:1; 14:4;
But Samson replied, "I only did to them what they did to me." 15:20

12 But the men of Judah told him, "We have come to tie you up and hand you over to the
Philistines."

15:1-5 In burning the wheat—both harvested and unharvested—and the vineyards and the olive trees, Samson wiped out the three main crops of the region. This act clearly designated Samson as a man to be reckoned with. He continued to establish this fact throughout the conflicts described over the rest of this chapter and the beginning of chapter 16.

15:11 In the case of Samson, it seems God sent a deliverer even before His people cried out for His aid. The men of Judah seem to have had no desire to back Samson's efforts to throw off the Philistine yoke. Instead, they were so content that they actually reproached Samson for defying the Philistines. And they were willing to hand him over without a fight in order to keep peace.

▸ WORSHIP

15:12 Watch your temper. Samson knew that he would lash out at whoever tried to kill him, and he didn't want it to be his own people. In a portrayal of Samson that is so far negative, Samson's commitment to killing Philistines instead of Israelites is a moral victory for him. Do you know yourself well enough to foresee when you will fall? Ask God to give you the grace to see your faults so you can protect others from their consequences. (***See Worship****> NT> Our Role> Attitude> Cooperative with other believers,* TopicGuide page A31.)

“All right,” Samson said. “But promise that you won’t kill me yourselves.”
13“We will only tie you up and hand you over to the Philistines,” they replied. “We won’t
kill you.” So they tied him up with two new ropes and brought him up from the rock.
15:14 14As Samson arrived at Lehi, the Philistines came shouting in triumph. But the Spirit of the
Judg 14:19 LORD came powerfully upon Samson, and he snapped the ropes on his arms as if they were
15:15 burnt strands of flax, and they fell from his wrists. 15Then he found the jawbone of a recently
Lev 26:8 killed donkey. He picked it up and killed 1,000 Philistines with it. 16Then Samson said,

“With the jawbone of a donkey,
I’ve piled them in heaps!
With the jawbone of a donkey,
I’ve killed a thousand men!”

17When he finished his boasting, he threw away the jawbone; and the place was named
Jawbone Hill.*
18Samson was now very thirsty, and he cried out to the LORD, “You have accomplished
this great victory by the strength of Your servant. Must I now die of thirst and fall into the
15:19 hands of these pagans?” 19So God caused water to gush out of a hollow in the ground at
Gen 45:27 Lehi, and Samson was revived as he drank. Then he named that place “The Spring of the
1 Sam 30:12 Isa 40:29 One Who Cried Out,”* and it is still in Lehi to this day.
15:20 20Samson judged Israel for twenty years during the period when the Philistines domi-
Heb 11:32 nated the land.

SAMSON CARRIES AWAY GAZA’S GATES

16:1 **16** One day Samson went to the Philistine town of Gaza and spent the night with a
Josh 15:47 prostitute. 2Word soon spread* that Samson was there, so the men of Gaza gath-
16:2 ered together and waited all night at the town gates. They kept quiet during the night, say-
Ps 118:10-12 ing to themselves, “When the light of morning comes, we will kill him.”
3But Samson stayed in bed only until midnight. Then he got up, took hold of the doors
of the town gate, including the two posts, and lifted them up, bar and all. He put them on
his shoulders and carried them all the way to the top of the hill across from Hebron.

15:17 Hebrew *Ramath-lehi.* 15:19 Hebrew *En-hakkore.* 16:2 As in Greek and Syriac versions and Latin Vulgate; Hebrew lacks *Word soon spread.*

15:14 Flax is a slender plant that grew to a height of three or four feet, with a blue flower. Its fibers are used to make linen cloth as well as linseed oil. The process of making linen requires soaking the flax in water to separate the fibers. The stalks are then spread out to dry in the sun. A woman named Rahab hid Israelite spies under piles of drying flax (Joshua 2). The comparison of the ropes to burnt flax, which would have been extremely fragile, indicated the ease with which Samson broke free.

▸GOD

15:18 Satisfied with God. Like ungrateful Israel, Samson beheld the wonder of God’s power to rescue him, but instead of responding with worship, he complained that he still had not received enough from God. The Spirit made Samson’s body strong, but his heart and mind remained weak in their understanding of God’s true nature (Romans 8:5-8). And yet, God graciously provided Samson with water, in spite of his ingratitude. Thank God for his mercy toward His ungrateful people! (***See God****> God’s Attributes> Merciful> God is merciful to sinners,* TopicGuide page A17.)

16:1-3 It is unclear whether Samson carried the Gaza gates all the way to Hebron, a distance of some 40 miles, or merely to a hill that faced Hebron. Certainly he could have carried the gates the whole distance by the power of the Spirit. However, the significance of this incident lies not in Samson’s display of strength but in what he lifted. By removing the gates, he took away Gaza’s security. While the men were planning his death, Samson removed the most basic form of protection that any city had—gates to guard the entrance.

16:3 Hebron was a place of great significance for the Israelites. It was near Hebron that Abraham first camped in the land of Canaan and received God’s promise that the land one day would belong to him (Genesis 13). It was also in this place that Abraham bought a cave that became his family burial plot (Genesis 23). Abraham’s grandson Jacob (the man whose 12 sons became the 12 tribes of Israel), made his home in Hebron before moving to Egypt in a famine (Genesis 35). When the great King David finally came to the throne, Hebron was his capital city for years before Jerusalem (2 Samuel 2:1-4). Later, David’s son Absalom launched a revolt against his father from Hebron.

SAMSON AND DELILAH

4Some time later Samson fell in love with a woman named Delilah, who lived in the valley
of Sorek. 5The rulers of the Philistines went to her and said, "Entice Samson to tell you
what makes him so strong and how he can be overpowered and tied up securely. Then
each of us will give you 1,100 pieces* of silver."
6So Delilah said to Samson, "Please tell me what makes you so strong and what it would
take to tie you up securely."
7Samson replied, "If I were tied up with seven new bowstrings that have not yet been
dried, I would become as weak as anyone else."
8So the Philistine rulers brought Delilah seven new bowstrings, and she tied Samson up
with them. 9She had hidden some men in one of the inner rooms of her house, and she
cried out, "Samson! The Philistines have come to capture you!" But Samson snapped the
bowstrings as a piece of string snaps when it is burned by a fire. So the secret of his
strength was not discovered.
10Afterward Delilah said to him, "You've been making fun of me and telling me lies!
Now please tell me how you can be tied up securely."
11Samson replied, "If I were tied up with brand-new ropes that had never been used, I
would become as weak as anyone else."
12So Delilah took new ropes and tied him up with them. The men were hiding in the in-
ner room as before, and again Delilah cried out, "Samson! The Philistines have come to
capture you!" But again Samson snapped the ropes from his arms as if they were thread.
13Then Delilah said, "You've been making fun of me and telling me lies! Now tell me
how you can be tied up securely."
Samson replied, "If you were to weave the seven braids of my hair into the fabric on
your loom and tighten it with the loom shuttle, I would become as weak as anyone else."
So while he slept, Delilah wove the seven braids of his hair into the fabric. 14Then she
tightened it with the loom shuttle.* Again she cried out, "Samson! The Philistines have
come to capture you!" But Samson woke up, pulled back the loom shuttle, and yanked his
hair away from the loom and the fabric.
15Then Delilah pouted, "How can you tell me, 'I love you,' when you don't share your
secrets with me? You've made fun of me three times now, and you still haven't told me
what makes you so strong!" 16She tormented him with her nagging day after day until he
was sick to death of it.
17Finally, Samson shared his secret with her. "My hair has never been cut," he con-
fessed, "for I was dedicated to God as a Nazirite from birth. If my head were shaved, my
strength would leave me, and I would become as weak as anyone else."
18Delilah realized he had finally told her the truth, so she sent for the Philistine rulers.
"Come back one more time," she said, "for he has finally told me his secret." So the Philis-
tine rulers returned with the money in their hands. 19Delilah lulled Samson to sleep with
his head in her lap, and then she called in a man to shave off the seven locks of his hair. In
this way she began to bring him down,* and his strength left him.

16:5 Judg 14:15
16:11 Judg 15:13
16:15 Judg 14:16
16:17 Num 6:2, 5; Judg 13:5

16:5 Hebrew *1,100 shekels,* about 28 pounds or 12.5 kilograms in weight. 16:13-14 As in Greek version and Latin Vulgate; Hebrew lacks *I would become as weak as anyone else. / So while he slept, Delilah wove the seven braids of his hair into the fabric. 14Then she tightened it with the loom shuttle.* 16:19 Or *she began to torment him.* Greek version reads *He began to grow weak.*

▶ GOD

16:17 Keeping secrets. What does it mean to be grateful? Is it as simple as saying "please" or "thank you," or is there something more? Samson demonstrated an ungrateful heart by showing disdain for the gifts of God and failing to keep his promises to God. By this time, Samson had failed to keep his Nazirite vow in every way except in the cutting of his hair. By sharing with Delilah the only thing holy left in his life with the knowledge that she would act as before and try to see him defiled and captured, Samson broke his covenant with God. As a result, his power was taken away. God finally allowed Samson to experience the consequences of his great ingratitude toward Him. Do you walk a path similar to Samson's? What can you do to avoid whining or complaining? (***See God****> God's Attributes> Faithful> God deserves thanks for His constant faithfulness,* TopicGuide page A16.)

16:20 20 Then she cried out, "Samson! The Philistines have come to capture you!"
1 Sam 16:14; 18:12 When he woke up, he thought, "I will do as before and shake myself free." But he didn't
realize the LORD had left him.
21 So the Philistines captured him and gouged out his eyes. They took him to Gaza,
where he was bound with bronze chains and forced to grind grain in the prison.
22 But before long, his hair began to grow back.

SAMSON'S FINAL VICTORY

16:23 23 The Philistine rulers held a great festival, offering sacrifices and praising their god, Da-
1 Sam 5:2 gon. They said, "Our god has given us victory over our enemy Samson!"
24 When the people saw him, they praised their god, saying, "Our god has delivered our
enemy to us! The one who killed so many of us is now in our power!"
25 Half drunk by now, the people demanded, "Bring out Samson so he can amuse us!" So
he was brought from the prison to amuse them, and they had him stand between the pil-
lars supporting the roof.
26 Samson said to the young servant who was leading him by the hand, "Place my hands
against the pillars that hold up the temple. I want to rest against them." 27 Now the temple
was completely filled with people. All the Philistine rulers were there, and there were
about 3,000 men and women on the roof who were watching as Samson amused them.
16:28 28 Then Samson prayed to the LORD, "Sovereign LORD, remember me again. O God,
Judg 15:18 please strengthen me just one more time. With one blow let me pay back the Philistines
for the loss of my two eyes." 29 Then Samson put his hands on the two center pillars that
held up the temple. Pushing against them with both hands, 30 he prayed, "Let me die with
the Philistines." And the temple crashed down on the Philistine rulers and all the people.
So he killed more people when he died than he had during his entire lifetime.
16:31 31 Later his brothers and other relatives went down to get his body. They took him back
Judg 15:20 home and buried him between Zorah and Eshtaol, where his father, Manoah, was buried.
Samson had judged Israel for twenty years.

MICAH'S IDOLS

17 There was a man named Micah, who lived in the hill country of Ephraim. 2 One
day he said to his mother, "I heard you place a curse on the person who stole
1,100 pieces* of silver from you. Well, I have the money. I was the one who took it."
17:3 "The LORD bless you for admitting it," his mother replied. 3 He returned the money to her,
Exod 20:4, 23; 34:17 and she said, "I now dedicate these silver coins to the LORD. In honor of my son, I will have
an image carved and an idol cast."

17:2 Hebrew *1,100 shekels,* about 28 pounds or 12.5 kilograms in weight.

▸ GOD
16:28 One last time. Selfishness can pollute even our finest moments. In Samson's second and final recorded prayer (see 15:18 for his first), he asked God to empower him to take revenge on those who had blinded him. But vengeance belongs to God, not to man (Psalm 94:1; Deuteronomy 32:34-35). God still used Samson to accomplish His overall goal for his life: divine judgment upon the Philistines for their abuse of God's people (Judges 13:5). (***See God****> God's Nature> Personality> Emotion> God executes vengeance on all disobedient nations,* TopicGuide page A14.)

17:1 The first 16 chapters of Judges contain a record of events in the nation of Israel that is roughly chronological. However, the language and circumstances of the last 5 chapters (17–21) reveal that these chapters probably happened before or during the events already described in this book. They reveal the deplorable state of the nation—the polytheism, the violence, and the lack of a sense of history.

▸ HOLINESS
17:2 Spare the rod. Is it such a bad thing to let your children get away with a few naughty behaviors? Such parental permissiveness was a prime example of why Israel needed a godly king. In this final section of Judges, we see that if life was bad with fallible judges like Samson, life without them was even worse. The story of Micah's home is a snapshot of terrible permissiveness, immorality, and idolatry. God is honored by the loving, firm approach to training children that is taught in Scripture. To allow children to go without proper discipline is, just as in the time of the judges, a sign that there is no godly leadership present (17:6). (***See Holiness****> Law and Grace> Law> Parents and children,* TopicGuide page A41.)

4So when he returned the money to his mother, she took 200 silver coins and gave
them to a silversmith, who made them into an image and an idol. And these were placed
in Micah's house. 5Micah set up a shrine for the idol, and he made a sacred ephod and **17:5**
some household idols. Then he installed one of his sons as his personal priest. Gen 31:19 Judg 8:27
6In those days Israel had no king; all the people did whatever seemed right in their own **17:6**
eyes. Deut 12:8
7One day a young Levite, who had been living in Bethlehem in Judah, arrived in that Judg 18:1; 19:1; 21:25
area. 8He had left Bethlehem in search of another place to live, and as he traveled, he
came to the hill country of Ephraim. He happened to stop at Micah's house as he was trav- **17:7** Judg 19:1
eling through. 9"Where are you from?" Micah asked him. He replied, "I am a Levite from Ruth 1:1-2
Bethlehem in Judah, and I am looking for a place to live." Mic 5:2 Matt 2:1
10"Stay here with me," Micah said, "and you can be a father and priest to me. I will give **17:10**
you ten pieces* of silver a year, plus a change of clothes and your food." 11The Levite Judg 18:19
agreed to this, and the young man became like one of Micah's sons.
12So Micah installed the Levite as his personal priest, and he lived in Micah's house. 13"I **17:12**
know the LORD will bless me now," Micah said, "because I have a Levite serving as my priest." Num 16:10 Judg 18:1-7

IDOLATRY IN THE TRIBE OF DAN

18 Now in those days Israel had no king. And the tribe of Dan was trying to find a **18:1**
place where they could settle, for they had not yet moved into the land assigned Josh 19:40-48
to them when the land was divided among the tribes of Israel. 2So the men of Dan chose Judg 17:6; 19:1 **18:2**
from their clans five capable warriors from the towns of Zorah and Eshtaol to scout out a Judg 13:25
land for them to settle in.
When these warriors arrived in the hill country of Ephraim, they came to Micah's house
and spent the night there. 3While at Micah's house, they recognized the young Levite's ac-
cent, so they went over and asked him, "Who brought you here, and what are you doing
in this place? Why are you here?" 4He told them about his agreement with Micah and that
he had been hired as Micah's personal priest. **18:4** Judg 17:10-12
5Then they said, "Ask God whether or not our journey will be successful."
6"Go in peace," the priest replied. "For the LORD is watching over your journey."
7So the five men went on to the town of Laish, where they noticed the people living **18:7**
carefree lives, like the Sidonians; they were peaceful and secure.* The people were also Josh 19:47

17:10 Hebrew *10 shekels,* about 4 ounces or 114 grams in weight. 18:7 The meaning of the Hebrew is uncertain.

17:5-6 This story of Micah reveals just how far the Israelites had fallen from their original vision of obedience. Moses and Joshua had instructed the people to worship only God, to use no images in their worship, and to make their sacrifices at one central place of worship (Exodus 20). But as the people began to do whatever seemed right to them, Micah made images or idols of numerous gods and turned his home into a shrine to them. He also made his son a priest, even though God said only the Levites should serve in ministry and only the descendants of Aaron should be priests (Exodus 28). Micah did at least recognize God's law when he stated that God would bless him once an actual Levite came to serve as priest (17:13).

17:5 An ephod was a ceremonial vest. The most famous ephod was the one worn by the high priest. It was highly decorative, with the names of the 12 tribes of Israel inscribed on precious stones. Gideon, a former judge, made his own ephod. Unfortunately it became an *object* of worship rather than a *tool* of worship. According to Judges 8:27, it even became a trap for Gideon and his family. Micah's creation of an ephod revealed that religious practices in Israel no longer conformed to any national understanding but were "up for grabs" for each citizen.

▸GOD

17:13 Sin blinds us. "I believe I am closer to God than ever," said a remorseless man who was explaining his abandonment of his family and marriage. It is a sad fact—just like Micah—when we are in our deepest sin, we often attempt to convince ourselves (and others around us) that we are doing God's will. But our feelings of happiness or sadness are not the ultimate guides to whether we are close to God. The fruit of the Holy Spirit being produced in our lives is a much better indicator of God's blessing on us. Trust God's ways of showing His blessing on your life, not your fickle feelings. (***See God****> God's Names> Holy Spirit> Produces spiritual fruit,* TopicGuide page A19.)

18:5-10 The warriors of Dan took advantage of their encounter with Micah's personal priest and had him ask God whether their search for a new home would be successful. Of course, as an improperly ordained priest using an unauthorized ephod, the Levite had no right to consult God, and he could not be depended upon to convey God's true answer. Nevertheless, he confidently assured the men of Dan that they would succeed, and they foolishly trusted him.

wealthy because their land was very fertile. And they lived a great distance from Sidon
and had no allies nearby.
8When the men returned to Zorah and Eshtaol, their relatives asked them, "What did
you find?"
9The men replied, "Come on, let's attack them! We have seen the land, and it is very
18:10 good. What are you waiting for? Don't hesitate to go and take possession of it. 10When
Deut 8:9 you get there, you will find the people living carefree lives. God has given us a spacious
and fertile land, lacking in nothing!"
11So 600 men from the tribe of Dan, armed with weapons of war, set out from Zorah
and Eshtaol. 12They camped at a place west of Kiriath-jearim in Judah, which is called
Mahaneh-dan* to this day. 13Then they went on from there into the hill country of Ephraim
and came to the house of Micah.
18:14 14The five men who had scouted out the land around Laish explained to the others,
Judg 17:5 "These buildings contain a sacred ephod, as well as some household idols, a carved im-
age, and a cast idol. What do you think you should do?" 15Then the five men turned off
the road and went over to Micah's house, where the young Levite lived, and greeted him
kindly. 16As the 600 armed warriors from the tribe of Dan stood at the entrance of the
gate, 17the five scouts entered the shrine and removed the carved image, the sacred
ephod, the household idols, and the cast idol. Meanwhile, the priest was standing at the
gate with the 600 armed warriors.
18When the priest saw the men carrying all the sacred objects out of Micah's shrine, he
said, "What are you doing?"
18:19 19"Be quiet and come with us," they said. "Be a father and priest to all of us. Isn't it
Judg 17:10 better to be a priest for an entire tribe and clan of Israel than for the household of just one
man?"
20The young priest was quite happy to go with them, so he took along the sacred
ephod, the household idols, and the carved image. 21They turned and started on their
way again, placing their children, livestock, and possessions in front of them.
22When the people from the tribe of Dan were quite a distance from Micah's house, the
people who lived near Micah came chasing after them. 23They were shouting as they
caught up with them. The men of Dan turned around and said to Micah, "What's the mat-
ter? Why have you called these men together and chased after us like this?"
24"What do you mean, 'What's the matter?'" Micah replied. "You've taken away all the
gods I have made, and my priest, and I have nothing left!"
25The men of Dan said, "Watch what you say! There are some short-tempered men
around here who might get angry and kill you and your family." 26So the men of Dan

18:12 *Mahaneh-dan* means "the camp of Dan."

▸ WORSHIP

18:20 Chaotic clergy. One of the signs of the deterioration of Israel under the judges was chaos among the clergy. This young Levite had long since given up worshiping God as he was commanded. Now his loyalties to Micah were tested and immediately revealed as lacking. Here was a member of the tribe of Levi who had no character whatsoever. Do you see godly men in leadership in your church or denomination? Where are the loyalties of those who stand as your spiritual leaders? Ask God to raise up people of character to shepherd His flock. (***See Worship****> NT> Church Government> Qualifications for elders,* TopicGuide page A30.)

▸ GOD

18:24 True values. "You've taken away all the gods I have made, and my priest, and I have nothing left!" When we love other things or people more than God, our values become confused. Micah put all his hope in his false god served by his false Levite priest. With those taken away, Micah was just an ordinary man. This is why Micah risked his life to save his worthless idols and no-good priest. Today, people live and die for new technology, the latest clothing, and other idols of materialism. But those who have Christ have everything, and God promises that while we may be poor in the eyes of the world, one day we will inherit the greatest blessings of God's creation (Psalm 2:8; Luke 12:21; Matthew 5:5). (***See God****> God's Nature> Alive> God lives; idols don't,* TopicGuide page A14.)

continued on their way. When Micah saw that there were too many of them for him to at-
tack, he turned around and went home.
27 Then, with Micah's idols and his priest, the men of Dan came to the town of Laish, 18:27
whose people were peaceful and secure. They attacked with swords and burned the Josh 19:47
town to the ground. 28 There was no one to rescue the people, for they lived a great
distance from Sidon and had no allies nearby. This happened in the valley near Beth- 18:28
rehob. 2 Sam 10:6
Then the people of the tribe of Dan rebuilt the town and lived there. 29 They renamed
the town Dan after their ancestor, Israel's son, but it had originally been called Laish.
30 Then they set up the carved image, and they appointed Jonathan son of Gershom, 18:30
son of Moses,* as their priest. This family continued as priests for the tribe of Dan until the Exod 2:22; 18:3
Exile. 31 So Micah's carved image was worshiped by the tribe of Dan as long as the Taber- 18:31
nacle of God remained at Shiloh. Josh 18:1

THE LEVITE AND HIS CONCUBINE

19 Now in those days Israel had no king. There was a man from the tribe of Levi liv- 19:1
ing in a remote area of the hill country of Ephraim. One day he brought home a Judg 18:1
woman from Bethlehem in Judah to be his concubine. 2 But she became angry with him*
and returned to her father's home in Bethlehem.
After about four months, 3 her husband set out for Bethlehem to speak personally to her 19:3
and persuade her to come back. He took with him a servant and a pair of donkeys. When Gen 34:3; 50:21
he arrived at* her father's house, her father saw him and welcomed him. 4 Her father urged
him to stay awhile, so he stayed three days, eating, drinking, and sleeping there.
5 On the fourth day the man was up early, ready to leave, but the woman's father said to 19:5
his son-in-law, "Have something to eat before you go." 6 So the two men sat down together Gen 18:5
and had something to eat and drink. Then the woman's father said, "Please stay another
night and enjoy yourself." 7 The man got up to leave, but his father-in-law kept urging him
to stay, so he finally gave in and stayed the night.
8 On the morning of the fifth day he was up early again, ready to leave, and again the
woman's father said, "Have something to eat; then you can leave later this afternoon." So
they had another day of feasting. 9 Later, as the man and his concubine and servant were
preparing to leave, his father-in-law said, "Look, it's almost evening. Stay the night and en-
joy yourself. Tomorrow you can get up early and be on your way." 19:10
10 But this time the man was determined to leave. So he took his two saddled donkeys Josh 15:8; 1 Chr 11:4-5
and his concubine and headed in the direction of Jebus (that is, Jerusalem). 11 It was late in 19:11
Judg 19:19

18:30 As in an ancient Hebrew tradition, some Greek manuscripts, and Latin Vulgate; Masoretic Text reads *son of Manasseh.* 19:2 Or *she was unfaithful to him.* 19:3 As in Greek version; Hebrew reads *When she brought him to.*

18:31 The author of Judges has already noted (18:1) that there was no king in Israel "in those days," meaning the time of the judges. By recounting the messy history of the judges, the author hoped to make the case for a monarchy in Israel. But not just any monarch would do—the author was a proponent of David. This historical notation is a subtle argument for David's moral leadership, for it was he who moved the Ark of the Covenant to its new location at Jerusalem, thus reestablishing proper worship of God in Israel.

▶ HOLINESS
19:1 Israel had no king. Have you ever had a job where the boss was never present? Or been in a church where the pastor was not really leading? The author of Judges repeats his theme—Israel is without a king—and tells another story to highlight how bad things could be without godly leadership. Our nations, our churches, and our families desperately need godly leaders if we are going to live dynamic lives that affect our world with the good news of the Gospel. Wherever you are, either follow the leader or be the leader. These are our only two choices. (***See Holiness*> *Law and Grace*> *Law*> *Leaders and followers,*** TopicGuide page A41.)

19:4-21 The Levite's father-in-law was exceedingly hospitable. But when the Levite finally started home with his concubine, he found no welcome. He rejected his servant's suggestion that they spend the night in Jerusalem because the Jebusites occupied it. Instead, he pressed on to Gibeah, an Israelite city in the territory of the tribe of Benjamin. He was counting on the people of Gibeah to obey God's command of hospitality to strangers (Exodus 23:9; Deuteronomy 10:19), but no one invited them in. Only the hospitality of one who was himself a stranger prevented them from sleeping in the open town square.

the day when they neared Jebus, and the man's servant said to him, "Let's stop at this Jeb-
usite town and spend the night there."
12"No," his master said, "we can't stay in this foreign town where there are no Israelites.
Instead, we will go on to Gibeah. 13Come on, let's try to get as far as Gibeah or Ramah, and
we'll spend the night in one of those towns." 14So they went on. The sun was setting as
they came to Gibeah, a town in the land of Benjamin, 15so they stopped there to spend the
night. They rested in the town square, but no one took them in for the night.
19:16 16That evening an old man came home from his work in the fields. He was from the hill
Ps 104:23 country of Ephraim, but he was living in Gibeah, where the people were from the tribe of
Benjamin. 17When he saw the travelers sitting in the town square, he asked them where
they were from and where they were going.
19:18 18"We have been in Bethlehem in Judah," the man replied. "We are on our way to a re-
Judg 18:31 mote area in the hill country of Ephraim, which is my home. I traveled to Bethlehem, and
now I'm returning home.* But no one has taken us in for the night, 19even though we have
everything we need. We have straw and feed for our donkeys and plenty of bread and
wine for ourselves."
20"You are welcome to stay with me," the old man said. "I will give you anything you might
19:21 need. But whatever you do, don't spend the night in the square." 21So he took them home
Gen 24:32-33 with him and fed the donkeys. After they washed their feet, they ate and drank together.
19:22 22While they were enjoying themselves, a crowd of troublemakers from the town sur-
Gen 19:4-5 rounded the house. They began beating at the door and shouting to the old man, "Bring
19:23 Gen 34:7 out the man who is staying with you so we can have sex with him."
2 Sam 13:12 23The old man stepped outside to talk to them. "No, my brothers, don't do such an evil
19:24 thing. For this man is a guest in my house, and such a thing would be shameful. 24Here, take
Gen 19:8 my virgin daughter and this man's concubine. I will bring them out to you, and you can
abuse them and do whatever you like. But don't do such a shameful thing to this man."
25But they wouldn't listen to him. So the Levite took hold of his concubine and pushed her
out the door. The men of the town abused her all night, taking turns raping her until morning.
Finally, at dawn they let her go. 26At daybreak the woman returned to the house where her
husband was staying. She collapsed at the door of the house and lay there until it was light.
27When her husband opened the door to leave, there lay his concubine with her hands
19:28 on the threshold. 28He said, "Get up! Let's go!" But there was no answer.* So he put her
Judg 20:5 body on his donkey and took her home.
19:29 29When he got home, he took a knife and cut his concubine's body into twelve pieces.
1 Sam 11:7 Then he sent one piece to each tribe throughout all the territory of Israel.
19:30 30Everyone who saw it said, "Such a horrible crime has not been committed in all the time
Judg 20:7 since Israel left Egypt. Think about it! What are we going to do? Who's going to speak up?"

19:18 As in Greek version (see also 19:29); Hebrew reads *now I'm going to the Tabernacle of the LORD.* 19:28 Greek version adds *for she was dead.*

19:12-13 There was more than one ancient town named Gibeah. This Gibeah was probably a town less than ten miles north of Jerusalem. It is mentioned in the book of Joshua as a part of the tribal region of Benjamin. Gibeah was the hometown of Israel's first king, Saul.

19:22-24 The horrendous trade-off proffered here—two women for one man—was reminiscent of the wickedness of Sodom and Gomorrah. Before the destruction of the two cities, angels of God appeared in Sodom to talk with Lot. The wicked men of the town came to Lot's house, demanding that he offer his guests to them. Lot negotiated with the men, offering his two virgin daughters instead of his two sacred houseguests. The angels intervened, saving Lot's life (Genesis 19:1-11). Unfortunately, the Levite's concubine had no such rescuers.

▸HOLINESS

19:25 Godless violence. This is one of the most brutal, shocking stories in the Bible, and the author intended it to be so. A Levite sacrificing his concubine to a rape gang, the murder of an innocent woman, dismemberment of her corpse—there was no end to the depths of unhindered human depravity. This was the author's final argument to prove that the lack of a godly king was devastating to the culture of Israel. And it is a horrifying warning that we need godly authority and accountability in our lives or we will be a force for chaos in the lives of those around us. (***See Holiness**> Set Apart> Religious Service> Priests and Levites,* TopicGuide page A40.)

ISRAEL'S WAR WITH BENJAMIN

20 Then all the Israelites were united as one man, from Dan in the north to Beer- 20:1
sheba in the south, including those from across the Jordan in the land of Gilead. 1 Sam 7:5
The entire community assembled in the presence of the LORD at Mizpah. 2The leaders of
all the people and all the tribes of Israel—400,000 warriors armed with swords—took their
positions in the assembly of the people of God. 3(Word soon reached the land of Benjamin
that the other tribes had gone up to Mizpah.) The Israelites then asked how this terrible
crime had happened.
4The Levite, the husband of the woman who had been murdered, said, "My concubine
and I came to spend the night in Gibeah, a town that belongs to the people of Benjamin.
5That night some of the leading citizens of Gibeah surrounded the house, planning to kill 20:5
me, and they raped my concubine until she was dead. 6So I cut her body into twelve Judg 19:22, 25-26
pieces and sent the pieces throughout the territory assigned to Israel, for these men have
committed a terrible and shameful crime. 7Now then, all of you—the entire community of 20:6-7
Israel—must decide here and now what should be done about this!" Judg 19:29-30
8And all the people rose to their feet in unison and declared, "None of us will return
home! No, not even one of us! 9Instead, this is what we will do to Gibeah; we will draw lots
to decide who will attack it. 10One tenth of the men* from each tribe will be chosen to sup-
ply the warriors with food, and the rest of us will take revenge on Gibeah* of Benjamin for
this shameful thing they have done in Israel." 11So all the Israelites were completely
united, and they gathered together to attack the town. 20:12
12The Israelites sent messengers to the tribe of Benjamin, saying, "What a terrible thing Deut 13:14
has been done among you! 13Give up those evil men, those troublemakers from Gibeah, 20:13
so we can execute them and purge Israel of this evil." 1 Cor 5:13
But the people of Benjamin would not listen. 14Instead, they came from their towns and
gathered at Gibeah to fight the Israelites. 15In all, 26,000 of their warriors armed with
swords arrived in Gibeah to join the 700 elite troops who lived there. 16Among Benjamin's 20:16
elite troops, 700 were left-handed, and each of them could sling a rock and hit a target Judg 3:15
within a hairsbreadth without missing. 17Israel had 400,000 experienced soldiers armed
with swords, not counting Benjamin's warriors.
18Before the battle the Israelites went to Bethel and asked God, "Which tribe should go 20:18
first to attack the people of Benjamin?" Num 27:21
The LORD answered, "Judah is to go first." Judg 1:1
19So the Israelites left early the next morning and camped near Gibeah. 20Then they ad-
vanced toward Gibeah to attack the men of Benjamin. 21But Benjamin's warriors, who
were defending the town, came out and killed 22,000 Israelites on the battlefield that
day.
22But the Israelites encouraged each other and took their positions again at the same 20:22
place they had fought the previous day. 23For they had gone up to Bethel and wept in the Josh 7:6-7

20:10a Hebrew *10 men from every hundred, 100 men from every thousand, and 1,000 men from every 10,000.* 20:10b Hebrew *Geba,* in this case a variant spelling of Gibeah; also in 20:33.

20:1 The phrase "from Dan in the north to Beersheba in the south" was a way of saying "the whole of Israel." Dan was the new name of the town that the tribe of Dan captured in the far northern territory of Israel; it formerly was named Laish. Beersheba was a town in the southernmost territory. Gilead was the collective name for the tribal territories east of the Jordan River.

▸ BIBLE
20:13 Protecting the guilty. A love for justice can save many lives. The tribe of Benjamin protected the gang of rapists and murderers in the town of Gibeah rather than surrender them for justice, sparking a civil war. The people of Israel cried out to the Lord for wisdom, and God eventually gave them victory (20:42). After killing more than 25,000 Benjamite warriors, the armies of Israel destroyed every town within marching distance (20:48). If you have an opportunity to aid in seeing justice done, do everything you can to help. (***See Bible***> *Power*> *Wisdom*> *Administer civil justice,* TopicGuide page A11.)

presence of the LORD until evening. They had asked the LORD, "Should we fight against our
relatives from Benjamin again?"
And the LORD had said, "Go out and fight against them."
24 So the next day they went out again to fight against the men of Benjamin, 25 but the
men of Benjamin killed another 18,000 Israelites, all of whom were experienced with the
sword.
20:26 26 Then all the Israelites went up to Bethel and wept in the presence of the LORD and
Judg 21:2-4 fasted until evening. They also brought burnt offerings and peace offerings to the LORD.
20:27 27 The Israelites went up seeking direction from the LORD. (In those days the Ark of the Cov-
Judg 20:18 enant of God was in Bethel, 28 and Phinehas son of Eleazar and grandson of Aaron was the
priest.) The Israelites asked the LORD, "Should we fight against our relatives from Benjamin
again, or should we stop?"
The LORD said, "Go! Tomorrow I will hand them over to you."
29 So the Israelites set an ambush all around Gibeah. 30 They went out on the third day
and took their positions at the same place as before. 31 When the men of Benjamin came
20:31 out to attack, they were drawn away from the town. And as they had done before, they be-
Josh 8:16 gan to kill the Israelites. About thirty Israelites died in the open fields and along the roads,
one leading to Bethel and the other leading back to Gibeah.
32 Then the warriors of Benjamin shouted, "We're defeating them as we did before!" But
the Israelites had planned in advance to run away so that the men of Benjamin would
chase them along the roads and be drawn away from the town.
20:33 33 When the main group of Israelite warriors reached Baal-tamar, they turned and took
Josh 8:19 up their positions. Meanwhile, the Israelites hiding in ambush to the west* of Gibeah
20:34 jumped up to fight. 34 There were 10,000 elite Israelite troops who advanced against Gibe-
Josh 8:14 ah. The fighting was so heavy that Benjamin didn't realize the impending disaster. 35 So
20:36 the LORD helped Israel defeat Benjamin, and that day the Israelites killed 25,100 of Benja-
Josh 8:15 min's warriors, all of whom were experienced swordsmen. 36 Then the men of Benjamin
saw that they were beaten.
The Israelites had retreated from Benjamin's warriors in order to give those hiding in
20:37-38 ambush more room to maneuver against Gibeah. 37 Then those who were hiding rushed
Josh 8:19-20 in from all sides and killed everyone in the town. 38 They had arranged to send up a large
cloud of smoke from the town as a signal. 39 When the Israelites saw the smoke, they
turned and attacked Benjamin's warriors.
By that time Benjamin's warriors had killed about thirty Israelites, and they shouted, "We're
20:40-41 defeating them as we did in the first battle!" 40 But when the warriors of Benjamin looked
Josh 8:20-21 behind them and saw the smoke rising into the sky from every part of the town, 41 the men of
Israel turned and attacked. At this point the men of Benjamin became terrified, because they
20:42 realized disaster was close at hand. 42 So they turned around and fled before the Israelites to-
Josh 8:15, 24 ward the wilderness. But they couldn't escape the battle, and the people who came out of the
nearby towns were also killed.* 43 The Israelites surrounded the men of Benjamin and chased
them relentlessly, finally overtaking them east of Gibeah.* 44 That day 18,000 of Benjamin's

20:33 As in Greek and Syriac versions and Latin Vulgate; Hebrew reads *hiding in the open space.* 20:42 Or *battle, for the people from the nearby towns also came out and killed them.* 20:43 The meaning of the Hebrew is uncertain.

20:27-28 The mention of Phinehas here is a reminder that these closing stories of Judges did not occur at the end of the time period. Given that Phinehas was Aaron's grandson, this battle probably took place within a generation or so after the people entered the land. Phinehas' leadership was first described in Numbers 25, when he killed a man who was about to incur God's further judgment on Israel. For many generations after, the high priest of the nation of Israel came through the family line of Phinehas.

20:27 The Ark of the Covenant was essentially a wooden chest made to strict specifications. It rested in the most holy inner chamber of the portable Tabernacle, then later in the Temple in Jerusalem. The lid of the Ark, sometimes translated "the mercy seat," represented God's throne. Stored inside the Ark were sacred relics such as a jar of manna and the tablets on which the Ten Commandments were inscribed. The Tabernacle and the Ark were at Bethel at this time, so the Israelites went there to seek the counsel of the high priest.

strongest warriors died in battle. 45The survivors fled into the wilderness toward the rock of 20:45
Rimmon, but Israel killed 5,000 of them along the road. They continued the chase until they Judg 21:13
had killed another 2,000 near Gidom.
46So that day the tribe of Benjamin lost 25,000 strong warriors armed with swords,
47leaving only 600 men who escaped to the rock of Rimmon, where they lived for four
months. 48And the Israelites returned and slaughtered every living thing in all the towns—
the people, the livestock, and everything they found. They also burned down all the towns
they came to.

ISRAEL PROVIDES WIVES FOR BENJAMIN

21 The Israelites had vowed at Mizpah, "We will never give our daughters in mar- 21:1
riage to a man from the tribe of Benjamin." 2Now the people went to Bethel and Judg 21:7, 18
sat in the presence of God until evening, weeping loudly and bitterly. 3"O LORD, God of Is- 21:2
rael," they cried out, "why has this happened in Israel? Now one of our tribes is missing Judg 20:18, 26
from Israel!"
4Early the next morning the people built an altar and presented their burnt offerings and 21:4
peace offerings on it. 5Then they said, "Who among the tribes of Israel did not join us at Deut 12:5
Mizpah when we held our assembly in the presence of the LORD?" At that time they had 2 Sam 24:25
taken a solemn oath in the LORD's presence, vowing that anyone who refused to come
would be put to death.
6The Israelites felt sorry for their brother Benjamin and said, "Today one of the tribes of
Israel has been cut off. 7How can we find wives for the few who remain, since we have
sworn by the LORD not to give them our daughters in marriage?"
8So they asked, "Who among the tribes of Israel did not join us at Mizpah when we as-
sembled in the presence of the LORD?" And they discovered that no one from Jabesh-
gilead had attended the assembly. 9For after they counted all the people, no one from
Jabesh-gilead was present.
10So the assembly sent 12,000 of their best warriors to Jabesh-gilead with orders to kill 21:10
everyone there, including women and children. 11"This is what you are to do," they said. Num 31:17-18
"Completely destroy* all the males and every woman who is not a virgin." 12Among the
residents of Jabesh-gilead they found 400 young virgins who had never slept with a man,
and they brought them to the camp at Shiloh in the land of Canaan.
13The Israelite assembly sent a peace delegation to the remaining people of Benjamin 21:13
who were living at the rock of Rimmon. 14Then the men of Benjamin returned to their Deut 20:10
homes, and the 400 women of Jabesh-gilead who had been spared were given to them as
wives. But there were not enough women for all of them.

21:11 The Hebrew term used here refers to the complete consecration of things or people to the LORD, either by destroying them or by giving them as an offering.

21:6 The nation of Israel had a tribal identity. There were 12 of these tribes, corresponding to the number of sons of Jacob (Abraham's grandson). Through the years, the configuration of the tribes had changed somewhat. God gave the tribe of Levi a religious role and scattered the people throughout Israel rather than granting them their own territory. However, the two sons of Joseph—Ephraim and Manasseh—both received territories, so the number of tribes with land remained at 12. Given this longstanding tribal structure, it grieved the Israelites to think that one of the 12 tribes was nearly wiped out.

▸ PURPOSE

21:7 No king from Benjamin. Have you ever made a promise that you later regretted? How did you deal with that? The people of Israel had pledged to keep their daughters from marrying the remaining men of Benjamin, but they regretted the consequences—the end of the tribe of Benjamin. So they reneged on their promise by finding a town that had not actually taken the pledge (they had previously declared such towns guilty of capital offense, as they had not assisted in punishing Benjamin's cruelty). Once they found such a town, they killed all the men and non-virgin women there and gave the virgin women to the men of Benjamin. As there were still not enough women for all the men of Benjamin, they allowed the Benjamites to kidnap women of Shiloh as they danced in a festival. This story is not only an argument for a godly king to guide Israel, but also an argument against that king being from the tribe of Benjamin—as King Saul was. This situation teaches us that we need to follow our King Jesus and be in complete submission to Him. (***See Purpose****> God's Means> God's Sovereignty> God is King over every nation,* TopicGuide page A52.)

15 The people felt sorry for Benjamin because the LORD had made this gap among the
tribes of Israel. 16 So the elders of the assembly asked, "How can we find wives for the few
who remain, since the women of the tribe of Benjamin are dead? 17 There must be heirs for
the survivors so that an entire tribe of Israel is not wiped out. 18 But we cannot give them
our own daughters in marriage because we have sworn with a solemn oath that anyone
who does this will fall under God's curse."

21:19 19 Then they thought of the annual festival of the LORD held in Shiloh, south of Lebonah
Josh 18:1 Judg 18:31 and north of Bethel, along the east side of the road that goes from Bethel to Shechem.
1 Sam 1:3 20 They told the men of Benjamin who still needed wives, "Go and hide in the vineyards.
21:21 21 When you see the young women of Shiloh come out for their dances, rush out from the
Exod 15:20 vineyards, and each of you can take one of them home to the land of Benjamin to be your
Judg 11:34 wife! 22 And when their fathers and brothers come to us in protest, we will tell them, 'Please
be sympathetic. Let them have your daughters, for we didn't find wives for all of them
when we destroyed Jabesh-gilead. And you are not guilty of breaking the vow since you
did not actually give your daughters to them in marriage.'"

21:23 23 So the men of Benjamin did as they were told. Each man caught one of the women as
Judg 20:48 she danced in the celebration and carried her off to be his wife. They returned to their own
land, and they rebuilt their towns and lived in them.

24 Then the people of Israel departed by tribes and families, and they returned to their
own homes.

25 In those days Israel had no king; all the people did whatever seemed right in their
own eyes.

RUTH

PURPOSE

To call the Israelites to faithfulness and loyalty to God by presenting the example of a foreign proselyte. Also to support David's kingship by showing that the foreign ancestor in his line was faithful to the God of Abraham, Isaac, and Jacob.

Like a silver thread running through a garment of plain, dark cloth, the book of Ruth stands as a glimmering testimony of love and devotion during the dark days of the judges in Israel.

Ruth, a recently widowed Moabite woman, leaves her family and her people to travel to Bethlehem in Judah, the homeland of her Israelite mother-in-law. Ruth's devotion is rewarded as she finds a new husband and becomes the great-grandmother of King David—and an ancestor of Jesus Christ (Matthew 1:5).

DISCOVER GOD IN RUTH

The book of Ruth illustrates one of the primary attributes of the character of God:

Redeemer: Ruth is the best illustration in Scripture of the Hebrew concept of the "kinsman-redeemer" (based on Leviticus 25:25-34). The kinsman-redeemer was a relative who had the ability and desire to redeem a family member who was in trouble. Perhaps the person had become enslaved due to debt, or, like Naomi or Ruth, was destitute because of the death of a husband. The person's name, reputation, and even life could be saved by the redemptive kindness of the kinsman-redeemer. Boaz qualified as a kinsman-redeemer, for he was a relative of Naomi (Ruth 2:1). By marrying Ruth, Boaz ensured that Naomi's property would not be passed on to another Israelite family and that the line of Naomi's deceased husband and son would continue. Boaz's selfless act is a picture of Jesus Christ, the divine Kinsman-Redeemer who came on our behalf. We were sold into slavery to sin, bound for destruction. Christ willingly became our human relative through the Incarnation and with His own blood paid the necessary price to redeem all of God's people in the world (1 John 2:2).

GROWING THROUGH RUTH

The small book of Ruth overflows with themes that apply to the disciple of Jesus Christ:

Loyalty: Naomi, her husband, and her two sons left Israel during a famine and journeyed to Moab in search of food. There her sons married Moabite women, Ruth and Orpah. Eventually, Naomi's husband and sons died. When Naomi prepared to return to Israel alone,

Ruth insisted on leaving her Moabite family and accompanying her elderly mother-in-law. Ruth demonstrated *hesed,* a Hebrew word for "loyal love"—the kind of love God has for His people.

Sacrifice: Ruth was not the only person who lived a sacrificial life in the book of Ruth. Commendably, she left the provision of her own family to help support her mother-in-law, and her reputation followed her (Ruth 3:10). But Boaz also sacrificed, as all kinsman-redeemers did, by marrying Ruth. The law provided for any children from their union to stand in the line of inheritance of Ruth's first husband, Naomi's son (Deuteronomy 25:5-6). There is no love or devotion without sacrifice.

Integrity: Both Ruth and Boaz demonstrated the highest levels of integrity and purity in their personal character (2:8-9; 3:11-12). They were lights of righteousness in an otherwise dark period in Israel's history. They had learned to live *in* the world without being *of* the world.

DISCOVERY VERSES

But Ruth replied, "Don't ask me to leave you and turn back. Wherever you go, I will go; wherever you live, I will live. Your people will be my people, and your God will be my God. Wherever you die, I will die, and there I will be buried. May the LORD punish me severely if I allow anything but death to separate us!" (Ruth 1:16-17)

Reward: Both Naomi's and Boaz's words indicate an understanding in Israel that righteousness is rewarded by God (1:8; 2:12)—and Ruth was indeed rewarded for her faithfulness. The New Testament expands that idea beyond the general "harvest what you plant" perspective (Galatians 6:7). Both Jesus and the apostles were very specific about the possibility of gaining—and losing—rewards in heaven based on choices made in this life (Matthew 5:12; 6:1-4; 1 Corinthians 3:14; Colossians 3:24; 1 Timothy 4:8; 1 Peter 1:17; 2 John 1:8). Ruth's rewards of marriage, security, and inclusion in the ancestry of Jesus Christ only foreshadow heavenly rewards that are to come.

RUTH FACTS

Author: Unknown.

Written to: No particular audience or recipient is suggested outside the general readership in Israel.

Date of writing: Sometime not long after the period of the judges, likely during David's reign.

Setting: Ruth opens in Moab, east of the Jordan River, but the majority of the story takes place in and around Bethlehem, 50 to 70 miles away.

OUTLINE

- **RUTH 1**—Naomi's bitterness
- **RUTH 2**—Ruth meets Boaz
- **RUTH 3**—Ruth seeks Boaz's help
- **RUTH 4:1-12**—Boaz becomes a kinsman-redeemer for Ruth
- **RUTH 4:13-17**—Naomi's bitterness turns to blessing

ELIMELECH MOVES HIS FAMILY TO MOAB

1:1 Judg 2:16-18 **1** In the days when the judges ruled in Israel, a severe famine came upon the land. So a
man from Bethlehem in Judah left his home and went to live in the country of Moab,
1:2 Gen 35:19 Judg 3:30 taking his wife and two sons with him. 2The man's name was Elimelech, and his wife was
Naomi. Their two sons were Mahlon and Kilion. They were Ephrathites from Bethlehem in
the land of Judah. And when they reached Moab, they settled there.
3Then Elimelech died, and Naomi was left with her two sons. 4The two sons married
Moabite women. One married a woman named Orpah, and the other a woman named
Ruth. But about ten years later, 5both Mahlon and Kilion died. This left Naomi alone, without her two sons or her husband.

NAOMI AND RUTH RETURN

1:6 Exod 4:31 6Then Naomi heard in Moab that the LORD had blessed His people in Judah by giving them
good crops again. So Naomi and her daughters-in-law got ready to leave Moab to return
to her homeland. 7With her two daughters-in-law she set out from the place where she
had been living, and they took the road that would lead them back to Judah.
1:8 2 Tim 1:16 8But on the way, Naomi said to her two daughters-in-law, "Go back to your mothers'
homes. And may the LORD reward you for your kindness to your husbands and to me.
1:9 Ruth 3:1 9May the LORD bless you with the security of another marriage." Then she kissed them
good-bye, and they all broke down and wept.
10"No," they said. "We want to go with you to your people."
1:11 Deut 25:5 11But Naomi replied, "Why should you go on with me? Can I still give birth to other sons
who could grow up to be your husbands? 12No, my daughters, return to your parents'

1:1 When God delivered the Israelites from Egypt, their government was a theocracy—God ruled them through Moses. Before Moses died, he gave the people guidelines for a king, should they choose one, but that didn't happen until centuries later. In the meantime, after the people partially settled the land, they cycled through periods of obeying God's law, thus becoming stronger as a nation; then living as they pleased, becoming weaker. Each time they despaired under the consequences of their disobedience, a national champion empowered by God arose to save Israel. The book of Judges and the first half of 1 Samuel give the accounts of those national champions, or judges. It was during the time of the judges that Ruth came to live in Israel.

1:1 The tribe of Judah was, perhaps, the most significant tribe of Israel. Israel's two greatest kings came from this tribe: David and the Messiah. After David's reign, Israel fell apart spiritually and politically, splitting into two kingdoms. The northern kingdom retained the name Israel. The southern kingdom took the name of Judah, its largest tribe. The citizens of Judah came to be known as *Jews.*

1:2 There were two cities named Bethlehem in Israel. The lesser known of the two, in the tribal region of Zebulun, was the home of the judge named Ibzan (Judges 12:8-9). The other, more prominent, Bethlehem, was in the tribal region of Judah. This Bethlehem was sometimes referred to as Ephrath (Genesis 48:7) or Bethlehem-judah to avoid confusion. The town was located less than ten miles south of Jerusalem. This Bethlehem was the hometown of Naomi, King David, and Jesus.

1:2 Moab was a small kingdom to the east of the Dead Sea. The original Moabites were descendants of Abraham's nephew, Lot. Lot's wife died when Sodom and Gomorrah were destroyed by God's judgment, but Lot and his two daughters survived. The two girls connived together to conceive babies by their father. Lot's older daughter had a son named Moab (Genesis 19:34-38). The Moabites settled in the land that had been occupied by people called the Emim. After the Israelites took possession of Canaan, Israel and Moab experienced periods of conflict and peace.

1:5 As a widow, Naomi's status was precarious. In this culture, a woman's rights were protected by the man in charge of her—most often her husband or her father. An older widow was likely to have lost both her father and her husband. To add to Naomi's dilemma, even her sons were gone. Her story reveals some of the extended-family customs and laws that would provide for widows for centuries to come. In the New Testament, care for widows was seen as a mark of true religion (James 1:27). Jesus pointed out the hypocrisy of the religious leaders by emphasizing the way they treated the widows of their community (Luke 20:45-47).

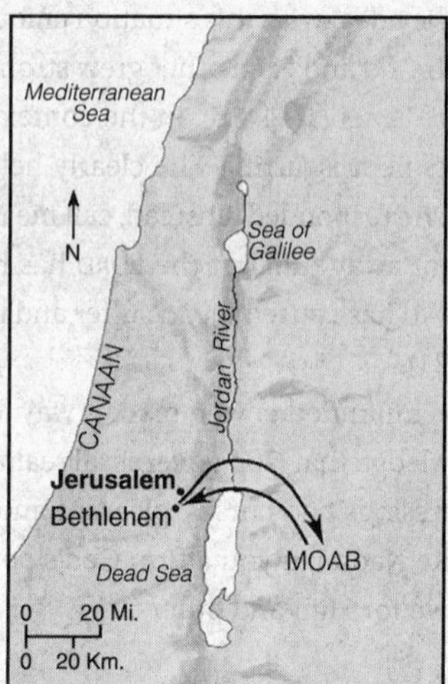

SETTING FOR THE STORY
Elimelech, Naomi, and their sons traveled from Bethlehem to Moab because of a famine. After her husband and sons died, Naomi returned to Bethlehem with her daughter-in-law Ruth.

homes, for I am too old to marry again. And even if it were possible, and I were to get mar-
ried tonight and bear sons, then what? 13 Would you wait for them to grow up and refuse **1:13** Judg 2:15
to marry someone else? No, of course not, my daughters! Things are far more bitter for me
than for you, because the LORD Himself has raised His fist against me."
14 And again they wept together, and Orpah kissed her mother-in-law good-bye. But
Ruth clung tightly to Naomi. 15 "Look," Naomi said to her, "your sister-in-law has gone back
to her people and to her gods. You should do the same." **1:16** 2 Kgs 2:2
16 But Ruth replied, "Don't ask me to leave you and turn back. Wherever you go, I will
go; wherever you live, I will live. Your people will be my people, and your God will be my
God. 17 Wherever you die, I will die, and there I will be buried. May the LORD punish me se-
verely if I allow anything but death to separate us!" 18 When Naomi saw that Ruth was de- **1:18** Acts 21:14
termined to go with her, she said nothing more.
19 So the two of them continued on their journey. When they came to Bethlehem, the
entire town was excited by their arrival. "Is it really Naomi?" the women asked.

▸ GOD

1:16 Deep relationships. In a world where people betray one another for 15 minutes of fame, true loyalty often shocks us. Ruth's circumstances dictated, "Get rid of the old woman and take care of yourself." But her heart told her that Naomi was a special woman with a God who could save her from her hopeless circumstances. So Ruth journeyed with Naomi to her ancestral home. Can you imagine a friendship that deep? Can you imagine having enough faith in a God you hardly knew to trust Him with your future? Faith in God and deep friendships with others are at the heart of the story of Ruth, and they are at the heart of your story as well. (***See God****> God's Nature> Personality> Relationships> He wants to be known,* TopicGuide page A14.)

MY RESPONSE TO GOD

Blaming God for Everything

RUTH 1:20-21

Ruth and her mother-in-law, Naomi, were both mourning the deaths of their husbands. Their future was bleak. As widows, they could lose their family's inheritance. Left alone, and with few tangible possessions, they would certainly join their husbands in death soon.

How did they deal with this situation emotionally? The first thing we see is that their relationship with God and each other grew strong: Ruth clung to Naomi and committed herself to the God of Israel (1:14, 16). In the context of this love for God and each other, Naomi's honest assessment is jarring. She clearly held God responsible for her tragedy: "'Don't call me Naomi,' she responded. 'Instead, call me Mara, for the Almighty has made life very bitter for me. I went away full, but the LORD has brought me home empty. Why call me Naomi when the LORD has caused me to suffer and the Almighty has sent such tragedy upon me?'" (Ruth 1:20-21).

God, in his unlimited power, made a way for Ruth and Naomi to survive and prosper. But if we acknowledge that God governs all reality, then, like Naomi, we must acknowledge that He sends blessings and curses, pleasant and unpleasant circumstances, and everything in between. Like Naomi, if you affirm God's power in all things, you will have the foundation for a new love for Him and others.

1:20 20"Don't call me Naomi," she responded. "Instead, call me Mara,* for the Almighty has
Exod 6:3 Job 6:4 made life very bitter for me. 21I went away full, but the LORD has brought me home empty.
1:21 Why call me Naomi when the LORD has caused me to suffer* and the Almighty has sent
Job 1:21 such tragedy upon me?"
1:22 22So Naomi returned from Moab, accompanied by her daughter-in-law Ruth, the young
Exod 9:31 Moabite woman. They arrived in Bethlehem in late spring, at the beginning of the barley
harvest.

RUTH WORKS IN BOAZ'S FIELD

2:1 **2** Now there was a wealthy and influential man in Bethlehem named Boaz, who was a
Ruth 1:2 relative of Naomi's husband, Elimelech.
2:2 Lev 19:9-10; 23:22 2One day Ruth the Moabite said to Naomi, "Let me go out into the harvest fields to pick
up the stalks of grain left behind by anyone who is kind enough to let me do it."
Naomi replied, "All right, my daughter, go ahead." 3So Ruth went out to gather grain
behind the harvesters. And as it happened, she found herself working in a field that be-
longed to Boaz, the relative of her father-in-law, Elimelech.
2:4 Ps 129:8 4While she was there, Boaz arrived from Bethlehem and greeted the harvesters. "The
Luke 1:28 LORD be with you!" he said.
"The LORD bless you!" the harvesters replied.
5Then Boaz asked his foreman, "Who is that young woman over there? Who does she
belong to?"
2:6 Ruth 1:22 6And the foreman replied, "She is the young woman from Moab who came back with
Naomi. 7She asked me this morning if she could gather grain behind the harvesters. She
has been hard at work ever since, except for a few minutes' rest in the shelter."
8Boaz went over and said to Ruth, "Listen, my daughter. Stay right here with us when
you gather grain; don't go to any other fields. Stay right behind the young women work-
ing in my field. 9See which part of the field they are harvesting, and then follow them. I
have warned the young men not to treat you roughly. And when you are thirsty, help
yourself to the water they have drawn from the well."
2:10 1 Sam 25:23 10Ruth fell at his feet and thanked him warmly. "What have I done to deserve such kind-
ness?" she asked. "I am only a foreigner."
11"Yes, I know," Boaz replied. "But I also know about everything you have done for your
mother-in-law since the death of your husband. I have heard how you left your father and
2:12 Ruth 1:16 mother and your own land to live here among complete strangers. 12May the LORD, the

1:20 *Naomi* means "pleasant"; *Mara* means "bitter." 1:21 Or *has testified against me.*

▶ WORSHIP
1:20 God in control. Believing that God is sovereign is all well and good when things are going fine, but what about when misery and tragedy strike? Is God in control over both pain and blessing? Naomi thought so, but she would soon discover God was busy bringing her into a place of blessing that she could not imagine. If you believe God is sovereign, you must use your eyes of faith to see Him in all your circumstances, working all things for your good (Romans 8:28). (***See Worship****> NT> Our Role> Attitude> Trusting in the midst of trials,* TopicGuide page A31.)

1:20 It was not surprising that grief drove Naomi to desire a name change. Names held great significance in ancient Hebrew culture. Abram's name, which meant "exalted father," was changed to Abraham, "father of many." This change reflected God's promise of many descendants. While subtle, this name change also reflected God's promise to enlarge their legacy (Genesis 17:15-16). Naomi's choice was to change her name, which meant "pleasant," to Mara, which meant "bitter."

2:3 In going to the fields, Ruth took advantage of a provision Moses made in some of his final instructions to the people of Israel. In Deuteronomy 24:19-22, Moses instructed the people to intentionally leave some of their harvest in the fields. In that way, foreigners, orphans, and widows would be saved from starving if they were willing to come and gather the leftovers. Moses' commands included not only grain crops, but also olives and grapes.

▶ CHURCH
2:10 Amazing grace. Were you surprised by Ruth's kindness to Naomi? Now it is Ruth's turn to be shocked at undeserved compassion. Boaz's kindness to Ruth flowed from his respect for her sacrifices for Naomi (2:11) and her faith in God (2:12). Like the first chapter of the book of Ruth, this part of the story illustrates the heart of the Christian life—sacrificial relationships and faith in God. (***See Church****> Role> Preach> Topics> Exhortations> Godly Lives> Kindness to neighbors,* TopicGuide page A50.)

God of Israel, under whose wings you have come to take refuge, reward you fully for what
you have done."
[13]"I hope I continue to please you, sir," she replied. "You have comforted me by speak-
ing so kindly to me, even though I am not one of your workers."
[14]At mealtime Boaz called to her, "Come over here, and help yourself to some food. You
can dip your bread in the sour wine." So she sat with his harvesters, and Boaz gave her
some roasted grain to eat. She ate all she wanted and still had some left over.
[15]When Ruth went back to work again, Boaz ordered his young men, "Let her gather
grain right among the sheaves without stopping her. [16]And pull out some heads of barley
from the bundles and drop them on purpose for her. Let her pick them up, and don't give
her a hard time!"
[17]So Ruth gathered barley there all day, and when she beat out the grain that evening, it
filled an entire basket.* [18]She carried it back into town and showed it to her mother-in-law.
Ruth also gave her the roasted grain that was left over from her meal.
[19]"Where did you gather all this grain today?" Naomi asked. "Where did you work?
May the LORD bless the one who helped you!"
So Ruth told her mother-in-law about the man in whose field she had worked. She said,
"The man I worked with today is named Boaz."
[20]"May the LORD bless him!" Naomi told her daughter-in-law. "He is showing his kind- **2:20** Ruth 3:9-10; 4:6
ness to us as well as to your dead husband.* That man is one of our closest relatives, one
of our family redeemers."
[21]Then Ruth* said, "What's more, Boaz even told me to come back and stay with his har-
vesters until the entire harvest is completed."
[22]"Good!" Naomi exclaimed. "Do as he said, my daughter. Stay with his young women
right through the whole harvest. You might be harassed in other fields, but you'll be safe
with him."
[23]So Ruth worked alongside the women in Boaz's fields and gathered grain with them
until the end of the barley harvest. Then she continued working with them through the
wheat harvest in early summer. And all the while she lived with her mother-in-law.

RUTH AT THE THRESHING FLOOR

3 One day Naomi said to Ruth, "My daughter, it's time that I found a permanent home **3:1** Ruth 1:9
for you, so that you will be provided for. [2]Boaz is a close relative of ours, and he's
been very kind by letting you gather grain with his young women. Tonight he will be win- **3:2** Deut 25:5-10
nowing barley at the threshing floor. [3]Now do as I tell you—take a bath and put on per-
fume and dress in your nicest clothes. Then go to the threshing floor, but don't let Boaz

2:17 Hebrew *it was about an ephah* [20 quarts or 22 liters]. 2:20 Hebrew *to the living and to the dead.* 2:21 Hebrew *Ruth the Moabite.*

2:20 To have an heir was a priority in this culture. If a man died without an heir, the closest male relative often married his widow. The first child they produced was considered the heir of the deceased, so the dead man's legacy could continue. The relative who took in the widow was referred to as the "family redeemer" because he redeemed the inheritance of that family line. The closest relative had the first opportunity to redeem the inheritance. If he did not take that opportunity, the next closest relative was considered, and on down the family line.

▸WORSHIP

2:23 Working in Boaz's fields. How many families survive because of a strong woman who tirelessly labors to support her family? God receives honor when strong women work hard for His glory (Proverbs 31). Boaz took every opportunity to support Ruth without patronizing her. How well do you and your church encourage the poor to work for their wages? Give freely to the poor (Proverbs 11:16), but always encourage them to work as much as possible (Proverbs 21:17; 2 Thessalonians 3:10). (***See Worship****> NT> Fellowship> Preserving> Look to the interests of one another,* TopicGuide page A31.)

3:3-9 Some parts of this courtship ritual are very familiar—cleaning up, dressing up, and wearing perfume. But the idea of Ruth sneaking into what was essentially a bunkhouse in order to make some kind of marriage proposal by rearranging blankets is a foreign concept. Nevertheless, for the day and time in which Ruth lived, her message was clearly conveyed—she had chosen Boaz for her husband and provider. For his part, Boaz did not hesitate to take care of the business at hand and deal with Ruth's more closely related family redeemer.

see you until he has finished eating and drinking. 4Be sure to notice where he lies down;
then go and uncover his feet and lie down there. He will tell you what to do."
5"I will do everything you say," Ruth replied. 6So she went down to the threshing floor
that night and followed the instructions of her mother-in-law.
3:7 7After Boaz had finished eating and drinking and was in good spirits, he lay down at the
Judg 19:6, 22 2 Sam 13:28 far end of the pile of grain and went to sleep. Then Ruth came quietly, uncovered his feet,
and lay down. 8Around midnight Boaz suddenly woke up and turned over. He was sur-
3:9 Ruth 2:20 prised to find a woman lying at his feet! 9"Who are you?" he asked.
"I am your servant Ruth," she replied. "Spread the corner of your covering over me, for
you are my family redeemer."
10"The LORD bless you, my daughter!" Boaz exclaimed. "You are showing even more
family loyalty now than you did before, for you have not gone after a younger man,
3:11 Prov 12:4; 31:10 whether rich or poor. 11Now don't worry about a thing, my daughter. I will do what is nec-
3:12 essary, for everyone in town knows you are a virtuous woman. 12But while it's true that I
Ruth 4:1 am one of your family redeemers, there is another man who is more closely related to you
3:13 than I am. 13Stay here tonight, and in the morning I will talk to him. If he is willing to re-
Ruth 4:5 Matt 22:24 deem you, very well. Let him marry you. But if he is not willing, then as surely as the LORD
lives, I will redeem you myself! Now lie down here until morning."
14So Ruth lay at Boaz's feet until the morning, but she got up before it was light enough
for people to recognize each other. For Boaz had said, "No one must know that a woman
was here at the threshing floor." 15Then Boaz said to her, "Bring your cloak and spread it
out." He measured six scoops* of barley into the cloak and placed it on her back. Then he*
returned to the town.
16When Ruth went back to her mother-in-law, Naomi asked, "What happened, my
daughter?"
Ruth told Naomi everything Boaz had done for her, 17and she added, "He gave me
these six scoops of barley and said, 'Don't go back to your mother-in-law empty-handed.'"
3:18 18Then Naomi said to her, "Just be patient, my daughter, until we hear what happens.
Ps 37:3-5 The man won't rest until he has settled things today."

BOAZ MARRIES RUTH

4:1 4 Boaz went to the town gate and took a seat there. Just then the family redeemer he
Ruth 3:12 had mentioned came by, so Boaz called out to him, "Come over here and sit down,
friend. I want to talk to you." So they sat down together. 2Then Boaz called ten leaders

3:15a Hebrew *six measures,* an unknown quantity. 3:15b Most Hebrew manuscripts read *he;* many Hebrew manuscripts, Syriac version, and Latin Vulgate read *she.*

▸ CHURCH
3:4 Initiating intimacy. This was quite a first date! We lack a clear understanding of ancient courtship rituals, but we assume that since both Ruth and Naomi were women of upright character, neither of them was guilty of sin in this matter, no matter what kind of sexual overtones this passage may have to modern eyes. Neither did Boaz engage in any impropriety. Instead, he responded to Ruth's entreaty in the socially appropriate manner by covering her with his garment and presenting her with a sizable amount of grain. God often uses odd circumstances to bring us into intimate relationships. But as with Ruth, go under counsel of a wise friend and be ready to take God-honoring risks to be with the one you love. (***See Church***> *What*> *Many Titles*> *Bride,* TopicGuide page A48.)

3:13 Boaz promised that if the other family redeemer would not marry Ruth, he would do so, and he sealed the promise with an oath: "as surely as the LORD lives." Among faithful Israelites, nothing was more certain than that God lived. Boaz was reassuring Ruth in the strongest possible terms that he would see her situation settled one way or the other.

4:1 In Boaz's time, the town gate was the place where most business transactions and disputes were handled. Most cities big enough to have a wall had two gates. One was larger and was located near the rear of the city, somewhat like a loading dock in the rear of a building. Large caravans could enter this way. The other gate was smaller; it provided a common entrance to the city.

4:2 By gathering ten witnesses, leaders of the town no less, Boaz ensured that the transaction would be settled and binding. While the Israelites had no formal, political hierarchy with a king at its head, since the earliest days of Moses there had been a formal decision-making and dispute-resolution process (Exodus 18:13-26). In the generations after Moses, judges like Deborah (Judges 4:4-5) served as chief mediators among the people, though their authority was not limited to only one city. The city leaders were leaders specifically over Bethlehem. They functioned somewhat like a board of directors made up of landowners and townsmen.

from the town and asked them to sit as witnesses. [3]And Boaz said to the family redeemer, **4:3**
"You know Naomi, who came back from Moab. She is selling the land that belonged to Lev 25:25
our relative Elimelech. [4]I thought I should speak to you about it so that you can redeem it **4:4**
if you wish. If you want the land, then buy it here in the presence of these witnesses. But if Lev 25:25; Jer 32:7-8
you don't want it, let me know right away, because I am next in line to redeem it after
you."
The man replied, "All right, I'll redeem it."
[5]Then Boaz told him, "Of course, your purchase of the land from Naomi also requires **4:5**
that you marry Ruth, the Moabite widow. That way she can have children who will carry Deut 25:5-6
on her husband's name and keep the land in the family."
[6]"Then I can't redeem it," the family redeemer replied, "because this might endanger **4:6**
my own estate. You redeem the land; I cannot do it." Lev 25:25; Ruth 3:12-13
[7]Now in those days it was the custom in Israel for anyone transferring a right of pur- **4:7**
chase to remove his sandal and hand it to the other party. This publicly validated the Deut 25:8-10
transaction. [8]So the other family redeemer drew off his sandal as he said to Boaz, "You
buy the land."
[9]Then Boaz said to the elders and to the crowd standing around, "You are wit-
nesses that today I have bought from Naomi all the property of Elimelech, Kilion, and
Mahlon. [10]And with the land I have acquired Ruth, the Moabite widow of Mahlon, to
be my wife. This way she can have a son to carry on the family name of her dead hus-
band and to inherit the family property here in his hometown. You are all witnesses
today."
[11]Then the elders and all the people standing in the gate replied, "We are witnesses! **4:11**
May the LORD make this woman who is coming into your home like Rachel and Leah, Gen 29:25-30
from whom all the nation of Israel descended! May you prosper in Ephrathah and be fa-
mous in Bethlehem. [12]And may the LORD give you descendants by this young woman **4:12**
who will be like those of our ancestor Perez, the son of Tamar and Judah." Gen 38:29; 46:12

4:3 The land that a person owned was of the greatest significance. When the people of Israel left Egypt and traveled to Canaan, they were banking on God's promise to Abraham that his descendants would have their own land to settle. The book of Joshua is the account of both the conquering and apportioning of that land. Thus, the piece of land that an Israelite owned was his or her piece of the promise of God. Even though Naomi was a widow with barely any rights, she did have the land that belonged to her family. It was this land that the family redeemer would purchase (or redeem), thus keeping the inheritance in the family and providing Naomi with some form of income.

4:4 To redeem something was to pay a price for it. This kind of redemption was a basic aspect of the sacrificial system. For instance, the firstborn of families and of flocks belonged to the Lord. Firstborn animals were offered as a sacrifice. However, there was the option to *redeem* the firstborn by making a monetary offering in its place. Leviticus 25; 27 give many scenarios in which a person could redeem an offering, a debt, or a piece of land. This understanding of redemption helps us understand Christ's redemption of us. He paid the price of our lives, setting us free.

4:7-8 The custom of offering a sandal to seal a deal may have evolved over the years. Deuteronomy 25:5-10 describes a scenario in which a man refused to marry the widow of his brother. In this case, the man's sandal was *taken* as a sign of dishonor. In fact, the widow was the one who took the man's sandal in the presence of the town leaders. She also was allowed to spit in the man's face. In Ruth's case, the reluctant kinsman-redeemer removed his own sandal to show that he was invoking his right of first refusal and transferring the purchasing rights to Boaz.

4:11 Rachel and Leah were the wives of Jacob, whose name was changed to Israel. Jacob's sons became the ancestors of the 12 tribes of Israel. Jacob first fell in love with Rachel. He worked seven years to earn the right to marry her. But in a last-minute deception, Rachel's father required that Jacob first marry Leah, Rachel's older sister, a woman whom Jacob did not love. Jacob did marry Leah, then worked seven more years in exchange for the right to marry Rachel also. Jacob's children were the product of his unions with these women and with their handmaidens, which was a custom of the day (Genesis 29:16–30:24).

4:12 The story of Tamar is the story of a family redeemer gone awry. Tamar married Er, the oldest son of Judah, one of the sons of Jacob. However, Er died before Tamar had any children. When Er died, Judah urged his second son, Onan, to marry Tamar as a family redeemer. Onan did so, but he died because he prevented any children from being conceived between them. Judah then told Tamar to go home and wait for his third son to grow up. But Judah was secretly afraid of losing another son, so he delayed the marriage. Tamar tricked Judah into fathering her twins, thus finally receiving the benefits of the family redeemer (Genesis 38). Her son Perez was an ancestor of Boaz (Ruth 4:18-22).

THE DESCENDANTS OF BOAZ

4:13 Gen 29:31; 33:5 — 4:14 Luke 1:58 — 4:15 Ruth 1:16-17; 2:11-12

13 So Boaz took Ruth into his home, and she became his wife. When he slept with her, the
LORD enabled her to become pregnant, and she gave birth to a son. 14 Then the women of
the town said to Naomi, "Praise the LORD, who has now provided a redeemer for your fami-
ly! May this child be famous in Israel. 15 May he restore your youth and care for you in
your old age. For he is the son of your daughter-in-law who loves you and has been better
to you than seven sons!"

16 Naomi took the baby and cuddled him to her breast. And she cared for him as if he
were her own. 17 The neighbor women said, "Now at last Naomi has a son again!" And
they named him Obed. He became the father of Jesse and the grandfather of David.

4:18-22 //1 Chr 2:5-15 //Matt 1:3-6 //Luke 3:31-33

18 This is the genealogical record of their ancestor Perez:

Perez was the father of Hezron.
19 Hezron was the father of Ram.
Ram was the father of Amminadab.
20 Amminadab was the father of Nahshon.
Nahshon was the father of Salmon.*
21 Salmon was the father of Boaz.
Boaz was the father of Obed.
22 Obed was the father of Jesse.
Jesse was the father of David.

4:20 As in some Greek manuscripts (see also 4:21); Hebrew reads *Salma*.

▸ GOD

4:13 The purpose of Ruth. Unlike many romances, this story comes to a happy ending. But only at the very end do we find out the historical reason why this story was written in the first place. It was written to explain why David, king of Israel, had a Moabite in his family tree (4:22). Those opposed to David's reign might have spread this information in an attempt to discredit him—"After all," they might have said, "he had enemies of Israel in his family" (Numbers 21:29). But David's ancestors were honorable people, faithful to God, and God used this true story to help secure David's claim to the throne of Israel. Do not judge a person by ancestry or nationality, but by faithfulness to God and to other people. These are the truest marks of maturity. (***See God****> God's Attributes> Just> God rightly judges heart, mind, and deeds,* TopicGuide page A17.)

4:17-22 Genealogies may not be page-turners to most of us today, but they connect the dots for people who find their identity in their family lines, as the people of Israel did. The reign of King David was a pinnacle in the history of Israel. To reveal here that he was actually born of the lineage of Boaz and Ruth the Moabite was to give incredible significance to this union. It was also through this family line that Jesus was born (Matthew 1; Luke 3).

KEY PLACES IN 1 SAMUEL

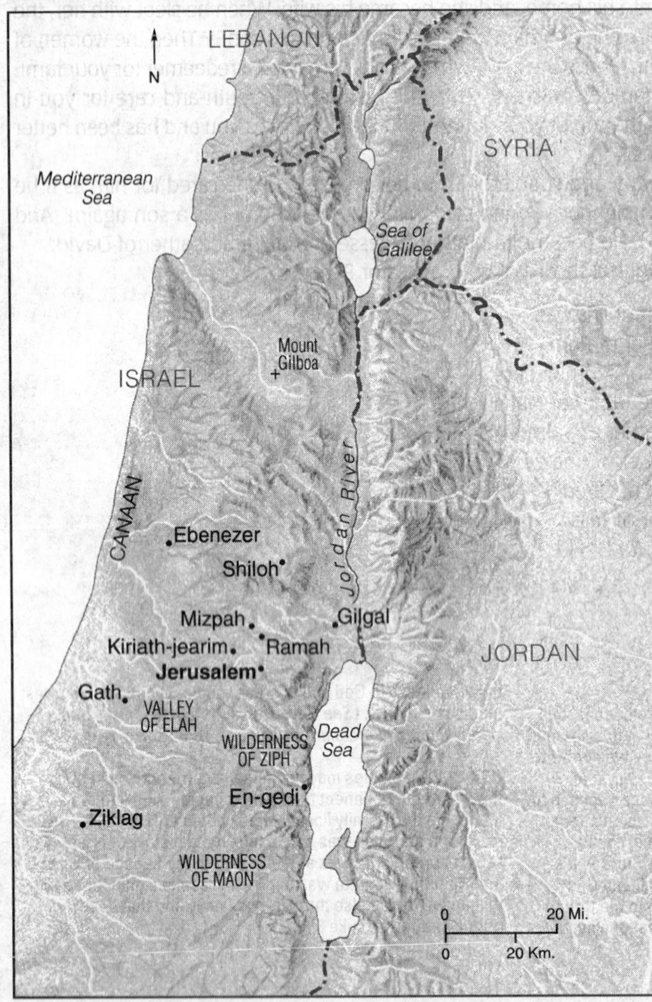

The broken lines (—·—) indicate modern boundaries.

1 Ramah Samuel was born in Ramah. Before his birth, Samuel's mother, Hannah, made a promise to God that she would dedicate her son to serve God alongside the priests in the Tabernacle at Shiloh (1:1–2:11).

2 Shiloh The focal point of Israel's worship was at Shiloh, where the Tabernacle and the Ark of the Covenant resided. Eli was the high priest, but his sons, Hophni and Phinehas, were evil men who took advantage of the people. Samuel, however, served God faithfully, and God blessed him as he grew (2:12–3:21).

3 Kiriath-jearim Israel was constantly at odds with the Philistines, and another battle was brewing. Hophni and Phinehas brought the Ark of the Covenant from Shiloh to the battlefield, believing that its mere presence would bring the Israelites victory. The Israelites were defeated by the Philistines at Ebenezer, and the Ark was captured. However, the Philistines soon found out that the Ark was not quite the great battle trophy they expected. For God sent plagues upon every Philistine city into which the Ark was brought. Finally, the Philistines sent it back to Kiriath-jearim in Israel (4:1–7:1).

4 Mizpah The Israelites' defeat made them realize that God was no longer blessing them. Samuel called the people together at Mizpah and asked them to fast and pray in sorrow for their sins. The assembly at Mizpah was a tempting target for the confident Philistines who advanced for an attack. But God intervened and routed their mighty army. Meanwhile, Samuel was judging cases throughout Israel. But as Samuel grew old, the people came to him at Ramah (his home base) demanding a king in order to be like the other nations. At Mizpah, Saul was chosen by sacred appointment to be Israel's first king with the blessing, but not the approval, of God and Samuel (7:2–10:27).

5 Gilgal A battle with the Ammonites proved Saul's leadership abilities to the people of Israel. He protected the people of Jabesh-gilead and scattered the Ammonite army. Samuel and the people crowned Saul as king of Israel at Gilgal (11:1-15).

6 Valley of Elah Saul won many other battles, but over time he proved to be arrogant, sinful, and rebellious, so God finally rejected him as king. Unknown to Saul, a young shepherd and musician named David was anointed to be Israel's next king. But it would be many years before David sat upon the throne. Ironically, Saul hired David to play the harp in his palace. Saul grew to like David so much that he made him his personal armor bearer. In one particular battle with the Philistines in the valley of Elah, David killed Goliath, the Philistines' mightiest soldier. But this victory was the beginning of the end of Saul's love for David. The Israelites praised David more than Saul, causing Saul to become so jealous that he plotted to kill David (12:1–22:23).

7 The Wilderness Even anointed kings are not exempt from troubles. David literally ran for his life from King Saul, hiding with his band of followers in the wilderness of Ziph (where the men of Ziph constantly betrayed him), the wilderness of Maon, and the wilderness of En-gedi. Though he had opportunities to kill Saul, David refused to do so because Saul was God's anointed king (23:1–26:25).

8 Gath David moved his men and family to Gath, the Philistine city where King Achish lived. Saul then stopped chasing him. The Philistines seemed to welcome this famous fugitive from Israel (27:1-4).

9 Ziklag Desiring privacy in return for his pretended loyalty to King Achish, David asked for a city in which to house his men and family. Achish gave him Ziklag. From there David conducted raids against the cities of the Geshurites, Girzites, and Amalekites, making sure no one escaped to tell the tale (27:5-12). David later conquered the Amalekites after they raided Ziklag (30:1-31).

10 Mount Gilboa War with the Philistines broke out again in the north, near Mount Gilboa. Saul, who no longer relied on God, consulted a medium in a desperate attempt to contact Samuel for help. In the meantime, David was sent back to Ziklag because the Philistine commanders did not trust his loyalty in battle against Israel. The Philistines slaughtered the Israelites on Mount Gilboa, killing King Saul and his three sons, including David's loyal friend Jonathan. Without God, Saul led a bitter and misguided life. The consequences of his sinful actions affected not only him but hurt his family and the entire nation as well (28:1–31:13).

1 SAMUEL

PURPOSE

To provide a historical record of the leaders God raised up from obscure places, and to encourage Israel to honor David and his descendants' claims to kingship.

God does not despise small things. In fact, in his letter to the Corinthian church, the apostle Paul reminded believers that God deliberately chooses people and things the world despises and considers foolish and powerless in order to shame the power structures of the world (see 1 Corinthians 1:26-29). And He does this so that He alone will receive the glory. This has already been seen with the way God used unlikely people like Abraham, Gideon, and others. First Samuel continues the theme: God raises up people from unlikely places and families and uses them to achieve His purposes among His people. Hannah, Samuel, Saul, and David all fit this pattern.

On the surface, it might seem that a paradigm shift—a momentous change—is taking place in Israel in 1 Samuel: rulers of Israel moving from judges to kings. But beneath this surface, the crucial question remains the same as before: Will the human king acknowledge God as the true king over Israel and maintain allegiance to His covenant? First Samuel is the story of how the first king, Saul, failed that test, and how a new king, David, was anointed to replace him.

DISCOVER GOD IN 1 SAMUEL

First Samuel is a type of biblical literature known as historical narrative; it reads much like a fast-paced novel. However, the accounts were arranged to support specific political purposes (such as support for the Davidic line of kings) and also theological ones. Threaded throughout the story are these insights about what God is like:

Kingship: While kingship may be an attribute of Saul and David in this story, 1 Samuel is really about the kingship of God—and whether Israel's earthly kings would acknowledge God's right to rule. Throughout Scripture, from Genesis to Revelation, a subtext of the redemption story is, "Who is in charge on planet Earth?" That was the issue in the Garden of Eden (Adam and Eve failed to live under God's rule), and that will be the issue in the final days of history, as many rise up in rebellion against God. God is the "great King" (Psalm 95:3) over the earth, a fact that is quickly established with the demise of Saul and the rise of David in 1 Samuel.

Values: It is plain in 1 Samuel that God focuses on different things than our world does. This is best illustrated by a comparison between Saul, the king who was after people's hearts, and David, the man who was after God's heart. Saul, the first king, was "the most handsome man in Israel—head and shoulders taller than anyone else in the land" (9:2). He was popular and charismatic, and he initially won the affections of the people. When God deposed Saul,

Samuel looked upon the distinguished sons of Jesse for a replacement, probably using Saul as a pattern. But God cautioned Samuel, "Don't judge by his appearance or height, for I have rejected him. The LORD doesn't see things the way you see them. People judge by outward appearance, but the LORD looks at the heart" (16:7). God's unchanging character, not man's superficial values, is the standard by which He chooses and acts in this world.

GROWING THROUGH 1 SAMUEL

In 1 Samuel there are good examples to follow and bad examples to avoid:

Obedience: When the prophet Samuel was just a child, he manifested the spirit that would make him a trusted prophet-servant of the Lord: "Speak, Your servant is listening" (3:10). Saul, on the other hand, lost his kingship because of a failure to obey God's commands, prompting this reprimand: "Obedience is better than sacrifice" (15:22). Step 1 in being a servant of God is learning to obey.

Ears to hear: In the Old Testament era, without the completed Word of God and the indwelling Holy Spirit to guide, God spoke directly to His prophets and leaders. But often even they needed clarification (16:6-7). Learning to discern the direction of the Lord requires a humble desire to be led, a willingness to be corrected and to repent, and a growing sensitivity to His "voice" (John 10:27).

Honor: One of the most amazing characteristics of David, the newly anointed king, was his unwillingness to dishonor the existing king, Saul, even though he knew Saul's days were numbered. David refused to act against Saul as long as he still occupied the throne of Israel (26:23-24). Learning to honor what God has established, and to wait upon His timing for change, is a sign of spiritual maturity.

DISCOVERY VERSES

No one is holy like the LORD! There is no one besides You; there is no Rock like our God.

(1 SAMUEL 2:2)

"It was the LORD who appointed Moses and Aaron," Samuel continued. "He brought your ancestors out of the land of Egypt. Now stand here quietly before the LORD as I remind you of all the great things the LORD has done for you and your ancestors."

(1 SAMUEL 12:6-7)

But Samuel replied, "What is more pleasing to the LORD: your burnt offerings and sacrifices or your obedience to His voice? Listen! Obedience is better than sacrifice, and submission is better than offering the fat of rams."

(1 SAMUEL 15:22)

1 SAMUEL FACTS

Author: Unknown. Samuel is a likely candidate, but his death before the end of the book (25:1) makes it impossible for him to be the sole author. It's likely that Samuel and others wrote various parts which were compiled by Samuel's associates among the prophets. In the Hebrew text, 1 and 2 Samuel were one large book. In the ancient Greek translation of the Old Testament, the Septuagint, these books were combined with 1 and 2 Kings and entitled "1-4 Kingdoms."

Written to: First Samuel was written to the internally divided and externally threatened covenant community of Israel.

Date of writing: Assuming 1 and 2 Samuel were written near the same time, they must have been completed after Solomon's death (931 BC) given the reference to the divided kingdom in 1 Samuel 27:6 (the united monarchy divided into Israel and Judah following Solomon's reign).

Setting: First Samuel covers almost 100 years following the period of the judges, from the birth of Samuel (approximately 1105 BC) to the death of Saul (approximately 1010 BC). This time frame is midway between the giving of the covenant promise to Abraham (around 2000 BC) and the fulfillment of the promise with the Messiah 1,000 years later. It is set primarily in the central hill country of the Promised Land.

OUTLINE

- **1 SAMUEL 1–7**—God establishes Samuel as the prophet for Israel
- **1 SAMUEL 8–14**—God establishes Saul as the king that Israel wanted
- **1 SAMUEL 15–31**—God establishes David as the king Israel needed

ELKANAH AND HIS FAMILY

1:1 **1** There was a man named Elkanah who lived in Ramah in the region of Zuph* in the
1 Chr 6:22-28, 33-38 hill country of Ephraim. He was the son of Jeroham, son of Elihu, son of Tohu, son of
1:2 Deut 21:15-17 Zuph, of Ephraim. 2 Elkanah had two wives, Hannah and Peninnah. Peninnah had children,
but Hannah did not.
1:3 3 Each year Elkanah would travel to Shiloh to worship and sacrifice to the LORD of
Exod 34:23 Heaven's Armies at the Tabernacle. The priests of the LORD at that time were the two sons
Deut 12:4-7 Josh 18:1 of Eli—Hophni and Phinehas. 4 On the days Elkanah presented his sacrifice, he would give
Luke 2:41-42 portions of the meat to Peninnah and each of her children. 5 And though he loved Hannah,
1:5 he would give her only one choice portion* because the LORD had given her no children.
Gen 30:1-2 6 So Peninnah would taunt Hannah and make fun of her because the LORD had kept her
from having children. 7 Year after year it was the same—Peninnah would taunt Hannah as
they went to the Tabernacle.* Each time, Hannah would be reduced to tears and would not
even eat.
1:8 8 "Why are you crying, Hannah?" Elkanah would ask. "Why aren't you eating? Why be
Ruth 4:15 downhearted just because you have no children? You have me—isn't that better than hav-
ing ten sons?"

HANNAH'S PRAYER FOR A SON

1:9 9 Once after a sacrificial meal at Shiloh, Hannah got up and went to pray. Eli the priest was
1 Sam 3:3 sitting at his customary place beside the entrance of the Tabernacle.* 10 Hannah was in
1:11 deep anguish, crying bitterly as she prayed to the LORD. 11 And she made this vow: "O LORD
Gen 29:32 Num 6:1-6; 30:6-11 of Heaven's Armies, if You will look upon my sorrow and answer my prayer and give me a
Judg 13:5 son, then I will give him back to You. He will be Yours for his entire lifetime, and as a sign
Luke 1:15 that he has been dedicated to the LORD, his hair will never be cut.*"

1:1 As in Greek version; Hebrew reads *in Ramathaim-zophim;* compare 1:19. 1:5 Or *And because he loved Hannah, he would give her a choice portion.* The meaning of the Hebrew is uncertain. 1:7 Hebrew *the house of the LORD;* also in 1:24. 1:9 Hebrew *the Temple of the LORD.* 1:11 Some manuscripts add *He will drink neither wine nor intoxicants.*

1:1 The nation of Israel was arranged by tribes named for the 12 sons of Jacob (whom God renamed Israel in Genesis 32:28). The tribal regions of Israel had been loosely divided into 12 territories. In the Ancient Near East, inheritance was divided between all sons with a double portion usually given to the eldest son. In Jacob's case the double portion went to his favorite son, Joseph. Joseph's two sons, Manasseh and Ephraim, received his inheritance (the tribe of Levi received no territory but instead received religious duties). The book of Samuel opens in the territory of Ephraim, the region allotted to Joseph's younger son. In some Old Testament prophecies the name *Ephraim* is used to identify the entire kingdom of the nation of Israel (Hosea 11–14).

1:2 Though foreign to modern people, polygamy was common in the Ancient Near East. Israelite law helped to regulate this practice (see Deuteronomy 21:15-17), but it was never endorsed. Hannah's inability to bear children would have brought her shame. But the Scriptures contain many accounts of barren women chosen for special motherhood in God's timing. Some examples are Sarah (Genesis 18), Rebekah (Genesis 25), Rachel (Genesis 30), Manoah's wife (Judges 13), and Elizabeth, mother of John the Baptist (Luke 1).

1:3 God gave the Israelites instructions at Mount Sinai on how to build a temporary place for worship, the Tabernacle. This was a portable tent structure, tended by the Levites, which moved with Israel for 40 years in the wilderness. After the people settled the Promised Land under the leadership of Joshua, the Tabernacle was set up permanently in the town of Shiloh. This town, located on the central ridge north of Jerusalem and south of Shechem, became a place of national significance for about 200 years. Once the Ark of the Covenant, the most sacred part of the Tabernacle, was taken from Shiloh (1 Samuel 4), the town began to lose its prominence.

1:3 According to God's instruction given through Moses, the priesthood was restricted to descendants of Aaron, the first high priest. Eli and his sons were descendants of Aaron.

1:4 God gave instructions in the Law concerning the use of sacrificial foods. The priest was allowed to use certain sacrifices for himself and his family's sustenance (see Numbers 18:8-11).

1:11 Vows were considered much more sacred in the biblical era than today. But in a real sense, Hannah was offering what God had already commanded. In the law He declared that all firstborns belonged to Him—firstborns of families, herds, and flocks. Bulls and sheep were often offered as sacrifices, though they could be redeemed, or bought back, for a price. A firstborn child was redeemed by a gift given at the Tabernacle (Exodus 13:10-16). In this way, Israel was to remember that their freedom from Egypt was achieved by the death of all firstborn males not protected by the Passover rituals (Exodus 12:1-13). Hannah was committing herself to follow the command to offer her firstborn back to God by allowing him to serve in the Tabernacle.

1:11 Hannah's description of her son's dedication followed the guidelines of the Nazirite vow outlined in Numbers 6:1-5. Samson was another famous Nazirite. His mother didn't drink wine while she was pregnant so that his vow might not be broken even in the womb; his long hair was associated with his commitment to his vow (Judges 13).

12As she was praying to the LORD, Eli watched her. 13Seeing her lips moving but hearing
no sound, he thought she had been drinking. 14"Must you come here drunk?" he de-
manded. "Throw away your wine!"

15"Oh no, sir!" she replied. "I haven't been drinking wine or anything stronger. But I am
very discouraged, and I was pouring out my heart to the LORD. 16Don't think I am a wicked
woman! For I have been praying out of great anguish and sorrow."

17"In that case," Eli said, "go in peace! May the God of Israel grant the request you have
asked of Him."

18"Oh, thank you, sir!" she exclaimed. Then she went back and began to eat again, and
she was no longer sad.

SAMUEL'S BIRTH AND DEDICATION

19The entire family got up early the next morning and went to worship the LORD once
more. Then they returned home to Ramah. When Elkanah slept with Hannah, the LORD re-
membered her plea, 20and in due time she gave birth to a son. She named him Samuel,*
for she said, "I asked the LORD for him."

21The next year Elkanah and his family went on their annual trip to offer a sacrifice to
the LORD. 22But Hannah did not go. She told her husband, "Wait until the boy is weaned.
Then I will take him to the Tabernacle and leave him there with the LORD permanently.*"

23"Whatever you think is best," Elkanah agreed. "Stay here for now, and may the LORD
help you keep your promise." So she stayed home and nursed the boy until he was
weaned.

24When the child was weaned, Hannah took him to the Tabernacle in Shiloh. They
brought along a three-year-old bull* for the sacrifice and a basket* of flour and some wine.
25After sacrificing the bull, they brought the boy to Eli. 26"Sir, do you remember me?"
Hannah asked. "I am the woman who stood here several years ago praying to the LORD. 27I
asked the LORD to give me this boy, and He has granted my request. 28Now I am giving
him to the LORD, and he will belong to the LORD his whole life." And they* worshiped the
LORD there.

1:14 Acts 2:13
1:15 Ps 42:4; Lam 2:19
1:17 Ps 20:3-5
1:18 Ruth 2:13
1:19 Gen 21:1-2; 30:22
1:21 Luke 2:22
1:24 Num 15:8-10

1:20 *Samuel* sounds like the Hebrew term for "asked of God" or "heard by God." 1:22 Some manuscripts add *I will offer him as a Nazirite for all time.* 1:24a As in Dead Sea Scrolls, Greek and Syriac versions; Masoretic Text reads *three bulls.* 1:24b Hebrew *and an ephah* [20 quarts or 22 liters]. 1:28 Hebrew *he.*

▸ WORSHIP

1:14 Harmful ministers. Is there a minister that you need to forgive for his sin against you? Ministers, like all fallen people, can say some very hurtful things. Sometimes, they say painful things that are correct—the command to repent can produce great sorrow, but a good preacher will tell you the truth about your sin. But at other times, ministers can say really stupid things, such as this charge of drunkenness made by Eli toward Hannah. Hannah had every reason to take offense, but instead, she corrected him. And Eli, being suitably reproved, pronounced God's blessing upon her. When she conceived, she did not hold Eli's previous sin against him, but entrusted the raising of her son to him. May God give you the grace to trust fallible ministers to care for you and your family. (***See Worship****> OT> Priesthood> Duties,* TopicGuide page A28.)

▸ HOLINESS

1:18 Free to rejoice. Though the reality of infertility weighed upon her, Eli's words caused Hannah to submit her feelings to her faith. Her depression began to lift, and she returned to her normal eating habits. As you root your life in what God says in His Word and as you walk in the Spirit, you can experience hope in the midst of (and even freedom from!) debilitating emotions. (***See Holiness****> Submission> Yielding to Spirit> Surrender your heart,* TopicGuide page A41.)

1:22 In the Ancient Near East, children nursed from their mother for as long as five years. In 2 Maccabees 7:27 (an apocryphal book from the biblical era) there is an explicit reference to at least three years of nursing before weaning.

1:24 A bull, some flour, and wine represented key ingredients for Tabernacle sacrifices. The book of Leviticus describes burnt offerings and sin offerings, which required sacrificed animals. The flour would have been for a grain or cereal offering. The wine would have been for a drink offering.

HANNAH'S PRAYER OF PRAISE

2:1 Luke 1:46-55
2:2 Exod 15:11; Deut 4:35; 32:30-31; 2 Sam 22:32
2:3 1 Sam 16:7; 1 Kgs 8:39; Prov 8:13; 16:2; 24:11-12
2:4 Pss 37:15; 46:7-9
2:5 Ps 113:9; Jer 15:9

2 Then Hannah prayed:

"My heart rejoices in the LORD!
The LORD has made me strong.*
Now I have an answer for my enemies;
I rejoice because You rescued me.
2 No one is holy like the LORD!
There is no one besides You;
there is no Rock like our God.

3 "Stop acting so proud and haughty!
Don't speak with such arrogance!
For the LORD is a God who knows what You have done;
He will judge your actions.
4 The bow of the mighty is now broken,
and those who stumbled are now strong.
5 Those who were well fed are now starving,
and those who were starving are now full.

2:1 Hebrew *has exalted my horn.*

▸ CHURCH

2:1 The joy of children. The birth of a child touches us all quite deeply. Hannah's prayer and the prayer of Mary (in Luke 1:46-55) are among the most beautiful and beloved by God's people. Both prayers are from godly women rejoicing in the child God had given them. Children are a blessing from the Lord and are one of the means God has ordained to bring His blessings to this world (Psalm 127:3; Genesis 12:1-3). Even when they drive you crazy, rejoice in the children God has given you! (***See Church***> *Who> From Every People> Children are included in the older covenants,* TopicGuide page A48.)

2:2 The "Rock" is a common description for God in biblical literature. It evokes the image of strength and immovability, something which you can depend upon not to change or break apart under pressure.

2:3-5 Like many of David's prayers (such as Psalm 69:22-28), a portion of Hannah's prayer is *imprecatory.* It is hopeful of the demise of the one who has inflicted harm (in this case Peninnah). The following note discusses how such prayers may apply to us.

▸ WORSHIP

2:5 Blessing and cursing. Have you ever hoped that God would judge someone who had hurt you or those you love? Jesus says we should love our enemies and pray forthose who persecute us (Matthew 5:44). But does that mean that our prayers may only be for the happiness or success of those who seek to harm us? Does Jesus' directive to love your enemies contradict a prayer like Hannah's, which calls curses on her enemy? The right answer to this lies in motive—those who prayed hoping for the destruction of God's enemies (Jesus, in Matthew 11:23-24; Paul in Galatians 1:8-9 and 2 Timothy 4:14; God's people in Revelation 6:10) were praying for God's justice to be made powerfully clear. These are not prayers of ungodly hatred or personal revenge, but are for God's glory to be made known through His justice and wrath. In this context, it is not contradictory to love your enemy and, at the same time, pray for God's enemies to have a hasty end rather than continue in their sin. (***See Worship***> *OT> Repentance> Nature> Obedience leads to blessing, failure to repent leads to curses,* TopicGuide page A29.)

BECAUSE GOD IS HOLY

I will devote myself to him in purity, worship and service.

No one is holy like the LORD!

1 SAMUEL 2:2

FOR THE NEXT *GOD IS HOLY* FEATURE SEE PAGE 493.

The childless woman now has seven children,
  and the woman with many children wastes away.
6 The LORD gives both death and life;
  He brings some down to the grave* but raises others up.
7 The LORD makes some poor and others rich;
  He brings some down and lifts others up.
8 He lifts the poor from the dust
  and the needy from the garbage dump.
He sets them among princes,
  placing them in seats of honor.
For all the earth is the LORD's,
  and He has set the world in order.

9 "He will protect His faithful ones,
  but the wicked will disappear in darkness.
No one will succeed by strength alone.
10 Those who fight against the LORD will be shattered.
He thunders against them from heaven;
  the LORD judges throughout the earth.
He gives power to His king;
  He increases the strength* of His anointed one."

11 Then Elkanah returned home to Ramah without Samuel. And the boy served the LORD
by assisting Eli the priest.

2:6 Deut 32:39
2:7 Deut 8:18; Job 1:21; 5:10-11; Ps 75:7
2:8 Job 36:7; 38:4-7; 42:10; Jas 2:5
2:9 Ps 91:11-12; Matt 8:12
2:10 Exod 15:6; 19:16; 1 Sam 7:10; Pss 18:13; 21:1, 7; 89:24; 96:13
2:11 1 Sam 3:1

ELI'S WICKED SONS

12 Now the sons of Eli were scoundrels who had no respect for the LORD 13 or for their duties
as priests. Whenever anyone offered a sacrifice, Eli's sons would send over a servant with
a three-pronged fork. While the meat of the sacrificed animal was still boiling, 14 the ser-
vant would stick the fork into the pot and demand that whatever it brought up be given to
Eli's sons. All the Israelites who came to worship at Shiloh were treated this way. 15 Some-
times the servant would come even before the animal's fat had been burned on the altar.
He would demand raw meat before it had been boiled so that it could be used for roasting.
16 The man offering the sacrifice might reply, "Take as much as you want, but the fat
must be burned first." Then the servant would demand, "No, give it to me now, or I'll take it
by force." 17 So the sin of these young men was very serious in the LORD's sight, for they
treated the LORD's offerings with contempt.
18 But Samuel, though he was only a boy, served the LORD. He wore a linen garment like
that of a priest.* 19 Each year his mother made a small coat for him and brought it to him
when she came with her husband for the sacrifice. 20 Before they returned home, Eli would

2:12 Jer 2:8; 9:3, 6
2:13 Lev 7:20, 28-36
2:15 Lev 3:2-5
2:17 Mal 2:7-9
2:18 1 Sam 2:11
2:19 1 Sam 1:3

2:6 Hebrew *to Sheol.* 2:10 Hebrew *he exalts the horn.* 2:18 Hebrew *He wore a linen ephod.*

▸ WORSHIP
2:12 Kids gone wild. It's not supposed to be this way, but sometimes the worst people in the church are the elders, pastors, or deacons—those entrusted with priestly duties. God warned Hophni and Phinehas through their feeble father, but they ignored his counsel, so God planned to end their ministry by ending their lives. Let this be a warning to all ministers who flaunt their position for personal gain—God is deadly serious about integrity among those who claim to be His ministers. (***See Worship****> NT> Reverence> We fear God because He has power over life and death,* TopicGuide page A32.)

2:12-17 Eli's sons, Hophni and Phinehas, showed complete disregard for both the sacrificial system given by God in the law and for their own role as priests within that system. Rather than bringing honor to their responsibilities, Hophni and Phinehas used their position to fulfill their own desires. The custom of reserving all the fat of a sacrifice for God is formalized in Leviticus. But God formalized this practice with His people in Leviticus 4:8-10. The fat of the animals represented flavor, opulence, and lavishness. It was supposed to be burned on the very day the animal was killed so that there was no temptation to use it any other way except to honor and acknowledge God's presence. The actions of Hophni and Phinehas involved more than just disregard for sacrificial customs—they were disregarding God Himself.

bless Elkanah and his wife and say, "May the LORD give you other children to take the
2:21 place of this one she gave to the LORD.*" 21And the LORD gave Hannah three sons and two
Gen 21:1 1 Sam 3:19-21 daughters. Meanwhile, Samuel grew up in the presence of the LORD.
Luke 2:40 22Now Eli was very old, but he was aware of what his sons were doing to the people of
2:22 Israel. He knew, for instance, that his sons were seducing the young women who assisted
Exod 38:8 at the entrance of the Tabernacle.* 23Eli said to them, "I have been hearing reports from all
2:23 the people about the wicked things you are doing. Why do you keep sinning? 24You must
Num 15:30 stop, my sons! The reports I hear among the LORD's people are not good. 25If someone sins
2:25 Josh 11:20 against another person, God* can mediate for the guilty party. But if someone sins against
the LORD, who can intercede?" But Eli's sons wouldn't listen to their father, for the LORD was
already planning to put them to death.
2:26 26Meanwhile, the boy Samuel grew taller and grew in favor with the LORD and with the
Luke 2:40, 52 people.

A WARNING FOR ELI'S FAMILY

2:27 27One day a man of God came to Eli and gave him this message from the LORD: "I revealed
Judg 13:6 Myself* to your ancestors when the people of Israel were slaves in Egypt. 28I chose your
2:28 Exod 28:1-4; 30:7-8 ancestor Aaron* from among all the tribes of Israel to be My priest, to offer sacrifices on My
altar, to burn incense, and to wear the priestly vest* as he served Me. And I assigned the
2:29 sacrificial offerings to you priests. 29So why do you scorn My sacrifices and offerings? Why
Matt 10:37 Deut 12:5 do you give your sons more honor than you give Me—for you and they have become fat
from the best offerings of My people Israel!
2:30 30"Therefore, the LORD, the God of Israel, says: I promised that your branch of the tribe
Num 25:12-13 of Levi* would always be My priests. But I will honor those who honor Me, and I will de-
Ps 50:23 Mal 2:7-9 spise those who think lightly of Me. 31The time is coming when I will put an end to your
2:31 family, so it will no longer serve as My priests. All the members of your family will die be-
1 Sam 4:11-18; fore their time. None will reach old age. 32You will watch with envy as I pour out prosperity
22:17-20 on the people of Israel. But no members of your family will ever live out their days.
33Those who survive will live in sadness and grief, and their children will die a violent
2:34 death.* 34And to prove that what I have said will come true, I will cause your two sons,
1 Sam 4:11, 17 1 Kgs 13:3 Hophni and Phinehas, to die on the same day!

2:20 As in Dead Sea Scrolls and Greek version; Masoretic Text reads *this one she requested of the LORD in prayer.* 2:22 Hebrew *Tent of Meeting.* Some manuscripts lack this entire sentence. 2:25 Or *the judges.* 2:27 As in Greek and Syriac versions; Hebrew reads *Did I reveal Myself.* 2:28a Hebrew *your father.* 2:28b Hebrew *an ephod.* 2:30 Hebrew *that your house and your father's house.* 2:33 As in Dead Sea Scrolls, which read *die by the sword;* Masoretic Text reads *die like mortals.*

2:22 Not only were Hophni and Phinehas treating the sacrificial system with contempt, they were involved in sexual scandal. Their actions were reminiscent of the worship practices in Egypt, Canaan, and other places in the Ancient Near East. Most pagan worship in this time involved fertility rites. Those who served in certain temples became sexually involved with the worshipers as part of the rituals. God explicitly prohibited this behavior as one way to set His people apart from the cultures around them.

2:26 In contrast to Eli's natural sons, who lacked character and vision, Samuel was described as a person of integrity and holiness. The language used to describe Samuel is very similar to that used to describe Jesus (see Luke 2:40, 52).

2:28 Aaron was the brother of Moses and the first high priest of Israel. Both were of the tribe of Levi. Only Aaron's descendants were designated as priests. The rest of the Levites were set apart to serve the Tabernacle in more general ways. The Levites and priests gave up land ownership as part of their inheritance, receiving instead the honor of service to the Lord. They also received a portion of the offerings that were brought by the other 11 tribes of Israelites. It was not wicked for Eli's sons to partake of the offerings. Their evil lay in the disregard they showed for the holiness of the offerings before they took their share.

▸ HOLINESS

2:29 Authority and responsibility. Eli bore great responsibility for the calamity in the clergy, because he was responsible for overseeing the entire priesthood. Those in authority bear responsibility for knowingly allowing misdeeds to continue under their oversight. But this is not an excuse to judge others—you must look at yourself. If you are in a position of authority, do you allow rampant sin to occur among those under your care? If you do, God will, one way or another, raise up someone else to oversee His work. (***See Holiness*****>** *Law and Grace*> *Law*> *Leaders and followers,* TopicGuide page A41.)

35"Then I will raise up a faithful priest who will serve Me and do what I desire. I will es-
tablish his family, and they will be priests to My anointed kings forever. 36Then all of your
surviving family will bow before him, begging for money and food. 'Please,' they will say,
'give us jobs among the priests so we will have enough to eat.' "

THE LORD SPEAKS TO SAMUEL

3 Meanwhile, the boy Samuel served the LORD by assisting Eli. Now in those days mes- **3:1**
sages from the LORD were very rare, and visions were quite uncommon. 1 Sam 2:11 Ps 74:9
2One night Eli, who was almost blind by now, had gone to bed. 3The lamp of God had Amos 8:11
not yet gone out, and Samuel was sleeping in the Tabernacle* near the Ark of God.
4Suddenly the LORD called out, "Samuel!"
"Yes?" Samuel replied. "What is it?" 5He got up and ran to Eli. "Here I am. Did you call me?"
"I didn't call you," Eli replied. "Go back to bed." So he did.
6Then the LORD called out again, "Samuel!"
Again Samuel got up and went to Eli. "Here I am. Did you call me?"
"I didn't call you, my son," Eli said. "Go back to bed."
7Samuel did not yet know the LORD because he had never had a message from the LORD **3:7**
before. 8So the LORD called a third time, and once more Samuel got up and went to Eli. Amos 3:7
"Here I am. Did you call me?"
Then Eli realized it was the LORD who was calling the boy. 9So he said to Samuel, "Go
and lie down again, and if someone calls again, say, 'Speak, LORD, your servant is listen-
ing.' " So Samuel went back to bed.
10And the LORD came and called as before, "Samuel! Samuel!"
And Samuel replied, "Speak, Your servant is listening." **3:11**
11Then the LORD said to Samuel, "I am about to do a shocking thing in Israel. 12I am go- 2 Kgs 21:12 Jer 19:3
ing to carry out all My threats against Eli and his family, from beginning to end. 13I have **3:12**
warned him that judgment is coming upon his family forever, because his sons are blas- 1 Sam 2:27-36
pheming God* and he hasn't disciplined them. 14So I have vowed that the sins of Eli and **3:14**
his sons will never be forgiven by sacrifices or offerings." Lev 15:31 1 Sam 2:25 Isa 22:14

SAMUEL SPEAKS FOR THE LORD

15Samuel stayed in bed until morning, then got up and opened the doors of the Taberna-
cle* as usual. He was afraid to tell Eli what the LORD had said to him. 16But Eli called out to
him, "Samuel, my son."
"Here I am," Samuel replied.
17"What did the LORD say to you? Tell me everything. And may God strike you and even
kill you if you hide anything from me!" 18So Samuel told Eli everything; he didn't hold any- **3:18**
thing back. "It is the LORD's will," Eli replied. "Let Him do what He thinks best." Job 2:10 Isa 39:8

3:3 Hebrew *the Temple of the LORD.* 3:13 As in Greek version; Hebrew reads *his sons have made themselves contemptible.*
3:15 Hebrew *the house of the LORD.*

▶ **BIBLE**

3:1 Healthy doubt. Have you ever thought you had a message directly from God? Rather than jump to conclusions, Samuel had healthy doubt about hearing directly from God. He sought counsel from his spiritual authority, and even the greatest priest of that time required several pieces of evidence before he thought it might be God at work. Always have a healthy skepticism about any apparent message from God except for the ones from His inerrant Word. There is no message more certain than God revealing His perfect will for you through His written Word. (***See Bible****> Uniqueness> Authoritative> Demands heart obedience,* TopicGuide page A10.)

3:1 Not too long before Samuel's time, God had manifested Himself in profound ways through pillars of smoke and fire. He spoke to Moses, giving him many messages. He showed Himself and spoke to leaders in the period of the judges. This description of Samuel's time stands in stark contrast to Israel's previous history.

3:5 The Hebrew term used here—*hineni*—carries the connotation of one who is not only present but one who is present with a readiness and willingness to serve with humility.

3:13-14 Think of how deplorable the blasphemy of Eli's sons must have been for God to vow that their sin would never be forgiven by sacrifices or offerings.

3:19 Gen 21:22 19As Samuel grew up, the LORD was with him, and everything Samuel said proved to be
Judg 13:24 reliable. 20And all Israel, from Dan in the north to Beersheba in the south, knew that Samu-
3:20 el was confirmed as a prophet of the LORD. 21The LORD continued to appear at Shiloh and
Judg 20:1 gave messages to Samuel there at the Tabernacle. 4:1And Samuel's words went out to all
the people of Israel.

THE PHILISTINES CAPTURE THE ARK

4:1 **4** At that time Israel was at war with the Philistines. The Israelite army was camped near
1 Sam 7:12; 29:1 Ebenezer, and the Philistines were at Aphek. 2The Philistines attacked and defeated
4:3 the army of Israel, killing 4,000 men. 3After the battle was over, the troops retreated to
Num 10:35 Josh 7:7 their camp, and the elders of Israel asked, "Why did the LORD allow us to be defeated by
the Philistines?" Then they said, "Let's bring the Ark of the Covenant of the LORD from Shi-
loh. If we carry it into battle with us, it* will save us from our enemies."
4:4 2 Sam 6:2 4So they sent men to Shiloh to bring the Ark of the Covenant of the LORD of Heaven's Ar-
Ps 80:1 mies, who is enthroned between the cherubim. Hophni and Phinehas, the sons of Eli, were
4:5 also there with the Ark of the Covenant of God. 5When all the Israelites saw the Ark of the
Josh 6:5 Covenant of the LORD coming into the camp, their shout of joy was so loud it made the
ground shake!
6"What's going on?" the Philistines asked. "What's all the shouting about in the Hebrew
4:7 camp?" When they were told it was because the Ark of the LORD had arrived, 7they pan-
Exod 14:25; 15:14 icked. "The gods have* come into their camp!" they cried. "This is a disaster! We have
never had to face anything like this before! 8Help! Who can save us from these mighty
gods of Israel? They are the same gods who destroyed the Egyptians with plagues when
4:9 Israel was in the wilderness. 9Fight as never before, Philistines! If you don't, we will be-
Judg 13:1 come the Hebrews' slaves just as they have been ours! Stand up like men and fight!"
4:10 10So the Philistines fought desperately, and Israel was defeated again. The slaughter was
Deut 28:15, 25 great; 30,000 Israelite soldiers died that day. The survivors turned and fled to their tents.
4:11 1 Sam 2:34 11The Ark of God was captured, and Hophni and Phinehas, the two sons of Eli, were killed.
Ps 78:60-61

4:3 Or *He.* 4:7 Or *A god has.*

▸ BIBLE

3:19-21 Discovering Jesus in the life of Samuel. The narrator comments twice on Samuel's early maturity as a confirmation of his special place in God's work, saying that he "grew taller and grew in favor with the LORD and with the people" (2:26; see also 3:19-21). In a similar way, Luke 2:52 says, "Jesus grew in wisdom and in stature and in favor with God and all the people." Luke demonstrates that Jesus had a unique place in God's kingdom at an early age, thus validating His later ministry. (***See Bible****> Unity> OT Types> Samuel,* TopicGuide page A11.)

4:1 The Philistines were a people who occupied the coastal plain on the southwestern part of the Promised Land. They troubled Israel for centuries, even ruling Israel for whole generations, at times (see Judges 13:1). A major trade route along the coastal area passed through Philistia. The word *Palestine,* though derived from the word *Philistine,* is a fairly recent term. Palestinians of modern times are not related to the Philistines from 3,000 years ago.

4:3 The Ark of the Covenant was essentially a wooden chest overlaid with gold and made to strict specifications (Exodus 25:10-14). The lid of the Ark is often translated "mercy seat," and it was a representation of God's throne. It was considered the place of atonement. The resting place of the Ark was in the most holy inner chamber of the portable Tabernacle. This Most Holy Place was seen as God's residence. The people associated God's presence with the Ark more than any other piece of the Tabernacle. They thought that to carry it into battle would be like carrying God Himself and His power with them.

4:6-9 The Philistines apparently knew something of Israel's Exodus from Egypt and journey to the Promised Land. They were aware of the role the Ark of the Covenant played in Israel's successes. The Philistines were motivated to fight desperately not because they believed in the God of Israel, but because they did not want to submit to the Israelites or their God. Archeological finds in the coastal plain of Israel confirm the Bible's testimony that the Philistines smelted iron weapons and controlled this industry during this time, giving them an advantage in armed conflict (1 Samuel 13:19-22; 17:7).

4:9 The Philistines had ruled the Israelites for at least 40 years (Judges 13:1). Other people groups had controlled Israel as well. One example is Moab (an 18-year occupation is described in Judges 3:12-14).

▸ GOD

4:11 The promise of judgment. It didn't take long for God's promise of judgment to come true against the house of Eli (3:14). One of the ways we know God's Word is true is that prophecies contained in it are fulfilled. Some prophecies may have contingencies (see the book of Jonah), but this one did not—God made a vow to judge the house of Eli, regardless of their repentance. Thank God that His Word is dependable! (***See God****> God's Attributes> Faithful> God is faithful to fulfill His promises,* TopicGuide page A16.)

THE DEATH OF ELI

12 A man from the tribe of Benjamin ran from the battlefield and arrived at Shiloh later that 4:12
same day. He had torn his clothes and put dust on his head to show his grief. 13 Eli was Josh 7:6
waiting beside the road to hear the news of the battle, for his heart trembled for the safety 2 Sam 1:2
of the Ark of God. When the messenger arrived and told what had happened, an outcry re- Neh 9:1
sounded throughout the town.
14 "What is all the noise about?" Eli asked.
The messenger rushed over to Eli, 15 who was ninety-eight years old and blind. 16 He said 4:15
to Eli, "I have just come from the battlefield—I was there this very day." Gen 27:1
"What happened, my son?" Eli demanded. 1 Sam 3:2
17 "Israel has been defeated by the Philistines," the messenger replied. "The people have 4:17 1 Sam 22:18
been slaughtered, and your two sons, Hophni and Phinehas, were also killed. And the Ark Ps 78:61, 64
of God has been captured."
18 When the messenger mentioned what had happened to the Ark of God, Eli fell back-
ward from his seat beside the gate. He broke his neck and died, for he was old and over-
weight. He had been Israel's judge for forty years.
19 Eli's daughter-in-law, the wife of Phinehas, was pregnant and near her time of deliv-
ery. When she heard that the Ark of God had been captured and that her father-in-law and
husband were dead, she went into labor and gave birth. 20 She died in childbirth, but be- 4:20
fore she passed away the midwives tried to encourage her. "Don't be afraid," they said. Gen 35:17-18
"You have a baby boy!" But she did not answer or pay attention to them.
21 She named the child Ichabod (which means "Where is the glory?"), for she said, "Isra- 4:21
el's glory is gone." She named him this because the Ark of God had been captured and be- Ps 106:20
cause her father-in-law and husband were dead. 22 Then she said, "The glory has departed
from Israel, for the Ark of God has been captured."

THE ARK IN PHILISTIA

5 After the Philistines captured the Ark of God, they took it from the battleground at 5:2 Judg 16:23
Ebenezer to the town of Ashdod. 2 They carried the Ark of God into the temple of Da- Ps 78:61

▸ GOD
4:12 God in a box. Sometimes we are tempted to think we have God all figured out. All we have to do is pray enough, have a daily quiet time, carry our Bible around, and things will go well for us in the battles of life. This was Israel's problem, too. They believed that if they took the Ark into battle, they couldn't lose. But God is bigger than that. He cannot be used like a good luck charm, nor is He merely at your disposal. (***See God****> God's Attributes> Infinite> He has no limits, boundaries, or end,* TopicGuide page A16.)

4:12 Grief and mourning was a public event in this ancient culture. When this man arrived from battle with dirt thrown on his head and his clothes torn, the people would have assumed he brought bad news. In times of mourning and grief in that day people didn't bathe, their hair was left loose, and clothing was torn. People would cover their faces and heads; wear sackcloth, a scratchy, uncomfortable fabric; and sit in the midst of ashes.

4:18 When he died, Eli was "old" and "overweight." The Hebrew term for "old" or "elder" (*zaqen*) was an honorable designation. The author may be using a word play with the term for "overweight" (*chabed*) since it is closely related to the term glory (*chabod*) used a couple of verses later. While Eli in his old age should have been respected for his age and glory, he was merely old and large.

4:21 On the surface, this looks as if God lost the battle and was taken captive by the Philistines. However, this captivity was God's way of beginning to restore glory to Himself and His people by cleansing Israel of sin and humbling their enemies.

▸ GOD
4:22 God has left. Have you ever felt as if God had abandoned you? Since God is everywhere (Psalm 139:7-10), He did not leave Israel completely; the glorious manifestation of His presence left Israel when the Ark was captured. When we sin, we experience a loss of fellowship, the relational manifestation of God's nearness to us. Repentance, however, restores our awareness of His abiding presence. (See Psalm 51; also ***see God****> God's Attributes> All-Present> All creation is dependent upon His presence,* TopicGuide page A16.)

4:22 Samuel had brought to the Tabernacle a new era of messages and visions from God (1 Samuel 3:21). The loss of the Ark of the Covenant, however, meant that God's powerful presence was no longer there. Psalm 78:56-64 confirms that the Lord allowed the Ark to be taken, and then His presence abandoned Shiloh. The Philistines only had the Ark for seven months before giving it up, but it was not officially returned to the Tabernacle until David returned it with great ceremony during his reign (2 Samuel 6).

5:1 The Philistine nation was a loose alliance of five city-states: Ashdod, Gaza, Ekron, Ashkelon, and Gath. All were located along or near the coast of the Mediterranean in the region now known as the Gaza Strip. When Joshua oversaw the allotment of land to the tribes of Israel, these cities were to have been part of Judah's land. According to Judges 1:19, though, Judah failed to drive the Philistines out because the iron chariots that the Philistines built and used in battle proved too much of an advantage.

5:3 gon and placed it beside an idol of Dagon. 3But when the citizens of Ashdod went to see it
Isa 19:1; 46:7 the next morning, Dagon had fallen with his face to the ground in front of the Ark of the
5:4 LORD! So they took Dagon and put him in his place again. 4But the next morning the same
Ezek 6:6 Mic 1:7 thing happened—Dagon had fallen face down before the Ark of the LORD again. This time
his head and hands had broken off and were lying in the doorway. Only the trunk of his
body was left intact. 5That is why to this day neither the priests of Dagon nor anyone who
enters the temple of Dagon in Ashdod will step on its threshold.

5:6 6Then the LORD's heavy hand struck the people of Ashdod and the nearby villages with
Exod 9:3 a plague of tumors.* 7When the people realized what was happening, they cried out, "We
1 Sam 6:4-5 can't keep the Ark of the God of Israel here any longer! He is against us! We will all be de-
5:8 Judg 16:18 stroyed along with Dagon, our god." 8So they called together the rulers of the Philistine
towns and asked, "What should we do with the Ark of the God of Israel?"

5:9 The rulers discussed it and replied, "Move it to the town of Gath." So they moved the Ark
1 Sam 7:13; 12:15 of the God of Israel to Gath. 9But when the Ark arrived at Gath, the LORD's heavy hand fell
on its men, young and old; He struck them with a plague of tumors, and there was a great
5:10 panic.

Josh 13:3 10So they sent the Ark of God to the town of Ekron, but when the people of Ekron saw
it coming they cried out, "They are bringing the Ark of the God of Israel here to kill us,
too!" 11The people summoned the Philistine rulers again and begged them, "Please send
the Ark of the God of Israel back to its own country, or it* will kill us all." For the deadly
plague from God had already begun, and great fear was sweeping across the town.
12Those who didn't die were afflicted with tumors; and the cry from the town rose to
heaven.

THE PHILISTINES RETURN THE ARK

6:2 Gen 41:8 **6** The Ark of the LORD remained in Philistine territory seven months in all. 2Then the
Exod 7:11 Philistines called in their priests and diviners and asked them, "What should we do
about the Ark of the LORD? Tell us how to return it to its own country."

6:3 3"Send the Ark of the God of Israel back with a gift," they were told. "Send a guilt offer-
Lev 5:15-16 ing so the plague will stop. Then, if you are healed, you will know it was His hand that
6:4 Josh 13:3 caused the plague."

1 Sam 5:6, 11; 6:5 5:6 Greek version and Latin Vulgate read *tumors; and rats appeared in their land, and death and destruction were throughout the city.* 5:11 Or *He.*

5:2 The Canaanite god, Dagon, was the principal idol of the Philistines. He was often portrayed as part fish and was seen as a god of agriculture. The worship practices of the followers of Dagon, similar to those of other Canaanite gods, involved behavior that God had banned from His people.

▸ GOD
5:4 Idols are weak. The Philistines thought they had the God of Israel under control. With His people defeated and His Ark captured, the great God of Israel, oppressor of mighty Egypt, was now under their boot. With delicious irony, the narrator demonstrates that it was the God of Israel, not Dagon, who reigned supreme. Not only was Dagon bowed low, but his priests and servants were struck with bubonic plague-like symptoms, causing them to shift the Ark around to various cities for seven months (5:10; 6:1-4). Those who appear to have the upper hand will be humbled by God's mighty hand. (***See God****> God's Nature> Alive> God lives, false gods don't,* TopicGuide page A14.)

5:6 The nature of the tumors mentioned here is uncertain. However, because the Philistines sent the Ark back with gold tumors accompanied by gold rats, many have held that the strange affliction was a type of bubonic plague spread by rat-borne fleas.

5:8 Gath was the home of Goliath, the giant warrior killed by young David with only a sling and a stone. In a historical twist, David defected to Gath when he fled from King Saul (1 Samuel 27). After his first failed attempt to return the Ark of the Covenant to the Tabernacle, David sent it to Gath, to the home of a man named Obed-edom (2 Samuel 6:10-12). Eventually David conquered Gath and brought it under his own rule (2 Samuel 8:1).

5:10 It was clear to the Philistines that the Ark, which they first thought was a prize to be kept, was now a pariah to be rid of. Each city was eager for the Ark to move on soon after it arrived.

4“What sort of guilt offering should we send?” they asked.
And they were told, “Since the plague has struck both you and your five rulers, make
five gold tumors and five gold rats, just like those that have ravaged your land. 5Make
these things to show honor to the God of Israel. Perhaps then He will stop afflicting you,
your gods, and your land. 6Don’t be stubborn and rebellious as Pharaoh and the Egyptians **6:6**
were. By the time God was finished with them, they were eager to let Israel go. Exod 8:15, 31-32; 12:31
7“Now build a new cart, and find two cows that have just given birth to calves. Make **6:7**
sure the cows have never been yoked to a cart. Hitch the cows to the cart, but shut their Deut 21:3
calves away from them in a pen. 8Put the Ark of the LORD on the cart, and beside it place a 2 Sam 6:3
chest containing the gold rats and gold tumors you are sending as a guilt offering. Then let
the cows go wherever they want. 9If they cross the border of our land and go to Beth- **6:9**
shemesh, we will know it was the LORD who brought this great disaster upon us. If they Josh 15:10
don’t, we will know it was not His hand that caused the plague. It came simply by chance.” 1 Sam 6:3
10So these instructions were carried out. Two cows were hitched to the cart, and their
newborn calves were shut up in a pen. 11Then the Ark of the LORD and the chest containing
the gold rats and gold tumors were placed on the cart. 12And sure enough, without veering
off in other directions, the cows went straight along the road toward Beth-shemesh, low-
ing as they went. The Philistine rulers followed them as far as the border of Beth-shemesh.
13The people of Beth-shemesh were harvesting wheat in the valley, and when they saw
the Ark, they were overjoyed! 14The cart came into the field of a man named Joshua and **6:14**
stopped beside a large rock. So the people broke up the wood of the cart for a fire and 2 Sam 24:22
killed the cows and sacrificed them to the LORD as a burnt offering. 15Several men of the **6:15** Josh 3:2-4
tribe of Levi lifted the Ark of the LORD and the chest containing the gold rats and gold tu-
mors from the cart and placed them on the large rock. Many sacrifices and burnt offerings
were offered to the LORD that day by the people of Beth-shemesh. 16The five Philistine rul-
ers watched all this and then returned to Ekron that same day.
17The five gold tumors sent by the Philistines as a guilt offering to the LORD were gifts **6:17** 1 Sam 6:4

▸ GOD

6:6 How to sin less. God does not send judgment on individuals or nations simply for punitive reasons. God is interested in promoting repentance, holiness, and joy in His people. In this case, God’s judgment on Egypt served as a warning that prevented the Philistines from committing greater atrocities against God and His people. God’s righteous punishment of the Egyptians encouraged the Philistines to sin less. Let God’s mighty power and commitment to justice warn you away from gossip, murder, divorce, homosexuality, and all other sins. (***See God****> God’s Nature> Personality> Emotion> Rebellion rightly angers God,* TopicGuide page A14.)

6:6 The priests and diviners were correct in their description of Pharaoh and his people. God sent ten plagues against Egypt: The water of the Nile turned to blood (Exodus 7), frogs covered the land, insects swarmed, flies descended (Exodus 8), livestock died, people suffered with boils, hail thundered down (Exodus 9), locusts destroyed crops, and complete darkness fell (Exodus 10). Finally, God sent the last plague in which the firstborn (both sons and livestock) died, including the firstborn of the royal family (Exodus 11–12). With each plague, Pharaoh would relent until the plague was gone; then he would betray his promises and refuse to allow Israel to leave.

6:10 Note that the priests of Dagon were trying to “stack the deck” against any possible sign that the Lord was involved in their situation. First, the cows chosen to pull the cart containing the Ark were unfamiliar with each other and so were not likely to make much progress together. Second, they both had new calves in pens nearby, further assuring they would not leave the area. What could be more unnatural than for a nursing mother animal to leave behind her newborn? The Philistines needed a success after such an affliction. They needed to know Dagon still mattered and was strong.

6:12 The town of Beth-shemesh is located in the Sorek Valley midway between Jerusalem on the central ridge and Ashdod on the coastal plain. This is the same valley where Samson found Delilah (Judges 16:4).

▸ GOD

6:13 Rejoice! God brings the Ark back to a people too foolish to keep it safe and too cowardly to risk their lives to get it back. Israel could have easily been shamed by the way the Ark was returned, but God used it to bring joy, not condemnation, to His broken people. When you see God entering into your life after you have failed Him, rejoice! He has come announcing the Good News of the Spirit-guided life through repentance and belief. (***See God****> God’s Nature> Personality> Relationships> He wants to be known,* TopicGuide page A14.)

6:15 Both Philistines and Israelites brought offerings and sacrifices in this episode. This reminds us that the system of offerings used by God was not unique—other Ancient Near Eastern religions had sacrificial systems as well (see, for example, 1 Kings 18 where both Elijah and the priests of Baal offer sacrifice on Mount Carmel). However, the system of sacrifice that God laid out for His people points to a Priest and Redeemer and admits that animal sacrifice is not sufficient for the remission of sin (Isaiah 52; Hebrews 8–9).

6:18 Deut 3:5 from the rulers of Ashdod, Gaza, Ashkelon, Gath, and Ekron. [18]The five gold rats represented the five Philistine towns and their surrounding villages, which were controlled by the five rulers. The large rock at Beth-shemesh, where they set the Ark of the LORD, still stands in the field of Joshua as a witness to what happened there.

THE ARK MOVED TO KIRIATH-JEARIM

6:19 2 Sam 6:7 6:20 Lev 11:44-45 2 Sam 6:9 Mal 3:2

[19]But the LORD killed seventy men* from Beth-shemesh because they looked into the Ark of the LORD. And the people mourned greatly because of what the LORD had done. [20]"Who is able to stand in the presence of the LORD, this holy God?" they cried out. "Where can we send the Ark from here?"

6:19 As in a few Hebrew manuscripts; most Hebrew manuscripts read *70 men, 50,000 men.* Perhaps the text should be understood to read *the LORD killed 70 men and 50 oxen.*

▸ WORSHIP

6:19 Forbidden knowledge. Our knowledge of God and our familiarity with Him must not breed a casual disrespect of Him. No matter how excited you get about God, and no matter how much you learn about Him, you must obey God's holy commands. In this case, God had forbidden laypeople to touch (and this included lifting up the lid and looking inside) the Ark. Remember, God is holy and must be given the deep respect He deserves in our worship. (***See Worship****> OT> Reverence> Fear Him because of what He has done,* TopicGuide page A28.)

6:19-20 The Ark of the Covenant (also called Ark of the Lord) was mysteriously powerful. When God gave Moses the instructions for building the Ark, metal loops were put on the sides so that poles could be used to carry the chest (Exodus 25:10-22). In this way, no one would have to touch it, because they would die if they did so. The people were to fear the power of God's presence. It is clear that such fear and reverence had disappeared in Israel since 70 men tried to look into the Ark. It would be 20 years before the Ark entered the narrative again, when David retrieved it in 2 Samuel 6.

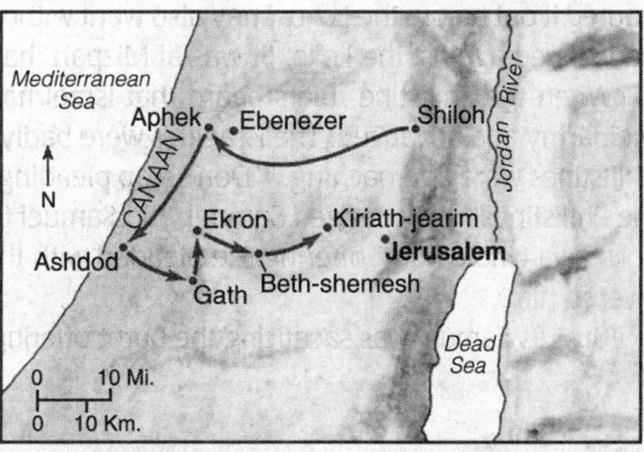

THE ARK'S TRAVELS

Eli's sons took the Ark from Shiloh to the battlefield on the lower plains at Ebenezer and Aphek. The Philistines captured the Ark and took it to Ashdod, Gath, and Ekron. Plagues forced the people to send the Ark back to Israel, where it finally was taken by cattle-drawn carts to Beth-shemesh and on to the home of Eleazar in Kiriath-jearim.

BECAUSE GOD IS HOLY

I will devote myself to him in purity, worship and service.

Who is able to stand in the presence of the LORD, this holy God?

1 SAMUEL 6:20

FOR THE NEXT *GOD IS HOLY* FEATURE SEE PAGE 1042.

21 So they sent messengers to the people at Kiriath-jearim and told them, "The Philis- 6:21
tines have returned the Ark of the LORD. Come here and get it!" Josh 15:9, 60

7

So the men of Kiriath-jearim came to get the Ark of the LORD. They took it to the hill- 7:1
side home of Abinadab and ordained Eleazar, his son, to be in charge of it. 2 The Ark 2 Sam 6:3-4
remained in Kiriath-jearim for a long time—twenty years in all. During that time all Israel
mourned because it seemed the LORD had abandoned them.

SAMUEL LEADS ISRAEL TO VICTORY

3 Then Samuel said to all the people of Israel, "If you are really serious about wanting to re- 7:3
turn to the LORD, get rid of your foreign gods and your images of Ashtoreth. Determine to Deut 6:13; 13:4 Josh 24:14, 23
obey only the LORD; then He will rescue you from the Philistines." 4 So the Israelites got rid Judg 2:12-13; 10:16
of their images of Baal and Ashtoreth and worshiped only the LORD. Joel 2:12-14
5 Then Samuel told them, "Gather all of Israel to Mizpah, and I will pray to the LORD for
you." 6 So they gathered at Mizpah and, in a great ceremony, drew water from a well and 7:6
poured it out before the LORD. They also went without food all day and confessed that they Judg 10:10 Neh 9:1
had sinned against the LORD. (It was at Mizpah that Samuel became Israel's judge.) Lam 2:19
7 When the Philistine rulers heard that Israel had gathered at Mizpah, they mobilized 7:8
their army and advanced. The Israelites were badly frightened when they learned that the Isa 37:4
Philistines were approaching. 8 "Don't stop pleading with the LORD our God to save us from 7:9
the Philistines!" they begged Samuel. 9 So Samuel took a young lamb and offered it to the Lev 22:26-27 Ps 99:6
LORD as a whole burnt offering. He pleaded with the LORD to help Israel, and the LORD an- Jer 15:1
swered him. 7:10
10 Just as Samuel was sacrificing the burnt offering, the Philistines arrived to attack Israel. 2 Sam 22:14 Ps 18:14

▸ GOD
7:2 Setting God aside. The Israelites' dancing (6:13) turned to mourning. After God reasserted Himself as holy and not subject to their human curiosity, Israel set His Ark aside, placing it in a private residence on the side of a remote hill. It is no surprise that they tried to distance themselves from God after disobeying His commands. You may try to set God aside, limiting your contact with Him until it is convenient and safe, but He will accept no such treatment. Repent, and you will enjoy intimacy with God. (***See God****> Relationship> Barriers> Disobedience,* TopicGuide page A14.)

▸ WORSHIP
7:3 Getting right with God. How do you get right with God? By going to church? That's not a bad start, but it doesn't make you holier any more than going to a bakery makes you a dessert. Repentance, an ongoing lifestyle of hating and forsaking sin, is one of the main ways God enables His people to draw near to Him. Samuel also instructed the people of Israel to sacrifice and fast (7:6). But our regular confession of the gospel's truths, both in action and word, and our lifestyle of repentance are the main ways God has ordained for us to grow spiritually. More specifically, examine your life for any idols that distract you from full-hearted worship of God. After you find them, determine to hate and forsake your sin, replacing it with the fruit of the Spirit (Galatians 5:22, 23). (***See Worship****> OT> Reverence> Put away idols,* TopicGuide page A28.)

7:3-4 The history of Israel (and indeed all humanity) is filled with struggle against the first two commandments: 1) Worship only the Lord God and 2) have no idols. Israel had already fallen down before the idol of a golden calf (Exodus 32) and worshiped foreign gods as they traveled toward the Promised Land (Numbers 25). When they settled the land, they failed to remove all other religions, which were constantly diluting their own religion. Ashtoreth (a Canaanite mother god figure) and Baal (the most prominent fertility god among the Canaanites) continued to woo God's people away from true worship throughout the Old Testament era.

7:5 Mizpah was an important center of worship, located north of Jerusalem and south of Bethel on the central ridge in Israel. Much later in Israel's history, the apocryphal book of 1 Maccabees (3:46) confirmed this: "Israel formerly had a place of prayer in Mizpah."

7:6 This action of pouring out water before the Lord has no parallel in Scripture. But perhaps it signifies repentance such as that seen in Lamentations 2:19: "Pour out your hearts like water to the Lord."

7:9 Whole burnt offerings were completely consumed by fire on the altar. None of the offering was set aside for the priests or the worshiper to eat. These offerings were given to please God and to consecrate the worshiper. In the original Israelite system of sacrifices, burnt offerings were offered daily, morning and evening. The animals used were required to be without defect (Numbers 28:3-8). For other sacrifices, such as sin offerings or peace offerings, only part of the animal was burned up completely. The remaining offering was given to the priests, or in some cases, returned to the family for a feast.

▸ SPIRITUAL WARFARE
7:10 Our warrior God. Our God is a mighty God! First, God rescued His Ark from the hands of His enemies—without any help from Israel. Then He subdued a large army with a thunderclap that made their brains rattle and their knees buckle as they fled before a smaller, less capable force. God is able to bring order to your circumstances and defeat those who oppress you—but He does it in His own time, in His own way, and for His own glory. Can you remain patient and await His victory? (***See Spiritual Warfare****> Resisting Sin and Evil> Trusting God> God as Warrior> God's fight to final victory,* TopicGuide page A46.)

But the LORD spoke with a mighty voice of thunder from heaven that day, and the Philistines
were thrown into such confusion that the Israelites defeated them. 11 The men of Israel
chased them from Mizpah to a place below Beth-car, slaughtering them all along the way.
12 Samuel then took a large stone and placed it between the towns of Mizpah and Jesha-
nah.* He named it Ebenezer (which means "the stone of help"), for he said, "Up to this point
the LORD has helped us!"
13 So the Philistines were subdued and didn't invade Israel again for some time. And
throughout Samuel's lifetime, the LORD's powerful hand was raised against the Philistines.
14 The Israelite villages near Ekron and Gath that the Philistines had captured were re-
stored to Israel, along with the rest of the territory that the Philistines had taken. And there
was peace between Israel and the Amorites in those days.
15 Samuel continued as Israel's judge for the rest of his life. 16 Each year he traveled
around, setting up his court first at Bethel, then at Gilgal, and then at Mizpah. He judged
the people of Israel at each of these places. 17 Then he would return to his home at Ramah,
and he would hear cases there, too. And Samuel built an altar to the LORD at Ramah.

ISRAEL REQUESTS A KING

8 As Samuel grew old, he appointed his sons to be judges over Israel. 2 Joel and Abijah,
his oldest sons, held court in Beersheba. 3 But they were not like their father, for they
were greedy for money. They accepted bribes and perverted justice.
4 Finally, all the elders of Israel met at Ramah to discuss the matter with Samuel. 5 "Look,"
they told him, "you are now old, and your sons are not like you. Give us a king to judge us
like all the other nations have."
6 Samuel was displeased with their request and went to the LORD for guidance. 7 "Do

7:12 Gen 35:13-15; Josh 4:9; 24:26
7:13 Judg 13:1; 1 Sam 13:5
7:15 1 Sam 7:6; 12:11
7:16 Gen 28:19; 1 Sam 7:5
7:17 1 Sam 1:1, 19; 2:11; 15:34
8:1 Deut 16:18-19
8:2 1 Kgs 19:3; Amos 5:5
8:3 Exod 23:6, 8; Deut 16:19
8:5 Deut 17:14-15
8:7 Exod 16:8

7:12 As in Greek and Syriac versions; Hebrew reads *Shen.*

7:12 *Ebenezer* is simply the combination of two Hebrew words: *eben* (meaning "stone") and *ezer* (meaning "help"). Notice the striking contrast between the name Samuel gave his altar and "Ichabod" (meaning "where is the glory?"), the name given to Eli's grandson on the day Eli and his sons died and the Ark fell into the Philistines' hands.

7:13-14 The Philistines and Amorites were forces to be reckoned with for much of Israel's early history. Moses led the people in a roundabout path to the Promised Land because of the Philistines (Exodus 13:17). Israel's unwillingness to trust God for the victory over the Amorites (Deuteronomy 1) resulted in 38 more years of wandering. The later defeat of Amorite kings Sihon and Og was crucial to entering the Promised Land. Young David's opponent, Goliath, was a Philistine. Throughout the reign of Israel's earliest kings, Saul and David, Israel fought the Philistines, at times overpowering them and at times being overpowered by them.

7:16-17 Samuel conducted a small circuit in central Israel. Bethel, Mizpah, and his home of Ramah are clustered together on the central ridge. The town of Gilgal is in the Jordan Valley closer to Jericho. It remained important to Israel since it was where the people first camped and erected the Tabernacle in the Promised Land (Joshua 4:19-20).

▸ HOLINESS
8:1 Godly leadership. Even wise Samuel, possibly the greatest of the judges, could not create judges merely by his own will. His sons did not bear the divine marks of God's chosen judges (8:5). The church today may choose elders or deacons, but unless God chooses them, their ministry will be in vain. Further, we see here the danger of considering church leadership an inherited right passed down from father to son. Pray that God will raise up loving, courageous church leaders. (***See Holiness****> Set Apart> Religious Service> Priests and Levites,* TopicGuide page A40.)

8:2 Beersheba (meaning, "well of the oath") was an important and ancient settlement around water in the south of Israel near the Negev. The patriarchs Isaac (Genesis 26:23-25) and Jacob (Genesis 46:1-4) both had crucial spiritual encounters with God near this city.

8:3 Samuel's sons, Joel and Abijah, mirrored the environment of Samuel's upbringing. Samuel was taken to the Tabernacle as a child to be raised by Eli, the priest there. Eli was a good man, though weak. His sons, Hophni and Phinehas, were priests but not good men. In fact, they were described as "scoundrels" who had no respect for their leadership roles (1 Samuel 2:12).

▸ MINISTRY
8:5 Right idea, wrong motive. Have you ever wanted something good, but for all the wrong reasons? Israel wanted something God had predicted and prepared Israel for—a king. The Bible teaches that God-honoring human kingship is a blessing that God ordained for His people (Genesis 17:16; Ecclesiastes 10:17; Hosea 3:4-5). This chapter shows that Israel's hasty decision, combined with the worldly attitude of the leaders, angered Samuel. But Samuel knew that God had made provisions in the law given by Moses for a king (Deuteronomy 17:14-20) and that he would eventually rejoice at what Moses wrote concerning a future king who would come from Israel to rule all of God's people (Numbers 24:17). Explore your motives for the leaders you choose in your church, community, and country. (***See Ministry****> Transformation> Vocations> King,* TopicGuide page A57.)

everything they say to you," the LORD replied, "for it is Me they are rejecting, not you. They
don't want Me to be their king any longer. [8]Ever since I brought them from Egypt they
have continually abandoned Me and followed other gods. And now they are giving you
the same treatment. [9]Do as they ask, but solemnly warn them about the way a king will
reign over them."

SAMUEL WARNS AGAINST A KINGDOM

[10]So Samuel passed on the LORD's warning to the people who were asking him for a king.
[11]"This is how a king will reign over you," Samuel said. "The king will draft your sons and
assign them to his chariots and his charioteers, making them run before his chariots.
[12]Some will be generals and captains in his army,* some will be forced to plow in his
fields and harvest his crops, and some will make his weapons and chariot equipment.
[13]The king will take your daughters from you and force them to cook and bake and make
perfumes for him. [14]He will take away the best of your fields and vineyards and olive
groves and give them to his own officials. [15]He will take a tenth of your grain and your
grape harvest and distribute it among his officers and attendants. [16]He will take your
male and female slaves and demand the finest of your cattle* and donkeys for his own
use. [17]He will demand a tenth of your flocks, and you will be his slaves. [18]When that day
comes, you will beg for relief from this king you are demanding, but then the LORD will
not help you."

[19]But the people refused to listen to Samuel's warning. "Even so, we still want a king,"
they said. [20]"We want to be like the nations around us. Our king will judge us and lead us
into battle."

[21]So Samuel repeated to the LORD what the people had said, [22]and the LORD replied, "Do
as they say, and give them a king." Then Samuel agreed and sent the people home.

SAUL MEETS SAMUEL

9 There was a wealthy, influential man named Kish from the tribe of Benjamin. He was
the son of Abiel, son of Zeror, son of Becorath, son of Aphiah, of the tribe of Benja-

8:9 1 Sam 8:11-18
8:11 Deut 17:16; 1 Sam 14:52; 2 Sam 15:1; 1 Kgs 1:5
8:12 1 Sam 22:7; 1 Kgs 4:7
8:14 1 Sam 22:7; 1 Kgs 21:7; Ezek 46:18
8:18 Job 27:9; Prov 1:25-28; Mic 3:4
8:19 Jer 44:16
8:22 1 Sam 8:7
9:1 1 Chr 8:33; 9:36-39

8:12 Hebrew *commanders of thousands and commanders of fifties.* 8:16 As in Greek version; Hebrew reads *young men.*

8:6-9 Israel's form of government changed as the nation grew. After leaving Egypt, the nation functioned as a theocracy, ruled by God through Moses and Aaron. After the Israelites settled their land, a series of national champions, or judges, led the people. Samuel is considered the last judge of Israel. His leadership was the transition between leadership by local champions and a formal monarchy for all the people. Samuel had access to God's guidelines about a king in the Law of Moses (Deuteronomy 17:14-20). In those writings, God instructed Israel that if they decided to be ruled by a king, that man must fear God, esteem God's Word, and consider himself a leader among peers rather than a leader above the citizens.

8:13 Perfumes were an integral part of Ancient Near Eastern culture. Because the land and climate were dry and dusty, the people's skin and hair became brittle unless they applied perfumed moisturizing oils to those areas. The story of Esther contains an example of these customs. Esther underwent months of beauty treatments using oil of myrrh and special perfumes (Esther 2:12) to prepare for a contest that determined the new queen of Persia. Ancient perfumes included cassia, cinnamon, frankincense, myrrh, and saffron. Exotic scents and spices were imported by traveling caravans between regions. When Joseph's brothers sold him into slavery, the Ishmaelite travelers he was sold to were carrying spices, balm, and myrrh (Genesis 37:25).

8:15-17 We think of a tenth as the tithe God demands of us, not as a standard for political purposes. But even before Moses formalized this amount in his law, a tenth or tithe was already seen as the appropriate gift to offer a deity, a monarch, or a person of honor. Evidence of tithes can be found in ancient cultures including China, Persia, Babylon, and Egypt. As early as Abraham's first days in Canaan, he offered the priest Melchizedek a tenth of the goods he recovered in a military victory (Genesis 14). Abraham's grandson, Jacob, made a commitment to God at Bethel that included a tenth of everything God gave him (Genesis 28:10-22).

8:20 God created Israel to be His own people, different and peculiar in comparison to the surrounding cultures. Their desires to conform to the world (and the terrible price they paid for conformity) warn us away from such longings (Romans 12:1-2). Even so, God occasionally gives us what we (wrongly) want in order to show us what we really need. Israel wanted a king. All they needed was to trust in the Lord, and the matter of the king would resolve itself in God's own time.

9:2 min. 2 His son Saul was the most handsome man in Israel—head and shoulders taller than
1 Sam 10:23-24 anyone else in the land.
2 Sam 14:25 3 One day Kish's donkeys strayed away, and he told Saul, "Take a servant with you, and
9:3 1 Sam 10:2, 14 go look for the donkeys." 4 So Saul took one of the servants and traveled through the hill
country of Ephraim, the land of Shalishah, the Shaalim area, and the entire land of Benja-
min, but they couldn't find the donkeys anywhere.
9:5 5 Finally, they entered the region of Zuph, and Saul said to his servant, "Let's go home.
1 Sam 1:1 By now my father will be more worried about us than about the donkeys!"
9:6 6 But the servant said, "I've just thought of something! There is a man of God who lives
Deut 33:1 1 Sam 3:19-20 here in this town. He is held in high honor by all the people because everything he says
2 Kgs 5:8 comes true. Let's go find him. Perhaps he can tell us which way to go."
7 "But we don't have anything to offer him," Saul replied. "Even our food is gone, and we
9:7 1 Kgs 14:3 don't have a thing to give him."
2 Kgs 5:15; 8:8-9 8 "Well," the servant said, "I have one small silver piece.* We can at least offer it to
Ezek 13:19 the man of God and see what happens!" 9 (In those days if people wanted a message
9:9 2 Sam 24:11 from God, they would say, "Let's go and ask the seer," for prophets used to be called seers.)
1 Chr 26:28 10 "All right," Saul agreed, "let's try it!" So they started into the town where the man of
God lived.
11 As they were climbing the hill to the town, they met some young women coming out
to draw water. So Saul and his servant asked, "Is the seer here today?"
9:12 12 "Yes," they replied. "Stay right on this road. He is at the town gates. He has just arrived
Luke 9:16 to take part in a public sacrifice up at the place of worship. 13 Hurry and catch him before he
John 6:11 goes up there to eat. The guests won't begin eating until he arrives to bless the food."
14 So they entered the town, and as they passed through the gates, Samuel was coming
out toward them to go up to the place of worship.
9:15 15 Now the LORD had told Samuel the previous day, 16 "About this time tomorrow I will
1 Sam 15:1 send you a man from the land of Benjamin. Anoint him to be the leader of My people,
9:16 Exod 3:7, 9 Israel. He will rescue them from the Philistines, for I have looked down on My people in
Acts 13:21 mercy and have heard their cry."

9:8 Hebrew *¼ shekel of silver,* about 0.1 ounces or 3 grams in weight.

9:4-5 The "hill country of Ephraim" describes the land of the central ridge in Israel. This central ridge runs like a backbone north to south through the Promised Land, just to the west of the Jordan River and valley. Flowing to the east and west of the ridge toward the Mediterranean Sea, these valleys were deep and sometimes impassible; it is of little wonder that these men had lost their donkeys in such a place. The district of Zuph was near Ramah and was likely named after Elkanah's son of the same name, also called Zophai (1 Chronicles 6:26). The location of Ramah is disputed, but it is most likely in the tribal territory of Benjamin (Joshua 18:21-25). The apocryphal history book 1 Maccabees (1:34) also places it on or near a mountain or "hill country" associated with Ephraim.

9:9 The word "seer" had a connotation of one who foretells the future. That was part of a prophet's role. The prophecies contained in Daniel in the Old Testament and Revelation in the New Testament often describe future events using apocalyptic and symbolic imagery. Old Testament prophets such as Isaiah foretold the coming of the Messiah. However, the Old Testament prophet's role included not merely foretelling the future, but also forth-telling God's message of truth. God directed prophets to speak, whether about future events or about the current state of the people's hearts.

9:15-17 These verses are an important interruption in the narrative, showing how God often works through the ordinary circumstances in our lives. Saul was merely searching for donkeys, a search that took him to an obscure village. But behind the mundane, God was orchestrating a crucial meeting with Samuel in order to benefit His people.

9:16 God "looked down" and "heard" His people; this reminds the reader of Exodus 3:7-9, where God "heard [His people's] cries of distress."

▶ BIBLE

9:16 Discovering God in His people's cry. God has mercy on His people. This is no mere pious platitude, but a historical fact: Since the beginning of time, God has heard and responded to His hurting people, and the Bible records many of these divine moments. Do you need God's mercy? There's no trick to it—it is part of God's nature to care for those who are broken and needy. But you can put yourself in a position where God has historically blessed His people; for instance, become part of a Bible-believing, God-honoring church. Or seek God through prayer and fasting. Or take a moral inventory of your life, repenting of every sin against God and man, and making amends where suitable. We can't manipulate God into immediate action, but we can position ourselves in the place where His mercy flows and rejoice when we experience His power to calm the storms of our lives. (***See Bible*> *Unity*> *Christ*> *Christ is "mercy,"* TopicGuide page A10.)

17 When Samuel saw Saul, the LORD said, "That's the man I told you about! He will rule 9:17
My people." 1 Sam 16:12
18 Just then Saul approached Samuel at the gateway and asked, "Can you please tell me
where the seer's house is?"
19 "I am the seer!" Samuel replied. "Go up to the place of worship ahead of me. We will
eat there together, and in the morning I'll tell you what you want to know and send you on
your way. 20 And don't worry about those donkeys that were lost three days ago, for they 9:20
have been found. And I am here to tell you that you and your family are the focus of all Is- 1 Sam 12:13
rael's hopes."
21 Saul replied, "But I'm only from the tribe of Benjamin, the smallest tribe in Israel, and 9:21
my family is the least important of all the families of that tribe! Why are you talking like Judg 20:46-48
this to me?" 1 Sam 15:17
22 Then Samuel brought Saul and his servant into the hall and placed them at the head of
the table, honoring them above the thirty special guests. 23 Samuel then instructed the cook to
bring Saul the finest cut of meat, the piece that had been set aside for the guest of honor. 24 So
the cook brought in the meat and placed it before Saul. "Go ahead and eat it," Samuel said. "I
was saving it for you even before I invited these others!" So Saul ate with Samuel that day.
25 When they came down from the place of worship and returned to town, Samuel took 9:25
Saul up to the roof of the house and prepared a bed for him there.* 26 At daybreak the next Deut 22:8 Acts 10:9-10
morning, Samuel called to Saul, "Get up! It's time you were on your way." So Saul got
ready, and he and Samuel left the house together. 27 When they reached the edge of town,
Samuel told Saul to send his servant on ahead. After the servant was gone, Samuel said,
"Stay here, for I have received a special message for you from God."

SAMUEL ANOINTS SAUL AS KING

10 Then Samuel took a flask of olive oil and poured it over Saul's head. He kissed 10:1
Saul and said, "I am doing this because the LORD has appointed you to be the ruler 1 Sam 9:16; 16:13; 26:9 2 Sam 1:14
over Israel, His special possession.* 2 When you leave me today, you will see two men be- 2 Kgs 9:3, 6

10:2 Gen 35:19; 48:7

9:25 As in Greek version; Hebrew reads *and talked with him there.* 10:1 Greek version reads *over Israel. And you will rule over the LORD's people and save them from their enemies around them. This will be the sign to you that the LORD has appointed you to be leader over His special possession.*

9:17 Samuel had a long history of hearing God's voice. As a child he served the Lord by assisting Eli the priest. It was an era in which God had been rather silent and dreams or visions were rare (3:1). But God revealed Himself to young Samuel, speaking to him several times, even revealing the sad fate that awaited Eli and his sons (3:2-14). This was the beginning of Samuel's ministry.

▸ PURPOSE

9:21 Small people, big God. God can do big things with small people. Saul clearly had no idea that God was in the business of doing the most with the least. But throughout the Scriptures and throughout the history of the church, God consistently uses the least expected, the weak, and the marginalized as His instruments. He does this so He will receive all the glory. God has big plans for you, and even shyness or fear can't stop God from using you to be a blessing to your friends, your family, and even the nations (Genesis 12:1-3). Embrace God's heroic calling on your life! (***See Purpose****> God's Means> Human Choice> Bringing our wills in subjection to God's will,* TopicGuide page A52.)

9:21 The tribe of Benjamin was made up of the descendants of Jacob's youngest son. Benjamin and Joseph were born to Jacob's most loved wife, Rachel. She died just after Benjamin was born. In Jacob's blessing over his sons he recognized Benjamin's warrior abilities (Genesis 49:27). This reputation was borne out in the tribe that descended from Benjamin. In fact, the tribe is most remembered for its participation in a highly violent incident with a traveling Levite. All eleven of the other tribes stood against this small tribe, and it was almost destroyed (Judges 19–20).

▸ WORSHIP

10:1 From anger to respect. Samuel kissed Saul on the cheek and said, "I am doing this because the LORD has appointed you to be the ruler over Israel, His special possession." Has God ever given you a love for someone you previously hated? While Samuel felt anger toward Israel's leaders for seeking a king (8:5), he showed affection for Saul as the time came to anoint him as Israel's king. Samuel anointed him with oil, symbolizing God's Spirit resting upon him, and gave him a brotherly kiss, demonstrating the love all Saul's subjects should have for him. (***See Worship****> NT> Prayer> Instructions> Pray for enemies,* TopicGuide page A33.)

10:1 Samuel's act, anointing Saul with oil, symbolized that Saul was set apart for special service. There are many examples of anointing in the Scriptures. Jacob anointed a stone at Bethel, a place where God met with him (Genesis 35:9-15). In this way he set that place apart as a holy place. Later, instructions for the Tabernacle included a recipe for holy anointing oil used to set apart priests, holy furniture, and utensils for the Tabernacle (Exodus 30:22-33). David was anointed with oil to set him apart to be king, as was Solomon (1 Samuel 16:13; 1 Kings 1:39). Psalm 23 describes God anointing His children with oil as special guests of His kingdom (Psalm 23:5).

side Rachel's tomb at Zelzah, on the border of Benjamin. They will tell you that the donkeys have been found and that your father has stopped worrying about them and is now worried about you. He is asking, 'Have you seen my son?'

RELIGIOUS AND POLITICAL CENTERS OF ISRAEL

During the period of the judges, Israel may have had more than one capital. This may explain why the Scriptures overlap with reference to some cities.

Gilgal	Joshua 4:19; Judges 2:1; Hosea 4:15; Micah 6:5
Shiloh	Joshua 18:1-10; 19:51; Judges 18:31; 1 Samuel 1:3; Jeremiah 7:12-14
Shechem	Joshua 24:1
Ramah	1 Samuel 7:17; 8:4
Mizpah	Judges 11:11; 20:1; 1 Samuel 10:17
Bethel	Judges 20:18, 26; 1 Samuel 10:3
Gibeah (political center only)	1 Samuel 10:26
Gibeon (religious center only)	1 Kings 3:4; 2 Chronicles 1:2, 3
Jerusalem	1 Kings 8:1ff; Psalm 51:16-19

Samuel called the Israelites together at Mizpah, where he would anoint Saul as their first king. Up to this point, the political seat of the nation seems to have been the religious center of the nation as well. Above are the cities which probably served as both the religious and political centers of Israel since the days of Joshua. Saul may have been the first Israelite leader to separate the nation's religious center (probably Mizpah at this time) from its political center (Gibeah—1 Samuel 11:4; 26:1). Politically, the nation grew strong for a while. But when Saul and his officials stopped seeking God's will, internal jealousies and strife soon began to decay the nation from within. When David became king, he brought the Ark of the Covenant back to Jerusalem, his capital. King Solomon then completely united the religious and political centers at Jerusalem.

10:3 3 "When you get to the oak of Tabor, you will see three men coming toward you who
Gen 35:1, 3, 7 10:5 are on their way to worship God at Bethel. One will be bringing three young goats, an-
1 Sam 19:20 other will have three loaves of bread, and the third will be carrying a wineskin full of wine.
2 Kgs 2:3, 5, 15 4 They will greet you and offer you two of the loaves, which you are to accept.
1 Chr 25:1 5 "When you arrive at Gibeah of God,* where the garrison of the Philistines is located,
10:6 Num 11:25, 29 you will meet a band of prophets coming down from the place of worship. They will be
Judg 3:10; 14:6 playing a harp, a tambourine, a flute, and a lyre, and they will be prophesying. 6 At that
1 Sam 19:23-24 time the Spirit of the LORD will come powerfully upon you, and you will prophesy with
10:8 them. You will be changed into a different person. 7 After these signs take place, do what
1 Sam 7:16; 11:14-15; 13:8 must be done, for God is with you. 8 Then go down to Gilgal ahead of me. I will join you

10:5 Hebrew *Gibeath-elohim.*

10:6-8 Notice that Samuel instructed Saul that after the Spirit came upon him, he woud receive further instructions from the prophet. This is a consistent pattern of God's work. He always accompanies the giving of spiritual power with divine instruction from His Word. God's children who seek the Spirit's power must also submit to His Word.

10:8 Gilgal held special significance for Israel. The Israelites first camped there after crossing the Jordan River and entering the Promised Land. Joshua created the memorial of 12 stones there to remind his people of all God had done to bring them into the land (Joshua 4). But later, prophets such as Hosea and Amos referred to Gilgal as a place where God was worshiped insincerely (Hosea 4:15; Amos 4:4).

10:8 Burnt offerings and sin offerings were given at designated times with careful instructions in order to make peace with God. Those already at peace with God offered fellowship or peace offerings. Given to show love and appreciation, these offerings were less restrictive and voluntary and could be given spontaneously.

there to sacrifice burnt offerings and peace offerings. You must wait for seven days until I
arrive and give you further instructions."

SAMUEL'S SIGNS ARE FULFILLED

9 As Saul turned and started to leave, God gave him a new heart, and all Samuel's signs — **10:9**
were fulfilled that day. 10 When Saul and his servant arrived at Gibeah, they saw a group of — 1 Sam 10:6
prophets coming toward them. Then the Spirit of God came powerfully upon Saul, and he, — **10:10**
too, began to prophesy. 11 When those who knew Saul heard about it, they exclaimed, — 1 Sam 10:5
"What? Is even Saul a prophet? How did the son of Kish become a prophet?" — **10:11** 1 Sam 19:24
12 And one of those standing there said, "Can anyone become a prophet, no matter who — Amos 7:14-15
his father is?"* So that is the origin of the saying "Is even Saul a prophet?" — Matt 13:54-57
13 When Saul had finished prophesying, he went up to the place of worship. 14 "Where — **10:14**
have you been?" Saul's uncle asked him and his servant. — 1 Sam 9:3
"We were looking for the donkeys," Saul replied, "but we couldn't find them. So we
went to Samuel to ask him where they were."
15 "Oh? And what did he say?" his uncle asked.
16 "He told us that the donkeys had already been found," Saul replied. But Saul didn't tell — **10:16**
his uncle what Samuel said about the kingdom. — 1 Sam 9:20

SAUL IS ACCLAIMED KING

17 Later Samuel called all the people of Israel to meet before the LORD at Mizpah. 18 And he — **10:17**
said, "This is what the LORD, the God of Israel, has declared: I brought you from Egypt and — Judg 20:1 1 Sam 7:5-6
rescued you from the Egyptians and from all of the nations that were oppressing you. — **10:18**
19 But though I have rescued you from your misery and distress, you have rejected your — Judg 6:8
God today and have said, 'No, we want a king instead!' Now, therefore, present yourselves — **10:19**
before the LORD by tribes and clans." — 1 Sam 8:5-7
20 So Samuel brought all the tribes of Israel before the LORD, and the tribe of Benjamin
was chosen by lot. 21 Then he brought each family of the tribe of Benjamin before the
LORD, and the family of the Matrites was chosen. And finally Saul son of Kish was chosen
from among them. But when they looked for him, he had disappeared! 22 So they asked
the LORD, "Where is he?"
And the LORD replied, "He is hiding among the baggage." 23 So they found him and — **10:23**
brought him out, and he stood head and shoulders above anyone else. — 1 Sam 9:2
24 Then Samuel said to all the people, "This is the man the LORD has chosen as your king. — **10:24**
No one in all Israel is like him!" — 2 Sam 21:6 1 Kgs 1:25, 34, 39
And all the people shouted, "Long live the king!" — 2 Kgs 11:12
25 Then Samuel told the people what the rights and duties of a king were. He wrote them — **10:25**
down on a scroll and placed it before the LORD. Then Samuel sent the people home again. — Deut 17:15 1 Sam 8:11-18

10:12 Hebrew *said, "Who is their father?"*

10:12 Though unfamiliar to modern readers, the question "Is even Saul a prophet?" must have been a familiar saying at that time.

▸ GOD
10:16 Are you shy? Why did Saul hide the greatest series of events of his life from his uncle? Probably for the same reason he hid from Samuel at his own coronation (10:22)—he doubted God's ability to make him into the man worthy to be the first king of Israel. God knows our insecurities, but He also knows the power He has placed within us—the power of the Holy Spirit. It is not by our might, nor by our power, but by God's Spirit that we can live beyond our mortal frailties. (***See God****> God's Names> Holy Spirit> Empowers us,* TopicGuide page A19.)

10:18 Israel should not have needed a reminder of God's great act of redeeming His people from bondage. But too often, those things that are most important are also taken for granted and drift from our thoughts. This is why the constant dual refrain in Deuteronomy was "remember what God has done" and "do not forget" (Deuteronomy 6:12; 8:2, 11, 19).

10:19 Earlier Samuel was foretelling the future with signs for Saul. Here he forth-tells the truth to Israel concerning their rejection of the Lord as their king. Both are roles of the biblical prophet.

26When Saul returned to his home at Gibeah, a group of men whose hearts God had
10:27 touched went with him. 27But there were some scoundrels who complained, "How can this
1 Kgs 10:24-25 man save us?" And they scorned him and refused to bring him gifts. But Saul ignored them.
[Nahash, king of the Ammonites, had been grievously oppressing the people of Gad
and Reuben who lived east of the Jordan River. He gouged out the right eye of each of the
Israelites living there, and he didn't allow anyone to come and rescue them. In fact, of all
the Israelites east of the Jordan, there wasn't a single one whose right eye Nahash had not
gouged out. But there were 7,000 men who had escaped from the Ammonites, and they
had settled in Jabesh-gilead.]*

SAUL DEFEATS THE AMMONITES

11:1 **11** About a month later,* King Nahash of Ammon led his army against the Israelite
Judg 11:4-6; 21:8 town of Jabesh-gilead. But all the citizens of Jabesh asked for peace. "Make a
1 Sam 12:12; 31:11 treaty with us, and we will be your servants," they pleaded.
11:2 1 Sam 17:26 2"All right," Nahash said, "but only on one condition. I will gouge out the right eye of
every one of you as a disgrace to all Israel!"
3"Give us seven days to send messengers throughout Israel!" replied the elders of Ja-
besh. "If no one comes to save us, we will agree to your terms."
11:4 1 Sam 10:26; 30:4 4When the messengers came to Gibeah of Saul and told the people about their plight,
11:5 everyone broke into tears. 5Saul had been plowing a field with his oxen, and when he re-
1 Kgs 19:19 turned to town, he asked, "What's the matter? Why is everyone crying?" So they told him
about the message from Jabesh.
11:6 6Then the Spirit of God came powerfully upon Saul, and he became very angry. 7He
Judg 3:10; 6:34 1 Sam 10:10 took two oxen and cut them into pieces and sent the messengers to carry them through-
out Israel with this message: "This is what will happen to the oxen of anyone who refuses
11:7 Judg 19:29; 20:1 to follow Saul and Samuel into battle!" And the LORD made the people afraid of Saul's an-
11:8 ger, and all of them came out together as one. 8When Saul mobilized them at Bezek, he
Judg 1:4-6 found that there were 300,000 men from Israel and 30,000* men from Judah.
9So Saul sent the messengers back to Jabesh-gilead to say, "We will rescue you by noon-
11:10 time tomorrow!" There was great joy throughout the town when that message arrived!
1 Sam 11:3 10The men of Jabesh then told their enemies, "Tomorrow we will come out to you, and
11:11 you can do to us whatever you wish." 11But before dawn the next morning, Saul arrived,
Judg 7:16 having divided his army into three detachments. He launched a surprise attack against the
Ammonites and slaughtered them the whole morning. The remnant of their army was so
badly scattered that no two of them were left together.

10:27 This paragraph, which is not included in the Masoretic Text, is found in Dead Sea Scroll 4QSam[a]. 11:1 As in Greek version; Hebrew lacks *About a month later.* 11:8 Dead Sea Scrolls and Greek version read *70,000.*

11:1 The original Ammonites were descendants of Abraham's nephew Lot. (see note at Genesis 19:30-38).

11:2 In the Ancient Near East, men in battle usually covered their left eye with their shield. Gouging out the right eye would make them unfit for battle and destined for lifelong disgrace.

11:4-8 In an earlier era (Judges 19–21), Gibeah was the setting for national disgrace (see note at 11:7). Now salvation comes to Gibeah at the hand of Saul. Israel did not fail to notice this reversal. Such a change could only be the result of God's Spirit moving in His chosen leader.

▸ GOD

11:6 The Spirit in action. Have you ever sensed a special presence of God's Spirit? There is nothing like it in this world. The first time Saul experienced it, he worshiped God as never before (10:9-10). But this time God's Spirit moved Saul to a holy anger—which immediately turned to an act of heroic mercy. He gathered all Israel to fight against those who would harm Jabesh-gilead. The Spirit of God moved him into action, from walking behind a plow (11:5) to walking in the Spirit. (***See God****> Salvation> Holy Spirit> Those who walk in the Spirit are led by the Spirit,* TopicGuide page A15.)

11:7 Saul's act of chopping up oxen and sending the pieces to all Israel reminds us—and perhaps helps us understand—the difficult account in Judges 19:22–20:48. Saul was sending a warning to Israel of what would happen to the nation if all did not come together against a danger to God's community. It could be that the Levite in Judges was sending the same signal, alerting Israel to join together in judgment against the sin of the tribe of Benjamin.

[12]Then the people exclaimed to Samuel, "Now where are those men who said, 'Why should Saul rule over us?' Bring them here, and we will kill them!"
[13]But Saul replied, "No one will be executed today, for today the LORD has rescued Israel!"
[14]Then Samuel said to the people, "Come, let us all go to Gilgal to renew the kingdom."
[15]So they all went to Gilgal, and in a solemn ceremony before the LORD they made Saul king. Then they offered peace offerings to the LORD, and Saul and all the Israelites were filled with joy.

11:12 1 Sam 10:27 Luke 19:27

11:13 Exod 14:13 1 Sam 19:5 2 Sam 19:22

11:14 1 Sam 10:1, 8

12:1 1 Sam 8:7, 9, 22

12:2 1 Sam 3:10, 19-20

SAMUEL'S FAREWELL ADDRESS

12 Then Samuel addressed all Israel: "I have done as you asked and given you a king. [2]Your king is now your leader. I stand here before you—an old, gray-haired

▸ **GOD**

11:13 A Spirit of mercy. In an act of mercy, Saul spares the lives of those who earlier spoke treason against his rule. Are you mature enough to have mercy on those who question your calling and try to destroy your life? You cannot grow spiritually on your own—you can only mature through the presence of the Spirit of God in your life. Read Ephesians 4:30-32 and ask yourself: "How can I welcome the Spirit of God into my life in a greater way?" (***See God***> *God's Attributes> Merciful> God gives mercy to those who are merciful,* TopicGuide page A17.)

11:14-15 In these two verses, the Hebrew text mentions Gilgal three times by name, and uses "there" four times in reference to Gilgal. This place was important for Israel, being the location where God constituted them as a new community as they entered the land. The Hebrew text here also quotes Samuel as saying, "Let us . . . renew the kingdom"; this quote, combined with the location of the coronation ceremony, leads some to think Samuel was giving Israel one last chance to reaffirm the kingship of the Lord instead of crowning a human king.

11:15 Peace offerings were instituted as a way for those in fellowship with God to express gratitude for God's goodness. These offerings may have involved drink, grain, or special offerings (see Leviticus 2; 3; Numbers 15:1-10). In this way they differed from burnt offerings for atonement and forgiveness.

MY RESPONSE TO GOD

God-centered, Biblical, Relevant

1 SAMUEL 12

Our corporate worship should reflect the message and values of the Bible. This message and these values may be summarized in three words:

1. Biblical—We ought to pattern our worship after how Scripture says God wants to be worshiped. We should never worship in ways the Bible forbids.
2. Relevant—The average layperson ought to be able to understand our worship. The language and music we choose should not be too difficult for others to understand or follow.
3. God-centered—Every facet of our worship of God ought to focus on His desires, rather than on ours.

Each of these three principles holds the others in balance. For instance, if we err in attempting to make worship too relevant, we may neglect scriptural guidelines for worship. If we focus too much on being God-centered in our worship, we may fail to facilitate ways for the other worshipers to participate. And worship that attempts to be woodenly biblical, down to mimicking the cultural circumstances of Bible times, draws our attention away from God and onto man-made rules.

Worship is giving God the glory He is due in response to what He has done for us in Jesus Christ. He has spoken in Scripture about the worship He wants from His people. Let us rejoice in the freedom and guidance God gives as we approach Him through biblical, relevant, and God-centered worship.

12:3 man—and my sons serve you. I have served as your leader from the time I was a boy to
Exod 23:8 this very day. 3Now testify against me in the presence of the LORD and before His anointed
Num 16:15 one. Whose ox or donkey have I stolen? Have I ever cheated any of you? Have I ever op-
Deut 16:19 pressed you? Have I ever taken a bribe and perverted justice? Tell me and I will make right
whatever I have done wrong."
4"No," they replied, "you have never cheated or oppressed us, and you have never
taken even a single bribe."
12:5 5"The LORD and His anointed one are my witnesses today," Samuel declared, "that my
Exod 22:4 hands are clean."
"Yes, He is a witness," they replied.
12:6 Exod 6:26 6"It was the LORD who appointed Moses and Aaron," Samuel continued. "He brought
12:7 your ancestors out of the land of Egypt. 7Now stand here quietly before the LORD as I re-
Judg 5:11 mind you of all the great things the LORD has done for you and your ancestors.
Ps 78:4 8"When the Israelites were* in Egypt and cried out to the LORD, He sent Moses and
Mic 6:4 Aaron to rescue them from Egypt and to bring them into this land. 9But the people soon
12:8 Exod 2:23-25; 3:10; forgot about the LORD their God, so He handed them over to Sisera, the commander of
4:14-16 Hazor's army, and also to the Philistines and to the king of Moab, who fought against
12:9 them.
Deut 32:18 10"Then they cried to the LORD again and confessed, 'We have sinned by turning away
Judg 3:7; 10:7; 13:1 from the LORD and worshiping the images of Baal and Ashtoreth. But we will worship You
12:10 Judg 10:10, 15-16 and You alone if You will rescue us from our enemies.' 11Then the LORD sent Gideon,* Be-
12:11 dan,* Jephthah, and Samuel* to save you, and you lived in safety.
Judg 4:6; 6:32; 11:1 12"But when you were afraid of Nahash, the king of Ammon, you came to me and said
12:12 that you wanted a king to reign over you, even though the LORD your God was already
Judg 8:22-23 your king. 13All right, here is the king you have chosen. You asked for him, and the LORD
12:13 has granted your request.
1 Sam 8:5; 10:24 14"Now if you fear and worship the LORD and listen to His voice, and if you do not rebel
Hos 13:11 against the LORD's commands, then both you and your king will show that you recognize

12:14 Josh 24:14, 20

12:8 Hebrew *When Jacob was.* The names "Jacob" and "Israel" are often interchanged throughout the Old Testament, referring sometimes to the individual patriarch and sometimes to the nation. 12:11a Hebrew *Jerub-baal,* another name for Gideon; see Judg 6:32. 12:11b Greek and Syriac versions read *Barak.* 12:11c Greek and Syriac versions read *Samson.*

12:7 People must be constantly reminded of what God has done. We are prone to forget (as seen in 12:9). So Samuel gives a five-verse capsulation of God's redemption of Israel. Samuel concludes in verse 24 by exhorting Israel to "think of all the wonderful things He has done for you." If we meditate upon God's goodness, we are less likely to forget and won't need to be reminded.

12:8 In the 400 years between the end of Genesis and the beginning of Exodus, Israel grew into a numerous people in Egypt. This verse summarizes Exodus through Deuteronomy. Hearing these brief words, the people would be reminded of slavery in Egypt, Moses' birth and rise to power in Pharaoh's house, and Moses' and Aaron's efforts to free the Israelites and lead them to the Promised Land.

12:9 This verse summarizes the books of Joshua and Judges. Sisera was a soldier under Jabin of Hazor. Jabin may have ruled all of Canaan, so Sisera probably had much power in the region. He had 900 iron chariots, which he used against Israel for 20 years. Judges 4–5 gives the account of Sisera's downfall in a battle led by Deborah, judge of Israel, and her military cohort, Barak.

12:10 Baal and Ashtoreth (also called Asherah) were Canaanite fertility gods. Worship of these gods involved sexual practices. Wooden poles or pillars represented Asherah, while Baal worship utilized altars. Throughout Israel's history, righteous leaders and kings periodically sought religious reform by tearing down the Asherah poles and Baal altars throughout the land.

12:10 Israel lived in a constant cycle of sin against God, resulting in judgment. When Israel repented, God would send a judge to deliver them. The problem here is that Israel promised to worship the Lord alone *if* He rescued them. The Lord alone is worthy of worship regardless of one's life situation.

12:11 These men represent the longer list of men God used to lead Israel before they were ruled by kings. Read about Gideon in Judges 6–9, Barak (or *Bedan*) in Judges 4–5, Jephthah in Judges 11–12, and Samuel, the last judge of Israel, in 1 Samuel.

12:14 In Hebrew, the phrase "listen to His voice" is an idiom that means "obey." When we hear the Lord speak, we must obey.

the LORD as your God. 15 But if you rebel against the LORD's commands and refuse to listen
to Him, then His hand will be as heavy upon you as it was upon your ancestors.
16 "Now stand here and see the great thing the LORD is about to do. 17 You know that it
does not rain at this time of the year during the wheat harvest. I will ask the LORD to send
thunder and rain today. Then you will realize how wicked you have been in asking the
LORD for a king!"
18 So Samuel called to the LORD, and the LORD sent thunder and rain that day. And all the
people were terrified of the LORD and of Samuel. 19 "Pray to the LORD your God for us, or we
will die!" they all said to Samuel. "For now we have added to our sins by asking for a king."
20 "Don't be afraid," Samuel reassured them. "You have certainly done wrong, but make
sure now that you worship the LORD with all your heart, and don't turn your back on Him.
21 Don't go back to worshiping worthless idols that cannot help or rescue you—they are to-
tally useless! 22 The LORD will not abandon His people, because that would dishonor His
great name. For it has pleased the LORD to make you His very own people.
23 "As for me, I will certainly not sin against the LORD by ending my prayers for you. And I
will continue to teach you what is good and right. 24 But be sure to fear the LORD and faith-
fully serve Him. Think of all the wonderful things He has done for you. 25 But if you con-
tinue to sin, you and your king will be swept away."

CONTINUED WAR WITH PHILISTIA

13 Saul was thirty* years old when he became king, and he reigned for forty-two
years.*
2 Saul selected 3,000 special troops from the army of Israel and sent the rest of the men

12:15 Josh 24:20; Isa 1:2, 20
12:16 Exod 14:13, 21, 31
12:17 1 Sam 7:10; 8:6-7
12:20 Exod 32:30; Deut 11:16
12:21 Deut 11:16; Hab 2:18
12:22 Exod 32:12; Num 14:13; Deut 7:6; 31:6; Josh 12:9; 1 Pet 2:9
12:23 1 Kgs 8:36; Prov 4:11; Rom 1:9; Col 1:9; 1 Thes 3:10
12:24 Deut 10:21; Eccl 12:13
12:25 Josh 24:20; 1 Sam 31:1-5; Isa 1:20
13:2 1 Sam 10:26

13:1a As in a few Greek manuscripts; the number is missing in the Hebrew. 13:1b Hebrew *reigned . . . and two;* the number is incomplete in the Hebrew. Compare Acts 13:21.

▸ MINISTRY
12:15 Great last words. Have you ever been fired? Or been forced to leave a position of authority? There can be hard feelings, tears, and regret. The honesty and emotions of the aged Samuel come through the text as he transferred his office of leadership to Saul. Now, the human representative of God to Israel would be a king, not a prophet or priest or judge. The people reaffirmed their covenant vows to God through the office of the king, acknowledging the blessings and responsibilities that having a king would bring to Israel. (***See Ministry***> *Transformation> Vocations> King,* TopicGuide page A57.)

▸ GOD
12:19 Bad motives. How does God communicate to you that you have sinned? Is the communication internal—through your conscience? Or external—through your circumstances? Or through His Word? Samuel explains to Israel that some aspects of their request for a king was wrong, and God followed up that point with peals of thunder and crashes of lightning. They cried out for mercy, and Samuel promised exactly that. It was God's will for Israel to have a king (see 1 Samuel 8:5 and note), but Israel's desire to be like the other nations and to rely on a person rather than God for salvation from their enemies—these were sinful motives. God cares about what we do—and He cares about why we do it as well. Ask God to give you insight into your motives. (***See God***> *God's Attributes> Just> God rightly judges heart, mind, and deeds,* TopicGuide page A17.)

12:22 The nation of Israel began as a promise from God to Abraham. God promised Abraham that his descendants would be many and that a land called Canaan would become their homeland (see Genesis 12 and 15). Throughout the history of this promise, the nation of Israel stood as a testimony to God's presence and faithfulness in the world. God's commitment to Israel is the result of a deeper commitment to the glory of His own name.

▸ WORSHIP
12:23 Lifetime of prayer. As the leader of Israel, Samuel's job description was to pray for God's people. But even though his job was changing, his responsibility to pray continued. Has God given every Christian a directive on what we are to pray for? Yes! He has commanded us that, first, we must pray for those who are our enemies (Luke 6:28). God wants us to bless them, not curse them. Second, God commands us to pray for His mercy upon all people (1 Timothy 2:1). Every person needs more of God's mercy than he knows. Third, God asks that we pray for other believers who are sick, that we might see them healed (James 5:16). It is simply our place to pray, not to fuss about how and when God answers. Finally, in 1 John 5:16, God commands that we should pray for believers who sin and have not yet repented, that they might quickly and fully forsake their sin. (***See Worship***> *OT> Fasting and Prayer> Prayer> Individual> Of Samuel,* TopicGuide page A26.)

12:23-25 Samuel's final address to God's people can be compared to Joshua's final address (Joshua 23–24) and Solomon's speech at the dedication of the Temple (1 Kings 8:12-61). All three look back at God's faithfulness, look forward anticipating God's blessings, and remind the people of God's ever-present grace.

13:2 The areas described here all fell in the tribal region of Benjamin just north of Jerusalem. Each location provided an advantage to Saul's soldiers. Micmash, less than ten miles north of Jerusalem, was near a pass through two cliffs. Whoever controlled it had an excellent military advantage. Gibeah was much closer to Jerusalem and on high ground. Saul eventually ruled from Gibeah because of the advantage this height gave him. He could look down over Jerusalem from his fortress in Gibeah.

home. He took 2,000 of the chosen men with him to Micmash and the hill country of Beth-
el. The other 1,000 went with Saul's son Jonathan to Gibeah in the land of Benjamin.
13:3 3 Soon after this, Jonathan attacked and defeated the garrison of Philistines at Geba. The
Judg 3:27; 6:34 news spread quickly among the Philistines. So Saul blew the ram's horn throughout the
1 Sam 10:5 land, saying, "Hebrews, hear this! Rise up in revolt!" 4 All Israel heard the news that Saul
2 Sam 2:28; 20:1 had destroyed the Philistine garrison at Geba and that the Philistines now hated the Israel-
ites more than ever. So the entire Israelite army was summoned to join Saul at Gilgal.
13:5 5 The Philistines mustered a mighty army of 3,000* chariots, 6,000 charioteers, and as
Josh 11:4 many warriors as the grains of sand on the seashore! They camped at Micmash east of
13:6 Beth-aven. 6 The men of Israel saw what a tight spot they were in; and because they were
Judg 6:2 hard pressed by the enemy, they tried to hide in caves, thickets, rocks, holes, and cisterns.
7 Some of them crossed the Jordan River and escaped into the land of Gad and Gilead.

SAUL'S DISOBEDIENCE AND SAMUEL'S REBUKE

13:8 Meanwhile, Saul stayed at Gilgal, and his men were trembling with fear. 8 Saul waited there
1 Sam 10:8 seven days for Samuel, as Samuel had instructed him earlier, but Samuel still didn't come.
13:9 Saul realized that his troops were rapidly slipping away. 9 So he demanded, "Bring me the
2 Sam 24:25 burnt offering and the peace offerings!" And Saul sacrificed the burnt offering himself.
1 Kgs 3:4
13:10 10 Just as Saul was finishing with the burnt offering, Samuel arrived. Saul went out to
1 Sam 15:13 meet and welcome him, 11 but Samuel said, "What is this you have done?"

Saul replied, "I saw my men scattering from me, and you didn't arrive when you said
you would, and the Philistines are at Micmash ready for battle. 12 So I said, 'The Philistines
are ready to march against us at Gilgal, and I haven't even asked for the LORD's help!' So I
felt compelled to offer the burnt offering myself before you came."

13:13 13 "How foolish!" Samuel exclaimed. "You have not kept the command the LORD your
1 Sam 15:23-24, 28 God gave you. Had you kept it, the LORD would have established your kingdom over Israel
2 Chr 16:9 forever. 14 But now your kingdom must end, for the LORD has sought out a man after His
13:14 own heart. The LORD has already appointed him to be the leader of His people, because
*Acts 13:22 you have not kept the LORD's command."

ISRAEL'S MILITARY DISADVANTAGE

13:15 15 Samuel then left Gilgal and went on his way, but the rest of the troops went with Saul to
1 Sam 14:2 meet the army. They went up from Gilgal to Gibeah in the land of Benjamin.* When Saul

13:5 As in Greek and Syriac versions; Hebrew reads *30,000.* 13:15 As in Greek version; Hebrew reads *Samuel then left Gilgal and went to Gibeah in the land of Benjamin.*

13:6 The hill country of Israel contains tremendously diverse terrain: deep valleys, odd caves and culverts, and some rock formations unique to the earth's surface. The variety of formations in this compact area makes this land a magnet for geological research even today.

13:7 Some of the land east of the Jordan River was Israelite land. As the people entered the Promised Land, the tribes of Gad, Reuben, and half of Manasseh chose to settle on this eastern side of the Jordan (sometimes referred to as Gilead). While the land east of the Jordan offered less protection from enemies farther east, it provided a safe place to hide from marauding Philistines from the west.

▸ WORSHIP
13:8-13 Respecting boundaries. Saul's grave error revealed a heart that was not permitted of a king. In modern circumstances, if the minister is late to church, God does not necessarily want us to start administering the sacraments or preaching the sermon. Those who are functioning as the mouth of the church should not decide that they have the right to take over the job of the ears, hands, or feet. If a sprinter runs in the lane of another runner, he is disqualified. God wants us to run in our lanes, to treat others with deference and love (Philippians 2:2). (***See Worship***> *OT> Prohibitions> Wrong Forms> Person not qualified,* TopicGuide page A28.)

13:9 God had given the Israelites very specific guidelines (within much of the book of Leviticus and portions of the other books of Moses) for the practice of sacrifices and offerings. In Samuel's absence, Saul usurped the role of priest for himself. He ignored God's law even as he gave offerings that were meant to acknowledge God's power and show gratitude.

▸ WORSHIP
13:12 Excuses, excuses. Is it a sin to offer excuses? In this case it was, because rather than repent of his sin, Saul tried to excuse his behavior. What are your favorite ways to put off accusations of sin—did your parents treat you poorly? Or are you from an ethnic background that genetically predisposes you to have a bad temper? Or do you have allergies? Or was traffic bad this morning? Whatever your favorite excuse is, stop using it now. "Let everything you say be good and helpful, so that your words will be an encouragement to those who hear them" (Ephesians 4:29). Let the gospel be the answer to dealing with your sin, not your defensive words. (***See Worship***> *OT> Repentance> Nature> Obedience leads to blessing, failure to repent leads to curses,* TopicGuide page A29.)

counted the men who were still with him, he found only 600 were left! [16]Saul and Jona- 13:16
than and the troops with them were staying at Geba in the land of Benjamin. The Philis- Josh 18:24
tines set up their camp at Micmash. [17]Three raiding parties soon left the camp of the
Philistines. One went north toward Ophrah in the land of Shual, [18]another went west to 13:18
Beth-horon, and the third moved toward the border above the valley of Zeboim near the Neh 11:31-35
wilderness.

[19]There were no blacksmiths in the land of Israel in those days. The Philistines wouldn't 13:19
allow them for fear they would make swords and spears for the Hebrews. [20]So whenever Judg 5:8 1 Sam 17:47
the Israelites needed to sharpen their plowshares, picks, axes, or sickles,* they had to take 2 Kgs 24:14
them to a Philistine blacksmith. [21](The charges were as follows: a quarter of an ounce of Jer 24:1
silver* for sharpening a plowshare or a pick, and an eighth of an ounce* for sharpening an
ax, a sickle, or an ox goad.) [22]So on the day of the battle none of the people of Israel had a
sword or spear, except for Saul and Jonathan.

[23]The pass at Micmash had meanwhile been secured by a contingent of the Philistine 13:23 1 Sam 14:4
army. Isa 10:28

JONATHAN'S DARING PLAN

14 One day Jonathan said to his armor bearer, "Come on, let's go over to where the
Philistines have their outpost." But Jonathan did not tell his father what he was
doing.

[2]Meanwhile, Saul and his 600 men were camped on the outskirts of Gibeah, around the 14:2
pomegranate tree* at Migron. [3]Among Saul's men was Ahijah the priest, who was wearing 1 Sam 13:15
the ephod, the priestly vest. Ahijah was the son of Ichabod's brother Ahitub, son of Phine- 14:3
has, son of Eli, the priest of the LORD who had served at Shiloh. 1 Sam 1:3; 22:11-12

No one realized that Jonathan had left the Israelite camp. [4]To reach the Philistine out-
post, Jonathan had to go down between two rocky cliffs that were called Bozez and Seneh.
[5]The cliff on the north was in front of Micmash, and the one on the south was in front of
Geba. [6]"Let's go across to the outpost of those pagans," Jonathan said to his armor bearer. 14:6
"Perhaps the LORD will help us, for nothing can hinder the LORD. He can win a battle Judg 7:4
whether He has many warriors or only a few!"

[7]"Do what you think is best," the armor bearer replied. "I'm with you completely, what-
ever you decide."

[8]"All right then," Jonathan told him. "We will cross over and let them see us. [9]If they say
to us, 'Stay where you are or we'll kill you,' then we will stop and not go up to them. [10]But 14:10
if they say, 'Come on up and fight,' then we will go up. That will be the LORD's sign that He Gen 24:14
will help us defeat them." Judg 6:36

[11]When the Philistines saw them coming, they shouted, "Look! The Hebrews are crawl-
ing out of their holes!" [12]Then the men from the outpost shouted to Jonathan, "Come on 14:11
up here, and we'll teach you a lesson!" 1 Sam 13:6

14:12 2 Sam 5:24

13:20 As in Greek version; Hebrew reads *or plowshares.* 13:21a Hebrew *1 pim* [8 grams]. 13:21b Hebrew *⅓ of a shekel* [4 grams]. 14:2 Or *around the rock of Rimmon;* compare Judg 20:45, 47; 21:13.

13:19-22 The Philistines had a reputation for the impressive stature and might of their warriors and for their ability to work with metal. In fact, they held a monopoly on iron during this era. This gave Philistia strategic control over weapons, tool manufacturing, and even the economy. While Saul and Jonathan had metal weapons, the rest of their army had to make do with slings, bows and arrows, and wooden spears like ox goads. Within a generation, during David's reign, Israel began to catch up in the area of metallurgy. These advances helped equip David to defeat the Philistines.

14:3 Ahijah's family line is recorded because only men descended from the first high priest, Aaron, could serve as priests. Eli and his sons were the last notable priests on record, so we are shown the link between them and Ahijah.

14:4 This Philistine outpost was in a strategic position because of the geography of the area. These two cliffs, Bozez and Seneh, were located near a pass (13:23). By controlling the pass, the Philistines controlled traffic through the area. As recently as 1918, a British general named Allenby read this account of Jonathan's attack and moved his army to this narrow pass, thereby defeating the Turks.

"Come on, climb right behind me," Jonathan said to his armor bearer, "for the LORD will
help us defeat them!"
13 So they climbed up using both hands and feet, and the Philistines fell before Jona-
than, and his armor bearer killed those who came behind them. 14 They killed some
twenty men in all, and their bodies were scattered over about half an acre.*
14:15 15 Suddenly, panic broke out in the Philistine army, both in the camp and in the field, in-
1 Sam 7:10 2 Kgs 7:6 cluding even the outposts and raiding parties. And just then an earthquake struck, and
everyone was terrified.

ISRAEL DEFEATS THE PHILISTINES

16 Saul's lookouts in Gibeah of Benjamin saw a strange sight—the vast army of Philistines
began to melt away in every direction. 17 "Call the roll and find out who's missing," Saul or-
14:18 dered. And when they checked, they found that Jonathan and his armor bearer were
1 Sam 23:9; 30:7 gone.
14:19 Num 27:21 18 Then Saul shouted to Ahijah, "Bring the ephod here!" For at that time Ahijah was wear-
14:20 ing the ephod in front of the Israelites.* 19 But while Saul was talking to the priest, the con-
Judg 7:21-22 fusion in the Philistine camp grew louder and louder. So Saul said to the priest, "Never
2 Chr 20:23 mind; let's get going!"*
14:21 1 Sam 29:4 20 Then Saul and all his men rushed out to the battle and found the Philistines killing
each other. There was terrible confusion everywhere. 21 Even the Hebrews who had previ-
14:22 1 Sam 13:6; 31:7 ously gone over to the Philistine army revolted and joined in with Saul, Jonathan, and the
rest of the Israelites. 22 Likewise, the men of Israel who were hiding in the hill country of
14:23 Exod 14:30 Ephraim joined the chase when they saw the Philistines running away. 23 So the LORD
2 Chr 32:22 saved Israel that day, and the battle continued to rage even beyond Beth-aven.

SAUL'S FOOLISH OATH

14:24 Josh 6:26 24 Now the men of Israel were pressed to exhaustion that day, because Saul had placed
them under an oath, saying, "Let a curse fall on anyone who eats before evening—before I
have full revenge on my enemies." So no one ate anything all day, 25 even though they
had all found honeycomb on the ground in the forest. 26 They didn't dare touch the honey
because they all feared the oath they had taken.
27 But Jonathan had not heard his father's command, and he dipped the end of his
stick into a piece of honeycomb and ate the honey. After he had eaten it, he felt re-
freshed.* 28 But one of the men saw him and said, "Your father made the army take a strict
oath that anyone who eats food today will be cursed. That is why everyone is weary and
faint."
14:29 1 Kgs 18:18 29 "My father has made trouble for us all!" Jonathan exclaimed. "A command like that
only hurts us. See how refreshed I am now that I have eaten this little bit of honey. 30 If the

14:14 Hebrew *half a yoke;* a "yoke" was the amount of land plowed by a pair of yoked oxen in one day. 14:18 As in some Greek manuscripts; Hebrew reads *"Bring the Ark of God." For at that time the Ark of God was with the Israelites.* 14:19 Hebrew *Withdraw your hand.* 14:27 Or *his eyes brightened;* similarly in 14:29.

14:15, 20 Panic and confusion had become a strategy in a Hebrew conflict. When the Hebrews first left Egypt in the great Exodus, God told Moses that Pharaoh would be confused and destroyed (Exodus 14). Gideon also preyed upon the panic of his enemies, the Midianites, causing them to turn on each other and give victory to Gideon (Judges 7:15-22).

▶ WORSHIP
14:24-46 A foolish vow. Have you ever made a foolish promise? Or made someone else take a foolish vow? Saul endangered the lives of all his troops by forcing them to abstain from food until he proclaimed victory over his enemies. Then he compounded his error by vowing to kill whoever had sinned, even if it was his own son (14:39). Saul then took another rash vow when Jonathan's deed (which was not a sin, see 14:27) was uncovered—he asked that God strike him down if Jonathan survived. But God did not strike down Saul, proving that not only were Jonathan's actions not deserving of death, but Saul's foolishness wasn't either. (***See Worship> Offerings> Other Sacrifices> Vows,*** TopicGuide page A27.)

men had been allowed to eat freely from the food they found among our enemies, think
how many more Philistines we could have killed!"
31 They chased and killed the Philistines all day from Micmash to Aijalon, growing more
and more faint. 32 That evening they rushed for the battle plunder and butchered the
sheep, goats, cattle, and calves, but they ate them without draining the blood. 33 Someone
reported to Saul, "Look, the men are sinning against the LORD by eating meat that still has
blood in it."
"That is very wrong," Saul said. "Find a large stone and roll it over here. 34 Then go out
among the troops and tell them, 'Bring the cattle, sheep, and goats here to me. Kill them
here, and drain the blood before you eat them. Do not sin against the LORD by eating meat
with the blood still in it.'"
So that night all the troops brought their animals and slaughtered them there. 35 Then
Saul built an altar to the LORD; it was the first of the altars he built to the LORD.
36 Then Saul said, "Let's chase the Philistines all night and plunder them until sunrise.
Let's destroy every last one of them."
His men replied, "We'll do whatever you think is best."
But the priest said, "Let's ask God first."
37 So Saul asked God, "Should we go after the Philistines? Will You help us defeat them?"
But God made no reply that day.
38 Then Saul said to the leaders, "Something's wrong! I want all my army commanders to
come here. We must find out what sin was committed today. 39 I vow by the name of the
LORD who rescued Israel that the sinner will surely die, even if it is my own son Jonathan!"
But no one would tell him what the trouble was.
40 Then Saul said, "Jonathan and I will stand over here, and all of you stand over there."
And the people responded to Saul, "Whatever you think is best."
41 Then Saul prayed, "O LORD, God of Israel, please show us who is guilty and who is in-
nocent.*" Then they cast sacred lots, and Jonathan and Saul were chosen as the guilty
ones, and the people were declared innocent.
42 Then Saul said, "Now cast lots again and choose between me and Jonathan." And Jon-
athan was shown to be the guilty one.
43 "Tell me what you have done," Saul demanded of Jonathan.
"I tasted a little honey," Jonathan admitted. "It was only a little bit on the end of my stick.
Does that deserve death?"
44 "Yes, Jonathan," Saul said, "you must die! May God strike me and even kill me if you
do not die for this."
45 But the people broke in and said to Saul, "Jonathan has won this great victory for Isra-
el. Should he die? Far from it! As surely as the LORD lives, not one hair on his head will be

14:31 Josh 10:12
14:32 Gen 9:4; Lev 17:10; 1 Sam 15:19; Acts 15:20
14:35 1 Sam 7:12, 17
14:37 1 Sam 28:5-6; 30:7-8
14:38 Josh 7:10-12
14:39 2 Sam 12:5
14:41 Acts 1:24
14:43 Josh 7:19; 1 Sam 14:27
14:44 Ruth 1:17; 1 Sam 3:17; 14:39; 25:22
14:45 2 Sam 14:11; Luke 21:18; Acts 27:34

14:41 Greek version adds *If the fault is with me or my son Jonathan, respond with Urim; but if the men of Israel are at fault, respond with Thummim.*

14:31 Micmash and Aijalon were both north of Jerusalem. Micmash was to the northeast in the tribal territory of Benjamin. Aijalon was to the northwest in the tribe of Dan. Saul's hungry and exhausted army traversed 15 miles chasing, running, and killing their enemies.

14:33 For an Israelite, one of the most important laws was the command to abstain from consuming or sacrificing animals without first draining the blood. Blood represented life, and life belonged to God. Therefore, draining the blood of animals before they were offered was an essential part of the sacrificial system. This practice foreshadowed the perfect sacrifice of Christ, who by His shed blood offers life to all who believe. For these Israelite soldiers to disregard this most essential custom was completely unacceptable, direct disobedience before God.

14:40-42 Saul determined the identity of the sinner by the ancient custom of casting lots. In some ways, casting lots was much like tossing a coin. This action prayerfully acknowledged that no person involved could sway the outcome. In that way, people believed, God would lead them. This custom was used for decisions as critical as dividing the Promised Land among the tribes (Joshua 18:10).

14:43-46 Saul's oath meant much more in his culture than a mere promise does in ours. Years earlier, a judge named Jephthah made a foolish oath that cost him the life of his own daughter (Judges 11:29-40). When the people stood against Saul and rescued Jonathan, they elevated life above tradition. In the New Testament, Jesus made a reputation for Himself by challenging tradition (Mark 2:23-28) that clashed with God's Word.

touched, for God helped him do a great deed today." So the people rescued Jonathan, and
he was not put to death.
46Then Saul called back the army from chasing the Philistines, and the Philistines re-
turned home.

SAUL'S MILITARY SUCCESSES

14:48 1 Sam 15:3, 7
14:49 1 Sam 18:17, 20, 27; 19:11-12; 31:2; 2 Sam 6:20; 1 Chr 8:33; 10:2
14:50 2 Sam 2:8
14:51 1 Sam 9:1
14:52 1 Sam 8:11

47Now when Saul had secured his grasp on Israel's throne, he fought against his enemies
in every direction—against Moab, Ammon, Edom, the kings of Zobah, and the Philistines.
And wherever he turned, he was victorious. 48He performed great deeds and conquered
the Amalekites, saving Israel from all those who had plundered them.
49Saul's sons included Jonathan, Ishbosheth,* and Malkishua. He also had two daugh-
ters: Merab, who was older, and Michal. 50Saul's wife was Ahinoam, the daughter of Ahim-
aaz. The commander of Saul's army was Abner, the son of Saul's uncle Ner. 51Saul's
father, Kish, and Abner's father, Ner, were both sons of Abiel.
52The Israelites fought constantly with the Philistines throughout Saul's lifetime. So
whenever Saul observed a young man who was brave and strong, he drafted him into his
army.

SAUL DESTROYS THE AMALEKITES

15:1 1 Sam 9:16; 10:1
15:2 Exod 17:8-16; Num 24:20; Deut 25:17
15:3 Deut 20:16-18; Josh 6:17-18

15 One day Samuel said to Saul, "It was the LORD who told me to anoint you as king
of His people, Israel. Now listen to this message from the LORD! 2This is what the
LORD of Heaven's Armies has declared: I have decided to settle accounts with the nation of
Amalek for opposing Israel when they came from Egypt. 3Now go and completely destroy*
the entire Amalekite nation—men, women, children, babies, cattle, sheep, goats, camels,
and donkeys."
4So Saul mobilized his army at Telaim. There were 200,000 soldiers from Israel and
10,000 men from Judah. 5Then Saul and his army went to a town of the Amalekites and

14:49 Hebrew *Ishvi*, a variant name for Ishbosheth; also known as Esh-baal. 15:3 The Hebrew term used here refers to the complete consecration of things or people to the LORD, either by destroying them or by giving them as an offering; also in 15:8, 9, 15, 18, 20, 21.

14:47-48 The peoples of Moab, Ammon, Edom, and Amalek were all distant relatives of the Israelites. The first two descended from Abraham's nephew Lot, who escaped from Sodom and Gomorrah. The Edomites descended from Abraham's grandson Esau, the twin brother of Jacob (whose name was changed to Israel). The Amalekites, descendants of Esau's grandson Amalek, were described as having no fear of God (Deuteronomy 25:18). The Amalekites continued to form alliances against Israel even into the days of King David.

14:47 This is the first time the kingdom of Zobah is mentioned in the Scriptures. This kingdom was in conflict with the Israelites during the reigns of Saul, David, and David's son Solomon. Their final mention is when Solomon defeated Hamath-zobah (2 Chronicles 8:3).

14:50 Saul's cousin Abner will be an important figure in coming chapters. He commanded the Israelite army throughout Saul's reign. He met David as a young boy, bringing him to Saul after David killed Goliath (17:55-57). Abner assisted Saul as he searched for David, jealous of David's accomplishments (1 Samuel 26). After Saul's death, Abner led Saul's son Ishbosheth in an attempt to gain Israel's throne. When that attempt failed, Abner negotiated with David to serve in David's kingdom. David agreed, but soon afterward, Abner was murdered by Joab in an act of revenge (2 Samuel 3:6-27).

14:47-52 From a literary standpoint, these verses conclude the focus on Saul. Though David is not mentioned by name until 16:13, the focus shifts to him with the next chapter.

15:2 The Amalekites assaulted Israel during the Exodus from Egypt when the Israelites were camped at Rephidim, between Egypt and Mount Sinai. During this battle Joshua first appeared as a future leader. Joshua led the army, while Moses stood on a hill with his staff raised. As long as Moses held his staff up, the Israelites had the advantage in battle. When Moses' arms grew weary, Aaron, his brother, and Hur, possibly a brother-in-law, helped to hold up his arms. Though the Israelites were victorious (Exodus 17:8-13), God held the Amalekites responsible for their actions and brought His vengeance in His time.

15:3 God often commanded the Israelites to destroy completely those they defeated. The concept of destroying cut two ways. At times they literally demolished the city or its inhabitants. At other times the word had a connotation of "complete dedication." Rather than destroying a herd, the Israelites may have brought that herd and offered it to God.

15:4 Telaim was probably a city in the southern part of the tribal land belonging to Judah.

lay in wait in the valley. 6Saul sent this warning to the Kenites: "Move away from where 15:6
the Amalekites live, or you will die with them. For you showed kindness to all the people Num 24:21-22 Judg 1:16; 4:11
of Israel when they came up from Egypt." So the Kenites packed up and left.
7Then Saul slaughtered the Amalekites from Havilah all the way to Shur, east of Egypt. 15:7 Gen 16:7; 25:18
8He captured Agag, the Amalekite king, but completely destroyed everyone else. 9Saul Exod 15:22
and his men spared Agag's life and kept the best of the sheep and goats, the cattle, the fat 1 Sam 27:8
calves, and the lambs—everything, in fact, that appealed to them. They destroyed only 15:8 Num 24:7
what was worthless or of poor quality. 15:9 1 Sam 15:15, 21

THE LORD REJECTS SAUL

10Then the LORD said to Samuel, 11"I am sorry that I ever made Saul king, for he has not 15:11 Gen 6:6-7
been loyal to Me and has refused to obey My command." Samuel was so deeply moved Exod 32:9, 11, 14
when he heard this that he cried out to the LORD all night. 2 Sam 24:16
12Early the next morning Samuel went to find Saul. Someone told him, "Saul went to the Luke 6:12
town of Carmel to set up a monument to himself; then he went on to Gilgal." 15:12 Josh 15:55
13When Samuel finally found him, Saul greeted him cheerfully. "May the LORD bless
you," he said. "I have carried out the LORD's command!"
14"Then what is all the bleating of sheep and goats and the lowing of cattle I hear?"
Samuel demanded.
15"It's true that the army spared the best of the sheep, goats, and cattle," Saul admitted. 15:15
"But they are going to sacrifice them to the LORD your God. We have destroyed everything Gen 3:12-13 1 Sam 15:9, 21
else."
16Then Samuel said to Saul, "Stop! Listen to what the LORD told me last night!"
"What did He tell you?" Saul asked.
17And Samuel told him, "Although you may think little of yourself, are you not the 15:17
leader of the tribes of Israel? The LORD has anointed you king of Israel. 18And the LORD sent 1 Sam 9:21; 10:22
you on a mission and told you, 'Go and completely destroy the sinners, the Amalekites,
until they are all dead.' 19Why haven't you obeyed the LORD? Why did you rush for the 15:19
plunder and do what was evil in the LORD's sight?" 1 Sam 14:32

15:6 The Kenites were a Canaanite tribe mentioned as early as Abraham's lifetime. Unlike some other Canaanite tribes, the Kenites aided Israel on several occasions. Saul's warning to them speaks to the mutually helpful relationship they had established. During the days of King David, Kenites still lived in Judah (1 Samuel 27:10).

▸ GOD

15:10-11 When God weeps. Some wonderful blessings God has for us are free, sent by God's grace, but contingent on our obedience. God's promises to bless Saul and his family were contingent on Saul's obedience as a king. When Saul refused to be obedient to the Lord in his duties as king, God sent Samuel to inform Saul that his kingdom would end. God hates sin and feels deep sorrow at the sinful behavior of His people. The more we seek to understand how God feels about our words, thoughts, and feelings, the more like Him we become (Psalm 139:23-25). (***See God****> God's Nature> Personality> Emotion> God can be moved to grief,* TopicGuide page A14.)

15:12 This Carmel is not the mountain in the northwest of Israel near the Mediterranean Sea. Rather, it is a mountain seven miles south of Hebron in Judah. This accounts for Saul's ability to go from there to Gilgal—not nearly as far away as the northern Carmel from Gilgal.

▸ GOD

15:12 VIP. Some people seem to change when they taste success. Saul previously thought little of himself, proceeding humbly into the role of king (15:17). But a season of victories on the battlefield revealed him to be a proud man. Now he journeyed to the top of sacred mountains, but not for God's glory—for his own. Are you more concerned with God's reputation, or your own? (***See God****> God's Attributes> Faithful> God deserves thanks for His constant faithfulness,* TopicGuide page A16.)

▸ GOD

15:15 Confronted by sin. When we are confronted with our sin, our inner character is immediately revealed. If we are liars, we lie. If we have a temper, we become angry. If we are violent, we fight. In this case, Saul was an excuse-making liar. He lied about obeying God (see 15:13), shifted blame to his troops, and made religious excuses for his cosmic treason (15:15). Samuel had heard enough—he could take no more. He pronounced the judgment of God upon Saul. Saul still was not humbled—he continued to make excuses (15:20). Like it or not, our life in God is deeply connected to our decision to admit our own sin and accept God's solution. Flee from the self-atonement scheme of excuse making and trust in Christ's gospel solution for your sin. (***See God****> Relationship> Barriers> Unconfessed transgressions,* TopicGuide page A14.)

20“But I did obey the LORD,” Saul insisted. “I carried out the mission He gave me. I
15:21 1 Sam 15:9, 15 brought back King Agag, but I destroyed everyone else. 21 Then my troops brought in the
best of the sheep, goats, cattle, and plunder to sacrifice to the LORD your God in Gilgal.”
15:22 Pss 40:6-8; 51:16-17 Isa 1:11-15 Jer 7:22-23 Hos 6:6 Mic 6:7-8 Mark 12:33 22But Samuel replied,

“What is more pleasing to the LORD:
your burnt offerings and sacrifices
or your obedience to His voice?
Listen! Obedience is better than sacrifice,
and submission is better than offering the fat of rams.
15:23 Deut 18:10 1 Sam 13:14 23 Rebellion is as sinful as witchcraft,
and stubbornness as bad as worshiping idols.
So because you have rejected the command of the LORD,
He has rejected you as king.”

SAUL PLEADS FOR FORGIVENESS

15:24 Num 22:34 2 Sam 12:13 Ps 51:4 Isa 51:12-13 24Then Saul admitted to Samuel, “Yes, I have sinned. I have disobeyed your instructions
and the LORD’S command, for I was afraid of the people and did what they demanded.
25But now, please forgive my sin and come back with me so that I may worship the LORD.”
15:25 Exod 10:17 26But Samuel replied, “I will not go back with you! Since you have rejected the LORD’S
command, He has rejected you as king of Israel.”
15:27 1 Kgs 11:30-31 27As Samuel turned to go, Saul tried to hold him back and tore the hem of his robe.
15:28 1 Sam 28:17-18 28And Samuel said to him, “The LORD has torn the kingdom of Israel from you today and
has given it to someone else—one who is better than you. 29And He who is the Glory of Is-
15:29 Num 23:19 Ezek 24:14 rael will not lie, nor will He change his mind, for He is not human that He should change
his mind!”
30Then Saul pleaded again, “I know I have sinned. But please, at least honor me before
15:30 Isa 29:13 the elders of my people and before Israel by coming back with me so that I may worship
the LORD your God.” 31 So Samuel finally agreed and went back with him, and Saul wor-
shiped the LORD.

▶ WORSHIP

15:22 Obedience is better than sacrifice. Nothing is worse than sin, and sin cloaked in religion is among the worst expressions of human rebellion against God. Even the holiest of sacrifices do not please God as much as the simplest obedience. Perhaps you think your sacrificial work in the church gives you the right to reward yourself with soul-searing pornography. Or you may think that the great expense you incurred to get your religious education entitles you to cheat on your taxes. Regardless of the details, sin that is sustained through claims of spirituality perverts the very reason for sacrificial obedience: the glory of God. (***See Worship***> *OT> Repentance> Nature> To obey is better than sacrifice,* TopicGuide page A29.)

▶ WORSHIP

15:24 Shut up and forgive me. Perhaps you have already figured this out—if you cannot excuse your actions and you cannot hide them, the next easiest defense is to admit you sinned, say you are sorry, then attack the person who will not immediately drop all discussion about the matter. Saul essentially said, “I’m sorry, I’m sorry, can’t we just move on now?!” Of course, if you do this consistently, you will likely die in your sins, never having known the forgiveness that God offers those who repent. True repentance and excuse making cannot exist together. (***See Worship***> *NT> Christ’s Supremacy> His sacrifice provides true cleansing from sin,* TopicGuide page A29.)

15:17, 24 We gain insight into Saul’s character in these verses. Saul was not raised among royalty. He went out looking for lost donkeys, and on the way was anointed king of Israel. In verse 17, Samuel notes that Saul thought little of himself. In verse 24, Saul admitted he was afraid of the people, so he sought to please them. It’s tempting to look back through history selectively freezing ancient men and women in molds created by their accomplishments. These insights remind us that leaders are human, with all the accompanying frailties.

15:27 The Hebrew text here says Saul “grabbed the hem of his robe,” which eventually ripped. Some say this was a humble gesture pleading for help. In Matthew 9:20-22 a woman reached out to touch the hem of Jesus’ garment, perhaps in a similar way.

15:29 Only here in Scripture are these words, “the Glory of Israel,” used to describe the Lord God, though a similar phrase appears in 1 Chronicles 29:11, rendering “glory” as “victory” or “splendor.”

SAMUEL EXECUTES KING AGAG

32Then Samuel said, "Bring King Agag to me." Agag arrived full of hope, for he thought,
"Surely the worst is over, and I have been spared!"* 33But Samuel said, "As your sword has
killed the sons of many mothers, now your mother will be childless." And Samuel cut Agag
to pieces before the LORD at Gilgal.
34Then Samuel went home to Ramah, and Saul returned to his house at Gibeah of Saul.
35Samuel never went to meet with Saul again, but he mourned constantly for him. And the
LORD was sorry He had ever made Saul king of Israel.

15:33 Gen 9:5-6; Judg 1:7
15:34 1 Sam 7:17; 11:4
15:35 1 Sam 16:1; 19:24

SAMUEL ANOINTS DAVID AS KING

16 Now the LORD said to Samuel, "You have mourned long enough for Saul. I have re-
jected him as king of Israel, so fill your flask with olive oil and go to Bethlehem.
Find a man named Jesse who lives there, for I have selected one of his sons to be My king."
2But Samuel asked, "How can I do that? If Saul hears about it, he will kill me."
"Take a heifer with you," the LORD replied, "and say that you have come to make a sacri-
fice to the LORD. 3Invite Jesse to the sacrifice, and I will show you which of his sons to
anoint for Me."
4So Samuel did as the LORD instructed. When he arrived at Bethlehem, the elders of the
town came trembling to meet him. "What's wrong?" they asked. "Do you come in peace?"
5"Yes," Samuel replied. "I have come to sacrifice to the LORD. Purify yourselves and
come with me to the sacrifice." Then Samuel performed the purification rite for Jesse and
his sons and invited them to the sacrifice, too.
6When they arrived, Samuel took one look at Eliab and thought, "Surely this is the
LORD's anointed!"
7But the LORD said to Samuel, "Don't judge by his appearance or height, for I have re-

16:1 1 Sam 9:16; 13:13-14; 2 Kgs 9:1-2
16:2 1 Sam 20:28-29
16:3 Deut 17:14-15
16:4 1 Kgs 2:13; Luke 2:4
16:5 Gen 35:2; Exod 19:10
16:6 1 Sam 17:13
16:7 1 Sam 9:2; 1 Kgs 8:39; 1 Chr 28:9; Luke 16:15

15:32 Dead Sea Scrolls and Greek version read *Agag arrived hesitantly, for he thought, "Surely this is the bitterness of death."*

15:35 Saul continued to reign in Israel even though he lost God's approval and access to Samuel's wisdom. Saul would rule for years under the oppressive knowledge that God had withdrawn His favor from him.

16:1 The horn of an animal (translated "flask" here) had many uses. In this case, the horn was used as a container to hold anointing oil. Ram's horns were also used as musical instruments to mark public occasions (Joshua 6:5). Some scribes used horns as kits to carry writing implements (Ezekiel 9:11).

16:1 Jesse, the father of the soon-to-be-anointed king, David, was the son of Obed and the grandson of Ruth and Boaz (Ruth 4:17-22).

▸ WORSHIP

16:2 Half truths. God wants our behavior to reflect His character. "Be holy as I am holy," He said to His people at Mount Sinai. Yet, in this passage, the Lord instructs Samuel to anoint one of Jesse's sons as king, with the explicit counsel that Samuel is to conceal the primary purpose of his visit. It appears as if the Scriptures teach that there are some situations of dire circumstances where God endorses giving incomplete or even superficially misleading information to others (Joshua 2:3-5; Judges 4:17–5:24; Exodus 1:15-21). In a modern war situation, a captured prisoner who tells the entire truth of what he or she knows would be a traitor, not a hero. Your motive, the situation, the possible violation of conscience, and the impression you receive from the indwelling Spirit—all these things must be taken into account before you consider anything other than being a strict truth-teller. Study and pray over this matter extensively and seek counsel before you even consider saying anything other than the plain truth. (***See Worship**> NT> Fellowship> Nature> Tell the unvarnished truth to each other,* TopicGuide page A30.)

16:4 There were two towns named Bethlehem in ancient Israel. This Bethlehem was in the region of Judah, six miles south of Jerusalem. The other was in Zebulun seven miles northwest of Nazareth in Galilee. Bethlehem of Judah was the location of Jesus' birth. This Bethlehem was also called Ephrath, so its inhabitants were sometimes called Ephrathites (Ruth 1:1; 1 Samuel 17:12).

16:5 Being clean, or pure, before God was an essential part of Israelite ritual. Some purification rites (especially involving birth, sexual activity, and death) took seven days of ritual cleansing (Leviticus 15). The people also purified themselves before meeting with God. Even in New Testament days a large complex of ritual baths was located just outside the main entrance to the Temple grounds so that people could fulfill these requirements before meeting with God.

16:6-9 Eliab, Jesse's oldest son, seems to have been an impressive man. He served in Saul's army, and later showed some resentment toward David when he arrived to check on his brothers and subsequently fought Goliath. Abinadab, Jesse's second son, served with his brothers in Saul's army. Shammah, Jesse's third son, was also called Shimea or Shimei.

16:7 Jeremiah 17:9 says, "The human heart is the most deceitful of all things, and desperately wicked. Who really knows how bad it is?" In this context, God was not looking for a good heart, since only God is good; He was looking for thoughts and intentions that could be inclined to His glory.

jected him. The LORD doesn't see things the way you see them. People judge by outward
appearance, but the LORD looks at the heart."
16:8 8 Then Jesse told his son Abinadab to step forward and walk in front of Samuel. But Sam-
1 Sam 17:13 uel said, "This is not the one the LORD has chosen." 9 Next Jesse summoned Shimea,* but
Samuel said, "Neither is this the one the LORD has chosen." 10 In the same way all seven of
Jesse's sons were presented to Samuel. But Samuel said to Jesse, "The LORD has not cho-
16:11 sen any of these." 11 Then Samuel asked, "Are these all the sons you have?"
2 Sam 7:8 "There is still the youngest," Jesse replied. "But he's out in the fields watching the sheep
and goats."
"Send for him at once," Samuel said. "We will not sit down to eat until he arrives."
16:12 Gen 39:6 12 So Jesse sent for him. He was dark and handsome, with beautiful eyes.
Exod 2:1-2 And the LORD said, "This is the one; anoint him."
1 Sam 9:17 Acts 7:20 13 So as David stood there among his brothers, Samuel took the flask of olive oil he had
brought and anointed David with the oil. And the Spirit of the LORD came powerfully upon
David from that day on. Then Samuel returned to Ramah.

DAVID SERVES IN SAUL'S COURT

16:14 14 Now the Spirit of the LORD had left Saul, and the LORD sent a tormenting spirit* that filled
Judg 16:20 1 Sam 11:6; 18:10- him with depression and fear.
12; 19:9 15 Some of Saul's servants said to him, "A tormenting spirit from God is troubling you.
1 Kgs 22:22 16 Let us find a good musician to play the harp whenever the tormenting spirit troubles
you. He will play soothing music, and you will soon be well again."
17 "All right," Saul said. "Find me someone who plays well, and bring him here."
16:18 18 One of the servants said to Saul, "One of Jesse's sons from Bethlehem is a talented
1 Sam 3:19; 17:32-37 harp player. Not only that—he is a brave warrior, a man of war, and has good judgment.
He is also a fine-looking young man, and the LORD is with him."
19 So Saul sent messengers to Jesse to say, "Send me your son David, the shepherd."
20 Jesse responded by sending David to Saul, along with a young goat, a donkey loaded
with bread, and a wineskin full of wine.
16:21 21 So David went to Saul and began serving him. Saul loved David very much, and Da-
Gen 41:46 vid became his armor bearer.

16:9 Hebrew *Shammah,* a variant spelling of Shimea; compare 1 Chr 2:13; 20:7. 16:14 Or *an evil spirit;* also in 16:15, 16, 23.

16:11 Sheep herding was a menial task given to someone who could not be trusted with much else. But God took this shepherd and raised him to be a shepherd for His people.

16:13 David's anointing in the midst of his brothers should remind the reader of other times in Scripture when God raises up an unexpected person for His purposes. Joseph (whose brothers eventually bowed before him) and Gideon (who was the least of his clan) are other examples.

▶ GOD

16:14 God as your enemy. Are you depressed? Are you afraid? Does it fill you with terror to think that, according to this passage, God could be the one tormenting you? The "Spirit" that left Saul should not be understood to be the indwelling Holy Spirit that secures and empowers all believers today. Nor was this "Spirit" an entity, such as an angel or demon. This was the royal anointing for ministry that God was removing from Saul. David received this same Spirit in the previous verse. This text is not saying that God sends demons upon His people whenever He feels like it—God does not do that (Luke 11:14-28). (***See God****> Salvation> Holy Spirit> Sealed by the Holy Spirit,* TopicGuide page A15.)

16:16 Servants in Saul's courts believed music could help Saul through his emotional difficulties, but the point of this narrative isn't musical, but political. The writer makes sure the reader knows that David never did anything to deserve the ill treatment doled out by the cursed, mad Saul.

16:19-20 The story of David and Saul lets us see God working behind the scenes to interweave these men's lives. The story of Joseph (Genesis 37–50) does this as well. These stories give us hope that while we may not see it, God's hand is working.

22 Then Saul sent word to Jesse asking, "Please let David remain in my service, for I am very pleased with him."

23 And whenever the tormenting spirit from God troubled Saul, David would play the harp. Then Saul would feel better, and the tormenting spirit would go away.

GOLIATH CHALLENGES THE ISRAELITES

17 The Philistines now mustered their army for battle and camped between Socoh in Judah and Azekah at Ephes-dammim. 2 Saul countered by gathering his Israelite troops near the valley of Elah. 3 So the Philistines and Israelites faced each other on opposite hills, with the valley between them.

4 Then Goliath, a Philistine champion from Gath, came out of the Philistine ranks to face the forces of Israel. He was over nine feet* tall! 5 He wore a bronze helmet, and his bronze coat of mail weighed 125 pounds.* 6 He also wore bronze leg armor, and he carried a bronze javelin on his shoulder. 7 The shaft of his spear was as heavy and thick as a weaver's beam, tipped with an iron spearhead that weighed 15 pounds.* His armor bearer walked ahead of him carrying a shield.

8 Goliath stood and shouted a taunt across to the Israelites. "Why are you all coming out to fight?" he called. "I am the Philistine champion, but you are only the servants of Saul. Choose one man to come down here and fight me! 9 If he kills me, then we will be your slaves. But if I kill him, you will be our slaves! 10 I defy the armies of Israel today! Send me a man who will fight me!" 11 When Saul and the Israelites heard this, they were terrified and deeply shaken.

17:1 1 Sam 13:5; 1 Chr 11:13
17:2 1 Sam 21:9
17:4 Josh 11:21-22; 2 Sam 21:19
17:9 2 Sam 2:12-16
17:10 1 Sam 17:26, 45

JESSE SENDS DAVID TO SAUL'S CAMP

12 Now David was the son of a man named Jesse, an Ephrathite from Bethlehem in the land of Judah. Jesse was an old man at that time, and he had eight sons. 13 Jesse's three oldest sons—Eliab, Abinadab, and Shimea*—had already joined Saul's army to fight the Philistines. 14 David was the youngest son. David's three oldest brothers stayed with Saul's army, 15 but David went back and forth so he could help his father with the sheep in Bethlehem.

16 For forty days, every morning and evening, the Philistine champion strutted in front of the Israelite army.

17:12 Gen 35:19; Ruth 4:18-22; 1 Chr 2:13
17:13 1 Sam 16:6-9
17:15 1 Sam 16:19

17:4 Hebrew *6 cubits and 1 span* [which totals about 9.75 feet or 3 meters]; Dead Sea Scrolls and Greek version read *4 cubits and 1 span* [which totals about 6.75 feet or 2 meters]. 17:5 Hebrew *5,000 shekels* [57 kilograms]. 17:7 Hebrew *600 shekels* [6.8 kilograms]. 17:13 Hebrew *Shammah,* a variant spelling of Shimea; compare 1 Chr 2:13; 20:7.

17:1-3 These verses describe an interesting location in the Elah Valley in the foothills below Bethlehem. This battlefield had two ridges on either side of a wadi, a creek bed that is dry for part of the year. With armies positioned on the hill on either side, David's fight with Goliath would have taken place in an arena-like environment with the opposing sides able to see and shout at each other from their respective hillsides.

17:4 Gath was one of five principal cities of Philistia, along with Ashdod, Gaza, Ekron, and Ashkelon. Gath was also the place David fled to when he feared for his life at the hands of King Saul (1 Samuel 27). David later took the Ark of the Covenant to Gath for safekeeping, to the home of a man named Obed-edom (2 Samuel 6).

17:4 Ancient texts differ concerning Goliath's height. Some say he was nine feet nine inches; others say he was six feet nine inches. Even with the lesser height, Goliath would have towered over the ancient Israelites who, because of diet and genetics, often stood just five feet tall.

17:5-6 Goliath's armor is further evidence that the Philistines surpassed Israel in metal-working abilities. Bearing bronze and iron weapons and armor gave a strategic advantage to Philistine warriors. In an earlier battle with the Philistines, only Saul and his son Jonathan, out of the whole Israelite army, even had a spear or a sword (1 Samuel 13:19-22).

17:7 A weaver's beam was the part of the loom that the weaver wrapped the finished fabric around. This spear shaft was substantial enough to carry a fifteen-pound spearhead, a daunting weapon that could pierce any ancient armor.

▸ WORSHIP

17:11 Shaken, but not stirred. Along with the rest of the warriors of Israel, Saul cowered in fear before the mighty Goliath. Their lack of faith in God, more than the size of their enemy, filled their hearts with terror. But focusing on the enormity of God's love for us drives out our fear (1 John 4:18). Pray that God will increase your understanding of His perfect love for you. (***See Worship****> OT> Reverence> Let the earth fear God,* TopicGuide page A29.)

17:17 17 One day Jesse said to David, "Take this basket* of roasted grain and these ten loaves
1 Sam 25:18 of bread, and carry them quickly to your brothers. 18 And give these ten cuts of cheese to
17:18 their captain. See how your brothers are getting along, and bring back a report on how
Gen 37:13-14 they are doing.*" 19 David's brothers were with Saul and the Israelite army at the valley of
Elah, fighting against the Philistines.

20 So David left the sheep with another shepherd and set out early the next morning
with the gifts, as Jesse had directed him. He arrived at the camp just as the Israelite army
was leaving for the battlefield with shouts and battle cries. 21 Soon the Israelite and Philis-
tine forces stood facing each other, army against army. 22 David left his things with the
17:23 keeper of supplies and hurried out to the ranks to greet his brothers. 23 As he was talking
1 Sam 17:8-10 with them, Goliath, the Philistine champion from Gath, came out from the Philistine ranks.
Then David heard him shout his usual taunt to the army of Israel.

17:25 24 As soon as the Israelite army saw him, they began to run away in fright. 25 "Have you
Josh 15:16
1 Sam 18:17 seen the giant?" the men asked. "He comes out each day to defy Israel. The king has of-
fered a huge reward to anyone who kills him. He will give that man one of his daughters
for a wife, and the man's entire family will be exempted from paying taxes!"

17:26 26 David asked the soldiers standing nearby, "What will a man get for killing this Philis-
1 Sam 11:2; 14:6 tine and ending his defiance of Israel? Who is this pagan Philistine anyway, that he is al-
2 Kgs 19:4 lowed to defy the armies of the living God?"

27 And these men gave David the same reply. They said, "Yes, that is the reward for kill-
ing him."

17:28 28 But when David's oldest brother, Eliab, heard David talking to the men, he was angry.
Gen 37:4, 8 "What are you doing around here anyway?" he demanded. "What about those few sheep
you're supposed to be taking care of? I know about your pride and deceit. You just want to
see the battle!"

29 "What have I done now?" David replied. "I was only asking a question!" 30 He walked
over to some others and asked them the same thing and received the same answer.
31 Then David's question was reported to King Saul, and the king sent for him.

DAVID KILLS GOLIATH

17:32 32 "Don't worry about this Philistine," David told Saul. "I'll go fight him!"
Deut 20:1 33 "Don't be ridiculous!" Saul replied. "There's no way you can fight this Philistine and
possibly win! You're only a boy, and he's been a man of war since his youth."

34 But David persisted. "I have been taking care of my father's sheep and goats," he said.
17:35 "When a lion or a bear comes to steal a lamb from the flock, 35 I go after it with a club and
Amos 3:12 rescue the lamb from its mouth. If the animal turns on me, I catch it by the jaw and club it
to death. 36 I have done this to both lions and bears, and I'll do it to this pagan Philistine,
17:37 too, for he has defied the armies of the living God! 37 The LORD who rescued me from the
1 Sam 20:13
2 Tim 4:17 claws of the lion and the bear will rescue me from this Philistine!"

17:17 Hebrew *ephah* [20 quarts or 22 liters]. 17:18 Hebrew *and take their pledge.*

17:17 In those times, as often through history, the families of fighting men, not their king or government, provided for their needs. David regularly ran supplies to his brothers.

17:28 Eliab's words revealed anger and resentment toward David. His accusations of pride and dishonesty offer insight into David's family as one that included conflicts, as most families do. While Eliab's issues may have to do with the fact that Samuel passed him over (at God's direction) for the eventual throne of Israel (1 Samuel 16:6-7), we can't know that for sure. During David's reign, Eliab, sometimes referred to as Elihu, was given leadership over the tribe of Judah (1 Chronicles 27:18).

▸ BIBLE

17:37 Only God can help. Have you ever experienced a crisis where only the power of the Almighty God could rescue you? In order to demonstrate that David bore God's kingly anointing, David defied the authority of his father and his brothers and joined the battle against the Philistine champion. Even Saul stood aside and David killed Goliath with an ease that only a sovereign God could accomplish. God specializes in using the weak and unexpected to accomplish His work. This forces the watching world to admit that God has displayed His power. Let God reveal your place in His kingdom through your submission to Him (Ephesians 4:30). (***See Bible*> *Unity*> *Christ*> *Christ is the "LORD of Heaven's Armies,"* TopicGuide page A10.)

Saul finally consented. "All right, go ahead," he said. "And may the LORD be with you!"
38Then Saul gave David his own armor—a bronze helmet and a coat of mail. 39David put
it on, strapped the sword over it, and took a step or two to see what it was like, for he had
never worn such things before.
"I can't go in these," he protested to Saul. "I'm not used to them." So David took them off
again. 40He picked up five smooth stones from a stream and put them into his shepherd's
bag. Then, armed only with his shepherd's staff and sling, he started across the valley to
fight the Philistine.
41Goliath walked out toward David with his shield bearer ahead of him, 42sneering in
contempt at this ruddy-faced boy. 43"Am I a dog," he roared at David, "that you come at
me with a stick?" And he cursed David by the names of his gods. 44"Come over here, and
I'll give your flesh to the birds and wild animals!" Goliath yelled.
45David replied to the Philistine, "You come to me with sword, spear, and javelin, but I
come to you in the name of the LORD of Heaven's Armies—the God of the armies of Israel,
whom you have defied. 46Today the LORD will conquer you, and I will kill you and cut off
your head. And then I will give the dead bodies of your men to the birds and wild animals,
and the whole world will know that there is a God in Israel! 47And everyone assembled
here will know that the LORD rescues His people, but not with sword and spear. This is the
LORD's battle, and He will give you to us!"
48As Goliath moved closer to attack, David quickly ran out to meet him. 49Reaching into
his shepherd's bag and taking out a stone, he hurled it with his sling and hit the Philistine
in the forehead. The stone sank in, and Goliath stumbled and fell face down on the
ground.
50So David triumphed over the Philistine with only a sling and a stone, for he had no
sword. 51Then David ran over and pulled Goliath's sword from its sheath. David used it to
kill him and cut off his head.

ISRAEL ROUTS THE PHILISTINES

When the Philistines saw that their champion was dead, they turned and ran. 52Then the
men of Israel and Judah gave a great shout of triumph and rushed after the Philistines,
chasing them as far as Gath* and the gates of Ekron. The bodies of the dead and
wounded Philistines were strewn all along the road from Shaaraim, as far as Gath and Ek-
ron. 53Then the Israelite army returned and plundered the deserted Philistine camp.
54(David took the Philistine's head to Jerusalem, but he stored the man's armor in his own
tent.)

17:42 1 Sam 16:12
17:43 1 Sam 24:14; 2 Sam 3:8; 9:8; 1 Kgs 20:10
17:45 2 Chr 32:8; Ps 124:8; Heb 11:32-34
17:46 Exod 7:5; Josh 4:24; 1 Kgs 18:36; 2 Kgs 19:19; Isa 37:20
17:47 1 Sam 14:6; 2 Chr 14:11; 20:15; Ps 44:6; Hos 1:7
17:50 1 Sam 25:29
17:52 Josh 15:11, 36

17:52 As in some Greek manuscripts; Hebrew reads *a valley*.

17:38-39 Saul's offer to allow David to wear his armor carried symbolism. A king's armor and weapons, particularly his sword, represented his position. David declined that honor. Later, when he met Jonathan, heir to the throne, Jonathan offered David his regalia (tunic, sword, bow, belt) as a commitment to their friendship (1 Samuel 18:3-4). That time, David accepted. This too was symbolic. David did not dethrone Saul as much as he did Saul's heir, Jonathan.

17:40 Slings originated among ancient shepherds as a weapon for protecting their herds against attacks from wild animals. David's sling gave him a decided distance advantage over Goliath's medium range weapons—a sword, a spear, and a javelin. Ancient slings were generally made from two leather straps with a pocket of leather tied in the middle. The thrower placed a tennis ball-sized stone in the leather pocket and, holding the ends, swung the sling around in circles. When ready to throw, he released one end of the straps, so that the stone was hurled toward the target at around 60 miles per hour. A well-trained slinger could hurl a stone over 1,000 feet.

17:47-49 David's powerful and pious speech not only defends the honor of Israel and the Almighty but also gives a rebuke to Saul. David declared that "the LORD rescues His people, but not with sword and spear," yet Saul attempted to cover him with armor and strap a sword to his side. This is one of the numerous unfavorable characterizations built into the Saul/David narrative (1 Samuel 17:55; 18:9, 25; 19:1; 22;16-17; and continuing until Saul's death in 1 Samuel 31.

17:52 Gath and Ekron were Philistine cities near the Mediterranean coast. Since the battle between David and Goliath took place to the east in the Elah Valley, the Israelites chased the Philistines down the valley, out of the foothills, and cross-country to the closest Philistine refuges; casualties of war were scattered over the ten to fifteen miles that the pursuit covered.

55 As Saul watched David go out to fight the Philistine, he asked Abner, the commander
of his army, "Abner, whose son is this young man?"
"I really don't know," Abner declared.
56 "Well, find out who he is!" the king told him.
57 As soon as David returned from killing Goliath, Abner brought him to Saul with the
Philistine's head still in his hand. 58 "Tell me about your father, young man," Saul said.
And David replied, "His name is Jesse, and we live in Bethlehem."

SAUL BECOMES JEALOUS OF DAVID

18:1 **18** After David had finished talking with Saul, he met Jonathan, the king's son.
Gen 44:30 There was an immediate bond between them, for Jonathan loved David. 2 From
2 Sam 1:26; 9:1 that day on Saul kept David with him and wouldn't let him return home. 3 And Jonathan
18:4 made a solemn pact with David, because he loved him as he loved himself. 4 Jonathan
Gen 41:42 sealed the pact by taking off his robe and giving it to David, together with his tunic,
Esth 6:8 sword, bow, and belt.
5 Whatever Saul asked David to do, David did it successfully. So Saul made him a com-
mander over the men of war, an appointment that was welcomed by the people and
18:6 Saul's officers alike.
Exod 15:20 Judg 11:34 6 When the victorious Israelite army was returning home after David had killed the Phi-
Pss 68:25; 149:3 listine, women from all the towns of Israel came out to meet King Saul. They sang and
18:7 1 Sam 21:11; 29:5 danced for joy with tambourines and cymbals.* 7 This was their song:

"Saul has killed his thousands,
and David his ten thousands!"

18:8 8 This made Saul very angry. "What's this?" he said. "They credit David with ten thou-
1 Sam 15:28-29 sands and me with only thousands. Next they'll be making him their king!" 9 So from that
time on Saul kept a jealous eye on David.
18:10 10 The very next day a tormenting spirit* from God overwhelmed Saul, and he began to
1 Sam 16:14 rave in his house like a madman. David was playing the harp, as he did each day. But Saul
18:11 had a spear in his hand, 11 and he suddenly hurled it at David, intending to pin him to the
1 Sam 19:10 wall. But David escaped him twice.
12 Saul was then afraid of David, for the LORD was with David and had turned away from
18:13 2 Sam 5:2 Saul. 13 Finally, Saul sent him away and appointed him commander over 1,000 men, and
David faithfully led his troops into battle.
18:14 Gen 39:3-4 14 David continued to succeed in everything he did, for the LORD was with him. 15 When
Saul recognized this, he became even more afraid of him. 16 But all Israel and Judah loved
David because he was so successful at leading his troops into battle.

18:6 The type of instrument represented by the word *cymbals* is uncertain. 18:10 Or *an evil spirit.*

▸ SALVATION

17:55 Details, details, details. Have you ever known someone (perhaps someone you look at in the mirror!) who conveniently forgets details when it would benefit him? Saul might have been engaging in this same sort of dishonesty when he attempted to shift the blame for his decision to choose David, rather than himself or his general (Abner), to lead the fight against the Philistines. It is as if Saul is saying, "How was I to know David was a great warrior? He just showed up, ran out on the field, and I've never even seen him before!" But we know that Saul did know who David was from 1 Samuel 16:18-22—David was Saul's official armor bearer. Never hide behind the excuse "I forgot!" Instead, acknowledge your decisions and be willing to live with the consequences. (***See Salvation*****>** *Receiving>* *How>* *Submit to God's grace/special favor,* TopicGuide page A22.)

18:1-4 Jonathan and David had one of the most famous friendships in the Bible. Jonathan's gifts to David were pledges to their vow of friendship. These gifts served a prophetic purpose as well. Jonathan was heir apparent to the throne of his father, Saul, yet he offered up his clothes and sword to David, the one who would actually ascend to the throne. Though Samuel had already privately anointed David, we don't know whether he shared that with Jonathan. Even though Jonathan's father quickly turned against David because of his growing fame and power in Israel, Jonathan remained an ally and protector of the future king.

18:5-10 Over the next few chapters, there are ten mentions of Saul's anger, suspicion, and the like, countered by almost as many mentions of David's godly character and response. The comparison is striking.

DAVID MARRIES SAUL'S DAUGHTER

17 One day Saul said to David, "I am ready to give you my older daughter, Merab, as your 18:17
wife. But first you must prove yourself to be a real warrior by fighting the LORD's battles." 1 Sam 17:25; 25:28
For Saul thought, "I'll send him out against the Philistines and let them kill him rather than
doing it myself."
18 "Who am I, and what is my family in Israel that I should be the king's son-in-law?" 18:18
David exclaimed. "My father's family is nothing!" 19 So* when the time came for Saul to 1 Sam 9:21 2 Sam 7:18
give his daughter Merab in marriage to David, he gave her instead to Adriel, a man from 18:19
Meholah. Judg 7:22
20 In the meantime, Saul's daughter Michal had fallen in love with David, and Saul was 2 Sam 21:8
delighted when he heard about it. 21 "Here's another chance to see him killed by the Philis- 18:20
tines!" Saul said to himself. But to David he said, "Today you have a second chance to be- 1 Sam 18:28
come my son-in-law!"
22 Then Saul told his men to say to David, "The king really likes you, and so do we. Why
don't you accept the king's offer and become his son-in-law?"
23 When Saul's men said these things to David, he replied, "How can a poor man from a 18:23
humble family afford the bride price for the daughter of a king?" Gen 29:20; 34:12
24 When Saul's men reported this back to the king, 25 he told them, "Tell David that all I
want for the bride price is 100 Philistine foreskins! Vengeance on my enemies is all I really
want." But what Saul had in mind was that David would be killed in the fight.
26 David was delighted to accept the offer. Before the time limit expired, 27 he and his 18:27
men went out and killed 200 Philistines. Then David fulfilled the king's requirement by 2 Sam 3:14
presenting all their foreskins to him. So Saul gave his daughter Michal to David to be his
wife.
28 When Saul realized that the LORD was with David and how much his daughter Michal
loved him, 29 Saul became even more afraid of him, and he remained David's enemy for
the rest of his life.
30 Every time the commanders of the Philistines attacked, David was more successful
against them than all the rest of Saul's officers. So David's name became very famous.

18:19 Or *But.*

18:6-7 The women's chanting was not an unusual event. Ancient Israelites celebrated many victories with songs, chants, and prayers. After God miraculously parted the sea for the people to escape from Egypt, Moses led them in a song (Exodus 15). Deborah, an Israelite judge, celebrated Israel's victory over Sisera with a song (Judges 5). King David himself sang after defeating the Philistines (2 Samuel 22).

▸ ADOPTION

18:9 Mental health. From this point on, Saul begins to act like a madman. But he made choices while he was in complete control of his faculties that would influence, perhaps even cause, his disturbed behavior. One flawed decision was to hate the future king of Israel, and this spun his heart and mind into an inescapable vortex of madness. Whether you suffer from a mental illness or are well, do your best to sustain your mental health through a life characterized by loving good and fleeing evil—following the direction of the Spirit (Galatians 5:16-18). This life of repentance is part of a healthy spiritual life (James 5:14-16). (***See Adoption****> With Christ> Supernatural> Freedom from envy and coveting,* TopicGuide page A37.)

18:14 David's story is one of several in the Old Testament in which a person rises to a position of power despite a lack of charisma, gifts, and worldly ability. In David's case, he was a man of humble origins hunted by the king. Joseph (Genesis 37; 39–41) and Daniel (Daniel 1–2) are other examples of men whose greatest asset was their faith in God, not any ability the world recognized.

18:25-27 These verses revealed the violence of this era. Bringing back body parts from battle was not an uncommon custom among many ancient nations. Often the heads of the defeated leaders were showcased after a battle. Just after the Israelites settled the land, a foreign king named Adoni-bezek was captured by the men of Judah. They cut off his thumbs and big toes . . . just as he had done to 70 other kings (Judges 1:6-7). In David's case, the grisly request held some symbolism. One of the distinctive characteristics of the Israelites was the custom of circumcision (Genesis 17:9-14). In essence, because of David's actions, the enemy had not only been conquered, but also brought into subjection: They were made like the Israelites.

▸ GOD

18:29 Enemy for life. Rage and hatred are hard to analyze logically—so difficult that we call them "madness." But Saul was not insane when he determined to kill the future king of Israel. He was not crazy before David's popularity drove him to violent jealousy. Out of the depths of our spirit come all sorts of evil deeds, and rarely can they be excused by pleading insanity. God looks at the heart and judges perfectly and at a depth that someday will surprise us. Rather than excusing your anger and violence, accept responsibility. Look carefully at the things that reveal rage and hatred in your heart and ask God to enable you to respond righteously to such strong feelings. (***See God****> God's Attributes> Patient> God is slow to anger,* TopicGuide page A17.)

SAUL TRIES TO KILL DAVID

19:1 1 Sam 18:1-3
19 Saul now urged his servants and his son Jonathan to assassinate David. But Jona-
than, because of his strong affection for David, 2told him what his father was plan-
ning. "Tomorrow morning," he warned him, "you must find a hiding place out in the fields.
19:3 1 Sam 20:9, 12
3I'll ask my father to go out there with me, and I'll talk to him about you. Then I'll tell you
everything I can find out."
4The next morning Jonathan spoke with his father about David, saying many good
things about him. "The king must not sin against his servant David," Jonathan said. "He's
19:5 Deut 19:10-13; 1 Sam 11:13; 17:49-50; Ps 94:21
never done anything to harm you. He has always helped you in any way he could.
5Have you forgotten about the time he risked his life to kill the Philistine giant and
how the LORD brought a great victory to all Israel as a result? You were certainly happy
about it then. Why should you murder an innocent man like David? There is no reason
for it at all!"
6So Saul listened to Jonathan and vowed, "As surely as the LORD lives, David will not be
19:7 1 Sam 16:21
killed."
7Afterward Jonathan called David and told him what had happened. Then he brought
David to Saul, and David served in the court as before.
8War broke out again after that, and David led his troops against the Philistines. He at-
19:9 1 Sam 16:14; 18:10-12
tacked them with such fury that they all ran away.
9But one day when Saul was sitting at home, with spear in hand, the tormenting spirit*
from the LORD suddenly came upon him again. As David played his harp, 10Saul hurled his
spear at David. But David dodged out of the way, and leaving the spear stuck in the wall,
he fled and escaped into the night.

MICHAL SAVES DAVID'S LIFE

19:11 Judg 16:2; Ps 59:TITLE, 3-4, 6
11Then Saul sent troops to watch David's house. They were told to kill David when he
came out the next morning. But Michal, David's wife, warned him, "If you don't escape to-
night, you will be dead by morning." 12So she helped him climb out through a window,
19:12 Josh 2:15; Acts 9:25
and he fled and escaped. 13Then she took an idol* and put it in his bed, covered it with
blankets, and put a cushion of goat's hair at its head.
19:13 Judg 18:14, 17
14When the troops came to arrest David, she told them he was sick and couldn't get out
of bed.
15But Saul sent the troops back to get David. He ordered, "Bring him to me in his bed so I
can kill him!" 16But when they came to carry David out, they discovered that it was only an
idol in the bed with a cushion of goat's hair at its head.
17"Why have you betrayed me like this and let my enemy escape?" Saul demanded of
Michal.
"I had to," Michal replied. "He threatened to kill me if I didn't help him."

19:9 Or *evil spirit.* **19:13** Hebrew *teraphim;* also in 19:16.

▸ BIBLE

19:2 Ethical wisdom. Just as truth telling demands a certain timing and wisdom to be most effective, so must obedience to superiors. Jonathan not only did not carry out his father's orders to kill David, but he also persuaded his father to abandon the idea himself. Jonathan's plan of action saved his friend David from death and his father Saul from sin (19:4); essentially he honored his father much more than if he had carried out his father's command. If someone in authority over you tells you to do something immoral or highly unwise, seek God's wisdom on the best way to honor your supervisor. (***See Bible> Power> Wisdom> Instruction through God's Word,*** TopicGuide page A11.)

19:7 This was one of the many times that Saul seemed to relent on his plan to destroy David (1 Samuel 24:16; 26:21). During the remainder of Saul's life, he fluctuated between a hateful, jealous rage toward David and a repentant understanding that David had no plans to harm him. Each time Saul relented, though, he eventually fell back into the hunt. He would get word of David's whereabouts (1 Samuel 26:1), or, as happened this time, he would simply experience one of the "spells" that filled him with anger and anxiety (19:9).

18So David escaped and went to Ramah to see Samuel, and he told him all that Saul had done to him. Then Samuel took David with him to live at Naioth. 19When the report reached Saul that David was at Naioth in Ramah, 20he sent troops to capture him. But when they arrived and saw Samuel leading a group of prophets who were prophesying, the Spirit of God came upon Saul's men, and they also began to prophesy. 21When Saul heard what had happened, he sent other troops, but they, too, prophesied! The same thing happened a third time. 22Finally, Saul himself went to Ramah and arrived at the great well in Secu. "Where are Samuel and David?" he demanded.

"They are at Naioth in Ramah," someone told him.

23But on the way to Naioth in Ramah the Spirit of God came even upon Saul, and he, too, began to prophesy all the way to Naioth! 24He tore off his clothes and lay naked on the ground all day and all night, prophesying in the presence of Samuel. The people who were watching exclaimed, "What? Is even Saul a prophet?"

JONATHAN HELPS DAVID

20 David now fled from Naioth in Ramah and found Jonathan. "What have I done?" he exclaimed. "What is my crime? How have I offended your father that he is so determined to kill me?"

2"That's not true!" Jonathan protested. "You're not going to die. He always tells me everything he's going to do, even the little things. I know my father wouldn't hide something like this from me. It just isn't so!"

3Then David took an oath before Jonathan and said, "Your father knows perfectly well about our friendship, so he has said to himself, 'I won't tell Jonathan—why should I hurt him?' But I swear to you that I am only a step away from death! I swear it by the LORD and by your own soul!"

4"Tell me what I can do to help you," Jonathan exclaimed.

5David replied, "Tomorrow we celebrate the new moon festival. I've always eaten with the king on this occasion, but tomorrow I'll hide in the field and stay there until the evening of the third day. 6If your father asks where I am, tell him I asked permission to go home to Bethlehem for an annual family sacrifice. 7If he says, 'Fine!' you will know all is well. But if he is angry and loses his temper, you will know he is determined to kill me. 8Show me this loyalty as my sworn friend—for we made a solemn pact before the LORD—or kill me yourself if I have sinned against your father. But please don't betray me to him!"

9"Never!" Jonathan exclaimed. "You know that if I had the slightest notion my father was planning to kill you, I would tell you at once."

10Then David asked, "How will I know whether or not your father is angry?"

11"Come out to the field with me," Jonathan replied. And they went out there together. 12Then Jonathan told David, "I promise by the LORD, the God of Israel, that by this time to-

19:18 1 Sam 7:17; 19:22-23
19:20 Num 11:24-25; 1 Sam 10:5-6, 10; Joel 2:28
19:23 1 Sam 10:13
19:24 1 Sam 10:10-12; 2 Sam 6:20; Mic 1:8
20:1 1 Sam 24:9
20:3 Deut 6:13; 2 Kgs 2:6-7
20:5 Num 10:10; 28:11-17; 1 Sam 19:2
20:6 1 Sam 16:2; 17:58
20:7 1 Sam 25:17
20:8 1 Sam 18:1-3; 2 Sam 1:26; 14:23

19:18-22 This is the only account in Scripture that mentions Naioth. Many have speculated about this place. From the passage here, we know it was a place that housed a band or even school of prophets, probably under the supervision of Samuel. It was within Ramah, and may have been similar to a sanctuary or cloister. In the prophet Elisha's day, other groups of prophets were from Bethel and Jericho (2 Kings 2). Obviously, from Saul's response (1 Samuel 19:23-24), Naioth was a place of great power where the spirit of God was free to move.

▸WORSHIP
19:23 Spiritual experiences. This odd scene testifies that even bad people can have authentic spiritual experiences. The ecstatic state that Saul entered into is common to many religions, not just Old Testament Judaism. This was not an emotional breakdown—it was from God (19:23). But the experience does not validate Saul's wicked life. You cannot base your standing with God on religious experiences, but only on the sure, unchanging foundation of God's Word. (***See Worship***> *OT*> *Reverence*> *Awe of God means obeying His commandments,* TopicGuide page A28.)

20:5 The New Moon Festival was celebrated monthly according to the lunar calendar. The feast involved special offerings, including a burnt offering with its accompanying grain and drink offering. It also involved a male goat offered as a sin offering. This was a time when all the people gathered together. Because of that, it was possibly a time when tribal business was attended to or prophets gave their most recent insights. It was a great reminder of God's faithfulness. The Old Testament prophet Amos railed against those who had no time to celebrate festivals such as the Sabbath and the New Moon festivals (Amos 8:5).

morrow, or the next day at the latest, I will talk to my father and let you know at once how
20:13 Ruth 1:17 he feels about you. If he speaks favorably about you, I will let you know. [13]But if he is an-
1 Sam 3:17; 14:44; 18:11-12 gry and wants you killed, may the LORD strike me and even kill me if I don't warn you so
you can escape and live. May the LORD be with you as He used to be with my father. [14]And
1 Chr 28:20 may you treat me with the faithful love of the LORD as long as I live. But if I die, [15]treat my
20:15 2 Sam 9:1 family with this faithful love, even when the LORD destroys all your enemies from the face
of the earth."

[16]So Jonathan made a solemn pact with David,* saying, "May the LORD destroy all your
enemies!" [17]And Jonathan made David reaffirm his vow of friendship again, for Jonathan
loved David as he loved himself.

[18]Then Jonathan said, "Tomorrow we celebrate the new moon festival. You will be
missed when your place at the table is empty. [19]The day after tomorrow, toward evening,
go to the place where you hid before, and wait there by the stone pile.* [20]I will come out
and shoot three arrows to the side of the stone pile as though I were shooting at a target.
[21]Then I will send a boy to bring the arrows back. If you hear me tell him, 'They're on this
side,' then you will know, as surely as the LORD lives, that all is well, and there is no trouble.
[22]But if I tell him, 'Go farther—the arrows are still ahead of you,' then it will mean that you
20:23 Gen 31:49-50, 53 must leave immediately, for the LORD is sending you away. [23]And may the LORD make us
keep our promises to each other, for He has witnessed them."

[24]So David hid himself in the field, and when the new moon festival began, the king sat
down to eat. [25]He sat at his usual place against the wall, with Jonathan sitting opposite
20:26 Lev 7:20-21 him* and Abner beside him. But David's place was empty. [26]Saul didn't say anything about
1 Sam 16:5 it that day, for he said to himself, "Something must have made David ceremonially un-
clean." [27]But when David's place was empty again the next day, Saul asked Jonathan,
"Why hasn't the son of Jesse been here for the meal either yesterday or today?"

20:28 1 Sam 20:6 [28]Jonathan replied, "David earnestly asked me if he could go to Bethlehem. [29]He said,
'Please let me go, for we are having a family sacrifice. My brother demanded that I be there.
So please let me get away to see my brothers.' That's why he isn't here at the king's table."

[30]Saul boiled with rage at Jonathan. "You stupid son of a whore!"* he swore at him. "Do
you think I don't know that you want him to be king in your place, shaming yourself and

20:16 Hebrew *with the house of David.* 20:19 Hebrew *the stone Ezel.* The meaning of the Hebrew is uncertain. 20:25 As in Greek version; Hebrew reads *with Jonathan standing.* 20:30 Hebrew *You son of a perverse and rebellious woman.*

▸ HOLINESS

20:13 Honor God first. Saul's own son recognized that God had removed His favor from Saul and placed it upon David. Jonathan recognized that he owed ultimate allegiance to God, and second to his friend and God's choice for the next king, David. Jonathan clearly chose his love for David over his love for his father as he planned to save David and when he prayed that God would destroy all David's enemies (20:15). There may be times in your life when you may be forced to ignore the wishes of a sinful parent in order for God's best to occur. Pray that this will not happen, but if it does, obey God first. His glory is more important than your relationship with your parents (Matthew 10:34-35). (***See Holiness****> Changed by God> The Father Foreordains> Follows allegiance to God,* TopicGuide page A41.)

20:13 Jonathan's comments revealed that he fully expected David to succeed his father, Saul, as king. Jonathan himself should have been heir to the throne since he was the king's son, yet from the beginning of his friendship with David, he seemed to lay down that expectation. Jonathan also trusted David. Often when a new dynasty took over the throne they killed all the heirs of the former dynasty so there would be less opportunity for a revolt. Jonathan's request was that David not only let his family survive, but that he care for them.

20:14-15 Jonathan's request was neither made lightly nor taken lightly by David. During David's reign he found Jonathan's sole survivor. Mephibosheth, Jonathan's son, had been hurt in childhood as he and his nurse escaped after a Philistine victory over Israel. Mephibosheth's injuries left him crippled for life and rejected. Yet David invited Mephibosheth to eat at the royal table and to receive his grandfather Saul's family land (2 Samuel 4:4; 9).

20:26 There could have been several reasons why a man would be ceremonially unclean. He may have been around something that was dead or a woman in childbirth. Some skin and health conditions also required a period of ceremonial uncleanness. Whatever the reason for David's possible uncleanness, it probably would have required him to stay in solitude for an amount of time defined by the laws of Moses. He then would have appeared before a priest and taken up his normal duties (see the many laws for ceremonial cleanliness found in Leviticus 13–15).

20:30-31 Saul's tirade revealed his awareness that David was a threat to his throne. This awareness first began after David returned from the famous battle with Goliath. Saul must have realized at that point that the people favored David over him. Although Saul realized God had blessed his successor, he failed to reconcile himself to that reality. Nor did he permanently reconcile with David, a soldier who had served him well.

your mother? 31As long as that son of Jesse is alive, you'll never be king. Now go and get
him so I can kill him!"
32"But why should he be put to death?" Jonathan asked his father. "What has he done?" **20:32** Matt 27:23
33Then Saul hurled his spear at Jonathan, intending to kill him. So at last Jonathan realized
that his father was really determined to kill David. **20:33** 1 Sam 18:11; 19:10-11
34Jonathan left the table in fierce anger and refused to eat on that second day of the fes-
tival, for he was crushed by his father's shameful behavior toward David.
35The next morning, as agreed, Jonathan went out into the field and took a young boy
with him to gather his arrows. 36"Start running," he told the boy, "so you can find the ar- **20:36** 1 Sam 20:20-21
rows as I shoot them." So the boy ran, and Jonathan shot an arrow beyond him. 37When
the boy had almost reached the arrow, Jonathan shouted, "The arrow is still ahead of you.
38Hurry, hurry, don't wait." So the boy quickly gathered up the arrows and ran back to his
master. 39He, of course, suspected nothing; only Jonathan and David understood the sig-
nal. 40Then Jonathan gave his bow and arrows to the boy and told him to take them back
to town.
41As soon as the boy was gone, David came out from where he had been hiding near
the stone pile.* Then David bowed three times to Jonathan with his face to the ground.
Both of them were in tears as they embraced each other and said good-bye, especially
David.
42At last Jonathan said to David, "Go in peace, for we have sworn loyalty to each other in **20:42** 1 Sam 20:14-15
the LORD's name. The LORD is the witness of a bond between us and our children forever."
Then David left, and Jonathan returned to the town.*

DAVID RUNS FROM SAUL

21 1*David went to the town of Nob to see Ahimelech the priest. Ahimelech trembled **21:1** 1 Sam 16:4; 22:19 Neh 11:32
when he saw him. "Why are you alone?" he asked. "Why is no one with you?"
2"The king has sent me on a private matter," David said. "He told me not to tell anyone
why I am here. I have told my men where to meet me later. 3Now, what is there to eat?
Give me five loaves of bread or anything else you have."

20:41 As in Greek version; Hebrew reads *near the south edge.* 20:42 This sentence is numbered 21:1 in Hebrew text.
21:1 Verses 21:1-15 are numbered 21:2-16 in Hebrew text.

▸ WORSHIP
20:41 Deep relationships. Some men get nervous when they read passages like this. But God displays for us in His Word intimate intra-gender relationships, not only between men like David and Jonathan, but more importantly between men and Christ. What can men do—pretend the center of the Christian faith isn't a deep love of a man? Should men not look forward to the day when they will hug Christ and rejoice that He returns our tiny affections with a love that wipes away every tear? If you are a man, bravely explore deeper relationships with godly men. (***See Worship****> NT> Fellowship> Preserving> Love one another,* TopicGuide page A31.)

20:42 The devotion between Jonathan and David affected their legacies for generations to come. Jonathan did not have the opportunity to make good on his promise to care for David's children, because he died with his father in a battle with the Philistines (1 Samuel 31:1-2). David did care for Jonathan's son, Mephibosheth, restoring to him his family's land and bestowing him with the honor to eat at the royal table (2 Samuel 9:1-10).

21:1 Nob was a town northeast of Jerusalem. It was located on a slope opposite the Mount of Olives. There were 86 priests living in Nob. It had become the central sanctuary after the Ark of the Covenant was taken from Shiloh. Nob was a place of refuge for David, but soon after it became a site of destruction. When Saul discovered how the priests from Nob had assisted David, he poured out his revenge on them, killing 86 priests and their families and animals (1 Samuel 22:11-23).

21:1 Ahimelech's decision to allow David's men to eat the holy bread was indirectly referred to by Jesus in the New Testament. Jesus allowed his disciples to eat some grain as they walked through a grain field on a Sabbath. The Pharisees criticized them, calling their actions of "harvesting grain" an illegal activity on the Sabbath. Jesus offered a rebuttal by referring to David's men eating the sacred bread. Jesus used this occasion to point out that there are some things greater than religious law. He, as the Christ, was one of them (Matthew 12:1-8).

▸ BIBLE
21:2 At war with God. Saul was attempting to kill the rightful king of Israel. His decision to be at war with God's purposes made David's subterfuge excusable based on his responsibility to preserve his men and himself. Anything else would have been traitorous and foolish, and God blessed David by arranging for the supplies that he needed and protecting him from King Achish. While the numerous lies that David tells throughout his escape from Saul may disturb us, God honored David's carefully crafted words. (***See Bible****> Power> Worldview> Offers God's perspective on issues,* TopicGuide page A12.)

21:4 4"We don't have any regular bread," the priest replied. "But there is the holy bread,
Exod 19:14-15 which you can have if your young men have not slept with any women recently."
Lev 24:5-9 Matt 12:4 5"Don't worry," David replied. "I never allow my men to be with women when they are on
a campaign. And since they stay clean even on ordinary trips, how much more on this one!"
21:6 6Since there was no other food available, the priest gave him the holy bread—the Bread
Matt 12:3-4 Mark 2:25-28 of the Presence that was placed before the LORD in the Tabernacle. It had just been re-
Luke 6:3-4 placed that day with fresh bread.
21:7 7Now Doeg the Edomite, Saul's chief herdsman, was there that day, having been de-
1 Sam 22:9, 22 tained before the LORD.*
Ps 52:1 8David asked Ahimelech, "Do you have a spear or sword? The king's business was so ur-
gent that I didn't even have time to grab a weapon!"
21:9 9"I only have the sword of Goliath the Philistine, whom you killed in the valley of Elah,"
1 Sam 17:2, 50-51 the priest replied. "It is wrapped in a cloth behind the ephod. Take that if you want it, for
there is nothing else here."
"There is nothing like it!" David replied. "Give it to me!"
21:10 10So David escaped from Saul and went to King Achish of Gath. 11But the officers of
1 Sam 27:2 Achish were unhappy about his being there. "Isn't this David, the king of the land?" they
21:11 1 Sam 18:7; 29:5 asked. "Isn't he the one the people honor with dances, singing,

'Saul has killed his thousands,
and David his ten thousands'?"

21:13 12David heard these comments and was very afraid of what King Achish of Gath might do
Ps 34:TITLE to him. 13So he pretended to be insane, scratching on doors and drooling down his beard.
14Finally, King Achish said to his men, "Must you bring me a madman? 15We already
have enough of them around here! Why should I let someone like this be my guest?"

DAVID AT THE CAVE OF ADULLAM

22:1-2 **22** So David left Gath and escaped to the cave of Adullam. Soon his brothers and all
2 Sam 23:13 his other relatives joined him there. 2Then others began coming—men who were
in trouble or in debt or who were just discontented—until David was the captain of about
400 men.

21:7 The meaning of the Hebrew is uncertain.

21:4-6 The "holy bread" or Bread of the Presence is sometimes translated *showbread*. Twelve large loaves were arranged in rows on a table outside of the innermost sanctuary of the Tabernacle (and later the Temple). Over two bushels of ground wheat were required to make this bread, which were considered a grain offering to God. The loaves were prepared weekly and replaced on the Sabbath. Typically no one but the priests ate this bread (Leviticus 24:5-9).

21:4-5 The sexual status of David's men was an issue because it was a component of being considered ceremonially clean. When the people prepared for a great event, they prepared themselves by washing their clothes and their bodies. They also abstained from sexual relations (Exodus 19:14-15).

21:9 After David defeated Goliath, he used the giant's own sword to behead him. Goliath's sword had made its way to the Tabernacle. David kept Goliath's armor and stored it in his tent. He carried Goliath's head to Jerusalem (1 Samuel 17:49-54) as a gruesome trophy of war. Imagine David's delight in the midst of running for his life, to reclaim the sword from his first victory on God's behalf.

21:9 The ephod was a part of the priest's clothing. It was similar to a breastplate with gemstones carved with the names of the twelve tribes of Israel (see Exodus 28). Kept within the ephod, and perhaps adding to its sanctity, were the Urim and Thummim, ancient tools for discerning God's will. While the high priest used the main ephod, there were others. Gideon, a judge of Israel, made an ephod of gold for his hometown, but the people unfortunately began to worship the ephod rather than the God of their faith (Judges 8:27).

21:10-14 Though David escaped in fear (22:1), later he returned to live under the rule of King Achish (1 Samuel 27:1-6). Achish even gave David the town of Ziklag to use as a headquarters.

21:15 Many of David's psalms were written about the events in the books of Samuel. David wrote psalm 34 about this very event with Achish, though the king is referred to in the psalm by the alternate name of Abimelech. Psalm 34 praises God for His protection and rescue.

22:1 Adullam was in the lowlands of the tribal territory of Judah between the city of Lacish on the plain and Hebron in the hill country. It was not far from where David fought Goliath. David's refuge in the cave at Adullam was the first of many. While he ran from Saul, he and his men often found refuge in caves in the area. The superscriptions at Psalms 57 and 142, written by David, mention the caves he used for safety.

3Later David went to Mizpeh in Moab, where he asked the king, "Please allow my fa-
ther and mother to live here with you until I know what God is going to do for me." 4So Da-
vid's parents stayed in Moab with the king during the entire time David was living in his
stronghold. **22:5**
5One day the prophet Gad told David, "Leave the stronghold and return to the land of 2 Sam 24:11
Judah." So David went to the forest of Hereth. 1 Chr 21:9; 29:29 2 Chr 29:25-26
6The news of his arrival in Judah soon reached Saul. At the time, the king was sitting **22:6**
beneath the tamarisk tree on the hill at Gibeah, holding his spear and surrounded by his Judg 4:5
officers. 1 Sam 14:2
7"Listen here, you men of Benjamin!" Saul shouted to his officers when he heard the **22:7** 1 Sam 8:12, 14
news. "Has that son of Jesse promised every one of you fields and vineyards? Has he 1 Chr 12:16-18
promised to make you all generals and captains in his army?* 8Is that why you have con- **22:8**
spired against me? For not one of you told me when my own son made a solemn pact with 1 Sam 23:21
the son of Jesse. You're not even sorry for me. Think of it! My own son—encouraging him
to kill me, as he is trying to do this very day!"
9Then Doeg the Edomite, who was standing there with Saul's men, spoke up. "When I **22:9**
was at Nob," he said, "I saw the son of Jesse talking to the priest, Ahimelech son of Ahitub. 1 Sam 21:1, 7
10Ahimelech consulted the LORD for him. Then he gave him food and the sword of Goliath **22:10** 1 Sam 21:6
the Philistine."

THE SLAUGHTER OF THE PRIESTS

11King Saul immediately sent for Ahimelech and all his family, who served as priests at
Nob. 12When they arrived, Saul shouted at him, "Listen to me, you son of Ahitub!"
"What is it, my king?" Ahimelech asked.
13"Why have you and the son of Jesse conspired against me?" Saul demanded. "Why
did you give him food and a sword? Why have you consulted God for him? Why have you
encouraged him to kill me, as he is trying to do this very day?"

22:7 Hebrew *commanders of thousands and commanders of hundreds?*

22:3 David's appeal to a Moabite king revealed an openness between the Moabites and the Israelites that had not been a reality in earlier times. But David would have had another connection to the Moabites. His grandmother, Ruth, was a Moabite. Her story is told in the book of Ruth. David could have had relatives in Moab on his grandmother's side.

22:5 The prophet and seer Gad interacted with David on several occasions. He and the prophet Nathan were evidently influential as David established order within worship in Jerusalem (see 2 Chronicles 29:25). Gad was referred to as "the king's seer." Gad's written record was mentioned as one of the three writings that together tell all the events of David's reign (1 Chronicles 29:29).

22:6 Since Saul was the first king of Israel, his was not a monarchy with palaces and thrones. His capital was his hometown of Gibeah about three and a half miles north of Jerusalem. The informality of his "royal court" is shown here. His spear denoted his position and his officers denoted his authority.

22:7 Saul spoke to the men of Benjamin because that was his own tribe. The tribal territory of Benjamin included Jerusalem, later claimed as David's capital, and Jericho, famous for Joshua's tumbling walls.

22:8 We are given no indication in Scripture that Saul's accusation against Jonathan was true. Jonathan did stand against his father's wish to have David killed (1 Samuel 19:1-6). He even went so far as to give David inside information to keep him from walking into a trap (1 Samuel 20). But nowhere was Jonathan described as plotting against his father. He did seem to accept, though, that David would be Saul's successor rather than anyone from his own family, including himself. In that sense, perhaps Saul had reason to feel that Jonathan had been unfaithful (1 Samuel 20:30).

▸ADOPTION
22:9 Gossip. Have you ever been a Doeg—a tattler? Someone who revels in the power to report the misdeeds of those around him, regardless of who is injured? All of Saul's men had the sense to withhold information about David's whereabouts, but the Edomite was happy to see Saul attempting to kill his best soldiers. Not only that, chaos-loving Doeg killed an entire priestly family with his own hands (22:18-19). Tattlers love the confusion and violence that a bad deed told at the worst time can bring. Close your mouth to inappropriate sharing of misdeeds and close your ears to gossip and slander. (***See Adoption***> *With Christ*> *Supernatural*> *Speak godly words,* TopicGuide page A37.)

22:13 Saul was either misinformed about Ahimelech or simply conjuring guilt for David. David had actually led Ahimelech to believe that he was on a mission *for* Saul. The priest allowed David to take some of the holy bread for his men to eat, in light of the urgency that David implied. In reality, David's urgency was to escape from Saul rather than to fulfill a mission given by Saul. Because of Doeg the Edomite, David's requests cost the priest his life.

22:14 1 Sam 19:4-5; 20:32
22:15 2 Sam 5:19, 23

14 "But sir," Ahimelech replied, "is anyone among all your servants as faithful as David, your son-in-law? Why, he is the captain of your bodyguard and a highly honored member of your household! 15 This was certainly not the first time I had consulted God for him! May the king not accuse me and my family in this matter, for I knew nothing at all of any plot against you."

22:17 1 Sam 14:45; 2 Kgs 10:25

16 "You will surely die, Ahimelech, along with your entire family!" the king shouted. 17 And he ordered his bodyguards, "Kill these priests of the LORD, for they are allies and conspirators with David! They knew he was running away from me, but they didn't tell me!" But Saul's men refused to kill the LORD's priests.

22:18 1 Sam 2:18, 30-33

18 Then the king said to Doeg, "You do it." So Doeg the Edomite turned on them and killed them that day, eighty-five priests in all, still wearing their priestly garments. 19 Then he went to Nob, the town of the priests, and killed the priests' families—men and women, children and babies—and all the cattle, donkeys, sheep, and goats.

22:20 1 Sam 2:30-33; 23:6; 30:7; 1 Kgs 2:26-27
22:22 1 Sam 21:7

20 Only Abiathar, one of the sons of Ahimelech, escaped and fled to David. 21 When he told David that Saul had killed the priests of the LORD, 22 David exclaimed, "I knew it! When I saw Doeg the Edomite there that day, I knew he was sure to tell Saul. Now I have caused the death of all your father's family. 23 Stay here with me, and don't be afraid. I will protect you with my own life, for the same person wants to kill us both."

DAVID PROTECTS THE TOWN OF KEILAH

23:1 Josh 15:44; Neh 3:17
23:2 1 Sam 23:4, 12; 30:8; 2 Sam 5:19, 23

23 One day news came to David that the Philistines were at Keilah stealing grain from the threshing floors. 2 David asked the LORD, "Should I go and attack them?"

"Yes, go and save Keilah," the LORD told him.

3 But David's men said, "We're afraid even here in Judah. We certainly don't want to go to Keilah to fight the whole Philistine army!"

23:4 Josh 8:7; Judg 7:7

4 So David asked the LORD again, and again the LORD replied, "Go down to Keilah, for I will help you conquer the Philistines."

23:6 1 Sam 22:20

5 So David and his men went to Keilah. They slaughtered the Philistines and took all their livestock and rescued the people of Keilah. 6 Now when Abiathar son of Ahimelech fled to David at Keilah, he brought the ephod with him.

7 Saul soon learned that David was at Keilah. "Good!" he exclaimed. "We've got him now! God has handed him over to me, for he has trapped himself in a walled town!" 8 So Saul mobilized his entire army to march to Keilah and besiege David and his men.

23:9 1 Sam 22:20; 30:7

9 But David learned of Saul's plan and told Abiathar the priest to bring the ephod and ask the LORD what he should do. 10 Then David prayed, "O LORD, God of Israel, I have heard that Saul is planning to come and destroy Keilah because I am here. 11 Will the leaders of Keilah betray me to him?* And will Saul actually come as I have heard? O LORD, God of Israel, please tell me."

23:11 Some manuscripts lack the first sentence of 23:11.

22:20 When he escaped the massacre at Nob, Abiathar was smart enough to bring David the ephod, a sacred garment used to discern God's will (1 Samuel 23:6). He stayed with David from this point on through David's reign as king of Israel.

23:1-2 Keilah was eight and a half miles northwest of Hebron, in the territory of Judah on the border between Israel and Philistia. Keilah's location made it an easy target for attack from the Philistines.

▸ PURPOSE

23:9 Discerning God's will. David was a man of action, but prayer preceded his decisions. In this case, he had a unique way of finding out God's will—his priest had the special ephod that was used in divining God's will. But how could a garment do that? Because it contained the Urim and Thummim in the pocket under its breastplate (Exodus 28:30). These were probably a bit like "holy dice" given by God to Israel for inquiring of God's will in a matter. If they had a question, they would use the objects to get an answer of yes or no, or to discern which of two options they should take. God gives modern Christians several ways to discern His will: The advice of past generations of Christians through various sorts of literature (past community), the counsel of our peers (the present community) and our own understanding of Scripture (personal conscience). We join David in the need to know God's will and to bathe our every decision in prayer. (***See Purpose***> *God's Means> Human Choice> Bringing our wills in subjection to God's will,* TopicGuide page A52.)

And the LORD said, "He will come."
12Again David asked, "Will the leaders of Keilah betray me and my men to Saul?"
And the LORD replied, "Yes, they will betray you."

DAVID HIDES IN THE WILDERNESS

13So David and his men—about 600 of them now—left Keilah and began roaming the 23:13
countryside. Word soon reached Saul that David had escaped, so he didn't go to Keilah af- 1 Sam 22:2; 25:13
ter all. 14David now stayed in the strongholds of the wilderness and in the hill country of 2 Sam 15:20
Ziph. Saul hunted him day after day, but God didn't let Saul find him. 23:14 Josh 15:55
15One day near Horesh, David received the news that Saul was on the way to Ziph to 2 Chr 11:8
search for him and kill him. 16Jonathan went to find David and encouraged him to stay
strong in his faith in God. 17"Don't be afraid," Jonathan reassured him. "My father will 23:17
never find you! You are going to be the king of Israel, and I will be next to you, as my fa- 1 Sam 20:31; 24:20
ther, Saul, is well aware." 18So the two of them renewed their solemn pact before the LORD. 23:18
Then Jonathan returned home, while David stayed at Horesh. 1 Sam 18:3 2 Sam 9:1
19But now the men of Ziph went to Saul in Gibeah and betrayed David to him. "We 23:19
know where David is hiding," they said. "He is in the strongholds of Horesh on the hill of 1 Sam 26:1
Hakilah, which is in the southern part of Jeshimon. 20Come down whenever you're ready,
O king, and we will catch him and hand him over to you!"
21"The LORD bless you," Saul said. "At last someone is concerned about me! 22Go and 23:21
check again to be sure of where he is staying and who has seen him there, for I know that 1 Sam 22:8
he is very crafty. 23Discover his hiding places, and come back when you are sure. Then I'll
go with you. And if he is in the area at all, I'll track him down, even if I have to search every
hiding place in Judah!" 24So the men of Ziph returned home ahead of Saul. 23:24
Meanwhile, David and his men had moved into the wilderness of Maon in the Arabah Josh 15:55
Valley south of Jeshimon. 25When David heard that Saul and his men were searching for
him, he went even farther into the wilderness to the great rock, and he remained there in
the wilderness of Maon. But Saul kept after him in the wilderness.
26Saul and David were now on opposite sides of a mountain. Just as Saul and his men 23:26
began to close in on David and his men, 27an urgent message reached Saul that the Philis- Ps 17:9

23:13 David's army had grown by half in a relatively small time frame. When he had escaped from King Achish in Gath and fled to the cave at Adullam, men began to join him there—400 of them. These men were "in trouble or in debt or who were just discontented" (1 Samuel 22:1-2). Such were the beginnings of the army that came to be known as David's mighty men (1 Chronicles 11:10).

23:14 Many of the psalms of David were written during his flight or about his flight from Saul. Psalm 63 was written about a time when David was in the Judean wilderness described here. It was a psalm of devotion and hope in God.

23:14-15 Hebron was about 25 miles southwest of Jerusalem. Ziph and its surrounding wilderness were farther south of Hebron in the Judean mountains. Horesh may have been a specific place within the wilderness of Ziph, or it may have simply referred to the wooded areas that David typically hid within.

23:19 We don't know a lot of specifics about this geography because words like Jeshimon ("wasteland") tend to describe just that: forests and hills and desert places familiar to those who traveled by foot over much of the area. The loosely charted nature of the land at this time was both an advantage to David and a disadvantage to Saul.

23:21 Saul's self-pity had been growing. It was evidenced by his exclamation, "At last someone is concerned about me!" In chapter 22 he berated his fellow tribesman and painted David—and Jonathan for that matter—in the worst light. Saul's paranoia was growing. Rather than submit to God and repent, Saul chose to shadowbox for the rest of his life against a fate that had already been determined.

23:23 Saul's tribal region, Benjamin, was a relatively small area: 28 miles by 12 miles. David's tribal region, Judah, on the other hand, was much larger: 50 miles by 20 miles. Though the lower half of Judah was desert, a large portion of the remainder is challenging mountainous terrain. Searching out every hiding place would have been a huge feat.

23:24 Maon was the southernmost point of David's escape route from Saul. The city was in the hill country of Judah, as was Ziph, but it was about eight miles south of Hebron. The Arabah Valley ran north to south the length of Israel from above the Sea of Galilee, along the Jordan River Valley and ending below the Dead Sea. David's earlier hiding places (the forests of Hereth, for example) were in the foothills toward the Mediterranean Sea. As Saul increased his search (and as his paranoia grew), David retreated to the region east of the central ridge toward the Arabah—treacherous, rocky, deep valleys that were much more difficult to travel through with large numbers.

23:29 tines were raiding Israel again. 28So Saul quit chasing David and returned to fight the Phi-
Josh 15:62 listines. Ever since that time, the place where David was camped has been called the Rock
2 Chr 20:2 of Escape.* 29*David then went to live in the strongholds of En-gedi.

DAVID SPARES SAUL'S LIFE

24 1*After Saul returned from fighting the Philistines, he was told that David had
24:2 gone into the wilderness of En-gedi. 2So Saul chose 3,000 elite troops from all Is-
1 Sam 26:2 rael and went to search for David and his men near the rocks of the wild goats.
24:3 3At the place where the road passes some sheepfolds, Saul went into a cave to relieve
Judg 3:24 himself. But as it happened, David and his men were hiding farther back in that very cave!
24:4 4"Now's your opportunity!" David's men whispered to him. "Today the LORD is telling
1 Sam 26:8, 11 you, 'I will certainly put your enemy into your power, to do with as you wish.'" So David
crept forward and cut off a piece of the hem of Saul's robe.
24:5 5But then David's conscience began bothering him because he had cut Saul's robe. 6"The
2 Sam 24:10 LORD knows I shouldn't have done that to my lord the king," he said to his men. "The LORD
24:6 1 Sam 26:11 forbid that I should do this to my lord the king and attack the LORD's anointed one, for the
LORD Himself has chosen him." 7So David restrained his men and did not let them kill Saul.
24:7 1 Kgs 1:31 After Saul had left the cave and gone on his way, 8David came out and shouted after
him, "My lord the king!" And when Saul looked around, David bowed low before him.
9Then he shouted to Saul, "Why do you listen to the people who say I am trying to harm
24:9 1 Sam 26:19 you? 10This very day you can see with your own eyes it isn't true. For the LORD placed you
at my mercy back there in the cave. Some of my men told me to kill you, but I spared you.
For I said, 'I will never harm the king—he is the LORD's anointed one.' 11Look, my father, at

24:11 1 Sam 23:14, 23; 26:20

23:28 Hebrew *Sela-hammahlekoth.* 23:29 Verse 23:29 is numbered 24:1 in Hebrew text. 24:1 Verses 24:1-22 are numbered 24:2-23 in Hebrew text.

▸ PURPOSE

23:28 Discovering God in Saul's retreat. God often protects us to allow us to complete His purpose for our lives. Saul's tactics were sound—he would split his larger force into two and encircle David's smaller group. But God ordained it so that Israel's enemies would attack at just the right moment so as to save David from death. God has ordained it so that all things happen for the good of those who love Him (Romans 8:28). Even terrible things like war are used by God to accomplish His highest glory and our highest good. (***See Purpose****> God's Means> God's Sovereignty> God has always had a plan,* TopicGuide page A52.)

23:29 En-gedi is an oasis on the western shore of the Dead Sea, about 23 miles directly southeast of Jerusalem. Hidden in the rough terrain, it has a hot water spring falling from the side of a limestone cliff. Because of this spring, vegetation—palms, vines, and balsam trees—that could not grow in the surrounding wilderness still flourishes there today.

▸ GOD

24:4 Tempted to violence. Have you ever wanted to kill someone? Or have you ever imagined how nice it would be if someone you were at odds with would "disappear"? David and his men thought about this regularly, and now that the opportunity presented itself, David backed away from the expedient, pragmatic murder of his king, instead showing him mercy. This act of mercy was one more reason the people should accept David as God's chosen king—God's leaders must be people of character who respect authority. David knew what Christ made so clear, "God blesses those who are merciful, for they will be shown mercy" (Matthew 5:7). (***See God****> God's Attributes> Merciful> God gives mercy to those who are merciful,* TopicGuide page A17.)

24:6 David's worldview centered on God's will and purposes. More than once David had the opportunity to harm Saul, but he didn't because he respected God's choice of when Saul's life would end. When Samuel confronted Saul about his sin (which was the reason his dynasty would end), he told Saul that God had sought out a man after His own heart. David's choice in the cave reveals why God chose to build a kingdom through David rather than Saul.

▸ GOD

24:10 Misuse of power. Pastors, like kings, will sometimes oppose you. How do you handle a situation where the person in authority, who is legitimately called by God to serve in that position, is misusing that power to hurt you? David's example is helpful to us, for he was in the same situation. First, David showed love and tried to help Saul (16:23). When his life was threatened, he either dodged the danger or completely fled the situation, but through Jonathan he continued to seek resolution (19:4). And when that was no longer possible, David left the situation entirely in God's hands, but he never struck back at God's anointed with his words or his sword. In fact, he continued to look out for Saul's best interest by serving as a mobile militia that kept the rural parts of Israel in order (1 Samuel 23:1-2). David believed that if God lifted Saul up without David's help, God could also remove him from power in the same manner. If you find yourself harassed by a pastor or another spiritual leader, look to David's example and find a way to escape the pain of an out-of-control spiritual leader, while honoring his unique position. (***See God****> God's Attributes> Forgiving> God's forgiveness leads believers to forgive others,* TopicGuide page A16.)

what I have in my hand. It is a piece of the hem of your robe! I cut it off, but I didn't kill you.
This proves that I am not trying to harm you and that I have not sinned against you, even
though you have been hunting for me to kill me.
12"May the LORD judge between us. Perhaps the LORD will punish you for what you are
trying to do to me, but I will never harm you. 13As that old proverb says, 'From evil people
come evil deeds.' So you can be sure I will never harm you. 14Who is the king of Israel try-
ing to catch anyway? Should he spend his time chasing one who is as worthless as a dead
dog or a single flea? 15May the LORD therefore judge which of us is right and punish the
guilty one. He is my advocate, and He will rescue me from your power!"
16When David had finished speaking, Saul called back, "Is that really you, my son Da-
vid?" Then he began to cry. 17And he said to David, "You are a better man than I am, for
you have repaid me good for evil. 18Yes, you have been amazingly kind to me today, for
when the LORD put me in a place where you could have killed me, you didn't do it. 19Who
else would let his enemy get away when he had him in his power? May the LORD reward
you well for the kindness you have shown me today. 20And now I realize that you are
surely going to be king, and that the kingdom of Israel will flourish under your rule. 21Now
swear to me by the LORD that when that happens you will not kill my family and destroy
my line of descendants!"
22So David promised this to Saul with an oath. Then Saul went home, but David and his
men went back to their stronghold.

THE DEATH OF SAMUEL

25 Now Samuel died, and all Israel gathered for his funeral. They buried him at his
house in Ramah.

NABAL ANGERS DAVID

Then David moved down to the wilderness of Maon.* 2There was a wealthy man from
Maon who owned property near the town of Carmel. He had 3,000 sheep and 1,000
goats, and it was sheep-shearing time. 3This man's name was Nabal, and his wife, Abigail,
was a sensible and beautiful woman. But Nabal, a descendant of Caleb, was crude and
mean in all his dealings.
4When David heard that Nabal was shearing his sheep, 5he sent ten of his young men
to Carmel with this message for Nabal: 6"Peace and prosperity to you, your family, and
everything you own! 7I am told that it is sheep-shearing time. While your shepherds
stayed among us near Carmel, we never harmed them, and nothing was ever stolen from
them. 8Ask your own men, and they will tell you this is true. So would you be kind to us,
since we have come at a time of celebration? Please share any provisions you might have

24:12 Gen 31:53; Judg 11:27
24:13 Matt 7:16-20
24:14 1 Sam 26:20
24:15 Ps 35:1
24:16 1 Sam 26:17
24:17 1 Sam 26:21; Matt 5:44
24:18 1 Sam 26:23
24:19 Ruth 2:12
24:20 1 Sam 13:14; 23:17
24:21 Gen 21:23; 1 Sam 20:14-17; 2 Sam 21:7
25:1 Deut 34:8; 1 Sam 7:17; 15:35; 28:3
25:2 Josh 15:55
25:3 Josh 15:13; 1 Sam 30:14
25:6 1 Chr 12:18
25:7 1 Sam 25:15
25:8 Neh 8:10

25:1 As in Greek version (see also 25:2); Hebrew reads *Paran.*

24:19 The crucial word in this verse is "power." The use or abuse of power will determine the character of a godly leader. David saw no need to use power for his advantage, especially against one he knew had been anointed by God.

▸ SPIRITUAL WARFARE
24:20 Shrewd and innocent. Mercy has a way of temporarily softening the hardened heart. David's show of mercy to Saul soothed his emotions and steadied his mind. But did David believe everything was fine? No, for after they parted, he didn't return to his home but went back to his stronghold in the wilderness. You need not be gullible, trusting that people always mean exactly what they say, just because you love Christ and His people. Be "as shrewd as snakes and harmless as doves" (Matthew 10:16). (***See Spiritual Warfare> God and Sin> Sin's Origin> The wise understand evil's source,*** TopicGuide page A45.)

24:20-21 Though Saul seemed to relent toward David, the two never reconciled. Saul acknowledged here that the throne would go to David, but he still continued to pursue him (1 Samuel 26:1). Saul (like Jonathan earlier) requested that David spare his descendants. In this ancient era when a new regime came into power, descendants of the old regime commonly were slaughtered so that none could contest the throne. David fulfilled this request with the one opportunity he had when he found Jonathan's son, Mephibosheth, and gave him a place at the royal table (2 Samuel 9).

on hand with us and with your friend David." [9]David's young men gave this message to
Nabal in David's name, and they waited for a reply.
25:10 [10]"Who is this fellow David?" Nabal sneered to the young men. "Who does this son of
Judg 9:28 Jesse think he is? There are lots of servants these days who run away from their masters.
[11]Should I take my bread and my water and my meat that I've slaughtered for my shear-
ers and give it to a band of outlaws who come from who knows where?"
25:13 [12]So David's young men returned and told him what Nabal had said. [13]"Get your
1 Sam 23:13 swords!" was David's reply as he strapped on his own. Then 400 men started off with Da-
vid, and 200 remained behind to guard their equipment.
[14]Meanwhile, one of Nabal's servants went to Abigail and told her, "David sent messen-
25:15 1 Sam 25:7 gers from the wilderness to greet our master, but he screamed insults at them. [15]These
men have been very good to us, and we never suffered any harm from them. Nothing was
25:16 Exod 14:22 stolen from us the whole time they were with us. [16]In fact, day and night they were like a
wall of protection to us and the sheep. [17]You need to know this and figure out what to do,
for there is going to be trouble for our master and his whole family. He's so ill-tempered
that no one can even talk to him!"
25:18 2 Sam 16:1 [18]Abigail wasted no time. She quickly gathered 200 loaves of bread, two wineskins full
1 Chr 12:40 of wine, five sheep that had been slaughtered, nearly a bushel* of roasted grain, 100 clus-
25:19 Gen 32:16, 20 ters of raisins, and 200 fig cakes. She packed them on donkeys [19]and said to her servants,
"Go on ahead. I will follow you shortly." But she didn't tell her husband Nabal what she
was doing.
[20]As she was riding her donkey into a mountain ravine, she saw David and his men
25:21 Ps 109:5 coming toward her. [21]David had just been saying, "A lot of good it did to help this fellow.
We protected his flocks in the wilderness, and nothing he owned was lost or stolen. But he
25:22 1 Sam 3:17 has repaid me evil for good. [22]May God strike me and kill me* if even one man of his
1 Kgs 14:10 household is still alive tomorrow morning!"

ABIGAIL INTERCEDES FOR NABAL

[23]When Abigail saw David, she quickly got off her donkey and bowed low before him.
[24]She fell at his feet and said, "I accept all blame in this matter, my lord. Please listen to
what I have to say. [25]I know Nabal is a wicked and ill-tempered man; please don't pay any
attention to him. He is a fool, just as his name suggests.* But I never even saw the young
men you sent.

25:18 Hebrew *5 seahs* [30 liters]. 25:22 As in Greek version; Hebrew reads *May God strike and kill the enemies of David.* 25:25 The name *Nabal* means "fool."

25:10 Nabal's characterization of David as a runaway servant with a band of outlaws may not have been far from the truth. Given David's contributions, though, such as his defeat of Goliath, coupled with his protective treatment of Nabal's shepherds, it was a foolish perspective for Nabal to take. While Nabal couldn't be expected to know that David was the future king of Israel, he should have known that David was no one to be trifled with. It is hard to believe, though, that Nabal was completely unaware of David's standing, given Abigail's words to David in 1 Samuel 25:28 regarding his lasting dynasty, which means that Nabal was both arrogant and disrespectful.

▶ SPIRITUAL WARFARE

25:11-35 A godly spouse. Sometimes even the best of us overreact. Not only did Nabal break Ancient Near Eastern rules of etiquette, but he refused to adequately reward David and his men, who served as a roving local militia protecting the countryside. David intended to kill Nabal for this insult. This does not appear to be a proportional response, no matter how deeply the insult may have cut David. God protected David from meaningless bloodshed (25:31) by inspiring the beautiful and wise Abigail (25:32) to intercede for her foolish husband. Are you more like the ungrateful and ill-tempered Nabal, the thin-skinned David, or the peacemaker Abigail? All of us could learn from her remarkable example. (***See Spiritual Warfare****> Resisting Sin and Evil> Resisting Temptation> How to Resist> By the help of our spouse,* TopicGuide page A45.)

25:18 The gifts Abigail prepared for David and his men were a good sampling of upscale travel foods of the day. Bread, wine, grain, and meat were foods that wouldn't last permanently, but if prepared appropriately could be carried on a journey. Raisins and dried figs were often pressed together into a non-baked fruit bar as opposed to being baked into modern floury cakes.

25:22 David's complaints offer us insight into the violent mindset of the day. Here was a man after God's own heart who vowed to kill every man of Nabal's household because Nabal refused to offer what David considered decent hospitality. It's easy to forget that while David was a musician and a shepherd, he was also a passionate warrior. This can be seen in a more sanctified manner in his psalms that cry out to God to protect him from his enemies (Psalm 3:6; 7:4-6; 13:2).

26“Now, my lord, as surely as the LORD lives and you yourself live, since the LORD has kept you from murdering and taking vengeance into your own hands, let all your enemies and those who try to harm you be as cursed as Nabal is. 27And here is a present that I, your servant, have brought to you and your young men. 28Please forgive me if I have offended you in any way. The LORD will surely reward you with a lasting dynasty, for you are fighting the LORD's battles. And you have not done wrong throughout your entire life.

29“Even when you are chased by those who seek to kill you, your life is safe in the care of the LORD your God, secure in his treasure pouch! But the lives of your enemies will disappear like stones shot from a sling! 30When the LORD has done all He promised and has made you leader of Israel, 31don't let this be a blemish on your record. Then your conscience won't have to bear the staggering burden of needless bloodshed and vengeance. And when the LORD has done these great things for you, please remember me, your servant!”

32David replied to Abigail, “Praise the LORD, the God of Israel, who has sent you to meet me today! 33Thank God for your good sense! Bless you for keeping me from murder and from carrying out vengeance with my own hands. 34For I swear by the LORD, the God of Israel, who has kept me from hurting you, that if you had not hurried out to meet me, not one of Nabal's men would still be alive tomorrow morning.” 35Then David accepted her present and told her, “Return home in peace. I have heard what you said. We will not kill your husband.”

36When Abigail arrived home, she found that Nabal was throwing a big party and was celebrating like a king. He was very drunk, so she didn't tell him anything about her meeting with David until dawn the next day. 37In the morning when Nabal was sober, his wife told him what had happened. As a result he had a stroke,* and he lay paralyzed on his bed like a stone. 38About ten days later, the LORD struck him, and he died.

25:26 2 Sam 18:32
25:27 Gen 33:11; 1 Sam 30:26
25:28 1 Sam 18:17; 2 Sam 7:11, 16
25:29 1 Sam 20:1; Jer 10:18
25:30 1 Sam 13:14
25:32 Exod 18:10
25:33 1 Sam 25:26
25:35 Gen 19:21

DAVID MARRIES ABIGAIL

39When David heard that Nabal was dead, he said, “Praise the LORD, who has avenged the insult I received from Nabal and has kept me from doing it myself. Nabal has received the punishment for his sin.” Then David sent messengers to Abigail to ask her to become his wife.

40When the messengers arrived at Carmel, they told Abigail, “David has sent us to take you back to marry him.”

41She bowed low to the ground and responded, “I, your servant, would be happy to marry David. I would even be willing to become a slave, washing the feet of his servants!” 42Quickly getting ready, she took along five of her servant girls as attendants, mounted her donkey, and went with David's messengers. And so she became his wife. 43David also married Ahinoam from Jezreel, making both of them his wives. 44Saul, meanwhile, had given his daughter Michal, David's wife, to a man from Gallim named Palti son of Laish.

25:42 Gen 24:61-67
25:43 1 Sam 27:2-3; 30:5
25:44 1 Sam 18:27; 2 Sam 3:14-15

25:37 Hebrew *his heart failed him.*

25:29 Abigail's word picture was an excellent choice to communicate with a man who spent his early life defending flocks of sheep with a sling. To envision David's enemies cast away as powerfully as a stone from a sling demonstrated that Abigail was an effective communicator.

25:44 Michal was first mentioned in 1 Samuel 18:20, where she is described as a woman in love with David. Unfortunately, what Michal is most remembered for is not her love for David, but her disdain. When David finally brought the Ark of the Covenant back to Jerusalem, he danced in the streets in celebration of the event. Michal watched her husband from her window and was “filled with contempt” (2 Samuel 6:15-16).

25:43 David married two different women here. Eventually his wife Michal was also returned to him. Later he married Bathsheba, a woman with whom he had an affair. He also married a foreign princess named Maacah, and women named Haggith, Abital, and Eglah. Polygamy was a custom of the day, but was not viewed as ideal in the eyes of God. Plus David had concubines (second wives), which, again, was a custom of the day, though not ordained by God as His chosen way of life. In fact, God warned the Israelites through Moses that their king should be careful in this regard (Deuteronomy 17:17). While a large family is a blessing, polygamy brought David much stress, heartbreak, and even political duress.

DAVID SPARES SAUL AGAIN

26:1 **26** Now some men from Ziph came to Saul at Gibeah to tell him, "David is hiding on
1 Sam 23:19 the hill of Hakilah, which overlooks Jeshimon."
26:2 1 Sam 13:2; 24:2 2 So Saul took 3,000 of Israel's elite troops and went to hunt him down in the wilderness
26:3 of Ziph. 3 Saul camped along the road beside the hill of Hakilah, near Jeshimon, where Da-
1 Sam 23:19 vid was hiding. When David learned that Saul had come after him into the wilderness, 4 he
sent out spies to verify the report of Saul's arrival.
26:5 5 David slipped over to Saul's camp one night to look around. Saul and Abner son of
1 Sam 14:50-51 Ner, the commander of his army, were sleeping inside a ring formed by the slumbering
26:6 warriors. 6 "Who will volunteer to go in there with me?" David asked Ahimelech the Hittite
1 Chr 2:16 and Abishai son of Zeruiah, Joab's brother.
"I'll go with you," Abishai replied. 7 So David and Abishai went right into Saul's camp and
found him asleep, with his spear stuck in the ground beside his head. Abner and the sol-
diers were lying asleep around him.
8 "God has surely handed your enemy over to you this time!" Abishai whispered to David.
26:9 "Let me pin him to the ground with one thrust of the spear; I won't need to strike twice!"
1 Sam 24:6 9 "No!" David said. "Don't kill him. For who can remain innocent after attacking the
2 Sam 1:14, 16 LORD's anointed one? 10 Surely the LORD will strike Saul down someday, or he will die of old
26:10 Deut 31:14 age or in battle. 11 The LORD forbid that I should kill the one He has anointed! But take his
1 Sam 25:38; 31:6 spear and that jug of water beside his head, and then let's get out of here!"
26:12 12 So David took the spear and jug of water that were near Saul's head. Then he and
Gen 2:21; 15:12 Isa 29:10 Abishai got away without anyone seeing them or even waking up, because the LORD had
put Saul's men into a deep sleep.
13 David climbed the hill opposite the camp until he was at a safe distance. 14 Then he
shouted down to the soldiers and to Abner son of Ner, "Wake up, Abner!"
"Who is it?" Abner demanded.
15 "Well, Abner, you're a great man, aren't you?" David taunted. "Where in all Israel is
there anyone as mighty? So why haven't you guarded your master the king when some-
one came to kill him? 16 This isn't good at all! I swear by the LORD that you and your men
deserve to die, because you failed to protect your master, the LORD's anointed! Look
around! Where are the king's spear and the jug of water that were beside his head?"
26:17 17 Saul recognized David's voice and called out, "Is that you, my son David?"
1 Sam 24:16 And David replied, "Yes, my lord the king. 18 Why are you chasing me? What have I
26:19 1 Sam 24:9 done? What is my crime? 19 But now let my lord the king listen to his servant. If the LORD
2 Sam 16:11 has stirred you up against me, then let Him accept my offering. But if this is simply a hu-
man scheme, then may those involved be cursed by the LORD. For they have driven me
from my home, so I can no longer live among the LORD's people, and they have said, 'Go,
26:20 1 Sam 24:14 worship pagan gods.' 20 Must I die on foreign soil, far from the presence of the LORD? Why
has the king of Israel come out to search for a single flea? Why does he hunt me down like
26:21 a partridge on the mountains?"
1 Sam 15:24, 30; 24:17 21 Then Saul confessed, "I have sinned. Come back home, my son, and I will no longer
try to harm you, for you valued my life today. I have been a fool and very, very wrong."

26:1-2 Ziph and its surrounding wilderness were three miles south of Hebron in the Judean mountains. Jeshimon was a wilderness area also a few miles south of Hebron. The hill of Hakilah was in the southern part of Jeshimon (1 Samuel 23:19).

26:5 Abner was Saul's cousin and his commander. Ner was Saul's uncle, his father's brother. After Saul's death, Abner first led Saul's son against David to fight for the throne. When that conflict was over, Abner negotiated with David to serve in David's kingdom. Before he could do so, Joab murdered Abner out of revenge (2 Samuel 3:6-27). At the end of David's reign, David warned Solomon about Joab, resulting in the warrior's execution (1 Kings 2:28-33).

26:17-18 This was not the first time David had the opportunity to hurt Saul. Earlier, as Saul was chasing David, he entered a cave in which David and his men were hiding. David's men encouraged him to take the king's life. Instead David cut a small piece of Saul's robe. When Saul was a safe distance, David called out to him making the same point as he did here: "Why do you listen to the people who say I am trying to harm you?" Saul seemed to repent then, just as he did here, but without a lasting effect (1 Samuel 24).

22"Here is your spear, O king," David replied. "Let one of your young men come over
and get it. 23The LORD gives His own reward for doing good and for being loyal, and I re-
fused to kill you even when the LORD placed you in my power, for you are the LORD's
anointed one. 24Now may the LORD value my life, even as I have valued yours today. May
He rescue me from all my troubles."
25And Saul said to David, "Blessings on you, my son David. You will do many heroic
deeds, and you will surely succeed." Then David went away, and Saul returned home.

DAVID AMONG THE PHILISTINES

27 But David kept thinking to himself, "Someday Saul is going to get me. The best
thing I can do is escape to the Philistines. Then Saul will stop hunting for me in Is-
raelite territory, and I will finally be safe."
2So David took his 600 men and went over and joined Achish son of Maoch, the king of
Gath. 3David and his men and their families settled there with Achish at Gath. David
brought his two wives along with him—Ahinoam from Jezreel and Abigail, Nabal's widow
from Carmel. 4Word soon reached Saul that David had fled to Gath, so he stopped hunting
for him.
5One day David said to Achish, "If it is all right with you, we would rather live in one of
the country towns instead of here in the royal city."
6So Achish gave him the town of Ziklag (which still belongs to the kings of Judah to this
day), 7and they lived there among the Philistines for a year and four months.
8David and his men spent their time raiding the Geshurites, the Girzites, and the Amalek-
ites—people who had lived near Shur, toward the land of Egypt, since ancient times. 9David

26:23 1 Sam 24:19
26:24 Ps 54:7
27:2 1 Sam 21:10; 2 Sam 2:2-3; 1 Kgs 2:39
27:3 1 Sam 25:43
27:6 Josh 15:31; 19:5; Neh 11:28
27:7 1 Sam 29:3
27:8 Exod 17:8; Josh 13:2-7, 13; 1 Sam 15:7-8
27:9 1 Sam 15:3

27:1 The Philistines had a long history with the Israelites, mostly as rivals and enemies. The Israelites had been subjects of the Philistines for 40 years during the time of the judges (Judges 13:1). David had a significant reputation as a warrior in both Philistia and Israel. After all, he had destroyed a mighty Philistine warrior, Goliath. Perhaps that reputation preceding David paved the way for his temporary defection.

27:2 Gath had already come into play in the history of the Israelites. It was a principal Philistine city located inland a little over ten miles from the Mediterranean coast. From an Israelite perspective, though, it was in the territory of Judah. Gath was one of the cities that held the Ark of the Covenant after the Philistines stole it during battle (1 Samuel 5:8). David had fled to Gath once before, but he did not receive a warm welcome (1 Samuel 21:10-15). It disappeared from historical significance in the eighth century when Sargon II conquered it.

27:2 This was not the first time David had approached King Achish, who was also known as Abimelech. During an earlier flight from Saul, David ran to Gath, to the court of Achish. He then overheard Achish's men and realized he was an unwanted guest. In order to be asked to leave, David began to act crazy, frothing at the mouth and scratching on doors. He was escorted out, and to safety (1 Samuel 21:10-15). On this next attempt to enter Gath, he was welcomed. Achish seemed to trust David implicitly once they formed an alliance. In fact, he gave David the town of Ziklag as a headquarters. During the time that David lived under Achish's authority, he led a double life, leading the king to believe that he was plundering Israelite towns when he was actually completely destroying the towns of Israel's enemies (1 Samuel 27:7-12).

27:6 Ziklag was located about 20 miles inland from the Mediterranean Sea, southeast of Gaza, a chief coastal city of Philistia. The Amalekites burned Ziklag to the ground while David was on a journey with Achish. During this attack the Amalekites took all the wives and children captive, causing dissension among David's ranks. Under God's guidance, David and his men retrieved their families and belongings and returned to Ziklag (1 Samuel 30).

27:8 There were two tribes of Geshurites. The first was east of the Jordan on the border of Bashan; their last king was Og, who suffered a notorious defeat at the hand of the Israelites. The other, mentioned here, was a neighbor to the Philistines in the western portion of Israel. These two tribes were related only by name and had vastly different relations to David. While a fugitive, David raided the western Geshurites; after he became king he married Maacah, the daughter of the king of the eastern tribe of Geshurites, forming an alliance with them (2 Samuel 3:3). Absalom, son of David and Maacah, eventually rebelled against his father's kingdom and found refuge among the eastern Geshurites (2 Samuel 13).

27:8 This is the only time the Girzites are mentioned in Scripture. While they were certainly a people group in southwest Canaan, there are two options for their origins. They may have been a tribe from the Mount Gerizim area, or they may have migrated from Gezer, a town in the foothills of Judah.

27:8 The Amalekites were distant relatives of the Israelites. Jacob, father of the 12 tribes of Israel, had a twin brother named Esau. One of Esau's grandsons was named Amalek, whose descendants were the Amalekites. The Amalekites were described as having no fear of God (Deuteronomy 25:18). These people were the first to block Israel's path out of Egypt during the great Exodus, and they harassed the Israelites as they journeyed to Canaan, the Promised Land (Exodus 17:8-16).

27:8-9 Shur was a wilderness area in the northern Sinai Peninsula. It lay between Egypt and Israel. Since David was deceiving the king, claiming to be destroying Israelite cities, Shur was an ideal location to attack: it was as far away from Gath as the Israelite cities that David claimed to destroy. David destroyed all enemies in the cities, so there was no one left to reveal his double life.

27:10 did not leave one person alive in the villages he attacked. He took the sheep, goats, cattle,
Judg 1:16; 4:11 1 Sam 30:27-31 donkeys, camels, and clothing before returning home to see King Achish.
1 Chr 2:9, 25 10"Where did you make your raid today?" Achish would ask.
And David would reply, "Against the south of Judah, the Jerahmeelites, and the Kenites."
11No one was left alive to come to Gath and tell where he had really been. This hap-
pened again and again while he was living among the Philistines. 12Achish believed David
and thought to himself, "By now the people of Israel must hate him bitterly. Now he will
have to stay here and serve me forever!"

SAUL CONSULTS A MEDIUM

28:1-2 **28** About that time the Philistines mustered their armies for another war with Israel.
1 Sam 29:1-2 King Achish told David, "You and your men will be expected to join me in battle."
2"Very well!" David agreed. "Now you will see for yourself what we can do."
Then Achish told David, "I will make you my personal bodyguard for life."
28:3 3Meanwhile, Samuel had died, and all Israel had mourned for him. He was buried in Ra-
Lev 19:31 Deut 18:10 mah, his hometown. And Saul had banned from the land of Israel all mediums and those
1 Sam 15:23; 25:1 who consult the spirits of the dead.
28:4 4The Philistines set up their camp at Shunem, and Saul gathered all the army of Israel
1 Sam 31:1, 3 and camped at Gilboa. 5When Saul saw the vast Philistine army, he became frantic with
2 Sam 1:6 28:6 fear. 6He asked the LORD what he should do, but the LORD refused to answer him, either by
Exod 28:30 dreams or by sacred lots* or by the prophets. 7Saul then said to his advisers, "Find a
28:7 woman who is a medium, so I can go and ask her what to do."
Ps 83:10 His advisers replied, "There is a medium at Endor."
Acts 16:16 8So Saul disguised himself by wearing ordinary clothing instead of his royal robes. Then
28:8 he went to the woman's home at night, accompanied by two of his men.
Isa 8:19 "I have to talk to a man who has died," he said. "Will you call up his spirit for me?"

28:6 Hebrew *by Urim.*

MINISTRY

27:10 Loyalty and trickery. David was a shrewd, convincing man. First, he took up residence in the capital city of Israel's greatest enemy. If that wasn't enough, he told Achish he was going out to raid the towns of Judah when in fact he was destroying isolated towns near Shur, allies of the Philistines in their hatred of Israel. And all during this time, none of David's men betrayed him—they all showed loyalty to their master, the rightful king of Israel. Whether you are in a battle or a mundane situation, whether at church or at home, show loyalty to those in authority over you and your family. Give respect to those who watch over both your body and soul. (***See Ministry****> Great Commission> Make Disciples> Disciples strategically use knowledge, skills, and abilities,* TopicGuide page A56.)

27:10 The Jerahmeelites were descendants of Judah through the family line of his son, Perez. They settled in a number of cities in the Negev region. The Negev was an arid desert in the southernmost region of Palestine. The Jerahmeelites didn't live as far away as the people David actually attacked, but they would have lived in a similar climate and culture.

27:10 The Kenites were a Canaanite tribe mentioned as early as Abraham's time. Evidently Moses' brother-in-law Hobab was a Kenite (Judges 4:11). In the days of Moses, Balaam, a diviner from Mesopotamia, prophesied the destruction of the Kenites at the hand of the Assyrians (Numbers 24:20-22). Unlike some other Canaanite tribes, the Kenites aided Israel on several occasions. David's claim to attack the Kenites indicated that he had no loyalty on behalf of Israel (which of course wasn't the case, as his claims were false). Later, during David's reign, Kenites were listed as inhabitants of Judah (1 Chronicles 2:55).

27:12 Achish was totally taken in by David's ruse. In fact, the king tried to take David into war *against* the Israelites. He referred to David as a defector, one who had totally changed allegiances (1 Samuel 29:3). Nothing could have been further from the truth. In fact, when he became king of Israel, David brought Gath under his own rule. Evidently Achish still ruled at that time, since he was still listed as the king of Gath years later when Solomon ruled after David (1 Kings 2:39).

28:3 Saul's ban fulfilled the Law of Moses. In Leviticus 19–20 Moses, under God's guidance, wrote that mediums and psychics were guilty of a capital offense. The people who consulted them were to be cut off from the community. The fact that Saul instigated the ban is a significant backdrop that highlights just how frantic his fear must have been to then disguise himself and seek out a medium to get advice from Samuel.

28:4 According to these locations, the Philistines would have been facing the Israelites across the Jezreel valley. The Philistines had set up camp at Shunem, at the outer hills of Mount Moreh. As described here, the Israelites were on Mount Gilboa. This site would have given Saul a good view of the vast Philistine army across the valley below. Saul would have had to circumvent the Philistine camp to reach Endor, the home of the medium.

28:7 This event was Endor's claim to fame. The town was mentioned only two other times in the Bible: in Joshua's list of cities given to Manasseh (Joshua 17:11) and then in Psalm 83 describing Barak's victory (Psalm 83:9-10). The city was located three miles south of Mount Tabor and less than fourteen miles southwest of the Sea of Galilee.

9 “Are you trying to get me killed?” the woman demanded. “You know that Saul has out- **28:9**
lawed all the mediums and all who consult the spirits of the dead. Why are you setting a 1 Sam 28:3
trap for me?”
10 But Saul took an oath in the name of the LORD and promised, “As surely as the LORD
lives, nothing bad will happen to you for doing this.”
11 Finally, the woman said, “Well, whose spirit do you want me to call up?”
“Call up Samuel,” Saul replied.
12 When the woman saw Samuel, she screamed, “You’ve deceived me! You are Saul!”
13 “Don’t be afraid!” the king told her. “What do you see?”
“I see a god* coming up out of the earth,” she said.
14 “What does he look like?” Saul asked. **28:14**
“He is an old man wrapped in a robe,” she replied. Saul realized it was Samuel, and he 1 Sam 15:27
fell to the ground before him.
15 “Why have you disturbed me by calling me back?” Samuel asked Saul. **28:15**
“Because I am in deep trouble,” Saul replied. “The Philistines are at war with me, and 1 Sam 16:14
God has left me and won’t reply by prophets or dreams. So I have called for you to tell me
what to do.”
16 But Samuel replied, “Why ask me, since the LORD has left you and has become your
enemy? 17 The LORD has done just as He said He would. He has torn the kingdom from you **28:17**
and given it to your rival, David. 18 The LORD has done this to you today because you re- 1 Sam 15:28
fused to carry out His fierce anger against the Amalekites. 19 What’s more, the LORD will **28:19**
hand you and the army of Israel over to the Philistines tomorrow, and you and your sons 1 Sam 31:2, 6
will be here with me. The LORD will bring down the entire army of Israel in defeat.”
20 Saul fell full length on the ground, paralyzed with fright because of Samuel’s words.
He was also faint with hunger, for he had eaten nothing all day and all night.
21 When the woman saw how distraught he was, she said, “Sir, I obeyed your command **28:21**
at the risk of my life. 22 Now do what I say, and let me give you a little something to eat so Judg 12:3
you can regain your strength for the trip back.”
23 But Saul refused. The men who were with him also urged him to eat, so he finally **28:23**
yielded and got up from the ground and sat on the couch. 2 Kgs 5:13 **28:24**
24 The woman had been fattening a calf, so she hurried out and killed it. She took some Gen 18:6-7
flour, kneaded it into dough and baked unleavened bread. 25 She brought the meal to Saul
and his men, and they ate it. Then they went out into the night.

THE PHILISTINES REJECT DAVID **29:1**

29 The entire Philistine army now mobilized at Aphek, and the Israelites camped at Josh 12:18 1 Sam 4:1
the spring in Jezreel. 2 As the Philistine rulers were leading out their troops in 2 Kgs 9:30
groups of hundreds and thousands, David and his men marched at the rear with King **29:2**
1 Sam 28:2

28:13 Or *gods.*

28:17-18 Samuel’s spirit only reminded Saul of what the king already knew. Saul had been commanded to defeat the Amalekites, destroying everything. That meant that everything would have either been physically destroyed or brought to the Tabernacle and dedicated to the Lord. Saul obeyed partially, but he and his men kept everything that “appealed to them” as well as Agag, King of the Amalekites (1 Samuel 15:9). When Samuel confronted Saul about his disobedience, Saul tried to skirt the issue. Because Saul was so casual about obeying God entirely, he was told from that point on that he would lose his kingdom.

▸ GOD
28:14 Do ghosts exist? Have you ever been to a fortune-teller? Or read your horoscope? It may be innocent or it may be an act of desperation—God knows. But regardless, Scripture forbids it (Leviticus 20:27; 1 Chronicles 10:13). There is a thorny problem in this chapter—was this medium truly empowered to speak to the dead? And if so, by whom—God or Satan? And was it really Samuel, or something else? We may never know. But we do know that the entire situation reeked of foolishness and Saul’s decision to allow women like her to stay in Israel meant that generations of kings after him would be tempted to seek spiritists for advice. (***See God***> *Relationship> Barriers> Demonic influence,* TopicGuide page A14.)

28:24 The medium prepared unleavened bread for two likely reasons—first, she wanted Saul to eat and leave quickly, and unleavened bread was quickly prepared and eaten. Second, the medium (perhaps unknowingly) honored Saul with a ceremonially clean final meal before he returned to what he had been told would be a fatal battle.

29:3 Achish. 3But the Philistine commanders demanded, "What are these Hebrews doing
1 Sam 27:1-7 here?"
1 Chr 12:19-20 And Achish told them, "This is David, the servant of King Saul of Israel. He's been with
me for years, and I've never found a single fault in him from the day he arrived until
today."
29:4 4But the Philistine commanders were angry. "Send him back to the town you've given
1 Sam 14:21 him!" they demanded. "He can't go into the battle with us. What if he turns against us in
battle and becomes our adversary? Is there any better way for him to reconcile himself
29:5 with his master than by handing our heads over to him? 5Isn't this the same David about
1 Sam 18:7; 21:11 whom the women of Israel sing in their dances,

'Saul has killed his thousands,
and David his ten thousands'?"

29:6 6So Achish finally summoned David and said to him, "I swear by the LORD that you have
1 Sam 27:12; 29:3 been a trustworthy ally. I think you should go with me into battle, for I've never found a
single flaw in you from the day you arrived until today. But the other Philistine rulers won't
hear of it. 7Please don't upset them, but go back quietly."
8"What have I done to deserve this treatment?" David demanded. "What have you ever
found in your servant, that I can't go and fight the enemies of my lord the king?"
29:9 9But Achish insisted, "As far as I'm concerned, you're as perfect as an angel of God. But
2 Sam 14:17, 20; 19:27 the Philistine commanders are afraid to have you with them in the battle. 10Now get up
early in the morning, and leave with your men as soon as it gets light."
11So David and his men headed back into the land of the Philistines, while the Philistine
army went on to Jezreel.

DAVID DESTROYS THE AMALEKITES

30:1 **30** Three days later, when David and his men arrived home at their town of Ziklag,
1 Sam 15:7; 27:6, 8 they found that the Amalekites had made a raid into the Negev and Ziklag; they
had crushed Ziklag and burned it to the ground. 2They had carried off the women and
children and everyone else but without killing anyone.
30:5 3When David and his men saw the ruins and realized what had happened to their fami-
1 Sam 25:39-43 lies, 4they wept until they could weep no more. 5David's two wives, Ahinoam from Jezreel
2 Sam 2:2 30:6 and Abigail, the widow of Nabal from Carmel, were among those captured. 6David was
Exod 17:4 now in great danger because all his men were very bitter about losing their sons and
1 Sam 23:16 daughters, and they began to talk of stoning him. But David found strength in the LORD his
Ps 18:2 God.

29:6-7 The government of the Philistines was based on city-states. There were five city-states joined together as a confederation. A lord or overseer, here referred to as rulers, controlled each city-state. Achish's interaction with the other rulers was a good example of how the Philistine lords interacted. Their city-states were autonomous, but when it came to a joint effort such as the battle before them, each ruler had a voice. The other lords didn't trust David as Achish did and voted him out of the battle.

▸ WORSHIP

29:8 Godly guile. We again see that David was one of the slyest people in the Bible. But he fell into in a trap and was about to be forced to attack his own people in battle. How could the future king of Israel attack fellow Israelites in the company of the Philistines? He could not. David arranged to be in the rear of the battle formation, a perfect place for an ambush against the Philistines, which forced the commanders of Philistia to ask to have him sent away. David then responded with mock indignation that only further convinced Achish of his allegiance. In the rare situation where righteousness requires you to deceive others, seek the council of godly friends and associates to make certain you are not in sin. (***See Worship***> *NT> Reverence> Jesus is our eternal Master*, TopicGuide page A32.)

30:1 David returned to utter destruction at the hands of the Amalekites. During David's stay in Ziklag, he had been ransacking and destroying Amalekite towns and villages, while claiming to King Achish that he had been attacking Israelite communities (1 Samuel 27:8-12). Given the violence of this era, it is not surprising that the people of Amalek sought revenge against David. What is surprising is that anyone was left alive, which suggests that the families would be used to prevent David from reprisal.

7 Then he said to Abiathar the priest, "Bring me the ephod!" So Abiathar brought it. 30:7
8 Then David asked the LORD, "Should I chase after this band of raiders? Will I catch them?" 1 Sam 23:9
And the LORD told him, "Yes, go after them. You will surely recover everything that was 30:8
taken from you!" 1 Sam 23:2, 4
9 So David and his 600 men set out, and they came to the brook Besor. 10 But 200 of the 30:9
men were too exhausted to cross the brook, so David continued the pursuit with 400 men. 1 Sam 27:2
11 Along the way they found an Egyptian man in a field and brought him to David. They
gave him some bread to eat and water to drink. 12 They also gave him part of a fig cake 30:12
and two clusters of raisins, for he hadn't had anything to eat or drink for three days and Judg 15:19
nights. Before long his strength returned.
13 "To whom do you belong, and where do you come from?" David asked him.
"I am an Egyptian—the slave of an Amalekite," he replied. "My master abandoned me
three days ago because I was sick. 14 We were on our way back from raiding the Kerethites 30:14 1 Sam 30:1
in the Negev, the territory of Judah, and the land of Caleb, and we had just burned Ziklag." 2 Sam 1:1; 15:17-18
15 "Will you lead me to this band of raiders?" David asked. 1 Chr 18:17
The young man replied, "If you take an oath in God's name that you will not kill me or 30:15
give me back to my master, then I will guide you to them." Deut 23:15
16 So he led David to them, and they found the Amalekites spread out across the fields,
eating and drinking and dancing with joy because of the vast amount of plunder they had
taken from the Philistines and the land of Judah. 17 David and his men rushed in among 30:17
them and slaughtered them throughout that night and the entire next day until evening. 1 Sam 15:3
None of the Amalekites escaped except 400 young men who fled on camels. 18 David got
back everything the Amalekites had taken, and he rescued his two wives. 19 Nothing was
missing: small or great, son or daughter, nor anything else that had been taken. David
brought everything back. 20 He also recovered all the flocks and herds, and his men drove
them ahead of the other livestock. "This plunder belongs to David!" they said.
21 Then David returned to the brook Besor and met up with the 200 men who had been 30:21
left behind because they were too exhausted to go with him. They went out to meet David 1 Sam 30:10-11
and his men, and David greeted them joyfully. 22 But some evil troublemakers among Da-
vid's men said, "They didn't go with us, so they can't have any of the plunder we recov-
ered. Give them their wives and children, and tell them to be gone."
23 But David said, "No, my brothers! Don't be selfish with what the LORD has given us. He
has kept us safe and helped us defeat the band of raiders that attacked us. 24 Who will lis- 30:24
ten when you talk like this? We share and share alike—those who go to battle and those Num 31:27
who guard the equipment." 25 From then on David made this a decree and regulation for Josh 22:7-8
Israel, and it is still followed today.
26 When he arrived at Ziklag, David sent part of the plunder to the elders of Judah, who 30:26
were his friends. "Here is a present for you, taken from the LORD's enemies," he said. Gen 33:11 1 Sam 25:27

30:7-8 Abiathar was the only priest who escaped Saul's attack on Ahimelech's family at Nob (1 Samuel 22:5-23). Abiathar brought the ephod, the sacred priestly breastplate, from Nob. This breastplate held the Urim and Thummim, used to discern guidance from God. We don't know exactly how they worked—probably as dice or tokens that were tossed. The inquirer asked a question, and then used the Urim and Thummim, which gave an answer that the user could not control.

30:14 The Kerethites were a people group associated with the Philistines. They settled near Hebron in southern Judah. In other contexts, they were associated with a group called the Pelethites, which may be another word for "Philistines." During David's reign, he hired both Kerethites and Pelethites as mercenaries in his army.

▸ WORSHIP

30:24-25 Share and share alike. "Life isn't fair," or so the saying goes. David attempted to show respect for the needs of both those who served as guards and the warriors. The text does not say that both groups were given equal amounts—only that those who were left behind received a cut of the booty. In your business relationships and all your dealings with others, attempt to treat people with at least the measure they deserve—if not more. (***See Worship***> *NT> Fellowship> Preserving> Honor one another,* TopicGuide page A31.)

30:26-30 David's actions of sharing the spoils with his Israelite brothers highlighted the irony of Achish's insistence that David go to war with him against the Israelites—rather than Israelites dying in battle under David's sword, God's people were blessed through his military prowess. His loyalties remained undivided (1 Samuel 29:1-6).

30:27 27The gifts were sent to the people of the following towns David had visited: Bethel,
Josh 15:48 Ramoth-negev, Jattir, 28Aroer, Siphmoth, Eshtemoa, 29Racal,* the towns of the Jerahmeel-
30:28 ites, the towns of the Kenites, 30Hormah, Bor-ashan, Athach, 31Hebron, and all the other
Josh 13:16 places David and his men had visited.

THE DEATH OF SAUL

31:1-13 **31** Now the Philistines attacked Israel, and the men of Israel fled before them. Many
//2 Sam 1:4-12 were slaughtered on the slopes of Mount Gilboa. 2The Philistines closed in on
//1 Chr 10:1-12
31:1 Saul and his sons, and they killed three of his sons—Jonathan, Abinadab, and Malkishua.
1 Sam 28:4 3The fighting grew very fierce around Saul, and the Philistine archers caught up with him
31:3 and wounded him severely.
2 Sam 1:6, 10 4Saul groaned to his armor bearer, "Take your sword and kill me before these pagan
31:4 Philistines come to run me through and taunt and torture me."
Judg 9:54 But his armor bearer was afraid and would not do it. So Saul took his own sword and fell
on it. 5When his armor bearer realized that Saul was dead, he fell on his own sword and
died beside the king. 6So Saul, his three sons, his armor bearer, and his troops all died to-
gether that same day.
7When the Israelites on the other side of the Jezreel Valley and beyond the Jordan saw
that the Israelite army had fled and that Saul and his sons were dead, they abandoned
their towns and fled. So the Philistines moved in and occupied their towns.
8The next day, when the Philistines went out to strip the dead, they found the bodies of
31:9 Saul and his three sons on Mount Gilboa. 9So they cut off Saul's head and stripped off his
Judg 16:23-24 armor. Then they proclaimed the good news of Saul's death in their pagan temple and to
2 Sam 1:20 the people throughout the land of Philistia. 10They placed his armor in the temple of the
31:10 Ashtoreths, and they fastened his body to the wall of the city of Beth-shan.
Josh 17:11
Judg 2:12-14 11But when the people of Jabesh-gilead heard what the Philistines had done to Saul,
1 Sam 7:3 12all their mighty warriors traveled through the night to Beth-shan and took the bodies of
31:11-12 Saul and his sons down from the wall. They brought them to Jabesh, where they burned
1 Sam 11:1-13 the bodies. 13Then they took their bones and buried them beneath the tamarisk tree at Ja-
2 Sam 2:4-7; 21:12-14 besh, and they fasted for seven days.

30:29 Greek version reads *Carmel*.

31:4 In the Ancient Near East, and to some extent in every culture, how a person dies is as important as whether and why death occurs. Saul's lack of character made his death as much a thing of grave shame as his life. Suicide is dishonorable; dying in combat for a righteous cause is honorable. This was a fitting, yet tragic end to the life of Saul.

31:10 The Ashtoreths were Canaanite gods. Ashtoreth, or Asherah, was the female counterpart to Baal. She was a fertility godess, and her worship practices were sexual and violent in nature. Saul's armor was hung in an Asherah temple, but his head was displayed in the temple of Dagon, a principal Philistine god. The city in which Saul's body was hung, Beth-shan, was located in the Jezreel Valley. Mount Gilboa, the site of Saul's headquarters for this battle, overlooked the valley in which his body was put on display as a trophy of war. Thus Saul's body hung before those who had previously served him.

▸WORSHIP

31:12 Honoring the dead. God's people give honor where honor is due. The people of Jabesh could not stand to see the king's body desecrated; they quietly traveled the 13 miles from their town, scaled the high hill, then the high walls of Beth-Shan, and pulled the royal family down for a proper burial. It pleased God to honor Saul and his sons at their deaths. Speak well of the dead, and attend the funerals of even those you didn't particularly like, for every person deserves a proper farewell. (***See Worship***> *OT> Reverence> For those who came before,* TopicGuide page A28.)

31:11-13 The people of Jabesh-gilead did save Saul and his sons some postmortem humiliation, but David went a step further. During his reign he retrieved the bones of Saul and his sons and buried them with Kish, Saul's father, in the family burial plot. Though Saul had hunted David as a fugitive and even planned his death, David continued to honor Saul as the man who at one time was God's anointed king of Israel.

KEY PLACES IN 2 SAMUEL

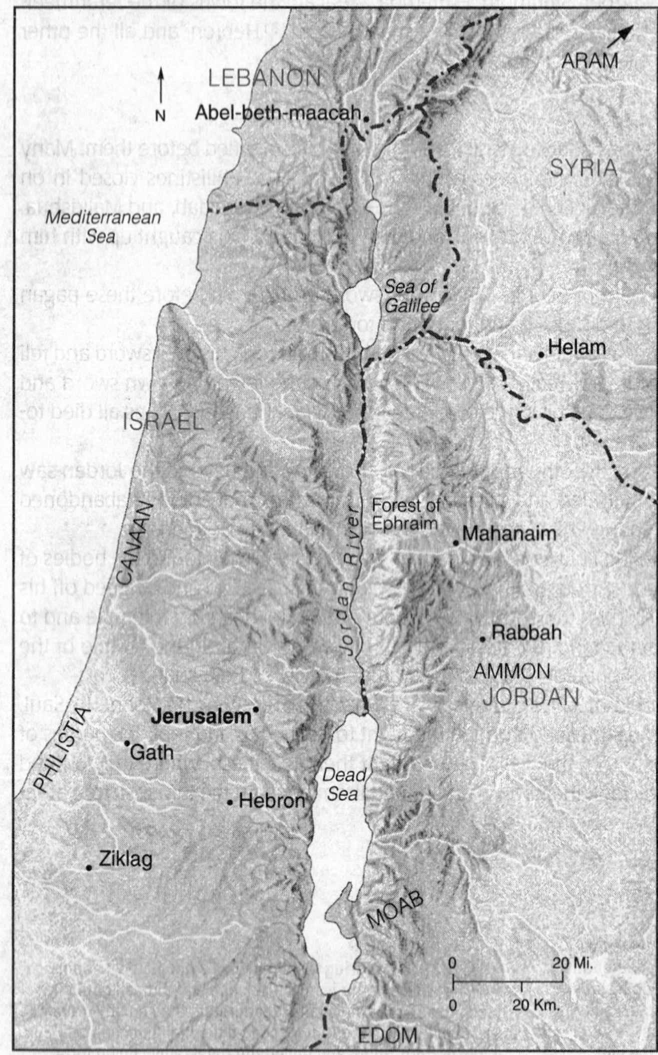

The broken lines (—·—·) indicate modern boundaries.

1 Hebron After Saul's death, David moved from the Philistine city of Ziklag to Hebron, where the tribe of Judah crowned him king. But the rest of Israel's tribes backed Saul's son Ishbosheth and crowned him king at Mahanaim. As a result, there was war between Judah and the rest of the tribes of Israel until Ishbosheth was assassinated. Then all of Israel pledged loyalty to David as their king (1:1–5:5).

2 Jerusalem One of David's first battles as king occurred at the fortress of Zion (Jerusalem). David and his troops took the city by surprise, and it became his capital. It was here that David brought the Ark of the Covenant and made a special covenant with God (5:6–7:29).

3 Gath The Philistines were Israel's constant enemy, though they did give David sanctuary when he was hiding from Saul (1 Samuel 27). But when Saul died and David became king, the Philistines planned to defeat him. In a battle near Jerusalem, David and his troops routed the Philistines (5:17-25), but they were not completely subdued until David conquered their largest city (8:1).

4 Moab During the time of the judges, Moab controlled many cities in Israel and demanded heavy taxes (Judges 3:12-30). David conquered Moab and, in turn, levied tribute from them (8:2).

5 Edom Though the Edomites and the Israelites traced their ancestry back to the same man, Isaac (Genesis 25:19-23), they were long-standing enemies. David defeated Edom and forced them to pay tribute also (8:14).

6 Rabbah The Ammonites insulted David's delegation and turned a peacemaking mission into angry warfare. The Ammonites called troops from Aram, but David defeated this alliance first at Helam, then at Rabbah, the capital city (10:1–12:31).

7 Mahanaim David had victory in the field, but problems at home. His son Absalom incited a rebellion and crowned himself king at Hebron. David and his men fled to Mahanaim. Acting on bad advice, Absalom mobilized his army to fight David (13:1–17:29).

8 Forest of Ephraim The armies of Absalom and David fought in the forest of Ephraim. Absalom's hair got caught in a tree, and Joab, David's general, found and killed him. With Absalom's death the rebellion died, and David was welcomed back to Jerusalem (18:1–19:43).

9 Abel-beth-maacah A man named Sheba also incited a rebellion against David. He fled to Abel-beth-maacah, but Joab and a small troop besieged the city. The citizens of Abel-beth-maacah killed Sheba themselves (20:1-26). David's victories laid the foundation for the peaceful reign of his son Solomon.

2 SAMUEL

PURPOSE

Second Samuel is a continuation of 1 Samuel, documenting David's rise from shepherd to king and God's plan to establish his dynasty forever.

Whether you are reading these words during daylight or darkness, if you turn your eyes to the sky, you will see something important regarding the events of the book of 2 Samuel. The Bible says that as long as the sun and moon are in the sky, David's dynasty of kings over Israel will continue (Psalm 89:36-37).

That's what 2 Samuel is about—the establishment of David as the true theocratic (God-centered) king over Israel, and the promise that rulers over Israel will come from David's "house" forever. Saul, the first king over Israel, failed to be God's faithful representative (1 Samuel). His rule became self-centered instead of God-centered, so God removed him from the kingship and established David, a man after His own heart (1 Samuel 13:14). David was not a perfect ruler; a significant part of 2 Samuel deals with David's sins and the resulting devastation, both personal and national. But David confessed his sins and was restored to fellowship with God, and God's promises to Him remained intact (7:4-16).

DISCOVER GOD IN 2 SAMUEL

Just as a person's character is clearly revealed in the give and take of real life, so is God's. The drama of 2 Samuel continues the revelation of God's attributes:

Loyal love: *Hesed* is an important Old Testament (Hebrew) word that can be translated as "mercy," "lovingkindness," or "loyal love." It is the kind of love that characterizes the covenants God makes with people. For instance, God said, "But My favor [*hesed*] will not be taken from him [David] as I took it from Saul, whom I removed from your sight" (2 Samuel 7:15). In response, David said, ". . . You show unfailing love [*hesed*] to Your anointed, to David and all his descendants forever" (2 Samuel 22:51b). At the heart of *hesed* is God's character. When He makes a promise, it is a promise forever—He does not lie or change His mind (1 Samuel 15:29). The prophet Isaiah foretold that "God will establish one of David's descendants as king. He will rule with mercy and truth. He will always do what is just and be eager to do what is right" (Isaiah 16:5; Luke 1:32). God's loyal love is a binding love, as secure as the character of God Himself.

Mercy: It was God's adherence to His own standards that caused Him to depose Saul as king over Israel and replace him with David. But the other side of the coin of judgment is mercy. Judgment is getting what we deserve, while mercy is not getting what we deserve.

When King David committed the dual sins of adultery (with Bathsheba) and murder (of Uriah), he deserved God's judgment (chapters 11–12). Instead, he received God's mercy—he didn't get what he deserved. Two factors were critical in God's extension of mercy: the promises God had made and David's repentance for his sins. While God is just, He is also merciful, and the mercy of God was intertwined with David's repentant heart. Centuries after David received mercy from God, Mary, the mother of Jesus, the Son of David praised God for it: "He shows mercy from generation to generation to all who fear Him" (Luke 1:50).

DISCOVERY VERSES

Then King David went in and sat before the LORD and prayed, "Who am I, O Sovereign LORD, and what is my family, that You have brought me this far? And now, Sovereign LORD, in addition to everything else, You speak of giving Your servant a lasting dynasty! Do You deal with everyone this way, O Sovereign LORD?" (2 SAMUEL 7:18-19)

"And now, O LORD God, I am Your servant; do as You have promised concerning me and my family. Confirm it as a promise that will last forever. And may Your name be honored forever so that everyone will say, 'The LORD of Heaven's Armies is God over Israel!' And may the house of Your servant David continue before You forever." (2 SAMUEL 7:25-26)

I called on the LORD, who is worthy of praise, and He saved me from my enemies. (2 SAMUEL 22:4)

GROWING THROUGH 2 SAMUEL

Numerous lessons await the careful student of David's life and experiences:

Worship as sacrifice: David refused to secure a place to worship God that cost him nothing. True worship always involves sacrifice (2 Samuel 24:24; Romans 12:1).

Loyalty to friends: David promised his friend Jonathan he would spare Jonathan's family any revenge against the house of Saul (1 Samuel 20:15, 42). When he became king, David sought out Jonathan's crippled son, Mephibosheth, and brought him to live in the royal court (2 Samuel 9). Real friends stick closer than a brother (Proverbs 18:24).

Honesty about sin: David concealed his adultery with Bathsheba for a year—and might have done so forever if God had not confronted him through Nathan the prophet. David was miserable for that year (Psalm 32), but he found freedom in confession and forgiveness (Psalm 51).

Willingness to wound: When God told Nathan the prophet to confront David about his sin, Nathan knew David might retaliate and have him killed. Fortunately, David had the sense to know that "wounds from a sincere friend are better than many kisses from an enemy" (Proverbs 27:6).

2 SAMUEL FACTS

Author: Anonymous (see 1 Samuel, Author). The books of 1 and 2 Samuel were compiled by an editor; they are probably not the product of a single author. Among the sources used to compile 1 and 2 Samuel were those listed in 2 Samuel 1:18 and 1 Chronicles 29:29.

Written to: Both books of Samuel were historical sources for the entire nation of Israel. As with all the history of the Old Testament, the arrangement or editing of the history shows both theological and political purposes.

Date of writing: See 1 Samuel, Date of Writing.

Setting: Hebron (chapters 1–5), where David ruled over the tribe of Judah for seven and a half years (1011–1004 BC); Jerusalem (chapters 6–24), where David reigned over all Israel for thirty-three years (1004–971 BC); and surrounding areas of Israel.

OUTLINE

- **2 SAMUEL 1–4**—David reigns over Judah
- **2 SAMUEL 5–20**—David reigns over all Israel
- **2 SAMUEL 21–24**—David's final years

DAVID LEARNS OF SAUL'S DEATH

1:1 1 Sam 30:1, 17
1 After the death of Saul, David returned from his victory over the Amalekites and
spent two days in Ziklag. [2]On the third day a man arrived from Saul's army camp. He
1:2 1 Sam 4:12
had torn his clothes and put dirt on his head to show that he was in mourning. He fell to
the ground before David in deep respect.
1:4-12 //1 Sam 31:1-13 //1 Chr 10:1-12
[3]"Where have you come from?" David asked.
"I escaped from the Israelite camp," the man replied.
[4]"What happened?" David demanded. "Tell me how the battle went."
1:4 1 Sam 4:16-17
The man replied, "Our entire army fled from the battle. Many of the men are dead, and
Saul and his son Jonathan are also dead."
[5]"How do you know Saul and Jonathan are dead?" David demanded of the young man.
1:6 1 Sam 28:4; 31:1-6
[6]The man answered, "I happened to be on Mount Gilboa, and there was Saul leaning on
his spear with the enemy chariots and charioteers closing in on him. [7]When he turned and
1:8 1 Sam 15:2-3; 30:1, 13, 17
saw me, he cried out for me to come to him. 'How can I help?' I asked him.
[8]"He responded, 'Who are you?'

1:1 The book of 2 Samuel is a continuation of the book of 1 Samuel. Originally they were one narrative, but when it was translated into Greek, it wouldn't all fit onto one scroll. Thus, the scribes divided the book into two parts. In order to represent the sequential nature of the books, they were designated very practically: 1 and 2 Samuel. First Samuel tells of the first king of Israel, Saul. Second Samuel records David's ascension to the throne and reign as king.

1:1 Saul, the first king of Israel, died in battle with the Philistines (1 Samuel 31). As far as we know, Saul's sons died in the fighting on Mount Gilboa, but Saul chose to end his own life rather than allow an enemy to claim that triumph. The Philistines displayed Saul's armor as a trophy in the temple of their fertility goddesses, the Ashtoreths, thereby crediting their idols with Saul's defeat. They also hung Saul's body on the wall of the city of Beth-shan, but the people of Jabesh-gilead recovered the bodies of Saul and his sons, burying them and mourning their passing.

1:1 Saul and David had been in conflict for years. Saul knew that David had been anointed as his successor. Because of that knowledge, Saul was prone to fits of jealousy and rage. He chased David through the forests and caves of the Judean hills. David eventually sought refuge among the Philistines, pretending to be a defector. David was nearly forced to fight against Israel in the battle in which Saul died. Instead, he returned to his camp in Ziklag, only to find that the Amalekites had ransacked it. David immediately set out to recover his men's families and goods. This was why, at the opening of 2 Samuel, David was returning from a battle with the Amalekites.

1:1 The Philistine town of Ziklag was David's headquarters for the 16 months he hid among the Philistines. King Achish of Gath had deeded the town over to David. Achish believed that David had truly defected, but David covertly led his men in regular raids against the towns in southern Philistia. Ziklag remained a territory of Judah even after David returned to Israel to become king.

1:2 Grief or mourning was often expressed in dramatic ways in this ancient culture. People in mourning didn't bathe. They left their hair loose. They tore their clothes. They covered their faces and heads. They wore sackcloth, or haircloth, a scratchy, uncomfortable fabric. They often sat in ashes or rolled around in dirt. Thus, when this man arrived from battle with dirt thrown on his head and his clothes torn, anyone who saw him knew that bad news was in store.

1:4 Jonathan was Saul's firstborn son and David's dearest friend. Throughout Saul and David's conflict-filled relationship, Jonathan stood between them, serving his father and protecting his friend. As Saul's eldest son, Jonathan was crown prince, the man who normally would succeed to the throne. But God had taken the kingdom away from Saul and anointed David to succeed him. Jonathan knew this and accepted it. What is more, Jonathan truly loved David and never wavered in his devotion to him. David would see Saul's death as the loss of God's anointed. But he would see Jonathan's death as the loss of his closest confidant. David later cared for Jonathan's only surviving son, Mephibosheth, in honor of their friendship.

1:6 Mount Gilboa was a limestone ridge south of Galilee. Its view over the Jezreel Valley made it an advantageous site for a battle headquarters. Scripture mentions Gilboa only in connection with Saul's battle with the Philistines, but several other biblical battles probably were fought in this area. Deborah, a judge of Israel, helped lead Israel to victory over Sisera near the Kishon River, which was in the vicinity (Judges 5:19-21). Gideon probably camped near Gilboa when he attacked the Midianites in the Jezreel Valley (Judges 6:32-33).

1:8 What was an Amalekite doing on the battlefield with Saul's Israelite army? The Amalekites were enemies of Israel; in fact, David had just returned from defeating a band of Amalekites. It is possible this man was a proselyte who had become a worshiper of the true God. In that case, he actually may have been fighting with Saul's men. It is also possible he was a mercenary. More likely he simply lived in Israelite territory. After all, the Israelites had failed to subdue certain Canaanite cities in the vicinity of Mount Gilboa. If the man who came to David was from one of these cities, he may well have been nothing more than a battlefield looter who found Saul's body before the Philistines did.

1:8 The fact that this man was an Amalekite is an ironic twist. Saul lost God's presence and power in his reign because he disobeyed God in a battle with the Amalekites (1 Samuel 15). God had instructed Saul to destroy the Amalekites because they had opposed the Israelites when they came out of Egypt en route to Canaan. But Saul spared the Amalekite king, Agag, and Saul and his men took whatever pleased them from the possessions of the Amalekites.

"'I am an Amalekite,' I told him.
9 "Then he begged me, 'Come over here and put me out of my misery, for I am in terrible
pain and want to die.'
10 "So I killed him," the Amalekite told David, "for I knew he couldn't live. Then I took his
crown and his armband, and I have brought them here to you, my lord."
11 David and his men tore their clothes in sorrow when they heard the news. 12 They 1:11
mourned and wept and fasted all day for Saul and his son Jonathan, and for the LORD's Gen 37:29, 34
army and the nation of Israel, because they had died by the sword that day.
13 Then David said to the young man who had brought the news, "Where are you from?" 1:14
And he replied, "I am a foreigner, an Amalekite, who lives in your land." 1 Sam 26:9-11
14 "Why were you not afraid to kill the LORD's anointed one?" David asked. 1:15 2 Sam 4:10, 12
15 Then David said to one of his men, "Kill him!" So the man thrust his sword into the 1:16
Amalekite and killed him. 16 "You have condemned yourself," David said, "for you yourself 1 Sam 26:9
confessed that you killed the LORD's anointed one." 2 Sam 1:10

DAVID'S SONG FOR SAUL AND JONATHAN

17 Then David composed a funeral song for Saul and Jonathan, 18 and he commanded that 1:17 2 Chr 35:27
it be taught to the people of Judah. It is known as the Song of the Bow, and it is recorded in 1:18
*The Book of Jashar.** Josh 10:13

19 Your pride and joy, O Israel, lies dead on the hills! 1:19 2 Sam 3:38
Oh, how the mighty heroes have fallen!

1:18 Or *The Book of the Upright.*

▸ GOD
1:10 Consequences of exaggeration. This Amalekite did not kill Saul—he found him dead on the battlefield (1 Samuel 31:5) after Saul fell on his sword. However, he knew that David would be the next king and saw a chance to ingratiate himself to the next monarch. He did not know that David was a man of character who loved Saul and respected God's calling on his life. Lying to make oneself or others appear better is a regular practice in our society. When we lie or slander to promote ourselves, we may increase ourselves in the eyes of others, but we decrease our heavenly reward (1 Corinthians 3), our love of truth, and the closeness of our walk with God. When is the last time you lied so others would think better of you? (***See God****> God's Attributes> True> God doesn't lie but keeps His word,* TopicGuide page A18.)

1:14 David showed time and again that no matter what he thought or felt about Saul, he respected the fact that God had chosen Saul as king. On one occasion, Saul entered a cave where David and his men were hiding. David's men urged him to take Saul's life. David's reply? "The LORD forbid that I should . . . attack the LORD's anointed one, for the LORD Himself has chosen him" (1 Samuel 24:6). On another occasion, David and Abishai entered Saul's camp at night. Abishai offered to kill Saul then and there. David's reply? "Who can remain innocent after attacking the LORD's anointed one?" (1 Samuel 26:9). In David's mind, only God had the right to end Saul's reign. Therefore, David could interpret this Amalekite's actions only as disrespect for God's sovereignty.

▸ SPIRITUAL WARFARE
1:16 The death penalty. This is an example of the trouble sinful communication can cause. David was not privy to the details of Saul's death as recorded in 1 Samuel 31, so he reacted as if the Amalekite's confession was authentic—and carried out the death penalty against him. The Amalekite's motive in his lie was to gain David's trust and favor, but he did not know David's heart, so the lie gained him a quick death. (***See Spiritual Warfare****> Resisting Sin and Evil> Consequences> Of Disobedience> Death,* TopicGuide page A46.)

1:17 While David was an accomplished warrior and an anointed king, he first appeared on the scene as a shepherd and a musician. In fact, his first role in Saul's kingdom was as a staff musician; his harp playing helped the king through periods of depression and rage. Thus, it is not surprising that David would process his grief through songwriting. He was responsible for at least seventy-three songs recorded in the Old Testament book of Psalms. Many believe, based on the superscription, that Psalm 18 may have been written partly in reference to Saul's death. This psalm appears almost in its entirety in 2 Samuel 22.

▸ WORSHIP
1:18 Spreading fame through song. David believed everyone would benefit from meditating on the deaths of Saul and Jonathan, so he sent musicians into the clans of Judah to teach an oral history of this sad event. In many societies today, people like to pretend they can be forever young. It is good, therefore, to take steps to remind yourself that we must die one day. And when we die, our opportunity to repent will have passed (Hebrews 9:27). Today, write a poem, a song, or a few paragraphs about how you want to be remembered when you die, or imagine what your first few moments before God will be like. (***See Worship****> OT> Music> David mourns Saul and Jonathan through song,* TopicGuide page A27.)

1:18 *The Book of Jashar* was a collection of poems and songs about Israelite heroes. Hebrew poetry was not defined so much by its rhyme scheme as by the writing style, the structure, and the use of imagery. Rather than rhyming with words, Hebrew poetry uses rhythms of thoughts or concepts to punctuate ideas. You can read some examples of Hebrew poetry (which some believe may have been a part of *The Book of Jashar* at one time) by reading Deborah's song (Judges 5) and Miriam's song (Exodus 15:21). Also, the book of Lamentations is basically a collection of poems or songs by the prophet Jeremiah.

1:20 1 Sam 31:8 Mic 1:10

20 Don't announce the news in Gath,
don't proclaim it in the streets of Ashkelon,
or the daughters of the Philistines will rejoice
and the pagans will laugh in triumph.

1:21 1 Sam 31:1 Ezek 31:15

21 O mountains of Gilboa,
let there be no dew or rain upon you,
nor fruitful fields producing offerings of grain.*
For there the shield of the mighty heroes was defiled;
the shield of Saul will no longer be anointed with oil.
22 The bow of Jonathan was powerful,
and the sword of Saul did its mighty work.
They shed the blood of their enemies
and pierced the bodies of mighty heroes.

1:23 Judg 14:18

23 How beloved and gracious were Saul and Jonathan!
They were together in life and in death.
They were swifter than eagles,
stronger than lions.
24 O women of Israel, weep for Saul,
for he dressed you in luxurious scarlet clothing,
in garments decorated with gold.

1:25 2 Sam 1:19

25 Oh, how the mighty heroes have fallen in battle!
Jonathan lies dead on the hills.

1:26 1 Sam 18:1

26 How I weep for you, my brother Jonathan!
Oh, how much I loved you!
And your love for me was deep,
deeper than the love of women!
27 Oh, how the mighty heroes have fallen!
Stripped of their weapons, they lie dead.

DAVID ANOINTED KING OF JUDAH

2:1 Josh 14:13-14 1 Sam 23:2, 4, 9-12

2 After this, David asked the LORD, "Should I move back to one of the towns of Judah?"
"Yes," the LORD replied.

1:21 The meaning of the Hebrew is uncertain.

1:20 Gath and Ashkelon were two of the five principal cities of Philistia. Philistia was a warrior nation recognized for its large, fierce soldiers and its accomplishments in metallurgy (resulting in iron chariots). Israel was in conflict with Philistia throughout most of its history. At one time, Philistia ruled Israel for a forty-year span. The Philistines certainly would have rejoiced over Saul's death if they thought it meant that they had a better chance of subjugating Saul's people.

▸ SPIRITUAL WARFARE

1:26 Loving our friends. Given the exaggerated language of this ancient requiem, it would be easy to pass over this part of the lament. But we must not miss the message of this verse. David asserts that Jonathan's love for him was "deeper than the love of women!" This reveals that God intends men to have deep, abiding relationships with one another, relationships that impact their lives perhaps even more than their relationships with women. Indeed, Proverbs 17:17 and 18:24 indicate that friends sometimes are more beloved than brothers. No doubt there are friends who impact us even more than our spouses. Some wrongly believe these words of David mean that Jonathan's love for David was greater than his love for women—which could mean that Jonathan preferred loving David over women. Some cite this as an example of homosexuality in the Bible. Yes, God intends men to love each other deeply—that is clear. But no, this passage in no sense gives permission to ignore God's wise guidelines for sexual relationships. Acting on homosexual urges is never the loving thing to do (Romans 1:24-27). (***See Spiritual Warfare**> Resisting Sin and Evil> Resisting Temptation> What to Resist> We are to resist sinful urges,* TopicGuide page A45.)

2:1 Israel was organized into 12 tribes, each of which was an extended family descended from a man named Jacob (later named Israel). David's tribe was Judah, the descendants of Jacob's fourth son. Judah remained a prominent tribe throughout history; Jesus Himself was of the tribe of Judah (Genesis 49:8-12). After the reigns of David and his son Solomon, Israel divided into two kingdoms (1 Kings 12–14).

Then David asked, "Which town should I go to?"
"To Hebron," the LORD answered.
2David's two wives were Ahinoam from Jezreel and Abigail, the widow of Nabal from 2:2
Carmel. So David and his wives 3and his men and their families all moved to Judah, and 1 Sam 25:39, 42-43
they settled in the villages near Hebron. 4Then the men of Judah came to David and 2:4
crowned him king over the people of Judah. 1 Sam 16:13; 31:11-13
When David heard that the men of Jabesh-gilead had buried Saul, 5he sent them this 2 Sam 5:3-5 2:5
message: "May the LORD bless you for being so loyal to your master Saul and giving him a 1 Sam 23:21; 24:19
decent burial. 6May the LORD be loyal to you in return and reward you with His unfailing 2:6
love! And I, too, will reward you for what you have done. 7Now that Saul is dead, I ask you Exod 34:5-6
to be my strong and loyal subjects like the people of Judah, who have anointed me as
their new king."

2:2 By the end of his life, David had many more wives than Moses' instructions for Israel's king allowed (Deuteronomy 17:14-17). At this point, though, he had only two wives. He met Abigail on his way to take vengeance against her husband, Nabal, for an insult; then married her after God caused Nabal's death (1 Samuel 25). We don't know much about Ahinoam. David's first wife was Michal, daughter of King Saul. Saul later took Michal away from David and gave her to a man named Palti. After Saul's death, David asked for Michal back. According to 2 Samuel 3:15-16, on Michal's return trip, Palti followed her for miles, "weeping as he went."

2:3 David had built a small army during his years of fleeing from Saul. When David first fled to escape Saul's wrath, he made one failed attempt to seek refuge with King Achish in the Philistine city of Gath. He then fled from there to a cave at Adullam. His family joined him there, along with 400 volunteer soldiers. These men were "in trouble or in debt or who were just discontented" (1 Samuel 22:2). In a relatively short time, that group grew by 50 percent to 600 men. The only time the men threatened revolt was when they returned to their headquarters in Ziklag to find the town burned and their families taken captive. David led them on a successful rescue mission against the Amalekites and regained their loyalty.

▸ CHURCH

2:4 Family feud. Has your family ever had a feud with another family? How did it start? Did it ever end? Did (or does!) your relationship with God influence your conflicts with others? After years of running and fighting, David was crowned king of Judah in the south. But there was no rest for David. Abner, the commander of Saul's army, rallied the rest of Israel around one of Saul's sons, Ishbosheth. This was the beginning of a two-year civil war that caused a long feud between the relatives of David and the family of Saul. Only death would end it, for Saul's relatives would not relent in their hatred of David's family. Be different from Saul's family—let God's Spirit have His way in resolving conflict, and do not resist God's will for peace in your life. (***See Church****> Role> Conflict> Peacemaking,* TopicGuide page A49.)

2:5-7 One of David's first acts as king of Judah was to praise the people of Jabesh-gilead for their gallantry in recovering and burying the bodies of Saul and his sons who had fallen in battle. There is little reason to doubt that David was completely sincere in expressing his appreciation to the people of Jabesh-gilead, for he recognized that God had anointed Saul for the kingship, and so Saul deserved all respect. However, this royal praise and promise of reward also had a political motive, as it probably went a long way toward winning the hearts of the people of Jabesh-gilead. After his compliment, David openly asked them to give their loyalty to him, not Ishbosheth.

BECAUSE GOD IS LOVE

He is unconditionally committed to my well-being.

May the LORD be loyal to you in return and reward you with His unfailing love!

2 SAMUEL 2:6

ISHBOSHETH CROWNED KING OF ISRAEL

2:8 8But Abner son of Ner, the commander of Saul's army, had already gone to Mahanaim
1 Sam 14:50 2 Sam 17:24 with Saul's son Ishbosheth.* 9There he proclaimed Ishbosheth king over Gilead, Jezreel,
Ephraim, Benjamin, the land of the Ashurites, and all the rest of Israel.
10Ishbosheth, Saul's son, was forty years old when he became king, and he ruled from
Mahanaim for two years. Meanwhile, the people of Judah remained loyal to David. 11David made Hebron his capital, and he ruled as king of Judah for seven and a half years.

WAR BETWEEN ISRAEL AND JUDAH

2:12 12One day Abner led Ishbosheth's troops from Mahanaim to Gibeon. 13About the same
Josh 10:12 time, Joab son of Zeruiah led David's troops out and met them at the pool of Gibeon. The
2:13 2 Sam 8:16 two groups sat down there, facing each other from opposite sides of the pool.
1 Chr 2:16; 11:5-6 14Then Abner suggested to Joab, "Let's have a few of our warriors fight hand to hand
here in front of us."
"All right," Joab agreed. 15So twelve men were chosen to fight from each side—twelve men
of Benjamin representing Ishbosheth son of Saul, and twelve representing David. 16Each one
grabbed his opponent by the hair and thrust his sword into the other's side so that all of them
died. So this place at Gibeon has been known ever since as the Field of Swords.*
2:17 17A fierce battle followed that day, and Abner and the men of Israel were defeated by
2 Sam 3:1 the forces of David.

THE DEATH OF ASAHEL

2:18 18Joab, Abishai, and Asahel—the three sons of Zeruiah—were among David's forces that
1 Chr 2:16; 11:26; 12:8 day. Asahel could run like a gazelle, 19and he began chasing Abner. He pursued him relentlessly, not stopping for anything. 20When Abner looked back and saw him coming, he
called out, "Is that you, Asahel?"
"Yes, it is," he replied.
21"Go fight someone else!" Abner warned. "Take on one of the younger men, and strip
him of his weapons." But Asahel kept right on chasing Abner.
2:22 22Again Abner shouted to him, "Get away from here! I don't want to kill you. How could I
2 Sam 3:27 ever face your brother Joab again?"
23But Asahel refused to turn back, so Abner thrust the butt end of his spear through Asahel's stomach, and the spear came out through his back. He stumbled to the ground and
died there. And everyone who came by that spot stopped and stood still when they saw
Asahel lying there.
24When Joab and Abishai found out what had happened, they set out after Abner. The
sun was just going down as they arrived at the hill of Ammah near Giah, along the road to
the wilderness of Gibeon. 25Abner's troops from the tribe of Benjamin regrouped there at
the top of the hill to take a stand.

2:8 *Ishbosheth* is another name for Esh-baal. 2:16 Hebrew *Helkath-hazzurim.*

2:12-13 Gibeon was a city just northwest of Jerusalem. When the Israelites first entered the land of Canaan, the Gibeonites duped Joshua into making an unlawful treaty with them (Joshua 9). Joshua, therefore, let the Gibeonites live, but as servants for the Israelites. These people were also identified as Hivites. The Hivites were descendants of Noah's grandson Canaan, the son of Ham.

2:14 When the army of David, led by Joab, met the army of Ishbosheth, led by Abner, in Gibeon, they did not immediately begin to fight. Instead, Abner suggested an "exhibition" by soldiers from each army. It is very possible that he was proposing a representative conflict—the army of the winning twelve-man team would be recognized as the winner of the "battle." Goliath proposed just such a conflict when he challenged the Israelites to send out a champion to face him, with the loser's army serving the winner's. David, of course, defeated Goliath, but the Philistines fled and did not follow through on Goliath's proposal. In this case, the exhibition ended in a draw and a full-fledged battle erupted.

2:18 As David's army gained the upper hand in the battle, Asahel doggedly pursued Abner, the commander of Ishbosheth's army. Asahel was a nephew of David, and he may have wanted to achieve a battlefield exploit that would somewhat rival his uncle's triumph over Goliath. Whatever his motives, they drove him to take on a warrior who was too experienced for him, and he lost his life.

[26]Abner shouted down to Joab, "Must we always be killing each other? Don't you realize 2:26 Deut 32:42
that bitterness is the only result? When will you call off your men from chasing their Israel-
ite brothers?"

[27]Then Joab said, "God only knows what would have happened if you hadn't spoken,
for we would have chased you all night if necessary." [28]So Joab blew the ram's horn, and
his men stopped chasing the troops of Israel.

[29]All that night Abner and his men retreated through the Jordan Valley.* They crossed 2:29 Deut 3:17
the Jordan River, traveling all through the morning,* and didn't stop until they arrived at
Mahanaim.

[30]Meanwhile, Joab and his men also returned home. When Joab counted his casualties,
he discovered that only 19 men were missing in addition to Asahel. [31]But 360 of Abner's
men had been killed, all from the tribe of Benjamin. [32]Joab and his men took Asahel's 2:32 Gen 49:29
body to Bethlehem and buried him there in his father's tomb. Then they traveled all night
and reached Hebron at daybreak.

3 That was the beginning of a long war between those who were loyal to Saul and 3:1 1 Kgs 14:30
those loyal to David. As time passed David became stronger and stronger, while
Saul's dynasty became weaker and weaker.

DAVID'S SONS BORN IN HEBRON

3:2-5 //1 Chr 3:1-4

[2]These are the sons who were born to David in Hebron:

3:2 1 Sam 25:43 2 Sam 13:1 1 Chr 3:1

The oldest was Amnon, whose mother was Ahinoam from Jezreel.
[3]The second was Daniel,* whose mother was Abigail, the widow of Nabal from Carmel.
The third was Absalom, whose mother was Maacah, the daughter of Talmai, king of Geshur.
[4]The fourth was Adonijah, whose mother was Haggith.
The fifth was Shephatiah, whose mother was Abital.
[5]The sixth was Ithream, whose mother was Eglah, David's wife.

3:3 1 Sam 25:42 1 Chr 3:2

3:4 1 Chr 3:2-3

3:5 1 Chr 3:3

These sons were all born to David in Hebron.

ABNER JOINS FORCES WITH DAVID

[6]As the war between the house of Saul and the house of David went on, Abner became a
powerful leader among those loyal to Saul. [7]One day Ishbosheth,* Saul's son, accused 3:7 2 Sam 21:8-11
Abner of sleeping with one of his father's concubines, a woman named Rizpah, daughter
of Aiah.

2:29a Hebrew *the Arabah.* 2:29b Or *continued on through the Bithron.* The meaning of the Hebrew is uncertain. 3:3 As in parallel text at 1 Chr 3:1 (see also Greek version, which reads *Daluia,* and Dead Sea Scrolls, which read *Dan[iel]*); Hebrew reads *Kileab.* 3:7 *Ishbosheth* is another name for Esh-baal.

▸ CHURCH

2:26 Violence and war. War is always destructive. Sometimes it is necessary, but it can degenerate into meaningless violence with no value to either side. In the middle of life-and-death combat, Abner suddenly understood how empty this conflict was and, seeing his men falling around him, pleaded with Joab to stop the deadly chase. You must have the courage to stop conflict when it is not producing the ultimate goal—the glory of God. Be God's peacemaker in contentious situations (James 3:18). (***See Church*** *> Role> Conflict> Restoration,* TopicGuide page A49.)

3:1 Saul's family grew weaker over time while David's grew stronger, so the advantage in the civil war gradually shifted to David. God had anointed David as the next king of Israel, but He brought His will to pass in a gradual manner, probably to refine David in order that he might be the prototype for all of Israel's future kings.

3:2-5 By taking multiple wives and concubines, and so producing many possible heirs to his throne (see the complete list of David's children in 1 Chronicles 3:1-9), David was following the royal tradition of the Ancient Near East. However, this behavior fell short of God's standard for Israel's kings (see Deuteronomy 17:17).

3:7 Ishbosheth's accusation was a serious one. In this culture, a concubine was a legitimate member of the family. More significantly, however, Rizpah was part of the royal harem. If Abner truly slept with her, he was making a claim to the throne, either purposely or inadvertently. Abner was the power behind Ishbosheth, but he had no legitimate claim to the kingship. Later, when David ascended to Israel's throne, Saul's harem became a part of his household (2 Samuel 12:8).

3:8 8Abner was furious. "Am I some Judean dog to be kicked around like this?" he shouted. "Af-
1 Sam 24:14; 2 Sam 9:8; 16:9 ter all I have done for your father, Saul, and his family and friends by not handing you over to
David, is this my reward—that you find fault with me about this woman? 9May God strike me
3:9 1 Sam 15:28 and even kill me if I don't do everything I can to help David get what the LORD has promised
him! 10I'm going to take Saul's kingdom and give it to David. I will establish the throne of Da-
vid over Israel as well as Judah, all the way from Dan in the north to Beersheba in the south."
11Ishbosheth didn't dare say another word because he was afraid of what Abner might do.
12Then Abner sent messengers to David, saying, "Doesn't the entire land belong to you?
Make a solemn pact with me, and I will help turn over all of Israel to you."
3:13 13"All right," David replied, "but I will not negotiate with you unless you bring back my
1 Sam 18:20 wife Michal, Saul's daughter, when you come."
3:14 14David then sent this message to Ishbosheth, Saul's son: "Give me back my wife Mi-
1 Sam 18:25-27 chal, for I bought her with the lives* of 100 Philistines."
3:15 1 Sam 25:44 15So Ishbosheth took Michal away from her husband, Palti* son of Laish. 16Palti followed
along behind her as far as Bahurim, weeping as he went. Then Abner told him, "Go back
3:16 2 Sam 16:5 home!" So Palti returned.
3:18 17Meanwhile, Abner had consulted with the elders of Israel. "For some time now," he told
1 Sam 9:16; 15:28 them, "you have wanted to make David your king. 18Now is the time! For the LORD has said,
3:19 'I have chosen David to save My people Israel from the hands of the Philistines and from all
1 Sam 10:20-21; 1 Chr 12:29 their other enemies.'" 19Abner also spoke with the men of Benjamin. Then he went to He-
bron to tell David that all the people of Israel and Benjamin had agreed to support him.
20When Abner and twenty of his men came to Hebron, David entertained them with a
3:21 great feast. 21Then Abner said to David, "Let me go and call an assembly of all Israel to sup-
1 Kgs 11:37 port my lord the king. They will make a covenant with you to make you their king, and you
will rule over everything your heart desires." So David sent Abner safely on his way.

JOAB MURDERS ABNER

3:22 22But just after David had sent Abner away in safety, Joab and some of David's troops
1 Sam 27:8 returned from a raid, bringing much plunder with them. 23When Joab arrived, he was told
that Abner had just been there visiting the king and had been sent away in safety.
3:24 24Joab rushed to the king and demanded, "What have you done? What do you mean
1 Sam 29:3 by letting Abner get away? 25You know perfectly well that he came to spy on you and find
out everything you're doing!"
26Joab then left David and sent messengers to catch up with Abner, asking him to
return. They found him at the well of Sirah and brought him back, though David knew

3:14 Hebrew *the foreskins.* 3:15 As in 1 Sam 25:44; Hebrew reads *Paltiel,* a variant spelling of Palti.

3:10 The phrase "from Dan in the north to Beersheba in the south" was used to refer to the whole nation of Israel.

▸ BIBLE

3:12 Political motives. Even in our best moments of obedience, we have mixed motives. For instance, perhaps you give money to the church, yet you secretly hope this will increase your standing with those who keep records of donations. Or you share the gospel boldly, not simply because you love Christ and want to see other people love Him, but because giving spiritual advice makes you feel powerful. Likewise, Abner did the right thing—he took steps to unify Israel and Judah—but he was motivated by revenge and embarrassment (3:7), and by a desire to end a violent period of Israelite history (2 Samuel 2:26). God has given us His Spirit and His Word to inform our consciences and help us to repent when we recognize sinful motives. By God's grace, continue to grow in your courageous repentance until you stand before Him, perfect and complete (1 John 4:17). (***See Bible****> Uniqueness> Authoritative> Demands repentance,* TopicGuide page A10.)

3:13-14 Michal is first mentioned in Scripture because of her love for David. At the time, David was not a rich man and could not pay a bride-price worth a king's daughter. Instead, Saul asked David for the foreskins of 100 Philistines, secretly hoping that David would be killed in the process of getting them. In his zeal, David brought Saul 200 Philistine foreskins rather than the 100 required and recorded here (1 Samuel 18:25-27).

3:17-19 Abner followed through on his threat to transfer his loyalties from Ishbosheth to David. His first step was to meet with the leaders of Israel and to urge them to join him in backing David. He grandiosely told the leaders that David was God's choice for the throne, conveniently overlooking the fact that he himself had been opposing David on Ishbosheth's behalf for years. Finally, he met with the leaders of Benjamin, the tribe of Saul, Ishbosheth, and Abner himself. When he finally went to David, he was conveying assurances that all the people of Israel, even the people of Benjamin, were on David's side.

nothing about it. 27 When Abner arrived back at Hebron, Joab took him aside at the gate- **3:27**
way as if to speak with him privately. But then he stabbed Abner in the stomach and 2 Sam 2:22-23; 20:8-10
killed him in revenge for killing his brother Asahel. 1 Kgs 2:5
28 When David heard about it, he declared, "I vow by the LORD that I and my kingdom are
forever innocent of this crime against Abner son of Ner. 29 Joab and his family are the **3:29**
guilty ones. May the family of Joab be cursed in every generation with a man who has Lev 13:45-46 Deut 21:7-8
open sores or leprosy* or who walks on crutches* or dies by the sword or begs for food!" 1 Kgs 2:31-33
30 So Joab and his brother Abishai killed Abner because Abner had killed their brother **3:30**
Asahel at the battle of Gibeon. 2 Sam 2:23

DAVID MOURNS ABNER'S DEATH

31 Then David said to Joab and all those who were with him, "Tear your clothes and put on **3:31**
burlap. Mourn for Abner." And King David himself walked behind the procession to the Gen 37:34 Judg 11:35
grave. 32 They buried Abner in Hebron, and the king and all the people wept at his **3:32**
graveside. 33 Then the king sang this funeral song for Abner: Prov 24:17

"Should Abner have died as fools die?
34 Your hands were not bound;
  your feet were not chained.
No, you were murdered—
  the victim of a wicked plot."

All the people wept again for Abner. 35 David had refused to eat anything on the day of **3:35**
the funeral, and now everyone begged him to eat. But David had made a vow, saying, 2 Sam 1:12; 12:17
"May God strike me and even kill me if I eat anything before sundown."
36 This pleased the people very much. In fact, everything the king did pleased them! 37 So
everyone in Judah and all Israel understood that David was not responsible for Abner's
murder.
38 Then King David said to his officials, "Don't you realize that a great commander has
fallen today in Israel? 39 And even though I am the anointed king, these two sons of Zerui- **3:39**
ah—Joab and Abishai—are too strong for me to control. So may the LORD repay these evil 2 Sam 19:5-7
men for their evil deeds."

THE MURDER OF ISHBOSHETH

4 When Ishbosheth,* Saul's son, heard about Abner's death at Hebron, he lost all **4:1**
courage, and all Israel became paralyzed with fear. 2 Now there were two brothers, 2 Sam 3:27
Baanah and Recab, who were captains of Ishbosheth's raiding parties. They were sons of **4:2**
Rimmon, a member of the tribe of Benjamin who lived in Beeroth. The town of Beeroth is Josh 9:17; 18:25
now part of Benjamin's territory 3 because the original people of Beeroth fled to Gittaim, **4:3**
where they still live as foreigners. Neh 11:33

3:29a Or *or a contagious skin disease.* The Hebrew word used here can describe various skin diseases. 3:29b Or *who is effeminate;* Hebrew reads *who handles a spindle.* 4:1 *Ishbosheth* is another name for Esh-baal.

3:27 David was willing to receive Abner and make peace, but Joab, David's nephew and commander of his army, was not. He bore a deep grudge against Abner for killing his younger brother, Asahel, in battle. Under certain circumstances, a family member could act as a "blood avenger" to retaliate for the murder of a family member. But Asahel had died in his role as a soldier after Abner had warned him to cease and desist. Joab had no right to take Abner's life, especially since David had received Abner in peace.

▸ WORSHIP

4:1 Frozen with fear. This section of the Old Testament has much to teach us about leadership. This text in particular reveals some of the differences between godly leadership and sinful, immature leadership. First, Ishbosheth panicked after hearing that his powerful general had died, for his means of controlling the military had died with Abner. Ishbosheth trusted in his own power and control, not God. Second, notice that all those surrounding Ishbosheth panicked as well. He had not chosen counselors with different perspectives to bring wisdom to his decisions. Instead, he had surrounded himself with people who were, sadly, as pathetic as himself. This foolish king of Israel had surrounded himself with other weaklings, and no one can continue to lead in such a tenuous situation. (***See Worship**> OT> Reverence> God helps those who fear Him,* TopicGuide page A29.)

4:1, 4 First Chronicles describes the same era as 2 Samuel. In Chronicles, though, Ishbosheth and Mephibosheth are called

4:4 [4](Saul's son Jonathan had a son named Mephibosheth,* who was crippled as a child. He
1 Sam 31:1-4 was five years old when the report came from Jezreel that Saul and Jonathan had been
2 Sam 9:3, 5-6; 1 Chr 8:34; 9:40 killed in battle. When the child's nurse heard the news, she picked him up and fled. But as
she hurried away, she dropped him, and he became crippled.)
4:5 [5]One day Recab and Baanah, the sons of Rimmon from Beeroth, went to Ishbosheth's
2 Sam 2:8 house around noon as he was taking his midday rest. [6]The doorkeeper, who had been sift-
4:6 2 Sam 2:23 ing wheat, became drowsy and fell asleep. So Recab and Baanah slipped past her.*
[7]They went into the house and found Ishbosheth sleeping on his bed. They struck and
killed him and cut off his head. Then, taking his head with them, they fled across the Jor-
dan Valley* through the night. [8]When they arrived at Hebron, they presented Ishbosheth's
head to David. "Look!" they exclaimed to the king. "Here is the head of Ishbosheth, the son
of your enemy Saul who tried to kill you. Today the LORD has given my lord the king re-
venge on Saul and his entire family!"
4:9 [9]But David said to Recab and Baanah, "The LORD, who saves me from all my enemies, is my
1 Kgs 1:29 witness. [10]Someone once told me, 'Saul is dead,' thinking he was bringing me good news. But
4:10 2 Sam 1:1-2, 4, 15 I seized him and killed him at Ziklag. That's the reward I gave him for his news! [11]How much
more should I reward evil men who have killed an innocent man in his own house and on his
4:11 Gen 9:5 own bed? Shouldn't I hold you responsible for his blood and rid the earth of you?"
Ps 9:12 [12]So David ordered his young men to kill them, and they did. They cut off their hands
4:12 and feet and hung their bodies beside the pool in Hebron. Then they took Ishbosheth's
2 Sam 1:15; 3:32 head and buried it in Abner's tomb in Hebron.

5:1-3 //1 Chr 11:1-3

DAVID BECOMES KING OF ALL ISRAEL

5 Then all the tribes of Israel went to David at Hebron and told him, "We are your own
5:2 1 Sam 18:5, 14; 25:30 flesh and blood. [2]In the past,* when Saul was our king, you were the one who really

4:4 *Mephibosheth* is another name for Merib-baal. 4:6 As in Greek version; Hebrew reads *So they went into the house pretending to fetch wheat, but they stabbed him in the stomach. Then Recab and Baanah escaped.* 4:7 Hebrew *the Arabah.* 5:2 Or *For some time.*

by what probably were their original names, Esh-Baal and Merib-Baal. The use of the word *baal* in Israelite names was common for a time, with *baal* meaning "master," but later generations frowned on the use of the word because of the god named Baal. Thus, the author of Samuel replaced the word *baal* in the names with the Hebrew word for shame, *bosheth.*

4:4 The mention of crippled Mephibosheth underlines the weakness of the house of Saul. Mephibosheth is mentioned throughout 2 Samuel to point out Saul's weakness and David's kindness (9:6-13; 16:1-4; 19:24-30; 21:7).

4:8-12 Recab and Baanah portrayed themselves as God's instruments to wreak vengeance on David's enemies. In all likelihood, they were only trying to obtain royal favor, but in a sense they were right—God certainly used the death of Ishbosheth to vindicate David and advance his cause. For this reason, David freely acknowledged that God was the One "who saves me from all my enemies." But God's use of Recab's and Baanah's sinful actions did not excuse them. David correctly judged them and required payment for their crime against Ishbosheth.

▸ SPIRITUAL WARFARE

4:11 No mourning allowed. David was a consistent man. He did not honor the man who claimed to have struck down the helpless Saul, and he refused to honor these cowards who had killed Ishbosheth. He found them guilty of a capital crime and had them executed. But why were the men's bodies mutilated? This question isn't directly answered in the Bible, but indirectly we have two clues. First, it made clear that David in no way approved of their assassination of Israel's king. Second, in David's time, murder was seen as a sin associated with the hands (Deuteronomy 21:7; Proverbs 6:16-17), so cutting off the hands symbolized their crime of murder. Similarly, uncovered or unkempt feet were often associated with mourning (2 Samuel 15:30; 19:24) in this part of Israel's history, so cutting off the feet communicated that no mourning was permitted for these scoundrels. No matter what the results, a godly leader will not honor cowardly and sinful tactics against those he opposes. Such behavior is unacceptable in Christian ministry and business, just as it was in David's royal court. (***See Spiritual Warfare****> Resisting Sin and Evil> Consequences> Of Disobedience> Death,* TopicGuide page A46.)

5:1-2 The leaders of Israel's tribes gave several reasons for anointing David as king. First, they declared that David was their kinsman and that they were his "own flesh and blood." Second, they acknowledged that David had functioned as Israel's leader even when Saul was still on the throne (5:2). Third, they cited the fact that God had told David, through the prophet and judge Samuel, that he would be king (1 Samuel 16).

▸ WORSHIP

5:1-3 Recognizing God's spokesman. God humbled rebellious Israel at last. The people finally recognized David as their true king, but that's not all. They also recognized him as a legitimate source of revelation from God—David was able to speak God's word. This affirmation caused future generations to gather and carefully preserve the poems and psalms of David, correctly treating them as special revelation from God. We can trust that God always gives His people the ability to recognize and receive His Word of truth. (***See Worship****> OT> Music> Psalms,* TopicGuide page A27.)

led the forces of Israel. And the LORD told you, 'You will be the shepherd of My people Isra-
el. You will be Israel's leader.'"
3 So there at Hebron, King David made a covenant before the LORD with all the elders of
Israel. And they anointed him king of Israel.
4 David was thirty years old when he began to reign, and he reigned forty years in all.
5 He had reigned over Judah from Hebron for seven years and six months, and from Jeru-
salem he reigned over all Israel and Judah for thirty-three years.

DAVID CAPTURES JERUSALEM

6 David then led his men to Jerusalem to fight against the Jebusites, the original inhabi-
tants of the land who were living there. The Jebusites taunted David, saying, "You'll never
get in here! Even the blind and lame could keep you out!" For the Jebusites thought they
were safe. 7 But David captured the fortress of Zion, which is now called the City of David.
8 On the day of the attack, David said to his troops, "I hate those 'lame' and 'blind' Jebu-
sites.* Whoever attacks them should strike by going into the city through the water tun-
nel.*" That is the origin of the saying, "The blind and the lame may not enter the house."*
9 So David made the fortress his home, and he called it the City of David. He extended
the city, starting at the supporting terraces* and working inward. 10 And David became
more and more powerful, because the LORD God of Heaven's Armies was with him.
11 Then King Hiram of Tyre sent messengers to David, along with cedar timber and car-
penters and stonemasons, and they built David a palace. 12 And David realized that the
LORD had confirmed him as king over Israel and had blessed his kingdom for the sake of
His people Israel.
13 After moving from Hebron to Jerusalem, David married more concubines and wives,
and they had more sons and daughters. 14 These are the names of David's sons who were
born in Jerusalem: Shammua, Shobab, Nathan, Solomon, 15 Ibhar, Elishua, Nepheg, Ja-
phia, 16 Elishama, Eliada, and Eliphelet.

DAVID CONQUERS THE PHILISTINES

17 When the Philistines heard that David had been anointed king of Israel, they mobilized all
their forces to capture him. But David was told they were coming, so he went into the strong-

5:3 1 Sam 16:1, 13; 2 Sam 2:4; 3:21
5:4 Gen 41:46; 1 Kgs 2:11; Luke 3:23
5:6-10 //1 Chr 11:4-9
5:7 1 Kgs 2:10
5:9 1 Kgs 9:15, 24
5:10 2 Sam 3:1
5:11-16 //1 Chr 3:5-9; 14:1-7
5:11 1 Kgs 5:10, 18; 1 Chr 14:1
5:12 Num 24:7
5:13 Deut 17:17; 1 Chr 3:9
5:14 1 Chr 3:5
5:17-25 //1 Chr 14:8-17

5:8a Or *Those 'lame' and 'blind' Jebusites hate me.* 5:8b Or *with scaling hooks.* The meaning of the Hebrew is uncertain. 5:8c The meaning of this saying is uncertain. 5:9 Hebrew *the millo.* The meaning of the Hebrew is uncertain.

5:3 One of many proofs of the supernatural inspiration of Scripture is the fulfillment of prophecies. Almost 1,000 years earlier, Jacob had prophesied that the dynastic kingship of Israel would fall to the tribe of his son Judah (Genesis 49:10). Now David, a member of that tribe, became king of Israel.

5:4-5 Numbers in the Bible are often rounded up or down, in sharp contrast to the concern in many Western cultures for exact figures. For example, David reigned 7½ years in Hebron plus 33 years in Jerusalem, for a total of 40½ years, but the length of his reign is rounded off to 40 years.

5:6-7 The "City of David," captured from the Jebusites, was very small, only 13 acres. However, it was to assume great importance in Israel's national life. Hebron, David's capital while he reigned over Judah, was too far south to serve as a center of government and commerce for all Israel. Shechem and Shiloh were both important cities, but were too far north for people from Judah to reach. Jerusalem was the most strategically located site for David's capital. Plus, it was still a stronghold for a pagan people, the Jebusites. In taking their city, David defeated some of God's enemies.

▶ BIBLE

5:12 God's promises come true. After years of running and hiding, finally it began to sink in—David was king! But it wasn't for David's sake that God was making Israel great; it was so that Israel would be blessed. A blessed Israel would function as a pulpit from which the kingdom rule and covenant blessings of God would overflow into all the nations. This would fulfill the promises God had made to Abraham (Genesis 12:1-3) and prepare the world for the coming Messiah, who would come from David's family to fulfill His kingly ministry. So rejoice: God's promises to Abraham came true through David; God's promises to David came true in Christ; and God's promises to Christ come true in you! (***See Bible***> *Unity*> *Christ*> *Christ in the promise to Abraham,* TopicGuide page A10.)

5:17-25 After David became king, the Philistines set out to dethrone him. They obviously did not like the prospect of a unified Israel and hoped to defeat David before he could consolidate his power. David carefully consulted God before taking any action against these enemies, but God assured him and even ordered the battle strategy in one instance. Then David gave praise to God for the victory, proclaiming, "The LORD did it!" God was using David to defeat Israel's enemies, just as Abner had foreseen (3:18).

5:18 Josh 15:8; 18:16 hold. [18]The Philistines arrived and spread out across the valley of Rephaim. [19]So David
asked the LORD, "Should I go out to fight the Philistines? Will You hand them over to me?"
5:19 1 Sam 23:2 The LORD replied to David, "Yes, go ahead. I will certainly hand them over to you."
[20]So David went to Baal-perazim and defeated the Philistines there. "The LORD did it!"
5:20 1 Chr 14:11 David exclaimed. "He burst through my enemies like a raging flood!" So he named that
place Baal-perazim (which means "the Lord who bursts through"). [21]The Philistines had
abandoned their idols there, so David and his men confiscated them.
[22]But after a while the Philistines returned and again spread out across the valley of
Rephaim. [23]And again David asked the LORD what to do. "Do not attack them straight on,"
the LORD replied. "Instead, circle around behind and attack them near the poplar* trees.
5:24 Judg 4:14 [24]When you hear a sound like marching feet in the tops of the poplar trees, be on the alert!
That will be the signal that the LORD is moving ahead of you to strike down the Philistine
5:25 Josh 12:12; 21:20-22 army." [25]So David did what the LORD commanded, and he struck down the Philistines all
the way from Gibeon* to Gezer.

MOVING THE ARK TO JERUSALEM

6:1-11 //1 Chr 13:1-14 **6** Then David again gathered all the elite troops in Israel, 30,000 in all. [2]He led them to
Baalah of Judah* to bring back the Ark of God, which bears the name of the LORD of
6:2 Lev 24:16 Heaven's Armies,* who is enthroned between the cherubim. [3]They placed the Ark of God
6:3 Num 7:4-9 on a new cart and brought it from Abinadab's house, which was on a hill. Uzzah and Ahio,
Abinadab's sons, were guiding the cart as it left the house, [4]carrying the Ark of God. Ahio
1 Sam 6:7 walked in front of the Ark. [5]David and all the people of Israel were celebrating before the
6:5 1 Chr 13:7-8; 16:5 LORD, singing songs* and playing all kinds of musical instruments—lyres, harps, tambourines, castanets, and cymbals.
6:6 Num 4:15 [6]But when they arrived at the threshing floor of Nacon, the oxen stumbled, and Uzzah
reached out his hand and steadied the Ark of God. [7]Then the LORD's anger was aroused
6:7 1 Sam 6:19 against Uzzah, and God struck him dead because of this.* So Uzzah died right there beside
the Ark of God.

5:23 Or *aspen,* or *balsam;* also in 5:24. The exact identification of this tree is uncertain. 5:25 As in Greek version (see also 1 Chr 14:16); Hebrew reads *Geba.* 6:2a *Baalah of Judah* is another name for Kiriath-jearim; compare 1 Chr 13:6. 6:2b Or *the Ark of God where the Name is proclaimed—the name of the LORD of Heaven's Armies.* 6:5 As in Greek version (see also 1 Chr 13:8); Hebrew reads *before the LORD with all manner of cypress trees.* 6:7 As in Dead Sea Scrolls; Masoretic Text reads *because of his irreverence.*

6:1 David mobilized all the elite troops in Israel, 30,000 in all, as if in preparation for a battle. However, he intended for them to serve as a military honor guard for Israel's God.

6:2 The "Ark of God" was also called the Ark of the Covenant. It was a wooden chest made to God's specifications (Exodus 25–26). Inside were national treasures: the tablets of the Ten Commandments, a jar of manna, and Aaron's rod that budded (Hebrews 9:4). The Hebrew term for the lid of the Ark is sometimes translated "the mercy seat"; it represented both God's heavenly throne and God's purpose to cleanse His people of their sins. The Ark had been in the home of Abinadab for 20 years following a brief capture by the Philistines (1 Samuel 4–7). David wanted to bring it to Jerusalem so that God's throne might rest in Israel's new capital.

6:3 Problems with the transfer of the Ark began to crop up almost immediately. First, it was brought out in plain view of the thousands of people who had gathered at Abinadab's home. But God had dictated that Israel's priests cover the Ark before it was moved so that even its carriers could not gaze upon it (Numbers 4:5, 20). Second, it was placed on a cart. But God had said the Ark was to be carried by men of the tribe of Levi using poles inserted through rings on the Ark (Numbers 7:9). David was attempting to do a good thing without proper regard for God-given procedures.

▶ GOD
6:5 How was your worship? The question to ask in the car after Sunday morning worship is not, "How was worship today?" but, "How was *your* worship today?" David and his people worshiped God with all their might—they gave every part of their bodies, every talent they possessed, to the almighty God. When is the last time you gave God everything in your worship? What would it look like if you were an active, selfless worshiper on the next Lord's day? (***See God****> Relationship> God Enables> Relationship with God requires worship,* TopicGuide page A14.)

6:6-7 When the oxen stumbled, Uzzah put out his hand to steady the Ark lest it tumble onto the ground. Instantly, God struck him dead. Was this an overreaction by God? Not at all. God already had tolerated the failure of the Israelites to cover the Ark and to use Levites to carry it. But He had said in His law that touching the Ark was punishable by death (Numbers 4:15). Uzzah's disregard for this clear command brought an outburst of holy wrath intended to remind the Israelites of the One with whom they were dealing.

8David was angry because the LORD's anger had burst out against Uzzah. He named that
place Perez-uzzah (which means "to burst out against Uzzah"), as it is still called today.
9David was now afraid of the LORD, and he asked, "How can I ever bring the Ark of the
LORD back into my care?" 10So David decided not to move the Ark of the LORD into the City **6:10**
of David. Instead, he took it to the house of Obed-edom of Gath. 11The Ark of the LORD re- 1 Chr 26:4-5
mained there in Obed-edom's house for three months, and the LORD blessed Obed-edom
and his entire household. **6:12-19**
12Then King David was told, "The LORD has blessed Obed-edom's household and every- 1 Chr 15:25–16:3 **6:12**
thing he has because of the Ark of God." So David went there and brought the Ark of God 1 Kgs 8:1
from the house of Obed-edom to the City of David with a great celebration. 13After the **6:13**
men who were carrying the Ark of the LORD had gone six steps, David sacrificed a bull and 1 Kgs 8:5
a fattened calf. 14And David danced before the LORD with all his might, wearing a priestly **6:14**
garment.* 15So David and all the people of Israel brought up the Ark of the LORD with Exod 15:20
shouts of joy and the blowing of rams' horns. 1 Sam 2:18, 28

MICHAL'S CONTEMPT FOR DAVID

16But as the Ark of the LORD entered the City of David, Michal, the daughter of Saul, looked **6:16**
down from her window. When she saw King David leaping and dancing before the LORD, 1 Sam 18:27
she was filled with contempt for him.
17They brought the Ark of the LORD and set it in its place inside the special tent David **6:17**
had prepared for it. And David sacrificed burnt offerings and peace offerings to the LORD. 1 Kgs 8:62-65 1 Chr 15:1
18When he had finished his sacrifices, David blessed the people in the name of the LORD of 2 Chr 1:4
Heaven's Armies. 19Then he gave to every Israelite man and woman in the crowd a loaf of
bread, a cake of dates,* and a cake of raisins. Then all the people returned to their homes.
20When David returned home to bless his own family, Michal, the daughter of Saul,

6:14 Hebrew *a linen ephod.* 6:19 Or *a portion of meat.* The meaning of the Hebrew is uncertain.

6:8 The words "as it is still called today" tell us that this material was composed at a significantly later time. Traditionally, it is said that 1 and 2 Samuel were composed hundreds of years later, but that its sources were the writings of Samuel and other prophets like Nathan. The books of Samuel were likely written before 1 and 2 Kings, which reached their final state approximately 500 years later.

▸ GOD

6:8 Great loss. Have you ever made a mistake in a relationship that resulted in a great loss? David made an enormous mistake in his relationship with God by disregarding His commandments about the treatment of the Ark. David may have been angry at God's judgment, Uzzah's irreverence, or himself as he realized the many ways he had disregarded God's instructions concerning the Ark. But our God is holy. We must not think that we can casually disregard His teachings concerning how He is to be served. Jesus is our Friend, God is our Father, and the Holy Spirit is the Comforter, but we must respect God's guidelines for His gracious relationship with us. (***See God****> God's Attributes> Just> God's law and judgments are completely righteous,* TopicGuide page A16.)

6:9-11 When David's anger cooled, it was replaced by fear that he or his people might be harmed if he brought the Ark to Jerusalem. He shelved his plan to move the Ark and left it in the care of a family living near the site of Uzzah's death. This family apparently treated the Ark with proper reverence, and God blessed them for it. Eventually, God's mercy toward this family restored David's confidence, and he resolved once again to move the Ark.

▸ BIBLE

6:13 Learning from our mistakes. A wise person learns from the past. When David made his second attempt to move the Ark, it was not pulled by oxen but carried by men (Levites, we assume) as God had commanded. Also, taking nothing for granted, solemn sacrifices were made along the way, symbolizing the people's need for atonement for the sins they had committed (and might still be committing) while moving the cart. All God's people should learn from their past sins, but take nothing for granted in the future. Wisdom gained from past transgressions does not rule out the possibility of future sin. (***See Bible****> Power> Wisdom> Instruction through God's Word,* TopicGuide page A11.)

6:17 David prepared a special tent for the Ark of the Covenant in Jerusalem. Of course, from the time of its construction under Moses 400 years earlier, the Ark was kept in a tent known as the Tabernacle (Exodus 40). Evidently the Tabernacle had been destroyed by David's time.

▸ WORSHIP

6:20 Making fun. Have you ever ridiculed people in your own church (or family) for the way they worship? Does that remind you of Michal's attitude toward David? As the procession entered the city, David was dancing breathlessly in an act of humble worship before the Lord. Michal was disgusted by this episode, but those who loved God and the king thought it was beautiful (6:22). We should be accepting of people who worship in a form different from us and be mindful that God looks at the heart when we sing, dance, play instruments, and pray. God does not have a worship style preference; He has a worship heart preference. Worship God with all your heart and according to Scriptural guidelines, and see how He blesses you. (***See Worship****> OT> Posture> Dancing> David danced before the Lord,* TopicGuide page A26.)

came out to meet him. She said in disgust, "How distinguished the king of Israel looked to-
day, shamelessly exposing himself to the servant girls like any vulgar person might do!"
6:21 21David retorted to Michal, "I was dancing before the LORD, who chose me above your
1 Sam 13:14 father and all his family! He appointed me as the leader of Israel, the people of the LORD,
so I celebrate before the LORD. 22Yes, and I am willing to look even more foolish than this,
even to be humiliated in my own eyes! But those servant girls you mentioned will indeed
think I am distinguished!" 23So Michal, the daughter of Saul, remained childless through-
out her entire life.

THE LORD'S COVENANT PROMISE TO DAVID

7:1-17 **7** When King David was settled in his palace and the LORD had given him rest from all
//1 Chr 17:1-15 the surrounding enemies, 2the king summoned Nathan the prophet. "Look," David
7:2 said, "I am living in a beautiful cedar palace,* but the Ark of God is out there in a tent!"
2 Sam 5:11
1 Kgs 1:22 3Nathan replied to the king, "Go ahead and do whatever you have in mind, for the LORD
1 Chr 29:29 is with you."
4But that same night the LORD said to Nathan,

7:5 5"Go and tell My servant David, 'This is what the LORD has declared: Are you the one
1 Kgs 5:3, 5; 8:17-19 to build a house for Me to live in? 6I have never lived in a house, from the day I
7:6 brought the Israelites out of Egypt until this very day. I have always moved from one
Exod 40:18, 34
1 Kgs 8:16 place to another with a tent and a Tabernacle as My dwelling. 7Yet no matter where
7:7 I have gone with the Israelites, I have never once complained to Israel's tribal leaders,
Lev 26:11-12 the shepherds of My people Israel. I have never asked them, "Why haven't you built
7:8 Me a beautiful cedar house?"'
1 Sam 16:10-11 8"Now go and say to My servant David, 'This is what the LORD of Heaven's Armies
Ps 78:70-71
*2 Cor 6:18 has declared: I took you from tending sheep in the pasture and selected you to be the
7:9 leader of My people Israel. 9I have been with you wherever you have gone, and I have
Ps 18:37-42 destroyed all your enemies before your eyes. Now I will make your name as famous
7:10 as anyone who has ever lived on the earth! 10And I will provide a homeland for My
Ps 89:22
Isa 60:18 7:2 Hebrew *a house of cedar.*

7:2 David's palace had been constructed for him as a goodwill gesture by King Hiram of Tyre (5:11), a city on the Mediterranean coast northwest of Jerusalem. The contrast between the ornate palace in which David lived and the simple tent in which the Ark of the Covenant was being kept made a strong impression on him. David believed that the Ark, which represented God's throne and hence God's presence, should have a better home than it did.

7:3-7 David wisely asked God's spokesman, the prophet Nathan, whether he should build a Temple for God, and Nathan gave the go-ahead. But God then intervened. Though He praised David for his desire to build a Temple (1 Kings 8:18), He rejected the plan for two reasons. First, God had not asked for a Temple. That did not mean that a Temple could never be built; God simply did not want one built yet. Second, David was not the man for the job. He was a warrior who had shed much blood (1 Chronicles 22:8-9), and the construction of the Temple would be accomplished by a "man of rest"—David's son Solomon, who would rule in the era of peace that David had won by the sword. Until then, God was content to dwell in a tent as His people had lived in tents for so long.

7:9 To ease David's disappointment over not being allowed to build the Temple, God first reminded him of past grace—that God had raised David up from tending sheep to ruling Israel, that He had been with David through all of his struggles, and that He had destroyed all of David's enemies. Then He promised continuing grace—that He would make David's name famous through all the earth.

▶ HOLINESS

7:10 Conditional blessing. God makes great promises to His people in Scripture. And God never falls short in His Word to us—His Word cannot fail. But that does not mean that all of God's promises are unconditional. God promised David, like Abraham and Moses before him, that Israel would enjoy the land God had given them. But after the death of Solomon (2 Samuel 7:14), Israel and Judah discarded these promises. God then allowed nations to oppress His people, even to the point of allowing Assyria to completely destroy the culture and government of the northern kingdom of Israel in 722 BC. Some of God's promises to us are contingent on our covenant faithfulness. The Beatitudes (Matthew 5) are a New Testament example of such promises—the merciful will receive mercy, the pure in heart will see God, and so on. But these promises of reward, even the promises of eternal life, are to those who repent and believe (Romans 10:9-10). If those responsibilities are ignored, the promised blessing is forfeited. (***See Holiness***> *Changed by God*> *The Spirit Enables*> *Seals believers,* TopicGuide page A41.)

people Israel, planting them in a secure place where they will never be disturbed. Evil
nations won't oppress them as they've done in the past, [11]starting from the time I ap-
pointed judges to rule My people Israel. And I will give you rest from all your enemies.
"'Furthermore, the LORD declares that He will make a house for you—a dynasty of
kings! [12]For when you die and are buried with your ancestors, I will raise up one of
your descendants, your own offspring, and I will make his kingdom strong. [13]He is
the one who will build a house—a temple—for My name. And I will secure his royal
throne forever. [14]I will be his father, and He will be My son. If He sins, I will correct
and discipline him with the rod, like any father would do. [15]But My favor will not be
taken from him as I took it from Saul, whom I removed from your sight. [16]Your
house and your kingdom will continue before Me* for all time, and your throne will
be secure forever.'"

[17]So Nathan went back to David and told him everything the LORD had said in this vision.

7:11 1 Sam 12:9-11; 25:28
7:12 1 Kgs 2:1; *Acts 2:30
7:13 1 Kgs 6:11-12; 8:19; Isa 9:7
7:14 Ps 89:26-27; Heb 1:5-6
7:15 1 Sam 15:23; 16:14; Ps 89:33
7:16 1 Sam 25:28; Ps 89:36-37

7:16 As in Greek version and some Hebrew manuscripts; Masoretic Text reads *before you.*

7:11-13 David wanted to build a Temple to house the Ark—essentially a house for God. God said no to that, but He then turned the tables and promised to build a "house" for David—not a house of wood and stone, but a kingly dynasty. First, He promised that one of David's sons would succeed him on the throne, a privilege God had denied to Saul. Then, stunningly, God promised that the line of that son of David—and, hence, David's line—would last *forever.* There was only one way this promise could be fulfilled—one of David's descendants would be the Messiah, who would reign forever. For this reason, the angel Gabriel told Mary that God would give her son "the throne of His ancestor David. And He will reign over Israel forever; His Kingdom will never end!" (Luke 1:32-33).

7:13 The phrase "a temple for [the LORD's] name" is another way of saying "a temple that honors [the LORD]."

MY RESPONSE TO GOD

How God Deals With People

2 SAMUEL 7:4-17

The Bible reveals that Christianity is a consistent religion. For many thousands of years, God has dealt with His people in the same way—through *covenants.* We see God making covenant agreements with people and groups throughout the Bible:

- Adam and Eve (Genesis 2:15-17; Hosea 6:7)
- Noah (Genesis 6:18; 9:9-17)
- Abraham (Genesis 15:18-21)
- The nation of Israel (Exodus 20)
- David and his descendants (2 Samuel 7:4-17)
- God speaks of ending His covenant with rebellious Israel and Judah (Jeremiah 31:31-34; Ezekiel 16:59-63), enabling God to establish a New Covenant with them—and with us—established by Jesus' perfect sacrifice on our behalf (Hebrews 7–10; Luke 22:20; Mark 14:24).

Just as with the older covenants, the new covenant is initiated by God, based on repentance and belief in God's promises, and sealed in blood. At the heart of the New Covenant is the same promise God made to His Old Covenant saints: He pledges to redeem all who place their faith in God's promise to save His people from their sin. God has never failed to keep His promises to any other person or group, and He will not fail to keep His covenant promises to you.

DAVID'S PRAYER OF THANKS

7:18-29 //1 Chr 17:16-27 [18]Then King David went in and sat before the LORD and prayed,

7:18 "Who am I, O Sovereign LORD, and what is my family, that You have brought me this
Exod 3:11 far? [19]And now, Sovereign LORD, in addition to everything else, You speak of giving
1 Sam 18:18 Your servant a lasting dynasty! Do You deal with everyone this way, O Sovereign
7:19 LORD?*
1 Chr 17:17 Isa 55:8-9 [20]"What more can I say to You? You know what Your servant is really like, Sover-
7:20 eign LORD. [21]Because of Your promise and according to Your will, You have done all
1 Sam 16:7 these great things and have made them known to Your servant.
John 21:17 [22]"How great You are, O Sovereign LORD! There is no one like You. We have never
7:22 Exod 10:2 even heard of another God like You! [23]What other nation on earth is like Your peo-
Deut 3:24 ple Israel? What other nation, O God, have You redeemed from slavery to be Your
1 Sam 2:2 Ps 44:1 own people? You made a great name for Yourself when You redeemed Your people
7:23 from Egypt. You performed awesome miracles and drove out the nations and gods
Deut 4:32; 9:26; that stood in their way.* [24]You made Israel Your very own people forever, and You,
10:21 O LORD, became their God.
7:24 [25]"And now, O LORD God, I am Your servant; do as You have promised concerning
Gen 17:7-8 Exod 6:7 me and my family. Confirm it as a promise that will last forever. [26]And may Your name
Deut 32:6 be honored forever so that everyone will say, 'The LORD of Heaven's Armies is God
Ps 48:14 over Israel!' And may the house of Your servant David continue before You forever.
[27]"O LORD of Heaven's Armies, God of Israel, I have been bold enough to pray this
prayer to You because You have revealed all this to Your servant, saying, 'I will build
7:28 a house for you—a dynasty of kings!' [28]For You are God, O Sovereign LORD. Your
Exod 34:5-6 John 17:17 words are truth, and You have promised these good things to Your servant. [29]And
7:29 now, may it please You to bless the house of Your servant, so that it may continue
Num 6:23-27 forever before You. For You have spoken, and when You grant a blessing to Your
servant, O Sovereign LORD, it is an eternal blessing!"

DAVID'S MILITARY VICTORIES

8:1-14 //1 Chr 18:1-13 **8** After this, David defeated and subdued the Philistines by conquering Gath, their larg-
8:2 est town.* [2]David also conquered the land of Moab. He made the people lie down on

2 Kgs 3:4; 17:3 7:19 Or *This is Your instruction for all humanity, O Sovereign LORD.* 7:23 As in Greek version (see also 1 Chr 17:21); Hebrew reads *You made a great name for Yourself and performed awesome miracles for Your land. You did this in the sight of Your people, whom You redeemed from Egypt, from nations and their gods.* 8:1 Hebrew *by conquering Metheg-ammah,* a name that means "the bridle," possibly referring to the size of the town or the tribute money taken from it. Compare 1 Chr 18:1.

7:18-21 When David heard God's incredible promise to him, he went humbly before God to give thanks. He freely confessed that he was unworthy to receive the blessing God planned to bestow upon him. But God was not making a mistake, as He already knew that David was a sinner. So this was an act of grace, but not only for David's sake. David acknowledged that God was making plans to send an eternal King, a Messiah, for the sake of His promise to bless all nations through David's ancestor Abraham (Genesis 12:3).

▸ BIBLE

7:29 Joy and sadness. We see good times come and go. We experience times of joy and times of sorrow. But just because some aspects of our lives still reflect the curse of living in this world does not mean that God is not filled with love for us and committed to our best. David knew that God's blessings on Israel would ebb and flow; there would be times of joy and times of sadness ahead (2 Samuel 7:14). But he knew that God had bestowed an unchanging blessing on Israel in general and more specifically on his family—from them would come the Messiah! In the person of Jesus Christ, an Israelite King would reign over all the world and a Son of David would have an eternal dynasty (7:27). If God can keep His promises to David, then He can keep His promises to you. (***See Bible**> Uniqueness> Inspired> His promises never fail,* TopicGuide page A10.)

8:1-17 This chapter is a summary of David's military accomplishments. Its parallel is 1 Chronicles 18. Repeatedly throughout this chapter, David's enemies are depicted as completely humbled but not completely destroyed (8:4, 6, 14). By the end of these operations, David's territory was much more vast and Israel was exponentially stronger. But the author is careful to note that "the LORD made David victorious wherever he went" (8:6).

8:2 David's harsh treatment of the Moabites, whom he previously trusted (1 Samuel 22:3), is not explained. He killed two-thirds of the Moabites and the remainder became his subjects and paid tribute. They remained in this state until after the death of Israel's King Ahab decades later (2 Kings 3:5).

the ground in a row, and he measured them off in groups with a length of rope. He mea-
sured off two groups to be executed for every one group to be spared. The Moabites who
were spared became David's subjects and paid him tribute money.
3 David also destroyed the forces of Hadadezer son of Rehob, king of Zobah, when Had-
adezer marched out to strengthen his control along the Euphrates River. 4 David captured
1,700 charioteers* and 20,000 foot soldiers. He crippled all the chariot horses except
enough for 100 chariots.
5 When Arameans from Damascus arrived to help King Hadadezer, David killed 22,000
of them. 6 Then he placed several army garrisons in Damascus, the Aramean capital, and
the Arameans became David's subjects and paid him tribute money. So the LORD made
David victorious wherever he went.
7 David brought the gold shields of Hadadezer's officers to Jerusalem, 8 along with a
large amount of bronze from Hadadezer's towns of Tebah* and Berothai.
9 When King Toi of Hamath heard that David had destroyed the entire army of Hadade-
zer, 10 he sent his son Joram to congratulate King David for his successful campaign. Had-
adezer and Toi had been enemies and were often at war. Joram presented David with
many gifts of silver, gold, and bronze.
11 King David dedicated all these gifts to the LORD, as he did with the silver and gold from
the other nations he had defeated—12 from Edom,* Moab, Ammon, Philistia, and Amalek—
and from Hadadezer son of Rehob, king of Zobah.

8:3 1 Sam 14:47; 2 Sam 10:16, 19
8:4 Josh 11:6, 9
8:5 1 Kgs 11:23-25
8:6 2 Sam 3:18
8:7 1 Kgs 10:16
8:8 Ezek 47:16
8:11 1 Kgs 7:51

8:4 Greek version reads *1,000 chariots and 7,000 charioteers;* compare 1 Chr 18:4. 8:8 As in some Greek manuscripts (see also 1 Chr 18:8); Hebrew reads *Betah.* 8:12 As in a few Hebrew manuscripts and Greek and Syriac versions (see also 8:14; 1 Chr 18:11); most Hebrew manuscripts read *Aram.*

8:3 Zobah was an Aramean kingdom to the north of Israel. At this time one king ruled it, but when it is first mentioned in Scripture it was said to have been under the rule of multiple kings (1 Samuel 14:47). Zobah was in conflict with the Israelites during the reigns of Saul, David, and David's son Solomon, but it is not mentioned after Solomon's defeat of Hamath-zobah (2 Chronicles 8:3).

8:4 David cut the hamstring tendons of most of the horses he captured from the king of Zobah, rendering them lame and therefore useless for war by his enemies or himself. He did this out of obedience to God, who had commanded that Israel's kings not build large stables of war horses (Deuteronomy 17:16). The king of Israel was to trust in God, not in his armies or weapons of war.

8:9-10 Even nations that he did not conquer paid David tribute money. Hamath was one of the kingdoms of upper Aram, located in the valley of Lebanon at the northern boundary of Palestine (Numbers 13:21; 34:8) at the foot of Hermon (Joshua 13:5).

8:11 When a thing was dedicated to God, it was set aside for special, holy use. David dedicated all this silver, gold, and bronze to God for use in the Temple that his son Solomon would build one day (1 Chronicles 18:8). Thus, by his wars, David not only secured the peace for the construction of the Temple; he acquired materials for its construction and adornment.

BECAUSE GOD IS SOVEREIGN

I will joyfully submit to His will.

How great You are, O Sovereign LORD! There is no one like You. We have never even heard of another God like You!

2 SAMUEL 7:22

FOR THE NEXT *GOD IS SOVEREIGN* FEATURE SEE PAGE 756.

13 So David became very famous. After his return he destroyed 18,000 Edomites* in the
Valley of Salt. 14 He placed army garrisons throughout Edom, and all the Edomites became
David's subjects. In fact, the LORD made David victorious wherever he went.
15 So David reigned over all Israel and did what was just and right for all his people.
16 Joab son of Zeruiah was commander of the army. Jehoshaphat son of Ahilud was the
royal historian. 17 Zadok son of Ahitub and Ahimelech son of Abiathar were the priests. Se-
raiah was the court secretary. 18 Benaiah son of Jehoiada was captain of the king's body-
guard.* And David's sons served as priestly leaders.*

8:13 2 Kgs 14:7; 1 Chr 18:12
8:14 Gen 27:30, 37-40
8:15-18 //1 Chr 18:14-17
8:18 2 Sam 20:7, 23; 1 Kgs 1:38, 44; 1 Chr 18:17

DAVID'S KINDNESS TO MEPHIBOSHETH

9 One day David asked, "Is anyone in Saul's family still alive—anyone to whom I can
show kindness for Jonathan's sake?" 2 He summoned a man named Ziba, who had
been one of Saul's servants. "Are you Ziba?" the king asked.
"Yes sir, I am," Ziba replied.
3 The king then asked him, "Is anyone still alive from Saul's family? If so, I want to show
God's kindness to them."
Ziba replied, "Yes, one of Jonathan's sons is still alive. He is crippled in both feet."
4 "Where is he?" the king asked.
"In Lo-debar," Ziba told him, "at the home of Makir son of Ammiel."
5 So David sent for him and brought him from Makir's home. 6 His name was Mephibo-
sheth*; he was Jonathan's son and Saul's grandson. When he came to David, he bowed
low to the ground in deep respect. David said, "Greetings, Mephibosheth."
Mephibosheth replied, "I am your servant."
7 "Don't be afraid!" David said. "I intend to show kindness to you because of my promise
to your father, Jonathan. I will give you all the property that once belonged to your grand-
father Saul, and you will eat here with me at the king's table!"
8 Mephibosheth bowed respectfully and exclaimed, "Who is your servant, that you
should show such kindness to a dead dog like me?"
9 Then the king summoned Saul's servant Ziba and said, "I have given your master's
grandson everything that belonged to Saul and his family. 10 You and your sons and ser-
vants are to farm the land for him to produce food for your master's household.* But

9:1 1 Sam 20:14-17, 42
9:2 2 Sam 16:1-4; 19:17
9:3 1 Sam 20:14-15; 2 Sam 4:4
9:4 2 Sam 17:27-29
9:7 2 Sam 19:28; 2 Kgs 25:29
9:9 2 Sam 16:4; 19:29
9:10 2 Sam 19:28

8:13 As in a few Hebrew manuscripts and Greek and Syriac versions (see also 8:14; 1 Chr 18:12); most Hebrew manuscripts read *Arameans.* 8:18a Hebrew *of the Kerethites and Pelethites.* 8:18b Hebrew *David's sons were priests;* compare parallel text at 1 Chr 18:17. 9:6 *Mephibosheth* is another name for Merib-baal. 9:10 As in Greek version; Hebrew reads *your master's grandson.*

▸ WORSHIP

9:1 Keeping our word. Do you keep your promises? Or do you avoid making promises altogether? Even after most others would have forgotten David's pledge to honor Saul's descendants, David remembered. More importantly, God remembered and was pleased when David reached out in covenant mercy to Mephibosheth. God is pleased when we keep our marriage vows, our membership vows to the church, and every other promise or contract we make. Make your word your bond—make any broken promise right with those you've dishonored. (***See Worship***> *OT> Offerings> Other Sacrifices> Vows,* TopicGuide page A27.)

9:4 In 2 Samuel, the writer characterized the people in the narrative by associating them with certain places—good people are associated with good places, and bad people are associated with bad places. In this case, Mephibosheth is associated with the town of Lo-debar, which was likely located about ten miles north of Mahanaim, Ishbosheth's capital across the Jordan River (2 Samuel 2:8). *Lo debar* is Hebrew for "no word," a shameful reminder to the original audience that the Word of God flowed forth from David's lineage in Jerusalem, not the cursed line of Saul.

9:6 Mephibosheth was Jonathan's son and Saul's grandson. He had been crippled (9:3) since he was five years old. Just after Saul and Jonathan died in battle, their families scattered in fear of retribution from Saul's enemies. During the flight, Mephibosheth's nurse fell and dropped him. The incident caused lifelong damage (2 Samuel 4:4). Mephibosheth was clearly terrified that David was seeking him for what he thought was the purpose of executing him as one of Saul's descendants, a potential rival for the throne.

9:7 David had promised Saul that he would not destroy Saul's descendants when God made him king (1 Samuel 24:21-22). That was why he asked whether any of Saul's descendants were still living (9:3). David had made a solemn covenant with Jonathan, promising to treat Jonathan's descendants with "faithful love" (1 Samuel 20:14-16). For this reason, when David learned that Mephibosheth was Jonathan's son, he restored Saul's former lands to Mephibosheth and brought him to the palace to live as if he were David's own son.

Mephibosheth, your master's grandson, will eat here at my table." (Ziba had fifteen sons
and twenty servants.)

Ziba replied, [11]"Yes, my lord the king; I am your servant, and I will do all that you have
commanded." And from that time on, Mephibosheth ate regularly at David's table,* like
one of the king's own sons.

[12]Mephibosheth had a young son named Mica. From then on, all the members of Ziba's
household were Mephibosheth's servants. [13]And Mephibosheth, who was crippled in both
feet, lived in Jerusalem and ate regularly at the king's table.

DAVID DEFEATS THE AMMONITES

10 Some time after this, King Nahash* of the Ammonites died, and his son Hanun be- **10:1-19**
came king. [2]David said, "I am going to show loyalty to Hanun just as his father, //1 Chr 19:1-19
Nahash, was always loyal to me." So David sent ambassadors to express sympathy to Ha-
nun about his father's death.

But when David's ambassadors arrived in the land of Ammon, [3]the Ammonite com-
manders said to Hanun, their master, "Do you really think these men are coming here to
honor your father? No! David has sent them to spy out the city so they can come in and
conquer it!" [4]So Hanun seized David's ambassadors and shaved off half of each man's **10:4**
beard, cut off their robes at the buttocks, and sent them back to David in shame. Isa 15:2; 20:4
[5]When David heard what had happened, he sent messengers to tell the men, "Stay at Jer 41:5
Jericho until your beards grow out, and then come back." For they felt deep shame be-
cause of their appearance.

[6]When the people of Ammon realized how seriously they had angered David, they sent **10:6**
and hired 20,000 Aramean foot soldiers from the lands of Beth-rehob and Zobah, 1,000 Gen 34:30
from the king of Maacah, and 12,000 from the land of Tob. [7]When David heard about this, 2 Kgs 7:6

9:11 As in Greek version; Hebrew reads *my table.* 10:1 As in parallel text at 1 Chr 19:1; Hebrew reads *the king.*

▸ SALVATION

9:13 Discovering God in David's choice of Mephibosheth. God saves us by His grace. David showed love not just to the poor and lame but also to his enemy! Saul's family hated David (2 Samuel 3:1), and we hated God before He showed us His life-giving love (Ephesians 2:1-6). God shows mercy to His enemies, for while we were still in cosmic rebellion against Him, Christ died for us (Romans 5:1-2). David's kindness toward Mephibosheth is a beautiful picture of God's love for helpless, angry sinners. (***See Salvation***> *Receiving> How> Submit to God's grace/special favor,* TopicGuide page A22.)

10:1 The Ammonites were descendants of Abraham's nephew Lot. In the divine destruction of Sodom and Gomorrah, Lot's wife died but Lot and his two daughters survived. The girls connived to conceive children by their father. From these unions, Lot's older daughter had a son named Moab (Genesis 19:34-38). His descendants, the Moabites, were occasionally enemies of Israel. Lot's younger daughter had a son named Ben-ammi. His descendants were the Ammonites, who were also enemies of Israel.

10:2-4 David had recently shown kindness to Mephibosheth. When King Nahash of the Ammonites died, David determined to act in kindness again. He sent a group of ambassadors to express sympathy to the king's son, Hanun. He was motivated by the fact that Nahash had been "always loyal" to him; possibly Nahash had submitted to David voluntarily as had King Toi of Hamath (2 Samuel 8:9-10). Sadly, Hanun received bad counsel from his advisers and took actions that completely spoiled Ammon's relations with Israel. Because ambassadors had the authority to speak for their king, any action toward them, good or evil, was treated as if it had been done to the king himself.

10:4 Israelite men ordinarily wore full beards and full-length robes, similar to modern desert-dwellers. By modern standards, Israelites were not prudish about nakedness, but this sort of humiliation was particularly severe in their culture. Beards were sometimes shaved to communicate deep mourning, so perhaps Hanun was making a mockery of David's intention to note the passing of his father.

▸ SPIRITUAL WARFARE

10:4 Shame and nakedness. Have you ever dreamed about being naked at an inappropriate time? We have associated nakedness with shame ever since the fall of man (Genesis 3:7). But shame is associated with much more than inopportune nakedness. It is attached to the way others have harmed us, the foolish things we have said and done, and sometimes to nothing at all—we simply feel ashamed and don't know why. But even better than wise King David (10:5), God offers a way to deal with our shame. Christ bore our shame on the dreadful cross (Hebrews 12:2). Those who live in an attitude of repentance and belief do not have to live in shame, for their nakedness is covered in Christ's righteousness (Ephesians 4:24). Let us rejoice and not be ashamed! (***See Spiritual Warfare***> *Origin of Sin> Humanity's Fall> Physical> Exposed and naked,* TopicGuide page A44.)

10:6 The Ammonites used the dispute with Israel as an excuse to go to war. They recruited large numbers of mercenaries to aid their cause. But in a series of battles, Joab and David defeated them all and actually extended David's rule to some of the mercenaries' homelands (10:19).

he sent Joab and all his warriors to fight them. 8The Ammonite troops came out and drew up
their battle lines at the entrance of the city gate, while the Arameans from Zobah and Rehob
and the men from Tob and Maacah positioned themselves to fight in the open fields.
9When Joab saw that he would have to fight on both the front and the rear, he chose
some of Israel's elite troops and placed them under his personal command to fight the Ar-
ameans in the fields. 10He left the rest of the army under the command of his brother
Abishai, who was to attack the Ammonites. 11"If the Arameans are too strong for me, then
come over and help me," Joab told his brother. "And if the Ammonites are too strong for
10:12 you, I will come and help you. 12Be courageous! Let us fight bravely for our people and the
Deut 31:6 1 Sam 3:18 cities of our God. May the LORD's will be done."
1 Cor 16:13 13When Joab and his troops attacked, the Arameans began to run away. 14And when
10:13 the Ammonites saw the Arameans running, they ran from Abishai and retreated into the
1 Kgs 20:13-21 city. After the battle was over, Joab returned to Jerusalem.
15The Arameans now realized that they were no match for Israel. So when they re-
grouped, 16they were joined by additional Aramean troops summoned by Hadadezer
from the other side of the Euphrates River.* These troops arrived at Helam under the com-
mand of Shobach, the commander of Hadadezer's forces.
17When David heard what was happening, he mobilized all Israel, crossed the Jordan
River, and led the army to Helam. The Arameans positioned themselves in battle forma-
10:18 tion and fought against David. 18But again the Arameans fled from the Israelites. This time
1 Chr 19:17-18 David's forces killed 700 charioteers and 40,000 foot soldiers,* including Shobach, the
10:19 2 Sam 8:6 commander of their army. 19When all the kings allied with Hadadezer saw that they had
been defeated by Israel, they surrendered to Israel and became their subjects. After that,
the Arameans were afraid to help the Ammonites.

11:1

DAVID AND BATHSHEBA

2 Sam 12:26-29 1 Chr 20:1 **11** In the spring of the year,* when kings normally go out to war, David sent Joab and
Amos 1:14 the Israelite army to fight the Ammonites. They destroyed the Ammonite army
11:2 and laid siege to the city of Rabbah. However, David stayed behind in Jerusalem.
Deut 22:8 2Late one afternoon, after his midday rest, David got out of bed and was walking on the
11:3 roof of the palace. As he looked out over the city, he noticed a woman of unusual beauty tak-
2 Sam 23:39 1 Chr 3:5 ing a bath. 3He sent someone to find out who she was, and he was told, "She is Bathsheba,
11:4 the daughter of Eliam and the wife of Uriah the Hittite." 4Then David sent messengers to

Lev 15:19; 18:20-28 10:16 Hebrew *the river.* 10:18 As in some Greek manuscripts (see also 1 Chr 19:18); Hebrew reads *charioteers.*
Ps 51:TITLE 11:1 Hebrew *At the turn of the year.* The first day of the year in the ancient Hebrew lunar calendar occurred in March or April.

10:12 Joab's words—"Let us fight bravely for our people and the cities of our God"—may indicate that the Ammonites' recruiting efforts had produced a legitimate threat to Israel. But Joab knew that the ultimate outcome of the battle did not rest with the armies but with the counsel of Israel's God.

11:1 The passing mention of David's decision to stay home during a time of war signals a change in the way the author presents the king. Up to this point, David essentially could do no wrong, but from this point on, his sins and mistakes are noted more frequently.

11:1 Spring was a good time to go to war because the land was drier and troops could move more easily. Also, since it was harvesttime, there was food for the armies to scavenge. Winter, on the other hand, was the rainy season in Israel. Wagons and chariots could not move well during these wet times.

▶ SALVATION
11:1-2 Lazy and lustful. David should have gone with his army, but instead he stayed in Jerusalem taking naps and looking at naked women. Besides being sins in their own right, laziness and lust often lead to even greater sins. David's laziness led to lust, and his lust led him to tell lie after lie to cover his transgression, and the lies led him to murder. Where does your laziness or lust lead you—to deception, or the foot of the cross in humble repentance? (***See Salvation> Our Need> Sinful> Enslaved to sin,*** TopicGuide page A22.)

11:3 Uriah was known as "the Hittite," but he had a Hebrew name meaning "the Lord is my light." He may have been born in Israel to foreign converts, or he may have converted as an adult and chosen a Hebrew name to commemorate the event. He was one of David's mighty men (2 Samuel 23:39), and, as his actions in this chapter show, he was intensely loyal to the king.

11:4 Israelite women had to go through ritual purification after menstruation and childbirth. During this process, they were required to refrain from sexual intercourse. By noting that Bathsheba had just completed the purification rites after her menstrual cycle when David took her, the author made it clear to his readers that David was the only man who could have fathered the baby.

get her; and when she came to the palace, he slept with her. She had just completed the puri-
fication rites after having her menstrual period. Then she returned home. 5Later, when Bath- 11:5 Lev 20:10
sheba discovered that she was pregnant, she sent David a message, saying, "I'm pregnant." Deut 22:22
6Then David sent word to Joab: "Send me Uriah the Hittite." So Joab sent him to David.
7When Uriah arrived, David asked him how Joab and the army were getting along and
how the war was progressing. 8Then he told Uriah, "Go on home and relax.*" David even
sent a gift to Uriah after he had left the palace. 9But Uriah didn't go home. He slept that
night at the palace entrance with the king's palace guard.
10When David heard that Uriah had not gone home, he summoned him and asked,
"What's the matter? Why didn't you go home last night after being away for so long?"
11Uriah replied, "The Ark and the armies of Israel and Judah are living in tents,* and 11:11
Joab and my master's men are camping in the open fields. How could I go home to wine 2 Sam 7:2
and dine and sleep with my wife? I swear that I would never do such a thing."
12"Well, stay here today," David told him, "and tomorrow you may return to the army."
So Uriah stayed in Jerusalem that day and the next. 13Then David invited him to dinner
and got him drunk. But even then he couldn't get Uriah to go home to his wife. Again he
slept at the palace entrance with the king's palace guard.

DAVID ARRANGES FOR URIAH'S DEATH

14So the next morning David wrote a letter to Joab and gave it to Uriah to deliver. 15The let- 11:14
ter instructed Joab, "Station Uriah on the front lines where the battle is fiercest. Then pull 1 Kgs 21:8-10
back so that he will be killed." 16So Joab assigned Uriah to a spot close to the city wall where 11:15
he knew the enemy's strongest men were fighting. 17And when the enemy soldiers came 2 Sam 12:9
out of the city to fight, Uriah the Hittite was killed along with several other Israelite soldiers.
18Then Joab sent a battle report to David. 19He told his messenger, "Report all the news of
the battle to the king. 20But he might get angry and ask, 'Why did the troops go so close to
the city? Didn't they know there would be shooting from the walls? 21Wasn't Abimelech son 11:21
of Gideon* killed at Thebez by a woman who threw a millstone down on him from the wall? Judg 9:50-54
Why would you get so close to the wall?' Then tell him, 'Uriah the Hittite was killed, too.'"
22So the messenger went to Jerusalem and gave a complete report to David. 23"The en-
emy came out against us in the open fields," he said. "And as we chased them back to the
city gate, 24the archers on the wall shot arrows at us. Some of the king's men were killed,
including Uriah the Hittite."
25"Well, tell Joab not to be discouraged," David said. "The sword devours this one today
and that one tomorrow! Fight harder next time, and conquer the city!"

11:8 Hebrew *and wash your feet*, an expression that may also have a connotation of ritualistic washing. 11:11 Or *at Succoth*. 11:21 Hebrew *son of Jerub-besheth*. Jerub-besheth is a variation on the name Jerub-baal, which is another name for Gideon; see Judg 6:32.

11:8 The phrase "go on home and relax" is more literally translated "go home and wash your feet." This expression may euphemistically refer to sexual intercourse, and the context seems to support this understanding.

▸ WORSHIP
11:11 Honor and sacrifice. The sterling qualities of Uriah's character are brought out more vividly by contrast with David, who not only was sleeping with his own wives while the men were at war, but with someone else's wife as well! Uriah's actions should have shamed David into repentance. His continuing efforts to cover his transgression only demonstrate how powerful sin can be and show that only the Holy Spirit can bring us to true repentance. Pray that God's convicting Spirit will reign in your life. (***See Worship****> NT> Our Role> Holiness> Sin not to reign in our bodies,* TopicGuide page A32.)

▸ SPIRITUAL WARFARE
11:15 Turning to murder. David's laziness and lust drove him to lies; when the lies failed, homicide was his final option. He successfully plotted to have Uriah killed in battle. Why do people's thoughts turn to murder when an unwanted pregnancy occurs? Very often, it is the baby who dies. Pray that God will turn fathers and mothers away from murderous thoughts when an unplanned child is conceived. (***See Spiritual Warfare****> Resisting Sin and Evil> Consequences> Of Disobedience> Further disobedience,* TopicGuide page A46.)

11:20, 25 David's mild reaction to the news of the death of many soldiers was uncharacteristic. Joab, in fact, expected the king to be angry—until he heard the news that his evil intention was accomplished and Uriah was dead. The fact that David could accept the loss of numerous loyal soldiers with no apparent pangs of conscience over his role in their deaths shows just how far from God his sin had taken him.

11:26 Gen 50:10; Deut 34:8
11:27 Ps 51:4-5

26 When Uriah's wife heard that her husband was dead, she mourned for him. 27 When the period of mourning was over, David sent for her and brought her to the palace, and she became one of his wives. Then she gave birth to a son. But the LORD was displeased with what David had done.

NATHAN REBUKES DAVID

12:1 2 Sam 7:2, 17; Ps 51:TITLE
12:5 1 Kgs 20:40
12:6 Exod 22:1
12:7 1 Sam 16:13; 1 Kgs 20:42
12:8 2 Sam 9:7
12:9 2 Sam 11:14-17, 27
12:10 2 Sam 13:28-29; 18:14; 1 Kgs 2:23
12:11 2 Sam 16:21-22

12 So the LORD sent Nathan the prophet to tell David this story: "There were two men in a certain town. One was rich, and one was poor. 2 The rich man owned a great many sheep and cattle. 3 The poor man owned nothing but one little lamb he had bought. He raised that little lamb, and it grew up with his children. It ate from the man's own plate and drank from his cup. He cuddled it in his arms like a baby daughter. 4 One day a guest arrived at the home of the rich man. But instead of killing an animal from his own flock or herd, he took the poor man's lamb and killed it and prepared it for his guest."

5 David was furious. "As surely as the LORD lives," he vowed, "any man who would do such a thing deserves to die! 6 He must repay four lambs to the poor man for the one he stole and for having no pity."

7 Then Nathan said to David, "You are that man! The LORD, the God of Israel, says: I anointed you king of Israel and saved you from the power of Saul. 8 I gave you your master's house and his wives and the kingdoms of Israel and Judah. And if that had not been enough, I would have given you much, much more. 9 Why, then, have you despised the word of the LORD and done this horrible deed? For you have murdered Uriah the Hittite with the sword of the Ammonites and stolen his wife. 10 From this time on, your family will live by the sword because you have despised Me by taking Uriah's wife to be your own.

11 "This is what the LORD says: Because of what you have done, I will cause your own household to rebel against you. I will give your wives to another man before your very eyes, and he will go to bed with them in public view. 12 You did it secretly, but I will make this happen to you openly in the sight of all Israel."

11:26 The period of mourning for the dead varied from 70 days for Jacob (Genesis 50:3) to 30 for Moses (Deuteronomy 34:8). Most mourning periods mentioned in Scripture lasted for 30 days (Deuteronomy 21:10-13), so Bathsheba likely mourned for one month.

▸ GOD
12:1-7 Repentance of the king. Some people associate stories with children and bedtime, but God can use stories to shock and surprise us into repentance. Jesus used punchy little stories called *parables* to spread His surprising message to the right ears. But a thousand years earlier, God used this story about a tiny lamb to break King David's hard heart and draw him to repentance. Let the stories of the Old and New Testaments tug at your heart, leading you to feel rightly about God and His people. (***See God****> God's Attributes> Patient> God patiently awaits repentance,* TopicGuide page A17.)

12:5-6 It is unlikely David was pronouncing the death penalty on this figuratively rich thief. Instead, he went on to pronounce a fine of four lambs, the precise penalty Moses laid down for this crime (Exodus 22:1).

12:7-12 Nathan, speaking for God, said that David's sins were rooted in dissatisfaction with God's blessings. God had been generous to David by every measure, but Nathan said that, in God's wisdom, He had given David only what He deemed appropriate for him. When David reached out to take more than what God had given, he was essentially despising God Himself. Thus, David's punishment was that his own household and all Israel would despise him.

▸ SPIRITUAL WARFARE
12:11 Free will and sin. Does God cause people to sin? Does He cause you to sin? If He does, then how could it be your fault, for how could you resist God's will? If He does not cause sin, what can we learn about God from this verse? God does not create sin. He creates good things (1 Timothy 4:4), and all good comes from Him (James 1:17). These and other parts of the Bible that explicitly teach about God's relationship to evil keep us from accusing Him of forcing the men and women of David's household into rebellion against Him. Of course, God does passively permit sin or it would not exist anywhere. But God does not compel it. You can trust that God is good, and His will is for your success in your battle against temptation and sin (Matthew 6:13). He never works against your obedience. (***See Spiritual Warfare****> God and Sin> Sin's Origin> Temptation not from God,* TopicGuide page A45.)

DAVID CONFESSES HIS GUILT

13 Then David confessed to Nathan, "I have sinned against the LORD." 12:13
Nathan replied, "Yes, but the LORD has forgiven you, and you won't die for this sin. Lev 20:10; 24:17
14 Nevertheless, because you have shown utter contempt for the LORD* by doing this, your Prov 28:13 Mic 7:18
child will die." Luke 18:13
15 After Nathan returned to his home, the LORD sent a deadly illness to the child of David 12:14
and Uriah's wife. 16 David begged God to spare the child. He went without food and lay all Isa 52:5
night on the bare ground. 17 The elders of his household pleaded with him to get up and Rom 2:23-24
eat with them, but he refused. 12:17 2 Sam 3:35
18 Then on the seventh day the child died. David's advisers were afraid to tell him. "He
wouldn't listen to reason while the child was ill," they said. "What drastic thing will he do
when we tell him the child is dead?"
19 When David saw them whispering, he realized what had happened. "Is the child
dead?" he asked.
"Yes," they replied, "he is dead."
20 Then David got up from the ground, washed himself, put on lotions,* and changed his
clothes. He went to the Tabernacle and worshiped the LORD. After that, he returned to the
palace and was served food and ate.
21 His advisers were amazed. "We don't understand you," they told him. "While the child
was still living, you wept and refused to eat. But now that the child is dead, you have 12:22
stopped your mourning and are eating again." Isa 38:1-5
22 David replied, "I fasted and wept while the child was alive, for I said, 'Perhaps the LORD Jon 3:9

12:14 As in Dead Sea Scrolls; Masoretic Text reads *the LORD's enemies.* 12:20 Hebrew *anointed himself.*

▸ GOD
12:13 Repentance by grace. David's will finally was broken. He no longer could resist God's call to repent. His verbal confession revealed a deep sorrow and a hatred of his sin. God graciously forgave David, not because David was such a nice fellow and deserved it, but because God has promised to forgive His people of their sin when they truly repent. David repented, and God responded as promised by forgiving him. God promises to forgive you—and always by His grace. (***See God***> *Forgiving> God forgives those who repent,* TopicGuide page A16.)

12:13 David penned Psalm 51 as an expression of his heartfelt repentance from his adultery, lies, and murder. In it, he pleaded that God would cleanse him, revive his love for God, and restore the joy he once had found in his salvation from God. Many scholars believe that Psalm 32 shows that God was faithful to answer David's prayer, for in it David declared, "Oh, what joy for those whose disobedience is forgiven, whose sin is put out of sight!" (Psalm 32:1).

12:13-14 God forgave David's sin, but He did not withhold all the consequences of it. God had already told David he would have unceasing family strife as a result of his rebellion (12:10-11). Now God announced that David's son by Bathsheba would die. The context of verse 14 indicates that God took the child's life because David had given God's enemies an opportunity to blaspheme, that is, to question God's holiness. God showed His grace in forgiving David and showed His righteousness in taking the child. We cannot be sure about the child's eternal home; David's statement (12:23) should be understood only as a reference to death in general. But we can rest assured that the Lord of life does all things justly, and all who are His will be with Him in death.

12:20 Shortly after David's ancestors left Egypt to travel to Canaan, God commanded them to build a Tabernacle, a large tent made of heavy curtains and poles. This became God's symbolic home in the midst of His people. After the people conquered the land under the leadership of Joshua, the Tabernacle was set up more permanently in the city of Shiloh. Once the Ark of the Covenant, the most sacred object in the Tabernacle, was taken from Shiloh (1 Samuel 4), that location lost its prominence. David later moved the Ark to Jerusalem and placed it in a tent, but it seems this was not the same Tabernacle the Israelites constructed in the wilderness (2 Samuel 6:17).

▸ CHURCH
12:22 Death and children. From this story of the death of David and Bathsheba's son, you can understand several important things about God. First, David recognized that God was merciful, and he understood that Nathan's prophecy (12:14) might not be absolute—God might change His mind. So David prayed and fasted until God's will was clear in the matter. We can do the same thing—if we are faced with loss and uncertainty, we can pray, fast, and inquire of God in the hope that the situation will change. Second, this story affirms that God alone is in charge of life and death. Sometimes God reveals His purposes in allowing human death to occur (such as the death of His perfect Son, Jesus), and sometimes He does not. In this case, it was God's purpose to underscore the gravity of judgment upon David's house by allowing this baby to die. Finally, we see that God fulfilled the prophecy of Nathan but graciously gave David and Bathsheba a new baby, Solomon, who would be one of the greatest kings the world has ever known. The death of someone we love can tear us apart emotionally. But this does not mean our faith in God must be torn apart, too. God shows that while He is in ultimate control of who lives and who dies, He is also a God of mercy who promises to treat children, both the living and the dead, in a way that honors His own love for them (Genesis 17:7; Mark 10:13-16; 2 Samuel 12:23). (***See Church***> *Who> From Every People> Children are blessed by inclusion in covenant community,* TopicGuide page A48.)

12:23 will be gracious to me and let the child live.' 23But why should I fast when he is dead? Can I
Gen 37:35 Job 7:9-10 bring him back again? I will go to him one day, but he cannot return to me."
12:24 24Then David comforted Bathsheba, his wife, and slept with her. She became pregnant
1 Chr 22:9 and gave birth to a son, and they named him Solomon. The LORD loved the child 25and
sent word through Nathan the prophet that they should name him Jedidiah (which means
"beloved of the LORD"), as the LORD had commanded.*

DAVID CAPTURES RABBAH

12:26 26Meanwhile, Joab was fighting against Rabbah, the capital of Ammon, and he captured
Deut 3:11 1 Chr 20:1-3 the royal fortifications.* 27Joab sent messengers to tell David, "I have fought against Rab-
bah and captured its water supply.* 28Now bring the rest of the army and capture the city.
Otherwise, I will capture it and get credit for the victory."

12:29-31 29So David gathered the rest of the army and went to Rabbah, and he fought against it
//1 Chr 20:1-3 and captured it. 30David removed the crown from the king's head,* and it was placed on
his own head. The crown was made of gold and set with gems, and it weighed seventy-
five pounds.* David took a vast amount of plunder from the city. 31He also made slaves of
the people of Rabbah and forced them to labor with* saws, iron picks, and iron axes, and
to work in the brick kilns.* That is how he dealt with the people of all the Ammonite towns.
Then David and all the army returned to Jerusalem.

THE RAPE OF TAMAR

13:1 **13** Now David's son Absalom had a beautiful sister named Tamar. And Amnon, her
2 Sam 3:2-3 1 Chr 3:1-2, 9 half brother, fell desperately in love with her. 2Amnon became so obsessed with
Tamar that he became ill. She was a virgin, and Amnon thought he could never have her.
13:3 3But Amnon had a very crafty friend—his cousin Jonadab. He was the son of David's
1 Sam 16:9 brother Shimea.* 4One day Jonadab said to Amnon, "What's the trouble? Why should the
son of a king look so dejected morning after morning?"
So Amnon told him, "I am in love with Tamar, my brother Absalom's sister."
5"Well," Jonadab said, "I'll tell you what to do. Go back to bed and pretend you are ill.
When your father comes to see you, ask him to let Tamar come and prepare some food
for you. Tell him you'll feel better if she prepares it as you watch and feeds you with her
own hands."
6So Amnon lay down and pretended to be sick. And when the king came to see him,
Amnon asked him, "Please let my sister Tamar come and cook my favorite dish* as I
watch. Then I can eat it from her own hands." 7So David agreed and sent Tamar to Am-
non's house to prepare some food for him.

12:25 As in Greek version; Hebrew reads *because of the LORD.* 12:26 Or *the royal city.* 12:27 Or *captured the city of water.* 12:30a Or *from the head of Milcom* (as in Greek version). Milcom, also called Molech, was the god of the Ammonites. 12:30b Hebrew *1 talent* [34 kilograms]. 12:31a Or *He also brought out the people of Rabbah and put them under.* 12:31b Or *and he made them pass through the brick kilns.* 13:3 Hebrew *Shimeah* (also in 13:32), a variant spelling of Shimea; compare 1 Chr 2:13. 13:6 Or *a couple of cakes;* also in 13:8, 10.

12:25 Although his parents named the baby Solomon, meaning "peaceful," the prophet Nathan came and told them to name him Jedidiah. This is one of the few instances in the Bible of God directly changing someone's name.

13:1-2 Nathan's prophecy (2 Samuel 12:10) began to come to fulfillment almost immediately. A sequence of events that would result in bloodshed in David's family was set in motion when David's son Amnon became obsessed with his half-sister.

▸GOD
13:5 Bad counsel. Have you ever given someone terrible advice? Or has someone else, perhaps trying to be helpful, said something perfectly awful to you? Amnon got the worst advice possible from Jonadab, who, in effect, said rape your sister and you'll feel better. And worse yet, Amnon followed that advice and brought untold trouble to Tamar and the entire house of David. Whenever you give counsel or receive counsel from others, carefully weigh it on the scale of conscience and Scripture. (***See God> God's Names> Holy Spirit> Guide/Counselor,*** TopicGuide page A19.)

8When Tamar arrived at Amnon's house, she went to the place where he was lying
down so he could watch her mix some dough. Then she baked his favorite dish for him.
9But when she set the serving tray before him, he refused to eat. "Everyone get out of 13:9 Gen 45:1
here," Amnon told his servants. So they all left.
10Then he said to Tamar, "Now bring the food into my bedroom and feed it to me here."
So Tamar took his favorite dish to him. 11But as she was feeding him, he grabbed her and 13:11 Gen 39:12
demanded, "Come to bed with me, my darling sister."
12"No, my brother!" she cried. "Don't be foolish! Don't do this to me! Such wicked 13:12 Lev 20:17
things aren't done in Israel. 13Where could I go in my shame? And you would be called
one of the greatest fools in Israel. Please, just speak to the king about it, and he will let
you marry me."
14But Amnon wouldn't listen to her, and since he was stronger than she was, he raped
her. 15Then suddenly Amnon's love turned to hate, and he hated her even more than he
had loved her. "Get out of here!" he snarled at her.
16"No, no!" Tamar cried. "Sending me away now is worse than what you've already
done to me."
But Amnon wouldn't listen to her. 17He shouted for his servant and demanded, "Throw
this woman out, and lock the door behind her!"
18So the servant put her out and locked the door behind her. She was wearing a long, 13:18 Gen 37:23
beautiful robe,* as was the custom in those days for the king's virgin daughters. 19But now
Tamar tore her robe and put ashes on her head. And then, with her face in her hands, she 13:19 Gen 37:29 2 Sam 1:11 Esth 4:1
went away crying.
20Her brother Absalom saw her and asked, "Is it true that Amnon has been with you?
Well, my sister, keep quiet for now, since he's your brother. Don't you worry about it." So
Tamar lived as a desolate woman in her brother Absalom's house.
21When King David heard what had happened, he was very angry.* 22And though Absa- 13:22 Gen 31:24 Lev 19:17-18 1 Jn 2:9-11
lom never spoke to Amnon about this, he hated Amnon deeply because of what he had
done to his sister.

ABSALOM'S REVENGE ON AMNON

23Two years later, when Absalom's sheep were being sheared at Baal-hazor near Ephraim,
Absalom invited all the king's sons to come to a feast. 24He went to the king and said, "My
sheep-shearers are now at work. Would the king and his servants please come to cele-
brate the occasion with me?"
25The king replied, "No, my son. If we all came, we would be too much of a burden on
you." Absalom pressed him, but the king would not come, though he gave Absalom his
blessing.
26"Well, then," Absalom said, "if you can't come, how about sending my brother Amnon
with us?"

13:18 Or *a robe with sleeves,* or *an ornamented robe.* The meaning of the Hebrew is uncertain. 13:21 Dead Sea Scrolls and Greek version add *But he did not punish his son Amnon, because he loved him, for he was his firstborn.*

13:12-13 Tamar attempted to reason her way out of this terrifying situation by appealing to high Israelite moral standards, to simple human kindness, to Amnon's own self-interest, and to the option of using marriage to obtain what he wanted. But Amnon's mind was made up.

13:14 In the Law of Moses, penalties for rape varied according to the situation. The narrative makes it clear that Amnon had removed everyone from the house who could hear Tamar scream (13:9) and that she resisted to the point that he was forced to overpower her. Under such circumstances, the law dictated that Amnon should receive the death penalty (Deuteronomy 22:25-27).

13:21-22 David was angry, but he did not render justice to Amnon. Perhaps this was because his own life was spared in the Bathsheba incident, but it may have resulted from David's general weakness toward disciplining his children. The latter tendency would manifest itself repeatedly in David's later years. David's son Absalom, Tamar's brother, was also upset and filled with hatred toward Amnon.

"Why Amnon?" the king asked. 27But Absalom kept on pressing the king until he finally
agreed to let all his sons attend, including Amnon. So Absalom prepared a feast fit for a king.*
28Absalom told his men, "Wait until Amnon gets drunk; then at my signal, kill him!
13:29 Don't be afraid. I'm the one who has given the command. Take courage and do it!" 29So at
2 Sam 18:9 Absalom's signal they murdered Amnon. Then the other sons of the king jumped on their
mules and fled.
30As they were on the way back to Jerusalem, this report reached David: "Absalom has
13:31 killed all the king's sons; not one is left alive!" 31The king got up, tore his robe, and threw
2 Sam 12:16 himself on the ground. His advisers also tore their clothes in horror and sorrow.
13:32 2 Sam 13:3-5 32But just then Jonadab, the son of David's brother Shimea, arrived and said, "No, don't
believe that all the king's sons have been killed! It was only Amnon! Absalom has been
13:34 plotting this ever since Amnon raped his sister Tamar. 33No, my lord the king, your sons
2 Sam 18:24 aren't all dead! It was only Amnon." 34Meanwhile Absalom escaped.
Then the watchman on the Jerusalem wall saw a great crowd coming toward the city
from the west. He ran to tell the king, "I see a crowd of people coming from the Horonaim
road* along the side of the hill."
35"Look!" Jonadab told the king. "There they are now! The king's sons are coming, just
as I said."
13:37 36They soon arrived, weeping and sobbing, and the king and all his servants wept bit-
2 Sam 3:3; 14:23, 32 terly with them. 37And David mourned many days for his son Amnon.
Absalom fled to his grandfather, Talmai son of Ammihud, the king of Geshur. 38He
13:39 stayed there in Geshur for three years. 39And King David, now reconciled to Amnon's
2 Sam 12:19-23 death, longed to be reunited with his son Absalom.*

JOAB ARRANGES FOR ABSALOM'S RETURN

14:2 14 Joab realized how much the king longed to see Absalom. 2So he sent for a
2 Chr 11:5-10 woman from Tekoa who had a reputation for great wisdom. He said to her, "Pre-
Amos 1:1 tend you are in mourning; wear mourning clothes and don't put on lotions.* Act like a
14:3 woman who has been mourning for the dead for a long time. 3Then go to the king and tell
2 Sam 14:19 him the story I am about to tell you." Then Joab told her what to say.
4When the woman from Tekoa approached the king, she bowed with her face to the
ground in deep respect and cried out, "O king! Help me!"

13:27 As in Greek and Latin versions (compare also Dead Sea Scrolls); the Hebrew text omits this sentence. 13:34 As in Greek version; Hebrew reads *from the road behind him.* 13:39 Or *no longer felt a need to go out after Absalom.* 14:2 Hebrew *don't anoint yourself with oil.*

13:28-29 When David failed to take action against Amnon, Absalom decided to take justice into his own hands. He carefully crafted a plot to take Amnon's life. This would gain justice for his sister—and would place him one step closer to the throne after David's death.

13:37 There were two tribes of Geshurites. One lived east of the Jordan River near Bashan. The other was a neighbor to the Philistines to the west and southwest of Israel. We don't have records to tell us whether these tribes were related. While he was a fugitive, David raided the western Geshurites (1 Samuel 27:8); after he became king, he married Maacah, the daughter of the king of the eastern Geshurites, forming an alliance with them (2 Samuel 3:3). It was among these eastern Geshurites that Absalom found refuge.

13:39 This verse is difficult to translate, and that makes David's attitude toward Absalom difficult to discern. According to the *New Living Translation,* the verse says David longed to be reunited with Absalom. Later events clearly reveal that David loved Absalom, supporting this translation. However, this verse may mean instead that David wanted nothing to do with Absalom because Absalom had murdered Amnon. As we will see, David let Absalom remain in exile in Geshur for three years before giving the order to have him brought home. That suggests that David had the power to bring Absalom home at any time but did not do so. Also, when David did bring Absalom home, he kept him at arm's length.

14:1 Joab, David's nephew and army commander, seems to have perceived a need for David to bring Absalom back from exile. Perhaps he feared that a lingering breach between the king and his charismatic son would split the nation. Small hints in this chapter suggest that Joab had been advising the king to bring Absalom home for some time, to no avail. Therefore, Joab resorted to a deceptive strategy to force David's hand.

5“What’s the trouble?” the king asked.
“Alas, I am a widow!” she replied. “My husband is dead. 6My two sons had a fight out in
the field. And since no one was there to stop it, one of them was killed. 7Now the rest of the
family is demanding, ‘Let us have your son. We will execute him for murdering his
brother. He doesn’t deserve to inherit his family’s property.’ They want to extinguish the
only coal I have left, and my husband’s name and family will disappear from the face of
the earth.”
8“Leave it to me,” the king told her. “Go home, and I’ll see to it that no one touches him.”
9“Oh, thank you, my lord the king,” the woman from Tekoa replied. “If you are criticized
for helping me, let the blame fall on me and on my father’s house, and let the king and his
throne be innocent.”
10“If anyone objects,” the king said, “bring him to me. I can assure you he will never
complain again!”
11Then she said, “Please swear to me by the LORD your God that you won’t let anyone
take vengeance against my son. I want no more bloodshed.”
“As surely as the LORD lives,” he replied, “not a hair on your son’s head will be disturbed!”
12“Please allow me to ask one more thing of my lord the king,” she said.
“Go ahead and speak,” he responded.
13She replied, “Why don’t you do as much for the people of God as you have promised
to do for me? You have convicted yourself in making this decision, because you have re-
fused to bring home your own banished son. 14All of us must die eventually. Our lives are
like water spilled out on the ground, which cannot be gathered up again. But God does not
just sweep life away; instead, he devises ways to bring us back when we have been sepa-
rated from him.
15“I have come to plead with my lord the king because people have threatened me. I
said to myself, ‘Perhaps the king will listen to me 16and rescue us from those who would
cut us off from the inheritance* God has given us. 17Yes, my lord the king will give us
peace of mind again.’ I know that you are like an angel of God in discerning good from
evil. May the LORD your God be with you.”
18“I must know one thing,” the king replied, “and tell me the truth.”
“Yes, my lord the king,” she responded.
19“Did Joab put you up to this?”
And the woman replied, “My lord the king, how can I deny it? Nobody can hide any-
thing from you. Yes, Joab sent me and told me what to say. 20He did it to place the matter
before you in a different light. But you are as wise as an angel of God, and you understand
everything that happens among us!”

14:7 Num 35:19; Deut 19:12-13
14:9 Gen 43:9; 1 Sam 25:24
14:11 Num 35:12, 19, 21; Deut 19:4-10; 1 Sam 14:45
14:13 2 Sam 13:37-39; 1 Kgs 20:40-42
14:14 Job 34:14-15; Heb 9:27
14:17 1 Sam 29:9; 2 Sam 19:27
14:19 2 Sam 14:3

14:16 Or *the property;* or *the people.*

14:5-11 The woman sent by Joab told David a fictional story concerning her two sons, one of whom murdered the other. Based on her appeal, David vowed to protect the surviving brother, the murderer, from vengeful family members. The woman even managed to induce David to commit himself to her son’s well-being with an oath (14:11).

14:13 As with Nathan’s parable (12:1-7), the woman’s story left David wide open for a rebuke based on words from his own lips. He declared that the woman’s son—and, by extension, her future descendants—would have his protection. The woman replied that Israel deserved the same consideration. Instead of letting a prince of Israel languish in a foreign land, she said, David ought to bring him home. Evidently, based on her argument, Absalom was now first in line for the throne, and the woman (whose words were supplied by Joab) was appealing for the return of the heir.

▸ HOLINESS

14:14 Disciplining our children. Do you find it difficult to punish your children? Do you think you would interfere with the process of justice if you could save your child from reprimand? David did nothing in response to Amnon’s rape of Tamar. Then, when Absalom killed Amnon, David’s only action was to let Absalom live in the exile he had imposed on himself, though David seems to have had the power to bring Absalom home at any time. In time, he allowed himself to be talked into letting Absalom return unpunished. If we fail to punish sin in our own households, it is a sign of weakness, not mercy. Failure to follow the biblical guidelines for maintaining discipline in your home only leads to greater sin and eventual calamity (Proverbs 29:15). (***See Holiness**> Submission> Learning God’s Word> Teaching your children,* TopicGuide page A40.)

21 So the king sent for Joab and told him, "All right, go and bring back the young man
Absalom."

22 Joab bowed with his face to the ground in deep respect and said, "At last I know that I
have gained your approval, my lord the king, for you have granted me this request!"

14:23 23 Then Joab went to Geshur and brought Absalom back to Jerusalem. 24 But the king
2 Sam 13:37-39 gave this order: "Absalom may go to his own house, but he must never come into my pres-
ence." So Absalom did not see the king.

ABSALOM RECONCILED TO DAVID

25 Now Absalom was praised as the most handsome man in all Israel. He was flawless from
head to foot. 26 He cut his hair only once a year, and then only because it was so heavy.
14:27 When he weighed it out, it came to five pounds!* 27 He had three sons and one daughter.
2 Sam 13:1 His daughter's name was Tamar, and she was very beautiful.

14:28 28 Absalom lived in Jerusalem for two years, but he never got to see the king. 29 Then Ab-
2 Sam 14:24 salom sent for Joab to ask him to intercede for him, but Joab refused to come. Absalom
sent for him a second time, but again Joab refused to come. 30 So Absalom said to his ser-
vants, "Go and set fire to Joab's barley field, the field next to mine." So they set his field on
fire, as Absalom had commanded.

31 Then Joab came to Absalom at his house and demanded, "Why did your servants set
my field on fire?"

14:32 32 And Absalom replied, "Because I wanted you to ask the king why he brought me back
1 Sam 20:8 from Geshur if he didn't intend to see me. I might as well have stayed there. Let me see the
king; if he finds me guilty of anything, then let him kill me."

14:33 33 So Joab told the king what Absalom had said. Then at last David summoned Absalom,
Gen 33:4 Luke 15:20 who came and bowed low before the king, and the king kissed him.

ABSALOM'S REBELLION

15:1 **15** After this, Absalom bought a chariot and horses, and he hired fifty bodyguards to
1 Kgs 1:5 run ahead of him. 2 He got up early every morning and went out to the gate of the
city. When people brought a case to the king for judgment, Absalom would ask where in
Israel they were from, and they would tell him their tribe. 3 Then Absalom would say,
"You've really got a strong case here! It's too bad the king doesn't have anyone to hear it.
15:4 Judg 9:29 4 I wish I were the judge. Then everyone could bring their cases to me for judgment, and I
would give them justice!"

15:5 2 Sam 14:33 5 When people tried to bow before him, Absalom wouldn't let them. Instead, he took
15:6 them by the hand and kissed them. 6 Absalom did this with everyone who came to the
Rom 16:18 king for judgment, and so he stole the hearts of all the people of Israel.

14:26 Hebrew *200 shekels* [2.3 kilograms] *by the royal standard.*

14:24 David allowed Absalom to return and live in Jerusalem as the heir to the throne. Daniel, son of Abigail, was actually older than Absalom, but he is mentioned only briefly (2 Samuel 3:3; 1 Chronicles 3:1) and evidently was never considered as an heir.

▸ HOLINESS

14:33 Getting away with murder. Our children can be highly skilled at getting their way. Absalom revealed himself to be a skilled manipulator. Using arson as a motivator, Absalom forced Joab to intercede on his behalf before David. And softhearted David, clearly willing to overlook anything, welcomed him back to the royal court. If we are willing to overlook every fault in our children for the sake of remaining emotionally close to them, we will never help them develop the moral compass they need to please God. Honor your God and your children by teaching them, through your example, that decisions have consequences. (***See Holiness****> Submission> Learning God's Word> Teaching your children,* TopicGuide page A40.)

15:1-6 Not content to be just the heir to Israel's throne, Absalom began plotting to seize his father's crown. First, he adopted a dashing lifestyle, complete with a chariot and an entourage—just the image of a king the people of Israel longed to see. Then he began to proclaim himself more concerned about the people's problems than their judges, including the ultimate human judge, King David. Soon, Absalom became wildly popular among the masses.

▸ WORSHIP

15:6 Submission to authority. Whether you are like Saul and attempt to kill your rivals, or like Absalom and try to take over through treachery, you are in sin when you refuse to function under divine and human authority (Romans 14). When confronted with leadership of which you disapprove, will you be like Saul or Absalom? Or will you be like David, who took God's difficult path to power? (***See Worship****> NT> Our Role> Attitude> Submissive before authority,* TopicGuide page A31.)

7After four years,* Absalom said to the king, "Let me go to Hebron to offer a sacrifice to
the LORD and fulfill a vow I made to Him. 8For while your servant was at Geshur in Aram, I
promised to sacrifice to the LORD in Hebron* if he would bring me back to Jerusalem."
9"All right," the king told him. "Go and fulfill your vow."
So Absalom went to Hebron. 10But while he was there, he sent secret messengers to all
the tribes of Israel to stir up a rebellion against the king. "As soon as you hear the ram's
horn," his message read, "you are to say, 'Absalom has been crowned king in Hebron.'"
11He took 200 men from Jerusalem with him as guests, but they knew nothing of his in-
tentions. 12While Absalom was offering the sacrifices, he sent for Ahithophel, one of Da-
vid's counselors who lived in Giloh. Soon many others also joined Absalom, and the
conspiracy gained momentum.

DAVID ESCAPES FROM JERUSALEM

13A messenger soon arrived in Jerusalem to tell David, "All Israel has joined Absalom in a
conspiracy against you!"
14"Then we must flee at once, or it will be too late!" David urged his men. "Hurry! If we
get out of the city before Absalom arrives, both we and the city of Jerusalem will be spared
from disaster."
15"We are with you," his advisers replied. "Do what you think is best."
16So the king and all his household set out at once. He left no one behind except ten of
his concubines to look after the palace. 17The king and all his people set out on foot, paus-
ing at the last house 18to let all the king's men move past to lead the way. There were
600 men from Gath who had come with David, along with the king's bodyguard.*
19Then the king turned and said to Ittai, a leader of the men from Gath, "Why are you
coming with us? Go on back to King Absalom, for you are a guest in Israel, a foreigner in
exile. 20You arrived only recently, and should I force you today to wander with us? I don't
even know where we will go. Go on back and take your kinsmen with you, and may the
LORD show you His unfailing love and faithfulness."*
21But Ittai said to the king, "I vow by the LORD and by your own life that I will go wher-
ever my lord the king goes, no matter what happens—whether it means life or death."
22David replied, "All right, come with us." So Ittai and all his men and their families went
along.
23Everyone cried loudly as the king and his followers passed by. They crossed the Kid-
ron Valley and then went out toward the wilderness.

15:7 As in Greek and Syriac versions; Hebrew reads *forty years.* 15:8 As in some Greek manuscripts; Hebrew lacks *in Hebron.* 15:18 Hebrew *the Kerethites and Pelethites.* 15:20 As in Greek version; Hebrew reads *and may unfailing love and faithfulness go with you.*

15:8 Gen 28:20; 2 Sam 13:37-39
15:10 1 Kgs 1:34; 2 Kgs 9:13
15:12 Josh 15:51; 2 Sam 17:14; Ps 3:1
15:13 Judg 9:3
15:14 2 Sam 12:11; Ps 3:TITLE
15:16 2 Sam 16:21-22
15:19 2 Sam 18:2
15:21 Ruth 1:16-17

15:7 Hebron was an important city in southern Israel, situated in the land of the tribe of Judah. After the death of Saul, the people of Judah recognized David as king, and he ruled from Hebron (2 Samuel 2:11) until he was crowned king of all Israel and captured Jerusalem as his capital (2 Samuel 5:6-7). This history made Hebron the perfect place for Absalom to launch his uprising against David.

15:11-12 Absalom took 200 leading citizens of Jerusalem with him to Hebron. They were not in on Absalom's plot, but Absalom knew that most Israelites would interpret their presence with him as support when his rebellion began. He also took Ahithophel, who had been a highly respected counselor to David (2 Samuel 16:23) but who apparently had been dismissed from the king's service; Ahithophel may have borne a grudge against David.

15:16 Some concubines remained to care for the needs of the elaborate palace. Perhaps these "second wives" were initially chosen for their domestic skills and not as life partners (Judges 8:31).

15:18 Gath was a Philistine city. David hid there while Saul, Israel's first king, hunted for him as if he was a criminal. Achish, the king of Gath, gave David and his men another Philistine town, Ziklag, to use as their headquarters. There, David pretended to have defected to the Philistines' side while he waited for the throne of Israel that God had promised him. These Gittites (the term for inhabitants of Gath), led by Ittai, may have entered David's service during this period.

24 Zadok and all the Levites also came along, carrying the Ark of the Covenant of God.
They set down the Ark of God, and Abiathar offered sacrifices* until everyone had passed
out of the city.
25 Then the king instructed Zadok to take the Ark of God back into the city. "If the LORD
sees fit," David said, "He will bring me back to see the Ark and the Tabernacle* again. 26 But
if He is through with me, then let Him do what seems best to Him."
27 The king also told Zadok the priest, "Look,* here is my plan. You and Abiathar* should
return quietly to the city with your son Ahimaaz and Abiathar's son Jonathan. 28 I will stop
at the shallows of the Jordan River* and wait there for a report from you." 29 So Zadok and
Abiathar took the Ark of God back to the city and stayed there.
30 David walked up the road to the Mount of Olives, weeping as he went. His head was
covered and his feet were bare as a sign of mourning. And the people who were with him
covered their heads and wept as they climbed the hill. 31 When someone told David that
his adviser Ahithophel was now backing Absalom, David prayed, "O LORD, let Ahithophel
give Absalom foolish advice!"
32 When David reached the summit of the Mount of Olives where people worshiped
God, Hushai the Arkite was waiting there for him. Hushai had torn his clothing and put dirt
on his head as a sign of mourning. 33 But David told him, "If you go with me, you will only
be a burden. 34 Return to Jerusalem and tell Absalom, 'I will now be your adviser, O king,
just as I was your father's adviser in the past.' Then you can frustrate and counter Ahitho-
phel's advice. 35 Zadok and Abiathar, the priests, will be there. Tell them about the plans
being made in the king's palace, 36 and they will send their sons Ahimaaz and Jonathan to
tell me what is going on."
37 So David's friend Hushai returned to Jerusalem, getting there just as Absalom arrived.

DAVID AND ZIBA

16 When David had gone a little beyond the summit of the Mount of Olives, Ziba, the
servant of Mephibosheth,* was waiting there for him. He had two donkeys loaded
with 200 loaves of bread, 100 clusters of raisins, 100 bunches of summer fruit, and a
wineskin full of wine.
2 "What are these for?" the king asked Ziba.
Ziba replied, "The donkeys are for the king's people to ride on, and the bread and sum-
mer fruit are for the young men to eat. The wine is for those who become exhausted in the
wilderness."

15:24 Num 4:15; 1 Sam 4:4-5; 2 Sam 8:17; 20:25
15:25 1 Sam 3:18; Ps 43:3
15:27 2 Sam 17:17
15:28 2 Sam 17:16
15:30 Esth 6:12; Ezek 24:23
15:31 2 Sam 15:12; 16:23; 17:14, 23
15:32 Josh 16:2
15:34 2 Sam 16:19
15:35 2 Sam 17:15-16
15:36 2 Sam 15:27
15:37 1 Chr 27:33
16:1 2 Sam 9:1-13
16:2 2 Sam 17:27-29

15:24 Or *Abiathar went up.* 15:25 Hebrew *and his dwelling place.* 15:27a As in Greek version; Hebrew reads *Are you a seer?* or *Do you see?* 15:27b Hebrew lacks *and Abiathar;* compare 15:29. 15:28 Hebrew *at the crossing points of the wilderness.* 16:1 *Mephibosheth* is another name for Merib-baal.

15:24-26 The high priests and the Levites were ready to evacuate Jerusalem with David, bringing the Ark of the Covenant along with them. But David refused to treat the Ark as a talisman or good-luck charm. Instead, he trusted in God to protect him.

15:30 The superscription on Psalm 3 indicates that David wrote it after he fled from Absalom. The grief David displayed as he left Jerusalem is mirrored in the opening of that poem, though David concludes with a reference to God's salvation and restoration.

▸ WORSHIP
15:37 Connected to others. Many of David's friends risked their lives to stay in Jerusalem to prepare a counterattack against Absalom. Do you have friends who would risk everything for you? Are you the sort of person who would do anything possible to help a friend in need? God uses the network of human relationships in your life to connect you even more deeply to Him. By loving one another, we grow in our love for God. (***See Worship****> NT> Our Role> Attitude> Cooperative with other believers,* TopicGuide page A31.)

16:1 Beverages were transported in the cured skins or stomachs of camels, goats, cows, or other animals. Depending on the size of the skin, the amount of wine could have been significant and comparable to the rest of the foodstuffs offered by Ziba.

3"And where is Mephibosheth, Saul's grandson?" the king asked him.
"He stayed in Jerusalem," Ziba replied. "He said, 'Today I will get back the kingdom of
my grandfather Saul.'"
4"In that case," the king told Ziba, "I give you everything Mephibosheth owns."
"I bow before you," Ziba replied. "May I always be pleasing to you, my lord the king."

16:3 2 Sam 9:9-10; 19:26-27

SHIMEI CURSES DAVID

5As King David came to Bahurim, a man came out of the village cursing them. It was
Shimei son of Gera, from the same clan as Saul's family. 6He threw stones at the king
and the king's officers and all the mighty warriors who surrounded him. 7"Get out
of here, you murderer, you scoundrel!" he shouted at David. 8"The LORD is paying you
back for all the bloodshed in Saul's clan. You stole his throne, and now the LORD has
given it to your son Absalom. At last you will taste some of your own medicine, for you
are a murderer!"
9"Why should this dead dog curse my lord the king?" Abishai son of Zeruiah de-
manded. "Let me go over and cut off his head!"
10"No!" the king said. "Who asked your opinion, you sons of Zeruiah! If the LORD has
told him to curse me, who are you to stop him?"
11Then David said to Abishai and to all his servants, "My own son is trying to kill me.
Doesn't this relative of Saul* have even more reason to do so? Leave him alone and let
him curse, for the LORD has told him to do it. 12And perhaps the LORD will see that I am be-
ing wronged and will bless me because of these curses today." 13So David and his men
continued down the road, and Shimei kept pace with them on a nearby hillside, cursing as
he went and throwing stones at David and tossing dust into the air.
14The king and all who were with him grew weary along the way, so they rested when
they reached the Jordan River.*

16:5 Exod 22:28; 1 Sam 17:43; 2 Sam 19:16-23; 1 Kgs 2:8
16:7 2 Sam 12:9
16:9 Exod 22:28; 1 Sam 26:8; 2 Sam 19:21
16:10 2 Sam 3:39; 19:22; John 18:11; Rom 9:20
16:11 Gen 45:5; 1 Sam 26:19; 2 Sam 12:11
16:12 Deut 23:5; Rom 8:28

AHITHOPHEL ADVISES ABSALOM

15Meanwhile, Absalom and all the army of Israel arrived at Jerusalem, accompanied by
Ahithophel. 16When David's friend Hushai the Arkite arrived, he went immediately to see
Absalom. "Long live the king!" he exclaimed. "Long live the king!"
17"Is this the way you treat your friend David?" Absalom asked him. "Why aren't you
with him?"
18"I'm here because I belong to the man who is chosen by the LORD and by all the men

16:15 2 Sam 15:12, 37
16:16 1 Sam 10:24; 2 Sam 15:33-34; 2 Kgs 11:12

16:11 Hebrew *this Benjaminite.* 16:14 As in Greek version (see also 17:16); Hebrew reads *when they reached their destination.*

16:4 David had made Ziba a servant of Mephibosheth (2 Samuel 9:10-12). Now, perhaps out of bitterness, Ziba lied about his master, saying that Mephibosheth was hoping Israel would turn to him, Saul's grandson, as a legitimate claimant to the throne. This would have been an act of deep treachery against David, who had treated Mephibosheth as his own son. In response, David gave Ziba all that belonged to Mephibosheth, but when he heard both sides of the story in chapter 19, he divided the disputed inheritance. David appears to have not fully believed either person.

▸ HOLINESS
16:4 Taking advantage. Ziba took advantage of the flurry of activity to attempt to advance his fortunes. He lied about Mephibosheth's words (see 2 Samuel 19:26) and capitalized on David's inability to double-check his charge. God does honor shrewdness in business (Luke 16:1-8), but this sort of behavior is forbidden. You are bound to honesty in the political and business worlds (Leviticus 19:36; Proverbs 16:11). (***See Holiness****> Disciplines> Of Engagement> Honesty,* TopicGuide page A42.)

16:5-13 Shimei may have held David responsible for the deaths of Saul, Abner, and Ishbosheth. His mock stoning of David was a grave insult, but David bore it because he sensed that he deserved it, and he thought it likely that God had inspired it.

▸ BIBLE
16:10 Receiving criticism. This experience of personal attack on David by Shimei apparently shocked David back into the man we know and love, the man after God's own heart. He revealed that he was no Saul, lashing out at those who appeared to oppose him. He could take criticism in stride, knowing it might very well be from God. Always accept criticism as a gift from God that allows you to see yourself as others do. (***See Bible****> Power> Wisdom> Instruction leads to wisdom,* TopicGuide page A11.)

16:19 of Israel," Hushai replied. 19"And anyway, why shouldn't I serve you? Just as I was your fa-
2 Sam 15:33-34 ther's adviser, now I will be your adviser!"
20Then Absalom turned to Ahithophel and asked him, "What should I do next?"
16:21 21Ahithophel told him, "Go and sleep with your father's concubines, for he has left them
2 Sam 15:16 here to look after the palace. Then all Israel will know that you have insulted your father
16:22 2 Sam 12:11; 20:3 beyond hope of reconciliation, and they will throw their support to you." 22So they set up a
tent on the palace roof where everyone could see it, and Absalom went in and had sex
with his father's concubines.
16:23 2 Sam 15:12; 23Absalom followed Ahithophel's advice, just as David had done. For every word Ahith-
17:14, 23 ophel spoke seemed as wise as though it had come directly from the mouth of God.

17 Now Ahithophel urged Absalom, "Let me choose 12,000 men to start out after
17:2 David tonight. 2I will catch up with him while he is weary and discouraged. He and
2 Sam 16:14 his troops will panic, and everyone will run away. Then I will kill only the king, 3and I will
1 Kgs 22:31 bring all the people back to you as a bride returns to her husband. After all, it is only one
man's life that you seek.* Then you will be at peace with all the people." 4This plan seemed
good to Absalom and to all the elders of Israel.

HUSHAI COUNTERS AHITHOPHEL'S ADVICE

17:5 5But then Absalom said, "Bring in Hushai the Arkite. Let's see what he thinks about this."
2 Sam 15:32-34 6When Hushai arrived, Absalom told him what Ahithophel had said. Then he asked, "What
is your opinion? Should we follow Ahithophel's advice? If not, what do you suggest?"
17:7 7"Well," Hushai replied to Absalom, "this time Ahithophel has made a mistake. 8You
2 Sam 16:21 know your father and his men; they are mighty warriors. Right now they are as enraged as
17:8 a mother bear who has been robbed of her cubs. And remember that your father is an ex-
Hos 13:8 perienced man of war. He won't be spending the night among the troops. 9He has proba-
bly already hidden in some pit or cave. And when he comes out and attacks and a few of
your men fall, there will be panic among your troops, and the word will spread that Absa-
17:10 lom's men are being slaughtered. 10Then even the bravest soldiers, though they have the
Josh 2:9, 11 heart of a lion, will be paralyzed with fear. For all Israel knows what a mighty warrior your
father is and how courageous his men are.
11"I recommend that you mobilize the entire army of Israel, bringing them from as far
away as Dan in the north and Beersheba in the south. That way you will have an army as
numerous as the sand on the seashore. And I advise that you personally lead the troops.
12When we find David, we'll fall on him like dew that falls on the ground. Then neither he
17:13 nor any of his men will be left alive. 13And if David were to escape into some town, you
Mic 1:6 will have all Israel there at your command. Then we can take ropes and drag the walls of
the town into the nearest valley until every stone is torn down."
17:14 2 Sam 15:31-34 14Then Absalom and all the men of Israel said, "Hushai's advice is better than Ahithophel's."

17:3 As in Greek version; Hebrew reads *like the return of all is the man whom you seek.*

16:22 This terrible act fulfilled the prophecy of Nathan (2 Samuel 12:11). Sleeping with David's concubines was a way for Absalom to proclaim that he was now king; the act said that what had been David's was now Absalom's. However, this behavior was clearly forbidden under the Mosaic law (Leviticus 18:7-8). Also, because of its personal nature, this course of action drove a permanent wedge between Absalom and his father.

17:14 The author of 2 Samuel declares that Ahithophel had come up with the better plan. It represented a lightning attack that might well have taken David by surprise and ended the civil war before it could get started. But Absalom listened to Hushai's advice because he believed that his father was still powerful and would be able to defeat a moderate force of 12,000 soldiers (alternate translation: 12 companies of soldiers). God allowed this delusion so He could bring defeat upon Absalom and his forces.

▸ GOD

17:14 The wisdom of the unwise. The enemies of God should never be underestimated. Many non-Christians are wise and thoughtful, and we would do well to consider, with discernment, their ideas. But God often delights to thwart the wisdom of mere humans to demonstrate that it is not by might or power but by His Spirit that kingdoms rise and fall. In difficult situations, trust in God and His Word, not in a so-called "no-lose" strategy from the world. (***See God****> God's Attributes> All-Knowing> His wisdom and knowledge are way beyond us,* TopicGuide page A15.)

For the LORD had determined to defeat the counsel of Ahithophel, which really was the
better plan, so that he could bring disaster on Absalom!

HUSHAI WARNS DAVID TO ESCAPE

15 Hushai told Zadok and Abiathar, the priests, what Ahithophel had said to Absalom and
the elders of Israel and what he himself had advised instead. 16 "Quick!" he told them.
"Find David and urge him not to stay at the shallows of the Jordan River* tonight. He must
go across at once into the wilderness beyond. Otherwise he will die and his entire army
with him."

17 Jonathan and Ahimaaz had been staying at En-rogel so as not to be seen entering and
leaving the city. Arrangements had been made for a servant girl to bring them the mes-
sage they were to take to King David. 18 But a boy spotted them at En-rogel, and he told
Absalom about it. So they quickly escaped to Bahurim, where a man hid them down inside
a well in his courtyard. 19 The man's wife put a cloth over the top of the well and scattered
grain on it to dry in the sun; so no one suspected they were there.

20 When Absalom's men arrived, they asked her, "Have you seen Ahimaaz and Jonathan?"

The woman replied, "They were here, but they crossed over the brook." Absalom's men
looked for them without success and returned to Jerusalem.

21 Then the two men crawled out of the well and hurried on to King David. "Quick!" they
told him, "cross the Jordan tonight!" And they told him how Ahithophel had advised that
he be captured and killed. 22 So David and all the people with him went across the Jordan
River during the night, and they were all on the other bank before dawn.

23 When Ahithophel realized that his advice had not been followed, he saddled his don-
key, went to his hometown, set his affairs in order, and hanged himself. He died there and
was buried in the family tomb.

24 David soon arrived at Mahanaim. By now, Absalom had mobilized the entire army of
Israel and was leading his troops across the Jordan River. 25 Absalom had appointed Ama-
sa as commander of his army, replacing Joab, who had been commander under David.
(Amasa was Joab's cousin. His father was Jether,* an Ishmaelite.* His mother, Abigail
daughter of Nahash, was the sister of Joab's mother, Zeruiah.) 26 Absalom and the Israelite
army set up camp in the land of Gilead.

27 When David arrived at Mahanaim, he was warmly greeted by Shobi son of Nahash,
who came from Rabbah of the Ammonites, and by Makir son of Ammiel from Lo-debar,
and by Barzillai of Gilead from Rogelim. 28 They brought sleeping mats, cooking pots, serv-
ing bowls, wheat and barley, flour and roasted grain, beans, lentils, 29 honey, butter, sheep,
goats, and cheese for David and those who were with him. For they said, "You must all be
very hungry and tired and thirsty after your long march through the wilderness."

17:15 2 Sam 15:35-36
17:16 2 Sam 15:28
17:17 Josh 15:7; 2 Sam 15:27, 35-36; 18:19
17:18 2 Sam 3:16; 16:5
17:19 Josh 2:4-6
17:20 Exod 1:19; Lev 19:11; 1 Sam 19:12-17
17:23 2 Sam 16:23; 2 Kgs 20:1; Matt 27:5
17:24 Gen 32:2; 2 Sam 2:8
17:25 2 Sam 19:13; 20:12; 1 Kgs 2:5; 1 Chr 2:16-17
17:27 2 Sam 9:4; 10:1-2; 12:26, 29; 1 Kgs 2:7
17:29 2 Sam 16:2

17:16 Hebrew *at the crossing points of the wilderness.* 17:25a Hebrew *Ithra,* a variant spelling of Jether. 17:25b As in some Greek manuscripts (see also 1 Chr 2:17); Hebrew reads *an Israelite.*

17:22 At this time in history, this area of the Jordan River ranged from 80 to 180 feet wide. It took all night for David's troops and family members to cross with all their supplies.

▸ ADOPTION

17:23 Rejection minus God. Ahithophel could not handle even the slightest rejection—one instance of the king's son listening to someone else and he killed himself. How do you handle failure or rejection? Do you spin into depression or take it in stride? There is a place for disappointment at personal failure, but our feelings must be connected to the reality of our standing with God—if God is for us, who can be against us? (***See Adoption*** *> With Christ> Supernatural> Freedom from rejection,* TopicGuide page A37.)

17:27 Three men—Shobi, Makir, and Barzillai—greeted David when he arrived in Mahanaim. They had collected food and other supplies for him and his men. This expression of support for the hard-pressed king was not without risk, for the area around Mahanaim had been a hotbed of support for Saul. Indeed, Saul's son Ishbosheth reigned from Mahanaim during his short-lived kingship after Saul's death. Makir himself cared for Saul's grandson Mephibosheth for many years prior to Mephibosheth's ascension to the royal court and the restoration of his lands (2 Samuel 9:4-5). That made him one of the few men who served Saul's family and David's with equal loyalty.

18:1 Exod 18:25 1 Sam 22:7
ABSALOM'S DEFEAT AND DEATH

18 David now mustered the men who were with him and appointed generals and
captains* to lead them. 2He sent the troops out in three groups, placing one group
18:2 1 Sam 11:11 under Joab, one under Joab's brother Abishai son of Zeruiah, and one under Ittai, the man
2 Sam 15:19-22 from Gath. The king told his troops, "I am going out with you."
18:3 3But his men objected strongly. "You must not go," they urged. "If we have to turn and
2 Sam 21:17 run—and even if half of us die—it will make no difference to Absalom's troops; they will be
looking only for you. You are worth 10,000 of us,* and it is better that you stay here in the
town and send help if we need it."
18:4 4"If you think that's the best plan, I'll do it," the king answered. So he stood alongside the
2 Sam 18:24 gate of the town as all the troops marched out in groups of hundreds and of thousands.
5And the king gave this command to Joab, Abishai, and Ittai: "For my sake, deal gently
with young Absalom." And all the troops heard the king give this order to his commanders.
18:6 6So the battle began in the forest of Ephraim, 7and the Israelite troops were beaten back
Josh 17:15 by David's men. There was a great slaughter that day, and 20,000 men laid down their
lives. 8The battle raged all across the countryside, and more men died because of the for-
est than were killed by the sword.
18:9 9During the battle, Absalom happened to come upon some of David's men. He tried
2 Sam 14:26 to escape on his mule, but as he rode beneath the thick branches of a great tree, his
hair* got caught in the tree. His mule kept going and left him dangling in the air. 10One
of David's men saw what had happened and told Joab, "I saw Absalom dangling from a
great tree."
11"What?" Joab demanded. "You saw him there and didn't kill him? I would have re-
warded you with ten pieces of silver* and a hero's belt!"
12"I would not kill the king's son for even a thousand pieces of silver,*" the man replied
to Joab. "We all heard the king say to you and Abishai and Ittai, 'For my sake, please spare
18:13 young Absalom.' 13And if I had betrayed the king by killing his son—and the king would
2 Sam 14:19-20 certainly find out who did it—you yourself would be the first to abandon me."
14"Enough of this nonsense," Joab said. Then he took three daggers and plunged them
into Absalom's heart as he dangled, still alive, in the great tree. 15Ten of Joab's young ar-
mor bearers then surrounded Absalom and killed him.
18:16 16Then Joab blew the ram's horn, and his men returned from chasing the army of Israel.
2 Sam 2:28; 20:22

18:1 Hebrew *appointed commanders of thousands and commanders of hundreds.* 18:3 As in two Hebrew manuscripts and some Greek and Latin manuscripts; most Hebrew manuscripts read *Now there are 10,000 like us.* 18:9 Hebrew *his head.* 18:11 Hebrew *10 shekels of silver,* about 4 ounces or 114 grams in weight. 18:12 Hebrew *1,000 shekels,* about 25 pounds or 11.4 kilograms in weight.

18:5 The theme of David's growing weakness, which began in chapter 12, continues as he wrongly asks his generals to not execute a traitor. The author of 2 Samuel has already told us that it was God's intention to bring disaster on Absalom (17:14). By commanding his men to spare Absalom, David was setting himself against God's justice.

▸ HOLINESS

18:5 All about us. Even in his most inexcusable act of misplaced protection of his son, David spoke the truth—it was all for him. All along, it was for David's sake, not Absalom's. If only parents could see how their "anything goes" child-rearing policies are all about them and their needs, not about their children's needs. Do not let your selfishness and sentimentality ruin your children. (***See Holiness****> Law and Grace> Law> Parents and children,* TopicGuide page A41.)

18:9-18 A mule was the ideal war steed in the rough terrain of the forest of Ephraim. But the mule could not deliver Absalom from God's pursuing justice. The fact that Absalom became stuck in a tree and eventually died there was a powerful symbol that he was under God's curse (Deuteronomy 21:22-23). Likewise, his burial was reminiscent of that of Achan, another Israelite who made himself an enemy of God and was laid to rest under a heap of stones (Joshua 7:26).

▸ GOD

18:9 Strength and weakness. Ironically, God used Absalom's point of personal pride, his beautiful hair, to end his patricidal campaign. Our greatest strengths are often our greatest weaknesses. Humble yourself before God and never grow arrogant about your strengths, for misplaced pride directly conflicts with God's best for you and those you love (Isaiah 2:12; Proverbs 3:34). (***See God****> Relationship> Barriers> Pride,* TopicGuide page A14.)

17 They threw Absalom's body into a deep pit in the forest and piled a great heap of stones **18:17**
over it. And all Israel fled to their homes. Josh 7:26; 8:29
18 During his lifetime, Absalom had built a monument to himself in the King's Valley, for **18:18**
he said, "I have no son to carry on my name." He named the monument after himself, and Gen 14:17 1 Sam 15:12
it is known as Absalom's Monument to this day. 2 Sam 14:27

DAVID MOURNS ABSALOM'S DEATH

19 Then Zadok's son Ahimaaz said, "Let me run to the king with the good news that the **18:19**
LORD has rescued him from his enemies." 2 Sam 15:36
20 "No," Joab told him, "it wouldn't be good news to the king that his son is dead. You
can be my messenger another time, but not today."
21 Then Joab said to a man from Ethiopia,* "Go tell the king what you have seen." The
man bowed and ran off.
22 But Ahimaaz continued to plead with Joab, "Whatever happens, please let me go,
too."
"Why should you go, my son?" Joab replied. "There will be no reward for your news."
23 "Yes, but let me go anyway," he begged.
Joab finally said, "All right, go ahead." So Ahimaaz took the less demanding route by
way of the plain and ran to Mahanaim ahead of the Ethiopian.
24 While David was sitting between the inner and outer gates of the town, the watchman **18:24**
climbed to the roof of the gateway by the wall. As he looked, he saw a lone man running 2 Sam 13:34; 19:8-10
toward them. 25 He shouted the news down to David, and the king replied, "If he is alone, 2 Kgs 9:17
he has news."
As the messenger came closer, 26 the watchman saw another man running toward
them. He shouted down, "Here comes another one!"
The king replied, "He also will have news."
27 "The first man runs like Ahimaaz son of Zadok," the watchman said. **18:27**
"He is a good man and comes with good news," the king replied. 1 Kgs 1:42
28 Then Ahimaaz cried out to the king, "Everything is all right!" He bowed before the king **18:28**
with his face to the ground and said, "Praise to the LORD your God, who has handed over 1 Sam 17:46; 25:23
the rebels who dared to stand against my lord the king."
29 "What about young Absalom?" the king demanded. "Is he all right?"
Ahimaaz replied, "When Joab told me to come, there was a lot of commotion. But I
didn't know what was happening."
30 "Wait here," the king told him. So Ahimaaz stepped aside.
31 Then the man from Ethiopia arrived and said, "I have good news for my lord the king.
Today the LORD has rescued you from all those who rebelled against you."
32 "What about young Absalom?" the king demanded. "Is he all right?" **18:32**
And the Ethiopian replied, "May all of your enemies, my lord the king, both now and in 1 Sam 25:26
the future, share the fate of that young man!"
33 *The king was overcome with emotion. He went up to the room over the gateway and **18:33**
burst into tears. And as he went, he cried, "O my son Absalom! My son, my son Absalom! If Exod 32:32 2 Sam 19:4
only I had died instead of you! O Absalom, my son, my son." Rom 9:1-3

18:21 Hebrew *from Cush;* similarly in 18:23, 31, 32. 18:33 Verse 18:33 is numbered 19:1 in Hebrew text.

18:18 This monument should not be confused with the highly visible Tomb of Absalom on the east side of the Kidron Valley in modern Jerusalem.

18:33 The writer of 2 Samuel went to great lengths to show just how anxious David was about Absalom. When the news finally reached him, David was "overcome with emotion." He mourned the loss of a son he truly loved, but his grief was heightened by the galling knowledge that Absalom's death was in part his own fault. His long-ago sin with Bathsheba brought God's judgment of rebellion and strife within his family (2 Samuel 12:11-12). That strife had now left a second son dead. No wonder David cried, "If only I had died instead of you!"

JOAB REBUKES THE KING

19:1 **19** 1*Word soon reached Joab that the king was weeping and mourning for Absalom.
2 Sam 18:5, 14 2As all the people heard of the king's deep grief for his son, the joy of that day's
victory was turned into deep sadness. 3They crept back into the town that day as though
19:4 they were ashamed and had deserted in battle. 4The king covered his face with his hands
2 Sam 15:30; 18:33 and kept on crying, "O my son Absalom! O Absalom, my son, my son!"
5Then Joab went to the king's room and said to him, "We saved your life today and the
lives of your sons, your daughters, and your wives and concubines. Yet you act like this,
making us feel ashamed of ourselves. 6You seem to love those who hate you and hate
those who love you. You have made it clear today that your commanders and troops
mean nothing to you. It seems that if Absalom had lived and all of us had died, you would
be pleased. 7Now go out there and congratulate your troops, for I swear by the LORD that if
you don't go out, not a single one of them will remain here tonight. Then you will be
worse off than ever before."
19:8 8So the king went out and took his seat at the town gate, and as the news spread
2 Sam 8:1; 15:2; 18:24 throughout the town that he was there, everyone went to him.
19:9 Meanwhile, the Israelites who had supported Absalom fled to their homes. 9And
2 Sam 8:1-14; 15:14 throughout all the tribes of Israel there was much discussion and argument going on. The
people were saying, "The king rescued us from our enemies and saved us from the Philis-
tines, but Absalom chased him out of the country. 10Now Absalom, whom we anointed to
rule over us, is dead. Why not ask David to come back and be our king again?"
19:11 11Then King David sent Zadok and Abiathar, the priests, to say to the elders of Judah,
2 Sam 15:24 "Why are you the last ones to welcome back the king into his palace? For I have heard that
all Israel is ready. 12You are my relatives, my own tribe, my own flesh and blood! So why
19:13 are you the last ones to welcome back the king?" 13And David told them to tell Amasa,
2 Sam 17:25 "Since you are my own flesh and blood, like Joab, may God strike me and even kill me if I
do not appoint you as commander of my army in his place."
14Then Amasa* convinced all the men of Judah, and they responded unanimously.
They sent word to the king, "Return to us, and bring back all who are with you."

DAVID'S RETURN TO JERUSALEM

19:15 15So the king started back to Jerusalem. And when he arrived at the Jordan River, the people
Josh 5:8-9 1 Sam 11:14-15 of Judah came to Gilgal to meet him and escort him across the river. 16Shimei son of Gera,
19:16 the man from Bahurim in Benjamin, hurried across with the men of Judah to welcome King
2 Sam 16:5-13 David. 17A thousand other men from the tribe of Benjamin were with him, including Ziba,
1 Kgs 2:8 the chief servant of the house of Saul, and Ziba's fifteen sons and twenty servants. They
19:17 rushed down to the Jordan to meet the king. 18They crossed the shallows of the Jordan to
2 Sam 9:2 bring the king's household across the river, helping him in every way they could.

19:1 Verses 19:1-43 are numbered 19:2-44 in Hebrew text. 19:14 As in Greek version; Hebrew reads *he*.

▸ SPIRITUAL WARFARE

19:6 Telling the hard truth. Joab had had enough of David's foolishness. He told David the hard truth about his shameful behavior. David responded in repentance, immediately changing his disposition toward those who had killed his son Absalom. Do you have someone in your life who can tell you the hard truth about your sin? Build accountable relationships through membership in a godly church and friendships with people who will tell you the truth in love. (***See Spiritual Warfare****> Resisting Sin and Evil> Resisting Temptation> How to Resist> By the help of our friends,* TopicGuide page A45.)

19:7 Joab all but threatened to lead another rebellion himself if David did not properly honor his fighting men. If David's own men were to desert him, he would indeed be worse off than ever, as Joab said.

19:13 David appointed Amasa, the man who commanded Absalom's army, as the new leader of his own army. This was politically astute, drawing fresh support from Judah for a Davidic kingdom. But it was also a harsh rebuke of Joab for killing Absalom and possibly for rebuking David so sternly.

19:18-23 Shimei, who cursed David as he fled from Jerusalem, came humbly to the king with an apparently genuine confession of wrongdoing and request for forgiveness. David chose not to take vengeance on him, apparently to promote national reconciliation. But he later told his son Solomon to pay Shimei back for his ill treatment of David (1 Kings 2:8-9, 36-46).

DAVID'S MERCY TO SHIMEI

As the king was about to cross the river, Shimei fell down before him. 19"My lord the king, **19:19**
please forgive me," he pleaded. "Forget the terrible thing your servant did when you left 2 Sam 16:6-9
Jerusalem. May the king put it out of his mind. 20I know how much I sinned. That is why I
have come here today, the very first person in all Israel* to greet my lord the king."
21Then Abishai son of Zeruiah said, "Shimei should die, for he cursed the LORD'S **19:21**
anointed king!" Exod 22:28
22"Who asked your opinion, you sons of Zeruiah!" David exclaimed. "Why have you **19:22**
become my adversary* today? This is not a day for execution but for celebration! Today I 1 Sam 11:13; 2 Sam 16:9-10
am once again the king of Israel!" 23Then, turning to Shimei, David vowed, "Your life will **19:23**
be spared." 1 Kgs 2:8

DAVID'S KINDNESS TO MEPHIBOSHETH

24Now Mephibosheth,* Saul's grandson, came down from Jerusalem to meet the king. He **19:24**
had not cared for his feet, trimmed his beard, or washed his clothes since the day the king 2 Sam 9:5-10
left Jerusalem. 25"Why didn't you come with me, Mephibosheth?" the king asked him. **19:25** 2 Sam 16:17
26Mephibosheth replied, "My lord the king, my servant Ziba deceived me. I told him,
'Saddle my donkey* so I can go with the king.' For as you know I am crippled. 27Ziba has **19:26** 2 Sam 9:2-3, 13
slandered me by saying that I refused to come. But I know that my lord the king is like an **19:27**
angel of God, so do what you think is best. 28All my relatives and I could expect only death 2 Sam 14:17, 20
from you, my lord, but instead you have honored me by allowing me to eat at your own **19:28**
table! What more can I ask?" 2 Sam 9:7
29"You've said enough," David replied. "I've decided that you and Ziba will divide your
land equally between you."
30"Give him all of it," Mephibosheth said. "I am content just to have you safely back
again, my lord the king!"

DAVID'S KINDNESS TO BARZILLAI

31Barzillai of Gilead had come down from Rogelim to escort the king across the Jordan. **19:31**
32He was very old, about eighty, and very wealthy. He was the one who had provided food 2 Sam 17:27-29; 1 Kgs 2:7
for the king during his stay in Mahanaim. 33"Come across with me and live in Jerusalem,"
the king said to Barzillai. "I will take care of you there."
34"No," he replied, "I am far too old to go with the king to Jerusalem. 35I am eighty years
old today, and I can no longer enjoy anything. Food and wine are no longer tasty, and I can- **19:35** Ps 90:10
not hear the singers as they sing. I would only be a burden to my lord the king. 36Just to go
across the Jordan River with the king is all the honor I need! 37Then let me return again to **19:37**
die in my own town, where my father and mother are buried. But here is your servant, my 1 Kgs 2:7
son Kimham. Let him go with my lord the king and receive whatever you want to give him." Jer 41:17
38"Good," the king agreed. "Kimham will go with me, and I will help him in any way you
would like. And I will do for you anything you want." 39So all the people crossed the Jor- **19:39** Gen 31:55
dan with the king. After David had blessed Barzillai and kissed him, Barzillai returned to Ruth 1:14
his own home. 2 Sam 14:33

19:20 Hebrew *in the house of Joseph.* 19:22 Or *my prosecutor.* 19:24 *Mephibosheth* is another name for Merib-baal.
19:26 As in Greek, Syriac, and Latin versions; Hebrew reads *I will saddle a donkey for myself.*

19:24-30 David appears to not have fully believed Mephibosheth's side of the story. Rather than punish Ziba for his apparent slander and betrayal, or punish Mephibosheth for his alleged treason, David ordered the disputed lands to be divided. Still, Mephibosheth's attitude of mourning and his willingness to yield all the land to Ziba argued for his faithfulness to David.

19:39 Barzillai was an elderly man who helped David when he fled from Absalom (2 Samuel 17:27-29). He came from his home to escort David back across the Jordan River, and David thanked him warmly for his service. Later, just as he had done for Shimei, David gave Solomon instructions on what to do for Barzillai. David told Solomon to take vengeance on Shimei, but he desired that Solomon would show continuing kindness to Barzillai and his family (1 Kings 2:7).

40The king then crossed over to Gilgal, taking Kimham with him. All the troops of Judah
and half the troops of Israel escorted the king on his way.

AN ARGUMENT OVER THE KING

41But all the men of Israel complained to the king, "The men of Judah stole the king and
didn't give us the honor of helping take you, your household, and all your men across the
Jordan."

42The men of Judah replied, "The king is one of our own kinsmen. Why should this
make you angry? We haven't eaten any of the king's food or received any special favors!"

19:43 43"But there are ten tribes in Israel," the others replied. "So we have ten times as much
2 Sam 5:1 right to the king as you do. What right do you have to treat us with such contempt?
Weren't we the first to speak of bringing him back to be our king again?" The argument
continued back and forth, and the men of Judah spoke even more harshly than the men
of Israel.

THE REVOLT OF SHEBA

20:1 **20** There happened to be a troublemaker there named Sheba son of Bicri, a man
1 Sam 22:7-8 1 Kgs 12:16 from the tribe of Benjamin. Sheba blew a ram's horn and began to chant:

2 Chr 10:16 "Down with the dynasty of David!
We have no interest in the son of Jesse.
Come on, you men of Israel,
back to your homes!"

2So all the men of Israel deserted David and followed Sheba son of Bicri. But the men of
Judah stayed with their king and escorted him from the Jordan River to Jerusalem.

20:3 3When David came to his palace in Jerusalem, he took the ten concubines he had left to
2 Sam 15:16; 16:21-22 look after the palace and placed them in seclusion. Their needs were provided for, but he
no longer slept with them. So each of them lived like a widow until she died.

20:4 4Then the king told Amasa, "Mobilize the army of Judah within three days, and report
2 Sam 17:25; 19:13 back at that time." 5So Amasa went out to notify Judah, but it took him longer than the
time he had been given.

20:6 6Then David said to Abishai, "Sheba son of Bicri is going to hurt us more than Absalom
2 Sam 21:17 did. Quick, take my troops and chase after him before he gets into a fortified town where
we can't reach him."

20:7 7So Abishai and Joab,* together with the king's bodyguard* and all the mighty warriors,
2 Sam 8:18; 15:17-18 1 Kgs 1:38 set out from Jerusalem to go after Sheba. 8As they arrived at the great stone in Gibeon,
20:8 Amasa met them. Joab was wearing his military tunic with a dagger strapped to his belt. As
2 Sam 2:18 he stepped forward to greet Amasa, he slipped the dagger from its sheath.*

9"How are you, my cousin?" Joab said and took him by the beard with his right hand as
20:10 1 Kgs 2:5 though to kiss him. 10Amasa didn't notice the dagger in his left hand, and Joab stabbed

20:7a Hebrew *So Joab's men.* 20:7b Hebrew *the Kerethites and Pelethites;* also in 20:23. 20:8 Hebrew *As he stepped forward, it fell out.*

20:1 Sheba, a member of Saul's clan, caused trouble and convinced the representatives of every tribe except Judah to withhold their affirmation of David's right to lead. The mention of him being a Benjamite reminds readers of historic troubles with the Benjamites (Judges 20) and thus discredits Sheba's call to civil war.

20:7 This elite guard is identified in the Hebrew with the proper nouns "Kerethites and Pelethites." They also accompanied David when he ran from Absalom, his son (2 Samuel 15:18). They were good companions for the king because they were loyal, yet they were foreign, so they would have no interest in challenging David for the throne.

20:10 Just as Joab had eliminated his rival before (3:27), he slyly kills Amasa. It is conceivable that David knew this would happen, and so he craftily gained the support of Judah by Amasa's appointment and then succeeded in punishing Amasa for leading the army of his rebellious son.

him in the stomach with it so that his insides gushed out onto the ground. Joab did not
need to strike again, and Amasa soon died. Joab and his brother Abishai left him lying
there and continued after Sheba.
11 One of Joab's young men shouted to Amasa's troops, "If you are for Joab and David,
come and follow Joab." 12 But Amasa lay in his blood in the middle of the road, and Joab's
man saw that everyone was stopping to stare at him. So he pulled him off the road into a
field and threw a cloak over him. 13 With Amasa's body out of the way, everyone went on
with Joab to capture Sheba son of Bicri.
14 Meanwhile, Sheba traveled through all the tribes of Israel and eventually came to the
town of Abel-beth-maacah. All the members of his own clan, the Bicrites,* assembled for bat-
tle and followed him into the town. 15 When Joab's forces arrived, they attacked Abel-beth- **20:15**
maacah. They built a siege ramp against the town's fortifications and began battering down Ezek 4:2
the wall. 16 But a wise woman in the town called out to Joab, "Listen to me, Joab. Come over **20:16**
here so I can talk to you." 17 As he approached, the woman asked, "Are you Joab?" 2 Sam 14:2
"I am," he replied.
So she said, "Listen carefully to your servant."
"I'm listening," he said.
18 Then she continued, "There used to be a saying, 'If you want to settle an argument,
ask advice at the town of Abel.' 19 I am one who is peace loving and faithful in Israel. But **20:19**
you are destroying an important town in Israel.* Why do you want to devour what belongs Deut 20:10
to the LORD?" 2 Sam 14:15-16
20 And Joab replied, "Believe me, I don't want to devour or destroy your town! 21 That's **20:21**
not my purpose. All I want is a man named Sheba son of Bicri from the hill country of Josh 24:33
Ephraim, who has revolted against King David. If you hand over this one man to me, I will 2 Sam 20:2
leave the town in peace."
"All right," the woman replied, "we will throw his head over the wall to you." 22 Then the **20:22**
woman went to all the people with her wise advice, and they cut off Sheba's head and Eccl 9:13
threw it out to Joab. So he blew the ram's horn and called his troops back from the attack.
They all returned to their homes, and Joab returned to the king at Jerusalem. **20:23**
23 Now Joab was the commander of the army of Israel. Benaiah son of Jehoiada was cap- 2 Sam 8:16-18
tain of the king's bodyguard. 24 Adoniram* was in charge of the labor force. Jehoshaphat **20:24**
son of Ahilud was the royal historian. 25 Sheva was the court secretary. Zadok and Abiathar 1 Kgs 12:18 **20:25**
were the priests. 26 And Ira, a descendant of Jair, was David's personal priest. 1 Sam 2:35

DAVID AVENGES THE GIBEONITES

21 There was a famine during David's reign that lasted for three years, so David **21:1**
asked the LORD about it. And the LORD said, "The famine has come because Saul Gen 12:10; 26:1; 42:5
and his family are guilty of murdering the Gibeonites."
2 So the king summoned the Gibeonites. They were not part of Israel but were all that **21:2** Josh 9:15-20

20:14 As in Greek and Latin versions; Hebrew reads *All the Berites.* 20:19 Hebrew *a town that is a mother in Israel.*
20:24 As in Greek version (see also 1 Kgs 4:6; 5:14); Hebrew reads *Adoram.*

20:16 One of several wise women in the story of David steps forward to save her city from destruction. After she bargains with Joab, the city takes her advice and executes the traitor, avoiding the destruction of their city and possible civil war.

▸ GOD
20:22 A wise use of violence. This elderly woman goes unnamed, but she is honored by inclusion in the Scriptures as an example of wisdom. She is much wiser than David, who could not bear to deal justly with those in his family. She is much wiser than Joab, who killed his own family with far too much pleasure (20:10). But this situation shows that violence is not always the refuge of the incompetent. Timing, acting in your sphere of authority, and intentions are key to the honorable use of violence. (***See God*****>** *God's Nature> Unique> He alone is completely wise,* TopicGuide page A15.)

21:2 The Gibeonites belonged to a larger ethnic group called the Hivites (see Joshua 9), although here they are classified as Amorites. Both groups are listed among the seven nations in Canaan that the Israelites were to remove from their property (Deuteronomy 7:1-2). But the Gibeonites tricked the Israelites into making a peace treaty with them and instead shared in the benefits of living among God's people.

was left of the nation of the Amorites. The people of Israel had sworn not to kill them, but
21:3 Saul, in his zeal for Israel and Judah, had tried to wipe them out. 3David asked them, "What
1 Sam 26:19 can I do for you? How can I make amends so that you will bless the LORD's people again?"
21:4 Num 35:33-34 4"Well, money can't settle this matter between us and the family of Saul," the Gibeon-
ites replied. "Neither can we demand the life of anyone in Israel."
21:5 "What can I do then?" David asked. "Just tell me and I will do it for you."
2 Sam 21:1 5Then they replied, "It was Saul who planned to destroy us, to keep us from having any
21:6 place at all in the territory of Israel. 6So let seven of Saul's sons be handed over to us, and
Num 25:4 we will execute them before the LORD at Gibeon, on the mountain of the LORD.*"
1 Sam 10:24 "All right," the king said, "I will do it." 7The king spared Jonathan's son Mephibosheth,*
21:7 1 Sam 18:1-3; 20:12- who was Saul's grandson, because of the oath David and Jonathan had sworn before the
17; 23:18 LORD. 8But he gave them Saul's two sons Armoni and Mephibosheth, whose mother was
2 Sam 4:4 Rizpah daughter of Aiah. He also gave them the five sons of Saul's daughter Merab,* the
21:8 wife of Adriel son of Barzillai from Meholah. 9The men of Gibeon executed them on the
1 Sam 18:19 2 Sam 3:7 mountain before the LORD. So all seven of them died together at the beginning of the bar-
ley harvest.
21:10 Deut 21:23 10Then Rizpah daughter of Aiah, the mother of two of the men, spread burlap on a rock
1 Sam 17:44 and stayed there the entire harvest season. She prevented the scavenger birds from tear-
ing at their bodies during the day and stopped wild animals from eating them at night.
21:12 11When David learned what Rizpah, Saul's concubine, had done, 12he went to the people
1 Sam 31:11-13 of Jabesh-gilead and retrieved the bones of Saul and his son Jonathan. (When the Philis-
tines had killed Saul and Jonathan on Mount Gilboa, the people of Jabesh-gilead stole
their bodies from the public square of Beth-shan, where the Philistines had hung them.)
13So David obtained the bones of Saul and Jonathan, as well as the bones of the men the
Gibeonites had executed.

14Then the king ordered that they bury the bones in the tomb of Kish, Saul's father, at
the town of Zela in the land of Benjamin. After that, God ended the famine in the land.

BATTLES AGAINST PHILISTINE GIANTS

21:15-22 15Once again the Philistines were at war with Israel. And when David and his men were in
//1 Chr 20:4-8 the thick of battle, David became weak and exhausted. 16Ishbi-benob was a descendant of
21:16 the giants*; his bronze spearhead weighed more than seven pounds,* and he was armed
Num 13:28 with a new sword. He had cornered David and was about to kill him. 17But Abishai son of
21:17 2 Sam 18:2-3; 20:6 Zeruiah came to David's rescue and killed the Philistine. Then David's men declared, "You
are not going out to battle with us again! Why risk snuffing out the light of Israel?"

21:6 As in Greek version (see also 21:9); Hebrew reads *at Gibeah of Saul, the chosen of the LORD.* 21:7 *Mephibosheth* is another name for Merib-baal. 21:8 As in a few Hebrew and Greek manuscripts and Syriac version (see also 1 Sam 18:19); most Hebrew manuscripts read *Michal.* 21:16a As in Greek version; Hebrew reads *a descendant of the Rephaites;* also in 21:18, 20, 22. 21:16b Hebrew *300 shekels* [3.4 kilograms].

21:14 The punishment of God upon Israel came because they had not punished those who broke a long-standing peace treaty (Joshua 9). Because David was too weak to punish the guilty, God assigned this duty to the Gibeonites. But the curse was not removed from Israel simply by executions. God only removed the curse when the dead had been properly honored with burial.

21:15 Continuing the theme of David's growing weakness, David's arms become too tired to lift the sword against the giant Philistines. While his killing of Goliath marked his entry into warfare, his inability to kill Ishbi-benob effectively marked the end of his military career.

▸ GOD

21:15 The next generation. Learning that we have come to the end of our youth can be a rude awakening. The mighty David finally began to show his age in battle so that his warriors rightly warned him against doing it again. Through this situation, God wanted a new generation of warriors to see God strike down Philistine giants. Can you pass on your skills to the next generation before time takes away the opportunity? One way is to step back and let God train them under your watchful eye. At some point, you need to step back from your children, your employees, and others under your authority and let them face the challenges that God uses to mature His people. (***See God***> *God's Attributes*> *Faithful*> *God faithfully matures believers,* TopicGuide page A16.)

18After this, there was another battle against the Philistines at Gob. As they fought, Sib-
becai from Hushah killed Saph, another descendant of the giants.
19During another battle at Gob, Elhanan son of Jair* from Bethlehem killed the brother
of Goliath of Gath.* The handle of his spear was as thick as a weaver's beam!
20In another battle with the Philistines at Gath, they encountered a huge man with six
fingers on each hand and six toes on each foot, twenty-four in all, who was also a descen-
dant of the giants. 21But when he defied and taunted Israel, he was killed by Jonathan, the
son of David's brother Shimea.*
22These four Philistines were descendants of the giants of Gath, but David and his war-
riors killed them.

DAVID'S SONG OF PRAISE

22 David sang this song to the LORD on the day the LORD rescued him from all his en-
emies and from Saul. 2He sang:

"The LORD is my rock, my fortress, and my savior;
3 my God is my rock, in whom I find protection.
He is my shield, the power that saves me,
and my place of safety.
He is my refuge, my savior,
the One who saves me from violence.
4 I called on the LORD, who is worthy of praise,
and He saved me from my enemies.

5 "The waves of death overwhelmed me;
floods of destruction swept over me.
6 The grave* wrapped its ropes around me;
death laid a trap in my path.
7 But in my distress I cried out to the LORD;
yes, I cried to my God for help.
He heard me from His sanctuary;
my cry reached His ears.

8 "Then the earth quaked and trembled.
The foundations of the heavens shook;
they quaked because of His anger.
9 Smoke poured from His nostrils;
fierce flames leaped from His mouth.
Glowing coals blazed forth from Him.
10 He opened the heavens and came down;
dark storm clouds were beneath His feet.

21:18 1 Chr 11:29; 20:4-8; 27:11
21:19 1 Sam 17:4-7
21:22 1 Chr 20:8
22:1-51 //Ps 18:1-50
22:1 Exod 15:1; Deut 31:30; Judg 5:1; Ps 18:TITLE
22:2 1 Sam 2:2; Pss 31:3; 71:3
22:3 Gen 15:1; Deut 33:29; Ps 3:3; Luke 1:69
22:4 Pss 48:1; 96:4
22:5 Pss 69:14; 93:4; Jon 2:3
22:6 Ps 116:3-4
22:7 Pss 116:4; 120:1
22:8 Judg 5:4; Job 26:11; Ps 97:4
22:9 Deut 32:22; Heb 12:29
22:10 Exod 20:21; 1 Kgs 8:12-13; Ps 97:2; Nah 1:3

21:19a As in parallel text at 1 Chr 20:5; Hebrew reads *son of Jaare-oregim.* 21:19b As in parallel text at 1 Chr 20:5; Hebrew reads *killed Goliath of Gath.* 21:21 As in parallel text at 1 Chr 20:7; Hebrew reads *Shimei*, a variant spelling of Shimea. 22:6 Hebrew *Sheol.*

▸ADOPTION

22:1 The song of a lifetime. This war song of praise to God cuts across the entire book of Psalms, picking up themes from each of the five sections. It covers a vast area of human emotion and experience. Perhaps it's time you sat back and considered the full picture of how God has dealt with you in your life. Would you write a song of victory, or of victimization? A song of triumph or tragedy? Or more likely, something in between? (***See Adoption**> With Christ> Supernatural> All things accomplished through Christ,* TopicGuide page A37.)

22:2 The image of God as a rock is a symbol of His protection (Deuteronomy 32:30; 1 Samuel 2:2; Psalm 18:2). The idea of God as a guardian forms the first section of this psalm of praise.

22:8 Through the metaphor of elemental wrath, this verse reveals God as coming in irresistible power upon His enemies when His people cry out to Him (1 Samuel 14:15; Psalm 18:7; Psalm 77:16).

11 Mounted on a mighty angelic being,* He flew,
soaring* on the wings of the wind.

22:12 Ps 104:3
12 He shrouded Himself in darkness,
veiling His approach with dense rain clouds.
13 A great brightness shone around Him,
and burning coals* blazed forth.

22:14 Job 37:2; Ps 29:3
14 The LORD thundered from heaven;
the voice of the Most High resounded.

22:15 Deut 32:23; Josh 10:10; 1 Sam 7:10
15 He shot arrows and scattered His enemies;
His lightning flashed, and they were confused.
16 Then at the command of the LORD,
at the blast of His breath,

22:16 Exod 15:8; Nah 1:4
the bottom of the sea could be seen,
and the foundations of the earth were laid bare.

22:17 Ps 144:7
17 "He reached down from heaven and rescued me;
He drew me out of deep waters.

22:18 Ps 23:4
18 He rescued me from my powerful enemies,
from those who hated me and were too strong for me.

22:19 Ps 23:4
19 They attacked me at a moment when I was in distress,
but the LORD supported me.

22:20 Pss 31:8; 118:5
20 He led me to a place of safety;
He rescued me because He delights in me.

22:21 1 Sam 26:23; Pss 24:4-5; 128:1
21 The LORD rewarded me for doing right;
He restored me because of my innocence.

22:22 Gen 18:19; Ps 128:1
22 For I have kept the ways of the LORD;
I have not turned from my God to follow evil.
23 I have followed all His regulations;

22:23 Deut 6:6-9
I have never abandoned His decrees.

22:24 Gen 6:9-10; 7:1; Eph 1:4
24 I am blameless before God;
I have kept myself from sin.
25 The LORD rewarded me for doing right.
He has seen my innocence.

22:26 Matt 5:7
26 "To the faithful You show Yourself faithful;
to those with integrity You show integrity.

22:27 Lev 26:23-24; Matt 5:8
27 To the pure You show Yourself pure,
but to the wicked You show Yourself hostile.

22:28 Exod 3:7-8; Ps 72:12-13; Isa 2:11-12, 17; 5:15
28 You rescue the humble,
but Your eyes watch the proud and humiliate them.
29 O LORD, You are my lamp.

22:29 Ps 27:1
The LORD lights up my darkness.
30 In Your strength I can crush an army;

22:31 Deut 32:4; 2 Sam 22:3; Pss 12:6; 119:140; Prov 30:5; Matt 5:48
with my God I can scale any wall.

31 "God's way is perfect.
All the LORD's promises prove true.
He is a shield for all who look to Him for protection.

22:11a Hebrew *a cherub.* 22:11b As in some Hebrew manuscripts (see also Ps 18:10); other Hebrew manuscripts read *appearing.* 22:13 Or *and lightning bolts.*

22:20 Through verse 29, David sings that God's rescue comes because of His joy in seeing His beloved walk in obedience and faithfulness. This poem is repeated in Psalm 18.

22:29 Through verse 49, David rejoices in the complete, utter victory God will give His people over those who persecute them.

32 For who is God except the LORD?
Who but our God is a solid rock? 22:32 1 Sam 2:2
33 God is my strong fortress,
and He makes my way perfect.
34 He makes me as surefooted as a deer,
enabling me to stand on mountain heights.
35 He trains my hands for battle; 22:35 Ps 144:1
He strengthens my arm to draw a bronze bow.
36 You have given me Your shield of victory; 22:36 Eph 6:16-17
Your help* has made me great.
37 You have made a wide path for my feet
to keep them from slipping.

38 "I chased my enemies and destroyed them;
I did not stop until they were conquered.
39 I consumed them; 22:39 Mal 4:3
I struck them down so they did not get up;
they fell beneath my feet.
40 You have armed me with strength for the battle;
You have subdued my enemies under my feet.
41 You placed my foot on their necks. 22:41 Exod 23:27
I have destroyed all who hated me.
42 They looked for help, but no one came to their rescue. 22:42 1 Sam 28:5-6 Isa 1:15
They even cried to the LORD, but He refused to answer.
43 I ground them as fine as the dust of the earth; 22:43 Isa 10:6 Mic 7:10
I trampled them* in the gutter like dirt.

22:36 As in Dead Sea Scrolls (see also Ps 18:35); Masoretic Text reads *Your answering.* 22:43 As in Dead Sea Scrolls (see also Ps 18:42); Masoretic Text reads *I crushed and trampled them.*

MY RESPONSE TO GOD

Culture Wars

2 SAMUEL 23:3

God, the Creator of all things, established three institutions for the ordering of His world—the civil government, the family, and the church. These institutions should work in harmony to glorify God, but they can be at odds when they supersede their boundaries. Above all, these institutions must be protected and defended.

- God's will for the family is that it would be the foundational institution of human society (Genesis 1:27; Genesis 2:18-25), a union of a man and woman in a lifelong commitment (Hebrews 13:4) to nurture all those under their care.
- God's will for the state is that it establish justice and restrain evil by penalizing lawbreakers (Deuteronomy 1:16-17; 1 Peter 2:14). All who serve in civil government must fear God (2 Samuel 23:3-4) and recognize that it is God who rules the universe, top to bottom (Daniel 4:25).
- God's will for the church is that it be a holy gathering of true Christians (Acts 2) who profess faith in Christ as their only hope for salvation (Galatians 5:11). Its mission is to establish and strengthen holiness in believers and their families (Acts 2:38-39; 16:31-34) and to penetrate the world with the gospel (Matthew 28:19-20).

Any idea that threatens the existence of these institutions is at war with the fabric of human culture. As you engage in this battle, focus your efforts on promoting godly government, strengthening families, and building the church.

22:44 2 Sam 3:1; 8:1-14; 19:8-10; Isa 55:5
22:45 Ps 66:3; Isa 55:5; 60:12
22:46 Mic 7:17
22:47 2 Sam 22:2, 32; Ps 89:26
22:48 1 Sam 24:12; 25:39; Pss 94:1; 144:2
22:49 Pss 44:5; 140:1, 4, 11
22:50 *Rom 15:9
22:51 2 Sam 7:12-16; Pss 89:20; 144:9-10

44 "You gave me victory over my accusers.
You preserved me as the ruler over nations;
people I don't even know now serve me.
45 Foreign nations cringe before me;
as soon as they hear of me, they submit.
46 They all lose their courage
and come trembling* from their strongholds.
47 "The LORD lives! Praise to my Rock!
May God, the Rock of my salvation, be exalted!
48 He is the God who pays back those who harm me;
He brings down the nations under me
49 and delivers me from my enemies.
You hold me safe beyond the reach of my enemies;
You save me from violent opponents.
50 For this, O LORD, I will praise You among the nations;
I will sing praises to Your name.
51 You give great victories to Your king;
You show unfailing love to Your anointed,
to David and all his descendants forever."

DAVID'S LAST WORDS

23:1 1 Sam 16:12-13; 2 Sam 7:8-9; Pss 78:70-72; 89:20
23:2 2 Pet 1:20-21
23:3 2 Sam 22:2, 32; 2 Chr 19:7, 9; Ps 72:1-3; Isa 11:1-5
23:4 Judg 5:31; Pss 72:6; 110:3
23:5 2 Sam 7:12; Ps 89:29; Isa 55:3

23 These are the last words of David:
"David, the son of Jesse, speaks—
David, the man who was raised up so high,
David, the man anointed by the God of Jacob,
David, the sweet psalmist of Israel.*
2 "The Spirit of the LORD speaks through me;
His words are upon my tongue.
3 The God of Israel spoke.
The Rock of Israel said to me:
'The One who rules righteously,
who rules in the fear of God,
4 is like the light of morning at sunrise,
like a morning without clouds,
like the gleaming of the sun
on new grass after rain.'
5 "Is it not my family God has chosen?
Yes, He has made an everlasting covenant with me.
His agreement is arranged and guaranteed in every detail.
He will ensure my safety and success.

22:46 As in parallel text at Ps 18:45; Hebrew reads *come girding themselves.* 23:1 Or *the favorite subject of the songs of Israel;* or *the favorite of the Strong One of Israel.*

22:50-51 In closing, David recalls a lifetime of great victories and looks forward to an eternity of unfaltering love for David's descendants, including Jesus Christ (Hosea 3:5; Matthew 1:1; Acts 2:30).

▶ HOLINESS
23:1-5 Chosen by the King. The warrior-poet David rejoiced in God's sovereign choice of his family to guide Israel. He wasn't speaking out of pride—his certitude came from his confidence in God's covenant with him. We can stand confident in God's choice of us. His New Covenant blessings flow through Christ, to the church, through our families, and into the world so that all can see the joy of living as a chosen child of God. (***See Holiness> Set Apart> Transforming> In the New Covenant,*** **TopicGuide page A40.**)

23:2 David's last words do not sound like what modern readers might expect. Instead, he repeats the general themes in chapter 22—God is a Rock (23:3) who protects His people as they are obedient to their covenant obligations (23:5) but destroys those who fail to cooperate with God's plan to bless His people (23:6-7).

6 But the godless are like thorns to be thrown away,
for they tear the hand that touches them.
7 One must use iron tools to chop them down;
they will be totally consumed by fire."

23:6 Matt 13:41-42

DAVID'S MIGHTIEST WARRIORS

8These are the names of David's mightiest warriors. The first was Jashobeam the Hac-
monite,* who was leader of the Three*—the three mightiest warriors among David's men.
He once used his spear to kill 800 enemy warriors in a single battle.*
9Next in rank among the Three was Eleazar son of Dodai, a descendant of Ahoah. Once
Eleazar and David stood together against the Philistines when the entire Israelite army
had fled. 10He killed Philistines until his hand was too tired to lift his sword, and the LORD
gave him a great victory that day. The rest of the army did not return until it was time to
collect the plunder!
11Next in rank was Shammah son of Agee from Harar. One time the Philistines gathered
at Lehi and attacked the Israelites in a field full of lentils. The Israelite army fled, 12but
Shammah* held his ground in the middle of the field and beat back the Philistines. So the
LORD brought about a great victory.

23:8 1 Chr 11:11-47
23:9 1 Chr 27:4

13Once during the harvest, when David was at the cave of Adullam, the Philistine army
was camped in the valley of Rephaim. The Three (who were among the Thirty—an elite
group among David's fighting men) went down to meet him there. 14David was staying in
the stronghold at the time, and a Philistine detachment had occupied the town of Bethlehem.
15David remarked longingly to his men, "Oh, how I would love some of that good water
from the well by the gate in Bethlehem." 16So the Three broke through the Philistine lines,
drew some water from the well by the gate in Bethlehem, and brought it back to David.
But he refused to drink it. Instead, he poured it out as an offering to the LORD. 17"The LORD
forbid that I should drink this!" he exclaimed. "This water is as precious as the blood of
these men* who risked their lives to bring it to me." So David did not drink it. These are ex-
amples of the exploits of the Three.

23:13 1 Sam 22:1; 2 Sam 5:18
23:14 1 Sam 22:4-5
23:16 Gen 35:13-14
23:17 Lev 17:10

DAVID'S THIRTY MIGHTY MEN

18Abishai son of Zeruiah, the brother of Joab, was the leader of the Thirty.* He once used
his spear to kill 300 enemy warriors in a single battle. It was by such feats that he became
as famous as the Three. 19Abishai was the most famous of the Thirty* and was their com-
mander, though he was not one of the Three.
20There was also Benaiah son of Jehoiada, a valiant warrior* from Kabzeel. He did many
heroic deeds, which included killing two champions* of Moab. Another time, on a snowy
day, he chased a lion down into a pit and killed it. 21Once, armed only with a club, he killed
a great Egyptian warrior who was armed with a spear. Benaiah wrenched the spear from
the Egyptian's hand and killed him with it. 22Deeds like these made Benaiah as famous as
the Three mightiest warriors. 23He was more honored than the other members of the
Thirty, though he was not one of the Three. And David made him captain of his bodyguard.
24Other members of the Thirty included:

Asahel, Joab's brother;
Elhanan son of Dodo from Bethlehem;
25 Shammah from Harod;
Elika from Harod;

23:18 2 Sam 10:10, 14; 18:2; 1 Chr 11:20-21
23:20 Josh 15:21; 2 Sam 8:18; 20:23
23:24 2 Sam 2:18
23:25 Judg 7:1

23:8a As in parallel text at 1 Chr 11:11; Hebrew reads *Josheb-basshebeth the Tahkemonite.* **23:8b** As in Greek and Latin versions (see also 1 Chr 11:11); the meaning of the Hebrew is uncertain. **23:8c** As in some Greek manuscripts (see also 1 Chr 11:11); the meaning of the Hebrew is uncertain, though it might be rendered *the Three. It was Adino the Eznite who killed 800 men at one time.* **23:12** Hebrew *he.* **23:17** Hebrew *Shall I drink the blood of these men?* **23:18** As in a few Hebrew manuscripts and Syriac version; most Hebrew manuscripts read *the Three.* **23:19** As in Syriac version; Hebrew reads *the Three.* **23:20a** Or *son of Jehoiada, son of Ish-hai.* **23:20b** Or *two sons of Ariel.*

26 Helez from Pelon*;
Ira son of Ikkesh from Tekoa;
23:27 Josh 21:18 27 Abiezer from Anathoth;
Sibbecai* from Hushah;
23:28 2 Kgs 25:23 28 Zalmon from Ahoah;
Maharai from Netophah;
29 Heled* son of Baanah from Netophah;
Ithai* son of Ribai from Gibeah (in the land of Benjamin);
23:30 Josh 24:30 30 Benaiah from Pirathon;
Hurai* from Nahale-gaash*;
31 Abi-albon from Arabah;
Azmaveth from Bahurim;
32 Eliahba from Shaalbon;
the sons of Jashen;
33 Jonathan son of Shagee* from Harar;
Ahiam son of Sharar from Harar;
23:34 2 Sam 11:3; 15:12 34 Eliphelet son of Ahasbai from Maacah;
Eliam son of Ahithophel from Giloh;
35 Hezro from Carmel;
Paarai from Arba;
36 Igal son of Nathan from Zobah;
Bani from Gad;
37 Zelek from Ammon;
Naharai from Beeroth, Joab's armor bearer;
23:38 1 Chr 2:53 38 Ira from Jattir;
Gareb from Jattir;
23:39 2 Sam 11:3 39 Uriah the Hittite.

There were thirty-seven in all.

24:1-17 1 Chr 21:1-17

DAVID TAKES A CENSUS

24:1 1 Chr 27:23

24 Once again the anger of the LORD burned against Israel, and he caused David to harm them by taking a census. "Go and count the people of Israel and Judah," the LORD told him.

23:26 As in parallel text at 1 Chr 11:27 (see also 1 Chr 27:10); Hebrew reads *from Palti.* 23:27 As in some Greek manuscripts (see also 1 Chr 11:29); Hebrew reads *Mebunnai.* 23:29a As in some Hebrew manuscripts (see also 1 Chr 11:30); most Hebrew manuscripts read *Heleb.* 23:29b As in parallel text at 1 Chr 11:31; Hebrew reads *Ittai.* 23:30a As in some Greek manuscripts (see also 1 Chr 11:32); Hebrew reads *Hiddai.* 23:30b Or *from the ravines of Gaash.* 23:33 As in parallel text at 1 Chr 11:34; Hebrew reads *Jonathan, Shammah;* some Greek manuscripts read *Jonathan son of Shammah.*

24:1 The author of the books of Samuel put some sections together topically, not necessarily in a chronological fashion. For instance, the previous chapter begins with David's last words followed by the names and deeds of David's mightiest warriors and the thirty mighty men (23:18-39). Chapter 24 returns to the previous theme of David's weakness being overshadowed by God's faithfulness to the covenant with him.

▸ GOD

24:1 The devil in the details. These verses present the same sort of tension we experience in our lives—why does God allow us to make bad decisions? And why does He sometimes appear to make the bad times even worse? Israel had sinned in some fashion and God wanted to discipline them. He chose to do so through David's census, and so when David thought of the prideful idea, God did not hinder it from coming to the surface—He passively allowed it. The confusing text in verse 1 is clarified by verse 10—God did not explicitly instruct David to take the census, or else David would have said in verse 10, "God, why did You tell me to do the census? That was a horrible idea!" And the punishment that follows (24:13) is connected to the initial rebellion of the nation of Israel at least as much as it is to David's prideful census. The ways of God are mysterious, and this passage raises more questions than it answers. God is not so actively involved in this census that God is the one who repents—it's David who repents. This is a mystery—the relationship between human sin and God's absolute control over all reality. We stand mute before such mysteries as this and await God's future clarification in heaven. (***See God****> God's Attributes> Sovereign> God is in control of all things,* TopicGuide page A17.)

2 So the king said to Joab and the commanders* of the army, "Take a census of all the 24:2
tribes of Israel—from Dan in the north to Beersheba in the south—so I may know how Judg 20:1
many people there are." 2 Sam 3:9-10
3 But Joab replied to the king, "May the LORD your God let you live to see a hundred 24:3
times as many people as there are now! But why, my lord the king, do you want to do Deut 1:11
this?"
4 But the king insisted that they take the census, so Joab and the commanders of the
army went out to count the people of Israel. 5 First they crossed the Jordan and camped at 24:5
Aroer, south of the town in the valley, in the direction of Gad. Then they went on to Jazer, Num 21:32; 32:34-36 Josh 13:9, 16
6 then to Gilead in the land of Tahtim-hodshi* and to Dan-jaan and around to Sidon. 7 Then 24:6
they came to the fortress of Tyre, and all the towns of the Hivites and Canaanites. Finally, Josh 19:28
they went south to Judah* as far as Beersheba.
8 Having gone through the entire land for nine months and twenty days, they returned
to Jerusalem. 9 Joab reported the number of people to the king. There were 800,000 capa- 24:9
ble warriors in Israel who could handle a sword, and 500,000 in Judah. Num 1:20-46 1 Chr 21:5

JUDGMENT FOR DAVID'S SIN

10 But after he had taken the census, David's conscience began to bother him. And he said 24:10
to the LORD, "I have sinned greatly by taking this census. Please forgive my guilt, LORD, for 1 Sam 24:5 2 Sam 12:13
doing this foolish thing."
11 The next morning the word of the LORD came to the prophet Gad, who was David's 24:11
seer. This was the message: 12 "Go and say to David, 'This is what the LORD says: I will give 1 Sam 9:9; 22:5
you three choices. Choose one of these punishments, and I will inflict it on you.'"
13 So Gad came to David and asked him, "Will you choose three* years of famine 24:13
throughout your land, three months of fleeing from your enemies, or three days of severe 1 Chr 21:12
plague throughout your land? Think this over and decide what answer I should give the
LORD who sent me."
14 "I'm in a desperate situation!" David replied to Gad. "But let us fall into the hands of 24:14
the LORD, for His mercy is great. Do not let me fall into human hands." Pss 51:1; 130:3-4, 7-8
15 So the LORD sent a plague upon Israel that morning, and it lasted for three days.* A to- 24:15
tal of 70,000 people died throughout the nation, from Dan in the north to Beersheba in 1 Chr 21:14; 27:24
the south. 16 But as the angel was preparing to destroy Jerusalem, the LORD relented and 24:16
said to the death angel, "Stop! That is enough!" At that moment the angel of the LORD was Exod 12:23
by the threshing floor of Araunah the Jebusite. 2 Kgs 19:35
17 When David saw the angel, he said to the LORD, "I am the one who has sinned and 24:17
done wrong! But these people are as innocent as sheep—what have they done? Let Your Ps 74:1
anger fall against me and my family."

DAVID BUILDS AN ALTAR

18 That day Gad came to David and said to him, "Go up and build an altar to the LORD on 24:18-25
the threshing floor of Araunah the Jebusite." //1 Chr 21:18-26

24:2 As in Greek version (see also 24:4 and 1 Chr 21:2); Hebrew reads *Joab the commander.* 24:6 Greek version reads *to Gilead and to Kadesh in the land of the Hittites.* 24:7 Or *they went to the Negev of Judah.* 24:13 As in Greek version (see also 1 Chr 21:12); Hebrew reads *seven.* 24:15 Hebrew *for the designated time.*

24:3 Even though there is no prohibition in Scripture concerning the counting of God's people, something about this plan deeply troubled Joab. But since David ordered it, Joab and his officers obeyed their king.

24:10-12 David's sin was internal, one of attitude or emotion. His sensitive conscience soon registered this breach of contract with God, and God brought a prophet his way to confirm his instincts.

24:15 The plague killed almost ten percent of the population.

24:17 David was carefully watching the plague progress, and so he saw the angel of death (or the effects of the angel) when it approached the outskirts of Jerusalem.

19So David went up to do what the LORD had commanded him. 20When Araunah saw
the king and his men coming toward him, he came and bowed before the king with his
24:21 Num 16:44-50 face to the ground. 21"Why have you come, my lord the king?" Araunah asked.
David replied, "I have come to buy your threshing floor and to build an altar to the LORD
there, so that he will stop the plague."
24:22 1 Sam 6:14 1 Kgs 19:21 22"Take it, my lord the king, and use it as you wish," Araunah said to David. "Here are
oxen for the burnt offering, and you can use the threshing boards and ox yokes for wood
to build a fire on the altar. 23I will give it all to you, Your Majesty, and may the LORD your
God accept your sacrifice."
24:24 Gen 23:16 24But the king replied to Araunah, "No, I insist on buying it, for I will not present burnt of-
ferings to the LORD my God that have cost me nothing." So David paid him fifty pieces of
silver* for the threshing floor and the oxen.
24:25 2 Sam 21:14 25David built an altar there to the LORD and sacrificed burnt offerings and peace offer-
ings. And the LORD answered his prayer for the land, and the plague on Israel was stopped.

24:24 Hebrew *50 shekels of silver*, about 20 ounces or 570 grams in weight.

24:21 David's story ends by featuring David's heroism, wisdom, and spirituality.

▶ WORSHIP

24:25 God hears our prayers. Even in the midst of discipline, God is gracious and hears our prayers. God is never blinded by anger, mindlessly carrying out His judgments. He is careful, aware of all the mitigating circumstances, and ever mindful of His praying saints. In some mysterious way, God gives us the means of prayer, bids us to pray, and conforms reality to our prayers that are according to His will. What a spiritual weapon God has given us—the power of prayer! (***See Worship****> OT> Fasting and Prayer> Prayer> God vows to answer according to His will,* TopicGuide page A26.)

KEY PLACES IN 1 KINGS

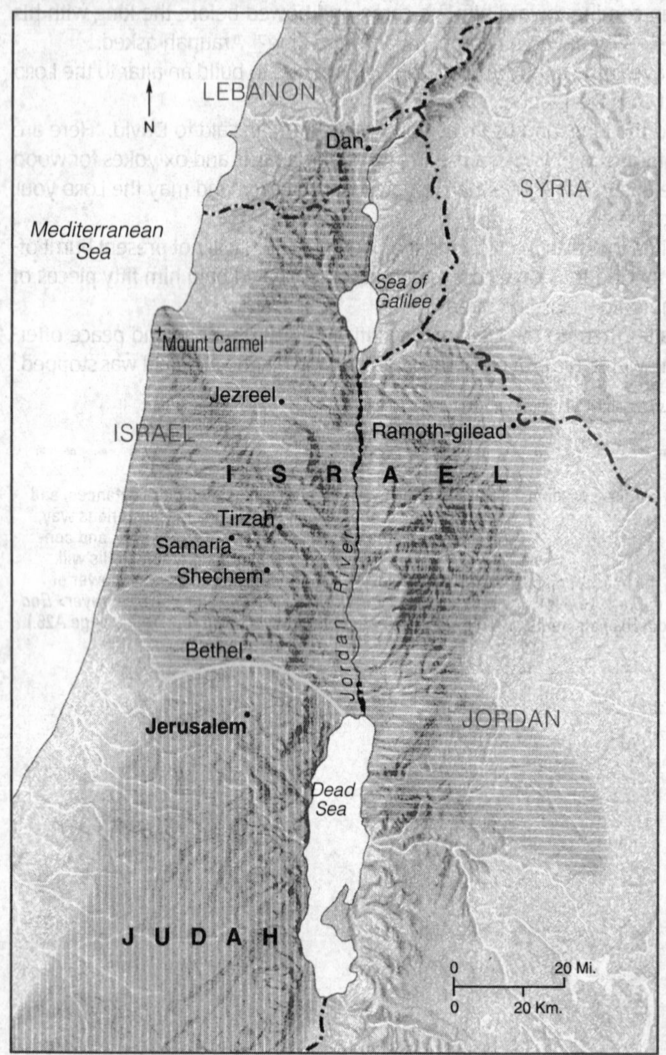

The broken lines (—·—·) indicate modern boundaries.

Solomon, David's son, brought Israel into its golden age. His wealth and wisdom were acclaimed worldwide. But he ignored God in his later years (1:1–11:43).

1 Shechem After Solomon's death, Israel assembled at Shechem to inaugurate his son Rehoboam. However, Rehoboam foolishly angered the people by threatening even heavier burdens, causing a revolt (12:1-19).

2 Israel Jeroboam, leader of the rebels, was made king of Israel, now called the northern kingdom. Jeroboam made Shechem his capital city (12:20, 25).

3 Judah Only the tribes of Judah and part of Benjamin remained loyal to Rehoboam. These two tribes became the southern kingdom. Rehoboam returned to Judah from Shechem and prepared to force the rebels into submission, but a prophet's message halted these plans (12:21-24).

4 Jerusalem Jerusalem was the capital city of Judah. Its Temple, built by Solomon, was the focal point of Jewish worship. This worried Jeroboam. How could he keep his people loyal if they were constantly going to Rehoboam's capital to worship (12:26, 27)?

5 Dan Jeroboam's solution was to set up his own worship centers. Two gold calves were made and proclaimed to be Israel's gods. One was placed in Dan, and the people were told that they could go there instead of to Jerusalem to worship (12:28, 29).

6 Bethel The other gold calf was placed in Bethel. The people of the northern kingdom had two convenient locations for worship in their own country, but their sin displeased God. In Jerusalem, meanwhile, Rehoboam was also allowing idolatry to creep in. The two nations were constantly at war (12:29–15:26).

7 Tirzah Jeroboam had moved the capital city to Tirzah (1 Kings 14:17). Next, Baasha became king of Israel after assassinating Nadab (15:27–16:22).

8 Samaria Israel continued to gain and lose kings through plots, assassinations, and warfare. When Omri became king, he bought a hill on which he built a new capital city, Samaria. Omri's son, Ahab, became the most wicked king of Israel. His wife, Jezebel, worshiped Baal. Ahab erected a temple to Baal in Samaria (16:23-34).

9 Mount Carmel Great evil often brings great people who oppose it. Elijah challenged the prophets of Baal and Asherah at Mount Carmel, where he would prove that they were false prophets. There Elijah humiliated these prophets and then executed them (17:1–18:46).

10 Jezreel Elijah returned to Jezreel. But Queen Jezebel, furious at the execution of her prophets, vowed to kill Elijah. He ran for his life, but God cared for and encouraged him. During his travels he anointed the future kings of Aram and Israel, as well as Elisha, his own replacement (19:1-21).

11 Ramoth-gilead The king of Aram declared war on Israel and was defeated in two battles. But the Arameans occupied Ramoth-gilead. Ahab and Jehoshaphat joined forces to recover the city. In this battle, Ahab was killed. Jehoshaphat later died (20:1–22:53).

1 KINGS

PURPOSE

To explain that the captivity of Israel by Assyria was due to its idolatry and apostasy; to call to repentance the exiled southern tribes of Judah, which had followed in Israel's apostasy; and to encourage the people to put their hope in kings from David's family.

The apostle James warned his readers not to be double-minded people who waver in everything and are unable to make up their minds (James 1:8). Unstable minds can lead to unstable lives—and, in the case of kings, unstable kingdoms.

Solomon, the son of David, was single-minded when he became king. He humbled himself before the Lord and asked for wisdom to govern God's people. God answered his prayer—and prospered him besides. But as Solomon's kingdom expanded and his fame, power, and wealth grew, his heart grew divided. As a result, when he died, the united kingdom of Israel divided into two kingdoms: ten tribes in the north, ruled by Jeroboam, and two tribes in the south, ruled by Rehoboam. Both kingdoms eventually slipped into idolatry and apostasy, and God allowed them to be conquered and exiled by their enemies.

DISCOVER GOD IN 1 KINGS

This book, which begins positively but ends negatively, displays seemingly contrasting attributes of God:

Generosity: Early in Solomon's reign, the Lord appeared to him in a dream and told the young king he could ask for whatever he wanted (1 Kings 3:5). Confessing he was like a "little child" when it came to being a king, Solomon asked for "an understanding heart" to know how to govern well and "know the difference between right and wrong" (1 Kings 3:9). God answered his prayer (1 Kings 3:11-12), but then, He granted even more than Solomon asked: "And I will also give you what you did not ask for—riches and fame!" (1 Kings 3:13). Solomon became the most famous king in the world because of God's generosity. God loves to exceed our greatest expectations (Ephesians 3:20).

Jealousy: In its negative manifestations, jealousy implies envy and is always self-centered, such as one person being jealous of another's skills, looks, or good fortune. But with God, jealousy implies zeal or righteous indignation. God's jealousy is for His glory—He becomes jealous for our holiness and righteousness when He sees us go after other "gods." When Jeroboam and Ahab led Israel into idolatry (Baal worship), God grew righteously jealous toward His people. When they failed to heed the warnings of Elijah the prophet, God sent invaders to discipline them, just as He did in the period of the judges—only this was much worse. God loves what is His and acts to keep it pure (Hebrews 12:5-11).

GROWING THROUGH 1 KINGS

As with all stories of spiritual victory and defeat, 1 Kings contains positive and negative examples for Christian disciples, specifically leaders:

Stewardship: The apostle Paul told the Corinthian church: "a person who is put in charge as a manager must be faithful" (1 Corinthians 4:2). First Kings is filled with examples of managers (kings) who failed in their task—beginning with Solomon. Ultimately, God severely judged both the northern and southern tribes because the shepherds of His people proved so unfaithful (Ezekiel 34).

Courage: The worship of the pagan god Baal became so dominant in Israel that God sent the prophet Elijah—alone—to confront King Ahab and 450 of his priests (1 Kings 18)! On top of Mount Carmel, Elijah challenged the priests to a contest, and God came through with fire from heaven. Confronting unrighteousness always requires courage and faith (Acts 4:19; 5:29).

Legacy: The only two kings in 1 Kings noted for walking in the ways of the Lord were both in Judah: Asa (15:9-24) and his son Jehoshaphat (22:41-50). They waged spiritual warfare against the idolatry in the land and restored Judah to the terms of God's covenant during their reigns. From one generation to the next, there are no spiritual guarantees. But setting a godly example is certainly the best way to establish a godly trend (Proverbs 22:6).

DISCOVERY VERSES

Take courage and be a man. Observe the requirements of the LORD your God, and follow all His ways. Keep the decrees, commands, regulations, and laws written in the Law of Moses so that you will be successful in all you do and wherever you go.

(1 KINGS 2:2-3)

Praise the LORD who has given rest to His people Israel, just as He promised. Not one word has failed of all the wonderful promises He gave through His servant Moses.

(1 KINGS 8:56)

Then Elijah stood in front of them and said, "How much longer will you waver, hobbling between two opinions? If the LORD is God, follow Him! But if Baal is God, then follow him!" But the people were completely silent.

(1 KINGS 18:21)

1 KINGS FACTS

Author: Unknown. Jewish tradition suggests that Jeremiah or one of his associates was the author. Several documents were available at the time for a writer/compiler to use (11:41; 14:19, 29; 15:7).

Written to: First and Second Kings were originally one book (like 1 and 2 Samuel and 1 and 2 Chronicles) that was addressed to the people of the southern kingdom of Judah, possibly already in exile in Babylon.

Date of writing: First and Second Kings began to be compiled prior to the invasion of Judah by Babylon in 586 BC (the northern ten tribes of Israel were conquered by Assyria in 722 BC). But the narrative goes to the middle of the Babylonian captivity, with 2 Kings ending during that time (2 Kings 25:27-30).

Setting: The narrative covers events in the northern ten tribes of Israel and in the two southern tribes of Judah, with much of the action happening in Jerusalem, the capital of Judah.

OUTLINE

- **1 KINGS 1–11**—The united reign of Solomon
- **1 KINGS 12–16**—The early divided kingdom
- **1 KINGS 17—2 KINGS 8:15**—Judah's faithfulness and fall
- **2 KINGS 8:16–17:41**—The late divided kingdom
- **2 KINGS 18–25**—Judah alone

DAVID IN HIS OLD AGE

1 King David was now very old, and no matter how many blankets covered him, he
could not keep warm. 2 So his advisers told him, "Let us find a young virgin to wait on
you and look after you, my lord. She will lie in your arms and keep you warm."
1:3 3 So they searched throughout the land of Israel for a beautiful girl, and they found Abi-
Josh 19:18 shag from Shunem and brought her to the king. 4 The girl was very beautiful, and she
1 Sam 28:4 looked after the king and took care of him. But the king had no sexual relations with her.

ADONIJAH CLAIMS THE THRONE

1:5 5 About that time David's son Adonijah, whose mother was Haggith, began boasting, "I will
2 Sam 3:4 make myself king." So he provided himself with chariots and charioteers and recruited
fifty men to run in front of him. 6 Now his father, King David, had never disciplined him at
any time, even by asking, "Why are you doing that?" Adonijah had been born next after
1:7 Absalom, and he was very handsome.
1 Sam 22:20, 23 7 Adonijah took Joab son of Zeruiah and Abiathar the priest into his confidence, and they
2 Sam 20:25 agreed to help him become king. 8 But Zadok the priest, Benaiah son of Jehoiada, Nathan
1 Kgs 2:22, 28 the prophet, Shimei, Rei, and David's personal bodyguard refused to support Adonijah.
1:8 2 Sam 8:18; 12:1; 20:25; 23:8-39 9 Adonijah went to the Stone of Zoheleth* near the spring of En-rogel, where he sacrificed

1:9 Or *to the Serpent's Stone;* Greek version supports reading *Zoheleth* as a proper name.

1:5 Adonijah was most likely the oldest of David's surviving sons (see 2 Samuel 3:2-5). David's third son, Absalom, died when he rebelled against his father (2 Samuel 18), while David's second son, Daniel, is never mentioned after 2 Samuel 3 and most likely died in his youth. Since this was the first ordinary succession in Israel's history, there was no established tradition regarding the rights to the throne. Adonijah, David's fourth son, seems to have assumed the right of the eldest living son to inherit the throne, although there was no law demanding such.

▶ HOLINESS

1:5 Dirty politics. Politics, even among God's people, can get messy. Now that David had grown weak, those who were impatient with his leadership (such as his long-time general Joab and powerful priest Abiathar) sided with the upstart Adonijah. The lust for power and impatience with God's timing can cloud our thinking. The Spirit of God should control us when we are involved in political situations. (***See Holiness****> Law and Grace> Law> Leaders and followers,* TopicGuide page A41.)

▶ HOLINESS

1:6 Should I spank my child? Children desperately need boundaries. The human heart is wicked, and that includes the hearts of children. They need to be kept safe from harming themselves and others, both physically and spiritually. But how should parents do this? Your answer to this question will not be found in King David's example. He failed to discipline his children, and his family was torn apart twice for that failure. Pray for the courage to restrain the misbehavior of your children. (***See Holiness****> Submission> Learning God's Word> Teaching your children,* TopicGuide page A40.)

1:7-8 Some of David's oldest associates aligned themselves with Adonijah. Joab had long served David as military commander (2 Samuel 2–3; 11–12; 14; 18). Abiathar joined David following Saul's slaughter of the priests (1 Samuel 22:20-23) and eventually became one of the leading priests. However, others from David's staff remained faithful. Benaiah was a high-ranking officer in David's army (2 Samuel 20:23). Zadok the priest is first introduced in 2 Samuel 8:17. Nathan is best remembered for his role in the establishment of the Davidic covenant and for confronting David with the murder of Uriah (2 Samuel 7; 12). Nothing more is known of Shimei and Rei (Shimei may be the Shimei mentioned in 1 Kings 4:18, but it is unlikely that he is the one referred to in 2 Samuel 16:5-8).

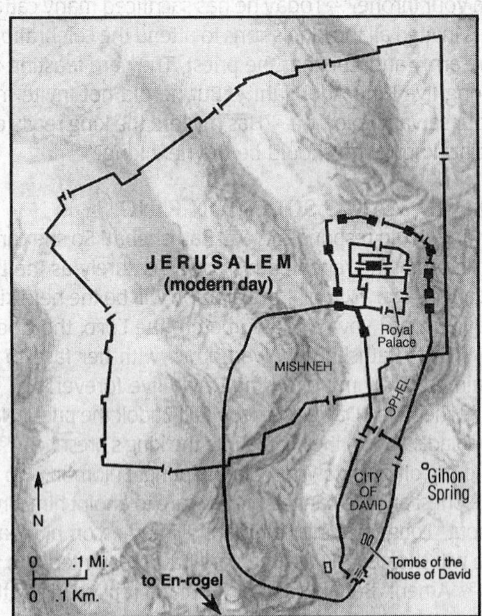

TWO CORONATIONS
As David lay on his deathbed, his son Adonijah crowned himself king at En-rogel outside Jerusalem. When the news reached David, he declared that Solomon was to be the next ruler. Solomon was anointed at Gihon. It may have been more than coincidence that Gihon was not only within shouting distance of En-rogel but also closer to the royal palace.

sheep, cattle, and fattened calves. He invited all his brothers—the other sons of King Da-
vid—and all the royal officials of Judah. 10But he did not invite Nathan the prophet or Bena- 1:10
iah or the king's bodyguard or his brother Solomon. 2 Sam 12:24
11Then Nathan went to Bathsheba, Solomon's mother, and asked her, "Haven't you
heard that Haggith's son, Adonijah, has made himself king, and our lord David doesn't
even know about it? 12If you want to save your own life and the life of your son Solomon,
follow my advice. 13Go at once to King David and say to him, 'My lord the king, didn't you 1:13
make a vow and say to me, "Your son Solomon will surely be the next king and will sit on 1 Chr 22:9-13
my throne"? Why then has Adonijah become king?' 14And while you are still talking with
him, I will come and confirm everything you have said."
15So Bathsheba went into the king's bedroom. (He was very old now, and Abishag was
taking care of him.) 16Bathsheba bowed down before the king.
"What can I do for you?" he asked her.
17She replied, "My lord, you made a vow before the LORD your God when you said to me,
'Your son Solomon will surely be the next king and will sit on my throne.' 18But instead,
Adonijah has made himself king, and my lord the king does not even know about it. 19He 1:19
has sacrificed many cattle, fattened calves, and sheep, and he has invited all the king's sons 1 Kgs 1:9
to attend the celebration. He also invited Abiathar the priest and Joab, the commander of
the army. But he did not invite your servant Solomon. 20And now, my lord the king, all Isra-
el is waiting for you to announce who will become king after you. 21If you do not act, my
son Solomon and I will be treated as criminals as soon as my lord the king has died."
22While she was still speaking with the king, Nathan the prophet arrived. 23The king's
officials told him, "Nathan the prophet is here to see you."
Nathan went in and bowed before the king with his face to the ground. 24Nathan asked,
"My lord the king, have you decided that Adonijah will be the next king and that he will sit 1:25
on your throne? 25Today he has sacrificed many cattle, fattened calves, and sheep, and he 1 Sam 10:24
has invited all the king's sons to attend the celebration. He also invited the commanders of 1 Kgs 1:9
the army and Abiathar the priest. They are feasting and drinking with him and shouting,
'Long live King Adonijah!' 26But he did not invite me or Zadok the priest or Benaiah or
your servant Solomon. 27Has my lord the king really done this without letting any of his of-
ficials know who should be the next king?"

DAVID MAKES SOLOMON KING

28King David responded, "Call Bathsheba!" So she came back in and stood before the king. 1:28-53
29And the king repeated his vow: "As surely as the LORD lives, who has rescued me from //1 Chr 29:21-25
every danger, 30your son Solomon will be the next king and will sit on my throne this very 1:29
day, just as I vowed to you before the LORD, the God of Israel." 2 Sam 4:9
31Then Bathsheba bowed down with her face to the ground before the king and ex-
claimed, "May my lord King David live forever!"
32Then King David ordered, "Call Zadok the priest, Nathan the prophet, and Benaiah son of
Jehoiada." When they came into the king's presence, 33the king said to them, "Take Solomon
and my officials down to Gihon Spring. Solomon is to ride on my own mule. 34There Zadok 1:34
the priest and Nathan the prophet are to anoint him king over Israel. Blow the ram's horn and 1 Sam 10:1; 16:3, 12
shout, 'Long live King Solomon!' 35Then escort him back here, and he will sit on my throne. 2 Sam 15:10
He will succeed me as king, for I have appointed him to be ruler over Israel and Judah."
36"Amen!" Benaiah son of Jehoiada replied. "May the LORD, the God of my lord the king,

1:10 Solomon is first introduced as Adonijah's brother and later as Bathsheba's son (1 Kings 1:12). As the story progresses, he is referred to as David's "servant" and then as his son (1 Kings 1:19, 26, 30). By the time the story concludes, he is explicitly called King Solomon by David, the people, Adonijah, and the narrator (1 Kings 1:34, 39, 46, 51, 53).

1:33 The powerful symbolism of Solomon riding upon the royal mule is lost on modern readers. Americans could compare the mule to Air Force One, the presidential aircraft, for mules and donkeys were used as mounts for royalty (2 Samuel 13:29; 18:9). This made a public declaration that Solomon was David's designated heir.

1:37 decree that it happen. 37And may the LORD be with Solomon as He has been with you, my
Josh 1:5, 17 1 Sam 20:13 lord the king, and may He make Solomon's reign even greater than yours!"
1 Kgs 1:47 38So Zadok the priest, Nathan the prophet, Benaiah son of Jehoiada, and the king's body-
1:39 guard* took Solomon down to Gihon Spring, with Solomon riding on King David's own mule.
1 Kgs 1:34 39There Zadok the priest took the flask of olive oil from the sacred tent and anointed Solomon
1 Chr 16:39; 29:22 with the oil. Then they sounded the ram's horn and all the people shouted, "Long live King
Ps 89:20 Solomon!" 40And all the people followed Solomon into Jerusalem, playing flutes and shouting
1:40 1 Sam 10:5 for joy. The celebration was so joyous and noisy that the earth shook with the sound.
41Adonijah and his guests heard the celebrating and shouting just as they were finish-
ing their banquet. When Joab heard the sound of the ram's horn, he asked, "What's going
on? Why is the city in such an uproar?"
1:42 42And while he was still speaking, Jonathan son of Abiathar the priest arrived. "Come
2 Sam 18:26-27 in," Adonijah said to him, "for you are a good man. You must have good news."
43"Not at all!" Jonathan replied. "Our lord King David has just declared Solomon king!
44The king sent him down to Gihon Spring with Zadok the priest, Nathan the prophet, and
Benaiah son of Jehoiada, protected by the king's bodyguard. They had him ride on the
king's own mule, 45and Zadok and Nathan have anointed him at Gihon Spring as the new
king. They have just returned, and the whole city is celebrating and rejoicing. That's what
1:47 all the noise is about. 46What's more, Solomon is now sitting on the royal throne as king.
1 Kgs 1:37 47And all the royal officials have gone to King David and congratulated him, saying, 'May
your God make Solomon's fame even greater than your own, and may Solomon's reign
1:48 be even greater than yours!' Then the king bowed his head in worship as he lay in his bed,
2 Sam 7:12 1 Kgs 3:6 48and he said, 'Praise the LORD, the God of Israel, who today has chosen a successor to sit
on my throne while I am still alive to see it.'"
1:50 49Then all of Adonijah's guests jumped up in panic from the banquet table and quickly
1 Kgs 2:28 scattered. 50Adonijah was afraid of Solomon, so he rushed to the sacred tent and grabbed
onto the horns of the altar. 51Word soon reached Solomon that Adonijah had seized the
horns of the altar in fear, and that he was pleading, "Let King Solomon swear today that he
will not kill me!"
52Solomon replied, "If he proves himself to be loyal, not a hair on his head will be
touched. But if he makes trouble, he will die." 53So King Solomon summoned Adonijah,

1:38 Hebrew *the Kerethites and Pelethites;* also in 1:44.

1:38 The king's guard was made up of Kerethites and Pelethites (see textual note). These two groups are typically mentioned together in Scripture (translated "the king's bodyguard" in the following passages: 2 Samuel 8:18; 15:18; 20:7, 23; 1 Chronicles 18:17; textual notes at each verse retain the Hebrew translation: "the Kerethites and Pelethites"). The Kerethites were likely Philistines who traveled from Crete and settled on the coast of Palestine. The identity of the Pelethites is uncertain, although the word may be a shortening of the Hebrew word for Philistines.

1:46 Here we find the key point of this chapter: "Solomon is now sitting on the royal throne as king." This phrase is used with slight variations three times for emphasis (1 Kings 1:35, 46, 48).

1:48 In verse 35, David emphasized his own choice of Solomon to succeed him as king. Here, however, David recognized that God had brought about Solomon's ascension. David acknowledged what Scripture consistently affirms: While humanity attempts to manipulate the unfolding of history, God is the One who holds ultimate control.

1:50-53 Adonijah's fear and panic contrast sharply with his earlier audacity (1 Kings 1:5-10). With Solomon's succession confirmed, Adonijah revealed his true self and confirmed that he would not have been an effective monarch. Solomon, on the other hand, took charge for the first time. His actions contrast with his earlier passivity as Nathan and Bathsheba propelled his ascent to power. He had assumed control of events and showed himself well fit for the throne.

▸ BIBLE

1:51 Responding to greed and grief. Many families are torn apart when it comes time to disperse an inheritance—greed and grief make a terrible combination. What would you have done if your brother had attempted to steal your most valuable possession—your father's throne? Solomon started his reign by showing the same mercy that had characterized his father; after Adonijah pledged loyalty, he was set free. (***See Bible****> Unity> Christ> Christ is "mercy,"* TopicGuide page A10.)

1:53 Earlier in the chapter, Nathan and Bathsheba bowed before David (1 Kings 1:16, 23, 31). Further on in the story, David bowed in worship, blessing God for the succession of Solomon to the throne. Finally, Adonijah bowed before Solomon. By recording these acts of obeisance, the author subtly demonstrates the transfer of power from David to Solomon.

and they brought him down from the altar. He came and bowed respectfully before King
Solomon, who dismissed him, saying, "Go on home."

DAVID'S FINAL INSTRUCTIONS TO SOLOMON

2 As the time of King David's death approached, he gave this charge to his son Solomon:
[2]"I am going where everyone on earth must someday go. Take courage and be a — 2:2 Josh 23:14
man. [3]Observe the requirements of the LORD your God, and follow all His ways. Keep the de- — 2:3
crees, commands, regulations, and laws written in the Law of Moses so that you will be suc- — Deut 18:18-19
cessful in all you do and wherever you go. [4]If you do this, then the LORD will keep the — Josh 1:6-7; 23:14 1 Chr 22:12
promise He made to me. He told me, 'If your descendants live as they should and follow Me — 2:4
faithfully with all their heart and soul, one of them will always sit on the throne of Israel.' — 2 Sam 7:12-13, 25
[5]"And there is something else. You know what Joab son of Zeruiah did to me when he — 1 Kgs 8:25; 9:5
murdered my two army commanders, Abner son of Ner and Amasa son of Jether. He pre- — 2:5
tended that it was an act of war, but it was done in a time of peace,* staining his belt and — 2 Sam 3:27; 20:10
sandals with innocent blood.* [6]Do with him what you think best, but don't let him grow
old and go to his grave in peace.*
[7]"Be kind to the sons of Barzillai of Gilead. Make them permanent guests at your table, — 2:7 2 Sam 17:27-29;
for they took care of me when I fled from your brother Absalom. — 19:31-38
[8]"And remember Shimei son of Gera, the man from Bahurim in Benjamin. He cursed me — 2:8
with a terrible curse as I was fleeing to Mahanaim. When he came down to meet me at the — 2 Sam 16:5-8;
Jordan River, I swore by the LORD that I would not kill him. [9]But that oath does not make him — 19:18-23
innocent. You are a wise man, and you will know how to arrange a bloody death for him.*"
[10]Then David died and was buried with his ancestors in the City of David. [11]David had — 2:10-12
reigned over Israel for forty years, seven of them in Hebron and thirty-three in Jerusalem. — //1 Chr 29:26-28
[12]Solomon became king and sat on the throne of David his father, and his kingdom was — 2:10 2 Sam 5:7
firmly established. — 1 Chr 29:28 Acts 2:29; 13:36

SOLOMON ESTABLISHES HIS RULE

— 2:11
[13]One day Adonijah, whose mother was Haggith, came to see Bathsheba, Solomon's — 2 Sam 5:4-5
mother. "Have you come with peaceful intentions?" she asked him. — 2:12 1 Chr 29:23 2 Chr 1:1

2:5a Or *He murdered them during a time of peace as revenge for deaths they had caused in time of war.* 2:5b As in some Greek and Old Latin manuscripts; Hebrew reads *with the blood of war.* 2:6 Hebrew *don't let his white head go down to Sheol in peace.* 2:9 Hebrew *how to bring his white head down to Sheol in blood.*

2:1 It seems that some kind of coregency existed between David and Solomon until David's death. However, the precise parameters of such an arrangement are not spelled out.

2:2-4 These verses echo God's words to Joshua as he succeeded Moses (Joshua 1:6-9) and recall the language of Deuteronomy (4:29; 6:2; 8:6; 11:1; 29:9). David's charge reminds Solomon that the king of Israel is not an absolute monarch but is limited by the law and bound to obey God. The writer of Kings consistently evaluates Solomon and the kings that follow him by the standard of God's law, especially as it is contained in the book of Deuteronomy.

▸ HOLINESS

2:2 "Be a man." How would you sum up your father's message to you on how to prosper in the world? Make it clear to those God puts under your care that you want them to be people of courage and people of God—there is little else that can compare to these traits. (***See Holiness*>** *Submission> Learning God's Word> Teaching your children,* TopicGuide page A40.)

2:5-6 Joab's murders are recorded in 2 Samuel 3:22-30 and 20:8-22. Neither case is clear-cut; Joab could not protest that he was acting in the best interests of David and the kingdom. This list of people that David perceived as a threat was conceived from a desire to secure Solomon's throne. This ruthless plan stands in contrast to David's lack of discipline of his children (2 Samuel 13) and his mercy on his enemies (2 Samuel 9:1-8).

2:8-9 Shimei's curse is recorded in 2 Samuel 16:5-13 and his change of heart in 2 Samuel 19:16-23. In the ancient world, oaths and vows carried an objective weight and could not simply be retracted. David was bound by his own oath to protect Shimei's life, but in David's literalistic interpretation of his oath Solomon was free to exact retribution. As with Joab, David likely perceived in Shimei a threat to Solomon's reign.

2:12-46 This section is bracketed by references to the establishment of Solomon's power. Within the section are four episodes (involving Adonijah, Abiathar, Joab, and Shimei) in which Solomon acted upon the advice of his father (1 Kings 2:1-9) and eliminated potential threats to his rule. Solomon consolidated his control through cunning and decisive action, but in the final analysis, the establishment of his kingdom was a work of God's grace and sovereignty.

2:13 As the queen mother, Bathsheba enjoyed unique access to and influence over the king. Solomon's courtesy to her (1 Kings 2:19) reflected the important status granted to the queen mother at the royal court in ancient Judah. One later queen mother, Athaliah, would even manage to become sole ruler of Judah through murder and intrigue (2 Kings 11).

"Yes," he said, "I come in peace. 14 In fact, I have a favor to ask of you."
"What is it?" she asked.
15 He replied, "As you know, the kingdom was rightfully mine; all Israel wanted me to be
the next king. But the tables were turned, and the kingdom went to my brother instead; for
that is the way the LORD wanted it. 16 So now I have just one favor to ask of you. Please
don't turn me down."
"What is it?" she asked.
2:17 17 He replied, "Speak to King Solomon on my behalf, for I know he will do anything you
1 Kgs 1:3 request. Ask him to let me marry Abishag, the girl from Shunem."
18 "All right," Bathsheba replied. "I will speak to the king for you."
2:19 19 So Bathsheba went to King Solomon to speak on Adonijah's behalf. The king rose from
Ps 45:9 his throne to meet her, and he bowed down before her. When he sat down on his throne
again, the king ordered that a throne be brought for his mother, and she sat at his right hand.
20 "I have one small request to make of you," she said. "I hope you won't turn me down."
"What is it, my mother?" he asked. "You know I won't refuse you."
21 "Then let your brother Adonijah marry Abishag, the girl from Shunem," she replied.
22 "How can you possibly ask me to give Abishag to Adonijah?" King Solomon de-
manded. "You might as well ask me to give him the kingdom! You know that he is my
2:23 older brother, and that he has Abiathar the priest and Joab son of Zeruiah on his side."
Ruth 1:17 23 Then King Solomon made a vow before the LORD: "May God strike me and even kill
me if Adonijah has not sealed his fate with this request. 24 The LORD has confirmed me and
placed me on the throne of my father, David; He has established my dynasty as He prom-
2:25 ised. So as surely as the LORD lives, Adonijah will die this very day!" 25 So King Solomon or-
2 Sam 8:18 dered Benaiah son of Jehoiada to execute him, and Adonijah was put to death.
2:26 Josh 21:17-18 26 Then the king said to Abiathar the priest, "Go back to your home in Anathoth. You de-
1 Sam 22:20; 26:16 serve to die, but I will not kill you now, because you carried the Ark of the Sovereign LORD
2 Sam 15:24 for David my father and you shared all his hardships." 27 So Solomon deposed Abiathar
Jer 1:1 from his position as priest of the LORD, thereby fulfilling the prophecy the LORD had given at
2:27 Shiloh concerning the descendants of Eli.
1 Sam 2:27-36 28 Joab had not joined Absalom's earlier rebellion, but he had joined Adonijah's rebel-
2:28 2 Sam 17:25 lion. So when Joab heard about Adonijah's death, he ran to the sacred tent of the LORD and
1 Kgs 1:49-50 grabbed onto the horns of the altar. 29 When this was reported to King Solomon, he sent
Benaiah son of Jehoiada to execute him.
30 Benaiah went to the sacred tent of the LORD and said to Joab, "The king orders you to
2:31 come out!"
Exod 21:14 But Joab answered, "No, I will die here."
Num 35:33 Deut 19:13 So Benaiah returned to the king and told him what Joab had said.
2:32 31 "Do as he said," the king replied. "Kill him there beside the altar and bury him. This will
Gen 9:5-6 remove the guilt of Joab's senseless murders from me and from my father's family. 32 The
Judg 9:24, 56-57 LORD will repay him* for the murders of two men who were more righteous and better than
2 Sam 3:27; 20:8-10 2 Chr 21:13 2:32 Hebrew *will return his blood on his own head.*

2:17 Adonijah's request appears innocent, but it actually was part of an oblique attempt to weaken Solomon's power and perhaps set the stage for a coup. Possessing the harem of the former king represented a claim to the throne (see 2 Samuel 3:6-7; 12:8; 16:21-22). Adonijah cunningly presented his request as a consolation for the loss of the kingdom, which he implied was rightly his. Solomon wisely saw through Adonijah's request and, heeding his father's advice (1 Kings 2:2), acted decisively to eliminate a threat to his kingdom.

2:26-35 Adonijah's second attempt to usurp Solomon's throne also led to the downfall of Abiathar and Joab. The author gives no indication of their complicity with Adonijah's request. Solomon, however, assumed their guilt, given their previous alliance with Adonijah (1 Kings 1:7-8). Solomon likely considered Abiathar a small threat to his kingdom and thus extended him leniency. His departure completed the fulfillment of the prophecy issued against the house of Eli in 1 Samuel 2:27-35 (the fulfillment of prophecy is a significant theme in the books of Kings). But Solomon showed no leniency toward Joab. Rather, he seized the opportunity to carry out David's dying wish for retribution (1 Kings 2:5-6). Solomon then rewarded Benaiah and Zadok for their support, naming them to replace Joab and Abiathar.

he. For my father knew nothing about the deaths of Abner son of Ner, commander of the 2:33
army of Israel, and of Amasa son of Jether, commander of the army of Judah. 33May their 2 Sam 3:29
blood be on Joab and his descendants forever, and may the LORD grant peace forever to
David, his descendants, his dynasty, and his throne."
34So Benaiah son of Jehoiada returned to the sacred tent and killed Joab, and he was
buried at his home in the wilderness. 35Then the king appointed Benaiah to command the 2:35
army in place of Joab, and he installed Zadok the priest to take the place of Abiathar. 1 Chr 29:22
36The king then sent for Shimei and told him, "Build a house here in Jerusalem and live 2:36
there. But don't step outside the city to go anywhere else. 37On the day you so much as 2 Sam 16:5; 1 Kgs 2:8
cross the Kidron Valley, you will surely die; and your blood will be on your own head." 2:37
38Shimei replied, "Your sentence is fair; I will do whatever my lord the king commands." 2 Sam 15:23
So Shimei lived in Jerusalem for a long time.
39But three years later two of Shimei's slaves ran away to King Achish son of Maacah of 2:39
Gath. When Shimei learned where they were, 40he saddled his donkey and went to Gath 1 Sam 27:2
to search for them. When he found them, he brought them back to Jerusalem.
41Solomon heard that Shimei had left Jerusalem and had gone to Gath and returned.
42So the king sent for Shimei and demanded, "Didn't I make you swear by the LORD and
warn you not to go anywhere else or you would surely die? And you replied, 'The sen-
tence is fair; I will do as you say.' 43Then why haven't you kept your oath to the LORD and
obeyed my command?" 2:44
44The king also said to Shimei, "You certainly remember all the wicked things you did to 1 Sam 25:39
my father, David. May the LORD now bring that evil on your own head. 45But may I, King 2 Sam 16:5-13
Solomon, receive the LORD's blessings, and may one of David's descendants always sit on 2:45 2 Sam 7:13
this throne in the presence of the LORD." 46Then, at the king's command, Benaiah son of Je- 2:46
hoiada took Shimei outside and killed him. 1 Kgs 2:12
So the kingdom was now firmly in Solomon's grip. 2 Chr 1:1

SOLOMON ASKS FOR WISDOM

3:1
3 Solomon made an alliance with Pharaoh, the king of Egypt, and married one of his 1 Kgs 7:8; 9:24
daughters. He brought her to live in the City of David until he could finish building his 3:2
palace and the Temple of the LORD and the wall around the city. 2At that time the people of Lev 17:3-5 Deut 12:13-14

2:36-46 Shimei's hometown, and possible source of support, was in the tribal region of Benjamin, across the Kidron Valley from Jerusalem (2 Samuel 16:5). By ordering Shimei to move to Jerusalem, Solomon may have been seeking to forestall his ability to foment a rebellion. Though Shimei's fateful venture from Jerusalem was in the opposite direction of the Kidron Valley, he had still defied Solomon's orders to not leave Jerusalem. Solomon seized on the opportunity to obey his father's request and eliminate another potential source of sedition. Verses 44-45 make Solomon's motives clear.

▸WORSHIP

2:46 Honoring our parents. Have your parents ever asked you to do something that you were not comfortable with? Of David's personal requests to his son Solomon, two seem a bit bloody and petty on the surface. David requested that Solomon carry out two acts of judgment: one on David's brilliant but unscrupulous general, Joab, and the other on Shimei, son of Gera, the Benjamite who cursed David as he was fleeing Absalom. But in both cases, a careful reading of the text shows Solomon carried out proper punishment against those who deserved it. When you are asked to perform an objectionable task, study the situation carefully before you object. God wants us to honor our parents and others in authority over us (Exodus 20:12). (***See Worship> OT> Reverence> Taught and modeled by Solomon,*** TopicGuide page A29.)

3:1 Here at the very outset of Solomon's reign the seeds of his later self-destruction appear. Deuteronomy 7:3-4 expressly forbade marriage to foreigners lest Israelites be led astray from the worship of the one true God. That is exactly what happened to Solomon (1 Kings 11:1-3). In fact, this marriage may have already distracted him from devotion to God. The books of 1 and 2 Kings tacitly censure Solomon for giving more attention to the building of his palace than the building of the Temple (see 1 Kings 6:38–7:1). The second half of this verse (1 Kings 3:1) implies that Solomon's preoccupation with his palace was to some degree motivated by the need to relocate his Egyptian wife.

3:2-3 In Deuteronomy 12, Moses defined pure worship as centralized worship. Decentralized and haphazard worship was considered a threat to the integrity of Israel's divinely given religion. Thus, worship at local altars (or "high places") is a key concern for the writer of 1 and 2 Kings, and he holds Solomon responsible for perpetuating this practice by participating in it. While Solomon is said to "love" God, the word translated "love" is used only here in 1 Kings of a ruler's relationship with God. However, it is used in 11:1-2 to describe Solomon's "love" of foreign women. Read together, these verses suggest that Solomon's "love" for God is not covenant loyalty (Deuteronomy 6:4-5) but at best divided affection.

Israel sacrificed their offerings at local places of worship, for a temple honoring the name
of the LORD had not yet been built.
3Solomon loved the LORD and followed all the decrees of his father, David, except that
Solomon, too, offered sacrifices and burned incense at the local places of worship. 4The
most important of these places of worship was at Gibeon, so the king went there and sacri-
ficed 1,000 burnt offerings. 5That night the LORD appeared to Solomon in a dream, and
God said, "What do you want? Ask, and I will give it to you!"
6Solomon replied, "You showed faithful love to Your servant my father, David, because
he was honest and true and faithful to You. And You have continued Your faithful love to
him today by giving him a son to sit on his throne.
7"Now, O LORD my God, You have made me king instead of my father, David, but I am
like a little child who doesn't know his way around. 8And here I am in the midst of Your
own chosen people, a nation so great and numerous they cannot be counted! 9Give me
an understanding heart so that I can govern Your people well and know the difference be-
tween right and wrong. For who by himself is able to govern this great people of Yours?"
10The Lord was pleased that Solomon had asked for wisdom. 11So God replied, "Be-
cause you have asked for wisdom in governing My people with justice and have not
asked for a long life or wealth or the death of your enemies—12I will give you what you
asked for! I will give you a wise and understanding heart such as no one else has had or
ever will have! 13And I will also give you what you did not ask for—riches and fame! No
other king in all the world will be compared to you for the rest of your life! 14And if you fol-
low Me and obey My decrees and My commands as your father, David, did, I will give you
a long life."
15Then Solomon woke up and realized it had been a dream. He returned to Jerusalem
and stood before the Ark of the LORD's Covenant, where he sacrificed burnt offerings and
peace offerings. Then he invited all his officials to a great banquet.

SOLOMON JUDGES WISELY

16Some time later two prostitutes came to the king to have an argument settled. 17"Please,
my lord," one of them began, "this woman and I live in the same house. I gave birth to a
baby while she was with me in the house. 18Three days later this woman also had a baby.
We were alone; there were only two of us in the house.
19"But her baby died during the night when she rolled over on it. 20Then she got up in
the night and took my son from beside me while I was asleep. She laid her dead child in

3:3 Deut 6:5; 1 Kgs 9:4; 11:4, 6, 38; Ps 31:23
3:4-15 //2 Chr 1:2-13
3:4 1 Chr 16:39; 21:29; 2 Chr 1:2-3
3:5 1 Kgs 9:2-3; Matt 1:20
3:6 2 Sam 7:8; 12:7; 1 Kgs 1:48; 9:4; 2 Chr 1:8
3:7 1 Chr 22:9-13; 29:1; Jer 1:6-7
3:8 Gen 13:16; 15:5; 22:17; Exod 19:6; Deut 7:6
3:9 2 Sam 14:17; 1 Kgs 3:12-13; 2 Chr 1:10; Ps 72:1; Prov 2:3-5, 9; Jas 1:5
3:12 1 Kgs 4:29-31; 1 Jn 5:14-15
3:13 1 Kgs 3:28; 4:20-24; 10:23
3:14 Ps 91:16; Prov 3:1-2, 16
3:15 1 Kgs 8:63, 65

3:5-15 This section addresses the nature of Solomon's kingdom. Would it be a kingdom of self-glorification or a kingdom dedicated to God's glory? Solomon wisely (but temporarily) rejected the kind of kingdom warned against in Deuteronomy 17:16-17 and 1 Samuel 8:11-18.

▸ PURPOSE
3:5 Whatever you wish. Imagine that God comes to you in a dream and offers you anything you want—quick, what is the first thing that comes to your mind? If nothing comes to mind, ask yourself, "What occupies most of my time, energy, thoughts, and prayers?" Still nothing? Then ask God to give you God-sized and God-centered desires that can be realized only through His power. (***See Purpose***> *God's Means> Human Choice> Bringing our wills in subjection to God's will,* TopicGuide page A52.)

▸ BIBLE
3:7-9 Give me wisdom. Solomon humbly referred to himself as a little child, even though he was almost 30 years old at his coronation. In line with this humility, Solomon saw the need for greater wisdom in dealing with God's people. After God granted his request and promised wealth and great renown, Solomon subsequently demonstrated God's gift of wisdom (see 1 Kings 3:16-28; 4:1-28; 4:29-34). God is faithful to do what He says. Pray that God will give you the gift of wisdom to enable you to complete the difficult tasks you face (James 3:13-17). (***See Bible***> *Power> Wisdom> Solomon's wisdom,* TopicGuide page A11; ***Worship***> *NT> Prayer> Instructions> Pray for wisdom,* TopicGuide page A33.)

3:11 "Death of your enemies" is not among the gifts God later granted to Solomon (1 Kings 3:12-14). God's words constituted a not-too-subtle critique of David's parting words to Solomon (1 Kings 2:6, 9).

3:15 Solomon's sacrifices at Jerusalem are significant. They suggest that Solomon had progressed beyond the lack of concern he showed earlier regarding the centralization of worship (see Deuteronomy 12). He had learned to discern right from wrong in his own life, an effect of the God-given wisdom he had been granted. The accounts that follow demonstrate his wisdom applied to the life of the nation.

my arms and took mine to sleep beside her. 21And in the morning when I tried to nurse my
son, he was dead! But when I looked more closely in the morning light, I saw that it wasn't
my son at all."

22Then the other woman interrupted, "It certainly was your son, and the living child is
mine."

"No," the first woman said, "the living child is mine, and the dead one is yours." And so
they argued back and forth before the king.

23Then the king said, "Let's get the facts straight. Both of you claim the living child is
yours, and each says that the dead one belongs to the other. 24All right, bring me a sword."
So a sword was brought to the king.

25Then he said, "Cut the living child in two, and give half to one woman and half to the
other!"

26Then the woman who was the real mother of the living child, and who loved him very
much, cried out, "Oh no, my lord! Give her the child—please do not kill him!"

But the other woman said, "All right, he will be neither yours nor mine; divide him be-
tween us!"

27Then the king said, "Do not kill the child, but give him to the woman who wants him to
live, for she is his mother!"

28When all Israel heard the king's decision, the people were in awe of the king, for they
saw the wisdom God had given him for rendering justice.

3:26 Isa 49:15; Jer 31:20; Hos 11:8

3:28 1 Kgs 3:9-12; 4:29

SOLOMON'S OFFICIALS AND GOVERNORS

4 King Solomon now ruled over all Israel, 2and these were his high officials:

Azariah son of Zadok was the priest.
3 Elihoreph and Ahijah, the sons of Shisha, were court secretaries.
Jehoshaphat son of Ahilud was the royal historian.

4:3 2 Sam 8:16

▸ BIBLE

3:24 Judging the heart. Judges need much wisdom, especially in a fallen world with an imperfect legal system and dishonest plaintiffs and defendants. The first sign of God's faithfulness to Solomon was in his ability to understand the right way to settle legal disputes. Solomon understood that he could properly judge between the two women by understanding the deepest desires of their hearts. Likewise, God gazes into the hearts of all people and can judge us perfectly. (***See Bible**> Unity> Christ> Christ in the wisdom of Solomon,* TopicGuide page A10.)

3:26-27 The reader has no way of knowing whether the first or the second woman protested the king's plan. The author meant to focus the reader's attention not on the women but on Solomon, who demonstrated his newfound wisdom by employing it in the service of his people.

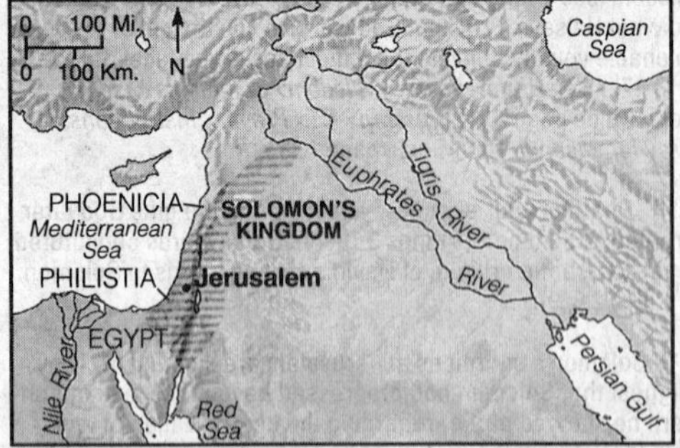

SOLOMON'S KINGDOM
Solomon's kingdom spread from the Euphrates River in the north to the borders of Egypt. The entire land was at peace under his rule.

▸ ADOPTION

4:1 Always late? Are you the one who plans events, finishes projects on time, and never loses your keys? Even if this describes you, you still need God's wisdom. The second way Solomon displayed God's gift of wisdom was in his organization of the domestic affairs of Israel and Judah (4:1-28). He chaired a committee of advisers and directed a dozen governors, all of whom advised Solomon of specific needs within the various tribes. Perhaps such large-scale administration feels out of your reach, but God's wisdom does bring a level of organization to mature people. He does not want us to live a life of chaos (1 Corinthians 14:33). (***See Adoption**> With Christ> Heirs of God> Spiritual blessing of wisdom,* TopicGuide page A36.)

4:2-4 Azariah's place of prominence within this list of high officials indicates that he is the high priest. Azariah is referred to as *the* priest, unlike Zadok and Abiathar, who are simply priests. Abiathar's reinstatement to the priesthood (compare 2:26-27) may have resulted from the change in Solomon following his dream (3:1-15). Likewise, Zadok may have been demoted from the high priesthood in favor of his son because of the questionable nature of his initial promotion in connection with the removal of Abiathar.

4:3 The roles of Solomon's royal historian and court secretaries are unclear. The secretaries may have been something like chiefs of staff or merely record keepers. The royal historian may have been a record keeper or perhaps a legal counsel to the throne.

4 Benaiah son of Jehoiada was commander of the army.
Zadok and Abiathar were priests.
5 Azariah son of Nathan was in charge of the district governors.
Zabud son of Nathan, a priest, was a trusted adviser to the king.
6 Ahishar was manager of the palace property.
Adoniram son of Abda was in charge of the labor force.

7 Solomon also had twelve district governors who were over all Israel. They were re-
sponsible for providing food for the king's household. Each of them arranged provisions
for one month of the year. 8 These are the names of the twelve governors:

4:9 Ben-hur, in the hill country of Ephraim.
Judg 1:35 9 Ben-deker, in Makaz, Shaalbim, Beth-shemesh, and Elon-bethhanan.
4:10 10 Ben-hesed, in Arubboth, including Socoh and all the land of Hepher.
Josh 12:17 11 Ben-abinadab, in all of Naphoth-dor.* (He was married to Taphath, one of Solomon's daughters.)
4:12 12 Baana son of Ahilud, in Taanach and Megiddo, all of Beth-shan* near Zarethan below
Josh 17:11 Jezreel, and all the territory from Beth-shan to Abel-meholah and over to Jokmeam.
4:13 13 Ben-geber, in Ramoth-gilead, including the Towns of Jair (named for Jair of the tribe
Num 32:41 of Manasseh*) in Gilead, and in the Argob region of Bashan, including sixty large
Deut 3:4 fortified towns with bronze bars on their gates.
14 Ahinadab son of Iddo, in Mahanaim.
15 Ahimaaz, in Naphtali. (He was married to Basemath, another of Solomon's daughters.)
16 Baana son of Hushai, in Asher and in Aloth.
17 Jehoshaphat son of Paruah, in Issachar.
18 Shimei son of Ela, in Benjamin.
4:19 19 Geber son of Uri, in the land of Gilead,* including the territories of King Sihon of the
Deut 3:8-10 Amorites and King Og of Bashan.
There was also one governor over the land of Judah.*

SOLOMON'S PROSPERITY AND WISDOM

4:20 20 The people of Judah and Israel were as numerous as the sand on the seashore. They
Gen 32:12 were very contented, with plenty to eat and drink. 21 *Solomon ruled over all the kingdoms
4:21 from the Euphrates River* in the north to the land of the Philistines and the border of Egypt
2 Sam 8:2, 6 in the south. The conquered peoples of those lands sent tribute money to Solomon and
2 Chr 9:26 continued to serve him throughout his lifetime.
Ps 72:10-11
22 The daily food requirements for Solomon's palace were 150 bushels of choice flour
and 300 bushels of meal*; 23 also 10 oxen from the fattening pens, 20 pasture-fed cattle,
100 sheep or goats, as well as deer, gazelles, roe deer, and choice poultry.*

4:11 Hebrew *Naphath-dor,* a variant spelling of Naphoth-dor. **4:12** Hebrew *Beth-shean,* a variant spelling of Beth-shan; also in 4:12b. **4:13** Hebrew *Jair son of Manasseh;* compare 1 Chr 2:22. **4:19a** Greek version reads *of Gad;* compare 4:13. **4:19b** As in some Greek manuscripts; Hebrew lacks *of Judah.* The meaning of the Hebrew is uncertain. **4:21a** Verses 4:21-34 are numbered 5:1-14 in Hebrew text. **4:21b** Hebrew *the river;* also in 4:24. **4:22** Hebrew *30 cors* [5.5 kiloliters] *of choice flour and 60 cors* [11 kiloliters] *of meal.* **4:23** Or *and fattened geese.*

4:5 Nathan was most likely the prophet who played a prominent role in securing the throne for Solomon (chapter 1). However, it is possible that Nathan, the son of David, is intended (2 Samuel 5:14). "Adviser to the king" literally means "friend" to the king (compare the role of Hushai in 2 Samuel 15:37; 16:16; 17:5-16).

4:20-21 In his dream, Solomon expressed his sense of inadequacy to rule over the numerous people of God (1 Kings 3:8-9). But through the wisdom given by God, Solomon showed himself adequate to the task, resulting in a prosperous and happy population. In saying the Israelites were as numerous as the sand on the seashore, the writer alludes to the promise made to Abraham in Genesis 22:17. Also, the dimensions of Solomon's kingdom corresponded to the extent of the land promised to Abraham (Genesis 15:18). The writer is suggesting that, under Solomon, Israel was enjoying the prosperity and security that were the fulfillment of God's covenant promises to Abraham.

24Solomon's dominion extended over all the kingdoms west of the Euphrates River,
from Tiphsah to Gaza. And there was peace on all his borders. 25During the lifetime of Sol-
omon, all of Judah and Israel lived in peace and safety. And from Dan in the north to Beer-
sheba in the south, each family had its own home and garden.*
26Solomon had 4,000* stalls for his chariot horses, and he had 12,000 horses.*
27The district governors faithfully provided food for King Solomon and his court; each
made sure nothing was lacking during the month assigned to him. 28They also brought
the necessary barley and straw for the royal horses in the stables.
29God gave Solomon very great wisdom and understanding, and knowledge as vast as
the sands of the seashore. 30In fact, his wisdom exceeded that of all the wise men of the
East and the wise men of Egypt. 31He was wiser than anyone else, including Ethan the Ez-
rahite and the sons of Mahol—Heman, Calcol, and Darda. His fame spread throughout all
the surrounding nations. 32He composed some 3,000 proverbs and wrote 1,005 songs.
33He could speak with authority about all kinds of plants, from the great cedar of Lebanon
to the tiny hyssop that grows from cracks in a wall. He could also speak about animals,
birds, small creatures, and fish. 34And kings from every nation sent their ambassadors to
listen to the wisdom of Solomon.

PREPARATIONS FOR BUILDING THE TEMPLE

5 1*King Hiram of Tyre had always been a loyal friend of David. When Hiram learned
that David's son Solomon was the new king of Israel, he sent ambassadors to con-
gratulate him.
2Then Solomon sent this message back to Hiram:

3"You know that my father, David, was not able to build a Temple to honor the name
of the LORD his God because of the many wars waged against him by surrounding
nations. He could not build until the LORD gave him victory over all his enemies. 4But
now the LORD my God has given me peace on every side; I have no enemies, and all
is well. 5So I am planning to build a Temple to honor the name of the LORD my God,

4:24 1 Chr 22:9
4:25 Jer 23:5-6; Mic 4:4; Zech 3:10
4:26 1 Kgs 10:26; 2 Chr 1:14
4:29 1 Kgs 3:12
4:30 Isa 19:11; Acts 7:22
4:31 1 Kgs 3:12
4:32 Prov 1:1; Eccl 12:9; Song 1:1
4:34 1 Kgs 10:1; 2 Chr 9:23
5:1-16 //2 Chr 2:1-18
5:1 2 Sam 5:11; 1 Chr 14:1
5:3 1 Chr 28:3
5:4 1 Kgs 4:24; 1 Chr 22:9
5:5 2 Sam 7:12-13; 1 Chr 17:12

4:25 Hebrew *each family lived under its own grapevine and under its own fig tree.* 4:26a As in some Greek manuscripts (see also 2 Chr 9:25); Hebrew reads *40,000.* 4:26b Or *12,000 charioteers.* 5:1 Verses 5:1-18 are numbered 5:15-32 in Hebrew text.

4:26-28 This record of the king's horses should be read in light of Deuteronomy 17:16, which forbade the king from accumulating many horses. The passage specifically barred the importation of horses from Egypt, which was precisely where Solomon's horses came from (1 Kings 10:28). Once again, the seeds of Solomon's later corruption appeared early in his reign. (See also 1 Samuel 8:10-18.)

▶ MINISTRY
4:29 Using what God gives you. Most modern cultures are preoccupied with who is the greatest. We want to know who is the fastest or strongest, both individually and as a team. This section shows how God's remarkable gift to Solomon put him far above every adviser in the known world. God quickly and permanently established Solomon as a supreme leader, one who made the nations marvel at the God of Israel and His wise servant. Make it your goal to make the people who know you praise God for your gifts and service to the world. You may not be considered as outstanding as Solomon, but you can be used by God to be a blessing to those around you. (***See Ministry****> Transformation> Fill and Subdue> Being salt and light in the world,* TopicGuide page A57.)

4:32-33 Solomon's wisdom encompassed more than judicial and administrative concerns. He also made observations and classifications of nature. This passage probably is not speaking of scientific observations, but observations that yielded moral and ethical wisdom for humanity, as demonstrated in various Proverbs (6:6; 24:30-34; 26:3; 30:15-31; compare also Job 38–41).

5:1 Hiram reigned over the prosperous port city of Tyre on the Mediterranean coast. He ascended to the throne around 970 BC and reigned for 34 years, according to the Jewish historian Josephus. David looked to Hiram for materials and workmen for his palace and the Temple (2 Samuel 5:11; 1 Chronicles 14:1; 22:4).

5:5 Solomon recalled God's promise to David (2 Samuel 7:1-17). David desired to build a Temple for God, but God did not allow him to do so. Instead, He promised David a son who would continue his dynasty and build the Temple. Solomon already had fulfilled one aspect of the promise, having perpetuated the Davidic dynasty. Here he set out to fulfill the second by building the Temple of God. These promises reached their ultimate fulfillment in Jesus Christ, who is both an heir of David and the embodiment of the Temple (Matthew 1:1; John 2:19).

▶ PURPOSE
5:5-7 Friends, or just friendly? What kind of relationships do you have with unbelievers? Do you love them or barely put up with them? Do you care for them or do you see your relationship with them as nothing more than a means to evangelize them? David and Solomon saw Hiram of Tyre as an ally and a friend. Solomon treated him fairly (1 Kings 5:6),

just as He had instructed my father, David. For the LORD told him, 'Your son, whom
I will place on your throne, will build the Temple to honor My name.'
6"Therefore, please command that cedars from Lebanon be cut for me. Let my men
work alongside yours, and I will pay your men whatever wages you ask. As you
know, there is no one among us who can cut timber like you Sidonians!"

7When Hiram received Solomon's message, he was very pleased and said, "Praise the
LORD today for giving David a wise son to be king of the great nation of Israel." 8Then he
sent this reply to Solomon:

5:9 "I have received your message, and I will supply all the cedar and cypress timber
2 Chr 2:16 you need. 9My servants will bring the logs from the Lebanon mountains to the
Ezra 3:7 Mediterranean Sea* and make them into rafts and float them along the coast to
Ezek 27:17 whatever place you choose. Then we will break the rafts apart so you can carry
the logs away. You can pay me by supplying me with food for my household."

10So Hiram supplied as much cedar and cypress timber as Solomon desired. 11In return,
5:12 Solomon sent him an annual payment of 100,000 bushels* of wheat for his household
1 Kgs 3:12 and 110,000 gallons* of pure olive oil. 12So the LORD gave wisdom to Solomon, just as He
had promised. And Hiram and Solomon made a formal alliance of peace.
5:14 13Then King Solomon conscripted a labor force of 30,000 men from all Israel. 14He sent
1 Kgs 4:6 them to Lebanon in shifts, 10,000 every month, so that each man would be one month in
Lebanon and two months at home. Adoniram was in charge of this labor force. 15Solomon
also had 70,000 common laborers, 80,000 quarry workers in the hill country, 16and 3,600*
5:17 foremen to supervise the work. 17At the king's command, they quarried large blocks of high-
2 Chr 22:2 quality stone and shaped them to make the foundation of the Temple. 18Men from the city of
Gebal helped Solomon's and Hiram's builders prepare the timber and stone for the Temple.

6:1-29
SOLOMON BUILDS THE TEMPLE

//2 Chr 3:1-14 **6** It was in midspring, in the month of Ziv,* during the fourth year of Solomon's reign,
that he began to construct the Temple of the LORD. This was 480 years after the peo-
ple of Israel were rescued from their slavery in the land of Egypt.

5:9 Hebrew *the sea.* 5:11a Hebrew *20,000 cors* [3,640 kiloliters]. 5:11b As in Greek version, which reads *20,000 baths* [420 kiloliters] (see also 2 Chr 2:10); Hebrew reads *20 cors,* about 800 gallons or 3.6 kiloliters in volume. 5:16 As in some Greek manuscripts (see also 2 Chr 2:2, 18); Hebrew reads *3,300.* 6:1 Hebrew *It was in the month of Ziv, which is the second month.* This month of the ancient Hebrew lunar calendar usually occurs within the months of April and May.

and spoke truthfully (5:5) and kindly (5:6) to him. Hiram may not have been a believer, but he at least respected God and the work He was doing in Israel. Build connections with unbelievers that count—that have substance—and see what else God does in those relationships to glorify His name. (***See Purpose***> *God's Deeds> Common Grace> Helps unbelievers do good without earning salvation,* TopicGuide page A54.)

5:6 Cedars from Lebanon were commonly used in the construction of temples and palaces. The Sidonians, or Phoenicians, were famous in antiquity for their work with timber. Sidon was a coastal city often linked with Tyre (see Jeremiah 25:22; Joel 3:4; Matthew 11:21).

5:7-12 Solomon's negotiations with Hiram and the resulting alliance confirmed his wisdom. The king procured the raw materials he sought through a mutually advantageous treaty that did not compromise Israel's covenantal obligations (contrast with 3:1).

5:11 The writer of Chronicles includes wine and barley in the deal, but he does not characterize the payment as an annual sum (2 Chronicles 2:10). Textual variants may have caused the discrepancy, or the Chronicler may have employed a different source that addressed another aspect of Solomon's arrangement with Hiram.

5:13-16 In 1 Kings 9:20-23 (compare 2 Chronicles 2:17-18), the writer indicates that no Israelites were part of the conscripted labor. There does appear to have been a workforce of Israelites who were not considered "forced labor" and who later formed the backbone of the rebellion against Judah (1 Kings 12:1-20). The revolving group of 30,000 workers may have constituted that workforce. Because they only worked one month in three, the author may have distinguished them from the foreign workers who labored permanently.

6:1 The building of the Temple was a momentous milestone in Israel's history. From the Exodus onward, Israel's history had been leading up to this moment when God's promises of land, peace, and His presence among the people would be solidified in the construction of the Temple. The salvation that began with deliverance from Egypt was being brought to its culmination. The number *480* may be symbolic, designating the passing of 12 generations (40 years represented an average generation).

2 The Temple that King Solomon built for the LORD was 90 feet long, 30 feet wide, and
45 feet high.* 3 The entry room at the front of the Temple was 30 feet* wide, running
across the entire width of the Temple. It projected outward 15 feet* from the front of the
Temple. 4 Solomon also made narrow recessed windows throughout the Temple. **6:4**
5 He built a complex of rooms against the outer walls of the Temple, all the way around Ezek 41:16
the sides and rear of the building. 6 The complex was three stories high, the bottom floor **6:5**
being 7½ feet wide, the second floor 9 feet wide, and the top floor 10½ feet wide.* The Ezek 41:5-6
rooms were connected to the walls of the Temple by beams resting on ledges built out
from the wall. So the beams were not inserted into the walls themselves.
7 The stones used in the construction of the Temple were finished at the quarry, so there **6:7** Exod 20:25
was no sound of hammer, ax, or any other iron tool at the building site. Deut 27:5-6
8 The entrance to the bottom floor* was on the south side of the Temple. There were
winding stairs going up to the second floor, and another flight of stairs between the sec- **6:9**
ond and third floors. 9 After completing the Temple structure, Solomon put in a ceiling 1 Kgs 6:14, 38
made of cedar beams and planks. 10 As already stated, he built a complex of rooms on
three sides of the building, attached to the Temple walls by cedar timbers. Each story of
the complex was 7½ feet* high. **6:12**
11 Then the LORD gave this message to Solomon: 12 "Concerning this Temple you are 2 Sam 7:12-16
building, if you keep all My decrees and regulations and obey all My commands, I will ful- 1 Kgs 9:4-5
fill through you the promise I made to your father, David. 13 I will live among the Israelites **6:13** Exod 25:8
and will never abandon My people Israel." Deut 31:6 Josh 1:5

THE TEMPLE'S INTERIOR

14 So Solomon finished building the Temple. 15 The entire inside, from floor to ceiling, was
paneled with wood. He paneled the walls and ceilings with cedar, and he used planks of **6:16**
cypress for the floors. 16 He partitioned off an inner sanctuary—the Most Holy Place—at the Exod 26:33 Lev 16:1-2
far end of the Temple. It was 30 feet deep and was paneled with cedar from floor to ceil- 2 Chr 3:8
ing. 17 The main room of the Temple, outside the Most Holy Place, was 60 feet* long.
18 Cedar paneling completely covered the stone walls throughout the Temple, and the
paneling was decorated with carvings of gourds and open flowers.
19 He prepared the inner sanctuary at the far end of the Temple, where the Ark of the
LORD's Covenant would be placed. 20 This inner sanctuary was 30 feet long, 30 feet wide,
and 30 feet high. He overlaid the inside with solid gold. He also overlaid the altar made of
cedar.* 21 Then Solomon overlaid the rest of the Temple's interior with solid gold, and he
made gold chains to protect the entrance* to the Most Holy Place. 22 So he finished over- **6:23**
laying the entire Temple with gold, including the altar that belonged to the Most Holy Place. Exod 25:20; 37:1-9
23 He made two cherubim of wild olive* wood, each 15 feet* tall, and placed them in the 2 Chr 3:10-12

6:2 Hebrew *60 cubits* [27.6 meters] *long, 20 cubits* [9.2 meters] *wide, and 30 cubits* [13.8 meters] *high.* **6:3a** Hebrew *20 cubits* [9.2 meters]; also in 6:16, 20. **6:3b** Hebrew *10 cubits* [4.6 meters]. **6:6** Hebrew *the bottom floor being 5 cubits* [2.3 meters] *wide, the second floor 6 cubits* [2.8 meters] *wide, and the top floor 7 cubits* [3.2 meters] *wide.* **6:8** As in Greek version; Hebrew reads *middle floor.* **6:10** Hebrew *5 cubits* [2.3 meters]. **6:17** Hebrew *40 cubits* [18.4 meters]. **6:20** Or *overlaid the altar with cedar.* The meaning of the Hebrew is uncertain. **6:21** Or *to draw curtains across.* The meaning of the Hebrew is uncertain. **6:23a** Or *pine;* Hebrew reads *oil tree;* also in 6:31, 33. **6:23b** Hebrew *10 cubits* [4.6 meters]; also in 6:24, 25.

6:8 The rooms around the outside of the Temple were used for storage.

6:16-22 The interior of the Temple was divided into three rooms: the foyer, a main hall, and an inner sanctuary. The inner sanctuary, or Most Holy Place, housed the Ark of the Covenant and represented the focal point of God's presence among His people. The most precious materials were reserved for the Most Holy Place; only the high priest entered the room, and even he only once a year on the Day of Atonement (Leviticus 16).

6:18 The carvings of gourds and open flowers evoked the Garden of Eden. In the Temple, God would live among His people as He had in the Garden. The presence of the cherubim (1 Kings 6:23-28, 29, 32) lends support to this association (Genesis 3:24).

6:23-28 Cherubim are angelic beings who guard access to God's presence (Genesis 3:24; Ezekiel 10). The 15-feet-tall cherubim served as impressive reminders of God's presence in the Temple. The cherubim also communicated the royalty of God, since kings in the ancient world often depicted themselves enthroned upon angelic wings. The abundant use of gold reinforced the theme of divine royalty.

inner sanctuary. 24 The wingspan of each of the cherubim was 15 feet, each wing being
7½ feet* long. 25 The two cherubim were identical in shape and size; 26 each was 15 feet
tall. 27 He placed them side by side in the inner sanctuary of the Temple. Their outspread
wings reached from wall to wall, while their inner wings touched at the center of the room.
28 He overlaid the two cherubim with gold.

29 He decorated all the walls of the inner sanctuary and the main room with carvings of
cherubim, palm trees, and open flowers. 30 He overlaid the floor in both rooms with gold.

31 For the entrance to the inner sanctuary, he made double doors of wild olive wood
with five-sided doorposts.* 32 These double doors were decorated with carvings of cheru-
bim, palm trees, and open flowers. The doors, including the decorations of cherubim and
palm trees, were overlaid with gold.

33 Then he made four-sided doorposts of wild olive wood for the entrance to the Tem-
6:34 Ezek 41:23-25 ple. 34 There were two folding doors of cypress wood, and each door was hinged to fold
back upon itself. 35 These doors were decorated with carvings of cherubim, palm trees, and
open flowers—all overlaid evenly with gold.

6:36 36 The walls of the inner courtyard were built so that there was one layer of cedar beams
1 Kgs 7:12 between every three layers of finished stone.

37 The foundation of the LORD's Temple was laid in midspring, in the month of Ziv,* dur-
ing the fourth year of Solomon's reign. 38 The entire building was completed in every detail
by midautumn, in the month of Bul,* during the eleventh year of his reign. So it took seven
years to build the Temple.

SOLOMON BUILDS HIS PALACE

7:1 1 Kgs 3:1; 9:10; 2 Chr 8:1 **7** Solomon also built a palace for himself, and it took him thirteen years to complete
the construction.

7:2 2 One of Solomon's buildings was called the Palace of the Forest of Lebanon. It was
1 Kgs 10:17 150 feet long, 75 feet wide, and 45 feet high.* There were four rows of cedar pillars, and
2 Chr 9:16 great cedar beams rested on the pillars. 3 The hall had a cedar roof. Above the beams on
the pillars were forty-five side rooms,* arranged in three tiers of fifteen each. 4 On each end

6:24 Hebrew *5 cubits* [2.3 meters]. 6:31 The meaning of the Hebrew is uncertain. 6:37 Hebrew *was laid in the month of Ziv.* This month of the ancient Hebrew lunar calendar usually occurs within the months of April and May. 6:38 Hebrew *by the month of Bul, which is the eighth month.* This month of the ancient Hebrew lunar calendar usually occurs within the months of October and November. 7:2 Hebrew *100 cubits* [46 meters] *long, 50 cubits* [23 meters] *wide, and 30 cubits* [13.5 meters] *high.* 7:3 Or *45 rafters,* or *45 beams,* or *45 pillars.* The architectural details in 7:2-6 can be interpreted in many different ways.

▸ WORSHIP

6:37-38 How big is too big? Christians argue about how big church buildings should be, or even whether churches ought to have buildings of their own. Are they too expensive? Or not expensive enough? These discussions have their place, but God is clearly not categorically opposed to extravagant structures—He commanded Solomon to build a lavish work of art to house the worship of God. If God asks you to do something for Him, no matter how excessive, do not hold back. Do it with all your might as an offering of love unto the Lord. (***See Worship****> OT> Place> Temple> Building of the Temple,* TopicGuide page A27.)

7:1-12 Rather than proceeding to the topic of furnishing of the Temple, the author interrupts his narrative to report on the construction of Solomon's palace complex. The author may have sought to minimize the palace by enveloping it with the construction and furnishing of the Temple, or he simply may have wanted to group building projects together. It is very likely, however, that the author intended to foreshadow Solomon's later preoccupation with his own glory. After all, this palace was much longer than the Temple and over twice as wide (compare with 1 Kings 6:2). In this way, Solomon is contrasted with David, who felt ashamed to live in a palace while the Ark had no permanent home (2 Samuel 7:1-2).

▸ SPIRITUAL WARFARE

7:1-2 Bigger than God. How can you tell when you are getting spiritually weak? When you are losing your spiritual vigor, you will show telltale signs. Solomon's first sign was that he married a pagan wife (1 Kings 3:1)—this was forbidden in the Law of Moses. Second, he began to acquire great numbers of horses (1 Kings 4:26; 10:26). This may seem innocent, but Moses forbade it as well (Deuteronomy 17:16); Israel's kings had to rely on God to save them, not their fleets of battle-steeds. After Solomon finished the Temple in seven years, he took almost twice as long to build his own home. And the honor of the name of his buildings went to those who supplied the materials, not to the Lord. These problems foreshadow Solomon's character failures that would plague Israel and play a great part in promoting civil war between northern Israel and southern Judah. What signs of spiritual weakness do you see in your past? What can you do to make the next phase of your life reflect maturity? (***See Spiritual Warfare****> Resisting Sin and Evil> Resisting Temptation> What to Resist> We are to resist worldly influences,* TopicGuide page A45.)

of the long hall were three rows of windows facing each other. 5All the doorways and
doorposts* had rectangular frames and were arranged in sets of three, facing each other.
6Solomon also built the Hall of Pillars, which was 75 feet long and 45 feet wide.* There
was a porch in front, along with a canopy supported by pillars.
7Solomon also built the throne room, known as the Hall of Justice, where he sat to hear 7:7
legal matters. It was paneled with cedar from floor to ceiling.* 8Solomon's living quarters 1 Kgs 6:9, 15-16
surrounded a courtyard behind this hall, and they were constructed the same way. He also 7:8 1 Kgs 3:1
built similar living quarters for Pharaoh's daughter, whom he had married. 2 Chr 8:11
9From foundation to eaves, all these buildings were built from huge blocks of high-
quality stone, cut with saws and trimmed to exact measure on all sides. 10Some of the
huge foundation stones were 15 feet long, and some were 12 feet* long. 11The blocks of
high-quality stone used in the walls were also cut to measure, and cedar beams were also 7:12
used. 12The walls of the great courtyard were built so that there was one layer of cedar 1 Kgs 6:36
beams between every three layers of finished stone, just like the walls of the inner court-
yard of the LORD's Temple with its entry room.

FURNISHINGS FOR THE TEMPLE

13King Solomon then asked for a man named Huram* to come from Tyre. 14He was half Is- 7:13
raelite, since his mother was a widow from the tribe of Naphtali, and his father had been a 2 Chr 2:13-14
craftsman in bronze from Tyre. Huram was extremely skillful and talented in any work in
bronze, and he came to do all the metal work for King Solomon.
15Huram cast two bronze pillars, each 27 feet tall and 18 feet in circumference.* 16For 7:15 2 Kgs 25:17
the tops of the pillars he cast bronze capitals, each 7½ feet* tall. 17Each capital was deco- 2 Chr 3:15; 4:12
rated with seven sets of latticework and interwoven chains. 18He also encircled the lattice-
work with two rows of pomegranates to decorate the capitals over the pillars. 19The
capitals on the columns inside the entry room were shaped like water lilies, and they were
six feet* tall. 20The capitals on the two pillars had 200 pomegranates in two rows around 7:20
them, beside the rounded surface next to the latticework. 21Huram set the pillars at the en- 2 Chr 3:16; 4:13
trance of the Temple, one toward the south and one toward the north. He named the one 7:21
on the south Jakin, and the one on the north Boaz.* 22The capitals on the pillars were 2 Chr 3:17
shaped like water lilies. And so the work on the pillars was finished.
23Then Huram cast a great round basin, 15 feet across from rim to rim, called the Sea. It 7:23-26
was 7½ feet deep and about 45 feet in circumference.* 24It was encircled just below its rim //2 Chr 4:2-5 7:23
by two rows of decorative gourds. There were about six gourds per foot* all the way 2 Kgs 25:13
around, and they were cast as part of the basin.
25The Sea was placed on a base of twelve bronze oxen,* all facing outward. Three
faced north, three faced west, three faced south, and three faced east, and the Sea

7:5 Greek version reads *windows.* 7:6 Hebrew *50 cubits* [23 meters] *long and 30 cubits* [13.8 meters] *wide.* 7:7 As in Syriac version and Latin Vulgate; Hebrew reads *from floor to floor.* 7:10 Hebrew *10 cubits* [4.6 meters] . . . *8 cubits* [3.7 meters]. 7:13 Hebrew *Hiram* (also in 7:40, 45); compare 2 Chr 2:13. This is not the same person mentioned in 5:1. 7:15 Hebrew *18 cubits* [8.3 meters] *tall and 12 cubits* [5.5 meters] *in circumference.* 7:16 Hebrew *5 cubits* [2.3 meters]. 7:19 Hebrew *4 cubits* [1.8 meters]; also in 7:38. 7:21 *Jakin* probably means "He establishes"; *Boaz* probably means "in Him is strength." 7:23 Hebrew *10 cubits* [4.6 meters] *across. . . . 5 cubits* [2.3 meters] *deep and 30 cubits* [13.8 meters] *in circumference.* 7:24 Or *20 gourds per meter;* Hebrew reads *10 per cubit.* 7:25 Hebrew *12 oxen;* compare 2 Kgs 16:17, which specifies *bronze oxen.*

7:15-22 Similar pillars were common in temples of the era, but their significance is uncertain. It is unclear whether the pillars were free standing or supported part of the roof structure. *Jakin* means "he establishes" and *Boaz* means "strength is in him." The names most likely reflect God's relationship to the Davidic dynasty.

7:23-26 The Sea replaced the bronze washbasin in the Tabernacle; priests used both for ritual cleansing (2 Chronicles 4:6). This piece of Temple furniture was rich in symbolism. In ancient mythology, the sea was a chaotic enemy of the gods. The still waters of the Sea before the Temple may have symbolized God's power over the chaotic elements of creation (compare Revelation 21:1). Likewise, the bull was a symbol of power and fertility in the ancient world. Setting the Sea on a base of twelve bulls facing the four points of the compass suggested God's power over all the earth.

rested on them. [26]The walls of the Sea were about three inches* thick, and its rim flared
out like a cup and resembled a water lily blossom. It could hold about 11,000 gallons*
of water.
7:27 2 Kgs 16:17 [27]Huram also made ten bronze water carts, each 6 feet long, 6 feet wide, and 4½ feet
tall.* [28]They were constructed with side panels braced with crossbars. [29]Both the panels
and the crossbars were decorated with carved lions, oxen, and cherubim. Above and be-
low the lions and oxen were wreath decorations. [30]Each of these carts had four bronze
wheels and bronze axles. There were supporting posts for the bronze basins at the corners
of the carts; these supports were decorated on each side with carvings of wreaths. [31]The
top of each cart had a rounded frame for the basin. It projected 1½ feet* above the cart's
top like a round pedestal, and its opening was 2¼ feet* across; it was decorated on the
outside with carvings of wreaths. The panels of the carts were square, not round. [32]Under
the panels were four wheels that were connected to axles that had been cast as one unit
with the cart. The wheels were 2¼ feet in diameter [33]and were similar to chariot wheels.
The axles, spokes, rims, and hubs were all cast from molten bronze.
[34]There were handles at each of the four corners of the carts, and these, too, were cast
as one unit with the cart. [35]Around the top of each cart was a rim nine inches wide.* The
corner supports and side panels were cast as one unit with the cart. [36]Carvings of cheru-
bim, lions, and palm trees decorated the panels and corner supports wherever there was
room, and there were wreaths all around. [37]All ten water carts were the same size and
were made alike, for each was cast from the same mold.
7:38-51 //2 Chr 4:6, 10–5:1 [38]Huram also made ten smaller bronze basins, one for each cart. Each basin was six feet
across and could hold 220 gallons* of water. [39]He set five water carts on the south side of
the Temple and five on the north side. The great bronze basin called the Sea was placed
near the southeast corner of the Temple. [40]He also made the necessary washbasins, shov-
els, and bowls.

So at last Huram completed everything King Solomon had assigned him to make for the
Temple of the LORD:

[41] the two pillars;
the two bowl-shaped capitals on top of the pillars;
the two networks of interwoven chains that decorated the capitals;
[42] the 400 pomegranates that hung from the chains on the capitals (two rows of
pomegranates for each of the chain networks that decorated the capitals on top of
the pillars);
[43] the ten water carts holding the ten basins;
[44] the Sea and the twelve oxen under it;
[45] the ash buckets, the shovels, and the bowls.

Huram made all these things of burnished bronze for the Temple of the LORD, just as King
Solomon had directed. [46]The king had them cast in clay molds in the Jordan Valley be-
7:47 1 Chr 22:3, 14 tween Succoth and Zarethan. [47]Solomon did not weigh all these things because there
were so many; the weight of the bronze could not be measured.

7:26a Hebrew *a handbreadth* [8 centimeters]. **7:26b** Hebrew *2,000 baths* [42 kiloliters]. **7:27** Hebrew *4 cubits* [1.8 meters] *long, 4 cubits wide, and 3 cubits* [1.4 meters] *high.* **7:31a** Hebrew *a cubit* [46 centimeters]. **7:31b** Hebrew *1½ cubits* [69 centimeters]; also in 7:32. **7:35** Hebrew *half a cubit wide* [23 centimeters]. **7:38** Hebrew *40 baths* [840 liters].

7:38-40 The priests used these large basins on movable carts to wash the portions of animals slaughtered for sacrifice (Leviticus 1:9; 2 Chronicles 4:6). The smaller basins had a different, unspecified purpose (compare 1 Kings 7:43, 45). The shovels were used to remove ashes from the altars. The bowls may have been employed to transport sacrificial blood or water for sprinkling.

48Solomon also made all the furnishings of the Temple of the LORD: 7:48 Exod 37:10-16
the gold altar;
the gold table for the Bread of the Presence;
49 the lampstands of solid gold, five on the south and five on the north, in front of the Most Holy Place; 7:49 Exod 25:31
the flower decorations, lamps, and tongs—all of gold;
50 the small bowls, lamp snuffers, bowls, dishes, and incense burners—all of solid gold; 7:50 2 Kgs 25:14-15
the doors for the entrances to the Most Holy Place and the main room of the Temple, with their fronts overlaid with gold.

51 So King Solomon finished all his work on the Temple of the LORD. Then he brought all 7:51 2 Sam 8:11 2 Chr 5:1
the gifts his father, David, had dedicated—the silver, the gold, and the various articles—and
he stored them in the treasuries of the LORD'S Temple.

THE ARK BROUGHT TO THE TEMPLE

8:1-21 2 Chr 5:2–6:11

8 Solomon then summoned to Jerusalem the elders of Israel and all the heads of the
tribes—the leaders of the ancestral families of the Israelites. They were to bring the 8:1 Num 7:2
Ark of the LORD'S Covenant to the Temple from its location in the City of David, also known 2 Sam 5:7; 6:17

7:48 Meals in the ancient world often symbolized political or spiritual fellowship (Genesis 14:18; 2 Kings 25:29). The Bread of the Presence symbolized God's fellowship with Israel (Exodus 24:9-11) and pointed to Christ, the Bread of Life (John 6:35).

7:49 Solomon constructed ten lampstands; the Tabernacle contained only one. The lampstands evoked the association between God and light (Genesis 1:3). God is light in the deepest sense (1 John 1:5).

MY RESPONSE TO GOD

The Mystery of His Magnificence

1 KINGS 8

"That's awesome!" we often exclaim. But what truly overwhelms us? What inspires our awe? Perhaps the grandeur of the Grand Canyon, or the sky-veiling Milky Way—yet these amazing sights contain only a speck of the glory of God.

Consider Psalm 104:2, where God is "dressed in a robe of light." Imagine a glory so bright that light—even a light as bright as the sun—could conceal it like a robe. The psalmist hints at what we clearly see in the New Testament—the glory of the sun is nothing compared to the glory of the Son (Matthew 17:2; Revelation 21:23). Now *that* is awesome!

King Solomon spent seven years building a massive, magnificent Temple for the worship of this holy God. Forty-five feet tall and overlaid with gold, the Temple was filled with the glory of the Lord (1 Kings 8:11). Solomon pondered how God, who cannot be contained even in the highest heaven, would dwell on earth (1 Kings 8:27). God revealed part of this mystery by Christ's incarnation (John 1:1), and He continues to give us reason to ponder how His Spirit dwells within our very bodies (Romans 8:9).

But the mystery of God is not yet fully revealed. Nor should it be, for it is through pondering God's majesty and glory that we worship Him as He deserves. Remain continually engaged with the majesty and mystery of our awesome God.

8:2 Lev 23:33-34; 2 Chr 5:3; 7:8-10
8:3 Num 7:9
8:5 2 Sam 6:13; 2 Chr 1:5-6
8:8 Exod 25:13-15; 37:4-5
8:9 Exod 24:7; 25:16; Deut 4:13-14; 10:2; Heb 9:4
8:10 Exod 40:34-35; 2 Chr 7:1-2
8:12 2 Chr 6:1; Ps 97:2
8:15 2 Sam 7:12-13; 1 Chr 22:10
8:16 Deut 12:4-5, 11; 1 Sam 16:1
8:17 2 Sam 7:2-3; 1 Chr 17:1-2
8:19 2 Sam 7:12-13; 1 Chr 17:11-12; 22:8-10
8:20 1 Chr 28:6

as Zion. 2So all the men of Israel assembled before King Solomon at the annual Festival of Shelters, which is held in early autumn in the month of Ethanim.*

3When all the elders of Israel arrived, the priests picked up the Ark. 4The priests and Levites brought up the Ark of the LORD along with the special tent* and all the sacred items that had been in it. 5There, before the Ark, King Solomon and the entire community of Israel sacrificed so many sheep, goats, and cattle that no one could keep count!

6Then the priests carried the Ark of the LORD's Covenant into the inner sanctuary of the Temple—the Most Holy Place—and placed it beneath the wings of the cherubim. 7The cherubim spread their wings over the Ark, forming a canopy over the Ark and its carrying poles. 8These poles were so long that their ends could be seen from the Temple's main room—the Holy Place—but not from the outside. They are still there to this day. 9Nothing was in the Ark except the two stone tablets that Moses had placed in it at Mount Sinai,* where the LORD made a covenant with the people of Israel when they left the land of Egypt.

10When the priests came out of the Holy Place, a thick cloud filled the Temple of the LORD. 11The priests could not continue their service because of the cloud, for the glorious presence of the LORD filled the Temple.

SOLOMON PRAISES THE LORD

12Then Solomon prayed, "O LORD, You have said that You would live in a thick cloud of darkness. 13Now I have built a glorious Temple for You, a place where You can live forever!*"

14Then the king turned around to the entire community of Israel standing before him and gave this blessing: 15"Praise the LORD, the God of Israel, who has kept the promise He made to my father, David. For He told my father, 16'From the day I brought My people Israel out of Egypt, I have never chosen a city among any of the tribes of Israel as the place where a Temple should be built to honor My name. But I have chosen David to be king over My people Israel.' "

17Then Solomon said, "My father, David, wanted to build this Temple to honor the name of the LORD, the God of Israel. 18But the LORD told him, 'You wanted to build the Temple to honor My name. Your intention is good, 19but you are not the one to do it. One of your own sons will build the Temple to honor Me.'

20"And now the LORD has fulfilled the promise He made, for I have become king in my father's place, and I now sit on the throne of Israel, just as the LORD promised. I have built this Temple to honor the name of the LORD, the God of Israel. 21And I have prepared a place there for the Ark, which contains the covenant that the LORD made with our ancestors when He brought them out of Egypt."

8:2 Hebrew *at the festival in the month Ethanim, which is the seventh month.* The Festival of Shelters began on the fifteenth day of the seventh month of the ancient Hebrew lunar calendar. This day occurred in late September, October, or early November. 8:4 Hebrew *the Tent of Meeting;* i.e., the tent mentioned in 2 Sam 6:17 and 1 Chr 16:1. 8:9 Hebrew *at Horeb,* another name for Sinai. 8:13 Some Greek texts add the line *Is this not written in the Book of Jashar?*

8:2 The Festival of Shelters commemorated Israel's nomadic period following the Exodus. Thus, it served as a significant context for a move into the permanence symbolized by the Temple. God had promised to give His people rest in the land of their inheritance (Exodus 33:12-17; Deuteronomy 12:10), and the completion of the Temple signaled to Solomon the fulfillment of those promises (1 Kings 8:56). The New Testament considers this rest a foreshadowing of the greater eternal rest of God's people (Hebrews 4:11)

8:10-11 God's presence among His people often took the form of a cloud. A cloud guided Israel through the wilderness and filled the Tabernacle when it was completed (Exodus 13:21-22; 19:9; 40:34-35). God spoke from a cloud at the transfiguration of Jesus, and Jesus ascended amid clouds (Matthew 17:5; Acts 1:9; Daniel 7:13).

8:14-21 Solomon addressed the people and gave praise to God for His faithfulness. He recalled the promises made to David (2 Samuel 7:1-17) and gave thanks for their fulfillment during his reign. Of course, those promises demanded faithful obedience on the part of David's sons. The author's audience may have been tempted to blame God for the Exile, but the author was aiming to show that the unfaithfulness of David's sons brought God's just judgment.

8:17 Solomon spoke of a house for the *"name* of the Lord." By using the word *name*, Solomon was avoiding the implication that the Temple contained God. The Temple would truly be a place where God's presence would reside, but His presence could not possibly be contained in it (see 1 Kings 8:27). Solomon clearly understood this paradox and displayed an understanding of God's transcendence and His immanence, both of which are essential to grasping the true nature of God.

SOLOMON'S PRAYER OF DEDICATION

22 Then Solomon stood before the altar of the LORD in front of the entire community of Israel. He lifted his hands toward heaven, 23 and he prayed,

"O LORD, God of Israel, there is no God like You in all of heaven above or on the earth below. You keep Your covenant and show unfailing love to all who walk before You in wholehearted devotion. 24 You have kept Your promise to Your servant David, my father. You made that promise with Your own mouth, and with Your own hands You have fulfilled it today.

25 "And now, O LORD, God of Israel, carry out the additional promise You made to Your servant David, my father. For You said to him, 'If your descendants guard their behavior and faithfully follow Me as you have done, one of them will always sit on the throne of Israel.' 26 Now, O God of Israel, fulfill this promise to Your servant David, my father.

27 "But will God really live on earth? Why, even the highest heavens cannot contain You. How much less this Temple I have built! 28 Nevertheless, listen to my prayer and my plea, O LORD my God. Hear the cry and the prayer that Your servant is making to You today. 29 May You watch over this Temple night and day, this place where You have said, 'My name will be there.' May You always hear the prayers I make toward this place. 30 May You hear the humble and earnest requests from me and Your people Israel when we pray toward this place. Yes, hear us from heaven where You live, and when You hear, forgive.

31 "If someone wrongs another person and is required to take an oath of innocence in front of Your altar in this Temple, 32 then hear from heaven and judge between Your servants—the accuser and the accused. Punish the guilty as they deserve. Acquit the innocent because of their innocence.

33 "If Your people Israel are defeated by their enemies because they have sinned against You, and if they turn to You and acknowledge Your name and pray to You here in this Temple, 34 then hear from heaven and forgive the sin of Your people Israel and return them to this land You gave their ancestors.

35 "If the skies are shut up and there is no rain because Your people have sinned against You, and if they pray toward this Temple and acknowledge Your name and turn from their sins because You have punished them, 36 then hear from heaven and forgive the sins of Your servants, Your people Israel. Teach them to follow the right path, and send rain on Your land that You have given to Your people as their special possession.

37 "If there is a famine in the land or a plague or crop disease or attacks of locusts or caterpillars, or if Your people's enemies are in the land besieging their towns—

8:23 Deut 7:9; Neh 1:5; 9:32
8:25 2 Sam 7:25; 1 Kgs 2:4; 1 Chr 17:23
8:27 2 Chr 2:6; Ps 139:7-16; Isa 66:1; Jer 23:24; Acts 7:48-49
8:29 Deut 12:11; 2 Chr 7:12, 15-16
8:30 Neh 1:5-7
8:31 Exod 22:8-11; Lev 5:1
8:32 Deut 25:1
8:33 Lev 26:14-17, 40-42; Deut 28:25, 47-48
8:35 Lev 26:19; Deut 11:16-17
8:36 1 Sam 12:23; Ps 27:11
8:37 Lev 26:16, 25-26; Deut 28:21-23

▸ WORSHIP

8:22 How to pray. Solomon was not a perfect man, but when he started praying, you would think he was. This is one of the most magnificent prayers in the Bible and we would do well to study its beauty and truth. As you read this prayer, you'll see a general flow—he prays for God's blessings based on the faithfulness of God. Using this prayer as your guide, celebrate the faithfulness of God to you, His promises to you, and the way you need Him to work out those promises in your circumstances. (***See Worship****> OT> Fasting and Prayer> Prayer> Individual> Of Solomon,* TopicGuide page A26.)

8:23-26 God's trustworthiness and love for His people set Him apart from the false gods of the world. Unlike false gods, past and present, the God of Israel has bound Himself to His people by His Word and has remained faithful to it. The past faithfulness of God serves as assurance in the present and provides hope for the future.

8:29-30 God was not contained by the Temple, but His attention was uniquely directed there. Because of this, a person did not have to be physically present at the Temple for God to hear him or her. But there was a physical requirement—facing the Temple during prayer—that shows the faithful obedience of the individual. God hears the prayer of His faithful.

8:33-40 Solomon's requests reflected the terms of God's covenant with Israel. Disobedience would result in the curses of the covenant, including drought, famine, military defeat, and exile (Leviticus 26:14-46; Deuteronomy 28:15-68). However, humble repentance would bring about healing and restoration. Throughout this section, Solomon anticipated disobedience on the part of Israel (see 1 Kings 8:46), so he reminded his audience (and the audience of 1 and 2 Kings) that the fulfillment of God's promises was ultimately an act of God's grace.

AN EVER-PRESENT FRIEND

LITTLE JESSICA HAD COMPLETED her first week in preschool. Each day, after her mother, Janice, picked her up, Jessica sat down at the table and ate a snack while Janice asked Jessica about her day.

The first day, when Jessica's mother asked her what the preschool had offered as a snack, Jessica looked oddly at her mother. "You know what it was," she said. The next day, when her mother asked what she did during free-play time, Jessica again replied with a sigh, "You know what I did, Mother."

After a week of hearing this answer, Janice finally figured out what her daughter was saying. This was Jessica's first experience away from her mother for hours at a time. Until this week, she had always had her mother beside her. Jessica had never experienced a time when her mother didn't know everything Jessica did, so Jessica continued to think that her mother knew all the details of her day. Janice chuckled as she gave Jessica a hug. Jessica would soon learn that her mother didn't know everything and that she wasn't beside her at every moment.

At times this life can be very lonely and terrifying. We may have many friends, relatives, or a loving spouse, but ultimately we still must face our problems on our own. No one can take our place. No one can be with us at all times. No one, except for One—God! He is present everywhere.

Because God is always present, we never have to wonder first thing in the morning: *Is God here in this room willing to start the day with me?* We do not have to ask ourselves: *Will God be with me tonight—even when I'm asleep?* We never have to worry: *Will God be with me tomorrow when I undertake a difficult task?*

Because God is ever-present, He is always with us. In Joshua 1:9, God promises, "This is My command—be strong and courageous. Do not be afraid or discouraged. For the Lord your God is with you wherever you go." With God's assurance of His continual presence, we can also be assured of several other truths:

- When I am confused, God will guide me (Psalm 32:8).
- When I am afraid, God will protect me (Isaiah 41:10).
- When I am tempted, God will help me resist (1 Corinthians 10:13).
- When I am hurting, God will comfort me (Psalm 34:18).
- When I am discouraged, God will encourage me (1 Peter 5:7).
- When I am lonely, God is my companion (Hebrews 13:5).

In joy, heartache, temptation, and peace, God is there. He is our ever-present friend.

whatever disaster or disease there is—38 and if Your people Israel pray about their
troubles, raising their hands toward this Temple, 39 then hear from heaven where You
live, and forgive. Give Your people what their actions deserve, for You alone know
each human heart. 40 Then they will fear You as long as they live in the land You
gave to our ancestors.
41 "In the future, foreigners who do not belong to Your people Israel will hear of
You. They will come from distant lands because of Your name, 42 for they will hear of
Your great name and Your strong hand and Your powerful arm. And when they pray
toward this Temple, 43 then hear from heaven where You live, and grant what they
ask of You. In this way, all the people of the earth will come to know and fear You,
just as Your own people Israel do. They, too, will know that this Temple I have built
honors Your name.
44 "If Your people go out where You send them to fight their enemies, and if they
pray to the LORD by turning toward this city You have chosen and toward this Temple
I have built to honor Your name, 45 then hear their prayers from heaven and uphold
their cause.
46 "If they sin against You—and who has never sinned?—You might become angry
with them and let their enemies conquer them and take them captive to their land
far away or near. 47 But in that land of exile, they might turn to You in repentance
and pray, 'We have sinned, done evil, and acted wickedly.' 48 If they turn to You with
their whole heart and soul in the land of their enemies and pray toward the land You
gave to their ancestors—toward this city You have chosen, and toward this Temple I
have built to honor Your name—49 then hear their prayers and their petition from
heaven where You live, and uphold their cause. 50 Forgive Your people who have
sinned against You. Forgive all the offenses they have committed against You. Make
their captors merciful to them, 51 for they are Your people—Your special possession—
whom You brought out of the iron-smelting furnace of Egypt.
52 "May Your eyes be open to my requests and to the requests of Your people Isra-
el. May You hear and answer them whenever they cry out to You. 53 For when You
brought our ancestors out of Egypt, O Sovereign LORD, You told Your servant Moses
that You had set Israel apart from all the nations of the earth to be Your own special
possession."

THE DEDICATION OF THE TEMPLE

54 When Solomon finished making these prayers and petitions to the LORD, he stood up in
front of the altar of the LORD, where he had been kneeling with his hands raised toward
heaven. 55 He stood and in a loud voice blessed the entire congregation of Israel:
56 "Praise the LORD who has given rest to His people Israel, just as He promised. Not one
word has failed of all the wonderful promises He gave through His servant Moses. 57 May
the LORD our God be with us as He was with our ancestors; may He never leave us or aban-
don us. 58 May He give us the desire to do His will in everything and to obey all the com-
mands, decrees, and regulations that He gave our ancestors. 59 And may these words that I
have prayed in the presence of the LORD be before Him constantly, day and night, so that

8:39 1 Sam 2:3; 1 Chr 28:9; Jer 17:10; John 2:24-25
8:42 Deut 3:24
8:43 1 Sam 17:46
8:44 2 Chr 14:11
8:46 2 Kgs 17:6, 18; 25:21; Prov 20:9; 1 Jn 1:8-10
8:47 Lev 26:40-42; Ezra 9:5-7; Neh 1:6-7; Ps 106:6-7; Dan 9:5
8:48 Deut 4:29; 1 Sam 7:3-4
8:50 2 Chr 30:9; Ps 106:46
8:51 Exod 32:11-12; Deut 4:20; 9:26-29; Jer 11:4
8:53 Exod 19:5-6
8:56 Josh 21:45; 23:14-15; 2 Kgs 10:9-10
8:57 Josh 1:5; 1 Sam 12:22; Heb 13:5
8:58 Ps 119:36; Jer 31:33

8:41-43 God promised Abraham that he would be a blessing to the nations (Genesis 12:3). In partial fulfillment of this promise, Solomon prayed that the Temple would bring Gentiles to worship the God of Israel. The spread of the gospel to all peoples following Pentecost fulfills God's promise to Abraham (Acts 10–11; 15; Galatians 3:24-29). Just as God could not physically reside wholly within the Temple, His spiritual blessings could not reside merely with the physical descendants of Abraham.

8:46-51 Solomon's prayer reflected the pattern of Israel's history first described by Moses (Deuteronomy 4:26-31) and later by the prophets of Israel. Disobedience would bring judgment, culminating in exile from the land, but repentance would bring restoration. The mention of the Exodus from Egypt suggested that a second deliverance from a powerful nation was entirely possible for God.

8:58 Solomon recognized that even the inclination to obey God's commands is a gift of His grace (compare Ephesians 2:8).

the LORD our God may give justice to me and to His people Israel, according to each day's
needs. [60]Then people all over the earth will know that the LORD alone is God and there is
no other. [61]And may you be completely faithful to the LORD our God. May you always
obey His decrees and commands, just as you are doing today."
[62]Then the king and all Israel with him offered sacrifices to the LORD. [63]Solomon offered
to the LORD a peace offering of 22,000 cattle and 120,000 sheep and goats. And so the
king and all the people of Israel dedicated the Temple of the LORD.
[64]That same day the king consecrated the central area of the courtyard in front of the
LORD's Temple. He offered burnt offerings, grain offerings, and the fat of peace offerings
there, because the bronze altar in the LORD's presence was too small to hold all the burnt
offerings, grain offerings, and the fat of the peace offerings.
[65]Then Solomon and all Israel celebrated the Festival of Shelters* in the presence of the
LORD our God. A large congregation had gathered from as far away as Lebo-hamath in the
north and the Brook of Egypt in the south. The celebration went on for fourteen days in
all—seven days for the dedication of the altar and seven days for the Festival of Shelters.*
[66]After the festival was over,* Solomon sent the people home. They blessed the king and
went to their homes joyful and glad because the LORD had been good to His servant David
and to His people Israel.

8:60 Deut 4:35; 1 Sam 17:46; 1 Kgs 18:39; Jer 10:10-12
8:61 Deut 18:13; 1 Kgs 11:4; 2 Kgs 20:3
8:62-66 2 Chr 7:1-10
8:64 2 Chr 4:1
8:65 Gen 15:18

THE LORD'S RESPONSE TO SOLOMON

9 So Solomon finished building the Temple of the LORD, as well as the royal palace. He
completed everything he had planned to do. [2]Then the LORD appeared to Solomon a
second time, as He had done before at Gibeon. [3]The LORD said to him,

"I have heard your prayer and your petition. I have set this Temple apart to be holy—
this place you have built where My name will be honored forever. I will always watch
over it, for it is dear to My heart.
[4]"As for you, if you will follow Me with integrity and godliness, as David your
father did, obeying all My commands, decrees, and regulations, [5]then I will establish
the throne of your dynasty over Israel forever. For I made this promise to your father,
David: 'One of your descendants will always sit on the throne of Israel.'
[6]"But if you or your descendants abandon Me and disobey the commands and
decrees I have given you, and if you serve and worship other gods, [7]then I will uproot
Israel from this land that I have given them. I will reject this Temple that I have made
holy to honor My name. I will make Israel an object of mockery and ridicule among

9:1-9 //2 Chr 7:11-22
9:1 1 Kgs 7:1-2; 2 Chr 8:6
9:2 1 Kgs 3:5; 11:9
9:3 2 Kgs 20:5
9:4 1 Kgs 3:14; 11:4
9:5 2 Sam 7:12
9:6 2 Sam 7:14-16; 1 Chr 28:9
9:7 Lev 18:24-29; Deut 4:26-27; 2 Kgs 17:23; Jer 7:4

8:65a Hebrew *the festival;* see note on 8:2. 8:65b Hebrew *seven days and seven days, fourteen days;* compare parallel text at 2 Chr 7:8-10. 8:66 Hebrew *On the eighth day,* probably referring to the day following the seven-day Festival of Shelters; compare parallel text at 2 Chr 7:9-10.

▸ CHURCH
8:60 Telling the world. God has always made evangelism an important part of the work of His people. It was Solomon's prayer that through Israel, God would spread His good news around the world. Join Solomon in praying that God would continue to use Christian Jews (and Gentiles!) to alert the world to God's glory and power. (***See Church****> Role> Preach> Topics> Evangelize> Around the world,* TopicGuide page A50.)

8:65-66 Lebo-hamath and the Brook of Egypt represented the northern and southern extent of Solomon's kingdom. People from all over his kingdom enjoyed Solomon's celebration, and they recognized the goodness of God toward the family of David and all of Israel.

9:2-9 God's response to Solomon's prayer reiterates the conditional nature of His promises to David. God would indeed consecrate the Temple by His presence and hear the prayers of His people as Solomon asked. Furthermore, He would perpetuate the dynasty of David as He had promised. Yet all of this was contingent upon the continued obedience of David's sons. Solomon would gradually leave the path of obedience and would be judged accordingly. Jesus, the great descendant of David, obediently kept the law of God perfectly and will reign over all creation forever (Matthew 1:1; Revelation 17:14).

9:6-9 The threats issued by God had already become a reality for the audience of 1 and 2 Kings. They had been exiled from the land and had seen the Temple destroyed by the Babylonians. No matter how beautiful the Temple was, it was no substitute for heartfelt obedience.

the nations. 8And though this Temple is impressive now, all who pass by will be 9:8 Deut 29:24-26
appalled and will shake their heads in amazement. They will ask, 'Why did the LORD 2 Chr 7:21
do such terrible things to this land and to this Temple?' Jer 22:8-9, 28
9"And the answer will be, 'Because His people abandoned the LORD their God, who 9:9
brought their ancestors out of Egypt, and they worshiped other gods instead and Deut 29:25-28
bowed down to them. That is why the LORD has brought all these disasters on them.'"

SOLOMON'S AGREEMENT WITH HIRAM

9:10-28 2 Chr 8:1-18

10It took Solomon twenty years to build the LORD's Temple and his own royal palace. At the
end of that time, 11he gave twenty towns in the land of Galilee to King Hiram of Tyre. (Hi- 9:10
ram had previously provided all the cedar and cypress timber and gold that Solomon had 1 Kgs 6:37-38
requested.) 12But when Hiram came from Tyre to see the towns Solomon had given him, 9:11 1 Kgs 5:1
he was not at all pleased with them. 13"What kind of towns are these, my brother?" he 2 Chr 2:4
asked. So Hiram called that area Cabul (which means "worthless"), as it is still known to- 9:13
day. 14Nevertheless, Hiram paid* Solomon 9,000 pounds* of gold. Josh 19:27

SOLOMON'S MANY ACHIEVEMENTS

15This is the account of the forced labor that King Solomon conscripted to build the LORD's 9:15
Temple, the royal palace, the supporting terraces,* the wall of Jerusalem, and the cities of 2 Sam 5:9
Hazor, Megiddo, and Gezer. 16(Pharaoh, the king of Egypt, had attacked and captured

9:14a Or *For Hiram had paid.* 9:14b Hebrew *120 talents* [4,000 kilograms]. 9:15 Hebrew *the millo;* also in 9:24. The meaning of the Hebrew is uncertain.

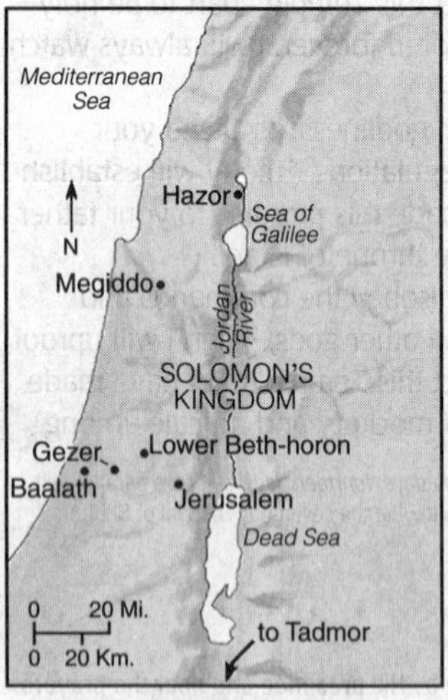

SOLOMON'S BUILDING PROJECTS
Solomon became known as one of the great builders in Israel's history. He built Hazor, Megiddo, and Gezer as fortress cities at key points during his reign. He also rebuilt the cities of lower Beth-horon, Baalath, and Tadmor.

▸ SPIRITUAL WARFARE
9:9 God is not mocked. The consequences associated with the Old Covenant sound confusing to our modern ears. God promised to keep the Temple safe (1 Kings 9:3), but later on He made it clear that if certain rules relating to repentance and obedience were not kept, He would allow the Temple to be destroyed and the land to be ravaged. Does this directly apply to us? Will God tear down our churches and take away our land if we do not have faith in Him? He might do just that (Revelation 1–3), but He makes no general promises to that effect. There are certainly many churches still standing today that have long since left the gospel behind. But this passage does remind us that God is not to be trifled with and that there are consequences for those who abandon God. If you see people drifting away, pray that God will quickly chase them back into full fellowship with Him. (***See Spiritual Warfare****> Resisting Sin and Evil> Consequences> Of Disobedience,* TopicGuide page A46.)

9:10-14 These are probably the towns that 2 Chronicles 8:2 records Hiram giving back to Solomon. This interaction demonstrates Hiram's vassal status. He was unable to press Solomon for better towns and had to provide even more gold for Solomon. Solomon's treatment of Hiram should perhaps be contrasted with his more equitable dealings with him in chapter 5 and taken as part of his downward slide toward self-glorification and idolatry.

▸ HOLINESS
9:10 Paying the piper. Have you ever entered into a business agreement that was good in the beginning but very bad in the long run? There are consequences for entering into long-term contracts, as Solomon learned. He was unable to continue making the regular payments of olive oil and wheat in exchange for Hiram's wood and gold, so he traded entire towns to this pagan king. Hiram was unhappy with the deal, and so was God, for while Solomon got the best of Hiram, Solomon dishonored God by giving away to an unbeliever a portion of God's gift of the Promised Land. Keep your agreements, and pay every cent that you owe to your creditors. This is God's will for us (Romans 13:8). (***See Holiness****> Maturing> Imitating God> His faithfulness,* TopicGuide page A40.)

9:15-28 Not all of Solomon's many achievements listed in this section should be understood as positive accomplishments. Following God's warning to remain faithful, many of these achievements suggest Solomon's decline into self-glorification. His use of forced labor sets the stage for the turmoil that resulted in the division of the kingdom (1 Kings 12). His accumulation of gold (1 Kings 9:28), chariots, horses (1 Kings 9:19), and foreign wives were all condemned in Deuteronomy 17:14-17.

Gezer, killing the Canaanite population and burning it down. He gave the city to his
daughter as a wedding gift when she married Solomon. 17 So Solomon rebuilt the city of
Gezer.) He also built up the towns of Lower Beth-horon, 18 Baalath, and Tamar* in the wil-
9:19 derness within his land. 19 He built towns as supply centers and constructed towns where
1 Kgs 4:26 his chariots and horses* could be stationed. He built everything he desired in Jerusalem
and Lebanon and throughout his entire realm.
20 There were still some people living in the land who were not Israelites, including Amo-
9:21 rites, Hittites, Perizzites, Hivites, and Jebusites. 21 These were descendants of the nations
Josh 15:63 whom the people of Israel had not completely destroyed.* So Solomon conscripted them
9:22 Lev 25:39 for his labor force, and they serve in the labor force to this day. 22 But Solomon did not con-
script any of the Israelites for forced labor. Instead, he assigned them to serve as fighting
men, government officials, officers and captains in his army, commanders of his chariots,
and charioteers. 23 Solomon appointed 550 of them to supervise the people working on
his various projects.
9:24 1 Kgs 3:1; 7:8; 24 Solomon moved his wife, Pharaoh's daughter, from the City of David to the new pal-
11:1, 27 ace he had built for her. Then he constructed the supporting terraces.
2 Chr 32:5 25 Three times each year Solomon presented burnt offerings and peace offerings on the
9:25 altar he had built for the LORD. He also burned incense to the LORD. And so he finished the
Exod 23:14-17 Deut 16:16 work of building the Temple.
9:26 26 King Solomon also built a fleet of ships at Ezion-geber, a port near Elath* in the land of
Num 33:35 Edom, along the shore of the Red Sea.* 27 Hiram sent experienced crews of sailors to sail
1 Kgs 22:48 the ships with Solomon's men. 28 They sailed to Ophir and brought back to Solomon some
9:27 1 Kgs 10:11 sixteen tons* of gold.

VISIT OF THE QUEEN OF SHEBA

10:1-13 //2 Chr 9:1-12 **10** When the queen of Sheba heard of Solomon's fame, which brought honor to the
10:1 name of the LORD,* she came to test him with hard questions. 2 She arrived in Jeru-
2 Chr 9:1 salem with a large group of attendants and a great caravan of camels loaded with spices,
Ps 72:10, 15 large quantities of gold, and precious jewels. When she met with Solomon, she talked with
Matt 12:42 him about everything she had on her mind. 3 Solomon had answers for all her questions;
nothing was too hard for the king to explain to her. 4 When the queen of Sheba realized
how very wise Solomon was, and when she saw the palace he had built, 5 she was over-
whelmed. She was also amazed at the food on his tables, the organization of his officials
and their splendid clothing, the cup-bearers, and the burnt offerings Solomon made at the
Temple of the LORD.

9:18 An alternate reading in the Masoretic Text reads *Tadmor.* 9:19 Or *and charioteers.* 9:21 The Hebrew term used here refers to the complete consecration of things or people to the LORD, either by destroying them or by giving them as an offering. 9:26a As in Greek version (see also 2 Kgs 14:22; 16:6); Hebrew reads *Eloth,* a variant spelling of Elath. 9:26b Hebrew *sea of reeds.* 9:28 Hebrew *420 talents* [14 metric tons]. 10:1 Or *which was due to the name of the LORD.* The meaning of the Hebrew is uncertain.

9:20 God had commanded Israel to destroy these nations as retribution for their sinfulness and to prevent them from corrupting Israel's worship (Deuteronomy 7:1; Joshua 3:10). Israel failed to do so effectively, and these nations plagued Israel for centuries. Their appearance here foreshadowed Solomon's slide into idolatry.

9:26-28 The coastal city of Ezion-geber on the Red Sea provided Solomon with an excellent port for his commercial fleet, which supplied him with vast amounts of gold from the region of Ophir. The location of Ophir is disputed, but it is probably somewhere along the western coast of Arabia. Experienced sailors, provided by Hiram, offered invaluable training for Israel's fledgling maritime force. Hiram also may have used ships of his own to transport Solomon's gold (1 Kings 10:11).

10:1 Sheba was located in the area of modern-day Yemen on the Arabian Peninsula. The queen journeyed fourteen hundred miles to witness Solomon's greatness and wisdom. She also may have wished to discuss trade with Solomon, who controlled the routes through which some of her nation's goods likely would have traveled. Ancient sources depict Sheba as a land of extravagant wealth derived from the trade of rare and precious spices. The queen's gifts to Solomon (1 Kings 10:10) reflect such wealth and opulence.

[6]She exclaimed to the king, "Everything I heard in my country about your achieve-
ments* and wisdom is true! [7]I didn't believe what was said until I arrived here and saw it
with my own eyes. In fact, I had not heard the half of it! Your wisdom and prosperity are far
beyond what I was told. [8]How happy your people* must be! What a privilege for your offi- **10:8** Prov 8:34
cials to stand here day after day, listening to your wisdom! [9]Praise the LORD your God, who
delights in you and has placed you on the throne of Israel. Because of the LORD's eternal **10:9** 2 Sam 8:15; 23:3
love for Israel, He has made you king so you can rule with justice and righteousness." 1 Kgs 5:7
[10]Then she gave the king a gift of 9,000 pounds* of gold, great quantities of spices, and 2 Chr 2:11
precious jewels. Never again were so many spices brought in as those the queen of Sheba
gave to King Solomon.
[11](In addition, Hiram's ships brought gold from Ophir, and they also brought rich car- **10:11**
goes of red sandalwood* and precious jewels. [12]The king used the sandalwood to make 1 Kgs 9:27
railings for the Temple of the LORD and the royal palace, and to construct lyres and harps
for the musicians. Never before or since has there been such a supply of sandalwood.)
[13]King Solomon gave the queen of Sheba whatever she asked for, besides all the cus-
tomary gifts he had so generously given. Then she and all her attendants returned to their
own land.

SOLOMON'S WEALTH AND SPLENDOR

[14]Each year Solomon received about 25 tons* of gold. [15]This did not include the addi- **10:14-29**
tional revenue he received from merchants and traders, all the kings of Arabia, and the //2 Chr 1:14-17; 9:13-28
governors of the land.
[16]King Solomon made 200 large shields of hammered gold, each weighing more than **10:16** 1 Kgs 14:26-28
fifteen pounds.* [17]He also made 300 smaller shields of hammered gold, each weighing 2 Chr 12:9-10
nearly four pounds.* The king placed these shields in the Palace of the Forest of Lebanon. **10:17**
[18]Then the king made a huge throne, decorated with ivory and overlaid with fine gold. 1 Kgs 7:2
[19]The throne had six steps and a rounded back. There were armrests on both sides of the
seat, and the figure of a lion stood on each side of the throne. [20]There were also twelve
other lions, one standing on each end of the six steps. No other throne in all the world
could be compared with it!
[21]All of King Solomon's drinking cups were solid gold, as were all the utensils in the Pal-
ace of the Forest of Lebanon. They were not made of silver, for silver was considered
worthless in Solomon's day!
[22]The king had a fleet of trading ships* that sailed with Hiram's fleet. Once every three
years the ships returned, loaded with gold, silver, ivory, apes, and peacocks.*

10:6 Hebrew *your words.* **10:8** Greek and Syriac versions and Latin Vulgate read *your wives.* **10:10** Hebrew *120 talents* [4,000 kilograms]. **10:11** Hebrew *almug wood;* also in 10:12. **10:14** Hebrew *666 talents* [23 metric tons]. **10:16** Hebrew *600 shekels* [6.8 kilograms]. **10:17** Hebrew *3 minas* [1.8 kilograms]. **10:22a** Hebrew *fleet of ships of Tarshish.* **10:22b** Or *and baboons.*

10:9 The queen not only praised Solomon but his God as well. She attributed Solomon's reign to God's eternal love for His people. However, it is questionable whether the queen's words in fact reflected reality. All of the marvels she noted were narrowly focused on Solomon and his personal grandeur. Would Solomon reign with justice and righteousness? The coming chapters offer a negative response to this question.

10:11-12 The note about Hiram's vessels returning with abundant precious cargo interrupts the account of the queen's visit. Hiram already had given Solomon as much gold as the queen presented to Solomon, and now Hiram's ships returned with more, as well as almug wood (possibly red sandalwood or juniper). Thus, while the queen's gifts were impressive, they did not significantly augment Solomon's already impressive wealth.

10:14-29 Gold is mentioned no fewer than eight times in these verses. Solomon collected vast quantities of gold, which he used to make extravagant and luxurious items, including decorative shields, his throne, and eating utensils. Read in light of Deuteronomy 17:16-17, this passage suggests that Solomon had turned his wisdom and God's blessing toward self-glorification and indulgence.

10:15 The revenue from merchants and traders came in the form of duties paid to Solomon for the right to transport goods across his territory. Israel lay at the crossroads of Africa and Asia, ensuring significant revenue from these sources.

10:23 23So King Solomon became richer and wiser than any other king on earth. 24People
1 Kgs 3:12-13; 4:30 from every nation came to consult him and to hear the wisdom God had given him. 25Year
after year everyone who visited brought him gifts of silver and gold, clothing, weapons,
spices, horses, and mules.
26Solomon built up a huge force of chariots and horses.* He had 1,400 chariots and
12,000 horses. He stationed some of them in the chariot cities and some near him in Jeru-
10:27 salem. 27The king made silver as plentiful in Jerusalem as stone. And valuable cedar tim-
2 Chr 1:14-17; 9:25, 27 ber was as common as the sycamore-fig trees that grow in the foothills of Judah.*
10:28 28Solomon's horses were imported from Egypt* and from Cilicia*; the king's traders ac-
2 Chr 1:16; 9:28 quired them from Cilicia at the standard price. 29At that time chariots from Egypt could be
10:29 purchased for 600 pieces of silver,* and horses for 150 pieces of silver.* They were then
2 Kgs 7:6-7 exported to the kings of the Hittites and the kings of Aram.

SOLOMON'S MANY WIVES

11:1 **11** Now King Solomon loved many foreign women. Besides Pharaoh's daughter, he
Neh 13:23-27 married women from Moab, Ammon, Edom, Sidon, and from among the Hittites.
11:2 2The LORD had clearly instructed the people of Israel, 'You must not marry them, because
Exod 23:31-33; 34:12-16 they will turn your hearts to their gods.' Yet Solomon insisted on loving them anyway. 3He
Deut 7:3-4 had 700 wives of royal birth and 300 concubines. And in fact, they did turn his heart away
11:3 from the LORD.
2 Sam 5:13-16 4In Solomon's old age, they turned his heart to worship other gods instead of being
11:5 completely faithful to the LORD his God, as his father, David, had been. 5Solomon wor-
Judg 2:12-14; 10:6 1 Sam 7:3-4 shiped Ashtoreth, the goddess of the Sidonians, and Molech,* the detestable god of the
Ammonites. 6In this way, Solomon did what was evil in the LORD's sight; he refused to fol-
low the LORD completely, as his father, David, had done.
11:7 7On the Mount of Olives, east of Jerusalem,* he even built a pagan shrine for Chemosh,
Lev 20:2-5 Num 21:27-30 the detestable god of Moab, and another for Molech, the detestable god of the Ammon-
Judg 11:24 2 Kgs 23:10, 13 ites. 8Solomon built such shrines for all his foreign wives to use for burning incense and
sacrificing to their gods.

10:26 Or *charioteers;* also in 10:26b. 10:27 Hebrew *the Shephelah.* 10:28a Possibly *Muzur,* a district near Cilicia; also in 10:29. 10:28b Hebrew *Kue,* probably another name for Cilicia. 10:29a Hebrew *600 shekels of silver,* about 15 pounds or 6.8 kilograms in weight. 10:29b Hebrew *150 [shekels],* about 3.8 pounds or 1.7 kilograms in weight. 11:5 Hebrew *Milcom,* a variant spelling of Molech; also in 11:33. 11:7 Hebrew *On the mountain east of Jerusalem.*

10:26-28 Deuteronomy 17:16 forbade kings from collecting large numbers of horses and chariots. The importation of horses from Egypt was expressly forbidden (see note at 1 Kings 4:26-28).

11:1-3 Deuteronomy 17:17 prohibited the king from accumulating many wives, and several passages warned the Israelites about taking foreign wives for themselves (Exodus 34:16; Deuteronomy 7:1-4; Joshua 23:12-13). While the figures given here (700 wives and 300 concubines, totaling 1,000) should perhaps not be understood in a strictly literal sense (compare Song of Songs 6:8-9), Solomon's numerous wives succeeded in doing exactly what God had warned about—they divided his loyalties and turned him away from God. On the use of the underlying Hebrew word for "love," see note at 1 Kings 3:2-3. Solomon failed to give God the kind of exclusive love and loyalty He deserved and demanded (Deuteronomy 6:5).

▸ HOLINESS

11:1 Looking for love. Have you ever known a Christian who fell into sexual sin? It happens to the intelligent, the skilled, and the mature—sexual sin tears the Christian life apart. And sexual sin is not terminal sin—it breeds greater sins. Solomon moved from serial polygamy to serial idolatry to complete disregard for his covenant with God (1 Kings 11:11). Never start down the path of sexual sin. You never know where you will end up at the end of your journey. (***See Holiness****> Disciplines> Of Abstinence> Chastity,* TopicGuide page A42.)

11:4 David is the standard against which all the kings of Judah are judged in the books of 1 and 2 Kings (1 Kings 3:14; 9:4; 14:8; 15:3; 2 Kings 8:18-19; 22:2). David committed grave sins, but he repented deeply and never turned away from God to worship idols (2 Samuel 11–12). In this sense, he always remained faithful. Solomon failed to follow his father's example.

11:5-8 Ashtoreth was a pagan mother-goddess widely worshiped throughout the ancient Near East (Judges 2:13; 1 Kings 11:33; 2 Kings 23:13). Molech, or Milcom (see textual note), was the national deity of Amon. Chemosh, the god of Moab, was associated with child sacrifice (2 Kings 3:27). It is tragically ironic that Solomon, who built the great Temple of the Lord, also constructed shrines to pagan gods and goddesses. Similar shrines and high places would plague Israel throughout her remaining history (1 Kings 14:23; 15:14; 16:31-33; 22:43).

[9]The LORD was very angry with Solomon, for his heart had turned away from the LORD,
the God of Israel, who had appeared to him twice. [10]He had warned Solomon specifically
about worshiping other gods, but Solomon did not listen to the LORD's command. [11]So
now the LORD said to him, "Since you have not kept My covenant and have disobeyed My
decrees, I will surely tear the kingdom away from you and give it to one of your servants.
[12]But for the sake of your father, David, I will not do this while you are still alive. I will take
the kingdom away from your son. [13]And even so, I will not take away the entire kingdom;
I will let him be king of one tribe, for the sake of My servant David and for the sake of Jerusalem, My chosen city."

11:9 1 Kgs 3:5; 9:2-3
11:10 1 Kgs 6:12; 9:6
11:11 1 Sam 2:30; 1 Kgs 6:11-12; 11:31
11:12 2 Sam 7:15

SOLOMON'S ADVERSARIES

[14]Then the LORD raised up Hadad the Edomite, a member of Edom's royal family, to be
Solomon's adversary. [15]Years before, David had defeated Edom. Joab, his army commander, had stayed to bury some of the Israelite soldiers who had died in battle. While
there, they killed every male in Edom. [16]Joab and the army of Israel had stayed there for
six months, killing them.

[17]But Hadad and a few of his father's royal officials escaped and headed for Egypt. (Hadad was just a boy at the time.) [18]They set out from Midian and went to Paran, where others joined them. Then they traveled to Egypt and went to Pharaoh, who gave them a
home, food, and some land. [19]Pharaoh grew very fond of Hadad, and he gave him his
wife's sister in marriage—the sister of Queen Tahpenes. [20]She bore him a son named Genubath. Tahpenes raised him* in Pharaoh's palace among Pharaoh's own sons.

[21]When the news reached Hadad in Egypt that David and his commander Joab were
both dead, he said to Pharaoh, "Let me return to my own country."

11:15 2 Sam 8:13-14; 1 Chr 18:12-13
11:21 1 Kgs 2:10, 34

11:20 As in Greek version; Hebrew reads *weaned him.*

FRIENDS AND ENEMIES Solomon's reputation brought acclaim and riches from many nations, but he disobeyed God, marrying pagan women and worshiping their gods. So God raised up enemies like Hadad from Edom and Rezon from Zobah (modern-day Syria). Jeroboam from Zeredah was another enemy who would eventually divide this mighty kingdom.

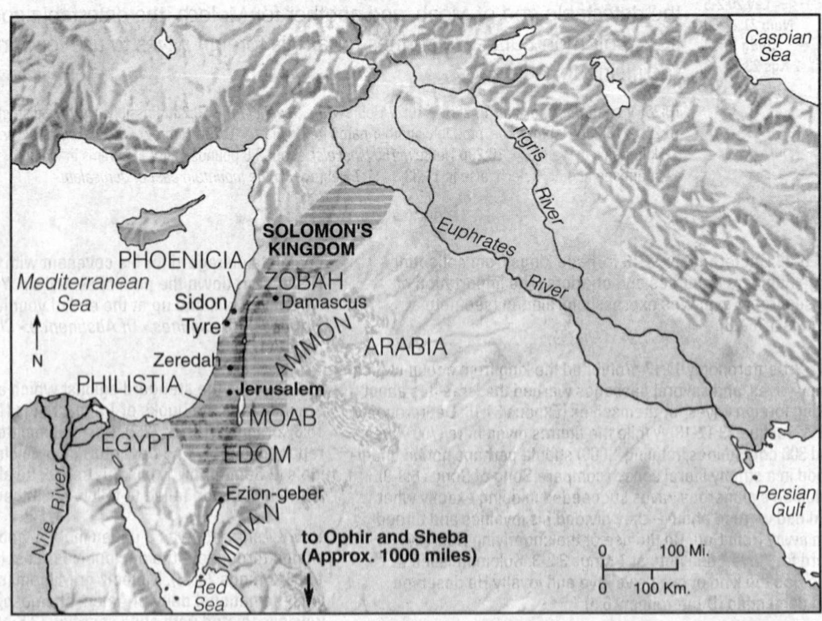

11:9-13 God responded to Solomon's apostasy with judgment and grace. The author reminds us that Solomon had been privileged with two appearances of God and had been specifically warned against idolatry, making his sin all the more reprehensible. Yet for the sake of David (that is, out of His mercy and grace), God mitigated His judgment against Solomon. He decreed that Solomon would not live to see the division of the kingdom, and the family of David would retain part of the kingdom. The one tribe in view was Judah. At least one other tribe, the tribe of Benjamin, would also remain under the Davidic dynasty, since only ten later rebelled (1 Kings 11:29-39).

22"Why?" Pharaoh asked him. "What do you lack here that makes you want to go home?"
"Nothing," he replied. "But even so, please let me return home."
11:23 23God also raised up Rezon son of Eliada as Solomon's adversary. Rezon had fled from
2 Sam 8:3; 10:15-16 his master, King Hadadezer of Zobah, 24and had become the leader of a gang of rebels. Af-
11:24 2 Sam 10:7-8, 18 ter David conquered Hadadezer, Rezon and his men fled to Damascus, where he became
king. 25Rezon was Israel's bitter adversary for the rest of Solomon's reign, and he made
trouble, just as Hadad did. Rezon hated Israel intensely and continued to reign in Aram.

JEROBOAM REBELS AGAINST SOLOMON

11:26 26Another rebel leader was Jeroboam son of Nebat, one of Solomon's own officials. He
2 Chr 13:6 came from the town of Zeredah in Ephraim, and his mother was Zeruah, a widow.
11:27 27This is the story behind his rebellion. Solomon was rebuilding the supporting terraces*
1 Kgs 9:24 and repairing the walls of the city of his father, David. 28Jeroboam was a very capable
young man, and when Solomon saw how industrious he was, he put him in charge of the
labor force from the tribes of Ephraim and Manasseh, the descendants of Joseph.
11:29 29One day as Jeroboam was leaving Jerusalem, the prophet Ahijah from Shiloh met him
1 Kgs 12:15; 14:2 along the way. Ahijah was wearing a new cloak. The two of them were alone in a field,
11:30 1 Sam 15:27-28 30and Ahijah took hold of the new cloak he was wearing and tore it into twelve pieces.
11:31 31Then he said to Jeroboam, "Take ten of these pieces, for this is what the LORD, the God of
1 Kgs 11:11-12 Israel, says: 'I am about to tear the kingdom from the hand of Solomon, and I will give ten
of the tribes to you! 32But I will leave him one tribe for the sake of My servant David and
11:33 for the sake of Jerusalem, which I have chosen out of all the tribes of Israel. 33For Solomon
1 Kgs 11:5-8 has* abandoned Me and worshiped Ashtoreth, the goddess of the Sidonians; Chemosh,
the god of Moab; and Molech, the god of the Ammonites. He has not followed My ways
and done what is pleasing in My sight. He has not obeyed My decrees and regulations as
David his father did.
34"'But I will not take the entire kingdom from Solomon at this time. For the sake of My
servant David, the one whom I chose and who obeyed My commands and decrees, I will
11:35 keep Solomon as leader for the rest of his life. 35But I will take the kingdom away from his
1 Kgs 12:16 son and give ten of the tribes to you. 36His son will have one tribe so that the descendants
11:36 of David My servant will continue to reign, shining like a lamp in Jerusalem, the city I have
1 Kgs 15:4 2 Kgs 8:19 chosen to be the place for My name. 37And I will place you on the throne of Israel, and you
2 Chr 21:7 will rule over all that your heart desires. 38If you listen to what I tell you and follow My
11:38 2 Sam 7:11, 27

11:27 Hebrew *the millo.* The meaning of the Hebrew is uncertain. 11:33 As in Greek, Syriac, and Latin Vulgate; Hebrew reads *For they have.*

11:25-28 Early in his reign, Solomon experienced peace on all sides (5:4), but now, as a consequence of his disobedience, God afflicted him with enemies. Rezon attacked him in the north, and Hadad troubled him in the south. Meanwhile, internal opposition to Solomon formed as disparate, malcontented people came together under Jeroboam, an Israelite from the tribe of Ephraim. Solomon named Jeroboam to supervise the workforce drafted from the tribes of Ephraim and Manasseh to continue Solomon's building projects in Jerusalem. This workforce apparently was distinct from the Canaanite workforce described in 5:13-14.

▸ PURPOSE
11:26-27 God's rebellion. Is God involved in politics? In a sense, there is no separation between God and state, for God is sovereign over all things. Elections, rebellions, taxes, war—nothing happens outside of God's permissive will. Jeroboam was a rebel, but at this point in his life (he later turned to idolatry), he was God's rebel, empowered to guide God's people away from Solomon's idolatry. In your places of influence, can you find ways to turn people toward the worship of the one true God? (***See Purpose> God's Means> God's Sovereignty> God decrees all,*** TopicGuide page A52.)

11:30 Throughout the Old Testament, prophets employed dramatic actions to convey their messages (compare 1 Kings 22:11; Isaiah 20; Jeremiah 13:1-11). Ahijah tore his cloak to represent the division of the kingdom. In Hebrew, the word *cloak* and the name *Solomon* are strikingly similar. Thus, the tearing of the cloak was a particularly strong visual and verbal image of the division of Solomon's kingdom. The ten pieces given to Jeroboam symbolized the ten tribes that would abandon the Davidic dynasty. (Compare with the prophetic confrontation of Saul, 1 Samuel 15:27-28.)

11:37-38 God entered into a conditional covenant with Jeroboam. If he would be obedient to God, his family would reign over the northern tribes of Israel perpetually. Jeroboam, however, quickly abandoned God's law and his dynasty ended following his son's murder (12:25–14:20; 15:25-31).

ways and do whatever I consider to be right, and if you obey My decrees and commands,
as My servant David did, then I will always be with you. I will establish an enduring dy-
nasty for you as I did for David, and I will give Israel to you. 39 Because of Solomon's sin I
will punish the descendants of David—though not forever.'"
40 Solomon tried to kill Jeroboam, but he fled to King Shishak of Egypt and stayed there 11:40 1 Kgs 14:25
until Solomon died. 2 Chr 12:2

SUMMARY OF SOLOMON'S REIGN

41 The rest of the events in Solomon's reign, including all his deeds and his wisdom, are re-
corded in *The Book of the Acts of Solomon.* 42 Solomon ruled in Jerusalem over all Israel for 11:41-43 //2 Chr 9:29-31
forty years. 43 When he died, he was buried in the City of David, named for his father. Then
his son Rehoboam became the next king.

THE NORTHERN TRIBES REVOLT

12 Rehoboam went to Shechem, where all Israel had gathered to make him king. 12:1-24 //2 Chr 10:1–11:4
2 When Jeroboam son of Nebat heard of this, he returned from Egypt,* for he had 12:1
fled to Egypt to escape from King Solomon. 3 The leaders of Israel summoned him, and Judg 9:1, 6
Jeroboam and the whole assembly of Israel went to speak with Rehoboam. 4 "Your father 2 Chr 10:1
was a hard master," they said. "Lighten the harsh labor demands and heavy taxes that 12:4
your father imposed on us. Then we will be your loyal subjects." 1 Sam 8:11-18
5 Rehoboam replied, "Give me three days to think this over. Then come back for my an- 12:5
swer." So the people went away. 1 Kgs 12:12
6 Then King Rehoboam discussed the matter with the older men who had counseled his
father, Solomon. "What is your advice?" he asked. "How should I answer these people?"
7 The older counselors replied, "If you are willing to be a servant to these people today
and give them a favorable answer, they will always be your loyal subjects."
8 But Rehoboam rejected the advice of the older men and instead asked the opinion of
the young men who had grown up with him and were now his advisers. 9 "What is your

12:2 As in Greek version and Latin Vulgate (see also 2 Chr 10:2); Hebrew reads *he lived in Egypt.*

11:39 The phrase "though not forever" engendered a longstanding hope for a reunion of the kingdom under a Davidic monarch. The prophets hoped for such a reunion under a messianic Davidic king (Amos 9:11-12; Hosea 3:5; Jeremiah 30:9), but it was not until the inauguration of the kingdom of Jesus, the Messiah, that such a hope begin to materialize (Matthew 1:1; 4:17).

11:40 It is unclear what actions Jeroboam took following his meeting with Ahijah, but judging from Solomon's response he certainly attempted to act on the words of the prophet. Shishak succeeded the pharaoh with whom Solomon had made an alliance and was the founder of the twenty-second dynasty of Egypt.

11:41-42 Kings provides formulaic conclusions to each ruler's reign, typically giving sources of information, the length of the reign, and burial and succession notices. The *Book of the Acts of Solomon* is a lost source used by the authors of Kings to compose their inspired history. Other such sources include *The Book of the History of the Kings of Israel* and *The Book of the History of the Kings of Judah* (1 Kings 14:19, 29). The dates of Solomon's reign have been estimated as 970–930 BC, and his son Rehoboam succeeded him.

▸ HOLINESS

11:42 Finishing strong. Many people start out their spiritual lives well but end poorly. Jesus spoke of such people in the parable of the soils (Mark 4:1-9)—they are those who sprout up quickly, but wilt just as quickly. What makes it harder, rather than easier, to remain faithful as you get older? What can you do to make sure you remain spiritually strong? (***See Holiness***> *Disciplines> Of Engagement> Endurance,* TopicGuide page A42.)

12:2-4 Solomon's expansive kingdom placed a heavy economic and physical burden on the tribes, a burden perhaps disproportionately shouldered by the northern tribes. Israel had been released from bondage in Egypt to be a free people, but now Solomon's policies had once again placed the people under a heavy yoke. In a case of historical irony that was almost certainly not missed by the author, Jeroboam emerged from Egypt as a new Moses to set the northern tribes free.

▸ BIBLE

12:6-11 Good advice. Getting advice is not just a good idea—it's biblical! God wants us to be deeply rooted in our present community so that it is entirely natural to seek guidance from those more mature than ourselves. But not all advice is created equal; as King Rehoboam learned, counsel stands or falls based on its foundation in God's Word. Compare the advice given by the older and younger advisers. How would you use God's Word to judge one over the other? (***See Bible***> *Power> Wisdom> Instruction through God's Word,* TopicGuide page A11.)

advice?" he asked them. "How should I answer these people who want me to lighten the
burdens imposed by my father?"
10 The young men replied, "This is what you should tell those complainers who want a
lighter burden: 'My little finger is thicker than my father's waist! 11 Yes, my father laid
heavy burdens on you, but I'm going to make them even heavier! My father beat you with
whips, but I will beat you with scorpions!' "
12:12 12 Three days later Jeroboam and all the people returned to hear Rehoboam's decision,
1 Kgs 12:5 just as the king had ordered. 13 But Rehoboam spoke harshly to the people, for he rejected
the advice of the older counselors 14 and followed the counsel of his younger advisers. He
told the people, "My father laid heavy burdens on you, but I'm going to make them even
12:15 heavier! My father beat you with whips, but I will beat you with scorpions!"
Deut 2:30 15 So the king paid no attention to the people. This turn of events was the will of the
Judg 14:4
2 Chr 10:15 LORD, for it fulfilled the LORD's message to Jeroboam son of Nebat through the prophet Ahi-
jah from Shiloh.
12:16 16 When all Israel realized that the king had refused to listen to them, they responded,
2 Sam 20:1

"Down with the dynasty of David!
We have no interest in the son of Jesse.
Back to your homes, O Israel!
Look out for your own house, O David!"

12:17
1 Kgs 11:13, 36 So the people of Israel returned home. 17 But Rehoboam continued to rule over the Isra-
12:18 elites who lived in the towns of Judah.
2 Sam 20:24 18 King Rehoboam sent Adoniram,* who was in charge of the labor force, to restore or-
der, but the people of Israel stoned him to death. When this news reached King Rehobo-
12:19 am, he quickly jumped into his chariot and fled to Jerusalem. 19 And to this day the
2 Kgs 17:21 northern tribes of Israel have refused to be ruled by a descendant of David.

12:18 As in some Greek manuscripts and Syriac version (see also 4:6; 5:14); Hebrew reads *Adoram*.

▸ADOPTION

12:10 Foul language. Do you casually use naughty or inappropriate words? Or do they slip out when something unexpected occurs? The young men advising Rehoboam most likely were making a phallic reference, thinking that if Rehoboam learned some racy rhetoric, his opponents would be impressed. But with God overhearing everything we say (and think!), some language must be set aside (Ephesians 4:29-32) as not worthy of God's children. Ask God to help you control your tongue (James 3:7-12). (***See Adoption****> With Christ> Supernatural> Speak godly words,* TopicGuide page A37.)

12:13-14 Although Rehoboam was 41 years old (1 Kings 14:21), he embodied the foolishness of youth. He arrogantly rejected the counsel of his elder statesmen in order to enforce his will upon the people. The elders of Israel exercised an important governing function throughout the nation's history (2 Samuel 3:17; 5:3; 17:4; 1 Kings 20:7-8). The younger men may have been civil servants who are sometimes distinguished from the elders (2 Kings 10:5). They also may have been Rehoboam's half-brothers from Solomon's multiple marriages. Rehoboam played the role of stubborn Pharaoh to the new Moses, Jeroboam (see note at 1 Kings 12:2-4).

12:15 The division of the kingdom is described as the will of God in fulfillment of prophecy, yet Rehoboam and his advisers were clearly held responsible for their poor judgment. God's sovereignty does not absolve men and women of responsibility for their actions.

12:18 Rehoboam signaled his determination to rule the people harshly by choosing Adoniram, the supervisor of forced labor, as an envoy to the disgruntled Israelites. The northern tribes immediately perceived this action as instigation and killed Adoniram, demonstrating their determination to resist Rehoboam's rule.

THE KINGDOM DIVIDES
Rehoboam's threat of heavier burdens caused a rebellion and divided the nation. Rehoboam ruled the southern kingdom; Jeroboam ruled the northern kingdom. Jeroboam set up idols in Dan and Bethel to discourage worship in Jerusalem. At the same time Aram, Ammon, Moab, and Edom claimed independence from the divided nation.

20 When the people of Israel learned of Jeroboam's return from Egypt, they called an assembly and made him king over all Israel. So only the tribe of Judah remained loyal to the family of David.

SHEMAIAH'S PROPHECY

21 When Rehoboam arrived at Jerusalem, he mobilized the men of Judah and the tribe of Benjamin—180,000 select troops—to fight against the men of Israel and to restore the kingdom to himself.

22 But God said to Shemaiah, the man of God, 23 "Say to Rehoboam son of Solomon, king of Judah, and to all the people of Judah and Benjamin, and to the rest of the people, 24 'This is what the LORD says: Do not fight against your relatives, the Israelites. Go back home, for what has happened is My doing!'" So they obeyed the message of the LORD and went home, as the LORD had commanded.

JEROBOAM MAKES GOLD CALVES

25 Jeroboam then built up the city of Shechem in the hill country of Ephraim, and it became his capital. Later he went and built up the town of Peniel.*

26 Jeroboam thought to himself, "Unless I am careful, the kingdom will return to the dynasty of David. 27 When these people go to Jerusalem to offer sacrifices at the Temple of the LORD, they will again give their allegiance to King Rehoboam of Judah. They will kill me and make him their king instead."

28 So on the advice of his counselors, the king made two gold calves. He said to the people,* "It is too much trouble for you to worship in Jerusalem. Look, Israel, these are the gods who brought you out of Egypt!"

29 He placed these calf idols in Bethel and in Dan—at either end of his kingdom. 30 But this became a great sin, for the people worshiped the idols, traveling as far north as Dan to worship the one there.

31 Jeroboam also erected buildings at the pagan shrines and ordained priests from the common people—those who were not from the priestly tribe of Levi. 32 And Jeroboam instituted a religious festival in Bethel, held on the fifteenth day of the eighth month,* in imitation of the annual Festival of Shelters in Judah. There at Bethel he himself offered sacrifices to the calves he had made, and he appointed priests for the pagan shrines he had made. 33 So on the fifteenth day of the eighth month, a day that he himself had designated, Jeroboam offered sacrifices on the altar at Bethel. He instituted a religious festival for Israel, and he went up to the altar to burn incense.

12:20 1 Kgs 11:13, 32
12:21 2 Chr 11:1
12:22 2 Chr 11:2; 12:5-7
12:25 Judg 8:8, 17
12:27 Deut 12:4-6, 14
12:28 Exod 32:4; 2 Kgs 10:29; 2 Chr 11:15; Hos 8:4-7
12:29 Gen 28:19; Judg 18:27-31
12:30 1 Kgs 13:34; 2 Kgs 17:21
12:31 1 Kgs 13:32; 2 Kgs 17:32; 2 Chr 11:13-15; 13:9
12:32 Lev 23:33-34; Num 29:12

12:25 Hebrew *Penuel,* a variant spelling of Peniel. 12:28 Hebrew *to them.* 12:32 This day of the ancient Hebrew lunar calendar occurred in late October or early November, exactly one month after the annual Festival of Shelters in Judah (see Lev 23:34).

12:26-28 God had promised to sustain Jeroboam's rule if he remained obedient to God's law (1 Kings 11:29-39), but Jeroboam chose not to place his confidence in God's promise. Jeroboam was concerned that continued worship at the Jerusalem Temple would lead the northern tribes to acknowledge Rehoboam's sovereignty once more, leading to the loss of his power and his life. So Jeroboam constructed an alternative system of worship that would not necessitate travel to Jerusalem. Having earlier played the part of Moses (see note at 1 Kings 12:2-4), Jeroboam now ominously uttered the words of Aaron in presenting the golden calf (Exodus 32:4).

▸ HOLINESS
12:27 Vote for Jesus! Manipulating people with religion never seems to go out of style. Jeroboam ignored God's Word, and, in the name of political expediency, officially instituted idol worship in Israel. Beware of political leaders who use watered-down religion to shore up their power base. (***See Holiness****> Law and Grace> Law> Leaders and followers,* TopicGuide page A41.)

12:29-30 In the ancient world, deities were often depicted enthroned upon bulls or calves. In biblical worship, the Ark of the Covenant functioned as the footstool of God (Psalm 132:6-8). Jeroboam perhaps intended the calves to function as the Ark did at Jerusalem, but this unsanctioned worship brought God's judgment upon Israel and opened the way for outright idolatry and polytheism.

12:31-33 Jeroboam went so far as to create a rival non-Levitical priesthood (Deuteronomy 18:1-8) and a new religious festival that was not divinely sanctioned. His festival was intended to rival the Festival of Shelters—ironically the very festival that marked the consecration of the Jerusalem Temple (see note at 1 Kings 8:2).

A PROPHET DENOUNCES JEROBOAM

13:1 2 Kgs 23:17 **13** At the LORD's command, a man of God from Judah went to Bethel, arriving there
just as Jeroboam was approaching the altar to burn incense. 2Then at the LORD's
13:2 2 Kgs 23:15-16, 20 command, he shouted, "O altar, altar! This is what the LORD says: A child named Josiah will
be born into the dynasty of David. On you he will sacrifice the priests from the pagan shrines
who come here to burn incense, and human bones will be burned on you." 3That same day
the man of God gave a sign to prove his message. He said, "The LORD has promised to give
this sign: This altar will split apart, and its ashes will be poured out on the ground."
4When King Jeroboam heard the man of God speaking against the altar at Bethel, he
pointed at him and shouted, "Seize that man!" But instantly the king's hand became para-
lyzed in that position, and he couldn't pull it back. 5At the same time a wide crack appeared
in the altar, and the ashes poured out, just as the man of God had predicted in his message
from the LORD.
13:6 6The king cried out to the man of God, "Please ask the LORD your God to restore my
Exod 8:8, 28; 9:28 Jer 37:3 hand again!" So the man of God prayed to the LORD, and the king's hand was restored and
Acts 8:24 he could move it again.
13:7 7Then the king said to the man of God, "Come to the palace with me and have some-
1 Sam 9:7 thing to eat, and I will give you a gift."
2 Kgs 5:15 8But the man of God said to the king, "Even if you gave me half of everything you own, I
13:8 Num 22:18 would not go with you. I would not eat or drink anything in this place. 9For the LORD gave me
13:9 this command: 'You must not eat or drink anything while you are there, and do not return
Num 22:18; 24:13 to Judah by the same way you came.'" 10So he left Bethel and went home another way.
11As it happened, there was an old prophet living in Bethel, and his sons* came home
and told him what the man of God had done in Bethel that day. They also told their father
what the man had said to the king. 12The old prophet asked them, "Which way did he go?"
So they showed their father* which road the man of God had taken. 13"Quick, saddle the
donkey," the old man said. So they saddled the donkey for him, and he mounted it.
14Then he rode after the man of God and found him sitting under a great tree. The old
prophet asked him, "Are you the man of God who came from Judah?"
"Yes, I am," he replied.
15Then he said to the man of God, "Come home with me and eat some food."
13:16 1 Kgs 13:8 16"No, I cannot," he replied. "I am not allowed to eat or drink anything here in this place.

13:11 As in Greek version; Hebrew reads *son.* 13:12 As in Greek version; Hebrew reads *They had seen.*

13:1-2 The words "man of God" often describe a prophet (1 Samuel 2:27; 1 Kings 12:22; 2 Kings 4:7). This unnamed prophet condemned Jeroboam's altar and, by association, his whole religious program. King Josiah would reign some three centuries after Jeroboam. His fulfillment of this prophecy is recorded in 2 Kings 23:15-20. The prophecy implicitly predicted the perpetuation of the Davidic dynasty.

▸ GOD
13:2 A word from God. God's message for us often does not come in a neat and tidy package. It can come through shouting ministers, screaming kids, bold headlines, or a general impression following a quiet walk. Look for God's guiding hand in everything—yes, everything—in your world. God is everywhere, speaking in all things, if we will only hear Him. (***See God****> God's Attributes> All-Present> God is everywhere,* TopicGuide page A16.)

13:3-6 God often gave signs in order to substantiate the words of His prophets (2 Kings 19:29; 20:8-9; Isaiah 38:22; Jeremiah 44:29). King Jeroboam received a double sign for his refusal to heed the prophecy and his attempt to seize the man of God. Not only did the altar split as the man of God had predicted, but Jeroboam's own hand dramatically shriveled (compare Exodus 4:6-7). In a show of mercy and a further demonstration of the authority of the man of God, God healed Jeroboam's hand through the intercession of the man of God.

13:9 The motivation for the instructions given to the man of God is not clear. Elsewhere, prophets refused to accept gifts in order to avoid the impression that God could be manipulated (2 Kings 5:16). The same principle may have been at work here; by avoiding circumstances that might compromise his message, the man of God would be better able to maintain his own integrity and God's freedom to act. Furthermore, to dine with Jeroboam might have been taken to imply the man of God's (and therefore God's) approval of Jeroboam.

13:11-15 The old prophet may have aligned himself with the worship institutions initiated by Jeroboam at Bethel. His hospitality, like Jeroboam's, may have been motivated by a desire to oblige the man of God to mitigate his message of condemnation.

17 For the LORD gave me this command: 'You must not eat or drink anything while you are there, and do not return to Judah by the same way you came.'"

18 But the old prophet answered, "I am a prophet, too, just as you are. And an angel gave me this command from the LORD: 'Bring him home with you so he can have something to eat and drink.'" But the old man was lying to him. 19 So they went back together, and the man of God ate and drank at the prophet's home.

20 Then while they were sitting at the table, a command from the LORD came to the old prophet. 21 He cried out to the man of God from Judah, "This is what the LORD says: You have defied the word of the LORD and have disobeyed the command the LORD your God gave you. 22 You came back to this place and ate and drank where He told you not to eat or drink. Because of this, your body will not be buried in the grave of your ancestors."

23 After the man of God had finished eating and drinking, the old prophet saddled his own donkey for him, 24 and the man of God started off again. But as he was traveling along, a lion came out and killed him. His body lay there on the road, with the donkey and the lion standing beside it. 25 People who passed by saw the body lying in the road and the lion standing beside it, and they went and reported it in Bethel, where the old prophet lived.

26 When the prophet heard the report, he said, "It is the man of God who disobeyed the LORD's command. The LORD has fulfilled His word by causing the lion to attack and kill him."

27 Then the prophet said to his sons, "Saddle a donkey for me." So they saddled a donkey, 28 and he went out and found the body lying in the road. The donkey and lion were still standing there beside it, for the lion had not eaten the body nor attacked the donkey. 29 So the prophet laid the body of the man of God on the donkey and took it back to the town to mourn over him and bury him. 30 He laid the body in his own grave, crying out in grief, "Oh, my brother!"

31 Afterward the prophet said to his sons, "When I die, bury me in the grave where the man of God is buried. Lay my bones beside his bones. 32 For the message the LORD told him to proclaim against the altar in Bethel and against the pagan shrines in the towns of Samaria will certainly come true."

33 But even after this, Jeroboam did not turn from his evil ways. He continued to choose priests from the common people. He appointed anyone who wanted to become a priest for the pagan shrines. 34 This became a great sin and resulted in the utter destruction of Jeroboam's dynasty from the face of the earth.

13:21 1 Sam 13:14
13:24 1 Kgs 20:36
13:31 2 Kgs 23:17-18
13:32 1 Kgs 16:24
13:33 1 Kgs 12:31; 2 Chr 13:9
13:34 1 Kgs 14:10; 15:29; 2 Kgs 17:21

AHIJAH'S PROPHECY AGAINST JEROBOAM

14 At that time Jeroboam's son Abijah became very sick. 2 So Jeroboam told his wife, "Disguise yourself so that no one will recognize you as my wife. Then go to the

14:2 1 Sam 28:7-8; 2 Sam 14:2-3; 2 Chr 18:29

13:20-24 The lying prophet now received a true word from God. The man of God was condemned for straying from the instructions God had given him. The gravity and timing of his mission warranted strict obedience, so his failure brought God's immediate judgment (compare Leviticus 10; 2 Samuel 6:1-8; Acts 5:1-11). The fact that the lion remained standing by the donkey, seemingly ignoring the easy prey, was a sign of the divine nature of the event.

▸ WORSHIP

13:21 The Word of the Lord? Have you ever had someone tell you something that they claimed was from the Lord, but actually it was not? How can you tell whether something is from God or not? Only by God's Word (Isaiah 8:19-20). Form your beliefs and actions in accordance to God's inerrant Word, harmonizing with Scripture, and you will not be led astray by other voices and opinions. (***See Worship****> OT> Prophets> Prophets are God's spokesmen,* TopicGuide page A28.)

13:34 The events that transpired regarding the man of God further confirmed the veracity of God's message of judgment, yet Jeroboam persisted with his unauthorized worship program. His refusal to abandon his false system of worship condemned his house and the northern tribes, who never abandoned Jeroboam's program. The idols, the alternative priesthood, and the new festival would henceforth be known as the sin of Jeroboam. Such practices would plague Israel throughout her existence and would ultimately bring about the destruction of the nation.

14:1-2 In the ancient world, prophets were often consulted in times of illness or distress (2 Kings 1:2-4; 4:17-30; 8:8). Jeroboam obviously recognized Ahijah's power and authority, but he was unwilling to submit himself to any possible reprimand for his actions, such as he had received from the unnamed prophet from Judah (1 Kings 13:2-6). The king demonstrated his spiritual blindness and folly by instructing his wife to disguise her appearance from a blind man (1 Kings 14:4). Ironically, this blind man would see through the king's deception.

14:3 prophet Ahijah at Shiloh—the man who told me I would become king. 3 Take him a gift of
1 Sam 9:7-8 ten loaves of bread, some cakes, and a jar of honey, and ask him what will happen to
2 Kgs 4:42 the boy."
14:4 4 So Jeroboam's wife went to Ahijah's home at Shiloh. He was an old man now and
1 Sam 3:2-3; 4:15 could no longer see. 5 But the LORD had told Ahijah, "Jeroboam's wife will come here, pre-
tending to be someone else. She will ask you about her son, for he is very sick. Give her
the answer I give you."
6 So when Ahijah heard her footsteps at the door, he called out, "Come in, wife of Jerobo-
am! Why are you pretending to be someone else?" Then he told her, "I have bad news for
14:7 you. 7 Give your husband, Jeroboam, this message from the LORD, the God of Israel: 'I pro-
1 Kgs 11:28, 31 moted you from the ranks of the common people and made you ruler over My people Is-
14:8 rael. 8 I ripped the kingdom away from the family of David and gave it to you. But you have
1 Kgs 11:33, 38; 15:5 not been like My servant David, who obeyed My commands and followed Me with all his
14:9 heart and always did whatever I wanted. 9 You have done more evil than all who lived be-
Exod 34:17 2 Chr 11:15 fore you. You have made other gods for yourself and have made Me furious with your
Ps 50:17 gold calves. And since you have turned your back on Me, 10 I will bring disaster on your dy-
Ezek 23:35 nasty and will destroy every one of your male descendants, slave and free alike, any-
14:10 where in Israel. I will burn up your royal dynasty as one burns up trash until it is all gone.
Deut 32:36 1 Kgs 15:29; 21:22 11 The members of Jeroboam's family who die in the city will be eaten by dogs, and those
2 Kgs 9:8-9 who die in the field will be eaten by vultures. I, the LORD, have spoken.'"
14:11 12 Then Ahijah said to Jeroboam's wife, "Go on home, and when you enter the city, the
1 Kgs 16:4-7; 21:24 child will die. 13 All Israel will mourn for him and bury him. He is the only member of your
14:12 1 Kgs 14:17 family who will have a proper burial, for this child is the only good thing that the LORD, the
14:14 God of Israel, sees in the entire family of Jeroboam.
1 Kgs 15:27, 29 14 "In addition, the LORD will raise up a king over Israel who will destroy the family of Jer-
14:15 oboam. This will happen today, even now! 15 Then the LORD will shake Israel like a reed
Deut 12:3-4 whipped about in a stream. He will uproot the people of Israel from this good land that He
Ps 52:5 gave their ancestors and will scatter them beyond the Euphrates River,* for they have an-
14:16 gered the LORD with the Asherah poles they have set up for worship. 16 He will abandon Is-
1 Kgs 12:30 rael because Jeroboam sinned and made Israel sin along with him."
14:17 17 So Jeroboam's wife returned to Tirzah, and the child died just as she walked through
1 Kgs 15:21, 33; 16:6-9 the door of her home. 18 And all Israel buried him and mourned for him, as the LORD had
promised through the prophet Ahijah.

14:15 Hebrew *the river.*

▶ SALVATION

14:3 A suffering child. Standing by helplessly while a child suffers—is there any worse feeling in the world? Jeroboam was obviously apprehensive about approaching Ahijah, but his apprehension was less than the pain of not knowing the future of his sick little boy. Ironically, Jeroboam figured that to get on Ahijah's good side, he should send him sweets (1 Kings 14:3), but Jeroboam refused to repent of his idolatry to gain God's favor. Even for the love of his son, Jeroboam would not repent of his reign of evil. Let your suffering and the pain of those around you drive you to the foot of the Cross, where our suffering Savior comforts His hurting people. (***See Salvation****> Receiving> How> Repent of/turn from sin,* TopicGuide page A22.)

14:7-11 The message Jeroboam's wife received was certainly not the one she anticipated. The prophet condemned Jeroboam for his failure to gratefully submit to God's law despite the magnitude of the grace shown to him. The prophet also condemned the king in the strongest language for his idolatrous system of worship. Consequently, Jeroboam's line would be wiped out and his dynasty abruptly terminated. Jeroboam, his wife, and his other children would even be denied proper burial, a great dishonor in ancient cultures (compare with 1 Samuel 31:8-13).

▶ GOD

14:13 Tender mercy. Sometimes God pulls back the curtain of mystery a bit, revealing His purposes to His puzzled people. This inconspicuous verse gives us rare insight into God's purposes in the wicked family of Jeroboam. It is hard to imagine that the death of a child could be anything but a curse, but God was actually demonstrating His special love for this young boy. By taking the boy's life, God spared him from the waves of judgment soon to fall upon the leadership of Israel. Can you think of situations where death is a way God shows mercy to His people? Thank God for all His tender mercies, and look for them in every circumstance. (***See God****> God's Attributes> Merciful> God is merciful according to His own purposes,* TopicGuide page A17.)

14:17-18 Tirzah was home to Jeroboam's palace; it lay about seven miles northeast of Shechem. The fulfillment of Ahijah's prophecy regarding the child's death served as a sign attesting to the validity of the remainder of the prophecy concerning the northern kingdom. The books of 1 and 2 Kings often stress the reliability of the prophetic word (1 Kings 16:12; 2 Kings 14:25).

[19]The rest of the events in Jeroboam's reign, including all his wars and how he ruled,
are recorded in *The Book of the History of the Kings of Israel.* [20]Jeroboam reigned in Israel
twenty-two years. When Jeroboam died, his son Nadab became the next king.

REHOBOAM RULES IN JUDAH

[21]Meanwhile, Rehoboam son of Solomon was king in Judah. He was forty-one years old
when he became king, and he reigned seventeen years in Jerusalem, the city the LORD had
chosen from among all the tribes of Israel as the place to honor His name. Rehoboam's
mother was Naamah, an Ammonite woman.
[22]During Rehoboam's reign, the people of Judah did what was evil in the LORD's sight,
provoking His anger with their sin, for it was even worse than that of their ancestors. [23]For
they also built for themselves pagan shrines and set up sacred pillars and Asherah poles
on every high hill and under every green tree. [24]There were even male and female shrine
prostitutes throughout the land. The people imitated the detestable practices of the pagan
nations the LORD had driven from the land ahead of the Israelites.
[25]In the fifth year of King Rehoboam's reign, King Shishak of Egypt came up and at-
tacked Jerusalem. [26]He ransacked the treasuries of the LORD's Temple and the royal pal-
ace; he stole everything, including all the gold shields Solomon had made. [27]King
Rehoboam later replaced them with bronze shields as substitutes, and he entrusted them
to the care of the commanders of the guard who protected the entrance to the royal pal-
ace. [28]Whenever the king went to the Temple of the LORD, the guards would also take the
shields and then return them to the guardroom.
[29]The rest of the events in Rehoboam's reign and everything he did are recorded in *The
Book of the History of the Kings of Judah.* [30]There was constant war between Rehoboam and
Jeroboam. [31]When Rehoboam died, he was buried among his ancestors in the City of David.
His mother was Naamah, an Ammonite woman. Then his son Abijam* became the next king.

ABIJAM RULES IN JUDAH

15 Abijam* began to rule over Judah in the eighteenth year of Jeroboam's reign in Is-
rael. [2]He reigned in Jerusalem three years. His mother was Maacah, the daughter
of Absalom.*

14:19 1 Kgs 14:29; 15:7, 23, 31; 16:4-7, 14, 20 1 Chr 9:1
14:21, 25-31 //2 Chr 12:9-16
14:21 1 Kgs 11:32, 36 2 Chr 12:13
14:22 Deut 32:21 2 Chr 12:1, 14
14:23 Deut 12:2; 16:22 2 Kgs 17:10 Jer 2:20 Ezek 16:24
14:24 Deut 23:17-18 2 Kgs 23:7
14:25 2 Chr 12:2, 9
14:26 1 Kgs 10:16-17; 15:18
14:30 1 Kgs 12:21; 15:6
15:1-2 //2 Chr 13:1-2

14:31 Also known as *Abijah.* 15:1 Also known as *Abijah.* 15:2 Hebrew *Abishalom* (also in 15:10), a variant spelling of Absalom; compare 2 Chr 11:20.

14:20 The date of Jeroboam's reign is approximately 930–909 BC.

14:21 Rehoboam's Ammonite mother is mentioned at the beginning and end of the account of his reign, perhaps to emphasize the idolatry into which Judah had sunk at the time of his kingship. Solomon's foreign wives had left their unfortunate mark on the worship of Israel. Rehoboam reigned from 930–913 BC.

14:22-24 During the reign of Rehoboam, Judah plunged into the detestable religious practices of the pagan nations that the Lord had previously driven out of Canaan. Solomon commenced this slide into idolatry by embracing the religious practices of his foreign wives (1 Kings 11:1-8). Sacred pillars were likely memorial stones erected to individual deities (Exodus 23:24; Leviticus 26:1). Asherah poles were wooden structures dedicated to the fertility goddess Asherah, a consort of Baal. Ritual prostitution, which was common in the ancient world, was condemned by Mosaic Law (Deuteronomy 23:17-18).

14:25-28 Judah's disobedience resulted in the successful invasion of Shishak, founder of Egypt's twenty-second dynasty. The terms of Israel's covenant with God threatened military defeat as a curse for disobedience (Deuteronomy 28:25). The replacement of Solomon's gold shields with shields made of bronze served as a poignant symbol of Israel's lost glory. The peace and prosperity that marked Solomon's early reign (1 Kings 5:4) were gone forever as a result of Judah's disobedience. Judah could only put on a show of prosperity for special occasions.

▸ CHURCH
14:31 The family of God. Are you very familiar with your family tree? Some people find great joy in searching out their genealogical records; others couldn't care less. But God often works through families, even more so than individuals, to accomplish His will. In the case of Rehoboam, the writer of 1 Kings was making sure that the audience knew the ancestry of Rehoboam was checkered. This made his reign and the reign of his son, Abijam, even more suspect. What can you do to make your family a fortress of faith? If your family has a suspect past, start anew and ask God to make your family a blessing to the nations. (***See Church*> *Who*> *From Every People*> *Children are blessed by inclusion in covenant community,* TopicGuide page A48.)

15:2 "Daughter" can more broadly designate a granddaughter, as it perhaps does here (see 2 Samuel 3:3; 14:27; 2 Chronicles 13:2). Abijam, who was also known as Abijah (2 Chronicles 13:1), reigned from 913–910 BC.

15:3 3He committed the same sins as his father before him, and he was not faithful to the
1 Kgs 11:4 LORD his God, as his ancestor David had been. 4But for David's sake, the LORD his God al-
15:4 lowed his descendants to continue ruling, shining like a lamp, and He gave Abijam a son
2 Chr 21:7 15:5 to rule after him in Jerusalem. 5For David had done what was pleasing in the LORD's sight
2 Sam 11:2-27 and had obeyed the LORD's commands throughout his life, except in the affair concerning
1 Kgs 9:4; 14:8 Uriah the Hittite.
15:6-8 6There was war between Abijam and Jeroboam* throughout Abijam's reign. 7The rest of
2 Chr 13:22–14:1 the events in Abijam's reign and everything he did are recorded in *The Book of the History*
of the Kings of Judah. There was constant war between Abijam and Jeroboam. 8When Abi-
jam died, he was buried in the City of David. Then his son Asa became the next king.

ASA RULES IN JUDAH

15:9-22 9Asa began to rule over Judah in the twentieth year of Jeroboam's reign in Israel. 10He
//2 Chr 14:2-3; 15:6–16:6 reigned in Jerusalem forty-one years. His grandmother* was Maacah, the daughter of Ab-
15:11 salom.
2 Chr 14:2; 15:17 11Asa did what was pleasing in the LORD's sight, as his ancestor David had done. 12He
15:12 banished the male and female shrine prostitutes from the land and got rid of all the idols*
Deut 23:17-18 his ancestors had made. 13He even deposed his grandmother Maacah from her position
1 Kgs 22:46 2 Chr 15:2-5 as queen mother because she had made an obscene Asherah pole. He cut down her ob-
scene pole and burned it in the Kidron Valley. 14Although the pagan shrines were not re-
15:13 1 Kgs 14:24 moved, Asa's heart remained completely faithful to the LORD throughout his life. 15He
2 Chr 15:16-18 brought into the Temple of the LORD the silver and gold and the various items that he and
15:14 his father had dedicated.
1 Kgs 8:61; 22:43 2 Kgs 12:3 16There was constant war between King Asa of Judah and King Baasha of Israel. 17King
15:17 Baasha of Israel invaded Judah and fortified Ramah in order to prevent anyone from en-
Josh 18:25 tering or leaving King Asa's territory in Judah.
2 Chr 16:1-6 18Asa responded by removing all the silver and gold that was left in the treasuries of the
15:18 Temple of the LORD and the royal palace. He sent it with some of his officials to Ben-hadad
1 Kgs 14:26 2 Kgs 12:17-18

15:6 As in a few Hebrew and Greek manuscripts; most Hebrew manuscripts read *between Rehoboam and Jeroboam.*
15:10 Or *The queen mother;* Hebrew reads *His mother* (also in 15:13); compare 15:2. 15:12 The Hebrew term (literally *round things*) probably alludes to dung.

▸ BIBLE
15:5 A life story. How would you briefly summarize your walk with the Lord? While we know of several of David's sins, this partial but legitimate summary of David's obedience only mentions his sins against Uriah (adultery and murder). But partially because David repented so effectively, his other misdeeds go unmentioned. Is your repentance so deep, so thorough, so quick, that the original sin is barely worth mentioning? Make it your goal to repent sincerely, escaping the snare of sin almost as soon as you fall into its trap. (***See Bible****> Unity> Kingdom of God> Repentance and faith embodies the kingdom,* TopicGuide page A11.)

15:11-15 Asa, who reigned from approximately 910–869 BC, was the first of several reforming Judean kings who sought to restore the worship of Judah to biblical standards (others included Jehoshaphat, Hezekiah, and Josiah). Asa's reforms aimed to undo the corruption that spread throughout the reign of Rehoboam (see note at 1 Kings 14:22-24.) He also tried to restore Judah's outward glory by replenishing the Temple, which had been plundered by Shishak (1 Kings 14:25-26).

▸ WORSHIP
15:13 Onto the trash heap. God ordered the destruction of the Canaanite religions not only because they were rivals to His own, but also because they were horrible. For instance, the worship of Molech involved offering live children as sacrifices (Leviticus 20:2-5). The Asherah pole was the center of highly sexualized worship, so for good reason Asa threw his grandmother's Asherah pole onto the trash heap. Make it your goal to cleanse the places under your authority of anything that smacks of idolatry and the occult. (***See Worship****> OT> Reverence> Put away idols,* TopicGuide page A28.)

15:17 Ramah lay a mere six miles north of Jerusalem, so its capture posed a grave threat to the security of the southern capital. Baasha was attempting to effectively seal off Judah from trade and supply.

15:18-21 Asa emptied the treasury of the Temple that he had earlier replenished (1 Kings 15:15) in order to bribe Ben-hadad, king of Aram, to abandon his treaty with Israel in favor of an alliance with Judah. These diplomatic maneuvers succeeded—Aram invaded Israel, causing Baasha to withdraw from Ramah. This Ben-hadad is not to be confused with the Ben-hadad who distressed Israel during the Omride dynasty (1 Kings 20—2 Kings 8). The biblical record gives no further description of the earlier treaty that existed between Tabrimmon and Abijam (1 Kings 15:19).

son of Tabrimmon, son of Hezion, the king of Aram, who was ruling in Damascus, along
with this message:

> 19"Let there be a treaty* between you and me like the one between your father and 15:19
> my father. See, I am sending you a gift of silver and gold. Break your treaty with King 2 Chr 16:7
> Baasha of Israel so that he will leave me alone."

20Ben-hadad agreed to King Asa's request and sent the commanders of his army to at-
tack the towns of Israel. They conquered the towns of Ijon, Dan, Abel-beth-maacah, and all
Kinnereth, and all the land of Naphtali. 21As soon as Baasha of Israel heard what was hap-
pening, he abandoned his project of fortifying Ramah and withdrew to Tirzah. 22Then 15:22
King Asa sent an order throughout Judah, requiring that everyone, without exception, Josh 18:24 2 Chr 16:6
help to carry away the building stones and timbers that Baasha had been using to fortify
Ramah. Asa used these materials to fortify the town of Geba in Benjamin and the town of
Mizpah.
23The rest of the events in Asa's reign—the extent of his power, everything he did, and 15:23-24 //2 Chr 16:11–17:1
the names of the cities he built—are recorded in *The Book of the History of the Kings of Ju-*
dah. In his old age his feet became diseased. 24When Asa died, he was buried with his an-
cestors in the City of David.

Then Jehoshaphat, Asa's son, became the next king.

NADAB RULES IN ISRAEL

25Nadab son of Jeroboam began to rule over Israel in the second year of King Asa's reign 15:25
in Judah. He reigned in Israel two years. 26But he did what was evil in the LORD's sight and 1 Kgs 14:20
followed the example of his father, continuing the sins that Jeroboam had led Israel to 15:26
commit. 1 Kgs 12:28-33; 13:33; 14:16
27Then Baasha son of Ahijah, from the tribe of Issachar, plotted against Nadab and as- 15:27
sassinated him while he and the Israelite army were laying siege to the Philistine town of Josh 19:44; 21:23-24
Gibbethon. 28Baasha killed Nadab in the third year of King Asa's reign in Judah, and he be-
came the next king of Israel.
29He immediately slaughtered all the descendants of King Jeroboam, so that not one of 15:29
the royal family was left, just as the LORD had promised concerning Jeroboam by the 1 Kgs 14:9-16
prophet Ahijah from Shiloh. 30This was done because Jeroboam had provoked the anger
of the LORD, the God of Israel, by the sins he had committed and the sins he had led Israel
to commit.
31The rest of the events in Nadab's reign and everything he did are recorded in *The* 15:31
Book of the History of the Kings of Israel. 1 Kgs 14:19

BAASHA RULES IN ISRAEL

32There was constant war between King Asa of Judah and King Baasha of Israel. 33Baasha 15:32
son of Ahijah began to rule over all Israel in the third year of King Asa's reign in Judah. 2 Chr 15:16
Baasha reigned in Tirzah twenty-four years. 34But he did what was evil in the LORD's sight

15:19 As in Greek version; Hebrew reads *There is a treaty.*

15:23 Gangrene, gout, and dropsy have all been proposed as the foot disease that afflicted Asa. It is unlikely the author knew the precise nature of the disease.

15:25–16:20 Beginning with Nadab, whose reign lasted from 909–908 BC, the books of 1 and 2 Kings trace a succession of northern kings that reigned briefly and ineffectively until the establishment of the Omride dynasty. This portion of Israel's history was marked by political violence and instability, along with continued religious apostasy.

15:28-30 Baasha assassinated Nadab and all of the descendants of Jeroboam. At that time, it was not uncommon for usurpers to kill all potential claimants to the throne. Baasha was unaware that he was acting as the agent of divine judgment, for his actions fulfilled Ahijah's prophecy (1 Kings 14:10). Still, he was held morally responsible for his actions (1 Kings 16:7; also see note at 12:15).

15:33 Tirzah served as Israel's capital until Omri built Samaria (1 Kings 16:24). Baasha reigned from 908–886 BC.

and followed the example of Jeroboam, continuing the sins that Jeroboam had led Israel
to commit.

16 This message from the LORD was delivered to King Baasha by the prophet Jehu son
of Hanani: 2"I lifted you out of the dust to make you ruler of My people Israel, but
you have followed the evil example of Jeroboam. You have provoked My anger by causing
My people Israel to sin. 3So now I will destroy you and your family, just as I destroyed the
descendants of Jeroboam son of Nebat. 4The members of Baasha's family who die in the
city will be eaten by dogs, and those who die in the field will be eaten by vultures."
5The rest of the events in Baasha's reign and the extent of his power are recorded in *The
Book of the History of the Kings of Israel.* 6When Baasha died, he was buried in Tirzah. Then
his son Elah became the next king.
7The message from the LORD against Baasha and his family came through the prophet
Jehu son of Hanani. It was delivered because Baasha had done what was evil in the LORD's
sight (just as the family of Jeroboam had done), and also because Baasha had destroyed
the family of Jeroboam. The LORD's anger was provoked by Baasha's sins.

ELAH RULES IN ISRAEL

8Elah son of Baasha began to rule over Israel in the twenty-sixth year of King Asa's reign in
Judah. He reigned in the city of Tirzah for two years.
9Then Zimri, who commanded half of the royal chariots, made plans to kill him. One day
in Tirzah, Elah was getting drunk at the home of Arza, the supervisor of the palace. 10Zimri
walked in and struck him down and killed him. This happened in the twenty-seventh year
of King Asa's reign in Judah. Then Zimri became the next king.
11Zimri immediately killed the entire royal family of Baasha, leaving him not even a sin-
gle male child. He even destroyed distant relatives and friends. 12So Zimri destroyed the
dynasty of Baasha as the LORD had promised through the prophet Jehu. 13This happened
because of all the sins Baasha and his son Elah had committed, and because of the sins
they led Israel to commit. They provoked the anger of the LORD, the God of Israel, with
their worthless idols.
14The rest of the events in Elah's reign and everything he did are recorded in *The Book
of the History of the Kings of Israel.*

ZIMRI RULES IN ISRAEL

15Zimri began to rule over Israel in the twenty-seventh year of King Asa's reign in Judah,
but his reign in Tirzah lasted only seven days. The army of Israel was then attacking the

16:1 1 Kgs 16:7; 2 Chr 19:2; 20:34
16:2 1 Sam 2:8; 1 Kgs 14:7-9
16:3 1 Kgs 14:10; 15:29; 21:21
16:4 1 Kgs 14:11
16:7 1 Kgs 16:1
16:9 2 Kgs 9:30-33
16:11 1 Kgs 15:29
16:13 Deut 32:21; 1 Kgs 15:30
16:14 1 Kgs 16:4-7, 20, 28, 30

16:2-4 Jehu's condemnation of Baasha echoes Ahijah's condemnation of Jeroboam (1 Kings 14:7-8). In both cases, the prophet opened by recalling the grace God had displayed in raising the king from obscurity to power. Yet both Jeroboam and Baasha responded with religious corruption that brought about the termination of their descendants and the desecration of their bodies.

▸ BIBLE
16:5 Ancient footnotes. Christians believe that God can speak to people through books other than the Bible. Other books, from Christians and non-Christians alike, contain information and ideas that are useful to us. One example is found in this ancient reference book used by the writers of 1 Kings. The books of 1 and 2 Samuel, 1 and 2 Kings, and 1 and 2 Chronicles show signs of being compiled from oral and written sources under the guidance of the Holy Spirit. Surely, if God saw fit to include ancient footnotes to secular sources in His Word, we are free to utilize other books for His glory and our good. (***See Bible*** *> Uniqueness> Authoritative> Demonstrates credibility,* TopicGuide page A10.)

16:8-13 Elah, Baasha's son. reigned from 886–885 BC. He was overthrown by Zimri. As was the case with the descendants of Jeroboam, the descendants of Baasha were slaughtered following Elah's assassination. (See note at 1 Kings 15:28-30.) As usual, the inspired historian does not hesitate to interpret the tragic events surrounding Israel's early monarchy. Here and elsewhere, the disobedience and idolatry of the kings caused the harm that befell their families.

16:15-16 Zimri seized the throne in the year 885 BC. But when the men of Israel's army, still embroiled in an extended siege of Gibbethon (1 Kings 15:27), heard of Zimri's coup, they responded with a revolt of their own. The biblical authors did not provide all of the details that must have surrounded the political intrigues of the era, but we can speculate that the army's action reflected existing tensions between the infantry and the charioteers, half of which Zimri commanded (1 Kings 16:9).

Philistine town of Gibbethon. 16When they heard that Zimri had committed treason and had assassinated the king, that very day they chose Omri, commander of the army, as the new king of Israel. 17So Omri led the entire army of Israel up from Gibbethon to attack Tirzah, Israel's capital. 18When Zimri saw that the city had been taken, he went into the citadel of the palace and burned it down over himself and died in the flames. 19For he, too, had done what was evil in the LORD's sight. He followed the example of Jeroboam in all the sins he had committed and led Israel to commit.

20The rest of the events in Zimri's reign and his conspiracy are recorded in *The Book of the History of the Kings of Israel.*

OMRI RULES IN ISRAEL

21But now the people of Israel were split into two factions. Half the people tried to make Tibni son of Ginath their king, while the other half supported Omri. 22But Omri's supporters defeated the supporters of Tibni. So Tibni was killed, and Omri became the next king.

23Omri began to rule over Israel in the thirty-first year of King Asa's reign in Judah. He reigned twelve years in all, six of them in Tirzah. 24Then Omri bought the hill now known as Samaria from its owner, Shemer, for 150 pounds of silver.* He built a city on it and called the city Samaria in honor of Shemer.

25But Omri did what was evil in the LORD's sight, even more than any of the kings before him. 26He followed the example of Jeroboam son of Nebat in all the sins he had committed and led Israel to commit. The people provoked the anger of the LORD, the God of Israel, with their worthless idols.

27The rest of the events in Omri's reign, the extent of his power, and everything he did are recorded in *The Book of the History of the Kings of Israel.* 28When Omri died, he was buried in Samaria. Then his son Ahab became the next king.

AHAB RULES IN ISRAEL

29Ahab son of Omri began to rule over Israel in the thirty-eighth year of King Asa's reign in Judah. He reigned in Samaria twenty-two years. 30But Ahab son of Omri did what was evil in the LORD's sight, even more than any of the kings before him. 31And as though it were not enough to follow the example of Jeroboam, he married Jezebel, the daughter of King Ethbaal of the Sidonians, and he began to bow down in worship of Baal. 32First Ahab built a temple and an altar for Baal in Samaria. 33Then he set up an Asherah pole. He did more to provoke the anger of the LORD, the God of Israel, than any of the other kings of Israel before him.

34It was during his reign that Hiel, a man from Bethel, rebuilt Jericho. When he laid its foundations, it cost him the life of his oldest son, Abiram. And when he completed it and set

16:18 1 Sam 31:4-5; 2 Sam 17:23
16:19 1 Kgs 12:28
16:20 1 Kgs 16:14, 27
16:24 1 Kgs 13:32
16:25 1 Kgs 14:9; Mic 6:16
16:26 1 Kgs 15:30
16:28 2 Chr 18:1
16:30 1 Kgs 14:9
16:31 Deut 7:3-4; 1 Kgs 11:5; 2 Kgs 10:18; 17:16
16:32 2 Kgs 10:21, 26-27
16:33 1 Kgs 21:19, 25; 2 Kgs 13:6
16:34 Josh 6:26

16:24 Hebrew *for 2 talents* [68 kilograms] *of silver.*

16:21-23 Following Zimri's death, two contestants emerged for the throne of Israel: Omri, who the army supported, and Tibni, of whom very little is known. Omri triumphed in the ensuing civil war, and Tibni was killed. The four-year struggle with Tibni is counted as part of Omri's reign (compare verses 15, 21, 29), which lasted from approximately 885–874 BC.

16:24 Samaria was located about ten miles west of the former capital, Tirzah. The name Samaria was sometimes used to refer to the whole of the northern kingdom (2 Kings 17:24).

16:29-31 Ahab reigned from approximately 874–853 BC. He followed in the wickedness of his father, Omri, but one of his worst mistakes was marrying Jezebel, the daughter of the king of the Sidonians. Through Jezebel's influence, the worship of Baal began to spread throughout Israel. Baal, whose name means "lord," was the most significant deity in Canaanite religion. He was a storm god, often pictured riding on the clouds and credited with bringing rain, fertility, and (by extension) life.

▸ CHURCH

16:30 A legacy of unbelief. Families can build a legacy of faithfulness or a legacy of sin. Every king in Israel was evil in God's sight. Is your family a household of faith, a bastion of unbelief, or somewhere in between? What would it look like if you took every opportunity to re-establish your family as a household of hope? Decide today to influence your family in the ways of righteousness. (***See Church**> Role> Church Community> Encouraging one another,* TopicGuide page A49.)

16:34 After destroying Jericho at the onset of the conquest of Canaan, Joshua pronounced a curse on anyone who rebuilt the city (Joshua 6:26). Treating Joshua's curse as a prophecy, the writer notes its precise fulfillment. The mention of Joshua's curse prepares the reader for the coming narrative by emphasizing the connection between disobedience and punishment and by invoking the memory of Moses and Joshua, who are paralleled by Elijah and Elisha.

up its gates, it cost him the life of his youngest son, Segub.* This all happened according to the message from the LORD concerning Jericho spoken by Joshua son of Nun.

ELIJAH FED BY RAVENS

17:1 Judg 12:4 1 Kgs 22:14 Luke 4:25 Jas 5:17

17 Now Elijah, who was from Tishbe in Gilead, told King Ahab, "As surely as the LORD, the God of Israel, lives—the God I serve—there will be no dew or rain during the next few years until I give the word!"
[2]Then the LORD said to Elijah, [3]"Go to the east and hide by Kerith Brook, near where it enters the Jordan River. [4]Drink from the brook and eat what the ravens bring you, for I have commanded them to bring you food."

16:34 An ancient Hebrew scribal tradition reads *He killed his oldest son when he laid its foundations, and he killed his youngest son when he set up its gates.*

KINGS TO DATE AND THEIR ENEMIES

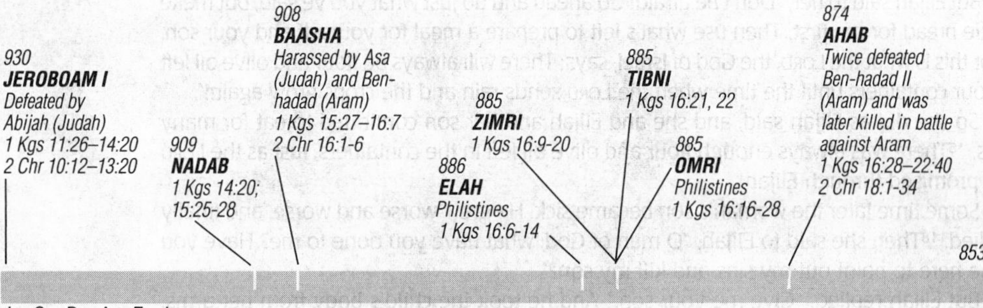

All dates are BC.
For all the kings of Israel and Judah, see the chart at the end of 1 Kings.

17:1-24 With minimal introduction, Elijah appears on the scene to lead Israel when her king does not. Elijah was one of the mightiest prophets of the Old Testament, but he was one of the last prophets of God left in the kingdom of Israel at this time. He often worked and lived in isolation and was sent by God to confront the corrupt king and the evil Baal cult. The three stories presented in this chapter—Elijah receiving food from ravens (1 Kings 17:1-7), Elijah feeding the widow at Zarephath (17:8-16), and Elijah raising the widow's son from death (17:17-24)—are tied together by the themes of famine and provision, faith and prophetic authority, and life and death. Elijah's deeds here legitimize his prophetic power.

17:1 Elijah lived in Tishbe, a town east of the Jordan River in the region of Gilead. Its exact location is unknown, and it is only mentioned in association with Elijah. His message to King Ahab recalled the covenant curses in Leviticus 26:14-39 and Deuteronomy 28:15-68, which Moses warned would befall God's people if they continued to disobey the Lord.

▸ SPIRITUAL WARFARE

17:1 No dew or rain. Is the sun shining today? Or is it raining? Did the forecaster get it right? The followers of Baal claimed that their god was the master of the weather, but God, through Elijah, demonstrated that He controlled the life-giving rain in Israel. It's no wonder weather forecasters sometimes fail to predict the future weather—such phenomena are only fully understood by the Creator of the universe. Thank God that neither the slightest sprinkle nor the smallest snowflake escapes His sovereign eye. (***See Spiritual Warfare****> God and Sin> Natural Disaster's Origin> God brings calamity,* TopicGuide page A45.)

17:4-6 Even during times of difficulty, God provides for His servants. This story recalls similar provisions received by the Israelites during their wilderness wanderings (Exodus 16:8, 12). Just as God regularly provides food to the ravens (Psalm 147:9; Job 38:41; Luke 12:24), so He used the ravens to provide food for Elijah, His servant. God was strengthening Elijah both physically and spiritually for the coming confrontation (1 Kings 18).

5 So Elijah did as the LORD told him and camped beside Kerith Brook, east of the Jordan.
6 The ravens brought him bread and meat each morning and evening, and he drank from the
brook. 7 But after a while the brook dried up, for there was no rainfall anywhere in the land.

THE WIDOW AT ZAREPHATH

8 Then the LORD said to Elijah, 9 "Go and live in the village of Zarephath, near the city of Si- 17:9
don. I have instructed a widow there to feed you." Obad 1:20 Luke 4:26
10 So he went to Zarephath. As he arrived at the gates of the village, he saw a widow 17:10
gathering sticks, and he asked her, "Would you please bring me a little water in a cup?" Gen 24:17
11 As she was going to get it, he called to her, "Bring me a bite of bread, too." John 4:7
12 But she said, "I swear by the LORD your God that I don't have a single piece of bread in 17:12
the house. And I have only a handful of flour left in the jar and a little cooking oil in the 2 Kgs 4:2-7
bottom of the jug. I was just gathering a few sticks to cook this last meal, and then my son
and I will die."
13 But Elijah said to her, "Don't be afraid! Go ahead and do just what you've said, but make
a little bread for me first. Then use what's left to prepare a meal for yourself and your son.
14 For this is what the LORD, the God of Israel, says: There will always be flour and olive oil left
in your containers until the time when the LORD sends rain and the crops grow again!"
15 So she did as Elijah said, and she and Elijah and her son continued to eat for many
days. 16 There was always enough flour and olive oil left in the containers, just as the LORD
had promised through Elijah.
17 Some time later the woman's son became sick. He grew worse and worse, and finally
he died. 18 Then she said to Elijah, "O man of God, what have you done to me? Have you
come here to point out my sins and kill my son?"
19 But Elijah replied, "Give me your son." And he took the child's body from her arms,
carried him up the stairs to the room where he was staying, and laid the body on his bed.
20 Then Elijah cried out to the LORD, "O LORD my God, why have You brought tragedy to this
widow who has opened her home to me, causing her son to die?"
21 And he stretched himself out over the child three times and cried out to the LORD, 17:21 2 Kgs 4:34
"O LORD my God, please let this child's life return to him." 22 The LORD heard Elijah's prayer, Acts 20:10-12
and the life of the child returned, and he revived! 23 Then Elijah brought him down from 17:23
the upper room and gave him to his mother. "Look!" he said. "Your son is alive!" Heb 11:35

17:9-10 Zarephath was northwest of Israel on the Phoenician coast, between Tyre and Sidon. Controlled by Sidon, it provided a safe haven for Elijah. This widow must have at one time been a woman of means, as she had an upper room (1 Kings 17:19). However, as a result of the famine and the death of her husband, she was extremely poor. Unless a widow had a relative who could provide for her, she had to live on what the Lord provided. Elijah arrived just in time—an encounter ordained by God. It was an honor that the prophet of God came to visit her, as Jesus pointed out in Luke 4:26 and Matthew 10:41-42.

▸ PURPOSE
17:15 Heeding God's prophet. What is faith? It is belief in God, sometimes in spite of circumstances that call His Word into question. In this case, the starving widow exercised her faith in a very practical way by taking the very last thing she had to feed her family . . . and giving it to a stranger who claimed to speak for God. God repeatedly confirmed His blessing on Elijah and that faithful woman by multiplying oil and flour for more than three years. Be adventurous in your faith, and do not miss an opportunity to take God at His Word. (***See Purpose***> *God's Deeds> Special Acts> Miracles> OT> Increase of oil,* TopicGuide page A53.)

17:18 The widow's exemplary faith in God and Elijah had diminished, and she thought the death of her son was retribution for her sins. Losing her beloved son was devastating for the widow—and her reaction is common among those who do not know God's ways when they are faced with personal tragedy.

▸ SPIRITUAL WARFARE
17:18 "What have you done to me?" One of the hazards of being a Christian is that some unbelievers vent their anger at God on us. Such was the case with Elijah. Elijah's reply to the widow: "Give me your son." He didn't defend himself or God, but immediately believed that God could raise this young man from the dead. After God revived the boy, the widow's doubting grief was replaced with a faith and respect for Elijah. Turn your persecution over to God and see if He arranges circumstances to bring glory to Himself and respect to you. (***See Spiritual Warfare***> *Resisting Sin and Evil> Consequences> Of Obedience> Persecution,* TopicGuide page A46.)

17:21 Elijah's strange action of stretching out over the boy was not an ancient form of mouth-to-mouth resuscitation. This action—which also occurred in 2 Kings 4:34-35—was simply an expression indicating that the power of God was passing from the healer to the healed (see also Matthew 8:3, 15; 9:20-22, 29). Because the boy was dead, Elijah needed the power of life to be transferred to every part of the boy's body. By placing Elijah's threefold intercession at the center of the narrative, the author strongly suggests that the miracle was a result of prayer.

17:24 John 2:11; 3:1-2; 16:30 [24]Then the woman told Elijah, "Now I know for sure that you are a man of God, and that
the LORD truly speaks through you."

THE CONTEST ON MOUNT CARMEL

18:1 Jas 5:17-18 **18** Later on, in the third year of the drought, the LORD said to Elijah, "Go and present
yourself to King Ahab. Tell him that I will soon send rain!" [2]So Elijah went to ap-
18:2 1 Kgs 16:24 pear before Ahab.
Meanwhile, the famine had become very severe in Samaria. [3]So Ahab summoned Oba-
18:3 1 Kgs 18:16 diah, who was in charge of the palace. (Obadiah was a devoted follower of the LORD. [4]Once
when Jezebel had tried to kill all the LORD's prophets, Obadiah had hidden 100 of them in
two caves. He put fifty prophets in each cave and supplied them with food and water.)
[5]Ahab said to Obadiah, "We must check every spring and valley in the land to see if we can
find enough grass to save at least some of my horses and mules." [6]So they divided the land
between them. Ahab went one way by himself, and Obadiah went another way by himself.
[7]As Obadiah was walking along, he suddenly saw Elijah coming toward him. Obadiah
recognized him at once and bowed low to the ground before him. "Is it really you, my lord
Elijah?" he asked.
[8]"Yes, it is," Elijah replied. "Now go and tell your master, 'Elijah is here.'"
[9]"Oh, sir," Obadiah protested, "what harm have I done to you that you are sending me to
my death at the hands of Ahab? [10]For I swear by the LORD your God that the king has
searched every nation and kingdom on earth from end to end to find you. And each time he
was told, 'Elijah isn't here,' King Ahab forced the king of that nation to swear to the truth of
18:12 2 Kgs 2:16 Ezek 3:12, 14 Acts 8:39 his claim. [11]And now you say, 'Go and tell your master, "Elijah is here."' [12]But as soon as I
leave you, the Spirit of the LORD will carry you away to who knows where. When Ahab comes
and cannot find you, he will kill me. Yet I have been a true servant of the LORD all my life.
18:13 1 Kgs 18:3-4 [13]Has no one told you, my lord, about the time when Jezebel was trying to kill the LORD's
prophets? I hid 100 of them in two caves and supplied them with food and water. [14]And now
you say, 'Go and tell your master, "Elijah is here."' Sir, if I do that, Ahab will certainly kill me."
[15]But Elijah said, "I swear by the LORD Almighty, in whose presence I stand, that I will
present myself to Ahab this very day."
[16]So Obadiah went to tell Ahab that Elijah had come, and Ahab went out to meet Elijah.
18:17 Josh 7:25 [17]When Ahab saw him, he exclaimed, "So, is it really you, you troublemaker of Israel?"
[18]"I have made no trouble for Israel," Elijah replied. "You and your family are the trouble-
18:18 1 Kgs 9:9; 21:25 makers, for you have refused to obey the commands of the LORD and have worshiped the
images of Baal instead. [19]Now summon all Israel to join me at Mount Carmel, along with
18:19 Josh 19:26 the 450 prophets of Baal and the 400 prophets of Asherah who are supported by Jezebel.*"

18:19 Hebrew *who eat at Jezebel's table.*

17:24 The widow who had doubted in 17:18 now had her faith restored by God's answer of prayer through Elijah. As the widow recognized Elijah as a "man of God," Elijah's credentials also become established in the eyes of the reader. Now he was ready for his confrontation with the prophets of Baal.

18:1-46 This chapter is one of the most dramatic in the entire Bible. God's defeat of Baal (who was really no god at all) on Mount Carmel engendered faith in the people who witnessed God's display of power. Likewise, the narrative would have strengthened the faith of those who first read the book (God's people exiled throughout the Babylonian empire), encouraging them to trust in the Lord rather than the impotent Babylonian god Marduk. God's people today should also respond in faith, forsaking such narcissistic, false gods of this age as wealth, power, sex, and comfort.

18:19 Mount Carmel is a part of a ridge northwest of Samaria, starting at the Mediterranean Sea and extending southeastward along the edge of the Jezreel Valley. The modern Israeli city of Haifa rises in tiers on the mountain's northwestern corner. Carmel means "vineyard" in Hebrew, which hints of the mountain's dense foliage and beauty (Isaiah 35:2; Song of Solomon 7:5). This mountain was a sacred worship site to Baal and served as a boundary marker between the Phoenicians and the people of Israel, so it was a perfect place for a showdown between God and Baal. It is possible that this episode took place at the foot of the mountain. Places of worship were usually not at the summit, because it would have been inaccessible to the common people. Elijah later ascended to the summit to pray for rain (1 Kings 18:42).

18:19 In Canaanite mythology, Asherah was one of the three consorts of Baal. These prophets (both male and female) included cult prostitutes whose job was to imitate the annual copulation of the gods, which was thought to bring rain and fertility. Jezebel's support, which involved financial backing and protection, was an overt religious endorsement.

20 So Ahab summoned all the people of Israel and the prophets to Mount Carmel.
21 Then Elijah stood in front of them and said, "How much longer will you waver, hobbling 18:21
between two opinions? If the LORD is God, follow Him! But if Baal is God, then follow him!" Josh 24:15 2 Kgs 17:41
But the people were completely silent.
22 Then Elijah said to them, "I am the only prophet of the LORD who is left, but Baal 18:22
has 450 prophets. 23 Now bring two bulls. The prophets of Baal may choose whichever 1 Kgs 19:10, 14
one they wish and cut it into pieces and lay it on the wood of their altar, but without set-
ting fire to it. I will prepare the other bull and lay it on the wood on the altar, but not set
fire to it. 24 Then call on the name of your god, and I will call on the name of the LORD. 18:24
The god who answers by setting fire to the wood is the true God!" And all the people 1 Sam 7:8 1 Kgs 18:38
agreed.
25 Then Elijah said to the prophets of Baal, "You go first, for there are many of you.
Choose one of the bulls, and prepare it and call on the name of your god. But do not set
fire to the wood."
26 So they prepared one of the bulls and placed it on the altar. Then they called on the 18:26 Ps 115:4-5
name of Baal from morning until noontime, shouting, "O Baal, answer us!" But there was Jer 10:5
no reply of any kind. Then they danced, hobbling around the altar they had made.
27 About noontime Elijah began mocking them. "You'll have to shout louder," he
scoffed, "for surely he is a god! Perhaps he is daydreaming, or is relieving himself.* Or
maybe he is away on a trip, or is asleep and needs to be wakened!"
28 So they shouted louder, and following their normal custom, they cut themselves with 18:28 Lev 19:28
knives and swords until the blood gushed out. 29 They raved all afternoon until the time Deut 14:1
of the evening sacrifice, but still there was no sound, no reply, no response. 18:30
30 Then Elijah called to the people, "Come over here!" They all crowded around him as 1 Kgs 19:10, 14
he repaired the altar of the LORD that had been torn down. 31 He took twelve stones, one 18:31 2 Kgs 17:34

18:27 Or *is busy somewhere else*, or *is engaged in business.*

THE SHOWDOWN AT CARMEL
In a showdown with the false prophets of Baal at Mount Carmel, Elijah set out to prove to evil Ahab that only the Lord is God. Elijah then killed the false prophets by the Kishon Valley and fled back to Jezreel.

18:23-24 Sacrifices were a common way to approach one's god in the ancient world. They could be offered to gain the favor of a god or to propitiate his wrath. A petition—symbolized by the aroma or smoke that rose to the deity's residence in the heavens—usually accompanied the sacrifice. Both parties in this contest wanted their god (or God) to show approval of their sacrifice in some way. Elijah was counting on God to respond with fire from heaven, which would also demonstrate His lordship over Baal, the so-called "god of the storm cloud."

▸ ADOPTION
18:24 The true God! This seemed like a no-lose situation for the followers of Baal. Even if their god didn't respond with flames (and they had no reason to believe he would), they still outnumbered that pest Elijah; the 450 prophets of Baal would kill him when he failed to call fire down from heaven. But God spoke clearly to Elijah (1 Kings 18:1) in order to establish the truth of God's Word against the lies of Baal and his prophets. This grand mountaintop stage was the perfect place to demonstrate God's power over those who sought to destroy God's voice in Israel. And though it was 450 against one, God secured Elijah's victory by His marvelous power. (***See Adoption****> With Christ> Supernatural> Victory over Satan,* TopicGuide page A37.)

▸ WORSHIP
18:27 Where is Baal? Did Elijah sin by using sarcasm against the prophets of Baal? Perhaps according to your mother he did, but the Bible tells a different story. Careful reason falls short in some situations (Proverbs 26:4). Other tools, such as sarcasm, can penetrate deeply where logic fails. But wait—isn't ridicule cruel? Good satire isn't cruel because the target needs it. God seems to honor careful ridicule of foolish behavior and ideas, especially in the ministries of Elijah, Jesus (Matthew 7:5), and Paul (Galatians 5:12). While your upbringing may forbid you from using this verbal skill, God's Word reveals that it is possible to be sarcastic and witty in good conscience. When in doubt, however, it is better to err on the side of mercy and kindness. (***See Worship****> NT> Fellowship> Nature> Tell the unvarnished truth to each other,* TopicGuide page A30.)

18:32 to represent each of the tribes of Israel,* 32 and he used the stones to rebuild the altar in
Col 3:17 the name of the LORD. Then he dug a trench around the altar large enough to hold about
18:33 three gallons.* 33 He piled wood on the altar, cut the bull into pieces, and laid the pieces
Gen 22:9 on the wood.

Then he said, "Fill four large jars with water, and pour the water over the offering and
the wood."

34 After they had done this, he said, "Do the same thing again!" And when they were fin-
ished, he said, "Now do it a third time!" So they did as he said, 35 and the water ran around
the altar and even filled the trench.

18:36 36 At the usual time for offering the evening sacrifice, Elijah the prophet walked up to the
Exod 3:6; 4:5 altar and prayed, "O LORD, God of Abraham, Isaac, and Jacob,* prove today that You are
Num 16:28-32 God in Israel and that I am Your servant. Prove that I have done all this at Your command.
37 O LORD, answer me! Answer me so these people will know that You, O LORD, are God and
that You have brought them back to Yourself."

18:38 Gen 15:17 38 Immediately the fire of the LORD flashed down from heaven and burned up the young
Lev 9:24; 10:1 bull, the wood, the stones, and the dust. It even licked up all the water in the trench! 39 And
2 Kgs 1:12 Job 1:16 when all the people saw it, they fell face down on the ground and cried out, "The LORD—He
is God! Yes, the LORD is God!"

18:40 40 Then Elijah commanded, "Seize all the prophets of Baal. Don't let a single one es-
Deut 13:5; 18:20 cape!" So the people seized them all, and Elijah took them down to the Kishon Valley and
2 Kgs 10:24 killed them there.

ELIJAH PRAYS FOR RAIN

41 Then Elijah said to Ahab, "Go get something to eat and drink, for I hear a mighty rain-
storm coming!"

18:42 42 So Ahab went to eat and drink. But Elijah climbed to the top of Mount Carmel and
Jas 5:18 bowed low to the ground and prayed with his face between his knees.
43 Then he said to his servant, "Go and look out toward the sea."

The servant went and looked, then returned to Elijah and said, "I didn't see anything."

Seven times Elijah told him to go and look. 44 Finally the seventh time, his servant told
him, "I saw a little cloud about the size of a man's hand rising from the sea."

Then Elijah shouted, "Hurry to Ahab and tell him, 'Climb into your chariot and go back
home. If you don't hurry, the rain will stop you!'"

45 And soon the sky was black with clouds. A heavy wind brought a terrific rainstorm,
18:46 and Ahab left quickly for Jezreel. 46 Then the LORD gave special strength to Elijah. He
2 Kgs 4:29 tucked his cloak into his belt* and ran ahead of Ahab's chariot all the way to the entrance
of Jezreel.

18:31 Hebrew *each of the tribes of the sons of Jacob to whom the LORD had said, "Your name will be Israel."* 18:32 Hebrew *2 seahs* [12 liters] *of seed.* 18:36 Hebrew *and Israel.* The names "Jacob" and "Israel" are often interchanged throughout the Old Testament, referring sometimes to the individual patriarch and sometimes to the nation. 18:46 Hebrew *He bound up his loins.*

▶ GOD

18:37 "Answer me . . . O LORD." Recall your own conversion—did you feel as if you were in charge of the situation or that God was? Elijah knew that people do not naturally drift toward God (1 Corinthians 2:14; Ephesians 2:1), but God brings rebellious people to Himself. God conquers the sinner's rebellion, enabling him to turn to Christ in genuine repentance and saving faith (John 6:45-65). When it comes to saving souls, it's our decision—but it's God who decides first (John 15:16). Thank God that He doesn't leave it up to us to turn to Him; instead He is actively involved in salvation. (***See God> Relationship> God's Desire> God pursues a relationship,*** TopicGuide page A14.)

18:40 Now that the people had stopped wavering and had chosen the true God, under Mosaic Law it was right to execute the leaders of the idolatrous Baal cult (Deuteronomy 13:5; 18:20). The prophets of Baal were executed in the Kishon Valley, which is northeast of the Carmel range. The Kishon River is fed by the Carmel range and flows into the Mediterranean just east of modern-day Haifa.

18:46 That Elijah ran ahead of Ahab's chariot could also mean he ran *with* the king's entourage, leading them, rather than outrunning them.

ELIJAH FLEES TO SINAI

19 When Ahab got home, he told Jezebel everything Elijah had done, including the
way he had killed all the prophets of Baal. 2So Jezebel sent this message to Elijah: 19:2
"May the gods strike me and even kill me if by this time tomorrow I have not killed you 2 Kgs 6:31
just as you killed them."
3Elijah was afraid and fled for his life. He went to Beersheba, a town in Judah, and he 19:3
left his servant there. 4Then he went on alone into the wilderness, traveling all day. He sat Gen 21:31
down under a solitary broom tree and prayed that he might die. "I have had enough, 19:4 Num 11:5
LORD," he said. "Take my life, for I am no better than my ancestors who have already Jer 20:14-18
died." Jon 4:3, 8
5Then he lay down and slept under the broom tree. But as he was sleeping, an angel
touched him and told him, "Get up and eat!" 6He looked around and there beside his head
was some bread baked on hot stones and a jar of water! So he ate and drank and lay
down again.
7Then the angel of the LORD came again and touched him and said, "Get up and eat
some more, or the journey ahead will be too much for you."
8So he got up and ate and drank, and the food gave him enough strength to travel forty 19:8
days and forty nights to Mount Sinai,* the mountain of God. 9There he came to a cave, Exod 3:1; 4:27; 24:18;
where he spent the night. 34:28 Deut 9:9 Matt 4:2

THE LORD SPEAKS TO ELIJAH

But the LORD said to him, "What are you doing here, Elijah?"
10Elijah replied, "I have zealously served the LORD God Almighty. But the people of Israel 19:10
have broken their covenant with You, torn down Your altars, and killed every one of Your *Rom 11:2-4
prophets. I am the only one left, and now they are trying to kill me, too." 19:11
11"Go out and stand before Me on the mountain," the LORD told him. And as Elijah stood Exod 19:16, 19-20;
there, the LORD passed by, and a mighty windstorm hit the mountain. It was such a terrible 24:12 Ezek 1:4
blast that the rocks were torn loose, but the LORD was not in the wind. After the wind there 19:12
was an earthquake, but the LORD was not in the earthquake. 12And after the earthquake Job 4:16

19:8 Hebrew *to Horeb,* another name for Sinai. 19:13 Exod 3:6

19:2-3 The seriousness of this threat is evident from the way Jezebel swore by her gods (similar oaths are uttered by Israelites in 1 Kings 2:23; 2 Samuel 3:35). Physically spent after the events on Mount Carmel, Elijah was frightened by Jezebel's threat. He immediately fled to Beersheba, which was in the southern part of Israel in the Negev. Three miles east of the modern city of Tell es-Seba, Beersheba is named for the wells dug there by Abraham and given to Abimelech (Genesis 21:31-32). Isaac also made an oath of nonaggression with Abimelech there (Genesis 26:23-33).

▸ GOD

19:4 "I have had enough, LORD." Do you feel this way right now: You are tired of running, tired of working, and, frankly, tired of God? God knew that Elijah was having a crisis of nutrition in addition to his crisis of faith, so He sent an angel to serve Elijah a hot meal. This may seem like an odd use of God's unlimited power, but God knows that sometimes we just need a good meal. When you feel depressed, attend to both your physical and spiritual needs. When other people around you are suffering, don't just pray for them—care for their obvious physical needs. (***See God*** > *God's Attributes* > *Merciful* > *God's mercy endures through trials,* TopicGuide page A17.)

19:8 Though the exact location of Mount Sinai (Horeb) on the Sinai Peninsula is not clear (see notes on Exodus 19:1), it is feasible that this journey of more than 200 miles could have taken 40 days. In Scripture, however, the number 40 is often associated with suffering, hardship, or punishment and should be understood primarily as symbolic. The number 40 was associated with the Flood (Genesis 7–8), the 40-year wilderness wandering, the 40-day exploration of the Promised Land (Numbers 14:34), Moses' time on Mount Sinai (Deuteronomy 9:9), and Moses' subsequent intercession for the Israelites (Deuteronomy 9:18). The writer of Kings probably included the number 40 here to call attention to the importance of Elijah's journey, placing it on the same level as the previously mentioned biblical events. Later, "forty days and forty nights" would be the length of Jesus' time in the wilderness (Matthew 4:2).

19:11-13 In the presence of the wind, earthquake, fire, and whisper, Elijah's complaints amounted to petulant whining. He wanted to quit the office of prophet, but then God revealed Himself to Elijah much like He did with Moses on the same mountain centuries earlier (Exodus 19:16-18). First, God dramatically displayed to Elijah His power over the other so-called gods (Psalm 29; Habakkuk 3:3-12). Then God, who is also relational, spoke in a gentle whisper to Elijah. In other words, God first got Elijah's attention, and then He ministered to him. God demonstrated that His gentle whisper is more powerful than the supposed thundering of Baal. God asked the same question of Elijah that He had asked before the wind, earthquake, fire, and whisper, and Elijah gave the same answer both times. God interacted with Jeremiah in a similar way at times (Jeremiah 11:18-23; 15:15-21).

there was a fire, but the LORD was not in the fire. And after the fire there was the sound of a
gentle whisper. 13 When Elijah heard it, he wrapped his face in his cloak and went out and
stood at the entrance of the cave.
And a voice said, "What are you doing here, Elijah?"
14 He replied again, "I have zealously served the LORD God Almighty. But the people of
19:15 Israel have broken their covenant with You, torn down Your altars, and killed every one of
2 Kgs 8:7-15 Your prophets. I am the only one left, and now they are trying to kill me, too."
19:16 15 Then the LORD told him, "Go back the same way you came, and travel to the wilder-
2 Kgs 2:9, 15; 9:1 ness of Damascus. When you arrive there, anoint Hazael to be king of Aram. 16 Then
19:17 2 Kgs 8:12-13, 29; anoint Jehu son of Nimshi to be king of Israel, and anoint Elisha son of Shaphat from the
9:14; 13:3 town of Abel-meholah to replace you as My prophet. 17 Anyone who escapes from Hazael
19:18 will be killed by Jehu, and those who escape Jehu will be killed by Elisha! 18 Yet I will pre-
Hos 13:2 *Rom 11:4 serve 7,000 others in Israel who have never bowed down to Baal or kissed him!"

THE CALL OF ELISHA

19:19 19 So Elijah went and found Elisha son of Shaphat plowing a field. There were twelve teams
2 Kgs 2:8, 13-14 of oxen in the field, and Elisha was plowing with the twelfth team. Elijah went over to him
and threw his cloak across his shoulders and then walked away. 20 Elisha left the oxen
standing there, ran after Elijah, and said to him, "First let me go and kiss my father and
mother good-bye, and then I will go with you!"
Elijah replied, "Go on back, but think about what I have done to you."
21 So Elisha returned to his oxen and slaughtered them. He used the wood from the
plow to build a fire to roast their flesh. He passed around the meat to the townspeople,
and they all ate. Then he went with Elijah as his assistant.

▸ GOD

19:13 The power of God's whisper. God reveals Himself in the remarkable power of nature. But He is also present—perhaps more so—in the still, quiet moments of life. Elijah sensed this as he hid his eyes from the majesty of God that was outside his cave. And the message of God was everything he could have hoped for: There would be victory in his struggle against Ahab and Jezebel, and he would be relieved of his duties as soon as Elisha was anointed as prophet. In your conflicts, God will always have the final victory and, if you are on His side, you will ultimately be vindicated as you enter into your deserved rest from your labors. (***See God****> God's Attributes> Sovereign> God has dominion over the affairs of people,* TopicGuide page A17.)

19:15-16 God put Elijah back to work, but Elijah only accomplished the third task God gave him here, performing the other two through Elisha, his successor. Elisha would travel all the way to the desert of Damascus, northeast of Israel. Hazael was a servant of Ben-hadad, the king of Aram, and would later assassinate him to claim the throne after his encounter with Elisha (2 Kings 8:7-15). Jehu, an army commander in Israel during the reign of Ahab, would eventually be anointed by a servant of Elisha (2 Kings 9–10) and exterminate the entire royal house of Omri, beginning a new, 100-year dynasty. Elisha was from Abel-meholah, south of Beth-shan. All of these men would continue the purge of Baal worship begun by Elijah, just as God promised.

19:18 Bowing down and kissing physical idols is a common act of submission offered to gods. God promised to preserve a remnant of those who had not submitted to Baal. Old Testament prophecies frequently affirm that the Lord always preserves a remnant of His people who are faithful to Him. This is evident in the Assyrian invasion (2 Kings 19:28-31), in the Babylonian invasion (2 Chronicles 36:20), after the exile (Ezra 9:14), in the time of Christ (Micah 2:12-13), and during our own time (Romans 9:27-29; 11:5; Isaiah 11; 1 Thessalonians 4:17).

▸ HOLINESS

19:19 Elijah found Elisha. It takes faith to pass on our responsibilities to someone else. You have to trust that they will take care of your work. After God hinted that he would be able to pass off his duties to Elisha, Elijah promptly commissioned him. Elijah was ready to delegate, ready to pass his ministry on to the next generation. This took faith in both God and Elisha. Show faith in God by passing on a legacy of ministry and life to those who follow you. (***See Holiness****> Submission> Trusting God> Obedience,* TopicGuide page A40.)

19:19-21 Elijah's gesture of throwing his cloak over Elisha was a call to the prophetic office. Little is known of what exactly is meant by the word "cloak," except that it is distinctive to the prophet (Zechariah 13:4). It may have been a hairy cloak (see textual note at 2 Kings 1:8). Elisha immediately asked to be allowed to kiss his parents goodbye, an understandable gesture that is seen in other passages in the context of receiving a blessing (Genesis 27:26; 31:28, 55; 48:10). Later, in an allusion to this act, Jesus' would not allow a potential disciple to turn back to his parents, because His ministry was far greater and more urgent than the disciple's desire to say goodbye (Luke 9:61-62). But Elisha had no intention of shirking his call. Rather, he forsook his former occupation and position, consecrating himself for the ministry by sacrificing his oxen and inviting his servants to feast with him as witnesses of this decision. Elisha made a complete break with his former life (compare Mark 1:18).

BEN-HADAD ATTACKS SAMARIA

20 About that time King Ben-hadad of Aram mobilized his army, supported by the 20:1
chariots and horses of thirty-two allied kings. They went to besiege Samaria, the 1 Kgs 15:18
capital of Israel, and launched attacks against it. [2]Ben-hadad sent messengers into the city 2 Kgs 6:24
to relay this message to King Ahab of Israel: "This is what Ben-hadad says: [3]'Your silver 20:2
and gold are mine, and so are your wives and the best of your children!'" 2 Chr 16:2
[4]"All right, my lord the king," Israel's king replied. "All that I have is yours!"
[5]Soon Ben-hadad's messengers returned again and said, "This is what Ben-hadad says:
'I have already demanded that you give me your silver, gold, wives, and children. [6]But
about this time tomorrow I will send my officials to search your palace and the homes of
your people. They will take away everything you consider valuable!'"
[7]Then Ahab summoned all the elders of the land and said to them, "Look how this man 20:7
is stirring up trouble! I already agreed with his demand that I give him my wives and chil- 2 Kgs 5:7
dren and silver and gold."
[8]"Don't give in to any more demands," all the elders and the people advised.
[9]So Ahab told the messengers from Ben-hadad, "Say this to my lord the king: 'I will give
you everything you asked for the first time, but I cannot accept this last demand of yours.'"
So the messengers returned to Ben-hadad with that response.
[10]Then Ben-hadad sent this message to Ahab: "May the gods strike me and even kill me if 20:10
there remains enough dust from Samaria to provide even a handful for each of my soldiers." 1 Kgs 19:2
[11]The king of Israel sent back this answer: "A warrior putting on his sword for battle should 2 Kgs 6:31
not boast like a warrior who has already won." 20:11 Prov 27:1
[12]Ahab's reply reached Ben-hadad and the other kings as they were drinking in their tents.*
"Prepare to attack!" Ben-hadad commanded his officers. So they prepared to attack the city.

AHAB'S VICTORY OVER BEN-HADAD

[13]Then a certain prophet came to see King Ahab of Israel and told him, "This is what the
LORD says: Do you see all these enemy forces? Today I will hand them all over to you.
Then you will know that I am the LORD."
[14]Ahab asked, "How will He do it?"
And the prophet replied, "This is what the LORD says: The troops of the provincial com-
manders will do it."
"Should we attack first?" Ahab asked.
"Yes," the prophet answered.
[15]So Ahab mustered the troops of the 232 provincial commanders. Then he called out
the rest of the army of Israel, some 7,000 men. [16]About noontime, as Ben-hadad and the 20:16
thirty-two allied kings were still in their tents drinking themselves into a stupor, [17]the 1 Kgs 16:9
troops of the provincial commanders marched out of the city as the first contingent.

20:12 Or *in Succoth;* also in 20:16.

20:1 The Arameans came from a larger people group later referred to collectively as Syrians. Conflicting genealogies make the origins of this people group difficult to determine (Genesis 10:20-23). They were no doubt Semitic, related to Laban (Genesis 25:20; 28:1-7) and therefore to Jacob (Deuteronomy 26:5). These Arameans settled in the central Euphrates region, where they spread out into separate kingdoms. David had conquered this group of kingdoms northeast of Israel (1 Chronicles 18:5–19:19), but they continued to trouble Israel during Solomon's reign (1 Kings 11:25) and the reigns of Baasha (of Israel) and Asa (of Judah) (1 Kings 15:16-22). Ahab took the brunt of the conflict during his reign. The name *Ben-hadad* simply means "son of Hadad," indicating he was named after the Syrian storm god. This was likely Ben-hadad II (see note at 1 Kings 20:34), who assembled a large force from other city-states to march against Israel.

20:3-4 By claiming Ahab's wealth, wives, and children, Ben-hadad was essentially calling for Ahab to be his vassal. Ahab immediately surrendered, using the address "my lord" and agreeing to meet the demands of tribute. It was a common practice of the time to take royal hostages to insure that the terms of surrender were met.

20:13 In Saul and David's time, it was common to consult the Lord concerning a coming battle, and this was done through various devices, such as the Urim and Thummim (1 Samuel 14:10; 22:10; 23:9-12). During this time, however, the prophet came to be seen as the means for consulting God's will. By the Lord's direction, this prophet arrived in the nick of time for God to give Israel a miraculous victory, resulting in the people giving their allegiance to Him.

As they approached, Ben-hadad's scouts reported to him, "Some troops are coming
from Samaria."
18"Take them alive," Ben-hadad commanded, "whether they have come for peace or
for war."
19But Ahab's provincial commanders and the entire army had now come out to fight.
20Each Israelite soldier killed his Aramean opponent, and suddenly the entire Aramean
army panicked and fled. The Israelites chased them, but King Ben-hadad and a few of his
charioteers escaped on horses. 21However, the king of Israel destroyed the other horses
and chariots and slaughtered the Arameans.
20:22 22Afterward the prophet said to King Ahab, "Get ready for another attack. Begin making
2 Sam 11:1 plans now, for the king of Aram will come back next spring.*"

BEN-HADAD'S SECOND ATTACK

23After their defeat, Ben-hadad's officers said to him, "The Israelite gods are gods of the
hills; that is why they won. But we can beat them easily on the plains. 24Only this time re-
place the kings with field commanders! 25Recruit another army like the one you lost. Give
us the same number of horses, chariots, and men, and we will fight against them on the
plains. There's no doubt that we will beat them." So King Ben-hadad did as they suggested.
20:26 26The following spring he called up the Aramean army and marched out against Israel,
2 Kgs 13:17 this time at Aphek. 27Israel then mustered its army, set up supply lines, and marched out
20:27 for battle. But the Israelite army looked like two little flocks of goats in comparison to the
Judg 6:3-5 1 Sam 13:5-8 vast Aramean forces that filled the countryside!
28Then the man of God went to the king of Israel and said, "This is what the LORD says:
The Arameans have said, 'The LORD is a god of the hills and not of the plains.' So I will de-
feat this vast army for you. Then you will know that I am the LORD."
20:30 29The two armies camped opposite each other for seven days, and on the seventh day
1 Kgs 22:25 the battle began. The Israelites killed 100,000 Aramean foot soldiers in one day. 30The
2 Chr 18:24 rest fled into the town of Aphek, but the wall fell on them and killed another 27,000. Ben-
hadad fled into the town and hid in a secret room.
20:31 31Ben-hadad's officers said to him, "Sir, we have heard that the kings of Israel are merci-
Gen 37:34 ful. So let's humble ourselves by wearing burlap around our waists and putting ropes on
our heads, and surrender to the king of Israel. Then perhaps he will let you live."
32So they put on burlap and ropes, and they went to the king of Israel and begged,
"Your servant Ben-hadad says, 'Please let me live!'"
The king of Israel responded, "Is he still alive? He is my brother!"
33The men took this as a good sign and quickly picked up on his words. "Yes," they said,
"your brother Ben-hadad!"

20:22 Hebrew *at the turn of the year;* similarly in 20:26. The first day of the year in the ancient Hebrew lunar calendar occurred in March or April.

20:22 Spring was the best time for kings to go to war (2 Samuel 11:1), because the mild weather contributed to easier travel and more favorable battle conditions. Even after this great victory, the prophet continued to declare God's mercy to Ahab by advising preparation for the predicted Aramean retaliation next spring.

20:25-26 Fighting Israel in the plains would allow the Arameans to take full advantage of their chariotry and cavalry, of which Israel had very little. Aphek was most likely a city just east of the Sea of Galilee on the main highway between Damascus and the Jezreel Valley. The city is called Fiq or Afiq today. Later, Elisha prophesied that King Jehoash (of Israel) would defeat the Arameans there, too (2 Kings 13:14-19).

20:31 Sackcloth, or burlap, was clothing made from goat or camel hair. It was worn to show sorrow and repentance (Genesis 37:34; 2 Kings 19:1; 2 Samuel 21:10; Esther 4:1; Nehemiah 9:1). Putting ropes on (over) one's head probably depicted mourning associated with captivity. Prisoners were usually led away by ropes, as seen in Assyrian and Egyptian reliefs.

20:32-34 After all the ways Ben-hadad had threatened King Ahab and all the trouble he had caused Israel, Ahab still treated him as an equal. It was customary in that society to treat a conquered king like a vassal; as such, Ben-hadad would have been forced to run next to the chariot. However, Ahab brought Ben-hadad up into his chariot, treating him as an honored equal and indicating his willingness to negotiate a treaty. Not only did this go against cultural expectations, but it is also apparent that God had instructed Ahab not to spare Ben-hadad (1 Kings 20:42). Ahab has shown himself to be a serious compromiser, unworthy to lead as Israel's anointed.

“Go and get him,” the king of Israel told them. And when Ben-hadad arrived, Ahab in-
vited him up into his chariot.
34 Ben-hadad told him, “I will give back the towns my father took from your father, and **20:34**
you may establish places of trade in Damascus, as my father did in Samaria.” 1 Kgs 15:20
Then Ahab said, “I will release you under these conditions.” So they made a new treaty,
and Ben-hadad was set free.

A PROPHET CONDEMNS AHAB

35 Meanwhile, the LORD instructed one of the group of prophets to say to another man, “Hit **20:35**
me!” But the man refused to hit the prophet. 36 Then the prophet told him, “Because you 1 Kgs 13:16-18
have not obeyed the voice of the LORD, a lion will kill you as soon as you leave me.” And **20:36**
when he had gone, a lion did attack and kill him. 1 Kgs 13:24
37 Then the prophet turned to another man and said, “Hit me!” So he struck the prophet
and wounded him.
38 The prophet placed a bandage over his eyes to disguise himself and then waited be- **20:38**
side the road for the king. 39 As the king passed by, the prophet called out to him, “Sir, I was 1 Kgs 14:2
in the thick of battle, and suddenly a man brought me a prisoner. He said, ‘Guard this man; **20:39**
if for any reason he gets away, you will either die or pay a fine of seventy-five pounds* of 2 Kgs 10:24
silver!’ 40 But while I was busy doing something else, the prisoner disappeared!”
“Well, it’s your own fault,” the king replied. “You have brought the judgment on yourself.”
41 Then the prophet quickly pulled the bandage from his eyes, and the king of Israel rec-
ognized him as one of the prophets. 42 The prophet said to him, “This is what the LORD
says: Because you have spared the man I said must be destroyed,* now you must die in
his place, and your people will die instead of his people.” 43 So the king of Israel went **20:43**
home to Samaria angry and sullen. 1 Kgs 21:4

NABOTH’S VINEYARD

21 Now there was a man named Naboth, from Jezreel, who owned a vineyard in Jez- **21:1**
reel beside the palace of King Ahab of Samaria. 2 One day Ahab said to Naboth, 2 Kgs 9:21
“Since your vineyard is so convenient to my palace, I would like to buy it to use as a vege-
table garden. I will give you a better vineyard in exchange, or if you prefer, I will pay you
for it.”
3 But Naboth replied, “The LORD forbid that I should give you the inheritance that was **21:3**
passed down by my ancestors.” Lev 25:23 Num 36:6-7
4 So Ahab went home angry and sullen because of Naboth’s answer. The king went to Ezek 46:18
bed with his face to the wall and refused to eat!
5 “What’s the matter?” his wife Jezebel asked him. “What’s made you so upset that
you’re not eating?”
6 “I asked Naboth to sell me his vineyard or trade it, but he refused!” Ahab told her.
7 “Are you the king of Israel or not?” Jezebel demanded. “Get up and eat something, and **21:7**
don’t worry about it. I’ll get you Naboth’s vineyard!” 1 Sam 8:14
8 So she wrote letters in Ahab’s name, sealed them with his seal, and sent them to the el- **21:8**
ders and other leaders of the town where Naboth lived. 9 In her letters she commanded: 2 Sam 11:14 2 Chr 32:17 Esth 3:12; 8:8

20:39 Hebrew *1 talent* [34 kilograms]. 20:42 The Hebrew term used here refers to the complete consecration of things or people to the LORD, either by destroying them or by giving them as an offering.

20:37-40 Prophets were known for performing symbolic acts (Hosea 1–3; Ezekiel 2:1–3:15; Isaiah 20:1-3) and using cunning parables to trap sinful kings (2 Samuel 12:1-14).

21:1-3 Jezreel was the site of King Ahab’s winter retreat, located at the foot of Mount Gilboah 15 to 20 miles west of Mount Carmel. It was a common practice among kings of other nations at this time to simply confiscate any land that they desired. But even though Ahab had shown evidence of being selfish and uncaring, he actually offered to pay Naboth for his vineyard instead of just taking it. Naboth refused on the grounds that he would lose the inheritance allotted to his family, which God had said should be kept within tribal bounds. The land was a gift of the covenant and was not to be permanently sold (Leviticus 25:23; Numbers 27:5-7).

"Call the citizens together for fasting and prayer, and give Naboth a place of honor. 10And
then seat two scoundrels across from him who will accuse him of cursing God and the
king. Then take him out and stone him to death."
11So the elders and other town leaders followed the instructions Jezebel had written in
the letters. 12They called for a fast and put Naboth at a prominent place before the people.
13Then the two scoundrels came and sat down across from him. And they accused Naboth
before all the people, saying, "He cursed God and the king." So he was dragged outside
the town and stoned to death. 14The town leaders then sent word to Jezebel, "Naboth has
been stoned to death."
15When Jezebel heard the news, she said to Ahab, "You know the vineyard Naboth
wouldn't sell you? Well, you can have it now! He's dead!" 16So Ahab immediately went
down to the vineyard of Naboth to claim it.
17But the LORD said to Elijah,* 18"Go down to meet King Ahab of Israel, who rules in Sa-
maria. He will be at Naboth's vineyard in Jezreel, claiming it for himself. 19Give him this
message: 'This is what the LORD says: Wasn't it enough that you killed Naboth? Must you
rob him, too? Because you have done this, dogs will lick your blood at the very place
where they licked the blood of Naboth!' "
20"So, my enemy, you have found me!" Ahab exclaimed to Elijah.
"Yes," Elijah answered, "I have come because you have sold yourself to what is evil in the
LORD's sight. 21So now the LORD says, 'I will bring disaster on you and consume you. I will
destroy every one of your male descendants, slave and free alike, anywhere in Israel! 22I
am going to destroy your family as I did the family of Jeroboam son of Nebat and the fami-
ly of Baasha son of Ahijah, for you have made Me very angry and have led Israel into sin.'
23"And regarding Jezebel, the LORD says, 'Dogs will eat Jezebel's body at the plot of land
in Jezreel.'*
24"The members of Ahab's family who die in the city will be eaten by dogs, and those
who die in the field will be eaten by vultures."
25(No one else so completely sold himself to what was evil in the LORD's sight as Ahab
did under the influence of his wife Jezebel. 26His worst outrage was worshiping idols* just
as the Amorites had done—the people whom the LORD had driven out from the land ahead
of the Israelites.)
27But when Ahab heard this message, he tore his clothing, dressed in burlap, and fasted.
He even slept in burlap and went about in deep mourning.
28Then another message from the LORD came to Elijah: 29"Do you see how Ahab has
humbled himself before Me? Because he has done this, I will not do what I promised dur-
ing his lifetime. It will happen to his sons; I will destroy his dynasty."

21:10 Exod 22:28; Lev 24:15-16; Acts 6:11
21:19 1 Kgs 22:38; 2 Kgs 9:26
21:20 1 Kgs 18:17; Rom 7:14
21:21 1 Kgs 14:10; 2 Kgs 9:8
21:22 1 Kgs 14:16; 15:29; 16:3
21:23 2 Kgs 9:10, 30-37
21:24 1 Kgs 14:11; 16:4-7
21:26 Gen 15:16; Lev 18:25-30; 2 Kgs 21:11
21:27 Gen 37:34; 2 Kgs 6:26-30
21:29 1 Kgs 22:38; 2 Kgs 9:25-37; 2 Chr 12:7; 34:27

21:17 Hebrew *Elijah the Tishbite;* also in 21:28. 21:23 As in several Hebrew manuscripts, Syriac, and Latin Vulgate (see also 2 Kgs 9:26, 36); most Hebrew manuscripts read *at the city wall.* 21:26 The Hebrew term (literally *round things*) probably alludes to dung.

21:10 For a true Israelite, loyalty to God was paramount, but loyalty to the king followed closely behind, since the king was the earthly representation of God (see Exodus 22:28). Therefore, cursing either God or the king was a very serious offense (2 Samuel 16:7-8). These "scoundrels" were literally called "sons of Belial" (again translated "troublemakers" and scoundrels" in Judges 20:13; 1 Samuel 10:27; 30:22), a name that later became identified with Satan (2 Corinthians 6:15). Jezebel specifically calls for two such people, because in capital offenses Mosaic Law required two witnesses for a conviction (Deuteronomy 17:6; 19:15; Numbers 35:30; Matthew 26:60).

21:19-24 What's worse than dying? In ancient Israel, dying without burial, being eaten by dogs and vultures, and having one's entire family destroyed were worse by far! Ahab knew about this kind of family extermination, because it had happened to two earlier Israelite dynasties: Jeroboam's (1 Kings 14:10-11; 15:29) and Baasha's (1 Kings 16:3-12). Elijah said that God was the one who destroyed them and that He would destroy Ahab's family, too, including Jezebel. Jehu was the man responsible for bringing forth God's justice (2 Kings 9–10).

21:25-26 To remove any doubt in the reader's mind as to why God was so unmerciful in this sentence of death, the author added this comment about Ahab's deeds. God's conviction of Ahab and Jezebel was just and fair because they had led Israel so far astray from God and perpetrated so much evil. That evil included the worship of idols in the manner of the Amorites, whom the Israelites had defeated in Joshua 10–11.

21:27-29 This is the first recorded sign of repentance by Ahab. Even after all the evil he had done, his sorrow and mourning were met with the mercy of God. Even after God had already promised a terrible fate for him and his family, God delayed the sentence for a generation (2 Kings 9:24-26; 10:17) in acknowledgment of Ahab's actions.

JEHOSHAPHAT AND AHAB

22 For three years there was no war between Aram and Israel. 2Then during the 22:1-28
third year, King Jehoshaphat of Judah went to visit King Ahab of Israel. 3During //2 Chr 18:1-27
the visit, the king of Israel said to his officials, "Do you realize that the town of Ramoth- 22:2
gilead belongs to us? And yet we've done nothing to recapture it from the king of Aram!" 1 Kgs 15:24
4Then he turned to Jehoshaphat and asked, "Will you join me in battle to recover 22:3 Deut 4:43
Ramoth-gilead?"
Jehoshaphat replied to the king of Israel, "Why, of course! You and I are as one. My 22:4 2 Kgs 3:6-8
troops are your troops, and my horses are your horses." 5Then Jehoshaphat added, "But 22:5
first let's find out what the LORD says." 2 Kgs 3:11
6So the king of Israel summoned the prophets, about 400 of them, and asked them,
"Should I go to war against Ramoth-gilead, or should I hold back?"
They all replied, "Yes, go right ahead! The Lord will give the king victory."
7But Jehoshaphat asked, "Is there not also a prophet of the LORD here? We should ask 22:7
him the same question." 2 Kgs 3:11
8The king of Israel replied to Jehoshaphat, "There is one more man who could consult
the LORD for us, but I hate him. He never prophesies anything but trouble for me! His name
is Micaiah son of Imlah."
Jehoshaphat replied, "That's not the way a king should talk! Let's hear what he has to say."
9So the king of Israel called one of his officials and said, "Quick! Bring Micaiah son of Imlah."

MICAIAH PROPHESIES AGAINST AHAB

10King Ahab of Israel and King Jehoshaphat of Judah, dressed in their royal robes, were sit-
ting on thrones at the threshing floor near the gate of Samaria. All of Ahab's prophets were 22:11
prophesying there in front of them. 11One of them, Zedekiah son of Kenaanah, made Deut 33:17
some iron horns and proclaimed, "This is what the LORD says: With these horns you will 2 Chr 18:10
gore the Arameans to death!" Zech 1:18-21
12All the other prophets agreed. "Yes," they said, "go up to Ramoth-gilead and be victori-
ous, for the LORD will give the king victory!"
13Meanwhile, the messenger who went to get Micaiah said to him, "Look, all the prophets
are promising victory for the king. Be sure that you agree with them and promise success."
14But Micaiah replied, "As surely as the LORD lives, I will say only what the LORD tells me 22:14 Num 22:18; 24:13
to say." 2 Chr 18:13
15When Micaiah arrived before the king, Ahab asked him, "Micaiah, should we go to
war against Ramoth-gilead, or should we hold back?"
Micaiah replied sarcastically, "Yes, go up and be victorious, for the LORD will give the
king victory!"

22:3 Ramoth-gilead was a northeastern city on the border between Israel and Aram, but its exact location is uncertain. Most accept it to be the modern-day Tell Ramith. If this is the case, it was about 45 miles east of Jezreel. Perhaps Ben-hadad never returned this city as promised in 20:34.

22:4-5 Though Jehoshaphat was considered one of Judah's good kings (2 Chronicles 17:3-6), Jehu the seer condemned him for assisting Ahab (2 Chronicles 19:1-3). Jehoshaphat's request for confirmation by a prophet before attacking Ramoth-gilead demonstrates the significance of the prophetic voice in Israel's armed conflicts (see note at 1 Kings 20:13).

22:8 Prophets employed in a royal court had a tendency to be "yes men," compromising the word of the Lord. Prophesying doom and destruction, inciting insurrection, or especially calling the king to account for his sin could get a prophet thrown into prison. But Micaiah, who is mentioned here for the first time in Scripture, was a prophet of integrity. He knew he must declare only what the Lord told him (1 Kings 22:14). This was the function of a prophet—to be the mouthpiece of the Lord, the covenant ambassador for God.

▸ PURPOSE
22:15 "Go right ahead!" Were all the prophets in Israel sassy (1 Kings 18:27)? Perhaps the situation called for it, for the foolish kings of Israel and Judah would hear nothing of God's truth told plainly. Perhaps the prophets thought that they had a chance to shock the kings into repentance with their sarcasm. When someone takes a sharp tone with you, do not ignore the truth behind his or her words. As the proverb says, "Wounds from a sincere friend are better than many kisses from an enemy" (Proverbs 27:6). (***See Purpose*> *God's Deeds*> *Judgment*> *Call to repentance*, TopicGuide page A54.)

16 But the king replied sharply, "How many times must I demand that you speak only the
22:17 Num 27:17 truth to me when you speak for the LORD?"
1 Kgs 22:33-37 17 Then Micaiah told him, "In a vision I saw all Israel scattered on the mountains, like
Matt 9:36 sheep without a shepherd. And the LORD said, 'Their master has been killed. Send them
*Mark 6:34 home in peace.'"
18 "Didn't I tell you?" the king of Israel exclaimed to Jehoshaphat. "He never prophesies
anything but trouble for me."
22:19 Isa 6:1 19 Then Micaiah continued, "Listen to what the LORD says! I saw the LORD sitting on His
Dan 7:9-10 throne with all the armies of heaven around Him, on His right and on His left. 20 And the LORD
said, 'Who can entice Ahab to go into battle against Ramoth-gilead so he can be killed?'
"There were many suggestions, 21 and finally a spirit approached the LORD and said, 'I
can do it!'
22:22 Judg 9:23 22 "'How will you do this?' the LORD asked.
2 Thes 2:11 "And the spirit replied, 'I will go out and inspire all of Ahab's prophets to speak lies.'
"'You will succeed,' said the LORD. 'Go ahead and do it.'
22:23 Ezek 14:9 23 "So you see, the LORD has put a lying spirit in the mouths of all your prophets. For the
LORD has pronounced your doom."
22:24 2 Chr 18:23 24 Then Zedekiah son of Kenaanah walked up to Micaiah and slapped him across the
face. "Since when did the Spirit of the LORD leave me to speak to you?" he demanded.
25 And Micaiah replied, "You will find out soon enough when you are trying to hide in
some secret room!"
26 "Arrest him!" the king of Israel ordered. "Take him back to Amon, the governor of the
22:27 2 Chr 16:10; 18:25-27 city, and to my son Joash. 27 Give them this order from the king: 'Put this man in prison,
22:28 and feed him nothing but bread and water until I return safely from the battle!'"
Deut 18:22 28 But Micaiah replied, "If you return safely, it will mean that the LORD has not spoken
through me!" Then he added to those standing around, "Everyone mark my words!"

THE DEATH OF AHAB

22:29-36 29 So King Ahab of Israel and King Jehoshaphat of Judah led their armies against Ramoth-
//2 Chr 18:28-34 gilead. 30 The king of Israel said to Jehoshaphat, "As we go into battle, I will disguise myself
22:30 2 Chr 35:22 so no one will recognize me, but you wear your royal robes." So the king of Israel dis-
22:31 guised himself, and they went into battle.
2 Chr 18:30 31 Meanwhile, the king of Aram had issued these orders to his thirty-two chariot com-
manders: "Attack only the king of Israel. Don't bother with anyone else!" 32 So when the
Aramean chariot commanders saw Jehoshaphat in his royal robes, they went after
him. "There is the king of Israel!" they shouted. But when Jehoshaphat called out, 33 the
chariot commanders realized he was not the king of Israel, and they stopped chasing him.
34 An Aramean soldier, however, randomly shot an arrow at the Israelite troops and hit
the king of Israel between the joints of his armor. "Turn the horses* and get me out of
here!" Ahab groaned to the driver of his chariot. "I'm badly wounded!"

22:17 Hebrew *These people have no master.* 22:34 Hebrew *Turn your hand.*

22:15-18 Micaiah's initial response to Ahab's request for divine guidance was sarcastic approval. Ahab, recognizing the prophet's sarcasm, piously demanded that he speak the truth. So Micaiah employed the imagery of sheep without a shepherd (Numbers 27:16-17; Isaiah 13:14; Zechariah 10:2) to predict the death of Ahab if he went to war. But despite having asked for the truth, Ahab was unwilling to abide by it. His response revealed his disdain for God's word.

22:30-33 Jehoshaphat's surprising willingness to go along with Ahab's scheme and put himself in harm's way has led some scholars to conclude that at this time Israel exercised some level of control over Judah. The scheme nearly cost him his life, an indication of God's displeasure.

22:34-38 The author employed a touch of irony when he described the random arrow that struck Ahab. Ahab's scheming to avoid the fate prophesied by Micaiah failed—he died in just the way Elijah had promised. God's sovereign control of history cannot be undone by man's clever attempts to determine his own fate.

35 The battle raged all that day, and the king remained propped up in his chariot facing
the Arameans. The blood from his wound ran down to the floor of his chariot, and as eve-
ning arrived he died. 36 Just as the sun was setting, the cry ran through his troops: "We're
done for! Run for your lives!"
37 So the king died, and his body was taken to Samaria and buried there. 38 Then his
chariot was washed beside the pool of Samaria, and dogs came and licked his blood at the **22:38**
place where the prostitutes bathed,* just as the LORD had promised. 1 Kgs 21:19
39 The rest of the events in Ahab's reign and everything he did, including the story of the
ivory palace and the towns he built, are recorded in *The Book of the History of the Kings of* **22:39**
Israel. 40 So Ahab died, and his son Ahaziah became the next king. Amos 3:15

JEHOSHAPHAT RULES IN JUDAH

41 Jehoshaphat son of Asa began to rule over Judah in the fourth year of King Ahab's reign **22:41-50**
in Israel. 42 Jehoshaphat was thirty-five years old when he became king, and he reigned in //2 Chr 20:31–21:1
Jerusalem twenty-five years. His mother was Azubah, the daughter of Shilhi.
43 Jehoshaphat was a good king, following the example of his father, Asa. He did what **22:43**
was pleasing in the LORD's sight. *During his reign, however, he failed to remove all the pa- 1 Kgs 15:14
gan shrines, and the people still offered sacrifices and burned incense there. 44 Jehosha- 2 Kgs 12:3
phat also made peace with the king of Israel.

22:38 Or *his blood, and the prostitutes bathed [in it];* or *his blood, and they washed his armor.* **22:43** Verses 22:43b-53 are numbered 22:44-54 in Hebrew text.

KINGS TO DATE AND THEIR ENEMIES

874
AHAB
Twice defeated Ben-hadad II (Aram) and was later killed in battle against Aram
1 Kgs 16:28–22:40
2 Chr 18:1-34

853
AHAZIAH
1 Kgs 22:40—
2 Kgs 1:18
2 Chr 20:350-37

852

ISRAEL

JUDAH

869

853 848 841

910
ASA
Defeated Zerah (the Ethiopian) and harassed Baasha
1 Kgs 15:8-24
2 Chr 14:1–16:14
Co-regency
872–869

872
JEHOSHAPHAT
Defeated by Ben-hadad II (Aram), gained miraculous victory over Moab and Ammon, and crushed a rebellion by Mesha (Moab)
1 Kgs 22:41-50
2 Chr 17:1–21:1
Co-regency
853–848

JEHORAM
Lost dominion over Edom, assaulted by Philistines and Arabs
2 Kgs 8:16-24
2 Chr 21:1-20

All dates are BC.
Solid section of the timeline indicates co-regency.
For all the kings of Israel and Judah, see the chart at the end of 1 Kings.

22:41-50 Jehoshaphat ruled from about 872–848 BC. Overall, he was considered a good king of Judah. Still, the writer of 1 and 2 Kings criticized him because of the book's emphasis on total devotion to the Lord. The writer of 1 and 2 Kings condemns Jehoshaphat specifically for making an alliance with Ahab, which included marrying his son Jehoram to Athaliah, Ahab's daughter; Athaliah followed Jezebel's wicked example (2 Kings 8:18; 11:1; 2 Chronicles 18:1-2). Jehoshaphat also allied himself with Ahab's son Ahaziah in order to launch a sailing expedition from Ezion-geber, but the ships were destroyed in a storm. After Ahaziah died, Jehoshaphat allied himself with another son of Ahab called Joram, and they fought against Mesha, the king of Moab (2 Kings 3:4-27).

22:46 Deut 23:17 45 The rest of the events in Jehoshaphat's reign, the extent of his power, and the wars he
1 Kgs 15:12 waged are recorded in *The Book of the History of the Kings of Judah.* 46 He banished from
22:47 the land the rest of the male and female shrine prostitutes, who still continued their prac-
2 Sam 8:14 2 Kgs 3:9 tices from the days of his father, Asa.
22:48 47 (There was no king in Edom at that time, only a deputy.)
1 Kgs 9:26-28 48 Jehoshaphat also built a fleet of trading ships* to sail to Ophir for gold. But the ships
never set sail, for they met with disaster in their home port of Ezion-geber. 49 At one time
22:50 Ahaziah son of Ahab had proposed to Jehoshaphat, "Let my men sail with your men in the
2 Chr 21:1 ships." But Jehoshaphat refused the request.
50 When Jehoshaphat died, he was buried with his ancestors in the City of David. Then
his son Jehoram became the next king.

AHAZIAH RULES IN ISRAEL

22:52 1 Kgs 15:26 51 Ahaziah son of Ahab began to rule over Israel in the seventeenth year of King Jehosha-
phat's reign in Judah. He reigned in Samaria two years. 52 But he did what was evil in the
LORD's sight, following the example of his father and mother and the example of Jerobo-
am son of Nebat, who had led Israel to sin. 53 He served Baal and worshiped him, provok-
ing the anger of the LORD, the God of Israel, just as his father had done.

22:48 Hebrew *fleet of ships of Tarshish.*

22:47-49 Traditionally the Israelites were not sailors, partially because the Philistines' coastal presence hindered Israel's access to the Mediterranean. Under Solomon, however, the Phoenicians taught some Israelites how to sail (1 Kings 9:27), and Solomon maintained a small fleet of ships on the Red Sea. Solomon brought back gold from Ophir, which was probably located near the southwest corner of the Arabian Peninsula (1 Kings 9:28; 10:11, 22). Because of the unstable political situation in Edom, Jehoshaphat was able to attempt a sailing expedition out of Ezion-geber on the northern tip of the modern-day Gulf of Aqaba. The ships met with disaster after the prophet Eliezer condemned Jehoshaphat for allying himself with Ahaziah (2 Chronicles 20:35-37).

22:50 The City of David is the southeastern part of Jerusalem. It is also called Zion (1 Kings 8:1).

22:51-53 Ahaziah, Ahab's son and successor, ruled for about two years. Evil kings were frequently compared to the prototypical evil king Jeroboam, who ruled Israel when it first broke away from Judah. The idolatry of Ahaziah's mother, Jezebel, was passed on to him as well. The events of Ahaziah's reign are recounted in 2 Kings 1 and 8:25–9:29.

A HARMONY OF THE BOOKS OF KINGS AND CHRONICLES

This chart gives a harmony of the history recorded in 1 & 2 Kings and 1 & 2 Chronicles. It provides you with the names of the kings listed chronologically (showing those in the northern kingdom at the top and the southern kingdom at the bottom), a brief overview of each king's reign, and where you can read about each king. The bold lines above and below the chart give you the names and timelines of prophets who prophesied during the reigns of particular kings.

AHIJAH 934–909

ELIJAH 875–848

930
JEROBOAM I
(22 years)
Fortified a capital city (Shechem), set up two golden calf-idols, led the nation into sin, allowed anyone to be a priest
1 Kgs 11:26–14:34
2 Chr 10:12–13:20

909
NADAB
(2 years)
1 Kgs 15:25-28

908
BAASHA
(24 years)
Led people into idol worship
1 Kgs 15:27–16:7
2 Chr 16:1-6

886
ELAH
(2 years)
Continued idol worship
1 Kgs 16:6-14

885
ZIMRI
(7 days)
1 Kgs 16:9-20

885
TIBNI
(4 years)
1 Kgs 16:21-22

885
OMRI
(12 years)
Built the capital city of Samaria, had great military power, but continued to lead Israel into idolatry
1 Kgs 16:16-28

874
AHAB
(22 years)
Married Jezebel (a non-Jew and extremely wicked woman), worshiped Baal, and suffered three years of famine caused by his consistent disobedience to God
1 Kgs 16:28–22:40
2 Chr 18:1-34

CAPITAL: SHECHEM, THEN TIRZAH, THEN SAMARIA
THE NORTHERN KINGDOM OF ISRAEL (TEN TRIBES)

THE SOUTHERN KINGDOM OF JUDAH (TWO TRIBES)
CAPITAL: JERUSALEM

930
REHOBOAM
(17 years)
Built many fortified cities, strengthened the economy (despite the tribute paid to Egypt), followed God for three years, but then set up idols and shrines to foreign gods
1 Kgs 11:43–14:31
2 Chr 9:31–12:16

913
ABIJAH
(3 years)
Despite his wickedness, he called for God's help to win the battle against Israel
1 Kgs 14:31–15:8
2 Chr 13:1–14:1

910
ASA
(41 years)
Destroyed pagan altars and rebuilt altar of God, built fortified cities, gained much wealth from plunder of foreign conquest, removed the queen mother for worshiping Asherah, led the people to worship God with their hearts, provided peace on home soil, was greatly loved and given a beautiful funeral
1 Kgs 15:8-24
2 Chr 14:1–16:14

872
JEHOSHAPHAT
(25 years)
Arranged for the marriage of his son to a daughter of Ahab (who made trouble later on), had a strong military (kept troops in cities of Israel his father had conquered), collected tribute from the Philistines, worshiped the Lord and destroyed idols, established education, and appointed judges and courts
1 Kgs 15:24; 22:41-50
2 Chr 17:1–21:1

All dates are BC. The total years of reign sometimes includes years of co-regency.

ELISHA 848–797

JONAH 793–753(?)

853
AHAZIAH
(2 years)
Proposed a joint trade venture with Judah
1 Kgs 22:40—2 Kgs 1:18
2 Chr 20:35-37

852
JORAM
(12 years)
Suffered famine and war during most of his reign
2 Kgs 3:1–8:25
2 Chr 22:5-7

841
JEHU
(28 years)
Was responsible for the deaths of Joram (king of Israel), Ahaziah (king of Judah), and Jezebel (wicked mother of Joram); destroyed the priests and temples of Baal but did not consistently follow God
2 Kgs 9:1–10:36
2 Chr 22:7-12

814
JEHOAHAZ
(17 years)
Evil reign included worship of Asherah, usually called "detestable"
2 Kgs 13:1-9

798
JEHOASH
(16 years)
Even though he was evil, he recognized the authority of Elisha as a prophet of God
2 Kgs 13:10–14:16
2 Chr 25:17-24

793
JEROBOAM II
(41 years)
Very evil but politically powerful; his nation enjoyed economic prosperity and military peace
2 Kgs 14:16-29

853
JEHORAM
(8 years)
Married a wicked daughter of Ahab, compelled the people to worship idols, and killed all his brothers
2 Kgs 8:16-24
2 Chr 21:1-20

841
AHAZIAH
(1 year)
Friend of Joram of Israel
2 Kgs 8:24–9:29
2 Chr 22:1-10

841
ATHALIAH (QUEEN)
(6 years)
Killed all her grandchildren except Joash, who was hidden by his nurse for six years, ravaged the Temple to furnish Baal's temple
2 Kgs 11:1-20
2 Chr 22:10–23:21

835
JOASH
(40 years)
Was crowned king at the age of seven by Jehoiada (the high priest), promoted peace and prosperity, repaired the Temple, and smashed the altars to Baal; abandoned God after Jehoiada died, and even had Jehoiada's son killed
2 Kgs 11:2–12:21
2 Chr 22:11–24:27

796
AMAZIAH
(29 years)
Was basically good but did not completely wipe out idol worship; organized and mustered the army
2 Kgs 14:1-20
2 Chr 25:1-28

792
UZZIAH
(52 years)
Rebuilt a city named Elath, owned many farms and vineyards, constructed water reservoirs and fortified towers, reorganized the army (so powerful that his fame spread to Egypt), but violated God's laws for priestly function—so God struck him with leprosy
2 Kgs 15:1-17
2 Chr 26:1-23

HOSEA 753–715

AMOS 760–750

753
ZECHARIAH
(6 months)
Encouraged idol worship
2 Kgs 14:29–15:11

752
SHALLUM
(1 month)
2 Kgs 15:10-15

752
MENAHEM
(10 years)
Imposed heavy taxes and oppressed his people
2 Kgs 15:14-22

742
PEKAHIAH
(2 years)
Continued idol worship
2 Kgs 15:22-26

740
PEKAH
(8 years)
During his reign many of the people were taken captive to Assyria
2 Kgs 15:25-31
2 Chr 28:5-8

732
HOSHEA
(9 years)
Suffered heavy taxation by Assyria and eventual conquest—bringing about Israelite captivity and resettlement of foreigners in Israel
2 Kgs 15:30; 17:1-6

722
END OF THE NORTHERN KINGDOM—Israel taken to Assyria by Shalmaneser

ISRAEL

JUDAH

750
JOTHAM
(16 years)
Rebuilt the upper gate of the Temple, rebuilt walls and cities, but still permitted idol worship
2 Kgs 15:32-38
2 Chr 27:1-9

735
AHAZ
(16 years)
Sacrificed his own son to pagan gods, nailed the Temple doors shut
2 Kgs 16:1-20
2 Chr 28:1-27

715
HEZEKIAH
(29 years)
Was a devoted follower of God, reopened the Temple doors, purified the Temple, reinstated priests and their duties, organized an orchestra to aid worship, destroyed idols (including the bronze serpent of Moses because people had begun to worship it), celebrated the Passover and even invited people who were living in the north to participate, constructed large public waterworks, was given 15 extra years of life, foolishly showed Babylonian messengers the wealth in the Temple
2 Kgs 16:20; 18:1–20:21
2 Chr 29:1–32:33

697
MANASSEH
(55 years)
Rebuilt all the pagan shrines, sacrificed one of his own sons, practiced sorcery, set up an idol right in the Temple, murdered many of his own people, but repented during his Assyrian captivity
2 Kgs 21:1-18
2 Chr 33:1-20

MICAH 742–687

ISAIAH 740–681

586
END OF THE SOUTHERN KINGDOM—carried off captive to Babylon by Nebuchadnezzar

642
AMON
(2 years)
2 Kgs 21:18-26
2 Chr 33:20-25

640
JOSIAH
(31 years)
Loved God with all his heart, repaired the Temple, found a lost scroll of the law (he promised to obey it, thus God delayed destruction for Judah until after his death), personally oversaw the major project of destroying idol shrines, reinstated the priests of God, celebrated the Passover with greater zeal than had been since Samuel's day, was greatly loved by his people
2 Kgs 21:26–23:30
2 Chr 33:25–35:27

609
JEHOAHAZ
(3 months)
Jailed and taken to Egypt, where he died
2 Kgs 23:30-34
2 Chr 36:1-4

609
JEHOIAKIM
(11 years)
Burned part of God's Word given to Jeremiah, was a puppet king for Egypt and then Babylon, watched gold and articles taken from the Temple to Babylon, saw first exile (in which Daniel was taken)
2 Kgs 23:34–24:6
2 Chr 36:5-8

598
JEHOIACHIN
(3 months)
Saw next exile to Babylon
2 Kgs 24:6-15; 25:27-30
2 Chr 36:8-10

597
ZEDEKIAH
(11 years)
Saw the Temple burned and Jerusalem destroyed, was tortured and carried away in the final exile to Babylon
2 Kgs 24:17–25:21
2 Chr 36:10-21

NAHUM 663–654

ZEPHANIAH 640–621

HULDAH 632

JEREMIAH 627–586

HABAKKUK 612–589

OBADIAH 598–580(?)

KEY PLACES IN 2 KINGS

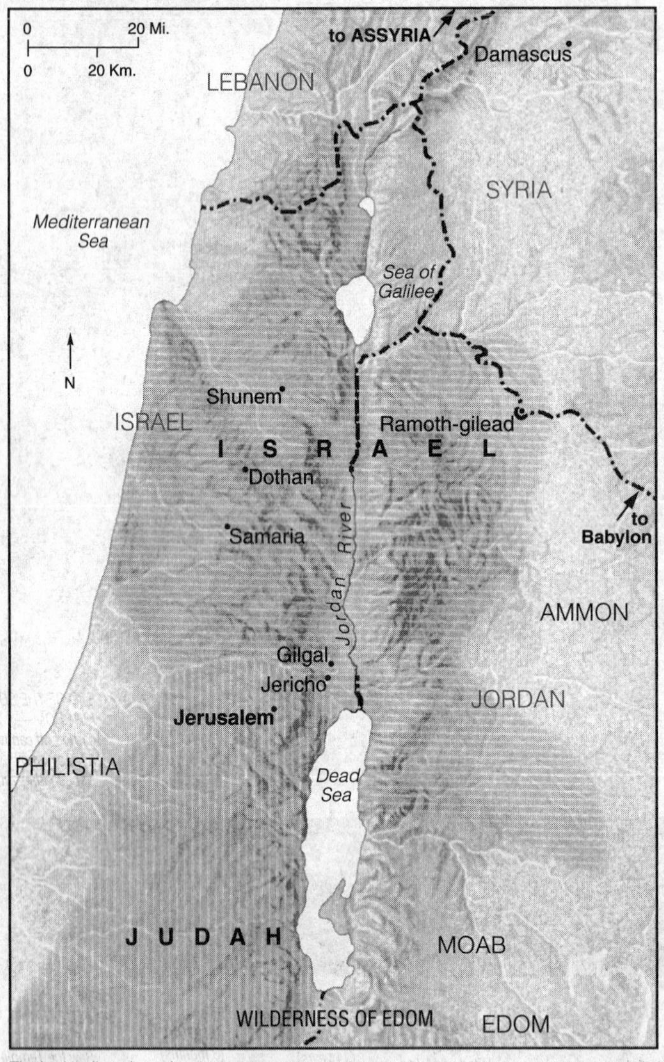

The broken lines (—·—) indicate modern boundaries.

The history of both Israel and Judah was much affected by the prophet Elisha's ministry. He served Israel for 50 years, fighting the idolatry of its kings and calling its people back to God.

1 Jericho Elijah's ministry had come to an end. He touched his cloak to the Jordan River, and he and Elisha crossed on dry ground. Elijah was taken by God in a whirlwind, and Elisha returned alone with the cloak. The prophets in Jericho realized that Elisha was Elijah's replacement (1:1–2:25).

2 Wilderness of Edom The king of Moab rebelled against Israel, so the nations of Israel, Judah, and Edom decided to attack from the wilderness of Edom but ran out of water. The kings consulted Elisha, who said God would send both water and victory (3:1-27).

3 Shunem Elisha cared for individuals and their needs. He helped a woman clear a debt by giving her a supply of oil to sell. For another family in Shunem, he raised a son from the dead (4:1-37).

4 Gilgal Elisha cared for the young prophets in Gilgal—he removed poison from a stew, made a small amount of food feed everyone, and even caused an ax head to float so it could be retrieved. It was to Elisha that Naaman, a commander in the Aramean army, came to be healed of leprosy (4:38–6:7).

5 Dothan Although he cured an Aramean commander's leprosy, Elisha was loyal to Israel. He knew the Aramean army's battle plans and kept Israel's king informed. The Aramean king tracked Elisha down in Dothan and surrounded the city, hoping to kill him. But Elisha prayed that the Arameans would be blinded; then he led the blinded army into Samaria, Israel's capital city (6:8-23).

6 Samaria But the Arameans didn't learn their lesson. They later besieged Samaria. Ironically, Israel's king thought it was Elisha's fault, but Elisha said food would be available in abundance the next day. True to Elisha's word, the Lord caused panic in the Aramean camp, and the enemy ran, leaving their supplies to Samaria's starving people (6:24–7:20).

7 Damascus Despite Elisha's loyalty to Israel, he obeyed God and traveled to Damascus, the capital of Aram. King Ben-hadad was sick, and he sent Hazael to ask Elisha if he would recover. Elisha knew the king would die and told this to Hazael. But Hazael then murdered Ben-hadad, making himself king. Later, Israel and Judah joined forces to fight this new Aramean threat (8:1-29).

8 Ramoth-gilead As Israel and Judah warred with Aram, Elisha sent a young prophet to Ramoth-gilead to anoint Jehu as Israel's next king. Jehu set out to destroy the wicked dynasties of Israel and Judah, killing kings Joram and Ahaziah, and wicked Queen Jezebel. He then destroyed King Ahab's family and all the Baal worshipers in Israel (9:1–11:1).

9 Jerusalem Power-hungry Athaliah became queen of Judah when her son Ahaziah was killed. She had all her grandsons killed except Joash, who was hidden by his aunt. Joash was crowned king at the age of seven and overthrew Athaliah. Meanwhile in Samaria, the Arameans continued to harass Israel. Israel's new king met with Elisha and was told that he would be victorious over Aram three times (11:2–13:19).

Following Elisha's death came a series of evil kings in Israel. Their idolatry and rejection of God caused their downfall. The Assyrian Empire captured Samaria and took most of the Israelites into captivity (13:20–17:41). Judah had a short reprieve because of a few good kings who destroyed idols and worshiped God. But many strayed from God. So Jerusalem fell to the next world power, Babylon (18:1–25:30).

2 KINGS

PURPOSE

To explain that the captivity of Israel by Assyria was due to its idolatry and apostasy; to call to repentance the exiled southern tribes of Judah, which had followed in Israel's apostasy; and to encourage the people to put their hope in kings from David's family.

Hamlet, Othello, Macbeth,* and *King Lear may be great tragedies of Western literature, but they've got nothing on what you are about to read. The assassinations, coups, and destruction in 2 Kings give credence to the saying that truth is often stranger—and more bloody—than fiction.

First Kings took us out of the united monarchy under King Solomon and into the divided monarchy of Jeroboam, king of Israel (the ten northern tribes), and Rehoboam, king of Judah (the two southern tribes of Benjamin and Judah plus the spiritual center of Jerusalem). If trouble was introduced in 1 Kings, tragedy becomes its ultimate result in 2 Kings. The northern kingdom of Israel never recovered from the idolatrous Baal worship introduced by Jeroboam and energized under wicked King Ahab. All of Israel's nineteen kings (part of nine separate dynasties, each inaugurated by the murder of the previous king) were wicked, which allowed for no brake on the nation's spiritual decline. Eight of Judah's twenty kings (all from a single dynasty) did what was right before God. That slowed Judah's decline, but Judah eventually succumbed to pagan ways as well.

The result? Israel was invaded and carried into captivity by the Assyrians in 722 BC, while Jerusalem and Judah fell to the Babylonians in 586 BC.

DISCOVER GOD IN 2 KINGS

The prophets Isaiah and Jeremiah, who ministered during the years covered in 2 Kings, give powerful perspectives on God during this time.

Sovereignty: Isaiah presented God as sovereign over the nations of the world. For instance, God treated the pagan nation of Assyria, a world power of the day, as a pet, whistling for it to come and discipline Judah: "In that day the LORD will whistle for the army of southern Egypt and the army of Assyria. They will swarm around you like flies and bees" (Isaiah 7:18). Later, God would summon the nations to return Judah home to Jerusalem (Isaiah 11:10, 12; 49:22; 62:10). The nations have been established by God for His purposes (see Acts 17:26), and He is sovereign over all their affairs.

Loyalty: Jeremiah presented contrasting messages to the nation of Judah. He told the people that their conquest by Babylon was imminent, but their permanence as a nation was not in question. God's purpose in taking Judah into captivity was *discipline*, not *destruction*:

"I am as likely to reject My people Israel as I am to abolish the laws of nature!" (Jeremiah 31:36). God used the sun, moon, and stars as testimony to His loyalty to Israel and Judah; He said that as long as the heavenly bodies existed, His chosen people would exist as a nation before Him (Jeremiah 31:35-37). God's promises to His people are as solid as the universe.

GROWING THROUGH 2 KINGS

The failures of the kings in Israel and Judah give fair warning to those who follow God today:

Reproof: All the kings of Israel and most of the kings of Judah failed to listen to the reproof of the prophets. God patiently reminded them of their covenant obligations, but they only lived for and ruled themselves. As a result, God brought conquest and death upon their kingdoms (Proverbs 10:10). It is much wiser, not to mention less painful, to heed a verbal reproof than receive a violent one.

Apprenticeship: In 1 Kings 19:16-21, Elijah called Elisha to be his assistant, apprentice, and eventual successor. Elisha continued Elijah's prophetic ministry to the northern nation of Israel (2 Kings 2–13). Much as John Mark did with Barnabas (Acts 15:39) and Timothy did with Paul (Acts 16:1-5), Elisha demonstrated humility and servanthood by playing second chair to a leader. Those unwilling to serve are rarely asked to lead.

The Glory of God: When Sennacherib, the king of Assyria, threatened King Hezekiah of Judah, Hezekiah went into the Temple in Jerusalem to pray for deliverance. He prayed, "Now, O Lord our God, rescue us from his power; then all the kingdoms of the earth will know that You alone, O Lord, are God" (2 Kings 19:19). We have a tendency, when we pray, to consider what's in it for us; Hezekiah's priority was how Judah's deliverance would reflect on God.

DISCOVERY VERSES

Then Naaman and his entire party went back to find the man of God. They stood before him, and Naaman said, "Now I know that there is no God in all the world except in Israel." (2 KINGS 5:15)

They rejected His decrees and the covenant He had made with their ancestors, and they despised all His warnings. They worshiped worthless idols, so they became worthless themselves. They followed the example of the nations around them, disobeying the LORD's command not to imitate them. (2 KINGS 17:15)

The king took his place of authority beside the pillar and renewed the covenant in the LORD's presence. He pledged to obey the LORD by keeping all His commands, laws, and decrees with all his heart and soul. In this way, he confirmed all the terms of the covenant that were written in the scroll, and all the people pledged themselves to the covenant. (2 KINGS 23:3)

2 KINGS FACTS

Author: Unknown. Jewish tradition suggests that Jeremiah or one of his associates was the author. Several documents were available at the time for a writer/compiler to use (2 Kings 11:41; 14:19, 29; 15:7).

Written to: First and Second Kings were originally one book that was addressed to the people of the southern kingdom of Judah, possibly already in exile in Babylon.

Date of writing: First and Second Kings began to be compiled prior to the invasion of Judah by Babylon in 586 BC (the northern ten tribes of Israel were conquered by Assyria in 722 BC). But the narrative goes to the middle of the Babylonian captivity, with 2 Kings ending during that time (2 Kings 25:27-30).

Setting: The narrative covers events in the northern ten tribes of Israel and in the two southern tribes of Judah, with much of the action happening in Jerusalem, the capital of Judah.

OUTLINE

- **1 KINGS 1–11**—The united reign of Solomon
- **1 KINGS 12–16**—The early divided kingdom
- **1 KINGS 17—2 KINGS 8:15**—Judah's faithfulness and fall
- **2 KINGS 8:16–17:41**—The late divided kingdom
- **2 KINGS 18–25**—Judah alone

ELIJAH CONFRONTS KING AHAZIAH

1:1 2 Sam 8:2 2 Kgs 3:5
1 After King Ahab's death, the land of Moab rebelled against Israel.
2One day Israel's new king, Ahaziah, fell through the latticework of an upper room
1:2 2 Kgs 1:16; 8:7-10 Mark 3:22
at his palace in Samaria and was seriously injured. So he sent messengers to the temple of
Baal-zebub, the god of Ekron, to ask whether he would recover.
3But the angel of the LORD told Elijah, who was from Tishbe, "Go and confront the mes-
1:3 1 Kgs 17:1
sengers of the king of Samaria and ask them, 'Is there no God in Israel? Why are you going
to Baal-zebub, the god of Ekron, to ask whether the king will recover? 4Now, therefore, this
1:4 2 Kgs 1:16-17
is what the LORD says: You will never leave the bed you are lying on; you will surely die.'"
So Elijah went to deliver the message.
5When the messengers returned to the king, he asked them, "Why have you returned
so soon?"
6They replied, "A man came up to us and told us to go back to the king and give him this
message. 'This is what the LORD says: Is there no God in Israel? Why are you sending men
to Baal-zebub, the god of Ekron, to ask whether you will recover? Therefore, because you
have done this, you will never leave the bed you are lying on; you will surely die.'"
7"What sort of man was he?" the king demanded. "What did he look like?"
1:8 Matt 3:4 Mark 1:6
8They replied, "He was a hairy man,* and he wore a leather belt around his waist."
"Elijah from Tishbe!" the king exclaimed.
9Then he sent an army captain with fifty soldiers to arrest him. They found him sitting
on top of a hill. The captain said to him, "Man of God, the king has commanded you to
come down with us."
1:10 1 Kgs 18:36-38 Job 1:16 Luke 9:54
10But Elijah replied to the captain, "If I am a man of God, let fire come down from heaven
and destroy you and your fifty men!" Then fire fell from heaven and killed them all.
11So the king sent another captain with fifty men. The captain said to him, "Man of God,
the king demands that you come down at once."
12Elijah replied, "If I am a man of God, let fire come down from heaven and destroy you
and your fifty men!" And again the fire of God fell from heaven and killed them all.
13Once more the king sent a third captain with fifty men. But this time the captain went
up the hill and fell to his knees before Elijah. He pleaded with him, "O man of God, please
spare my life and the lives of these, your fifty servants. 14See how the fire from heaven
1:15 2 Kgs 1:3 Isa 51:12 Jer 1:17 Ezek 2:6
came down and destroyed the first two groups. But now please spare my life!"
15Then the angel of the LORD said to Elijah, "Go down with him, and don't be afraid of
him." So Elijah got up and went with him to the king.

1:8 Or *He was wearing clothing made of hair.*

1:1 It was typical for vassal kingdoms to declare independence when the ruling kingdom went through leadership transitions. In this case, King Mesha of Moab renounced the burden of taxation that Ahaziah's grandfather, Omri, had imposed on them.

1:2 Samaria was the capital city of Israel. Gridlike latticework was used for the upper floor of buildings to offer shade below and ventilation above. Excavations in Samaria have shown that there were indeed two stories in the royal palace.

1:2 Baal-zebub, literally "lord of the flies," was a Philistine idol. Ekron was a Philistine city 60 miles southwest of Samaria. The Ark of the Covenant was kept at Ekron for a time after it was stolen from Israel (1 Samuel 5:1-12). Ekron was located at the site of Tel Miqne.

1:10 A "man of God" or prophet was dangerous. At any time, he could pronounce a curse over the disobedient (see 1 Kings 20:35-36). Centuries later in this same region, Jesus' apostles asked him whether they could call down fire from heaven like Elijah, but Jesus rebuked them because He had come to save lives, not take them.

▸ PURPOSE

1:14 "Please spare my life!" Ahaziah fundamentally misunderstood his relationship to God and His covenant relationship with Israel. He perceived that Elijah's prophecy was a political threat to him—and that's all he could see. Rather than surrender to the God of Israel (as even his common soldiers had the sense to do (2 Kings 1:13), Ahaziah continued to distance himself from the only God who could save him and his kingdom. If you think you may be under discipline from God, fall on your face before Him. Humble yourself before the Almighty God—and stay there. God will lift up the humble. (***See Purpose****> God's Deeds> Special Acts> Miracles> OT> Ahaziah's captains and men consumed by fire,* TopicGuide page A53.)

1:15 Elijah was not obliged to obey the demands of an evil king. He left only when God told him to go.

[16]And Elijah said to the king, "This is what the LORD says: Why did you send messengers to Baal-zebub, the god of Ekron, to ask whether you will recover? Is there no God in Israel to answer your question? Therefore, because you have done this, you will never leave the bed you are lying on; you will surely die."

[17]So Ahaziah died, just as the LORD had promised through Elijah. Since Ahaziah did not
have a son to succeed him, his brother Joram* became the next king. This took place in the
second year of the reign of Jehoram son of Jehoshaphat, king of Judah.

[18]The rest of the events in Ahaziah's reign are recorded in *The Book of the History of the Kings of Israel.*

1:17 2 Kgs 3:1; 8:16

ELIJAH TAKEN INTO HEAVEN

2 When the LORD was about to take Elijah up to heaven in a whirlwind, Elijah and Elisha
were traveling from Gilgal. [2]And Elijah said to Elisha, "Stay here, for the LORD has told
me to go to Bethel."

But Elisha replied, "As surely as the LORD lives and you yourself live, I will never leave you!" So they went down together to Bethel.

[3]The group of prophets from Bethel came to Elisha and asked him, "Did you know that the LORD is going to take your master away from you today?"

"Of course I know," Elisha answered. "But be quiet about it."

[4]Then Elijah said to Elisha, "Stay here, for the LORD has told me to go to Jericho."

2:1 Gen 5:23-24; 1 Kgs 19:16-21; Heb 11:5

1:17 Hebrew *Jehoram,* a variant spelling of Joram.

KINGS TO DATE AND THEIR ENEMIES

ISRAEL

853 **AHAZIAH** *1 Kgs 22:40—2 Kgs 1:18; 2 Chr 20:35-37*

852 **JORAM** *With Judah, defeated Mesha (Moab), and was miraculously delivered from Ben-hadad II (Aram); 2 Kgs 1:17; 3:1–8:25; 2 Chr 22:5-7*

841

JUDAH

872 **JEHOSHAPHAT** *Defeated by Ben-hadad II (Aram), gained miraculous victory over Moab and Ammon, and crushed a rebellion by Mesha (Moab); 2 Kgs 22:41-50; 2 Chr 17:1–21:1; Co-regency 853–848*

853 **JEHORAM** *Lost dominion over Edom, assaulted by Philistines and Arabs; 2 Kgs 8:16-24; 2 Chr 21:1-20*

848 *841*

All dates are BC.
Solid section of the timeline indicates co-regency.
For all the kings of Israel and Judah, see the chart at the end of 1 Kings.

1:17 Ahaziah's brother Joram (sometimes referred to as Jehoram), reigned from about 852 to 841 BC, which means that, for a time, Israel and Judah had kings with the same name.

2:2 By stating, "As surely as the LORD lives," Elisha was declaring an oath. Since oaths were treated with grave seriousness in ancient times, the elder prophet did not contest Elisha's determination to stay with him.

But Elisha replied again, "As surely as the LORD lives and you yourself live, I will never
leave you." So they went on together to Jericho.
5 Then the group of prophets from Jericho came to Elisha and asked him, "Did you know
that the LORD is going to take your master away from you today?"
"Of course I know," Elisha answered. "But be quiet about it."
2:6 6 Then Elijah said to Elisha, "Stay here, for the LORD has told me to go to the Jordan River."
Ruth 1:16 But again Elisha replied, "As surely as the LORD lives and you yourself live, I will never
2 Kgs 2:1-2 leave you." So they went on together.
7 Fifty men from the group of prophets also went and watched from a distance as Elijah
2:8 and Elisha stopped beside the Jordan River. 8 Then Elijah folded his cloak together and
Exod 14:21 1 Kgs 19:19 struck the water with it. The river divided, and the two of them went across on dry ground!
9 When they came to the other side, Elijah said to Elisha, "Tell me what I can do for you
before I am taken away."
And Elisha replied, "Please let me inherit a double share of your spirit and become your
successor."
10 "You have asked a difficult thing," Elijah replied. "If you see me when I am taken from
2:11 you, then you will get your request. But if not, then you won't."
2 Kgs 6:17 11 As they were walking along and talking, suddenly a chariot of fire appeared, drawn by
2:12 horses of fire. It drove between the two men, separating them, and Elijah was carried by a
2 Kgs 13:14 whirlwind into heaven. 12 Elisha saw it and cried out, "My father! My father! I see the chari-
ots and charioteers of Israel!" And as they disappeared from sight, Elisha tore his clothes in
distress.
13 Elisha picked up Elijah's cloak, which had fallen when he was taken up. Then Elisha re-
2:14 turned to the bank of the Jordan River. 14 He struck the water with Elijah's cloak and cried
2 Kgs 2:8 out, "Where is the LORD, the God of Elijah?" Then the river divided, and Elisha went across.
15 When the group of prophets from Jericho saw from a distance what happened, they
exclaimed, "Elijah's spirit rests upon Elisha!" And they went to meet him and bowed to the
2:16 ground before him. 16 "Sir," they said, "just say the word and fifty of our strongest men will
1 Kgs 18:12 search the wilderness for your master. Perhaps the Spirit of the LORD has left him on some
Acts 8:39 mountain or in some valley."
"No," Elisha said, "don't send them." 17 But they kept urging him until they shamed him
into agreeing, and he finally said, "All right, send them." So fifty men searched for three
days but did not find Elijah. 18 Elisha was still at Jericho when they returned. "Didn't I tell
you not to go?" he asked.

2:8 Elijah dividing the water recalls similar deeds by Moses (Exodus 14:21-22) and Joshua (Joshua 3).

2:9 In ancient Israel, the eldest son (or often the favored one) received a double share of the inheritance from the father's estate (see Deuteronomy 21:17). This tradition regarding inheritance was seen in Israel's distribution of tribal lands. Each tribe received land (except the Levites, who received the service of God). The tribe of Joseph, however, received two allotments of land, one for each of Joseph's sons, Manasseh and Ephraim. Though not the oldest of Jacob's sons, Joseph was Jacob's favorite and thus received the double blessing. Elisha's request is a bold one when seen in this light.

▸ GOD

2:10 Uncertainty at the end. You would think that if Elijah knew that his time on earth was done, he would also have known that Elisha would succeed him. But Elijah admitted his uncertainty over the will of God in this matter just moments before he came face to face with God. If Elijah himself was uncertain about the will of God, surely it is acceptable for us to be unclear about God's will in many areas. Even to the most spiritual of God's people, His ways are mysterious, and the future ultimately belongs solely to God. (***See God*****> *God's Attributes> All-Knowing> His wisdom and knowledge are way beyond us,*** TopicGuide page A15.)

2:12 To tear, or rend, a garment was a sign of grief and mourning in the ancient Near East. In fact, this symbolic gesture is still practiced in parts of the Middle East even in the twenty-first century.

▸ GOD

2:14 Elisha's sorrow. Grief can make us all temporarily appear as raving unbelievers. You can almost hear Elisha shouting at God as he helplessly struck the water. But when the water roared to a stop, you can imagine that Elisha was quickly shocked back to his senses. Elijah may have been gone, but Elisha learned that God was still with him. God knows your fears, your shock, and even in your most out-of-control emotional moments, He knows and loves you just as He did before. God dwells with His people, and the depths of human emotion do not put Him off. (***See God****> God's Attributes> All-Present> God's continual presence brings contentment,* TopicGuide page A16.)

ELISHA'S FIRST MIRACLES

19 One day the leaders of the town of Jericho visited Elisha. "We have a problem, my lord,"
they told him. "This town is located in pleasant surroundings, as you can see. But the wa-
ter is bad, and the land is unproductive."
20 Elisha said, "Bring me a new bowl with salt in it." So they brought it to him. 21 Then he — **2:21**
went out to the spring that supplied the town with water and threw the salt into it. And he — Exod 15:25-26
said, "This is what the LORD says: I have purified this water. It will no longer cause death or — 2 Kgs 4:41; 6:6
infertility.*" 22 And the water has remained pure ever since, just as Elisha said.
23 Elisha left Jericho and went up to Bethel. As he was walking along the road, a group of
boys from the town began mocking and making fun of him. "Go away, baldy!" they
chanted. "Go away, baldy!" 24 Elisha turned around and looked at them, and he cursed
them in the name of the LORD. Then two bears came out of the woods and mauled forty- — **2:25**
two of them. 25 From there Elisha went to Mount Carmel and finally returned to Samaria. — 1 Kgs 18:20

WAR BETWEEN ISRAEL AND MOAB

3 Ahab's son Joram* began to rule over Israel in the eighteenth year of King Jehosha- — **3:1**
phat's reign in Judah. He reigned in Samaria twelve years. 2 He did what was evil in — 2 Kgs 1:17; 8:16
the LORD's sight, but not to the same extent as his father and mother. He at least tore down — **3:2** 1 Kgs 16:30-32
the sacred pillar of Baal that his father had set up. 3 Nevertheless, he continued in the sins — 2 Kgs 10:25-26
that Jeroboam son of Nebat had committed and led the people of Israel to commit. — **3:3**
4 King Mesha of Moab was a sheep breeder. He used to pay the king of Israel an annual — 1 Kgs 12:28; 14:16
tribute of 100,000 lambs and the wool of 100,000 rams. 5 But after Ahab's death, the king — **3:4**
of Moab rebelled against the king of Israel. 6 So King Joram promptly mustered the army — 2 Sam 8:2
of Israel and marched from Samaria. 7 On the way, he sent this message to King Jehosha- — Isa 16:1-2
phat of Judah: "The king of Moab has rebelled against me. Will you join me in battle — **3:5** 2 Kgs 1:1
against him?" — **3:7**
And Jehoshaphat replied, "Why, of course! You and I are as one. My troops are your troops, — 1 Kgs 22:4
and my horses are your horses." 8 Then Jehoshaphat asked, "What route will we take?"
"We will attack from the wilderness of Edom," Joram replied.
9 The king of Edom and his troops joined them, and all three armies traveled along a — **3:9**
roundabout route through the wilderness for seven days. But there was no water for the — 1 Kgs 22:47
men or their animals.

2:21 Or *or make the land unproductive;* Hebrew reads *or barrenness.* 3:1 Hebrew *Jehoram,* a variant spelling of Joram; also in 3:6.

▸ PURPOSE

2:21 Water made wholesome. There are few things in life as critical as the need for water. We can do without most things for varying lengths of time, but no one can live without water for very long. During the time of Elisha, the water supply for Jericho was cursed with some impurity that occasionally caused infertility and death. But Elisha demonstrated God's care for His people by healing the tainted waters and restoring the city of Jericho to health. God may not function as your water purifier, but He does promise to protect you from any harm or danger that will keep you from accomplishing His plan for your life. God's will for you is not threatened by sickness or accidents—all things, even tragedy, are ordained by God and fits into His plan (Romans 8:28). (***See Purpose**> God's Deeds> Special Acts> Miracles> OT> Waters of Jericho,* TopicGuide page A53.)

▸ SPIRITUAL WARFARE

2:23 "Go away, baldy!" Have you ever mocked anyone for the way they looked? If so, did you fear that bears might actually appear out of nowhere and attack you? As strange as this sounds, this is exactly what happened here. Upon closer study, however, we see that these youths were using the same language that described Elijah's ascension on the chariot, so the kids may have been saying, "We've heard your crazy story about Elijah, so why don't you just join him in the sky?" But the mauling—wasn't that a little harsh? The youths' rejection of Elisha as God's primary mouthpiece was no joking matter. Elisha may have called down judgment upon them, but he was likely as surprised as anyone to see bears attacking them. This only underscores that God is not mocked without grave consequences (Proverbs 24:9). (***See Spiritual Warfare**> Resisting Sin and Evil> Consequences> Of Disobedience> God is not mocked,* TopicGuide page A46.)

3:4 Moab was a tribal kingdom located east of Israel across the Dead Sea. The people of Israel traveled through this land en route to inherit the Promised Land. Along the way, they were hindered by the king of this area. This began a long-standing grudge between these peoples.

3:7 After many years of strife between Israel and Judah, King Joram of the northern kingdom made an alliance with the southern kingdom. This alliance was mutually beneficial, since both kingdoms needed security against aggression from neighboring kingdoms.

10 “What should we do?” the king of Israel cried out. “The LORD has brought the three of
us here to let the king of Moab defeat us.”
3:11 11 But King Jehoshaphat of Judah asked, “Is there no prophet of the LORD with us? If there
1 Kgs 19:21; 22:7 is, we can ask the LORD what to do through him.”
One of King Joram’s officers replied, “Elisha son of Shaphat is here. He used to be Eli-
jah’s personal assistant.*”
12 Jehoshaphat said, “Yes, the LORD speaks through him.” So the kings of Israel, Judah,
and Edom went to consult with Elisha.
3:13 13 “Why are you coming to me?”* Elisha asked the king of Israel. “Go to the pagan proph-
1 Kgs 22:6-11, 22-25 ets of your father and mother!”
But King Joram of Israel said, “No! For it was the LORD who called us three kings here—
only to be defeated by the king of Moab!”
14 Elisha replied, “As surely as the LORD Almighty lives, whom I serve, I wouldn’t even
3:15 bother with you except for my respect for King Jehoshaphat of Judah. 15 Now bring me
1 Sam 16:23 someone who can play the harp.”
While the harp was being played, the power* of the LORD came upon Elisha, 16 and he
said, “This is what the LORD says: This dry valley will be filled with pools of water! 17 You
will see neither wind nor rain, says the LORD, but this valley will be filled with water. You
will have plenty for yourselves and your cattle and other animals. 18 But this is only a sim-
ple thing for the LORD, for He will make you victorious over the army of Moab! 19 You will
conquer the best of their towns, even the fortified ones. You will cut down all their good
trees, stop up all their springs, and ruin all their good land with stones.”
3:20 20 The next day at about the time when the morning sacrifice was offered, water sud-
Exod 29:39-40 denly appeared! It was flowing from the direction of Edom, and soon there was water
everywhere.
21 Meanwhile, when the people of Moab heard about the three armies marching against
them, they mobilized every man who was old enough to strap on a sword, and they sta-
tioned themselves along their border. 22 But when they got up the next morning, the sun
was shining across the water, making it appear red to the Moabites—like blood. 23 “It’s
blood!” the Moabites exclaimed. “The three armies must have attacked and killed each
other! Let’s go, men of Moab, and collect the plunder!”
24 But when the Moabites arrived at the Israelite camp, the army of Israel rushed out and
attacked them until they turned and ran. The army of Israel chased them into the land of
3:25 Isa 16:7 Moab, destroying everything as they went.* 25 They destroyed the towns, covered their
Jer 48:31, 36 good land with stones, stopped up all the springs, and cut down all the good trees. Finally,
only Kir-hareseth and its stone walls were left, but men with slings surrounded and at-
tacked it.

3:11 Hebrew *He used to pour water on the hands of Elijah.* 3:13 Hebrew *What is there in common between you and me?* 3:15 Hebrew *the hand.* 3:24 The meaning of the Hebrew is uncertain.

3:13-14 Elisha’s responses to the king of Israel revealed his utter contempt for those who had rejected God’s law and turned to pagan worship. Elisha recognized that the king in Judah, though not perfect, still acknowledged the Lord as God.

▶ BIBLE
3:17 Pools in the desert. God can use any means He chooses to rescue His people. The mountain water not only gave drink to the armies, but it allowed the armies to approach Moab without detection, for the dampness kept the dust raised by approaching armies to a minimum. The water also formed a fearsome illusion as it reflected the red mountains of Edom (*edom* means “red” in Hebrew). The Moabites thought they saw their enemy’s blood, when in fact their mistake cost them their own blood spilled on that plain. God knows exactly how to befuddle our enemies and save us from defeat. Trust that God’s people will never taste ultimate defeat with Christ as our mighty Warrior. (***See Bible***> *Unity> Christ> Christ is the “LORD God of Heaven’s Armies,”* TopicGuide page A10.)

3:20 The morning sacrifice was a daily ritual specified by God in Numbers 28:3-4. Elisha’s prediction of water from God came to pass at this time. It is interesting to note that when Elijah confronted the prophets of Baal at Mount Carmel, his prayer came at the time of the corresponding evening offering and was accompanied not by water but by fire from heaven.

26When the king of Moab saw that he was losing the battle, he led 700 of his swords-
men in a desperate attempt to break through the enemy lines near the king of Edom, but
they failed. 27Then the king of Moab took his oldest son, who would have been the next 3:27
king, and sacrificed him as a burnt offering on the wall. So there was great anger against Mic 6:7
Israel,* and the Israelites withdrew and returned to their own land.

ELISHA HELPS A POOR WIDOW

4 One day the widow of a member of the group of prophets came to Elisha and cried 4:1
out, "My husband who served you is dead, and you know how he feared the LORD. Lev 25:39-41, 48
But now a creditor has come, threatening to take my two sons as slaves." Neh 5:2-5
2"What can I do to help you?" Elisha asked. "Tell me, what do you have in the house?" 4:2
"Nothing at all, except a flask of olive oil," she replied. 1 Kgs 17:12
3And Elisha said, "Borrow as many empty jars as you can from your friends and neigh-
bors. 4Then go into your house with your sons and shut the door behind you. Pour olive
oil from your flask into the jars, setting each one aside when it is filled."
5So she did as she was told. Her sons kept bringing jars to her, and she filled one after
another. 6Soon every container was full to the brim!
"Bring me another jar," she said to one of her sons.
"There aren't any more!" he told her. And then the olive oil stopped flowing.
7When she told the man of God what had happened, he said to her, "Now sell the olive 4:7
oil and pay your debts, and you and your sons can live on what is left over." 1 Kgs 12:22

ELISHA AND THE WOMAN FROM SHUNEM

8One day Elisha went to the town of Shunem. A wealthy woman lived there, and she 4:8
urged him to come to her home for a meal. After that, whenever he passed that way, he Josh 19:18
would stop there for something to eat.
9She said to her husband, "I am sure this man who stops in from time to time is a holy
man of God. 10Let's build a small room for him on the roof and furnish it with a bed, a ta- 4:10
ble, a chair, and a lamp. Then he will have a place to stay whenever he comes by." Matt 10:41
11One day Elisha returned to Shunem, and he went up to this upper room to rest. 12He Rom 12:13
said to his servant Gehazi, "Tell the woman from Shunem I want to speak to her." When
she appeared, 13Elisha said to Gehazi, "Tell her, 'We appreciate the kind concern you have
shown us. What can we do for you? Can we put in a good word for you to the king or to the
commander of the army?'"
"No," she replied, "my family takes good care of me."

3:27 Or *So Israel's anger was great.* The meaning of the Hebrew is uncertain.

▸ **HOLINESS**
3:27 Sacrificing a child. Why is it that some people think that killing their children will make things better? In Elisha's day, the god Chemosh received human sacrifice and, in exchange, promised blessing and military victory. Child sacrifice was forbidden in Israel (Exodus 34:20), but the foolish Israelite armies were still impressed enough with this horrible spectacle that they withdrew from the city that held the rest of the royal family of Moab. But we should fear only God and not be intimidated by those who destroy their children. (***See Holiness****> Law and Grace> Law> Parents and children,* TopicGuide page A41.)

4:1-44 In this chapter, Elisha performs four miracles of mercy for the needy: providing oil to meet the financial needs of a poverty-stricken woman; providing a son (later brought back from death) for a childless woman; rendering poisonous food edible for famine-stricken people; and providing food for more than 100 people from a small amount of grain.

▸ **GOD**
4:2 "What can I do to help you?" Mercy should be a defining characteristic of God's people. Just as Elisha's mentor showed mercy to widows (1 Kings 17:15), Elisha himself demonstrated that he was called to a prophetic ministry that was defined by both kindness and sternness by caring for the widow and her son. Do not let your ministry be unbalanced—demonstrate the love of God by a constant flow of compassion (2 Corinthians 8:7). (***See God****> God's Nature> Personality> Emotion> God is compassionate and loving,* TopicGuide page A14.)

4:8 The village of Shunem, located on an important route through the Jezreel Valley, was 20 miles or more east of Mount Carmel toward the Jordan Valley. The location was so important that this small village is listed in ancient writings of foreign powers that sought to control this trade route.

14 Later Elisha asked Gehazi, "What can we do for her?"
Gehazi replied, "She doesn't have a son, and her husband is an old man."
4:15 15 "Call her back again," Elisha told him. When the woman returned, Elisha said to her as
Gen 18:14 she stood in the doorway, 16 "Next year at this time you will be holding a son in your
arms!"
"No, my lord!" she cried. "O man of God, don't deceive me and get my hopes up like that."
17 But sure enough, the woman soon became pregnant. And at that time the following
year she had a son, just as Elisha had said.
18 One day when her child was older, he went out to help his father, who was working
with the harvesters. 19 Suddenly he cried out, "My head hurts! My head hurts!"
His father said to one of the servants, "Carry him home to his mother."
20 So the servant took him home, and his mother held him on her lap. But around noon-
4:21 time he died. 21 She carried him up and laid him on the bed of the man of God, then shut
2 Kgs 4:32 the door and left him there. 22 She sent a message to her husband: "Send one of the ser-
vants and a donkey so that I can hurry to the man of God and come right back."
23 "Why go today?" he asked. "It is neither a new moon festival nor a Sabbath."
But she said, "It will be all right."
24 So she saddled the donkey and said to the servant, "Hurry! Don't slow down unless I
tell you to."
25 As she approached the man of God at Mount Carmel, Elisha saw her in the distance.
He said to Gehazi, "Look, the woman from Shunem is coming. 26 Run out to meet her and
ask her, 'Is everything all right with you, your husband, and your child?'"
"Yes," the woman told Gehazi, "everything is fine."
27 But when she came to the man of God at the mountain, she fell to the ground before
him and caught hold of his feet. Gehazi began to push her away, but the man of God said,
"Leave her alone. She is deeply troubled, but the LORD has not told me what it is."
28 Then she said, "Did I ask you for a son, my lord? And didn't I say, 'Don't deceive me
and get my hopes up'?"
4:29 29 Then Elisha said to Gehazi, "Get ready to travel*; take my staff and go! Don't talk to
Exod 4:17; 7:19; 14:16 anyone along the way. Go quickly and lay the staff on the child's face."
1 Kgs 18:46 30 But the boy's mother said, "As surely as the LORD lives and you yourself live, I won't go
home unless you go with me." So Elisha returned with her.
31 Gehazi hurried on ahead and laid the staff on the child's face, but nothing hap-
pened. There was no sign of life. He returned to meet Elisha and told him, "The child is
still dead."
32 When Elisha arrived, the child was indeed dead, lying there on the prophet's bed.
4:34 33 He went in alone and shut the door behind him and prayed to the LORD. 34 Then he lay
1 Kgs 17:21-23 down on the child's body, placing his mouth on the child's mouth, his eyes on the child's
eyes, and his hands on the child's hands. And as he stretched out on him, the child's body
began to grow warm again! 35 Elisha got up, walked back and forth across the room once,
and then stretched himself out again on the child. This time the boy sneezed seven times
and opened his eyes!

4:29 Hebrew *Bind up your loins.*

4:14 Ancient Near Eastern culture placed great weight on a male heir. To be without an heir was to be without future sustenance and without hope. The text says only that the woman had no son, but it seems to imply she was childless. Though this wealthy woman expressed no need, her need was great in the eyes of the culture of that day.

4:23 Most modern calendars are solar-based, but Israel's calendar was based on the phases of the moon (a lunar calendar). Each new moon was to be accompanied by a feast or festival. The Sabbath was the weekly observance instituted by God for rest and worship. As the apostle Paul points out, such outward ceremonies and rituals were shadows of the real thing—Jesus Christ (Colossians 2:16-17).

36Then Elisha summoned Gehazi. "Call the child's mother!" he said. And when she came
in, Elisha said, "Here, take your son!" 37She fell at his feet and bowed before him, over- 4:37
whelmed with gratitude. Then she took her son in her arms and carried him downstairs. Heb 11:35

MIRACLES DURING A FAMINE

38Elisha now returned to Gilgal, and there was a famine in the land. One day as the group 4:38
of prophets was seated before him, he said to his servant, "Put a large pot on the fire, and 2 Kgs 2:1; 8:1
make some stew for the rest of the group."

39One of the young men went out into the field to gather herbs and came back with a
pocketful of wild gourds. He shredded them and put them into the pot without realizing they
were poisonous. 40Some of the stew was served to the men. But after they had eaten a bite
or two they cried out, "Man of God, there's poison in this stew!" So they would not eat it.

41Elisha said, "Bring me some flour." Then he threw it into the pot and said, "Now it's all 4:41
right; go ahead and eat." And then it did not harm them. Exod 15:25 2 Kgs 2:21-22

42One day a man from Baal-shalishah brought the man of God a sack of fresh grain and
twenty loaves of barley bread made from the first grain of his harvest. Elisha said, "Give it
to the people so they can eat." 4:43

43"What?" his servant exclaimed. "Feed a hundred people with only this?" Luke 9:13

But Elisha repeated, "Give it to the people so they can eat, for this is what the LORD says: John 6:9, 12
Everyone will eat, and there will even be some left over!" 44And when they gave it to the 4:44
people, there was plenty for all and some left over, just as the LORD had promised. Matt 14:16, 20

THE HEALING OF NAAMAN

5 The king of Aram had great admiration for Naaman, the commander of his army, be- 5:1
cause through him the LORD had given Aram great victories. But though Naaman was Luke 4:27
a mighty warrior, he suffered from leprosy.*

2At this time Aramean raiders had invaded the land of Israel, and among their captives 5:2
was a young girl who had been given to Naaman's wife as a maid. 3One day the girl said 2 Kgs 6:23
to her mistress, "I wish my master would go to see the prophet in Samaria. He would heal
him of his leprosy."

4So Naaman told the king what the young girl from Israel had said. 5"Go and visit the 5:5
prophet," the king of Aram told him. "I will send a letter of introduction for you to take to the 1 Sam 9:7-8
king of Israel." So Naaman started out, carrying as gifts 750 pounds of silver, 150 pounds

5:1 Or *from a contagious skin disease.* The Hebrew word used here and throughout this passage can describe various skin diseases.

▶ GOD

4:36 God and miracles. Why does God perform miracles? In this case, many reasons are evident. First, God's character demanded it—He desired to demonstrate His mercy so that all would know that He was full of compassion. Second, God wanted to confirm that Elisha was His true prophet, speaking God's Word without error. Third, God wanted to draw Israel—the rich, the poor, the young, and the old—to Himself. Gracious miracles prove God's love and concern for His people. (***See God****> God's Nature> Unique> His miracles show that He alone is God,* TopicGuide page A15.)

▶ PURPOSE

4:38 Famine in the land. In homes that overflow with food, making a spoiled kettle of stew palatable (2 Kings 4:40) and making bread multiply (2 Kings 4:43) might not seem impressive. But if we were starving and there was very little food or water available, this type of miracle might be the most glorious thing we had ever seen. Live in gratitude for God's present blessing of food, clothing, and shelter. (***See Purpose****> God's Deeds> Judgment> Famine,* TopicGuide page A53.)

4:42-44 As with other miracles in this chapter, this miracle of multiplying food looked forward to Jesus and His miracles with bread and fish (the only miracle recorded by all four Gospels—see Matthew 14:13-21; Mark 6:32-44; Luke 9:10-17; and John 6:5-14). As Jesus raised people from the dead and multiplied food, all who saw and heard immediately thought of Elijah and Elisha. The miracles of Jesus served notice that One greater than these prophets had arrived in Israel.

5:1 Aram was a territory northeast of Israel in present-day Syria. This king was probably Ben-hadad II (see 2 Kings 8:7).

5:5 Even though Aram and Israel engaged in continual skirmishes and aggression, diplomatic practice in the ancient Near East allowed one king to send a messenger to a rival king with a letter of introduction. This letter allowed the messenger to carry on important business, whether personal or national.

of gold,* and ten sets of clothing. 6The letter to the king of Israel said: "With this letter I pre-
sent my servant Naaman. I want you to heal him of his leprosy."
5:7 7When the king of Israel read the letter, he tore his clothes in dismay and said, "This
Gen 30:2; 37:29 man sends me a leper to heal! Am I God, that I can give life and take it away? I can see that
1 Kgs 20:7 he's just trying to pick a fight with me."
8But when Elisha, the man of God, heard that the king of Israel had torn his clothes in
dismay, he sent this message to him: "Why are you so upset? Send Naaman to me, and he
will learn that there is a true prophet here in Israel."
9So Naaman went with his horses and chariots and waited at the door of Elisha's house.
5:10 John 9:7 10But Elisha sent a messenger out to him with this message: "Go and wash yourself seven
times in the Jordan River. Then your skin will be restored, and you will be healed of your
leprosy."
11But Naaman became angry and stalked away. "I thought he would certainly come out
to meet me!" he said. "I expected him to wave his hand over the leprosy and call on the
5:12 Prov 14:17; 19:11 name of the LORD his God and heal me! 12Aren't the rivers of Damascus, the Abana and the
Pharpar, better than any of the rivers of Israel? Why shouldn't I wash in them and be
healed?" So Naaman turned and went away in a rage.
13But his officers tried to reason with him and said, "Sir,* if the prophet had told you to
do something very difficult, wouldn't you have done it? So you should certainly obey him
5:14 Job 33:23-25 when he says simply, 'Go and wash and be cured!'" 14So Naaman went down to the Jor-
Luke 4:27; 5:13 dan River and dipped himself seven times, as the man of God had instructed him. And his
skin became as healthy as the skin of a young child's, and he was healed!
5:15 15Then Naaman and his entire party went back to find the man of God. They stood be-
1 Sam 17:46-47 fore him, and Naaman said, "Now I know that there is no God in all the world except in Is-
rael. So please accept a gift from your servant."
5:16 Gen 14:22-23 16But Elisha replied, "As surely as the LORD lives, whom I serve, I will not accept any
2 Kgs 3:14 gifts." And though Naaman urged him to take the gift, Elisha refused.
5:17 17Then Naaman said, "All right, but please allow me to load two of my mules with
Exod 20:24 earth from this place, and I will take it back home with me. From now on I will never
5:18 again offer burnt offerings or sacrifices to any other god except the LORD. 18However, may
2 Kgs 7:2 the LORD pardon me in this one thing: When my master the king goes into the temple
of the god Rimmon to worship there and leans on my arm, may the LORD pardon me
when I bow, too."
19"Go in peace," Elisha said. So Naaman started home again.

5:5 Hebrew *10 talents* [340 kilograms] *of silver, 6,000 shekels* [68 kilograms] *of gold.* 5:13 Hebrew *My father.*

▸ MINISTRY
5:8 "Send Naaman to me." For better or for worse, God's people attract attention. The way we speak and act—it's different from those around us. One reason why God wants you to perform excellent, Spirit-empowered ministry is to demonstrate to the watching and skeptical world that there are true people of God. God wants Spirit-controlled ambassadors shutting the accusing mouths of the wicked, instead filling them with blessing to God for sending us their way. Be a blessing to those around you. (***See Ministry****> Transformation> Fill and Subdue> Being salt and light in the world,* TopicGuide page A57.)

5:11-12 Naaman's reaction to the prospect of bathing in the Jordan is understandable. Through much of the year, this river is shallow and muddy. In comparison, the rivers of Aram, flowing from the snow-capped Mount Hermon, were beautiful and appealing.

5:16 Again we see that when one takes an oath ("as surely as the LORD lives"), there is no persuading the person to compromise.

▸ WORSHIP
5:17 Earth from Israel. What on earth did Naaman want with two loads of dirt? It was common for non-Israelites to believe that all gods were to be worshiped locally, in a holy place associated with their mightiest acts. Not wanting to disrespect God by worshiping Him in a totally foreign place, Naaman requested a supply of earth from Israel. Elisha did not discourage this culturally based sign of respect, but other passages of Scripture make it clear that God accepts people's worship from every mountain, hill, and valley (Psalm 67; 96; 1 Chronicles 16:23-33; John 4:21-24). (***See Worship****> NT> Our Role> Mind and Heart> Must be in respect and holy fear,* TopicGuide page A32.)

THE GREED OF GEHAZI

20 But Gehazi, the servant of Elisha, the man of God, said to himself, "My master should not 5:20
have let this Aramean get away without accepting any of his gifts. As surely as the LORD 2 Kgs 4:11-12, 31, 36
lives, I will chase after him and get something from him." 21 So Gehazi set off after Naaman.
When Naaman saw Gehazi running after him, he climbed down from his chariot and
went to meet him. "Is everything all right?" Naaman asked.
22 "Yes," Gehazi said, "but my master has sent me to tell you that two young prophets 5:22
from the hill country of Ephraim have just arrived. He would like 75 pounds* of silver and 2 Kgs 5:5
two sets of clothing to give to them."
23 "By all means, take twice as much* silver," Naaman insisted. He gave him two sets of
clothing, tied up the money in two bags, and sent two of his servants to carry the gifts for
Gehazi. 24 But when they arrived at the citadel,* Gehazi took the gifts from the servants and
sent the men back. Then he went and hid the gifts inside the house.
25 When he went in to his master, Elisha asked him, "Where have you been, Gehazi?"
"I haven't been anywhere," he replied.
26 But Elisha asked him, "Don't you realize that I was there in spirit when Naaman 5:26
stepped down from his chariot to meet you? Is this the time to receive money and cloth- 2 Kgs 5:16
ing, olive groves and vineyards, sheep and cattle, and male and female servants? 27 Be- 5:27
cause you have done this, you and your descendants will suffer from Naaman's leprosy Exod 4:6 Num 12:10
forever." When Gehazi left the room, he was covered with leprosy; his skin was white as
snow.

THE FLOATING AX HEAD

6 One day the group of prophets came to Elisha and told him, "As you can see, this 6:1
place where we meet with you is too small. 2 Let's go down to the Jordan River, where 2 Kgs 2:3, 5, 7
there are plenty of logs. There we can build a new place for us to meet."
"All right," he told them, "go ahead."
3 "Please come with us," someone suggested.
"I will," he said. 4 So he went with them.
When they arrived at the Jordan, they began cutting down trees. 5 But as one of them
was cutting a tree, his ax head fell into the river. "Oh, sir!" he cried. "It was a borrowed ax!"
6 "Where did it fall?" the man of God asked. When he showed him the place, Elisha cut a 6:6
stick and threw it into the water at that spot. Then the ax head floated to the surface. Exod 15:25
7 "Grab it," Elisha said. And the man reached out and grabbed it. 2 Kgs 2:21; 4:41

ELISHA TRAPS THE ARAMEANS

8 When the king of Aram was at war with Israel, he would confer with his officers and say,
"We will mobilize our forces at such and such a place."
9 But immediately Elisha, the man of God, would warn the king of Israel, "Do not go near 6:9 1 Kgs 20:13, 28 2 Kgs 6:12

5:22 Hebrew *1 talent* [34 kilograms]. 5:23 Hebrew *take 2 talents* [68 kilograms]. 5:24 Hebrew *the Ophel.*

5:20-27 Elisha refused monetary gifts and clothing in order to show that God's mercy cannot be bought and that grace is free. Though it may seem that God's judgment of Gehazi is harsh here, remember that his greed might have allowed someone to believe he or she could purchase God's favor.

▸ HOLINESS

5:26 Dangers in the pursuit of wealth. Love of money can make even the spiritually rich feel like paupers. Elisha turned down the fortune offered to him from Naaman, but Gehazi could not bear watching those two loaded donkeys waltz away with his retirement fund. But his immoral pursuit of personal wealth brought a curse upon him and his family. Take great care that your pursuit of financial security does not endanger you and your family, both physically and spiritually. (***See Holiness*** *> Disciplines> Of Abstinence> Stewardship,* TopicGuide page A42.)

6:1-7 It is tempting to conclude that this passage teaches us that we must be careful with borrowed tools or some similar moralism. But a closer look reveals that this passage is speaking about God rather than people. We are reminded that God not only sees and controls national affairs and armies, but He also knows the needs of people in their work. God helps the weak and broken, exerts control over even the laws of nature, and brings good out of apparent loss.

that place, for the Arameans are planning to mobilize their troops there." [10]So the king of
Israel would send word to the place indicated by the man of God. Time and again Elisha
warned the king, so that he would be on the alert there.
[11]The king of Aram became very upset over this. He called his officers together and de-
manded, "Which of you is the traitor? Who has been informing the king of Israel of my
plans?"
[12]"It's not us, my lord the king," one of the officers replied. "Elisha, the prophet in Israel,
tells the king of Israel even the words you speak in the privacy of your bedroom!"
6:13 [13]"Go and find out where he is," the king commanded, "so I can send troops to seize him."
Gen 37:17 And the report came back: "Elisha is at Dothan." [14]So one night the king of Aram sent a
great army with many chariots and horses to surround the city.
[15]When the servant of the man of God got up early the next morning and went outside,
there were troops, horses, and chariots everywhere. "Oh, sir, what will we do now?" the
6:16 young man cried to Elisha.
Exod 14:13 [16]"Don't be afraid!" Elisha told him. "For there are more on our side than on theirs!"
2 Chr 32:7 [17]Then Elisha prayed, "O LORD, open his eyes and let him see!" The LORD opened the
Rom 8:31 young man's eyes, and when he looked up, he saw that the hillside around Elisha was
6:17 2 Kgs 2:11-12 filled with horses and chariots of fire.
6:18 [18]As the Aramean army advanced toward him, Elisha prayed, "O LORD, please make
Gen 19:11 them blind." So the LORD struck them with blindness as Elisha had asked.
6:19 [19]Then Elisha went out and told them, "You have come the wrong way! This isn't the
1 Kgs 20:1 2 Kgs 3:1 right city! Follow me, and I will take you to the man you are looking for." And he led them
to the city of Samaria.
[20]As soon as they had entered Samaria, Elisha prayed, "O LORD, now open their eyes
and let them see." So the LORD opened their eyes, and they discovered that they were in
the middle of Samaria.
6:21 [21]When the king of Israel saw them, he shouted to Elisha, "My father, should I kill them?
1 Sam 24:4, 19; 26:8 Should I kill them?"
6:22 [22]"Of course not!" Elisha replied. "Do we kill prisoners of war? Give them food and drink
Deut 20:11 2 Chr 28:8-15 Rom 12:20 and send them home again to their master."

ELISHA AND THE ARAMEANS Elisha knew Aram's battle plans and kept Israel's king informed. The Aramean king tracked down Elisha at Dothan, but Elisha prayed that the Aramean army would be blinded. He then led the blind army into Samaria, Israel's capital city!

6:13-14 The village of Dothan was located southeast of Meggido toward Samaria in the central part of the northern kingdom of Israel.

▸ CHURCH

6:16 "There are more on our side than on theirs!" Do you sometimes wonder whether the church will survive the secular forces that attempt to snuff it out? God assures us that this will never happen (Matthew 16:18), but we tend to see this promise fulfilled through natural rather than supernatural means. But don't limit God's power simply to providence—God can protect His people in ways that boggle our imagination. (***See Church****> What> Many Titles> Sheep> The sheep trust the protection of the shepherd,* TopicGuide page A48.)

6:19 The city of Samaria was located on the northern edge of the central ridge in Israel, about 13 miles south of Dothan toward Jerusalem.

▸ GOD

6:22 Treatment of prisoners. Throughout these stories, the Bible repeats the theme that mercy marks authentic ministry. Elisha had as much to gain as anyone by slaughtering Israel's enemies—they had been sent to capture him. But God confirmed Elisha's calling by giving him a spirit of mercy toward those who sought to harm him. Remember—the merciful will obtain mercy (Matthew 5:7). (***See God****> God's Attributes> Merciful> God gives mercy to those who are merciful,* TopicGuide page A17.)

23 So the king made a great feast for them and then sent them home to their master. 6:23
After that, the Aramean raiders stayed away from the land of Israel. 2 Kgs 5:2

BEN-HADAD BESIEGES SAMARIA

24 Some time later, however, King Ben-hadad of Aram mustered his entire army and be- 6:24
sieged Samaria. 25 As a result, there was a great famine in the city. The siege lasted so long 1 Kgs 20:1
that a donkey's head sold for eighty pieces of silver, and a cup of dove's dung sold for five
pieces* of silver.
26 One day as the king of Israel was walking along the wall of the city, a woman called to
him, "Please help me, my lord the king!"
27 He answered, "If the LORD doesn't help you, what can I do? I have neither food from
the threshing floor nor wine from the press to give you." 28 But then the king asked, "What 6:28
is the matter?" Lev 26:29
She replied, "This woman said to me: 'Come on, let's eat your son today, then we will Deut 28:53-55
eat my son tomorrow.' 29 So we cooked my son and ate him. Then the next day I said to 6:29
her, 'Kill your son so we can eat him,' but she has hidden her son." Lev 26:29; Deut 28:53
30 When the king heard this, he tore his clothes in despair. And as the king walked along
the wall, the people could see that he was wearing burlap under his robe next to his skin.*
31 "May God strike me and even kill me if I don't separate Elisha's head from his shoulders 6:31
this very day," the king vowed. 1 Kgs 19:2
32 Elisha was sitting in his house with the elders of Israel when the king sent a messenger 6:32
to summon him. But before the messenger arrived, Elisha said to the elders, "A murderer 1 Kgs 18:3-4, 14
has sent a man to cut off my head. When he arrives, shut the door and keep him out. We Ezek 8:1; 14:1; 20:1
will soon hear his master's steps following him."
33 While Elisha was still saying this, the messenger arrived. And the king* said, "All this 6:33
misery is from the LORD! Why should I wait for the LORD any longer?" Isa 8:21

7 Elisha replied, "Listen to this message from the LORD! This is what the LORD says:
By this time tomorrow in the markets of Samaria, five quarts of choice flour will
cost only one piece of silver,* and ten quarts of barley grain will cost only one piece of
silver.*"
2 The officer assisting the king said to the man of God, "That couldn't happen even if 7:2 Gen 7:11
the LORD opened the windows of heaven!" 2 Kgs 5:18
But Elisha replied, "You will see it happen with your own eyes, but you won't be able to Mal 3:10
eat any of it!"

LEPERS VISIT THE ENEMY CAMP

3 Now there were four men with leprosy* sitting at the entrance of the city gates. "Why 7:3
should we sit here waiting to die?" they asked each other. 4 "We will starve if we stay here, Lev 13:45-46
but with the famine in the city, we will starve if we go back there. So we might as well go Num 5:1-4
out and surrender to the Aramean army. If they let us live, so much the better. But if they 7:4
kill us, we would have died anyway." 2 Kgs 6:24

6:25 Hebrew *sold for 80 shekels* [2 pounds, or 0.9 kilograms] *of silver, and ¼ of a cab* [0.3 liters] *of dove's dung sold for 5 shekels* [2 ounces, or 57 grams]. *Dove's dung* may be a variety of wild vegetable. **6:30** As in Greek version; Hebrew reads *wearing burlap next to his skin from the house.* **6:33** Hebrew *he.* **7:1a** Hebrew *1 seah* [6 liters] *of choice flour will cost 1 shekel* [0.4 ounces, or 11 grams]; also in 7:16, 18. **7:1b** Hebrew *2 seahs* [12 liters] *of barley grain will cost 1 shekel* [0.4 ounces, or 11 grams]; also in 7:16, 18. **7:3** Or *with a contagious skin disease.* The Hebrew word used here and throughout this passage can describe various skin diseases.

6:25 The Aramean siege of Samaria led to famine and desperation. People were paying high prices to obtain even the unclean parts of animals as food. And dung (usually free for the taking to be used as fuel for fires) became so scarce that it was bought and sold.

7:1 The prices Elisha prophesied for basic goods reflected more normal values. Thus, he was predicting that the severe conditions of famine and deprivation that the people were experiencing were about to suddenly end, and the economy would return to normal.

5 So at twilight they set out for the camp of the Arameans. But when they came to the
7:6 2 Sam 5:24 2 Chr 12:2-3 edge of the camp, no one was there! 6 For the Lord had caused the Aramean army to hear
the clatter of speeding chariots and the galloping of horses and the sounds of a great army
7:7 Ps 48:4-6 Prov 28:1 approaching. "The king of Israel has hired the Hittites and Egyptians* to attack us!" they
cried to one another. 7 So they panicked and ran into the night, abandoning their tents,
horses, donkeys, and everything else, as they fled for their lives.
8 When the lepers arrived at the edge of the camp, they went into one tent after another,
eating and drinking wine; and they carried off silver and gold and clothing and hid it.
9 Finally, they said to each other, "This is not right. This is a day of good news, and we
aren't sharing it with anyone! If we wait until morning, some calamity will certainly fall
upon us. Come on, let's go back and tell the people at the palace."
10 So they went back to the city and told the gatekeepers what had happened. "We went
out to the Aramean camp," they said, "and no one was there! The horses and donkeys
were tethered and the tents were all in order, but there wasn't a single person around!"
11 Then the gatekeepers shouted the news to the people in the palace.

ISRAEL PLUNDERS THE CAMP

7:12 Josh 8:6-12 2 Kgs 6:25-29 12 The king got out of bed in the middle of the night and told his officers, "I know what has
happened. The Arameans know we are starving, so they have left their camp and have
hidden in the fields. They are expecting us to leave the city, and then they will take us
alive and capture the city."
13 One of his officers replied, "We had better send out scouts to check into this. Let them
take five of the remaining horses. If something happens to them, it will be no worse than if
they stay here and die with the rest of us."
14 So two chariots with horses were prepared, and the king sent scouts to see what had
happened to the Aramean army. 15 They went all the way to the Jordan River, following a
trail of clothing and equipment that the Arameans had thrown away in their mad rush to es-
7:16 2 Kgs 7:1 cape. The scouts returned and told the king about it. 16 Then the people of Samaria rushed
out and plundered the Aramean camp. So it was true that five quarts of choice flour were
sold that day for one piece of silver, and ten quarts of barley grain were sold for one piece of
7:17 2 Kgs 7:2 silver, just as the LORD had promised. 17 The king appointed his officer to control the traffic at
the gate, but he was knocked down and trampled to death as the people rushed out.
So everything happened exactly as the man of God had predicted when the king came
to his house. 18 The man of God had said to the king, "By this time tomorrow in the markets
of Samaria, five quarts of choice flour will cost one piece of silver, and ten quarts of barley
grain will cost one piece of silver."
7:19 2 Kgs 7:2 19 The king's officer had replied, "That couldn't happen even if the LORD opened the win-
dows of heaven!" And the man of God had said, "You will see it happen with your own

7:6 Possibly *and the people of Muzur,* a district near Cilicia.

▶ HOLINESS

7:6 A clatter of chariots. What do you fear the most? Is it national disaster or personal misfortune? Mental or physical illness? Dying of old age? This passage shows two groups of people—lepers and the Aramean army. One group was powerless and thus feared nothing, not even death. The other was powerful, yet they fled at what they thought was the sound of chariots and horses. When we take a position of weakness and admit our utter lack of resources, we can experience the freedom those lepers felt as they marched into the Aramean camp. But if we feign strength and rely on our own resources, our courage will fail us, and we will never know the strength that God gives to those who trust in Him alone. (***See Holiness***> *Submission> Trusting God> Overcoming,* TopicGuide page A40.)

7:15 The route from the city of Samaria to the Jordan River went southeast, down from the central ridge through tight and often quite steep valleys—a route difficult to manage with loads of gear. It was also a considerable distance—at least 25 miles.

▶ WORSHIP

7:19 "That couldn't happen!" You can disbelieve politicians and mistrust your friends' fish stories with few ill effects. Ministers will even say things that need to be questioned. But doubting God's Word is a dangerous decision. The longer you live in doubt of God, the longer you risk the consequences. Make a list of all the things you struggle to believe in the Bible, and pray that God will give you the insight and faith to trust every word in His book. (***See Worship***> *NT> Reverence> Fear/awe of God is characteristic of faith,* TopicGuide page A32.)

eyes, but you won't be able to eat any of it!" 20And so it was, for the people trampled him
to death at the gate!

THE WOMAN FROM SHUNEM RETURNS HOME

8 Elisha had told the woman whose son he had brought back to life, "Take your family
and move to some other place, for the LORD has called for a famine on Israel that will
last for seven years." 2So the woman did as the man of God instructed. She took her family
and settled in the land of the Philistines for seven years.
3After the famine ended she returned from the land of the Philistines, and she went to
see the king about getting back her house and land. 4As she came in, the king was talking
with Gehazi, the servant of the man of God. The king had just said, "Tell me some stories
about the great things Elisha has done." 5And Gehazi was telling the king about the time
Elisha had brought a boy back to life. At that very moment, the mother of the boy walked
in to make her appeal to the king about her house and land.
"Look, my lord the king!" Gehazi exclaimed. "Here is the woman now, and this is her
son—the very one Elisha brought back to life!"
6"Is this true?" the king asked her. And she told him the story. So he directed one of his
officials to see that everything she had lost was restored to her, including the value of any
crops that had been harvested during her absence.

HAZAEL MURDERS BEN-HADAD

7Elisha went to Damascus, the capital of Aram, where King Ben-hadad lay sick. When
someone told the king that the man of God had come, 8the king said to Hazael, "Take
a gift to the man of God. Then tell him to ask the LORD, 'Will I recover from this illness?'"
9So Hazael loaded down forty camels with the finest products of Damascus as a gift for
Elisha. He went to him and said, "Your servant Ben-hadad, the king of Aram, has sent me
to ask, 'Will I recover from this illness?'"
10And Elisha replied, "Go and tell him, 'You will surely recover.' But actually the LORD has
shown me that he will surely die!" 11Elisha stared at Hazael* with a fixed gaze until Hazael
became uneasy.* Then the man of God started weeping.
12"What's the matter, my lord?" Hazael asked him.
Elisha replied, "I know the terrible things you will do to the people of Israel. You will
burn their fortified cities, kill their young men with the sword, dash their little children to
the ground, and rip open their pregnant women!"
13Hazael responded, "How could a nobody like me* ever accomplish such great
things?"
Elisha answered, "The LORD has shown me that you are going to be the king of Aram."
14When Hazael left Elisha and went back, the king asked him, "What did Elisha tell you?"
And Hazael replied, "He told me that you will surely recover."
15But the next day Hazael took a blanket, soaked it in water, and held it over the king's
face until he died. Then Hazael became the next king of Aram.

8:1 Gen 41:27; Ps 105:16; Hag 1:11
8:2 2 Kgs 4:18, 31-35
8:4 2 Kgs 4:11-12; 5:20-27
8:5 2 Kgs 4:34-35
8:7 2 Kgs 6:24
8:8 1 Kgs 14:3; 19:15
8:11 Luke 19:41
8:12 2 Kgs 10:32-33; 12:17; 13:3; 15:16
8:13 1 Sam 17:43; 2 Sam 9:8; 1 Kgs 19:15

8:11a Hebrew *He stared at him.* 8:11b The meaning of the Hebrew is uncertain. 8:13 Hebrew *a dog.*

8:2 The land of the Philistines lay along the Mediterranean coastal plain well to the south of Mount Carmel. This was a fertile area, less susceptible to famine than areas further inland.

▸ SALVATION
8:6 "Is this true?" Elisha's reputation gave a leper (Gehazi, see 2 Kings 5:20-28) entrance to the king's court and a displaced woman the welcome of a queen. God's favor on us will sometimes translate into favor with others, and we should use that for His glory (Luke 2:52). Who knows what doors God may open for you? (***See Salvation***> *Receiving*> *How*> *Submit to God's grace/special favor,* TopicGuide page A22.)

8:7 The city of Damascus is about 135 miles north of Jerusalem. It is one of the oldest continuously inhabited cities in the world. During the biblical era, Damascus was located on a major trade route from Egypt toward Asia, so whoever controlled this city controlled much wealth and power.

JEHORAM RULES IN JUDAH

8:16-24 16 Jehoram son of King Jehoshaphat of Judah began to rule over Judah in the fifth year of
//2 Chr 21:5-20 the reign of Joram son of Ahab, king of Israel. 17 Jehoram was thirty-two years old when he
8:17 became king, and he reigned in Jerusalem eight years. 18 But Jehoram followed the exam-
2 Chr 21:5-10 ple of the kings of Israel and was as wicked as King Ahab, for he had married one of
8:19 Ahab's daughters. So Jehoram did what was evil in the LORD's sight. 19 But the LORD did not
2 Sam 7:12-15 want to destroy Judah, for He had made a covenant with David and promised that his de-
1 Kgs 11:36 scendants would continue to rule, shining like a lamp forever.
8:20 20 During Jehoram's reign, the Edomites revolted against Judah and crowned their own
1 Kgs 22:47 king. 21 So Jehoram* went with all his chariots to attack the town of Zair.* The Edomites sur-
2 Kgs 3:9, 26 rounded him and his chariot commanders, but he went out at night and attacked them*
8:22 under cover of darkness. But Jehoram's army deserted him and fled to their homes. 22 So
Gen 27:39-40 Edom has been independent from Judah to this day. The town of Libnah also revolted
Josh 21:13 about that same time.
8:24 23 The rest of the events in Jehoram's reign and everything he did are recorded in *The*
2 Chr 21:20; 22:1 *Book of the History of the Kings of Judah.* 24 When Jehoram died, he was buried with his an-
cestors in the City of David. Then his son Ahaziah became the next king.

AHAZIAH RULES IN JUDAH

8:25-29 25 Ahaziah son of Jehoram began to rule over Judah in the twelfth year of the reign of Jo-
//2 Chr 22:1-6 8:26 ram son of Ahab, king of Israel.
2 Kgs 11:1 26 Ahaziah was twenty-two years old when he became king, and he reigned in Jerusa-
8:27 lem one year. His mother was Athaliah, a granddaughter of King Omri of Israel. 27 Ahaziah
1 Kgs 16:30 followed the evil example of King Ahab's family. He did what was evil in the LORD's sight,
just as Ahab's family had done, for he was related by marriage to the family of Ahab.
28 Ahaziah joined Joram son of Ahab, the king of Israel, in his war against King Hazael of
8:29 Aram at Ramoth-gilead. When the Arameans wounded King Joram in the battle, 29 he re-
2 Kgs 9:14-15 turned to Jezreel to recover from the wounds he had received at Ramoth.* Because Joram
2 Chr 22:5-6 was wounded, King Ahaziah of Judah went to Jezreel to visit him.

JEHU ANOINTED KING OF ISRAEL

9:1 **9** Meanwhile, Elisha the prophet had summoned a member of the group of prophets.
1 Sam 10:1; 16:1 1 Kgs 1:39 "Get ready to travel,"* he told him, "and take this flask of olive oil with you. Go to
2 Kgs 8:28 Ramoth-gilead, 2 and find Jehu son of Jehoshaphat, son of Nimshi. Call him into a private
9:3 1 Kgs 19:16 room away from his friends, 3 and pour the oil over his head. Say to him, 'This is what
the LORD says: I anoint you to be the king over Israel.' Then open the door and run for
your life!"

8:21a Hebrew *Joram,* a variant spelling of Jehoram; also in 8:23, 24. 8:21b Greek version reads *Seir.* 8:21c Or *he went out and escaped.* The meaning of the Hebrew is uncertain. 8:29 Hebrew *Ramah,* a variant spelling of Ramoth. 9:1 Hebrew *Bind up your loins.*

8:19 The covenant with David was a reaffirmation by God of the promises made to Abraham, Isaac, and Jacob. God reiterated these promises to Moses and then extended them to David in 2 Samuel 7:12-16. In declaring the first covenant with Abraham in Genesis 15, God took an oath that He would uphold the promise on penalty of His own death (an impossibility). Judah was the continuing remnant of David's kingdom.

8:20-22 The Edomites were related to the people of Israel and lived in a region southeast of the Dead Sea on the Transjordanian plateau. The comment here that the area of Edom was free "to this day" is an indication that 2 Kings was written to a specific people at a specific time.

8:25 If Joram's ascension year is included in his 12 years, then the tension regarding the length of his reign given in 9:29 is resolved.

9:2-3 It fell to Elisha to fulfill a task first given to Elijah (1 Kings 19:16). Jehu was to be anointed as an instrument of God's judgment on the house of Ahab. Anointing people set them apart for specific tasks and offices (1 Samuel 10:1; 2 Samuel 2:7; 1 Kings 19:15; 2 Kings 11:12; 23:30). Jehu's father, Jehoshaphat, was not the king of Judah by the same name.

[4]So the young prophet did as he was told and went to Ramoth-gilead. [5]When he arrived
there, he found Jehu sitting around with the other army officers. "I have a message for
you, Commander," he said.
"For which one of us?" Jehu asked.
"For you, Commander," he replied.
[6]So Jehu left the others and went into the house. Then the young prophet poured the oil
over Jehu's head and said, "This is what the LORD, the God of Israel, says: I anoint you king
over the LORD's people, Israel. [7]You are to destroy the family of Ahab, your master. In this
way, I will avenge the murder of My prophets and all the LORD's servants who were killed
by Jezebel. [8]The entire family of Ahab must be wiped out. I will destroy every one of his
male descendants, slave and free alike, anywhere in Israel. [9]I will destroy the family of
Ahab as I destroyed the families of Jeroboam son of Nebat and of Baasha son of Ahijah.
[10]Dogs will eat Ahab's wife Jezebel at the plot of land in Jezreel, and no one will bury her."
Then the young prophet opened the door and ran.
[11]Jehu went back to his fellow officers, and one of them asked him, "What did that mad-
man want? Is everything all right?"
"You know how a man like that babbles on," Jehu replied.
[12]"You're hiding something," they said. "Tell us."
So Jehu told them, "He said to me, 'This is what the LORD says: I have anointed you to be
king over Israel.'"
[13]Then they quickly spread out their cloaks on the bare steps and blew the ram's horn,
shouting, "Jehu is king!"

9:6 1 Kgs 19:16
9:7 Deut 32:35; 1 Sam 25:22; 1 Kgs 18:3-4; 21:15, 21; 2 Kgs 10:17
9:9 1 Kgs 14:10; 15:29; 16:3, 11
9:10 1 Kgs 21:23; 2 Kgs 9:35-36
9:13 2 Sam 15:10; 1 Kgs 1:34, 39; Matt 21:8

JEHU KILLS JORAM AND AHAZIAH

[14]So Jehu son of Jehoshaphat, son of Nimshi, led a conspiracy against King Joram.
(Now Joram had been with the army at Ramoth-gilead, defending Israel against the
forces of King Hazael of Aram. [15]But King Joram* was wounded in the fighting and re-
turned to Jezreel to recover from his wounds.) So Jehu told the men with him, "If you want
me to be king, don't let anyone leave town and go to Jezreel to report what we have
done."
[16]Then Jehu got into a chariot and rode to Jezreel to find King Joram, who was lying
there wounded. King Ahaziah of Judah was there, too, for he had gone to visit him. [17]The
watchman on the tower of Jezreel saw Jehu and his company approaching, so he shouted
to Joram, "I see a company of troops coming!"
"Send out a rider to ask if they are coming in peace," King Joram ordered.
[18]So a horseman went out to meet Jehu and said, "The king wants to know if you are
coming in peace."
Jehu replied, "What do you know about peace? Fall in behind me!"
The watchman called out to the king, "The messenger has met them, but he's not
returning."
[19]So the king sent out a second horseman. He rode up to them and said, "The king
wants to know if you come in peace."

9:14-15 2 Kgs 8:28-29

9:15 Hebrew *Jehoram*, a variant spelling of Joram; also in 9:17, 21, 22, 23, 24.

9:7-10 Ahab and his wife, Jezebel, actively persecuted the prophets of God and sought to eliminate them from the nation of Israel (1 Kings 18:4, 13; 19:2). For that reason, God determined to bring judgment upon them. Elijah had pronounced these judgments earlier (1 Kings 21:21-23). Ahab had already died in battle, but now his family would be wiped out, just as the dynasties of Jeroboam and Baasha were overthrown and eradicated for their unfaithfulness and idolatry (1 Kings 14:7-18; 16:1-4). Jezebel would suffer a grotesque fate and be denied a proper burial—a sign of disgrace (Jeremiah 8:2; 16:4). Elijah did not explicitly mention the lack of burial, but it was certainly implied by his words about the fate of her body.

9:11-13 As Jehu spoke with his officers, he attempted to casually dismiss the prophet as a madman. But his officers, perhaps noticing the oil dripping from his head, pressed Jehu to reveal the prophet's words. Upon hearing the content of the message, they threw their support to Jehu and entered into open revolt.

Again Jehu answered, "What do you know about peace? Fall in behind me!"
9:20 20The watchman exclaimed, "The messenger has met them, but he isn't returning ei-
2 Sam 18:27 ther! It must be Jehu son of Nimshi, for he's driving like a madman."
9:21-29 21"Quick! Get my chariot ready!" King Joram commanded.
1 Kgs 21:1 //2 Chr 22:7-9 Then King Joram of Israel and King Ahaziah of Judah rode out in their chariots to meet
9:22 Jehu. They met him at the plot of land that had belonged to Naboth of Jezreel. 22King Jo-
1 Kgs 16:31; 18:19 ram demanded, "Do you come in peace, Jehu?"
Jehu replied, "How can there be peace as long as the idolatry and witchcraft of your
mother, Jezebel, are all around us?"
9:23 23Then King Joram turned the horses around* and fled, shouting to King Ahaziah, "Trea-
2 Kgs 11:14 son, Ahaziah!" 24But Jehu drew his bow and shot Joram between the shoulders. The arrow
9:24 1 Kgs 22:34 pierced his heart, and he sank down dead in his chariot.
25Jehu said to Bidkar, his officer, "Throw him into the plot of land that belonged to Na-
9:25 1 Kgs 21:1, 19 both of Jezreel. Do you remember when you and I were riding along behind his father,
Ahab? The LORD pronounced this message against him: 26'I solemnly swear that I will re-
9:26 1 Kgs 21:19 pay him here on this plot of land, says the LORD, for the murder of Naboth and his sons that
9:27 I saw yesterday.' So throw him out on Naboth's property, just as the LORD said."
Josh 17:11 Judg 1:27 27When King Ahaziah of Judah saw what was happening, he fled along the road to
2 Chr 22:7, 9 Beth-haggan. Jehu rode after him, shouting, "Shoot him, too!" So they shot Ahaziah in his
9:28 chariot at the Ascent of Gur, near Ibleam. He was able to go on as far as Megiddo, but he
2 Kgs 23:30 died there. 28His servants took him by chariot to Jerusalem, where they buried him with
9:29 his ancestors in the City of David. 29Ahaziah had become king over Judah in the eleventh
2 Kgs 8:25, 28 year of the reign of Joram son of Ahab.

THE DEATH OF JEZEBEL

9:30 30When Jezebel, the queen mother, heard that Jehu had come to Jezreel, she painted her
Jer 4:30 Ezek 23:40 eyelids and fixed her hair and sat at a window. 31When Jehu entered the gate of the pal-
9:31 ace, she shouted at him, "Have you come in peace, you murderer? You're just like Zimri,
1 Kgs 16:9-20 who murdered his master!"*
32Jehu looked up and saw her at the window and shouted, "Who is on my side?" And
two or three eunuchs looked out at him. 33"Throw her down!" Jehu yelled. So they threw
her out the window, and her blood spattered against the wall and on the horses. And Jehu
trampled her body under his horses' hooves.
9:34 1 Kgs 16:30-31 34Then Jehu went into the palace and ate and drank. Afterward he said, "Someone go
and bury this cursed woman, for she is the daughter of a king." 35But when they went out
to bury her, they found only her skull, her feet, and her hands.

9:23 Hebrew *turned his hands.* 9:31 See 1 Kgs 16:9-10, where Zimri killed his master, King Elah.

9:20 Jehu was identified by his reckless driving. Ironically, the Hebrew word translated "like a madman" is derived from the same root used to describe the prophet in 9:11.

9:21 These events transpired in the field that had belonged to Naboth—an instance of poetic justice, since Joram's parents, Ahab and Jezebel, conspired against Naboth and plotted his murder in order to confiscate his land. It was at this same place that Elijah prophesied the destruction of Ahab's family (1 Kings 21).

▸ SPIRITUAL WARFARE

9:22 Surrendering to evil. Too often we make an uneasy peace with the idolatry and evil around (and inside) us. Rather than take up the sword of the Spirit and put on the helmet of salvation, we prefer to relax and hope our own sins and the ones around us don't cause too much trouble. We must not be satisfied with the status quo. We must not be satisfied with simply not getting any worse. God empowers us to grow in grace, and that means sinning less and loving more (2 Corinthians 13:7, 9). (***See Spiritual Warfare****> Resisting Sin and Evil> Standing Firm> Empowered to obey,* TopicGuide page A46.)

9:27 King Ahaziah of Judah was related to the family of Ahab through his marriage to Ahab's daughter, Athaliah. Ahaziah was not, however, a descendant of Ahab. His murder commenced Jehu's ruthless rampage, during which he drastically exceeded his prophetic mandate. The locations mentioned suggest that Ahaziah was fleeing south toward Samaria or Jerusalem.

9:31 Zimri assassinated his king (1 Kings 16:8-15) only to reign in his place for a mere seven days before suffering a similar fate.

36When they returned and told Jehu, he stated, "This fulfills the message from the LORD, 9:36
which he spoke through His servant Elijah from Tishbe: 'At the plot of land in Jezreel, dogs 1 Kgs 21:23
will eat Jezebel's body. 37Her remains will be scattered like dung on the plot of land in Jez- 9:37
reel, so that no one will be able to recognize her.'" Jer 8:2

JEHU KILLS AHAB'S FAMILY

10 Ahab had seventy sons living in the city of Samaria. So Jehu wrote letters and sent 10:1
them to Samaria, to the elders and officials of the city,* and to the guardians of King 1 Kgs 16:24-29
Ahab's sons. He said, 2"The king's sons are with you, and you have at your disposal chariots,
horses, a fortified city, and weapons. As soon as you receive this letter, 3select the best quali-
fied of your master's sons to be your king, and prepare to fight for Ahab's dynasty."
4But they were paralyzed with fear and said, "We've seen that two kings couldn't stand
against this man! What can we do?"
5So the palace and city administrators, together with the elders and the guardians of the 10:5
king's sons, sent this message to Jehu: "We are your servants and will do anything you tell Josh 9:8, 11
us. We will not make anyone king; do whatever you think is best."
6Jehu responded with a second letter: "If you are on my side and are going to obey
me, bring the heads of your master's sons to me at Jezreel by this time tomorrow." Now
the seventy sons of the king were being cared for by the leaders of Samaria, where they
had been raised since childhood. 7When the letter arrived, the leaders killed all seventy 10:7
of the king's sons. They placed their heads in baskets and presented them to Jehu at Judg 9:5
Jezreel. 2 Kgs 11:1
8A messenger went to Jehu and said, "They have brought the heads of the king's sons."
So Jehu ordered, "Pile them in two heaps at the entrance of the city gate, and leave
them there until morning."
9In the morning he went out and spoke to the crowd that had gathered around them.
"You are not to blame," he told them. "I am the one who conspired against my master and
killed him. But who killed all these? 10You can be sure that the message of the LORD that 10:10
was spoken concerning Ahab's family will not fail. The LORD declared through His servant 1 Kgs 21:29
Elijah that this would happen." 11Then Jehu killed all who were left of Ahab's relatives liv- 2 Kgs 9:7-10
ing in Jezreel and all his important officials, his personal friends, and his priests. So Ahab
was left without a single survivor.
12Then Jehu set out for Samaria. Along the way, while he was at Beth-eked of the Shep-
herds, 13he met some relatives of King Ahaziah of Judah. "Who are you?" he asked them. 10:13
And they replied, "We are relatives of King Ahaziah. We are going to visit the sons of 2 Kgs 8:24, 29
King Ahab and the sons of the queen mother." 2 Chr 22:8
14"Take them alive!" Jehu shouted to his men. And they captured all forty-two of them
and killed them at the well of Beth-eked. None of them escaped.

10:1 As in some Greek manuscripts and Latin Vulgate (see also 10:6); Hebrew reads *of Jezreel*.

▶ SPIRITUAL WARFARE

9:39 Rejoicing in pain. When it's time for budget cuts again at your job and people you have known for years are laid off, do you secretly rejoice at such an occurrence, knowing you may get a promotion from it? Jezebel thought that she was now the sole ruler of Israel, so she dressed in her finest and prepared to deal with the rebel who stood in her way. But her cruelty meant the palace staff hated her, so they joined Jehu's rebellion and threw her down to the street below. She received the dishonor that she deserved for promoting such idolatry among God's people. (***See Spiritual Warfare****> Resisting Sin and Evil> Consequences> Of Disobedience> God may allow consequences to run their course,* TopicGuide page A46.)

10:2-4 Jehu's letter was a sarcastic challenge to the leaders of the city. He dared them to employ their military advantage against his forces. The rub to the challenge may have been the charge to fight for Ahab's dynasty. The leaders proved unwilling to do that, which may indicate that loyalty to Ahab's corrupt dynasty was already wavering. They were probably also keenly aware that Jehu had already dispatched two kings: Joram and Ahaziah.

10:11 Jehu exceeded the commission given to him by God through Elijah and Elisha (1 Kings 21:21-24; 2 Kings 9:7-10) by executing anyone who had the slightest connection to Ahab and his administration. Jehu's ruthless extermination of Ahab's government sent the nation into a period of instability and disorder.

10:15 15 When Jehu left there, he met Jehonadab son of Recab, who was coming to meet him.
2 Kgs 10:23 After they had greeted each other, Jehu said to him, "Are you as loyal to me as I am to you?"
Jer 35:6-19 "Yes, I am," Jehonadab replied.
"If you are," Jehu said, "then give me your hand." So Jehonadab put out his hand, and
Jehu helped him into the chariot. 16 Then Jehu said, "Now come with me, and see how de-
voted I am to the LORD." So Jehonadab rode along with him.
10:17 17 When Jehu arrived in Samaria, he killed everyone who was left there from Ahab's
2 Kgs 9:8 family, just as the LORD had promised through Elijah.

JEHU KILLS THE PRIESTS OF BAAL

10:18 18 Then Jehu called a meeting of all the people of the city and said to them, "Ahab's wor-
1 Kgs 16:31-32 ship of Baal was nothing compared to the way I will worship him! 19 Therefore, summon
all the prophets and worshipers of Baal, and call together all his priests. See to it that
every one of them comes, for I am going to offer a great sacrifice to Baal. Anyone who
fails to come will be put to death." But Jehu's cunning plan was to destroy all the worship-
ers of Baal.
10:20 20 Then Jehu ordered, "Prepare a solemn assembly to worship Baal!" So they did. 21 He
Exod 32:5 sent messengers throughout all Israel summoning those who worshiped Baal. They all
came—not a single one remained behind—and they filled the temple of Baal from one end
to the other. 22 And Jehu instructed the keeper of the wardrobe, "Be sure that every wor-
shiper of Baal wears one of these robes." So robes were given to them.
23 Then Jehu went into the temple of Baal with Jehonadab son of Recab. Jehu said to the
worshipers of Baal, "Make sure no one who worships the LORD is here—only those who
worship Baal." 24 So they were all inside the temple to offer sacrifices and burnt offerings.
Now Jehu had stationed eighty of his men outside the building and had warned them, "If
you let anyone escape, you will pay for it with your own life."
10:25 25 As soon as Jehu had finished sacrificing the burnt offering, he commanded his guards
1 Sam 22:17 and officers, "Go in and kill all of them. Don't let a single one escape!" So they killed them
1 Kgs 18:40 all with their swords, and the guards and officers dragged their bodies outside.* Then
10:26 1 Kgs 14:23 Jehu's men went into the innermost fortress* of the temple of Baal. 26 They dragged out the
2 Kgs 3:2 sacred pillar* used in the worship of Baal and burned it. 27 They smashed the sacred pillar
and wrecked the temple of Baal, converting it into a public toilet, as it remains to this day.

10:25a Or *they left their bodies lying there;* or *they threw them out into the outermost court.* 10:25b Hebrew *city.* 10:26 As in Greek and Syriac versions and Latin Vulgate; Hebrew reads *sacred pillars.*

10:15 Jehonadab was the leader of a religious order called Recabites (named after Jehonadab's father, Recab), who maintained a strict nomadic tradition (see Jeremiah 35). Jehonadab apparently shared Jehu's reforming zeal, and his support must have added some legitimacy to Jehu's actions.

▶ ADOPTION
10:16 Outside of our authority. Is this how those who are zealous for God's will should act? Jehu acted as prophesied, but not as God wanted. The prophet Hosea later criticized him for his tactics (Hosea 1:4). God no longer calls us to take up actual swords against idolaters; instead He gives us greater weapons: prayer, fasting, and all the spiritual weapons the church has to batter down the very gates of hell (Matthew 16:18). (***See Adoption****> With Christ> Servants> Provided spiritual weapons,* TopicGuide page A37.)

10:18-27 Jehu proceeded to purge Israel of the worship of Baal (see note at 1 Kings 16:29-31), but his actions once again were devious, calculated, and ruthless. He secured the trust of the priests and lured them into a trap by feigning deep devotion to Baal. Jehu employed a clever—and morbid—play on words: the word translated "sacrifice" (2 Kings 10:19) can also refer to the "slaughter" of apostates (1 Kings 13:2; 2 Kings 23:20). Not only did he slaughter the followers and priests of Baal, he also demolished all of the structures associated with Baal worship. By converting the temple of Baal into a public toilet, Jehu defiled it, heaped scorn on Baal, and made sure that the site was never used for the worship of Baal again.

▶ SPIRITUAL WARFARE
10:27 God's enemies are humiliated. God has always been merciful to His enemies—the fact that you are reading this study Bible and not suffering eternal punishment for your sins is all the proof you should need. Yet there are times when God decides that the time for judgment has come, and that time was fast approaching for the followers of Baal. They bragged that Baal was the master of all, but Jehu demonstrated that the flimsiest of lies could completely destroy Baal and his followers. Pray for the enemies of God's kingdom that they will turn to God before it is too late. (***See Spiritual Warfare****> Resisting Sin and Evil> Consequences> Of Disobedience> Death,* TopicGuide page A46.)

28In this way, Jehu destroyed every trace of Baal worship from Israel. 29He did not, how- 10:29
ever, destroy the gold calves at Bethel and Dan, with which Jeroboam son of Nebat had 1 Kgs 12:28-30;
caused Israel to sin. 13:33-34
30Nonetheless the LORD said to Jehu, "You have done well in following My instructions 10:30 2 Kgs 15:12
to destroy the family of Ahab. Therefore, your descendants will be kings of Israel down to
the fourth generation." 31But Jehu did not obey the Law of the LORD, the God of Israel, with
all his heart. He refused to turn from the sins that Jeroboam had led Israel to commit.

THE DEATH OF JEHU

32At about that time the LORD began to cut down the size of Israel's territory. King Hazael 10:32
conquered several sections of the country 33east of the Jordan River, including all of Gile- 2 Kgs 8:12; 13:22, 25
ad, Gad, Reuben, and Manasseh. He conquered the area from the town of Aroer by the
Arnon Gorge to as far north as Gilead and Bashan.
34The rest of the events in Jehu's reign—everything he did and all his achievements—are
recorded in *The Book of the History of the Kings of Israel.*
35When Jehu died, he was buried in Samaria. Then his son Jehoahaz became the next
king. 36In all, Jehu reigned over Israel from Samaria for twenty-eight years.

QUEEN ATHALIAH RULES IN JUDAH

11 When Athaliah, the mother of King Ahaziah of Judah, learned that her son was 11:1-21
dead, she began to destroy the rest of the royal family. 2But Ahaziah's sister Jehosh- //2 Chr 22:10–23:21
eba, the daughter of King Jehoram,* took Ahaziah's infant son, Joash, and stole him away 11:2
from among the rest of the king's children, who were about to be killed. She put Joash and 2 Kgs 12:1
his nurse in a bedroom to hide him from Athaliah, so the child was not murdered. 3Joash re-
mained hidden in the Temple of the LORD for six years while Athaliah ruled over the land.

REVOLT AGAINST ATHALIAH

4In the seventh year of Athaliah's reign, Jehoiada the priest summoned the commanders, 11:4
the Carite mercenaries, and the palace guards to come to the Temple of the LORD. He 2 Kgs 11:19
made a solemn pact with them and made them swear an oath of loyalty there in the 2 Chr 23:1
LORD's Temple; then he showed them the king's son.

11:2 Hebrew *Joram,* a variant spelling of Jehoram.

10:28-31 These concluding statements exhibit ambivalence toward Jehu on the part of the author of 1 and 2 Kings. Jehu carried out his commission to eliminate the family of Ahab, yet he overstepped his bounds by extending his slaughter beyond Ahab's male descendants. He successfully exterminated Baal worship in Israel, but he did nothing to undo the corrupt worship of God established by Jeroboam (see note at 1 Kings 13:34).

▸ SPIRITUAL WARFARE
10:31 Less than perfect. Are you perfect? Do you always obey everything God commands? It should bring us some degree of hope when we see that someone of mixed character such as Jehu can accomplish much when God favors him. We are much more like Jehu than Jesus, yet God can still draw straight lines with crooked sticks. Don't wait to become perfect to get involved in building God's kingdom. (***See Spiritual Warfare***> *Resisting Sin and Evil> Standing Firm> Empowered to obey,* TopicGuide page A46.)

10:34-36 Kings provides a formulaic conclusion to each king's reign, typically giving sources of information, length of reign, and burial and succession notices. *The Book of the History of the Kings of Israel* is a lost source used by the author of 1 and 2 Kings to compose his inspired history. Other such sources include *The Book of the Acts of Solomon* and *The Book of the History of the Kings of Judah* (2 Kings 14:19, 29). Jehu reigned from approximately 841–814 BC.

11:1 Athaliah, the daughter of King Ahab of Israel (2 Kings 8:26-27), married into the royal family of Judah. She seized the opportunity provided by her son Ahaziah's death to violently assume control of Judah and promote Baal worship throughout the land. It cannot be said with certainty that Athaliah was Jezebel's daughter, but she certainly exhibited some of the same characteristics.

11:2-3 Jehosheba was likely Ahaziah's half-sister by a wife other than Athaliah. According to 2 Chronicles 22:11, she married a priest named Jehoiada. This explains the use of the Temple as a place of hiding for the young prince. The murder of Joash's brothers reduced the royal family to one legitimate heir, which appeared to place the Davidic covenant in grave danger.

11:4 Jehoiada enlisted the support of various military units present in Jerusalem. The Carites operated as a royal guard. The origin of their name is uncertain. They may have been the group called "Kerethites" in 1 Kings 1:38 (see textual note) or mercenaries from the region of Caria in Asia Minor.

11:5 5 Jehoiada told them, "This is what you must do. A third of you who are on duty on the Sab-
1 Chr 9:25 bath are to guard the royal palace itself. 6 Another third of you are to stand guard at the Sur
Gate. And the final third must stand guard behind the palace guard. These three groups will all
guard the palace. 7 The other two units who are off duty on the Sabbath must stand guard for
the king at the LORD's Temple. 8 Form a bodyguard around the king and keep your weapons in
hand. Kill anyone who tries to break through. Stay with the king wherever he goes."

9 So the commanders did everything as Jehoiada the priest ordered. The commanders
took charge of the men reporting for duty that Sabbath, as well as those who were going
11:10 off duty. They brought them all to Jehoiada the priest, 10 and he supplied them with the
2 Sam 8:7 spears and small shields that had once belonged to King David and were stored in the
1 Chr 18:7-8 Temple of the LORD. 11 The palace guards stationed themselves around the king, with their
weapons ready. They formed a line from the south side of the Temple around to the north
side and all around the altar.

11:12 12 Then Jehoiada brought out Joash, the king's son, placed the crown on his head, and
Exod 25:16; 31:18 presented him with a copy of God's laws.* They anointed him and proclaimed him king,
1 Sam 10:24 and everyone clapped their hands and shouted, "Long live the king!"

THE DEATH OF ATHALIAH

11:13 13 When Athaliah heard all the noise made by the palace guards and the people, she hur-
2 Chr 23:12 ried to the LORD's Temple to see what was happening. 14 When she arrived, she saw the
11:14 newly crowned king standing in his place of authority by the pillar, as was the custom at
Gen 37:29 1 Kgs 1:39 times of coronation. The commanders and trumpeters were surrounding him, and people
2 Kgs 9:23 from all over the land were rejoicing and blowing trumpets. When Athaliah saw all this,
she tore her clothes in despair and shouted, "Treason! Treason!"

15 Then Jehoiada the priest ordered the commanders who were in charge of the troops,
"Take her to the soldiers in front of the Temple,* and kill anyone who tries to rescue her." For
the priest had said, "She must not be killed in the Temple of the LORD." 16 So they seized her
and led her out to the gate where horses enter the palace grounds, and she was killed there.

JEHOIADA'S RELIGIOUS REFORMS

11:17 17 Then Jehoiada made a covenant between the LORD and the king and the people that
Josh 24:25 they would be the LORD's people. He also made a covenant between the king and the peo-
2 Sam 5:3 2 Chr 15:12-14; 34:31 ple. 18 And all the people of the land went over to the temple of Baal and tore it down. They
11:18 demolished the altars and smashed the idols to pieces, and they killed Mattan the priest of
Deut 12:2-3 1 Kgs 18:40 Baal in front of the altars.

11:12 Or *a copy of the covenant.* 11:15 Or *Bring her out from between the ranks;* or *Take her out of the Temple precincts.* The meaning of the Hebrew is uncertain.

11:12 The dramatic events surrounding the overthrow of Athaliah climaxed with the crowning of Joash and his acclamation by those present. The covenant placed in the king's hands may have been a copy of the Mosaic covenant as a whole, a section of the Mosaic covenant detailing the responsibilities of kingship (Deuteronomy 17:14-20), or the covenant mentioned in 2 Kings 11:17.

11:13-14 The noise of the celebration alerted Athaliah to the coronation of Joash (compare with Solomon's coronation and Adonijah's response, 1 Kings 1:41-51). She arrived much too late to counter the coup, however, and her cry of "treason" was tragically ironic given her own treacherous rise to power (2 Kings 11:1). The pillar by which Joash stood was likely one of the two great pillars called Jakin and Boaz (see note at 1 Kings 7:15-22). Josiah also stood by the pillar when he led the nation in covenant renewal (2 Kings 23:3).

11:17 Athaliah's reign represented a time of religious infidelity and political irregularity. Jehoiada wisely addressed both of these concerns by leading a ceremony of covenant renewal. During this ceremony, the people's faithfulness to God and the king's relationship with the people were reaffirmed along lines consistent with God's law. For similar ceremonies of covenant renewal, see Joshua 8:30-35; 24:1-28; 2 Samuel 5:3; and 2 Chronicles 15:12; 23:3; 29:10; 34:31-32.

▸ SPIRITUAL WARFARE

11:18 Sin comes back. Sin, once chased away, does not typically stay away. Jesus remarked that demons will come back after a time, sometimes even worse than before (Matthew 12:43-45). We must remain vigilant against sin, ever walking in the Spirit. As we deepen our trust in God, we'll more quickly see sin coming and be able to avoid it more effectively. Our ability to avoid and repent of sin is the truest sign of spiritual maturity. (***See Spiritual Warfare> Resisting Sin and Evil> Trusting God> Faithful Soldiers> Be alert,*** TopicGuide page A46.)

Jehoiada the priest stationed guards at the Temple of the LORD. [19]Then the command- 11:19
ers, the Carite mercenaries, the palace guards, and all the people of the land escorted the 2 Kgs 11:4
king from the Temple of the LORD. They went through the gate of the guards and into the
palace, and the king took his seat on the royal throne. [20]So all the people of the land re- 11:20
joiced, and the city was peaceful because Athaliah had been killed at the king's palace. Prov 11:10
[21]*Joash* was seven years old when he became king. 11:21 2 Chr 24:1-14

JOASH REPAIRS THE TEMPLE

12 [1]*Joash* began to rule over Judah in the seventh year of King Jehu's reign in Isra- 12:1-21
el. He reigned in Jerusalem forty years. His mother was Zibiah from Beersheba. //2 Chr 24:1-14,
[2]All his life Joash did what was pleasing in the LORD'S sight because Jehoiada the priest in- 23-27
structed him. [3]Yet even so, he did not destroy the pagan shrines, and the people still of- 12:3
fered sacrifices and burned incense there. 2 Kgs 14:4; 15:34-35
[4]One day King Joash said to the priests, "Collect all the money brought as a sacred offer- 12:4
ing to the LORD'S Temple, whether it is a regular assessment, a payment of vows, or a vol- Exod 35:5-9, 22, 29
untary gift. [5]Let the priests take some of that money to pay for whatever repairs are 2 Kgs 22:3-6 1 Chr 29:3-9
needed at the Temple."
[6]But by the twenty-third year of Joash's reign, the priests still had not repaired the Tem-
ple. [7]So King Joash called for Jehoiada and the other priests and asked them, "Why haven't
you repaired the Temple? Don't use any more money for your own needs. From now on, it
must all be spent on Temple repairs." [8]So the priests agreed not to accept any more money
from the people, and they also agreed to let others take responsibility for repairing the
Temple.
[9]Then Jehoiada the priest bored a hole in the lid of a large chest and set it on the right- 12:9
hand side of the altar at the entrance of the Temple of the LORD. The priests guarding the Mark 12:41
entrance put all of the people's contributions into the chest. [10]Whenever the chest became Luke 21:1
full, the court secretary and the high priest counted the money that had been brought to
the LORD'S Temple and put it into bags. [11]Then they gave the money to the construction
supervisors, who used it to pay the people working on the LORD'S Temple—the carpenters,
the builders, [12]the masons, and the stonecutters. They also used the money to buy the
timber and the finished stone needed for repairing the LORD'S Temple, and they paid any
other expenses related to the Temple's restoration.

11:21a Verse 11:21 is numbered 12:1 in Hebrew text. 11:21b Hebrew *Jehoash,* a variant spelling of Joash. 12:1a Verses 12:1-21 are numbered 12:2-22 in Hebrew text. 12:1b Hebrew *Jehoash,* a variant spelling of Joash; also in 12:2, 4, 6, 7, 18.

11:19-20 This chapter begins with the line of David on the brink of extinction but concludes with a legitimate heir of David on the throne. God providentially preserved the family of David and his kingdom.

12:1 Joash reigned from approximately 835–796 BC. Beersheba was located in southern Judah.

12:4 Joash listed three classes of revenue. The first was the regular assessment, which referred to money collected as part of a periodic census of male Israelites (Exodus 30:11-16). The second was money associated with vows (see Leviticus 27:1-25). The third class of revenue, voluntary gifts, may have referred to ordinary gifts or to a special fund-raising effort specifically for the repair of the Temple (compare Exodus 35:5, 21-22).

12:6-8 It is not clear when Joash issued his initial command that money be raised, but it seems that a good deal of time passed with no work being done. Finally, the king was forced to exercise his authority in a more tangible way: He denied the priests access to their income and implemented a system of collection under royal supervision (2 Kings 12:10-11).

▶ CHURCH

12:7 Pay to pray. Ordinarily, ministers deserve payment for their work of prayer, preaching, and devotion to God and His people. But Joash believed the priests should tighten their belts until the Temple was repaired, so the priests immediately took steps to repair God's house. In the end, a portion of the ordinary donations was set aside for the priests (2 Kings 12:16) due to the length of the project and the diligence they had shown in managing the task. If you are in a church where the pastor is paid little, make sure your church pays your minister a salary to match his needs as soon as possible. (***See Church****> Role> Preach> Topics> Collect Resources> For salaries of ministers,* TopicGuide page A50.)

12:11-14 Apparently the Temple had fallen into considerable disrepair by this time. The workforce that Joash assembled to work on the Temple resembled those of both Solomon (1 Kings 5) and Josiah (2 Kings 22:3-6). The extent of Joash's repairs seems to have precluded the use of funds for implements of worship. Unlike in the days of Solomon, silver was no longer considered cheap (1 Kings 10:21).

12:13 13The money brought to the Temple was not used for making silver bowls, lamp
1 Kgs 7:48-51 snuffers, basins, trumpets, or other articles of gold or silver for the Temple of the LORD. 14It
12:15 was paid to the workmen, who used it for the Temple repairs. 15No accounting of this
2 Kgs 22:7 money was required from the construction supervisors, because they were honest and
trustworthy men. 16However, the money that was contributed for guilt offerings and sin of-
ferings was not brought into the LORD'S Temple. It was given to the priests for their own use.

THE END OF JOASH'S REIGN

12:17 17About this time King Hazael of Aram went to war against Gath and captured it. Then he
2 Kgs 8:12; 10:32-33 turned to attack Jerusalem. 18King Joash collected all the sacred objects that Jehoshaphat,
12:18 Jehoram, and Ahaziah, the previous kings of Judah, had dedicated, along with what he
1 Kgs 15:18 2 Kgs 16:8; 18:15-16 himself had dedicated. He sent them all to Hazael, along with all the gold in the treasuries
of the LORD'S Temple and the royal palace. So Hazael called off his attack on Jerusalem.
19The rest of the events in Joash's reign and everything he did are recorded in *The Book*
of the History of the Kings of Judah.
12:20 20Joash's officers plotted against him and assassinated him at Beth-millo on the road to
2 Sam 5:9 Silla. 21The assassins were Jozacar* son of Shimeath and Jehozabad son of Shomer—both
2 Chr 24:25-27 trusted advisers. Joash was buried with his ancestors in the City of David. Then his son
Amaziah became the next king.

JEHOAHAZ RULES IN ISRAEL

13:2 **13** Jehoahaz son of Jehu began to rule over Israel in the twenty-third year of King
1 Kgs 12:26-33 Joash's reign in Judah. He reigned in Samaria seventeen years. 2But he did what
13:3 Judg 2:12-14 was evil in the LORD'S sight. He followed the example of Jeroboam son of Nebat, continu-
2 Kgs 12:17 ing the sins that Jeroboam had led Israel to commit. 3So the LORD was very angry with Is-
rael, and he allowed King Hazael of Aram and his son Ben-hadad to defeat them
repeatedly.
13:4 4Then Jehoahaz prayed for the LORD'S help, and the LORD heard his prayer, for He could
Exod 3:7-9 Num 21:7-9 see how severely the king of Aram was oppressing Israel. 5So the LORD provided some-
13:5 one to rescue the Israelites from the tyranny of the Arameans. Then Israel lived in safety
Judg 2:18 Neh 9:27 again as they had in former days.
6But they continued to sin, following the evil example of Jeroboam. They also allowed
13:6 the Asherah pole in Samaria to remain standing. 7Finally, Jehoahaz's army was reduced to
1 Kgs 16:33 50 charioteers, 10 chariots, and 10,000 foot soldiers. The king of Aram had killed the oth-
ers, trampling them like dust under his feet.
8The rest of the events in Jehoahaz's reign—everything he did and the extent of his

12:21 As in Greek and Syriac versions; Hebrew reads *Jozabad.*

12:17-18 Gath was one of five major Philistine cities to the west of Judah. The Aramean army's presence along Judah's western flank presented a serious threat to Judah's trade and security. Joash drew from the Temple and palace treasuries to bribe Hazael and purchase peace during his reign. According to the Chronicler, however, the Arameans did not withdraw before inflicting significant damage and wounding Joash in battle (2 Chronicles 24:23-25).

12:20 Beth-millo, or House of Millo, may refer to a site in Jerusalem, northwest of the City of David. The location of Silla is unknown.

13:1 Jehoahaz reigned from approximately 814–798 BC.

13:3 This Ben-hadad was the third monarch by that name to rule Aram (see 1 Kings 15:18-22 for Ben-hadad I; see 1 Kings 20:1 and 2 Kings 6:24; 8:7 for Ben-hadad II). The oppression of Israel by the kings of Aram formed part of the background for the ministry of the prophet Amos (see Amos 1:3-5).

13:4-5 The pattern and language of these verses is reminiscent of the Exodus and the period of the judges (compare Deuteronomy 26:7-9 and Judges 2:18-19). God was moved by mercy to alleviate the suffering of His people. The identity of the deliverer is uncertain, but there are two credible possibilities: Adad-nirari III, a king of Assyria who campaigned against Aram, or the prophet Elisha, who re-enters the narrative in this chapter.

13:6-7 Israel spurned God's grace and continued in their idolatrous rebellion rather than humbly repenting of their sin and obeying the Lord's commands. The sin of Jeroboam consisted of unauthorized worship (see note at 1 Kings 13:34). Israel's renewed disobedience brought about the severe reduction of the nation's military forces.

power—are recorded in *The Book of the History of the Kings of Israel.* 9 When Jehoahaz died,
he was buried in Samaria. Then his son Jehoash* became the next king.

JEHOASH RULES IN ISRAEL

10 Jehoash son of Jehoahaz began to rule over Israel in the thirty-seventh year of King Jo-
ash's reign in Judah. He reigned in Samaria sixteen years. 11 But he did what was evil in the
LORD's sight. He refused to turn from the sins that Jeroboam son of Nebat had led Israel to
commit.

12 The rest of the events in Jehoash's reign and everything he did, including the extent 13:12
of his power and his war with King Amaziah of Judah, are recorded in *The Book of the His-* 2 Kgs 14:8, 15, 28
tory of the Kings of Israel. 13 When Jehoash died, he was buried in Samaria with the kings of
Israel. Then his son Jeroboam II became the next king.

ELISHA'S FINAL PROPHECY

14 When Elisha was in his last illness, King Jehoash of Israel visited him and wept over him. 13:14
"My father! My father! I see the chariots and charioteers of Israel!" he cried. 2 Kgs 2:12

15 Elisha told him, "Get a bow and some arrows." And the king did as he was told. 16 Elisha
told him, "Put your hand on the bow," and Elisha laid his own hands on the king's hands.

17 Then he commanded, "Open that eastern window," and he opened it. Then he said, 13:17
"Shoot!" So he shot an arrow. Elisha proclaimed, "This is the LORD's arrow, an arrow of vic- 1 Kgs 20:26
tory over Aram, for you will completely conquer the Arameans at Aphek."

18 Then he said, "Now pick up the other arrows and strike them against the ground." So
the king picked them up and struck the ground three times. 19 But the man of God was an-
gry with him. "You should have struck the ground five or six times!" he exclaimed. "Then
you would have beaten Aram until it was entirely destroyed. Now you will be victorious
only three times."

20 Then Elisha died and was buried. 13:20

Groups of Moabite raiders used to invade the land each spring. 21 Once when some Isra- 2 Kgs 3:7; 24:2
elites were burying a man, they spied a band of these raiders. So they hastily threw the 13:21
corpse into the tomb of Elisha and fled. But as soon as the body touched Elisha's bones, Matt 27:52
the dead man revived and jumped to his feet!

13:9 Hebrew *Joash,* a variant spelling of Jehoash; also in 13:10, 12, 13, 14, 25.

13:10 Jehoash reigned from approximately 798–782 BC. Chapter 14 records further information regarding his reign.

▸ HOLINESS
13:10 Stand and lead! The leadership in Israel had sunk so low that God returned to the way He dealt with His people during the period of the judges. He sent a special military leader or deliverer to rescue God's people from their enemies and stimulate repentance. This wasn't the ideal, but sometimes second best is exactly what the situation requires. You may not be the wisest person in the room or the one who is officially in charge, but sometimes God will call you—yes, you!—to resolve conflict and give direction. (***See Holiness****> Law and Grace> Law> Leaders and followers,* TopicGuide page A41.)

13:14 Elisha last appeared in the narrative at the anointing of Jehu some 50 years earlier (9:1-10). Jehoash used the very words Elisha did when Elijah was taken to heaven in a whirlwind (2:11-12).

▸ GOD
13:14 Waiting for direction. What or whom do you depend on for rescue? King Jehoash recognized that Elisha, not his own military might, was the hope of Israel's survival. The distraught king wept over the dying prophet because he feared utter defeat by the forces of Aram. Completely outnumbered by the Arameans, Jehoash had little hope of defending his nation without the guidance of a prophet who could command God's power to strike his enemies. Do you value spiritual counsel from others? Decide to seek counsel from God and your mature Christian friends before making significant decisions about yourself and your family. (***See God****> God's Names> Holy Spirit> Guide/Counselor,* TopicGuide page A19.)

13:17-19 The arrow symbolized military victory over Aram, which lay to the east of Israel, the direction in which the arrow was shot. The arrow functioned as a sign of the promise that followed, confirming God's intention to fulfill His word. Sadly, Jehoash responded to the prophetic word with insufficient zeal, revealing a lack of faith. As a result, the promise of complete victory was reduced. Jehoash would enjoy only three victories against Aram (2 Kings 13:25).

13:21 This unusual incident may be best understood as a symbolic expression of hope in the power of God to restore His people from the "death" of exile that was drawing near. The same Hebrew word underlies both the throwing of the body here and the banishment of Israel in 2 Kings 13:23. Ezekiel 37 employs similar imagery to describe the restoration of Israel.

13:22 22King Hazael of Aram had oppressed Israel during the entire reign of King Jehoahaz.
2 Kgs 8:12 23But the LORD was gracious and merciful to the people of Israel, and they were not to-
13:23 tally destroyed. He pitied them because of His covenant with Abraham, Isaac, and Jacob.
Gen 13:16; 17:2-5 2 Kgs 14:27 And to this day He still has not completely destroyed them or banished them from His
presence.

13:25 24King Hazael of Aram died, and his son Ben-hadad became the next king. 25Then Jeho-
2 Kgs 10:32-33; 14:25 ash son of Jehoahaz recaptured from Ben-hadad son of Hazael the towns that had been
taken from Jehoash's father, Jehoahaz. Jehoash defeated Ben-hadad on three occasions,
and he recovered the Israelite towns.

AMAZIAH RULES IN JUDAH

14:1-7 //2 Chr 25:1-4, 11-12 **14** Amaziah son of Joash began to rule over Judah in the second year of the reign of
King Jehoash* of Israel. 2Amaziah was twenty-five years old when he became
king, and he reigned in Jerusalem twenty-nine years. His mother was Jehoaddin from Je-
rusalem. 3Amaziah did what was pleasing in the LORD's sight, but not like his ancestor Da-
14:4 vid. Instead, he followed the example of his father, Joash. 4Amaziah did not destroy the
2 Kgs 12:3 pagan shrines, and the people still offered sacrifices and burned incense there.
14:5 2 Kgs 12:20 5When Amaziah was well established as king, he executed the officials who had assas-
sinated his father. 6However, he did not kill the children of the assassins, for he obeyed the
14:6 Deut 24:16 command of the LORD as written by Moses in the Book of the Law: "Parents must not be put
Jer 31:30 Ezek 18:4, 20 to death for the sins of their children, nor children for the sins of their parents. Those de-
serving to die must be put to death for their own crimes."*

14:7 2 Sam 8:13 7Amaziah also killed 10,000 Edomites in the Valley of Salt. He also conquered Sela and
1 Chr 18:12 changed its name to Joktheel, as it is called to this day.
2 Chr 25:11 Isa 16:1 8One day Amaziah sent messengers with this challenge to Israel's king Jehoash, the son
of Jehoahaz and grandson of Jehu: "Come and meet me in battle!"*
14:8-22 //2 Chr 25:17–26:2 9But King Jehoash of Israel replied to King Amaziah of Judah with this story: "Out in the
14:9 Lebanon mountains, a thistle sent a message to a mighty cedar tree: 'Give your daughter
Judg 9:8-15 in marriage to my son.' But just then a wild animal of Lebanon came by and stepped on
the thistle, crushing it!

10"You have indeed defeated Edom, and you are very proud of it. But be content with
your victory and stay at home! Why stir up trouble that will only bring disaster on you and
the people of Judah?"

14:11 11But Amaziah refused to listen, so King Jehoash of Israel mobilized his army against
Josh 19:35-39 King Amaziah of Judah. The two armies drew up their battle lines at Beth-shemesh in Ju-
dah. 12Judah was routed by the army of Israel, and its army scattered and fled for home.

14:1 Hebrew *Joash*, a variant spelling of Jehoash; also in 14:13, 23, 27. 14:6 Deut 24:16. 14:8 Hebrew *Come, let us look one another in the face.*

14:3 The authors evaluated only a few kings of Judah by comparison with David. Solomon and Rehoboam were unfavorably compared (1 Kings 11:4; 15:3), while Asa, Hezekiah, and Josiah received favorable comparisons to David (1 Kings 15:11; 2 Kings 18:3; 22:1-2). Amaziah here received a mixed evaluation (see note at 1 Kings 11:4). The pagan shrines that Amaziah failed to remove would not be thoroughly eliminated until the reign of Josiah.

14:8-10 King Jehoash used a parable to try to dissuade the less powerful King Amaziah of Judah from challenging Israel to battle. The details of the parable should not be pressed too strictly for meaning. For instance, the wild animal does not necessarily represent a third party—Jehoash himself would crush Amaziah. The parable's main point was simply that a puny thistle (Amaziah) should not challenge a mighty cedar (Jehoash).

▸SPIRITUAL WARFARE

14:10 Be content with your victory. It makes sense that you shouldn't start a fight unless it is absolutely necessary. King Jehoash, the peacemaker, understood this. He knew that violence could accomplish good or evil, and in this case a battle between Israel and Judah would bring only harm to God's people. But Amaziah refused to listen to God speaking through Jehoash. As a result, Judah suffered greatly—Jerusalem most of all. Be very careful in your use of violence, and always use it as a last resort for defending those you love. (***See Spiritual Warfare***> *Resisting Sin and Evil*> *Trusting God*> *God as Warrior,* TopicGuide page A46.)

13King Jehoash of Israel captured Judah's king, Amaziah son of Joash and grandson of 14:13
Ahaziah, at Beth-shemesh. Then he marched to Jerusalem, where he demolished 2 Chr 25:23
600 feet* of Jerusalem's wall, from the Ephraim Gate to the Corner Gate. 14He carried off Neh 8:16; 12:39
all the gold and silver and all the articles from the Temple of the LORD. He also seized the 14:14 2 Kgs 12:18
treasures from the royal palace, along with hostages, and then returned to Samaria.

15The rest of the events in Jehoash's reign and everything he did, including the extent 14:15
of his power and his war with King Amaziah of Judah, are recorded in *The Book of the His-* 2 Kgs 13:12-13
tory of the Kings of Israel. 16When Jehoash died, he was buried in Samaria with the kings of
Israel. And his son Jeroboam II became the next king.

17King Amaziah of Judah lived for fifteen years after the death of King Jehoash of Israel. 14:17
18The rest of the events in Amaziah's reign are recorded in *The Book of the History of the* 2 Chr 25:25-28
Kings of Judah.

19There was a conspiracy against Amaziah's life in Jerusalem, and he fled to Lachish. But 14:19
his enemies sent assassins after him, and they killed him there. 20They brought his body 2 Kgs 12:20
back to Jerusalem on a horse, and he was buried with his ancestors in the City of David. 14:20 2 Kgs 9:28

21All the people of Judah had crowned Amaziah's sixteen-year-old son, Uzziah,* as king 14:21
in place of his father, Amaziah. 22After his father's death, Uzziah rebuilt the town of Elath 2 Chr 26:23
and restored it to Judah. Hos 1:1 Matt 1:9

14:13 Hebrew *400 cubits* [180 meters]. 14:21 Hebrew *Azariah,* a variant spelling of Uzziah.

KINGS TO DATE AND THEIR ENEMIES

ISRAEL

841
JEHU
Lost a large portion of northern Israel to Hazael (Aram)
2 Kgs 9:1–10:36
2 Chr 22:7-9

814
JEHOAHAZ
Continually defeated by Hazael (Aram)
2 Kgs 10:35; 13:1-9

798
JEHOASH
2 Kgs 13:10–14:16
2 Chr 25:17-24
Co-regency 793–782

793
JEROBOAM II
Recaptured Israel's former territories from Aram
2 Kgs 14:16-29

782 *753*

JUDAH

841
AHAZIAH
Hazael (Aram)
2 Kgs 8:24–9:29
2 Chr 22:1-9

841
ATHALIAH (QUEEN)
2 Kgs 11:1-20
2 Chr 22:10–23:21

835
JOASH
Averted Hazael's attack by paying tribute, and later was defeated by Aram
2 Kgs 11:2–12:21
2 Chr 22:11–24:27

796
AMAZIAH
Defeated by Jehoash and Jeroboam II (Israel)
2 Kgs 14:1-20
2 Chr 24:27–25:28

767

All dates are BC.
Solid section of the timeline indicates co-regency.
For all the kings of Israel and Judah, see the chart at the end of 1 Kings.

14:13-14 Judah's humiliating defeat and the ensuing looting and deportation constituted the first of several such incidents, culminating with the destruction of Jerusalem by Babylon (2 Kings 23:33-34; 24:10-17; 25:1-21). The Ephraim Gate was located on the north wall, and the Corner Gate occupied the northwest corner of the city (compare Jeremiah 31:38 and Nehemiah 8:16). Amaziah apparently was released upon Jehoash's death (2 Kings 14:17).

14:22 Amaziah's defeat of Edom (2 Kings 14:7) allowed Uzziah to rebuild the important port city of Elath on the Gulf of Aqaba. The city previously had served as a port for Solomon's naval ventures (1 Kings 9:26-28).

JEROBOAM II RULES IN ISRAEL

14:23 23 Jeroboam II, the son of Jehoash, began to rule over Israel in the fifteenth year of King
2 Kgs 13:13 Amaziah's reign in Judah. Jeroboam reigned in Samaria forty-one years. 24 He did what
Amos 1:1 was evil in the LORD's sight. He refused to turn from the sins that Jeroboam son of Nebat
14:24 1 Kgs 15:30 had led Israel to commit. 25 Jeroboam II recovered the territories of Israel between Lebo-
14:25 hamath and the Dead Sea,* just as the LORD, the God of Israel, had promised through Jo-
Deut 3:17 nah son of Amittai, the prophet from Gath-hepher.
2 Kgs 13:25 Jon 1:1 26 For the LORD saw the bitter suffering of everyone in Israel, and that there was no one in
14:26 Israel, slave or free, to help them. 27 And because the LORD had not said He would blot out
Deut 32:36 the name of Israel completely, He used Jeroboam II, the son of Jehoash, to save them.
2 Kgs 13:4 28 The rest of the events in the reign of Jeroboam II and everything he did—including the
14:27 extent of his power, his wars, and how he recovered for Israel both Damascus and
2 Kgs 13:5, 23 Hamath, which had belonged to Judah*—are recorded in *The Book of the History of the
Kings of Israel.* 29 When Jeroboam II died, he was buried in Samaria* with the kings of Isra-
el. Then his son Zechariah became the next king.

UZZIAH RULES IN JUDAH

15:1 **15** Uzziah* son of Amaziah began to rule over Judah in the twenty-seventh year of the
2 Kgs 14:21; 15:13, 17 reign of King Jeroboam II of Israel. 2 He was sixteen years old when he became
king, and he reigned in Jerusalem fifty-two years. His mother was Jecoliah from Jerusalem.
3 He did what was pleasing in the LORD's sight, just as his father, Amaziah, had done. 4 But
he did not destroy the pagan shrines, and the people still offered sacrifices and burned in-
cense there. 5 The LORD struck the king with leprosy,* which lasted until the day he died. He
15:5 Lev 13:46 lived in isolation in a separate house. The king's son Jotham was put in charge of the royal
palace, and he governed the people of the land.
6 The rest of the events in Uzziah's reign and everything he did are recorded in *The Book
of the History of the Kings of Judah.* 7 When Uzziah died, he was buried with his ancestors in
the City of David. And his son Jotham became the next king.

ZECHARIAH RULES IN ISRAEL

8 Zechariah son of Jeroboam II began to rule over Israel in the thirty-eighth year of King Uz-
15:8 ziah's reign in Judah. He reigned in Samaria six months. 9 Zechariah did what was evil in
2 Kgs 14:29 the LORD's sight, as his ancestors had done. He refused to turn from the sins that Jeroboam

14:25 Hebrew *the sea of the Arabah.* 14:28 Or *to Yaudi.* The meaning of the Hebrew is uncertain. 14:29 As in some Greek manuscripts; Hebrew omits *in Samaria.* 15:1 Hebrew *Azariah,* a variant spelling of Uzziah; also in 15:6, 7, 8, 17, 23, 27. 15:5 Or *with a contagious skin disease.* The Hebrew word used here and throughout this passage can describe various skin diseases.

14:23-24 Jeroboam II reigned from approximately 793–753 BC. For the sin of Jeroboam I, see 1 Kings 13:34.

14:25-27 Both Israel under Jeroboam II and Judah under Uzziah enjoyed periods of territorial and economic expansion. The writers saw these respites as gifts of God's grace. However, that grace was not met with repentance and grateful obedience.

14:28 Jeroboam gained control of Damascus, the capital of Aram, and Hamath, 125 miles north of Damascus. These cities had once been under David and Solomon's control during the united monarchy (2 Samuel 8:6; 1 Kings 8:65).

15:1 Uzziah began his reign as coregent upon his father's capture (2 Kings 14:13). Uzziah reigned from approximately 792–740 BC.

▸ CHURCH
15:4 Leading away from danger. It's tempting to allow the people under your leadership to do whatever they want, as long as they do not cause serious problems. But we must realize that there are things worse than being an unpopular leader—such as being a poor leader! Be courageous and merciful in your leadership, but above all, love those under your care enough to lead them away from sin and into righteousness (1 Samuel 2:24; 1 Corinthians 5:1-2). (***See Church***> *Role> Church Government> Local> To spiritually lead,* TopicGuide page A49.)

15:5 Uzziah was struck with a skin disease (see textual note) because he attempted to offer incense in the Temple. The chronicler attributed Uzziah's actions to pride and recorded the king's confrontation with the priests who attempted to stop him (2 Chronicles 26:16-21). Old Testament law required that those affected by skin disease be removed from the community (Leviticus 13:46; Numbers 5:1-4; 12:15), so Uzziah was forced to live by himself for the rest of his days. At this time, Jotham began to rule as coregent with his father, who was unable to fully carry out his royal responsibilities.

15:8-10 Zechariah's reign likely occurred during 753 BC. His assassination triggered a period of intense instability marked by constant revolution and counterrevolution. Within thirteen years, five kings took the throne in Israel. Zechariah's death brought to fulfillment the Lord's message to Jehu (see 2 Kings 15:12; 10:30).

son of Nebat had led Israel to commit. [10]Then Shallum son of Jabesh conspired against 15:10
Zechariah, assassinated him in public,* and became the next king. Amos 7:9
[11]The rest of the events in Zechariah's reign are recorded in *The Book of the History of*
the Kings of Israel. [12]So the LORD's message to Jehu came true: "Your descendants will be 15:12
kings of Israel down to the fourth generation." 2 Kgs 10:30

SHALLUM RULES IN ISRAEL

[13]Shallum son of Jabesh began to rule over Israel in the thirty-ninth year of King Uzzi- 15:13
ah's reign in Judah. Shallum reigned in Samaria only one month. [14]Then Menahem son of 2 Kgs 15:1, 8
Gadi went to Samaria from Tirzah and assassinated him, and he became the next king.
[15]The rest of the events in Shallum's reign, including his conspiracy, are recorded in
The Book of the History of the Kings of Israel.

MENAHEM RULES IN ISRAEL

[16]At that time Menahem destroyed the town of Tappuah* and all the surrounding country- 15:16
side as far as Tirzah, because its citizens refused to surrender the town. He killed the entire 2 Kgs 8:12
population and ripped open the pregnant women. Hos 13:16
[17]Menahem son of Gadi began to rule over Israel in the thirty-ninth year of King Uzzi-
ah's reign in Judah. He reigned in Samaria ten years. [18]But Menahem did what was evil in
the LORD's sight. During his entire reign, he refused to turn from the sins that Jeroboam son
of Nebat had led Israel to commit.
[19]Then King Tiglath-pileser* of Assyria invaded the land. But Menahem paid him thirty- 15:19
seven tons* of silver to gain his support in tightening his grip on royal power. [20]Menahem 1 Chr 5:26
extorted the money from the rich of Israel, demanding that each of them pay fifty pieces*
of silver to the king of Assyria. So the king of Assyria turned from attacking Israel and did
not stay in the land.
[21]The rest of the events in Menahem's reign and everything he did are recorded in *The*
Book of the History of the Kings of Israel. [22]When Menahem died, his son Pekahiah became
the next king.

PEKAHIAH RULES IN ISRAEL

[23]Pekahiah son of Menahem began to rule over Israel in the fiftieth year of King Uzziah's reign
in Judah. He reigned in Samaria two years. [24]But Pekahiah did what was evil in the LORD's
sight. He refused to turn from the sins that Jeroboam son of Nebat had led Israel to commit.
[25]Then Pekah son of Remaliah, the commander of Pekahiah's army, conspired against
him. With fifty men from Gilead, Pekah assassinated the king, along with Argob and Arieh,
in the citadel of the palace at Samaria. And Pekah reigned in his place.
[26]The rest of the events in Pekahiah's reign and everything he did are recorded in *The*
Book of the History of the Kings of Israel.

15:10 Or *at Ibleam.* 15:16 As in some Greek manuscripts; other Greek manuscripts read *at Ibleam.* Hebrew reads *Tiphsah.* 15:19a Hebrew *Pul,* another name for Tiglath-pileser. 15:19b Hebrew *1,000 talents* [34 metric tons]. 15:20 Hebrew *50 shekels* [20 ounces, or 570 grams].

15:13 Shallum probably took the throne in 752 BC.

15:17-20 Menahem reigned from approximately 752–742 BC, a very turbulent period in Israel's history. He struggled with internal dissent and the external threat of the Assyrian empire. The Assyrians, under Tiglath-pileser (745–727 BC), expanded their sphere of domination westward, coming into contact with Israel and later Judah (2 Kings 16:7). Rather than resist Assyria and face certain defeat, Menahem accepted vassal status. Assyrian records confirm Menahem's payment of tribute.

▸ CHURCH
15:19 Pay or die. There is not necessarily anything wrong with bribing an army not to destroy your nation. Menahem should be praised for his quick thinking. But Scripture condemned his method of gathering the bribe from the people. Each wealthy person in Israel was required to pay the equivalent of the price of a male slave (Leviticus 27:3). While unfair taxes are evil, condemned both here and throughout the Scriptures (Matthew 17:24-27; 2 Kings 23:35-37), God does call us to pay our taxes (Romans 13:6-7). Do everything within your power as a citizen to make the tax laws of your country equitable, but when they are not, pay them and rejoice in God's provision, for God's Word is clear regarding our response to unfair taxation. (***See Church*>** *Role> Church Government> Society> Church honors authority of government,* TopicGuide page A49.)

15:23 Pekahiah reigned from approximately 742–740 BC.

PEKAH RULES IN ISRAEL

15:27 [27]Pekah son of Remaliah began to rule over Israel in the fifty-second year of King Uzziah's
2 Kgs 15:32; 16:5 reign in Judah. He reigned in Samaria twenty years. [28]But Pekah did what was evil in the
2 Chr 28:6 LORD's sight. He refused to turn from the sins that Jeroboam son of Nebat had led Israel to
commit.
15:29 [29]During Pekah's reign, King Tiglath-pileser of Assyria attacked Israel again, and he cap-
2 Kgs 17:6 tured the towns of Ijon, Abel-beth-maacah, Janoah, Kedesh, and Hazor. He also conquered
the regions of Gilead, Galilee, and all of Naphtali, and he took the people to Assyria as
15:30 captives. [30]Then Hoshea son of Elah conspired against Pekah and assassinated him. He
2 Kgs 12:20 began to rule over Israel in the twentieth year of Jotham son of Uzziah.

KINGS TO DATE AND THEIR ENEMIES

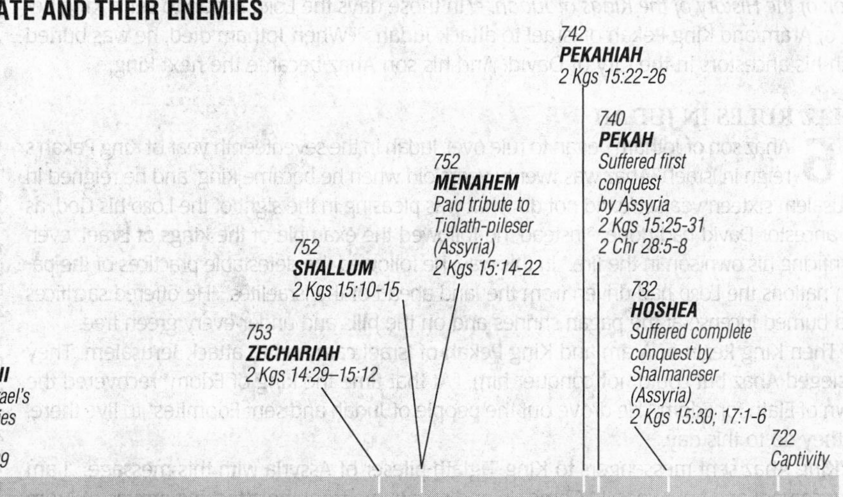

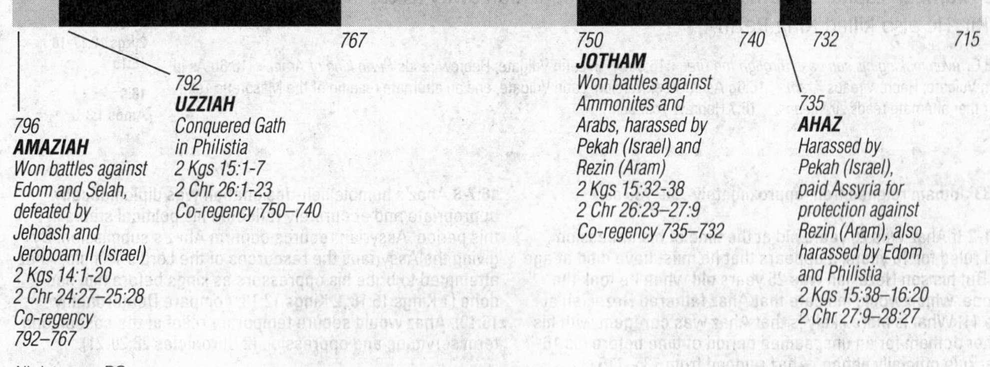

All dates are BC.
Solid section of the timeline indicates co-regency.
For all the kings of Israel and Judah, see the chart at the end of 1 Kings.

15:27-29 Pekah reigned approximately 740–720 BC. His anti-Assyrian policies brought about Tiglath-pileser's military retaliation in 733 BC. The cities and regions listed represent the northern and northwestern portions of Israel. See also note at 2 Kings 16:7-9.

15:30 Assyrian records indicate that Hoshea's coup enjoyed the support of Tiglath-pileser. Hoshea likely served as a puppet king under the Assyrian monarch. The placement of Pekah's murder during Jotham's reign appears problematic because Pekah is known to have played a significant role during the Aramean-Israelite crisis during the reign of Jotham's son Ahaz (2 Kings 16:5; Isaiah 7). Once again, this descrepancy may be resolved if there was a coregency between Ahaz and Jotham (see note at 2 Kings 16:1-2).

31 The rest of the events in Pekah's reign and everything he did are recorded in *The Book
of the History of the Kings of Israel.*

JOTHAM RULES IN JUDAH

32 Jotham son of Uzziah began to rule over Judah in the second year of King Pekah's reign
in Israel. 33 He was twenty-five years old when he became king, and he reigned in Jerusa-
lem sixteen years. His mother was Jerusha, the daughter of Zadok.
34 Jotham did what was pleasing in the LORD's sight. He did everything his father, Uzziah,
had done. 35 But he did not destroy the pagan shrines, and the people still offered sacri-
fices and burned incense there. He rebuilt the upper gate of the Temple of the LORD.
36 The rest of the events in Jotham's reign and everything he did are recorded in *The
Book of the History of the Kings of Judah.* 37 In those days the LORD began to send King Re-
zin of Aram and King Pekah of Israel to attack Judah. 38 When Jotham died, he was buried
with his ancestors in the City of David. And his son Ahaz became the next king.

15:32 2 Chr 27:1; Matt 1:9
15:33-38 //2 Chr 27:1-4, 7-9
15:34 2 Chr 26:4-5
15:36 2 Kgs 15:6; 16:19; 20:20

AHAZ RULES IN JUDAH

16 Ahaz son of Jotham began to rule over Judah in the seventeenth year of King Pekah's
reign in Israel. 2 Ahaz was twenty years old when he became king, and he reigned in
Jerusalem sixteen years. He did not do what was pleasing in the sight of the LORD his God, as
his ancestor David had done. 3 Instead, he followed the example of the kings of Israel, even
sacrificing his own son in the fire.* In this way, he followed the detestable practices of the pa-
gan nations the LORD had driven from the land ahead of the Israelites. 4 He offered sacrifices
and burned incense at the pagan shrines and on the hills and under every green tree.
5 Then King Rezin of Aram and King Pekah of Israel came up to attack Jerusalem. They
besieged Ahaz but could not conquer him. 6 At that time the king of Edom* recovered the
town of Elath for Edom.* He drove out the people of Judah and sent Edomites* to live there,
as they do to this day.
7 King Ahaz sent messengers to King Tiglath-pileser of Assyria with this message: "I am
your servant and your vassal.* Come up and rescue me from the attacking armies of Aram
and Israel." 8 Then Ahaz took the silver and gold from the Temple of the LORD and the pal-
ace treasury and sent it as a payment to the Assyrian king. 9 So the king of Assyria attacked
the Aramean capital of Damascus and led its population away as captives, resettling them
in Kir. He also killed King Rezin.

16:1-20 //2 Chr 28:1-27
16:2 2 Kgs 14:3
16:3 Lev 18:21; Deut 12:31; 2 Kgs 17:17; 21:6
16:4 Deut 12:2
16:5 2 Kgs 15:37; 2 Chr 28:5; Isa 7:1-6
16:6 2 Kgs 14:22; 2 Chr 26:2
16:7 2 Kgs 15:29
16:8 2 Kgs 12:17-18; 18:15
16:9 Amos 1:3-5

16:3 Or *even making his son pass through the fire.* 16:6a As in Latin Vulgate; Hebrew reads *Rezin king of Aram.* 16:6b As in Latin Vulgate; Hebrew reads *Aram.* 16:6c As in Greek version, Latin Vulgate, and an alternate reading of the Masoretic Text; the other alternate reads *Arameans.* 16:7 Hebrew *your son.*

15:33 Jotham reigned from approximately 750–735 BC.

16:1-2 If Ahaz was 20 years old at the time of his accession and ruled for 16 years, it appears that he must have died at age 36. But his son Hezekiah was 25 years old when he took the throne, which would indicate that Ahaz fathered Hezekiah at age 11. What is more likely is that Ahaz was coregent with his father Jotham for an unspecified period of time before his 16-year rule officially began. Ahaz reigned from 735–715 BC.

16:3 Jehoram is the only other king of Judah besides Ahaz to be explicitly likened to the kings of Israel (2 Kings 8:18). (See note at 1 Kings 13:34.) Child sacrifice was the most detestable of the pagan rituals practiced by Israel's neighbors, and it was particularly associated with the worship of Molech (Leviticus 20:1-5; Deuteronomy 18:10; 2 Kings 3:26-27; Micah 6:7). The reign of Ahaz marked a clear return to the practices of the Canaanite nations that inhabited the land before the conquest.

16:7-8 Ahaz's humble self-designation was diplomatically appropriate and accurately reflected his political status in this period. Assyrian records confirm Ahaz's submission. By giving the Assyrians the resources of the Lord's Temple, Ahaz attempted to bribe his oppressors as kings before him had done (1 Kings 15:18; 2 Kings 12:18; compare Deuteronomy 16:19). Ahaz would secure temporary relief at the cost of long-term servitude and oppression (2 Chronicles 28:20-21).

▸ SPIRITUAL WARFARE

16:7-8 Crying out for help. You can always ask God for help. You should never feel as if you have sinned too much or gone too far to submit yourself to God's solution for your problem. King Ahaz sacrificed the holiest treasures of his people and his God (2 Kings 16:8) to gain the support of the pagan king. In what ways does it cost you when you refuse to turn to God for salvation? In what ways does it cost you when you try to do everything yourself? (***See Spiritual Warfare**> Resisting Sin and Evil> Consequences> Of Disobedience> God may allow consequences to run their course,* TopicGuide page A46.)

16:10 [10]King Ahaz then went to Damascus to meet with King Tiglath-pileser of Assyria. While
Isa 8:2 he was there, he took special note of the altar. Then he sent a model of the altar to Uriah
the priest, along with its design in full detail. [11]Uriah followed the king's instructions and
built an altar just like it, and it was ready before the king returned from Damascus.
16:12 [12]When the king returned, he inspected the altar and made offerings on it. [13]He presented
2 Chr 26:16, 19 a burnt offering and a grain offering, he poured out a liquid offering, and he sprinkled the
blood of peace offerings on the altar.

16:14 [14]Then King Ahaz removed the old bronze altar from its place in front of the LORD's Tem-
Exod 40:6 1 Kgs 8:64 ple, between the entrance and the new altar, and placed it on the north side of the new al-
16:15 tar. [15]He told Uriah the priest, "Use the new altar* for the morning sacrifices of burnt
Exod 29:38-41 offering, the evening grain offering, the king's burnt offering and grain offering, and the
burnt offerings of all the people, as well as their grain offerings and liquid offerings. Sprin-
kle the blood from all the burnt offerings and sacrifices on the new altar. The bronze altar
will be for my personal use only." [16]Uriah the priest did just as King Ahaz commanded him.

16:17 [17]Then the king removed the side panels and basins from the portable water carts. He
1 Kgs 7:23, 25, 27 also removed the great bronze basin called the Sea from the backs of the bronze oxen and
placed it on the stone pavement. [18]In deference to the king of Assyria, he also removed
the canopy that had been constructed inside the palace for use on the Sabbath day,* as
well as the king's outer entrance to the Temple of the LORD.

[19]The rest of the events in Ahaz's reign and everything he did are recorded in *The Book*
16:20 *of the History of the Kings of Judah.* [20]When Ahaz died, he was buried with his ancestors in
2 Chr 28:27; 29:1 the City of David. Then his son Hezekiah became the next king.

HOSHEA RULES IN ISRAEL

17:1 **17** Hoshea son of Elah began to rule over Israel in the twelfth year of King Ahaz's
2 Kgs 15:30 reign in Judah. He reigned in Samaria nine years. [2]He did what was evil in the
LORD's sight, but not to the same extent as the kings of Israel who ruled before him.

17:3-7 [3]King Shalmaneser of Assyria attacked King Hoshea, so Hoshea was forced to pay
//2 Kgs 18:9-12 heavy tribute to Assyria. [4]But Hoshea stopped paying the annual tribute and conspired
17:4 2 Kgs 18:20-21 against the king of Assyria by asking King So of Egypt* to help him shake free of Assyria's

16:15 Hebrew *the great altar.* 16:18 The meaning of the Hebrew is uncertain. 17:4 Or *by asking the king of Egypt at Sais.*

16:10 Ahaz's visit to his new overlord resulted in a new altar for the Temple. His motive for building the altar is unclear. The altar may have reflected Ahaz's new vassal status, but that is not indicated by the text. Most likely Ahaz simply liked the unusual design and desired a replica for aesthetic purposes. The prophet Isaiah spoke positively of the priest Uriah, who built the altar for Ahaz (Isaiah 8:2).

16:15 It is interesting to note the distinction between the offerings of the king and the offerings of the people (1 Kings 8:62-64). The same distinction is made in Ezekiel 46:2, 12. The old bronze altar was reserved for Ahaz's personal use. The underlying Hebrew phrase is obscure but may suggest that Ahaz used the altar for divination. Discerning the future by examining the entrails of sacrificial animals was practiced by some of Israel's neighbors but forbidden in Leviticus 19:26 and Deuteronomy 18:10.

16:17 As with his design for the new altar, Ahaz's other changes to the Temple courtyard may have been motivated by nothing more than aesthetic considerations. This would explain the acquiescence of Uriah the priest (2 Kings 16:16). (See 1 Kings 7:27-37 regarding the portable water carts and 1 Kings 7:23-26 regarding the Sea.) Ahaz would later take much more damaging action against the Temple (2 Chronicles 28:24).

16:18 "Canopy" translates an obscure Hebrew word. The exact nature of this Sabbath structure is uncertain, as is the reason it would give offense to the Assyrian king. What is clear is Ahaz's subservience to the Assyrian king.

▸ GOD

16:18 Showing deference. To whom do you show respect? Ahaz had respect for his rescuer, so he made a copy of his altar (2 Kings 16:10) and replaced the original altar with it (2 Kings 16:14). Ahaz's lack of respect for God, however, is evidenced by his removal of the reminders of God from the Temple and the palace. Honor God by treasuring the traditions, ideas, holidays, and other things that God has given His people. (***See God***> *God's Attributes*> *Holy*> *The most holy One deserves constant honor,* TopicGuide page A16.)

17:1-2 Hoshea reigned from approximately 732–723 BC. He received the only positive comment afforded the kings of Israel in this book. But slight reform at the end of Israel's history could not undo generations of wickedness and idolatry.

17:4-6 Hoshea's refusal to pay his annual tribute resulted in his removal by his Assyrian overlord, who then besieged Samaria and captured it in "the ninth year of King Hoshea's reign," probably in 722 BC. The fall of Samaria marked the end of the northern kingdom as an independent political entity. Assyrian sources record the deportation of 27,290 people. Gozan was located on the Habor River, a northern tributary of the Euphrates. The exact location of Halah is uncertain.

power. When the king of Assyria discovered this treachery, he seized Hoshea and put him
in prison.

SAMARIA FALLS TO ASSYRIA

5 Then the king of Assyria invaded the entire land, and for three years he besieged the city
of Samaria. 6 Finally, in the ninth year of King Hoshea's reign, Samaria fell, and the people
of Israel were exiled to Assyria. They were settled in colonies in Halah, along the banks of
the Habor River in Gozan, and in the cities of the Medes.
7 This disaster came upon the people of Israel because they worshiped other gods.
They sinned against the LORD their God, who had brought them safely out of Egypt and
had rescued them from the power of Pharaoh, the king of Egypt. 8 They had followed the
practices of the pagan nations the LORD had driven from the land ahead of them, as well
as the practices the kings of Israel had introduced. 9 The people of Israel had also secretly
done many things that were not pleasing to the LORD their God. They built pagan shrines
for themselves in all their towns, from the smallest outpost to the largest walled city.
10 They set up sacred pillars and Asherah poles at the top of every hill and under every
green tree. 11 They offered sacrifices on all the hilltops, just like the nations the LORD had
driven from the land ahead of them. So the people of Israel had done many evil things,
arousing the LORD's anger. 12 Yes, they worshiped idols,* despite the LORD's specific and
repeated warnings.
13 Again and again the LORD had sent His prophets and seers to warn both Israel and Ju-
dah: "Turn from all your evil ways. Obey My commands and decrees—the entire law that
I commanded your ancestors to obey, and that I gave you through My servants the
prophets."
14 But the Israelites would not listen. They were as stubborn as their ancestors who had
refused to believe in the LORD their God. 15 They rejected His decrees and the covenant
He had made with their ancestors, and they despised all His warnings. They worshiped
worthless idols, so they became worthless themselves. They followed the example of the
nations around them, disobeying the LORD's command not to imitate them.

17:6 Deut 28:64; 29:27-28; 2 Kgs 18:11; 1 Chr 5:26; Hos 13:16
17:7 Josh 23:15-16
17:8 Lev 18:3; Deut 18:9
17:9 2 Kgs 18:8
17:12 Exod 20:4
17:13 Neh 9:29-30; Jer 7:5-6; 18:11; Acts 7:51-52
17:14 Exod 32:9; 33:3
17:15 Exod 24:6-8; Deut 12:30-31; 29:25; 32:21

17:12 The Hebrew term (literally *round things*) probably alludes to dung.

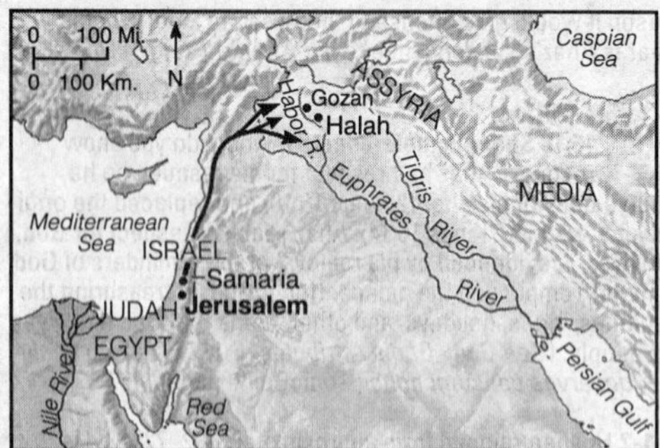

ISRAEL TAKEN CAPTIVE
Finally the sins of Israel's people caught up with them. God allowed Assyria to defeat and disperse the people. They were led into captivity, swallowed up by the mighty, evil Assyrian Empire. Sin always brings discipline, and the consequences of that sin are sometimes irreversible.

▶ SPIRITUAL WARFARE
17:7 God is not mocked. In the form of a legal edict, the writers announce that Israel, the northern portion of God's covenant people (Judah was the southern section) perished as a nation. Again and again, God sent prophets to warn Israel of the coming judgment, but they would not listen (2 Kings 17:14). God swept them away (2 Kings 17:18) and assimilated those ten tribes into Assyria. Both here and throughout Scripture (Revelation 1–3, for instance), you can see that God will not tolerate complete rebellion from His covenant people. He will destroy churches, denominations, and whatever else is called by His name if they remain in full rebellion against His purposes. God's love for His glory is too great to endure mocking (Mark 15:32). (***See Spiritual Warfare****> Resisting Sin and Evil> Consequences> Of Disobedience> God is not mocked,* TopicGuide page A46.)

17:13 Prophets functioned as emissaries from God. Their role is best understood within the context of Israel's covenant relationship with God. When a vassal state began to violate the terms of its covenant with its sovereign nation, an emissary would often be sent to demand renewed obedience and threaten the nation with the curses stipulated by the covenant. The prophets sent by God performed this same role for God and Israel regarding their covenant relationship (Deuteronomy 28; Leviticus 26). Israel failed to heed the prophets' warnings and brought God's just punishment upon themselves.

17:16 16 They rejected all the commands of the LORD their God and made two calves from
1 Kgs 12:28; 16:31 metal. They set up an Asherah pole and worshiped Baal and all the forces of heaven.
17:17 17 They even sacrificed their own sons and daughters in the fire.* They consulted fortune-
Lev 19:26 Deut 18:10-12 tellers and practiced sorcery and sold themselves to evil, arousing the LORD's anger.
2 Kgs 3:27; 16:3; 21:6 18 Because the LORD was very angry with Israel, He swept them away from His presence.
17:19 Only the tribe of Judah remained in the land. 19 But even the people of Judah refused to
1 Kgs 14:22-24 obey the commands of the LORD their God, for they followed the evil practices that Israel
17:21 had introduced. 20 The LORD rejected all the descendants of Israel. He punished them by
1 Kgs 11:11, 31; 12:20 handing them over to their attackers until He had banished Israel from His presence.
17:23 21 For when the LORD* tore Israel away from the kingdom of David, they chose Jeroboam
2 Kgs 18:11-12 son of Nebat as their king. But Jeroboam drew Israel away from following the LORD and
made them commit a great sin. 22 And the people of Israel persisted in all the evil ways of
Jeroboam. They did not turn from these sins 23 until the LORD finally swept them away from
His presence, just as all His prophets had warned. So Israel was exiled from their land to
Assyria, where they remain to this day.

FOREIGNERS SETTLE IN ISRAEL

17:24 24 The king of Assyria transported groups of people from Babylon, Cuthah, Avva, Hamath,
2 Kgs 18:34 Ezra 4:2, 10 and Sepharvaim and resettled them in the towns of Samaria, replacing the people of Isra-
el. They took possession of Samaria and lived in its towns. 25 But since these foreign set-
tlers did not worship the LORD when they first arrived, the LORD sent lions among them,
which killed some of them.
26 So a message was sent to the king of Assyria: "The people you have sent to live in the
towns of Samaria do not know the religious customs of the God of the land. He has sent
lions among them to destroy them because they have not worshiped Him correctly."
27 The king of Assyria then commanded, "Send one of the exiled priests back to Samaria.
Let him live there and teach the new residents the religious customs of the God of the
land." 28 So one of the priests who had been exiled from Samaria returned to Bethel and
taught the new residents how to worship the LORD.
17:29 29 But these various groups of foreigners also continued to worship their own gods. In town
1 Kgs 12:31; 13:32 after town where they lived, they placed their idols at the pagan shrines that the people of Sa-
maria had built. 30 Those from Babylon worshiped idols of their god Succoth-benoth. Those
17:31 from Cuthah worshiped their god Nergal. And those from Hamath worshiped Ashima. 31 The
2 Kgs 17:24; 19:37

17:17 Or *They even made their sons and daughters pass through the fire.* 17:21 Hebrew *He;* compare 1 Kgs 11:31-32.

17:16-17 Jeroboam set up gold calves in Dan and Bethel as part of his unauthorized system of worship. Mosaic Law condemned the worship of heavenly bodies (Deuteronomy 4:19; 17:3) and the practices of child sacrifice, fortune-telling, and sorcery (Deuteronomy 18:9-13).

17:18-19 The destruction of Israel became a warning to the remaining tribe of Judah. Prophets warned Judah that they would suffer a fate like Israel's if they continued to behave like Israel (see Micah 1; Jeremiah 2–3; Ezekiel 16).

17:24-41 This section describes how the Assyrian policy of deportation and repopulation was applied to Israel. The resulting amalgamation of ethnicities, cultures, and religions eventually gave rise to the people referred to in the New Testament as Samaritans. By dislocating people groups and replacing them with other displaced groups, the Assyrians sought to prevent uprisings.

17:25-27 Lions were not uncommon in ancient Israel, yet the authors identify this outbreak as the work of God (see also Deuteronomy 32:24; 1 Kings 13:24; 20:36; Amos 3:12). These attacks were reported to the Assyrian king, who responded by sending an Israelite priest to teach the people how to worship God correctly. The king's action stemmed from the common belief in the ancient world that the deities of local regions needed to be accorded a measure of respect, or they would lash out against the inhabitants of the land.

▸ WORSHIP

17:26 Respect the Temple. It dishonored God for people to worship other gods in the land of Israel. The Assyrian king understood this and sent a priest back to teach the people how to worship God, but the idolatry continued. Does God have holy places today? He does—our very bodies are the temples where God dwells, and they are to be honored (Ephesians 4:30; 1 Corinthians 6:15, 19). Keep your body pure and holy, and worship God alone. (***See Worship****> OT> Reverence> Awe of God means obeying His commandments,* TopicGuide page A28.)

17:30-31 Nergal was the god of the underworld in Mesopotamian mythology. Anammelech was another name for the Mesopotamian sun god Anu. The rest of the idols mentioned here were local deities of which we know little.

Avvites worshiped their gods Nibhaz and Tartak. And the people from Sepharvaim even
burned their own children as sacrifices to their gods Adrammelech and Anammelech.
32 These new residents worshiped the LORD, but they also appointed from among them- **17:32**
selves all sorts of people as priests to offer sacrifices at their places of worship. 33 And 1 Kgs 12:31
though they worshiped the LORD, they continued to follow their own gods according to the
religious customs of the nations from which they came. 34 And this is still going on today. **17:34**
They continue to follow their former practices instead of truly worshiping the LORD and Gen 32:28; 35:10
obeying the decrees, regulations, instructions, and commands He gave the descendants
of Jacob, whose name He changed to Israel.
35 For the LORD had made a covenant with the descendants of Jacob and commanded **17:35**
them: "Do not worship any other gods or bow before them or serve them or offer sacrifices Exod 20:5
to them. 36 But worship only the LORD, who brought you out of Egypt with great strength
and a powerful arm. Bow down to Him alone, and offer sacrifices only to Him. 37 Be careful **17:37**
at all times to obey the decrees, regulations, instructions, and commands that He wrote for Deut 5:32
you. You must not worship other gods. 38 Do not forget the covenant I made with you, and **17:38**
do not worship other gods. 39 You must worship only the LORD your God. He is the One Deut 4:23; 6:10-12
who will rescue you from all your enemies."
40 But the people would not listen and continued to follow their former practices. 41 So **17:41**
while these new residents worshiped the LORD, they also worshiped their idols. And to this Zeph 1:5
day their descendants do the same. Matt 6:24

HEZEKIAH RULES IN JUDAH

18 Hezekiah son of Ahaz began to rule over Judah in the third year of King Hoshea's **18:1**
reign in Israel. 2 He was twenty-five years old when he became king, and he 2 Chr 28:27
reigned in Jerusalem twenty-nine years. His mother was Abijah,* the daughter of Zechari- **18:2-4**
ah. 3 He did what was pleasing in the LORD's sight, just as his ancestor David had done. 4 He //2 Chr 29:1-2; 31:1
removed the pagan shrines, smashed the sacred pillars, and cut down the Asherah poles. **18:4** Num 21:8-9
He broke up the bronze serpent that Moses had made, because the people of Israel had 2 Chr 31:1
been offering sacrifices to it. The bronze serpent was called Nehushtan.*

18:2 As in parallel text at 2 Chr 29:1; Hebrew reads *Abi,* a variant spelling of Abijah. 18:4 *Nehushtan* sounds like the Hebrew terms that mean "snake," "bronze," and "unclean thing."

▸ MINISTRY

17:41 Praying for the Samaritans. In Jesus' day, the group of people mentioned in these verses was known as the Samaritans. But within a few hundred years of Jesus' talk with the Samaritan woman at Jacob's Well (John 4), Samaritan society began to disintegrate due to pressures and hardships created by various ruling empires. Today only 600 descendants of those ancient Samaritans remain, with 400 of this number living at the top of Mount Gerizim. They believe they worship God rightly and believe in a messiah that is yet to come. Pray for people like the Samaritans that they will recognize that the Messiah has come and welcomes them into His kingdom. (***See Ministry****> Great Commission> Make Disciples> Prayers> That they would confess Christ as Lord,* TopicGuide page A56.)

18:1 Hezekiah reigned from approximately 715–686 BC.

18:4 Moses crafted the bronze serpent according to God's instructions during a plague of serpents in the wilderness (Numbers 21:6-9). This incident demonstrates humanity's unfortunate propensity for idolatry (see Romans 1:18-32).

▸ WORSHIP

18:4 Renewal and destruction. Bringing reformation and renewal to your family and church may mean abandoning some traditions that have become unhealthy. Even the most biblical of traditions can be misapplied. The yearly Jewish Passover was transformed into daily communion meals (Acts 2:42, 46) and then into the weekly Agape Feast (1 Corinthians 9). Due to abuses, however, the tradition was modified between the sixth and eighth centuries to a weekly representative feast with only wine and bread. Ask God for the wisdom to renew or restore traditions that have ceased to honor God. Seek to make the worship at your church or small group both biblical and relevant. (***See Worship****> OT> Repentance> Nature> To obey is better than sacrifice,* TopicGuide page A29.)

▸ WORSHIP

18:4 Tear down your idols. What would people today call someone who, if he became king, told his soldiers to destroy all the other religions in the nation except for one? Would we call him faithful (2 Kings 18:6) and successful (2 Kings 18:7), or small-minded, bigoted, violent, and dangerous? Yet this was what God judged as righteous in that situation. In modern nations, this type of behavior by a ruler is not constitutionally acceptable. But God has called us to eradicate, with great enthusiasm, all paganism and unbelief in those areas in which we do have authority. In your workplace, in your home, in your church, in your very heart—what can you do or stop doing to establish a right worship of God? (***See Worship****> OT> Repentance> Nature> Repentance is characterized as turning from idols to the living God,* TopicGuide page A29.)

18:5-7 //2 Chr 31:20-21
18:5 2 Kgs 19:10; 23:25
18:6 Deut 10:20
18:7 Gen 39:2-3; 1 Sam 18:14
18:8 2 Kgs 17:9; 2 Chr 28:18
18:9-12 //2 Kgs 17:3-7
18:12 1 Kgs 9:6; Dan 9:6, 10

5 Hezekiah trusted in the LORD, the God of Israel. There was no one like him among all the kings of Judah, either before or after his time. 6 He remained faithful to the LORD in everything, and he carefully obeyed all the commands the LORD had given Moses. 7 So the LORD was with him, and Hezekiah was successful in everything he did. He revolted against the king of Assyria and refused to pay him tribute. 8 He also conquered the Philistines as far distant as Gaza and its territory, from their smallest outpost to their largest walled city.

9 During the fourth year of Hezekiah's reign, which was the seventh year of King Hoshea's reign in Israel, King Shalmaneser of Assyria attacked the city of Samaria and began a siege against it. 10 Three years later, during the sixth year of King Hezekiah's reign and the ninth year of King Hoshea's reign in Israel, Samaria fell. 11 At that time the king of Assyria exiled the Israelites to Assyria and placed them in colonies in Halah, along the banks of the Habor River in Gozan, and in the cities of the Medes. 12 For they refused to listen to the LORD their God and obey Him. Instead, they violated His covenant—all the laws that Moses the LORD's servant had commanded them to obey.

ASSYRIA INVADES JUDAH

18:13 2 Chr 32:1; Isa 36:1
18:15 1 Kgs 15:18-19; 2 Kgs 12:18

13 In the fourteenth year of King Hezekiah's reign,* King Sennacherib of Assyria came to attack the fortified towns of Judah and conquered them. 14 King Hezekiah sent this message to the king of Assyria at Lachish: "I have done wrong. I will pay whatever tribute money you demand if you will only withdraw." The king of Assyria then demanded a settlement of more than eleven tons of silver and one ton of gold.* 15 To gather this amount, King Hezekiah used all the silver stored in the Temple of the LORD and in the palace treasury. 16 Hezekiah even stripped the gold from the doors of the LORD's Temple and from the doorposts he had overlaid with gold, and he gave it all to the Assyrian king.

18:17-37 //2 Chr 32:9-19; //Isa 36:1-22
18:18 2 Kgs 19:2; Isa 22:15-16, 20

17 Nevertheless, the king of Assyria sent his commander in chief, his field commander, and his chief of staff* from Lachish with a huge army to confront King Hezekiah in Jerusalem. The Assyrians took up a position beside the aqueduct that feeds water into the upper pool, near the road leading to the field where cloth is washed.* 18 They summoned King Hezekiah, but the king sent these officials to meet with them: Eliakim son of Hilkiah, the palace administrator; Shebna the court secretary; and Joah son of Asaph, the royal historian.

SENNACHERIB THREATENS JERUSALEM

19 Then the Assyrian king's chief of staff told them to give this message to Hezekiah:

"This is what the great king of Assyria says: What are you trusting in that makes you so confident? 20 Do you think that mere words can substitute for military skill and strength? Who are you counting on, that you have rebelled against me? 21 On Egypt? If you lean on Egypt, it will be like a reed that splinters beneath your weight and pierces your hand. Pharaoh, the king of Egypt, is completely unreliable!

18:13 The fourteenth year of Hezekiah's reign was 701 B.C. 18:14 Hebrew *300 talents* [10 metric tons] *of silver and 30 talents* [1 metric ton] *of gold.* 18:17a Or *the rabshakeh;* also in 18:19, 26, 27, 28, 37. 18:17b Or *bleached.*

18:14-16 Hezekiah's initial response to the Assyrian threat was not what we might have expected of him (2 Kings 18:7). His behavior was sadly reminiscent of his father Ahaz (2 Kings 16:8-9) and others who plundered the Temple to appease foreign enemies (1 Kings 14:25-28; 2 Kings 12:17-18). This early timidity in Hezekiah may have been recorded to emphasize the strengthening effect of the word of God through the prophet Isaiah (2 Kings 19:5-7, 20-34).

18:19-25 The initial speech by Sennacherib's representative revolved around the theme of trust. Would Judah trust in her allies, particularly Egypt? Would she trust in her God? Or would she surrender to the Assyrians, failing to trust in anyone? In this cunning piece of psychological warfare, the Assyrian representative naturally suggested that the third alternative was the only reasonable choice.

22“But perhaps you will say to me, ‘We are trusting in the LORD our God!’ But isn’t He the One who was insulted by Hezekiah? Didn’t Hezekiah tear down His shrines and altars and make everyone in Judah and Jerusalem worship only at the altar here in Jerusalem?

23“I’ll tell you what! Strike a bargain with my master, the king of Assyria. I will give you 2,000 horses if you can find that many men to ride on them! 24With your tiny army, how can you think of challenging even the weakest contingent of my master’s troops, even with the help of Egypt’s chariots and charioteers? 25What’s more, do you think we have invaded your land without the LORD’s direction? The LORD Himself told us, ‘Attack this land and destroy it!’”

26Then Eliakim son of Hilkiah, Shebna, and Joah said to the Assyrian chief of staff, “Please speak to us in Aramaic, for we understand it well. Don’t speak in Hebrew,* for the people on the wall will hear.”

18:26
Ezra 4:7
Dan 2:4

27But Sennacherib’s chief of staff replied, “Do you think my master sent this message only to you and your master? He wants all the people to hear it, for when we put this city under siege, they will suffer along with you. They will be so hungry and thirsty that they will eat their own dung and drink their own urine.”

28Then the chief of staff stood and shouted in Hebrew to the people on the wall, “Listen to this message from the great king of Assyria! 29This is what the king says: Don’t let Hezekiah deceive you. He will never be able to rescue you from my power. 30Don’t let him fool you into trusting in the LORD by saying, ‘The LORD will surely rescue us. This city will never fall into the hands of the Assyrian king!’

31“Don’t listen to Hezekiah! These are the terms the king of Assyria is offering: Make peace with me—open the gates and come out. Then each of you can continue eating from your own grapevine and fig tree and drinking from your own well. 32Then I will arrange to take you to another land like this one—a land of grain and new wine, bread and vineyards, olive groves and honey. Choose life instead of death!

18:31
Deut 8:7-9
1 Kgs 4:25

“Don’t listen to Hezekiah when he tries to mislead you by saying, ‘The LORD will rescue us!’ 33Have the gods of any other nations ever saved their people from the king of Assyria? 34What happened to the gods of Hamath and Arpad? And what about the gods of Sepharvaim, Hena, and Ivvah? Did any god rescue Samaria from my power? 35What god of any nation has ever been able to save its people from my power? So what makes you think that the LORD can rescue Jerusalem from me?”

18:33
2 Kgs 19:12

18:34
2 Kgs 17:24; 19:13

36But the people were silent and did not utter a word because Hezekiah had commanded them, “Do not answer him.”

37Then Eliakim son of Hilkiah, the palace administrator; Shebna the court secretary; and Joah son of Asaph, the royal historian, went back to Hezekiah. They tore their clothes in despair, and they went in to see the king and told him what the Assyrian chief of staff had said.

HEZEKIAH SEEKS THE LORD’S HELP

19:1-13
//Isa 37:1-13

19:1
2 Chr 32:20-22

19 When King Hezekiah heard their report, he tore his clothes and put on burlap and went into the Temple of the LORD. 2And he sent Eliakim the palace administrator,

18:26 Hebrew *in the dialect of Judah;* also in 18:28.

18:22 The Assyrian representative wrongly assumed that Hezekiah’s reforms (2 Kings 18:4) must have angered the God of Israel. At the same time, he expected, perhaps correctly, that the population must have been angered by the removal of their shrines and idols and therefore would be swayed by his theological argument.

18:23-25 Having dismissed Judah’s military might and Judah’s God, the Assyrian representative followed with taunting sarcasm and outright deception to convince Jerusalem to surrender (2 Kings 18:23-25).

18:31-32 These words ironically echo the language of Deuteronomy 30:15-20. Hezekiah was faced with a critical decision: trust in God or capitulate to the Assyrian monarch. Both demanded ultimate allegiance, but only One possessed the right and power to demand such allegiance.

19:1-4 Hezekiah dressed in clothing that reflected the perilous circumstances. He then sought help from God through the prophet Isaiah. He framed his petition in terms of Jerusalem’s plight and God’s own offended honor.

19:2 Shebna the court secretary, and the leading priests, all dressed in burlap, to the prophet
Isa 1:1 Isaiah son of Amoz. [3]They told him, "This is what King Hezekiah says: Today is a day of
trouble, insults, and disgrace. It is like when a child is ready to be born, but the mother has
19:4 no strength to deliver the baby. [4]But perhaps the LORD your God has heard the Assyrian
2 Sam 16:12 2 Kgs 18:35 chief of staff,* sent by the king to defy the living God, and will punish him for his words.
Isa 1:9 Oh, pray for those of us who are left!"

[5]After King Hezekiah's officials delivered the king's message to Isaiah, [6]the prophet re-
plied, "Say to your master, 'This is what the LORD says: Do not be disturbed by this blasphe-
19:7 mous speech against Me from the Assyrian king's messengers. [7]Listen! I Myself will move
2 Kgs 19:37 against him,* and the king will receive a message that he is needed at home. So he will re-
turn to his land, where I will have him killed with a sword.'"

19:8 [8]Meanwhile, the Assyrian chief of staff left Jerusalem and went to consult the king of As-
2 Kgs 18:14 syria, who had left Lachish and was attacking Libnah.

[9]Soon afterward King Sennacherib received word that King Tirhakah of Ethiopia* was
leading an army to fight against him. Before leaving to meet the attack, he sent messen-
gers back to Hezekiah in Jerusalem with this message:

> 19:10 [10]"This message is for King Hezekiah of Judah. Don't let your God, in whom you
> 2 Kgs 18:5, 30 trust, deceive you with promises that Jerusalem will not be captured by the king of
> Assyria. [11]You know perfectly well what the kings of Assyria have done wherever
> 19:12 they have gone. They have completely destroyed everyone who stood in their way!
> 2 Kgs 17:6; 18:33 Why should you be any different? [12]Have the gods of other nations rescued them—
> Isa 37:12 such nations as Gozan, Haran, Rezeph, and the people of Eden who were in Tel-
> 19:13 assar? My predecessors destroyed them all! [13]What happened to the king of
> 2 Kgs 18:34 Hamath and the king of Arpad? What happened to the kings of Sepharvaim,
> Hena, and Ivvah?"

19:14-19 [14]After Hezekiah received the letter from the messengers and read it, he went up to the
//Isa 37:14-20 LORD's Temple and spread it out before the LORD. [15]And Hezekiah prayed this prayer be-
fore the LORD: "O LORD, God of Israel, You are enthroned between the mighty cherubim!
You alone are God of all the kingdoms of the earth. You alone created the heavens and
19:16 the earth. [16]Bend down, O LORD, and listen! Open Your eyes, O LORD, and see! Listen to
1 Kgs 8:29-30 2 Chr 6:40 Sennacherib's words of defiance against the living God.

[17]"It is true, LORD, that the kings of Assyria have destroyed all these nations. [18]And they
19:18 Isa 44:9-20 have thrown the gods of these nations into the fire and burned them. But of course the As-
Acts 17:29 syrians could destroy them! They were not gods at all—only idols of wood and stone
19:19 shaped by human hands. [19]Now, O LORD our God, rescue us from his power; then all the
1 Kgs 8:42-43 kingdoms of the earth will know that You alone, O LORD, are God."

19:4 Or *the rabshakeh;* also in 19:8. 19:7 Hebrew *I will put a spirit in him.* 19:9 Hebrew *of Cush.*

19:6-7 The Lord's response to Hezekiah evoked the holy war traditions of Israel. Faced with an overwhelming enemy, Judah was not to fear but instead to rely on God, who would fight for His people (compare with Exodus 14:13-14 and Joshua 1:6; 10:1; 11:6).

▶ HOLINESS

19:7 Surrender to God. If you were faced with the threat of utter desolation, what would your first thoughts be? One option is surrender, but Hezekiah didn't prostrate himself before Assyria. He surrendered to God, the only One who could save his nation. God responded by promising to lure the Assyrian army away from Jerusalem, leaving the city unharmed. For His own glory and honor, God swore to rescue Judah from the world's greatest army (2 Kings 19:17-19). Hezekiah's surrender to God was the perfect plan to defeat his enemies. (***See Holiness*** > *Submission* > *Yielding to Spirit* > *Surrender your heart,* TopicGuide page A41.)

19:9 Ethiopia (literally, Cush) is best associated with present-day Sudan. Tirhakah was not officially made king until shortly after the Sennacherib invasion, yet it was appropriate to refer to him as king, since the readers would have known him as such. He later became Pharaoh in Egypt's twenty-fifth dynasty.

19:14-19 Hezekiah's prayer resembled the prayer of Solomon at the dedication of the Temple (1 Kings 8:23-53, especially verses 33-34). Hezekiah's prayer was profound in its grasp of God's uniqueness, majesty, and sovereignty, and it was passionate in its appeals to God's compassion. Not surprisingly, the prayer also reflected the theology of Isaiah (Isaiah 42:8; 43:13; 44:6).

ISAIAH PREDICTS JUDAH'S DELIVERANCE

20Then Isaiah son of Amoz sent this message to Hezekiah: "This is what the LORD, the God of Israel, says: I have heard your prayer about King Sennacherib of Assyria. 21And the LORD has spoken this word against him:

"The virgin daughter of Zion
despises you and laughs at you.
The daughter of Jerusalem
shakes her head in derision as you flee.

22 "Whom have you been defying and ridiculing?
Against whom did you raise your voice?
At whom did you look with such haughty eyes?
It was the Holy One of Israel!
23 By your messengers you have defied the Lord.
You have said, 'With my many chariots
I have conquered the highest mountains—
yes, the remotest peaks of Lebanon.
I have cut down its tallest cedars
and its finest cypress trees.
I have reached its farthest corners
and explored its deepest forests.
24 I have dug wells in many foreign lands
and refreshed myself with their water.
With the sole of my foot
I stopped up all the rivers of Egypt!'

25 "But have you not heard?
I decided this long ago.
Long ago I planned it,
and now I am making it happen.
I planned for you to crush fortified cities
into heaps of rubble.
26 That is why their people have so little power
and are so frightened and confused.
They are as weak as grass,
as easily trampled as tender green shoots.
They are like grass sprouting on a housetop,
scorched before it can grow lush and tall.

27 "But I know you well—
where you stay
and when you come and go.
I know the way you have raged against Me.
28 And because of your raging against Me
and your arrogance, which I have heard for Myself,
I will put My hook in your nose
and My bit in your mouth.
I will make you return
by the same road on which you came."

29Then Isaiah said to Hezekiah, "Here is the proof that what I say is true:

19:20-37 //Isa 37:21-38
19:21 Lam 2:13
19:22 Exod 5:2; Isa 5:24; 30:10-15
19:25 Isa 10:5-7; 45:5-7
19:26 Ps 129:6-7
19:27 Ps 139:1-4
19:28 2 Kgs 19:33; Ezek 29:4
19:29 Exod 3:12; 2 Kgs 20:8-9

19:29-31 This second section of Isaiah's prophecy promised the king and his people recovery and healing. While initial conditions would be bleak, they would improve, and the remnant of Judah's population would take root and flourish. The experience of this remnant anticipated and perhaps informed the remnant theology of the book of Isaiah, which looked forward to the remnant that would survive the Babylonian exile (see Isaiah 6:13; 11:11).

"This year you will eat only what grows up by itself,
and next year you will eat what springs up from that.
But in the third year you will plant crops and harvest them;
you will tend vineyards and eat their fruit.
19:30 2 Chr 32:22-23 [30] And you who are left in Judah,
who have escaped the ravages of the siege,
will put roots down in your own soil
and will grow up and flourish.
19:31 Isa 9:7 [31] For a remnant of My people will spread out from Jerusalem,
a group of survivors from Mount Zion.
The passionate commitment of the LORD of Heaven's Armies*
will make this happen!

[32] "And this is what the LORD says about the king of Assyria:
"His armies will not enter Jerusalem.
They will not even shoot an arrow at it.
They will not march outside its gates with their shields
nor build banks of earth against its walls.
19:33 2 Kgs 19:28 [33] The king will return to his own country
by the same road on which he came.
He will not enter this city,
says the LORD.
19:34 1 Kgs 11:12-13 2 Kgs 20:6 [34] For My own honor and for the sake of My servant David,
I will defend this city and protect it."
19:35-37 //2 Chr 32:20-21 [35] That night the angel of the LORD went out to the Assyrian camp and killed 185,000
Assyrian soldiers. When the surviving Assyrians* woke up the next morning, they found
19:36 Jon 1:2 corpses everywhere. [36] Then King Sennacherib of Assyria broke camp and returned to his
own land. He went home to his capital of Nineveh and stayed there.
19:37 Gen 8:4 Ezra 4:2 [37] One day while he was worshiping in the temple of his god Nisroch, his sons* Adram-
melech and Sharezer killed him with their swords. They then escaped to the land of Ararat,
and another son, Esarhaddon, became the next king of Assyria.

HEZEKIAH'S SICKNESS AND RECOVERY

20:1-11 //2 Chr 32:24-26 //Isa 38:1-8 **20** About that time Hezekiah became deathly ill, and the prophet Isaiah son of
Amoz went to visit him. He gave the king this message: "This is what the LORD

19:31 As in Greek and Syriac versions, Latin Vulgate, and an alternate reading of the Masoretic Text (see also Isa 37:32); the other alternate reads *the LORD*. 19:35 Hebrew *When they*. 19:37 As in Greek version and an alternate reading of the Masoretic Text (see also Isa 37:38); the other alternate reading lacks *his sons*.

19:32-34 The final portion of Isaiah's oracle announced God's intention to defend Jerusalem for the sake of His own honor and His servant David. Hezekiah's prayer had previously invoked God's concern for His own glory (2 Kings 19:16, 19). The appeal to the Davidic covenant, even in the context of Hezekiah's highly regarded reign, reminds us that even the most righteous still must rely on God's grace.

19:35 The destroying angel is also associated with the last of the ten plagues that God sent upon Egypt (Exodus 12:21-23) and David's infamous census (2 Samuel 24). The Greek historian Herodotus and the Jewish historian Josephus both recorded Sennacherib's withdrawal under disastrous circumstances. In his own account, Sennacherib boasted of trapping Hezekiah in Jerusalem, but he said nothing of attacking the city and remained glaringly silent on why he retreated.

20:1-19 Hezekiah reigned for 29 years. Subtracting the 15 years of life that God granted him (2 Kings 20:6), the events described here took place in or around Hezekiah's fourteenth year, the year of the Assyrian attack (2 Kings 18:13). Given the presence of substantial wealth in Judah's treasuries (compare 2 Kings 20:13 with 18:14-16), it is likely that these events took place before the siege of Jerusalem. If this is the case, these events have been arranged topically rather than chronologically.

▸ BIBLE
20:1-6 Unspoken possibilities. Why did the Lord change what he said to Hezekiah regarding his imminent death (2 Kings 20:5)? God's Word is true, but there are unspoken contingencies built into some of His prophecies. We also see this when God relented from destroying Nineveh (Jonah 4:11) and from destroying all Israel after their worship of the gold calf (Exodus 32:4). When God threatens disaster or suffering for sin, He often allows the possibility of mercy for those who repent. When we repent and believe the gospel, all believers move from condemnation to favor and forgiveness. (***See Bible***> *Unity*> *Kingdom of God*> *Kingdom is associated with forgiveness of sins,* TopicGuide page A11.)

says: Set your affairs in order, for you are going to die. You will not recover from this
illness."
2 When Hezekiah heard this, he turned his face to the wall and prayed to the LORD,
3 "Remember, O LORD, how I have always been faithful to You and have served You single- **20:3**
mindedly, always doing what pleases You." Then he broke down and wept bitterly. 2 Kgs 18:3-6
4 But before Isaiah had left the middle courtyard, this message came to him from the
LORD: 5 "Go back to Hezekiah, the leader of My people. Tell him, 'This is what the LORD, the **20:5**
God of your ancestor David, says: I have heard your prayer and seen your tears. I will heal 2 Kgs 19:20 Ps 39:12
you, and three days from now you will get out of bed and go to the Temple of the LORD. 6 I **20:6**
will add fifteen years to your life, and I will rescue you and this city from the king of Assyr- 2 Kgs 19:34
ia. I will defend this city for My own honor and for the sake of My servant David.'"
7 Then Isaiah said, "Make an ointment from figs." So Hezekiah's servants spread the
ointment over the boil, and Hezekiah recovered!
8 Meanwhile, Hezekiah had said to Isaiah, "What sign will the LORD give to prove that He
will heal me and that I will go to the Temple of the LORD three days from now?"
9 Isaiah replied, "This is the sign from the LORD to prove that He will do as He promised.
Would you like the shadow on the sundial to go forward ten steps or backward ten steps?*" **20:9** Isa 38:7-8
10 "The shadow always moves forward," Hezekiah replied, "so that would be easy. Make **20:11**
it go ten steps backward instead." 11 So Isaiah the prophet asked the LORD to do this, and Josh 10:12-14
He caused the shadow to move ten steps backward on the sundial* of Ahaz!

ENVOYS FROM BABYLON

12 Soon after this, Merodach-baladan son of Baladan, king of Babylon, sent Hezekiah his **20:12-19**
best wishes and a gift, for he had heard that Hezekiah had been very sick. 13 Hezekiah re- //Isa 39:1-8
ceived the Babylonian envoys and showed them everything in his treasure-houses—the **20:13**
silver, the gold, the spices, and the aromatic oils. He also took them to see his armory and 2 Chr 32:27
showed them everything in his royal treasuries! There was nothing in his palace or king-
dom that Hezekiah did not show them.
14 Then Isaiah the prophet went to King Hezekiah and asked him, "What did those men
want? Where were they from?"
Hezekiah replied, "They came from the distant land of Babylon."
15 "What did they see in your palace?" Isaiah asked.
"They saw everything," Hezekiah replied. "I showed them everything I own—all my
royal treasuries."
16 Then Isaiah said to Hezekiah, "Listen to this message from the LORD: 17 The time is **20:17**
coming when everything in your palace—all the treasures stored up by your ancestors un- 2 Kgs 24:13; 25:13-15
til now—will be carried off to Babylon. Nothing will be left, says the LORD. 18 Some of your Jer 52:17-23

20:9 Or *The shadow on the sundial has gone forward ten steps; do you want it to go backward ten steps?* 20:11 Hebrew *the steps.*

20:8 Isaiah's ministry often included signs to authenticate his prophecies (2 Kings 19:29; Isaiah 7:11). Hezekiah's request for a sign should probably be interpreted negatively, since his healing had already begun. He lacked faith in God's Word (compare Matthew 12:38-39).

20:9-11 The use of a sundial may have had symbolic weight. The shadow of death had crept up on Hezekiah, but God had "turned the clock back," as we might say, and death had retreated. Hezekiah's recovery mirrored the salvation of Jerusalem from the brink of destruction at the hands of Sennacherib (2 Kings 20:6).

▸ GOD
20:11 Tick-tock. While the sundial was invented in Egypt around the time of the Exodus, it was likely not introduced to Israel's society until the reign of Ahaz. Until then, time was measured in larger, more casual units. Today, every second seems to count. In a day when time is the master of so many, make sure that God, not time, rules your life. God is most certainly the master of time! (***See God**> God's Attributes> Infinite> God, who exists before and after time, deserves honor,* TopicGuide page A16.)

20:13 Regarding when this event occurred, see note at 2 Kings 20:1-19. Hezekiah was not merely providing an entertaining tour for his guests, he was consenting to an alliance with Babylon and offering the resources at his disposal. Isaiah condemned this course of action in Isaiah 30–31. Relying on foreign allies suggested a failure to rely on God for Judah's security.

20:16-18 Within 100 years, the Babylonians overthrew the Assyrians and established themselves as the leading power of the region. By 586 BC, the Temple lay in ruins.

very own sons will be taken away into exile. They will become eunuchs who will serve in
the palace of Babylon's king."
19 Then Hezekiah said to Isaiah, "This message you have given me from the LORD is
good." For the king was thinking, "At least there will be peace and security during my
lifetime."
20 The rest of the events in Hezekiah's reign, including the extent of his power and how
he built a pool and dug a tunnel* to bring water into the city, are recorded in *The Book of
the History of the Kings of Judah*. 21 Hezekiah died, and his son Manasseh became the next
king.

MANASSEH RULES IN JUDAH

21 Manasseh was twelve years old when he became king, and he reigned in Jerusa-
lem fifty-five years. His mother was Hephzibah. 2 He did what was evil in the
LORD's sight, following the detestable practices of the pagan nations that the LORD had
driven from the land ahead of the Israelites. 3 He rebuilt the pagan shrines his father, Heze-
kiah, had destroyed. He constructed altars for Baal and set up an Asherah pole, just as
King Ahab of Israel had done. He also bowed before all the powers of the heavens and
worshiped them.
4 He built pagan altars in the Temple of the LORD, the place where the LORD had said, "My
name will remain in Jerusalem forever." 5 He built these altars for all the powers of the
heavens in both courtyards of the LORD's Temple. 6 Manasseh also sacrificed his own son in
the fire.* He practiced sorcery and divination, and he consulted with mediums and psy-
chics. He did much that was evil in the LORD's sight, arousing His anger.
7 Manasseh even made a carved image of Asherah and set it up in the Temple, the very
place where the LORD had told David and his son Solomon: "My name will be honored
forever in this Temple and in Jerusalem—the city I have chosen from among all the tribes
of Israel. 8 If the Israelites will be careful to obey My commands—all the laws My servant
Moses gave them—I will not send them into exile from this land that I gave their ances-
tors." 9 But the people refused to listen, and Manasseh led them to do even more evil
than the pagan nations that the LORD had destroyed when the people of Israel entered
the land.
10 Then the LORD said through His servants the prophets: 11 "King Manasseh of Judah has
done many detestable things. He is even more wicked than the Amorites, who lived in this
land before Israel. He has caused the people of Judah to sin with his idols.* 12 So this is
what the LORD, the God of Israel, says: I will bring such disaster on Jerusalem and Judah
that the ears of those who hear about it will tingle with horror. 13 I will judge Jerusalem by

20:18 2 Kgs 24:12, 15; 2 Chr 33:11
20:20-21 //2 Chr 32:32-33
20:21 2 Chr 32:33
21:1-10 //2 Chr 33:1-10
21:2 2 Kgs 16:3
21:3 Lev 18:25; Deut 12:31; 17:3; 1 Kgs 16:29-33; 2 Kgs 18:4
21:4 2 Sam 7:13
21:6 Lev 18:21; 19:26, 31; Deut 18:10; 2 Kgs 16:3; 17:17
21:7 Deut 16:21; 1 Kgs 9:3; 2 Kgs 23:6
21:8 2 Sam 7:10; 2 Kgs 18:11-12; 2 Chr 15:2
21:11 Gen 15:16; 1 Kgs 21:26; 2 Kgs 24:3-4
21:12 Jer 19:3
21:13 Isa 34:11; Amos 7:7-8

20:20 Hebrew *watercourse*. 21:6 Or *also made his son pass through the fire*. 21:11 The Hebrew term (literally *round things*) probably alludes to dung; also in 21:21.

▸ GOD
20:19 Double talk. Do you often say one thing but mean another and hope that no one catches you? Hezekiah forgot that God, who knows every thought, knows when we deceive one another. Be appropriately transparent with those God brings into your life. (***See God****> God's Attributes> All-Knowing> God misses nothing about us,* TopicGuide page A15.)

20:20-21 The tunnel mentioned here extended 1,700 feet from the Gihon Spring outside the walls of Jerusalem to the Pool of Siloam inside the city. It is a marvel of ancient water systems and can still be seen today in Jerusalem.

21:1 Chronological difficulties regarding Manasseh's reign lead many scholars to suggest that he served a ten-year co-regency with Hezekiah. Manasseh reigned from approximately 697–642 BC.

21:2-6 Judah was now engaged in the practices that led God to drive the Canaanites from the Promised Land at the time of the conquest (Deuteronomy 9:4; 18:9). Judah soon would face a similar fate as those Canaanites. (On child sacrifice, see note at 16:3. On sorcery, see note at 17:16-17.)

21:7-9 The audacity of Manasseh's wickedness, epitomized by the establishment of a pagan shrine within the Temple itself, is set in sharp contrast to the Lord's words to David and Solomon. The specter of an exile is now brought forcefully to the forefront (Deuteronomy 4:25-26; Leviticus 26:27-35).

21:10-15 None of the prophets mentioned in the Bible ministered during the reign of Manasseh. These verses are more a summary of the prophetic message than the precise words of any one prophet.

the same standard I used for Samaria and the same measure* I used for the family of Ahab. I will wipe away the people of Jerusalem as one wipes a dish and turns it upside down. 14 Then I will reject even the remnant of My own people who are left, and I will hand them over as plunder for their enemies. 15 For they have done great evil in My sight and have angered Me ever since their ancestors came out of Egypt."

16 Manasseh also murdered many innocent people until Jerusalem was filled from one end to the other with innocent blood. This was in addition to the sin that he caused the people of Judah to commit, leading them to do evil in the LORD's sight.

17 The rest of the events in Manasseh's reign and everything he did, including the sins he committed, are recorded in *The Book of the History of the Kings of Judah.* 18 When Manasseh died, he was buried in the palace garden, the garden of Uzza. Then his son Amon became the next king.

AMON RULES IN JUDAH

19 Amon was twenty-two years old when he became king, and he reigned in Jerusalem two years. His mother was Meshullemeth, the daughter of Haruz from Jotbah. 20 He did what was evil in the LORD's sight, just as his father, Manasseh, had done. 21 He followed the example of his father, worshiping the same idols his father had worshiped. 22 He abandoned the LORD, the God of his ancestors, and he refused to follow the LORD's ways.

23 Then Amon's own officials conspired against him and assassinated him in his palace. 24 But the people of the land killed all those who had conspired against King Amon, and they made his son Josiah the next king.

25 The rest of the events in Amon's reign and what he did are recorded in *The Book of the History of the Kings of Judah.* 26 He was buried in his tomb in the garden of Uzza. Then his son Josiah became the next king.

JOSIAH RULES IN JUDAH

22 Josiah was eight years old when he became king, and he reigned in Jerusalem thirty-one years. His mother was Jedidah, the daughter of Adaiah from Bozkath. 2 He did what was pleasing in the LORD's sight and followed the example of his ancestor David. He did not turn away from doing what was right.

3 In the eighteenth year of his reign, King Josiah sent Shaphan son of Azaliah and grandson of Meshullam, the court secretary, to the Temple of the LORD. He told him, 4 "Go to Hilkiah the high priest and have him count the money the gatekeepers have collected from the people at the LORD's Temple. 5 Entrust this money to the men assigned to supervise the Temple's restoration. Then they can use it to pay workers to repair the Temple of the LORD. 6 They will need to hire carpenters, builders, and masons. Also have them buy the timber and the finished stone needed to repair the Temple. 7 But don't require the construction supervisors to keep account of the money they receive, for they are honest and trustworthy men."

HILKIAH DISCOVERS GOD'S LAW

8 Hilkiah the high priest said to Shaphan the court secretary, "I have found the Book of the Law in the LORD's Temple!" Then Hilkiah gave the scroll to Shaphan, and he read it.

21:16 2 Kgs 24:3-4
21:17-18 //2 Chr 33:18-20
21:18 2 Kgs 21:26
21:22 2 Kgs 22:17
21:23 2 Kgs 12:20; 14:19
21:26 2 Kgs 21:18
22:1-20 //2 Chr 34:1-2, 8-28
22:1 Josh 15:39
22:3 2 Chr 34:8-9
22:4 2 Kgs 12:4
22:5 2 Kgs 12:11-14
22:7 2 Kgs 12:15
22:8 Deut 31:24-26; 2 Chr 34:14-16

21:13 Hebrew *the same plumb line I used for Samaria and the same plumb bob.*

▸ WORSHIP
21:13 Remove the unrepentant. God's people must act to remove corrupt leadership in their midst. The Bible gives us directions on how to do this (1 Samuel 2:24; Acts 11:1-18). But why should we care? Why not just let God deal with the problem? Because when God's people allowed corrupt Manasseh to remain in power, everyone suffered. Men, women, children—aside from a faithful remnant God preserved for Himself (Isaiah 65:9), Judah would perish in the same way as Israel had generations before. Do not allow the unrepentant to lead you and your family into ruin. (***See Worship****> OT> Repentance> Nature> Obedience leads to blessings, failure to repent leads to curses,* TopicGuide page A29.)

21:17 Manasseh's exile, repentance, and restoration are recorded in 2 Chronicles 33:11-17.

21:19 Amon reigned from approximately 642–640 BC.

22:1 Josiah reigned from approximately 640–609 BC.

22:8 There is a general consensus that the Book of the Law found in the Temple was the book of Deuteronomy, in whole or in part. Deuteronomy commands many of the reforms undertaken by Josiah, and Josiah's celebration of the Passover (2 Kings 23:21-23; 2 Chronicles 35:1-19) was in keeping with the standards set down in Deuteronomy 12 and 16.

9 Shaphan went to the king and reported, "Your officials have turned over the money col-
lected at the Temple of the LORD to the workers and supervisors at the Temple." 10 Shaphan
also told the king, "Hilkiah the priest has given me a scroll." So Shaphan read it to the king.
22:11 11 When the king heard what was written in the Book of the Law, he tore his clothes in
Josh 7:6 despair. 12 Then he gave these orders to Hilkiah the priest, Ahikam son of Shaphan, Acbor
22:12 2 Kgs 25:22 son of Micaiah, Shaphan the court secretary, and Asaiah the king's personal adviser: 13 "Go
2 Chr 34:20 to the Temple and speak to the LORD for me and for the people and for all Judah. Inquire
Jer 26:24 about the words written in this scroll that has been found. For the LORD's great anger is
22:13 burning against us because our ancestors have not obeyed the words in this scroll. We
Deut 29:23-28 have not been doing everything it says we must do."
22:14 14 So Hilkiah the priest, Ahikam, Acbor, Shaphan, and Asaiah went to the New Quarter*
2 Chr 34:22 of Jerusalem to consult with the prophet Huldah. She was the wife of Shallum son of
Tikvah, son of Harhas, the keeper of the Temple wardrobe.
15 She said to them, "The LORD, the God of Israel, has spoken! Go back and tell the man
22:16 who sent you, 16 'This is what the LORD says: I am going to bring disaster on this city* and its
Dan 9:11 people. All the words written in the scroll that the king of Judah has read will come true.
17 For My people have abandoned Me and offered sacrifices to pagan gods, and I am very
angry with them for everything they have done. My anger will burn against this place, and
it will not be quenched.'
18 "But go to the king of Judah who sent you to seek the LORD and tell him: 'This is what
22:19 the LORD, the God of Israel, says concerning the message you have just heard: 19 You were
Lev 26:31 Jer 26:6 sorry and humbled yourself before the LORD when you heard what I said against this city
and its people—that this land would be cursed and become desolate. You tore your cloth-
ing in despair and wept before Me in repentance. And I have indeed heard you, says the
LORD. 20 So I will not send the promised disaster until after you have died and been buried
in peace. You will not see the disaster I am going to bring on this city.'"
So they took her message back to the king.

JOSIAH'S RELIGIOUS REFORMS

23:1-3 **23** Then the king summoned all the elders of Judah and Jerusalem. 2 And the king
//2 Chr 34:29-32 went up to the Temple of the LORD with all the people of Judah and Jerusalem,

23:2 Deut 31:11

22:14 Or *the Second Quarter*, a newer section of Jerusalem. Hebrew reads *the Mishneh*. 22:16 Hebrew *this place;* also in 22:19, 20.

22:13 Josiah apparently associated the numerous curses in the book of Deuteronomy with the recent wickedness of the nation and its socio-political struggles (Deuteronomy 27–28).

22:14 Nothing is known about Huldah beyond what is related here. She was one of several women designated as prophets in the Old Testament (Exodus 15:20; Judges 4:4; Nehemiah 6:14). Her husband's office was associated with the Temple (compare 2 Kings 10:22).

▶ SPIRITUAL WARFARE

22:19 Threats and promises. The eternal punishment of hell, terrible wars, and other punishments sent by God upon those who refuse to repent can make us feel troubled when we are confronted by these parts of Scripture. But these warnings have a gracious purpose—to lead us to repentance. Such warnings should make us all the more grateful for the good news of the gospel. When you are sharing the gospel, find appropriate ways to tell unbelievers of the damnation that awaits those who refuse to repent. As uncomfortable as it may make us feel, this is part of the gospel, too. (***See Spiritual Warfare****> Resisting Sin and Evil> Consequences> Of Disobedience> Falling under discipline,* TopicGuide page A46.)

22:20 Despite this promise of a peaceful burial, Josiah eventually died a violent death in the heat of battle (2 Kings 23:29). The peace in view here, however, meant that Josiah would be spared the sight of Jerusalem's destruction (compare 1 Kings 14:12-13).

23:1-3 Unlike Hezekiah, who remained selfishly content by the assurance that Jerusalem would escape judgment in his lifetime (2 Kings 20:19), Josiah vigorously undertook a program of reform initiated by a national ceremony of covenant renewal. He was the antithesis of Manasseh, who led the people into all manner of wickedness (2 Kings 21:9). Asa (2 Chronicles 15:10-15) and Joash (2 Kings 11:12, 17-18) celebrated similar covenant renewals, as did Moses (Deuteronomy 29–30) and Joshua (Joshua 24:1-25).

▶ HOLINESS

23:2 Covenant renewal. Josiah called the nation to renew their covenant with God. What happens in your church on Sunday? Songs? Preaching? Skits? Are you aware that every Sunday morning, we also renew our covenant with the Lord? Especially when we partake of the Lord's Supper, we confirm all the terms of the new covenant, in which God has promised to save and sanctify us and we have promised to live surrendered lives under His law of love toward us (Luke 22:19-20; 1 Corinthians 11:25; James 2:8). Remain faithful to God and know that God will always keep His side of the new covenant. (***See Holiness****> Maturing> Conformity to Christ> Following the Royal Law of love,* TopicGuide page A40.)

along with the priests and the prophets—all the people from the least to the greatest.
There the king read to them the entire Book of the Covenant that had been found in the
LORD's Temple. 3The king took his place of authority beside the pillar and renewed the
covenant in the LORD's presence. He pledged to obey the LORD by keeping all His com-
mands, laws, and decrees with all his heart and soul. In this way, he confirmed all the
terms of the covenant that were written in the scroll, and all the people pledged them-
selves to the covenant.
4Then the king instructed Hilkiah the high priest and the priests of the second rank and
the Temple gatekeepers to remove from the LORD's Temple all the articles that were used
to worship Baal, Asherah, and all the powers of the heavens. The king had all these things
burned outside Jerusalem on the terraces of the Kidron Valley, and he carried the ashes
away to Bethel. 5He did away with the idolatrous priests, who had been appointed by the
previous kings of Judah, for they had offered sacrifices at the pagan shrines throughout
Judah and even in the vicinity of Jerusalem. They had also offered sacrifices to Baal, and
to the sun, the moon, the constellations, and to all the powers of the heavens. 6The king
removed the Asherah pole from the LORD's Temple and took it outside Jerusalem to the
Kidron Valley, where he burned it. Then he ground the ashes of the pole to dust and threw
the dust over the graves of the people. 7He also tore down the living quarters of the male
and female shrine prostitutes that were inside the Temple of the LORD, where the women
wove coverings for the Asherah pole.
8Josiah brought to Jerusalem all the priests who were living in other towns of Judah. He
also defiled the pagan shrines, where they had offered sacrifices—all the way from Geba
to Beersheba. He destroyed the shrines at the entrance to the gate of Joshua, the governor
of Jerusalem. This gate was located to the left of the city gate as one enters the city. 9The
priests who had served at the pagan shrines were not allowed* to serve at the LORD's altar
in Jerusalem, but they were allowed to eat unleavened bread with the other priests.
10Then the king defiled the altar of Topheth in the valley of Ben-Hinnom, so no one
could ever again use it to sacrifice a son or daughter in the fire* as an offering to Molech.
11He removed from the entrance of the LORD's Temple the horse statues that the former
kings of Judah had dedicated to the sun. They were near the quarters of Nathan-melech
the eunuch, an officer of the court.* The king also burned the chariots dedicated to the
sun.
12Josiah tore down the altars that the kings of Judah had built on the palace roof above
the upper room of Ahaz. The king destroyed the altars that Manasseh had built in the two
courtyards of the LORD's Temple. He smashed them to bits* and scattered the pieces in the
Kidron Valley. 13The king also desecrated the pagan shrines east of Jerusalem, to the
south of the Mount of Corruption, where King Solomon of Israel had built shrines for Ash-
toreth, the detestable goddess of the Sidonians; and for Chemosh, the detestable god of
the Moabites; and for Molech,* the vile god of the Ammonites. 14He smashed the sacred
pillars and cut down the Asherah poles. Then he desecrated these places by scattering hu-
man bones over them.
15The king also tore down the altar at Bethel—the pagan shrine that Jeroboam son of
Nebat had made when he caused Israel to sin. He burned down the shrine and ground it to

23:3 Deut 13:4; 2 Kgs 11:14, 17
23:6 2 Chr 34:4
23:7 1 Kgs 14:24; 15:12; 22:46; Ezek 16:16
23:8 1 Kgs 15:22
23:9 Ezek 44:9-14
23:10 Lev 18:21; 1 Kgs 11:7; Jer 7:31-32
23:12 2 Kgs 21:3-5; 2 Chr 33:4-5; Jer 19:13; Zeph 1:5
23:13 1 Kgs 11:7; Jer 48:7
23:14 Deut 7:5, 25
23:15 1 Kgs 12:28-33

23:9 Hebrew *did not come up.* 23:10 Or *to make a son or daughter pass through the fire.* 23:11 The meaning of the Hebrew is uncertain. 23:12 Or *He quickly removed them.* 23:13 Hebrew *Milcom,* a variant spelling of Molech.

23:6 King Manasseh had set up the Asherah pole in the Temple (2 Kings 21:7). Grinding the pole to dust suggested its absolute destruction. Spreading the dust on the cemetery simultaneously desecrated the Asherah pole and signaled the death of its worship.

23:15-18 Josiah's attention turned next to the corrupt worship established by Jeroboam I of Israel. Jeroboam made Bethel the principal location of his idolatrous system by placing one of two gold calves there for the people to worship (see 1 Kings 12:25-30). A similar shrine was established in northern Israel in the territory of Dan. A prophet from Judah had condemned Jeroboam's altar and predicted its desecration (1 Kings 13:2).

23:16 dust, and he burned the Asherah pole. 16Then Josiah turned around and noticed several
1 Kgs 13:2, 32 tombs in the side of the hill. He ordered that the bones be brought out, and he burned
them on the altar at Bethel to desecrate it. (This happened just as the LORD had promised
through the man of God when Jeroboam stood beside the altar at the festival.)
Then Josiah turned and looked up at the tomb of the man of God* who had predicted
23:17 these things. 17"What is that monument over there?" Josiah asked.
1 Kgs 13:1-2, 30-31 And the people of the town told him, "It is the tomb of the man of God who came from
Judah and predicted the very things that you have just done to the altar at Bethel!"
23:18 18Josiah replied, "Leave it alone. Don't disturb his bones." So they did not burn his
1 Kgs 13:11, 31 bones or those of the old prophet from Samaria.
23:19 19Then Josiah demolished all the buildings at the pagan shrines in the towns of Samar-
2 Chr 34:6-7 ia, just as he had done at Bethel. They had been built by the various kings of Israel and
23:20 had made the LORD* very angry. 20He executed the priests of the pagan shrines on their
2 Kgs 11:18 own altars, and he burned human bones on the altars to desecrate them. Finally, he re-
turned to Jerusalem.

JOSIAH CELEBRATES PASSOVER

23:21-23 21King Josiah then issued this order to all the people: "You must celebrate the Passover to
//2 Chr 35:1, 18-19 the LORD your God, as required in this Book of the Covenant." 22There had not been a Pass-
23:21 Num 9:2-4 over celebration like that since the time when the judges ruled in Israel, nor throughout all
Deut 16:2-8 the years of the kings of Israel and Judah. 23This Passover was celebrated to the LORD in Je-
23:22 rusalem in the eighteenth year of King Josiah's reign.
2 Chr 35:18-19 24Josiah also got rid of the mediums and psychics, the household gods, the idols,* and
23:24 every other kind of detestable practice, both in Jerusalem and throughout the land of Ju-
Lev 19:31 Deut 18:10-12 dah. He did this in obedience to the laws written in the scroll that Hilkiah the priest had
2 Kgs 21:6; 22:8 found in the LORD's Temple. 25Never before had there been a king like Josiah, who turned
23:25 to the LORD with all his heart and soul and strength, obeying all the laws of Moses. And
2 Kgs 18:5 there has never been a king like him since.
23:26 26Even so, the LORD was very angry with Judah because of all the wicked things Manas-
2 Kgs 21:11-13; 22:15-16 seh had done to provoke Him. 27For the LORD said, "I will also banish Judah from My pres-
23:27 ence just as I have banished Israel. And I will reject My chosen city of Jerusalem and the
2 Kgs 21:13-14 Temple where My name was to be honored."
23:28-30 28The rest of the events in Josiah's reign and all his deeds are recorded in *The Book of*
2 Chr 35:20–36:1 *the History of the Kings of Judah.*
23:29 29While Josiah was king, Pharaoh Neco, king of Egypt, went to the Euphrates River to
2 Chr 35:20-24 help the king of Assyria. King Josiah and his army marched out to fight him,* but King
23:30 Neco* killed him when they met at Megiddo. 30Josiah's officers took his body back in a
2 Chr 36:1-4 chariot from Megiddo to Jerusalem and buried him in his own tomb. Then the people of
the land anointed Josiah's son Jehoahaz and made him the next king.

23:16 As in Greek version; Hebrew lacks *when Jeroboam stood beside the altar at the festival. Then Josiah turned and looked up at the tomb of the man of God.* 23:19 As in Greek and Syriac versions and Latin Vulgate; Hebrew lacks *the LORD.* 23:24 The Hebrew term (literally *round things*) probably alludes to dung. 23:29a Or *Josiah went out to meet him.* 23:29b Hebrew *he.*

23:21-23 Hezekiah also celebrated Passover during his reign (2 Chronicles 30). The significance of Josiah's celebration lay in its conformity to the Deuteronomic practice. Deuteronomy envisioned a centralized celebration of the Passover once Israel settled into the land (Deuteronomy 16). Prior to this, the Passover had been celebrated in households with fathers officiating (Exodus 12).

23:29 The battle against Neco took place in 609 BC. The Babylonians were challenging the Assyrians for dominance in the Near East. The Egyptians under Pharaoh Neco were advancing to aid the Assyrians when Josiah challenged them; he might have been motivated either by an alliance with Babylon against Assyria or by his own refusal to allow Judah's territorial integrity to be compromised. See 2 Chronicles 35:20-27 for additional information.

JEHOAHAZ RULES IN JUDAH

31 Jehoahaz was twenty-three years old when he became king, and he reigned in Jerusa-
lem three months. His mother was Hamutal, the daughter of Jeremiah from Libnah. 32 He
did what was evil in the LORD's sight, just as his ancestors had done.
33 Pharaoh Neco put Jehoahaz in prison at Riblah in the land of Hamath to prevent him
from ruling* in Jerusalem. He also demanded that Judah pay 7,500 pounds of silver and
75 pounds of gold* as tribute.

23:31-34 //2 Chr 36:2-4
23:31 2 Kgs 24:18; Jer 22:11
23:33 2 Kgs 23:29

JEHOIAKIM RULES IN JUDAH

34 Pharaoh Neco then installed Eliakim, another of Josiah's sons, to reign in place of his fa-
ther, and he changed Eliakim's name to Jehoiakim. Jehoahaz was taken to Egypt as a pris-
oner, where he died.
35 In order to get the silver and gold demanded as tribute by Pharaoh Neco, Jehoiakim
collected a tax from the people of Judah, requiring them to pay in proportion to their wealth.
36 Jehoiakim was twenty-five years old when he became king, and he reigned in Jerusa-
lem eleven years. His mother was Zebidah, the daughter of Pedaiah from Rumah. 37 He did
what was evil in the LORD's sight, just as his ancestors had done.

23:34 1 Chr 3:15; 2 Chr 36:4-8; Jer 22:12; Ezek 19:3-4
23:36–24:6 //2 Chr 36:5-8; Jer 1:3; 26:21

24 During Jehoiakim's reign, King Nebuchadnezzar of Babylon invaded the land of
Judah. Jehoiakim surrendered and paid him tribute for three years but then re-
belled. 2 Then the LORD sent bands of Babylonian,* Aramean, Moabite, and Ammonite raid-
ers against Judah to destroy it, just as the LORD had promised through His prophets.
3 These disasters happened to Judah because of the LORD's command. He had decided to
banish Judah from His presence because of the many sins of Manasseh, 4 who had filled
Jerusalem with innocent blood. The LORD would not forgive this.
5 The rest of the events in Jehoiakim's reign and all his deeds are recorded in *The Book
of the History of the Kings of Judah.* 6 When Jehoiakim died, his son Jehoiachin became the
next king.
7 The king of Egypt did not venture out of his country after that, for the king of Babylon
captured the entire area formerly claimed by Egypt—from the Brook of Egypt to the Eu-
phrates River.

24:1 2 Chr 36:6; Jer 25:1, 9
24:2 2 Kgs 13:20-21; 23:27
24:3 2 Kgs 18:25; 23:26
24:4 2 Kgs 21:16
24:6 Jer 22:19, 24-25
24:7 Jer 37:5, 7; 46:2

JEHOIACHIN RULES IN JUDAH

8 Jehoiachin was eighteen years old when he became king, and he reigned in Jerusalem
three months. His mother was Nehushta, the daughter of Elnathan from Jerusalem. 9 Je-
hoiachin did what was evil in the LORD's sight, just as his father had done.
10 During Jehoiachin's reign, the officers of King Nebuchadnezzar of Babylon came up

24:8-17 //2 Chr 36:9-10

23:33a The meaning of the Hebrew is uncertain. 23:33b Hebrew *100 talents* [3,400 kilograms] *of silver and 1 talent* [34 kilograms] *of gold.* 24:2 Or *Chaldean.*

23:31 Jehoahaz was Josiah's fourth son (1 Chronicles 3:15) and reigned in 609 BC. The Jeremiah mentioned here was not the prophet of the same name (compare Jeremiah 1:1). The prophet Jeremiah gave a highly critical assessment of Jehoahaz's brief reign (Jeremiah 22:11-17).

23:36 Jehoiakim reigned from approximately 609–598 BC. Further information regarding Jehoiakim is provided by Jeremiah (Jeremiah 22:18-23; 25–26; 36:1-32).

24:1 Pharaoh Neco's control over Judah was short lived. Nebuchadnezzar defeated Neco at the battle of Carchemish (605 BC), and Judah became a vassal state of Babylon.

24:2-4 God directed the waves of assault upon Judah. The nations that attacked Judah acted as instruments of divine judgment. Judah had broken covenant with God, so now the nation faced the consequences of their unfaithfulness (see Deuteronomy 28 and Leviticus 26). The exiled readers of 1 and 2 Kings may have been tempted to blame God for their plight, but the authors made clear the people's own sins were to blame. On the sins of Manasseh, see 2 Kings 21:1-18.

24:7 Ironically, these geographic markers previously designated the extent of Solomon's glorious kingdom (1 Kings 4:21, 24; 8:65).

24:8 Jehoiachin reigned from approximately 598–597 BC.

24:10-12 Nebuchadnezzar's actions against Jehoiachin may have been prompted by the rebellion of Jehoiachin's father, Jehoiakim, prior to his death (2 Kings 24:1). Babylonian records attest to Jehoiachin's exile in significant detail.

against Jerusalem and besieged it. [11]Nebuchadnezzar himself arrived at the city during
24:12 2 Chr 36:10 Jer 24:1; 29:1-2 — the siege. [12]Then King Jehoiachin, along with the queen mother, his advisers, his com-
manders, and his officials, surrendered to the Babylonians.
In the eighth year of Nebuchadnezzar's reign, he took Jehoiachin prisoner. [13]As the
24:13 1 Kgs 7:48-50 2 Kgs 20:17; 25:13-15 Isa 39:6 — LORD had said beforehand, Nebuchadnezzar carried away all the treasures from the LORD's
Temple and the royal palace. He stripped away* all the gold objects that King Solomon of
Israel had placed in the Temple. [14]King Nebuchadnezzar took all of Jerusalem captive, in-
24:14 2 Kgs 25:12 Jer 24:1; 52:28 — cluding all the commanders and the best of the soldiers, craftsmen, and artisans—10,000
in all. Only the poorest people were left in the land.
[15]Nebuchadnezzar led King Jehoiachin away as a captive to Babylon, along with the
queen mother, his wives and officials, and all Jerusalem's elite. [16]He also exiled 7,000 of
the best troops and 1,000 craftsmen and artisans, all of whom were strong and fit for war.
24:17 2 Chr 36:10-13 Jer 37:1 — [17]Then the king of Babylon installed Mattaniah, Jehoiachin's* uncle, as the next king, and
he changed Mattaniah's name to Zedekiah.

ZEDEKIAH RULES IN JUDAH

24:18-20 //2 Chr 36:11-13 //Jer 52:1-3 — [18]Zedekiah was twenty-one years old when he became king, and he reigned in Jerusalem
eleven years. His mother was Hamutal, the daughter of Jeremiah from Libnah. [19]But Zed-
ekiah did what was evil in the LORD's sight, just as Jehoiakim had done. [20]These things
24:20 2 Chr 36:13 Jer 27:12; 38:17, 21-22; 39:1 — happened because of the LORD's anger against the people of Jerusalem and Judah, until
He finally banished them from His presence and sent them into exile.

24:13 Or *He cut apart.* 24:17 Hebrew *his.*

KINGS TO DATE AND THEIR ENEMIES

722 Captivity in Assyria

ISRAEL

JUDAH

686 *586*

715 ***HEZEKIAH*** *Miraculously delivered from Sennacherib's (Assyria) attack, conquered Gaza in Philistia 2 Kgs 18:1–20:21 2 Chr 28:27–32:33 Co-regency 697–686*

697 ***MANASSEH*** *Taken captive by Assyria, imprisoned in Babylon and later released 2 Kgs 20:21–21:18 2 Chr 32:33–33:20*

642 ***AMON*** *2 Kgs 21:18-26 2 Chr 33:20-24*

640 ***JOSIAH*** *Died in battle against Neco (Egypt) 2 Kgs 22:1–23:30 2 Chr 33:25–35:27*

609 ***JEHOAHAZ*** *Neco (Egypt) 2 Kgs 23:30-34 2 Chr 36:1-4*

609 ***JEHOIAKIM*** *2 Kgs 23:34–24:6 2 Chr 36:4-8*

598 ***JEHOIACHIN*** *Rebelled against Babylon and was taken captive 2 Kgs 24:6-16; 25:27-30 2 Chr 36:8-10*

597 ***ZEDEKIAH*** *Rebelled, completely conquered by Babylon 2 Kgs 24:17–25:21 2 Chr 36:10-20*

735 ***AHAZ*** *Harassed by Pekah (Israel), paid Assyria for protection against Rezin (Aram), also harassed by Edom and Philistia 2 Kgs 15:38–16:20 2 Chr 27:9–28:27*

All dates are BC.
Solid section of the timeline indicates co-regency.
For all the kings of Israel and Judah, see the chart at the end of 1 Kings.

24:13-16 **The last remains of Solomon's glorious kingdom were finally undone. The gold was gone, the army depleted, and the population purged of the upper echelons of citizens. Nebuchadnezzar's actions accurately reflected Babylonian patterns of deportation designed to cripple a nation's economy and leadership base in order to preempt rebellions.**

24:18 **Zedekiah reigned from approximately 597–586 BC.**

THE FALL OF JERUSALEM

Zedekiah rebelled against the king of Babylon.

25 So on January 15,* during the ninth year of Zedekiah's reign, King Nebuchadnez- 25:1-12
zar of Babylon led his entire army against Jerusalem. They surrounded the city //Jer 39:1-7
and built siege ramps against its walls. [2]Jerusalem was kept under siege until the eleventh 25:1
year of King Zedekiah's reign. 2 Chr 36:17-20 Ezek 21:22; 24:2
[3]By July 18 in the eleventh year of Zedekiah's reign,* the famine in the city had become 25:3
very severe, and the last of the food was entirely gone. [4]Then a section of the city wall was 2 Kgs 6:24-25
broken down, and all the soldiers fled. Since the city was surrounded by the Babylonians,* Lam 4:9-10
they waited for nightfall. Then they slipped through the gate between the two walls be-
hind the king's garden and headed toward the Jordan Valley.*
[5]But the Babylonian* troops chased the king and caught him on the plains of Jericho, for
his men had all deserted him and scattered. [6]They took him to the king of Babylon at Rib- 25:6
lah, where they pronounced judgment upon Zedekiah. [7]They made Zedekiah watch as Jer 32:4
they slaughtered his sons. Then they gouged out Zedekiah's eyes, bound him in bronze 25:7
chains, and led him away to Babylon. Jer 39:6-7 Ezek 12:13

THE TEMPLE DESTROYED

[8]On August 14 of that year,* which was the nineteenth year of King Nebuchadnezzar's 25:8
reign, Nebuzaradan, the captain of the guard and an official of the Babylonian king, ar- Jer 52:12
rived in Jerusalem. [9]He burned down the Temple of the LORD, the royal palace, and all the 25:9
houses of Jerusalem. He destroyed all the important buildings* in the city. [10]Then he su- 2 Chr 36:19 Ps 74:3-8
pervised the entire Babylonian army as they tore down the walls of Jerusalem on every Amos 2:5
side. [11]Nebuzaradan, the captain of the guard, then took as exiles the rest of the people 25:10
who remained in the city, the defectors who had declared their allegiance to the king of Neh 1:3
Babylon, and the rest of the population. [12]But the captain of the guard allowed some of the 25:11
poorest people to stay behind in Judah to care for the vineyards and fields. 2 Chr 36:20
[13]The Babylonians broke up the bronze pillars in front of the LORD's Temple, the bronze 25:12 2 Kgs 24:14
water carts, and the great bronze basin called the Sea, and they carried all the bronze Jer 40:7; 52:16
away to Babylon. [14]They also took all the ash buckets, shovels, lamp snuffers, dishes, and 25:13
all the other bronze articles used for making sacrifices at the Temple. [15]Nebuzaradan, the 1 Kgs 7:15-22
captain of the guard, also took the incense burners and basins, and all the other articles 2 Chr 36:18
made of pure gold or silver. 25:14
[16]The weight of the bronze from the two pillars, the Sea, and the water carts was too great 1 Kgs 7:47-50 2 Chr 24:14
to be measured. These things had been made for the LORD's Temple in the days of King Solo- 25:17
mon. [17]Each of the pillars was 27 feet* tall. The bronze capital on top of each pillar was 1 Kgs 7:15-22
7½ feet* high and was decorated with a network of bronze pomegranates all the way around.
[18]Nebuzaradan, the captain of the guard, took with him as prisoners Seraiah the high 25:18
priest, Zephaniah the priest of the second rank, and the three chief gatekeepers. [19]And 1 Chr 6:14 Ezra 7:1
from among the people still hiding in the city, he took an officer who had been in charge Jer 29:25-26, 29

25:1 Hebrew *on the tenth day of the tenth month,* of the ancient Hebrew lunar calendar. A number of events in 2 Kings can be cross-checked with dates in surviving Babylonian records and related accurately to our modern calendar. This day was January 15, 588 B.C. **25:3** Hebrew *By the ninth day of the [fourth] month* [in the eleventh year of Zedekiah's reign] (compare Jer 52:6 and the note there). This day was July 18, 586 B.C.; also see note on 25:1. **25:4a** Or *the Chaldeans;* also in 25:13, 25, 26. **25:4b** Hebrew *the Arabah.* **25:5** Or *Chaldean;* also in 25:10, 24. **25:8** Hebrew *On the seventh day of the fifth month,* of the ancient Hebrew lunar calendar. This day was August 14, 586 B.C.; also see note on 25:1. **25:9** Or *destroyed the houses of all the important people.* **25:17a** Hebrew *18 cubits* [8.1 meters]. **25:17b** As in parallel texts at 1 Kgs 7:16, 2 Chr 3:15, and Jer 52:22, all of which read *5 cubits* [2.3 meters]; Hebrew reads *3 cubits,* which is 4.5 feet or 1.4 meters.

25:10 In keeping with the warnings of God and His prophets, Jerusalem was desolated (1 Kings 9:6-9; 2 Kings 21:10-15). Walls provided vital security to ancient cities. By destroying Jerusalem's walls, the Babylonians made it virtually impossible for the city to be a center of organized resistance to Babylonian power.

25:13-15 Descriptions of these Temple furnishings are found in 1 Kings 7:15-50. See also Jeremiah 27:19-22.

of the Judean army; five of the king's personal advisers; the army commander's chief sec-
25:20 2 Kgs 23:33 retary, who was in charge of recruitment; and sixty other citizens. [20]Nebuzaradan, the cap-
tain of the guard, took them all to the king of Babylon at Riblah. [21]And there at Riblah, in
25:21 Deut 28:64 the land of Hamath, the king of Babylon had them all put to death. So the people of Judah
2 Kgs 23:27 were sent into exile from their land.

GEDALIAH GOVERNS IN JUDAH

25:22-26 [22]Then King Nebuchadnezzar appointed Gedaliah son of Ahikam and grandson of Shaphan
//Jer 40:7-9; 41:1-3, 16-18 as governor over the people he had left in Judah. [23]When all the army commanders and their
men learned that the king of Babylon had appointed Gedaliah as governor, they went to see
25:23 Jer 40:7-9 him at Mizpah. These included Ishmael son of Nethaniah, Johanan son of Kareah, Seraiah son
of Tanhumeth the Netophathite, and Jezaniah* son of the Maacathite, and all their men.
[24]Gedaliah vowed to them that the Babylonian officials meant them no harm. "Don't be
afraid of them. Live in the land and serve the king of Babylon, and all will go well for you,"
he promised.
25:25 Jer 41:1-2 [25]But in midautumn of that year,* Ishmael son of Nethaniah and grandson of Elishama,
who was of the royal family, went to Mizpah with ten men and killed Gedaliah. He also
killed all the Judeans and Babylonians who were with Gedaliah at Mizpah.
25:26 Jer 43:5-7 [26]Then all the people of Judah, from the least to the greatest, as well as the army com-
manders, fled in panic to Egypt, for they were afraid of what the Babylonians would do to
them.

HOPE FOR ISRAEL'S ROYAL LINE

25:27 2 Kgs 24:12 Jer 52:31-34 [27]In the thirty-seventh year of the exile of King Jehoiachin of Judah, Evil-merodach as-
cended to the Babylonian throne. He was kind to* Jehoiachin and released him from
prison on April 2 of that year.* [28]He spoke kindly to Jehoiachin and gave him a higher
place than all the other exiled kings in Babylon. [29]He supplied Jehoiachin with new clothes
to replace his prison garb and allowed him to dine in the king's presence for the rest of his
life. [30]So the Babylonian king gave him a regular food allowance as long as he lived.

25:23 As in parallel text at Jer 40:8; Hebrew reads *Jaazaniah,* a variant spelling of Jezaniah. **25:25** Hebrew *in the seventh month,* of the ancient Hebrew lunar calendar. This month occurred within the months of October and November 586 B.C.; also see note on 25:1. **25:27a** Hebrew *He raised the head of.* **25:27b** Hebrew *on the twenty-seventh day of the twelfth month,* of the ancient Hebrew lunar calendar. This day was April 2, 561 B.C.; also see note on 25:1.

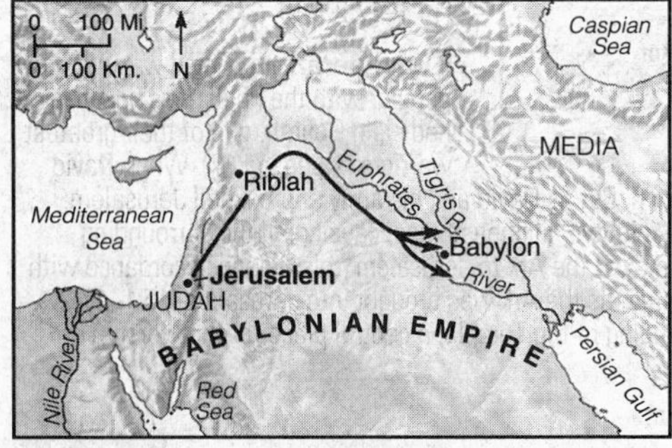

JUDAH EXILED
Evil permeated Judah, and God's anger flared against his rebellious people. Babylon conquered Assyria and became the new world power. The Babylonian army marched into Jerusalem, burned the Temple, tore down the city's massive walls, and carried off the people into captivity.

25:23 Mizpah lay approximately eight miles north of Jerusalem. See also Jeremiah 40:10-12.

25:27-30 With the death of Zedekiah's sons (2 Kings 25:7), it seemed that the Davidic line had come to an end. But Jehoiachin's surprising reappearance in the narrative suggested that the line was not yet undone. The survival and release of Jehoiachin provided a poignant, if subdued, note of hope with which to conclude this book. Jehoiachin enjoyed mercy from his captors as Solomon had requested of God centuries earlier (1 Kings 8:50).

▸ HOLINESS
25:27 The kindness of God. From the midst of the darkest times, the light of hope springs forth. Our God of grace and love granted Judah's former king, Jehoiachin, favor with the new king of Babylon. You may be in an extremely dark time of your life, even under the judgment of God, but keep looking for God's grace. It often appears when we least expect it. (***See Holiness***> *Changed by God*> *God Provides*> *Extending grace to us,* TopicGuide page A41.)

KEY PLACES IN 1 CHRONICLES

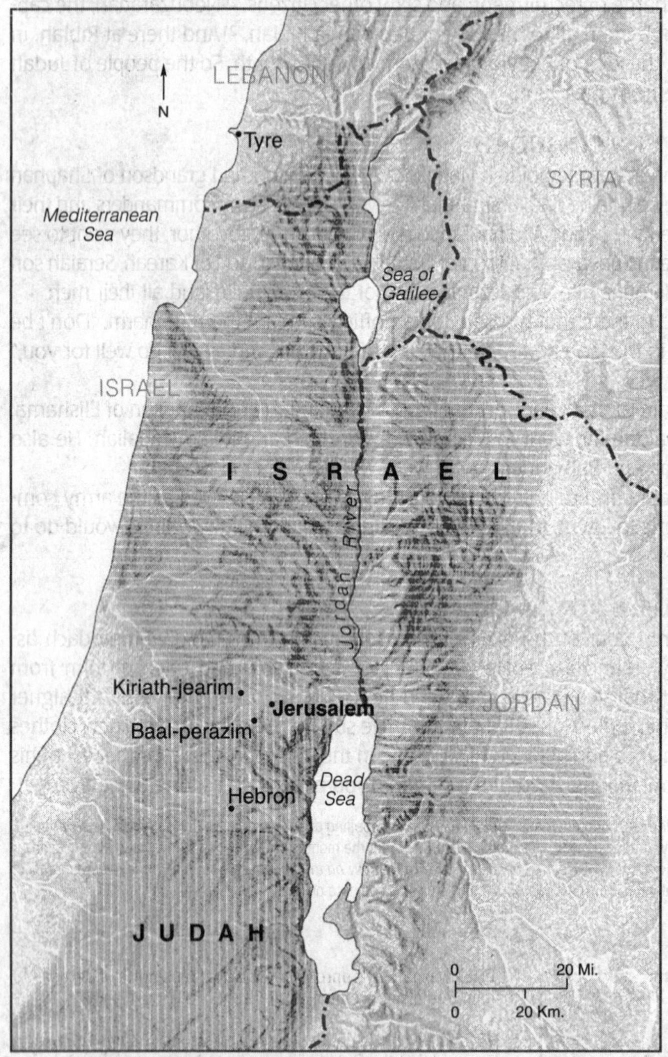

The broken lines (—·—·) indicate modern boundaries.

The genealogies of 1 Chronicles present an overview of Israel's history. The first nine chapters are filled with genealogies tracing the lineages of people from the Creation to the exile in Babylon. Saul's death is recorded in chapter 10. Chapter 11 begins the history of David's reign over Israel.

1 Hebron Although David had been anointed king years earlier, his reign began when the leaders of Israel accepted him as king at Hebron (11:1-3).

2 Jerusalem David set out to complete the conquest of the land begun by Joshua. He attacked Jerusalem, captured it, and made it his capital (11:4–12:40).

3 Kiriath-jearim The Ark of the Covenant, which had been captured by the Philistines in battle and returned (1 Samuel 4–6), was in safekeeping in Kiriath-jearim. David summoned all Israel to this city to join in bringing the Ark to Jerusalem. Unfortunately, it was not moved according to God's instructions, and as a result, one man died. David left the Ark in the home of Obed-edom until he could discover how to transport it correctly (13:1-14).

4 Tyre David did much building in Jerusalem. King Hiram of Tyre sent workers and supplies to help build David's palace. Cedar, abundant in the mountains north of Israel, was a valuable and hardy wood for the beautiful buildings in Jerusalem (14:1–17:27).

5 Baal-perazim David was not very popular with the Philistines because he had slain Goliath, one of their greatest warriors (1 Samuel 17). When David began to rule over a united Israel, the Philistines set out to capture him. But as David and his army approached Jerusalem, they attacked the Philistines at Baal-perazim. His army defeated the mighty Philistines twice, causing all the surrounding nations to fear David's power (14:11-17). After these battles, David moved the Ark to Jerusalem (this time in accordance with God's instructions for transporting the Ark). There was great celebration as the Ark was brought into Jerusalem (15:1–17:27). David spent the remainder of his life making preparations for the building of the Temple, a central place for the worship of God (18:1–29:30).

1 CHRONICLES

PURPOSE

To direct the obedience of God's people as they return from captivity in Babylon.

Few books in the Old Testament are as ignored by Bible readers as 1 Chronicles. Why? Because the first nine chapters are genealogy. Few people wade through those chapters, and after they decide that the first nine chapters are not so interesting, it's only natural to decide that the rest of the book may be just as unpleasant and seemingly useless to read. But this was not uninteresting material for the author or the original audience—it was actually motivational.

The chronicler included family records in his book to establish that his readers were the legitimate continuation of God's elect people. By reporting the segregation of Israel from all of humanity (1 Chronicles 1:2–2:2), the assembly of the tribes of Israel (1 Chronicles 2:3–9:1), and the tribal leaders that returned from Babylon (1 Chronicles 9:14-34), the writer pieced together the most important thing his audience needed to hear—"You are God's chosen people!" And as the readers (who had recently returned from captivity in Babylon) accepted the responsibility of being the continuation of the people of God, they could then read and understand the following history in 1 Chronicles 10 through the end of 2 Chronicles as *their* history, *their* story, a preamble to a new beginning of covenant faithfulness.

DISCOVER GOD IN 1 CHRONICLES

In the pages of 1 Chronicles, the returning Jews found what they needed—assurance that God had not changed.

Steadfastness: Jerusalem was a city without walls (a sign of complete and utter destruction in biblical days), and the Temple, the dwelling place of God, was no more. All the visible signs of the presence and power of God were missing from Jerusalem. It would have been easy for the Jews to imagine that their role as the people of God ended with their captivity. How could a disheveled and disorganized remnant legitimately call themselves the people of God? Answer: God's steadfastness. God's promises are not dependent on circumstances. His program of redemption for the world, stated generally in Genesis 3:15 and made specific with the promises to Abraham (Genesis 12:1-3), was still in motion. God's steadfastness is not determined by external appearances but by the integrity of His word.

Willingness: Many people have an idea that God spends most of His time trying to catch human beings doing something wrong. In reality, the opposite is true—God wants to enter into partnership with those who are eager to do what is right (2 Chronicles 16:9). When David was preparing Solomon to become king and build the first Temple in Jerusalem, he told Solomon, "The LORD sees every heart and knows every plan and thought. If you seek Him, you will find Him" (1 Chronicles 28:9). God is willing to be found by those who seek Him! God is a personal God, not a distant, impersonal deity. Since the fellowship in Eden was broken by sin, God has been reaching out, making Himself available to all who seek to know Him.

GROWING THROUGH 1 CHRONICLES

First Chronicles presents lessons in overcoming adversity and standing firm when things have fallen apart around you:

DISCOVERY VERSES

[Jabez] was the one who prayed to the God of Israel, "Oh, that you would bless me and expand my territory! Please be with me in all that I do, and keep me from all trouble and pain!" And God granted him his request.

(1 CHRONICLES 4:10)

"And Solomon, my son, learn to know the God of your ancestors intimately. Worship and serve Him with your whole heart and a willing mind. For the LORD sees every heart and knows every plan and thought. If you seek Him, you will find Him. But if you forsake Him, He will reject you forever."

(1 CHRONICLES 28:9)

"Yours, O LORD, is the greatness, the power, the glory, the victory, and the majesty. Everything in the heavens and on earth is Yours, O LORD, and this is Your kingdom. We adore You as the One who is over all things."

(1 CHRONICLES 29:11)

Walk by Faith: The essence of a successful spiritual life is walking by faith, not by sight (2 Corinthians 5:7). Often there will be benchmarks and mile markers that let us know we are building our life true to form and that we are on the right road. But sometimes all external guides disappear. When the Jews returned from exile, they had to live by the old saying, "Don't doubt in the darkness what God has revealed in the light." They needed to cling to the promises of God about the lineage of David and the permanence of Israel's place in God's sight. We walk by faith the same way—in reliance on the promises of God.

The "Findability" of God: Hebrews 11:6 says, "Anyone who wants to come to [God] must believe that God exists and that He rewards those who sincerely seek Him." Jesus said that wanting to know the will of God is in the first step to discovering it (John 7:17). And David told Solomon if he would seek God he would find Him (1 Chronicles 28:9). Solomon was at a place in life where he definitely needed God's help. It is good to know that God does not hide Himself from His people.

Status and Stewardship: It's not hard to see why David was considered a man after God's heart (1 Samuel 13:14). He confessed to being a visitor and a stranger on earth: "Our days on earth are like a passing shadow, gone so soon without a trace" (1 Chronicles 29:15). David saw his status as "just passing through"—this earth was not his permanent home. As such, he was the owner of nothing: "O LORD our God, even this material we have gathered to build a Temple to honor Your holy name comes from You! It all belongs to You!" (1 Chronicles 29:16). David's title and treasure were temporary, but his hope in God was permanent.

1 CHRONICLES FACTS

Author: Unknown, but strong Jewish tradition suggests Ezra was the author. Ezra's role as priest matches well with the priestly perspective of Chronicles. The author of Chronicles compiled his work from various historical documents and records and added a priestly perspective to the material (1 Chronicles 29:29; 2 Chronicles 9:29; 12:15; 13:22; 26:22; 33:19).

Written to: The immediate audience was the group of Jewish exiles returning from Babylon to Judah to rebuild Jerusalem and the Temple and to repopulate the Promised Land.

Date of Writing: Probably written in the latter half of the fifth century BC, when the exiles were returning from Babylon.

Setting: The first nine chapters establish the right of the Davidic dynasty to rule over Israel, tracing the lineage all the way back to Adam (1:1). Chapters 10–29 cover the reign of David.

OUTLINE

- ▸**1 CHRONICLES 1:1–9:34**—The genealogy of God's people
- ▸**1 CHRONICLES 9:35—2 CHRONICLES 9:31**—The united monarchy
- ▸**2 CHRONICLES 10–28**—The divided kingdom
- ▸**2 CHRONICLES 29–36**—The reunited kingdom

FROM ADAM TO NOAH'S SONS

1:1 Gen 5:1-32 Luke 3:36-38 **1** The descendants of Adam were Seth, Enosh, [2]Kenan, Mahalalel, Jared,
[3]Enoch, Methuselah, Lamech, [4]and Noah.
The sons of Noah were* Shem, Ham, and Japheth.

DESCENDANTS OF JAPHETH

1:5-7 //Gen 10:2-5 [5]The descendants of Japheth were Gomer, Magog, Madai, Javan, Tubal,
Meshech, and Tiras.
[6]The descendants of Gomer were Ashkenaz, Riphath,* and Togarmah.
[7]The descendants of Javan were Elishah, Tarshish, Kittim, and Rodanim.

DESCENDANTS OF HAM

1:8-16 //Gen 10:6-20 [8]The descendants of Ham were Cush, Mizraim,* Put, and Canaan.
[9]The descendants of Cush were Seba, Havilah, Sabtah, Raamah, and Sabteca. The
descendants of Raamah were Sheba and Dedan. [10]Cush was also the ancestor of
Nimrod, who was the first heroic warrior on earth.
1:11 Gen 10:13-18 [11]Mizraim was the ancestor of the Ludites, Anamites, Lehabites, Naphtuhites,
[12]Pathrusites, Casluhites, and the Caphtorites, from whom the Philistines came.*
1:13 Gen 15:19-21 [13]Canaan's oldest son was Sidon, the ancestor of the Sidonians. Canaan was also the
ancestor of the Hittites, [14]Jebusites, Amorites, Girgashites, [15]Hivites, Arkites, Sinites,
[16]Arvadites, Zemarites, and Hamathites.

DESCENDANTS OF SHEM

1:17-23 //Gen 10:21-31; 11:10-27 Luke 3:36 [17]The descendants of Shem were Elam, Asshur, Arphaxad, Lud, and Aram.
The descendants of Aram were* Uz, Hul, Gether, and Mash.*
[18]Arphaxad was the father of Shelah.
Shelah was the father of Eber.
1:19 Gen 11:16 [19]Eber had two sons. The first was named Peleg (which means "division"), for during his
lifetime the people of the world were divided into different language groups. His
brother's name was Joktan.
[20]Joktan was the ancestor of Almodad, Sheleph, Hazarmaveth, Jerah, [21]Hadoram, Uzal,

1:4 As in Greek version (see also Gen 5:3-32); Hebrew lacks *The sons of Noah were.* 1:6 As in some Hebrew manuscripts and Greek version (see also Gen 10:3); most Hebrew manuscripts read *Diphath.* 1:8 Or *Egypt;* also in 1:11. 1:12 Hebrew *Casluhites, from whom the Philistines came, Caphtorites.* See Jer 47:4; Amos 9:7. 1:17a As in one Hebrew manuscript and some Greek manuscripts (see also Gen 10:23); most Hebrew manuscripts lack *The descendants of Aram were.* 1:17b As in parallel text at Gen 10:23; Hebrew reads *and Meshech.*

1:1 Through an extensive series of genealogies, the chronicler (the anonymous author of 1 and 2 Chronicles) traces the work of God since the beginning of the human race through specific families. This is intended to be an argument in favor of God's choice of the family of David to rule Israel.

1:1 See Genesis 2–4 for a discussion of the direct descendants of Adam.

1:4 See Genesis 5 for a discussion of the ancestors of Noah and Genesis 9:18–10:32 for a better look at Shem, Ham and Japheth.

1:5 Seven sons of Japheth are mentioned, but only two receive additional attention. This demonstrates the selectivity of the author—his genealogies are summaries, not precise reproductions, of the descendants of important people in Old Testament history.

Diklah, 22 Obal,* Abimael, Sheba, 23 Ophir, Havilah, and Jobab. All these were
descendants of Joktan.
24 So this is the family line descended from Shem: Arphaxad, Shelah,* 25 Eber, Peleg, **1:24** Gen 11:10-26
Reu, 26 Serug, Nahor, Terah, 27 and Abram, later known as Abraham. Luke 3:34-36

DESCENDANTS OF ABRAHAM

28 The sons of Abraham were Isaac and Ishmael. 29 These are their genealogical records: **1:29-31**
The sons of Ishmael were Nebaioth (the oldest), Kedar, Adbeel, Mibsam, 30 Mishma, //Gen 25:12-16
Dumah, Massa, Hadad, Tema, 31 Jetur, Naphish, and Kedemah. These were the sons
of Ishmael.

32 The sons of Keturah, Abraham's concubine, were Zimran, Jokshan, Medan, Midian, **1:32-33**
Ishbak, and Shuah. //Gen 25:1-4
The sons of Jokshan were Sheba and Dedan.
33 The sons of Midian were Ephah, Epher, Hanoch, Abida, and Eldaah.
All these were descendants of Abraham through his concubine Keturah.

DESCENDANTS OF ISAAC

34 Abraham was the father of Isaac. The sons of Isaac were Esau and Israel.* **1:34** Gen 25:25-26; 32:28
Matt 1:2

DESCENDANTS OF ESAU

35 The sons of Esau were Eliphaz, Reuel, Jeush, Jalam, and Korah. **1:35**
36 The sons of Eliphaz were Teman, Omar, Zepho,* Gatam, Kenaz, and Amalek, who was Gen 36:4, 19
born to Timna.* **1:35-37**
37 The sons of Reuel were Nahath, Zerah, Shammah, and Mizzah. //Gen 36:10-14

ORIGINAL PEOPLES OF EDOM

38 The sons of Seir were Lotan, Shobal, Zibeon, Anah, Dishon, Ezer, and Dishan. **1:38-42**
39 The sons of Lotan were Hori and Heman.* Lotan's sister was named Timna. //Gen 36:20-28
40 The sons of Shobal were Alvan,* Manahath, Ebal, Shepho,* and Onam.
The sons of Zibeon were Aiah and Anah.
41 The son of Anah was Dishon.
The sons of Dishon were Hemdan,* Eshban, Ithran, and Keran.
42 The sons of Ezer were Bilhan, Zaavan, and Akan.*
The sons of Dishan* were Uz and Aran.

RULERS OF EDOM

43 These are the kings who ruled in Edom before there were kings in Israel*: **1:43-54**
//Gen 36:31-43
Bela son of Beor, who ruled from his city of Dinhabah.
44 When Bela died, Jobab son of Zerah from Bozrah became king.
45 When Jobab died, Husham from the land of the Temanites became king.
46 When Husham died, Hadad son of Bedad became king and ruled from the city of **1:45** Job 2:11
Avith. He was the one who destroyed the Midianite army in the land of Moab.
47 When Hadad died, Samlah from the city of Masrekah became king.

1:22 As in some Hebrew manuscripts and Syriac version (see also Gen 10:28); most Hebrew manuscripts read *Ebal.* **1:24** Some Greek manuscripts read *Arphaxad, Cainan, Shelah.* See notes on Gen 10:24; 11:12-13. **1:34** *Israel* is the name that God gave to Jacob. **1:36a** As in many Hebrew manuscripts and a few Greek manuscripts (see also Gen 36:11); most Hebrew manuscripts read *Zephi.* **1:36b** As in some Greek manuscripts (see also Gen 36:12); Hebrew reads *Kenaz, Timna, and Amalek.* **1:39** As in parallel text at Gen 36:22; Hebrew reads *and Homam.* **1:40a** As in many Hebrew manuscripts and a few Greek manuscripts (see also Gen 36:23); most Hebrew manuscripts read *Alian.* **1:40b** As in some Hebrew manuscripts (see also Gen 36:23); most Hebrew manuscripts read *Shephi.* **1:41** As in many Hebrew manuscripts and some Greek manuscripts (see also Gen 36:26); most Hebrew manuscripts read *Hamran.* **1:42a** As in many Hebrew and Greek manuscripts (see also Gen 36:27); most Hebrew manuscripts read *Jaakan.* **1:42b** Hebrew *Dishon;* compare 1:38 and parallel text at Gen 36:28. **1:43** Or *before an Israelite king ruled over them.*

48When Samlah died, Shaul from the city of Rehoboth on the river became king.
49When Shaul died, Baal-hanan son of Acbor became king.
50When Baal-hanan died, Hadad became king and ruled from the city of Pau.* His wife
was Mehetabel, the daughter of Matred and granddaughter of Me-zahab. 51Then
Hadad died.

The clan leaders of Edom were Timna, Alvah,* Jetheth, 52Oholibamah, Elah, Pinon,
53Kenaz, Teman, Mibzar, 54Magdiel, and Iram. These were the clan leaders of Edom.

DESCENDANTS OF ISRAEL

2:1-2 //Gen 35:23-26; 46:8-25 Exod 1:1-4 Num 1:2-15 Rev 7:4-8

2 The sons of Israel* were Reuben, Simeon, Levi, Judah, Issachar, Zebulun, 2Dan,
Joseph, Benjamin, Naphtali, Gad, and Asher.

DESCENDANTS OF JUDAH

3Judah had three sons from Bathshua, a Canaanite woman. Their names were Er, Onan,
2:3 Gen 38:2-10 and Shelah. But the LORD saw that the oldest son, Er, was a wicked man, so He killed
him. 4Later Judah had twin sons from Tamar, his widowed daughter-in-law. Their
2:4 Gen 38:13-30 names were Perez and Zerah. So Judah had five sons in all.
2:5-15 //Ruth 4:18-22 Matt 1:3-6 5The sons of Perez were Hezron and Hamul.
6The sons of Zerah were Zimri, Ethan, Heman, Calcol, and Darda*—five in all.
7The son of Carmi (a descendant of Zimri) was Achan,* who brought disaster on Israel
2:7 Josh 7:1 by taking plunder that had been set apart for the LORD.*
8The son of Ethan was Azariah.

FROM JUDAH'S GRANDSON HEZRON TO DAVID

9The sons of Hezron were Jerahmeel, Ram, and Caleb.*
2:10 Num 1:7 10Ram was the father of Amminadab.
Amminadab was the father of Nahshon, a leader of Judah.
11Nahshon was the father of Salmon.*
Salmon was the father of Boaz.
2:12 Ruth 4:17 Matt 1:5 12Boaz was the father of Obed.
Obed was the father of Jesse.
2:13 1 Sam 16:6 13Jesse's first son was Eliab, his second was Abinadab, his third was Shimea, 14his
fourth was Nethanel, his fifth was Raddai, 15his sixth was Ozem, and his seventh was
David.
2:16 1 Sam 26:6 2 Sam 2:18 16Their sisters were named Zeruiah and Abigail. Zeruiah had three sons named
Abishai, Joab, and Asahel. 17Abigail married a man named Jether, an Ishmaelite, and
2:17 2 Sam 17:25 they had a son named Amasa.

1:50 As in many Hebrew manuscripts, some Greek manuscripts, Syriac version, and Latin Vulgate (see also Gen 36:39); most Hebrew manuscripts read *Pai.* **1:51** As in parallel text at Gen 36:40; Hebrew reads *Aliah.* **2:1** *Israel* is the name that God gave to Jacob. **2:6** As in many Hebrew manuscripts, some Greek manuscripts, and Syriac version (see also 1 Kgs 4:31); Hebrew reads *Dara.* **2:7a** Hebrew *Achar;* compare Josh 7:1. *Achar* means "disaster." **2:7b** The Hebrew term used here refers to the complete consecration of things or people to the LORD, either by destroying them or by giving them as an offering. **2:9** Hebrew *Kelubai,* a variant spelling of Caleb; compare 2:18. **2:11** As in Greek version (see also Ruth 4:21); Hebrew reads *Salma.*

2:3 God sovereignly chose David as king, but not because he came from the perfect family. David's ancestor Judah began his dynasty by producing heirs through an illegitimate marriage to a Canaanite and an affair with his dead son's widow. His sons Er (Genesis 38:7) and Onan (Genesis 38:10) were struck down by God for their sins. Moreover, Achan (1 Chronicles 2:7) was executed for thievery (Joshua 7:1). This level of honesty on the part of the writer demonstrates that, even with the political goal of endorsing a continuing Davidic monarchy, he was not interested in whitewashing David's history.

2:9 As the genealogy continues, it begins to narrow its scope. From chosen nations to chosen tribes, now the chronicler traces the work of God from Hezron, grandson of Judah, to David.

OTHER DESCENDANTS OF HEZRON

18 Hezron's son Caleb had sons from his wife Azubah and from Jerioth.* Her sons were
named Jesher, Shobab, and Ardon. 19 After Azubah died, Caleb married Ephrathah,* and
they had a son named Hur. 20 Hur was the father of Uri. Uri was the father of Bezalel.
21 When Hezron was sixty years old, he married Gilead's sister, the daughter of Makir.
They had a son named Segub. 22 Segub was the father of Jair, who ruled twenty-three
towns in the land of Gilead. 23 (But Geshur and Aram captured the Towns of Jair* and
also took Kenath and its sixty surrounding villages.) All these were descendants of
Makir, the father of Gilead.
24 Soon after Hezron died in the town of Caleb-ephrathah, his wife Abijah gave birth to a
son named Ashhur (the father of* Tekoa).

DESCENDANTS OF HEZRON'S SON JERAHMEEL

25 The sons of Jerahmeel, the oldest son of Hezron, were Ram (the firstborn), Bunah,
Oren, Ozem, and Ahijah. 26 Jerahmeel had a second wife named Atarah. She was the
mother of Onam.
27 The sons of Ram, the oldest son of Jerahmeel, were Maaz, Jamin, and Eker.
28 The sons of Onam were Shammai and Jada.
The sons of Shammai were Nadab and Abishur.
29 The sons of Abishur and his wife Abihail were Ahban and Molid.
30 The sons of Nadab were Seled and Appaim. Seled died without children, 31 but
Appaim had a son named Ishi. The son of Ishi was Sheshan. Sheshan had a
descendant named Ahlai.
32 The sons of Jada, Shammai's brother, were Jether and Jonathan. Jether died without
children, 33 but Jonathan had two sons named Peleth and Zaza.
These were all descendants of Jerahmeel.
34 Sheshan had no sons, though he did have daughters. He also had an Egyptian
servant named Jarha. 35 Sheshan gave one of his daughters to be the wife of Jarha,
and they had a son named Attai.
36 Attai was the father of Nathan. **2:36** 1 Chr 11:41
Nathan was the father of Zabad.
37 Zabad was the father of Ephlal.
Ephlal was the father of Obed.
38 Obed was the father of Jehu.
Jehu was the father of Azariah.
39 Azariah was the father of Helez.
Helez was the father of Eleasah.
40 Eleasah was the father of Sismai.
Sismai was the father of Shallum.
41 Shallum was the father of Jekamiah.
Jekamiah was the father of Elishama.

DESCENDANTS OF HEZRON'S SON CALEB

42 The descendants of Caleb, the brother of Jerahmeel, included Mesha (the firstborn),
who became the father of Ziph. Caleb's descendants also included the sons of
Mareshah, the father of Hebron.*

2:18 Or *Caleb had a daughter named Jerioth from his wife, Azubah.* The meaning of the Hebrew is uncertain. **2:19** Hebrew *Ephrath,* a variant spelling of Ephrathah; compare 2:50 and 4:4. **2:23** Or *captured Havvoth-jair.* **2:24** Or *the founder of;* also in 2:42, 45, 49. **2:42** Or *who founded Hebron.* The meaning of the Hebrew is uncertain.

2:42-55 Many proper names from this section correspond to towns and cities. In this case, "father of" could be translated "founder of," and "sons of" should be understood as a similar reference to the founders of the settlement. This would have reminded the original audience that God's will for them was to return from exile into the land God had prepared for them.

43 The sons of Hebron were Korah, Tappuah, Rekem, and Shema. 44 Shema was the
father of Raham. Raham was the father of Jorkeam. Rekem was the father of
2:45 Shammai. 45 The son of Shammai was Maon. Maon was the father of Beth-zur.
Josh 15:55 46 Caleb's concubine Ephah gave birth to Haran, Moza, and Gazez. Haran was the father
of Gazez.
47 The sons of Jahdai were Regem, Jotham, Geshan, Pelet, Ephah, and Shaaph.
48 Another of Caleb's concubines, Maacah, gave birth to Sheber and Tirhanah. 49 She
also gave birth to Shaaph (the father of Madmannah) and Sheva (the father of
Macbenah and Gibea). Caleb also had a daughter named Acsah.
2:50 50 These were all descendants of Caleb.
1 Chr 4:4

DESCENDANTS OF CALEB'S SON HUR

The sons of Hur, the oldest son of Caleb's wife Ephrathah, were Shobal (the founder
of Kiriath-jearim), 51 Salma (the founder of Bethlehem), and Hareph (the founder of
Beth-gader).
52 The descendants of Shobal (the founder of Kiriath-jearim) were Haroeh, half the
Manahathites, 53 and the families of Kiriath-jearim—the Ithrites, Puthites, Shumathites,
and Mishraites, from whom came the people of Zorah and Eshtaol.
54 The descendants of Salma were the people of Bethlehem, the Netophathites,
2:55 2 Kgs 10:15 Atroth-beth-joab, the other half of the Manahathites, the Zorites, 55 and the families
of scribes living at Jabez—the Tirathites, Shimeathites, and Sucathites. All these were
Kenites who descended from Hammath, the father of the family of Recab.*

DESCENDANTS OF DAVID

3:1-4 3 These are the sons of David who were born in Hebron:
//2 Sam 3:2-5
3:1 The oldest was Amnon, whose mother was Ahinoam from Jezreel.
1 Sam 25:43 The second was Daniel, whose mother was Abigail from Carmel.
3:2 2 The third was Absalom, whose mother was Maacah, the daughter of Talmai, king of
2 Sam 3:4; 13:20; 14:23 Geshur.
The fourth was Adonijah, whose mother was Haggith.
3 The fifth was Shephatiah, whose mother was Abital.
The sixth was Ithream, whose mother was Eglah, David's wife.
3:4 2 Sam 5:4-5 4 These six sons were born to David in Hebron, where he reigned seven and a half years.

3:5-8 Then David reigned another thirty-three years in Jerusalem. 5 The sons born to David in
//2 Sam 5:14-16 Jerusalem included Shammua,* Shobab, Nathan, and Solomon. Their mother was Bath-
sheba,* the daughter of Ammiel. 6 David also had nine other sons: Ibhar, Elishua,* Elpelet,*
7 Nogah, Nepheg, Japhia, 8 Elishama, Eliada, and Eliphelet.
3:9 9 These were the sons of David, not including his sons born to his concubines. Their sis-
2 Sam 13:1 ter was named Tamar.

3:10 1 Kgs 15:1, 8, 24

DESCENDANTS OF SOLOMON

3:11 10 The descendants of Solomon were Rehoboam, Abijah, Asa, Jehoshaphat, 11 Jehoram,*
2 Kgs 8:24-25; 11:21 Ahaziah, Joash, 12 Amaziah, Uzziah,* Jotham, 13 Ahaz, Hezekiah, Manasseh, 14 Amon,
3:13 2 Kgs 16:1; 18:1 2 Chr 29:1; 33:1 and Josiah.

3:14 2 Kgs 21:19-26

2:55 Or *the founder of Beth-recab.* **3:5a** As in Syriac version (see also 14:4; 2 Sam 5:14); Hebrew reads *Shimea.* **3:5b** Hebrew *Bathshua,* a variant spelling of Bathsheba. **3:6a** As in some Hebrew and Greek manuscripts (see also 14:5-7 and 2 Sam 5:15); most Hebrew manuscripts read *Elishama.* **3:6b** Hebrew *Eliphelet;* compare parallel text at 14:5-7. **3:11** Hebrew *Joram,* a variant spelling of Jehoram. **3:12** Hebrew *Azariah,* a variant spelling of Uzziah.

3:1 Chapter 3 begins the most important part of the genealogy: the descendants of David. This was intended to clarify who could—and could not—have a legitimate claim to the throne of Israel in the future.

3:10 By continuing the genealogy past David's lifetime into the time of Judah's exile to Babylon (722 BC), the writer reveals that this record was completed long after that time, and the purpose and audience would have been affected by that event.

15 The sons of Josiah were Johanan (the oldest), Jehoiakim (the second), Zedekiah (the **3:15**
third), and Jehoahaz* (the fourth). 2 Kgs 23:34
16 The successors of Jehoiakim were his son Jehoiachin and his brother Zedekiah.*

DESCENDANTS OF JEHOIACHIN

17 The sons of Jehoiachin,* who was taken prisoner by the Babylonians, were Shealtiel,
18 Malkiram, Pedaiah, Shenazzar, Jekamiah, Hoshama, and Nedabiah.
19 The sons of Pedaiah were Zerubbabel and Shimei.
The sons of Zerubbabel were Meshullam and Hananiah. (Their sister was Shelomith.)
20 His five other sons were Hashubah, Ohel, Berekiah, Hasadiah, and Jushab-hesed.
21 The sons of Hananiah were Pelatiah and Jeshaiah. Jeshaiah's son was Rephaiah.
Rephaiah's son was Arnan. Arnan's son was Obadiah. Obadiah's son was Shecaniah.
22 The descendants of Shecaniah were Shemaiah and his sons, Hattush, Igal, Bariah, **3:22**
Neariah, and Shaphat—six in all. Ezra 8:2-3
23 The sons of Neariah were Elioenai, Hizkiah, and Azrikam—three in all.
24 The sons of Elioenai were Hodaviah, Eliashib, Pelaiah, Akkub, Johanan, Delaiah, and
Anani—seven in all.

OTHER DESCENDANTS OF JUDAH

4 The descendants of Judah were Perez, Hezron, Carmi, Hur, and Shobal. **4:1**
2 Shobal's son Reaiah was the father of Jahath. Jahath was the father of Ahumai Num 26:21
and Lahad. These were the families of the Zorathites. 1 Chr 2:3
3 The descendants of* Etam were Jezreel, Ishma, Idbash, their sister Hazzelelponi,
4 Penuel (the father of* Gedor), and Ezer (the father of Hushah). These were the
descendants of Hur (the firstborn of Ephrathah), the ancestor of Bethlehem.
5 Ashhur (the father of Tekoa) had two wives, named Helah and Naarah. 6 Naarah gave
birth to Ahuzzam, Hepher, Temeni, and Haahashtari. 7 Helah gave birth to Zereth,
Izhar, Ethnan, 8 and Koz, who became the ancestor of Anub, Zobebah, and all the
families of Aharhel son of Harum.
9 There was a man named Jabez who was more honorable than any of his brothers. His
mother named him Jabez* because his birth had been so painful. 10 He was the one

3:15 Hebrew *Shallum,* another name for Jehoahaz. **3:16** Hebrew *The sons of Jehoiakim were his son Jeconiah* [a variant spelling of Jehoiachin] *and his son Zedekiah.* **3:17** Hebrew *Jeconiah,* a variant spelling of Jehoiachin. **4:3** As in Greek version; Hebrew reads *father of.* The meaning of the Hebrew is uncertain. **4:4** Or *the founder of;* also in 4:5, 12, 14, 17, 18, and perhaps other instances where the text reads *the father of.* **4:9** *Jabez* sounds like a Hebrew word meaning "distress" or "pain."

3:17-24 The royal line continued through Jehoiachin, but not without great trouble. Jeremiah, a prophet contemporary with the writing of Chronicles (2 Chronicles 35:25; 36:12-22), told Jehoiachin that God would remove his family from the throne (Jeremiah 22:28-30), but God mercifully removed that judgment and had Jehoiachin released from captivity (2 Kings 25:27-30). In the first few chapters of the Gospels of Matthew and Luke, Jesus' royal lineage is traced through this restored royal family.

3:22 The record of Shecaniah's direct descendants includes one son and five grandchildren, revealing that the concerns of ancient genealogies are different from modern ones. They occasionally insert political, geographical, and other social connections without reference to kinship. In these cases, the expressions "son of" and "father of" had a meaning other than immediate biological descent. For instance, this section of families is preceded by a description of political relations (1 Chronicles 2:24, 42, 45, 49-52), and followed by a list of trade guilds (4:14, 21-23).

4:1 This summary of the rest of the family of Judah includes those outside David's direct line of descendants, and the closely associated tribe of Simeon (See Genesis 34:25-31; 1 Chronicles 4:24-43). The names in this chapter are a mixture of personal, clan, and settlement names, showing that the tribe of Judah was more than individuals—it included their associations and lands.

4:9 This is an example of a godly man in the line of Judah. Receiving God's blessing through prayerful reliance on Him is a common theme in Chronicles (1 Chronicles 5:18-22; 17:16-27; 21:1–22:1; 2 Chronicles 6:12-42; 7:11-16; 13:14; 14:11-13; 18:31; 20:5-30; 30:18-20; 32:20-24; 33:12-13). Jabez's mention of land continues the message of this chapter that Judah's identity was closely associated with territory.

▸ SALVATION
4:9 A blessing, not a bother. Does this prayer sound familiar? Jabez, who was apparently famous for causing his mother great pain in childbirth, cried out to God to cause pleasure and blessing, not pain and cursing, to flow through the rest of his life. God granted his request, and He can grant yours, too. Ask God to make you a source of bliss, not bother, to those in your life. (***See Salvation***> *Receiving*> *Results*> *Works*> *Bring God's blessing,* TopicGuide page A23.)

who prayed to the God of Israel, "Oh, that You would bless me and expand my
territory! Please be with me in all that I do, and keep me from all trouble and pain!"
And God granted him his request.
11 Kelub (the brother of Shuhah) was the father of Mehir. Mehir was the father of Eshton.
12 Eshton was the father of Beth-rapha, Paseah, and Tehinnah. Tehinnah was the
father of Ir-nahash. These were the descendants of Recah.
4:13 Josh 15:17 13 The sons of Kenaz were Othniel and Seraiah. Othniel's sons were Hathath and
Meonothai.* 14 Meonothai was the father of Ophrah. Seraiah was the father of Joab,
the founder of the Valley of Craftsmen,* so called because they were craftsmen.
15 The sons of Caleb son of Jephunneh were Iru, Elah, and Naam. The son of Elah was
Kenaz.
16 The sons of Jehallelel were Ziph, Ziphah, Tiria, and Asarel.
17 The sons of Ezrah were Jether, Mered, Epher, and Jalon. One of Mered's wives
became* the mother of Miriam, Shammai, and Ishbah (the father of Eshtemoa). 18 He
married a woman from Judah, who became the mother of Jered (the father of Gedor),
Heber (the father of Soco), and Jekuthiel (the father of Zanoah). Mered also married
Bithia, a daughter of Pharaoh, and she bore him children.
19 Hodiah's wife was the sister of Naham. One of her sons was the father of Keilah the
Garmite, and another was the father of Eshtemoa the Maacathite.
20 The sons of Shimon were Amnon, Rinnah, Ben-hanan, and Tilon.
The descendants of Ishi were Zoheth and Ben-zoheth.

DESCENDANTS OF JUDAH'S SON SHELAH

21 Shelah was one of Judah's sons. The descendants of Shelah were Er (the father of
Lecah); Laadah (the father of Mareshah); the families of linen workers at Beth-ashbea;
22 Jokim; the men of Cozeba; and Joash and Saraph, who ruled over Moab and
Jashubi-lehem. These names all come from ancient records. 23 They were the pottery
makers who lived in Netaim and Gederah. They lived there and worked for the king.

DESCENDANTS OF SIMEON

24 The sons of Simeon were Jemuel,* Jamin, Jarib, Zohar,* and Shaul.
25 The descendants of Shaul were Shallum, Mibsam, and Mishma.
26 The descendants of Mishma were Hammuel, Zaccur, and Shimei.
27 Shimei had sixteen sons and six daughters, but none of his brothers had large
families. So Simeon's tribe never grew as large as the tribe of Judah.
28 They lived in Beersheba, Moladah, Hazar-shual, 29 Bilhah, Ezem, Tolad, 30 Bethuel,
4:28-33 //Josh 19:2-10 Hormah, Ziklag, 31 Beth-marcaboth, Hazar-susim, Beth-biri, and Shaaraim. These
towns were under their control until the time of King David. 32 Their descendants also
lived in Etam, Ain, Rimmon, Token, and Ashan—five towns 33 and their surrounding
villages as far away as Baalath.* This was their territory, and these names are listed
in their genealogical records.

4:13 As in some Greek manuscripts and Latin Vulgate; Hebrew lacks *and Meonothai.* 4:14 Or *Joab, the father of Ge-harashim.* 4:17 Or *Jether's wife became;* Hebrew reads *She became.* 4:24a As in Syriac version (see also Gen 46:10; Exod 6:15); Hebrew reads *Nemuel.* 4:24b As in parallel texts at Gen 46:10 and Exod 6:15; Hebrew reads *Zerah.* 4:33 As in some Greek manuscripts (see also Josh 19:8); Hebrew reads *Baal.*

▸ BIBLE

4:22 The Bible is accurate. Do you believe the Bible is God's Word? Do you believe the Bible essentially fell from heaven, already bound in leather, or did it develop over time through many authors? Regardless of exactly what you believe about how the Bible came to be, it is apparent from passages like these that some portions of the Bible were carefully researched from oral and written records. This does not invalidate the protective care that the Holy Spirit took in assembling God's Word, but it confirms that God's Word was established on real history, using the best research but wholly protected from error by God's Spirit. (***See Bible****> Uniqueness> Authoritative> Demonstrates credibility,* TopicGuide page A10.)

[34]Other descendants of Simeon included Meshobab, Jamlech, Joshah son of Amaziah,
[35]Joel, Jehu son of Joshibiah, son of Seraiah, son of Asiel, [36]Elioenai, Jaakobah,
Jeshohaiah, Asaiah, Adiel, Jesimiel, Benaiah, [37]and Ziza son of Shiphi, son of Allon,
son of Jedaiah, son of Shimri, son of Shemaiah.

[38]These were the names of some of the leaders of Simeon's wealthy clans. Their fami-
lies grew, [39]and they traveled to the region of Gerar,* in the east part of the valley, seeking
pastureland for their flocks. [40]They found lush pastures there, and the land was quiet and **4:40** Judg 18:7-10
peaceful.

Some of Ham's descendants had been living in that region. [41]But during the reign of
King Hezekiah of Judah, these leaders of Simeon invaded the region and completely de-
stroyed* the homes of the descendants of Ham and of the Meunites. No trace of them re-
mains today. They killed everyone who lived there and took the land for themselves,
because they wanted its good pastureland for their flocks. [42]Five hundred of these invad- **4:42**
ers from the tribe of Simeon went to Mount Seir, led by Pelatiah, Neariah, Rephaiah, and Gen 36:8-9 **4:43**
Uzziel—all sons of Ishi. [43]They destroyed the few Amalekites who had survived, and they 1 Sam 15:7-8; 30:16-
have lived there ever since. 17

DESCENDANTS OF REUBEN

5 The oldest son of Israel* was Reuben. But since he dishonored his father by sleeping **5:1**
with one of his father's concubines, his birthright was given to the sons of his brother Gen 29:32; 35:22;
Joseph. For this reason, Reuben is not listed in the genealogical records as the firstborn 48:15-22; 49:4 1 Chr 2:1
son. [2]The descendants of Judah became the most powerful tribe and provided a ruler for **5:2**
the nation,* but the birthright belonged to Joseph. Gen 49:8-10, 12 Mic 5:2 Matt 2:6

[3]The sons of Reuben, the oldest son of Israel, were Hanoch, Pallu, Hezron, and Carmi.
[4]The descendants of Joel were Shemaiah, Gog, Shimei, [5]Micah, Reaiah, Baal, [6]and **5:3**
Beerah. Beerah was the leader of the Reubenites when they were taken into captivity Gen 46:9 Exod 6:14
by King Tiglath-pileser* of Assyria. Num 26:5
[7]Beerah's* relatives are listed in their genealogical records by their clans: Jeiel (the **5:6**
leader), Zechariah, [8]and Bela son of Azaz, son of Shema, son of Joel. 2 Kgs 15:19
The Reubenites lived in the area that stretches from Aroer to Nebo and Baal-meon. **5:7-8**
[9]And since they had so many livestock in the land of Gilead, they spread east toward Num 32:34 Josh 12:2
the edge of the desert that stretches to the Euphrates River. **5:9**
[10]During the reign of Saul, the Reubenites defeated the Hagrites in battle. Then they Josh 22:8-9
moved into the Hagrite settlements all along the eastern edge of Gilead. **5:10** 1 Chr 5:18-21

DESCENDANTS OF GAD

[11]Next to the Reubenites, the descendants of Gad lived in the land of Bashan as far east **5:11**
as Salecah. [12]Joel was the leader in the land of Bashan, and Shapham was second-in- Josh 13:11, 24-28
command, followed by Janai and Shaphat.
[13]Their relatives, the leaders of seven other clans, were Michael, Meshullam, Sheba,

4:39 As in Greek version; Hebrew reads *Gedor.* 4:41 The Hebrew term used here refers to the complete consecration of things or people to the LORD, either by destroying them or by giving them as an offering. 5:1 *Israel* is the name that God gave to Jacob. 5:2 Or *and from Judah came a prince.* 5:6 Hebrew *Tilgath-pilneser,* a variant spelling of Tiglath-pileser; also in 5:26. 5:7 Hebrew *His.*

4:40 Continuing the association of God's blessings with those who live in the lands promised to them, the author reported that Simeonites dwelt in spacious pasturelands. The New Covenant reveals the full reward God has for His people—an inheritance of much greater portion, extending to the entire world (Matthew 5:5; 2 Peter 3:13) and every spiritual blessing (Ephesians 1:3) through Christ (Psalm 2:8).

5:1 In the Old Testament, the covenant blessings of God were handed down through families, usually from the father to the eldest son. But due to immorality or foolishness (as with Esau, see Genesis 25:34) the blessing could go to a younger man. This explanation of God's work in Israel's (Jacob's) family explains how Judah (David's ancestor), not Reuben, had a special place of blessing and responsibility in God's pact with His people.

Jorai, Jacan, Zia, and Eber. 14 These were all descendants of Abihail son of Huri, son
of Jaroah, son of Gilead, son of Michael, son of Jeshishai, son of Jahdo, son of Buz.
15 Ahi son of Abdiel, son of Guni, was the leader of their clans.

5:16 16 The Gadites lived in the land of Gilead, in Bashan and its villages, and throughout all
1 Chr 27:29 the pasturelands of Sharon. 17 All of these were listed in the genealogical records during
5:17 the days of King Jotham of Judah and King Jeroboam of Israel.
2 Kgs 14:16, 28; 15:5, 32-33

THE TRIBES EAST OF THE JORDAN

5:18 18 There were 44,760 capable warriors in the armies of Reuben, Gad, and the half-tribe of
Num 1:3 Manasseh. They were all skilled in combat and armed with shields, swords, and bows.
5:19 19 They waged war against the Hagrites, the Jeturites, the Naphishites, and the Nodabites.
Gen 25:15 1 Chr 1:31; 5:10 20 They cried out to God during the battle, and He answered their prayer because they
5:20 trusted in Him. So the Hagrites and all their allies were defeated. 21 The plunder taken
2 Chr 14:11-13 from the Hagrites included 50,000 camels, 250,000 sheep and goats, 2,000 donkeys,
Ps 9:10 and 100,000 captives. 22 Many of the Hagrites were killed in the battle because God was
5:22 fighting against them. The people of Reuben, Gad, and Manasseh lived in their land until
Josh 23:10 2 Kgs 15:29; 17:6 they were taken into exile.
2 Chr 32:8 23 The half-tribe of Manasseh was very large and spread through the land from Bashan
5:23 to Baal-hermon, Senir, and Mount Hermon. 24 These were the leaders of their clans: Epher,*
Deut 3:9 Ishi, Eliel, Azriel, Jeremiah, Hodaviah, and Jahdiel. These men had a great reputation as
mighty warriors and leaders of their clans.
5:25 25 But these tribes were unfaithful to the God of their ancestors. They worshiped the
Exod 34:15 2 Kgs 17:7 gods of the nations that God had destroyed. 26 So the God of Israel caused King Pul of As-
5:26 syria (also known as Tiglath-pileser) to invade the land and take away the people of Reu-
2 Kgs 15:19, 29 ben, Gad, and the half-tribe of Manasseh as captives. The Assyrians exiled them to Halah,
Habor, Hara, and the Gozan River, where they remain to this day.

THE PRIESTLY LINE

6:1 **6** 1* The sons of Levi were Gershon, Kohath, and Merari.
Gen 46:11 Exod 6:16-25 2 The descendants of Kohath included Amram, Izhar, Hebron, and Uzziel.
3 The children of Amram were Aaron, Moses, and Miriam.
6:3 The sons of Aaron were Nadab, Abihu, Eleazar, and Ithamar.
Lev 10:1 4 Eleazar was the father of Phinehas.
Phinehas was the father of Abishua.

5:24 As in Greek version and Latin Vulgate; Hebrew reads *and Epher.* 6:1 Verses 6:1-15 are numbered 5:27-41 in Hebrew text.

5:16-17 The mention of larger geographical areas such as the "pasturelands of Sharon" signals one of the differences between ancient genealogical records and modern ones. The chronicler in particular combined agreeable descriptions of the land with declarations of tribal affiliation to establish a sense of ownership and pride among the exiles. His purpose was to convince the exiles to return to the land God had set aside for them.

5:18 The rest of the chapter moves from discussing certain families to discussing a region—the east side of the Jordan, where some of the Israelite tribes lived. They are alternately depicted as covenant keepers (1 Chronicles 5:20) and covenant breakers (1 Chronicles 5:25). They eventually fell under the same punishment suffered by those on the west side of the Jordan—exile.

5:21 Hebrew numbers present translation challenges throughout the Old Testament. The numbers in this section could be taken in three ways. First, they could be taken literally as translated. This presents some problems in that during this period of history, armies and herds of livestock of these numbers were unheard of—analysis of buildings, trash, skeletons, traces of ancient farms and fields, clothing, and documents show that the land of Israel was not highly populated until modern times. Second, these numbers may also be understood as hyperbole, purposefully inflated to generally communicate the vast amount of plunder God granted His faithful armies over a mighty enemy. Third, these numbers may be understood if the term for "thousand" is interpreted as "unit." Since we have no clues in Scripture of the size of these military units, we can only guess as to the resulting number of troops except that the number of soldiers would be markedly reduced.

6:1 This chapter records the genealogy of the tribe of Levi. A clear history of the families who could perform religious functions in Israel was critical for restoring proper worship after the people of Israel returned from exile. See the books of Nehemiah and Ezra for records of the return of God's people to their land.

[5] Abishua was the father of Bukki.
Bukki was the father of Uzzi.
[6] Uzzi was the father of Zerahiah.
Zerahiah was the father of Meraioth.
[7] Meraioth was the father of Amariah.
Amariah was the father of Ahitub.
[8] Ahitub was the father of Zadok. 6:8 Ezra 7:2
Zadok was the father of Ahimaaz.
[9] Ahimaaz was the father of Azariah.
Azariah was the father of Johanan.
[10] Johanan was the father of Azariah, the high priest at the Temple* built by Solomon in Jerusalem.
[11] Azariah was the father of Amariah.
Amariah was the father of Ahitub.
[12] Ahitub was the father of Zadok.
Zadok was the father of Shallum.
[13] Shallum was the father of Hilkiah.
Hilkiah was the father of Azariah.
[14] Azariah was the father of Seraiah.
Seraiah was the father of Jehozadak, [15]who went into exile when the LORD sent the people of Judah and Jerusalem into captivity under Nebuchadnezzar. 6:15 Neh 12:1 Hag 1:1, 14 Zech 6:11

THE LEVITE CLANS

[16]*The sons of Levi were Gershon,* Kohath, and Merari.
[17]The descendants of Gershon included Libni and Shimei.
[18]The descendants of Kohath included Amram, Izhar, Hebron, and Uzziel.
[19]The descendants of Merari included Mahli and Mushi. 6:19 1 Chr 23:21

The following were the Levite clans, listed according to their ancestral descent:

[20]The descendants of Gershon included Libni, Jahath, Zimmah, [21]Joah, Iddo, Zerah, and Jeatherai.
[22]The descendants of Kohath included Amminadab, Korah, Assir, [23]Elkanah, Abiasaph,* Assir, [24]Tahath, Uriel, Uzziah, and Shaul.
[25]The descendants of Elkanah included Amasai, Ahimoth, [26]Elkanah, Zophai, Nahath,
[27]Eliab, Jeroham, Elkanah, and Samuel.* 6:27 1 Sam 1:1, 20
[28]The sons of Samuel were Joel* (the older) and Abijah (the second). 6:28 1 Sam 8:2 1 Chr 6:33
[29]The descendants of Merari included Mahli, Libni, Shimei, Uzzah, [30]Shimea, Haggiah, and Asaiah.

THE TEMPLE MUSICIANS

[31]David assigned the following men to lead the music at the house of the LORD after the Ark was placed there. [32]They ministered with music at the Tabernacle* until Solomon built 6:31 2 Sam 6:17 1 Chr 15:16-22, 27; 16:4-6

6:10 Hebrew *the house.* **6:16a** Verses 6:16-81 are numbered 6:1-66 in Hebrew text. **6:16b** Hebrew *Gershom,* a variant spelling of Gershon (see 6:1); also in 6:17, 20, 43, 62, 71. **6:23** Hebrew *Ebiasaph,* a variant spelling of Abiasaph (also in 6:37); compare parallel text at Exod 6:24. **6:27** As in some Greek manuscripts (see also 6:33-34); Hebrew lacks *and Samuel.* **6:28** As in some Greek manuscripts and the Syriac version (see also 6:33 and 1 Sam 8:2); Hebrew lacks *Joel.* **6:32** Hebrew *the Tabernacle, the Tent of Meeting.*

6:31 Knowing that there could be controversy regarding who performed what duties in postexilic Israel, the writer notes that King David specifically assigned worship leaders their roles. This clarified the division of responsibilities in the restored Temple after the readers returned from captivity.

▸ CHURCH
6:32 Tradition of worship. What part does tradition play in your church? Is it viewed as a good thing, a bad thing, or something else? Tradition can be a wonderful part of the church. For instance, the worship leaders under

the Temple of the LORD in Jerusalem. They carried out their work, following all the regula-
tions handed down to them. 33These are the men who served, along with their sons:

Heman the musician was from the clan of Kohath. His genealogy was traced back
through Joel, Samuel, 34Elkanah, Jeroham, Eliel, Toah, 35Zuph, Elkanah, Mahath,
Amasai, 36Elkanah, Joel, Azariah, Zephaniah, 37Tahath, Assir, Abiasaph, Korah,
38Izhar, Kohath, Levi, and Israel.*

39Heman's first assistant was Asaph from the clan of Gershon.* Asaph's genealogy was
traced back through Berekiah, Shimea, 40Michael, Baaseiah, Malkijah, 41Ethni, Zerah,
Adaiah, 42Ethan, Zimmah, Shimei, 43Jahath, Gershon, and Levi.

44Heman's second assistant was Ethan from the clan of Merari. Ethan's genealogy was
traced back through Kishi, Abdi, Malluch, 45Hashabiah, Amaziah, Hilkiah, 46Amzi,
Bani, Shemer, 47Mahli, Mushi, Merari, and Levi.

48Their fellow Levites were appointed to various other tasks in the Tabernacle, the house
of God.

AARON'S DESCENDANTS

49Only Aaron and his descendants served as priests. They presented the offerings on the
altar of burnt offering and the altar of incense, and they performed all the other duties re-
lated to the Most Holy Place. They made atonement for Israel by doing everything that
Moses, the servant of God, had commanded them.

6:50 50The descendants of Aaron were Eleazar, Phinehas, Abishua, 51Bukki, Uzzi, Zerahiah,
1 Chr 6:4-8 52Meraioth, Amariah, Ahitub, 53Zadok, and Ahimaaz.

TERRITORY FOR THE LEVITES

6:54 54This is a record of the towns and territory assigned by means of sacred lots to the descen-
Josh 21:4, 10 dants of Aaron, who were from the clan of Kohath. 55This territory included Hebron and its
6:55-56 surrounding pasturelands in Judah, 56but the fields and outlying areas belonging to the city
Josh 14:13; 15:13 were given to Caleb son of Jephunneh. 57So the descendants of Aaron were given the follow-
6:58 ing towns, each with its pasturelands: Hebron (a city of refuge),* Libnah, Jattir, Eshtemoa, 58Ho-
Josh 10:3 lon,* Debir, 59Ain,* Juttah,* and Beth-shemesh. 60And from the territory of Benjamin they were
6:61 given Gibeon,* Geba, Alemeth, and Anathoth, each with its pasturelands. So thirteen towns
Josh 21:5 were given to the descendants of Aaron. 61The remaining descendants of Kohath received
1 Chr 6:66-70 ten towns from the territory of the half-tribe of Manasseh by means of sacred lots.
62The descendants of Gershon received by sacred lots thirteen towns from the territories
of Issachar, Asher, Naphtali, and from the Bashan area of Manasseh, east of the Jordan.
6:63 63The descendants of Merari received by sacred lots twelve towns from the territories of
Josh 21:7, 34-40 Reuben, Gad, and Zebulun.
6:64 64So the people of Israel assigned all these towns and pasturelands to the Levites. 65The

Num 35:1-8
Josh 21:3, 41-42
1 Chr 6:57-60

6:38 *Israel* is the name that God gave to Jacob. **6:39** Hebrew lacks *from the clan of Gershon;* see 6:43. **6:57** As in parallel text at Josh 21:13; Hebrew reads *were given the cities of refuge: Hebron, and the following towns, each with its pasturelands.* **6:58** As in parallel text at Josh 21:15; Hebrew reads *Hilen.* **6:59a** As in parallel text at Josh 21:16; Hebrew reads *Ashan.* **6:59b** As in Syriac version (see also Josh 21:16); Hebrew lacks *Juttah.* **6:60** As in parallel text at Josh 21:17; Hebrew lacks *Gibeon.*

David's instruction trained those who led worship in Solomon's Temple. Who wouldn't want a worship leader to be trained by King David? Through tradition, we can enjoy the wisdom and gifts that God's Spirit gave to past generations. Do not reject all tradition out of hand, but respect the work of God's Spirit in your past community. (*See Church*> *Role> Church Community> Using their gifts to build up the body,* TopicGuide page A49.)

6:49 Only descendants from Aaron could serve as priests in Israel. The Levites performed other functions, ranging from leading others in music to baking the bread used in the Temple.

6:54 It may be surprising to modern readers that "sacred lots" were used in assigning property, discerning guilt (Joshua 7:16-18), or even picking apostles (Acts 1:26). The Urim and Thumim, which had been carried by the high priest since Moses' time (Exodus 28:30), were the first of such devices.

towns in the territories of Judah, Simeon, and Benjamin, mentioned above, were assigned
to them by means of sacred lots.
66The descendants of Kohath were given the following towns from the territory of **6:66**
Ephraim, each with its pasturelands: 67Shechem (a city of refuge in the hill country of Josh 21:20-26
Ephraim),* Gezer, 68Jokmeam, Beth-horon, 69Aijalon, and Gath-rimmon. 70The remaining
descendants of Kohath were assigned the towns of Aner and Bileam from the territory of
the half-tribe of Manasseh, each with its pasturelands.
71The descendants of Gershon received the towns of Golan (in Bashan) and Ashtaroth
from the territory of the half-tribe of Manasseh, each with its pasturelands. 72From the terri-
tory of Issachar, they were given Kedesh, Daberath, 73Ramoth, and Anem, each with its
pasturelands. 74From the territory of Asher, they received Mashal, Abdon, 75Hukok, and Re-
hob, each with its pasturelands. 76From the territory of Naphtali, they were given Kedesh in
Galilee, Hammon, and Kiriathaim, each with its pasturelands.
77The remaining descendants of Merari received the towns of Jokneam, Kartah,* Rimmon,*
and Tabor from the territory of Zebulun, each with its pasturelands. 78From the territory of
Reuben, east of the Jordan River opposite Jericho, they received Bezer (a desert town), Jahaz,*
79Kedemoth, and Mephaath, each with its pasturelands. 80And from the territory of Gad, they
received Ramoth in Gilead, Mahanaim, 81Heshbon, and Jazer, each with its pasturelands.

DESCENDANTS OF ISSACHAR

7 The four sons of Issachar were Tola, Puah, Jashub, and Shimron. **7:1** Gen 46:13
2The sons of Tola were Uzzi, Rephaiah, Jeriel, Jahmai, Ibsam, and Shemuel. Each **7:2**
of them was the leader of an ancestral clan. At the time of King David, the total 2 Sam 24:1-9
number of mighty warriors listed in the records of these clans was 22,600.
3The son of Uzzi was Izrahiah. The sons of Izrahiah were Michael, Obadiah, Joel, and
Isshiah. These five became the leaders of clans. 4All of them had many wives and
many sons, so the total number of men available for military service among their
descendants was 36,000.
5The total number of mighty warriors from all the clans of the tribe of Issachar was
87,000. All of them were listed in their genealogical records.

DESCENDANTS OF BENJAMIN

6Three of Benjamin's sons were Bela, Beker, and Jediael. **7:6** 1 Chr 8:1-40
7The five sons of Bela were Ezbon, Uzzi, Uzziel, Jerimoth, and Iri. Each of them was the
leader of an ancestral clan. The total number of mighty warriors from these clans was
22,034, as listed in their genealogical records.
8The sons of Beker were Zemirah, Joash, Eliezer, Elioenai, Omri, Jeremoth, Abijah,
Anathoth, and Alemeth. 9Each of them was the leader of an ancestral clan. The total
number of mighty warriors and leaders from these clans was 20,200, as listed in
their genealogical records.
10The son of Jediael was Bilhan. The sons of Bilhan were Jeush, Benjamin, Ehud,
Kenaanah, Zethan, Tarshish, and Ahishahar. 11Each of them was the leader of an
ancestral clan. From these clans the total number of mighty warriors ready for war
was 17,200.
12The sons of Ir were Shuppim and Huppim. Hushim was the son of Aher.

6:66-67 As in parallel text at Josh 21:21. Hebrew text reads *were given the cities of refuge: Shechem in the hill country of Ephraim, and the following towns, each with its pasturelands.* **6:77a** As in Greek version (see also Josh 21:34); Hebrew lacks *Jokneam, Kartah.* **6:77b** As in Greek version (see also Josh 19:13); Hebrew reads *Rimmono.* **6:78** Hebrew *Jahzah,* a variant spelling of Jahaz.

7:6-12 Among the tribes detailed in this chapter, the most important to the chronicler was Benjamin. The chronicler returns to the details of this tribe in 8:1-40 to trace the lineage of Saul.

DESCENDANTS OF NAPHTALI

7:13 13 The sons of Naphtali were Jahzeel,* Guni, Jezer, and Shillem.* They were all
Gen 30:8 descendants of Jacob's concubine Bilhah.

DESCENDANTS OF MANASSEH

7:14 14 The descendants of Manasseh through his Aramean concubine included Asriel. She
Gen 50:23 also bore Makir, the father of Gilead. 15 Makir found wives for* Huppim and Shuppim.
Num 26:29-30 Makir had a sister named Maacah. One of his descendants was Zelophehad, who had
only daughters.
16 Makir's wife, Maacah, gave birth to a son whom she named Peresh. His brother's name
was Sheresh. The sons of Peresh were Ulam and Rakem. 17 The son of Ulam was
Bedan. All these were considered Gileadites, descendants of Makir son of Manasseh.
18 Makir's sister Hammoleketh gave birth to Ishhod, Abiezer, and Mahlah.
19 The sons of Shemida were Ahian, Shechem, Likhi, and Aniam.

DESCENDANTS OF EPHRAIM

7:20 20 The descendants of Ephraim were Shuthelah, Bered, Tahath, Eleadah, Tahath,
Num 26:35-36 21 Zabad, Shuthelah, Ezer, and Elead. These two were killed trying to steal livestock
from the local farmers near Gath. 22 Their father, Ephraim, mourned for them a long
time, and his relatives came to comfort him. 23 Afterward Ephraim slept with his wife,
and she became pregnant and gave birth to a son. Ephraim named him Beriah*
7:24 because of the tragedy his family had suffered. 24 He had a daughter named Sheerah.
Josh 16:3, 5 She built the towns of Lower and Upper Beth-horon and Uzzen-sheerah.
7:25-27 25 The descendants of Ephraim included Rephah, Resheph, Telah, Tahan, 26 Ladan,
Exod 17:9-14; 24:13 Ammihud, Elishama, 27 Nun, and Joshua.

28 The descendants of Ephraim lived in the territory that included Bethel and its sur-
rounding towns to the south, Naaran to the east, Gezer and its villages to the west, and
7:29 Shechem and its surrounding villages to the north as far as Ayyah and its towns. 29 Along
Josh 17:7-11 the border of Manasseh were the towns of Beth-shan,* Taanach, Megiddo, Dor, and their
surrounding villages. The descendants of Joseph son of Israel* lived in these towns.

DESCENDANTS OF ASHER

7:30 30 The sons of Asher were Imnah, Ishvah, Ishvi, and Beriah. They had a sister named
Gen 46:17 Serah.
Num 26:44-46 31 The sons of Beriah were Heber and Malkiel (the father of Birzaith).
32 The sons of Heber were Japhlet, Shomer, and Hotham. They had a sister named Shua.
33 The sons of Japhlet were Pasach, Bimhal, and Ashvath.
34 The sons of Shomer were Ahi,* Rohgah, Hubbah, and Aram.
35 The sons of his brother Helem* were Zophah, Imna, Shelesh, and Amal.
36 The sons of Zophah were Suah, Harnepher, Shual, Beri, Imrah, 37 Bezer, Hod, Shamma,
Shilshah, Ithran,* and Beera.
38 The sons of Jether were Jephunneh, Pispah, and Ara.
39 The sons of Ulla were Arah, Hanniel, and Rizia.
40 Each of these descendants of Asher was the head of an ancestral clan. They were all
select men—mighty warriors and outstanding leaders. The total number of men available
for military service was 26,000, as listed in their genealogical records.

7:13a As in parallel text at Gen 46:24; Hebrew reads *Jahziel,* a variant spelling of Jahzeel. **7:13b** As in some Hebrew and Greek manuscripts (see also Gen 46:24; Num 26:49); most Hebrew manuscripts read *Shallum.* **7:15** Or *Makir took a wife from.* The meaning of the Hebrew is uncertain. **7:23** *Beriah* sounds like a Hebrew term meaning "tragedy" or "misfortune." **7:29a** Hebrew *Beth-shean,* a variant spelling of Beth-shan. **7:29b** *Israel* is the name that God gave to Jacob. **7:34** Or *The sons of Shomer, his brother, were.* **7:35** Possibly another name for *Hotham;* compare 7:32. **7:37** Possibly another name for *Jether;* compare 7:38.

DESCENDANTS OF BENJAMIN

8 Benjamin's first son was Bela, the second was Ashbel, the third was Aharah, [2]the fourth was Nohah, and the fifth was Rapha. 8:1 Gen 46:21 1 Chr 7:6-12
[3]The sons of Bela were Addar, Gera, Abihud,* [4]Abishua, Naaman, Ahoah, [5]Gera,
Shephuphan, and Huram.
[6]The sons of Ehud, leaders of the clans living at Geba, were exiled to Manahath.
[7]Ehud's sons were Naaman, Ahijah, and Gera. Gera, who led them into exile, was the
father of Uzza and Ahihud.*
[8]After Shaharaim divorced his wives Hushim and Baara, he had children in the land of
Moab. [9]Hodesh, his new wife, gave birth to Jobab, Zibia, Mesha, Malcam, [10]Jeuz,
Sakia, and Mirmah. These sons all became the leaders of clans.
[11]Shaharaim's wife Hushim had already given birth to Abitub and Elpaal. [12]The sons of 8:12 Ezra 2:33 Neh 6:2; 7:37; 11:35
Elpaal were Eber, Misham, Shemed (who built the towns of Ono and Lod and their
nearby villages), [13]Beriah, and Shema. They were the leaders of the clans living in 8:13 Josh 10:12; 11:22
Aijalon, and they drove out the inhabitants of Gath.
[14]Ahio, Shashak, Jeremoth, [15]Zebadiah, Arad, Eder, [16]Michael, Ishpah, and Joha were
the sons of Beriah.
[17]Zebadiah, Meshullam, Hizki, Heber, [18]Ishmerai, Izliah, and Jobab were the sons of
Elpaal.
[19]Jakim, Zicri, Zabdi, [20]Elienai, Zillethai, Eliel, [21]Adaiah, Beraiah, and Shimrath were the
sons of Shimei.
[22]Ishpan, Eber, Eliel, [23]Abdon, Zicri, Hanan, [24]Hananiah, Elam, Anthothijah, [25]Iphdeiah,
and Penuel were the sons of Shashak.
[26]Shamsherai, Shehariah, Athaliah, [27]Jaareshiah, Elijah, and Zicri were the sons of
Jeroham.
[28]These were the leaders of the ancestral clans; they were listed in their genealogical
records, and they all lived in Jerusalem.

THE FAMILY OF SAUL

[29]Jeiel* (the father of* Gibeon) lived in the town of Gibeon. His wife's name was 8:29 Josh 9:3
Maacah, [30]and his oldest son was named Abdon. Jeiel's other sons were Zur, Kish,
Baal, Ner,* Nadab, [31]Gedor, Ahio, Zechariah,* [32]and Mikloth, who was the father of
Shimeam.* All these families lived near each other in Jerusalem.
[33] Ner was the father of Kish. 8:33 1 Sam 9:1; 14:49-50 1 Chr 9:39-44
Kish was the father of Saul.
Saul was the father of Jonathan, Malkishua, Abinadab, and Esh-baal.
[34] Jonathan was the father of Merib-baal. 8:34 2 Sam 4:4
Merib-baal was the father of Micah.
[35] Micah was the father of Pithon, Melech, Tahrea,* and Ahaz.
[36] Ahaz was the father of Jadah.*
Jadah was the father of Alemeth, Azmaveth, and Zimri.
Zimri was the father of Moza.

8:3 Possibly *Gera the father of Ehud;* compare 8:6. **8:7** Or *Gera, that is Heglam, was the father of Uzza and Ahihud.* **8:29a** As in some Greek manuscripts (see also 9:35); Hebrew lacks *Jeiel.* **8:29b** Or *the founder of.* **8:30** As in some Greek manuscripts (see also 9:36); Hebrew lacks *Ner.* **8:31** As in parallel text at 9:37; Hebrew reads *Zeker,* a variant spelling of Zechariah. **8:32** As in parallel text at 9:38; Hebrew reads *Shimeah,* a variant spelling of Shimeam. **8:35** As in parallel text at 9:41; Hebrew reads *Tarea,* a variant spelling of Tahrea. **8:36** As in parallel text at 9:42; Hebrew reads *Jehoaddah,* a variant spelling of Jadah.

8:1 The author closes the survey of the tribes of Israel by giving additional details of Saul's lineage, which descends from the tribe of Benjamin. Though it isn't until 8:33 that Saul's name is mentioned, it is the preeminent name in the list.

8:8-13 The origin of the relationship between Israel and Moab is found in Genesis 7, where the nation can be traced to the sinful behavior of Lot's daughters with their father. See 1 Samuel 22:3-5 for a mention of Israelites honorably dwelling within Moab.

37 Moza was the father of Binea.
Binea was the father of Rephaiah.*
Rephaiah was the father of Eleasah.
Eleasah was the father of Azel.
38 Azel had six sons: Azrikam, Bokeru, Ishmael, Sheariah, Obadiah, and Hanan. These
were the sons of Azel.
39 Azel's brother Eshek had three sons: the first was Ulam, the second was Jeush, and
the third was Eliphelet. 40 Ulam's sons were all mighty warriors and expert archers.
They had many sons and grandsons—150 in all.

All these were descendants of Benjamin.

9 So all Israel was listed in the genealogical records in *The Book of the Kings of Israel.*

THE RETURNING EXILES

9:1 1 Chr 5:25 — The people of Judah were exiled to Babylon because they were unfaithful to the LORD.
2 The first of the exiles to return to their property in their former towns were priests, Levites,
9:2 Ezra 2:43, 58, 70; 8:20 Neh 11:3-22 — Temple servants, and other Israelites. 3 Some of the people from the tribes of Judah, Benja-
min, Ephraim, and Manasseh came and settled in Jerusalem.
4 One family that returned was that of Uthai son of Ammihud, son of Omri, son of Imri,
9:4 Gen 46:12 — son of Bani, a descendant of Perez son of Judah.
5 Others returned from the Shilonite clan, including Asaiah (the oldest) and his sons.
6 From the Zerahite clan, Jeuel returned with his relatives.
In all, 690 families from the tribe of Judah returned.

7 From the tribe of Benjamin came Sallu son of Meshullam, son of Hodaviah, son of
Hassenuah; 8 Ibneiah son of Jeroham; Elah son of Uzzi, son of Micri; and Meshullam
son of Shephatiah, son of Reuel, son of Ibnijah.
9:9 Neh 11:8 — 9 These men were all leaders of clans, and they were listed in their genealogical records. In
all, 956 families from the tribe of Benjamin returned.

THE RETURNING PRIESTS

9:10 Neh 11:10-14 — 10 Among the priests who returned were Jedaiah, Jehoiarib, Jakin, 11 Azariah son of
Hilkiah, son of Meshullam, son of Zadok, son of Meraioth, son of Ahitub. Azariah
was the chief officer of the house of God.
12 Other returning priests were Adaiah son of Jeroham, son of Pashhur, son of Malkijah,
and Maasai son of Adiel, son of Jahzerah, son of Meshullam, son of Meshillemith,
son of Immer.
13 In all, 1,760 priests returned. They were heads of clans and very able men. They were
responsible for ministering at the house of God.

THE RETURNING LEVITES

9:14 Neh 11:15-19 — 14 The Levites who returned were Shemaiah son of Hasshub, son of Azrikam, son of
Hashabiah, a descendant of Merari; 15 Bakbakkar; Heresh; Galal; Mattaniah son of Mica,
son of Zicri, son of Asaph; 16 Obadiah son of Shemaiah, son of Galal, son of Jeduthun;
and Berekiah son of Asa, son of Elkanah, who lived in the area of Netophah.

8:37 As in parallel text at 9:43; Hebrew reads *Raphah,* a variant spelling of Rephaiah.

9:1 This reference to "The Book of the Kings of Israel" is not a reference to the books of 1 and 2 Kings, but to a royal genealogy now lost to us.

9:2 The chronicler emphasizes that the returnees should repossess land that was rightfully theirs. This explains the mention of towns and tribal areas in the preceding genealogical lists.

9:3-4 Special attention is given to Judah in this chapter. Judah and Benjamin are given lengthy treatment in these genealogies, reminding the reader of respect due to the faithful southern tribes of Israel. King David, the second ruler of Israel, came from the tribe of Judah, as did Jesus Christ (Hebrews 7:14).

17The gatekeepers who returned were Shallum, Akkub, Talmon, Ahiman, and their **9:17**
relatives. Shallum was the chief gatekeeper. 18Prior to this time, they were Ezek 46:1-2
responsible for the King's Gate on the east side. These men served as gatekeepers
for the camps of the Levites. 19Shallum was the son of Kore, a descendant of
Abiasaph,* from the clan of Korah. He and his relatives, the Korahites, were
responsible for guarding the entrance to the sanctuary, just as their ancestors had
guarded the Tabernacle in the camp of the LORD.

20Phinehas son of Eleazar had been in charge of the gatekeepers in earlier times, **9:20**
and the LORD had been with him. 21And later Zechariah son of Meshelemiah was Num 25:7-13
responsible for guarding the entrance to the Tabernacle.* **9:21** 1 Chr 26:2, 14

22In all, there were 212 gatekeepers in those days, and they were listed according to the
genealogies in their villages. David and Samuel the seer had appointed their ancestors be-
cause they were reliable men. 23These gatekeepers and their descendants, by their divi-
sions, were responsible for guarding the entrance to the house of the LORD when that
house was a tent. 24The gatekeepers were stationed on all four sides—east, west, north,
and south. 25Their relatives in the villages came regularly to share their duties for seven- **9:25**
day periods. 2 Kgs 11:5, 7 2 Chr 23:8

26The four chief gatekeepers, all Levites, were trusted officials, for they were responsible
for the rooms and treasuries at the house of God. 27They would spend the night around **9:27**
the house of God, since it was their duty to guard it and to open the gates every morning. 1 Chr 23:30-32

28Some of the gatekeepers were assigned to care for the various articles used in wor-
ship. They checked them in and out to avoid any loss. 29Others were responsible for the **9:29**
furnishings, the items in the sanctuary, and the supplies, such as choice flour, wine, olive 1 Chr 23:29
oil, frankincense, and spices. 30But it was the priests who blended the spices. 31Mattithiah, **9:30**
a Levite and the oldest son of Shallum the Korahite, was entrusted with baking the bread Exod 30:23-25
used in the offerings. 32And some members of the clan of Kohath were in charge of pre- **9:32**
paring the bread to be set on the table each Sabbath day. Lev 24:5-8

33The musicians, all prominent Levites, lived at the Temple. They were exempt from **9:33**
other responsibilities since they were on duty at all hours. 34All these men lived in Jerusa- 1 Chr 6:31-47;
lem. They were the heads of Levite families and were listed as prominent leaders in their 25:1-31 Ps 134:1
genealogical records.

KING SAUL'S FAMILY TREE

35Jeiel (the father of* Gibeon) lived in the town of Gibeon. His wife's name was Maacah, **9:35**
36and his oldest son was named Abdon. Jeiel's other sons were Zur, Kish, Baal, Ner, 1 Chr 8:29-32
Nadab, 37Gedor, Ahio, Zechariah, and Mikloth. 38Mikloth was the father of Shimeam.
All these families lived near each other in Jerusalem.

39 Ner was the father of Kish. **9:39**
Kish was the father of Saul. 1 Chr 8:33-38
Saul was the father of Jonathan, Malkishua, Abinadab, and Esh-baal.
40 Jonathan was the father of Merib-baal.
Merib-baal was the father of Micah.
41 The sons of Micah were Pithon, Melech, Tahrea, and Ahaz.* **9:41**
42 Ahaz was the father of Jadah.* 1 Chr 8:35-37
Jadah was the father of Alemeth, Azmaveth, and Zimri.
Zimri was the father of Moza.

9:19 Hebrew *Ebiasaph,* a variant spelling of Abiasaph; compare Exod 6:24. **9:21** Hebrew *Tent of Meeting.* **9:35** Or *the founder of.* **9:41** As in Syriac version and Latin Vulgate (see also 8:35); Hebrew lacks *and Ahaz.* **9:42** As in some Hebrew manuscripts and Greek version (see also 8:36); Hebrew reads *Jarah.*

9:31 This is an example of the various duties of a Levite as distinguished from the work of the priests.

43 Moza was the father of Binea.
Binea's son was Rephaiah.
Rephaiah's son was Eleasah.
Eleasah's son was Azel.
44 Azel had six sons, whose names were Azrikam, Bokeru, Ishmael, Sheariah, Obadiah,
and Hanan. These were the sons of Azel.

THE DEATH OF KING SAUL

10:1 **10** Now the Philistines attacked Israel, and the men of Israel fled before them. Many
1 Sam 31:1-13 were slaughtered on the slopes of Mount Gilboa. 2 The Philistines closed in on
10:2 Saul and his sons, and they killed three of his sons—Jonathan, Abinadab, and Malkishua.
1 Sam 31:2, 4 3 The fighting grew very fierce around Saul, and the Philistine archers caught up with him
and wounded him.
4 Saul groaned to his armor bearer, "Take your sword and kill me before these pagan
Philistines come to taunt and torture me."
But his armor bearer was afraid and would not do it. So Saul took his own sword and fell
on it. 5 When his armor bearer realized that Saul was dead, he fell on his own sword and
died. 6 So Saul and his three sons died there together, bringing his dynasty to an end.
7 When all the Israelites in the Jezreel Valley saw that their army had fled and that Saul
and his sons were dead, they abandoned their towns and fled. So the Philistines moved in
and occupied their towns.
8 The next day, when the Philistines went out to strip the dead, they found the bodies of
10:9 Saul and his sons on Mount Gilboa. 9 So they stripped off Saul's armor and cut off his head.
1 Sam 31:9 Then they proclaimed the good news of Saul's death before their idols and to the people
throughout the land of Philistia. 10 They placed his armor in the temple of their gods, and
they fastened his head to the temple of Dagon.
10:13 11 But when everyone in Jabesh-gilead heard about everything the Philistines had done to
Lev 19:31 Saul, 12 all their mighty warriors brought the bodies of Saul and his sons back to Jabesh. Then
1 Sam 13:13-14; 15:23; 28:7 they buried their bones beneath the great tree at Jabesh, and they fasted for seven days.
13 So Saul died because he was unfaithful to the LORD. He failed to obey the LORD's com-
10:14 1 Sam 15:28 mand, and he even consulted a medium 14 instead of asking the LORD for guidance. So the
1 Chr 12:23 LORD killed him and turned the kingdom over to David son of Jesse.

10:1 The sudden shift from genealogy to narrative implies a tight connection between history and an understanding of the family of God. The following narrative shows the unity of Israel under the reign of David, starting with the death of Saul.

10:1-2 Mount Gilboa is a barren ridge on the southeastern end of the Jezreel Valley between Galilee and Samaria. Gideon selected his 300 warriors to battle the Midianites at the foot of this mountain (Judges 7:5-7). Where God had previously given Israel miraculous victory, now Saul ended that tradition in a tragic defeat.

10:4 From a human perspective, suicide seems appropriate for a king on the verge of utter defeat by his life-long enemies. But the chronicler uses this account to point out Saul's moral failure (1 Chronicles 10:13-14). Suicide, while not an unpardonable sin, should be understood as included in the command against murder (Exodus 20:13) and forever ranks Saul among those such as Abimelech (Judges 9:54), a wicked ruler who died in a similar fashion.

10:7 As a result of the Philistines' victory, the Philistines controlled a sizeable portion of Palestine west of the Jordan until David was made king over Israel (14:8-17).

10:11-12 The warriors of Jabesh-gilead marched about 13 miles to the wall of Beth-shan to show honor to Saul, who rescued them from the Ammonites (see 1 Samuel 11). Centuries earlier, Jabesh-gilead had been derided by the other tribes for not sending a contingent to fight against the Benjamites after men from Gibeah (Saul's hometown) raped and killed a Levite's concubine (Judges 21:8-25). By recording the rescue of Saul's and his son's bodies, the chronicler shows how brave acts of honor can rectify years of hostile internal division.

10:13-14 The chronicler concludes with an explanation of why Saul's dynasty came to an end, providing encouragement for God's people to obey the Lord and contrasting Saul's kingship against David's.

▸ WORSHIP
10:13 God controls life and death. Does the God you worship kill people? How can we believe God is a God of love if He does that? First, because God's love is perfect and not merely sentimental, God is not paralyzed by His genuine love for us. He is free to act in our best interest and His—even when that action is punitive. Second, God's perfect plan for our salvation involves the death of His perfect Son—Jesus Christ. We cannot be saved unless we embrace the sacrificial death (and resurrection!) of God's Son for us. So while it may make us nervous to worship a God who wields the power of life and death, He uses His power for the good of all who love Him (Romans 8:28). (***See Worship****> NT> Reverence> We fear God because He has power over life and death,* TopicGuide page A32.)

DAVID BECOMES KING OF ALL ISRAEL

11 Then all Israel gathered before David at Hebron and told him, "We are your own 11:1-3
flesh and blood. 2 In the past,* even when Saul was king, you were the one who //2 Sam 5:1-3
really led the forces of Israel. And the LORD your God told you, 'You will be the shepherd of 11:2
My people Israel. You will be the leader of My people Israel.'" 2 Sam 5:2; 7:7
3 So there at Hebron, David made a covenant before the LORD with all the elders of Israel. 11:3
And they anointed him king of Israel, just as the LORD had promised through Samuel. 1 Sam 16:1-13

DAVID CAPTURES JERUSALEM

4 Then David and all Israel went to Jerusalem (or Jebus, as it used to be called), where the 11:4-9
Jebusites, the original inhabitants of the land, were living. 5 The people of Jebus taunted //2 Sam 5:6-10
David, saying, "You'll never get in here!" But David captured the fortress of Zion, which is 11:4
now called the City of David. Josh 15:8, 63 Judg 1:21
6 David had said to his troops, "Whoever is first to attack the Jebusites will become the 11:6
commander of my armies!" And Joab, the son of David's sister Zeruiah, was first to attack, 2 Sam 8:16
so he became the commander of David's armies.
7 David made the fortress his home, and that is why it is called the City of David. 8 He ex-
tended the city from the supporting terraces* to the surrounding area, while Joab rebuilt
the rest of Jerusalem. 9 And David became more and more powerful, because the LORD of 11:9
Heaven's Armies was with him. 2 Sam 3:1

11:2 Or *For some time.* 11:8 Hebrew *the millo.* The meaning of the Hebrew is uncertain.

11:1 After Saul's death, seven and a half years passed before the entire kingdom was united under David around 1003 BC. Initially David was anointed king over Judah and ruled from Hebron (2 Samuel 2:1-4). Ishbosheth (Saul's son) reigned over the northern tribes of Israel for two years and waged an unsuccessful civil war against the house of David (2 Samuel 2:8–3:1). After Ishbosheth's death (2 Samuel 4:1-7), the representatives of Israel finally sought unity. The chronicler reports the coronation of David in Chapters 11–12 to show that all 12 tribes recognized David's kingship.

11:2 There is no other record of this promise, but as suggested in the next verse, it probably refers to David's private anointing by Samuel in 1 Samuel 16:13, which was made public at a later time.

11:3 Just as they did for Saul (1 Samuel 10:24-25), the people confirmed their loyalty to David by establishing a covenant with him. The responsibilities of the king according to God's Word were demanding (see Deuteronomy 17:14-20), and the chronicler is holding up David as the model king.

▸WORSHIP

11:3 The chain of command. Who is in charge? In many situations this is unclear; more often, it is simply too inconvenient for us to follow the chain of command. In either case, we are unable to get things done in an orderly way. Our general mistrust of authority makes it hard for us to submit to those to whom we owe respect, especially God. David did it right: He met with the elders of Israel, thus avoiding as much confusion as possible as to who was in charge of Israel. On your job, in your church, and in your home, submit to those in authority, for God is pleased when we learn to obey those who are in charge (Ephesians 5:21-24; Titus 3:1; Hebrews 12:9). (***See Worship****> NT> Our Role> Attitude> Submissive before authority,* TopicGuide page A31.)

11:4 Jerusalem was the perfect political and military choice for David's new capital from which to reign over all of Israel. Located in the center of Palestine on the Benjamin/Judah tribal boundary, it sat on a ridge with high walls, making it especially difficult to overtake. It favored neither the northern nor the southern tribes, which reduced the already-existing tension between the two areas.

11:5 The Jebusites were a Canaanite tribe that the Benjamites failed to drive out after the conquest—another selective comment by the chronicler favoring David's tribe of Judah over Saul's tribe of Benjamin (compare Judges 1:21 with Joshua 15:63).

11:5 The history of the word *Zion* is unclear. Its root likely means "dry," in reference to the lack of rain in the area. Geographically, it refers to the entire raised area upon which Jerusalem sat, but it also referred to the 13-acre City of David. The Temple was eventually built adjacent to the City of David (2 Chronicles 5:2). The Old Testament also uses the term *Zion* symbolically to refer to the dwelling place of God in the midst of His people—His holy hill (Psalm 99:9). In the New Testament, it is a symbol of heaven (Hebrews 12:18-24), where God forever will be with all his people (Revelation 14:1-5).

11:6 David's men captured Zion by climbing up the city's water tunnel (2 Samuel 5:8).

11:6 Jerusalem means "city of peace" and was important to the chronicler and his readers. The city was in ruins during the exile, and now God's people needed to rebuild it as their royal capital. David's aggressive construction provided the perfect example for those who read this book after the exile.

11:9 The Hebrew words translated "Lord Almighty" portray God as the leader of the armies of heaven, literally the "Lord of Hosts." This image of God was important to God's people during this time because they faced wild animals, internal divisions, and hostilities from neighboring people groups that had been brought into Palestine by Babylon. They needed the Lord to fight for them like He did for David.

DAVID'S MIGHTIEST WARRIORS

11:10 10These are the leaders of David's mighty warriors. Together with all Israel, they decided
2 Sam 23:8-39 1 Chr 11:3 to make David their king, just as the LORD had promised concerning Israel.
11:11 11Here is the record of David's mightiest warriors: The first was Jashobeam the Hac-
2 Sam 23:8 monite, who was leader of the Three—the mightiest warriors among David's men.* He
11:12 once used his spear to kill 300 enemy warriors in a single battle.
1 Chr 27:4 12Next in rank among the Three was Eleazar son of Dodai,* a descendant of Ahoah.
11:13 13He was with David in the battle against the Philistines at Pas-dammim. The battle took
2 Sam 23:11-12 place in a field full of barley, and the Israelite army fled. 14But Eleazar and David* held
their ground in the middle of the field and beat back the Philistines. So the LORD saved
them by giving them a great victory.
11:15 15Once when David was at the rock near the cave of Adullam, the Philistine army was
1 Chr 14:9 camped in the valley of Rephaim. The Three (who were among the Thirty—an elite group
11:16 1 Sam 10:5 among David's fighting men) went down to meet him there. 16David was staying in the
stronghold at the time, and a Philistine detachment had occupied the town of Bethlehem.
17David remarked longingly to his men, "Oh, how I would love some of that good water
from the well by the gate in Bethlehem." 18So the Three broke through the Philistine lines,
drew some water from the well by the gate in Bethlehem, and brought it back to David.
But David refused to drink it. Instead, he poured it out as an offering to the LORD. 19"God
forbid that I should drink this!" he exclaimed. "This water is as precious as the blood of
these men* who risked their lives to bring it to me." So David did not drink it. These are ex-
amples of the exploits of the Three.

DAVID'S THIRTY MIGHTY MEN

20Abishai, the brother of Joab, was the leader of the Thirty.* He once used his spear to kill
300 enemy warriors in a single battle. It was by such feats that he became as famous as
the Three. 21Abishai was the most famous of the Thirty and was their commander, though
he was not one of the Three.
11:22 22There was also Benaiah son of Jehoiada, a valiant warrior from Kabzeel. He did many
2 Sam 8:18 heroic deeds, which included killing two champions* of Moab. Another time, on a snowy
11:23 1 Sam 17:7 day, he chased a lion down into a pit and killed it. 23Once, armed only with a club, he

11:11 As in some Greek manuscripts (see also 2 Sam 23:8); Hebrew reads *leader of the Thirty,* or *leader of the captains.* 11:12 As in parallel text at 2 Sam 23:9 (see also 1 Chr 27:4); Hebrew reads *Dodo,* a variant spelling of Dodai. 11:14 Hebrew *they.* 11:19 Hebrew *Shall I drink the lifeblood of these men?* 11:20 As in Syriac version; Hebrew reads *the Three;* also in 11:21. 11:22 Or *two sons of Ariel.*

11:10 The chronicler continues his positive portrayal of David by listing the warriors present at David's coronation, both his mighty men (1 Chronicles 11:10–12:22) and regular troops (1 Chronicles 12:23-37). They, "together with all Israel," demonstrated David's breadth of support (repeated in 1 Chronicles 12:38).

11:10-47 Totaling 400–600 warriors, David's mighty men are an outgrowth of the small band of family, clansmen, and others who served with him during his flight from Saul (1 Samuel 22:1-2; 27:2). These warriors continued to perform courageous deeds in battle after David's coronation. What follows are vignettes of those exploits, presented in three classes. "The Three" highest were Jashobeam, Eleazer, and Shammah. The second class of three was Abishai, Benaiah, and Amasai (1 Chronicles 12:18), who commanded the third class, called "The Thirty."

11:12-14 Eleazer, the second of "the Three," is famous for his bravery in a battle against the Philistines when David was a general under Saul. But when we compare this passage with 2 Samuel 23:9-12, we see the third of "the Three," Shammah being credited for this same battle. Apparently, Shammah secured the lentil field after Eleazer gave up from exhaustion (see 2 Samuel 23:11-12). Pas-dammim is in the western foothills of Judah between Socoh and Azekah.

11:15 These exploits were performed by those in the second-class of 30 mighty men mentioned in 11:20-25.

11:15-16 During the first defensive campaign against the Philistines after David became king over all Israel, the Philistines camped in the valley of Rephaim, a broad valley southwest of Jerusalem named after a race of giants that lived in Abraham's time (Gen 15:20). David had established a stronghold in caves near Adullam (1 Chronicles 14:8-9; 2 Samuel 5:17-18), where he had fled from Saul (1 Samuel 22:1) and where he wrote Psalms 57 and 142.

11:17-19 In this covert operation, the three mighty men traveled approximately 14 miles, infiltrated an enemy garrison, and took water from a well in Bethlehem (David's birthplace).

killed an Egyptian warrior who was 7½ feet* tall and whose spear was as thick as a
weaver's beam. Benaiah wrenched the spear from the Egyptian's hand and killed him with
it. 24 Deeds like these made Benaiah as famous as the three mightiest warriors. 25 He was
more honored than the other members of the Thirty, though he was not one of the Three.
And David made him captain of his bodyguard.

26 David's mighty warriors also included:

Asahel, Joab's brother;
Elhanan son of Dodo from Bethlehem;
27 Shammah from Harod;*
Helez from Pelon;
28 Ira son of Ikkesh from Tekoa;
Abiezer from Anathoth;
29 Sibbecai from Hushah;
Zalmon* from Ahoah;
30 Maharai from Netophah;
Heled son of Baanah from Netophah;
31 Ithai son of Ribai from Gibeah (in the land of Benjamin);
Benaiah from Pirathon;
32 Hurai from near Nahale-gaash*;
Abi-albon* from Arabah;
33 Azmaveth from Bahurim*;
Eliahba from Shaalbon;
34 the sons of Jashen* from Gizon;
Jonathan son of Shagee from Harar;
35 Ahiam son of Sharar* from Harar;
Eliphal son of Ur;
36 Hepher from Mekerah;
Ahijah from Pelon;
37 Hezro from Carmel;
Paarai* son of Ezbai;
38 Joel, the brother of Nathan;
Mibhar son of Hagri;
39 Zelek from Ammon;
Naharai from Beeroth, Joab's armor bearer;
40 Ira from Jattir;
Gareb from Jattir;
41 Uriah the Hittite;
Zabad son of Ahlai;
42 Adina son of Shiza, the Reubenite leader who had thirty men with him;
43 Hanan son of Maacah;
Joshaphat from Mithna;

11:23 Hebrew *5 cubits* [2.3 meters]. 11:27 As in parallel text at 2 Sam 23:25; Hebrew reads *Shammoth from Haror.* 11:29 As in parallel text at 2 Sam 23:28; Hebrew reads *Ilai.* 11:32a Or *from the ravines of Gaash.* 11:32b As in parallel text at 2 Sam 23:31; Hebrew reads *Abiel.* 11:33 As in parallel text at 2 Sam 23:31; Hebrew reads *Baharum.* 11:34 As in parallel text at 2 Sam 23:32; Hebrew reads *sons of Hashem.* 11:35 As in parallel text at 2 Sam 23:33; Hebrew reads *son of Sacar.* 11:37 As in parallel text at 2 Sam 23:35; Hebrew reads *Naarai.*

11:25 Benaiah was a strong supporter of David. He commanded David's elite troops (2 Samuel 8:18; 1 Chronicles 27:6) and was Temple commander during the third month of the year (27:5). He remained loyal to David through Absalom's rebellion (2 Samuel 15:18) and Adonijah's rebellion (1 Kings 1:8), and he was eventually appointed commander of Israel's standing army under Solomon (1 Kings 2:35).

11:41-47 The list of mighty men from Judah and Benjamin in 11:26-41 comes directly from 2 Samuel 23:24-29. The chronicler adds to this list men from unknown parts and areas east of the Jordan to show the extent of David's rule and the widespread allegiance that he inspired.

44 Uzzia from Ashtaroth;
Shama and Jeiel, the sons of Hotham, from Aroer;
45 Jediael son of Shimri;
Joha, his brother, from Tiz;
46 Eliel from Mahavah;
Jeribai and Joshaviah, the sons of Elnaam;
Ithmah from Moab;
47 Eliel and Obed;
Jaasiel from Zobah.*

WARRIORS JOIN DAVID'S ARMY

12:1 1 Sam 27:2-6 **12** The following men joined David at Ziklag while he was hiding from Saul son of
Kish. They were among the warriors who fought beside David in battle. 2All of them
12:2 Judg 3:15; 20:16 were expert archers, and they could shoot arrows or sling stones with their left hand as well
as their right. They were all relatives of Saul from the tribe of Benjamin. 3Their leader was
Ahiezer son of Shemaah from Gibeah; his brother Joash was second-in-command. These
were the other warriors:

Jeziel and Pelet, sons of Azmaveth;
Beracah;
Jehu from Anathoth;
4 Ishmaiah from Gibeon, a famous warrior and leader among the Thirty;
*Jeremiah, Jahaziel, Johanan, and Jozabad from Gederah;
5 Eluzai, Jerimoth, Bealiah, Shemariah, and Shephatiah from Haruph;
6 Elkanah, Isshiah, Azarel, Joezer, and Jashobeam, who were Korahites;
7 Joelah and Zebadiah, sons of Jeroham from Gedor.

12:8 2 Sam 2:18 8Some brave and experienced warriors from the tribe of Gad also defected to David
while he was at the stronghold in the wilderness. They were expert with both shield and
spear, as fierce as lions and as swift as deer on the mountains.

9 Ezer was their leader.
Obadiah was second.
Eliab was third.
10 Mishmannah was fourth.
Jeremiah was fifth.
11 Attai was sixth.
Eliel was seventh.
12 Johanan was eighth.
Elzabad was ninth.
13 Jeremiah was tenth.
Macbannai was eleventh.

11:47 Or *the Mezobaite.* 12:4 Verses 12:4b-40 are numbered 12:5-41 in Hebrew text.

12:1-7 Some Benjamite warriors had defected to David long ago while he dwelt in the Canaanite city of Ziklag (1 Samuel 27:2-6), which King Achish of Gath had given to him. This list of supporters is not found in 2 Samuel; the chronicler is adding this data to show his audience that even former supporters of Saul joined themselves to David, the true king.

12:2 The chronicler notes the curiously common trait of ambidexterity among Benjamites (Judges 3:15; 20:16), which was extremely helpful in battle.

12:8-15 Some experienced warriors from the tribe of Gad (east of the Jordan) joined David earlier when he fled from Saul in the wilderness of Judah, and they are compared to lions and deer in their abilities as warriors (see also 2 Samuel 1:23).

14These warriors from Gad were army commanders. The weakest among them could 12:14
take on a hundred regular troops, and the strongest could take on a thousand! 15These Deut 32:30
were the men who crossed the Jordan River during its seasonal flooding at the beginning of 12:15
the year and drove out all the people living in the lowlands on both the east and west banks. Josh 3:15; 4:18
16Others from Benjamin and Judah came to David at the stronghold. 17David went out
to meet them and said, "If you have come in peace to help me, we are friends. But if you
have come to betray me to my enemies when I am innocent, then may the God of our an-
cestors see it and punish you."
18Then the Spirit came upon Amasai, the leader of the Thirty, and he said, 12:18 Judg 3:10; 6:34

"We are yours, David! 1 Chr 2:17
We are on your side, son of Jesse.
Peace and prosperity be with you,
and success to all who help you,
for your God is the One who helps you."

So David let them join him, and he made them officers over his troops.
19Some men from Manasseh defected from the Israelite army and joined David when he 12:19
set out with the Philistines to fight against Saul. But as it turned out, the Philistine rulers re- 1 Sam 29:2-9
fused to let David and his men go with them. After much discussion, they sent them back, for
they said, "It will cost us our heads if David switches loyalties to Saul and turns against us."
20Here is a list of the men from Manasseh who defected to David as he was returning to
Ziklag: Adnah, Jozabad, Jediael, Michael, Jozabad, Elihu, and Zillethai. Each commanded
1,000 troops from the tribe of Manasseh. 21They helped David chase down bands of raid- 12:21
ers, for they were all brave and able warriors who became commanders in his army. 22Day 1 Sam 30:1
after day more men joined David until he had a great army, like the army of God. 12:22 Josh 5:13-15
23These are the numbers of armed warriors who joined David at Hebron. They were all 12:23
eager to see David become king instead of Saul, just as the Lord had promised. 2 Sam 2:3-4

24From the tribe of Judah, there were 6,800 warriors armed with shields and spears. 1 Chr 10:14; 11:10
25From the tribe of Simeon, there were 7,100 brave warriors.
26From the tribe of Levi, there were 4,600 warriors. 27This included Jehoiada, leader of
the family of Aaron, who had 3,700 under his command. 28This also included Zadok, 12:28
a brave young warrior, with 22 members of his family who were all officers. 1 Chr 6:8

▸ADOPTION
12:14 Overstating the truth. God uses all the tools of language to communicate His truths. The writer of this section of Chronicles uses hyperbole, or purposeful overstatement, to communicate the greatness of David's army. His heroes can kill a hundred or thousand men by themselves (1 Chronicles 12:14). David's army is numbered like the angelic forces of God (1 Chronicles 12:22). Your skillful use of humor, irony, overstatement, understatement, and other tools of speech can be used to honor God and help you convince more people of His truth. (***See Adoption**> With Christ> Supernatural> Speak godly words,* TopicGuide page A37.)

12:16-18 These verses give evidence of David's increasing human support and the divine aid of God, two key ways the writer demonstrates God's favor on David.

12:18 In Chronicles, the Spirit came upon people primarily to enable them to speak authorized words from the Lord (1 Chronicles 12:18; 28:12; 2 Chronicles 15:1; 18:22; 20:14; 24:20).

12:19 The historical events behind this passage are recorded in 1 Samuel 29. Like the prophets before him, the chronicler warns his audience against alliances with the surrounding nations (2 Chronicles 16:1-9; 28:16-21), and for this reason he is careful to show that David and his troops did not participate in the war against Israel.

12:20 The chronicler sometimes uses the word that is translated here as "thousand," but it is probably best understood as referring to a division or a unit, rather than the number 1,000 (1 Chronicles 5:21; 12:23-27; 13:1; 27:1-15; see also Numbers 31:48). However the word should be translated, it is plain that these warriors were brave and able captains of many (12:21).

12:21 The bands of raiders mentioned here were the Amalekites, who lived south of Ziklag. David destroyed the Amalekites in 1 Samuel 30.

12:22 The chronicler uses hyperbole again (1 Chronicles 12:14) to show David's army was unimaginably large.

12:23-37 The warriors listed here were the regular troops at David's coronation. The number of troops, their readiness for battle, and full representation from all the tribes give strong evidence of the widespread support for David's kingship.

12:24 Or "6 divisions with 800 warriors armed for battle," see also 12:25 and following through the end of the chapter.

12:29 2 Sam 2:8-9 [29]From the tribe of Benjamin, Saul's relatives, there were 3,000 warriors. Most of the
men from Benjamin had remained loyal to Saul until this time.
[30]From the tribe of Ephraim, there were 20,800 brave warriors, each highly respected
in his own clan.
[31]From the half-tribe of Manasseh west of the Jordan, 18,000 men were designated by
name to help David become king.
12:32 Esth 1:13 Ps 12:2 [32]From the tribe of Issachar, there were 200 leaders of the tribe with their relatives. All these
men understood the signs of the times and knew the best course for Israel to take.
[33]From the tribe of Zebulun, there were 50,000 skilled warriors. They were fully armed
and prepared for battle and completely loyal to David.
[34]From the tribe of Naphtali, there were 1,000 officers and 37,000 warriors armed with
shields and spears.
[35]From the tribe of Dan, there were 28,600 warriors, all prepared for battle.
[36]From the tribe of Asher, there were 40,000 trained warriors, all prepared for battle.
[37]From the east side of the Jordan River—where the tribes of Reuben and Gad and the half-
tribe of Manasseh lived—there were 120,000 troops armed with every kind of weapon.

12:38 2 Sam 5:1-3 1 Chr 12:33 [38]All these men came in battle array to Hebron with the single purpose of making David
the king over all Israel. In fact, everyone in Israel agreed that David should be their king.
[39]They feasted and drank with David for three days, for preparations had been made by
12:40 1 Sam 25:18 their relatives for their arrival. [40]And people from as far away as Issachar, Zebulun, and
Naphtali brought food on donkeys, camels, mules, and oxen. Vast supplies of flour, fig
cakes, clusters of raisins, wine, olive oil, cattle, sheep, and goats were brought to the cele-
bration. There was great joy throughout the land of Israel.

DAVID ATTEMPTS TO MOVE THE ARK

13:1-4 //2 Sam 6:1-11 **13** David consulted with all his officials, including the generals and captains of his
army.* [2]Then he addressed the entire assembly of Israel as follows: "If you approve
and if it is the will of the LORD our God, let us send messages to all the Israelites throughout
the land, including the priests and Levites in their towns and pasturelands. Let us invite them

13:1 Hebrew *the commanders of thousands and of hundreds.*

12:29 Or "3 divisions." The relatively small number of Benjamite warriors as compared to the rest of the tribes indicates the lack of support from the family of Saul and his son, Ishbosheth.

12:32 These men knew that joining David was the best course for Israel. The chronicler wanted his people to understand the temper of the times, too.

12:34 Or "some division commanders and 37 divisions."

12:38 See note on 11:10.

12:39-41 A king's coronation was a time of national celebration. In addition to the religious feasts appointed by the Lord through Moses in Leviticus 23, community feasts and celebrations also occurred for weddings, birthdays, farewells, dedications, and other special occasions. An important expression of the community's identity, these celebrations commemorated events, encouraged cohesiveness, and symbolized religious and political ideals. Similar joyful celebrations were held during Solomon's coronation (1 Kings 1:40) and the dedication of the new Temple (Nehemiah 12:43). One day God's people will find everlasting joy at the final restoration when King Jesus will gather all the redeemed together for the final feast (Isaiah 51:11).

13:1-4 The Ark of the Covenant had been at Abinadab's house in Kiriath-jearim for about 20 years (1 Samuel 7:1-2). The Philistines suffered plagues and calamity by capturing it and sent it back to Israel by way of Beth-shemesh (1 Samuel 5–6). Why it was not immediately transported to the Tabernacle at Shiloh may be explained by some scholars' suggestion that the Philistines controlled Shiloh at that time.

▶ BIBLE

13:1 Bad advice. Have you ever gone to someone looking for counsel and received poor advice? David wanted to move the Ark of the Covenant (Exodus 25:16-22) into Jerusalem, so he asked everyone (1 Chronicles 13:1-4) for feedback on how to do this. But someone neglected to tell David to transport the Ark in the approved fashion—with Levites carrying it using special poles through the carrying rings (Exodus 35:5). David did the right thing by seeking counsel, but evidently no one told him about the special rules for transporting it, causing the frightening death of Uzzah (1 Chronicles 13:7-10). Even though you may get advice that sounds good, still consult God's Word as the final answer to your deepest questions. (***See Bible****> Power> Wisdom> Instruction through God's Word,* TopicGuide page A11.)

13:2, 4 Though he was king, David consulted with the people to garner their support for this task. Jehoshephat (2 Chronicles 20:17) and Hezekiah (2 Chronicles 30:2, 4, 12, 23) would also appeal to popular consent. By recording this action, the chronicler aims to teach the leaders of God how to administrate wisely.

to come and join us. 3It is time to bring back the Ark of our God, for we neglected it during
the reign of Saul."
4The whole assembly agreed to this, for the people could see it was the right thing to do.
5So David summoned all Israel, from the Shihor Brook of Egypt in the south all the way to
the town of Lebo-hamath in the north, to join in bringing the Ark of God from Kiriath-
jearim. 6Then David and all Israel went to Baalah of Judah (also called Kiriath-jearim) to
bring back the Ark of God, which bears the name* of the LORD who is enthroned between
the cherubim. 7They placed the Ark of God on a new cart and brought it from Abinadab's
house. Uzzah and Ahio were guiding the cart. 8David and all Israel were celebrating before
God with all their might, singing songs and playing all kinds of musical instruments—lyres,
harps, tambourines, cymbals, and trumpets.
9But when they arrived at the threshing floor of Nacon,* the oxen stumbled, and Uzzah
reached out his hand to steady the Ark. 10Then the LORD's anger was aroused against Uz-
zah, and He struck him dead because he had laid his hand on the Ark. So Uzzah died there
in the presence of God.
11David was angry because the LORD's anger had burst out against Uzzah. He named
that place Perez-uzzah (which means "to burst out against Uzzah"), as it is still called today.
12David was now afraid of God, and he asked, "How can I ever bring the Ark of God back
into my care?" 13So David did not move the Ark into the City of David. Instead, he took it to
the house of Obed-edom of Gath. 14The Ark of God remained there in Obed-edom's
house for three months, and the LORD blessed the household of Obed-edom and every-
thing he owned.

DAVID'S PALACE AND FAMILY

14 Then King Hiram of Tyre sent messengers to David, along with cedar timber, and
stonemasons and carpenters to build him a palace. 2And David realized that the

13:3 1 Sam 7:1-2
13:5 1 Sam 6:21; 7:1; 2 Sam 6:1; 1 Kgs 8:65; 1 Chr 15:3
13:6 Josh 15:9; 2 Kgs 19:15
13:7 1 Sam 7:1
13:8 1 Chr 15:13-16
13:9 2 Sam 6:6
13:10 Lev 10:2; 1 Chr 15:13, 15
13:13 2 Chr 25:24-25
13:14 1 Chr 26:4-5
14:1-7 //2 Sam 5:11-16; //1 Chr 3:5-8
14:1 2 Sam 5:11

13:6 Or *the Ark of God, where the Name is proclaimed—the name.* 13:9 As in parallel text at 2 Sam 6:6; Hebrew reads *Kidon.*

13:6 Kiriath-jearim (Baalah) was a village about 10 miles northwest of Jerusalem. Named Abu Ghosh today, this village was mistakenly identified as Emmaus during the Crusades.

13:7 Uzzah and Ahio were Abinadab's sons.

13:9-10 Uzzah died because touching the Ark was a violation of the instructions in Numbers 4:15, for it was holy and represented the presence of the Lord. A similar fate befell Nadab and Abihu when they presented "strange fire" in the wilderness Tabernacle (Leviticus 10:1-3). Despite Uzzah's good intention to keep the Ark from falling, this act so violated its holiness that God killed him. David later explains (1 Chronicles 15:13) the Ark should have been carried by Levites with poles as prescribed in the Law (Exodus 25:12-15).

▸ WORSHIP
13:12 Do you fear God? The Bible speaks very highly of fearing God. Fear can mean respect or honor, as we would give a king. Fear can mean awe, as we would feel viewing a powerful storm or looking out an airplane window for the first time. But it also can mean fright and dread, and this passage, among others (Acts 5:11; Isaiah 8:13), teaches that God deserves that sort of fear, too. Love God with all your heart, but fear Him as well (Ecclesiastes 12:13). (***See Worship****> OT> Reverence> God requires us to fear Him,* TopicGuide page A28.)

13:13-14 Obed-edom lived in the town of Gath-rimmon in the territory of Dan, close to where Uzzah died. This verse shows that God was not against Israel. On the contrary, a reverent attitude and proper procedure concerning the holy God results in blessing. The blessing spoken of here is one of many descendants (Psalm 127:3-5). The Bible records 72 of Obed-edom's descendants.

14:1-17 The first attempt to move the Ark ended with David in fear (13:12) because the Lord acted against Israel (13:11). In this chapter, the chronicler uses events from 2 Samuel 5:11-25 to show that the Lord had acted against David's enemies (14:11), and all the nations feared David (14:17). Because David realized that God had made his kingdom great (14:2), he had the courage to finish the task of bringing the Ark to Jerusalem. The chronicler wanted the leaders of God's people to have that same courage in their day, so he took an event that 2 Samuel places before the moving of the Ark and places it afterward, almost the way modern writers use a "flashback," to emphasize his point.

14:1-2 Hiram was king of the coastal Phoenician city of Tyre, northwest of Israel. Hiram remained on friendly terms with David and Solomon throughout his 34-year reign, providing a tribute of artisans and materials for David's palace (2 Samuel 5:11), trading food for artisans and materials for the Temple (2 Chronicles 2:3-16), paying money for 20 cities in Galilee (1 Kings 9:10-14), and providing sailors and maritime assistance to Solomon's mini-fleet in Ezion-geber (1 Kings 10:22; 2 Chronicles 8:17-18). Phoenician historians even record that Hiram gave his daughter to Solomon in marriage. These political honors are an indication of how great Israel had grown under David's reign.

14:2-3 David's kingship became the ideal pattern for all future kings of Israel. David's kingship points to Jesus (Hebrews 2:9-10), who rules and reigns for His glory and our good.

LORD had confirmed him as king over Israel and had greatly blessed his kingdom for the
sake of His people Israel.
3 Then David married more wives in Jerusalem, and they had more sons and daughters.
14:4 4 These are the names of David's sons who were born in Jerusalem: Shammua, Shobab,
1 Chr 3:5-9 Nathan, Solomon, 5 Ibhar, Elishua, Elpelet, 6 Nogah, Nepheg, Japhia, 7 Elishama, Eliada,*
and Eliphelet.

DAVID CONQUERS THE PHILISTINES

14:8-17 8 When the Philistines heard that David had been anointed king over all Israel, they mobi-
//2 Sam 5:17-25 lized all their forces to capture him. But David was told they were coming, so he marched
14:9 out to meet them. 9 The Philistines arrived and made a raid in the valley of Rephaim. 10 So
1 Chr 11:15; 14:13 David asked God, "Should I go out to fight the Philistines? Will You hand them over to me?"
The LORD replied, "Yes, go ahead. I will hand them over to you."
11 So David and his troops went up to Baal-perazim and defeated the Philistines there.
"God did it!" David exclaimed. "He used me to burst through my enemies like a raging
flood!" So they named that place Baal-perazim (which means "the Lord who bursts through").
12 The Philistines had abandoned their gods there, so David gave orders to burn them.
14:13 13 But after a while the Philistines returned and raided the valley again. 14 And once again
1 Chr 14:9 David asked God what to do. "Do not attack them straight on," God replied. "Instead, circle
around behind and attack them near the poplar* trees. 15 When you hear a sound like
marching feet in the tops of the poplar trees, go out and attack! That will be the signal that
God is moving ahead of you to strike down the Philistine army." 16 So David did what God
commanded, and they struck down the Philistine army all the way from Gibeon to Gezer.
14:17 17 So David's fame spread everywhere, and the LORD caused all the nations to fear David.
Exod 15:14-16
Deut 2:25

14:7 Hebrew *Beeliada*, a variant spelling of Eliada; compare 3:8 and parallel text at 2 Sam 5:16. 14:14 Or *aspen*, or *balsam*; also in 14:15. The exact identification of this tree is uncertain.

14:3 Polygamy is not endorsed in the Bible (See Mark 10:2-9, where Jesus comments on Genesis 2:24), but David succumbed to the practices of his day. There was a specific prohibition for the king against having many wives (Deuteronomy 17:17). Consequently, the writer of Samuel presents this parallel passage (2 Samuel 5:13) in a tone that emphasizes David's faithlessness. Here however, the chronicler's emphasis was not on David's shame but that his royal family was growing, a sign of favor from God.

14:8 This incident actually occurred much earlier than the present context—right after David's coronation over the northern tribes (Israel) at Hebron (11:1-3; 12:38-40).

14:8-16 David handled these two battles in the ideal way, according to the chronicler. He went out to meet them instead of fleeing (14:8); he inquired of God in both battles (14:10, 14); he obeyed the word of the Lord (14:11, 16); and he relied on and acknowledged that it was God's divine power that attained the victory (14:11, 15).

14:9 The Valley of Rephaim is a broad valley southwest of Jerusalem named after a race of giants that lived during Abraham's time (Gen 15:20).

14:11 The word "Baal" here is used simply as "master" or "lord." It was a generic term for Yahweh used before Israel fell into the problem of Baal worship under Ahab (1 Kings 19:29-33).

14:11 Various forms of the Hebrew word translated "burst" or "outbreak" are used several times here (1 Chronicles 13:2, 10, 11; 15:13). The chronicler is using this play on words to draw attention to the theme of appropriate fear of God and His people.

14:14 The exact identification of these trees is uncertain. Some have translated this as "mulberry trees," but this is improbable because, although plentiful today, they had not yet been introduced into Palestine during this time. Arabic writers maintain the trees mentioned here are similar to balsam trees that grow near Mecca, but they are not found in Palestine either. Most likely these are poplar trees, which can grow tall and exude a milky-white gum.

14:15 The sound like marching feet in the tops of the trees is caused by the wind. God's presence is often sensed as wind in the Bible (Genesis 1:2; Hosea 13:15; Ezekiel 37:9-10; John 3:8; Acts 2:1-4). When God showed Israel His favor, God went before them in battle with the armies of heaven (Joshua 6:1-21; Judges 7:1-25; 2 Kings 7:6-7; 2 Kings 19:35). God's presence was an essential and miraculous part of holy war. Today, holy war takes the form of the spreading the gospel of God's love, and He leads the way (2 Corinthians 10:3-5; Revelation 6:2; Matthew 24:12).

14:17 The chronicler added this verse to the parallel text in 2 Samuel 5:17-25 to encourage the people of his day to remain dependent on God. If they acted like David concerning the surrounding nations, every nation would fear them too.

▶ CHURCH

14:17 Restraining fear. Of what are you most afraid? God taught David to fear Him (1 Chronicles 13:12), then restrained the evil activity of the surrounding nations through a holy fear of God and His people (Psalm 36:1). Today, the world rightly fears the church, for the very gates of hell will not stop its progress (Matthew 16:18). Pray that the entire world will grow to wonder at, respect, and fear those God has raised up to lead His people (Psalm 61:5). (***See Church***> *Role> Church Government> Society> Government should honor the spiritual authority of the church,* TopicGuide page A49.)

PREPARING TO MOVE THE ARK

15 David now built several buildings for himself in the City of David. He also pre-
pared a place for the Ark of God and set up a special tent for it. [2]Then he com-
manded, "No one except the Levites may carry the Ark of God. The LORD has chosen them
to carry the Ark of the LORD and to serve Him forever."

[3]Then David summoned all Israel to Jerusalem to bring the Ark of the LORD to the place
he had prepared for it. [4]This is the number of the descendants of Aaron (the priests) and
the Levites who were called together:

[5]From the clan of Kohath, 120, with Uriel as their leader.
[6]From the clan of Merari, 220, with Asaiah as their leader.
[7]From the clan of Gershon,* 130, with Joel as their leader.
[8]From the descendants of Elizaphan, 200, with Shemaiah as their leader.
[9]From the descendants of Hebron, 80, with Eliel as their leader.
[10]From the descendants of Uzziel, 112, with Amminadab as their leader.

[11]Then David summoned the priests, Zadok and Abiathar, and these Levite leaders: Uri-
el, Asaiah, Joel, Shemaiah, Eliel, and Amminadab. [12]He said to them, "You are the leaders
of the Levite families. You must purify yourselves and all your fellow Levites, so you can
bring the Ark of the LORD, the God of Israel, to the place I have prepared for it. [13]Because
you Levites did not carry the Ark the first time, the anger of the LORD our God burst out
against us. We failed to ask God how to move it properly." [14]So the priests and the Levites
purified themselves in order to bring the Ark of the LORD, the God of Israel, to Jerusalem.
[15]Then the Levites carried the Ark of God on their shoulders with its carrying poles, just as
the LORD had instructed Moses.

15:1 1 Chr 16:1; 17:1-5
15:2 Num 4:15; Deut 10:8
15:3 2 Sam 6:12, 17; 1 Kgs 8:1; 1 Chr 13:5; 15:1, 12
15:4 1 Chr 6:16-30; 12:26
15:11 1 Sam 22:20-23; 1 Kgs 2:26, 35; 1 Chr 12:28
15:12 Exod 19:14-15; 2 Chr 35:6
15:13 1 Chr 13:7
15:15 Exod 25:14

15:7 Hebrew *Gershom,* a variant spelling of Gershon.

15:1 The Ark had been left at the house of Obed-Edom after the Lord struck Uzzah dead (13:13-14). It is not certain why David constructed a new Tabernacle in Jerusalem instead of having the old Tabernacle brought from Gibeon (See note on 16:39). But by reporting that David was preparing a place for the Ark, the chronicler is showing that David never abandoned his plan to bring the Ark to Jerusalem.

▸BIBLE
15:2 Learning from our mistakes. Repenting of your past sins does not mean forgetting them. David would never transport the Ark in a disrespectful way again (1 Chronicles 13:7-10). He issues clear instructions to the Levites, and they carried the Ark without error (1 Chronicles 12:13-15). How well have you learned from your past mistakes? Review your biggest mistakes and ask God to help you move past regret to maturity. (***See Bible****> Unity> OT Types> Ark of the Covenant,* TopicGuide page A11.)

15:3 The chronicler uses the term translated "all the Israelites" or "all Israel" several times (1 Chronicles 11:1; 12:38; 13:5; 14:8; 15:28; 18:14; 28:4; 29:23-26). He was deeply concerned to show that representatives from all the tribes participated in these major national events. This encouraged God's people in his day—including those still in exile—to have unity. The desire for a restored people of God is fully realized in Christ Jesus (Galatians 3:28).

15:5-10 The three divisions of the tribe of Levi (Kohathites, Merarites, and Gershonites) were included in David's worship organization. Including these sorts of details shows the chronicler's interest in restoring proper worship in the postexilic period.

15:11 Zadok and Abiathar were the two high priests during David's reign. It was unusual to have two high priests. Zadok was from the line of Eleazar, the eldest son of Aaron (6:1-8), and he officiated over the Tabernacle at Gibeon. Abiathar was from the line of Ithamar (Aaron's other son), and he represented the old tribal league over which Eli was high priest. After escaping from the massacre at Nob, Abiathar had been a trusted priest for David through his flight from Saul and rise to kingship (1 Samuel 22:19-23). Both priests were given high priestly duties in Jerusalem under David's new worship system (1 Samuel 15:24-29; 1 Chronicles 18:16; 24:1-19). However, Abiathar would later support Adonijah's attempt to take the throne during David's last days and would be deposed by Solomon (1 Kings 2:26-27). This fulfilled a prophetic curse on Eli's house (1 Samuel 2:27-36). Zadok's line continued to the Exile (1 Kings 2:35) and beyond. The chronicler takes care to emphasize the Zadokite line throughout Chronicles as the legitimate priesthood (23:13; 24:1-3; 29:22) in order to counter other claims to the high priestly office as God's people returned to Israel after the Exile (see note on 23:28-32).

15:12 Ritual purification is important for any involvement in the worship of the living God. The priests and Levites of Israel followed prescribed ritual washings and avoided ceremonial defilement in order to consecrate themselves to God's service. These included both one-time purification (Exodus 29:1-37) and continuous purification (Exodus 30:19-21). David called the Levites to perform these rituals before they attempted to transport the Ark to Jerusalem the second time.

15:15 This is a summary statement showing that the Levites did everything in accordance with the Law (Exodus 25:12-15). David and Israel modeled the kind of behavior the chronicler wanted the people of God to have. The chronicler jumps ahead chronologically to events he expands upon in 15:25-28.

15:16 16 David also ordered the Levite leaders to appoint a choir of Levites who were singers
1 Chr 13:8; 25:1 and musicians to sing joyful songs to the accompaniment of harps, lyres, and cymbals.
15:17 17 So the Levites appointed Heman son of Joel along with his fellow Levites: Asaph son of
1 Chr 25:1 Berekiah, and Ethan son of Kushaiah from the clan of Merari. 18 The following men were
chosen as their assistants: Zechariah, Jaaziel,* Shemiramoth, Jehiel, Unni, Eliab, Benaiah,
Maaseiah, Mattithiah, Eliphelehu, Mikneiah, and the gatekeepers—Obed-edom and Jeiel.
19 The musicians Heman, Asaph, and Ethan were chosen to sound the bronze cymbals.
20 Zechariah, Aziel, Shemiramoth, Jehiel, Unni, Eliab, Maaseiah, and Benaiah were chosen
to play the harps.* 21 Mattithiah, Eliphelehu, Mikneiah, Obed-edom, Jeiel, and Azaziah
were chosen to play the lyres.* 22 Kenaniah, the head Levite, was chosen as the choir
leader because of his skill.
15:24 23 Berekiah and Elkanah were chosen to guard* the Ark. 24 Shebaniah, Joshaphat, Ne-
1 Chr 16:6 thanel, Amasai, Zechariah, Benaiah, and Eliezer—all of whom were priests—were chosen
to blow the trumpets as they marched in front of the Ark of God. Obed-edom and Jehiah
were chosen to guard the Ark.

MOVING THE ARK TO JERUSALEM

15:25–16:3 25 Then David and the elders of Israel and the generals of the army* went to the house of
//2 Sam 6:12-19 Obed-edom to bring the Ark of the LORD's Covenant up to Jerusalem with a great celebra-
15:25 tion. 26 And because God was clearly helping the Levites as they carried the Ark of the
1 Chr 13:13 LORD's Covenant, they sacrificed seven bulls and seven rams.
15:26 27 David was dressed in a robe of fine linen, as were all the Levites who carried the Ark,
Num 23:1-4, 29 and also the singers, and Kenaniah the choir leader. David was also wearing a priestly

15:18 Or *Zechariah son of Jaaziel;* or *Zechariah, Ben, Jaaziel.* 15:20 Hebrew adds *according to Alamoth,* which is probably a musical term. The meaning of the Hebrew is uncertain. 15:21 Hebrew adds *according to the Sheminith,* which is probably a musical term. The meaning of the Hebrew is uncertain. 15:23 Hebrew *chosen as gatekeepers for;* also in 15:24. 15:25 Hebrew *the commanders of thousands.*

15:16-24 Before he recounts the actual moving of the Ark, the chronicler records the joyful music that accompanied the process. Music is a necessary and joyful display of worship, and the chronicler loves to highlight such worship in his retelling of Israel's history. In 2 Samuel 6:12, this event is a personal delight for David, but in Chronicles, it is a grand celebration for all Israel. The Levites rejoiced with singing, lyres, harps, cymbals, trumpets, and the horn (1 Chronicles 15:28), played by those who were skilled in singing and music. Note that the Hebrew word translated "to sing" in these verses also includes the playing of musical instruments. Most of these appointed Levites appear in other lists of official musicians in the Jerusalem Tabernacle (1 Chronicles 6:31-48; 16:5-6; 25:1-31).

15:19 The Hebrew word translated "bronze cymbals" is from a root word meaning "to tingle." Musicians played them by crashing pairs together.

15:20 The Hebrew word translated "lyre" here may be better translated as "harp," as this instrument belonged to the harp family (Amos 6:5).

15:23 The guards (literally "gatekeepers") and musicians were mentioned together because music was later performed at the gates of the Temple (1 Chronicles 23:5; Nehemiah 7:1; 12:45).

15:24 The trumpet (Numbers 10:2) was used for war, gatherings, and music, and would become an important part of the Temple service. Seven trumpets are mentioned here. The triumphal Arch in Rome built by Titus depicts trumpets captured from the Temple.

15:25 While 2 Samuel 6:12 mentions only David, the chronicler emphasizes the large, representative number of people (see note on 15:3) involved in transporting the Ark to Jerusalem: the king, the religious leaders (Levites and priests), the political leaders, and the military leaders. The Hebrew word translated "generals" here refers to the leader or "captain of a division" (see note on 12:20).

15:26 Here the chronicler further elaborates on the account in 2 Samuel 6:13 by mentioning the sacrifice of seven bulls and lambs. In Hebrew, the number seven commonly represents completeness or perfection (Genesis 2:2; Exodus 21:2; Leviticus 18:14, 19; 25:4, 10; Judges 16:13; Zechariah 4:10; Matthew 18:22; Revelation 1:4; 3:1; 4:5; 5:6; 12:3; 13:1; 17:3, 9-11). The Levites therefore offered the perfect amount of sacrifices to God along the stretch of road between Gath-rimmon and Jerusalem, signifying their devotion to God. The meat from the sacrifices was likely distributed to the public (see 1 Chronicles 16:1-3).

15:27 That David was dressed in a robe of fine linen like the Levites was appropriate for such a grand occasion. But the ephod of linen was normally reserved only for the priests (1 Samuel 2:28). During this ceremony David wore the garb of a priest because he was worthy to assume the role of a special "priest-king." This is evidenced in his performance of priestlike duties: playing music, psalm writing, and worship leading. David was a king who completely reformed worship for Israel, setting out the priestly patterns for generations to come (2 Chronicles 8:14). This dual office was only occupied by Melchizedek before him and Jesus after him (read Hebrews 7–11). Jesus Christ as the God-Man uniquely fills the triple office of "Prophet-Priest-King" and was the true Son of David (Matthew 22:41-45).

garment.* 28So all Israel brought up the Ark of the LORD's Covenant with shouts of joy, the
blowing of rams' horns and trumpets, the crashing of cymbals, and loud playing on harps
and lyres.
29But as the Ark of the LORD's Covenant entered the City of David, Michal, the daughter
of Saul, looked down from her window. When she saw King David skipping about and
laughing with joy, she was filled with contempt for him.

16 They brought the Ark of God and placed it inside the special tent David had pre- **16:1**
pared for it. And they presented burnt offerings and peace offerings to God. 1 Chr 15:1
2When he had finished his sacrifices, David blessed the people in the name of the LORD.
3Then he gave to every man and woman in all Israel a loaf of bread, a cake of dates,* and
a cake of raisins. **16:4**
4David appointed the following Levites to lead the people in worship before the Ark of 1 Chr 15:2
the LORD—to invoke His blessings, to give thanks, and to praise the LORD, the God of Israel.
5Asaph, the leader of this group, sounded the cymbals. Second to him was Zechariah, fol-
lowed by Jeiel, Shemiramoth, Jehiel, Mattithiah, Eliab, Benaiah, Obed-edom, and Jeiel.
They played the harps and lyres. 6The priests, Benaiah and Jahaziel, played the trumpets
regularly before the Ark of God's Covenant.

DAVID'S SONG OF PRAISE

7On that day David gave to Asaph and his fellow Levites this song of thanksgiving to the
LORD:

8 Give thanks to the LORD and proclaim His greatness. **16:8-22**
Let the whole world know what He has done. //Ps 105:1-15
9 Sing to Him; yes, sing His praises. **16:8** 1 Kgs 8:43
Tell everyone about His wonderful deeds. 2 Kgs 19:19

15:27 Hebrew *a linen ephod.* 16:3 Or *a portion of meat.* The meaning of the Hebrew is uncertain.

15:28 Psalm 24 may have been composed for this occasion. It is an advent hymn commemorating God (and His Ark) coming into His Temple.

▸ WORSHIP
15:29 Celebration. When God has done great things for you, don't forget to celebrate. The chronicler's treatment of this passage is different from that of the writer of Samuel (2 Samuel 6:16), who was justifying King David's actions. The chronicler is focused on the wondrous joy and celebration in Israel associated with moving the Ark of God, and he uses Michal's negative reaction to teach us what not to do in times of great national and religious commemoration. Do you easily give God great praise when He does something incredible? Remember that the phrase "Praise the LORD" in the psalms is a command. (***See Worship****> OT> Posture> Dancing> David danced before the Lord,* TopicGuide page A28.)

16:1 Burnt offerings were for devotion and were entirely consumed by the fire, whereas large portions of the peace offering (for fellowship) were returned to the people (Leviticus 7:11-36). The chronicler's focus on the large amount of peace offerings shows that this was a national religious celebration in Israel (1 Chronicles 16:3).

16:2 Blessing the people is another act of worship performed by David that was usually reserved for the high priest (see note on 15:27). Solomon did the same thing at the dedication of the Temple (2 Chronicles 6:3).

16:3 Gifts of food or feasts were given at the high points of David's reign (1 Chronicles 12:39; see also 29:22). The grand scale of the celebration is shown by the fact that every person received a gift of food. Raisin cakes were an expensive delicacy, and they may have also symbolized a blessing of fertility upon each house (Song of Solomon 2:5; Hosea 3:1, see text note). These gifts were to be eaten together with the peace offerings (see note on 16:1).

16:4-7 The account continues with more of David's appointments to the ministry of the Temple. These were permanent arrangements concerning the Levites' ongoing tasks. The chronicler reported them to reestablish ministerial patterns for Israel after the Exile.

16:4 The Hebrew phrase translated "to invoke His blessings" is better translated "to make remembrance," "memorialize," or "commemorate," which was done with music. Commemorating God's mighty works is the subject of the following hymn (1 Chronicles 16:8, 12, 15, 24).

16:5-6 These Levites were chosen from those who had taken part in the procession of the Ark (15:19-21).

16:7-36 This is a hymn of thanksgiving that David commissioned for the occasion, and apparently he composed much of it himself. Verses 8-22 parallel Psalm 105:1-15. Verses 23-33 parallel the whole of Psalm 96. Verses 34-36 parallel Psalm 106:1, 47-48 (refer to the corresponding notes for each Psalm). It is not clear whether David or the chronicler combined the three psalms into one, but taken in the form in which it appears here, the hymn has three stanzas: Remembrance (16:8-22), Praise (16:23-33), and Petition (16:34-36). The hymn is enclosed by the command to give thanks (16:8, 34).

10 Exult in His holy name;
rejoice, you who worship the LORD.

16:11 Ps 24:6
11 Search for the LORD and for His strength;
continually seek Him.

16:12 Pss 78:43; 103:2
12 Remember the wonders He has performed,
His miracles, and the rulings He has given,
13 you children of His servant Israel,
you descendants of Jacob, His chosen ones.

16:14 Ps 48:10
14 He is the LORD our God.
His justice is seen throughout the land.
15 Remember His covenant forever—
the commitment He made to a thousand generations.

16:16 Gen 17:2; 22:16-18; 26:3
16 This is the covenant He made with Abraham
and the oath He swore to Isaac.

16:17 Gen 35:9-12
17 He confirmed it to Jacob as a decree,
and to the people of Israel as a never-ending covenant:

16:18 Gen 13:14-17
18 "I will give you the land of Canaan
as your special possession."

16:19 Gen 34:30; Deut 7:7
19 He said this when you were few in number,
a tiny group of strangers in Canaan.
20 They wandered from nation to nation,
from one kingdom to another.

16:21 Gen 12:17; 20:3; Exod 7:15-18
21 Yet He did not let anyone oppress them.
He warned kings on their behalf:

16:22 Gen 20:7
22 "Do not touch My chosen people,
and do not hurt My prophets."

16:23-33 //Ps 96:1-13
23 Let the whole earth sing to the LORD!
Each day proclaim the good news that He saves.
24 Publish His glorious deeds among the nations.
Tell everyone about the amazing things He does.

16:25 Pss 89:7; 144:3-6
25 Great is the LORD! He is most worthy of praise!
He is to be feared above all gods.

16:26 Lev 19:4; Ps 102:25
26 The gods of other nations are mere idols,
but the LORD made the heavens!
27 Honor and majesty surround Him;
strength and joy fill His dwelling.

28 O nations of the world, recognize the LORD,
recognize that the LORD is glorious and strong.

16:29 Ps 29:2
29 Give to the LORD the glory He deserves!
Bring your offering and come into His presence.
Worship the LORD in all His holy splendor.
30 Let all the earth tremble before Him.
The world stands firm and cannot be shaken.

16:31 Pss 93:1; 96:10; Isa 44:23; 49:13
31 Let the heavens be glad, and the earth rejoice!
Tell all the nations, "The LORD reigns!"

16:13 The word "Israel" is substituted here for "Abraham" (see parallel passage in Psalm 105:6) in order to make the hymn more appropriate for the worship that is being described here.

16:19 The phrase "when they were few in number" from Psalm 105:12 is changed here to read, "when you were few in number." This change helps the chronicler's audience identify with an earlier Israel.

32 Let the sea and everything in it shout His praise!
Let the fields and their crops burst out with joy!
33 Let the trees of the forest rustle with praise,
for the LORD is coming to judge the earth.

34 Give thanks to the LORD, for He is good!
His faithful love endures forever.
35 Cry out, "Save us, O God of our salvation!
Gather and rescue us from among the nations,
so we can thank Your holy name
and rejoice and praise You."

36 Praise the LORD, the God of Israel,
who lives from everlasting to everlasting!

And all the people shouted "Amen!" and praised the LORD.

WORSHIP AT JERUSALEM AND GIBEON

37 David arranged for Asaph and his fellow Levites to serve regularly before the Ark of the
LORD's Covenant, doing whatever needed to be done each day. 38 This group included
Obed-edom (son of Jeduthun), Hosah, and sixty-eight other Levites as gatekeepers.
39 Meanwhile, David stationed Zadok the priest and his fellow priests at the Tabernacle
of the LORD at the place of worship in Gibeon, where they continued to minister before the
LORD. 40 They sacrificed the regular burnt offerings to the LORD each morning and evening
on the altar set aside for that purpose, obeying everything written in the Law of the LORD,
as He had commanded Israel. 41 David also appointed Heman, Jeduthun, and the others
chosen by name to give thanks to the LORD, for "His faithful love endures forever." 42 They
used their trumpets, cymbals, and other instruments to accompany their songs of praise to
God.* And the sons of Jeduthun were appointed as gatekeepers.

16:32 Ps 98:7
16:34-36 //Ps 106:1, 47-48
16:34 Ezra 3:11; Pss 106:1; 136:1; Jer 33:11
16:35 Ps 106:47-48
16:36 Deut 27:15; 1 Kgs 8:15, 56; Neh 8:6; Ps 72:18-19
16:37 2 Chr 8:14; Ezra 3:4
16:38 1 Chr 13:13-14; 26:10
16:39 1 Kgs 3:4
16:40 Exod 29:38-42; Num 28:1-8
16:41 1 Chr 6:33; 25:1-6; 2 Chr 5:13
16:42 2 Chr 7:6; 29:27

16:42 Or *to accompany the sacred music;* or *to accompany singing to God.*

▸ GOD
16:32 All creation worships God. The Bible tell us of three kinds of worship: liturgical worship, which all God's people perform as they worship together (Acts 2:43-47; Hebrews 10:25); living worship, which individuals do as they offer up their lives as a sacrifice to God (Romans 12:1); and lasting worship, which is forever offered up to God by all things as they rightly follow His precise commands (Psalm 19; 1 Chronicles 16:32-33). The entire universe praises God—let us join in the chorus! (***See God****> God's Attributes> All-Powerful> His creation reflects His power,* TopicGuide page A15.)

16:34 This phrase is a liturgical formula for thanksgiving used by Israel. It is found in many psalms and passages after the Exile (Jeremiah 33:11; Psalm 118; 136; Ezra 3:11) and was recited or sung responsively in worship. It is representative of Old Testament praise, which is focused on God's love.

16:35 The chronicler added "cry out" to the parallel passage in Psalm 106:47 to direct his audience to make this prayer their own. God's people today should also "cry out" for God to complete His plan to save people from every nation (Revelation 5:9-10).

16:36 The chronicler recorded the enthusiasm and joy of the people because he desired the people of God to express the same emotions in their worship.

16:38 Different than the Obed-edom in whose house the Ark stayed (1 Chronicles 13:14), this Obed-edom was a gatekeeper (1 Chronicles 15:21, 24; 26:4, 8, 15).

16:39 Although David had brought the Ark into Jerusalem, Israel's worship was not completely centralized yet. Musical and sacrificial ceremonies were performed in both Jerusalem (1 Chronicles 16:4-6; 18:16, 40) and Gibeon (1 Chronicles 16:39-42; 1 Kings 3:4-5). David was reforming Israel's worship in stages. After hundreds of years with no precedent, combining the political center with the religious center must have been a difficult and sensitive undertaking. Nevertheless, David was sure this was the place where God had chosen to live among His people (Psalm 76:2; 78:68; 132:13).

16:40 These words demonstrated that God approved of David's arrangements. The commands are spelled out in Exodus 29:38; Numbers 28.

16:41 The chronicler embraces the liturgical response "His faithful love endures forever" (1 Chronicles 16:34) in this report. This emphasizes God's generous, eternal affection for His chosen people. The audience could then take courage that, even after the judgment of the Exile, God's love for them would continue.

43 Then all the people returned to their homes, and David turned and went home to
bless his own family.

THE LORD'S COVENANT PROMISE TO DAVID

17:1-15 **17** When David was settled in his palace, he summoned Nathan the prophet. "Look,"
//2 Sam 7:1-17 David said, "I am living in a beautiful cedar palace,* but the Ark of the LORD's Cov-
enant is out there under a tent!"
2 Nathan replied to David, "Do whatever you have in mind, for God is with you."
3 But that same night God said to Nathan,

17:4 4 "Go and tell My servant David, 'This is what the LORD has declared: You are not the
1 Chr 28:2-3 one to build a house for Me to live in. 5 I have never lived in a house, from the day
17:5 I brought the Israelites out of Egypt until this very day. My home has always been
Exod 40:2-3 a tent, moving from one place to another in a Tabernacle. 6 Yet no matter where I
2 Sam 7:6 have gone with the Israelites, I have never once complained to Israel's leaders,* the
17:6 shepherds of My people. I have never asked them, "Why haven't you built Me
2 Sam 7:7 a beautiful cedar house?"'

7 "Now go and say to My servant David, 'This is what the LORD of Heaven's Armies
has declared: I took you from tending sheep in the pasture and selected you to be the
leader of My people Israel. 8 I have been with you wherever you have gone, and I have
destroyed all your enemies before your eyes. Now I will make your name as famous as
anyone who has ever lived on the earth! 9 And I will provide a homeland for My people
Israel, planting them in a secure place where they will never be disturbed. Evil nations

17:1 Hebrew *a house of cedar.* 17:6 As in Greek version (see also 2 Sam 7:7); Hebrew reads *judges.*

16:43 This sentence closes the whole Ark episode of chapters 13–16. The chronicler concludes his narrative on a note of joy by reporting that David returned to bless his family, and he leaves out the encounter with his discontented wife, Michal (2 Samuel 6:20-23).

17:1-15 This passage recounts David's desire to build a Temple for the Ark of the Covenant. Royal inscriptions of surrounding nations show that this was a common practice of powerful, successful kings. A temple built for God shows a king's acknowledgement of the source of his power and his reverence for his God. But David is called not to build the Temple, but to prepare for its building (see 2 Samuel 7).

17:1 By this time, David had built his palace (with cedar from King Hiram of Tyre), defended Israel against the Philistines, and moved the Ark to Jerusalem (2 Samuel 7:1-2).

17:2 Nathan was a prophet in Jerusalem at the time of David. As an official spokesperson for God, he functioned both as a prophet to the king (2 Chronicles 29:25) and a writing prophet (1 Chronicles 29:29; 2 Chronicles 9:29). He was the one who helped to open David's eyes to his sin of adultery with Bathsheba, and he predicted trouble in David's household (2 Samuel 12:1-14).

17:2-4 Nathan apparently didn't feel the need to inquire of the Lord about his first response because his common sense told him the Lord was "with" David (1 Chronicles 11:9; 17:8). The chronicler often described divine favor for Israel in this way (1 Chronicles 4:10; 9:20; 22:11; 22:18; 28:20; 2 Chronicles 1:1; 13:12; 15:2, 9; 17:3; 20:17; 25:7; 32:7; 35:21; 36:23). For God to be "with" His people meant that He fought for them. God's favor was the basis for David's success.

▸ WORSHIP

17:3 God speaks through us. It's very unlikely that God will speak through you in a literal way as He did with Nathan. But God's Word still applies to you and to those around you, and you can find a loving, truthful way to communicate how the Bible applies to your neighbor. If Nathan had the courage to speak to a king, you can speak to your spouse, your children, your workmate, or your neighbor about God's love and truth for them. But make sure you practice what you preach (Matthew 7:3-5). (***See Worship**> OT> Prophets> Prophets are God's spokesmen,* TopicGuide page A28.)

17:4-6 God had never asked for a permanent Temple, but He did not entirely reject David's proposal to build Him one. God wanted Solomon to carry out the actual building of the Temple (1 Chronicles 28:6) instead of David. At a later time, God apparently communicated the reason: David was a man of war and Solomon a man of peace, as his name implies (1 Chronicles 22:8; 28:3). Further, it was important that the establishment of the Temple was not just based on David's realization that the Lord needed a house (out of guilt for his own palace). The Temple must be built because of God's heavenly initiative.

17:7-8 This is a reference to the nations David had already subdued (1 Chronicles 14:8-17) and to others that were still to be conquered (1 Chronicles 18–20).

17:9-10 This promise does not apply to modern-day Israelis, but to all God's people—that is, those who have placed their faith in God and His true King, Jesus Christ. Both the place and the time of rest promised here are ultimately a heavenly destination (Hebrews 4; 11:8-18).

won't oppress them as they've done in the past, 10starting from the time I appointed
judges to rule My people Israel. And I will defeat all your enemies.

THE DAVIDIC DYNASTY

The Lord promised David that his kingdom would endure and his throne would be established forever (2 Samuel 7:16). As a partial fulfillment of this promise, David and his descendants ruled Judah for over 400 years. Jesus Christ was a direct descendant of David and was the ultimate fulfillment of this promise (Acts 2:22-36).

David	1009–971	1 Chronicles 10–29
Solomon	971–931	2 Chronicles 1–9
Rehoboam	930–913	2 Chronicles 10–12
Abijah	913–910	2 Chronicles 13
Asa	910–869	2 Chronicles 14–16
Jehoshaphat	872–848	2 Chronicles 17–20
Jehoram	848–841	2 Chronicles 21
Ahaziah	841–842	2 Chronicles 22:1–9
Athaliah	841–835	2 Chronicles 22:10–23:21
Joash	835–796	2 Chronicles 24
Amaziah	796–767	2 Chronicles 25
Uzziah	792–740	2 Chronicles 26
Jotham	750–735	2 Chronicles 27
Ahaz	735–715	2 Chronicles 27
Hezekiah	715–686	2 Chronicles 29–32
Manasseh	697–642	2 Chronicles 33:1-20
Amon	642–640	2 Chronicles 33:21-25
Josiah	640–609	2 Chronicles 34–35
Jehoahaz	609 (3 months)	2 Chronicles 36:1-4
Jehoiakim	609–620	2 Chronicles 36:5-8
Jehoiachin	597 (3 months)	2 Chronicles 36:9-10
Zedekiah	597–586	2 Chronicles 36:11-16

17:10-14 God established a solemn agreement with David and his descendants, which is often referred to as the Davidic Covenant (also in Psalms 89 and 132). God plays on the Hebrew word translated as "house" to tell David He will give him an everlasting dynasty. This promise is eternal, but conditional. Future sons may fail, in which case God would discipline them and raise up another son (2 Samuel 7:14), but the emphasis in Chronicles is on God's sovereign establishment of the Davidic dynasty and its eternal rule over the whole of God's kingdom (see 1 Chronicles 17:9, 23, 27). Consequently, the passage is usually taken to have a double meaning. It speaks of both David's earthly sons (particularly Solomon) and Jesus Christ, the heavenly Son of David, who is the messianic King (Matthew 22:41-46). The promises of the Davidic Covenant were completely fulfilled only in Christ (Acts 2:25-36), who was Himself divine (John 1:1-18; 17:1; Luke 1:35). The Davidic Covenant was important to the chronicler's audience because it was the basis for their national unity and security. It is important to God's people today because it is the basis for the heavenly Kingdom of God, which was established once-for-all when Christ entered the world (Matthew 4:17; 12:22-29; Mark 1:15; Luke 4:14-19).

"'Furthermore, I declare that the LORD will build a house for you—a dynasty of
kings! 11 For when you die and join your ancestors, I will raise up one of your
descendants, one of your sons, and I will make his kingdom strong. 12 He is the
17:13 one who will build a house—a temple—for Me. And I will secure his throne forever.
1 Chr 10:14 13 I will be his father, and he will be My son. I will never take My favor from him as
Heb 1:5 I took it from the one who ruled before you. 14 I will confirm him as king over My
house and My kingdom for all time, and his throne will be secure forever.'"

15 So Nathan went back to David and told him everything the LORD had said in this vision.

DAVID'S PRAYER OF THANKS

17:16-27 16 Then King David went in and sat before the LORD and prayed,
//2 Sam 7:18-29

"Who am I, O LORD God, and what is my family, that You have brought me this far?
17:17 17 And now, O God, in addition to everything else, You speak of giving Your servant
2 Sam 7:19 a lasting dynasty! You speak as though I were someone very great,* O LORD God!
18 "What more can I say to You about the way You have honored me? You know
17:19 what Your servant is really like. 19 For the sake of Your servant, O LORD, and according
2 Sam 7:21, 25
Isa 37:35 to Your will, You have done all these great things and have made them known.
20 "O LORD, there is no One like You. We have never even heard of another God
like You! 21 What other nation on earth is like Your people Israel? What other nation,
O God, have You redeemed from slavery to be Your own people? You made a great
name for Yourself when You redeemed Your people from Egypt. You performed
17:22 awesome miracles and drove out the nations that stood in their way. 22 You chose
Exod 19:5-6 Israel to be Your very own people forever, and You, O LORD, became their God.
23 "And now, O LORD, I am Your servant; do as You have promised concerning me
and my family. May it be a promise that will last forever. 24 And may Your name be
established and honored forever so that everyone will say, 'The LORD of Heaven's
Armies, the God of Israel, is Israel's God!' And may the house of Your servant David
continue before You forever.
25 "O my God, I have been bold enough to pray to You because You have revealed
to Your servant that You will build a house for him—a dynasty of kings! 26 For You are
God, O LORD. And You have promised these good things to Your servant. 27 And now,
it has pleased You to bless the house of Your servant, so that it will continue forever
before You. For when You grant a blessing, O LORD, it is an eternal blessing!"

17:17 The meaning of the Hebrew is uncertain.

17:16-27 David eloquently praises God for what He has done and what He will do. His prayer of praise to the Lord is mixed with astonishment and humility. David refers to himself as "Your servant" eight times and to God as "O LORD God" (literally "Lord Yahweh") seven times. The rhetorical question "Who am I?" sets the tone of this prayer, showing David knew he did not deserve God's blessings (29:14-16). The audience of Chronicles also had cause to praise God, having just returned from Babylonian captivity, and the chronicler wanted them to follow David's example of humility and praise.

▸PURPOSE

17:18 God knows our heart. David rejoiced at how God could bless someone like him—a former shepherd boy, a soldier, a singer, a poet, and a big sinner. God knew David's deeds and his thoughts, but God still saw fit to work through him by blessing him and his family. God can work through anyone to accomplish His will—even you! (***See Purpose**> God's Means> God's Sovereignty> God knows all,* TopicGuide page A52.)

17:20 This verse is reminiscent of the central confession of Israel from Deuteronomy 6:4-5, called "the Shema," which emphasizes the uniqueness and supremacy of God and expresses one's full devotion to Him.

17:23 David is not telling God what to do here or giving God permission. David would not even presume to ask this blessing of God (17:25). Rather, this is a confirmation, or ratification of the covenant that God already offered in 17:10-14.

17:27 The promise of an eternal blessing on David's dynasty is an incredible gift. Whereas David was planning to build a house for God, God would build an eternal house for David. Consequently, it is God's actions (not David's) that would eternally assure that God would be with His people forever. It is no wonder David is honored.

DAVID'S MILITARY VICTORIES

18 After this, David defeated and subdued the Philistines by conquering Gath and its surrounding towns. 2David also conquered the land of Moab, and the Moabites who were spared became David's subjects and paid him tribute money. 18:1-13 //2 Sam 8:1-14

3David also destroyed the forces of Hadadezer, king of Zobah, as far as Hamath,* when Hadadezer marched out to strengthen his control along the Euphrates River. 4David captured 1,000 chariots, 7,000 charioteers, and 20,000 foot soldiers. He crippled all the chariot horses except enough for 100 chariots.

5When Arameans from Damascus arrived to help King Hadadezer, David killed 22,000 of them. 6Then he placed several army garrisons* in Damascus, the Aramean capital, and the Arameans became David's subjects and paid him tribute money. So the LORD made David victorious wherever he went.

7David brought the gold shields of Hadadezer's officers to Jerusalem, 8along with a large amount of bronze from Hadadezer's towns of Tebah* and Cun. Later Solomon melted the bronze and molded it into the great bronze basin called the Sea, the pillars, and the various bronze articles used at the Temple.

9When King Toi* of Hamath heard that David had destroyed the entire army of King Hadadezer of Zobah, 10he sent his son Joram* to congratulate King David for his successful

18:3 The meaning of the Hebrew is uncertain. 18:6 As in Greek version and Latin Vulgate (see also 2 Sam 8:6); Hebrew lacks *several army garrisons.* 18:8 Hebrew reads *Tibhath,* a variant spelling of Tebah; compare parallel text at 2 Sam 8:8. 18:9 As in parallel text at 2 Sam 8:9; Hebrew reads *Tou;* also in 18:10. 18:10 As in parallel text at 2 Sam 8:10; Hebrew reads *Hadoram,* a variant spelling of Joram.

18:1-13 The chronicler returns to an overview of David's later military exploits in order to immediately show that God kept the promise He made in 17:10. The word translated "defeated and subdued" does not mean that David completely conquered and enslaved the surrounding nations as he did the Amalekites (1 Samuel 27:9; 30:17). Rather, he defeated them in battle to the point where they surrendered and agreed to pay tribute to King David. These nations were notorious enemies of Israel and had troubled them for centuries. The chronicler is encouraging his people that they can do the same after returning from exile.

18:1 Gath was one of the five Philistine cities near the southwest coast of Palestine, on the northwestern border of Judah's territory. It was the home of the giant Goliath, whom David killed in his youth, and there were still some giants left there (20:4-8). David had taken refuge in Gath twice before when he was being pursued by Saul (1 Samuel 21:10; 27:2-4), but now it came under the control of Israel. Gath has been destroyed and restored so many times that its location can only be estimated to be the modern-day Tell es Safi.

18:2 Moab was a kingdom east of Israel on the southeast shore of the Dead Sea. The Moabites were descendants of Abraham's nephew, Lot (Genesis 19:30-37), but they were a menace to Israel during the Conquest (Numbers 22–25) and hired Balaam to curse them. During the time of the Judges, the Moabites oppressed Israel until God provided a deliverer named Ehud to deliver the Israelites (Judges 3:12-30). We know from the book of Ruth that Moab lived in peace with Israel before Israel had a king. Though Saul unsuccessfully tried to subdue Moab, David swiftly subjugated them (2 Samuel 8:2). Moab would fall in and out of Israel's control in the later years of the kingdom. The enmity between Moab and Israel ran deep; this is evidenced by God's words through the prophets (Isaiah 15–16; Jeremiah 9:25-26, 48; Amos 2:1-3; Zephaniah 2:8-11).

18:3 Zobah was a kingdom of the Arameans (Syrians) and ruled by Hadadezer. It lay northeast of Israel and was defeated by Saul previously (1 Samuel 14:47). For David to defeat them (2 Samuel 9:3-5; see also Psalm 60 superscription), he had to battle a large coalition of Arameans and warriors from Zobah (see 19:16-19). Hamath was a city on the Orontes River in the northern part of Aram, and the Euphrates River marked the northern boundary of Aram.

18:4 Though this passage reports 1,000 chariots and 7,000 horsemen, the parallel text of 2 Samuel 8:4 only mentions 1,700 horsemen. It is likely that the Samuel text has suffered from transcribing errors, and this is the better text. Whatever plunder was saved might have been used in a triumphal procession back in Jerusalem and then destroyed. David, knowing the word of the Lord against having many horses (Deuteronomy 17:16; Psalm 20:7; Isaiah 31:1) hamstrung the horses that were captured.

18:5-6 The Arameans came from a larger people group later referred to collectively as Syrians. Conflicting genealogies make the origins of this people group difficult to determine (Genesis 10:20-23). They are no doubt Semitic, related to Laban (Genesis 25:20; 28:1-7), and therefore Jacob (Deuteronomy 26:5). These Arameans settled in the central Euphrates region, where they then spread out. After David defeated them, he established an occupation force throughout the region and received tribute from the people.

18:7-11 David gained many spoils from his exploits and vassal kingdoms. The chronicler added the comments about the great amount of bronze taken, showing another of his underlying reasons for recounting David's battles: The spoils from all his battles were being saved in preparation for Solomon to build the Temple.

18:10 Following a common way to make peace with a stronger nation, the king of Hamath sent his son to David with valuable gifts. The king's tribute, and his willingness to risk his heir to the throne, showed submission to David's authority and an invitation to initiate a bilateral treaty.

campaign. Hadadezer and Toi had been enemies and were often at war. Joram presented
David with many gifts of gold, silver, and bronze.

18:11 Num 24:18-20 [11]King David dedicated all these gifts to the LORD, along with the silver and gold he had
taken from the other nations—from Edom, Moab, Ammon, Philistia, and Amalek.
[12]Abishai son of Zeruiah destroyed 18,000 Edomites in the Valley of Salt. [13]He placed
army garrisons in Edom, and all the Edomites became David's subjects. In fact, the LORD
made David victorious wherever he went.

18:14-17 //2 Sam 8:15-18 [14]So David reigned over all Israel and did what was just and right for all his people.
18:15 1 Chr 11:6 [15]Joab son of Zeruiah was commander of the army. Jehoshaphat son of Ahilud was the
royal historian. [16]Zadok son of Ahitub and Ahimelech* son of Abiathar were the priests.
Seraiah* was the court secretary. [17]Benaiah son of Jehoiada was captain of the king's
bodyguard.* And David's sons served as the king's chief assistants.

DAVID DEFEATS THE AMMONITES

19:1-19 //2 Sam 10:1-19 **19** Some time after this, King Nahash of the Ammonites died, and his son Hanun* became king. [2]David said, "I am going to show loyalty to Hanun because his father,
Nahash, was always loyal to me." So David sent messengers to express sympathy to Hanun about his father's death.

But when David's ambassadors arrived in the land of Ammon, [3]the Ammonite commanders said to Hanun, "Do you really think these men are coming here to honor your father? No! David has sent them to spy out the land so they can come in and conquer it!" [4]So

18:16a As in some Hebrew manuscripts, Syriac version, and Latin Vulgate (see also 2 Sam 8:17); most Hebrew manuscripts read *Abimelech.* 18:16b As in parallel text at 2 Sam 8:17; Hebrew reads *Shavsha.* 18:17 Hebrew *of the Kerethites and Pelethites.* 19:1 As in parallel text at 2 Sam 10:1; Hebrew lacks *Hanun.*

18:11-13 The Valley of Salt is probably modern-day es-Sebka, the salt plain south of the Dead Sea. This valley marked the location of another of David's battles with the surrounding nations. Abishai, David's nephew (1 Chronicles 2:16) and one of his mighty men (1 Chronicles 11:21) commanded the army that killed 18,000 Edomites. The superscription of Psalm 60 attributes 12,000 of them to Joab, who undoubtedly was also a commander in the fray. The people of Edom were descendants of Esau (Genesis 36), and their territory was outside the Promised Land to the southeast. Consequently, Israel was to show them kindness during the conquest of Canaan (Deuteronomy 2:4-5; 23:7). The Edomites lost this protected status, however, by troubling Israel (Numbers 20:14-21; 1 Samuel 14:47; Amos 9:11-12).

▸ HOLINESS

18:14 Powerful, yet fair. You would think that as David grew in political and military power he would also grow in cruelty toward his enemies. But power did not corrupt David; he remained a just king throughout his reign. He could have easily justified crushing any who showed disrespect or destroying entire towns for the slightest offense, but he only fought when necessary. Leadership has its temptations, but you do not have to succumb to them. Wherever you have authority, lead evenhandedly. (***See Holiness***> *Law and Grace> Law> Leaders and followers,* TopicGuide page A41.)

18:15-17 This is the typical way for the chronicler to summarize the administration of a particular king. These well-known officials provided an excellent bureaucracy for Solomon, preparing the way for the building of the Temple. The chronicler expected that the leadership of his community would do the same.

18:15 Joab became commander by his valiant capture of Jebus, later renamed Jerusalem (1 Chronicles 11:6).

18:16 Zadok and Abimelech were valued priests to David, serving at Gibeon and Jerusalem, respectively (see note on 15:11).

18:17 Benaiah was one of David's mighty men (1 Chronicles 11:22-25) and served as commander of David's special guard (Hebrew, of the Kerethites and Pelethites. The Kerethites were the men who had accompanied David while he was with the Philistines (1 Samuel 30:1-15; see also Ezekiel 25:16). The Pelethites were the men who joined Benaiah at Ziklag; their name is derived from Pelet, their chief (1 Chronicles 12:3).

19:1-19 This chapter details the Aramean-Ammonite war with Israel that was summarized in 18:3-6.

19:1 The Ammonites were descendants of Lot (Genesis 19:38), and therefore Israel was ordered to keep at peace with them during the Conquest (Deuteronomy 2:19; Joshua 13:25). At the time of the Conquest, the Ammonites were oppressed by the Hittites and Amorites (Numbers 21:21-31). As Israel came into the land, they defeated the Hittites and Amorites, thereby freeing the Ammonites to settle directly east of Israel between the Arnon River and the Jabbok River. From this location, the Ammonites launched an unsuccessful military campaign against the Israelites (Judges 11:1-28). Despite their defeat, they continued their hostility and made enemies of themselves with the God of Israel (Jeremiah 49:1-6; Ezekiel 21:20; 25:1-7; Amos 1:14).

19:2-3 Considering the past hostility of Ammon, this was a kind offer from King David. Even Hanan's advisers suspected retribution from Israel.

19:4-5 The beard was a sign of maturity, wisdom, and affluence among ancient Semitic people. Israelites were prohibited from trimming facial hair for religious reasons (Leviticus 19:27; 21:5-6). Consequently, it was humiliating for a man's beard to be mutilated (Isaiah 7:20; 50:6). To have one's nakedness exposed was also an embarrassment (Jeremiah 13:22, 26; Nahum 3:5). The actions of Hanun were extremely disgraceful and tantamount to a declaration of war, since to mistreat the representatives of the king was to mistreat the king himself.

Hanun seized David's ambassadors and shaved them, cut off their robes at the buttocks,
and sent them back to David in shame.
5 When David heard what had happened to the men, he sent messengers to tell them,
"Stay at Jericho until your beards grow out, and then come back." For they felt deep shame
because of their appearance.
6 When the people of Ammon realized how seriously they had angered David, Hanun
and the Ammonites sent 75,000 pounds* of silver to hire chariots and charioteers from
Aram-naharaim, Aram-maacah, and Zobah. 7 They also hired 32,000 chariots and secured **19:7**
the support of the king of Maacah and his army. These forces camped at Medeba, where Num 21:30
they were joined by the Ammonite troops that Hanun had recruited from his own towns. Josh 13:9, 16
8 When David heard about this, he sent Joab and all his warriors to fight them. 9 The Am-
monite troops came out and drew up their battle lines at the entrance of the city, while the
other kings positioned themselves to fight in the open fields.
10 When Joab saw that he would have to fight on both the front and the rear, he chose
some of Israel's elite troops and placed them under his personal command to fight the Ar-
ameans in the fields. 11 He left the rest of the army under the command of his brother
Abishai, who was to attack the Ammonites. 12 "If the Arameans are too strong for me, then
come over and help me," Joab told his brother. "And if the Ammonites are too strong for
you, I will help you. 13 Be courageous! Let us fight bravely for our people and the cities of
our God. May the LORD's will be done."
14 When Joab and his troops attacked, the Arameans began to run away. 15 And when **19:14**
the Ammonites saw the Arameans running, they also ran from Abishai and retreated into 2 Sam 10:14
the city. Then Joab returned to Jerusalem.
16 The Arameans now realized that they were no match for Israel, so they sent messen- **19:16**
gers and summoned additional Aramean troops from the other side of the Euphrates 2 Sam 10:15-16
River.* These troops were under the command of Shobach,* the commander of Hadade-
zer's forces.
17 When David heard what was happening, he mobilized all Israel, crossed the Jordan
River, and positioned his troops in battle formation. Then David engaged the Arameans in
battle, and they fought against him. 18 But again the Arameans fled from the Israelites. This
time David's forces killed 7,000 charioteers and 40,000 foot soldiers, including Shobach,
the commander of their army. 19 When Hadadezer's allies saw that they had been de-
feated by Israel, they surrendered to David and became his subjects. After that, the Arame-
ans were no longer willing to help the Ammonites.

19:6 Hebrew *1,000 talents* [34,000 kilograms]. 19:16a Hebrew *the river.* 19:16b As in parallel text at 2 Sam 10:16; Hebrew reads *Shophach;* also in 19:18.

19:6-9 The Ammonites called for help from their allies, the Aramean kingdoms in the north (see note on 18:5-6). The chronicler not only added to the record the outrageous price paid for these troops, he also included the number of chariot forces (see also 2 Samuel 10:6). These combined forces met David's army in Israelite territory just south of Ammon on a plain northeast of the Dead Sea. The town of Medeba is on the King's Highway 25 miles south of the modern-day town of Amman (see 1 Chronicles 19:7).

19:10-15 Joab's strategy of splitting Israel's forces with his brother Abishai was innovative and risky, but the Lord was on their side. This ended the first battle of the Aramean-Ammonite war.

19:16-19 The second stage of the Aramean-Ammonite war took place the next year. Forces from Aram-naharim (Mesopotamia in the far northeast), joined those from Zobah and Aram-damascus (1 Chronicles 18:5-6), engaging David's army at Helam, an unknown site east of the Jordan (2 Samuel 10:17). After they were defeated, the Arameans were made vassals to Israel, and the king of Hamath in the north pledged his submission to David (1 Chronicles 18:9-10).

▸ HOLINESS
19:19 Defeating two enemies at once. David found that when he destroyed the Ammonites, he also ended his troubles with the Arameans. When we defeat one sin—stealing, for instance—it conquers many other sins in our lives: the lies to cover up the sin stop, and the promise breaking stops. Many smaller sins quickly disperse when we chase the main sin away. Discover a fundamental sin in your life and focus your efforts on defeating it. When it falls, many others will fall with it. (***See Holiness***> *Changed by God> God Provides> Conviction of sin,* TopicGuide page A41.)

DAVID CAPTURES RABBAH

20:1-3 //2 Sam 11:1; 12:29-31

20 In the spring of the year,* when kings normally go out to war, Joab led the
Israelite army in successful attacks against the land of the Ammonites. In
the process he laid siege to the city of Rabbah. However, David stayed behind in Je-
rusalem.
[2]When David arrived at Rabbah, he removed the crown from the king's head,* and it
was placed on his own head. The crown was made of gold and set with gems, and he
found that it weighed seventy-five pounds.* David took a vast amount of plunder from the
city. [3]He also made slaves of the people of Rabbah and forced them to labor with* saws,
iron picks, and iron axes.* That is how David dealt with the people of all the Ammonite
towns. Then David and all the army returned to Jerusalem.

BATTLES AGAINST PHILISTINE GIANTS

20:4-8 //2 Sam 21:15-22

20:5 1 Sam 17:4-7; 2 Sam 21:19; 1 Chr 11:23

[4]After this, war broke out with the Philistines at Gezer. As they fought, Sibbecai from Hu-
shah killed Saph,* a descendant of the giants,* and so the Philistines were subdued.
[5]During another battle with the Philistines, Elhanan son of Jair killed Lahmi, the
brother of Goliath of Gath. The handle of Lahmi's spear was as thick as a weaver's
beam!
[6]In another battle with the Philistines at Gath, they encountered a huge man with six fin-
gers on each hand and six toes on each foot, twenty-four in all, who was also a descen-
dant of the giants. [7]But when he defied and taunted Israel, he was killed by Jonathan, the
son of David's brother Shimea.
[8]These Philistines were descendants of the giants of Gath, but David and his warriors
killed them.

20:1 Hebrew *At the turn of the year.* The first day of the year in the ancient Hebrew lunar calendar occurred in March or April. 20:2a Or *from the head of Milcom* (as in Greek version and Latin Vulgate). Milcom, also called Molech, was the god of the Ammonites. 20:2b Hebrew *1 talent* [34 kilograms]. 20:3a Or *He also brought out the people of Rabbah and cut them with.* 20:3b As in parallel text at 2 Sam 12:31; Hebrew reads *and saws.* 20:4a As in parallel text at 2 Sam 21:18; Hebrew reads *Sippai.* 20:4b Hebrew *descendant of the Rephaites;* also in 20:6, 8.

20:1-8 At this point, the chronicler chooses to omit David's sin with Bathsheba and Nathan's rebuke (2 Samuel 11–12). He includes battling the Ammonites (see note on 19:1-19), but discards the embarrassment of Joab sending for David on the verge of sacking the city (2 Samuel 12:26-28). Trouble in David's house is omitted (2 Samuel 13:1–21:14). David's rescue from the Philistine battle is omitted (2 Samuel 21:15-17), but the actual victory is reported. It is clear that the chronicler is focusing his historic presentation on only the exemplary aspects of David's reign in order to present him as the ideal king for his audience.

▸ BIBLE
20:1 What really happened that spring? The Bible doesn't include every detail about the events it describes—or even the details we may really want to know. Each author had his own Holy-Spirit-guided goals and chose his material accordingly. For instance, we know from 2 Samuel 11 that David did more than stay home and rest that spring—he dallied with Bathsheba, killed her husband, and lost his infant son. But the interests of the author of Chronicles lay elsewhere—he mainly told stories that built David up as a leader and downplayed David's faults. The goals and perspectives of Samuel's and Chronicles' authors were slightly different, but they both told the truth about David's life. As you read the Scriptures, trust that God gave each author the ability to perfectly arrange and summarize his material. (***See Bible*> *Uniqueness*> *Authoritative*> *All-sufficient,*** TopicGuide page A10.)

20:2 The crown belonged to Milcom (also called Molech), the god of the Ammonites, whom Solomon later worshiped (1 Kings 11:5). Again, the emphasis here is on the vast amounts of valuables David gathered in preparation to build the Temple.

20:3 In repayment for so much violence against Israel in the past, David enslaved the Ammonites (see note on 19:1). Second Samuel 12:31 also mentions that David forced the Ammonites to make bricks.

20:4-8 Gezer (Gob) was the northernmost of the largest Philistine cities. The fact that Gezer was located well within Israel's territory (only 20 miles northwest of Jerusalem) indicates that David no doubt was having trouble with encroaching Philistine aggression (14:16). Although Israel was never able to completely dominate the Philistines, the chronicler reported that they were subdued, recalling the promise God gave David in 17:10.

DAVID TAKES A CENSUS

21 Satan rose up against Israel and caused David to take a census of the people of Israel. [2]So David said to Joab and the commanders of the army, "Take a census of all the people of Israel—from Beersheba in the south to Dan in the north—and bring me a report so I may know how many there are."

[3]But Joab replied, "May the LORD increase the number of His people a hundred times over! But why, my lord the king, do you want to do this? Are they not all your servants? Why must you cause Israel to sin?"

[4]But the king insisted that they take the census, so Joab traveled throughout all Israel to count the people. Then he returned to Jerusalem [5]and reported the number of people to David. There were 1,100,000 warriors in all Israel who could handle a sword, and 470,000 in Judah. [6]But Joab did not include the tribes of Levi and Benjamin in the census because he was so distressed at what the king had made him do.

JUDGMENT FOR DAVID'S SIN

[7]God was very displeased with the census, and He punished Israel for it. [8]Then David said to God, "I have sinned greatly by taking this census. Please forgive my guilt for doing this foolish thing."

21:1-26 //2 Sam 24:1-25
21:2 1 Chr 27:23-24
21:3 Deut 1:11
21:5 2 Sam 24:9
21:6 1 Chr 27:24
21:8 2 Sam 12:13

21:1–22:1 The chronicler expands the account of David's census from 2 Samuel 24 in order to set up the selection of the Temple site and to lead into reporting of the Temple arrangements (1 Chronicles 22:2–29:25). David's selection of the Temple site is probably the most dramatic episode of 1 Chronicles, and it follows on the heels of one of David's great sins, beautifully showing how the Sovereign Lord can use evil for good. This is the longest original contribution of the chronicler, showing how he valued holy worship practices.

▸ **WORSHIP**

21:1 Sin and the census. Don't worry—it's not a sin to be counted in a census (Exodus 30:11-16). But while it's not clear exactly what sin he committed, David did something very wrong. He refused to obey God in this matter and would not repent until those around him began to suffer. Do you sometimes do the right things for the wrong reasons? God is not interested in delays or excuses—He wants repentance. He wants us to listen when people tell us we are in sin. Heed the warnings of God's people and God's Spirit. (***See Worship****> OT> Prophets> Israel to listen and obey God's prophets,* TopicGuide page A28.)

21:1 The parallel text in 2 Samuel says God caused David to take the census because He was angry at Israel (2 Samuel 24:1). Does this mean David had no choice but to sin? Also, doesn't this contradict the apostle James's statement that God does not tempt anyone (James 1:13)? There is no contradiction if we maintain a biblical understanding of the complete sovereignty of God. Humans and angels are free, but not as free as God. He accomplishes His good will through primary causes (creation and miracles) and secondary causes (providence and free choices). Further, God's control (which extends over all things) rightly uses all free actions (good or evil) for His glory. The chronicler here merely clarified that God let Satan tempt David to call for the census in order to accomplish His divine purpose, much like He let Satan attack Job (Job 1:12).

21:2-4 Taking a census is not wrong by itself. Moses did it (Exodus 30:11-16; Numbers 3:40-43; Numbers 26). Solomon did it (2 Chronicles 2:17). Ezra 2 and Nehemiah 7 also record census reports. David's order to take a census, however, was likely motivated by a desire to size up his military strength (1 Chronicles 21:5) and to build a standing army (1 Chronicles 27:1-15). In doing so, David was relying on his own strength, instead of the Lord's. This sin of self-reliance often plagued the leaders of God's people (Isaiah 31:1-9; 2 Kings 18:20-25; 2 Chronicles 16:7-9). This sin was painfully obvious even to someone like Joab (see 1 Chronicles 21:6), and the chronicler wanted to teach the people of God during his time that they must learn from David's mistake as they face threats from the surrounding nations.

21:5 There is a discrepancy between the total number of fighting men listed here and the total given in 2 Samuel 24:9, which reports 800,000 Israelites and 500,000 Judahites. Scholars suggest the problem is probably with a corruption of one or both texts. Whatever the case, 1.1 million fighting men seems very large. Estimates of population in the Iron Age do not match this figure. Indeed, it would be almost impossible to quarter this many fighting troops. Most modern military forces today do not have this many people in their entire organization. Further, casualties today come nowhere close to what the chronicler reports (1 Chronicles 11:21; 2 Chronicles 13:3), even with weapons of mass destruction. As with most of the chronicler's reports (2 Chronicles 13:3; 14:7-9; 17:12-19), many scholars think this is a likely a case where the chronicler uses hyperbole to encourage his audience to be bold and defend themselves against the aggressive surrounding nations.

21:6 The law prohibited counting the Levites (Numbers 1:49), which may be why Joab objected so strongly to David. The Hebrew text literally says, "Joab abhorred the word of the king." From the way Joab conducted the census (see 2 Samuel 24:1-9), it seems the task was cut short before he could get to the territory of Benjamin (1 Chronicles 27:24).

21:7 As the king of Israel, David played a special representative role in God's relationship with His people. When David sinned, the people bore some of the responsibility, and vice versa (1 Chronicles 21:3). This is also a key principle in understanding the nature of our salvation in Christ, of whom David was a type. King Jesus, the true son of David, represents before God all those who have placed their faith in Him. Since Christ was perfect, we are represented as perfect. Since we are sinful, Christ suffered the punishment for our sin. "For God made Christ, who never sinned, to be the offering for our sin, so that we could be made right with God through Christ" (2 Corinthians 5:21).

21:8-9 David humbly repented, which is what the chronicler wants the people of God to do when they sin. Because of David's response, God graciously gave David a choice in the administration of Israel's punishment. The offer came through

21:9 9 Then the LORD spoke to Gad, David's seer. This was the message: 10 "Go and say to Da-
1 Sam 9:9 vid, 'This is what the LORD says: I will give you three choices. Choose one of these punish-
2 Sam 24:11 1 Chr 29:29 ments, and I will inflict it on you.' "
21:12 11 So Gad came to David and said, "These are the choices the LORD has given you. 12 You
2 Sam 24:13 may choose three years of famine, three months of destruction by the sword of your ene-
mies, or three days of severe plague as the angel of the LORD brings devastation through-
out the land of Israel. Decide what answer I should give the LORD who sent me."
21:13 13 "I'm in a desperate situation!" David replied to Gad. "But let me fall into the hands of
Pss 51:1; 130:4, 7 the LORD, for His mercy is very great. Do not let me fall into human hands."
21:14 14 So the LORD sent a plague upon Israel, and 70,000 people died as a result. 15 And God
1 Chr 27:24 **21:15** sent an angel to destroy Jerusalem. But just as the angel was preparing to destroy it, the
Exod 32:14 LORD relented and said to the death angel, "Stop! That is enough!" At that moment the an-
1 Sam 15:11 gel of the LORD was standing by the threshing floor of Araunah* the Jebusite.
Jon 3:10 16 David looked up and saw the Angel of the LORD standing between heaven and earth
21:16 with his sword drawn, reaching out over Jerusalem. So David and the leaders of Israel put
1 Kgs 21:27 **21:17** on burlap to show their deep distress and fell face down on the ground. 17 And David said
2 Sam 7:8 to God, "I am the one who called for the census! I am the one who has sinned and done
Ps 74:1 wrong! But these people are as innocent as sheep—what have they done? O LORD my God,
let Your anger fall against me and my family, but do not destroy Your people."

21:15 As in parallel text at 2 Sam 24:16; Hebrew reads *Ornan,* another name for Araunah; also in 21:18-28.

Gad, another prophet (formerly called a seer; 1 Samuel 9:9) in David's service. Gad had advised David while David was fleeing Saul (1 Samuel 22:5) and would assist David in musical arrangements (2 Chronicles 29:25). He is also said to have kept a record of all the events of David's reign (1 Chronicles 29:29). Gad is a decisive character in the background of this episode (1 Chronicles 21:18).

21:11-13 It is hard to know why God gave David these choices. The threats are clearly divine punishment and bear a strong resemblance to the six seals of Revelation (Revelation 6). The duration of the punishments follows a pattern (three years, months, or days), which seems to indicate the punishments are of the same severity. The means of the punishment is what is truly different. The natural world brings famine, military enemies bring destruction, and the Lord Himself brings devastation through plague. God was teaching David a lesson in the midst of his punishment. Though David had distrusted God by determining his military strength through a census, his choice of punishment showed a renewed trust in God. David chose a punishment directly from God because he believed that God is merciful. Indeed, God did cut the punishment short (1 Chronicles 21:15) after David and the leaders prayed (1 Chronicles 21:16-17).

21:14 This time David's sin cost him more than one of his men and his son (2 Samuel 11–12)—it cost 70,000 people. Though God graciously curtailed the punishment, the consequences of sin remained. But why were the people punished for David's crime? The answer lies partly in the corporate understanding of life in the ancient world. Ancient peoples viewed themselves as connected to their leaders in a stronger way than many do today. Second, David was a type of King Jesus, and he performed a special representative (Messianic) role in Israel (see note on 21:7).

21:15 The Hebrew text actually says "angel of the LORD," which is a manifestation of God Himself. Appearing throughout the Old Testament (Genesis 21:17; 22:11-18; 24:7, 40; 31:11-13; 48:16; Exodus 3:2-10; Numbers 22:21-22; 1 Kings 19:7; 2 Chronicles 32:21), this figure is God's special messenger who accomplished special functions during the history of Israel. Sometimes He was a guide and protector (Genesis 16:7-13; Exodus 14:19; 23:20; 33:2; Numbers 20:16), and sometimes He was a destroyer (Exodus 23:23; Joshua 5:13–6:2; 2 Samuel 24:16; 2 Kings 19:35). Whatever His function, His purpose was to preserve Israel's special relationship with God. He was a physical incarnation of God's grace to His people. Because of this and the fact that John 1:14-18 says Jesus Christ is the unique Son of God—the glory of the Father revealed to us—we can identify the angel of the Lord as the pre-incarnate Christ.

21:15 The Hebrew word translated "relented" is most often used to describe God ceasing a particular course of action because of human obedience or disobedience (Jonah 3:10; Jeremiah 26:3, 19; Amos 7:3, 6). Other translations have rendered the word "repent," but that implies that God changed His mind or regretted His intentions. God is not sinful, so relenting involves God changing His plans according to His overarching sovereign purpose. This may seem contradictory, since other passages state that He does not change His mind (1 Samuel 15:29; Psalm 110:4; Isaiah 46:10; Ephesians 1:11; Hebrews 6:17; James 1:17). But these passages refer to God's eternal character and plan, which is to save His people. It is God's unchangeability that prevents Him from destroying sinful Judah—He shows mercy and keeps His covenant (Malachi 3:6). To be true to this purpose, God must at times threaten disaster upon His people so that they will turn from their sin and trust in Him. When this does happen, God "relents" from the disaster He planned. Jeremiah 18:7-10 is a clear reminder that prophecy is conditional upon the response of those to whom it is directed.

21:16-17 This dramatic scene clearly happened before verse 15, or else God would not have stopped the angel's hand. The chronicler is using the art of storytelling to dramatically portray the imminent danger Israel was in. David's humble prayer for mercy in the face of his sin's consequences is striking. Even though Israel sinned too (2 Samuel 24:1), David selflessly offers to take the punishment. In his kingly role as representative of Israel (see note on 1 Chronicles 21:7), David is reminiscent of Jesus Christ, who sacrificed Himself for his people (Luke 23:34).

DAVID BUILDS AN ALTAR

18Then the angel of the LORD told Gad to instruct David to go up and build an altar to the 21:18 2 Chr 3:1
LORD on the threshing floor of Araunah the Jebusite. 19So David went up to do what the LORD
had commanded him through Gad. 20Araunah, who was busy threshing wheat at the time,
turned and saw the angel there. His four sons, who were with him, ran away and hid.
21When Araunah saw David approaching, he left his threshing floor and bowed before Da-
vid with his face to the ground.

22David said to Araunah, "Let me buy this threshing floor from you at its full price. Then I
will build an altar to the LORD there, so that He will stop the plague."

23"Take it, my lord the king, and use it as you wish," Araunah said to David. "I will give
the oxen for the burnt offerings, and the threshing boards for wood to build a fire on the
altar, and the wheat for the grain offering. I will give it all to you."

24But King David replied to Araunah, "No, I insist on buying it for the full price. I will not
take what is yours and give it to the LORD. I will not present burnt offerings that have cost me
nothing!" 25So David gave Araunah 600 pieces of gold* in payment for the threshing floor.

26David built an altar there to the LORD and sacrificed burnt offerings and peace offer- 21:26 Lev 9:24
ings. And when David prayed, the LORD answered him by sending fire from heaven to burn Judg 6:21
up the offering on the altar. 27Then the LORD spoke to the angel, who put the sword back
into its sheath.

28When David saw that the LORD had answered his prayer, he offered sacrifices there at
Araunah's threshing floor. 29At that time the Tabernacle of the LORD and the altar of burnt 21:29 1 Kgs 3:4
offering that Moses had made in the wilderness were located at the place of worship in 1 Chr 16:39
Gibeon. 30But David was not able to go there to inquire of God, because he was terrified by
the drawn sword of the angel of the LORD.

22 Then David said, "This will be the location for the Temple of the LORD God and 22:1 1 Chr 21:18-28
the place of the altar for Israel's burnt offerings!" 2 Chr 3:1

21:25 Hebrew *600 shekels of gold,* about 15 pounds or 6.8 kilograms in weight.

21:18-19 In the Bible, atonement requires that sacrifices be made to pay for sin's guilt (Hebrews 9:22). Since the threshing floor of Araunah was where the sword of the angel of the Lord was stopped, it became the place where God's mercy was poured forth. It became holy ground—a place of forgiveness (Genesis 22:2; 2 Chronicles 3:1; Hebrews 13:12). Today, forgiveness is attained through the sacrifice of Jesus Christ (Ephesians 5:2; John 1:29; Hebrews 7:27; 9:26; 10:12). He is the superior way to God, and He is God with us (Matthew 12:6; Hebrews 6:19–7:28; Revelation 21:22).

21:20-21 Araunah (the Hebrew reads by Ornan) was processing harvested wheat by dragging a wooden sledge behind oxen to break the grain off the shaft, then throwing it in the air to separate the grain from the chaff (Isaiah 30:24). A threshing floor was usually a level, elevated place for performing this process.

21:22-24 Araunah is presented here as honorable, and David as even more honorable. An original inhabitant of Jerusalem (Jebus), Araunah gave literally everything he owned there for the sacrifice. David's purchase of the land resembles Abraham's purchase of Sarah's burial plot (Genesis 23:1-20). The chronicler was encouraging his readers to respond in complete devotion to God when it comes to worship.

21:25 This large amount was probably the cost for the entire land purchase, rather than just the threshing floor and oxen, as reported in 2 Samuel 24:24.

21:26-27 When God consumed the sacrifice with fire, it was a sign of His presence and pleasure in the worship (Leviticus 9:24; Judges 6:21; 1 Kings 18:38; 2 Chronicles 7:1). By showing God's approval of David's sacrifices and the angel's withdrawing of his sword, the chronicler made clear to his people that the place of the Temple was instituted by none other than God Himself.

21:28-30 The chronicler presents a reason for why David performed sacrifices here instead of following Mosaic instructions. Recall that after David brought the Ark to Jerusalem, he left Zadok in charge of the Tabernacle at Gibeon to continue to offer sacrifices for Israel (16:39-40). This was an emergency situation, however, for Israel was in imminent danger, so David offered the sacrifice. The Lord approved other modified worship practices in Israel arising from unusual circumstances (2 Chronicles 5:11-12; 30:2-3). Further, David knew that Israel's worship would eventually be centralized at this location (Deuteronomy 12:8-11), so he ordered the first of many sacrifices to come at this newly instituted Temple site.

22:1 This is the climactic ending of the census episode. The discovery of the central, permanent place of Israel's worship was a dramatic and glorious event. It represented God resting with his people in the Promised Land (Joshua 23:1). The chronicler's message was clear: The people must reestablish the Temple in Jerusalem after the Exile. It is also a foreshadowing of the deeper reality of Christ inhabiting His people "in these final days" (Hebrews 1:1-2), and it is symbolic of God being fully with His people in the age to come (Revelation 21:3, 22).

PREPARATIONS FOR THE TEMPLE

2So David gave orders to call together the foreigners living in Israel, and he assigned
them the task of preparing finished stone for building the Temple of God. 3David pro-
vided large amounts of iron for the nails that would be needed for the doors in the gates
and for the clamps, and he gave more bronze than could be weighed. 4He also provided
innumerable cedar logs, for the men of Tyre and Sidon had brought vast amounts of ce-
dar to David.
5David said, "My son Solomon is still young and inexperienced. And since the Temple
to be built for the LORD must be a magnificent structure, famous and glorious throughout
the world, I will begin making preparations for it now." So David collected vast amounts of
building materials before his death.
6Then David sent for his son Solomon and instructed him to build a Temple for the LORD,
the God of Israel. 7"My son, I wanted to build a Temple to honor the name of the LORD my
God," David told him. 8"But the LORD said to me, 'You have killed many men in the battles
you have fought. And since you have shed so much blood in My sight, you will not be the
one to build a Temple to honor My name. 9But you will have a son who will be a man of
peace. I will give him peace with his enemies in all the surrounding lands. His name will be
Solomon,* and I will give peace and quiet to Israel during his reign. 10He is the one who
will build a Temple to honor My name. He will be My son, and I will be his father. And I will
secure the throne of his kingdom over Israel forever.'
11"Now, my son, may the LORD be with you and give you success as you follow His direc-
tions in building the Temple of the LORD your God. 12And may the LORD give you wisdom
and understanding, that you may obey the Law of the LORD your God as you rule over Isra-
el. 13For you will be successful if you carefully obey the decrees and regulations that the
LORD gave to Israel through Moses. Be strong and courageous; do not be afraid or lose
heart!

22:2 1 Kgs 5:17-18; 9:20-21; 2 Chr 2:17-18
22:4 1 Kgs 5:6-10
22:5 1 Kgs 3:7; 1 Chr 29:1
22:7 2 Sam 7:2-3; 1 Chr 17:1-2
22:8 1 Chr 28:3
22:9 2 Sam 12:24-25; 1 Kgs 4:20, 25
22:10 2 Sam 7:13; 1 Chr 17:12
22:11 1 Chr 22:16
22:12 1 Kgs 3:9-12; 2 Chr 1:10
22:13 Josh 1:6-9; 1 Chr 28:7

22:9 *Solomon* sounds like and is probably derived from the Hebrew word for "peace."

22:2-19 The text implies that David immediately and decisively went about the task of Temple preparation after discovering the Temple site. Chapter 22 is basically a summary of the rest of 1 Chronicles, which details what David did, his counsel and commission to Solomon, and the materials he gathered for the Temple.

22:2 Foreigners in David's day were conscripted to cut stone (2 Chronicles 2:7; 8:7-10; 1 Kings 5:13-18). This set a precedent for the chronicler's audience, who were surrounded by foreigners in postexilic Israel.

22:3-4 The chronicler may be using hyperbole again (see note on 1 Chronicles 21:5) to create a sense of wonder and astonishment in his readers. In this way they would be encouraged to gather many supplies in their day.

22:4 Recall that the Phoenician King Hiram of Tyre was David's ally (1 Chronicles 14:1) and would continue to be an ally to Solomon (1 Kings 5:1-12).

22:5 This verse is better translated "David had said," showing that he likely said this before he began gathering materials. Commenting to himself, David realized that the Temple would require massive amounts of fine materials and that he must be the one to make the preparations, or else Solomon would not succeed. The grandness of Solomon's Temple would later be compared to the lesser Temple foundation built by Zerubbabel (Ezra 3:12-13). The chronicler was pushing his audience to build a grand Temple in their day, no matter how much the effort cost.

▸ SALVATION

22:5 Fathers and sons. What father doesn't want his son to succeed? David wanted to help his young son Solomon in his first kingly task. He gathered the materials and workmen who would build the Temple that God required. He also ordered all the leaders to obey Solomon in the vast building project. But then David stopped—he didn't do the job for Solomon. He simply gave him a good start. Fathers, don't take away the ability of your children to succeed by doing tasks for them. Love them, prepare them, but then let them go. God will be with them. (***See Salvation***> *Our Need*> *Sinful*> *Influence of father,* TopicGuide page A22.)

22:8-10 A man of war cannot build a house of peace. The Temple was the place where God lived among His people and where eventually all the nations were to come (Psalm 96; 102:12-22; 117; Isaiah 2:2-4). The idea that a man of war like David would build a temple in a city whose name is rooted in the Hebrew word for "peace" created a tension. God resolved that Solomon, whose name is also rooted in the Hebrew word for "peace," would be the one to build such a monument to peace. Christ came as a man of peace (Isaiah 9:6; Luke 2:14; 4:18-19), but will come again as a warrior (Isaiah 61:2; Revelation 19:11-21), signaling that there is a time for peace and war in God's ways.

22:12-13 David's advice to Solomon is reminiscent of God's charge to Joshua (Joshua 1:1-9). The chronicler needed God's people in his day to be strong and courageous, too.

[14]"I have worked hard to provide materials for building the Temple of the LORD—nearly
4,000 tons of gold, 40,000 tons of silver,* and so much iron and bronze that it cannot be
weighed. I have also gathered timber and stone for the walls, though you may need to
add more. [15]You have a large number of skilled stonemasons and carpenters and crafts-
men of every kind. [16]You have expert goldsmiths and silversmiths and workers of bronze
and iron. Now begin the work, and may the LORD be with you!"

[17]Then David ordered all the leaders of Israel to assist Solomon in this project. [18]"The
LORD your God is with you," he declared. "He has given you peace with the surrounding
nations. He has handed them over to me, and they are now subject to the LORD and His
people. [19]Now seek the LORD your God with all your heart and soul. Build the sanctuary of
the LORD God so that you can bring the Ark of the LORD's Covenant and the holy vessels of
God into the Temple built to honor the LORD's name."

22:14 1 Chr 22:3; 29:4
22:16 1 Chr 22:11
22:17 1 Chr 28:1-6
22:18 1 Chr 22:9; 23:25
22:19 1 Kgs 8:6, 21; 1 Chr 28:9; 2 Chr 5:7

DUTIES OF THE LEVITES

23 When David was an old man, he appointed his son Solomon to be king over Isra-
el. [2]David summoned all the leaders of Israel, together with the priests and Le-
vites. [3]All the Levites who were thirty years old or older were counted, and the total came
to 38,000. [4]Then David said, "From all the Levites, 24,000 will supervise the work at the
Temple of the LORD. Another 6,000 will serve as officials and judges. [5]Another 4,000 will
work as gatekeepers, and 4,000 will praise the LORD with the musical instruments I have
made." [6]Then David divided the Levites into divisions named after the clans descended
from the three sons of Levi—Gershon, Kohath, and Merari.

THE GERSHONITES

[7]The Gershonite family units were defined by their lines of descent from Libni* and
Shimei, the sons of Gershon. [8]Three of the descendants of Libni were Jehiel (the
family leader), Zetham, and Joel. [9]These were the leaders of the family of Libni.

23:1 1 Chr 28:5; 29:22, 28
23:3 Num 4:3-49; 1 Chr 23:24
23:4 1 Chr 26:29; Ezra 3:8-9
23:5 1 Chr 15:16
23:6 1 Chr 6:1

22:14 Hebrew *100,000 talents* [3,400 metric tons] *of gold, 1,000,000 talents* [34,000 metric tons] *of silver.* 23:7 Hebrew *Ladan* (also in 23:8, 9), a variant spelling of Libni; compare 6:17.

22:14 The amounts of these precious metals are enormous and are another case of intentional exaggeration by the chronicler to show that David provided much of the Temple materials (see note on 22:3-4). Solomon's annual income was only 25 tons of gold (1 Kings 10:14).

22:17-19 By asking for their help, David obtains assistance for Solomon and a "buy-in" on this project from the leaders of Israel. He was rather overt about the reason they were blessed with this opportunity—because he had conquered all the surrounding enemies! This political appeal is combined with the fact that Israel had inherited their rest, and God had designated the place where He would dwell permanently (Deuteronomy 12:8-11). The chronicler is using politics here, too, in order to inspire the leaders and people of his day to seek the Lord God with all their heart. Whoever opposed the efforts to rebuild the Temple opposed King David's orders.

23:1 The record of this coronation ceremony extends from 23:1–29:25. The first section provides a summary of David's appointees (1 Chronicles 23:2–27:34). The second section records what happened at the assembly (1 Chronicles 28:1–29:25). The coronation was the last great assembly under David's reign and was likely the same event reported in 1 Kings 1:38-53.

23:3 This census was acceptable because it was done for the purpose of organizing the work of the Temple—not to number the fighting men out of self-reliance (1 Chronicles 21:1-3). The unusually large number of Levites can be explained by translating the text "38 divisions" (see notes on 12:20 and 21:5). Compare the 4,000 musicians (1 Chronicles 23:5) with "288 in all" (1 Chronicles 25:7).

23:4-5 The verses that follow detail the divisions of Levites that David established here: "24 divisions" of Temple supervisors (23:6–24:31), "6 divisions" of officials and judges (26:20-32), "4 divisions" of gatekeepers (26:1-19), and "4 divisions" of singers and musicians (25:1-31).

23:6–24:31 This section regarding Levites and priests who worked closely together is further divided into the descendents of Levi (1 Chronicles 23:6-27), Levites who worked closely with the priests (1 Chronicles 23:28-32), the priests themselves (1 Chronicles 24:1-19), and another list of Levites (1 Chronicles 24:20-31).

23:6-23 These three clans were mentioned during the transportation of the Ark (15:5-7). Traditionally they were charged with attending to the worship of God (Numbers 3:5-39), and the Kohathites were usually given special duties. Though many of the names listed here are not in the chronicler's genealogies (chapter 6), remember that it is not uncommon for genealogies in the Bible to skip generations. The point the chronicler is making here is that all the Levitical clans took part in the work of the Temple, and their representatives supported the transfer of the kingship to Solomon.

Three of the descendants of Shimei were Shelomoth, Haziel, and Haran. 10Four other
descendants of Shimei were Jahath, Ziza,* Jeush, and Beriah. 11Jahath was the family
leader, and Ziza was next. Jeush and Beriah were counted as a single family because
neither had many sons.

THE KOHATHITES

23:13 12Four of the descendants of Kohath were Amram, Izhar, Hebron, and Uzziel.
Exod 6:20; 28:1; 13The sons of Amram were Aaron and Moses. Aaron and his descendants were set
30:6-10 apart to dedicate the most holy things, to offer sacrifices in the LORD's presence, to
serve the LORD, and to pronounce blessings in His name forever.
23:14 Deut 33:1 14As for Moses, the man of God, his sons were included with the tribe of Levi.
15The sons of Moses were Gershom and Eliezer. 16The descendants of Gershom
included Shebuel, the family leader. 17Eliezer had only one son, Rehabiah, the family
leader. Rehabiah had numerous descendants.
18The descendants of Izhar included Shelomith, the family leader.
19The descendants of Hebron included Jeriah (the family leader), Amariah (the second),
Jahaziel (the third), and Jekameam (the fourth).
20The descendants of Uzziel included Micah (the family leader) and Isshiah (the second).

THE MERARITES

23:21 21The descendants of Merari included Mahli and Mushi.
1 Chr 6:19 The sons of Mahli were Eleazar and Kish. 22Eleazar died with no sons, only daughters.
His daughters married their cousins, the sons of Kish.
23Three of the descendants of Mushi were Mahli, Eder, and Jerimoth.

23:24 24These were the descendants of Levi by clans, the leaders of their family groups, regis-
Num 10:17, 21 tered carefully by name. Each had to be twenty years old or older to qualify for service in
1 Chr 23:3 the house of the LORD. 25For David said, "The LORD, the God of Israel, has given us peace,
23:25 1 Chr 22:18 and He will always live in Jerusalem. 26Now the Levites will no longer need to carry the
23:26 Tabernacle and its furnishings from place to place." 27In accordance with David's final in-
Num 4:5, 15; 7:9 structions, all the Levites twenty years old or older were registered for service.
Deut 10:8 28The work of the Levites was to assist the priests, the descendants of Aaron, as they
served at the house of the LORD. They also took care of the courtyards and side rooms,
helped perform the ceremonies of purification, and served in many other ways in the
23:29 house of God. 29They were in charge of the sacred bread that was set out on the table, the
Lev 6:20-21; choice flour for the grain offerings, the wafers made without yeast, the cakes cooked in ol-
19:35-36; 24:5-9 1 Chr 9:29, 32 ive oil, and the other mixed breads. They were also responsible to check all the weights
and measures. 30And each morning and evening they stood before the LORD to sing songs
23:31 of thanks and praise to Him. 31They assisted with the burnt offerings that were presented
Lev 23:2-4 to the LORD on Sabbath days, at new moon celebrations, and at all the appointed festivals.
Isa 1:13-14 The required number of Levites served in the LORD's presence at all times, following all the
procedures they had been given.

23:10 As in Greek version and Latin Vulgate (see also 23:11); Hebrew reads *Zina.*

23:24-27 The chronicler points out that at some point later, the king changed the minimum registration age from 30 (1 Chronicles 23:3) as outlined by Moses (Numbers 4:3) to 20 years old. While there was no need for Levites to carry the Tabernacle and utensils, the Levitical duties no doubt expanded when the Ark was placed in Jerusalem because there were now two worship sites. The chronicler mentions "David's final instructions" to establish Levitical policy in his day.

23:28-32 The Levites who helped the priests did a variety of Temple service duties. For a description of the Temple and its furnishings, refer to 2 Chronicles 3–4. The subordination of the Levites under the priests is an important issue to the chronicler. After the Exile, disagreements arose over who would be in charge of Israel's worship duties. Should it be Joshua (the returning high priest) and his Zadokite relatives (who were descendants of Aaron), or other prominent Levites? The chronicler, who follows the prophet Ezekiel (Ezekiel 40:46; 44:10-16; 48:11), was making it clear that the Zadokite line had been set apart especially for this task (1 Chronicles 23:13; 24:1-3; 29:22). For background on Zadok, see the note on 1 Chronicles 15:11.

32 And so, under the supervision of the priests, the Levites watched over the Tabernacle 23:32
and the Temple* and faithfully carried out their duties of service at the house of the LORD. Num 1:53; 3:6-9, 38

DUTIES OF THE PRIESTS

24 This is how Aaron's descendants, the priests, were divided into groups for ser- 24:1
vice. The sons of Aaron were Nadab, Abihu, Eleazar, and Ithamar. 2 But Nadab Exod 6:23
and Abihu died before their father, and they had no sons. So only Eleazar and Ithamar 24:2
were left to carry on as priests. Lev 10:1-2

3 With the help of Zadok, who was a descendant of Eleazar, and of Ahimelech, who was
a descendant of Ithamar, David divided Aaron's descendants into groups according to
their various duties. 4 Eleazar's descendants were divided into sixteen groups and Itha-
mar's into eight, for there were more family leaders among the descendants of Eleazar.

5 All tasks were assigned to the various groups by means of sacred lots so that no prefer- 24:5
ence would be shown, for there were many qualified officials serving God in the sanctuary 1 Chr 24:31
from among the descendants of both Eleazar and Ithamar. 6 Shemaiah son of Nethanel, a
Levite, acted as secretary and wrote down the names and assignments in the presence of 24:6
the king, the officials, Zadok the priest, Ahimelech son of Abiathar, and the family leaders 1 Chr 18:16
of the priests and Levites. The descendants of Eleazar and Ithamar took turns casting lots.

7 The first lot fell to Jehoiarib. 24:7
The second lot fell to Jedaiah. Neh 12:6
8 The third lot fell to Harim.
The fourth lot fell to Seorim.
9 The fifth lot fell to Malkijah.
The sixth lot fell to Mijamin.
10 The seventh lot fell to Hakkoz. 24:10
The eighth lot fell to Abijah. Neh 12:4
11 The ninth lot fell to Jeshua. Luke 1:5
The tenth lot fell to Shecaniah.
12 The eleventh lot fell to Eliashib.
The twelfth lot fell to Jakim.
13 The thirteenth lot fell to Huppah.
The fourteenth lot fell to Jeshebeab.
14 The fifteenth lot fell to Bilgah.
The sixteenth lot fell to Immer.
15 The seventeenth lot fell to Hezir.
The eighteenth lot fell to Happizzez.
16 The nineteenth lot fell to Pethahiah.
The twentieth lot fell to Jehezkel.
17 The twenty-first lot fell to Jakin.
The twenty-second lot fell to Gamul.
18 The twenty-third lot fell to Delaiah.
The twenty-fourth lot fell to Maaziah.

23:32 Hebrew *the Tent of Meeting and the sanctuary.*

24:2 Nadab and Abihu died during Moses' time for presenting "the wrong kind of fire, different than [the Lord] commanded" in Leviticus 10:1-3 and Numbers 3:2-4.

24:3-6 Eleazer had twice as many descendants as Ithamar, but his family was not twice as powerful; the duties of the priests were determined by sacred lot, not by family size. The chronicler was meticulous in his recording of this event so that his audience would know that God ordained the division of priestly duties and that they were free from human prejudice.

24:7-18 A regular annual rotation of 24 priestly families was established to perform duties at the Temple (see Luke 1:8-9). These divisions corresponded to the rotating 24 Levitical "divisions" (1 Chronicles 23:4-6), 24 musician clans (1 Chronicles 25:9-31), and 12 army "divisions" (1 Chronicles 27:1-15).

19 Each group carried out its appointed duties in the house of the LORD according to the
procedures established by their ancestor Aaron in obedience to the commands of the
LORD, the God of Israel.

FAMILY LEADERS AMONG THE LEVITES

20 These were the other family leaders descended from Levi:

From the descendants of Amram, the leader was Shebuel.*
From the descendants of Shebuel, the leader was Jehdeiah.
21 From the descendants of Rehabiah, the leader was Isshiah.
22 From the descendants of Izhar, the leader was Shelomith.*
From the descendants of Shelomith, the leader was Jahath.
24:23 1 Chr 23:19 23 From the descendants of Hebron, Jeriah was the leader,* Amariah was second,
Jahaziel was third, and Jekameam was fourth.
24 From the descendants of Uzziel, the leader was Micah.
From the descendants of Micah, the leader was Shamir, 25 along with Isshiah, the
brother of Micah.
From the descendants of Isshiah, the leader was Zechariah.
26 From the descendants of Merari, the leaders were Mahli and Mushi.
From the descendants of Jaaziah, the leader was Beno.
27 From the descendants of Merari through Jaaziah, the leaders were Beno, Shoham,
Zaccur, and Ibri.
28 From the descendants of Mahli, the leader was Eleazar, though he had no sons.
29 From the descendants of Kish, the leader was Jerahmeel.
30 From the descendants of Mushi, the leaders were Mahli, Eder, and Jerimoth.

24:31 These were the descendants of Levi in their various families. 31 Like the descendants of
1 Chr 24:5-6 Aaron, they were assigned to their duties by means of sacred lots, without regard to age or
rank. Lots were drawn in the presence of King David, Zadok, Ahimelech, and the family
leaders of the priests and the Levites.

DUTIES OF THE MUSICIANS

25:1 2 Kgs 3:15 1 Chr 6:33, 39; 15:16 **25** David and the army commanders then appointed men from the families of
Asaph, Heman, and Jeduthun to proclaim God's messages to the accompani-
ment of lyres, harps, and cymbals. Here is a list of their names and their work:

2 From the sons of Asaph, there were Zaccur, Joseph, Nethaniah, and Asarelah. They
worked under the direction of their father, Asaph, who proclaimed God's messages
by the king's orders.
25:3 3 From the sons of Jeduthun, there were Gedaliah, Zeri, Jeshaiah, Shimei,* Hashabiah,
1 Chr 16:41-42 and Mattithiah, six in all. They worked under the direction of their father, Jeduthun,

24:20 Hebrew *Shubael* (also in 24:20b), a variant spelling of Shebuel; compare 23:16 and 26:24. 24:22 Hebrew *Shelomoth* (also in 24:22b), a variant spelling of Shelomith; compare 23:18. 24:23 Hebrew *From the descendants of Jeriah;* compare 23:19. 25:3 As in one Hebrew manuscript and some Greek manuscripts (see also 25:17); most Hebrew manuscripts lack *Shimei*.

24:20-31 These other Levites were clearly connected with the Levites that worked closely with the priests, because some names are the same. However, some names are from the next generation. These details and the Levites' assignment by sacred lots likely resolved disputes over equality of worship duties in the chronicler's day.

25:1-5 The commanders of the army assisted David in appointing musicians, since Levitical music was also performed in battle (Joshua 6:4-20; Judges 7:17-20; 2 Chronicles 20:22, 27-28). These Levites also prophesied with music (1 Chronicles 25:3; 2 Chronicles 20:14; 35:15), a practice that has other precedents in Scripture (1 Samuel 10:5; 2 Kings 3:15). Heman is actually called the king's seer (1 Chronicles 25:5), as is Jeduthun (2 Chronicles 35:15).

who proclaimed God's messages to the accompaniment of the lyre, offering thanks
and praise to the LORD.
4 From the sons of Heman, there were Bukkiah, Mattaniah, Uzziel, Shubael,* Jerimoth, **25:4**
Hananiah, Hanani, Eliathah, Giddalti, Romamti-ezer, Joshbekashah, Mallothi, Hothir, 2 Sam 24:11
and Mahazioth. 5 All these were the sons of Heman, the king's seer, for God had
honored him with fourteen sons and three daughters.

6 All these men were under the direction of their fathers as they made music at the **25:6**
house of the LORD. Their responsibilities included the playing of cymbals, harps, and lyres 1 Chr 15:16, 19
at the house of God. Asaph, Jeduthun, and Heman reported directly to the king. 7 They and
their families were all trained in making music before the LORD, and each of them—288 in
all—was an accomplished musician. 8 The musicians were appointed to their term of ser- **25:8**
vice by means of sacred lots, without regard to whether they were young or old, teacher or 1 Chr 26:13
student.

9 The first lot fell to Joseph of the Asaph clan and twelve of his sons and relatives.*
The second lot fell to Gedaliah and twelve of his sons and relatives.
10 The third lot fell to Zaccur and twelve of his sons and relatives.
11 The fourth lot fell to Zeri* and twelve of his sons and relatives.
12 The fifth lot fell to Nethaniah and twelve of his sons and relatives.
13 The sixth lot fell to Bukkiah and twelve of his sons and relatives.
14 The seventh lot fell to Asarelah* and twelve of his sons and relatives.
15 The eighth lot fell to Jeshaiah and twelve of his sons and relatives.
16 The ninth lot fell to Mattaniah and twelve of his sons and relatives.
17 The tenth lot fell to Shimei and twelve of his sons and relatives.
18 The eleventh lot fell to Uzziel* and twelve of his sons and relatives.
19 The twelfth lot fell to Hashabiah and twelve of his sons and relatives.
20 The thirteenth lot fell to Shubael and twelve of his sons and relatives.
21 The fourteenth lot fell to Mattithiah and twelve of his sons and relatives.
22 The fifteenth lot fell to Jerimoth* and twelve of his sons and relatives.
23 The sixteenth lot fell to Hananiah and twelve of his sons and relatives.
24 The seventeenth lot fell to Joshbekashah* and twelve of his sons and relatives.
25 The eighteenth lot fell to Hanani and twelve of his sons and relatives.
26 The nineteenth lot fell to Mallothi and twelve of his sons and relatives.
27 The twentieth lot fell to Eliathah and twelve of his sons and relatives.
28 The twenty-first lot fell to Hothir and twelve of his sons and relatives.
29 The twenty-second lot fell to Giddalti and twelve of his sons and relatives.
30 The twenty-third lot fell to Mahazioth and twelve of his sons and relatives.
31 The twenty-fourth lot fell to Romamti-ezer and twelve of his sons and relatives. **25:31** 1 Chr 9:33

25:4 Hebrew *Shebuel,* a variant spelling of Shubael; compare 25:20. 25:9 As in Greek version; Hebrew lacks *and twelve of his sons and relatives.* 25:11 Hebrew *Izri,* a variant spelling of Zeri; compare 25:3. 25:14 Hebrew *Jesarelah,* a variant spelling of Asarelah; compare 25:2. 25:18 Hebrew *Azarel,* a variant spelling of Uzziel; compare 25:4. 25:22 Hebrew *Jeremoth,* a variant spelling of Jerimoth; compare 25:4. 25:24 Hebrew *Joshbekasha,* a variant spelling of Joshbekashah; compare 25:4.

25:6-7 Levitical musicians were able to devote their whole lives to worshiping God through music, so many became very skillful in their craft (1 Chronicles 15:22; 2 Chronicles 34:12). As apprentices, Levites had to memorize vast amounts of sacred music and liturgy (Nehemiah 11:23). After the return from exile, they lived together in communities when they were not on duty (Nehemiah 12:29). The Levite musicians were on a rotation of serving in the Temple; during times of service, the Levites would remain and live in the Temple around the clock (1 Chronicles 9:33; 25:8). The Levites were considered a critical part of Temple worship.

25:8-31 This is not just a record of names. The designation of 24 clan divisions by sacred lot set forth godly patterns for the post-exilic worship community. The chronicler emphasizes that reformation of a proper music ministry is key to restoring proper worship.

DUTIES OF THE GATEKEEPERS

26 These are the divisions of the gatekeepers:

From the Korahites, there was Meshelemiah son of Kore, of the family of Abiasaph.*

2 The sons of Meshelemiah were Zechariah (the oldest), Jediael (the second), Zebadiah (the third), Jathniel (the fourth), 3 Elam (the fifth), Jehohanan (the sixth), and Eliehoenai (the seventh).

4 The sons of Obed-edom, also gatekeepers, were Shemaiah (the oldest), Jehozabad (the second), Joah (the third), Sacar (the fourth), Nethanel (the fifth), 5 Ammiel (the sixth), Issachar (the seventh), and Peullethai (the eighth). God had richly blessed Obed-edom.

6 Obed-edom's son Shemaiah had sons with great ability who earned positions of great authority in the clan. 7 Their names were Othni, Rephael, Obed, and Elzabad. Their relatives, Elihu and Semakiah, were also very capable men.

8 All of these descendants of Obed-edom, including their sons and grandsons—sixty-two of them in all—were very capable men, well qualified for their work.

9 Meshelemiah's eighteen sons and relatives were also very capable men.

26:10 1 Chr 16:38

10 Hosah, of the Merari clan, appointed Shimri as the leader among his sons, though he was not the oldest. 11 His other sons included Hilkiah (the second), Tebaliah (the third), and Zechariah (the fourth). Hosah's sons and relatives, who served as gatekeepers, numbered thirteen in all.

26:13 1 Chr 24:5, 31; 25:8

12 These divisions of the gatekeepers were named for their family leaders, and like the other Levites, they served at the house of the LORD. 13 They were assigned by families for guard duty at the various gates, without regard to age or training, for it was all decided by means of sacred lots.

14 The responsibility for the east gate went to Meshelemiah* and his group. The north gate was assigned to his son Zechariah, a man of unusual wisdom. 15 The south gate went to Obed-edom, and his sons were put in charge of the storehouse. 16 Shuppim and Hosah were assigned the west gate and the gateway leading up to the Temple.* Guard duties were divided evenly. 17 Six Levites were assigned each day to the east gate, four to the north gate, four to the south gate, and two pairs at the storehouse. 18 Six were assigned each day to the west gate, four to the gateway leading up to the Temple, and two to the courtyard.*

19 These were the divisions of the gatekeepers from the clans of Korah and Merari.

TREASURERS AND OTHER OFFICIALS

26:20 1 Chr 26:22, 24; 28:12

20 Other Levites, led by Ahijah, were in charge of the treasuries of the house of God and the treasuries of the gifts dedicated to the LORD. 21 From the family of Libni* in the clan of Gershon, Jehiel* was the leader. 22 The sons of Jehiel, Zetham and his brother Joel, were in charge of the treasuries of the house of the LORD.

23 These are the leaders that descended from Amram, Izhar, Hebron, and Uzziel:

26:1 As in Greek version (see also Exod 6:24); Hebrew reads *Asaph.* **26:14** Hebrew *Shelemiah,* a variant spelling of Meshelemiah; compare 26:2. **26:16** Or *the gate of Shalleketh on the upper road* (also in 26:18). The meaning of the Hebrew is uncertain. **26:18** Or *the colonnade.* The meaning of the Hebrew is uncertain. **26:21a** Hebrew *Ladan,* a variant spelling of Libni; compare 6:17. **26:21b** Hebrew *Jehieli* (also in 26:22), a variant spelling of Jehiel; compare 23:8.

26:1-13 Gatekeepers were assigned by sacred lots as well. The two family divisions of Korahites and Merarites were assigned evenly among the different gates and Temple areas. This Obed-edom is the same one who kept the Ark for a time (13:13-14).

26:14-19 This gate description is similar to Ezekiel's description of the rebuilt Temple (Ezekiel 40). These 24 guards enforced religious restrictions at the Temple and protected the Temple's physical edifice. In addition to the duties described here, the Levites who returned from exile were in charge of equipment, treasuries, worship utensils, furnishings, and food supplies (1 Chronicles 9:23-29).

26:20-28 In the tradition of Moses' son Gershom, Libni and other families kept the treasuries of the Temple. The treasury contained the vast resources that David collected for the future Temple: plunder from battle, relics from famous Israelites, and any valuable items sanctified for Temple use.

24From the clan of Amram, Shebuel was a descendant of Gershom son of Moses. He
was the chief officer of the treasuries. 25His relatives through Eliezer were Rehabiah,
Jeshaiah, Joram, Zicri, and Shelomoth.
26Shelomoth and his relatives were in charge of the treasuries containing the gifts 26:26
that King David, the family leaders, and the generals and captains* and other officers 2 Sam 8:11
of the army had dedicated to the LORD. 27These men dedicated some of the plunder
they had gained in battle to maintain the house of the LORD. 28Shelomoth* and his
relatives also cared for the gifts dedicated to the LORD by Samuel the seer, Saul son
of Kish, Abner son of Ner, and Joab son of Zeruiah. All the other dedicated gifts were
in their care, too.
29From the clan of Izhar came Kenaniah. He and his sons were given administrative 26:29
responsibilities* over Israel as officials and judges. 1 Chr 23:4
30From the clan of Hebron came Hashabiah. He and his relatives—1,700 capable men— 26:30
were put in charge of the Israelite lands west of the Jordan River. They were 1 Chr 27:17
responsible for all matters related to the things of the LORD and the service of the
king in that area.
31Also from the clan of Hebron came Jeriah,* who was the leader of the Hebronites 26:31
according to the genealogical records. (In the fortieth year of David's reign, a search 1 Chr 23:19
was made in the records, and capable men from the clan of Hebron were found at
Jazer in the land of Gilead.) 32There were 2,700 capable men among the relatives of
Jeriah. King David sent them to the east side of the Jordan River and put them in
charge of the tribes of Reuben and Gad and the half-tribe of Manasseh. They were
responsible for all matters related to God and to the king.

MILITARY COMMANDERS AND DIVISIONS

27 This is the list of Israelite generals and captains,* and their officers, who served
the king by supervising the army divisions that were on duty each month of the
year. Each division served for one month and had 24,000 troops.
2Jashobeam son of Zabdiel was commander of the first division of 24,000 troops, 27:2
which was on duty during the first month. 3He was a descendant of Perez and was in 2 Sam 23:8
charge of all the army officers for the first month. 1 Chr 11:11-31

26:26 Hebrew *the commanders of thousands and of hundreds.* 26:28 Hebrew *Shelomith,* a variant spelling of Shelomoth. 26:29 Or *were given outside work;* or *were given work away from the Temple area.* 26:31 Hebrew *Jerijah,* a variant spelling of Jeriah; compare 23:19. 27:1 Hebrew *commanders of thousands and of hundreds.*

▸ WORSHIP

26:27 Offerings to God from our excess. As an act of gratitude, God's people give out of their plenty, perhaps to missionaries, local charities, or their local church. God has blessed us so that we might be a blessing to others. But no matter how much we give, there are always people in need around us—how do we decide when to stop giving? Set specific goals for your gifts beyond your regular tithe to your church—and increase them as the Lord gives you ability. Stretch yourself, weaning yourself and your family from the desire to upgrade your lifestyle. Give liberally of your time, your prayers, and your finances to all who need it, for God has given so much to you. (***See Worship****> NT> Offerings> Be faithful with riches,* TopicGuide page A31.)

26:29-32 Other Levites were appointed throughout Israel to teach and judge (see Deuteronomy 33:10; 17:9; 2 Chronicles 19:10). The wide range of duties performed by the Levites in David's day set the pattern for post-exilic Israel.

26:32 The word translated "thousand" in this context may also mean a division or group, in this case two groups with 700 each. The chronicler may also have been using hyperbole to demonstrate the over-abundance of qualified magistrates. See notes on 12:20 and 21:5 for more discussions on the difficulties in translating larger numbers in the Old Testament.

27:1-34 This chapter is concerned with the military and civilian leadership present at Solomon's coronation. The numerical parallels of 12 army divisions, 12 tribal leaders, and 12 overseers of royal property help make the chronicler's point: The leadership of all Israel supported the transfer of authority to Solomon and the plans to build the Temple.

27:1-15 The militia of David's fighting days was now reorganized as a standing army. A rotation of men was on call every month. These leaders mentioned here are heads of families, probably responsible for the activation of troops. Joab was the general of the army (1 Chronicles 27:34). Under him were commanders of "thousands" and officers of "hundreds." Again we are faced with the translation problem of oddly large military numbers. There is an apparent total of more than 288,000 trained fighting men in Israel. But the word "thousand" is probably a military term for a group of soldiers less than a thousand men (see note on 12:20). For each division, instead of "24,000 troops," a better translation might be, "He had 24 units."

[4]Dodai, a descendant of Ahoah, was commander of the second division of
24,000 troops, which was on duty during the second month. Mikloth was his
chief officer.
[5]Benaiah son of Jehoiada the priest was commander of the third division of 24,000
troops, which was on duty during the third month. [6]This was the Benaiah who
commanded David's elite military group known as the Thirty. His son Ammizabad
was his chief officer.
[7]Asahel, the brother of Joab, was commander of the fourth division of 24,000 troops,
which was on duty during the fourth month. Asahel was succeeded by his son
Zebadiah.
[8]Shammah* the Izrahite was commander of the fifth division of 24,000 troops, which
was on duty during the fifth month.
[9]Ira son of Ikkesh from Tekoa was commander of the sixth division of 24,000 troops,
which was on duty during the sixth month.
[10]Helez, a descendant of Ephraim from Pelon, was commander of the seventh division
of 24,000 troops, which was on duty during the seventh month.
[11]Sibbecai, a descendant of Zerah from Hushah, was commander of the eighth division
of 24,000 troops, which was on duty during the eighth month.
[12]Abiezer from Anathoth in the territory of Benjamin was commander of the ninth
division of 24,000 troops, which was on duty during the ninth month.
[13]Maharai, a descendant of Zerah from Netophah, was commander of the tenth division
of 24,000 troops, which was on duty during the tenth month.
[14]Benaiah from Pirathon in Ephraim was commander of the eleventh division of
24,000 troops, which was on duty during the eleventh month.
[15]Heled,* a descendant of Othniel from Netophah, was commander of the twelfth
division of 24,000 troops, which was on duty during the twelfth month.

LEADERS OF THE TRIBES

[16]The following were the tribes of Israel and their leaders:

Tribe	*Leader*
Reuben	Eliezer son of Zicri
Simeon	Shephatiah son of Maacah
[17] Levi	Hashabiah son of Kemuel
Aaron (the priests)	Zadok
[18] Judah	Elihu (a brother of David)
Issachar	Omri son of Michael
[19] Zebulun	Ishmaiah son of Obadiah
Naphtali	Jeremoth son of Azriel
[20] Ephraim	Hoshea son of Azaziah
Manasseh (west)	Joel son of Pedaiah
[21] Manasseh in Gilead (east)	Iddo son of Zechariah
Benjamin	Jaasiel son of Abner
[22] Dan	Azarel son of Jeroham

27:17 1 Chr 12:28

These were the leaders of the tribes of Israel.

27:8 Hebrew *Shamhuth,* a variant spelling of Shammah; compare 11:27 and 2 Sam 23:25. 27:15 Hebrew *Heldai,* a variant spelling of Heled; compare 11:30 and 2 Sam 23:29.

27:16-23 These leaders (literally, "chief officers") of Israel were probably royal appointees. Tribal leaders were not usually referred to in this way. Combined with the rest of the retinue, this chapter shows Israel growing into a centralized bureaucracy. Gad and Asher are not included in this list for unknown reasons. In an effort to maintain the ideal number 12, Aaron (a Levite) is listed separately, and Manasseh is listed twice, as the tribe is divided in half by the Jordan River.

23 When David took his census, he did not count those who were younger than twenty **27:23**
years of age, because the LORD had promised to make the Israelites as numerous as the stars 2 Sam 24:1
in heaven. 24 Joab son of Zeruiah began the census but never finished it because* the anger **27:24**
of God fell on Israel. The total number was never recorded in King David's official records. 2 Sam 24:12-15 1 Chr 21:1-7

OFFICIALS OF DAVID'S KINGDOM

25 Azmaveth son of Adiel was in charge of the palace treasuries.
Jonathan son of Uzziah was in charge of the regional treasuries throughout the towns, villages, and fortresses of Israel.
26 Ezri son of Kelub was in charge of the field workers who farmed the king's lands.
27 Shimei from Ramah was in charge of the king's vineyards.
Zabdi from Shepham was responsible for the grapes and the supplies of wine.
28 Baal-hanan from Geder was in charge of the king's olive groves and sycamore-fig trees in the foothills of Judah.* **27:28** 1 Kgs 10:27 2 Chr 1:15
Joash was responsible for the supplies of olive oil.
29 Shitrai from Sharon was in charge of the cattle on the Sharon Plain. **27:29**
Shaphat son of Adlai was responsible for the cattle in the valleys. 1 Chr 5:16
30 Obil the Ishmaelite was in charge of the camels.
Jehdeiah from Meronoth was in charge of the donkeys.
31 Jaziz the Hagrite was in charge of the king's flocks of sheep and goats. **27:31**
All these officials were overseers of King David's property. 1 Chr 5:10

32 Jonathan, David's uncle, was a wise counselor to the king, a man of great insight, and a
scribe. Jehiel the Hacmonite was responsible for teaching the king's sons. 33 Ahithophel was **27:33**
the royal adviser. Hushai the Arkite was the king's friend. 34 Ahithophel was succeeded by 2 Sam 15:12, 32, 37
Jehoiada son of Benaiah and by Abiathar. Joab was commander of the king's army. **27:34** 1 Kgs 1:7 1 Chr 11:6; 27:5

DAVID'S INSTRUCTIONS TO SOLOMON

28 David summoned all the officials of Israel to Jerusalem—the leaders of the tribes, **28:1**
the commanders of the army divisions, the other generals and captains,* the 1 Chr 11:10-47; 23:2; 27:1-31
overseers of the royal property and livestock, the palace officials, the mighty men, and all
the other brave warriors in the kingdom. 2 David rose to his feet and said: "My brothers and **28:2** 1 Chr 17:1-2 Ps 132:7 Isa 66:1

27:24 Or *never finished it, and yet.* 27:28 Hebrew *the Shephelah.* 28:1 Hebrew *the commanders of thousands and commanders of hundreds.*

27:23-24 Recalling the events in chapter 21, the chronicler must explain why he does not report the total population, which would normally be expected from a chronicle such as this.

27:25-34 Kings like David often had vast royal possessions and resources. Whether obtained by annexation, conquest, or cultivation, these resources must have been great and were managed by 12 officials.

27:33-34 Notice the chronicler is selectively choosing historical material to reinforce his point that all Israel supported this transition of power. He did not mention Absalom's rebellion, which occurred before Solomon came to the throne (2 Samuel 15–18). He also did not mention that Ahithophel betrayed David by helping Absalom and later hung himself in disgrace (2 Samuel 17:23). Hushai, David's friend, was a key player in bringing defeat to Absalom (2 Samuel 17:14).

28:1–29:22 Finally we witness the coronation ceremony of Solomon. This section consists of David's speech and charge to the people (28:2-8), his public charge to Solomon and the transfer of the Temple plans (28:9-20), an appeal for dedicatory contributions (29:1-5), the contributions made by the people (29:6-9), David's prayer of praise (29:10-19), the people's response of praise (29:20), and the next day's sacrifices (29:21-22).

28:1 Though David was still very much alive, this ceremony transferred power to Solomon and retained David as a sort of "executive king." Coregency was a common occurrence both in Israel and among the surrounding nations. A king would crown his son before he was incapacitated to ensure that the dynasty would continue as planned. Coregency explains why there appear to be overlapping reigns in the later accounts of the kings (2 Chronicles 27:8–28:1), and it also explains why Solomon was crowned again after David died (1 Chronicles 29:22-25).

28:2 The Ark of the Lord's covenant so symbolized God's presence that it was understood to be the footstool of God (2 Kings 19:15; Psalms 99:5; 132:7). God's glory was believed to dwell between the two cherubim (angels who attended to God) that were fashioned above the Ark (Exodus 25:22). Because of Christ (God incarnate), who "tabernacled among us" (a literal rending of John 1:14), we have access to God's holy presence (Matthew 27:51; Hebrews 9:11-12) and will one day live permanently in His presence (Revelation 11:15-19).

my people! It was my desire to build a temple where the Ark of the LORD's Covenant, God's
28:3 1 Chr 17:4; 22:8 footstool, could rest permanently. I made the necessary preparations for building it, [3]but
God said to me, 'You must not build a temple to honor My name, for you are a warrior and
have shed much blood.'
28:4 Gen 49:8-10 [4]"Yet the LORD, the God of Israel, has chosen me from among all my father's family to be
1 Sam 16:1-6 king over Israel forever. For He has chosen the tribe of Judah to rule, and from among the
1 Chr 5:2; 17:23, 27 families of Judah He chose my father's family. And from among my father's sons the LORD
28:5 was pleased to make me king over all Israel. [5]And from among my sons—for the LORD has
1 Chr 3:1-9; 14:3-7; 22:9-10 given me many—He chose Solomon to succeed me on the throne of Israel and to rule over
28:6 the LORD's kingdom. [6]He said to me, 'Your son Solomon will build My Temple and its court-
2 Sam 7:13-14 yards, for I have chosen him as My son, and I will be his father. [7]And if he continues to obey
28:7 My commands and regulations as he does now, I will make his kingdom last forever.'
1 Chr 22:13 [8]"So now, with God as our witness, and in the sight of all Israel—the LORD's assembly—I
give you this charge. Be careful to obey all the commands of the LORD your God, so that
you may continue to possess this good land and leave it to your children as a permanent
inheritance.
28:9 [9]"And Solomon, my son, learn to know the God of your ancestors intimately. Worship
1 Kgs 8:61 and serve Him with your whole heart and a willing mind. For the LORD sees every heart
2 Chr 15:2 Jer 29:13 and knows every plan and thought. If you seek Him, you will find Him. But if you forsake
28:10 Him, He will reject you forever. [10]So take this seriously. The LORD has chosen you to build a
1 Chr 22:13 Temple as His sanctuary. Be strong, and do the work."
28:11 [11]Then David gave Solomon the plans for the Temple and its surroundings, including the
Exod 25:17-22, 40 entry room, the storerooms, the upstairs rooms, the inner rooms, and the inner sanctuary—
28:12 which was the place of atonement. [12]David also gave Solomon all the plans he had in mind*
1 Chr 26:20, 28 for the courtyards of the LORD's Temple, the outside rooms, the treasuries, and the rooms for

28:12 Or *the plans of the spirit that was with him.*

28:3 See notes on 17:4-6 and 22:8.

28:4-6 This recalls promises of the Davidic Covenant in 17:10-14. The ceremony likely took place after Solomon had already been anointed king amidst an attempt by Adonijah to ascend first (1 Kings 1). The chronicler didn't mention these events; evidently, they did not serve the specific lessons he hoped his audience would learn from his writings.

28:7 Though the special relationship between God and the future king (Solomon, then his descendants) is forever, it is conditional (17:15-17; 2 Samuel 7:14-16; Psalm 89:30-34; 132:12). Solomon would succeed only if he obeyed the Lord.

28:8 David's charge was directed to all the people of Israel, Solomon included. David echoed the same charge God gave to the people in Deuteronomy before they entered the land (Deuteronomy 4:26-31, 40). This charge is even more significant for the people of Israel in the chronicler's day because it foresaw that Israel would be scattered in exile on account of their disobedience. But they would return to the Lord, and God would not abandon them (Deuteronomy 4:31). This is exactly what the people of God needed in the chronicler's day to motivate them to rebuild the Temple.

28:9 This moment overflows with dramatic tenderness, as David charges his son to have a deep, sincere, inward devotion to God. As one who had had a long, transparent walk with the Lord, David knew that one must live "coram Deo"—before the face of God, because God looks at the thoughts and intentions of the heart (Psalm 139:1; Jeremiah 11:20). This standard for assessing a person was how God, through Samuel, chose David from the beginning (1 Samuel 16:7).

▸ BIBLE

28:9 Seeking God. What does it mean to "seek God"? What could David mean, especially in light of Romans 3:11, which says that no one seeks after God? In this context, David seems to be contrasting faithfulness with unfaithfulness to God. If you seek God, David says, you will find Him waiting for you with open arms. But if you do not, that is, if you reject God, you will find judgment (Deuteronomy 4:29; 2 Chronicles 15:2; Jeremiah 29:12-14). Christians can seek God by studying His Word, by coming before Him in prayer, and by contemplating His works in this world. (***See Bible****> Unity> Kingdom of God> Seeking the Kingdom is highest priority,* TopicGuide page A11.)

28:10 Inscriptions from ancient temples at this time praised kings for their great victories and achievements, but David charged Solomon to build the Temple out of right motives: to glorify God, not Solomon.

28:11-19 David gave Solomon the plans for the Temple, which the Lord had given to David. This recalls Moses' plans for the Tabernacle, which followed both the pattern of the heavenly Tabernacle (Exodus 25:9) and Ezekiel's plans for the post-exilic Temple (Ezekiel 40:1–43:10).

28:11 The place of atonement is where God's wrath against sin is satisfied and the worshiper is cleansed of that sin (Romans 3:22-25; see notes on 1 Chronicles 21:7 and 21:18-19).

28:18 The Hebrew text here calls the Ark the LORD's "chariot." This imagery is drawn from earlier times when the Levites carried the Ark before the Israelite army into battle (Numbers 10:33-36; see also Psalm 18:10).

the gifts dedicated to the LORD. 13The king also gave Solomon the instructions concerning **28:13**
the work of the various divisions of priests and Levites in the Temple of the LORD. And he 1 Chr 23:6; 24:1
gave specifications for the items in the Temple that were to be used for worship.
14David gave instructions regarding how much gold and silver should be used to make
the items needed for service. 15He told Solomon the amount of gold needed for the gold **28:15**
lampstands and lamps, and the amount of silver for the silver lampstands and lamps, de- Exod 25:31
pending on how each would be used. 16He designated the amount of gold for the table on
which the Bread of the Presence would be placed and the amount of silver for other tables.
17David also designated the amount of gold for the solid gold meat hooks used to han-
dle the sacrificial meat and for the basins, pitchers, and dishes, as well as the amount of sil-
ver for every dish. 18He designated the amount of refined gold for the altar of incense. **28:18**
Finally, he gave him a plan for the LORD's "chariot"—the gold cherubim* whose wings were Exod 25:18-22; 30:1
stretched out over the Ark of the LORD's Covenant. 19"Every part of this plan," David told **28:19**
Solomon, "was given to me in writing from the hand of the LORD.*" 1 Chr 28:11-12
20Then David continued, "Be strong and courageous, and do the work. Don't be afraid or
discouraged, for the LORD God, my God, is with you. He will not fail you or forsake you. He **28:20** Josh 1:5
will see to it that all the work related to the Temple of the LORD is finished correctly. 21The 1 Chr 22:13
various divisions of priests and Levites will serve in the Temple of God. Others with skills of Heb 13:5
every kind will volunteer, and the officials and the entire nation are at your command." **28:21** Exod 35:25-35; 36:1-2

GIFTS FOR BUILDING THE TEMPLE

29 Then King David turned to the entire assembly and said, "My son Solomon,
whom God has clearly chosen as the next king of Israel, is still young and inexpe- **29:1** 1 Chr 22:5
rienced. The work ahead of him is enormous, for the Temple he will build is not for mere **29:2**
mortals—it is for the LORD God Himself! 2Using every resource at my command, I have 1 Chr 22:2-5
gathered as much as I could for building the Temple of my God. Now there is enough
gold, silver, bronze, iron, and wood, as well as great quantities of onyx, other precious
stones, costly jewels, and all kinds of fine stone and marble.
3"And now, because of my devotion to the Temple of my God, I am giving all of my
own private treasures of gold and silver to help in the construction. This is in addition to **29:4**
the building materials I have already collected for His holy Temple. 4I am donating more 1 Kgs 9:28 1 Chr 22:14

28:18 Hebrew *for the gold cherub chariot.* 28:19 Or *was written under the direction of the LORD.*

28:19 David specifically states that the Temple instructions were given to him "from the hand of the LORD." This is one of the clearest expressions of 2 Timothy 3:16—that all Scripture is inspired by God. This shows the chronicler's readers that David didn't just make all this up—these instructions came from God. And since David is the ideal king, they should follow God's instructions to rebuild according to the same patterns.

28:20 David returns to his charge to Solomon (some of which he had already done in private; see 1 Chronicles 22:11-14), using language that is strikingly similar to what God spoke to Joshua. Both Joshua and Solomon had large tasks to do. David was implying that building the Temple would be as tough as conquering the Promised Land (Joshua 1:6-9; 2 Chronicles 15:7; 32:7). It would not be an easy task, but God would be with Solomon. Therefore, Solomon just needed to be strong and courageous to do the work

▸ GOD

28:20 A God who doesn't quit. Solomon had a head start at finishing the Temple, but would he finish well? The writer of Chronicles assures Solomon that God would ensure that he accomplished this great task. Many times we aim to do our best at something, and we start out very well, but often we fail in the end. But the Christian life is not like that—even when we do our worst, God remains faithful. We may fail, but God will complete the work of salvation He began in us (Philippians 1:6). (***See God> God's Attributes> Faithful> His faithfulness endures,*** TopicGuide page A16.)

28:21 In this verse the chronicler implies that the people of post-exilic Israel should volunteer to join in the rebuilding of the Temple.

29:1-5 David was a good fund-raiser. His appeal here is backed with both state funds and his own funds, which most likely came from his past conquests (1 Chronicles 18:7-11). David's call for the people to contribute was persuasive and direct. This manner of making an appeal wasn't wrong; David was wise, and he simply knew how to motivate his people. Paul did some of the same kind of fund raising among the Jews in Jerusalem and the Gentiles in Asia Minor (Romans 15:25-29; 1 Corinthians 16:1-4; 2 Corinthians 9). As a leader, the ability to be effective with fund-raising campaigns can go far in accomplishing big projects for the Lord.

29:4 The large amounts of precious metals that David contributed from his own treasuries are enormous. Today, this amount of gold and silver is valued at over 1.6 billion dollars! While intentional exaggeration cannot be ruled out (see note on 12:14), the Temple needs were also enormous. Nevertheless, the chronicler is making the point that David had extreme enthusiasm for this landmark project.

TWO-YEAR-OLD MELODY HOPPED into the house after preschool, her eyes eagerly scanning the living room. Today was the day when Mommy and Daddy were going to set up the forty-gallon fresh-water aquarium. And there it was, bubbling and sparkling in the corner near the front window!

Melody hurried over to stare deep into the aquarium. A shimmering treasure chest lying on the bottom opened its lid all on its own. Seaweed swayed as angelfish and neon tetras flitted by.

Melody gazed at the fish for a few moments, awed at what she saw. The clean water in the tank was almost colorless. Then she turned to her mother, who was standing behind her, pointed at the angelfish, and said, "Mommy, those butterflies can swim."

Seeing life through the eyes of a toddler is an amazing experience. Everything looks bigger, brighter, scarier, and more wonderful. Toddlers don't take anything for granted—not the ant crawling on the sidewalk or the moon in the night sky or the shimmer on a bubble. What we don't even notice, they see, hear, taste, smell, and touch.

Sometimes we are also guilty of taking God for granted, as if we have lost the wonder of His majesty. When was the last time that some quality of God's magnificent character took your breath away? Have you thought about how He really is? About the height of His love for you? About the purity of His holiness?

More important, has the beauty of God's majesty transformed your daily life? Are you living in the radiance of God's presence moment by moment? Do other people see your awe of His majesty? First Chronicles 29:10-11 says, "O Lord, the God of our ancestor Israel, may You be praised forever and ever! Yours, O Lord, is the greatness, the power, the glory, the victory, and the majesty. . . . We adore You as the One who is over all things."

Praising God and exalting Him for His eternal attributes is an excellent way to rekindle the sense of God's majesty in your life. When you grasp the wonder of God's majesty, your life will be transformed. Paul writes about this process of transformation: "I plead with you to give your bodies to God because of all He has done for you. Let them be a living and holy sacrifice—the kind He will find acceptable. This is truly the way to worship Him" (Romans 12:1). As you are changed, others will see the gospel alive in you, and God's family will grow as a result.

than 112 tons of gold* from Ophir and 262 tons of refined silver* to be used for over-
laying the walls of the buildings 5and for the other gold and silver work to be done by
the craftsmen. Now then, who will follow my example and give offerings to the LORD
today?"

6Then the family leaders, the leaders of the tribes of Israel, the generals and captains 29:6
of the army,* and the king's administrative officers all gave willingly. 7For the construc- 1 Chr 27:1, 25; 28:1
tion of the Temple of God, they gave about 188 tons of gold,* 10,000 gold coins,*
375 tons of silver,* 675 tons of bronze,* and 3,750 tons of iron.* 8They also contributed 29:8
numerous precious stones, which were deposited in the treasury of the house of the 1 Chr 23:8
LORD under the care of Jehiel, a descendant of Gershon. 9The people rejoiced over the 29:9 1 Kgs 8:61
offerings, for they had given freely and wholeheartedly to the LORD, and King David was 2 Cor 9:7
filled with joy.

29:4a Hebrew *3,000 talents* [102 metric tons] *of gold.* 29:4b Hebrew *7,000 talents* [238 metric tons] *of silver.* 29:6 Hebrew *the commanders of thousands and commanders of hundreds.* 29:7a Hebrew *5,000 talents* [170 metric tons] *of gold.* 29:7b Hebrew *10,000 darics* [a Persian coin] *of gold,* about 185 pounds or 84 kilograms in weight. 29:7c Hebrew *10,000 talents* [340 metric tons] *of silver.* 29:7d Hebrew *18,000 talents* [612 metric tons] *of bronze.* 29:7e Hebrew *100,000 talents* [3,400 metric tons] *of iron.*

29:5 The Hebrew text literally reads that David asked who is willing to "fill his hands," or "consecrate himself" to the Lord. This implies that the actual giving of offerings was an act of consecration to God (performing ritual cleansings to be set apart for worship or service), teaching the chronicler's audience not to be satisfied with half-hearted devotion. Consecration, which is necessary for proper worship, appears often in Chronicles (1 Chronicles 15:12; 23:13; 2 Chronicles 5:11; 7:7; 26:18; 29:5, 34; 30:17).

29:7 More exaggerations are possible here, since these amounts are enormous. The chronicler could be using hyperbole (see comments on 29:4 and 12:14) to motivate the post-exilic community.

29:9 Giving willingly in the face of valid needs results in joy (2 Corinthians 9:7). Chronicles, as opposed to the books of Samuel or Kings, often stressed the people's joy as a result of a unified response to God (1 Chronicles 12:20, 38-40; 16:3; 29:22; 2 Chronicles 7:10; 15:15; 23:21; 29:36; 30:23-26). A restored sense of national unity was important for the post-exilic returnees if they were to finish rebuilding the Temple (Haggai 1:3-6; Malachi 3:8-12). The lesson they needed to learn from Chronicles was that wholehearted devotion to the Lord brings joy!

BECAUSE GOD IS SOVEREIGN

I will joyfully submit to His will.

Power and might are in Your hand, and at Your discretion people are made great and given strength.

1 CHRONICLES 29:12

FOR THE NEXT *GOD IS SOVEREIGN* FEATURE SEE PAGE 938.

DAVID'S PRAYER OF PRAISE

10 Then David praised the LORD in the presence of the whole assembly:

"O LORD, the God of our ancestor Israel,* may You be praised forever and ever!
29:11 Rev 5:12-13 11 Yours, O LORD, is the greatness, the power, the glory, the victory, and the majesty.
Everything in the heavens and on earth is Yours, O LORD, and this is Your kingdom.
29:12 2 Chr 1:12; 20:6 We adore You as the One who is over all things. 12 Wealth and honor come from You
alone, for You rule over everything. Power and might are in Your hand, and at Your
discretion people are made great and given strength.

13 "O our God, we thank You and praise Your glorious name! 14 But who am I, and
who are my people, that we could give anything to You? Everything we have has
29:15 come from You, and we give You only what You first gave us! 15 We are here for only
Lev 25:23 a moment, visitors and strangers in the land as our ancestors were before us. Our
Job 14:2, 10-12 days on earth are like a passing shadow, gone so soon without a trace.

16 "O LORD our God, even this material we have gathered to build a Temple to honor
29:17 1 Chr 28:9 Your holy name comes from You! It all belongs to You! 17 I know, my God, that You
examine our hearts and rejoice when You find integrity there. You know I have done
all this with good motives, and I have watched Your people offer their gifts willingly
and joyously.

18 "O LORD, the God of our ancestors Abraham, Isaac, and Israel, make Your people
29:19 1 Chr 28:9 always want to obey You. See to it that their love for You never changes. 19 Give my son
Ps 72:1 Solomon the wholehearted desire to obey all Your commands, laws, and decrees, and to
do everything necessary to build this Temple, for which I have made these preparations."

29:20 20 Then David said to the whole assembly, "Give praise to the LORD your God!" And the
Josh 22:33 entire assembly praised the LORD, the God of their ancestors, and they bowed low and knelt
before the LORD and the king.

SOLOMON NAMED AS KING

29:21 21 The next day they brought 1,000 bulls, 1,000 rams, and 1,000 male lambs as burnt of-
1 Kgs 8:62-63 ferings to the LORD. They also brought liquid offerings and many other sacrifices on behalf
29:22 1 Kgs 1:33-34 of all Israel. 22 They feasted and drank in the LORD's presence with great joy that day.
1 Chr 29:1 And again they crowned David's son Solomon as their new king. They anointed him be-
fore the LORD as their leader, and they anointed Zadok as priest. 23 So Solomon took the
throne of the LORD in place of his father, David, and he succeeded in everything, and all

29:10 *Israel* is the name that God gave to Jacob.

29:10-19 David's prayer is the climax of the coronation ceremony. It reveals the power of God that guided David's successful preparations. The three-part prayer consists of praise (1 Chronicles 29:10-13), acknowledgment (1 Chronicles 29:14-16), and petition (1 Chronicles 29:17-19). It is obviously a prayer from the heart, and it is directed toward the people's hearts. Because the prayer focuses on God's sovereignty, our dependence upon Him, and our desire to honor Him, God's people in any day should be able to emulate this attitude of prayer in their quest to have wholehearted devotion to the Lord.

▸ WORSHIP

29:14 Giving back to God. In a sense, we own nothing. God has loaned us everything we have for a brief time (1 Chronicles 29:15) to see how we will use it for His glory (Matthew 25:15). What have you done with your time? Your words? Your finances? Take a strict account of what you are doing with the things God has given you. Do not allow yourself to treat anything in this world as an end in itself—everything we do and think and feel is an act of worship toward God or toward another god. (***See Worship****> NT> Prohibitions> Wrong Objects> Money,* TopicGuide page A33.)

29:21-22 The next day's sacrifices totaled 3,000 animals. In comparison with the moving of the Ark, this amount seems reasonable and appropriate considering the number of people present (but see note on 15:26 for a figurative view of the sacrifice numbers). The chronicler probably included peace or fellowship offerings, the meat of which was shared with the people (16:1).

29:22-25 The crowning of Solomon this second time is really just the succession of Solomon's kingship after David died (See note on co-regency in 28:1). That is why this statement appears so close to the final report of David's reign (as in 1 Kings 2:10-12). Both of these ceremonies occurred after Solomon's anointing by Zadok (1 Kings 1:38-42).

Israel obeyed him. [24]All the officials, the warriors, and the sons of King David pledged their
loyalty to King Solomon. [25]And the LORD exalted Solomon in the sight of all Israel, and He
gave Solomon greater royal splendor than any king in Israel before him.

29:25 2 Chr 1:1, 12

29:26-28 //1 Kgs 2:10-12

SUMMARY OF DAVID'S REIGN

[26]So David son of Jesse reigned over all Israel. [27]He reigned over Israel for forty years,
seven of them in Hebron and thirty-three in Jerusalem. [28]He died at a ripe old age, having
enjoyed long life, wealth, and honor. Then his son Solomon ruled in his place.
[29]All the events of King David's reign, from beginning to end, are written in *The Record
of Samuel the Seer, The Record of Nathan the Prophet,* and *The Record of Gad the Seer.*
[30]These accounts include the mighty deeds of his reign and everything that happened to
him and to Israel and to all the surrounding kingdoms.

29:26 1 Chr 18:14

29:27 2 Sam 5:4-5

29:28 1 Chr 23:1 Acts 13:36

29:29 1 Sam 9:9; 22:5 2 Sam 7:2

29:24 All pledged their loyalty to Solomon, but perhaps not freely—Solomon began to kill those who threatened him (1 Kings 2:5-46).

29:26-30 The chronicler emphasized David as the ideal king in order that his descendants would follow his example. These are the typical end-credits for a king as they would be found in the literary form of a chronicle (1 Kings 2:10-11): a summary of rule, his successor, and other records.

PURPOSE

To place the Temple and covenant obligations in their proper place for the generation returning from captivity in Babylon, just as Deuteronomy provided a "refresher" on the law for the second generation of Israelites about to occupy the Promised Land.

Some people we meet in life are consumed with a single passion—a hobby, a sport, a ministry, or a business. Whatever their passion, you can't be around them very long without knowing who or what they love the most.

The writer of 2 Chronicles had a passion as well: the Temple in Jerusalem. From his priestly perspective, he wrote the history of Judah from Solomon to the Exile. The book begins with Solomon building the Temple in Jerusalem and ends four centuries later with Cyrus, the king of Persia, issuing a decree for the Temple to be rebuilt in Jerusalem. The Temple was not just a priestly passion; it was the focal point for all Israel—the dwelling place of God. Second Chronicles pays little attention to the ten northern tribes of Israel, because they broke away from Judah and established a separate capital in Shechem (1 Kings 12:25). Because they failed to worship at the Temple in Jerusalem, they were cut off from God's blessings (Deuteronomy 12:13-14).

DISCOVER GOD IN 2 CHRONICLES

Second Chronicles paints a picture of a nation in upheaval. Yet in the midst of national turmoil, God's attributes remain unchanged:

Intimacy: The apostle John says Jesus Christ came and "made His home among us" (John 1:14). The word John used for "made His home" is the Greek verb *skenoo,* which means to dwell in a tent or tabernacle. It is a clear reference to the Old Testament when God first established His presence among the Israelites by dwelling in the tabernacle built for Him in the Sinai desert. Solomon built the Temple, a permanent dwelling place for God, in Jerusalem. Sadly, the prophet Ezekiel saw in a vision the presence of the Lord depart from the Temple in Jerusalem (Ezekiel 11:23), but in another vision he saw that it would return (43:2-5). God's search for intimacy with humanity is clearly pictured in 2 Chronicles by His blessing of the meticulous efforts the Israelites made to provide a dwelling place for Him.

Goodness and Power: A consistent attack upon the character of God goes like this: since there is evil in the world, God is either not good enough or not powerful enough to eradicate it. But a constant refrain of worship in Scripture seems to suggest that God is both good and powerful: "He is so good! His faithful love endures forever!" (2 Chronicles 5:13; 7:3; see also 1 Chronicles 16:34; Psalm 106:1; 107:1; 118:1, 29; 136:1; Jeremiah 33:11). God could easily have gotten rid of the evil in Israel and Judah during the period of 2 Chronicles. But He is seeking a people who will choose to put aside evil out of love for Him. When the redemption story is complete, evil will be eradicated forever (Revelation 20:10; 22:3). Until then, we live in a world where evil exists, but where the love and power of God are greater (2 Chronicles 32:7).

GROWING THROUGH 2 CHRONICLES

A number of themes surface in 2 Chronicles that bear directly on the spiritual success of the follower of Christ today:

Purity of the Temple: Only twenty-five years old when he became king, Hezekiah immediately sought to cleanse the Temple and restore the worship that God deserved. It took over two weeks to haul out of the Temple all the refuse and junk that had been allowed to accumulate over the years (2 Chronicles 29:15-17). The apostle Peter says that followers of Christ are the new temple of the Lord—the place of His habitation. We function as "holy priests" who offer the "spiritual sacrifices that please God" (1 Peter 2:5). Because our bodies are the "temple of the Holy Spirit" (1 Corinthians 6:19), we have no less an obligation to remain pure than the Old Testament priests had to keep the Jerusalem Temple pure.

DISCOVERY VERSES

Solomon decided to build a Temple to honor the name of the LORD, and also a royal palace for himself." (2 CHRONICLES 2:1)

"This is what King Cyrus of Persia says: The LORD, the God of heaven, has given me all the kingdoms of the earth. He has appointed me to build him a Temple at Jerusalem, which is in Judah. Any of you who are the LORD's people may go there for this task. And may the LORD your God be with you!" (2 CHRONICLES 36:23)

Our Greater Power: When Sennacherib and his Assyrian army surrounded Jerusalem, Hezekiah undertook all the physical and military preparations he could (2 Chronicles 32:1-5). But in the final analysis he relied on a different defense: "Don't be afraid or discouraged because of the king of Assyria or his mighty army, for there is a power far greater on our side! He may have a great army, but they are merely men. We have the LORD our God to help us and to fight our battles for us!" (2 Chronicles 32:7-8). This sounds suspiciously like the truth written by the apostle John concerning our spiritual battles: "You have already won a victory over those people [false prophets], because the Spirit who lives in you is greater than the spirit who lives in the world" (1 John 4:4). In every battle, there is our part and God's part. But ultimately it is God's part that makes the difference.

Centrality of the Word: During King Josiah's reign, a priest discovered a scroll, which had been lost, containing the Law of God. When Josiah heard what it said, he "tore his clothes in despair"! (2 Chronicles 34:19). He learned that God promised curses on all who failed to walk in His laws (see Deuteronomy 28:15-68), and called Judah to renew their faithfulness to the covenant stipulations given by God through Moses. "And throughout the rest of [Josiah's] lifetime, they did not turn away from the LORD, the God of their ancestors" (2 Chronicles 34:33). Knowledge of the requirements of God brings with it an obligation to walk in them.

2 CHRONICLES FACTS

Author: Perhaps Ezra. See 1 Chronicles Introduction, Author.

Written to: Jewish exiles returning from captivity in Babylon.

Date of writing: The latter half of the fifth century BC.

Setting: Judah and Jerusalem.

OUTLINE

- **1 CHRONICLES 1:1–9:34**—The genealogy of God's people
- **1 CHRONICLES 9:35—2 CHRONICLES 9:31**—The united monarchy
- **2 CHRONICLES 10–28**—The divided kingdom

KEY PLACES IN 2 CHRONICLES

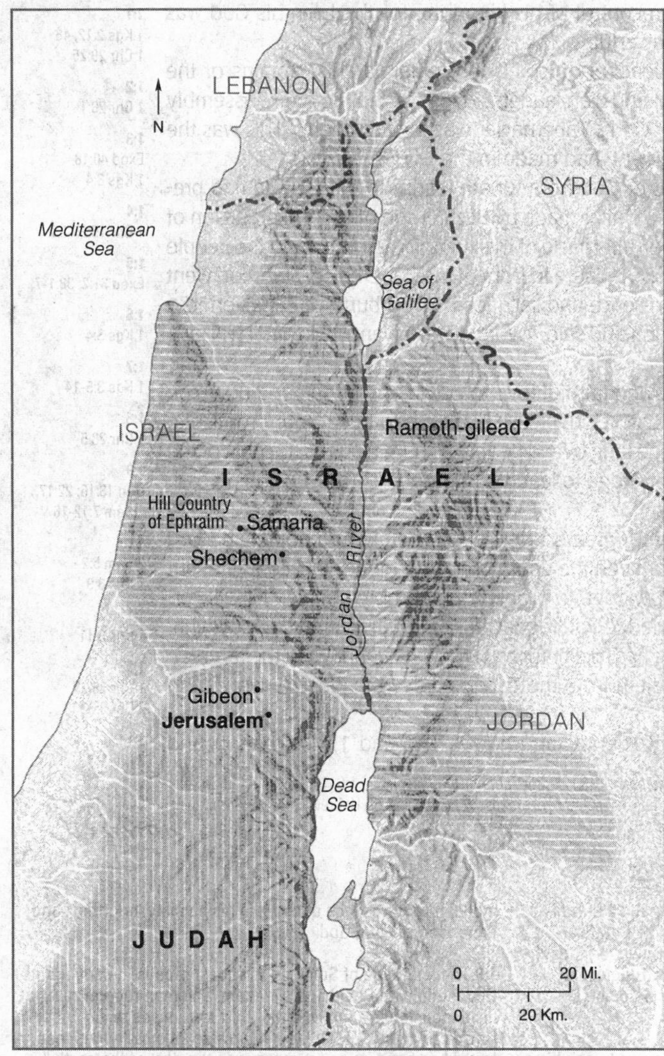

The broken lines (—·—) indicate modern boundaries.

1 Gibeon David's son Solomon became king over Israel. He summoned the nation's leaders to a ceremony in Gibeon. Here God told Solomon to ask for whatever he desired. Solomon asked for wisdom and knowledge to rule Israel (1:1-12).

2 Jerusalem After the ceremony in Gibeon, Solomon returned to the capital city, Jerusalem. His reign began a golden age for Israel. Solomon implemented the plans for the Temple, which had been drawn up by his father, David. It was a magnificent construction. It symbolized Solomon's wealth and wisdom, which became known worldwide (1:13–9:31).

3 Shechem After Solomon's death, his son Rehoboam was ready to be crowned in Shechem. However, his promise of higher taxes and harder work for the people led to rebellion. Everyone but the tribes of Judah and Benjamin deserted Rehoboam and set up their own kingdom to the north called Israel. Rehoboam returned to Jerusalem as ruler over the southern kingdom called Judah (10:1–12:16). The remainder of 2 Chronicles records the history of Judah.

4 Hill Country of Ephraim Abijah became the next king of Judah, and soon war broke out between Israel and Judah. When the armies of the two nations arrived for battle in the hill country of Ephraim, Israel had twice as many troops as Judah. It looked like Judah's defeat was certain. But they cried out to God, and God gave them victory over Israel. In their history as separate nations, Judah had a few godly kings, who instituted reforms and brought the people back to God. Israel, however, had a succession of only evil kings (13:1-22).

5 Aram (Syria) Asa, a godly king, removed every trace of pagan worship from Judah and renewed the people's covenant with God in Jerusalem. But King Baasha of Israel built a fortress to control traffic into Judah. Instead of looking to God for guidance, Asa took the silver and gold from the Temple and sent it to the king of Aram, requesting his help against King Baasha. As a result, God became angry with Judah (14:1–16:14).

6 Samaria Although Jehoshaphat was a godly king, he allied himself with Israel's most evil king, Ahab. Ahab's capital was Samaria. Ahab wanted help fighting against Ramoth-gilead. Jehoshaphat wanted advice, but rather than listening to God's prophet who had promised defeat, he joined Ahab in battle (17:1–18:27).

7 Ramoth-gilead The alliance with Israel against Ramoth-gilead ended in defeat and Ahab's death. Shaken by his defeat, Jehoshaphat returned to Jerusalem and to God. But his son Jehoram was a wicked king, as was his son Ahaziah, and history repeated itself. Ahaziah formed an alliance with Israel's king Joram to do battle with the Arameans at Ramoth-gilead. This led to the death of both kings (18:28–22:9).

8 Jerusalem The rest of Judah's history recorded in 2 Chronicles centers on Jerusalem. Some kings caused Judah to sin by bringing idol worship into their midst. Others cleaned up the idol worship, reopened and restored the Temple, and in the case of Josiah, tried to follow God's laws as they were written by Moses. In spite of the few good influences, a series of evil kings sent Judah into a downward spiral that ended with the Babylonian Empire overrunning the country. The Temple was burned, the walls of the city were broken down, and the people were deported to Babylon.

SOLOMON ASKS FOR WISDOM

1 Solomon son of David took firm control of his kingdom, for the LORD his God was with him and made him very powerful.
2Solomon called together all the leaders of Israel—the generals and captains of the army,* the judges, and all the political and clan leaders. 3Then he led the entire assembly to the place of worship in Gibeon, for God's Tabernacle* was located there. (This was the Tabernacle that Moses, the LORD's servant, had made in the wilderness.)
4David had already moved the Ark of God from Kiriath-jearim to the tent he had prepared for it in Jerusalem. 5But the bronze altar made by Bezalel son of Uri and grandson of Hur was there* at Gibeon in front of the Tabernacle of the LORD. So Solomon and the people gathered in front of it to consult the LORD.* 6There in front of the Tabernacle, Solomon went up to the bronze altar in the LORD's presence and sacrificed 1,000 burnt offerings on it.
7That night God appeared to Solomon and said, "What do you want? Ask, and I will give it to you!"
8Solomon replied to God, "You showed faithful love to David, my father, and now You have made me king in his place. 9O LORD God, please continue to keep Your promise to David my father, for You have made me king over a people as numerous as the dust of the earth! 10Give me the wisdom and knowledge to lead them properly,* for who could possibly govern this great people of Yours?"
11God said to Solomon, "Because your greatest desire is to help your people, and you did not ask for wealth, riches, fame, or even the death of your enemies or a long life, but rather you asked for wisdom and knowledge to properly govern My people—12I will certainly give you the wisdom and knowledge you requested. But I will also give you wealth, riches, and fame such as no other king has had before you or will ever have in the future!"
13Then Solomon returned to Jerusalem from the Tabernacle at the place of worship in Gibeon, and he reigned over Israel.
14Solomon built up a huge force of chariots and horses.* He had 1,400 chariots and

1:1 1 Kgs 2:12, 46; 1 Chr 29:25
1:2 1 Chr 28:1
1:3 Exod 40:18; 1 Kgs 3:4
1:4 1 Chr 15:25-28
1:5 Exod 31:2; 38:1-7
1:6 1 Kgs 3:4
1:7 1 Kgs 3:5-14
1:8 1 Chr 28:5
1:9 Gen 13:16; 22:17; 2 Sam 7:12-16
1:10 2 Sam 5:2; 1 Kgs 3:9
1:11 1 Kgs 3:11
1:12 1 Chr 29:25; 2 Chr 9:22
1:13 2 Chr 1:3
1:14 1 Kgs 4:26; 9:19; 10:26-29

1:2 Hebrew *the commanders of thousands and of hundreds.* 1:3 Hebrew *Tent of Meeting;* also in 1:6, 13. 1:5a As in Greek version and Latin Vulgate, and some Hebrew manuscripts. Masoretic Text reads *he placed.* 1:5b Hebrew *to consult Him.* 1:10 Hebrew *to go out and come in before this people.* 1:14 Or *charioteers;* also in 1:14b.

1:1 The chronicler (the anonymous author of 1 and 2 Chronicles) omits the 1 Kings 1–2 account of the intrigue that surrounded Solomon's ascension to the throne. However; though the language of this verse hints at the power struggle; the focus is on the ways God was responsible for Solomon's success.

1:2-3 Like David (see 1 Chronicles 13:1-6), Solomon began his reign by leading his people to seek God. First Kings 3:4-15 presents Solomon's visit to Gibeon as a personal pilgrimage, while the chronicler depicts this event as a national gathering of "all Israel" in order to emphasize to his audience the ideal of a unified kingdom (1 Chronicles 11:1; 14:8; 2 Chronicles 7:8; 9:30).

1:3-6 Solomon demonstrates his piety by commencing his reign with an act of worship. For the chronicler, seeking or consulting God was an essential element of personal and national righteousness (2 Chronicles 7:14).

1:5 Bezalel was the chief architect of the Tabernacle (Exodus 31:2; 35:30-35). Exodus indicates that God blessed Bezalel with the gift of wisdom in order to accomplish his task. His mention foreshadows God's gift of wisdom to Solomon, the builder of the Temple.

1:7-12 The divine gift of wisdom prepared Solomon to rule God's people and build His Temple. Solomon is portrayed as a model for future kings of Israel in his humility, priorities, and dependence upon God.

1:9 The language of Solomon's request recalls the covenants God made with David and Abraham. Solomon recognizes that his ascension is a fulfillment of God's promises to his father David (2 Samuel 7:12-16). Solomon also acknowledges that Israel has become as "numerous as the dust of the earth," fulfilling the promise made to Abraham (Genesis 13:16). The faithfulness of God in the past provides hope for the future of Israel under Solomon, the son of David.

▸ HOLINESS
1:11 A leader's heart. We generally judge rulers by their basic fairness to us and to the nation as a whole. We tend to assess equity and justice externally, by the actions and reactions of the one in charge. But Solomon found favor with God by his desires—when confronted with the ultimate offer of any type of gift he chose, he wanted wisdom. Solomon's greatest desire was to help his people by leading them wisely. Ask God to grant your desires that honor Him (Psalm 37:3-5). (***See Holiness***> *Law and Grace> Law> Leaders and followers,* TopicGuide page A41.)

1:14-17 The writer of Chronicles gives a similar record of Solomon's trading activities at 9:13-28. Together they serve as literary bookends for the chronicler's account of Solomon's reign.

12,000 horses. He stationed some of them in the chariot cities and some near him in Jeru-
1:15 salem. 15 The king made silver and gold as plentiful in Jerusalem as stone. And valuable
1 Kgs 10:27 cedar timber was as common as the sycamore-fig trees that grow in the foothills of Judah.*
16 Solomon's horses were imported from Egypt* and from Cilicia*; the king's traders ac-
quired them from Cilicia at the standard price. 17 At that time chariots from Egypt could be
purchased for 600 pieces of silver,* and horses for 150 pieces of silver.* They were then
exported to the kings of the Hittites and the kings of Aram.

PREPARATIONS FOR BUILDING THE TEMPLE

2:1 **2** 1*Solomon decided to build a Temple to honor the name of the LORD, and also a royal
1 Kgs 5:5 2:2 palace for himself. 2*He enlisted a force of 70,000 laborers, 80,000 men to quarry
1 Kgs 5:15-16 stone in the hill country, and 3,600 foremen.
2 Chr 2:18 3 Solomon also sent this message to King Hiram* at Tyre:

2:3 1 Kgs 5:2-11 "Send me cedar logs as you did for my father, David, when he was building his
1 Chr 14:1 palace. 4 I am about to build a Temple to honor the name of the LORD my God. It will
2:4 be a place set apart to burn fragrant incense before Him, to display the special
Exod 25:30; sacrificial bread, and to sacrifice burnt offerings each morning and evening, on the
29:38-42; 30:7 Num 28:9-10 Sabbaths, at new moon celebrations, and at the other appointed festivals of the LORD
our God. He has commanded Israel to do these things forever.
2:5 5 "This must be a magnificent Temple because our God is greater than all other
Exod 15:11 gods. 6 But who can really build Him a worthy home? Not even the highest heavens
1 Chr 16:25 can contain Him! So who am I to consider building a Temple for Him, except as a
2:6 1 Kgs 8:27 place to burn sacrifices to Him?
2 Chr 6:18 7 "So send me a master craftsman who can work with gold, silver, bronze, and iron,
2:7 as well as with purple, scarlet, and blue cloth. He must be a skilled engraver who can
Exod 31:3-5 1 Chr 22:15 work with the craftsmen of Judah and Jerusalem who were selected by my father,
2 Chr 2:13-15 David.
2:8 8 "Also send me cedar, cypress, and red sandalwood* logs from Lebanon, for I
2 Chr 9:10-11 know that your men are without equal at cutting timber in Lebanon. I will send my

1:15 Hebrew *the Shephelah.* **1:16a** Possibly *Muzur,* a district near Cilicia; also in 1:17. **1:16b** Hebrew *Kue,* probably another name for Cilicia. **1:17a** Hebrew *600 shekels of silver,* about 15 pounds or 6.8 kilograms in weight. **1:17b** Hebrew *150 shekels,* about 3.8 pounds or 1.7 kilograms in weight. **2:1** Verse 2:1 is numbered 1:18 in Hebrew text. **2:2** Verses 2:2-18 are numbered 2:1-17 in Hebrew text. **2:3** Hebrew *Huram,* a variant spelling of Hiram; also in 2:11. **2:8** Or *juniper;* Hebrew reads *algum,* perhaps a variant spelling of *almug;* compare 9:10-11 and parallel text at 1 Kgs 10:11-12.

1:15 The chronicler depicts Solomon's reign as a golden era, serving as a model for the restoration of Israel following their defeat and exile in 586 BC. His detailed description of Solomon's wealth serves to emphasize the glory of the kingdom.

1:16-17 Israel's location allowed Solomon to control trade routes on land between three continents: Europe, Asia, and Africa. The absence of a formidable power among the surrounding nations (Egypt was in decline; Assyria was on the rise) allowed Solomon to exercise military and economic mastery over the lucrative region. This prosperity was a fulfillment of God's promise (2 Chronicles 1:12) and provided Solomon the resources to build the Temple.

2:1 The chronicler focuses attention on the Temple by omitting any details about the construction of the royal palace (1 Kings 7:1-12).

2:3 Tyre prospered as a port city on the Mediterranean coast. According to the Jewish historian Josephus, Hiram ascended to the throne around 970 BC and reigned for 34 years. Earlier, Hiram had also provided materials and workmen for David's palace and preparations for the Temple (1 Chronicles 14:1; 22:4).

2:4 God established the sacrifices and practices noted here through Moses (Exodus 25:6, 30; 30:7-8; 40:23; Leviticus 24:5-9; and Numbers 28–29). Solomon's words instruct the chronicler's audience about their need to rebuild the Temple and renew their worship as God instructed.

2:5-6 Solomon was building a Temple worthy of God, but he also recognized that even the whole of creation could not contain God. Yet in His grace God condescends to meet His people. This concept of a sacred space where God meets His people points to Jesus Christ (John 1:14), the Spirit's indwelling of believers (1 Corinthians 6:19), and the church (Ephesians 2:21).

2:7 The master craftsman's list of skills closely resembles that of Bezalel, the architect of the Tabernacle (Exodus 31:3-5).

2:8 Algum, translated here as sandalwood or juniper, is the Hebrew name for an unidentified type of wood. Its name also appears in Assyrian documents from the same period.

men to help them. [9]An immense amount of timber will be needed, for the Temple
I am going to build will be very large and magnificent. [10]In payment for your wood- **2:10**
cutters, I will send 100,000 bushels of crushed wheat, 100,000 bushels of barley,* 1 Kgs 5:11
110,000 gallons of wine, and 110,000 gallons of olive oil.*"

[11]King Hiram sent this letter of reply to Solomon: **2:11** 1 Kgs 10:9 2 Chr 9:8

"It is because the LORD loves His people that He has made you their king! [12]Praise the **2:12**
LORD, the God of Israel, who made the heavens and the earth! He has given King 2 Chr 2:1
David a wise son, gifted with skill and understanding, who will build a Temple for the Pss 33:6; 102:25
LORD and a royal palace for himself.

[13]"I am sending you a master craftsman named Huram-abi, who is extremely
talented. [14]His mother is from the tribe of Dan in Israel, and his father is from Tyre. **2:14**
He is skillful at making things from gold, silver, bronze, and iron, and he also works 1 Kgs 7:14
with stone and wood. He can work with purple, blue, and scarlet cloth and fine linen.
He is also an engraver and can follow any design given to him. He will work with
your craftsmen and those appointed by my lord David, your father.

[15]"Send along the wheat, barley, olive oil, and wine that my lord has mentioned. **2:15**
[16]We will cut whatever timber you need from the Lebanon mountains and will float 2 Chr 2:10
the logs in rafts down the coast of the Mediterranean Sea* to Joppa. From there you **2:16**
can transport the logs up to Jerusalem." 1 Kgs 5:8-9

[17]Solomon took a census of all foreigners in the land of Israel, like the census his father **2:17**
had taken, and he counted 153,600. [18]He assigned 70,000 of them as common laborers, 1 Chr 22:2
80,000 as quarry workers in the hill country, and 3,600 as foremen. **2:18** 2 Chr 2:2

SOLOMON BUILDS THE TEMPLE

3 So Solomon began to build the Temple of the LORD in Jerusalem on Mount Moriah, **3:1-14**
where the LORD had appeared to David, his father. The Temple was built on the 1 Kgs 6:1-29
threshing floor of Araunah* the Jebusite, the site that David had selected. [2]The construc- **3:1**
tion began in midspring,* during the fourth year of Solomon's reign. 1 Chr 21:18

2:10a Hebrew *20,000 cors* [3,640 kiloliters] *of crushed wheat, 20,000 cors of barley.* **2:10b** Hebrew *20,000 baths* [420 kiloliters] *of wine, and 20,000 baths of olive oil.* **2:16** Hebrew *the sea.* **3:1** Hebrew reads *Ornan,* a variant spelling of Araunah; compare 2 Sam 24:16. **3:2** Hebrew *on the second day of the second month.* This day of the ancient Hebrew lunar calendar occurred in April or May.

2:10 First Kings 5:11 makes no mention of wine or barley, and it lists the payments as being made annually. Textual variants may have caused the apparent discrepancy here, or the chronicler may have drawn from a different source that addressed another aspect of Solomon's arrangement with Hiram.

▸ WORSHIP

2:11 Politics and God's love. God's mercy flows in every area of life, including politics. A good leader is a blessing from the Lord, while wicked rulers are sent to punish rebellion against God (1 Peter 2:13-17). Whether essentially good or bad people are in charge, we should always obey all types of authority (Romans 13:1-7), except when that authority specifically forbids what God requires or requires what God forbids. Pray regularly for those in authority, that they may allow you to live a godly life without persecution. (***See Worship****> NT> Prohibitions> Wrong Objects> Political leaders,* TopicGuide page A33.)

2:12 God answered David's prayer for Solomon (1 Chronicles 22:12). Hiram's praise of God need not imply conversion; Hiram probably understood the God of Solomon to be one more deity among many.

2:13-14 First Kings 7:14 indicates that Huram-abi's mother belonged to the tribe of Naphtali rather than Dan. It is possible that she either resided geographically in one tribe while belonging by descent to the other, or her parents may have been from different tribes. The chronicler may have chosen Dan to connect Huram-abi to Oholiab, Bezalel's assistant in building the Tabernacle (Exodus 31:6). Solomon and Huram-abi emerge as the new Bezalel and Oholiab, emphasizing the continuity between the Tabernacle and the Temple.

2:16 Joppa was about 35 miles northwest of Jerusalem and served as its major seaport.

2:17-18 The census of foreigners indicates that the laborers for the construction of the Temple were drawn from among that group. First Kings 5:13-18, however, seems to indicate that Israelites were also employed for the task.

3:1 The site of the Temple possessed historical and theological significance. Abraham brought Isaac to be sacrificed at Mount Moriah (Genesis 22), and David saw the angel of the Lord there after his ill-fated census (1 Chronicles 21:1–22:1).

3These are the dimensions Solomon used for the foundation of the Temple of God (us-
3:4 ing the old standard of measurement).* It was 90 feet long and 30 feet wide.* 4The entry
1 Kgs 6:3 room at the front of the Temple was 30 feet* wide, running across the entire width of the
Temple, and 30 feet* high. He overlaid the inside with pure gold.
3:5 5He paneled the main room of the Temple with cypress wood, overlaid it with fine gold,
1 Kgs 6:17 and decorated it with carvings of palm trees and chains. 6He decorated the walls of the
3:7 Temple with beautiful jewels and with gold from the land of Parvaim. 7He overlaid the
1 Kgs 6:20-22, 29-35 beams, thresholds, walls, and doors throughout the Temple with gold, and he carved fig-
ures of cherubim on the walls.
3:8 8He made the Most Holy Place 30 feet wide, corresponding to the width of the Temple,
Exod 26:33 1 Kgs 6:16 and 30 feet deep. He overlaid its interior with 23 tons* of fine gold. 9The gold nails that
3:9 were used weighed 20 ounces* each. He also overlaid the walls of the upper rooms with
1 Chr 28:11 gold.
3:10 10He made two figures shaped like cherubim, overlaid them with gold, and placed them
1 Kgs 6:23-28 in the Most Holy Place. 11The total wingspan of the two cherubim standing side by side
was 30 feet. One wing of the first figure was 7½ feet* long, and it touched the Temple
wall. The other wing, also 7½ feet long, touched one of the wings of the second figure.
12In the same way, the second figure had one wing 7½ feet long that touched the oppo-
site wall. The other wing, also 7½ feet long, touched the wing of the first figure. 13So the
wingspan of the two cherubim side by side was 30 feet. They stood on their feet and faced
out toward the main room of the Temple.
3:14 14Across the entrance of the Most Holy Place he hung a curtain made of fine linen, deco-
Exod 26:31 rated with blue, purple, and scarlet thread and embroidered with figures of cherubim.
3:15 15For the front of the Temple, he made two pillars that were 27 feet* tall, each topped by a
1 Kgs 7:15-20 capital extending upward another 7½ feet. 16He made a network of interwoven chains and
used them to decorate the tops of the pillars. He also made 100 decorative pomegranates

3:3a The "old standard of measurement" was a cubit equal to 18 inches [46 centimeters]. The new standard was a cubit of approximately 21 inches [53 centimeters]. 3:3b Hebrew *60 cubits* [27.6 meters] *long and 20 cubits* [9.2 meters] *wide.* 3:4a Hebrew *20 cubits* [9.2 meters]; also in 3:8, 11, 13. 3:4b As in some Greek and Syriac manuscripts, which read *20 cubits* [9.2 meters]; Hebrew reads *120 cubits,* which is 180 feet or 55 meters. 3:8 Hebrew *600 talents* [20.4 metric tons]. 3:9 Hebrew *50 shekels* [570 grams]. 3:11 Hebrew *5 cubits* [2.3 meters]; also in 3:11b, 12, 15. 3:15 As in Syriac version (see also 1 Kgs 7:15; 2 Kgs 25:17; Jer 52:21), which reads *18 cubits* [8.3 meters]; Hebrew reads *35 cubits,* which is 52.5 feet or 16.5 meters.

▶ MINISTRY

3:5 Revealing heaven and earth. Are you a Christian Gnostic? That is, are you someone who sees religion as relating only to the spiritual—God, heaven, angels—and not the physical world of family or food? But the design of the Temple honored both heaven and earth, with some rooms decorated by cherubic angels and others by everyday fruits and flowers. God rules the realms above and the realms below with equal authority. Mature Christians show Jesus' impact in every area of their lives. Make your walk with God one that acknowledges the reality of earth and heaven. (***See Ministry> Transformation> Fill and Subdue> Influencing every sphere of life,*** TopicGuide page A57.)

3:5 The Temple was divided into two parts: the main room (or Holy Place) and the Most Holy Place where the Ark of the Covenant resided. A curtain of fine linen barred access to the Most Holy Place and God's presence (2 Chronicles 3:14). When Christ's death secured access to God's presence, the curtain in the Temple was torn (Matthew 27:51).

3:5-7 The carvings of palm trees and cherubim seem to have been designed to evoke images of the Garden of Eden. Palm trees gave the interior of the Temple the appearance of a garden, and cherubim guarded the garden following the expulsion of Adam and Eve (Genesis 3:24). In the Temple God lived among His people as He had in the garden.

3:5-14 The grandeur of the Temple testified to the holiness and majesty of God, but most Israelites never even saw its interior. By reading the chronicler's description, however, the readers could glimpse both the interior of the Temple and what it intended to communicate about God's nature. The three-story vaulted ceilings (1 Kings 6), for instance, communicated a sense of God's transcendence. Architecture, both then and now, can artistically represent the grandeur of both the creation and the Creator.

3:6 The location of Parvaim is unknown. The name may simply signify "finest gold."

3:10-13 Cherubim are angelic beings who guard access to God's presence (Genesis 3:24; Ezekiel 10). The carved cherubim were impressive reminders of God's presence in the Temple.

and attached them to the chains. 17Then he set up the two pillars at the entrance of the Tem-
ple, one to the south of the entrance and the other to the north. He named the one on the
south Jakin, and the one on the north Boaz.*

FURNISHINGS FOR THE TEMPLE

4 Solomon* also made a bronze altar 30 feet long, 30 feet wide, and 15 feet high.*
2Then he cast a great round basin, 15 feet across from rim to rim, called the Sea. It
was 7½ feet deep and about 45 feet in circumference.* 3It was encircled just below its rim
by two rows of figures that resembled oxen. There were about six oxen per foot* all the
way around, and they were cast as part of the basin.

4The Sea was placed on a base of twelve bronze oxen, all facing outward. Three faced
north, three faced west, three faced south, and three faced east, and the Sea rested on
them. 5The walls of the Sea were about three inches* thick, and its rim flared out like a cup
and resembled a water lily blossom. It could hold about 16,500 gallons* of water.

6He also made ten smaller basins for washing the utensils for the burnt offerings. He set
five on the south side and five on the north. But the priests washed themselves in the Sea.

7He then cast ten gold lampstands according to the specifications that had been given,
and he put them in the Temple. Five were placed against the south wall, and five were
placed against the north wall.

8He also built ten tables and placed them in the Temple, five along the south wall and
five along the north wall. Then he molded 100 gold basins.

9He then built a courtyard for the priests, and also the large outer courtyard. He made
doors for the courtyard entrances and overlaid them with bronze. 10The great bronze ba-
sin called the Sea was placed near the southeast corner of the Temple.

11Huram-abi also made the necessary washbasins, shovels, and bowls.

So at last Huram-abi completed everything King Solomon had assigned him to make for
the Temple of God:

12 the two pillars;
the two bowl-shaped capitals on top of the pillars;
the two networks of interwoven chains that decorated the capitals;
13 the 400 pomegranates that hung from the chains on the capitals (two rows of
pomegranates for each of the chain networks that decorated the capitals on top of
the pillars);

3:17 1 Kgs 7:21
4:1 Exod 27:1-2; 2 Kgs 16:14
4:2 1 Kgs 7:23-26
4:5 1 Kgs 7:26
4:6 1 Kgs 7:38, 40
4:7 Exod 25:31-40; 1 Kgs 7:49
4:8 1 Kgs 7:48
4:9 1 Kgs 6:36
4:10 1 Kgs 7:39
4:11 1 Kgs 7:14, 40
4:12 1 Kgs 20:27-43; 2 Chr 2:13
4:13 1 Kgs 7:20

3:17 *Jakin* probably means "He establishes"; *Boaz* probably means "in Him is strength." 4:1a Or *Huram-abi;* Hebrew reads *He.* 4:1b Hebrew *20 cubits* [9.2 meters] *long, 20 cubits wide, and 10 cubits* [4.6 meters] *high.* 4:2 Hebrew *10 cubits* [4.6 meters] *across . . . 5 cubits* [2.3 meters] *deep and 30 cubits* [13.8 meters] *in circumference.* 4:3 Or *20 oxen per meter;* Hebrew reads *10 per cubit.* 4:5a Hebrew *a handbreadth* [8 centimeters]. 4:5b Hebrew *3,000 baths* [63 kiloliters].

3:17 Pillars such as those set up at the entrance to the Temple were common in temples of the era, but their significance is uncertain. Jakin means "he establishes" and Boaz means "strength is in him." God is most likely the subject of both words, and reference to His relationship to the Davidic dynasty may have been intended.

4:1 These measurements probably apply to the base of the altar. The priests offered sacrifices on this altar in front of the Temple.

4:2 The Sea replaced the bronze washbasin in the Tabernacle; the priests used both objects for ritual cleansing. In ancient mythology the sea was a chaotic enemy of the gods. The still waters of the Sea before the Temple may have symbolized God's power over creation (compare Revelation 21:1).

4:7 Solomon constructed ten lampstands; the Tabernacle contained only one. The lampstands spoke of God as the source of light, literally and spiritually, and pointed to Christ, the Light of the world (John 8:12).

4:8 The function of the ten tables is uncertain. They may have been used to support the lampstands, or they may have been tables for the Bread of the Presence. There are indications, however, that only one table was used for the Bread of the Presence (2 Chronicles 13:11). The Bread of the Presence symbolized God's fellowship with Israel (Exodus 24:9-11) and pointed to Christ, the Bread of Life (John 6:35).

4:9 The Temple complex was arranged according to three degrees of holiness: the outer courtyard, the main room (or Holy Place), and the Most Holy Place. The outer courtyard was accessible to all male Israelites who were ceremonially clean, and its furnishings were made of bronze. Furnishings for the inner two levels were made of gold. Access to the main room was limited to the priesthood, while access to the Most Holy Place was restricted to the high priest once a year.

4:14 14 the water carts holding the basins;
1 Kgs 7:27 15 the Sea and the twelve oxen under it;
4:16 16 the ash buckets, the shovels, the meat hooks, and all the related articles.
1 Kgs 7:14

Huram-abi made all these things of burnished bronze for the Temple of the LORD, just as
4:17-18 King Solomon had directed. 17 The king had them cast in clay molds in the Jordan Valley
1 Kgs 7:47 between Succoth and Zarethan.* 18 Solomon used such great quantities of bronze that its
weight could not be determined.

19 Solomon also made all the furnishings for the Temple of God:

the gold altar;
the tables for the Bread of the Presence;
4:20 20 the lampstands and their lamps of solid gold, to burn in front of the Most Holy Place
Exod 25:31-37 as prescribed;
21 the flower decorations, lamps, and tongs—all of the purest gold;
22 the lamp snuffers, bowls, dishes, and incense burners—all of solid gold;
the doors for the entrances to the Most Holy Place and the main room of the Temple, overlaid with gold.

5 So Solomon finished all his work on the Temple of the LORD. Then he brought all the
5:1 gifts his father, David, had dedicated—the silver, the gold, and the various articles—
1 Kgs 7:51 and he stored them in the treasuries of the Temple of God.

THE ARK BROUGHT TO THE TEMPLE

5:2–6:11 2 Solomon then summoned to Jerusalem the elders of Israel and all the heads of tribes—
//1 Kgs 8:1-21 the leaders of the ancestral families of Israel. They were to bring the Ark of the LORD's
5:2 2 Sam 6:12 Covenant to the Temple from its location in the City of David, also known as Zion. 3 So all
2 Chr 1:4 the men of Israel assembled before the king at the annual Festival of Shelters, which is
held in early autumn.*

5:4 4 When all the elders of Israel arrived, the Levites picked up the Ark. 5 The priests and
2 Chr 5:7 Levites brought up the Ark along with the special tent* and all the sacred items that had
been in it. 6 There, before the Ark, King Solomon and the entire community of Israel sacri-
ficed so many sheep, goats, and cattle that no one could keep count!

7 Then the priests carried the Ark of the LORD's Covenant into the inner sanctuary of
the Temple—the Most Holy Place—and placed it beneath the wings of the cherubim. 8 The
5:9 cherubim spread their wings over the Ark, forming a canopy over the Ark and its carry-
1 Kgs 8:8-9 ing poles. 9 These poles were so long that their ends could be seen from the Temple's
5:10 main room—the Holy Place*—but not from the outside. They are still there to this day.
Deut 10:2-5
Heb 9:4

4:17 As in parallel text at 1 Kgs 7:46; Hebrew reads *Zeredah.* 5:3 Hebrew *at the festival that is in the seventh month.* The Festival of Shelters began on the fifteenth day of the seventh month of the ancient Hebrew lunar calendar. This day occurred in late September, October, or early November. 5:5 Hebrew *the Tent of Meeting;* i.e., the tent mentioned in 2 Sam 6:17 and 1 Chr 16:1. 5:9 As in parallel text at 1 Kgs 8:8; Hebrew reads *from the Ark in front of the Most Holy Place.*

5:2-6 This gathering embodies a number of the chronicler's hopes for his audience: all Israel led by a faithful king gathered to worship God at His Temple. Likewise today, this gathering points to the church as it gathers to worship God through Jesus Christ, our faithful King and Temple (Revelation 21:5, 22).

5:3 The Festival of Shelters took place during the seventh month (Leviticus 23:34). According to 1 Kings 6:38, the Temple was completed in the eighth month. Either the ceremony took place during the month prior to the Temple's completion or it took place 11 months later. Eleven months would provide ample time for the preparations and travel involved in the inauguration ceremony.

5:4, 7 The Levites were assigned the duty of transporting the Ark and here performed this task for the last time (Numbers 1:50-51). Only the priests, however, were allowed to enter the Temple, and they carried the Ark to its place within the Most Holy Place. Solomon obediently observes these regulations (compare David's initial carelessness in 1 Chronicles 13).

5:9 The Ark and the poles had been lost by the chronicler's time, presumably during the destruction of Jerusalem by the Babylonians in 587 BC. The note regarding their continuing presence belonged to an older source quoted by the chronicler to compile his inspired history.

[10]Nothing was in the Ark except the two stone tablets that Moses had placed in it at Mount Sinai,* where the LORD made a covenant with the people of Israel when they left Egypt.

[11]Then the priests left the Holy Place. All the priests who were present had purified themselves, whether or not they were on duty that day. [12]And the Levites who were musicians—Asaph, Heman, Jeduthun, and all their sons and brothers—were dressed in fine linen robes and stood at the east side of the altar playing cymbals, lyres, and harps. They were joined by 120 priests who were playing trumpets. [13]The trumpeters and singers performed together in unison to praise and give thanks to the LORD. Accompanied by trumpets, cymbals, and other instruments, they raised their voices and praised the LORD with these words:

5:11 1 Chr 24:1-5
5:12 1 Chr 25:1-4; 2 Chr 7:6
5:13 1 Chr 16:34, 42; 2 Chr 7:3

"He is good!
His faithful love endures forever!"

At that moment a thick cloud filled the Temple of the LORD. [14]The priests could not continue their service because of the cloud, for the glorious presence of the LORD filled the Temple of God.

5:14 1 Kgs 8:11

SOLOMON PRAISES THE LORD

6 Then Solomon prayed, "O LORD, You have said that You would live in a thick cloud of darkness. [2]Now I have built a glorious Temple for You, a place where You can live forever!"

6:1 1 Kgs 8:12-50

[3]Then the king turned around to the entire community of Israel standing before him and gave this blessing: [4]"Praise the LORD, the God of Israel, who has kept the promise He made to my father, David. For He told my father, [5]'From the day I brought My people out of the land of Egypt, I have never chosen a city among any of the tribes of Israel as the place where a Temple should be built to honor My name. Nor have I chosen a king to lead

5:10 Hebrew *Horeb,* another name for Sinai.

▸ **WORSHIP**
5:10 Losing value. Have you ever lost something extremely important to you? The people of Israel grieved deeply over the loss of their religious artifacts and treasures. You may lose tangible items, and these may bring genuine sorrow to your heart. You may also lose the intangible—the respect of your family, for instance. In both categories, there are some things that, once lost, can never be replaced. Guard your relationships, your family, and your faith with all diligence. (***See Worship****> OT> Reverence> Compared to treasure,* TopicGuide page A29.)

5:10 At one point the Ark also contained Aaron's rod and a jar of manna in addition to the two stone tablets bearing the Ten Commandments (Hebrews 9:4; Exodus 16:32-34; Numbers 17:10-11).

5:11-13 The chronicler takes special interest in the worship music of Israel (2 Chronicles 20:19; 29:25-29; 35:15). Because the Ark would no longer be moved, praising God in music and song would be the Levites' main duty. The words they sang are found often in the Psalms (107:1; 118:1) and celebrate the character of God.

▸ **WORSHIP**
5:13 Music in the Old Testament. What did this magnificent group of instruments and singers sound like? Modern four-part choral music did not exist until the sixteenth century, but we do have evidence of the use of scales in the ancient Near East that were roughly equivalent to our own. They produced music in unison, with all participants singing the same note at the same time. Ancient records show references to fast, slow, loud, and soft songs, so the songs had many modern dynamics. But God did not leave us the tunes or music theory behind Israelite music, suggesting that these issues were not what God was most concerned about. Likewise today, we may be dogmatic on the lyrics of our songs—striving for beautiful, biblical lyrics—but we should be gracious to one another concerning the form of music we use in the church. (***See Worship****> OT> Music,* TopicGuide page A27.)

5:13-14 God's presence among His people often took the form of a cloud. A cloud guided Israel through the wilderness and filled the Tabernacle when it was completed. God spoke from a cloud at the transfiguration of Jesus, and Jesus ascended amid clouds (see Exodus 13:21-22; 19:9; 40:34-35; Daniel 7:13; Matthew 17:5; Acts 1:9).

6:1-2 Solomon's opening statement introduces the themes of transcendence and immanence, which recur throughout the chapter. God fills the universe, but he will dwell in the Temple among His people. God knows and orders all things, but He responds to the prayers of His people. "Thick cloud of . . . darkness" recalls God's descent on Mt. Sinai (Exodus 19:16).

6:4-9 Solomon's blessing blends earlier accounts of the promises God made to David regarding his dynasty and the Temple (1 Chronicles 17; 22:7-10; 28:3-6).

6:6 My people Israel. 6 But now I have chosen Jerusalem as the place for My name to be hon-
1 Chr 28:4 2 Chr 12:13 ored, and I have chosen David to be king over My people Israel.'"
7 Then Solomon said, "My father, David, wanted to build this Temple to honor the name
6:7 1 Chr 28:2 of the LORD, the God of Israel. 8 But the LORD told him, 'You wanted to build the Temple to
6:8 honor My name. Your intention is good, 9 but you are not the one to do it. One of your own
1 Kgs 5:3 sons will build the Temple to honor Me.'
10 "And now the LORD has fulfilled the promise He made, for I have become king in my
father's place, and now I sit on the throne of Israel, just as the LORD promised. I have built
6:11 this Temple to honor the name of the LORD, the God of Israel. 11 There I have placed the
2 Chr 5:7, 10 Ark, which contains the covenant that the LORD made with the people of Israel."

SOLOMON'S PRAYER OF DEDICATION

6:12-40 12 Then Solomon stood before the altar of the LORD in front of the entire community of Isra-
//1 Kgs 8:22-53 el, and he lifted his hands in prayer. 13 Now Solomon had made a bronze platform 7½ feet
6:12 Neh 8:4 long, 7½ feet wide, and 4½ feet high* and had placed it at the center of the Temple's
outer courtyard. He stood on the platform, and then he knelt in front of the entire commu-
6:14 nity of Israel and lifted his hands toward heaven. 14 He prayed,

Exod 15:11 Deut 3:24; 7:9 "O LORD, God of Israel, there is no God like You in all of heaven and earth. You keep
Your covenant and show unfailing love to all who walk before You in wholehearted
6:15 devotion. 15 You have kept Your promise to Your servant David, my father. You made
1 Chr 22:9-10 that promise with Your own mouth, and with Your own hands You have fulfilled it
today.
6:16 16 "And now, O LORD, God of Israel, carry out the additional promise You made to
1 Kgs 2:4 Your servant David, my father. For You said to him, 'If your descendants guard their
2 Chr 7:18 behavior and faithfully follow My Law as you have done, one of them will always sit
on the throne of Israel.' 17 Now, O LORD, God of Israel, fulfill this promise to Your ser-
vant David.
6:18 18 "But will God really live on earth among people? Why, even the highest heavens
2 Chr 2:6 cannot contain You. How much less this Temple I have built! 19 Nevertheless, listen to
my prayer and my plea, O LORD my God. Hear the cry and the prayer that Your ser-
vant is making to You. 20 May You watch over this Temple day and night, this place

6:13 Hebrew *5 cubits* [2.3 meters] *long, 5 cubits wide, and 3 cubits* [1.4 meters] *high.*

6:10-11 Solomon emphasizes God's faithfulness to His word. From the time He led them out of Egypt, God had been faithful to His people Israel, and He had kept His word to David. In the aftermath of the Exile, it was vital that the chronicler's audience remember the past faithfulness of God so that they would believe His promises of restoration for them. We, too, must be reminded of God's past faithfulness to His people so that we might hold fast to the promises He has made to us.

6:14 God's trustworthiness and love for His people set Him apart from the false gods of the world. Unlike false gods, past and present, the God of Israel has bound Himself to His people by His word and has remained faithful.

6:14-42 Solomon's prayer can be divided into three parts: prayer for the Davidic dynasty (2 Chronicles 6:14-17), various occasions for prayer (6:18-40), and prayer for God's enduring presence (6:41-42). The prayer is paralleled in 1 Kings 8:22-53.

6:16 God's promises to the line of David were not unconditional; they required faithful obedience on the part of David's descendants. The chronicler's audience may have wondered if God had broken His promise to David's descendants, but it was David's descendants who had been unfaithful.

▸ GOD

6:18 Where does God live? Both children and adults wonder about where God lives. Solomon understood that even the entire universe could not contain God, so he asked how God could be located in the Temple. This mystery becomes even more puzzling when we realize that God's presence appeared in the Temple (2 Chronicles 7:1), but it reached its fullest expression in Jesus, who took on human nature and was born the son of Mary. If the physical universe cannot contain God, then how can He be born in human flesh? We can but marvel and ponder such mysteries of God. (***See God**> God's Attributes> Infinite> Heaven and earth cannot contain Him,* TopicGuide page A16.)

6:18-21 Solomon presented a paradox of the Temple: God would be truly present there, but the Temple could not contain Him. God chose the Temple as the place where His people would have access to His heavenly court (2 Chronicles 6:21, 30, 33, 39).

where You have said You would put Your name. May You always hear the prayers I
make toward this place. 21 May You hear the humble and earnest requests from me **6:21** Mic 7:18
and Your people Israel when we pray toward this place. Yes, hear us from heaven
where You live, and when You hear, forgive.
22 "If someone wrongs another person and is required to take an oath of innocence
in front of Your altar at this Temple, 23 then hear from heaven and judge between
Your servants—the accuser and the accused. Pay back the guilty as they deserve.
Acquit the innocent because of their innocence.
24 "If Your people Israel are defeated by their enemies because they have sinned
against You, and if they turn back and acknowledge Your name and pray to You
here in this Temple, 25 then hear from heaven and forgive the sin of Your people
Israel and return them to this land You gave to them and to their ancestors.
26 "If the skies are shut up and there is no rain because Your people have sinned **6:26**
against You, and if they pray toward this Temple and acknowledge Your name and 1 Kgs 17:1
turn from their sins because You have punished them, 27 then hear from heaven and
forgive the sins of Your servants, Your people Israel. Teach them to follow the right
path, and send rain on Your land that You have given to Your people as their special
possession.
28 "If there is a famine in the land or a plague or crop disease or attacks of locusts **6:28**
or caterpillars, or if Your people's enemies are in the land besieging their towns— 2 Chr 20:9
whatever disaster or disease there is—29 and if Your people Israel pray about their
troubles or sorrow, raising their hands toward this Temple, 30 then hear from heaven **6:30**
where You live, and forgive. Give Your people what their actions deserve, for You 1 Sam 16:7
alone know each human heart. 31 Then they will fear You and walk in Your ways as 1 Chr 28:9
long as they live in the land You gave to our ancestors.
32 "In the future, foreigners who do not belong to Your people Israel will hear of
You. They will come from distant lands when they hear of Your great name and Your
strong hand and Your powerful arm. And when they pray toward this Temple, 33 then
hear from heaven where You live, and grant what they ask of You. In this way, all **6:33**
the people of the earth will come to know and fear You, just as Your own people 2 Chr 7:14
Israel do. They, too, will know that this Temple I have built honors Your name.
34 "If Your people go out where You send them to fight their enemies, and if they
pray to You by turning toward this city You have chosen and toward this Temple I
have built to honor Your name, 35 then hear their prayers from heaven and uphold
their cause.
36 "If they sin against You—and who has never sinned?—You might become angry **6:36** Job 15:14-16
with them and let their enemies conquer them and take them captive to a foreign 1 Jn 1:8-10

▸ GOD

6:24 God disciplines His people. Throughout his prayer (2 Chronicles 6:24-39), Solomon asked God to cease disciplining His people when they turned to Him in repentance. God promises to restrain His people from sin through the holy threat of punishment (2 Chronicles 7:12-22; Hebrews 12:6; Revelation 3:19). God is not angry with us—His wrath against us was satisfied in the sacrifice of His Son (Romans 3:25). His punishment is intended to save us from the danger of spiritual destruction and apostasy, which is much more dangerous than any physical harm. So after you fail Him, flee to God for the restoration that He offers all who repent. (***See God**> God's Attributes> Faithful> God forgives the repentant,* TopicGuide page A16.)

6:24-39 Solomon's request for God to hear the repentant cries of His people reflects the terms of the covenant God made with Israel. Disobedience would bring the curses of the covenant, including drought, famine, military defeat, and exile (Leviticus 26:14-46; Deuteronomy 28:15-68).

6:32-33 God promised Abraham that he would be a blessing to the nations (Genesis 12:3). In partial fulfillment of this promise, Solomon prayed that the Temple would bring Gentiles to worship the God of Israel. The spread of the gospel to all peoples following Pentecost fulfilled God's promise to Abraham (Acts 10–11; 15; Galatians 3:24-29).

6:36-39 Moses was the first to speak about the pattern of disobedience, exile, and restoration following repentance (Deuteronomy 4:26-31), and the prophets (particularly Amos, Hosea, Micah, Isaiah, Nahum, Zephaniah, Habakkuk, and Jeremiah) reflected the same understanding of Israel's history. We see a similar pattern in the cycles of disobedience, punishment, and restoration in the book of Judges.

land far away or near. 37 But in that land of exile, they might turn to You in repentance
and pray, 'We have sinned, done evil, and acted wickedly.' 38 If they turn to You with
their whole heart and soul in the land of their captivity and pray toward the land You
gave to their ancestors—toward this city You have chosen, and toward this Temple
I have built to honor Your name— 39 then hear their prayers and their petitions from
heaven where You live, and uphold their cause. Forgive Your people who have
sinned against You.

6:40 2 Chr 7:15; Neh 1:6, 11; Ps 17:1

40 "O my God, may Your eyes be open and Your ears attentive to all the prayers
made to You in this place.

6:41-42 //Ps 132:8-10

41 "And now arise, O LORD God, and enter Your resting place,
along with the Ark, the symbol of Your power.
May Your priests, O LORD God, be clothed with salvation;
may Your loyal servants rejoice in Your goodness.
42 O LORD God, do not reject the king You have anointed.
Remember Your unfailing love for Your servant David."

THE DEDICATION OF THE TEMPLE

7:1-10 1 Kgs 8:62-66

7:1 1 Kgs 8:54; 18:24, 38

7:3 2 Chr 5:13; 20:21

7 When Solomon finished praying, fire flashed down from heaven and burned up the
burnt offerings and sacrifices, and the glorious presence of the LORD filled the Tem-
ple. 2 The priests could not enter the Temple of the LORD because the glorious presence of
the LORD filled it. 3 When all the people of Israel saw the fire coming down and the glorious
presence of the LORD filling the Temple, they fell face down on the ground and worshiped
and praised the LORD, saying,

"He is good!
His faithful love endures forever!"

7:4 1 Kgs 8:62-63

7:6 1 Chr 15:16-21; 2 Chr 5:12

4 Then the king and all the people offered sacrifices to the LORD. 5 King Solomon offered a
sacrifice of 22,000 cattle and 120,000 sheep and goats. And so the king and all the peo-
ple dedicated the Temple of God. 6 The priests took their assigned positions, and so did the
Levites who were singing, "His faithful love endures forever!" They accompanied the sing-
ing with music from the instruments King David had made for praising the LORD. Across
from the Levites, the priests blew the trumpets, while all Israel stood.

7:7 1 Kgs 8:64-66

7 Solomon then consecrated the central area of the courtyard in front of the LORD's Tem-
ple. He offered burnt offerings and the fat of peace offerings there, because the bronze al-
tar he had built could not hold all the burnt offerings, grain offerings, and sacrificial fat.

7:8 1 Kgs 8:65

8 For the next seven days Solomon and all Israel celebrated the Festival of Shelters.* A

7:8 Hebrew *the festival* (also in 7:9); see note on 5:3.

7:1 Fire from heaven, such as Solomon witnessed here, also signaled God's approval of the first sacrifices made by Aaron (Leviticus 9:24), the sacrifices David made following his ill-fated census (1 Chronicles 21:26), and Elijah's sacrifice on Mount Carmel (1 Kings 18:38).

▸ WORSHIP

7:3 Responding to God's glory. Since God no longer seems to signal His presence with clouds of glory and fire from heaven, how do we recognize God's special blessings? Are they as ordinary as a good meal? Or as extraordinary as the birth of a baby? Or as miraculous as a healed body? God is everywhere in the life of a believer—nothing happens outside His permission (Hebrews 6:3; Acts 16:7). Such a realization calls believers to a constant state of gratitude to God for His provision (Ephesians 5:20). (***See Worship****> NT> To the Father> God is to receive all praise and glory,* TopicGuide page A29.)

7:4-7 The dedication ceremony continued with sacrifices and jubilation. The celebration was well ordered, with the priests and Levites fulfilling their appointed duties and Solomon dedicating the Temple's central courtyard before proceeding with the overflow of sacrifices. Solomon balanced passionate worship with obedience to God's law.

7:8-9 The Festival of Shelters (or Tabernacles) commemorated Israel's years of wandering in the wilderness (Leviticus 23:33-44). The Temple's dedication spilled over into the festival, resulting in two weeks of celebration. The chronicler records that all Israel was represented from north to south—a hopeful model for those returning from exile in Babylon.

large congregation had gathered from as far away as Lebo-hamath in the north and the
Brook of Egypt in the south. 9 On the eighth day they had a closing ceremony, for they had 7:9
celebrated the dedication of the altar for seven days and the Festival of Shelters for seven Lev 23:26
days. 10 Then at the end of the celebration,* Solomon sent the people home. They were all
joyful and glad because the LORD had been so good to David and to Solomon and to His
people Israel.

THE LORD'S RESPONSE TO SOLOMON

11 So Solomon finished the Temple of the LORD, as well as the royal palace. He completed 7:11-22
everything he had planned to do in the construction of the Temple and the palace. 12 Then //1 Kgs 9:1-9
one night the LORD appeared to Solomon and said,

"I have heard your prayer and have chosen this Temple as the place for making 7:13
sacrifices. 13 At times I might shut up the heavens so that no rain falls, or command 2 Chr 6:26-28
grasshoppers to devour your crops, or send plagues among you. 14 Then if My people 7:14
who are called by My name will humble themselves and pray and seek My face and 2 Chr 6:37-39
turn from their wicked ways, I will hear from heaven and will forgive their sins and
restore their land. 15 My eyes will be open and My ears attentive to every prayer 7:15
made in this place. 16 For I have chosen this Temple and set it apart to be holy—a 2 Chr 6:20, 40
place where My name will be honored forever. I will always watch over it, for it is 7:16 2 Chr 7:12
dear to My heart.

17 "As for you, if you faithfully follow Me as David your father did, obeying all My 7:18
commands, decrees, and regulations, 18 then I will establish the throne of your 2 Chr 6:16
dynasty. For I made this covenant with your father, David, when I said, 'One of your
descendants will always rule over Israel.'

19 "But if you or your descendants abandon Me and disobey the decrees and 7:19 Lev 26:14, 33
commands I have given you, and if you serve and worship other gods, 20 then I will Deut 28:15
uproot the people from this land that I have given them. I will reject this Temple that 7:20
I have made holy to honor My name. I will make it an object of mockery and ridicule Deut 28:37; 29:28 1 Kgs 14:15
among the nations. 21 And though this Temple is impressive now, all who pass by will 7:21
be appalled. They will ask, 'Why did the LORD do such terrible things to this land and Deut 29:24-27
to this Temple?'

22 "And the answer will be, 'Because His people abandoned the LORD, the God of

7:10 Hebrew *Then on the twenty-third day of the seventh month.* This day of the ancient Hebrew lunar calendar occurred in October or early November.

7:11-12 Solomon completed his palace 13 years after the completion of the Temple (1 Kings 7:1; 9:10). The chronicler chooses not to make reference to that time gap in order to link God's message more closely with Solomon's prayer at the Temple dedication.

7:12-22 God's response to Solomon's prayer reiterates the conditionality of God's promises to David. If David's descendants disobeyed, God's justice would impose punishment. In His mercy, however, God promised healing and restoration if the people repented of their sins and sought God's forgiveness.

▸ SALVATION

7:14 A promise in a dream. God came to Solomon in a dream and reaffirmed the covenant He made with his father, David. God promised to bless Israel if they lived in obedience and repentance (2 Chronicles 7:14) and to curse them if they forgot God's claim on them (2 Chronicles 7:19). God has made a covenant with all who believe in Jesus Christ—a New Covenant—whereby we may approach God and find blessings in Christ's perfect obedience. We will never face God's covenant wrath again, for Jesus bore that once and for all on the Cross. Instead of God abandoning us when we disobey, God abandoned Christ as He bore our sin (Mark 15:34). Thank God for the new and better covenant whereby all may find salvation! (***See Salvation*****>** *Receiving***>** *When***>** *Delivered or rescued,* TopicGuide page A22.)

7:14 This verse encapsulates the major themes of Chronicles and speaks very clearly to the chronicler's audience returning from exile. The hope of healing is held out on the condition of humility, repentance, and prayer. The reigns of Israel's and Judah's kings as recorded by the chronicler powerfully illustrate this verse. Those kings who displayed humility, sought God, and turned from their wickedness found God's mercy and blessing (2 Chronicles 12:6-7; 15:4; 32:20-21).

7:16 God's promise of His abiding presence should be read along with God's threat of abandonment in verse 20. God reserved the right to remove His presence from the Temple as punishment for Israel's disobedience.

their ancestors, who brought them out of Egypt, and they worshiped other gods
instead and bowed down to them. That is why He has brought all these disasters
on them.'"

SOLOMON'S MANY ACHIEVEMENTS

8:1-18 //1 Kgs 9:10-28 **8** It took Solomon twenty years to build the LORD's Temple and his own royal palace. At
the end of that time, 2Solomon turned his attention to rebuilding the towns that King
Hiram* had given him, and he settled Israelites in them.
3Solomon also fought against the town of Hamath-zobah and conquered it. 4He rebuilt
8:5 Tadmor in the wilderness and built towns in the region of Hamath as supply centers. 5He
1 Chr 7:24 fortified the towns of Upper Beth-horon and Lower Beth-horon, rebuilding their walls and
2 Chr 14:7 installing barred gates. 6He also rebuilt Baalath and other supply centers and constructed
towns where his chariots and horses* could be stationed. He built everything he desired in
Jerusalem and Lebanon and throughout his entire realm.
7There were still some people living in the land who were not Israelites, including the
8:8 1 Kgs 4:6; 9:21 Hittites, Amorites, Perizzites, Hivites, and Jebusites. 8These were descendants of the na-
tions whom the people of Israel had not destroyed. So Solomon conscripted them for his
labor force, and they serve in the labor force to this day. 9But Solomon did not conscript
any of the Israelites for his labor force. Instead, he assigned them to serve as fighting men,
officers in his army, commanders of his chariots, and charioteers. 10King Solomon ap-
pointed 250 of them to supervise the people.
8:11 1 Kgs 3:1; 7:8 11Solomon moved his wife, Pharaoh's daughter, from the City of David to the new pal-
ace he had built for her. He said, "My wife must not live in King David's palace, for the Ark
of the LORD has been there, and it is holy ground."
8:12 2 Chr 4:1 12Then Solomon presented burnt offerings to the LORD on the altar he had built for Him
8:13 Exod 23:14-17; 29:38-42 in front of the entry room of the Temple. 13He offered the sacrifices for the Sabbaths, the
new moon festivals, and the three annual festivals—the Passover celebration, the Festival
Num 28:3 of Harvest,* and the Festival of Shelters—as Moses had commanded.

8:2 Hebrew *Huram,* a variant spelling of Hiram; also in 8:18. 8:6 Or *and charioteers.* 8:13 Or *Festival of Weeks.*

8:2 In 1 Kings 9:10-14 Solomon gave these towns to Hiram. Hiram, however, was displeased with the towns. Hiram's displeasure may have led him to return the towns to Solomon, which is what the chronicler records here.

8:3-4 Hamath and Tadmor lie to the north and east of Israel. Significant trade routes run through both towns. By possessing these towns, Solomon effectively controlled the trade through the region.

8:3-6 The chronicler portrays Solomon as a man of peace (1 Chronicles 22:9), unlike his father David, but here he briefly records some of Solomon's military activities and the expansion of Israel's borders.

8:5 Upper and Lower Beth-horon sit on a ridge rising from the Valley of Aijalon north of Jerusalem. The towns are crucial to the security of a key road that gave Jerusalem access to the major trade route along the coast of the Mediterranean. From ancient times to World War I, invading armies have also used the road to gain access to Jerusalem.

8:7-10 The chronicler indicates that no Israelites were used as forced labor, but 1 Kings 5:13-16 states that Israelites were conscripted to labor. Because the Israelites only worked one month in three the chronicler may have considered their status distinct from that of the foreign workers who labored permanently.

8:8 "To this day" and expressions like it are not used consistently throughout Chronicles. At times they may refer to the chronicler's own time (1 Chronicles 5:26; 2 Chronicles 20:26; 35:25). At other times, they seem to be direct transcriptions of the words of the chronicler's sources (1 Chronicles 13:11; 2 Chronicles 5:9; 8:8; 10:19; 21:10). It is also possible to understand the expression as an idiom for "from then on."

▸ SPIRITUAL WARFARE

8:11 Compromise and the Christian. Concessions must sometimes be made when Christians have dealings with non-Christians. Some tensions are unavoidable—a non-Christian business associate needs to meet you on Sunday before he leaves town—what do you do? Or your non-Christian husband sees no need to go to church or have the children go to Sunday School—what now? Solomon realized that he had a delicate situation: His foreign (and likely pagan, see 1 Kings 11:8) wife was living in what Israelites considered a holy place. His solution—go to the extra expense of building her a special palace to protect the sanctity of the City of David. When you are forced to compromise in your dealings with non-Christians, make sure those compromises are wise and do not violate your conscience. (***See Spiritual Warfare**> Resisting Sin and Evil> Resisting Temptation> What to Resist> We are to resist worldly influences,* TopicGuide page A45.)

8:11 The books of 1 Kings and 2 Chronicles both record Solomon's relocation of his Egyptian wife, but only 2 Chronicles adds the theological justification in order to further enhance Solomon's reputation.

[14]In assigning the priests to their duties, Solomon followed the regulations of his father,
David. He also assigned the Levites to lead the people in praise and to assist the priests in
their daily duties. And he assigned the gatekeepers to their gates by their divisions, follow-
ing the commands of David, the man of God. [15]Solomon did not deviate in any way from
David's commands concerning the priests and Levites and the treasuries.
[16]So Solomon made sure that all the work related to building the Temple of the LORD
was carried out, from the day its foundation was laid to the day of its completion.
[17]Later Solomon went to Ezion-geber and Elath,* ports along the shore of the Red Sea*
in the land of Edom. [18]Hiram sent him ships commanded by his own officers and manned
by experienced crews of sailors. These ships sailed to Ophir with Solomon's men and
brought back to Solomon almost seventeen tons* of gold.

8:14 1 Chr 24:1; 25:1; 26:1; Neh 12:24, 36
8:17 1 Kgs 9:26; 2 Kgs 14:22
8:18 2 Chr 9:10, 13

VISIT OF THE QUEEN OF SHEBA

9 When the queen of Sheba heard of Solomon's fame, she came to Jerusalem to test
him with hard questions. She arrived with a large group of attendants and a great car-
avan of camels loaded with spices, large quantities of gold, and precious jewels. When she
met with Solomon, she talked with him about everything she had on her mind. [2]Solomon
had answers for all her questions; nothing was too hard for him to explain to her. [3]When
the queen of Sheba realized how wise Solomon was, and when she saw the palace he had
built, [4]she was overwhelmed. She was also amazed at the food on his tables, the organiza-
tion of his officials and their splendid clothing, the cup-bearers and their robes, and the
burnt offerings Solomon made at the Temple of the LORD.
[5]She exclaimed to the king, "Everything I heard in my country about your achieve-
ments* and wisdom is true! [6]I didn't believe what was said until I arrived here and saw it
with my own eyes. In fact, I had not heard the half of your great wisdom! It is far beyond
what I was told. [7]How happy your people must be! What a privilege for your officials to
stand here day after day, listening to your wisdom! [8]Praise the LORD your God, who de-
lights in you and has placed you on the throne as king to rule for Him. Because God loves

9:1 1 Kgs 10:1-13; Matt 12:42; Luke 11:31
9:8 Deut 7:8; 1 Chr 28:5; 29:23; 2 Chr 2:11

8:17a As in Greek version (see also 2 Kgs 14:22; 16:6); Hebrew reads *Eloth,* a variant spelling of Elath. 8:17b As in parallel text at 1 Kgs 9:26; Hebrew reads *the sea.* 8:18 Hebrew *450 talents* [15.3 metric tons]. 9:5 Hebrew *your words.*

8:12-15 The Temple was one of the chronicler's chief concerns. Solomon paid careful attention to the commands of Moses and David regarding the Temple and worship. In his obedience and zeal Solomon was a model for the chronicler's audience, who struggled with rebuilding the Temple and renewing a worshiping community.

▸ GOD
8:14 Following regulations. Do you like innovative and creative approaches to worship? Or do you prefer the standard hymns and creeds? Solomon contributed to the worship of God with creative architecture and new facilities, but he gratefully received the forms of worship passed down from God, through Moses, and finally through his father. He honored the work of the Holy Spirit in his spiritual ancestors by not re-creating all aspects of worship. We should not quickly cast aside all traditions as we form our own tradition. Judge everything in your worship service by Scripture, and see if God might be honored to keep some of the traditions passed down from the previous generations of believers. (***See God**> God's Names> Holy Spirit> Enables true worship,* TopicGuide page A19.)

9:1 Sheba was probably located in the area of modern-day Yemen on the Arabian Peninsula. The queen journeyed across 1,400 miles of arduous terrain to witness Solomon's greatness and wisdom firsthand. She may also have wished to discuss trade with Solomon, who controlled the routes through which her nation's goods would have likely traveled.

9:1-12 The chronicler employs the praise of foreign rulers to magnify the greatness of Solomon's kingdom. The queen of Sheba's visit is positioned like a bookend to Solomon's correspondence with another prominent Gentile, King Hiram (2 Chronicles 2:1-16). With both of them mentioned, it shows that foreign honors for Solomon were not a fluke, but a trend.

▸ SPIRITUAL WARFARE
9:5 Unbelievers' attitudes. Sometimes unbelievers have a great deal of respect for the morality, philosophy, and values of Christians, but they still do not trust in Christ. We have no evidence that the queen of Sheba or Hiram or the other peaceful pagans Solomon worked with ever humbled themselves before God alone, but they did respect Solomon and his God. Do you live the sort of life that makes unbelievers respect you? Seek to be at peace with everyone, if possible (Romans 12:18). (***See Spiritual Warfare**> Resisting Sin and Evil> Consequences> Of Obedience> Potential for a more peaceable life,* TopicGuide page A46.)

9:8 The queen's praises extended beyond Solomon to the God of Israel. Like Hiram (2 Chronicles 2:11), the queen attributed Solomon's reign to the love of God for His people. The blessings God granted His people resulted in praise and glory returned to Him. The original Hebrew is not worded "the throne" but "His throne"—that is, God's throne—thus making a powerful statement about God's sovereignty and kingship.

Israel and desires this kingdom to last forever, He has made you king over them so you
can rule with justice and righteousness."
9 Then she gave the king a gift of 9,000 pounds* of gold, great quantities of spices, and
precious jewels. Never before had there been spices as fine as those the queen of Sheba
gave to King Solomon.
9:10 10 (In addition, the crews of Hiram and Solomon brought gold from Ophir, and they also
2 Chr 8:18 brought red sandalwood* and precious jewels. 11 The king used the sandalwood to make
steps* for the Temple of the LORD and the royal palace, and to construct lyres and harps for
the musicians. Never before had such beautiful things been seen in Judah.)
12 King Solomon gave the queen of Sheba whatever she asked for—gifts of greater
value than the gifts she had given him. Then she and all her attendants returned to their
own land.

SOLOMON'S WEALTH AND SPLENDOR

9:13-28 13 Each year Solomon received about 25 tons* of gold. 14 This did not include the addi-
//1 Kgs 10:14-28 tional revenue he received from merchants and traders. All the kings of Arabia and the
//2 Chr 1:14-17 governors of the provinces also brought gold and silver to Solomon.
15 King Solomon made 200 large shields of hammered gold, each weighing more than
15 pounds.* 16 He also made 300 smaller shields of hammered gold, each weighing more
than 7½ pounds.* The king placed these shields in the Palace of the Forest of Lebanon.
17 Then the king made a huge throne, decorated with ivory and overlaid with pure gold.
18 The throne had six steps, with a footstool of gold. There were armrests on both sides of
the seat, and the figure of a lion stood on each side of the throne. 19 There were also
twelve other lions, one standing on each end of the six steps. No other throne in all the
world could be compared with it!
20 All of King Solomon's drinking cups were solid gold, as were all the utensils in the Pal-
ace of the Forest of Lebanon. They were not made of silver, for silver was considered
worthless in Solomon's day!
21 The king had a fleet of trading ships* manned by the sailors sent by Hiram.* Once
every three years the ships returned, loaded with gold, silver, ivory, apes, and peacocks.*
9:22 22 So King Solomon became richer and wiser than any other king on earth. 23 Kings
1 Kgs 3:13 from every nation came to consult him and to hear the wisdom God had given him.
2 Chr 1:12 24 Year after year everyone who visited brought him gifts of silver and gold, clothing,
weapons, spices, horses, and mules.
9:25 25 Solomon had 4,000 stalls for his horses and chariots, and he had 12,000 horses.* He
Deut 17:16 1 Kgs 4:26; 10:26 stationed some of them in the chariot cities, and some near him in Jerusalem. 26 He ruled
2 Chr 1:14 over all the kings from the Euphrates River* in the north to the land of the Philistines
9:26 1 Kgs 4:21, 24 and the border of Egypt in the south. 27 The king made silver as plentiful in Jerusalem
as stone. And valuable cedar timber was as common as the sycamore-fig trees that
9:27 2 Chr 1:15-17 grow in the foothills of Judah.* 28 Solomon's horses were imported from Egypt* and many
9:28 2 Chr 1:16 other countries.

9:9 Hebrew *120 talents* [4,000 kilograms]. **9:10** Hebrew *algum wood* (also in 9:11); perhaps a variant spelling of *almug*. Compare parallel text at 1 Kgs 10:11-12. **9:11** Or *gateways*. The meaning of the Hebrew is uncertain. **9:13** Hebrew *666 talents* [23 metric tons]. **9:15** Hebrew *600 shekels* [6.8 kilograms]. **9:16** Hebrew *300 shekels* [3.4 kilograms]. **9:21a** Hebrew *fleet of ships that could sail to Tarshish*. **9:21b** Hebrew *Huram*, a variant spelling of Hiram. **9:21c** Or *and baboons*. **9:25** Or *12,000 charioteers*. **9:26** Hebrew *the river*. **9:27** Hebrew *the Shephelah*. **9:28** Possibly *Muzur*, a district near Cilicia.

9:9 The queen's extravagant gifts are not surprising, since it is known from ancient sources that the region of Sheba possessed vast wealth, particularly from the trade of rare spices.

9:13-28 This final summary of Solomon's splendor reinforces the impression of his reign as a golden era for Israel. In this way the kingdom of Solomon becomes a model for the chronicler's audience, which is faced with the task of rebuilding the nation following the Babylonian exile.

SUMMARY OF SOLOMON'S REIGN

29 The rest of the events of Solomon's reign, from beginning to end, are recorded in *The* 9:29-31
Record of Nathan the Prophet, and *The Prophecy of Ahijah from Shiloh,* and also in *The Vi-* //1 Kgs 11:41-43
sions of Iddo the Seer, concerning Jeroboam son of Nebat. 30 Solomon ruled in Jerusalem 9:30
over all Israel for forty years. 31 When he died, he was buried in the City of David, named 1 Kgs 11:42-43
for his father. Then his son Rehoboam became the next king. 9:31 1 Kgs 2:10

THE NORTHERN TRIBES REVOLT

10 Rehoboam went to Shechem, where all Israel had gathered to make him king. 10:1
2 When Jeroboam son of Nebat heard of this, he returned from Egypt, for he had 1 Kgs 12:1-20
fled to Egypt to escape from King Solomon. 3 The leaders of Israel summoned him, and 10:2
Jeroboam and all Israel went to speak with Rehoboam. 4 "Your father was a hard master," 1 Kgs 11:40
they said. "Lighten the harsh labor demands and heavy taxes that your father imposed on
us. Then we will be your loyal subjects."
5 Rehoboam replied, "Come back in three days for my answer." So the people went away.
6 Then King Rehoboam discussed the matter with the older men who had counseled his
father, Solomon. "What is your advice?" he asked. "How should I answer these people?"
7 The older counselors replied, "If you are good to these people and do your best to
please them and give them a favorable answer, they will always be your loyal subjects."
8 But Rehoboam rejected the advice of the older men and instead asked the opinion of
the young men who had grown up with him and were now his advisers. 9 "What is your
advice?" he asked them. "How should I answer these people who want me to lighten the
burdens imposed by my father?"
10 The young men replied, "This is what you should tell those complainers who want a
lighter burden: 'My little finger is thicker than my father's waist! 11 Yes, my father laid
heavy burdens on you, but I'm going to make them even heavier! My father beat you with
whips, but I will beat you with scorpions!' "
12 Three days later Jeroboam and all the people returned to hear Rehoboam's decision,
just as the king had ordered. 13 But Rehoboam spoke harshly to them, for he rejected the
advice of the older counselors 14 and followed the counsel of his younger advisers. He told
the people, "My father laid* heavy burdens on you, but I'm going to make them even
heavier! My father beat you with whips, but I will beat you with scorpions!"

10:14 As in Greek version and many Hebrew manuscripts (see also 1 Kgs 12:14); Masoretic Text reads *I will lay.*

9:29-30 The chronicler skips to the conclusion of Solomon's reign without mentioning Solomon's multiple foreign wives and his idolatry (1 Kings 11:1-13) or his struggles with enemies, foreign (1 Kings 11:14-25) and domestic (1 Kings 11:26-40). The books of 1 and 2 Kings were written to those in exile and focuses on the sins of the people as the cause of the Exile. The books of 1 and 2 Chronicles were written to those returning from exile and presented a vision of the past that was also a hope for the future.

9:29 The chronicler employed the writings of various prophets as sources for his history. The ministries of Nathan and Ahijah are confirmed in the books of 1 and 2 Samuel and 1 and 2 Kings (2 Samuel 7; 1 Kings 11:29-30), but nothing is known of the work of Iddo.

10:1 The long political and religious history of Shechem dates back to the time of Abraham and made the city a favored place for significant gatherings (Genesis 12:6-7; Joshua 24). The nature of the demands of the northern tribes likely made them wary of traveling to Jerusalem.

10:4 See comment on 2 Chronicles 2:17-18 and 8:7-10 for a discussion of Israelite laborers.

▸ CHURCH

10:5 Waiting for answers. Truth takes time. Even the immature Rehoboam wisely set aside three days to make this important decision. Waiting can be a spiritual exercise—David often spoke of the difficult, yet rewarding practice of waiting on God (Psalms 38:15; 69:3). Isaiah wrote that without waiting, Israel would never experience the rescue of God (Isaiah 30:15). How can you practice the art of waiting on God? (***See Church****> What> Many Titles> Bride> Who joyfully awaits the wedding day,* TopicGuide page A48.)

10:6-10 The elders of Israel exercised an important governing function throughout the nation's history (2 Samuel 3:17; 5:3; 17:4; 1 Kings 20:7-8). Rehoboam's younger advisers may have been civil servants who are sometimes distinguished from the elders (2 Kings 10:5) or Rehoboam's half-brothers from Solomon's multiple marriages.

10:8 Despite being 41 years old, Rehoboam presents a case study in the foolishness of youth. He failed to heed the wisdom of experienced counselors and allowed his unchecked impetuosity to lead him and his nation into a civil war. Compare Abijah's denunciation of Rehoboam (2 Chronicles 13:7).

10:15 [15]So the king paid no attention to the people. This turn of events was the will of God, for
1 Kgs 11:29-39 it fulfilled the LORD's message to Jeroboam son of Nebat through the prophet Ahijah from
Shiloh.

10:16 [16]When all Israel realized* that the king had refused to listen to them, they responded,
2 Sam 20:1
2 Chr 10:19 "Down with the dynasty of David!

We have no interest in the son of Jesse.

Back to your homes, O Israel!

Look out for your own house, O David!"

So all the people of Israel returned home. [17]But Rehoboam continued to rule over the Is-
raelites who lived in the towns of Judah.

10:18 [18]King Rehoboam sent Adoniram,* who was in charge of the labor force, to restore or-
1 Kgs 4:6; 5:14 der, but the people of Israel stoned him to death. When this news reached King Rehobo-
am, he quickly jumped into his chariot and fled to Jerusalem. [19]And to this day the
10:19 1 Kgs 12:19 northern tribes of Israel have refused to be ruled by a descendant of David.

SHEMAIAH'S PROPHECY

11:1 **11** When Rehoboam arrived at Jerusalem, he mobilized the men of Judah and Benja-
1 Kgs 12:21-24 min—180,000 select troops—to fight against Israel and to restore the kingdom to
himself.

11:2 [2]But the LORD said to Shemaiah, the man of God, [3]"Say to Rehoboam son of Solomon,
2 Chr 12:5-7, 15 king of Judah, and to all the Israelites in Judah and Benjamin: [4]'This is what the LORD says:
11:4 2 Chr 10:15; 28:8-11 Do not fight against your relatives. Go back home, for what has happened is My doing!'"
So they obeyed the message of the LORD and did not fight against Jeroboam.

REHOBOAM FORTIFIES JUDAH

11:5 [5]Rehoboam remained in Jerusalem and fortified various towns for the defense of Judah.
2 Chr 8:2-6; 11:23 [6]He built up Bethlehem, Etam, Tekoa, [7]Beth-zur, Soco, Adullam, [8]Gath, Mareshah, Ziph,
[9]Adoraim, Lachish, Azekah, [10]Zorah, Aijalon, and Hebron. These became the fortified

10:16 As in Syriac version, Latin Vulgate, and many Hebrew manuscripts (see also 1 Kgs 12:16); Masoretic Text lacks *realized.*
10:18 Hebrew *Hadoram,* a variant spelling of Adoniram; compare 1 Kgs 4:6; 5:14; 12:18.

▶ GOD
10:15 The Lord's message fulfilled. It is possible to emphasize God's control over a certain situation to the point that it appears as if the people involved are merely puppets. It is also possible to describe a situation in such a way that people appear to be completely autonomous, almost limitless in their potential. In this passage, God's involvement and control are highlighted. God does not restrain the immaturity and foolishness in Rehoboam's heart but allows it to take its course into civil war. Prophecy (2 Chronicles 11:4) was fulfilled by the withdrawal of God's favor from Rehoboam, and he quickly drifted into sin. Pray for the sustaining power of God's Spirit in the lives of our leaders. (***See God****> God's Nature> Personality> Will> He accomplishes His purposes and good pleasure,* TopicGuide page A14.)

10:15 The chronicler has no difficulty describing the split of the kingdom as the will of God in fulfillment of prophecy, and yet he clearly holds Rehoboam and his advisers responsible for their poor judgment. God's sovereignty does not absolve men and women of the responsibility for their actions.

10:16 This four-part poetic rejection of David's royal line is the counterpart to the similarly arranged acceptance of David in 1 Chronicles 12:18.

10:18 Adoniram became an unwitting means of communication between Rehoboam and the northern tribes. Rehoboam signaled to the northern tribes his unwillingness to back down by his choice of Adoniram, the supervisor of forced labor, who served as an envoy to the disgruntled Israelites. This action was immediately perceived as an instigation, and the northern tribes killed Adoniram to communicate their unwillingness to recognize Rehoboam's sovereignty.

11:1-4 Through the words of the prophet Shemaiah the chronicler again presents the division of the kingdom as the will of God. Rehoboam heeds the words of the prophet both here and in 2 Chronicles 12:5-7. The fortifications listed below and the migration of the Levitical priests are portrayed as blessings resulting from Rehoboam's obedience. Although civil war is averted at this juncture, it would characterize the early history of the divided kingdom (2 Chronicles 12:15).

11:5-12 Most of the cities listed here are located in the south of Judah, suggesting that Rehoboam anticipated an invasion from Egypt. Jeroboam had been sheltered in Egypt during Solomon's final years (2 Chronicles 10:2). Rehoboam may have suspected a joint effort between Jeroboam and Egypt against his kingdom.

towns of Judah and Benjamin. 11Rehoboam strengthened their defenses and stationed
commanders in them, and he stored supplies of food, olive oil, and wine. 12He also put
shields and spears in these towns as a further safety measure. So only Judah and Benja-
min remained under his control.

13But all the priests and Levites living among the northern tribes of Israel sided with Re-
hoboam. 14The Levites even abandoned their pasturelands and property and moved to **11:14**
Judah and Jerusalem, because Jeroboam and his sons would not allow them to serve the Num 35:2-5
LORD as priests. 15Jeroboam appointed his own priests to serve at the pagan shrines, **11:15**
where they worshiped the goat and calf idols he had made. 16From all the tribes of Israel, 1 Kgs 12:31; 13:33
those who sincerely wanted to worship the LORD, the God of Israel, followed the Levites to **11:16** 2 Chr 15:9
Jerusalem, where they could offer sacrifices to the LORD, the God of their ancestors. 17This
strengthened the kingdom of Judah, and for three years they supported Rehoboam son **11:17** 2 Chr 12:1
of Solomon, for during those years they faithfully followed in the footsteps of David and
Solomon.

REHOBOAM'S FAMILY

18Rehoboam married his cousin Mahalath, the daughter of David's son Jerimoth and of **11:18**
Abihail, the daughter of Eliab son of Jesse. 19Mahalath had three sons—Jeush, Shemariah, 1 Sam 16:6
and Zaham.

20Later Rehoboam married another cousin, Maacah, the daughter of Absalom. Maacah
gave birth to Abijah, Attai, Ziza, and Shelomith. 21Rehoboam loved Maacah more than **11:21**
any of his other wives and concubines. In all, he had eighteen wives and sixty concubines, Deut 17:17
and they gave birth to twenty-eight sons and sixty daughters.

22Rehoboam appointed Maacah's son Abijah as leader among the princes, making it **11:22**
clear that he would be the next king. 23Rehoboam also wisely gave responsibilities to his Deut 21:15-17
other sons and stationed some of them in the fortified towns throughout the land of Judah
and Benjamin. He provided them with generous provisions, and he found many wives for
them.

11:13-16 In an effort to solidify his control over the northern tribes, Jeroboam established a system of worship independent of the Temple in Jerusalem (1 Kings 12:25–14:20). He built two altars—one at Bethel and the other at Dan—where gold calves were placed for worship, and he enlisted priests who were not Levites. Levites who remained faithful to the Lord abandoned their homes and moved to Judah.

11:15 In the ancient Middle East deities are not typically portrayed in animal form. However, both instances featuring calf idols in the Bible are connected with Egypt where the practice of depicting deities in animal form is common. Aaron and the Israelites (Exodus 33), like Jeroboam, had recently left Egypt when they fashioned their gold calves.

▸ MINISTRY

11:15 Religious power. Jeroboam knew that if he allowed worship of the one true God to continue in Israel, each year his people would be forced to leave his nation and travel to Jerusalem. Jeroboam feared that this would undermine his political and military power, so he immediately created another religion with his own ministers that would bind his nation together and set them in opposition to Judah. We must be wary of leaders who use corrupt religion to manipulate entire nations. Pray for nations that are held captive by false religion, that Christ will come and set them free. (***See Ministry*** *> Great Commission> Make Disciples> Prayers> That they would believe in Christ as Savior,* TopicGuide page A56.)

▸ WORSHIP

11:16 Changing churches. How often do you change churches? Are you dissatisfied in your current church for no good reason? Or are you satisfied in a church that no longer preaches the Word? Both are terrible errors. The Levites and laypeople who left decaying Israel for Judah did so because Jeroboam would not allow biblical worship of God. Those who sincerely worship God will find a church that preaches the Word, serves the sacraments rightly, and enforces biblical, loving church discipline. These Israelites show us that we should be willing to take drastic steps to be with God's people in a biblical church. (***See Worship*** *>NT Church Government> Local church,* TopicGuide page A30.)

11:22 Perhaps aware of the struggles his father Solomon had faced as he ascended to the throne of Israel (1 Kings 1), Rehoboam clearly established Abijah as his successor.

11:23 By dispersing his sons throughout the kingdom, Rehoboam not only bolstered his defenses but also heightened his personal control of Judah and rendered hostile acts against the dynasty more difficult.

EGYPT INVADES JUDAH

12:1 2 Chr 11:17 **12** But when Rehoboam was firmly established and strong, he abandoned the Law of
the LORD, and all Israel followed him in this sin. [2]Because they were unfaithful to
the LORD, King Shishak of Egypt came up and attacked Jerusalem in the fifth year of King
12:3 2 Chr 16:8 Rehoboam's reign. [3]He came with 1,200 chariots, 60,000 horses,* and a countless army
Nah 3:9 of foot soldiers, including Libyans, Sukkites, and Ethiopians.* [4]Shishak conquered Judah's
12:4 fortified towns and then advanced to attack Jerusalem.
2 Chr 11:5-12 [5]The prophet Shemaiah then met with Rehoboam and Judah's leaders, who had all fled
12:5 to Jerusalem because of Shishak. Shemaiah told them, "This is what the LORD says: You
Deut 28:15 have abandoned Me, so I am abandoning you to Shishak."
2 Chr 11:2; 15:2 [6]Then the leaders of Israel and the king humbled themselves and said, "The LORD is
12:6 Exod 9:27 right in doing this to us!"
Dan 9:14 [7]When the LORD saw their change of heart, he gave this message to Shemaiah: "Since
12:7 the people have humbled themselves, I will not completely destroy them and will soon
1 Kgs 21:29 2 Chr 34:25-27 give them some relief. I will not use Shishak to pour out My anger on Jerusalem. [8]But they
Ps 78:38 will become his subjects, so they will know the difference between serving Me and serving
12:8 earthly rulers."
Deut 28:47-48 [9]So King Shishak of Egypt came up and attacked Jerusalem. He ransacked the treasur-
12:9-16 ies of the LORD's Temple and the royal palace; he stole everything, including all the gold
//1 Kgs 14:25-31 2 Chr 9:15-16 shields Solomon had made. [10]King Rehoboam later replaced them with bronze shields as
substitutes, and he entrusted them to the care of the commanders of the guard who pro-
tected the entrance to the royal palace. [11]Whenever the king went to the Temple of the
12:12 LORD, the guards would also take the shields and then return them to the guardroom.
2 Chr 12:6-7; 19:3 [12]Because Rehoboam humbled himself, the LORD's anger was turned away, and He did not
destroy him completely. There were still some good things in the land of Judah.

SUMMARY OF REHOBOAM'S REIGN

12:13 [13]King Rehoboam firmly established himself in Jerusalem and continued to rule. He was
1 Kgs 14:21 forty-one years old when he became king, and he reigned seventeen years in Jerusalem,
the city the LORD had chosen from among all the tribes of Israel as the place to honor His
12:14 name. Rehoboam's mother was Naamah, a woman from Ammon. [14]But he was an evil
2 Chr 19:3 king, for he did not seek the LORD with all his heart.

12:3a Or *charioteers,* or *horsemen.* 12:3b Hebrew *and Cushites.*

12:1-2 The chronicler carefully crafted his narratives to illustrate a theology of retribution. He explicitly ties disobedience to punishment and obedience to blessing. Hence here Rehoboam is said to abandon the law of the Lord only to find himself immediately under threat from Egypt.

12:1, 4 Rehoboam resorted to a kind of hubris that cost him the kingdom. Overconfident in his defenses, Rehoboam lapsed in his obedience to the law of God (the precise nature of his disobedience is unknown, but see 1 Kings 14:22-24). The fortified cities proved useless against Shishak's onslaught. The author does not fail to note the irony.

12:2 Shishak was the founder of Egypt's twenty-second dynasty, and the record of his campaign against Israel is found inscribed on the walls of a temple in the Egyptian city of Karnak. Jerusalem is not named among the towns Shishak destroyed, corroborating the biblical record.

12:5-7 In keeping with the principle expressed in 2 Chronicles 7:14, God extended His mercy to Judah because they humbled themselves and acknowledged their guilt.

▸ SPIRITUAL WARFARE

12:8 Servants of sin. Under the Old Covenant, God did not ultimately desert sinful Israel but always cared for a faithful remnant. Under the New Covenant that we have with God through Jesus Christ, God will never completely abandon us to our sin. There will be consequences—our marriage, our job, our friendships—all could be forfeited if we choose to live in our sin. God may allow sin to gain its horrible mastery in our lives to show us how foolish we were to think we could try to live without Him as our King. (***See Spiritual Warfare**> Resisting Sin and Evil> Consequences> Of Disobedience> God may allow consequences to run their course,* TopicGuide page A46.)

12:9-11 While enormous amounts of gold symbolized the grandeur of Solomon's kingdom, the replacement of the gold with bronze ceremonial shields signaled the decline of the kingdom. Rehoboam attempted to maintain a façade of glory, but the chronicler reckoned his efforts unimpressive.

12:14 The chronicler evaluated Rehoboam negatively despite his flashes of repentance. The chronicler often displays a concern for wholehearted obedience, and he judges partial attempts to seek after God to be significant failures.

15The rest of the events of Rehoboam's reign, from beginning to end, are recorded in
The Record of Shemaiah the Prophet and *The Record of Iddo the Seer,* which are part of the
genealogical record. Rehoboam and Jeroboam were continually at war with each other.
16When Rehoboam died, he was buried in the City of David. Then his son Abijah became
the next king.

ABIJAH'S WAR WITH JEROBOAM

13 Abijah began to rule over Judah in the eighteenth year of Jeroboam's reign in Is-
rael. 2He reigned in Jerusalem three years. His mother was Maacah,* the daughter
of Uriel from Gibeah.

Then war broke out between Abijah and Jeroboam. 3Judah, led by King Abijah, fielded
400,000 select warriors, while Jeroboam mustered 800,000 select troops from Israel.
4When the army of Judah arrived in the hill country of Ephraim, Abijah stood on Mount
Zemaraim and shouted to Jeroboam and all Israel: "Listen to me! 5Don't you realize that
the LORD, the God of Israel, made a lasting covenant* with David, giving him and his de-
scendants the throne of Israel forever? 6Yet Jeroboam son of Nebat, a mere servant of Da-
vid's son Solomon, rebelled against his master. 7Then a whole gang of scoundrels joined
him, defying Solomon's son Rehoboam when he was young and inexperienced and could
not stand up to them.
8"Do you really think you can stand against the kingdom of the LORD that is led by the
descendants of David? You may have a vast army, and you have those gold calves that
Jeroboam made as your gods. 9But you have chased away the priests of the LORD (the de-
scendants of Aaron) and the Levites, and you have appointed your own priests, just like
the pagan nations. You let anyone become a priest these days! Whoever comes to be
dedicated with a young bull and seven rams can become a priest of these so-called gods
of yours!
10"But as for us, the LORD is our God, and we have not abandoned Him. Only the descen-
dants of Aaron serve the LORD as priests, and the Levites alone may help them in their
work. 11They present burnt offerings and fragrant incense to the LORD every morning and
evening. They place the Bread of the Presence on the holy table, and they light the gold
lampstand every evening. We are following the instructions of the LORD our God, but you
have abandoned Him. 12So you see, God is with us. He is our leader. His priests blow their
trumpets and lead us into battle against you. O people of Israel, do not fight against the
LORD, the God of your ancestors, for you will not succeed!"

12:15 1 Kgs 14:29; 2 Chr 9:29; 12:5
12:16 2 Chr 11:20
13:1-2 //1 Kgs 15:1-2; 2 Chr 11:20
13:2 1 Kgs 15:6
13:4 Josh 18:22
13:5 Num 18:19; 2 Sam 7:12-16
13:6 1 Kgs 11:26
13:7 2 Chr 12:13
13:8 1 Kgs 12:28; 2 Chr 11:15
13:9 Exod 29:29-33; 2 Chr 11:14-15; Jer 2:11; 5:7
13:11 Exod 25:30-39; 29:38-39; Lev 24:5-9; 2 Chr 2:4
13:12 Num 10:8-9

13:2 As in most Greek manuscripts and Syriac version (see also 2 Chr 11:20-21; 1 Kgs 15:2); Hebrew reads *Micaiah,* a variant spelling of Maacah. 13:5 Hebrew *a covenant of salt.*

13:1 Abijah is called Abijam in 1 Kings 15:1. It is possible that a textual difficulty caused the variation. It is also possible that the chronicler changed Abijam, "My father is Yam" (a pagan deity), to Abijah, "My father is Yah" (a shortened form of Yahweh) to reflect his more positive account of Abijah's reign.

13:4-8 In making his appeal to the army of the northern kingdom, Abijah assigned blame to Jeroboam for the rebellion, and he may have suggested that the troops would find amnesty if they abandon Jeroboam and recognized the legitimacy of the Davidic dynasty.

13:4-12 Abijah's speech is clearly employed by the chronicler to address two of his major themes: the superiority of the Davidic dynasty and the Levitical priesthood. Abijah's speech defends these two institutions against Jeroboam's rebellion and religious innovations.

13:8 The chronicler again (see 2 Chronicles 9:8) assigns ownership of the kingdom of Israel to God Himself. David and his descendants were vassals reigning under the authority of God, who is ultimately the King of Israel.

▸ADOPTION

13:12 Try to avoid violence. Have you ever been forced to defend yourself? Abijah readied himself for battle, but he issued words of peace. It's a complicated balance—God calls us to live lives of peace (James 3:18), yet we should be prepared to defend those under our care (Deuteronomy 33:7). Be ready for difficult circumstances, but be an instrument of God's peace wherever possible. (***See Adoption****> With Christ> Supernatural> A life of everlasting peace,* TopicGuide page A37.)

13:12 This verse alludes to Israel's holy war tradition. God was with Israel not merely in a metaphysical sense; He was present to fight for them (compare Exodus 14:13-14 and Deuteronomy 20).

13:13 Josh 8:4-9
13:14 2 Chr 14:11
13:15 2 Chr 14:12
13:18 2 Chr 14:11
13:20 1 Sam 25:38; 1 Kgs 14:20
13:22–14:1 1 Kgs 15:6-8; 2 Chr 24:27

13Meanwhile, Jeroboam had secretly sent part of his army around behind the men of Ju-
dah to ambush them. 14When Judah realized that they were being attacked from the front
and the rear, they cried out to the LORD for help. Then the priests blew the trumpets, 15and
the men of Judah began to shout. At the sound of their battle cry, God defeated Jeroboam
and all Israel and routed them before Abijah and the army of Judah.
16The Israelite army fled from Judah, and God handed them over to Judah in defeat. 17Abi-
jah and his army inflicted heavy losses on them; 500,000 of Israel's select troops were killed
that day. 18So Judah defeated Israel on that occasion because they trusted in the LORD, the
God of their ancestors. 19Abijah and his army pursued Jeroboam's troops and captured some
of his towns, including Bethel, Jeshanah, and Ephron, along with their surrounding villages.
20So Jeroboam of Israel never regained his power during Abijah's lifetime, and finally the
LORD struck him down and he died. 21Meanwhile, Abijah of Judah grew more and more
powerful. He married fourteen wives and had twenty-two sons and sixteen daughters.
22The rest of the events of Abijah's reign, including his words and deeds, are recorded in
The Commentary of Iddo the Prophet.

EARLY YEARS OF ASA'S REIGN

14:2-3 //1 Kgs 15:11-12
14:3 Exod 34:13; Deut 7:5; 1 Kgs 15:12-14
14:5 2 Chr 34:4, 7
14:6 2 Chr 11:5; 15:15
14:7 2 Chr 8:5

14 1*When Abijah died, he was buried in the City of David. Then his son Asa became
the next king. There was peace in the land for ten years. 2*Asa did what was pleas-
ing and good in the sight of the LORD his God. 3He removed the foreign altars and the pagan
shrines. He smashed the sacred pillars and cut down the Asherah poles. 4He commanded
the people of Judah to seek the LORD, the God of their ancestors, and to obey His law and His
commands. 5Asa also removed the pagan shrines, as well as the incense altars from every
one of Judah's towns. So Asa's kingdom enjoyed a period of peace. 6During those peaceful
years, he was able to build up the fortified towns throughout Judah. No one tried to make
war against him at this time, for the LORD was giving him rest from his enemies.
7Asa told the people of Judah, "Let us build towns and fortify them with walls, towers,
gates, and bars. The land is still ours because we sought the LORD our God, and He has
given us peace on every side." So they went ahead with these projects and brought them
to completion.

14:1 Verse 14:1 is numbered 13:23 in the Hebrew text. 14:2 Verses 14:2-15 are numbered 14:1-14 in Hebrew text.

13:19 The captured town of Bethel was one of the two cities used by Jeroboam as centers for his calf worship. Apparently the calves were with the army at the time of the battle mentioned in 2 Chronicles 13:8 and were not captured. Some time later, however, Bethel fell under the control of the northern kingdom once again, and calf worship was reinstated (see 2 Kings 10:28-29).

13:20-21 The chronicler contrasts the fates of Jeroboam and Abijah to further emphasize the blessings that flow from trusting in the Lord.

14:1 The chronicler employs a number of chronological divisions in Asa's reign. Here he records ten years of peace, and in the fifteenth year there is covenant renewal. Then there is peace until the thirty-fifth year, invasion in the thirty-sixth year, foot disease in the thirty-ninth year, and death in the forty-first year.

14:1–16:14 The chronicler presents the reign of Asa in far more detail than the author of Kings. In so doing the chronicler fashions his account of Asa in keeping with his theological outlook. Asa's reign is divided into two major sections displaying God's blessing for obedience and curses for disobedience.

14:3 This verse appears to be in tension with 2 Chronicles 15:17, which claims that Asa did not successfully remove the pagan altars from the land. It is possible that 14:3 is concerned with Asa's earlier reign and 15:17 with his later reign. It is also possible that the qualifying phrase "from Israel" in 15:17 indicates that Asa did not remove the shrines from lands he took over from the northern kingdom during his reign.

14:3-5 Asa's reform activities included the removal of pagan elements of worship. The sacred pillars were likely memorial stones erected to various deities. The Asherah poles were wooden structures dedicated to the fertility goddess Asherah, a consort of Baal.

14:6 The rest that Asa enjoyed evokes the peace and prosperity in the land God promised to the Israelites. Building and fortification, as well as times of peace, are blessings from God for faithfulness and obedience (see also 2 Chronicles 17:12; 26:6-10). But this rest had to be vigilantly maintained. In Christ, the church receives the promise of complete rest without the threat of loss (Hebrews 3–4).

14:7 Evidencing his devotion, Asa ascribes praise and glory to God for His blessings. Asa's use of the plural in his speech testifies to his bond with his people and his willingness to identify himself with his subjects as joint recipients of God's grace (on seeking the Lord, see note at 7:14).

8King Asa had an army of 300,000 warriors from the tribe of Judah, armed with large 14:8
shields and spears. He also had an army of 280,000 warriors from the tribe of Benjamin, 2 Chr 13:3
armed with small shields and bows. Both armies were composed of well-trained fighting
men.
9Once an Ethiopian* named Zerah attacked Judah with an army of 1,000,000 men* and 14:9
300 chariots. They advanced to the town of Mareshah, 10so Asa deployed his armies for 2 Chr 11:8; 12:2-3; 16:8
battle in the valley north of Mareshah.* 11Then Asa cried out to the LORD his God, "O LORD, 14:11
no one but You can help the powerless against the mighty! Help us, O LORD our God, for 2 Chr 13:14, 18
we trust in You alone. It is in Your name that we have come against this vast horde.
O LORD, You are our God; do not let mere men prevail against You!"
12So the LORD defeated the Ethiopians* in the presence of Asa and the army of Judah, 14:12
and the enemy fled. 13Asa and his army pursued them as far as Gerar, and so many Ethio- 2 Chr 13:15
pians fell that they were unable to rally. They were destroyed by the LORD and His army, 14:13 Gen 10:19
and the army of Judah carried off a vast amount of plunder.
14While they were at Gerar, they attacked all the towns in that area, and terror from the 14:14 2 Chr 17:10
LORD came upon the people there. As a result, a vast amount of plunder was taken from
these towns, too. 15They also attacked the camps of herdsmen and captured many sheep,
goats, and camels before finally returning to Jerusalem.

ASA'S RELIGIOUS REFORMS

15 Then the Spirit of God came upon Azariah son of Oded, 2and he went out to meet 15:1 2 Chr 20:14; 24:20
King Asa as he was returning from the battle. "Listen to me, Asa!" he shouted. "Lis- 15:2
ten, all you people of Judah and Benjamin! The LORD will stay with you as long as you stay 2 Chr 15:4, 15; 20:17
with Him! Whenever you seek Him, you will find Him. But if you abandon Him, He will 15:3
abandon you. 3For a long time Israel was without the true God, without a priest to teach Lev 10:8-11
them, and without the Law to instruct them. 4But whenever they were in trouble and 1 Kgs 12:28-33 2 Chr 17:9
turned to the LORD, the God of Israel, and sought Him out, they found Him.
5"During those dark times, it was not safe to travel. Problems troubled the people of 15:4 Deut 4:29
every land. 6Nation fought against nation, and city against city, for God was troubling 15:5 Judg 5:6

15:6 Matt 24:7

14:9a Hebrew *a Cushite.* 14:9b Or *an army of thousands and thousands;* Hebrew reads *an army of a thousand thousands.* 14:10 Or *in the Zephathah Valley near Mareshah.* 14:12 Hebrew *Cushites;* also in 14:13.

14:8-9 The numbers for Asa and Zerah's armies seem remarkably large. Some have suggested that the word signifying "thousand" may be better rendered "unit" or "officer." This would mean Asa's army was composed of 580 units of unknown size to Zerah's army of 1000 units. It is also possible the numbers are exaggerated to magnify the nature of God's intervention. In any case, Zerah's army was nearly twice as large as Asa's army.

14:11 Asa responded in ideal fashion to the crisis before him. Despite being outnumbered nearly 2 to 1, he committed himself and his army to God and trusted in God for a dramatic victory. For the chronicler's audience, who was no doubt the underdog in any military contest, this story inspired hope.

14:12-15 The language of Israel's holy war tradition (see Exodus 15; Deuteronomy 20) dominates this battle account—"the LORD defeated," "destroyed by the LORD," and "terror from the LORD." The decisive victory and resulting plunder all indicate that God fought for Israel.

▸ SPIRITUAL WARFARE
14:14 Aiding and abetting. Aiding others in commiting sin is a serious matter. In this context, Judah appeared to be securing an area from which invasions were launched. Armies would march north and south, parallel to the Mediterranean Sea, and when they reached Gerar, the geography allowed them to cut east and quickly strike western Judah. The residents of Gerar seem to have been complicit in this tactic, allowing free access to Judah through their region. Judah subjugated those who aided their enemies. God is not pleased with those who purposely act in such a way as to encourage sin against Him and His people. God's final vengeance against them will come (Revelation 6:9-17). (***See Spiritual Warfare****> Resisting Sin and Evil> Standing Firm> Empowered to help others see their sin,* TopicGuide page A46.)

15:1 Azariah the prophet is otherwise unknown outside of Chronicles.

15:1-7 Azariah's speech as recorded by the chronicler would have immediate relevance to the chronicler's audience. They, too, were living in times similar to those described by Azariah. Yet if they sought God and obeyed His law, they would find God and be rewarded for their work.

15:3-6 The exact time period described by Azariah is unknown. Some have taken it to be a generalized description applicable at various points in Israel's history. Others have found verse 5 to be highly compatible with the time of the Judges.

15:7 them with every kind of problem. 7But as for you, be strong and courageous, for your
Josh 1:7, 9 work will be rewarded."
15:8 8When Asa heard this message from Azariah the prophet,* he took courage and re-
2 Chr 4:1; 8:12 moved all the detestable idols from the land of Judah and Benjamin and in the towns he
had captured in the hill country of Ephraim. And he repaired the altar of the LORD, which
stood in front of the entry room of the LORD's Temple.
15:9 9Then Asa called together all the people of Judah and Benjamin, along with the people
2 Chr 11:16 of Ephraim, Manasseh, and Simeon who had settled among them. For many from Israel
had moved to Judah during Asa's reign when they saw that the LORD his God was with
him. 10The people gathered at Jerusalem in late spring,* during the fifteenth year of Asa's
reign.
15:11 11On that day they sacrificed to the LORD 700 cattle and 7,000 sheep and goats from
2 Chr 14:13-15 the plunder they had taken in the battle. 12Then they entered into a covenant to seek the
15:12 2 Chr 23:16 LORD, the God of their ancestors, with all their heart and soul. 13They agreed that anyone
15:13 who refused to seek the LORD, the God of Israel, would be put to death—whether young or
Exod 22:20 old, man or woman. 14They shouted out their oath of loyalty to the LORD with trumpets
Deut 13:6-9, 15 blaring and rams' horns sounding. 15All in Judah were happy about this covenant, for they
15:15 2 Chr 14:7 had entered into it with all their heart. They earnestly sought after God, and they found
15:16-19 Him. And the LORD gave them rest from their enemies on every side.
//1 Kgs 15:13-15 2 Chr 14:2-5 16King Asa even deposed his grandmother* Maacah from her position as queen mother

15:8 As in Syriac version and Latin Vulgate (see also 15:1); Hebrew reads *from Oded the prophet.* 15:10 Hebrew *in the third month.* This month of the ancient Hebrew lunar calendar usually occurs within the months of May and June. 15:16 Hebrew *his mother.*

15:8 Asa's reforms extended not only to Judah and Benjamin, but also to the captured towns of Israel. This seems to indicate that there was at least minor conflict between Asa and Israel prior to the 35th year of Asa (2 Chronicles 15:19). The repairs to the altar probably refer to ordinary refurbishing, since no damage to the altar is recorded in the previous reigns.

15:9 The chronicler is concerned to show that the ideal Israelite community was composed of "all Israel," not just the southern tribes. Throughout his account he highlights various instances when residents of the north came to Judah out of faithfulness to Temple worship. This unity was grounded in the true worship of God according to His law and centered at His Temple.

15:10 The celebration of covenant renewal probably took place during the Harvest Festival (Exodus 23:16; 34:22; Leviticus 23:15-21), when Jerusalem would have been filled with pilgrims coming to worship at the Temple as required by the Law of Moses.

15:10-15 Asa is one of several faithful kings of Judah who held covenant renewal celebrations (2 Chronicles 29:10; 34:30-32). The celebration featured sacrifices and a rededication of the community to seek after God. Covenant renewal also emphasized God's continuing faithfulness and the people's continuity with their ancestors in the faith.

▸ CHURCH

15:12 Reentering the covenant. Every time you attend church, you reaffirm your covenant with God. Especially when we partake of the Lord's Supper, we renew our covenant with God, who sent Jesus Christ to live a perfect life and die a sacrificial death for us. Just as we continually repent and believe the gospel, we should continually confirm God's promises to us and reaffirm our promises to Him in our worship. Keep on believing, keep on repenting, and keep on rehearsing the promises and warnings found in the Word of God. (***See Church**> Role> Sacraments> As a covenant-renewal ceremony,* TopicGuide page A50.)

15:12 For the chronicler, mere rote performance of religious rituals was not sufficient; the people needed to seek God with "all their heart and soul." This emphasis on wholehearted obedience recurs throughout 1 and 2 Chronicles (2 Chronicles 6:14; 19:9; 25:2).

▸ HOLINESS

15:13 To seek or not to seek. Reading the Bible isn't always easy. For instance, you might not know that the phrase "seeking God" isn't used in a consistent manner throughout the Bible. The chronicler used it to mean obedience to the Law (2 Chronicles 15:13). But the Psalmist lamented that the wicked do not seek God and inferred that no one naturally seeks Him (Psalm 53:2), and Paul used the same verses to discuss the fallen nature of all humanity (Romans 3:9-18). What do these differences mean? It means that we must always look at the context to define biblical words and concepts. Ask God to make you more than a reader of Scripture—He wants you to be a student of it. (***See Holiness**> Submission> Learning God's Word> Glorifying God with the mind,* TopicGuide page A40.)

15:15 Again the chronicler draws an explicit connection between the people's fidelity and God's blessing. As a result of the wholehearted covenant renewal celebration, God grants His people rest from their enemies. The message to the chronicler's audience is quite clear: wholeheartedly seek God and receive His blessings.

▸ WORSHIP

15:16 Take out the garbage. King Asa knew that idols deserved to be thrown onto the trash heap, so he had the ornate Asherah pole of Maacah thrown into the Kidron Valley, a smoldering garbage dump. Are there items in your home or office that would best be destroyed? Treat items strongly associated with witchcraft, paganism, or idolatry the same way—throw them into the trash. (***See Worship**> OT> Prohibitions> Wrong Preparation> Not holy due to unrepentant idolatry,* TopicGuide page A28.)

because she had made an obscene Asherah pole. He cut down her obscene pole, broke it up,
and burned it in the Kidron Valley. 17Although the pagan shrines were not removed from Is-
rael, Asa's heart remained completely faithful throughout his life. 18He brought into the Tem-
ple of God the silver and gold and the various items that he and his father had dedicated.
19So there was no more war until the thirty-fifth year of Asa's reign.

FINAL YEARS OF ASA'S REIGN

16 In the thirty-sixth year of Asa's reign, King Baasha of Israel invaded Judah and for- 16:1-6
tified Ramah in order to prevent anyone from entering or leaving King Asa's terri- //1 Kgs 15:17-22
tory in Judah.
2Asa responded by removing the silver and gold from the treasuries of the Temple of
the LORD and the royal palace. He sent it to King Ben-hadad of Aram, who was ruling in Da-
mascus, along with this message:

3"Let there be a treaty between you and me like the one between your father and
my father. See, I am sending you silver and gold. Break your treaty with King Baasha
of Israel so that he will leave me alone."

4Ben-hadad agreed to King Asa's request and sent the commanders of his army to attack 16:4
the towns of Israel. They conquered the towns of Ijon, Dan, Abel-beth-maacah,* and all the Exod 1:11
store cities in Naphtali. 5As soon as Baasha of Israel heard what was happening, he aban-
doned his project of fortifying Ramah and stopped all work on it. 6Then King Asa called out
all the men of Judah to carry away the building stones and timbers that Baasha had been 16:7
using to fortify Ramah. Asa used these materials to fortify the towns of Geba and Mizpah. 1 Kgs 16:1 2 Chr 14:11; 19:2;
7At that time Hanani the seer came to King Asa and told him, "Because you have put 32:7-8
your trust in the king of Aram instead of in the LORD your God, you missed your chance to 16:8
destroy the army of the king of Aram. 8Don't you remember what happened to the Ethio- 2 Chr 12:3; 13:16, 18;
pians* and Libyans and their vast army, with all of their chariots and charioteers?* At that 14:9
time you relied on the LORD, and He handed them over to you. 9The eyes of the LORD 16:9 2 Chr 15:17 Prov 15:3 Zech 4:10

16:4 As in parallel text at 1 Kgs 15:20; Hebrew reads *Abel-maim,* a variant spelling of Abel-beth-maacah. 16:8a Hebrew *Cushites.* 16:8b Or *and horsemen?*

15:17 Regarding the incompleteness of Asa's purge, see note at 14:3.

15:19 This verse seems to contradict 1 Kings 15:16, which indicates that there was constant warfare between Asa and King Baasha of the northern kingdom. However, the chronicler may only have had large-scale engagements in mind. The more serious difficulty arises from the placement of Baasha's invasion in Asa's 36th year, when according to 1 Kings 15:33 Baasha had died by Asa's 26th year. It may be that the chronicler calculated the 35th year from the division of the kingdom, but this solution also has problems.

16:1 Ramah was located on a key north-south ridge about five miles north of Jerusalem. Its strategic position made it well suited for Baasha's goal of cutting off Judah.

16:2 The Arameans were constant enemies of the northern kingdom throughout their history. This Ben-hadad is not to be confused with the Ben-hadad who distressed Israel during the rule of the Omride dynasty (1 Kings 20—2 Kings 8).

16:3 While Asa's diplomatic maneuvers appear wise and effective, the chronicler viewed alliances with other nations as symptomatic of a lack of trust in God's protection. This will become clear from Hanani's condemnation in 16:8.

16:7 Asa may have succeeded in diverting Baasha's advances on his territory, but the prophet Hanani indicates that Asa's self-reliance caused him to miss out on a larger potential victory over both Israel and the Arameans.

16:8 The language of "chariots and charioteers" belongs to Israel's holy war tradition going back to the Red Sea crossing (Exodus 14–15) and further condemns Asa's lack of trust. If God defeated the armies of Egypt for Israel, could he not have done the same against the Arameans?

▸ ADOPTION

16:9 A life without power. When the electricity goes out in a home, sometimes it takes a while to restore the power. An impatient homeowner might begin to try and repair the problem himself, but that usually results in even more problems—no power and serious injury! King Asa saw that the power of God had departed from his rule, so he tried to strengthen his political power with his own methods. That doomed his rule to even greater weakness. God strengthens His people, but He also allows us to be weakened when we fight against His will (Deuteronomy 28:43; Psalm 32:3). Submit to the Lord, and you will find strength (Isaiah 40:28-31; Hebrews 12:9), but if you attempt to live by your own might, you will get exactly what you wished for—life without God's power. (***See Adoption*** > *With Christ* > *Supernatural* > *A life of supernatural power,* TopicGuide page A37.)

search the whole earth in order to strengthen those whose hearts are fully committed to
Him. What a fool you have been! From now on you will be at war."
10 Asa became so angry with Hanani for saying this that he threw him into prison and
put him in stocks. At that time Asa also began to oppress some of his people.

SUMMARY OF ASA'S REIGN

16:11–17:1 //1 Kgs 15:23-24; 16:12 Jer 17:5; 16:14 Gen 50:2, John 19:39-40

11 The rest of the events of Asa's reign, from beginning to end, are recorded in *The Book of the
Kings of Judah and Israel.* 12 In the thirty-ninth year of his reign, Asa developed a serious foot
disease. Yet even with the severity of his disease, he did not seek the LORD's help but turned
only to his physicians. 13 So he died in the forty-first year of his reign. 14 He was buried in the
tomb he had carved out for himself in the City of David. He was laid on a bed perfumed with
sweet spices and fragrant ointments, and the people built a huge funeral fire in his honor.

JEHOSHAPHAT RULES IN JUDAH

17:1 1 Kgs 15:24; 17:2 2 Chr 11:5; 15:8

17 Then Jehoshaphat, Asa's son, became the next king. He strengthened Judah to
stand against any attack from Israel. 2 He stationed troops in all the fortified towns

16:10 The imprisonment of Hanani marks the first instance of persecution of a prophet of God by a king of Israel or Judah. The oppressed people were likely followers of the prophet who echoed Hanani's critique of Asa.

▸ WORSHIP
16:10 Angry at God. The persecution faced by God's people is often misdirected. In this case, Asa wasn't angry with Hanani so much as he was with God. Putting Hanani into a cruel dungeon was the means to Asa's end—living apart from the Word and the presence of God. Yet even as Asa lay suffering for two years of a wasting disease, he did not seek God's help. Look in your heart and repent of any anger against God you find. (***See Worship**> NT> Our Role> Attitude> Willing to repent of bad attitude,* TopicGuide page A32.)

16:12 Gangrene, gout, and dropsy have all been proposed as the foot disease that afflicted Asa. It is likely that the chronicler himself did not know the precise nature of the disease. What was important for the chronicler is that in this case, disease revealed God's displeasure with Asa's lack of trust during the conflict with Israel.

16:14 The elaborate funeral indicates that, despite his later failures, Asa was rightly reckoned a godly king of Judah. The fire was a sign of honor and was not used to cremate the body.

▸ HOLINESS
17:1 A father's example. Asa's son Jehoshaphat followed his father's example in both the good and the bad, and he served God in his kingly duties. Jehoshaphat loved God, hated sin, and financed a government-sponsored teaching ministry that filled his people with a holy fear (2 Chronicles 17:10). Thank God that He uses fathers, even inconsistent ones like Asa, to teach sons to obey Him. (***See Holiness**> Submission> Learning God's Word> Teaching your children,* TopicGuide page A40.)

17:1-2 It is possible that Jehoshaphat served as co-regent during the final years of his father's reign due to Asa's illness. The recurring conflict with the northern kingdom spurs Jehoshaphat to solidify his defenses and prepare Judah to withstand an attack from Israel.

BECAUSE GOD IS A PERSONAL SPIRIT

I will seek intimate fellowship with Him.

The eyes of the LORD search the whole earth in order to strengthen those whose hearts are fully committed to Him.

2 CHRONICLES 16:9

FOR THE NEXT *GOD IS A PERSONAL SPIRIT* FEATURE SEE PAGE 1059.

of Judah, and he assigned additional garrisons to the land of Judah and to the towns of
Ephraim that his father, Asa, had captured.
3The LORD was with Jehoshaphat because he followed the example of his father's early
years* and did not worship the images of Baal. 4He sought his father's God and obeyed His 17:4
commands instead of following the evil practices of the kingdom of Israel. 5So the LORD es- 1 Kgs 12:28
tablished Jehoshaphat's control over the kingdom of Judah. All the people of Judah 17:5
brought gifts to Jehoshaphat, so he became very wealthy and highly esteemed. 6He was 2 Chr 18:1
deeply committed to* the ways of the LORD. He removed the pagan shrines and Asherah 17:6 2 Chr 15:17
poles from Judah. 17:7
7In the third year of his reign Jehoshaphat sent his officials to teach in all the towns of 2 Chr 15:3; 19:8; 35:3
Judah. These officials included Ben-hail, Obadiah, Zechariah, Nethanel, and Micaiah. 8He 17:8
sent Levites along with them, including Shemaiah, Nethaniah, Zebadiah, Asahel, Shemira- 2 Chr 19:8
moth, Jehonathan, Adonijah, Tobijah, and Tob-adonijah. He also sent out the priests Elish-
ama and Jehoram. 9They took copies of the Book of the Law of the LORD and traveled 17:9
around through all the towns of Judah, teaching the people. Deut 6:4-9
10Then the fear of the LORD fell over all the surrounding kingdoms so that none of them 17:10 2 Chr 14:14
wanted to declare war on Jehoshaphat. 11Some of the Philistines brought him gifts and sil-
ver as tribute, and the Arabs brought 7,700 rams and 7,700 male goats. 17:11 2 Chr 9:14; 26:8
12So Jehoshaphat became more and more powerful and built fortresses and storage cit-
ies throughout Judah. 13He stored numerous supplies in Judah's towns and stationed an
army of seasoned troops at Jerusalem. 14His army was enrolled according to ancestral
clans.

From Judah there were 300,000 troops organized in units of 1,000, under the
command of Adnah. 15Next in command was Jehohanan, who commanded 280,000
troops. 16Next was Amasiah son of Zicri, who volunteered for the LORD's service, with 17:16
200,000 troops under his command. Judg 5:2, 9
17From Benjamin there were 200,000 troops equipped with bows and shields. They 1 Chr 29:9
were under the command of Eliada, a veteran soldier. 18Next in command was
Jehozabad, who commanded 180,000 armed men.

19These were the troops stationed in Jerusalem to serve the king, besides those Jehosha- 17:19
phat stationed in the fortified towns throughout Judah. 2 Chr 17:2

17:3 Some Hebrew manuscripts read *the example of his father, David.* 17:6 Hebrew *His heart was courageous in.*

17:3 The chronicler draws a positive comparison between Jehoshaphat and his father Asa. Their two reigns are patterned similarly by the chronicler: reforms and building projects (2 Chronicles 14:2-8; 17:1-19), battle report (2 Chronicles 14:9-15; 18:1–19:3), further reforms (2 Chronicles 15:1-19; 19:4-11), second battle report (2 Chronicles 16:1-9; 20:1-30), and failure and death (2 Chronicles 16:10-14; 20:31–21:1). The theme of foreign alliances is also common to both.

17:4-5 These verses demonstrate the chronicler's principle that God blesses obedience. Jehoshaphat sought God and obeyed His commands and as a result God strengthened Jehoshaphat's kingdom and blessed him with wealth and prestige (compare 1 Chronicles 29:2-5; 2 Chronicles 9:13-27).

17:6 For Asherah poles, see note at 2 Chronicles 14:3-5.

17:8 Although Jehoshaphat's educational program seems to be under the administration of lay officials, the priests and Levites played a crucial role as well. The teaching function of the Levites and priests is also attested to in Leviticus 10:11; Deuteronomy 33:10; Hosea 4:6; Jeremiah 18:18; and Malachi 2:7.

17:9 The precise content of the Book of the Law cannot be known for certain, but it is likely that at least the five books of Moses are in view. The phrase establishes the notion of a canon of authoritative books early in Israel's history.

17:10-19 The chronicler notes once again how blessing follows obedience. Jehoshaphat's attentiveness to the law of the Lord brought subsequent peace and tribute from his enemies, strong fortifications, and a large, well-supplied army.

17:14 Judah's army was still organized according to clan structure, much as it had been in Judges 6:15; Numbers 1:16; 1 Samuel 10:19; and 2 Chronicles 1:2.

17:14-18 Regarding the large numbers given in these verses, see note at 2 Chronicles 14:8-9. However these figures are to be interpreted, it is clear that the chronicler saw large armies as a sign of God's blessing. The size of Jehoshaphat's army exceeded that of other righteous kings, including Abijah, Asa, Amaziah, and Uzziah (13:3; 14:8; 25:5; 26:11-15).

JEHOSHAPHAT AND AHAB

18:1-27 //1 Kgs 22:1-28 **18** Jehoshaphat enjoyed great riches and high esteem, and he made an alliance with
Ahab of Israel by having his son marry Ahab's daughter. 2A few years later he
18:1 2 Chr 17:5 went to Samaria to visit Ahab, who prepared a great banquet for him and his officials.
They butchered great numbers of sheep, goats, and cattle for the feast. Then Ahab enticed
18:2 1 Kgs 22:2-35 Jehoshaphat to join forces with him to recover Ramoth-gilead.

3"Will you go with me to Ramoth-gilead?" King Ahab of Israel asked King Jehoshaphat
of Judah.

Jehoshaphat replied, "Why, of course! You and I are as one, and my troops are your
troops. We will certainly join you in battle." 4Then Jehoshaphat added, "But first let's find
out what the LORD says."

5So the king of Israel summoned the prophets, 400 of them, and asked them, "Should
we go to war against Ramoth-gilead, or should I hold back?"

They all replied, "Yes, go right ahead! God will give the king victory."

6But Jehoshaphat asked, "Is there not also a prophet of the LORD here? We should ask
him the same question."

7The king of Israel replied to Jehoshaphat, "There is one more man who could consult
the LORD for us, but I hate him. He never prophesies anything but trouble for me! His name
is Micaiah son of Imlah."

Jehoshaphat replied, "That's not the way a king should talk! Let's hear what he has to
say."

8So the king of Israel called one of his officials and said, "Quick! Bring Micaiah son of
Imlah."

MICAIAH PROPHESIES AGAINST AHAB

9King Ahab of Israel and King Jehoshaphat of Judah, dressed in their royal robes, were sit-
ting on thrones at the threshing floor near the gate of Samaria. All of Ahab's prophets were
prophesying there in front of them. 10One of them, Zedekiah son of Kenaanah, made
some iron horns and proclaimed, "This is what the LORD says: With these horns you will
gore the Arameans to death!"

11All the other prophets agreed. "Yes," they said, "go up to Ramoth-gilead and be victori-
ous, for the LORD will give the king victory!"

12Meanwhile, the messenger who went to get Micaiah said to him, "Look, all the proph-
ets are promising victory for the king. Be sure that you agree with them and promise suc-
cess."

18:13 13But Micaiah replied, "As surely as the LORD lives, I will say only what my God says."
Num 22:18-20, 35 14When Micaiah arrived before the king, Ahab asked him, "Micaiah, should we go to
war against Ramoth-gilead, or should I hold back?"

Micaiah replied sarcastically, "Yes, go up and be victorious, for you will have victory
over them!"

18:1 Like his father Asa, Jehoshaphat unwisely entered into a foreign alliance. Ahab, the most infamous king of the northern kingdom, and his Sidonian wife Jezebel plunged Israel into rampant Baal worship and persecuted the prophets of God (1 Kings 16:28–22:40).

▶ CHURCH
18:1 Giving our children away. Have you ever tried to help someone, but it backfired? Jehoshaphat sinned by allying himself with King Ahab of Israel (2 Chronicles 18:1), but more specifically he arranged for his son to marry a non-Israelite (which was forbidden, see Deuteronomy 7:3; Joshua 23:12; Nehemiah 13:25) from the unbelieving household of Ahab. Jehoshaphat may have thought this was helpful to his family or politically expedient, but because he forgot the counsel of the Word of God, he doomed his family to shame. Be very careful how you guide your children or those under your care. (***See Church****> Role> Preach> Instructions> Train in godly behavior and thinking,* TopicGuide page A49.)

18:6 The chronicler does not indicate how Jehoshaphat knew that the prophets of Ahab were not prophets of the Lord. One characteristic of the prophetic voice, however, is that it tended to run counter to popular opinion (Nehemiah 9:26; Jeremiah 25:4; 26:4-5; 29:24-32). It is possible that the prophets' unanimous support for Ahab's venture appropriately raised suspicion in Jehoshaphat's mind.

15But the king replied sharply, "How many times must I demand that you speak only the
truth to me when you speak for the LORD?"
16Then Micaiah told him, "In a vision I saw all Israel scattered on the mountains, like
sheep without a shepherd. And the LORD said, 'Their master has been killed.* Send them
home in peace.'"
17"Didn't I tell you?" the king of Israel exclaimed to Jehoshaphat. "He never prophesies
anything but trouble for me."
18Then Micaiah continued, "Listen to what the LORD says! I saw the LORD sitting on His
throne with all the armies of heaven around Him, on His right and on His left. 19And the
LORD said, 'Who can entice King Ahab of Israel to go into battle against Ramoth-gilead so
he can be killed?'
"There were many suggestions, 20and finally a spirit approached the LORD and said, 'I
can do it!'
"'How will you do this?' the LORD asked.
21"And the spirit replied, 'I will go out and inspire all of Ahab's prophets to speak lies.'
"'You will succeed,' said the LORD. 'Go ahead and do it.'
22"So you see, the LORD has put a lying spirit in the mouths of your prophets. For the
LORD has pronounced your doom."
23Then Zedekiah son of Kenaanah walked up to Micaiah and slapped him across the
face. "Since when did the Spirit of the LORD leave me to speak to you?" he demanded.
24And Micaiah replied, "You will find out soon enough when you are trying to hide in
some secret room!"
25"Arrest him!" the king of Israel ordered. "Take him back to Amon, the governor of the
city, and to my son Joash. 26Give them this order from the king: 'Put this man in prison,
and feed him nothing but bread and water until I return safely from the battle!'"
27But Micaiah replied, "If you return safely, it will mean that the LORD has not spoken
through me!" Then he added to those standing around, "Everyone mark my words!"

THE DEATH OF AHAB

28So King Ahab of Israel and King Jehoshaphat of Judah led their armies against Ramoth-
gilead. 29The king of Israel said to Jehoshaphat, "As we go into battle, I will disguise myself
so no one will recognize me, but you wear your royal robes." So the king of Israel dis-
guised himself, and they went into battle.

18:16 Num 27:17; Ezek 34:4-8; *Mark 6:34; Matt 9:36
18:18 Isa 6:1-5; Dan 7:9-10
18:20 Job 1:6
18:22 Ezek 14:9
18:23 Jer 20:2; Mark 14:65; Acts 23:2
18:25 2 Chr 18:8
18:26 2 Chr 16:10
18:28-34 //1 Kgs 22:29-36

18:16 Hebrew *These people have no master.*

18:10 Symbolic gestures were sometimes part of prophetic messages (compare with Jeremiah 28:1-17).

18:14 Micaiah knew what Ahab wanted to hear and sarcastically echoed the self-serving message of the false prophets (2 Chronicles 18:11).

18:16-17 Micaiah's second message employs the imagery of sheep without a shepherd (Numbers 27:16-17; Isaiah 13:14; Zechariah 10:2) to predict the death of Ahab if he went to war. Ahab's response reveals his disdain for God's word. Having demanded the truth, Ahab was unable to abide by it.

18:18-22 The throne room of God and the armies of heaven are common elements of prophetic visions (2 Kings 6:15-19; Isaiah 6). Typically the prophetic visions reveal God assembling forces to fight on behalf of Israel (Isaiah 13:1-13; Joel 3:9-12), but here God is seen ordaining defeat for Ahab.

▸ GOD

18:21 God is in control of all things. Does God force people to sin? Other passages of Scripture make it clear that God neither forced these false prophets to sin nor did he tempt them to do so (James 1:13). Instead, God allowed these prophets to follow through with their own sinful actions—and it led to Ahab's downfall. Those who make war with God must be prepared for the awful consequences (Genesis 6:13; Deuteronomy 8:20; Revelation 19). But those who repent will find forgiveness and peace with God through Jesus Christ (Romans 5:1). (***See God*** *> God's Attributes> Sovereign,* TopicGuide page A17.)

18:25 Imprisoning Micaiah seems to be an attempt to prevent the fulfillment of his message. Ahab would also join the battle in disguise, apparently hoping this would also prevent Micaiah's message from coming to pass (2 Chronicles 18:29).

18:29 Jehoshaphat's surprising willingness to go along with Ahab's scheme and put himself in harm's way has led some scholars to conclude that Israel must have exercised some level of control over Judah at this time.

[30]Meanwhile, the king of Aram had issued these orders to his chariot commanders: "At-
18:31 tack only the king of Israel! Don't bother with anyone else." [31]So when the Aramean chari-
2 Chr 13:14-15 ot commanders saw Jehoshaphat in his royal robes, they went after him. "There is the
king of Israel!" they shouted. But Jehoshaphat called out, and the LORD saved him. God
helped him by turning the attackers away from him. [32]As soon as the chariot commanders
realized he was not the king of Israel, they stopped chasing him.

[33]An Aramean soldier, however, randomly shot an arrow at the Israelite troops and hit
the king of Israel between the joints of his armor. "Turn the horses* and get me out of
here!" Ahab groaned to the driver of the chariot. "I'm badly wounded!"

[34]The battle raged all that day, and the king of Israel propped himself up in his chariot
facing the Arameans. In the evening, just as the sun was setting, he died.

19:2
JEHOSHAPHAT APPOINTS JUDGES

1 Kgs 16:1 **19** When King Jehoshaphat of Judah arrived safely home in Jerusalem, [2]Jehu son of
2 Chr 18:1, 3; 20:34; Hanani the seer went out to meet him. "Why should you help the wicked and love
24:18 19:3 those who hate the LORD?" he asked the king. "Because of what you have done, the LORD is
2 Chr 12:12; 17:6 very angry with you. [3]Even so, there is some good in you, for you have removed the Ashe-
rah poles throughout the land, and you have committed yourself to seeking God."

19:4 [4]Jehoshaphat lived in Jerusalem, but he went out among the people, traveling from
Deut 16:18-20 Beersheba to the hill country of Ephraim, encouraging the people to return to the LORD, the
2 Chr 15:8-13 God of their ancestors. [5]He appointed judges throughout the nation in all the fortified
19:6 towns, [6]and he said to them, "Always think carefully before pronouncing judgment. Re-
Lev 19:15 Deut 1:17 member that you do not judge to please people but to please the LORD. He will be with you
19:7 when you render the verdict in each case. [7]Fear the LORD and judge with integrity, for the
Gen 18:25 LORD our God does not tolerate perverted justice, partiality, or the taking of bribes."
Deut 10:17-18; 32:4

18:33 Hebrew *Turn your hand.*

18:30-32 Jehoshaphat's ill-advised alliance with Ahab nearly cost him his life, an indication of God's displeasure. In the parallel account in 1 Kings, there is no indication that Jehoshaphat's cry was directed to God (1 Kings 22:32). The chronicler has added the detail that when Jehoshaphat cried out God saved him to reinforce his overall positive portrait of Jehoshaphat.

▸ GOD
18:33 Random arrows and the will of God. We know this arrow wasn't as "random" as it seemed, for Micaiah had predicted this exact end—the death of Ahab (2 Chronicles 18:27). Even those incidents that appear indiscriminate are under the complete control or permission of God. How would our relationship to God be different if we believed that He is sovereign over all things? How would our outlook on life be different? (***See God****> God's Attributes> Sovereign> God is in control of all things,* TopicGuide page A17.)

19:1-3 These verses present the chronicler's rationale for including the lengthy battle report in 2 Chronicles 18: Jehoshaphat erred in allying himself with the wicked king of Israel. The chronicler reinforces his negative view of foreign alliances, which was already made evident in the account of Asa's reign (2 Chronicles 16:1-10).

19:3 Seeking God (or not seeking God) is a central theme for the chronicler and a standard means by which the chronicler evaluates the kings. Those who seek after God find blessing, while those who fail to seek after God find curses (2 Chronicles 12:14; 14:4, 7; 15:2, 4, 12, 13, 15; 16:12; 17:4; 18:4; 20:4; etc.).

19:4-11 This section narrates a second round of reforms led by Jehoshaphat, supplementing the initial reforms described in chapter 17. These reforms may be described as largely judicial, while the former were largely educational.

19:5 The choice of fortified cities as centers of judicial reform is logical, since the need to enforce judicial verdicts by force of arms is always a possibility. Presumably, the fortified cities would also already be centers of royal power and administration.

19:6-7 The king's injunction eloquently testifies to the real source of power and authority in Judah. Though the king was sending and directing these judges, they were ultimately responsible to God and were to execute His justice. In modern terminology, Israel exhibited a limited monarchy subject to the rule of law—God's law.

▸ BIBLE
19:7 God judges the judges. God holds judges accountable for their decisions (Psalm 82:1). Judges must fear God and know that He is the Great Judge who will judge all who sin against Him. Pray that judges and lawyers will seek God's will as they carry out their duties, knowing that God honors those who do what is right (2 Chronicles 19:11). (***See Bible****> Power> Wisdom> Administer civil justice,* TopicGuide page A11.)

8In Jerusalem, Jehoshaphat appointed some of the Levites and priests and clan leaders 19:8
in Israel to serve as judges for cases involving the LORD's regulations and for civil disputes. 2 Chr 17:8-9
9These were his instructions to them: "You must always act in the fear of the LORD, with
faithfulness and an undivided heart. 10Whenever a case comes to you from fellow citizens 19:10
in an outlying town, whether a murder case or some other violation of God's laws, com- Deut 17:8; 2 Chr 19:2
mands, decrees, or regulations, you must warn them not to sin against the LORD, so that He
will not be angry with you and them. Do this and you will not be guilty.
11"Amariah the high priest will have final say in all cases involving the LORD. Zebadiah 19:11
son of Ishmael, a leader from the tribe of Judah, will have final say in all civil cases. The Le- 1 Chr 28:20; 2 Chr 19:8
vites will assist you in making sure that justice is served. Take courage as you fulfill your
duties, and may the LORD be with those who do what is right."

WAR WITH SURROUNDING NATIONS

20 After this, the armies of the Moabites, Ammonites, and some of the Meunites* de- 20:2
clared war on Jehoshaphat. 2Messengers came and told Jehoshaphat, "A vast Gen 14:7
army from Edom* is marching against you from beyond the Dead Sea.* They are already
at Hazazon-tamar." (This was another name for En-gedi.)
3Jehoshaphat was terrified by this news and begged the LORD for guidance. He also or- 20:3
dered everyone in Judah to begin fasting. 4So people from all the towns of Judah came to 1 Sam 7:6; 2 Chr 19:3
Jerusalem to seek the LORD's help. Ezra 8:21
5Jehoshaphat stood before the community of Judah and Jerusalem in front of the new 20:6
courtyard at the Temple of the LORD. 6He prayed, "O LORD, God of our ancestors, You alone Deut 4:39
are the God who is in heaven. You are ruler of all the kingdoms of the earth. You are power- 1 Chr 29:11
ful and mighty; no one can stand against You! 7O our God, did You not drive out those who 20:7
lived in this land when Your people Israel arrived? And did You not give this land forever to Isa 41:8
the descendants of Your friend Abraham? 8Your people settled here and built this Temple
to honor Your name. 9They said, 'Whenever we are faced with any calamity such as war,* 20:9; 2 Chr 6:20, 28-30
plague, or famine, we can come to stand in Your presence before this Temple where Your
name is honored. We can cry out to You to save us, and You will hear us and rescue us.'
10"And now see what the armies of Ammon, Moab, and Mount Seir are doing. You 20:10; Num 20:17-21
would not let our ancestors invade those nations when Israel left Egypt, so they went 2 Chr 20:1, 22

20:1 As in some Greek manuscripts (see also 26:7); Hebrew repeats *Ammonites.* 20:2a As in one Hebrew manuscript; most Hebrew manuscripts and ancient versions read *Aram.* 20:2b Hebrew *the sea.* 20:9 Or *sword of judgment;* or *sword, judgment.*

19:8-11 While the boundaries between the religious and civic aspects of Israel's law were unclear, there was some distinction between the throne and the Temple—though they were both ultimately under God. The distinction may have been especially important for the chronicler's audience, for whom the king was not a Davidic monarch but a pagan ruler.

20:1 Moab and Ammon lay to the east and north of Judah across the Dead Sea. The Meunites are later (2 Chronicles 20:10, 22, 23) identified with Mount Seir, which is typically associated with Edom to the south and east of Judah.

▸WORSHIP

20:3 A national fast. When times get hard and stress is high, what is the first thing you do? Many people deal with the stress by eating, drinking, or becoming highly emotional. But God's people can live differently. The king of Judah commanded a time of fasting and worship, and God's people responded. They pronounced their helplessness (2 Chronicles 20:12) and put their hope in God. God responded by sending a special visitation of His Spirit upon His people (2 Chronicles 20:13). Decide now: How will you respond during times of crisis or doubt—by yelling at the people around you or crying out to God? (***See Worship****> OT> Fasting and Prayer> Fasting> Occasions> Fasting when facing impending danger,* TopicGuide page A26.)

20:3-4 Jehoshaphat modeled godly leadership by remaining calm in the face of disturbing opposition and seeking the help of God. This inspired his people to do the same. See also note at 2 Chronicles 19:3.

20:6-7 The first part of Jehoshaphat's prayer focuses on God's sovereignty over the nations and His past faithfulness to the people of Israel. These two aspects of God's character were demonstrated in the conquest of the Promised Land under Joshua.

20:8-9 Jehoshaphat recalled Solomon's prayer of dedication, in which Solomon asked God to be attentive to the prayers of His people in precisely such circumstances as Judah now found itself (2 Chronicles 6:28, 34). Jehoshaphat could rest in God's promise to Solomon that He would indeed hear the prayers of His people (2 Chronicles 7:12-14).

20:10-11 Deuteronomy 2 and Judges 11:14-27 summarize Israel's interaction with these nations. God had instructed the Israelites not to attack these peoples as they made their way to the Promised Land.

20:11 around them and did not destroy them. 11 Now see how they reward us! For they have
Ps 83:12 come to throw us out of Your land, which You gave us as an inheritance. 12 O our God,
20:12 won't You stop them? We are powerless against this mighty army that is about to attack
Judg 11:27 Pss 25:15; 121:1-2 us. We do not know what to do, but we are looking to You for help."
13 As all the men of Judah stood before the LORD with their little ones, wives, and chil-
20:14 dren, 14 the Spirit of the LORD came upon one of the men standing there. His name was Ja-
2 Chr 15:1; 24:20 haziel son of Zechariah, son of Benaiah, son of Jeiel, son of Mattaniah, a Levite who was a
descendant of Asaph.
20:15 15 He said, "Listen, all you people of Judah and Jerusalem! Listen, King Jehoshaphat!
Exod 14:13 This is what the LORD says: Do not be afraid! Don't be discouraged by this mighty army, for
1 Sam 17:47 2 Chr 32:7-8 the battle is not yours, but God's. 16 Tomorrow, march out against them. You will find them
coming up through the ascent of Ziz at the end of the valley that opens into the wilderness
20:17 of Jeruel. 17 But you will not even need to fight. Take your positions; then stand still and
Exod 14:13 watch the LORD's victory. He is with you, O people of Judah and Jerusalem. Do not be
2 Chr 15:2 afraid or discouraged. Go out against them tomorrow, for the LORD is with you!"
18 Then King Jehoshaphat bowed low with his face to the ground. And all the people of
Judah and Jerusalem did the same, worshiping the LORD. 19 Then the Levites from the clans
of Kohath and Korah stood to praise the LORD, the God of Israel, with a very loud shout.
20:20 20 Early the next morning the army of Judah went out into the wilderness of Tekoa. On
Isa 7:9 the way Jehoshaphat stopped and said, "Listen to me, all you people of Judah and Jerusa-
lem! Believe in the LORD your God, and you will be able to stand firm. Believe in His proph-
ets, and you will succeed."
20:21 21 After consulting the people, the king appointed singers to walk ahead of the army,
1 Chr 16:29, 34, 41 Ps 29:2 singing to the LORD and praising Him for His holy splendor. This is what they sang:

> "Give thanks to the LORD;
> His faithful love endures forever!"

20:22 22 At the very moment they began to sing and give praise, the LORD caused the armies of
2 Chr 13:13; 20:10 Ammon, Moab, and Mount Seir to start fighting among themselves. 23 The armies of Moab
20:23 and Ammon turned against their allies from Mount Seir and killed every one of them. After
Judg 7:22 1 Sam 14:20 they had destroyed the army of Seir, they began attacking each other. 24 So when the army
of Judah arrived at the lookout point in the wilderness, all they saw were dead bodies lying
on the ground as far as they could see. Not a single one of the enemy had escaped.
25 King Jehoshaphat and his men went out to gather the plunder. They found vast
amounts of equipment, clothing,* and other valuables—more than they could carry. There
was so much plunder that it took them three days just to collect it all! 26 On the fourth day
they gathered in the Valley of Blessing,* which got its name that day because the people
praised and thanked the LORD there. It is still called the Valley of Blessing today.

20:25 As in some Hebrew manuscripts and Latin Vulgate; most Hebrew manuscripts read *corpses*. 20:26 Hebrew *valley of Beracah.*

20:15-17 Jahaziel's oracle of salvation employs the imagery and language of holy war and follows the prescribed speech that a priest was to give the army of Israel before battle (Deuteronomy 20:2-4). Compare Jahaziel's command to "stand still and watch the Lord's victory" with Moses' identical command to Israel on the shores of the Red Sea with the Egyptian army bearing down on them (Exodus 14:13-14).

20:21 Military bands have an established place in the history of warfare. The place of music in the history of Israel's battle is well attested throughout the Old Testament (Joshua 6:4-20; Judges 7:18-20; 2 Chronicles 13:12). God Himself is often described as coming in judgment accompanied by the sounds of song and music (Psalms 47; 96; 98).

▸ SPIRITUAL WARFARE

20:22 God confuses our enemies. As God's people marched out, ready for battle, God went before them, scattering their enemies like dust in the wind (2 Chronicles 20:26-30). How often does God go before us, turning aside dangers and snares? We may never know how gracious God is to us. Thank God for His great care for His people. (***See Spiritual Warfare****> Resisting Sin and Evil> Trusting God> God as Warrior,* TopicGuide page A46.)

20:22-23 Confusion among the enemy, resulting in their own self-destruction, is a recurring feature of Israel's military history (Judges 7:22; 1 Samuel 14:20; 2 Kings 3:23; Ezekiel 38:21; Haggai 2:22).

27Then all the men returned to Jerusalem, with Jehoshaphat leading them, overjoyed 20:27
that the Lord had given them victory over their enemies. 28They marched into Jerusalem Neh 12:43
to the music of harps, lyres, and trumpets, and they proceeded to the Temple of the Lord.
29When all the surrounding kingdoms heard that the Lord Himself had fought against
the enemies of Israel, the fear of God came over them. 30So Jehoshaphat's kingdom was at 20:30
peace, for his God had given him rest on every side. 2 Chr 14:6-7, 14; 15:15; 17:10

SUMMARY OF JEHOSHAPHAT'S REIGN

31So Jehoshaphat ruled over the land of Judah. He was thirty-five years old when he be- 20:31–21:1
came king, and he reigned in Jerusalem twenty-five years. His mother was Azubah, the //1 Kgs 22:41-50 2 Chr 17:6
daughter of Shilhi.
32Jehoshaphat was a good king, following the ways of his father, Asa. He did what was
pleasing in the Lord's sight. 33During his reign, however, he failed to remove all the pagan 20:33
shrines, and the people never fully committed themselves to follow the God of their an- 2 Chr 17:6; 19:3
cestors.
34The rest of the events of Jehoshaphat's reign, from beginning to end, are recorded in 20:34
The Record of Jehu Son of Hanani, which is included in *The Book of the Kings of Israel.* 1 Kgs 16:1, 7
35Some time later King Jehoshaphat of Judah made an alliance with King Ahaziah of Is- 20:35
rael, who was very wicked.* 36Together they built a fleet of trading ships* at the port of 1 Kgs 22:48-49
Ezion-geber. 37Then Eliezer son of Dodavahu from Mareshah prophesied against Jehosha- 20:36 2 Chr 9:21
phat. He said, "Because you have allied yourself with King Ahaziah, the Lord will destroy
your work." So the ships met with disaster and never put out to sea.*

JEHORAM RULES IN JUDAH

21 When Jehoshaphat died, he was buried with his ancestors in the City of David. 21:1
Then his son Jehoram became the next king. 1 Kgs 22:50
2Jehoram's brothers—the other sons of Jehoshaphat—were Azariah, Jehiel, Zechariah,
Azariahu, Michael, and Shephatiah; all these were the sons of Jehoshaphat king of Judah.*
3Their father had given each of them valuable gifts of silver, gold, and costly items, and 21:3
also some of Judah's fortified towns. However, he designated Jehoram as the next king 2 Chr 11:5
because he was the oldest. 4But when Jehoram had become solidly established as king, he
killed all his brothers and some of the other leaders of Judah.

20:35 Or *who made him do what was wicked.* 20:36 Hebrew *fleet of ships that could go to Tarshish.* 20:37 Hebrew *never set sail for Tarshish.* 21:2 Hebrew *of Israel;* also in 21:4. The author of Chronicles sees Judah as representative of the true Israel. See also some Hebrew manuscripts, Greek and Syriac versions, and Latin Vulgate.

20:27-30 The chronicler once again highlights his theme of how faithfulness to God is rewarded with peace from enemies.

20:31 The Chronicler records a reign of 25 years for Jehoshaphat, while the author of Kings records a reign of 22 years (see 2 Kings 3:1 and 8:16). This discrepancy is resolved if the Chronicler included a co-regency of 3 years with his father Asa, who suffered from disease during his final years as king (2 Chronicles 16:10-14).

20:33 Like Asa, Jehoshaphat is said to have removed the pagan shrines, yet elsewhere it is said that he did not remove all the pagan shrines (2 Chronicles 14:2-5; 15:17; 17:6; 20:33). See note at 2 Chronicles 14:3.

▸WORSHIP
20:35 Partnering with unbelievers. Scripture passages indicate that God has concerns about covenant partnerships with unbelievers. The Old Testament warns against marrying outside of God's covenant people (Deuteronomy 7:3; Nehemiah 13:25), and the New Testament echoes this teaching (2 Corinthians 6:15). In what other circumstances would it be unwise to partner with unbelievers? Ask God to give you wisdom on how to fearlessly interact with unbelievers, yet not to "stand around with sinners, or join in with mockers" (Psalm 1:1). (***See Worship***> *NT> Our Role> Holiness> Flee immorality,* TopicGuide page A32.)

20:35-37 Once again Jehoshaphat agreed to an alliance with the wicked kings of the north. This time he agreed to a joint maritime venture with Ahab's son, Ahaziah. The ships sank before leaving port, however, indicating God's displeasure over the alliance. Jehoshaphat took the prophet's message to heart and refused an offer for a second venture (1 Kings 22:49).

21:1–22:12 These chapters tell the story of a dark period in Judah's history when the nation's affairs were tragically impacted by the northern dynasty of Ahab. Unfortunately this dark time was introduced by the otherwise righteous King Jehoshaphat, who entered into unwise alliances with King Ahab.

21:5-10 5 Jehoram was thirty-two years old when he became king, and he reigned in Jerusalem
//2 Kgs 8:16-24 eight years. 6 But Jehoram followed the example of the kings of Israel and was as wicked
21:6 as King Ahab, for he had married one of Ahab's daughters. So Jehoram did what was evil
1 Kgs 12:28-30 2 Chr 18:1 in the LORD's sight. 7 But the LORD did not want to destroy David's dynasty, for He had made
21:7 a covenant with David and promised that his descendants would continue to rule, shining
2 Sam 7:12-17 like a lamp forever.
1 Kgs 11:13 8 During Jehoram's reign, the Edomites revolted against Judah and crowned their own
21:8 2 Chr 20:22-23; 21:10 king. 9 So Jehoram went out with his full army and all his chariots. The Edomites sur-
rounded him and his chariot commanders, but he went out at night and attacked them*
under cover of darkness. 10 Even so, Edom has been independent from Judah to this day.
The town of Libnah also revolted about that same time. All this happened because Jeho-
21:11 Lev 20:5 ram had abandoned the LORD, the God of his ancestors. 11 He had built pagan shrines in
1 Kgs 11:7 the hill country of Judah and had led the people of Jerusalem and Judah to give them-
selves to pagan gods and to go astray.
21:12 2 Chr 14:2-5; 17:3-4 12 Then Elijah the prophet wrote Jehoram this letter:

"This is what the LORD, the God of your ancestor David, says: You have not followed
the good example of your father, Jehoshaphat, or your grandfather King Asa of
21:13 Judah. 13 Instead, you have been as evil as the kings of Israel. You have led the
1 Kgs 16:31-33 2 Chr 21:4, 6, 11 people of Jerusalem and Judah to worship idols, just as King Ahab did in Israel. And
you have even killed your own brothers, men who were better than you. 14 So now
the LORD is about to strike you, your people, your children, your wives, and all that is
21:15 yours with a heavy blow. 15 You yourself will suffer with a severe intestinal disease
2 Chr 21:18-19 that will get worse each day until your bowels come out."

21:16 16 Then the LORD stirred up the Philistines and the Arabs, who lived near the Ethiopians,*
2 Chr 17:11; 22:1; to attack Jehoram. 17 They marched against Judah, broke down its defenses, and carried
33:11 away everything of value in the royal palace, including the king's sons and his wives. Only
21:17 2 Chr 25:23 his youngest son, Ahaziah,* was spared.
18 After all this, the LORD struck Jehoram with the severe intestinal disease. 19 The disease
21:18 2 Chr 21:15 grew worse and worse, and at the end of two years it caused his bowels to come out, and
21:19 he died in agony. His people did not build a great funeral fire to honor him as they had
2 Chr 16:14 done for his ancestors.

21:9 Or *he went out and escaped.* The meaning of the Hebrew is uncertain. 21:16 Hebrew *the Cushites.* 21:17 Hebrew *Jehoahaz,* a variant spelling of Ahaziah; compare 22:1.

21:5 A co-regency between Jehoshaphat and Jehoram is likely, given the fact that the writer of Kings records the ascension of King Joram of Israel in the 18th year of Jehoshaphat and the 2nd year of Jehoram (2 Kings 1:17; 3:1).

21:7 God withholds immediate and definitive judgment upon the house of Jehoram for the sake of His promises to David. The covenant with David was conditional, depending on the continued obedience of David's descendants (2 Chronicles 6:16), so God here is extending mercy and grace.

21:8 Edom was subjected to Israelite control under the reign of David (2 Samuel 8:13-14). It is likely that control of Edom was initially lost during the reign of Rehoboam but reestablished during the reigns of Asa or Jehoshaphat (compare 1 Kings 22:47).

21:8-10 While the Davidic dynasty would be spared, Jehoram still faced God's discipline. The successful revolts of Edom and Libnah are directly attributed to Jehoram's abandonment of God.

21:10 Libnah lay to the west of Judah on the border with Philistia. Therefore, Jehoram faced dangerous conflict on two fronts.

21:12 The prophet Elijah plays a major role in the history of the northern kingdom as recorded in 1 Kings 17—2 Kings 2. This is the only mention of the prophet's interaction with the kings of Judah, although such an interaction is not surprising, since Jehoram was the son-in-law of Elijah's nemesis King Ahab.

21:18 In fulfillment of the word of Elijah (21:15), Jehoram is struck with an intestinal disease. The precise nature of the disease is uncertain. Ulcers, colitis, prolapse, and dysentery have all been suggested.

21:19-20 For Jehoram there was no great fire, no sympathy, and no burial in the royal cemetery—a fitting end to a wicked reign. Notice also that the chronicler makes no mention of sources where further information regarding Jehoram's reign were available.

20 Jehoram was thirty-two years old when he became king, and he reigned in Jerusalem **21:20**
eight years. No one was sorry when he died. They buried him in the City of David, but not 2 Chr 24:25; 28:27
in the royal cemetery. Jer 22:18, 28

AHAZIAH RULES IN JUDAH

22 Then the people of Jerusalem made Ahaziah, Jehoram's youngest son, their next **22:1-6**
king, since the marauding bands who came with the Arabs* had killed all the //2 Kgs 8:25-29
older sons. So Ahaziah son of Jehoram reigned as king of Judah. **22:1**
2 Ahaziah was twenty-two* years old when he became king, and he reigned in Jerusalem 2 Chr 21:16-17
one year. His mother was Athaliah, a granddaughter of King Omri. 3 Ahaziah also followed
the evil example of King Ahab's family, for his mother encouraged him in doing wrong. **22:3** 2 Chr 21:6-7
4 He did what was evil in the LORD's sight, just as Ahab's family had done. They even be-
came his advisers after the death of his father, and they led him to ruin.
5 Following their evil advice, Ahaziah joined King Joram,* the son of King Ahab of Israel, **22:5**
in his war against King Hazael of Aram at Ramoth-gilead. When the Arameans wounded 2 Kgs 8:28
Joram in the battle, 6 he returned to Jezreel to recover from the wounds he had received at
Ramoth.* Because Joram was wounded, King Ahaziah* of Judah went to Jezreel to visit him.
7 But God had decided that this visit would be Ahaziah's downfall. While he was there, **22:7-9**
Ahaziah went out with Joram to meet Jehu son of Nimshi, whom the LORD had appointed //2 Kgs 9:21-29
to destroy the dynasty of Ahab.
8 While Jehu was executing judgment against the family of Ahab, he happened to meet **22:8**
some of Judah's officials and Ahaziah's relatives* who were traveling with Ahaziah. So Jehu 2 Kgs 10:13-14
killed them all. 9 Then Jehu's men searched for Ahaziah, and they found him hiding in the **22:9**
city of Samaria. They brought him to Jehu, who killed him. Ahaziah was given a decent 2 Kgs 9:27-28 2 Chr 17:4

22:1 Or *marauding bands of Arabs.* 22:2 As in some Greek manuscripts and Syriac version (see also 2 Kgs 8:26); Hebrew reads *forty-two.* 22:5 Hebrew *Jehoram,* a variant spelling of Joram; also in 22:6, 7. 22:6a Hebrew *Ramah,* a variant spelling of Ramoth. 22:6b As in some Hebrew manuscripts, Greek and Syriac versions, and Latin Vulgate (see also 2 Kgs 8:29); most Hebrew manuscripts read *Azariah.* 22:8 As in Greek version (see also 2 Kgs 10:13); Hebrew reads *and sons of the brothers of Ahaziah.*

22:1 Due to the death of his older brothers, Ahaziah, Jehoram's youngest son, is named king of Judah.

22:3 Queen mothers played an important role in the kingdoms of the ancient world, including Israel and Judah (1 Kings 1:11-31; 2:13-21; 15:13; 21:5-7; Jeremiah 13:18). Athaliah emulated her mother Jezebel (see note at 2 Kings 11:1) in her pernicious influence upon the king's policies.

22:4 Ahab's family extended their influence over the affairs of Judah through a network of advisers to the king. Some have suggested that the northern kingdom exercised significant power over Judah during the years of kings Omri and Ahab, and Ahab's immediate successors.

22:5 King Joram of Israel enlisted the military aid of Ahaziah against King Hazael of Aram in order to recapture the city of Ramoth-gilead. Joram's father, Ahab, had been killed in his ill-fated attempt to recapture the same city (2 Chronicles 18), which had originally been assigned to the tribe of Gad and was designated a Levitical city (Deuteronomy 4:43). Ramoth-gilead's strategic location along the King's Highway made it a source of continual struggle between Israel and Aram.

22:5-9 In 2 Kings 9, the death of Ahaziah is attributed to Jehu's overstepping his commission to terminate the family of Ahab. In Chronicles, Ahaziah's death is portrayed as a providential outworking of God's displeasure. Both perspectives are valid and demonstrate the differences in the authors' audiences and concerns.

22:6 The city of Jezreel was a favorite residence of the Omride dynasty. It lay in the valley of Jezreel near Mt. Gilboa.

22:8 The parallel account in 2 Kings 10:13-14 places the death of Ahaziah's relatives after the death of Ahaziah. The chronological discrepancy may be explained by the chronicler's desire to focus attention on the death of Ahaziah.

▸ HOLINESS
22:9 Capable of ruling. A leader is someone who can take a group of people from one place to the next with the least amount of friction and the most amount of joy. Leaders may be good, evil, or a mix of both in their behavior, but to be effective leaders, they must manifest a group of gifts that enable them to direct and inspire people. Without these gifts and talents from God, a person may wish to lead, but the people around them will simply not follow them. If you are a leader, use your gifts and lead with all your might! If you are a follower, then do what you can to accomplish the goals at hand with joy. (***See Holiness****> Law and Grace> Law> Leaders and followers,* TopicGuide page A41.)

22:9 The chronicler does not mention the place of Ahaziah's burial, but this should not be taken as a discrepancy with 2 Kings 9:28, which gives Jerusalem as a place of burial. The chronicler's ambiguity is consistent with his use of burial notices to evaluate the king's reign. The nondescript burial notice signals the author's disapproval.

burial because the people said, "He was the grandson of Jehoshaphat—a man who sought
the LORD with all his heart." But none of the surviving members of Ahaziah's family was ca-
pable of ruling the kingdom.

QUEEN ATHALIAH RULES IN JUDAH

22:10–23:21 [10]When Athaliah, the mother of King Ahaziah of Judah, learned that her son was dead, she
2 Kgs 11:1-21 began to destroy the rest of Judah's royal family. [11]But Ahaziah's sister Jehosheba,* the
daughter of King Jehoram, took Ahaziah's infant son, Joash, and stole him away from
among the rest of the king's children, who were about to be killed. She put Joash and his
nurse in a bedroom. In this way, Jehosheba, wife of Jehoiada the priest and sister of Ahazi-
ah, hid the child so that Athaliah could not murder him. [12]Joash remained hidden in the
Temple of God for six years while Athaliah ruled over the land.

REVOLT AGAINST ATHALIAH

23:1 23 In the seventh year of Athaliah's reign, Jehoiada the priest decided to act. He
2 Kgs 11:4-20 summoned his courage and made a pact with five army commanders: Azariah
son of Jeroham, Ishmael son of Jehohanan, Azariah son of Obed, Maaseiah son of Adaiah,
and Elishaphat son of Zicri. [2]These men traveled secretly throughout Judah and sum-
23:3 moned the Levites and clan leaders in all the towns to come to Jerusalem. [3]They all gath-
2 Sam 7:12 ered at the Temple of God, where they made a solemn pact with Joash, the young king.
2 Chr 21:7 Jehoiada said to them, "Here is the king's son! The time has come for him to reign! The
23:4 LORD has promised that a descendant of David will be our king. [4]This is what you must do.
1 Chr 9:26 When you priests and Levites come on duty on the Sabbath, a third of you will serve as
gatekeepers. [5]Another third will go over to the royal palace, and the final third will be at
23:6 the Foundation Gate. Everyone else should stay in the courtyards of the LORD's Temple.
1 Sam 10:24 [6]Remember, only the priests and Levites on duty may enter the Temple of the LORD, for
1 Chr 23:28-32 they are set apart as holy. The rest of the people must obey the LORD's instructions and
stay outside. [7]You Levites, form a bodyguard around the king and keep your weapons in
hand. Kill anyone who tries to enter the Temple. Stay with the king wherever he goes."
23:8 [8]So the Levites and all the people of Judah did everything as Jehoiada the priest or-
1 Chr 24:1 dered. The commanders took charge of the men reporting for duty that Sabbath, as well
as those who were going off duty. Jehoiada the priest did not let anyone go home after
their shift ended. [9]Then Jehoiada supplied the commanders with the spears and the large
and small shields that had once belonged to King David and were stored in the Temple
of God. [10]He stationed all the people around the king, with their weapons ready. They

22:11 As in parallel text at 2 Kgs 11:2; Hebrew omits *Ahaziah's sister* and reads *Jehoshabeath* [a variant spelling of Jehosheba].

22:10 The chronicler omits his typical introductory formula for a new king. By doing so, the chronicler challenges the legitimacy of Athaliah's rule. Similarly, there is no concluding summary.

22:10-12 The royal family is once again reduced to one legitimate heir (2 Chronicles 21:4), this time by Athaliah's murder of Ahaziah's children. Jehosheba was likely Ahaziah's half-sister by a wife other than Athaliah.

23:1 The coup against Athaliah included both military and religious leaders. The reign of Athaliah had sunk Judah into a period of military weakness and religious syncretism. It is little wonder that the religious and military leaders would plot together to remove the illegitimate monarch.

23:2 The organizers of the coup also enlisted the support of local leaders throughout Judah. Popular support for righteous leaders is a recurring theme in Chronicles (1 Chronicles 11:1; 28:1; 2 Chronicles 1:2; 11:13-17; 15:9; 17:5).

23:3 The chronicler inserts Jehoiada's appeal to the Davidic covenant, which is not found in the parallel account in 2 Kings 11. This insertion demonstrates the chronicler's concerns and communicates to his audience the need to restore not only the Temple but also the Davidic monarchy.

23:4-10 The chronicler emphasized the role of the Levites in staging the coup against Athaliah. The Levites had always been a quasi-military force employed as guardians of the Ark of the Covenant and the Temple precincts. (Compare Exodus 32:26-29.)

23:6-7 Even as these extraordinary circumstances transpired, Jehoiada continued to respect the sanctity of the Temple and ensured that only consecrated personnel entered the sacred areas.

23:9 The chronicler brings to light the historically ironic use of Davidic weaponry for the reestablishment of the Davidic monarchy.

formed a line from the south side of the Temple around to the north side and all around
the altar.
[11]Then Jehoiada and his sons brought out Joash, the king's son, placed the crown on
his head, and presented him with a copy of God's laws.* They anointed him and pro-
claimed him king, and everyone shouted, "Long live the king!"

THE DEATH OF ATHALIAH

[12]When Athaliah heard the noise of the people running and the shouts of praise to the
king, she hurried to the LORD's Temple to see what was happening. [13]When she arrived,
she saw the newly crowned king standing in his place of authority by the pillar at the Tem-
ple entrance. The commanders and trumpeters were surrounding him, and people from
all over the land were rejoicing and blowing trumpets. Singers with musical instruments
were leading the people in a great celebration. When Athaliah saw all this, she tore her
clothes in despair and shouted, "Treason! Treason!"
[14]Then Jehoiada the priest ordered the commanders who were in charge of the troops,
"Take her to the soldiers in front of the Temple,* and kill anyone who tries to rescue her."
For the priest had said, "She must not be killed in the Temple of the LORD." [15]So they seized **23:15**
her and led her out to the entrance of the Horse Gate on the palace grounds, and they Neh 3:28
killed her there.

JEHOIADA'S RELIGIOUS REFORMS

[16]Then Jehoiada made a covenant between himself and the king and the people that they
would be the LORD's people. [17]And all the people went over to the temple of Baal and tore **23:17**
it down. They demolished the altars and smashed the idols, and they killed Mattan the Deut 13:9
priest of Baal in front of the altars.
[18]Jehoiada now put the priests and Levites in charge of the Temple of the LORD, follow- **23:18** 1 Chr 23:6, 25-31
ing all the directions given by David. He also commanded them to present burnt offerings 2 Chr 5:5
to the LORD, as prescribed by the Law of Moses, and to sing and rejoice as David had in-
structed. [19]He also stationed gatekeepers at the gates of the LORD's Temple to keep out **23:19**
those who for any reason were ceremonially unclean. 1 Chr 9:22
[20]Then the commanders, nobles, rulers, and all the people of the land escorted the king **23:20**
from the Temple of the LORD. They went through the upper gate and into the palace, and 2 Kgs 11:19
they seated the king on the royal throne. [21]So all the people of the land rejoiced, and the
city was peaceful because Athaliah had been killed.

23:11 Or *a copy of the covenant.* 23:14 Or *Bring her out from between the ranks;* or *Take her out of the Temple precincts.* The meaning of the Hebrew is uncertain.

23:11 The word translated as "a copy of God's laws" is better rendered simply "a copy of the covenant," as in 23:16. The covenant placed in Joash's hand is probably the "solemn pact" of 23:3 that likely stipulated the terms of the king's restoration.

▸ HOLINESS
23:13 A place of authority. The newly crowned king, Joash, likely stood in a place that symbolized authority and respect—to the outside of the right pillar marking the Temple's entrance. This visually illustrated his standing as a mediator and leader established by God. The New Testament follows this theme by speaking of Jesus seated at the right hand of God (Acts 2:34; Ephesians 1:20) and—miracle of miracles—we are seated with Him (Ephesians 2:6). We have been raised by God and seated with Christ in a place of authority and honor so that we may glorify Him. What difference would it make if you truly believed that you are a coheir with Christ and lived accordingly? (***See Holiness****> Submission> Identifying with Christ> Living as an adopted son,* TopicGuide page A40.)

23:13 The pillar is likely one of the two great pillars called Jakin and Boaz (see note at 3:17). Athaliah's cry of "treason" is full of irony given her own treacherous rise to power.

23:18-19 The chronicler positively portrays Jehoiada's reforming activities and emphasizes his fidelity to the Law of Moses and instructions of David. Jehoiada is once again a model for the chronicler's audience as they sought to rebuild their society after returning from exile.

▸ GOD
23:21 Life from death. It is sad when people, even bad people, perish. But when a person brings great harm to society, as Athaliah did, it provides an opportunity to rejoice in God's victory over those who would destroy His people. We do not rejoice over death, but we do rejoice over the hope of new life and freedom from oppression (Proverbs 29:2). (***See God****> God's Attributes> Self-Sufficient> God supplies all things their life and breath,* TopicGuide page A17.)

JOASH REPAIRS THE TEMPLE

24:1-14 //2 Kgs 12:1-16 **24** Joash was seven years old when he became king, and he reigned in Jerusalem
24:1 forty years. His mother was Zibiah from Beersheba. [2]Joash did what was pleasing
2 Kgs 11:21 in the LORD's sight throughout the lifetime of Jehoiada the priest. [3]Jehoiada chose two
wives for Joash, and he had sons and daughters.
[4]At one point Joash decided to repair and restore the Temple of the LORD. [5]He sum-
24:4 2 Chr 24:7 moned the priests and Levites and gave them these instructions: "Go to all the towns of Ju-
dah and collect the required annual offerings, so that we can repair the Temple of your
God. Do not delay!" But the Levites did not act immediately.
24:6 [6]So the king called for Jehoiada the high priest and asked him, "Why haven't you de-
Exod 30:12-16 manded that the Levites go out and collect the Temple taxes from the towns of Judah and
from Jerusalem? Moses, the servant of the LORD, levied this tax on the community of Israel
in order to maintain the Tabernacle of the Covenant.*"
24:7 [7]Over the years the followers of wicked Athaliah had broken into the Temple of God,
2 Chr 21:17 and they had used all the dedicated things from the Temple of the LORD to worship the im-
ages of Baal.
24:9 [8]So now the king ordered a chest to be made and set outside the gate leading to the
2 Chr 24:6; 36:22 Temple of the LORD. [9]Then a proclamation was sent throughout Judah and Jerusalem, tell-
ing the people to bring to the LORD the tax that Moses, the servant of God, had required of
the Israelites in the wilderness. [10]This pleased all the leaders and the people, and they
gladly brought their money and filled the chest with it.
24:11 [11]Whenever the chest became full, the Levites would carry it to the king's officials. Then
2 Kgs 12:10 the court secretary and an officer of the high priest would come and empty the chest and
take it back to the Temple again. This went on day after day, and a large amount of
money was collected. [12]The king and Jehoiada gave the money to the construction super-
visors, who hired masons and carpenters to restore the Temple of the LORD. They also
hired metalworkers, who made articles of iron and bronze for the LORD's Temple.
[13]The men in charge of the renovation worked hard and made steady progress. They
restored the Temple of God according to its original design and strengthened it. [14]When

24:6 Hebrew *Tent of the Testimony.*

24:2 The chronicler presents Joash's reign in two parts. The first, largely positive segment coincided with Jehoiada's lifetime. The second, largely negative segment commences with the death of Jehoiada.

24:4 The first part of the chronicler's account of Joash's reign (which is bracketed by the words "repair" and "restore" here and "renovation" in 2 Chronicles 24:13) is dominated by the restoration of the Temple. Presumably the Temple fell into disrepair during the troubled reigns of Jehoram, Ahaziah, and Athaliah, when the worship of Baal flourished.

24:5 The inaction of the priests in response to Joash's instructions may reflect that Joash was attempting to use funds ordinarily used to support the priests, the Levites, and their families to repair the Temple. The lack of immediate cooperation may also reflect rising tensions between the crown and the Temple.

24:6 According to 2 Kings 12:6, Joash called for Jehoiada in his 23rd year, so some time has elapsed between Joash's initial order and this summons of Jehoiada.

24:8-10 Joash abandoned his first plan to raise money for the Temple and established a place for the collection of voluntary funds for the restoration. This second effort proved much more successful and may represent a compromise between the king and the priesthood. The monies raised were above and beyond the monies contributed for the welfare of the priesthood.

24:10 The abundant and voluntary giving to the Temple is reminiscent of earlier days when the people gave to the building of the Tabernacle and the initial construction of the Temple (Exodus 36:4-7; 1 Chronicles 29:1-9).

24:11 The appointment of both a royal and a priestly official to count and transport the collected funds further suggests the compromising nature of the new arrangement.

▸ WORSHIP
24:13 Restoring the Temple. Jehoiada wasn't blind to other needs in Israel—poverty, a lack of education, economic challenges—Israel had many deficits. But nothing was more important to Jehoiada than restoring the proper ministry of the Temple in Israel. By King David's time, the Old Covenant was based on the existence and proper function of the Temple, and no time or money could be spared in repairing it. Does your church look a little ragged? Does it need physical repair? Or are there other needs that are causing the church to fail in its ministry? Pay attention to external problems in the church that may be causing it to struggle in ministry. (***See Worship****> OT> Place> Temple,* TopicGuide page A28.)

24:14 In contrast with this verse, the account in 2 Kings indicates that the collected funds were used to pay the workers and were not used to pay for the implements of worship (2 Kings 12:11-14). These accounts may be reconciled by noting that the chronicler had surplus funds in view.

all the repairs were finished, they brought the remaining money to the king and Jehoiada.
It was used to make various articles for the Temple of the LORD—articles for worship ser-
vices and for burnt offerings, including ladles and other articles made of gold and silver.
And the burnt offerings were sacrificed continually in the Temple of the LORD during the
lifetime of Jehoiada the priest.
15 Jehoiada lived to a very old age, finally dying at 130. 16 He was buried among the kings
in the City of David, because he had done so much good in Judah* for God and His Temple.

JEHOIADA'S REFORMS REVERSED

17 But after Jehoiada's death, the leaders of Judah came and bowed before King Joash and 24:18
persuaded him to listen to their advice. 18 They decided to abandon the Temple of the Exod 34:12-14
LORD, the God of their ancestors, and they worshiped Asherah poles and idols instead! Be- Josh 24:20
cause of this sin, divine anger fell on Judah and Jerusalem. 19 Yet the LORD sent prophets to 24:19
bring them back to Him. The prophets warned them, but still the people would not listen. Jer 7:25
20 Then the Spirit of God came upon Zechariah son of Jehoiada the priest. He stood be- 24:20 Num 14:41
fore the people and said, "This is what God says: Why do you disobey the LORD's com- 2 Chr 15:2; 20:14
mands and keep yourselves from prospering? You have abandoned the LORD, and now He
has abandoned you!" 24:21
21 Then the leaders plotted to kill Zechariah, and King Joash ordered that they stone him Neh 9:26
to death in the courtyard of the LORD's Temple. 22 That was how King Joash repaid Jehoia- Matt 23:35
da for his loyalty—by killing his son. Zechariah's last words as he died were, "May the LORD 24:22
see what they are doing and avenge my death!" Gen 9:5

THE END OF JOASH'S REIGN

23 In the spring of the year* the Aramean army marched against Joash. They invaded Ju- 24:23-27
dah and Jerusalem and killed all the leaders of the nation. Then they sent all the plunder //2 Kgs 12:17-21
back to their king in Damascus. 24 Although the Arameans attacked with only a small 24:24
army, the LORD helped them conquer the much larger army of Judah. The people of Judah 2 Chr 16:7-8
had abandoned the LORD, the God of their ancestors, so judgment was carried out against
Joash.

24:16 Hebrew *in Israel.* The author of Chronicles sees Judah as representative of the true Israel. 24:23 Hebrew *At the turn of the year.* The first day of the year in the ancient Hebrew lunar calendar occurred in March or April.

24:15-16 Jehoiada's age is the oldest recorded since the days of the patriarchs. Both his old age and his burial among the kings testify to his obedient service to God and His people. Contrast this with Athaliah, whose burial is not even recorded by the chronicler.

24:17-18 Jehoiada's death marked a drastic transition for Joash and the nation. The radical shift in policy suggests that Joash's leadership was dependent more on his advisers than on his own convictions. The return to idolatry likewise indicates that the reforms under Jehoiada did not turn the hearts of the people.

▸ SPIRITUAL WARFARE

24:18 Abandoning God. What does apostasy look like? Is it always as obvious as bowing down to other gods, or can abandoning the worship of God be subtler? Joash ceased to worship God and thus exposed himself and his kingdom to the wrath of God. God will discipline His people when we publicly abandon Him (Deuteronomy 8:5). And since leaders are more accountable, God is even quicker to discipline them (James 3:1). Take a close look at yourself and those for whom you are responsible—are you wandering away from God? Warn those who wander from God of the grave consequences. (***See Spiritual Warfare***> *Resisting Sin and Evil*> *Consequences*> *Of Disobedience*> *Falling under discipline,* TopicGuide page A46.)

24:19-20 The warnings of the prophets were evidence of God's mercy and patience. Zechariah's message echoes Numbers 14:41.

24:21-22 The treatment of Zechariah is marked by tragic irony. Joash orders the death of the son of the man who saved his life. He kills Zechariah in the very place where as a boy he had been protected and established as king. Despite Jehoiada's efforts to keep the Temple grounds undefiled by bloodshed, his own son was murdered there.

24:23 In keeping with the theme of immediate retribution, the chronicler records the invasion of Aram on the heels of Joash's rebellion.

24:24 Previously, the Lord had granted Judah unlikely victories in the face of overwhelming odds (2 Chronicles 13:3-18; 14:8-15). Here, however, that pattern is reversed. Despite fielding a much larger army, Judah is defeated in battle, demonstrating that the course of Judah's history was determined by God's providential outworking of His covenant relationship with His people.

24:25 25The Arameans withdrew, leaving Joash severely wounded. But his own officials plot-
2 Kgs 12:20-21 ted to kill him for murdering the son* of Jehoiada the priest. They assassinated him as he
lay in bed. Then he was buried in the City of David, but not in the royal cemetery. 26The as-
sassins were Jozacar,* the son of an Ammonite woman named Shimeath, and Jehozabad,
the son of a Moabite woman named Shomer.*
24:27 27The account of the sons of Joash, the prophecies about him, and the record of his res-
2 Chr 13:22; 24:12 toration of the Temple of God are written in *The Commentary on the Book of the Kings.* His
son Amaziah became the next king.

AMAZIAH RULES IN JUDAH

25:1-4 **25** Amaziah was twenty-five years old when he became king, and he reigned in Je-
//2 Kgs 14:1-6 rusalem twenty-nine years. His mother was Jehoaddin* from Jerusalem. 2Ama-
25:2 ziah did what was pleasing in the LORD's sight, but not wholeheartedly.
2 Chr 24:2 3When Amaziah was well established as king, he executed the officials who had assas-
25:4 sinated his father. 4However, he did not kill the children of the assassins, for he obeyed the
Deut 24:16 command of the LORD as written by Moses in the Book of the Law: "Parents must not be put
to death for the sins of their children, nor children for the sins of their parents. Those de-
25:5 serving to die must be put to death for their own crimes."*
Num 1:3 5Then Amaziah organized the army, assigning generals and captains* for all Judah and
2 Chr 26:13 Benjamin. He took a census and found that he had an army of 300,000 select troops,
twenty years old and older, all trained in the use of spear and shield. 6He also paid about
7,500 pounds* of silver to hire 100,000 experienced fighting men from Israel.
7But a man of God came to him and said, "Your Majesty, do not hire troops from Israel,
25:8 for the LORD is not with Israel. He will not help those people of Ephraim! 8If you let them go
2 Chr 14:11; 20:6 with your troops into battle, you will be defeated by the enemy no matter how well you
fight. God will overthrow you, for He has the power to help you or to trip you up."
9Amaziah asked the man of God, "But what about all that silver I paid to hire the army of
Israel?"
The man of God replied, "The LORD is able to give you much more than this!" 10So Ama-
ziah discharged the hired troops and sent them back to Ephraim. This made them very an-
gry with Judah, and they returned home in a great rage.
25:11-12 11Then Amaziah summoned his courage and led his army to the Valley of Salt, where
//2 Kgs 14:7 they killed 10,000 Edomite troops from Seir. 12They captured another 10,000 and took
them to the top of a cliff and threw them off, dashing them to pieces on the rocks below.

24:25 As in Greek version and Latin Vulgate; Hebrew reads *sons.* 24:26a As in parallel text at 2 Kgs 12:21; Hebrew reads *Zabad.* 24:26b As in parallel text at 2 Kgs 12:21; Hebrew reads *Shimrith,* a variant spelling of Shomer. 25:1 As in parallel text at 2 Kgs 14:2; Hebrew reads *Jehoaddan,* a variant spelling of Jehoaddin. 25:4 Deut 24:16. 25:5 Hebrew *commanders of thousands and commanders of hundreds.* 25:6 Hebrew *100 talents* [3,400 kilograms].

24:25 According to 2 Kings 12:18, the Arameans abandoned their attack after Joash paid them off with the Temple funds. The chronicler adds that Joash was assassinated for the murder of Zechariah. The chronicler once again uses the burial notice to emphasize his evaluation of the king. Righteous kings are buried in honor, while the unrighteous suffer humiliation even in death (2 Chronicles 16:14; 21:19-20; 26:23).

25:2 Wholehearted obedience is an important theme for the chronicler (1 Chronicles 28:9; 29:9; 2 Chronicles 6:14; 19:9; 31:21).

25:4 This verse refers to Deuteronomy 24:16. The Old Testament establishes both individual and corporate responsibility. For examples of situations in which the Lord assigns guilt to others because of the actions of one person, consider both the story of Achan (Joshua 7:24) and the Lord's threat to punish the children for their parents' idolatry (Deuteronomy 5:9). Ezekiel (Ezekiel 18:1, 19-24) emphasized individual responsibility, but ironically in the context of a community that was in exile because of the sins of prior generations.

25:5 Amaziah's military organization was similar to that of David's (1 Chronicles 21; 27), Solomon's (2 Chronicles 1:14), Asa's (2 Chronicles 14:8) and Jehoshaphat's (2 Chronicles 17:14-19). Amaziah's force, however, was smaller in size than the previous armies.

25:6-8 The chronicler's disapproval of foreign alliances is once again displayed. Such alliances were considered evidence of a failure to trust in God (2 Chronicles 16:2-9; 19:1-3; 20:15-17; 32:7-8).

25:10 The Israelite mercenaries likely received their promised fee (25:9), however, their resentment may be due to the inability to profit from the spoils of battle or enjoy the glory of victory.

[13]Meanwhile, the hired troops that Amaziah had sent home raided several of the towns
of Judah between Samaria and Beth-horon. They killed 3,000 people and carried off great
quantities of plunder.
[14]When King Amaziah returned from slaughtering the Edomites, he brought with him idols
taken from the people of Seir. He set them up as his own gods, bowed down in front of them, 25:14
and offered sacrifices to them! [15]This made the LORD very angry, and He sent a prophet to ask, 2 Chr 28:23
"Why do you turn to gods who could not even save their own people from you?" 25:15
[16]But the king interrupted him and said, "Since when have I made you the king's coun- 2 Chr 25:11-12
selor? Be quiet now before I have you killed!"

So the prophet stopped with this warning: "I know that God has determined to destroy
you because you have done this and have refused to accept my counsel."
[17]After consulting with his advisers, King Amaziah of Judah sent this challenge to Israel's
king Jehoash,* the son of Jehoahaz and grandson of Jehu: "Come and meet me in battle!"* 25:17-28
[18]But King Jehoash of Israel replied to King Amaziah of Judah with this story: "Out in the //2 Kgs 14:8-20
Lebanon mountains, a thistle sent a message to a mighty cedar tree: 'Give your daughter 25:18 Judg 9:8-15
in marriage to my son.' But just then a wild animal of Lebanon came by and stepped on
the thistle, crushing it!
[19]"You are saying, 'I have defeated Edom,' and you are very proud of it. But my advice
is to stay at home. Why stir up trouble that will only bring disaster on you and the people 25:19 2 Chr 26:16; 32:25
of Judah?"
[20]But Amaziah refused to listen, for God was determined to destroy him for turning to the
gods of Edom. [21]So King Jehoash of Israel mobilized his army against King Amaziah of Ju-
dah. The two armies drew up their battle lines at Beth-shemesh in Judah. [22]Judah was
routed by the army of Israel, and its army scattered and fled for home. [23]King Jehoash of Is-
rael captured Judah's king, Amaziah son of Joash and grandson of Ahaziah, at Beth- 25:23 2 Chr 21:17
shemesh. Then he brought him to Jerusalem, where he demolished 600 feet* of Jerusa-
lem's wall, from the Ephraim Gate to the Corner Gate. [24]He carried off all the gold and silver
and all the articles from the Temple of God that had been in the care of Obed-edom. He also 25:24 1 Chr 26:15
seized the treasures of the royal palace, along with hostages, and then returned to Samaria.
[25]King Amaziah of Judah lived on for fifteen years after the death of King Jehoash of Is-
rael. [26]The rest of the events in Amaziah's reign, from beginning to end, are recorded in 25:25
The Book of the Kings of Judah and Israel. 2 Kgs 14:17-22

25:17a Hebrew *Joash*, a variant spelling of Jehoash; also in 25:18, 21, 23, 25. **25:17b** Hebrew *Come, let us look one another in the face.* **25:23** Hebrew *400 cubits* [180 meters].

▸ CHURCH

25:14 Starting well, finishing poorly. Many run the first few laps of a race well, but at the end, they are nowhere in sight. Amaziah began his reign as king of Judah well, but his downfall began as he hired out apostate Israelites to fight for him. His fall was complete when he turned to worshiping the gods of the very people God had allowed him to defeat. How often do you worship the gods of materialism or sensuality, from whom God has set you free? Flee from the disaster of worshiping other gods by repenting and believing, by constantly walking in the Spirit, and by rejoicing in God's great promise of heaven for those who persevere until the end (Revelation 3:10). (***See Church***> *Who> From Every People> Those who have persevered until the end,* TopicGuide page A48.)

25:14 In the ancient Near East, the gods of nations defeated in battle were sometimes understood to have abandoned their people in favor of the invaders. Amaziah may have been reflecting such an understanding when he brought the Edomite gods to Judah and offered homage to them.

25:16-17 The prophet's departure may reflect the recent memory of Zechariah's murder by Amaziah's father, Joash (24:17-22).

25:18-19 Jehoash's parable is similar to Jotham's in Judges 9:7-15.

▸ SPIRITUAL WARFARE

25:20 God's discipline through human circumstances. God judged Amaziah by ceasing to restrain his pride and arrogance, thus allowing him to completely underestimate his enemy, Israel. God did not force Amaziah to be prideful, nor did He force Amaziah to decide to attack Israel. Amaziah's decisions were free and unforced. But God used Amaziah's stubbornness to punish him. Are there behaviors or thoughts you engage in which place you in great danger of discipline? Flee from illegal and immoral activities, for you never know when God may allow circumstances to take their course and bring great consequences to you and those around you. (***See Spiritual Warfare***> *Resisting Sin and Evil> Consequences> Of Disobedience> God may allow consequences to run their course,* TopicGuide page A46.)

25:25 The chronicler seems to imply that Amaziah was released at the time of Jehoash's death and then lived for an additional 15 years.

[27]After Amaziah turned away from the LORD, there was a conspiracy against his life in Je-
rusalem, and he fled to Lachish. But his enemies sent assassins after him, and they killed
him there. [28]They brought his body back on a horse, and he was buried with his ancestors
in the City of David.*

UZZIAH RULES IN JUDAH

26 All the people of Judah had crowned Amaziah's sixteen-year-old son, Uzziah, as
26:1-4 king in place of his father. [2]After his father's death, Uzziah rebuilt the town of
//2 Kgs 14:21-22; Elath* and restored it to Judah.
15:1-3 [3]Uzziah was sixteen years old when he became king, and he reigned in Jerusalem fifty-
two years. His mother was Jecoliah from Jerusalem. [4]He did what was pleasing in the
LORD's sight, just as his father, Amaziah, had done. [5]Uzziah sought God during the days of
26:5 Zechariah, who taught him to fear God.* And as long as the king sought guidance from the
2 Chr 15:2; 24:2 LORD, God gave him success.
Dan 1:17 [6]Uzziah declared war on the Philistines and broke down the walls of Gath, Jabneh, and
Ashdod. Then he built new towns in the Ashdod area and in other parts of Philistia. [7]God
26:6 Isa 14:29 helped him in his wars against the Philistines, his battles with the Arabs of Gur,* and his
26:7 wars with the Meunites. [8]The Meunites* paid annual tribute to him, and his fame spread
2 Chr 21:16 even to Egypt, for he had become very powerful.
26:8 [9]Uzziah built fortified towers in Jerusalem at the Corner Gate, at the Valley Gate, and at
2 Chr 17:11 the angle in the wall. [10]He also constructed forts in the wilderness and dug many water cis-
26:9 terns, because he kept great herds of livestock in the foothills of Judah* and on the plains.
2 Chr 25:23 Neh 3:13 He was also a man who loved the soil. He had many workers who cared for his farms and
26:10 vineyards, both on the hillsides and in the fertile valleys.
Gen 26:18-21 [11]Uzziah had an army of well-trained warriors, ready to march into battle, unit by unit.
This army had been mustered and organized by Jeiel, the secretary of the army, and his
assistant, Maaseiah. They were under the direction of Hananiah, one of the king's officials.
[12]These regiments of mighty warriors were commanded by 2,600 clan leaders. [13]The
26:13 army consisted of 307,500 men, all elite troops. They were prepared to assist the king
2 Chr 25:5 against any enemy.
[14]Uzziah provided the entire army with shields, spears, helmets, coats of mail, bows,
and sling stones. [15]And he built structures on the walls of Jerusalem, designed by experts
to protect those who shot arrows and hurled large stones* from the towers and the corners

25:28 As in some Hebrew manuscripts and other ancient versions (see also 2 Kgs 14:20); most Hebrew manuscripts read *the city of Judah.* 26:2 As in Greek version (see also 2 Kgs 14:22; 16:6); Hebrew reads *Eloth*, a variant spelling of Elath. 26:5 As in Syriac and Greek versions; Hebrew reads *who instructed him in divine visions.* 26:7 As in Greek version; Hebrew reads *Gurbaal.* 26:8 As in Greek version; Hebrew reads *Ammonites.* Compare 26:7. 26:10 Hebrew *the Shephelah.* 26:15 Or *to shoot arrows and hurl large stones.*

26:1 Uzziah began his reign as co-regent upon his father's capture (2 Chronicles 25:23). This explains the unusual formula "the people of Judah had crowned." According to 2 Kings 15:1, Uzziah assumed the throne in the 27th year of Jeroboam II. However, when Jeroboam died 14 years later in his 41st year, Uzziah is said to have already been reigning for 38 years (2 Kings 15:8). A co-regency of 24 years is assumed. Uzziah is also known as Azariah in 2 Kings.

26:5 The Zechariah mentioned here is not mentioned elsewhere in the Old Testament, unless he is to be equated with the Zechariah mentioned in Isaiah 8:2. Zechariah functioned for Uzziah as Jehoiada did for Joash (2 Chronicles 24:2). Seeking the Lord is an essential characteristic of a righteous king (2 Chronicles 11:17; 14:7; 15:4; 17:4; 31:21).

26:6-8 These verses summarize Uzziah's military endeavors, which focused on areas generally to the west and south of Judah. His activities may reflect an attempt to control the leading commercial highways of the time such as the Way of the Sea, which ran along the Mediterranean coast.

26:9 Uzziah's building projects were likely efforts to repair the damage caused by Jehoash when he attacked Amaziah (2 Chronicles 25:23-24) and the damage caused by an earthquake, which is mentioned in the books of Amos (Amos 1:1) and Zechariah (Zechariah 14:5).

26:9-10 These verses summarize Uzziah's domestic affairs. Expansive building projects are a sign of divine blessing for the chronicler, and he typically included them only for the reigns of righteous kings (2 Chronicles 14:6; 17:12; 27:3).

26:15 Since catapults and other similar weapons did not appear until 500 BC at the earliest, the devices described here are likely protective structures that allowed archers and soldiers with similar weapons to fire without being exposed. Such devices are attested to in murals depicting battles from the period.

of the wall. His fame spread far and wide, for the LORD gave him marvelous help, and he
became very powerful.

UZZIAH'S SIN AND PUNISHMENT

16 But when he had become powerful, he also became proud, which led to his downfall. He 26:16
sinned against the LORD his God by entering the sanctuary of the LORD's Temple and per- Deut 32:15 1 Kgs 13:1-4
sonally burning incense on the incense altar. 17 Azariah the high priest went in after him 2 Chr 25:19
with eighty other priests of the LORD, all brave men. 18 They confronted King Uzziah and 26:17
said, "It is not for you, Uzziah, to burn incense to the LORD. That is the work of the priests 1 Chr 6:10
alone, the descendants of Aaron who are set apart for this work. Get out of the sanctuary, 26:18
for you have sinned. The LORD God will not honor you for this!" Exod 30:7-8 Num 16:39-40
19 Uzziah, who was holding an incense burner, became furious. But as he was standing 26:19
there raging at the priests before the incense altar in the LORD's Temple, leprosy* suddenly 2 Kgs 5:25-27
broke out on his forehead. 20 When Azariah the high priest and all the other priests saw the
leprosy, they rushed him out. And the king himself was eager to get out because the LORD
had struck him. 21 So King Uzziah had leprosy until the day he died. He lived in isolation in 26:21-23
a separate house, for he was excluded from the Temple of the LORD. His son Jotham was //2 Kgs 15:5-7
put in charge of the royal palace, and he governed the people of the land.
22 The rest of the events of Uzziah's reign, from beginning to end, are recorded by the 26:22
prophet Isaiah son of Amoz. 23 When Uzziah died, he was buried with his ancestors; his Isa 1:1
grave was in a nearby burial field belonging to the kings, for the people said, "He had lep- 26:23
rosy." And his son Jotham became the next king. 2 Chr 21:20; 28:27 Isa 6:1

JOTHAM RULES IN JUDAH

27 Jotham was twenty-five years old when he became king, and he reigned in Jeru- 27:1-9
salem sixteen years. His mother was Jerusha, the daughter of Zadok. //2 Kgs 15:33-38
2 Jotham did what was pleasing in the LORD's sight. He did everything his father, Uzziah, 27:2 2 Chr 26:16
had done, except that Jotham did not sin by entering the Temple of the LORD. But the peo-
ple continued in their corrupt ways.
3 Jotham rebuilt the upper gate of the Temple of the LORD. He also did extensive rebuilding 27:3 2 Chr 33:14
on the wall at the hill of Ophel. 4 He built towns in the hill country of Judah and constructed Neh 3:26
fortresses and towers in the wooded areas. 5 Jotham went to war against the Ammonites and 27:4
conquered them. Over the next three years he received from them an annual tribute of 2 Chr 11:5
7,500 pounds* of silver, 50,000 bushels of wheat, and 50,000 bushels of barley.*

26:19 Or *a contagious skin disease.* The Hebrew word used here and throughout this passage can describe various skin diseases. 27:5a Hebrew *100 talents* [3,400 kilograms]. 27:5b Hebrew *10,000 cors* [1,820 kiloliters] *of wheat, and 10,000 cors of barley.*

▸ GOD

26:16 Pride and power. "Success!" Many people live to hear that word, craving the admiration of their peers. But as few people know how to succeed, fewer still know how to handle victory gracefully. But mature Christians know that they have no right to feel proud in their accomplishments—it's all from God. Even our best efforts are made possible by God's sustaining power (James 1:17). Ask God to help you turn from any self-importance and smugness to a humble, God-centered understanding of achievement. (***See God****> Relationship> Barriers> Pride,* TopicGuide page A14.)

26:16 Numbers 16:40 specifies that only descendants of Aaron were allowed to burn incense before the Lord.

26:19 Disease was also a mark of God's displeasure toward Asa (2 Chronicles 16:12-13) and Jehoram (2 Chronicles 21:12-19). The Hebrew word translated "leprosy" here included various diseases, such as psoriasis and fungal infections.

26:21 Old Testament law required that those affected by skin disease be removed from the community (Leviticus 13:46; Numbers 5:1-4; 12:15). At this time, Jotham began to rule as co-regent with his father, who was unable to fully carry out his royal duties.

27:1 The book of 2 Kings records that Hoshea of Israel came to power in the twentieth year of Jotham's reign (2 Kings 15:30). The 16-year reign recorded here by the chronicler may not include a period of co-regency with Jotham's son Ahaz.

27:2 The chronicler treats Jotham's reign as an uncorrupted continuation of Uzziah's rule. Despite the righteousness of the king, we know from the testimonies of Isaiah and Micah (who ministered during this time) that the people of Judah continued to exhibit moral and religious corruption (Isaiah 8:6-8; Micah 1:13).

27:3-4 On building projects, see note at 26:9-10. The location of Ophel is uncertain. Jotham's construction continued and supplemented the projects begun by Uzziah (compare with 2 Chronicles 26:9-10).

6King Jotham became powerful because he was careful to live in obedience to the LORD
his God.
7The rest of the events of Jotham's reign, including all his wars and other activities, are
recorded in *The Book of the Kings of Israel and Judah.* 8He was twenty-five years old when
he became king, and he reigned in Jerusalem sixteen years. 9When Jotham died, he was
buried in the City of David. And his son Ahaz became the next king.

27:6 2 Chr 26:5
27:7 2 Kgs 15:36
27:8 2 Chr 27:1

AHAZ RULES IN JUDAH

28 Ahaz was twenty years old when he became king, and he reigned in Jerusalem
sixteen years. He did not do what was pleasing in the sight of the LORD, as his an-
cestor David had done. 2Instead, he followed the example of the kings of Israel. He cast
metal images for the worship of Baal. 3He offered sacrifices in the valley of Ben-Hinnom,
even sacrificing his own sons in the fire.* In this way, he followed the detestable practices of
the pagan nations the LORD had driven from the land ahead of the Israelites. 4He offered sac-
rifices and burned incense at the pagan shrines and on the hills and under every green tree.
5Because of all this, the LORD his God allowed the king of Aram to defeat Ahaz and to exile
large numbers of his people to Damascus. The armies of the king of Israel also defeated
Ahaz and inflicted many casualties on his army. 6In a single day Pekah son of Remaliah, Is-
rael's king, killed 120,000 of Judah's troops, all of them experienced warriors, because they
had abandoned the LORD, the God of their ancestors. 7Then Zicri, a warrior from Ephraim,
killed Maaseiah, the king's son; Azrikam, the king's palace commander; and Elkanah, the
king's second-in-command. 8The armies of Israel captured 200,000 women and children
from Judah and seized tremendous amounts of plunder, which they took back to Samaria.
9But a prophet of the LORD named Oded was there in Samaria when the army of Israel
returned home. He went out to meet them and said, "The LORD, the God of your ancestors,

28:1-27 //2 Kgs 16:1-20
28:2 Exod 34:17; 2 Chr 22:3
28:3 Lev 18:21; Josh 15:8; 2 Chr 33:2, 6
28:5 2 Kgs 16:5; 2 Chr 24:24; Isa 7:1
28:6 2 Kgs 16:5
28:8 Deut 28:25, 41; 2 Chr 11:4
28:9 2 Chr 25:15; Ezra 9:6; Isa 47:6; Rev 18:5

28:3 Or *even making his sons pass through the fire.*

▸ HOLINESS

27:6 Blessing the faithful. The faithful sometimes seem to have it worse than the faithless. In fact, God revealed early on that it was His will that the faithful face trials on this earth (Job 1–2; 2 Thessalonians 1:5). The chronicler, however, promises that covenant obedience will bring God's favor. God gave the writer special insight to see that in this instance, there was a connection between the blessings of God and Jotham's obedience. Like Job, we may never see the connection between our deeds and God's providence. Nevertheless, God encourages us to obey and to expect a reward (Hebrews 11:6). Seek and serve God, and humbly wait and see how He rewards your diligence. (***See Holiness****> God's Blessing> Obedience brings God's favor,* TopicGuide page A42.)

27:6 Jotham was uncorrupted by his power, unlike his father, Uzziah. This comment underscores once again the chronicler's theology that obedience is met with blessing and disobedience with curses.

28:1 If Ahaz was 20 years old at the time of his accession and ruled for 16 years, it appears that he must have died at age 36. But his son Hezekiah was 25 years old when he took the throne, which would indicate that Ahaz fathered Hezekiah at age 11. While this is not impossible, co-regency, or shared power, was not uncommon in ancient times. Ahaz likely shared power with his father Jotham for a period of time, and adding that tenure to his 16-year reign would theoretically move Hezekiah's birth date up into Ahaz's adult years.

28:3 Child sacrifice was the most detestable of the pagan rituals practiced by Israel's neighbors and was particularly associated with the worship of Molech (Leviticus 20:1-5; Deuteronomy 18:10; 2 Kings 3:26-27; Micah 6:7). The valley of Ben-Hinnom is associated with child sacrifice in 2 Chronicles 33:6 and Jeremiah 7:31-32. It was there that the refuse of Jerusalem was burned, and its Hebrew name, *Gehenna*, has come to designate hell.

28:5-8 These verses articulate the chronicler's theology of immediate retribution clearly and forcefully. Ahaz's apostasy brought upon him repeated and severe military catastrophes.

28:6-8 The large casualty numbers are problematic. In 480 BC, Xerxes attacked Greece with forces that for the first time in history approached 100,000. As with the inordinately large armies mentioned elsewhere in 2 Chronicles (13:3-4; 14:9; 17:12-19; 25:5-6), it is possible to read the Hebrew as 120 military units rather than 120,000 soldiers, and people from 200 families rather than 200,000 individuals. The figures may also represent the author's use of hyperbole to communicate his point.

▸ GOD

28:9 All is fair in love and war. Have you ever had someone at your mercy? Pekah, the king of Israel, soundly defeated Judah because they had been unfaithful to God (2 Chronicles 28:5; also see Deuteronomy 8:19-20). But as He punished Judah, God still had mercy on His people. He sent Oded to warn Israel to not completely annihilate Judah and to keep the laws that forbade the enslavement of other Israelites (see note at 2 Chronicles 28:10). War is an awful thing—whether it be in your home, your church, or on the battlefield—but God's Word reminds us to be merciful and obey His Word in the midst of it. Even the worst horrors of conflict don't do away with the need to show restraint at the end of the battle. After a quarrel, big or small, show mercy and love toward those whom you've battled. (***See God****> God's Attributes> Merciful> God is merciful,* TopicGuide page A17.)

was angry with Judah and let you defeat them. But you have gone too far, killing them
without mercy, and all heaven is disturbed. [10]And now you are planning to make slaves of 28:10
these people from Judah and Jerusalem. What about your own sins against the LORD your Lev 25:39
God? [11]Listen to me and return these prisoners you have taken, for they are your own rel- 28:11
atives. Watch out, because now the LORD's fierce anger has been turned against you!" 2 Chr 28:8

[12]Then some of the leaders of Israel*—Azariah son of Jehohanan, Berekiah son of Me-
shillemoth, Jehizkiah son of Shallum, and Amasa son of Hadlai—agreed with this and
confronted the men returning from battle. [13]"You must not bring the prisoners here!"
they declared. "We cannot afford to add to our sins and guilt. Our guilt is already great,
and the LORD's fierce anger is already turned against Israel."

[14]So the warriors released the prisoners and handed over the plunder in the sight of the
leaders and all the people. [15]Then the four men just mentioned by name came forward 28:15
and distributed clothes from the plunder to the prisoners who were naked. They provided Deut 34:3 2 Kgs 6:22
clothing and sandals to wear, gave them enough food and drink, and dressed their Prov 25:21-22
wounds with olive oil. They put those who were weak on donkeys and took all the prison-
ers back to their own people in Jericho, the city of palms. Then they returned to Samaria.

AHAZ CLOSES THE TEMPLE

[16]At that time King Ahaz of Judah asked the king of Assyria for help. [17]The armies of Edom 28:16
had again invaded Judah and taken captives. [18]And the Philistines had raided towns lo- 2 Kgs 16:7
cated in the foothills of Judah* and in the Negev of Judah. They had already captured and 28:18
occupied Beth-shemesh, Aijalon, Gederoth, Soco with its villages, Timnah with its villages, Ezek 16:57
and Gimzo with its villages. [19]The LORD was humbling Judah because of King Ahaz of Ju- 28:19
dah,* for he had encouraged his people to sin and had been utterly unfaithful to the LORD. 2 Chr 21:2

[20]So when King Tiglath-pileser* of Assyria arrived, he attacked Ahaz instead of helping 28:20 1 Chr 5:26
him. [21]Ahaz took valuable items from the LORD's Temple, the royal palace, and from the 28:21
homes of his officials and gave them to the king of Assyria as tribute. But this did not help 2 Kgs 16:8-9
him.

[22]Even during this time of trouble, King Ahaz continued to reject the LORD. [23]He offered 28:23
sacrifices to the gods of Damascus who had defeated him, for he said, "Since these gods 2 Chr 25:14 Jer 44:17-18
helped the kings of Aram, they will help me, too, if I sacrifice to them." But instead, they led
to his ruin and the ruin of all Judah.

[24]The king took the various articles from the Temple of God and broke them into pieces. 28:24 2 Kgs 16:17
He shut the doors of the LORD's Temple so that no one could worship there, and he set up 2 Chr 29:7; 30:14;
altars to pagan gods in every corner of Jerusalem. [25]He made pagan shrines in all the 33:3-5

28:12 Hebrew *Ephraim,* referring to the northern kingdom of Israel. 28:18 Hebrew *the Shephelah.* 28:19 Hebrew *of Israel;* also in 28:23, 27. The author of Chronicles sees Judah as representative of the true Israel. See also some Hebrew manuscripts, Greek and Syriac versions, and Latin Vulgate. 28:20 Hebrew *Tilgath-pilneser,* a variant spelling of Tiglath-pileser.

28:10 The Law of Moses forbade Israelites to enslave their fellow countrymen (Leviticus 25:42-43, 46).

28:15 It seems likely that this passage may have been in Jesus' mind as He told the parable of the Good Samaritan (Luke 10:25-37).

28:16-25 The key word "help" runs throughout this unit and alerts the reader to the chronicler's main point: Ahaz's search for help apart from God proved futile. The places where he turned for help ironically became channels of further trouble.

▶ CHURCH

28:21 Giving the church away. Faced with pressure from the world, churches and denominations have sometimes compromised. Some have compromised in the manner of Ahaz, who gave away the greatest treasures of the Temple to the king of Assyria. When the result didn't suit him, he began to worship other gods (2 Chronicles 28:22). He destroyed many of the important objects associated with Temple worship and shut the doors to the Temple, encouraging the people to worship other gods (2 Chronicles 28:25). Today, some places that look like churches on the outside no longer worship God—except in a vague, general fashion. They don't believe the Bible. They tell their members that other religions offer as much truth as Christianity and even incorporate their practices into their worship. This sort of apostasy makes God furious (2 Chronicles 28:25; Revelation 2:15-16). Pray, even with fasting, that true Christians will come out of untrue churches or denominations and will find refreshing preaching and fellowship in Bible-based churches. (***See Church****> Who> From Every People> Those who are tempted to apostasy by suffering,* TopicGuide page A48.)

towns of Judah for offering sacrifices to other gods. In this way, he aroused the anger of
the LORD, the God of his ancestors.
28:26 26The rest of the events of Ahaz's reign and everything he did, from beginning to end,
2 Kgs 16:19-20 are recorded in *The Book of the Kings of Judah and Israel.* 27When Ahaz died, he was bur-
28:27 2 Chr 24:25 ied in Jerusalem but not in the royal cemetery of the kings of Judah. Then his son Hezeki-
ah became the next king.

HEZEKIAH RULES IN JUDAH

29:1-2 //2 Kgs 18:1-3 **29** Hezekiah was twenty-five years old when he became the king of Judah, and he
29:2 reigned in Jerusalem twenty-nine years. His mother was Abijah, the daughter of
2 Chr 34:2 Zechariah. 2He did what was pleasing in the LORD's sight, just as his ancestor David had
done.

HEZEKIAH REOPENS THE TEMPLE

29:3 2 Chr 28:24; 29:7 3In the very first month of the first year of his reign, Hezekiah reopened the doors of the
Temple of the LORD and repaired them. 4He summoned the priests and Levites to meet
29:5 him at the courtyard east of the Temple. 5He said to them, "Listen to me, you Levites! Pu-
2 Chr 29:15, 34; 35:6 rify yourselves, and purify the Temple of the LORD, the God of your ancestors. Remove all
29:6 the defiled things from the sanctuary. 6Our ancestors were unfaithful and did what was
Ezek 8:16 evil in the sight of the LORD our God. They abandoned the LORD and His dwelling place;
they turned their backs on Him. 7They also shut the doors to the Temple's entry room, and
they snuffed out the lamps. They stopped burning incense and presenting burnt offerings
at the sanctuary of the God of Israel.
29:8 8"That is why the LORD's anger has fallen upon Judah and Jerusalem. He has made them
Deut 28:25 2 Chr 24:18; 28:5 an object of dread, horror, and ridicule, as you can see with your own eyes. 9Because of
Jer 25:9, 18 this, our fathers have been killed in battle, and our sons and daughters and wives have
29:9 been captured. 10But now I will make a covenant with the LORD, the God of Israel, so that
2 Chr 28:5-8, 17 His fierce anger will turn away from us. 11My sons, do not neglect your duties any longer!
29:10 2 Chr 23:16 The LORD has chosen you to stand in His presence, to minister to Him, and to lead the peo-
29:11 ple in worship and present offerings to Him."
Num 3:6; 8:6, 14 12Then these Levites got right to work:
29:12 Num 3:19-20 2 Chr 31:13

From the clan of Kohath: Mahath son of Amasai and Joel son of Azariah.
From the clan of Merari: Kish son of Abdi and Azariah son of Jehallelel.
From the clan of Gershon: Joah son of Zimmah and Eden son of Joah.
13 From the family of Elizaphan: Shimri and Jeiel.
From the family of Asaph: Zechariah and Mattaniah.
14 From the family of Heman: Jehiel and Shimei.
From the family of Jeduthun: Shemaiah and Uzziel.

29:15 15These men called together their fellow Levites, and they all purified themselves. Then
1 Chr 23:28 2 Chr 29:5; 30:12 they began to cleanse the Temple of the LORD, just as the king had commanded. They

▸ WORSHIP
29:2 Tradition is good. "It's the way we've always done it!" can either be good or bad news. It can mean an inflexible, unchanging commitment to a doomed strategy or it can be common sense borne out and tested by time. In Hezekiah's day all subsequent kings were measured by Hezekiah's ancestor, David. If you wanted to know what a great king was like, it wasn't necessary to be too creative—David had already set the standard. In this case tradition is good. At the bare minimum, it gives a healthy goal to keep in mind during a time of recovery from sin or weakness. At its best, it's the starting point for continued growth and maturity. God wants us to honor the work of those who have gone before us and to stand on the shoulders of the giants of the faith. Learn from the healthy traditions passed down from your spiritual fathers and mothers. (***See Worship****> OT> Reverence> For those who came before,* TopicGuide page A29.)

29:2 Abijah (also known as Abi; see textual note at 2 Kings 18:2), the daughter of Zechariah, is mentioned in verse 1 to hint that she was partially the reason for Hezekiah's mature leadership, not his godless father, Ahaz. Jewish apocryphal literature tells how Abijah miraculously saved the life of her son from her husband.

were careful to follow all the LORD's instructions in their work. [16]The priests went into the 29:16
sanctuary of the Temple of the LORD to cleanse it, and they took out to the Temple court- 2 Chr 15:16
yard all the defiled things they found. From there the Levites carted it all out to the Kidron
Valley.
[17]They began the work in early spring, on the first day of the new year,* and in eight 29:17
days they had reached the entry room of the LORD's Temple. Then they purified the Tem- 2 Chr 29:3
ple of the LORD itself, which took another eight days. So the entire task was completed in
sixteen days.

THE TEMPLE REDEDICATION

[18]Then the Levites went to King Hezekiah and gave him this report: "We have cleansed
the entire Temple of the LORD, the altar of burnt offering with all its utensils, and the table
of the Bread of the Presence with all its utensils. [19]We have also recovered all the items 29:19
discarded by King Ahaz when he was unfaithful and closed the Temple. They are now in 2 Chr 28:24
front of the altar of the LORD, purified and ready for use."
[20]Early the next morning King Hezekiah gathered the city officials and went to the Tem-
ple of the LORD. [21]They brought seven bulls, seven rams, and seven male lambs as a burnt 29:21
offering, together with seven male goats as a sin offering for the kingdom, for the Temple, Lev 4:3-14
and for Judah. The king commanded the priests, who were descendants of Aaron, to sacri-
fice the animals on the altar of the LORD.
[22]So they killed the bulls, and the priests took the blood and sprinkled it on the altar. 29:22
Next they killed the rams and sprinkled their blood on the altar. And finally, they did the Lev 4:18
same with the male lambs. [23]The male goats for the sin offering were then brought before 29:23
the king and the assembly of people, who laid their hands on them. [24]The priests then Lev 4:15 29:24
killed the goats as a sin offering and sprinkled their blood on the altar to make atonement Lev 4:26
for the sins of all Israel. The king had specifically commanded that this burnt offering and
sin offering should be made for all Israel. 29:25
[25]King Hezekiah then stationed the Levites at the Temple of the LORD with cymbals, 2 Sam 7:2; 24:11
lyres, and harps. He obeyed all the commands that the LORD had given to King David 1 Chr 25:6 2 Chr 8:14
through Gad, the king's seer, and the prophet Nathan. [26]The Levites then took their posi- 29:26
tions around the Temple with the instruments of David, and the priests took their positions 1 Chr 23:5
with the trumpets. 2 Chr 5:12
[27]Then Hezekiah ordered that the burnt offering be placed on the altar. As the burnt of- 29:27
fering was presented, songs of praise to the LORD were begun, accompanied by the trum- 2 Chr 23:18
pets and other instruments of David, the former king of Israel. [28]The entire assembly
worshiped the LORD as the singers sang and the trumpets blew, until all the burnt offerings
were finished. [29]Then the king and everyone with him bowed down in worship. [30]King 29:29
Hezekiah and the officials ordered the Levites to praise the LORD with the psalms written by 2 Chr 20:18
David and by Asaph the seer. So they offered joyous praise and bowed down in worship.
[31]Then Hezekiah declared, "Now that you have consecrated yourselves to the LORD, 29:31 Exod 35:5, 22

29:17 Hebrew *on the first day of the first month.* This day in the ancient Hebrew lunar calendar occurred in March or early April, 715 B.C.

29:17 The work of sanctifying the Temple began on the first day of the first month (see textual note) and continued for 16 days. The work was then completed 2 days after the feast of Passover should have begun (Numbers 9:1-11).

29:21 The chronicler distinguishes between the burnt offerings and the sin offerings. The bulls, rams, and lambs belonged to the burnt offerings, and the goats were offered as sin offerings. For a description of the burnt and sin offerings see Leviticus 1 and 4.

29:23-24 The sin offering, which was also the principle offering of the Day of Atonement (Leviticus 16), was an offering of purification. The offering did not typically purify the one bringing the sacrifice—in this case the king and the people—but the sanctuary of God (Leviticus 4:3-7). However, showing the flexibility of the law of Moses that Christ would rebuke the Pharisees for not understanding (Matthew 12:1-14; John 7:21-24), this sacrifice purified the guilty covenant community.

29:31 The description of the people's sacrifices is consciously reminiscent of similar offerings in the days of Moses, David, and Solomon (Exodus 36:6-7; 1 Chronicles 29:6-9; 2 Chronicles 7:7).

bring your sacrifices and thanksgiving offerings to the Temple of the LORD." So the people
brought their sacrifices and thanksgiving offerings, and all whose hearts were willing
brought burnt offerings, too. 32The people brought to the LORD 70 bulls, 100 rams, and
200 male lambs for burnt offerings. 33They also brought 600 cattle and 3,000 sheep and
goats as sacred offerings.
29:34 34But there were too few priests to prepare all the burnt offerings. So their relatives the
2 Chr 30:3; 35:11 Levites helped them until the work was finished and more priests had been purified, for
the Levites had been more conscientious about purifying themselves than the priests had
29:35 been. 35There was an abundance of burnt offerings, along with the usual liquid offerings,
Lev 3:16 Num 15:5-10 and a great deal of fat from the many peace offerings.
2 Chr 29:32 So the Temple of the LORD was restored to service. 36And Hezekiah and all the people re-
joiced because of what God had done for the people, for everything had been accom-
plished so quickly.

PREPARATIONS FOR PASSOVER

30:2 **30** King Hezekiah now sent word to all Israel and Judah, and he wrote letters of invi-
Num 9:10-11 2 Chr 30:13, 15 tation to the people of Ephraim and Manasseh. He asked everyone to come to
the Temple of the LORD at Jerusalem to celebrate the Passover of the LORD, the God of Isra-
el. 2The king, his officials, and all the community of Jerusalem decided to celebrate Pass-
30:3 over a month later than usual.* 3They were unable to celebrate it at the prescribed time
2 Chr 29:34 because not enough priests could be purified by then, and the people had not yet assem-
bled at Jerusalem.
30:5 4This plan for keeping the Passover seemed right to the king and all the people. 5So they
Judg 20:1 sent a proclamation throughout all Israel, from Beersheba in the south to Dan in the north,
inviting everyone to come to Jerusalem to celebrate the Passover of the LORD, the God of Is-
rael. The people had not been celebrating it in great numbers as required in the Law.
30:6 6At the king's command, runners were sent throughout Israel and Judah. They carried
2 Chr 28:20 Esth 8:14 Jer 51:31 letters that said:

"O people of Israel, return to the LORD, the God of Abraham, Isaac, and Israel,* so that
He will return to the few of us who have survived the conquest of the Assyrian kings.
30:7 7Do not be like your ancestors and relatives who abandoned the LORD, the God of
2 Chr 29:8 Ezek 20:13, 18 their ancestors, and became an object of derision, as you yourselves can see. 8Do not
30:8 be stubborn, as they were, but submit yourselves to the LORD. Come to His Temple,
Exod 32:9 2 Chr 29:10 which He has set apart as holy forever. Worship the LORD your God so that His fierce
anger will turn away from you.

30:2 Hebrew *in the second month.* Passover was normally observed in the first month (of the ancient Hebrew lunar calendar). 30:6 *Israel* is the name that God gave to Jacob.

▸ MINISTRY
29:34 Making allowances. When David was fleeing Saul, he and his men happened upon the Tabernacle, the mobile sanctuary of God, located then in the city of Nob. David's men were hungry and unequipped, and David asked for the holy bread to be served to his men. Even then, David understood that God placed mercy and kindness above the ceremonial law (see Jesus' commentary in Matthew 12:3-8). Hezekiah, exhibiting the same wisdom as David, allowed the Levites to help prepare the burnt offering (which contradicts the normal rules of sacrifice found in Numbers 18), thereby enabling the Temple to be fully and quickly restored to service. Hezekiah demonstrated the biblical principle that God values people over process. He values mercy and love more than rigid rule keeping. Show love and mercy as you help people to obey God's rules and thus become more like the Lord they serve. (***See Ministry*> *Great Commission> Make Disciples> Disciples strategically use knowledge, skills, and abilities,* TopicGuide page A56.)

30:1 Hezekiah's invitation assumed that the northern kingdom of Israel had already collapsed or was on the verge of doing so. He extended the invitation to all Israel, the large tribes of Ephraim and Manasseh representing the whole (see 2 Chronicles 30:5). All Israel is an important theme for the chronicler and a central element of his vision for his audience, the restoration community (1 Chronicles 9:1; 11:1; 29:23; 2 Chronicles 7:8; 13:4; 28:23; 35:3).

30:2-3 Numbers 9:9-11 allowed for the celebration of Passover in the second month for those who were ritually unclean at the ordinary time of Passover. This provision, originally intended for individuals, was extended to the whole community.

9"For if you return to the LORD, your relatives and your children will be treated **30:9**
mercifully by their captors, and they will be able to return to this land. For the LORD Exod 34:6-7 Deut 30:2
your God is gracious and merciful. If you return to Him, He will not continue to turn Mic 7:18
His face from you."

CELEBRATION OF PASSOVER

10The runners went from town to town throughout Ephraim and Manasseh and as far as **30:10**
the territory of Zebulun. But most of the people just laughed at the runners and made fun 2 Chr 36:16
of them. 11However, some people from Asher, Manasseh, and Zebulun humbled them- **30:11** 2 Chr 30:18, 21
selves and went to Jerusalem.
12At the same time, God's hand was on the people in the land of Judah, giving them all
one heart to obey the orders of the king and his officials, who were following the word of
the LORD. 13So a huge crowd assembled at Jerusalem in midspring* to celebrate the Festi- **30:13** 2 Chr 30:2
val of Unleavened Bread. 14They set to work and removed the pagan altars from Jerusa- **30:14**
lem. They took away all the incense altars and threw them into the Kidron Valley. 2 Chr 28:24; 29:16
15On the fourteenth day of the second month, one month later than usual,* the people **30:15**
slaughtered the Passover lamb. This shamed the priests and Levites, so they purified 2 Chr 29:34; 30:2-3
themselves and brought burnt offerings to the Temple of the LORD. 16Then they took their **30:16**
places at the Temple as prescribed in the Law of Moses, the man of God. The Levites 2 Chr 35:10, 15
brought the sacrificial blood to the priests, who then sprinkled it on the altar.
17Since many of the people had not purified themselves, the Levites had to slaughter
their Passover lamb for them, to set them apart for the LORD. 18Most of those who came **30:18**
from Ephraim, Manasseh, Issachar, and Zebulun had not purified themselves. But King Exod 12:43-49 Num 9:6-10
Hezekiah prayed for them, and they were allowed to eat the Passover meal anyway, even
though this was contrary to the requirements of the Law. For Hezekiah said, "May the
LORD, who is good, pardon those 19who decide to follow the LORD, the God of their ances-
tors, even though they are not properly cleansed for the ceremony." 20And the LORD lis-
tened to Hezekiah's prayer and healed the people.
21So the people of Israel who were present in Jerusalem joyously celebrated the Festival **30:21**
of Unleavened Bread for seven days. Each day the Levites and priests sang to the LORD, Exod 12:15; 13:6
accompanied by loud instruments.* 22Hezekiah encouraged all the Levites regarding the **30:22** 2 Chr 32:6 Ezra 10:11

30:13 Hebrew *in the second month.* The second month of the ancient Hebrew lunar calendar usually occurs within the months of April and May. 30:15 Hebrew *On the fourteenth day of the second month.* Passover normally began on the fourteenth day of the first month (see Lev 23:5). 30:21 Or *sang to the LORD with all their strength.*

30:9 The hope of a return from exile conditioned on repentance was not new but was first articulated by Moses in Deuteronomy 4:26-29. Hezekiah's words applied directly to the chronicler's audience: Repentance was critical to the success of the restoration.

▸ WORSHIP

30:10-12 Laughing at the messenger. People don't always respond well to the good news of the gospel. Some may be openly hostile, but as in this case, some may simply laugh and make fun of God's messengers. But the verbal ridicule is worth the results—some people respond (see Romans 10:14-17). Jesus said that His prophets had been persecuted since the beginning, and His faithful followers would experience the same (Matthew 5:10-12). Have you ever been ridiculed for spreading the gospel or giving your testimony? If you haven't, then perhaps you have not witnessed enough! Make it your goal to tell others about the good news of your rescue through faith in Jesus Christ, and get ready to receive the blessings—and ridicule—that accompany the gospel. (***See Worship****> NT> Teaching and Preaching> Persecution for preaching the Word,* TopicGuide page A34.)

30:17 The one bringing the offering would typically be the one to slaughter the animal for the Passover sacrifice. The ritual uncleanness of so many of the worshipers, however, necessitated the Levites' assistance (Exodus 12:3-6, 21).

30:17-20 As in the previous chapter with the untrained Levites serving in the Temple, further allowances were made to enable the northern tribes to immediately participate in the Passover. God heard the prayers of Hezekiah and did not discipline the people for failing to strictly follow God's ceremonial laws (Leviticus 23; Numbers 9).

30:18-20 Hezekiah's prayer and God's response is reminiscent of Solomon's prayer at the Temple dedication (2 Chronicles 6:14-42; 7:12-22). Hezekiah was the first sole monarch over all the tribes of Israel since Solomon, and the chronicler depicts his reign as a rebirth of Solomon's glory and a model for the restoration community. The comparison is made explicit in 2 Chronicles 30:26.

30:20 The use of the word "healed" echoes 2 Chronicles 7:14, which operates as a theme verse for the chronicler.

30:23 skill they displayed as they served the LORD. The celebration continued for seven days.
1 Kgs 8:65 Peace offerings were sacrificed, and the people gave thanks to the LORD, the God of their
30:24 ancestors.
2 Chr 29:34; 30:3; 23The entire assembly then decided to continue the festival another seven days, so they
35:7-8 30:25 celebrated joyfully for another week. 24King Hezekiah gave the people 1,000 bulls and
2 Chr 30:11, 18 7,000 sheep and goats for offerings, and the officials donated 1,000 bulls and 10,000
30:26 sheep and goats. Meanwhile, many more priests purified themselves.
2 Chr 7:8-10 25The entire assembly of Judah rejoiced, including the priests, the Levites, all who
30:27 Num 6:23 came from the land of Israel, the foreigners who came to the festival, and all those who
Deut 26:15 lived in Judah. 26There was great joy in the city, for Jerusalem had not seen a celebration
2 Chr 23:18 like this one since the days of Solomon, King David's son. 27Then the priests and Levites
Ps 68:5 stood and blessed the people, and God heard their prayer from His holy dwelling in
heaven.

HEZEKIAH'S RELIGIOUS REFORMS

31:1 **31** When the festival ended, the Israelites who attended went to all the towns of Ju-
2 Kgs 18:4 dah, Benjamin, Ephraim, and Manasseh, and they smashed all the sacred pillars,
cut down the Asherah poles, and removed the pagan shrines and altars. After this, the Isra-
elites returned to their own towns and homes.
31:2 2Hezekiah then organized the priests and Levites into divisions to offer the burnt offer-
1 Chr 23:28-32; 24:1 ings and peace offerings, and to worship and give thanks and praise to the LORD at the
31:3 Num 28:1-29 gates of the Temple. 3The king also made a personal contribution of animals for the daily
2 Chr 35:7 morning and evening burnt offerings, the weekly Sabbath festivals, the monthly new
31:4 moon festivals, and the annual festivals as prescribed in the Law of the LORD. 4In addition,
Num 18:8 he required the people in Jerusalem to bring a portion of their goods to the priests and Le-
vites, so they could devote themselves fully to the Law of the LORD.

▸ WORSHIP

30:22 Repentance in worship. Certain themes in the worship of God have continued across the millennia, and one such theme is repentance. Even today, whether you are in a charismatic, Anglican, or Baptist church, every Bible-based church will include turning from sin as a necessary component of worship. As a wise pastor said, "The only thing we have to offer God is our sin." Confess your sins to God regularly, but make it a special part of your weekly worship to thoroughly repent of your sins—remember, even your imperfect repentance needs to be forgiven! Empower your worship with thorough, holy repentance. (***See Worship****> OT> Music> Psalms> Lament> Repentance,* TopicGuide page A27.)

30:22 Hezekiah praised the Levites, who had shown exceptional skill and attention to detail under very difficult circumstances.

30:27 The blessing that the priests and Levites were instructed to give is recorded in Numbers 6:22-27.

▸ WORSHIP

31:1 Smashing idols. Has the Holy Spirit ever convicted you of something that you needed to get rid of in your life? Perhaps alcohol or certain types of entertainment were influencing you too strongly, and God showed you that you needed to be completely free of it. As Hezekiah's people reformed their worship, they took action against the articles of idol worship that had poisoned Israel for many years. Only after they destroyed the various pagan shrines around Israel did they feel free to return to their homes. Perhaps there's something from which you need to free yourself or your family—too much cable TV? Inappropriate language in the home? Too much time on the Internet? Ask God to make your home and church a holy place and to give you the courage to destroy anything that comes between you, your family, and your God. (***See Worship****> OT> Reverence> Put away idols,* TopicGuide page A28.)

31:1 The reform program initiated by Hezekiah expanded in concentric circles beginning with the Temple (2 Chronicles 29:3-36), Jerusalem (2 Chronicles 30:13-14), then the rest of Judah, and even into Israel (2 Chronicles 31:1).

31:2-4 Having restored the Temple and celebrated its rededication in grand fashion, Hezekiah now made provisions for the continued, ordinary operations of the Temple. As elsewhere in Scripture, the extraordinary moment prepares for the sustained obedience of everyday life (compare Acts 2:41-42).

31:3 David and Solomon also gave to the Temple from their own wealth (1 Chronicles 29:1-5; 2 Chronicles 9:10-11).

▸ HOLINESS

31:3-5 Follow the leader. Some leaders motivate their followers by exercising power—they command obedience and punish the disobedient. While this is not foreign to the Scriptures, Hezekiah also led by example, showing the people how to obey and inviting them to follow his lead. Godly leaders need a careful mix of power and persuasion in order to get the most people to follow their instructions. In your leadership areas, do you struggle with getting people to follow you? Follow Hezekiah's example and use a wise combination of power and influence. (***See Holiness****> Law and Grace> Law> Leaders and followers,* TopicGuide page A41.)

5 The people of Israel responded immediately and generously by bringing the first of 31:5
their crops and grain, new wine, olive oil, honey, and all the produce of their fields. They Neh 13:12
brought a large quantity—a tithe of all they produced. 6 The people who had moved to Ju- 31:6
dah from Israel, and the people of Judah themselves, brought in the tithes of their cattle, Lev 27:30 Deut 14:28
sheep, and goats and a tithe of the things that had been dedicated to the LORD their God,
and they piled them up in great heaps. 7 They began piling them up in late spring, and the
heaps continued to grow until early autumn.* 8 When Hezekiah and his officials came and
saw these huge piles, they thanked the LORD and His people Israel!
9 "Where did all this come from?" Hezekiah asked the priests and Levites.
10 And Azariah the high priest, from the family of Zadok, replied, "Since the people be- 31:10
gan bringing their gifts to the LORD's Temple, we have had enough to eat and plenty to 1 Chr 6:8-9 Mal 3:10
spare. The LORD has blessed His people, and all this is left over."
11 Hezekiah ordered that storerooms be prepared in the Temple of the LORD. When this 31:11
was done, 12 the people faithfully brought all the tithes and gifts to the Temple. Conaniah 1 Kgs 6:5
the Levite was put in charge, assisted by his brother Shimei. 13 The supervisors under them
were Jehiel, Azaziah, Nahath, Asahel, Jerimoth, Jozabad, Eliel, Ismakiah, Mahath, and Be-
naiah. These appointments were made by King Hezekiah and Azariah, the chief official in
the Temple of God.
14 Kore son of Imnah the Levite, who was the gatekeeper at the East Gate, was put in
charge of distributing the voluntary offerings given to God, the gifts, and the things that
had been dedicated to the LORD. 15 His faithful assistants were Eden, Miniamin, Jeshua, 31:15
Shemaiah, Amariah, and Shecaniah. They distributed the gifts among the families of Josh 21:9-19 2 Chr 29:12
priests in their towns by their divisions, dividing the gifts fairly among old and young alike.
16 They distributed the gifts to all males three years old or older, regardless of their place in
the genealogical records. The distribution went to all who would come to the LORD's Tem-
ple to perform their daily duties according to their divisions. 17 They distributed gifts to the 31:17
priests who were listed by their families in the genealogical records, and to the Levites 1 Chr 23:24
twenty years old or older who were listed according to their jobs and their divisions.
18 Food allotments were also given to the families of all those listed in the genealogical rec-
ords, including their little babies, wives, sons, and daughters. For they had all been faithful
in purifying themselves.
19 As for the priests, the descendants of Aaron, who were living in the open villages 31:19
around the towns, men were appointed by name to distribute portions to every male Lev 25:34 Num 35:2
among the priests and to all the Levites listed in the genealogical records. 2 Chr 31:12-15
20 In this way, King Hezekiah handled the distribution throughout all Judah, doing what 31:20-21
was pleasing and good in the sight of the LORD his God. 21 In all that he did in the service of //2 Kgs 18:5-7
the Temple of God and in his efforts to follow God's laws and commands, Hezekiah
sought his God wholeheartedly. As a result, he was very successful.

ASSYRIA INVADES JUDAH

32 After Hezekiah had faithfully carried out this work, King Sennacherib of Assyria 32:1
invaded Judah. He laid siege to the fortified towns, giving orders for his army to Isa 36:1–37:37

31:7 Hebrew *in the third month . . . until the seventh month.* The third month of the ancient Hebrew lunar calendar usually occurs within the months of May and June; the seventh month usually occurs within September and October.

31:5-6 Gifts were brought to the priests and Levites in accordance with the Law of Moses (Numbers 18:12-13, 21). Those who lived away from the city were likewise obedient in bringing their offerings and gifts to the Temple (Deuteronomy 12:17-18; 14:24-26).

31:9-10 The Israelites gave with overabundant generosity to aid in the construction of both the Tabernacle and the Temple (Exodus 36:2-7; 1 Chronicles 29:6-9). In similar fashion, the rededication of the Temple under Hezekiah was met by remarkable generosity on the part of the people. The chronicler was sending an important message to his audience as they struggled with the rebuilding of the Temple and walls of the city in their own day.

31:20-21 Prior to this summary evaluation, the chronicler employed material that was largely unique to his record. Following this summary he more closely follows the parallel account in 2 Kings 18–20.

break through their walls. 2 When Hezekiah realized that Sennacherib also intended to at-
tack Jerusalem, 3 he consulted with his officials and military advisers, and they decided to
32:4 stop the flow of the springs outside the city. 4 They organized a huge work crew to stop the
2 Kgs 20:20 2 Chr 32:30 flow of the springs, cutting off the brook that ran through the fields. For they said, "Why
32:5 should the kings of Assyria come here and find plenty of water?"
1 Kgs 9:24 5 Then Hezekiah worked hard at repairing all the broken sections of the wall, erecting
2 Kgs 25:4 2 Chr 25:23 towers, and constructing a second wall outside the first. He also reinforced the supporting
terraces* in the City of David and manufactured large numbers of weapons and shields.
32:6 2 Chr 30:22 6 He appointed military officers over the people and assembled them before him in the
32:7 square at the city gate. Then Hezekiah encouraged them by saying: 7 "Be strong and cou-
2 Kgs 6:16 rageous! Don't be afraid or discouraged because of the king of Assyria or his mighty army,
1 Chr 22:13 for there is a power far greater on our side! 8 He may have a great army, but they are
32:8 merely men. We have the LORD our God to help us and to fight our battles for us!" Hezeki-
2 Chr 20:17 Jer 17:5 ah's words greatly encouraged the people.

SENNACHERIB THREATENS JERUSALEM

32:9-19 //2 Kgs 18:17-35 9 While King Sennacherib of Assyria was still besieging the town of Lachish, he sent his of-
//Isa 36:2-20 ficers to Jerusalem with this message for Hezekiah and all the people in the city:

10 "This is what King Sennacherib of Assyria says: What are you trusting in that makes you
think you can survive my siege of Jerusalem? 11 Hezekiah has said, 'The LORD our God will
rescue us from the king of Assyria.' Surely Hezekiah is misleading you, sentencing you
32:12 to death by famine and thirst! 12 Don't you realize that Hezekiah is the very person who
2 Chr 31:1 destroyed all the LORD's shrines and altars? He commanded Judah and Jerusalem to
worship only at the altar at the Temple and to offer sacrifices on it alone.

32:13 13 "Surely you must realize what I and the other kings of Assyria before me have
2 Kgs 18:33-35 done to all the people of the earth! Were any of the gods of those nations able to
32:14 rescue their people from my power? 14 Which of their gods was able to rescue its
Isa 10:9-11 people from the destructive power of my predecessors? What makes you think your

32:5 Hebrew *the millo.* The meaning of the Hebrew is uncertain.

32:3-4 During a siege, the enemy would often poison or otherwise divert the city's water supply. Cutting off the obvious supply of water would render the invader's task more difficult. Hezekiah's famous tunnel mentioned in 2 Chronicles 32:30 was constructed and would provide water for the city during the siege.

THE ASSYRIAN EMPIRE
The mighty Assyrian Empire extended from the Persian Gulf, across the Fertile Crescent, and south to Egypt. Shalmaneser III extended the empire toward the Mediterranean Sea by conquering cities as far west as Qarqar. Tiglath-pileser extended the empire south into Aram, Israel, Judah, and Philistia. It was Shalmaneser V who destroyed Samaria, Israel's capital.

32:5 Hezekiah's fortifications signaled his intent to resist the invasion rather than capitulate and submit to Assyrian domination. Archaeologists have uncovered portions of a wall that was seven meters thick, which may date to Hezekiah's reign. Compare with Isaiah 22:8-11.

▸ CHURCH
32:5-8 Pray and prepare. Preparation should never be separated from faith in God. Hezekiah knew that King Sennacherib would soon attack his people, thus he knew that simply telling God's people to "have faith in God" would not do. He prepared them for war and encouraged them to fear God, not the men who would threaten them. If you suspect that difficulties are in your future, ground yourself in God and then do your homework—get ready for the likely future. God will honor faith and hard work as the means He uses to protect His people (James 2:21-24). (***See Church***> *What> Many Titles> Servants> Servants must be prepared to work,* TopicGuide page A48.)

32:7-8 Hezekiah's speech contains a classic statement of Israel's holy war theology (Deuteronomy 7; 20). It is delivered in the face of an overwhelming enemy and focuses on the power of God. Compare with Joshua 10:25; Deuteronomy 31:6; 2 Kings 6:16; Isaiah 8:8-10; and Jeremiah 17:5.

32:9-18 The Assyrian officials engaged in psychological warfare. They attempted to shake the people's confidence in Hezekiah through misinformation (2 Chronicles 32:9-12) and propaganda (2 Chronicles 32:13-15).

God can rescue you from me? [15]Don't let Hezekiah deceive you! Don't let him fool
you like this! I say it again—no god of any nation or kingdom has ever yet been able
to rescue his people from me or my ancestors. How much less will your God rescue
you from my power!"

[16]And Sennacherib's officers further mocked the LORD God and His servant Hezekiah,
heaping insult upon insult. [17]The king also sent letters scorning the LORD, the God of Israel. **32:17** 2 Chr 32:14
He wrote, "Just as the gods of all the other nations failed to rescue their people from my
power, so the God of Hezekiah will also fail." [18]The Assyrian officials who brought the let-
ters shouted this in Hebrew* to the people gathered on the walls of the city, trying to terrify
them so it would be easier to capture the city. [19]These officers talked about the God of Je-
rusalem as though He were one of the pagan gods, made by human hands.

[20]Then King Hezekiah and the prophet Isaiah son of Amoz cried out in prayer to God in **32:20-21** //2 Kgs 19:35-37 //Isa 37:36-38
heaven. [21]And the LORD sent an angel who destroyed the Assyrian army with all its command-
ers and officers. So Sennacherib was forced to return home in disgrace to his own land. And
when he entered the temple of his god, some of his own sons killed him there with a sword.

[22]That is how the LORD rescued Hezekiah and the people of Jerusalem from King Sen-
nacherib of Assyria and from all the others who threatened them. So there was peace
throughout the land. [23]From then on King Hezekiah became highly respected among all **32:23** 2 Sam 8:10
the surrounding nations, and many gifts for the LORD arrived at Jerusalem, with valuable
presents for King Hezekiah, too.

HEZEKIAH'S SICKNESS AND RECOVERY

[24]About that time Hezekiah became deathly ill. He prayed to the LORD, who healed him and **32:24-33** //2 Kgs 20:1-21 //Isa 37:21-38; 38:1-8
gave him a miraculous sign. [25]But Hezekiah did not respond appropriately to the kindness
shown him, and he became proud. So the LORD's anger came against him and against Ju-
dah and Jerusalem. [26]Then Hezekiah humbled himself and repented of his pride, as did the **32:25** 2 Chr 24:18; 26:16
people of Jerusalem. So the LORD's anger did not fall on them during Hezekiah's lifetime.

[27]Hezekiah was very wealthy and highly honored. He built special treasury buildings for **32:26** Jer 26:18-19
his silver, gold, precious stones, and spices, and for his shields and other valuable items.
[28]He also constructed many storehouses for his grain, new wine, and olive oil; and he **32:29** 1 Chr 29:12
made many stalls for his cattle and pens for his flocks of sheep and goats. [29]He built many
towns and acquired vast flocks and herds, for God had given him great wealth. [30]He **32:30** 1 Kgs 1:33 2 Kgs 20:20
blocked up the upper spring of Gihon and brought the water down through a tunnel to the
west side of the City of David. And so he succeeded in everything he did. **32:31** Deut 8:16 2 Kgs 20:12 2 Chr 32:24 Isa 38:7-8; 39:1

[31]However, when ambassadors arrived from Babylon to ask about the remarkable

32:18 Hebrew *in the dialect of Judah.*

32:21 The exact nature of the miraculous intervention is not specified. The destroying angel is also associated with the last plague (Exodus 12) and David's infamous census (2 Samuel 24). The Greek historian Herodotus and the Jewish historian Josephus both record Sennacherib's withdrawal under disastrous circumstances. Assyria's own history records Sennacherib's later assassination by his sons, Adrammelech and Sharezer.

32:24-26 This event is also recorded in 2 Kings 20:1-11 and Isaiah 38:1-22. The chronicler assumes that his readers are familiar with the earlier accounts and does not explain the nature of the sign (see 2 Kings 20:9-11). Hezekiah and the people displayed the humility and repentance called for in 2 Chronicles 7:14, and as a result they received mercy and healing.

▸ PURPOSE

32:31 God withdrew. Have you ever had the sense that God was testing you? Using similar language as with Job (Job 1–2), the chronicler records that God withdrew His protection from Hezekiah to demonstrate the true qualities in the heart of Hezekiah. But we are also shown the critical difference between Hezekiah and Job: pride (2 Chronicles 32:26). The test revealed that, even at the end of his life, the great King Hezekiah could still be foolish and proud. In the parallel passage in 2 Kings 20, Isaiah announced the consequences of Hezekiah's failure: "The time is coming when everything in your palace—all the treasures stored up by your ancestors until now—will be carried off to Babylon." When God tests us, it is never to gain insight Himself, for He already knows everything. Testing shows God's people who they are without Him. Has God sent circumstances or people your way that bring out your worst? Or your best? Thank God for testing you and revealing the true nature of your heart. (***See Purpose**> God's Means> God's Sovereignty> God knows all,* TopicGuide page A52.)

events that had taken place in the land, God withdrew from Hezekiah in order to test him and to see what was really in his heart.

SUMMARY OF HEZEKIAH'S REIGN

32The rest of the events in Hezekiah's reign and his acts of devotion are recorded in *The Vision of the Prophet Isaiah Son of Amoz,* which is included in *The Book of the Kings of Judah and Israel.* 33When Hezekiah died, he was buried in the upper area of the royal cemetery, and all Judah and Jerusalem honored him at his death. And his son Manasseh became the next king.

MANASSEH RULES IN JUDAH

33:1-10 **33** Manasseh was twelve years old when he became king, and he reigned in Jerusa-
//2 Kgs 21:1-10 33:2 lem fifty-five years. 2He did what was evil in the LORD's sight, following the detest-
2 Chr 28:3 able practices of the pagan nations that the LORD had driven from the land ahead of the
33:3 Israelites. 3He rebuilt the pagan shrines his father, Hezekiah, had broken down. He con-
Deut 16:21 2 Kgs 23:5-6 structed altars for the images of Baal and set up Asherah poles. He also bowed before all
2 Chr 31:1 the powers of the heavens and worshiped them.
4He built pagan altars in the Temple of the LORD, the place where the LORD had said, "My
33:4 name will remain in Jerusalem forever." 5He built these altars for all the powers of the
2 Chr 7:16; 28:24 heavens in both courtyards of the LORD's Temple. 6Manasseh also sacrificed his own sons
33:5 2 Chr 4:9 in the fire* in the valley of Ben-Hinnom. He practiced sorcery, divination, and witchcraft,
and he consulted with mediums and psychics. He did much that was evil in the LORD's
33:6 Lev 19:31; 20:27 sight, arousing His anger.
2 Chr 28:3 7Manasseh even took a carved idol he had made and set it up in God's Temple, the very
place where God had told David and his son Solomon: "My name will be honored forever
in this Temple and in Jerusalem—the city I have chosen from among all the tribes of Israel.
33:8 8If the Israelites will be careful to obey My commands—all the laws, decrees, and regula-
2 Sam 7:10 tions given through Moses—I will not send them into exile from this land that I set aside for
your ancestors." 9But Manasseh led the people of Judah and Jerusalem to do even more
evil than the pagan nations that the LORD had destroyed when the people of Israel entered
the land.
33:11 10The LORD spoke to Manasseh and his people, but they ignored all His warnings. 11So
Deut 28:36 2 Chr 36:6 the LORD sent the commanders of the Assyrian armies, and they took Manasseh prisoner.
They put a ring through his nose, bound him in bronze chains, and led him away to Bab-
33:12 2 Chr 32:26 ylon. 12But while in deep distress, Manasseh sought the LORD his God and sincerely hum-
33:13 bled himself before the God of his ancestors. 13And when he prayed, the LORD listened to
Ezra 8:23 him and was moved by his request. So the LORD brought Manasseh back to Jerusalem and
Dan 4:25, 32 to his kingdom. Then Manasseh finally realized that the LORD alone is God!

33:6 Or *also made his sons pass through the fire.*

32:33 The "upper area" of the cemetery indicates a place of greater honor or prominence.

33:2-9 Manasseh's reign plunged Judah to the depth of apostasy experienced under Ahaz (2 Chronicles 28:2-4). The nation engaged in the same practices that brought God's judgment upon the Canaanite inhabitants of the land at the time of the Conquest. The same fate, therefore, that met the Canaanites also awaited Judah.

33:7 In 2 Kings 21:7 the carved idol is identified as an Asherah pole (see note at 2 Chronicles 14:3-5). It is singled out because of its presence in the Temple itself.

33:7-8 These verses are derived largely from God's covenant with David's family as presented in 2 Chronicles 7:12-22. Manasseh's reign demonstrates the necessity of obedience as a condition of the promises made to David and the reality of exile as a curse for disobedience. Manasseh's reign therefore foreshadows Judah's experience as a nation.

33:12-13 Manasseh's response to his captivity was a model for the people of Judah. It follows the pattern commended by Moses (Deuteronomy 4:26-31) and by Solomon in his prayer at the dedication of the Temple (2 Chronicles 6:36-39). Humility and a desire to seek the Lord are two key qualities throughout Chronicles (see note at 2 Chronicles 7:14).

14 After this Manasseh rebuilt the outer wall of the City of David, from west of the Gihon
Spring in the Kidron Valley to the Fish Gate, and continuing around the hill of Ophel. He
built the wall very high. And he stationed his military officers in all of the fortified towns of
Judah. 15 Manasseh also removed the foreign gods and the idol from the LORD's Temple.
He tore down all the altars he had built on the hill where the Temple stood and all the al-
tars that were in Jerusalem, and he dumped them outside the city. 16 Then he restored the
altar of the LORD and sacrificed peace offerings and thanksgiving offerings on it. He also
encouraged the people of Judah to worship the LORD, the God of Israel. 17 However, the
people still sacrificed at the pagan shrines, though only to the LORD their God.

18 The rest of the events of Manasseh's reign, his prayer to God, and the words the seers
spoke to him in the name of the LORD, the God of Israel, are recorded in *The Book of the
Kings of Israel.* 19 Manasseh's prayer, the account of the way God answered him, and an ac-
count of all his sins and unfaithfulness are recorded in *The Record of the Seers.** It includes
a list of the locations where he built pagan shrines and set up Asherah poles and idols be-
fore he humbled himself and repented. 20 When Manasseh died, he was buried in his pal-
ace. Then his son Amon became the next king.

AMON RULES IN JUDAH

21 Amon was twenty-two years old when he became king, and he reigned in Jerusalem two
years. 22 He did what was evil in the LORD's sight, just as his father, Manasseh, had done. He
worshiped and sacrificed to all the idols his father had made. 23 But unlike his father, he did
not humble himself before the LORD. Instead, Amon sinned even more.

24 Then Amon's own officials conspired against him and assassinated him in his palace.
25 But the people of the land killed all those who had conspired against King Amon, and
they made his son Josiah the next king.

JOSIAH RULES IN JUDAH

34 Josiah was eight years old when he became king, and he reigned in Jerusalem
thirty-one years. 2 He did what was pleasing in the LORD's sight and followed the
example of his ancestor David. He did not turn away from doing what was right.

3 During the eighth year of his reign, while he was still young, Josiah began to seek the
God of his ancestor David. Then in the twelfth year he began to purify Judah and Jerusa-
lem, destroying all the pagan shrines, the Asherah poles, and the carved idols and cast im-
ages. 4 He ordered that the altars of Baal be demolished and that the incense altars which
stood above them be broken down. He also made sure that the Asherah poles, the carved
idols, and the cast images were smashed and scattered over the graves of those who had
sacrificed to them. 5 He burned the bones of the pagan priests on their own altars, and so
he purified Judah and Jerusalem.

33:14 1 Kgs 1:33; 2 Chr 27:3; Neh 3:3
33:15 2 Chr 33:3-7
33:17 2 Chr 32:12
33:18-20 //2 Kgs 21:17-18
33:19 2 Chr 33:3, 13
33:21-25 //2 Kgs 21:19-24
33:23 2 Chr 33:12, 19
33:24 2 Chr 25:27
34:1-2 //2 Kgs 22:1-2
34:2 2 Chr 29:2
34:3 1 Kgs 13:2; 2 Chr 15:2; 33:17, 22
34:4 Exod 32:20; 2 Kgs 23:4-5, 11
34:5 1 Kgs 13:2; 2 Kgs 23:20

33:19 Or *The Record of Hozai.*

33:14 Upon returning from his exile Manasseh engaged in a program of rebuilding and fortification. The chronicler portrayed such activity as evidence of God's blessings (see notes at 2 Chronicles 14:6 and 17:1-2). In his rebuilding and his repentance, Manasseh was a model for the chronicler's audience.

▸ PURPOSE

33:17 Never too late. Complete and thorough repentance seems rare in the Christian life. Like Hezekiah in the previous chapter, we often repent of a sin only to have it crop up soon afterward. But it's never too late for God to break into our lives and grant us victory over a sinful thought or deed. God spoke to Manasseh and all Israel about their covenant-breaking ways, but they didn't listen. Finally, Manasseh got the message (2 Chronicles 33:11) and responded in humble faith to God's offer of salvation (2 Chronicles 33:13). Manasseh never fully recovered his tarnished reputation (notice the mixed review of his reign in 2 Chronicles 33:19), but he did demonstrate to God's people that change is possible. You may be in deep sin right now. You may know someone who is trapped in a maze of unbelief. Read the story of Manasseh along with Luke 15 and you'll discover that God always delights in repentance—whether early or late—but that it's much better for us if it's early. It's never too late to repent. (***See Purpose****> God's Deeds> Judgment> Call to repentance,* TopicGuide page A54.)

34:2 The chronicler compares other kings to David, but only of Josiah is it said that he did not deviate from David's example (2 Chronicles 11:17; 29:1-2).

34:6 [6]He did the same thing in the towns of Manasseh, Ephraim, and Simeon, even as far as
2 Kgs 23:15, 19 Naphtali, and in the regions* all around them. [7]He destroyed the pagan altars and the
34:7 Asherah poles, and he crushed the idols into dust. He cut down all the incense altars
2 Chr 31:1 throughout the land of Israel. Finally, he returned to Jerusalem.
[8]In the eighteenth year of his reign, after he had purified the land and the Temple, Josiah
34:8-13 appointed Shaphan son of Azaliah, Maaseiah the governor of Jerusalem, and Joah son of
//2 Kgs 22:3-7 Joahaz, the royal historian, to repair the Temple of the LORD his God. [9]They gave Hilkiah the
34:9 2 Chr 30:10, 18; 35:8 high priest the money that had been collected by the Levites who served as gatekeepers at
the Temple of God. The gifts were brought by people from Manasseh, Ephraim, and from all
the remnant of Israel, as well as from all Judah, Benjamin, and the people of Jerusalem.

[10]He entrusted the money to the men assigned to supervise the restoration of the LORD's
Temple. Then they paid the workers who did the repairs and renovation of the Temple.
[11]They hired carpenters and builders, who purchased finished stone for the walls and tim-
34:11 2 Chr 33:4-7 ber for the rafters and beams. They restored what earlier kings of Judah had allowed to fall
into ruin.

34:12 [12]The workers served faithfully under the leadership of Jahath and Obadiah, Levites of
1 Chr 25:1 the Merarite clan, and Zechariah and Meshullam, Levites of the Kohathite clan. Other Le-
34:13 vites, all of whom were skilled musicians, [13]were put in charge of the laborers of the vari-
Neh 4:10 ous trades. Still others assisted as secretaries, officials, and gatekeepers.

HILKIAH DISCOVERS GOD'S LAW

34:14-28 [14]While they were bringing out the money collected at the LORD's Temple, Hilkiah the
//2 Kgs 22:8-20 priest found the Book of the Law of the LORD that was written by Moses. [15]Hilkiah said to
34:14 Shaphan the court secretary, "I have found the Book of the Law in the LORD's Temple!"
2 Chr 34:9 Then Hilkiah gave the scroll to Shaphan.

[16]Shaphan took the scroll to the king and reported, "Your officials are doing everything
they were assigned to do. [17]The money that was collected at the Temple of the LORD has
been turned over to the supervisors and workmen." [18]Shaphan also told the king, "Hilkiah
the priest has given me a scroll." So Shaphan read it to the king.

34:19 [19]When the king heard what was written in the Law, he tore his clothes in despair.
Josh 7:6 [20]Then he gave these orders to Hilkiah, Ahikam son of Shaphan, Acbor son of Micaiah,*
34:21 Shaphan the court secretary, and Asaiah the king's personal adviser: [21]"Go to the Temple
2 Chr 29:8 and speak to the LORD for me and for all the remnant of Israel and Judah. Inquire about the
words written in the scroll that has been found. For the LORD's great anger has been

34:6 As in Syriac version. Hebrew reads *in their temples,* or *in their ruins.* The meaning of the Hebrew is uncertain. 34:20 As in parallel text at 2 Kgs 22:12; Hebrew reads *Abdon son of Micah.*

34:9 The chronicler specifically points to the participation of the tribes of Manasseh, Ephraim, and the remnant of Israel in the collection for the Temple (compare 2 Kings 22:4; see also Joshua 22:10-34). Once more the ideal of all Israel in unity is held up as a model for the chronicler's audience (see note at 2 Chronicles 1:2-3).

34:14-28 The writer of 1 and 2 Kings placed the discovery of the Book of the Law at the head of his account of Josiah's reign (2 Kings 22:3–23:23). The writer of 1 and 2 Kings seems to have ordered the events geographically: reformation first in the Temple, then the city, and then the nation. The chronicler most likely preserves a chronological ordering of the events.

▸ BIBLE
34:16-28 Finding the truth. Imagine that all the Bibles in the world have been lost or destroyed—this is what happened in Josiah's time. For generations, the books of Moses had been lost, leaving only oral tradition to keep God's Word alive in Israel. After the Book of the Law was read, he did not trust Shaphan alone but gave orders to him and four others to contact the prophet Huldah. As an expert in the oral tradition, she confirmed that everything in the scroll was true (2 Chronicles 34:23) and that God would bless Josiah for his faithfulness in restoring God's written Word to His people. How do you feel knowing that many people groups around the world do not have the Bible in their language? Pray and act in such a way that builds a passion for God's Word in your heart and that seeks to spread God's Word around the world. (***See Bible*>** *Power> Equip> Delivers from bondage,* TopicGuide page A11.)

34:21 There is a general consensus that the Book of the Law found in the Temple was the book of Deuteronomy in whole or in part. Deuteronomy commands many of the reforms carried out by Josiah, and Josiah's celebration of the Passover is in keeping with the stipulations found in Deuteronomy (Deuteronomy 12; 16). Deuteronomy features an extended section of curses (compare 2 Chronicles 34:24 with Deuteronomy 27–28), and it resembles ancient covenants (2 Chronicles 34:30).

poured out on us because our ancestors have not obeyed the word of the LORD. We have
not been doing everything this scroll says we must do."
22 So Hilkiah and the other men went to the New Quarter* of Jerusalem to consult with
the prophet Huldah. She was the wife of Shallum son of Tikvah, son of Harhas,* the keeper
of the Temple wardrobe.
23 She said to them, "The LORD, the God of Israel, has spoken! Go back and tell the man
who sent you, 24 'This is what the LORD says: I am going to bring disaster on this city* and its
people. All the curses written in the scroll that was read to the king of Judah will come true.
25 For My people have abandoned Me and offered sacrifices to pagan gods, and I am very
angry with them for everything they have done. My anger will be poured out on this place,
and it will not be quenched.'
26 "But go to the king of Judah who sent you to seek the LORD and tell him: 'This is what
the LORD, the God of Israel, says concerning the message you have just heard: 27 You were
sorry and humbled yourself before God when you heard His words against this city and its
people. You humbled yourself and tore your clothing in despair and wept before Me in re-
pentance. And I have indeed heard you, says the LORD. 28 So I will not send the promised
disaster until after you have died and been buried in peace. You yourself will not see the
disaster I am going to bring on this city and its people.' "
So they took her message back to the king.

34:24 Deut 28:15-68; 2 Chr 36:14-20
34:25 2 Chr 33:3
34:27 2 Chr 12:7; 32:26

JOSIAH'S RELIGIOUS REFORMS

29 Then the king summoned all the elders of Judah and Jerusalem. 30 And the king went up
to the Temple of the LORD with all the people of Judah and Jerusalem, along with the
priests and the Levites—all the people from the greatest to the least. There the king read to
them the entire Book of the Covenant that had been found in the LORD's Temple. 31 The
king took his place of authority beside the pillar and renewed the covenant in the LORD's
presence. He pledged to obey the LORD by keeping all His commands, laws, and decrees
with all his heart and soul. He promised to obey all the terms of the covenant that were
written in the scroll. 32 And he required everyone in Jerusalem and the people of Benjamin
to make a similar pledge. The people of Jerusalem did so, renewing their covenant with
God, the God of their ancestors.
33 So Josiah removed all detestable idols from the entire land of Israel and required
everyone to worship the LORD their God. And throughout the rest of his lifetime, they did
not turn away from the LORD, the God of their ancestors.

34:29-32 //2 Kgs 23:1-3
34:30 Neh 8:1-3
34:31 2 Chr 23:16; 29:10
34:33 2 Kgs 23:3; 2 Chr 34:3-7

JOSIAH CELEBRATES PASSOVER

35 Then Josiah announced that the Passover of the LORD would be celebrated in Je-
rusalem, and so the Passover lamb was slaughtered on the fourteenth day of the
first month.* 2 Josiah also assigned the priests to their duties and encouraged them in their
work at the Temple of the LORD. 3 He issued this order to the Levites, who were to teach all
Israel and who had been set apart to serve the LORD: "Put the holy Ark in the Temple that

35:1 Exod 12:6; Num 9:3; 2 Kgs 23:21-22
35:2 2 Chr 29:11
35:3 1 Chr 23:26; 2 Chr 17:7-9; Neh 8:7

34:22a Or *the Second Quarter*, a newer section of Jerusalem. Hebrew reads *the Mishneh*. 34:22b As in parallel text at 2 Kgs 22:14; Hebrew reads *son of Tokhath, son of Hasrah*. 34:24 Hebrew *this place;* also in 34:27, 28. 35:1 This day in the ancient Hebrew lunar calendar was April 5, 622 B.C.

34:28 Josiah eventually died in battle, hardly a peaceful death (2 Chronicles 35:22-24). The peace in view, however, is defined in terms of not witnessing the destruction of Jerusalem. In this respect Josiah did die in peace.

▶ GOD

34:32 Covenant renewal. Every week God's people meet and renew their covenant with God. Through Christ, we are bound to God, and He to us, by a series of promises and responsibilities outlined in the basic gospel message. And every time we meet—especially when we baptize or partake of the Lord's Supper—we renew our vows of repentance and belief to God (Matthew 26:28; 1 Corinthians 11:25; 2 Corinthians 3:6-14). Our relationship with God must be intimate and not mechanical, yet it must also include covenant obedience. This obedience in turn demonstrates our heartfelt faith in God (James 2:25-26). Fulfill your vows—whether associated with marriage, baptism, or ordination—in a way that shows your love and devotion to Christ. (***See God***> *Relationship> God Enables> Relationship with God requires obedience,* TopicGuide page A14.)

was built by Solomon son of David, the king of Israel. You no longer need to carry it back
and forth on your shoulders. Now spend your time serving the LORD your God and His peo-
35:4 ple Israel. 4Report for duty according to the family divisions of your ancestors, following
1 Chr 9:10-13 2 Chr 8:14 the directions of King David of Israel and the directions of his son Solomon.
5"Then stand in the sanctuary at the place appointed for your family division and help
35:6 the families assigned to you as they bring their offerings to the Temple. 6Slaughter the
2 Chr 29:5, 15; 35:1 Passover lambs, purify yourselves, and prepare to help those who come. Follow all the di-
rections that the LORD gave through Moses."
7Then Josiah provided 30,000 lambs and young goats for the people's Passover offer-
35:8 ings, along with 3,000 cattle, all from the king's own flocks and herds. 8The king's officials
2 Chr 31:13 also made willing contributions to the people, priests, and Levites. Hilkiah, Zechariah, and
Jehiel, the administrators of God's Temple, gave the priests 2,600 lambs and young goats
35:9 and 300 cattle as Passover offerings. 9The Levite leaders—Conaniah and his brothers She-
2 Chr 31:12 maiah and Nethanel, as well as Hashabiah, Jeiel, and Jozabad—gave 5,000 lambs and
young goats and 500 cattle to the Levites for their Passover offerings.
35:10 10When everything was ready for the Passover celebration, the priests and the Levites
2 Chr 35:4-5 35:11 took their places, organized by their divisions, as the king had commanded. 11The Levites
2 Chr 29:22, 34; then slaughtered the Passover lambs and presented the blood to the priests, who sprinkled
35:1, 6 the blood on the altar while the Levites prepared the animals. 12They divided the burnt of-
35:13 ferings among the people by their family groups, so they could offer them to the LORD as
Exod 12:8-9 Lev 6:25 prescribed in the Book of Moses. They did the same with the cattle. 13Then they roasted the
Passover lambs as prescribed; and they boiled the holy offerings in pots, kettles, and pans,
and brought them out quickly so the people could eat them.
14Afterward the Levites prepared Passover offerings for themselves and for the priests—
the descendants of Aaron—because the priests had been busy from morning till night of-
fering the burnt offerings and the fat portions. The Levites took responsibility for all these
preparations.
35:15 15The musicians, descendants of Asaph, were in their assigned places, following the
1 Chr 25:1; 26:12-19 commands that had been given by David, Asaph, Heman, and Jeduthun, the king's seer.
The gatekeepers guarded the gates and did not need to leave their posts of duty, for their
Passover offerings were prepared for them by their fellow Levites.
16The entire ceremony for the LORD's Passover was completed that day. All the burnt of-
35:17 ferings were sacrificed on the altar of the LORD, as King Josiah had commanded. 17All the
Exod 12:15 2 Chr 30:21 Israelites present in Jerusalem celebrated Passover and the Festival of Unleavened Bread
35:18-19 for seven days. 18Never since the time of the prophet Samuel had there been such a Pass-
//2 Kgs 23:21-23 over. None of the kings of Israel had ever kept a Passover as Josiah did, involving all the
priests and Levites, all the people of Jerusalem, and people from all over Judah and Israel.
19This Passover celebration took place in the eighteenth year of Josiah's reign.

35:6-14 During Hezekiah's Passover celebration, the king ordered the Levites to slay the offerings because the people were unclean and thus unable to do so for themselves as commanded in Deuteronomy 16:5-6 (2 Chronicles 30:17). Josiah continued this practice, showing that the ceremonial laws of the Old Testament could be altered under certain unusual circumstances (such as by David in 1 Samuel 21:1-6). These alterations foreshadowed the day when Christ would do away with the requirements to maintain the ceremonial law (Hebrews 8:7-13; 9:9-28).

35:7-9 Similar voluntary and joyful giving by the king and the people is recorded in 1 Chronicles 29:3-9 and 2 Chronicles 24:8-14; 29:31-36; 31:3-21, providing the chronicler's audience with encouragement toward similar generosity. The offerings totaled 37,600 lambs and goats and 3,800 bulls. These totals exceeded those sacrificed during Hezekiah's reign (2 Chronicles 30:24).

▸ GOD

35:19 Slow change. We live in a time of instant coffee, microwave ovens, and jet airplanes. We want everything now! But sometimes change comes slowly. God's truth takes time to sink into our thick skulls and hard hearts. It took 18 years to get to the point where the nation of Judah could rightly celebrate the Passover. Even then, allowances had to be made (2 Chronicles 35:6) to enable the ceremony to occur. God is working on your church, your nation, and your heart, but even His goals are not reached overnight. Be patient as you work toward holy change in your life and in the lives of those around you. (***See God***> *God's Attributes> True> His Spirit guides believers into all truth,* TopicGuide page A18.)

JOSIAH DIES IN BATTLE

[20]After Josiah had finished restoring the Temple, King Neco of Egypt led his army up from Egypt to do battle at Carchemish on the Euphrates River, and Josiah and his army marched out to fight him.* [21]But King Neco sent messengers to Josiah with this message:

35:20–36:1 //2 Kgs 23:28-30

> "What do you want with me, king of Judah? I have no quarrel with you today! I am on my way to fight another nation, and God has told me to hurry! Do not interfere with God, who is with me, or He will destroy you."

[22]But Josiah refused to listen to Neco, to whom God had indeed spoken, and he would not turn back. Instead, he disguised himself and led his army into battle on the plain of Megiddo. [23]But the enemy archers hit King Josiah with their arrows and wounded him. He cried out to his men, "Take me from the battle, for I am badly wounded!"

35:22 Judg 5:19; 2 Chr 18:29; 35:21

[24]So they lifted Josiah out of his chariot and placed him in another chariot. Then they brought him back to Jerusalem, where he died. He was buried there in the royal cemetery. And all Judah and Jerusalem mourned for him. [25]The prophet Jeremiah composed funeral songs for Josiah, and to this day choirs still sing these sad songs about his death. These songs of sorrow have become a tradition and are recorded in *The Book of Laments.*

35:25 Jer 22:10-13; Lam 4:20; Zech 12:11

[26]The rest of the events of Josiah's reign and his acts of devotion (carried out according to what was written in the Law of the LORD), [27]from beginning to end—all are recorded in *The Book of the Kings of Israel and Judah.*

JEHOAHAZ RULES IN JUDAH

36 Then the people of the land took Josiah's son Jehoahaz and made him the next king in Jerusalem.

36:1 Jer 22:11

[2]Jehoahaz* was twenty-three years old when he became king, and he reigned in Jerusalem three months.

36:2-4 //2 Kgs 23:31-34

[3]Then he was deposed by the king of Egypt, who demanded that Judah pay 7,500 pounds of silver and 75 pounds of gold* as tribute.

35:20 Or *Josiah went out to meet him.* 36:2 Hebrew *Joahaz,* a variant spelling of Jehoahaz; also in 36:4. 36:3 Hebrew *100 talents* [3,400 kilograms] *of silver and 1 talent* [34 kilograms] *of gold.*

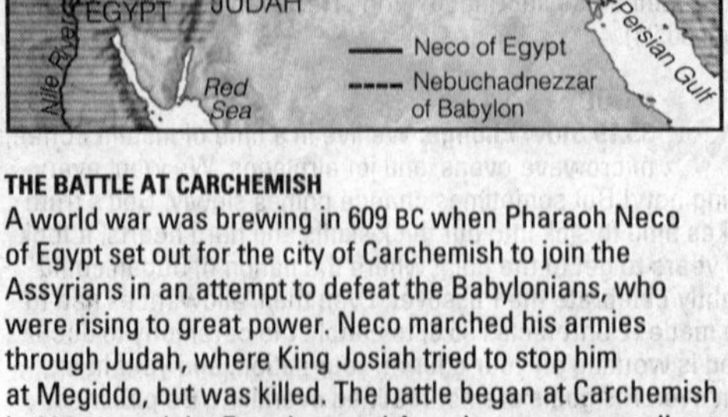

THE BATTLE AT CARCHEMISH

A world war was brewing in 609 BC when Pharaoh Neco of Egypt set out for the city of Carchemish to join the Assyrians in an attempt to defeat the Babylonians, who were rising to great power. Neco marched his armies through Judah, where King Josiah tried to stop him at Megiddo, but was killed. The battle began at Carchemish in 605 BC, and the Egyptians and Assyrians were soundly defeated, chased to Hamath, and defeated again. Babylon was now the new world power.

35:20 Judah was but a very small player on the world scene at this time. In 609 BC, the Babylonians were challenging the Assyrians for domination of the ancient Near Eastern world. The Egyptians under Pharaoh Neco were headed to the Euphrates River to aid the Assyrians when Josiah challenged them.

35:22 Josiah was motivated either by an alliance with Babylon against Assyria or by a refusal to allow Judah's territorial integrity to be challenged. In either case, Josiah failed to heed the warnings of God relayed by Neco's own messengers. The apocryphal work of 1 Esdras 1:26 suggests that Jeremiah the prophet validated Neco's warning, thus explaining why Josiah should have listened to the Egyptian pharaoh. Another example of nonbelievers delivering God's Word is found in the story of Balaam (Numbers 22; also see Jude 1:11).

36:2 Jehoahaz was Josiah's fourth son (1 Chronicles 3:15). Jeremiah (Jeremiah 22:11-17) gave a negative portrayal of Jehoahaz's brief reign. The rest of the chapter is a dirge, repeating the phrase "he did what was evil" until God was ready to judge Judah for their sin (2 Chronicles 36:16). The almost unbelievable disaster of the destruction of Jerusalem is firmly blamed on the downward spiral of leadership in the religious and political realms (2 Chronicles 36:14-15).

JEHOIAKIM RULES IN JUDAH

36:4 4 The king of Egypt then installed Eliakim, the brother of Jehoahaz, as the next king of Ju-
Jer 22:10, 12 dah and Jerusalem, and he changed Eliakim's name to Jehoiakim. Then Neco took Jehoa-
haz to Egypt as a prisoner.
36:5-8 5 Jehoiakim was twenty-five years old when he became king, and he reigned in Jerusa-
//2 Kgs 23:36–24:6 lem eleven years. He did what was evil in the sight of the LORD his God.
36:5 Jer 22:13-19 6 Then King Nebuchadnezzar of Babylon came to Jerusalem and captured it, and he
36:6 bound Jehoiakim in bronze chains and led him away to Babylon. 7 Nebuchadnezzar also
2 Kgs 24:1 took some of the treasures from the Temple of the LORD, and he placed them in his palace*
2 Chr 33:11 Jer 22:19-20 in Babylon.
36:7 8 The rest of the events in Jehoiakim's reign, including all the evil things he did and
2 Kgs 24:13 everything found against him, are recorded in *The Book of the Kings of Israel and Judah.*
36:8 Then his son Jehoiachin became the next king.
2 Kgs 24:5

JEHOIACHIN RULES IN JUDAH

36:9-10 9 Jehoiachin was eighteen* years old when he became king, and he reigned in Jerusalem
//2 Kgs 24:8-17 three months and ten days. Jehoiachin did what was evil in the LORD's sight.
36:10 10 In the spring of the year* King Nebuchadnezzar took Jehoiachin to Babylon. Many trea-
Jer 37:1 sures from the Temple of the LORD were also taken to Babylon at that time. And Nebuchad-
nezzar installed Jehoiachin's uncle,* Zedekiah, as the next king in Judah and Jerusalem.

ZEDEKIAH RULES IN JUDAH

36:11-16 11 Zedekiah was twenty-one years old when he became king, and he reigned in Jerusalem
//2 Kgs 24:18-20 //Jer 52:1-3 eleven years. 12 He did what was evil in the sight of the LORD his God, and he refused to hum-
36:12 ble himself when the prophet Jeremiah spoke to him directly from the LORD. 13 He also rebelled
2 Chr 33:23 against King Nebuchadnezzar, even though he had taken an oath of loyalty in God's name.
Jer 21:3-7 Zedekiah was a hard and stubborn man, refusing to turn to the LORD, the God of Israel.
36:13 14 Likewise, all the leaders of the priests and the people became more and more unfaith-
2 Chr 30:8 Jer 52:3 ful. They followed all the pagan practices of the surrounding nations, desecrating the Tem-
Ezek 17:15 ple of the LORD that had been consecrated in Jerusalem.
36:15 15 The LORD, the God of their ancestors, repeatedly sent His prophets to warn them, for
Jer 7:13; 25:3-4 He had compassion on His people and His Temple. 16 But the people mocked these mes-
36:16 sengers of God and despised their words. They scoffed at the prophets until the LORD's an-
2 Chr 30:10 Ezra 5:12 ger could no longer be restrained and nothing could be done.
Prov 1:24-32 Jer 5:12-13

THE FALL OF JERUSALEM

36:17-20 17 So the LORD brought the king of Babylon against them. The Babylonians* killed Judah's
//2 Kgs 25:1-21 //Jer 52:4-27

36:7 Or *temple.* 36:9 As in one Hebrew manuscript, some Greek manuscripts, and Syriac version (see also 2 Kgs 24:8); most Hebrew manuscripts read *eight.* 36:10a Hebrew *At the turn of the year.* The first day of this year in the ancient Hebrew lunar calendar was April 13, 597 B.C. 36:10b As in parallel text at 2 Kgs 24:17; Hebrew reads *brother,* or *relative.* 36:17 Or *Chaldeans.*

36:7 The vessels of the Temple were brought back from Babylon by the Judean exiles and provided a crucial link between the postexilic community and ancient Israel (Ezra 1:7).

▸ BIBLE

36:17 Total destruction. What if every church in the world was destroyed? And all the ministers killed or scattered? And every city in which there was a church was razed? How would you feel about your faith, your religion . . . your God? This is the crisis that confronted ancient Judah. The faithful remnant of God's people accepted God's judgment upon their sinful nation, but they had no idea exactly how the worship of God would continue. But the promise of a Davidic king who would reign forever (2 Samuel 7:1-17) was still in place. Like the faithful left in Judah, we sometimes come to points in our lives where there are only a few promises left that seem to make sense. When everything we thought would last forever is gone, God's promises to His people remain. Stay focused on the basic truths of the gospel—memorize them, meditate on them, study them—for in difficult times, these may be the only promises that still make sense. (***See Bible***> *Uniqueness> Inspired> His promises never fail,* TopicGuide page A10.)

36:17-20 Nebuchadnezzar destroyed Jerusalem in 586 BC after laying siege to the city for two years. Jeremiah 52 provides a more detailed account of the final tragic years of Zedekiah's reign.

young men, even chasing after them into the Temple. They had no pity on the people, kill-
ing both young men and young women, the old and the infirm. God handed all of them
over to Nebuchadnezzar. 18The king took home to Babylon all the articles, large and
small, used in the Temple of God, and the treasures from both the LORD's Temple and from
the palace of the king and his officials. 19Then his army burned the Temple of God, tore
down the walls of Jerusalem, burned all the palaces, and completely destroyed everything
of value.* 20The few who survived were taken as exiles to Babylon, and they became ser-
vants to the king and his sons until the kingdom of Persia came to power.
21So the message of the LORD spoken through Jeremiah was fulfilled. The land finally
enjoyed its Sabbath rest, lying desolate until the seventy years were fulfilled, just as the
prophet had said.

36:18 2 Chr 36:7, 10
36:19 2 Kgs 25:9; Jer 52:13
36:20 2 Kgs 25:11; Jer 27:7
36:21 Lev 25:4; 26:33-34; Jer 29:10

CYRUS ALLOWS THE EXILES TO RETURN

22In the first year of King Cyrus of Persia,* the LORD fulfilled the prophecy He had given
through Jeremiah.* He stirred the heart of Cyrus to put this proclamation in writing and to
send it throughout his kingdom:

23"This is what King Cyrus of Persia says:

"The LORD, the God of heaven, has given me all the kingdoms of the earth. He has appointed me to build Him a Temple at Jerusalem, which is in Judah. Any of you who are the LORD's people may go there for this task. And may the LORD your God be with you!"

36:22-23 //Ezra 1:1-3
36:22 Isa 44:28; Jer 29:10

36:19 Or *destroyed all the valuable articles from the Temple.* 36:22a The first year of Cyrus's reign over Babylon was 538 B.C. 36:22b See Jer 25:11-12; 29:10.

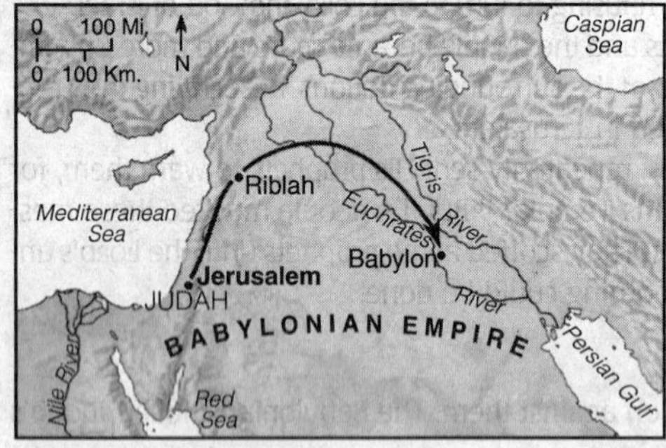

EXILE TO BABYLON
Despite Judah's few good kings and timely reforms, the people never truly changed. Their evil continued, and finally God used the Babylonian Empire, under Nebuchadnezzar, to conquer Judah, destroy Jerusalem, and take the people captive to Babylon.

36:21 Regarding the length of the Babylonian exile, the chronicler cites Jeremiah 25:1-14 (see also Daniel 9). There have been several attempts to reckon the precise chronological parameters of the 70 years. It seems more probable though that the 70 years are not an exact time frame but rather a symbolic designation referring to the fullness of judgment.

36:22 The chronicler marks the Cyrus Edict as the end of the exile (compare Zechariah 1:12 where the 70 years appear to continue into the prophet's own day). The Cyrus Edict was issued in 538 BC, and a historical inscription on the Cyrus Cylinder, discovered in Iraq in 1879, confirms this date for the edict.

36:23 The Cyrus Edict is also recorded in Ezra 1:1-4. The edict reflected Cyrus' generous foreign policy to his new subjects inherited from his conquest of the former Babylonian empire. The chronicler closes his account on a note of hope with Israel poised to embark on a second Exodus.

PURPOSE

To demonstrate how God kept His promise to bring His exiled people home (Jeremiah 29:14), and to show how God sovereignly led pagan kings to provide what His people needed to rebuild the Temple and to reestablish themselves in their homeland.

Ezra is a small book that covers big issues—it comes as close to picturing the spiritual dynamics and realities of life as any book in the Bible.

The Jews spent 70 years as captives in Babylon—one year for every seven-year period in which they failed to give the land its Sabbath rest from farming, as stipulated by God's laws (Leviticus 25:2-4; 26:34; 2 Chronicles 36:21). The Jews had been brought there by the king of Babylon, who was then conquered by the king of Persia. God later moved the king of Persia to allow the Jewish captives to return home to Jerusalem. But when they returned, they were a generation that was unschooled in the ways of the Lord. The task of rebuilding the Temple fell to Zerubbabel, and the task of rebuilding the people fell, 80 years later, to Ezra, who led a second return of Jews. Nehemiah, who rebuilt the wall around Jerusalem, led a third return following Ezra.

DISCOVER GOD IN EZRA

The greater the challenges to our spiritual life, the more likely the attributes of God will stand out as problems are solved with His guidance:

Sufficiency: Who would have thought that the smallest portion of an internally divided nation could survive 70 years in captivity in a culture far different and distant from their own—and then return to their homeland to live again? If that was improbable enough, these survivors, who were sent back with the Persian king's blessing, were opposed anew by local residents once they arrived back in Judea and didn't know enough of God's statutes to live righteously. Yet, in the words of Jesus Himself, "Humanly speaking, it is impossible. But with God everything is possible" (Matthew 19:26). As is evident by God's work in the hearts of kings (Ezra 7:27; see also 2 Chronicles 36:22-23), the more complicated and unlikely life becomes, the clearer His attributes are seen. God's sufficiency is best defined in His own words: "My grace is all you need. My power works best in weakness" (2 Corinthians 12:9).

Protector: An expression that grew out of wartime experiences says, "There are no atheists in foxholes." When faced with life-or-death circumstances, almost everyone calls out to God for protection. It's in our hearts to do so (Ecclesiastes 3:11). But some people, like Ezra, make a lifestyle of calling on God, because they know His character. When Ezra prepared to lead 2,000 men, women, and children back to Jerusalem, he called out to God for protection.

And God answered his prayer (Ezra 8:21-23). There may be more words in the Bible used to describe God as protector than for any other role: He is called a sword, shield, rock, fortress, tower, and other names. There is no reason to live in fear when we have a divine shield about us (Psalm 3:3).

GROWING THROUGH EZRA

Ezra provides warnings and lessons for living successfully in a setting characterized by opposition and temptation:

Separation from the World: On two separate occasions, the opportunity to form unequal spiritual partnerships arose. The Jews resisted the first one but succumbed to the second. First, they resisted the offer of pagan rulers in Judea to help rebuild the Temple (4:1-3). These people worshiped many gods, including the God of Israel—and Zerubbabel sent them away. Second, when Ezra returned, he found that many in the first wave of returnees had married pagan wives, in clear violation of Moses' direction (Exodus 34:15). Thankfully, the people repented of this sin. But because their temptations are common ones, we are warned against them as well (2 Corinthians 6:14-18).

DISCOVERY VERSES

This was because Ezra had determined to study and obey the Law of the LORD and to teach those decrees and regulations to the people of Israel. (EZRA 7:10)

So we fasted and earnestly prayed that our God would take care of us, and he heard our prayer. (EZRA 8:23)

Spiritual Warfare: When those living in Judea were rebuffed in their attempts to form alliances with the Jews, they devised different strategies and were successful for a time (4:4-24). A Persian king briefly stopped the rebuilding of the Temple. Fortunately, it was restarted when yet another Persian king gained the throne. The apostle Paul says we live in the midst of spiritual warfare; we are targets of the schemes of the devil (2 Corinthians 2:11; Ephesians 6:11). To be ignorant of the realities of such scheming is to be vulnerable to defeat.

Prayer and Fasting: When Ezra needed protection for his journey from Persia to Jerusalem, he called the people to fast and pray (Ezra 8:21). Note that the fasting and prayer were corporate and public—"by the Ahava Canal." These actions provided evidence of humility, earnest supplication, and immediate need. These corporate disciplines of fasting and prayer are all but unknown in the modern, Western church. Modern appetites have become strong competitors to ancient disciplines.

Confession and Repentance: Ezra learned of the inter-marriages between Jewish men and pagan women and entered into a prolonged prayer of confession. Though Ezra himself had not done anything wrong, his prayer expressed his solidarity with the people, and his confession was made on their behalf (Ezra 9:5–10:1). The people were so moved by Ezra's contrition that they, too, were immediately convicted of their sin and "wept bitterly with him" (Ezra 10:1). They then confessed their sins and repented, putting away their foreign wives (Ezra 10:2-17). Confession without repentance is not true sorrow for sin; it is merely regret at having been caught (2 Corinthians 7:10-11).

EZRA FACTS

Author: While not named specifically, Ezra is probably the author. Second Chronicles and Ezra flow together like Luke and Acts in the New Testament, both of which were written by Luke. Ezra was a scribe and a priest, and he possessed the character necessary to be a spiritual leader and reformer. Part of the book (7:28–9:15) is written from a first-person viewpoint with Ezra as the speaker.

Written to: Israel in general, but specifically for the returning exiles as a chronicle of how God prospered and protected them.

Date of writing: Around the middle of the fifth century BC.

Setting: Ezra takes place in two major movements: the return of nearly 50,000 Jews from Persia to Judea under Zerubbabel (chapters 1–6), and the return of just under 2,000 Jews with Ezra 80 years later (chapters 7–10). The events of the book of Esther took place in the period between these two movements.

OUTLINE

- **EZRA 1–6**—Return of the exiles and rebuilding of the Temple
- **EZRA 7–10**—Return of Ezra and rebuilding of the community

CYRUS ALLOWS THE EXILES TO RETURN

1:1-3 **1** In the first year of King Cyrus of Persia,* the LORD fulfilled the prophecy He had given
//2 Chr 36:22-23 through Jeremiah.* He stirred the heart of Cyrus to put this proclamation in writing
1:1 Jer 25:11-12; 29:10-14 and to send it throughout his kingdom:

1:2 Isa 44:28; 45:1-13 2 "This is what King Cyrus of Persia says:
"The LORD, the God of heaven, has given me all the kingdoms of the earth. He has
1:3 Dan 6:26 appointed me to build Him a Temple at Jerusalem, which is in Judah. 3 Any of you
who are His people may go to Jerusalem in Judah to rebuild this Temple of the LORD,
the God of Israel, who lives in Jerusalem. And may your God be with you! 4 Wherever
this Jewish remnant is found, let their neighbors contribute toward their expenses by
giving them silver and gold, supplies for the journey, and livestock, as well as a
voluntary offering for the Temple of God in Jerusalem."

1:5 2 Chr 36:22 5 Then God stirred the hearts of the priests and Levites and the leaders of the tribes of Ju-
dah and Benjamin to go to Jerusalem to rebuild the Temple of the LORD. 6 And all their
neighbors assisted by giving them articles of silver and gold, supplies for the journey, and
livestock. They gave them many valuable gifts in addition to all the voluntary offerings.

1:1a The first year of Cyrus's reign over Babylon was 538 B.C. **1:1b** See Jer 25:11-12; 29:10.

▸ GOD

1:1 God brings about change. Trapped in a foreign nation, cut off from family and friends, under the rule of a godless king—it would be easy to feel hopeless in such a situation. But God is not limited—by anything! In Ezra, we read the story of God stirring the heart of a powerful political leader who acted kindly toward the Jews. Perhaps there's someone or something in your life that appears to be an immovable obstacle, but God is not troubled. He can change anyone or any circumstance. Don't be afraid to pray to God to overcome any situation. (***See God****> God's Names> God> King,* TopicGuide page A18.)

1:1-4 The three themes found in these verses echo throughout the book of Ezra: 1) The divine authorization of the restoration programs of Zerubbabel, Ezra, and Nehemiah; 2) the importance of rebuilding the Temple; and 3) the cooperation of all God's people in the project.

1:2 Other official correspondence beyond this famous decree is included in Ezra, and much of it was not even translated into Hebrew but was left in its original Aramaic, the language of international diplomacy at that time in the Near East. Some of this correspondence includes: 1) the letter of Rehum to Artaxerxes (Ezra 4:11-16); 2) the reply of Artaxerxes (4:17-22); 3) the letter of Tattenai to Darius (Ezra 5:7-17); 4) the memorandum regarding the decree of Cyrus (Ezra 6:3-5); 5) the reply of Darius to Tattenai (Ezra 6:6-12); and 6) the letter of Artaxerxes on behalf of Ezra (Ezra 7:12-26). Also included are memoirs of Ezra (Ezra 7:27–9:15). Concerning Cyrus's decree, it is doubtful that he actually understood or believed his own testimony about God's involvement in his rule, since he said similar things about Marduk on the ancient Cylinder of Cyrus. Cyrus's purpose was to enlist the gods of these peoples in his own service.

1:5 The return of God's people is described in three parts: the Cyrus edict (1:1-4), the Jews' preparations (1:5-11), and a list of returnees (2:1-70). The valuable items donated by Cyrus were a sign of his favor on the project as well as a sign of God's blessing upon it.

▸ WORSHIP

1:6 Giving our valuable gifts. When God is at work in an area of ministry, those who love Him are responsible to give toward His purposes. The Jewish people gave "many valuable gifts," not their leftovers. They were enthused about what they could contribute. Are you giving toward God's purposes in your area of service? Is your attitude one of "how much can I give?" rather than "how much can I keep for myself?" Wholeheartedly work to build up ministries that God is using around you. (***See Worship****> NT> Sacrificial Living> Sacrificial living is pleasing to God,* TopicGuide page A34.)

7King Cyrus himself brought out the articles that King Nebuchadnezzar had taken from the LORD'S Temple in Jerusalem and had placed in the temple of his own gods. 8Cyrus directed Mithredath, the treasurer of Persia, to count these items and present them to Sheshbazzar, the leader of the exiles returning to Judah.* 9This is a list of the items that were returned:

1:7 2 Kgs 24:13; 25:13-16 2 Chr 36:7-18 Ezra 6:5

1:8 Ezra 5:14-16

gold basins 30
silver basins 1,000
silver incense burners* 29
10 gold bowls 30
silver bowls 410
other items 1,000

11In all, there were 5,400 articles of gold and silver. Sheshbazzar brought all of these along when the exiles went from Babylon to Jerusalem.

1:8 Hebrew *Sheshbazzar, the prince of Judah.* 1:9 The meaning of this Hebrew word is uncertain.

THE PERSIAN KINGS OF EZRA'S DAY

Name	Date of Reign	Relationship to Israel
Cyrus	559–530 BC	Conquered Babylon. Established a policy of returning exiles to their homelands. Sent Zerubbabel to Jerusalem, financed his project, and returned the gold and silver articles that Nebuchadnezzar had taken from the Temple. He probably knew Daniel.
Darius	522–486 BC	Supported construction of the Temple in Jerusalem.
Xerxes (Ahasuerus)	486–465 BC	Was Esther's husband. Allowed the Jews to protect themselves against Haman's attempt to eliminate their people.
Artaxerxes I	465–424 BC	Had Nehemiah as his cup-bearer. Allowed both Ezra and Nehemiah to return to Jerusalem.

1:7 In 597 BC (see 2 Chronicles 36:7), Nebuchadnezzar carried away many precious objects from Jerusalem. It was normal for victorious armies to carry away the religious artifacts from the temples of their enemies.

▸ MINISTRY
1:8 Using our talents for God. Mithredath, the Persian official, fulfilled an essential role in the rebuilding of the Temple. As treasurer, he utilized his expertise to make sure the exiles had all the materials they needed. The talents and education you have are also valuable in your service to God. Sometimes we only think of those talents we consider "spiritual," such as singing in church or teaching a Sunday school class, but many more areas are needed for God's kingdom. Can you fix the plumbing at your church? Do you know how to balance a ledger for your mission committee? Can you cater an event for the congregation? Examine your strengths and ask God how you can use them for His glory. (***See Ministry****> Transformation> Vocations> Treasurer,* TopicGuide page A57.)

1:8 Sheshbazzar may be a Persian name for Zerubbabel (mentioned in Ezra 2:2). He may also be the official governor of the territory, with Zerubbabel holding the informal role of Jewish representative.

1:9-11 The total of the numbers in Ezra 1:9-10 is 2,499, not the 5,400 of Ezra 1:11. For some reason, not all of the articles are included in the count. The problem is compounded by not knowing exactly what the "basins" and "bowls" and "incense burners" were (Ezra 1:9, 10). These may have been stackable units that held many items, which, when added together, equaled the 5,400 in Ezra 1:11.

EXILES WHO RETURNED WITH ZERUBBABEL

2:1-70 //Neh 7:6-73 **2** Here is the list of the Jewish exiles of the provinces who returned from their captiv-
2:1 2 Kgs 24:14-16; 25:11 2 Chr 36:20 ity. King Nebuchadnezzar had deported them to Babylon, but now they returned to
Jerusalem and the other towns in Judah where they originally lived. 2 Their leaders were
Zerubbabel, Jeshua, Nehemiah, Seraiah, Reelaiah, Mordecai, Bilshan, Mispar, Bigvai, Re-
hum, and Baanah.

2:2 Neh 7:7 This is the number of the men of Israel who returned from exile:

3 The family of Parosh	2,172
4 The family of Shephatiah	372
5 The family of Arah	775
2:5-6 Neh 7:10-11 6 The family of Pahath-moab (descendants of Jeshua and Joab)	2,812
7 The family of Elam	1,254
8 The family of Zattu	945
9 The family of Zaccai	760
10 The family of Bani	642
11 The family of Bebai	623
12 The family of Azgad	1,222
13 The family of Adonikam	666
14 The family of Bigvai	2,056
15 The family of Adin	454
16 The family of Ater (descendants of Hezekiah)	98
17 The family of Bezai	323
18 The family of Jorah	112
19 The family of Hashum	223
20 The family of Gibbar	95
21 The people of Bethlehem	123
22 The people of Netophah	56
23 The people of Anathoth	128
24 The people of Beth-azmaveth*	42
25 The people of Kiriath-jearim,* Kephirah, and Beeroth	743
26 The people of Ramah and Geba	621
27 The people of Micmash	122
28 The people of Bethel and Ai	223
29 The citizens of Nebo	52
30 The citizens of Magbish	156
31 The citizens of Elam	1,254
32 The citizens of Harim	320
33 The citizens of Lod, Hadid, and Ono	725

2:24 As in parallel text at Neh 7:28; Hebrew reads *Azmaveth*. 2:25 As in some Hebrew manuscripts and Greek version (see also Neh 7:29); Hebrew reads *Kiriath-arim*.

2:1-70 This list is repeated with some variations in Nehemiah 7:6-73 (and the non-canonical 1 Esdras 5:4-46). The many numerical differences between these three lists can be explained as scribal errors as the text was copied down through the ages.

2:2-25 The first group listed here is the laity. This keeps with Ezra's emphasis on the significance of the common people in rebuilding.

▸ CHURCH

2:3 The importance of the family. The family was the central unit of Jewish society. A person's heritage and future was tied to his or her family line. That's one way God protects people and builds a strong nation. Our family and heritage can be either a hindrance to ministry (Mark 3:21; 6:4; Luke 9:61) or a blessing (Philippians 3:5). In the New Covenant, the church also functions as our family (Ephesians 2:19) and becomes the central unit of life in the Kingdom (Matthew 16:18). How can you show God's love to those in your families? How can you care for the children in your families? (***See Church**> Role> Church Community> Living as a family,* TopicGuide page A49; ***See Holiness**> Submission> Learning God's Word> Teaching your children,* TopicGuide page A40.)

34 The citizens of Jericho 345
35 The citizens of Senaah 3,630

36 These are the priests who returned from exile: 2:36 1 Chr 24:7-18
The family of Jedaiah (through the line of Jeshua) 973
37 The family of Immer .... 1,052 2:38 1 Chr 9:12
38 The family of Pashhur 1,247
39 The family of Harim .... 1,017 2:39 1 Chr 24:8

40 These are the Levites who returned from exile: 2:40 Neh 12:24
The families of Jeshua and Kadmiel (descendants of Hodaviah) 74
41 The singers of the family of Asaph 128
42 The gatekeepers of the families of Shallum, Ater, Talmon, Akkub, Hatita, and Shobai 139

43 The descendants of the following Temple servants returned from exile: 2:43 1 Chr 9:2
Ziha, Hasupha, Tabbaoth,
44 Keros, Siaha, Padon,
45 Lebanah, Hagabah, Akkub,
46 Hagab, Shalmai,* Hanan,
47 Giddel, Gahar, Reaiah,
48 Rezin, Nekoda, Gazzam,
49 Uzza, Paseah, Besai,
50 Asnah, Meunim, Nephusim,
51 Bakbuk, Hakupha, Harhur,
52 Bazluth, Mehida, Harsha,
53 Barkos, Sisera, Temah,
54 Neziah, and Hatipha.

2:46 As in an alternate reading of the Masoretic Text (see also Neh 7:48); the other alternate reads *Shamlai.*

THE RETURN FROM EXILE

Year	Number of People Returned	Persian King	Jewish Leader	Main Accomplishment
538 BC	50,000	Cyrus	Zerubbabel	They rebuilt the Temple, but only after a 20-year struggle. The work was halted for several years but was finally finished.
458 BC	2,000 men and their families	Artaxerxes	Ezra	Ezra confronted the spiritual disobedience of the people, and they repented and established worship at the Temple. But the wall of Jerusalem remained in ruins.
445 BC	Small group	Artaxerxes	Nehemiah	The city was rebuilt, and a spiritual awakening followed. But the people still struggled with ongoing disobedience.

2:36-58 In the next group of returnees are those who served in the Temple.

2:55-57 55 The descendants of these servants of King Solomon returned from exile:
Neh 7:57-60 Sotai, Hassophereth, Peruda,
56 Jaalah, Darkon, Giddel,
57 Shephatiah, Hattil, Pokereth-hazzebaim, and Ami.

58 In all, the Temple servants and the descendants of Solomon's servants numbered 392.

59 Another group returned at this time from the towns of Tel-melah, Tel-harsha, Kerub,
Addan, and Immer. However, they could not prove that they or their families were descen-
dants of Israel. 60 This group included the families of Delaiah, Tobiah, and Nekoda—a total
of 652 people.
61 Three families of priests—Hobaiah, Hakkoz, and Barzillai—also returned. (This Barzillai
2:61 2 Sam 17:27 had married a woman who was a descendant of Barzillai of Gilead, and he had taken her
2:62 family name.) 62 They searched for their names in the genealogical records, but they were
Num 3:10; 16:39-40 not found, so they were disqualified from serving as priests. 63 The governor told them not
Ezra 2:59 to eat the priests' share of food from the sacrifices until a priest could consult the LORD
2:63 Exod 28:30 about the matter by using the Urim and Thummim—the sacred lots.
Lev 2:3, 10 64 So a total of 42,360 people returned to Judah, 65 in addition to 7,337 servants and
2:64 200 singers, both men and women. 66 They took with them 736 horses, 245 mules,
Neh 7:66-67 67 435 camels, and 6,720 donkeys.
68 When they arrived at the Temple of the LORD in Jerusalem, some of the family leaders
2:69 made voluntary offerings toward the rebuilding of God's Temple on its original site, 69 and
Ezra 8:25-34 each leader gave as much as he could. The total of their gifts came to 61,000 gold coins,*
6,250 pounds* of silver, and 100 robes for the priests.
2:70 Neh 7:73 70 So the priests, the Levites, the singers, the gatekeepers, the Temple servants, and
some of the common people settled in villages near Jerusalem. The rest of the people re-
turned to their own towns throughout Israel.

THE ALTAR IS REBUILT

3:1 Neh 7:73; 8:1 **3** In early autumn,* when the Israelites had settled in their towns, all the people assem-
bled in Jerusalem with a unified purpose. 2 Then Jeshua son of Jehozadak* joined his

3:2 Lev 1:1-17; 6:8-13 Deut 12:5-6

2:69a Hebrew *61,000 darics of gold,* about 1,100 pounds or 500 kilograms in weight. 2:69b Hebrew *5,000 minas* [3,000 kilograms]. 3:1 Hebrew *in the seventh month.* The year is not specified, so it may have been during Cyrus's first year (538 B.C.) or second year (537 B.C.). The seventh month of the ancient Hebrew lunar calendar occurred within the months of September/October 538 B.C. and October/November 537 B.C. 3:2 Hebrew *Jozadak,* a variant spelling of Jehozadak; also in 3:8.

2:59-63 The final grouping is made up of those who could not prove their ancestry. Of this group, the laity is listed first (Ezra 2:60) and the priests second (Ezra 2:61), once again demonstrating Ezra's emphasis on the contribution of the commoner.

2:63 Only a priest or a member of his household could eat the portion of the sacrifice allotted to the priests (see Leviticus 22:10). Concerning the "*sacred lots,*" or "*Urim and Thummim,*" these objects were the special means by which the Jewish leaders were able to seek God's will. *Urim* is derived from the Hebrew for "light," or "to give light," and *Thummim* from "completeness" or "perfection." In this case, the sacred lots enabled them to determine those of proper ancestry to serve in the Temple.

2:64 This is the same total as the amount listed in Nehemiah 7:66. The sum of the figures in the list in Ezra is only 29,818. The sum of the list in Nehemiah 7 is 31,089. Either certain groups were counted but not listed, or the numbers in the text suffered corruption as they were transmitted through the ages.

2:68 The first Temple was also built with freewill offerings (see 1 Chronicles 29:1-9), not from the general funds. The principle of giving beyond the tithe and according to one's ability is still applicable in building the kingdom in the New Covenant (see 2 Corinthians 8:11).

WORSHIP
2:68 Giving to immediate needs. How's your budget? Are you spending too much money on unnecessary things? Or too little on investing? The families who saw the great needs of the Temple in Jerusalem didn't necessarily have a perfect budget—they were former political exiles—but they gave whatever they could where it was needed. Make a sizeable niche in your budget for giving to the needy around you. (***See Worship****> NT> Sacrificial Living> Planning and budgeting part of sacrificial living,* TopicGuide page A34.)

3:1 The rebuilding of the Temple occurred in stages, thus these chapters divide into two main sections: rebuilding the altar (Ezra 3:1-6) and rebuilding the Temple proper (Ezra 3:7–6:22). The altar came first due to the centrality of regularly offered sacrifices under the Old Covenant. It also likely came first because the Festival of Shelters was approaching (see Ezra 3:4; also Leviticus 23:33-40).

fellow priests and Zerubbabel son of Shealtiel with his family in rebuilding the altar of the
God of Israel. They wanted to sacrifice burnt offerings on it, as instructed in the Law of
Moses, the man of God. [3]Even though the people were afraid of the local residents, they
rebuilt the altar at its old site. Then they began to sacrifice burnt offerings on the altar to
the LORD each morning and evening.
[4]They celebrated the Festival of Shelters as prescribed in the Law, sacrificing the num-
ber of burnt offerings specified for each day of the festival. [5]They also offered the regular
burnt offerings and the offerings required for the new moon celebrations and the annual
festivals as prescribed by the LORD. The people also gave voluntary offerings to the LORD.
[6]Fifteen days before the Festival of Shelters began,* the priests had begun to sacrifice
burnt offerings to the LORD. This was even before they had started to lay the foundation of
the LORD's Temple.

3:3 Num 28:1-8
3:4 Exod 23:16; Num 29:12; Neh 8:14
3:5 Exod 29:38, 42; Num 28:11-14; 29:39

THE PEOPLE BEGIN TO REBUILD THE TEMPLE

[7]Then the people hired masons and carpenters and bought cedar logs from the people of
Tyre and Sidon, paying them with food, wine, and olive oil. The logs were brought down
from the Lebanon mountains and floated along the coast of the Mediterranean Sea* to
Joppa, for King Cyrus had given permission for this.
[8]The construction of the Temple of God began in midspring,* during the second year af-
ter they arrived in Jerusalem. The work force was made up of everyone who had returned
from exile, including Zerubbabel son of Shealtiel, Jeshua son of Jehozadak and his fellow
priests, and all the Levites. The Levites who were twenty years old or older were put in
charge of rebuilding the LORD's Temple. [9]The workers at the Temple of God were super-
vised by Jeshua with his sons and relatives, and Kadmiel and his sons, all descendants of
Hodaviah.* They were helped in this task by the Levites of the family of Henadad.
[10]When the builders completed the foundation of the LORD's Temple, the priests put on

3:7 1 Kgs 5:9-11; 2 Chr 2:10-16; Ezra 1:2; 6:3
3:8 Num 4:3; Ezra 3:2; 4:2
3:9 Ezra 2:40
3:10 1 Chr 6:31; 25:1

3:6 Hebrew *On the first day of the seventh month.* This day in the ancient Hebrew lunar calendar occurred in September or October. The Festival of Shelters began on the fifteenth day of the seventh month. 3:7 Hebrew *the sea.* 3:8 Hebrew *in the second month.* This month in the ancient Hebrew lunar calendar occurred within the months of April and May 536 B.C. 3:9 Hebrew *sons of Judah* (i.e., *bene Yehudah*). *Bene* might also be read here as the proper name Binnui; *Yehudah* is probably another name for Hodaviah. Compare 2:40; Neh 7:43; 1 Esdras 5:58.

▸ MINISTRY
3:3 Having a bold witness. Fear did not keep the Jewish people from rebuilding the altar. Even though they were the minority in the land, they stuck to their mandate to follow God's plan. Sometimes we may feel intimidated by those living around us and feel tempted to hide our faith. But that's not the way of blessing. Just as the Jews of Nehemiah's day gave evidence of their faith by burning sacrifices every morning and evening, we should not be afraid to consistently witness about our faith in our neighborhoods and workplaces. (***See Ministry***> *Great Commission*> *Witness,* TopicGuide page A56.)

▸ WORSHIP
3:6 Putting God first. Before the Jewish people began the project of rebuilding the Temple, they sacrificed burnt offerings to the Lord. They laid the worship of God as a foundation for everything else. Whatever your church is planning, whether a building or a program or anything else, make the first step one of worship. The focus of God's people should always be on God rather than on a project. God always comes first. (***See Worship***> *OT*> *God's Supremacy,* TopicGuide page A27.)

3:7 No sooner had the first sacrifices been offered than provisions were made to begin rebuilding the Temple. Nevertheless, many opposed the construction of the Temple, and the work required perseverance. These next few chapters alternate stories about rebuilding (Ezra 3:7-13; 5:1-2; 6:13-22) and opposition to the rebuilding (Ezra 4:1-24; 5:3–6:12).

3:8 The concept or image of the Temple is an important one in the Christian faith. Not only did Christ cleanse the Temple (Matthew 21:12-13; John 2:13-17), He became the Temple (John 2:19-22). Christ also established the church as the Temple of God (1 Corinthians 3:16-17; 2 Corinthians 6:16), and He now ministers in the heavenly Temple (Hebrews 9:11-12, 24). When Christ returns, He will create a new heaven and earth as the holy city of God, with Himself and the Father as the Temple (Revelation 21:22). The themes of the presence of God, holiness, the priesthood, sacrifices, prayers, and forgiveness all begin with the Temple, and they are all fulfilled in Christ.

3:8 Midspring, or Iyyar (April-May), is the same month in which Solomon began building the original Temple (see 2 Chronicles 3:2). Whether intentional on the part of the builders or simply ordained by God, the original reader knew that this was another confirmation of God's blessing on this Temple.

▸ WORSHIP
3:10 The least of them. Each person who participated in the rebuilding of the Temple played an important part. The builders worked first; then the priests performed their duties. Each type of worker was given his own recognition in the book of Ezra. Strive to recognize those who work at your church but who are often ignored, such as the janitor, the handyman, or the church secretary. They are all part of God's team as they serve the mission of your church. (***See Worship***> *NT*> *Fellowship*> *Preserving*> *Honor one another,* TopicGuide page A30.)

their robes and took their places to blow their trumpets. And the Levites, descendants of
3:11 1 Chr 16:34, 41; 2 Chr 7:3; Neh 12:24, 40; Ps 106:1 Asaph, clashed their cymbals to praise the LORD, just as King David had prescribed. [11]With
praise and thanks, they sang this song to the LORD:

"He is so good!
His faithful love for Israel endures forever!"

Then all the people gave a great shout, praising the LORD because the foundation of the
LORD's Temple had been laid.
3:12 Hag 2:3 [12]But many of the older priests, Levites, and other leaders who had seen the first Tem-
ple wept aloud when they saw the new Temple's foundation. The others, however, were
shouting for joy. [13]The joyful shouting and weeping mingled together in a loud noise that
could be heard far in the distance.

ENEMIES OPPOSE THE REBUILDING

4:1 Ezra 4:7-10 **4** The enemies of Judah and Benjamin heard that the exiles were rebuilding a Temple
to the LORD, the God of Israel. [2]So they approached Zerubbabel and the other leaders
4:2 2 Kgs 17:32; 19:37 and said, "Let us build with you, for we worship your God just as you do. We have sacri-
4:3 Ezra 1:1-4; 6:3-5; Neh 2:20 ficed to Him ever since King Esarhaddon of Assyria brought us here."
[3]But Zerubbabel, Jeshua, and the other leaders of Israel replied, "You may have no part
in this work. We alone will build the Temple for the LORD, the God of Israel, just as King Cy-
rus of Persia commanded us."
4:4 Ezra 3:3 [4]Then the local residents tried to discourage and frighten the people of Judah to keep
them from their work. [5]They bribed agents to work against them and to frustrate their
plans. This went on during the entire reign of King Cyrus of Persia and lasted until King Da-
rius of Persia took the throne.*

4:5 Darius reigned 521–486 B.C.

▸ WORSHIP
3:12 Faith and feelings. Have you ever experienced something that caused both happiness and sadness? The people of Israel experienced this upon completion of the new Temple. Some people praised God for what He had done, while others mourned over how humble this new Temple was in comparison with Solomon's Temple. The Christian life is often a mixture of burdens and freedom, happiness and grief. God's people are not bonded together by common emotion but a common faith. Make your church a place where people of common faith can come together to both rejoice and weep. (***See Worship****> NT> Fellowship> Fellowship based on one faith one body,* TopicGuide page A31.)

3:12-13 Moses had promised that the returnees would be blessed beyond previous generations (Deuteronomy 30:5), but the older members of the community were shedding tears of disappointment. These older members remembered the glory of Solomon's Temple, and they were saddened to see such a humble replacement (see Zechariah 4:10). Similar disappointment would later need to be rebuked (see Haggai 2:1-5).

4:1-24 The story continues to turn darker, moving from disappointment by some to rising opposition by others. The writer lists in chronological order the major attempts to stop the reconstruction effort. They occurred during the reign of Cyrus (559–530 BC, Ezra 4:1-5), Xerxes (486–465 BC, Ezra 4:6), and Artaxerxes I (465–424 BC, Ezra 4:7-23). Ezra then goes back and picks up his story during the reign of Darius I (522–486 BC, Ezra 4:24).

4:2 Though on the surface the enemies came with good intentions, we know that their real purpose was to undermine the work of restoring the true worship of God. The enemies were the Samaritans, who were a mixture of different peoples who had been transplanted to Samaria, the area just north of Judah, after the destruction of the northern kingdom of Israel in 722 BC. These peoples worshiped many gods and incorporated the Lord into their polytheism (see 2 Kings 17:24-41). The animosity between the Jews and the Samaritans formed an important part of the background of Jesus' ministry (see John 4:1-42; Luke 10:30-37).

▸ CHURCH
4:5 God will lead us into battle. We should not be surprised when we encounter opposition to God's work. In fact, we should expect a battle to ensue when we begin to make inroads into Satan's territory. The exiles experienced hostility the entire time they were rebuilding the Temple, but they didn't let their enemies deter them from their work. We should take on the same attitude and carefully, consistently, and patiently complete the tasks that God gives us. God will lead us in the battle to accomplish His work. (***See Church****> What> Many Titles> Servants> Servants must be prepared to work,* TopicGuide page A48.)

LATER OPPOSITION UNDER XERXES AND ARTAXERXES

6 Years later when Xerxes* began his reign, the enemies of Judah wrote a letter of accusation against the people of Judah and Jerusalem.

7 Even later, during the reign of King Artaxerxes of Persia,* the enemies of Judah, led by Bishlam, Mithredath, and Tabeel, sent a letter to Artaxerxes in the Aramaic language, and it was translated for the king.

8 *Rehum the governor and Shimshai the court secretary wrote the letter, telling King Artaxerxes about the situation in Jerusalem. 9 They greeted the king for all their colleagues—the judges and local leaders, the people of Tarpel, the Persians, the Babylonians, and the people of Erech and Susa (that is, Elam). 10 They also sent greetings from the rest of the people whom the great and noble Ashurbanipal* had deported and relocated in Samaria and throughout the neighboring lands of the province west of the Euphrates River.* 11 This is a copy of their letter:

> "To King Artaxerxes, from your loyal subjects in the province west of the Euphrates River.
>
> 12 "The king should know that the Jews who came here to Jerusalem from Babylon are rebuilding this rebellious and evil city. They have already laid the foundation and will soon finish its walls. 13 And the king should know that if this city is rebuilt and its walls are completed, it will be much to your disadvantage, for the Jews will then refuse to pay their tribute, customs, and tolls to you.
>
> 14 "Since we are your loyal subjects* and do not want to see the king dishonored in this way, we have sent the king this information. 15 We suggest that a search be made in your ancestors' records, where you will discover what a rebellious city this has been in the past. In fact, it was destroyed because of its long and troublesome history of revolt against the kings and countries who controlled it. 16 We declare to the king that if this city is rebuilt and its walls are completed, the province west of the Euphrates River will be lost to you."

17 Then King Artaxerxes sent this reply:

> "To Rehum the governor, Shimshai the court secretary, and their colleagues living in Samaria and throughout the province west of the Euphrates River. Greetings.
>
> 18 "The letter you sent has been translated and read to me. 19 I ordered a search of the records and have found that Jerusalem has indeed been a hotbed of insurrection against many kings. In fact, rebellion and revolt are normal there! 20 Powerful kings have ruled over Jerusalem and the entire province west of the Euphrates River, receiving tribute,

4:6 Esth 1:1; Dan 9:1
4:7 2 Kgs 18:26; Isa 36:11; Dan 2:4
4:8 Ezra 5:6
4:12 Ezra 5:3, 9
4:13 Ezra 7:24; Neh 5:4
4:18 Neh 8:8
4:20 1 Kgs 4:21, 24; 1 Chr 18:3; Ezra 4:13

4:6 Hebrew *Ahasuerus,* another name for Xerxes. He reigned 486–465 B.C. 4:7 Artaxerxes reigned 465–424 B.C. 4:8 The original text of 4:8–6:18 is in Aramaic. 4:10a Aramaic *Osnappar,* another name for Ashurbanipal. 4:10b Aramaic *the province beyond the river;* also in 4:11, 16, 17, 20. 4:14 Aramaic *Since we eat the salt of the palace.*

▸ PURPOSE

4:6 Don't become discouraged. Sometimes, the enemies of God seem to accomplish their purposes in spite of our best efforts. In this case, they brought up old accusations against the Jews in order to halt the rebuilding of the Temple. The accusations worked, and the people had to put down their tools. How discouraged the people must have felt at this moment. But God knows the past and the future. He knew that the rebuilding would resume at the right time. We can be assured that He also knows what is happening around us. When it seems as if all we are doing is fruitless, we must put our plans into God's hands and let Him guide the future. (***See Purpose****> God's Means> God's Sovereignty> God decrees all,* TopicGuide page A52.)

4:6-23 In Ezra 4:1-5 we read the first account of opposition experienced by the returnees in the days of Cyrus (559–530 BC), but we are not told the result of that opposition until 4:24. The opposition caused work on the Temple to cease until the second year of the reign of Darius (522–486 BC). After work had resumed during Darius's reign, there was further opposition during the reigns of Xerxes (486–465 BC) and Artaxerxes I (464–424 BC). By holding off until verse 24 to explain the results of the opposition, Ezra links the rebuilding of the Temple with the rebuilding of the wall.

4:7 Artaxerxes I was the successor to Xerxes, and he reigned from 464–424 BC.

4:8–6:18 This section is not written in Hebrew but in Aramaic, the language in which the recorded documents were originally written.

4:16 This verse is obviously an overstatement, bordering on ridiculous, and is intended to sway the mind of the king.

customs, and tolls. 21Therefore, issue orders to have these men stop their work. That city must not be rebuilt except at my express command. 22Be diligent, and don't neglect this matter, for we must not permit the situation to harm the king's interests."

23When this letter from King Artaxerxes was read to Rehum, Shimshai, and their colleagues, they hurried to Jerusalem. Then, with a show of strength, they forced the Jews to stop building.

THE REBUILDING RESUMES

4:24 Hag 1:1, 15 24So the work on the Temple of God in Jerusalem had stopped, and it remained at a stand-
Zech 1:1 still until the second year of the reign of King Darius of Persia.*

5:1 Ezra 6:14 **5** At that time the prophets Haggai and Zechariah son of Iddo prophesied to the Jews in
Hag 1:1 Judah and Jerusalem. They prophesied in the name of the God of Israel who was
Zech 1:1 over them. 2Zerubbabel son of Shealtiel and Jeshua son of Jehozadak* responded by start-
5:2 ing again to rebuild the Temple of God in Jerusalem. And the prophets of God were with
Ezra 3:2 them and helped them.
5:3 3But Tattenai, governor of the province west of the Euphrates River,* and Shethar-
Ezra 1:3; 5:6, 9, 17; bozenai and their colleagues soon arrived in Jerusalem and asked, "Who gave you per-
6:6, 13 5:4 mission to rebuild this Temple and restore this structure?" 4They also asked for the names
Ezra 5:10 of all the men working on the Temple. 5But because their God was watching over them,
5:5 the leaders of the Jews were not prevented from building until a report was sent to Darius
Ezra 7:6, 28 Ps 33:18 and he returned his decision.

TATTENAI'S LETTER TO KING DARIUS

6This is a copy of the letter that Tattenai the governor, Shethar-bozenai, and the other officials of the province west of the Euphrates River sent to King Darius:

7"To King Darius. Greetings.

8"The king should know that we went to the construction site of the Temple of the great God in the province of Judah. It is being rebuilt with specially prepared stones, and timber is being laid in its walls. The work is going forward with great energy and success.

9"We asked the leaders, 'Who gave you permission to rebuild this Temple and restore this structure?' 10And we demanded their names so that we could tell you who the leaders were.

5:11 1 Kgs 6:1-38 2 Chr 3:1-2 11"This was their answer: 'We are the servants of the God of heaven and earth, and

4:24 The second year of Darius's reign was 520 B.C. The narrative started in 4:1-5 is resumed at verse 24. 5:2 Aramaic *Jozadak,* a variant spelling of Jehozadak. 5:3 Aramaic *the province beyond the river;* also in 5:6.

5:1-2 The year in which Haggai and Zechariah began to prophesy was the same year referred to in 4:24, the second year of Darius (see Haggai 1:1; Zechariah 1:1).

5:3–6:12 As soon as work on the Temple was renewed, opposition came from the zealous Persian officials of the area. But this time, God chose to immediately intervene, and the officials permitted the work to continue until they heard from Darius. Here, as throughout Ezra and Nehemiah, God intervened through the actions of people, revealing His power over them.

▸ GOD

5:5 God watches over us. Sometimes we feel helpless before people with political or legal or religious authority, especially when they abuse their power. How comforting to know that God is watching over us regardless of who has authority over us. If we are accomplishing His will, God is working on our behalf, even when we don't visibly see it. If you are discouraged in your ministry, take comfort that God is using His mighty hand to make sure that you will succeed in fulfilling His will. (***See God***> *Attributes of God> Sovereign> The Creator looks after His creation,* TopicGuide page A17.)

5:9 This question underscores the lack of authority and independence that the returning Jewish exiles had in Judah.

▸ MINISTRY

5:11 Claim allegiance to God. Even though they faced opposition, the Jewish people were proud to declare themselves in the service of God. Today, we have more freedoms than these people had, yet many times we are less bold in claiming allegiance to God. Do you tell people that you are a servant of the God of heaven and earth? Do you give Him credit for who you are and what you have? Decide today to make sure everyone knows who is Lord of your life. (***See Ministry***> *Great Commission> Make Disciples> Disciples are obligated to share Christ with others,* TopicGuide page A56.)

we are rebuilding the Temple that was built here many years ago by a great king of
Israel. 12But because our ancestors angered the God of heaven, He abandoned them
to King Nebuchadnezzar of Babylon,* who destroyed this Temple and exiled the
people to Babylonia. 13However, King Cyrus of Babylon,* during the first year of his
reign, issued a decree that the Temple of God should be rebuilt. 14King Cyrus returned
the gold and silver cups that Nebuchadnezzar had taken from the Temple of God in
Jerusalem and had placed in the temple of Babylon. These cups were taken from that
temple and presented to a man named Sheshbazzar, whom King Cyrus appointed
as governor of Judah. 15The king instructed him to return the cups to their place
in Jerusalem and to rebuild the Temple of God there on its original site. 16So this
Sheshbazzar came and laid the foundations of the Temple of God in Jerusalem. The
people have been working on it ever since, though it is not yet completed.'

17"Therefore, if it pleases the king, we request that a search be made in the royal
archives of Babylon to discover whether King Cyrus ever issued a decree to rebuild
God's Temple in Jerusalem. And then let the king send us his decision in this matter."

5:12 2 Kgs 24:2, 10; 25:1, 8-11; 2 Chr 36:6-20
5:13 Ezra 1:1-8
5:14 Ezra 1:7-8, 11; 5:16; 6:3-5; Dan 5:2
5:17 Ezra 6:1-2

DARIUS APPROVES THE REBUILDING

6 So King Darius issued orders that a search be made in the Babylonian archives,
which were stored in the treasury. 2But it was at the fortress at Ecbatana in the prov-
ince of Media that a scroll was found. This is what it said:

"Memorandum:

3"In the first year of King Cyrus's reign, a decree was sent out concerning the
Temple of God at Jerusalem.

6:1 Ezra 5:17
6:3 Ezra 3:10

5:12 Aramaic *Nebuchadnezzar the Chaldean.* 5:13 King Cyrus of Persia is here identified as the king of Babylon because Persia had conquered the Babylonian Empire.

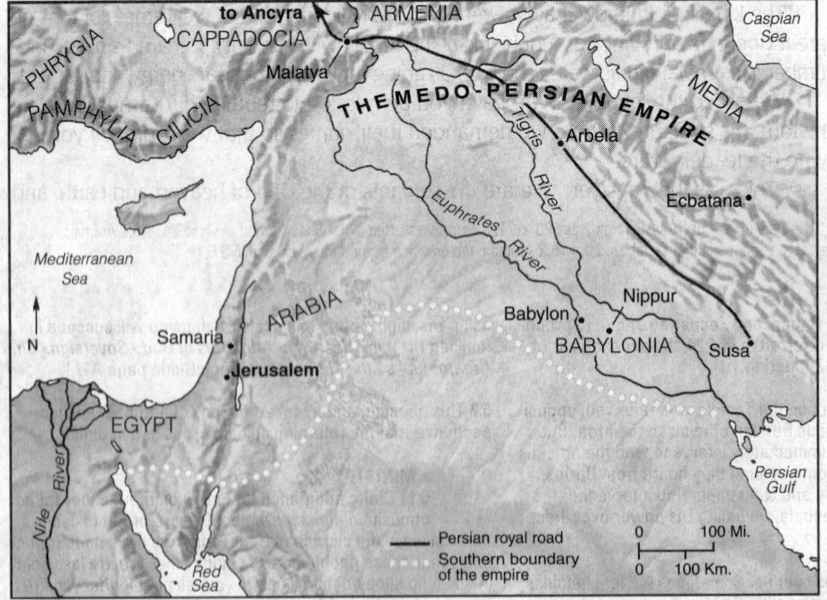

THE MEDO-PERSIAN EMPIRE
The Medo-Persian Empire included the lands of Media and Persia, much of the area shown on this map and more. The Jewish exiles were concentrated in the area around Nippur in the Babylonian province. The decree by King Cyrus that allowed the Israelites to return to their homeland and rebuild the Temple was discovered in the palace at Ecbatana.

5:12 Nebuchadnezzar destroyed the Temple and deported the people, but only as the human agent of the sovereign God, who had handed His people over to Nebuchadnezzar's army.

6:3 These dimensions are larger than those of Solomon's Temple (see 1 Kings 6:2). They likely do not specify the actual size of the Temple building but perhaps set an outer limit on the size of a Temple that Cyrus was willing to subsidize.

"Let the Temple be rebuilt on the site where Jews used to offer their sacrifices,
using the original foundations. Its height will be ninety feet, and its width will be
ninety feet.* 4Every three layers of specially prepared stones will be topped by a layer
6:4 of timber. All expenses will be paid by the royal treasury. 5Furthermore, the gold and
1 Kgs 6:36 silver cups, which were taken to Babylon by Nebuchadnezzar from the Temple of
God in Jerusalem, must be returned to Jerusalem and put back where they belong.
Let them be taken back to the Temple of God."

6So King Darius sent this message:

6:6 "Now therefore, Tattenai, governor of the province west of the Euphrates River,* and
Ezra 5:3; 6:13 Shethar-bozenai, and your colleagues and other officials west of the Euphrates
River—stay away from there! 7Do not disturb the construction of the Temple of God.
Let it be rebuilt on its original site, and do not hinder the governor of Judah and the
elders of the Jews in their work.

8"Moreover, I hereby decree that you are to help these elders of the Jews as they
rebuild this Temple of God. You must pay the full construction costs, without delay,
from my taxes collected in the province west of the Euphrates River so that the work
will not be interrupted.

9"Give the priests in Jerusalem whatever is needed in the way of young bulls,
rams, and male lambs for the burnt offerings presented to the God of heaven. And
without fail, provide them with as much wheat, salt, wine, and olive oil as they need
each day. 10Then they will be able to offer acceptable sacrifices to the God of heaven
6:10 and pray for the welfare of the king and his sons.

Ezra 7:23 11"Those who violate this decree in any way will have a beam pulled from their
6:11 house. Then they will be tied to it and flogged, and their house will be reduced to a
Ezra 7:26 Dan 2:5; 3:29 pile of rubble.* 12May the God who has chosen the city of Jerusalem as the place to
6:12 honor His name destroy any king or nation that violates this command and destroys
Deut 12:4-5, 11 this Temple.

1 Kgs 9:2-3 "I, Darius, have issued this decree. Let it be obeyed with all diligence."

THE TEMPLE'S DEDICATION

13Tattenai, governor of the province west of the Euphrates River, and Shethar-bozenai and
6:13 their colleagues complied at once with the command of King Darius. 14So the Jewish el-
Ezra 6:6 ders continued their work, and they were greatly encouraged by the preaching of the
6:14 prophets Haggai and Zechariah son of Iddo. The Temple was finally finished, as had been
Ezra 5:1-2; 6:12; 7:1, commanded by the God of Israel and decreed by Cyrus, Darius, and Artaxerxes, the kings
7-9, 11 Zech 4:9 of Persia. 15The Temple was completed on March 12,* during the sixth year of King Dari-
us's reign.

6:3 Aramaic *Its height will be 60 cubits* [27.6 meters], *and its width will be 60 cubits.* It is commonly held that this verse should be emended to read: "Its height will be 30 cubits [45 feet, or 13.8 meters], its length will be 60 cubits [90 feet, or 27.6 meters], and its width will be 20 cubits [30 feet, or 9.2 meters]"; compare 1 Kgs 6:2. The emendation regarding the width is supported by the Syriac version. **6:6** Aramaic *the province beyond the river;* also in 6:6b, 8, 13. **6:11** Aramaic *a dunghill.* **6:15** Aramaic *on the third day of the month Adar,* of the ancient Hebrew lunar calendar. A number of events in Ezra can be cross-checked with dates in surviving Persian records and related accurately to our modern calendar. This day was March 12, 515 B.C.

6:12 To pronounce curses on any who would challenge an official document was customary (see Revelation 22:18-19). This verified that God's people were granted complete support to rebuild the Temple.

6:14 The preaching of the prophets motivated the people to start the work again (see Ezra 5:1-2) and to complete it.

6:15 Rounded numbers and general dates were common in ancient literature. But these sorts of specifics show how important this date was to Israel. It was 4 years after the work was renewed (see Haggai 1:15), 20 years after the work was begun (see Ezra 3:8), and almost exactly 70 years after Solomon's Temple was destroyed in 586 BC.

16The Temple of God was then dedicated with great joy by the people of Israel, the
priests, the Levites, and the rest of the people who had returned from exile. 17During the
dedication ceremony for the Temple of God, 100 young bulls, 200 rams, and 400 male
lambs were sacrificed. And 12 male goats were presented as a sin offering for the twelve
tribes of Israel. 18Then the priests and Levites were divided into their various divisions to
serve at the Temple of God in Jerusalem, as prescribed in the Book of Moses.

6:16 1 Kgs 8:63; 2 Chr 7:5
6:18 Num 3:6; 1 Chr 23:6; 2 Chr 35:4-5

CELEBRATION OF PASSOVER

19On April 21* the returned exiles celebrated Passover. 20The priests and Levites had puri-
fied themselves and were ceremonially clean. So they slaughtered the Passover lamb for
all the returned exiles, for their fellow priests, and for themselves. 21The Passover meal
was eaten by the people of Israel who had returned from exile and by the others in the
land who had turned from their immoral customs to worship the LORD, the God of Israel.
22Then they celebrated the Festival of Unleavened Bread for seven days. There was great
joy throughout the land because the LORD had caused the king of Assyria* to be favorable
to them, so that he helped them to rebuild the Temple of God, the God of Israel.

6:19 Exod 12:6
6:20 2 Chr 29:34; 30:15-17; 35:11
6:21 Num 9:6-7, 10-14
6:22 Exod 12:15

EZRA ARRIVES IN JERUSALEM

7 Many years later, during the reign of King Artaxerxes of Persia,* there was a man
named Ezra. He was the son* of Seraiah, son of Azariah, son of Hilkiah, 2son of Shal-
lum, son of Zadok, son of Ahitub, 3son of Amariah, son of Azariah, son* of Meraioth, 4son
of Zerahiah, son of Uzzi, son of Bukki, 5son of Abishua, son of Phinehas, son of Eleazar,
son of Aaron the high priest.* 6This Ezra was a scribe who was well versed in the Law of
Moses, which the LORD, the God of Israel, had given to the people of Israel. He came up to
Jerusalem from Babylon, and the king gave him everything he asked for, because the gra-
cious hand of the LORD his God was on him. 7Some of the people of Israel, as well as some
of the priests, Levites, singers, gatekeepers, and Temple servants, traveled up to Jerusalem
with him in the seventh year of King Artaxerxes' reign.

7:1 1 Chr 6:9-14; Ezra 7:12, 21; 8:1–10:44; Neh 8:1-18
7:6 Ezra 7:10-11, 21-29; Neh 8:9, 13
7:7 Ezra 8:1-20

6:19 Hebrew *On the fourteenth day of the first month,* of the ancient Hebrew lunar calendar. This day was April 21, 515 B.C.; also see note on 6:15. 6:22 King Darius of Persia is here identified as the king of Assyria because Persia had conquered the Babylonian Empire, which included the earlier Assyrian Empire. 7:1a Artaxerxes reigned 465–424 B.C. 7:1b Or *descendant;* see 1 Chr 6:14. 7:3 Or *descendant;* see 1 Chr 6:6-10. 7:5 Or *the first priest.*

▸ CHURCH
6:16 Celebrate! God's people have always known how to have a real party, but sometimes we don't celebrate the right thing. Following the example of this text, when was the last time you celebrated something that God had done? Does your church arrange for congregational rejoicing when a ministry milestone is achieved? Many times we come together to pray when things look ominous—and that is important. But expressing joy with other believers is just as essential for building up the body of Christ. (***See Church****> Role> Glorify God> As a community,* TopicGuide page A49.)

6:19 This precise dating of the Passover showed how important the sacred day was to Israel. It had been almost 70 years since the exiles had celebrated Passover in Jerusalem.

▸ WORSHIP
6:22 Rescue of God. Like the modern-day Lord's Supper, the Passover is a celebration of God's rescue of sinners. In this case, those who traveled to Jerusalem with Ezra were celebrating how God rescued them from exile. Now they were home and able to worship God exactly as they pleased. If you live in a situation where you are free to worship God, repent and rejoice with all your might, letting everyone know of the privilege of worshiping God! But if you are in a place where open worship of God is not permitted, pray and act in a way that will make it possible in the future to have religious freedom. Pray that God will rescue His people again. (***See Worship****> OT> Festivals> Passover,* TopicGuide page A26.)

7:1–10:44 Attention shifts from the initial reconstruction effort under Zerubabbel to the revival work of Ezra. About 60 years passed between the events at the end of chapter 6 and those at the beginning of chapter 7. The lack of intervening material portrays Ezra's ministry as the legitimate continuation of Zerubabbel's work. These chapters divide into two main parts: Ezra's return (7:1–8:36) and Ezra's rebuilding of the community (9:1–10:44).

7:1-10 Ezra was a descendant of Aaron (Ezra 7:5) and therefore had priestly authority, and God's hand (and the king's) was upon him (Ezra 7:9).

▸ WORSHIP
7:7 Coming alongside others. When Ezra went to meet the king, many people accompanied him on the journey. Any mission we undertake is so much easier when others come alongside us. Do you look for ways to come alongside others in their work for God? Are you an encourager who doesn't need to be first, but can you help others succeed? Do not allow Christians around you to walk alone. (***See Worship****> NT> Fellowship> Preserving> Encourage one another,* TopicGuide page A31.)

8 Ezra arrived in Jerusalem in August* of that year. 9 He had arranged to leave Babylon on
7:9 Ezra 7:6 April 8, the first day of the new year,* and he arrived at Jerusalem on August 4,* for the
7:10 gracious hand of his God was on him. 10 This was because Ezra had determined to study
Neh 8:1 and obey the Law of the LORD and to teach those decrees and regulations to the people of
Israel.

ARTAXERXES' LETTER TO EZRA

11 King Artaxerxes had given a copy of the following letter to Ezra, the priest and scribe
who studied and taught the commands and decrees of the LORD to Israel:

12*"From Artaxerxes, the king of kings, to Ezra the priest, the teacher of the law of the
7:12 God of heaven. Greetings.
Ezek 26:7 13 "I decree that any of the people of Israel in my kingdom, including the priests
Dan 2:37, 47 and Levites, may volunteer to return to Jerusalem with you. 14 I and my council of
7:14 seven hereby instruct you to conduct an inquiry into the situation in Judah and
Ezra 7:15, 28 Jerusalem, based on your God's law, which is in your hand. 15 We also commission
you to take with you silver and gold, which we are freely presenting as an offering
to the God of Israel who lives in Jerusalem.
16 "Furthermore, you are to take any silver and gold that you may obtain from the
7:16 1 Chr 29:6 province of Babylon, as well as the voluntary offerings of the people and the priests
Ezra 8:25 that are presented for the Temple of their God in Jerusalem. 17 These donations are
7:17 to be used specifically for the purchase of bulls, rams, male lambs, and the
Num 15:4-13 appropriate grain offerings and liquid offerings, all of which will be offered on the
Deut 12:4-11 altar of the Temple of your God in Jerusalem. 18 Any silver and gold that is left over
may be used in whatever way you and your colleagues feel is the will of your God.
19 "But as for the cups we are entrusting to you for the service of the Temple of
your God, deliver them all to the God of Jerusalem. 20 If you need anything else for
7:20 your God's Temple or for any similar needs, you may take it from the royal treasury.
Ezra 6:4 21 "I, Artaxerxes the king, hereby send this decree to all the treasurers in the
7:21 Ezra 7:6 province west of the Euphrates River*: 'You are to give Ezra, the priest and teacher of
the law of the God of heaven, whatever he requests of you. 22 You are to give him up

7:8 Hebrew *in the fifth month.* This month in the ancient Hebrew lunar calendar occurred within the months of August and September 458 B.C. **7:9a** Hebrew *on the first day of the first month,* of the ancient Hebrew lunar calendar. This day was April 8, 458 B.C.; also see note on 6:15. **7:9b** Hebrew *on the first day of the fifth month,* of the ancient Hebrew lunar calendar. This day was August 4, 458 B.C.; also see note on 6:15. **7:12** The original text of 7:12-26 is in Aramaic. **7:21** Aramaic *the province beyond the river;* also in 7:25.

7:9 Ezra's trip took place in the spring, when water and food would be plentiful.

▸ HOLINESS

7:10 Have a plan to study God's Word. Ezra did not leave his education to chance. He determined to study God's Word. He had a plan to make the Bible the center of his life and to teach others to value it. Do you have a plan to become a student of God's Word? There is no book in the world that is more important to your soul than the Bible. Keep reading, meditating, and studying His Word! (***See Holiness> Submission> Learning God's Word> Public teaching,*** TopicGuide page A40.)

7:10 The characterizations of Zerubbabel, Ezra, and Nehemiah as leaders anticipate the work of Christ. As they devoted their lives to leading God's people toward the blessings of God, Christ leads us toward ultimate and eternal blessings. Like Christ, Ezra and Nehemiah confronted and corrected sin within Israel (Ezra 9:1-15; 10:10-14; Nehemiah 1:6-7; 9:1-3, 26-38; 13:15-27; Matthew 23:1-39). Like Christ, they identified themselves with God's sinful people and prayed for them (Ezra 9:6-15; Nehemiah 1:4-11; John 17:1-26).

7:12 The "king of kings" title used by Ezra to the Persian monarch was common court language of the time. God's title as the true king of kings is also implicit in the book of Ezra and explicit elsewhere in Scripture (see Daniel 2:37; Revelation 17:14; 19:16).

7:14 Whereas Cyrus commissioned the first returnees to rebuild the Temple, Artaxerxes commissioned Ezra "to conduct an inquiry" regarding the spiritual condition of the people—in other words, rebuild the community.

7:18 Conformity to God's will is a major theme in the rest of the book because all that is done in this restoration program is authorized by God, which is one of the main themes of Ezra.

to 7,500 pounds* of silver, 500 bushels* of wheat, 550 gallons of wine, 550 gallons
of olive oil,* and an unlimited supply of salt. 23Be careful to provide whatever the God
of heaven demands for His Temple, for why should we risk bringing God's anger
against the realm of the king and his sons? 24I also decree that no priest, Levite,
singer, gatekeeper, Temple servant, or other worker in this Temple of God will be
required to pay tribute, customs, or tolls of any kind.'
25"And you, Ezra, are to use the wisdom your God has given you to appoint
magistrates and judges who know your God's laws to govern all the people in the
province west of the Euphrates River. Teach the law to anyone who does not know it.
26Anyone who refuses to obey the law of your God and the law of the king will be
punished immediately, either by death, banishment, confiscation of goods, or
imprisonment."

7:25 Exod 18:21-25 Deut 16:18 Ezra 7:6, 10

7:26 Ezra 6:11-12

EZRA PRAISES THE LORD

27Praise the LORD, the God of our ancestors, who made the king want to beautify the Tem-
ple of the LORD in Jerusalem! 28And praise Him for demonstrating such unfailing love to

7:27 Ezra 6:22

7:28 Ezra 9:9

7:22a Aramaic *100 talents* [3,400 kilograms]. 7:22b Aramaic *100 cors* [18.2 kiloliters]. 7:22c Aramaic *100 baths* [2.1 kiloliters] *of wine, 100 baths of olive oil.*

▶ SALVATION

7:28 Thank God for the victory. When Ezra saw the mission he put before the king succeed, his reaction was to praise God for His unfailing love. He didn't pat himself on the back, but he moved from personal success to personal intimacy with God. We pray fervently before we step out in faith, but once the situation is over we sometimes forget it was God, not our efforts, that brought success. Make a practice of praising God for each event in which you have seen His help. (***See Salvation***> *Receiving> Results> Works> Have the glory and praise of God as their object,* TopicGuide page A23.)

MY RESPONSE TO GOD

Where Is Your Bible?

EZRA 7:25

We've all misplaced our keys. If you have toddlers in your home, anything can disappear! But what if everyone, even ministers, lost their Bibles—for 50 years?

That's what happened during the dark decades before the ministries of Ezra and Nehemiah (450 BC). During their years in exile, most Jewish people had forgotten God's Word, their culture, and even how to read Hebrew. But in 438 BC, many years after King Cyrus of Persia had decreed that Jews could return to their land, a renewal and revival began, and eventually God's people recovered His Word.

After the Temple was rebuilt, Ezra studied the law carefully (Ezra 7:10). He then began to reeducate the Jews. He stood before the people and taught them from the Scripture. The Levites helped translate and interpret. For the first time in many years, God's covenant people heard God's will for their lives (Nehemiah 8:8; Ezra 6:18).

Many of us have forgotten the Bible, too. We have not searched God's Word for His will in 5, 10, even 50 years, so we hardly know how to respond to it.

Commit to connecting to the Bible in such a way that you don't need to actually have it in your hands. Receive God's Word eagerly through reading, meditation, prayerful study, and memorization. Then even if you misplace your Bible, you will still have it with you—written on your heart.

me by honoring me before the king, his council, and all his mighty nobles! I felt encour-
8:1 Ezra 7:7 aged because the gracious hand of the LORD my God was on me. And I gathered some of
the leaders of Israel to return with me to Jerusalem.

EXILES WHO RETURNED WITH EZRA

8 Here is a list of the family leaders and the genealogies of those who came with me
from Babylon during the reign of King Artaxerxes:

2 From the family of Phinehas: Gershom.
From the family of Ithamar: Daniel.
From the family of David: Hattush, 3 a descendant of Shecaniah.
8:3 Ezra 2:3 From the family of Parosh: Zechariah and 150 other men were registered.
4 From the family of Pahath-moab: Eliehoenai son of Zerahiah and 200 other men.
5 From the family of Zattu*: Shecaniah son of Jahaziel and 300 other men.
6 From the family of Adin: Ebed son of Jonathan and 50 other men.
7 From the family of Elam: Jeshaiah son of Athaliah and 70 other men.
8 From the family of Shephatiah: Zebadiah son of Michael and 80 other men.
9 From the family of Joab: Obadiah son of Jehiel and 218 other men.
10 From the family of Bani*: Shelomith son of Josiphiah and 160 other men.
11 From the family of Bebai: Zechariah son of Bebai and 28 other men.
12 From the family of Azgad: Johanan son of Hakkatan and 110 other men.
13 From the family of Adonikam, who came later*: Eliphelet, Jeuel, Shemaiah, and
60 other men.
14 From the family of Bigvai: Uthai, Zaccur,* and 70 other men.

EZRA'S JOURNEY TO JERUSALEM

15 I assembled the exiles at the Ahava Canal, and we camped there for three days while I
8:15 Ezra 8:21, 31 went over the lists of the people and the priests who had arrived. I found that not one Le-
vite had volunteered to come along. 16 So I sent for Eliezer, Ariel, Shemaiah, Elnathan, Ja-
rib, Elnathan, Nathan, Zechariah, and Meshullam, who were leaders of the people. I also
sent for Joiarib and Elnathan, who were men of discernment. 17 I sent them to Iddo, the
8:17 Ezra 2:43-54 leader of the Levites at Casiphia, to ask him and his relatives and the Temple servants to
send us ministers for the Temple of God at Jerusalem.
18 Since the gracious hand of our God was on us, they sent us a man named Sherebiah,
along with eighteen of his sons and brothers. He was a very astute man and a descendant
of Mahli, who was a descendant of Levi son of Israel.* 19 They also sent Hashabiah, together
with Jeshaiah from the descendants of Merari, and twenty of his sons and brothers, 20 and
8:20 Ezra 2:43 220 Temple servants. The Temple servants were assistants to the Levites—a group of Tem-
ple workers first instituted by King David and his officials. They were all listed by name.
21 And there by the Ahava Canal, I gave orders for all of us to fast and humble ourselves

8:21 2 Chr 20:3 Ezra 8:15, 31 Ps 27:11

8:5 As in some Greek manuscripts (see also 1 Esdras 8:32); Hebrew lacks *Zattu.* 8:10 As in some Greek manuscripts (see also 1 Esdras 8:36); Hebrew lacks *Bani.* 8:13 Or *who were the last of his family.* 8:14 As in Greek and Syriac versions and an alternate reading of the Masoretic Text; the other alternate reads *Zabbud.* 8:18 *Israel* is the name that God gave to Jacob.

8:1-12 Not all the exiles returned in response to the decree of Cyrus in 538 BC. With Ezra, a second but smaller group returned about 80 years after the first return.

8:18-20 Ezra always ascribed his success to God's providential control (see Ezra 7:6). God's gracious support legitimized Ezra's actions. Just as the Lord had stirred the hearts of Cyrus (Ezra 1:1), the first returnees (Ezra 1:5), and Artaxerxes (Ezra 7:27), so His gracious hand moved this company of Levites to accept Ezra's daring call.

▸ WORSHIP
8:21 Preparing for the journey. When we get up in the morning, we wash, put on clothes, and generally prepare ourselves to meet the day—at least physically. The people, led by Ezra, prepared themselves for the journey ahead by fasting and praying. When we undertake something for God, we also need to prepare thoroughly. Fasting and prayer is an excellent way to take your eyes off the difficulties of the task and fix them on God's magnificent power and wisdom. When you begin a project with this kind of preparation, you will often find the situation much easier and more joyful. Prepare yourself spiritually for your future. (***See Worship****> OT> Fasting and Prayer> Fasting> Occasions> Return from exile,* TopicGuide page A26.)

before our God. We prayed that He would give us a safe journey and protect us, our children, and our goods as we traveled. 22For I was ashamed to ask the king for soldiers and horsemen* to accompany us and protect us from enemies along the way. After all, we had told the king, "Our God's hand of protection is on all who worship Him, but His fierce anger rages against those who abandon Him." 23So we fasted and earnestly prayed that our God would take care of us, and He heard our prayer.

24I appointed twelve leaders of the priests—Sherebiah, Hashabiah, and ten other priests—25to be in charge of transporting the silver, the gold, the gold bowls, and the other items that the king, his council, his officials, and all the people of Israel had presented for the Temple of God. 26I weighed the treasure as I gave it to them and found the totals to be as follows:

24 tons* of silver,
7,500 pounds* of silver articles,
7,500 pounds of gold,
27 20 gold bowls, equal in value to 1,000 gold coins,*
2 fine articles of polished bronze, as precious as gold.

28And I said to these priests, "You and these treasures have been set apart as holy to the LORD. This silver and gold is a voluntary offering to the LORD, the God of our ancestors. 29Guard these treasures well until you present them to the leading priests, the Levites, and the leaders of Israel, who will weigh them at the storerooms of the LORD's Temple in Jerusalem." 30So the priests and the Levites accepted the task of transporting these treasures of silver and gold to the Temple of our God in Jerusalem.

31We broke camp at the Ahava Canal on April 19* and started off to Jerusalem. And the gracious hand of our God protected us and saved us from enemies and bandits along the way. 32So we arrived safely in Jerusalem, where we rested for three days.

33On the fourth day after our arrival, the silver, gold, and other valuables were weighed at the Temple of our God and entrusted to Meremoth son of Uriah the priest and to Eleazar son of Phinehas, along with Jozabad son of Jeshua and Noadiah son of Binnui—both of whom were Levites. 34Everything was accounted for by number and weight, and the total weight was officially recorded.

35Then the exiles who had come out of captivity sacrificed burnt offerings to the God of Israel. They presented twelve bulls for all the people of Israel, as well as ninety-six rams

Isa 58:3, 5
8:22 2 Chr 15:2; Ezra 7:6, 9, 28
8:23 2 Chr 33:13
8:25 Ezra 7:15-16
8:28 Lev 21:6-8; 22:2-3; Isa 52:11
8:29 Ezra 8:33-34
8:31 Ezra 7:9
8:32 Neh 2:11
8:33 Ezra 8:30
8:35 Ezra 2:1; 6:17

8:22 Or *charioteers*. **8:26a** Hebrew *650 talents* [22 metric tons]. **8:26b** Hebrew *100 talents* [3,400 kilograms]; also in 8:26c. **8:27** Hebrew *1,000 darics,* about 19 pounds or 8.6 kilograms in weight. **8:31** Hebrew *on the twelfth day of the first month,* of the ancient Hebrew lunar calendar. This day was April 19, 458 B.C.; also see note on 6:15.

▶ WORSHIP

8:23 A hunger for God. Ezra and the other travelers were in a difficult spot—they worried that the journey would be unsafe for their children, but they had just finished bragging about how God could protect them from anything. Their prayers became serious, and when that happens, God's people join fasting with prayer. Fasting helps us put aside our daily distractions and concentrate solely on God. Fasting allows us to spend more time in prayer. It's a time to emphasize our spiritual dependence on God rather than our physical dependence on food. Undertake a fast and see how this spiritual discipline can lead you to a deeper prayer life. (***See Worship****> OT> Fasting and Prayer> Fasting> Occasions> Fasting as a means to receive God's favor,* TopicGuide page A26.)

8:26-27 The total listed contributions to the Temple are enormous, such that some have doubted the accuracy of the list. The Persian kings were, however, known for their great wealth and generosity toward the religions of subject peoples; there were also wealthy Jewish families in Babylon by this time who may also have contributed.

▶ HOLINESS

8:28 A holy vessel. Just as the Old Testament priests set apart treasures to be used in God's service, God wants us to set apart our bodies as holy vessels for Him to use in His service. These Temple utensils were a freewill offering to God, given with a heart of gratitude and thanksgiving. That's how we are to offer ourselves to God. Open yourself up to being totally filled with God. (***See Holiness****> Set Apart> Religious Service> The Temple and its articles,* TopicGuide page A40.)

8:32 The theme of three days of rest is repeated throughout Scripture, including Nehemiah's rest (Nehemiah 2:11), the Israelites' rest (Joshua 3:1-2), Jesus' three days in the tomb (1 Corinthians 15:3-4), and Jonah's three days in the belly of the giant fish (Jonah 1:17).

and seventy-seven male lambs. They also offered twelve male goats as a sin offering. All
8:36 this was given as a burnt offering to the LORD. 36The king's decrees were delivered to his
Ezra 7:21 highest officers and the governors of the province west of the Euphrates River,* who then
cooperated by supporting the people and the Temple of God.

EZRA'S PRAYER CONCERNING INTERMARRIAGE

9 When these things had been done, the Jewish leaders came to me and said, "Many of
9:1 the people of Israel, and even some of the priests and Levites, have not kept them-
Exod 23:28 Lev 18:24-30 selves separate from the other peoples living in the land. They have taken up the detestable
Deut 20:17 practices of the Canaanites, Hittites, Perizzites, Jebusites, Ammonites, Moabites, Egyptians,
and Amorites. 2For the men of Israel have married women from these people and have
9:2 taken them as wives for their sons. So the holy race has become polluted by these mixed
Exod 34:16 marriages. Worse yet, the leaders and officials have led the way in this outrage."
3When I heard this, I tore my cloak and my shirt, pulled hair from my head and beard,
9:3 and sat down utterly shocked. 4Then all who trembled at the words of the God of Israel
Neh 1:4 came and sat with me because of this outrage committed by the returned exiles. And I sat
9:4 Exod 29:38-39 there utterly appalled until the time of the evening sacrifice.
5At the time of the sacrifice, I stood up from where I had sat in mourning with my clothes
torn. I fell to my knees and lifted my hands to the LORD my God. 6I prayed,

9:5 Exod 9:29, 33 "O my God, I am utterly ashamed; I blush to lift up my face to You. For our sins are
9:6 piled higher than our heads, and our guilt has reached to the heavens. 7From the
2 Chr 28:9 Rev 18:5 days of our ancestors until now, we have been steeped in sin. That is why we and
our kings and our priests have been at the mercy of the pagan kings of the land. We
have been killed, captured, robbed, and disgraced, just as we are today.
8"But now we have been given a brief moment of grace, for the LORD our God has
allowed a few of us to survive as a remnant. He has given us security in this holy
place. Our God has brightened our eyes and granted us some relief from our slavery.
9For we were slaves, but in His unfailing love our God did not abandon us in our
slavery. Instead, He caused the kings of Persia to treat us favorably. He revived us
9:9 so we could rebuild the Temple of our God and repair its ruins. He has given us a
Exod 1:11-14 Neh 9:36-37 protective wall in Judah and Jerusalem.
Ps 106:45-46 10"And now, O our God, what can we say after all of this? For once again we have
abandoned Your commands! 11Your servants the prophets warned us when they
said, 'The land you are entering to possess is totally defiled by the detestable

8:36 Hebrew *the province beyond the river.*

9:1 The issue raised by the Jewish leaders was not simply about racial separation, but religious separation, as the following verses indicate (Ezra 9:10-12; see also 4:3) and the New Testament confirms (1 Corinthians 7:39). See Exodus 34:10-16 and Deuteronomy 7:1-4 for the original prohibitions against intermarriage.

9:1–10:44 Having set the Temple into fuller operation, Ezra turned to the purification of the returnees. These chapters divide into two sections: Ezra's response to widespread intermarriage with unbelievers (Ezra 9:1-15) and the people's reaction to Ezra (10:1-44).

9:3-4 Ezra's first response to corporate sin wasn't anger or judgment, but grief and sadness. Tearing a garment or pulling out hair demonstrated grief in ancient times (2 Samuel 13:19). Oddly, Nehemiah is recorded as pulling out the hair of the offenders (Nehemiah 13:25). Perhaps both point to their frustration over externals, such as hairstyles, that had been borrowed from surrounding cultures.

▸ WORSHIP
9:5 Expressing the depth of our prayer. When Ezra expressed deep sorrow before the Lord, he knelt and lifted his hands in prayer. Kneeling helps us express the depth of our repentance or sorrow in prayer. It shows that we are coming before the almighty God, who deserves honor from those He created. By kneeling in prayer, we show that we mean business with God. (***See Worship****> OT> Posture> Kneeling,* TopicGuide page A28.)

9:8 Justice demanded the absolute end of the Jewish people, but grace preserved a remnant. Through this remnant the Messiah would come, and redemption would be accomplished (see Isaiah 1:9; 10:20-22). God would continue to work through a remnant of godly Jews (Romans 11:1-5). The phrase "brightened our eyes" is an idiom for increased vigor (Psalm 13:3; see also 1 Samuel 14:25-30).

practices of the people living there. From one end to the other, the land is filled with
corruption. 12 Don't let your daughters marry their sons! Don't take their daughters as 9:12
wives for your sons. Don't ever promote the peace and prosperity of those nations. If Deut 7:3
you follow these instructions, you will be strong and will enjoy the good things the
land produces, and you will leave this prosperity to your children forever.'
13 "Now we are being punished because of our wickedness and our great guilt. But
we have actually been punished far less than we deserve, for You, our God, have
allowed some of us to survive as a remnant. 14 But even so, we are again breaking 9:14
Your commands and intermarrying with people who do these detestable things. Deut 9:7-8, 13-14
Won't Your anger be enough to destroy us, so that even this little remnant no longer
survives? 15 O LORD, God of Israel, You are just. We come before You in our guilt as 9:15
nothing but an escaped remnant, though in such a condition none of us can stand in Neh 9:33-34 Ps 130:3
Your presence." Dan 9:7-11

THE PEOPLE CONFESS THEIR SIN

10 While Ezra prayed and made this confession, weeping and lying face down on the 10:1
ground in front of the Temple of God, a very large crowd of people from Israel— 2 Chr 20:9
men, women, and children—gathered and wept bitterly with him. 2 Then Shecaniah son of Dan 9:20
Jehiel, a descendant of Elam, said to Ezra, "We have been unfaithful to our God, for we 10:2 Ezra 9:2; 10:11
have married these pagan women of the land. But in spite of this there is hope for Israel. Neh 13:27
3 Let us now make a covenant with our God to divorce our pagan wives and to send them 10:3 Deut 7:2-3
away with their children. We will follow the advice given by you and by the others who re- 2 Chr 34:31
spect the commands of our God. Let it be done according to the Law of God. 4 Get up, for it
is your duty to tell us how to proceed in setting things straight. We are behind you, so be
strong and take action."
5 So Ezra stood up and demanded that the leaders of the priests and the Levites and all 10:5 Neh 5:12; 13:25
the people of Israel swear that they would do as Shecaniah had said. And they all swore 10:6
a solemn oath. 6 Then Ezra left the front of the Temple of God and went to the room of Deut 9:18

▸ WORSHIP

9:15 Repentance is necessary. Is your heart sorrowful at seeing the sin around you? Our society is rampant with the most atrocious deeds and attitudes. Like Ezra, we need to come before God and plead for our nation, our state, and our city. None of us, without exception, could stand before God in our own righteousness apart from Christ. We are all guilty of sin. But thank God that He has offered us forgiveness, and we can approach Him because of Christ's death on the cross. In grateful response to His grace, we should continually repent of the sins that we continue to commit. This repentance will lead to a deeper fellowship with God and joy in our heart. (***See Worship****> OT> Repentance> Examples> Ezra intercedes for the exiles,* TopicGuide page A29.)

▸ WORSHIP

10:1 Practice repentance. Repentance opens the door for God to cleanse the heart. But true repentance is more than just saying, "I'm sorry," and then going on your way. True repentance means feeling genuine sorrow for sin and its effect on others. True repentance means throwing yourself at God's mercy and asking Him to forgive you, specifically naming what you have done. Practice repentance on a consistent basis to keep your fellowship with God deep and personal. (***See Worship****> OT> Repentance> Nature> Contriteness before the Law ensures God's blessings,* TopicGuide page A29.)

10:1-44 Previously leaders had set the pace for sin (see Ezra 9:2). Here Ezra set the pace for repentance, not by exhorting the people to mourn but by mourning himself. The greatest leaders in the Bible have been people marked by repentance (for instance, David in Psalm 51 and Josiah in 2 Kings 22).

10:3 This was not the making of an entirely new covenant, but the renewal of the Mosaic covenant in terms of an oath (see Ezra 10:5) to keep the stipulation regarding intermarriage (see Deuteronomy 7:3; see also Jeremiah 34:8-9 for a similar covenant renewal). The Hebrew for "divorce" used here is not the word that is translated "divorce" elsewhere—it is only used here. Moreover, the Hebrew used in Ezra 10:2 for "married" is not that normally used for marriage and is used in the same way only in Nehemiah 13:23 in a similar situation. Also, the word for "pagan women" is used in Proverbs for harlots and prostitutes. All these choices of wording by the author suggest that he did not regard the unions as legitimate marriages and therefore the sending away not as true divorces.

10:5 The reforms that Ezra and Nehemiah brought to the nation find their ultimate fulfillment in Christ. Christ also called God's covenant people to turn back to the Lord and His law (Matthew 5:17-19). Through Christ's death and resurrection and the empowerment of the Spirit, Christ cleanses those who believe in Him from unrighteousness and leads them into faithful living (1 John 1:7-9) so that they may inherit the blessings of God (Matthew 25:34-40; Romans 6:1-23; 1 Peter 3:9-12).

10:6 A total fast was rare (see Deuteronomy 9:18). The fast indicates that Ezra did not believe the exiles were safe from the covenant curses on the basis of their oath alone.

Jehohanan son of Eliashib. He spent the night* there without eating or drinking any-
thing. He was still in mourning because of the unfaithfulness of the returned exiles.
[7]Then a proclamation was made throughout Judah and Jerusalem that all the exiles
should come to Jerusalem. [8]Those who failed to come within three days would, if the lead-
ers and elders so decided, forfeit all their property and be expelled from the assembly of
the exiles.
10:9 [9]Within three days, all the people of Judah and Benjamin had gathered in Jerusalem.
1 Sam 12:17-18 This took place on December 19,* and all the people were sitting in the square before the
Ezra 9:4 Temple of God. They were trembling both because of the seriousness of the matter and
because it was raining. [10]Then Ezra the priest stood and said to them: "You have commit-
10:11 ted a terrible sin. By marrying pagan women, you have increased Israel's guilt. [11]So now
Lev 26:40 confess your sin to the LORD, the God of your ancestors, and do what He demands. Sepa-
Ezra 10:3 rate yourselves from the people of the land and from these pagan women."
[12]Then the whole assembly raised their voices and answered, "Yes, you are right; we
must do as you say!" [13]Then they added, "This isn't something that can be done in a day
or two, for many of us are involved in this extremely sinful affair. And this is the rainy sea-
10:14 son, so we cannot stay out here much longer. [14]Let our leaders act on behalf of us all. Let
2 Chr 29:10; 30:8 everyone who has a pagan wife come at a scheduled time, accompanied by the leaders
and judges of his city, so that the fierce anger of our God concerning this affair may be
turned away from us."
[15]Only Jonathan son of Asahel and Jahzeiah son of Tikvah opposed this course of ac-
tion, and they were supported by Meshullam and Shabbethai the Levite.
[16]So this was the plan they followed. Ezra selected leaders to represent their families,
designating each of the representatives by name. On December 29,* the leaders sat down
to investigate the matter. [17]By March 27, the first day of the new year,* they had finished
dealing with all the men who had married pagan wives.

THOSE GUILTY OF INTERMARRIAGE

[18]These are the priests who had married pagan wives:
From the family of Jeshua son of Jehozadak* and his brothers: Maaseiah, Eliezer, Jarib,
10:19 and Gedaliah. [19]They vowed to divorce their wives, and they each acknowledged
Lev 5:15 their guilt by offering a ram as a guilt offering.
[20]From the family of Immer: Hanani and Zebadiah.
[21]From the family of Harim: Maaseiah, Elijah, Shemaiah, Jehiel, and Uzziah.
[22]From the family of Pashhur: Elioenai, Maaseiah, Ishmael, Nethanel, Jozabad, and Elasah.

[23]These are the Levites who were guilty: Jozabad, Shimei, Kelaiah (also called Kelita),
Pethahiah, Judah, and Eliezer.

[24]This is the singer who was guilty: Eliashib.

These are the gatekeepers who were guilty: Shallum, Telem, and Uri.

10:6 As in parallel text at 1 Esdras 9:2; Hebrew reads *He went.* **10:9** Hebrew *on the twentieth day of the ninth month,* of the ancient Hebrew lunar calendar. This day was December 19, 458 B.C.; also see note on 6:15. **10:16** Hebrew *On the first day of the tenth month,* of the ancient Hebrew lunar calendar. This day was December 29, 458 B.C.; also see note on 6:15. **10:17** Hebrew *By the first day of the first month,* of the ancient Hebrew lunar calendar. This day was March 27, 457 B.C.; also see note on 6:15. **10:18** Hebrew *Jozadak,* a variant spelling of Jehozadak.

10:9 Why were the people "trembling . . . because it was raining"? Most likely it was because torrential rains with much lightning and thunder was sometimes a sign of God's wrath (see Psalm 83:15; Ezekiel 13:10-13; Isaiah 24:20). It was highly unusual to be distressed by normal rain, which was regarded as a blessing (see Deuteronomy 11:13-15; 28:12).

10:18-44 From this list of those guilty of intermarriage it is evident that the individual who sins cannot find sanctuary within the larger community (see Deuteronomy 29:19-21).

[25]These are the other people of Israel who were guilty:
From the family of Parosh: Ramiah, Izziah, Malkijah, Mijamin, Eleazar, Hashabiah,* and
Benaiah.
[26]From the family of Elam: Mattaniah, Zechariah, Jehiel, Abdi, Jeremoth, and Elijah.
[27]From the family of Zattu: Elioenai, Eliashib, Mattaniah, Jeremoth, Zabad, and Aziza.
[28]From the family of Bebai: Jehohanan, Hananiah, Zabbai, and Athlai.
[29]From the family of Bani: Meshullam, Malluch, Adaiah, Jashub, Sheal, and Jeremoth.
[30]From the family of Pahath-moab: Adna, Kelal, Benaiah, Maaseiah, Mattaniah, Bezalel,
Binnui, and Manasseh.
[31]From the family of Harim: Eliezer, Ishijah, Malkijah, Shemaiah, Shimeon, [32]Benjamin,
Malluch, and Shemariah.
[33]From the family of Hashum: Mattenai, Mattattah, Zabad, Eliphelet, Jeremai, Manasseh,
and Shimei.
[34]From the family of Bani: Maadai, Amram, Uel, [35]Benaiah, Bedeiah, Keluhi, [36]Vaniah,
Meremoth, Eliashib, [37]Mattaniah, Mattenai, and Jaasu.
[38]From the family of Binnui*: Shimei, [39]Shelemiah, Nathan, Adaiah, [40]Macnadebai, Sha-
shai, Sharai, [41]Azarel, Shelemiah, Shemariah, [42]Shallum, Amariah, and Joseph.
[43]From the family of Nebo: Jeiel, Mattithiah, Zabad, Zebina, Jaddai, Joel, and Benaiah.

[44]Each of these men had a pagan wife, and some even had children by these wives.* **10:44** Ezra 10:3

10:25 As in parallel text at 1 Esdras 9:26; Hebrew reads *Malkijah.* **10:37-38** As in Greek version; Hebrew reads *Jaasu,* [38]*Bani, Binnui.* **10:44** Or *and they sent them away with their children.* The meaning of the Hebrew is uncertain.

NEHEMIAH

PURPOSE

To record how God kept His promise to bring His exiled people back to Jerusalem (Jeremiah 29:14). Nehemiah also shows how God protected His people during the rebuilding of Jerusalem's city wall.

Bookstores are filled with volumes on the subjects of leadership and management. But one of the best small books ever penned on the subject is missing from those collections. Yet, it's been available in Scripture for centuries.

Nehemiah was a gifted leader. Though the exiles who returned from Persia under Zerubbabel had been in Jerusalem nearly a hundred years, the city was still without walls. Nehemiah, still in Persia, wept when he heard this news. As a member of King Artaxerxes' court, he petitioned the king for permission to return and rebuild the gates and walls of the city (Nehemiah 2:7-9). Permission was granted, and Nehemiah did in fifty-two days what hadn't been done in a century: He rebuilt the walls around Jerusalem, which gave the city a measure of security from her enemies. He went on to implement civil and social reforms among the returned exiles, to bring life in post-exilic Jerusalem into agreement with the laws of God.

DISCOVER GOD IN NEHEMIAH

Nehemiah is a book about physical, political, social, and spiritual building and transformation, all of which is consistent with the character of God.

Progress: God is a builder and transformer. And in a world devastated by sin, there is plenty of building to do. In Jerusalem, the walls and gates were burned and torn down, just as Nebuchadnezzar had left them. To a godly man like Nehemiah, destruction was not consistent with the blessing of God. After praying and fasting for several days, he became convinced that God was calling him to turn destruction into deliverance. God honored his desire and gave him favor with the king—and the gates and walls were rebuilt. Rebuilding the walls of a small city is a micro-example of the building God is doing today: His church (Matthew 16:18); His kingdom (Matthew 13:31-33); individuals to Christ-likeness (Romans 8:29); and an eternal habitation for the saints (John 14:2-3). With God, there is no neutrality; we're either working with Him or against Him (Luke 11:23).

Order: The reforms instituted by Ezra and Nehemiah upon their return from Persia presuppose one thing: a preferred way of doing things. In short, the kingdom of God is not everyone doing "whatever seem[s] right in their own eyes" (Judges 21:25). Some people do not like order of any sort, believing order is little more than a constraint upon the creativity of the human spirit. But creation itself suggests that without order in the universe and in our world, there would be no life at all. It takes firmness and resolve to bring the order of God to bear upon socially and civilly chaotic conditions. The direction and organization employed by Nehemiah to rebuild the city wall in less than two months reflected orderly thinking. And the stern measures employed by Nehemiah (Nehemiah 13:17-18, 21, 25), reminiscent of stern measures taken by another young Reformer a few centuries later (Mark 11:15-17), suggest that sometimes God uses disorder to bring about order—always His ultimate purpose.

GROWING THROUGH NEHEMIAH

The themes of practicality and spirituality are balanced beautifully in the book of Nehemiah:

Asking and Receiving: Nehemiah had no resources to accomplish his goal, but the king he served had everything he needed. Solution? He would ask for help. With a request couched in a prayer, Nehemiah asked and received (Nehemiah 2:4-5). It's possible that the walls of Jerusalem wouldn't have been rebuilt except for Nehemiah's boldness. How many goals go unfulfilled in our lives because we do not ask for what we need—either from God or from others (James 4:2)?

Sovereignty vs. Responsibility: The opponents of the Jews hounded them day and night as Nehemiah worked to get the walls around Jerusalem rebuilt. Nehemiah exercised the ideal balance between faith and works, between divine sovereignty and human responsibility: "But we prayed to our God and guarded the city day and night to protect ourselves" (Nehemiah 4:9). Praying and guarding: a balanced approach to kingdom building.

DISCOVERY VERSES

When our enemies and the surrounding nations heard about it, they were frightened and humiliated. They realized this work had been done with the help of our God.

(NEHEMIAH 6:16)

Leading by Example: In a day when the lifestyle of some ministry leaders might be confused with that of extravagant corporate CEO's, Nehemiah would probably stand out in the crowd. He led by example. In his 24/7 approach to wall-building, he was on the front line with his troops at all times: "During this time, none of us—not I, nor my relatives, nor my servants, nor the guards who were with me—ever took off our clothes. We carried our weapons with us at all times, even when we went for water" (Nehemiah 4:23). Nehemiah's dirty and thirsty troops probably worked as hard as they did because they saw their leader on the wall with them.

Accountability: Accountability means stepping forward and being counted. That's what eighty-four leaders in Jerusalem did when they signed a covenant renewal document drawn up by the Levites (Nehemiah 9:38–10:27). As a result of their willingness to be accountable, the rest of the people bound themselves to the same agreement (10:28-29). For things to change, someone has to step forward, count the cost and make a commitment. Accountability is the backbone of spiritual discipleship (Luke 14:25-33).

NEHEMIAH FACTS

Author: The first verse names Nehemiah as the author of the "memoirs" that follow. Consensus holds that Nehemiah wrote most of the book, with some sections possibly being compiled from other sources; an example is Nehemiah 7:5-73, the list of returning exiles.

Written to: Like Ezra, Nehemiah is written for all Israel in general, but for the returned community specifically, as evidence of the blessing of God in restoring the Jews to their land and to Jerusalem.

Date of writing: Probably in the latter years of the 5th century BC, after Nehemiah's second trip from Persia to Jerusalem.

Setting: The book of Nehemiah takes place first in exile in Persia, but then moves to Jerusalem.

OUTLINE

- **NEHEMIAH 1:1–7:3**—Return of Nehemiah and rebuilding of the wall
- **NEHEMIAH 7:4–13:31**—Return of the exiles and rebuilding the community

1:1 Neh 2:1; 10:1 **1** These are the memoirs of Nehemiah son of Hacaliah.

Esth 1:2 Dan 8:2

NEHEMIAH'S CONCERN FOR JERUSALEM

Zech 7:1 In late autumn, in the month of Kislev, in the twentieth year of King Artaxerxes' reign,* I
1:2 was at the fortress of Susa. 2 Hanani, one of my brothers, came to visit me with some other
Neh 7:2 men who had just arrived from Judah. I asked them about the Jews who had returned
there from captivity and about how things were going in Jerusalem.

1:3 3 They said to me, "Things are not going well for those who returned to the province of
Neh 2:3, 17; 7:6 Judah. They are in great trouble and disgrace. The wall of Jerusalem has been torn down,
and the gates have been destroyed by fire."

1:4 4 When I heard this, I sat down and wept. In fact, for days I mourned, fasted, and prayed
Ezra 9:3; 10:1 to the God of heaven. 5 Then I said,

1:5 Exod 20:6 "O LORD, God of heaven, the great and awesome God who keeps His covenant
Neh 4:14; 9:32 of unfailing love with those who love Him and obey His commands, 6 listen to
1:6 2 Chr 29:6 my prayer! Look down and see me praying night and day for Your people Israel.
Ezra 10:1 I confess that we have sinned against You. Yes, even my own family and I have
Dan 9:20 sinned! 7 We have sinned terribly by not obeying the commands, decrees, and
1:7 Deut 28:14 regulations that You gave us through Your servant Moses.

Dan 9:5 8 "Please remember what You told Your servant Moses: 'If you are unfaithful to
1:8 Me, I will scatter you among the nations. 9 But if you return to Me and obey My
Lev 26:33 commands and live by them, then even if you are exiled to the ends of the earth,
1:9 I will bring you back to the place I have chosen for My name to be honored.'

Deut 12:5; 30:2-4

1:1 Hebrew *In the month of Kislev of the twentieth year.* A number of dates in the book of Nehemiah can be cross-checked with dates in surviving Persian records and related accurately to our modern calendar. This month of the ancient Hebrew lunar calendar occurred within the months of November and December 446 B.C. The *twentieth year* probably refers to the reign of King Artaxerxes I; compare 2:1; 5:14.

1:1 Originally the book of Nehemiah was most likely a continuation of the book of Ezra. The name Nehemiah means "the Lord has comforted."

▸ CHURCH

1:2 The responsibility continues. In our transitory society, we get used to friends and family members moving away from us. Sometimes our Christian family—fellow believers in Christ—becomes separated. What is our responsibility when these loved ones are no longer near us? We can take an example from Nehemiah and keep informed about those who are living far away from us. We need to keep them in our prayers and strive to keep in touch with how they are doing. Continuing to invest ourselves in others' lives helps maintain strong bonds and deepens support among the body of Christ. (***See Church****> Who> From Every People> The community of the saved,* TopicGuide page A48.)

1:2 Hanani is a variation of the name Hananiah, meaning "the Lord is gracious." A certain Hananiah who was head of Jewish affairs is mentioned in the Elephantine papyri (Aramaic texts discovered in a sixth century Jewish settlement in southern Egypt). This same Hanani is believed by some to have been the brother of Nehemiah (see Nehemiah 7:2).

▸ WORSHIP

1:4 Pray for the nations. Do you pay attention to national or international news? Nehemiah heard more international news than most due to his position in the royal court, and when he heard stories about his home, he listened even closer. The sad news about his home drove him to grief, which then drove him to God. Use the sad things in the daily news to turn you to God in prayer. Pray regularly for those things that deeply touch you, and follow the story to see how God is answering your prayer. (***See Worship****> OT> Fasting and Prayer> Fasting> Occasions> Nehemiah fasted when he heard of the state of Jerusalem,* TopicGuide page A26.)

1:4 Fasting is here connected both with mourning (see 1 Samuel 31:13) and with making a request of God (see Ezra 8:21; Isaiah 58:3).

1:5 In this address Nehemiah acknowledged both the transcendence and immanence of Israel's God. The true God is not only far above His people as the "God of heaven," He is also near His people as the God of the covenant. Jesus Christ is Emmanuel, "God is with us" (Matthew 1:23; Isaiah 7:14).

1:7 The covenant relationship between God and His people made blessings and curses dependent on the faithfulness of the people. The Lord would have kept His promises if Israel had obeyed His commands (see Nehemiah 1:5), but Israel had failed to obey His commands, and so they were sent into exile (see Ezra 9:7).

1:8 Does God forget things? Asking God to remember His promises is a common petition in Scripture (see Deuteronomy 9:27; Jeremiah 14:21; Psalm 132:1), particularly in Nehemiah (5:19; 6:14; 13:14, 22, 29, 31). Such pleas do not indicate that God forgets things, for He knows everything. Instead, it is simply a passionate plea for God to do what He has promised.

10"The people You rescued by Your great power and strong hand are Your
servants. 11O Lord, please hear my prayer! Listen to the prayers of those of us who
delight in honoring You. Please grant me success today by making the king favorable
to me.* Put it into his heart to be kind to me."

In those days I was the king's cup-bearer.

NEHEMIAH GOES TO JERUSALEM

2 Early the following spring, in the month of Nisan,* during the twentieth year of King
Artaxerxes' reign, I was serving the king his wine. I had never before appeared sad in
his presence. 2So the king asked me, "Why are you looking so sad? You don't look sick to
me. You must be deeply troubled."

Then I was terrified, 3but I replied, "Long live the king! How can I not be sad? For the city
where my ancestors are buried is in ruins, and the gates have been destroyed by fire."

4The king asked, "Well, how can I help you?"

With a prayer to the God of heaven, 5I replied, "If it please the king, and if you are
pleased with me, your servant, send me to Judah to rebuild the city where my ancestors
are buried."

6The king, with the queen sitting beside him, asked, "How long will you be gone? When
will you return?" After I told him how long I would be gone, the king agreed to my request.

7I also said to the king, "If it please the king, let me have letters addressed to the gover-
nors of the province west of the Euphrates River,* instructing them to let me travel safely
through their territories on my way to Judah. 8And please give me a letter addressed to
Asaph, the manager of the king's forest, instructing him to give me timber. I will need it to
make beams for the gates of the Temple fortress, for the city walls, and for a house for my-
self." And the king granted these requests, because the gracious hand of God was on me.

1:10 Exod 32:11 Deut 9:29
1:11 Gen 40:21 Neh 1:6
2:1 Ezra 7:1 Neh 1:1, 11
2:2 Prov 15:13
2:3 Neh 1:3 Dan 2:4
2:4 Neh 1:4
2:6 Neh 13:6
2:7 Ezra 7:21; 8:36 Neh 2:9
2:8 Eccl 2:5-6

1:11 Hebrew *today in the sight of this man.* 2:1 Hebrew *In the month of Nisan.* This month of the ancient Hebrew lunar calendar occurred within the months of April and May 445 B.C. 2:7 Hebrew *the province beyond the river;* also in 2:9.

▸ MINISTRY
1:10 We are rescued. Nehemiah believed in God's power to rescue His people. God still performs miracles on behalf of those who love and serve Him. We can ask for great and mighty things from Him, yet we need to accept His answer as His will. Whether we are praying for some corporate request on behalf of a group or a private request of our own, God will use His mighty power on our behalf. Do not be afraid to pray big prayers. (***See Ministry***> *Great Commission> Risk> Stepping outside of your "comfort zone,"* TopicGuide page A56.)

1:11 The cup-bearer was a favored member of the royal court. His responsibility was to select wine for the king (see 2:1) and safeguard it from poison. Such free access to the king entailed prestige and influence at the royal court.

2:1-8 God's authorization of Nehemiah's return was affirmed by the king's response.

2:2 Why was Nehemiah afraid? Perhaps he feared the king's wrath (see Proverbs 16:14), either because he was sad on a festive occasion or because he was about to ask the king to reverse a previous decision (see Ezra 4:21). Perhaps Nehemiah feared he would fail in his attempt to gain permission to rebuild Jerusalem. Regardless, he admitted his fear and went forward with his divine mission.

▸ MINISTRY
2:4 Prayer in the midst. Nehemiah didn't wait to pray until he had a moment in private; he prayed as he went. In the midst of his dialogue with the king, he sent up a prayer for help. We, too, can come before God's throne as we are "going along." If you are speaking to someone and need wisdom in your answer, breathe a silent prayer. Any time or place, you can access God's throne and receive His help. The key to answered prayer is faith, not location. (***See Ministry***> *Transformation> Fill and Subdue> Influencing every sphere of life,* TopicGuide page A57.)

2:5 Rebuilding the city is one aspect of rebuilding the "house of God," a major theme in Ezra-Nehemiah (See Introduction to Ezra, TopicGuide page 823.).

2:7-8 Here the scope of the building project becomes clear: fortress, walls, and a small governor's palace. Nehemiah's success was due to God's gracious character (see Ezra 7:6), which demonstrated His approval of Nehemiah's role in the broader restoration program under Ezra and Zerubbabel.

▸ PURPOSE
2:8 God's gracious hand. God will graciously answer our requests when we do His will. He often calls us to step out in faith, and then He rewards us for taking the step. Nehemiah took a chance by approaching the king; consequently God's blessing was upon him. What do you desire to do for God but are afraid to undertake? God will be with you just as He was with Nehemiah. Take the story of Nehemiah as your encouragement to act in faith knowing that God will be with you. (***See Purpose***> *God's Means> Human Choice> Bringing our wills in subjection to God's will,* TopicGuide page A52.)

2:9 9When I came to the governors of the province west of the Euphrates River, I delivered the
Ezra 8:22 Neh 2:7 king's letters to them. The king, I should add, had sent along army officers and horsemen* to
2:10 protect me. 10But when Sanballat the Horonite and Tobiah the Ammonite official heard of
Neh 2:19; 4:1-3 my arrival, they were very displeased that someone had come to help the people of Israel.

NEHEMIAH INSPECTS JERUSALEM'S WALL

11So I arrived in Jerusalem. Three days later, 12I slipped out during the night, taking only
a few others with me. I had not told anyone about the plans God had put in my heart for
2:13 Neh 1:3; 3:13 Jerusalem. We took no pack animals with us except the donkey I was riding. 13After dark I
2:14 went out through the Valley Gate, past the Jackal's Well,* and over to the Dung Gate to in-
2 Kgs 20:20 spect the broken walls and burned gates. 14Then I went to the Fountain Gate and to the
Neh 3:15 King's Pool, but my donkey couldn't get through the rubble. 15So, though it was still dark,
I went up the Kidron Valley* instead, inspecting the wall before I turned back and entered
again at the Valley Gate.

16The city officials did not know I had been out there or what I was doing, for I had not
yet said anything to anyone about my plans. I had not yet spoken to the Jewish leaders—
2:17 the priests, the nobles, the officials, or anyone else in the administration. 17But now I said
Neh 1:3 to them, "You know very well what trouble we are in. Jerusalem lies in ruins, and its gates
have been destroyed by fire. Let us rebuild the wall of Jerusalem and end this disgrace!"
18Then I told them about how the gracious hand of God had been on me, and about my
conversation with the king.

They replied at once, "Yes, let's rebuild the wall!" So they began the good work.

2:19 19But when Sanballat, Tobiah, and Geshem the Arab heard of our plan, they scoffed
Neh 6:6 contemptuously. "What are you doing? Are you rebelling against the king?" they asked.

2:20 Ezra 4:3 20I replied, "The God of heaven will help us succeed. We, His servants, will start rebuild-
Neh 2:4 ing this wall. But you have no share, legal right, or historic claim in Jerusalem."

REBUILDING THE WALL OF JERUSALEM

3:1 Neh 3:20, 32; 6:1; **3** Then Eliashib the high priest and the other priests started to rebuild at the Sheep
7:1; 12:39; 13:28 Jer 31:38 Gate. They dedicated it and set up its doors, building the wall as far as the Tower of

2:9 Or *charioteers.* 2:13 Or *Serpent's Well.* 2:15 Hebrew *the valley.*

2:10 Sanballat was governor of Samaria, the area immediately north of Judah. His name, Babylonian in origin, means "Sin (the moon god) gives life." It is likely, however, that Sanballat worshiped the God of Israel in some fashion (see 2 Kings 17:24-41), because his sons were named Deliah and Shelemiah, both of which contain a short form of "Yahweh." Tobiah was the governor of Ammon, the area east of Judah. His name means "the Lord is good," likely indicating that his parents worshiped the God of Israel, and perhaps he did too (see Nehemiah 6:17-18; 13:4). References to Nehemiah's enemies having "heard" will punctuate the rest of Nehemiah 1:1–7:3 like a refrain (see Nehemiah 2:19; 4:1; 4:5; 4:15; 6:1; 6:16). Each time, the conflict escalates until it is resolved in Nehemiah 6:16.

2:11 Nehemiah's decision was carefully considered. Nehemiah's three-day wait after arriving in Jerusalem compares with Ezra and his three-day wait (see Ezra 8:32). While Ezra acted publicly, Nehemiah acted secretly (note the emphasis on "had not told any one" in Nehemiah 2:12, 16).

2:11–7:3 Nehemiah devoted himself to building the walls of Jerusalem not only to bring political stability but also to create a holy city for the Temple of God. These chapters alternate between Nehemiah's efforts to rebuild (Nehemiah 2:11-18; 3:1-32; 4:15-23; 6:15–7:3) and the opposition he overcame (Nehemiah 2:19-20; 4:1-15; 5:1-19; 6:1-14). Similar tensions and resolutions occur throughout Ezra.

2:13 This section of Scripture gives us the most complete description of the walls and gates of Jerusalem from this time. Archaeologists who followed the steps of Nehemiah have uncovered gates from the Persian period. This evidence is among thousands of confirmed archeological finds that demonstrate the truths of Scripture.

2:17 Jerusalem had lain in ruins for almost 150 years. An earlier attempt to rebuild the wall had been stopped (see Ezra 4:7-23).

2:19 Geshem, the third opponent of Nehemiah, along with Sanballat and Tobiah (see Nehemiah 2:10). Geshem was probably an Arab chief controlling the area to the south of Judah. Nehemiah is pictured as virtually surrounded by opponents: Sanballat to the north, Tobiah to the east, and Geshem to the south (see Nehemiah 4:7-8).

3:1 The Sheep Gate was located at the northeast corner of the city (see John 5:2). The description in the following verses moves counterclockwise, returning to the Sheep Gate in Nehemiah 1:32.

3:1-32 The reconstruction of the wall proceeded with a list of various people responsible for different portions of the wall. The entire perimeter of the city was covered while underscoring the involvement of all the people of God (especially the laity) in the project.

the Hundred, which they dedicated, and the Tower of Hananel. 2People from the town of 3:2
Jericho worked next to them, and beyond them was Zaccur son of Imri. Neh 7:36
3The Fish Gate was built by the sons of Hassenaah. They laid the beams, set up its 3:3
doors, and installed its bolts and bars. 4Meremoth son of Uriah and grandson of Hakkoz Neh 12:39
repaired the next section of wall. Beside him were Meshullam son of Berekiah and grand-
son of Meshezabel, and then Zadok son of Baana. 5Next were the people from Tekoa,
though their leaders refused to work with the construction supervisors.
6The Old City Gate* was repaired by Joiada son of Paseah and Meshullam son of Beso- 3:6
deiah. They laid the beams, set up its doors, and installed its bolts and bars. 7Next to them Neh 12:39
were Melatiah from Gibeon, Jadon from Meronoth, people from Gibeon, and people from
Mizpah, the headquarters of the governor of the province west of the Euphrates River.*
8Next was Uzziel son of Harhaiah, a goldsmith by trade, who also worked on the wall. Be- 3:8
yond him was Hananiah, a manufacturer of perfumes. They left out a section of Jerusalem Neh 3:31-32; 12:38
as they built the Broad Wall.*
9Rephaiah son of Hur, the leader of half the district of Jerusalem, was next to them on 3:9
the wall. 10Next Jedaiah son of Harumaph repaired the wall across from his own house, Neh 3:12, 17
and next to him was Hattush son of Hashabneiah. 11Then came Malkijah son of Harim
and Hasshub son of Pahath-moab, who repaired another section of the wall and the Tower 3:11
of the Ovens. 12Shallum son of Hallohesh and his daughters repaired the next section. He Neh 12:38
was the leader of the other half of the district of Jerusalem. 3:12 Neh 3:9
13The Valley Gate was repaired by the people from Zanoah, led by Hanun. They set up 3:13
its doors and installed its bolts and bars. They also repaired the 1,500 feet* of wall to the Neh 2:13
Dung Gate.

3:6 Or *The Mishneh Gate,* or *The Jeshanah Gate.* 3:7 Hebrew *the province beyond the river.* 3:8 Or *They fortified Jerusalem up to the Broad Wall.* 3:13 Hebrew *1,000 cubits* [450 meters].

THE RESTORATION OF THE CITY WALLS
Nehemiah takes us on a counterclockwise tour around Jerusalem (beginning with the Sheep Gate). He describes for us each section, gate, and tower on the wall and who worked to rebuild it.

▸ ADOPTION
3:5 Working with the laborers. Have you ever worked on a church committee or with another group where the leadership stood aloof from the regular members when it came to the in-the-trenches work? The book of Nehemiah gives us the standard for leaders: They should labor shoulder-to-shoulder with those they lead. Each of us is of equal value to God, no matter what position we have. Just as Jesus humbled Himself for our sakes, we need to keep a proper perspective of ourselves as leaders and work side by side with our brothers and sisters in Christ. (***See Adoption****> With Christ> Servants> Unified community of believers,* TopicGuide page A37.)

▸ MINISTRY
3:8 Side by side. One of the joys of working within the church is that we are able to work side by side with people of so many different stations in life. In Nehemiah's day, various tradespeople banded together to build the wall. Likewise, the church should not show favoritism, and we should band together to build up God's kingdom. A carpenter and a nurse may cooperate in teaching a children's program. An accountant and a trucker may work together on a missions project. As others join you in ministry, welcome them as fellow team members in building the wall of God's kingdom. (***See Ministry****> Great Commission> Make Disciples> Disciples are team-players,* TopicGuide page A56.)

3:12 Shallum's daughters joined him in his repairs. This shows that all of God's people, including women, were involved in the task of rebuilding the ancient walls (see Nehemiah 5:1; 12:43).

3:14 14 The Dung Gate was repaired by Malkijah son of Recab, the leader of the Beth-
Neh 2:13 hakkerem district. He rebuilt it, set up its doors, and installed its bolts and bars.
3:15 15 The Fountain Gate was repaired by Shallum* son of Col-hozeh, the leader of the
2 Kgs 25:4-5 Neh 2:14; 12:37 Mizpah district. He rebuilt it, roofed it, set up its doors, and installed its bolts and bars. Then
he repaired the wall of the pool of Siloam* near the king's garden, and he rebuilt the wall as
3:16 far as the stairs that descend from the City of David. 16 Next to him was Nehemiah son of
2 Kgs 20:20 Azbuk, the leader of half the district of Beth-zur. He rebuilt the wall from a place across from
Neh 2:14; 3:9, 12, 17 the tombs of David's family as far as the water reservoir and the House of the Warriors.
17 Next to him, repairs were made by a group of Levites working under the supervision of Re-
hum son of Bani. Then came Hashabiah, the leader of half the district of Keilah, who super-
vised the building of the wall on behalf of his own district. 18 Next down the line were his
countrymen led by Binnui* son of Henadad, the leader of the other half of the district of Keilah.
3:19 19 Next to them, Ezer son of Jeshua, the leader of Mizpah, repaired another section of
2 Chr 26:9 wall across from the ascent to the armory near the angle in the wall. 20 Next to him was
Neh 3:15-16 Baruch son of Zabbai, who zealously repaired an additional section from the angle to the
3:20 Neh 3:1 door of the house of Eliashib the high priest. 21 Meremoth son of Uriah and grandson of
Hakkoz rebuilt another section of the wall extending from the door of Eliashib's house to
the end of the house.
3:22 22 The next repairs were made by the priests from the surrounding region. 23 After them,
Neh 12:28 Benjamin and Hasshub repaired the section across from their house, and Azariah son of
3:24 Neh 3:19 Maaseiah and grandson of Ananiah repaired the section across from his house. 24 Next was
Binnui son of Henadad, who rebuilt another section of the wall from Azariah's house to the
3:25 Jer 32:2 angle and the corner. 25 Palal son of Uzai carried on the work from a point opposite the an-
3:26 gle and the tower that projects up from the king's upper house beside the court of the
Neh 7:46; 8:1, 3; guard. Next to him were Pedaiah son of Parosh, 26 with the Temple servants living on the
11:21 hill of Ophel, who repaired the wall as far as a point across from the Water Gate to the east
3:27 Neh 3:5 and the projecting tower. 27 Then came the people of Tekoa, who repaired another section
3:28 across from the great projecting tower and over to the wall of Ophel.
2 Kgs 11:16 28 Above the Horse Gate, the priests repaired the wall. Each one repaired the section im-
2 Chr 23:15 mediately across from his own house. 29 Next Zadok son of Immer also rebuilt the wall
Jer 31:40 across from his own house, and beyond him was Shemaiah son of Shecaniah, the gate-
keeper of the East Gate. 30 Next Hananiah son of Shelemiah and Hanun, the sixth son of
Zalaph, repaired another section, while Meshullam son of Berekiah rebuilt the wall across
3:31 from where he lived. 31 Malkijah, one of the goldsmiths, repaired the wall as far as the
Neh 3:1, 8 housing for the Temple servants and merchants, across from the Inspection Gate. Then he
3:32 continued as far as the upper room at the corner. 32 The other goldsmiths and merchants
Neh 3:1; 12:39 repaired the wall from that corner to the Sheep Gate.

ENEMIES OPPOSE THE REBUILDING

4:1 Neh 2:10, 19 **4** 1* Sanballat was very angry when he learned that we were rebuilding the wall. He flew
into a rage and mocked the Jews, 2 saying in front of his friends and the Samarian

3:15a As in Syriac version; Hebrew reads *Shallun.* 3:15b Hebrew *pool of Shelah,* another name for the pool of Siloam.
3:18 As in a few Hebrew manuscripts, some Greek manuscripts, and Syriac version (see also 3:24; 10:9); most Hebrew manuscripts read *Bavvai.* 4:1 Verses 4:1-6 are numbered 3:33-38 in Hebrew text.

3:15 Though in disrepair, Jerusalem was still viewed as the City of David, where the Son of David would reign in the future (1 Chronicles 17; see also Mark 10:48; Luke 18:38).

▸ SPIRITUAL WARFARE

4:2 Never underestimate God's servants. The world has always underestimated God's servants. In Nehemiah's day, Sanballat disparaged the Jews who were building the walls, claiming that they would never be successful. Today, people who oppose the gospel make the same charges. Because they don't understand or accept God's methods and power, they expect and desire Christians to fail at ministry, in their vocations, and in their marriages. Do not let opposition discourage you. God is in the business of using you—even with your weaknesses—to astound the so-called strong. With God on your side, you will have the wisdom and strength to do His will. (***See Spiritual Warfare****> Resisting Sin and Evil> Standing Firm> Empowered to obey,* TopicGuide page A46.)

army officers, "What does this bunch of poor, feeble Jews think they're doing? Do they
think they can build the wall in a single day by just offering a few sacrifices?* Do they actu-
ally think they can make something of stones from a rubbish heap—and charred ones at
that?"
3 Tobiah the Ammonite, who was standing beside him, remarked, "That stone wall 4:3
would collapse if even a fox walked along the top of it!" Neh 2:10
4 Then I prayed, "Hear us, our God, for we are being mocked. May their scoffing fall back 4:4
on their own heads, and may they themselves become captives in a foreign land! 5 Do not Pss 79:12; 123:3-4
ignore their guilt. Do not blot out their sins, for they have provoked You to anger here in 4:5 Ps 69:27-28
front of* the builders." Jer 18:23
6 At last the wall was completed to half its height around the entire city, for the people
had worked with enthusiasm.
7 *But when Sanballat and Tobiah and the Arabs, Ammonites, and Ashdodites heard that
the work was going ahead and that the gaps in the wall of Jerusalem were being repaired,
they were furious. 8 They all made plans to come and fight against Jerusalem and throw us
into confusion. 9 But we prayed to our God and guarded the city day and night to protect
ourselves.
10 Then the people of Judah began to complain, "The workers are getting tired, and
there is so much rubble to be moved. We will never be able to build the wall by ourselves."
11 Meanwhile, our enemies were saying, "Before they know what's happening, we will
swoop down on them and kill them and end their work."
12 The Jews who lived near the enemy came and told us again and again, "They will
come from all directions and attack us!"* 13 So I placed armed guards behind the lowest 4:13
parts of the wall in the exposed areas. I stationed the people to stand guard by families, Neh 4:9, 17-18
armed with swords, spears, and bows.
14 Then as I looked over the situation, I called together the nobles and the rest of the 4:14
people and said to them, "Don't be afraid of the enemy! Remember the Lord, who is great Num 14:9 Deut 1:29-30
and glorious, and fight for your brothers, your sons, your daughters, your wives, and your 2 Sam 10:12
homes!"
15 When our enemies heard that we knew of their plans and that God had frustrated 4:15
them, we all returned to our work on the wall. 16 But from then on, only half my men 2 Sam 17:14
worked while the other half stood guard with spears, shields, bows, and coats of mail. The
leaders stationed themselves behind the people of Judah 17 who were building the wall.

4:2 The meaning of the Hebrew is uncertain. 4:5 Or *for they have thrown insults in the face of.* 4:7 Verses 4:7-23 are numbered 4:1-17 in Hebrew text. 4:12 The meaning of the Hebrew is uncertain.

4:4-5 This is the first of three such imprecatory prayers, which justly called down curses on the enemies of God (see Nehemiah 6:14; 13:29). Such prayers took place in the extreme circumstances of Israel's conflicts with aggressive enemies (see Psalms 79:12; 89:49-51; 94:1-3; 137:7-9). This kind of prayer must be understood within the framework of Israel's wars to reclaim the Promised Land (Exodus 15:3-5; Joshua 5:13-15) and must be balanced with mercy and kindness toward others (see Matthew 5:43-45; Romans 12:14-21). Today Christians pray for Christ's victory, which will one day entail eternal judgment against His enemies.

4:7-8 One more group is added to the list of enemies: the men of Ashdod. Nehemiah is now completely encircled by opponents, as Ashdod lies to his west (see note at Nehemiah 2:19).

4:10-11 The second part of Nehemiah 4:10: "there is so much rubble . . ." and the reply of God's enemies in verse 11: "before they know what's happening . . ." are a poetic couplet with similar rhythms and sounds. Perhaps this was a depressing song sung by the workers or used as a taunt by God's enemies.

▸ MINISTRY

4:15 Work smarter. When Nehemiah encountered problems in his effort to rebuild the wall around Jerusalem, he surveyed the situation and changed his plans. God expects us to work smarter, too, when we encounter difficulties in His work. Our message never changes, but our methods do. When you run into obstacles in your ministry, evaluate where you find the roadblocks and what you can do to eliminate them. Work together with your co-laborers to resolve the problems and be more effective in how you spread the gospel. (***See Ministry*****>** *Great Commission> Make Disciples> Disciples strategically use knowledge, skills, and abilities,* TopicGuide page A56.)

The laborers carried on their work with one hand supporting their load and one hand
holding a weapon. [18]All the builders had a sword belted to their side. The trumpeter
stayed with me to sound the alarm.
[19]Then I explained to the nobles and officials and all the people, "The work is very
spread out, and we are widely separated from each other along the wall. [20]When you
4:20 hear the blast of the trumpet, rush to wherever it is sounding. Then our God will fight
Exod 14:14 for us!"
Deut 1:30 [21]We worked early and late, from sunrise to sunset. And half the men were always on
guard. [22]I also told everyone living outside the walls to stay in Jerusalem. That way they
and their servants could help with guard duty at night and work during the day. [23]During
this time, none of us—not I, nor my relatives, nor my servants, nor the guards who were
with me—ever took off our clothes. We carried our weapons with us at all times, even
when we went for water.*

NEHEMIAH DEFENDS THE OPPRESSED

5 About this time some of the men and their wives raised a cry of protest against their
5:1-2 fellow Jews. [2]They were saying, "We have such large families. We need more food to
Lev 25:35 survive."
Deut 15:7 [3]Others said, "We have mortgaged our fields, vineyards, and homes to get food during
the famine."
[4]And others said, "We have had to borrow money on our fields and vineyards to pay
5:4 our taxes. [5]We belong to the same family as those who are wealthy, and our children are
Ezra 4:13; 7:24 just like theirs. Yet we must sell our children into slavery just to get enough money to live.
5:5 We have already sold some of our daughters, and we are helpless to do anything about it,
Gen 37:27 Lev 25:39 for our fields and vineyards are already mortgaged to others."
[6]When I heard their complaints, I was very angry. [7]After thinking it over, I spoke out
5:7 against these nobles and officials. I told them, "You are hurting your own relatives by

Exod 22:25 Lev 25:36 4:23 Or *Each carried his weapon in his right hand.* Hebrew reads *Each his weapon the water.* The meaning of the Hebrew is uncertain.

▸ **CHURCH**

4:20 When you hear the trumpet. Nehemiah worked out a plan where each person could call for help from all the others when necessary. Do you have such a plan in your ministry or church? When one member suffers, can he or she easily contact other members to receive help? Sometimes we may experience such a devastating blow that we can barely call out for help. In those times, we need to have a plan that allows us to come alongside each other, pray for each other, and meet each other's needs. A prayer chain or a prayer group could be the answer to helping each other in times of need. (***See Church****> Role> Church Community> Encouraging one another,* TopicGuide page A49.)

4:21 Work usually ended at sundown, but the laborers' commitment went beyond the ordinary.

▸ **SPIRITUAL WARFARE**

4:23 Wearing the armor. Since we are also in a battle that never lets up, we need to wear our spiritual armor night and day so that we are ready to battle at a moment's notice. Our enemy, Satan, is waiting for us to put down our weapons and take off our armor so that he can attack. Keep your sword, God's Word, always at your side and prepare yourself by donning your spiritual armor on a daily basis. (See Ephesians 6:10-18; also ***see Spiritual Warfare****> Resisting Sin and Evil> Putting On and Off> Putting On> The whole armor of God,* TopicGuide page A46.)

5:1-19 Digressing from the main topic of opposition from outsiders, this section draws attention to internal problems. There were economic problems for at least four reasons: 1) Judah was cut off commercially from the neighboring peoples; 2) the effort to rebuild the wall resulted in a decrease in grain production, since the farmers were staying in Jerusalem (see Nehemiah 4:22); 3) climatic factors contributed to the famine (Nehemiah 5:3); and 4) the previous administrators had placed heavy burdens on the people (Nehemiah 5:15). As a result, some had no money to buy grain (Nehemiah 5:2), some had to mortgage their property to buy it (Nehemiah 5:3), and some had to borrow money to pay taxes to the Persian king (Nehemiah 5:4). The lending of money at perhaps excessive interest made the situation intolerable. When some of the above were unable to pay their debts, their children were taken into slavery (Nehemiah 5:5). The economic and social fabric was in danger of completely unraveling.

5:5 According to Leviticus 25:39-43, a man who became poor could sell himself, along with his family, to a fellow Israelite in order to get back on his feet financially. But he was to be treated as a hired worker, not as a slave. The error in Nehemiah's day seems to have been twofold: 1) Only the children were being sold, resulting in the breakup of family units; and 2) the children were being treated as slaves, not as hired workers.

5:7 The Law of Moses not only prohibited excessive interest, but interest of any kind (see Exodus 22:25-27; Leviticus 25:36; Deuteronomy 23:20).

charging interest when they borrow money!" Then I called a public meeting to deal with
the problem.
8 At the meeting I said to them, "We are doing all we can to redeem our Jewish relatives **5:8**
who have had to sell themselves to pagan foreigners, but you are selling them back into slav- Lev 25:48
ery again. How often must we redeem them?" And they had nothing to say in their defense.
9 Then I pressed further, "What you are doing is not right! Should you not walk in the
fear of our God in order to avoid being mocked by enemy nations? 10 I myself, as well as
my brothers and my workers, have been lending the people money and grain, but now let
us stop this business of charging interest. 11 You must restore their fields, vineyards, olive
groves, and homes to them this very day. And repay the interest you charged when you
lent them money, grain, new wine, and olive oil."
12 They replied, "We will give back everything and demand nothing more from the peo- **5:12**
ple. We will do as you say." Then I called the priests and made the nobles and officials Ezra 10:5
swear to do what they had promised. Neh 10:31
13 I shook out the folds of my robe and said, "If you fail to keep your promise, may God **5:13**
shake you like this from your homes and from your property!" Neh 8:6 Acts 18:6
The whole assembly responded, "Amen," and they praised the LORD. And the people did
as they had promised.
14 For the entire twelve years that I was governor of Judah—from the twentieth year to the **5:14**
thirty-second year of the reign of King Artaxerxes*—neither I nor my officials drew on our of- Neh 1:1; 13:6
ficial food allowance. 15 The former governors, in contrast, had laid heavy burdens on the **5:15** Neh 5:9
people, demanding a daily ration of food and wine, besides forty pieces* of silver. Even their
assistants took advantage of the people. But because I feared God, I did not act that way.
16 I also devoted myself to working on the wall and refused to acquire any land. And I re-
quired all my servants to spend time working on the wall. 17 I asked for nothing, even **5:17** 1 Kgs 18:19
though I regularly fed 150 Jewish officials at my table, besides all the visitors from other
lands! 18 The provisions I paid for each day included one ox, six choice sheep or goats, and **5:18**
a large number of poultry. And every ten days we needed a large supply of all kinds of 1 Kgs 4:22-23 2 Thes 3:8
wine. Yet I refused to claim the governor's food allowance because the people already car-
ried a heavy burden.

19 Remember, O my God, all that I have done for these people, and bless me for it. **5:19** Neh 13:14, 22, 31

CONTINUED OPPOSITION TO REBUILDING

6 Sanballat, Tobiah, Geshem the Arab, and the rest of our enemies found out that I had **6:1**
finished rebuilding the wall and that no gaps remained—though we had not yet set Neh 3:1, 3
up the doors in the gates. 2 So Sanballat and Geshem sent a message asking me to meet **6:2**
them at one of the villages* in the plain of Ono. 1 Chr 8:12

5:14 That is, 445–433 B.C. 5:15 Hebrew *40 shekels* [1 pound, or 456 grams]. 6:2 As in Greek version; Hebrew reads *at Kephirim*.

▸ HOLINESS

5:12 Corrupt business practices. Some of the people involved in the rebuilding project were overcharging their own people. When Nehemiah learned about their deeds, he pointed out that what they were doing was wrong. They immediately repented of their wrongdoing and vowed to correct it. How are you treating your brothers and sisters in Christ? Is your motivation to make as big a profit as possible or are you handling your business with them fairly? God holds us to a high standard in our business dealings. Be sure that you are maintaining God's standards, not the world's. (***See Holiness****> Disciplines> Of Abstinence> Resisting worldly influences,* TopicGuide page A42.)

5:13 Nehemiah dramatized the curses that would fall on those who did not keep their oaths (Jeremiah 34:8-22).

5:18 Nehemiah was a man of considerable wealth and a sacrificial spirit. The food provided at his expense could have fed approximately 700 people.

5:19 This is the second use of "remember" in a prayer (see note at Nehemiah 1:8) and the first of four prayers that take the form of remembering a particular deed. (see Nehemiah 13:14, 22, 31).

6:1-14 The main cycle of conflict and resolution now returns. The conflict that has been steadily escalating here reaches its climax, as the wall is virtually complete. This final attempt to stop the work involves three methods: to harm (Nehemiah 6:2-4), to frighten (Nehemiah 6:5-9), and to discredit (Nehemiah 6:10-13).

But I realized they were plotting to harm me, [3]so I replied by sending this message to
them: "I am engaged in a great work, so I can't come. Why should I stop working to come
and meet with you?"
[4]Four times they sent the same message, and each time I gave the same reply. [5]The fifth
6:6 time, Sanballat's servant came with an open letter in his hand, [6]and this is what it said:
Neh 2:19

"There is a rumor among the surrounding nations, and Geshem* tells me it is true,
that you and the Jews are planning to rebel and that is why you are building the
wall. According to his reports, you plan to be their king. [7]He also reports that you
have appointed prophets in Jerusalem to proclaim about you, 'Look! There is a king
in Judah!'
"You can be very sure that this report will get back to the king, so I suggest that
you come and talk it over with me."

[8]I replied, "There is no truth in any part of your story. You are making up the whole thing."
[9]They were just trying to intimidate us, imagining that they could discourage us and
stop the work. So I continued the work with even greater determination.*
6:10 [10]Later I went to visit Shemaiah son of Delaiah and grandson of Mehetabel, who was
Jer 36:5 confined to his home. He said, "Let us meet together inside the Temple of God and bolt the
doors shut. Your enemies are coming to kill you tonight."
[11]But I replied, "Should someone in my position run from danger? Should someone in
my position enter the Temple to save his life? No, I won't do it!" [12]I realized that God had
not spoken to him, but that he had uttered this prophecy against me because Tobiah and
6:13 Sanballat had hired him. [13]They were hoping to intimidate me and make me sin. Then
Neh 6:6 they would be able to accuse and discredit me.

[14]Remember, O my God, all the evil things that Tobiah and Sanballat have done.
6:14 Neh 13:29 And remember Noadiah the prophet and all the prophets like her who have tried to
Ezek 13:17 intimidate me.

6:15 Neh 4:1-2

THE BUILDERS COMPLETE THE WALL

[15]So on October 2* the wall was finished—just fifty-two days after we had begun. [16]When
6:16 Neh 2:10; 4:1, 7

6:6 Hebrew *Gashmu*, a variant spelling of Geshem. 6:9 As in Greek version; Hebrew reads *But now to strengthen my hands.* 6:15 Hebrew *on the twenty-fifth day of the month Elul*, of the ancient Hebrew lunar calendar. This day was October 2, 445 B.C.; also see note on 1:1.

6:5 The usual custom was for letters to be sealed. Sanballat wanted the negative content of the note to be known so as to discourage the completion of the project.

▸ SPIRITUAL WARFARE

6:9 Praying for strength. If you encounter opposition from the world in your ministry, the pattern given in Nehemiah is to go to the Lord and ask for strength. Sometimes, even when we do good, the world can misrepresent our deeds. But God knows our hearts and our actions. Do not feel intimidated; break out in the strength of the Lord. (***See Spiritual Warfare****> Resisting Sin and Evil> Embracing Christ> Entrust yourself to God's care,* TopicGuide page A45.)

6:10 Shemaiah plays a part in a plot to discredit Nehemiah. While finding asylum at the altar in the courtyard may have been a legitimate option for Nehemiah (see Exodus 21:12-14), entering the Temple proper was not, since Nehemiah was not a priest (see Numbers 18:7).

▸ SALVATION

6:13 No intimidation. Occasionally, we will find ourselves in a whirlwind of erroneous accusations just because we have aligned ourselves with God's purposes. But we should understand that these are Satan's tactics to defeat God's people, and we should not be intimidated. Satan will take every opportunity to sabotage God's work. Don't let him succeed. Recognize Satan's handiwork in these situations and call upon God for help. He will come to your rescue. (***See Salvation****> Receiving> When> Delivered or rescued,* TopicGuide page A22.)

6:13 The final ploy was to frighten Nehemiah into taking a sinful course of action so that his reputation would be ruined, which would prevent him from completing the building project.

6:14 In the Old Testament, women were called to be God's mouth in the world, on an equal footing with male prophets. Miriam (Exodus 15:20) was the first of several who are named, including Deborah (Judges 4:4-7), Huldah (2 Kings 22:13-20), and the false prophetess, Noadiah. Joel (Joel 2:28) predicts that in the last days, God will fulfill Moses' prayer that all the Lord's people, men and women alike, will prophesy (Numbers 11:29). At Pentecost, the Holy Spirit empowered both men and women to proclaim boldly the good news that Jesus is Lord of all and to build His Church (Acts 2).

6:15 This verse forms the conclusion to the previous section that began in 6:1, with 6:16 opening the final episode of 1:1–7:3. The last of six attempts to stop the work had failed.

our enemies and the surrounding nations heard about it, they were frightened and humili-
ated. They realized this work had been done with the help of our God.
[17]During those fifty-two days, many letters went back and forth between Tobiah and
the nobles of Judah. [18]For many in Judah had sworn allegiance to him because his
father-in-law was Shecaniah son of Arah, and his son Jehohanan was married to the
daughter of Meshullam son of Berekiah. [19]They kept telling me about Tobiah's good
deeds, and then they told him everything I said. And Tobiah kept sending threatening
letters to intimidate me.

7 After the wall was finished and I had set up the doors in the gates, the gatekeepers, **7:1** Neh 6:1, 15
singers, and Levites were appointed. [2]I gave the responsibility of governing Jerusa-
lem to my brother Hanani, along with Hananiah, the commander of the fortress, for he **7:2** Neh 1:2; 10:23
was a faithful man who feared God more than most. [3]I said to them, "Do not leave the
gates open during the hottest part of the day.* And even while the gatekeepers are on
duty, have them shut and bar the doors. Appoint the residents of Jerusalem to act as
guards, everyone on a regular watch. Some will serve at sentry posts and some in front of
their own homes."

NEHEMIAH REGISTERS THE PEOPLE

[4]At that time the city was large and spacious, but the population was small, and none of
the houses had been rebuilt. [5]So my God gave me the idea to call together all the nobles
and leaders of the city, along with the ordinary citizens, for registration. I had found the
genealogical record of those who had first returned to Judah. This is what was written
there:

> [6]Here is the list of the Jewish exiles of the provinces who returned from their **7:6-73** //Ezra 2:1-70
> captivity. King Nebuchadnezzar had deported them to Babylon, but now they
> returned to Jerusalem and the other towns in Judah where they originally lived. **7:7** Ezra 2:2
> [7]Their leaders were Zerubbabel, Jeshua, Nehemiah, Seraiah,* Reelaiah,* Nahamani,
> Mordecai, Bilshan, Mispar,* Bigvai, Rehum,* and Baanah.

7:3 Or *Keep the gates of Jerusalem closed until the sun is hot.* **7:7a** As in parallel text at Ezra 2:2; Hebrew reads *Azariah.* **7:7b** As in parallel text at Ezra 2:2; Hebrew reads *Raamiah.* **7:7c** As in parallel text at Ezra 2:2; Hebrew reads *Mispereth.* **7:7d** As in parallel text at Ezra 2:2; Hebrew reads *Nehum.*

▸ HOLINESS
7:2 Select good leaders. When the wall was completed, Nehemiah selected certain men to serve as governors of Jerusalem. The quality he looked for in these leaders was faithfulness and fear of God. How do you select the leaders in your church? Are you looking for these same qualities? Many times we judge potential leaders by their outward appearance and not by the attitude of their hearts. Get to know those who may become leaders in your church and evaluate them according to God's standards. (***See Holiness****> Law and Grace> Law> Leaders and followers,* TopicGuide page A41.)

7:3 Nehemiah's concerns for the security of Jerusalem meant taking precautions. Even the custom of letting the breeze blow through an open gate on a hot afternoon was forbidden.

7:4-5 Although a number of people had returned to the land by this time, Jerusalem was still relatively unpopulated, perhaps because it was the center of international tensions. The prophetic expectation was that Jerusalem would be overflowing with people (see Zechariah 8:4-8). Nehemiah pressed for more returnees to come to the city.

7:4–13:31 The final major section of Ezra-Nehemiah focuses on rebuilding the community, which forms one aspect of rebuilding the "house of God." This same theme is evident in Ezra 7–10. These chapters divide into two main parts: More exiles return to the land (7:4-73a), and Nehemiah rebuilds the community (7:73b–13:31). Simply having Jerusalem fortified was not enough to bring the blessings of God. The people needed to be rebuilt into a holy community as well. This aspect of the restoration program divides into three main parts: the renewal of covenant commitments (7:73b–10:39), the dedication of the wall (11:1–12:47), and the reform of the people (13:1-31).

▸ SPIRITUAL WARFARE
7:5 Following God's leading. When doing God's work, we must allow God to lead us. That doesn't mean that we wait for some audible voice before we step out in faith. It means that we are in constant prayer over each step of ministry that we take. We also search the Scripture to learn the principles that will help us keep on the right track. Through God's Word and prayer, we can be assured that we are walking in the right pathway. (See Titus 1:9; also ***see Spiritual Warfare****> Resisting Sin and Evil> Trusting God> Faithful Soldiers> Hold firmly to the truth,* TopicGuide page A46.)

This is the number of the men of Israel who returned from exile:
8 The family of Parosh ... 2,172
9 The family of Shephatiah ... 372
10 The family of Arah ... 652
11 The family of Pahath-moab (descendants of Jeshua and Joab) ... 2,818
12 The family of Elam ... 1,254
13 The family of Zattu ... 845
14 The family of Zaccai ... 760
15 The family of Bani* ... 648
16 The family of Bebai ... 628
17 The family of Azgad ... 2,322
18 The family of Adonikam ... 667
19 The family of Bigvai ... 2,067
20 The family of Adin ... 655
21 The family of Ater (descendants of Hezekiah) ... 98
22 The family of Hashum ... 328
23 The family of Bezai ... 324
24 The family of Jorah* ... 112
25 The family of Gibbar* ... 95
26 The people of Bethlehem and Netophah ... 188
27 The people of Anathoth ... 128
28 The people of Beth-azmaveth ... 42
29 The people of Kiriath-jearim, Kephirah, and Beeroth ... 743
30 The people of Ramah and Geba ... 621
31 The people of Micmash ... 122
32 The people of Bethel and Ai ... 123
33 The people of Nebo ... 52
34 The citizens of Elam ... 1,254
35 The citizens of Harim ... 320
36 The citizens of Jericho ... 345
37 The citizens of Lod, Hadid, and Ono ... 721
38 The citizens of Senaah ... 3,930

7:39 Ezra 2:36-39

39 These are the priests who returned from exile:
The family of Jedaiah (through the line of Jeshua) ... 973
40 The family of Immer ... 1,052
41 The family of Pashhur ... 1,247
42 The family of Harim ... 1,017

7:43 Ezra 2:40-42

43 These are the Levites who returned from exile:
The families of Jeshua and Kadmiel (descendants of Hodaviah*) ... 74
44 The singers of the family of Asaph ... 148
45 The gatekeepers of the families of Shallum, Ater, Talmon, Akkub, Hatita, and Shobai ... 138

7:46 Ezra 2:43-54

46 The descendants of the following Temple servants returned from exile:
Ziha, Hasupha, Tabbaoth,
47 Keros, Siaha,* Padon,
48 Lebanah, Hagabah, Shalmai,
49 Hanan, Giddel, Gahar,
50 Reaiah, Rezin, Nekoda,

7:15 As in parallel text at Ezra 2:10; Hebrew reads *Binnui*. **7:24** As in parallel text at Ezra 2:18; Hebrew reads *Hariph*. **7:25** As in parallel text at Ezra 2:20; Hebrew reads *Gibeon*. **7:43** As in parallel text at Ezra 2:40; Hebrew reads *Hodevah*. **7:47** As in parallel text at Ezra 2:44; Hebrew reads *Sia*.

51 Gazzam, Uzza, Paseah,
52 Besai, Meunim, Nephusim,*
53 Bakbuk, Hakupha, Harhur,
54 Bazluth,* Mehida, Harsha,
55 Barkos, Sisera, Temah,
56 Neziah, and Hatipha.

57 The descendants of these servants of King Solomon returned from exile:
Sotai, Hassophereth, Peruda,*
58 Jaalah,* Darkon, Giddel,
59 Shephatiah, Hattil, Pokereth-hazzebaim, and Ami.*

7:57 Ezra 2:55-57

60 In all, the Temple servants and the descendants of Solomon's servants numbered 392.

61 Another group returned at this time from the towns of Tel-melah, Tel-harsha,
Kerub, Addan,* and Immer. However, they could not prove that they or their families
were descendants of Israel. 62 This group included the families of Delaiah, Tobiah,
and Nekoda—a total of 642 people.

63 Three families of priests—Hobaiah, Hakkoz, and Barzillai—also returned. (This
Barzillai had married a woman who was a descendant of Barzillai of Gilead, and he
had taken her family name.) 64 They searched for their names in the genealogical
records, but they were not found, so they were disqualified from serving as priests.

7:63 Ezra 2:61

7:52 As in parallel text at Ezra 2:50; Hebrew reads *Nephushesim.* **7:54** As in parallel text at Ezra 2:52; Hebrew reads *Bazlith.* **7:57** As in parallel text at Ezra 2:55; Hebrew reads *Sotai, Sophereth, Perida.* **7:58** As in parallel text at Ezra 2:56; Hebrew reads *Jaala.* **7:59** As in parallel text at Ezra 2:57; Hebrew reads *Amon.* **7:61** As in parallel text at Ezra 2:59; Hebrew reads *Addon.*

MY RESPONSE TO GOD

Responding to God's Word

NEHEMIAH 8

Lecturing isn't a very effective teaching method. Even if you listened to a fascinating speaker teach about your favorite topic, you would still forget most of what you heard.

Preachers face two challenges: Our ears don't retain all we hear, and our hearts don't want to obey it. But God commands us to listen to preaching as a part of our weekly attentiveness to God in worship (1 Timothy 4:13; Romans 10:14).

Nehemiah describes the Israelites passionately worshiping God through listening. "Ezra praised the LORD, the great God, and all the people chanted, 'Amen! Amen!' as they lifted their hands. Then they bowed down and worshiped the LORD with their faces to the ground" (Nehemiah 8:6). When Ezra the priest read the Book of the Law to the people, they wept (Nehemiah 8:3, 9), because they had not followed God's commands.

When we hear God's Word, we too should humbly weep over our sin. But we shouldn't stop there. Nehemiah went on to tell the people, "Go and celebrate with a feast of rich foods and sweet drinks, and share gifts of food with people who have nothing prepared" (Nehemiah 8:10). They celebrated and shared their joy because they had heard and understood the Word of God. Likewise, when we hear God's Word, we should not linger in grief over our sins. We should rejoice in knowing that Christ's perfect sacrifice has paid for our sins (1 Peter 1:18).

65 The governor told them not to eat the priests' share of food from the sacrifices
until a priest could consult the LORD about the matter by using the Urim and
Thummim—the sacred lots.
66 So a total of 42,360 people returned to Judah, 67 in addition to 7,337 servants
and 245 singers, both men and women. 68 They took with them 736 horses,
245 mules,* 69 435 camels, and 6,720 donkeys.
7:70 70 Some of the family leaders gave gifts for the work. The governor gave to the
Neh 8:9 treasury 1,000 gold coins,* 50 gold basins, and 530 robes for the priests. 71 The
other leaders gave to the treasury a total of 20,000 gold coins* and some 2,750
pounds* of silver for the work. 72 The rest of the people gave 20,000 gold coins,
about 2,500 pounds* of silver, and 67 robes for the priests.
7:73 73 So the priests, the Levites, the gatekeepers, the singers, the Temple servants, and
Ezra 3:1 some of the common people settled near Jerusalem. The rest of the people returned
to their own towns throughout Israel.

EZRA READS THE LAW

8:1 **8** In October,* when the Israelites had settled in their towns, 8:1 all the people assem-
2 Chr 34:15 bled with a unified purpose at the square just inside the Water Gate. They asked Ezra
Ezra 7:6 Neh 3:26 the scribe to bring out the Book of the Law of Moses, which the LORD had given for Israel to
8:2 obey.
Lev 23:24 2 So on October 8* Ezra the priest brought the Book of the Law before the assembly,
Deut 31:9-12 which included the men and women and all the children old enough to understand. 3 He
faced the square just inside the Water Gate from early morning until noon and read aloud
to everyone who could understand. All the people listened closely to the Book of the Law.
4 Ezra the scribe stood on a high wooden platform that had been made for the occasion.
To his right stood Mattithiah, Shema, Anaiah, Uriah, Hilkiah, and Maaseiah. To his left
stood Pedaiah, Mishael, Malkijah, Hashum, Hashbaddanah, Zechariah, and Meshullam.
5 Ezra stood on the platform in full view of all the people. When they saw him open the
8:6 book, they all rose to their feet.
Exod 4:31 6 Then Ezra praised the LORD, the great God, and all the people chanted, "Amen! Amen!"
Neh 5:13 1 Tim 2:8 as they lifted their hands. Then they bowed down and worshiped the LORD with their faces
8:7 to the ground.
Lev 10:11 7 The Levites—Jeshua, Bani, Sherebiah, Jamin, Akkub, Shabbethai, Hodiah, Maaseiah,
Deut 33:10 Kelita, Azariah, Jozabad, Hanan, and Pelaiah—then instructed the people in the Law while

7:68 As in some Hebrew manuscripts (see also Ezra 2:66); most Hebrew manuscripts lack this verse. Verses 7:69-73 are numbered 7:68-72 in Hebrew text. **7:70** Hebrew *1,000 darics of gold,* about 19 pounds or 8.6 kilograms in weight. **7:71a** Hebrew *20,000 darics of gold,* about 375 pounds or 170 kilograms in weight; also in 7:72. **7:71b** Hebrew *2,200 minas* [1,300 kilograms]. **7:72** Hebrew *2,000 minas* [1,200 kilograms]. **7:73** Hebrew *in the seventh month.* This month of the ancient Hebrew lunar calendar occurred within the months of October and November 445 B.C. **8:2** Hebrew *on the first day of the seventh month,* of the ancient Hebrew lunar calendar. This day was October 8, 445 B.C.; also see note on 1:1.

7:73 True to the directions of Moses' law, Nehemiah led the people to renew their covenant commitments. Three steps were taken: the law was read (7:73b–8:18), sins were confessed (9:1-37), and an oath was taken (9:38–10:39).

▸ BIBLE
8:1 Assembling for reading the Word. Reading the Word of God should be a holy practice. When you assemble to read God's Word, make it a solemn occasion. Bring together your entire family, people of all ages, even the little ones. To make the occasion more memorable, ask people to stand while the Bible is read. Give prominence to the person who reads. If you treat the reading of God's Word with the gravity that it deserves, its message will carry more import for the listeners. (***See Bible****> Power> Wisdom> Instruction through God's Word,* TopicGuide page A11.)

8:3 For the public reading of the Law of Moses in the context of covenant ratification or renewal, see Exodus 24:7; Deuteronomy 11:29; Joshua 8:30-35; and 2 Kings 23:1-3.

8:5-6 *Amen* here means the people concurred in the praise offered by Ezra. By repeating the phrase, the people expressed that they strongly agreed with Ezra's praise. Their reverence for God's law was expressed in a physical manner through standing (Nehemiah 8:5), lifting their hands, bowing down (Nehemiah 8:6), and celebrating (Nehemiah 8:10).

everyone remained in their places. 8They read from the Book of the Law of God and clearly explained the meaning of what was being read, helping the people understand each passage.

9Then Nehemiah the governor, Ezra the priest and scribe, and the Levites who were interpreting for the people said to them, "Don't mourn or weep on such a day as this! For today is a sacred day before the LORD your God." For the people had all been weeping as they listened to the words of the Law.

8:9 Deut 12:7, 12; Neh 8:2

10And Nehemiah* continued, "Go and celebrate with a feast of rich foods and sweet drinks, and share gifts of food with people who have nothing prepared. This is a sacred day before our Lord. Don't be dejected and sad, for the joy of the LORD is your strength!"

8:10 Deut 26:11-13; Esth 9:22

11And the Levites, too, quieted the people, telling them, "Hush! Don't weep! For this is a sacred day." 12So the people went away to eat and drink at a festive meal, to share gifts of food, and to celebrate with great joy because they had heard God's words and understood them.

8:12 Neh 8:7-8, 10

THE FESTIVAL OF SHELTERS

13On October 9* the family leaders of all the people, together with the priests and Levites, met with Ezra the scribe to go over the Law in greater detail. 14As they studied the Law, they discovered that the LORD had commanded through Moses that the Israelites should live in shelters during the festival to be held that month.* 15He had said that a proclamation should be made throughout their towns and in Jerusalem, telling the people to go to the hills to get branches from olive, wild olive,* myrtle, palm, and other leafy trees. They were to use these branches to make shelters in which they would live during the festival, as prescribed in the Law.

8:14 Lev 23:34, 40, 42

16So the people went out and cut branches and used them to build shelters on the roofs of their houses, in their courtyards, in the courtyards of God's Temple, or in the squares just inside the Water Gate and the Ephraim Gate. 17So everyone who had returned from captivity lived in these shelters during the festival, and they were all filled with great joy! The Israelites had not celebrated like this since the days of Joshua* son of Nun.

8:16 2 Kgs 14:13; Neh 8:1; 12:39; Jer 32:29

8:17 2 Chr 7:8; 8:13; 30:21

18Ezra read from the Book of the Law of God on each of the seven days of the festival. Then on the eighth day they held a solemn assembly, as was required by law.

8:18 Lev 23:36; Num 29:35; Deut 31:11

THE PEOPLE CONFESS THEIR SINS

9 On October 31* the people assembled again, and this time they fasted and dressed in burlap and sprinkled dust on their heads. 2Those of Israelite descent separated themselves from all foreigners as they confessed their own sins and the sins of their ancestors. 3They remained standing in place for three hours* while the Book of the Law of the LORD their God was read aloud to them. Then for three more hours they confessed

9:1 1 Sam 4:12; Ezra 8:23; Neh 8:2; Job 2:12

9:2 Ezra 10:11; Neh 13:3

8:10 Hebrew *he.* 8:13 Hebrew *On the second day,* of the seventh month of the ancient Hebrew lunar calendar. This day was October 9, 445 B.C.; also see notes on 1:1 and 8:2. 8:14 Hebrew *in the seventh month.* This month of the ancient Hebrew lunar calendar usually occurs within the months of September and October. See Lev 23:39-43. 8:15 Or *pine;* Hebrew reads *oil tree.* 8:17 Hebrew *Jeshua,* a variant spelling of Joshua. 9:1 Hebrew *On the twenty-fourth day of that same month,* the seventh month of the ancient Hebrew lunar calendar. This day was October 31, 445 B.C.; also see notes on 1:1 and 8:2. 9:3 Hebrew *for a quarter of a day.*

8:10 Those who had were to share with those who did not have, as in Psalm 22:26. Here lies the background for understanding the sin at the Lord's Table in 1 Corinthians 11:17-34.

▸ BIBLE
8:12 Joy in God's Word. What reaction do you have when you hear the reading of God's Word aloud—ho-hum or hallelujah? The people in Ezra's day rejoiced because they had heard and understood God's Words, some of them for the first time in their lives. The Bible is the most holy and life-changing book in history. We should never take its words for granted. (***See Bible****> Power> Worldview> Eternal truth,* TopicGuide page A12.)

8:14 These shelters referred to those of the Feast of Tabernacles or Shelters (see Leviticus 23:37-40).

9:1-37 As God's law was received by faith, the people confessed their sin and found grace and mercy in God's forgiveness. This revival soon turned to jubilant song (Nehemiah 9:7-37).

9:4 their sins and worshiped the LORD their God. 4The Levites—Jeshua, Bani, Kadmiel, Shebani-
Neh 8:7 ah, Bunni, Sherebiah, Bani, and Kenani—stood on the stairway of the Levites and cried out
to the LORD their God with loud voices.
5Then the leaders of the Levites—Jeshua, Kadmiel, Bani, Hashabneiah, Sherebiah, Hodi-
9:6 ah, Shebaniah, and Pethahiah—called out to the people: "Stand up and praise the LORD
Gen 1:1 Deut 6:4 your God, for He lives from everlasting to everlasting!" Then they prayed:

2 Kgs 19:15 Ps 103:20 "May Your glorious name be praised! May it be exalted above all blessing and praise!
Col 1:16-17 6"You alone are the LORD. You made the skies and the heavens and all the stars.
9:7 Gen 11:31; 12:1; You made the earth and the seas and everything in them. You preserve them all, and
15:7; 17:5 the angels of heaven worship You.
9:8 7"You are the LORD God, who chose Abram and brought him from Ur of the
Gen 15:6, 18-21 Chaldeans and renamed him Abraham. 8When he had proved himself faithful,
Josh 21:43-45 You made a covenant with him to give him and his descendants the land of the
9:9 Canaanites, Hittites, Amorites, Perizzites, Jebusites, and Girgashites. And You have
Exod 14:10-14 done what You promised, for You are always true to Your word.
9:10 9"You saw the misery of our ancestors in Egypt, and You heard their cries from
Exod 3:7; 5:2; 9:16 beside the Red Sea.* 10You displayed miraculous signs and wonders against Pharaoh,
9:11 Exod 14:21; 15:1, his officials, and all his people, for You knew how arrogantly they were treating our
5, 10 ancestors. You have a glorious reputation that has never been forgotten. 11You
9:12 divided the sea for Your people so they could walk through on dry land! And then
Exod 13:21-22 You hurled their enemies into the depths of the sea. They sank like stones beneath
9:13 Exod 19:11, 18-20 the mighty waters. 12You led our ancestors by a pillar of cloud during the day and a
Ps 19:7-9 pillar of fire at night so that they could find their way.
9:14 13"You came down at Mount Sinai and spoke to them from heaven. You gave them
Exod 16:23; 20:8 regulations and instructions that were just, and decrees and commands that were good.
9:15 Exod 16:4, 14-15; 14You instructed them concerning Your holy Sabbath. And You commanded them,
17:6 through Moses Your servant, to obey all Your commands, decrees, and instructions.
Num 20:7-13 15"You gave them bread from heaven when they were hungry and water from the
Deut 1:8, 21 rock when they were thirsty. You commanded them to go and take possession of the
Josh 1:2-4 land You had sworn to give them.
9:16 Deut 31:27 16"But our ancestors were proud and stubborn, and they paid no attention to Your
Neh 9:10, 29 commands. 17They refused to obey and did not remember the miracles You had
9:17 Exod 34:6-7 done for them. Instead, they became stubborn and appointed a leader to take them
Num 14:4 back to their slavery in Egypt! But You are a God of forgiveness, gracious and
Ps 78:11 merciful, slow to become angry, and rich in unfailing love. You did not abandon
9:18 them, 18even when they made an idol shaped like a calf and said, 'This is your god
Exod 32:4-8, 31 who brought you out of Egypt!' They committed terrible blasphemies.
9:19 19"But in Your great mercy You did not abandon them to die in the wilderness. The
Neh 9:12, 27, 31 pillar of cloud still led them forward by day, and the pillar of fire showed them the
9:20 Num 11:17 way through the night. 20You sent Your good Spirit to instruct them, and You did not
Neh 9:15, 30 stop giving them manna from heaven or water for their thirst. 21For forty years You
Isa 63:11-14 sustained them in the wilderness, and they lacked nothing. Their clothes did not
9:21 Deut 2:7 wear out, and their feet did not swell!

9:9 Hebrew *sea of reeds.*

9:7-8 This covenant with Abraham (see Genesis 15) is the basis upon which God's grace is extended time and again to His unfaithful people, and this is highlighted in the remainder of the song.

9:13 God's law was not perceived to be a burden but a delight. This connects to Jesus' statement that His teachings bring freedom and rest (Matthew 11:28-30).

9:14 In many respects, the Sabbath stood as the apex of the Law (see Isaiah 56:2, 4, 6; Ezekiel 20–23).

22 “Then You helped our ancestors conquer kingdoms and nations, and You placed
Your people in every corner of the land.* They took over the land of King Sihon of
Heshbon and the land of King Og of Bashan. 23 You made their descendants as
numerous as the stars in the sky and brought them into the land You had promised
to their ancestors.

24 “They went in and took possession of the land. You subdued whole nations
before them. Even the Canaanites, who inhabited the land, were powerless! Your
people could deal with these nations and their kings as they pleased. 25 Our ancestors
captured fortified cities and fertile land. They took over houses full of good things,
with cisterns already dug and vineyards and olive groves and fruit trees in
abundance. So they ate until they were full and grew fat and enjoyed themselves
in all Your blessings.

26 “But despite all this, they were disobedient and rebelled against You. They
turned their backs on Your Law, they killed Your prophets who warned them to
return to You, and they committed terrible blasphemies. 27 So You handed them over
to their enemies, who made them suffer. But in their time of trouble they cried to
You, and You heard them from heaven. In Your great mercy, You sent them
liberators who rescued them from their enemies.

28 “But as soon as they were at peace, Your people again committed evil in Your
sight, and once more You let their enemies conquer them. Yet whenever Your people
turned and cried to You again for help, You listened once more from heaven. In Your
wonderful mercy, You rescued them many times!

29 “You warned them to return to Your Law, but they became proud and obstinate
and disobeyed Your commands. They did not follow Your regulations, by which
people will find life if only they obey. They stubbornly turned their backs on You
and refused to listen. 30 In Your love, You were patient with them for many years.
You sent Your Spirit, who warned them through the prophets. But still they wouldn't
listen! So once again You allowed the peoples of the land to conquer them. 31 But in
Your great mercy, You did not destroy them completely or abandon them forever.
What a gracious and merciful God You are!

32 “And now, our God, the great and mighty and awesome God, who keeps his
covenant of unfailing love, do not let all the hardships we have suffered seem
insignificant to You. Great trouble has come upon us and upon our kings and leaders
and priests and prophets and ancestors—all of Your people—from the days when the
kings of Assyria first triumphed over us until now. 33 Every time You punished us You
were being just. We have sinned greatly, and You gave us only what we deserved.
34 Our kings, leaders, priests, and ancestors did not obey Your Law or listen to the
warnings in Your commands and laws. 35 Even while they had their own kingdom,
they did not serve You, though You showered Your goodness on them. You gave
them a large, fertile land, but they refused to turn from their wickedness.

36 “So now today we are slaves in the land of plenty that You gave our ancestors
for their enjoyment! We are slaves here in this good land. 37 The lush produce of this
land piles up in the hands of the kings whom You have set over us because of our
sins. They have power over us and our livestock. We serve them at their pleasure,
and we are in great misery.”

9:22 Num 21:21-35; Deut 2:26–3:11
9:23 Gen 15:5
9:24 Josh 18:1; 21:43
9:25 Num 13:27; Deut 3:5; 6:11; 32:15; 1 Kgs 8:66
9:26 Judg 2:11; 1 Kgs 14:9; 2 Chr 36:16
9:27 Judg 2:14, 16, 18
9:28 Judg 3:11; Ps 106:43
9:29 Lev 18:5; Zech 7:11
9:30 2 Kgs 17:13; Neh 9:20
9:31 Neh 9:17; Jer 4:27
9:32 2 Kgs 15:19, 29; 17:3-6
9:33 Gen 18:25; Jer 12:1
9:35 Deut 28:45-47
9:36 Deut 28:48
9:37 Deut 28:33

9:22 The meaning of the Hebrew is uncertain.

9:29 Like all biblical covenants, the Mosaic covenant required loyalty (see Leviticus 18:5; Romans 7:10; 10:5). Israel's failure to keep their covenant vows in the land, which resulted in their loss of the land, testifies to the universal need for someone through whom God's requirements of the law might be fully met. No one could meet the requirements of the Old Covenant on their own (Romans 2:17-29; 3:19). No one could meet the requirements of the New Covenant (Romans 3:21-24) on their own. In both cases, God gives the faith to obey (Romans 4:16; Ephesians 2:8-10).

THE PEOPLE AGREE TO OBEY

[38]*The people responded, "In view of all this,* we are making a solemn promise and putting it in writing. On this sealed document are the names of our leaders and Levites and priests."

10

[1]*The document was ratified and sealed with the following names:

The governor:

Nehemiah son of Hacaliah, and also Zedekiah.

[2]The following priests:

Seraiah, Azariah, Jeremiah, [3]Pashhur, Amariah, Malkijah, [4]Hattush, Shebaniah,
Malluch, [5]Harim, Meremoth, Obadiah, [6]Daniel, Ginnethon, Baruch, [7]Meshullam,
10:8-9 Abijah, Mijamin, [8]Maaziah, Bilgai, and Shemaiah. These were the priests.
Neh 12:1 [9]The following Levites:

Jeshua son of Azaniah, Binnui from the family of Henadad, Kadmiel, [10]and their
fellow Levites: Shebaniah, Hodiah, Kelita, Pelaiah, Hanan, [11]Mica, Rehob, Hashabiah,
[12]Zaccur, Sherebiah, Shebaniah, [13]Hodiah, Bani, and Beninu.

[14]The following leaders:

Parosh, Pahath-moab, Elam, Zattu, Bani, [15]Bunni, Azgad, Bebai, [16]Adonijah, Bigvai,
Adin, [17]Ater, Hezekiah, Azzur, [18]Hodiah, Hashum, Bezai, [19]Hariph, Anathoth, Nebai,
[20]Magpiash, Meshullam, Hezir, [21]Meshezabel, Zadok, Jaddua, [22]Pelatiah, Hanan,
Anaiah, [23]Hoshea, Hananiah, Hasshub, [24]Hallohesh, Pilha, Shobek, [25]Rehum,
Hashabnah, Maaseiah, [26]Ahiah, Hanan, Anan, [27]Malluch, Harim, and Baanah.

THE VOW OF THE PEOPLE

[28]Then the rest of the people—the priests, Levites, gatekeepers, singers, Temple servants,
10:28 Ezra 2:36-58 and all who had separated themselves from the pagan people of the land in order to obey
Neh 9:2 the Law of God, together with their wives, sons, daughters, and all who were old enough
10:29 to understand—[29]joined their leaders and bound themselves with an oath. They swore a
Neh 5:12 curse on themselves if they failed to obey the Law of God as issued by His servant Moses.
They solemnly promised to carefully follow all the commands, regulations, and decrees of
the LORD our Lord:

[30]"We promise not to let our daughters marry the pagan people of the land, and not
10:30 Exod 34:16 Deut 7:3 to let our sons marry their daughters.

9:38a Verse 9:38 is numbered 10:1 in Hebrew text. 9:38b Or *In spite of all this.* 10:1 Verses 10:1-39 are numbered 10:2-40 in Hebrew text.

10:1-29 This list of people who, for the most part, are unknown reinforces one of the major themes of Ezra-Nehemiah: The people of God as a whole, not just the great leaders, are vital for accomplishing God's redemptive plan.

10:28-29 This covenant affirmation wasn't simply accepted by the leaders and then begrudgingly accepted by the rest, but by "all who were old enough to understand," from the oldest to the youngest.

▸ WORSHIP

10:29 The oath to obey. The people of Nehemiah's day bound themselves with an oath to obey the law of God. We should have the same depth of purpose in obeying God's Word as they had. When we "carefully follow all the commands, regulations, and decrees" that God has given us, we enter into God's blessings. Our obedience is a sign of our love for Him. We obey not merely because we are afraid of God but because we want to serve Him out of love. Do you have that single-minded dedication to God in your life? (***See Worship> OT> Reverence> Awe of God means obeying His commandments,*** TopicGuide page A28.)

10:30-39 Pledges of covenant faithfulness focused on key problems related to the exile community—marriage (Nehemiah 10:30), Sabbath keeping (Nehemiah 10:31), and financial responsibility (Nehemiah 10:32). The marriage clause had an impact on infants and those not yet conceived. Even those who did not actively pledge on that day would enjoy the benefits and responsibilities of the covenant. We find no historical evidence that Israel as a whole practiced the *Shmita*, or the principle of resting from agricultural work every Sabbatical (seventh) year (Leviticus 25:1-7), although the Jews practice this infrequently in modern times. The oath concerning financial responsibility consisted of two parts—the standard Temple tax and the donation of a tenth of all agricultural produce (Nehemiah 10:37).

[31] "We also promise that if the people of the land should bring any merchandise or
grain to be sold on the Sabbath or on any other holy day, we will refuse to buy it.
Every seventh year we will let our land rest, and we will cancel all debts owed to us.
[32] "In addition, we promise to obey the command to pay the annual Temple tax
of one-eighth of an ounce of silver* for the care of the Temple of our God. [33] This
will provide for the Bread of the Presence; for the regular grain offerings and burnt
offerings; for the offerings on the Sabbaths, the new moon celebrations, and the
annual festivals; for the holy offerings; and for the sin offerings to make atonement
for Israel. It will provide for everything necessary for the work of the Temple of
our God.
[34] "We have cast sacred lots to determine when—at regular times each year—the
families of the priests, Levites, and the common people should bring wood to God's
Temple to be burned on the altar of the LORD our God, as is written in the Law.
[35] "We promise to bring the first part of every harvest to the LORD's Temple year
after year—whether it be a crop from the soil or from our fruit trees. [36] We agree to
give God our oldest sons and the firstborn of all our herds and flocks, as prescribed in
the Law. We will present them to the priests who minister in the Temple of our God.
[37] We will store the produce in the storerooms of the Temple of our God. We will bring
the best of our flour and other grain offerings, the best of our fruit, and the best of our
new wine and olive oil. And we promise to bring to the Levites a tenth of everything
our land produces, for it is the Levites who collect the tithes in all our rural towns.
[38] "A priest—a descendant of Aaron—will be with the Levites as they receive these
tithes. And a tenth of all that is collected as tithes will be delivered by the Levites to
the Temple of our God and placed in the storerooms. [39] The people and the Levites
must bring these offerings of grain, new wine, and olive oil to the storerooms and
place them in the sacred containers near the ministering priests, the gatekeepers,
and the singers.
"We promise together not to neglect the Temple of our God."

10:31 Exod 23:10-11; Lev 25:1-7; Deut 15:1-2; Neh 13:15-22
10:32 Exod 30:11-16; Matt 17:24
10:33 Lev 23:1-44; 24:5-7
10:34 Neh 11:1; 13:31
10:35 Exod 23:19; Deut 26:2
10:36 Exod 13:2
10:37 Lev 23:17; 27:30; Neh 13:5, 9
10:38 Num 18:26; Neh 13:12-13
10:39 Deut 12:6; Neh 13:10-11

THE PEOPLE OCCUPY JERUSALEM

11 The leaders of the people were living in Jerusalem, the holy city. A tenth of the
people from the other towns of Judah and Benjamin were chosen by sacred lots to

11:1 Neh 7:4; 10:34; 11:18; Isa 48:2

10:32 Hebrew *tax of 1/3 of a shekel* [4 grams].

▸ MINISTRY
10:31 Honor in business. When it comes to everyday life, many people leave their Christian principles at the door of the church. But our responsibility is to represent Christ at the office as much as we do at church. We influence many more people who don't know Christ in our business dealings than we do when we fellowship with our brothers and sisters in Christ. Our witness depends on our honesty, lack of greediness, and compassion in the workplace. (***See Ministry****> Transformation> Fill and Subdue> Influencing every sphere of life,* TopicGuide page A57.)

▸ WORSHIP
10:35 Giving the first fruits. Why does God call us to give the first of what we earn? When we give the first 10 percent of our income, we acknowledge that all we have comes from God. We show that we are merely stewards of what we own, managers of what God has given us. Check through your budget today to see if you are giving with the enthusiasm and the honesty that God requires. (***See Worship****> NT> Offerings> God loves a cheerful giver,* TopicGuide page A31.)

10:39 Rebuilding the house of God is a major theme in Ezra-Nehemiah.

11:1 The phrase "the holy city" is very rare, used in the Old Testament only in Nehemiah 11:18; Isaiah 48:2; 52:1. In the New Testament, it is found in Matthew 27:53 and twice in Revelation (11:2; 21:2). Holiness had been expanding from holy vessels (Ezra 1:7; see 8:28) to holy priests (Ezra 8:28) to holy people (Ezra 9:2) to the holy place/sanctuary (Ezra 9:8) to holy Sabbaths (Nehemiah 9:14) to the point that the entire city became holy. The *sacred lots* mentioned at the end of this verse may have been the same Urim and Thummim referenced in Ezra 2:63.

11:1–12:47 The dedication of the wall of Jerusalem was closely tied to the reordering of the community. These chapters divide into three parts: preparations (11:1–12:26), the dedication itself (12:27-43), and provisions made for the clergy (12:44-47).

live there, too, while the rest stayed where they were. [2]And the people commended every-
one who volunteered to resettle in Jerusalem.

11:3-19 //1 Chr 9:1-17 Ezra 2:43-57 Neh 7:57-59; 11:20

[3]Here is a list of the names of the provincial officials who came to live in Jerusalem.
(Most of the people, priests, Levites, Temple servants, and descendants of Solomon's ser-
vants continued to live in their own homes in the various towns of Judah, [4]but some of the
people from Judah and Benjamin resettled in Jerusalem.)

From the tribe of Judah:

Athaiah son of Uzziah, son of Zechariah, son of Amariah, son of Shephatiah, son of
Mahalalel, of the family of Perez. [5]Also Maaseiah son of Baruch, son of Col-hozeh,
son of Hazaiah, son of Adaiah, son of Joiarib, son of Zechariah, of the family of
Shelah.* [6]There were 468 descendants of Perez who lived in Jerusalem—all
outstanding men.

[7]From the tribe of Benjamin:

Sallu son of Meshullam, son of Joed, son of Pedaiah, son of Kolaiah, son of
Maaseiah, son of Ithiel, son of Jeshaiah. [8]After him were Gabbai and Sallai and a
total of 928 relatives. [9]Their chief officer was Joel son of Zicri, who was assisted by
Judah son of Hassenuah, second-in-command over the city.

[10]From the priests:

Jedaiah son of Joiarib; Jakin; [11]and Seraiah son of Hilkiah, son of Meshullam, son of
Zadok, son of Meraioth, son of Ahitub, the supervisor of the Temple of God. [12]Also
822 of their associates, who worked at the Temple. Also Adaiah son of Jeroham, son
of Pelaliah, son of Amzi, son of Zechariah, son of Pashhur, son of Malkijah, [13]along
with 242 of his associates, who were heads of their families. Also Amashsai son of
Azarel, son of Ahzai, son of Meshillemoth, son of Immer, [14]and 128 of his*
outstanding associates. Their chief officer was Zabdiel son of Haggedolim.

[15]From the Levites:

Shemaiah son of Hasshub, son of Azrikam, son of Hashabiah, son of Bunni. [16]Also
Shabbethai and Jozabad, who were in charge of the work outside the Temple of God.
[17]Also Mattaniah son of Mica, son of Zabdi, a descendant of Asaph, who led in
thanksgiving and prayer. Also Bakbukiah, who was Mattaniah's assistant, and Abda
son of Shammua, son of Galal, son of Jeduthun. [18]In all, there were 284 Levites in
the holy city.

11:18 Neh 11:1, 3

[19]From the gatekeepers:

Akkub, Talmon, and 172 of their associates, who guarded the gates.

[20]The other priests, Levites, and the rest of the Israelites lived wherever their family in-
heritance was located in any of the towns of Judah. [21]The Temple servants, however,
whose leaders were Ziha and Gishpa, all lived on the hill of Ophel.

11:21 Neh 3:26

11:5 Hebrew *son of the Shilonite.* 11:14 As in Greek version; Hebrew reads *their.*

▸ HOLINESS

11:2 The courage of the faithful. Consider how difficult it must have been for people to resettle Jerusalem. They faced a hostile population, austere conditions, and separation from family and friends. Yet many of the Jews willingly obeyed, packed up their belongings, and moved. What is God asking you to do for Him? Perhaps He wants you to minister in an area that might cause you real loss for a time. Maybe God is calling you to serve overseas or in a difficult part of your city. Just as God has empowered people in the past to help build His kingdom in difficult places, He will enable you to accomplish the tasks He gives you. (***See Holiness***> *Changed by God> God Provides> Empowering us,* TopicGuide page A41.)

11:4–12:26 These lists of people connect the goals of Ezra (see Ezra 2:21-35) and Nehemiah.

▸ ADOPTION

11:20 Our inheritance. The Levites were anxious to rebuild Jerusalem because the land was their families' inheritance. They had a vested interest in seeing the land prosper. Our inheritance is the kingdom of God, not our material wealth. If we focus on our true inheritance, we will put our hearts into building up our brothers and sisters in Christ and seeing people come to Christ. Then we will be storing up a treasure in heaven, not in an earthly bank, and we will inherit blessings from God that we cannot receive any other way. (See Matthew 19:21; also ***see Adoption***> *With Christ> Heirs of God> Inheritance reserved in heaven,* TopicGuide page A36.)

[22]The chief officer of the Levites in Jerusalem was Uzzi son of Bani, son of Hashabiah, 11:22 Neh 11:9, 14, 17, 23
son of Mattaniah, son of Mica, a descendant of Asaph, whose family served as singers at
God's Temple. [23]Their daily responsibilities were carried out according to the terms of a
royal command.

[24]Pethahiah son of Meshezabel, a descendant of Zerah son of Judah, was the royal ad-
viser in all matters of public administration.

[25]As for the surrounding villages with their open fields, some of the people of Judah lived 11:25 Josh 13:9, 17; 14:15
in Kiriath-arba with its settlements, Dibon with its settlements, and Jekabzeel with its vil-
lages. [26]They also lived in Jeshua, Moladah, Beth-pelet, [27]Hazar-shual, Beersheba with its
settlements, [28]Ziklag, and Meconah with its settlements. [29]They also lived in En-rimmon,
Zorah, Jarmuth, [30]Zanoah, and Adullam with their surrounding villages. They also lived in
Lachish with its nearby fields and Azekah with its surrounding villages. So the people of Ju-
dah were living all the way from Beersheba in the south to the valley of Hinnom.

[31]Some of the people of Benjamin lived at Geba, Micmash, Aija, and Bethel with its set-
tlements. [32]They also lived in Anathoth, Nob, Ananiah, [33]Hazor, Ramah, Gittaim, [34]Hadid,
Zeboim, Neballat, [35]Lod, Ono, and the Valley of Craftsmen.* [36]Some of the Levites who
lived in Judah were sent to live with the tribe of Benjamin.

A HISTORY OF THE PRIESTS AND LEVITES

12 Here is the list of the priests and Levites who returned with Zerubbabel son of She- 12:1 Ezra 2:1-2
altiel and Jeshua the high priest:

Seraiah, Jeremiah, Ezra,
[2] Amariah, Malluch, Hattush,
[3] Shecaniah, Harim,* Meremoth,
[4] Iddo, Ginnethon,* Abijah,
[5] Miniamin, Moadiah,* Bilgah,
[6] Shemaiah, Joiarib, Jedaiah,
[7] Sallu, Amok, Hilkiah, and Jedaiah.

These were the leaders of the priests and their associates in the days of Jeshua.

[8]The Levites who returned with them were Jeshua, Binnui, Kadmiel, Sherebiah, Judah,
and Mattaniah, who with his associates was in charge of the songs of thanksgiving. [9]Their 12:8 Ezra 2:2 Neh 11:17
associates, Bakbukiah and Unni, stood opposite them during the service.

[10] Jeshua the high priest was the father of Joiakim.
Joiakim was the father of Eliashib.
Eliashib was the father of Joiada.
[11] Joiada was the father of Johanan.*
Johanan was the father of Jaddua.

11:35 Or *and Ge-harashim.* 12:3 Hebrew *Rehum;* compare 7:42; 12:15; Ezra 2:39. 12:4 As in some Hebrew manuscripts and Latin Vulgate (see also 12:16); most Hebrew manuscripts read *Ginnethoi.* 12:5 Hebrew *Mijamin, Maadiah;* compare 12:17. 12:11 Hebrew *Jonathan;* compare 12:22.

12:1-10 The list of priests and Levites who returned under Zerubbabel binds the end of Nehemiah to the beginning of Ezra, thus uniting the work of Zerubbabel, Ezra, and Nehemiah.

▸ WORSHIP
12:8 The importance of thanksgiving. Sometimes in our worship we just go through the motions, feeling weighed down with the responsibilities and cares of our daily lives. But giving thanks to God through songs and prayers of praise will lift our spirits and help us to focus on God. Such praise can be drawn from a wealth of different sources, such as older hymns, newer praise songs, or Scripture psalms. Make sure that in your worship you establish a practice of thanking God for all He has done for you. (***See Worship***> *OT> Music> Psalms> Thanksgiving,* TopicGuide page A27.)

12:9 These Levites stood opposite each other to facilitate call-and-response musical forms.

[12]Now when Joiakim was high priest, the family leaders of the priests were as follows:
Meraiah was leader of the family of Seraiah.
Hananiah was leader of the family of Jeremiah.
[13] Meshullam was leader of the family of Ezra.
Jehohanan was leader of the family of Amariah.
[14] Jonathan was leader of the family of Malluch.*
Joseph was leader of the family of Shecaniah.*
[15] Adna was leader of the family of Harim.
Helkai was leader of the family of Meremoth.*
[16] Zechariah was leader of the family of Iddo.
Meshullam was leader of the family of Ginnethon.
[17] Zicri was leader of the family of Abijah.
There was also a* leader of the family of Miniamin.
Piltai was leader of the family of Moadiah.
[18] Shammua was leader of the family of Bilgah.
Jehonathan was leader of the family of Shemaiah.
[19] Mattenai was leader of the family of Joiarib.
Uzzi was leader of the family of Jedaiah.
[20] Kallai was leader of the family of Sallu.*
Eber was leader of the family of Amok.
[21] Hashabiah was leader of the family of Hilkiah.
Nethanel was leader of the family of Jedaiah.

[22]A record of the Levite families was kept during the years when Eliashib, Joiada, Joha-
nan, and Jaddua served as high priest. Another record of the priests was kept during the
reign of Darius the Persian.* [23]A record of the heads of the Levite families was kept in *The
Book of History* down to the days of Johanan, the grandson* of Eliashib.

12:24 Neh 11:17 [24]These were the family leaders of the Levites: Hashabiah, Sherebiah, Jeshua, Binnui,*
Kadmiel, and other associates, who stood opposite them during the ceremonies of praise
and thanksgiving, one section responding to the other, as commanded by David, the man
12:25 1 Chr 26:15-16 of God. [25]This included Mattaniah, Bakbukiah, and Obadiah.

12:26 Meshullam, Talmon, and Akkub were the gatekeepers in charge of the storerooms at
Neh 8:9 the gates. [26]These all served in the days of Joiakim son of Jeshua, son of Jehozadak,* and
in the days of Nehemiah the governor and of Ezra the priest and scribe.

DEDICATION OF JERUSALEM'S WALL

12:27 [27]For the dedication of the new wall of Jerusalem, the Levites throughout the land were
1 Chr 15:16, 28 asked to come to Jerusalem to assist in the ceremonies. They were to take part in the joyous

12:14a As in Greek version (see also 10:4; 12:2); Hebrew reads *Malluchi.* 12:14b As in many Hebrew manuscripts, some Greek manuscripts, and Syriac version (see also 12:3); most Hebrew manuscripts read *Shebaniah.* 12:15 As in some Greek manuscripts (see also 12:3); Hebrew reads *Meraioth.* 12:17 Hebrew lacks the name of this family leader. 12:20 Hebrew *Sallai;* compare 12:7. 12:22 *Darius the Persian* is probably Darius II, who reigned 423–404 B.C., or possibly Darius III, who reigned 336–331 B.C. 12:23 Hebrew *son;* compare 12:10-11. 12:24 Hebrew *son of* (i.e., *ben*), which should probably be read here as the proper name Binnui; compare Ezra 3:9 and the note there. 12:26 Hebrew *Jozadak,* a variant spelling of Jehozadak.

12:22 This is a reference to either Darius II Nothus (423–404 BC) or Darius III Codamannus (336–331 BC).

▸ WORSHIP
12:27 Singing from the heart. Music was an essential part of the worship services in the Old Testament. People used musical instruments, dance, and vocal music to praise God for what He had done for them. This facet of worship was considered so important that some Levites were dedicated fully to service in these areas. We can enjoy giving praise to God through the talents God has given us. Find out how you can best use your abilities to praise God. Perhaps you can join the choir or play an instrument in the worship service. Or maybe you can join the congregation in singing praise choruses. However you contribute, sing to God from your heart. (***See Worship****> OT> Music> Psalms> Thanksgiving psalms> Reliance,* TopicGuide page A27.)

12:27-43 This dedication ceremony was for the rebuilt wall, but by extension for the whole "house of God" (Temple, community, and city), which was now complete (Ezra 6:14). This material was probably part of Nehemiah's memoirs, since Nehemiah speaks in the first person here.

occasion with their songs of thanksgiving and with the music of cymbals, harps, and lyres.
28The singers were brought together from the region around Jerusalem and from the vil- 12:28 1 Chr 9:16
lages of the Netophathites. 29They also came from Beth-gilgal and the rural areas near Geba
and Azmaveth, for the singers had built their own settlements around Jerusalem. 30The 12:30 Neh 13:22, 30
priests and Levites first purified themselves; then they purified the people, the gates, and the
wall.

31I led the leaders of Judah to the top of the wall and organized two large choirs to give 12:31 Neh 2:13; 3:13-14
thanks. One of the choirs proceeded southward* along the top of the wall to the Dung
Gate. 32Hoshaiah and half the leaders of Judah followed them, 33along with Azariah, Ezra,
Meshullam, 34Judah, Benjamin, Shemaiah, and Jeremiah. 35Then came some priests who
played trumpets, including Zechariah son of Jonathan, son of Shemaiah, son of Mattaniah,
son of Micaiah, son of Zaccur, a descendant of Asaph. 36And Zechariah's colleagues were
Shemaiah, Azarel, Milalai, Gilalai, Maai, Nethanel, Judah, and Hanani. They used the mu-
sical instruments prescribed by David, the man of God. Ezra the scribe led this procession.
37At the Fountain Gate they went straight up the steps on the ascent of the city wall toward 12:37 Neh 2:14; 3:15, 26
the City of David. They passed the house of David and then proceeded to the Water Gate
on the east.

38The second choir giving thanks went northward* around the other way to meet them. 12:38 Neh 3:8, 11
I followed them, together with the other half of the people, along the top of the wall past
the Tower of the Ovens to the Broad Wall, 39then past the Ephraim Gate to the Old City 12:39 Neh 3:1, 3, 6, 25, 31-32; 8:16 Jer 31:38
Gate,* past the Fish Gate and the Tower of Hananel, and on to the Tower of the Hundred.
Then we continued on to the Sheep Gate and stopped at the Guard Gate.

40The two choirs that were giving thanks then proceeded to the Temple of God, where
they took their places. So did I, together with the group of leaders who were with me.
41We went together with the trumpet-playing priests—Eliakim, Maaseiah, Miniamin, Mica-
iah, Elioenai, Zechariah, and Hananiah—42and the singers—Maaseiah, Shemaiah, Eleazar,
Uzzi, Jehohanan, Malkijah, Elam, and Ezer. They played and sang loudly under the direc-
tion of Jezrahiah the choir director.

43Many sacrifices were offered on that joyous day, for God had given the people cause
for great joy. The women and children also participated in the celebration, and the joy of
the people of Jerusalem could be heard far away.

PROVISIONS FOR TEMPLE WORSHIP

44On that day men were appointed to be in charge of the storerooms for the offerings, the 12:44 Neh 13:4-5, 12-13
first part of the harvest, and the tithes. They were responsible to collect from the fields out-
side the towns the portions required by the Law for the priests and Levites. For all the peo-
ple of Judah took joy in the priests and Levites and their work. 45They performed the 12:45 1 Chr 25:1-8; 26:1-32
service of their God and the service of purification, as commanded by David and his son
Solomon, and so did the singers and the gatekeepers. 46The custom of having choir direc- 12:46 2 Chr 29:30
tors to lead the choirs in hymns of praise and thanksgiving to God began long ago in the
days of David and Asaph. 47So now, in the days of Zerubbabel and of Nehemiah, all Israel 12:47 Num 18:21-29
brought a daily supply of food for the singers, the gatekeepers, and the Levites. The Levites,
in turn, gave a portion of what they received to the priests, the descendants of Aaron.

12:31 Hebrew *to the right.* 12:38 Hebrew *to the left.* 12:39 Or *the Mishneh Gate,* or *the Jeshanah Gate.*

12:30 Observing ceremonial purity provided a context for teaching moral purity (see Leviticus 16:30).

12:31-39 A procession took place, which apparently began at the Valley Gate (see Nehemiah 2:13, 15; 3:13). Part of the procession (Nehemiah 12:31-37), led by Ezra (Nehemiah 12:36), moved counterclockwise (Nehemiah 12:31), passing the Dung Gate (12:31), the Fountain Gate (12:37) and the Water Gate (12:37), before proceeding to the Temple. The other part of the procession (12:38-39), accompanied by Nehemiah (12:38), moved clockwise (12:38), passing the gates on the northwest and north sides of the city before proceeding to the Temple. From an archaeological perspective, this is an important record of the placement of ancient gates and their subsequent discovery shows the preservation and perfections of God's Word.

NEHEMIAH'S VARIOUS REFORMS

13:1 Deut 23:3-5 Neh 13:23 **13** On that same day, as the Book of Moses was being read to the people, the pas-
sage was found that said no Ammonite or Moabite should ever be permitted to
13:2 Num 22:3-11 enter the assembly of God.* 2For they had not provided the Israelites with food and water
in the wilderness. Instead, they hired Balaam to curse them, though our God turned the
13:3 Neh 9:2; 10:28 curse into a blessing. 3When this passage of the Law was read, all those of foreign descent
were immediately excluded from the assembly.

13:4 Neh 6:17-19; 12:44 4Before this had happened, Eliashib the priest, who had been appointed as supervisor of
13:5 Num 18:21 the storerooms of the Temple of our God and who was also a relative of Tobiah, 5had con-
verted a large storage room and placed it at Tobiah's disposal. The room had previously
been used for storing the grain offerings, the frankincense, various articles for the Temple,
and the tithes of grain, new wine, and olive oil (which were prescribed for the Levites, the
singers, and the gatekeepers), as well as the offerings for the priests.

13:6 Neh 5:14 6I was not in Jerusalem at that time, for I had returned to King Artaxerxes of Babylon in
13:7 Neh 13:5 the thirty-second year of his reign,* though I later asked his permission to return. 7When I
arrived back in Jerusalem, I learned about Eliashib's evil deed in providing Tobiah with a
room in the courtyards of the Temple of God. 8I became very upset and threw all of Tobi-
13:9 2 Chr 29:5, 15-19 ah's belongings out of the room. 9Then I demanded that the rooms be purified, and I
brought back the articles for God's Temple, the grain offerings, and the frankincense.

13:10 Neh 10:37; 12:28-29 10I also discovered that the Levites had not been given their prescribed portions of food,
so they and the singers who were to conduct the worship services had all returned to work
their fields. 11I immediately confronted the leaders and demanded, "Why has the Temple
of God been neglected?" Then I called all the Levites back again and restored them to their
13:12 Neh 10:37-39; 12:44 proper duties. 12And once more all the people of Judah began bringing their tithes of
grain, new wine, and olive oil to the Temple storerooms.

13:13 Neh 7:2 13I assigned supervisors for the storerooms: Shelemiah the priest, Zadok the scribe, and
Pedaiah, one of the Levites. And I appointed Hanan son of Zaccur and grandson of Matta-
niah as their assistant. These men had an excellent reputation, and it was their job to
make honest distributions to their fellow Levites.

13:14 Neh 5:19; 13:22, 31 14Remember this good deed, O my God, and do not forget all that I have faithfully
done for the Temple of my God and its services.

13:15 Exod 20:8-11; 34:21 Neh 13:21 15In those days I saw men of Judah treading out their winepresses on the Sabbath. They
were also bringing in grain, loading it on donkeys, and bringing their wine, grapes, figs,
and all sorts of produce to Jerusalem to sell on the Sabbath. So I rebuked them for selling

13:1 See Deut 23:3-6. 13:6 King Artaxerxes of Persia is here identified as the king of Babylon because Persia had conquered the Babylonian Empire. The thirty-second year of Artaxerxes was 433 B.C.

13:1-31 Nehemiah's final act in this book is to bring reform to the community. This sanctification of the people took place in four ways: expelling foreigners from the assembly (Nehemiah 13:1-3), attending to the Temple (Nehemiah 13:4-14), observing the Sabbath (Nehemiah 13:15-22), and divorcing foreign wives (Nehemiah 13:23-31).

▸ CHURCH

13:10 Give what is due. When a person serves in the church on a full-time basis, we must be sure that they are as well paid as possible. If we do not pay our ministers a fair wage, the work (and the minister) suffers. Many times pastors or other workers are paid so little that they cannot sufficiently support their family. Make a decision that you will not require your ministers to live in poverty, but that you will adequately reward them for their labors (1 Corinthians 9:9; 1 Timothy 5:18). (***See Church****> Role> Preach> Topics> Collect Resources> For salaries of ministers,* TopicGuide page A50.)

13:10 This situation links this section to the pledge in Nehemiah 10:37. The Levites possessed no land (see Numbers 18:20-24), though some may have had private income (see Deuteronomy 18:8). The dependence of the Levites on the support of the people may explain the reluctance of many Levites to leave Babylon (see Ezra 8:15-20). They did not believe they could survive in Jerusalem.

13:14 This is the fifth use of "remember" in a prayer (see Nehemiah 1:8; 5:19; 6:14) and the second of four such prayers by Nehemiah (see Nehemiah 5:19).

their produce on that day. 16Some men from Tyre, who lived in Jerusalem, were bringing
in fish and all kinds of merchandise. They were selling it on the Sabbath to the people of
Judah—and in Jerusalem at that!
17So I confronted the nobles of Judah. "Why are you profaning the Sabbath in this evil
way?" I asked. 18"Wasn't it just this sort of thing that your ancestors did that caused our
God to bring all this trouble upon us and our city? Now you are bringing even more wrath
upon Israel by permitting the Sabbath to be desecrated in this way!"
19Then I commanded that the gates of Jerusalem should be shut as darkness fell every
Friday evening,* not to be opened until the Sabbath ended. I sent some of my own ser-
vants to guard the gates so that no merchandise could be brought in on the Sabbath day.
20The merchants and tradesmen with a variety of wares camped outside Jerusalem once
or twice. 21But I spoke sharply to them and said, "What are you doing out here, camping
around the wall? If you do this again, I will arrest you!" And that was the last time they
came on the Sabbath. 22Then I commanded the Levites to purify themselves and to guard
the gates in order to preserve the holiness of the Sabbath.

Remember this good deed also, O my God! Have compassion on me according to
Your great and unfailing love.

23About the same time I realized that some of the men of Judah had married women
from Ashdod, Ammon, and Moab. 24Furthermore, half their children spoke the language
of Ashdod or of some other people and could not speak the language of Judah at all. 25So
I confronted them and called down curses on them. I beat some of them and pulled out
their hair. I made them swear in the name of God that they would not let their children
intermarry with the pagan people of the land.
26"Wasn't this exactly what led King Solomon of Israel into sin?" I demanded. "There
was no king from any nation who could compare to him, and God loved him and made
him king over all Israel. But even he was led into sin by his foreign wives. 27How could you
even think of committing this sinful deed and acting unfaithfully toward God by marrying
foreign women?"
28One of the sons of Joiada son of Eliashib the high priest had married a daughter of
Sanballat the Horonite, so I banished him from my presence.

29Remember them, O my God, for they have defiled the priesthood and the solemn
vows of the priests and Levites.

30So I purged out everything foreign and assigned tasks to the priests and Levites, mak-
ing certain that each knew his work. 31I also made sure that the supply of wood for the al-
tar and the first portions of the harvest were brought at the proper times.

Remember this in my favor, O my God.

13:17 Neh 13:11, 15
13:18 Jer 17:21
13:19 Lev 23:32
13:21 Neh 13:15
13:22 Neh 13:14, 31
13:23 Ezra 9:2; Neh 10:30
13:25 Deut 25:2; Neh 10:29-30; 13:11, 17
13:26 1 Kgs 3:13; 11:1-8; 2 Chr 1:12
13:27 Ezra 10:2; Neh 13:23
13:28 Neh 2:10, 19
13:29 Num 25:13; Neh 6:14
13:30 Neh 10:30
13:31 Neh 10:34; 13:14, 22

13:19 Hebrew *on the day before the Sabbath.*

13:19 The Israelites at times reckoned the day from sunset to sunset, as indicated by the phrases "night or day" (Esther 4:16) and "evenings and mornings" (Daniel 8:14), and at times from morning to morning, as indicated by the phrase "day and night" (Deuteronomy 28:66-67). Here the Sabbath began at sunset.

▸ WORSHIP

13:22 Respect the Lord's Day. Do you set aside one day a week to worship God? Throughout the Old and New Testaments, the people considered one day a week as sacred to God, a time to worship and focus on Him. Today, many have turned their attention from God on that one day to recreation and other activities. We have lost the reverence we once paid to God each week. Check your family calendar to set aside time to worship God on the Lord's Day. (***See Worship****> OT> Festivals> Sabbath,* TopicGuide page A26.)

13:22 This is the sixth use of "remember" in a prayer (see note at Nehemiah 1:8) and the third of four such prayers by Nehemiah (see note at Nehemiah 5:19).

13:23-31 The pledge in Nehemiah 10:30 had been violated. Nehemiah understood that reformation that begins in the heart bears fruit in the home. The New Testament makes it clear that God's people may marry any race they choose, but they remain barred from marrying those outside the covenant community (1 Corinthians 7:39). See also Ezra 10 for a similar situation and explanation.

ESTHER

PURPOSE

To document God's preservation of the Jews from genocide at the hands of Haman, and to record the origins of the annual Jewish Feast of Purim, which celebrates the Jews' deliverance.

In some people's minds, chance and coincidence, fate and fortune determine how life turns out. The book of Esther, however, refutes that notion. Life is providential, not coincidental.

When King Cyrus of Persia gave permission for Jews to return to their homeland after living in captivity for seventy years, not all Jews returned. Many remained in Persia, since they had been born there and had established roots in that land. A young Jewish woman named Esther was elevated to a place of influence in King Xerxes' court—and when opposition against the Jews arose, she managed to save the Persian Jews from extinction. This book highlights the fact that God is in the details; that nothing in life is coincidental; that He is behind the scenes working out His purposes in every area of life. Through seemingly mundane, everyday, unpredictable events, God preserved His people in Persia—a victory still celebrated annually by Jews the world over in the Feast of Purim.

The Book of Esther contains no explicit references to God, yet God is still prominent throughout the book. The reason the author chose not to mention God explicitly may be that he intended his book to become part of the royal archives of the Persian kings (see notes on Esther 2:21-23 and 10:2), and references to the God of the monotheistic Jews would have hindered such a goal in the polytheistic Persian culture.

DISCOVER GOD IN ESTHER

In a book where God is not mentioned a single time, His presence is seen everywhere:

Trustworthiness: Many see the historic existence of the Jews as evidence of the character and purposes of God. God promised Abraham that his descendants would be "like the stars in the sky and the sand on the seashore" (Genesis 22:17). Many times the future of God's people seemed doubtful, and no more so than in Persia during the reign of Xerxes. Had Haman's genocidal plan worked, a large portion of the descendants of Abraham would have been killed. The nation would have been reduced to a fraction of its size. But God is trustworthy. He is still committed to showing grace to the Jewish people by saving those who repent and believe in their Messiah, Jesus Christ (Romans 11:1-5).

Faithfulness: In our relationships with others, we are tempted to distance ourselves from those with whom we've experienced conflict, so it is easy to think of God distancing Himself from the Jews during their captivity in Babylon and Persia. We may think He stayed in the land of promise while His people languished in the land of punishment. But God is like a loving parent—His love for His children isn't determined by their behavior. His promise to His chosen people was that they were His forever (Jeremiah 31:35-37). So when they went to Babylon in captivity, He went with them to oversee their lives and to ensure their preservation. The evidence of God's presence was the Jews' deliverance. And the lack of His name anywhere in the book demonstrates that God was working behind the scenes, rather than in overt ways. Whether seen or not seen, God is faithful to stay close to those He loves (Psalm 139:7-12).

GROWING THROUGH ESTHER

Because every follower of Christ undergoes times of testing—times when God seems distant—there are lessons from the book of Esther:

Circumstantial Evidence: Circumstances as a way of discerning God's will should not be discounted. In Esther's case, an opportunity slowly unfolded that put her in a place of influence to help her people. As events and relationships unfold in our lives, discernment is the watchword: "Lord, are these circumstances something You are doing? Please give me wisdom and care as I walk through the doors that You are opening."

Godly Promotions: There is a false sense of humility that can short-circuit God's plans if we are not careful. What if Esther had thought, "The role of queen is too prideful and worldly a position for me"? What if Abraham, Moses, Joseph, Daniel, and others had thought similar things? God's promotions to places of influence should be received with gratitude and with a view toward discovering how to advance God's purposes in that place. Queen Esther recognized why God promoted her and used her influence accordingly.

Righteousness and Risk-Taking: When Esther discovered the plot against her people, she knew the right thing to do: tell the king and ask for his intervention. But asking an ancient Near Eastern king for favors was risky—even for a queen (Esther 1:16-18). Scripture is filled with examples of people who did the right thing in the face of harm, the greatest example being Jesus Christ. Esther illustrated what Jesus Christ later taught, that the greatest love is the one that is willing to risk life and limb for others (John 15:13).

Righteousness vs. Recognition: Mordecai was a modest layman, a single Jew among thousands in Persia. When he discovered a secret plot among Xerxes' subjects to kill the king, he sent word to Esther, who told the king, saving his life. Later, Mordecai's deed came to the attention of the king, and he was rewarded for his loyalty. Mordecai did not seek recognition or favor; rather he acted out of respect for a king. Acts motivated by a desire for recognition may be rewarded immediately by others, but acts motivated by righteousness will be rewarded by God in His time and in His way (Galatians 6:7).

DISCOVERY VERSES

"If you keep quiet at a time like this, deliverance and relief for the Jews will arise from some other place, but you and your relatives will die. Who knows if perhaps you were made queen for just such a time as this?" (ESTHER 4:14)

"Go and gather together all the Jews of Susa and fast for me. Do not eat or drink for three days, night or day. My maids and I will do the same. And then, though it is against the law, I will go in to see the king. If I must die, I must die." (ESTHER 4:16)

ESTHER FACTS

Author: Unknown. The intimate knowledge of Persian life indicates the author was probably a Jew living in Persia at the time of the events.

Written to: Probably initially written to the Jewish population in Persia as a historical account, but also for the returned exiles in Judea.

Date of writing: The events of Esther occur approximately 483 BC. The story could have been put to writing any time after that up to 100 BC.

Setting: The setting is Susa, an important city in the Persian Empire.

OUTLINE

- ▸ **ESTHER 1–2**—Esther chosen as queen
- ▸ **ESTHER 3–4**—Haman plots to destroy the Jews
- ▸ **ESTHER 5:1–9:15**—Esther saves the Jews
- ▸ **ESTHER 9:16-32**—Establishment of the feast
- ▸ **ESTHER 10**—Epilogue

THE KING'S BANQUET

1:1 **1** These events happened in the days of King Xerxes,* who reigned over 127 provinces
Ezra 4:6 Esth 8:9-10 stretching from India to Ethiopia.* 2At that time Xerxes ruled his empire from his royal
Dan 8:2 throne at the fortress of Susa. 3In the third year of his reign, he gave a banquet for all his
1:2 nobles and officials. He invited all the military officers of Persia and Media as well as the
Neh 1:1 princes and nobles of the provinces. 4The celebration lasted 180 days—a tremendous dis-
1:3 Esth 2:18 play of the opulent wealth of his empire and the pomp and splendor of his majesty.
5When it was all over, the king gave a banquet for all the people, from the greatest to
1:5 Esth 7:7-8 the least, who were in the fortress of Susa. It lasted for seven days and was held in the
1:6 courtyard of the palace garden. 6The courtyard was beautifully decorated with white cot-
Ezek 23:41 ton curtains and blue hangings, which were fastened with white linen cords and purple
Amos 6:4 ribbons to silver rings embedded in marble pillars. Gold and silver couches stood on a mo-
saic pavement of porphyry, marble, mother-of-pearl, and other costly stones.
1:7 7Drinks were served in gold goblets of many designs, and there was an abundance of
Esth 2:18 royal wine, reflecting the king's generosity. 8By edict of the king, no limits were placed on
the drinking, for the king had instructed all his palace officials to serve each man as much
as he wanted.
9At the same time, Queen Vashti gave a banquet for the women in the royal palace of
King Xerxes.

QUEEN VASHTI DEPOSED

1:10 10On the seventh day of the feast, when King Xerxes was in high spirits because of the
Judg 16:25 Dan 5:1-4 wine, he told the seven eunuchs who attended him—Mehuman, Biztha, Harbona, Bigtha,
Abagtha, Zethar, and Carcas—11to bring Queen Vashti to him with the royal crown on her
head. He wanted the nobles and all the other men to gaze on her beauty, for she was a

1:1a Hebrew *Ahasuerus,* another name for Xerxes; also throughout the book of Esther. Xerxes reigned 486–465 B.C.
1:1b Hebrew *to Cush.*

1:1 *Xerxes* in Hebrew is *Ahasuerus,* who reigned over the Persian Empire from 486–464 BC. He was the son of Darius and grandson of Cyrus the Great (see Daniel 10:1), the founder of the Medo-Persian Empire. The events of the book of Esther likely occurred in the first half of King Xerxes' reign.

1:2-3 *Susa* was the winter capital city of ancient Persia (modern Iran). See Nehemiah 1:1; Daniel 8:2.

▸ PURPOSE
1:3 God's providence in crisis. When the book of Esther opens, King Xerxes is hosting a huge party for his kingdom's officials. The overwhelming opulence of his party displayed the greatest treasures in the world. It may have seemed as if the king lived a life outside of God's providence—the king could do and have whatever he wanted. However, a humble young woman, Esther, with no treasure but her God, was about to take the center stage. In her weakness and in the weakness of her Jewish family, God would display His sovereign plan. God has our future in His hands in a similar way. We may feel as if we have no power to effect change, but God is working out circumstances to complete His plan for our lives. Our role is to be willing to be used by Him in His master plan. (***See Purpose***> *God's Means> God's Sovereignty> God's people are chosen for service,* TopicGuide page A52.)

1:3 The author does not give the reason for King Xerxes' banquet, but it seems likely that he used this event to plan his military campaigns in the west (482–479 BC), which were successful until the Greeks stopped him at the battle of Salamis in 480 BC.

1:9 *Vashti* is Persian for "beloved," or perhaps "beautiful." Queen Vashti is not mentioned anywhere in ancient literature except Esther 1–2, unless she is the Queen Amestris mentioned by some ancient historians. Polygamy was so common in the ancient world, especially among royalty, that it was common for many of the women in a king's harem to remain shrouded in virtual anonymity—even if she was the favorite at one time.

very beautiful woman. 12But when they conveyed the king's order to Queen Vashti, she refused to come. This made the king furious, and he burned with anger.

13He immediately consulted with his wise advisers, who knew all the Persian laws and customs, for he always asked their advice. 14The names of these men were Carshena, Shethar, Admatha, Tarshish, Meres, Marsena, and Memucan—seven nobles of Persia and Media. They met with the king regularly and held the highest positions in the empire.

1:13
1 Chr 12:32

15"What must be done to Queen Vashti?" the king demanded. "What penalty does the law provide for a queen who refuses to obey the king's orders, properly sent through his eunuchs?"

16Memucan answered the king and his nobles, "Queen Vashti has wronged not only the king but also every noble and citizen throughout your empire. 17Women everywhere will begin to despise their husbands when they learn that Queen Vashti has refused to appear before the king. 18Before this day is out, the wives of all the king's nobles throughout Persia and Media will hear what the queen did and will start treating their husbands the same way. There will be no end to their contempt and anger.

19"So if it please the king, we suggest that you issue a written decree, a law of the Persians and Medes that cannot be revoked. It should order that Queen Vashti be forever banished from the presence of King Xerxes, and that the king should choose another queen more worthy than she. 20When this decree is published throughout the king's vast empire, husbands everywhere, whatever their rank, will receive proper respect from their wives!"

1:19
Esth 8:8
Dan 6:8, 15

21The king and his nobles thought this made good sense, so he followed Memucan's

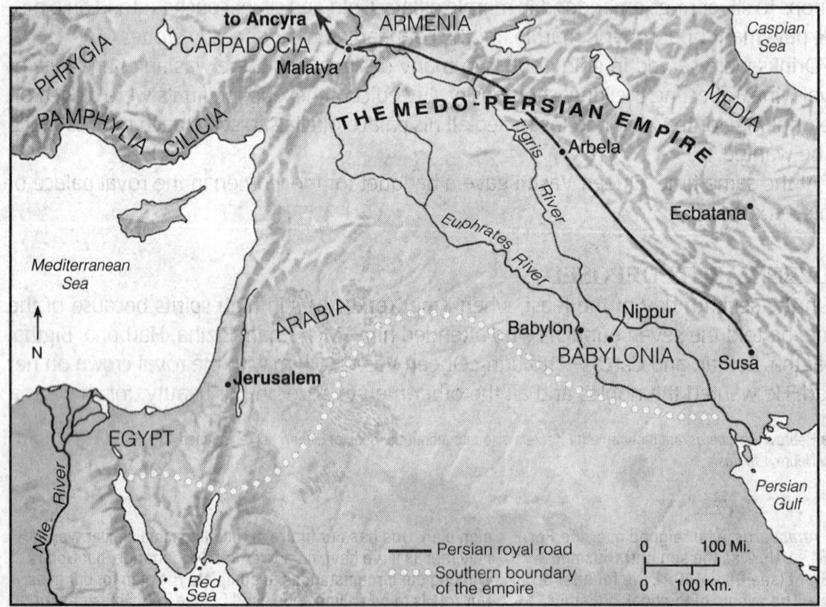

THE WORLD OF ESTHER'S DAY
Esther lived in the capital of the vast Medo-Persian Empire, which incorporated the provinces of Media and Persia, as well as the previous empires of Assyria and Babylon. Esther, a Jew, was chosen by King Xerxes to be his queen. The story of how she saved her people takes place in the palace in Susa.

1:12 Queen Vashti's refusal to follow the king's orders took a lot of courage and could have resulted in much worse than just being deposed and banished (Esther 1:19). Her fall from the king's favor made possible Esther's ascension to the throne as queen (Esther 2). However, if Vashti is equated with Amestris, then she regained her power after the death of Xerxes when their son Artaxerxes became king in 464 BC.

1:19 The Medo-Persian Empire was the first empire to emphasize rule by law rather than royal decree. Even the king could not veto a Medo-Persian law, and this fact is particularly important in the unfolding drama of Esther and her people, the Jews. This aspect of Medo-Persian law is also significant in the events of Daniel 6.

▸ GOD

1:21 Making decisions at the wrong time. King Xerxes made a decision in high spirits and in a partying state of mind. Therefore, he quickly grew angry when Queen Vashti ignored his request. He consulted his advisers, who were also at the party. The result: the queen was deposed. Have you ever made decisions based on emotion (anger, pride, depression) and later regretted what you had done? Have you ever put yourself in a situation where you were acting outside of God's will and then made choices that affected your future and the future of those around you? As believers, we are called to live pure lives and make informed choices in the power of the Holy Spirit. (***See God****> God's Names> Holy Spirit> Guide/ Counselor,* TopicGuide page A19.)

1:22 counsel. 22He sent letters to all parts of the empire, to each province in its own script and
Esth 3:12; 8:9-10 language, proclaiming that every man should be the ruler of his own home and should
say whatever he pleases.*

ESTHER BECOMES QUEEN

2:1 **2** But after Xerxes' anger had subsided, he began thinking about Vashti and what she
Esth 1:19-20; 7:10 had done and the decree he had made. 2So his personal attendants suggested, "Let
us search the empire to find beautiful young virgins for the king. 3Let the king appoint
2:3 Esth 2:8-9, 15 agents in each province to bring these beautiful young women into the royal harem at the
fortress of Susa. Hegai, the king's eunuch in charge of the harem, will see that they are all
given beauty treatments. 4After that, the young woman who most pleases the king will be
made queen instead of Vashti." This advice was very appealing to the king, so he put the
plan into effect.
2:5 5At that time there was a Jewish man in the fortress of Susa whose name was Mordecai
Esth 3:2-6 son of Jair. He was from the tribe of Benjamin and was a descendant of Kish and Shimei.
6His family* had been among those who, with King Jehoiachin* of Judah, had been exiled
2:6 2 Kgs 24:14-15 from Jerusalem to Babylon by King Nebuchadnezzar. 7This man had a very beautiful and
lovely young cousin, Hadassah, who was also called Esther. When her father and mother
2:7-8 Esth 2:15 died, Mordecai adopted her into his family and raised her as his own daughter.
8As a result of the king's decree, Esther, along with many other young women, was
2:9 brought to the king's harem at the fortress of Susa and placed in Hegai's care. 9Hegai was
Esth 2:3, 12 very impressed with Esther and treated her kindly. He quickly ordered a special menu for
her and provided her with beauty treatments. He also assigned her seven maids specially
chosen from the king's palace, and he moved her and her maids into the best place in the
harem.
2:10 10Esther had not told anyone of her nationality and family background, because Mordecai
Esth 2:20

1:22 Or *and should speak in the language of his own people.* 2:6a Hebrew *He.* 2:6b Hebrew *Jeconiah,* a variant spelling of Jehoiachin.

1:22 Sending out a decree written in the numerous languages of the 127 provinces (see Esther 1:1) would have taken many months, perhaps over a year. But this was the primary means of international communication at the time.

2:1-4 Kings in the ancient world rarely went to such lengths to find a queen. This search was for Vashti's replacement as the king's favorite, not for just another wife to add to his harem. It is possible that King Xerxes' main purpose was to regain some of the honor and dignity he had lost after the unsuccessful military campaigns against the Greeks.

2:5 The name Mordecai came from Marduk, the chief god of the Babylonians. We are not given Mordecai's Hebrew name. An exiled Jew named Mordecai returned to Jerusalem from Babylon with Zerubbabel (Ezra 2:2; Nehemiah 7:7), but this is probably not the Mordecai of Esther. Jewish tradition names Mordecai as the author of the book of Esther (see note on 9:20).

▸ SALVATION

2:7 God uses the insignificant. Have you ever felt as if you were the least likely person God would choose to accomplish His will? Do you ever feel too weak or powerless to make a difference for God? Look at Esther's qualifications for her job. She was an orphan. She came from a race of people who were living in exile in a foreign land. She had no wealth and lacked any sort of "royal" education. But she was the person God chose to become queen and save her people from genocide. God still uses the weak and the powerless today to change the world. All He requires is a willing heart and obedience to His commands. If you place yourself in God's hands, He can use you in ways you may never expect in order to accomplish amazing things for His glory. (***See Salvation**> Receiving> Results> Works> Produced in us by God,* TopicGuide page A23.)

2:7 *Hadassah* is Hebrew for "myrtle," and *Esther* is probably Persian for "star." However, it is possible that the name Esther came from Ishtar, the name of the Egyptian goddess of love and fertility.

2:7 "*Cousin*" is literally "daughter of his uncle," so Esther and Mordecai were first cousins. Apparently, Mordecai was much older than Esther.

2:8 The women selected to be brought before Xerxes were probably not given a choice, and likely neither was Esther.

2:9 The phrase "special menu" is literally "her foods." Daniel and his three friends refused to eat the unclean food of the Babylonians (Daniel 1:8-16), but the food mentioned here for Esther may not have been unclean. Esther was also careful to conceal her national identity, as the next few verses show.

2:10 Mordecai wisely told Esther to conceal the fact that she was a Jew (see also Esther 2:20). If King Xerxes or even Hegai had known, it is very likely that she would have been dismissed at once to return to her home.

had directed her not to do so. 11 Every day Mordecai would take a walk near the courtyard of the harem to find out about Esther and what was happening to her.

12 Before each young woman was taken to the king's bed, she was given the prescribed twelve months of beauty treatments—six months with oil of myrrh, followed by six months with special perfumes and ointments. 13 When it was time for her to go to the king's palace, she was given her choice of whatever clothing or jewelry she wanted to take from the harem. 14 That evening she was taken to the king's private rooms, and the next morning she was brought to the second harem,* where the king's wives lived. There she would be under the care of Shaashgaz, the king's eunuch in charge of the concubines. She would never go to the king again unless he had especially enjoyed her and requested her by name.

15 Esther was the daughter of Abihail, who was Mordecai's uncle. (Mordecai had adopted his younger cousin Esther.) When it was Esther's turn to go to the king, she accepted the advice of Hegai, the eunuch in charge of the harem. She asked for nothing except what he suggested, and she was admired by everyone who saw her.

2:15 Esth 9:29

2:14 Or *to another part of the harem.*

▸ CHURCH

2:11 Mordecai's faithfulness. Even when Esther moved out of Mordecai's household, he kept watching out for her. Even though she wasn't his own daughter, he kept on loving her. We can have that same dedication to people in our household of faith. When we know of a sister or brother in the faith who is going through a difficult time, we can take an intimate interest in what happens to her or him. We should take the initiative to find out what's going on in the lives of those near to us in the faith, particularly those in our family. (***See Church***> *Role> Church Community> Living as family,* TopicGuide page A49.)

2:14 The numerous young women who were not chosen to replace Vashti as the king's favorite were relegated to Xerxes' large harem for the rest of their lives, which was basically the same as lifelong widowhood. Coming before Xerxes' presence again was possible only if he specifically requested her. Women endured great indignity in a royal harem.

MY RESPONSE TO GOD

No Chance with God

ESTHER 3

Most religions teach some sort of doctrine of providence—that a deity generally guides people and events. Some religions reduce the idea of providence to a mere knowledge of the future. But the God of the Bible is capable of much more.

Providence is the omnipresent power of God that plans and upholds all circumstances in heaven and earth so that nothing comes by chance, but from His loving hand.

For instance, Haman, a high-ranking Persian official, plotted to destroy the Jews (Esther 3:6). He convinced King Xerxes to issue a decree "that all Jews—young and old, including women and children—must be killed, slaughtered, and annihilated on a single day" (Esther 3:13). If Haman's wish had come true, Jesus may have never been born—His ancestors might have perished. The best schemes of the wicked could not stop God's plan.

Since God controls all things, and since He does so for His glory and for our good, we can accept our past, take courage in our present, and be hopeful about our future. No creature, including ourselves, may separate us from the love and care of God (Romans 8:35-39).

2:17 [16]Esther was taken to King Xerxes at the royal palace in early winter* of the seventh
Esth 1:11 year of his reign. [17]And the king loved Esther more than any of the other young women.
2:18 Esth 1:3-8 He was so delighted with her that he set the royal crown on her head and declared her
queen instead of Vashti. [18]To celebrate the occasion, he gave a great banquet in Esther's
honor for all his nobles and officials, declaring a public holiday for the provinces and giv-
ing generous gifts to everyone.
2:20 Esth 2:10 [19]Even after all the young women had been transferred to the second harem* and Mor-
decai had become a palace official,* [20]Esther continued to keep her family background
and nationality a secret. She was still following Mordecai's directions, just as she did when
she lived in his home.

2:21 Esth 1:10; 6:2

MORDECAI'S LOYALTY TO THE KING

[21]One day as Mordecai was on duty at the king's gate, two of the king's eunuchs, Bigtha-
na* and Teresh—who were guards at the door of the king's private quarters—became an-
2:22 Esth 6:1-2 gry at King Xerxes and plotted to assassinate him. [22]But Mordecai heard about the plot
2:23 and gave the information to Queen Esther. She then told the king about it and gave Mor-
Esth 10:2 decai credit for the report. [23]When an investigation was made and Mordecai's story was
found to be true, the two men were impaled on a sharpened pole. This was all recorded in
The Book of the History of King Xerxes' Reign.

3:1 Esth 3:10; 5:11

HAMAN'S PLOT AGAINST THE JEWS

3:2 **3** Some time later King Xerxes promoted Haman son of Hammedatha the Agagite
Esth 5:9 over all the other nobles, making him the most powerful official in the empire. [2]All
the king's officials would bow down before Haman to show him respect whenever he
passed by, for so the king had commanded. But Mordecai refused to bow down or show
3:3 Esth 3:2 him respect.
[3]Then the palace officials at the king's gate asked Mordecai, "Why are you disobeying
the king's command?" [4]They spoke to him day after day, but still he refused to comply
with the order. So they spoke to Haman about this to see if he would tolerate Mordecai's
conduct, since Mordecai had told them he was a Jew.

2:16 Hebrew *in the tenth month, the month of Tebeth.* A number of dates in the book of Esther can be cross-checked with dates in surviving Persian records and related accurately to our modern calendar. This month of the ancient Hebrew lunar calendar occurred within the months of December 479 B.C. and January 478 B.C. **2:19a** The meaning of the Hebrew is uncertain. **2:19b** Hebrew *and Mordecai was sitting in the gate of the king.* **2:21** Hebrew *Bigthan;* compare 6:2.

2:19 "Had become a palace official" is literally "sitting at the king's gate." The gate of a city or palace was a place of commerce and government activity, so this indicates that Mordecai had attained a high position of authority, though the writer does not explain what that position was or how he got it.

2:21-23 Mordecai saved the king's life by thwarting the guards' plot against him, and Mordecai's loyalty was recorded in the official records of the empire. These two events become significant in Esther 6 (see note at 6:1).

▸ ADOPTION
2:22 Telling the truth wisely. It's not enough to simply tell the truth. Paul knew this and told the Ephesians, "Instead, we will speak the truth in love" (Ephesians 4:15). There are proper affections and proper actions that should accompany truth. Mordecai knew the truth—that the king's life was in danger. By passing the information along through Esther, the truth combined with wise obedience had its effect: the king's life was saved, and, in God's providence, all the exiled Jews were saved (Esther 4). Wisely use the truth so that it will have the maximum positive impact. (***See Adoption***> *With Christ> Supernatural> Speak godly words,* TopicGuide page A37.)

3:1 About four years had elapsed since the events in chapter 2 occurred. *Haman* means "magnificent," an ironic name in light of his character.

▸ MINISTRY
3:2 True colors. Haman and Mordecai came into conflict because their ultimate loyalties were different. Mordecai had determined to serve God, while Haman served himself. As we live our daily lives, we will also encounter situations where we will have to oppose others to stand up for God. This may be difficult for those who don't like conflict. But following God completely requires determining ahead of time to obey Him no matter what it costs. Perhaps it means visualizing a difficult situation and deciding what to do before you are challenged with the problem. At times, that may also mean we must be willing to gain an enemy that doesn't like our stance. Yet we can be sure that God is with us and will protect us. (***See Ministry***> *Great Commission> Risk> Stepping outside of your "comfort zone,"* TopicGuide page A56.)

3:2-4 Haman was an Agagite, a descendant of King Agag of the Amalakites whom God had placed under a curse (see Exodus 17:14-16; Numbers 24:7; 1 Samuel 15:1-33). Thus Mordecai was justified in his refusal to honor Haman.

5 When Haman saw that Mordecai would not bow down or show him respect, he was 3:5 Esth 5:9
filled with rage. 6 He had learned of Mordecai's nationality, so he decided it was not
enough to lay hands on Mordecai alone. Instead, he looked for a way to destroy all the 3:6 Ps 83:4
Jews throughout the entire empire of Xerxes.
7 So in the month of April,* during the twelfth year of King Xerxes' reign, lots were cast in 3:7
Haman's presence (the lots were called *purim*) to determine the best day and month to Esth 9:24-26
take action. And the day selected was March 7, nearly a year later.*
8 Then Haman approached King Xerxes and said, "There is a certain race of people scat- 3:8
tered through all the provinces of your empire who keep themselves separate from every- Ezra 4:12-15
one else. Their laws are different from those of any other people, and they refuse to obey Acts 16:20-21
the laws of the king. So it is not in the king's interest to let them live. 9 If it please the king,
issue a decree that they be destroyed, and I will give 10,000 large sacks* of silver to the
government administrators to be deposited in the royal treasury."
10 The king agreed, confirming his decision by removing his signet ring from his finger 3:10
and giving it to Haman son of Hammedatha the Agagite, the enemy of the Jews. 11 The Gen 41:42 Esth 8:2
king said, "The money and the people are both yours to do with as you see fit."
12 So on April 17* the king's secretaries were summoned, and a decree was written ex- 3:12 1 Kgs 21:8
actly as Haman dictated. It was sent to the king's highest officers, the governors of the re- Esth 8:8-10
spective provinces, and the nobles of each province in their own scripts and languages.
The decree was written in the name of King Xerxes and sealed with the king's signet ring.
13 Dispatches were sent by swift messengers into all the provinces of the empire, giving the 3:13
order that all Jews—young and old, including women and children—must be killed, Esth 8:9-14; 9:2,
slaughtered, and annihilated on a single day. This was scheduled to happen on March 7 of 7-10, 17
the next year.* The property of the Jews would be given to those who killed them. 3:14
14 A copy of this decree was to be issued as law in every province and proclaimed to all Esth 4:8; 8:13-14
peoples, so that they would be ready to do their duty on the appointed day. 15 At the 3:15 Esth 8:15

3:7a Hebrew *in the first month, the month of Nisan.* This month of the ancient Hebrew lunar calendar occurred within the months of April and May 474 B.C.; also see note on 2:16. 3:7b As in Greek version, which reads *the thirteenth day of the twelfth month, the month of Adar* (see also 3:13). Hebrew reads *in the twelfth month,* of the ancient Hebrew lunar calendar. The date selected was March 7, 473 B.C.; also see note on 2:16. 3:9 Hebrew *10,000 talents,* about 375 tons or 340 metric tons in weight. 3:12 Hebrew *On the thirteenth day of the first month,* of the ancient Hebrew lunar calendar. This day was April 17, 474 B.C.; also see note on 2:16. 3:13 Hebrew *on the thirteenth day of the twelfth month, the month of Adar,* of the ancient Hebrew lunar calendar. The date selected was March 7, 473 B.C.; also see note on 2:16.

3:5-6 Haman's hatred of Mordecai caused him to attempt genocide of all Jewish people in King Xerxes' empire. Thus Haman became the prototype of the wicked Greek king Antiochus IV (about 165 BC).

3:7 The casting of lots (called *purim*) was a common way in the ancient world to determine the will of the gods even into New Testament times (see Acts 1:26). The casting of *purim* was intended to mark the annihilation of the Jewish people, but chapter 9 explains why it became a celebration of their salvation instead. The Jewish people still celebrate the Feast of Purim every spring in commemoration of their deliverance from Haman's plot.

3:8 Haman correctly stated that the laws of the Jews were different from those of other nations, but he lied about the Jews being unwilling to obey even the laws of the king. The Jews normally obeyed the laws of those in authority over them unless such laws were in conflict with God's law. Haman, of course, was thinking specifically about Mordecai's refusal to honor him as the king had commanded (but see note on 3:2-4).

3:9-11 Haman attempted to bribe the king with the enormous amount of silver. But the bribery wasn't necessary since the king trusted Haman's judgment, and though the king refused the money, he still gave Haman permission to do as he pleased against the Jews. It is doubtful that Haman owned this amount of silver, so the money would likely have come from the plunder of the Jews' possessions after they had been destroyed (as 3:13 implies).

3:13 The fact that the decree to kill all the Jews in the empire would not be enforced for almost a year gave Mordecai time to put his own plan into action on behalf of his people, which he did immediately (see Esther 4:1). Haman's decree to kill all the Jews in the empire was the counterpoint of God's command to Saul to kill all the Amalekites (1 Samuel 15:3).

▶HOLINESS

3:15 The author of confusion. Why was the city of Susa in confusion? Because the king and Haman had proclaimed a decree that perpetrated evil behavior. Whenever Satan is involved with those in power, confusion reigns. This principle is still true today. When those who have power do not use their authority for good, everyone suffers. When children fight, often the source of their conflict is a parent's sour attitude. If employees are disheartened and the work isn't getting done, it is not uncommon that a harsh or lazy supervisor is to blame. If you are in a position of power, make sure that you are handling your responsibilities God's way. This will alleviate much confusion and oil the wheels of good management. (***See Holiness*****> *Law and Grace*> *Law*> *Leaders and followers,* TopicGuide page A41.)

king's command, the decree went out by swift messengers, and it was also proclaimed in
the fortress of Susa. Then the king and Haman sat down to drink, but the city of Susa fell
into confusion.

MORDECAI REQUESTS ESTHER'S HELP

4:1 **4** When Mordecai learned about all that had been done, he tore his clothes, put on bur-
2 Sam 1:11 lap and ashes, and went out into the city, crying with a loud and bitter wail. 2He went
Esth 3:8-10 Ezek 27:30 as far as the gate of the palace, for no one was allowed to enter the palace gate while
Jon 3:4-9 wearing clothes of mourning. 3And as news of the king's decree reached all the provinces,
there was great mourning among the Jews. They fasted, wept, and wailed, and many peo-
ple lay in burlap and ashes.
4When Queen Esther's maids and eunuchs came and told her about Mordecai, she was
deeply distressed. She sent clothing to him to replace the burlap, but he refused it. 5Then
Esther sent for Hathach, one of the king's eunuchs who had been appointed as her atten-
dant. She ordered him to go to Mordecai and find out what was troubling him and why he
was in mourning. 6So Hathach went out to Mordecai in the square in front of the palace
4:7 gate.
Esth 3:9 7Mordecai told him the whole story, including the exact amount of money Haman had
4:8 promised to pay into the royal treasury for the destruction of the Jews. 8Mordecai gave Ha-
Esth 3:14-15 thach a copy of the decree issued in Susa that called for the death of all Jews. He asked Ha-
thach to show it to Esther and explain the situation to her. He also asked Hathach to direct
her to go to the king to beg for mercy and plead for her people. 9So Hathach returned to
Esther with Mordecai's message.
4:11 10Then Esther told Hathach to go back and relay this message to Mordecai: 11"All the
Esth 5:1-2; 6:4; 8:4 king's officials and even the people in the provinces know that anyone who appears be-
Dan 2:9 fore the king in his inner court without being invited is doomed to die unless the king
holds out his gold scepter. And the king has not called for me to come to him for thirty
days." 12So Hathach* gave Esther's message to Mordecai.
13Mordecai sent this reply to Esther: "Don't think for a moment that because you're in the
palace you will escape when all other Jews are killed. 14If you keep quiet at a time like this,
deliverance and relief for the Jews will arise from some other place, but you and your rela-
tives will die. Who knows if perhaps you were made queen for just such a time as this?"

4:12 As in Greek version; Hebrew reads *they.*

3:15 For the king and his prime minister (see Esther 3:1) to plan the deaths of millions of people—including women and children (see Esther 3:13)—and then to calmly sit down to drink is hard to fathom. This is just one instance of many great evils that God's people have faced throughout human history at the hands of those in high places of authority. Xerxes and Haman enjoyed a drink together, but Mordecai and the Jewish people mourned (Esther 4:1-3).

4:1 In ancient times, people demonstrated great mourning by tearing their clothing and throwing dirt or ash on themselves.

▸ WORSHIP

4:3 Mourning together. When the Jews heard about the decree of death pronounced by the king, they began to fast, weep, and pray. In their sorrow, they banded together. This reaction is not always true of believers. When you hear of persecution of brothers and sisters in the Lord somewhere in the world, do you fall on your knees and plead for them? If a group of believers in your community is facing hard times, are you there to comfort them and pray with them? Does the sorrow of another Christian motivate you to help him? We can encourage each other in times of great suffering by joining with those who are hurting and providing help when we are able. (***See Worship***> *OT> Fasting and Prayer> Fasting> Occasions> The Jews fasted when they heard of the king's decree,* TopicGuide page A26.)

4:11 This is no exaggeration on Esther's part, for it is confirmed by the Greek historian Herodotus. This is yet another example in Esther of the abuse of royal power so common to ancient monarchies: A king's wife could die if she approached him without being summoned. A wife in a harem could spend great lengths of time without being summoned by the king—even an entire lifetime.

4:14 Mordecai knew that God's timing was perfect and that He did everything for a purpose (compare Genesis 45:5-8). God had providentially placed Esther in a position of authority, and Mordecai urged her to act quickly on behalf of her people. Failing to act meant going against the very reason God had made Esther queen.

15Then Esther sent this reply to Mordecai: 16"Go and gather together all the Jews of
Susa and fast for me. Do not eat or drink for three days, night or day. My maids and I will 4:16 2 Chr 20:3
do the same. And then, though it is against the law, I will go in to see the king. If I must die,
I must die." 17So Mordecai went away and did everything as Esther had ordered him.

ESTHER'S REQUEST TO THE KING

5 On the third day of the fast, Esther put on her royal robes and entered the inner court 5:1 Esth 4:11, 16; 6:4
of the palace, just across from the king's hall. The king was sitting on his royal throne,
facing the entrance. 2When he saw Queen Esther standing there in the inner court, he wel-
comed her and held out the gold scepter to her. So Esther approached and touched the 5:2 Esth 4:11; 8:4
end of the scepter.
3Then the king asked her, "What do you want, Queen Esther? What is your request? I 5:3 Esth 5:6; 7:2 Mark 6:23 Luke 18:41
will give it to you, even if it is half the kingdom!"
4And Esther replied, "If it please the king, let the king and Haman come today to a ban-
quet I have prepared for the king."
5The king turned to his attendants and said, "Tell Haman to come quickly to a banquet, 5:5 Esth 6:14
as Esther has requested." So the king and Haman went to Esther's banquet.
6And while they were drinking wine, the king said to Esther, "Now tell me what you 5:6 Esth 5:3; 7:2
really want. What is your request? I will give it to you, even if it is half the kingdom!"
7Esther replied, "This is my request and deepest wish. 8If I have found favor with the king, 5:8 Esth 6:14; 7:3; 8:5
and if it pleases the king to grant my request and do what I ask, please come with Haman
tomorrow to the banquet I will prepare for you. Then I will explain what this is all about."

HAMAN'S PLAN TO KILL MORDECAI

9Haman was a happy man as he left the banquet! But when he saw Mordecai sitting at the 5:9 Esth 3:2, 5
palace gate, not standing up or trembling nervously before him, Haman became furious.
10However, he restrained himself and went on home. 5:10 Esth 6:13

▸ WORSHIP

4:16 Gathering for fasting and prayer. Esther's reaction when she heard the news of the king's decree of death for her people was to call the Jews to fast and pray. For three days, they implored God to save them. She also asked them to pray for her as she approached the king. In recent years, many Christian groups have sprung up to advocate fasting and prayer for national well-being. They are calling on believers to ask God to turn away the evil that is spreading throughout the land and to restore a spirit of godliness. Are you involved with any large movements of fasting and prayer? Have you taken time from your schedule to plead with God about the issues that are weighing heavily on your heart? Each of us can effect change in our communities and even our nation as we join with others in fasting and prayer. (***See Worship****> OT> Fasting and Prayer> Fasting> Occasions> Esther and Mordecai fasted before she went before the king,* TopicGuide page A26; ***Worship****> OT> Fasting and Prayer> Fasting> Length> Day and night,* TopicGuide page A26.)

4:16 Esther knew that for such an undertaking she would need the support of God's people; the fasting Esther requested likely included prayer as well. Esther showed great bravery in being willing to approach the king without being summoned, since she could be executed if the king did not wish to see her.

5:2 The raising of the royal staff indicated that the king would allow someone to see him without an official summons (see Esther 4:11).

5:3 The phrase "even if it is half the kingdom" likely is an exaggeration on the king's part to show how pleased he was to see Esther and that he would grant practically any request she made.

5:4 Esther seems to have used this banquet simply as preparation for the banquet she planned for the next day. Esther wanted to soften the king before voicing her request at the next banquet. However, God uses the extra day to exalt Mordecai (Esther 6) and prepare events for Haman's downfall (Esther 7).

▸ SPIRITUAL WARFARE

5:9 The bubble bursts. Haman appeared happy; everything seemed to be going his way. The king and Esther were giving him special attention. But all his apparent happiness was destroyed by one glimpse of Mordecai, his avowed enemy. Haman couldn't enjoy even a brief moment of his success because of the jealousy and hatred that ruled his heart (Proverbs 10:12). It had such a grip on him that it intruded on every situation in his life. Are you letting destructive emotions control you? One little seed of sin sown deep in your heart can reap a harvest of unhappiness. If you don't deal with it, that tiny seed will eventually dominate your thought life, your emotions, your entire inner world. Through faithful repentance, purge your life of destructive thoughts as soon as you discover them. (***See Spiritual Warfare****> Resisting Sin and Evil> Resisting Temptation> What to Resist> We are to resist sinful urges,* TopicGuide page A45.)

5:9 Haman's arrogance about being summoned to Esther's banquet with the king led to his decision to get rid of Mordecai once and for all.

Then Haman gathered together his friends and Zeresh, his wife, 11and boasted to them
about his great wealth and his many children. He bragged about the honors the king had
given him and how he had been promoted over all the other nobles and officials.
12Then Haman added, "And that's not all! Queen Esther invited only me and the king
himself to the banquet she prepared for us. And she has invited me to dine with her and
the king again tomorrow!" 13Then he added, "But this is all worth nothing as long as I see
Mordecai the Jew just sitting there at the palace gate."
5:14 14So Haman's wife, Zeresh, and all his friends suggested, "Set up a sharpened pole that
Esth 5:10; 6:4; 7:9-10 stands seventy-five feet* tall, and in the morning ask the king to impale Mordecai on it.
When this is done, you can go on your merry way to the banquet with the king." This
pleased Haman, and he ordered the pole set up.

THE KING HONORS MORDECAI

6:1 6 That night the king had trouble sleeping, so he ordered an attendant to bring the book of
Esth 2:21-23; 10:2 the history of his reign so it could be read to him. 2In those records he discovered an ac-
Dan 6:18 count of how Mordecai had exposed the plot of Bigthana and Teresh, two of the eunuchs who
6:2 Esth 2:21-22 guarded the door to the king's private quarters. They had plotted to assassinate King Xerxes.
3"What reward or recognition did we ever give Mordecai for this?" the king asked.
His attendants replied, "Nothing has been done for him."
6:4 4"Who is that in the outer court?" the king inquired. As it happened, Haman had just ar-
Esth 4:11; 5:14 rived in the outer court of the palace to ask the king to impale Mordecai on the pole he had
prepared.
5So the attendants replied to the king, "Haman is out in the court."
6:6 "Bring him in," the king ordered. 6So Haman came in, and the king said, "What should I
Esth 6:7, 9, 11 do to honor a man who truly pleases me?"

5:14 Hebrew *50 cubits* [22.5 meters].

▸ **CHURCH**
5:14 The influence of friends. Haman certainly didn't surround himself with people who gave him good advice. Even his wife suggested that he erect a sharpened pole on which to impale his enemy, Mordecai. And Haman eagerly listened to this bad advice. What kind of advice are you receiving? Do you allow people who have evil intentions to advise you on what you should do? Or do you bring your problems before God and seek out godly counselors? The advice you receive could determine your future. (***See Church****> Role> Conflict> General Counsel> Go to Your Elders for Counsel,* TopicGuide page A49.)

5:14 The sharpened pole Haman erected for Mordecai would eventually serve another very significant purpose (see Esther 7:10).

▸ **SALVATION**
6:1 A record of good deeds. Have you ever felt impatient because someone failed to recognize a good deed you did? Do you sometimes get discouraged because you don't receive the honor you feel you deserve? When Mordecai saved the king's life by informing him about the plot to assassinate him, he wasn't acting out of a desire to be honored. In fact, Mordecai's good deed went unrecognized for a long time. But God hadn't forgotten. When the time was right, the king remembered what Mordecai had done. God will not forget what you have done either. Even if you are never rewarded in this life for any sacrifice or good deed you perform, God has a record of your work and will reward you in heaven. And who knows, He may bring reward for your good deed at a time you least expect it. (***See Salvation****> Receiving> Results> Works> Bring God's blessing,* TopicGuide page A23.)

6:1 The king's insomnia was providential, since God used it to promote Mordecai. Ancient monarchs had historical records made of the major events of their reigns and placed in archives. The document here is referred to as *The Book of the History of Xerxes' Reign* in Esther 2:23.

6:4 With skillful use of irony, the author reveals that at the very moment that Xerxes decided to reward Mordecai, Haman arrived to see the king—after he had just finished erecting the sharpened pole for Mordecai's execution. The king's question to Haman (Esther 6:6) revealed Haman's heart—he wanted honor and fame more than anything else. In another ironic twist, Haman is then forced to give honor and fame to the hated Mordecai.

▸ **SALVATION**
6:6 Avoid false honor. Haman was a bee who got trapped in his own honey. When the king asked Haman how he should honor a man who pleased him, Haman immediately assumed that the king was referring to him. So Haman suggested the very glory that he wished for himself. But, of course, the king intended to honor Haman's enemy, Mordecai. Haman's pride led to his own humiliation. This incident is an example of "pride goes before destruction" (see Proverbs 16:18). When we try to grab onto honor for ourselves, we often end up being dishonored. Just as the king honored Mordecai, God will honor us for what we do for Him. (***See Salvation****> Receiving> Results> Works> Bring God's blessing,* TopicGuide page A23.)

Haman thought to himself, “Whom would the king wish to honor more than me?” 7So
he replied, “If the king wishes to honor someone, 8he should bring out one of the king’s 6:8
own royal robes, as well as a horse that the king himself has ridden—one with a royal em- 1 Kgs 1:33
blem on its head. 9Let the robes and the horse be handed over to one of the king’s most 6:9 Gen 41:43
noble officials. And let him see that the man whom the king wishes to honor is dressed in
the king’s robes and led through the city square on the king’s horse. Have the official
shout as they go, ‘This is what the king does for someone he wishes to honor!’ ”
10“Excellent!” the king said to Haman. “Quick! Take the robes and my horse, and do just
as you have said for Mordecai the Jew, who sits at the gate of the palace. Leave out noth-
ing you have suggested!”
11So Haman took the robes and put them on Mordecai, placed him on the king’s own
horse, and led him through the city square, shouting, “This is what the king does for some- 6:12
one he wishes to honor!” 12Afterward Mordecai returned to the palace gate, but Haman 2 Sam 15:30 Esth 7:8
hurried home dejected and completely humiliated. Jer 14:3
13When Haman told his wife, Zeresh, and all his friends what had happened, his wise advis- 6:13
ers and his wife said, “Since Mordecai—this man who has humiliated you—is of Jewish birth, Esth 5:10, 14
you will never succeed in your plans against him. It will be fatal to continue opposing him.”
14While they were still talking, the king’s eunuchs arrived and quickly took Haman to
the banquet Esther had prepared. 6:14 Esth 5:5-8

THE KING EXECUTES HAMAN

7 So the king and Haman went to Queen Esther’s banquet. 2On this second occasion,
while they were drinking wine, the king again said to Esther, “Tell me what you want, 7:2
Queen Esther. What is your request? I will give it to you, even if it is half the kingdom!” Esth 5:3, 6
3Queen Esther replied, “If I have found favor with the king, and if it pleases the king to
grant my request, I ask that my life and the lives of my people will be spared. 4For my peo- 7:3
ple and I have been sold to those who would kill, slaughter, and annihilate us. If we had Esth 5:7-8; 8:5
merely been sold as slaves, I could remain quiet, for that would be too trivial a matter to 7:4 Esth 3:9; 4:7
warrant disturbing the king.”
5“Who would do such a thing?” King Xerxes demanded. “Who would be so presumptu-
ous as to touch you?”
6Esther replied, “This wicked Haman is our adversary and our enemy.” Haman grew 7:6 Esth 3:10

6:12-13 This verse shows the great difference in character between Haman and Mordecai. Mordecai did not let all the royal pomp go to his head, so he simply returned to his job at the palace. Haman, however, went home dejected and humiliated, since he had wanted the rewards Mordecai had received. The comment made by Haman’s wife and friends turned out to be quite insightful (Esther 7:10).

6:14 Eunuchs served in the king’s courts. These castrated men were household officers of the king, with frequent duties pertaining to overseeing the king’s wives and his harem.

▸ SALVATION
7:1 The queen is rewarded. Esther had taken a daring step. She approached the king even though he hadn’t requested her presence. In ancient Persia, that could mean a sentence of death. But God saw Esther’s plight, and she was rewarded with the king’s favor. The king thwarted Haman’s plans, and the Jews were saved. Sometimes when we step out for God, we may risk unpleasant consequences. The believer who witnesses to a coworker could end up being shunned by that person. The employee who refuses to cooperate with corruption may lose his job. The citizen who speaks up for morality in the community may be ridiculed. In what ways is God asking you to take a daring step for Him? Whether you see immediate dividends or not, your stance for what’s right will be rewarded by God. (***See Salvation****> Receiving> Results> Works> God remembers them,* TopicGuide page A23.)

7:2 Regarding the king’s comments, see note on 5:3.

7:3-7 Xerxes had already been made aware of Haman’s plot and had even approved it (see Esther 3:11, 15). But now that the king saw that Haman’s plans were affecting someone he cared about, he became very upset.

▸ SPIRITUAL WARFARE
7:6 Sowing and reaping. The story of Haman is yet another example of the biblical principle of reaping what you sow. Haman tried to sow death among the Jews, but it turned back on his own head in the end. Likewise today, if we sow seeds such as anger, jealousy, dishonesty, or selfishness, one day we will reap a harvest of sad consequences. What seeds are you sowing right now? Ask God to help you sow seeds of righteousness and obedience (***See Spiritual Warfare****> Resisting Sin and Evil> Consequences> Of Disobedience> God may allow consequences to run their course,* TopicGuide page A46.)

pale with fright before the king and queen. 7Then the king jumped to his feet in a rage and
went out into the palace garden.
Haman, however, stayed behind to plead for his life with Queen Esther, for he knew that
the king intended to kill him. 8In despair he fell on the couch where Queen Esther was re-
7:8 clining, just as the king was returning from the palace garden.
Esth 1:6 The king exclaimed, "Will he even assault the queen right here in the palace, before my
very eyes?" And as soon as the king spoke, his attendants covered Haman's face, signal-
ing his doom.
9Then Harbona, one of the king's eunuchs, said, "Haman has set up a sharpened pole
7:9 that stands seventy-five feet* tall in his own courtyard. He intended to use it to impale
Esth 5:14 Mordecai, the man who saved the king from assassination."
"Then impale Haman on it!" the king ordered. 10So they impaled Haman on the pole he
7:10 Esth 9:25 had set up for Mordecai, and the king's anger subsided.
Pss 7:16; 94:23

A DECREE TO HELP THE JEWS

8:1 **8** On that same day King Xerxes gave the property of Haman, the enemy of the Jews,
Esth 2:7; 7:6 to Queen Esther. Then Mordecai was brought before the king, for Esther had told the
8:2 king how they were related. 2The king took off his signet ring—which he had taken back
Esth 3:10 from Haman—and gave it to Mordecai. And Esther appointed Mordecai to be in charge of
Haman's property.
3Then Esther went again before the king, falling down at his feet and begging him with
8:4 Esth 4:11; 5:2 tears to stop the evil plot devised by Haman the Agagite against the Jews. 4Again the king
8:5 held out the gold scepter to Esther. So she rose and stood before him.
Esth 3:13; 5:7-8; 7:3 5Esther said, "If it please the king, and if I have found favor with him, and if he thinks it is
right, and if I am pleasing to him, let there be a decree that reverses the orders of Haman
8:6 son of Hammedatha the Agagite, who ordered that Jews throughout all the king's prov-
Esth 3:13; 7:4; 9:1 inces should be destroyed. 6For how can I endure to see my people and my family slaugh-
8:7 tered and destroyed?"
Esth 7:10 7Then King Xerxes said to Queen Esther and Mordecai the Jew, "I have given Esther the
8:8 property of Haman, and he has been impaled on a pole because he tried to destroy the
Esth 1:19; 3:12; 8:2, Jews. 8Now go ahead and send a message to the Jews in the king's name, telling them
9-10, 14 Dan 6:15 whatever you want, and seal it with the king's signet ring. But remember that whatever
has already been written in the king's name and sealed with his signet ring can never be
revoked."
8:9 9So on June 25* the king's secretaries were summoned, and a decree was written ex-
Esth 1:1, 2, 22; 3:12 actly as Mordecai dictated. It was sent to the Jews and to the highest officers, the gover-
nors, and the nobles of all the 127 provinces stretching from India to Ethiopia.* The decree

7:9 Hebrew *50 cubits* [22.5 meters]. 8:9a Hebrew *on the twenty-third day of the third month, the month of Sivan,* of the ancient Hebrew lunar calendar. This day was June 25, 474 B.C.; also see note on 2:16. 8:9b Hebrew *to Cush.*

7:10 The author uses irony to highlight God's way of resolving the injustice of the situation. Haman erected a sharpened pole intended for Mordecai, but Haman was impaled on his own sharpened pole, while Mordecai enjoyed honor.

8:1 Haman's family was also punished, since the king gave Esther all of Haman's wealth, which was likely considerable. Ancient sources confirm that the estate of someone guilty of treason (or other high crimes) would be taken over by the king. See 1 Kings 21:15 for a biblical example.

8:2 The fact that the king gave Mordecai his signet ring meant that Mordecai could act on the king's behalf in making laws and policies. Ironically, this privilege had previously belonged to Haman, and Mordecai was placed in charge of Haman's property.

8:3-8 Although Haman was dead, his plot against the Jews was not. Esther's plea for the king to reverse the orders was necessary, since the law to kill all the Jews in the empire was still in force, and, according to Medo-Persian law, it could not be revoked (see note on 1:19).

8:9-10 Although the law to kill all the Jews in the empire would not go into effect for about nine more months (see 9:1), Mordecai acted swiftly in the king's name to save the Jewish people throughout the empire from annihilation.

was written in the scripts and languages of all the peoples of the empire, including that of
the Jews. 10The decree was written in the name of King Xerxes and sealed with the king's
signet ring. Mordecai sent the dispatches by swift messengers, who rode fast horses espe-
cially bred for the king's service.
11The king's decree gave the Jews in every city authority to unite to defend their lives.
They were allowed to kill, slaughter, and annihilate anyone of any nationality or province 8:11
who might attack them or their children and wives, and to take the property of their ene- Esth 3:13; 9:2, 10
mies. 12The day chosen for this event throughout all the provinces of King Xerxes was
March 7 of the next year.* 8:12 Esth 3:13; 9:1
13A copy of this decree was to be issued as law in every province and proclaimed to all
peoples, so that the Jews would be ready to take revenge on their enemies on the appointed 8:13
day. 14So urged on by the king's command, the messengers rode out swiftly on fast horses Esth 3:14
bred for the king's service. The same decree was also proclaimed in the fortress of Susa.
15Then Mordecai left the king's presence, wearing the royal robe of blue and white, the
great crown of gold, and an outer cloak of fine linen and purple. And the people of Susa cele-
brated the new decree. 16The Jews were filled with joy and gladness and were honored every-
where. 17In every province and city, wherever the king's decree arrived, the Jews rejoiced and
had a great celebration and declared a public festival and holiday. And many of the people of
the land became Jews themselves, for they feared what the Jews might do to them.

THE VICTORY OF THE JEWS

9 So on March 7* the two decrees of the king were put into effect. On that day, the ene- 9:1
mies of the Jews had hoped to overpower them, but quite the opposite happened. It Esth 3:13; 8:11-12; 9:17
was the Jews who overpowered their enemies. 2The Jews gathered in their cities through-
out all the king's provinces to attack anyone who tried to harm them. But no one could 9:2 Esth 8:11, 17; 9:15-18
make a stand against them, for everyone was afraid of them. 3And all the nobles of the 9:3
provinces, the highest officers, the governors, and the royal officials helped the Jews for Esth 8:17
fear of Mordecai. 4For Mordecai had been promoted in the king's palace, and his fame
spread throughout all the provinces as he became more and more powerful.

8:12 Hebrew *the thirteenth day of the twelfth month, the month of Adar,* of the ancient Hebrew lunar calendar. The date selected was March 7, 473 B.C.; also see note on 2:16. 9:1 Hebrew *on the thirteenth day of the twelfth month, the month of Adar,* of the ancient Hebrew lunar calendar. This day was March 7, 473 B.C.; also see note on 2:16.

▸ WORSHIP

8:10 A new day. At the beginning of this story, Mordecai was just an exile who had little standing in the kingdom of Susa. But by some extraordinary events, he became one of the most powerful men in all of Persia. God had turned a hopeless situation into one of glory and joy. Are you involved in a situation right now that seems hopeless? Does it seem as if the end result cannot be changed for good? Put your circumstances in God's hands. He controls the entire universe, including everything that happens to you, and God's plans for you are good. Take heart from Mordecai's story and trust God with your life. (***See Worship****> NT> Our Role> Attitude> Trusting in the midst of trials,* TopicGuide page A31.)

8:11-12 Since the law to kill all the Jews in the empire could not be revoked, Mordecai did the next best thing. He sent out a new decree in the king's name that the Jews could defend themselves against those who tried to kill them. This new law would go into effect on the same day as the previous one: March 7 (see Esther 3:13; 9:1).

▸ WORSHIP

8:17 A change of attitude. What was the greatest result of the story of Esther? This verse tells us that many people converted to Judaism because of what had happened, and the Jewish people rejoiced, celebrated, and opened their arms to those who joined them. This is the pattern that we see throughout the Bible. God works through His people so that those who do not know Him come into His kingdom. People are attracted to a group that exudes joy and hope. Like the Jews of Esther's day, we have much to celebrate. Let's open our arms, rejoice, and proclaim God's goodness and works so that the world can see! (***See Worship****> OT> God's Supremacy> God delivered/saved in order to be worshiped and served,* TopicGuide page A27.)

8:17 God providentially turned Haman's plot upside down. Instead of all the Jews in the empire being killed, many Gentiles became Jews (technically proselytes, who accepted the Jewish religion and way of life) because they feared what the Jews might do to them.

9:1-4 The two opposing laws went into effect on the same day, but only a small percentage of the Gentiles in the empire actually tried to kill the Jews, because they feared Mordecai (see Esther 9:16; the Jews killed 75,000 of their enemies).

9:5 [5]So the Jews went ahead on the appointed day and struck down their enemies with the
Esth 3:13 sword. They killed and annihilated their enemies and did as they pleased with those who
hated them. [6]In the fortress of Susa itself, the Jews killed 500 men. [7]They also killed Par-
shandatha, Dalphon, Aspatha, [8]Poratha, Adalia, Aridatha, [9]Parmashta, Arisai, Aridai, and
9:10 Vaizatha—[10]the ten sons of Haman son of Hammedatha, the enemy of the Jews. But they
Esth 5:11; 8:11 did not take any plunder.

[11]That very day, when the king was informed of the number of people killed in the for-
9:12 tress of Susa, [12]he called for Queen Esther. He said, "The Jews have killed 500 men in the
Esth 7:2 fortress of Susa alone, as well as Haman's ten sons. If they have done that here, what has
happened in the rest of the provinces? But now, what more do you want? It will be granted
to you; tell me and I will do it."

9:13 [13]Esther responded, "If it please the king, give the Jews in Susa permission to do again
Esth 8:11 tomorrow as they have done today, and let the bodies of Haman's ten sons be impaled on
a pole."

[14]So the king agreed, and the decree was announced in Susa. And they impaled the
9:15 bodies of Haman's ten sons. [15]Then the Jews at Susa gathered together on March 8* and
Esth 9:10 killed 300 more men, and again they took no plunder.

[16]Meanwhile, the other Jews throughout the king's provinces had gathered together to
9:16 Esth 9:2 defend their lives. They gained relief from all their enemies, killing 75,000 of those who
9:17-18 hated them. But they did not take any plunder. [17]This was done throughout the provinces
Esth 9:1-2, 21 on March 7, and on March 8 they rested,* celebrating their victory with a day of feasting
and gladness. [18](The Jews at Susa killed their enemies on March 7 and again on March 8,
9:19 then rested on March 9,* making that their day of feasting and gladness.) [19]So to this day,
Neh 8:10 rural Jews living in remote villages celebrate an annual festival and holiday on the ap-
Esth 9:20-31 pointed day in late winter,* when they rejoice and send gifts of food to each other.

THE FESTIVAL OF PURIM

[20]Mordecai recorded these events and sent letters to the Jews near and far, throughout all
the provinces of King Xerxes, [21]calling on them to celebrate an annual festival on these

9:15 Hebrew *the fourteenth day of the month of Adar,* of the Hebrew lunar calendar. This day was March 8, 473 B.C.; also see note on 2:16. 9:17 Hebrew *on the thirteenth day of the month of Adar, and on the fourteenth day they rested.* These days were March 7 and 8, 473 B.C.; also see note on 2:16. 9:18 Hebrew *killed their enemies on the thirteenth day and the fourteenth day, and then rested on the fifteenth day,* of the Hebrew month of Adar. 9:19 Hebrew *on the fourteenth day of the month of Adar.* This day of the Hebrew lunar calendar occurs in February or March.

9:7-10 God's final judgment on Haman's family was that the Jews killed his ten sons on the very day that Haman had planned for all the Jews in the empire to be killed. This clearly demonstrates that God will keep His promise to Abraham: "I will bless those who bless you and curse those who treat you with contempt" (Genesis 12:3). The Jews did not take any plunder (see also Esther 9:15), unlike Saul, who lost the kingship for taking plunder from the Amalekites (1 Samuel 15:17-19).

9:13-14 Perhaps as a final warning to those who would plan such evil against the Jewish people, Esther asked that the bodies of Haman's ten sons be impaled on the sharpened pole the same way that Haman was.

9:18-19 This verse explains why the Festival of Purim lasts for two days. All the Jews in the Persian Empire celebrated the festival on the fourteenth, except those in Susa (the Persian capital) who celebrated it on the fifteenth. Today, the Jews celebrate this same festival on the fourteenth, except those in Jerusalem (Israel's capital), who celebrate it on the fifteenth.

▶ WORSHIP
9:19 Celebrating God's deliverance. The Jewish people gathered to celebrate what God had done in their midst. He had not only preserved them as a people but had also destroyed their enemies. Just as the Jewish people continue to celebrate their past victories during the Festival of Purim, we, too, can celebrate the victories God has given us. Do you set aside time to thank Him for how He helped you yesterday? last week? last year? Keeping a prayer journal is a good way to help you remember what God has done for you each day. From time to time (perhaps including Thanksgiving), you can look back and remind yourself of the victories God has given you and thank Him. Celebrating God's work in the past will help you face the future. (***See Worship****> OT> Festivals> Purim,* TopicGuide page A26.)

9:19-23 One of the purposes of the book of Esther is to document the origin of the Festival of Purim, which originated with Mordecai's decree to all the Jews in the empire to commemorate their deliverance from Haman's plot.

9:20 This verse lends support to the view that Mordecai wrote the book of Esther, although this statement could be understood as a reference to the content of the letters Mordecai sent throughout all the king's provinces.

two days.* 22 He told them to celebrate these days with feasting and gladness and by giving gifts of food to each other and presents to the poor. This would commemorate a time when the Jews gained relief from their enemies, when their sorrow was turned into gladness and their mourning into joy.

23 So the Jews accepted Mordecai's proposal and adopted this annual custom. 24 Haman son of Hammedatha the Agagite, the enemy of the Jews, had plotted to crush and destroy them on the date determined by casting lots (the lots were called *purim*). 25 But when Esther came before the king, he issued a decree causing Haman's evil plot to backfire, and Haman and his sons were impaled on a sharpened pole. 26 That is why this celebration is called Purim, because it is the ancient word for casting lots.

So because of Mordecai's letter and because of what they had experienced, 27 the Jews throughout the realm agreed to inaugurate this tradition and to pass it on to their descendants and to all who became Jews. They declared they would never fail to celebrate these two prescribed days at the appointed time each year. 28 These days would be remembered and kept from generation to generation and celebrated by every family throughout the provinces and cities of the empire. This Festival of Purim would never cease to be celebrated among the Jews, nor would the memory of what happened ever die out among their descendants.

29 Then Queen Esther, the daughter of Abihail, along with Mordecai the Jew, wrote another letter putting the queen's full authority behind Mordecai's letter to establish the Festival of Purim. 30 Letters wishing peace and security were sent to the Jews throughout the 127 provinces of the empire of Xerxes. 31 These letters established the Festival of Purim—an annual celebration of these days at the appointed time, decreed by both Mordecai the Jew and Queen Esther. (The people decided to observe this festival, just as they had decided for themselves and their descendants to establish the times of fasting and mourning.) 32 So the command of Esther confirmed the practices of Purim, and it was all written down in the records.

9:24 Esth 3:1, 6-7
9:25 Esth 3:6-15; 7:4-10; Ps 7:16
9:26 Esth 3:7; 9:20
9:27 Esth 8:17; 9:20-21
9:29 Esth 2:15; 9:20-21
9:30 Esth 1:1
9:31 Esth 4:3

THE GREATNESS OF XERXES AND MORDECAI

10 King Xerxes imposed a tribute throughout his empire, even to the distant coastlands. 2 His great achievements and the full account of the greatness of Mordecai, whom the king had promoted, are recorded in *The Book of the History of the Kings of Media and Persia.* 3 Mordecai the Jew became the prime minister, with authority next to that of King Xerxes himself. He was very great among the Jews, who held him in high esteem, because he continued to work for the good of his people and to speak up for the welfare of all their descendants.

10:1 Isa 24:15
10:2 Esth 2:23; 8:15; 9:4
10:3 Gen 41:43-44; Neh 2:10

9:21 Hebrew *on the fourteenth and fifteenth days of Adar,* of the Hebrew lunar calendar.

9:24-28 These verses provide a succinct summary of the entire book, ending with the origin of the Festival of Purim.

9:29-32 Queen Esther provided royal authority for the annual celebration of the Festival of Purim, which is still celebrated today by Jews throughout the world.

10:2 Part, if not all, of the book of Esther was included in King Xerxes' archives as recorded in *The Book of the History of the Kings of Media and Persia* (see note on Esther 2:23).

▸ WORSHIP
10:3 Serving those under you. Mordecai ruled with the people in mind; therefore, his people held him in high esteem. As you look back over the rulers of the past, can you see this same principle at work? People love rulers who act on their behalf. The same is true for any person in power. Have you ever sat under a committee chairperson who was more interested in promoting their own agenda rather than serving those under him or her? Have you ever worked for a boss who was mostly interested in making himself look good before his superiors? If you are in a position of power, remember Mordecai's example and work for the good of those you serve. (***See Worship****> NT> Fellowship> Preserving> Serve one another,* TopicGuide page A31.)

10:3 As a final point of irony, King Xerxes appointed Mordecai to replace Haman as prime minister (see Esther 3:1). Mordecai's role as prime minister is reminiscent of Joseph's relationship to Pharaoh (Genesis 41:39-44) and Daniel's relationship to Darius (Daniel 6:3). In all three instances, one of God's people, a lowly slave or exile, was providentially promoted until he became the king's second-in-command. Both Joseph and Mordecai were placed in positions of authority by God to keep His chosen people from extinction.

JOB

PURPOSE

To demonstrate the hidden purposes of God in tragedy and the humble response required of His people.

Who hasn't heard of "the patience of Job"? Actually, Job was not a very patient man. He grew quite impatient with God for failing to relieve what he considered to be unjust suffering, or explain what he had done to deserve his plight.

The book of Job takes us through several cycles of debates between Job and three friends over the cause of his suffering. He never learned the reason for his trials—but he did learn that life is not about comfort, but about God's control; not about suffering but about God's sovereignty; not about questions but about God's answers. Job's story teaches us that even at the center of suffering we find God, who wisely plans its beginning and end (Ephesians 1:11). Job learned what Adam and Eve forgot—spiritual maturity comes not when we know everything God knows, but when we are willing to trust God to guide our search for knowledge.

In the end, God led Job to a deeper respect and awe of Him. The result of Job's expanded view of God was that he understood that God was worthy of his trust, even when the answers he desired were not present.

DISCOVER GOD IN JOB

In Job, some of what is said about God is wrong—Job's counselors were not very good theologians. Nonetheless, several of God's attributes are plainly evident:

Justice: Job's friends held the view that suffering was evidence of sin. They believed that God causes the guilty to suffer and spares the innocent from trials. Therefore, since Job was suffering, his friends reasoned, he must have sinned. Job's friends were wrong in their conclusion: Job's suffering was not divine retribution. Still, it is true that God, being just, must punish sin. How, then, can God ever justify (that is, declare righteous) a sinner? This question was answered in the person of Jesus Christ (Romans 3:25-26). In short, God punished Himself for our sins. Since sins were paid for in Jesus, suffering could be separated from sin, but God reserved the prerogative to allow suffering for other reasons: testing, training, fostering maturity, developing wisdom, and revealing more of Himself.

Sovereignty: We could point to numerous people or other forces as the reasons for Job's suffering: Sabeans, Chaldean raiders, fire from heaven, wind, and Satan. In truth, all of these *were* responsible for his problems. But none of them could have touched Job had God not given the go-ahead. In the book of Job, the curtain that veils God's omnipotent rule over all things is pulled back as nowhere else. The early chapters reveal that even the most powerful enemy of the human race, Satan, can do nothing without God's permission. Then, in the closing chapters, God's challenge to Job makes clear the awesome power that He alone possesses.

GROWING THROUGH JOB

While it is easy to identify with Job's suffering, our greater need is to identify with Job's ultimate response to God:

Suffering: Eliphaz was right on at least one point: "People are born for trouble as readily as sparks fly up from a fire" (Job 5:7). Job learned that suffering is a reality of life, something that everyone experiences for often-untold reasons. After spending fruitless time trying to justify himself, Job learned to let God be God. If God was allowing him to suffer, there must have been a good reason. If God is in suffering, only good can come out of it (Romans 8:28).

Spiritual Realities: The book of Job (chapters 1–2) and the book of Daniel (10:1-14) reveal the realities of heavenly places. In a world that believes only in what can be seen and experienced, disciples today must not forget that we live in a spiritual world. Satan, while always under the control of God, is often free to do his will in the earth—and that can result in suffering. To be forewarned about spiritual realities is to be forearmed with the truth.

Creature vs. Creator: When Job was finally all talked out, God spoke (Job 38:1–40:2)—and Job was, for the first time, speechless (Job 40:3-5). After listening to a description of the power and wisdom of God in creation, Job realized that God could take away and restore anything at His command—which is exactly what He did for Job (Job 42:10-17). Job learned that neither His possessions nor His suffering were as important as knowing God, the Creator of all things.

Friendship: Job's friends did one thing right and one thing wrong. The first thing they did was what all good friends should do: They grieved with him and sat silently with him for a whole week, just to identify with his suffering (Job 2:11-13; Romans 12:15). Unfortunately, they then proceeded to try to explain Job's experience to him—a fruitless endeavor. Grieving people don't need lectures; they need compassion and understanding most of all—regardless of who's at fault.

DISCOVERY VERSES

He said, "I came naked from my mother's womb, and I will be naked when I leave. The LORD gave me what I had, and the LORD has taken it away. Praise the name of the LORD!"

(JOB 1:21)

"I had only heard about You before, but now I have seen You with my own eyes. I take back everything I said, and I sit in dust and ashes to show my repentance."

(JOB 42:5-6)

JOB FACTS

Author: Unknown. There is linguistic evidence to suggest the author was an Israelite who lived long after Job.

Written to: The nation of Israel.

Date of writing: Although the book is set during the era of the patriarchs (Abraham and his immediate descendants), various linguistic features of the book suggest that it was written later. If it was written as late as the period of national distress following the invasion by Babylon, it may have been intended as a defense of God in light of Israel's suffering.

Setting: The land of Uz was east of the Jordan River, extending toward Edom and Arabia in the south. Job's friends came from areas surrounding Uz.

OUTLINE

- **JOB 1:1–2:13**—Prologue
- **JOB 3:1–21:34**—Dialogues
- **JOB 28:1–42:6**—Monologues
- **JOB 42:7-17**—Epilogue

PROLOGUE

1:1
Gen 6:9; 17:1; 22:12 **1** There once was a man named Job who lived in the land of Uz. He was blameless—a
Jer 25:20 man of complete integrity. He feared God and stayed away from evil. 2He had seven
Lam 4:21 Ezek 14:14 sons and three daughters. 3He owned 7,000 sheep, 3,000 camels, 500 teams of oxen,
Jas 5:11 and 500 female donkeys. He also had many servants. He was, in fact, the richest person in
1:2 that entire area.
Job 42:13 4Job's sons would take turns preparing feasts in their homes, and they would also invite
1:5 Gen 8:20 their three sisters to celebrate with them. 5When these celebrations ended—sometimes af-
1 Kgs 21:10-11 ter several days—Job would purify his children. He would get up early in the morning and
Job 8:4; 42:8 offer a burnt offering for each of them. For Job said to himself, "Perhaps my children have
sinned and have cursed God in their hearts." This was Job's regular practice.

JOB'S FIRST TEST

1:6 6One day the members of the heavenly court* came to present themselves before the
Job 38:7 LORD, and the Accuser, Satan,* came with them. 7"Where have you come from?" the LORD
1:7 1 Pet 5:8 asked Satan.
Satan answered the LORD, "I have been patrolling the earth, watching everything that's
going on."
1:8 Num 12:7 8Then the LORD asked Satan, "Have you noticed My servant Job? He is the finest man in
Josh 1:2, 7 all the earth. He is blameless—a man of complete integrity. He fears God and stays away
Job 1:1; 7:8; 42:7-8 from evil."
1:10 9Satan replied to the LORD, "Yes, but Job has good reason to fear God. 10You have al-
Job 29:2-6; 31:25 ways put a wall of protection around him and his home and his property. You have made

1:6a Hebrew *the sons of God.* 1:6b Hebrew *and the satan;* similarly throughout this chapter.

1:1 Uz was located east of Israel (see Job 1:3) near the desert (1:15). If Uz is an ancient name for Edom (the land of Esau's descendants) as Lamentations 4:21 seems to indicate, then Uz was likely in modern Jordan.

1:1 The author's fourfold description of Job as "blameless—a man of complete integrity" and one who "feared God and stayed away from evil" is also reflected in God's two conversations with Satan about Job (see Job 1:8; 2:3; the Hebrew wording in all three is almost identical). This indicates that the sufferings Job endured as recounted in chapters 1–2 were not the result of sin in his life, a truth his three friends Eliphaz, Bildad, and Zophar could not accept.

1:2-3 Job was the richest person in the entire area, a fact that Satan tries to use against Job (Job 1:9-11).

1:4-5 Job's godliness can also be seen in his role as priest and intercessor for his family. The fact that Job would offer a burnt offering indicates that the setting of Job is prior to the time of Moses. Most scholars place the events of Job in the patriarchal period (early second millennium BC), around the time of Abraham.

▸ SPIRITUAL WARFARE
1:6 Satan is subject to God. This verse describes a fascinating scene in heaven, where a drama plays out that affects our lives today. Satan was unable to touch Job's life without the permission of God. If God has put a hedge of protection around you, Satan cannot penetrate it. Only what God wills for your life will be able to touch you. You can live with the assurance that Satan's power is limited and that he is no match for God. Use this knowledge to work boldly for our Lord Jesus Christ. (***See Spiritual Warfare****> Originator of Sin> Satan's Character> Slanderous,* TopicGuide page A44.)

1:6 In the Old Testament "Satan" occurs only in Job 1–2 (14 times), 1 Chronicles 21:1, and Zechariah 3:1-2 as a reference to the archenemy of God and the leader of the demons. In the New Testament the title "Satan" occurs 36 times. The Greek term "devil" refers to this same person 34 times in the New Testament. Both terms are used in Revelation 12:9.

1:6-7 "Members of the heavenly court" is literally "the sons of God," but angels are clearly in view, although some see the phrase as a reference to dead believers already in heaven. Apparently, the angels and Satan came to present themselves before the Lord to give an account of their activities (also in Job 2:1-2).

1:8 The Lord, not Satan, took the initiative in this conversation by calling Satan's attention to Job's fourfold character (see note at Job 1:1). One of the main themes of the book of Job is that the Lord is all-powerful and all-wise, and He sovereignly controls everything that happens to Job, a truth most clearly seen in the Lord's speech (Job 38–41).

▸ SPIRITUAL WARFARE
1:9 Resisting temptation. When Satan comes before God, he asks if Job will continue to serve God if God no longer blesses him. Satan is your accuser. He wants to present you before God in the worst light possible. How would you answer Satan's question if he said that about you? It's easy for us to worship and serve God when He blesses us, but when trials and temptations surround us, can we still serve Him wholeheartedly? Not without the grace of God. Depend on God's power—not your own—to sustain you during difficult times. (***See Spiritual Warfare****> Resisting Sin and Evil> Resisting Temptation> Examples> Satan's Schemes> Against Job,* TopicGuide page A45.)

him prosper in everything he does. Look how rich he is! 11 But reach out and take away
everything he has, and he will surely curse You to Your face!"
12 "All right, you may test him," the LORD said to Satan. "Do whatever you want with
everything he possesses, but don't harm him physically." So Satan left the LORD's presence.
13 One day when Job's sons and daughters were feasting at the oldest brother's house,
14 a messenger arrived at Job's home with this news: "Your oxen were plowing, with the
donkeys feeding beside them, 15 when the Sabeans raided us. They stole all the animals
and killed all the farmhands. I am the only one who escaped to tell you."
16 While he was still speaking, another messenger arrived with this news: "The fire of
God has fallen from heaven and burned up your sheep and all the shepherds. I am the
only one who escaped to tell you."
17 While he was still speaking, a third messenger arrived with this news: "Three bands of
Chaldean raiders have stolen your camels and killed your servants. I am the only one who
escaped to tell you."
18 While he was still speaking, another messenger arrived with this news: "Your sons
and daughters were feasting in their oldest brother's home. 19 Suddenly, a powerful wind
swept in from the wilderness and hit the house on all sides. The house collapsed, and all
your children are dead. I am the only one who escaped to tell you."
20 Job stood up and tore his robe in grief. Then he shaved his head and fell to the ground
to worship. 21 He said,

"I came naked from my mother's womb,
  and I will be naked when I leave.
The LORD gave me what I had,
  and the LORD has taken it away.
Praise the name of the LORD!"

22 In all of this, Job did not sin by blaming God.

1:11 Job 2:5; 19:21
1:15 Job 6:19
1:16 Gen 19:24; Lev 10:2; Num 11:1-3
1:17 Gen 11:28, 31
1:20 Gen 37:29, 34
1:21 1 Sam 2:7-8; Job 2:10; Eccl 5:15; 1 Tim 6:7
1:22 Job 2:10

MY RESPONSE TO GOD

The King of Pain

JOB 1

Physical, emotional, and spiritual pain do not necessarily occur because we have sinned. Jesus' sufferings certainly didn't occur because of His sin—He was perfect. Likewise, blessings and happiness are not necessarily the result of our good deeds, either. In Matthew 5:45, Jesus said, "He sends rain on the just and the unjust alike."

While suffering's origin may not be rooted in our sin, its purpose is not disconnected from it. Pain sends us running to God for safety and comfort (Psalms 41:3; 69:29). Pain sends us running from a sin-ravaged world to a merciful God who oversees the outcome of every illness, natural disaster, and even the occasional flat tire.

As C. S. Lewis said, "God whispers to us in our pleasures, speaks in our conscience, but shouts in our pain: it is His megaphone to rouse a deaf world." Every bit of pain and suffering in this world serves to rouse humanity from its sinful slumber to seek its sole hope of salvation. Listen closely to the discomforts in your life—what is God saying?

JOB'S SECOND TEST

2:1 Job 1:6-8
2:3 Job 27:5-6
2:5 Job 1:11
2:7 Deut 28:35; Job 7:5; 13:28
2:8 Job 42:6; Jer 6:26; Ezek 27:30; Jon 3:6; Matt 11:21
2:10 Job 1:21-22; Ps 39:1

2 One day the members of the heavenly court* came again to present themselves be-
fore the LORD, and the Accuser, Satan,* came with them. 2"Where have you come
from?" the LORD asked Satan.
Satan answered the LORD, "I have been patrolling the earth, watching everything that's
going on."
3Then the LORD asked Satan, "Have you noticed My servant Job? He is the finest man in
all the earth. He is blameless—a man of complete integrity. He fears God and stays away
from evil. And he has maintained his integrity, even though you urged Me to harm him
without cause."
4Satan replied to the LORD, "Skin for skin! A man will give up everything he has to save
his life. 5But reach out and take away his health, and he will surely curse You to Your
face!"
6"All right, do with him as you please," the LORD said to Satan. "But spare his life." 7So Sa-
tan left the LORD's presence, and he struck Job with terrible boils from head to foot.
8Job scraped his skin with a piece of broken pottery as he sat among the ashes. 9His
wife said to him, "Are you still trying to maintain your integrity? Curse God and die."
10But Job replied, "You talk like a foolish woman. Should we accept only good things
from the hand of God and never anything bad?" So in all this, Job said nothing wrong.

JOB'S THREE FRIENDS SHARE HIS ANGUISH

2:12 Josh 7:6; Job 1:20; Lam 2:10; Ezek 27:30
2:13 Gen 50:10; Ezek 3:15

11When three of Job's friends heard of the tragedy he had suffered, they got together and
traveled from their homes to comfort and console him. Their names were Eliphaz the Te-
manite, Bildad the Shuhite, and Zophar the Naamathite. 12When they saw Job from a dis-
tance, they scarcely recognized him. Wailing loudly, they tore their robes and threw dust
into the air over their heads to show their grief. 13Then they sat on the ground with him for
seven days and nights. No one said a word to Job, for they saw that his suffering was too
great for words.

2:1a Hebrew *the sons of God.* 2:1b Hebrew *and the satan;* similarly throughout this chapter.

2:1-6 The pattern of 1:6-12 is repeated.

▸ SPIRITUAL WARFARE

2:2 Satan is a formidable foe. Satan is watching God's people. He is irritated when one of God's children walks in the path of righteousness. We must never forget that he is a formidable enemy who wants to defeat us. That alone should bring us even closer to the arms of our almighty God. Watch those areas of temptation that afflict you. Ask the Holy Spirit to enable you to walk in God's way at all times to foil the plans of Satan. (***See Spiritual Warfare****> Resisting Sin and Evil> Resisting Temptation> Examples> Satan's Schemes> Against Job,* TopicGuide page A45.)

▸ HOLINESS

2:5 God is in charge. Are you a fair-weather Christian? Do you say good things about God when He blesses you but keep quiet about Him when trials afflict you? The temptation to cast aside our intimacy with God during difficult times comes from Satan, who wants to damage our relationship with God. Remember that God is always in charge—even when life looks bleak. Thank Him in the hard times as well as the good times. Both times are designed to draw us closer to God. (***See Holiness****> Changed by God> God Provides> Temporal misery,* TopicGuide page A41.)

2:8 Scraping the skin provided some relief from the pain of the boils and helped cleanse the wound.

2:9 Satan had claimed that Job would curse God (Job 2:5), but Job did not do so—even at the urging of his wife. One can understand, though not excuse, Job's wife, for she had suffered greatly also. The ten children were hers also; Job's possessions and servants were hers also; and even more, her husband was stricken with an awful disease.

2:11 One of Job's friends was Eliphaz the Temanite. Teman was the principal city of Edom, the land of Esau's descendants (see note on Uz at 1:1). Since the setting of these events is likely the patriarchal period, it is possible that this Eliphaz is the same person as Esau's oldest son, who had a son named Teman (Genesis 36:4-16, 42; 1 Chronicles 1:35-36, 53), who was most likely the founder of the city of Teman. Because of the longevity of life of those living in the patriarchal period, it is possible for Eliphaz to have lived in a town founded by his son, Teman.

2:11 Another of Job's friends was Bildad the Shuhite, who may have been a descendent of Shuah, one of Abraham's sons through his second wife Keturah (Genesis 25:1-2). This would be consistent with the fact that Abraham sent all of his sons by Keturah eastward away from Isaac (Genesis 25:5-6), and the land east of Israel is the setting of the book of Job (see note on Uz at 1:1).

2:11 Another of Job's friends was Zophar the Naamathite, who was likely from the city of Naamah in northwest Arabia.

JOB'S FIRST SPEECH

3 At last Job spoke, and he cursed the day of his birth. [2]He said:

[3] "Let the day of my birth be erased,
and the night I was conceived.
[4] Let that day be turned to darkness.
Let it be lost even to God on high,
and let no light shine on it.
[5] Let the darkness and utter gloom claim that day for its own.
Let a black cloud overshadow it,
and let the darkness terrify it.
[6] Let that night be blotted off the calendar,
never again to be counted among the days of the year,
never again to appear among the months.
[7] Let that night be childless.
Let it have no joy.
[8] Let those who are experts at cursing—
whose cursing could rouse Leviathan*—
curse that day.
[9] Let its morning stars remain dark.
Let it hope for light, but in vain;
may it never see the morning light.
[10] Curse that day for failing to shut my mother's womb,
for letting me be born to see all this trouble.

[11] "Why wasn't I born dead?
Why didn't I die as I came from the womb?
[12] Why was I laid on my mother's lap?
Why did she nurse me at her breasts?
[13] Had I died at birth, I would now be at peace.
I would be asleep and at rest.
[14] I would rest with the world's kings and prime ministers,
whose great buildings now lie in ruins.
[15] I would rest with princes, rich in gold,
whose palaces were filled with silver.
[16] Why wasn't I buried like a stillborn child,
like a baby who never lives to see the light?

3:3 Jer 20:14
3:8 Job 41:1, 10, 25
3:9 Job 41:18
3:11 Job 10:18-19
3:13 Job 14:10-15; 19:25-27

3:8 The identification of Leviathan is disputed, ranging from an earthly creature to a mythical sea monster in ancient literature.

3:1 When Job broke the weeklong silence, he cursed the day of his birth. Job's response to his sufferings should be interpreted in light of the following: 1) Job knew nothing about the two conversations between God and Satan (chapters 1–2). 2) Job did not have any Scripture to help him understand God's ways, since no Scripture had yet been written. He only had limited revelation from God. 3) Job knew that the sufferings he had experienced were not because God was punishing him for sin in his life. These three facts presented Job with a paradox: How could God be just if He sent such great sufferings into Job's life that he did not deserve? This paradox is the theme of the dialogues between Job and his three friends and explains Job's strong words in this chapter.

▶ GOD
3:3 God is with you. Have you ever felt as low as Job did when he expressed these words? Discouragement can be a formidable foe. Whenever you feel that cold flood of discouragement engulfing you, read Isaiah 41:10, where God tells us, "Don't be afraid, for I am with you." Also pray, share your situation with Christian friends, seeking godly counsel. God will strengthen and uphold you throughout your discouraging time, but avail yourself of the means He has given His people for their encouragement. (***See God***> *God's Attributes*> *All-Present*> *God is everywhere,* TopicGuide page A16.)

3:11 Job continued his monologue by suggesting that he would have been better off if he had died at birth, a theme that continues through verse 19. In his mind, this would have been the next best thing to not being born at all (Job 3:3-10).

[17] For in death the wicked cause no trouble,
and the weary are at rest.
[18] Even captives are at ease in death,
with no guards to curse them.
[19] Rich and poor are both there,
and the slave is free from his master.

[20] "Oh, why give light to those in misery,
and life to those who are bitter?
3:21 Rev 9:6 [21] They long for death, and it won't come.
They search for death more eagerly than for hidden treasure.
[22] They're filled with joy when they finally die,
3:23 Job 19:6, 8, 12 and rejoice when they find the grave.
Ps 88:8 [23] Why is life given to those with no future,
Lam 3:7 those God has surrounded with difficulties?
3:24 [24] I cannot eat for sighing;
Job 6:7; 33:20 Ps 42:3-4 my groans pour out like water.
3:25 [25] What I always feared has happened to me.
Job 9:28; 30:15 What I dreaded has come true.
3:26 [26] I have no peace, no quietness.
Job 7:13-14 I have no rest; only trouble comes."

ELIPHAZ'S FIRST RESPONSE TO JOB

4 Then Eliphaz the Temanite replied to Job:

4:2 [2] "Will you be patient and let me say a word?
Job 32:18-20 For who could keep from speaking out?

4:3 [3] "In the past you have encouraged many people;
Job 29:21, 25 you have strengthened those who were weak.
[4] Your words have supported those who were falling;
you encouraged those with shaky knees.
4:5 [5] But now when trouble strikes, you lose heart.
Job 6:14; 19:21 You are terrified when it touches you.

3:20 Job finished his monologue by longing for death and identifying himself with others who had suffered greatly and wanted to die.

▶ GOD
3:25 Fear of the future. Many of us spend our days fearing what the future may hold. We are afraid of what may be lurking just around the corner: Will one of my loved ones be injured in an accident? Will I have enough income when I'm elderly? Do I have an incurable illness? Undoubtedly, each of us will face trouble if the Lord allows us to live long lives, but James 1:3 helps us understand the purpose for some of these trials: God is building patience in our lives. After suffering more than any of us ever has, Job was struggling to trust God. But we can cling to God's promises. God is faithful, and if we are willing, He can use our times of testing to forge godly character in us. (***See God***> *God's Attributes> Faithful> God is faithful through calamity,* TopicGuide page A16.)

4:1 In the three cycles of dialogue between Job and his three friends (4:1–31:39), Eliphaz always speaks first, followed by Bildad and then Zophar. Job always responds to each one before the next one speaks. Zophar does not speak in the third cycle.

4:2 Eliphaz's request that Job be patient was probably made in light of Job's strong words in chapter 3.

4:3-4 Eliphaz comforts Job by pointing out that he had encouraged, supported, strengthened, and steadied others in the past, so Job should allow Eliphaz to do the same for him.

▶ WORSHIP
4:4 Looking to help. What does it mean to truly help those who are suffering? What does it mean to steady those who waver? Around us are other believers who need help staying on the path of righteousness. Christian friends may be struggling under a heavy burden and need someone to come alongside them to share the load (Galatians 6:2). Look for brothers and sisters in Christ whose hands God may be asking you to hold. (***See Worship***> *OT> Fasting and Prayer> Prayer> Bear with one another,* TopicGuide page A26.)

4:5-6 Eliphaz begins offering his solution to Job's paradox by accusing him of having no confidence in God to care for those who are upright, implying both that Job lacked faith and that he was not upright. Eliphaz is convinced from the outset that Job was suffering because of sin in his life.

6 Doesn't your reverence for God give you confidence?
Doesn't your life of integrity give you hope?

7 "Stop and think! Do the innocent die?
When have the upright been destroyed?
8 My experience shows that those who plant trouble
and cultivate evil will harvest the same.
9 A breath from God destroys them.
They vanish in a blast of His anger.
10 The lion roars and the wildcat snarls,
but the teeth of strong lions will be broken.
11 The fierce lion will starve for lack of prey,
and the cubs of the lioness will be scattered.

12 "This truth was given to me in secret,
as though whispered in my ear.
13 It came to me in a disturbing vision at night,
when people are in a deep sleep.
14 Fear gripped me,
and my bones trembled.
15 A spirit* swept past my face,
and my hair stood on end.*
16 The spirit stopped, but I couldn't see its shape.
There was a form before my eyes.
In the silence I heard a voice say,
17 'Can a mortal be innocent before God?
Can anyone be pure before the Creator?'

18 "If God does not trust His own angels
and has charged His messengers with foolishness,
19 how much less will He trust people made of clay!
They are made of dust, crushed as easily as a moth.
20 They are alive in the morning but dead by evening,
gone forever without a trace.
21 Their tent-cords are pulled and the tent collapses,
and they die in ignorance.

4:6
Job 1:1
Prov 3:26

4:7-8
Job 8:20
Ps 37:25
Prov 22:8
Gal 6:7-8

4:9
Job 15:30
Isa 30:33
2 Thes 2:8

4:11
Job 5:4
Ps 34:10

4:12
Job 26:14; 33:15-18

4:17
Job 9:2; 35:10

4:19
Gen 2:7; 3:19
Job 10:9; 15:15; 22:16

4:20
Job 14:2, 20; 20:7

4:21
Job 8:22

ELIPHAZ'S RESPONSE CONTINUES

5 1 "Cry for help, but will anyone answer you?
Which of the angels* will help you?

5:1
Job 15:15

4:15a Or *wind;* also in 4:16. 4:15b Or *its wind sent shivers up my spine.* 5:1 Hebrew *the holy ones.*

4:7-17 Eliphaz presents a cause and effect argument using the imagery of planting and harvesting (Job 4:8). If someone does evil, then God will judge him for it. The innocent do not perish and the upright are not destroyed (4:7). Thus, Job must be experiencing God's judgment for sin in his life; after all, no one can be pure before the Creator (4:17).

4:19 Eliphaz argues that since man originated from dust (see Genesis 2:7) he is frail and quickly disappears from this life. Although this is true (see James 4:14), it does nothing to explain Job's sufferings. Eliphaz seems to be accusing Job of making too big an issue out of what happened to him.

▸ GOD

4:20 A breath of wind. We must always remember that we are mortal. Our lives are like a breath of wind compared to God's eternity, and we have no guarantee of seeing another day. As Eliphaz says, even the holiest of people may disappear without a trace. Psalm 39:5 tells us that because we are mortal, we must remember that our days are numbered and use them wisely. How are you using your days? Do you waste time with too much recreation? Take an inventory of the minutes you spend each day and see how many you are wasting and how many you are using for God's glory. (***See God**> God's Attributes> Eternal> God is timeless,* TopicGuide page A15.)

5:2 Prov 12:16; 27:3
[2] Surely resentment destroys the fool,
and jealousy kills the simple.
5:3 Job 24:18
[3] I have seen that fools may be successful for the moment,
but then comes sudden disaster.
[4] Their children are abandoned far from help;
they are crushed in court with no one to defend them.
5:5 Job 18:8-10
[5] The hungry devour their harvest,
even when it is guarded by brambles.*
The thirsty pant after their wealth.
[6] But evil does not spring from the soil,
and trouble does not sprout from the earth.
5:7 Job 14:1
[7] People are born for trouble
as readily as sparks fly up from a fire.

[8] "If I were you, I would go to God
and present my case to Him.
5:9 Job 9:10; 37:14, 16; 42:3
[9] He does great things too marvelous to understand.
He performs countless miracles.
5:10 Job 36:27-29; 37:6-11 Ps 65:9
[10] He gives rain for the earth
and water for the fields.
[11] He gives prosperity to the poor
5:11 Job 22:29; 36:7
and protects those who suffer.
[12] He frustrates the plans of schemers
so the work of their hands will not succeed.
5:13 *1 Cor 3:19
[13] He traps the wise in their own cleverness
so their cunning schemes are thwarted.
5:14 Deut 28:29
[14] They find it is dark in the daytime,
and they grope at noon as if it were night.
[15] He rescues the poor from the cutting words of the strong,
and rescues them from the clutches of the powerful.
5:16 Ps 107:42
[16] And so at last the poor have hope,
and the snapping jaws of the wicked are shut.

5:17 Ps 94:12 Heb 12:5-11
[17] "But consider the joy of those corrected by God!
Do not despise the discipline of the Almighty when you sin.

5:5 The meaning of the Hebrew for this phrase is uncertain.

▸ HOLINESS

5:3 The easy way out. Have you seen the truth in this statement by Eliphaz? People who turn away from God may be successful at first, but eventually their lives accumulate many more troubles. This is hard to remember when temptation comes and the pressure to do wrong seems overwhelming because sin can be fun for a season. Whenever you are tempted to turn away from doing what's right, remember the truth of this verse. Responding to that first flirtation leads to the breakup of a home. That one little bet in the casino paves the way to a life of addiction. That first fit of anger is the foreshadowing of a habitual short temper. Resistance may be hard in the moment, but it leads to joy and peace. (***See Holiness****> Disciplines> Of Abstinence> Resisting sinful urges,* TopicGuide page A41.)

5:3 Eliphaz warns Job not to be a fool by turning against God. He may have thought Job's sufferings would cause him to do so, or he may have been concerned that Job would not listen to him. In Eliphaz's view, Job's refusal to listen would be the same as turning against God, since he considered his explanation of Job's sufferings to be the correct one.

5:7 A second line of reasoning Eliphaz used is that Job's sufferings were just part of being human. But this didn't really explain the intense sufferings Job was enduring, which were not at all what most everyone else experiences.

▸ HOLINESS

5:8 Presenting our case to God. We can always go to God and present our case to Him. He wants us to place our burdens in His hands. What insurmountable problem do you need to bring to Him? A wayward child? A habit you need to break? A health need? He understands what you are going through and will either give you the strength to go through the testing or show you a way to avoid it. (***See Holiness****> Submission> Trusting God> Overcoming,* TopicGuide page A40.)

5:8-16 Eliphaz urged Job to ask God for an answer about why he was suffering so much. Eliphaz was correct about many things he said about God in these verses, but he was incorrect to assume that because these things are true, God was therefore obligated to give Job an explanation for what happened.

18 For though He wounds, He also bandages.
He strikes, but His hands also heal.
19 From six disasters He will rescue you;
even in the seventh, He will keep you from evil.
20 He will save you from death in time of famine,
from the power of the sword in time of war.
21 You will be safe from slander
and have no fear when destruction comes.
22 You will laugh at destruction and famine;
wild animals will not terrify you.
23 You will be at peace with the stones of the field,
and its wild animals will be at peace with you.
24 You will know that your home is safe.
When you survey your possessions, nothing will be missing.
25 You will have many children;
your descendants will be as plentiful as grass!
26 You will go to the grave at a ripe old age,
like a sheaf of grain harvested at the proper time!

27 "We have studied life and found all this to be true.
Listen to my counsel, and apply it to yourself."

5:18 Deut 32:39; Isa 30:26; Hos 6:1
5:20 Pss 33:19; 144:10
5:23 Isa 11:6-9; 65:25
5:24 Job 8:6
5:26 Gen 15:15; Job 42:17; Prov 9:11

JOB'S SECOND SPEECH: A RESPONSE TO ELIPHAZ

6 Then Job spoke again:

2 "If my misery could be weighed
and my troubles be put on the scales,
3 they would outweigh all the sands of the sea.
That is why I spoke impulsively.
4 For the Almighty has struck me down with His arrows.
Their poison infects my spirit.
God's terrors are lined up against me.
5 Don't I have a right to complain?
Don't wild donkeys bray when they find no grass,
and oxen bellow when they have no food?
6 Don't people complain about unsalted food?
Does anyone want the tasteless white of an egg?*
7 My appetite disappears when I look at it;
I gag at the thought of eating it!

6:2 Job 31:6
6:3 Job 23:2
6:4 Job 16:13; 21:20; 30:15; Ps 38:2
6:5 Job 39:5-8

6:6 Or *the tasteless juice of the mallow plant?*

5:17-18 Eliphaz closed his first speech by urging Job to accept God's chastening for his sin, which shows once again that Eliphaz believed Job's sufferings were because of personal sin in his life. Eliphaz believed that if Job would just accept this, God would restore and heal him (Job 5:19-26). But Job 2:10 makes it clear that Eliphaz was wrong.

▸ PURPOSE
5:19 God rescues us. Eliphaz's response was part truth, part fiction. God obviously doesn't rescue His people from every problem in life—look at the struggles of God's prophets and of His own Son! But on the other hand, God sometimes does rescue His children in dramatic fashion. The Israelites were saved from the Egyptian army at the Red Sea. Daniel's three friends were saved from the burning furnace in Babylon. Mary, Joseph, and the baby Jesus were rescued from Herod's evil scheme to kill all the baby boys in the Bethlehem area. God is still in the business of rescuing lives. His greatest rescue was when He sent His Son to die on a cross to save us from eternal destruction. Knowing how God delights in rescuing His people, you can pray to Him, boldly asking assistance, yet trusting that God causes everything to work together for our good. (***See Purpose****> God's Deeds> Special Acts> Saving acts/deliverance,* TopicGuide page A52.)

6:2-3 Eliphaz's argument did nothing to ease Job's pain, since Job's sadness outweighed all the sands of the sea.

8 "Oh, that I might have my request,
that God would grant my desire.
6:9 1 Kgs 19:4 9 I wish He would crush me.
I wish He would reach out His hand and kill me.
6:10 Job 23:11-12 10 At least I can take comfort in this:
Despite the pain,
I have not denied the words of the Holy One.
6:11 Job 21:4 11 But I don't have the strength to endure.
I have nothing to live for.
12 Do I have the strength of a stone?
Is my body made of bronze?
6:13 Job 26:2-3 13 No, I am utterly helpless,
without any chance of success.

6:14 Job 1:5; 4:5 14 "One should be kind to a fainting friend,
but you accuse me without any fear of the Almighty.*
6:15 Jer 15:18 15 My brothers, you have proved as unreliable as a seasonal brook
that overflows its banks in the spring
16 when it is swollen with ice and melting snow.
6:17 Job 24:19 17 But when the hot weather arrives, the water disappears.
The brook vanishes in the heat.
18 The caravans turn aside to be refreshed,
but there is nothing to drink, so they die.
6:19 Gen 25:15 Job 1:15 Isa 21:14 19 The caravans from Tema search for this water;
the travelers from Sheba hope to find it.
20 They count on it but are disappointed.
6:20 Jer 14:3 When they arrive, their hopes are dashed.
21 You, too, have given no help.
You have seen my calamity, and you are afraid.
22 But why? Have I ever asked you for a gift?
Have I begged for anything of yours for myself?
23 Have I asked you to rescue me from my enemies,
or to save me from ruthless people?

6:14 Or *friend, / or he might lose his fear of the Almighty.*

6:8-9 Job returned to his melancholy desire of chapter 3 and longed for death. Eliphaz's argument did nothing to alleviate Job's mental anguish about his sufferings.

6:10 Job was certain that he had not sinned against God, so he knew that there must have been another reason for his sufferings.

▸ WORSHIP

6:10 Emotions or faith? No matter how difficult the trials became for Job, he didn't deny God or God's Word. Sometimes, in the midst of a severe trial, we may feel as if we are barely hanging on to our sanity, but if we can keep our trust in God, we will make it through. Our emotions may be stretched so thin that they feel like a rubber band just before it snaps, but our faith holds us together. In dire times, immerse yourself in God's Word, prayer, fasting, and every means of grace God has given His people. (***See Worship****> OT> Teaching and preaching> Learning to trust God,* TopicGuide page A29.)

6:14 Job pointed out that Eliphaz had accused him without the slightest fear of the Almighty, that is, without concern for the fact that he was sinning by making false accusations against him.

6:19 *Tema* was a town in Edom (modern Teima), and *Sheba* (modern Saba) was a territory in southwestern Arabia (modern Saudi Arabia).

▸ CHURCH

6:21 Coming alongside. What kinds of trials make you shrink in fear? If a friend developed AIDS, would you desert him? If a neighbor lost all his financial assets, would you help him? If a sister in Christ went through a divorce, would you comfort her? We should love our brothers and sisters in Christ so that we help them recover from the frightening events that can occur in this world. Don't be quick to judge, like Job's "friends," but be quick to comfort. (***See Church****> Role> Preach> Topics> Godly Lives> Kindness to neighbors,* TopicGuide page A50.)

[24] Teach me, and I will keep quiet.
Show me what I have done wrong.
[25] Honest words can be painful,
but what do your criticisms amount to?
[26] Do you think your words are convincing
when you disregard my cry of desperation?
[27] You would even send an orphan into slavery*
or sell a friend.
[28] Look at me!
Would I lie to your face?
[29] Stop assuming my guilt,
for I have done no wrong.
[30] Do you think I am lying?
Don't I know the difference between right and wrong?

7 [1] "Is not all human life a struggle?
Our lives are like that of a hired hand,
[2] like a worker who longs for the shade,
like a servant waiting to be paid.
[3] I, too, have been assigned months of futility,
long and weary nights of misery.
[4] Lying in bed, I think, 'When will it be morning?'
But the night drags on, and I toss till dawn.
[5] My body is covered with maggots and scabs.
My skin breaks open, oozing with pus.

JOB CRIES OUT TO GOD

[6] "My days fly faster than a weaver's shuttle.
They end without hope.
[7] O God, remember that my life is but a breath,
and I will never again feel happiness.
[8] You see me now, but not for long.
You will look for me, but I will be gone.

6:26 Job 8:2
6:27 Job 22:9; 24:9; Joel 3:3; Nah 3:10; 2 Pet 2:3
6:29 Job 13:18; 27:5-6; 42:1-6
6:30 Job 12:11
7:1 Lev 25:50; Job 14:6, 14
7:4 Deut 28:67; Job 7:13-14
7:7 Job 7:16; 9:25; Ps 78:39
7:8 Job 7:21; 20:9

6:27 Hebrew *even gamble over an orphan.*

6:24 Job returned to his great dilemma—he still sought a reasonable answer for what happened to him. Eliphaz had not provided one, for Job still asked what he had done wrong.

6:28-29 Twice Job challenged Eliphaz's assumption that he was lying.

▸ CHURCH
7:1 Expect hard times. We expect to encounter hard times in this life. No one escapes the valleys. Believers over the ages have faced torture and sickness and hardship. The godly have been forced from their homes for the sake of their faith. Many have endured ridicule and loss for Christ's sake. Yet through it all, God is with His people. You can count on Him to bear you up under times of persecution and struggle. Even as Stephen was being stoned by those to whom he taught the truth (Acts 7:54-58), he rejoiced to see a vision of God welcoming him to heaven. Know that even in the darkest times, Jesus is cheering you on and waiting for you at the finish line. (***See Church****> Role> Preach> Topics> Godly Lives> Kindness to neighbors,* TopicGuide page A50.)

7:1-6 These verses describe the futility of life, a theme developed more fully in the book of Ecclesiastes. Job was still responding to Eliphaz, who thought he had everything neatly figured out with his belief that God blesses good people but curses bad ones. Job knew this was not so, however, for life is full of unexplainable elements, citing the lifelong struggle to survive, the endlessness of the workday, the futility and misery of each day, sleeplessness at night, sickness, and the days that fly by without hope.

▸ GOD
7:6 The swiftness of our days. Those who are young tend to think they have an endless supply of days available to them. But as we grow older, we realize that our days fly by swiftly. What stage of this process are you in right now? Are your days just a whirl of activity, with one hardly distinguishable from the next? If you don't have a sense of the briefness of life, you will be more likely to misuse or waste your days. But if you keep in mind the shortness of your days, you will desire to use them in God's service. (***See God****> God's Nature> Unique> God alone possesses immortality in Himself,* TopicGuide page A15.)

9 Just as a cloud dissipates and vanishes,
those who die* will not come back.
7:10 Ps 103:16 — 10 They are gone forever from their home—
never to be seen again.

11 "I cannot keep from speaking.
I must express my anguish.
My bitter soul must complain.
12 Am I a sea monster or a dragon
that You must place me under guard?
7:13 Job 7:4; Ps 6:6 — 13 I think, 'My bed will comfort me,
and sleep will ease my misery,'
14 but then You shatter me with dreams
and terrify me with visions.
15 I would rather be strangled—
rather die than suffer like this.
7:16 Job 6:9; 7:7; 9:21; 10:1 — 16 I hate my life and don't want to go on living.
Oh, leave me alone for my few remaining days.

7:17 Job 22:2; Heb 2:6 — 17 "What are people, that You should make so much of us,
that You should think of us so often?
18 For You examine us every morning
and test us every moment.
19 Why won't You leave me alone,
at least long enough for me to swallow!
7:20 Job 35:3, 6 — 20 If I have sinned, what have I done to You,
O Watcher of all humanity?
Why make me Your target?
Am I a burden to You?
7:21 Job 10:9, 14 — 21 Why not just forgive my sin
and take away my guilt?
For soon I will lie down in the dust and die.
When You look for me, I will be gone."

BILDAD'S FIRST RESPONSE TO JOB

8 Then Bildad the Shuhite replied to Job:
2 "How long will you go on like this?
You sound like a blustering wind.

7:9 Hebrew *who go down to Sheol.*

7:7-10 Job addressed God in a prayer that continues through verse 21. His tone was still full of sadness at his plight, for he thought his opportunities for enjoying life were over since he would die soon (7:8-10; but see 42:10-17).

7:11-15 Once again Job returned to his theme of longing for death, which he saw as the only escape from his dilemma.

7:17-19 Job asked God why He takes such an interest in mere mortals by constantly examining and testing them. Job insisted that God doesn't leave humans alone even for a moment. Job knew that God is actively involved in human affairs, but this means his dilemma was still unsolved: If God was involved in Job's life, what was His purpose for Job's sufferings?

▸ GOD

7:17 God knows and cares for you. Does it amaze you that God cares—actually thinks about—you? That's a humbling thought. God, who uses the earth as His footstool (Isaiah 66:1), knows how many hairs are on your head (Matthew 10:30)! His eyes are always on you. Thank Him for how intimately He cares for you. (***See God*** > *God's Attributes* > *All-Knowing* > *God misses nothing about us,* TopicGuide page A15.)

7:20-21 "O watcher of all humanity" refers to God, who sees all and knows all. Although Job admitted that there had been sin in his life, he was convinced that he had not sinned in a way that deserved such severe punishment.

[3] Does God twist justice?
Does the Almighty twist what is right?
[4] Your children must have sinned against Him,
so their punishment was well deserved.
[5] But if you pray to God
and seek the favor of the Almighty,
[6] and if you are pure and live with integrity,
He will surely rise up and restore your happy home.
[7] And though you started with little,
you will end with much.

[8] "Just ask the previous generation.
Pay attention to the experience of our ancestors.
[9] For we were born but yesterday and know nothing.
Our days on earth are as fleeting as a shadow.
[10] But those who came before us will teach you.
They will teach you the wisdom of old.

[11] "Can papyrus reeds grow tall without a marsh?
Can marsh grass flourish without water?
[12] While they are still flowering, not ready to be cut,
they begin to wither more quickly than grass.
[13] The same happens to all who forget God.
The hopes of the godless evaporate.
[14] Their confidence hangs by a thread.
They are leaning on a spider's web.
[15] They cling to their home for security, but it won't last.
They try to hold it tight, but it will not endure.
[16] The godless seem like a lush plant growing in the sunshine,
its branches spreading across the garden.
[17] Its roots grow down through a pile of stones;
it takes hold on a bed of rocks.
[18] But when it is uprooted,
it's as though it never existed!
[19] That's the end of its life,
and others spring up from the earth to replace it.

[20] "But look, God will not reject a person of integrity,
nor will He lend a hand to the wicked.

8:3 Gen 18:25; Deut 32:4; 2 Chr 19:7; Job 34:10, 12; 36:23; Rom 3:5
8:4 Job 1:5, 18-19
8:5 Job 5:17-27
8:6 Job 22:27; Ps 7:6
8:7 Job 42:12
8:8 Deut 4:32; 32:7; Job 15:18
8:13 Ps 9:17
8:15 Job 27:18; Ps 49:11
8:16 Pss 37:35; 80:11
8:19 Job 20:5

8:3 Bildad made basically the same argument Eliphaz did: Since God does not twist justice or twist what is right, then Job's sufferings must have been due to sin in his life.

8:5-7 Bildad assured Job that if he started living as he should, God would bless him again. This is the cause and effect argument in reverse: If someone sins, God punishes him; if someone is righteous, God will bless him. This viewpoint falsely assumes that these are the only two ways God works in people's lives.

8:6 The Hebrew word for complete integrity that Bildad used here is the same word already used of Job three times earlier in the book (1:1, 8; 2:3; see note at 1:1). Bildad challenged Job to become something the text has already said that he was—a man of integrity.

8:8-10 Like Eliphaz, Bildad used experience to validate his argument.

▶ MINISTRY

8:15 The vanity of material wealth. Have you noticed how hard we often try to hang on to our material possessions? When we buy something new, we take pleasure in it for a time. But then the new car gets its first dent. A new article of clothing gets stained. A new home soon needs a paint job or a furnace repair. How much do you rely on your material possessions for your happiness? Make the joy you get from a new possession pale in comparison to the joy you have from knowing God and making Him known. (***See Ministry***> *Great Commission> Make Disciples> Disciples strategically use material wealth,* TopicGuide page A56.)

8:21 Pss 126:1-2; 132:16
[21] He will once again fill your mouth with laughter
and your lips with shouts of joy.
8:22 Job 8:15 Ps 132:18
[22] Those who hate you will be clothed with shame,
and the home of the wicked will be destroyed."

JOB'S THIRD SPEECH: A RESPONSE TO BILDAD

9 Then Job spoke again:

9:2 Job 4:17; 25:4
[2] "Yes, I know all this is true in principle.
But how can a person be declared innocent in God's sight?
9:3 Job 10:2; 40:2
[3] If someone wanted to take God to court,*
would it be possible to answer Him even once in a thousand times?
[4] For God is so wise and so mighty.
Who has ever challenged Him successfully?

9:5 Job 26:6-14
[5] "Without warning, He moves the mountains,
overturning them in His anger.
9:6 Isa 2:19, 21; 13:13 Hag 2:6 Heb 12:26
[6] He shakes the earth from its place,
and its foundations tremble.
[7] If He commands it, the sun won't rise
9:7 Isa 13:10
and the stars won't shine.
[8] He alone has spread out the heavens
9:8 Gen 1:1 Pss 77:19; 104:2 Isa 40:22
and marches on the waves of the sea.
[9] He made all the stars—the Bear and Orion,
the Pleiades and the constellations of the southern sky.
9:9 Job 38:31-32
[10] He does great things too marvelous to understand.
He performs countless miracles.

9:11 Job 23:8-9
[11] "Yet when He comes near, I cannot see Him.
When He moves by, I do not see Him go.
9:12 Job 10:7; 11:10 Isa 45:9
[12] If He snatches someone in death, who can stop Him?
Who dares to ask, 'What are You doing?'
[13] And God does not restrain His anger.
9:13 Job 26:12 Ps 89:10
Even the monsters of the sea* are crushed beneath His feet.

[14] "So who am I, that I should try to answer God
or even reason with Him?

9:3 Or *If God wanted to take someone to court.* 9:13 Hebrew *the helpers of Rahab,* the name of a mythical sea monster that represents chaos in ancient literature.

9:2 Job recognized that much of what Bildad said was true in principle.

9:3-4 Job knew that God is so wise and mighty that no one can succeed in bringing a case against Him (see 9:32), but this did not keep Job from asking several questions that he wished God would answer (see chapter 10).

9:5-10 Job acknowledged God's sovereignty over nature as its Creator, which anticipates many of the things God will say to him later (see Job 38:4-6, 12-15, 31).

▸ GOD
9:9 Considering the awesome Creator God. Standing on a hilltop on a star-filled night can fill you with a sense of God's awesomeness. Just the thought of how huge and unfathomable the universe is compared with our small lives can give you the chills. God spread beauty in the sky with the sound of His voice (Genesis 1:14). Because of Him, the oceans stay in their place. Should we stand against the will of a God who can create whole worlds with a thought? Or should we stand in awe and give Him the worship He deserves? (***See God*** *> God's Attributes> Self-Sufficient> The One Creator originates and controls His creation,* TopicGuide page A17.)

9:9 The Bear, Orion, and Pleiades are three of many constellations that were identified by astrologers in ancient times (see also 38:31). The Bear is better known today as the Big Dipper.

9:11-20 Job also acknowledged God's sovereignty over human affairs, even when God's actions do not seem just. Both elements of Job's paradox are here: God's justice and Job's innocence.

[15] Even if I were right, I would have no defense.
I could only plead for mercy.
[16] And even if I summoned Him and He responded,
I'm not sure He would listen to me.
[17] For He attacks me with a storm
and repeatedly wounds me without cause.
[18] He will not let me catch my breath,
but fills me instead with bitter sorrows.
[19] If it's a question of strength, He's the strong One.
If it's a matter of justice, who dares to summon Him to court?
[20] Though I am innocent, my own mouth would pronounce me guilty.
Though I am blameless, it* would prove me wicked.

[21] "I am innocent,
but it makes no difference to me—
I despise my life.
[22] Innocent or wicked, it is all the same to God.
That's why I say, 'He destroys both the blameless and the wicked.'
[23] When a plague* sweeps through,
He laughs at the death of the innocent.
[24] The whole earth is in the hands of the wicked,
and God blinds the eyes of the judges.
If He's not the One who does it, who is?

[25] "My life passes more swiftly than a runner.
It flees away without a glimpse of happiness.
[26] It disappears like a swift papyrus boat,
like an eagle swooping down on its prey.
[27] If I decided to forget my complaints,
to put away my sad face and be cheerful,
[28] I would still dread all the pain,
for I know You will not find me innocent, O God.
[29] Whatever happens, I will be found guilty.
So what's the use of trying?
[30] Even if I were to wash myself with soap
and clean my hands with lye,
[31] You would plunge me into a muddy ditch,
and my own filthy clothing would hate me.

[32] "God is not a mortal like me,
so I cannot argue with Him or take Him to trial.

9:15 Job 8:5; 10:15
9:17 Job 16:12, 14
9:18 Job 27:2
9:20 Job 9:15, 29
9:21 Job 1:1; 7:16
9:22 Eccl 9:2-3
9:24 Job 12:6, 17; 16:11
9:25 Job 7:6-7
9:26 Hab 1:8
9:28 Job 3:25; 7:21; 10:14
9:29 Ps 37:33
9:30 Job 31:7 Jer 2:22
9:32 1 Sam 2:25 Rom 9:20

9:20 Or *He*. 9:23 Or *disaster*.

9:21-24 Job saw another dilemma in the way God works: He seems to treat the innocent and the wicked the same—even favoring the wicked at times. This made Job's paradox even more difficult to solve.

9:25-31 Job lamented that the futility of life is made even more miserable when God allows the innocent to be condemned as guilty.

▶ SALVATION
9:29 Oh, what's the use? Job's cry in this verse is the same as those who do not know about God's plan to set His people free from sin and death. Those who do not know Christ or understand His act of substitution when He died for us on the cross do not have any hope. But we can say with Peter, "All praise to God, the Father of our Lord Jesus Christ. It is by his great mercy that we have been born again, because God raised Jesus Christ from the dead" (1 Peter 1:3). This is the Good News that we can hang on to no matter what happens, no matter how dark the days. Are you hanging on to the hope of your new life in Christ? (***See Salvation****> Receiving> When> Born to a living hope,* TopicGuide page A22.)

9:32-35 Job wished for a mediator who could make God stop beating him and allow him to plead his case.

9:33 33 If only there were a mediator between us,
1 Sam 2:25 someone who could bring us together.
9:34 34 The mediator could make God stop beating me,
Ps 39:10 and I would no longer live in terror of His punishment.
35 Then I could speak to Him without fear,
but I cannot do that in my own strength.

JOB FRAMES HIS PLEA TO GOD

10:1 **10** 1 "I am disgusted with my life.
1 Kgs 19:4 Let me complain freely.
Job 7:11, 16 My bitter soul must complain.
10:2 2 I will say to God, 'Don't simply condemn me—
Job 9:29 tell me the charge You are bringing against me.
10:3 3 What do You gain by oppressing me?
Job 9:22-24; 10:8; 19:6; 21:16; 22:18 Why do You reject me, the work of Your own hands,
while smiling on the schemes of the wicked?
10:4 4 Are Your eyes like those of a human?
1 Sam 16:7 Job 9:12; 36:26 Do You see things only as people see them?
5 Is Your lifetime only as long as ours?
Is Your life so short
6 that You must quickly probe for my guilt
and search for my sin?
7 Although You know I am not guilty,
no one can rescue me from Your hands.

10:8 8 "'You formed me with Your hands; You made me,
Job 9:22 Ps 119:73 yet now You completely destroy me.
9 Remember that You made me from dust—
10:9 Job 4:19; 7:21; 33:6 will You turn me back to dust so soon?
10 You guided my conception
and formed me in the womb.*
11 You clothed me with skin and flesh,
and You knit my bones and sinews together.
10:12 12 You gave me life and showed me Your unfailing love.
Job 33:4 My life was preserved by Your care.

10:13 13 "'Yet Your real motive—
Job 23:13 Your true intent—
10:14 14 was to watch me, and if I sinned,
Job 9:28 You would not forgive my guilt.

10:10 Hebrew *You poured me out like milk / and curdled me like cheese.*

10:1 Job again spoke of the futility of life (see notes at 3:3, 11, 20; 9:25-31).

10:2-6 Job declared that he wanted God to tell him the charge He was bringing against him, and then he voiced the questions that had been on his mind since his sufferings began.

▸ GOD
10:11 "You clothed me with skin." The Bible is clear about who created you—God. He regards each of us as His precious creation. In Psalm 139:13, David describes his own creation: "You made all the delicate, inner parts of my body and knit me together in my mother's womb." We are not an accident of nature. Each of us is a planned, carefully constructed work of beauty. Each time you feel insecure about yourself, remind yourself of these verses and thank God for making you so wonderfully complex. (***See God***> *God's Names> Father> Creates,* TopicGuide page A18.)

10:13-17 Job set the good things he received from God in stark contrast to God's awesome power that seemed to be bringing an ever-increasing volume of anger against him.

[15] If I am guilty, too bad for me;
and even if I'm innocent, I can't hold my head high,
because I am filled with shame and misery.
[16] And if I hold my head high, You hunt me like a lion
and display Your awesome power against me.
[17] Again and again You witness against me.
You pour out Your growing anger on me
and bring fresh armies against me.

10:15 Job 6:29; Isa 3:11
10:16 Job 5:9
10:17 Job 16:8

[18] "'Why, then, did You deliver me from my mother's womb?
Why didn't You let me die at birth?
[19] It would be as though I had never existed,
going directly from the womb to the grave.
[20] I have only a few days left, so leave me alone,
that I may have a moment of comfort
[21] before I leave—never to return—
for the land of darkness and utter gloom.
[22] It is a land as dark as midnight,
a land of gloom and confusion,
where even the light is dark as midnight.'"

10:18 Job 3:11-13
10:20 Job 7:19; 14:1
10:21 Ps 23:4; 88:12

ZOPHAR'S FIRST RESPONSE TO JOB

11 Then Zophar the Naamathite replied to Job:

[2] "Shouldn't someone answer this torrent of words?
Is a person proved innocent just by a lot of talking?
[3] Should I remain silent while you babble on?
When you mock God, shouldn't someone make you ashamed?
[4] You claim, 'My beliefs are pure,'
and 'I am clean in the sight of God.'
[5] If only God would speak;
if only He would tell you what He thinks!
[6] If only He would tell you the secrets of wisdom,
for true wisdom is not a simple matter.
Listen! God is doubtless punishing you
far less than you deserve!

[7] "Can you solve the mysteries of God?
Can you discover everything about the Almighty?

11:2 Job 8:2; 15:2
11:3 Job 17:2; 21:3
11:4 Job 6:10; 10:7
11:6 Job 22:5
11:7 Job 33:12-13; 36:26; 37:5

▸ **GOD**
10:15 Having a pity party. Have you ever felt as low as Job felt at this moment? We all go through times when guilt overwhelms us and our circumstances seem so dire that we don't think we can go on. But these times are just a natural product of our human emotions. God is still beside us, even when we don't feel He's there. Cling to God's promise that He will never forsake us (Hebrews 13:5). He was with Job at that moment in time. He is with you in your darkest hour also. (***See God****> God's Attributes> All-Present> God's continual presence brings contentment*, TopicGuide page A15.)

10:18-22 Without an answer to his paradox, Job wished once again that he had died at birth (see note at 3:11), despite his description of death as a place of gloom from which no one ever returns.

11:2-4 Like Eliphaz and Bildad before him, Zophar rebuked Job for his claim of innocence (compare 4:2, 7-8; 8:2-6).

▸ **WORSHIP**
11:5 Why, God? Have you ever cried to God with words such as those in this verse? Sometimes it may seem as if our prayers are going no further than the ceiling. Yet God desires to give us wisdom and show us His will. We must remember that God's timing is perfect. He doesn't always answer immediately when we call on Him. He knows just when to act and when to withhold His actions. Consider how long the Israelites waited to see the fulfillment of prophecy in Jesus Christ! God always acts on our behalf when circumstances are just right. We must trust God's timing and His perfect answer. (***See Worship****> OT> Fasting and Prayer> Prayer> God does not always say yes*, TopicGuide page A26.)

11:8 Job 22:12; 38:17
8 Such knowledge is higher than the heavens—
and who are you?
It is deeper than the underworld*—
what do you know?
9 It is broader than the earth
and wider than the sea.
11:10 Job 9:12
10 If God comes and puts a person in prison
or calls the court to order, who can stop Him?
11:11 Job 34:21-25
11 For He knows those who are false,
and He takes note of all their sins.
11:12 Ps 62:9
12 An empty-headed person won't become wise
any more than a wild donkey can bear a human child.*

11:13 Pss 78:8; 88:9
13 "If only you would prepare your heart
and lift up your hands to Him in prayer!
11:14 Job 22:23
14 Get rid of your sins,
and leave all iniquity behind you.
11:15 Pss 27:3; 46:2
15 Then your face will brighten with innocence.
You will be strong and free of fear.
11:16 Job 22:11 Isa 65:16
16 You will forget your misery;
it will be like water flowing away.
11:17 Ps 37:6
17 Your life will be brighter than the noonday.
Even darkness will be as bright as morning.
18 Having hope will give you courage.
11:19 Lev 26:6 Zeph 3:13
You will be protected and will rest in safety.
19 You will lie down unafraid,
11:20 Deut 28:65 Job 6:9; 34:22
and many will look to you for help.
20 But the wicked will be blinded.
They will have no escape.
Their only hope is death."

JOB'S FOURTH SPEECH: A RESPONSE TO ZOPHAR

12 Then Job spoke again:

12:2 Job 17:10
2 "You people really know everything, don't you?
And when you die, wisdom will die with you!
12:3 Job 13:2
3 Well, I know a few things myself—
and you're no better than I am.
Who doesn't know these things you've been saying?
12:4 Job 6:29; 17:6; 30:1, 9-10
4 Yet my friends laugh at me,
for I call on God and expect an answer.

11:8 Hebrew *than Sheol.* 11:12 Or *than a wild male donkey can bear a tame colt.*

11:7-9 Although Zophar correctly stated that God's ways are beyond comprehension and higher than the heavens, he drew the wrong conclusion about Job (see note at 11:13-14).

11:10-11 In a subtle way Zophar accused Job of being false and guilty of sin, which, in his view, showed that Job deserved his sufferings.

11:13-14 Zophar's solution was for Job to repent and stop sinning. If Job would do this, God would reward him with a happy life once again (11:15-19). But Jesus' sufferings, despite His perfect life, reveal that even when we are doing the right thing, we may still face tragedy.

11:20 In a subtle way once again (see note at 11:10-11) Zophar accused Job of being wicked and with no escape or hope.

12:2 Job's sarcasm showed his frustration with Zophar, who basically used the same line of reasoning that Eliphaz and Bildad had used: Job was suffering because of sin in his life.

12:3 Job pointed out that Zophar's solution to his sufferings lacked any new insight.

I am a just and blameless man,
yet they laugh at me.
5 People who are at ease mock those in trouble.
They give a push to people who are stumbling.
6 But robbers are left in peace,
and those who provoke God live in safety—
though God keeps them in His power.

7 "Just ask the animals, and they will teach you.
Ask the birds of the sky, and they will tell you.
8 Speak to the earth, and it will instruct you.
Let the fish in the sea speak to you.
9 For they all know
that my disaster* has come from the hand of the LORD.
10 For the life of every living thing is in His hand,
and the breath of every human being.
11 The ear tests the words it hears
just as the mouth distinguishes between foods.
12 Wisdom belongs to the aged,
and understanding to the old.

13 "But true wisdom and power are found in God;
counsel and understanding are His.
14 What He destroys cannot be rebuilt.
When He puts someone in prison, there is no escape.
15 If He holds back the rain, the earth becomes a desert.
If He releases the waters, they flood the earth.
16 Yes, strength and wisdom are His;
deceivers and deceived are both in His power.
17 He leads counselors away, stripped of good judgment;
wise judges become fools.
18 He removes the royal robe of kings.
They are led away with ropes around their waist.
19 He leads priests away, stripped of status;
He overthrows those with long years in power.

12:6 Job 9:24; 21:7-9
12:9 Isa 41:20
12:10 Job 33:4; 34:3
12:12 Job 32:7
12:13 Job 9:4; 11:6
12:14 Job 19:10; Isa 25:2
12:15 Gen 7:11-24; Deut 11:17; 1 Kgs 8:35
12:16 Job 13:7, 9; 37:7
12:17 Job 3:14
12:18 Ps 116:16
12:19 Job 34:24-28

12:9 Hebrew *that this.*

12:7-11 Job pointed out that all of creation testifies to God's sovereignty—even human activity, since the life of every living thing is in His hand.

▸GOD
12:13 The wisdom of fear. We've all known people who have an abundance of knowledge but very little wisdom. Don't most of us have that same problem? Proverbs 9:10 says, "Fear of the LORD is the foundation of wisdom." The secret to being wise (indeed, to having almost everything God offers) is having a respectful, intimate relationship with Him (Isaiah 33:6). Humble yourself before your fearsome, awesome God and then you will find the treasures sought by wise people in every age. (***See God****> God's Attributes> All-Knowing> His wisdom and knowledge are way beyond us,* TopicGuide page A15.)

▸GOD
12:16 God's dominion. Whom does God control? Job rightly believed that no person is outside of God's directives. Sometimes we think that He controls the affairs only of those who love Him, but His power extends over those who oppose Him also. He gives us examples in His Word of people who opposed Him but who still became part of His completed plans. Think of the actions of the Pharisees of Jesus' day. They opposed God's plan of redemption, yet their efforts to put Jesus to death brought about that very redemption. They couldn't thwart God's plan; rather, they unwittingly advanced it. This raises some hard questions about human freedom, but it also gives us comfort that no one—absolutely no one—can do or say anything that God has not foreseen. He can prepare you for anything because He knows and controls the future. (***See God****> God's Attributes> Sovereign> God has dominion over the affairs of people,* TopicGuide page A17.)

12:16-25 Job also explains that since strength and wisdom are with God alone, God can and often does thwart the plans of those who ignore or defy him. Job seems to have been warning Zophar not to presume that he has God all figured out, which is the thrust of Job's rebuttal to Zophar in 13:1-19.

12:20 Job 32:9
[20] He silences the trusted adviser
and removes the insight of the elders.
12:21 Job 12:18; 34:19 Ps 107:40
[21] He pours disgrace upon princes
and disarms the strong.
12:22 Dan 2:22 1 Cor 4:5
[22] "He uncovers mysteries hidden in darkness;
He brings light to the deepest gloom.
12:23 Isa 9:3
[23] He builds up nations, and He destroys them.
He expands nations, and He abandons them.
12:24 Job 12:20
[24] He strips kings of understanding
and leaves them wandering in a pathless wasteland.
[25] They grope in the darkness without a light.
He makes them stagger like drunkards.

JOB WANTS TO ARGUE HIS CASE WITH GOD

13 [1] "Look, I have seen all this with my own eyes
and heard it with my own ears, and now I understand.
13:2 Job 12:3
[2] I know as much as you do.
You are no better than I am.
13:3 Job 13:22; 23:4
[3] As for me, I would speak directly to the Almighty.
I want to argue my case with God Himself.
13:4 Ps 119:69 Jer 23:32
[4] As for you, you smear me with lies.
As physicians, you are worthless quacks.
13:5 Prov 17:28
[5] If only you could be silent!
That's the wisest thing you could do.
[6] Listen to my charge;
pay attention to my arguments.

13:7 Job 27:4
[7] "Are you defending God with lies?
Do you make your dishonest arguments for His sake?
[8] Will you slant your testimony in His favor?
Will you argue God's case for Him?
[9] What will happen when He finds out what you are doing?
Can you fool Him as easily as you fool people?
13:10 Job 32:21
[10] No, you will be in trouble with Him
if you secretly slant your testimony in His favor.
13:11 Job 31:23
[11] Doesn't His majesty terrify you?
Doesn't your fear of Him overwhelm you?
13:12 Job 15:3
[12] Your platitudes are as valuable as ashes.
Your defense is as fragile as a clay pot.

13:13 Job 13:5
[13] "Be silent now and leave me alone.
Let me speak, and I will face the consequences.

▸ GOD
12:23 God controls the destiny of nations. In our day, we have seen the rise and fall of atheistic governments. Their leaders foolishly discount the power of God, believing that they alone rule the people and that no higher power opposes them. Job reminds us, however, that God raises up certain nations for a time and then causes them to fall. He is not frustrated by any politician—God, not people, controls the future. If God controls entire nations, can't you trust Him to guide your life? Rejoice that God can guide you through anything. (***See God****> God's Nature> Personality> Will> No one obstructs God or can question His actions,* TopicGuide page A14.)

13:7-12 Job warned Zophar that his attempt to defend God's actions could actually get him in trouble, since his explanations of Job's sufferings were lies and dishonest arguments. The end of the book vindicates Job's warning (see 42:7-9).

▸ WORSHIP
13:11 Respect for God. Reverence and awe for God are often not popular. Instead, many people like to think of God as their "buddy." But even though God is our Father, He is also the Creator and Judge of the world, and we must have a healthy and reverent fear of Him. Give Him the respect that He deserves. (***See Worship****> OT> Reverence> God requires us to fear Him,* TopicGuide page A28.)

14 Yes, I will take my life in my hands
and say what I really think.
15 God might kill me, but I have no other hope.
I am going to argue my case with Him.
16 But this is what will save me—I am not godless.
If I were, I could not stand before Him.

17 "Listen closely to what I am about to say.
Hear me out.
18 I have prepared my case;
I will be proved innocent.
19 Who can argue with me over this?
And if you prove me wrong, I will remain silent and die.

13:15 Job 7:6; 27:5; 34:21-23

13:18 Job 9:21; 23:4

13:19 Job 7:21 Isa 50:8

JOB ASKS HOW HE HAS SINNED

20 "O God, grant me these two things,
and then I will be able to face You.
21 Remove Your heavy hand from me,
and don't terrify me with Your awesome presence.
22 Now summon me, and I will answer!
Or let me speak to You, and You reply.
23 Tell me, what have I done wrong?
Show me my rebellion and my sin.
24 Why do You turn away from me?
Why do You treat me as Your enemy?
25 Would You terrify a leaf blown by the wind?
Would You chase dry straw?

26 "You write bitter accusations against me
and bring up all the sins of my youth.
27 You put my feet in stocks.
You examine all my paths.
You trace all my footprints.
28 I waste away like rotting wood,
like a moth-eaten coat.

13:21 Job 9:34 Ps 39:10

13:22 Job 14:15

13:24 Job 19:11; 33:10 Ps 13:1

13:25 Lev 26:36

13:26 Job 9:18 Ps 25:7

13:27 Job 33:11

14 1 "How frail is humanity!
How short is life, how full of trouble!
2 We blossom like a flower and then wither.
Like a passing shadow, we quickly disappear.

14:1 Job 5:7 Eccl 2:23

14:2 Job 8:9

13:21-23 Job's prayer continues through this section (13:21–14:22). His lengthy prayer begins by expressing his desire for intimacy with God—he doesn't want to know God's fearsome qualities, but His tenderness. Job wanted God to summon him into His presence so that he could find out what he had done wrong.

13:28 This is another of the many times that Job expressed the futility of his life, mainly because he still had no answer to his paradox articulated first in 3:1. It essentially is, "How could God be just if He sent such great sufferings into Job's life that he did not deserve?"

▸ GOD

14:2 Life is short. Have you ever visited an old cemetery? It's a humbling experience to realize that all the people lying there in the ground once had dreams, ambitions, and hopes. If you examine the dates on the headstones, you will probably see that some of those buried there died many years ago. Does anyone alive today remember what they looked like, how they smiled, how their voice sounded? Where is all that they worked for in their lifetimes? We must remember the fact that we are here on earth for a short time, and then we pass on to the next part of our existence. How short a time we have to honor God and do His will in this life! Let's make the most of our time. (***See God****> God's Attributes> Self-Sufficient> God supplies all things their life and breath,* TopicGuide page A17.)

14:3 Pss 143:2; 144:3
3 Must You keep an eye on such a frail creature
and demand an accounting from me?
14:4 Job 15:14; 25:4
4 Who can bring purity out of an impure person?
No one!
14:5 Job 21:21
5 You have decided the length of our lives.
You know how many months we will live,
and we are not given a minute longer.
6 So leave us alone and let us rest!
We are like hired hands, so let us finish our work in peace.

7 "Even a tree has more hope!
If it is cut down, it will sprout again
and grow new branches.
8 Though its roots have grown old in the earth
and its stump decays,
9 at the scent of water it will bud
and sprout again like a new seedling.

14:10 Job 13:19
10 "But when people die, their strength is gone.
They breathe their last, and then where are they?
14:11 Isa 19:5
11 As water evaporates from a lake
and a river disappears in drought,
12 people are laid to rest and do not rise again.
Until the heavens are no more, they will not wake up
nor be roused from their sleep.

14:13 Isa 26:20
13 "I wish You would hide me in the grave*
and forget me there until Your anger has passed.
But mark Your calendar to think of me again!
14 Can the dead live again?
If so, this would give me hope through all my years of struggle,
and I would eagerly await the release of death.
15 You would call and I would answer,
and You would yearn for me, Your handiwork.
14:16 Job 10:6; 31:4; 34:21 Prov 5:21
16 For then You would guard my steps,
instead of watching for my sins.
14:17 Deut 32:32-34
17 My sins would be sealed in a pouch,
and You would cover my guilt.

14:13 Hebrew *in Sheol.*

▶ GOD

14:5 God knows the length of our days. This verse gives those who believe in God and His Son Jesus Christ the confidence that, no matter what happens to us, God determines the length of our days. No enemy or disaster can shorten our days without God's permission. He is the One who decides how long we will live, so we can serve God with boldness. Don't be afraid of sickness or an accident. Of course, we shouldn't act foolishly, but because our God holds us in His hands, we can pursue His will without fear. (***See God**> God's Attributes> Self-Sufficient> God supplies all things their life and breath,* TopicGuide page A17.)

14:7-12 When Job commented that people do not rise again after they have died, he was not denying the resurrection (see note at 14:14 and 19:25); he was describing the common perspective of life in a fallen world—people die, and they are gone.

14:13-15 Job longed to hide from God until He called for him. Job was afraid of fellowship with God unless he knew that his sufferings were over, for what if he did something in God's presence that made his sufferings worse?

14:14 Job referred to the resurrection here, which would give him hope (see note at 19:25 also) as he faced sufferings and death. God's people may not have always known as much about the afterlife as we do today, having God's completed Word to teach us, but they always seemed to look forward to a resurrection of the dead.

14:15 Job referred to another aspect of the futility of human existence: the brevity of a person's life on earth (see notes at 3:3, 11, 20; 9:25-31). This caused him to wonder why God is so concerned about what people do during their time on earth.

18 "But instead, as mountains fall and crumble
and as rocks fall from a cliff,
19 as water wears away the stones — 14:19 Job 7:6
and floods wash away the soil,
so You destroy people's hope.
20 You always overpower them, and they pass from the scene. — 14:20 Job 20:7; 34:20
You disfigure them in death and send them away.
21 They never know if their children grow up in honor — 14:21 Eccl 9:5
or sink to insignificance.
22 They suffer painfully;
their life is full of trouble."

ELIPHAZ'S SECOND RESPONSE TO JOB

15 Then Eliphaz the Temanite replied:

2 "A wise man wouldn't answer with such empty talk! — 15:2 Job 6:26
You are nothing but a windbag.
3 The wise don't engage in empty chatter.
What good are such words?
4 Have you no fear of God,
no reverence for Him?
5 Your sins are telling your mouth what to say. — 15:5 Job 5:12-13
Your words are based on clever deception.
6 Your own mouth condemns you, not I. — 15:6 Job 9:20
Your own lips testify against you.

7 "Were you the first person ever born? — 15:7 Job 38:4, 21 Prov 8:25
Were you born before the hills were made?
8 Were you listening at God's secret council? — 15:8 Rom 11:34
Do you have a monopoly on wisdom?
9 What do you know that we don't? — 15:9 Job 12:3; 13:2
What do you understand that we do not?
10 On our side are aged, gray-haired men — 15:10 Job 12:12
much older than your father!

11 "Is God's comfort too little for you? — 15:11 Job 6:10
Is His gentle word not enough?
12 What has taken away your reason? — 15:12 Job 36:13
What has weakened your vision,*
13 that you turn against God
and say all these evil things?
14 Can any mortal be pure? — 15:14 Job 14:4; 25:4 Prov 20:9 Eccl 7:20
Can anyone born of a woman be just?

15:12 Or *Why do your eyes flash with anger;* Hebrew reads *Why do your eyes blink.*

14:18-22 Job interpreted the unpredictability of life as a sign of God's harshness with people. No one can anticipate or explain the severe problems they face in life.

15:2-6 The second cycle of dialogue (see note at 4:1) begins with Eliphaz's second speech. Eliphaz uses a much harsher tone than in the first cycle to rebuke Job for talking too much and for allowing his sins to determine what he says. Job's first response to his friends made no impression on Eliphaz.

15:7-8 Eliphaz's questions anticipate what God will ask Job later (see 38:2, 4).

15:10 The fact that Eliphaz, Bildad, and Zophar were much older than Job's father made Job's refusal to accept their counsel even more grievous in Eliphaz's opinion, since ancient cultures revered the elderly and their wisdom.

15:15 Job 4:18; 25:5
15 Look, God does not even trust the angels.*
Even the heavens are not absolutely pure in His sight.
15:16 Job 34:7 Ps 14:1, 3
16 How much less pure is a corrupt and sinful person
with a thirst for wickedness!

17 "If you will listen, I will show you.
I will answer you from my own experience.
15:18 Job 8:8
18 And it is confirmed by the reports of wise men
who have heard the same thing from their fathers—
19 from those to whom the land was given
long before any foreigners arrived.

20 "The wicked writhe in pain throughout their lives.
Years of trouble are stored up for the ruthless.
15:21 Job 18:11; 20:21, 25
21 The sound of terror rings in their ears,
and even on good days they fear the attack of the destroyer.
15:22 Job 15:30; 19:29; 27:14
22 They dare not go out into the darkness
for fear they will be murdered.
23 They wander around, saying, 'Where can I find bread?'*
They know their day of destruction is near.
24 That dark day terrifies them.
They live in distress and anguish,
like a king preparing for battle.
15:25 Job 36:9
25 For they shake their fists at God,
defying the Almighty.
26 Holding their strong shields,
they defiantly charge against Him.

15:27 Pss 73:7; 119:70
27 "These wicked people are heavy and prosperous;
their waists bulge with fat.
28 But their cities will be ruined.
They will live in abandoned houses
that are ready to tumble down.
15:29 Job 27:16-17
29 Their riches will not last,
and their wealth will not endure.
Their possessions will no longer spread across the horizon.

15:30 Job 4:9; 5:14; 22:20
30 "They will not escape the darkness.
The burning sun will wither their shoots,
and the breath of God will destroy them.

15:15 Hebrew *the holy ones.* 15:23 Greek version reads *He is appointed to be food for a vulture.*

15:16 Eliphaz continued his line of reasoning from the first speech by insisting even more strongly that Job was a corrupt and sinful person with a thirst for wickedness (see note at 15:20-35)!

15:17-19 Once again Eliphaz appealed to his and others' experiences to provide the answer to Job's sufferings. Appealing to experience as the final arbiter of truth will continue to lead Job's accusers astray.

▶ HOLINESS

15:20 The pain of sin. Ever since the beginning, sin has brought pain. Just look around. Sex outside of marriage can lead to disease, broken relationships, or heartache. Uncontrolled anger shatters friendships and damages the confidence of others; sometimes it even leads to murder. Yet we go on dabbling (and more!) in sin as if there are no consequences. When faced with temptation, remember the inevitability of consequences. Doing what's right may be hard in the moment, but living a life of purity helps us avoid greater pain in the end. (***See Holiness***> *Submission> Trusting God> Obedience,* TopicGuide page A40.)

15:20-35 Eliphaz considered Job one of the wicked people that he described in the rest of this speech. Eliphaz knew that Job had refused to admit that his sufferings were the result of sin in his life, and Eliphaz did not think that God would restore Job until he did admit it (see notes at 4:5-6; 4:7-17; 5:17-18).

31 Let them no longer fool themselves by trusting in empty riches,
for emptiness will be their only reward.
32 Like trees, they will be cut down in the prime of life;
their branches will never again be green.
33 They will be like a vine whose grapes are harvested too early,
like an olive tree that loses its blossoms before the fruit can form.
34 For the godless are barren.
Their homes, enriched through bribery, will burn.
35 They conceive trouble and give birth to evil.
Their womb produces deceit."

15:31 Isa 59:4
15:32 Job 18:16; 22:16
15:34 Job 8:22
15:35 Ps 7:14 Isa 59:4

JOB'S FIFTH SPEECH: A RESPONSE TO ELIPHAZ

16 Then Job spoke again:
2 "I have heard all this before.
What miserable comforters you are!
3 Won't you ever stop blowing hot air?
What makes you keep on talking?
4 I could say the same things if you were in my place.
I could spout off criticism and shake my head at you.
5 But if it were me, I would encourage you.
I would try to take away your grief.
6 Instead, I suffer if I defend myself,
and I suffer no less if I refuse to speak.

7 "O God, You have ground me down
and devastated my family.
8 As if to prove I have sinned, You've reduced me to skin and bones.
My gaunt flesh testifies against me.
9 God hates me and angrily tears me apart.
He snaps His teeth at me
and pierces me with His eyes.
10 People jeer and laugh at me.
They slap my cheek in contempt.
A mob gathers against me.
11 God has handed me over to sinners.
He has tossed me into the hands of the wicked.

12 "I was living quietly until He shattered me.
He took me by the neck and broke me in pieces.
Then He set me up as His target,

16:2 Job 13:4; 21:34
16:3 Job 6:26
16:4 Pss 22:7; 109:25
16:6 Job 9:27-28
16:7 Job 7:3; 16:20; 19:13-15
16:8 Job 10:17; 19:20
16:9 Job 13:24; 33:10
16:10 Job 30:12
16:12 Job 7:20; 9:17

16:2-6 Job's friends had not comforted him at all about his sufferings. Their words, in fact, have forced him to defend himself, which is why he could not refuse to speak.

▸ CHURCH
16:5 The comfort of a friend. Have you ever felt like Job—has a friend ever spoken discouraging words when you needed comfort? Or have you played the role of "Job's comforter" and hurt someone that was already suffering? That hurts! God has given us the ability to soothe the hearts of those who are being tossed in life's storms (Proverbs 25:11). When you encounter a friend in need of comfort, let your words be rich, nourishing—like a gift from God. Be realistic about the circumstances, but be realistic about the hope we have in God and His promises to us, too. (***See Church> Role> Preach> Topics> Consolation and comfort,*** TopicGuide page A50.)

16:7-8 Through a lament prayer, Job summarized what happened to him in chapters 1–2. He correctly saw that his sufferings were part of God's sovereign will, but he concluded incorrectly that this was evidence that God hated him.

16:10-11 Job recounted another aspect of his sufferings that continued after the events of chapters 1–2: the way other people are treating him. Job thought this too came unfairly from God.

16:12-17 Job returned to his description of his sufferings. His happy life was interrupted when God broke him apart even though he was innocent.

16:13 Job 6:4; 19:12
13 and now His archers surround me.
His arrows pierce me without mercy.
The ground is wet with my blood.*

16:14 Job 9:17 Joel 2:7
14 Again and again He smashes against me,
charging at me like a warrior.

16:15 Gen 37:34 Job 30:19 Ps 69:11 Jon 3:8
15 I wear burlap to show my grief.
My pride lies in the dust.
16 My eyes are red with weeping;
dark shadows circle my eyes.

16:16 Job 16:20; 24:17
17 Yet I have done no wrong,
and my prayer is pure.

16:17 Job 27:4
18 "O earth, do not conceal my blood.
Let it cry out on my behalf.

16:19 Job 19:25-27; 31:2
19 Even now my witness is in heaven.
My advocate is there on high.
20 My friends scorn me,
but I pour out my tears to God.
21 I need someone to mediate between God and me,
as a person mediates between friends.

16:22 Job 3:13
22 For soon I must go down that road
from which I will never return.

JOB CONTINUES TO DEFEND HIS INNOCENCE

17:1 Ps 88:3-4
17 1 "My spirit is crushed,
and my life is nearly snuffed out.
The grave is ready to receive me.

17:2 Job 12:4; 17:6
2 I am surrounded by mockers.
I watch how bitterly they taunt me.

17:3 Ps 119:122
3 "You must defend my innocence, O God,
since no one else will stand up for me.

17:4 Job 12:20
4 You have closed their minds to understanding,
but do not let them triumph.

16:13 Hebrew *my gall.*

▸ **GOD**
16:17 A broken heart. Sometimes our trials are so severe that we feel as if we are like Job, broken and bleeding from the buffeting we have received from God. But Job said our goal should be to remain innocent and pray purely. Can you pray for those who hurt you? Will you continue to thank God when financial difficulties seem like insurmountable mountains? Will your testimony for Christ be strong when illness strikes without warning? During difficult times, keep your prayer life more active than ever. Cry out to God and have faith that He hears your cries (2 Samuel 22:7). (***See God****> God's Attributes> Merciful> God's mercy endures through trials,* TopicGuide page A16.)

16:18-22 Job again longed for an advocate or mediator (see note at 9:32-35) to explain the paradox of unjust suffering in his life, but he feared that he would not get an answer before he went down that road from which he would never return (physical death).

▸ **ADOPTION**
16:19 A witness in heaven. Job was confident that he had a witness in heaven, someone who knew the true status of his heart and would defend him. The New Testament affirms that Jesus is our witness in heaven, where He acts as our Advocate and waits to welcome us home. All of those who endure suffering for Jesus' sake will receive the prize at the end of the race (Hebrews 11:39-40). As you pass through suffering, keep your eyes on Christ and the prize that awaits you. (***See Adoption****> In Heaven> Rewarded saints,* TopicGuide page A38.)

▸ **GOD**
17:3 "Defend my innocence." We all have a time when we need a good lawyer. If you have ever stood before a judge's bench, you know how valuable it can be to have an able lawyer standing beside you. You do not need to stand alone before the bar of God's judgment; Jesus is your defender (1 John 2:1-2). He will attest that He has paid the penalty for your sins; you have no guilt because of Him (Romans 3:22). Thank God that Jesus is your defender and that He has made it possible for you to come before God confidently. (***See God****> God's Attributes> Just> Jesus, our righteous defender before the Father,* TopicGuide page A16.)

17:3-5 In this brief lament prayer, Job called on God to defend his innocence—which He had not done so far—and not to let Job's critics think they were correct about him all along.

[5] They betray their friends for their own advantage,
so let their children faint with hunger. 17:5 Job 11:20

[6] "God has made a mockery of me among the people;
they spit in my face. 17:6 Job 30:9-10
[7] My eyes are swollen with weeping,
and I am but a shadow of my former self.
[8] The virtuous are horrified when they see me.
The innocent rise up against the ungodly. 17:8 Job 22:19
[9] The righteous keep moving forward,
and those with clean hands become stronger and stronger. 17:9 Job 22:30

[10] "As for all of you, come back with a better argument,
though I still won't find a wise man among you. 17:10 Job 12:2
[11] My days are over.
My hopes have disappeared.
My heart's desires are broken. 17:11 Job 7:6
[12] These men say that night is day;
they claim that the darkness is light.
[13] What if I go to the grave*
and make my bed in darkness? 17:13 Job 3:13
[14] What if I call the grave my father,
and the maggot my mother or my sister? 17:14 Job 21:26
[15] Where then is my hope?
Can anyone find it? 17:15 Job 7:6
[16] No, my hope will go down with me to the grave.
We will rest together in the dust!" 17:16 Job 3:17; 21:33

BILDAD'S SECOND RESPONSE TO JOB

18 Then Bildad the Shuhite replied:

[2] "How long before you stop talking?
Speak sense if you want us to answer!

17:13 Hebrew *to Sheol;* also in 17:16.

17:6-8 Job described some of the most difficult consequences of his sufferings. The events of chapters 1–2 were not the only sufferings Job had to endure.

▸ SPIRITUAL WARFARE

17:9 The path of the righteous. Generally, the Bible promises many blessings for those who walk in the path of righteousness. For instance, Proverbs 11:28 compares the righteous to leaves in the spring, and Proverbs 13:9 tells us that the godly are full of light and joy. Just like a plant in springtime, we grow stronger when we live in righteousness. But our righteous deeds are hardly enough to merit God's blessings—the New Testament explains that we now have Christ's righteousness. Romans 5:17 traces God's greatest blessings to us being clothed in the rewards earned by Christ's perfect life and death. Keep obeying and keep trusting that God gives life to all those who have Christ's merit as their own. (***See Spiritual Warfare*****>** *Resisting Sin and Evil> Embracing Christ> Clothed in Christ's righteousness,* TopicGuide page A45.)

17:10 Job was confident that even if his three critics came back and tried again to persuade him to their way of thinking, there still would not have been a wise man among them—that is, they would never provide the right answer.

17:11-16 Three times in these verses Job stated that he had lost all hope of being vindicated before he died.

▸ SPIRITUAL WARFARE

17:12 Perverting the truth. Times have not changed too much. In Job's day, some people were perverting the truth, calling good bad and bad good. We see the same thing happening today. The idea that truth is relative is just another way of making sin acceptable. The unrighteous declare, "I should be able to do it if it feels good," or "In my situation, this really isn't sinful." Don't let the world's excuses become an avenue to carry you into sin. God's truth is absolute. Sin is sin. Take your temptations to Him rather than letting the world give you excuses for improper behavior. (***See Spiritual Warfare*****>** *Resisting Sin and Evil> Resisting Temptation> How to Resist> By the help of God,* TopicGuide page A45.)

18:2-3 Like Eliphaz before him, Bildad began his second speech by complaining that Job talked too much (see note at 15:2-6).

18:3 Ps 73:22
3 Do you think we are mere animals?
Do you think we are stupid?
4 You may tear out your hair in anger,
but will that destroy the earth?
Will it make the rocks tremble?

18:5 Job 21:17
5 "Surely the light of the wicked will be snuffed out.
The sparks of their fire will not glow.
18:6 Job 12:25
6 The light in their tent will grow dark.
The lamp hanging above them will be quenched.
7 The confident stride of the wicked will be shortened.
Their own schemes will be their downfall.
18:8 Job 22:10
8 The wicked walk into a net.
They fall into a pit.
9 A trap grabs them by the heel.
A snare holds them tight.
10 A noose lies hidden on the ground.
A rope is stretched across their path.

18:11 Job 15:21; 18:18
11 "Terrors surround the wicked
and trouble them at every step.
12 Hunger depletes their strength,
and calamity waits for them to stumble.
18:14 Job 8:22; 15:21
13 Disease eats their skin;
death devours their limbs.
18:16 Job 15:30, 32 Isa 5:24 Hos 9:1-16 Amos 2:9
14 They are torn from the security of their homes
and are brought down to the king of terrors.
15 The homes of the wicked will burn down;
burning sulfur rains on their houses.
18:17 Job 24:20 Ps 34:16 Prov 10:7
16 Their roots will dry up,
and their branches will wither.
17 All memory of their existence will fade from the earth,
18:18 Job 5:14; 27:21-23
No one will remember their names.
18 They will be thrust from light into darkness,
18:19 Job 27:14-15 Isa 14:22 Jer 22:30
driven from the world.
19 They will have neither children nor grandchildren,
nor any survivor in the place where they lived.
18:20 Jer 50:27 Obad 1:12
20 People in the west are appalled at their fate;
people in the east are horrified.

18:5-7 Also like Eliphaz, Bildad spoke in harsher terms in his second speech when he accused Job of being one of the wicked whose doom was certain.

▸ GOD
18:8 The fate of the wicked. In the 1940s, Adolf Hitler nearly conquered all of Europe. In his heyday, he commanded a fierce army with tremendous power. At the time, he seemed unstoppable. But soon, all he had built fell into ruin, and now his name is synonymous with evil. When it seems as if the wicked have their way in our world, be encouraged by this verse. God will not allow the wicked to prosper indefinitely. And when they fall, they will disappear into a pit of their own making. Thank God that His justice is at work in the world in spite of the evil around us. (***See God***> *God's Attributes*> *Just*> *God judges all people with justice,* TopicGuide page A16.)

18:8-21 Bildad's description of a series of calamities that befall the wicked were intended to apply to Job, revealing the harshness of Bildad's attitude toward Job at this point—that he is trapped, afraid, ill, homeless, forgotten, and alone—all culminating in the conclusion that the person who suffered such things had rejected God.

▸ SALVATION
18:11 Terrors afflict the wicked. Terror and trouble plague the sinner. That's the way this world is designed—it generally causes more pain to those who break God's laws. And generally, when we confess our sins to Him, when we make amends to those we've hurt, our hearts are freed from guilt; we are at peace. Do your best to make sure that your heart is not harboring any sin and that you confess any wrongdoing you are trying to cover up. It always helps to have a clean slate with God. (***See Salvation***> *Receiving*> *How*> *Repent of/turn from sin,* TopicGuide page A22.)

21 They will say, 'This was the home of a wicked person,
the place of one who rejected God.'"

JOB'S SIXTH SPEECH: A RESPONSE TO BILDAD

19 Then Job spoke again:
2 "How long will you torture me?
How long will you try to crush me with your words?
3 You have already insulted me ten times.
You should be ashamed of treating me so badly.
4 Even if I have sinned,
that is my concern, not yours.
5 You think you're better than I am,
using my humiliation as evidence of my sin.
6 But it is God who has wronged me,
capturing me in His net.*

7 "I cry out, 'Help!' but no one answers me.
I protest, but there is no justice.
8 God has blocked my way so I cannot move.
He has plunged my path into darkness.
9 He has stripped me of my honor
and removed the crown from my head.
10 He has demolished me on every side, and I am finished.
He has uprooted my hope like a fallen tree.
11 His fury burns against me;
He counts me as an enemy.
12 His troops advance.
They build up roads to attack me.
They camp all around my tent.

13 "My relatives stay far away,
and my friends have turned against me.
14 My family is gone,
and my close friends have forgotten me.
15 My servants and maids consider me a stranger.
I am like a foreigner to them.
16 When I call my servant, he doesn't come;
I have to plead with him!
17 My breath is repulsive to my wife.
I am rejected by my own family.
18 Even young children despise me.
When I stand to speak, they turn their backs on me.

19:5 Pss 35:26; 38:16; 55:12-13

19:6 Job 16:11; 18:8-10; 27:2; Ps 66:11

19:7 Job 30:20, 24; Hab 1:2

19:8 Job 3:23; 30:26; Lam 3:7, 9

19:9 Job 12:17, 19; Ps 89:39, 44; Lam 5:16

19:10 Job 7:6; 12:14; 24:20

19:11 Job 13:24; 16:9

19:12 Job 16:13; 30:12

19:13 Job 16:7, 20; Pss 69:8; 88:8, 18

19:14 Job 19:19

19:6 Or *for I am like a city under siege.*

19:2-3 Job once again rebuked his critics for their harsh and false words about him. The verbs in these verses are plural, indicating that Job was referring to all three of his critics, not just Bildad. When Job accused them of insulting him "ten times," he was using intentional hyperbole. Bildad's speech was actually the fifth response to Job thus far.

19:6 Job's only wrongdoing was when he claimed that God had wronged him. This is likely what God was referring to in His speech to Job (see note at 40:7-14; compare 42:7).

19:10 Once again Job said he had lost hope (see note at 17:11-16), but his words at the close of this speech were full of hope (see note at 19:25-27).

19:13-20 Job's three critics were not the only ones who had turned against him (see note at 17:6-8); all his other friends, relatives, and even his wife had also.

19:19 Pss 38:11; 55:12-13
19 My close friends detest me.
Those I loved have turned against me.
19:20 Job 33:21 Ps 102:5 Lam 4:8
20 I have been reduced to skin and bones
and have escaped death by the skin of my teeth.
21 "Have mercy on me, my friends, have mercy,
19:21 Job 1:11
for the hand of God has struck me.
19:22 Ps 69:26
22 Must you also persecute me, like God does?
Haven't you chewed me up enough?

19:23 Isa 30:8 Jer 36:2
23 "Oh, that my words could be recorded.
Oh, that they could be inscribed on a monument,
24 carved with an iron chisel and filled with lead,
engraved forever in the rock.

19:25 Job 16:19 Ps 78:35 Isa 43:14 Jer 50:34
25 "But as for me, I know that my Redeemer lives,
and He will stand upon the earth at last.
26 And after my body has decayed,
yet in my body I will see God!*
19:26 Matt 5:8 1 Cor 13:12 1 Jn 3:2
27 I will see Him for myself.
Yes, I will see Him with my own eyes.
I am overwhelmed at the thought!

19:28 Job 19:22
28 "How dare you go on persecuting me,
saying, 'It's his own fault'?
19:29 Job 15:22; 22:4 Ps 9:7 Eccl 12:14
29 You should fear punishment yourselves,
for your attitude deserves punishment.
Then you will know that there is indeed a judgment."

ZOPHAR'S SECOND RESPONSE TO JOB

20 Then Zophar the Naamathite replied:
2 "I must reply
because I am greatly disturbed.

19:26 Or *without my body I will see God!* The meaning of the Hebrew is uncertain.

19:23-24 Since the book of Job is part of Scripture, God honored Job's request that his "words could be recorded" and "engraved forever"—and to a degree Job never imagined.

▸ GOD
19:25 Christ is our Redeemer. Thousands of years before Christ was born in Bethlehem, Job prophesied that Jesus would come and stand on the earth. The Old Testament is filled with such prophecies that made it clear that the Messiah would come and even prophesies how the Messiah should be welcomed. Centuries after Job, the prophet Isaiah described in detail how the Messiah would die (Isaiah 53). And even the sacrificial system in the Temple illustrated how the Messiah would become the Redeemer for the sins of His people. Today we can read in the New Testament exactly how those prophecies were fulfilled in Jesus Christ. Praise the Father for His Son, Jesus Christ, our Redeemer, and give thanks that He lives today! (***See God**> God's Names> Son> Redeemer,* TopicGuide page A19.)

19:25-27 These verses show that Job had not completely lost hope (see note at 19:10). "My Redeemer lives, and He will stand upon the earth at last" (19:25) refers to Job's hope that someone would vindicate him in the eyes of his critics. Furthermore, Job had the hope of the resurrection, since he believed that he would one day see God with his own eyes in a physical body even after his earthly body had decayed.

▸ ADOPTION
19:26 I will see God! Job was thrilled that he would one day see God. In the midst of his pain and suffering, he could look forward to a time when he would be free of his maladies and would be in the presence of God. That idea overwhelmed him. Are you excited about seeing Jesus? Jesus promises us that we will see Him (John 16:16). That is our glorious hope. Keep your eyes focused on the future when you will be united with your Savior, Jesus Christ. (***See Adoption**> In Heaven> Eternally with Christ,* TopicGuide page A38.)

19:28-29 Job's words of warning to his three critics were prophetic (see 42:7-10).

20:2-3 Like Eliphaz and Bildad before him, Zophar became harsher in his tone with Job. All three lost their patience with Job the longer the dialogue continued.

[3] I've had to endure your insults,
but now my spirit prompts me to reply.

[4] "Don't you realize that from the beginning of time,
ever since people were first placed on the earth,
[5] the triumph of the wicked has been short lived
and the joy of the godless has been only temporary?
[6] Though the pride of the godless reaches to the heavens
and their heads touch the clouds,
[7] yet they will vanish forever,
thrown away like their own dung.
Those who knew them will ask,
'Where are they?'
[8] They will fade like a dream and not be found.
They will vanish like a vision in the night.
[9] Those who once saw them will see them no more.
Their families will never see them again.
[10] Their children will beg from the poor,
for they must give back their stolen riches.
[11] Though they are young,
their bones will lie in the dust.

[12] "They enjoyed the sweet taste of wickedness,
letting it melt under their tongue.
[13] They savored it,
holding it long in their mouths.
[14] But suddenly the food in their bellies turns sour,
a poisonous venom in their stomach.
[15] They will vomit the wealth they swallowed.
God won't let them keep it down.
[16] They will suck the poison of cobras.
The viper will kill them.
[17] They will never again enjoy streams of olive oil
or rivers of milk and honey.
[18] They will give back everything they worked for.
Their wealth will bring them no joy.
[19] For they oppressed the poor and left them destitute.
They foreclosed on their homes.
[20] They were always greedy and never satisfied.
Nothing remains of all the things they dreamed about.

20:3 Job 19:3
20:5 Job 8:12-13; Ps 37:35-36
20:6 Isa 14:13-14; Obad 1:3-4
20:7 Job 4:20; 7:10; 8:18; 14:20
20:8 Job 18:18; Pss 73:20; 90:5
20:9 Job 7:8, 10; 8:18
20:10 Job 5:4; 27:16-17
20:11 Job 13:26
20:12 Job 15:16
20:16 Deut 32:24, 33
20:17 Deut 32:13-14; Job 29:6
20:18 Job 20:10, 15
20:19 Job 24:2-4; 35:9
20:20 Eccl 5:13-15

20:4-21 As Zophar described the fate of the wicked, he repeatedly noted how a wicked person loses his wealth (see 1:1-3, 13-19). Zophar's words imply that he regarded Job as one of those who were wicked, because his words do not make sense unless he has Job in mind. Zophar's accusation about Job's mistreatment of the poor in 20:19 is particularly strange and unfounded, which shows how far he was willing to go to prove his point about the reason for Job's sufferings.

▸ HOLINESS
20:14 The taste of sin. In this verse, Job's friend described the ultimate "taste" of sin. At first, sin can seem sweet and fulfilling, but it soon turns into poison in the stomach. A lie can feel good at first, especially if it gets you out of a difficult position. But later, the lie can bite you when the truth comes out. Anger feels sweet when you strike at someone who irritates you, but later, when your relationship suffers, you feel the poison of regret and loneliness. Make sure you understand the lingering effects of sin and avoid areas of temptation that entrap you. Pray that God will send His Holy Spirit to help you resist these sins. (***See Holiness*****>** *Disciplines> Of Abstinence> Resisting sinful urges,* TopicGuide page A42.)

20:21 Job 15:29
[21] Nothing is left after they finish gorging themselves.
Therefore, their prosperity will not endure.

20:22 Job 5:5
[22] "In the midst of plenty, they will run into trouble
and be overcome by misery.
20:23 Num 11:18-20, 33; Ps 78:30-31
[23] May God give them a bellyful of trouble.
May God rain down His anger upon them.
20:24 Isa 24:18; Amos 5:19
[24] When they try to escape an iron weapon,
a bronze-tipped arrow will pierce them.
[25] The arrow is pulled from their back,
20:25 Job 16:13; 18:11, 14
and the arrowhead glistens with blood.*
The terrors of death are upon them.
20:26 Job 15:30; 18:18; Ps 21:9
[26] Their treasures will be thrown into deepest darkness.
A wildfire will devour their goods,
consuming all they have left.
20:27 Deut 31:28
[27] The heavens will reveal their guilt,
and the earth will testify against them.
20:28 Deut 28:31; Job 21:30
[28] A flood will sweep away their house.
God's anger will descend on them in torrents.
20:29 Job 27:13; 31:2-3
[29] This is the reward that God gives the wicked.
It is the inheritance decreed by God."

JOB'S SEVENTH SPEECH: A RESPONSE TO ZOPHAR

21 Then Job spoke again:

[2] "Listen closely to what I am saying.
That's one consolation you can give me.
[3] Bear with me, and let me speak.
After I have spoken, you may resume mocking me.

21:4 Job 6:11; 7:11
[4] "My complaint is with God, not with people.
I have good reason to be so impatient.
21:5 Judg 18:19; Job 29:9; 40:4
[5] Look at me and be stunned.
Put your hand over your mouth in shock.
21:6 Ps 55:5
[6] When I think about what I am saying, I shudder.
My body trembles.

20:25 Hebrew *with gall.*

▶ MINISTRY
20:21 What is true wealth? Many people spend their lives amassing wealth by any means possible, only to die and leave it all as an inheritance. What good did their wealth do for them? And what good does it actually do to have inherited wealth? Does money make us happy? Or holy? As rich as Job was (Job 1:3), he knew that if he didn't focus on God and His priorities, he could get caught up in materialism and greed. Human life is more than possessions and the empty soul can't be filled with money. Memorize Matthew 6:33 to help you keep your priorities straight. (***See Ministry****> Great Commission> Make Disciples> Disciples strategically use material wealth,* TopicGuide page A56.)

20:22-25 Zophar insisted that God brings judgment on the wicked in this life, which implied that Job should recognize that his sufferings were God's judgment on him for his sins.

20:26-29 Zophar concluded his speech by warning Job of the final judgment, when God's anger will descend on the wicked as decreed by God.

▶ ADOPTION
21:2 The comfort of listening. Job pleaded with his friends to listen to him. Many times we are guilty of not listening when our friends try to share their burdens with us. Instead, we think about our own problems or get distracted while they are talking. We may even fail to listen to our friends because we have preconceived ideas about what they are experiencing or why it is happening to them. Proverbs 18:13 says, "Spouting off before listening to the facts is both shameful and foolish." Be the first to listen and the last to speak when your friend seeks you out for comfort. (***See Adoption****> With Christ> Supernatural> Quick to listen,* TopicGuide page A37.)

21:6-33 Job's words about God's ways were so disturbing to him that thinking about them made him shudder. Once again Job referred to how unfair it was for God to allow the wicked to prosper (see note at 9:21-24)—an observation that stands in great contrast to what Zophar said about the wicked in the previous chapter.

7 "Why do the wicked prosper,
growing old and powerful?
8 They live to see their children grow up and settle down,
and they enjoy their grandchildren.
9 Their homes are safe from every fear,
and God does not punish them.
10 Their bulls never fail to breed.
Their cows bear calves and never miscarry.
11 They let their children frisk about like lambs.
Their little ones skip and dance.
12 They sing with tambourine and harp.
They celebrate to the sound of the flute.
13 They spend their days in prosperity,
then go down to the grave* in peace.
14 And yet they say to God, 'Go away.
We want no part of you and your ways.
15 Who is the Almighty, and why should we obey Him?
What good will it do us to pray?'
16 (They think their prosperity is of their own doing,
but I will have nothing to do with that kind of thinking.)

17 "Yet the light of the wicked never seems to be extinguished.
Do they ever have trouble?
Does God distribute sorrows to them in anger?
18 Are they driven before the wind like straw?
Are they carried away by the storm like chaff?
Not at all!

19 "'Well,' you say, 'at least God will punish their children!'
But I say He should punish the ones who sin,
so that they understand His judgment.
20 Let them see their destruction with their own eyes.
Let them drink deeply of the anger of the Almighty.
21 For they will not care what happens to their family
after they are dead.

22 "But who can teach a lesson to God,
since He judges even the most powerful?

21:7 Ps 73:3; Jer 12:1
21:8 Ps 17:14
21:9 Job 12:6; Ps 73:5
21:13 Job 36:11
21:14 Job 22:17
21:15 Job 22:17; 34:9
21:17 Job 18:5-6
21:18 Job 13:25; Pss 1:4; 35:5; 83:13; Isa 17:13
21:19 Exod 20:5; Ezek 18:4
21:20 Isa 51:17; Jer 25:15; Rev 14:10
21:22 Job 36:22; Ps 82:1; Isa 40:13-14; Rom 11:34

21:13 Hebrew *to Sheol.*

▶ HOLINESS

21:16 The prosperity of the wicked. It's not a problem when the rich get richer—that's often a function of good investments. But when the wicked rich get richer, it bothers us. When immoral nations prosper, something in us wonders if God is really in charge. Job looked at his rich friends, some of them wicked, and he knew many who were happy and appeared blessed (21:7). Even if they blasphemed God, they seemed to not suffer (21:14). With this observation, Job countered the popular arguments of his counselors, and we should receive this correction as well. If you know people who are prosperous, do not necessarily think that they got that way by evil doings. Do not draw conclusions about people's spirituality because of what they own, but by who they love. (***See Holiness***> *Submission> Delighting in God> Gladness in God,* TopicGuide page A40.)

▶ GOD

21:22 Do not doubt God's justice. The Bible tells us that God will judge the whole earth (Genesis 18:25; Psalm 96:13). He can do this accurately because He knows every detail of every action on earth. Many people fail to realize this and behave as if God were uninformed or ignorant of their actions. Such people need to join Job's counselors and receive Job's rebuke—stop pronouncing judgments on people whom you know little about! Just because people suffer doesn't mean they are guilty, and just because people are happy doesn't mean they are godly! Besides that, God has called us to judge those in the church (1 Corinthians 5:1-2), but God says He will judge those outside the church (1 Corinthians 5:12-13). So we are not to be busy deciding the fate of those outside the church anyhow, rich or poor. Pray that God will help you mind your own business—the glory of God in His church. (***See God***> *God's Nature> Unique> He is the final lawgiver and judge,* TopicGuide page A15.)

23 One person dies in prosperity,
completely comfortable and secure,
24 the picture of good health,
vigorous and fit.
25 Another person dies in bitter poverty,
never having tasted the good life.
21:26 Job 3:13; 20:11; 24:20
26 But both are buried in the same dust,
both eaten by the same maggots.

27 "Look, I know what you're thinking.
I know the schemes you plot against me.
21:28 Job 1:3
28 You will tell me of rich and wicked people
whose houses have vanished because of their sins.
29 But ask those who have been around,
and they will tell you the truth.
21:30 Job 20:29 Prov 16:4 Rom 2:5 2 Pet 2:9
30 Evil people are spared in times of calamity
and are allowed to escape disaster.
31 No one criticizes them openly
or pays them back for what they have done.
32 When they are carried to the grave,
an honor guard keeps watch at their tomb.
21:33 Job 3:19, 22; 17:16; 24:24
33 A great funeral procession goes to the cemetery.
Many pay their respects as the body is laid to rest,
and the earth gives sweet repose.

21:34 Job 16:2
34 "How can your empty clichés comfort me?
All your explanations are lies!"

ELIPHAZ'S THIRD RESPONSE TO JOB

22 Then Eliphaz the Temanite replied:
22:2 Job 35:7 Luke 17:10
2 "Can a person do anything to help God?
Can even a wise person be helpful to Him?
3 Is it any advantage to the Almighty if you are righteous?
Would it be any gain to Him if you were perfect?
22:4 Job 14:3
4 Is it because you're so pious that He accuses you
and brings judgment against you?
22:5 Job 11:6; 15:5
5 No, it's because of your wickedness!
There's no limit to your sins.

22:6 Exod 22:26 Deut 24:6, 17 Job 24:3, 9; 31:19-20 Ezek 18:16
6 "For example, you must have lent money to your friend
and demanded clothing as security.
Yes, you stripped him to the bone.

21:34 After the second cycle of dialogue (see note at 4:1) ended, Job summarized what he thought about his three critics' explanations of his sufferings thus far: They cannot comfort him, because all their explanations are wrong. (The Hebrew for "you" and for "your" is plural, so Job is not talking just to Zophar.)

22:1 The third cycle of dialogue begins with Eliphaz's third and last speech (see note at 4:1).

22:2-5 This series of rhetorical questions is laced with sarcasm, and in Eliphaz's mind the answer to each one was "Not at all!" Eliphaz claimed that Job's sufferings were because his sins had no limit.

22:6-9 Eliphaz raised his charges against Job to a new level even though he had no evidence that Job did any of the things he mentioned, such as dealing dishonestly with a friend about money (see 22:24), withholding water and food from the needy, and mistreating widows and orphans.

[7] You must have refused water for the thirsty
and food for the hungry.
[8] You probably think the land belongs to the powerful
and only the privileged have a right to it!
[9] You must have sent widows away empty-handed
and crushed the hopes of orphans.
[10] That is why you are surrounded by traps
and tremble from sudden fears.
[11] That is why you cannot see in the darkness,
and waves of water cover you.

[12] "God is so great—higher than the heavens,
higher than the farthest stars.
[13] But you reply, 'That's why God can't see what I am doing!
How can He judge through the thick darkness?
[14] For thick clouds swirl about Him, and He cannot see us.
He is way up there, walking on the vault of heaven.'

[15] "Will you continue on the old paths
where evil people have walked?
[16] They were snatched away in the prime of life,
the foundations of their lives washed away.
[17] For they said to God, 'Leave us alone!
What can the Almighty do to us?'
[18] Yet He was the One who filled their homes with good things,
so I will have nothing to do with that kind of thinking.

[19] "The righteous will be happy to see the wicked destroyed,
and the innocent will laugh in contempt.
[20] They will say, 'See how our enemies have been destroyed.
The last of them have been consumed in the fire.'

[21] "Submit to God, and you will have peace;
then things will go well for you.
[22] Listen to His instructions,
and store them in your heart.
[23] If you return to the Almighty, you will be restored—
so clean up your life.
[24] If you give up your lust for money
and throw your precious gold into the river,
[25] the Almighty Himself will be your treasure.
He will be your precious silver!

22:7 Job 31:31; Matt 10:42
22:8 Job 9:24; 12:19
22:9 Job 6:27; 24:3, 21
22:12 Job 11:7-9
22:13 Pss 10:11; 64:5; 94:7; Isa 29:15
22:14 Job 26:9
22:16 Job 14:14; 15:32; Matt 7:26-27
22:17 Job 21:14-15
22:18 Job 12:6; 21:16
22:19 Pss 58:10; 107:42
22:20 Job 15:30
22:22 Job 6:10; 23:12; Prov 2:6
22:23 Job 8:5; 11:14; Isa 19:22; Zech 1:3
22:24 Job 31:24-25

22:12-14 Eliphaz basically accused Job of being an agnostic in his worldview and believing that people can do anything they wish since God cannot see them.

▸ GOD
22:15 Two paths. The Bible tells us that life has two paths—the narrow and the wide (Matthew 7:13). The narrow path is followed by those who love and follow God. The wide path is followed by those who follow their own way. People don't wander onto these paths by accident—we each choose the direction we take. Jesus tells us that He is at the very center of the narrow way (John 14:6). The most important decision you will make in your lifetime is whether you will take the path less traveled, the narrow road accompanied by Christ, or whether you will walk the wide path of human autonomy. Make the right choice. (***See God****> God's Names> Son> The Way,* TopicGuide page A18.)

22:15 Eliphaz considered Job one of the evil people who lost everything he had because he forgot about God.

22:21-30 Once again Eliphaz called on Job to return to God and pray, and then God would provide light for the life that lies ahead (see note at 5:17-18).

22:26 Isa 58:14
[26] "Then you will take delight in the Almighty
and look up to God.
22:27 Isa 58:9
[27] You will pray to Him, and He will hear you,
and you will fulfill your vows to Him.
22:28 Ps 112:4
[28] You will succeed in whatever you choose to do,
and light will shine on the road ahead of you.
22:29 Job 5:11
[29] If people are in trouble and you say, 'Help them,'
God will save them.
22:30 Pss 18:20; 24:3-4
[30] Even sinners will be rescued;
they will be rescued because your hands are pure."

JOB'S EIGHTH SPEECH: A RESPONSE TO ELIPHAZ

23 Then Job spoke again:

23:2 Job 6:2-3; 7:11
[2] "My complaint today is still a bitter one,
and I try hard not to groan aloud.
[3] If only I knew where to find God,
I would go to His court.
23:4 Job 13:18
[4] I would lay out my case
and present my arguments.
[5] Then I would listen to His reply
and understand what He says to me.
23:6 Job 9:4
[6] Would He use His great power to argue with me?
No, He would give me a fair hearing.
23:7 Job 13:3, 16
[7] Honest people can reason with Him,
so I would be forever acquitted by my judge.
23:8 Job 9:11
[8] I go east, but He is not there.
I go west, but I cannot find Him.
[9] I do not see Him in the north, for He is hidden.
I look to the south, but He is concealed.

23:10 Job 7:18 Pss 7:9; 11:5
[10] "But He knows where I am going.
And when He tests me, I will come out as pure as gold.

▸ HOLINESS

22:26 Delight in God. What does it mean to "take delight in God," as Eliphaz mentioned? Eliphaz was a little confused—he thought that giving up all desires and all possessions would be the key. But the Bible says that delighting in God means eagerly anticipating your time with Him. It means experiencing joy as you open His book and read what He says to you (Nehemiah 8:12). It means feeling the thrill of hurrying to obey God's will. Delighting in God is savoring His love and His comfort and doing everything you can to keep delighting in it. Take time right now to focus on Him and how much He means to you—it's the greatest joy God offers you this side of heaven. (***See Holiness****> Submission> Delighting in God> Rejoicing in repentance,* TopicGuide page A40.)

23:3 Despite what Eliphaz said about Job, the problem was not that Job didn't want to talk to God or that he refused to listen to Him. The problem, as Job explained, was that God has been silent during the entire ordeal, and he didn't know where to find Him. But Job's three critics thought they had everything all figured out about Job's sufferings.

23:4-5 Given the opportunity, Job would have been glad to present his case to God, and then he would have listen to God's reply. Job had been eager all along to hear from God, but God doesn't always respond in the way or at the time that we desire.

23:7 Job was still confident that he would be acquitted by the Judge if he were allowed to argue his case before Him.

▸ WORSHIP

23:10 God tests His own. We are often surprised when trials come upon us. But both here and throughout the Bible, God promises to test us (see James 1:12; 1 Peter 1:7). Although we should seek the reason for our problems and correct what is causing them if necessary, we should not fault God for allowing difficult circumstances into our lives. The Old and New Testament saints faced enemies or problems that seemed unsolvable at the time (Genesis 22:1). Joseph was sold as a slave (Genesis 37). David had to hide in caves for years. Isaiah was asked to preach to people who would not listen to him (Isaiah 6:9). The leaders in the early church endured persecution and even martyrdom for the gospel's sake. God has His plan for our lives—and it's a good plan. But it will certainly involve times of testing and trial (Acts 14:22). Can you thank Him for these times as well as the good ones? (***See Worship****> OT> God's Supremacy> Required obedience in daily life and affairs,* TopicGuide page A26.)

[11] For I have stayed on God's paths;
I have followed His ways and not turned aside.
[12] I have not departed from His commands,
but have treasured His words more than daily food.
[13] But once He has made His decision, who can change His mind?
Whatever He wants to do, He does.
[14] So He will do to me whatever He has planned.
He controls my destiny.
[15] No wonder I am so terrified in His presence.
When I think of it, terror grips me.
[16] God has made me sick at heart;
the Almighty has terrified me.
[17] Darkness is all around me;
thick, impenetrable darkness is everywhere.

JOB ASKS WHY THE WICKED ARE NOT PUNISHED

24 [1] "Why doesn't the Almighty bring the wicked to judgment?
Why must the godly wait for Him in vain?
[2] Evil people steal land by moving the boundary markers.
They steal livestock and put them in their own pastures.
[3] They take the orphan's donkey
and demand the widow's ox as security for a loan.
[4] The poor are pushed off the path;
the needy must hide together for safety.
[5] Like wild donkeys in the wilderness,
the poor must spend all their time looking for food,
searching even in the desert for food for their children.
[6] They harvest a field they do not own,
and they glean in the vineyards of the wicked.
[7] All night they lie naked in the cold,
without clothing or covering.
[8] They are soaked by mountain showers,
and they huddle against the rocks for want of a home.

[9] "The wicked snatch a widow's child from her breast,
taking the baby as security for a loan.
[10] The poor must go about naked, without any clothing.
They harvest food for others while they themselves are starving.
[11] They press out olive oil without being allowed to taste it,
and they tread in the winepress as they suffer from thirst.

23:11
Job 31:7
Pss 17:5; 44:18

23:12
Job 6:10

23:16
Deut 20:3
Jer 51:46

23:17
Job 10:18-19; 19:8

24:1
Isa 2:12
Jer 46:10

24:2
Deut 19:14; 27:17

24:3
Exod 22:26
Deut 24:17

24:4
Job 29:16; 30:25
Prov 14:31
Amos 8:4

24:5
Job 39:5-8
Ps 104:23

24:7
Exod 22:26

24:8
Lam 4:5

24:9
Job 6:27

23:15-17 Job considered God elusive and terrifying. This is often the response of those who expect God to act a certain way—only to discover that He doesn't.

24:1-25 This chapter records Job's puzzlement at why God doesn't bring immediate judgment on the wicked.

24:2-21 Job complained that evil people take advantage of the helpless to increase their own wealth. Contrary to Eliphaz's accusations (see note at 22:6-9), Job *is* concerned about the well-being of the poor, orphans, and widows.

▸ CHURCH
24:3 God sees the poor. The Bible repeatedly tells us that God has a special place in His heart for the poor, the fatherless, and widows (Psalm 68:5; Proverbs 22:22). Many people fit these categories today. Homeless families crowd into shelters, many children live in foster care, and single mothers struggle to raise their children. Are you part of God's army in reaching out to those who are needy? Perhaps you can befriend a fatherless child in your church or neighborhood or begin a support group to help single parents or volunteer at a homeless shelter. When you care for those who are bereft, you are acting on God's behalf, showing His love to those who need it most. (***See Church****> Role> Preach> Topics> Godly Lives> Care for their poor, widows, and orphans,* TopicGuide page A50.)

24:12 Job 9:23-24
12 The groans of the dying rise from the city,
and the wounded cry for help,
yet God ignores their moaning.

13 "Wicked people rebel against the light.
They refuse to acknowledge its ways
or stay in its paths.
24:14 Ps 10:8 Mic 2:1
14 The murderer rises in the early dawn
to kill the poor and needy;
at night he is a thief.
24:15 Prov 7:9
15 The adulterer waits for the twilight,
saying, 'No one will see me then.'
He hides his face so no one will know him.
24:16 Exod 22:2 Matt 6:19
16 Thieves break into houses at night
and sleep in the daytime.
They are not acquainted with the light.
24:17 Ps 91:5
17 The black night is their morning.
They ally themselves with the terrors
of the darkness.

24:18 Job 5:3; 22:11, 16; 27:20
18 "But they disappear like foam down a river.
Everything they own is cursed,
and they are afraid to enter their own vineyards.
24:19 Job 6:16-17; 21:13
19 The grave* consumes sinners
24:20 Job 18:17; 19:10; 21:26 Prov 10:7 Isa 49:15 Dan 4:14
just as drought and heat consume snow.
20 Their own mothers will forget them.
Maggots will find them sweet to eat.
No one will remember them.
Wicked people are broken like a tree in the storm.
24:21 Job 22:9
21 They cheat the woman who has no son to help her.
They refuse to help the needy widow.

24:22 Job 9:4; 12:6
22 "God, in His power, drags away the rich.
They may rise high, but they have no
assurance of life.
24:23 Job 11:11; 12:6
23 They may be allowed to live in security,
but God is always watching them.
24:24 Job 14:21 Ps 37:10
24 And though they are great now,
in a moment they will be gone like all others,
cut off like heads of grain.
24:25 Job 6:28; 27:4
25 Can anyone claim otherwise?
Who can prove me wrong?"

24:19 Hebrew *Sheol*.

▸ GOD

24:22-25 The fate of the wicked. Have you ever attended the funeral of someone who publicly rejected God? Compare that to the funeral of a saint who served God. In both instances, the body is destined for burial and decay. Yet there is a vast difference in the hope! For those who love the Lord, a funeral signifies the beginning of eternal glory. Paul writes these inspiring words: "But thank God! He gives us victory over sin and death through our Lord Jesus Christ" (1 Corinthians 15:57). We may mourn over losing a Christian loved one in this life, but we know that we will see them again in heaven one day. Keep this hope close to your heart when you are in the midst of sorrow over the passing of a loved one. (***See God**> God's Attributes> All-Powerful> He has power over death,* TopicGuide page A15.)

BILDAD'S THIRD RESPONSE TO JOB

25 Then Bildad the Shuhite replied:

2 "God is powerful and dreadful.
He enforces peace in the heavens.
3 Who is able to count His heavenly army?
Doesn't His light shine on all the earth?
4 How can a mortal be innocent before God?
Can anyone born of a woman be pure?
5 God is more glorious than the moon;
He shines brighter than the stars.
6 In comparison, people are maggots;
we mortals are mere worms."

25:2 Job 9:4; 16:19; 31:2; 36:5; 37:23
25:4 Job 4:17; 9:2
25:5 Job 15:15; 31:26
25:6 Job 7:17

JOB'S NINTH SPEECH: A RESPONSE TO BILDAD

26 Then Job spoke again:

2 "How you have helped the powerless!
How you have saved the weak!
3 How you have enlightened my stupidity!
What wise advice you have offered!
4 Where have you gotten all these wise sayings?
Whose spirit speaks through you?

5 "The dead tremble—
those who live beneath the waters.
6 The underworld* is naked in God's presence.
The place of destruction* is uncovered.
7 God stretches the northern sky over empty space
and hangs the earth on nothing.
8 He wraps the rain in His thick clouds,
and the clouds don't burst with the weight.
9 He covers the face of the moon,*
shrouding it with His clouds.
10 He created the horizon when He separated the waters;
He set the boundary between day and night.
11 The foundations of heaven tremble;
they shudder at His rebuke.

26:2 Ps 71:9
26:5 Job 3:13 Ps 88:10
26:7 Job 9:8
26:8 Job 37:11 Prov 30:4
26:9 Job 22:14 Pss 97:2; 105:39
26:10 Job 38:1-11, 19-20, 24 Prov 8:29

26:6a Hebrew *Sheol.* **26:6b** Hebrew *Abaddon.* **26:9** Or *covers His throne.*

25:1-6 Bildad's third and final speech was the briefest one from the four speakers. He reiterated a common theme mentioned in the three cycles of dialogue by the four men: God is greater than all, and all are but worms in his sight. Apparently Bildad was surprised at Eliphaz's wild accusations against Job in his previous speech, and Bildad was not willing to continue with that line of argument.

▸ WORSHIP
25:5 God's glory. If you live in a metropolitan area, you cannot see the stars clearly because the city lights interfere with their glow. But if you travel to a rural area and walk under a starry sky, you can appreciate the beauty of the light-studded canopy. The stars twinkle with a sharp, clear light. Their beauty can take your breath away. Yet even the heavens in all their glory are nothing compared to the glory of their Creator. Look to the Scriptures and to creation to gain a deeper appreciation of the awe and majesty of the God you serve. (***See Worship****> OT> Reverence> Let the earth fear God,* TopicGuide page A29.)

26:2-4 Job used sarcasm to rebuke Bildad for the weakness of his last speech (see note at 25:1-6).

26:5-14 Job referred to God's many acts in creation as some of the minor things He does, which shows that no one can understand the thunder of God's power. Job's point seems to be that if we cannot understand God's creation, which we can see and are a part of, we are certainly not able to explain His unseen actions either.

12 By His power the sea grew calm.
By His skill He crushed the great sea monster.*

26:13 Job 9:8 Isa 27:1

13 His Spirit made the heavens beautiful,
and His power pierced the gliding serpent.

26:14 Job 36:29; 37:4-5

14 These are just the beginning of all that He does,
merely a whisper of His power.
Who, then, can comprehend the thunder of His power?"

JOB'S FINAL SPEECH

27:1 Job 29:1

27 Job continued speaking:

27:2 Job 9:18; 16:11

2 "I vow by the living God, who has taken away my rights,
by the Almighty who has embittered my soul—

27:3 Job 32:8; 33:4

3 As long as I live,
while I have breath from God,

27:4 Job 6:28; 33:3

4 my lips will speak no evil,
and my tongue will speak no lies.
5 I will never concede that you are right;
I will defend my integrity until I die.

27:6 Job 2:3; 13:18

6 I will maintain my innocence without wavering.
My conscience is clear for as long as I live.

7 "May my enemy be punished like the wicked,
my adversary like those who do evil.

27:8 Job 8:13; 11:20

8 For what hope do the godless have when God cuts them off
and takes away their life?

27:9 Job 35:12-13 Prov 1:27-28 Isa 1:15

9 Will God listen to their cry
when trouble comes upon them?
10 Can they take delight in the Almighty?
Can they call to God at any time?

27:10 Job 22:26-27

11 I will teach you about God's power.
I will not conceal anything concerning the Almighty.
12 But you have seen all this,
yet you say all these useless things to me.

27:13 Job 15:20; 20:29

13 "This is what the wicked will receive from God;
this is their inheritance from the Almighty.

26:12 Hebrew *Rahab,* the name of a mythical sea monster that represents chaos in ancient literature.

▶ GOD

26:14 Merely a whisper of God's power! In this chapter, Job described the Creator's awesome power. And yet, Job said, these mighty acts are only a whisper of His power, a mere hint of what God is capable of doing, and God's true power goes well beyond our comprehension. Likewise, God's holiness and goodness cannot be fully grasped by our minds. But while such things are only partially known through head knowledge, we can gain heart knowledge about them. Through holy meditation, that is, to "wait quietly before God" (see Psalm 62:1, 5), we can silently and intimately commune with God. The psalmist encourages us to meditate on God's love (Psalm 48:9), on His Word (Psalm 119:27), and on God's royal beauty (Psalm 145:5). Take the time, be patient, and meditate on the immensity of God's power. (***See God***> *God's Attributes> All-Powerful> God has the power to create anything from nothing,* TopicGuide page A15.)

27:1 The comment about Job's continuation in speaking probably indicates that Job paused briefly in his speech, probably to allow Zophar a chance to respond. Zophar did not say anything in this last cycle of dialogue (see note at 4:1), so Job kept going (see note at 29:1).

27:2-6 In very strong terms Job once again declared his innocence and insisted that his sufferings were not the result of great sins in his life—as his three critics were insisting all along.

▶ WORSHIP

27:8-10 Does God hear us? In times of dire crisis, even the wicked or the godless might cry out to God. But does God listen to their cries for help? The answer to Job's rhetorical questions is no. Children of God, however, have an assurance—"And we are confident that He hears us whenever we ask for anything that pleases Him" (1 John 5:14). How does it feel to know that God will hear you when you call to Him? Take advantage of God's listening ear and spend more time in honest, worshipful prayer. (***See Worship***> *OT> Fasting and Prayer> Prayer> Devote yourselves to prayer,* TopicGuide page A26.)

14 They may have many children,
but the children will die in war or starve to death.
15 Those who survive will die of a plague,
and not even their widows will mourn them.

16 "Evil people may have piles of money
and may store away mounds of clothing.
17 But the righteous will wear that clothing,
and the innocent will divide that money.
18 The wicked build houses as fragile as a spider's web,*
as flimsy as a shelter made of branches.
19 The wicked go to bed rich
but wake to find that all their wealth is gone.
20 Terror overwhelms them like a flood,
and they are blown away in the storms of the night.
21 The east wind carries them away, and they are gone.
It sweeps them away.
22 It whirls down on them without mercy.
They struggle to flee from its power.
23 But everyone jeers at them
and mocks them.

27:14 Job 20:18-21
27:15 Ps 78:64
27:18 Job 8:15
27:19 Job 7:8, 21
27:20 Job 15:21; 20:8
27:21 Job 7:10; 18:18; 20:8; 21:18
27:22 Job 11:20; Jer 13:14; Ezek 5:11; 24:14

JOB SPEAKS OF WISDOM AND UNDERSTANDING

28 1 "People know where to mine silver
and how to refine gold.
2 They know where to dig iron from the earth
and how to smelt copper from rock.
3 They know how to shine light in the darkness
and explore the farthest regions of the earth
as they search in the dark for ore.
4 They sink a mine shaft into the earth
far from where anyone lives.
They descend on ropes, swinging back and forth.
5 Food is grown on the earth above,
but down below, the earth is melted as by fire.
6 Here the rocks contain precious lapis lazuli,
and the dust contains gold.
7 These are treasures no bird of prey can see,
no falcon's eye observe.
8 No wild animal has walked upon these treasures;
no lion has ever set his paw there.

28:5 Ps 104:14

27:18 As in Greek and Syriac versions (see also 8:14); Hebrew reads *a moth.*

27:12 Job realized that much of what his three critics had said about God was true, but they had also said many useless things about Job. People may have good theology, but it also takes wisdom to correctly apply our knowledge about God to people and situations.

▸ ADOPTION
27:18 Wealth is fragile. In Job's final speech, he uses the metaphor of a flimsy house to describe the precarious situation of those who trust in material blessings to demonstrate their spiritual blessings. But what (or who!) is the foundation of spiritual maturity? Second Samuel 22:3 says, "My God is my rock, in whom I find protection." Where are you placing your trust—on shaky foundations of wealth or in our mighty God? Your trust in Christ and your intimacy with Him is the only trustworthy measure of your spiritual maturity. (***See Adoption****> With Christ> Supernatural> A life of immeasurable riches,* TopicGuide page A37.)

28:1-28 In this chapter Job described wisdom and humanity's futile attempts to discover it apart from God.

28:1-11 Job explained how people go to great lengths to search for valuable things hidden in the recesses of the earth, such as silver and gold, iron and copper, sapphires and precious stones, and other hidden treasures.

28:9 Deut 8:15; 32:13
9 People know how to tear apart flinty rocks
and overturn the roots of mountains.
10 They cut tunnels in the rocks
and uncover precious stones.
11 They dam up the trickling streams
and bring to light the hidden treasures.

28:12 Job 28:23, 28
12 "But do people know where to find wisdom?
Where can they find understanding?
13 No one knows where to find it,
for it is not found among the living.
14 'It is not here,' says the ocean.
'Nor is it here,' says the sea.
15 It cannot be bought with gold.
It cannot be purchased with silver.
16 It's worth more than all the gold of Ophir,
greater than precious onyx or lapis lazuli.
28:17 Prov 8:10; 16:16
17 Wisdom is more valuable than gold and crystal.
It cannot be purchased with jewels mounted in fine gold.
28:18 Prov 8:11
18 Coral and jasper are worthless in trying to get it.
The price of wisdom is far above rubies.
28:19 Prov 8:19
19 Precious peridot from Ethiopia* cannot be exchanged for it.
It's worth more than the purest gold.

28:20 Job 28:23, 28
20 "But do people know where to find wisdom?
Where can they find understanding?
21 It is hidden from the eyes of all humanity.
Even the sharp-eyed birds in the sky cannot discover it.
28:22 Job 26:6
22 Destruction* and Death say,
'We've heard only rumors of where
wisdom can be found.'

28:23 Prov 8:22-36
23 "God alone understands the way to wisdom;
He knows where it can be found,
28:24 Ps 33:13-14 Prov 15:3
24 for He looks throughout the whole earth
and sees everything under the heavens.
28:25 Job 12:15; 38:8-11 Ps 135:7
25 He decided how hard the winds should blow
and how much rain should fall.
28:26 Job 37:3, 6, 11-12; 38:25
26 He made the laws for the rain
and laid out a path for the lightning.
27 Then He saw wisdom and evaluated it.
He set it in place and examined it thoroughly.

28:19 Hebrew *from Cush.* 28:22 Hebrew *Abaddon.*

▶ BIBLE
28:12 Where do you go to find wisdom? Job spent the first part of this chapter describing how people ingeniously mine the earth for its riches. He notes, however, that people show no such aptness for finding wisdom. In our own time, technological advances have extended life spans and brought a higher standard of living, but people still lack true wisdom. Proverbs 2:6-7 says, "The Lord grants wisdom! From His mouth come knowledge and understanding. He grants a treasure of common sense to the honest." Be diligent to mine God's Word for the greatest treasure—the wisdom of God. (***See Bible****> Power> Wisdom> Instruction leads to wisdom,* TopicGuide page A11.)

28:12-22 Job explained that no one knows where to find wisdom even though it is more valuable than anything found in or on the earth.

28 And this is what He says to all humanity: 28:28 Ps 111:10 Prov 1:7; 9:10
'The fear of the Lord is true wisdom;
to forsake evil is real understanding.'"

JOB SPEAKS OF HIS FORMER BLESSINGS

29 Job continued speaking: 29:1 Job 27:1

2 "I long for the years gone by 29:2 Jer 31:28
when God took care of me,
3 when He lit up the way before me 29:3 Job 11:17
and I walked safely through the darkness.
4 When I was in my prime,
God's friendship was felt in my home.
5 The Almighty was still with me,
and my children were around me.
6 My cows produced milk in abundance, 29:6 Deut 32:13 Ps 81:16
and my groves poured out streams of olive oil.

7 "Those were the days when I went to the city gate
and took my place among the honored leaders.
8 The young stepped aside when they saw me,
and even the aged rose in respect at my coming.
9 The princes stood in silence 29:9 Job 21:5; 29:21
and put their hands over their mouths.
10 The highest officials of the city stood quietly,
holding their tongues in respect.

11 "All who heard me praised me. 29:11 Job 4:3-4
All who saw me spoke well of me.
12 For I assisted the poor in their need 29:12 Job 24:4, 9; 31:16-17, 21; 34:28
and the orphans who required help.
13 I helped those without hope, and they blessed me. 29:13 Job 31:19-20
And I caused the widows' hearts to sing for joy.

▸ WORSHIP
28:28 Flee from evil. If you came upon a dangerous situation, such as a robbery in progress or a riot, you would flee from the danger. Your heart would pound and your mouth would become dry. We should have the same reactions when we recognize that we are being tempted to sin. When Joseph faced sexual temptation, he didn't fight it internally. He didn't pray about it. He ran! (Genesis 39:10-12). There's no shame in fleeing temptation—it's the first step in Job's advice to "forsake evil." (***See Worship****> OT> Reverence> Flee from evil,* TopicGuide page A28.)

28:28 The fear of the Lord and forsaking evil is a fair summary of the ancient faith of Job.

29:1 Apparently, Job paused to give his three critics a chance to respond, and he continued when they remained silent (see note at 27:1).

29:2-5 Job reminisced about the happy life he enjoyed before his sufferings began, a theme that continues through the end of this chapter. In these first few verses Job remembered how close his relationship with God was—a relationship that seems to have been lost.

29:5-11 Job fondly recalled his children, his wealth, and his great reputation as a leader among the people—from "the young" to "the aged", even to "princes" and the "highest officials."

▸ CHURCH
29:11 Praise from God and people. In chapter 1 of this book, God praised Job's righteousness. Here, Job noted that people also spoke well of him because his faith was expressed in actions that represented God's heart. He helped the poor, the orphans, and the widows. He encouraged the despondent. He helped the disabled and stood up for those who were oppressed. When we are truly following God, our actions will reflect God's character, and we will develop a good reputation. Personal righteousness may not silence every critic, but it certainly doesn't hurt. When you are criticized by others, instead of striking back, show them the love that flows from a God-centered life. (***See Church****> Role> Preach> Topics> Disciple> Encourage the saints to love and good deeds,* TopicGuide page A50.)

29:12-17 Job listed several things he did that caused people to praise him, including helping those who were poor, orphans, widows, blind, lame, and strangers. Some of these are the same people that Eliphaz claimed Job had oppressed (see note at 22:6-9).

29:14 Job 27:5-6; Ps 132:9; Isa 59:17; 61:10; Eph 6:14

[14] Everything I did was honest.
Righteousness covered me like a robe,
and I wore justice like a turban.
[15] I served as eyes for the blind
and feet for the lame.

29:16 Prov 29:7

[16] I was a father to the poor
and assisted strangers who needed help.

29:17 Ps 3:7

[17] I broke the jaws of godless oppressors
and plucked their victims from their teeth.

[18] "I thought, 'Surely I will die surrounded by my family
after a long, good life.*

29:19 Jer 17:8; Hos 14:5

[19] For I am like a tree whose roots reach the water,
whose branches are refreshed with the dew.

29:20 Gen 49:24; Ps 18:34

[20] New honors are constantly bestowed on me,
and my strength is continually renewed.'

29:21 Job 4:3; 29:9

[21] "Everyone listened to my advice.
They were silent as they waited for me to speak.
[22] And after I spoke, they had nothing to add,
for my counsel satisfied them.
[23] They longed for me to speak as people long for rain.
They drank my words like a refreshing spring rain.
[24] When they were discouraged, I smiled at them.
My look of approval was precious to them.

29:25 Job 1:3; 4:4; 16:5; 31:37

[25] Like a chief, I told them what to do.
I lived like a king among his troops
and comforted those who mourned.

JOB SPEAKS OF HIS ANGUISH

30:1 Job 12:4

30 [1] "But now I am mocked by people younger than I,
by young men whose fathers are not worthy to run with my sheepdogs.
[2] A lot of good they are to me—
those worn-out wretches!
[3] They are gaunt with hunger
and flee to the deserts,
to desolate and gloomy wastelands.
[4] They pluck wild greens from among the bushes
and eat from the roots of broom trees.
[5] They are driven from human society,
and people shout at them as if they were thieves.

29:18 Hebrew *after I have counted my days like sand.*

29:18-20 Before his sufferings began, Job thought that he would enjoy all those blessings of life detailed in 29:2-17 without interruption until the day he died.

29:21-25 Job's nostalgic look back at his former life concludes with a description of his role as counselor and guide to those who needed his insights and advice—an indication of the great respect and admiration that Job formerly garnered.

▸ GOD
29:23 Words as refreshing as rain. After a time of drought, rain can feel refreshing, cleansing, like a blessing straight from God to the dry earth. Our words can have the quality of refreshing rain for others. Proverbs 13:14 says, "The instruction of the wise is like a life-giving fountain." Are you giving out streams of sweet water that help soothe the souls of hurting friends, or are your words caustic? Choose your words and actions like Job did so that others will benefit from being in your presence. (***See God***> *God's Attributes> True> God's words are faithful and true,* TopicGuide page A18.)

30:1-15 In contrast to his former life, Job was now mocked by everyone—young and old alike—even to his face. Job saw God's hand in this (30:11), but he didn't understand why.

6 So now they live in frightening ravines,
in caves and among the rocks.
7 They sound like animals howling among the bushes,
huddled together beneath the nettles.
8 They are nameless fools,
outcasts from society.

9 "And now they mock me with vulgar songs!
They taunt me!
10 They despise me and won't come near me,
except to spit in my face.
11 For God has cut my bowstring.
He has humbled me,
so they have thrown off all restraint.
12 These outcasts oppose me to my face.
They send me sprawling
and lay traps in my path.
13 They block my road
and do everything they can to destroy me.
They know I have no one to help me.
14 They come at me from all directions.
They jump on me when I am down.
15 I live in terror now.
My honor has blown away in the wind,
and my prosperity has vanished like a cloud.

16 "And now my life seeps away.
Depression haunts my days.
17 At night my bones are filled with pain,
which gnaws at me relentlessly.
18 With a strong hand, God grabs my shirt.
He grips me by the collar of my coat.
19 He has thrown me into the mud.
I'm nothing more than dust and ashes.

20 "I cry to You, O God, but You don't answer.
I stand before You, but You don't even look.

30:9 Job 12:4; 17:6 Ps 69:11-12

30:10 Num 12:14 Deut 25:9 Isa 50:6 Matt 26:67

30:11 Ruth 1:21 Ps 88:7

30:12 Job 19:12 Ps 140:4-5 Isa 3:5

30:15 Job 3:25; 7:9; 31:23 Ps 55:3-5 Hos 13:3

30:16 Pss 22:14; 42:4

30:17 Job 30:30

30:19 Ps 69:2, 14

30:20 Job 19:7

▸ HOLINESS

30:13 Championing the weak. While Job's life was being blessed, people honored him. As soon as he was devastated by calamity, these same people took advantage of him. Today, the wicked still seek to pounce on the weak, as is shown by such blatant exploitation and inhumanity as the Holocaust, genocide in Sudan, and slavery in Thailand. As Christians, we need to stand up for those who cannot fight for themselves. Jesus loved the lepers, the outcasts of His society. What you do for the downtrodden will testify to how God is at work in your life. Find ways to bless the poor around you, then around the world. (***See Holiness****> Disciplines> Of Abstinence> Resisting worldly influences,* TopicGuide page A42.)

▸ ADOPTION

30:16 Focus on God. At this point, Job seems to have lost sight of God's comfort. Depression is a common reaction to sustained adverse circumstances, but as believers we don't need to wallow in our sad feelings. Paul writes, "Don't worry about anything; instead, pray about everything" (Philippians 4:6). Prayer is an antidote to depression, for we know that our prayers do reach God's throne. Fellowship with God's people is also part of God's solution for depression (1 John 1:7). Repenting of any lingering sin (Psalm 51:7-8) or confused ideas about God or yourself is also important to help you escape debilitating feelings. In every situation, talk to God and stay focused on Him. (***See Adoption****> With Christ> Redemption> Freedom from meaninglessness and despair,* TopicGuide page A37.)

30:16-19 As he had done many times before, Job described the anguish his sufferings had brought: He was brokenhearted, depressed, weary, and in pain. He also knew that God was the one who brought him so low—nothing more than "dust and ashes"—yet once again he doesn't know why God had done this to him.

30:20-23 In this prayer Job once again cried out to God for an answer for his sufferings, but he didn't receive one. Job wasn't afraid to repeat himself if he didn't hear an answer from God.

30:21 Job 16:9, 14
30:22 Job 9:17; 10:3; 27:21
30:23 Job 3:19; 9:22; 10:8
30:24 Job 19:7
30:26 Job 3:25-26; 19:8 Jer 8:15
30:28 Job 19:7 Pss 38:6; 42:9; 43:2
30:29 Mic 1:8
30:30 Job 2:7 Ps 102:3

21 You have become cruel toward me.
You use Your power to persecute me.
22 You throw me into the whirlwind
and destroy me in the storm.
23 And I know You are sending me to my death—
the destination of all who live.

24 "Surely no one would turn against the needy
when they cry for help in their trouble.
25 Did I not weep for those in trouble?
Was I not deeply grieved for the needy?
26 So I looked for good, but evil came instead.
I waited for the light, but darkness fell.
27 My heart is troubled and restless.
Days of suffering torment me.
28 I walk in gloom, without sunlight.
I stand in the public square and cry for help.
29 Instead, I am considered a brother to jackals
and a companion to owls.
30 My skin has turned dark,
and my bones burn with fever.
31 My harp plays sad music,
and my flute accompanies those who weep.

JOB'S FINAL PROTEST OF INNOCENCE

31:1 2 Sam 11:2-4 Matt 5:28
31:2 Job 20:29
31:3 Job 18:12; 21:30
31:4 2 Chr 16:9 Job 14:16; 28:24; 34:21 Prov 5:21

31 1 "I made a covenant with my eyes
not to look with lust at a young woman.
2 For what has God above chosen for us?
What is our inheritance from the Almighty on high?
3 Isn't it calamity for the wicked
and misfortune for those who do evil?
4 Doesn't He see everything I do
and every step I take?

5 "Have I lied to anyone
or deceived anyone?

30:24-30 Job did not understand how he could help the needy and those in trouble and then end up ostracized and sick himself.

▸ PURPOSE
30:26 Darkness and light. After the first messenger arrived with bad news, Job probably thought that was the worst of it. But then, one by one, other messengers came with sad tidings. Finally, Job was struck with a painful disease. Job didn't understand why all this had happened to him. But we have the advantage of being able to see the scene in heaven and the conversation between God and Satan. This helps us know that more is at stake in our struggles and sufferings than what we see on the surface. God gives us the story of Job's life to help us understand that He is sovereign and He has a plan for our lives, though we may not understand it. So when troubles seem to pile up on your doorstep, have confidence that God is doing something marvelous in your life. (***See Purpose****> God's Means> God's Sovereignty> God has always had a plan,* TopicGuide page A52.)

31:1 In this chapter Job finished his defense of his integrity by pointing out his refusal "to look with lust at a young woman" (see also 31:9-12). Job knew that it would be futile to make such a claim if it were untrue, since God could see everything Job did (31:4).

▸ GOD
31:4 "Every step I take." How do you feel when you see a policeman in the rearview mirror? Likewise, how do you feel when you realize God sees everything you do? Just as with the policeman, your emotional reaction depends on the state of your heart. When we desire to serve God and freely confess our sins to Him, we welcome His presence and His help every moment of every day. But when we hang onto sin or seek to live our own way, we fear God's attention toward us and the punishment that it might bring. If the thought of God's eyes upon you brings you joy, thank Him for His love. If you feel fear, confess your sins right away to restore your joy. (***See God****> God's Attributes> All-Present> God is everywhere,* TopicGuide page A15.)

6 Let God weigh me on the scales of justice,
for He knows my integrity.
7 If I have strayed from His pathway,
or if my heart has lusted for what my eyes have seen,
or if I am guilty of any other sin,
8 then let someone else eat the crops I have planted.
Let all that I have planted be uprooted.

9 "If my heart has been seduced by a woman,
or if I have lusted for my neighbor's wife,
10 then let my wife belong to* another man;
let other men sleep with her.
11 For lust is a shameful sin,
a crime that should be punished.
12 It is a fire that burns all the way to hell.*
It would wipe out everything I own.

13 "If I have been unfair to my male or female servants
when they brought their complaints to me,
14 how could I face God?
What could I say when He questioned me?
15 For God created both me and my servants.
He created us both in the womb.

16 "Have I refused to help the poor,
or crushed the hopes of widows?

31:6 Job 6:2-3; Isa 26:7
31:7 Job 9:30; 23:11
31:8 Lev 26:16; Job 20:18
31:10 Deut 28:30; Jer 8:10
31:11 Deut 22:24
31:12 Job 15:30
31:13 Deut 24:14-15
31:15 Job 10:3
31:16 Exod 22:22-24; Job 20:19

31:10 Hebrew *grind for.* 31:12 Hebrew *to Abaddon.*

31:13-23 Job insisted that he treated his servants fairly, knowing that "God created both me and my servants." Job also helped others in need, despite Eliphaz's claim that Job mistreated people who were low on the social scale (see note at 22:6-9).

▸ HOLINESS
31:15 The role of employers. The principles stated in verses 13-15 apply not only to masters of servants but also to modern employers. If you are an employer, you can be sure that God will question you about your business practices. He does not regard an employer as more important than an employee, so you have a responsibility to treat your employees fairly (Ephesians 6:9). If they have complaints, you must listen to them, and if their concerns are legitimate, you must address them. (***See Holiness**> Maturing> Obeying God's Word> Obedience to God's Word is empowered by and demonstrates love,* TopicGuide page A40.)

BECAUSE GOD IS EVER-PRESENT

He is always with me.

Doesn't He see everything I do and every step I take?

JOB 31:4

FOR THE NEXT *GOD IS EVER-PRESENT* FEATURE SEE PAGE 1802.

31:17 Job 22:7-9; 29:12
[17] Have I been stingy with my food
and refused to share it with orphans?
[18] No, from childhood I have cared for orphans like a father,
and all my life I have cared for widows.

31:19 Job 22:6; 29:13
[19] Whenever I saw the homeless without clothes
and the needy with nothing to wear,
[20] did they not praise me
for providing wool clothing to keep them warm?

[21] "If I raised my hand against an orphan,
knowing the judges would take my side,

31:22 Job 38:15
[22] then let my shoulder be wrenched out of place!
Let my arm be torn from its socket!

31:23 Job 13:11; 31:3
[23] That would be better than facing God's judgment.
For if the majesty of God opposes me, what hope is there?

31:24 Job 22:23-25; Mark 10:23
[24] "Have I put my trust in money
or felt secure because of my gold?

31:25 Ps 62:10
[25] Have I gloated about my wealth
and all that I own?

[26] "Have I looked at the sun shining in the skies,
or the moon walking down its silver pathway,
[27] and been secretly enticed in my heart
to throw kisses at them in worship?
[28] If so, I should be punished by the judges,
for it would mean I had denied the God of heaven.

[29] "Have I ever rejoiced when disaster struck my enemies,
or become excited when harm came their way?

31:30 Job 5:3
[30] No, I have never sinned by cursing anyone
or by asking for revenge.

31:31 Job 22:7
[31] "My servants have never said,
'He let others go hungry.'
[32] I have never turned away a stranger
but have opened my doors to everyone.

[33] "Have I tried to hide my sins like other people do,
concealing my guilt in my heart?

31:34 Prov 29:25
[34] Have I feared the crowd
or the contempt of the masses,
so that I kept quiet and stayed indoors?

31:24-28 Job rejected the accusation that he had ever been guilty of coveting money (which Eliphaz claimed in 22:8, 24) or of committing idolatry.

▶ GOD

31:29 Love your enemies. How many times have you heard the expression "sweet revenge"? Perhaps you didn't take revenge yourself, but you felt satisfaction when someone who opposed or hurt you got what he deserved. God says that we are not to indulge in these feelings (Matthew 5:44). No matter how much someone has hurt us, we should not feel glad when trouble comes his or her way. Do you remember what Jesus said in His last moments? As He looked down from the cross at those who had accused and crucified Him, He said, "Father, forgive these people, for they don't know what they are doing" (Luke 23:34). His enemies deserved instant punishment, yet Jesus still loved them. The fruit of the Spirit in your life will be particularly evident when you show love to those who have hurt you. (***See God****> God's Attributes> Loving> To love enemies and the wicked is to be like God,* TopicGuide page A17.)

31:29-34 Job explains that he had always treated his servants, his enemies, and strangers with integrity.

35 "If only someone would listen to me!
Look, I will sign my name to my defense.
Let the Almighty answer me.
Let my Accuser write out the charges against me.
36 I would face the accusation proudly.
I would wear it like a crown.
37 For I would tell Him exactly what I have done.
I would come before Him like a prince.

38 "If my land accuses me
and all its furrows cry out together,
39 or if I have stolen its crops
or murdered its owners,
40 then let thistles grow on that land instead of wheat,
and weeds instead of barley."

Job's words are ended.

31:35 Job 19:7; 27:7; 30:20, 24, 28; 35:14 Ps 26:1
31:37 Job 1:3; 29:25; 31:4
31:38 Job 24:2, 6, 10-12
31:40 Isa 5:6

ELIHU RESPONDS TO JOB'S FRIENDS

32 Job's three friends refused to reply further to him because he kept insisting on his
innocence.
2 Then Elihu son of Barakel the Buzite, of the clan of Ram, became angry. He was angry
because Job refused to admit that he had sinned and that God was right in punishing him.
3 He was also angry with Job's three friends, for they made God* appear to be wrong by
their inability to answer Job's arguments. 4 Elihu had waited for the others to speak to Job
because they were older than he. 5 But when he saw that they had no further reply, he
spoke out angrily. 6 Elihu son of Barakel the Buzite said,

"I am young and you are old,
so I held back from telling you what I think.
7 I thought, 'Those who are older should speak,
for wisdom comes with age.'

32:1 Job 10:7; 13:18; 31:6; 33:9
32:2 Gen 22:21
32:6 Job 15:10

32:3 As in ancient Hebrew scribal tradition; the Masoretic Text reads *Job.*

31:35-40 One last time Job calls on his critics to take his claims of innocence seriously. He includes the possibility of facing accusations from "the Almighty," for Job is confident that God would exonerate him.

31:40 "Job's words are ended" refers to the end of Job's defenses of his integrity in the three cycles of dialogue, though Job does speak briefly later in response to God's speeches (see 40:3-5; 42:1-6).

32:1 After Job's lengthy final speech (chapters 26–31), his "three friends" decided not to respond again because Job "kept insisting on his innocence." Ironically, at the conclusion of the story the Lord rebuked the three friends—not Job—since they were wrong in what they said about Him (42:7).

32:2 A new speaker is introduced at this point. Elihu was the "son of Barakel the Buzite," meaning either that he was a descendant of Buz, Abraham's nephew (see Genesis 22:21), or that he was from the city of Buz in Arabia (see Jeremiah 25:23). Neither Elihu nor his father Barakel are mentioned anywhere else in the Bible. Chapters 32–37 record Elihu's four speeches: 32–33; 34; 35; and 36–37.

32:2-4 Elihu was wrong about God's punishing Job for his sins (see note at 1:1), but he was right that "Job's three friends" had not been able "to answer Job's arguments." The reason that Elihu waited so long to speak is that all four men "were older than he," and ancient custom was to allow the elders to speak first.

▸ HOLINESS

32:5 The danger of anger. Anger is a common emotion, yet it can have devastating effects. Anger can quickly cause a person's thinking to become clouded, which often leads to harmful decisions. Elihu waited for some time to speak, but as he waited, his anger began to boil. He heard all the arguments of Job and his friends, but all that he heard was filtered through his anger. Therefore, his judgment was distorted, and he spoke with undue passion when his opportunity to speak came. The Bible does not tell us we cannot get angry. But it does give us this warning: "Don't sin by letting anger control you" (Psalm 4:4). Deal with your anger as soon as it enters your heart so that it will not cause you to act in a destructive way. (***See Holiness****> Submission> Delighting in God> Rejoicing in repentance,* TopicGuide page A40.)

32:6-10 Elihu allowed the other four men to speak first because of their age but concluded that they weren't so wise after all.

32:8
Job 33:4; 38:36
Prov 2:6
1 Cor 2:11

8 But there is a spirit* within people,
the breath of the Almighty within them,
that makes them intelligent.
9 Sometimes the elders are not wise.
Sometimes the aged do not understand justice.
10 So listen to me,
and let me tell you what I think.

32:11
Prov 18:17

11 "I have waited all this time,
listening very carefully to your arguments,
listening to you grope for words.
12 I have listened,
but not one of you has refuted Job
or answered his arguments.

32:13
Jer 9:23

13 And don't tell me, 'He is too wise for us.
Only God can convince him.'
14 If Job had been arguing with me,
I would not answer with your kind of logic!
15 You sit there baffled,
with nothing more to say.
16 Should I continue to wait, now that you are silent?
Must I also remain silent?
17 No, I will say my piece.
I will speak my mind.
18 For I am full of pent-up words,
and the spirit within me urges me on.
19 I am like a cask of wine without a vent,
like a new wineskin ready to burst!
20 I must speak to find relief,
so let me give my answers.

32:21
Lev 19:15
Job 13:8, 10; 34:19

21 I won't play favorites
or try to flatter anyone.
22 For if I tried flattery,
my Creator would soon destroy me.

ELIHU PRESENTS HIS CASE AGAINST JOB

33 1 "Listen to my words, Job;
pay attention to what I have to say.
2 Now that I have begun to speak,
let me continue.

32:8 Or *Spirit;* also in 32:18.

32:11-22 Elihu rebuked Job's three friends for not being able to refute Job's arguments, and then he prepared to offer his own answers to Job's paradox of suffering more at God's hands than the wicked around him.

▸ ADOPTION
32:18 Speaking out of turn. Elihu spoke his mind, but his words were seasoned not with kindness or wisdom but with anger. We rarely speak words of wisdom when we are angry. Instead, we usually accuse and blame. Proverbs 15:23 says, "Everyone enjoys a fitting reply; it is wonderful to say the right thing at the right time!" Elihu was so busy thinking of the right arguments to make that he missed the point—consoling his hurting friend. When you find yourself in a situation where you want to speak your mind, stop and examine your heart first. Make sure the words you speak are appropriate for the issue at hand. (***See Adoption****> With Christ> Supernatural> Speak godly words,* TopicGuide page A37.)

3 I speak with all sincerity;
I speak the truth.
4 For the Spirit of God has made me,
and the breath of the Almighty gives me life.
5 Answer me, if you can;
make your case and take your stand.
6 Look, you and I both belong to God.
I, too, was formed from clay.
7 So you don't need to be afraid of me.
I won't come down hard on you.

8 "You have spoken in my hearing,
and I have heard your very words.
9 You said, 'I am pure; I am without sin;
I am innocent; I have no guilt.
10 God is picking a quarrel with me,
and He considers me His enemy.
11 He puts my feet in the stocks
and watches my every move.'

12 "But you are wrong, and I will show you why.
For God is greater than any human being.
13 So why are you bringing a charge against Him?
Why say He does not respond to people's complaints?
14 For God speaks again and again,
though people do not recognize it.
15 He speaks in dreams, in visions of the night,
when deep sleep falls on people
as they lie in their beds.
16 He whispers in their ears
and terrifies them with warnings.
17 He makes them turn from doing wrong;
He keeps them from pride.
18 He protects them from the grave,
from crossing over the river of death.

19 "Or God disciplines people with pain on their sickbeds,
with ceaseless aching in their bones.
20 They lose their appetite
for even the most delicious food.
21 Their flesh wastes away,
and their bones stick out.
22 They are at death's door;
the angels of death wait for them.

33:3 Job 6:28; 27:4; 36:4
33:4 Job 10:3; 27:3; 32:8
33:5 Job 33:32
33:7 Job 13:22
33:9 Job 7:21; 9:21; 10:7, 14; 13:23; 16:17
33:10 Job 13:23-24
33:11 Job 13:27
33:13 Job 40:2 Isa 45:9
33:14 Job 40:5 Ps 62:11
33:15 Job 4:12-17
33:16 Job 36:10, 15
33:18 Job 33:24, 28, 30
33:19 Job 30:17
33:20 Job 3:24; 6:7 Ps 107:18
33:21 Job 16:8; 19:20 Ps 22:17

33:5 Elihu was rather arrogant to imply that Job would not be able to refute his arguments as he did the arguments of the other three.

33:8-11 Elihu doesn't always quote Job verbatim but simply gives the substance of his statements (also in 33:12-13; 34:5-6, 9; 35:2, 3).

33:12-30 Elihu claimed that Job was wrong about his innocence and God's severity in bringing suffering into his life. Eliphaz's argument seems to have been that God speaks to people in a variety of ways, so Job should have considered that God was trying to speak to him through his sufferings. Elihu was wrong to deny Job's innocence but right to see Job's sufferings as part of God's discipline to enable him to know God better (see 33:19). Thus Elihu provided a partial solution to Job's paradox (that is, he suffered more at God's hands than the wicked around him), though he was not completely right about Job. Although Job had not sinned in such a way as to deserve such great sufferings, God was not unjust in bringing these sufferings into his life, since Job would learn more about God and his relationship to Him through them.

23 "But if an angel from heaven appears—
a special messenger to intercede for a person
and declare that he is upright—
33:24 Isa 38:17 24 he will be gracious and say,
'Rescue him from the grave,
for I have found a ransom for his life.'
25 Then his body will become as healthy as a child's,
firm and youthful again.
33:26 Job 22:26-27; 34:28 26 When he prays to God,
he will be accepted.
And God will receive him with joy
and restore him to good standing.
33:27 2 Sam 12:13 Luke 15:21 Rom 6:21 27 He will declare to his friends,
'I sinned and twisted the truth,
but it was not worth it.*
33:28 Job 22:28 28 God rescued me from the grave,
and now my life is filled with light.'

33:29 Eph 1:11 Phil 2:13 29 "Yes, God does these things
again and again for people.
30 He rescues them from the grave
so they may enjoy the light of life.
31 Mark this well, Job. Listen to me,
for I have more to say.
32 But if you have anything to say, go ahead.
Speak, for I am anxious to see you justified.
33:33 Ps 34:11 33 But if not, then listen to me.
Keep silent and I will teach you wisdom!"

ELIHU ACCUSES JOB OF ARROGANCE

34 Then Elihu said:
2 "Listen to me, you wise men.
Pay attention, you who have knowledge.
34:3 Job 12:11 3 Job said, 'The ear tests the words it hears
just as the mouth distinguishes between foods.'
4 So let us discern for ourselves what is right;
let us learn together what is good.
34:5 Job 27:2; 33:9 5 For Job also said, 'I am innocent,
but God has taken away my rights.
6 I am innocent, but they call me a liar.
My suffering is incurable, though I have not sinned.'

33:27 Greek version reads *but He* [God] *did not punish me as my sin deserved.*

▸ SPIRITUAL WARFARE
33:28 Rescue from the grave. Just like Job, God's people have always known God could rescue His people from any circumstance. A man was given two weeks to live. His family was shocked, but they had enough sense to dedicate a day to fasting and prayer for his recovery. Even the grandchildren participated in simple ways. In this case, the family asked God to heal their loved one, and he recovered from his illness and went home from the hospital. The family was willing to accept God's will if He saw fit to take their loved one home to heaven, but they also had confidence that God would hear their prayers. If you or someone you love is facing a life-or-death crisis, trust God's will. Place yourself or your dear one's life in God's hands. You will receive a response from the God who hears His people's prayers. (***See Spiritual Warfare****> Resisting Sin and Evil> Consequences> Of Obedience> Potential for a more peaceable life,* TopicGuide page A46.)

33:31–34:1 Elihu paused to give Job a chance to respond, but he does not—perhaps because he recognized that there was an element of truth in what Elihu was saying (see note at 33:12-30). So Elihu continued his argument. A similar pause is likely indicated at 35:1 and 36:1.

7 "Tell me, has there ever been a man like Job,
with his thirst for irreverent talk?
8 He chooses evil people as companions.
He spends his time with wicked men.
9 He has even said, 'Why waste time
trying to please God?'

10 "Listen to me, you who have understanding.
Everyone knows that God doesn't sin!
The Almighty can do no wrong.
11 He repays people according to their deeds.
He treats people as they deserve.
12 Truly, God will not do wrong.
The Almighty will not twist justice.
13 Did someone else put the world in His care?
Who set the whole world in place?
14 If God were to take back His spirit
and withdraw His breath,
15 all life would cease,
and humanity would turn again to dust.

34:7 Job 15:16
34:9 Job 21:15; 35:3
34:11 Ps 62:12; Prov 24:12; Matt 16:27; Rom 2:6; 2 Cor 5:10; Rev 22:12
34:15 Gen 3:19; 7:21; Job 9:22; 10:9

34:7-9 With these unfounded accusations, Elihu lapsed into the arguments of Job's three friends.

▶ SPIRITUAL WARFARE
34:10 God never does anything wrong. To Job, it's one of the elementary teachings about God—He is morally perfect. It's tempting to blame God when things do not go well in our lives—after all, He is in control of everything. "God put this terrible temptation in my path," we may say. However, the Bible teaches us that everything God does is right; He never sins, and He never tempts us. James 1:13 says, "Remember, when you are being tempted, do not say, 'God is tempting me.' God is never tempted to do wrong, and he never tempts anyone else." Temptations come from Satan. When you face temptations, make sure that you see them for what they are—Satan's tools—and do not accuse God of wrongdoing. (***See Spiritual Warfare***> *God and Sin*> *Sin's Origin*> *The wise understand evil's source,* TopicGuide page A45.)

34:10-15 Elihu was correct that "God doesn't sin," but he was incorrect that God immediately punishes sin. Job challenged the idea that God always works that way in his second response to Zophar (chapter 21).

▶ GOD
34:14-15 "Life would cease." Before Creation, before Genesis 1:1, what existed in this universe? Nothing. Not a speck. Not until God spoke matter and life into existence could anything come to be. And in turn, if God ever removed His life-giving power from the universe, what would happen? The universe would go back to nothing, for God sustains the universe. We serve a powerful God, who is thinking about every aspect of the universe, holding it in existence. Do you relate to God with the respect and fear that He deserves? You can trust Him with anything, for He created and sustains everything. (***See God***> *God's Attributes*> *Self-Sufficient*> *God supplies all things their life and breath,* TopicGuide page A17.)

BECAUSE GOD IS SOVEREIGN

I will joyfully submit to His will.

If God were to take back His spirit and withdraw His breath, all life would cease, and humanity would turn again to dust.

JOB 34:14-15

FOR THE NEXT *GOD IS SOVEREIGN* FEATURE SEE PAGE 2038.

16 "Now listen to me if you are wise.
Pay attention to what I say.
34:17 Job 40:8
17 Could God govern if He hated justice?
Are you going to condemn the almighty judge?
18 For He says to kings, 'You are wicked,'
34:19 Deut 10:17; Acts 10:34; Rom 2:11; Gal 2:6; Eph 6:9; 1 Pet 1:17
and to nobles, 'You are unjust.'
19 He doesn't care how great a person may be,
and He pays no more attention to the rich than to the poor.
He made them all.
20 In a moment they die.
34:20 Exod 12:29; Job 12:19; 36:20
In the middle of the night they pass away;
the mighty are removed without human hand.

34:21 Prov 5:21; 15:3
21 "For God watches how people live;
He sees everything they do.
34:22 Ps 139:11-12; Amos 9:2-3
22 No darkness is thick enough
to hide the wicked from His eyes.
23 We don't set the time
when we will come before God in judgment.
34:24 Job 12:19
24 He brings the mighty to ruin without asking anyone,
and He sets up others in their place.
34:25 Job 34:11, 20
25 He knows what they do,
and in the night He overturns and destroys them.
26 He strikes them down because they are wicked,
doing it openly for all to see.
34:27 1 Sam 15:11
27 For they turned away from following Him.
They have no respect for any of His ways.
34:28 Exod 22:23; Job 22:27; 35:9
28 They cause the poor to cry out, catching God's attention.
He hears the cries of the needy.
34:29 Job 5:15
29 But if He chooses to remain quiet,
who can criticize Him?
When He hides His face, no one can find Him,
whether an individual or a nation.
34:30 Job 34:17
30 He prevents the godless from ruling
so they cannot be a snare to the people.

31 "Why don't people say to God, 'I have sinned,
but I will sin no more'?
32 Or 'I don't know what evil I have done—tell me.
If I have done wrong, I will stop at once'?

34:16-20 Elihu pointed out that God does not play favorites according to social status. He may have been implying that Job had no right to expect special favors from God because of his wealth and standing in the community prior to his sufferings.

34:21-30 Elihu provided a list of ways God's justice prevails, though it is clearly not true that God "prevents the godless from ruling" (34:30).

▶ ADOPTION

34:31 Why do people keep sinning? Do you know people who repeat their sins? No matter what consequences they suffer when they sin, they do it all over again. We may think of alcoholics or compulsive liars, but to some degree this is true of all of us—we are not terribly creative in our sin. However, the Lord Jesus Christ, through the power of the Holy Spirit, can change our hearts. When we receive a new nature by being born again, Christ gives us power to say no to temptation. Jesus Christ is the only answer to habitual sin. Have you made the decision to allow Him to control your life? The holy pattern of belief and repentance can set you free from the frustration of habitual sin. (***See Adoption***> *With Christ*> *Supernatural*> *Controlled by Christ,* TopicGuide page A37.)

34:31-32 Elihu, like Job's three friends before him, believed that Job should either admit that he has sinned or ask God to show him in what way he had sinned.

33 "Must God tailor His justice to your demands?
But you have rejected Him!
The choice is yours, not mine.
Go ahead, share your wisdom with us.
34 After all, bright people will tell me,
and wise people will hear me say,
35 'Job speaks out of ignorance;
his words lack insight.'
36 Job, you deserve the maximum penalty
for the wicked way you have talked.
37 For you have added rebellion to your sin;
you show no respect,
and you speak many angry words against God."

34:35 Job 35:16
34:36 Job 22:15 Pss 17:3; 26:2

ELIHU REMINDS JOB OF GOD'S JUSTICE

35 Then Elihu said:
2 "Do you think it is right for you to claim,
'I am righteous before God'?
3 For you also ask, 'What's in it for me?
What's the use of living a righteous life?'

4 "I will answer you
and all your friends, too.
5 Look up into the sky,
and see the clouds high above you.
6 If you sin, how does that affect God?
Even if you sin again and again,
what effect will it have on Him?
7 If you are good, is this some great gift to Him?
What could you possibly give Him?
8 No, your sins affect only people like yourself,
and your good deeds also affect only humans.

9 "People cry out when they are oppressed.
They groan beneath the power of the mighty.
10 Yet they don't ask, 'Where is God my Creator,
the One who gives songs in the night?
11 Where is the One who makes us smarter than the animals
and wiser than the birds of the sky?'
12 And when they cry out, God does not answer
because of their pride.

35:2 Job 27:2
35:3 Job 9:30-31; 34:9
35:5 Job 22:11
35:6 Job 7:20 Prov 8:36 Jer 7:19
35:7 Job 22:2-3 Prov 9:12 Luke 17:10 Rom 11:35
35:9 Exod 2:23
35:10 Job 27:10 Pss 42:8; 149:5 Acts 16:25
35:11 Ps 94:12 Jer 32:33
35:12 Prov 1:28

34:33-37 Like Eliphaz before him (see note at 22:6-9), Elihu raised his charges against Job to a new level by accusing him of rejecting God, lacking wisdom, deserving "the maximum penalty" for his wickedness, and adding "rebellion" to his other sins.

35:1-8 Elihu challenged Job's claim that he was "righteous before God" and then he pointed out that committing a sin affects "only people like yourself" but not God. Elihu was wrong about Job but right that nothing changes God's essence or nature.

35:9-11 Elihu stated that people may "groan" because of suffering, but they do not question God's presence in their lives, implying that Job should not question God about his sufferings.

▸ GOD

35:12 God hates pride and arrogance. Elihu understood in 2100 BC what Amos would say almost 1500 years later: "The Sovereign LORD has sworn by His own name, and this is what He, the LORD God of Heaven's Armies, says: 'I despise the arrogance of Israel'" (Amos 6:8). Why does God hate pride so much? Because the proud person is so puffed up with his own importance that he will not submit to God. His prayers are all talk, but no listening. Ask God to show you your prideful areas so that you can confess them and allow God to take control. Rather than telling God your plans, search for His will. Rather than preaching, learn. Rather than talking, listen. (***See God****> Relationship> Barriers> Pride,* TopicGuide page A14.)

35:13 Job 27:9 Isa 1:15 Jer 11:11 Jas 4:3
13 But it is wrong to say God doesn't listen,
to say the Almighty isn't concerned.
14 You say you can't see Him,
but He will bring justice if you will only wait.*
35:14 Job 31:35 Ps 37:5-6
15 You say He does not respond to sinners with anger
and is not greatly concerned about wickedness.*
35:16 Job 34:35; 38:2
16 But you are talking nonsense, Job.
You have spoken like a fool."

36 Elihu continued speaking:
2 "Let me go on, and I will show you the truth.
For I have not finished defending God!
36:3 Job 8:3; 37:23
3 I will present profound arguments
for the righteousness of my Creator.
36:4 Job 33:3; 37:16
4 I am telling you nothing but the truth,
for I am a man of great knowledge.

36:5 Pss 22:24; 69:33; 102:17
5 "God is mighty, but He does not despise anyone!
He is mighty in both power and understanding.
36:6 Job 5:15; 8:22; 34:26
6 He does not let the wicked live
but gives justice to the afflicted.
36:7 Pss 33:18; 34:15; 113:8
7 He never takes His eyes off the innocent,
but He sets them on thrones with kings
and exalts them forever.
36:8 Job 36:10
8 If they are bound in chains
and caught up in a web of trouble,
36:9 Job 15:25
9 He shows them the reason.
He shows them their sins of pride.
36:10 2 Kgs 17:13 Job 33:16; 36:21 Jon 3:8
10 He gets their attention
and commands that they turn from evil.

11 "If they listen and obey God,
they will be blessed with prosperity throughout their lives.
All their years will be pleasant.
36:12 Job 4:21; 15:22
12 But if they refuse to listen to Him,
they will be killed by the sword*
and die from lack of understanding.
13 For the godless are full of resentment.
Even when He punishes them,
they refuse to cry out to Him for help.

35:13-14 These verses can also be translated as follows: [13]*Indeed, God doesn't listen to their empty plea; / the Almighty is not concerned. /* [14]*How much less will He listen when you say you don't see Him, / and that your case is before Him and you're waiting for justice.* 35:15 As in Greek and Latin versions; the meaning of this Hebrew word is uncertain. 36:12 Or *they will cross the river* [of death].

35:12-14 Elihu claimed that God doesn't answer people because of their pride, which in his view was yet another sin of Job. Yet Job never said God "isn't concerned" and "doesn't listen" to His people's cries. Another problem with Elihu's argument is that although he was correct that God "will bring about justice," he was incorrect that one can see justice "if you will only wait"—as if justice will always occur in this life.

36:2-4 Elihu's arrogance (see note at 33:5) was revealed as he began his final speech, and this arrogance may be why Job chose not to respond to his arguments.

36:5-15 Elihu attempted to describe the ways God deals with people in this life, but his descriptions of the ways God works were not without exceptions, which Job pointed out in his response to Eliphaz in chapter 24.

[14] They die when they are young,
after wasting their lives in immoral living.
[15] But by means of their suffering, He rescues those who suffer.
For He gets their attention through adversity.

36:15 Job 36:10

[16] "God is leading you away from danger, Job,
to a place free from distress.
He is setting your table with the best food.
[17] But you are obsessed with whether the godless will be judged.
Don't worry, judgment and justice will be upheld.
[18] But watch out, or you may be seduced by wealth.*
Don't let yourself be bribed into sin.
[19] Could all your wealth*
or all your mighty efforts
keep you from distress?
[20] Do not long for the cover of night,
for that is when people will be destroyed.*
[21] Be on guard! Turn back from evil,
for God sent this suffering
to keep you from a life of evil.

36:17 Job 22:5, 10-11; 33:24; 34:33 Jon 4:4, 9

36:20 Job 34:20, 25

36:21 Ps 66:18

ELIHU REMINDS JOB OF GOD'S POWER

[22] "Look, God is all-powerful.
Who is a teacher like Him?
[23] No one can tell Him what to do,
or say to Him, 'You have done wrong.'
[24] Instead, glorify His mighty works,
singing songs of praise.
[25] Everyone has seen these things,
though only from a distance.

36:22 Job 35:11

36:23 Job 8:3

36:24 Ps 59:16

[26] "Look, God is greater than we can understand.
His years cannot be counted.
[27] He draws up the water vapor
and then distills it into rain.
[28] The rain pours down from the clouds,
and everyone benefits.
[29] Who can understand the spreading of the clouds
and the thunder that rolls forth from heaven?

36:26 Job 11:7-9; 37:23 Pss 90:2; 102:24, 27

36:27 Job 5:10; 37:6, 11 Ps 147:8

36:29 Job 26:14; 37:11, 16

36:18 Or *But don't let your anger lead you to mockery.* 36:19 Or *Could all your cries for help.* 36:16-20 The meaning of the Hebrew in this passage is uncertain.

▸ WORSHIP

36:18 Seduced by wealth. Everywhere we look, we are being marketed. People are no longer referred to as citizens, but consumers. We are offered more credit and get-rich-quick schemes, and people uproot their families to move halfway across the world for a job that pays just a little more. How do we keep from buying too many things and becoming obsessed with money? The only way is to walk closely with the Lord. When we focus on Him, material possessions don't seem so important (Matthew 6:33). Then we can focus on how to use our money to build the kingdom rather than how to buy more. In your daily prayer, ask God to help you keep your eyes on Him rather than on new possessions. Seeking Him will cultivate a joy that wealth cannot provide. (***See Worship****> OT> Offerings> Other sacrifices> Tithing> A tithe should be used properly,* TopicGuide page A27.)

36:18-19 Elihu warned Job not to let his wealth become a problem in his life. Apparently, Elihu had forgotten that Job had lost all of his wealth.

36:21 Elihu warned Job to "turn back from evil" and claimed that "God sent this suffering" to keep him from "a life of evil." But the author's description of Job as a righteous man indicates that Elihu's explanation can hardly be the reason for Job's sufferings (see note at 1:1).

36:26-33 Elihu correctly stated that "God is greater than we can understand," and this in part explains Job's dilemma—as God's speech to Job later made clear (chapters 38–41). Early in His speech to Job, God also refers to His control of the weather (see 38:22-30).

[30] See how He spreads the lightning around Him
and how it lights up the depths of the sea.
[31] By these mighty acts He nourishes* the people,
giving them food in abundance.
[32] He fills His hands with lightning bolts
and hurls each at its target.
[33] The thunder announces His presence;
the storm announces His indignant anger.*

36:31 Job 37:13; Acts 14:17
36:32 Job 37:11-12, 15
36:33 Job 37:2

37

[1] "My heart pounds as I think of this.
It trembles within me.
[2] Listen carefully to the thunder of God's voice
as it rolls from His mouth.
[3] It rolls across the heavens,
and His lightning flashes in every direction.
[4] Then comes the roaring of the thunder—
the tremendous voice of His majesty.
He does not restrain it when He speaks.
[5] God's voice is glorious in the thunder.
We can't even imagine the greatness of His power.

[6] "He directs the snow to fall on the earth
and tells the rain to pour down.
[7] Then everyone stops working
so they can watch His power.
[8] The wild animals take cover
and stay inside their dens.
[9] The stormy wind comes from its chamber,
and the driving winds bring the cold.
[10] God's breath sends the ice,
freezing wide expanses of water.
[11] He loads the clouds with moisture,
and they flash with His lightning.
[12] The clouds churn about at His direction.
They do whatever He commands throughout the earth.
[13] He makes these things happen either to punish people
or to show His unfailing love.

[14] "Pay attention to this, Job.
Stop and consider the wonderful miracles of God!
[15] Do you know how God controls the storm
and causes the lightning to flash from His clouds?

37:2 Job 36:33
37:5 Job 5:9; 26:14; Rom 11:33
37:6 Job 36:27; 38:22
37:7 Job 12:14
37:8 Job 38:40; Ps 104:21-22
37:9 Job 9:9
37:10 Job 38:29; Ps 147:17
37:11 Job 36:27, 29; 37:15
37:12 Ps 148:8
37:13 Exod 9:18-19; 1 Kgs 18:45; Job 38:26

36:31 Or *He governs.* 36:33 Or *even the cattle know when a storm is coming.* The meaning of the Hebrew is uncertain.

37:2-5 Elihu called attention to God's majesty as displayed through lightning and thunder, both of which are under His control.

37:6-18 Elihu once again referred to God's control of the weather (see note at 36:26-33).

▸ SPIRITUAL WARFARE
37:14 Stop and consider God's majesty. Meditation is an act of contemplation where you intentionally fix your mind upon one idea. As Elihu advised Job, it is helpful to stop and meditate on God's magnificence. Chapter 37 of Job can be very helpful in this. Job 37:14-18 describes the glories of God's creative power. Job 37:19-20 tells of His wisdom. The remaining verses touch on His splendor. Later chapters, in which God Himself challenges Job to consider what He is like and what He can do, are also helpful in this regard. As you meditate on aspects of God's majesty, praise Him and thank Him for being your heavenly Father. (***See Spiritual Warfare***> *Origin of Sin> Creation in Bondage> God Created,* TopicGuide page A44.)

[16] Do you understand how He moves the clouds
with wonderful perfection and skill?
[17] When you are sweltering in your clothes
and the south wind dies down and everything is still,
[18] He makes the skies reflect the heat like a bronze mirror.
Can you do that?

[19] "So teach the rest of us what to say to God.
We are too ignorant to make our own arguments.
[20] Should God be notified that I want to speak?
Can people even speak when they are confused?*
[21] We cannot look at the sun,
for it shines brightly in the sky
when the wind clears away the clouds.
[22] So also, golden splendor comes from the mountain of God.*
He is clothed in dazzling splendor.
[23] We cannot imagine the power of the Almighty;
but even though He is just and righteous,
He does not destroy us.
[24] No wonder people everywhere fear Him.
All who are wise show Him reverence."

37:16 Job 36:4; 37:5, 14, 23
37:18 Job 9:8-9; Ps 104:2; Isa 44:24; 45:12; Jer 10:12
37:23 Job 8:3; Isa 63:9
37:24 Job 5:13; Matt 10:28; 11:25; 1 Cor 1:26

THE LORD CHALLENGES JOB

38 Then the LORD answered Job from the whirlwind:
[2] "Who is this that questions My wisdom
with such ignorant words?
[3] Brace yourself like a man,
because I have some questions for you,
and you must answer them.

38:1 Job 40:6
38:2 Job 35:16; 42:3
38:3 Job 40:7; 42:4

37:20 Or *speak without being swallowed up?* 37:22 Or *from the north;* or *from the abode.*

37:19-24 Elihu concluded his speech by pointing out how little people really understand about God's power, majesty, and splendor.

▸ MINISTRY
37:24 People everywhere are turning to God. Today you can find believers on every inhabited continent. In many places, Christianity is thriving like never before. People by the millions are coming to know God through Jesus Christ. There can be only one explanation for the phenomenon of the Christian faith: God is at work! Is He busy converting people in your neighborhood? Or in your city? Start praying for local, national, and international missionaries who are spreading God's Good News. Start praying that you and your friends will start seeing more and more conversions to Christ among those you know. (***See Ministry****> Great Commission> Witness> Locally, regionally, worldwide,* TopicGuide page A56.)

38:1 At last the Lord manifested His presence to Job in a whirlwind, perhaps in keeping with Elihu's many references to His power over nature. The Lord's speech in chapters 38–41 is interrupted only once (40:3-5) and contains a series of rhetorical questions for Job, interspersed with various comments about the subjects the Lord addresses. Each rhetorical question emphasizes the Lord's greatness, power, majesty, and sovereignty over all affairs—even Job's life. Incredibly, when the Lord condescended to speak to Job, He didn't even acknowledge that Job had suffered. But this speaks to Job's paradox of suffering without knowing why—although the sufferings he endured were not the result of sins in his life, the Lord was not evil for allowing those sufferings into Job's life. The Lord has His own infinitely wise plans that He will carry out, and He doesn't owe anyone an explanation for His actions or anyone's approval before He does them.

38:2-3 The Lord pointed out that Job's biggest mistake in his attempt to explain his sufferings was that he questioned the Lord's actions (see note at 19:6). The Lord then turned the tables on Job and asked him numerous questions that he either couldn't answer or that emphasized God's greatness compared to humanity.

▸ ADOPTION
38:3 God questions Job. Can you imagine how Job must have felt when God began to question him? Job must have been shaking in his sandals! We all will have to stand before God one day and answer His questions about our lives. Revelation 20:12 says: "I saw the dead, both great and small, standing before God's throne. And the books were opened, including the Book of Life. And the dead were judged according to what they had done, as recorded in the books." That will be the day when all humanity has to answer the Lord's questions. We must be ready to give an account for how we have lived. Make certain that you are standing with Christ on that day—His presence will take away the fear of judgment day. (***See Adoption****> Without Christ> Separated from God> Facing judgment,* TopicGuide page A36.)

38:4 Job 15:7 Ps 104:5 Prov 8:29; 30:4

4 "Where were you when I laid the foundations of the earth?
Tell Me, if you know so much.
5 Who determined its dimensions
and stretched out the surveying line?
6 What supports its foundations,
and who laid its cornerstone
7 as the morning stars sang together
and all the angels* shouted for joy?

38:7 Job 1:6

38:8 Gen 1:9

8 "Who kept the sea inside its boundaries
as it burst from the womb,
9 and as I clothed it with clouds
and wrapped it in thick darkness?
10 For I locked it behind barred gates,
limiting its shores.
11 I said, 'This far and no farther will you come.
Here your proud waves must stop!'

38:10 Gen 1:9 Ps 33:7 Prov 8:29 Jer 5:22

12 "Have you ever commanded the morning to appear
and caused the dawn to rise in the east?
13 Have you made daylight spread to the ends of the earth,
to bring an end to the night's wickedness?
14 As the light approaches,
the earth takes shape like clay pressed beneath a seal;
it is robed in brilliant colors.*
15 The light disturbs the wicked
and stops the arm that is raised in violence.

38:13 Job 37:3; 34:25-26

38:15 Job 5:14 Pss 10:15; 37:17

16 "Have you explored the springs from which the seas come?
Have you explored their depths?
17 Do you know where the gates of death are located?
Have you seen the gates of utter gloom?
18 Do you realize the extent of the earth?
Tell Me about it if you know!

38:16 Gen 7:11; 8:2 Prov 8:24, 28

38:17 Job 28:24; 33:22 Ps 9:13

19 "Where does light come from,
and where does darkness go?
20 Can you take each to its home?
Do you know how to get there?
21 But of course you know all this!
For you were born before it was all created,
and you are so very experienced!

38:20 Job 26:10

38:21 Job 15:7

38:7 Hebrew *the sons of God.* 38:14 Or *its features stand out like folds in a robe.*

▸ GOD

38:4 Unknown God. Since the Garden of Eden and Eve's desire for forbidden knowledge, God has reminded His people that they don't know everything—and He wants it to stay that way. Using rhetorical questions, God strips Job of any hope of winning an argument with Him. God's questioning rebuke reminds us of His piercing questions to Adam and Eve after their desire for forbidden knowledge ended in disaster (Genesis 3:8, 11, 13). Learn as much as possible about God and His Word, but do not seek knowledge in a prideful manner, either to justify your failings or accuse God. (***See God****> God's Attributes> All-Powerful> God's creative power is beyond our comprehension,* TopicGuide page A15.)

38:4-21 These questions refer to the Lord's power as Creator of the world and His wisdom in making the various parts of the world work together. The word "angels" (38:7) is literally "the sons of God," but the phrase clearly refers to angels, as in 1:6-7 (see note) and 2:1-2. "Morning stars" (38:7) may also refer to angels, but it could refer to literal stars that are personified as singing God's praises (compare Psalm 50:6). The Lord's creative power includes control of the seas (38:8-11, 16) and the establishment of light and darkness (38:19-20).

22 "Have you visited the storehouses of the snow
or seen the storehouses of hail?
23 (I have reserved them as weapons for the time of trouble,
for the day of battle and war.)
24 Where is the path to the source of light?
Where is the home of the east wind?

25 "Who created a channel for the torrents of rain?
Who laid out the path for the lightning?
26 Who makes the rain fall on barren land,
in a desert where no one lives?
27 Who sends rain to satisfy the parched ground
and make the tender grass spring up?

28 "Does the rain have a father?
Who gives birth to the dew?
29 Who is the mother of the ice?
Who gives birth to the frost from the heavens?
30 For the water turns to ice as hard as rock,
and the surface of the water freezes.

31 "Can you direct the movement of the stars—
binding the cluster of the Pleiades
or loosening the cords of Orion?
32 Can you direct the sequence of the seasons
or guide the Bear with her cubs across the heavens?
33 Do you know the laws of the universe?
Can you use them to regulate the earth?

34 "Can you shout to the clouds
and make it rain?
35 Can you make lightning appear
and cause it to strike as you direct?
36 Who gives intuition to the heart
and instinct to the mind?
37 Who is wise enough to count all the clouds?
Who can tilt the water jars of heaven
38 when the parched ground is dry
and the soil has hardened into clods?

39 "Can you stalk prey for a lioness
and satisfy the young lions' appetites

38:22 Exod 9:18 Job 37:6 Isa 30:30 Ezek 13:11, 13 Rev 16:21

38:24 Job 26:10

38:26 Job 36:27

38:27 Ps 104:13-14

38:29 Job 37:10 Pss 104:13-14; 147:16-17

38:31 Job 9:9

38:34 Job 22:11; 36:27-28

38:35 Job 36:32; 37:3

38:36 Job 32:8 Ps 51:6 Eccl 2:26

38:39 Job 37:8 Ps 104:21

38:22-30 These questions exalt the Lord's power to establish various weather patterns involving precipitation, something humans would like to do but cannot (see also 38:34-38).

38:31-33 The Lord called Job's attention to His great power in placing the stars in the sky in constellations, three of which are called by name (Pleiades, Orion, and the Bear; see note at 9:9).

▸ GOD

38:33 The laws of the universe. Amazingly, the majority of the scientists who uncover the laws of the universe with their years of study refuse to acknowledge that a supreme being had to establish those laws! How does gravity work so perfectly? How did the planets come to orbit the sun? Where do an animal's instincts come from? Satisfying answers to these questions do not come from nature, but they do come from God's Word. We can use science to broaden our understanding of the greatness of God and His creation, but it's good to know that many of the questions unanswered by modern science are easily answered by God in His Word. Read Genesis 1–3 very carefully and take notes on all the difficult scientific questions God answers there. (***See God**> God's Attributes> Sovereign> God controls time and seasons,* TopicGuide page A18.)

38:39-41 From here to the end of the Lord's speech (41:34), the Lord overwhelmed Job with the marvels of the animal world He created. He referred to the animals' strengths, special needs, and uniqueness, none of which can be controlled or fully fathomed by human beings. The first two examples the Lord gave from the animal world refer to His provision of food for lions and ravens.

38:41 Ps 147:9 Luke 12:24

40 as they lie in their dens
or crouch in the thicket?
41 Who provides food for the ravens
when their young cry out to God
and wander about in hunger?

THE LORD'S CHALLENGE CONTINUES

39:1 Deut 14:5

39 1"Do you know when the wild goats give birth?
Have you watched as deer are born in the wild?
2 Do you know how many months they carry their young?
Are you aware of the time of their delivery?
3 They crouch down to give birth to their young
and deliver their offspring.
4 Their young grow up in the open fields,
then leave home and never return.

39:5 Job 6:5; 11:12; 24:5
39:6 Job 24:5 Jer 2:24

5 "Who gives the wild donkey its freedom?
Who untied its ropes?
6 I have placed it in the wilderness;
its home is the wasteland.
7 It hates the noise of the city
and has no driver to shout at it.
8 The mountains are its pastureland,
where it searches for every blade of grass.

39:9 Num 23:22 Deut 33:17 Ps 92:10

9 "Will the wild ox consent to being tamed?
Will it spend the night in your stall?
10 Can you hitch a wild ox to a plow?
Will it plow a field for you?
11 Given its strength, can you trust it?
Can you leave and trust the ox to do your work?
12 Can you rely on it to bring home your grain
and deliver it to your threshing floor?

13 "The ostrich flaps her wings grandly,
but they are no match for the feathers of the stork.
14 She lays her eggs on top of the earth,
letting them be warmed in the dust.
15 She doesn't worry that a foot might crush them
or a wild animal might destroy them.

39:1-12, 19-25 The wonders of land animals are the focus of these verses. The special characteristics of mountain goats, wild deer, wild donkeys, wild ox, and horses are used as lessons for Job to learn about the Lord's greatness, wisdom, and creativity.

▶ HOLINESS
39:9 The untamable nature. From time to time, a trainer of wild animals is attacked by one of his animals. In such instances, the wild nature of the beast asserts itself without warning. No matter what kind of relationship the trainer has developed with the animal, it can still have a core of wildness in its being. As humans, we have only so much control over the natural world. We can often predict an earthquake or a storm, but we cannot stop it. Only God contains and controls nature. We observe and take care of the natural world that God has created (Genesis 1:28). Being conformed to the image of His Son (Romans 8:29), building faithful families (Ephesians 5:31-33), being good stewards of all that He has made—this is how we tame the created order for the glory of God. (***See Holiness***> *Disciplines> Of Abstinence> Stewardship,* TopicGuide page A41.)

39:13-18, 26-30 In these verses the Lord called Job's attention to three unusual birds. Each has a particular strength that puts them beyond man, and a particular weakness that places them far beneath man. Yet they function very well in their context, thus revealing the wisdom of God.

16 She is harsh toward her young,
as if they were not her own.
She doesn't care if they die.
17 For God has deprived her of wisdom.
He has given her no understanding.
18 But whenever she jumps up to run,
she passes the swiftest horse with its rider.

19 "Have you given the horse its strength
or clothed its neck with a flowing mane?
20 Did you give it the ability to leap like a locust?
Its majestic snorting is terrifying!
21 It paws the earth and rejoices in its strength
when it charges out to battle.
22 It laughs at fear and is unafraid.
It does not run from the sword.
23 The arrows rattle against it,
and the spear and javelin flash.
24 It paws the ground fiercely
and rushes forward into battle when the ram's horn blows.
25 It snorts at the sound of the horn.
It senses the battle in the distance.
It quivers at the captain's commands and the noise of battle.

26 "Is it your wisdom that makes the hawk soar
and spread its wings toward the south?
27 Is it at your command that the eagle rises
to the heights to make its nest?
28 It lives on the cliffs,
making its home on a distant, rocky crag.
29 From there it hunts its prey,
keeping watch with piercing eyes.
30 Its young gulp down blood.
Where there's a carcass, there you'll find it."

39:16 Lam 4:3
39:20 Jer 8:16; Joel 2:5
39:21 Jer 8:6
39:27 Jer 49:16; Obad 1:4
39:29 Job 9:26
39:30 Matt 24:28; Luke 17:37

40

Then the LORD said to Job,
2 "Do you still want to argue with the Almighty?
You are God's critic, but do you have the answers?"

40:2 Job 9:3; 10:2; 13:3; 23:4; 31:35; 33:13

JOB RESPONDS TO THE LORD

3 Then Job replied to the LORD,
4 "I am nothing—how could I ever find the answers?
I will cover my mouth with my hand.

40:4 Job 21:5; 29:9

40:1-2 The Lord paused to ask Job two direct questions, and apparently He expected an answer from Job. Both of them emphasized that a godly man like Job should have known better than to question the Lord's actions—as if the Lord could ever make a mistake.

40:3-5 Job was so overwhelmed by all that the Lord said that he could only acknowledge his own insignificance. Surrendering to God is often the wisest thing we can say to Him.

▸ GOD

40:4 Job's silence. When Job heard what the Lord said about His majesty and power, Job had no response. He realized what he was compared to the holy, all-knowing, all-powerful God. Has God's majesty ever so overwhelmed you that you sat in stunned silence? Have you ever been so impressed with God's glory that you were stripped of words? Prayerfully read Psalm 95 to remind yourself of how God is bigger than anything you can imagine. Use the chapter as a prayer to God, giving Him praise for who He is. (***See God***> *God's Attributes*> *All-Powerful*> *No one can challenge what God does,* TopicGuide page A15.)

40:5 Job 9:3, 15
[5] I have said too much already.
I have nothing more to say."

THE LORD CHALLENGES JOB AGAIN

40:6 Job 38:1
[6]Then the LORD answered Job from the whirlwind:

40:7 Job 38:3; 42:4
[7] "Brace yourself like a man,
because I have some questions for you,
and you must answer them.

40:8 Job 10:3, 7; 13:18; 27:2, 6 Rom 3:4
[8] "Will you discredit My justice
and condemn Me just to prove you are right?
[9] Are you as strong as God?
40:9 Job 37:5
Can you thunder with a voice like His?
[10] All right, put on your glory and splendor,
40:10 Pss 93:1; 104:1
your honor and majesty.
[11] Give vent to your anger.
40:11 Isa 2:12; 42:25 Dan 4:37 Nah 1:6, 8
Let it overflow against the proud.
[12] Humiliate the proud with a glance;
walk on the wicked where they stand.
40:12 Isa 13:11; 63:3
[13] Bury them in the dust.
40:13 Isa 2:10-12
Imprison them in the world of the dead.
[14] Then even I would praise you,
for your own strength would save you.

[15] "Take a look at Behemoth,*
which I made, just as I made you.
It eats grass like an ox.
[16] See its powerful loins
and the muscles of its belly.
[17] Its tail is as strong as a cedar.
The sinews of its thighs are knit tightly together.
[18] Its bones are tubes of bronze.
Its limbs are bars of iron.
40:19 Job 40:15; 41:33
[19] It is a prime example of God's handiwork,
and only its Creator can threaten it.
[20] The mountains offer it their best food,
where all the wild animals play.
[21] It lies under the lotus plants,*
hidden by the reeds in the marsh.
[22] The lotus plants give it shade
among the willows beside the stream.
[23] It is not disturbed by the raging river,
not concerned when the swelling Jordan rushes around it.

40:15 The identification of Behemoth is disputed, ranging from an earthly creature to a mythical sea monster in ancient literature. **40:21** Or *bramble bushes;* also in 40:22.

40:7-14 The Lord rebukes Job for concluding that He must have made a mistake since Job knew his sufferings were not the result of sin (see note at 19:6). The Lord also challenged Job to demonstrate his powers as God if he really thought he could run the universe better. If Job could do so, he would be worthy of the praise that belongs only to God.

40:15-24 The rest of the Lord's speech (ending at 41:34) focuses on two very large, strong, and dangerous animals as evidences of the Lord's greatness and power. The powerful animal described in 40:15-24 is called "Behemoth." Some have suggested that the term refers to a hippopotamus, but the description of the animal in the rest of the chapter indicates a much larger creature (see especially 40:17-18, 23). Such a powerful animal terrified those who saw it, but Job needed to remember that the Lord is infinitely more powerful (40:19). In fact, the Lord created this incredible animal just as surely as He created Job (40:15).

24 No one can catch it off guard
or put a ring in its nose and lead it away.

THE LORD'S CHALLENGE CONTINUES

41 1*"Can you catch Leviathan* with a hook
or put a noose around its jaw?
2 Can you tie it with a rope through the nose
or pierce its jaw with a spike?
3 Will it beg you for mercy
or implore you for pity?
4 Will it agree to work for you,
to be your slave for life?
5 Can you make it a pet like a bird,
or give it to your little girls to play with?
6 Will merchants try to buy it
to sell it in their shops?
7 Will its hide be hurt by spears
or its head by a harpoon?
8 If you lay a hand on it,
you will certainly remember the battle that follows.
You won't try that again!
9* No, it is useless to try to capture it.
The hunter who attempts it will be knocked down.
10 And since no one dares to disturb it,
who then can stand up to Me?
11 Who has given Me anything that I need to pay back?
Everything under heaven is Mine.

12 "I want to emphasize Leviathan's limbs
and its enormous strength and graceful form.
13 Who can strip off its hide,
and who can penetrate its double layer of armor?*
14 Who could pry open its jaws?
For its teeth are terrible!
15 Its scales are like rows of shields
tightly sealed together.
16 They are so close together
that no air can get between them.

41:1
Job 3:8
Pss 74:14; 104:26
Isa 27:1

41:2
2 Kgs 19:28
Isa 37:29

41:10
Job 3:8

41:11
Exod 19:5
Deut 10:14
Pss 24:1; 50:12
Rom 11:35
1 Cor 10:26

41:1a Verses 41:1-8 are numbered 40:25-32 in Hebrew text. 41:1b The identification of Leviathan is disputed, ranging from an earthly creature to a mythical sea monster in ancient literature. 41:9 Verses 41:9-34 are numbered 41:1-26 in Hebrew text. 41:13 As in Greek version; Hebrew reads *its bridle?*

41:1 This entire chapter describes a creature called "Leviathan." Some have suggested that the term may refer to a crocodile, but the description seems to indicate an animal much larger than and quite different from a crocodile (see especially 41:7, 12-17, 22-32). It may have been a genuine animal, such as a plesiosaur, that God had in mind. Or it may have been a well-known mythical animal that God was using as an example.

41:11 The point to this fierce description was to build awe and respect for God, for if no one can safely challenge God's creation, how can we safely challenge the Creator, who is even more imposing?

▸ GOD

41:11 Speaking our mind. How mad can you get with God? How playful can you act before Him? Are there any boundaries in how we may speak to God? Perhaps not outward boundaries, but there are certainly boundaries of attitude, and that was God's concern about Job. In Job 42 and many other passages (at least 25 others) in Scripture, God says that we should approach him with a healthy fear (Ecclesiastes 12:13; Jeremiah 2:19; Luke 12:5; Acts 10:2; 2 Corinthians 5:11; Hebrews 12:28). Nothing you do or say can make God love you any more or any less than He does—but mature believers approach God with a healthy fear. Give your King all the royal respect He deserves. (***See God****> Relationship> God Enables> Relationship with God requires obedience,* TopicGuide page A14.)

[17] Each scale sticks tight to the next.
They interlock and cannot be penetrated.

41:18 Job 3:9
[18] "When it sneezes, it flashes light!
Its eyes are like the red of dawn.
[19] Lightning leaps from its mouth;
flames of fire flash out.
[20] Smoke streams from its nostrils
like steam from a pot heated over burning rushes.
[21] Its breath would kindle coals,
for flames shoot from its mouth.

[22] "The tremendous strength in Leviathan's neck
strikes terror wherever it goes.
[23] Its flesh is hard and firm
and cannot be penetrated.
[24] Its heart is hard as rock,
hard as a millstone.
[25] When it rises, the mighty are afraid,
gripped by terror.
[26] No sword can stop it,
no spear, dart, or javelin.
[27] Iron is nothing but straw to that creature,
and bronze is like rotten wood.
[28] Arrows cannot make it flee.
Stones shot from a sling are like bits of grass.
[29] Clubs are like a blade of grass,
and it laughs at the swish of javelins.
[30] Its belly is covered with scales as sharp as glass.
It plows up the ground as it drags through the mud.

[31] "Leviathan makes the water boil with its commotion.
It stirs the depths like a pot of ointment.
[32] The water glistens in its wake,
making the sea look white.

41:33 Job 40:19
[33] Nothing on earth is its equal,
no other creature so fearless.

41:34 Job 28:8
[34] Of all the creatures, it is the proudest.
It is the king of beasts."

JOB RESPONDS TO THE LORD

42 Then Job replied to the LORD:

42:2 Gen 18:14 Matt 19:26
[2] "I know that You can do anything,
and no one can stop You.

42:3 Job 38:2 Pss 40:5; 131:1; 139:6
[3] You asked, 'Who is this that questions My wisdom with such ignorance?'
It is I—and I was talking about things I knew nothing about,
things far too wonderful for me.

42:4 Job 38:3; 40:7
[4] You said, 'Listen and I will speak!
I have some questions for you,
and you must answer them.'

42:5 Job 26:14 Isa 6:5
[5] I had only heard about You before,
but now I have seen You with my own eyes.

6 I take back everything I said,
and I sit in dust and ashes to show my repentance."

CONCLUSION: THE LORD BLESSES JOB

7After the LORD had finished speaking to Job, He said to Eliphaz the Temanite: "I am angry **42:7**
with you and your two friends, for you have not spoken accurately about Me, as My ser- Job 40:3-5
vant Job has. 8So take seven bulls and seven rams and go to My servant Job and offer a **42:8**
burnt offering for yourselves. My servant Job will pray for you, and I will accept his prayer Job 1:5; 22:30
on your behalf. I will not treat you as you deserve, for you have not spoken accurately Jas 5:16
about Me, as My servant Job has." 9So Eliphaz the Temanite, Bildad the Shuhite, and Zo-
phar the Naamathite did as the LORD commanded them, and the LORD accepted Job's
prayer.

10When Job prayed for his friends, the LORD restored his fortunes. In fact, the LORD gave **42:10**
him twice as much as before! 11Then all his brothers, sisters, and former friends came and Pss 14:7; 85:1-3; 126:1-6
feasted with him in his home. And they consoled him and comforted him because of all **42:11**
the trials the LORD had brought against him. And each of them brought him a gift of Job 2:11; 19:13
money* and a gold ring.

12So the LORD blessed Job in the second half of his life even more than in the beginning. **42:12**
For now he had 14,000 sheep, 6,000 camels, 1,000 teams of oxen, and 1,000 female Job 1:3, 10; 8:7
donkeys. 13He also gave Job seven more sons and three more daughters. 14He named his 1 Tim 6:17
first daughter Jemimah, the second Keziah, and the third Keren-happuch. 15In all the land
no women were as lovely as the daughters of Job. And their father put them into his will
along with their brothers.

16Job lived 140 years after that, living to see four generations of his children and grand-
children. 17Then he died, an old man who had lived a long, full life. **42:17** Gen 15:15; 25:8

42:11 Hebrew *a kesitah;* the value or weight of the kesitah is no longer known.

▸ WORSHIP
42:6 The importance of repentance. What was Job's reaction to the Lord's voice? He repented in dust and ashes. When he saw the glory of the Lord and heard God's voice, he was humbled. That is the reaction that pleases God. Until we turn from our stubbornness and pride to acknowledge that God is ruler over all, we will be confused in our understanding of God. Why else would God call Himself King (Psalm 47:7) and Creator (Genesis 14:19-22) and Lord (Genesis 3:24; Revelation 19:16) and heavenly Father (Luke 11:13) if He didn't intend for us to give Him the respect those titles deserve? Kneel in repentance before God and acknowledge the sins that keep you from giving Him the praise He deserves. (***See Worship****> OT> Repentance> Examples> Job repents in dust and ashes,* TopicGuide page A29.)

42:7-10 The Lord's vindication of Job began with His rebuke of Eliphaz, Bildad, and Zophar. God intended to humble them by requiring these sacrifices in Job's presence, by having Job pray to the Lord on their behalf, and by hearing the Lord say that they were wrong about Him and Job was right.

▸ WORSHIP
42:8 Pray for your friends. God rebuked Job's three friends for the bad advice they gave him. He then instructed Job to pray for them. God asks us to do the same for those we love. We will not always see eye to eye with our friends and loved ones, but God asks us to love them and pray for them always. Job did what God asked of him, and when he did, God blessed him. We also receive blessings as we bring our friends—and our enemies—before God's throne. (***See Worship****> OT> Posture> Kneeling,* TopicGuide page A28.)

42:10-16 The Lord further vindicated Job by restoring his wealth "twice as much as before," by restoring fellowship with his friends and relatives, by giving Job as many children as he had before, and by allowing Job to enjoy his renewed happy life for "140 years," which may be double what he had lived previously—meaning he was 70 years old at the time his sufferings occurred and lived a total of 210 years.

42:17 God restored Job's life, but He does not always work this way. Sometimes it is God's sovereign will for His people to remain faithful through continued suffering (see 2 Corinthians 11:23-28; 2 Timothy 4:6-7).

PURPOSE

To provide Israel with a collection of songs for worship that are appropriate for a variety of situations.

The whole world loves the 23rd Psalm. It cuts across most religious and cultural boundaries because it addresses the common human experience of fear and offers the comfort of God's presence even in "the darkest valley" (see NLT textual note).

The universal appeal of Psalm 23—its connection with life's high points and low points, dangers and deliverances, pleasures and pains—can be found throughout the Psalms. And in the midst of it all is God, worthy to be praised for who He is and what He does for those who cling to Him by faith. There are psalms to read in worship, in prayer, in sorrow, in confession, in danger, and in celebration. This Psalms help us to think and meditate about the goodness and greatness of God in the midst of the human condition, whatever it might be.

DISCOVER GOD IN PSALMS

The Psalms are a poetic prism, revealing the character of God in a seemingly limitless array of attributes. Three of the most significant attributes of God's character in Psalms are:

Worthiness: The modern English word *worship* derives from the Old English word *worthship*. That is, worship is a matter of proclaiming the worth of the person who is worshiped. The psalmists did this by recounting their experiences with God. For example, Psalm 18:3 says, "I called on the LORD, who is worthy of praise, and He saved me from my enemies." In recounting what God had done for him, the psalmist was led to declare God worthy of praise. As entire congregations recite the psalms in worship, they affirm for themselves the psalmist's proclamations of God's worthiness. God's worthiness is the grandest theme of the Psalms.

Imminence: We know something of how worthy God truly is because He demonstrates His character to us in ways that we can understand. God is close to us—imminent—and therefore worthy to be praised (Hebrews 2:18; 4:15). He goes everywhere we go (Psalm 139:7-12); He refuses to allow us to cover up our sins (Psalm 32:3-5); He remains with us even when we do sin (Psalm 51:11-12); He guards us while we sleep (Psalm 4:8); and He knows about our broken hearts (Psalm 6:3). God is big enough for our greatest needs and personal enough to care.

Glory: The apostle Paul gives us one of the best descriptions of the glory of God in 1 Timothy 6:16: "He lives in light so brilliant that no human can approach Him. No human eye has ever seen Him, nor ever will." Metaphorically, to stand in the presence of the glory of God would be like standing on the surface of the sun. Such glory consumes everything that approaches it. The psalmists recognized that God's glory was greater than the heavens and earth (Psalm 113:4), that He deserves to be glorified (Psalm 96:8), and that the universe speaks of His glory (Psalm 19:1). God is worthy to be praised because His glory exceeds all other glory.

GROWING THROUGH PSALMS

The Psalms are quoted or referenced more times in the New Testament than any other Old Testament book. It is a treasure of timeless themes for the follower of Christ:

Difficulties and Dependence: It is not the kinds of difficulties we have that cause us to flee to the Psalms, it is their intensity. In the Psalms, we find people in life-or-death situations, and our own circumstances can seem equally serious at times. The psalmists call out to God in the plainest and most emotional of terms, giving us permission to do likewise. Our cries for help do not inform God of our need (Matthew 6:8); they inform us of our need for God.

Public Praise: On one occasion, David called out to God, "Save me so I can praise You publicly at Jerusalem's gates" (Psalm 9:14). Another time he reasoned with God: "What will You gain if I die, if I sink into the grave? Can my dust praise You? Can it tell of Your faithfulness?" (Psalm 30:9). And again, "Then I will thank You in front of the great assembly. I will praise You before all the people" (Psalm 35:18). Again and again, the psalmists stress the central place of public praise in the life of the believer.

DISCOVERY VERSES

Create in me a clean heart, O God. Renew a loyal spirit within me. (PSALM 51:10)

Enter His gates with thanksgiving; go into His courts with praise. Give thanks to Him and praise His name. For the LORD is good. His unfailing love continues forever, and His faithfulness continues to each generation. (PSALM 100:4-5)

How can a young person stay pure? By obeying Your word. I have tried hard to find You—don't let me wander from Your commands. (PSALM 119:9-10)

Gratitude: The psalmists express heartfelt thankfulness for a wide range of God's gifts: for guidance, for strength, for victory over enemies, for comfort amid trials, and for forgiveness from sin. The Psalms teach that a relationship with God is filled with benefits for the believer and that it is fitting to express thanks for those benefits. As Christians, our prayers should overflow with expressions of gratitude to God.

PSALMS FACTS

Authors: David wrote seventy-three psalms; Asaph, a priest, wrote twelve; the sons (or descendants) of Korah wrote nine; Solomon wrote two; and Moses, Heman, and Ethan each wrote one; fifty-one psalms are anonymous.

Written to: As the "hymn book" of Israel, the Psalms generally were written for the worshiping community of Israel.

Dates of writing: The dates of various psalms correlate with the dates of their authors, beginning with Moses. The Psalms were collected, arranged, and rearranged over several centuries, with the Psalter reaching its final form around the third century BC, about 250 years after Israel returned from exile.

Setting: The setting of the Psalms is life itself; they flow out of the personal experiences of those who wrote them.

OUTLINE

- **PSALMS 1–41**—Book one
- **PSALMS 42–72**—Book two
- **PSALMS 73–89**—Book three
- **PSALMS 90–106**—Book four
- **PSALMS 107–150**—Book five

BOOK ONE (PSALMS 1–41)

PSALM 1

1 Oh, the joys of those who do not
follow the advice of the wicked,
or stand around with sinners,
or join in with mockers.
2 But they delight in the law of the LORD,
meditating on it day and night.
3 They are like trees planted along the riverbank,
bearing fruit each season.
Their leaves never wither,
and they prosper in all they do.

4 But not the wicked!
They are like worthless chaff, scattered by the wind.
5 They will be condemned at the time of judgment.
Sinners will have no place among the godly.
6 For the LORD watches over the path of the godly,
but the path of the wicked leads to destruction.

1:1 Pss 17:4; 26:5 Prov 4:14 Jer 15:17
1:2 Pss 25:5; 63:5-6; 119:13-16
1:3 Gen 39:3 Jer 17:7-8 Ezek 47:12
1:4 Job 21:18 Ps 35:5 Isa 17:13
1:6 Neh 1:7 Pss 9:5-6; 11:6 John 10:14 2 Tim 2:19

PSALM 2

1 Why are the nations so angry?
Why do they waste their time with futile plans?
2 The kings of the earth prepare for battle;
the rulers plot together
against the LORD
and against His anointed one.
3 "Let us break their chains," they cry,
"and free ourselves from slavery to God."

2:1 Pss 21:11; 46:6 Acts 4:25-26
2:2 Pss 48:4-6; 74:18, 23 Jer 5:5 John 1:41

1:1 This psalm is an introduction to the entire book. It is less a prayer itself than a preparation for prayer.

▸ HOLINESS
1:2 My delight. Have you ever had something that entranced you so much that it flitted through your mind again and again? Perhaps it was the taste of fine chocolate or a fragment of a favorite song. Does God's Word delight you as much as these things? God's Word is so vital that we should bathe our thoughts constantly in its principles. Memorizing Bible verses is a way to achieve this. Pick out a verse that touches your life right now and think over its refrains during your day. (***See Holiness***> *Law and Grace> Law> God's Law is good,* TopicGuide page A41; also ***see Worship***> *OT> Fasting and Prayer> Prayer> Psalms> Wisdom poems,* TopicGuide page A26.)

1:4-5 The contrast between the wicked and the obedient is strong. The wicked are described as "worthless chaff," discarded by God and excluded from the covenant community.

▸ WORSHIP
1:6 The place for sinners. God's Word is very clear about the destination of those who do not follow God. That's why it is so essential to study God's Word to find God's answers to life. The dividing line between those who enjoy God's protection and those who will face destruction is plain. Where do you stand? Second Timothy 2:19 says that the righteous "must turn away from evil." This is the wise choice. (***See Worship***> *OT> Music> Psalms> Special> Law,* TopicGuide page A27.)

▸ WORSHIP
2:2 The kings rebel. What a rebellious lot are the rulers of nations! Look back over history: Nero, Hitler, and Stalin (to name just a few) all proclaimed themselves against God and His plans. We can see the same thinking in today's world. Many leaders, large and small, oppose what's right. Whenever a ruler chooses evil, he opposes God. The Bible promises that these rulers will earn just consequences. We can rest in the fact that God will prevail, no matter how bleak current political situations may look. (***See Worship***> *OT> Fasting and Prayer> Prayer> Psalms> Royal psalms,* TopicGuide page A26.)

2:2 In its Old Testament context, "anointed one" referred to the Davidic king. The Davidic monarchy anticipated the kingly ministry of the coming Messiah (Matthew 27:11).

4 But the One who rules in heaven laughs.
The Lord scoffs at them.
5 Then in anger He rebukes them,
terrifying them with His fierce fury.
6 For the Lord declares, "I have placed My chosen king
on the throne
in Jerusalem,* on My holy mountain."

7 The king proclaims the LORD's decree:
"The LORD said to me, 'You are My son.*
Today I have become your Father.*
8 Only ask, and I will give you the nations as your inheritance,
the whole earth as your possession.
9 You will break* them with an iron rod
and smash them like clay pots.'"

10 Now then, you kings, act wisely!
Be warned, you rulers of the earth!
11 Serve the LORD with reverent fear,
and rejoice with trembling.
12 Submit to God's royal son,* or He will become angry,
and you will be destroyed in the midst of all your activities—
for His anger flares up in an instant.
But what joy for all who take refuge in him!

2:4 Pss 37:12-13; 59:8
2:5 Pss 76:7; 78:49-50
2:6 Pss 3:4; 45:6; 48:1-2
2:7 *Acts 13:32-33 *Heb 1:5-6; 5:5
2:8 Pss 21:1-2; 22:27
2:9 Pss 28:5; 110:5-6 Rev 2:26-27; 12:5; 19:15
2:10 Prov 8:14-15
2:11 Pss 5:7; 119:119-120 Heb 12:28
2:12 Pss 5:11; 34:8, 22 John 5:23 Rom 9:33 Rev 6:16

PSALM 3

A psalm of David, regarding the time David fled from his son Absalom.

1 O LORD, I have so many enemies;
so many are against me.
2 So many are saying,
"God will never rescue him!"
*Interlude**

3 But you, O LORD, are a shield around me;
You are my glory, the One who holds my head high.
4 I cried out to the LORD,
and He answered me from His holy mountain.
Interlude

3:1 2 Sam 15:12 Ps 69:4
3:2 Pss 22:7-8; 71:11
3:3 Pss 5:12; 27:5-6; 28:7; 62:7
3:4 Pss 4:3; 34:4; 99:9

2:6 Hebrew *on Zion.* 2:7a Or *Son;* also in 2:12. 2:7b Or *Today I reveal you as My son.* 2:9 Greek version reads *rule.* Compare Rev 2:27. 2:12 The meaning of the Hebrew is uncertain. 3:2 Hebrew *Selah.* The meaning of this word is uncertain, though it is probably a musical or literary term. It is rendered *Interlude* throughout the Psalms.

▸ WORSHIP

2:12 Submit to the Son. In centuries past, when kings and queens ruled, the king's son had a pre-eminent place in the kingdom. He was the heir to the throne, so he received honor for his place in the kingly line. Whatever the son said was followed as if it were law. As a sign of submission, a person would kiss the ring or the feet of his ruler. That's the kind of humility we need to have before Jesus Christ, God's Son. When we honor Him, we honor God. Try kneeling as you pray so that you can give the Lord Jesus the reverence He is due. (***See Worship****> OT> Reverence> Kiss the Son,* TopicGuide page A29.)

▸ WORSHIP

3:1 A lament to God. Have things ever seemed so dark you felt like giving up? The Psalms help us express these feelings. In this poem, David cries to God out of his pain. He feels overwhelmed by his circumstances and his enemies. (See 2 Samuel 15:12-14 to read about his dilemma.) We can also take our deepest sorrows to God. He will listen to our cries. We can follow David's example in crying out to God. (***See Worship****> OT> Music> Psalms> Lament> Individual,* TopicGuide page A27.)

3:4 The "holy mountain" referenced here is Zion, which was prepared for the Temple during David's lifetime. It was the primary place God chose to reveal Himself to His people in David's time.

3:5 Lev 26:6; Pss 4:8; 139:17-18; Prov 3:24-26
3:6 Pss 23:4; 27:3; 118:10-13
3:8 Pss 28:8; 29:11; Isa 43:11; Jer 3:23

5 I lay down and slept,
yet I woke up in safety,
for the LORD was watching over me.
6 I am not afraid of ten thousand enemies
who surround me on every side.

7 Arise, O LORD!
Rescue me, my God!
Slap all my enemies in the face!
Shatter the teeth of the wicked!
8 Victory comes from You, O LORD.
May You bless Your people. *Interlude*

PSALM 4

For the choir director: A psalm of David, to be accompanied by stringed instruments.

4:1 Pss 3:4; 17:6; 18:6, 18-19; 25:16

1 Answer me when I call to You,
O God who declares me innocent.
Free me from my troubles.
Have mercy on me and hear my prayer.

4:2 Pss 31:6, 18; 69:7-10, 19-20
4:3 Pss 6:8-9; 17:6; 31:23; 50:5; 135:4
4:4 Ps 77:6; Eph 4:26
4:5 Pss 37:3, 5; 50:14; 51:19
4:6 Num 6:26; Job 7:7; 9:25; Ps 80:3, 7, 19

2 How long will you people ruin my reputation?
How long will you make groundless accusations?
How long will you continue your lies? *Interlude*
3 You can be sure of this:
The LORD set apart the godly for Himself.
The LORD will answer when I call to Him.

4 Don't sin by letting anger control you.
Think about it overnight and remain silent. *Interlude*
5 Offer sacrifices in the right spirit,
and trust the LORD.

6 Many people say, "Who will show us better times?"
Let Your face smile on us, LORD.

▸ GOD
3:5 Peace and quiet. Do you know someone who can sleep through almost any calamity? As in Psalm 91, David is able to sleep peacefully in the middle of a battle zone because he knows that God, the Divine Warrior, protects him. Even when it is very quiet, you may struggle to have a restful night because of emotional or physical pain. If so, God knows. He watches over you and reassures His people that they can rest peacefully with Him in charge. (***See God****> God's Attributes> True> God doesn't lie but keeps His word,* TopicGuide page A18.)

3:7 The psalmist's request for God to "arise" is a plea for Him to stand up from His royal throne and strike His enemies down (Psalm 94:1; Romans 12:19).

▸ WORSHIP
4:1 Take away my distress. What distress are you facing at this moment? It may be as simple as a burned pie in the oven or as crippling as a stroke. God hears us when we call upon Him for mercy. He's not too busy to listen to our small concerns and He's not too weak to handle our greatest needs. He was with Corrie ten Boom in the center of a Nazi death camp. He was with Amy Carmichael when she rescued children from prostitution in India. He is with you when you pray for your family. Seek Him first in your distress. (***See Worship****> OT> Music> Psalms> Lament> Individual,* TopicGuide page A27.)

4:1 David confidently addresses God and His people. He knows that God has set him in a right relationship with Himself by declaring David innocent and taking away the guilt and distress that come from living in sin.

▸ GOD
4:4 The answer to anger. All of us have faced circumstances in which anger has robbed us of our self-control. That anger may have been expressed in a temper tantrum, caustic remarks, avoiding a friend, or inner seething. When anger becomes uncontrolled, it becomes sin. Those who walk in godliness will not allow anger to maintain control or to linger. Take the problem to God immediately, asking Him to help you stay cool. Pray about it overnight, and He'll help you keep your joy. (***See God****> Relationship> God Enables> Relationship with God requires a right heart,* TopicGuide page A14.)

4:6-7 The psalmist looks forward to the time when God's "smile," or His blessing, will drive every shameful word away and fill God's people with joy and peace. The words "Let your face smile on us, LORD" reminds us of the priestly blessing found in Numbers 6:25-26.

7 You have given me greater joy
than those who have abundant harvests of grain and new wine.
8 In peace I will lie down and sleep,
for You alone, O LORD, will keep me safe.

4:7 Acts 14:17
4:8 Lev 25:18; Deut 12:10; Job 11:19

PSALM 5

For the choir director: A psalm of David, to be accompanied by the flute.

1 O LORD, hear me as I pray;
pay attention to my groaning.
2 Listen to my cry for help, my King and my God,
for I pray to no one but You.
3 Listen to my voice in the morning, LORD.
Each morning I bring my requests to You
and wait expectantly.

4 O God, You take no pleasure in wickedness;
You cannot tolerate the sins of the wicked.
5 Therefore, the proud may not stand in Your presence,
for You hate all who do evil.
6 You will destroy those who tell lies.
The LORD detests murderers and deceivers.

7 Because of Your unfailing love, I can enter Your house;
I will worship at Your Temple with deepest awe.
8 Lead me in the right path, O LORD,
or my enemies will conquer me.
Make Your way plain for me to follow.

9 My enemies cannot speak a truthful word.
Their deepest desire is to destroy others.
Their talk is foul, like the stench from an open grave.
Their tongues are filled with flattery.*
10 O God, declare them guilty.
Let them be caught in their own traps.
Drive them away because of their many sins,
for they have rebelled against You.

11 But let all who take refuge in You rejoice;
let them sing joyful praises forever.

5:1 Ps 54:2
5:2 Ps 84:3
5:3 Pss 88:13; 130:5
5:4 Pss 11:5; 34:16; 92:15
5:5 Pss 1:5; 11:5; 45:7; 75:4
5:6 Pss 52:4-5; 55:23
5:7 Pss 69:13; 115:11, 13
5:8 Pss 27:11; 31:1, 3
5:9 *Rom 3:13; Luke 11:44
5:10 Pss 9:16; 36:12; 107:10-11
5:11 Pss 2:12; 12:7; 33:1; 64:10; Isa 65:13

5:9 Greek version reads *with lies.* Compare Rom 3:12.

5:1 In this lament, the psalmist uses imperatives to communicate the urgency of his requests. Even though his "groaning" makes his words almost inaudible, he knows God will hear, in contrast to the empty speech of his enemies.

▸ WORSHIP
5:3 Morning supplication. In this verse, David tells us that he spends his first moments of the day coming before God's throne. First, he cries out to God with his requests. Then, rather than rushing through his morning devotions, he waits on God to answer. This means taking time to pray and meditate. What a great pattern to follow! Make the most of your morning by spending unhurried moments with God, refreshing your soul. (***See Worship****> OT> Music> Psalms> Lament> Individual,* TopicGuide page A27.)

5:7 "Unfailing love" is a love grounded in God's promises to Israel. It is a love that reflects God's choice of Israel and His faithfulness to His people. It was on the basis of this love that the Israelites could worship before God. We, too, come before God in worship because of His unfailing love for us (1 John 4:10).

▸ SPIRITUAL WARFARE
5:10 It'll be okay. What is the prevailing wisdom of our generation about committing sin? "It'll be okay. God is love. I'll get by because I'm not too bad." Wrong! God's love does not mitigate His demand for righteousness. Not only will we reap consequences here and now for our sins, but we will have to face God's throne and answer to Him about them. Make sure you're not in the sin trap. Sin is *not* okay. And God's judgment will not be waylaid forever! (***See Spiritual Warfare****> Resisting Sin and Evil> Consequences> Of Disobedience> Guilt,* TopicGuide page A46.)

Spread Your protection over them,
that all who love Your name may be filled with joy.
12 For You bless the godly, O LORD;
You surround them with Your shield of love.

5:12 Pss 29:11; 32:7, 10

PSALM 6

*For the choir director: A psalm of David, to be accompanied by an eight-stringed instrument.**

1 O LORD, don't rebuke me in Your anger
or discipline me in Your rage.
2 Have compassion on me, LORD, for I am weak.
Heal me, LORD, for my bones are in agony.
3 I am sick at heart.
How long, O LORD, until You restore me?

4 Return, O LORD, and rescue me.
Save me because of Your unfailing love.
5 For the dead do not remember You.
Who can praise You from the grave?*

6 I am worn out from sobbing.
All night I flood my bed with weeping,
drenching it with my tears.
7 My vision is blurred by grief;
my eyes are worn out because of all my enemies.

8 Go away, all you who do evil,
for the LORD has heard my weeping.
9 The LORD has heard my plea;
the LORD will answer my prayer.
10 May all my enemies be disgraced and terrified.
May they suddenly turn back in shame.

6:1 Pss 2:5; 38:1
6:2 Ps 22:14
6:3 Pss 88:3; 90:13; John 12:27
6:4 Ps 17:13
6:5 Ps 30:9; Isa 38:18
6:6 Pss 42:3; 69:3
6:7 Ps 31:9
6:10 Pss 71:24; 73:19

6:TITLE Hebrew *with stringed instruments; according to the sheminith.* 6:5 Hebrew *from Sheol?*

6:1-3 The petition is prefaced by a cry for mercy. This cry of the psalmist may be motivated by the sense that his illness is the result of sin or that his request is inappropriate. In either case, David recognizes, as we all must, that he is perpetually in need of God's grace. The illness has affected the psalmist both physically and spiritually.

6:4 The psalmist's expression suggests that he considers himself abandoned by God, but he pleads for deliverance on the basis of God's unfailing love, a love intimately tied to God's covenantal faithfulness to His people.

▸ SALVATION

6:5 The resurrection in Psalms. How unified the Bible is! From Genesis to Revelation, God's holy Word proclaims the same theme—God is our Savior! This verse foretells the greatest miracle in history—the resurrection of Jesus Christ. He conquered the grave. Death could not imprison Him for He is more powerful than the grave. Just as David does here, we can place our hope in Jesus in the midst of sorrows, pain, and grief because He has conquered all of them. (***See Salvation***> *Jesus' Work*> *Resurrection*> *Old Testament points to resurrection,* TopicGuide page A22.)

6:6-7 Clear and keen eyesight was associated with vitality and health (Deuteronomy 34:7), so David's words refer generally to his failing health.

6:8-10 The tone of the psalm changes dramatically in verse 8 as David concludes with a flourish triumphantly proclaiming his confidence in God. The change in tone may reflect the growing confidence David experiences as he prays and renews his communion with God. The act of prayer restores David's spirit and gives him new hope.

▸ WORSHIP

6:9 The Lord hears. This psalm is a song of David in which he cries out to God about all the hardships he is enduring. Do you ever call out to God in a similar way? When you are hurting, do you bring your grief to God? He is our greatest comfort. We are promised that when we cry out to Him, He hears and answers. Whatever we entrust to Him, He will turn to His glory and our benefit. (***See Worship***> *OT*> *Music*> *Psalms*> *Lament*> *Repentance,* TopicGuide page A27.)

PSALM 7

A psalm of David, which he sang to the LORD concerning Cush of the tribe of Benjamin.

[1] I come to You for protection, O LORD my God.
Save me from my persecutors—rescue me!
[2] If You don't, they will maul me like a lion,
tearing me to pieces with no one to rescue me.
[3] O LORD my God, if I have done wrong
or am guilty of injustice,
[4] if I have betrayed a friend
or plundered my enemy without cause,
[5] then let my enemies capture me.
Let them trample me into the ground
and drag my honor in the dust. *Interlude*

[6] Arise, O LORD, in anger!
Stand up against the fury of my enemies!
Wake up, my God, and bring justice!
[7] Gather the nations before You.
Rule over them from on high.
[8] The LORD judges the nations.
Declare me righteous, O LORD,
for I am innocent, O Most High!
[9] End the evil of those who are wicked,
and defend the righteous.
For You look deep within the mind and heart,
O righteous God.

[10] God is my shield,
saving those whose hearts are true and right.
[11] God is an honest judge.
He is angry with the wicked every day.

[12] If a person does not repent,
God* will sharpen His sword;
He will bend and string His bow.

7:1 Pss 11:1; 31:1, 14-15
7:2 Pss 17:12; 57:4
7:3 1 Sam 24:11
7:4 1 Sam 24:7; 26:9
7:6 Pss 3:7; 35:23; 94:2; 138:7
7:8 Pss 18:20; 35:24; 96:13
7:9 1 Chr 28:9; Pss 11:4-5; 34:21; 94:23; Jer 11:20; Rev 2:23
7:10 Pss 18:2, 30; 97:10-11; 125:4
7:11 Pss 50:6; 90:9
7:12 Deut 32:41; Ps 64:7; Ezek 33:9

7:12 Hebrew *He.*

▸ **GOD**

7:1 Protection from the Lord. Our society is big on protecting people from possible danger. For example, children's toys have been changed in recent years to make sure little ones aren't harmed by their playthings. Automobile designers try to ensure safer driving. In spite of these gains, our world is still marred by tragedies and calamities. Plus, we face spiritual forces that desire our downfall. But we don't need to fear. We are not the prisoners of some terrible fate. God protects us. He will not allow anything to occur that is not in His will for us. We can count on Him. Are you going to Him for protection? Have you placed your life in His care? Just as He rescued David from his circumstances, He will help you. (***See God***> *God's Attributes> All-Powerful> God has power to deliver,* TopicGuide page A15.)

7:1-2 David vividly portrays himself as a lion's prey being hunted down by his false accusers. Lions were common in the ancient Middle East and served as powerful symbols of violence and avarice. David is alone and unable to defend himself against attacks, so he turns to God for refuge.

7:6-9 In language that evokes images of God as Warrior and Judge, David calls upon God to arbitrate his case from His heavenly throne room. David is fully confident that what transpires before the throne of God resonates in the earthly realm. If the just God of all the earth will hear his case, he will be found innocent in heaven and on earth.

▸ **WORSHIP**

7:9 God looks at the heart. How aware are you that God knows your deepest thoughts? God understands the meaning and attitudes behind everything we do and say. He knows how insincere you were when you praised your friend. He sees how well you have covered up your envy or dislike. He weighs the dissatisfaction you have pushed aside. First Chronicles 28:9 says, "The LORD sees every heart and knows every plan and thought." That's why it's so vital that we stay honest with Him and bring our attitudes to Him so that He can help us deal with them. (***See Worship***> *OT> Music> Psalms> Lament> Individual,* TopicGuide page A27.)

7:12-14 The metaphors employed by David depict God as a warrior preparing for battle. The sword is sharpened before

7:13 Pss 18:14; 45:5; 64:7
13 He will prepare His deadly weapons
and shoot His flaming arrows.

7:14 Job 15:35 Isa 59:4 Jas 1:15
14 The wicked conceive evil;
they are pregnant with trouble
and give birth to lies.

7:15 Job 4:7-8 Ps 57:6
15 They dig a deep pit to trap others,
then fall into it themselves.

7:16 Esth 9:24-25 Ps 140:9, 11
16 The trouble they make for others backfires on them.
The violence they plan falls on their own heads.

7:17 Pss 9:2; 66:1-2, 4; 71:15-16
17 I will thank the LORD because He is just;
I will sing praise to the name of the LORD Most High.

PSALM 8

*For the choir director: A psalm of David, to be accompanied by a stringed instrument.**

8:1 Pss 57:5, 11; 66:2; 113:4; 148:13
1 O LORD, our Lord, Your majestic name fills the earth!
Your glory is higher than the heavens.

8:2 Matt 21:16
2 You have taught children and infants
to tell of Your strength,*
silencing Your enemies
and all who oppose You.

8:3 Pss 89:11; 136:9
3 When I look at the night sky and see the work of Your fingers—
the moon and the stars You set in place—

8:4 Job 7:17 Ps 144:3 Heb 2:6-8
4 what are mere mortals that You should think about them,
human beings that You should care for them?*

8:5 Pss 21:5; 82:6; 103:4
5 Yet You made them only a little lower than God*
and crowned them* with glory and honor.

8:TITLE Hebrew *according to the gittith.* 8:2 Greek version reads *to give You praise.* Compare Matt 21:16. 8:4 Hebrew *what is man that You should think of him, / the son of man that You should care for him?* 8:5a Or *Yet You made them only a little lower than the angels;* Hebrew reads *Yet You made him* [i.e., man] *a little lower than Elohim.* 8:5b Hebrew *him* [i.e., man]; similarly in 8:6.

the fight; the bent bow is equivalent to a cocked pistol ready to shoot. But God does not act against the wicked until they have given birth to their mischief. The metaphor of childbirth conveys the malicious forethought with which the wicked effect their plots against the righteous.

8:1 "LORD" translates God's covenant name, Yahweh. This is the name by which God revealed Himself to His people (Exodus 3:14). The Sovereign of Israel is also the Creator of all things. The name of God is synonymous with His glory; the glory of God fills all of creation. This psalm is a response to the glory of God permeating creation.

▸ WORSHIP

8:1-3 Creation sings! In the language of a poet, the psalmist reveals that every molecule of creation points to God's power, creativity, and wisdom. The flowers open with a foretaste of His beauty. The mountains stand firm as a reflection of His strength. The stars twinkle, reminding us of the revealed-yet-hidden nature of our knowledge of God. Everywhere we look, creation praises Him. Are you doing the same? As you discover the wonders of creation, point others to the God who created them all. (***See Worship***> *OT*> *Music*> *Psalms*> *Praise,* TopicGuide page A27.)

8:2 The contrast is between the weak and the strong. The weak have found strength in God, whom they praise and thus silence their enemies. For all of their relative strength, the strong are unable to overcome those who trust in God (see Matthew 21:16).

8:5-8 Instead of despairing at the apparent insignificance of mankind on earth, the psalmist reflects on the Creation account (Genesis 1:26-31) and finds that God has invested humanity with remarkable significance. Our glory and honor derive from our creation in the image of God. Yet sin has tarnished the image and prevented us from achieving the glory for which we were made. Christ, the perfect man and second Adam, restores the image and receives dominion over all things for the sake of His church (Hebrews 2:6-8; 1 Corinthians 15:21-28; Ephesians 1:22).

[6] You gave them charge of everything You made,
putting all things under their authority–
[7] the flocks and the herds
and all the wild animals,
[8] the birds in the sky, the fish in the sea,
and everything that swims the ocean currents.

[9] O LORD, our Lord, Your majestic name fills the earth!

8:6 Gen 1:26, 28 *1 Cor 15:27

PSALM 9

For the choir director: A psalm of David, to be sung to the tune "Death of the Son."

[1] I will praise You, LORD, with all my heart;
I will tell of all the marvelous things You have done.
[2] I will be filled with joy because of You.
I will sing praises to Your name, O Most High.

9:1 Pss 26:7; 86:12

9:2 Pss 66:2, 4; 92:1; 104:34

▸ MINISTRY

8:6 Subduing the earth. Charles handed the car keys to his son, Robbie. Robbie would be operating the vehicle alone for the first time. Charles could feel the tension creeping up his neck as Robbie got behind the wheel. How would his son handle the responsibility? Psalm 8:6 says that God has given the human race authority over more than a car—we have authority over His entire creation. God has given us a responsibility to manage His creation. Your yard, your fields, your pets—God wants you to love and care for them all. How are you handling your responsibility? Do you see yourself as a steward of the land? (***See Ministry***> *Transformation> Fill and Subdue> Caretakers of the earth's resources,* TopicGuide page A56.)

9:1-2 David's praise expresses gratitude, rejoices in God with both word and song, and brings him deep joy. The two principal objects of David's praise are the works of God and the name of God. These are intimately connected: God revealed His name to Israel in the context of the Exodus, His greatest work of salvation in the Old Testament (Exodus 3:14). To praise the name of God is to acknowledge His reputation earned through His mighty works.

MY RESPONSE TO GOD

A Reflection of God

PSALM 8:5

Are humans merely hairless apes? Grownup germs? Or are we something more?

God designed the entire universe, but He crafted only one thing after His own image: people. He formed the first man out of the dust of the ground and breathed life into him (Genesis 2:7). But far from being just another animal, God placed in Adam and Eve some qualities that were previously reserved only for Himself–thus, we are made in God's image.

God's image in us consists of our innate knowledge of morality, our rationality, and attributes such as the ability to love (Ephesians 4:24; Colossians 3:10). Before the Fall, our first parents were happy, productive, and complete. The primary reason why things were so good was not that they were without sin, for perfect satisfaction isn't gained merely by the absence of sin. Life was so good because Adam and Eve perfectly reflected the image of God in humanity.

This is why all types of murder, including abortion, are so horrible–they are a destruction of God's image, an attack against God's revelation of Himself. This is why the entire moral law is summed up in the dual command to love God and our neighbor. You cannot love God and hate your neighbor, who bears God's image (1 John 4:20-21).

9:3 Pss 27:2; 56:9
9:4 Pss 47:8; 140:12; 1 Pet 2:23
9:5 Pss 69:28; 119:21
9:6 Pss 34:16; 40:15

3 My enemies retreated;
they staggered and died when You appeared.
4 For You have judged in my favor;
from Your throne You have judged with fairness.
5 You have rebuked the nations and destroyed the wicked;
You have erased their names forever.
6 The enemy is finished, in endless ruins;
the cities You uprooted are now forgotten.

9:7 Pss 10:16; 89:14-15
9:8 Ps 96:13
9:9 Pss 18:2; 37:39; 59:9, 16-17
9:10 Pss 37:28; 91:14; 94:14

7 But the LORD reigns forever,
executing judgment from His throne.
8 He will judge the world with justice
and rule the nations with fairness.
9 The LORD is a shelter for the oppressed,
a refuge in times of trouble.
10 Those who know Your name trust in You,
for You, O LORD, do not abandon those who search for You.

9:11 Pss 76:2; 105:1
9:12 Gen 9:5-6; Ps 72:14

11 Sing praises to the LORD who reigns in Jerusalem.*
Tell the world about His unforgettable deeds.
12 For He who avenges murder cares for the helpless.
He does not ignore the cries of those who suffer.

9:13 Pss 30:3; 38:19; 86:13
9:14 Pss 13:5; 20:5; 35:9; 51:12; 106:2

13 LORD, have mercy on me.
See how my enemies torment me.
Snatch me back from the jaws of death.
14 Save me so I can praise You publicly at Jerusalem's gates,
so I can rejoice that You have rescued me.

9:15 Pss 7:15; 35:8

15 The nations have fallen into the pit they dug for others.
Their own feet have been caught in the trap they set.
16 The LORD is known for His justice.
The wicked are trapped by their own deeds. *Quiet Interlude**

9:17 Pss 49:14; 50:22

17 The wicked will go down to the grave.*
This is the fate of all the nations who ignore God.

9:11 Hebrew *Zion;* also in 9:14. 9:16 Hebrew *Higgaion Selah.* The meaning of this phrase is uncertain. 9:17 Hebrew *to Sheol.*

9:3-4, 7-8 David confidently expects his enemies' defeat because God has rendered a favorable judgment on his behalf. David's confidence is the result of his recognition of God's intimate involvement with His creation and His people. What transpires in heaven, the divine throne room, has repercussions in human history. God's just judgment from heaven will deliver David on earth.

▶ GOD

9:8 God judges rightly. As we look at world events, it sometimes seems that good people are losing. Over the centuries, many evil rulers have acted without enduring consequences. Why was Hitler allowed to wreak havoc for so many years? Why weren't Lenin and Stalin brought down before millions endured horrible deaths? Thankfully, Christians have the assurance that God will judge all actions—every one. No one is getting away with anything. A time is coming when God will make everything right. Put your trust in the fact that, in time, God will either punish or forgive every sin. (***See God****> God's Attributes> Just> God judges all people with justice,* TopicGuide page A16.)

▶ SPIRITUAL WARFARE

9:10 Trust in God's name. Today, we don't name people after their roles in life. But in earlier times, this was common. The last name *Baker* was given to those people who baked for a living. *Smith* came from blacksmith, a person who made things from metal. It's obvious how the names *Cook* and *Shoemaker* may have been derived. But what about God's names? What do they say about Him? *Yahweh-Sabbaoth* means the captain of our salvation, the warrior who fights against an enemy (see Jeremiah 11:20; Zechariah 4:6). As His name implies, He protects us from anyone who would harm us. Place your trust in God, for His very name offers protection. (***See Spiritual Warfare****> Resisting Sin and Evil> Embracing Christ> Entrust yourself to God's care,* TopicGuide page A45.)

9:17-18 These verses are framed around the concept of memory. Those who ignore (literally, forget) God will go down to the grave, where they will be forgotten and where there is no memory of God (see Psalm 6:5). But the afflicted who trust in God will not be forgotten; their hope will endure.

[18] But the needy will not be ignored forever;
the hopes of the poor will not always be crushed.

[19] Arise, O LORD!
Do not let mere mortals defy You!
Judge the nations!
[20] Make them tremble in fear, O LORD.
Let the nations know they are merely human. *Interlude*

9:18 Pss 9:12; 62:5; 71:5
9:19 Num 10:35; 2 Chr 14:11
9:20 Ps 62:9

PSALM 10

1 O LORD, why do You stand so far away?
Why do You hide when I am in trouble?
2 The wicked arrogantly hunt down the poor.
Let them be caught in the evil they plan for others.
3 For they brag about their evil desires;
they praise the greedy and curse the LORD.

4 The wicked are too proud to seek God.
They seem to think that God is dead.
5 Yet they succeed in everything they do.
They do not see Your punishment awaiting them.
They sneer at all their enemies.
6 They think, "Nothing bad will ever happen to us!
We will be free of trouble forever!"

7 Their mouths are full of cursing, lies, and threats.*
Trouble and evil are on the tips of their tongues.
8 They lurk in ambush in the villages,
waiting to murder innocent people.
They are always searching for helpless victims.
9 Like lions crouched in hiding,
they wait to pounce on the helpless.
Like hunters they capture the helpless
and drag them away in nets.
10 Their helpless victims are crushed;
they fall beneath the strength of the wicked.

10:1 Pss 13:1; 22:1; 55:1
10:2 Pss 7:15; 9:16; 73:6, 8
10:3 Pss 49:6; 94:3-4
10:4 Pss 14:1; 36:1-2
10:5 Pss 28:5; 52:7
10:6 Pss 30:6-7; 49:11
10:7 Pss 59:12; 73:8; 140:3; *Rom 3:14
10:8 Pss 11:2; 94:6-7
10:9 Pss 10:2; 17:12; 59:3; 140:5

10:7 Greek version reads *cursing and bitterness.* Compare Rom 3:14.

9:19-20 The cry for God to arise employs language with military overtones. David calls on God to fight for His people to vindicate His name. David's desire is not so much for the undoing of His enemies as for the glory of God. If God would display His power, the people of the nations would rightly fear Him and acknowledge their status as finite creatures.

10:1-2 The psalmist cries in desperation, not because of his own troubles but because of the apparent absence of God. While God has remained silent, the wicked have arrogantly oppressed the defenseless. The psalmist does not understand why God has not acted, but now he implores God to judge the wicked by allowing them to succumb to their own plots.

▸ SPIRITUAL WARFARE

10:2 God defends the poor. The poor and powerless need God's help. Programs have been put into place in an effort to feed the poor, only to be used as get-rich-quick schemes. People feign poverty in order to get donations, but secretly live like kings. How can we help the poor without wondering whether we are wasting our money? We can't. But we can give them the gospel in addition to the resources and protection they need to survive. With both the gospel and necessary goods, even the poorest among us can know true riches. (***See Spiritual Warfare**> Resisting Sin and Evil> Resisting Temptation> Examples> Worldly Influences> On the poor,* TopicGuide page A45.)

10:3-6 The ungodly defy God because they do not believe He will judge them. They are convinced that their present success signals God's ignorance, apathy, or impotence. The psalmist hints at the end that awaits the wicked (10:5) before continuing with his description of their arrogance.

10:11 Ps 10:4 — 11 The wicked think, "God isn't watching us!
He has closed His eyes and won't even see what we do!"

10:12 Pss 9:12; 17:7 — 12 Arise, O LORD!
Punish the wicked, O God!
Do not ignore the helpless!
13 Why do the wicked get away with despising God?
They think, "God will never call us to account."

10:14 Pss 9:12; 22:9-11; 37:5 — 14 But You see the trouble and grief they cause.
You take note of it and punish them.
The helpless put their trust in You.
You defend the orphans.

10:15 Pss 37:17; 140:11 — 15 Break the arms of these wicked, evil people!
10:16 Deut 8:20 — Go after them until the last one is destroyed.
Ps 29:10 — 16 The LORD is king forever and ever!
The godless nations will vanish from the land.
10:17 Pss 9:18; 34:15; 145:19 — 17 LORD, You know the hopes of the helpless.
Surely You will hear their cries and comfort them.
10:18 Pss 9:9; 74:21; 146:9 Isa 29:20 — 18 You will bring justice to the orphans and the oppressed,
so mere people can no longer terrify them.

PSALM 11

For the choir director: A psalm of David.

11:1 Ps 121:1-2 — 1 I trust in the LORD for protection.
So why do you say to me,
"Fly like a bird to the mountains for safety!

11:2 Pss 7:12; 64:3-4 — 2 The wicked are stringing their bows
and fitting their arrows on the bowstrings.
They shoot from the shadows
at those whose hearts are right.
11:3 Ps 82:5 — 3 The foundations of law and order have collapsed.
What can the righteous do?"
11:4 Pss 34:15-16; 103:19 — 4 But the LORD is in His holy Temple;
the LORD still rules from heaven.
He watches everyone closely,
examining every person on earth.

10:15-16 The arm symbolized the power of the man. With this plea, the psalmist is calling on God to break the power of the wicked. He triumphantly urges God to pursue the wicked to their end and thus vindicate His rule on earth. The psalmist expresses the same sentiment that is found in the Lord's Prayer: "May Your will be done on earth, as it is in heaven" (Matthew 6:10).

▸ WORSHIP

10:17 The hopes of the hopeless. A recurrent theme in God's Word is that He helps the helpless, even when no one else can. But before we turn our eyes toward others we consider helpless, let's remember that we are all hopeless and helpless in God's eyes because of our sin. No one is strong enough or pure enough to conquer his or her problem with sin. Yet understanding our hopelessness is the greatest step we can take. Jesus said in His Sermon on the Mount, "God blesses those who are poor and realize their need for Him, for the Kingdom of Heaven is theirs" (Matthew 5:3). If you understand your helplessness, you are on the brink of blessings. Offer yourself to God in true humility so that He can give you eternal hope. (***See Worship****> OT> Music> Psalms> Lament> Individual,* TopicGuide page A27.)

11:1 Do advisers counsel David to flee or is it his own fear that urges him to run for shelter? In either case, David refuses to capitulate; his trust is in the Lord and he knows he need not run.

11:2-3 The tactics of the wicked are cowardly and treacherous, and the righteous expose them by virtue of their own character. Society itself crumbles as trust and confidence in an ordered and secure world collapse. "What will the righteous do?" Will they run and hide, thus speeding the slide to chaos? David's response is already implicit in 11:1 and further developed in 11:4-7.

[5] The LORD examines both the righteous and the wicked.
He hates those who love violence.
[6] He will rain down blazing coals and burning sulfur on the wicked,
punishing them with scorching winds.
[7] For the righteous LORD loves justice.
The virtuous will see His face.

11:5 Gen 22:1; Ps 5:5
11:6 Jer 4:11-12; Ezek 38:22
11:7 Pss 7:9-11; 17:15; 33:5

PSALM 12

*For the choir director: A psalm of David, to be accompanied by an eight-stringed instrument.**

[1] Help, O LORD, for the godly are fast disappearing!
The faithful have vanished from the earth!
[2] Neighbors lie to each other,
speaking with flattering lips and deceitful hearts.
[3] May the LORD cut off their flattering lips
and silence their boastful tongues.
[4] They say, "We will lie to our hearts' content.
Our lips are our own—who can stop us?"

[5] The LORD replies, "I have seen violence done to the helpless,
and I have heard the groans of the poor.
Now I will rise up to rescue them,
as they have longed for Me to do."
[6] The LORD's promises are pure,
like silver refined in a furnace,
purified seven times over.

12:1 Mic 7:1-2
12:2 Pss 28:3; 41:6; Jer 9:8; Rom 16:18
12:3 Pss 55:21; 73:8-9
12:5 Pss 3:7; 34:6; 35:10
12:6 Pss 19:8-10; 119:140; Prov 30:5

12:TITLE Hebrew *according to the sheminith.*

▸ GOD
11:4 The place of God. The Temple in Jerusalem functioned as the center of Israel's national life. It was the place where God's presence could be found. However, this Temple was just a shadow of the place where God dwells in heaven. From this vantage point, He sees all and rules over all. His throne is truly the center of the universe. If God is above all, why are we so timid about giving Him control over every part of our lives? Keep an image of God's throne in His glorious heavenly Temple in your mind whenever you are tempted to run your own life. Give God control instead. (***See God****> God's Nature> Unique> He alone is God, the only sovereign,* TopicGuide page A15.)

11:6 The language of judgment is reminiscent of the destruction of Sodom and Gomorrah (Genesis 19:24).

▸ WORSHIP
11:7 Doing what is right. We are not saved by our good deeds (Ephesians 2:8-10), but we are not saved without them. There is no such thing as a true saving faith that does not stimulate obedience and repentance (James 2:14). But what about babies or those who are unable to obey prior to salvation? They are still saved by grace, through faith, apart from good works (Ephesians 2:8-10). The only works that save us are the works of Jesus Christ, who lived a perfect life, died a sacrificial death, and rose triumphant from the grave. Rejoice in the works of Jesus that make our good works possible! (***See Worship****> OT> Music> Psalms> Thanksgiving> Reliance,* TopicGuide page A27.)

11:7 To see the face of God is to experience His blessing and enjoy His salvation (Numbers 6:25).

▸ WORSHIP
12:1 Where are the godly? In this day, the lament of this verse echoes across the land. So many people claim the name of the Lord only to betray Him. Many of those we count on to help us with spiritual strength fall away. Some succumb to sexual temptation; others to materialism. Some tire of the spiritual battle and give up. That's why we need to derive our spiritual strength from the Lord alone. He never fails. When someone you counted on proves unfaithful, keep your eyes on Jesus. He will always help. (***See Worship****> OT> Music> Psalms> Lament> Community,* TopicGuide page A27.)

12:1 The cry of the psalmist recalls the words of Elijah when he was hunted by Jezebel. He felt as though there was no one else who resisted the idols of the day (1 Kings 19).

▸ GOD
12:6 The purity of God's promises. In some cultures, silver is considered more precious than gold. Silver is used to make coins, ornaments, jewelry, and royal crowns. Until the time of Solomon, silver was more valuable than gold (1 Kings 10:21). But even silver looks tarnished compared to God's promises. Without God's precious promises, we would be destitute and doomed. His gift of eternal life through Jesus Christ must be the most precious promise to believers, but what comes next? His promises of His presence, His protection, His love? Thank Him for the promises that mean most to you. (***See God****> God's Attributes> Faithful> God is faithful to fulfill His promises,* TopicGuide page A16.)

12:7 Pss 37:28; 97:10 7 Therefore, LORD, we know You will protect the oppressed,
preserving them forever from this lying generation,
12:8 Ps 55:10-11 8 even though the wicked strut about,
and evil is praised throughout the land.

PSALM 13

For the choir director: A psalm of David.

13:1 Job 13:24 Pss 44:24; 89:46 1 O LORD, how long will You forget me? Forever?
How long will You look the other way?
13:2 Ps 42:4-5, 9 2 How long must I struggle with anguish in my soul,
with sorrow in my heart every day?
How long will my enemy have the upper hand?

13:3 Ezra 9:8 Job 33:29-30 Ps 5:1 3 Turn and answer me, O LORD my God!
Restore the sparkle to my eyes, or I will die.
4 Don't let my enemies gloat, saying, "We have defeated him!"
13:4 Pss 25:2; 38:16 Don't let them rejoice at my downfall.

13:5 Pss 9:14; 52:8 5 But I trust in Your unfailing love.
I will rejoice because You have rescued me.
13:6 Ps 116:7 6 I will sing to the LORD
because He is good to me.

PSALM 14

For the choir director: A psalm of David.

14:1-7 //Ps 53:1-6 1 Only fools say in their hearts,
"There is no God."
14:1 Pss 10:4; 53:1 *Rom 3:10-12 They are corrupt, and their actions are evil;
not one of them does good!

14:2 Pss 33:13-15; 102:19 2 The LORD looks down from heaven
on the entire human race;

12:7-8 It is important to note that the circumstances have not necessarily changed for David; the wicked still strut about as if they ruled without opposition (2:4). However, David has changed. His confidence in the truth of God's words has been renewed.

▶ WORSHIP

13:1 Cry out to God. This psalm begins with a cry to God because the psalmist feels as if he has been forsaken. Yet by the time David concludes his song of lament, he expresses confidence in God's power to rescue him. Have you ever experienced this transition? Whenever your circumstances seem about to overwhelm you, cry out to God. Honestly express your feelings to Him; He knows them anyway. Repeat this psalm when you are afraid, and know that God hears your cries and tears (Psalm 56:8), and He will never forsake you. (***See Worship***> *OT> Music> Psalms> Lament> Individual,* TopicGuide page A27.)

13:1-2 Occurring four times, David's cry of "How long?" expresses profound anxiety and desperation. David feels alienated from God's presence and blessing. Yet the phrase suggests hope, as well; implicit in the cry of "How long?" is the hope that an answer will be forthcoming in time. Lament does not necessarily imply doubt.

13:5-6 David now reflects on the past faithfulness of God in order to deal with his present experience and gain hope for the future. *Unfailing love* designates God's faithfulness to His people grounded in His covenant with them. David's lament is turned to song because he remembers the goodness of God.

▶ ADOPTION

14:1 The real fool. We've all heard people say about someone, "He's a real fool!" The comment might be made about a person who doesn't handle his money wisely, can't manage a situation appropriately, or has problems with relationships. We've all felt like a fool. But who does the Bible label as a fool? The atheist. Without acknowledging God, our lives are foolish—without meaning. How thankful we can be that God does not consider us fools! Even the least of us has been given wisdom from the Rock of Ages. Knowing Christ is our source of wisdom. (***See Adoption***> *Without Christ> Separated from God> Bad spiritual heart,* TopicGuide page A36.)

14:2-3 It may be tempting to view the fool only as the defiant atheist who mocks God and His people. The psalmist, however, encompasses all of humanity in his appraisal of foolishness. The apostle Paul confirms this evaluation by using these verses to build his case against humanity (Romans 3:10-18). Any attempt to live independently of God is folly, and we are all guilty. The wisdom needed to counter this folly can be found only in Christ, who grants it to His people (1 Corinthians 1:30–2:16).

He looks to see if anyone is truly wise,
if anyone seeks God.
3 But no, all have turned away;
all have become corrupt.*
No one does good,
not a single one!

4 Will those who do evil never learn?
They eat up my people like bread
and wouldn't think of praying to the LORD.
5 Terror will grip them,
for God is with those who obey Him.
6 The wicked frustrate the plans of the oppressed,
but the LORD will protect His people.

7 Who will come from Mount Zion to rescue Israel?
When the LORD restores His people,
Jacob will shout with joy, and Israel will rejoice.

14:3 Pss 58:3; 143:2
14:4 Isa 64:7
14:6 Pss 9:9; 40:17
14:7 Job 42:10; Pss 53:6; 85:1-2

PSALM 15

A psalm of David.

1 Who may worship in Your sanctuary, LORD?
Who may enter Your presence on Your holy hill?
2 Those who lead blameless lives and do what is right,
speaking the truth from sincere hearts.
3 Those who refuse to gossip
or harm their neighbors
or speak evil of their friends.

15:1 Pss 24:3; 27:5-6
15:2 Ps 24:4; Eph 4:25
15:3 Exod 23:1; Ps 28:3

14:3 Greek version reads *have become useless.* Compare Rom 3:12.

▸ WORSHIP
14:4 Those who do evil. In this psalm, David laments about the power of the wicked. Why does it seem that those who perpetrate evil achieve success? We can see this same pattern at work today. It doesn't matter which arena of life you experience—political, business, even the spiritual—ruthless people tend to dominate. They boast that their success is the result of their own efforts alone. But their success is limited. The most ruthless person ages and eventually loses his power. No one can hang on forever. And that day comes for everyone when they have to face their last master—death. No one escapes. We do not envy the wicked their success because we know what the end of their pathway will bring. (***See Worship****> OT> Music> Psalms> Lament> Individual,* TopicGuide page A27.)

14:4-6 The foolish express their folly by living as if there is no God and oppressing the people of God. Yet the very One they deny is working against them and defending His people. Verse 5 suggests that even the foolish may not be convinced by their denials of God. They are haunted by the fear that the God they deny exists and has taken note of their folly.

▸ WORSHIP
15:1 Who may worship You, God? Imagine you are standing in an enormous, ancient building. You hear these words being chanted in the Temple in the time of the Old Testament kingdom of Israel. The sight of the priests, the sound of chanting, the smell of incense—you would quickly make certain you were suitably dressed. If you were dirty, you would want to clean up. If you were smelly, you would want to freshen up. It is only natural to become sensitive to our appearance when we are in a majestic, holy place. In the same way, when we are worshiping God, each of us should be attentive to the state of his or her soul. Is it smeared with a dirty conscience? Is it foul with unconfessed sin? Before you approach God, especially in the taking of the Lord's Supper (1 Corinthians 11:28, 31), repent of all known sins. Through Christ, we can repent and stand spotless before God. (***See Worship****> OT> Fasting and Prayer> Prayer> Psalms> Liturgies,* TopicGuide page A26.)

15:1 God's sanctuary—the tent of the Lord and later the Temple—was situated atop the hill known as Mount Zion, just north of Jerusalem. Those who enter the presence of God must have certain characteristics, as described below. Sinless perfection is not expected, but rather a disposition toward obedience.

15:2-5 While not exhaustive, this list intends to encompass the whole person, including deeds and speech. The requirements are moral in nature, suggesting that ritual purity is not sufficient for those who seek God. And the requirements are both positive and negative. The one who worships God must not just avoid evil but pursue goodness as well.

15:4 Judg 11:35 Acts 28:10

4 Those who despise flagrant sinners,
and honor the faithful followers of the LORD,
and keep their promises even when it hurts.

15:5 Exod 22:25; 23:8 Deut 16:19

5 Those who lend money without charging interest,
and who cannot be bribed to lie about the innocent.
Such people will stand firm forever.

PSALM 16

A psalm of David.

16:1 Pss 7:1; 17:8

1 Keep me safe, O God,
for I have come to You for refuge.

16:2 Ps 73:25

2 I said to the LORD, "You are my Master!
Every good thing I have comes from You."

16:3 Pss 101:6; 119:63

3 The godly people in the land
are my true heroes!
I take pleasure in them!

16:4 Exod 23:13 Josh 23:7 Pss 32:10; 106:37-38

4 Troubles multiply for those who chase after other gods.
I will not take part in their sacrifices of blood
or even speak the names of their gods.

5 LORD, You alone are my inheritance, my cup of blessing.
You guard all that is mine.

16:6 Ps 78:55 Jer 3:19

6 The land You have given me is a pleasant land.
What a wonderful inheritance!

16:7 Pss 73:24; 77:6

7 I will bless the LORD who guides me;
even at night my heart instructs me.

16:8 Pss 27:8; 73:23; 110:5; 123:1-2

8 I know the LORD is always with me.
I will not be shaken, for He is right beside me.

9 No wonder my heart is glad, and I rejoice.*
My body rests in safety.

16:10 Pss 49:15; 86:13 *Acts 2:25-28; 13:35

10 For You will not leave my soul among the dead*
or allow Your holy one* to rot in the grave.

16:11 Ps 36:7-8

11 You will show me the way of life,
granting me the joy of Your presence
and the pleasures of living with You forever.*

16:9 Greek version reads *and my tongue shouts His praises.* Compare Acts 2:26. 16:10a Hebrew *in Sheol.* 16:10b Or *Your Holy One.* 16:11 Greek version reads *You have shown me the way of life, / and You will fill me with the joy of Your presence.* Compare Acts 2:28.

▸ GOD

16:1-11 God is my refuge. This song describes several ways in which God is our refuge. He gives us good things. He is our inheritance and blessing. He guides us. He is always with us. He protects our bodies for future resurrection. He promises that we will live with Him forever. These verses give us a new appreciation for our safety and pleasure in Him. (***See God***> *God's Names> God> Refuge,* TopicGuide page A18; also ***see Worship***> *OT> Music> Psalms> Thanksgiving> Reliance,* TopicGuide page A27.)

16:5-6 David reflects on the gifts of God. "Inheritance," "cup of blessing," and "the land" designate all of the blessings God has showered on him throughout his life. The providence of God has ordered David's life in goodness and joy.

16:9-10 David speaks here of his deliverance from the immediate danger he is facing. God has saved him from the danger of death. These words, however, also speak prophetically of Jesus' triumph over the grave (Acts 2:25-28; 13:35). While David is delivered from death without experiencing it, Jesus is delivered from death itself, ending its power over Him and all of those who are united to Him (Romans 6:1-5).

▸ ADOPTION

16:10 Promise of resurrection. When Peter preached his tremendous sermon on the Day of Pentecost (Acts 2:25-28), he quoted these words from this psalm. Peter attributed these facts to Jesus. He is the Holy One whom God would not abandon in the grave. Therefore, in this psalm, written hundreds of years before Jesus died, David perfectly predicted Jesus' resurrection. This is proof of how the Bible's theme is unified in the life of Jesus Christ. No other explanation can describe the accuracy of this verse. Jesus has risen—just as was predicted so long ago. (See Acts 2:25-28; also ***see Adoption***> *In Heaven> Bodily resurrection,* TopicGuide page A37.)

PSALM 17

A prayer of David.

1 O LORD, hear my plea for justice.
Listen to my cry for help.
Pay attention to my prayer,
for it comes from honest lips.
2 Declare me innocent,
for You see those who do right.

3 You have tested my thoughts and examined
my heart in the night.
You have scrutinized me and found nothing wrong.
I am determined not to sin in what I say.
4 I have followed Your commands,
which keep me from following cruel and evil people.
5 My steps have stayed on Your path;
I have not wavered from following You.

6 I am praying to You because I know You will answer, O God.
Bend down and listen as I pray.
7 Show me Your unfailing love in wonderful ways.
By Your mighty power You rescue
those who seek refuge from their enemies.
8 Guard me as You would guard Your own eyes.*
Hide me in the shadow of Your wings.
9 Protect me from wicked people who attack me,
from murderous enemies who surround me.
10 They are without pity.
Listen to their boasting!
11 They track me down and surround me,
watching for the chance to throw me to the ground.
12 They are like hungry lions, eager to tear me apart—
like young lions hiding in ambush.

13 Arise, O LORD!
Stand against them, and bring them to their knees!
Rescue me from the wicked with Your sword!
14 By the power of Your hand, O LORD,
destroy those who look to this world for their reward.

17:1 Pss 61:1; 88:2; 142:6
17:2 Pss 98:8-9; 99:4; 103:6
17:3 Job 23:10; Pss 26:1-2; 39:1; 66:10; Jer 50:20
17:4 Pss 10:5-11; 119:9, 101
17:5 Pss 18:36; 37:30-31; 44:18
17:8 Deut 32:10; Ruth 2:12; Pss 36:7; 91:1, 4
17:10 1 Sam 2:3; Pss 31:18; 73:7-8
17:11 Pss 37:14; 88:17
17:12 Pss 7:2; 10:9
17:13 Ps 22:20
17:14 Ps 73:3-7

17:8 Hebrew *as the pupil of Your eye.*

17:2-5 David is not claiming absolute sinlessness. Rather, he is affirming his innocence of the particular charges being made against him. God has searched his heart in the stillness of the night and found him innocent. In language reminiscent of Psalm 1, David attributes his innocence to his commitment to God's law.

▶ WORSHIP
17:8 Our importance to God. David gives us two powerful images to describe how much God loves us. As the apple of His eye, we are the center of His focus. Nothing distracts Him from caring for us. He provides shelter for us like a mother hen does for her chicks. We are safe and warm under His protection. Do you feel important to God? Do you visualize yourself as a duckling under His wing for protection? God gives us these word pictures so that we can trust in Him. (***See Worship****> OT> Music> Psalms> Lament> Individual,* TopicGuide page A27.)

17:9-12 David cites the wickedness and ruthlessness of his enemies as a reason for God to act decisively in his defense. The lion is an apt symbol of the avarice of David's enemies, who track him like prey.

17:13 David invokes military terminology to call upon God to act on his behalf (Numbers 10:35). In the Old Testament, God is often portrayed as a warrior, fighting to defend and uphold His people (Exodus 14:14; Isaiah 59:16-19).

But satisfy the hunger of Your treasured ones.
May their children have plenty,
leaving an inheritance for their descendants.

17:15 Pss 4:6-7; 16:11; 140:13

15 Because I am righteous, I will see You.
When I awake, I will see You face to face and be satisfied.

PSALM 18

18:TITLE //2 Sam 22:1-51

For the choir director: A psalm of David, the servant of the LORD. He sang this song to the LORD on the day the LORD rescued him from all his enemies and from Saul. He sang:

18:1 Ps 59:17

1 I love You, LORD;
You are my strength.

18:2 1 Sam 2:2 Pss 19:14; 28:1; 59:9, 11; 71:3; 75:10; 144:2

2 The LORD is my rock, my fortress, and my savior;
my God is my rock, in whom I find protection.
He is my shield, the power that saves me,
and my place of safety.

18:3 Num 10:9 Pss 34:6; 96:4

3 I called on the LORD, who is worthy of praise,
and He saved me from my enemies.

18:4 Pss 69:1-2; 116:3; 124:2-5

4 The ropes of death entangled me;
floods of destruction swept over me.

18:5 Ps 116:3

5 The grave* wrapped its ropes around me;
death laid a trap in my path.

18:6 Pss 3:4; 34:15

6 But in my distress I cried out to the LORD;
yes, I prayed to my God for help.
He heard me from His sanctuary;
my cry to Him reached His ears.

18:7 Ps 114:4, 6-7

7 Then the earth quaked and trembled.
The foundations of the mountains shook;
they quaked because of His anger.
8 Smoke poured from His nostrils;
fierce flames leaped from His mouth.
Glowing coals blazed forth from Him.

18:9 Exod 20:21 Pss 97:2; 144:5

9 He opened the heavens and came down;
dark storm clouds were beneath His feet.

18:10 Pss 80:1; 99:1

10 Mounted on a mighty angelic being,* He flew,
soaring on the wings of the wind.
11 He shrouded Himself in darkness,
veiling His approach with dark rain clouds.

18:5 Hebrew *Sheol.* 18:10 Hebrew *a cherub.*

17:15 Throughout the night, David pours himself out before God, pleading for vindication. The psalm closes with David's assurance that morning will bring God's deliverance. David's satisfaction derives from his anticipation of God's presence. God's face represents blessing and protection.

18:1 The psalm opens with an unusually personal statement of David's intimate love for God. David's love springs from an awareness of God's presence with him in times of trouble and danger. During these times, God upholds and defends David.

▸ GOD

18:2 What's in a name? A study of God's names will reveal the strong character of our God. In this verse, He is called a fortress and a rock. As a fortress, He protects us from the guiles of our enemy, Satan. No one can pull down this fortress, so we are eternally protected. As the rock, He provides the only sure foundation. With a fortress and a rock, we have complete assurance in Him. Research the self-designations of God to see how He wants us to understand Him. (***See God****> God's Names> God> Fortress,* TopicGuide page A18; also ***see God****> God's Names> God> Rock,* TopicGuide page A18.)

18:7-15 These verses powerfully depict God as a mighty warrior moved to action by the cry of His servant. The description contains images that are characteristic of God's appearance as a warrior throughout the Old Testament, such as fire, earthquakes, smoke, and clouds (Exodus 19:18; Daniel 7:13; Nahum 1:3-6).

[12] Thick clouds shielded the brightness around Him
and rained down hail and burning coals.*
[13] The LORD thundered from heaven;
the voice of the Most High resounded
amid the hail and burning coals.
[14] He shot His arrows and scattered His enemies;
His lightning flashed, and they were greatly confused.
[15] Then at Your command, O LORD,
at the blast of Your breath,
the bottom of the sea could be seen,
and the foundations of the earth were laid bare.

[16] He reached down from heaven and rescued me;
He drew me out of deep waters.
[17] He rescued me from my powerful enemies,
from those who hated me and were too strong for me.
[18] They attacked me at a moment when I was in distress,
but the LORD supported me.
[19] He led me to a place of safety;
He rescued me because He delights in me.
[20] The LORD rewarded me for doing right;
He restored me because of my innocence.
[21] For I have kept the ways of the LORD;
I have not turned from my God to follow evil.
[22] I have followed all His regulations;
I have never abandoned His decrees.
[23] I am blameless before God;
I have kept myself from sin.
[24] The LORD rewarded me for doing right.
He has seen my innocence.

[25] To the faithful You show Yourself faithful;
to those with integrity You show integrity.
[26] To the pure You show Yourself pure,
but to the wicked You show Yourself hostile.
[27] You rescue the humble,
but You humiliate the proud.
[28] You light a lamp for me.
The LORD, my God, lights up my darkness.
[29] In Your strength I can crush an army;
with my God I can scale any wall.

[30] God's way is perfect.
All the LORD's promises prove true.
He is a shield for all who look to Him for protection.
[31] For who is God except the LORD?
Who but our God is a solid rock?

18:12 Pss 97:2; 104:1-2
18:13 Pss 29:3; 104:7-8
18:14 Ps 144:6
18:15 Exod 15:8; Ps 106:9
18:16 Ps 144:7
18:17 Ps 35:10
18:18 Pss 16:8; 59:16
18:19 Pss 31:8; 37:23; 41:1, 11; 118:5
18:20 Pss 7:8; 24:4
18:21 2 Chr 34:33; Pss 37:34; 119:33, 102-103
18:25 Ps 62:12; Matt 5:7
18:27 Pss 72:12; 101:5; Prov 6:16-19
18:28 Job 18:6; Ps 27:1
18:29 Ps 118:10-12; 2 Cor 12:9
18:30 Pss 12:6; 19:7
18:31 Deut 32:31, 39; Pss 62:2; 86:8-10

18:12 Or *and lightning bolts;* also in 18:13.

18:15-17 In the ancient world, the sea was a metaphor for the chaotic elements of creation that threatened the order of the world, but the elements were powerless against the command of God. The image of parted seas recalls the Israelites' miraculous crossing of the Red Sea, when God revealed Himself as a warrior fighting for His people (Exodus 14:14).

18:20-24 The righteousness David claims is not an absolute righteousness. David was righteous in the particular circumstances that gave rise to this psalm. His sin had not brought about the crisis. Furthermore, his righteousness is construed as a disposition; in other words, he walks with integrity. His commitment to obedience does not waver.

18:32 Isa 45:5
32 God arms me with strength,
and He makes my way perfect.
18:33 Deut 32:13 Hab 3:19
33 He makes me as surefooted as a deer,
enabling me to stand on mountain heights.
34 He trains my hands for battle;
He strengthens my arm to draw a bronze bow.
18:35 Pss 33:20; 63:8; 119:117
35 You have given me Your shield of victory.
Your right hand supports me;
Your help has made me great.
18:36 Pss 31:8; 66:9
36 You have made a wide path for my feet
to keep them from slipping.

18:37 Ps 44:5
37 I chased my enemies and caught them;
I did not stop until they were conquered.
18:38 Pss 36:12; 47:3
38 I struck them down so they could not get up;
they fell beneath my feet.
39 You have armed me with strength for the battle;
You have subdued my enemies under my feet.
18:40 Pss 21:12; 94:23
40 You placed my foot on their necks.
I have destroyed all who hated me.
18:41 Ps 50:22
41 They called for help, but no one came to their rescue.
They even cried to the LORD, but He refused to answer.
18:42 Ps 83:13
42 I ground them as fine as dust in the wind.
I swept them into the gutter like dirt.
18:43 2 Sam 3:1 Ps 89:27 Isa 55:5
43 You gave me victory over my accusers.
You appointed me ruler over nations;
people I don't even know now serve me.
18:44 Ps 66:3
44 As soon as they hear of me, they submit;
foreign nations cringe before me.
45 They all lose their courage
and come trembling from their strongholds.

46 The LORD lives! Praise to my Rock!
May the God of my salvation be exalted!
18:47 Pss 47:3; 94:1-2; 144:2
47 He is the God who pays back those who harm me;
He subdues the nations under me
48 and rescues me from my enemies.
18:48 Pss 3:7; 27:5-6
You hold me safe beyond the reach of my enemies;
You save me from violent opponents.
18:49 Ps 108:1 *Rom 15:9
49 For this, O LORD, I will praise You among the nations;
I will sing praises to Your name.
18:50 Pss 21:1; 28:8; 89:4
50 You give great victories to Your king;
You show unfailing love to Your anointed,
to David and all his descendants forever.

▸ WORSHIP
18:46 The Lord lives! Every interaction we have with God—ones of love or hate, of trust or mistrust—presupposes a belief that a God exists to have these feelings toward. Those who approach God must believe that He is (Hebrews 11:6). Every benefit we obtain comes because God is real. Because God exists, we have life—abundant and eternal. We have joined the family of God and have the assurance that God lives—within us, of all places! Because God lives in intimate, personal union with us, we know that He will not allow us to be destroyed. God, through Christ, is in such union with us that our destruction would mean His destruction. Thus, we can rejoice that "The LORD Lives!" (***See Worship**> OT> Music> Psalms> Thanksgiving> Individual,* TopicGuide page A27.)

18:49 David's response to God's protection is praise. He is determined to praise God even among the Gentiles. Paul cites this verse to explain how the work of Christ united Jews and Gentiles into one body committed to the worship of God (Romans 15:9).

PSALM 19

For the choir director: A psalm of David.

1 The heavens proclaim the glory of God. 19:1 Gen 1:6-8 Rom 1:19-20
The skies display His craftsmanship.
2 Day after day they continue to speak; 19:2 Ps 74:16
night after night they make Him known.
3 They speak without a sound or word;
their voice is never heard.*
4 Yet their message has gone throughout the earth, 19:4 *Rom 10:18
and their words to all the world.

God has made a home in the heavens for the sun.
5 It bursts forth like a radiant bridegroom after his wedding.
It rejoices like a great athlete eager to run the race.
6 The sun rises at one end of the heavens 19:6 Ps 113:3
and follows its course to the other end.
Nothing can hide from its heat.

7 The instructions of the LORD are perfect, 19:7 Pss 23:3; 36:9; 111:7; 119:14, 98-100, 160
reviving the soul.
The decrees of the LORD are trustworthy,
making wise the simple.
8 The commandments of the LORD are right, 19:8 Pss 12:6; 119:128
bringing joy to the heart.
The commands of the LORD are clear,
giving insight for living.
9 Reverence for the LORD is pure, 19:9 Ps 119:138, 142
lasting forever.
The laws of the LORD are true;
each one is fair.
10 They are more desirable than gold, 19:10 Ps 119:127
even the finest gold.
They are sweeter than honey,
even honey dripping from the comb.

19:3 Or *There is no speech or language where their voice is not heard.*

▶ **GOD**

19:1-4 We see God everywhere. Have you heard a thunderstorm speak about God? Have you seen something of Him revealed in a fluttering butterfly? For the psalmist, it was not necessary to look down at his scroll to learn about God—he could look into the sky and hear a sermon on the power of his Creator God. This message goes out to the whole earth (19:4) with the rising and setting of the sun. Look up and marvel at God's power as He sustains His creation and commit to making your life speak of the greatness of God. (***See God****> God's Attributes> All-Powerful> His creation reflects His power,* TopicGuide page A15.)

19:1-2 All of nature reveals the glory of God, but the psalmist focuses on one part—the sky. The heavens and skies of 19:1 recall the Creation story (Genesis 1:1-8), as do the day and night of 19:2. Day and night provide the two perspectives from which we observe different dimensions of God's glory.

19:3-4 The heavens bear a message without sound. They constantly bear witness to the glory and majesty of God. It is a witness that humanity's sin muffles and distorts, but it is always present, silently pointing to the Creator (compare Romans 1:20).

▶ **GOD**

19:7 The law is perfect. Whatever you think about the way the Old Testament law applies to us today, it remains God's perfect revelation of who He is, who we are, and how God views the world. You certainly can't rely on the good works of the law to justify you before God (Galatians 2:6), but God's law can revive you, give you wisdom and joy (19:8), and reward you if you obey (19:11). If you need more joy or more wisdom, then read and prayerfully apply God's law to your life. (***See God****> God's Attributes> True> God doesn't lie but keeps His word,* TopicGuide page A18.)

19:7-11 The several terms used for the law of God essentially overlap. Taken together, they designate the whole of God's revealed instructions to mankind. The law of God is pure, true, and eternal; it animates the soul, imparts wisdom, and brings deep joy.

19:11 Ps 17:4 Prov 29:18-19

[11] They are a warning to Your servant,
a great reward for those who obey them.

19:12 Pss 51:1-2; 90:8; 139:23-24

[12] How can I know all the sins lurking in my heart?
Cleanse me from these hidden faults.

19:13 Pss 25:11; 32:2

[13] Keep Your servant from deliberate sins!
Don't let them control me.
Then I will be free of guilt
and innocent of great sin.

19:14 Pss 18:2; 104:34

[14] May the words of my mouth
and the meditation of my heart
be pleasing to You,
O LORD, my rock and my redeemer.

PSALM 20

For the choir director: A psalm of David.

20:1 Ps 46:7, 11

[1] In times of trouble, may the LORD answer your cry.
May the name of the God of Jacob keep you safe from all harm.

20:2 Pss 3:4; 110:2

[2] May He send you help from His sanctuary
and strengthen you from Jerusalem.*

20:3 Ps 51:19 Acts 10:4

[3] May He remember all your gifts
and look favorably on your burnt offerings. *Interlude*

20:4 Pss 21:2; 145:19

[4] May He grant your heart's desires
and make all your plans succeed.

20:2 Hebrew *Zion.*

19:11-14 The psalmist is moved to reflect on his failure to abide by the perfect law of God and recognizes that his only help is God, who alone can cleanse him. He follows the law of Moses in distinguishing between conscious ("deliberate") and unconscious ("hidden") sins while accepting responsibility for both (see Numbers 15:27-36). David concludes by joining the heavens in praise of his God.

20:1 The trouble in view is imminent battle. This is made clear by the expected victory and victory banner of verse 5 and the chariots and horses of verse 7. The congregation is pleading that the life of the king be spared in battle.

20:2-3 Solomon prayed for God to hear from His Temple His people when they marched to war (1 Kings 8:44-45). Praying in like manner, the congregation expresses the hope that God will look favorably upon the king's sacrifices.

FOR THE NEXT *GOD IS ABSOLUTE TRUTH* FEATURE SEE PAGE 1200.

BECAUSE GOD IS ABSOLUTE TRUTH

I will believe what He says and live accordingly.

The commandments of the LORD are right, bringing joy to the heart. . . .
The laws of the LORD are true; each one is fair.

PSALM 19:8, 9

5 May we shout for joy when we hear of your victory
and raise a victory banner in the name of our God.
May the LORD answer all your prayers.

6 Now I know that the LORD rescues His anointed king.
He will answer him from His holy heaven
and rescue him by His great power.
7 Some nations boast of their chariots and horses,
but we boast in the name of the LORD our God.
8 Those nations will fall down and collapse,
but we will rise up and stand firm.

9 Give victory to our king, O LORD!
Answer our cry for help.

20:5 1 Sam 1:17; Pss 9:14; 60:4
20:6 Pss 28:8; 41:11; Isa 58:9
20:7 2 Chr 32:8; Ps 33:16-17
20:9 Ps 17:6

PSALM 21

For the choir director: A psalm of David.

1 How the king rejoices in Your strength, O LORD!
He shouts with joy because You give him victory.
2 For You have given him his heart's desire;
You have withheld nothing he requested. *Interlude*

3 You welcomed him back with success and prosperity.
You placed a crown of finest gold on his head.
4 He asked You to preserve his life,
and You granted his request.
The days of his life stretch on forever.

21:1 Ps 59:16-17
21:2 Ps 37:4
21:4 Pss 61:6; 91:16; 133:3

▸ MINISTRY
20:5 Fly your banner. Before the age of innovation changed the way people waged war, soldiers looked to the banner. In battle, one soldier was assigned to carry the flag, or guidon. This flag allowed the soldiers to see where their company was fighting. They rallied 'round the flag. But the one who carried the flag was most vulnerable because he was a likely target of the enemy. "Flying the flag" for Jesus can also make us a target—of those who resent our Leader. Are you willing to fly your banner by telling others that you serve Jesus—even if that means that you might draw discrimination? Honor our God by flying His banner everywhere you go. (***See Ministry****> Great Commission> Witness> Christ issues the call of the gospel,* TopicGuide page A56.)

20:6 Now an individual (perhaps the king) or the people with one voice affirm that God has heard from His holy heaven, of which the sanctuary in Jerusalem (20:2) is only a shadow.

▸ GOD
20:7 Boasting in our God. In what do you feel pride? Your physical appearance? Your paycheck? What would it look like to boast in God? He is our great Provider, yet we usually fail to acknowledge this fact. We are rarely too busy or too shy to let other people know about our various successes and witty comments. Why, therefore, are we always too busy or too shy to spread the good news about our great God? Value God. Value His Word. Take pride in God's work in your life, and don't be shy to tell others about it. (***See God****> Relationship> Barriers> Refusing to honor God as God,* TopicGuide page A14.)

20:7-8 Israel's success in war is based not on its resources or numbers but on the strength of God, who fights for the people. This was clear from the very beginning of Israel's history (Exodus 14–15).

21:1-2 The king rejoices because God has heard his request and the request of his people (Psalm 20). In 20:4, the desire of the king's heart was victory in battle, and God has granted that desire. The king's praise acknowledges that the victory belonged to God (compare 20:6-8).

▸ GOD
21:2 The true desires of our heart. In this passage, does God say He will give the king anything his heart desires or does He promise to give the king new desires? In this psalm, God promises the former—to give the king all the blessings that the king can imagine, even "eternal" blessings that are beyond his ability to fully understand (21:6; see also 20:2). These grand blessings include the destruction of every enemy who would so much as plan to attack the king (21:11). It may be hard to believe, but all these blessings are yours, too—God promises to bless all those who are born again with every imaginable spiritual blessing (Ephesians 1:3), including the destruction of our enemies (Revelation 6:9-11). Praise the Lord for the blessings He pours out on His persevering people! (***See God****> God's Attributes> True> God doesn't lie but keeps His word,* TopicGuide page A18.)

21:3-7 The context of these verses is the king's return from battle. Victory and salvation characterize the king's life. Psalm 21:4 either speaks hyperbolically or envisions the eternal character of David's dynasty. God's victory has brought honor, splendor, and majesty to the king. These are qualities of God reflected by the king, who has been in God's presence and basks in His love.

21:5 Pss 8:5; 96:6
5 Your victory brings him great honor,
and You have clothed him with splendor and majesty.
6 You have endowed him with eternal blessings
and given him the joy of Your presence.
21:7 Pss 112:6; 125:1
7 For the king trusts in the LORD.
The unfailing love of the Most High will keep him from stumbling.

21:8 Isa 10:10
8 You will capture all Your enemies.
Your strong right hand will seize all who hate You.
21:9 Lam 2:2 Mal 4:1
9 You will throw them in a flaming furnace
when You appear.
The LORD will consume them in His anger;
fire will devour them.
10 You will wipe their children from the face of the earth;
they will never have descendants.
21:11 Ps 2:1-3
11 Although they plot against You,
their evil schemes will never succeed.
21:12 Pss 7:12-13; 18:40
12 For they will turn and run
when they see Your arrows aimed at them.
21:13 Pss 59:16; 81:1
13 Rise up, O LORD, in all Your power.
With music and singing we celebrate Your mighty acts.

PSALM 22

For the choir director: A psalm of David, to be sung to the tune "Doe of the Dawn."

22:1 *Matt 27:46 *Mark 15:34
1 My God, my God, why have You abandoned me?
Why are You so far away when I groan for help?
22:2 Pss 42:3; 88:1
2 Every day I call to You, my God, but You do not answer.
Every night You hear my voice, but I find no relief.

22:3 Pss 99:9; 148:14
3 Yet You are holy,
enthroned on the praises of Israel.
4 Our ancestors trusted in You,
and You rescued them.
5 They cried out to You and were saved.
They trusted in You and were never disgraced.

▶ **GOD**

21:5 Godly rulers and great reward. Have you ever had a godly boss? Happy are those who have leaders who make God's strength their confidence and God's salvation their joy, and are as pleased with the advance of God's kingdom as the advance of their careers. God richly blesses those who serve Him with distinction. Those blessings may not be great power or pay raises, for those things are minor trinkets compared with the spiritual blessings God has for His faithful people (21:6). Serve God, and you will find great reward waiting for you in heaven (1 Corinthians 3:10-14). (***See God****> God's Attributes> True> God doesn't lie but keeps His word,* TopicGuide page A18.)

21:8-12 It is not clear whether God or the king is the subject of these verses; most likely, both are in view. The king must fight, but the victory belongs to God. The scope of this victory, however, surpasses the power of an ordinary king. Therefore, the psalm anticipates the reign of the Messiah and His final triumph over all the enemies of God (2 Thessalonians 1:7-9).

▶ **GOD**

22:1 God never leaves us. From being picked last to play in a grade-school game to being abandoned by a parent or spouse, everybody experiences pain. Is there anyone who has not felt deserted by those they hold dear? David felt this way as he awaited God's response to the trial that initiated his cry for relief. Jesus experienced this sense of abandonment when He accepted separation from God on behalf of all God's people (Galatians 3:5); thus, Jesus quoted this verse as He hung on the cross (Matthew 27:46). You can cry out to God—it's no sin to tell Him exactly how lonely, how empty, how distant you feel from Him. Stop pretending your relationship with God is always perfect; cry out to God when you feel empty of Him, and experience the comfort of God (22:19-22). (***See God****> God's Attributes> True> God doesn't lie but keeps His word,* TopicGuide page A18.)

22:1-5 The psalmist is troubled more by the seeming absence of God than by his actual affliction. The God of Israel was always faithful to His people; the first Israelites trusted Him and were not disappointed. But the psalmist feels abandoned by God in his plight.

[6] But I am a worm and not a man.
I am scorned and despised by all!
[7] Everyone who sees me mocks me.
They sneer and shake their heads, saying,
[8] "Is this the one who relies on the LORD?
Then let the LORD save him!
If the LORD loves him so much,
let the LORD rescue him!"

[9] Yet You brought me safely from my mother's womb
and led me to trust You at my mother's breast.
[10] I was thrust into Your arms at my birth.
You have been my God from the moment
I was born.

[11] Do not stay so far from me,
for trouble is near,
and no one else can help me.
[12] My enemies surround me like a herd of bulls;
fierce bulls of Bashan have hemmed me in!
[13] Like lions they open their jaws against me,
roaring and tearing into their prey.
[14] My life is poured out like water,
and all my bones are out of joint.
My heart is like wax,
melting within me.
[15] My strength has dried up like sunbaked clay.
My tongue sticks to the roof of my mouth.
You have laid me in the dust and left me for dead.
[16] My enemies surround me like a pack of dogs;
an evil gang closes in on me.
They have pierced my hands and feet.
[17] I can count all my bones.
My enemies stare at me and gloat.
[18] They divide my garments among themselves
and throw dice* for my clothing.

[19] O LORD, do not stay far away!
You are my strength; come quickly to my aid!
[20] Save me from the sword;
spare my precious life from these dogs.
[21] Snatch me from the lion's jaws
and from the horns of these wild oxen.

22:6 Job 25:6; Ps 31:11; Isa 41:14; 49:7
22:7 Isa 53:3; Matt 27:39; Mark 15:29-30
22:8 Matt 27:43
22:10 Isa 46:3
22:11 Ps 72:12
22:13 Ps 17:12
22:14 Job 30:16; Ps 31:9-10
22:15 Pss 38:10; 104:29; *John 19:28
22:16 Ps 59:6-7; Matt 27:35; John 20:25
22:18 *Matt 27:35; *Mark 15:24; Luke 23:34; John 19:23-24
22:19 Pss 22:11; 70:5
22:20 Pss 35:17; 37:14
22:21 Pss 34:4; 118:5; 120:1

22:18 Hebrew *cast lots.*

22:12-18 Bulls from the territory of Bashan were known to be the largest bulls of the region.

▶ GOD
22:18 Why believe Jesus? Many people wonder why Christians trust the words of Jesus more than those attributed to Mohammad, Buddha, or any other religious figure. It's a fair question that deserves an answer. One reason is that many years before Jesus came to earth, God left clues about the future Messiah in His Word. This verse is an example of one of those clues, as it gives a preview of what happened at the foot of Jesus' cross a thousand years prior to the event (Luke 23:34). We can trust that Jesus truly is the Son of God because of the clues that God left foretelling Jesus' birth, death, and resurrection. (***See God****> God's Attributes> True> God doesn't lie but keeps His word,* TopicGuide page A18.)

22:22 *Heb 2:12

22 I will proclaim Your name to my brothers and sisters.*
I will praise You among your assembled people.

22:23 Pss 33:8; 86:12; 135:19-20

23 Praise the LORD, all you who fear Him!
Honor Him, all you descendants of Jacob!
Show Him reverence, all you descendants of Israel!

22:24 Pss 27:9; 31:22 Heb 5:7

24 For He has not ignored or belittled the suffering of the needy.
He has not turned His back on them,
but has listened to their cries for help.

22:25 Pss 35:18; 40:9-10

25 I will praise You in the great assembly.
I will fulfill my vows in the presence of those who worship You.

22:26 Pss 40:16; 69:32; 107:9

26 The poor will eat and be satisfied.
All who seek the LORD will praise Him.
Their hearts will rejoice with everlasting joy.
27 The whole earth will acknowledge the LORD and return to Him.
All the families of the nations will bow down before Him.

22:28 Ps 47:6-8

28 For royal power belongs to the LORD.
He rules all the nations.

29 Let the rich of the earth feast and worship.
Bow before Him, all who are mortal,
all whose lives will end as dust.

22:30 Ps 102:18, 28

30 Our children will also serve Him.
Future generations will hear about the wonders of the Lord.
31 His righteous acts will be told to those not yet born.
They will hear about everything He has done.

PSALM 23

A psalm of David.

23:1 John 10:11 1 Pet 2:25

1 The LORD is my shepherd;
I have all that I need.

23:2 Pss 5:8; 46:4 Ezek 34:14 Rev 7:17

2 He lets me rest in green meadows;
He leads me beside peaceful streams.
3 He renews my strength.

23:3 Pss 5:8; 19:7; 85:13

He guides me along right paths,
bringing honor to His name.

22:22 Hebrew *my brothers.*

22:22-24 The circumstances of 22:1-18 are now reversed. No longer does the psalmist despair at the apparent absence of God. Once again he revels in the presence of God and praises Him before the people. And now the people who surround him are not those who mock, but those who join him in praising God.

22:27-31 The psalmist's deliverance leads him to announce the reign of God that will extend throughout the whole earth, encompassing both rich and poor, and, in fact, all mortals past and present. This is a fitting end to a psalm that points so vividly to the suffering of Christ. His suffering was merely the prelude to His now-and-future reign.

▶GOD

23:1 Under His care. Psalm 23 is most often read at funerals or in times of crisis, but it fits right wherever you are. In a world that seeks to mold us into its image through dissatisfaction and fear, we need to be constantly reminded of God's provision and protection. When we live in God's embrace, we can walk through the darkest valley and not fear, for we know God is close to us, protecting and comforting us (23:4). You can live every moment beneath His guardian staff, unafraid in times of danger and comforted in times of loss. (***See God*> *God's Attributes*> *True*> *God doesn't lie but keeps His word,* TopicGuide page A18.)

23:1 The shepherd is Yahweh, the faithful God of Israel who guided His people out of Egypt and provided for them through the wilderness. This psalm allows an individual to claim the Lord as his or her own shepherd. The protection and provision evoked by the image of the shepherd belong to all of God's people.

4 Even when I walk
through the darkest valley,*
I will not be afraid,
for You are close beside me.
Your rod and Your staff
protect and comfort me.
5 You prepare a feast for me
in the presence of my enemies.
You honor me by anointing my head with oil.
My cup overflows with blessings.
6 Surely Your goodness and unfailing love will pursue me
all the days of my life,
and I will live in the house of the LORD
forever.

23:4 Pss 27:1; 107:14
23:5 Pss 16:5; 78:19; 92:10
23:6 Pss 25:6-7, 10; 27:4-6

PSALM 24

A psalm of David.

1 The earth is the LORD's, and everything in it.
The world and all its people belong to Him.
2 For He laid the earth's foundation on the seas
and built it on the ocean depths.

3 Who may climb the mountain of the LORD?
Who may stand in His holy place?
4 Only those whose hands and hearts are pure,
who do not worship idols
and never tell lies.
5 They will receive the LORD's blessing
and have a right relationship with God their savior.

24:1 Ps 89:11; *1 Cor 10:26
24:3 Pss 15:1; 65:4
24:4 Job 17:9; Pss 51:10; 73:1; Matt 5:8
24:5 Deut 11:26-27

23:4 Or *the dark valley of death.*

▸ GOD
23:4 Walking in the shadows. There is no passage in the Bible that promises that Christians will live easy lives. In fact, the Bible teaches the exact opposite. The psalmist assumes that God's people will walk through dark valleys, face fearsome evil, and have enemies (23:5). The apostle Paul echoed this sentiment as he taught the new followers of Jesus that "we must suffer many hardships to enter the Kingdom of God" (Acts 14:22). Do not be surprised when you face trials, gain enemies, and taste death (1 Peter 4:12). If you are not experiencing much trouble in this life, then you should ask yourself whether you are really walking the narrow path of faith, truly confronting sin, and honestly seeking to engage this wicked world with the glorious gospel. Trust God and risk it all—then you will know the comfort of God. (***See God***> *God's Attributes> True> God doesn't lie but keeps His word,* TopicGuide page A18.)

23:4 To this day, a shepherd in the Middle East carries a rod as a weapon against animals that would harm his sheep and a staff to guide the sheep. In the psalm, the rod and staff represent God's constant protection and guidance. Psalm 23:2, 3 describe the rest and peace that come from being led and protected by the heavenly Shepherd.

23:5 The imagery now shifts from the shepherd's field to the banquet table, but the message remains the same: God defends His people and provides for them. The overflowing cup and anointing oil suggest the great joy that comes with God's care.

23:6 "Unfailing love" refers to God's covenant faithfulness to His people. This faithfulness is experienced most profoundly when we are welcomed to worship God.

24:1-2 All things on earth belong to the Lord because He is the Creator of all things. In ancient creation myths, the seas and depths (literally, rivers) were monstrous opponents of the gods. For the psalmist, however, they are mere elements of creation ordered by God without struggle or resistance.

24:3-6 The Temple was situated atop the hill known as Mount Zion, just north of Jerusalem. Moral purity was required of those who would ascend to worship God. Only one man has met the requirement of absolute moral purity—Christ Jesus. He entered the Most Holy Place through His death and righteousness to secure right standing with God for His people, thus becoming their Savior (Hebrews 9:11-28).

▸ GOD
24:4 Coming before God. Just for a moment, visualize yourself coming physically into God's presence and standing before His holy throne. What would you do? His holy presence would immediately remind you of your sinfulness. If you are smart, you would throw yourself at His feet in repentance and awe. But we are always in God's presence. That's why we need to repent of our sin continually. To further your relationship with Him, there is nothing better than developing a lifestyle of turning from sin to God. (***See God***> *Relationship> God Enables> Relationship with God requires purity,* TopicGuide page A14.)

24:6 Ps 27:8
6 Such people may seek You
and worship in Your presence, O God of Jacob. *Interlude*

7 Open up, ancient gates!
Open up, ancient doors,
and let the King of glory enter.
24:8 Exod 15:3, 6 Ps 76:3-6
8 Who is the King of glory?
The LORD, strong and mighty;
the LORD, invincible in battle.
24:9 Zech 9:9 Matt 21:5
9 Open up, ancient gates!
Open up, ancient doors,
and let the King of glory enter.
10 Who is the King of glory?
The LORD of Heaven's Armies—
He is the King of glory. *Interlude*

PSALM 25*

A psalm of David.

1 O LORD, I give my life to You.
2 I trust in You, my God!
Do not let me be disgraced,
or let my enemies rejoice in my defeat.
25:3 Pss 37:9; 40:1 Isa 49:23
3 No one who trusts in You will ever be disgraced,
but disgrace comes to those who try to deceive others.

25:4 Pss 5:8; 86:11
4 Show me the right path, O LORD;
point out the road for me to follow.
25:5 Pss 24:5; 40:1
5 Lead me by Your truth and teach me,
for You are the God who saves me.
All day long I put my hope in You.
25:6 Ps 103:17
6 Remember, O LORD, Your compassion and unfailing love,
which You have shown from long ages past.
25:7 Job 13:26 Ps 51:1
7 Do not remember the rebellious sins of my youth.
Remember me in the light of Your unfailing love,
for You are merciful, O LORD.

25 This psalm is a Hebrew acrostic poem; each verse begins with a successive letter of the Hebrew alphabet.

▸ WORSHIP
24:10 The King of Glory. The psalmist has a grand vision of God—a mighty warrior, striding in from battle, welcomed by the inhabitants of the city as their great defender. This psalm may be sung by Christians to celebrate their Divine Warrior, Jesus Christ, who has defeated our enemies and is worthy to receive all glory, honor, and praise. Is God your defender, or do you fight your battle against sin and the world by yourself? Stand up and celebrate the rescue of all God's people from the clutches of Satan. (***See Worship****> OT> Fasting and Prayer> Prayer> Psalms> Liturgies,* TopicGuide page A26; also ***see Worship****> OT> Music> Psalms> Liturgy> Temple Liturgy,* TopicGuide page A27.)

25:1-3 David gives an intensely personal statement of his trust in God. He knows God will not allow those who trust in Him to be shamed. This confidence, however, does not preclude David from petitioning the Lord to uphold his cause.

25:4-5 David's trust (25:1-2) expresses itself in a fervent desire to walk in God's ways. The faithful seek God not only in trust but also in submission. Recognizing his own inability, David prays for guidance and strength, confident that God is inclined to honor such requests (25:8-9, 12).

▸ WORSHIP
25:7 "Do not remember the . . . sins of my youth." No matter what age you are, when you look back, you can remember sins that you committed. Do these sins haunt you? Perhaps you strayed from your moral commitments, dishonored your parents, or brought shame on yourself. Perhaps your sin was as simple as ignoring God for a few months, a few years—or a few decades. Whatever your sins, God will forgive them when you confess them to Him. You can live free from the gnawing guilt of the past. God doesn't want you to limp along with a guilty conscience; He wants you to walk in boldness and confidence that you are forgiven. Do a moral inventory, writing down all your sins. Confess any nagging sins, and if possible make restitution. (***See Worship****> OT> Music> Psalms> Lament> Individual,* TopicGuide page A27.)

8 The LORD is good and does what is right;
He shows the proper path to those who go astray.
9 He leads the humble in doing right,
teaching them His way.
10 The LORD leads with unfailing love and faithfulness
all who keep His covenant and obey His demands.

11 For the honor of Your name, O LORD,
forgive my many, many sins.
12 Who are those who fear the LORD?
He will show them the path they should choose.
13 They will live in prosperity,
and their children will inherit the land.
14 The LORD is a friend to those who fear Him.
He teaches them His covenant.
15 My eyes are always on the LORD,
for He rescues me from the traps of my enemies.

16 Turn to me and have mercy,
for I am alone and in deep distress.
17 My problems go from bad to worse.
Oh, save me from them all!
18 Feel my pain and see my trouble.
Forgive all my sins.
19 See how many enemies I have
and how viciously they hate me!
20 Protect me! Rescue my life from them!
Do not let me be disgraced, for in You I take refuge.
21 May integrity and honesty protect me,
for I put my hope in You.

22 O God, ransom Israel
from all its troubles.

25:8 Ps 86:5
25:9 Pss 23:3; 32:8
25:10 Pss 40:11; 103:17-18
25:11 Ps 79:9
25:13 Pss 37:11; 69:36
25:14 Prov 3:32; John 7:17
25:15 Pss 31:4; 123:2; 141:8
25:16 Ps 69:16
25:17 Pss 40:12; 107:6
25:18 Pss 31:7; 103:3
25:19 Pss 3:1; 9:13
25:20 Pss 25:2; 86:2
25:21 Pss 25:3; 41:12

PSALM 26

A psalm of David.

1 Declare me innocent, O LORD,
for I have acted with integrity;
I have trusted in the LORD without wavering.

26:1 Pss 7:8; 13:5; Heb 10:23

▶ **GOD**

25:14 Friendship with God. Just think about what it means to be a friend of God! What do friends do for each other? This verse mentions that God reveals mysteries to us—has He done that for you? He has shown those who fear Him the depths of His promises and the heights of His love. Because the Holy Spirit lives inside you as a believer, He will help you to understand the mysteries of God's Word. How amazing that God chooses to reveal His secrets to us! Thank Him for His friendship. (***See God****> God's Names> Son> Friend of sinners,* TopicGuide page A18.)

25:15-21 This psalm of confident praise turns into a lament as David expresses his deep distress over the enemies who seek his harm and over his sin. However, his loneliness and fear have served to heighten his dependence on God, so his distress has not become despair. He is able to conclude with strong affirmations of his trust and hope in God.

26:1-3 The psalmist is not affirming sinlessness but rather his wholehearted trust in the Lord, which is required of those who would enter God's presence. In fact, David acknowledges his constant need of God's covenantal love and mercy. "Truth" may be better rendered "faithfulness," further grounding the psalmist's confidence in God, not himself.

26:2 Pss 7:9; 139:23 — 2 Put me on trial, LORD, and cross-examine me.
Test my motives and my heart.
26:3 Pss 1:2; 48:9 — 3 For I am always aware of Your unfailing love,
and I have lived according to Your truth.
26:4 Ps 1:1 — 4 I do not spend time with liars
or go along with hypocrites.
26:5 Pss 1:1; 31:6; 139:21 — 5 I hate the gatherings of those who do evil,
and I refuse to join in with the wicked.
26:6 Ps 43:3-4 — 6 I wash my hands to declare my innocence.
I come to Your altar, O LORD,
26:7 Ps 9:1 — 7 singing a song of thanksgiving
and telling of all Your wonders.
26:8 Ps 27:4 — 8 I love Your sanctuary, LORD,
the place where Your glorious presence dwells.

26:9 Ps 28:3 — 9 Don't let me suffer the fate of sinners.
Don't condemn me along with murderers.
10 Their hands are dirty with evil schemes,
and they constantly take bribes.
26:11 Pss 26:1; 69:18 — 11 But I am not like that; I live with integrity.
So redeem me and show me mercy.
26:12 Pss 22:22; 27:11; 40:2 — 12 Now I stand on solid ground,
and I will publicly praise the LORD.

PSALM 27

A psalm of David.

27:1 Pss 18:28; 118:6, 14 — 1 The LORD is my light and my salvation—
so why should I be afraid?
The LORD is my fortress, protecting me from danger,
so why should I tremble?
2 When evil people come to devour me,
when my enemies and foes attack me,
they will stumble and fall.

▸ WORSHIP

26:2 Test me, O God. Most of us shy away from asking God to test our souls. After all, we know the darkness we have inside—the sins we haven't confessed, the thoughts that aren't godly, the attitudes that don't measure up to God's standards. Yet God's testing is one of the most helpful things He can do to reveal our need of Him. When God tests our motives and affections, He reveals what doesn't meet His criteria. He exposes those areas that we have covered up or that we don't realize are sinful. He purifies our hearts. Asking God to put you on trial may be painful in the short run, but in the long run it will bring joy and fulfillment. (***See Worship***> *OT> Music> Psalms> Lament> Individual,* TopicGuide page A27.)

26:4-5 The pursuit of righteousness is accompanied by contempt for evil (compare Psalm 1:1).

26:11-12 The psalmist is not asserting sinlessness; that is clear from his cry for mercy. He is affirming his commitment to the Lord, which leads him to abandon the way of the wicked (26:9-10) and publicly praise his God.

▸ ADOPTION

26:12 Take a stand for the Lord. There are many places in our lives where we may find it difficult to take a stand for the Lord. For some people, the workplace can be a hostile environment for expressing the faith. Others may find resistance within their own extended families. But no matter where we are, we must put God first. Ask God to show you how to best stand up for Him. He may lead you to be bold and forthright. He may also lead you to be gentle and tactful. Each situation is different. We never change the message—the gospel of Jesus Christ—but we do change how we present it to maximize its power. Make this a matter of special prayer as you decide to stand up for the Lord in those difficult places. (***See Adoption***> *With Christ> Servants> Witness for Christ,* TopicGuide page A37.)

27:1-3 Light is an image frequently associated with God (Psalms 18:28; 44:3; 56:13; Isaiah 9:2; 49:6; John 1:4; 8:12). Light has the ability to dispel darkness instantaneously, and the psalmist is confident that God will dispel the darkness enveloping him as his enemies surround him.

3 Though a mighty army surrounds me,
my heart will not be afraid.
Even if I am attacked,
I will remain confident.

27:3
Pss 3:6-7; 14:4

4 The one thing I ask of the LORD—
the thing I seek most—
is to live in the house of the LORD all the days
of my life,
delighting in the LORD's perfections
and meditating in His Temple.

27:4
Pss 23:6; 26:8

5 For He will conceal me there when troubles come;
He will hide me in His sanctuary.
He will place me out of reach on a high rock.

27:5
Pss 17:8; 31:20

6 Then I will hold my head high
above my enemies who surround me.
At His sanctuary I will offer sacrifices with shouts of joy,
singing and praising the LORD with music.

27:6
Pss 13:6; 107:22

7 Hear me as I pray, O LORD.
Be merciful and answer me!

27:7
Ps 13:3

8 My heart has heard You say, "Come and talk with Me."
And my heart responds, "LORD, I am coming."

27:8
Ps 105:4

9 Do not turn Your back on me.
Do not reject Your servant in anger.
You have always been my helper.
Don't leave me now; don't abandon me,
O God of my salvation!

27:9
Pss 6:1; 40:17; 69:17; 94:14

10 Even if my father and mother abandon me,
the LORD will hold me close.

27:10
Isa 40:11; 49:15

11 Teach me how to live, O LORD.
Lead me along the right path,
for my enemies are waiting for me.

27:11
Pss 5:8; 25:4; 86:11

12 Do not let me fall into their hands.
For they accuse me of things I've never done;
with every breath they threaten me with violence.

27:12
Ps 35:11
Matt 26:60
Acts 9:1

▶ GOD

27:4 One thing. If you could ask God for one thing for yourself, what would it be? Wisdom? Long life? World peace? The psalmist tells God he wants only one thing—to live in the Temple. He wants to live in God's presence with God's people and worship God with every fiber of his being. What distracts you from the joys of worshiping God? What keeps you from delighting in everything that God is? Set it aside and take God as your highest passion. (***See God***> *God's Attributes> True> God doesn't lie but keeps His word,* TopicGuide page A18.)

27:4-6 The psalmist draws his strength from the presence of the Lord. The presence of God was located most emphatically within His sanctuary. Within the sanctuary, the psalmist worships and reflects on God's beauty, finding strength to face whatever troubles or enemies await him. Troubles and enemies shrink by comparison when God's people take in His perfections.

27:7-10 The psalmist prefaces his specific requests (27:11-12) by expressing the more general desire to be heard by God. He recognizes that God's hearing is an act of mercy because his sinfulness deserves God's anger.

▶ GOD

27:10 Abandoned by family. By the end of his days, David's family had seen its share of troubles. Fussing with his brothers (1 Samuel 17:28) was the least of his worries. His wife had been torn away from him (1 Samuel 25:44), then returned, only to turn against him (2 Samuel 6:16). David had sons die prematurely (2 Samuel 12:15-19) and one attempt to kill him (2 Samuel 18). Perhaps people, even your own relatives, have discarded you. God has a message for you—He will hold you close. He will never, ever reject you. Nothing can separate God's people from His love (Romans 8:31-39). (***See God***> *God's Attributes> True> God doesn't lie but keeps His word,* TopicGuide page A18.)

27:13 Pss 116:9; 142:5 Isa 38:11
13 Yet I am confident I will see the LORD's goodness
while I am here in the land of the living.

27:14 Pss 31:24; 37:34
14 Wait patiently for the LORD.
Be brave and courageous.
Yes, wait patiently for the LORD.

PSALM 28

A psalm of David.

28:1 Pss 18:2; 35:22; 83:1; 88:4-5
1 I pray to you, O LORD, my rock.
Do not turn a deaf ear to me.
For if You are silent,
I might as well give up and die.

28:2 Ps 141:2 Lam 2:19 1 Tim 2:8
2 Listen to my prayer for mercy
as I cry out to You for help,
as I lift my hands toward Your holy sanctuary.

28:3 Pss 26:9-10; 55:21; 62:4 Jer 9:8
3 Do not drag me away with the wicked—
with those who do evil—
those who speak friendly words to their neighbors
while planning evil in their hearts.

28:4 Ps 62:12 2 Tim 4:14 Rev 18:6
4 Give them the punishment they so richly deserve!
Measure it out in proportion to their wickedness.
Pay them back for all their evil deeds!
Give them a taste of what they have done to others.

28:5 Isa 5:12
5 They care nothing for what the LORD has done
or for what His hands have made.
So He will tear them down,
and they will never be rebuilt!

28:6 Ps 116:1
6 Praise the LORD!
For He has heard my cry for mercy.

27:13-14 The psalm concludes with an honest affirmation of the tensions that accompany belief. The psalmist is confident God's goodness will prevail, but he acknowledges the need to endure courageously while God unfolds His will.

▸ WORSHIP
28:1 Is this really true? Are there some mornings when you wake up and wonder whether you've been lied to about God? Whether the whole Jesus thing is just a fabrication? Whether or not God exists? Well, you aren't crazy. Everyone has these moments. David expresses these sorts of questions in the Psalms—"God, where are you? Are you there? Prove it by saving me!" God does not reject this honest articulation of our greatest fears—He respects it. According to the Psalms, He hears our cries for answers, for mercy, and for faith. And rather than reject us, He becomes our shield and fills our empty hearts with joy and trust (28:7). Be honest with God about your thoughts and feelings, and you will discover He is more than able to hold you securely in His arms of love (28:9). (***See Worship****> OT> Posture> Hands uplifted,* TopicGuide page A28.)

28:1 God is described as a rock, a metaphor that communicates a sense of God's strength, stability, and ability to offer security for the believer. David's language suggests that he has been making his request for some time without response. David prefers death to such silence. For him, life loses its meaning if communion with God is not possible.

▸ WORSHIP
28:5 God's justice. King David felt a deep sense of injustice over the way his enemies treated him. But he didn't take that sense and inflict judgment on them. Instead, he cried out to God and asked Him to make things right. He understood the motives of the wicked, that they weren't afraid of God. Today, Jesus has given us an even greater command—to love our enemies. After all, we were once enemies of God also, before we received Him as our Savior and Lord. God will ensure justice. We don't need to worry about what people have inflicted on us. Instead, we turn those hurts over to God and pray for those who are against Him. (***See Worship****> OT> Music> Psalms> Lament> Individual,* TopicGuide page A27.)

28:5 These words may have been spoken by a priest in response to the request of the previous verses. This would explain the sudden change in tone in the following verses. The wicked were guilty of disregarding God's words and deeds.

7 The LORD is my strength and shield.
I trust Him with all my heart.
He helps me, and my heart is filled with joy.
I burst out in songs of thanksgiving.

8 The LORD gives His people strength.
He is a safe fortress for His anointed king.
9 Save Your people!
Bless Israel, Your special possession.*
Lead them like a shepherd,
and carry them in Your arms forever.

28:7 Pss 13:5-6; 16:9; 40:3; 59:17

28:8 Ps 20:6

28:9 Deut 9:29; 32:9 Pss 33:12; 80:1 Isa 40:11

PSALM 29

A psalm of David.

1 Honor the LORD, you heavenly beings*;
honor the LORD for His glory and strength.
2 Honor the LORD for the glory of His name.
Worship the LORD in the splendor of His holiness.

3 The voice of the LORD echoes above the sea.
The God of glory thunders.
The LORD thunders over the mighty sea.
4 The voice of the LORD is powerful;
the voice of the LORD is majestic.
5 The voice of the LORD splits the mighty cedars;
the LORD shatters the cedars of Lebanon.
6 He makes Lebanon's mountains skip like a calf;
He makes Mount Hermon* leap like a young wild ox.
7 The voice of the LORD strikes
with bolts of lightning.
8 The voice of the LORD makes the barren wilderness quake;
the LORD shakes the wilderness of Kadesh.

29:1 1 Chr 16:28-29 Ps 96:7-9

29:4 Ps 68:33

29:5 Isa 2:13

29:6 Deut 3:9 Ps 114:4

29:8 Num 13:26

28:9 Hebrew *Bless Your inheritance.* **29:1** Hebrew *you sons of God.* **29:6** Hebrew *Sirion,* another name for Mount Hermon.

▸ SPIRITUAL WARFARE

28:7 "The LORD is my . . . shield." When King David wrote these words, he had experienced God's deliverance. As a young man, he had to run from King Saul, who was trying to destroy him. David had to sleep in caves, eating whatever he could find on the run. But God protected him, and David eventually was crowned king of all Israel. Yet even before God elevated him, David trusted in God. Before he saw answers to his pleas, he gave thanks to God. We can follow the example of David by singing for joy and giving thanks to God in the midst of our troubles. Trust God with all your heart. (***See Spiritual Warfare**> Resisting Sin and Evil> Embracing Christ> Entrust yourself to God's care*, TopicGuide page A45)

28:8-9 David was not merely a private citizen; he was the anointed king of Israel. As such, his fate was intimately connected to that of the nation. His victories were victories for the nation. This principle anticipates the connection between Jesus, the Davidic King of kings, and His people (Romans 6:3-5; Ephesians 1:3).

29:1-2 The psalm begins with a call to worship addressed to the heavenly assembly of angels that attends God's throne. The call resonates with military overtones. The name of the Lord was a source of strength and victory in battle (Exodus 15:3).

29:3 In the ancient world, the sea was associated with chaos and evil that the gods must defeat to bring order to the created world. The psalmist, however, recognizes that God created the world and everything in it, including the sea. The sea does not rage against God but is merely a work of His hands over which He rules.

29:3-9 The voice of the Lord is likened to the sound of thunder. In Canaanite mythology, it was Baal, the god of storms who controlled the rhythms of nature, whose voice was linked with thunder. But the psalmist counters this fable.

29:5-6 Lebanon was famous for its imposing cedars, yet these impressive trees are metaphorically shattered by the voice of the Lord. Likewise, the mountains of this region, seemingly immovable, spring into motion at the sound of God's powerful voice. The Canaanite symbols of power and strength cannot compare with the God of Israel.

29:9 Ps 26:8
[9] The voice of the LORD twists mighty oaks*
and strips the forests bare.
29:10 Gen 6:17 Ps 10:16
In His Temple everyone shouts, "Glory!"
[10] The LORD rules over the floodwaters.
29:11 Pss 28:8; 37:11 Isa 40:29
The LORD reigns as king forever.
[11] The LORD gives His people strength.
The LORD blesses them with peace.

PSALM 30

A psalm of David. A song for the dedication of the Temple.

30:1 Pss 25:2; 35:19, 24; 118:28; 145:1
[1] I will exalt You, LORD, for You rescued me.
You refused to let my enemies triumph over me.
30:2 Pss 6:2; 88:13
[2] O LORD my God, I cried to You for help,
and You restored my health.
30:3 Pss 28:1; 86:13
[3] You brought me up from the grave,* O LORD.
You kept me from falling into the pit of death.

30:4 Pss 97:12; 149:1
[4] Sing to the LORD, all you godly ones!
Praise His holy name.
30:5 Pss 103:9; 118:1
[5] For His anger lasts only a moment,
but His favor lasts a lifetime!
Weeping may last through the night,
but joy comes with the morning.

30:6 Ps 10:6
[6] When I was prosperous, I said,
"Nothing can stop me now!"
30:7 Ps 104:29
[7] Your favor, O LORD, made me as secure as a mountain.
Then You turned away from me, and I was shattered.

[8] I cried out to You, O LORD.
I begged the Lord for mercy, saying,
30:9 Ps 6:5
[9] "What will You gain if I die,
if I sink into the grave?
Can my dust praise You?
Can it tell of Your faithfulness?
30:10 Pss 4:1; 27:7, 9
[10] Hear me, LORD, and have mercy on me.
Help me, O LORD."

29:9 Or *causes the deer to writhe in labor.* 30:3 Hebrew *from Sheol.*

▸ WORSHIP

29:10 God in the storm. What do you think of when you see lightning blaze from cloud to cloud? Hear thunder roar? Watch hurricanes spin and grow? We worship the God who rules over nature. Even the most powerful and deadly natural phenomena are not outside God's control. We may rightly question how God can allow tornadoes, tidal waves, and floods to cause such damage, but these questions must be addressed in context of honoring God (Psalm 29:1). It is in a context of God-centered worship that such puzzling questions are resolved into peaceful trust. (***See Worship****> OT> God's Supremacy> Glorified and Blessed God,* TopicGuide page A27.)

29:10-11 Once again, the psalmist alludes to the mythology of the time (Psalm 29:3), but also to the flood account (Genesis 7). The floodwaters are not God's opponents; they are His creation and He uses them as He pleases. Thus, God is greater than all the false gods of the ancient world. He alone is King and His people enjoy the benefits of His reign.

30:1-3 David thanks God for His deliverance from an illness that brought him near death. The enemies of 30:1 are most likely illness and death, which threatened David. The verb translated "rescued me" is typically used to speak of something being lifted out of a well—an appropriate metaphor for deliverance from death, which is spoken of as a pit.

30:8-10 David modeled the ideal response to God's chastening—he acknowledged his sin and repented (compare Hebrews 12:5-11). Not all illness is a sign of God's displeasure (consider Job), but David recognized that it was in his case and responded appropriately by seeking mercy from the Lord.

11 You have turned my mourning into joyful dancing.
You have taken away my clothes of mourning and clothed me with joy,
12 that I might sing praises to You and not be silent.
O LORD my God, I will give You thanks forever!

30:11 Jer 31:4, 13
30:12 Pss 44:8; 57:8; 108:1

PSALM 31

For the choir director: A psalm of David.

1 O LORD, I have come to You for protection;
don't let me be disgraced.
Save me, for You do what is right.
2 Turn Your ear to listen to me;
rescue me quickly.
Be my rock of protection,
a fortress where I will be safe.
3 You are my rock and my fortress.
For the honor of Your name, lead me out of this danger.
4 Pull me from the trap my enemies set for me,
for I find protection in You alone.
5 I entrust my spirit into Your hand.
Rescue me, LORD, for You are a faithful God.

6 I hate those who worship worthless idols.
I trust in the LORD.
7 I will be glad and rejoice in Your unfailing love,
for You have seen my troubles,
and You care about the anguish of my soul.
8 You have not handed me over to my enemies
but have set me in a safe place.

9 Have mercy on me, LORD, for I am in distress.
Tears blur my eyes.
My body and soul are withering away.

31:1-4 //Ps 71:1-3
31:1 Pss 25:2; 143:1
31:2 Pss 71:3; 86:1; 102:2
31:3 Pss 18:2; 23:2-3
31:4 Ps 25:15
31:5 Luke 23:46 Acts 7:59
31:6 Jon 2:8-9
31:7 Pss 10:14; 90:14
31:8 Deut 32:30
31:9 Pss 6:7; 32:3; 38:3-4; 39:11; 63:1; 69:17; 102:1, 3-4

▸ WORSHIP

30:11 Mourning into joy. At the writing of this psalm, the Israelites had come a long way—from slavery to the dedication of the Temple. God had taken them through many dark times in the more than 400 years since they had left Egypt. Their joy at this moment was complete. They were in possession of their own land and now could worship God in the Temple built by King Solomon. How has God turned your mourning into joy? When have you experienced times when He has brought you through them? Take time to praise and thank Him for being a faithful presence in your life. Specifically thank Him for each time He brought joy out of a painful situation. (***See Worship****> OT> Music> Psalms> Lament> Individual,* TopicGuide page A27.)

31:2-3 The metaphors of rock and fortress describe God in terms of His power and steadfastness. As a warrior, David knows the advantage a fortress can provide. He is counting on God to provide protection and safety from his enemies.

▸ GOD

31:3 You are my Rock! We've all seen pictures of a home suspended over a raging flood because the soil underneath the home has been eroded away. Within hours, the house may be swept away. Surely, at such a moment, the homeowner must regret building on such soft soil. We never have to worry about our spiritual foundation when we build our lives on God. He never changes. His truth never shifts. In times of stress, He's always there. Are you clinging to the Rock? Seek God's will and truth first in every situation and God will become a fortress for you. (***See God****> God's Names> God> Fortress,* TopicGuide page A18.)

▸ GOD

31:5 God is faithful and true. In what ways is God faithful? He keeps His promises (Deuteronomy 9:5). He is faithful through His Son (1 Corinthians 1:9). He always tells the truth (Hebrews 6:18). He keeps our souls forever (1 Peter 4:19). What other ways can you think of that God shows His faithfulness? Do a search in your Bible concordance for the word *faithful.* Write down additional ways God is faithful. Then thank Him for each one. (***See God****> God's Attributes> True> He is "the God of truth,"* TopicGuide page A18.)

31:5 David expresses his confidence in God by entrusting his life to Him in a time of crisis. Facing certain death, Jesus employed David's words to express His own confidence in His Father (Luke 23:46).

31:10 Ps 13:2 — 10 I am dying from grief;
my years are shortened by sadness.
Sin has drained my strength;
I am wasting away from within.
31:11 Pss 38:11; 88:8, 18 Isa 53:3 — 11 I am scorned by all my enemies
and despised by my neighbors—
even my friends are afraid to come near me.
When they see me on the street,
they run the other way.
31:12 Ps 88:5 — 12 I am ignored as if I were dead,
as if I were a broken pot.
31:13 Ps 41:7 Jer 20:10 Matt 27:1 — 13 I have heard the many rumors about me,
and I am surrounded by terror.
My enemies conspire against me,
plotting to take my life.

31:14 Pss 140:6; 143:9 — 14 But I am trusting You, O LORD,
saying, "You are my God!"
31:15 Ps 143:9 — 15 My future is in Your hands.
Rescue me from those who hunt me down relentlessly.
31:16 Num 6:24-26 Ps 6:4 — 16 Let Your favor shine on Your servant.
In Your unfailing love, rescue me.
31:17 1 Sam 2:9 Ps 25:2-3, 20 — 17 Don't let me be disgraced, O LORD,
for I call out to You for help.
Let the wicked be disgraced;
let them lie silent in the grave.*
31:18 1 Sam 2:3 Pss 94:4; 120:2 — 18 Silence their lying lips—
those proud and arrogant lips that accuse the godly.

31:19 Ps 5:11 Rom 11:22 — 19 How great is the goodness
You have stored up for those who fear You.
You lavish it on those who come to You for protection,
blessing them before the watching world.

31:20 Job 5:21 Pss 27:5; 31:13 — 20 You hide them in the shelter of Your presence,
safe from those who conspire against them.
You shelter them in Your presence,
far from accusing tongues.

31:21 Ps 17:7 — 21 Praise the LORD,
for He has shown me the wonders of His unfailing love.
He kept me safe when my city was under attack.
31:22 Pss 66:19; 116:11-12; 145:19 Lam 3:54-56 — 22 In panic I cried out,
"I am cut off from the LORD!"
But You heard my cry for mercy
and answered my call for help.

31:17 Hebrew *in Sheol.*

31:14 David's affirmation of faith is strikingly personal and covenantal. The emphasis lies on the pronouns "I" and "You." David's strength grows out of his relationship with God, which is grounded in God's covenant with His people (Genesis 17:8).

31:19-23 The tone of the psalm changes dramatically as David breaks into jubilant thanksgiving. David's thanksgiving reflects his earlier petitions. God has heard his prayer for deliverance and shown Himself to be a rock and a fortress to David (31:2-3). He has protected David from the slander of his enemies (31:13, 18). He has displayed His covenantal love and confirmed David in his trust (31:14, 16).

23 Love the LORD, all you godly ones!
For the LORD protects those who are loyal to Him,
but He harshly punishes the arrogant.
24 So be strong and courageous,
all you who put your hope in the LORD!

31:23 Deut 32:40-41; Ps 37:28
31:24 Ps 27:14

PSALM 32

A psalm of David.*

1 Oh, what joy for those
whose disobedience is forgiven,
whose sin is put out of sight!
2 Yes, what joy for those
whose record the LORD has cleared of guilt,*
whose lives are lived in complete honesty!
3 When I refused to confess my sin,
my body wasted away,
and I groaned all day long.
4 Day and night Your hand of discipline was heavy on me.
My strength evaporated like water in the summer heat. *Interlude*

5 Finally, I confessed all my sins to You
and stopped trying to hide my guilt.
I said to myself, "I will confess my rebellion to the LORD."
And You forgave me! All my guilt is gone. *Interlude*

6 Therefore, let all the godly pray to You while there is still time,
that they may not drown in the floodwaters of judgment.
7 For You are my hiding place;
You protect me from trouble.
You surround me with songs of victory. *Interlude*

32:2 Ps 85:2; *Rom 4:7-8
32:3 Pss 31:10; 39:2
32:4 Pss 22:15; 39:10
32:5 Lev 26:40; Job 31:33; Ps 38:18; 1 Jn 1:9
32:6 Pss 69:13; Isa 43:2
32:7 Exod 15:1; Pss 31:20; 40:3; 121:7

32:TITLE Hebrew *maskil.* This may be a literary or musical term. 32:2 Greek version reads *of sin.* Compare Rom 4:7.

32:1-2 "Joy" (literally, blessedness) comes to those who sincerely confess their wrongdoing and receive forgiveness. These verses employ three different Hebrew words for sin, but because they are used poetically they probably should be understood as synonyms.

▸ HOLINESS

32:3 The consequences of unconfessed sin. David knew firsthand the consequences of hidden sin when he had his adulterous relationship with Bathsheba. He cries out to God regarding the inner turmoil that his unconfessed sin caused him. Refusing to deal with sin problems leads us into many consequences, including loss of joy and peace. Unconfessed sin eats away at us like a cancer, making us weak and miserable. But what an easy remedy we have—to admit to God what we have done wrong and ask for His forgiveness. As long as we are sincere in our confession and desire to turn away from sin, He will forgive us and restore our joy. What's eating at you right now? Deal with your unconfessed sin right away. (***See Holiness***> *Changed by God> God Provides> Conviction of sin,* TopicGuide page A41.)

▸ SPIRITUAL WARFARE

32:5 The guilt trip. Once guilt grabs us, it takes us for an unpleasant ride to an unpleasant destination. We can't reason away guilt or lessen it by doing something good. We only have one solution for guilt—confessing our wrongdoing to God. Only He can wipe our slate clean—only because of the sacrifice of His Son, Jesus. Are you on a guilt trip right now? God doesn't want you to stay on it. Change your direction, turn to Jesus, and you'll experience freedom from guilt. (***See Spiritual Warfare***> *Resisting Sin and Evil> Consequences> Of Disobedience> Guilt,* TopicGuide page A46.)

32:5 David says that he finally acknowledged and confessed his sin. He employs the same three Hebrew words used to describe sin in 32:1-2 to indicate his complete repentance. His sincere and deep repentance immediately led to forgiveness and restoration. God is eager and willing to forgive those who come to Him in faith and repentance.

32:6-7 David's experience of mercy leads him to call all the godly to acknowledge their sin and enjoy the joy that accompanies forgiveness (32:1). David and the godly then join their voices in praising the Lord, who has saved them from judgment and delivered them from the troubles that accompany unconfessed sin.

32:8 Pss 25:8; 33:18-19
8 The LORD says, "I will guide you along the best pathway for your life.
I will advise you and watch over you.
9 Do not be like a senseless horse or mule
that needs a bit and bridle to keep it under control."

32:10 Ps 16:4 Prov 16:20 Rom 2:9-10
10 Many sorrows come to the wicked,
but unfailing love surrounds those who trust the LORD.
11 So rejoice in the LORD and be glad, all you who obey Him!
Shout for joy, all you whose hearts are pure!

PSALM 33

33:1 Pss 32:11; 147:1
1 Let the godly sing for joy to the LORD;
it is fitting for the pure to praise Him.
33:2 Ps 92:3
2 Praise the LORD with melodies on the lyre;
make music for Him on the ten-stringed harp.
33:3 Pss 96:1; 98:1 Rev 5:9
3 Sing a new song of praise to Him;
play skillfully on the harp, and sing with joy.
33:4 Ps 19:8
4 For the word of the LORD holds true,
and we can trust everything He does.
33:5 Pss 11:7; 119:64
5 He loves whatever is just and good;
the unfailing love of the LORD fills the earth.

33:6 Gen 1:6-7 Ps 148:5 Heb 11:3
6 The LORD merely spoke,
and the heavens were created.
He breathed the word,
and all the stars were born.

32:10-11 The purity of heart that is in view here cannot be sinlessness given the earlier content of the psalm (32:5). Purity of heart arises out of God's forgiveness and cleansing of the sinner. God's mercy is grounded in His covenantal ("unfailing") love for His people and appropriated by faith ("trust").

33:1-3 The lyre and harp were but two of the musical instruments available to accompany the praise of God's people in ancient Israel (see Psalm 150).

33:4-9 The language used here alludes to the Red Sea crossing, when God revealed Himself as a mighty warrior and delivered His people, giving birth to a new nation (Exodus 15:1-18).

BECAUSE GOD IS MERCIFUL

He forgives me of my sins when I sincerely confess them.

Oh, what joy for those whose disobedience is forgiven, whose sin is put out of sight! Yes, what joy for those whose record the LORD has cleared of guilt, whose lives are lived in complete honesty!

PSALM 32:1-2, 6

FOR THE NEXT *GOD IS MERCIFUL* FEATURE SEE PAGE 1750.

[7] He assigned the sea its boundaries
and locked the oceans in vast reservoirs.
[8] Let the whole world fear the LORD,
and let everyone stand in awe of Him.
[9] For when He spoke, the world began!
It appeared at His command.

[10] The LORD frustrates the plans of the nations
and thwarts all their schemes.
[11] But the LORD's plans stand firm forever;
His intentions can never be shaken.

[12] What joy for the nation whose God is the LORD,
whose people He has chosen as His inheritance.

[13] The LORD looks down from heaven
and sees the whole human race.
[14] From His throne He observes
all who live on the earth.
[15] He made their hearts,
so He understands everything they do.
[16] The best-equipped army cannot save a king,
nor is great strength enough to save a warrior.
[17] Don't count on your warhorse to give you victory—
for all its strength, it cannot save you.

[18] But the LORD watches over those who fear Him,
those who rely on His unfailing love.
[19] He rescues them from death
and keeps them alive in times of famine.

[20] We put our hope in the LORD.
He is our help and our shield.
[21] In Him our hearts rejoice,
for we trust in His holy name.
[22] Let Your unfailing love surround us, LORD,
for our hope is in You alone.

33:7 Exod 15:8
33:8 Pss 67:7; 96:9
33:9 Gen 1:3; Ps 148:5
33:10 Isa 8:9-10; 19:3
33:12 Exod 19:5; Ps 144:15
33:16 Pss 44:6; 147:10
33:17 Ps 20:7; Prov 21:31
33:18 Ps 34:15
33:19 Ps 37:19
33:20 Ps 115:9; Isa 8:17

▸ WORSHIP
33:8 Stand in awe of God. In the military, whenever a general enters the room, all the soldiers stand at attention. They are honoring the rank before them. At some point in time, all the earth will stand at attention in God's honor (Revelation 20:12). This will be the moment when all are judged for their works. So the question is not *if* you will stand in awe of God, but *when.* Are you giving Him His due respect and glory now? Now is the time to acknowledge His place as ruler of the universe. (***See Worship****> OT> Reverence> Let the earth fear God,* TopicGuide page A29.)

33:10-12 The psalmist turns his attention from Creation to history. The Word of God brought about Creation and the plans of God direct history. Just as God's creative word could not be resisted, His plans in history cannot fail. God's plan is focused on the formation of His people.

33:13-15 The Creator of all things (33:6-9), the One who directs history by His plan (33:10-12), is also the Judge of His creatures. God's vision extends to all humanity and yet can focus on an individual human heart; nothing escapes His gaze. He sees from His throne, suggesting His right to rule and judge His creatures as their King and Creator.

33:16-17 Earlier Israelite hymns celebrated the power of God in the face of powerful enemies equipped with the best military technology (Exodus 15:1-4; Judges 5:19-22). The psalmist borrows their language to affirm God's strength.

▸ WORSHIP
33:18 God delivers us. When the three young Jewish men stood before the king, facing a horrible death in the fiery furnace for standing up for their faith, they confidently said, "If we are thrown into the blazing furnace, the God whom we serve is able to save us. He will rescue us from your power, Your Majesty" (Daniel 3:17). God has delivered us from our most fearsome enemy—Satan (2 Timothy 4:18). No matter what Satan tries, he cannot prevail against us because of Jesus Christ. Go boldly into the spiritual battles you face, knowing that God will deliver you. (***See Worship****> OT> Reverence> God delivers those who fear Him,* TopicGuide page A29.)

PSALM 34*

A psalm of David, regarding the time he pretended to be insane in front of Abimelech, who sent him away.

34:1 [1] I will praise the LORD at all times.
Ps 71:6 I will constantly speak His praises.
Eph 5:20 [2] I will boast only in the LORD;
34:2 Jer 9:24 let all who are helpless take heart.
[3] Come, let us tell of the LORD's greatness;
let us exalt His name together.

[4] I prayed to the LORD, and He answered me.
He freed me from all my fears.
34:5 Ps 36:9 [5] Those who look to Him for help will be radiant with joy;
no shadow of shame will darken their faces.
[6] In my desperation I prayed, and the LORD listened;
He saved me from all my troubles.
34:7 Dan 6:22 [7] For the angel of the LORD is a guard;
he surrounds and defends all who fear Him.

34:8 1 Pet 2:3 [8] Taste and see that the LORD is good.
Oh, the joys of those who take refuge in Him!
34:9 Pss 23:1; 31:23 [9] Fear the LORD, you His godly people,
for those who fear Him will have all they need.
34:10 Ps 84:11 [10] Even strong young lions sometimes go hungry,
but those who trust in the LORD will lack no good thing.

34:11 Ps 111:10 [11] Come, my children, and listen to me,
and I will teach you to fear the LORD.
34:12 1 Pet 3:10-12 [12] Does anyone want to live a life
that is long and prosperous?
34:13 Jas 1:26 [13] Then keep your tongue from speaking evil
1 Pet 2:22 and your lips from telling lies!
34:14 Ps 37:27 [14] Turn away from evil and do good.
Rom 14:18-19 Search for peace, and work to maintain it.
Heb 12:14
34:15 Job 36:7 [15] The eyes of the LORD watch over those who do right;
His ears are open to their cries for help.
Ps 33:18-19 [16] But the LORD turns His face against those who do evil;
34:16 He will erase their memory from the earth.
Pss 9:6; 109:15

34 This psalm is a Hebrew acrostic poem; each verse begins with a successive letter of the Hebrew alphabet.

34:2 Boasting is typically an offensive practice, but not when it is boasting in God rather than oneself. To boast in God is to recognize His greatness and praise Him for it. Boasting in God alone means that we recognize that there is nothing we can boast of in ourselves (Jeremiah 9:24).

▸ WORSHIP

34:3 Exalt God together. "How was church?" This question reveals more about us than the quality of our worship experience. At church, we aren't the audience, critiquing every moment. We are the performers, and God is the audience. No matter how well the sermon went or how poorly the songs were chosen, it is our job to humbly gather with God's people and worship Him with all our hearts. (***See Worship****> OT> God's Supremacy> Was God-centered (not worshiper-centered),* TopicGuide page A27.)

34:7 "The angel of the LORD" is a representative of God so closely associated with Him that he is often described in language typically reserved for God Himself. The angel of the LORD appeared to Joshua before battle, suggesting that he plays a militaristic role (Joshua 5:13-14), but in the context of the psalm the language extends to God's general protection of His people.

34:11-16 These verses exhibit many characteristics of Israel's wisdom literature. The fear of God is the beginning of wisdom and essential to a life well lived (Proverbs 1:7). Instruction is directed from father to child (Proverbs 1:8). Two paths are set before the reader: one of godliness and subsequent blessing, the other of wickedness and subsequent curse (compare Psalm 1).

17 The LORD hears His people when they call to Him for help.
He rescues them from all their troubles.
18 The LORD is close to the brokenhearted;
He rescues those whose spirits are crushed.

34:18 Pss 51:17; 145:18 Isa 57:15

19 The righteous person faces many troubles,
but the LORD comes to the rescue each time.
20 For the LORD protects the bones of the righteous;
not one of them is broken!

34:19 Ps 71:20 Prov 24:16

21 Calamity will surely overtake the wicked,
and those who hate the righteous will be punished.
22 But the LORD will redeem those who serve Him.
No one who takes refuge in Him will be condemned.

34:21 Ps 94:23

34:22 Ps 71:23

PSALM 35

A psalm of David.

1 O LORD, oppose those who oppose me.
Fight those who fight against me.
2 Put on Your armor, and take up Your shield.
Prepare for battle, and come to my aid.
3 Lift up Your spear and javelin
against those who pursue me.
Let me hear You say,
"I will give you victory!"
4 Bring shame and disgrace on those trying to kill me;
turn them back and humiliate those who want to harm me.
5 Blow them away like chaff in the wind—
a wind sent by the angel of the LORD.
6 Make their path dark and slippery,
with the angel of the LORD pursuing them.
7 I did them no wrong, but they laid a trap for me.
I did them no wrong, but they dug a pit to catch me.
8 So let sudden ruin come upon them!
Let them be caught in the trap they set for me!
Let them be destroyed in the pit they dug for me.

9 Then I will rejoice in the LORD.
I will be glad because He rescues me.
10 With every bone in my body I will praise Him:
"LORD, who can compare with You?
Who else rescues the helpless from the strong?
Who else protects the helpless and poor from those who rob them?"

35:1 Ps 56:1-2 Isa 49:25

35:2 Ps 91:4

35:3 Ps 62:2

35:4 Pss 40:14; 70:2-3

35:5 Job 21:18 Pss 1:4; 83:13 Isa 29:5

35:6 Ps 73:18 Jer 23:12

35:7 Pss 69:4; 109:3

35:8 Ps 9:15 Isa 47:11 1 Thes 5:3

35:9 Isa 61:10 Luke 1:47

35:10 Exod 15:11-12 Pss 18:17; 37:14

▸ HOLINESS

34:20 God is our keeper. Jesus once prayed, "Now I am departing from the world; they are staying in this world, but I am coming to You. Holy Father, You have given Me Your name; now protect them by the power of Your name so that they will be united just as We are" (John 17:11). What comfort to know that our heavenly Father will protect us as one of His own. Are you risking enough so that you need God to protect you? Have you ever risked comfort, possessions, or relationships? Live a faithful life and you will discover that those united with Christ will indeed require the protection of God. (***See Holiness*> *God's Blessing*> *Obedience improves our relationship with God,* TopicGuide page A42.)

35:1-3 David describes the Lord as a divine warrior armed with the weapons of the infantry. The word translated "oppose" typically denotes the action of bringing a case against someone in a court of law.

35:4-6 The "angel of the LORD" is associated with God's warfare on behalf of His people (Joshua 5:14). Lightweight "chaff" is separated from edible grains by tossing the two into the sky, with the breeze blowing away the chaff, allowing the grains to fall into a container.

35:11 Ps 27:12 — 11 Malicious witnesses testify against me.
They accuse me of crimes I know nothing about.
35:12 Ps 38:20; John 10:32 — 12 They repay me evil for good.
I am sick with despair.
35:13 Job 30:25; Ps 69:10 — 13 Yet when they were ill, I grieved for them.
I denied myself by fasting for them,
but my prayers returned unanswered.
14 I was sad, as though they were my friends or family,
as if I were grieving for my own mother.
15 But they are glad now that I am in trouble;
they gleefully join together against me.
I am attacked by people I don't even know;
they slander me constantly.
35:16 Lam 2:16 — 16 They mock me and call me names;
they snarl at me.

35:17 Pss 13:1; 22:20-21; Hab 1:13 — 17 How long, O Lord, will You look on and do nothing?
Rescue me from their fierce attacks.
Protect my life from these lions!
35:18 Ps 22:23, 25 — 18 Then I will thank You in front of the great assembly.
I will praise You before all the people.
35:19 Pss 13:4; 38:16, 19; 69:4; *John 15:25 — 19 Don't let my treacherous enemies rejoice over my defeat.
Don't let those who hate me without cause gloat over my sorrow.
20 They don't talk of peace;
they plot against innocent people who mind their own business.
35:21 Pss 22:13; 40:15 — 21 They shout, "Aha! Aha!
With our own eyes we saw him do it!"
35:22 Exod 3:7; Ps 10:14 — 22 O LORD, You know all about this.
Do not stay silent.
Do not abandon me now, O Lord.
23 Wake up! Rise to my defense!
Take up my case, my God and my Lord.
35:24 Pss 9:4; 43:1 — 24 Declare me not guilty, O LORD my God, for You give justice.
Don't let my enemies laugh about me in my troubles.
35:25 Ps 56:1; Lam 2:16 — 25 Don't let them say, "Look, we got what we wanted!
Now we will eat him alive!"
35:26 Pss 38:16; 40:14 — 26 May those who rejoice at my troubles
be humiliated and disgraced.
May those who triumph over me
be covered with shame and dishonor.

35:11-13 Legal terminology ("witnesses," "testify," "accuse") appears again. The psalm may be describing the rupture of a treaty relationship. If that is the case, David is being accused of breaking the terms of the treaty even though he has remained loyal to his treaty partner.

▸ WORSHIP
35:13 A change of heart. Why would David fast and pray when it seemed as if his prayers were not being answered? Because fasting and prayer affect the soul of the person. Fasting directs our attention to God, and therefore we are humbled before His power. In our state of humility, we will open our ears and hearts to Him. The next time you see those who oppose you or the God you worship suffering, do not take delight in it. Instead, fast and pray, and ask God to give you a love for their souls. (***See Worship****> OT> Fasting and Prayer> Fasting> Occasions> Fasting as a means to afflict or humble the soul,* TopicGuide page A26.)

▸ WORSHIP
35:26 Pray for your enemies. Do you pray for those who attempt to harm God's people around the world? In this psalm, David cries out to God for the destruction of God's (and his) enemies. This may sound odd to our ears, particularly as Jesus reminded us to love our enemies (Matthew 5:43-44). But David demonstrates that we can love our enemies while praying for God to take vengeance on them. Looking ahead to the book of Revelation, we see that people even more sanctified than David—people in heaven—pray for God to take vengeance on the wicked. (***See Worship****> OT> Music> Psalms> Lament> Retaliation,* TopicGuide page A27.)

27 But give great joy to those who came to my defense.
Let them continually say, "Great is the LORD,
who delights in blessing His servant with peace!"
28 Then I will proclaim Your justice,
and I will praise You all day long.

35:27 Pss 40:16; 70:4; 149:4-5
35:28 Ps 51:14-15

PSALM 36

For the choir director: A psalm of David, the servant of the LORD.

1 Sin whispers to the wicked, deep within their hearts.
They have no fear of God at all.
2 In their blind conceit,
they cannot see how wicked they really are.
3 Everything they say is crooked and deceitful.
They refuse to act wisely or do good.
4 They lie awake at night, hatching sinful plots.
Their actions are never good.
They make no attempt to turn from evil.

5 Your unfailing love, O LORD, is as vast as the heavens;
Your faithfulness reaches beyond the clouds.
6 Your righteousness is like the mighty mountains,
Your justice like the ocean depths.
You care for people and animals alike, O LORD.
7 How precious is Your unfailing love, O God!
All humanity finds shelter
in the shadow of Your wings.
8 You feed them from the abundance of Your own house,
letting them drink from Your river of delights.
9 For You are the fountain of life,
the light by which we see.

10 Pour out Your unfailing love on those who love You;
give justice to those with honest hearts.
11 Don't let the proud trample me
or the wicked push me around.
12 Look! Those who do evil have fallen!
They are thrown down, never to rise again.

36:1 *Rom 3:18
36:3 Ps 10:7; Jer 4:22
36:4 Prov 4:16; Isa 65:2; Mic 2:1
36:5 Pss 57:10; 103:11; 108:4
36:6 Pss 104:14-15; 145:16-17; Rom 11:33
36:7 Ruth 2:12; Pss 91:4; 139:17-18
36:8 Isa 25:6; Rev 22:1
36:9 1 Pet 2:9
36:12 Ps 140:10

35:27-28 David anticipates the praise that will resound to God from himself and those who have stood with him—the congregation of Psalm 35:18.

▸ WORSHIP
36:1 Sin whispers softly. Sin can be quite sneaky. To those without God's Spirit, sin becomes a constant companion who whispers temptations to them. "Just one more time" comes the voice. "It won't hurt anything. No one will know." Without Christ, sinners find only temporary freedom from the constant whisper of sin. Using the strength that Christ supplies, you can run away from temptation. Flee from sin's soft voice and listen to the Word of God. God gives grace to flee from the temptation and sin that haunt His people. (***See Worship****> OT> Music> Psalms> Lament> Individual,* TopicGuide page A27.)

36:1-2 Sin resides deep within the heart and mind, wielding enormous power over an individual. The fear of God is the beginning of true wisdom (Proverbs 1:7). Without the fear of God, a person becomes his own standard of morality and is unable to discern whether his actions are right or wrong. He is blinded to his own condition.

36:3-4 The ungodly are so obsessed with their wickedness they would rather scheme than sleep. Their refusal to act wisely is linked to their refusal to do good. True wisdom is ethical; it produces righteousness, not merely cleverness.

36:7 As a mother bird protects her young under her wing, so God shelters His people. Deuteronomy 32:11 employs similar imagery to describe God's care for Israel following the Exodus.

36:10 God's unfailing love is experienced by all in some sense (Psalm 36:7), but it is showered on those who love Him in an intensified manner (compare 1 Timothy 4:10).

PSALM 37*

A psalm of David.

1 Don't worry about the wicked
or envy those who do wrong.
2 For like grass, they soon fade away.
Like spring flowers, they soon wither.

3 Trust in the LORD and do good.
Then you will live safely in the land and prosper.
4 Take delight in the LORD,
and He will give you your heart's desires.

5 Commit everything you do to the LORD.
Trust Him, and He will help you.
6 He will make your innocence radiate like the dawn,
and the justice of your cause will shine like the noonday sun.

7 Be still in the presence of the LORD,
and wait patiently for Him to act.
Don't worry about evil people who prosper
or fret about their wicked schemes.

8 Stop being angry!
Turn from your rage!
Do not lose your temper—
it only leads to harm.
9 For the wicked will be destroyed,
but those who trust in the LORD will possess the land.

10 Soon the wicked will disappear.
Though you look for them, they will be gone.
11 The lowly will possess the land
and will live in peace and prosperity.

12 The wicked plot against the godly;
they snarl at them in defiance.
13 But the Lord just laughs,
for He sees their day of judgment coming.

14 The wicked draw their swords
and string their bows
to kill the poor and the oppressed,
to slaughter those who do right.
15 But their swords will stab their own hearts,
and their bows will be broken.

16 It is better to be godly and have little
than to be evil and rich.

37:1 Ps 73:3; Prov 3:31
37:2 Job 14:2; Ps 90:5-6
37:3 Deut 30:20; Ps 62:8; Isa 40:11
37:4 Ps 145:19; Isa 58:14
37:5 Ps 55:22; Prov 16:3; 1 Pet 5:7
37:6 Isa 58:8, 10; Mic 7:9
37:7 Pss 40:1; 62:5; Jer 12:1
37:8 Eph 4:31; Col 3:8
37:9 Ps 25:13; Isa 60:21
37:10 Job 24:24
37:11 Matt 5:3, 5
37:12 Ps 35:16
37:13 Ps 2:4
37:14 Pss 11:2; 35:10
37:15 Pss 9:16; 46:9
37:16 Prov 15:16; 16:8

37 This psalm is a Hebrew acrostic poem; each stanza begins with a successive letter of the Hebrew alphabet.

37:1-4 These four verses provide a dual response to the apparent prosperity of the wicked. First, the believer is not to envy the wicked because their advantage is ephemeral. Second, the believer is to trust in the Lord and delight in Him, particularly reflecting upon His goodness. All the while the believer is to continue on the path of righteousness, not allowing distress to deter obedience.

37:12-13 The prosperity of the wicked is often achieved at the expense of the righteous. But the psalmist unveils to the righteous the divine perspective: God mocks the rantings of the wicked because He knows He will hold them accountable (compare to Psalm 2).

[17] For the strength of the wicked will be shattered,
but the LORD takes care of the godly.

37:17 Job 38:15 Ps 10:15

[18] Day by day the LORD takes care of the innocent,
and they will receive an inheritance that lasts forever.
[19] They will not be disgraced in hard times;
even in famine they will have more than enough.

37:19 Job 5:20 Ps 33:18-19

[20] But the wicked will die.
The LORD's enemies are like flowers in a field—
they will disappear like smoke.

37:20 Pss 68:2; 73:27; 102:3

[21] The wicked borrow and never repay,
but the godly are generous givers.
[22] Those the LORD blesses will possess the land,
but those He curses will die.

37:22 Job 5:3 Prov 3:33

[23] The LORD directs the steps of the godly.
He delights in every detail of their lives.
[24] Though they stumble, they will never fall,
for the LORD holds them by the hand.

37:23 1 Sam 2:9 Pss 40:2; 147:11

37:24 Pss 145:14; 147:6 Prov 24:15-16

[25] Once I was young, and now I am old.
Yet I have never seen the godly abandoned
or their children begging for bread.
[26] The godly always give generous loans to others,
and their children are a blessing.

37:25 Isa 41:17 Heb 13:5

37:26 Ps 37:21

[27] Turn from evil and do good,
and you will live in the land forever.
[28] For the LORD loves justice,
and He will never abandon the godly.

37:27 Ps 34:14

37:28 Pss 11:7; 21:10

He will keep them safe forever,
but the children of the wicked will die.
[29] The godly will possess the land
and will live there forever.

37:29 Ps 37:9, 18

[30] The godly offer good counsel;
they teach right from wrong.
[31] They have made God's law their own,
so they will never slip from His path.

37:31 Ps 40:8 Isa 51:7

[32] The wicked wait in ambush for the godly,
looking for an excuse to kill them.

37:32 Pss 10:8; 37:14

▸GOD

37:25 The truth about poverty? Have you ever seen a poor Christian? The writer of this psalm testifies that in his entire life, he has never seen the godly destitute. We have no reason to doubt his personal testimony, but we also have no reason to think that he believed that God's people never experience what his culture defined as "poverty." Verse 16 makes it clear that it is better to be poor and godly than to be rich and evil, so we know that God might allow poverty to touch His people for their own eternal good. So how do we interpret this verse? You can trust that while God's people may experience earthly poverty, the humble faithful are promised great blessing and ultimate victory over their enemies (37:10, 13, 18). God has everything—your finances, your sex life, your doctrine—under His watchful eye (37:23). (***See God***> *God's Attributes> True> God doesn't lie but keeps His word,* TopicGuide page A18.)

37:35-36 The image is similar to that of Psalm 1, but reversed. There the righteous are pictured as a tree flourishing by a stream; here it is the wicked who appear to be thriving like mighty trees. But their thriving is temporary. Unlike the godly, their source of strength dries up and leaves them to wither. The godly, however, are sustained by the eternal strength of God, who does not fail, and so their flourishing is perpetual.

37:33 2 Pet 2:9 33 But the LORD will not let the wicked succeed
or let the godly be condemned when
they are put on trial.

37:34 Pss 27:14; 37:9 34 Put your hope in the LORD.
Travel steadily along His path.
He will honor you by giving you the land.
You will see the wicked destroyed.

37:35 Job 5:3 35 I have seen wicked and ruthless people
flourishing like a tree in its native soil.
36 But when I looked again, they were gone!
Though I searched for them, I could
not find them!

37 Look at those who are honest and good,
for a wonderful future awaits those
who love peace.
37:38 Pss 1:1; 73:19 38 But the rebellious will be destroyed;
they have no future.

37:39 Pss 3:8; 9:9 39 The LORD rescues the godly;
He is their fortress in times of trouble.
40 The LORD helps them,
rescuing them from the wicked.
He saves them,
and they find shelter in Him.

PSALM 38

A psalm of David, asking God to remember him.
38:1 Ps 6:1 1 O LORD, don't rebuke me in Your anger
or discipline me in Your rage!
38:2 Job 6:4 2 Your arrows have struck deep,
Ps 32:4 and Your blows are crushing me.
38:3 3 Because of Your anger, my whole body is sick;
Pss 6:2; 31:9-10 my health is broken because of my sins.
Isa 1:5-6 4 My guilt overwhelms me—
38:4 Ezra 9:6 it is a burden too heavy to bear.

38:1-3 David assumes that his sickness is God's judgment on his sinfulness. However, it is not always true that illness is God's discipline for particular sins. Job, for example, suffered enormously, but his suffering was not specifically correlated to his sin (Job 1–2). Still, while our sicknesses may not be connected to particular sins, it is never a bad thing to search our hearts and repent of all known sin.

▸ WORSHIP
38:3-8 The crushing weight of sin. Here David describes the physical and emotional effects of harboring unconfessed sin. When we ignore the presence of sin in our lives, our bodies may suffer, guilt may become our companion, and agony may be present around the clock. Most people suffer under these symptoms every day. But God has given us a remedy for our anguish—repentance. To repent is to humble ourselves before God by turning away from sin, replacing the false beliefs about God and self that underlie sin, and surrendering ourselves to the promptings and protection of the Holy Spirit. Pray for a greater understanding and more effective practice of repentance. (***See Worship****> OT> Music> Psalms> Lament> Repentance*, TopicGuide page A27.)

38:4 Sin, guilt, and physical suffering plague David. He is physically and spiritually overwhelmed. The body and soul are intimately bound together and suffering in one can affect the other. See Psalm 32:3-4 for another example of this interrelationship.

[5] My wounds fester and stink
because of my foolish sins.
[6] I am bent over and racked with pain.
All day long I walk around filled with grief.
[7] A raging fever burns within me,
and my health is broken.
[8] I am exhausted and completely crushed.
My groans come from an anguished heart.

[9] You know what I long for, Lord;
You hear my every sigh.
[10] My heart beats wildly, my strength fails,
and I am going blind.
[11] My loved ones and friends stay away,
fearing my disease.
Even my own family stands at a distance.
[12] Meanwhile, my enemies lay traps to kill me.
Those who wish me harm make plans to ruin me.
All day long they plan their treachery.

[13] But I am deaf to all their threats.
I am silent before them as one
who cannot speak.
[14] I choose to hear nothing,
and I make no reply.
[15] For I am waiting for You, O LORD.
You must answer for me, O Lord my God.
[16] I prayed, "Don't let my enemies gloat over me
or rejoice at my downfall."

[17] I am on the verge of collapse,
facing constant pain.
[18] But I confess my sins;
I am deeply sorry for what I have done.
[19] I have many aggressive enemies;
they hate me without reason.
[20] They repay me evil for good
and oppose me for pursuing good.
[21] Do not abandon me, O LORD.
Do not stand at a distance, my God.
[22] Come quickly to help me,
O Lord my savior.

38:5 Ps 69:5
38:6 Ps 35:14
38:7 Ps 102:3-4
38:8 Job 3:24; Ps 22:1
38:9 Ps 10:17
38:10 Pss 6:7; 31:10
38:12 Pss 35:20; 54:3; 140:5
38:15 Ps 17:6
38:16 Pss 13:4; 35:26
38:17 Ps 13:2
38:18 2 Cor 7:9-10
38:19 Pss 18:17; 35:19
38:20 Ps 35:12; 1 Jn 3:12
38:21 Pss 22:19; 35:22
38:22 Pss 27:1; 40:13, 17

38:5-10 It is difficult to link David's catalog of maladies with any particular disease. It is more likely a list of symptoms experienced over a lifetime of physical suffering. This generality allows the psalm to have a wide relevance to those who suffer from many types of sickness.

38:15 David is unwilling to even attempt to defend himself (38:13-14). Instead, he decides to rely on God, even though he carries a powerful awareness of his sinfulness. David can do nothing except cast himself on God's mercy. The Lord "must" answer him, not because God is compelled to do so, but because David has no other source of help. If God does not rescue him, he has no hope.

▸ SPIRITUAL WARFARE
38:18 Depth of confession. We must be sorry enough for our sin to hate it and forsake it. When David, our role model for repentance, confessed his sin to God, he was "deeply sorry." If we do not regret the wrong we have done, we clearly do not understand the depth of our sin against God and man. The deep sorrow experienced by David is not a terminal emotion, but it leads to trusting Christ, following the guidance of the Spirit, and fearing God. (**See Spiritual Warfare**> *Resisting Sin and Evil> Consequences> Of Disobedience> Conviction of the Spirit/lack of joy,* TopicGuide page A46.)

PSALM 39

For Jeduthun, the choir director: A psalm of David.

39:1 Pss 34:13; 141:3 Jas 3:2, 5-12

1 I said to myself, "I will watch what I do
and not sin in what I say.
I will hold my tongue
when the ungodly are around me."
2 But as I stood there in silence—
not even speaking of good things—
the turmoil within me grew worse.
3 The more I thought about it,
the hotter I got,
igniting a fire of words:

39:4 Pss 78:39; 90:12; 103:14-15
39:5 Job 14:2 Pss 62:9; 89:47; 144:4

4 "LORD, remind me how brief my time on earth will be.
Remind me that my days are numbered—
how fleeting my life is.
5 You have made my life no longer than the width of my hand.
My entire lifetime is just a moment to You;
at best, each of us is but a breath." *Interlude*

39:6 Ps 127:2 Luke 12:20 1 Pet 1:24

6 We are merely moving shadows,
and all our busy rushing ends in nothing.
We heap up wealth,
not knowing who will spend it.
7 And so, Lord, where do I put my hope?
My only hope is in You.

39:8 Pss 51:9; 79:4, 9
39:9 Job 2:10
39:10 Job 9:34 Ps 32:4
39:11 Job 13:27-28 Ps 90:7 2 Pet 2:16

8 Rescue me from my rebellion.
Do not let fools mock me.
9 I am silent before You; I won't say a word,
for my punishment is from You.
10 But please stop striking me!
I am exhausted by the blows from Your hand.
11 When You discipline us for our sins,
You consume like a moth what is precious to us.
Each of us is but a breath. *Interlude*

▸ HOLINESS
39:1 Curbing our tongues. Sometimes when we are around unbelievers, we may be tempted to lower our standards to fit in. We may think, "If all my friends are going to use colorful language, why can't I? After all, they won't know the difference, will they?" Yes, they will, especially if they know that you are a follower of Christ. It's amazing how unbelievers watch and listen to a Christian to see whether his faith is genuine. Guard yourself from hypocrisy and your standing with non-Christians will increase. (***See Holiness****> Changed by God> God Provides> Restricting our choices,* TopicGuide page A41.)

39:1-3 In the company of wicked people, David says he found himself tempted to speak out in a sinful manner, perhaps by questioning God's justice or goodness. However, he committed himself to a discipline of silence, refraining even from appropriate statements for fear his speech would get away from him. Yet his best efforts to "hold" (literally, muzzle) his tongue failed and he spoke.

39:4-6 When David did speak, he asked for perspective. His request was already pointed toward the answer, and David himself provides the response. The width of the hand was one of smallest units in the Hebrew system of measurement. The life of an individual and even the existence of humanity is a fleeting moment to God. Hence, it follows that the apparent prosperity of the wicked is transitory; they will not enjoy their wealth. David begins to find relief by viewing his circumstances from God's perspective.

▸ WORSHIP
39:6 Lamenting the rush of life. The older a person gets, the more he understands the futility of life. For example, an actor gets a starring role in a television comedy, but ten years later he's seen only in those reruns. A mother clears her toddler's play area, but in an hour the mess has returned. Without God, these setbacks would rightly leave us depressed. But with His hope (39:7), we can experience failure and learn from it, knowing that God has a plan that will glorify Him and help us. When you are grieved by the busy, chaotic nature of this world, put your hope in God and His plan to rescue you and the entire universe from futility (Romans 8:18-28). (***See Worship****> OT> Music> Psalms> Lament> Individual,* TopicGuide page A27.)

12 Hear my prayer, O LORD!
Listen to my cries for help!
Don't ignore my tears.
For I am Your guest—
a traveler passing through,
as my ancestors were before me.
13 Leave me alone so I can smile again
before I am gone and exist no more.

39:12 Ps 102:1 Heb 11:13 1 Pet 2:11

39:13 Job 10:20; 14:6

PSALM 40

For the choir director: A psalm of David.

1 I waited patiently for the LORD to help me,
and He turned to me and heard my cry.
2 He lifted me out of the pit of despair,
out of the mud and the mire.
He set my feet on solid ground
and steadied me as I walked along.
3 He has given me a new song to sing,
a hymn of praise to our God.
Many will see what He has done and be amazed.
They will put their trust in the LORD.

4 Oh, the joys of those who trust the LORD,
who have no confidence in the proud
or in those who worship idols.
5 O LORD my God, You have performed many wonders for us.
Your plans for us are too numerous to list.
You have no equal.
If I tried to recite all Your wonderful deeds,
I would never come to the end of them.

6 You take no delight in sacrifices or offerings.
Now that You have made me listen, I finally understand*—
You don't require burnt offerings or sin offerings.

40:1 Pss 27:14; 34:15

40:2 Pss 27:5; 69:1-2 Jer 38:6

40:3 Pss 32:7; 33:3; 64:9

40:4 Ps 84:12

40:5 Job 5:9 Pss 136:4; 139:17-18 Isa 55:8

40:6-8 1 Sam 15:22 Jer 7:22-23 Mic 6:6-8 *Heb 10:5-7

40:6 Greek text reads *You have given me a body.* Compare Heb 10:5.

39:12-13 David concludes with a prayer for mercy. Once again he reflects on the brevity of human life, this time through the metaphor of a traveler. We pass through life as people on a journey. Only those who know God's grace can face this reality with confidence and even joy. The New Testament seizes upon the image of a traveler or sojourner to describe the Christian (Hebrews 11:13; 1 Peter 2:11) and gives a fuller picture of the destination (Revelation 21–22).

40:1-3 David recounts a past instance of God's deliverance, probably a military victory snatched from apparent defeat. The "pit" is a frequent metaphor for death, probably death on the battlefield where bodies are tossed into a mass grave. The "new song" is typically associated with praise following a victory in battle.

▸ WORSHIP

40:3 Sing loudly! When we experience a miraculous event—such as an answer to prayer, the touch of God's hand in healing, or comfort in a time of trial—what is its effect? We are encouraged and our faith is strengthened, but God intends for His work to have a wider impact. When we praise God for what He has done for us, others can share in our blessing. When we praise Him, our words act as messengers of God's truth to others. Don't keep God's miracles to yourself—tell others about the ways God has dealt with you. (***See Worship***> *OT> Music> Psalms> Thanksgiving> Individual,* TopicGuide page A27.)

40:6-8 These verses are not a condemnation of Israel's sacrificial system, which was, after all, established by God. David is simply indicating that mere ritual observance is insufficient to please God. The law written for the king required a spirit of humble obedience beyond, but not apart from, ritual purity (Deuteronomy 17:14-20).

7 Then I said, "Look, I have come.
As is written about me in the Scriptures:
40:8 Ps 37:31; 2 Cor 3:3; John 4:34; Rom 7:22
8 I take joy in doing Your will, my God,
for Your instructions are written on my heart."
40:9 Pss 22:25; 119:13
9 I have told all Your people about Your justice.
I have not been afraid to speak out,
as You, O LORD, well know.
40:10 Ps 89:1; Acts 20:20, 27
10 I have not kept the good news of Your justice
hidden in my heart;
I have talked about Your faithfulness
and saving power.
I have told everyone in the great assembly
of Your unfailing love and faithfulness.

40:11 Ps 61:7
11 LORD, don't hold back Your tender mercies from me.
Let Your unfailing love and faithfulness always
protect me.
40:12 Pss 18:5; 38:4; 73:26; 116:3
12 For troubles surround me—
too many to count!
My sins pile up so high
I can't see my way out.
They outnumber the hairs on my head.
I have lost all courage.

40:13-17 //Ps 70:1-5
13 Please, LORD, rescue me!
Come quickly, LORD, and help me.
40:14 Pss 35:4, 26; 70:2-3
14 May those who try to destroy me
be humiliated and put to shame.
May those who take delight in my trouble
be turned back in disgrace.
15 Let them be horrified by their shame,
for they said, "Aha! We've got him now!"

40:16 Pss 35:27; 70:4
16 But may all who search for You
be filled with joy and gladness in You.
May those who love Your salvation
repeatedly shout, "The LORD is great!"
40:17 Ps 70:5
17 As for me, since I am poor and needy,
let the Lord keep me in His thoughts.
You are my helper and my savior.
O my God, do not delay.

40:11-13 The tone of the psalm now changes dramatically. Having celebrated God's past faithfulness, David now calls upon God to deliver him from a present crisis. He knows no hope other than God's faithfulness to His word and love for His people. David's enemies encircle him and he has no escape if God will not help him. David pleads simply and forthrightly for God to come to his aid. The apostle John will echo this sentiment at the close of the Christian canon by inviting the soon return of our Lord (Revelation 22:20).

40:16-17 David returns to a tone of confidence and exultation. His confidence is grounded in God's character and his assurance of God's intimate concern for His people.

▶ WORSHIP

40:17 I am poor and needy. All of us fit into the category of the poor and needy. Even if a person is wealthy, famous, and healthy, he doesn't necessarily have the kind of riches that really matter. For example, look at the lives of movie stars or business tycoons. Many wallow in depression and loneliness. David was a person who obtained high regard in this life as the king of Israel. But he recognized that apart from God, he was poor and needy. Understanding this fact is the first step to gaining spiritual riches—the only wealth that lasts. (***See Worship***> *OT> Music> Psalms> Lament> Individual,* TopicGuide page A27.)

PSALM 41

For the choir director: A psalm of David.

1 Oh, the joys of those who are kind to the poor!
The LORD rescues them when they are in trouble.
2 The LORD protects them
and keeps them alive.
He gives them prosperity in the land
and rescues them from their enemies.
3 The LORD nurses them when they are sick
and restores them to health.

4 "O LORD," I prayed, "have mercy on me.
Heal me, for I have sinned against You."
5 But my enemies say nothing but evil about me.
"How soon will he die and be forgotten?" they ask.
6 They visit me as if they were my friends,
but all the while they gather gossip,
and when they leave, they spread it everywhere.
7 All who hate me whisper about me,
imagining the worst.
8 "He has some fatal disease," they say.
"He will never get out of that bed!"
9 Even my best friend, the one I trusted completely,
the one who shared my food, has turned against me.

10 LORD, have mercy on me.
Make me well again, so I can pay them back!
11 I know You are pleased with me,
for You have not let my enemies triumph over me.
12 You have preserved my life because I am innocent;
You have brought me into Your presence forever.

13 Praise the LORD, the God of Israel,
who lives from everlasting to everlasting.
Amen and amen!

41:1 Pss 37:19; 82:3-4 Prov 14:21
41:2 Ps 37:22, 28
41:4 Pss 6:2; 51:4; 103:3
41:5 Ps 38:12
41:6 Ps 12:2
41:7 Ps 56:5
41:9 Job 19:19 Ps 55:12-13, 20 Jer 20:10 *Mark 14:18 *John 13:18
41:10 Ps 3:3
41:11 Pss 25:2; 37:23-24; 147:11
41:12 Job 36:7 Pss 21:6; 37:17
41:13 Pss 72:18-19; 106:48

▶ CHURCH
41:1 Be kind to the poor. Any reputable church must do more than preach God's Word. The ministry must also address the needs of those they serve, even those too weak to cry out for help. Paul reported that the elders in Jerusalem had advised him to continue his ministry, adding, "Their only suggestion was that we keep on helping the poor, which I have always been eager to do" (Galatians 2:10). Are you involved in ministry to the poor, particularly the Christian poor (Acts 4:34)? How can you take care of the "least of these" (Matthew 25:40, 45)? Your actions will bring you much joy and reflect God's heart toward the poor. (***See Church***> *Role> Preach> Topics> Godly Lives> Make the most of opportunities for kindness,* TopicGuide page A50.)

41:1-3 This portion of the psalm may have been spoken by a priest to a worshiper coming in distress. The blessing assumes that those who would receive kindness from the hand of God in their time of need should exhibit kindness to others in their need. Verses 2 and 3 provide specific examples of the blessedness described in verse 1.

41:4 David expresses his urgent petition. He seeks healing of body and spirit—deliverance from illness and forgiveness of sins. As in Psalms 32 and 38, David assumes that in these specific circumstances, there is a link between sin and physical suffering. He would have been well aware that sickness is not necessarily the result of particular sins (consider Job 1–2).

41:5-8 The majority of David's lament focuses not on the symptoms of his illness but on the enemies who are taking advantage of his weakness. They take pleasure in speaking of his impending demise, perhaps also spreading rumors of sins for which they suppose David is being punished.

▶ GOD
41:13 God is eternal. After eight decades, the human body begins to tire. So when the Bible says that God is eternal, within that concept lies the fact that God never "wears out." Isaiah writes, "Have you never heard? Have you never understood? The LORD is the everlasting God, the Creator of all the earth. He never grows weak or weary" (Isaiah 40:28). Place your trust in His eternal nature, for He will always be present to help you. He will never grow tired of loving you and shaping you into someone who can love Him to your fullest. (***See God***> *God's Nature> Eternal> He precedes all else that exists,* TopicGuide page A14.)

BOOK TWO (PSALMS 42–72)

PSALM 42

For the choir director: A psalm of the descendants of Korah.*

42:1 Ps 63:1 — 1 As the deer longs for streams of water,
so I long for You, O God.
2 I thirst for God, the living God.
When can I go and stand before Him?
42:2 Pss 43:4; 84:2; 143:6; Jer 10:10; Rom 9:26 — 3 Day and night I have only tears for food,
while my enemies continually taunt me, saying,
"Where is this God of yours?"

42:3 Pss 79:10; 80:5; Joel 2:17 — 4 My heart is breaking
as I remember how it used to be:
42:4 Job 30:16; Ps 100:4; Isa 30:29 — I walked among the crowds of worshipers,
leading a great procession to the house of God,
singing for joy and giving thanks
amid the sound of a great celebration!

42:5 Pss 38:6; 77:3; Lam 3:24 — 5 Why am I discouraged?
Why is my heart so sad?
I will put my hope in God!
I will praise Him again—
42:6 Ps 61:2; *Mark 14:34 — my Savior and 6 my God!

Now I am deeply discouraged,
but I will remember You—
even from distant Mount Hermon, the source of the Jordan,
from the land of Mount Mizar.
42:7 Ps 88:7; Jon 2:3 — 7 I hear the tumult of the raging seas
as Your waves and surging tides sweep over me.
42:8 Job 35:10; Pss 16:7; 57:3; 77:6; 149:4-5 — 8 But each day the LORD pours His unfailing love upon me,
and through each night I sing His songs,
praying to God who gives me life.

42:9 Pss 17:9; 38:6 — 9 "O God my rock," I cry,
"Why have You forgotten me?

42:TITLE Hebrew *maskil.* This may be a literary or musical term.

42:1-2 The psalmist seizes upon an image from nature, a thirsty deer in a dry land, to describe his deep longing for the Lord. The specific desire of the psalmist is to worship the Lord before His presence in the Temple. The metaphor of thirst for spiritual longing is taken up by Jesus on the cross as He faces alienation from the Father (John 19:28).

▸ SALVATION

42:2 Thirsting for God. Life is like running a long-distance race. It takes training and determination to keep up the pace. When a racer runs in the hot sun, he soon feels the clutching grasp of thirst. The feeling can become so strong that it can make the runner focus all his attention on quenching that thirst. The thought of water becomes all-encompassing. As believers, we should feel that same sort of desperate need for God. Our complete attention should be focused on Him. Walk with God, spend time with God's people, and nourish yourself on God's Word, always praying (1 Thessalonians 5:17). (***See Salvation****> Receiving> Results> Perseverance,* TopicGuide page A23.)

▸ GOD

42:4 The broken heart. Contrary to popular opinion, it's not unusual for a Christian, even a joyful one, to have a broken heart. The sin in this world is enough to sadden anyone; then there's the sin in our own hearts. Loved ones betray us, spouses die, and churches we love fall apart due to unspiritual leadership. Rather than cover up the reality of emotional pain in this world, we should bring it to God. By faith, we can receive the hope that God offers (42:5). We will find that while we may still feel sad, we can now praise God in the midst of the pain that often accompanies real life in the real world. (***See God****> God's Attributes> Loving> God deserves thanks because of His perpetual love,* TopicGuide page A16.)

Why must I wander around in grief,
oppressed by my enemies?"
10 Their taunts break my bones.
They scoff, "Where is this God of yours?"

11 Why am I discouraged?
Why is my heart so sad?
I will put my hope in God!
I will praise Him again—
my Savior and my God!

PSALM 43

1 Declare me innocent, O God!
Defend me against these ungodly people.
Rescue me from these unjust liars.
2 For You are God, my only safe haven.
Why have You tossed me aside?
Why must I wander around in grief,
oppressed by my enemies?
3 Send out Your light and Your truth;
let them guide me.
Let them lead me to Your holy mountain,
to the place where You live.
4 There I will go to the altar of God,
to God—the source of all my joy.
I will praise You with my harp,
O God, my God!

5 Why am I discouraged?
Why is my heart so sad?

43:1
1 Sam 24:15
Pss 26:1; 35:24

43:2
Pss 42:9; 44:9

43:3
Pss 36:9; 84:1

43:4
Pss 26:6; 33:2

42:4 The psalmist tries to find comfort in memories of experiences of worship amid the pilgrim throngs that traveled to the Temple during the great feasts of Israel. Such memories, however, only aggravate his sense of alienation. The memories taunt him rather than comfort him.

42:5-6 This refrain will occur twice more (42:11; 43:5). The psalmist attempts to balance the emotions of his circumstances with his faith that God can transform them. Present distress tends to overwhelm, but reflecting on God can combat the tyranny of the present by providing a transcendent perspective.

42:6-7 Once again, the psalmist seeks refuge in memory. The locations he mentions appear to be places where he had experienced God's blessing. But relief does not accompany his remembrance; rather, he employs the familiar imagery of tumultuous waters to describe his continuing despair.

▸ GOD
43:1 Our Defender. What if you were on trial and had no one to defend you? You would be ill-prepared for the accusations thrown at you at the legal proceedings—even the truth might not save you. The good news is that God, who is the perfect Judge, has appointed His Son, Jesus Christ, as our defender. As the apostle John writes, "My dear children, I am writing this to you so that you will not sin. But if anyone does sin, we have an advocate who pleads our case before the Father. He is Jesus Christ, the One who is truly righteous" (1 John 2:1). His advocacy enables you to stand guiltless before God. (***See God***> *God's Names> Son> Advocate/ Intercessor,* TopicGuide page A18.)

43:1 Rather than follow the refrain of 42:11 with another lament focusing on efforts to revive his spirits through introspection and memory, the psalmist now turns explicitly to prayer. He does not address himself, but God. This marks the transition from lament and discouragement to praise and joy.

43:3-4 The psalmist no longer wallows in remembrances or seeks to strengthen himself. Now he acknowledges his need of God's grace and direction. Furthermore, he is no longer content to remember past experiences of worship before the Lord; he will now go to the Temple and worship God anew.

▸ WORSHIP
43:4 A musical offering. Everywhere we go, we can hear music from stringed instruments. This is nothing new—in Old Testament times, the harp was used for a variety of purposes. It was used in Temple worship (Psalm 33:2-3), in the royal court (1 Samuel 16:16), in battle, and in civil ceremonies (Nehemiah 12:27). In all these cases, music allowed the musician and audience to turn their focus to God. Whatever style of music you enjoy, use it to direct your thoughts and feelings to God. (***See Worship***> *OT> Music> Psalms> Lament> Individual,* TopicGuide page A27.)

I will put my hope in God!
  I will praise Him again—
  my Savior and my God!

PSALM 44

For the choir director: A psalm of the descendants of Korah.*

44:1 Exod 12:26-27
1 O God, we have heard it with our own ears—
  our ancestors have told us
of all You did in their day,
  in days long ago:
44:2 Pss 78:55; 80:8
2 You drove out the pagan nations by Your power
  and gave all the land to our ancestors.
You crushed their enemies
  and set our ancestors free.
44:3 Deut 4:37; Josh 24:12; Ps 77:15
3 They did not conquer the land with their swords;
  it was not their own strong arm that gave them victory.
It was Your right hand and strong arm
  and the blinding light from Your face that
    helped them,
  for You loved them.

44:4 Ps 74:12
4 You are my King and my God.
  You command victories for Israel.*
44:5 Ps 60:12
5 Only by Your power can we push back our enemies;
  only in Your name can we trample our foes.
6 I do not trust in my bow;
  I do not count on my sword to save me.
44:7 Pss 53:5; 136:24
7 You are the One who gives us victory over our enemies;
  You disgrace those who hate us.
44:8 Pss 30:12; 34:2
8 O God, we give glory to You all day long
  and constantly praise Your name. *Interlude*

44:9 Pss 43:2; 60:10; 74:1
9 But now You have tossed us aside in dishonor.
  You no longer lead our armies to battle.
44:10 Josh 7:8, 12; Ps 89:41
10 You make us retreat from our enemies
  and allow those who hate us to plunder our land.
44:11 Deut 4:27; 28:64; Ps 106:27; Ezek 20:23-24
11 You have butchered us like sheep
  and scattered us among the nations.
44:12 Isa 52:3-4
12 You sold Your precious people for a pittance,
  making nothing on the sale.
44:13 Pss 79:4; 80:6
13 You let our neighbors mock us.
  We are an object of scorn and derision to those around us.
44:14 Ps 109:25; Jer 24:9
14 You have made us the butt of their jokes;
  they shake their heads at us in scorn.
15 We can't escape the constant humiliation;
  shame is written across our faces.

44:TITLE Hebrew *maskil.* This may be a literary or musical term. **44:4** Hebrew *for Jacob.* The names "Jacob" and "Israel" are often interchanged throughout the Old Testament, referring sometimes to the individual patriarch and sometimes to the nation.

44:4-8 The psalmist appropriates the past for the present. He knows that the God of Israel is not a relic of the past but is still at work in Israel's history. The armies of Joshua relied on God, and so does the psalmist. He confesses his dependence on God's strength and attributes all glory to God for the expected victory.

44:9-16 The tone of the psalm changes dramatically. The remembrance of past victories (44:1-3) and present reliance on God's strength (44:4-8) do not result in victory. Israel's army is defeated and the psalmist expresses a sense of abandonment. The glory that would have belonged to the Lord is now reversed, and the enemies of Israel mock God's people.

[16] All we hear are the taunts of our mockers.
All we see are our vengeful enemies.

[17] All this has happened though we have not forgotten You.
We have not violated Your covenant.
[18] Our hearts have not deserted You.
We have not strayed from Your path.
[19] Yet You have crushed us in the jackal's desert home.
You have covered us with darkness and death.
[20] If we had forgotten the name of our God
or spread our hands in prayer to foreign gods,
[21] God would surely have known it,
for He knows the secrets of every heart.
[22] But for Your sake we are killed every day;
we are being slaughtered like sheep.
[23] Wake up, O Lord! Why do You sleep?
Get up! Do not reject us forever.
[24] Why do You look the other way?
Why do You ignore our suffering and oppression?
[25] We collapse in the dust,
lying face down in the dirt.
[26] Rise up! Help us!
Ransom us because of Your unfailing love.

44:17 Pss 119:61, 83, 109, 141, 153, 176
44:18 Job 23:11 Ps 119:51, 157
44:19 Job 3:5 Ps 51:8
44:20 Ps 81:9
44:22 Isa 53:7 *Rom 8:36
44:23 Pss 7:6; 77:7; 78:65
44:24 Job 13:24 Pss 42:9; 88:14
44:25 Ps 119:25

PSALM 45

For the choir director: A love song to be sung to the tune "Lilies." A psalm of the descendants of Korah.*

[1] Beautiful words stir my heart.
I will recite a lovely poem about the king,
for my tongue is like the pen of a skillful poet.

45:TITLE Hebrew *maskil.* This may be a literary or musical term.

44:17-21 The language used to describe Israel's defeat is similar to the curses for disobedience attached to the covenant (Deuteronomy 28:15-69). The psalmist, however, is deeply troubled because Israel has been faithful. Defeat amid disobedience would make sense. But defeat despite faithfulness produces despair and confusion.

▸ WORSHIP
44:18 Finding the right path. One day while Jason and his mother were walking together to preschool, Jason's eye caught sight of a frog in the gutter. Without warning, he slipped his hand out of his mother's and dashed into the street after the frog. Reacting quickly, his mother grabbed him by the back of the shirt and pulled him back onto the sidewalk. Many times, we react to situations around us and take action without thinking about God's will or the consequences. God wants us to use reason and consult Him and His Word first because they are our guide to keeping on the right road. They protect us from getting off the path. Keep in constant prayer over the decisions you make each day—big or small—so that you do not stray from God's path. (***See Worship****> OT> Music> Psalms> Lament> Community,* TopicGuide page A27.)

44:23-26 The psalmist never arrives at a solution to his conflict, but his faith in God remains. The psalmist employs battlefield language ("Wake up!"; "Rise up!"), perhaps because the war still rages, to move God to action. He grounds his appeal for help in God's covenantal ("unfailing") love.

▸ GOD
44:26 Hope in discouragement. A renowned writer found himself facing a debilitating illness and the ravages of aging. All the fame and accolades he had received in his lifetime couldn't push away the despair he felt. Without God and without hope, he committed suicide. In a similar position, the faithful believer has reason to hope. One Christian man amazed those around him with his intractable hope in the midst of the trial of incurable cancer. He knew that God's strength was sufficient for that and any other situation. He knew a glorious future awaited him. You can put your hope in God, too. He can give you the courage to face any foe—even death. (***See God****> God's Attributes> Faithful> God is faithful through calamity,* TopicGuide page A16.)

▸ MINISTRY
45:1 A poem to the King. Have you ever considered using poetry in your public and private worship? People often don't regard poetry with the high esteem it received in the past. Yet reading or writing poetry is a marvelous way to express our feelings to God. Singing excellent song lyrics is another way we can use the beauty of language to praise God. The ancient poetry of the psalms shows us that God intends Christians to use poetry to inspire and to focus our worship. (***See Ministry****> Transformation> Vocations> Writer,* TopicGuide page A57.)

45:2 Ps 21:6 Luke 4:22	[2] You are the most handsome of all. Gracious words stream from your lips. God himself has blessed you forever. [3] Put on your sword, O mighty warrior! You are so glorious, so majestic!
45:4 Rev 6:2	[4] In your majesty, ride out to victory, defending truth, humility, and justice. Go forth to perform awe-inspiring deeds!
45:5 Ps 120:4 Isa 5:28	[5] Your arrows are sharp, piercing your enemies' hearts. The nations fall beneath your feet.
45:6 Pss 93:2; 98:8-9 *Heb 1:8-9	[6] Your throne, O God,* endures forever and ever. You rule with a scepter of justice. [7] You love justice and hate evil.
45:7 Pss 11:7; 21:6; 33:5	Therefore God, your God, has anointed you, pouring out the oil of joy on you more than on anyone else.
45:8 Song 1:3; 4:13-14	[8] Myrrh, aloes, and cassia perfume your robes. In ivory palaces the music of strings entertains you.
45:9 1 Kgs 2:19; 9:28 Song 6:8 Isa 13:12	[9] Kings' daughters are among your noble women. At your right side stands the queen, wearing jewelry of finest gold from Ophir!
45:10 Deut 21:13	[10] Listen to me, O royal daughter; take to heart what I say. Forget your people and your family far away. [11] For your royal husband delights in your beauty; honor him, for he is your lord.
45:12 Ps 72:10-11	[12] The princess of Tyre* will shower you with gifts. The wealthy will beg your favor.
45:13 Isa 61:10	[13] The bride, a princess, looks glorious in her golden gown.
45:14 Song 1:4 Ezek 16:9-13	[14] In her beautiful robes, she is led to the king, accompanied by her bridesmaids. [15] What a joyful and enthusiastic procession as they enter the king's palace! [16] Your sons will become kings like their father. You will make them rulers over many lands.
45:17 Ps 138:4 Mal 1:11	[17] I will bring honor to your name in every generation. Therefore, the nations will praise you forever and ever.

45:6 Or *Your divine throne.* 45:12 Hebrew *The daughter of Tyre.*

45:2-5 The psalmist first extols the beauty of the king. This beauty is not primarily physical, as the following verses make clear. And the king's blessedness is not inherent to him; it is God's gift. God had promised to uphold and bless David's dynasty forever (2 Samuel 7). The psalmist then exalts the king by calling attention to his virtues as a warrior. The king defeats the enemies of his people and fights on behalf of justice. In this way, the king reflects God, the divine Warrior, fighting for His people (Exodus 14:14). He also anticipates Christ, the King of kings, conquering all the forces of evil in this world (Revelation 19:11-16).

45:6 The psalmist equates the throne of Israel with the throne of God (2 Chronicles 9:8). The Davidic king was God's representative on earth; he was a vice-regent under God. The temporal and temporary reign of the Davidic king foreshadowed the cosmic and eternal reign of Christ (Ephesians 1:19-23).

45:10-11 The bride apparently is from a foreign land. It would be natural for her to miss her home, but the psalmist encourages her to forsake her past and cling to the king and her new future. It should be noted that marriage to foreign wives often led Israelite kings astray (1 Kings 11:1-8; 16:31).

▸ ADOPTION

45:13 A bride dressed in gold. Picture a bride waiting for her groom. She's dressed in a gorgeous bridal gown and she's looking forward to a new life with her husband-to-be. And if her husband is part of the royal family, what a future awaits her! She will receive a new title and will inherit the riches (and responsibilities) of her new station. How does she feel? Excited, a little nervous, perhaps even a little impatient. It might surprise you to know that you are that bride. If you are a part of the church, the Bible describes you as the bride of Christ (Ephesians 5:22-32; Revelation 21:9). We are waiting for Him to end this long engagement. Are you excited? A little impatient? Are your thoughts about Him and your future together? Look forward to holy intimacy with Christ. (***See Adoption**> In Heaven> Married to Christ*, TopicGuide page A37.)

PSALM 46

*For the choir director: A song of the descendants of Korah, to be sung by soprano voices.**

1 God is our refuge and strength,
always ready to help in times of trouble.
2 So we will not fear when earthquakes come
and the mountains crumble into the sea.
3 Let the oceans roar and foam.
Let the mountains tremble as the waters surge! *Interlude*

4 A river brings joy to the city of our God,
the sacred home of the Most High.
5 God dwells in that city; it cannot be destroyed.
From the very break of day, God will protect it.
6 The nations are in chaos,
and their kingdoms crumble!
God's voice thunders,
and the earth melts!
7 The LORD of Heaven's Armies is here among us;
the God of Israel* is our fortress. *Interlude*

8 Come, see the glorious works of the LORD:
See how He brings destruction upon the world.
9 He causes wars to end throughout the earth.
He breaks the bow and snaps the spear;
He burns the shields with fire.

10 "Be still, and know that I am God!
I will be honored by every nation.
I will be honored throughout the world."

11 The LORD of Heaven's Armies is here among us;
the God of Israel is our fortress. *Interlude*

46:1 Deut 4:7; Pss 9:9; 14:6; 62:7-8; 145:18
46:2 Pss 18:7; 23:4; 82:5
46:4 Ps 87:3; Rev 3:12; 22:1
46:5 Isa 12:6; 41:14; Ezek 43:7; Luke 1:54
46:6 Ps 2:1; Mic 1:4
46:7 Num 14:9; 2 Chr 13:12; Ps 9:9
46:8 Ps 66:5; Isa 61:4; Jer 51:43
46:9 Isa 2:4; 9:5; Mic 4:3
46:10 Ps 100:3; Isa 2:11, 17

46:TITLE Hebrew *according to alamoth.* **46:7** Hebrew *of Jacob;* also in 46:11. See note on 44:4.

46:1-3 The opening verse announces the theme of the psalm—God is a source of protection in times of crisis. Such times are described in language that alludes to the mythology of the ancient world. The tumultuous waters represented the forces of chaos that threatened to overturn the order of creation. The psalmist envisions just such a descent into primordial chaos, yet he refuses to fear because God is his refuge. This theme is echoed in Psalm 46:7, 11.

▸ PURPOSE
46:2 Fear no evil. One of the most beloved verses in the Bible, Psalm 23:4 says, "Even when I walk through the darkest valley, I will not be afraid, for You are close beside me." That's the secret to conquering our fear in any situation—knowing that God is beside us. An earthquake cannot shake God. A mud slide cannot sweep away His strength. A hurricane cannot match His mighty arm. Anything we experience is nothing compared to His wisdom and might. Fear nothing—but God. (***See Purpose****> God's Deeds> Judgment> Mountains quake/earthquake,* TopicGuide page A53.)

46:4-6 The psalmist now shifts the imagery to Jerusalem, the city God chose as His dwelling. The language associates Jerusalem (which has no rivers) with Eden, through which a river ran (Genesis 2:10). His presence assures the safety of the city, even though invading armies threatened disorder. The Edenic imagery reappears in Ezekiel's Temple vision and in the image of the New Jerusalem (Ezekiel 47; Revelation 22:1).

46:8-10 The psalmist draws the main themes of the psalm together by inviting his readers to witness the power of God over the chaos inherent in natural cataclysm and war. God is able to defeat the powers of disorder in nature and the power of Israel's enemies.

▸ WORSHIP
46:10 Silence! Walking into the chaotic classroom, the teacher had one word that solved the problem: "Quiet!" Students scattered like cockroaches under a bright light, into their seats and into obedience. This is the equivalent of what God is saying to the upstart nations (46:6) and the warring factions (46:9). In this psalm, God demands the quiet submission of all nations to His supreme authority. The psalmist dreams of the day when every nation will honor God as the one true God, just as He is honored by His covenant people. Until then, let all who would oppose God hide their shamed faces and quietly consider the fate of those who rebel against Him. (***See Worship****> OT> Music> Psalms> Liturgy> Songs of Zion,* TopicGuide page A27.)

PSALM 47

For the choir director: A psalm of the descendants of Korah.

47:1 Pss 98:8-9; 106:47
1 Come, everyone! Clap your hands!
Shout to God with joyful praise!
47:2 Deut 7:21
2 For the LORD Most High is awesome.
He is the great King of all the earth.
47:3 Ps 18:47
3 He subdues the nations before us,
putting our enemies beneath our feet.
47:4 1 Pet 1:4
4 He chose the Promised Land as our inheritance,
the proud possession of Jacob's descendants, whom He loves. *Interlude*

47:5 Pss 68:18, 25, 33; 98:6
5 God has ascended with a mighty shout.
The LORD has ascended with trumpets blaring.
47:6 Ps 68:4
6 Sing praises to God, sing praises;
sing praises to our King, sing praises!
7 For God is the King over all the earth.
Praise Him with a psalm!
47:8 1 Chr 16:31
8 God reigns above the nations,
sitting on His holy throne.
47:9 Pss 72:11; 89:18; 97:9; Isa 49:7, 23; Rom 4:11-12
9 The rulers of the world have gathered together
with the people of the God of Abraham.
For all the kings of the earth belong to God.
He is highly honored everywhere.

PSALM 48

A song. A psalm of the descendants of Korah.

48:1 1 Chr 16:25; Pss 87:1; 96:4; 145:3; Zech 8:3
1 How great is the LORD,
how deserving of praise,
in the city of our God,
which sits on His holy mountain!

47:1 *Everyone* literally means "nations." God is not merely a local deity as the ancient nations envisioned their gods. He is the God of all the earth and ought to be praised by all peoples. The psalm may be envisioning a gathering where representatives of nations subject to Israel are present.

▸ GOD
47:2 King of the earth. The pomp and ceremony surrounding a king is intended to elevate him among his people. Usually, the king's throne sits higher than the floor so that visitors have to look up at him when they approach. The jewel-studded crown is a symbol of the king's authority. His royal robes show his richness. The guards around him signify his military might. His words are written as law. These honors describe kings who merely rule a portion of land on this earth. How much more magnificent is the God of the universe! All heaven falls at His feet in worship. Countless choirs of angels sing His praises. Even the most honored of saints bow before Him. All nature obeys His voice. Praise our awesome God. (***See God****> God's Names> God> King,* TopicGuide page A18.)

47:3-4 God's rule was exhibited in His military victories on Israel's behalf, by which the land of Canaan was secured as Israel's inheritance. The record of the conquest and all subsequent reflections on it attribute Israel's success to God's aid in battle (Deuteronomy 7:7-11; Joshua 5:13-15).

47:5 The ascension described here may be that of the Ark of the Covenant in a procession to the Temple following a victory in battle. Or it may metaphorically depict the ascent of God to His throne.

▸ WORSHIP
47:9 Rulers praise God. Although God is still sovereign over all events on the earth, most rulers don't respect Him. In fact, some are hostile toward God. But when Christ's kingdom is manifested on earth as it is in heaven, all leaders will submit to His authority. As the psalmist says, "Now then, you kings, act wisely! Be warned, you rulers of the earth! Serve the LORD with reverent fear, and rejoice with trembling. Submit to God's royal son, or He will become angry" (Psalm 2:10-12). Do you want to see the day when Jesus will reign over the entire world? If not, why? (***See Worship****> OT> Music> Psalms> Liturgy> Royal,* TopicGuide page A27.)

48:1-3 The opening verse sets the tone for the psalm. The city in view is Jerusalem, which God chose to be His dwelling place on earth. The holy mountain is Mount Zion, the particular hill on which the Temple was located. The psalm celebrates God's presence in Jerusalem and His protection of the city. The psalm also anticipates the day Gentiles will worship the God of Israel. The fulfillment of this vision commences with the work of Christ, who brings Jews and Gentiles together into one body (Ephesians 2:11-22; Revelation 21:10-27).

[2] It is high and magnificent;
the whole earth rejoices to see it!
Mount Zion, the holy mountain,*
is the city of the great King!
[3] God Himself is in Jerusalem's towers,
revealing Himself as its defender.

[4] The kings of the earth joined forces
and advanced against the city.
[5] But when they saw it, they were stunned;
they were terrified and ran away.
[6] They were gripped with terror
and writhed in pain like a woman in labor.
[7] You destroyed them like the mighty
ships of Tarshish
shattered by a powerful east wind.

[8] We had heard of the city's glory,
but now we have seen it ourselves—
the city of the LORD of Heaven's Armies.
It is the city of our God;
He will make it safe forever. *Interlude*

[9] O God, we meditate on Your unfailing love
as we worship in Your Temple.
[10] As Your name deserves, O God,
You will be praised to the ends of the earth.
Your strong right hand is filled with victory.
[11] Let the people on Mount Zion rejoice.
Let all the towns of Judah be glad
because of Your justice.

[12] Go, inspect the city of Jerusalem.*
Walk around and count the many towers.
[13] Take note of the fortified walls,
and tour all the citadels,
that You may describe them
to future generations.
[14] For that is what God is like.
He is our God forever and ever,
and He will guide us until we die.

48:2 Ps 50:2; Lam 2:15; Matt 5:35
48:3 Ps 46:7
48:4 2 Sam 10:6-19
48:5 Exod 15:15
48:6 Isa 13:8
48:8 Ps 87:5
48:9 Pss 26:3; 40:10
48:10 Josh 7:9; Isa 41:10; Mal 1:11
48:11 Ps 97:8
48:13 Ps 78:5-7
48:14 Ps 23:4; Isa 58:11

48:2 Or *Mount Zion, in the far north;* Hebrew reads *Mount Zion, the heights of Zaphon.* 48:12 Hebrew *Zion.*

48:4-7 For the time being, the nations come not to worship but to invade. But their combined strength is thwarted by the awe-inspiring power of God. Their fear and retreat is described by the metaphors of childbirth and a great storm (compare Isaiah 13:8; 21:3). Tarshish most likely refers simply to the open sea.

48:8 The reaction of a faithful pilgrim is a sharp contrast to that of an invading army. Both see the same sight, Jerusalem, but while the invader runs in fear, the pilgrim is overwhelmed by joy and security. "The LORD of Heaven's Armies" is a military term, which accords well with the imagery of the psalm.

▸ GOD

48:14 Our faithful Guide. Finding and keeping a full-time, long-term job seems more difficult than ever. Business downturns eliminate jobs. Illnesses or family problems limit the energy for hard work. Technology changes the skills needed for continued productivity. Yet one thing is constant in our vocations—God's commands. God knows that times change, but God's Word gives principles for vocational faithfulness (1 Timothy 5:8; Proverbs 18:9). (***See God*****> *God's Attributes> Faithful> His faithfulness endures,* TopicGuide page A16.)

PSALM 49

For the choir director: A psalm of the descendants of Korah.

49:1 Pss 33:8; 78:1

1 Listen to this, all you people!
Pay attention, everyone in the world!
2 High and low,
rich and poor—listen!

49:3 Pss 37:30; 119:130

3 For my words are wise,
and my thoughts are filled with insight.

49:4 Num 12:8; 2 Kgs 3:15; Ps 78:2

4 I listen carefully to many proverbs
and solve riddles with inspiration from a harp.

49:5 Pss 23:4; 27:1

5 Why should I fear when trouble comes,
when enemies surround me?

49:6 Ps 52:7; Mark 10:24-25

6 They trust in their wealth
and boast of great riches.

49:7 Job 36:18

7 Yet they cannot redeem themselves from death*
by paying a ransom to God.

49:8 Matt 16:26

8 Redemption does not come so easily,
for no one can ever pay enough

49:9 Pss 22:29; 89:48

9 to live forever
and never see the grave.

49:10 Ps 39:6; Luke 12:20-21

10 Those who are wise must finally die,
just like the foolish and senseless,
leaving all their wealth behind.

49:11 Deut 3:14; Ps 10:6

11 The grave is their eternal home,
where they will stay forever.
They may name their estates after themselves,
12 but their fame will not last.
They will die, just like animals.

49:13 Jer 17:11

13 This is the fate of fools,
though they are remembered as being wise.* *Interlude*

49:14 Ps 9:17; Dan 7:18; Mal 4:3; 1 Cor 6:2; Rev 2:26

14 Like sheep, they are led to the grave,*
where death will be their shepherd.
In the morning the godly will rule over them.
Their bodies will rot in the grave,
far from their grand estates.

49:7 Or *no one can redeem the life of another.* 49:13 The meaning of the Hebrew is uncertain. 49:14 Hebrew *Sheol;* also in 49:14b, 15.

49:1-2 In a manner characteristic of wisdom literature, the psalmist addresses himself to humanity in a broad sense. His insights have application across ethnic and social boundaries. However, the psalm seems addressed particularly to the oppressed poor.

49:5-9 The psalmist offers perspective for the oppressed. It appears that he speaks to those who are poor and threatened by the power of the wealthy. However, the powerful have an enemy they cannot overcome by their wealth—death. All the money in the world cannot hold off death.

▸ SPIRITUAL WARFARE

49:7 Riches are no guarantee. In this world, wealth brings great advantages. You've probably noticed how this works. When you meet others, they often assess you by the quality of the clothes you wear or the status of the job you hold. When you need medical care, you receive the services that you can afford. When you apply for a loan, you are dealt with according to the size of your accounts. We can be so thankful that God does not favor one person over another. No one can buy his own redemption. We must all come to the cross with empty hands, but a repentant heart. (***See Spiritual Warfare****> Resisting Sin and Evil> Embracing Christ> Entrust yourself to God's care,* TopicGuide page A45.)

49:14-15 The psalmist employs two metaphors to contrast the fate of the wicked with that of the righteous. The wicked are like sheep being led away by death personified as a shepherd. They never see the light after they enter the grave. The righteous, however, survive the night of death. No one possesses enough wealth to redeem himself from death (49:7), but the righteous can trust in God to be their Redeemer.

15 But as for me, God will redeem my life.
He will snatch me from the power of the grave. *Interlude*

16 So don't be dismayed when the wicked grow rich
and their homes become ever more splendid.
17 For when they die, they take nothing with them.
Their wealth will not follow them into the grave.
18 In this life they consider themselves fortunate
and are applauded for their success.
19 But they will die like all before them
and never again see the light of day.
20 People who boast of their wealth don't understand;
they will die, just like animals.

49:15 Ps 16:10-11
49:16 Ps 37:7
49:17 Ps 17:14; 1 Tim 6:7
49:18 Ps 10:3; Luke 12:19
49:19 Job 33:29-30
49:20 Ps 49:12

PSALM 50

A psalm of Asaph.

1 The LORD, the Mighty One, is God,
and He has spoken;
He has summoned all humanity
from where the sun rises to where it sets.
2 From Mount Zion, the perfection of beauty,
God shines in glorious radiance.
3 Our God approaches,
and He is not silent.
Fire devours everything in His way,
and a great storm rages around Him.
4 He calls on the heavens above and earth below
to witness the judgment of His people.
5 "Bring My faithful people to Me—
those who made a covenant with Me by giving sacrifices."
6 Then let the heavens proclaim His justice,
for God Himself will be the judge. *Interlude*

7 "O My people, listen as I speak.
Here are My charges against you, O Israel:
I am God, your God!
8 I have no complaint about your sacrifices
or the burnt offerings you constantly offer.
9 But I do not need the bulls from your barns
or the goats from your pens.

50:1 Josh 22:22; Ps 113:3
50:2 Deut 33:2; Pss 48:2; 80:1
50:3 Ps 18:12-13; Dan 7:10
50:4 Deut 4:26; 32:1; Isa 1:2
50:5 Exod 24:7
50:6 Pss 75:7; 96:13; 97:6
50:8 Ps 40:6
50:9 Ps 69:31

▸ WORSHIP
49:18 Fading success. What is the world's definition of success? We can see it splashed over newspaper headlines, magazine covers, and book jackets. Those who have wealth (no matter how they got it), fame (in whatever area, good or bad), or position (the amount of power they hold) are admired by many. In spite of leading immoral lives, they are honored. Yet their success fades when they grow old and die. Then they must measure up to God's standard of success—righteousness. Whenever you find yourself drawn to the world's version of success, reread this psalm and remember the ultimate riches that will never fade away. (***See Worship****> OT> Music> Psalms> Lament> Individual,* TopicGuide page A27.)

50:1-6 God is portrayed descending from heaven to address and judge His people. The Lord's descent is described in language that is reminiscent of God's appearance at Mount Sinai (Exodus 19:16-19). He calls the world to observe what will transpire, and He calls heaven and earth to be witnesses of the proceedings. Finally, He calls His people to come before Him, that their faithfulness to the covenant may be judged. When all is done, all present will praise God's justice.

50:7-15 God now addresses His people on the meaning of sacrifices. The people performed their sacrifices, but they apparently misunderstood the purpose. Their misunderstanding was grounded in false assumptions about the nature of God and what He required. Sacrifices were not intended to supply God with something He lacked.

50:10 Ps 104:24
10 For all the animals of the forest are Mine,
and I own the cattle on a thousand hills.
11 I know every bird on the mountains,
and all the animals of the field are Mine.
50:12 Exod 19:5
12 If I were hungry, I would not tell you,
for all the world is Mine and everything in it.
50:13 Hos 6:6
13 Do I eat the meat of bulls?
Do I drink the blood of goats?
50:14 Deut 23:21 Hos 14:2 Rom 12:1 Heb 13:15
14 Make thankfulness your sacrifice to God,
and keep the vows you made to the Most High.
15 Then call on Me when you are in trouble,
and I will rescue you,
and you will give Me glory."

50:16 Isa 29:13
16 But God says to the wicked:
"Why bother reciting My decrees
and pretending to obey My covenant?
50:17 Neh 9:26 Rom 2:21-22
17 For you refuse My discipline
and treat My words like trash.
50:18 Rom 1:32 1 Tim 5:22
18 When you see thieves, you approve of them,
and you spend your time with adulterers.
50:19 Pss 10:7; 36:3
19 Your mouth is filled with wickedness,
and your tongue is full of lies.
50:20 Matt 10:21
20 You sit around and slander your brother—
your own mother's son.
50:21 Ps 90:8 Eccl 8:11 Isa 42:14
21 While you did all this, I remained silent,
and you thought I didn't care.
But now I will rebuke you,
listing all My charges against you.
50:22 Job 8:13 Ps 9:17
22 Repent, all of you who forget Me,
or I will tear you apart,
and no one will help you.
50:23 Pss 50:14; 85:13; 91:16
23 But giving thanks is a sacrifice that truly honors Me.
If you keep to My path,
I will reveal to you the salvation of God."

▸ GOD

50:12 God is self-sufficient. As humans, we are terribly dependent on each other. We need help in gathering our food, keeping healthy, addressing our emotional needs, and meeting our sexual needs. We could list countless other areas. But God is different. He needs nothing from us. Everything He needs He provides. No one can influence Him because He is self-sufficient. He can't be tempted by anything because He owns everything. He can't be swayed because He is unchanging. We are not like this—and God doesn't want us to be! But we should be grateful that God is God, and that He doesn't lack anything He needs to keep on being God. (***See God****> God's Attributes> Self-Existent> We have nothing materially that God needs or wants,* TopicGuide page A17.)

▸ BIBLE

50:13 Sacrifice is not sufficient. Many religions of the world teach the same concept: deities require sacrifices in order to be satisfied. Whether it's vowing to avoid certain foods, killing an animal, or performing certain deeds, the devout must work to meet certain standards. But in Christianity, we admit that our sacrifices and obedience are not good enough for our great God—only through the faithful Son, Jesus Christ, can we be saved from our sins. Rejoice in the perfect sacrifice of Jesus, setting you free from the treadmill of ceremonial law keeping and into a life of relying on Christ's once-and-for-all sacrifice to make us right with God! (***See Bible****> Unity> Salvation> Old Testament Sacrificial system cannot save,* TopicGuide page A11.)

50:16-20 The psalmist now turns his attention to those within the covenant community who know the law but do not obey it. The wicked violate the law of God, specifically the seventh, eighth, and ninth commandments (Exodus 20:14-16). The violations appear to involve a failure to grasp the full range of application for each commandment.

50:22-23 The psalm concludes with a call for repentance. A failure to repent will result in God's judgment, which is described graphically as being torn to pieces (compare Hosea 5:14).

PSALM 51

For the choir director: A psalm of David, regarding the time Nathan the prophet came to him after David had committed adultery with Bathsheba.

1 Have mercy on me, O God,
because of Your unfailing love.
Because of Your great compassion,
blot out the stain of my sins.
2 Wash me clean from my guilt.
Purify me from my sin.
3 For I recognize my rebellion;
it haunts me day and night.
4 Against You, and You alone, have I sinned;
I have done what is evil in Your sight.
You will be proved right in what You say,
and Your judgment against me is just.*
5 For I was born a sinner—
yes, from the moment my mother conceived me.
6 But You desire honesty from the womb,*
teaching me wisdom even there.

7 Purify me from my sins,* and I will be clean;
wash me, and I will be whiter than snow.
8 Oh, give me back my joy again;
You have broken me—
now let me rejoice.
9 Don't keep looking at my sins.
Remove the stain of my guilt.
10 Create in me a clean heart, O God.
Renew a loyal spirit within me.
11 Do not banish me from Your presence,
and don't take Your Holy Spirit* from me.

12 Restore to me the joy of Your salvation,
and make me willing to obey You.

51:1 Ps 4:1; Acts 3:19
51:2 Jer 33:8; Acts 22:16; Heb 9:13-14; 1 Jn 1:7, 9
51:3 Isa 59:12
51:4 Gen 20:6; Luke 15:21; *Rom 3:4
51:5 Ps 58:3; Job 14:4; Eph 2:3
51:7 Exod 12:22; Isa 1:18
51:9 Jer 16:17
51:10 Ps 78:37; Matt 5:8; Acts 15:9; Eph 2:10
51:11 Eph 4:30

51:4 Greek version reads *and You will win Your case in court.* Compare Rom 3:4. 51:6 Or *from the heart;* Hebrew reads *in the inward parts.* 51:7 Hebrew *Purify me with the hyssop branch.* 51:11 Or *your spirit of holiness.*

51:1-2 David casts himself on the mercy of God. He can make no claim on God's favor, but God has committed Himself to David in a covenant relationship ("unfailing love"), and David grounds his plea in that relationship. The expression *blot out* is usually associated with striking words from a scroll or tablet (Psalm 69:28). The words "wash" and "purify" are connected with washing clothes and ritual cleansing, respectively (Exodus 19:10; Leviticus 11:32).

▸ GOD
51:4 All sin is against God. Sometimes we consider certain sins to be insignificant or explainable—the "white" lie we tell, the grudge that seems justified, or the private sins about which no one knows. The problem is that all sin is committed against God, a God who will not be defied, publicly or privately. In that light, consider anew your actions and attitudes. (***See God****> God's Attributes> Just> All sin is ultimately against a righteous God,* TopicGuide page A16.)

51:5 David acknowledges the deep roots of sin in his being. He sees that sin is not an accidental feature of his otherwise good character. Instead, sin has been endemic to his being from conception. Far from excusing David, this indicates his (and our) desperate need of God's mercy and grace.

▸ HOLINESS
51:8 Rejoicing after repentance. Some of the most painful moments we can experience are times when God reveals the blackness of our sin to us. Our hearts break over the ugliness of what we have done and its consequences—the people we have hurt, the ways in which we have failed, the lack we see in our character. But out of the valley of repentance, God raises us up to a time of rejoicing. We once again have the joy of walking in step with God's Spirit (Galatians 5:25). Ask God to restore your joy through heartfelt repentance. He will! (***See Holiness****> Submission> Delighting in God> Rejoicing in repentance,* TopicGuide page A40.)

▸ SPIRITUAL WARFARE
51:12 Make me willing to obey. All our intimacy with God can dissipate like sugar in hot water when we are depressed. Perhaps you can see it coming—does it start with irritability or a short fuse? What can you do when you sense depres-

51:13 Ps 22:27 13 Then I will teach Your ways to rebels,
and they will return to You.
51:14 2 Sam 12:9 Pss 9:14; 25:5; 71:15 14 Forgive me for shedding blood, O God who saves;
then I will joyfully sing of Your forgiveness.
15 Unseal my lips, O Lord,
that my mouth may praise You.

51:16 1 Sam 15:22 Ps 40:6 16 You do not desire a sacrifice, or I would offer one.
You do not want a burnt offering.
51:17 Ps 34:18 17 The sacrifice You desire is a broken spirit.
You will not reject a broken and repentant heart, O God.
51:18 Isa 51:3 18 Look with favor on Zion and help her;
rebuild the walls of Jerusalem.
51:19 Pss 4:5; 66:13, 15 19 Then You will be pleased with sacrifices offered in the right spirit—
with burnt offerings and whole burnt offerings.
Then bulls will again be sacrificed on Your altar.

PSALM 52

For the choir director: A psalm of David, regarding the time Doeg the Edomite said to Saul, "David has gone to see Ahimelech."*

52:1 Ps 94:4 1 Why do you boast about your crimes, great warrior?
Don't you realize God's justice continues forever?
52:2 Pss 5:9; 57:4; 59:7 2 All day long you plot destruction.
Your tongue cuts like a sharp razor;
you're an expert at telling lies.
52:3 Pss 36:4; 58:3 Jer 9:4-5 3 You love evil more than good
and lies more than truth. *Interlude*

52:4 Ps 120:3 4 You love to destroy others with your words,
you liar!
52:5 Prov 2:22 Isa 22:18-19 5 But God will strike you down once and for all.
He will pull you from your home
and uproot you from the land of the living. *Interlude*

52:6 Job 22:19 Ps 40:3 6 The righteous will see it and be amazed.
They will laugh and say,

52:TITLE Hebrew *maskil.* This may be a literary or musical term.

sion coming on? Go back to the fundamentals of your faith by thanking God for the incredible price He paid for our salvation (Romans 5:6-10). Realizing how valuable God considers your life will help you focus on His love rather than on your inadequacies. Then ask a loving God to give you a willing heart to obey Him. (***See Spiritual Warfare****> Resisting Sin and Evil> Consequences> Of Disobedience> Conviction of the Spirit/Lack of Joy,* TopicGuide page A46.)

51:16-17 David is not condemning the sacrificial system as such, as 51:19 indicates. Rather, he is saying that sacrifices without heartfelt repentance and devotion are of no value. David understands the futility of going through the motions of worship if his heart is not right with God (compare Micah 6:6-8).

52:1-4 The wicked man who thinks he's a mighty warrior has inverted all values. He values lies over truth and evil over goodness. He has rejected God's moral order. His sins are verbal in nature; his plots consist of lies designed to entrap innocent people.

▸ HOLINESS

52:3 Hating evil. Do you really hate evil? Is it something that makes your blood boil? Many times we compromise by shrugging off evil. A little lie is all right as long as it doesn't hurt anyone. A moment of flirting with someone other than your spouse is okay as long as it goes no further. Your sharp-tongued response to your friend is all right because she actually deserves it. When we do this, we are like princes or princesses dressed in royal robes standing in a pool of barnyard muck. Make sure that you hate your sin enough to forsake it. (***See Holiness****> Law and Grace> Law> Hate evil,* TopicGuide page A42.)

52:5 David describes the judgment that awaits the wicked man through a series of metaphors that suggest the decisiveness and finality of God's punishment. "Uproot" contrasts the fate of the wicked with that of David, who is planted firmly like an olive tree (52:8).

7 "Look what happens to mighty warriors
who do not trust in God.
They trust their wealth instead
and grow more and more bold in their wickedness."

8 But I am like an olive tree, thriving in the house of God.
I will always trust in God's unfailing love.
9 I will praise You forever, O God,
for what You have done.
I will trust in Your good name
in the presence of Your faithful people.

52:8 Pss 13:5; 128:3 Jer 11:16

52:9 Pss 30:12; 54:6

PSALM 53

For the choir director: A meditation; a psalm of David.*

1 Only fools say in their hearts,
"There is no God."
They are corrupt, and their actions are evil;
not one of them does good!

2 God looks down from heaven
on the entire human race;
He looks to see if anyone is truly wise,
if anyone seeks God.
3 But no, all have turned away;
all have become corrupt.*
No one does good,
not a single one!

4 Will those who do evil never learn?
They eat up my people like bread
and wouldn't think of praying to God.
5 Terror will grip them,
terror like they have never known before.

53:1-6 //Ps 14:1-7

53:2 Ps 33:13-15

53:3 Rom 3:10, 12

53:5 Lev 26:17, 36 Ps 44:7 Jer 6:30; 8:1-2 Ezek 6:5

53:TITLE Hebrew *maskil.* This may be a literary or musical term. 53:3 Greek version reads *have become useless.* Compare Rom 3:12.

▸ ADOPTION
52:8 Thriving in love. Nothing makes us thrive more than love. Loving relationships energize us; hateful relationships drain us of life. Why, then, would we want to live anywhere other than in the center of God's love and care? It's the place where we will grow the best. But how do we experience the benefits of God's love? The same way we experience every blessing of the Christian life—believing and repenting (Matthew 4:17, 23). (***See Adoption****> With Christ> United with Christ> Loved by God,* TopicGuide page A37.)

52:8-9 While the wicked are uprooted and left to wander without a home (52:5), the righteous enjoy the stability and sustenance of a relationship with God. The wicked are characterized by their lack of trust in God (52:7), but the righteous are known for trusting God's faithfulness to His people.

53:1-3 The psalmist encompasses all of humanity in his appraisal of foolishness. The apostle Paul confirms this appraisal by using these verses to build his case against all mankind (Romans 3:10-18). Any attempt to live independently of God is folly, and we are all guilty. The wisdom needed to counter this folly can be found only in Christ, who grants it to His people (1 Corinthians 1:30–2:16).

▸ ADOPTION
53:2 What does God see? When God looks down from heaven, what does He see? Not an earth full of people who live to serve Him. Instead, He sees a depraved human race that murders its own, abuses the gift of sex, hangs on to material wealth, and spurns Him. But He also sees a growing church, a redeemed people, and the answer to Jesus' prayer: "May Your Kingdom come soon. May Your will be done on earth, as it is in heaven" (Matthew 6:10). Let us pray that more and more sinners come to repent, believe, and rejoice in the good news of the gospel. (***See Adoption****> Without Christ> Separated from God> A world of lost sinners,* TopicGuide page A36.)

53:4-5 The foolish express their folly by oppressing the people of God. Yet the very person they deny will defend His people against these attacks and destroy the foolish. The scattering of their bones suggests the disdain with which they will be treated.

God will scatter the bones of your enemies.
You will put them to shame, for God has rejected them.

53:6 Ps 14:7
6 Who will come from Mount Zion to rescue Israel?
When God restores His people,
Jacob will shout with joy, and Israel will rejoice.

PSALM 54

For the choir director: A psalm of David, regarding the time the Ziphites came and said to Saul, "We know where David is hiding." To be accompanied by stringed instruments.*

54:1 2 Chr 20:6 Ps 20:1
1 Come with great power, O God, and rescue me!
Defend me with Your might.
2 Listen to my prayer, O God.
Pay attention to my plea.
54:3 1 Sam 20:1 Pss 36:1; 40:14; 86:14; 140:1, 4
3 For strangers are attacking me;
violent people are trying to kill me.
They care nothing for God. *Interlude*

54:4 Ps 37:24, 40
4 But God is my helper.
The Lord keeps me alive!
5 May the evil plans of my enemies be turned against them.
Do as You promised and put an end to them.

54:6 Ps 50:14
6 I will sacrifice a voluntary offering to You;
I will praise Your name, O LORD,
for it is good.
54:7 Pss 34:6; 59:10
7 For You have rescued me from my troubles
and helped me to triumph over my enemies.

PSALM 55

For the choir director: A psalm of David, to be accompanied by stringed instruments.*

55:1 Pss 27:9; 61:1
1 Listen to my prayer, O God.
Do not ignore my cry for help!
55:2 1 Sam 1:16 Pss 77:3; 86:6-7 Isa 38:14
2 Please listen and answer me,
for I am overwhelmed by my troubles.

54:TITLE Hebrew *maskil.* This may be a literary or musical term. 55:TITLE Hebrew *maskil.* This may be a literary or musical term.

▸ ADOPTION
54:1 God's rescuing power. In what ways have you seen God use His power on your behalf? Sometimes we take these ways for granted. We don't acknowledge answers to prayer or thank God for the blessings He has provided at just the right time. We forget about the wisdom He has taught us that keeps us from harm. Make a list of the ways God has rescued you, and thank Him for each one. (***See Adoption****> With Christ> Redemption> Promise of rescue from trouble,* TopicGuide page A36.)

54:4-5 David remains confident in the face of his violent oppressors because he relies on God. He calls on God to act according to His promises by causing the schemes of his enemies to backfire. Such a hope is expressed often in the Psalms (Psalms 7:15-16; 9:15-16).

54:6-7 David anticipates God's help and pledges his gratitude and praise. To speak of God's name was a reverential way of referring to God's presence (compare 1 Kings 8:17-20).

55:1-3 It appears David's prayers have gone unanswered for some time. He feels ignored by God and pleads for God to hear him. As with most lament psalms, the nature of the attacks by the psalmist's enemies is ambiguous.

▸ WORSHIP
55:2 Help me, God! What sort of prayer do you pray when the very worst thing happens? Tom and Karen cried out to God when their three-month-old son died in an accident. All they could do to keep going was to ask God to help them say good-bye to their little baby. God gave them peace and strength that, before, they could not have imagined existed. He can do this for you, too. Call out to God when you experience the deepest of sorrows and God will hear your cry. (***See Worship****> OT> Music> Psalms> Lament> Individual,* TopicGuide page A27.)

3 My enemies shout at me,
making loud and wicked threats.
They bring trouble on me
and angrily hunt me down.
4 My heart pounds in my chest.
The terror of death assaults me.
5 Fear and trembling overwhelm me,
and I can't stop shaking.
6 Oh, that I had wings like a dove;
then I would fly away and rest!
7 I would fly far away
to the quiet of the wilderness. *Interlude*
8 How quickly I would escape—
far from this wild storm of hatred.

9 Confuse them, Lord, and frustrate their plans,
for I see violence and conflict in the city.
10 Its walls are patrolled day and night against invaders,
but the real danger is wickedness within the city.
11 Everything is falling apart;
threats and cheating are rampant in the streets.

12 It is not an enemy who taunts me—
I could bear that.
It is not my foes who so arrogantly insult me—
I could have hidden from them.
13 Instead, it is you—my equal,
my companion and close friend.
14 What good fellowship we once enjoyed
as we walked together to the house of God.

15 Let death stalk my enemies;
let the grave* swallow them alive,
for evil makes its home within them.

16 But I will call on God,
and the LORD will rescue me.
17 Morning, noon, and night
I cry out in my distress,
and the LORD hears my voice.
18 He ransoms me and keeps me safe
from the battle waged against me,
though many still oppose me.
19 God, who has ruled forever,
will hear me and humble them. *Interlude*
For my enemies refuse to change their ways;
they do not fear God.

20 As for my companion, he betrayed his friends;
he broke his promises.

55:3 2 Sam 16:7-8; Pss 17:9; 71:11
55:4 Ps 116:3
55:5 Job 21:6
55:6 Job 3:13
55:8 Isa 4:6
55:9 Jer 6:7
55:11 Pss 5:9; 10:7
55:12-13 Ps 41:9
55:14 Ps 42:4
55:15 Num 16:30, 33; Ps 64:7
55:16 Ps 57:2-3
55:17 Pss 5:3; 88:13; 141:2; Dan 6:10; Acts 3:1
55:18 Ps 103:4
55:19 Pss 36:1; 93:2
55:20 Num 30:2; Pss 7:3-4; 89:34

55:15 Hebrew *let Sheol.*

55:9-11 David calls on God to judge the wicked city in language that alludes to the Tower of Babel narrative (Genesis 11:1-9). It is unclear which city is in view, but it is full of corruption and violence. David's language suggests continuous, widespread, and unchecked wickedness.

55:16-19 The far-reaching wickedness of David's enemies (55:10-11) is contrasted with the scope of God's power to save His people. David's confidence is grounded in his conviction of God's just rule. He pictures God seated on His throne as King and Judge, prepared to dispense justice and defend His people.

55:21 Pss 12:2; 28:3 Prov 5:3-4

21 His words are as smooth as butter,
but in his heart is war.
His words are as soothing as lotion,
but underneath are daggers!

55:22 Pss 37:5; 112:6 1 Pet 5:7

22 Give your burdens to the LORD,
and He will take care of you.
He will not permit the godly to slip and fall.

55:23 Pss 5:6; 56:3-4; 73:18

23 But You, O God, will send the wicked
down to the pit of destruction.
Murderers and liars will die young,
but I am trusting You to save me.

PSALM 56

For the choir director: A psalm of David, regarding the time the Philistines seized him in Gath. To be sung to the tune "Dove on Distant Oaks."

56:1 Pss 17:9; 35:1, 25

1 O God, have mercy on me,
for people are hounding me.
My foes attack me all day long.
2 I am constantly hounded by those who slander me,
and many are boldly attacking me.

56:3 Pss 11:1; 56:10-11

3 But when I am afraid,
I will put my trust in You.

56:4 Ps 118:6 Heb 13:6

4 I praise God for what He has promised.
I trust in God, so why should I be afraid?
What can mere mortals do to me?

56:5 Ps 41:7 2 Pet 3:15-16

5 They are always twisting what I say;
they spend their days plotting to harm me.

56:6 Pss 17:11; 59:3

6 They come together to spy on me—
watching my every step, eager to kill me.

56:7 Pss 36:12; 55:23

7 Don't let them get away with their wickedness;
in Your anger, O God, bring them down.

56:8 Pss 39:12; 139:3 Mal 3:16

8 You keep track of all my sorrows.*
You have collected all my tears in Your bottle.
You have recorded each one in Your book.

56:8 Or *my wanderings.*

56:1 The words "hounding me" may also be rendered "panting after me," suggesting the image of wild beasts pursuing their prey.

▸ WORSHIP

56:4 Praise and fear. Each of us has different areas of fear. Some people are terrified of illness; others shrink from job stress. No matter what you fear, the solution is the same—praising God. When we fear, we fix our attention on our circumstances. When we praise, we turn our eyes to God. When you feel that first prickle of fear, begin to praise our almighty God. (***See Worship****> OT> Reverence> God requires us to fear him,* TopicGuide page A28.)

▸ GOD

56:8 Tears in a bottle. What a picture this verse gives us of the completeness of God's compassion. He doesn't overlook one of your tears. He records all your sorrows. Whenever you feel that no one pays attention to your heartaches or knows what you are going through, reread this psalm. You never cry alone! (***See God****> God's Nature> Personality> Emotion> God is compassionate and loving,* TopicGuide page A14.)

56:8-9 God's care for His people is described in vivid metaphors that suggest deep and intimate concern. David is supremely confident that God has heard his cry and will act decisively on his behalf. And when God acts, not one of His enemies can stand against Him. Christians can express similar confidence because Christ is for us and has conquered His enemies and ours (Romans 8:31).

[9] My enemies will retreat when I call to You for help.
This I know: God is on my side!
[10] I praise God for what He has promised;
Yes, I praise the LORD for what He has promised.
[11] I trust in God, so why should I be afraid?
What can mere mortals do to me?

[12] I will fulfill my vows to You, O God,
and will offer a sacrifice of thanks for Your help.
[13] For You have rescued me from death;
You have kept my feet from slipping.
So now I can walk in Your presence, O God,
in Your life-giving light.

56:9 Pss 41:11; 118:6 Rom 8:31

56:12 Ps 50:14-15

56:13 Job 33:30 Pss 33:19; 86:13; 116:8-9

PSALM 57

For the choir director: A psalm of David, regarding the time he fled from Saul and went into the cave. To be sung to the tune "Do Not Destroy!"

[1] Have mercy on me, O God, have mercy!
I look to You for protection.
I will hide beneath the shadow of Your wings
until the danger passes by.
[2] I cry out to God Most High,*
to God who will fulfill His purpose for me.
[3] He will send help from heaven to rescue me,
disgracing those who hound me. *Interlude*
My God will send forth His unfailing love and faithfulness.

[4] I am surrounded by fierce lions
who greedily devour human prey—
whose teeth pierce like spears and arrows,
and whose tongues cut like swords.

[5] Be exalted, O God, above the highest heavens!
May Your glory shine over all the earth.

[6] My enemies have set a trap for me.
I am weary from distress.
They have dug a deep pit in my path,
but they themselves have fallen into it. *Interlude*

[7] My heart is confident in You, O God;
my heart is confident.
No wonder I can sing Your praises!

57:1 Ruth 2:12 Pss 36:7; 91:4 Isa 26:20

57:2 Ps 138:8

57:3 Pss 18:16; 25:10; 56:2; 144:5, 7

57:4 Pss 58:6; 64:3 Prov 30:13-14

57:5 Ps 108:5

57:6 Pss 10:9; 35:7; 140:5 Prov 26:27

57:7-11 //Ps 108:1-5

57:2 Hebrew *El-Elyon*.

56:12-13 In times of trouble, it was not uncommon for believers to make vows contingent upon deliverance. Such vows could reflect a mechanical and utilitarian view of God, but they also could reflect a sincere desire to thank God for His salvation.

57:1 David's imagery may allude to the wings of the cherubim that were depicted in the Tabernacle and on the Ark of the Covenant. Or he may simply have the image of a mother bird caring for her young in mind. In either case, the emphasis is on the shelter God provides for His people.

▸ GOD

57:2 God's purpose for me. Do you realize that God has a purpose for your life? We may not understand where He is leading us, but we can have confidence that He knows the way. Whenever we feel as if the path is not clear, we can cry out to Him. His Spirit is our guide (Galatians 5:16). (***See God****> God's Names> Holy Spirit> Guide/Counselor,* TopicGuide page A19.)

57:4 Lions are ruthless and violent predators. Throughout the Psalms, they are used to represent the enemies who pursue God's people (for example, Psalms 7:2; 10:9; 17:12). Here the metaphor is blended with images of battle, suggesting a military context.

57:8 Pss 16:9; 30:12; 150:3

8 Wake up, my heart!
Wake up, O lyre and harp!
I will wake the dawn with my song.
9 I will thank You, Lord, among all the people.
I will sing Your praises among the nations.

57:10 Ps 36:5

10 For Your unfailing love is as high as the heavens.
Your faithfulness reaches to the clouds.

11 Be exalted, O God, above the highest heavens.
May Your glory shine over all the earth.

PSALM 58

For the choir director: A psalm of David, to be sung to the tune "Do Not Destroy!"

58:1 Ps 82:2

1 Justice—do you rulers* know the meaning of the word?
Do you judge the people fairly?

58:2 Ps 94:20

2 No! You plot injustice in your hearts.
You spread violence throughout the land.

58:3 Ps 53:3; Isa 48:8

3 These wicked people are born sinners;
even from birth they have lied and gone their own way.

58:4 Deut 32:33; Pss 81:11; 140:3

4 They spit venom like deadly snakes;
they are like cobras that refuse to listen,
5 ignoring the tunes of the snake charmers,
no matter how skillfully they play.

58:6 Job 4:10; Ps 3:7

6 Break off their fangs, O God!
Smash the jaws of these lions, O LORD!

58:7 Josh 7:5; Pss 64:3; 112:10

7 May they disappear like water into thirsty ground.
Make their weapons useless in their hands.*

58:8 Job 3:16

8 May they be like snails that dissolve into slime,
like a stillborn child who will never see the sun.

58:9 Job 27:21; Ps 118:12; Prov 10:25

9 God will sweep them away, both young and old,
faster than a pot heats over burning thorns.

58:10 Pss 32:11; 64:10; 68:22-23; 91:8

10 The godly will rejoice when they see injustice avenged.
They will wash their feet in the blood of the wicked.

58:1 Or *you gods.* 58:7 Or *Let them be trodden down and wither like grass.* The meaning of the Hebrew is uncertain.

▸ WORSHIP

57:8 Wake up and sing. What good advice David gives us in this psalm! If we make it a habit to sing praises to God when we first wake up, we will set the tone for our day. This could mean listening to worshipful music, singing as part of your morning devotions, reciting the lyrics of a praise song, or writing a poem of praise. Start your day with praise! (***See Worship****> OT> Music> Praise> Praise psalms,* TopicGuide page A27.)

57:8 David is not awakened by the dawn; rather, his praise calls forth the dawn. The dawning of a new day symbolized hope, rejuvenation, and the triumph of God over the wickedness embodied in the darkness of night. Elsewhere in the Psalms, dawn is identified as the time of God's appearing to rescue His people (Psalms 46:5; 90:14).

▸ GOD

58:1 Value justice. God values justice (Deuteronomy 32:4). He sees when the defenseless are downtrodden by the strong and the wealthy. He notices when people defraud their neighbors. He condemns the ruler who misjudges his own people. Do you display God's justice? Do you deal fairly with everyone—your coworkers, your neighbors, your loved ones? Ask God to give you a love for justice. (***See God****> God's Attributes> Just> The Messiah will judge all with complete justice,* TopicGuide page A17.)

58:1-2 The psalm is addressed to those rulers in the land who are entrusted with the responsibility of administering justice. They occupy a position of great power, often issuing life-or-death verdicts. These rulers, however, abuse their power and pervert rather than uphold justice. (Compare Amos 5:7; Isaiah 1:23; 5:23; Micah 3:11.)

58:3 David recognized that he was not altogether different from the wicked judges (Psalm 51:5). All men are wicked from birth. However, some actualize that wickedness more thoroughly than others.

58:10-11 Injustice and oppression are grievous sins that bring much sorrow and pain. Sometimes these sins lead the faithful to question God's just rule. This is because the godly long for the day when God's justice will prevail over all the earth. They rightly rejoice when they see partial expressions of that justice.

[11] Then at last everyone will say,
"There truly is a reward for those who live for God;
surely there is a God who judges justly here on earth."

59:11 Pss 9:8; 18:20 Luke 6:23, 35

PSALM 59

For the choir director: A psalm of David, regarding the time Saul sent soldiers to watch David's house in order to kill him. To be sung to the tune "Do Not Destroy!"

[1] Rescue me from my enemies, O God.
Protect me from those who have come to destroy me.
[2] Rescue me from these criminals;
save me from these murderers.
[3] They have set an ambush for me.
Fierce enemies are out there waiting, LORD,
though I have not sinned or offended them.
[4] I have done nothing wrong,
yet they prepare to attack me.
Wake up! See what is happening and help me!
[5] O LORD God of Heaven's Armies, the God of Israel,
wake up and punish those hostile nations.
Show no mercy to wicked traitors. *Interlude*

[6] They come out at night,
snarling like vicious dogs
as they prowl the streets.
[7] Listen to the filth that comes from their mouths;
their words cut like swords.
"After all, who can hear us?" they sneer.
[8] But LORD, You laugh at them.
You scoff at all the hostile nations.
[9] You are my strength; I wait for You to rescue me,
for You, O God, are my fortress.
[10] In His unfailing love, my God will stand with me.
He will let me look down in triumph on all my enemies.

59:1 Pss 20:1; 143:9
59:2 Pss 14:4; 28:3; 94:16; 139:19
59:3 Pss 7:3-4; 56:6; 69:4
59:4 Ps 35:19, 23
59:5 Pss 9:5; 84:8 Jer 18:23
59:7 Job 22:13 Pss 10:11; 73:11; 94:4-7
59:8 Pss 2:4; 37:13
59:9 Ps 9:9
59:10 Ps 54:7

▶ ADOPTION
58:11 Leap for joy! In Luke 6, Jesus tells us that when we persevere for the Lord, our reward will be great in heaven. In fact, He says, "Leap for joy" (Luke 6:23). Our rewards are absolutely sure, and because they come from our loving God, we can be sure that they will be fantastic. Keep your eyes on the prize—the reward God has promised. (***See Adoption****> With Christ> Supernatural> A life of infinite joy,* TopicGuide page A37.)

▶ SPIRITUAL WARFARE
59:1 God is our Protector. The prophet Elijah was in a terrible predicament. The powerful Queen Jezebel had vowed to kill him (1 Kings 19). Depressed, he fled into the wilderness, where he sat under a broom tree. The world looked bleak to him at that moment. But the Lord saw him and comforted him. Angels ministered to him and brought him food. That's the kind of God we serve. He protects us from all kinds of enemies and helps us in the midst of our worst depression. Ask Him to protect and comfort you, too. (***See Spiritual Warfare****> Resisting Sin and Evil> Trusting God> God as Warrior> God's fight against the enemies of Israel,* TopicGuide page A46.)

59:4-5 David claims innocence with respect to the enemies who seek to harm him. He has done nothing to justify their attacks, so he calls on the "LORD God of Heaven's Armies" to defend him.

59:6-7 David portrays his enemies as a pack of wild dogs wandering the streets and biting with teeth like swords. Dogs were disparaged in the ancient world and only rarely domesticated. Thus, David's image is at once descriptive and disdainful. The arrogance of the attackers is a recurring theme throughout the Psalms (compare Psalms 10:3-6; 12:4). It is an arrogance that both the psalmists and God despise. (See also 59:14-15.)

59:8 God's derision undermines the arrogance of the wicked. They only appear to go unpunished; in reality, their continued insolence actually compounds the wrath of God against them. Their noise and fury merely elicit disdainful laughter from God, who is not at all unnerved by their plots (compare Psalm 2).

59:10 God's "unfailing love" is His love for His people grounded in His promises to them. This love, which is a theme of this psalm (see also 59:16-17), is the basis for God's deliverance.

59:11 Deut 4:9 Pss 106:27; 144:6
[11] Don't kill them, for my people soon forget such lessons;
stagger them with Your power, and bring them to their knees,
O Lord our shield.

59:12 Ps 10:7 Prov 12:13 Zeph 3:11
[12] Because of the sinful things they say,
because of the evil that is on their lips,
let them be captured by their pride,
their curses, and their lies.

59:13 Pss 83:18; 104:35
[13] Destroy them in Your anger!
Wipe them out completely!
Then the whole world will know
that God reigns in Israel.*

Interlude

59:14 Ps 59:6
[14] My enemies come out at night,
snarling like vicious dogs
as they prowl the streets.
[15] They scavenge for food
but go to sleep unsatisfied.*

59:16 Pss 21:13; 46:1; 101:1
[16] But as for me, I will sing about Your power.
Each morning I will sing with joy about Your unfailing love.
For You have been my refuge,
a place of safety when I am in distress.

59:17 Ps 59:9-10
[17] O my Strength, to You I sing praises,
for You, O God, are my refuge,
the God who shows me unfailing love.

PSALM 60

For the choir director: A psalm of David useful for teaching, regarding the time David fought Aram-naharaim and Aram-zobah, and Joab returned and killed 12,000 Edomites in the Valley of Salt. To be sung to the tune "Lily of the Testimony."

60:1 Pss 44:9; 79:5; 80:3
[1] You have rejected us, O God, and broken our defenses.
You have been angry with us; now restore us to Your favor.

60:2 2 Chr 7:14 Ps 18:7
[2] You have shaken our land and split it open.
Seal the cracks, for the land trembles.

60:3 Ps 66:12
[3] You have been very hard on us,
making us drink wine that sent us reeling.

59:13 Hebrew *in Jacob.* See note on 44:4. 59:15 Or *and growl if they don't get enough.*

▸ GOD
59:16 A place of safety. Years ago, armies built forts to protect the soldiers from their enemies. Inside the walls of a fort, an army stockpiled everything it needed to survive if it was attacked—ammunition, water, and food. This is a picture of our position as God's child. He builds a fortress around us to protect us. He provides everything we need. His power and love shelter us. Sing for joy because of the safety we have in God. (***See God****> God's Names> God> Fortress,* TopicGuide page A18.)

▸ GOD
60:1 Restore us, God. David understood the position of one who disobeys God (Psalm 32). He felt the sting of guilt and the loneliness of a broken relationship with God. But David also experienced the quickness with which God restored His communion with David when David repented of his sin. Have you let unconfessed sin come between you and God? Ask for His forgiveness and see how quickly your relationship with Him is restored. (***See God****> Relationship> Barriers> Unconfessed transgressions,* TopicGuide page A14.)

60:1-2 David describes a series of military setbacks. In the Old Testament, Israel's victories are attributed to God's presence in the midst of His people. Conversely, defeat in battle is said to result from God's abandonment. Typically, though not exclusively, such abandonment followed Israel's unfaithfulness (Deuteronomy 28:25). David metaphorically describes the damage inflicted by the enemy as an earthquake that shakes the land.

60:3 The shock of defeat is likened to a drunken stupor. For the image of wine as judgment, see Isaiah 51:17-22; Jeremiah 25:15-38; and Nahum 3:11.

4 But You have raised a banner for those who fear You—
a rallying point in the face of attack. *Interlude*

5 Now rescue Your beloved people.
Answer and save us by Your power.
6 God has promised this by His holiness*:
"I will divide up Shechem with joy.
I will measure out the valley of Succoth.
7 Gilead is Mine,
and Manasseh, too.
Ephraim, My helmet, will produce My warriors,
and Judah, My scepter, will produce My kings.
8 But Moab, My washbasin, will become My servant,
and I will wipe My feet on Edom
and shout in triumph over Philistia."

9 Who will bring me into the fortified city?
Who will bring me victory over Edom?
10 Have You rejected us, O God?
Will You no longer march with our armies?
11 Oh, please help us against our enemies,
for all human help is useless.
12 With God's help we will do mighty things,
for He will trample down our foes.

60:5-12 //Ps 108:6-13
60:6 Gen 33:17; Josh 17:7; Ps 89:35
60:7 Gen 49:10; Deut 33:17; Josh 13:31
60:8 2 Sam 8:1-2, 14
60:9 Ps 44:9
60:10 Ps 60:1
60:11 Ps 146:3
60:12 Num 24:15-19; Pss 44:5; 118:16

PSALM 61

For the choir director: A psalm of David, to be accompanied by stringed instruments.

1 O God, listen to my cry!
Hear my prayer!
2 From the ends of the earth,
I cry to You for help
when my heart is overwhelmed.
Lead me to the towering rock of safety,
3 for You are my safe refuge,
a fortress where my enemies cannot reach me.

61:1 Pss 64:1; 86:6
61:2 Pss 18:2; 77:3
61:3 Ps 62:7; Prov 18:10

60:6 Or *in His sanctuary.*

60:6-7 These verses recall the division of Canaan among the people of Israel following the conquest of the land. Shechem and Succoth lay on either side of the Jordan in central Israel; both were associated with Jacob (Genesis 33:17-20). Gilead was a fertile region on the east bank of the Jordan River. The tribal lands of Manasseh and Ephraim were in central and northern Israel. Judah's region was in southern Israel.

▸ ADOPTION
60:12 Doing mighty things. King David conquered many foes in the strength of the Lord. Second Samuel 8 describes how David's army defeated nations who made alliances against Israel, "The LORD made David victorious wherever he went" (8:14). We have different foes from the ones David faced. Our battle is against Satan's armies. In community (Matthew 16:17-18) and in Christ (Ephesians 6:10-18), you can be a victorious soldier in God's advancing kingdom. Ask God to help you do mighty things in His name. (***See Adoption***> *With Christ> Supernatural> Victory over Satan,* TopicGuide page A37.)

▸ GOD
61:2 From the ends of the earth. Isn't it amazing that we can count on God no matter where we are? There is no place on earth we can go and be out of touch with Him. He sees everything (2 Chronicles 16:9). If you travel in a submarine to the depths of the ocean, God is there. If you take a rocket ship into outer space, He is there. If you travel to Antarctica, He is there. We can rely on God at all times and in all places. This frees us up to risk everything and go anywhere to accomplish His will for our lives. (***See God***> *God's Nature> Personality> Intellect> God knows everything there is to know,* TopicGuide page A14.)

61:2-3 The phrase "the ends of the earth" may be taken literally to mean remote regions or metaphorically to describe emotional isolation. The mention of "enemies" suggests David is engaged in a military campaign far from Jerusalem. David recognizes that under such conditions, he needs a refuge that he cannot construct—God must be his fortress.

61:4 Pss 17:8; 23:6; 27:4; 91:4
4 Let me live forever in Your sanctuary,
safe beneath the shelter of Your wings! *Interlude*

61:5 Ps 56:12 Mal 2:5; 4:2
5 For You have heard my vows, O God.
You have given me an inheritance reserved for those
who fear Your name.
6 Add many years to the life of the king!
May his years span the generations!

61:7 Pss 40:11; 41:12
7 May he reign under God's protection forever.
May Your unfailing love and faithfulness watch over him.

61:8 Pss 30:4; 65:1; 71:22
8 Then I will sing praises to Your name forever
as I fulfill my vows each day.

PSALM 62

For Jeduthun, the choir director: A psalm of David.

62:1 Pss 33:20
1 I wait quietly before God,
for my victory comes from Him.

62:2 Pss 37:39; 59:17; 89:26
2 He alone is my rock and my salvation,
my fortress where I will never be shaken.

62:3 Isa 30:13
3 So many enemies against one man—
all of them trying to kill me.
To them I'm just a broken-down wall
or a tottering fence.

62:4 Pss 4:2; 28:3
4 They plan to topple me from my high position.
They delight in telling lies about me.
They praise me to my face
but curse me in their hearts. *Interlude*

5 Let all that I am wait quietly before God,
for my hope is in Him.
6 He alone is my rock and my salvation,
my fortress where I will not be shaken.

62:7 Ps 46:1
7 My victory and honor come from God alone.
He is my refuge, a rock where no enemy can reach me.

62:8 Ps 42:4 Lam 2:19
8 O my people, trust in Him at all times.
Pour out your heart to Him,
for God is our refuge. *Interlude*

61:5 Vows were often offered along with prayers, committing the petitioner to acts of worship if the prayers were answered (compare Psalms 50:14; 65:1). (See also 61:8.)

61:6-7 In the ancient world, the fate of the king and the fate of his people were seen as intimately connected. Success and health for the king signaled prosperity and stability for the nation. It is in Jesus Christ, however, that the hopes the psalmist expresses find their fulfillment. As David's greater Son, Christ will reign eternally at His Father's right hand (Acts 2:29-36).

▸ HOLINESS
62:1 Wait quietly before the Lord. One aspect of life in the twenty-first century is that everyone is busy. People stream to work, then hurry home again, exhausted. Even with all our modern conveniences, we fill our time with activities. We have lost the ability to sit quietly before God. We want answers to prayer now! We skip our times with God in the morning so that we can fit one more thing into our schedules. What joy we are missing! Today, commit yourself to waiting on the Lord, meditating on His Word, praying and listening for His answer, praising Him for an extended period of time. (***See Holiness****> Submission> Delighting in God> Joy in Discovering God,* TopicGuide page A40.)

62:1-2 The opening verses express a calm and studied assurance. God is described with metaphors that suggest strength and stability. The words are those of someone who has experienced God's protection and deliverance. The sentiment is repeated and intensified in 62:5-6.

9 Common people are as worthless as a puff of wind,
and the powerful are not what they appear to be.
If you weigh them on the scales,
together they are lighter than a breath of air.

10 Don't make your living by extortion
or put your hope in stealing.
And if your wealth increases,
don't make it the center of your life.

11 God has spoken plainly,
and I have heard it many times:
Power, O God, belongs to You;
12 unfailing love, O Lord, is Yours.
Surely You repay all people
according to what they have done.

62:9 Isa 40:15

62:10 Ps 49:6 Isa 61:8 Mark 10:25 Luke 12:15 1 Tim 6:10

62:12 Job 34:11 Matt 16:27 *Rom 2:6

PSALM 63

A psalm of David, regarding a time when David was in the wilderness of Judah.

1 O God, You are my God;
I earnestly search for You.
My soul thirsts for You;
my whole body longs for You
in this parched and weary land
where there is no water.
2 I have seen You in Your sanctuary
and gazed upon Your power and glory.
3 Your unfailing love is better than life itself;
how I praise You!
4 I will praise You as long as I live,
lifting up my hands to You in prayer.
5 You satisfy me more than the richest feast.
I will praise You with songs of joy.

63:1 Pss 42:2; 84:2

63:2 Ps 27:4

63:3 Ps 69:16

63:4 Pss 28:2; 104:33

63:5 Pss 36:8; 71:23

▸ GOD

62:9 Weighing our worth. What are you worth? If we compare ourselves to God, we are worth nothing. Nothing we do lasts. Our lives are a mere puff of air when measured against God's eternal nature. Yet we often consider ourselves as the center of the universe. We see all of life from our own viewpoint. We can never succeed if we don't understand how insignificant we are next to God's worth. We gain a greater grasp of the magnificence of God's love when we realize that He sent His Son to die for us. Why would God sacrifice so much for a human race that is rebellious and sinful? Because of His love, we are now priceless to Him. Praise God for His love that has given us our worth. (***See God**> Relationship> God Enables> God accepts us through Christ,* TopicGuide page A14.)

62:9-10 The language and tone of these verses is similar to that of Ecclesiastes. David's point is that men and women are nothing without God. In particular, he is concerned to show that the apparent prosperity of the wicked is transitory and ultimately meaningless.

62:11-12 David concludes by bringing together the main themes of the psalm—God's power and justice. These two qualities are linked by the love of God, which directs God's strength and justice toward His people. These divine characteristics are the source of David's calm and confidence in the face of danger and corruption.

▸ ADOPTION

63:1 Refreshment in the desert. If you travel through the desert, you understand more clearly what it means to be thirsty. As you walk each dusty mile, you see nothing but more sand, dirt, and an arid horizon. Your mouth becomes parched. The air feels scratchy and dry. The plant life is scarce. The ground feels hot under your feet. In this psalm, David is comparing this world to a desert. We cannot quench our spiritual thirst through anything this world has to offer. When our souls thirst, we can find relief only in God's love. His compassion toward us is like a running stream, cool and refreshing. Are you drinking from the waters of God's love? Or are you trying to find satisfaction in the world's way of doing things? Set your eyes upon God's love through His Son, Jesus Christ, and you will quench your soul's thirst. (***See Adoption**> With Christ> In Heaven> Living water,* TopicGuide page A38.)

63:6 Pss 4:4; 16:7; 42:8
6 I lie awake thinking of You,
meditating on You through the night.
7 Because You are my helper,
I sing for joy in the shadow of Your wings.
63:8 Ps 18:35
8 I cling to You;
Your strong right hand holds me securely.

63:9 Pss 40:14; 55:15
9 But those plotting to destroy me will come to ruin.
They will go down into the depths of the earth.
10 They will die by the sword
and become the food of jackals.
63:11 Deut 6:13 Isa 45:23
11 But the king will rejoice in God.
All who trust in Him will praise Him,
while liars will be silenced.

PSALM 64

For the choir director: A psalm of David.

1 O God, listen to my complaint.
Protect my life from my enemies' threats.
64:2 Pss 56:6; 59:2
2 Hide me from the plots of this evil mob,
from this gang of wrongdoers.
64:3 Ps 140:3
3 They sharpen their tongues like swords
and aim their bitter words like arrows.
64:4 Pss 10:8; 11:2
4 They shoot from ambush at the innocent,
attacking suddenly and fearlessly.
64:5 Ps 140:5
5 They encourage each other to do evil
and plan how to set their traps in secret.
"Who will ever notice?" they ask.
6 As they plot their crimes, they say,
"We have devised the perfect plan!"
Yes, the human heart and mind are cunning.

64:7 Ps 7:12-13
7 But God Himself will shoot them with
His arrows,
suddenly striking them down.

63:7 The Tabernacle and the Ark of the Covenant featured artistic representations of cherubim with outstretched wings (Exodus 25:20). It is also possible the image is that of an eagle or hen protecting her young (Exodus 19:4). In either case, the metaphor clearly communicates God's care and protection.

▶ GOD
63:8 Following God. When the young boy went with his father into the haunted house at the amusement park, he followed his father step by step. He grabbed onto his father's pant leg to make sure he wouldn't get lost. At each scary moment, he sidled up closer to his father's leg and hung on. What a picture of how we should handle life! The closer we walk with God, the more security we will have. The more we talk to Him, the less scary the world will seem. How close can you walk to God? Keep Him in your sights at all times. (***See God***> *God's Nature> Personality> Relationships> God walks and lives with His people,* TopicGuide page A14.)

63:9-11 David is faced with enemies who seek his life, but his prior experiences of God's blessing fill him with confidence. He vividly contrasts his fate with that of his enemies. They will be undone and even denied the honor of a proper burial. David, however, rejoices in God, implying that he will be delivered.

64:2-4 The nature of the threat posed by David's enemies is not specified, but verbal attacks seem to be in view. Military imagery conveys the intensity and violence of the attacks leveled against David.

▶ ADOPTION
64:3 Sharp tongues and bitter words. Do you notice in this verse that David considered those who used sharp tongues and bitter words as his enemies? He called these tactics weapons of war. These enemies used their weapons in ambush. They purposefully devised their plans for destruction. Do you use these weapons? Do you often flay someone with words? Has your tongue become someone's enemy? We must be careful about what we say because sharp tongues and bitter words are tactics that God dislikes. (***See Adoption***> *With Christ> Supernatural> Speak godly words,* TopicGuide page A37.)

8 Their own tongues will ruin them,
and all who see them will shake their
heads in scorn.
9 Then everyone will be afraid;
they will proclaim the mighty acts of God
and realize all the amazing things He does.
10 The godly will rejoice in the LORD
and find shelter in Him.
And those who do what is right
will praise Him.

64:8
Ps 9:3
Prov 18:6-7

64:10
Pss 11:1; 25:20; 32:11

PSALM 65

For the choir director: A song. A psalm of David.

1 What mighty praise, O God,
belongs to You in Zion.
We will fulfill our vows to You,
2 for You answer our prayers.
All of us must come to You.
3 Though we are overwhelmed by our sins,
You forgive them all.
4 What joy for those You choose to bring near,
those who live in Your holy courts.
What festivities await us
inside Your holy Temple.

5 You faithfully answer our prayers with awesome deeds,
O God our savior.
You are the hope of everyone on earth,
even those who sail on distant seas.
6 You formed the mountains by Your power
and armed Yourself with mighty strength.
7 You quieted the raging oceans
with their pounding waves
and silenced the shouting of the nations.
8 Those who live at the ends of the earth
stand in awe of Your wonders.
From where the sun rises to where it sets,
You inspire shouts of joy.

65:1
Pss 86:9; 116:18

65:2
Isa 66:23

65:3
Ps 40:12
Heb 9:14

65:4
Pss 4:3; 33:12; 36:8

65:5
Pss 45:4; 48:10

65:6
Pss 93:1; 95:4

65:7
Ps 89:9
Isa 17:12-13
Matt 8:26

65:8
Ps 139:9-10

65:1-2 Worshipers often made vows in times of distress to be fulfilled when God sent deliverance (Leviticus 7:16-21).

▸ GOD
65:5 God answers prayer. Here is another precious biblical promise—that God answers prayers. No matter whether you live in a mansion in Beverly Hills, in a jungle in South America, on a ship in the Indian Ocean, or on a mountain in Tibet, God still answers the prayers of His children. Without Him, we would have no hope. With Him, we know that He will hear and help us when we pray. But this only happens when we have the faith to pray. Act on your beliefs in a powerful and loving God and pray—pray! (***See God> God's Attributes> True> God follows through on His promises,*** TopicGuide page A18.)

65:5-8 The language of the psalm emphatically declares God's rule over all creation. "Distant seas," "the ends of the earth," "from where the sun rises to where it sets"—each of these phrases is designed to designate the whole earth as the region of God's domain. The result is an expectation for the expansion of God's people throughout the world. This hope, expressed elsewhere in the Old Testament, finds fulfillment in the spread of the gospel of Christ to all nations and peoples (Isaiah 55:5-7; 60:3; Romans 1:16; Revelation 5:9; 7:9).

65:6-7 The mountains and the seas were chaotic components of ancient mythologies in which the gods battled to bring order to creation. In the biblical worldview, however, these forces are entirely subservient to God because it is He who brought them into existence. There is no element of creation that stands outside of God's rule or presents a challenge to His power. (Compare Psalm 29:3.)

65:9 Pss 104:13-14, 24 [9] You take care of the earth and water it,
making it rich and fertile.
The river of God has plenty of water;
it provides a bountiful harvest of grain,
for You have ordered it so.
[10] You drench the plowed ground with rain,
melting the clods and leveling the ridges.
You soften the earth with showers
and bless its abundant crops.
[11] You crown the year with a bountiful harvest;
even the hard pathways overflow with abundance.
65:12 Job 38:26-27 [12] The grasslands of the wilderness become a lush pasture,
and the hillsides blossom with joy.
65:13 Pss 98:8; 144:13 Isa 30:23; 55:12 [13] The meadows are clothed with flocks of sheep,
and the valleys are carpeted with grain.
They all shout and sing for joy!

PSALM 66

For the choir director: A song. A psalm.

[1] Shout joyful praises to God, all the earth!
[2] Sing about the glory of His name!
Tell the world how glorious He is.
66:3 Pss 18:44; 47:2 [3] Say to God, "How awesome are Your deeds!
Your enemies cringe before Your mighty power.
66:4 Pss 22:27; 67:4 [4] Everything on earth will worship You;
they will sing Your praises,
shouting Your name in glorious songs." *Interlude*

66:5 Ps 46:8 [5] Come and see what our God has done,
what awesome miracles He performs for people!
66:6 Exod 14:21 Ps 105:43 [6] He made a dry path through the Red Sea,*
and His people went across on foot.
There we rejoiced in Him.

66:6 Hebrew *the sea.*

▸ SPIRITUAL WARFARE

65:9 God takes care of the earth. God takes care of His creation. For example, He created the water cycle in which rain drenches the earth, rises up through evaporation, and comes back down again as rain. This process not only waters the earth, it keeps the water supply purified. We could say that God was the first conservationist, for He created and sustains His creation. Are you following God's lead? Do you care for your corner of the earth? (***See Spiritual Warfare****> Origin of Sin> Creation in Bondage> God sustains,* TopicGuide page A44.)

65:9-13 David praises God for His providential care of the land and, consequently, His people. Unfortunately, the force of the metaphor is lost on city people, who fail to recognize the absolute necessity of rain for survival. The welfare of Israel depended on bountiful rains to water the land, and the psalmist acknowledges God as the source of this indispensable blessing.

▸ HOLINESS

66:1 Consider God's miracles. When the people of Israel came out of Egypt, they traveled to the edge of the Red Sea. It was an impassable barrier. What could they do? Pharaoh's forces were behind them. Then God told Moses to hold his staff over the water. When he did, the water parted and the people crossed the Red Sea on dry ground (Exodus 14). Since that day, the Jewish people have remembered the miracle of His rescue from Egypt through celebrating the Passover. We can do the same. Not only can we remember the great moments recorded in the Bible, we must keep in mind the wonderful things God has done for us. Has He answered your fervent prayers? Has He given you special blessings? Write these things down for a remembrance, and read through them often. Think of them when you partake of the Lord's Supper. (***See Holiness****> Submission> Delighting in God> Joy in Discovering God,* TopicGuide page A40.)

66:1-4 The psalmist calls on all the inhabitants of the earth to join him in praising the God of Israel. Specifically, God is to be praised for His mighty deeds in battle. God is the divine Warrior who fights on behalf of His people, striking fear into the hearts of Israel's enemies (Joshua 2:8-13).

7 For by His great power He rules forever.
He watches every movement of the nations;
let no rebel rise in defiance. *Interlude*

8 Let the whole world bless our God
and loudly sing His praises.
9 Our lives are in His hands,
and He keeps our feet from stumbling.
10 You have tested us, O God;
You have purified us like silver.
11 You captured us in Your net
and laid the burden of slavery on our backs.
12 Then You put a leader over us.*
We went through fire and flood,
but You brought us to a place of great abundance.

13 Now I come to Your Temple with burnt offerings
to fulfill the vows I made to You—
14 yes, the sacred vows that I made
when I was in deep trouble.
15 That is why I am sacrificing burnt offerings to You—
the best of my rams as a pleasing aroma,
and a sacrifice of bulls and male goats. *Interlude*

16 Come and listen, all you who fear God,
and I will tell you what He did for me.
17 For I cried out to Him for help,
praising Him as I spoke.
18 If I had not confessed the sin in my heart,
the Lord would not have listened.
19 But God did listen!
He paid attention to my prayer.
20 Praise God, who did not ignore my prayer
or withdraw His unfailing love from me.

66:7 Pss 11:4; 140:8; 145:13
66:9 Ps 30:3
66:10 Ps 17:3; Zech 13:9; 1 Pet 1:6-7
66:11 Lam 1:13
66:12 Ps 18:19; Isa 43:2; 51:23
66:13 Ps 22:25; Eccl 5:4
66:14 Ps 18:6
66:15 Num 6:14; Ps 51:19
66:16 Ps 34:11; 71:15, 24
66:18 Job 36:21; Ps 18:41; Isa 1:15; Jas 4:3
66:19 Ps 116:1-2
66:20 Ps 22:24

PSALM 67

For the choir director: A song. A psalm, to be accompanied by stringed instruments.

1 May God be merciful and bless us.
May His face smile with favor on us. *Interlude*

67:1 Num 6:25; Pss 4:6; 80:3, 7, 19

66:12 Or *You made people ride over our heads.*

▸ GOD
66:10 God tests us. When a silversmith processes silver ore, he applies high heat. This heat separates the silver from the impurities in the ore. Then the silversmith skims off the purified metal, with which he makes beautiful objects such as jewelry. God tells us that this process is similar to how He purifies our lives (1 Peter 1:7). The difficult experiences we face are the heat of purification. This heat reveals our failings and sins. Then God helps us to eliminate those areas of our lives that give us trouble. Easy times don't help us see our weaknesses and sins. So God tests us through trials so that we will turn to Him and let Him mold our character to be like His. (***See God***> *God's Attributes*> *Faithful*> *God faithfully matures believers,* TopicGuide page A16.)

66:10-12 The psalmist recalls a painful defeat in battle, interpreting it as an instance of God testing Israel in order to purify the nation. Scripture frequently employs the purification of metals by fire as a metaphor for the refinement of God's people by trial (Isaiah 48:10; 1 Peter 1:6-7).

66:18-19 The psalms frequently recognize sin as a significant barrier to effective prayer. Thus, many psalms contain proclamations of innocence or prayers of confession (compare Psalms 17:1-2; 26:1-3; 32:1-4).

67:1 The psalmist adopts the language of the priestly blessing recorded in Numbers 6:22-27. God's face symbolizes His favorable disposition toward His people; in other words, the face of God represents the blessing of God.

67:2 Acts 18:25 Titus 2:11 — [2] May Your ways be known throughout the earth,
Your saving power among people everywhere.
67:3 Ps 66:4 — [3] May the nations praise You, O God.
Yes, may all the nations praise You.
67:4 Ps 96:10, 13 — [4] Let the whole world sing for joy,
because You govern the nations with justice
and guide the people of the whole world. *Interlude*

67:5 Ps 22:27 — [5] May the nations praise You, O God.
Yes, may all the nations praise You.
67:6 Lev 26:4 Ezek 34:27 — [6] Then the earth will yield its harvests,
and God, our God, will richly bless us.
67:7 Ps 33:8 — [7] Yes, God will bless us,
and people all over the world will fear Him.

PSALM 68

For the choir director: A song. A psalm of David.

68:1 Num 10:35 — [1] Rise up, O God, and scatter Your enemies.
Let those who hate God run for their lives.
68:2 Ps 37:20 Isa 9:18 Hos 13:3 Mic 1:4 — [2] Blow them away like smoke.
Melt them like wax in a fire.
Let the wicked perish in the presence of God.
[3] But let the godly rejoice.
Let them be glad in God's presence.
Let them be filled with joy.
68:4 Pss 40:3; 68:33 — [4] Sing praises to God and to His name!
Sing loud praises to Him who rides the clouds.
His name is the LORD—
rejoice in His presence!

68:5 Deut 10:18; 26:15 — [5] Father to the fatherless, defender of widows—
this is God, whose dwelling is holy.
[6] God places the lonely in families;
He sets the prisoners free and gives them joy.
But He makes the rebellious live in a sun-scorched land.

▸ CHURCH
67:2 God's message spread throughout the earth. Titus 2:11 says, "The grace of God has been revealed, bringing salvation to all people." That's the message of hope that God has given us through His Son, Jesus Christ. We have the responsibility of carrying this message to the ends of the earth. Every person needs to know how he or she can have eternal life through faith in Jesus Christ. When the nations turn to God, they will praise Him, and He will be honored everywhere. We can all participate in this task through giving to missions programs, telling our neighbors and friends about Jesus, and praying that God's message will be accepted everywhere. (***See Church****> Role> Preach> Topics> Evangelize> Around the world,* TopicGuide page A50.)

67:2-5 The Old Testament writers often expressed the hope that the nations would come to worship the God of Israel (Genesis 12:3; Isaiah 55:5-7; 60:3). This hope finds fulfillment in the spread of the gospel of Christ to all nations and peoples (Romans 1:16; Revelation 5:9; 7:9). The psalmist fully expects that submission to the rule of God will be a source of great joy to the nations.

67:6 The psalmist recognizes God as the source of abundant harvests. The blessing of God (67:1) is reflected in His providential care for His people. It is not surprising to find the evangelization of the nations and the abundance of creation linked together. Both were hopes associated with the era of the Messiah (for example, see Isaiah 55:5-13).

68:1-3 David invokes military terminology to call upon God to defeat His enemies (Numbers 10:35). Just as smoke is powerless to resist the wind and wax melts before the fire, so the enemies of God are impotent to resist His power. The godly, by contrast, find joy in God's presence.

7 O God, when You led your people out from Egypt,
when You marched through the dry wasteland, *Interlude* 68:7 Exod 13:21
8 the earth trembled, and the heavens poured down rain 68:8 Exod 19:18 Judg 5:4-5
before You, the God of Sinai,
before God, the God of Israel.
9 You sent abundant rain, O God, 68:9 Deut 11:11
to refresh the weary land.
10 There Your people finally settled,
and with a bountiful harvest, O God,
You provided for Your needy people.

11 The Lord gives the word, 68:11 Exod 15:20
and a great army* brings the good news.
12 Enemy kings and their armies flee,
while the women of Israel divide the plunder.

68:11 Or *a host of women.*

68:7-10 David recalls the Exodus from Egypt, God's appearance at Mount Sinai, and the inheritance of the Promised Land. In each of these events, God led and provided for His people. The natural phenomena described here often accompanied appearances of God (Exodus 19:16-18; 1 Kings 19:11-13; Habakkuk 3:3-12).

68:11-13 When soldiers returned victorious from battle, the women of the city celebrated their triumph. This imagery is employed to describe the joy God's people experience when He defeats His enemies and establishes peace. The mention of a dove may allude to the ancient practice of releasing doves to signal a victory on the battlefield.

MY RESPONSE TO GOD

The Gospel and Guilt

PSALM 67:4

As Christians, we know that the most important thing we can do for others is to help them know Christ. But relatively few of us actively engage in evangelism. We focus most of our attention on our families, our church friends, and our jobs. We may feel guilty about our failure to evangelize, but that's the extent of our emotional involvement.

If this describes you, what should you do about it?

First, make sure you are a Christian. If you have no interest in evangelism and no interest in repenting of this failure, then you may not be filled with the Holy Spirit—you may not be converted. But listen: "Today is the day of salvation" (2 Corinthians 6:2). Immediately turn to page 1907 and read the Gospel of John, which was designed to teach us how to believe that Jesus Christ is the Son of God (John 20:31).

Even if you are a Christian, you may not be prepared for evangelism. A tool such as "The Four Spiritual Laws" or some other summary of the gospel may be helpful. But more importantly, you need to be spiritually prepared through prayer, fasting, Scripture meditation, the sacraments, preaching and fellowship. You also need to be able to simply and clearly articulate your own experience with God. As God's power and presence shine through us, and He brings us opportunities to reach out to others, the gospel will flow out of us.

God doesn't want you to live in a state of guilt for more than the moment it takes to repent. Life is too short to live under the burden of neurotic, useless guilt. The motivation to share the gospel—and to live every moment of the Christian life—is found in the past, present and future grace of God (Acts 13:43; Galatians 2:21).

68:13 Gen 49:14 | [13] Even those who lived among the sheepfolds found treasures—
doves with wings of silver
and feathers of gold.
68:14 Josh 10:10 | [14] The Almighty scattered the enemy kings
like a blowing snowstorm on Mount Zalmon.

68:15 Ps 36:6 | [15] The mountains of Bashan are majestic,
with many peaks stretching high into the sky.
[16] Why do you look with envy, O rugged mountains,
at Mount Zion, where God has chosen to live,
where the LORD Himself will live forever?

68:17 Deut 33:2 Dan 7:10 | [17] Surrounded by unnumbered thousands of chariots,
the Lord came from Mount Sinai into His sanctuary.
68:18 *Eph 4:8 | [18] When You ascended to the heights,
You led a crowd of captives.
You received gifts from the people,
even from those who rebelled against You.
Now the LORD God will live among us there.

68:19 Pss 55:22; 65:5 Isa 46:4 | [19] Praise the Lord; praise God our savior!
For each day He carries us in His arms. *Interlude*
68:20 Ps 56:13 | [20] Our God is a God who saves!
The Sovereign LORD rescues us from death.
68:21 Ps 110:6 Hab 3:13 | [21] But God will smash the heads of His enemies,
crushing the skulls of those who love their guilty ways.
68:22 Amos 9:1-3 | [22] The Lord says, "I will bring My enemies down from Bashan;
I will bring them up from the depths of the sea.
68:23 1 Kgs 21:19 Ps 58:10 Jer 15:3 | [23] You, My people, will wash your feet in their blood,
and even your dogs will get their share!"

68:24 Ps 63:2 | [24] Your procession has come into view, O God—
the procession of my God and King as He goes
into the sanctuary.
68:25 Exod 15:20 Judg 11:34 1 Chr 13:8 | [25] Singers are in front, musicians behind;
between them are young women playing tambourines.
68:26 Deut 33:28 Pss 22:22-23; 26:12 | [26] Praise God, all you people of Israel;
praise the LORD, the source of Israel's life.
[27] Look, the little tribe of Benjamin leads the way.
Then comes a great throng of rulers from Judah
and all the rulers of Zebulun and Naphtali.

68:16-18 God chose Mount Zion, a hill outside of Jerusalem, as the place where His Temple would be built and His presence symbolized. It was on Mount Sinai that God appeared to give His law to Israel. The psalmist alludes to these two mountains to create the image of God the King leading a triumphant procession in the wake of a victorious battle. Behind Him trailed His captives; before Him waited His people with gifts and rejoicing. The imagery is further developed in 68:24-27. Much later, the image is borrowed and transformed by Paul to describe Christ's ascension (Ephesians 4:8-10).

▸ MINISTRY
68:25 Singing to the Lord. This psalm shows us the importance of using our talents in worship. One of the most dynamic ways we can offer praise to God is through music. Whether you like to sing, play an instrument, or hum along, music helps you focus on God and praise Him for His awesome character. Many psalms have instructions to use instruments in singing the verses. David was known as a musician. What do you use to worship God? You don't need to have the talent of an opera singer; you just need to have a heart of love for Him. Sing along with praise songs, repeat the words of a favorite hymn, or just listen to inspirational music while focusing on God's attributes. (***See Ministry**> Transformation> Vocations> Musician,* TopicGuide page A57.)

28 Summon Your might, O God.
Display Your power, O God, as You have in the past.
29 The kings of the earth are bringing tribute
to Your Temple in Jerusalem.
30 Rebuke these enemy nations—
these wild animals lurking in the reeds,
this herd of bulls among the weaker calves.
Make them bring bars of silver in humble tribute.
Scatter the nations that delight in war.
31 Let Egypt come with gifts of precious metals*;
let Ethiopia* bow in submission to God.
32 Sing to God, you kingdoms of the earth.
Sing praises to the Lord. *Interlude*
33 Sing to the One who rides across the ancient heavens,
His mighty voice thundering from the sky.
34 Tell everyone about God's power.
His majesty shines down on Israel;
His strength is mighty in the heavens.
35 God is awesome in His sanctuary.
The God of Israel gives power and strength to His people.

Praise be to God!

68:28 Pss 29:11; 44:4
68:29 Ps 72:10
68:30 Ps 89:10
68:31 Isa 19:19-21; 45:14
68:32 Ps 102:21-22
68:33 Pss 18:10; 29:4
68:35 Deut 10:17; Pss 29:11; 47:2

PSALM 69

For the choir director: A psalm of David, to be sung to the tune "Lilies."

1 Save me, O God,
for the floodwaters are up to my neck.
2 Deeper and deeper I sink into the mire;
I can't find a foothold.
I am in deep water,
and the floods overwhelm me.
3 I am exhausted from crying for help;
my throat is parched.
My eyes are swollen with weeping,
waiting for my God to help me.
4 Those who hate me without cause
outnumber the hairs on my head.
Many enemies try to destroy me with lies,
demanding that I give back what I didn't steal.

5 O God, You know how foolish I am;
my sins cannot be hidden from You.

69:2 Jon 2:3
69:3 Pss 6:6; 119:82, 123; Isa 38:14
69:4 Pss 35:11; 59:3; *John 15:25
69:5 Ps 44:21

68:31a Or *of rich cloth.* 68:31b Hebrew *Cush.*

68:28-32 Having celebrated God's great power and recalled His past triumphs, David now calls on God to defeat the present enemies of Israel. Egypt is often associated with reeds (Isaiah 19:6; 36:6; Ezekiel 29:6). The animals lurking in the reeds are likely crocodiles, which are also linked with Egypt.

69:1-3 In the ancient world, the sea embodied the forces of chaos that threatened to overwhelm the order of creation. David's poetic language draws on a sense of fearful foreboding associated with the deep waters in the ancient Near Eastern mind. When the language of 69:3 is compared to that of 69:1-2, it becomes evident David is speaking of his suffering metaphorically, yet no less meaningfully. (See also 69:14-15.)

69:5-12 The threat posed by David's enemies is not described in great detail, but the language seems to suggest false accusations within a judicial context. However, David says his suffering is linked directly to his piety. His enemies oppose him precisely because of his zeal for God. David's plight is familiar to God's people throughout the ages, who find their efforts to obey God met by hostility and scorn. It should be noted, however, that David also acknowledges his own sinfulness (69:5).

69:6 2 Sam 12:14 — 6 Don't let those who trust in You be ashamed because of me,
O Sovereign LORD of Heaven's Armies.
Don't let me cause them to be humiliated,
O God of Israel.
7 For I endure insults for Your sake;
humiliation is written all over my face.
69:8 Pss 31:11; 38:11 — 8 Even my own brothers pretend they don't know me;
they treat me like a stranger.

69:9 *John 2:17 *Rom 15:3 — 9 Passion for Your house has consumed me,
and the insults of those who insult You have fallen on me.
10 When I weep and fast,
they scoff at me.
11 When I dress in burlap to show sorrow,
they make fun of me.
69:12 Job 30:9 — 12 I am the favorite topic of town gossip,
and all the drunks sing about me.

69:13 Ps 32:6 Isa 49:8 2 Cor 6:2 — 13 But I keep praying to You, LORD,
hoping this time You will show me favor.
In Your unfailing love, O God,
answer my prayer with Your sure salvation.
69:14 Ps 144:7 — 14 Rescue me from the mud;
don't let me sink any deeper!
Save me from those who hate me,
and pull me from these deep waters.
69:15 Num 16:33 Ps 124:4-5 — 15 Don't let the floods overwhelm me,
or the deep waters swallow me,
or the pit of death devour me.

69:16 Pss 25:16; 51:1; 63:3 — 16 Answer my prayers, O LORD,
for Your unfailing love is wonderful.
Take care of me,
for Your mercy is so plentiful.
17 Don't hide from Your servant;
answer me quickly, for I am in deep trouble!
69:18 Pss 49:15; 119:134 — 18 Come and redeem me;
free me from my enemies.

▸ **MINISTRY**

69:6 Let me be a consistent witness. David was concerned that his failings in life would be a stumbling block to others. He probably was thinking about his bad moments. He committed adultery with Bathsheba and caused her husband to be killed in battle. He was pressed on every side by his enemies and had to flee into the wilderness. During these times, he despaired for his life. We all have times when we think life's circumstances are going to defeat us. Our consistent walk with God becomes essential then. Many people are watching us to see how God works in our lives. Our children, coworkers, neighbors, and friends all expect to see our relationship with God stand the test. This week, ask God to help you be a consistent witness for Him. (***See Ministry****> Great Commission> Witness> Witness in the power of the Holy Spirit,* TopicGuide page A56.)

▸ **WORSHIP**

69:10 Fasting through it all. The world doesn't understand what fasting signifies. People in the world are mostly interested in fulfilling their own pleasures, not limiting their intake. But for a believer, fasting expresses a desire to know God better. The fast helps us take our eyes off our physical needs and place them on God. When we fast, we discipline our bodies. The world will never understand why we fast, but God often uses it to revive our souls and find closer communion with Him. Try fasting and prayer to see how your relationship with God will deepen. (***See Worship****> OT> Fasting and Prayer> Fasting> Occasions> Afflicting one's soul was understood to refer to fasting,* TopicGuide page A26.)

69:13-18 David does not allow the hostility of his enemies to destroy his faith. He finds hope in God's faithfulness and calls on God to turn toward him in favor and mercy. To speak of God's face turned toward His people is to speak of God's favorable disposition experienced through His blessing (Numbers 6:25).

19 You know of my shame, scorn, and disgrace.
You see all that my enemies are doing.
20 Their insults have broken my heart,
and I am in despair.
If only one person would show some pity;
if only one would turn and comfort me.
21 But instead, they give me poison* for food;
they offer me sour wine for my thirst.

22 Let the bountiful table set before them become a snare
and their prosperity become a trap.*
23 Let their eyes go blind so they cannot see,
and make their bodies shake continually.*
24 Pour out Your fury on them;
consume them with Your burning anger.
25 Let their homes become desolate
and their tents be deserted.
26 To the one You have punished, they add
insult to injury;
they add to the pain of those You have hurt.
27 Pile their sins up high,
and don't let them go free.
28 Erase their names from the Book of Life;
don't let them be counted among the righteous.

29 I am suffering and in pain.
Rescue me, O God, by Your saving power.

30 Then I will praise God's name with singing,
and I will honor Him with thanksgiving.
31 For this will please the LORD more than sacrificing cattle,
more than presenting a bull with its horns
and hooves.
32 The humble will see their God at work and be glad.
Let all who seek God's help be encouraged.
33 For the LORD hears the cries of the needy;
He does not despise His imprisoned people.

34 Praise Him, O heaven and earth,
the seas and all that move in them.
35 For God will save Jerusalem*
and rebuild the towns of Judah.
His people will live there
and settle in their own land.
36 The descendants of those who obey Him will
inherit the land,
and those who love Him will live there in safety.

69:19 Ps 22:6-7 Isa 53:3
69:21 *Matt 27:48 *John 19:29
69:23 *Rom 11:9-10
69:25 Matt 23:38 Luke 13:35 *Acts 1:20
69:26 2 Chr 28:9 Isa 53:4
69:28 Exod 32:32-33 Luke 10:20 Rev 3:5; 13:8; 20:15
69:30 Pss 28:7; 50:14-15
69:31 Ps 50:13-14
69:32 Pss 22:26; 34:2
69:34 Ps 148:1-13
69:35 Ps 147:2 Isa 44:26
69:36 Ps 25:13

69:21 Or *gall.* 69:22 Greek version reads *Let their bountiful table set before them become a snare, / a trap that makes them think all is well. / Let their blessings cause them to stumble, / and let them get what they deserve.* Compare Rom 11:9.
69:23 Greek version reads *and let their backs be bent forever.* Compare Rom 11:10. 69:35 Hebrew *Zion.*

69:34-36 David calls on all of creation to rejoice over the deliverance of God's people. The apostle Paul echoes this thought when he speaks of creation groaning for its redemption, awaiting the glorification of God's children (Romans 8:19-22).

PSALM 70

For the choir director: A psalm of David, asking God to remember him.

70:1-5 //Ps 40:13-17 [1] Please, God, rescue me!
Come quickly, LORD, and help me.
70:2 Ps 35:4, 26 [2] May those who try to kill me
be humiliated and put to shame.
May those who take delight in my trouble
be turned back in disgrace.
[3] Let them be horrified by their shame,
for they said, "Aha! We've got him now!"
[4] But may all who search for You
be filled with joy and gladness in You.
May those who love Your salvation
repeatedly shout, "God is great!"
[5] But as for me, I am poor and needy;
please hurry to my aid, O God.
You are my helper and my savior;
O LORD, do not delay.

PSALM 71

71:1 Pss 25:2-3; 31:1-3 [1] O LORD, I have come to You for protection;
don't let me be disgraced.
71:2 Pss 17:6; 31:1 [2] Save me and rescue me,
for You do what is right.
Turn Your ear to listen to me,
and set me free.
71:3 Deut 33:27 Ps 18:2 [3] Be my rock of safety
where I can always hide.
Give the order to save me,
for You are my rock and my fortress.
[4] My God, rescue me from the power of the wicked,
from the clutches of cruel oppressors.
71:5 Ps 22:9-11 Jer 17:7, 17 [5] O Lord, You alone are my hope.
I've trusted You, O LORD, from childhood.
71:6 Pss 22:9-10; 34:1 Isa 46:3 [6] Yes, You have been with me from birth;
from my mother's womb You have cared for me.
No wonder I am always praising You!

70:1-3 The psalmist urgently cries to God for deliverance from enemies who seek to destroy him. He hopes his enemies will be undone in the same way that they seek to harm him.

▸ HOLINESS
70:4 Divine gladness. If you ask a person on the street to describe his present disposition, would he say, "I'm glad today"? What do we have to be glad about? Psalm 70 says that our joy and gladness are in God. He fills us with His joy. Our supreme "gladness" results from us knowing about His love for us through the gift of His Son. Do you shout, "God is great!" when you think about His salvation? Before we ever knew Him, He revealed Himself to us. The Creator of the universe took the time to reach down to you. Isn't that amazing? We can never express the depths of God's greatness, but we can praise Him for the joy and gladness that He has given us. (***See Holiness***> *Submission*> *Delighting in God*> *Gladness in God,* TopicGuide page A40.)

71:4-8 The psalmist finds hope for his present crises from the remembrance of his long-standing relationship with the Lord. It is a relationship that has encompassed the psalmist's whole life and has led him to praise God continually. The life and praise of the psalmist consequently have become signs to others of God's grace and mercy. This theme recurs throughout this psalm.

[7] My life is an example to many,
because You have been my strength
and protection.
[8] That is why I can never stop praising You;
I declare Your glory all day long.
[9] And now, in my old age, don't set me aside.
Don't abandon me when my strength is failing.
[10] For my enemies are whispering against me.
They are plotting together to kill me.
[11] They say, "God has abandoned him.
Let's go and get him,
for no one will help him now."

[12] O God, don't stay away.
My God, please hurry to help me.
[13] Bring disgrace and destruction on my accusers.
Humiliate and shame those who want
to harm me.
[14] But I will keep on hoping for Your help;
I will praise You more and more.
[15] I will tell everyone about Your righteousness.
All day long I will proclaim Your saving power,
though I am not skilled with words.*
[16] I will praise Your mighty deeds, O Sovereign LORD.
I will tell everyone that You alone are just.

[17] O God, You have taught me from my
earliest childhood,
and I constantly tell others about the wonderful
things You do.
[18] Now that I am old and gray,
do not abandon me, O God.
Let me proclaim Your power to this new
generation,
Your mighty miracles to all who come after me.

[19] Your righteousness, O God, reaches to the
highest heavens.
You have done such wonderful things.
Who can compare with You, O God?

71:7 Ps 61:3
71:9 Ps 92:14
71:10 Matt 27:1
71:11 Pss 3:2; 7:2
71:12 Ps 22:9-11
71:13 Ps 35:4, 26
71:15 Pss 35:28; 40:5
71:16 Ps 106:2
71:18 Pss 22:31; 78:4, 6
71:19 Deut 3:24 Pss 35:10; 57:10 Luke 1:49

71:15 Or *though I cannot count it.*

▸ WORSHIP
71:7 Be an example to many. What do people compliment you for? Your kindness? Patience? A listening ear? Any positive quality we display is a result of God's work in our lives, and we should give Him the credit. The times when God has helped us should be the place we praise Him to others. In what ways has God protected and strengthened you? Tell your friends about it. (***See Worship****> OT> God's Supremacy> Was God-centered (not worshiper-centered),* TopicGuide page A27.)

71:11 The wicked continually misinterpret God's apparent silence (Psalm 50:21). Here they wrongly assume God has abandoned His child.

▸ GOD
71:19 God's righteousness. Walking in the countryside after a new snowfall is a thrilling experience. The hills are swathed in a blanket of pure white. Everywhere you look, the snowy landscape rises and falls, covered with countless sparkles gleaming in the sunshine. Nowhere can you see a splotch of mud. God's righteousness is that complete. He has no blot of sin anywhere in His character. The beauty of His righteousness sparkles. He deserves our utmost praise for His awesome nature. (***See God****> God's Attributes> Righteous> His righteousness is absolute,* TopicGuide page A17.)

71:20 Pss 23:4; 60:3-4; 119:25 Hos 6:2
20 You have allowed me to suffer much hardship,
but You will restore me to life again
and lift me up from the depths of the earth.
21 You will restore me to even greater honor
and comfort me once again.

71:22 Pss 33:2; 89:18; 147:7
22 Then I will praise You with music
on the harp,
because You are faithful to Your promises,
O my God.
I will sing praises to You with a lyre,
O Holy One of Israel.
71:23 Pss 5:11; 103:4
23 I will shout for joy and sing Your praises,
for You have ransomed me.
71:24 Pss 35:28; 71:13
24 I will tell about Your righteous deeds
all day long,
for everyone who tried to hurt me
has been shamed and humiliated.

PSALM 72

A psalm of Solomon.

72:1 1 Kgs 3:9
1 Give Your love of justice to the king, O God,
and righteousness to the king's son.
72:2 Ps 82:3 Isa 9:7; 11:2-5
2 Help him judge Your people in the right way;
let the poor always be treated fairly.
72:3 Isa 9:5-6 Mic 4:3-4 Zech 9:10
3 May the mountains yield prosperity for all,
and may the hills be fruitful.
4 Help him to defend the poor,
72:4 Isa 11:4
to rescue the children of the needy,
and to crush their oppressors.
72:5 Ps 89:36-37
5 May they fear You as long as the sun shines,
as long as the moon remains in the sky.
Yes, forever!

72:6 Deut 32:2 Ps 65:10 Hos 6:3
6 May the king's rule be refreshing like spring rain
on freshly cut grass,
like the showers that water the earth.
72:7 Ps 92:12
7 May all the godly flourish during his reign.
May there be abundant prosperity until the moon
is no more.
72:8 Exod 23:31 Zech 9:10
8 May he reign from sea to sea,
and from the Euphrates River* to the
ends of the earth.

72:8 Hebrew *the river.*

72:1-4 The king is God's representative on earth. God's passion for justice and concern for the needy are to be characteristics of the king, as well (compare Psalm 68:5-6). The psalm expresses the hope that, in the king, the justice and compassion of God will be embodied and carried out. (See also 72:6-7, 12-14.)

72:5 It was not uncommon to speak in hyperbolic terms about the duration of the king's reign. However, such language anticipates the eternal reign of the last Davidic king, Jesus Christ.

72:8-11 "From sea to sea" alludes to the promised extent of Israel's kingdom (Exodus 23:31). However, the language also depicts a universal kingdom. Tarshish, Sheba, and Seba were all distant lands representing the extent of the known world.

9 Desert nomads will bow before him;
his enemies will fall before him in the dust.
10 The western kings of Tarshish and other
distant lands
will bring him tribute.
The eastern kings of Sheba and Seba
will bring him gifts.
11 All kings will bow before him,
and all nations will serve him.

12 He will rescue the poor when they cry to him;
he will help the oppressed, who have no one
to defend them.
13 He feels pity for the weak and the needy,
and he will rescue them.
14 He will redeem them from oppression
and violence,
for their lives are precious to him.

15 Long live the king!
May the gold of Sheba be given to him.
May the people always pray for him
and bless him all day long.
16 May there be abundant grain throughout the land,
flourishing even on the hilltops.
May the fruit trees flourish like the trees of Lebanon,
and may the people thrive like grass in a field.

72:9 Isa 49:23; Mic 7:17
72:10 Pss 45:12; 68:29; Isa 42:4, 10; 60:6
72:11 Pss 86:9; 138:4; Isa 49:23
72:12 Job 29:12
72:14 Ps 116:15
72:15 Isa 60:6
72:16 Job 5:25

72:15-19 The major themes of the psalm are threaded together in verses 15-17: the prosperity and joy of a just king's reign, an eternal dominion, and the submission of the nations to the king's rule. The psalm then concludes with the recognition that such a kingdom is possible only through the work of God. It is in the reign of the God-Man, Jesus Christ, that the kingdom described in this psalm becomes a reality.

72:20 At one point during the development of the Psalter, this psalm was the final song in that collection. It now closes the second of five sections of the Psalms.

BECAUSE GOD IS HOLY

I will devote myself to him in purity, worship and service.

Praise His glorious name forever! Let the whole earth be filled with His glory. Amen and amen!

PSALM 72:19

FOR THE NEXT *GOD IS HOLY* FEATURE SEE PAGE 1160.

72:17 Gen 12:3; 22:18 Ps 89:36
17 May the king's name endure forever;
may it continue as long as the sun shines.
May all nations be blessed through him
and bring him praise.

72:18 Exod 15:11 Pss 41:13; 77:14
18 Praise the LORD God, the God of Israel,
who alone does such wonderful things.
72:19 Num 14:20-21 Neh 9:5
19 Praise His glorious name forever!
Let the whole earth be filled with His glory.
Amen and amen!

20 (This ends the prayers of David son of Jesse.)

BOOK THREE (PSALMS 73–89)

PSALM 73

A psalm of Asaph.

73:1 Pss 24:3-4; 51:10 Matt 5:8
1 Truly God is good to Israel,
to those whose hearts are pure.
73:2 Ps 94:18
2 But as for me, I almost lost my footing.
My feet were slipping, and I was almost gone.
73:3 Ps 37:1, 7 Jer 12:1
3 For I envied the proud
when I saw them prosper despite their wickedness.
4 They seem to live such painless lives;
their bodies are so healthy and strong.
73:5 Job 21:9-10
5 They don't have troubles like other people;
they're not plagued with problems like everyone else.
73:6 Ps 109:18
6 They wear pride like a jeweled necklace
and clothe themselves with cruelty.
73:7 Job 15:27-28 Ps 17:10
7 These fat cats have everything
their hearts could ever wish for!
73:8 Pss 1:1; 17:10 Jude 1:16
8 They scoff and speak only evil;
in their pride they seek to crush others.
9 They boast against the very heavens,
and their words strut throughout the earth.
10 And so the people are dismayed and confused,
drinking in all their words.
73:11 Job 22:13
11 "What does God know?" they ask.
"Does the Most High even know what's happening?"
73:12 Ps 49:6
12 Look at these wicked people—
enjoying a life of ease while their riches multiply.
73:13 Job 21:15; 34:9 Ps 26:6
13 Did I keep my heart pure for nothing?
Did I keep myself innocent for no reason?
73:14 Pss 38:5-6; 118:18
14 I get nothing but trouble all day long;
every morning brings me pain.
15 If I had really spoken this way to others,
I would have been a traitor to Your people.

73:4-9 The psalmist describes the prosperity of the wicked in hyperbolic terms. He says that from his perspective, it appeared as though the ungodly experience no distress and enjoy uninterrupted blessing despite their wickedness. Also, their prosperity produces pride and arrogance directed against God Himself.

73:15-16 The psalmist says he recognized the impropriety of the approach just outlined. He knew that he must not abandon his faith, but he would not abandon the question either. He determined to pursue the matter while humbly recognizing the difficulty of the issue.

16 So I tried to understand why the wicked prosper.
But what a difficult task it is!
17 Then I went into Your sanctuary, O God,
and I finally understood the destiny of the wicked.
18 Truly, You put them on a slippery path
and send them sliding over the cliff to destruction.
19 In an instant they are destroyed,
completely swept away by terrors.
20 When You arise, O Lord,
You will laugh at their silly ideas
as a person laughs at dreams in the morning.

21 Then I realized that my heart was bitter,
and I was all torn up inside.
22 I was so foolish and ignorant—
I must have seemed like a senseless animal to You.
23 Yet I still belong to You;
You hold my right hand.
24 You guide me with Your counsel,
leading me to a glorious destiny.
25 Whom have I in heaven but You?
I desire You more than anything on earth.
26 My health may fail, and my spirit may grow weak,
but God remains the strength of my heart;
He is mine forever.

27 Those who desert Him will perish,
for You destroy those who abandon You.
28 But as for me, how good it is to be near God!
I have made the Sovereign LORD my shelter,
and I will tell everyone about the wonderful things You do.

73:16 Eccl 8:16-17
73:17 Ps 27:4
73:19 Num 16:21; Isa 47:11
73:22 Eccl 3:18
73:24 Pss 32:8; 48:14
73:26 Pss 16:5; 38:10
73:27 Ps 37:20
73:28 Pss 40:5; 71:7; Heb 10:22

PSALM 74

A psalm of Asaph.*

1 O God, why have You rejected us so long?
Why is Your anger so intense against the sheep of Your own pasture?

74:1 Deut 29:20; Pss 44:9; 89:46

74:TITLE Hebrew *maskil.* This may be a literary or musical term.

73:17-20 The psalmist came to the sanctuary of God and found a new angle of vision. In the presence of God, the psalmist assumed a transcendent perspective to consider the fate of the wicked. In so doing, he realized the transitory nature of the prosperity enjoyed by the wicked. Their bliss is temporary and they will be held responsible for their wickedness.

▸ ADOPTION
73:24 God holds our hands. Can you picture a child walking with his father through a dark alley? The child reaches up and grabs his father's hand. The feel of those huge fingers and strong muscles gives the child all the confidence he needs to keep going. That's similar to how we relate to God. He is leading us to a destiny—heaven—but we don't know the way. Our job is to just keep our hand in His. We do that through prayer and trust. God has promised that He will lead us to our sure destiny—a life forever with Him in heaven. Count on Him! (***See Adoption**> In Heaven> Immortal,* TopicGuide page A38.)

73:25 The attitude expressed here contrasts sharply with the self-interest that motivated the faithless response described in 73:10-14. Faith recognizes fellowship with God as the highest reward of the righteous, and such fellowship is not contingent upon earthly prosperity.

74:1-3 In 586 BC, the Babylonians destroyed Jerusalem, including the Temple, and took a large portion of the population captive. The psalmist cries to God, invoking the memory of God's special relationship with Israel. God chose Israel as His special people and Jerusalem as the place of His dwelling. The language of remembrance, however, involves more than mere mental recall; the psalmist is calling on God to fulfill His promises and save His people (Genesis 8:1; Leviticus 26:42).

74:2 [2] Remember that we are the people You chose long ago,
Deut 32:6, 9 the tribe You redeemed as Your own special possession!
Ps 68:16 And remember Jerusalem,* Your home here on earth.
74:3 [3] Walk through the awful ruins of the city;
Ps 79:1 / Isa 61:4 see how the enemy has destroyed Your sanctuary.
[4] There Your enemies shouted their victorious battle cries;
there they set up their battle standards.
74:5 [5] They swung their axes
Jer 46:22 like woodcutters in a forest.
[6] With axes and picks,
they smashed the carved paneling.
74:7 [7] They burned Your sanctuary to the ground.
2 Kgs 25:9 They defiled the place that bears Your name.
74:8 [8] Then they thought, "Let's destroy everything!"
Ps 83:4 So they burned down all the places where God was worshiped.

74:9 [9] We no longer see Your miraculous signs.
Lev 24:16 All the prophets are gone,
Ps 78:43 and no one can tell us when it will end.
74:10 [10] How long, O God, will You allow our enemies to insult You?
Ps 44:16 Will You let them dishonor Your name forever?
74:11 [11] Why do You hold back Your strong right hand?
Ps 59:13 Unleash Your powerful fist and destroy them.

74:12 [12] You, O God, are my king from ages past,
Ps 44:4 bringing salvation to the earth.
74:13 [13] You split the sea by Your strength
Exod 14:21 and smashed the heads of the sea monsters.
[14] You crushed the heads of Leviathan*
and let the desert animals eat him.
74:15 [15] You caused the springs and streams to gush forth,
Exod 14:21-22; 17:5-6 and You dried up rivers that never run dry.
74:16 [16] Both day and night belong to You;
Gen 1:14-18 You made the starlight* and the sun.
Ps 136:7-8 [17] You set the boundaries of the earth,
74:17 and You made both summer and winter.
Gen 8:22
Acts 17:26 [18] See how these enemies insult You, LORD.
74:18 A foolish nation has dishonored Your name.
Deut 32:6 / Pss 39:8; 74:10

74:2 Hebrew *Mount Zion.* 74:14 The identification of Leviathan is disputed, ranging from an earthly creature to a mythical sea monster in ancient literature. 74:16 Or *moon;* Hebrew reads *light.*

74:4-8 Following Judah's rebellion against Nebuchadnezzar, the Babylonian king laid siege to Jerusalem. When the city fell, the Babylonians destroyed the walls of the city and leveled the Temple. The destruction of the city and the Temple was God's just punishment for Judah's persistent and pervasive unfaithfulness (see 2 Kings 25).

74:15-17 The psalmist alludes to the Creation story of Genesis 1 (compare Job 38:8-11; Jeremiah 5:22). The Old Testament portrays the Exile as a return to the state of chaos (Jeremiah 4:23-26). Not surprisingly, the psalmist praises God's creative power from amid the ruins because an act of re-creation is now necessary.

▸ SPIRITUAL WARFARE
74:16 It belongs to God. When you stand out in the sunshine drinking in the warm rays do you think, "This sunshine belongs to God"? Usually, we just take for granted the brightness of our daytimes and the quietness of our nights. But the psalmist remembers to give God the glory due Him as Creator. We have no claim to His world—the daylight and the moonlight. He is the owner. He sustains it all (Nehemiah 9:6). Praise Him for all He has created by enjoying the gifts of creation. (***See Spiritual Warfare**> Origin of Sin> Creation in Bondage> God Created,* TopicGuide page A44.)

74:18-23 The psalmist calls on God to rescue Israel and offers reasons to persuade God to act. God should act to vindicate His glory, fulfill His covenantal commitments, and demonstrate His compassion. The calls to "arise" and "defend" are part of the language of battle; the psalmist envisions God as a divine warrior (Numbers 10:35).

19 Don't let these wild beasts destroy Your turtledoves.
Don't forget Your suffering people forever.

20 Remember Your covenant promises,
for the land is full of darkness and violence! 74:20 Gen 17:7 Ps 106:45
21 Don't let the downtrodden be humiliated again.
Instead, let the poor and needy praise Your name. 74:21 Ps 35:10 Isa 41:17

22 Arise, O God, and defend Your cause.
Remember how these fools insult You all day long. 74:22 Ps 43:1
23 Don't overlook what Your enemies have said
or their growing uproar. 74:23 Ps 65:7

PSALM 75

For the choir director: A psalm of Asaph. A song to be sung to the tune "Do Not Destroy!"

1 We thank You, O God!
We give thanks because You are near. 75:1 Pss 44:1; 71:17
People everywhere tell of Your wonderful deeds.

2 God says, "At the time I have planned,
I will bring justice against the wicked.
3 When the earth quakes and its people live in turmoil, 75:3 1 Sam 2:8 Ps 46:6
I am the One who keeps its foundations firm. *Interlude*

4 "I warned the proud, 'Stop your boasting!'
I told the wicked, 'Don't raise your fists!
5 Don't raise your fists in defiance at the heavens 75:5 Ps 94:4
or speak with such arrogance.'"
6 For no one on earth—from east or west,
or even from the wilderness—
should raise a defiant fist.*
7 It is God alone who judges; 75:7 1 Sam 2:7
He decides who will rise and who will fall.
8 For the LORD holds a cup in His hand
that is full of foaming wine mixed with spices.
He pours out the wine in judgment,
and all the wicked must drink it,
draining it to the dregs.

9 But as for me, I will always proclaim what God has done; 75:9 Ps 40:10
I will sing praises to the God of Jacob.

75:6 Hebrew *should lift.*

75:1 The opening verse sets the psalm in the context of corporate worship. Corporate worship was rare under the Old Covenant, with much of the formal practice of faith done in private or at the Temple with your immediate family and a priest.

75:2-3 The world exhibits natural and moral orders, both established by God. Evil threatens to undo the moral order, but God acts to prevent the world from falling into utter chaos. Yet He does so when and where He pleases.

▶ PURPOSE
75:3 Our fragile life. When the tsunami of 2004 traversed the Indian Ocean, the damage to South Asian coastal cities and villages was horrific. A 9.0 earthquake under the water triggered the tsunami. This one natural event sent the lives of hundreds of thousands of people into turmoil. Could something worse happen? What keeps our world from cracking into a thousand pieces? God does. He "keeps its foundations firm." That is such a comforting thought. Even though major disasters hit different parts of the world with devastating results, God keeps the earth firmly on its course. Thank God for how He takes care of His creation. (***See Purpose**> God's Deeds> Judgment> Mountains quake/earthquake,* TopicGuide page A53.)

75:8 The wrath of God is also symbolized by a cup in Isaiah 51:17 and Jeremiah 25:15-17.

75:10 Pss 89:17; 148:14
10 For God says, "I will break the strength of the wicked,
but I will increase the power of the godly."

PSALM 76

For the choir director: A psalm of Asaph. A song to be accompanied by stringed instruments.

1 God is honored in Judah;
His name is great in Israel.
76:2 Pss 48:2-3; 132:13; 135:21
2 Jerusalem* is where He lives;
Mount Zion is His home.
76:3 Ps 46:9
3 There He has broken the fiery arrows of the enemy,
the shields and swords and weapons of war. *Interlude*

4 You are glorious and more majestic
than the everlasting mountains.*
76:5 Isa 10:12
5 Our boldest enemies have been plundered.
They lie before us in the sleep of death.
No warrior could lift a hand against us.
76:6 Exod 15:1, 21
6 At the blast of Your breath, O God of Jacob,
their horses and chariots lay still.
76:7 Ps 89:7 Nah 1:6 Rev 6:17
7 No wonder You are greatly feared!
Who can stand before You when Your anger explodes?
76:8 1 Chr 16:30
8 From heaven You sentenced Your enemies;
the earth trembled and stood silent before You.
76:9 Pss 9:7-9; 72:4
9 You stand up to judge those who do evil, O God,
and to rescue the oppressed of the earth. *Interlude*
76:10 Exod 9:16 Rom 9:17
10 Human defiance only enhances Your glory,
for You use it as a weapon.*

11 Make vows to the LORD your God, and keep them.
Let everyone bring tribute to the Awesome One.

76:2 Hebrew *Salem,* another name for Jerusalem. **76:4** As in Greek version; Hebrew reads *than mountains filled with beasts of prey.* **76:10** The meaning of the Hebrew is uncertain.

76:2 The tent of the Lord, and later the first and second Temple, was situated atop the hill known as Mount Zion, just north of Jerusalem. Jerusalem and Zion came to embody and symbolize the presence of God on earth.

76:3 The weaponry metaphors establish the principle imagery of the psalm—God as a warrior. God breaks the enemy's weapons, rendering them useless as instruments of violence and war. The imagery suggests God's victory over the enemies of Israel and the establishment of peace (compare Psalm 46:9; Micah 5:10).

▸ GOD

76:4 God's majesty. The mountains are truly some of the most majestic objects on earth. Whether the mountain is rounded and green or stark and rocky, its face is something to behold. Amazing stands of pine trees cover their sides; snow blankets their tops. Huge boulders and gaping ravines cling to the slopes. Yet the beauty of the Alps or the Andes cannot match the glorious majesty of our God. He is their Creator; He formed them by His wisdom and imagination. The next time you see the mountains, let them remind you of God's majesty. (***See God***> *God's Attributes> Infinite> Heaven and earth cannot contain Him,* TopicGuide page A16.)

▸ ADOPTION

76:7 The Judgment Day. What do you think it will be like on the day when God's anger explodes? Can you imagine what will happen at that moment? In Revelation 20:11-12, the apostle John describes the Judgment Day: "I saw a great white throne and the One sitting on it. The earth and sky fled from His presence, but they found no place to hide. I saw the dead, both great and small, standing before God's throne." How wonderful that we don't have to face God's exploding anger because of Jesus Christ! Thank God for salvation in His Son, the hope we have for the future. (***See Adoption***> *Without Christ> Separated from God> Facing judgment,* TopicGuide page A36.)

76:11 Worshipers often made vows in times of distress to be fulfilled when God sent deliverance (Leviticus 7:16-21). Weaker nations that were defeated in battle were often subjected to the payment of tribute (or tax) to the conquerors. The psalmist depicts God as the conquering Sovereign.

12 For He breaks the pride of princes,
and the kings of the earth fear Him.

PSALM 77

For Jeduthun, the choir director: A psalm of Asaph.

1 I cry out to God; yes, I shout.
Oh, that God would listen to me!
2 When I was in deep trouble,
I searched for the Lord.
All night long I prayed, with hands lifted toward heaven,
but my soul was not comforted.
3 I think of God, and I moan,
overwhelmed with longing for His help. *Interlude*

4 You don't let me sleep.
I am too distressed even to pray!
5 I think of the good old days,
long since ended,
6 when my nights were filled with joyful songs.
I search my soul and ponder the difference now.
7 Has the Lord rejected me forever?
Will He never again be kind to me?
8 Is His unfailing love gone forever?
Have His promises permanently failed?
9 Has God forgotten to be gracious?
Has He slammed the door on His compassion? *Interlude*

10 And I said, "This is my fate;
the Most High has turned His hand against me."
11 But then I recall all You have done, O LORD;
I remember Your wonderful deeds of long ago.
12 They are constantly in my thoughts.
I cannot stop thinking about Your mighty works.

13 O God, Your ways are holy.
Is there any god as mighty as You?
14 You are the God of great wonders!
You demonstrate Your awesome power among the nations.
15 By Your strong arm, You redeemed Your people,
the descendants of Jacob and Joseph. *Interlude*

16 When the Red Sea* saw You, O God,
its waters looked and trembled!
The sea quaked to its very depths.

77:16 Hebrew *the waters.*

77:2 Job 11:13; Pss 50:15; 88:9; Isa 26:9, 16
77:3 Pss 43:5; 61:2; 142:2-3
77:5 Ps 143:5
77:6 Ps 42:8
77:8 Ps 89:49
77:9 Ps 25:6
77:11 Exod 15:11; Ps 86:8
77:13 Exod 15:11; Ps 86:8
77:15 Exod 6:6; Deut 9:29
77:16 Exod 14:21

77:1-3 The psalmist describes his spiritual suffering with intense and vivid language that reflects his complete dependence on God for sustenance and joy. Crying through the night with uplifted hands is a recurring theme in the psalms of lament (Psalms 6:6; 22:2; 88:9; 141:2). The posture of uplifted hands suggests complete dependence.

77:11-15 A change occurs in the tone of the psalm. The psalmist commits himself to rehearse the past triumphs of God in the hope that God will perform mighty deeds to rescue His people once again. The psalmist's commitment to praise God in his pain suggests a profound transforming and sustaining role for praise.

77:16-20 The Red Sea crossing demonstrated God's awesome power and marked the inception of the frequently used image of God as a warrior (Exodus 14–15). The psalmist employs language typically associated with the appearance of God on

77:17 Ps 68:33
[17] The clouds poured down rain;
the thunder rumbled in the sky.
Your arrows of lightning flashed.
77:18 Judg 5:4
[18] Your thunder roared from the whirlwind;
the lightning lit up the world!
The earth trembled and shook.
77:19 Hab 3:15
[19] Your road led through the sea,
Your pathway through the mighty waters—
a pathway no one knew was there!
77:20 Exod 6:26; 13:21 Ps 78:52 Isa 63:11-13
[20] You led Your people along that road like
a flock of sheep,
with Moses and Aaron as their shepherds.

PSALM 78

A psalm of Asaph.*

[1] O my people, listen to my instructions.
Open your ears to what I am saying,
78:2 *Matt 13:34-35
[2] for I will speak to you in a parable.
I will teach you hidden lessons from our past—
78:3 Ps 44:1
[3] stories we have heard and known,
stories our ancestors handed down to us.
78:4 Deut 11:19 Ps 22:30
[4] We will not hide these truths from our children;
we will tell the next generation
about the glorious deeds of the LORD,
about His power and His mighty wonders.
78:5 Deut 6:4-9
[5] For He issued His laws to Jacob;
He gave His instructions to Israel.
He commanded our ancestors
to teach them to their children,

78:TITLE Hebrew *maskil.* This may be a literary or musical term.

earth (compare Exodus 19:9, 11, 16). He also borrows imagery drawn from ancient myths that spoke of the gods' cosmic struggle against chaotic seas to bring order to creation. By doing so, the psalmist is affirming the unique sovereignty of God as Creator and Redeemer.

▸ PURPOSE
77:18 Creation is evidence of God's existence. Whenever we stand under the fury of a thunderstorm, it reminds us of our Creator God. The flash of lightning across a stormy sky shows us the power of our God. The tremble of a thunderstorm takes us back to the fact that if we feel small next to it. How tiny are we in comparison to God? All creation shouts out the wonder of God's power and strength. If creation gives this kind of praise to God, how much more should we honor Him with our voices and our deeds? (***See Purpose****> God's Deeds> Judgment> Mountains quake/earthquake,* TopicGuide page A53.)

▸ CHURCH
77:20 God led the people. When a shepherd moves his flock, he goes in front of them, leading them rather than herding them from the rear. When the Hebrew people left Egypt to go into the wilderness, God led them through a pillar of cloud that went ahead of them (Exodus 13:21). That's a picture of how God leads us. He goes before us, not behind us. He shows us the way. Because He knows all, He helps us with our problems and trials. The next time you experience a heavy time in your life, picture God as a shepherd going ahead of you. Rely on Him to show you the way. (***See Church****> What> Many Titles> Sheep> The sheep trust the protection of the shepherd,* TopicGuide page A48.)

▸ BIBLE
78:1 God's instructions to us. God has provided an immense treasure of help for us—His Word. Stories from the past teach us how to serve Him. Examples of the mighty acts God has performed give us confidence in His strength. His decrees and commandments keep us on the right pathway. How do we find all these treasures? Just like a treasure seeker, we must search for them. We do this by faithfully studying God's Word. Daily turn to the Scriptures to find new treasure. (***See Bible****> Power> Wisdom> Instruction through God's Word,* TopicGuide page A11.)

78:1-4 The events to be retold are parables in the sense that they are presented as lessons for the audience. The faith of Israel was a historical faith. The God of Israel acted in human history on behalf of His people. If the Israelites were to retain their integrity as God's people, it was crucial that they remember their history.

6 so the next generation might know them—
even the children not yet born—
and they in turn will teach their own children.

78:6 Deut 11:19; Ps 102:18

7 So each generation should set its hope anew on God,
not forgetting His glorious miracles
and obeying His commands.

78:7 Deut 4:2, 9; Josh 22:5

8 Then they will not be like their ancestors—
stubborn, rebellious, and unfaithful,
refusing to give their hearts to God.

78:8 Exod 32:9; Ezek 20:18

9 The warriors of Ephraim, though armed with bows,
turned their backs and fled on the day of battle.
10 They did not keep God's covenant
and refused to live by His instructions.

78:10 2 Kgs 18:12

11 They forgot what He had done—
the great wonders He had shown them,

78:11 Ps 106:13

12 the miracles He did for their ancestors
on the plain of Zoan in the land of Egypt.

78:12 Num 13:22; Isa 19:11

13 For He divided the sea and led them through,
making the water stand up like walls!

78:13 Exod 14:21; 15:18

14 In the daytime He led them by a cloud,
and all night by a pillar of fire.

78:14 Exod 13:21

15 He split open the rocks in the wilderness
to give them water, as from a gushing spring.

78:15 Exod 17:5-6; *1 Cor 10:4

16 He made streams pour from the rock,
making the waters flow down like a river!

78:16 Num 20:8, 10-11

17 Yet they kept on sinning against Him,
rebelling against the Most High in the desert.

78:17 Heb 3:16

18 They stubbornly tested God in their hearts,
demanding the foods they craved.

78:18 Num 11:4-5; *1 Cor 10:9-10

19 They even spoke against God Himself, saying,
"God can't give us food in the wilderness.

78:19 Exod 16:3; Num 21:5

20 Yes, He can strike a rock so water gushes out,
but He can't give His people bread and meat."

78:20 Num 20:11

21 When the LORD heard them, He was furious.
The fire of His wrath burned against Jacob.
Yes, His anger rose against Israel,

78:21 Num 11:1

22 for they did not believe God
or trust Him to care for them.

78:22-23 Heb 3:19

23 But He commanded the skies to open;
He opened the doors of heaven.

78:23 Mal 3:10

24 He rained down manna for them to eat;
He gave them bread from heaven.

78:24 Exod 16:4; *John 6:30-31

25 They ate the food of angels!
God gave them all they could hold.
26 He released the east wind in the heavens
and guided the south wind by His mighty power.

78:26 Num 11:31

78:5-8 Faithful Israelites perpetuated their faith by retelling their story to their children and grandchildren. God specifically instructed His people to do so (Deuteronomy 6:4-9). The goal of such instruction was faith and obedience.

78:12-16 The foundational event in Israel's history was the Exodus from Egypt. God revealed Himself to Israel through His mighty deeds, chief of which was the parting of the Red Sea. He then continued to guide Israel toward the Promised Land, miraculously providing for the people along the way. (See Exodus 7–15; Numbers 20:8-11.)

78:27 Exod 16:13 Ps 105:40
27 He rained down meat as thick as dust—
birds as plentiful as the sand on the seashore!
28 He caused the birds to fall within their camp
and all around their tents.
78:29 Num 11:19-20
29 The people ate their fill.
He gave them what they craved.
30 But before they satisfied their craving,
while the meat was yet in their mouths,
78:31 Num 11:33-34
31 the anger of God rose against them,
and He killed their strongest men.
He struck down the finest of Israel's young men.

78:32 Num 14:11
32 But in spite of this, the people kept sinning.
Despite His wonders, they refused to trust Him.
78:33 Num 14:29, 34-35
33 So He ended their lives in failure,
their years in terror.
78:34 Hos 5:15
34 When God began killing them,
they finally sought Him.
They repented and took God seriously.
78:35 Deut 9:26; 32:4
35 Then they remembered that God was their rock,
that God Most High* was their redeemer.
78:36 Exod 32:7-8 Ezek 33:31
36 But all they gave Him was lip service;
they lied to Him with their tongues.
37 Their hearts were not loyal to Him.
They did not keep His covenant.
78:38 Exod 34:5-6 Num 14:18-20
38 Yet He was merciful and forgave their sins
and did not destroy them all.
Many times He held back His anger
and did not unleash His fury!
78:39 Job 7:16-17 Jas 4:14
39 For He remembered that they were merely mortal,
gone like a breath of wind that never returns.

40 Oh, how often they rebelled against Him
in the wilderness
and grieved His heart in that dry wasteland.
78:41 2 Kgs 19:22
41 Again and again they tested God's patience
and provoked the Holy One of Israel.
78:42 Judg 8:34
42 They did not remember His power
and how He rescued them from their enemies.
78:43 Exod 7:3
43 They did not remember His miraculous signs in Egypt,
His wonders on the plain of Zoan.
78:44 Exod 7:20 Ps 105:29
44 For He turned their rivers into blood,
so no one could drink from the streams.
78:45 Exod 8:6, 24 Ps 105:30-31
45 He sent vast swarms of flies to consume them
and hordes of frogs to ruin them.

78:35 Hebrew *El-Elyon.*

▸ **GOD**
78:35 The Most High God. Psalm 47:2 says, "The LORD Most High is awesome. He is the great King of all the earth." "Most High" is one of God's names. It describes His position compared to everything else in the universe. No one can reach Him because He is not physical—so we can never climb to His height. We are not simply insignificant and small compared to Him: We are utterly unable to approach Him on our own. This is why we must trust Christ, Immanuel, "God with us." There is only one way to God, and that is through Christ alone. (***See God***> *God's Names*> *God*> *God Most High (El Elyon),* TopicGuide page A18.)

46 He gave their crops to caterpillars;
their harvest was consumed by locusts.
47 He destroyed their grapevines with hail
and shattered their sycamore-figs with sleet.
48 He abandoned their cattle to the hail,
their livestock to bolts of lightning.
49 He loosed on them His fierce anger—
all His fury, rage, and hostility.
He dispatched against them
a band of destroying angels.
50 He turned His anger against them;
He did not spare the Egyptians' lives
but ravaged them with the plague.
51 He killed the oldest son in each Egyptian family,
the flower of youth throughout the land of Egypt.*
52 But He led His own people like a flock of sheep,
guiding them safely through the wilderness.
53 He kept them safe so they were not afraid;
but the sea covered their enemies.
54 He brought them to the border of His holy land,
to this land of hills He had won for them.
55 He drove out the nations before them;
He gave them their inheritance by lot.
He settled the tribes of Israel into their homes.

56 But they kept testing and rebelling against God Most High.
They did not obey His laws.
57 They turned back and were as faithless as their parents.
They were as undependable as a crooked bow.
58 They angered God by building shrines to other gods;
they made Him jealous with their idols.
59 When God heard them, He was very angry,
and He completely rejected Israel.
60 Then He abandoned His dwelling at Shiloh,
the Tabernacle where He had lived among the people.
61 He allowed the Ark of His might to be captured;
He surrendered His glory into enemy hands.
62 He gave His people over to be butchered by the sword,
because He was so angry with His own people—His special possession.
63 Their young men were killed by fire;
their young women died before singing their wedding songs.
64 Their priests were slaughtered,
and their widows could not mourn their deaths.

65 Then the Lord rose up as though waking from sleep,
like a warrior aroused from a drunken stupor.

78:46 Exod 10:14
78:47 Exod 9:23-25; Ps 105:32
78:48 Exod 9:19
78:49 Exod 15:7
78:51 Exod 12:29-30; Ps 105:36
78:52 Ps 77:20
78:53 Exod 14:19-20, 27-28
78:54 Exod 15:17
78:55 Josh 23:4-5; Pss 44:1-2; 105:10-11
78:58 Lev 26:1; Deut 32:16, 21
78:59 Lev 26:30; Deut 32:19
78:60 1 Sam 4:11
78:61 1 Sam 4:17
78:62 Judg 20:21; 1 Sam 4:10
78:63 Num 11:1; Jer 7:34; 16:9
78:64 1 Sam 22:18
78:65 Isa 42:13

78:51 Hebrew *in the tents of Ham.*

78:52-55 The contrast with God's treatment of Egypt could not be more stark. Israel enjoyed God's blessing to a remarkable degree. He sheltered the nation and provided for Israel in the wilderness until they finally came to the Promised Land. Once there, He delivered the people of Canaan into the Israelites' hands and divided the land among them as their inheritance (Joshua 13–19).

78:56-64 Israel persisted in its recurring rebellion. Throughout the period of the judges, the people's worship of false gods brought God's judgment through surrounding nations. Israel cried out for deliverance and, in His mercy, the Lord complied, only to see Israel abandon Him once more. The capture of the Ark by the Philistines (78:61) is recorded in 1 Samuel 4–5.

78:66 1 Sam 5:6
66 He routed His enemies
and sent them to eternal shame.
67 But He rejected Joseph's descendants;
He did not choose the tribe of Ephraim.

78:68 Ps 87:1-2
68 He chose instead the tribe of Judah,
and Mount Zion, which He loved.

78:69 1 Kgs 6:1-38
69 There He built His sanctuary as high as the heavens,
as solid and enduring as the earth.

78:70 1 Sam 16:10-12
70 He chose His servant David,
calling him from the sheep pens.

78:71 2 Sam 5:2; 7:8 1 Chr 11:2
71 He took David from tending the ewes and lambs
and made him the shepherd of Jacob's descendants—
God's own people, Israel.

78:72 1 Kgs 9:4
72 He cared for them with a true heart
and led them with skillful hands.

PSALM 79

A psalm of Asaph.

79:1 Ps 74:2-7 Jer 26:18 Lam 1:10
1 O God, pagan nations have conquered Your land,
Your special possession.
They have defiled Your holy Temple
and made Jerusalem a heap of ruins.

79:2 Deut 28:26 Jer 7:33; 16:4
2 They have left the bodies of Your servants
as food for the birds of heaven.
The flesh of Your godly ones
has become food for the wild animals.

79:3 Jer 14:16
3 Blood has flowed like water all around Jerusalem;
no one is left to bury the dead.

79:4 Ps 44:13
4 We are mocked by our neighbors,
an object of scorn and derision to those around us.

79:5 Ps 74:1, 9-10 Zeph 3:8
5 O LORD, how long will You be angry with us? Forever?
How long will Your jealousy burn like fire?

79:6 Jer 10:25 2 Thes 1:8
6 Pour out Your wrath on the nations that refuse to acknowledge You—
on kingdoms that do not call upon Your name.

79:7 Ps 53:4
7 For they have devoured Your people Israel,*
making the land a desolate wilderness.

79:8 Pss 106:6; 142:6 Isa 26:5; 64:9
8 Do not hold us guilty for the sins of our ancestors!
Let Your compassion quickly meet our needs,
for we are on the brink of despair.

79:7 Hebrew *devoured Jacob.* See note on 44:4.

78:70-72 God established David and his family as the rulers of His people forever (2 Samuel 7). The psalmist plays on David's past as a shepherd and a musician to describe his reign over Israel.

79:1 The psalmist describes the fall of Jerusalem to the Babylonian armies in 586 BC. Nebuchadnezzar destroyed the city and the Temple while taking a large portion of the population captive. The psalm reflects the sorrow of one left behind amid the ruins.

79:2-3 In the ancient world, it was considered a great disgrace when a body was left to decay and become food for wild animals.

79:5 The psalmist rightly recognizes the destruction of Jerusalem as an act of God's judgment. God's covenant with His people threatened exile as the final punishment for continued disobedience (Deuteronomy 28:63-65). Despite repeated warnings from God's prophets, the people persisted in their unfaithfulness and received God's just punishment (2 Chronicles 36:14-21).

9 Help us, O God of our salvation!
Help us for the glory of Your name.
Save us and forgive our sins
for the honor of Your name.
10 Why should pagan nations be allowed to scoff,
asking, "Where is their God?"
Show us Your vengeance against the nations,
for they have spilled the blood of Your servants.
11 Listen to the moaning of the prisoners.
Demonstrate Your great power by saving those condemned
to die.

12 O Lord, pay back our neighbors seven times
for the scorn they have hurled at You.
13 Then we Your people, the sheep of Your pasture,
will thank You forever and ever,
praising Your greatness from generation to generation.

79:9 2 Chr 14:11; Jer 14:7
79:10 Ps 115:2
79:12 Gen 4:15; Ps 74:10, 18, 22
79:13 Pss 74:1; 95:7; 100:3; Isa 43:21

PSALM 80

For the choir director: A psalm of Asaph, to be sung to the tune "Lilies of the Covenant."

1 Please listen, O Shepherd of Israel,
You who lead Joseph's descendants like a flock.
O God, enthroned above the cherubim,
display Your radiant glory
2 to Ephraim, Benjamin, and Manasseh.
Show us Your mighty power.
Come to rescue us!

3 Turn us again to Yourself, O God.
Make Your face shine down upon us.
Only then will we be saved.
4 O LORD God of Heaven's Armies,
how long will You be angry with our prayers?
5 You have fed us with sorrow
and made us drink tears by the bucketful.

80:1 Exod 25:22; Pss 23:1; 77:20
80:2 Ps 35:23
80:3 Num 6:24-26; Pss 31:16; 60:1; Lam 5:21
80:4 Pss 79:5; 84:8
80:5 Pss 42:3; 102:9

▸ **GOD**

79:9 For the sake of God's name. Why does the psalmist plead with God to help His people for the sake of His name? One of God's names is "Savior of the world" (John 4:42). This name was realized through the life and death of His Son, Jesus Christ. Because of Jesus, we can have our sins forgiven. How amazing that our salvation secures the honor of God's name! If He cannot save, His name is besmirched. Therefore, we can be sure that He will save. Praise Him for His name, God Most High. (***See God****> God's Names> God> Deliverer/Savior,* TopicGuide page A18.)

79:12 The number seven suggests completeness in Scripture. The psalmist is asking for thorough judgment.

▸ **GOD**

79:13 Thank Him forever. When we think of what God has done for us, we can never thank Him enough. As we live and walk in His grace, we see more and more of what He has done for us. This gives us the privilege of thanking Him continually. We will have all of eternity to give Him His due. Psalm 100:3 urges us to "acknowledge that the LORD is God!" What would it be like to live a life based on thankfulness to God for what He has done for you? (***See God****> God's Attributes> Good> God deserves thanks for His goodness,* TopicGuide page A16.)

80:1 The image of God as a Shepherd and His people as a flock occurs frequently throughout Scripture (Psalm 23:1-4; Ezekiel 34:11-16; John 10:1-18). The metaphor conveys a sense of God's tender care and guidance. Two golden cherubim with outstretched wings topped the Ark of the Covenant (Exodus 25:20). Scripture envisions God enthroned above these two angelic representations, thus mirroring the heavenly throne, which is surrounded by seraphim (Isaiah 6).

80:4 The psalms of lament often ask, "How long?" The question admits the justice of the punishment being experienced, yet pleads for its termination. It longs for the end of God's discipline and the renewal of His favor and blessing.

80:6 Pss 44:13; 79:4
6 You have made us the scorn* of neighboring nations.
Our enemies treat us as a joke.

7 Turn us again to Yourself, O God of Heaven's Armies.
Make Your face shine down upon us.
Only then will we be saved.

80:8 2 Chr 20:7; Ps 44:2; Isa 5:2, 7; Jer 2:21; 11:17; Ezek 17:6, 23; Amos 9:15
8 You brought us from Egypt like a grapevine;
You drove away the pagan nations and transplanted
us into Your land.

80:9 Exod 23:28; Isa 5:2; Hos 14:5
9 You cleared the ground for us,
and we took root and filled the land.
10 Our shade covered the mountains;
our branches covered the mighty cedars.

80:11 Ps 72:8
11 We spread our branches west to the Mediterranean Sea;
our shoots spread east to the Euphrates River.*

80:12 Ps 89:40; Isa 5:5
12 But now, why have You broken down our walls
so that all who pass by may steal our fruit?

80:13 Jer 5:6
13 The wild boar from the forest devours it,
and the wild animals feed on it.

14 Come back, we beg You, O God of Heaven's Armies.
Look down from heaven and see our plight.
Take care of this grapevine
15 that You Yourself have planted,
this son You have raised for Yourself.

80:16 2 Chr 36:19; Ps 39:11; Jer 52:13
16 For we are chopped up and burned by our enemies.
May they perish at the sight of Your frown.

80:17 Ps 89:21
17 Strengthen the man You love,
the son of Your choice.

80:18 Ps 71:20; Isa 50:5
18 Then we will never abandon You again.
Revive us so we can call on Your name once more.

19 Turn us again to Yourself, O LORD God
of Heaven's Armies.
Make Your face shine down upon us.
Only then will we be saved.

80:6 As in Syriac version; Hebrew reads *the strife.* 80:11 Hebrew *west to the sea, . . . east to the river.*

80:8-11 The psalmist portrays God as a vinedresser who takes the vine (Israel) from the ground of Egypt and replants it in the Promised Land. He then nurtures the vine until it spreads throughout the land. The historical events described here are recorded in Exodus through Joshua. The vine and vinedresser imagery also occurs in Isaiah 5:1-7; Ezekiel 15:1-8; Hosea 10:1; and John 15:1-6.

▶GOD

80:14 We are God's vine. In both the Old Testament and the New Testament, God refers to His people as a vine. In the Old Testament, the nation of Israel is called the vine. In the New Testament, the worldwide church is called the branches. In a vineyard, the vinedresser cares for the grape vines by watering, fertilizing, and pruning. A neglected vine does not bear fruit, but a well-cared-for vine produces much fruit. In John 15:1-2, Jesus explains, "I am the true grapevine, and My Father is the gardener. He cuts off every branch of Mine that doesn't produce fruit, and He prunes the branches that do bear fruit so they will produce even more." The Father will care for us like a gardener tends his vines. He pays attention to everything that happens to us, and He is involved in our lives. Allow that fact to give you great comfort as you walk through your daily life—the Father is busy caring for you, making sure you grow into a fruitful vine. (See John 15:1-2; also ***see God*> *God's Names*> *Father*> *Gardener (Vinedresser),* TopicGuide page A18.)

80:14-18 In calling on God in His mercy to restore Israel, the psalmist blends the language of adoption with that of the vine. Both images communicate the intimate nature of God's relationship with His people and recur in the New Testament to describe God's relationship to the church (John 1:12; 15:1-6).

PSALM 81

*For the choir director: A psalm of Asaph, to be accompanied by a stringed instrument.**

1 Sing praises to God, our strength.
Sing to the God of Jacob.
2 Sing! Beat the tambourine.
Play the sweet lyre and the harp.
3 Blow the ram's horn at new moon,
and again at full moon to call a festival!
4 For this is required by the decrees of Israel;
it is a regulation of the God of Jacob.
5 He made it a law for Israel*
when He attacked Egypt to set us free.

I heard an unknown voice say,
6 "Now I will take the load from your shoulders;
I will free your hands from their heavy tasks.
7 You cried to Me in trouble, and I saved you;
I answered out of the thundercloud
and tested your faith when there was
no water at Meribah. *Interlude*

8 "Listen to Me, O My people, while I give
you stern warnings.
O Israel, if you would only listen to Me!
9 You must never have a foreign god;
you must not bow down before a false god.
10 For it was I, the LORD your God,
who rescued you from the land of Egypt.
Open your mouth wide, and I will fill it
with good things.

11 "But no, My people wouldn't listen.
Israel did not want Me around.
12 So I let them follow their own stubborn desires,
living according to their own ideas.
13 Oh, that My people would listen to Me!
Oh, that Israel would follow Me, walking
in My paths!
14 How quickly I would then subdue their enemies!
How soon My hands would be upon their foes!

81:1 Pss 46:1; 59:16; 66:1; 95:1-2
81:2 Pss 108:2; 144:9; 149:3
81:3 Lev 23:24 Num 10:10
81:5 Exod 11:4
81:6 Isa 9:4; 10:27
81:7 Exod 2:23; 17:5-7; 19:19 Pss 50:15; 95:8
81:8 Ps 50:7
81:9 Exod 20:3 Isa 43:12
81:10 Exod 20:2 Pss 78:25; 103:5
81:11 Exod 32:1
81:12 Acts 7:42 Rom 1:24, 26
81:13 Deut 5:29 Isa 48:18 Jer 7:23
81:14 Ps 47:3 Amos 1:8

81:TITLE Hebrew *according to the gittith.* 81:5 Hebrew *for Joseph.*

81:1-5 The setting of the psalm is one of Israel's great feasts, probably the Feast of Tabernacles (or Booths). The feast began with a trumpet blast on the fifteenth day of the seventh month during a full moon (Leviticus 23:33-43; Numbers 10:10). The festival commemorated the deliverance of Israel from Egypt and its subsequent wanderings in the wilderness. The psalms often call upon God's people to praise God accompanied by musical instruments (Psalms 98:5-6; 150:3).

▸ WORSHIP
81:7 God is supreme. In Exodus 17:1-7 we find the story of how God provided water for the Israelite people as they traveled through the Sin Desert. God instructed Moses to strike a rock with his staff. When he did, the rock gushed forth streams of water. First Corinthians 10:4 tells us that this rock symbolizes Jesus Christ. He is the spiritual water that quenches our spiritual thirst. With His strength and power, we can survive in the desertlike experiences of life. God has provided Jesus Christ as your source of spiritual nourishment. By faith, drink of Him. (***See Worship****> OT> God's Supremacy> Required personal and ritual cleanliness,* TopicGuide page A27.)

81:9-10 The language is patterned after the prologue to the Ten Commandments and the first two commands (Exodus 20:2-4). In both instances, obedience is encouraged by the past experience of deliverance. Grateful obedience should naturally follow God's gracious salvation.

81:15 [15] Those who hate the LORD would cringe before Him;
they would be doomed forever.
81:16 Deut 32:13-14 [16] But I would feed you with the finest wheat.
I would satisfy you with wild honey
from the rock."

PSALM 82

A psalm of Asaph.

82:1 Ps 58:11 Isa 3:13 [1] God presides over heaven's court;
He pronounces judgment on the heavenly beings:
82:2 Deut 1:17 Ps 58:1-2 Prov 18:5 [2] "How long will you hand down unjust decisions
by favoring the wicked? *Interlude*
[3] "Give justice to the poor and the orphan;
82:3 Deut 24:17 uphold the rights of the oppressed and the destitute.
[4] Rescue the poor and helpless;
82:4 Job 29:12 deliver them from the grasp of evil people.
[5] But these oppressors know nothing;
they are so ignorant!
They wander about in darkness,
while the whole world is shaken to the core.
82:6 *John 10:34 [6] I say, 'You are gods;
you are all children of the Most High.
82:7 Pss 49:12; 83:11 [7] But you will die like mere mortals
and fall like every other ruler.'"

82:8 Pss 2:8; 12:5 Rev 11:15 [8] Rise up, O God, and judge the earth,
for all the nations belong to You.

PSALM 83

A song. A psalm of Asaph.

83:1 Pss 28:1; 109:1 [1] O God, do not be silent!
Do not be deaf.
Do not be quiet, O God.

82:1-2 The picture here is primarily of an assembly of angelic beings before the throne of God. The same kind of divine council is portrayed in the story of Job (Job 1–2) and in Micaiah's vision of the heavenly court (1 Kings 22:19-23; see also Deuteronomy 32:8-9). These beings function in some sense as judges who are themselves judged by God for failing to administer justice. But because Scripture presupposes an interaction between the heavenly and earthly realms, the judgment issued against these angelic beings applies equally to corrupt human judges (compare Daniel 8:10-11; Revelation 1:20).

▸ CHURCH

82:3 Look out for the rights of others. Sometimes we let our politicians handle the issue of other people's rights. Yet God has given us believers the responsibility of seeing that the helpless are defended. The poor and destitute cannot defend themselves; they need an advocate. We see that everywhere. For example, during a famine, heartless merchants sell food at exorbitant prices. After a natural disaster, greedy people take advantage of the needs of the victims for their own benefit. In the midst of a medical emergency, the rich receive life-saving treatment but the poor are left to die. But we are to act differently. Our goal is to see to the rights of those who cannot help themselves. Demonstrate God's compassion by helping to protect the orphans, the poor, and the oppressed in your area. (***See Church****> Role> Preach> Topics> Godly Lives> Care for their poor, widows, and orphans,* TopicGuide page A50.)

82:3-4 The requirements for judges are reflections of God's character. God frequently is portrayed as the only hope of the weak and oppressed. The law of God embodies this care through legislation designed to shelter helpless members of society, such as widows and orphans.

82:6-7 These verses further reflect the interplay between the visible and invisible, the heavenly and the earthly (see note at 82:1-2). Both officers are condemned to lose their dignity for their failure to execute their offices justly.

[2] Don't You hear the uproar of Your enemies?
Don't You see that Your arrogant enemies are rising up?
[3] They devise crafty schemes against Your people;
they conspire against Your precious ones.
[4] "Come," they say, "let us wipe out Israel as a nation.
We will destroy the very memory of its existence."
[5] Yes, this was their unanimous decision.
They signed a treaty as allies against You—
[6] these Edomites and Ishmaelites;
Moabites and Hagrites;
[7] Gebalites, Ammonites, and Amalekites;
and people from Philistia and Tyre.
[8] Assyria has joined them, too,
and is allied with the descendants of Lot. *Interlude*

[9] Do to them as You did to the Midianites
and as You did to Sisera and Jabin at the Kishon River.
[10] They were destroyed at Endor,
and their decaying corpses fertilized the soil.
[11] Let their mighty nobles die as Oreb and Zeeb did.
Let all their princes die like Zebah and Zalmunna,
[12] for they said, "Let us seize for our own use
these pasturelands of God!"
[13] O my God, scatter them like tumbleweed,
like chaff before the wind!
[14] As a fire burns a forest
and as a flame sets mountains ablaze,
[15] chase them with Your fierce storm;
terrify them with Your tempest.
[16] Utterly disgrace them
until they submit to Your name, O LORD.
[17] Let them be ashamed and terrified forever.
Let them die in disgrace.
[18] Then they will learn that You alone are called the LORD,
that You alone are the Most High,
supreme over all the earth.

83:2 Pss 2:1; 81:15 Isa 17:12
83:3 Ps 31:20
83:4 Esth 3:5-6
83:5 Ps 2:2
83:6 Gen 25:12-16 2 Chr 20:1, 10 Ps 137:7
83:7 1 Sam 4:1; 15:2 2 Chr 20:10 Ezek 27:2-3, 9
83:9 Judg 4:22-23
83:11 Judg 7:25; 8:21
83:12 2 Chr 20:11
83:14 Deut 32:22 Isa 9:18
83:15 Job 9:17 Ps 58:9
83:16 Ps 109:29
83:18 Ps 59:13 Isa 45:21

83:6-8 The nations mentioned here surrounded Israel geographically and were all enemies of Israel at one point or another, although there is no record of a combined action on their part (see Genesis 37:25-28; Judges 3:13; 1 Samuel 14:47; 1 Chronicles 5:10; Isaiah 15–17; 34:5-6). The "descendants of Lot" are traditionally the Moabites and Ammonites, but the term may refer generally to the various nations of the region (Genesis 19:36-38).

83:9-12 Israel defeated each of the enemies listed during the era of the judges (Judges 4–8).

83:13-18 In these verses, the psalmist draws together several cultural expressions to call on God to defeat the enemies of Israel. The psalmist is most concerned with the honor of God. He longs for the day when all nations will recognize the sovereignty that belongs to God alone. Lightweight chaff is separated from edible grains by the wind blowing through it. For similar imagery, see Deuteronomy 4:11; Isaiah 9:18-19; 40:24; Jeremiah 13:24; and Hosea 13:3. For the motif of the elements of nature as weapons of the divine Warrior, see Joshua 10:11; Isaiah 29:6; Hosea 8:7; Amos 1:14; and Nahum 1:3.

83:16 The psalmist hopes God's enemies will submit to Him as a result of their defeat (compare Jeremiah 46:12; Ezekiel 7:18; Obadiah 1:10; and Micah 7:10).

▸ WORSHIP
83:18 God's enemies acknowledge Him. The end of all life will be the same—people will acknowledge that God is the Lord. Even God's enemies will bow before Him and give Him honor (Philippians 2:10-11). Therefore, we can rejoice that we know Him and honor Him today. Our joy is in giving Him the glory that He deserves. We can also praise God that He is the Most High and that no one on earth can do anything to thwart His complete sovereignty. God is supreme. Praise Him for His utmost power and glory. (***See Worship**> OT> God's Supremacy> God alone was to be worshiped—no one else,* TopicGuide page A26.)

PSALM 84

*For the choir director: A psalm of the descendants of Korah, to be accompanied by a stringed instrument.**

84:1 Ps 27:4
[1] How lovely is Your dwelling place,
O LORD of Heaven's Armies.

84:2 Pss 42:1-2; 63:1
[2] I long, yes, I faint with longing
to enter the courts of the LORD.
With my whole being, body and soul,
I will shout joyfully to the living God.

84:3 Ps 43:4
[3] Even the sparrow finds a home,
and the swallow builds her nest and raises her young
at a place near your altar,
O LORD of Heaven's Armies, my King and my God!

84:4 Ps 65:4
[4] What joy for those who can live in Your house,
always singing Your praises. *Interlude*

84:5 Ps 81:1
[5] What joy for those whose strength comes from the LORD,
who have set their minds on a pilgrimage to Jerusalem.

84:6 Ps 107:35
[6] When they walk through the Valley of Weeping,*
it will become a place of refreshing springs.
The autumn rains will clothe it with blessings.

84:7 Deut 16:16 Isa 40:31
[7] They will continue to grow stronger,
and each of them will appear before God in Jerusalem.*

84:TITLE Hebrew *according to the gittith.* **84:6** Or *Valley of Poplars;* Hebrew reads *valley of Baca.* **84:7** Hebrew *Zion.*

84:1-2 The psalmist passionately articulates his desire to enter God's presence in the Temple. The Temple symbolized and embodied the presence of God on earth. The psalmist similarly expresses a unity of body and soul. The Temple was and our bodies are composed of spiritual and bodily elements that naturally interact.

84:3-4 The psalmist expresses his longing for the presence of God by calling attention to the birds that make nests in the Temple. These birds make their homes in proximity to God's presence, symbolizing the spiritual nearness the psalmist desires. Their songs fill the Temple like the songs of the worshipers who praise God with their voices.

▸ WORSHIP

84:5 Taking a pilgrimage. In Old Testament times, the Jewish people made pilgrimages to Jerusalem to worship at the Temple. They came weeping because their journey to God's holy seat caused them to repent of their sins. When they brought sacrifices of blood offerings, the Lord forgave them and their hearts were restored in their relationship to Him. We make a similar pilgrimage today—not by traveling to Jerusalem but by repenting of our sins. When we realize the holiness of God, we find ourselves lacking in purity. We ask God to forgive us and to help us grow to be like Him. Make your prayers as sweet incense to God through your repentance. (***See Worship****> OT> Fasting and Prayer> Prayer> Psalms> Songs for pilgrimage,* TopicGuide page A26.)

BECAUSE GOD IS A PERSONAL SPIRIT

I will seek intimate fellowship with Him.

I faint with longing to enter the courts of the LORD.

PSALM 84:2

8 O LORD God of Heaven's Armies, hear my prayer.
Listen, O God of Jacob. *Interlude*
9 O God, look with favor upon the king, our shield!
Show favor to the one You have anointed.

10 A single day in Your courts
is better than a thousand anywhere else!
I would rather be a gatekeeper in the house of my God
than live the good life in the homes of the wicked.
11 For the LORD God is our sun and our shield.
He gives us grace and glory.
The LORD will withhold no good thing
from those who do what is right.
12 O LORD of Heaven's Armies,
what joy for those who trust in You.

84:9 Gen 15:1; 2 Sam 19:21; Ps 115:9-11
84:10 1 Chr 23:5; Ps 27:4
84:11 Ps 2:12
84:12 Ps 2:12

PSALM 85

For the choir director: A psalm of the descendants of Korah.

1 LORD, You poured out blessings on Your land!
You restored the fortunes of Israel.*
2 You forgave the guilt of Your people—
yes, You covered all their sins. *Interlude*
3 You held back Your fury.
You kept back Your blazing anger.

4 Now restore us again, O God of our salvation.
Put aside Your anger against us once more.
5 Will You be angry with us always?
Will You prolong Your wrath to all generations?
6 Won't You revive us again,
so Your people can rejoice in You?

85:1 Jer 30:18; Joel 3:1
85:2 Num 14:19; Ps 32:1; Jer 31:34
85:3 Exod 32:12; Deut 13:17; Ps 78:38
85:4 Ps 80:3, 7
85:5 Pss 74:1; 79:5; 80:4
85:6 Ps 149:2

85:1 Hebrew *of Jacob.* See note on 44:4.

84:9 The psalmist petitions the Lord on behalf of the king. The king played a central role in Israel's political and religious life. As the covenant leader of God's people, he enjoyed a unique relationship with God (Psalm 2:7) and embodied the rule of God on earth. Notice that the psalmist speaks of both the king and God (84:11) as his protector.

▸ HOLINESS
84:12 True happiness. How would you define true happiness? For many people, this means having wealth and health. They focus on what they can obtain and the fun they can have. But no one has achieved true happiness through these things. Making more money makes us want even more money. Having good health is only a temporary state of being; eventually all of us will age and our bodies will deteriorate. Possessions wear out and become useless. Fun only lasts for a moment, and then we must once again face our problems. But when we trust in God, He gives us joy and happiness that circumstances can't change. Depend on God for your true happiness. Nothing or no one else will do. (***See Holiness****> Submission> Trusting God> True happiness,* TopicGuide page A40.)

85:1-3 The remembrance of God's past salvation and blessing is the foundation for the psalmist's call for help in the present. He attributes both spiritual and earthly blessing to God's goodness. Note that the psalmist declares that the land belongs to the Lord. While the land has been entrusted to Israel (see 85:12), God retains ultimate ownership.

▸ GOD
85:2 Our guilt is gone. In this verse, the psalmist says that all our sins are covered. What does that mean? Micah 7:19 says, "You will trample our sins under Your feet and throw them into the depths of the ocean!" In that time, divers could only go down 100 feet or so. If God throws our sin into the deepest part of the ocean, in that context, they are forever gone. That's how complete God's forgiveness is. This is our wonderful assurance of freedom in Christ! Thank Him for His complete forgiveness of your sin. (***See God****> God's Attributes> Forgiving> God forgives those who repent,* TopicGuide page A16.)

85:4-7 The psalmist pleads with God to remove His anger and renew His blessing. He calls on God to do what God had done in the past (85:3). Speaking for a community that has long suffered under God's anger, he throws himself on God's compassion. He calls on God to express His "unfailing love," which is a love based on God's covenantal relationship with Israel.

7 Show us Your unfailing love, O LORD,
and grant us Your salvation.

85:8 Pss 29:11; 78:57
8 I listen carefully to what God the LORD is saying,
for He speaks peace to His faithful people.
But let them not return to their foolish ways.
85:9 Ps 84:11 Isa 46:13 John 1:14
9 Surely His salvation is near to those who fear Him,
so our land will be filled with His glory.

85:10 Ps 72:3 Prov 3:3 Isa 32:17
10 Unfailing love and truth have met together.
Righteousness and peace have kissed!
11 Truth springs up from the earth,
85:11 Isa 45:8
and righteousness smiles down from heaven.
12 Yes, the LORD pours down His blessings.
85:12 Ps 84:11 Jas 1:17
Our land will yield its bountiful harvest.
13 Righteousness goes as a herald before Him,
preparing the way for His steps.

PSALM 86

A prayer of David.

86:1 Pss 17:6; 40:17
1 Bend down, O LORD, and hear my prayer;
answer me, for I need Your help.
86:2 Pss 4:3; 25:20
2 Protect me, for I am devoted to You.
Save me, for I serve You and trust You.
You are my God.
3 Be merciful to me, O Lord,
for I am calling on You constantly.
4 Give me happiness, O Lord,
for I give myself to You.

86:5 Pss 103:8; 130:4
5 O Lord, You are so good, so ready to forgive,
so full of unfailing love for all who ask for Your help.
86:6 Ps 55:1
6 Listen closely to my prayer, O LORD;
hear my urgent cry.
86:7 Ps 50:14-15
7 I will call to You whenever I'm in trouble,
and You will answer me.
86:8 Exod 15:11 Deut 3:24
8 No pagan god is like You, O Lord.
None can do what You do!

▸ ADOPTION
85:8 Listening carefully to God. Does this verse express the attitude of your heart? Do you listen to God's words as you live your daily life? Do you listen to Him carefully or are you only hearing Him halfheartedly? We listen to God through reading His Word and applying what we learn, and by praying to Him often. When we listen to Him, we avoid the foolish acts that we have committed in the past. Instead, we live by His wisdom. Are your ears open to Him? (***See Adoption****> With Christ> Supernatural> Quick to listen,* TopicGuide page A37.)

85:8 The word *peace* functioned as a technical term in ancient treaties, such as God's covenant with Israel. In this context, it means He is favorably disposed to His people.

86:1-4 David's opening petition calls on God to protect and bless him. These petitions are bound together with reasons God ought to grant the petitions, reasons that convey David's dependence on and devotion to God.

▸ GOD
86:5 Ready to forgive. As humans, we often are slow to forgive. When someone hurts us, we usually hold a grudge and keep anger in our hearts toward that person. But God is always ready to forgive. His mercy is always available. Lamentations 3:23 describes God's forgiveness: "Great is His faithfulness; His mercies begin fresh each day." No matter what we have done, we can find room at the mercy seat. (***See God****> God's Attributes> Forgiving> God is ready to forgive,* TopicGuide page A16.)

86:5-7 David continues to plead with God for salvation, grounding his petitions in God's character.

86:8-10 David confesses God's uniqueness. The gods of the other nations are silent while the God of Israel is actively engaged in the nation's history. Their silence, of course, stems from their nonexistence.

9 All the nations You made
will come and bow before You, Lord;
they will praise Your holy name.
10 For You are great and perform wonderful deeds.
You alone are God.

11 Teach me Your ways, O LORD,
that I may live according to Your truth!
Grant me purity of heart,
so that I may honor You.
12 With all my heart I will praise You, O Lord my God.
I will give glory to Your name forever,
13 for Your love for me is very great.
You have rescued me from the depths of death.*

14 O God, insolent people rise up against me;
a violent gang is trying to kill me.
You mean nothing to them.
15 But You, O Lord,
are a God of compassion and mercy,
slow to get angry
and filled with unfailing love and faithfulness.
16 Look down and have mercy on me.
Give Your strength to Your servant;
save me, the son of Your servant.
17 Send me a sign of Your favor.
Then those who hate me will be put to shame,
for You, O LORD, help and comfort me.

86:9 Isa 66:23; Rev 15:3-4
86:10 Deut 32:39; Isa 44:6, 8; Mark 12:29; 1 Cor 8:4
86:11 Ps 25:5; Jer 32:39
86:12 Ps 111:1
86:13 Ps 30:3
86:14 Ps 54:3
86:16 Ps 68:35
86:17 Pss 112:10; 118:13; 119:122

PSALM 87

A song. A psalm of the descendants of Korah.

1 On the holy mountain
stands the city founded by the LORD.
2 He loves the city of Jerusalem
more than any other city in Israel.*

87:1 Ps 78:68-69; Isa 28:16
87:2 Ps 78:67-68

86:13 Hebrew *of Sheol.* 87:2 Hebrew *He loves the gates of Zion more than all the dwellings of Jacob.* See note on 44:4.

▶ **GOD**

86:15 Slow to anger. What does this verse mean when it says that God is slow to anger? Well, we aren't dead yet—that's at least part of it. As depraved, sinful humans, we do not deserve any mercy from God. If justice were served, we would all be condemned to physical and spiritual death immediately. We would have no hope because our actions are sinful. Yet God doesn't destroy us as soon as we sin. He is patient, waiting for us to come to repentance. In fact, Jesus says that God waits patiently to see the lost found and brought into the kingdom of God (Luke 15:1-10). Let's thank Him for His patient mercy. (***See God****> God's Attributes> Patient> Believers can appeal to their patient God,* TopicGuide page A17; also ***see God****> God's Attributes> Merciful> God is merciful,* TopicGuide page A17.)

▶ **BIBLE**

86:15 An everlasting love. When this verse says that God's love is unfailing, we know that He loves us forever because of His everlasting nature. Have you ever thought about how long everlasting is? We are so conditioned to think in terms of minutes, days, and years that we rarely expand our minds to consider God's everlasting nature. God has always existed and will always exist. His reign is like the turn of a ring. A ring has no end; it just goes on and on. We cannot even describe its end because it has no end. Like the turn of a ring, God's love for us will never end. (***See Bible****> Unity> Salvation> God's everlasting love,* TopicGuide page A11.)

87:1-2 The holy mountain is Mount Zion, the hill just north of Jerusalem on which the Temple was located. God chose Jerusalem as the place where His presence would reside among His people. In this sense, Jerusalem and Mount Zion were "holy," or "set apart" (compare Isaiah 14:32).

87:3 Pss 46:4; 48:8 Isa 60:1 3 O city of God,
what glorious things are said of you! *Interlude*

87:4 Pss 45:12; 68:31 Isa 19:23-25 4 I will count Egypt* and Babylon among those who know Me—
also Philistia and Tyre, and even distant Ethiopia.*
They have all become citizens of Jerusalem!

87:5 Ps 48:8 5 Regarding Jerusalem* it will be said,
"Everyone enjoys the rights of citizenship there."
And the Most High will personally bless this city.

87:6 Isa 4:2-4 6 When the LORD registers the nations, He will say,
"They have all become citizens of Jerusalem." *Interlude*

87:7 Ps 36:9 7 The people will play flutes* and sing,
"The source of my life springs from Jerusalem!"

PSALM 88

For the choir director: A psalm of the descendants of Korah. A song to be sung to the tune "The Suffering of Affliction." A psalm of Heman the Ezrahite.*

88:1 Ps 22:2 Luke 18:7 1 O LORD, God of my salvation,
I cry out to You by day.
I come to You at night.

88:2 Pss 18:6; 86:1 2 Now hear my prayer;
listen to my cry.

88:3 Pss 107:18; 116:3 3 For my life is full of troubles,
and death* draws near.

88:4 Ps 28:1 4 I am as good as dead,
like a strong man with no strength left.

88:5 Ps 31:12 Isa 53:8 5 They have left me among the dead,
and I lie like a corpse in a grave.
I am forgotten,
cut off from Your care.

87:4a Hebrew *Rahab,* the name of a mythical sea monster that represents chaos in ancient literature. The name is used here as a poetic name for Egypt. **87:4b** Hebrew *Cush.* **87:5** Hebrew *Zion.* **87:7** Or *will dance.* **88:TITLE** Hebrew *maskil.* This may be a literary or musical term. **88:3** Hebrew *Sheol.*

87:4-6 Citizenship in Jerusalem is a metaphor for religious kinship with Israel and the Lord. The psalmist anticipates the day when all nations will acknowledge the Lord as their God. Egypt and Babylon were two major powers of the ancient world to the east and to the west of Israel. Philistia and Tyre lay to the east of Israel along the Mediterranean coast. Ethiopia, literally "Cush," was located in North Africa and was associated with Egypt (Nahum 3:8). They are not natural-born citizens, but are granted citizenship by an act of God—as such, disobedience and faithlessness could revoke the citizenship (compare Exodus 32:32; Ezekiel 13:9). The work of Christ secures the conversion of the Gentiles (Ephesians 2:11-18). Pentecost inaugurates the fulfillment of the hope of the conversion of the nations (Acts 2; compare Galatians 4:26).

▸ WORSHIP

87:7 Rejoicing together. In the Old Testament, the Israelites gathered to celebrate spiritual festivals and holy days. During these celebrations, they sang and danced to the Lord (see Exodus 15:20-21; 2 Samuel 6:13-14). They expressed the love and joy they felt during their worship. How do you express your joy in His salvation? Music and dance are wonderful ways to do just that. Integrate holy singing and dancing into your worship of God. (***See Worship****> OT> Posture> Dancing> Singers and dancers celebrate the glory of Zion,* TopicGuide page A28.)

88:1-2 The psalmist cries out in anguish to his Savior. This is the only touch of hope offered by the psalm. The psalmist acknowledges that the One to whom he prays is a God who saves. It is a mark of the faithful that even in their deepest dejection they know on whom to cast themselves.

▸ ADOPTION

88:3 Death draws near. Death is a fact each of us must face. Al experienced this when the doctor told him he had only four months to live. At eighty-four years old, he knew that death would not be far away. But hearing the doctor's pronouncement still had an impact. Suddenly, death was no longer *in* the future—it *was* the future. This was the time when Al's faith meant so much to him; he knew the Lord would walk with him through this valley But do you have this assurance? Just as David cried out to God during his troubles, you can do the same. He promises that He will be with you during your last struggle in life (Romans 8:35-37). (***See Adoption****> Without Christ> Separated from God> Facing physical death,* TopicGuide page A36.)

6 You have thrown me into the lowest pit,
into the darkest depths.
7 Your anger weighs me down;
with wave after wave You have engulfed me. *Interlude*

8 You have driven my friends away
by making me repulsive to them.
I am in a trap with no way of escape.
9 My eyes are blinded by my tears.
Each day I beg for Your help, O LORD;
I lift my hands to You for mercy.
10 Are Your wonderful deeds of any use to the dead?
Do the dead rise up and praise You? *Interlude*

11 Can those in the grave declare Your unfailing love?
Can they proclaim Your faithfulness in the place of destruction?*
12 Can the darkness speak of Your wonderful deeds?
Can anyone in the land of forgetfulness talk about Your righteousness?
13 O LORD, I cry out to You.
I will keep on pleading day by day.
14 O LORD, why do You reject me?
Why do You turn Your face from me?

15 I have been sick and close to death since my youth.
I stand helpless and desperate before Your terrors.
16 Your fierce anger has overwhelmed me.
Your terrors have paralyzed me.
17 They swirl around me like floodwaters all day long.
They have engulfed me completely.
18 You have taken away my companions and loved ones.
Darkness is my closest friend.

PSALM 89

A psalm of Ethan the Ezrahite.*

1 I will sing of the LORD's unfailing love forever!
Young and old will hear of Your faithfulness.
2 Your unfailing love will last forever.
Your faithfulness is as enduring as the heavens.
3 The LORD said, "I have made a covenant with David, My chosen servant.
I have sworn this oath to him:

88:6 Pss 32:4; 69:15; 143:3; Lam 3:55
88:7 Ps 42:7
88:8 Job 19:19; 30:10; Ps 31:11
88:9 Job 11:13; Pss 6:7; 22:2
88:10 Ps 6:5
88:12 Job 10:20-21
88:13 Pss 5:3; 119:147
88:14 Job 13:24; Ps 13:1
88:15 Job 6:4
88:17 Ps 22:12, 16
88:18 Job 19:13; Pss 31:11; 38:11
89:1 Pss 40:10; 59:16
89:2 Ps 36:5
89:3 2 Sam 7:16; Ps 132:11; Isa 9:7; Luke 1:31-33

88:11 Hebrew *in Abaddon?* 89:TITLE Hebrew *maskil.* This may be a literary or musical term.

88:6-8 In his distress, the psalmist accuses God of bringing about his suffering. In some ultimate sense, this is true. But we do not know if the psalmist's suffering was brought about by sin or if it was like that of Job, who had done no wrong. The psalmist, however, rightly recognizes God's sovereignty even over his suffering. It is better to cry out before God in frustration than to dismiss God or think Him irrelevant.

88:10-12 At this point in the history of God's revelation, God's people had a limited knowledge of what transpired after death. This limitation caused God's people to value life as a time when they knew with certainty that they could praise God and experience His blessing.

88:15-18 The psalm closes with a painful description of suffering that matches the realities of this life. Sometimes situations do not end pleasantly. This writer has suffered for an extended time and his suffering has consumed him. His life has sunk into primordial chaos, as symbolized by the floodwaters and darkness (Genesis 1:1-2).

89:1-4 The main themes of the psalm are set forth in these opening verses. The psalmist praises God's faithfulness to His people, particularly to David's family. God entered into a covenant with David and his descendants, promising to sustain the rule of David's sons over the people of Israel (1 Samuel 7).

89:4 2 Sam 7:16 Isa 9:7 Luke 1:33

4 'I will establish your descendants as kings forever;
they will sit on your throne from now until eternity.'" *Interlude*
5 All heaven will praise Your great wonders, LORD;
myriads of angels will praise You for Your faithfulness.

89:6 Pss 29:1; 96:4

6 For who in all of heaven can compare with the LORD?
What mightiest angel is anything like the LORD?

89:7 Pss 47:2; 96:4

7 The highest angelic powers stand in awe of God.
He is far more awesome than all who surround His throne.

89:8 Pss 35:10; 71:19

8 O LORD God of Heaven's Armies!
Where is there anyone as mighty as You, O LORD?
You are entirely faithful.

89:9 Pss 65:7; 107:29

9 You rule the oceans.
You subdue their storm-tossed waves.

89:10 Ps 18:14

10 You crushed the great sea monster.*
You scattered Your enemies with Your mighty arm.

89:11 Gen 1:1 1 Chr 29:11 Ps 24:1

11 The heavens are Yours, and the earth is Yours;
everything in the world is Yours—You created it all.
12 You created north and south.

89:12 Josh 12:1; 19:22

Mount Tabor and Mount Hermon praise Your name.
13 Powerful is Your arm!

89:13 Ps 118:16

Strong is Your hand!
Your right hand is lifted high in glorious strength.

89:14 Ps 97:2

14 Righteousness and justice are the foundation of Your throne.
Unfailing love and truth walk before You as attendants.

89:15 Num 10:10

15 Happy are those who hear the joyful call to worship,
for they will walk in the light of Your presence, LORD.
16 They rejoice all day long in Your wonderful reputation.
They exult in Your righteousness.

89:17 Pss 44:3; 75:10; 148:14

17 You are their glorious strength.
It pleases You to make us strong.

89:18 Ps 47:9

18 Yes, our protection comes from the LORD,
and He, the Holy One of Israel, has given us our king.

89:19 2 Sam 17:10 1 Kgs 11:34

19 Long ago You spoke in a vision to Your faithful people.
You said, "I have raised up a warrior.
I have selected him from the common people to be king.

89:20 1 Sam 16:13 *Acts 13:22

20 I have found My servant David.
I have anointed him with My holy oil.
21 I will steady him with My hand;
with My powerful arm I will make him strong.

89:22 2 Sam 7:10-11

22 His enemies will not defeat him,
nor will the wicked overpower him.

89:23 2 Sam 7:9

23 I will beat down his adversaries before him
and destroy those who hate him.

89:10 Hebrew *Rahab,* the name of a mythical sea monster that represents chaos in ancient literature.

89:9-13 The Canaanites believed the world arose from the struggle of the gods (notably Baal) to establish order out of the chaos symbolized by the sea and the sea monster Rahab (see textual note). By applying this language to the Lord, the psalmist affirms that God is the sole Creator of the world without assenting to the details of the Canaanite story (compare Genesis 1–2). God's sovereignty is grounded in His creation of all things. Mount Tabor and Mount Hermon are two impressive peaks in the north and northwest of Israel.

89:19-23 The psalmist alludes to both the anointing of David (1 Samuel 16:1-13) and the establishment of the Davidic covenant (2 Samuel 7). God chose David to be the king over His people and empowered him as a warrior (compare Psalm 2).

24 My faithfulness and unfailing love will be with him,
and by My authority he will grow in power.
25 I will extend his rule over the sea,
his dominion over the rivers.
26 And he will call out to Me, 'You are my Father,
my God, and the Rock of my salvation.'
27 I will make him My firstborn son,
the mightiest king on earth.
28 I will love him and be kind to him forever;
My covenant with him will never end.
29 I will preserve an heir for him;
his throne will be as endless as the
days of heaven.
30 But if his descendants forsake My instructions
and fail to obey My regulations,
31 if they do not obey My decrees
and fail to keep My commands,
32 then I will punish their sin with the rod,
and their disobedience with beating.
33 But I will never stop loving him
nor fail to keep My promise to him.
34 No, I will not break My covenant;
I will not take back a single word I said.
35 I have sworn an oath to David,
and in My holiness I cannot lie:
36 His dynasty will go on forever;
his kingdom will endure as the sun.
37 It will be as eternal as the moon,
My faithful witness in the sky!"
Interlude

38 But now You have rejected him and cast him off.
You are angry with Your anointed king.
39 You have renounced Your covenant with him;
You have thrown his crown in the dust.
40 You have broken down the walls protecting him
and ruined every fort defending him.
41 Everyone who comes along has robbed him,
and he has become a joke to his neighbors.

89:26 2 Sam 7:14; 1 Chr 22:10
89:27 Pss 2:7; 72:11; Rev 19:16
89:29 1 Kgs 2:4; Isa 9:7; Jer 33:17
89:30 2 Sam 7:14
89:33 2 Sam 7:15
89:34 Num 23:19; Jer 33:20-21
89:36 Ps 72:5
89:38 1 Chr 28:9
89:39 Ps 78:59; Lam 2:7; 5:16
89:40 Ps 80:12; Lam 2:2, 5

▸ GOD
89:26 Father means love. What kind of a name is *father*? It is a name that expresses love. If someone asks to be called "father," he wants to emphasize the close relationship between him and his child. Calling someone "father" shows that you have a special feeling for that person. You are connected to him by more than just friendship. Isn't it amazing that God wants us—even commands us—to call Him Father? Thank Him for extending to us the love of a holy father's heart. (***See God***> *God's Names*> *God*> *Father,* TopicGuide page A18.)

89:30-37 David and his sons would not be exempt from correction. The covenant included conditional elements. As a good father chastises his sons for their own good, so the Lord would punish David and his sons when they went astray in the hope of restoring them to obedience and blessing. But punishment would not overwhelm grace. David and his sons did fail, of course, and they experienced God's anger even to the point of exile. However, God's love to David triumphed in the life and reign of Jesus Christ. As the heir of David and Son of God, Jesus reigns now and forever.

89:38-48 The psalm now takes the form of a lament. The psalmist earlier alluded to the threat of punishment facing David and his sons if they rebelled against God (89:30-32). Now the nation faces such a time of chastisement. The king has rebelled and God's hand of displeasure is being felt through military defeat and humiliation. The promised blessings are reversed. The cry *How long?* is characteristic of lament psalms (for example, see Psalms 6:3; 13:1; 79:5; 82:2; 88:10). The psalmist calls on God to relent from His anger by invoking the frailty of human existence and God's own compassion.

89:42 Pss 13:2; 80:6
42 You have strengthened his enemies
and made them all rejoice.
89:43 Ps 44:10
43 You have made his sword useless
and refused to help him in battle.
89:44 Ezek 28:7
44 You have ended his splendor
and overturned his throne.
89:45 Ps 44:15-16
45 You have made him old before his time
and publicly disgraced him. *Interlude*

89:46 Pss 13:1; 79:5
46 O LORD, how long will this go on?
Will You hide Yourself forever?
How long will Your anger burn like fire?
89:47 Job 7:7; 14:1 Ps 39:5-6 Eccl 1:2; 2:11
47 Remember how short my life is,
how empty and futile this human existence!
48 No one can live forever; all will die.
89:48 Ps 22:29 Heb 11:5
No one can escape the power of the grave.* *Interlude*
49 Lord, where is Your unfailing love?
89:49 2 Sam 7:15
You promised it to David with a faithful pledge.
50 Consider, Lord, how Your servants are disgraced!
I carry in my heart the insults of so many people.
89:51 Ps 74:9-10, 18, 22
51 Your enemies have mocked me, O LORD;
they mock Your anointed king wherever he goes.

89:52 Pss 41:13; 106:48
52 Praise the LORD forever!
Amen and amen!

BOOK FOUR (PSALMS 90–106)

PSALM 90

A prayer of Moses, the man of God.

90:1 Deut 33:27 Ezek 11:16 Rev 21:3
1 Lord, through all the generations
You have been our home!
90:2 Gen 1:1 Ps 102:24-25, 27 Prov 8:22-26
2 Before the mountains were born,
before You gave birth to the earth and the world,
from beginning to end, You are God.
90:3 Job 34:14-15
3 You turn people back to dust, saying,
"Return to dust, you mortals!"

89:48 Hebrew *of Sheol.*

90:1-2 Moses opens with a hymn of praise celebrating God's eternal nature and His creation of the world. The eternal Creator is also the shelter of His people.

▶ GOD

90:2 God is timeless. As humans, we love clocks. We have them all over our homes: on the VCR, on the microwave, and on the walls. We put them everywhere at work: on our telephones, on our office machines, and on our desks. We so love our timepieces that we carry them everywhere we go by wearing watches. Why are we so dependent on time? Because our lives are limited. We have only so many days to live, then comes the final act—death. We only have so much time to do what we desire to do. But God has no limits. He is timeless. He doesn't need to divide His time into portions because He has all the time in eternity. Praise God for His timeless nature. (***See God****> God's Attributes> Eternal> God is timeless,* TopicGuide page A16; also ***see God****> God's Attributes> Infinite> He is not limited by time,* TopicGuide page A16.)

▶ SPIRITUAL WARFARE

90:3 Consider the end of it all. When was the last time you attended a funeral? The ceremony makes us face an unalterable fact—we will all die. The view of the casket underscores the frailty of life. But why doesn't the fact of death affect our way of living? Most of us leave the funeral and continue ignoring our destiny. We live as if we will go on forever. The wise person understands that this physical life will end, and that each person will face judgment. This realization takes us to Christ's cross and our need of salvation from our sins (Hebrews 9:27). He is the only One who can secure eternal life for us. Have you asked Him to be your Savior and Lord? (***See Spiritual Warfare****> Origin of Sin> Humanity's Fall> Physical> End of perpetual physical life,* TopicGuide page A44.)

[4] For You, a thousand years are as a passing day,
as brief as a few night hours.
[5] You sweep people away like dreams that disappear.
They are like grass that springs up in the morning.
[6] In the morning it blooms and flourishes,
but by evening it is dry and withered.
[7] We wither beneath Your anger;
we are overwhelmed by Your fury.
[8] You spread out our sins before You—
our secret sins—and You see them all.
[9] We live our lives beneath Your wrath,
ending our years with a groan.

[10] Seventy years are given to us!
Some even live to eighty.
But even the best years are filled with pain and trouble;
soon they disappear, and we fly away.
[11] Who can comprehend the power of Your anger?
Your wrath is as awesome as the fear You deserve.
[12] Teach us to realize the brevity of life,
so that we may grow in wisdom.

[13] O LORD, come back to us!
How long will You delay?
Take pity on Your servants!
[14] Satisfy us each morning with Your unfailing love,
so we may sing for joy to the end of our lives.
[15] Give us gladness in proportion to our former misery!
Replace the evil years with good.
[16] Let us, Your servants, see You work again;
let our children see Your glory.
[17] And may the Lord our God show us His approval
and make our efforts successful.
Yes, make our efforts successful!

90:4 Ps 39:5; 2 Pet 3:8
90:5 Job 14:2; 20:8; Isa 40:6; Matt 6:30
90:6 Ps 92:7
90:9 Ps 78:33
90:10 Ps 78:39; Eccl 12:2-7
90:11 Ps 76:7
90:12 Ps 39:4
90:13 Deut 32:36
90:14 Pss 36:8; 103:5; Jer 31:14
90:15 Pss 31:10; 86:4
90:16 Ps 44:1
90:17 Ps 27:4; Isa 26:12

PSALM 91

[1] Those who live in the shelter of the Most High
will find rest in the shadow of the Almighty.
[2] This I declare about the LORD:
He alone is my refuge, my place of safety;
He is my God, and I trust Him.
[3] For He will rescue you from every trap
and protect you from deadly disease.
[4] He will cover you with His feathers.
He will shelter you with His wings.
His faithful promises are your armor and protection.

91:1 Isa 25:4; 32:2
91:2 Pss 18:2; 142:5; Jer 16:19
91:3 2 Chr 20:9; Ps 124:7
91:4 Pss 35:2; 57:1; 63:7

90:3-6 The brevity of human existence is described by the images of dust blown away and grass withered by evening. This is contrasted to the permanence of God, to whom a thousand years are as a day gone by. The imagery of dust alludes to the account of man's creation in Genesis 2:7.

91:1-2 The opening verses set the tone for the psalm by employing a series of metaphors to express utmost confidence in God's care. The language of verse 1 suggests the image of a bird providing shelter for her young. Verse 2 employs the imagery of military fortifications. Both of these images are developed further in 91:3-8.

91:5 Job 5:19-23 Ps 23:4	[5] Do not be afraid of the terrors of the night, nor the arrow that flies in the day.
91:6 Job 5:22	[6] Do not dread the disease that stalks in darkness, nor the disaster that strikes at midday. [7] Though a thousand fall at your side, though ten thousand are dying around you, these evils will not touch you.
91:8 Ps 37:34	[8] Just open your eyes, and see how the wicked are punished.
	[9] If you make the LORD your refuge, if you make the Most High your shelter,
91:10 Prov 12:21	[10] no evil will conquer you; no plague will come near your home.
91:11 Ps 34:7 *Matt 4:6 *Luke 4:9-11	[11] For He will order His angels to protect you wherever you go. [12] They will hold you up with their hands so you won't even hurt your foot on a stone.
91:13 Judg 14:6 Luke 10:19	[13] You will trample upon lions and cobras; you will crush fierce lions and serpents under your feet!
	[14] The LORD says, "I will rescue those who love Me. I will protect those who trust in My name.
91:15 1 Sam 2:30 Ps 50:15 John 12:26	[15] When they call on Me, I will answer; I will be with them in trouble. I will rescue and honor them. [16] I will reward them with a long life and give them My salvation."

PSALM 92

A psalm. A song to be sung on the Sabbath Day.

[1] It is good to give thanks to the LORD,
to sing praises to the Most High.
[2] It is good to proclaim Your unfailing love in the morning,
Your faithfulness in the evening,

▸ **PURPOSE**

91:2 God is my Refuge. When a storm comes, animals run for safety. They snuggle under the brush, slip into a cave, or slither into their holes. Where do we go when the storms of life descend? We find refuge in God's loving arms. Our refuge even includes deliverance from eternal death. Through Jesus Christ, God delivered us from the judgment for our sins. When He sacrificed Himself on the cross, Jesus Christ took on the judgment for sin on our behalf. When we repent and believe the gospel, we find safety in God's arms. Truly, God is our shelter from the eternal consequences of our sin. (***See Purpose****> God's Deeds> Judgment> Deliverance from judgment,* TopicGuide page A54.)

91:5-7 By mentioning both day and night, the psalmist suggests God's total and continuous protection. The numeric references indicate God's ability to protect His people in the face of massive danger.

91:11-12 God employs His angels to protect His people from stumbling along the journey of life. Stumbling serves as a metaphor for any number of troubles or dangers that God's people may encounter throughout their lives. However, it should be remembered that God's people are not exempted from suffering. (See Matthew 4:6 to see how Satan used these verses to tempt Jesus.)

91:13 Cobras and lions were not uncommon in ancient Israel and the surrounding areas. Both were considered dangerous and ruthless, making them suitable metaphors for the enemies of God's people.

92:1-3 It is the high calling of God's people to lift their voices in praise. The psalmist extols God's love for His people and His faithfulness to His promises. The imagery in these verses reflects the worship of God in the Jerusalem Temple, where morning and evening sacrifices were offered. As priests and worshipers offered their sacrifices, Levitical singers played music and sang praises to God (compare Psalms 98:5-6; 150:3).

3 accompanied by the ten-stringed harp
and the melody of the lyre.
4 You thrill me, LORD, with all You have done for me!
I sing for joy because of what You have done.
5 O LORD, what great works You do!
And how deep are Your thoughts.
6 Only a simpleton would not know,
and only a fool would not understand this:
7 Though the wicked sprout like weeds
and evildoers flourish,
they will be destroyed forever.

8 But You, O LORD, will be exalted forever.
9 Your enemies, LORD, will surely perish;
all evildoers will be scattered.
10 But You have made me as strong as a wild ox.
You have anointed me with the finest oil.
11 My eyes have seen the downfall of my enemies;
my ears have heard the defeat of my wicked opponents.
12 But the godly will flourish like palm trees
and grow strong like the cedars of Lebanon.
13 For they are transplanted to the LORD's own house.
They flourish in the courts of our God.
14 Even in old age they will still produce fruit;
they will remain vital and green.
15 They will declare, "The LORD is just!
He is my rock!
There is no evil in Him!"

92:3 1 Sam 10:5; 1 Chr 13:8; Neh 12:27
92:5 Pss 40:5; 139:17; Rom 11:33
92:6 Ps 73:22
92:7 Ps 37:38
92:9 Pss 37:20; 68:1
92:10 Pss 23:5; 75:10
92:11 Ps 54:7
92:14 Isa 37:31; John 15:2
92:15 Rom 9:14

PSALM 93

1 The LORD is king! He is robed in majesty.
Indeed, the LORD is robed in majesty and armed with strength.
The world stands firm
and cannot be shaken.

93:1 Pss 65:6; 96:10; 97:1; 99:1; 104:1; Isa 51:9

▶ **GOD**
92:2 Proclaiming our love for God. How often should we proclaim our love for God? In this verse, the psalmist tells us to do so both in the morning and at night. The act of thanking God for His love helps us bookend our days with joy and gladness. In the morning, our thanksgiving reminds us that our day is the Lord's and that He is with us. In the evening, our thanksgiving helps us express gratitude for what He has done for us during the day. (***See God****> God's Attributes> Faithful> God deserves thanks for His constant faithfulness,* TopicGuide page A16.)

92:4-5 The psalmist turns his attention to God's mighty acts of salvation. God is not just the Creator, but also the sovereign God who providentially and miraculously works in history to effect His purposes.

92:10-11 The psalmist speaks now from personal experience. He has been strengthened by the Lord and has witnessed the downfall of the wicked. Not all of God's oppressed people will live to be vindicated in this life, but we are assured in faith that God ultimately will judge the wicked and reward His children.

92:12-14 The psalmist moves from personal observations to more general pronouncements about the blessedness of the righteous. Unlike the wicked, who are but weeds to be uprooted (92:7), the righteous are mighty trees made to thrive in the presence of God and permanently bear fruit (compare Psalm 1).

▶ **GOD**
92:15 The Rock. When we see a rock, we know that it will remain the same for a long, long time. It doesn't change its shape or its makeup. It doesn't move. Day after day, it stays the same. That is a metaphor to help explain God's changeless nature. When the psalmist says that He is just, we can depend on that. His justice will never fail. Aren't you glad that God is our Rock, our sure foundation? (***See God****> God's Names> God> Rock,* TopicGuide page A18.)

93:2 Lam 5:19
2 Your throne, O LORD, has stood from time immemorial.
You Yourself are from the everlasting past.
93:3 Ps 98:7-8
3 The floods have risen up, O LORD.
The floods have roared like thunder;
the floods have lifted their pounding waves.
93:4 Ps 65:7
4 But mightier than the violent raging of the seas,
mightier than the breakers on the shore—
93:5 Ps 19:7
the LORD above is mightier than these!
1 Cor 3:17
5 Your royal laws cannot be changed.
Your reign, O LORD, is holy forever and ever.

PSALM 94

94:1 Deut 32:35 Isa 35:4 Nah 1:2 Rom 12:19
1 O LORD, the God of vengeance,
O God of vengeance, let Your glorious justice shine forth!
2 Arise, O judge of the earth.
Give the proud what they deserve.
3 How long, O LORD?
How long will the wicked be allowed to gloat?
94:4 Pss 31:18; 52:1
4 How long will they speak with arrogance?
How long will these evil people boast?
5 They crush Your people, LORD,
hurting those You claim as Your own.
94:6 Isa 10:2
6 They kill widows and foreigners
and murder orphans.
7 "The LORD isn't looking," they say,
"and besides, the God of Israel* doesn't care."

8 Think again, you fools!
When will you finally catch on?
94:9 Exod 4:11 Prov 20:12
9 Is He deaf—the One who made your ears?
Is He blind—the One who formed your eyes?
94:10 Ps 44:2
10 He punishes the nations—won't He also punish you?
He knows everything—doesn't He also know what you are doing?

94:7 Hebrew *of Jacob.* See note on 44:4.

93:2 The Lord's eternal reign contrasts sharply with the pagan gods of the ancient Near East who were seen as susceptible to being overthrown and destroyed, which would result in chaos upon the earth. God is not threatened by other beings or by the forces of creation. As both Creator and King, His reign is eternal.

93:3-4 In the ancient worldview, the tumultuous sea embodied chaotic forces that threatened to undo the order of the world. In ancient creation myths, the gods battled against the sea in order to subdue it before creating the world. Yet the God of Israel knew of no such challenge. As mighty and foreboding as the sea appeared, it was as nothing compared to the power of God.

▶ GOD
93:4 Mightier than the raging seas. If you have experienced a night out on the ocean when a storm is raging, you understand the power of the sea. The waves crashing against the bow of the ship underscore the fragility of human handiwork. The roar and the hiss of the water shake the boat's sides. The timbers shudder under the assault. Yet the power of the sea cannot begin to be compared to the power of God. It just gives us a taste of God's might. Bow before the God who is the master of His creation. (***See God****> God's Attributes> All-Powerful> His creation reflects His power,* TopicGuide page A15.)

93:5 The psalm concludes by linking the moral order to God's reign. Just as God established a natural order in creation, He established a moral order described in His commandments. While the ideal natural order reflects God's power and strength, the ideal moral order reflects His holiness.

94:2 The call for God to "arise" is the language of the battlefield, envisioning God as the divine warrior (Numbers 10:35).

94:8-10 Through a series of rhetorical questions playing off God's creation of mankind, the psalmist demonstrates the foolishness of the wicked who believe they will escape judgment.

[11] The LORD knows people's thoughts;
He knows they are worthless!

[12] Joyful are those You discipline, LORD,
those You teach with Your instructions.
[13] You give them relief from troubled times
until a pit is dug to capture the wicked.
[14] The LORD will not reject His people;
He will not abandon His special possession.
[15] Judgment will again be founded on justice,
and those with virtuous hearts will pursue it.

[16] Who will protect me from the wicked?
Who will stand up for me against evildoers?
[17] Unless the LORD had helped me,
I would soon have settled in the silence of the grave.
[18] I cried out, "I am slipping!"
but Your unfailing love, O LORD, supported me.
[19] When doubts filled my mind,
Your comfort gave me renewed hope and cheer.

[20] Can unjust leaders claim that God is on their side—
leaders whose decrees permit injustice?
[21] They gang up against the righteous
and condemn the innocent to death.
[22] But the LORD is my fortress;
my God is the mighty rock where I hide.
[23] God will turn the sins of evil people back on them.
He will destroy them for their sins.
The LORD our God will destroy them.

94:11 *1 Cor 3:20
94:12 Deut 8:5; Heb 12:5-6
94:14 1 Sam 12:22; Rom 11:2
94:15 Isa 42:3; Mic 7:9
94:16 Num 10:35; Isa 33:10
94:17 Ps 124:1-2
94:19 Isa 57:18; 66:13
94:20 Ps 58:2
94:21 Exod 23:7; Matt 27:4
94:22 Pss 59:9; 71:7
94:23 Pss 7:16; 140:9, 11

PSALM 95

[1] Come, let us sing to the LORD!
Let us shout joyfully to the Rock of our salvation.
[2] Let us come to Him with thanksgiving.
Let us sing psalms of praise to Him.
[3] For the LORD is a great God,
a great King above all gods.
[4] He holds in His hands the depths of the earth
and the mightiest mountains.

95:2 Mic 6:6-8
95:4 Ps 135:5-6

▸ SPIRITUAL WARFARE
94:12 Experiencing God's discipline. Going through a time of discipline is not a pleasant experience. How, then, can those who receive discipline feel happy? It's like the child who welcomes discipline because by it his parent helps him curtail wrongful behavior. His parent is setting limits on his behavior so that he will grow in the right ways. That's what God does for us. Our sin displeases God; therefore, God acts to restrict our wrong behavior. He allows us to suffer consequences so that we will not repeat our actions. Hebrews 12:5-6 says, "My child, don't make light of the LORD's discipline, and don't give up when He corrects you. For the LORD disciplines those He loves, and He punishes each one He accepts as His child." Are you grateful to God for His discipline? (See Hebrews 12:5-6; also ***see Spiritual Warfare**> Resisting Sin and Evil> Consequences> Of Disobedience> Falling under discipline,* TopicGuide page A46.)

94:16-19 The psalmist expresses complete dependence on God's grace. If not for God's deliverance, he would be overwhelmed by wickedness from without and fear from within.

95:3 The psalmist is not affirming the existence of rival gods. He merely acknowledges the belief in other gods by Israel's neighbors. God stands alone as the one true deity.

95:4-6 The psalmist celebrates God's kingship in the context of creation. God is the Maker of the seas and the dry land. From the highest peak to the lowest depth, He formed it all. He is our Maker as well, and as such He deserves our praise and obedience.

95:5 Gen 1:9-10
5 The sea belongs to Him, for He made it.
His hands formed the dry land, too.

6 Come, let us worship and bow down.
Let us kneel before the LORD our maker,
95:7-11 *Heb 3:7-11, 15; 4:7
7 for He is our God.
We are the people He watches over,
the flock under His care.

If only you would listen to His voice today!
95:8 Num 20:13 Deut 6:16
8 The LORD says, "Don't harden your hearts as Israel did at Meribah,
as they did at Massah in the wilderness.
95:9 Num 14:22
9 For there your ancestors tested and tried My patience,
even though they saw everything I did.
95:10 Acts 7:36; 13:18 Heb 3:10, 17
10 For forty years I was angry with them, and I said,
'They are a people whose hearts turn away from Me.
They refuse to do what I tell them.'
95:11 Deut 1:35 *Heb 4:3, 5
11 So in My anger I took an oath:
'They will never enter My place of rest.'"

PSALM 96

96:1-13 //1 Chr 16:23-33
1 Sing a new song to the LORD!
Let the whole earth sing to the LORD!
96:2 Ps 71:15
2 Sing to the LORD; praise His name.
Each day proclaim the good news that He saves.
96:3 Ps 145:12
3 Publish His glorious deeds among the nations.
Tell everyone about the amazing things He does.

▸ WORSHIP
95:6 Kneeling before God. When you worship God, do you often kneel? The position in which we come before God can help us acknowledge His sovereignty. By kneeling, we recognize His Lordship and His authority over our lives. This stance helps us focus on God and take our minds off ourselves. Try kneeling in your devotional time today. (***See Worship****> OT> Posture> Kneeling,* TopicGuide page A28.)

95:7 The image of God as a Shepherd and His people as a flock occurs frequently throughout Scripture (Psalm 23:1-4; Ezekiel 34:11-16; John 10:1-18). The metaphor conveys a sense of God's tender care and guidance.

95:8-11 The psalmist refers to incidents during Israel's wilderness journey following the Exodus from Egypt. Meribah and Massah were places of "arguing" and "test," respectively, where God's patience was tried when Israel rebelled against God (Exodus 17:1-7; Numbers 20:1-13). Together, they symbolized Israel's recurring faithlessness and ingratitude throughout its time in the wilderness.

▸ SALVATION
95:10 The sin of ungratefulness. What sin did the Israelite people commit for 40 years? While they traveled through the wilderness, God led them. He provided for all their needs. Yet they grumbled and complained about His care. When Moses climbed Mount Sinai to receive the Ten Commandments, they worshiped an idol (Exodus 32). Time after time, they disobeyed God even though He showed them miracles and provided for them. They were ungrateful for what God had done for them. Do we do the same thing to God? He has given us salvation through the sacrifice of His Son. Our lives should be continually filled with gratitude to Him. (***See Salvation****> Receiving> Results> Works> Expression of gratitude,* TopicGuide page A23.)

95:11 The generation that escaped Egypt failed to enter the Promised Land because of their persistent unbelief (Numbers 14:23). In the New Testament, their experience becomes a warning to professing believers who must persevere in their faith if they will enter God's eternal rest (Hebrews 3:7-19).

96:1-3 Three calls to "sing to the LORD" are balanced by three imperatives: "praise," "proclaim," and "publish." The precise significance of "a new song" is uncertain, but other references are associated with God's victories in battle, perhaps in anticipation of His final victory (Psalms 33:3; 98:1; 149:1; Revelation 5:9; 14:3). The specific act of deliverance the psalmist has in mind is not clear.

▸ MINISTRY
96:2 Proclaim His salvation! Every morning as we wake, we should begin the day by praising God for His salvation. Throughout each day, our lips should proclaim what He has done for us—not mechanically, but naturally. How many people do you meet who may have never heard about how God has been merciful to you? In every place we go, we should prayerfully spread the news about God's love and Christ's sacrifice. Let others know about how good God has been to you. (***See Ministry****> Great Commission> Witness> Witness in the power of the Holy Spirit,* TopicGuide page A56.)

4 Great is the LORD! He is most worthy of praise!
He is to be feared above all gods.
5 The gods of other nations are mere idols,
but the LORD made the heavens!
6 Honor and majesty surround Him;
strength and beauty fill His sanctuary.

7 O nations of the world, recognize the LORD;
recognize that the LORD is glorious and strong.
8 Give to the LORD the glory He deserves!
Bring your offering and come into His courts.
9 Worship the LORD in all His holy splendor.
Let all the earth tremble before Him.
10 Tell all the nations, "The LORD reigns!"
The world stands firm and cannot be shaken.
He will judge all peoples fairly.

11 Let the heavens be glad, and the earth rejoice!
Let the sea and everything in it shout His praise!
12 Let the fields and their crops burst out with joy!
Let the trees of the forest rustle with praise
13 before the LORD, for He is coming!
He is coming to judge the earth.
He will judge the world with justice,
and the nations with His truth.

96:5 1 Chr 16:26; Isa 42:5
96:6 Ps 104:1
96:8 Ps 115:1
96:9 1 Chr 16:29; 2 Chr 20:21
96:10 Pss 58:11; 67:4; 93:1
96:11 Pss 97:1; 98:7; Isa 49:13
96:12 Isa 35:1; 44:23; 55:12-13

PSALM 97

1 The LORD is king!
Let the earth rejoice!
Let the farthest coastlands be glad.
2 Dark clouds surround Him.
Righteousness and justice are the
foundation of His throne.

97:1 Ps 96:10-11
97:2 Exod 19:9; Deut 4:11; 1 Kgs 8:12; Pss 18:11; 89:14

96:4-5 Far from affirming the existence of other gods, the psalmist explicitly relegates them to the status of idols. The nations worship false gods in ignorance and rebellion. These false gods are powerless, but the God of Israel is the Creator who brought all things into existence.

96:11-13 The psalmist portrays all of creation in eager expectation of the coming of God to establish His rule. The apostle Paul also describes creation's anticipation of the consummation of the Creator's kingdom (Romans 8:19-22).

▸ GOD
96:12 Creation praises God. When you take a walk in the woods in the early morning, can you hear the trees praising God? When you stroll along the seashore, do you hear the waves singing about His magnificence? If you fly over fruitful croplands, do they express God's awesome nature? All nature shows God's strength and beauty (Job 38:1-11). As a result of His creativity, the universe shows us His character. Praise Him for His wondrous works. (***See God****> God's Attributes> All-Powerful> God's creative power is beyond our comprehension,* TopicGuide page A16.)

97:1 Most ancient cultures conceived of their gods as local deities. The Lord, however, claimed not just Israel as His own, but the whole of creation.

▸ GOD
97:2 The foundation of God's rule. Every leader on earth has principles from which he rules. Some act out of greed and selfishness. They make decisions that benefit themselves, not their subjects. Others rule with viciousness or callousness, disregarding the needs of others. A few rule from good motives, trying to help those they serve. But the basis of God's rule is righteousness and justice. Whatever He does stems from these characteristics. Rest in the fact that He will always act with goodness and fairness. (***See God****> God's Attributes> Righteous> He rules out of righteousness,* TopicGuide page A17.)

97:2-5 The psalmist employs language frequently used to describe the appearance of God in the Old Testament. The prototype for such appearances was the giving of the law from Mount Sinai (Exodus 19; compare Deuteronomy 4:9-12). Such language was used frequently to describe the coming of the Lord in judgment (Joel 2:2; Zephaniah 1:15; Nahum 1:5; compare Psalm 18).

97:3 Heb 12:29 [3] Fire spreads ahead of Him
and burns up all His foes.
[4] His lightning flashes out across the world.
The earth sees and trembles.
97:5 Josh 3:11 Amos 9:5 [5] The mountains melt like wax before the LORD,
before the Lord of all the earth.
97:6 Ps 50:6 [6] The heavens proclaim His righteousness;
every nation sees His glory.
97:7 Jer 10:14 *Heb 1:6 [7] Those who worship idols are disgraced—
all who brag about their worthless gods—
for every god must bow to Him.
97:8 Zeph 3:14 [8] Jerusalem* has heard and rejoiced,
and all the towns of Judah are glad
because of Your justice, O LORD!
97:9 Exod 18:11 Pss 83:18; 95:3 [9] For You, O LORD, are supreme over all the earth;
You are exalted far above all gods.
97:10 Dan 3:28 Rom 12:9 [10] You who love the LORD, hate evil!
He protects the lives of His godly people
97:11 Job 22:28 and rescues them from the power of the wicked.
[11] Light shines on the godly,
and joy on those whose hearts are right.
97:12 Ps 32:11 [12] May all who are godly rejoice in the LORD
and praise His holy name!

97:8 Hebrew *Zion*.

▶ HOLINESS

97:10 Hate evil! What characteristics should we exhibit if we hate evil? Hatred of evil should drive us to prayer, asking God to keep us from sin. We should have such a sense of God's holiness that we run from temptation and wrongdoing. We should continually ask God to reveal in us what displeases Him so that we may repent of our sin. Make a commitment today to keep your sin accounts short, taking every wrongdoing immediately to God. (***See Holiness****> Law and Grace> Law> Hate evil,* TopicGuide page A42.)

BECAUSE GOD IS JUST

He will always treat me fairly.

He is coming to judge the earth. He will judge the world with justice, and the nations with His truth.

PSALM 96:13

FOR THE NEXT *GOD IS JUST* FEATURE SEE PAGE 1396.

PSALM 98

A psalm.

[1] Sing a new song to the LORD,
for He has done wonderful deeds.
His right hand has won a mighty victory;
His holy arm has shown His saving power!
[2] The LORD has announced His victory
and has revealed His righteousness to every nation!
[3] He has remembered His promise to love and be faithful to Israel.
The ends of the earth have seen the victory of our God.

[4] Shout to the LORD, all the earth;
break out in praise and sing for joy!
[5] Sing your praise to the LORD with the harp,
with the harp and melodious song,
[6] with trumpets and the sound of the ram's horn.
Make a joyful symphony before the LORD, the King!

[7] Let the sea and everything in it shout His praise!
Let the earth and all living things join in.
[8] Let the rivers clap their hands in glee!
Let the hills sing out their songs of joy
[9] before the LORD.
For the LORD is coming to judge the earth.
He will judge the world with justice,
and the nations with fairness.

98:1 Exod 15:6; Isa 52:10
98:3 Luke 1:54, 72
98:4 Ps 100:1
98:6 Num 10:10; 2 Chr 15:14
98:7 Pss 24:1; 96:11
98:9 Ps 96:10, 13

PSALM 99

[1] The LORD is king!
Let the nations tremble!
He sits on His throne between the cherubim.
Let the whole earth quake!
[2] The LORD sits in majesty in Jerusalem,*
exalted above all the nations.
[3] Let them praise Your great and awesome name.
Your name is holy!
[4] Mighty King, lover of justice,
You have established fairness.

99:1 Exod 25:22; 1 Sam 4:4
99:3 Deut 28:58; Josh 24:19; 1 Sam 2:2
99:4 Ps 17:2

99:2 Hebrew *Zion.*

▸ WORSHIP

98:1 Sing a new song to God. Whenever God does something wonderful for you, what's your reaction? How do you express your thankfulness and gratitude? One way we can articulate our feelings is by singing songs that put into words how we feel. We can search our hymnbook for old favorites that help us say what our hearts feel. Listening to Christian radio stations allows us to hear new songs that help us worship Him. Congregational singing allows us to express with others what God has done for us. Let your mind wander and think of ways to worship God that come uniquely from your mind and heart and body. (***See Worship****> OT> Music> Psalms> Liturgy> Royal,* TopicGuide page A27.*)*

98:4-6 The psalms often call upon God's people to praise Him accompanied by musical instruments (Psalms 81:1-5; 150:3). Here, all the earth is called upon to celebrate God's kingship.

98:7-9 The earlier portion of the psalm celebrated a past victory of God. Now the psalmist looks forward to God's future acts of salvation. He enjoins all of creation to vibrantly praise the Lord, whose coming will establish justice among the nations.

99:1 Two golden cherubim with outstretched wings topped the Ark of the Covenant (Exodus 25:20). Scripture envisions God enthroned above these two angelic representations, mirroring the heavenly throne, which is surrounded by seraphim (Isaiah 6).

99:3-5 The psalmist keys in on the holiness and justice of God. Unlike the rule of so many human leaders, the rule of God is marked by fairness and equity. It is among God's people, whether Israel in the Old Testament or the church in the New, that the world sees most clearly the rule of God embodied.

You have acted with justice
and righteousness throughout Israel.*
5 Exalt the LORD our God!
Bow low before His feet, for He is holy!

99:6 Exod 15:25 1 Sam 7:9
6 Moses and Aaron were among His priests;
Samuel also called on His name.
They cried to the LORD for help,
and He answered them.

99:7 Exod 33:9 Num 12:5
7 He spoke to Israel from the pillar of cloud,
and they followed the laws and decrees He gave them.

99:8 Num 14:20
8 O LORD our God, You answered them.
You were a forgiving God to them,
but You punished them when they went wrong.

9 Exalt the LORD our God,
and worship at His holy mountain in Jerusalem,
for the LORD our God is holy!

PSALM 100

A psalm of thanksgiving.

100:1 Ps 98:4
1 Shout with joy to the LORD, all the earth!
100:2 Deut 28:47
2 Worship the LORD with gladness.
Come before Him, singing with joy.
100:3 1 Kgs 18:39 Ezek 34:30-31 Mark 14:27 John 10:11
3 Acknowledge that the LORD is God!
He made us, and we are His.
We are His people, the sheep of His pasture.
100:4 Pss 95:2; 96:2
4 Enter His gates with thanksgiving;
go into His courts with praise.
Give thanks to Him and praise His name.
100:5 Pss 25:8; 119:90
5 For the LORD is good.
His unfailing love continues forever,
and His faithfulness continues to each generation.

99:4 Hebrew *Jacob.* See note on 44:4.

99:7 A pillar of cloud was God's chosen method of revealing His presence during Israel's wilderness wandering (Numbers 10:12).

▸ WORSHIP

99:9 God is holy. In Isaiah 6, the prophet tells of a vision he saw of God's throne in heaven. Angels were worshiping God, singing, "Holy, holy, holy is the Lord of Heaven's Armies! The whole earth is filled with His glory!" (Isaiah 6:3). When Isaiah saw God's holiness, he recognized his own sinfulness. He immediately knew that he was a guilty man and in need of forgiveness. When we worship God, our attention should be on Him, not on ourselves. We should focus first on His holiness. This helps us put our own insignificance in perspective. Then we see our sin as God sees it and we seek His forgiveness. (***See Worship**> OT> God's Supremacy> Was God-centered (not worshiper-centered),* TopicGuide page A27.)

100:1 The scope of the kingship of God is not limited to the nation of Israel. It encompasses the whole earth.

▸ GOD

100:5 God is good. Do you know someone whom you would describe as "good"? We judge goodness by external actions, but we cannot see the heart, where the blackest of sins may lie. God not only does what is good, He *is* good. Whether we look into His being, His doing, or His saying, every aspect of God is good. People, however, are not good at this level. We all have flaws and faults (Romans 3:23). This is why only God's Spirit can develop true goodness in our lives, not the flawed version promised through other sources. Today, thank God for His goodness and rely on the Holy Spirit to develop goodness in your life. (***See God**> God's Attributes> Good> God deserves thanks for His goodness,* TopicGuide page A16.)

▸ GOD

100:5 God is love. Love is not an action that can be taken alone. Love must have an object. A mother loves her baby. A grandparent loves his grandchildren. A ruler loves his subjects. Since God is love, who is the object of God's love? We are. He bestows on us the depth of His love, which is infinite. He proved His love when He sent Jesus Christ to die on the cross. That is the ultimate example of love. Thank God for His unfailing love for you. (***See God**> God's Attributes> Loving> God deserves thanks because of His perpetual love,* TopicGuide page A17.)

100:5 God's "unfailing love" is best understood as His covenantal loyalty to His people. God bound Himself to His people by His word and will remain faithful to them eternally, even if they prove unfaithful.

PSALM 101

A psalm of David.

1 I will sing of Your love and justice, LORD.
I will praise You with songs.
2 I will be careful to live a blameless life—
when will You come to help me?
I will lead a life of integrity
in my own home.
3 I will refuse to look at
anything vile and vulgar.
I hate all who deal crookedly;
I will have nothing to do with them.
4 I will reject perverse ideas
and stay away from every evil.
5 I will not tolerate people who slander
their neighbors.
I will not endure conceit and pride.

6 I will search for faithful people
to be my companions.
Only those who are above reproach
will be allowed to serve me.
7 I will not allow deceivers to serve in my house,
and liars will not stay in my presence.
8 My daily task will be to ferret out the wicked
and free the city of the LORD from their grip.

101:1 Pss 89:1; 145:7

101:4 Prov 11:20

101:5 Ps 50:20; Prov 6:16-19

101:6 Ps 119:1

101:8 Pss 46:4; 75:10; 118:10-12

PSALM 102

A prayer of one overwhelmed with trouble, pouring out problems before the LORD.

1 LORD, hear my prayer!
Listen to my plea!

102:1 Exod 2:23; 1 Sam 9:16

101:1 David praises the qualities of God that he seeks to emulate as ruler of God's people. The king of Israel was a representative of God to the people. As such, his rule needed to reflect the love and justice that would characterize the rule of God.

▸ HOLINESS

101:2 Integrity at home. Oftentimes, we exhibit less integrity at home than anywhere else. We let our guard down and slip into habits that do not please God—swearing behind closed doors, snapping at family members, grumbling at our chores. Having integrity at home means living as close to God as possible, even in our most private moments. A life of integrity glorifies God before those we love the most. What would your family say about your character? Do they think you honor God? What do you need to change to glorify Him in your home? (***See Holiness***> *Submission*> *Learning God's Word*> *Teaching your children,* TopicGuide page A40.)

▸ SPIRITUAL WARFARE

101:3-4 Keeping our eyes pure. Isn't it amazing how little human life has changed over the centuries? Even in the days of King David, visual temptations were a problem. In fact, King David himself sinned after he watched his neighbor's wife bathing (2 Samuel 11–12). And yet, no matter where we go today, our eyes see things they never would have been exposed to in days gone by. Risqué billboard signs, TV commercials, and magazine ads all tempt us to sin. It's almost impossible to avoid all these areas completely. Yet we can refuse to look at vulgar and vile things wherever and whenever they accost us. Keep your eyes pure. Reject perverse images and avoid evil. (***See Spiritual Warfare***> *Resisting Sin and Evil*> *Resisting Temptation*> *What to Resist*> *We are to resist sinful urges,* TopicGuide page A45.)

101:5-7 The king seeks to implement justice amid his people. The pursuit of justice results in the punishment of the wicked and the protection of the righteous. To aid him in administering a just society, the king plans to surround himself only with men of character and integrity. His concern for justice begins with his own court.

102:1-2 The psalmist uses a collage of phrases to express his intense desire to be heard by God. To have the Lord turn His face toward you is to experience His blessing and enjoy His salvation (Numbers 6:25).

102:2 Ps 69:17
[2] Don't turn away from me
in my time of distress.
Bend down to listen,
and answer me quickly when I call
to You.

102:3 Job 30:30 Jas 4:14
[3] For my days disappear like smoke,
and my bones burn like red-hot coals.
[4] My heart is sick, withered like grass,
and I have lost my appetite.

102:5 Lam 4:8
[5] Because of my groaning,
I am reduced to skin and bones.
[6] I am like an owl in the desert,
like a little owl in a far-off wilderness.

102:7 Ps 77:4
[7] I lie awake,
lonely as a solitary bird on the roof.

102:8 2 Sam 16:5 Isa 65:15 Luke 23:11 Acts 26:11
[8] My enemies taunt me day after day.
They mock and curse me.
[9] I eat ashes for food.
My tears run down into my drink
[10] because of Your anger and wrath.
For You have picked me up and thrown
me out.
[11] My life passes as swiftly as the evening
shadows.
I am withering away like grass.

102:12 Exod 3:15 Lam 5:19
[12] But You, O LORD, will sit on Your throne forever.
Your fame will endure to every generation.

102:13 Isa 60:10 Zech 1:12
[13] You will arise and have mercy on Jerusalem*—
and now is the time to pity her,
now is the time You promised to help.
[14] For Your people love every stone in her walls
and cherish even the dust in her streets.

102:15 1 Kgs 8:41-42
[15] Then the nations will tremble before the LORD.
The kings of the earth will tremble before
His glory.

102:16 Isa 60:1-2
[16] For the LORD will rebuild Jerusalem.
He will appear in His glory.

102:17 Neh 1:6
[17] He will listen to the prayers of the destitute.
He will not reject their pleas.

102:18 Deut 31:19 1 Cor 10:11
[18] Let this be recorded for future generations,
so that a people not yet born will praise
the LORD.

102:19 Deut 26:15
[19] Tell them the LORD looked down
from His heavenly sanctuary.
He looked down to earth from heaven

102:13 Hebrew *Zion;* also in 102:16.

102:13-17 The Babylonians destroyed Jerusalem and sent its people into exile. Evoking the language of the battlefield (Numbers 10:35), the psalmist calls on God to deliver His people and restore their beloved city.

20 to hear the groans of the prisoners,
to release those condemned to die.
21 And so the LORD's fame will be celebrated in Zion,
His praises in Jerusalem,
22 when multitudes gather together
and kingdoms come to worship the LORD.

23 He broke my strength in midlife,
cutting short my days.
24 But I cried to Him, "O my God, who lives forever,
don't take my life while I am so young!
25 Long ago You laid the foundation of the earth
and made the heavens with Your hands.
26 They will perish, but You remain forever;
they will wear out like old clothing.
You will change them like a garment
and discard them.
27 But You are always the same;
You will live forever.
28 The children of Your people
will live in security.
Their children's children
will thrive in Your presence."

102:21 Zech 8:20-23
102:22 Ps 86:9
102:24 Isa 38:10
102:25-27 Gen 1:1; *Heb 1:10-12
102:26 Matt 24:35; 2 Pet 3:10; Rev 20:11
102:27 Mal 3:6; Jas 1:17

PSALM 103

A psalm of David.

1 Let all that I am praise the LORD;
with my whole heart, I will praise His holy name.
2 Let all that I am praise the LORD;
may I never forget the good things He does for me.

103:1 Pss 33:21; 104:1

102:23-28 The psalmist returns to his earlier tone of lament. He contrasts the brevity of his life with the permanence of creation and of God Himself. Yet the psalmist draws strength from the fact of God's permanence. God's love for His children withstands the vicissitudes of historical change.

▸ GOD
102:25 God is unchanging. Creativity is built into human nature. Preschoolers love to work with modeling clay. Kindergarten children love to finger paint and color with crayons. Teenagers write romantic poems and sing songs of passion. Adults find many kinds of creativity through which to express their feelings and ideas. But none of these can come close to the creativity of God. He created brightly colored fish that live deep within the ocean. He planned each melting snowflake to have a unique structure. He foreordained the clouds that form and re-form in the sky in countless wonderful shapes. Yet through all His creative works, His personality is still the same. The hands that formed Adam from the dust still work on our behalf today. Thank God for His unchanging, creative nature. (***See God****> God's Attributes> Unchanging> Though the universe will change, God never will,* TopicGuide page A18.)

▸ GOD
102:27 How many birthdays have you had? When we were in elementary school, we could hardly wait for our birthdays to roll around. Many of us measured time by the half-year ("I'm five and a half!"). But when we reached a certain age, we quit announcing our age. As each year creeps by, we realize even more completely how short life really is. The higher our age, the shorter a year seems. But God doesn't measure His age. He is eternal. No one can count the number of days He has lived. He is beyond time. He is always there. When you feel threatened by the fragility of life, turn to God. (***See God****> God's Attributes> Eternal> God has no end of days,* TopicGuide page A16.)

▸ WORSHIP
103:1 With your whole heart. When you are with someone—fully present with that person—you sense a unity that goes beyond words. Worship of God is just this way. Every aspect of our being should tremble in His presence, undergo His care, bow before His majesty. Any corner of our lives that we have kept from Him, we will turn over to Him. Are you worshiping God with your whole heart? Give Him every part of yourself in worship. (***See Worship****> OT> God's Supremacy> Glorified and Blessed God,* TopicGuide page A27.)

103:3 Exod 34:7; Jer 30:17
103:4 Ps 49:15
103:5 Isa 40:31
103:7 Exod 33:13
103:8 Num 14:18; Neh 9:17; Joel 2:13; Jon 4:2; Nah 1:3
103:9 Ps 30:5; Isa 57:16; Jer 3:5
103:10 Lam 3:22
103:11 Ps 36:5
103:12 Isa 38:17; Heb 9:26
103:13 Mal 3:17
103:14 Gen 3:19; Eccl 12:7; Isa 29:16
103:15 Jas 1:10-11; 1 Pet 1:24
103:18 Deut 7:9

3 He forgives all my sins
 and heals all my diseases.
4 He redeems me from death
 and crowns me with love and tender mercies.
5 He fills my life with good things.
 My youth is renewed like the eagle's!

6 The LORD gives righteousness
 and justice to all who are treated unfairly.

7 He revealed His character to Moses
 and His deeds to the people of Israel.
8 The LORD is compassionate and merciful,
 slow to get angry and filled with unfailing love.
9 He will not constantly accuse us,
 nor remain angry forever.
10 He does not punish us for all our sins;
 He does not deal harshly with us, as we deserve.
11 For His unfailing love toward those who fear Him
 is as great as the height of the heavens above the earth.
12 He has removed our sins as far from us
 as the east is from the west.
13 The LORD is like a father to His children,
 tender and compassionate to those who fear Him.
14 For He knows how weak we are;
 He remembers we are only dust.
15 Our days on earth are like grass;
 like wildflowers, we bloom and die.
16 The wind blows, and we are gone—
 as though we had never been here.
17 But the love of the LORD remains forever
 with those who fear Him.
 His salvation extends to the children's children
18 of those who are faithful to His covenant,
 of those who obey His commandments!

19 The LORD has made the heavens His throne;
 from there He rules over everything.

103:3-5 The psalmist enumerates the wealth of blessings that belong to God's people. The kindness of God extends to both the spiritual and physical spheres of life, but this is not always manifested in the way that conforms to our cultural definition of wealth.

▸ WORSHIP
103:13 Fearing God. The word *fear* in the Old Testament means "to have reverence and respect" for someone. Many people have never experienced fearing God. Instead, they take God for granted, expecting Him to be like a soft-spoken grandfather who will let them get away with anything. When we truly fear God, our lives change. We become more concerned about pleasing Him than about fitting in with the crowd. We understand how much we need His mercy for our sins. We gain a more accurate picture of His ways of disciplining His disobedient children. Today, fear God by giving Him your deep respect and reverence, and depend on His mercy.
(***See Worship****> OT> Reverence> God shows mercy to those who fear Him,* TopicGuide page A28.)

103:17-18 The love of God that the psalmist has described in such lavish language is not indiscriminate. It is reserved for His people, for those who fearfully seek to obey the Lord. Obedience itself, however, is not the ground of God's love. In the context of the psalm, humanity's need of God's mercy due to sin is assumed.

103:19-22 After beginning his psalm on a very personal note (103:1-6) and then expanding his focus to the covenant community (103:7-18), the psalmist now extends his scope to encompass the whole created order. The praise of the individual, however, is not lost within the chorus of universal praise.

20 Praise the LORD, you angels,
you mighty ones who carry out His plans,
listening for each of His commands.
21 Yes, praise the LORD, you armies of angels
who serve Him and do His will!
22 Praise the LORD, everything He has created,
everything in all His kingdom.

Let all that I am praise the LORD.

103:20 Matt 6:10 Heb 1:14

PSALM 104

1 Let all that I am praise the LORD.

O LORD my God, how great You are!
You are robed with honor and majesty.
2 You are dressed in a robe of light.
You stretch out the starry curtain of the heavens;
3 You lay out the rafters of Your home in the rain clouds.
You make the clouds Your chariot;
You ride upon the wings of the wind.
4 The winds are Your messengers;
flames of fire are Your servants.*

5 You placed the world on its foundation
so it would never be moved.
6 You clothed the earth with floods of water,
water that covered even the mountains.
7 At Your command, the water fled;
at the sound of Your thunder, it hurried away.
8 Mountains rose and valleys sank
to the levels You decreed.
9 Then You set a firm boundary for the seas,
so they would never again cover the earth.

10 You make springs pour water into the ravines,
so streams gush down from the mountains.
11 They provide water for all the animals,
and the wild donkeys quench their thirst.
12 The birds nest beside the streams
and sing among the branches of the trees.
13 You send rain on the mountains from Your heavenly home,
and You fill the earth with the fruit of Your labor.

104:2 Dan 7:9
104:3 Ps 18:10 Amos 9:6
104:4 2 Kgs 2:11; 6:17 *Heb 1:7
104:5 Job 38:4
104:6 Gen 1:2
104:7 Pss 18:15; 29:3
104:9 Job 38:10-11 Jer 5:22
104:10 Isa 41:18
104:12 Matt 8:20

104:4 Greek version reads *He sends His angels like the winds, / His servants like flames of fire.* Compare Heb 1:7.

104:1-4 The psalmist praises God as the Creator and King of the universe. Verse 2 alludes to the first two days of Creation, as recorded in Genesis 1. The chariot and messenger imagery suggests the servant role of Creation. God employs all elements of Creation to accomplish His purposes.

▸ GOD
104:9 A worldwide flood. Verses 6-9 of this psalm reaffirm the accuracy of Genesis 6–9, the story of Noah's flood. These two passages give us a clear picture of how completely God controls nature. He caused the water to cover even the highest mountains. It was through His command that the water receded. God also gives us a promise in verse 9—that never again will a worldwide flood afflict the earth. His power is so complete that He can make this promise. The Bible consistently shows us that God directly and actively controls the universe. Are you honoring Him as the almighty Creator? (***See God**> God's Attributes> Sovereign> The Creator looks after His creation,* TopicGuide page A17.)

104:10-18 Through His providential ordering of nature, the Lord has provided shelter and sustenance for all creatures. In this way, creation demonstrates the Lord's compassionate care.

104:14 Gen 1:29-30 Job 28:5
14 You cause grass to grow for the livestock
and plants for people to use.
You allow them to produce food from the earth—
104:15 Judg 9:13; 19:5, 8 Prov 31:6 Eccl 10:19 Luke 7:46
15 wine to make them glad,
olive oil to soothe their skin,
and bread to give them strength.
16 The trees of the LORD are well cared for—
the cedars of Lebanon that He planted.
104:17 Lev 11:19
17 There the birds make their nests,
and the storks make their homes
in the cypresses.
104:18 Lev 11:5 Prov 30:26
18 High in the mountains live the wild goats,
and the rocks form a refuge for the hyraxes.*

104:19 Gen 1:14
19 You made the moon to mark the seasons,
and the sun knows when to set.
104:20 Isa 45:7; 56:9
20 You send the darkness, and it becomes night,
when all the forest animals prowl about.
21 Then the young lions roar for their prey,
stalking the food provided by God.
104:22 Job 37:8
22 At dawn they slink back
into their dens to rest.
104:23 Gen 3:19
23 Then people go off to their work,
where they labor until evening.

104:24 Pss 40:5; 65:9 Jer 10:12; 51:15
24 O LORD, what a variety of things
You have made!
In wisdom You have made them all.
The earth is full of Your creatures.
25 Here is the ocean, vast and wide,
teeming with life of every kind,
both large and small.
104:26 Job 41:1
26 See the ships sailing along,
and Leviathan,* which You made to play
in the sea.

104:27 Ps 136:25
27 They all depend on You
to give them food as they need it.
28 When You supply it, they gather it.
You open Your hand to feed them,
and they are richly satisfied.
104:29 Gen 3:19
29 But if You turn away from them,
they panic.
When You take away their breath,
they die and turn again to dust.

104:18 Or *coneys*, or *rock badgers*. 104:26 The identification of Leviathan is disputed, ranging from an earthly creature to a mythical sea monster in ancient literature.

104:19-24 The Lord has established the rhythms of creation, from the movement of the heavenly bodies to the patterns of human life. The wisdom of God displayed by creation is a significant theme in Scripture, particularly in the wisdom literature (see Proverbs 8:22-31; Job 38–41).

104:27-30 The psalmist once more reflects on creation's total dependence on God. The Spirit is the agent of God in creation (Genesis 1:2; 2:4-8).

30 When You give them Your breath,* life is created,
and You renew the face of the earth.

31 May the glory of the LORD continue forever!
The LORD takes pleasure in all He has made!
32 The earth trembles at His glance;
the mountains smoke at His touch.

33 I will sing to the LORD as long as I live.
I will praise my God to my last breath!
34 May all my thoughts be pleasing to Him,
for I rejoice in the LORD.
35 Let all sinners vanish from the face of the earth;
let the wicked disappear forever.

Let all that I am praise the LORD.

Praise the LORD!

104:30 Ezek 37:9
104:31 Gen 1:31
104:32 Exod 19:18; Judg 5:5
104:35 Pss 37:10; 59:13

PSALM 105

1 Give thanks to the LORD and proclaim His greatness.
Let the whole world know what He has done.
2 Sing to Him; yes, sing His praises.
Tell everyone about His wonderful deeds.
3 Exult in His holy name;
rejoice, you who worship the LORD.
4 Search for the LORD and for His strength;
continually seek Him.
5 Remember the wonders He has performed,
His miracles, and the rulings He has given,
6 you children of His servant Abraham,
you descendants of Jacob, His chosen ones.

7 He is the LORD our God.
His justice is seen throughout the land.

105:1-15 //1 Chr 16:8-22
105:2 Ps 98:5
105:3 Ps 33:21
105:4 Ps 27:8
105:7 Isa 26:9

104:30 Or *When You send Your Spirit.*

▸ GOD
104:30 The Holy Spirit in creation. The Bible tells us that God's relationship to His creation continues up to and beyond today. In the beginning, He made everything (104:24). Since then, all creation has depended on God for everything it needs—food, water, air to breathe. Without His support, all life dies (104:29). God's Spirit is the One who sustains this life; He constantly replenishes life. He is the reason you are alive today. Not only has He created you, but He also upholds your life. Thank Him for every breath you take. Place your life in His hands because He is the One who gives you life. (***See God***> *God's Names> Holy Spirit> Gives Life,* TopicGuide page A19.)

105:1 The Lord is the Creator and Ruler of all nations, not merely Israel. It is the psalmist's hope that all nations will recognize the rule of God and praise Him accordingly. This hope is realized in the breaking forth of the gospel to the Gentiles following the death and resurrection of Jesus Christ.

▸ GOD
105:4 Search for God. What does it mean to "search for the LORD"? It means that we have a heart that continually desires His will and His ways. It means studying the Word to find out what He is like and how we can serve Him. It means going to Him in prayer many times a day, asking for His guidance, repenting of our sins, and adoring Him in worship. Our life's task is to walk more closely with Him each day. That search for a deeper relationship with Him is a never-ending joy. Make your search a one-step-at-a-time experience. Begin by dedicating your waking moments to communicating with Him. Be sure that a major part of this interaction is spent in awe of Him. (***See God***> *Relationship> God Enables> Relationship with God requires worship,* TopicGuide page A14.)

105:7-11 The Lord is faithful to His word. He keeps the promises He makes to His people. The Lord entered into a covenant relationship with Abraham and his descendants through whom the whole earth would be blessed (Genesis 12:1-3). The Lord fulfilled (and is still fulfilling) all the promises He made to Abraham.

105:8 Gen 22:16-18 Deut 7:9 Luke 1:72

8 He always stands by His covenant—
the commitment He made to a thousand generations.
9 This is the covenant He made with Abraham
and the oath He swore to Isaac.

105:10 Gen 28:13-15 Josh 23:4

10 He confirmed it to Jacob as a decree,
and to the people of Israel as a never-ending covenant:

105:11 Gen 13:15; 15:18

11 "I will give you the land of Canaan
as your special possession."

105:12 Gen 34:30 Heb 11:9

12 He said this when they were few in number,
a tiny group of strangers in Canaan.
13 They wandered from nation to nation,
from one kingdom to another.

105:14 Gen 12:17; 35:5

14 Yet He did not let anyone oppress them.
He warned kings on their behalf:
15 "Do not touch My chosen people,
and do not hurt My prophets."

105:16 Lev 26:26 Isa 3:1 Ezek 4:16

16 He called for a famine on the land of Canaan,
cutting off its food supply.
17 Then He sent someone to Egypt ahead of them—
Joseph, who was sold as a slave.

105:17 Gen 37:28, 36 Acts 7:9

18 They bruised his feet with fetters
and placed his neck in an iron collar.

105:19 Ps 66:10

19 Until the time came to fulfill his dreams,*
the LORD tested Joseph's character.

105:20 Gen 41:14

20 Then Pharaoh sent for him and set him free;
the ruler of the nation opened his prison door.
21 Joseph was put in charge of all the king's household;
he became ruler over all the king's possessions.
22 He could instruct the king's aides as he pleased
and teach the king's advisers.

23 Then Israel arrived in Egypt;
Jacob lived as a foreigner in the land of Ham.

105:24 Exod 1:7, 9

24 And the LORD multiplied the people of Israel
until they became too mighty for their enemies.

105:25 Exod 1:8 Acts 7:19

25 Then He turned the Egyptians against the Israelites,
and they plotted against the LORD's servants.

105:26 Exod 3:10 Num 16:5

26 But the LORD sent His servant Moses,
along with Aaron, whom He had chosen.

105:19 Hebrew *his word.*

▸ PURPOSE

105:15 God's promise to the people. In Old Testament days, God sent prophets to His people. These prophets warned the people to turn from their sins. If the people repented, God delivered them from judgment. If the people didn't repent, they faced judgment. Many times, God's people rejected the prophets' stern message from God and even harmed the prophets. That meant they had to stand before God's justice and answer for their rejection of God's messengers. God offers us the same promise. If we repent of our sins and receive God's final messenger—Jesus Christ—God will deliver us from judgment (see Romans 8:1-2). It's our choice.

(***See Purpose**> God's Deeds> Judgment> Deliverance from judgment,* TopicGuide page A54.)

105:16-22 Through Joseph, the Lord prepared in Egypt a refuge for the family of Abraham during a time of famine. During his time in Egypt, Joseph was protected and blessed by the Lord in spite of numerous ordeals and hardships (Genesis 38–50).

27 They performed miraculous signs among the Egyptians,
and wonders in the land of Ham.
28 The LORD blanketed Egypt in darkness,
for they had defied His commands to let His people go.
29 He turned their water into blood,
poisoning all the fish.
30 Then frogs overran the land
and even invaded the king's bedrooms.
31 When the LORD spoke, flies descended on the Egyptians,
and gnats swarmed across Egypt.
32 He sent them hail instead of rain,
and lightning flashed over the land.
33 He ruined their grapevines and fig trees
and shattered all the trees.
34 He spoke, and hordes of locusts came—
young locusts beyond number.
35 They ate up everything green in the land,
destroying all the crops in their fields.
36 Then He killed the oldest son in each Egyptian home,
the pride and joy of each family.

37 The LORD brought His people out of Egypt, loaded
with silver and gold;
and not one among the tribes of Israel even stumbled.
38 Egypt was glad when they were gone,
for they feared them greatly.
39 The LORD spread a cloud above them as a covering
and gave them a great fire to light the darkness.
40 They asked for meat, and He sent them quail;
He satisfied their hunger with manna—bread from heaven.
41 He split open a rock, and water gushed out
to form a river through the dry wasteland.
42 For He remembered His sacred promise
to His servant Abraham.
43 So He brought His people out of Egypt with joy,
His chosen ones with rejoicing.
44 He gave His people the lands of pagan nations,
and they harvested crops that others had planted.
45 All this happened so they would follow His decrees
and obey His instructions.

Praise the LORD!

105:27 Ps 78:43-51
105:28 Exod 10:22
105:29 Exod 7:20
105:30 Exod 8:6
105:31 Exod 8:16, 21
105:32 Exod 9:23
105:36 Exod 12:29-30
105:37 Exod 12:33
105:39 Neh 9:12; Isa 4:5
105:40 Num 11:31; John 6:31
105:41 Exod 17:6; Ps 78:15; 1 Cor 10:4
105:43 Exod 15:1
105:44 Josh 13:7
105:45 Deut 4:40

PSALM 106

1 Praise the LORD!

Give thanks to the LORD, for He is good!
His faithful love endures forever.

106:1 1 Chr 16:34, 41; Pss 100:4-5; 105:1

105:42 The language of remembrance involves more than mere mental recall; it is language that calls on God to fulfill His promises and save His people (Genesis 8:1; Leviticus 26:42). The mighty acts of God for His people, so eloquently recounted by the psalmist, flowed from God's faithfulness to His word.

106:1-2 The psalm opens and closes with a call to praise God. The impetus to praise Him arises from the remembrance of His mighty acts. The psalmist recounts the many ways in which God actively intervened in the history of Israel. These mighty acts of deliverance flowed from God's goodness and love.

2 Who can list the glorious miracles of the LORD?
Who can ever praise Him enough?
106:3 Ps 15:2 — 3 There is joy for those who deal justly with others
and always do what is right.

106:4 Ps 44:3 — 4 Remember me, LORD, when You show favor to Your people;
come near and rescue me.
106:5 Pss 1:3; 118:15 — 5 Let me share in the prosperity of Your chosen ones.
Let me rejoice in the joy of Your people;
let me praise You with those who are Your heritage.

106:6 2 Chr 30:7 Ezra 9:7 Neh 1:7 Zech 1:4 — 6 Like our ancestors, we have sinned.
We have done wrong! We have acted wickedly!
7 Our ancestors in Egypt
were not impressed by the LORD's miraculous deeds.
106:7 Judg 3:7 — They soon forgot His many acts of kindness to them.
Instead, they rebelled against Him at the Red Sea.*
106:8 Ezek 20:9 — 8 Even so, He saved them—
to defend the honor of His name
and to demonstrate His mighty power.
106:9 Exod 14:21 Isa 63:11-13 — 9 He commanded the Red Sea* to dry up.
He led Israel across the sea as if it were a desert.
10 So He rescued them from their enemies
and redeemed them from their foes.
106:11 Exod 15:5 — 11 Then the water returned and covered their enemies;
not one of them survived.
12 Then His people believed His promises.
Then they sang His praise.

13 Yet how quickly they forgot what He had done!
They wouldn't wait for His counsel!
106:14 Num 11:4 — 14 In the wilderness their desires ran wild,
testing God's patience in that dry wasteland.
106:15 Ps 78:29-31 — 15 So He gave them what they asked for,
but He sent a plague along with it.
106:16 Num 16:1-3 — 16 The people in the camp were jealous of Moses
and envious of Aaron, the LORD's holy priest.
106:17 Deut 11:6 — 17 Because of this, the earth opened up;
it swallowed Dathan
and buried Abiram and the other rebels.
106:18 Num 16:35 — 18 Fire fell upon their followers;
a flame consumed the wicked.

106:19 Acts 7:41 — 19 The people made a calf at Mount Sinai*;
they bowed before an image made of gold.
106:20 Jer 2:11 Rom 1:23 — 20 They traded their glorious God
for a statue of a grass-eating bull.
106:21 Deut 10:21 — 21 They forgot God, their savior,
who had done such great things in Egypt—

106:7 Hebrew *at the sea, the sea of reeds.* 106:9 Hebrew *sea of reeds;* also in 106:22. 106:19 Hebrew *at Horeb,* another name for Sinai.

106:19-23 The Israelites substituted the glory of the invisible God for an idol made of gold (Deuteronomy 9:7-29). Their idolatry was all the more shameful in that it followed so closely their miraculous deliverance from Egypt and the giving of the law, which forbade the making of images to represent God (Exodus 20:4-6). Moses bravely interceded for Israel and secured God's mercy toward the nation.

22 such wonderful things in the land of Ham,
such awesome deeds at the Red Sea.
23 So He declared He would destroy them.
But Moses, His chosen one, stepped between the LORD
and the people.
He begged Him to turn from His anger and
not destroy them.

24 The people refused to enter the pleasant land,
for they wouldn't believe His promise to care for them.
25 Instead, they grumbled in their tents
and refused to obey the LORD.
26 Therefore, He solemnly swore
that He would kill them in the wilderness,
27 that He would scatter their descendants among the nations,
exiling them to distant lands.

28 Then our ancestors joined in the worship of Baal at Peor;
they even ate sacrifices offered to the dead!
29 They angered the LORD with all these things,
so a plague broke out among them.
30 But Phinehas had the courage to intervene,
and the plague was stopped.
31 So he has been regarded as a righteous man
ever since that time.

32 At Meribah, too, they angered the LORD,
causing Moses serious trouble.
33 They made Moses angry,*
and he spoke foolishly.

34 Israel failed to destroy the nations in the land,
as the LORD had commanded them.
35 Instead, they mingled among the pagans
and adopted their evil customs.
36 They worshiped their idols,
which led to their downfall.

106:22 Ps 105:27
106:23 Exod 32:10-14
106:24 Jer 3:19
106:26 Heb 3:11
106:28 Hos 9:10
106:30 Num 25:7-13
106:32 Ps 78:40
106:34 Judg 1:21, 27-36

106:33 Hebrew *They embittered his spirit.*

▸ PURPOSE
106:28 Deliverance from judgment. What is the most devastating sin you have committed? Do you think God has forgiven you for it? By faith, He has! We can see this through the lives of the Hebrew people. They committed a sin that seemed unforgivable—the Israelite men married women who worshiped idols. Then they began bowing to the idols along with their wives. God sent a plague upon the people as an act of judgment. Phinehas, a high priest, rid the camp of two offending people, and because of his zealous action God stopped the plague (Numbers 25). When we cleanse our lives of sin, God also delivers us from judgment. Our cleansing comes through the actions of Jesus Christ, our Deliverer. Have you accepted God's deliverance through trust in Jesus Christ? (***See Purpose****> God's Deeds> Judgment> Deliverance from judgment,* TopicGuide page A54.)

106:34-39 Once they entered Canaan, the Israelites failed to drive out all of the inhabitants of the land as they had been instructed (Joshua 13:1-7; Judges 2:1-3). Israel's accommodation to surrounding pagan cultures inevitably resulted in apostasy and corruption. Israel adopted the very practices that had condemned the previous inhabitants of the land in the eyes of God.

▸ SPIRITUAL WARFARE
106:36 False worship. Did you know that a person can participate in false worship? When we worship anything other than God, we are honoring Satan, God's enemy. In Old Testament times, the people bowed down before idols and adopted the religious customs of people living around them. We do the same thing today. We may not worship physical idols of wood and stone, but we do bow down before the world's ideas. We make materialism our central goal or unquestionably accept evolutionary theory. Anything we believe that takes the place of God in our lives becomes an idol. Any sinful behavior allows Satan influence over us. Search your life. Are you participating in false worship? Repent right now of anything that serves Satan's purposes. (***See Spiritual Warfare****> Originator of Sin> Satan's Domain> Receives false worship,* TopicGuide page A44.)

106:37 2 Kgs 17:17
[37] They even sacrificed their sons
and their daughters to the demons.
[38] They shed innocent blood,
the blood of their sons and daughters.
By sacrificing them to the idols of Canaan,
they polluted the land with murder.
106:39 Hos 4:12
[39] They defiled themselves by their evil deeds,
and their love of idols was adultery in the LORD's sight.

106:40 Judg 2:12-14
[40] That is why the LORD's anger burned against His people,
and He abhorred His own special possession.
106:41 Neh 9:27
[41] He handed them over to pagan nations,
and they were ruled by those who hated them.
[42] Their enemies crushed them
and brought them under their cruel power.
106:43 Judg 6:6 Ps 81:12
[43] Again and again He rescued them,
but they chose to rebel against Him,
and they were finally destroyed by their sin.
[44] Even so, He pitied them in their distress
and listened to their cries.
106:45 Lev 26:42
[45] He remembered His covenant with them
and relented because of His unfailing love.
106:46 2 Chr 30:9 Ezra 9:9
[46] He even caused their captors
to treat them with kindness.

106:47-48 //1 Chr 16:34-36
[47] Save us, O LORD our God!
Gather us back from among the nations,
so we can thank Your holy name
and rejoice and praise You.

[48] Praise the LORD, the God of Israel,
who lives from everlasting to everlasting!
Let all the people say, "Amen!"

Praise the LORD!

BOOK FIVE (PSALMS 107–150)

PSALM 107

107:1 Ps 106:1
[1] Give thanks to the LORD, for He is good!
His faithful love endures forever.
107:2 Isa 35:9-10
[2] Has the LORD redeemed you? Then speak out!
Tell others He has redeemed you from your enemies.
107:3 Neh 1:9 Ps 106:47 Ezek 20:34
[3] For He has gathered the exiles from many lands,
from east and west,
from north and south.

▸ MINISTRY
107:2 Speak out for God! Why do we witness for Christ? Because He has redeemed us. That is our motivation for telling the world the Good News. We want to share with everyone our joy and our relationship with God. He has saved us from our greatest enemies—Satan and eternal death. How can we do any less than spread the message about God's love to everyone we know? Just as God delivered the Israelites from their enemies in the Promised Land, He has given us victory through Jesus Christ (1 Corinthians 15:57). Thank Him for His mighty deliverance by telling others about Jesus. (***See Ministry***> *Great Commission*> *Witness*> *Turn others from Satan to God,* TopicGuide page A56.)

4 Some wandered in the wilderness,
lost and homeless.
5 Hungry and thirsty,
they nearly died.
6 "LORD, help!" they cried in their trouble,
and He rescued them from their distress.
7 He led them straight to safety,
to a city where they could live.
8 Let them praise the LORD for His great love
and for the wonderful things He has done
for them.
9 For He satisfies the thirsty
and fills the hungry with good things.

10 Some sat in darkness and deepest gloom,
imprisoned in iron chains of misery.
11 They rebelled against the words of God,
scorning the counsel of the Most High.
12 That is why He broke them with hard labor;
they fell, and no one was there to help them.
13 "LORD, help!" they cried in their trouble,
and He saved them from their distress.
14 He led them from the darkness and deepest gloom;
He snapped their chains.
15 Let them praise the LORD for His great love
and for the wonderful things He has done for them.
16 For He broke down their prison gates of bronze;
He cut apart their bars of iron.

17 Some were fools; they rebelled
and suffered for their sins.
18 They couldn't stand the thought of food,
and they were knocking on death's door.
19 "LORD, help!" they cried in their trouble,
and He saved them from their distress.
20 He sent out His word and healed them,
snatching them from the door of death.
21 Let them praise the LORD for His great love
and for the wonderful things He has done
for them.
22 Let them offer sacrifices of thanksgiving
and sing joyfully about His glorious acts.

107:4 Josh 5:6
107:7 Jer 31:9
107:9 Matt 5:6; Luke 1:53
107:10 Mic 7:8-9; Luke 1:79
107:11 Num 15:31
107:14 Ps 116:16; Acts 12:7
107:16 Isa 45:1-2
107:17 Isa 65:6-7; Ezek 24:23
107:18 Job 33:19-22; Pss 9:13; 88:3
107:20 2 Kgs 20:5; Matt 8:8
107:22 Lev 7:12; Pss 9:11; 50:14; 73:28; 118:17

107:4-9 This is the first of four stanzas illustrating God's ability and willingness to deliver those who call on His name. The psalmist may be envisioning the Exile as a time of aimless wandering through a wasteland or he may be describing the return journey through the deserts of the Middle East. When the lost cried out to God, He provided a path to safety. (See Isaiah 58:10-11 for God's promise of guidance and satisfaction.) In 107:8, the psalmist calls on those who experienced God's salvation to praise and glorify the Lord publicly. "Great love" (elsewhere translated "unfailing love") refers to God's faithfulness to the promises made to His people. (See also 107:15, 21, and 31.)

107:10-16 It was not clear that those who wandered in the wilderness in the first stanza did so because of their sin, but that is explicitly stated to be the case for the prisoners in the second stanza. But their hardship caused them to repent, and when they cried out to God He heard their prayers (see Isaiah 42:6-8).

107:17-22 In the third stanza, the people's suffering is linked once again to their sin. Rebellion against God is the ultimate act of foolishness. But even these fools were brought to repentance by the experience of God's judgment, and God in His great love heard their cries and saved them from death.

23 Some went off to sea in ships,
plying the trade routes of the world.
24 They, too, observed the LORD's power in action,
His impressive works on the deepest seas.
107:25 25 He spoke, and the winds rose,
Ps 93:3-4 stirring up the waves.
26 Their ships were tossed to the heavens
and plunged again to the depths;
the sailors cringed in terror.
27 They reeled and staggered like drunkards
and were at their wits' end.
28 "LORD, help!" they cried in their trouble,
and He saved them from their distress.
107:29 29 He calmed the storm to a whisper
Matt 8:26 and stilled the waves.
Luke 8:24
30 What a blessing was that stillness
as He brought them safely into harbor!
31 Let them praise the LORD for His great love
and for the wonderful things He has done
for them.
107:32 32 Let them exalt Him publicly before the congregation
Ps 22:22, 25 and before the leaders of the nation.
Isa 25:1

33 He changes rivers into deserts,
and springs of water into dry, thirsty land.
107:34 34 He turns the fruitful land into salty wastelands,
Gen 19:24-25 because of the wickedness of those who live there.
107:35 35 But He also turns deserts into pools of water,
Isa 35:6-7; 41:18 the dry land into springs of water.
36 He brings the hungry to settle there
and to build their cities.
107:37 37 They sow their fields, plant their vineyards,
2 Kgs 19:29 and harvest their bumper crops.
Amos 9:14
38 How He blesses them!
107:38 They raise large families there,
Gen 12:2
Exod 1:7 and their herds of livestock increase.

39 When they decrease in number and become impoverished
through oppression, trouble, and sorrow,
40 the LORD pours contempt on their princes,
causing them to wander in trackless wastelands.
41 But He rescues the poor from trouble
107:42 and increases their families like flocks of sheep.
Job 22:19
Ps 52:6 42 The godly will see these things and be glad,
Rom 3:19 while the wicked are struck silent.
107:43 43 Those who are wise will take all this to heart;
Ps 64:9
Jer 9:12 they will see in our history the faithful love
Hos 14:9 of the LORD.

107:23-32 The fourth stanza returns to the experience of peril not directly linked to disobedience. The psalmist dramatically portrays the danger of those cast about by the raging seas. In their fear, they called out to God, and He calmed the seas and led them safely to port. These verses are reminiscent of the experience of Jonah and the disciples (Jonah 1–2; Matthew 8:23-27).

PSALM 108

A song. A psalm of David.

1 My heart is confident in You, O God;
no wonder I can sing Your praises with
all my heart!
2 Wake up, lyre and harp!
I will wake the dawn with my song.
3 I will thank You, LORD, among all the people.
I will sing Your praises among the nations.
4 For Your unfailing love is higher than the heavens.
Your faithfulness reaches to the clouds.
5 Be exalted, O God, above the highest heavens.
May Your glory shine over all the earth.

6 Now rescue Your beloved people.
Answer and save us by Your power.
7 God has promised this by His holiness*:
"I will divide up Shechem with joy.
I will measure out the valley of Succoth.
8 Gilead is Mine,
and Manasseh, too.
Ephraim, My helmet, will produce My warriors,
and Judah, My scepter, will produce My kings.
9 But Moab, My washbasin, will become My servant,
and I will wipe My feet on Edom
and shout in triumph over Philistia."

10 Who will bring me into the fortified city?
Who will bring me victory over Edom?
11 Have You rejected us, O God?
Will You no longer march with our armies?
12 Oh, please help us against our enemies,
for all human help is useless.
13 With God's help we will do mighty things,
for He will trample down our foes.

108:1-5 //Ps 57:7-11

108:4 Ps 113:4

108:6-13 //Ps 60:5-12

108:11 Ps 44:9

108:7 Or *in His sanctuary.*

▸ WORSHIP
108:2 Awake the dawn. Have you ever opened your eyes from a night of sleep and immediately started worshiping God? The moment we open our eyes, we can begin to tell Him how much we love Him. You could pray something like this: "Oh, Lord, you have given me another day. I appreciate every breath of life You allow me to have. You have provided me with another opportunity to walk with You. How much I love You! You are the center of my heart!" If this sort of expression sounds a little strange to you, ask yourself why it seems so. (***See Worship****> OT> God's Supremacy> Was God-centered (not worshiper-centered),* TopicGuide page A27.)

108:2 David is not awakened by the dawn; rather, his praise calls the dawn forth. The dawning of a new day symbolized the triumph of God over the wickedness embodied in the darkness of night. Elsewhere in the Psalms, dawn is the time of God's appearing to rescue His people (46:5; 90:13).

108:7 "By His holiness" is also rendered "in His sanctuary" (see textual note). The song of victory that follows is the word of God delivered by a prophet or priest from the sanctuary in response to David's plea for help.

108:7-8 These verses recall the division of Canaan among the tribes of Israel following the conquest of the land. Shechem and Succoth lay on either side of the Jordan in central Israel (both were associated with Jacob, Genesis 33:17-20). Gilead, Manasseh, and Ephraim were all located in northern Israel and partially across the Jordan. Judah lay in southern Israel.

108:9 Moab, Edom, and Philistia were minor kingdoms that surrounded Israel from the southeast to the west. These nations were subjected to Israel during the reigns of David and Solomon.

PSALM 109

For the choir director: A psalm of David.

109:1 Ps 83:1 [1] O God, whom I praise,
don't stand silent and aloof
109:2 Pss 52:4; 120:2 [2] while the wicked slander me
and tell lies about me.
109:3 Ps 69:4 [3] They surround me with hateful words
and fight against me for no reason.
109:4 Ps 38:20 [4] I love them, but they try to destroy me with accusations
even as I am praying for them!
109:5 John 7:7 [5] They repay evil for good,
and hatred for my love.

109:6 Zech 3:1 [6] They say,* "Get an evil person to turn against him.
Send an accuser to bring him to trial.
109:7 Prov 28:9 [7] When his case comes up for judgment,
let him be pronounced guilty.
Count his prayers as sins.
109:8 *Acts 1:20 [8] Let his years be few;
let someone else take his position.
109:9 Exod 22:24 [9] May his children become fatherless,
and his wife a widow.
[10] May his children wander as beggars
and be driven from their ruined homes.
109:11 Isa 1:7 [11] May creditors seize his entire estate,
and strangers take all he has earned.
109:12 Isa 9:17 [12] Let no one be kind to him;
let no one pity his fatherless children.
[13] May all his offspring die.
May his family name be blotted out in a single generation.
109:14 Neh 4:5 Isa 65:6-7 [14] May the LORD never forget the sins of his fathers;
may his mother's sins never be erased from the record.
109:15 Jer 16:17 [15] May the LORD always remember these sins,
and may his name disappear from human memory.
109:16 Ps 37:32 [16] For he refused all kindness to others;
he persecuted the poor and needy,
and he hounded the brokenhearted to death.

109:6 Hebrew lacks *They say.*

▸ WORSHIP

109:4-5 Love your enemies. In this psalm, David shows us how he applied a biblical principle—loving one's enemies—in his life. Even though he cried out to God about what others were doing to him, he still prayed for them. In doing so, David was reflecting the kind of love God has for us. When we were His enemies and didn't accept His love for us, He still loved us. That's how He expects us to treat our enemies. Who has returned evil for your good in your life? What was your reaction? Ask God to give you a love for your enemies and an honest prayer for their improvement. (***See Worship***> *OT> Music> Psalms> Lament> Retaliation,* TopicGuide page A27.)

109:6-20 David recounts the curses called against him by his accuser. This section fleshes out the "evil" spoken against David in 109:5.

109:6-15 David's accuser calls for covenant curses to be activated against him. The curses extend to the man's wife and children, his possessions, his place in the memory of the community, and the spiritual state of his family. These have some historic similarities to the condition of Saul and his family after his downfall (1 Samuel 31; 1 Chronicles 10).

109:16-20 The accuser continues his smear campaign by claiming that David cruelly oppressed the poor and needy. He claimed David lived a life animated by hate rather than love. By contrast, God loved David deeply (109:21) and when He vindicated him, it moved David to joy (109:28).

17 He loved to curse others;
now you curse him.
He never blessed others;
now don't you bless him.
18 Cursing is as natural to him as his clothing,
or the water he drinks,
or the rich food he eats.
19 Now may his curses return and cling to him
like clothing;
may they be tied around him like a belt."

20 May those curses become the LORD's punishment
for my accusers who speak evil of me.
21 But deal well with me, O Sovereign LORD,
for the sake of Your own reputation!
Rescue me
because You are so faithful and good.
22 For I am poor and needy,
and my heart is full of pain.
23 I am fading like a shadow at dusk;
I am brushed off like a locust.
24 My knees are weak from fasting,
and I am skin and bones.
25 I am a joke to people everywhere;
when they see me, they shake their heads
in scorn.

26 Help me, O LORD my God!
Save me because of Your unfailing love.
27 Let them see that this is Your doing,
that You Yourself have done it, LORD.
28 Then let them curse me if they like,
but You will bless me!
When they attack me, they will be disgraced!
But I, Your servant, will go right on rejoicing!
29 May my accusers be clothed with disgrace;
may their humiliation cover them like a cloak.
30 But I will give repeated thanks to the LORD,
praising Him to everyone.
31 For He stands beside the needy,
ready to save them from those who
condemn them.

109:17 Matt 7:2
109:18 Ps 73:6
109:19 Ezek 7:27
109:20 Isa 3:11; 2 Tim 4:14
109:21 Ps 25:11; Ezek 36:22
109:22 Ps 40:17; Prov 18:14
109:24 Heb 12:12
109:26 Ps 119:86
109:28 2 Sam 16:11-12
109:29 Job 8:22; Ps 35:26
109:30 Ps 35:18
109:31 Pss 16:8; 37:33

▶ WORSHIP
109:24 Dealing with the impossible. At times, David despaired of his very life. When his enemies were hunting him, he had to hide in caves to thwart their aim to kill him. The future looked bleak. He had been anointed king, but he had no kingdom to rule (1 Samuel 23:14). How did David respond to his situation? He fasted and prayed, asking God to help him. And God did! Eventually, David served as king over the whole nation. What in your future seems unsolvable? God knows about it and wants to give you the wisdom and strength to deal with the problem. If God could help David, He can help you, too! Begin by undertaking a fast for your situation. During your fast, pray for your enemies and trust God for the solution to your problem. (See 1 Samuel 23:14; also ***see Worship****> OT> Fasting and Prayer> Fasting> Occasions> Fasting for enemies,* TopicGuide page A26.)

109:27-29 David confidently expects God to reverse all the harm done by his enemies. They are seeking to humiliate David, but it is they who ultimately will be shamed by God's judgment. The language of curse and blessing is reminiscent of God's promise to Abraham: "I will bless those who bless you and curse those who treat you with contempt" (Genesis 12:3).

PSALM 110

A psalm of David.

110:1 *Matt 22:44 *Mark 12:36; 14:62 *Luke 20:42 *Acts 2:34 *Heb 1:13

1 The LORD said to my Lord,
"Sit in the place of honor at My right hand
until I humble Your enemies,
making them a footstool under Your feet."

110:2 Ps 45:6 Dan 7:13-14

2 The LORD will extend Your powerful kingdom from Jerusalem*;
You will rule over Your enemies.

110:3 Judg 5:2 Ps 96:9

3 When You go to war,
Your people will serve You willingly.
You are arrayed in holy garments,
and Your strength will be renewed each day like the morning dew.

110:4 *Heb 5:6; 7:17, 21

4 The LORD has taken an oath and will not break His vow:
"You are a priest forever in the order of Melchizedek."

110:5 Pss 2:5, 12; 16:8 Rom 2:5 Rev 6:17

5 The Lord stands at Your right hand to protect You.
He will strike down many kings when His anger erupts.
6 He will punish the nations
and fill their lands with corpses;
He will shatter heads over the whole earth.
7 But He Himself will be refreshed from brooks along the way.
He will be victorious.

PSALM 111*

111:1 Ps 138:1

1 Praise the LORD!

I will thank the LORD with all my heart
as I meet with His godly people.

111:2 Ps 92:5

2 How amazing are the deeds of the LORD!
All who delight in Him should ponder them.

110:2 Hebrew *Zion.* 111 This psalm is a Hebrew acrostic poem; after the introductory note of praise, each line begins with a successive letter of the Hebrew alphabet.

110:1a God is referred to by His divine name, *Yahweh,* which is translated "LORD." God addresses the Davidic king, who is designated by a title of honor translated "Lord." The New Testament makes clear that this passage found its fulfillment in Jesus Christ, whom David rightly recognized as Lord even though he himself was a king (Mark 12:35-37).

110:1b God promised to establish the rule of the Davidic king. The right hand was a place of honor and privilege. The enemies of the king would be thoroughly subjugated. The footstool image is derived from the practice of Near Eastern monarchs placing their feet on the necks of defeated enemies. In the psalm's immediate context, the enemies were the hostile nations that surrounded Israel. In its fullest sense, however, the psalm envisions the complete subjugation of all creation to the messianic King, Christ Jesus (1 Corinthians 15:25; Ephesians 1:20-23).

▶ GOD

110:4 Jesus is our High Priest. Whenever Scripture tells us that the Lord takes a vow, we can be assured that the promise is secure. Hebrews 7:21-22 says that Jesus is the High Priest spoken about in this psalm. He guarantees our salvation because He lives forever. The other priests in the Old Testament Temple system served until they died. Then their position passed on to their sons. Because Christ rose again from the dead, He lives forever. His position never passes on. Right now, He is before God's throne, serving as your Advocate. Keep this in mind as you confront your daily struggles: Jesus is praying for you. (See Hebrews 7:21-22; also ***see God****> God's Names> Son> Advocate/Intercessor,* TopicGuide page A19.)

110:4 Melchizedek functioned as both a priest and king of the ancient city of Salem (Genesis 14:18-20). The psalmist envisions the blending of the offices of king and priest in one person. This expectation could be applied rightly to David, who dressed in the garb of the priesthood and officiated as a priest (2 Samuel 6:14-18). However, David was merely a shadow of Christ, in whom the two offices would be united forever (Hebrews 5:6-10; 7:22).

110:5-6 The messianic Priest-King will be God's instrument of judgment against the nations (compare Psalm 2:5, 12; Isaiah 13:9, 13; Zephaniah 2:3). The fulfillment of this hope will take place when Christ returns to establish His kingdom.

111:2-3 The praise of God's people centers on the great works of God. The Lord is no distant deity without care or concern for His people. He is a God of righteous compassion who actively intervenes in history for His people. The mighty acts of God reveal His character and elicit wonder from His own.

3 Everything He does reveals His glory and majesty.
His righteousness never fails.
4 He causes us to remember His wonderful works.
How gracious and merciful is our LORD!
5 He gives food to those who fear Him;
He always remembers His covenant.
6 He has shown His great power to His people
by giving them the lands of other nations.
7 All He does is just and good,
and all His commandments are trustworthy.
8 They are forever true,
to be obeyed faithfully and with integrity.
9 He has paid a full ransom for His people.
He has guaranteed His covenant with them forever.
What a holy, awe-inspiring name He has!
10 Fear of the LORD is the foundation of true wisdom.
All who obey His commandments will grow in wisdom.

Praise Him forever!

111:3 Pss 96:6; 145:5
111:4 Pss 86:15; 103:8
111:5 Matt 6:31-33
111:7 Ps 19:7-9; Rev 15:3-4
111:8 Isa 40:8; Matt 5:18
111:9 Ps 99:3; Luke 1:68
111:10 Prov 1:7, 9; 3:4-5; 9:10

PSALM 112*

1 Praise the LORD!

How joyful are those who fear the LORD
and delight in obeying His commands.
2 Their children will be successful everywhere;
an entire generation of godly people will be blessed.

112:1 Ps 119:16
112:2 Ps 25:13

112 This psalm is a Hebrew acrostic poem; after the introductory note of praise, each line begins with a successive letter of the Hebrew alphabet.

111:4-6 The psalmist seems to have the Exodus, the wilderness wandering, and the conquest of Canaan in mind when he calls on the people to memorialize the wonders of God. Through awe-inspiring wonders God rescued Israel from Egypt. The attributes of mercy and grace are particularly associated with God's revelation to Moses (Exodus 34:6). He fed them as they wandered through the wilderness. And He led them in the conquest of Canaan.

111:7-8 God reveals Himself through His law as well as through His acts in history. The law of God is holy, righteous, and true, and it reveals God to be the same (Romans 7:12).

▶ BIBLE
111:10 The beginning of wisdom. Wisdom is something on which the world thinks it has a corner. If a person graduates with a Ph.D., the world considers him wise. A business tycoon is given special honors for the same reason. Parents tell their children, "Get an education and you'll make something of yourself." But none of the world's ways produce real wisdom. An esteemed professor may be a poor spouse and parent. A CEO can end up bankrupt. Educated children may ruin their lives with substance abuse. Go to God's Word. It teaches us to honor and obey God. He will lead us to be wise and understanding. (***See Bible****> Power> Wisdom> The beginning of wisdom is obedience to Scripture,* TopicGuide page A11.)

▶ WORSHIP
111:10 Awe and obedience. Jeffrey played Little League baseball after school. Each day when he arrived at practice, he ran up to his coach with a question. To Jeffrey, his coach was a source of awe. Everything the coach did, Jeffrey imitated. He watched his coach during each practice session. We can take a lesson from Jeffrey by developing an awe for our Lord and Savior. He is so much more than a coach to us—He is our source of everything. Our awe leads us to obey Him in everything. Are you obeying God out of a sense of awe? Approach Him in prayer, asking Him to give you a heart of obedience springing from your wonder of Him. (***See Worship****> OT> Reverence> Awe of God means obeying His commandments,* TopicGuide page A28.)

▶ HOLINESS
112:1 How to find happiness. What do people do to find happiness? They try to make more money. They buy coveted possessions. They travel the world. They plan for early retirement. But this kind of happiness only lasts for a season. True happiness comes from obeying God's moral laws. These moral laws, found in the Bible, are as important as scientific laws. For example, a person may be wealthy yet find himself in terrible physical shape because of immoral living. Someone may own many homes and cars and yet be lonely because he has alienated his family and friends. God gave us His moral laws because they work for our benefit. Read the Ten Commandments in Exodus 20 to find the basis for God's moral laws. Make yourself happy by delighting in God's commands. (***See Holiness****> Law and Grace> Law> The moral law of God,* TopicGuide page A41.)

112:3 Prov 3:16-17; 8:18
3 They themselves will be wealthy,
and their good deeds will last forever.
112:4 Job 11:17 Ps 97:11
4 Light shines in the darkness for the godly.
They are generous, compassionate, and righteous.
112:5 Ps 37:21, 26
5 Good comes to those who lend money generously
and conduct their business fairly.
112:6 Pss 15:5; 55:22
6 Such people will not be overcome by evil.
Those who are righteous will be long remembered.
112:7 Ps 56:4
7 They do not fear bad news;
they confidently trust the LORD to care for them.
112:8 Ps 56:10-11
8 They are confident and fearless
and can face their foes triumphantly.
112:9 Ps 148:14 *2 Cor 9:9
9 They share freely and give generously to those in need.
Their good deeds will be remembered forever.
They will have influence and honor.
112:10 Matt 8:12 Luke 13:28
10 The wicked will see this and be infuriated.
They will grind their teeth in anger;
they will slink away, their hopes thwarted.

PSALM 113

113:1 Ps 135:1
1 Praise the LORD!

Yes, give praise, O servants of the LORD.
Praise the name of the LORD!
113:2 Dan 2:20
2 Blessed be the name of the LORD
now and forever.
113:3 Ps 50:1
3 Everywhere—from east to west—
praise the name of the LORD.
113:4 Pss 8:1; 97:9; 99:2
4 For the LORD is high above the nations;
His glory is higher than the heavens.

113:5 Pss 89:6; 103:19
5 Who can be compared with the LORD our God,
who is enthroned on high?

112:4 Darkness serves as an evocative metaphor for trouble and tribulation. Yet darkness does not have the final word. The light of God's salvation ultimately will triumph. This verse also could be translated to suggest the righteous are the light in darkness, offering hope in troubled times by their compassion and generosity.

▸ GOD
112:5-7 Be generous. The psalmist tells us that generosity makes our lives run better. People will remember our generosity and think well of us. The generous won't have to look behind themselves to see if others who were hurt by their ungenerous acts are coming after them. The generous can face their foes because their consciences are clear. The generous also will receive honor for their good deeds. How generous are you? Will you reap the reward of the generous? (***See God****> God's Attributes> Good> All good comes from God,* TopicGuide page A16.)

112:9 The righteous freely share their blessedness with those who are needy and poor. The apostle Paul cited this verse when he encouraged believers to give liberally to the poor (2 Corinthians 9:9).

113:2 The praise of God focuses on His name. "The name of the LORD" is a reverential way of speaking of the various forms of God's self-revelation to His people, whether in His words or deeds. To praise the name of God is to praise Him for who He is and what He has done.

▸ MINISTRY
113:3 Praise the Lord everywhere. What are some places where you can praise God? Praise Him for His presence when you are alone in your bed. Praise Him for being the Creator in the morning when you wake up to the light of day. Praise Him for being the Provider when you are at your job. Praise Him for His protection when you travel on the freeway. Praise Him for good health when you are in the gym. Make it your practice to praise Him everywhere. (***See Ministry****> Transformation> Fill and Subdue> Influencing every sphere of life,* TopicGuide page A57.)

113:3 "From east to west" is a figure of speech intended to encompass the whole earth. The praise of God is not limited to the land of Israel. As the people of God expand throughout the world, so does the praise of God.

113:4-6 The God of Israel far transcends any earthly or even heavenly boundaries. The psalmist employs a rhetorical question to communicate the grandeur of God. The implied response is that no one can be compared to the Lord, for He is unique in His power and glory.

6 He stoops to look down
on heaven and on earth.
7 He lifts the poor from the dust
and the needy from the garbage dump.
8 He sets them among princes,
even the princes of His own people!
9 He gives the childless woman a family,
making her a happy mother.

Praise the LORD!

113:6 Ps 11:4; Isa 57:15
113:7 1 Sam 2:8
113:8 Job 36:7
113:9 1 Sam 2:5; Ps 68:6; Isa 54:1

PSALM 114

1 When the Israelites escaped from Egypt—
when the family of Jacob left that foreign land—
2 the land of Judah became God's sanctuary,
and Israel became His kingdom.

3 The Red Sea* saw them coming and hurried out of their way!
The water of the Jordan River turned away.
4 The mountains skipped like rams,
the hills like lambs!
5 What's wrong, Red Sea, that made you hurry out of their way?
What happened, Jordan River, that you turned away?
6 Why, mountains, did you skip like rams?
Why, hills, like lambs?

7 Tremble, O earth, at the presence of the Lord,
at the presence of the God of Jacob.
8 He turned the rock into a pool of water;
yes, a spring of water flowed from solid rock.

114:1 Exod 13:3
114:2 Exod 19:6; 29:45-46; Ps 78:68-69
114:3 Exod 14:21; Josh 3:13-14, 16
114:4 Ps 29:5-6; Hab 3:6
114:5 Hab 3:8
114:7 Ps 96:9
114:8 Exod 17:5-6; Deut 8:15

PSALM 115

1 Not to us, O LORD, not to us,
but to Your name goes all the glory
for Your unfailing love and faithfulness.
2 Why let the nations say,
"Where is their God?"

115:1 Ps 29:2; Isa 48:11; Ezek 36:22, 32
115:2 Pss 42:3; 79:10

114:3 Hebrew *the sea;* also in 114:5.

113:7-9 The transcendence of God does not render Him detached from His creation. God, who is above all things, condescends in His compassion to attend to the needs of the poor. Verses 7-8 are taken from Hannah's song (1 Samuel 2:8). Hannah was unable to bear children until God granted her a son, Samuel.

114:3-6 The Lord miraculously allowed Israel to cross over the Red Sea and the Jordan River on dry ground (Exodus 14–15; Joshua 3). The psalmist depicts the waters running away as a foe vanquished in battle. The mountains allude to the events at Mount Sinai (Exodus 19). The psalmist personifies the Red Sea, the Jordan River, and the mountains in order to express God's power over creation in the service of redemption.

▸ PURPOSE
114:7 Creation obeys God. Isn't it amazing how all of creation obeys God? We have some wonderful examples in Scripture. The Red Sea and the Jordan River parted at His command (114:3). The weather is at Jesus' command (Luke 8:22-25). The only part of creation that doesn't obey God without question is mankind. We are rebellious and hard-hearted, bent on rebellion. Yet if all the rest of creation obeys God, how much more should we do so? Let all creation inspire you to deeper obedience. (***See Purpose***> *God's Deeds*> *Special Acts*> *Miracles*> *OT*> *Red Sea divided,* TopicGuide page A52.)

114:8 At Horeb and Kadesh, the Lord miraculously provided water for His people as they journeyed through the wilderness (Exodus 17:6; Numbers 20:1-13).

115:1 The psalmist rightly makes the glory of God his preeminent concern. The love and faithfulness of God are character traits particularly related to His covenant with Israel. God's affection and loyalty to His people are everlasting because He remains true to His word.

115:3 3 Our God is in the heavens,
Pss 103:19; 135:6 and He does as He wishes.
Dan 4:35 4 Their idols are merely things of silver and gold,
115:4-11 //Ps 135:15-20 shaped by human hands.
115:5 5 They have mouths but cannot speak,
Jer 10:5 and eyes but cannot see.
6 They have ears but cannot hear,
and noses but cannot smell.
7 They have hands but cannot feel,
and feet but cannot walk,
and throats but cannot make a sound.
115:8 8 And those who make idols are just like them,
Ps 135:18 as are all who trust in them.

115:9 9 O Israel, trust the LORD!
Pss 33:20; 62:8 He is your helper and your shield.
10 O priests, descendants of Aaron, trust the LORD!
He is your helper and your shield.
115:11 11 All you who fear the LORD, trust the LORD!
Pss 103:11; 135:20 He is your helper and your shield.

115:12 12 The LORD remembers us and will bless us.
Ps 98:3 He will bless the people of Israel
and bless the priests, the descendants of Aaron.
115:13 13 He will bless those who fear the LORD,
Ps 128:1, 4 both great and lowly.

115:14 14 May the LORD richly bless
Deut 1:11 both you and your children.
115:15 15 May you be blessed by the LORD,
Gen 1:1; 14:19 who made heaven and earth.
115:16 16 The heavens belong to the LORD,
Pss 8:6; 89:11 but He has given the earth to all humanity.
115:17 17 The dead cannot sing praises to the LORD,
Pss 6:5; 31:17 for they have gone into the silence of the grave.
115:18 18 But we can praise the LORD
Ps 113:2 both now and forever!

Praise the LORD!

▸ GOD

115:3 It's God's prerogative. Have you ever questioned something God has allowed to happen in your life? Perhaps it was the death of a loved one, a serious accident, or a job reversal. It's not our place to inform God of our plans. We must be willing to accept His will for our lives. God rebuked Job, saying, "Who is this that questions My wisdom with such ignorant words?" (Job 38:2). God doesn't come to us for counsel on what to do. He is the source of wisdom and He acts on His own will. He does what He pleases. Allow God to be the Lord of your life and over all your circumstances. (***See God**> God's Nature> Personality> Will> God does whatever He pleases,* TopicGuide page A15.)

115:4-8 The psalmist lays bare the worthlessness of foreign gods. They are fashioned by human hands and are entirely powerless. Those who worship such idols are condemned to futility. The psalmist's stinging critique of idolatry echoes similar condemnations in Isaiah 44:9-20, Jeremiah 10:1-9, and Habakkuk 2:18-19.

115:9-11 At this point in the psalm, the one leading worship, most likely a priest, speaks directly to the people. He instructs them to place their trust in the Lord while reminding them the Lord is their source of strength and shelter. It is possible that "all you who fear the LORD" is a technical phrase designating Gentiles who have acknowledged the God of Israel.

▸ WORSHIP

115:13 Receiving blessings. Everyone wants to be blessed by God. But how can we receive that blessing? By giving God respect and reverence. When we honor God, our attitude opens channels of blessing for us. Our holy fear of Him enables us to live wisely (Job 28:28; Ecclesiastes 12:13). That also brings blessing. Practice reverence and respect for God throughout your day. (***See Worship**> OT> Reverence> He blesses those who revere Him,* TopicGuide page A29.)

PSALM 116

[1] I love the LORD because He hears my voice
and my prayer for mercy.
[2] Because He bends down to listen,
I will pray as long as I have breath!
[3] Death wrapped its ropes around me;
the terrors of the grave* overtook me.
I saw only trouble and sorrow.
[4] Then I called on the name of the LORD:
"Please, LORD, save me!"
[5] How kind the LORD is! How good He is!
So merciful, this God of ours!
[6] The LORD protects those of childlike faith;
I was facing death, and He saved me.
[7] Let my soul be at rest again,
for the LORD has been good to me.
[8] He has saved me from death,
my eyes from tears,
my feet from stumbling.
[9] And so I walk in the LORD's presence
as I live here on earth!
[10] I believed in You, so I said,
"I am deeply troubled, LORD."
[11] In my anxiety I cried out to You,
"These people are all liars!"
[12] What can I offer the LORD
for all He has done for me?
[13] I will lift up the cup of salvation
and praise the LORD's name for saving me.
[14] I will keep my promises to the LORD
in the presence of all His people.

[15] The LORD cares deeply
when His loved ones die.
[16] O LORD, I am Your servant;
yes, I am Your servant, born into Your household;
You have freed me from my chains.
[17] I will offer You a sacrifice of thanksgiving
and call on the name of the LORD.

116:1 Pss 18:1; 66:19
116:2 Pss 17:6; 31:2
116:3 Ps 18:4-6
116:4 Pss 22:20; 118:5
116:5 Exod 34:6
116:6 Ps 142:6
116:7 Ps 13:6; Matt 11:29
116:8 Pss 49:15; 56:13
116:10 *2 Cor 4:13
116:12 2 Chr 32:25; 1 Thes 3:9
116:14 Pss 22:25; 50:14
116:15 Ps 72:14

116:3 Hebrew *of Sheol.*

WORSHIP

116:1 God answers prayer. Can you affirm this verse? What prayers has God answered for you? Each of us can remember answers to prayer that touched our hearts deeply. Perhaps it was a time when God comforted you during a dark period. Some look back on a trail of events that has God's hand written all over it. Write down three or four answers to prayer that mean the most to you. Attach that to your bathroom mirror, and every morning, tell God how much you love Him for hearing your prayers. (***See Worship****> OT> Fasting and Prayer> Prayer> Devote yourselves to prayer,* TopicGuide page A26.)

116:5 The psalmist's profound experience of God's salvation moves him to praise the kindness, goodness, and mercy of God. These characteristics closely mirror those mentioned in God's own description of Himself to Moses in Exodus 34:5-7.

116:17-19 The psalmist sets his commitment to praise and obedience within the context of the community of God's people. In their midst he would praise the Lord and fulfill his vows. Individuals are never saved out of their sin into isolation; they are saved into the people of God, where they become part of God's larger work in the history of humanity.

[18] I will fulfill my vows to the LORD
in the presence of all His people—
[19] in the house of the LORD
in the heart of Jerusalem.

Praise the LORD!

PSALM 117

117:1 *Rom 15:11 [1] Praise the LORD, all you nations.
Praise Him, all you people of the earth.
117:2 Ps 100:5 [2] For He loves us with unfailing love;
the LORD's faithfulness endures forever.

Praise the LORD!

PSALM 118

118:1 Ps 136:1-26 [1] Give thanks to the LORD, for He is good!
His faithful love endures forever.
118:2 Ps 115:9 [2] Let all Israel repeat:
"His faithful love endures forever."
[3] Let Aaron's descendants, the priests, repeat:
"His faithful love endures forever."
[4] Let all who fear the LORD repeat:
"His faithful love endures forever."
118:5 Pss 18:19; 120:1 [5] In my distress I prayed to the LORD,
and the LORD answered me and set me free.
118:6 Job 19:27 *Heb 13:6 [6] The LORD is for me, so I will have no fear.
What can mere people do to me?
118:7 Ps 54:7 [7] Yes, the LORD is for me; He will help me.
I will look in triumph at those who hate me.

▸ **WORSHIP**
116:18 My promise. Does this verse express your commitment to honor those things that God has led you to do? This should be the desire of your heart. The psalmist also makes a similar statement in verse 14, making it the central theme of his psalm. How can you be sure to keep your promises to God? Take them to Him in prayer frequently, asking Him to enable you to keep your integrity. (***See Worship***> *OT> Fasting and Prayer> Prayer> Prophets pray unceasingly,* TopicGuide page A26.)

117:1 The Old Testament frequently expresses hope for the conversion of the nations. The apostle Paul quoted this verse as he reflected on the fulfillment of this hope in the building of the church (Romans 15:11).

▸ **GOD**
117:2 God's truth is everlasting. What words describe the longevity of God's truth? *Everlasting, forever, eternal, infinite, unfailing.* Truth can be only as accurate and enduring as the person who gives it. God's truth is everlasting because God is eternal. In Revelation 1:8, God says, "'I am the One who is, who always was, and who is still to come—the Almighty One.'" Because God's truth is so indestructible, we can use it to guide our lives. But we can't use it unless we know it. Make the Bible the instruction manual for this life. (***See God***> *God's Attributes> True> God's truth is everlasting,* TopicGuide page A18.)

118:1-4 Thanksgiving is the theme of the psalm. God's faithful love is the consistent expression of His commitment to His people and to His word, by which He has bound Himself to His people. The psalmist exhorts God's people to offer the Lord thanksgiving for His faithfulness to them. It is possible that "all who fear the LORD" is a technical phrase designating Gentiles who have acknowledged the God of Israel.

▸ **MINISTRY**
118:6 Suffering for Jesus. The long annals of Christian history show us that believers can stand up for Jesus through persecution. Athanasius, who lived in the third century, was banished from his home five times for the sake of the gospel. John Wycliffe faced the burning stake for his witness. Jim Elliot was martyred when he brought the gospel to tribal people in South America. Believers are still being persecuted for their faith today. Some persecution is minor—a snide remark about Christians in the workplace, gentle teasing by unbelieving members of your family, ridicule in a college classroom for your beliefs. Whatever we face, the Lord is with us. Therefore, we can be bold in our witness for Him. We will all face persecution of some degree. Will you be ready when the time comes for you? (***See Ministry***> *Great Commission> Risk> Opposition and ill-treatment,* TopicGuide page A56.)

118:6 The presence of God among His people is their abiding source of hope and strength, and the essence of His promises to them (Exodus 29:43-45; Revelation 21:3).

8 It is better to take refuge in the LORD
than to trust in people.
9 It is better to take refuge in the LORD
than to trust in princes.

10 Though hostile nations surrounded me,
I destroyed them all with the authority of the LORD.
11 Yes, they surrounded and attacked me,
but I destroyed them all with the authority of the LORD.
12 They swarmed around me like bees;
they blazed against me like a crackling fire.
But I destroyed them all with the authority of the LORD.
13 My enemies did their best to kill me,
but the LORD rescued me.
14 The LORD is my strength and my song;
He has given me victory.
15 Songs of joy and victory are sung in the camp of the godly.
The strong right arm of the LORD has done glorious things!
16 The strong right arm of the LORD is raised in triumph.
The strong right arm of the LORD has done glorious things!
17 I will not die; instead, I will live
to tell what the LORD has done.
18 The LORD has punished me severely,
but He did not let me die.

19 Open for me the gates where the righteous enter,
and I will go in and thank the LORD.
20 These gates lead to the presence of the LORD,
and the godly enter there.
21 I thank You for answering my prayer
and giving me victory!

22 The stone that the builders rejected
has now become the cornerstone.
23 This is the LORD's doing,
and it is wonderful to see.
24 This is the day the LORD has made.
We will rejoice and be glad in it.
25 Please, LORD, please save us.
Please, LORD, please give us success.
26 Bless the one who comes in the name of the LORD.
We bless you from the house of the LORD.
27 The LORD is God, shining upon us.
Take the sacrifice and bind it with cords on the altar.

118:8 2 Chr 32:7-8; Isa 57:13
118:10 Ps 18:40
118:12 Deut 1:44
118:14 Exod 15:2; Isa 12:2
118:15 Ps 89:13; Luke 1:51
118:18 Jer 31:18; 1 Cor 11:32; 2 Cor 6:9
118:19 Isa 26:2
118:22 Matt 21:42; Mark 12:10-11; *Luke 20:17; *Acts 4:11; *1 Pet 2:7
118:23 *Matt 21:42; *Mark 12:11
118:26 *Matt 21:9; *Mark 11:9; *Luke 13:35; 19:38; *John 12:13
118:27 1 Pet 2:9

118:10-13 The immediate context of the psalm is the battlefield. The king of Israel, the representative of God and His people, invoked the Lord's aid against the enemies of Israel.

118:15-16 The king and his army appropriately respond to the Lord's victory with praise and thanksgiving. The Lord's "right arm" is a metaphor for His strength and power.

118:22 The image suggests the raising of someone from defeat to victory or from dishonor to glory. The stone in the psalm is most likely the king, and his rejection may have been an earlier defeat in battle. The New Testament frequently cites this verse to describe Christ's humiliation and exaltation (Matthew 21:42; Acts 4:11; Ephesians 2:20; 1 Peter 2:7).

118:27 The shining light of God's face metaphorically describes His favorable disposition toward His people.

118:28 Exod 15:2 Isa 25:1 [28] You are my God, and I will praise You!
You are my God, and I will exalt You!
[29] Give thanks to the LORD, for He is good!
His faithful love endures forever.

PSALM 119

*Aleph**

119:1 Prov 11:20; 13:6 [1] Joyful are people of integrity,
who follow the instructions of the LORD.
119:2 Deut 4:29; 10:12; 11:13; 30:2 [2] Joyful are those who obey His laws
and search for Him with all their hearts.
[3] They do not compromise with evil,
and they walk only in His paths.
119:4 Deut 4:13 [4] You have charged us
to keep Your commandments carefully.
119:5 2 Chr 7:17 Prov 4:26 [5] Oh, that my actions would consistently
reflect Your decrees!
[6] Then I will not be ashamed
when I compare my life with Your commands.
[7] As I learn Your righteous regulations,
I will thank You by living as I should!
119:8 Ps 71:9, 18 [8] I will obey Your decrees.
Please don't give up on me!

Beth

119:9 1 Kgs 8:25 2 Chr 6:16 [9] How can a young person stay pure?
By obeying Your word.
[10] I have tried hard to find You—
don't let me wander from Your commands.
119:11 Luke 2:19, 51 [11] I have hidden Your word in my heart,
that I might not sin against You.
[12] I praise You, O LORD;
teach me Your decrees.
119:13 Ps 40:9 [13] I have recited aloud
all the regulations You have given us.

119 This psalm is a Hebrew acrostic poem; there are twenty-two stanzas, one for each successive letter of the Hebrew alphabet. Each of the eight verses within each stanza begins with the Hebrew letter named in its heading.

119:1-8 The psalmist begins with a reflection on the happiness (literally "blessedness") of those who live according to the law of God. The psalmist acknowledges his duty to obey God's law faithfully and his failure to do so. But he is committed in his effort to live righteously while relying on God's mercy.

▸ SPIRITUAL WARFARE
119:3 Never compromise with sin. Most of the time, Christians don't set out to sin. But what trips us up is that we compromise with evil. We allow ourselves to watch that movie with unnecessary sexual displays because "It's art!" We take equipment home from the office because "no one will miss them." We hold a grudge because "you just don't know what that person did to me." What compromises are you making with sin? Obey God's Word completely to avoid sin. (***See Spiritual Warfare****> Resisting Sin and Evil> Embracing Christ> Obey His Word,* TopicGuide page A45.)

▸ BIBLE
119:11 Hide God's word in your heart. Many of us read this verse and think, "I can't memorize verses. That's too hard for me." But think about your memorization skills. You've probably memorized something this week—a telephone number, the words to a song, an advertising slogan. How did you memorize it? Apply the same method to your Bible memorization. Write a verse out on an index card or put it on your PDA. Whenever you have a break, read it over. After several days, you will know the verse. (***See Bible****> Power> Equip> To be hidden in the heart,* TopicGuide page A11.)

14 I have rejoiced in Your laws
as much as in riches.
15 I will study Your commandments
and reflect on Your ways.
16 I will delight in Your decrees
and not forget Your word.

Gimel

17 Be good to Your servant,
that I may live and obey Your word.
18 Open my eyes to see
the wonderful truths in Your instructions.
19 I am only a foreigner in the land.
Don't hide Your commands from me!
20 I am always overwhelmed
with a desire for Your regulations.
21 You rebuke the arrogant;
those who wander from Your commands are cursed.
22 Don't let them scorn and insult me,
for I have obeyed Your laws.
23 Even princes sit and speak against me,
but I will meditate on Your decrees.
24 Your laws please me;
they give me wise advice.

Daleth

25 I lie in the dust;
revive me by Your word.
26 I told You my plans, and You answered.
Now teach me Your decrees.
27 Help me understand the meaning of Your commandments,
and I will meditate on Your wonderful deeds.
28 I weep with sorrow;
encourage me by Your word.
29 Keep me from lying to myself;
give me the privilege of knowing Your instructions.
30 I have chosen to be faithful;
I have determined to live by Your regulations.
31 I cling to Your laws.
LORD, don't let me be put to shame!
32 I will pursue Your commands,
for You expand my understanding.

119:15 Isa 58:2
119:19 1 Chr 29:15; Heb 11:13
119:20 Ps 42:1-2
119:21 Deut 27:26; Ps 37:22
119:25 Ps 44:25
119:28 Ps 22:14; 1 Pet 5:10
119:31 Deut 11:22

119:17-24 The psalmist expresses his dependence on God's grace to illuminate and empower him as he seeks to obey God's law. He desires such grace because he has a deep desire to please the Lord and he understands that God punishes the wicked. Thus, regardless of opposition, the psalmist will live according to God's word with joy.

▸ HOLINESS
119:18 "Open my eyes." Sometimes, having your eyes open doesn't mean that you see what's there. If you have been a parent of a grade-schooler, you understand this fact. If you send the child into a room to look for an item, he probably will come back and say, "I looked everywhere, but I couldn't find it." Then, when you go into the room to search, you see the item in plain sight. We do this same thing to God's moral laws. We know what they are, but we overlook them. We read the words, but we don't obey them. Ask God to help you open your eyes to see His commandments and obey them. (***See Holiness***> *Law and Grace*> *Law*> *The moral law of God,* TopicGuide page A41.)

119:25-32 The tone of this stanza is that of a lament. The circumstances of life often tend to overwhelm God's people, so that remaining faithful to God's law becomes increasingly difficult. Yet in those times, it is especially important to cling to God's word and remain steadfast in the pursuit of obedience. Engaged in such a struggle, the psalmist depends on God to sustain and deliver him.

He

119:33 1 Chr 22:12 Ezek 44:24

33 Teach me Your decrees, O LORD;
I will keep them to the end.
34 Give me understanding and I will obey Your instructions;
I will put them into practice with all my heart.

119:35 Pss 25:4; 112:1

35 Make me walk along the path of Your commands,
for that is where my happiness is found.

119:36 Luke 12:15 Heb 13:5

36 Give me an eagerness for Your laws
rather than a love for money!

119:37 Ps 71:20 Isa 33:15

37 Turn my eyes from worthless things,
and give me life through Your word.*

119:38 2 Sam 7:25

38 Reassure me of Your promise,
made to those who fear You.
39 Help me abandon my shameful ways;
for Your regulations are good.
40 I long to obey Your commandments!
Renew my life with Your goodness.

Waw

41 LORD, give me Your unfailing love,
the salvation that You promised me.
42 Then I can answer those who taunt me,
for I trust in Your word.
43 Do not snatch Your word of truth from me,
for Your regulations are my only hope.

119:44 Acts 26:1-2

44 I will keep on obeying Your instructions
forever and ever.
45 I will walk in freedom,
for I have devoted myself to Your commandments.

119:46 Matt 10:18 Acts 26:1-2

46 I will speak to kings about Your laws,
and I will not be ashamed.
47 How I delight in Your commands!
How I love them!
48 I honor and love Your commands.
I meditate on Your decrees.

Zayin

49 Remember Your promise to me;
it is my only hope.

119:50 Rom 15:4

50 Your promise revives me;
it comforts me in all my troubles.

119:51 Job 23:11 Jer 20:7

51 The proud hold me in utter contempt,
but I do not turn away from Your instructions.

119:52 Ps 103:18

52 I meditate on Your age-old regulations;
O LORD, they comfort me.

119:53 Exod 32:19 Neh 13:25

53 I become furious with the wicked,
because they reject Your instructions.

119:37 Some manuscripts read *in Your ways.*

119:49-56 Through trial and persecution, the psalmist finds strength in God's promises. Regardless of external circumstances, the promises of God hold true and inspire unfailing hope in those who know Him. In the psalmist's poetic imagination, the law of God provides the rhythms by which the faithful order their journey through life.

54 Your decrees have been the theme of my songs
wherever I have lived.
55 I reflect at night on who You are, O LORD;
therefore, I obey Your instructions.
56 This is how I spend my life:
obeying Your commandments.

119:55 Pss 42:8; 63:6; 92:2 Acts 16:25

Heth

57 LORD, You are mine!
I promise to obey Your words!
58 With all my heart I want Your blessings.
Be merciful as You promised.
59 I pondered the direction of my life,
and I turned to follow Your laws.
60 I will hurry, without delay,
to obey Your commands.
61 Evil people try to drag me into sin,
but I am firmly anchored to Your instructions.
62 I rise at midnight to thank You
for Your just regulations.
63 I am a friend to anyone who fears You—
anyone who obeys Your commandments.
64 O LORD, Your unfailing love fills the earth;
teach me Your decrees.

119:57 Deut 33:9 Ps 16:5
119:58 Ps 41:4
119:59 Mark 14:72 Luke 15:17
119:61 Ps 140:5
119:63 Ps 101:6
119:64 Ps 33:5

Teth

65 You have done many good things for me, LORD,
just as You promised.
66 I believe in Your commands;
now teach me good judgment and knowledge.
67 I used to wander off until You disciplined me;
but now I closely follow Your word.
68 You are good and do only good;
teach me Your decrees.
69 Arrogant people smear me with lies,
but in truth I obey Your commandments with all my heart.
70 Their hearts are dull and stupid,
but I delight in Your instructions.
71 My suffering was good for me,
for it taught me to pay attention to Your decrees.
72 Your instructions are more valuable to me
than millions in gold and silver.

119:66 Phil 1:9
119:67 Jer 31:18-19 Heb 12:5-11
119:68 Pss 86:5; 125:4
119:70 Ps 17:10 Isa 6:10 Jer 5:28
119:72 Prov 8:10-11, 19

Yodh

73 You made me; You created me.
Now give me the sense to follow Your commands.
74 May all who fear You find in me a cause for joy,
for I have put my hope in Your word.
75 I know, O LORD, that Your regulations are fair;
You disciplined me because I needed it.
76 Now let Your unfailing love comfort me,
just as You promised me, Your servant.
77 Surround me with Your tender mercies so I may live,
for Your instructions are my delight.

119:73 Job 31:15 Ps 139:15-16
119:74 Ps 35:27
119:75 Heb 12:10

HE WAS ATTRACTIVE, INTELLIGENT, and he had enough money and talent to get into (and get out of) almost any trouble. He moved easily from one philosophy school to the next, learning and teaching as he went, and life was grand. But even these sorts of advantages couldn't keep our friend from the eventual consequences of a careless life. Petty theft, mistress after mistress, broken engagements, a life of carousing—even with all his learning, he was a slave to his baser desires.

But slowly, things changed, for this young man had a godly mother who prayed for him constantly. She threw him out of her home for boasting about his sinful lifestyle—but she still prayed for him every day. He broke the engagement his mother had arranged with a Christian woman—but she still prayed for him. It looked as if his mother's prayers would go unanswered, but the death of a friend shook the young man to his core. Perplexingly, this friend had converted to Christianity before his death, and this motivated the young man—Augustine—to search for freedom from his debauchery. Beneath a fig tree in the summer of AD 386, God spoke to Augustine through Romans 13:13-14 and set him free to pursue God. In that moment, Augustine was truly free!

Only God's truth can set a person free. Even in the fourth century, the lie had already been spread that education and wealth could liberate the soul. Augustine had believed that lie, but he was in chains until he met Christ. You can lean on the words of Jesus: "And you will know the truth, and the truth will set you free" (John 8:32).

78 Bring disgrace upon the arrogant people who lied about me; **119:78**
meanwhile, I will concentrate on Your commandments. Jer 50:32
79 Let me be united with all who fear You,
with those who know Your laws.
80 May I be blameless in keeping Your decrees;
then I will never be ashamed.

Kaph

81 I am worn out waiting for Your rescue,
but I have put my hope in Your word.
82 My eyes are straining to see Your promises come true. **119:82**
When will You comfort me? Isa 38:14 Lam 2:11
83 I am shriveled like a wineskin in the smoke,
but I have not forgotten to obey Your decrees.
84 How long must I wait? **119:84** Rev 6:10
When will You punish those who persecute me?
85 These arrogant people who hate Your instructions **119:85**
have dug deep pits to trap me. Pss 35:19; 57:6 Jer 18:22
86 All Your commands are trustworthy.
Protect me from those who hunt me down without cause.
87 They almost finished me off,
but I refused to abandon Your commandments.
88 In Your unfailing love, spare my life;
then I can continue to obey Your laws.

119:81-88 This stanza arises out of a time of crisis. The psalmist is nearly overwhelmed by his enemies. But even in his dire situation, he remains steadfastly committed to God's law. He has not lost faith in the virtue of obedience or in the truth of God's word. He will remain faithful while he waits expectantly for deliverance.

MY RESPONSE TO GOD

Lighting the Path

PSALM 119:103-105, 130, 133

Standing in the darkness of a moonless, cloudy night, the ancient fishermen and shepherds knew the importance of light. Without it, they were helpless and easy prey for a stray wave or a hungry lion. Psalm 119 compares God's Word to just this sort of situation. Just as a physical light could reveal whether someone was an intruder sneaking in or a friend coming to visit, the light of Scripture reveals both the snares of Satan and the means of redemption that God has provided. The Scriptures chase away the darkness and chaos, enabling us to see the world, God, and ourselves more clearly. Without God's Word, we would not know how to be saved from God's righteous wrath. We would not know how to avoid Satan's traps and tricks. And just like a lamp could enable us to explore a dark cave, the light of God's Word also allows us to explore any place God wants us to go, from the darkest corners of this world to the darkest corners of our hearts.

Do you want to see God's will more clearly and to find your way in this world? Then read God's Word. Do you want to discover how remarkable the Bible truly is? Read it. Do you want to see God, yourself, and this world revealed most clearly? Read God's Word.

Lamedh

119:89 Isa 40:8 Matt 24:35 1 Pet 1:25
89 Your eternal word, O LORD,
stands firm in heaven.
119:90 Pss 89:1-2; 148:6
90 Your faithfulness extends to every generation,
as enduring as the earth You created.
119:91 Jer 31:35
91 Your regulations remain true to this day,
for everything serves Your plans.
92 If Your instructions hadn't sustained me with joy,
I would have died in my misery.
93 I will never forget Your commandments,
for by them You give me life.
94 I am Yours; rescue me!
For I have worked hard at obeying Your commandments.
119:95 Ps 40:14 Isa 32:7
95 Though the wicked hide along the way to kill me,
I will quietly keep my mind on Your laws.
96 Even perfection has its limits,
but Your commands have no limit.

Mem

97 Oh, how I love Your instructions!
I think about them all day long.
119:98 Deut 4:6
98 Your commands make me wiser than my enemies,
for they are my constant guide.
99 Yes, I have more insight than my teachers,
for I am always thinking of Your laws.
119:100 Job 32:7-9
100 I am even wiser than my elders,
for I have kept Your commandments.
101 I have refused to walk on any evil path,
so that I may remain obedient to Your word.
119:102 Deut 17:20 Josh 23:6
102 I haven't turned away from Your regulations,
for You have taught me well.
119:103 Ps 19:10
103 How sweet Your words taste to me;
they are sweeter than honey.
104 Your commandments give me understanding;
no wonder I hate every false way of life.

Nun

105 Your word is a lamp to guide my feet
and a light for my path.

▸ BIBLE

119:89 The enduring book. When a publishing company releases a book, the book probably has a shelf life of six months or so. When the sales dwindle, the publisher drops the book from the catalog. That's not true of God's Word. Not only is it the best-selling book of all time, the Bible will last forever. It has no limit to its "shelf life." Psalm 119 tells us that the Bible transcends our world and inhabits heaven. Our world has no effect on it. In fact, the Bible will go on forever. It's the only book we can rely on completely. If you haven't done so already, commit yourself to reading your Bible fifteen minutes per day. It will change your life—eternally. (***See Bible> Power> Wisdom> His Word Forever settled,*** TopicGuide page A11.)

119:89-96 The psalmist celebrates the eternal character of God's word and takes comfort in the enduring value of God's law. By His word God created the heavens and the earth, and by His word the Lord delivered the psalmist. Once again, the psalmist commits himself to the Lord and His word in the face of trouble and opposition.

▸ BIBLE

119:105 A good light. A camper knows the importance of having a good flashlight. He has no light switch to flip on when the sun goes down. He can't rely on streetlights for safety. But a flashlight lights up the path before him so that he doesn't trip or lose his way. That beam of light, spreading out before his feet, is his lifeline. That's how we should consider the Bible's wisdom. In this life, we constantly travel down roads we've never been before. A sickness strikes. We start a new job. A loved one comes to us for advice. A son or daughter poses a challenge. As verse 104 says, our understanding of life's principles comes from God's Word. But we can use it only if we "turn it on" by studying it and applying its truths. Do you have a plan for Bible study? Adopt one today. (***See Bible> Power> Wisdom> Guidance for life,*** TopicGuide page A11.)

106 I've promised it once, and I'll promise it again:
I will obey Your righteous regulations.
107 I have suffered much, O LORD;
restore my life again as You promised.
108 LORD, accept my offering of praise,
and teach me Your regulations.
109 My life constantly hangs in the balance,
but I will not stop obeying Your instructions.
110 The wicked have set their traps for me,
but I will not turn from Your commandments.
111 Your laws are my treasure;
they are my heart's delight.
112 I am determined to keep Your decrees
to the very end.

Samekh

113 I hate those with divided loyalties,
but I love Your instructions.
114 You are my refuge and my shield;
Your word is my source of hope.
115 Get out of my life, you evil-minded people,
for I intend to obey the commands of my God.
116 LORD, sustain me as You promised, that I may live!
Do not let my hope be crushed.
117 Sustain me, and I will be rescued;
then I will meditate continually on Your decrees.
118 But You have rejected all who stray from Your decrees.
They are only fooling themselves.
119 You skim off the wicked of the earth like scum;
no wonder I love to obey Your laws!
120 I tremble in fear of You;
I stand in awe of Your regulations.

Ayin

121 Don't leave me to the mercy of my enemies,
for I have done what is just and right.
122 Please guarantee a blessing for me.
Don't let the arrogant oppress me!
123 My eyes strain to see Your rescue,
to see the truth of Your promise fulfilled.
124 I am Your servant; deal with me in unfailing love,
and teach me Your decrees.
125 Give discernment to me, Your servant;
then I will understand Your laws.
126 LORD, it is time for You to act,
for these evil people have violated Your instructions.

119:108 Hos 14:2 Heb 13:15
119:110 Pss 91:3; 140:5
119:111 Deut 33:4
119:113 1 Kgs 18:21 Jas 1:8; 4:8
119:114 Pss 31:20; 61:4
119:115 Pss 6:8; 139:19 Matt 7:23
119:116 Pss 25:2, 20; 31:1, 17 Rom 5:5; 9:33 Phil 1:20
119:117 Ps 12:5 Prov 29:25
119:119 Isa 1:22, 25 Ezek 22:18-19
119:120 Job 4:14 Hab 3:16
119:121 2 Sam 8:15 Job 29:14
119:124 Pss 51:1; 106:45; 109:26
119:126 Jer 18:23 Ezek 31:11

119:105-112 In the face of unspecified danger, the psalmist reaffirms his commitment to God and His Word. He acknowledges the law of God as his guide and asserts that he will not be dissuaded by the peril posed by his enemies. Throughout his life, he has sought to remain faithful to the Lord, and no new danger will make him change his course.

119:114-128 The psalmist is faced with enemies who oppress him. Desperate for deliverance, he calls on God to show Himself faithful to His promises by saving him from the danger that threatens to undo him. However, the psalmist never conditions his obedience upon God's deliverance; he remains God's servant no matter what transpires.

¹²⁷Truly, I love Your commands
more than gold, even the finest gold.

119:128 Ps 19:8
¹²⁸Each of Your commandments is right.
That is why I hate every false way.

Pe

¹²⁹Your laws are wonderful.
No wonder I obey them!

119:130 Prov 6:23
¹³⁰The teaching of Your word gives light,
so even the simple can understand.

¹³¹I pant with expectation,
longing for Your commands.

¹³²Come and show me Your mercy,
as You do for all who love Your name.

119:133 Ps 19:13
¹³³Guide my steps by Your word,
so I will not be overcome by evil.

119:134 Ps 142:6
¹³⁴Ransom me from the oppression of evil people;
then I can obey Your commandments.

119:135 Num 6:25 Ps 67:1
¹³⁵Look upon me with love;
teach me Your decrees.

119:136 Jer 9:1, 18; 14:17 Lam 3:48
¹³⁶Rivers of tears gush from my eyes
because people disobey Your instructions.

Tsadhe

119:137 Ezra 9:15 Jer 12:1 Dan 9:7, 14
¹³⁷O LORD, You are righteous,
and Your regulations are fair.

¹³⁸Your laws are perfect
and completely trustworthy.

119:139 Ps 69:9
¹³⁹I am overwhelmed with indignation,
for my enemies have disregarded Your words.

119:140 Ps 12:6
¹⁴⁰Your promises have been thoroughly tested;
that is why I love them so much.

119:141 Ps 22:6
¹⁴¹I am insignificant and despised,
but I don't forget Your commandments.

¹⁴²Your justice is eternal,
and Your instructions are perfectly true.

¹⁴³As pressure and stress bear down on me,
I find joy in Your commands.

119:144 Ps 19:9
¹⁴⁴Your laws are always right;
help me to understand them so I may live.

119:129-136 To those who know the Lord, His law is full of wisdom and truth. However, no one obeys God's law perfectly, and thus all stand in need of God's mercy, as the psalmist acknowledges. He petitions God not only for mercy but for strength to obey and for protection from the ungodly. The final verse of this stanza reveals the heart of one who loves the Lord and desires to see Him honored by all.

▶ BIBLE

119:130 You can understand God's Word. In this world, we are divided into groups. Some of us attend college and become experts in a field such as history, law, or politics. Others go to a technical school and learn a trade such as plumbing or electrical work. Still others learn on the job. Our jobs are distinct. We wouldn't think of asking our doctor to fix a leaky faucet or our gardener to wire a new outlet. Each person has his own expertise, and we don't expect to understand everyone's job. Wouldn't it be tragic if God expected something like that of us when we read His Word? What if we had to be an "expert" to open His Word? What if we had to go to school to learn about salvation? But God has made His message of love through Jesus Christ so simple that we all can understand it. Thank Him for he simplicity and purity of His message. (***See Bible***> *Power*> *Wisdom*> *Gives light to the simple,* TopicGuide page A11.)

119:137-144 The law of God flows from His character and thus reflects His righteousness. The psalmist, however, finds a world unwilling to obey God's law, and he is exasperated by their rebellion. But even though he finds himself in the minority, his loyalty does not waver and his commitment does not shrink.

Qoph

145 I pray with all my heart; answer me, LORD!
I will obey Your decrees.
146 I cry out to You; rescue me,
that I may obey Your laws.
147 I rise early, before the sun is up;
I cry out for help and put my hope in Your words.
148 I stay awake through the night,
thinking about Your promise.
149 In Your faithful love, O LORD, hear my cry;
let me be revived by following Your regulations.
150 Lawless people are coming to attack me;
they live far from Your instructions.
151 But You are near, O LORD,
and all Your commands are true.
152 I have known from my earliest days
that Your laws will last forever.

Resh

153 Look upon my suffering and rescue me,
for I have not forgotten Your instructions.
154 Argue my case; take my side!
Protect my life as You promised.
155 The wicked are far from rescue,
for they do not bother with Your decrees.
156 LORD, how great is Your mercy;
let me be revived by following Your regulations.
157 Many persecute and trouble me,
yet I have not swerved from Your laws.
158 Seeing these traitors makes me sick at heart,
because they care nothing for Your word.
159 See how I love Your commandments, LORD.
Give back my life because of Your unfailing love.
160 The very essence of Your words is truth;
all Your just regulations will stand forever.

Shin

161 Powerful people harass me without cause,
but my heart trembles only at Your word.
162 I rejoice in Your word
like one who discovers a great treasure.
163 I hate and abhor all falsehood,
but I love Your instructions.
164 I will praise You seven times a day
because all Your regulations are just.
165 Those who love Your instructions have
great peace
and do not stumble.
166 I long for Your rescue, LORD,
so I have obeyed Your commands.
167 I have obeyed Your laws,
for I love them very much.
168 Yes, I obey Your commandments and laws
because You know everything I do.

119:146 Ps 3:7
119:147 Ps 108:2
119:151 Ps 34:18; Isa 50:8
119:152 Luke 21:33
119:154 Ps 35:1; Mic 7:9
119:156 2 Sam 24:14
119:158 Ps 139:21
119:162 1 Sam 30:16; Isa 9:3
119:163 Ps 31:6; Prov 13:5
119:165 Prov 3:23; 1 Jn 2:10
119:166 Gen 49:18
119:168 Ps 139:3; Prov 5:21

Taw

119:169 Ps 18:6 — 169 O LORD, listen to my cry;
give me the discerning mind You promised.
119:170 Pss 22:20; 31:2; 140:6 — 170 Listen to my prayer;
rescue me as You promised.
119:171 Isa 2:3; Mic 4:2 — 171 Let praise flow from my lips,
for You have taught me Your decrees.
119:172 Ps 51:14 — 172 Let my tongue sing about Your word,
for all Your commands are right.
119:173 Josh 24:22; Ps 37:24 — 173 Give me a helping hand,
for I have chosen to follow Your commandments.
174 O LORD, I have longed for Your rescue,
and Your instructions are my delight.
119:175 Isa 55:3 — 175 Let me live so I can praise You,
and may Your regulations help me.
119:176 Isa 53:6; Luke 15:4 — 176 I have wandered away like a lost sheep;
come and find me,
for I have not forgotten Your commands.

PSALM 120

A song for pilgrims ascending to Jerusalem.

120:1 Pss 18:6; 102:2 — 1 I took my troubles to the LORD;
I cried out to Him, and He answered my prayer.
120:2 Ps 52:4; Prov 12:22 — 2 Rescue me, O LORD, from liars
and from all deceitful people.
3 O deceptive tongue, what will God do to you?
How will He increase your punishment?
120:4 Ps 140:10 — 4 You will be pierced with sharp arrows
and burned with glowing coals.

120:5 Gen 10:2; 25:13; Jer 2:10; 49:28 — 5 How I suffer in far-off Meshech.
It pains me to live in distant Kedar.
6 I am tired of living
among people who hate peace.

▸ WORSHIP

119:170 Pray for deliverance. One of the most difficult battles we have in life is fighting against temptation and the power of sin. Each of us has an area of temptation that is especially difficult. For James, it was his temper. Most of the time, his anger was triggered by frustration. Traffic jams on the freeway, computer malfunctions, or disagreements with his brother set him off. The only way we can conquer these problems is by asking God to deliver us. He will rescue us from the power of sin in our lives. Look at your life and see where you need God's deliverance. Ask Him to help you conquer these areas. (***See Worship***> *OT> God's Supremacy> God delivered/saved in order to be worshiped and served,* TopicGuide page A27.)

120:1-7 The psalmist cries out to God, certain that his prayer will be heard. He requires rescue from pagans who, through gossip and deceit, provoke violence against him. The greatest fear of a lone traveler in the psalmist's time would have been violent bandits.

120:3 Lying creates a ripple effect beyond an initial sin. The psalmist notes that God gives greater punishment to those who lie (Psalm 5:6; Proverbs 25:18; Revelation 21:8). God's people are to tell the truth to one another (Ephesians 4:25).

120:5 The psalmist cites two large regions, Meshech (Genesis 10:2; Ezekiel 38:2) and Kedar (Isaiah 21:16; Ezekiel 27:21). Meshech was near modern Turkey and Kedar was in modern Saudi Arabia. These distant and very large pagan cultures emphasize the breadth of opposition the psalmist faces.

▸ ADOPTION

120:6 God understands your discomfort in this life. When a vacationer travels to other parts of the world, he feels excited when leaving home. He has made plans to see exotic places and experience unusual things. But at some point in his travels, the yearning for home can overpower him. He longs for the comfort of his own bed, the softness of his favorite chair, and the company of friends and loved ones. The sights and smells of strange places become odious to him. This reminds us of our sojourn on earth. We are just pilgrims in this life. Our real home is with Christ (Philippians 1:23). The conflicts and sufferings of this world make us lonesome to be with Him, where we will experience perfect peace. When this life seems too much to bear, take your feelings to Jesus. Ask Him to help you endure your earthly travels for His sake. (***See Adoption***> *With Christ> Supernatural> A life of everlasting peace,* TopicGuide page A37.)

[7] I search for peace;
but when I speak of peace, they want war!

120:7 Pss 55:21; 109:4

PSALM 121

A song for pilgrims ascending to Jerusalem.

[1] I look up to the mountains—
does my help come from there?
[2] My help comes from the LORD,
who made heaven and earth!

[3] He will not let you stumble;
the One who watches over you will not slumber.
[4] Indeed, He who watches over Israel
never slumbers or sleeps.

[5] The LORD Himself watches over you!
The LORD stands beside you as your protective shade.
[6] The sun will not harm you by day,
nor the moon at night.

[7] The LORD keeps you from all harm
and watches over your life.
[8] The LORD keeps watch over you as you come and go,
both now and forever.

121:2 Pss 115:15; 124:8
121:3 Pss 66:9; 127:1
121:5 Ps 91:4
121:6 Isa 49:10 Rev 7:16
121:7 Ps 91:10-12

PSALM 122

A song for pilgrims ascending to Jerusalem. A psalm of David.

[1] I was glad when they said to me,
"Let us go to the house of the LORD."
[2] And now here we are,
standing inside your gates, O Jerusalem.
[3] Jerusalem is a well-built city;
its seamless walls cannot be breached.

122:1 Isa 2:3 Zech 8:21
122:3 Ps 48:13

120:7 God's people prefer peace (Matthew 5:9), looking forward to the day when all will live in harmony (Hebrews 10:13; 13:20). However, there is an appropriate time for conflict (Ecclesiastes 3:8; Matthew 10:34).

▸ BIBLE

121:1 Look to the mountain. If you live close to a mountain or even a high hill, that elevated land becomes a point of reference. When driving on unfamiliar streets, you keep the mountain to one side to maintain your direction. When giving directions to your home, you use the mountain as a guide: "Go north three blocks toward the mountain." That's similar to how we look to God. He is our reference point. Whenever we don't know where to go, we look to Him. Whenever we want to explain how to live abundantly, we look to Him. He is the point from which we derive our moral direction. Is God your point of moral reference? Do you consistently look to Him for where you are going? Ask Him frequently to help you find the right direction in life. (***See Bible> Power> Wisdom> Guidance for life,*** TopicGuide page A11.)

121:1 Jerusalem and the Temple sat at an elevation of 2,550 feet above sea level. Although there were higher places in Israel, someone traveling to Jerusalem always spoke of going "up" out of respect for the city God had chosen as the place of His presence (see 1 Chronicles 15:25; Ezra 7:7; Galatians 1:17).

121:3 The slippery and rocky terrain of ancient Israel made roads quite dangerous. Thus, safety was a matter of prayer for all who traveled.

121:4 This statement recalls the prophet Elijah's mockery of the pagan god Baal, whom Elijah accused of falling asleep when his prophets needed him (1 Kings 18:27).

122:2 The journey to Jerusalem happens without comment between verses 1 and 2. To the pilgrim, the journey pales before the glories of Jerusalem.

122:4 Deut 16:16 — 4 All the tribes of Israel—the LORD's people—
make their pilgrimage here.
They come to give thanks to the name of the LORD,
as the law requires of Israel.
122:5 Deut 17:8; 2 Chr 19:8 — 5 Here stand the thrones where judgment is given,
the thrones of the dynasty of David.

122:6 Ps 102:14 — 6 Pray for peace in Jerusalem.
May all who love this city prosper.
122:7 Isa 62:6 — 7 O Jerusalem, may there be peace within your walls
and prosperity in your palaces.
122:8 Ps 133:1 — 8 For the sake of my family and friends, I will say,
"May you have peace."
9 For the sake of the house of the LORD our God,
I will seek what is best for you, O Jerusalem.

PSALM 123

A song for pilgrims ascending to Jerusalem.

123:1 Pss 11:4; 141:8 — 1 I lift my eyes to You,
O God, enthroned in heaven.
123:2 Mal 1:6 — 2 We keep looking to the LORD our God for His mercy,
just as servants keep their eyes on their master,
123:3 Neh 4:4; Pss 4:1; 51:1; 79:4; 119:22 — as a slave girl watches her mistress for the slightest signal.
3 Have mercy on us, LORD, have mercy,
for we have had our fill of contempt.
123:4 Ps 79:4 — 4 We have had more than our fill of the scoffing
of the proud
and the contempt of the arrogant.

122:4 Israelites were required to travel to Jerusalem yearly for worship (see Exodus 23:14-19; Deuteronomy 12).

▸ WORSHIP
122:6 Pray for Jerusalem. If you have read any newspapers lately or tuned into your favorite newscast, you know Jerusalem has a prominent role in the news. It seems that the whole earth has focused on that one small city in the Middle East. In fact, Jerusalem is the center of Bible history and prophecy. It is the spiritual focus of the Jewish nation. Worldwide conflict perches on the edge of Jerusalem. Many wars have been fought on that city's behalf over the last several thousand years, and the current skirmishes suggest the last war for Jerusalem has not been fought. This verse tells us to pray for the peace of Jerusalem. Ask God to preserve the lives of the people within this historic city. (***See Worship****> OT> Fasting and Prayer> Prayer> Psalms> Songs for pilgrimage,* TopicGuide page A26.)

122:7 The ultimate glory of Jerusalem was not its bricks and mortar, but the people of God living in harmony with one another and God.

122:9 The Babylonians ransacked Jerusalem and destroyed Solomon's Temple in 586 BC (2 Kings 25). The thorough destruction of Jerusalem and the second Temple (or Herod's Temple) by Titus and the Romans in AD 70 ended the possibility of Israelites fulfilling the ceremonial laws pertaining to sacrifice. This makes modern Judaism a significant departure from the commands of the law.

123:1 References to God's heavenly throne fill the Scriptures (Matthew 5:34; Hebrews 12:2; Revelation 20:12), but God's people understood that He cannot be contained (1 Kings 8:27).

▸ ADOPTION
123:2 Look to God for mercy. In the days when slavery was common, the relationship between a slave and his master was clearly defined. The slave had no rights. He had to do what the master said immediately and thoroughly. Any laxity could bring severe punishment. The slave studied the master's wants so that he could respond promptly and correctly. That's how we should look to the Lord. He grants us mercy out of His loving heart; therefore, we should look for His slightest signal. We should respond to His every desire for us. We should jump to do His command. Dedicate yourself to be a slave for Jesus. (***See Adoption****> With Christ> United with Christ> Enslaved to God,* TopicGuide page A37.)

123:2 A servant might watch the hand of his or her master for commands, punishment, or provision. All three could be in mind here, as God's people depend on Him for everything.

PSALM 124

A song for pilgrims ascending to Jerusalem. A psalm of David.

1 What if the LORD had not been on our side?
Let all Israel repeat: 124:1 Pss 94:17; 129:1
2 What if the LORD had not been on our side
when people attacked us?
3 They would have swallowed us alive
in their burning anger. 124:3 Pss 56:1; 57:3
4 The waters would have engulfed us; 124:4 Pss 18:16; 69:2
a torrent would have overwhelmed us.
5 Yes, the raging waters of their fury
would have overwhelmed our very lives.

6 Praise the LORD,
who did not let their teeth tear us apart!
7 We escaped like a bird from a hunter's trap.
The trap is broken, and we are free! 124:7 Pss 91:3; 141:10 Prov 6:5
8 Our help is from the LORD,
who made heaven and earth. 124:8 Gen 1:1 Ps 121:2

PSALM 125

A song for pilgrims ascending to Jerusalem.

1 Those who trust in the LORD are as secure as Mount Zion; 125:1 Ps 46:5
they will not be defeated but will endure forever.
2 Just as the mountains surround Jerusalem, 125:2 Ps 121:8 Zech 2:5
so the LORD surrounds His people, both now and forever.
3 The wicked will not rule the land of the godly, 125:3 1 Sam 24:10 Prov 22:8 Isa 14:5
for then the godly might be tempted to do wrong.
4 O LORD, do good to those who are good,
whose hearts are in tune with You. 125:4 Pss 7:10; 94:15; 119:68

124:1 The liturgical instruction "Let all Israel repeat" shows that the recitation of this psalm was begun by a priest or leader, followed by a response from the congregation of travelers.

124:3 The fiery dangers here compare with the waters of verses 4-5, the ravaging of wild beasts in verse 6, and the trap of the hunter in verse 7. God rescued them from every imaginable disaster.

124:4 The deluge of this verse could refer to Israel's crossing of the Red Sea (Exodus 14:22) or to a metaphorical flood (see Psalms 18:4; 29:3, 10; 32:6; 42:7; 46:2-4; 114:3).

▸ WORSHIP
124:8 God is our help. When her husband died, Martha was left with an empty house, medical bills, and an inadequate income. Because she was elderly, Martha didn't have the ability to work at a job. Her situation seemed hopeless. But she had spent a lifetime trusting God for her needs, so she went to Him with her concerns. She believed that God owned heaven and earth—He could easily help her. Month by month, He did meet her needs. Your problem may not resemble Martha's, but you can expect that God will help you. Go to Him with your problems today. Remember that He owns the universe, so He is able to help you go from where you are to where He wants you to be. (***See Worship**> OT> Reverence> God helps those who fear Him,* TopicGuide page A28.)

▸ GOD
125:1 Our trust is secure. If you live close to a mountain, take a few moments to view the scene. Or look at a picture of the Rockies or Alps. What do you see? The mountain stands tall and immovable, with big shoulders and a lofty beauty. It doesn't change from day to day. The weather around it may change, but the mountain stays the same. This mountain is like the person who puts his trust in God. He won't be moved. The person who trusts in God lives securely through all kinds of trials and turmoil. Is that true of you? Do you place your trust in God for everything? Turn it all over to Him. (***See God**> God's Attributes> Eternal> The eternal God is the believer's source of security,* TopicGuide page A16.)

125:1 Mount Zion was the hill on which the Temple was built. As the place of God's earthly dwelling, it represented holiness and stability. These traits belong to those who put their trust in God (James 1:2-8).

125:2 Jerusalem was in the mountainous region that ran from north to south through central Israel. The mountain closest to Jerusalem was the Mount of Olives, set east of Jerusalem (see 2 Kings 6:17).

125:4-5 The pilgrim/psalmist reminds God to keep His covenant promises to bless those who obey the law, repent of their sins, and believe His promises (Deuteronomy 28:1-14). On the other hand, he calls on God to curse those who do not keep the covenant.

125:5 Gal 6:16
5 But banish those who turn to crooked ways, O LORD.
Take them away with those who do evil.

May Israel have peace!

PSALM 126

A song for pilgrims ascending to Jerusalem.

126:1 Jer 29:14
1 When the LORD brought back His exiles to Jerusalem,*
it was like a dream!
126:2 Job 8:21 Ps 51:14
2 We were filled with laughter,
and we sang for joy.
And the other nations said,
"What amazing things the LORD has done for them."
126:3 Isa 25:9
3 Yes, the LORD has done amazing things for us!
What joy!

126:4 Isa 35:6; 43:19
4 Restore our fortunes, LORD,
as streams renew the desert.
126:5 Ps 80:5 Gal 6:9
5 Those who plant in tears
will harvest with shouts of joy.
6 They weep as they go to plant their seed,
but they sing as they return with the harvest.

PSALM 127

A song for pilgrims ascending to Jerusalem. A psalm of Solomon.

127:1 Ps 78:69
1 Unless the LORD builds a house,
the work of the builders is wasted.
Unless the LORD protects a city,
guarding it with sentries will do no good.
127:2 Gen 3:17 Job 11:18-19 Eccl 5:12
2 It is useless for you to work so hard
from early morning until late at night,

126:1 Hebrew *Zion.*

126:1 The decision of King Cyrus of Persia to allow the Jews to return to Israel (see the books of Ezra and Nehemiah, as well as 2 Chronicles 36) was not political but providential. Therefore, the pilgrim/psalmist renders praise not to Cyrus but to God.

126:4 The reference to streams in this verse can be translated literally as "streams in the Negev." In south Israel, the arid Negev region is riven with gullies and dry riverbeds. At the slightest downpour, these ditches stream with rushing water. During the rainy season, this arid land becomes green and full of life.

▶ HOLINESS

126:5 The law of sowing and reaping. Imagine how the Jewish people felt when they saw Jerusalem. They had been in exile for years, and then the king allowed them to return to their homeland. Their joy was overwhelming. Why did God allow them to go home? They had obeyed Him, so He blessed them. They were rewarded for trusting God—even when their circumstances were discouraging. Galatians 6:9 says, "Let's not get tired of doing what is good. At just the right time we will reap a harvest of blessing if we don't give up." Do you get tired of doing what you know is right? Are you tired of forging ahead in your area of ministry? Keep in mind what God did for His people when they trusted and obeyed Him. God will bless you for doing what's right, too. (***See Holiness**> Changed by God> God Provides> Rewarding us,* TopicGuide page A41.)

▶ SPIRITUAL WARFARE

127:1 Building a godly home. If you go into a bookstore, you will find many books on how to build a strong marriage and raise good children. Some of the advice is bizarre; other authors use common sense in their writing. But when it comes down to the facts, only those who trust God to build their homes have lasting results. God is the Creator of the home. He knows the hearts of each individual. He can see the future. And through His Holy Spirit, we can have the power to build our homes on His principles. What does it mean to allow the Lord to build your home? You must go to Him with all your concerns and problems. You must talk to Him daily and read His Word. And you must apply each principle that you find in His Word. When you do, your work will be rewarded with eternal effects. (***See Spiritual Warfare**> Resisting Sin and Evil> Trusting God> Obeying God,* TopicGuide page A46.)

127:1 Solomon's association with this psalm makes it natural to think that the building mentioned here was the Temple. The security of the city, specifically Jerusalem, was another of Solomon's concerns.

anxiously working for food to eat;
for God gives rest to His loved ones.

3 Children are a gift from the LORD;
they are a reward from Him. 127:3 Deut 28:4
4 Children born to a young man
are like arrows in a warrior's hands.
5 How joyful is the man whose quiver is full of them!
He will not be put to shame when he confronts his accusers at the city gates.

PSALM 128

A song for pilgrims ascending to Jerusalem.

1 How joyful are those who fear the LORD—
all who follow His ways! 128:1 Pss 112:1; 119:3
2 You will enjoy the fruit of your labor. 128:2 Eccl 8:12
How joyful and prosperous you will be!
3 Your wife will be like a fruitful grapevine, 128:3 Ps 52:8
flourishing within your home.
Your children will be like vigorous young olive trees
as they sit around your table.
4 That is the LORD's blessing
for those who fear Him.

5 May the LORD continually bless you from Zion. 128:5 Pss 122:9; 134:3
May you see Jerusalem prosper as long as you live.
6 May you live to enjoy your grandchildren. 128:6 Gen 48:11
May Israel have peace!

PSALM 129

A song for pilgrims ascending to Jerusalem.

1 From my earliest youth my enemies have persecuted me. 129:1 Exod 1:11
Let all Israel repeat this:

127:3 No matter what parents may feel or the state may proclaim, all children should be treated as precious gifts of God.

127:4 Children, particularly sons, were viewed as weapons that could rally to the aid of their parents in times of crisis.

127:5 God's protection of His people included providing strong sons, who would rally to the gates of the city to defend it and their families' lives.

128:1 The book of Psalms begins (1:1) with the theme of God's blessing on those who keep covenant with Him. Those who fear God live obedient, courageous lives (Psalms 34:7; 36:1; 119:63).

128:2 An obvious sign of God's blessing is enjoyment of the results of one's labor. When sin entered the world, the negative effects included the necessity of great labor to secure sustenance (Genesis 3:17-19). In an agrarian culture, it was not rare for a man to work so hard for food and water that he was unable to enjoy it. The fruits of his labor might even be taken away before he could consume them (Ecclesiastes 5:8–6:12).

▸ WORSHIP
128:3 The advantage of revering God in your home. This passage gives us a picture of a godly home. Each person in the household contributes to the atmosphere of harmony and peace. The members are content and eager for the future. Of course, no one can guarantee that our family members will revere God, because we each have our own wills, but the spouses who build their relationship on God will experience blessings, joy, and fulfillment. If they revere God, they will avoid many of the pitfalls that sin brings into a home. Does your family resemble this picture? If not, why not? If the problem is that you don't revere God, change this right now. You can't afford to spend one more day building on the wrong foundation. (***See Worship****> OT> Reverence> He blesses those who revere Him,* TopicGuide page A29.)

128:3 Both wine (Psalm 104:15) and family can bring sorrow as well as joy. In this case, a wine-producing vine and a child-producing wife are acknowledged as blessings of God on those who obey Him.

128:5 "From Zion" refers to Mount Zion, the hill just north of Jerusalem that was the site of the Temple. "From Zion" is a poetic way of celebrating the blessings of God that flow from His presence (Psalms 2:6; 50:2).

129:1-3 These images of oppression remind the traveler and his companions of their slave origins in Egypt.

129:2 Jer 15:20 Matt 16:18
2 From my earliest youth my enemies have persecuted me,
but they have never defeated me.
3 My back is covered with cuts,
as if a farmer had plowed long furrows.
4 But the LORD is good;
He has cut me free from the ropes of the ungodly.

129:5 Ps 71:13 Mic 4:11
5 May all who hate Jerusalem*
be turned back in shameful defeat.
129:6 2 Kgs 19:26 Ps 37:2
6 May they be as useless as grass on a rooftop,
turning yellow when only half grown,
7 ignored by the harvester,
despised by the binder.
129:8 Ruth 2:4 Ps 118:26
8 And may those who pass by
refuse to give them this blessing:
"The LORD bless you;
we bless you in the LORD's name."

PSALM 130

A song for pilgrims ascending to Jerusalem.

130:1 Pss 42:7; 69:2
1 From the depths of despair, O LORD,
I call for Your help.
130:2 2 Chr 6:40 Pss 28:2; 64:1
2 Hear my cry, O Lord.
Pay attention to my prayer.

130:3 Pss 76:7; 86:5
3 LORD, if You kept a record of our sins,
who, O Lord, could ever survive?
130:4 Exod 34:7
4 But You offer forgiveness,
that we might learn to fear You.

130:5 Ps 40:1 Isa 8:17
5 I am counting on the LORD;
yes, I am counting on Him.
I have put my hope in His word.

129:5 Hebrew *Zion.*

129:4-8 These images of military assault and discourtesy remind the pilgrim of the days when the Babylonians attacked Jerusalem (in 586 BC), only to then be conquered by the Persian king Cyrus the Great in 539 BC.

129:6-7 Every bit of vegetation was used to improve life in ancient Israel. But the psalmist declares that those who hate God's earthly throne are like stunted grass and deserve to be treated as unworthy of any use whatsoever.

129:8 No benediction or parting blessing exists for those who work against God (Ruth 2:4) or ignore His people.

130:1 The psalm begins with a confession of deep anguish. Only the Master of the depths (Psalm 77:16; Romans 8:39) can save the pilgrim/psalmist from this crisis. The word translated here as "depths" is also found in Psalm 69:2, with closely related expressions in Psalms 18:4; 29:3, 10; 32:6; 42:7; 46:2, 4; 114:3.

130:2-3 The pilgrim/psalmist is certain that even though he is submerged beneath the greatest of emotional pain, God will hear his prayer (Psalms 119:149; 142:6). Yet he remains puzzled as to how God can hear his prayers in light of his numerous sins (Psalm 53:1-3; Romans 3:9-20).

▸ GOD

130:3 The joy of forgiveness. Consider what you have done today. Think of all the acts you have performed. Include your interactions with people, your secret deeds, and your reactions to your circumstances. How many of them were displeasing to God? Now recall your attitudes. How many of those were sinful? Ponder your discontent with your situation, your selfishness, and your impatience. Just imagine if God held every one of these against you. How big of a pile did you accumulate today? Now multiply that by 365 days. Are you worried yet? And that's only for one year. Aren't you glad that God has forgiven you? What a miracle of grace that is! Our only hope of heaven is in the forgiveness of God made possible through Jesus Christ. Thank Him today for the complete forgiveness He offers to you. (***See God**> God's Attributes> Forgiving> God's forgiveness clears one's record,* TopicGuide page A16.)

130:4 God regularly offered forgiveness to Old Testament saints who, by faith, offered the sacrifices God required (1 Kings 8:46-51; Nehemiah 9:17; Jeremiah 36:7).

130:5 Though the pilgrim/psalmist lives in the depths of despair (130:1), he can wait patiently for God's promises to come true.

6 I long for the Lord
more than sentries long for the dawn,
yes, more than sentries long for the dawn.

7 O Israel, hope in the LORD;
for with the LORD there is unfailing love.
His redemption overflows.
8 He Himself will redeem Israel
from every kind of sin.

130:6 Ps 63:6
130:7 Pss 103:4; 131:3
130:8 Luke 1:68

PSALM 131

A song for pilgrims ascending to Jerusalem. A psalm of David.

1 LORD, my heart is not proud;
my eyes are not haughty.
I don't concern myself with matters too great
or too awesome for me to grasp.
2 Instead, I have calmed and quieted myself,
like a weaned child who no longer cries for its mother's milk.
Yes, like a weaned child is my soul within me.

3 O Israel, put your hope in the LORD—
now and always.

131:1 Rom 12:16
131:2 Ps 62:1
131:3 Ps 130:7

PSALM 132

A song for pilgrims ascending to Jerusalem.

1 LORD, remember David
and all that he suffered.
2 He made a solemn promise to the LORD.
He vowed to the Mighty One of Israel,*
3 "I will not go home;
I will not let myself rest.
4 I will not let my eyes sleep
nor close my eyelids in slumber

132:2 Gen 49:24 Isa 49:26
132:4 Prov 6:4

132:2 Hebrew *of Jacob;* also in 132:5. See note on 44:4.

130:8 The pilgrim/psalmist lifts his voice loud enough for the entire nation to hear his story of forgiveness through repentance and faith in God's promises.

▸ BIBLE
131:2 Be quiet before God. If you are a parent, you can relate to the image in this verse. Who is safer than a baby being held by his mother? He has every need supplied, including his desire for comfort and love. To him, the world is not a scary place because he feels his mother's loving arms around him. Whenever he cries, she's there to see to his discomfort. What a picture of the intimacy God wants to have with us. He wants us to come to Him like a baby who snuggles up to his mother. We can have such rich times reading God's Word and praying. But we must come before God in quietness and meditation, shutting out the world and concentrating on Him. In your devotions this week, spend a few extra minutes just telling God how much you appreciate His comfort and love. Quietly meditate on the verses you read. (*See **Bible**> Unity> God's Message> Devotion to God,* TopicGuide page A11.)

131:2 God is not a sexual being, so Scripture freely uses male and, in this case, female images to describe Him. Other female images include those of a mother birthing and feeding her children (Isaiah 46:3-4; 49:14-15; 66:12-13), a midwife (Psalm 22:9-10; Isaiah 66:9), a housewife looking for a coin (Luke 15:8-10), and many others (Deuteronomy 32:11-12; Matthew 23:37; Hosea 13:8).

132:2-5 The psalmist recalls David's commitment to build a Temple for the Lord (2 Samuel 7). Although David was denied the honor, the Lord established a covenant with David and his family, ensuring that one of David's descendants would rule over the people of God forever (see 2 Samuel 7:10-12). David's son Solomon eventually built a Temple for the Lord.

THE BROKEN RECORD OF SIN

RONNIE WAS SIXTEEN YEARS OLD, and the highlight of his year—perhaps even his life—was a trip to Hawaii with his youth group. After all the fund-raisers and planning meetings, the thrilling day finally arrived. Ronnie waved to his mother at the airport and then boarded the plane for the time of his life.

But during the trip, Ronnie gave in to temptation and stole some items from the other students' belongings. He was caught with the items, and when he returned home, his mother was told what he had done. His mother punished him by grounding him for a month. But even after Ronnie had served his punishment and demonstrated that he really had repented of stealing, his mother brought up the incident again and again. She mentioned his stealing when he didn't complete his chores, when he got a bad grade in school, or when they argued about the least thing. Ronnie felt like he could never get away from that sin.

What would your life be like if, each time you sinned, God brought up everything you had ever done wrong in the past? You would feel like Ronnie did—unable to move beyond the guilt of your past. But God is not like an imperfect parent. The psalmist wrote, "LORD, if You kept a record of our sins, who, O LORD, could ever survive? But You offer forgiveness, that we might learn to fear You" (Psalm 130:3-4).

God's mercy is complete. When He forgives, He refuses to continue to hold our sin against us in any way. Then God uses our sin and His great mercy as an example to bless others. Paul wrote, "'Christ Jesus came into the world to save sinners'—and I am the worst of them all. But God had mercy on me so that Christ Jesus could use me as a prime example of His great patience with even the worst sinners. Then others will realize that they, too, can believe in Him and receive eternal life" (1 Timothy 1:15-16).

Many people continue to live under the fear that God is counting up the sins He has forgiven until the number gets too high—and then He'll lash out and punish us for all those past sins. But God truly forgives when we repent. In His mercy, He doesn't hold grudges; He holds the perfect sacrifice of His Son as evidence that the punishment for our sins has been accomplished. All God is concerned about is His glory and your glorious future.

[5] until I find a place to build a house for the LORD,
a sanctuary for the Mighty One of Israel." 132:5 Acts 7:46

[6] We heard that the Ark was in Ephrathah;
then we found it in the distant countryside of Jaar. 132:6 Gen 35:19 1 Sam 7:1; 17:12
[7] Let us go to the sanctuary of the LORD;
let us worship at the footstool of His throne. 132:7 1 Chr 28:2 Pss 5:7; 99:5
[8] Arise, O LORD, and enter Your resting place,
along with the Ark, the symbol of Your power. 132:8-10 //2 Chr 6:41-42
[9] May Your priests be clothed in godliness;
may Your loyal servants sing for joy. 132:8 Num 10:35 Ps 78:61
[10] For the sake of Your servant David,
do not reject the king You have anointed. 132:9 Ps 149:5
[11] The LORD swore an oath to David
with a promise He will never take back: 132:11 2 Sam 7:12-16 2 Chr 6:16 *Acts 2:30
"I will place one of your descendants
on your throne.
[12] If your descendants obey the terms of My covenant
and the laws that I teach them, 132:12 Luke 1:32
then your royal line
will continue forever and ever."

[13] For the LORD has chosen Jerusalem*;
He has desired it for His home. 132:13 Ps 78:68
[14] "This is My resting place forever," He said.
"I will live here, for this is the home I desired. 132:14 Matt 23:21
[15] I will bless this city and make it prosperous;
I will satisfy its poor with food. 132:15 Ps 107:9
[16] I will clothe its priests with godliness;
its faithful servants will sing for joy.
[17] Here I will increase the power of David;
My anointed one will be a light for My people.

132:13 Hebrew *Zion*.

WORSHIP

132:5 Love for God's house. David had a desire that consumed him. He wanted to build a Temple for the Lord, a place that would honor God and where the people could worship. God gave David his desire by allowing him to prepare all the materials for building the Temple. Then his son Solomon completed the building. Today we don't have a Temple at which to worship like the Israelites did, but we have our churches, where we can gather to honor God. The church is now the center of the Christian community. We minister; we fellowship with other believers; we study the Scriptures; and we sing and pray together there. But do we desire to be in church with the same fervor that David had for the Temple? Or do we take for granted the many blessings we experience through the local church? Ask God to give you a love for His house like David had for the Temple. (***See Worship****> OT> Place> Temple> God's promise to build the Temple through Solomon,* TopicGuide page A27.)

132:8-9 Solomon spoke these words at the inauguration of the Temple (2 Chronicles 6:41).

132:10-12 The Lord promised David that one of his descendants would always reign over God's people (2 Samuel 7). The promise, however, required faithfulness on the part of David's sons. When those descendants were unfaithful, God's love for David caused Him to extend grace to them. God's promise was ultimately fulfilled in Christ, David's faithful Son, whose reign will never end.

GOD

132:11 The promise of a future King. This verse is a prophecy about a future King who will reign forever on David's throne. In Acts 2:32-33, Luke explains, "God raised Jesus from the dead, and we are all witnesses of this. Now He is exalted to the place of highest honor in heaven, at God's right hand." Jesus fulfilled all the requirements in the Old Testament for this King. Someday He will return and become the flesh-and-blood King of Israel and the world. His reign will never end. What does this fact mean to us? It means we can place our lives in His hands and trust His mighty power. We need never be afraid of other people or our circumstances because Jesus rules it all. Hang onto this promise. Jesus reigns in heaven today and He will reign on earth soon. (***See God****> God's Attributes> Eternal> The Son's reign will have no end,* TopicGuide page A16.)

132:13 God chose the city of Jerusalem as the focal point of His presence on earth. It was there that the Temple was built as the focal point of ancient Israel's worship.

18 I will clothe his enemies with shame,
but he will be a glorious king."

PSALM 133

A song for pilgrims ascending to Jerusalem. A psalm of David.

1 How wonderful and pleasant it is
when brothers live together in harmony!
133:2 Exod 30:25, 30 Lev 8:12
2 For harmony is as precious as the anointing oil
that was poured over Aaron's head,
that ran down his beard
and onto the border of his robe.
133:3 Deut 4:48
3 Harmony is as refreshing as the dew from Mount Hermon
that falls on the mountains of Zion.
And there the LORD has pronounced His blessing,
even life everlasting.

PSALM 134

A song for pilgrims ascending to Jerusalem.

134:1 Deut 10:8 1 Chr 9:33 2 Chr 29:11
1 Oh, praise the LORD, all you servants of the LORD,
you who serve at night in the house of the LORD.
2 Lift up holy hands in prayer,
and praise the LORD.
134:2 Ps 28:2 1 Tim 2:8
134:3 Pss 124:8; 128:5
3 May the LORD, who made heaven and earth,
bless you from Jerusalem.*

PSALM 135

1 Praise the LORD!

Praise the name of the LORD!
Praise Him, you who serve the LORD,
135:2 Ps 116:19
2 you who serve in the house of the LORD,
in the courts of the house of our God.

134:3 Hebrew *Zion.*

▸ HOLINESS
133:1 The refreshing nature of harmony. If you live in a house where people are feuding, you understand the truth of this psalm. Whenever people quarrel, the atmosphere becomes charged, and no one can rest. Our tendency is to have conflict with the people we love most because we are so close to them. Yet this conflict causes much more harm than we are willing to admit. Our homes are embedded in turmoil. Peace is nowhere to be found. People become distant to each other. But how pleasant we feel when everyone gets along. True harmony can be achieved only through the power of the Holy Spirit. So much of our conflict comes from selfishness and a lack of compassion for others—set aside your own rights and embrace those who have offended you. (***See Holiness****> Disciplines> Of Engagement> Fellowship,* TopicGuide page A42.)

133:1 "Brothers" most likely encompasses all of God's people as they are united in the family of God.

133:2 At their ordination, Aaron and his sons were anointed with oil (Exodus 30:22-33; Leviticus 8:30). The luxuriant oil marked the priests as consecrated for their service to the Lord.

133:3 Mount Hermon in northern Israel was well known for heavy dew. Mount Zion outside of Jerusalem was the site of the Temple. As with the sacred oil, unity among God's people is symbolized by a liquid flowing downward. In much the same way, the Holy Spirit, the source of unity, is described as being poured out upon God's people (Acts 2:17-18; 10:45; Ephesians 4:3).

134:1 The "servants of the LORD" are most likely the priests and Levites who serve in the Temple of Jerusalem.

▸ WORSHIP
134:2 Lift up your hands. What is the best way to praise the Lord? God does not mandate any certain position, but in this verse we can see that He encourages us to express our love and awe of Him by lifting up our hands in prayer. When we lift our hands toward heaven, we turn our focus on God. As we concentrate on Him, we filter out the distractions around us. For some people, this position expresses their sense of worship. But whatever position we take during our prayer, our motive should be to surrender to God's will for our lives. (***See Worship****> OT> Posture> Hands uplifted,* TopicGuide page A28.)

[3] Praise the LORD, for the LORD is good;
celebrate His lovely name with music.
[4] For the LORD has chosen Jacob for Himself,
Israel for His own special treasure.

[5] I know the greatness of the LORD—
that our Lord is greater than any other god.
[6] The LORD does whatever pleases Him
throughout all heaven and earth,
and on the seas and in their depths.
[7] He causes the clouds to rise over the whole earth.
He sends the lightning with the rain
and releases the wind from His storehouses.

[8] He destroyed the firstborn in each Egyptian home,
both people and animals.
[9] He performed miraculous signs and wonders in Egypt
against Pharaoh and all his people.
[10] He struck down great nations
and slaughtered mighty kings—
[11] Sihon king of the Amorites,
Og king of Bashan,
and all the kings of Canaan.
[12] He gave their land as an inheritance,
a special possession to His people Israel.

[13] Your name, O LORD, endures forever;
Your fame, O LORD, is known to every generation.
[14] For the LORD will give justice to His people
and have compassion on His servants.

[15] The idols of the nations are merely things of silver and gold,
shaped by human hands.
[16] They have mouths but cannot speak,
and eyes but cannot see.
[17] They have ears but cannot hear,
and noses but cannot smell.

135:3 Pss 68:4; 100:5
135:4 Exod 19:5; Deut 7:6; 10:15; 1 Pet 2:9
135:5 Pss 48:1; 97:9
135:6 Ps 115:3
135:7 Job 38:25-26; Jer 51:16; Zech 10:1
135:8 Ps 78:51
135:9 Deut 6:22
135:10 Ps 136:17-21
135:11 Num 21:33-35; Josh 12:7-24
135:12 Ps 78:55
135:13 Exod 3:15; Ps 102:12
135:14 Deut 32:36; Ps 106:45
135:15-20 //Ps 115:4-11

135:3-4 The call to praise the Lord is grounded in the Lord's character ("the LORD is good") and in the grace He showed when He chose the Israelites to be His people. The people of Israel in no way deserved such an honor; their position was entirely due to God's grace (Exodus 19:5-6; Deuteronomy 7:7-11).

135:5-7 The psalmist approaches the greatness of God from two perspectives: His rule over creation and His deliverance of Israel (see 135:8-13). His rule over creation is described in a way that directly challenges the assumptions of the local pagan mythologies. The God of Israel tames the chaos symbolized by the raging seas and controls the weather.

▸ PURPOSE
135:7 The grandeur of God's creation. First comes a strange stillness. The sky darkens with low-hanging clouds. The humidity rises. Lightning flashes over the horizon. You know that a thunderstorm is approaching rapidly. The signs are clear. Then the wind begins to blow and the rain pours down. The thunder crashes as the lightning comes nearer. The sky darkens even more. Do these things remind you of God's grandeur? Does a thunderstorm show you God's power? None of these natural forces would behave as they do if God wasn't in charge. He sends them for our good and He keeps them in check for our safety. All of God's creation tells of His majesty. Praise God for each thing in nature that reminds you of His attributes. Praise God for the wind because it reminds us of God's Spirit. Praise God for the earthquake because it reminds us of His strength. Praise God for the snow because it reminds us of God's purity. (***See Purpose****> God's Means> God's Sovereignty> God sustains His creation,* TopicGuide page A52.)

135:8-12 The Exodus and the conquest of Canaan marked the birth of Israel as a nation. They were the most significant and dramatic events in the Old Testament history of salvation. The events in Egypt are recorded in Exodus 7–15. The victories over Sihon and Og are recorded in Numbers 21:21-35.

135:15-18 Idols fashioned by human hands are entirely powerless and worthless. Those who worship such idols are condemned to futility. The psalmist's stinging critique of idolatry echoes similar condemnations in Isaiah 44:9-20, Jeremiah 10:1-9, and Habakkuk 2:18-19.

[18] And those who make idols are just like them,
as are all who trust in them.

[19] O Israel, praise the LORD!
O priests—descendants of Aaron—praise the LORD!

135:20 Ps 118:4

[20] O Levites, praise the LORD!
All you who fear the LORD, praise the LORD!
[21] The LORD be praised from Zion,
for He lives here in Jerusalem.

Praise the LORD!

PSALM 136

136:1 1 Chr 16:41 2 Chr 20:21 Ps 107:1

[1] Give thanks to the LORD, for He is good!
His faithful love endures forever.
[2] Give thanks to the God of gods.
His faithful love endures forever.

136:2 Deut 10:17

[3] Give thanks to the Lord of lords.
His faithful love endures forever.

136:4 Ps 72:18

[4] Give thanks to Him who alone does mighty miracles.
His faithful love endures forever.

136:5 Prov 3:19

[5] Give thanks to Him who made the heavens so skillfully.
His faithful love endures forever.

136:6 Ps 24:2

[6] Give thanks to Him who placed the earth among the waters.
His faithful love endures forever.

136:7 Ps 74:16

[7] Give thanks to Him who made the heavenly lights—
His faithful love endures forever.

136:8 Gen 1:16

[8] the sun to rule the day,
His faithful love endures forever.
[9] and the moon and stars to rule the night.
His faithful love endures forever.

136:10 Exod 12:29 Ps 78:51

[10] Give thanks to Him who killed the firstborn of Egypt.
His faithful love endures forever.

▸ GOD

136:1 God's faithful love. It's so true that faithfulness and love go together. If a person has love but is not faithful, his love is not consistent. Think of a husband who is not faithful to his wife. He does not really love her. He is not thinking of her welfare above all. But God's love is completely faithful. That means His love will never diminish or fail. His love lasts forever. He always looks to our welfare and benefit. That gives us great confidence. Paul writes, "I am convinced that nothing can ever separate us from God's love. Neither death nor life, neither angels nor demons, neither our fears for today nor our worries about tomorrow—not even the powers of hell can separate us from God's love" (Romans 8:38). When you begin doubting God's love, go back to this verse in Psalms. The refrain is repeated 25 times throughout this chapter. Use it as your chorus to keep your eyes on God's love. (***See God***> *God's Attributes> Loving> Nothing can separate the believer from His love,* TopicGuide page A17.)

136:1-3 Thanksgiving is the theme of this psalm. Verses 1-3, 26 direct the thanksgiving to the Lord. The remainder of the psalm focuses on the works of the Lord for which He is to be thanked. God's faithful love is the expression of His commitment to the people to whom He has bound Himself in a covenant relationship.

136:4-9 God's creation is the initial focus of the psalmist's calls for thanksgiving. God is to be thanked because He alone brought all things into existence (see Genesis 1).

▸ GOD

136:7 The heavenly lights shine on. What would happen if you walked outside tonight and the sky was entirely black—you could not see a star twinkling anywhere and the moon did not rise? You wait for the clouds to part, but . . . nothing. This is unimaginable, because the stars are consistent. But they are just a shadow of God's faithfulness. He made the stars so consistent, and He is the One who promises that His faithfulness will go beyond every physical thing. The next time you doubt God's faithfulness, take a walk in the night air and look up into the sky. What a great reminder of God's faithfulness! (***See God***> *God's Attributes> All-Powerful> His creation reflects His power,* TopicGuide page A15.)

136:10-16 The second focus of the thanksgiving directed toward the Lord is His deliverance of Israel from Egyptian slavery. The psalmist specifically commemorates the tenth plague (Exodus 11), the Red Sea crossing (Exodus 14–15), and the Lord's provision for Israel through the wilderness (Exodus 16–17).

11 He brought Israel out of Egypt.
His faithful love endures forever.
12 He acted with a strong hand and powerful arm.
His faithful love endures forever.
13 Give thanks to Him who parted the Red Sea.*
His faithful love endures forever.
14 He led Israel safely through,
His faithful love endures forever.
15 but He hurled Pharaoh and his army into the Red Sea.
His faithful love endures forever.
16 Give thanks to Him who led His people through the wilderness.
His faithful love endures forever.
17 Give thanks to Him who struck down mighty kings.
His faithful love endures forever.
18 He killed powerful kings—
His faithful love endures forever.
19 Sihon king of the Amorites,
His faithful love endures forever.
20 and Og king of Bashan.
His faithful love endures forever.
21 God gave the land of these kings as an inheritance—
His faithful love endures forever.
22 a special possession to His servant Israel.
His faithful love endures forever.
23 He remembered us in our weakness.
His faithful love endures forever.
24 He saved us from our enemies.
His faithful love endures forever.
25 He gives food to every living thing.
His faithful love endures forever.
26 Give thanks to the God of heaven.
His faithful love endures forever.

136:11 Exod 12:51; 13:3 Deut 9:29
136:12 Deut 4:34 Ps 44:3
136:13 Exod 14:21 Ps 78:13
136:14 Ps 106:9
136:16 Exod 13:18 Deut 8:15
136:17 Ps 135:10-12
136:21 Josh 12:1
136:22 Isa 41:8; 45:4
136:23 Pss 9:12; 106:45
136:24 Judg 6:9
136:25 Pss 104:27; 145:15
136:26 2 Chr 36:23 Ezra 3:11

PSALM 137

1 Beside the rivers of Babylon, we sat and wept
as we thought of Jerusalem.*
2 We put away our harps,
hanging them on the branches of poplar trees.
3 For our captors demanded a song from us.
Our tormentors insisted on a joyful hymn:
"Sing us one of those songs of Jerusalem!"
4 But how can we sing the songs of the LORD
while in a pagan land?

137:1 Neh 1:4 Ezek 1:1, 3
137:2 Ezek 26:13
137:3 2 Chr 29:27 Neh 12:46

136:13 Hebrew *sea of reeds;* also in 136:15. 137:1 Hebrew *Zion;* also in 137:3.

137:2-3 Song and music were expressions of joy and happiness. Examples of "songs of Jerusalem" (or "songs of Zion") include Psalms 46; 48; 76; 84; 87; 122. Such songs celebrated Jerusalem and the Temple. However, both had been destroyed by the Babylonians, who now tormented their captives with this cruel request.

▶ SALVATION
137:4 Singing songs in a foreign land. At times, the Israelites were taken into captivity and many of the Jewish people were transported to a foreign land. They no longer could worship at the Temple or breathe the air of their homeland. In some ways, we are like those Israelites. Our true homeland is not this world but heaven. This world is filled with pain and suffering. Even

5 If I forget you, O Jerusalem,
let my right hand forget how to play the harp.
137:6 Ezek 3:26
6 May my tongue stick to the roof of my mouth
if I fail to remember you,
if I don't make Jerusalem my greatest joy.
137:7 Jer 49:7-22 Ezek 25:12-14 Obad 1:10-14
7 O LORD, remember what the Edomites did
on the day the armies of Babylon captured Jerusalem.
"Destroy it!" they yelled.
"Level it to the ground!"
137:8 Isa 13:1-22; 47:1-15 Jer 50:1-46; 51:1-64
8 O Babylon, you will be destroyed.
Happy is the one who pays you back
for what you have done to us.
9 Happy is the one who takes your babies
and smashes them against the rocks!

PSALM 138

A psalm of David.

138:1 Pss 95:3; 96:4; 111:1
1 I give You thanks, O LORD, with all my heart;
I will sing Your praises before the gods.
138:2 Ps 5:7
2 I bow before Your holy Temple as I worship.
I praise Your name for Your unfailing love and faithfulness;
for Your promises are backed
by all the honor of Your name.
138:3 Pss 28:7; 46:1; 118:5
3 As soon as I pray, You answer me;
You encourage me by giving me strength.
138:4 Ps 102:15
4 Every king in all the earth will thank You, LORD,
for all of them will hear Your words.
138:6 Pss 101:5; 113:4-7 Prov 3:34 Jas 4:6
5 Yes, they will sing about the LORD's ways,
for the glory of the LORD is very great.
6 Though the LORD is great, He cares for the humble,
but He keeps His distance from the proud.
138:7 Exod 15:12 Ezra 9:8-9 Pss 20:6; 23:4; 71:20
7 Though I am surrounded by troubles,
You will protect me from the anger of my enemies.

the most fortunate of people face trials and sickness. As believers, we endure a world system that's foreign to us. In Philippians 3:20, Paul says that our citizenship is in heaven. We are just sojourners here. Are you living as a citizen of heaven or are you weighed down with this world's concerns? Confront your problems in life with that in mind. You are just here for a while. Endure them with joy, knowing that the best is yet to come! (***See Salvation****> Receiving> When> Heir and citizen of heaven,* TopicGuide page A23.)

137:8-9 The warfare of the ancient world was harsh. When the Babylonians conquered Judah, they most likely killed innocent women and children. Here the psalmist expresses his desire for just retribution against Babylon, which would include similar treatment of the Babylonian population.

▸ GOD

138:1 With all your heart. What does it mean to give God thanks with all your heart? It means that we thank Him for everything. Sometimes it's very difficult to do that. Can you thank God when cancer strikes? Can you thank God when your child runs away? Can you thank God when depression hits? First Thessalonians 5:18 says, "Be thankful in all circumstances, for this is God's will for you who belong to Christ Jesus." Thanking God doesn't mean that we like these difficult situations, but it does acknowledge that we know God is in charge of our lives. Begin right now to thank Him for all the difficulties in your life. Name them one by one and thank God for them. Then you will know what it means to thank God with all your heart. (***See God****> God's Attributes> Faithful> God deserves thanks for His constant faithfulness,* TopicGuide page A16.)

138:4 The Old Testament often expresses the expectation of universal worship being offered to the God of Israel. This expectation was never realized in ancient Israel, but the coming of Christ and the spread of the gospel among the Gentiles initiated the fulfillment of that hope (Isaiah 55:5-7; 60:3; Romans 1:16; Revelation 5:9; 7:9).

138:6 God's transcendence does not render Him removed from His creation. Although far above creation in power and glory, the Lord is intimately concerned with even the lowliest of His creatures. The proud, however, forfeit the benefits of God's kindness (compare James 4:6).

You reach out Your hand,
and the power of Your right hand saves me.
8 The LORD will work out His plans for my life—
for Your faithful love, O LORD, endures forever.
Don't abandon me, for You made me.

138:8 Job 10:3; Pss 27:9; 71:9; Phil 1:6

PSALM 139

For the choir director: A psalm of David.

1 O LORD, You have examined my heart
and know everything about me.
2 You know when I sit down or stand up.
You know my thoughts even when I'm far away.
3 You see me when I travel
and when I rest at home.
You know everything I do.
4 You know what I am going to say
even before I say it, LORD.
5 You go before me and follow me.
You place Your hand of blessing on my head.
6 Such knowledge is too wonderful for me,
too great for me to understand!

7 I can never escape from Your Spirit!
I can never get away from Your presence!
8 If I go up to heaven, You are there;
if I go down to the grave,* You are there.
9 If I ride the wings of the morning,
if I dwell by the farthest oceans,
10 even there Your hand will guide me,
and Your strength will support me.

139:1 Ps 44:21
139:2 Ps 94:11
139:3 Job 14:16
139:4 Heb 4:13
139:5 Ps 34:7
139:6 Job 42:3; Rom 11:33
139:7 Jer 23:24
139:8 Prov 15:11; Amos 9:2-4
139:10 Ps 23:2-3

139:8 Hebrew *to Sheol.*

▸ **GOD**
138:8 God's plans for my life. What assurance we have in this verse! God has not created us and then left us to manage on our own. If we love Him, He has plans for our lives. These plans are so much greater than any we could devise for ourselves. He not only plans for our lives, but He will also guide us into His plans and give us the strength and ability to accomplish them. Verse 3 says that when we pray, God will answer and give us strength. Does this describe your pattern for living? Do you first ask God for His plans and then for His strength to work out what He has for you to do? Put this on the top of your daily prayer list. God will guide you into great and mighty work for Him. (***See God****> God's Attributes> Sovereign> He has a plan for His people and will carry it out,* TopicGuide page A17.)

▸ **GOD**
139:1 What God knows about you. Before you read this verse, what did you think God knew about you? Did you think He saw only what you did in church? Or that He didn't see the innermost secrets in your heart? He knows more about you than you do. He understands your motives and your intentions. He knows what you did yesterday and what you are going to do tomorrow. That is either encouraging or frightening. Because God knows everything about us, we can bring all our problems to Him. We also need to confess every sin immediately because we cannot hide them from Him. (***See God****> God's Attributes> All-Knowing> God's unfathomable knowledge of His people,* TopicGuide page A15.)

139:1 God possesses intimate knowledge of all things, including the lives of His people. As the following verses make clear, nothing escapes the Lord's eye. He perceives and understands all things. Such knowledge ought to inspire both reverent fear and comfort in the Lord's people.

▸ **GOD**
139:7 You cannot escape from God. Jonah felt that he could escape from God, so he hopped on a ship and slipped down into the hold. But Jonah was terribly mistaken. God could see his every move. God sent a storm that caused the sailors to throw Jonah overboard. A great fish swallowed Jonah. Then Jonah wanted God to see him! He prayed for God to rescue him. And God did. We cannot hide from God either. When God asks us to do something that seems more than we can manage, we cannot slip away. Instead, we must rely on God to give us the wisdom and strength to accomplish what He has set before us. If you are facing something that seems insurmountable, take it to God. Don't try to run away. (***See God****> God's Attributes> All-Knowing> One cannot escape God,* TopicGuide page A15.)

139:8 David establishes the Lord's omniscience through a series of contrasts. Each of them has the effect of encompassing all of reality within the reach of God's vision. The first contrast is perhaps the most dramatic. God's sight not only takes in His abode in heaven, but the realm of death, as well.

[139:11 Job 22:13] 11 I could ask the darkness to hide me
and the light around me to become night—
[139:12 Job 34:22; Dan 2:22; 1 Jn 1:5] 12 but even in darkness I cannot hide from You.
To You the night shines as bright as day.
Darkness and light are the same to You.

[139:13 Ps 119:73] 13 You made all the delicate, inner parts of my body
and knit me together in my mother's womb.
14 Thank You for making me so wonderfully complex!
Your workmanship is marvelous—how well I know it.
[139:15 Job 10:8-10; Eccl 11:5] 15 You watched me as I was being formed in utter seclusion,
as I was woven together in the dark of the womb.
[139:16 Job 14:5; Ps 56:8] 16 You saw me before I was born.
Every day of my life was recorded in Your book.
Every moment was laid out
before a single day had passed.

[139:17 Ps 40:5] 17 How precious are Your thoughts about me,* O God.
They cannot be numbered!
18 I can't even count them;
they outnumber the grains of sand!
And when I wake up,
You are still with me!

19 O God, if only You would destroy the wicked!
[139:19 Isa 11:4] Get out of my life, you murderers!
[139:20 Exod 20:7; Deut 5:11] 20 They blaspheme You;
Your enemies misuse Your name.
21 O LORD, shouldn't I hate those who hate You?
Shouldn't I despise those who oppose You?
22 Yes, I hate them with total hatred,
for Your enemies are my enemies.

[139:23 Ps 26:2] 23 Search me, O God, and know my heart;
test me and know my anxious thoughts.
[139:24 Pss 5:8; 16:11; 143:10] 24 Point out anything in me that offends You,
and lead me along the path of everlasting life.

PSALM 140

For the choir director: A psalm of David.

[140:1 Ps 17:13] 1 O LORD, rescue me from evil people.
Protect me from those who are violent,

139:17 Or *How precious to me are Your thoughts.*

139:19-22 David expresses his desire to see God's justice and will accomplished on earth. His hope is not motivated by vengefulness or self-righteousness, but by a sincere and deep regard for God's honor. With the coming of Christ, the warfare of God's people has been directed toward heavenly foes and powers (Ephesians 6:12). However, when Christ returns, God's justice will be dispensed as David prays here.

▸ GOD
139:23 Search me, O God. Have you prayed this prayer—"Search me, O God"—today? Sometimes sin hides in our hearts, deceiving us about what we are thinking and doing. Sins can be such a part of our lives that we don't even recognize them as sins. But when we ask God to search our hearts, He begins to reveal these areas so that we can repent and turn from them. Make this one of the first prayers you pray each day, but be prepared to hear His answer. It may not be what you expected. (***See God*****>** *God's Attributes> All-Knowing> God knows the believer's heart,* TopicGuide page A15.)

140:1-3 David turns to God for help as wicked men seek to harm him. The metaphors of verse 3 suggest they are employing slanderous lies to destroy David's reputation.

2 those who plot evil in their hearts
and stir up trouble all day long.
3 Their tongues sting like a snake;
the venom of a viper drips from their lips. *Interlude*

4 O LORD, keep me out of the hands of the wicked.
Protect me from those who are violent,
for they are plotting against me.
5 The proud have set a trap to catch me;
they have stretched out a net;
they have placed traps all along the way. *Interlude*

6 I said to the LORD, "You are my God!"
Listen, O LORD, to my cries for mercy!
7 O Sovereign LORD, the strong One who rescued me,
You protected me on the day of battle.
8 LORD, do not let evil people have their way.
Do not let their evil schemes succeed,
or they will become proud. *Interlude*

9 Let my enemies be destroyed
by the very evil they have planned for me.
10 Let burning coals fall down on their heads.
Let them be thrown into the fire
or into watery pits from which they can't escape.
11 Don't let liars prosper here in our land.
Cause great disasters to fall on the violent.

12 But I know the LORD will help those they persecute;
He will give justice to the poor.
13 Surely righteous people are praising Your name;
the godly will live in Your presence.

140:2 Ps 56:6; Prov 6:14; Isa 59:4
140:3 Rom 3:13; Jas 3:8
140:4 Ps 71:4
140:5 Job 18:9; Pss 35:7; 57:6
140:6 Esth 9:25; Ps 112:10
140:7 Pss 28:8; 144:10
140:8 Ps 112:10
140:9 Ps 7:16
140:10 Pss 11:6; 21:9; Matt 3:10
140:11 Ps 34:21
140:12 Pss 9:4; 35:10
140:13 Pss 16:11; 17:15; 97:12

PSALM 141

A psalm of David.

1 O LORD, I am calling to You. Please hurry!
Listen when I cry to You for help!

141:1 Ps 70:5

▸ WORSHIP

140:6 A cry to God. In this psalm, David cried out to God during a dark time in his life. Because he was hounded by his enemies, he had to hide in caves and eat on the run. His enemies, including King Saul, wanted to kill him. Yet he still placed his faith in God. In time, God delivered David, and he became king of all Israel. If you are in a dark time right now, you may feel as David did when his enemies seemed to have the upper hand. You think: "I can't imagine how my situation could ever turn out for the good." You may wonder if God is really interested in your situation. When the situation seems the most hopeless, that's the time to say, "You are my God!" The women at the cross certainly didn't see any hope, yet the Resurrection was only days away. If God can do that for them, He can bless your situation. Give Him your trust to handle it in His way. (***See Worship***> *OT> Music> Psalms> Lament> Retaliation,* TopicGuide page A27.)

140:9 The psalmists often envision God's judgment coming upon the wicked in ironic fashion. David prays for the plots of his wicked enemies to backfire upon them. Such an outcome reflects the self-destructive nature of sin.

▸ MINISTRY

140:13 Live in God's presence. Carol was devastated by the news. The doctors had told her that her cancer had been eliminated. But later, it returned. This time, the treatments would be even more difficult. And she knew from experience how sick she would become. But she was determined to go through this trial in God's strength. She began praying right away for God to stave off the depression that was threatening to overcome her. Sometimes she had to pray moment by moment to bring her focus back onto God and off her illness. But day by day she lived in God's presence, and He gave her a joy and fulfillment she initially couldn't imagine that she would experience through her treatment. Living in God's presence means relying on Him for your every need. Prayer is a vital part of this intimate relationship with God. When you start to think and feel as if God isn't near, pray and ask God to help you feel, think, and act like He's right there—because He is. (***See Ministry***> *Great Commission> Make Disciples> Disciples enjoy God's presence,* TopicGuide page A56.)

141:2 Exod 29:41; 30:8 Rev 5:8; 8:3-4
[2] Accept my prayer as incense offered to You,
and my upraised hands as an evening offering.
141:3 Ps 39:1 Prov 13:3; 21:23
[3] Take control of what I say, O LORD,
and guard my lips.
141:4 Ps 119:36 Prov 23:6 Mal 3:15
[4] Don't let me drift toward evil
or take part in acts of wickedness.
Don't let me share in the delicacies
of those who do wrong.

141:5 Ps 23:5 Prov 9:8; 19:25; 27:6 Gal 6:1
[5] Let the godly strike me!
It will be a kindness!
If they correct me, it is soothing medicine.
Don't let me refuse it.

But I pray constantly
against the wicked and their deeds.
[6] When their leaders are thrown down from a cliff,
the wicked will listen to my words and find them true.
141:7 Ps 53:5
[7] Like rocks brought up by a plow,
the bones of the wicked will lie scattered without burial.*

141:8 Ps 11:1
[8] I look to You for help, O Sovereign LORD.
You are my refuge; don't let them kill me.
141:9 Ps 91:3
[9] Keep me from the traps they have set for me,
from the snares of those who do wrong.
141:10 Ps 35:8
[10] Let the wicked fall into their own nets,
but let me escape.

PSALM 142

A psalm of David, regarding his experience in the cave. A prayer.*

142:1 Pss 30:8; 77:1
[1] I cry out to the LORD;
I plead for the LORD's mercy.

141:7 Hebrew *scattered at the mouth of Sheol.* 142:TITLE Hebrew *maskil.* This may be a literary or musical term.

▶ WORSHIP

141:2 The sweet smell of prayer. David describes his prayers as incense that floats up to God and likens them to the offerings he presents on the altar in the Tabernacle. Have you thought of your prayers as a sweet-smelling offering to God? In Psalm 42:8, the psalmist describes prayer this way: "But each day the LORD pours His unfailing love upon me, and through each night I sing His songs, praying to God who gives me life." When our day ends, we can offer up to God the thanksgiving He deserves for bringing us through another day. As you pray in the evening, visualize your prayers as incense floating up before God's throne. (***See Worship****> OT> Music> Psalms> Lament> Individual,* TopicGuide page A27.)

141:2 The language of the psalm reflects the sacrificial worship of Israel. Incense was offered inside the Tabernacle and the Temple (Exodus 30:34-38). Its pleasing aroma rising toward heaven was a symbol of the pleasing worship of God's people coming before His throne. Evening sacrifices were offered at the close of each day (Exodus 29:41; see also Revelation 8:3-5).

▶ ADOPTION

141:3 Keep my lips sealed. One of the most difficult problems we face in life is controlling our tongues. When someone angers us, we blurt out unloving words. When we get frustrated, we lash out at the people closest to us. Only God's Holy Spirit can enable us to control our words. But how do we tie into the power of His Spirit? When tempted to say unrighteous words, we can echo David's prayer. Write this verse out on a card and place it somewhere in plain view so that you can use it when you need to control your speech. Repeat it as a prayer from your heart as often as necessary. (***See Adoption****> With Christ> Supernatural> Speak godly words,* TopicGuide page A37.)

141:3-5 David invokes the aid of the Lord and the community of the godly in his pursuit of holiness. We are ultimately powerless to obey God's law apart from the grace of God's Spirit, but for those who receive that grace, strength to obey can be found in communion with the people of God.

141:7 It was a great dishonor in ancient Israel to be denied a proper burial.

141:9-10 David calls on God to frustrate the schemes of his enemies by causing them to backfire. Such a hope is expressed often in the Psalms (7:15-16; 9:15-16; 140:9).

142:1-3 David's language conveys a sense of desperation and fatigue. David pleads with God for deliverance and guidance.

[2] I pour out my complaints before Him
and tell Him all my troubles.
[3] When I am overwhelmed,
you alone know the way I should turn.
Wherever I go,
my enemies have set traps for me.
[4] I look for someone to come and help me,
but no one gives me a passing thought!
No one will help me;
no one cares a bit what happens to me.
[5] Then I pray to You, O LORD.
I say, "You are my place of refuge.
You are all I really want in life.
[6] Hear my cry,
for I am very low.
Rescue me from my persecutors,
for they are too strong for me.
[7] Bring me out of prison
so I can thank You.
The godly will crowd around me,
for You are good to me."

142:3 Ps 140:5
142:4 Ps 88:8; Jer 30:17
142:5 Ps 91:2, 9
142:6 Pss 18:17; 79:8
142:7 Ps 13:6

PSALM 143

A psalm of David.

[1] Hear my prayer, O LORD;
listen to my plea!
Answer me because You are faithful and righteous.
[2] Don't put Your servant on trial,
for no one is innocent before You.
[3] My enemy has chased me.
He has knocked me to the ground
and forces me to live in darkness like those in the grave.
[4] I am losing all hope;
I am paralyzed with fear.
[5] I remember the days of old.
I ponder all Your great works
and think about what You have done.

143:1 Ps 140:6
143:2 Job 14:3; 22:4
143:3 Lam 3:6
143:4 Lam 3:11
143:5 Ps 77:5, 10-11

▸ WORSHIP

142:2 Pour your complaints out to God. Sometimes we feel as if we have to hide our true feelings from God. After all, we don't want Him to know about the secret bad attitudes we harbor about our lot in life! But God already knows about these feelings. He sees the innermost part of our hearts. We might as well be honest with Him. If you are frustrated or depressed about your circumstances, tell that to God. He will listen to your complaints. Many times, David expressed to God the hurts and fears he felt. You can do the same. Tell Him your troubles, asking Him to help you accept His will and to endure for His sake. (***See Worship**> OT> Music> Psalms> Lament> Individual,* TopicGuide page A27.)

142:3-4 David has been isolated by his enemies. He has no one to whom he can turn for help. He feels threatened from every side.

▸ HOLINESS

142:5 All I want. Can you say with David that God is all you really want in life? That should be our goal. Nothing else compares with our God. He is not only a place of refuge, but also our comfort, guide, and Savior. He's everything we need to live an abundant, joyful life. Yet many times we fail to make Him the center of our lives. We have so many distractions and entertainments. We relegate Him to a corner in our lives, brought out only on Sundays. Make this verse your prayer today. Don't let anything else take the place of God in your life. (***See Holiness**> Submission> Yielding to Spirit> Surrender your heart,* TopicGuide page A40.)

143:1-2 While confident in God's character, David is painfully aware of his faults. David knows his sin well. If God answers his prayer, it will be an act of mercy and grace.

143:6 Ps 63:1
[6] I lift my hands to You in prayer.
I thirst for You as parched land thirsts for rain. *Interlude*

143:7 Pss 69:17; 88:4
[7] Come quickly, LORD, and answer me,
for my depression deepens.
Don't turn away from me,
or I will die.

143:8 Ps 32:8
[8] Let me hear of Your unfailing love each morning,
for I am trusting You.
Show me where to walk,
for I give myself to You.

143:9 Ps 59:1
[9] Rescue me from my enemies, LORD;
I run to You to hide me.

143:10 Neh 9:20 Pss 23:3; 119:12
[10] Teach me to do Your will,
for You are my God.
May Your gracious Spirit lead me forward
on a firm footing.
[11] For the glory of Your name, O LORD, preserve my life.
Because of Your faithfulness, bring me out
of this distress.

143:12 Pss 52:5; 116:16
[12] In Your unfailing love, silence all my enemies
and destroy all my foes,
for I am Your servant.

PSALM 144

A psalm of David.

144:1 Ps 18:2
[1] Praise the LORD, who is my rock.
He trains my hands for war
and gives my fingers skill for battle.
[2] He is my loving ally and my fortress,
my tower of safety, my rescuer.
He is my shield, and I take refuge in Him.
He makes the nations* submit to me.

144:2 Some manuscripts read *my people.*

143:6 The powerful metaphor of the "thirst" of a dry land describes David's longing after God. This metaphor for spiritual longing is taken up by Jesus on the cross as He faces alienation from the Father (John 19:28).

▶ HOLINESS

143:7 God's help in depressing times. Does it surprise you that David struggled with depression? Look how God brought him through his experiences. David was anointed king of Israel by Samuel, God's prophet. But then David had to flee for his life and lived in caves while trying to avoid his enemies. It certainly didn't seem as if he were heading down the royal lane! But when the time was right, God instated David as the king (see 2 Samuel 2). David reigned for a long time. Remember David's story when you confront your own depression. What God did for David, He will do for you. He will stick by you during your deepest down times. He knows the way out of your situation. He will not turn away from you. (***See Holiness****> Submission> Trusting God> Overcoming,* TopicGuide page A40.)

143:9-10 David binds salvation and obedience together. He prays not only for deliverance, but for the strength to obey God's law. The people of God should desire both to experience God's salvation and to live according to His commands.

144:1 In the Old Testament, warfare played a crucial role in the history of God's people. The Lord's aid in battle was one of the chief blessings of His covenant with Israel (Deuteronomy 28:7). The church also is engaged in warfare, though its fight is not against armies and nations but against Satan and his power on earth (Ephesians 6:10-20). Just as God's aid was crucial to Israel's victory in battle, so the church depends on God's strength to succeed in its warfare against spiritual darkness.

144:2 David describes God with a flurry of images drawn from the field of battle. The metaphors communicate God's power to protect and defend David in battle.

3 O LORD, what are human beings that You should notice them,
mere mortals that You should think about them?
4 For they are like a breath of air;
their days are like a passing shadow.
5 Open the heavens, LORD, and come down.
Touch the mountains so they billow smoke.
6 Hurl Your lightning bolts and scatter Your enemies!
Shoot Your arrows and confuse them!
7 Reach down from heaven and rescue me;
rescue me from deep waters,
from the power of my enemies.
8 Their mouths are full of lies;
they swear to tell the truth, but they lie instead.

9 I will sing a new song to You, O God!
I will sing Your praises with a ten-stringed harp.
10 For You grant victory to kings!
You rescued Your servant David from the fatal sword.
11 Save me!
Rescue me from the power of my enemies.
Their mouths are full of lies;
they swear to tell the truth, but they lie instead.

12 May our sons flourish in their youth
like well-nurtured plants.
May our daughters be like graceful pillars,
carved to beautify a palace.
13 May our barns be filled
with crops of every kind.
May the flocks in our fields multiply by the thousands,
even tens of thousands,
14 and may our oxen be loaded down with produce.
May there be no enemy breaking through our walls,
no going into captivity,
no cries of alarm in our town squares.
15 Yes, joyful are those who live like this!
Joyful indeed are those whose God is the LORD.

144:3 Ps 8:4
144:4 Job 8:9; 14:2 Pss 39:11; 109:23
144:5 Ps 18:9 Isa 64:1
144:6 Hab 3:11 Zech 9:14
144:7 Pss 18:44; 69:1, 14
144:8 Deut 32:40 Pss 12:2; 41:6 Isa 44:20
144:9 Ps 40:3
144:10 2 Sam 18:7 Ps 140:7
144:11 Ps 12:2 Isa 44:20
144:12 Ps 92:12-14 Prov 3:9-10 Song 4:4; 7:4
144:14 2 Kgs 25:11 Isa 24:11 Jer 14:2

▸ GOD

144:3 Who are you to God? We know that God is the Ruler of the universe. With just the power of His voice, He created everything (see Genesis 1). He knows everything; He has all power. Why, then, would He want to have anything to do with you and me? We are so insignificant in the scheme of the universe. Our lives are so brief compared to the span of history. Yet God demonstrated His eternal attention to our plight when He sent His Son to die on the cross for each one of us. Paul says in 1 Timothy 1:15, "'Christ Jesus came into the world to save sinners'—and I am the worst of them all." Your life is extremely valuable to God. He paid for it with His Son's life. So you can answer the question that David posed. You can say with confidence, "I am the one that God sent His Son to die for!" (***See God***> *Salvation*> *Father*> *Sent His only Son,* TopicGuide page A15.)

144:5-7 David prays for God's aid in battle in language that is reminiscent of descriptions of God's earlier appearances in the Old Testament, particularly His appearance at Mount Sinai (Exodus 19:16-19). In Psalm 18, David describes God's past deliverance in very similar language. Lightning bolts are described frequently as the arrows of God (2 Samuel 22:15; Psalm 18:14; Habakkuk 3:11).

144:12-14 The blessings described here are those that were promised to Israel if the people remained obedient and faithful to the law of God (Leviticus 26:1-13; Deuteronomy 28:1-14). David envisions these blessings arising out of the victory he prays God will grant His people in battle.

▸ HOLINESS

144:15 The root of happiness. Most people are on a quest to be happy. In this psalm, David tells how he found happiness—the source is God. As a result of this discovery, he was victorious over his enemies, his children flourished, and his farms were bountiful with crops. He attributes all his success to the Lord. We also can achieve happiness through our relationship with God. When we commit ourselves to Him and His Word with all our hearts, He floods our lives with joy and fulfillment. Even when things go wrong, His strong arm helps us. The world cannot give us joy. Only a deep trust in God can. Determine today that you will place your future in His hands and

PSALM 145*

A psalm of praise of David.

1 I will exalt You, my God and King,
and praise Your name forever and ever.
2 I will praise You every day;
yes, I will praise You forever.
145:3 — 3 Great is the LORD! He is most worthy of praise!
Rom 11:33 — No one can measure His greatness.

145:4 Isa 38:19 — 4 Let each generation tell its children of Your mighty acts;
let them proclaim Your power.
145:5 — 5 I will meditate* on Your majestic, glorious splendor
Ps 119:27 — and Your wonderful miracles.
145:6 Deut 10:21; 32:3 — 6 Your awe-inspiring deeds will be on every tongue;
I will proclaim Your greatness.
145:7 Ps 51:14 — 7 Everyone will share the story of Your wonderful goodness;
Isa 63:7 — they will sing with joy about Your righteousness.

145:8 Exod 34:6 — 8 The LORD is merciful and compassionate,
145:9 — slow to get angry and filled with unfailing love.
Ps 100:5 Nah 1:7 — 9 The LORD is good to everyone.
Matt 19:17 — He showers compassion on all His creation.
Mark 10:18 — 10 All of Your works will thank You, LORD,
145:10 — and Your faithful followers will praise You.
Pss 19:1; 68:26 — 11 They will speak of the glory of Your kingdom;
they will give examples of Your power.
145:12 — 12 They will tell about Your mighty deeds
Ps 105:1 Isa 2:10, 19, 21 — and about the majesty and glory of Your reign.
145:13 — 13 For Your kingdom is an everlasting kingdom.
2 Pet 1:11 — You rule throughout all generations.

The LORD always keeps His promises;
He is gracious in all He does.*
14 The LORD helps the fallen
and lifts those bent beneath their loads.

145 This psalm is a Hebrew acrostic poem; each verse (including 13b) begins with a successive letter of the Hebrew alphabet. 145:5 Some manuscripts read *They will speak.* 145:13 The last two lines of 145:13 are not found in many of the ancient manuscripts.

you will find joy. (***See Holiness****> Submission> Delighting in God> Joy in Discovering God,* TopicGuide page A40.)

145:1-3 The opening verses of the psalm set the exuberant and celebratory tone of the whole psalm. The kingship of God is the primary focus of David's praise. He is overwhelmed by the sheer grandeur and incomprehensibility of the Lord.

145:4-7 David praises God for His works in human history. The particular works in view are probably those surrounding the Exodus from Egypt. In the Exodus and in Israel's subsequent history, the Lord showed Himself to be a God who actively directs and intervenes in human history for the sake of His people. It was the task of each generation to entrust to the next the stories of God's mighty deeds.

▸ PURPOSE
145:9 God's grace to all. God has every right to run the world the way He sees fit. He has chosen to bless us all with His many blessings. We all receive rain. We all sleep when darkness falls. We all breathe the fresh air and bask under the sunshine. God provides all these things because of His grace. We certainly don't deserve any of them. God created the natural laws and He sees to it that they continue on the earth. We are beneficiaries of His master plan for His creation. Do you thank Him for what He has made that gives you life? Make that a regular practice. (***See Purpose****> God's Deeds> Common Grace> On creation,* TopicGuide page A54.)

145:9-13 While God's redeeming grace is reserved for His people, all of creation enjoys God's goodness to some degree (Genesis 9:8-11; Matthew 5:45).

145:14 God's special concern for the poor, oppressed, and needy is emphasized throughout Scripture (Deuteronomy 15:7; 1 Samuel 2:8; Isaiah 61:1; Luke 6:20).

[15] The eyes of all look to You in hope;
You give them their food as they need it.
[16] When You open your hand,
You satisfy the hunger and thirst of every living thing.
[17] The LORD is righteous in everything He does;
He is filled with kindness.
[18] The LORD is close to all who call on Him,
yes, to all who call on Him in truth.
[19] He grants the desires of those who fear Him;
He hears their cries for help and rescues them.
[20] The LORD protects all those who love Him,
but He destroys the wicked.

[21] I will praise the LORD,
and may everyone on earth bless His holy name
forever and ever.

145:15 Ps 104:27
145:18 Deut 4:7; John 4:24
145:19 Ps 10:17; Prov 15:29
145:20 Pss 31:23; 37:38
145:21 Pss 71:8; 150:6

PSALM 146

[1] Praise the LORD!

Let all that I am praise the LORD.
[2] I will praise the LORD as long as I live.
I will sing praises to my God with my dying breath.

[3] Don't put your confidence in powerful people;
there is no help for you there.
[4] When they breathe their last, they return to the earth,
and all their plans die with them.
[5] But joyful are those who have the God of Israel* as their helper,
whose hope is in the LORD their God.
[6] He made heaven and earth,
the sea, and everything in them.
He keeps every promise forever.
[7] He gives justice to the oppressed
and food to the hungry.
The LORD frees the prisoners.
[8] The LORD opens the eyes of the blind.
The LORD lifts up those who are weighed down.
The LORD loves the godly.

146:1 Ps 103:1
146:2 Pss 63:4; 104:33
146:3 Ps 60:11
146:4 Pss 33:10; 104:29; Eccl 12:7
146:5 Ps 71:5
146:6 Acts 14:15
146:7 Ps 68:6
146:8 Matt 9:30; John 9:7

146:5 Hebrew *of Jacob.* See note on 44:4.

146:1 "Praise the LORD" is a translation of *hallelu* (meaning "praise") and *Yah* (a shortened form of God's name, Yahweh, which is translated as "LORD"). (See also 146:10.)

▸ ADOPTION
146:2 Praise the Lord all your life. We all think about our last days at some time. Perhaps in a quiet moment, you consider what your future holds. When you picture yourself in the future, do you find yourself praising God? We can determine to praise God until we take our last breath. That's the commitment that God wants from us. Even when we struggle through those last moments of life, we can praise God for bringing us into the world and walking with us through to the end. Praise God for who He is. Tell Him how much you appreciate Him and His love. Keep praising—all your life. (***See Adoption***> *In Heaven> Future full of spiritual riches,* TopicGuide page A38.)

146:3-4 At various junctures in Israel's history, the people were tempted to put their confidence in powerful men, often foreign leaders, rather than trust in the Lord to meet their needs. The psalmist, however, emphasizes the fleeting nature of even the most powerful man's life in order to highlight the foolishness of such misplaced trust.

▸ BIBLE
146:6 God's forever promises. Do you really believe that God keeps His promises forever? If you do, does your life reflect your belief? His promises are recorded in His Word. To find them, we must study and read the Scriptures. Set up a plan to read and study God's Word starting now. Each time you read a promise, underline it or write it down. See how many promises God has given you. (***See Bible***> *Uniqueness> Inspired> His promises never fail,* TopicGuide page A10.)

146:9 Exod 22:21 Lev 19:34 Deut 10:18
9 The LORD protects the foreigners among us.
He cares for the orphans and widows,
but He frustrates the plans of the wicked.

146:10 Ps 10:16
10 The LORD will reign forever.
He will be your God, O Jerusalem,* throughout the generations.

Praise the LORD!

PSALM 147

147:1 Pss 33:1; 135:3
1 Praise the LORD!

How good to sing praises to our God!
How delightful and how fitting!

147:2 Isa 11:12; 56:8 Ezek 39:28
2 The LORD is rebuilding Jerusalem
and bringing the exiles back to Israel.
3 He heals the brokenhearted
and bandages their wounds.

147:4 Gen 15:5 Isa 40:26
4 He counts the stars
and calls them all by name.

147:5 Ps 98:1 Isa 40:28
5 How great is our Lord! His power is absolute!
His understanding is beyond comprehension!
6 The LORD supports the humble,
but He brings the wicked down into the dust.

7 Sing out your thanks to the LORD;
sing praises to our God with a harp.

147:8 Job 5:10; 26:8; 38:26
8 He covers the heavens with clouds,
provides rain for the earth,
and makes the grass grow in mountain pastures.

147:9 Job 38:41 Ps 104:27
9 He gives food to the wild animals
and feeds the young ravens when they cry.

147:10 1 Sam 16:7 Ps 33:17
10 He takes no pleasure in the strength of a horse
or in human might.
11 No, the LORD's delight is in those who fear Him,
those who put their hope in His unfailing love.

146:10 Hebrew *Zion.*

▶ GOD

147:1 Fill your life with praise. God has created us with a way to give Him beautiful praise—through song. When we sing to Him, our hearts are uplifted and we can repeat with the psalmist, "How delightful and how fitting!" One song of praise can express what's on our hearts that we haven't been able to communicate. Through song, we can lift our hearts heavenward. Instrumental music can aid in our meditation. Choirs help us glorify God today just as they will in heaven (Revelation 5:11-14). Are you participating in worshipful song? Check your schedule and see if you need to set aside time to worship God in song. (***See God***> *Relationship> God Enables> Relationship with God requires worship,* TopicGuide page A14.)

147:2-6 The psalm most likely is set during the time of restoration following the return from the Babylonian Exile (2 Chronicles 36:22-23). The story of the return and the rebuilding of Jerusalem is recorded in the books of Ezra and Nehemiah. The psalmist considered the release from bondage and the rebuilding of Jerusalem to be a testimony to God's great power and wisdom (compare Isaiah 61:1).

▶ PURPOSE

147:8 God's creative power. What is your favorite place in nature? Some people love to walk through the grasslands, feeling the wind at their backs. Others love the beach, stretching out beneath the sunshine. Still others prefer the mountains, standing under the majesty of a towering pine tree. Some love the desert with its stark beauty. It's amazing how different nature is from place to place! Each corner of the world has its own habitat, animals, and plants. Not only has God created all these wonderful diversities, He also sustains them. They continue to exist because He oversees the whole universe. This week, take a few moments to enjoy the natural world around you. Praise God for what you see and enjoy, looking forward to the day when it will all be made perfect (Revelation 21:1-2). (***See Purpose***> *God's Means> God's Sovereignty> God sustains His creation,* TopicGuide page A52.)

12 Glorify the LORD, O Jerusalem!
Praise your God, O Zion!
13 For He has strengthened the bars of your gates
and blessed your children within your walls.
14 He sends peace across your nation
and satisfies your hunger with the finest wheat.
15 He sends His orders to the world—
how swiftly His word flies!
16 He sends the snow like white wool;
He scatters frost upon the ground like ashes.
17 He hurls the hail like stones.*
Who can stand against His freezing cold?
18 Then, at His command, it all melts.
He sends His winds, and the ice thaws.
19 He has revealed His words to Jacob,
His decrees and regulations to Israel.
20 He has not done this for any other nation;
they do not know His regulations.

Praise the LORD!

147:13 Neh 3:3; 7:3
147:14 Deut 32:14; Isa 54:13; 60:17-18
147:15 Job 37:12; Ps 104:4
147:19 Deut 33:3-4; Mal 4:4
147:20 Deut 4:7-8; Ps 79:6

PSALM 148

1 Praise the LORD!

Praise the LORD from the heavens!
Praise Him from the skies!
2 Praise Him, all His angels!
Praise Him, all the armies of heaven!
3 Praise Him, sun and moon!
Praise Him, all you twinkling stars!
4 Praise Him, skies above!
Praise Him, vapors high above the clouds!
5 Let every created thing give praise to the LORD,
for He issued His command, and they came into being.
6 He set them in place forever and ever.
His decree will never be revoked.

148:1 Ps 102:19
148:2 Ps 103:20-21
148:4 Gen 1:7; Deut 10:14
148:5 Gen 1:1
148:6 Job 38:33

147:17 Hebrew *like bread crumbs.*

147:12-14 God had provided security for His people, as symbolized here by the bars on the city gates, and prosperity, represented by children and abundant crops.

147:15-18 The realm of nature once more provides the psalmist with compelling examples of God's power and sovereignty. The very rhythms of the seasons are at God's command.

▶ GOD

148:1 Praise God at all times. This psalm shows us the magnitude of praise due to God. All the angels and the armies of heaven praise Him. Everything in the sky praises Him. All the animals on the land and in the oceans praise Him. The weather praises Him. How about us? Do we give Him the praise He is due? If all creation praises Him, we should do no less. Begin a lifestyle of praise today. Make it a habit to look for ways to glorify His name. When you get up, praise God for being the weather-maker. When you go to bed, praise Him for being above the night skies. During your day, stop and praise Him for being present everywhere. Find new ways to praise Him each day. (***See God*> *God's Attributes> Just> All God's ways are righteous and deserve praise,* TopicGuide page A16.)

148:1-4 In the first section of the psalm, the psalmist addresses the heavenly realm, where the angels, stars, and other heavenly bodies reside. The mention of vapors (literally "waters") above the clouds reflects Genesis 1:7.

148:2 "Angels" and "armies of heaven" are synonymous. The angelic host is often described as the army of God waiting to do His bidding (compare 2 Kings 6:17).

148:7 Gen 1:21 Ps 74:13 Hab 3:10

7 Praise the LORD from the earth,
you creatures of the ocean depths,
8 fire and hail, snow and clouds,*
wind and weather that obey Him,

148:9 Isa 44:23; 49:13; 55:12

9 mountains and all hills,
fruit trees and all cedars,
10 wild animals and all livestock,
small scurrying animals and birds,
11 kings of the earth and all people,
rulers and judges of the earth,
12 young men and young women,
old men and children.

148:13 Pss 8:1; 113:4 Rev 5:12

13 Let them all praise the name of the LORD.
For His name is very great;
His glory towers over the earth and heaven!

148:14 Deut 10:21 1 Sam 2:1 Eph 2:17

14 He has made His people strong,
honoring His faithful ones—
the people of Israel who are close to Him.

Praise the LORD!

PSALM 149

1 Praise the LORD!

149:1 Pss 33:3; 89:5

Sing to the LORD a new song.
Sing His praises in the assembly of the faithful.

149:2 Judg 8:23 Ps 47:6

2 O Israel, rejoice in your Maker.
O people of Jerusalem,* exult in your King.

149:3 Exod 15:20

3 Praise His name with dancing,
accompanied by tambourine and harp.

148:8 Or *mist,* or *smoke.*

148:7 "Creatures of the ocean depths" may be a reference to the mythical creatures that were thought to embody chaos and evil, and which challenged the gods in ancient Canaanite creation myths. By borrowing this imagery, the psalmist is suggesting that there is no power in all of creation that challenges the Lord. All creation, even the apparently chaotic elements, glorifies God.

148:7-12 In the second section of the psalm, the psalmist addresses the earthly realm. The physical features and inhabitants of the earth are invited to join their voices to those of the heavenly realm in praise to God.

▸ GOD

148:8 Nature's cycles come from God. Do you know the weather patterns in your area? What happens during the spring? During the summer? In the fall? How is the weather different in the winter? We can plan on certain weather events during each season. Perhaps you enjoy snow in winter. Maybe your area sees temperatures in the 100-degree range and above for most of the summer. God provided them all. We count on these patterns to run our lives—the plants we grow in our gardens, the activities we plan for recreation, the kind of clothing we buy. Without these natural cycles, our lives would be unmanageable. Do you appreciate the order God has built into nature? Thank Him for each kind of weather you enjoy this week. (***See God****> God's Attributes> Sovereign> God controls time and seasons,* TopicGuide page A17.)

149:1 The precise significance of "a new song" is uncertain, but such songs typically are associated with God's victories in battle, perhaps in anticipation of His final victory (Psalms 33:3; 96:1; 98:1; 144:9; Revelation 5:9; 14:3). Note the language of warfare in 149:6-9.

▸ WORSHIP

149:3 Praise God with your body. God has created each one of us to praise Him. How we do this is an individual preference. But we should use our bodies to praise Him. This may be simply through using our voices in singing. We have many wonderful praise songs and hymns for this purpose. Some people like to raise their hands in worship. Others like to bow their heads or even kneel. And some people enjoy expressing their praise through worshipful dance. Which of these describes your method of worship? Praise God today with your body. (***See Worship****> OT> Posture> Dancing> Dance in corporate worship,* TopicGuide page A28.)

149:3 The tambourine and harp were but two of the musical instruments available to accompany the praise of God's people (compare Psalms 98:5-6; 81:1-5; 150:3-5).

4 For the LORD delights in His people; **149:4** Ps 35:27
He crowns the humble with victory.
5 Let the faithful rejoice that He honors them. **149:5** Job 35:10
Let them sing for joy as they lie on their beds.

6 Let the praises of God be in their mouths, **149:6** Ps 66:17
and a sharp sword in their hands—
7 to execute vengeance on the nations
and punishment on the peoples,
8 to bind their kings with shackles **149:8** Nah 3:10
and their leaders with iron chains,
9 to execute the judgment written against them. **149:9** Ps 148:14; Ezek 28:26
This is the glorious privilege of His faithful ones.

Praise the LORD!

PSALM 150

1 Praise the LORD! **150:1** Pss 19:1; 73:17; 102:19

Praise God in His sanctuary;
praise Him in His mighty heaven!
2 Praise Him for His mighty works; **150:2** Deut 3:24
praise His unequaled greatness!
3 Praise Him with a blast of the ram's horn; **150:3** Ps 98:6
praise Him with the lyre and harp!
4 Praise Him with the tambourine and dancing; **150:4** Isa 38:20
praise Him with strings and flutes!
5 Praise Him with a clash of cymbals; **150:5** 1 Chr 13:8; 15:16
praise Him with loud clanging cymbals.
6 Let everything that breathes sing praises to the LORD! **150:6** Ps 145:21

Praise the LORD!

149:2 Hebrew *Zion.*

▸ HOLINESS
149:4 God delights in you. How reassuring it is to know that God delights in each one of us. The word *delight* has such a wonderful connotation. It means "to savor," letting the pleasure of the moment roll around on your tongue. It means "to enjoy something immensely," appreciating everything about it. Imagine that God feels that way about you! He wants to spend time with you, talk to you, help and guide you. When He thinks about your name, He feels pleased. What a God we serve! Today, think of ways that He delights you. Tell Him about each of these ways. (***See Holiness****> Submission> Delighting in God> Gladness in God,* TopicGuide page A40.)

149:6-9 In the Old Testament era, the Lord employed Israel as an instrument of judgment against wickedness and evil (see, for example, Deuteronomy 9:4-5). When Israel became intolerably wicked, God used other nations to judge it. The church, unlike Israel, is not a nation and is not called to wage physical war (Ephesians 6:12). However, when Christ returns, He Himself will judge all the nations and their inhabitants.

▸ WORSHIP
150:2 Praise God for His greatness. How do you praise God for His greatness? Plan to do so each day. First, take out a sheet of paper and a pencil and brainstorm ways God has helped you. Then write down the characteristics of God that enabled Him to help you. You might write words such as *powerful, kind,* or *knows all my problems.* Praise God for each one of these. Then go outside and notice God's creation. Again, write down characteristics of God that made what you see possible. Praise God for these characteristics also. Keep your sheet to use for praise on other days. (***See Worship****> OT> Posture> Dancing> Praise Him with timbrel and dance,* TopicGuide page A28.)

▸ WORSHIP
150:6 Praise the Lord! What a wonderful way to end the book of Psalms—"Praise the LORD!" This encapsulates so much of what the psalmists are writing about throughout the book. If you were to examine your day, how much of it is devoted to praising God? How often do you stop your activities to praise Him? How many times a day do you think about how wonderful God is? Make praising God your lifestyle. Think of new ways to praise Him. As you read your Bible, jot down attributes of God for which you want to praise Him. Keep expanding that list. Soon you will have a page full of ways to praise Him. (***See Worship****> OT> Music> Psalms> Praise,* TopicGuide page A27.)

PROVERBS

PURPOSE

To impart skills for living wisely in a fallen world.

One of the biggest differences between biblical and modern society is the status of those considered to be wise. Today, it is seen as more important to be wealthy, smart, popular, or widely known than to be wise. Perhaps the reason wisdom appears to be largely absent from modern culture is because the very source of wisdom is missing: the fear of the Lord.

Proverbs exists as a testimony to the belief among God's people that success in life comes from fearing the Lord, and that skill in living can be taught and transferred from one generation to the next. The most important concept in the book is the Hebrew idea of "skill." This term was used in a variety of ways, such as describing the excellence necessary to sew the high priest's garments (Exodus 28:3), build the Tabernacle (Exodus 31:3), govern a nation (1 Kings 4:29), and live life (Proverbs 2:2). The skill of living learned in context of a reverence for God—this is the heart of biblical wisdom.

DISCOVER GOD IN PROVERBS

Wisdom is based on awe and respect for God (Proverbs 1:7; 9:10), so God demonstrates perfect wisdom in His:

Unfolding Plan: The apostle Paul referred to God as "the only wise God" (Romans 16:27). The Scriptures extol God's wisdom in His work of creation (Psalm 104:24), His providential governing of the universe, and in His unfolding plan of redemption (1 Corinthians 1:21-24). The wisdom of God was gloriously displayed in the God-man, Jesus Christ (1 Corinthians 1:24, 30). By His questions, His answers, and His parables and sayings, Jesus confounded critics and amazed adherents wherever He went. God's plan was to display His wisdom in the flesh: "For our benefit God made Him to be wisdom itself" (1 Corinthians 1:30). This explains why an entire book in the Old Testament is devoted to wisdom—it's part of God's plan to prepare us for Christ and enable us to live well in His kingdom.

Perfect Parenting: Moses made it clear that parents are to impart wisdom and knowledge to their children (Deuteronomy 6:4-9), and Proverbs continues and builds on that command (Proverbs 2:1; 3:1; 4:1; 5:1; 6:1, 20; 7:1; 31:1). The wise child listens to the instruction of parents (Proverbs 1:8-9), while the foolish child rejects their teaching. God, our heavenly Father, regards His people as His children: "When Israel was a child, I loved him, and I called my son out of Egypt" (Hosea 11:1). God's desire for His people is that they will become so skilled in reflecting His glory that the world will be drawn to Him through them. Parents who need wisdom can turn to their heavenly Parent—the source of true wisdom, God Himself.

GROWING THROUGH PROVERBS

True Wisdom: The church at Corinth made a mistake that is common among young Christians: equating knowledge with wisdom. Paul wrote, "Knowledge makes us feel important" (1 Corinthians 8:1), but it is not the same thing as wisdom. True wisdom grows out of fear (respect, awe) of God, not infatuation with self or others. True wisdom leads to skills such as humility, fruitful relationships, sound financial practices, and gainful vocations. Therefore, wisdom is practical—it is the expression of knowledge, not the possession of it for its own sake.

The Role of Discipline: Throughout Proverbs, the person who rejects wisdom receives discipline (Proverbs 13:24; 15:10; 22:15). But discipline in this context should not be understood as merely punishment. Instead, it should be equated with training. Discipline has skillful living as its goal, whereas punishment inflicts discomfort as payment for incorrect behavior. While discipline can be uncomfortable at times, its motive is love and transformation of character. The goal of a parent's discipline should be the same as God's when He disciplines His spiritual children: a harvest of righteousness and peace (Hebrews 12:11).

The Place of Practicality: It has been said that Christians can become so heavenly minded that they are of no earthly good. While we are indeed called to be heavenly minded (Philippians 3:20), Proverbs is a book that equips us to live successfully while on our way "home." Most of life is lived in the valley, not on the mountaintop. Families, finances, faith, friendships—these are the "stuff" of life, day in and day out. The journey to heaven will be more fruitful if we employ wisdom in managing the affairs of our life on earth.

DISCOVERY VERSES

Fear of the LORD is the foundation of true knowledge, but fools despise wisdom and discipline. (PROVERBS 1:7)

Without wise leadership, a nation falls; there is safety in having many advisers. (PROVERBS 11:14)

Pride goes before destruction, and haughtiness before a fall. (PROVERBS 16:18)

PROVERBS FACTS

Authors: King Solomon wrote around ninety percent of the nearly nine-hundred proverbs (1 Kings 4:32; Ecclesiastes 12:9), but there are also collections from other sources: thirty anonymous wise sayings (22:17–24:22), the sayings of Agur (chapter 30), and the wisdom of Lemuel (chapter 31).

Written to: The families of Israel.

Date of writing: From the time of Solomon (930 BC) to the time of Hezekiah (700 BC), who collected the proverbs of Solomon in chapters 25–29.

Setting: The proverbs were written in ancient Israel, and many of them bear marks of being written from the royal courts of Solomon.

OUTLINE

- **PROVERBS 1:1–9:18**—Fatherly wisdom
- **PROVERBS 10:1–22:16**—Solomon's wisdom
- **PROVERBS 22:17–24:34**—Sages' wisdom
- **PROVERBS 25:1–29:27**—More of Solomon's wisdom
- **PROVERBS 30:1-33**—Agur's wisdom
- **PROVERBS 31:1-31**—Lemuel's wisdom

THE PURPOSE OF PROVERBS

1:1 1 Kgs 4:32 Prov 25:1 Eccl 1:1; 12:9

1 These are the proverbs of Solomon, David's son, king of Israel.

2 Their purpose is to teach people wisdom and discipline,
to help them understand the insights of the wise.

1:3 Prov 2:9; 19:20

3 Their purpose is to teach people to live disciplined and successful lives,
to help them do what is right, just, and fair.

1:4 Prov 2:10-11; 8:5, 12

4 These proverbs will give insight to the simple,
knowledge and discernment to the young.

1:5 Prov 9:9; 14:6 Eccl 9:1

5 Let the wise listen to these proverbs and become even wiser.
Let those with understanding receive guidance
6 by exploring the meaning in these proverbs and parables,
the words of the wise and their riddles.

1:7 Prov 9:10; 15:33 Eccl 12:13

7 Fear of the LORD is the foundation of true knowledge,
but fools despise wisdom and discipline.

▸ WORSHIP
1:1 The wisdom of Solomon. God honored Solomon by endowing him with great wisdom. In his early days, Solomon lived faithfully by his God-given wisdom, which he shared here in the book of Proverbs. Proverbs 1:2 tells us that Solomon gave us his proverbs to teach us wisdom and discipline. These characteristics go hand in hand. Have you ever known someone who had the right knowledge but lacked the discipline to follow through with it? Or do you know someone who has great discipline but not the wisdom to know when to exercise it? By daily walking in God's Spirit and following His Word, we will have both discipline and wisdom. (***See Worship***> *OT> Reverence> Taught and modeled by Solomon,* TopicGuide page A28.)

1:1 Solomon is credited with writing Proverbs (1:1; 10:1; 25:1), but it is clear that others also had a minor hand in its composition. Two unknown men named Agur (30:1) and Lemuel (31:1), as well as "the wise" (22:17; 24:23), are credited with small portions. Clearly, someone else must have arranged what we presently read, possibly adding the introduction (1:1-7) by King Hezekiah's time (c. 700 BC) at the earliest.

1:1-7 As a collection of wise sayings, the book of Proverbs was used in the tutelage of princes, the training of court advisers, or the rearing of children (Proverbs 8:15-16). As 1 Kings 4:30-34 tells us, Solomon was wiser than the wisest in the surrounding nations. He probably interacted with wise men from other nations, and he even claimed and adapted some pagan formulations and sayings for the service of the LORD. Indeed, much of the knowledge contained in Proverbs is observable by anyone who is wise. However, Proverbs affirms that fear of the Lord is the beginning of knowledge, and this marks Hebrew wisdom literature as unique and superior in the ancient world.

▸ WORSHIP
1:2 What kind of instruction? Many parents are anxious when their sons and daughters begin school. It's not just the separation or the financial challenges; Christian children are often negatively influenced by worldly philosophies taught in many schools. In many schools, learning is no longer tied to true wisdom—the fear of the Lord. What can parents do to give their children the ability to get an education in a world that is opposed to their faith? First, find a school that will, as much as possible, affirm your values. Second, ground your children in a fear of God. Fearing God means submitting to God and giving holy defiance to the lies of this world. It means turning away from lies and toward truth. With practical and spiritual preparation, your children can be ready to begin a lifetime journey of learning about God and His creation. (***See Worship***> *OT> Reverence> The beginning of knowledge,* TopicGuide page A29.)

▸ WORSHIP
1:7 The fear of the Lord. When you hear the word *fear,* the fear of God most likely is not the concept that automatically pops into your mind. We fear death, disease, speaking in public, and many other things—and we do everything we can to avoid them. But fear of God draws us to Him. Fear of God is a worshipful reverence for who He is and what He can do. When we focus on His might and His character, we live our lives according to what He deems to be right. Our fear is comparable to a child who shuns acts of disobedience because he respects and loves his parents. If you fear God, you will be wise, because your heart will be turned toward God and His wisdom. (***See Worship***> *OT> Reverence> The beginning of knowledge,* TopicGuide page A29.)

1:7 "Fear of the LORD," arguably the theme of Proverbs, is mentioned throughout the book (Proverbs 2:5; 8:13; 9:10; 10:27; 14:27; 15:33; 19:23; 22:4; 31:30). Success and wisdom in the Bible are inextricably tied to a vibrant faith in the living God. James 3:13-18 confirms this when it condemns "earthly" wisdom and commends "wisdom from above." The so-called wisdom of the secular world can be deceiving and can become a barrier to faith in the Lord. True wisdom is God's wisdom, but it only takes root in a changed heart and a mind enlightened by the Holy Spirit (1 Corinthians 2:14). Fools show that their hearts are not changed when they despise or fail to discern this godly wisdom. In fact, the gospel seems foolish to the world (1 Corinthians 1:18-27). Proverbs constantly contrasts the fool and the wise, prompting the reader to choose the path he or she will follow in everyday life. This is not just helpful advice, but a matter of spiritual life and death.

A FATHER'S EXHORTATION: ACQUIRE WISDOM

8 My child,* listen when your father corrects you.
Don't neglect your mother's instruction.
9 What you learn from them will crown you with grace
and be a chain of honor around your neck.

10 My child, if sinners entice you,
turn your back on them!
11 They may say, "Come and join us.
Let's hide and kill someone!
Just for fun, let's ambush the innocent!
12 Let's swallow them alive, like the grave*;
let's swallow them whole, like those who go down to the pit of death.
13 Think of the great things we'll get!
We'll fill our houses with all the stuff we take.
14 Come, throw in your lot with us;
we'll all share the loot."

15 My child, don't go along with them!
Stay far away from their paths.
16 They rush to commit evil deeds.
They hurry to commit murder.
17 If a bird sees a trap being set,
it knows to stay away.
18 But these people set an ambush for themselves;
they are trying to get themselves killed.
19 Such is the fate of all who are greedy for money;
it robs them of life.

WISDOM SHOUTS IN THE STREETS

20 Wisdom shouts in the streets.
She cries out in the public square.

1:8-9 Prov 6:20
1:10 Ps 1:1; Prov 7:21; 13:20
1:11 Prov 1:18
1:15 Pss 1:1; 119:101; Prov 4:14
1:16 Isa 59:7; *Rom 3:15-17
1:19 Prov 15:27
1:20 Prov 8:1-5; 9:3

1:8 Hebrew *My son;* also in 1:10, 15. 1:12 Hebrew *like Sheol.*

▸ HOLINESS

1:8 Listen to others. Many teenagers refuse to listen to their parents. In fact, they bristle when they are encouraged to follow the advice of any elder. Even as adults, some refuse to take advice or follow orders. Justifying this attitude with "I'm too old to follow orders." or "I know!" is not the solution—it's just rebellion. God calls us to take seriously all the words that come from our elders—both those in the faith and those outside of it (1 Timothy 6:2). Are you listening—to anyone? Listen to God when He says, "give respect and honor to those who are in authority" (Romans 13:7). (***See Holiness***> *Disciplines> Of Engagement> Call to study,* TopicGuide page A42.)

1:8–9:18 The first large section of Proverbs consists of 12 fatherly lectures (Proverbs 1:8-19; 2:1-22; 3:1-12; 3:13-35; 4:1-9; 4:10-19; 4:20-27; 5:1-23; 6:1-19; 6:20-35; 7:1-27; 9:1-18) interspersed with two interludes by a personified Wisdom (1:20-33; 8:1-36). These lectures are addressed to the son who someday will be a leader, presumably in the context of the royal family, and who is most vulnerable at a young age to "easy sex," "easy money," and "thinking himself wise." While the Hebrew literally says "son," it can be understood to apply to anyone with child/student/apprentice status. This exhortation for the child to listen is an extension of the fifth commandment, which promises a prosperous and long life to those who obey (Exodus 20:12; Deuteronomy 5:16).

1:10-19 This lecture is an exhortation to stay away from those who ambush the innocent for selfish gain. A similar ambush occurred in the story of the Good Samaritan (Luke 10:30). Throughout the first nine chapters of Proverbs, the imagery of two paths is placed before the child. One leads to life and the other to death. The "admonition to stay on the right path" is employed extensively throughout Proverbs to illustrate growing up in the Lord (Proverbs 1:15, 30-31; 2:8, 13, 18-20; 3:5-6, 21-26; 4:11-14, 25-26; 5:5-6, 21; 7:8; 8:20, 32). Those who choose the path of wickedness will be led to sin, calamity, and death (see also Psalm 1).

1:20-33 The previous call from the murderous gang to "come, throw in your lot with us" (1:8-19) is contrasted here with an interlude by Wisdom personified, who gives an infinitely better call. Personified as a wise sisterly woman (see note on Proverbs 7:4), Wisdom calls from out in the open rather than in secret. Wisdom offers to be the gullible child's personal guide on the path of life, while the other path is led by false guides and evil influences that will end in utter ruin (1:27). Wisdom is kind, loving, and seeking, but when completely rejected, she leaves her pupils to their own foolish way (1:24-33), because the problem is not a pupil's mental capacity but the orientation of the heart.

21 She calls to the crowds along the main street,
to those gathered in front of the city gate:
22 "How long, you simpletons,
will you insist on being simpleminded?
How long will you mockers relish your mocking?
How long will you fools hate knowledge?
23 Come and listen to my counsel.
I'll share my heart with you
and make you wise.

24 "I called you so often, but you wouldn't come.
I reached out to you, but you paid no attention.
25 You ignored my advice
and rejected the correction I offered.
26 So I will laugh when you are in trouble!
I will mock you when disaster overtakes you—
27 when calamity overtakes you like a storm,
when disaster engulfs you like a cyclone,
and anguish and distress overwhelm you.

28 "When they cry for help, I will not answer.
Though they anxiously search for me, they will not find me.
29 For they hated knowledge
and chose not to fear the LORD.
30 They rejected my advice
and paid no attention when I corrected them.
31 Therefore, they must eat the bitter fruit of living their own way,
choking on their own schemes.
32 For simpletons turn away from me—to death.
Fools are destroyed by their own complacency.
33 But all who listen to me will live in peace,
untroubled by fear of harm."

1:22 Prov 9:4; 14:15
1:23 Joel 2:28
1:24 Isa 65:12; 66:4
1:25 2 Chr 36:16; Ps 107:11
1:26 Ps 2:4
1:27 Prov 10:25
1:28 Job 27:9; Ps 18:41; Ezek 8:18; Zech 7:13
1:29 Job 21:14
1:30 Ps 81:11
1:31 Job 4:8; Prov 5:22; 22:8
1:32 Jer 2:19
1:33 Pss 23:4; Prov 3:24-26

THE BENEFITS OF WISDOM

2 1 My child,* listen to what I say,
and treasure my commands.
2 Tune your ears to wisdom,
and concentrate on understanding.
3 Cry out for insight,
and ask for understanding.
4 Search for them as you would for silver;
seek them like hidden treasures.
5 Then you will understand what it means to fear the LORD,
and you will gain knowledge of God.

2:1 Prov 3:1; 4:10
2:4 Prov 3:14; Matt 13:44

2:1 Hebrew *My son.*

2:1-22 This carefully written speech proclaims the benefits of wisdom. In the first half (Proverbs 2:1-11), wisdom is described metaphorically as a shield that equips the child with common sense and a sense of justice. In this translation, the primary metaphor may seem to be treasure, but the Hebrew text shows that the child should seek after wisdom *as* he would seek for treasure. The first half of the chapter emphasizes seeking and storing wisdom. In the second half (2:12-22), implanted wisdom is said to protect the child from schemers, the immoral woman, the path of unrighteousness, and ultimately, death. So wisdom is a shield to those who seek it—it protects them from attack.

6 For the LORD grants wisdom!
From His mouth come knowledge and understanding.
7 He grants a treasure of common sense to the honest.
He is a shield to those who walk with integrity.
8 He guards the paths of the just
and protects those who are faithful to Him.

9 Then you will understand what is right, just, and fair,
and you will find the right way to go.
10 For wisdom will enter your heart,
and knowledge will fill you with joy.
11 Wise choices will watch over you.
Understanding will keep you safe.

12 Wisdom will save you from evil people,
from those whose words are twisted.
13 These men turn from the right way
to walk down dark paths.
14 They take pleasure in doing wrong,
and they enjoy the twisted ways of evil.
15 Their actions are crooked,
and their ways are wrong.

16 Wisdom will save you from the immoral woman,
from the seductive words of the promiscuous woman.
17 She has abandoned her husband
and ignores the covenant she made before God.
18 Entering her house leads to death;
it is the road to the grave.*
19 The man who visits her is doomed.
He will never reach the paths of life.

20 Follow the steps of good men instead,
and stay on the paths of the righteous.
21 For only the godly will live in the land,
and those with integrity will remain in it.
22 But the wicked will be removed from the land,
and the treacherous will be uprooted.

2:6 Job 32:8; Jas 1:5
2:8 1 Sam 2:9
2:9 Prov 8:20
2:10 Prov 14:33; 22:18
2:11 Ps 82:5; Prov 6:22
2:14 Prov 10:23; Hab 1:15
2:15 Ps 125:5
2:16 Prov 6:24; 23:27
2:17 Mal 2:14-15
2:18 Prov 7:27
2:20 Prov 13:20
2:21 Ps 37:9, 29; Prov 10:30
2:22 Deut 28:63; Ps 37:38; Prov 10:30

2:18 Hebrew *to the spirits of the dead.*

▸ WORSHIP
2:6 The wisdom of God. Many people constantly run around trying to "fix" all the difficulties in their lives, bringing their problems to God only when things seem hopeless. But all that time, God is willing to grant us wisdom (2:6). How much better off would we be if we brought problems to God as soon as we recognized them? We would avoid many of the consequences we suffer for wrong actions. The world's wisdom cannot measure up to God's. Turn to Him—quickly—in every crisis. (***See Worship***> *OT*> *Reverence*> *The beginning of wisdom,* TopicGuide page A29.)

▸ WORSHIP
2:20 Practical advice for living. God gives us practical steps for living good lives. In this verse, He shows us two ways to keep our steps from sin. The first is to "follow the steps of good men," or follow the example of godly Christians you know. The second is to "stay on the paths of the righteous," or follow the law of God. Any failure to do what's right could lead to disaster. But following conscience (Romans 2:15; 1 Timothy 1:19) and Scripture will keep you in the safety of God's will. (***See Worship***> *OT*> *Reverence*> *The beginning of knowledge,* TopicGuide page A29.)

2:21-22 The Hebrew word translated "land" here can refer to either the known regions of the earth or the Promised Land of the nation of Israel. The point here is that the righteous live and prosper, while the wicked die. They are cut off from the earth (Deuteronomy 28:63).

3:1-12 This speech lists four blessings of wisdom when it is used properly. After the familiar appeal to the child (3:1-2), each of four commands is followed by a reward. The rewards are collectively referred to with the Hebrew word *shalom* (3:2), which means not just "peace of mind" but complete wellness in body and spirit. This includes long life, prosperity, purpose and direction, health, wholeness, and harmony with God and people. This *shalom* is not guaranteed, however, but is prom-

TRUSTING IN THE LORD

3:1 Exod 20:6 Deut 30:16 | 3:2 Pss 91:16; 119:93 Prov 9:11 | 3:3 Prov 6:21; 7:3 2 Cor 3:3 | 3:4 1 Sam 2:26 Prov 8:35 Jer 9:23-24 Luke 2:52 | 3:5 Prov 22:19 | 3:6 1 Chr 28:9 Prov 16:3 | 3:7 Job 1:1; 28:28 Prov 4:21; 8:13; 16:6 | 3:9 Exod 23:19 Isa 43:23 Mal 3:10 | 3:11 Job 5:17 *Heb 12:5-6

3 1 My child,* never forget the things I have taught you.
Store my commands in your heart.
2 If you do this, you will live many years,
and your life will be satisfying.
3 Never let loyalty and kindness leave you!
Tie them around your neck as a reminder.
Write them deep within your heart.
4 Then you will find favor with both God and people,
and you will earn a good reputation.
5 Trust in the LORD with all your heart;
do not depend on your own understanding.
6 Seek His will in all you do,
and He will show you which path to take.
7 Don't be impressed with your own wisdom.
Instead, fear the LORD and turn away from evil.
8 Then you will have healing for your body
and strength for your bones.
9 Honor the LORD with your wealth
and with the best part of everything you produce.
10 Then He will fill your barns with grain,
and your vats will overflow with good wine.
11 My child, don't reject the LORD's discipline,
and don't be upset when He corrects you.
12 For the LORD corrects those He loves,
just as a father corrects a child in whom he delights.*

3:1 Hebrew *My son;* also in 3:11, 21. 3:12 Greek version reads *And He punishes those He accepts as His children.* Compare Heb 12:6.

ised upon the condition of obedience to the four commands: trust Him, fear Him, honor Him, and accept His discipline.

3:3 The words of this verse recall the exhortation to the Israelites in Deuteronomy 6:4-9 to remember God's most important teachings. The idea to "write them deep within your heart" also looks forward to the New Covenant, mentioned in Jeremiah 31:33 and explained in Hebrews 8:10 and 10:16. It is God's desire that His people internalize His law, making His commands a part of their inner life.

▸ BIBLE

3:9 What do you give to God? What is the biblical principle for giving? God's people give the first and best to Him because we love Him. After all, He gave the best He had—His Son, Jesus Christ—for our sakes. How can we do less? What you give to Him of your money, possessions, time, and talents will show your devotion to Him. Don't be limited by ideas of "tithes" or "offerings" belonging to God—all our resources belong to him (Psalm 24:1; John 3:27). Be a good steward of every penny you have. (***See Bible****> Unity> God's Message> Devotion to God,* TopicGuide page A10.)

3:9-10 In ancient agrarian societies, barns filled with grain, produce, much livestock, and vats of "good wine" were a blessing. God promised to increase the wealth of His people if they honored Him by offering the first of the produce of the land (Deuteronomy 26:1-3, 9-11).

▸ ADOPTION

3:11 The encouragement of discipline. Most of us don't feel encouraged when we are disciplined. If our bosses reprimand us, we bristle. If friends correct our behavior, we see red. And if God uses circumstances to shape our behavior, we cry out, "Why me, God?" But God only disciplines us for our own good. He never corrects us out of revenge or spite. So if you are speeding on the freeway and a policeman gives you a ticket, think: "God is trying to slow me down. He wants me to obey the rules of the road." If you cheat on your taxes and the government finds you out, think, "God is keeping me from going farther in my habit of cheating." Don't be discouraged when God corrects you , but know that God is making sure you become a mature child of God. (***See Adoption****> With Christ> Children of God> God disciplines His children,* TopicGuide page A36.)

▸ GOD

3:12 Heavenly sandpaper. When the antiques collector begins refinishing the piece of furniture, he takes note of all the lumps and bumps that have accumulated in the wood over the years. Carefully, he sands the wood until it feels as smooth as silk. That's what God does in our lives. The rough times we suffer through are like heavenly sandpaper, rubbing off the rough edges that harm those around us. He does this because He considers us valuable, treasured, and worth the time to restore. Be patient when you encounter difficulties, and view them as God's heavenly sandpaper. (***See God****> God's Attributes> Loving> As a father, God corrects His beloved children,* TopicGuide page A17.)

13 Joyful is the person who finds wisdom,
the one who gains understanding.
14 For wisdom is more profitable than silver,
and her wages are better than gold.
15 Wisdom is more precious than rubies;
nothing you desire can compare with her.
16 She offers you long life in her right hand,
and riches and honor in her left.
17 She will guide you down delightful paths;
all her ways are satisfying.
18 Wisdom is a tree of life to those who embrace her;
happy are those who hold her tightly.

19 By wisdom the LORD founded the earth;
by understanding He created the heavens.
20 By His knowledge the deep fountains of the earth burst forth,
and the dew settles beneath the night sky.

21 My child, don't lose sight of common sense and discernment.
Hang on to them,
22 for they will refresh your soul.
They are like jewels on a necklace.
23 They keep you safe on your way,
and your feet will not stumble.
24 You can go to bed without fear;
you will lie down and sleep soundly.
25 You need not be afraid of sudden disaster
or the destruction that comes upon the wicked,
26 for the LORD is your security.
He will keep your foot from being caught in a trap.

27 Do not withhold good from those who deserve it
when it's in your power to help them.

3:13 Job 28:17
3:14 Prov 8:10, 19
3:16 Ps 21:4; Prov 3:2; 8:18; 16:7; 22:4
3:18 Gen 2:9; Prov 11:30; Rev 2:7
3:19 Prov 8:27-28
3:20 Gen 7:11
3:21 Prov 4:21
3:22 Deut 32:47; Prov 1:9; 4:22
3:23 Prov 4:12; 10:9
3:24 Job 5:21; 11:19; Ps 3:5; Prov 1:33; 6:22
3:25 Ps 91:5
3:27 Deut 24:15

3:13-18 Wisdom is personified as a sisterly woman who is better than riches and treasures because she brings blessing. "Joyful," or "blessed," is the Hebrew description for those who experience life as God intended—they are blessed not only when seemingly good things happen, but also when the "bad" things come (Job 5:17; Matthew 5:3-12).

3:16 In ancient cultures, depictions of deities sometimes included objects in their hands as symbols of honor. The right hand had more honor than the left (Genesis 35:19; 45:14; Matthew 25:33), suggesting that God considers long life a greater blessing than wealth.

▸ MINISTRY
3:21 Is planning important? Have you ever heard a preacher urge people to be totally "led by the Spirit"? While this aspect of our walk with God is important, these verses show us that planning is also important. Noah began building the ark years before a drop of rain fell. David began planning the construction of the Temple even though he knew his son Solomon would actually be the one to build it. As you begin a project, pray and plan your steps. Then listen for God's voice as you move ahead with your plans. The Spirit may change your direction as He sees fit, and He can often do so through some commonsense planning. (***See Ministry****> Great Commission> Make Disciples> Disciples strategically use knowledge, skills, and abilities,* TopicGuide page A56.)

▸ CHURCH
3:27 Doing good to others. Luke 6:36 says, "You must be compassionate, just as your Father is compassionate." "Sure," you may say, "but God doesn't have to live with my husband!" But kindness is most needed where it is most difficult to give. Is your neighbor grouchy with your children? Show him kindness. Does your boss irk you? Find ways to show him kindness. Do you have a relative who gossips about your family? Go out of your way to show love. Use kindness, not anger, as your reaction to the grumpy people in your life. Remember, God is kind to you, and you certainly haven't deserved the half of it! (***See Church****> Role> Preach> Topics> Godly Lives> Kindness to neighbors,* TopicGuide page A50.)

3:27 The Hebrew text implies that the "good" already belongs to the neighbor (Deuteronomy 24:19-22). Thus, to withhold it from him when you have the ability to give it is a sin (2 Corinthians 8:12; Galatians 6:10).

• • • DISCOVER

PROOF OF THE PUDDING

"THE PROOF OF THE PUDDING IS IN THE EATING." What does that English proverb from the 1300s mean? It announces that the best test of whether a dish is done properly is in the tasting of the food.

This proverb is rarely truer than when applied to trusting God. We can read about faith, and still remain faithless. We can pray for more faith, but still not trust God any more than before we prayed. It is in the act of trusting God, relying on God to keep His covenant with us through Christ, that we discover that God is able to guide us. It is by faith in God and renouncing confidence in our own sinful strategies (Proverbs 18:10-11; 28:11, 26) that we discover God's wise plans for our life.

As with faith, we do not experience God's direction by passively waiting for His will to be revealed to us. It is by actively seeking God's will that we experience the joy of walking in His way. As the Psalmist says, "Taste and see that the LORD is good. Oh, the joys of those who take refuge in him!" (Psalm 34:8).

28 If you can help your neighbor now, don't say,
"Come back tomorrow, and then I'll help you." Rom 13:8

29 Don't plot harm against your neighbor,
for those who live nearby trust you. 3:29 Prov 14:22
30 Don't pick a fight without reason,
when no one has done you harm. 3:30 Prov 26:17 Rom 12:18

31 Don't envy violent people
or copy their ways. 3:31 Ps 37:1 Prov 24:1
32 Such wicked people are detestable to the LORD,
but He offers His friendship to the godly. 3:32 Ps 25:14
33 The LORD curses the house of the wicked,
but He blesses the home of the upright. 3:33 Deut 11:28 Job 8:6 Mal 2:2
34 The LORD mocks the mockers
but is gracious to the humble.* 3:34 Jas 4:6 *1 Pet 5:5
35 The wise inherit honor,
but fools are put to shame!

A FATHER'S WISE ADVICE

4 1 My children,* listen when your father corrects you.
Pay attention and learn good judgment, 4:1 Prov 1:8
2 for I am giving you good guidance.
Don't turn away from my instructions.
3 For I, too, was once my father's son,
tenderly loved as my mother's only child.

4 My father taught me,
"Take my words to heart.
Follow my commands, and you will live. 4:4 Prov 3:1; 4:10; 9:11
5 Get wisdom; develop good judgment.
Don't forget my words or turn away from them. 4:5 Prov 4:7; 16:16
6 Don't turn your back on wisdom, for she will protect you.
Love her, and she will guard you. 4:6 Prov 2:11 2 Thes 2:10
7 Getting wisdom is the wisest thing you can do!
And whatever else you do, develop good judgment. 4:7 Prov 23:23

3:34 Greek version reads *The LORD opposes the proud / but favors the humble.* Compare Jas 4:6; 1 Pet 5:5. 4:1 Hebrew *My sons.*

▸ HOLINESS
3:31 Don't imitate violence. The Bible does not shrink from showing just how brutal people can be. In the Bible, people die—in the worst case of all, God's perfect Son was tortured to death. This proverb tells us not to imitate the violent—but what does that mean? First, do not imitate the quickness to violence that is at the heart of the violent. Be slow to wrath, and slow to do harm to another unless absolutely necessary. Second, take an inventory of the entertainment you and your family like to enjoy. Are you and yours drawn to sadistic people? Or to cruel, brutal stories? Are your children exposed to cartoons that solve every problem with a fight? Use the wisdom of the Proverbs to help you become a person of peace (Matthew 5:9). (***See Holiness****> Law and Grace> Law> A window to view the world,* TopicGuide page A42.)

4:1-25 This chapter contains three more lectures from the father. He exhorts his children to embrace wisdom as he had once received teaching from his father (4:1-9), to follow the way of righteousness (4:10-19), and to guard their hearts tenaciously.

4:6-9 Again wisdom is personified as a woman, and the child is exhorted to "love her." The image is not so much that of a wise wife, to whom one would give romantic love, but of an older, sisterly patroness (see note on 7:4). "Love her," then, is legal and familial language (Deuteronomy 6:5); it describes a sentiment that is akin to esteem and obedience.

▸ BIBLE
4:7 Finding wisdom. Where can we find wisdom? Everywhere! When should we be seeking it? All the time! But certain people are to be heeded above others—fathers and mothers are featured here. All of life exists to teach us about God and His way of doing things, with even the wicked showing us how *not* to live. But wisdom is hard to find if we are not looking for it through the lens of the Word of God. Whenever you lack wisdom, ask God to give you understanding from and through His Word. God promises to answer your prayers for wisdom (James 1:5). (***See Bible****> Unity> Christ> Christ in the wisdom of Solomon,* TopicGuide page A10.)

4:8 Prov 3:18

[8] If you prize wisdom, she will make you great.
Embrace her, and she will honor you.
[9] She will place a lovely wreath on your head;
she will present you with a beautiful crown."

4:10 Prov 2:1; 9:11; 10:27; 22:4

[10] My child,* listen to me and do as I say,
and you will have a long, good life.
[11] I will teach you wisdom's ways
and lead you in straight paths.
[12] When you walk, you won't be held back;
when you run, you won't stumble.

4:13 Prov 3:18, 22

[13] Take hold of my instructions; don't let them go.
Guard them, for they are the key to life.

4:14 Ps 1:1 Prov 1:15

[14] Don't do as the wicked do,
and don't follow the path of evildoers.
[15] Don't even think about it; don't go that way.
Turn away and keep moving.

4:16 Ps 36:4 Mic 2:1

[16] For evil people can't sleep until they've done their evil deed for the day.
They can't rest until they've caused someone to stumble.
[17] They eat the food of wickedness
and drink the wine of violence!

4:18 2 Sam 23:4 Dan 12:3

[18] The way of the righteous is like the first gleam of dawn,
which shines ever brighter until the full light of day.

4:19 Job 18:5 Isa 59:9-10

[19] But the way of the wicked is like total darkness.
They have no idea what they are stumbling over.

4:20 Prov 2:1; 5:1

[20] My child, pay attention to what I say.
Listen carefully to my words.

4:21 Prov 3:21; 7:1

[21] Don't lose sight of them.
Let them penetrate deep into your heart,

4:22 Prov 3:8, 22

[22] for they bring life to those who find them,
and healing to their whole body.

4:23 Luke 6:45

[23] Guard your heart above all else,
for it determines the course of your life.

4:24 Job 11:14

[24] Avoid all perverse talk;
stay away from corrupt speech.

4:25 Job 31:1

[25] Look straight ahead,
and fix your eyes on what lies before you.

4:26 *Heb 12:13

[26] Mark out a straight path for your feet;
stay on the safe path.

4:10 Hebrew *My son;* also in 4:20.

4:10-19 The imagery of the path is presented again in this lecture as the father exhorts his child to travel in the company and in the way of the righteous, not the wicked. Specific images of traveling on a journey are presented: straight (upright) paths, hampered steps, stumbling, avoiding the entrance to the wicked way, sleepless nights, eating and drinking, light in the day, and stumbling in the darkness.

4:23 In ancient cultures, the heart was thought to be the center of the emotions (Proverbs 14:10), intellect (1 Kings 3:9), habits (Psalm 86:11), morality (Jeremiah 17:9), and will (Exodus 35:22).

WORSHIP

4:26 Fixing our eyes on Jesus. When a runner begins his race, where does he set his eyes? He doesn't look back—that distracts him from his goal. He looks ahead, toward the finish line. Hebrews 12:1-2 tells us that Jesus is our focus. When we set our eyes on Him, we don't look back over the sins we have committed in the past. Furthermore, we don't stray from the path of righteousness because we see where He is leading us. Are you focusing on Jesus? Begin each morning by setting your thoughts on Jesus. Ask for His guidance and follow through with a runner's determination. (***See Worship****> OT> Reverence> Taught and modeled by Solomon,* TopicGuide page A28.)

27 Don't get sidetracked;
keep your feet from following evil.

4:27 Deut 5:32; 28:14

AVOID IMMORAL WOMEN

5 1 My son, pay attention to my wisdom;
listen carefully to my wise counsel.
2 Then you will show discernment,
and your lips will express what you've learned.
3 For the lips of an immoral woman are as sweet as honey,
and her mouth is smoother than oil.
4 But in the end she is as bitter as poison,
as dangerous as a double-edged sword.
5 Her feet go down to death;
her steps lead straight to the grave.*
6 For she cares nothing about the path to life.
She staggers down a crooked trail and doesn't realize it.

7 So now, my sons, listen to me.
Never stray from what I am about to say:
8 Stay away from her!
Don't go near the door of her house!
9 If you do, you will lose your honor
and will lose to merciless people all you have achieved.
10 Strangers will consume your wealth,
and someone else will enjoy the fruit of your labor.
11 In the end you will groan in anguish
when disease consumes your body.
12 You will say, "How I hated discipline!
If only I had not ignored all the warnings!
13 Oh, why didn't I listen to my teachers?
Why didn't I pay attention to my instructors?
14 I have come to the brink of utter ruin,
and now I must face public disgrace."

15 Drink water from your own well—
share your love only with your wife.*

5:1 Prov 4:20
5:3 Ps 55:21 Prov 5:20; 7:5
5:4 Ps 57:4 Eccl 7:26
5:5 Prov 2:18; 7:27
5:6 2 Pet 2:14
5:7 Prov 7:24
5:8 Prov 7:25; 9:14
5:12 Prov 1:22, 25
5:13 Prov 1:8

5:5 Hebrew *to Sheol.* 5:15 Hebrew *Drink water from your own cistern, / flowing water from your own well.*

5:1-23 In ancient Israel, sexual sin was seen as an attack on someone's household by disrupting procreation and inheritance (Exodus 20:14). In addition, it defiled the participants (Leviticus 18:20) and was disrespectful to one's neighbor (Exodus 20:17). For this reason, sexual sin was punishable by death. Proverbs 5 exposes the folly of this behavior by showing that adultery leads to death, wandering, weakness, disease, regret, and punishment. The vulnerable son is warned to avoid the immoral woman at all costs (5:3-14) and instead to delight in his own wife (5:15-20), for God will hold him to account (5:21-23). This metaphor of faithful love is not simply a moral tale but is a part of a larger comparison between the joys of union with wisdom and the agony of union with folly.

5:6 In ancient Israel, good roads were not common. A maze of trails often connected homes with the main village or surrounding orchards and pastures. Folly, personified as the immoral woman, picks random trails to follow, stumbling foolishly along to no place in particular.

▸ ADOPTION
5:12-13 Too late. It's painful to even think about, but there are grave consequences for sexual sin. The male character in this narrative now lies dying, considering that others will inherit his belongings as the disease he is experiencing will surely kill him. He is filled with regret that he did not heed the wisdom of his parents and now it is too late—what he did in private will now destroy his family, his body, and his reputation. The story doesn't have a happy ending—"He will die for lack of self-control" (5:23). Do we serve a God of second chances? Yes. But we also serve a God who will allow us to experience the full consequences of sexual sin. By God's grace, flee the foolishness of sexual sin. (***See Adoption***> *With Christ*> *Supernatural*> *Controlled by Christ,* TopicGuide page A37.)

5:15-20 The sexual connotations in these verses are poetic and vivid. The uninhibited, intoxicating lovemaking between husband and wife is contrasted with the wasteful lack of self-control of the foolish man. The husband should be delighted only by his wife, who evokes the grace of a deer (Song of Solomon 2:9, 17; 4:5; 7:3). This is a strong call for privacy and monogamy in the marriage relationship.

5:16 Prov 5:18 16 Why spill the water of your springs in the streets,
having sex with just anyone?*
17 You should reserve it for yourselves.
Never share it with strangers.

5:18 Eccl 9:9 Mal 2:14 18 Let your wife be a fountain of blessing for you.
Rejoice in the wife of your youth.
5:19 Song 4:5; 7:3 19 She is a loving deer, a graceful doe.
Let her breasts satisfy you always.
May you always be captivated by her love.
5:20 Prov 2:16; 5:3 20 Why be captivated, my son, by an immoral woman,
or fondle the breasts of a promiscuous woman?
5:21 Job 14:16 Ps 119:168 21 For the LORD sees clearly what a man does,
examining every path he takes.
5:22 Num 32:23 22 An evil man is held captive by his own sins;
they are ropes that catch and hold him.
5:23 Job 4:21; 36:12 Prov 10:21 23 He will die for lack of self-control;
he will be lost because of his great foolishness.

LESSONS FOR DAILY LIFE

6:1 Prov 11:15; 17:18; 20:16; 22:26; 27:13 **6** 1 My child,* if you have put up security for a friend's debt
or agreed to guarantee the debt of a stranger—
2 if you have trapped yourself by your agreement
and are caught by what you said—
3 follow my advice and save yourself,
for you have placed yourself at your friend's mercy.
Now swallow your pride;
go and beg to have your name erased.
4 Don't put it off; do it now!
Don't rest until you do.
6:5 Pss 91:3; 124:7 5 Save yourself like a gazelle escaping from a hunter,
like a bird fleeing from a net.

6:6 Prov 10:26; 13:4; 30:24-25 6 Take a lesson from the ants, you lazybones.
Learn from their ways and become wise!

5:16 Hebrew *Why spill your springs in the streets, / your streams in the city squares?* 6:1 Hebrew *My son.*

▸ BIBLE
5:18 A fountain of joy. Magazines rarely print articles about the joys of sex with your spouse. If you look through the magazine rack at your local store, you'll find them virtual evangelists for a culture of sex outside of marriage. But this verse calls us to rejoice in our spouse, to delight in their physical pleasures and be captivated by their beauty. This advice is a great comfort when couples hit those inevitable rough places in marital relationships. Sexual pleasure isn't everything; it doesn't solve every problem of marriage. But it certainly helps to be thoroughly smitten and completely attracted to the person with whom you are experiencing conflict. (***See Bible****> Unity> Doctrines> Principles of marriage,* TopicGuide page A10.)

6:1-5 The ancients relied on collateral to secure debts, just as we do today. This was usually symbolized by pledging a garment (Genesis 38:17-18; Exodus 22:26-27; Deuteronomy 24:10-13, 17). But Proverbs always warns against securing the debt of a stranger (Proverbs 11:15; 17:18; 20:16; 22:26; 27:13). To avoid ruin, the father urgently warns his child to get out of the arrangement as soon as possible and with all effort to avoid entrapment.

6:1-19 This lecture describes three people: the one who pledges to secure another's debt, the sluggard, and the troublemaker. The last one is the worst, and the Lord detests him for it. All three of these character shortcomings lead to destruction.

▸ ADOPTION
6:6 Learn from the ants. With the plethora of entertainment choices we have today—computers, television, videos, movies, books—we all face the temptation to put off work and simply entertain ourselves. God wants us to have balance in our lives, but some people spend hours playing with the computer, while others have stacks of movies. God tells us to look at the industry of the ants. They consistently work at finding food and building their homes. The Bible says, "You have six days each week for your ordinary work, but on the seventh day you must stop working" (Exodus 23:12). Is that a description of your life? Then get busy, and then your rest will be more energizing than you could imagine. (***See Adoption****> With Christ> Servants> Created to do good works,* TopicGuide page A37.)

[7] Though they have no prince
or governor or ruler to make them work,
[8] they labor hard all summer,
gathering food for the winter.
[9] But you, lazybones, how long will you sleep?
When will you wake up?
[10] A little extra sleep, a little more slumber,
a little folding of the hands to rest—
[11] then poverty will pounce on you like a bandit;
scarcity will attack you like an armed robber.

[12] What are worthless and wicked people like?
They are constant liars,
[13] signaling their deceit with a wink of the eye,
a nudge of the foot, or the wiggle of fingers.
[14] Their perverted hearts plot evil,
and they constantly stir up trouble.
[15] But they will be destroyed suddenly,
broken in an instant beyond all hope of healing.

[16] There are six things the LORD hates—
no, seven things He detests:
[17] haughty eyes,
a lying tongue,
hands that kill the innocent,
[18] a heart that plots evil,
feet that race to do wrong,
[19] a false witness who pours out lies,
a person who sows discord in a family.

[20] My son, obey your father's commands,
and don't neglect your mother's instruction.
[21] Keep their words always in your heart.
Tie them around your neck.
[22] When you walk, their counsel will lead you.
When you sleep, they will protect you.
When you wake up, they will advise you.
[23] For their command is a lamp
and their instruction a light;
their corrective discipline
is the way to life.

6:8 Prov 10:5
6:10 Prov 24:33
6:13 Ps 35:19; Prov 10:10
6:14 Prov 6:19; Mic 2:1
6:15 2 Chr 36:16; Prov 24:22; Jer 19:11
6:16-19 Gen 6:5; Prov 1:16; 6:14; 19:5, 9; 21:4; 24:2; 28:17; Isa 1:15
6:21 Prov 3:3
6:22 Prov 3:23
6:23 Ps 119:105; Prov 13:9

6:12-13 The kind of people these verses refer to could also be translated as "troublemakers," "insurrectionists," or "malevolent people" who maliciously wink. (See also 16:30.)

▸ SPIRITUAL WARFARE
6:14 Stirring up trouble. Have you ever known a person who constantly stirs up trouble? Perhaps that person spreads gossip or argues with others over minor matters. Some people look for ways to put down their "friends" or get their own way, no matter what it costs. What about you? Do you stir up trouble often? Psalm 34:14 tells us how we ought to conduct ourselves: "Search for peace, and work to maintain it." (***See Spiritual Warfare****> Resisting Sin and Evil> Consequences> Of Obedience> Potential for a more peaceable life,* TopicGuide page A46.)

6:16-19 The form of this proverb follows an interesting pattern that is observed in Semitic and Homeric poetry (see Proverbs 30:15-16, 18-19, 21-31). The list of seven things the Lord hates is a catalog of misused body parts, all of which are disruptive. These verses are a poetic pronouncement upon the malevolent troublemaker described in 6:12-15.

6:20-35 The subject of this lecture is the high price of adultery. The body of the warning (6:25-35) is prefaced by the typical introductory exhortation for the son to heed the father's words (6:20-25). Expanding upon Proverbs 2:16-19 and 5:1-23, the father vividly portrays the consequences of adultery: the capture of one's heart, the civil punishment, the public shame, the legal fines, and the vengeful pursuit by the woman's husband.

6:24 Prov 2:16; 5:3
6:25 2 Kgs 9:30; Matt 5:28
6:26 Prov 5:9-10; 29:3
6:29 Ezek 18:6
6:31 Ezek 22:1-4
6:32 Prov 7:7, 22-23; 9:15-18
6:34 Prov 11:4; 27:4; Song 8:6

24 It will keep you from the immoral woman,
from the smooth tongue of a promiscuous woman.
25 Don't lust for her beauty.
Don't let her coy glances seduce you.
26 For a prostitute will bring you to poverty,*
but sleeping with another man's wife will cost you your life.
27 Can a man scoop a flame into his lap
and not have his clothes catch on fire?
28 Can he walk on hot coals
and not blister his feet?
29 So it is with the man who sleeps with another man's wife.
He who embraces her will not go unpunished.

30 Excuses might be found for a thief
who steals because he is starving.
31 But if he is caught, he must pay back seven times what he stole,
even if he has to sell everything in his house.
32 But the man who commits adultery is an utter fool,
for he destroys himself.
33 He will be wounded and disgraced.
His shame will never be erased.
34 For the woman's jealous husband will be furious,
and he will show no mercy when he takes revenge.
35 He will accept no compensation,
nor be satisfied with a payoff of any size.

ANOTHER WARNING ABOUT IMMORAL WOMEN

7:1 Prov 2:1; 4:1
7:2 Deut 32:10; Ps 17:8; Prov 4:4; 9:11
7:3 Deut 6:8; Prov 3:3; 6:21
7:5 Prov 6:24

7 1 Follow my advice, my son;
always treasure my commands.
2 Obey my commands and live!
Guard my instructions as you guard your own eyes.*
3 Tie them on your fingers as a reminder.
Write them deep within your heart.

4 Love wisdom like a sister;
make insight a beloved member of your family.
5 Let them protect you from an affair with an immoral woman,
from listening to the flattery of a promiscuous woman.

6:26 Hebrew *to a loaf of bread.* 7:2 Hebrew *as the pupil of your eye.*

6:25 The Hebrew is better translated, "Don't let her capture you with her eyes." This vividly describes how a woman's beautiful eyes, probably enhanced with makeup (2 Kings 9:30; Jeremiah 4:30; Ezekiel 23:40), can entrance a man.

7:1-27 By way of story, this lecture vividly portrays an eyewitness account of the encounter between an ignorant fool and an adulteress (7:6-23), and then it concludes with some final, sobering admonitions (7:24-27).

7:3 The phrase "tie them on your fingers" speaks of the phylactery, first mentioned in Deuteronomy (Deuteronomy 6:8; 11:18). At this time, it was a strip of parchment with several passages written on it (Exodus 13:1-16; Deuteronomy 6:4-9; 11:13-21). As noted in Proverbs 3:3, the binding was symbolic for the actual writing of God's Law on the heart of the individual Israelite, but as an act of piety, some Jews took God's command literally. Jesus spoke of the Pharisees' pride and hypocrisy when He said they made their phylacteries "extra wide" (Matthew 23:5). However, in this verse, the father is encouraging the son to do whatever is necessary to emblazon wise teaching indelibly on his heart.

7:4 Wisdom is again portrayed as a dear sister (also see notes on Proverbs 1:20-33 and 3:13-18) who offers faithfulness if the son will but claim it. She appeals to the son spiritually, but the immoral woman appeals to the son erotically. They are contrasted in previous verses (Proverbs 1:16-19, 20-33; 3:13-18; 4:6-9; 5:3-15; 6:24-29), and this episode sets up a final contest between the two (Proverbs 8:1-21; 9:1-18).

6 While I was at the window of my house,
looking through the curtain,
7 I saw some naive young men,
and one in particular who lacked common sense.
8 He was crossing the street near the house of an immoral woman,
strolling down the path by her house.
9 It was at twilight, in the evening,
as deep darkness fell.
10 The woman approached him,
seductively dressed and sly of heart.
11 She was the brash, rebellious type,
never content to stay at home.
12 She is often in the streets and markets,
soliciting at every corner.
13 She threw her arms around him and kissed him,
and with a brazen look she said,
14 "I've just made my peace offerings
and fulfilled my vows.
15 You're the one I was looking for!
I came out to find you, and here you are!
16 My bed is spread with beautiful blankets,
with colored sheets of Egyptian linen.
17 I've perfumed my bed
with myrrh, aloes, and cinnamon.
18 Come, let's drink our fill of love until morning.
Let's enjoy each other's caresses,
19 for my husband is not home.
He's away on a long trip.
20 He has taken a wallet full of money with him
and won't return until later this month.*"

21 So she seduced him with her pretty speech
and enticed him with her flattery.
22 He followed her at once,
like an ox going to the slaughter.
He was like a stag caught in a trap,
23 awaiting the arrow that would pierce its heart.
He was like a bird flying into a snare,
little knowing it would cost him his life.

24 So listen to me, my sons,
and pay attention to my words.

7:7 Prov 1:22; 6:32
7:8 Prov 7:12
7:9 Job 24:15
7:10 Gen 38:14-15
7:11 Prov 9:13
7:12 Prov 23:28
7:16 Prov 31:22; Ezek 27:7
7:21 Prov 5:3; 6:24
7:23 Eccl 9:12
7:24 Prov 4:1

7:20 Hebrew *until the moon is full.*

7:6-23 The adulteress stalks the ignorant fool, and his many mistakes allow her to lure him. He is naive and ignorant, while she is sly and cunning (Proverbs 7:7, 10, 23). He passes by her house (7:8) when he should steer clear. He is out at the wrong time, passing by at dusk—prime time in Israel for "night life" (7:9). He does not run when she meets him (7:10), like Joseph did with Potiphar's wife (Genesis 39:6-18). He does not have a plan of defense when she tempts him (7:21). Finally, he falls suddenly because he has no discipline (7:22). He is no match for the scheming sexual predator, who vanquishes him like a skillful hunter making a quick kill (7:21-23).

7:14 The Hebrew indicates this is a fellowship offering, which involves a sacrificed animal, with some portions offered to God and other portions cooked and consumed by the worshiper and priestly officials (Leviticus 3:1-17; 7:11-21). Having made such an offering, she is free and clear of any sin, and is ready to sin again. This is a disgusting display of dead religiosity, akin to going to the confession booth to get a clean bill and then sinning as soon as one walks out.

7:25 Prov 5:8
25 Don't let your hearts stray away toward her.
Don't wander down her wayward path.
26 For she has been the ruin of many;
many men have been her victims.
7:27 Prov 2:18; 9:18
27 Her house is the road to the grave.*
Her bedroom is the den of death.

WISDOM CALLS FOR A HEARING

8:1 Prov 1:20-21
8 1 Listen as Wisdom calls out!
Hear as understanding raises her voice!
2 On the hilltop along the road,
she takes her stand at the crossroads.
3 By the gates at the entrance to the town,
on the road leading in, she cries aloud,
4 "I call to you, to all of you!
I raise my voice to all people.
8:5 Prov 1:4, 22, 32
5 You simple people, use good judgment.
You foolish people, show some understanding.
6 Listen to me! For I have important things to tell you.
Everything I say is right,
7 for I speak the truth
and detest every kind of deception.
8 My advice is wholesome.
There is nothing devious or crooked in it.
8:9 Prov 3:13; 14:6
9 My words are plain to anyone with understanding,
clear to those with knowledge.
10 Choose my instruction rather than silver,
and knowledge rather than pure gold.
8:11 Prov 3:14-15; 16:16; 20:15
11 For wisdom is far more valuable than rubies.
Nothing you desire can compare with it.
8:12 Prov 1:4; 8:5
12 "I, Wisdom, live together with good judgment.
I know where to discover knowledge and discernment.
8:13 Prov 3:7; 6:12; 15:9
13 All who fear the LORD will hate evil.
Therefore, I hate pride and arrogance,
corruption and perverse speech.

7:27 Hebrew *to Sheol.*

▸ HOLINESS
7:27 Immorality: the door to death. Never in human history has it been so evident as now that immorality leads to death. Sexually transmitted diseases cause the deaths of millions of people worldwide each year. Many more endure a lifetime of suffering and embarrassment because of their rash behavior. God's Word always tells the stark truth—sexual sin is a doorway to doom. That's not saying God can't rescue us, or that sexual sin is somehow the worst of all sins—far from it. But the danger should be a warning to us and those we love—flee sexual immorality! (***See Holiness****> Disciplines> Of Abstinence> Resisting worldy influences,* TopicGuide page A42.)

8:1-36 This second interlude by Wisdom (for the first, see 1:20-33) is a hymn of self-praise divided into Wisdom's call (8:1-6), Wisdom's counsel to the son (8:7-21), Wisdom's counsel in creation (8:22-31), and Wisdom's concluding invitation (8:32-36). Similar hymns of self-praise have been found in Mesopotamian writings, and the use of this literary form by the compiler of Proverbs is both poetic and convincing.

8:2-3 Wisdom passionately pleads and takes her stand in open places, because it is there that people begin journeys, conduct business, make decisions, and live life. The harlot, on the other hand, makes her appeal in secret (Proverbs 7:12-20; 9:13-18).

▸ HOLINESS
8:13 Hate evil. The evils mentioned in this verse are all sins we can easily overlook in our lives. In the world's eyes, they don't seem as terrible as murder, robbery, or other sins. But God sees things differently. Pride affects our attitude toward everything we do. When we are arrogant, we treat people badly. When we are corrupt and use perverted speech, we use what we have for the wrong purposes. To what degree are these sins present in your life? With God's help, root them out. Then set up a prayer firewall to keep them away. (***See Holiness****> Law and Grace> Law> Hate evil,* TopicGuide page A42.)

14 Common sense and success belong to me.
Insight and strength are mine.
15 Because of me, kings reign,
and rulers make just decrees.
16 Rulers lead with my help,
and nobles make righteous judgments.

17 "I love all who love me.
Those who search will surely find me.
18 I have riches and honor,
as well as enduring wealth and justice.
19 My gifts are better than gold, even the purest gold,
my wages better than sterling silver!
20 I walk in righteousness,
in paths of justice.
21 Those who love me inherit wealth.
I will fill their treasuries.

22 "The LORD formed me from the beginning,
before He created anything else.
23 I was appointed in ages past,
at the very first, before the earth began.
24 I was born before the oceans were created,
before the springs bubbled forth their waters.
25 Before the mountains were formed,
before the hills, I was born—
26 before He had made the earth and fields
and the first handfuls of soil.
27 I was there when He established the heavens,
when He drew the horizon on the oceans.
28 I was there when He set the clouds above,
when He established springs deep in the earth.
29 I was there when He set the limits of the seas,
so they would not spread beyond their boundaries.
And when He marked off the earth's foundations,
30 I was the architect at His side.
I was His constant delight,
rejoicing always in His presence.
31 And how happy I was with the world He created;
how I rejoiced with the human family!

32 "And so, my children,* listen to me,
for all who follow my ways are joyful.
33 Listen to my instruction and be wise.
Don't ignore it.
34 Joyful are those who listen to me,
watching for me daily at my gates,
waiting for me outside my home!

8:32 Hebrew *my sons.*

8:14 Prov 1:25; 2:7
8:17 1 Sam 2:30; Ps 91:14; Prov 2:4-5; 4:6; John 14:21
8:18 Ps 112:3; Prov 3:16; 22:4; Matt 6:33; Jas 2:5
8:19 Prov 3:14; 10:20
8:20 Pss 23:3; 25:4
8:21 Prov 3:19
8:22 Job 28:27
8:23 John 17:5, 24
8:24 Job 38:16
8:25 Ps 90:2
8:27 Job 26:10; Prov 3:19
8:29 Job 38:6, 10; Ps 104:9
8:32 Ps 119:1-2; Prov 5:7; 29:18
8:33 Prov 4:1
8:34 Ps 27:4; Prov 3:13, 18; Jas 1:22

8:22-31 Expanding upon 3:19-20, this poem shows Wisdom's knowledge and participation in Creation. The fact that Wisdom existed before Creation implies her standing above it—it is divine and eternal, not material and subject to the ravages of time. The order that Wisdom imposed upon chaos in the Creation is the same order that Wisdom gives to family and society (8:12-21).

8:27-31 Wisdom's role during Creation and afterward is one of giving advice and support at God's side (see 3:19-20). She was a craftsman who took the basic creation and did the "finishing" as a contractor would finish the walls and woodwork in a new house. Finally, she rejoiced over the created world and humanity in particular.

8:35 Prov 3:4; 4:22; 12:2; John 17:3
8:36 Prov 1:31-32; 5:12; 15:32

35 For whoever finds me finds life
and receives favor from the LORD.
36 But those who miss me injure themselves.
All who hate me love death."

9:1 Eph 2:20-22; 1 Pet 2:5
9:2 Matt 22:4
9:3 Prov 1:20; 8:1-2; Matt 22:3
9:4 Ps 19:7; Prov 8:5
9:5 Song 5:1; Isa 55:1; John 6:27
9:6 Prov 9:11; 16:22

9

1 Wisdom has built her house;
she has carved its seven columns.
2 She has prepared a great banquet,
mixed the wines, and set the table.
3 She has sent her servants to invite everyone to come.
She calls out from the heights overlooking the city.
4 "Come in with me," she urges the simple.
To those who lack good judgment, she says,
5 "Come, eat my food,
and drink the wine I have mixed.
6 Leave your simple ways behind, and begin to live;
learn to use good judgment."

9:7 Prov 23:9
9:9 Prov 1:5
9:10 Job 28:28; Ps 111:10; Prov 1:7
9:11 Prov 3:2, 16; 9:6; 10:27
9:12 Job 22:2

7 Anyone who rebukes a mocker will get
an insult in return.
Anyone who corrects the wicked will get hurt.
8 So don't bother correcting mockers;
they will only hate you.
But correct the wise,
and they will love you.
9 Instruct the wise,
and they will be even wiser.
Teach the righteous,
and they will learn even more.
10 Fear of the LORD is the foundation of wisdom.
Knowledge of the Holy One results in
good judgment.
11 Wisdom will multiply your days
and add years to your life.
12 If you become wise, you will be the one to benefit.
If you scorn wisdom, you will be the one to suffer.

9:1-6 Wisdom's metaphorical home is a seven-pillared house in the heights. The number seven has long been symbolic for perfection (Genesis 2:1-3; Proverbs 6:16; 24:16; 26:16). The house on the heights was usually the temple or the place of learning in an area. Wisdom's banquet foreshadows the great wedding feast that God makes possible through Jesus Christ (Matthew 22:2-14).

9:1-18 This is the last lecture in the first section of Proverbs (see note on 1:8–9:18). It is the culminating presentation of two invitations: one from Wisdom (9:1-6) and one from the immoral woman (9:13-18), with a short section between them that deals with the scoffer (9:7-12). The warning to the scoffer corresponds to the introductory exhortation to listen (1:5-7). It repeats the theme of Proverbs from 1:7—"Fear of the LORD is the foundation of wisdom" (9:10)—giving unity to this section of Proverbs.

▸ GOD

9:10 Attractive misinformation. What did Saint Augustine mean when he said, "I believe, that I may understand." There are a myriad of opinions flying around regarding the universe and the way things work, and many of them intentionally exclude belief in God: Is matter all that is (materialism)? Does God exist (atheism)? Did people come to exist by random forces (evolution)? On the other hand, if we presume that God exists, then it's possible to cut through many of these foolish ideas and make progress on some of life's true mysteries. Pursue learning, and pursue answers to life's moral and scientific mysteries, but never lose sight of the fact that knowledge of God provides the foundation of all intellectual pursuit. (***See God****> God's Attributes> True> God's truth can be suppressed to our peril,* TopicGuide page A18.)

FOLLY CALLS FOR A HEARING

13 The woman named Folly is brash.
She is ignorant and doesn't know it.
14 She sits in her doorway
on the heights overlooking the city.
15 She calls out to men going by
who are minding their own business.
16 "Come in with me," she urges the simple.
To those who lack good judgment, she says,
17 "Stolen water is refreshing;
food eaten in secret tastes the best!"
18 But little do they know that the dead are there.
Her guests are in the depths of the grave.*

9:13 Prov 5:6; 7:11
9:16 Prov 9:4
9:17 Prov 20:17
9:18 Prov 7:27

THE PROVERBS OF SOLOMON

10 The proverbs of Solomon:

A wise child* brings joy to a father;
a foolish child brings grief to a mother.

10:1 Prov 15:20; 17:25; 29:3, 15

9:18 Hebrew *in Sheol.* 10:1 Hebrew *son;* also in 10:1b.

▸ HOLINESS
9:13 Folly calls out to us. Proverbs gives us a picture of an enticing woman named Folly. She is still hard at work today. But she no longer sits on her doorstep; instead, we have invited her into our homes. Day and night, we allow her to indoctrinate us through mass media. The philosophy that sex is free and that we should indulge our desires comes through clearly in movies, television programs, music, and Internet content. We allow into our homes material that just a few decades ago would have been considered pornographic. But the Bible tells us, "God's will is for you to be holy, so stay away from all sexual sin" (1 Thessalonians 4:3). Be careful of bringing Folly into your home. Carefully evaluate all the media to which you expose yourself and your family. (***See Holiness****> Law and Grace> Law> Hate evil,* TopicGuide page A42.)

9:13-18 The immoral woman is presented as the opposite of Wisdom (9:1-6). Instead of calling to all humanity, she calls only to the men going by her as she stands in the doorway of her house. The offer to drink stolen water and eat food in secrecy seeks to appeal to youthful lust.

10:1–22:16 This extended section of Proverbs is attributed to Solomon, David's son and the builder of the Temple in Israel. It is probably no coincidence that the number of proverbs in this section, 375, corresponds to the numerical value of Solomon's name in Hebrew. This portion of Proverbs seems to have two sections: Chapters 10 to 15 contain primarily "antithetical" proverbs contrasting two relative opposites, while chapters 16 to 22 contain almost no antithetical proverbs. These later chapters use primarily (though not exclusively) synonymous or "synthetic" structures in the sayings.

BECAUSE GOD IS HOLY

I will devote myself to him in purity, worship and service.

Fear of the LORD is the foundation of wisdom.
Knowledge of the Holy One results in good judgment.

PROVERBS 9:10

FOR THE NEXT *GOD IS HOLY* FEATURE SEE PAGE 1516.

10:2 Ps 49:6-7; Prov 11:4; 21:6; Eccl 2:4

2 Tainted wealth has no lasting value,
but right living can save your life.

10:3 Pss 34:9-10; 37:25; Matt 6:33

3 The LORD will not let the godly go hungry,
but He refuses to satisfy the craving of the wicked.

10:4 Prov 13:4

4 Lazy people are soon poor;
hard workers get rich.

5 A wise youth harvests in the summer,
but one who sleeps during harvest is a disgrace.

10:6 Prov 28:20

6 The godly are showered with blessings;
the words of the wicked conceal violent intentions.

10:7 Ps 9:5-6

7 We have happy memories of the godly,
but the name of a wicked person rots away.

10:8 Prov 9:8; Matt 7:24

8 The wise are glad to be instructed,
but babbling fools fall flat on their faces.

10:9 Ps 23:4; Prov 3:23; Isa 33:15-16; Matt 10:26

9 People with integrity walk safely,
but those who follow crooked paths will slip and fall.

10:10 Prov 6:13

10 People who wink at wrong cause trouble,
but a bold reproof promotes peace.*

10:11 Ps 37:30; Prov 13:14; 18:4

11 The words of the godly are a life-giving fountain;
the words of the wicked conceal violent intentions.

10:12 Prov 17:9; 1 Cor 13:4-7; *1 Pet 4:8

12 Hatred stirs up quarrels,
but love makes up for all offenses.

10:13 Prov 10:31; 26:3

13 Wise words come from the lips of people with understanding,
but those lacking sense will be beaten with a rod.

10:14 Prov 9:9; 13:3; 18:7; Jas 3:2, 5

14 Wise people treasure knowledge,
but the babbling of a fool invites disaster.

10:15 Ps 52:7; Prov 18:11; 19:7

15 The wealth of the rich is their fortress;
the poverty of the poor is their destruction.

10:16 Prov 11:18-19

16 The earnings of the godly enhance their lives,
but evil people squander their money on sin.

10:17 Prov 6:23

17 People who accept discipline are on the pathway to life,
but those who ignore correction will go astray.

10:10 As in Greek version; Hebrew reads *but babbling fools fall flat on their faces.*

10:2-5, 14-16 This chapter contains about a dozen references to wealth. One primary teaching is that righteousness (right living) is a better security than earthly wealth.

10:3 In this collection of Solomon's sayings (Proverbs 10–15), the LORD gives life and blessing to those whose character honors Him. Their deeds do not earn favor so much as God-given virtue.

10:15 A "fortress" is technically a fortified city, which in the biblical era was a place of security against assault. But the force of the proverb is that while wealth may seem to bring security, trusting in walls and external protection is ultimately foolish. After all, how many ancient fortified cities still stand?

▶ BIBLE

10:17 Accepting correction. Being rebuked for something we are doing can be very difficult to handle. Sometimes our first reaction is to explode in anger—even if we respect the person who is rebuking us. We think, "Who is he to criticize me?" But as this verse says, the wise person listens to the correction and evaluates its substance. You should always bring a rebuke before the Lord because some criticism is unfounded. But when you find that a rebuke is accurate, take it to heart. This will help you to stay on the pathway of righteousness and to keep your example for Christ clear and unhindered. (***See Bible> Power> Convict> Cuts through deception,*** TopicGuide page A11.)

18 Hiding hatred makes you a liar;
slandering others makes you a fool.

19 Too much talk leads to sin.
Be sensible and keep your mouth shut.

20 The words of the godly are like sterling silver;
the heart of a fool is worthless.

21 The words of the godly encourage many,
but fools are destroyed by their lack of common sense.

22 The blessing of the LORD makes a person rich,
and He adds no sorrow with it.

23 Doing wrong is fun for a fool,
but living wisely brings pleasure to the sensible.

24 The fears of the wicked will be fulfilled;
the hopes of the godly will be granted.

25 When the storms of life come, the wicked are whirled away,
but the godly have a lasting foundation.

26 Lazy people irritate their employers,
like vinegar to the teeth or smoke in the eyes.

27 Fear of the LORD lengthens one's life,
but the years of the wicked are cut short.

28 The hopes of the godly result in happiness,
but the expectations of the wicked come to nothing.

29 The way of the LORD is a stronghold to those with integrity,
but it destroys the wicked.

30 The godly will never be disturbed,
but the wicked will be removed from the land.

31 The mouth of the godly person gives wise advice,
but the tongue that deceives will be cut off.

32 The lips of the godly speak helpful words,
but the mouth of the wicked speaks perverse words.

11

1 The LORD detests the use of dishonest scales,
but He delights in accurate weights.

2 Pride leads to disgrace,
but with humility comes wisdom.

10:18 Prov 26:24
10:19 Job 11:2; Prov 18:21; Eccl 5:3; Jas 3:2
10:20 Prov 8:19
10:21 Prov 5:23; 10:11
10:22 Gen 24:35; 26:12; Deut 8:18; Prov 8:21
10:23 Prov 15:21
10:24 Ps 145:19; Prov 1:27; 15:8; Matt 5:6
10:25 Ps 15:1-5; Prov 12:3; Matt 7:24-25
10:27 Ps 55:23; Prov 3:2; 9:11; 14:27
10:28 Job 11:20; Prov 11:7, 23
10:29 Prov 21:15
10:30 Ps 37:29
10:31 Prov 11:20
10:32 Prov 6:12; Eccl 12:10
11:1 Deut 25:13-16; Prov 16:11
11:2 Prov 16:18; 18:12; 29:23

▸ SPIRITUAL WARFARE
10:18 Hiding hatred. Christians have devised all kinds of ways to hide their true feelings. When we dislike a person, we don't say, "I hate him." Instead, we cover our feelings with platitudes: "I just don't like the way he lives his life"; "I don't think God approves of her"; "That person just doesn't have the 'right' attitude"; or "If I have anything to do with him, he'll just hurt me again." This verse makes it clear that hiding hatred is lying—to ourselves and to God. Whom do you dislike? Are you truthful with yourself about your feelings? How will you deal with your true attitude? (***See Spiritual Warfare**> Originator of Sin> Satan's Titles> Father of lies,* TopicGuide page A44.)

10:31-32 Both of these verses contrast the upright with the perverse with respect to their speech. The righteous speak life-giving words, but the tongue of the perverse will be cut out. While cutting out the tongue may seem to be a hyperbole, such a drastic penalty was not entirely uncommon in ancient days.

11:1-8 Since wealth is not a reliable source of security, these verses hold up honesty, integrity, and righteousness as sources of more lasting protection. Notice especially the antithetical parallels: good people/honesty vs. treacherous people/dishonesty; godly/honesty vs. wicked/sin.

11:3 Prov 13:6; 22:12
3 Honesty guides good people;
dishonesty destroys treacherous people.

11:4 Prov 10:2 Ezek 7:19
4 Riches won't help on the day of judgment,
but right living can save you from death.

11:5 Prov 3:6; 5:22
5 The godly are directed by honesty;
the wicked fall beneath their load of sin.

11:6 Pss 7:15-16; 9:15
6 The godliness of good people rescues them;
the ambition of treacherous people traps them.

11:7 Prov 10:28
7 When the wicked die, their hopes die with them,
for they rely on their own feeble strength.

8 The godly are rescued from trouble,
and it falls on the wicked instead.

9 With their words, the godless destroy their friends,
but knowledge will rescue the righteous.

11:10 Prov 28:12
10 The whole city celebrates when the godly succeed;
they shout for joy when the wicked die.

11 Upright citizens are good for a city and make it prosper,
but the talk of the wicked tears it apart.

12 It is foolish to belittle one's neighbor;
a sensible person keeps quiet.

11:13 Lev 19:16 Prov 19:11; 20:19 1 Tim 5:13
13 A gossip goes around telling secrets,
but those who are trustworthy can keep a confidence.

11:14 Prov 15:22; 20:18; 24:6
14 Without wise leadership, a nation falls;
there is safety in having many advisers.

11:15 Prov 6:1; 27:13
15 There's danger in putting up security for a stranger's debt;
it's safer not to guarantee another person's debt.

11:16 Prov 31:28, 30
16 A gracious woman gains respect,
but ruthless men gain only wealth.

11:17 Matt 5:7; 25:34-36
17 Your kindness will reward you,
but your cruelty will destroy you.

11:18 Hos 10:12 Gal 6:8-9
18 Evil people get rich for the moment,
but the reward of the godly will last.

11:19 Prov 10:16; 19:23; 21:16 Rom 6:23 Jas 1:15
19 Godly people find life;
evil people find death.

▸ SPIRITUAL WARFARE

11:9 The power of evil words. The proliferation of communication media in our day has made it temptingly easy to pass along gossip and slander. As Christians, we must resist this temptation. When we say something nasty about someone, we fail to heed God's command to act lovingly toward all people, and such actions cause deep hurts and destroy friendships, as these verses point out. The wise person chooses his or her words carefully, judging them by God's standards. In this way we can avoid many hurtful situations and preserve our friendships. (***See Spiritual Warfare****> Resisting Sin and Evil> Consequences> Of Disobedience> Broken relationships,* TopicGuide page A46.)

11:10-15 These verses show how a person's speech can affect a community. Notice the references to the city, neighbors, gossip (which involves networks of people), and the nation.

11:16-22 This brief section focuses on benevolence—the disposition to do good and show kindness to others. Again, all the comparisons are antithetical.

[20] The LORD detests people with crooked hearts,
but He delights in those with integrity.

11:20 Prov 13:6

[21] Evil people will surely be punished,
but the children of the godly will go free.

11:21 Prov 16:5

[22] A beautiful woman who lacks discretion
is like a gold ring in a pig's snout.

[23] The godly can look forward to a reward,
while the wicked can expect only judgment.

11:23 Prov 10:28; Rom 2:8-9

[24] Give freely and become more wealthy;
be stingy and lose everything.

[25] The generous will prosper;
those who refresh others will themselves be refreshed.

11:25 Matt 5:7; 2 Cor 9:6-7

[26] People curse those who hoard their grain,
but they bless the one who sells in time of need.

11:26 Job 29:13

[27] If you search for good, you will find favor;
but if you search for evil, it will find you!

11:27 Ps 7:15

[28] Trust in your money and down you go!
But the godly flourish like leaves in spring.

11:28 Pss 1:2-3; 92:12; Jer 17:7-8; Mark 10:24-25; 1 Tim 6:17

[29] Those who bring trouble on their families inherit the wind.
The fool will be a servant to the wise.

11:29 Prov 14:19; 15:27

[30] The seeds of good deeds become a tree of life;
a wise person wins friends.*

11:30 Prov 3:18; Jas 5:20

[31] If the righteous are rewarded here on earth,
what will happen to wicked sinners?*

11:31 2 Sam 22:21; *1 Pet 4:18

12

[1] To learn, you must love discipline;
it is stupid to hate correction.

12:1 Prov 1:5; 9:9; 25:12

[2] The LORD approves of those who are good,
but He condemns those who plan wickedness.

12:2 Prov 3:4; 8:35-36

11:30 Or *and those who win souls are wise.* 11:31 Greek version reads *If the righteous are barely saved, / what will happen to godless sinners?* Compare 1 Pet 4:18.

11:28-31 This chapter concludes with proverbs about the certainty of gain through righteousness and integrity compared to the certainty of loss from money, foolishness, and wickedness.

▸ ADOPTION

11:30 Bearing fruit. If you plant a fruit tree in your backyard, you expect to reap a harvest in the future. The tree begins to grow, the branches spread out, and soon the springtime blossoms are nestled among the leaves. From those blossoms come the much-anticipated fruit. The tree doesn't strain to produce its crop; the fruit comes naturally through growth and nurturing. That's the way the Holy Spirit works in our lives to bring forth mature fruit in our lives. It's synergistic—we work together with God as we bear fruit—but our participation is characterized more by trusting than trying, more by waiting than working (John 15:4). (***See Adoption****> With Christ> Servants> Appointed to bear fruit,* TopicGuide page A37.)

12:1 This verse seeks to remind the reader of the book's beginning. The elements of instruction, discipline, and correction are fundamental to a life well lived.

12:1-28 Proverbs 12 focuses on speech and deeds. The lesson is that the wise are teachable but the foolish are stubborn in their ignorance. These traits are seen in the way people talk and live.

12:3 Ps 15:1-5; Prov 10:25; 11:5

3 Wickedness never brings stability,
but the godly have deep roots.

12:4 Prov 14:1; 19:13; 21:9; 27:15; 31:10; 1 Cor 11:7

4 A worthy wife is a crown for her husband,
but a disgraceful woman is like cancer in his bones.

12:5 Prov 16:23; Matt 12:34; 15:18

5 The plans of the godly are just;
the advice of the wicked is treacherous.

12:6 Ps 35:11; Prov 14:3; 31:8

6 The words of the wicked are like a murderous ambush,
but the words of the godly save lives.

12:7 Prov 11:21; 14:11; Isa 3:10-11; Matt 7:24-27

7 The wicked die and disappear,
but the family of the godly stands firm.

12:8 Eccl 8:1

8 A sensible person wins admiration,
but a warped mind is despised.

12:9 Luke 14:11

9 Better to be an ordinary person with a servant
than to be self-important but have no food.

12:10 Gen 33:13

10 The godly care for their animals,
but the wicked are always cruel.

12:11 Prov 9:6; 14:24

11 A hard worker has plenty of food,
but a person who chases fantasies has no sense.

12:12 Prov 1:18-19; 11:24-25; 21:10

12 Thieves are jealous of each other's loot,
but the godly are well rooted and bear their own fruit.

12:13 Prov 11:8; 13:5; 25:18

13 The wicked are trapped by their own words,
but the godly escape such trouble.

12:14 Prov 12:24, 27; 13:11; 14:11; 24:12; Isa 3:10

14 Wise words bring many benefits,
and hard work brings rewards.

12:15 Prov 14:12; 16:2

15 Fools think their own way is right,
but the wise listen to others.

12:16 Prov 19:11; 29:11

16 A fool is quick-tempered,
but a wise person stays calm when insulted.

12:17 Prov 12:13; 14:3, 23; 25:18

17 An honest witness tells the truth;
a false witness tells lies.

12:18 Ps 57:4; Prov 8:6-7; 15:4

18 Some people make cutting remarks,
but the words of the wise bring healing.

12:19 Prov 19:9

19 Truthful words stand the test of time,
but lies are soon exposed.

▸ BIBLE

12:4 Affecting each other. The unity shared with a spouse can work for good . . . or for bad. When a husband or wife fails to live as he or she ought, the other spouse may suffer embarrassment, grow bitter, and lose heart through struggling to hold the marriage together. One spouse's failure to walk with God can have a great effect on the relationship. But the other is true as well—success and joy strengthens the other spouse. If this is true in marriage, imagine how your union with Christ affects you! Colossians 2:10 says, "you also are complete through your union with Christ." If you are one with the victorious Lord of the universe, then you have every reason to celebrate as you continue on your journey. (***See Bible****> Unity> Doctrines> Principles of marriage,* TopicGuide page A10.)

12:17 Justice requires truth. This verse uses legal language to show that without truthfulness, justice is threatened. In the biblical era, long before modern scientific forensic evidence, witnesses determined truth. Inner character was and continues to be fundamental to societal justice.

20 Deceit fills hearts that are plotting evil;
joy fills hearts that are planning peace!

21 No harm comes to the godly,
but the wicked have their fill of trouble.

22 The LORD detests lying lips,
but He delights in those who tell the truth.

23 The wise don't make a show of their knowledge,
but fools broadcast their foolishness.

24 Work hard and become a leader;
be lazy and become a slave.

25 Worry weighs a person down;
an encouraging word cheers a person up.

26 The godly give good advice to their friends;*
the wicked lead them astray.

27 Lazy people don't even cook the game they catch,
but the diligent make use of everything they find.

28 The way of the godly leads to life;
that path does not lead to death.

12:20 Prov 2:10; 26:24-26
12:21 Ps 121:7 Prov 1:33 1 Pet 3:13
12:22 Eccl 5:2 Isa 19:21
12:23 Prov 10:14; 13:16
12:24 Prov 12:11; 14:11; 22:29
12:25 Prov 15:13; 17:22
12:26 Prov 6:21; 12:15; 18:15
12:27 Prov 10:4; 13:4
12:28 Prov 8:35; 9:11 Ezek 18:9, 20 Rom 5:21

13

1 A wise child accepts a parent's discipline;*
a mocker refuses to listen to correction.

2 Wise words will win you a good meal,
but treacherous people have an appetite for violence.

3 Those who control their tongue will have a long life;
opening your mouth can ruin everything.

4 Lazy people want much but get little,
but those who work hard will prosper.

13:1 Prov 10:1; 15:12, 20
13:3 Prov 18:7, 21; 20:19; 21:23 Jas 3:2

12:26 Or *The godly are cautious in friendship;* or *The godly are freed from evil.* The meaning of the Hebrew is uncertain.
13:1 Hebrew *A wise son accepts his father's discipline.*

▸ ADOPTION
12:20 What fills your heart? For pioneers who first move into unsettled territories, finding good sources of water is vital. Many homesteaders must dig wells, and what each well yields often means the difference between failure and survival. Our hearts are like those wells. Whatever flows from our hearts shows what we have deep inside. No matter how we try to cover our inner dispositions by looking good on the outside, eventually our attitudes reveal themselves. What do you have in your heart? Underneath the exterior "good" person you try to display, what attitudes do you harbor? Be honest with God about those areas you know are deceitful. Ask Him to cleanse your heart and to cause it to overflow with joy. (***See Adoption****> Without Christ> Separated from God> Bad spiritual heart,* TopicGuide page A36.)

▸ BIBLE
12:25 The unbearable load. Years ago, when pack animals transported goods, the animals' handlers had to know just how much each animal could carry. They knew that if they tried to load their animals with one pack too many, the animals could be injured or eventually would lose their strength. As this verse suggests, worry can be like that final pack for us. Taking on worries as we go along in life will eventually cause our spirits to collapse. We can shed our worrisome burdens, however, by trusting God and calling on Him for help, because we know that He cares for us (1 Peter 5:7). Look for ways you can encourage others when they are burdened with cares. One word in the right place is like removing the pack from an overburdened animal trying to climb a mountainside. (***See Bible****> Power> Equip> Lightens the heart,* TopicGuide page A11.)

12:28 This closing verse is another example of synthetic parallelism: A truth is stated and is then followed by another truth that is related to or extended from the first. This proverb reminds the reader again of the book's recurring message: Godliness and wise living lead to life, while the opposite leads to death. "Life" and "death" in this context refer to physical life, but they can also be applied to spiritual, moral, and emotional life as well.

13:5 Prov 3:35

5 The godly hate lies;
the wicked cause shame and disgrace.

13:6 Prov 6:15

6 Godliness guards the path of the blameless,
but the evil are misled by sin.

13:7 Prov 11:24; Luke 12:20-21; 2 Cor 6:10; Jas 2:5

7 Some who are poor pretend to be rich;
others who are rich pretend to be poor.

8 The rich can pay a ransom for their lives,
but the poor won't even get threatened.

13:9 Job 18:5; 29:3; Prov 4:18; 24:20

9 The life of the godly is full of light and joy,
but the light of the wicked will be snuffed out.

10 Pride leads to conflict;
those who take advice are wise.

11 Wealth from get-rich-quick schemes quickly disappears;
wealth from hard work grows over time.

12 Hope deferred makes the heart sick,
but a dream fulfilled is a tree of life.

13:13 2 Chr 36:16

13 People who despise advice are asking for trouble;
those who respect a command will succeed.

13:14 Ps 18:5; Prov 10:11

14 The instruction of the wise is like a life-giving fountain;
those who accept it avoid the snares of death.

13:15 Prov 3:4

15 A person with good sense is respected;
a treacherous person is headed for destruction.*

13:16 Prov 12:23

16 Wise people think before they act;
fools don't—and even brag about their foolishness.

13:17 Prov 25:13

17 An unreliable messenger stumbles into trouble,
but a reliable messenger brings healing.

13:18 Prov 15:5, 32

18 If you ignore criticism, you will end in poverty and disgrace;
if you accept correction, you will be honored.

19 It is pleasant to see dreams come true,
but fools refuse to turn from evil to attain them.

13:15 As in Greek version; Hebrew reads *the way of the treacherous is lasting.*

▸ GOD

13:10 The result of pride. Have you ever had a friend who had to be right about everything? How about you? Have you ever argued a point you knew was wrong just because you couldn't admit you were wrong? Sometimes the desire to justify our viewpoint makes us blind to the truth. When that happens, we become like the Pharisees, who thought they were right and wouldn't listen to Jesus, the Son of God (Matthew 9:34; 12:10). This verse makes it clear that we need to be willing to live in humility and accept wise counsel on any subject from any source. Ask God to reveal any pride you may be concealing in your heart and to help you welcome the advice of others. (***See God****> Relationship> Barriers> Pride,* TopicGuide page A14.)

13:12 The loss of hope is demoralizing to the soul. When a promise remains unfulfilled over time, the heart may come to despair. Christian hope, though, is based on the unchangeable God, so it serves as an anchor for the soul (Hebrews 6:16-19).

13:13-18 These verses highlight advice, good sense, and criticism. Wisdom is the accumulation of experience and input from those older and wiser. Good advice is indispensable for gaining wisdom.

20 Walk with the wise and become wise;
associate with fools and get in trouble.

21 Trouble chases sinners,
while blessings reward the righteous.

22 Good people leave an inheritance to their grandchildren,
but the sinner's wealth passes to the godly.

23 A poor person's farm may produce much food,
but injustice sweeps it all away.

24 Those who spare the rod of discipline hate their children.
Those who love their children care enough to discipline them.

25 The godly eat to their hearts' content,
but the belly of the wicked goes hungry.

13:20 Prov 2:20
13:21 Ps 32:10; Prov 11:31; Isa 3:10
13:22 Ezra 9:12; Ps 37:25; Prov 28:8
13:24 Prov 19:18; 22:15; 23:13
13:25 Ps 34:10; Prov 10:3

14

1 A wise woman builds her home,
but a foolish woman tears it down with her own hands.

2 Those who follow the right path fear the LORD;
those who take the wrong path despise Him.

3 A fool's proud talk becomes a rod that beats him,
but the words of the wise keep them safe.

4 Without oxen a stable stays clean,
but you need a strong ox for a large harvest.

5 An honest witness does not lie;
a false witness breathes lies.

6 A mocker seeks wisdom and never finds it,
but knowledge comes easily to those with understanding.

7 Stay away from fools,
for you won't find knowledge on their lips.

8 The prudent understand where they are going,
but fools deceive themselves.

9 Fools make fun of guilt,
but the godly acknowledge it and seek reconciliation.

10 Each heart knows its own bitterness,
and no one else can fully share its joy.

14:1 Prov 31:10-27
14:3 Prov 12:6
14:5 Prov 6:19; 12:17; Rev 3:14
14:7 Prov 23:9
14:8 Prov 15:28

▸ SPIRITUAL WARFARE
13:20 Walking with the wise. Many people have not yet learned the extent to which their companion's behavior will influence them. Many feel that they can enjoy the company of sinful friends and yet remain unaffected. The office worker who spends time with gossiping employees will likely find gossip becoming a problem in his or her own life. The person who spends time with those whose driving ambition is to obtain better houses, cars, and jewelry will eventually begin to desire these things, too. But notice that this verse also mentions that the person who enjoys the company of a godly friend can benefit from this, too. Glorify God with your choices of companions, knowing your choices have an impact on your spiritual life. (***See Spiritual Warfare**> God and Sin> Sin's Origin> The wise understand evil's source,* TopicGuide page A45.)

13:24 The writer observes that people who let their children run wild don't love them as they should. Godly discipline, on the other hand, springs from affection.

14:1-9 "Fools" take center stage in this chapter. More than merely people who are ignorant, fools in the book of Proverbs are those who are morally and religiously the opposite of the righteous. A primary characteristic of biblical fools is certainty that they think they are right in their stance, for which reason they refuse correction or advice. They are stubborn against the truth, which makes them stubborn against the living God.

14:11 Prov 12:7 [11] The house of the wicked will be destroyed,
but the tent of the godly will flourish.

14:12 Prov 16:25 Rom 6:21 [12] There is a path before each person that seems right,
but it ends in death.

14:13 Eccl 2:1-2 [13] Laughter can conceal a heavy heart,
but when the laughter ends, the grief remains.

14:14 Prov 1:31; 12:14, 21 [14] Backsliders get what they deserve;
good people receive their reward.

[15] Only simpletons believe everything they're told!
The prudent carefully consider their steps.

14:16 Prov 22:3 [16] The wise are cautious* and avoid danger;
fools plunge ahead with reckless confidence.

14:17 Prov 14:29 [17] Short-tempered people do foolish things,
and schemers are hated.

[18] Simpletons are clothed with foolishness,*
but the prudent are crowned with knowledge.

14:19 1 Sam 2:36 Prov 11:29 [19] Evil people will bow before good people;
the wicked will bow at the gates of the godly.

14:20 Prov 19:4, 7 [20] The poor are despised even by their neighbors,
while the rich have many "friends."

14:21 Ps 41:1 Prov 11:12 [21] It is a sin to belittle one's neighbor;
blessed are those who help the poor.

14:22 Prov 12:2 Gal 6:7 [22] If you plan to do evil, you will be lost;
if you plan to do good, you will receive unfailing love and faithfulness.

[23] Work brings profit,
but mere talk leads to poverty!

[24] Wealth is a crown for the wise;
the effort of fools yields only foolishness.

14:25 Prov 14:5 [25] A truthful witness saves lives,
but a false witness is a traitor.

14:26 Prov 19:23 [26] Those who fear the LORD are secure;
He will be a refuge for their children.

14:27 Prov 13:14 [27] Fear of the LORD is a life-giving fountain;
it offers escape from the snares of death.

14:16 Hebrew *The wise fear.* 14:18 Or *inherit foolishness.*

14:12 In biblical lands, the topography in many places is so steep and treacherous that taking the wrong path can lead one to fall into a deep ravine or off a cliff. This provided a powerful metaphor for living righteously or sinfully.

▶ GOD
14:26 Security in the Lord. Those of us who live in free societies are often deluded by a false sense of security. We feel sympathy for our brothers and sisters who live in places where persecution of Christians is common, and we wonder how they can raise their children there. The truth, of course, is that no place on earth is perfectly safe. Even in free societies, we must face the threat of accidents, disease, natural disasters, crime, and terrorism. In this way we can learn from believers in less-secure places, who must find their security in Jesus Christ, not in their social situation. Instead of worrying, follow this verse and place your life and the lives of those you love in God's hands. He is our only real security. (***See God**> God's Attributes> Eternal> The eternal God is the believer's source of security,* TopicGuide page A16.)

28 A growing population is a king's glory;
a prince without subjects has nothing.

29 People with understanding control their anger;
a hot temper shows great foolishness.

30 A peaceful heart leads to a healthy body;
jealousy is like cancer in the bones.

31 Those who oppress the poor insult their Maker,
but helping the poor honors Him.

32 The wicked are crushed by disaster,
but the godly have a refuge when they die.

33 Wisdom is enshrined in an understanding heart;
wisdom is not* found among fools.

34 Godliness makes a nation great,
but sin is a disgrace to any people.

35 A king rejoices in wise servants
but is angry with those who disgrace him.

15 1 A gentle answer deflects anger,
but harsh words make tempers flare.

2 The tongue of the wise makes knowledge appealing,
but the mouth of a fool belches out foolishness.

3 The LORD is watching everywhere,
keeping His eye on both the evil and the good.

4 Gentle words are a tree of life;
a deceitful tongue crushes the spirit.

5 Only a fool despises a parent's* discipline;
whoever learns from correction is wise.

14:29 Prov 16:32; 19:11 Jas 1:19

14:31 Ps 12:5 Prov 14:21; 17:5; 22:2, 16

14:32 2 Cor 1:9

14:35 Matt 24:45

15:1 Judg 8:1-3 1 Sam 25:10-13 Prov 15:18; 25:10, 15

15:2 Prov 12:23; 13:16; 15:28 Eccl 12:10

15:3 Job 31:4; 34:21 Heb 4:13

15:5 Prov 13:1

14:33 As in Greek and Syriac versions; Hebrew lacks *not*. 15:5 Hebrew *father's*.

14:28 In ancient times, population growth meant strength while dwindling populations meant weakness. But while there is strength in numbers, Scripture also teaches that we cannot rely on numerical strength alone for deliverance (Psalm 33:16, 17; Jeremiah 9:23-24; Zechariah 4:6).

▸ WORSHIP
14:34 Pray for nations. This verse shows us why it is essential to pray for our nation, and 1 Timothy 2:1-2 reminds us to pray for those who have authority over us so that we may live in peace and quietness. We can do this by making a prayer list that includes governmental leaders, keeping in mind that it is just as important to pray for those who don't agree with us politically as for those who do. Then spread the names over a month's time, perhaps even writing the names on a calendar to remind you to pray for them. As you follow the news, note any information you might need to include in your prayers. (***See Worship****> OT> Fasting and Prayer> Prayer> Prayer for those in authority,* TopicGuide page A26.)

▸ GOD
15:3 What does God see? Before Christmas, parents sometimes say to their children, "Be good or Santa won't bring you any gifts." Where did the idea come from that Santa Claus can see every child and know whether he or she is naughty or nice? Such all-encompassing knowledge is possessed by God alone. Only He sees it all. He knows what you are thinking. He even knows the attitude of your heart. He sees the bad attitude you have pasted over with a seemingly good one. He also understands when you hurt and when you are confused. God rejoices in your joy and notices your accomplishments. Most of all, if you are a Christian, God sees you as His child, loved, wanted, and cared for. Praise God for this wonderful attribute. (***See God****> God's Attributes> All-Knowing> God sees it all,* TopicGuide page A15.)

15:5 With this verse, a subtle shift occurs in the style of the proverbial sayings. The previous five chapters have offered mainly antithetical parallelisms; that is, the proverbs contain two opposite ideas. From this point on, however, we begin to see more comparative parallel and synthetic parallel structure. The first occurs when the primary idea in the verse is compared or mildly contrasted with another idea in the second clause (see, for example, Proverbs 15:4, 7, 16, etc.). Synthetic parallelism occurs when the idea in the first clause is developed or extended in some manner by the second clause (see 15:10-12).

15:6 Prov 8:21

6 There is treasure in the house of the godly,
but the earnings of the wicked bring trouble.

15:7 Prov 10:13

7 The lips of the wise give good advice;
the heart of a fool has none to give.

15:8 Prov 21:27; Isa 1:11

8 The LORD detests the sacrifice of the wicked,
but He delights in the prayers of the upright.

15:9 Prov 11:20

9 The LORD detests the way of the wicked,
but He loves those who pursue godliness.

10 Whoever abandons the right path will be severely disciplined;
whoever hates correction will die.

15:11 1 Sam 16:7; 2 Chr 6:30; Job 26:6; Acts 1:24

11 Even Death and Destruction* hold no secrets from the LORD.
How much more does He know the human heart!

15:12 Prov 9:7; 13:1; 19:25; 24:9

12 Mockers hate to be corrected,
so they stay away from the wise.

15:13 Prov 17:22; Eccl 8:1

13 A glad heart makes a happy face;
a broken heart crushes the spirit.

15:14 Prov 18:15

14 A wise person is hungry for knowledge,
while the fool feeds on trash.

15 For the despondent, every day brings trouble;
for the happy heart, life is a continual feast.

15:16 Ps 37:16; Prov 16:8; 1 Tim 6:6

16 Better to have little, with fear for the LORD,
than to have great treasure and inner turmoil.

15:17 Prov 17:1

17 A bowl of vegetables with someone you love
is better than steak with someone you hate.

15:18 Prov 14:29; 16:28; 26:21; Eccl 10:4

18 A hot-tempered person starts fights;
a cool-tempered person stops them.

19 A lazy person's way is blocked with briers,
but the path of the upright is an open highway.

15:20 Prov 10:1; 29:3; 30:17

20 Sensible children bring joy to their father;
foolish children despise their mother.

15:21 Eph 5:15

21 Foolishness brings joy to those with no sense;
a sensible person stays on the right path.

15:11 Hebrew *Sheol and Abaddon.*

15:8-9 While all people come to God as sinners, the "wicked" in Proverbs are those whose inner disposition is evil and self-centered. They are described in Proverbs as "violent," "greedy," "cruel," and "perverse." When such people participate in the worship of God, they are only trying to manipulate Him. The Lord hates their duplicity and their empty offerings. But those who pursue godliness, while still sinners, are seeking to worship God in spirit and truth (see John 4:23-24).

15:11 In Hebrew culture, the mysterious places of death, *Sheol* and *Abaddon* (see NLT textual note), were thought to be deep in the darkness of the earth. This proverb reminds us that if God knows, sees, and in some sense is present even there in judgment, surely He also knows and sees those things "hidden" in the human heart.

15:13-15 The heart continues to be the focus here (and through 15:18). A "glad" or "happy" heart is said to triumph over outer circumstances. The apostle Paul taught the same, saying that he had learned to be content in all situations, whether in plenty or in want. When the heart knows God and is at peace, outer circumstances beyond control have less of an effect on the emotional well-being of a person.

22 Plans go wrong for lack of advice;
many advisers bring success.

23 Everyone enjoys a fitting reply;
it is wonderful to say the right thing at the right time!

24 The path of life leads upward for the wise;
they leave the grave* behind.

25 The LORD tears down the house of the proud,
but He protects the property of widows.

26 The LORD detests evil plans,
but He delights in pure words.

27 Greed brings grief to the whole family,
but those who hate bribes will live.

28 The heart of the godly thinks carefully before speaking;
the mouth of the wicked overflows with evil words.

29 The LORD is far from the wicked,
but He hears the prayers of the righteous.

30 A cheerful look brings joy to the heart;
good news makes for good health.

31 If you listen to constructive criticism,
you will be at home among the wise.

32 If you reject discipline, you only harm yourself;
but if you listen to correction, you grow in understanding.

33 Fear of the LORD teaches wisdom;
humility precedes honor.

15:22 Prov 11:14
15:23 Prov 25:11
15:25 Pss 68:5; 146:9; Prov 14:11
15:27 Exod 23:8; Deut 16:19; Prov 28:25
15:28 Prov 10:19, 32; 1 Pet 3:15
15:29 Ps 145:18-19; Prov 1:28; 15:8
15:31 Prov 15:5
15:33 Prov 1:7

16

1 We can make our own plans,
but the LORD gives the right answer.

2 People may be pure in their own eyes,
but the LORD examines their motives.

3 Commit your actions to the LORD,
and your plans will succeed.

4 The LORD has made everything for His own purposes,
even the wicked for a day of disaster.

5 The LORD detests the proud;
they will surely be punished.

16:1 Prov 16:9; 19:21
16:2 Prov 21:2
16:3 Pss 37:5; 55:22; Prov 3:6
16:4 Job 38:23; Eccl 3:11; Isa 43:7
16:5 Prov 6:16-17; 8:13; 11:21

15:24 Hebrew *Sheol.*

▸ ADOPTION
15:28 Think before you speak. How many times have you spoken like the wicked in this verse and then regretted what you said? Sometimes it seems as if harsh words crouch at the ends of our tongues, just waiting to slip out the moment we let down our guard. To keep those words from escaping our lips, we must strive to bring our hearts and tongues under the control of the Holy Spirit. With His help, we can gain the discipline to think before we speak. Read James 3 prayerfully and pursue this discipline in your life this week. (***See Adoption> With Christ> Supernatural> Speak godly words,*** TopicGuide page A37.)

16:4-6 Proverbs 16 opens by focusing on the Lord's sovereign power over all things. In particular, we are reminded that He has power over the wicked, even to the point of setting the time and manner of their judgment. In verse 6 we see the other side, that love and faithfulness cover (the verb can also be translated "to atone for") sin.

16:6 Prov 8:13; 14:27
6 Unfailing love and faithfulness make atonement for sin.
By fearing the LORD, people avoid evil.

16:7 2 Chr 17:10
7 When people's lives please the LORD,
even their enemies are at peace with them.

8 Better to have little, with godliness,
than to be rich and dishonest.

16:9 Ps 37:23 Prov 16:1; 19:21; 20:24 Jer 10:23
9 We can make our plans,
but the LORD determines our steps.

16:10 1 Kgs 3:28
10 The king speaks with divine wisdom;
he must never judge unfairly.

16:11 Prov 11:1
11 The LORD demands accurate scales and balances;
He sets the standards for fairness.

16:12 Prov 25:5
12 A king detests wrongdoing,
for his rule is built on justice.

16:13 Prov 14:35
13 The king is pleased with words from righteous lips;
he loves those who speak honestly.

16:14 Prov 19:12
14 The anger of the king is a deadly threat;
the wise will try to appease it.

16:15 Job 29:23
15 When the king smiles, there is life;
his favor refreshes like a spring rain.

16:16 Prov 8:10, 19
16 How much better to get wisdom than gold,
and good judgment than silver!

17 The path of the virtuous leads away from evil;
whoever follows that path is safe.

16:18 Jer 49:16
18 Pride goes before destruction,
and haughtiness before a fall.

16:19 Isa 57:15
19 Better to live humbly with the poor
than to share plunder with the proud.

16:20 Pss 2:12; 34:8 Jer 17:7
20 Those who listen to instruction will prosper;
those who trust the LORD will be joyful.

16:21 Prov 16:23
21 The wise are known for their understanding,
and pleasant words are persuasive.

16:9, 25, 33 In these verses sprinkled through the chapter, we see God's control over our lives. We are free beings, making thousands of decisions daily with our wills (the Hebrew text says "the heart of man devises his path"). Still, in some mysterious way, God is orchestrating the outcomes. For the follower of Christ, there is great comfort in this (see Romans 8:28). When we seize control, however, disaster soon follows.

▸ GOD

16:18 Pride before a fall. The truth of this frequently quoted passage can be seen in the life of King Saul. At God's command the prophet Samuel anointed Saul as Israel's king, but Saul died in a battle with Israel's enemies, the Philistines. First Chronicles 10:13 says that Saul died because he was unfaithful to God's commands. Saul's pride led him to follow his own impulses rather than God's will. That's pride in a nutshell—considering ourselves more than God. In which areas of your life do you struggle with pride? Pray that God will give you the humility to follow His way, lest you stumble and fall. (***See God****> Relationship> Barriers> Pride,* TopicGuide page A14.)

16:20-24 This small collection of proverbs says that prudent speech benefits all the people in a community. Good words (including instruction, understanding, discretion, wise speech, and kind words) bring prosperity, understanding, persuasion, and a sweetness to life.

22 Discretion is a life-giving fountain to those who possess it,
but discipline is wasted on fools.

23 From a wise mind comes wise speech;
the words of the wise are persuasive.

16:23 Ps 37:30 Prov 15:18, 28

24 Kind words are like honey—
sweet to the soul and healthy for the body.

16:24 Prov 4:22; 15:26; 17:22; 24:13

25 There is a path before each person that seems right,
but it ends in death.

16:25 Prov 14:12

26 It is good for workers to have an appetite;
an empty stomach drives them on.

27 Scoundrels create trouble;
their words are a destructive blaze.

16:27 Prov 6:14, 18 Jas 3:6

28 A troublemaker plants seeds of strife;
gossip separates the best of friends.

29 Violent people mislead their companions,
leading them down a harmful path.

16:29 Prov 1:10

30 With narrowed eyes, people plot evil;
with a smirk, they plan their mischief.

31 Gray hair is a crown of glory;
it is gained by living a godly life.

16:31 Prov 20:29

32 Better to be patient than powerful;
better to have self-control than to conquer a city.

16:32 Prov 19:11

33 We may throw the dice,*
but the LORD determines how they fall.

17

1 Better a dry crust eaten in peace
than a house filled with feasting—and conflict.

17:1 Prov 15:17

2 A wise servant will rule over the master's disgraceful son
and will share the inheritance of the master's children.

16:33 Hebrew *We may cast lots.*

▸ ADOPTION

16:24 Sweet words. In the Old Testament world, honey was the common sweetener for foods. Without honey, there was often no other way to make some foods palatable. Have you ever tasted the "honey" of kind words that this verse mentions? When we are pressed by despair, threatened by a crisis, or faced with long days in a boring job, a friend's soothing words can make all the difference in our attitude. Such words are like honey poured over a bland biscuit—the dry bread is turned into a dessertlike treat. Are kind words a necessary part of your speech? Sprinkle your daily life with kind words, and sweeten the lives of those around you. (***See Adoption*** > *With Christ*> *Supernatural*> *Speak godly words,* TopicGuide page A37.)

16:31-32 In a world where power, youthful vigor, and strength are glorified and the body is exalted, these words stand out. In God's mind, power and conquest are not as virtuous as patience and self-control. Old age and godly living are significant blessings from God. God treasures character and other attributes frequently disparaged by the world.

16:33 An example of God controlling even the casting of lots is found in the story of Jonah. The sailors, not believers in God, used lots to determine the cause of their trouble. God displayed sovereign control over this, as the lot pointed to Jonah (see Jonah 1:7-10).

17:3 1 Chr 29:17; Ps 26:2
3 Fire tests the purity of silver and gold,
but the LORD tests the heart.

17:4 Prov 1:10; 16:29
4 Wrongdoers eagerly listen to gossip;
liars pay close attention to slander.

17:5 Job 31:29; Prov 14:31; 24:17
5 Those who mock the poor insult their Maker;
those who rejoice at the misfortune of others will be punished.

17:6 Gen 48:11; Prov 13:22
6 Grandchildren are the crowning glory of the aged;
parents* are the pride of their children.

17:7 Prov 12:22; 24:7
7 Eloquent words are not fitting for a fool;
even less are lies fitting for a ruler.

17:8 Prov 21:14; Isa 1:23; Amos 5:12
8 A bribe is like a lucky charm;
whoever gives one will prosper!

17:9 Prov 10:12; Jas 5:20
9 Love prospers when a fault is forgiven,
but dwelling on it separates close friends.

10 A single rebuke does more for a person of understanding
than a hundred lashes on the back of a fool.

11 Evil people are eager for rebellion,
but they will be severely punished.

17:12 Prov 29:9; Hos 13:8
12 It is safer to meet a bear robbed of her cubs
than to confront a fool caught in foolishness.

17:13 Ps 109:5; Prov 13:21; Jer 18:20
13 If you repay good with evil,
evil will never leave your house.

17:6 Hebrew *fathers.*

▸ BIBLE
17:3 The test of the heart. God allows tests in our lives to show us where our hearts stray from His standards (Deuteronomy 13:3). If we don't undergo the tests, we won't know where we are lacking. When you are entering a time of trial, start looking for how God is testing you. Look for the cracks that may begin to appear in your character during difficult times. When you find that weakness, ask God to help you develop spiritual fruit and thank Him that He has shown you the truth about your sinful heart. If you cannot find any weaknesses, then pray that God will reveal the sin in your life. (***See Bible****> Power> Convict> Compared to fire and a hammer,* TopicGuide page A11.)

17:3 In the ancient world, precious metals such as gold and silver were refined by heating them beyond their melting points and removing the impurities that rose to the surface (see 1 Peter 1:6-7). God sees all impurities—even in the depths of the heart.

17:5 This proverb highlights God's concern for justice, especially for those who are often marginalized in society. God holds special affection for the poor, the weak, and the disabled, and He commands His people to imitate Him by showing similar concern for those the world often rejects.

▸ HOLINESS
17:6 Parents are our pride. Grandparents often brag about their grandchildren. They pull out pictures and show them to every person who shows the slightest interest. But what about the second half of this verse? Are children proud of their parents? Do we brag about what our parents have done for us? Tragically, many people, especially young people, are embarrassed by their parents. They don't want to be seen in the company of older people. We don't respect the aged; rather, we make fun of them or shun them. Even in churches, generations often don't mix because younger people don't feel they can learn much from their elders. Spiritual leaders must teach the younger generations how valuable older people are to us. How are you displaying respect for your elders? This week, go out of your way at least once to show respect for your elders. (***See Holiness****> Law and Grace > Law> Parents and children,* TopicGuide page A41.)

17:10 Most societies today no longer give public "lashes" to punish rebellion. But the idea of this proverb is that a fool feels no shame at any sort of public punishment, and it brings no change in his behavior. The wise person, on the other hand, seeks to change his behavior rather than receive a second word of correction. Some have pointed out that just a glance from Jesus was enough punishment to cause Peter to change (see Luke 22:61-62).

14 Starting a quarrel is like opening a floodgate,
so stop before a dispute breaks out.

15 Acquitting the guilty and condemning the innocent—
both are detestable to the LORD.

16 It is senseless to pay tuition to educate a fool,
since he has no heart for learning.

17 A friend is always loyal,
and a brother is born to help in time of need.

18 It's poor judgment to guarantee another person's debt
or put up security for a friend.

19 Anyone who loves to quarrel loves sin;
anyone who trusts in high walls invites disaster.

20 The crooked heart will not prosper;
the lying tongue tumbles into trouble.

21 It is painful to be the parent of a fool;
there is no joy for the father of a rebel.

22 A cheerful heart is good medicine,
but a broken spirit saps a person's strength.

23 The wicked take secret bribes
to pervert the course of justice.

24 Sensible people keep their eyes glued on wisdom,
but a fool's eyes wander to the ends of the earth.

25 Foolish children* bring grief to their father
and bitterness to the one who gave them birth.

26 It is wrong to punish the godly for being good
or to flog leaders for being honest.

27 A truly wise person uses few words;
a person with understanding is even-tempered.

28 Even fools are thought wise when they keep silent;
with their mouths shut, they seem intelligent.

18

1 Unfriendly people care only about themselves;
they lash out at common sense.

2 Fools have no interest in understanding;
they only want to air their own opinions.

17:14 Prov 20:3; 25:8

17:15 Exod 23:7; Prov 24:24; Isa 5:23

17:17 Ruth 1:16; Prov 18:24

17:18 Prov 6:1; 11:15; 22:26

17:19 Prov 13:2; 16:18; 29:22-23

17:20 Jas 3:8

17:21 Prov 10:1; 17:25; 19:13

17:22 Prov 15:13

17:23 Exod 23:8

17:24 Eccl 2:14

17:25 Prov 10:1

17:26 Prov 18:5

17:27 Prov 10:19; Jas 1:19

17:28 Job 13:5

18:2 Prov 12:23

17:25 Hebrew *A foolish son.*

17:15 The Lord is not only concerned for the downtrodden (see note at 17:5), His justice demands that the innocent not be wrongly punished or the guilty released. Because God despises injustice, His people are commanded to do what is right (see Micah 6:8). This saying challenges the notion that it is better to let the guilty go free than to incarcerate one innocent person. Both injustices, say the Scriptures, are an abomination to God.

17:17 Jesus may have been thinking of this proverb ("a friend is always loyal") as he spoke to His disciples in John 15:12-15. This verse also describes Ruth, the Moabite woman (see Ruth 1:16-17).

3 Doing wrong leads to disgrace,
and scandalous behavior brings contempt.

18:4 Prov 20:5

4 Wise words are like deep waters;
wisdom flows from the wise like a bubbling brook.

18:5 Prov 17:15; 24:23

5 It is not right to acquit the guilty
or deny justice to the innocent.

18:6 Prov 10:14; 13:3

6 Fools' words get them into constant quarrels;
they are asking for a beating.

7 The mouths of fools are their ruin;
they trap themselves with their lips.

8 Rumors are dainty morsels
that sink deep into one's heart.

9 A lazy person is as bad as
someone who destroys things.

18:10 2 Sam 22:2 Pss 18:2; 61:3; 91:2 Prov 29:25

10 The name of the LORD is a strong fortress;
the godly run to Him and are safe.

18:11 Prov 10:15

11 The rich think of their wealth as a strong defense;
they imagine it to be a high wall of safety.

18:12 Prov 11:2; 16:18; 29:23

12 Haughtiness goes before destruction;
humility precedes honor.

18:13 Prov 20:25 John 7:51

13 Spouting off before listening to the facts
is both shameful and foolish.

14 The human spirit can endure a sick body,
but who can bear a crushed spirit?

18:15 Prov 15:14

15 Intelligent people are always ready to learn.
Their ears are open for knowledge.

18:16 Gen 32:20 1 Sam 25:27

16 Giving a gift can open doors;
it gives access to important people!

17 The first to speak in court sounds right—
until the cross-examination begins.

18:4 The power of words is again the focus here. In the arid Middle East, streams are rare and many are only seasonal. To find a "bubbling brook" is indeed refreshing. In such places, water literally can be lifesaving. So it is with well-spoken words: They can bring refreshment and life.

▸ ADOPTION

18:13 Listen first. We give this verse's advice to children, but we don't always follow it ourselves. We are prone to think that we understand others' situations much more clearly than we usually do. As a result, we quickly pigeonhole their problems and offer a bit of canned advice. As Proverbs tells us, this is folly, for it can lead those we advise into deeper troubles and can cause hurt feelings among those who realize we have not taken the time to truly listen (consider Job's counselors in Job 3–25). As believers, we must be quick to listen and slow to come to conclusions (James 1:19). To do anything less fails to show others the love our Lord Jesus Christ expects of us. (***See Adoption*** *> With Christ> Supernatural> Quick to listen,* TopicGuide page A37.)

18:17 This proverb uses legal language to remind us that both sides should be heard before a matter is judged. Dishonest people become well trained in convincing others of their lies. A wise person always hears both sides of a story before taking sides.

18 Flipping a coin* can end arguments;
it settles disputes between powerful opponents.

19 An offended friend is harder to win back than a fortified city.
Arguments separate friends like a gate locked with bars.

20 Wise words satisfy like a good meal;
the right words bring satisfaction.

21 The tongue can bring death or life;
those who love to talk will reap the consequences.

22 The man who finds a wife finds a treasure,
and he receives favor from the LORD.

23 The poor plead for mercy;
the rich answer with insults.

24 There are "friends" who destroy each other,
but a real friend sticks closer than a brother.

18:18 Prov 16:33
18:20 Prov 12:14
18:21 Prov 13:3; Matt 12:37
18:22 Prov 12:4; 19:14; 31:10-31
18:23 Prov 19:7; Jas 2:3

19

1 Better to be poor and honest
than to be dishonest and a fool.

2 Enthusiasm without knowledge is no good;
haste makes mistakes.

3 People ruin their lives by their own foolishness
and then are angry at the LORD.

4 Wealth makes many "friends";
poverty drives them all away.

5 A false witness will not go unpunished,
nor will a liar escape.

6 Many seek favors from a ruler;
everyone is the friend of a person who gives gifts!

7 The relatives of the poor despise them;
how much more will their friends avoid them!
Though the poor plead with them,
their friends are gone.

8 To acquire wisdom is to love oneself;
people who cherish understanding will prosper.

19:1 Prov 20:7; 28:6
19:3 Isa 8:21
19:4 Prov 14:20
19:5 Exod 23:1; Deut 19:16-19; Prov 19:9
19:6 Prov 18:16; 29:26
19:7 Ps 38:11; Prov 18:23
19:8 Prov 16:20

18:18 Hebrew *Casting lots.*

18:18 Even in the biblical era, wise people recognized that there are times when both sides of a conflict present compelling arguments (these are "powerful opponents"). In some cases, when it seemed impossible to render a verdict, people were taught to depend on God to settle the dispute by the casting of lots. If God controlled even the outcome of the lot, then His decision could be relied upon by faith.

18:24 The "real friend" presented in Proverbs is one who demonstrates the godly virtues of honesty and integrity, and who is a part of the community of God's people. This is contrasted with other so-called friends that are simply wealthy, influential, or powerful people seeking their own gain. In Proverbs, friends are measured not in number, but in quality.

19:3 This example of synthetic parallelism says first that foolish people routinely reap a natural harvest of pain or loss by their unwise choices. But then the proverb goes a step further to say such people commonly shake a fist at God as if He is at fault. Fools hate to take responsibility for their sorry state and love to shift blame.

19:9 Prov 19:5
9 A false witness will not go unpunished,
and a liar will be destroyed.

19:10 Prov 26:1 Eccl 10:6-7
10 It isn't right for a fool to live in luxury
or for a slave to rule over princes!

19:11 Prov 14:29; 16:32
11 Sensible people control their temper;
they earn respect by overlooking wrongs.

19:12 Gen 27:28 Prov 16:14-15
12 The king's anger is like a lion's roar,
but his favor is like dew on the grass.

19:13 Prov 17:25; 21:9, 19
13 A foolish child* is a calamity to a father;
a quarrelsome wife is as annoying as constant dripping.

19:14 Prov 18:22 2 Cor 12:14
14 Fathers can give their sons an inheritance of houses and wealth,
but only the LORD can give an understanding wife.

19:15 Prov 6:9; 16:26; 24:33
15 Lazy people sleep soundly,
but idleness leaves them hungry.

19:16 Prov 16:17 Luke 10:28; 11:28
16 Keep the commandments and keep your life;
despising them leads to death.

19:17 Deut 15:7 Prov 14:31; 28:27 Luke 6:38
17 If you help the poor, you are lending to the LORD—
and He will repay you!

19:18 Prov 13:24
18 Discipline your children while there is hope.
Otherwise you will ruin their lives.

19 Hot-tempered people must pay the penalty.
If you rescue them once, you will have to do it again.

19:20 Prov 4:1; 8:33; 12:15
20 Get all the advice and instruction you can,
so you will be wise the rest of your life.

19:21 Ps 33:10-11 Prov 16:1, 9
21 You can make many plans,
but the LORD's purpose will prevail.

19:13 Hebrew *son;* also in 19:27.

▶ **CHURCH**

19:11 Overlooking wrongs. Standing on a balcony can give a person a good view of the countryside by allowing him or her to overlook what is underneath the balcony. This may be a picture of how this verse urges us to treat some wrongs we experience. We must not keep them in front of our eyes or they will block the scenery and the broader picture. If you are wronged by another person, sometimes it's better to act as if you are on a balcony looking over that person's personality. Concentrate on the beauty and the fullness of that person's attractiveness, and overlook the faults. In some situations, however, it is best to confront faults (Proverbs 27:5). Ask God for wisdom regarding when to overlook minor faults. (***See Church****> Role> Conflict> General Counsel> Overlook another's faults,* TopicGuide page A49.)

19:13 The "constant dripping" is that from a leaking roof. In the ancient Near East, roofs consisted of multiple layers of boards, branches, clay, and other materials, and leaks were common.

19:16, 23 These two proverbs are examples of sayings that are generally true, but not always. Some people who fear and serve God lose everything (see Hebrews 10:32-34), even their lives. While such proverbs are not hard-and-fast promises in our fallen world, they do speak truth concerning God's ultimate salvation, safety, and security. For those who trust in God, there is no ultimate danger (see Romans 8:38-39).

▶ **WORSHIP**

19:17 Always serving the poor. More than likely, in comparison to other people in the world, you are wealthy. You have been given a unique gift—material resources—that God calls you to use in the right way and for the right reason. Jesus taught His disciples that whatever they did to help those who were hungry, thirsty, lonely, unclothed, or imprisoned, they did to Him (Matthew 25:35-36). We can give food—to Jesus! We can give clothing—to Jesus! From the Old Testament to the New, God strongly encourages Christians to lead the way in works of charity and mercy (Deuteronomy 15:4, 11). Consider setting aside a set amount of money and time each month to serve those who cannot help themselves, and do it with joy, for God loves a joyful giver (2 Corinthians 8:9). (***See Worship****> OT> God's Supremacy> God delivered/saved in order to be worshiped and served,* TopicGuide page A27.)

22 Loyalty makes a person attractive.
It is better to be poor than dishonest.

23 Fear of the LORD leads to life,
bringing security and protection from harm.

24 Lazy people take food in their hand
but don't even lift it to their mouth.

25 If you punish a mocker, the simpleminded will learn a lesson;
if you correct the wise, they will be all the wiser.

26 Children who mistreat their father or chase away their mother
are an embarrassment and a public disgrace.

27 If you stop listening to instruction, my child,
you will turn your back on knowledge.

28 A corrupt witness makes a mockery of justice;
the mouth of the wicked gulps down evil.

29 Punishment is made for mockers,
and the backs of fools are made to be beaten.

19:23 Ps 25:13 Prov 14:27 1 Tim 4:8
19:24 Prov 26:15
19:25 Prov 9:7-8; 21:11
19:26 Prov 20:20; 28:24
19:28 Job 15:16
19:29 Prov 9:12; 10:13; 26:3

20

1 Wine produces mockers; alcohol leads to brawls.
Those led astray by drink cannot be wise.

2 The king's fury is like a lion's roar;
to rouse his anger is to risk your life.

3 Avoiding a fight is a mark of honor;
only fools insist on quarreling.

4 Those too lazy to plow in the right season
will have no food at the harvest.

5 Though good advice lies deep within the heart,
a person with understanding will draw it out.

6 Many will say they are loyal friends,
but who can find one who is truly reliable?

7 The godly walk with integrity;
blessed are their children who follow them.

8 When a king sits in judgment, he weighs all the evidence,
distinguishing the bad from the good.

9 Who can say, "I have cleansed my heart;
I am pure and free from sin"?

20:1 Prov 31:4 Isa 5:22; 56:12
20:2 1 Kgs 2:23 Prov 8:36; 19:12
20:3 Prov 14:29; 16:32; 19:11
20:5 Prov 18:4
20:7 Pss 37:26; 112:2
20:8 Prov 20:26
20:9 2 Chr 6:36 Job 14:4

▶ GOD

20:6 A faithful friend. All people experience times of betrayal by close friends. Such actions hurt us deeply and make us wonder whether we should trust anyone ever again. But just like any other problem in our lives, we can take this concern to Jesus. Nothing you have experienced with your friends compares to the rejection Jesus faced. One of His 12 closest disciples, Judas Iscariot, gave Him up to the chief priests by betraying Him with a kiss (Matthew 26:25, 47-49). Another, Simon Peter, denied knowing Him (Matthew 26:70-72). Unlike them, however, Jesus never turned His back on His friends or rejected them. And you can be sure He will not reject you once He has set His love upon you (Hebrews 13:5). Turn to Jesus when everyone else seems to desert you. (***See God> God's Names> Son> Friend of sinners,*** TopicGuide page A18.)

20:9 The form of this proverb is rare: It speaks forth universal truth through a question. The question expects the answer given in Psalm 53:3 and quoted later by Paul (see Romans 3:9-18): No one is pure of heart; no one is free from sin. All alike need the cleansing work of Christ. God foresaw this when He said in Deuteronomy 30:6 that He would be the One to cleanse the hearts of His people.

20:10 Prov 11:1; 20:23

10 False weights and unequal measures*—
the LORD detests double standards of every kind.

20:11 Matt 7:16

11 Even children are known by the way they act,
whether their conduct is pure, and whether it is right.

20:12 Exod 4:11

12 Ears to hear and eyes to see—
both are gifts from the LORD.

20:13 Prov 6:9-10; 19:15; 24:32-33

13 If you love sleep, you will end in poverty.
Keep your eyes open, and there will be plenty to eat!

14 The buyer haggles over the price, saying, "It's worthless,"
then brags about getting a bargain!

15 Wise words are more valuable
than much gold and many rubies.

16 Get security from someone who guarantees a stranger's debt.
Get a deposit if he does it for foreigners.*

20:17 Prov 9:17-18

17 Stolen bread tastes sweet,
but it turns to gravel in the mouth.

20:18 Prov 15:22; 24:6; Luke 14:31

18 Plans succeed through good counsel;
don't go to war without wise advice.

20:19 Prov 11:13

19 A gossip goes around telling secrets,
so don't hang around with chatterers.

20:20 Exod 21:17; Lev 20:9; Prov 30:11; Matt 15:4

20 If you insult your father or mother,
your light will be snuffed out in total darkness.

21 An inheritance obtained too early in life
is not a blessing in the end.

20:22 Ps 27:14; Prov 24:28-29; Matt 5:39; Rom 12:17

22 Don't say, "I will get even for this wrong."
Wait for the LORD to handle the matter.

20:23 Prov 11:1; 20:10

23 The LORD detests double standards;
He is not pleased by dishonest scales.

20:24 Ps 37:23; Prov 16:9

24 The LORD directs our steps,
so why try to understand everything along the way?

20:25 Eccl 5:4-5

25 Don't trap yourself by making a rash promise to God
and only later counting the cost.

20:10 Hebrew *A stone and a stone, an ephah and an ephah.* 20:16 An alternate reading in the Hebrew text is *for a promiscuous woman.*

20:12 In Proverbs, people who are teachable often are said to have "ears to hear" while those with the virtue of moral discernment are said to have "eyes to see." The Lord reminded Moses that God is the one who created eyes and ears (see Exodus 4:11), and both Isaiah and Jesus used the same truth to speak about spiritual seeing and hearing (see Isaiah 6:9-10 and Matthew 13:13-16).

20:20 God's law in Leviticus 20:9 condemns a child for cursing his parents. This law essentially equates such sin with blasphemy against God Himself, because the child is rebelling against God-ordained authority. The warning in this proverb emphasizes the curses given for disobeying the fifth commandment (see Exodus 20:12).

20:21 Coming into vast wealth, especially at an early age, is rarely a blessing. Throughout the Western world, "winners" of huge lottery prizes routinely end up destitute—if not monetarily, at least in terms of relationships and contentment.

20:24 Though we may have maps and directions to help us get from one place to another, we have no reliable road map of the future. This proverb reminds the wise person that the Lord is the one who keeps His people in His sight and on the road toward Him (see also Psalm 119:105 and Proverbs 3:5-6).

26 A wise king scatters the wicked like wheat,
then runs his threshing wheel over them.

27 The LORD's light penetrates the human spirit,*
exposing every hidden motive.

28 Unfailing love and faithfulness protect the king;
his throne is made secure through love.

29 The glory of the young is their strength;
the gray hair of experience is the splendor of the old.

30 Physical punishment cleanses away evil;*
such discipline purifies the heart.

20:26 Prov 20:8
20:27 1 Cor 2:11
20:28 Prov 29:14
20:29 Prov 16:31

21

1 The king's heart is like a stream of water directed by the LORD;
He guides it wherever He pleases.

2 People may be right in their own eyes,
but the LORD examines their heart.

3 The LORD is more pleased when we do what is right and just
than when we offer Him sacrifices.

4 Haughty eyes, a proud heart,
and evil actions are all sin.

5 Good planning and hard work lead to prosperity,
but hasty shortcuts lead to poverty.

6 Wealth created by a lying tongue
is a vanishing mist and a deadly trap.*

7 The violence of the wicked sweeps them away,
because they refuse to do what is just.

8 The guilty walk a crooked path;
the innocent travel a straight road.

9 It's better to live alone in the corner of an attic
than with a quarrelsome wife in a lovely home.

10 Evil people desire evil;
their neighbors get no mercy from them.

11 If you punish a mocker, the simpleminded become wise;
if you instruct the wise, they will be all the wiser.

21:1 Ezra 6:21, 22
21:2 Prov 16:2; 24:11-12; Luke 16:15
21:3 Prov 15:8; Isa 1:11; Mic 6:6-8
21:4 Prov 6:17; 30:13; Luke 11:34
21:5 Prov 10:4; 28:22
21:6 Prov 10:2; 13:11
21:10 Prov 2:14
21:11 Prov 19:25

20:27 Or *The human spirit is the LORD's light.* 20:30 The meaning of the Hebrew is uncertain. 21:6 As in Greek version; Hebrew reads *mist for those who seek death.*

PURPOSE

21:1 God's prerogative. God is involved in everything. God sent Moses to Pharaoh to demand that he let the Israelites leave Egypt. But God also told Moses that He would harden Pharaoh's heart, so that he would refuse to heed Moses (Exodus 4:21). Why did God do this? God wanted to display His mighty power, both as a judgment on Egypt and as a means to bolster the faith of His people. God planned to establish for Himself a reputation that would serve His people well when they invaded Canaan. God's ways of dealing with Pharaoh must have baffled Moses and Aaron, but they remained faithful and obedient nonetheless. God's purposes in modern politics are equally baffling, but we have the assurance that He is always in control and is working for His glory. Fulfill your obligations as a citizen, but trust Him as the ultimate guide of the political forces of this world. (***See Purpose**> God's Means> Human Choice> God's View,* TopicGuide page A52.)

12 The Righteous One* knows what is going on in the homes of the wicked;
He will bring disaster on them.

21:13 Matt 18:30-34 Luke 16:19-31 Jas 2:13 1 Jn 3:17

13 Those who shut their ears to the cries of the poor
will be ignored in their own time of need.

21:14 Prov 17:8; 19:6

14 A secret gift calms anger;
a bribe under the table pacifies fury.

21:15 Prov 10:29

15 Justice is a joy to the godly,
but it terrifies evildoers.

21:16 Ps 49:14

16 The person who strays from common sense
will end up in the company of the dead.

21:17 Prov 23:19-21

17 Those who love pleasure become poor;
those who love wine and luxury will never be rich.

21:18 Prov 11:8 Isa 43:3-4

18 The wicked are punished in place of the godly,
and traitors in place of the honest.

21:19 Prov 21:9

19 It's better to live alone in the desert
than with a quarrelsome, complaining wife.

21:20 Job 20:15, 18 Prov 8:21

20 The wise have wealth and luxury,
but fools spend whatever they get.

21:21 Matt 5:6

21 Whoever pursues righteousness and unfailing love
will find life, righteousness, and honor.

21:22 2 Sam 5:6-9 Prov 24:5 Eccl 9:15-16

22 The wise conquer the city of the strong
and level the fortress in which they trust.

21:23 Prov 12:13; 13:3 Jas 3:2

23 Watch your tongue and keep your mouth shut,
and you will stay out of trouble.

21:24 Ps 1:1 Prov 1:22

24 Mockers are proud and haughty;
they act with boundless arrogance.

21:25 Prov 13:4

25 Despite their desires, the lazy will come to ruin,
for their hands refuse to work.

26 Some people are always greedy for more,
but the godly love to give!

21:27 Prov 15:8

27 The sacrifice of an evil person is detestable,
especially when it is offered with wrong motives.

21:12 Or *The righteous man.*

21:13 Deuteronomy 25:15 serves as the basis for this proverb, and Jesus told an expansive parable based on this proverb in Matthew 25:31-46. This concept of God hearing the cry of the poor but commanding us to respond is an important one to God-fearers in all times (Psalm 72:12).

▸ GOD

21:15 When justice is an enemy. Do you ever wonder why so many people oppose the law? One reason is given here: Some don't want justice. Sinners do not want to face the consequences of their sin. At some point in our lives (like when we are breaking the law!) we are all in this position. But when God brings us to Himself through Christ, we know with certainty that our sin is forgiven, and we no longer need to fear justice—of any kind. When you are tempted to hide from justice, remember that hiding from true justice is the same thing as hiding from God. (***See God***> *God's Attributes*> *Just*> *God judges all people with justice,* TopicGuide page A16.)

21:21 This saying summarizes much of Proverbs. Righteousness and unfailing, covenantal love are the height of biblical virtue. The pursuit of these virtues promises life, righteousness (which was sought), and honor.

[28] A false witness will be cut off,
but a credible witness will be allowed to speak.

[29] The wicked bluff their way through,
but the virtuous think before they act.

[30] No human wisdom or understanding or plan
can stand against the LORD.

21:30 Isa 8:9; 14:27 Acts 5:38-39

[31] The horse is prepared for the day of battle,
but the victory belongs to the LORD.

21:31 Ps 20:7 Isa 31:1-3 1 Cor 15:57

22

[1] Choose a good reputation over great riches;
being held in high esteem is better than silver or gold.

[2] The rich and poor have this in common:
The LORD made them both.

22:2 Job 31:15 Prov 14:31

[3] A prudent person foresees danger and takes precautions.
The simpleton goes blindly on and suffers the consequences.

22:3 Prov 14:16; 27:12

[4] True humility and fear of the LORD
lead to riches, honor, and long life.

22:4 Prov 3:16; 4:4

[5] Corrupt people walk a thorny, treacherous road;
whoever values life will avoid it.

22:5 Prov 15:19

[6] Direct your children onto the right path,
and when they are older, they will not leave it.

22:6 Eph 6:4

[7] Just as the rich rule the poor,
so the borrower is servant to the lender.

22:7 Jas 2:6

[8] Those who plant injustice will harvest disaster,
and their reign of terror will come to an end.*

22:8 Job 4:8 Prov 24:16

[9] Blessed are those who are generous,
because they feed the poor.

22:9 Prov 19:17 Luke 14:13 2 Cor 9:6

[10] Throw out the mocker, and fighting goes, too.
Quarrels and insults will disappear.

22:10 Prov 24:9

22:8 The Greek version includes an additional proverb: *God blesses a man who gives cheerfully, / but his worthless deeds will come to an end.* Compare 2 Cor 9:7.

21:30-31 The hundreds of sayings that comprise the book of Proverbs have been arranged in a careful manner, not haphazardly. One example of this care is that this chapter opens with two verses that speak of God's sovereignty over governing rulers and then more generally over the hearts and motives of people. The chapter concludes with these two verses restating the same truths in reverse. They speak first of the Lord ruling over every human plan, and second of the Lord being sovereign over governing powers.

22:1-9 This section of verses focuses particularly on wealth. The Lord is portrayed as the One who is sovereign even over riches and possessions.

22:3 The word translated here as "simpleton" (a term used about 15 times in Proverbs) may also be rendered "gullible." This person is not yet wicked or rebelliously foolish but is easily persuaded by those with whom he walks. Since the simpleton is intellectually impressionable, there is still hope that he may begin to walk with the wise and learn from them. The opposite of the simpleton, the "prudent" person is one who has learned discretion and discernment.

22:6 This famous proverb is another example of how the book of Proverbs supplies principles for living, not life-long promises. Many Christian parents who read this verse condemn themselves because their children have wandered from the faith, even though they faithfully sought to raise their children under the promises and claims of the gospel. In fact, the Hebrew sense of the verse allows it to be as much a warning as a promise. If parents allow a child to walk in his own way (characterized by the folly of youth), they should not be surprised when he continues to walk that way as he grows older.

22:11 Ps 24:4 Prov 14:35 Matt 5:8
11 Whoever loves a pure heart and gracious speech
will have the king as a friend.

12 The LORD preserves those with knowledge,
but He ruins the plans of the treacherous.

22:13 Rom 12:11
13 The lazy person claims, "There's a lion out there!
If I go outside, I might be killed!"

22:14 Eccl 7:26
14 The mouth of an immoral woman is a dangerous trap;
those who make the LORD angry will fall into it.

22:15 Prov 13:24; 23:14
15 A youngster's heart is filled with foolishness,
but physical discipline will drive it far away.

22:16 Prov 14:31; 28:3
16 A person who gets ahead by oppressing the poor
or by showering gifts on the rich will end in poverty.

SAYINGS OF THE WISE

22:17 Prov 5:1
17 Listen to the words of the wise;
apply your heart to my instruction.
18 For it is good to keep these sayings in your heart
and always ready on your lips.
19 I am teaching you today—yes, you—
so you will trust in the LORD.
20 I have written thirty sayings* for you,
filled with advice and knowledge.
21 In this way, you may know the truth
and take an accurate report to those who sent you.

22:22 Zech 7:10 Mal 3:5
22 Don't rob the poor just because you can,
or exploit the needy in court.
23 For the LORD is their defender.
He will ruin anyone who ruins them.

22:24 Prov 29:22
24 Don't befriend angry people
or associate with hot-tempered people,

22:20 Or *excellent sayings;* the meaning of the Hebrew is uncertain.

▸ CHURCH

22:15 Discipline is the answer. Parents see the foolishness of children, whose lack of experience causes them to misjudge many situations. From the two-year-old child who eats too many cookies to the teenager who believes his life will be happier if he has no rules, children bristle against authority. This proverb states that the parents' role is to provide discipline to help them curtail foolish desires. This discipline includes guidelines to help them lead balanced lives, as well as punishment for infractions. An out-of-control child is miserable; a well-disciplined child feels secure. If God entrusts the life of a child to your care, work hard to enforce the kind of discipline that honors God. (***See Church****> Mission> Nurture> Developing maturity,* TopicGuide page A49.)

22:17 This is the first of several subsections or collections of sayings in the book of Proverbs. This collection (22:17–24:22) is comprised of 30 sayings that are framed at beginning and end with admonitions to "trust in the LORD" (22:19) and to "fear the LORD" (24:21). Some scholars see similarities between the opening verses of this collection (22:17–23:11) and an ancient Egyptian collection of wisdom sayings titled *Instruction of Amenemope.*

▸ HOLINESS

22:26 Business sense. Although the Bible's main purpose is to reveal God and His plan for our lives, it's an immensely practical document as well. This verse warns, in the same general sense of other proverbs, that the only person you can truly vouch for is yourself. While this shouldn't be taken as an absolute command, it certainly should be taken as a warning to be prepared to pay in full every penny of that debt you've cosigned. Be extremely cautious when taking on the debts of others and be hesitant to ask others to secure your debt. (***See Holiness****> Disciplines> Of Abstinence> Stewardship,* TopicGuide page A42.)

25 or you will learn to be like them
and endanger your soul.

26 Don't agree to guarantee another person's debt
or put up security for someone else.
27 If you can't pay it,
even your bed will be snatched from under you.

28 Don't cheat your neighbor by moving the ancient boundary markers
set up by previous generations.

29 Do you see any truly competent workers?
They will serve kings
rather than working for ordinary people.

22:26 Prov 6:1-5
22:28 Deut 19:14; 27:17
22:29 1 Kgs 10:8; 11:28

23

1 While dining with a ruler,
pay attention to what is put before you.
2 If you are a big eater,
put a knife to your throat;
3 don't desire all the delicacies,
for he might be trying to trick you.

4 Don't wear yourself out trying to get rich.
Be wise enough to know when to quit.
5 In the blink of an eye wealth disappears,
for it will sprout wings
and fly away like an eagle.

6 Don't eat with people who are stingy;
don't desire their delicacies.
7 They are always thinking about how much it costs.*
"Eat and drink," they say, but they don't mean it.
8 You will throw up what little you've eaten,
and your compliments will be wasted.

9 Don't waste your breath on fools,
for they will despise the wisest advice.

10 Don't cheat your neighbor by moving the ancient boundary markers;
don't take the land of defenseless orphans.
11 For their Redeemer* is strong;
He Himself will bring their charges against you.

23:2 Prov 23:20
23:3 Ps 141:4
23:4 Prov 15:27; 28:20 Matt 6:19 1 Tim 6:9
23:6 Ps 141:4 Prov 1:15; 4:14; 23:1
23:9 Prov 1:7
23:10 Deut 19:14 Prov 22:28 Jer 22:3 Zech 7:10

23:7 The meaning of the Hebrew is uncertain. 23:11 Or *redeemer.*

22:28 The book of Joshua tells how the land of Canaan was divided among Israel's tribes and clans by sacred lot (Joshua 14–19). The boundaries that were established were considered protected by the Law of Moses (see Deuteronomy 19:14; 27:17). These boundaries were marked by stones or even pillars. This proverb speaks to God's sense of justice in that He sought to protect the land for each family, lest dishonesty over time should leave a family without means to support itself.

▸ PURPOSE
23:2-8 Smart Eating. Yes, gluttony is a sin, but these verses have nothing to do with gaining weight. They are about being lured into an obligation by a powerful person's overtures of generosity (in this case, food). How often have you been enticed by a mixture of power and physical pleasure to do things you should not have done? It's a common deceptive practice in almost every society. Don't be moved to unwise behavior by a nice dessert or an expensive glass of wine—be smarter than that. (***See Purpose**> God's Means> Human Choice> Bringing our wills in subjection to God's will,* TopicGuide page A52.)

23:4 Notice here and throughout these "thirty sayings" (see note at 22:17) the presence of imperatives of prohibition (negative commands). In fact, more than 20 times in these 30 sayings we read "do not" or "don't." Just as the apostle Paul had to describe love as much by what it was not as by what it was (1 Corinthians 13:4-7), teaching positive virtue and character often requires negative prohibitions.

23:12 Prov 22:17
[12] Commit yourself to instruction;
listen carefully to words of knowledge.

23:13 Prov 13:24; 19:18 1 Cor 5:5
[13] Don't fail to discipline your children.
They won't die if you spank them.
[14] Physical discipline
may well save them from death.*

23:15 Prov 15:20; 27:11; 29:3
[15] My child,* if your heart is wise,
my own heart will rejoice!
[16] Everything in me will celebrate
when you speak what is right.

23:17 Pss 37:1; 73:3 Prov 24:1, 14, 19
[17] Don't envy sinners,
but always continue to fear the LORD.
[18] You will be rewarded for this;
your hope will not be disappointed.

23:19 Prov 23:29
[19] My child, listen and be wise:
Keep your heart on the right course.
[20] Do not carouse with drunkards
or feast with gluttons,
23:21 Prov 21:17
[21] for they are on their way to poverty,
and too much sleep clothes them in rags.

23:22 Prov 1:8; 30:17
[22] Listen to your father, who gave you life,
and don't despise your mother when she is old.
23:23 Prov 4:7; 18:15
[23] Get the truth and never sell it;
also get wisdom, discipline, and good judgment.
23:24 Prov 10:1
[24] The father of godly children has cause for joy.
What a pleasure to have children who are wise.*
[25] So give your father and mother joy!
May she who gave you birth be happy.

23:26 Prov 3:1; 4:4
[26] O my son, give me your heart.
May your eyes take delight in following my ways.
[27] A prostitute is a dangerous trap;
a promiscuous woman is as dangerous as falling into a narrow well.
[28] She hides and waits like a robber,
eager to make more men unfaithful.

23:14 Hebrew *from Sheol.* 23:15 Hebrew *My son;* also in 23:19. 23:24 Hebrew *to have a wise son.*

▶ HOLINESS
23:12 Study God's Word. People can learn and memorize all kinds of knowledge. Sports fans can spout off statistics and scores. A history buff can remember dates and place names. A chef has many recipes memorized. Do we come to the Bible with the same enthusiasm for learning? Are we so entranced with God's Word that we memorize its contents? Take this verse to heart and treat God's Word as the most important source of knowledge in your life, then commit yourself to study it. (***See Holiness****> Disciplines> Of Engagement> Call to study,* TopicGuide page A42.)

23:15, 19, 22, 26 These verses are further evidence that the intended audience for the book of Proverbs was young people in their morally and intellectually formative years. The opening nine chapters are more specific in that direction, but the rest of the book is also indispensable for young people who wish to gain not just knowledge of how the world works, but wisdom for living in the world.

▶ HOLINESS
23:23 "Buying" wisdom. We sometimes hear about an investor who buys shares of a fledgling company and becomes incredibly wealthy as the value of the stock multiplies many times. None of us knows for certain which stocks will rise or fall in the future, but we do know where lasting value lies—in the truth of God's Word. It will lead us to wisdom, discipline, and discernment. These are more precious than wealth. Are you working diligently to acquire the treasure of truth in God's Word? (***See Holiness****> Disciplines> Of Engagement> Call to study,* TopicGuide page A42.)

[29] Who has anguish? Who has sorrow?
Who is always fighting? Who is always complaining?
Who has unnecessary bruises? Who has bloodshot eyes?
[30] It is the one who spends long hours in the taverns,
trying out new drinks.
[31] Don't gaze at the wine, seeing how red it is,
how it sparkles in the cup, how smoothly it goes down.
[32] For in the end it bites like a poisonous snake;
it stings like a viper.
[33] You will see hallucinations,
and you will say crazy things.
[34] You will stagger like a sailor tossed at sea,
clinging to a swaying mast.
[35] And you will say, "They hit me, but I didn't feel it.
I didn't even know it when they beat me up.
When will I wake up
so I can look for another drink?"

23:29 Isa 5:11, 22
23:35 Isa 56:12

24

[1] Don't envy evil people
or desire their company.
[2] For their hearts plot violence,
and their words always stir up trouble.

[3] A house is built by wisdom
and becomes strong through good sense.
[4] Through knowledge its rooms are filled
with all sorts of precious riches and valuables.

[5] The wise are mightier than the strong,*
and those with knowledge grow stronger and stronger.
[6] So don't go to war without wise guidance;
victory depends on having many advisers.

[7] Wisdom is too lofty for fools.
Among leaders at the city gate, they have nothing to say.

[8] A person who plans evil
will get a reputation as a troublemaker.
[9] The schemes of a fool are sinful;
everyone detests a mocker.

[10] If you fail under pressure,
your strength is too small.
[11] Rescue those who are unjustly sentenced to die;
save them as they stagger to their death.

24:1 Pss 1:1; 37:1 Prov 1:15; 23:17; 24:19
24:2 Ps 10:7 Jer 22:17
24:5 Prov 21:22
24:6 Prov 11:14; 20:18
24:7 Prov 14:6; 17:16, 24
24:8 Prov 6:14; 14:22 Rom 1:30
24:10 Job 4:5 Heb 12:3
24:11 Ps 82:4

24:5 As in Greek version; Hebrew reads *A wise man is strength.*

23:29-35 These verses warn about the ill effects of drunkenness. Though written some 3,000 years ago, they accurately portray the kinds of physiological changes that occur through abuse of alcohol: bloodshot eyes, staggering and imbalance, hallucinations and impaired judgment, and a craving for more drink. See Song of Songs 8:2; Luke 22:20; John 2 for examples of the proper use of alcohol.

24:5 This proverb about wisdom and strength likely gave rise to the modern proverb, "The pen is mightier than the sword." The true measure of might is not brute strength, as the world so often believes, but lasting change in people and cultures. Ideas well-stated and communicated are stronger than mere physical strength.

24:12 *Rom 2:6
[12] Don't excuse yourself by saying, "Look, we didn't know."
For God understands all hearts, and He sees you.
He who guards your soul knows you knew.
He will repay all people as their actions deserve.

24:13 Ps 19:10 Prov 25:16
[13] My child,* eat honey, for it is good,
and the honeycomb is sweet to the taste.
24:14 Prov 2:10
[14] In the same way, wisdom is sweet to your soul.
If you find it, you will have a bright future,
and your hopes will not be cut short.

[15] Don't wait in ambush at the home of the godly,
and don't raid the house where the godly live.
[16] The godly may trip seven times, but they will get up again.
But one disaster is enough to overthrow the wicked.

24:17 Ps 35:15 Rom 11:18-21
[17] Don't rejoice when your enemies fall;
don't be happy when they stumble.
[18] For the LORD will be displeased with you
and will turn His anger away from them.

24:19 Job 15:31 Prov 13:9; 24:1
[19] Don't fret because of evildoers;
don't envy the wicked.
[20] For evil people have no future;
the light of the wicked will be snuffed out.

24:21 Rom 13:4 1 Pet 2:17
[21] My child, fear the LORD and the king.
Don't associate with rebels,
[22] for disaster will hit them suddenly.
Who knows what punishment will come
from the LORD and the king?

MORE SAYINGS OF THE WISE

[23]Here are some further sayings of the wise:

It is wrong to show favoritism when passing judgment.

24:13 Hebrew *My son;* also in 24:21.

▸ HOLINESS

24:12 Admit your sins. Parents of large families know this situation well: Someone disobeys and when caught, they exclaim, "I didn't know it was wrong!" As Christians, we may offer the same response when we are accused of some sin. But God knows the truth. If we are guilty, we cannot claim ignorance before Him. He wants us to confess our faults to Him and ask for forgiveness from those we have wronged. You should never prolong your sin with the lie of ignorance. (***See Holiness****> Disciplines> Of Abstinence> Resisting sinful urges,* TopicGuide page A42.)

24:12 This proverb tells us that God not only knows what we have done, He knows what we should have done but didn't (in the Hebrew text of this verse, He is called "the One who weighs motives"). God knows every thought, and even every intention and motive. His wisdom and knowledge are unfathomable.

24:13-14 This simile between honey and wisdom resembles that found in Psalm 19:9-10, which boasts that the law of the Lord is sweeter than honey. Even Ezekiel, whose message was woe and lament, said that God's Word became like honey in his mouth (see Ezekiel 2:9–3:3). In all cases, the instruction is to consume the Word of wisdom, to digest it, to not just take note of it from a distance.

▸ MINISTRY

24:17 Don't gloat. We like to see bad people get what's coming to them. If we get fired, we want the company to struggle because of our departure. If we get cut off in traffic, we sometimes hope that the person who did it gets a ticket (or worse!). We always face the strong temptation to rejoice when our enemies fall into trouble. But when we react this way, we miss a golden opportunity to demonstrate the reality of God's mercy in our lives. How many times would God have been justified to let you fall under the weight of your own sin? Think about that the next time you are tempted to hope for the worst for those who cross you. Show them the same love God has shown you. (***See Ministry****> Transformation> Fill and Subdue> Influencing every sphere of life,* TopicGuide page A57.)

24:23-34 Immediately following the collection of "thirty sayings" is another, even briefer set of "sayings of the wise." Though the writer is not identified, we can presume that, as with other sayings, Solomon collected these for training young leaders. This section seems to contrast two scenarios: the person who speaks well and works hard and one who speaks poorly and is lazy.

24 A judge who says to the wicked, "You are innocent,"
will be cursed by many people and denounced by the nations.
25 But it will go well for those who convict the guilty;
rich blessings will be showered on them.

26 An honest answer
is like a kiss of friendship.

27 Do your planning and prepare your fields
before building your house.

28 Don't testify against your neighbors without cause;
don't lie about them.
29 And don't say, "Now I can pay them back for what they've done to me!
I'll get even with them!"

30 I walked by the field of a lazy person,
the vineyard of one with no common sense.
31 I saw that it was overgrown with nettles.
It was covered with weeds,
and its walls were broken down.
32 Then, as I looked and thought about it,
I learned this lesson:
33 A little extra sleep, a little more slumber,
a little folding of the hands to rest—
34 then poverty will pounce on you like a bandit;
scarcity will attack you like an armed robber.

24:24 Prov 17:15
24:28 Prov 25:18
24:29 Prov 20:22; Matt 5:39
24:30 Prov 6:6-11
24:31 Prov 6:10; 12:24; 23:21

MORE PROVERBS OF SOLOMON

25 These are more proverbs of Solomon, collected by the advisers of King Hezekiah of Judah.

2 It is God's privilege to conceal things
and the king's privilege to discover them.
3 No one can comprehend the height of heaven, the depth of the earth,
or all that goes on in the king's mind!

4 Remove the impurities from silver,
and the sterling will be ready for the silversmith.
5 Remove the wicked from the king's court,
and his reign will be made secure by justice.
6 Don't demand an audience with the king
or push for a place among the great.
7 It's better to wait for an invitation to the head table
than to be sent away in public disgrace.

25:1 Prov 1:1
25:2 Deut 29:29; Ezra 6:1; Rom 11:33
25:4 Ezek 22:18; Mal 3:2-3

25:1 This verse tells us that the next collection (Proverbs 25–29) is composed of more proverbs attributed to King Solomon, the second son of David and Bathsheba. He reigned in Jerusalem from approximately 970–930 BC. This collection, however, while originating with Solomon (a portion of the three thousand proverbs mentioned in 1 Kings 4:32), was gathered and organized by wise men during the time of King Hezekiah. This king, who ruled from 715–686 BC, was one of very few deemed to have been faithful in God's sight (see 2 Kings 18:1-5).

25:2-15 Notice that the focus of the first several verses is on the king, while verses 7-15 speak to people subject to authority, telling them how they should conduct themselves. The theme of this portion of Solomon's proverbs is that citizens owe a certain respect to authority, whether it be the king, the judge (15:8), or a prince (25:15).

Just because you've seen something,
25:8 Prov 17:14 8 don't be in a hurry to go to court.
For what will you do in the end
if your neighbor deals you a shameful defeat?

9 When arguing with your neighbor,
don't betray another person's secret.
10 Others may accuse you of gossip,
and you will never regain your good reputation.

25:11 Prov 15:23 11 Timely advice is lovely,
like golden apples in a silver basket.

25:12 Prov 15:31; 20:12 12 To one who listens, valid criticism
is like a gold earring or other gold jewelry.

25:13 Prov 13:17 13 Trustworthy messengers refresh like snow in summer.
They revive the spirit of their employer.

14 A person who promises a gift but doesn't give it
is like clouds and wind that bring no rain.

25:15 Prov 15:1 Eccl 10:4 15 Patience can persuade a prince,
and soft speech can break bones.

25:16 Prov 25:27 16 Do you like honey?
Don't eat too much, or it will make you sick!

17 Don't visit your neighbors too often,
or you will wear out your welcome.

25:18 Ps 57:4 Prov 12:18; 24:28 Jer 9:8 18 Telling lies about others
is as harmful as hitting them with an ax,
wounding them with a sword,
or shooting them with a sharp arrow.

25:19 Job 6:15 19 Putting confidence in an unreliable person in times of trouble
is like chewing with a broken tooth or walking on a lame foot.

20 Singing cheerful songs to a person with a heavy heart
is like taking someone's coat in cold weather
or pouring vinegar in a wound.*

25:21 Exod 23:4-5 2 Kgs 6:22 2 Chr 28:15 Matt 5:44 Rom 12:20 21 If your enemies are hungry, give them food to eat.
If they are thirsty, give them water to drink.

25:20 As in Greek version; Hebrew reads *pouring vinegar on soda.*

25:14, 23 These two proverbs make their point through the use of climatic conditions familiar to the original readers. In many areas of Israel, rain is scarce. Hope and expectation rise when clouds arrive, with even stronger expectations placed on clouds moving in from the north.

▸ CHURCH

25:18 The power of lies. Receiving criticism can cause us pain, but as this verse shows, we can be harmed even more severely by words that are not spoken to our faces. For instance, a rumor can devastate a person's reputation. Sadly, Western culture is so charmed by gossip that it has magazines, television shows, and Internet sites dedicated to spreading vicious information about people. But God's standard for His people is different from the world's standards. We must be honest when talking about others. Gossip should not be found in our churches. Make a commitment today to tell the truth in love about others. (***See Church****> Mission> Nurture> True teaching,* TopicGuide page A49.)

▸ MINISTRY

25:21 Witness through your actions. You don't need to look very hard to find suffering in the world. It could be something large, like an earthquake, a flood, or a famine; or something small, such as a neighbor's child being killed in a car accident. All of these are opportunities for God's people to spread His love. It is not enough merely to sympathize with those who hurt; we must act to ease their suffering. Even those who oppose us should receive our aid if they need it. Do you have a plan to help others in crisis? Look over your schedule and your finances to see whether you are being salt and light here at home and to faraway places. (***See Ministry****> Transformation> Fill and Subdue> Being salt and light in the world,* TopicGuide page A57.)

22 You will heap burning coals of shame on their heads,
and the LORD will reward you.

23 As surely as a north wind brings rain,
so a gossiping tongue causes anger!

24 It's better to live alone in the corner of an attic
than with a quarrelsome wife in a lovely home.

25 Good news from far away
is like cold water to the thirsty.

26 If the godly give in to the wicked,
it's like polluting a fountain or muddying a spring.

27 It's not good to eat too much honey,
and it's not good to seek honors for yourself.

28 A person without self-control
is like a city with broken-down walls.

25:22 *Rom 12:20
25:23 Prov 13:3; 26:20
25:24 Prov 21:9
25:25 Prov 15:30
25:26 Ezek 32:2; 34:18
25:27 Prov 25:16; 27:2
25:28 2 Chr 32:5 Prov 16:32

26

1 Honor is no more associated with fools
than snow with summer or rain with harvest.

2 Like a fluttering sparrow or a darting swallow,
an undeserved curse will not land on its intended victim.

3 Guide a horse with a whip, a donkey with a bridle,
and a fool with a rod to his back!

4 Don't answer the foolish arguments of fools,
or you will become as foolish as they are.

5 Be sure to answer the foolish arguments of fools,
or they will become wise in their own estimation.

6 Trusting a fool to convey a message
is like cutting off one's feet or drinking poison!

7 A proverb in the mouth of a fool
is as useless as a paralyzed leg.

8 Honoring a fool
is as foolish as tying a stone to a slingshot.

9 A proverb in the mouth of a fool
is like a thorny branch brandished by a drunk.

10 An employer who hires a fool or a bystander
is like an archer who shoots at random.

26:1 1 Sam 12:17
26:2 Num 23:8 2 Sam 16:12
26:3 Ps 32:9 Prov 10:13
26:4 Prov 23:9; 29:9

25:28 This verse begins a section dealing with seven kinds of people—all held up as negative examples of character. Here we see the person who lacks self-control. Without discipline, passions and sin run rampant, and the person becomes as vulnerable as an unguarded city.

26:1-12 The second negative character example is the fool. This person is stubborn in his rebellion and his refusal to receive wise counsel or correction. Contrary to the wise person, the fool is convinced he is right even though the product of his actions is harmful to him and to the community around him.

26:4-5 On the surface these two proverbs seem contradictory. However, the aim of both is to help the reader to stop the spread of foolishness. In the first, the point is to not become like the fool by resorting to his style of speech. In the second, the point is that the fool must be answered lest his ideas and actions spread further. In each situation, one must have the wisdom to keep foolishness from spreading, but each fool must be judged individually to make that decision properly.

26:11 Exod 8:15 *2 Pet 2:22
11 As a dog returns to its vomit,
so a fool repeats his foolishness.

26:12 Prov 3:7; 29:20
12 There is more hope for fools
than for people who think they are wise.

26:13 Prov 22:13
13 The lazy person claims, "There's a lion on the road!
Yes, I'm sure there's a lion out there!"

26:14 Prov 6:9
14 As a door swings back and forth on its hinges,
so the lazy person turns over in bed.

26:15 Prov 19:24
15 Lazy people take food in their hand
but don't even lift it to their mouth.

16 Lazy people consider themselves smarter
than seven wise counselors.

26:17 Prov 3:30; 20:3
17 Interfering in someone else's argument
is as foolish as yanking a dog's ears.

26:18 Prov 24:12, 28 Isa 50:11
18 Just as damaging
as a madman shooting a deadly weapon
19 is someone who lies to a friend
and then says, "I was only joking."

26:20 Prov 16:28; 22:10; 24:28
20 Fire goes out without wood,
and quarrels disappear when gossip stops.

26:21 Prov 15:18; 29:22
21 A quarrelsome person starts fights
as easily as hot embers light charcoal
or fire lights wood.

26:22 Prov 18:8
22 Rumors are dainty morsels
that sink deep into one's heart.

26:23 Luke 11:39
23 Smooth* words may hide a wicked heart,
just as a pretty glaze covers a clay pot.

26:23 As in Greek version; Hebrew reads *Burning.*

▸ HOLINESS

26:11 Repeating folly. As disgusting as it is, a dog returning to its vomit is only doing what comes naturally. Likewise, we should not be surprised when a sinner follows his nature and sins repeatedly. The apostle Peter acknowledged this truth as well, and he went on to warn that those who learn of God's ways and reject them are worse off than they were before (2 Peter 2:20-21). Through Christ, He has broken the power of sin in your life and daily He gives you strength to stand firm against temptations. Pray that He will deliver your friends and relatives who are still captives to their sinful natures. Directly attack the false ideas and feelings that often trap us in repetitive sins by immersing yourself in God's Word. (See 2 Peter 2:21-22; also ***see Holiness****> Submission> Learning God's Word> Makes us aware of worldly ideas to beware of their sin,* TopicGuide page A40.)

26:12-16 These proverbs present the third negative example—the lazy person. Also called a "sluggard," such a person is both unreliable and a danger to himself and those around him. He does not contribute to the community's good. There is an important difference between the "poor" and the "lazy"—the poor have no control over their difficult circumstances, but the sluggard causes his own plight.

26:17 Someone who interferes in the affairs of others is often called a "busybody"—the fourth negative example. Such people hurt only themselves by becoming involved in matters that should not concern them.

26:18-22 These proverbs depict two more types of morally deficient people. One lies and jests, making mischief; the other uses words as a weapon, starting quarrels and rumors. The first enjoys causing pain for his neighbor; the second slanders his neighbor for personal gain. Both types of people are dangerously self-centered.

26:23-28 This section presents the final of seven negative examples: one who is a deceitful person. This person is characterized by his wicked heart, filled with hatred and evil.

24 People may cover their hatred with pleasant words,
but they're deceiving you.
25 They pretend to be kind, but don't believe them.
Their hearts are full of many evils.*
26 While their hatred may be concealed by trickery,
their wrongdoing will be exposed in public.

27 If you set a trap for others,
you will get caught in it yourself.
If you roll a boulder down on others,
it will crush you instead.

28 A lying tongue hates its victims,
and flattering words cause ruin.

26:24 Ps 41:6; Prov 12:20
26:27 Ps 7:15
26:28 Prov 28:23

27

1 Don't brag about tomorrow,
since you don't know what the day will bring.

2 Let someone else praise you, not your own mouth—
a stranger, not your own lips.

3 A stone is heavy and sand is weighty,
but the resentment caused by a fool is even heavier.

4 Anger is cruel, and wrath is like a flood,
but jealousy is even more dangerous.

5 An open rebuke
is better than hidden love!

6 Wounds from a sincere friend
are better than many kisses from an enemy.

7 A person who is full refuses honey,
but even bitter food tastes sweet to the hungry.

8 A person who strays from home
is like a bird that strays from its nest.

9 The heartfelt counsel of a friend
is as sweet as perfume and incense.

10 Never abandon a friend—
either yours or your father's.

27:1 Luke 12:19-20; Jas 4:13-16
27:2 Prov 25:27; 2 Cor 10:12, 18
27:4 Prov 6:34
27:5 Prov 25:12
27:6 Ps 141:5; Matt 26:49
27:10 1 Kgs 12:6; 2 Chr 10:6-8; Prov 17:17; 18:24

26:25 Hebrew *seven evils.*

▶ SPIRITUAL WARFARE

26:24 Hateful people. Many people succeed for a time in camouflaging deep hatred. Some people nurse prejudices that lead them to treat people unfairly. Others wield revenge like a fearsome weapon. Still others spread the poison of gossip about others. In all these cases, the offenders may offer smooth explanations for their behavior, but their actions reveal the truth of what is concealed in their heart. Hatred in any form is evil. When you see hatred, prayerfully point it out and call the hateful one to repent of it. (***See Spiritual Warfare****> God and Sin> Sin's Origin> The wise understand evil's source,* TopicGuide page A45.)

27:1-22 Repetition of words often communicates a theme in Scripture. In this case, the words *friend* and *neighbor* regularly occur here, showing that this group of proverbs is generally concerned with right relationships.

▶ HOLINESS

27:2 Don't praise yourself! A ring of children begins bragging about what they can do. One statement leads to another until the claims are outlandish. "I'm so strong I can lift a table with one hand." "If I try hard enough, I can lift a car." "That's nothing. I can lift an elephant!" We laugh at these children, yet we often give in to the temptation to brag about ourselves, too. But what do bragging words say about us? That we are insecure and need to puff ourselves up? Or that we have a desire to look better than our neighbors? We do better to follow the example of Jesus. He never sought the praise and honor of other people, only that of His Father. Remember that our greatest praise will come from our heavenly Father as we serve Him and others. (***See Holiness****> Law and Grace> Law> A mirror to view ourselves,* TopicGuide page A41.)

When disaster strikes, you won't have to ask your brother for assistance.
It's better to go to a neighbor than to a brother who lives far away.

27:11 Prov 10:1; 23:15

11 Be wise, my child,* and make my heart glad.
Then I will be able to answer my critics.

27:12 Prov 22:3

12 A prudent person foresees danger and takes precautions.
The simpleton goes blindly on and suffers the consequences.

27:13 Prov 20:16

13 Get security from someone who guarantees a stranger's debt.
Get a deposit if he does it for foreigners.*

14 A loud and cheerful greeting early in the morning
will be taken as a curse!

27:15 Prov 19:13

15 A quarrelsome wife is as annoying
as constant dripping on a rainy day.
16 Stopping her complaints is like trying to stop the wind
or trying to hold something with greased hands.

17 As iron sharpens iron,
so a friend sharpens a friend.

27:18 Luke 12:42-44; 1 Cor 9:7; 2 Tim 2:6

18 As workers who tend a fig tree are allowed to eat the fruit,
so workers who protect their employer's interests will be rewarded.
19 As a face is reflected in water,
so the heart reflects the real person.

27:20 Prov 30:15; Eccl 1:8-11; Hab 2:5

20 Just as Death and Destruction* are never satisfied,
so human desire is never satisfied.

27:21 Prov 17:3; Zech 13:9; Luke 6:26

21 Fire tests the purity of silver and gold,
but a person is tested by being praised.*

27:22 Prov 23:35; 26:11; Jer 5:3

22 You cannot separate fools from their foolishness,
even though you grind them like grain with mortar and pestle.

27:23 Ezek 34:12; John 10:3

23 Know the state of your flocks,
and put your heart into caring for your herds,
24 for riches don't last forever,
and the crown might not be passed to the next generation.
25 After the hay is harvested and the new crop appears
and the mountain grasses are gathered in,

27:11 Hebrew *my son.* 27:13 As in Greek and Latin versions (see also 20:16); Hebrew reads *for a promiscuous woman.* 27:20 Hebrew *Sheol and Abaddon.* 27:21 Or *by flattery.*

27:12 The comparison between the "prudent person" and the "simpleton" may be seen as one between a careful, discriminating thinker and a gullible person who is easily swayed by others.

▸ SPIRITUAL WARFARE

27:17 The value of friends. One important aspect of friendship is the accountability it provides. If you stray from the path of righteousness, an acquaintance, a colleague, or a classmate might say nothing. But if that person is a true friend, he or she will remind you of what is right. In this way, your friend will help you discover areas of weakness in your life and show you what you need to overcome. In short, a true friend will help you grow as a Christian. Ask God to help you find godly friends who will help you grow in His grace. (***See Spiritual Warfare> Resisting Sin and Evil> Resisting Temptation> How to Resist> By the help of our friends,*** TopicGuide page A45.)

27:20 "Death and Destruction" (or *Sheol* and *Abaddon* in Hebrew; see NLT textual note) were shadowy realms of the dead in ancient Hebrew thought. The Hebrew text here literally says, "the eyes of man are not satisfied." The comparison shows that just as the underworld of death seems never to stop consuming more and more, so our eyes are ever feeding our desires. These desires may be God-given, but they can develop into sin if left unchecked by godly restraint and virtue (see James 1:12-15).

26 your sheep will provide wool for clothing,
and your goats will provide the price of a field.
27 And you will have enough goats' milk for yourself,
your family, and your servant girls.

28

1 The wicked run away when no one is chasing them,
but the godly are as bold as lions. 28:1 Lev 26:17, 36

2 When there is moral rot within a nation, its government topples easily.
But wise and knowledgeable leaders bring stability. 28:2 1 Kgs 16:8-28; 2 Kgs 15:8-15

3 A poor person who oppresses the poor
is like a pounding rain that destroys the crops. 28:3 Matt 18:28

4 To reject the law is to praise the wicked;
to obey the law is to fight them. 28:4 Rom 1:32; Eph 5:11

5 Evil people don't understand justice,
but those who follow the LORD understand completely. 28:5 Ps 92:6-7; Prov 2:9

6 Better to be poor and honest
than to be dishonest and rich. 28:6 Prov 19:1

7 Young people who obey the law are wise;
those with wild friends bring shame to their parents.* 28:7 Prov 23:20

8 Income from charging high interest rates
will end up in the pocket of someone who is kind to the poor. 28:8 Exod 22:25; Deut 23:19-20

9 God detests the prayers
of a person who ignores the law. 28:9 Pss 66:18; 109:7; Prov 15:8

10 Those who lead good people along an evil path
will fall into their own trap,
but the honest will inherit good things. 28:10 Prov 26:27; Heb 6:12

11 Rich people may think they are wise,
but a poor person with discernment can see right through them. 28:11 Prov 26:12

12 When the godly succeed, everyone is glad.
When the wicked take charge, people go into hiding. 28:12 Eccl 10:5-6

13 People who conceal their sins will not prosper,
but if they confess and turn from them, they will receive mercy. 28:13 Ps 32:1-11; 1 Jn 1:6-9

28:7 Hebrew *their father.*

PURPOSE

28:4 Rejecting the law. As Christians, we must be careful to be on the right side of the law. We should be model citizens. Romans 13:1-2 explains: "Everyone must submit to governing authorities. For all authority comes from God, and those in positions of authority have been placed there by God." In other words, when we violate the speed limits set by our governments or cheat on taxes, we disobey God. And when we do that, we declare by our actions that we believe the way of wickedness is best. On the other hand, when we take a stand for God by submitting to all lawful authorities, we strike a blow for what is right against those who disregard the law. Resolve today, with God's help, to stand for what is right. (***See Purpose*****> *God's Means> Human Choice> Human view,* TopicGuide page A52.)

28:4 "The law" mentioned here is the Law of Moses, the entire legal code of Israel. This would include ceremonial, civil, and moral laws.

28:9 The Hebrew of this verse literally says, "The one who turns his ear from hearing Torah [the law], even his prayers are detestable." Proverbs already has taught that God despises the false piety of the wicked. A person who stubbornly refuses to hear and obey God's rules should not expect to be heard by God (1 Peter 3:7).

28:11 This proverb teaches that the rich too often mistakenly think they are wise. But in fact, a person may be nearly destitute financially ("the poor") and be wiser than the wealthy, since he can see the rich person's empty duplicity and self-deception. Such wisdom is better than wealth.

28:14 Rom 2:5
[14] Blessed are those who fear to do wrong,*
but the stubborn are headed for serious trouble.

28:15 Prov 19:12 Matt 2:16 1 Pet 5:8
[15] A wicked ruler is as dangerous to the poor
as a roaring lion or an attacking bear.

28:16 Eccl 10:16 Isa 3:12
[16] A ruler with no understanding will oppress his people,
but one who hates corruption will have a long life.

28:17 Gen 9:6 Exod 21:14
[17] A murderer's tormented conscience will drive him into the grave.
Don't protect him!

[18] The blameless will be rescued from harm,
but the crooked will be suddenly destroyed.

28:19 Prov 12:11
[19] A hard worker has plenty of food,
but a person who chases fantasies ends up in poverty.

28:20 Matt 25:21
[20] The trustworthy person will get a rich reward,
but a person who wants quick riches will get into trouble.

28:21 Ezek 13:19
[21] Showing partiality is never good,
yet some will do wrong for a mere piece of bread.

[22] Greedy people try to get rich quick
but don't realize they're headed for poverty.

[23] In the end, people appreciate honest criticism
far more than flattery.

28:24 Prov 19:26; 20:20
[24] Anyone who steals from his father and mother
and says, "What's wrong with that?"
is no better than a murderer.

[25] Greed causes fighting;
trusting the LORD leads to prosperity.

28:26 Prov 3:5
[26] Those who trust their own insight are foolish,
but anyone who walks in wisdom is safe.

28:27 Prov 11:24; 19:17
[27] Whoever gives to the poor will lack nothing,
but those who close their eyes to poverty will be cursed.

[28] When the wicked take charge, people go into hiding.
When the wicked meet disaster, the godly flourish.

28:14 Or *those who fear the LORD;* Hebrew reads *those who fear.*

28:14 The person with a tender conscience (literally, "one who trembles continually" in the sense of fearing God) is compared in this proverb with the stubborn person (literally, "one who hardens his heart"). The hardened heart cannot feel or respond and is in danger of becoming increasingly hardened against God (Zechariah 7:12). The tender-hearted person feels compassion for God's people (1 Peter 3:8).

28:18-28 This extended section of proverbs focuses on people who are self-centered. They are described as crooked, greedy, robbers, foolish, and wicked. Such self-centered people also seek an easy route to monetary "wealth," thinking it will satisfy their selfishness. The antithesis is that hard work, integrity, and honesty bring true satisfaction and peace.

▸ SPIRITUAL WARFARE

28:22 Greediness brings poverty. A woman learned of a scheme to make 100 percent on an investment. The deal was supposed to be fail-safe, though a little on the shady side. You probably can guess what happened—she lost the entire $20,000 she invested. This scenario is repeated time and again. The dishonest keep coming up with attractive deals that trap the greedy. Just when you think that you cannot be fooled, someone will lure you into some scheme—greed turns even the wisest into fools. But when our goal is to serve God as stewards of our wealth, we are less likely to be enticed by greed. Remind yourself often that all you have is God's and should be used in ways that honor Him. (***See Spiritual Warfare****> Resisting Sin and Evil> Resisting Temptation> Examples> Worldly Influences> On the affluent,* TopicGuide page A45.)

29 1 Whoever stubbornly refuses to accept criticism
will suddenly be destroyed beyond recovery.

2 When the godly are in authority, the people rejoice.
But when the wicked are in power, they groan.

3 The man who loves wisdom brings joy to his father,
but if he hangs around with prostitutes, his wealth is wasted.

4 A just king gives stability to his nation,
but one who demands bribes destroys it.

5 To flatter friends
is to lay a trap for their feet.

6 Evil people are trapped by sin,
but the righteous escape, shouting for joy.

7 The godly care about the rights of the poor;
the wicked don't care at all.

8 Mockers can get a whole town agitated,
but the wise will calm anger.

9 If a wise person takes a fool to court,
there will be ranting and ridicule but no satisfaction.

10 The bloodthirsty hate blameless people,
but the upright seek to help them.*

11 Fools vent their anger,
but the wise quietly hold it back.

12 If a ruler pays attention to liars,
all his advisers will be wicked.

13 The poor and the oppressor have this in common—
the LORD gives sight to the eyes of both.

14 If a king judges the poor fairly,
his throne will last forever.

15 To discipline a child produces wisdom,
but a mother is disgraced by an undisciplined child.

29:1 1 Sam 2:25; 2 Chr 36:16; Prov 1:24-31; 13:18; 15:31-32
29:2 Esth 8:15-16; Prov 11:10; 28:12, 28
29:3 Prov 6:26; 10:1; 28:7; Luke 15:13
29:4 Prov 8:15; 15:27; 29:14
29:5 Ps 5:9
29:7 Ps 41:1; Prov 31:8-9
29:8 Prov 11:11; 16:14
29:10 1 Jn 3:12
29:12 1 Kgs 12:14
29:13 Ps 13:3
29:14 Ps 72:4; Prov 16:12

29:10 Or *The bloodthirsty hate blameless people, / and they seek to kill the upright;* Hebrew reads *The bloodthirsty hate blameless people; / as for the upright, they seek their life.*

29:3-6 This short set of proverbs presents the truth that righteousness yields a life of joy and stability. The wicked life, on the other hand, brings immorality, instability, and entrapment to sin.

29:8 We learn from this proverb that foolishness and rebellion lead to chaos but wisdom leads to peace. Jesus Christ affirmed this truth in the Sermon on the Mount when He said, "God blesses those who work for peace" (Matthew 5:9).

29:13 This proverb teaches that God "gives sight" to all. The Hebrew term translated as "light to the eyes" in Proverbs signifies more than mere physical eyesight. It connotes life itself, and even spiritual illumination and moral guidance. This gift to all is an example of God's "common grace"—that is, a gift given to all people in all places throughout time.

▸ HOLINESS

29:15 Undisciplined children. In a roomful of young children, it is not difficult to pick out ones who have little discipline at home. Such children are used to having their way. They need the grace of discipline so that they might learn wisdom. A lack of godly discipline results in children who are frustrating and embarrassing, as this verse attests. But if children continue without discipline, they will grow into foolish teenagers and adults who will likely bring deeper shame upon their parents. If you are a parent (or you anticipate becoming one someday), make it your aim to discipline your children from their earliest years. The wisdom your loving discipline instills will stand them in good stead through all their years. (***See Holiness**> Law and Grace> Law> Parents and children,* TopicGuide page A41.)

29:16 Ps 37:34-38

[16] When the wicked are in authority, sin flourishes,
but the godly will live to see their downfall.

[17] Discipline your children, and they will give you peace of mind
and will make your heart glad.

29:18 Exod 32:25 Pss 1:1-2; 119:2-3

[18] When people do not accept divine guidance, they run wild.
But whoever obeys the law is joyful.

[19] Words alone will not discipline a servant;
the words may be understood, but they are not heeded.

29:20 Prov 26:12 Jas 1:19

[20] There is more hope for a fool
than for someone who speaks without thinking.

[21] A servant pampered from childhood
will become a rebel.

[22] An angry person starts fights;
a hot-tempered person commits all kinds of sin.

29:23 Prov 15:33; 22:4 Dan 4:30 Matt 23:12 Jas 4:6

[23] Pride ends in humiliation,
while humility brings honor.

29:24 Lev 5:1

[24] If you assist a thief, you only hurt yourself.
You are sworn to tell the truth, but you dare not testify.

29:25 Gen 12:11-13 Luke 12:4

[25] Fearing people is a dangerous trap,
but trusting the LORD means safety.

29:26 Isa 49:4

[26] Many seek the ruler's favor,
but justice comes from the LORD.

29:27 Pss 69:4; 139:21-22 Matt 10:22; 24:9

[27] The righteous despise the unjust;
the wicked despise the godly.

THE SAYINGS OF AGUR

30 The sayings of Agur son of Jakeh contain this message.*

I am weary, O God;
I am weary and worn out, O God.*

30:2 Job 42:3-6 Ps 49:10

[2] I am too stupid to be human,
and I lack common sense.

30:1a Or *son of Jakeh from Massa;* or *son of Jakeh, an oracle.* 30:1b The Hebrew can also be translated *The man declares this to Ithiel, / to Ithiel and to Ucal.*

29:23 This proverb is stated in various ways throughout Scripture. Generally, God exalts the humble but humbles the prideful. Pride is the attitude of self-sufficiency that shakes a fist at God, saying there is no need of Him. What the proud want to avoid, they receive: humiliation. The humble, however, receive what they least demand: honor.

▸ MINISTRY

29:27 Persecution will come. Why do the wicked hate the godly? It is because the actions and attitudes of those who serve God illuminate the depravity of sinners, reminding them of how dark their deeds truly are. In their anger over this exposure, the sinful lash out at believers. Jesus warns, "You will be arrested, persecuted, and killed. You will be hated all over the world because you are My followers" (Matthew 24:9). Be prepared for opposition as you go out to serve God. Some will hear your message and joyfully turn to Christ. But many others will spurn you because of Jesus. When this happens, remind yourself that Jesus endured the same rejection and much worse on your behalf. (***See Ministry****> Great Commission> Witness> Locally, regionally, worldwide,* TopicGuide page A56.)

30:1 Though there have been numerous creative attempts to identify Agur, the writer's roots are unknown. An oracle (see NLT textual note) is usually a prophetic statement of judgment (see Zechariah 9:1; Malachi 1:1; Habakkuk 1:1 for other examples), but numerous Hebrew words have different senses in the different types of literature. In this case, the term "oracle" underscores that this is from God, through Agur.

3 I have not mastered human wisdom,
nor do I know the Holy One.

4 Who but God goes up to heaven and comes back down?
Who holds the wind in His fists?
Who wraps up the oceans in His cloak?
Who has created the whole wide world?
What is His name—and His Son's name?
Tell me if you know!

5 Every word of God proves true.
He is a shield to all who come to Him for protection.
6 Do not add to His words,
or He may rebuke you and expose you as a liar.

7 O God, I beg two favors from You;
let me have them before I die.
8 First, help me never to tell a lie.
Second, give me neither poverty nor riches!
Give me just enough to satisfy my needs.

30:4 Exod 15:10 Job 26:8; 38:8-9 Pss 24:2; 68:18; 135:7 Isa 45:18 Rev 19:12

30:5 Pss 3:3; 12:6; 18:30; 84:11 Prov 2:7-8

30:6 Deut 4:2; 12:32 Rev 22:18

30:8 Matt 6:11

30:4 This verse is reminiscent of material from the book of Job. The nature of the questions has caused some to propose that Agur's statement ends with this verse, with the following verses being added by someone else to answer his skepticism. However, there is no reason to read multiple authors into this section. In his honesty, Agur asks universal questions, then lays out the answers.

▸ BIBLE

30:5 Every word is true. Do you believe that every word of the Bible is true? Beginning with the Renaissance and the Enlightenment in the West, people doubted the accuracy of the Bible's historical accounts. Today, archaeologists are discovering artifacts that show that the Bible has been right all along. The Old Testament predicted many details about the first coming of the Messiah. All of these prophecies were fulfilled in Jesus Christ. In every area, the Bible has been found to be accurate and true. How could it be otherwise when the Bible comes from the God who embodies truth? Since you can trust the Bible's authenticity, you can stand on its promises. (***See Bible****> Uniqueness> Flawless> Scripture is sure and convincing,* TopicGuide page A10.)

▸ SPIRITUAL WARFARE

30:8 "Satisfy my needs." In your private prayers, what request do you bring to God about your financial situation? Do you ask to be rich? God says we should ask Him to meet our needs. There is nothing wrong with wealth, and we should rejoice when God chooses to bless individuals abundantly. But all too often we pursue riches out of a desire for the security we believe they provide. When we do this, we fail to trust God as we should. He has promised to meet all our needs and even to give us the desires of our heart. But we must seek Him above all things. Pursue God and trust Him to care for you. He is your ever-faithful Provider. (***See Spiritual Warfare****> Resisting Sin and Evil> Resisting Temptation> Examples> Worldly Influences> On the poor,* TopicGuide page A45.)

FOR THE NEXT *GOD IS ABSOLUTE TRUTH* FEATURE SEE PAGE 1327.

BECAUSE GOD IS ABSOLUTE TRUTH

I will believe what He says and live accordingly.

Every word of God proves true.

PROVERBS 30:5

30:9 Deut 8:12; 31:20 Neh 9:25 Hos 13:6

9 For if I grow rich, I may deny You and say, "Who is the LORD?"
And if I am too poor, I may steal and thus insult God's holy name.

30:10 Eccl 7:21

10 Never slander a worker to the employer,
or the person will curse you, and you will pay for it.

30:11 Exod 21:17 Prov 20:20

11 Some people curse their father
and do not thank their mother.
12 They are pure in their own eyes,
but they are filthy and unwashed.
13 They look proudly around,
casting disdainful glances.

30:14 Job 29:17 Ps 14:4

14 They have teeth like swords
and fangs like knives.
They devour the poor from the earth
and the needy from among humanity.

30:15 Prov 27:20

15 The leech has two suckers
that cry out, "More, more!"*

There are three things that are never satisfied—
no, four that never say, "Enough!":
16 the grave,*
the barren womb,
the thirsty desert,
the blazing fire.

30:17 Gen 9:22

17 The eye that mocks a father
and despises a mother's instructions
will be plucked out by ravens of the valley
and eaten by vultures.

18 There are three things that amaze me—
no, four things that I don't understand:
19 how an eagle glides through the sky,
how a snake slithers on a rock,
how a ship navigates the ocean,
how a man loves a woman.

30:20 Prov 5:6

20 An adulterous woman consumes a man,
then wipes her mouth and says, "What's wrong with that?"

21 There are three things that make the earth tremble—
no, four it cannot endure:
22 a slave who becomes a king,
an overbearing fool who prospers,

30:15 Hebrew *two daughters who cry out, "Give, give!"* 30:16 Hebrew *Sheol.*

30:10-33 Beginning with verse 10, Agur's message breaks into numbered groups, all on the topic of social order.

30:10-16 This first set of numerical sayings focuses on pride and greed as vices that will destroy a people or a generation. Pride never remains simply a sin of self-reliance. It moves into slander of others, disdain and disrespect for others, and finally, even disdain for the poor and helpless.

30:17-33 These four sets of numerical sayings focus on the social order: the beautiful compared with the crass (30:18-20); four examples of broken social order (30:21-23); four small and vulnerable creatures that succeed (30:24-28); and four large and strong creatures that rule (30:29-33).

23 a bitter woman who finally gets a husband,
a servant girl who supplants her mistress.

24 There are four things on earth that are small but unusually wise:
25 Ants—they aren't strong,
but they store up food all summer. 30:25 Prov 6:6
26 Hyraxes*—they aren't powerful,
but they make their homes among the rocks.
27 Locusts—they have no king,
but they march in formation.
28 Lizards—they are easy to catch,
but they are found even in kings' palaces.

29 There are three things that walk with stately stride—
no, four that strut about:
30 the lion, king of animals, who won't turn aside for anything,
31 the strutting rooster,
the male goat,
a king as he leads his army.

32 If you have been a fool by being proud or plotting evil, 30:32 Job 21:5; 40:4 Mic 7:16
cover your mouth in shame.

33 As the beating of cream yields butter 30:33 Prov 10:12; 29:22
and striking the nose causes bleeding,
so stirring up anger causes quarrels.

THE SAYINGS OF KING LEMUEL

31 The sayings of King Lemuel contain this message,* which his mother taught him.

2 O my son, O son of my womb, 31:2 1 Sam 1:11 Isa 49:15
O son of my vows,
3 do not waste your strength on women, 31:3 Deut 17:17 1 Kgs 11:1 Prov 5:9
on those who ruin kings.

4 It is not for kings, O Lemuel, to guzzle wine. 31:4 Prov 20:1 Eccl 10:16-17 Isa 5:22-23 Hos 4:11
Rulers should not crave alcohol.
5 For if they drink, they may forget the law 31:5 Deut 16:19 Prov 17:15
and not give justice to the oppressed.
6 Alcohol is for the dying,
and wine for those in bitter distress.
7 Let them drink to forget their poverty
and remember their troubles no more.

30:26 Or *Coneys,* or *Rock badgers.* 31:1 Or *of Lemuel, king of Massa;* or *of King Lemuel, an oracle.*

31:1-9 Though credited to Lemuel, these proverbs were taught to him by his mother. So Proverbs begins (Proverbs 1–9) with a father teaching wisdom to his son, and the final chapter closes with a mother's wisdom for a son who would be a king: a description of a noble wife.

31:1-30 The sayings of King Lemuel resemble sayings that were used in both Egypt and Babylon to equip future rulers to live and reign properly. Though some people credit Lemuel with only the first nine verses, there are thematic and grammatical consistencies that support Lemuel as the source for the entire chapter.

▸ CHURCH
31:9 Speak up for the helpless. We should take the time to speak up for the helpless because that is exactly what Jesus did for us. When we were deep in sin and enemies of God, He died for us. He gave His lifeblood so that His people would have eternal life. If He sacrificed that much for us, how can we do less for others? Who is helpless around you? A fatherless child? A single mother trying to raise children on her own? Someone who is disabled and cannot work? A person beaten down by prejudice? Ask God to lead you to someone you can help in Jesus' name. (***See Church****> Mission> Nurture> Fostering community,* TopicGuide page A49.)

31:8 Job 29:12-17 Isa 58:9-10 Ps 82:3-5

8 Speak up for those who cannot speak for themselves;
ensure justice for those being crushed.
9 Yes, speak up for the poor and helpless,
and see that they get justice.

31:9 Lev 19:15 Isa 1:17

A WIFE OF NOBLE CHARACTER

31:10 Ruth 3:11 Prov 12:4; 19:14

10*Who can find a virtuous and capable wife?
She is more precious than rubies.
11 Her husband can trust her,
and she will greatly enrich his life.
12 She brings him good, not harm,
all the days of her life.

31:13 1 Tim 2:9-10

13 She finds wool and flax
and busily spins it.
14 She is like a merchant's ship,
bringing her food from afar.

31:15 Rom 12:11

15 She gets up before dawn to prepare breakfast
for her household
and plan the day's work for her servant girls.

16 She goes to inspect a field and buys it;
with her earnings she plants a vineyard.
17 She is energetic and strong,
a hard worker.
18 She makes sure her dealings are profitable;
her lamp burns late into the night.

19 Her hands are busy spinning thread,
her fingers twisting fiber.

31:20 Deut 15:11 Eph 4:28

20 She extends a helping hand to the poor
and opens her arms to the needy.
21 She has no fear of winter for her household,
for everyone has warm* clothes.

22 She makes her own bedspreads.
She dresses in fine linen and purple gowns.
23 Her husband is well known at the city gates,
where he sits with the other civic leaders.

31:10 Verses 10-31 comprise a Hebrew acrostic poem; each verse begins with a successive letter of the Hebrew alphabet.
31:21 As in Greek and Latin versions; Hebrew reads *scarlet*.

▸ HOLINESS

31:10 Finding a worthy wife. The world tells young men who are seeking wives to look at the outward appearance. Inner character is not deemed important. And the world doesn't even consider spiritual qualities. To counter this message, the church and parents must give thorough guidance regarding the qualities of a noble woman. They must point out the consequences of choosing a bad marriage partner, plus the benefits of choosing well. Godly characteristics must be held in high esteem. Have a plan—they won't learn God's message about marriage unless you make an effort to teach them to resist the world's message and embrace God's. By God's grace, they'll raise a godly generation who will embrace biblical values, filling God's world with men and women who love one another God's way. (***See Holiness**> Submission> Yielding to Spirit> Resist the world's influence,* TopicGuide page A41.)

31:10-31 These verses in Hebrew are arranged as an acrostic poem. The first word of verse 10 begins with *aleph*, the first letter of the Hebrew alphabet. Then each following verse begins with the next letter in the alphabet. This literary form is not uncommon in the Hebrew text of the Old Testament. Numerous psalms are acrostic (Psalm 119 is the largest), and each chapter in Lamentations is set up this way. In a sense, the verses here present the noble wife "from A to Z."

24 She makes belted linen garments
and sashes to sell to the merchants.

25 She is clothed with strength and dignity,
and she laughs without fear of the future.
26 When she speaks, her words are wise,
and she gives instructions with kindness.
27 She carefully watches everything in her household
and suffers nothing from laziness.

28 Her children stand and bless her.
Her husband praises her:
29 "There are many virtuous and capable women in the world,
but you surpass them all!"

30 Charm is deceptive, and beauty does not last;
but a woman who fears the LORD will be greatly praised.
31 Reward her for all she has done.
Let her deeds publicly declare her praise.

31:26
Prov 10:31

31:27
Prov 19:15

31:30
Prov 22:4

31:31
Prov 11:16

ECCLESIASTES

PURPOSE

To demonstrate the foolishness of secular thinking and the rewards of fearing God.

It's easy to be cynical about life these days: the bad guys often finish first, leaders let us down, and efforts at virtue seem to go unrewarded. Everywhere we look we see abundant reasons to be cynical and apathetic. If we are to live successfully in a world gone bad, we must learn to live by faith.

Ecclesiastes (meaning "preacher") is a book that applies wisdom to a world gone awry—a world that doesn't seem to be governed by a God of justice or equity. The author recounts his efforts to find fulfillment in life through the best the world has to offer. He discovers that "everything is meaningless . . . completely meaningless!" (1:2). This is the perspective of a secular man, possessing no fear of the Lord. By the end of the book, it is written: "Fear God and obey His commands, for this is everyone's duty" (12:13). Nothing else gives the proper perspective on work, pleasure, family, or education except the fear of God.

DISCOVER GOD IN ECCLESIASTES

Even though life can seem meaningless, Ecclesiastes presents God as the constant—the one reality that gives meaning to all things.

Timelessness: The ever-present reality of time adds a measure of futility to human life: Things happen at the "wrong time"; we work for a "long time" to succeed, and then our hard work is undone by circumstances beyond our control; we don't have "adequate time" to accomplish what we desire; and time "drags" when we are in the midst of suffering. Time is an antagonist because we have no control over it; it is an unrelenting governor over our lives. But it is not so with God. The Scriptures teach us that God is eternal (Deuteronomy 33:27; Psalm 41:13; 1 Timothy 1:17), unaffected by the passage of time on earth. God sees everything at once: past, present, and future. From His perspective, "For everything there is a season, a time for every activity under heaven" (3:1). We see only individual events and don't understand their connection, whereas God sees all events as a whole. We see the pieces of the puzzle, whereas God views the completed puzzle. God's timelessness inspires faith and gives meaning to every moment of our lives.

Benevolence: Ecclesiastes recaptures the theme of the benevolence of God from the first two chapters of Genesis. In His benevolence—His generosity and goodwill—God created people to live in enjoyment of Him forever. However, sin's entrance into the world (Genesis 3) spoiled that design. Instead of enjoying life in response to a benevolent Creator, we use and abuse life as a source of pleasure—enjoyment as an end in itself. However, Ecclesiastes points out that God is still benevolent; despite our abuse of the privilege of living in His world,

He offers us great joy. In numerous passages, Solomon exhorts his readers to enjoy life to the fullest, for it is for our pleasure that God made it enjoyable (3:13; 5:18; 8:15; 9:7). And yet, God's benevolence in this sin-stained world is only a foretaste of the joy that is yet to be revealed (Revelation 19:7).

GROWING THROUGH ECCLESIASTES

Like Proverbs, Ecclesiastes touches on the gritty realities of life in a fallen and frustrating world—and provides the solution.

Finding Meaning in Life: The idea that life is meaningless is expressed more than twenty times in Ecclesiastes, and life "under the sun" is mentioned almost thirty times. The point is that life, viewed from a human perspective, seems to be nothing but unending cycles of meaningless events; that there is nothing new under the sun. The Teacher is saying, "I've looked everywhere and can find nothing new or meaningful in and of itself." This is a message of realism, for life can indeed seem futile and meaningless apart from God. Therefore, to find true meaning in life, we have to begin and end with God. As a Protestant confession of faith puts it, "The chief end of man is to glorify God and enjoy Him forever."

DISCOVERY VERSES

For everything there is a season, a time for every activity under heaven.
(ECCLESIASTES 3:1)

Here now is my final conclusion: Fear God and obey His commands, for this is everyone's duty. God will judge us for everything we do, including every secret thing, whether good or bad.
(ECCLESIASTES 12:13-14)

Learning to Enjoy Life: Jesus Christ echoed the message of Ecclesiastes when He declared that He had come to give "a rich and satisfying life" (John 10:10b). Unfortunately, many Christians seem to live by an Eleventh Commandment: "Thou shalt not enjoy life." If life is not to be full and abundant, to what are we inviting those who do not know Christ? As the great English evangelist John Wesley said, "Sour godliness is the Devil's religion." Enjoyment, on the other hand, is the natural overflow of a life lived in reverence to God.

ECCLESIASTES FACTS

Author: While Solomon is not named as the author, numerous clues in the book point to his material: The author claims to be the king of Israel and the son of David (1:1, 12); the great wisdom of the author is a theme (1:16). The author wrote and collected many proverbs (12:9); and the description of the author's lifestyle parallels that of Solomon (2:4-9). However, the book was not fully completed until sometime after Solomon's lifetime (see editorial note at Ecclesiastes 12:9).

Written to: Like Proverbs, Ecclesiastes was written for the Israelite community at large. But there are special sections addressing students and young men in chapters 11–12.

Date of writing: Ecclesiastes was likely written sometime between the latter years of Solomon's life and reign (which ended 930 BC) and the fall of Jerusalem (586 BC).

Setting: Ancient Israel during the chaotic times after Solomon.

OUTLINE

- **ECCLESIASTES 1:1-2**—Prologue
- **ECCLESIASTES 1:3–3:8**—Shortcomings of Human Work and Wisdom
- **ECCLESIASTES 3:9–6:7**—Enduring Quality of God's Work
- **ECCLESIASTES 6:8–12:7**—Unfathomable Quality of God's Wisdom
- **ECCLESIASTES 12:8-14**—Epilogue

1:2 Pss 39:5-6; 62:9; 144:4 Eccl 12:8 Rom 8:20
1:3 Eccl 2:11; 3:9; 5:16
1:4 Pss 104:5; 119:90
1:6 Eccl 11:5 John 3:8
1:8 Prov 27:20 Eccl 4:8
1:11 Eccl 2:16; 9:5
1:12 Eccl 1:1; 7:27; 12:8-10
1:13 Eccl 1:17; 3:10-11; 7:25; 8:17
1:14 Eccl 2:11; 4:4; 6:9
1:15 Eccl 7:13

1 These are the words of the Teacher,* King David's son, who ruled in Jerusalem.

EVERYTHING IS MEANINGLESS

2"Everything is meaningless," says the Teacher, "completely meaningless!"
3What do people get for all their hard work under the sun? 4Generations come and gen-
erations go, but the earth never changes. 5The sun rises and the sun sets, then hurries
around to rise again. 6The wind blows south, and then turns north. Around and around it
goes, blowing in circles. 7Rivers run into the sea, but the sea is never full. Then the water
returns again to the rivers and flows out again to the sea. 8Everything is wearisome be-
yond description. No matter how much we see, we are never satisfied. No matter how
much we hear, we are not content.
9History merely repeats itself. It has all been done before. Nothing under the sun is truly
new. 10Sometimes people say, "Here is something new!" But actually it is old; nothing is
ever truly new. 11We don't remember what happened in the past, and in future genera-
tions, no one will remember what we are doing now.

THE TEACHER SPEAKS: THE FUTILITY OF WISDOM

12I, the Teacher, was king of Israel, and I lived in Jerusalem. 13I devoted myself to search
for understanding and to explore by wisdom everything being done under heaven. I soon
discovered that God has dealt a tragic existence to the human race. 14I observed every-
thing going on under the sun, and really, it is all meaningless—like chasing the wind.

15What is wrong cannot be made right.
What is missing cannot be recovered.

1:1 Hebrew *Qoheleth;* this term is rendered "the Teacher" throughout this book.

1:1 The author is called "the Teacher" and "David's son" (see also Ecclesiastes 1:12). His royal position, as well as the title he had been given, gives great weight to his advice to the godly and to his critique of secular, godless thinking. His words are not to be ignored any more than you would ignore the words of the king.

1:2 The Hebrew word for "meaningless" occurs 36 times in Ecclesiastes. It comes from a root meaning "breath" or "vapor." It could also be translated "absurd," "futile," "transitory," "temporary," or "ridiculous." It describes various aspects of life that are not the way they ought to be, and for this reason they are beyond explanation—at least for human beings who are not nearly as smart as they think they are.

▶ ADOPTION
1:2 Life is meaningless without God. Have you ever been depressed? As the Teacher begins his sermon, he sounds like he's depressed, but he is not—he is building a case for how life without God is futile. The Teacher is not satisfied until he makes us downright nervous about how far he will go to build his case. The Teacher wants us to taste the bitterness of lost love, to see the dark cloud of despair, to smell death itself; only then does he suggest that God might be the answer (see chapter 3). Don't be afraid to look at the dark chaos of this world, for only then will you truly appreciate the light and life offered through the good news of the gospel (Matthew 4:15-17). (***See Adoption****> With Christ> Redemption> Freedom from meaninglessness and despair,* TopicGuide page A37.)

1:3 The phrase "under the sun" occurs 29 times in Ecclesiastes, though it is occasionally omitted by the NLT to reduce repetition. The equivalent phrase "under heaven" occurs three times (see 1:13; 3:1; and 2:3 where the NLT reads "in this world"). These repeated phrases reveal a theme—the wise understand that life may be viewed from different perspectives; in this case, from earthly and heavenly perspectives.

1:4-8 The earth, the sun, the wind, the rivers, and the sea are aspects of God's creation that are fixed in a "wearisome" cycle of doing the same monotonous things over and over again—just like humanity, it would seem.

1:9-11 The Teacher warns that seeking fame by being the first to say, do, or invent something will end in frustration, for most people will fail in such pursuits, and those who are successful will not find ultimate satisfaction in it.

1:12-18 Solomon was uniquely qualified to find life's fulfillment in intellectual pursuits (see note at 1:1), but he found such an endeavor burdensome and unfulfilling.

▶ ADOPTION
1:14 A wild goose chase. Not every topic of study results in useful knowledge. In Ecclesiastes 1:12–2:24, the Teacher reviews various topics and reports that none of them provide meaning in life. Reason, unreason, pleasure, and pain—none of these can provide the fulfilling life that the Teacher believes exists. While some of the Teacher's studies prove more rewarding than others (wisdom is better than folly, see 2:13), nothing fills the God-shaped hole in his soul. If you have searched religion, relationships, or knowledge for a way to find God, stop looking around and start looking up—to God. (***See Adoption****> In Heaven> Complete in knowledge,* TopicGuide page A38.)

16 I said to myself, "Look, I am wiser than any of the kings who ruled in Jerusalem before
me. I have greater wisdom and knowledge than any of them." 17 So I set out to learn every-
thing from wisdom to madness and folly. But I learned firsthand that pursuing all this is
like chasing the wind.

18 The greater my wisdom, the greater my grief.
To increase knowledge only increases sorrow.

THE FUTILITY OF PLEASURE

2 I said to myself, "Come on, let's try pleasure. Let's look for the 'good things' in life."
But I found that this, too, was meaningless. 2 So I said, "Laughter is silly. What good
does it do to seek pleasure?" 3 After much thought, I decided to cheer myself with wine.
And while still seeking wisdom, I clutched at foolishness. In this way, I tried to experience
the only happiness most people find during their brief life in this world.

4 I also tried to find meaning by building huge homes for myself and by planting beautiful
vineyards. 5 I made gardens and parks, filling them with all kinds of fruit trees. 6 I built reser-
voirs to collect the water to irrigate my many flourishing groves. 7 I bought slaves, both men
and women, and others were born into my household. I also owned large herds and flocks,
more than any of the kings who had lived in Jerusalem before me. 8 I collected great sums of
silver and gold, the treasure of many kings and provinces. I hired wonderful singers, both
men and women, and had many beautiful concubines. I had everything a man could desire!

9 So I became greater than all who had lived in Jerusalem before me, and my wisdom
never failed me. 10 Anything I wanted, I would take. I denied myself no pleasure. I even
found great pleasure in hard work, a reward for all my labors. 11 But as I looked at every-
thing I had worked so hard to accomplish, it was all so meaningless—like chasing the
wind. There was nothing really worthwhile anywhere.

THE WISE AND THE FOOLISH

12 So I decided to compare wisdom with foolishness and madness (for who can do this
better than I, the king?*). 13 I thought, "Wisdom is better than foolishness, just as light is
better than darkness. 14 For the wise can see where they are going, but fools walk in the
dark." Yet I saw that the wise and the foolish share the same fate. 15 Both will die. So I said
to myself, "Since I will end up the same as the fool, what's the value of all my wisdom?
This is all so meaningless!" 16 For the wise and the foolish both die. The wise will not be re-
membered any longer than the fool. In the days to come, both will be forgotten.

17 So I came to hate life because everything done here under the sun is so troubling.
Everything is meaningless—like chasing the wind.

THE FUTILITY OF WORK

18 I came to hate all my hard work here on earth, for I must leave to others everything I
have earned. 19 And who can tell whether my successors will be wise or foolish? Yet they

1:16 1 Kgs 3:12; 4:30; 10:23
1:17 Eccl 2:12; 7:25
1:18 Eccl 12:12
2:1 Eccl 7:4, 6; 8:15
2:3 Judg 9:13; Eccl 6:12; 8:15; 12:13
2:4 1 Kgs 7:1-12; Song 8:10-11
2:5 Neh 2:8; Song 4:16; 5:1
2:6 Neh 2:14; 3:15-16
2:7 Gen 14:14; 15:3; 1 Kgs 4:23
2:8 1 Kgs 9:28; 10:10, 14
2:9 1 Chr 29:25; Eccl 1:16
2:10 Eccl 3:22; 5:18; 6:2; 9:9
2:11 Eccl 1:3, 14; 2:22; 3:9; 5:16
2:12 Eccl 1:9-10, 17; 7:25
2:13 Eccl 7:11-12, 19
2:14 Ps 49:10; Eccl 9:2-3
2:15 Eccl 2:16; 6:8, 11
2:16 Eccl 1:11; 2:14; 9:5
2:18 Pss 39:6; 49:10; Eccl 2:11

2:12 The meaning of the Hebrew is uncertain.

2:1 The Teacher either imagines or actually puts himself to the test to see if "pleasure" brings fulfillment. The verses that follow (2:2-11) show that the pleasures he had in mind were the luxuries that great wealth can buy (regarding Solomon's wealth, see 1 Kings 10:10-29). Such a pursuit turned out to be "meaningless."

2:2-3 "Laughter" and "wine" have been means of searching for happiness for many people since the beginning of human existence, but the Teacher learned very quickly that such happiness was temporary and thus "foolishness." The basic problem of life—human mortality ("during their brief life in this world")—remained unsolved.

2:4-11 The Teacher attempted to find real significance in life through vast building projects, amassing great wealth (see note at 2:1), and attaining an impressive harem (see 1 Kings 11:3), but they proved to be "meaningless" since none of it was "really worthwhile."

2:19 Another frustrating aspect of life for the Teacher was that after he died he would have no control over what his "successors" would do with all that he had accomplished in his life (see also 2:21).

2:21 Eccl 2:18; 4:4 will control everything I have gained by my skill and hard work under the sun. How
meaningless! 20So I gave up in despair, questioning the value of all my hard work in this
2:22 Eccl 1:3 world.
21Some people work wisely with knowledge and skill, then must leave the fruit of their
2:23 Job 5:7; 14:1 Ps 127:2 Eccl 1:18 efforts to someone who hasn't worked for it. This, too, is meaningless, a great tragedy. 22So
what do people get in this life for all their hard work and anxiety? 23Their days of labor are
filled with pain and grief; even at night their minds cannot rest. It is all meaningless.
2:24 Eccl 2:3; 3:12, 22; 5:18; 6:12; 8:15; 9:7 24So I decided there is nothing better than to enjoy food and drink and to find satisfac-
tion in work. Then I realized that these pleasures are from the hand of God. 25For who can
2:26 Job 27:16-17; 32:8 Eccl 1:14 eat or enjoy anything apart from Him?* 26God gives wisdom, knowledge, and joy to those
who please Him. But if a sinner becomes wealthy, God takes the wealth away and gives it
to those who please Him. This, too, is meaningless—like chasing the wind.

A TIME FOR EVERYTHING

3:1 Eccl 3:17; 8:6 **3** 1 For everything there is a season,
a time for every activity under heaven.
3:2 Heb 9:27 2 A time to be born and a time to die.
A time to plant and a time to harvest.
3 A time to kill and a time to heal.
A time to tear down and a time to build up.
3:4 Exod 15:20 Ps 126:2 Rom 12:15 4 A time to cry and a time to laugh.
A time to grieve and a time to dance.
5 A time to scatter stones and a time to gather stones.
A time to embrace and a time to turn away.
6 A time to search and a time to quit searching.
A time to keep and a time to throw away.
3:7 Amos 5:13 7 A time to tear and a time to mend.
A time to be quiet and a time to speak.
3:8 Ps 101:3 8 A time to love and a time to hate.
A time for war and a time for peace.

2:25 As in Greek and Syriac versions; Hebrew reads *apart from Me?*

2:24-26 The phrase "there is nothing better" (2:24) does not mean that enjoying food, drink, and work is the ultimate good, but that determining to enjoy God's provisions in life is the proper attitude to have. It is both "meaningless" and "chasing the wind" (2:26) to make the enjoyment of such pleasures one's primary purpose in life. Realizing that these are gifts from God keeps life's priorities in order and in proper perspective.

▸ MINISTRY
2:25 The God life. Many people strive for the good life, but when the good life is separated from the "God life," it's meaningless. Like water to a thirsty man, pleasure is diminished if it's not a relief from the hard work with which God has honored us. Every nap, every game, every bite of food—it's all better when taken in the context of hard work for God's glory (1 Corinthians 10:31). (***See Ministry****> Transformation> Fill and Subdue> Influencing every sphere of life,* TopicGuide page A57.)

▸ PURPOSE
3:1 The rhythm of life. If you've ever had someone close to you die, you no doubt felt like it was too soon. There never seems to be a "best" time to die, to go to war, or to cry (3:1-9). Yet this ancient poem speaks deeply to us because, while our emotions may not easily adapt to it, our minds know that there is a season for all things. And while the "Why?" may escape us (see 3:11), the undulation of life and death is as dependable as the rising and setting of the sun (1:5). The wise person is flexible—not fighting the inescapable cadence of life, but holding on loosely to pleasure, good health, and peace, for such things will not last. When you are facing a difficult time of transition or loss, trust God's perfect timing. (***See Purpose****> God's Means> God's Sovereignty> God has always had a plan,* TopicGuide page A52.)

3:1-8 In this poetic masterpiece about the nature of life "under heaven," the Teacher explains that various things in life are certain to happen. Events in our world are not random, but neither are they under human control, and recognizing this will help us cope with life's inevitable difficulties. Each occurs as part of human existence and reminds us as humans that we are limited by time, though fit for eternity (see note at 3:11-13).

3:8 The Teacher is not advocating hate or war but simply recognizing that they are inevitable results of living in a corrupt, sinful world.

9 What do people really get for all their hard work? 10 I have seen the burden God has
placed on us all. 11 Yet God has made everything beautiful for its own time. He has planted
eternity in the human heart, but even so, people cannot see the whole scope of God's
work from beginning to end. 12 So I concluded there is nothing better than to be happy and
enjoy ourselves as long as we can. 13 And people should eat and drink and enjoy the fruits
of their labor, for these are gifts from God.

14 And I know that whatever God does is final. Nothing can be added to it or taken from
it. God's purpose is that people should fear Him. 15 What is happening now has happened
before, and what will happen in the future has happened before, because God makes the
same things happen over and over again.

THE INJUSTICES OF LIFE

16 I also noticed that under the sun there is evil in the courtroom. Yes, even the courts of
law are corrupt! 17 I said to myself, "In due season God will judge everyone, both good and
bad, for all their deeds."

3:11 Gen 1:31; Job 5:9; Eccl 8:17; Rom 11:33
3:14 Eccl 5:7; 7:18; 8:12-13; 12:13
3:16 Eccl 4:1; 5:8; 8:9
3:17 Gen 18:25; Pss 96:13; 98:9; Eccl 3:1; 8:6; Matt 16:27; Rom 2:6-10; 2 Thes 1:6-9

▸ **GOD**

3:11 Beautiful tragedy. How does God do it? How does everything, even loss, end up beautiful through God? It's His commitment to bring beauty out of even the worst circumstances that should cause us to worship Him with even more awe. Look at the death of Christ: There is no greater tragedy than the death of Christ, yet there is no greater beauty than the salvation that it purchased for all God's people. Learn to look for His glory; it shines through the ugliest of circumstances. (***See God****> God's Nature> Personality> Will> He accomplishes His purposes and good pleasure,* TopicGuide page A14.)

▸ **GOD**

3:11 Eternity in our heart. Have you ever tried to think about "forever"? Did it make your head hurt? It should. But the fact that you can think about it at all hints at the fact that God has "planted eternity in the human heart." By definition, eternity is a duration of time that cannot be measured. God is called eternal (Genesis 21:33; Isaiah 26:4; 40:28) in the sense that He always was and always will be. And while God has given us the ability to contemplate eternity, this still doesn't mean we can truly understand it. God gives you the capacity to look into the vastness of His being. You may not understand Him, but that doesn't mean you can't be filled with wonder (and perhaps feel a bit dizzy) at the immensity of His being. Worship your awesome God today! (***See God****> God's Attributes> Eternal> God is eternal,* TopicGuide page A16.)

3:11-13 Humans long for things that last, especially a legacy for themselves and their loved ones after them. This longing exists because God "has planted eternity in the human heart." Since God has done this, humans can never be fully satisfied with things that are temporal, existing only in time on this side of eternity (see note at 3:1-8). Regarding the phrase "nothing better," see note at 2:24-26.

3:14-15 The Teacher provides a divine perspective on the frustration that comes from events that are beyond your control (see note at 3:1-8). All events are under God's control; they always have been and always will be.

3:16-17 Despite the fact that our world is full of injustice—even "in the courtroom"—the Teacher reminds us that God will have the final word by bringing judgment on everyone "for all their deeds," sometimes in this life but certainly in the next.

MY RESPONSE TO GOD

Two Are Better Than One

ECCLESIASTES 4:9-12

Have you ever tried to relocate all your possessions all by yourself? Or to drop your car off for repairs and then get back to work without some assistance? When we are overwhelmed with difficult tasks, we discover how important it is to have friends who can help us. "Two people are better off than one, for they can help each other succeed" (Ecclesiastes 4:9). The same is true for our Christian journey. Jesus told His disciples to love one another, to pray together, and to serve one another. We face temptations daily, and on our own we can quickly fall. We need others to support us, counsel us, and encourage us to stand strong in our faith. "A person standing alone can be attacked and defeated, but two can stand back-to-back and conquer. Three are even better, for a triple-braided cord is not easily broken" (Ecclesiastes 4:12).

Who stands with you during your struggles? Who encourages you in your faith and life? If you are not sure, perhaps this is why you feel incomplete and lonely, for God designed us to function best in community.

3:18 18 I also thought about the human condition—how God proves to people that they are
Pss 49:12, 20; 73:22 like animals. 19 For people and animals share the same fate—both breathe* and both must
3:20 Gen 3:19 die. So people have no real advantage over the animals. How meaningless! 20 Both go to
Ps 103:14 the same place—they came from dust and they return to dust. 21 For who can prove that
Eccl 12:7 the human spirit goes up and the spirit of animals goes down into the earth? 22 So I saw
3:22 Eccl 2:18, 24; 6:12; that there is nothing better for people than to be happy in their work. That is why we are
8:7; 10:14 here! No one will bring us back from death to enjoy life after we die.

4:1 Eccl 3:16; 5:8 **4** Again, I observed all the oppression that takes place under the sun. I saw the tears of
Isa 5:7 the oppressed, with no one to comfort them. The oppressors have great power, and
Lam 1:9 their victims are helpless. 2 So I concluded that the dead are better off than the living. 3 But
4:2 Job 3:11-26 most fortunate of all are those who are not yet born. For they have not seen all the evil
Eccl 2:17 that is done under the sun.
4 Then I observed that most people are motivated to success because they envy their
neighbors. But this, too, is meaningless—like chasing the wind.

4:5 Prov 6:10; 24:33 5 "Fools fold their idle hands,
Isa 9:20 leading them to ruin."

4:6 Prov 15:16-17; 16:8 6 And yet,
"Better to have one handful with quietness
than two handfuls with hard work
and chasing the wind."

THE ADVANTAGES OF COMPANIONSHIP

4:8 Prov 27:20 7 I observed yet another example of something meaningless under the sun. 8 This is the
Eccl 1:8; 2:21; 5:10 case of a man who is all alone, without a child or a brother, yet who works hard to gain as
much wealth as he can. But then he asks himself, "Who am I working for? Why am I giving
up so much pleasure now?" It is all so meaningless and depressing.
9 Two people are better off than one, for they can help each other succeed. 10 If one person
4:11 1 Kgs 1:1-4 falls, the other can reach out and help. But someone who falls alone is in real trouble. 11 Like-
wise, two people lying close together can keep each other warm. But how can one be warm
alone? 12 A person standing alone can be attacked and defeated, but two can stand back-to-
back and conquer. Three are even better, for a triple-braided cord is not easily broken.

THE FUTILITY OF POLITICAL POWER

4:13 Eccl 7:19; 9:15 13 It is better to be a poor but wise youth than an old and foolish king who refuses all ad-
4:14 Gen 41:14, 41-43 vice. 14 Such a youth could rise from poverty and succeed. He might even become king,

3:19 Or *both have the same spirit.*

▶ GOD

4:1 Political uncertainty. Misrule and poor leadership frustrate the writer of Ecclesiastes, as they do us. The Teacher takes solace in the future judgment of evil politicians (3:16-17; 8:10-13) but also anguishes over the oppression of the poor, political intrigue (5:8), and the misuse of power (8:9). Governments prosper under virtuous leadership (10:17), but nothing is certain—at any moment, fools can overwhelm a nation (10:5-6, 16). In the end, we must trust that God holds the hearts of even the greatest kings in His mighty hands (Proverbs 21:1), and we must do all we can as citizens and Christians to see justice done (1 Peter 3:12). Investigate how you could be more involved in promoting responsible political service. (***See God*** > *God's Attributes* > *Sovereign* > *He raises and removes rulers,* TopicGuide page A17.)

4:1-3 The Teacher observes another of life's great inequalities: the oppressed have no one to help them. This, of course, is not always the case, but it is the case much too often. The Teacher explains that those who are dead—better yet, those who never lived—are much better off than those who live now and have to see such unfair suffering.

4:5-6 The Teacher warns against two extreme attitudes about work: being too lazy to work or being too obsessed with work to enjoy life.

4:7-8 Acquiring great wealth is "meaningless and depressing" if the wealthy person has no one to share it with.

4:9-12 Being a loner can be frustrating and dangerous since one can accomplish more if he has help and since a partner can help to protect him from adversaries if trouble comes.

4:13-16 Wise living involves the willingness to take advice, whether you are poor, young, rich, or privileged.

though he has been in prison. 15But then everyone rushes to the side of yet another
youth* who replaces him. 16Endless crowds stand around him,* but then another genera-
tion grows up and rejects him, too. So it is all meaningless—like chasing the wind.

APPROACHING GOD WITH CARE

5 1*As you enter the house of God, keep your ears open and your mouth shut. It is evil
to make mindless offerings to God. 2*Don't make rash promises, and don't be hasty
in bringing matters before God. After all, God is in heaven, and you are here on earth. So
let your words be few.
3Too much activity gives you restless dreams; too many words make you a fool.
4When you make a promise to God, don't delay in following through, for God takes no
pleasure in fools. Keep all the promises you make to Him. 5It is better to say nothing than
to make a promise and not keep it. 6Don't let your mouth make you sin. And don't defend
yourself by telling the Temple messenger that the promise you made was a mistake. That
would make God angry, and He might wipe out everything you have achieved.
7Talk is cheap, like daydreams and other useless activities. Fear God instead.

THE FUTILITY OF WEALTH

8Don't be surprised if you see a poor person being oppressed by the powerful and if justice
is being miscarried throughout the land. For every official is under orders from higher up,
and matters of justice get lost in red tape and bureaucracy. 9Even the king milks the land
for his own profit!*
10Those who love money will never have enough. How meaningless to think that
wealth brings true happiness! 11The more you have, the more people come to help you
spend it. So what good is wealth—except perhaps to watch it slip through your fingers!
12People who work hard sleep well, whether they eat little or much. But the rich seldom
get a good night's sleep.
13There is another serious problem I have seen under the sun. Hoarding riches harms
the saver. 14Money is put into risky investments that turn sour, and everything is lost. In

4:16 Eccl 1:14
5:1 Exod 3:5; 30:18-20; 1 Sam 15:22; Prov 15:8; 21:27; Isa 1:12
5:2 Prov 10:19; 20:25; Matt 6:7
5:4 Num 30:2; Pss 50:14; 66:13-14; 76:11
5:5 Prov 20:25; Acts 5:4
5:6 Lev 4:2, 22; Num 15:25
5:7 Eccl 3:14; 12:13
5:8 Ps 12:5; Eccl 4:1; Ezek 18:18; 1 Pet 4:12
5:11 Eccl 2:9
5:12 Prov 3:24

4:15 Hebrew *the second youth.* 4:16 Hebrew *There is no end to all the people, to all those who are before them.* 5:1 Verse 5:1 is numbered 4:17 in Hebrew text. 5:2 Verses 5:2-20 are numbered 5:1-19 in Hebrew text. 5:9 The meaning of the Hebrew in verses 8 and 9 is uncertain.

5:1-7 The Teacher gives some advice about worship (here "the house of God" is the Temple). We need to enter God's presence with quiet reverence, preparing ourselves to listen to Him instead of talking. We also need to be careful about making "rash promises" to God, since we don't know what the future holds or whether we can follow through on what we told Him we would do. Yet we must keep whatever promises we do make. Reverence before God and submission to His sovereignty are key elements of true worship.

▶ ADOPTION
5:2 Much talk, much sin. How many times have you said, "Why did I say that?" Our holy fear of God should first move us to quietness and humility, not jabbering. Too many Christians, even the most mature, think it is a sign of spirituality to talk about God—and everything else—constantly. But this book of wisdom advises us to cultivate a spiritual life that is not based on our words, but God's. God often wants us to keep our ears open and our mouths shut (5:1)—for our own sake (5:6) and for His glory. (See Psalm 39:1; Proverbs 10:19; and James 1:19; also ***see Adoption****> With Christ> Supernatural> No foolish talk,* TopicGuide page A37.)

▶ CHURCH
5:7 Dreaming away our lives. Another way that life is rendered meaningless is when we spend too much time daydreaming or living in a fantasy world. In general, we should not waste our lives with meaningless or escapist activities—our lives should make a positive difference. Specifically, we should avoid wasting time when we should be working. Following the wishes of our employer and respecting those in authority over us go hand in hand with fearing God. Instead of spending time playing games or surfing the Internet or daydreaming (or even reading your *Discover God Study Bible*!), be diligent during your time at work. (***See Church****> Role> Preach> Topics> Godly Lives> Live quietly and work hard,* TopicGuide page A50.)

5:8-9 Corruption in government is so common that no one should be surprised when it happens. The pursuit of a perfect government, like the pursuit of ultimate riches, is futile.

5:10-15 The Teacher gives seven warnings about wealth: First, loving money brings a desire for more than you already have; second, loving money results in the absurd belief that more of it will make you happy; third, other people will want the money you have; fourth, money easily disappears; fifth, wealthy people have worries in life that others do not have; sixth, hoarding wealth can be destructive to the owner; and seventh, bad investments can cause a wealthy person to lose everything and end up with nothing.

5:15 the end, there is nothing left to pass on to one's children. 15We all come to the end of our
Job 1:21 Ps 49:17 lives as naked and empty-handed as on the day we were born. We can't take our riches
1 Tim 6:7 with us.
5:16 16And this, too, is a very serious problem. People leave this world no better off than
Prov 11:29 when they came. All their hard work is for nothing—like working for the wind. 17Through-
Eccl 1:3; 2:11; 3:9 out their lives, they live under a cloud—frustrated, discouraged, and angry.
5:17 18Even so, I have noticed one thing, at least, that is good. It is good for people to eat,
Eccl 2:23 drink, and enjoy their work under the sun during the short life God has given them, and to
5:18 Eccl 2:10, 24 accept their lot in life. 19And it is a good thing to receive wealth from God and the good
5:19 health to enjoy it. To enjoy your work and accept your lot in life—this is indeed a gift from
2 Chr 1:12 God. 20God keeps such people so busy enjoying life that they take no time to brood over
Eccl 3:13; 6:2 the past.

6:1 **6** There is another serious tragedy I have seen under the sun, and it weighs heavily on
Eccl 5:13 humanity. 2God gives some people great wealth and honor and everything they
6:2 1 Kgs 3:13 could ever want, but then He doesn't give them the chance to enjoy these things. They
Pss 17:14; 73:7 die, and someone else, even a stranger, ends up enjoying their wealth! This is meaning-
less—a sickening tragedy.
6:3 3A man might have a hundred children and live to be very old. But if he finds no satis-
Job 3:16 Eccl 4:3 faction in life and doesn't even get a decent burial, it would have been better for him to be
Isa 14:20 born dead. 4His birth would have been meaningless, and he would have ended in dark-
Matt 26:24 ness. He wouldn't even have had a name, 5and he would never have seen the sun or
known of its existence. Yet he would have had more peace than in growing up to be an
6:6 unhappy man. 6He might live a thousand years twice over but still not find contentment.
Eccl 2:14 And since he must die like everyone else—well, what's the use?
6:7 7All people spend their lives scratching for food, but they never seem to have enough.
Prov 16:26 8So are wise people really better off than fools? Do poor people gain anything by being
6:8 Eccl 2:15 wise and knowing how to act in front of others?
9Enjoy what you have rather than desiring what you don't have. Just dreaming about
6:9 Eccl 1:14; 11:9 nice things is meaningless—like chasing the wind.

▸ **BIBLE**

5:15 Certain death. Of all the misfortune and chaos the writer of Ecclesiastes spotlights, one thing is certain: death. Even mighty wisdom is cut short by death (2:13-17), and riches are stripped away by our demise. In a godless world, adding up everything we have ever done comes to the same result at death—zero. In a godless world, there is no one keeping count of good or bad. There is no justice except that the evil (as well as the good) die. In a world without God, death is the ultimate leveler, breaking down every difference in humanity until we are all the same—dust. But the resurrection of Christ (1 Corinthians 15:12-20) and the promised resurrection of all humanity (Daniel 12:2; John 5:28; Acts 24:15) show us that death does not have the final word—God does. How can you prepare yourself for your death? What practical and spiritual steps must you take to be ready for that day? (***See Bible****> Unity> Doctrines> Principle of death,* TopicGuide page A10.)

5:16-17 The very things that people sacrifice and sweat and work for are often the least valuable at death. If we realize this and still do not make the necessary changes in our lives, we will encounter grief and remorse.

5:18-20 One aspect of a life well lived is the ability to enjoy the things God has provided. The person who does this avoids regret (5:17, 20) because he accepts health and wealth as gracious gifts from God, not as expected rewards based on hard work.

6:1-2 One of the ironies of being wealthy is that—despite their riches—wealthy people are often unable to enjoy what they have.

6:3-6 Numerous children and a long life do not guarantee satisfaction or fulfillment in life, for death will eventually claim everyone.

▸ **GOD**

6:9 Contentment is everything. From the Ten Commandments (Exodus 20:1-17) to the New Testament (Hebrews 13:5), God warns us against the sin of greed and covetousness and encourages us to be satisfied with what we have. But that sounds hollow, especially against the daily assault of mass marketing schemes designed to cause us to feel empty, ugly, or stupid without a certain product. Yet we can learn to take pleasure in the joys of this world by valuing God more. Without God, even the fastest cars and the sweetest perfume are meaningless, for in the end, who cares if your hearse drives fast, or if your decaying body smells like roses? Being filled with God is the only way to live—and die—with a satisfied mind. (***See God****> God's Attributes> All-Present> God's continual presence brings contentment,* TopicGuide page A15.)

THE FUTURE—DETERMINED AND UNKNOWN

10Everything has already been decided. It was known long ago what each person would
be. So there's no use arguing with God about your destiny.
11The more words you speak, the less they mean. So what good are they?
12In the few days of our meaningless lives, who knows how our days can best be spent?
Our lives are like a shadow. Who can tell what will happen on this earth after we are gone?

6:10 Gen 3:17-19; Job 9:32; 40:2; Eccl 1:9; 3:15; Isa 45:9
6:11 Hos 12:1

WISDOM FOR LIFE

7 1 A good reputation is more valuable than costly perfume.
And the day you die is better than the day you are born.
2 Better to spend your time at funerals than at parties.
After all, everyone dies—
so the living should take this to heart.
3 Sorrow is better than laughter,
for sadness has a refining influence on us.
4 A wise person thinks a lot about death,
while a fool thinks only about having a good time.

5 Better to be criticized by a wise person
than to be praised by a fool.
6 A fool's laughter is quickly gone,
like thorns crackling in a fire.
This also is meaningless.

7 Extortion turns wise people into fools,
and bribes corrupt the heart.

8 Finishing is better than starting.
Patience is better than pride.

9 Control your temper,
for anger labels you a fool.

10 Don't long for "the good old days."
This is not wise.

11 Wisdom is even better when you have money.
Both are a benefit as you go through life.
12 Wisdom and money can get you almost anything,
but only wisdom can save your life.

13 Accept the way God does things,
for who can straighten what He has made crooked?

7:1 Prov 22:1; Eccl 4:2; 7:8
7:2 Ps 90:12; Eccl 2:16; 3:19-20; 9:2-3
7:3 Eccl 2:2; 2 Cor 7:10
7:5 Ps 141:5; Prov 6:23; 13:18; 15:31-32; 25:12; Eccl 9:17
7:6 Pss 58:9; 118:12; Eccl 2:2
7:7 Exod 23:8; Deut 16:19; Prov 17:23; Eccl 4:1; 5:8
7:8 Prov 14:29; 16:32; Eccl 7:1; Gal 5:22; Eph 4:2
7:9 Prov 14:17; Jas 1:19
7:11 Prov 8:10-11
7:12 Prov 3:18; 8:35; Eccl 9:18
7:13 Eccl 1:15; 3:11; 8:17

6:10-12 "Decided" is literally translated "named." That everything has already been named probably refers to Adam's naming of all the animals (Genesis 2:19-20), which showed Adam's authority over them. In the Hebrew underlying these verses, there are four occurrences of the Hebrew word *adam* (meaning "man" or "Adam"). The Teacher's point is that the father of all, Adam, sinned against God in the Garden of Eden in search of knowledge. The rest of humanity will also fail if they attempt to speak where they should be silent and attempt to know what is intended to be mystery.

7:1-4 A person who thinks seriously about death knows what is important in this life: a good reputation (literally "name") that continues after death. Also important is a determination to learn from sorrow instead of feigning tranquility.

7:5-6 A fool's praise is worthless, but often people want to hear what makes them feel better about themselves instead of what is true.

7:10 People tend to look on former days as so much better than what they are going through in the present, but every generation has their own difficulties, tragedies, and sorrows to deal with.

7:11-12 Conventional wisdom states that being wealthy is better than wisdom, but the Teacher denies this. The reason for wisdom's superiority is that it alone can save one's life; that is, wisdom preserves us so we can enjoy life as God intended His people to do.

7:13-14 Enjoying life is impossible without acknowledging God's sovereignty over all things and accepting both the prosperous times and the hard times that He sends our way.

14 Enjoy prosperity while you can,
but when hard times strike, realize that both come from God.
Remember that nothing is certain in this life.

THE LIMITS OF HUMAN WISDOM

15 I have seen everything in this meaningless life, including the death of good young people and the long life of wicked people. 16 So don't be too good or too wise! Why destroy yourself? 17 On the other hand, don't be too wicked either. Don't be a fool! Why die before your time? 18 Pay attention to these instructions, for anyone who fears God will avoid both extremes.*

19 One wise person is stronger than ten leading citizens of a town!

20 Not a single person on earth is always good and never sins.

21 Don't eavesdrop on others—you may hear your servant curse you. 22 For you know how often you yourself have cursed others.

23 I have always tried my best to let wisdom guide my thoughts and actions. I said to myself, "I am determined to be wise." But it didn't work. 24 Wisdom is always distant and difficult to find. 25 I searched everywhere, determined to find wisdom and to understand the reason for things. I was determined to prove to myself that wickedness is stupid and that foolishness is madness.

26 I discovered that a seductive woman* is a trap more bitter than death. Her passion is a snare, and her soft hands are chains. Those who are pleasing to God will escape her, but sinners will be caught in her snare.

27 "This is my conclusion," says the Teacher. "I discovered this after looking at the matter from every possible angle. 28 Though I have searched repeatedly, I have not found what I was looking for. Only one out of a thousand men is virtuous, but not one woman! 29 But I did find this: God created people to be virtuous, but they have each turned to follow their own downward path."

8

1 How wonderful to be wise,
to analyze and interpret things.

7:14 Deut 8:5; 26:11; Eccl 3:22; 9:7; 11:9
7:15 Eccl 6:12; 8:12-14; 9:9
7:16 Rom 12:3
7:17 Ps 55:23; Prov 10:27
7:18 Eccl 3:14; 5:7; 8:12-13
7:20 1 Kgs 8:46; 2 Chr 6:36; Ps 143:2; Prov 20:9; Rom 3:23
7:24 Deut 30:11-14; Job 11:7; 37:23; Rom 11:33
7:25 Eccl 1:17
7:26 Prov 5:4; 6:23-24; 7:23; 22:14
7:28 1 Kgs 11:3
7:29 Gen 1:27
8:1 Exod 34:29-30

7:18 Or *will follow them both.* 7:26 Hebrew *a woman.*

▸ HOLINESS

7:14 Everything from God. Have you ever, literally or figuratively, looked up at the sky and shaken your fist at God? If you did, even in your anger, you were acknowledging a theological truth—God is in control. Even our negative emotions testify that we believe God rules everything. While this may trouble us, perplex us, or go against everything we believe, we must honestly acknowledge that this is precisely what the author of Ecclesiastes teaches (1:13; 2:24-26; 3:14) and what the rest of the Bible echoes—God rules and sustains the universe, including a free humanity (Philippians 2:12-13; Proverbs 16:9; Psalm 103:19). The Teacher knows that those who look carefully at the world will see both blessing and chaos. The Teacher also knows that trusting in God's care and control gives us the emotional strength to live wisely in a world of both beauty and ugliness. (***See Holiness****> Changed by God> God provides> Temporal misery,* TopicGuide page A41.)

7:15-18 The Teacher is not downplaying the importance of goodness and wisdom. Instead, he is warning that an overemphasis on them can lead to a wasteful, falsely spiritual lifestyle that has no practical value. "Anyone who fears God" in verse 18 occurs close to the middle of the book and anticipates the Teacher's conclusion of all he says about life and its meaning (see note at 12:13-14).

▸ BIBLE

7:24 The great unknown. God wants us to know Him, but He can't be discovered by mere observation (Ecclesiastes 8:17). Yet true worship is, at least in part, listening carefully to God (Ecclesiastes 5:1). The Teacher exposes us to this tension: The unsearchable God reveals Himself, not by sight, but by faith, to those who humble themselves in worship before Him. It may be temporarily fulfilling to poke around in the darkness, going from one doctrine or one religion to the next, but we may only approach God by faith, in an attitude of humility. God will make Himself known to those who approach Him by faith. (***See Bible****> Unity> Salvation> Old Testament and New Testament teach salvation by faith,* TopicGuide page A11.)

7:26-27 The Teacher warns men that "a seductive woman" brings death and that it is better to simply avoid being around her. This theme is also common in Proverbs (2:16-19; 6:26; 7:6-27; 23:27-28; 29:3).

7:28 The Teacher does not mean that men are superior to women but that, as a man, he found a few lasting friendships with other men, but never with a woman. A woman teacher would be able to say the same thing in reverse. "One out of a thousand" is hyperbole for effect.

7:29 This verse is a clear allusion to Genesis 1–3, the creation and fall of humanity (literally *adam*). God created Adam "virtuous," but he rebelled against God to follow his "own downward path"—thus taking all humanity *(adam)* with him.

Wisdom lights up a person's face,
softening its harshness.

OBEDIENCE TO THE KING

2Obey the king since you vowed to God that you would. 3Don't try to avoid doing your
duty, and don't stand with those who plot evil, for the king can do whatever he wants. 4His
command is backed by great power. No one can resist or question it. 5Those who obey
him will not be punished. Those who are wise will find a time and a way to do what is
right, 6for there is a time and a way for everything, even when a person is in trouble.
7Indeed, how can people avoid what they don't know is going to happen? 8None of us
can hold back our spirit from departing. None of us has the power to prevent the day of
our death. There is no escaping that obligation, that dark battle. And in the face of death,
wickedness will certainly not rescue the wicked.

THE WICKED AND THE RIGHTEOUS

9I have thought deeply about all that goes on here under the sun, where people have the
power to hurt each other. 10I have seen wicked people buried with honor. Yet they were
the very ones who frequented the Temple and are now praised* in the same city where
they committed their crimes! This, too, is meaningless. 11When a crime is not punished
quickly, people feel it is safe to do wrong. 12But even though a person sins a hundred
times and still lives a long time, I know that those who fear God will be better off. 13The
wicked will not prosper, for they do not fear God. Their days will never grow long like the
evening shadows.
14And this is not all that is meaningless in our world. In this life, good people are often
treated as though they were wicked, and wicked people are often treated as though they
were good. This is so meaningless!
15So I recommend having fun, because there is nothing better for people in this world
than to eat, drink, and enjoy life. That way they will experience some happiness along
with all the hard work God gives them under the sun.
16In my search for wisdom and in my observation of people's burdens here on earth, I
discovered that there is ceaseless activity, day and night. 17I realized that no one can dis-
cover everything God is doing under the sun. Not even the wisest people discover every-
thing, no matter what they claim.

DEATH COMES TO ALL

9 This, too, I carefully explored: Even though the actions of godly and wise people are
in God's hands, no one knows whether God will show them favor. 2The same destiny

8:2 Exod 22:11; 2 Sam 21:7; Ezek 17:18
8:4 Job 9:12; Dan 4:35
8:5 Exod 1:17-21; Prov 12:21
8:8 Deut 20:5-8; Ps 49:7-9; Eccl 8:13
8:11 Exod 34:6; Ps 86:15; Rom 2:4-5; 2 Pet 3:9
8:12 Deut 4:40; Ps 37:11; Prov 1:33; Eccl 7:15; Isa 3:10
8:13 Eccl 6:12; 8:8; Isa 3:11
8:14 Job 21:7; Ps 73:3, 12; Eccl 7:15; Jer 12:1; Mal 3:15
8:15 Eccl 2:24; 3:12-13; 5:18; 9:7
9:1 Deut 33:3; Eccl 9:6; 10:14
9:2 Job 9:22; Eccl 2:14; 3:19; 6:6; 7:2

8:10 As in some Hebrew manuscripts and Greek version; many Hebrew manuscripts read *and are forgotten.*

8:2-6 The Teacher advocates careful timing in dealing with the powerful if one wants to influence the decisions these officials make.

8:12-14 Despite appearances to the contrary, the wicked do not prosper since their days are limited by God's will. But it is also true that—at least in this life—the righteous do not always receive a reward for following God.

▸ GOD

8:13 Everything matters. From the secular perspective, nothing matters. People are just grown-up germs, and germs are just a random arrangement of molecules, and the downward spiral of meaninglessness continues to the quantum level. But in the real world, where God exists, everything matters. God's sense of justice tells us what is good and bad, valuable and trash. The wicked hear this and fear, while others hear it and are warned (11:9), but no one can face God's justice and merely shrug. In the context of life's appalling lack of fairness, God promises that a final tally will be made (8:10-13; 12:14). Even the craftiest criminal that manages to avoid earthly detection will face the certain judgment of God. For this reason, everything we do, both good and evil, matters. (***See God****> God's Attributes> Just> God rightly judges heart, mind, and deeds,* TopicGuide page A17.)

8:15-17 One way to enjoy the good things in life that God has provided is to admit that we do not have all the answers to the problems of the world. God does, but we don't and never will, so we must be willing to let some problems go and leave them in God's mighty hands. On "nothing better" see note at 2:24-26.

9:1-2 The Teacher argues that without a God-centered view of life, it is reasonable to assume that death destroys the value of life. Death can appear at any time and immediately destroy any glimpse of blessing.

ultimately awaits everyone, whether righteous or wicked, good or bad,* ceremonially clean or unclean, religious or irreligious. Good people receive the same treatment as sinners, and people who make promises to God are treated like people who don't.

3It seems so tragic that everyone under the sun suffers the same fate. That is why people are not more careful to be good. Instead, they choose their own mad course, for they have no hope. There is nothing ahead but death anyway. 4There is hope only for the living. As they say, "It's better to be a live dog than a dead lion!"

5The living at least know they will die, but the dead know nothing. They have no further reward, nor are they remembered. 6Whatever they did in their lifetime—loving, hating, envying—is all long gone. They no longer play a part in anything here on earth. 7So go ahead. Eat your food with joy, and drink your wine with a happy heart, for God approves of this! 8Wear fine clothes, with a splash of cologne!

9Live happily with the woman you love through all the meaningless days of life that God has given you under the sun. The wife God gives you is your reward for all your earthly toil. 10Whatever you do, do well. For when you go to the grave,* there will be no work or planning or knowledge or wisdom.

11I have observed something else under the sun. The fastest runner doesn't always win the race, and the strongest warrior doesn't always win the battle. The wise sometimes go hungry, and the skillful are not necessarily wealthy. And those who are educated don't always lead successful lives. It is all decided by chance, by being in the right place at the right time.

12People can never predict when hard times might come. Like fish in a net or birds in a trap, people are caught by sudden tragedy.

THOUGHTS ON WISDOM AND FOLLY

13Here is another bit of wisdom that has impressed me as I have watched the way our world works. 14There was a small town with only a few people, and a great king came with his army and besieged it. 15A poor, wise man knew how to save the town, and so it was rescued. But afterward no one thought to thank him. 16So even though wisdom is better than strength, those who are wise will be despised if they are poor. What they say will not be appreciated for long.

17 Better to hear the quiet words of a wise person
than the shouts of a foolish king.
18 Better to have wisdom than weapons of war,
but one sinner can destroy much that is good.

9:5 Job 14:21; Ps 88:12; Eccl 1:11; 2:16; 8:10; Isa 26:14
9:8 Ps 23:5; Rev 3:4
9:9 Eccl 6:12; 7:15
9:10 Gen 37:35; Job 21:13; Eccl 9:5; 11:6; Rom 12:11; Col 3:23
9:11 Deut 8:17-18; 1 Sam 6:9; 2 Chr 20:15; Ps 76:5; Amos 2:14-15; Zech 4:6
9:12 Eccl 8:7; Isa 24:18; Hos 9:8; Luke 21:34-35
9:15 2 Sam 20:22; Eccl 2:16; 4:13; 8:10
9:16 Prov 21:22; Eccl 7:12, 19
9:17 Eccl 7:5; 10:12
9:18 Josh 7:1-26; 2 Kgs 21:2-17; Eccl 9:16

9:2 As in Greek and Syriac versions and Latin Vulgate; Hebrew lacks *or bad.* 9:10 Hebrew *to Sheol.*

9:3-6 "Everyone under the sun suffers the same fate" means that everyone dies. The Teacher leaves difficult statements hanging for the godly and the ungodly to consider—"How are we supposed to make sense of the fact that the righteous and the unrighteous seem to suffer the same fate, regardless of their actions?" The Teacher wants all to see that the ungodly have no answer to the problems of life and death, while the faithful fear God and trust Him in the midst of the difficulties of this world.

9:7-10 Once again the Teacher returns to his theme of enjoying the good things in this life that God has provided, such as food, drink, and marriage. Once in the grave it is too late to enjoy them. The godly and the ungodly must wrestle with the transience of life, but only the godly can truly enjoy the common blessings of food and drink. Even the simple pleasures of a good meal are muted without a God-centered life.

▶ GOD
9:11 Blind luck. In a universe without a sovereign God, people look for ways to manipulate reality. Some keep symbols of luck nearby, like a rabbit's foot. Others wear "charm bracelets" with astrological symbols—"lucky stars"—attached. Some Christians treat the Bible like a good-luck charm, frequently quoting certain passages or "claiming" certain verses to attempt to change their situations. But in a universe where God exists, luck doesn't. If there is one atom running around loose outside the scope or the sphere of God's divine direction, then that autonomous atom may change the entire course of human history. It might obstruct God, stopping Him from keeping the promises He has made to His people. If there is any ingredient of God's creation that is outside of His authority, then He no longer is God over all. God owns what He makes, and He rules what He owns. Put your trust in God, not in luck. (***See God*** *> God's Attributes> Sovereign> God has dominion over the affairs of people,* TopicGuide page A17.)

9:13-18 The power of a foolish king is compared to the wisdom of a poor man. People tend to forget the wise person who helped them at a critical time in their lives, but such a person is still preferred more than an arrogant king. This proverbial advice, along with the rest of Ecclesiastes, continues to accomplish its real purpose: to assault a secular worldview and advance the effectiveness of a worldview powered by belief in a God who is worthy of our respect.

10 [1]As dead flies cause even a bottle of perfume to stink,
so a little foolishness spoils great wisdom and honor.

[2] A wise person chooses the right road;
a fool takes the wrong one.

[3] You can identify fools
just by the way they walk down the street!

[4] If your boss is angry at you, don't quit!
A quiet spirit can overcome even great mistakes.

THE IRONIES OF LIFE

[5]There is another evil I have seen under the sun. Kings and rulers make a grave mistake
[6]when they give great authority to foolish people and low positions to people of proven
worth. [7]I have even seen servants riding horseback like princes—and princes walking like
servants!

[8] When you dig a well,
you might fall in.
When you demolish an old wall,
you could be bitten by a snake.

[9] When you work in a quarry,
stones might fall and crush you.
When you chop wood,
there is danger with each stroke of your ax.

[10] Using a dull ax requires great strength,
so sharpen the blade.
That's the value of wisdom;
it helps you succeed.

[11] If a snake bites before you charm it,
what's the use of being a snake charmer?

[12] Wise words bring approval,
but fools are destroyed by their own words.

[13] Fools base their thoughts on foolish assumptions,
so their conclusions will be wicked madness;
[14] they chatter on and on.

No one really knows what is going to happen;
no one can predict the future.

[15] Fools are so exhausted by a little work
that they can't even find their way home.

[16] What sorrow for the land ruled by a servant,*
the land whose leaders feast in the morning.

10:1 Exod 30:25
10:3 Prov 13:16; 18:2
10:4 1 Sam 25:24-33; Prov 25:15; Eccl 8:3
10:6 Esth 3:1; Prov 28:12; 29:2
10:7 Esth 6:8; Prov 19:10
10:8 Ps 7:15; Prov 26:27; Amos 5:19
10:11 Ps 58:45; Jer 8:17
10:12 Prov 10:14, 32; 22:11
10:14 Prov 15:2; Eccl 3:22; 5:3; 6:12; 7:14; 8:7
10:16 Isa 3:4-5, 12; 5:11

10:16 Or *a child.*

10:1 Using the sense of smell to make his point, the Teacher explains that it doesn't take much foolishness to overwhelm wisdom. In other words, one or two stupid mistakes can destroy numerous good decisions in a very short period of time.

10:2-3 Both wise and foolish actions are often revealed very quickly for what they are.

10:5-7 All too often, people in the highest positions of governmental authority elevate unqualified personnel to high positions, which keeps those truly qualified in the lower positions. Unless we trust in a God who controls kings and princes, there is no reason to be hopeful about the future of government.

10:8-9 The point of these verses is that anything you do in this life involves risks, so nothing can be taken for granted.

10:16-17 A person with political power can use it for good, but if he uses it as an opportunity merely to indulge himself, then the people in his realm will suffer.

17 Happy is the land whose king is a noble leader
and whose leaders feast at the proper time
to gain strength for their work, not to get drunk.

10:18 Prov 24:30-34 18 Laziness leads to a sagging roof;
idleness leads to a leaky house.

10:19 Judg 9:13 Ps 104:15 Eccl 2:3; 7:12 19 A party gives laughter,
wine gives happiness,
and money gives everything!

10:20 Exod 22:28 2 Kgs 6:12 Luke 12:3 Acts 23:5 20 Never make light of the king, even in your thoughts.
And don't make fun of the powerful, even in your own bedroom.
For a little bird might deliver your message
and tell them what you said.

THE UNCERTAINTIES OF LIFE

11:1 Deut 15:7-11 Prov 19:17 Isa 32:20 Matt 10:42 2 Cor 9:8 Gal 6:9 Heb 6:10

11 1 Send your grain across the seas,
and in time, profits will flow back to you.*
2 But divide your investments among many places,*
for you do not know what risks might lie ahead.

3 When clouds are heavy, the rains come down.
Whether a tree falls north or south, it stays where it falls.

11:2 Ps 112:9 1 Tim 6:18-19 4 Farmers who wait for perfect weather never plant.
If they watch every cloud, they never harvest.

11:5 Ps 139:13-16 Eccl 1:15; 3:10; 8:17 John 3:8 5 Just as you cannot understand the path of the wind or the mystery of a tiny baby growing
in its mother's womb,* so you cannot understand the activity of God, who does all things.
6 Plant your seed in the morning and keep busy all afternoon, for you don't know if
11:6 Eccl 9:10 profit will come from one activity or another—or maybe both.

ADVICE FOR YOUNG AND OLD

11:7 Eccl 6:5; 7:11 7 Light is sweet; how pleasant to see a new day dawning.
11:8 Eccl 9:7; 12:1 8 When people live to be very old, let them rejoice in every day of life. But let them also
remember there will be many dark days. Everything still to come is meaningless.

11:1 Or *Give generously, / for your gifts will return to you later.* Hebrew reads *Throw your bread on the waters, / for after many days you will find it again.* 11:2 Hebrew *among seven or even eight.* 11:5 Some manuscripts read *Just as you cannot understand how breath comes to a tiny baby in its mother's womb.*

10:19 Proverbs such as this are designed to dare the ungodly to disagree with this crass secular saying. If they do attempt to prove that people and relationships and love are more valuable than money, then the ungodly will be forced to admit that there is something beyond this world. The godly are challenged by this secular proverb as well, as it may uncomfortably reveal a worldly lifestyle.

11:1-6 These verses contain the Teacher's advice on how to handle money. First, invest and diversify. Second, recognize that people cannot always predict whether an investment is sound (clouds that bring rain and trees that fall refer to inevitable events), but this should not keep them from making investments anyway. Third, just as couples have children even though only God truly understands the reproductive process, so people should not be afraid to make investments they don't fully understand—though again, diversification of assets is critical for success.

▸ CHURCH
11:5 Work hard. The author of Ecclesiastes, the Teacher, repeatedly argues that everything is uncertain in a worldview with no God. But in 11:1-6, he turns this upside down, arguing that since life (even with God) is mysterious, we should work harder. Yes, obscurity abounds, but that doesn't mean we have to know the answer to every question to accomplish important tasks. For instance, we don't need to solve the mystery of life to procreate. So ask your questions, but don't be paralyzed when you don't get them all answered. Live in the fear of God, walk humbly before Him, and stay busy—you never know when your time of labors will be over. (***See Church****> What> Many Titles> Servants> Servants must be prepared to work,* TopicGuide page A48.)

11:7-8 People should enjoy life while they can—whether young or old—before the "dark days" of death come. The days of life are far fewer in number than the days after death.

9Young people,* it's wonderful to be young! Enjoy every minute of it. Do everything you
want to do; take it all in. But remember that you must give an account to God for every-
thing you do. 10So refuse to worry, and keep your body healthy. But remember that youth,
with a whole life before you, is meaningless.

12 Don't let the excitement of youth cause you to forget your Creator. Honor Him in
your youth before you grow old and say, "Life is not pleasant anymore."
2Remember Him before the light of the sun, moon, and stars is dim to your old eyes, and
rain clouds continually darken your sky. 3Remember Him before your legs—the guards of
your house—start to tremble; and before your shoulders—the strong men—stoop. Remem-
ber Him before your teeth—your few remaining servants—stop grinding; and before your
eyes—the women looking through the windows—see dimly.
4Remember Him before the door to life's opportunities is closed and the sound of work
fades. Now you rise at the first chirping of the birds, but then all their sounds will grow faint.
5Remember Him before you become fearful of falling and worry about danger in the
streets; before your hair turns white like an almond tree in bloom, and you drag along
without energy like a dying grasshopper, and the caperberry no longer inspires sexual de-
sire. Remember Him before you near the grave, your everlasting home, when the mourn-
ers will weep at your funeral.
6Yes, remember your Creator now while you are young, before the silver cord of life

11:9 Ps 81:12; Acts 21:25; Rom 14:10
11:10 2 Cor 7:1; 2 Tim 2:22
12:1 Deut 8:18; 2 Sam 19:35; Pss 63:6; 119:55
12:2 Isa 13:10; Ezek 32:7-8; Joel 3:15; Matt 24:29
12:3 Gen 27:1; 1 Sam 3:2; Ps 35:14
12:4 2 Sam 19:35; Rev 18:22
12:5 Gen 50:10; Job 17:13; Jer 9:17

11:9 Hebrew *Young man.*

▸ WORSHIP
11:9 Simple pleasures. It's good to be young and full of life. For all the vanity and emptiness of human existence without God, the author finds some fulfillment in the joys of youth. These joys are from the hand of God (9:7) and can brighten the gray life without God (5:18; 9:9). Thank God that He gives common pleasures to all people, regardless of their spirituality, and thus makes this world of sin a brighter place. Never be so "spiritual" that you miss the ordinary delights that come from God's hand. It is no sign of spiritual maturity when we fail to thank God for simple pleasures like a starry night, a warm hug, or a red-striped sunset (11:7). Encourage those around you to have the wisdom to slow down and honestly appreciate the common joys God has given us. (***See Worship***> *OT> God's Supremacy> Glorified and blessed God,* TopicGuide page A27.)

11:9-10 The Teacher advises the young not to let the sorrows of life overwhelm them to the point that they cannot enjoy life. But they must also keep their youthful desires in check, since God will call every action into account.

▸ GOD
12:1 Discovering God in Ecclesiastes. How does God's creation of the universe shape our daily lives? The Old Testament uses this strong word *Creator* to speak of God—and no one else. The title occurs only once in Ecclesiastes, but the writer, just as in the rest of the Bible, grounds all reality in God. The Creator is the one who has made everything, and He begins and ends every life (11:5; 12:7). The timing of all things belongs to Him (3:11). God made people perfect in the beginning (7:29) and thus cannot be held responsible for the fall of humanity. While the world comes up with theories about life coming from nothing, firmly establish in your mind and heart that God is your Creator. Your life began when God said so, and your life will end when He decides it. (***See God***> *God's Attributes> Self-Sufficient> The One Creator originates and controls His creation,* TopicGuide page A17.)

12:1-7 The Teacher addresses the young, who can so easily forget God in their "excitement" about life. When they get older, they will look back at the wasted years of their youth and be disappointed with what they did or did not do. But by then the limitations of old age will not let them do anything about the wasted time and opportunities. Even more devastating is the fact that death ("dust" in 12:7 is an echo of Genesis 3:19) will make it impossible to correct past mistakes.

▸ BIBLE
12:2 Forgetting God. The Bible assumes that young people understand that God created them—how else could they forget Him if they did not already know Him (Romans 1:18-20)? The consequence of forgetting God is that when we are old, we will have nothing left of any eternal value. In the end, if we don't have God, we don't have anything. If we don't see God reflected in creation, then the created order appears increasingly chaotic and random. In a world that seeks to deny that God is revealed in creation (Romans 1:18-25) and that God is sovereign over all things (Romans 8:28), take active steps to base your emotions and your thoughts on God's existence. Look for Him and His hand of providence in all things, and as you get older, you'll be surprised at what the eyes of faith can see! (***See Bible***> *Unity> Doctrines> Doctrine of natural revelation,* TopicGuide page A10.)

▸ WORSHIP
12:6 Everything is not meaningless! The full beauty of a diamond is revealed only when it is placed on a dark surface. Likewise, the author of Ecclesiastes puts God on the dark surface of nihilism, the philosophy that everything is meaningless, so that we can see Him in His full glory. Only after the author has explained the emptiness of life without God does he fully reveal God to us—a God who deserves to be feared and obeyed (12:13), for He will judge everything we think, say, or do (12:14). There is only one answer to secularism, nihilism, and all the other philosophies that lie about God—God Himself. God will have the last word, not death. Do not spend your time trying not to die, but spend your time trying to live! God has made you invincible until your work on earth is done. Finish well! (***See Worship***> *OT> Reverence> Our duty,* TopicGuide page A29.)

▪ ▪ ▪ DISCOVER

TO FEAR OR NOT TO FEAR?

***WHEN YOU HEAR THE WORD* FEAR**, what pops into your mind? We fear crime, cancer, public speaking, darkness—but fear God? Why would the writer of Ecclesiastes *encourage* us—God's covenant people—to fear God?

We can all agree that there are those who do not love God. They have every reason to live in unrelenting terror of God, for God promises that all who live in rebellion against Him will suffer eternally (2 Thessalonians 1:6-9; Matthew 5:29; 10:28; 13:49; 18:8; 25:46; Revelation 14:9-11; 20:10).

But the puzzle remains: In what sense should God's people live in fear of God? In Christians, the fear of God prompts worship and reverence for who He is and what He can do. Sometimes our fear is like that of a child who shuns acts of disobedience because he respects and loves his parents. Other times it is a holy fright—no one in his right mind would be calm and settled in the presence of the most powerful being in the universe. God's people also have a healthy fear of coming under His divine discipline (Acts 5:11). It's natural and appropriate to fear the consequences of disobedience (Hebrews 12:4-11).

A healthy fear of God can also stem from His attributes, such as God's complete knowledge of all things. Many people often wonder, *If God knows everything about me, how can He still love me?* But it doesn't matter what you have done in the past—God is willing to forgive those who repent in faith. Those who put their faith in Christ never have to worry about whether God will find out about their past and strike them down (Romans 5:1-10). He already knows everything we've done and everything we will do—and He loves us forever (John 16:27). Through Christ's sacrifice, God accepts us as we are, so we can go to God with all our questions and concerns.

For most of us, fear is something we try to avoid. But the fear of God opens the door to true knowledge of Him and to the riches of the promises of God. Fear God and it will change your relationship with Him—for the better.

snaps and the golden bowl is broken. Don't wait until the water jar is smashed at the
spring and the pulley is broken at the well. 7For then the dust will return to the earth, and
the spirit will return to God who gave it.

12:7 Gen 3:19 Job 34:14 Ps 104:29 Isa 57:16 Zech 12:1 Luke 23:46 Acts 7:59

CONCLUDING THOUGHTS ABOUT THE TEACHER

8"Everything is meaningless," says the Teacher, "completely meaningless."
9Keep this in mind: The Teacher was considered wise, and he taught the people every-
thing he knew. He listened carefully to many proverbs, studying and classifying them.
10The Teacher sought to find just the right words to express truths clearly.*
11The words of the wise are like cattle prods—painful but helpful. Their collected say-
ings are like a nail-studded stick with which a shepherd* drives the sheep.
12But, my child,* let me give you some further advice: Be careful, for writing books is
endless, and much study wears you out.
13That's the whole story. Here now is my final conclusion: Fear God and obey His com-
mands, for this is everyone's duty. 14God will judge us for everything we do, including
every secret thing, whether good or bad.

12:10 Prov 10:32; 22:20-21

12:11 Isa 22:23 Acts 2:37

12:13 Deut 4:2; 6:2; 10:12 Mic 6:8

12:14 Matt 10:26 Rom 2:16 1 Cor 4:5

12:10 Or *sought to write what was upright and true.* 12:11 Or *one shepherd.* 12:12 Hebrew *my son.*

12:8 The Hebrew of this verse is almost identical with 1:2 (see note there). The Teacher closes by reminding his readers that "everything is meaningless," just as he has demonstrated throughout the book—at least that is the case without God in one's life (see note at 12:13-14). This is likely the final comment from the hand of the Teacher himself; Ecclesiastes 12:9-14 appear to be the comments of an editor.

▶ MINISTRY

12:9 Knowledge isn't everything. It is possible to know too much. We can fill our minds with so much trivia and opinion and factoids that we lose sight of the fundamental—and exhaust ourselves in the process. At some point, it is wise to focus less on learning more and focus more on doing more; strive to change yourself and your world for the better by applying what you know. Learn everything worth knowing, but then move on to action, achievement, and making a difference in this chaotic world. Be strategic in the books you read, the movies you watch, and your educational choices. (***See Ministry>*** *Great Commission> Make Disciples> Disciples strategically use knowledge, skills, and abilities,* TopicGuide page A56.)

12:9-12 These verses appear to be written by an editor as a salute to the Teacher and an encouragement and warning to the student.

12:13-14 The editor's summation of all the Teacher has said in the book is that everyone must "fear God and obey His commands." Anyone can restore his or her true humanity through a trusting relationship with God. This breaks the cycle of a meaningless life and enables God's people to stand before Him and accept His judgment.

SONG OF SONGS

PURPOSE

To celebrate sexuality that has been redeemed through harmony with God and with your beloved.

Some who read the Song of Songs for the first time cannot believe they're reading from the Bible! Human love and sexuality have been so twisted in our modern world that many have forgotten, or never knew to begin with, that they are wonderful gifts from God. But the Song of Songs unashamedly celebrates these gifts. At its heart, this book is a love story—a picture of the passions and perils in courtship and marriage. But marriage itself is a picture of the relationship of God and His people (Ephesians 5:25-30). Thus, the Song of Songs reflects God's love for His bride (2 Corinthians 11:2), too. Just as the zenith of human love is that between a man and wife, the zenith of spiritual love is that between God and His people.

DISCOVER GOD IN SONG OF SONGS

Various dimensions of the love of God are seen in the Song of Songs:

Passion: First and foremost, the Song of Songs is an account of the love between a man and a woman—indeed, their *passionate* love. While much is made (correctly) of the fact that love is a choice that is reflected in actions (see 1 Corinthians 13), it is also true that love is passionate. The truth is, however, that human beings didn't invent passion. Humans are able to display passionate love for one another only because we are made in the image of a passionate God—one who loves ardently, boundlessly, and with complete abandon. What does this look like? Think of the love God displayed when Jesus Christ went to the cross. We even refer to Jesus' sufferings between the Last Supper and the Crucifixion as His "Passion," and dramas about the Crucifixion are called "passion plays." The way Solomon loved his bride gives us a hint as to how God loves His bride: passionately.

Expression: Modern books on marriage have cited the Song of Songs as a template for how to show love to a spouse. Depending on which Bible translation one uses, the word *like* occurs nearly fifty times in the book (e.g., "your eyes are like doves," 1:15), demonstrating the prolific use of word pictures by the two lovers to describe each other. These images of idealized human love, however, only mirror the love God expresses toward us in Christ. The Scriptures say, "But God showed His great love for us by sending Christ to die for us while we were still sinners" (Romans 5:8) and "God showed how much He loved us by sending His one and only Son into the world" (1 John 4:9). True love is communicated to the beloved through every opportunity, in both words and actions.

Celebration: Love in the Song of Songs is nothing if not a celebration. With typical Solomonic extravagance, the wedding procession up to Jerusalem was grandiose; the Songs of Songs describes the aromas, the appearance, the armed escorts, the elaborate carriage, and the "young women of Jerusalem" (3:6-11). It was a light and sound show, a celebration of love. But celebrations were nothing new in Jerusalem. Three times a year (Passover, Pentecost, and the Feast of Tabernacles), Israel gathered in Jerusalem to remember and celebrate God's love, deliverance, and protection. Scripture says God delights in such righteous revelries by His people (Psalm 150). Whether it is love for a person or for God, our celebration of love is a reflection of God's celebratory nature.

GROWING THROUGH SONG OF SONGS

Being the Lover: It is difficult to read the Song of Songs without becoming envious of the proactive personalities of Solomon and his bride. They were uninhibited, unrestrained, and unashamed of their love for one another. While Solomon initiated their relationship, there was no lack of activism on his bride's part. Every person who has known the proactive love of God—a love that reached out to redeem us—should be a proactive lover of both God and other people. Solomon and his bride are examples for married lovers everywhere—and for all who love God—of how to throw off restraint and demonstrate, in word and deed, love for one's beloved.

DISCOVERY VERSES

My lover is mine, and I am his. (SONG OF SONGS 2:16)

Many waters cannot quench love, nor can rivers drown it. (SONG OF SONGS 8:7)

Being the Beloved: Some people are more comfortable showing love than receiving it. Interestingly, God is not: He desires the worship and adoration of His people, but not in a self-serving way. Solomon and his bride gave and received love freely—it flowed between them like a current, saturating their hearts with mutual security and pleasure. This is how we ought to receive God's love. The one who will not willingly receive His love is not truly ready to love God or others.

Being the Encourager: The "women of Jerusalem" (1:5; 2:7; 3:5, 10; 5:8, 16; 8:4) serve more than a literary purpose—they play a vital role in the courtship of Solomon and his bride, encouraging the couple in their pursuit of joy. Love, especially the love that develops in courtship, may not come easily. It involves learning to trust and communicate, learning to handle misunderstandings, and learning to give and receive forgiveness. All who are learning to love (a lifelong task!) need encouragement and affirmation from others. Learn to promote commitment and passion in those around you.

SONG OF SONGS FACTS

Author: Solomon traditionally has been regarded as the author (1:1). First Kings 4:29-34 records that Solomon was a prolific writer. However, the language of 1:1 may intend to communicate that it was written in Solomon's honor by an anonymous author.

Written to: Song of Songs was most likely originally written to educate young students in the royal courts, but it eventually made its way into study in the Temple and synagogues.

Date of writing: The work likely began early in Solomon's reign as king (970–930 BC), but like Psalms and Proverbs, it may contain compositions and edits from different periods.

Settings: Jerusalem, Solomon's home and royal court.

OUTLINE

- **SONG OF SONGS 1:1–2:17**—Opening words and a young man's invitation
- **SONG OF SONGS 3:1-5**—The young woman's nighttime search
- **SONG OF SONGS 3:6–5:1**—The wedding day
- **SONG OF SONGS 5:2–7:11**—The young woman's nighttime search
- **SONG OF SONGS 7:12–8:14**—The young woman's invitation and closing words

1:1 1 Kgs 4:32
1 This is Solomon's song of songs, more wonderful than any other.
*Young Woman**
1:2 Song 1:4; 4:10
2 Kiss me and kiss me again,
for your love is sweeter than wine.
1:3 Eccl 7:1 Song 4:10 John 12:3
3 How fragrant your cologne;
your name is like its spreading fragrance.
No wonder all the young women love you!
1:4 Ps 45:14-15
4 Take me with you; come, let's run!
The king has brought me into his bedroom.

Young Women of Jerusalem
How happy we are for you, O king.
We praise your love even more than wine.

Young Woman
How right they are to adore you.

1:5 Song 2:7, 14; 4:3; 5:8; 6:4
5 I am dark but beautiful,
O women of Jerusalem—
dark as the tents of Kedar,
dark as the curtains of Solomon's tents.
1:6 Ps 69:8 Song 8:11
6 Don't stare at me because I am dark—
the sun has darkened my skin.
My brothers were angry with me;
they forced me to care for their vineyards,
so I couldn't care for myself—my own vineyard.

1:7 Song 2:16; 3:1-4; 8:13
7 Tell me, my love, where are you leading your flock today?
Where will you rest your sheep at noon?
For why should I wander like a prostitute*
among your friends and their flocks?

Young Man
1:8 Song 5:9; 6:1
8 If you don't know, O most beautiful woman,
follow the trail of my flock,
and graze your young goats by the shepherds' tents.

1:1 The headings identifying the speakers are not in the original text, though the Hebrew usually gives clues by means of the gender of the person speaking. 1:7 Hebrew *like a veiled woman.*

1:1 The name of the book comes from the first two words of the book written in Hebrew, translated here *song of songs.* This phrase means that this poem is intended to be the finest song about the finest topic—love.

1:2-3 It is impossible to understand this book without knowing the identities of the speaker and the one spoken to. The NLT has helpfully inserted identifications to indicate a change of speaker(s), although they are not part of the Hebrew text. The first one to speak is the bride, who praises the way her groom kisses and smells. She also eagerly anticipates their wedding night together, which indicates that at the time the love poem begins, the bride and groom are legally married but the ceremony and consummation have not yet taken place. This was a normal custom in ancient Israel.

1:5 The fact that the bride is "dark" indicates that she is from the sun-tanned working class and not of noble or royal blood as the groom is. Her low social status does not keep the king from loving and wanting her.

▸ GOD

1:7 The love of the shepherd. Some occupations are more family-friendly than others. It's hard to carry on a relationship with someone if you are traveling all over the world or always working late. In this story, the ideal husband's profession is a shepherd-king. The watchful care and authority his vocation hones is the perfect preparation for marriage. The Bible describes Jesus as our Shepherd-King (John 10:11). Read Psalm 23 and reflect on how Jesus is the perfect Shepherd-King to care for His people. Learn to use His Word to guide you through your relationships. (***See God*****>** *God's Names> God> Shepherd,* TopicGuide page A18.)

1:7-8 Pastoral imagery, which occurs frequently in the Song of Songs (see 2:8-17; 3:5; 4:8, 12-16; 5:1; 6:2-3, 11; 7:10-13; 8:5, 11-14), was common in ancient Semitic love poetry, for such locations provide an ideal setting for romance.

9 You are as exciting, my darling,
as a mare among Pharaoh's stallions.
10 How lovely are your cheeks;
your earrings set them afire!
How lovely is your neck,
enhanced by a string of jewels.
11 We will make for you earrings of gold
and beads of silver.

Young Woman

12 The king is lying on his couch,
enchanted by the fragrance of my perfume.
13 My lover is like a sachet of myrrh
lying between my breasts.
14 He is like a bouquet of sweet henna blossoms
from the vineyards of En-gedi.

Young Man

15 How beautiful you are, my darling,
how beautiful!
Your eyes are like doves.

Young Woman

16 You are so handsome, my love,
pleasing beyond words!
The soft grass is our bed;
17 fragrant cedar branches are the beams of our house,
and pleasant smelling firs are the rafters.

1:9 2 Chr 1:16-17
1:10 Gen 24:53; Song 5:13
1:12 Song 4:13-14; Mark 14:3
1:13 Ps 45:8; John 19:39
1:14 1 Sam 23:29; Song 4:13
1:15 Song 1:16; 2:10, 13; 4:1
1:17 1 Kgs 6:9-10; 2 Chr 3:5; Jer 22:14; Ezek 41:16

2

Young Woman

1 I am the spring crocus blooming on the Sharon Plain,*
the lily of the valley.

Young Man

2 Like a lily among thistles
is my darling among young women.

Young Woman

3 Like the finest apple tree in the orchard
is my lover among other young men.

2:1 Isa 33:9; 35:2; Hos 14:5
2:3 Song 8:5

2:1 Traditionally rendered *I am the rose of Sharon.* Sharon Plain is a region in the coastal plain of Palestine.

1:9-11 The groom compliments his bride for her beauty, which is enhanced by the lovely and exquisite jewelry she wears—just as Pharaoh's horses looked so impressive when bedecked with ornaments while pulling the royal chariot.

1:12-13 The bride anticipates the consummation of their love as she describes her sensual smell and her groom's enjoyment of her breasts.

1:15 Song of Songs reveals God's view of the sexual relationship that is enjoyed in its fullness during marriage. When we honor God by following God's standards, our sexual intimacy is a holy and wonderful thing. He planned it for our pleasure and growth as marriage partners. If you are dating, guard your body from sexual sin. If you are married, commit yourself to reveling in your partner's beauty and sexuality no matter how long you have been together.

2:1-2 The bride refers to herself as a "crocus" and a "lily," common flowers throughout Israel. This serves as a modest appraisal of her beauty compared to other girls. The groom, however, sees her as a "lily among thistles," that is, the one with the greatest beauty.

2:3-9 The bride describes the virtues of her groom and how she longs to be with him. Their wedding brings them together at last, and it was just in time since she was "weak with love" (2:5). She describes their lovemaking and how much she enjoys being with him.

I sit in his delightful shade
and taste his delicious fruit.

2:4 Ps 63:2-5 · Song 1:4
4 He escorts me to the banquet hall;
it's obvious how much he loves me.

2:5 Song 5:8; 7:8
5 Strengthen me with raisin cakes,
refresh me with apples,
for I am weak with love.

2:6 Prov 4:8 · Song 8:3
6 His left arm is under my head,
and his right arm embraces me.

2:7 Gen 49:21 · Song 3:5; 5:8; 8:14 · Hab 3:19
7 Promise me, O women of Jerusalem,
by the gazelles and wild deer,
not to awaken love until the time is right.*

2:8 Song 2:17 · Isa 52:7
8 Ah, I hear my lover coming!
He is leaping over the mountains,
bounding over the hills.

2:9 Judg 5:28 · Prov 6:5 · Song 2:17; 3:5; 8:14
9 My lover is like a swift gazelle
or a young stag.
Look, there he is behind the wall,
looking through the window,
peering into the room.

10 My lover said to me,
"Rise up, my darling!
Come away with me, my fair one!
11 Look, the winter is past,
and the rains are over and gone.

2:12 Gen 15:9 · Ps 74:19
12 The flowers are springing up,
the season of singing birds* has come,
and the cooing of turtledoves fills the air.

2:13 Matt 24:32
13 The fig trees are forming young fruit,
and the fragrant grapevines are blossoming.
Rise up, my darling!
Come away with me, my fair one!"

Young Man

2:14 Song 5:2; 6:9 · Jer 48:28
14 My dove is hiding behind the rocks,
behind an outcrop on the cliff.
Let me see your face;
let me hear your voice.
For your voice is pleasant,
and your face is lovely.

2:7 Or *not to awaken love until it is ready.* 2:12 Or *the season of pruning vines.*

▸ CHURCH

2:8 Watching for my lover. Have you ever had feelings for someone such that you looked for that person everywhere you went? In the New Testament, Jesus is pictured as the bridegroom who will come for His bride, the worldwide church. Are you longing for His return like a bride longs for her future husband? Do you constantly look for Him, anxious to see what life will be like with Him? Jesus said, "So you, too, must keep watch! For you do not know the day or hour of My return" (Matthew 25:13). Keep watch—stay prepared! (***See Church****> What> Many Titles> Bride> Who joyfully awaits the wedding day,* TopicGuide page A48.)

2:10-17 The groom is possibly the speaker in 2:10-15. If so, he invites his bride to go away with him to enjoy the pastoral scenery, the perfect setting for lovemaking. He eagerly seeks his bride who is playfully "hiding behind the rocks" (2:14), and the bride encourages him to hurry and find her.

Young Women of Jerusalem

15 Catch all the foxes,
those little foxes,
before they ruin the vineyard of love,
for the grapevines are blossoming! 2:15 Song 2:13

Young Woman

16 My lover is mine, and I am his.
He browses among the lilies. 2:16 Song 4:5; 6:2-3; 7:10
17 Before the dawn breezes blow
and the night shadows flee, 2:17 Song 2:8-9; 4:6
return to me, my love, like a gazelle
or a young stag on the rugged mountains.*

3

Young Woman

1 One night as I lay in bed, I yearned for my lover.
I yearned for him, but he did not come. 3:1 Song 1:7; 5:6
2 So I said to myself, "I will get up and roam the city,
searching in all its streets and squares. 3:2 Jer 5:1
I will search for the one I love."
So I searched everywhere but did not find him.
3 The watchmen stopped me as they made their rounds,
and I asked, "Have you seen the one I love?" 3:3 Song 5:7
4 Then scarcely had I left them
when I found my love! 3:4 Song 8:2
I caught and held him tightly,
then I brought him to my mother's house,
into my mother's bed, where I had been conceived.

5 Promise me, O women of Jerusalem,
by the gazelles and wild deer, 3:5 Song 2:7; 8:2
not to awaken love until the time is right.*

Young Women of Jerusalem

6 Who is this sweeping in from the wilderness
like a cloud of smoke? 3:6 Exod 13:21-22 Song 1:13; 4:12-14 Rev 5:8; 18:13

2:17 Or *on the hills of Bether.* 3:5 Or *not to awaken love until it is ready.*

▸ BIBLE

2:16 My lover is mine. The Bible is very clear about the type of intimacy that a husband and wife should share. Ephesians 5:31 says, "A man leaves his father and mother and is joined to his wife, and the two are united into one." This oneness includes every part of the marital relationship—the spiritual, emotional, and the physical union. The husband and wife belong to each other, with nothing held back. This closeness takes time and maturity, but it is the most satisfying human relationship we can experience. This doesn't mean either spouse loses his or her individuality, but they fit together like two pieces of a puzzle. Take a moment to reflect on how you can foster this oneness in your marriage. (***See Bible****> Unity> Doctrines> Principles of marriage,* TopicGuide page A10.)

3:1-5 The bride recalls a time before their wedding when she "yearned" (3:1) for her groom so they could consummate their marriage. She searched for him and found him and then gave her virginity to him on their wedding night. She then makes the "women of Jerusalem" promise that they too would not "awaken love" (enjoy sexual union) "until the time is right" (in marriage) (3:5).

▸ WORSHIP

3:6 The light of my lover. In past centuries, some theologians have downplayed sex and everything related to a married couple's physical union. Yet this verse tells us the opposite story. Sensual attraction is presented as a beautiful part of the marital experience. From the days of courtship to the time of marital consummation, and on to the continuing sexual relationship, a couple's physical feelings are to be honored and enjoyed. How do you view a sexual relationship? Are you committed to following God's plan for sex? Do you rejoice in the pleasure that God has provided for you and your spouse? Ask God to give you a sense of the joy and unity with your spouse that sex can bring. (***See Worship****> OT> Reverence> The sanctity of physical love,* TopicGuide page A29.)

3:6-10 Solomon is described as the quintessential groom who comes majestically to the wedding ceremony. He is desirable, strong, and ready for his bride. The chronology of this book is complex in that it shifts from pre-wedding scenes to wedding scenes to post-wedding scenes quite often. This explains the reference to the wedding here after descriptions of sexual interactions (see note at Song of Songs 2:3-9).

Who is it, fragrant with myrrh and frankincense
and every kind of spice?
[7] Look, it is Solomon's carriage,
surrounded by sixty heroic men,
the best of Israel's soldiers.
3:8 Pss 45:3; 91:5 Jer 50:9
[8] They are all skilled swordsmen,
experienced warriors.
Each wears a sword on his thigh,
ready to defend the king against an attack in the night.
[9] King Solomon's carriage is built
of wood imported from Lebanon.
[10] Its posts are silver,
its canopy gold;
its cushions are purple.
It was decorated with love
by the young women of Jerusalem.

Young Woman

3:11 Isa 62:5
[11] Come out to see King Solomon,
young women of Jerusalem.*
He wears the crown his mother gave him on his wedding day,
his most joyous day.

4

Young Man

4:1 Song 1:15; 5:12; 6:5, 7
[1] You are beautiful, my darling,
beautiful beyond words.
Your eyes are like doves
behind your veil.
Your hair falls in waves,
like a flock of goats winding down the slopes of Gilead.
[2] Your teeth are as white as sheep,
recently shorn and freshly washed.
Your smile is flawless,
each tooth matched with its twin.*

3:11 Hebrew *of Zion.* 4:2 Hebrew *Not one is missing; each has a twin.*

▸ BIBLE
3:11 The crown of marriage. During Jewish weddings in Old Testament times, both the bride and the groom wore crowns. The crowns signified building a new covenant home, where they would reign as king and queen. We still use symbols to celebrate the marriage union in our wedding ceremonies today—rings, change of name, and vows. God can use these to strengthen your passion and commitment to one another (Numbers 30:1-13; Psalm 61:8). God can use symbols and vows as a means to strengthen the bond with those you love (Mark 10:38-39). But as in all things, Christ, not symbols nor even your beloved, must be at the center of your relationship (Ephesians 1:9-11). If you both put Him first, your spiritual unity will mirror your physical unity. (***See Bible*>** *Unity> Doctrines> Principles of marriage,* TopicGuide page A10.)

3:11 The bride calls on her attendants ("young women of Jerusalem") to admire her groom, King Solomon, who is there for "his wedding day." The flashback that began in 3:1 has come full circle to the present, and the bride and groom enjoy each other sexually once again (chapter 4).

▸ MINISTRY
4:1 A poem to your lover. Song of Songs isn't a literal story or historical account of a couple's experiences. It is poetry, with lyrical lines and vivid images. When is the last time you used poetry, flowers, or beauty to woo your spouse? The young man in this verse delightfully describes his lover in beautiful words, thereby fanning the flames of passion and sacred intimacy between the two of them. Express to your marital partner the passion of your heart in a way that's meaningful to him or her. See how your expression will enliven the relationship you now enjoy. (***See Ministry*>** *Transformation> Vocations> Poet,* TopicGuide page A57.)

4:1 In 4:1-7, the groom describes his bride's physical appearance by starting at the head and working his way down her body. He uses a variety of similes and metaphors (see notes at Song of Songs 5:10-16 and 7:1-5). In 4:1 the bride's eyes are gentle like doves, and her long hair cascades down her shoulders in waves—a description that evokes images of numerous goats descending from a mountain.

3 Your lips are like scarlet ribbon;
your mouth is inviting.
Your cheeks are like rosy pomegranates
behind your veil.
4 Your neck is as beautiful as the tower of David,
jeweled with the shields of a thousand heroes.
5 Your breasts are like two fawns,
twin fawns of a gazelle grazing among the lilies.
6 Before the dawn breezes blow
and the night shadows flee,
I will hurry to the mountain of myrrh
and to the hill of frankincense.
7 You are altogether beautiful, my darling,
beautiful in every way.

8 Come with me from Lebanon, my bride,
come with me from Lebanon.

4:3 Song 5:13, 16; 6:7

4:4 Neh 3:19; Song 7:4

4:5 Song 2:16; 6:2-3; 7:3

4:6 Song 2:17; 4:14

4:8 Deut 3:9; 1 Kgs 4:33; 1 Chr 5:23; Song 5:1; Isa 62:5

4:3 The veil both hides the beauty of the bride and mysteriously increases it (as in 4:1). Her cheeks are red and perfectly proportioned "like rosy pomegranates."

4:4 This verse does not mean that the bride has an unusually long neck. It indicates that her neck is as majestic in appearance as "the tower of David."

4:5-6 The groom admires his bride's breasts, which remind him of the tenderness of "twin fawns" (4:5). He then voices his intention to enjoy her breasts (one is "the mountain of myrrh" and the other is "the hill of frankincense") before sunset ("dawn breezes blow" and "night shadows flee"). Compare Proverbs 5:18-19.

4:8 The groom invites his bride to go away with him again. In verses 9-15 the groom describes the pleasures of intimacy with his bride.

MY RESPONSE TO GOD

Intimacy with God

SONG OF SONGS 4:12

How's your love life?

We usually think of our love life in terms of romantic relationships and the intimate moments we share with another person. But what about your love life with God? Do you spend intimate time alone with Him?

This doesn't downplay the role of public worship—gathering with God's people is vital and commanded (Hebrews 10:25). The time we spend with God and His people on the Sabbath is critical to our spiritual growth. But private worship—our intimate time with God—is an equally vital part of our Christian experience.

When we see Jesus worshiping in the Scriptures, we often see Him going to lonely places (Mark 1:35), up quiet mountains (Mark 6:45-46; Luke 6:12), and into the wilderness (Luke 5:16). Jesus once spent forty days alone, fasting and praying and battling with Satan (Matthew 4:1-11). Jesus demonstrated for His people that going further with God often requires spending time alone with Him.

Perhaps you need to rent a hotel room and unplug the television. Or clear out the floor of a closet, and sit in the dark for an hour to pray. Whatever it takes, spend secret time with God. Develop an intimacy with Him that rivals the passion any man and wife have ever shared.

Come down* from Mount Amana,
from the peaks of Senir and Hermon,
where the lions have their dens
and leopards live among the hills.

4:9 Ezek 16:11
9 You have captured my heart,
my treasure,* my bride.
You hold it hostage with one glance of your eyes,
with a single jewel of your necklace.
10 Your love delights me,
my treasure, my bride.
Your love is better than wine,
your perfume more fragrant than spices.

4:11 Gen 27:27 Prov 24:13-14 Hos 14:6
11 Your lips are as sweet as nectar, my bride.
Honey and milk are under your tongue.
Your clothes are scented
like the cedars of Lebanon.

4:12 Gen 29:3 Prov 5:15-18
12 You are my private garden, my treasure, my bride,
a secluded spring, a hidden fountain.
13 Your thighs shelter a paradise of pomegranates
with rare spices—
henna with nard,

4:14 Exod 30:23 Song 1:12; 4:6 John 19:39
14 nard and saffron,
fragrant calamus and cinnamon,
with all the trees of frankincense, myrrh, and aloes,
and every other lovely spice.

4:15 Zech 14:8 John 4:10, 14; 7:38
15 You are a garden fountain,
a well of fresh water
streaming down from Lebanon's mountains.

Young Woman

4:16 Song 1:13; 2:3; 5:1; 6:2
16 Awake, north wind!
Rise up, south wind!
Blow on my garden
and spread its fragrance all around.
Come into your garden, my love;
taste its finest fruits.

4:8 Or *Look down.* 4:9 Hebrew *my sister;* also in 4:10, 12.

4:9-10 The groom is captivated by his bride's beauty and declares that her "love is better than wine," meaning their physical love together is better than the most pleasant drink God's earth has to offer.

▶ BIBLE

4:12 The exclusivity of marriage. The Bible explicitly tells us that a husband and wife are to reserve themselves for each other. The marital relationship is like having a private garden where you can walk in security and enjoy the fruits all to yourself. That's why infidelity is so destructive to a marriage—one spouse gives away to another person the exclusive property and rights of his or her spouse. The security once felt by the other partner vanishes. Guard the privacy of your marriage, and you will find in your spouse a treasure that grows richer with time. (***See Bible***> *Unity*> *Creation*> *Creation and marriage,* TopicGuide page A10.)

4:12-15 The groom mixes three metaphors to describe intimacy with his bride: enjoying the fruits from a garden or orchard, enjoying the smells of rare perfumes, and enjoying the refreshing taste of fresh water.

4:16 The bride calls on the wind to send her sensual scents to the groom as an invitation to be intimate with her.

5

Young Man

1 I have entered my garden, my treasure,* my bride!
I gather myrrh with my spices
and eat honeycomb with my honey.
I drink wine with my milk.

5:1 Prov 9:5 Song 1:13; 4:9; 6:2 Isa 55:1 John 3:29

Young Women of Jerusalem

Oh, lover and beloved, eat and drink!
Yes, drink deeply of your love!

Young Woman

2 I slept, but my heart was awake,
when I heard my lover knocking and calling:
"Open to me, my treasure, my darling,
my dove, my perfect one.
My head is drenched with dew,
my hair with the dampness of the night."

5:2 Song 2:14; 4:9; 6:9

3 But I responded,
"I have taken off my robe.
Should I get dressed again?
I have washed my feet.
Should I get them soiled?"

5:3 Gen 19:2 Luke 11:7

4 My lover tried to unlatch the door,
and my heart thrilled within me.
5 I jumped up to open the door for my love,
and my hands dripped with perfume.
My fingers dripped with lovely myrrh
as I pulled back the bolt.

5:5 Song 5:13

6 I opened to my lover,
but he was gone!
My heart sank.
I searched for him
but could not find him anywhere.
I called to him,
but there was no reply.

5:6 Prov 1:28 Song 3:1; 5:2; 6:1

7 The night watchmen found me
as they made their rounds.
They beat and bruised me
and stripped off my veil,
those watchmen on the walls.

5:7 Song 3:3

5:1 Hebrew *my sister;* also in 5:2.

▶ GOD

5:1 Eat and drink deeply. As the Lover of our soul, Jesus Christ offers us a gift we cannot refuse. He is the Living Water and the Bread of Life. Everything we need He will supply freely. Isaiah prophesies, "Is anyone thirsty? Come and drink—even if you have no money! Come, take your choice of wine or milk—it's all free! . . . Listen to me, and you will eat what is good. You will enjoy the finest food" (Isaiah 55:1-2). Are you drinking deeply from the blessings that Jesus offers? His hand is out; His love is unending. (***See God****> God's Attributes> Unchanging> His love is never-ending,* TopicGuide page A18.)

5:1 The groom accepts his bride's invitation (see note at Song of Songs 4:16). In the latter part of the verse, the "young women of Jerusalem" encourage the bride and groom to enjoy their sexual union to the fullest ("drink deeply of your love").

5:2-8 These verses are parallel to 3:1-5 and describe in highly symbolic language the wedding night. As in real life, this encounter, even between two people who love each other dearly, ends in some degree of frustration. But her disappointment only heightens her desire for her beloved (5:10-16).

5:8 Song 2:5, 7; 3:5
[8] Make this promise, O women of Jerusalem—
If you find my lover,
tell him I am weak with love.

Young Women of Jerusalem

5:9 Song 1:8; 6:1
[9] Why is your lover better than all others,
O woman of rare beauty?
What makes your lover so special
that we must promise this?

Young Woman

5:10 1 Sam 16:12 Ps 45:2
[10] My lover is dark and dazzling,
better than ten thousand others!
[11] His head is finest gold,
his wavy hair is black as a raven.

5:12 Song 1:15; 4:1
[12] His eyes sparkle like doves
beside springs of water;
they are set like jewels
washed in milk.

5:13 Song 2:1; 5:5; 6:2
[13] His cheeks are like gardens of spices
giving off fragrance.
His lips are like lilies,
perfumed with myrrh.

5:14 Exod 24:10; 28:18, 20 Job 28:16 Isa 54:11 Ezek 1:16 Dan 10:6
[14] His arms are like rounded bars of gold,
set with beryl.
His body is like bright ivory,
glowing with lapis lazuli.

5:15 1 Kgs 4:33 Song 7:4
[15] His legs are like marble pillars
set in sockets of finest gold.
His posture is stately,
like the noble cedars of Lebanon.

5:16 2 Sam 1:23 Song 7:9
[16] His mouth is sweetness itself;
he is desirable in every way.
Such, O women of Jerusalem,
is my lover, my friend.

6

Young Women of Jerusalem

6:1 Song 1:8; 5:6
[1] Where has your lover gone,
O woman of rare beauty?
Which way did he turn
so we can help you find him?

Young Woman

6:2 Song 1:7; 2:1; 4:16; 5:1, 13
[2] My lover has gone down to his garden,
to his spice beds,
to browse in the gardens
and gather the lilies.

5:9 This question is in response to the bride's song in verses 2-8 and prepares for her next song of love about her groom (5:10-16).

5:10-16 The bride describes her groom by starting with his head and working downward (except for his mouth in 5:16; see notes at Song of Songs 4:1 and 7:1-5). She delights in every part of his physical appearance, and she concludes by calling him "my lover, my friend"—both of which every man should be to his wife.

6:1-3 The bride is no longer looking for her groom (compare 5:6). The "young women of Jerusalem" are eager to help the beautiful bride search for him, but she assures them that she knows where he is. The groom is in bed with her. Once again (see note at 4:16) metaphors are used to describe their sexual union: "garden," "spice beds," and "lilies"—climaxed by the bride's declaration of their mutual ownership of each other: "I am my lover's, and my lover is mine" (see also Song of Songs 2:16; 7:10).

[3] I am my lover's, and my lover is mine.
He browses among the lilies.

6:3 Song 2:16; 4:5; 7:10

Young Man

[4] You are beautiful, my darling,
like the lovely city of Tirzah.
Yes, as beautiful as Jerusalem,
as majestic as an army with billowing banners.

6:4 1 Kgs 14:17 Pss 48:2; 50:2 Song 1:15; 6:10

[5] Turn your eyes away,
for they overpower me.
Your hair falls in waves,
like a flock of goats winding down the slopes of Gilead.

6:5 Song 4:1

[6] Your teeth are as white as sheep
that are freshly washed.
Your smile is flawless,
each tooth matched with its twin.*

6:6-7 Song 4:2-3

[7] Your cheeks are like rosy pomegranates
behind your veil.

[8] Even among sixty queens
and eighty concubines
and countless young women,

6:8 1 Kgs 11:3 Song 1:3

[9] I would still choose my dove, my perfect one—
the favorite of her mother,
dearly loved by the one who bore her.
The young women see her and praise her;
even queens and royal concubines sing her praises:

6:9 Gen 30:13 Song 2:14; 5:2

[10] "Who is this, arising like the dawn,
as fair as the moon,
as bright as the sun,
as majestic as an army with billowing banners?"

6:10 Job 31:26 Song 6:4 Matt 17:2 Rev 1:16

[11] I went down to the grove of walnut trees
and out to the valley to see the new spring growth,
to see whether the grapevines had budded
or the pomegranates were in bloom.

6:11 Song 4:13; 7:12

[12] Before I realized it,
I found myself in the royal chariot with my beloved.*

Young Women of Jerusalem

[13]*Return, return to us, O maid of Shulam.
Come back, come back, that we may see you again.

6:13 Gen 32:2 Judg 21:21 2 Sam 17:24

6:6 Hebrew *Not one is missing; each has a twin.* 6:12 Or *among the royal chariots of my people,* or *among the chariots of Amminadab.* The meaning of the Hebrew is uncertain. 6:13a Verse 6:13 is numbered 7:1 in Hebrew text.

▶ BIBLE

6:3 The gift of love. The principles of marriage in the Bible are not random—they are intended to make marriage strong. One such principle is the taking on of vows, in which we pledge ourselves to another person. That means that we give ownership of our rights to our spouse. No longer do we hold on to pure personal autonomy, but we first regard the interests and well-being of our mate (1 Corinthians 7:1-7). We give everything we are—our talents, possessions, and physical being—to our lover. What are you holding back from your spouse? Make a list of the things that you uniquely hold that your spouse needs. Show your spouse your willingness to serve him or her. (***See Bible> Unity> Doctrines> Principles of marriage,*** TopicGuide page A10.)

6:4-10 In verses 4-7 the groom once again extols the beauty of his bride, much of it similar to Song of Songs 4:1-7 (see note). He sees her as "perfect" and prefers her to the numerous others ("queens," "concubines," or "young women") he could have chosen. In fact, these women are also overwhelmed by her beauty and wonder who she is.

6:11-12 The bride may be the speaker here and not the groom. The metaphors of "walnut trees," "the valley," "grapevines" and "pomegranates" likely describe the groom's body and her sexual union with him.

6:13 The "young women of Jerusalem" call to the bride to return to them so they can see her again, but the groom gently

Young Man

Why do you stare at this young woman of Shulam,
as she moves so gracefully between two lines
of dancers?*

7:1 Ps 45:13

7 1*How beautiful are your sandaled feet,
O queenly maiden.
Your rounded thighs are like jewels,
the work of a skilled craftsman.
2 Your navel is perfectly formed
like a goblet filled with mixed wine.
Between your thighs lies a mound of wheat
bordered with lilies.

7:3 Song 4:5

3 Your breasts are like two fawns,
twin fawns of a gazelle.

7:4 Num 21:26 Song 4:4

4 Your neck is as beautiful as an ivory tower.
Your eyes are like the sparkling pools in Heshbon
by the gate of Bath-rabbim.
Your nose is as fine as the tower of Lebanon
overlooking Damascus.

7:5 Isa 35:2

5 Your head is as majestic as Mount Carmel,
and the sheen of your hair radiates royalty.
The king is held captive by its tresses.

7:6 Song 1:15-16

6 Oh, how beautiful you are!
How pleasing, my love, how full of delights!
7 You are slender like a palm tree,
and your breasts are like its clusters of fruit.

7:8 Song 2:5

8 I said, "I will climb the palm tree
and take hold of its fruit."
May your breasts be like grape clusters,
and the fragrance of your breath like apples.

7:9 Prov 23:31 Song 5:16

9 May your kisses be as exciting as the best wine,
flowing gently over lips and teeth.*

6:13b Or *as you would at the movements of two armies?* or *as you would at the dance of Mahanaim?* The meaning of the Hebrew is uncertain. 7:1 Verses 7:1-13 are numbered 7:2-14 in Hebrew text. 7:9 As in Greek and Syriac versions and Latin Vulgate; Hebrew reads *over lips of sleepers.*

rebukes them for wanting her back. She is forever his. He then turns his attention to her beauty once again (see Song of Songs 7:1-9). "Maid of Shulam" may be a play on Solomon's name (the Hebrew consonants are the same), or it could be a title meaning "she who is perfect."

▸ HOLINESS

7:1 The joy of beauty. **Did you know that the Bible teaches us that physical attractiveness to your mate is important? In this verse, a young man extols the wonder of his bride. He revels in her sensuousness. Sometimes, as believers, we get so concerned about our society's promiscuous attitudes about sex that we forget the importance of physical attraction. We should appreciate the beauty of our mate, and in doing so we will find joy and more complete satisfaction. Do your best to make sure that your mate is not interested in rejoicing in the beauty of anyone but you.** **(*See Holiness*> *Law and Grace*> *Law*> *Marriage*, TopicGuide page A41.)**

7:1-5 **In verses 1-5 the groom once again describes his beautiful bride's physical appearance, this time starting at the feet and working his way up her body (see notes at Song of Songs 4:1 and 5:10-16). Each of their descriptions refers to things that remind them in some way of each other.**

7:6-9 **The groom finds his bride's body "full of delights" (7:6). He then returns to describing her breasts (7:3; see note at Song of Songs 4:5-6), which he here compares to "clusters of fruit" and "grape clusters." He anticipates the excitement of her kisses, which are as intoxicating as wine (see note at Song of Songs 4:9-10).**

Young Woman

10 I am my lover's,
and he claims me as his own. 7:10 Ps 45:11 Song 2:16; 6:3
11 Come, my love, let us go out to the fields
and spend the night among the wildflowers.*
12 Let us get up early and go to the vineyards 7:12 Song 6:11
to see if the grapevines have budded,
if the blossoms have opened,
and if the pomegranates have bloomed.
There I will give you my love.
13 There the mandrakes give off their fragrance, 7:13 Gen 30:14 Song 2:3; 4:13, 16
and the finest fruits are at our door,
new delights as well as old,
which I have saved for you, my lover.

8 *Young Woman*
1 Oh, I wish you were my brother,
who nursed at my mother's breasts.
Then I could kiss you no matter who was watching,
and no one would criticize me.
2 I would bring you to my childhood home, 8:2 Song 3:4
and there you would teach me.*
I would give you spiced wine to drink,
my sweet pomegranate wine.
3 Your left arm would be under my head, 8:3 Song 2:6
and your right arm would embrace me.

4 Promise me, O women of Jerusalem, 8:4 Song 2:7; 3:5
not to awaken love until the time is right.*

7:11 Or *in the villages.* 8:2 Or *there she will teach me;* or *there she bore me.* 8:4 Or *not to awaken love until it is ready.*

7:10-13 The bride invites her groom to a pastoral setting to enjoy intimacy with her—"there I will give you my love" (7:12). Previously, the groom had invited his bride to go away with him, and now she becomes the aggressor in pursuing him (see note at Song of Songs 2:10-17). The mandrake is a vegetable that was considered an aphrodisiac in the ancient world (see Genesis 30:14-16). The reference to it here is to enhance the romantic setting.

▶ **BIBLE**

7:12 Take time to be together. When is the last time you arose early with your spouse and spent time in a garden, enjoying nature, worshiping God, and celebrating your love for one another? In this chapter, Solomon gives us a picture of the joy we can have when we spend time building our marital relationship. Those times alone are essential to our unity as spouses. Do you set aside time to enjoy those moments alone with your mate? If the busyness of life has squeezed out the joy of being together, plan for a date night or for a walk in the garden. Read this chapter together, and, in an appropriate way, plan to show your affection for your spouse. (***See Bible***> *Unity*> *Doctrines*> *Principles of marriage,* TopicGuide page A10.)

8:1 The bride's wish for her groom to be her brother does not imply an incestuous relationship, but simply indicates that she would like to express her affections for him openly. In ancient Israel a woman could kiss her father, brother, or some other close male relative in public, but no one else—not even her husband.

8:2-3 The bride's reference to her brother (see note at 8:1) does not carry over to these verses. "I would bring" and "I would give" are literally translated "I will bring" and "I will give." She plans to take her groom to a private place where she can show her love for him fully and passionately.

▶ **HOLINESS**

8:4 The right time. There is a right time for allowing physical passion and longing to flower into sexual activity. But how do you get the timing right? How do you build your desire for the one you love without becoming overpowered by that same desire—particularly as a single person? Avoiding sin means avoiding temptation. If you are dating or spending significant private time with someone to whom you are attracted, that may mean taking some precautions. Acknowledging that we have physical urges that may waylay us and compromise our standards is the first step in this planning. The next step is accountability—spend time together in groups, not always alone. Finally, keep God at the center of every relationship—our mutual love for Him helps keep our passion in its place. (***See Holiness***> *Disciplines*> *Of Abstinence*> *Resisting sinful urges,* TopicGuide page A42.)

Young Women of Jerusalem

8:5 Song 2:3; 3:6
[5] Who is this sweeping in from the desert,
leaning on her lover?

Young Woman

I aroused you under the apple tree,
where your mother gave you birth,
where in great pain she delivered you.

8:6 Prov 6:34 Isa 49:16 Jer 22:24 Hag 2:23
[6] Place me like a seal over your heart,
like a seal on your arm.
For love is as strong as death,
its jealousy* as enduring as the grave.*
Love flashes like fire,
the brightest kind of flame.
[7] Many waters cannot quench love,
nor can rivers drown it.
If a man tried to buy love
with all his wealth,
his offer would be utterly scorned.

The Young Woman's Brothers

8:8 Ezek 16:7
[8] We have a little sister
too young to have breasts.
What will we do for our sister
if someone asks to marry her?

8:9 1 Kgs 6:15
[9] If she is a virgin, like a wall,
we will protect her with a silver tower.
But if she is promiscuous, like a swinging door,
we will block her door with a cedar bar.

Young Woman

[10] I was a virgin, like a wall;
now my breasts are like towers.
When my lover looks at me,
he is delighted with what he sees.

8:11 Eccl 2:4 Song 1:6; 2:3; 8:12 Isa 7:23 Matt 21:33
[11] Solomon has a vineyard at Baal-hamon,
which he leases out to tenant farmers.
Each of them pays a thousand pieces of silver*
for harvesting its fruit.

8:6a Or *its passion.* **8:6b** Hebrew *as Sheol.* **8:11** Hebrew *1,000 shekels of silver.*

8:5 In Song of Songs 3:6, the "young women of Jerusalem" had admired the groom with similar wording, but now they admire the bride as she arrives with "her lover."

8:5-7 The bride "aroused" her groom so they could enjoy sexual relations with each other, and she declares that their devotion to each other is permanent, like a "seal" over the heart and on the arm. "Jealousy" is literally translated "passion" (see textual note), which seems to provide a better parallel with "love." Their love for each other as strong as death and the grave, that is, it will not end.

8:8-9 Since the bride's brothers have not spoken elsewhere, it is likely that the "young women of Jerusalem" are the speakers here. (They are mentioned in 1:6 but do not speak.) They protest that the bride (their "little sister") is too young to get married ("too young to have breasts") and should remain a virgin until the proper time.

8:10-12 The bride explains that her "breasts are like towers" (sexually mature) and that her groom ("Solomon") is, in fact, in her vineyard; that is, they are being physically intimate. Thus, the "young women of Jerusalem" were wrong to protest her marriage, for the bride is both ready for her groom and happy to be intimate with him.

[12] But my vineyard is mine to give,
and Solomon need not pay a thousand pieces of silver.
But I will give two hundred pieces
to those who care for its vines.

Young Man

[13] O my darling, lingering in the gardens,
your companions are fortunate to hear your voice.
Let me hear it, too!

8:13 Song 1:7; 2:14

Young Woman

[14] Come away, my love! Be like a gazelle
or a young stag on the mountains of spices.

8:14 Song 2:7, 9, 17; 4:6

▸ CHURCH

8:13 Lingering with Christ. The Bible pictures Christ as our bridegroom, the lover of our soul. He is the One who loves us in a way no one else ever will. He is beside us when everyone else leaves. He protects, saves, comforts, and guides us. Do you linger with Him as a bride would with her bridegroom? Do you wake every morning eager to hear His voice? Is the thought of His love the last thing on your mind at night? He will never disappoint you. Make Him the center of your life. (***See Church***> *What> Many Titles> Bride> Who rejoices and fasts,* TopicGuide page A48.)

8:13 The groom knows that many others are noticing his bride, and he longs to hear her voice again.

8:14 The book closes with the bride's invitation to the groom to go away with her to enjoy life and love together. The poem ends with every sense involved, every sensual tension brought to bear—being apart from one another, hearing the voice of the beloved (8:13), coming together again to touch one another, with the scent of spiced perfume rising like an offering to God, the giver of physical love.

ISAIAH

PURPOSE

To announce God's forthcoming judgment upon Judah for following Israel into idolatry and to console the condemned nation with the promise of salvation and restoration.

Most people who read the Bible are familiar with the four Gospels of the New Testament—the books of Matthew, Mark, Luke, and John. Fewer, however, are acquainted with the "Gospel of Isaiah." Though this book was written hundreds of years before Jesus' birth, no other book in the Old Testament presents such clear and compelling prophecies about the salvation to come through the Servant of the Lord, Jesus Christ.

Isaiah is the longest of the Old Testament prophetic books and is widely regarded as the most beautifully written and theologically profound. Its sixty-six chapters are divided in a similar fashion as the Bible's sixty-six books (thirty-nine Old Testament books, twenty-seven New Testament). The first thirty-nine chapters of Isaiah are a message of *condemnation and deportation* directed toward Judah for her failure to be faithful to God. But the last twenty-seven chapters are a message of *consolation and restoration*. Though Israel's sins were like scarlet, after the washing of the Lord they would be white as snow (1:18).

DISCOVER GOD IN ISAIAH

Three attributes of God frame the book of Isaiah: He is Judge (mentioned most often in chapters 1–39), Servant (mentioned mostly in chapters 49–55), and Healer (mentioned mostly in chapters 53–66).

Judge: From the earliest days of their relationship, God told Israel what would happen if they rejected Him and His statutes. Moses put it this way: "You will watch as your sons and daughters are taken away as slaves. Your heart will break for them, but you won't be able to help them. A foreign nation you have never heard about will eat the crops you worked so hard to grow. You will suffer under constant oppression and harsh treatment" (Deuteronomy 28:32-33). As Israel's sins mounted, Isaiah pictured God calling pagan nations to carry out the wounding of His people (5:25-30; 7:18-21). Why did God wound those He loved? The answer lies in God's covenant relationship with His people. He promised to bless their faithful obedience and to punish their rebellion. Because God is holy, He must judge sin, and because God is always true to Himself, He must fulfill His covenant promises—and His covenant threats. But while God wounded His people Israel, He did not kill them. He wounds those He loves to bring them to repentance, that He might win them back to Himself.

Healer: The first words of Isaiah 40 reveal the healing character of the God who wounds: " 'Comfort, comfort My people,' says your God. 'Speak tenderly to Jerusalem. Tell her that her sad days are gone and her sins are pardoned. Yes, the LORD has punished her twice over for all her sins' " (40:1-2). It is easy to see why Isaiah is often referred to as "the Gospel of Isaiah." In fact, in the New Testament, the apostle Peter quotes another passage from Isaiah that contains the heart of the gospel: "He personally carried our sins in his body on the cross so that we can be dead to sin and live for what is right. By His wounds you are healed" (1 Peter 2:24; see Isaiah 53:5). The healing ministry prophesied by Isaiah was fulfilled in Jesus' ministry (forgiving and healing) and consummated on the cross when Jesus died to heal the sins of "all the world" (1 John 2:2).

DISCOVERY VERSES

For a Child is born to us, a Son is given to us. The government will rest on His shoulders. And He will be called: Wonderful Counselor, Mighty God, Everlasting Father, Prince of Peace. His government and its peace will never end. He will rule with fairness and justice from the throne of His ancestor David for all eternity. The passionate commitment of the LORD of Heaven's Armies will make this happen! (ISAIAH 9:6-7)

But those who trust in the LORD will find new strength. They will soar high on wings like eagles. They will run and not grow weary. They will walk and not faint. (ISAIAH 40:31)

"My thoughts are nothing like your thoughts," says the LORD. "And My ways are far beyond anything you could imagine. For just as the heavens are higher than the earth, so My ways are higher than your ways and My thoughts higher than your thoughts." (ISAIAH 55:8-9)

Servant: Much is made today of the notion of "servant leadership"—leading by serving instead of dictating. The nation of Israel was God's original servant-leader, commissioned to reveal the glory of God to the nations (Isaiah 44:21; 45:4; 49:3). But Israel forfeited the right to lead by being unwilling to serve, so God took on the role of Servant-Leader Himself through the person of the Messiah, Jesus Christ (Isaiah 42:1-4; 49:5; 49:7; 53:2, 11). Jesus Christ served the whole world by His voluntary submission to death on the cross. Among all the religions of the world, no demonstration of service has ever surpassed that seen on Calvary. It was God's attribute of servanthood that motivated Jesus to say, "There is no greater love than to lay down one's life for one's friends" (John 15:13).

GROWING THROUGH ISAIAH

Two themes stand out in Isaiah for the follower of Christ:

Suffering: It is impossible to read Isaiah 53 without concluding that, from God's perspective, suffering plays an integral part in His plan to save sinful humanity. Isaiah 53 says, "It was the LORD's good plan to crush Him and cause Him grief" (Isaiah 53:10). This chapter is not just powerful Hebrew poetry—it speaks of the need for all God's people to recognize suffering as one of God's means to accomplish His will. The suffering of this Servant would not be in vain—no one can be saved unless he believes by faith that Jesus suffered on his behalf. The message of Isaiah is that the Lord is the God who ordains suffering as a means to some of His most glorious ends.

Trust in the Lord: In Isaiah 36, we meet a noble king named Hezekiah. There was much to commend in the rule of Hezekiah, king of Judah. For instance, he reopened the Temple in Jerusalem and restored worship there. But when enemies came near his gate, Hezekiah's faith failed, and he engaged in alliances with pagan nations—even though the Lord had promised him deliverance from Assyria (Isaiah 38:6-7). Though Jerusalem was saved from Assyria, Isaiah prophesied her destruction by Babylon because of Hezekiah's lack of faithfulness (39:5-7). There is a price to be paid for failing to be loyal to the Lord who is loyal to us—and often the price must be paid not only by us, but also by those under our care.

ISAIAH FACTS

Author: Isaiah (1:1). Appropriately for his ultimate message, *Isaiah* means "the LORD saves."

Written to: The nation of Judah.

Date of writing: Isaiah's prophetic words were written during the years of his ministry, 740 to 680 BC.

Setting: Isaiah prophesied in Jerusalem and in Judah at large. However, the book also addresses Assyria, Babylon, and other nearby pagan nations that were in line for God's judgment.

OUTLINE

- **ISAIAH 1:1–6:13**—Judgment and comfort
- **ISAIAH 7:1–39:8**—Warnings amid Assyrian judgment
- **ISAIAH 40:1–66:24**—Comfort amid Babylonian judgment

1:1 2 Kgs 15:1, 13; 16:1; 18:1 Isa 2:1; 40:9

1 These are the visions that Isaiah son of Amoz saw concerning Judah and Jerusalem. He saw these visions during the years when Uzziah, Jotham, Ahaz, and Hezekiah were kings of Judah.*

A MESSAGE FOR REBELLIOUS JUDAH

1:2 Deut 32:1 Isa 65:2 Jer 3:22 Mic 1:2

2 Listen, O heavens! Pay attention, earth!
This is what the LORD says:
"The children I raised and cared for
have rebelled against Me.

1:3 Jer 8:7; 9:3, 6

3 Even an ox knows its owner,
and a donkey recognizes its master's care—
but Israel doesn't know its Master.
My people don't recognize My care for them."

1:4 Isa 1:28; 5:24; 14:20

4 Oh, what a sinful nation they are—
loaded down with a burden of guilt.
They are evil people,
corrupt children who have rejected the LORD.
They have despised the Holy One of Israel
and turned their backs on Him.

1:5 Isa 31:6; 33:24

5 Why do you continue to invite punishment?
Must you rebel forever?
Your head is injured,
and your heart is sick.

1:6 Ps 38:3

6 You are battered from head to foot—
covered with bruises, welts, and infected wounds—
without any soothing ointments or bandages.

1:7 Lev 26:33 Jer 44:6

7 Your country lies in ruins,
and your towns are burned.
Foreigners plunder your fields before your eyes
and destroy everything they see.

1:1 These kings reigned from 792 to 686 B.C.

1:2–5:30 The collection of oracles in chapters 1–5 was most likely delivered after Isaiah's call to service, but was placed before the record of his vision (chapter 6) as an introduction to the book. (See Introduction to Isaiah for a simple outline of the book.)

1:2-3 Isaiah opens with an indictment of Israel presented in the language of a courtroom. Heaven and earth are symbolically called as witnesses against God's people. Israel is charged with rebellion. She rejected God's care and provision. Even the ox and the donkey, known for their stubbornness and stupidity, do not reject their owners; yet Israel rejected the Lord.

GOD

1:3 The gratitude of a donkey. When a farmer treats his animals well, they usually respond to his kindness with hard work. But people are more complicated. Many people will admit that God gives us good things. Yet few respond to God's kindness by listening to Him. Instead, they take God's blessings for granted and go their own way. They rebel against the One that has done so much for them. Which attitude describes your behavior toward God—gratitude or ingratitude? Begin your day by thanking God for the blessings He has given you. (***See God***> *Relationship> God's Desire> God loves and wants to be loved,* TopicGuide page A14.)

1:4 The Lord is referred to as the "Holy One of Israel" 26 times in the book of Isaiah (for example, 5:19; 12:6; 30:11; 41:14). The title emphasizes not only God's righteousness and purity but also His transcendence. God is distinct and unique; there is none like Him.

THE WRITING PROPHETS

The following chart lists details about the Old Testament prophetic books. Each book is named after the prophet who wrote it. The dates of ministry listed are for the spoken ministries of the prophets, and are often associated with the dates of kings during whose lives the prophets ministered. The final dates of writing are probable ranges for the completion of the written books as they now exist in the Old Testament. All dates are BC. The original audiences include both audiences of ministry and of writing.

Name	Date of Ministry	Final Date of Writing	Original Audience	Message
Isaiah	740–686	686–650	Israel and Judah	Remain loyal to God, repent of sin, and hope for blessings in the restoration after exile.
Jeremiah	626–586	580–539	Judah	Remember reasons for exile, repent of sin, and hope for blessings in restoration after exile.
Ezekiel	593–573	573–570	Judah	Remain faithful to God so that God will fulfill his offers of restoration with a new temple.
Daniel	605–539	539	Judah	God is in control of history, but there will be a long period of trouble before God's kingdom is manifested on earth.
Hosea	760–722	724–722	Israel	God's judgment and exile of Israel was just, but God would restore them in the future.
Joel	unknown	unknown	Judah	Repent of sin in order to avoid judgment and obtain blessings on the Day of the Lord.
Amos	793–740	760–750	Israel	Divine judgment against infidelity would be severe, but there was hope for restoration after exile.
Obadiah	586	586	Edom and Judah	Hope in God's justice for victory over enemies.
Jonah	786–746	750–613	Assyria and Israel	Extend the gospel to the nations.
Micah	742–686	715–686	Israel and Judah	Repent of sin, and hope in God for restoration after exile.
Nahum	663–627	663–612	Assyria and Judah	Take comfort in God's coming judgment against Assyria.
Habakkuk	605	605–600	Judah	Remain faithful to God even while suffering conquest and exile.
Zephaniah	640–609	640–621	Judah	Repent before exile, and hope for restoration after exile.
Haggai	520	520–516	Judah	Reconstruct the temple and hope for God's blessing.
Zechariah	520–475	480–475	Judah	Hope in God through trials, and for great blessings in the restoration of the kingdom.
Malachi	458–433	458–433	Judah	Renew faith in God and trust in His coming messiah.

8 Beautiful Jerusalem* stands abandoned
like a watchman's shelter in a vineyard,
like a lean-to in a cucumber field after the harvest,
like a helpless city under siege.
1:9 9 If the LORD of Heaven's Armies
Isa 10:20-22; 11:11, 16 had not spared a few of us,*
*Rom 9:29 we would have been wiped out like Sodom,
destroyed like Gomorrah.

1:10 10 Listen to the LORD, you leaders of "Sodom."
Ezek 16:46 Listen to the law of our God, people of "Gomorrah."
Rev 11:8 11 "What makes you think I want all your sacrifices?"
1:11 says the LORD.
Jer 6:20
Mal 1:10 "I am sick of your burnt offerings of rams
and the fat of fattened cattle.
I get no pleasure from the blood
of bulls and lambs and goats.
12 When you come to worship Me,
who asked you to parade through My courts with all your ceremony?
1:13 13 Stop bringing Me your meaningless gifts;
1 Chr 23:31 the incense of your offerings disgusts Me!
As for your celebrations of the new moon and the Sabbath
and your special days for fasting—
they are all sinful and false.
I want no more of your pious meetings.
1:14 14 I hate your new moon celebrations and your annual festivals.
Isa 43:24 They are a burden to Me. I cannot stand them!
1:15 15 When you lift up your hands in prayer, I will not look.
Isa 59:2 Though you offer many prayers, I will not listen,
Mic 3:4 for your hands are covered with the blood of innocent victims.
1:16 16 Wash yourselves and be clean!
Ps 26:6 Get your sins out of My sight.
Isa 52:11
Jer 25:5 Give up your evil ways.
1:17 17 Learn to do good.
Jer 22:3 Seek justice.
Help the oppressed.
Defend the cause of orphans.
Fight for the rights of widows.

1:18 18 "Come now, let's settle this,"
Ps 51:7 says the LORD.
Isa 43:26; 44:22
Rev 7:14

1:8 Hebrew *The daughter of Zion.* 1:9 Greek version reads *a few of our children.* Compare Rom 9:29.

1:9-10 The Lord completely destroyed the cities of Sodom and Gomorrah because of their unspeakable wickedness (see Genesis 18:20-21; 19:24-25). The allusion to these infamous cities suggests both the abject level of wickedness that filled Judah, as well as the judgment that threatened to overwhelm the nation.

1:11-17 Judah's sacrifices, worship, and prayers were rejected because they were offered hypocritically by people whose hearts were far from God. The Lord is never satisfied with mere external conformity to the law; He desires wholehearted love and obedience, which results in justice in the public sphere. Compare Psalm 40:6-8 and Micah 6:6-8.

▶ GOD

1:16 A right heart. People in a crisis often cry out for God's help, but then go right back to their earlier behavior once their situation resolves itself. Isaiah tells us that our relationship to God requires repentance. That means turning from our sins to God. To have an intimate walk with God, search your heart for any wrong attitudes or for any secret sin. Confess these to God, asking Him to help you give up your wicked ways and embrace His holy ways. (***See God**> Relationship> God Enables> Relationship with God requires a right heart,* TopicGuide page A14.)

"Though your sins are like scarlet,
I will make them as white as snow.
Though they are red like crimson,
I will make them as white as wool.
19 If you will only obey Me,
you will have plenty to eat.
20 But if you turn away and refuse to listen,
you will be devoured by the sword of your enemies.
I, the LORD, have spoken!"

1:19 Deut 30:15-16
1:20 Isa 3:25

UNFAITHFUL JERUSALEM

21 See how Jerusalem, once so faithful,
has become a prostitute.
Once the home of justice and righteousness,
she is now filled with murderers.
22 Once like pure silver,
you have become like worthless slag.
Once so pure,
you are now like watered-down wine.
23 Your leaders are rebels,
the companions of thieves.
All of them love bribes
and demand payoffs,
but they refuse to defend the cause of orphans
or fight for the rights of widows.
24 Therefore, the Lord, the LORD of Heaven's Armies,
the Mighty One of Israel, says,
"I will take revenge on My enemies
and pay back My foes!
25 I will raise My fist against you.
I will melt you down and skim off your slag.
I will remove all your impurities.
26 Then I will give you good judges again
and wise counselors like you used to have.
Then Jerusalem will again be called the Home of Justice
and the Faithful City."

27 Zion will be restored by justice;
those who repent will be revived by righteousness.
28 But rebels and sinners will be completely destroyed,
and those who desert the LORD will be consumed.

29 You will be ashamed of your idol worship
in groves of sacred oaks.
You will blush because you worshiped
in gardens dedicated to idols.

1:21 Jer 2:20
1:23 Exod 23:8; Jer 5:28; Ezek 22:7; Mic 7:3
1:24 Isa 35:4; 49:26
1:25 Ezek 22:19-22; Mal 3:3
1:26 Isa 33:5; Zech 8:3
1:28 Ps 9:5; 2 Thes 1:8-9
1:29 Isa 65:3

1:21-23 Through a series of similes, Isaiah described Jerusalem's moral and religious decline. The specific examples of wickedness center on the perversion of justice and oppression of the helpless. The Law of Moses contains provisions aimed at the relief and protection of orphans and widows who were particularly vulnerable to abuse (Deuteronomy 10:18; 17:19; 24:17-19; 26:12-13).

1:29-30 God's people engaged in pagan fertility rituals in groves of oak trees and gardens (compare 65:3 and 66:17). Isaiah transformed the oaks and gardens into metaphors of God's impending judgment.

30 You will be like a great tree with withered leaves,
like a garden without water.

1:31 Isa 5:24; 33:11-14; 66:24 Matt 3:12

31 The strongest among you will disappear like straw;
their evil deeds will be the spark that sets it on fire.
They and their evil works will burn up together,
and no one will be able to put out the fire.

THE LORD'S FUTURE REIGN

2:1-4 //Mic 4:1-3

2 This is a vision that Isaiah son of Amoz saw concerning Judah and Jerusalem:

2 In the last days, the mountain of the LORD's house
will be the highest of all—
the most important place on earth.
It will be raised above the other hills,
and people from all over the world will stream there to worship.

2:3 Isa 51:4-5 Luke 24:47

3 People from many nations will come and say,
"Come, let us go up to the mountain of the LORD,
to the house of Jacob's God.
There He will teach us His ways,
and we will walk in His paths."
For the LORD's teaching will go out from Zion;
His word will go out from Jerusalem.

2:4 Isa 32:17-18 Hos 2:18

4 The LORD will mediate between nations
and will settle international disputes.
They will hammer their swords into plowshares
and their spears into pruning hooks.
Nation will no longer fight against nation,
nor train for war anymore.

A WARNING OF JUDGMENT

2:5 Isa 58:1; 60:1-2, 19-20 1 Jn 1:5, 7

5 Come, descendants of Jacob,
let us walk in the light of the LORD!

2:6 Deut 31:17 2 Kgs 1:2; 16:7-8

6 For the LORD has rejected His people,
the descendants of Jacob,
because they have filled their land with practices from the East
and with sorcerers, as the Philistines do.
They have made alliances with pagans.

2:7 Deut 17:16

7 Israel is full of silver and gold;
there is no end to its treasures.
Their land is full of warhorses;
there is no end to its chariots.

2:1–4:6 This passage, which begins with a new title, is composed of four sections. The opening and closing sections are hymns of Zion that celebrate what Jerusalem was meant to be (2:2-4) and what she could yet become (4:2-6). Within these hymns, however, are two oracles that denounce the religious (2:5-22) and social (3:1–4:1) sins of the people of Judah.

2:1 The new title suggests that 2:1–4:6 circulated as an independent composition before being brought into the present collection of Isaiah's work.

2:2 The phrase "last days" is derived from Moses' outline of Israel's history in Deuteronomy 4:30, but, depending on the context, can mean several things in Scripture. Here the "last days" is a technical designation for the time of Israel's restoration following an exile from the land. The "last days" following a return from exile would mark a return to the land, the renewal of the Davidic line, and innumerable blessings (Hosea 3:5; Micah 4:1). According to the New Testament, the "last days" were inaugurated by the work of Christ and will continue until His return (Acts 2:17; 2 Timothy 3:1; Hebrews 1:2; 2 Peter 3:3).

2:6-9 Isaiah frequently ridiculed idols as the work of human hands (see 17:7-8; 30:22; 31:7; 40:19-20).

8 Their land is full of idols;
the people worship things they have made
with their own hands.
9 So now they will be humbled,
and all will be brought low—
do not forgive them.
10 Crawl into caves in the rocks.
Hide in the dust
from the terror of the LORD
and the glory of His majesty.
11 Human pride will be brought down,
and human arrogance will be humbled.
Only the LORD will be exalted
on that day of judgment.

12 For the LORD of Heaven's Armies
has a day of reckoning.
He will punish the proud and mighty
and bring down everything that is exalted.
13 He will cut down the tall cedars of Lebanon
and all the mighty oaks of Bashan.
14 He will level all the high mountains
and all the lofty hills.
15 He will break down every high tower
and every fortified wall.
16 He will destroy all the great trading ships*
and every magnificent vessel.
17 Human pride will be humbled,
and human arrogance will be brought down.
Only the LORD will be exalted
on that day of judgment.

18 Idols will completely disappear.
19 When the LORD rises to shake the earth,
His enemies will crawl into holes in the ground.
They will hide in caves in the rocks
from the terror of the LORD
and the glory of His majesty.
20 On that day of judgment they will abandon the gold and silver idols
they made for themselves to worship.
They will leave their gods to the rodents and bats,

2:8 Ps 115:4-8; Isa 10:11; 17:8; 44:17
2:9 Neh 4:5; Isa 5:15
2:10 2 Thes 1:9; Rev 6:15-16
2:11 Isa 13:11
2:12 Job 40:11-12; Mal 4:1
2:13 Isa 10:33-34; Zech 11:2
2:16 1 Kgs 10:22; Isa 23:1, 14
2:18 Isa 21:9; Mic 1:7
2:19 Ps 18:7; Hag 2:6-7; Heb 12:26
2:20 Isa 30:22

2:16 Hebrew *every ship of Tarshish.*

▸ WORSHIP
2:8 Setting up idols. In the days of Isaiah, the people set up idols and worshiped them instead of honoring God. Today, those ancient gods are rarely worshiped. But we have our own idols; anything we put in God's place is an idol. Some people worship material possessions. Others worship their children or their career. Even honorable work, such as helping your church, can become an idol if it becomes more important than God. Examine your loves and activities. Are any of them assuming more devotion than God receives? Make God the first priority in your life. (***See Worship****> OT> Reverence> Put away idols,* TopicGuide page A28.)

2:11 The "day of judgment" or "day of the LORD" is a recurring theme throughout the prophetic books. The "day of the LORD" in the Old Testament may be any day in which God acts in judgment either against His enemies or against His people for their sins. There is also the hope of a great and final "day of judgment" when He will permanently defeat all evil in the world.

2:12-18 The Lord's judgment against the proud and the arrogant is symbolized by the destruction of awe-inspiring features of the natural world and the great works of human hands.

2:21 Isa 2:10, 19

21 while they crawl away into caverns
and hide among the jagged rocks in the cliffs.
They will try to escape the terror of the LORD
and the glory of His majesty
as He rises to shake the earth.

2:22 Pss 8:4; 144:3-4; 146:3 Jer 17:5 Jas 4:14

22 Don't put your trust in mere humans.
They are as frail as breath.
What good are they?

JUDGMENT AGAINST JUDAH

3:1 Lev 26:26 Ezek 4:16

3 1 The Lord, the LORD of Heaven's Armies,
will take away from Jerusalem and Judah
everything they depend on:
every bit of bread
and every drop of water,

3:2 Isa 9:14-15

2 all their heroes and soldiers,
judges and prophets,
fortune-tellers and elders,
3 army officers and high officials,
advisers, skilled craftsmen, and astrologers.

3:4 Eccl 10:16

4 I will make boys their leaders,
and toddlers their rulers.

3:5 Isa 9:19 Jer 9:3-8 Mic 7:3-6

5 People will oppress each other—
man against man,
neighbor against neighbor.
Young people will insult their elders,
and vulgar people will sneer at the honorable.

6 In those days a man will say to his brother,
"Since you have a coat, you be our leader!
Take charge of this heap of ruins!"

3:7 Ezek 34:4

7 But he will reply,
"No! I can't help.
I don't have any extra food or clothes.
Don't put me in charge!"

3:8 Isa 1:7; 6:11; 9:17; 65:3, 5

8 For Jerusalem will stumble,
and Judah will fall,

▸ HOLINESS

2:22 Trust in God, not in humans. As humans, our tendency is to turn to other people in times of stress rather than turning to God. When illness strikes, we hurry to the doctor. When we are depressed, we cry on a friend's shoulder or go to a counselor or pastor. Looking to such people for help is not wrong, but it can become sinful if we place more trust in them than in God. Who do you turn to when a problem strikes? Do you go to God first? Do you feel the greatest comfort in His presence? If not, ask God to help you rely on Him as your most trusted friend. (***See Holiness****> Submission> Trusting God> Trust in God, not humans,* TopicGuide page A41.)

3:1-5 The Lord would bring judgment against Judah, resulting in complete anarchy and the overthrow of the traditional order of society. The ruling class would be done away with and the young and inexperienced would lead society. In the wake of God's judgment, the moral restraints of a stable society would crumble, opening the door for increased violence and crime.

3:6 Following God's judgment, conditions would deteriorate to the point where the mere possession of clothing would qualify a person to rule.

▸ WORSHIP

3:8 Pray for your country. Isaiah predicted the fall of Judah and its capital city, Jerusalem, because the people rebelled against God and chose their sinful ways. Their certain downfall didn't require Isaiah's prophecy to come true—God had already promised discipline if they turned against Him (Deuteronomy 7:7-10). Under the New Covenant, God requires that we pray for our nation. (1 Timothy 2:2). Specifically pray for your political leaders, your employer, and anyone else in authority over you, that they may allow you to live a godly, humble life. (***See Worship****> NT> Prayer> Instructions> Pray for those in authority,* TopicGuide page A33.)

because they speak out against the LORD and refuse to obey Him.
They provoke Him to His face.
9 The very look on their faces gives them away.
They display their sin like the people of Sodom
and don't even try to hide it.
They are doomed!
They have brought destruction upon themselves.

10 Tell the godly that all will be well for them.
They will enjoy the rich reward they have earned!
11 But the wicked are doomed,
for they will get exactly what they deserve.

12 Childish leaders oppress My people,
and women rule over them.
O My people, your leaders mislead you;
they send you down the wrong road.

13 The LORD takes His place in court
and presents His case against His people!
14 The LORD comes forward to pronounce judgment
on the elders and rulers of His people:
"You have ruined Israel, My vineyard.
Your houses are filled with things stolen from the poor.
15 How dare you crush My people,
grinding the faces of the poor into the dust?"
demands the Lord, the LORD of Heaven's Armies.

A WARNING TO JERUSALEM

16 The LORD says, "Beautiful Zion* is haughty:
craning her elegant neck,
flirting with her eyes,
walking with dainty steps,
tinkling her ankle bracelets.
17 So the Lord will send scabs on her head;
the LORD will make beautiful Zion bald."

18 On that day of judgment
the Lord will strip away everything that makes her beautiful:
ornaments, headbands, crescent necklaces,

3:9 Gen 13:13; Prov 8:36
3:10 Deut 28:1-14
3:11 Deut 28:15-68
3:12 Isa 9:16
3:13 Hos 4:1; Mic 6:2
3:14 Job 24:9, 14; Pss 10:9; 14:4; Ezek 18:12; 20:35-36; Jas 2:6
3:15 Ps 94:5
3:16 Isa 4:4
3:18 Judg 8:21

3:16 Or *The women of Zion* (with corresponding changes to plural forms through verse 24); Hebrew reads *The daughters of Zion;* also in 3:17.

3:12 The traditional social structure of Judah had been reversed. Judah was forced to rely on inexperienced youths and brazen women (3:16).

3:13-15 Isaiah again used the courtroom imagery to describe God's judgment against His people. The vineyard is a metaphor for Israel and anticipates the extended allegory of chapter 5.

▶ GOD
3:13 Your day in court. Imagine yourself accused in court of a terrible crime, and the verdict is returned: "Guilty." Dread fills your heart as the reality of your judgment sinks in. Now think of how it would feel to hear that same verdict from God on Judgment Day. In that court God will serve as both the prosecuting attorney and the judge. Since He knows everything, nothing you have done will miss His eye, and since He judges the heart, every motive and attitude will show through. The only way we can escape this dreadful day is to embrace the forgiveness offered through faith in Jesus Christ. Have you made the decision to trust Christ for your salvation? If not, do so right now and experience freedom from your guilt before God. (***See God****> God's Names> God> Judge,* TopicGuide page A18.)

19 earrings, bracelets, and veils;
20 scarves, ankle bracelets, sashes,
perfumes, and charms;
21 rings, jewels,
22 party clothes, gowns, capes, and purses;
23 mirrors, fine linen garments,
head ornaments, and shawls.

3:24 Esth 2:12 Isa 15:3; 22:12 1 Pet 3:3

24 Instead of smelling of sweet perfume, she will stink.
She will wear a rope for a sash,
and her elegant hair will fall out.
She will wear rough burlap instead of rich robes.
Shame will replace her beauty.*

3:25 Isa 1:20; 65:12

25 The men of the city will be killed with the sword,
and her warriors will die in battle.

3:26 Jer 14:2 Lam 2:10

26 The gates of Zion will weep and mourn.
The city will be like a ravaged woman,
huddled on the ground.

4:1 Isa 13:12; 54:4

4 In that day so few men will be left that seven women will fight for each man, saying, "Let us all marry you! We will provide our own food and clothing. Only let us take your name so we won't be mocked as old maids."

A PROMISE OF RESTORATION

4:2 Isa 11:1-5; 52:13; 53:2 Jer 23:5-6 Zech 3:8; 6:12

2 But in that day, the branch* of the LORD
will be beautiful and glorious;
the fruit of the land will be the pride and glory
of all who survive in Israel.

4:3 Isa 28:5 Luke 10:20

3 All who remain in Zion
will be a holy people—
those who survive the destruction of Jerusalem
and are recorded among the living.
4 The Lord will wash the filth from beautiful Zion*
and cleanse Jerusalem of its bloodstains
with the hot breath of fiery judgment.

4:5 Num 9:15-23

5 Then the LORD will provide shade for Mount Zion
and all who assemble there.
He will provide a canopy of cloud during the day
and smoke and flaming fire at night,
covering the glorious land.

3:24 As in Dead Sea Scrolls; Masoretic Text reads *robes / because instead of beauty.* **4:2** Or *the Branch.* **4:4** Or *from the women of Zion;* Hebrew reads *from the daughters of Zion.*

4:2-6 The judgment of the day of the Lord would purge the evil from Judah and produce a glorious renewal of Jerusalem. This restoration would be effected by the "branch of the LORD," a metaphorical title for the messianic Son of David, who would lead in the rebuilding of God's people (compare 11:1-5; Zechariah 3:8-10). Jesus, the eternal Son of David, ultimately fulfills this promised renewal along with His people, the sons and daughters of a heavenly Jerusalem (Galatians 4:26).

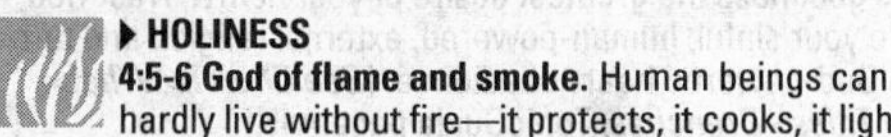

▸ HOLINESS
4:5-6 God of flame and smoke. Human beings can hardly live without fire—it protects, it cooks, it lights the darkness—but it endangers all who trifle with it. As Moses watched his sheep, God surprised him by revealing Himself through a blazing bush. As the people of Israel journeyed from Egypt to Canaan, God manifested Himself as smoke and fire (Exodus 13:20-22; 19:18-19; Numbers 9:15-23). Early in God's interaction with Israel, fire was the primary vessel of God's presence among His people. Isaiah prophesied that God's fiery presence would continue to protect and bless His people but would be a constant threat to His enemies. Live fearlessly, trusting in God's power to protect you as you boldly obey Him. (***See Holiness*** *> Submission> Trusting God> Overcoming,* TopicGuide page A40.)

[6] It will be a shelter from daytime heat
and a hiding place from storms and rain.

4:6
Ps 27:5
Isa 25:4; 32:1-2

A SONG ABOUT THE LORD'S VINEYARD

5 [1] Now I will sing for the One I love
a song about His vineyard:
My beloved had a vineyard
on a rich and fertile hill.
[2] He plowed the land, cleared its stones,
and planted it with the best vines.
In the middle He built a watchtower
and carved a winepress in the nearby rocks.
Then He waited for a harvest of sweet grapes,
but the grapes that grew were bitter.

5:1
Ps 80:8-9
Jer 12:10
Matt 21:33
Mark 12:1
Luke 20:9

5:2
Jer 2:21
Matt 21:19
Mark 11:13
Luke 13:6

[3] Now, you people of Jerusalem and Judah,
you judge between Me and My vineyard.
[4] What more could I have done for My vineyard
that I have not already done?
When I expected sweet grapes,
why did My vineyard give Me bitter grapes?

5:4
Jer 7:25-26
Matt 23:37

[5] Now let Me tell you
what I will do to My vineyard:
I will tear down its hedges
and let it be destroyed.
I will break down its walls
and let the animals trample it.
[6] I will make it a wild place
where the vines are not pruned and the ground is not hoed,
a place overgrown with briers and thorns.
I will command the clouds
to drop no rain on it.

5:5
Ps 80:12
Lam 1:15
Luke 21:24
Rev 11:2

5:6
Isa 24:3
Jer 14:1-22; 25:11

[7] The nation of Israel is the vineyard of the LORD
of Heaven's Armies.
The people of Judah are His pleasant garden.
He expected a crop of justice,
but instead He found oppression.
He expected to find righteousness,
but instead He heard cries of violence.

5:1-2 Isaiah's song allegorically depicts the relationship between his beloved (the Lord) and the beloved's vineyard (Israel, see 5:7). God cared for and protected Israel, and He provided for His people. Rather than receiving gracious obedience in return for His tender love, God was rejected by His own people.

▶ CHURCH

5:7 God's vineyard. Isaiah described the nation of Israel as the Lord's vineyard. Jesus tells us that Christians are branches in God's vineyard. He says, "Yes, I am the vine; you are the branches. Those who remain in Me, and I in them, will produce much fruit. For apart from Me you can do nothing" (John 15:5). Because Israel produced the fruit of wickedness, they were disciplined by being taken into captivity. Are you producing the fruit of the Spirit (Galatians 5:22-23)? Is godliness the greatest desire of your heart? Trust God to take your sinful, human-powered, external religion and turn it into God-powered heart-obedience. (***See Church*** *> What> Many Titles> Branches,* TopicGuide page A48.)

JUDAH'S GUILT AND JUDGMENT

5:8 Jer 22:13-17 Mic 2:2
8 What sorrow for you who buy up house after house and field after field,
until everyone is evicted and you live alone in the land.
9 But I have heard the LORD of Heaven's Armies
5:9 Isa 6:11-12 Matt 23:38
swear a solemn oath:
"Many houses will stand deserted;
even beautiful mansions will be empty.
5:10 Hag 1:6; 2:16
10 Ten acres* of vineyard will not produce even six gallons* of wine.
Ten baskets of seed will yield only one basket* of grain."

5:11 Prov 23:29-30 Isa 28:1, 3, 7-8
11 What sorrow for those who get up early in the morning
looking for a drink of alcohol
and spend long evenings drinking wine
to make themselves flaming drunk.
5:12 Ps 28:5
12 They furnish wine and lovely music at their grand parties—
lyre and harp, tambourine and flute—
but they never think about the LORD
or notice what He is doing.

5:13 Isa 1:3; 3:3 Hos 4:6
13 So My people will go into exile far away
because they do not know Me.
Those who are great and honored will starve,
and the common people will die of thirst.
5:14 Prov 30:16
14 The grave* is licking its lips in anticipation,
opening its mouth wide.
The great and the lowly
and all the drunken mob will be swallowed up.
5:15 Isa 2:11
15 Humanity will be destroyed, and people brought down;
even the arrogant will lower their eyes in humiliation.
5:16 Isa 33:5, 10
16 But the LORD of Heaven's Armies will be exalted by His justice.
The holiness of God will be displayed by His righteousness.
5:17 Isa 29:23 Zeph 2:6
17 In that day lambs will find good pastures,
and fattened sheep and young goats* will feed among the ruins.

5:18 Jer 23:10-14
18 What sorrow for those who drag their sins behind them
with ropes made of lies,
who drag wickedness behind them like a cart!
5:19 2 Pet 3:3-4
19 They even mock God and say,
"Hurry up and do something!
We want to see what You can do.
Let the Holy One of Israel carry out His plan,
for we want to know what it is."

5:10a Hebrew *A ten yoke,* that is, the area of land plowed by ten teams of oxen in one day. 5:10b Hebrew *a bath* [21 liters]. 5:10c Hebrew *A homer* [5 bushels or 182 liters] *of seed will yield only an ephah* [20 quarts or 22 liters]. 5:14 Hebrew *Sheol.* 5:17 As in Greek version; Hebrew reads *and strangers.*

5:8-30 Isaiah pronounced six oracles of judgment against Judah, each beginning with the words "what sorrow" (literally "woe").

5:8-10 The first pronouncement of certain judgment condemned those who accrued their wealth through the acquisition of land at the expense of the poor. In ancient Israel, land was not merely private property; it was an inheritance from God intimately bound with the Lord's redemption of Israel (see Leviticus 25:23; Numbers 27:1-11).

5:11-17 The second pronouncement of certain judgment condemned drunkards, who embodied the corruption of society in general. Isaiah described those whose only concern was to chase after fleeting pleasure and celebration with no regard for the Lord.

5:18-19 The third pronouncement of certain judgment was issued against those who spoke contemptuously against the Lord. They wrongly interpreted God's patience as indifference or even absence, but they would soon experience the wrath of the One they mocked.

20 What sorrow for those who say
that evil is good and good is evil,
that dark is light and light is dark,
that bitter is sweet and sweet is bitter.
21 What sorrow for those who are wise in their own eyes
and think themselves so clever.
22 What sorrow for those who are heroes at drinking wine
and boast about all the alcohol they can hold.
23 They take bribes to let the wicked go free,
and they punish the innocent.

24 Therefore, just as fire licks up stubble
and dry grass shrivels in the flame,
so their roots will rot
and their flowers wither.
For they have rejected the law of the LORD of Heaven's Armies;
they have despised the word of the Holy One of Israel.
25 That is why the LORD's anger burns against His people,
and why He has raised His fist to crush them.
The mountains tremble,
and the corpses of His people litter the streets like garbage.
But even then the LORD's anger is not satisfied.
His fist is still poised to strike!

26 He will send a signal to distant nations far away
and whistle to those at the ends of the earth.
They will come racing toward Jerusalem.
27 They will not get tired or stumble.
They will not stop for rest or sleep.
Not a belt will be loose,
not a sandal strap broken.
28 Their arrows will be sharp
and their bows ready for battle.
Sparks will fly from their horses' hooves,
and the wheels of their chariots will spin like a whirlwind.
29 They will roar like lions,
like the strongest of lions.
Growling, they will pounce on their victims and carry them off,
and no one will be there to rescue them.
30 They will roar over their victims on that day of destruction
like the roaring of the sea.
If someone looks across the land,
only darkness and distress will be seen;
even the light will be darkened by clouds.

5:20 Job 17:12; Prov 17:15; Matt 6:22-23; Luke 11:34-35
5:21 Prov 3:7; Rom 12:16; 1 Cor 3:18-20
5:22 Isa 5:11; 56:12; Hab 2:15
5:23 Ps 94:21; Mic 3:11; Jas 5:6
5:24 Isa 9:18-19; 30:12
5:25 2 Kgs 22:13, 17; Isa 9:12, 17, 21; 10:4; 66:15
5:26 Isa 13:2-3
5:27 Joel 2:7-8
5:28 Ps 7:12-13; Jer 4:13
5:29 Isa 42:22; Zeph 3:3
5:30 Isa 8:22; 17:12; Jer 4:23-28; 6:23; Joel 2:10

5:20 The fourth pronouncement of certain judgment condemned those who sought to overturn the moral order established by God. They consciously inverted God's standard of good and evil.

5:21 The fifth pronouncement of certain judgment indicted those who foolishly presumed to be wise and full of knowledge. They established their own reason as the standard of truth, but true knowledge and wisdom is dependent on God's revelation (Proverbs 3:7; 26:5, 12).

5:22-25 The sixth pronouncement of certain judgment was again directed against those who overindulged in alcohol and perverted justice in the courts. Because they had forsaken God's law, God's wrath would come upon them.

5:26-30 Assyria used the lion as a national symbol of might and power.

ISAIAH'S CLEANSING AND CALL

6:1 **6** It was in the year King Uzziah died* that I saw the Lord. He was sitting on a lofty
2 Kgs 15:7 throne, and the train of His robe filled the Temple. 2Attending Him were mighty sera-
Isa 1:1 John 12:41 phim, each having six wings. With two wings they covered their faces, with two they cov-
6:2 ered their feet, and with two they flew. 3They were calling out to each other,

Rev 4:8 "Holy, holy, holy is the LORD of Heaven's Armies!
6:3 Ps 72:19 The whole earth is filled with His glory!"

Rev 4:8 4Their voices shook the Temple to its foundations, and the entire building was filled with
smoke.
6:5 5Then I said, "It's all over! I am doomed, for I am a sinful man. I have filthy lips, and I live
Jer 9:3-8; 51:57 Luke 5:8 among a people with filthy lips. Yet I have seen the King, the LORD of Heaven's Armies."
6Then one of the seraphim flew to me with a burning coal he had taken from the altar
6:7 Isa 40:2 with a pair of tongs. 7He touched my lips with it and said, "See, this coal has touched your
Jer 1:9 lips. Now your guilt is removed, and your sins are forgiven."
1 Jn 1:7 8Then I heard the Lord asking, "Whom should I send as a messenger to this people?
Who will go for us?"
I said, "Here I am. Send me."
6:9 9And He said, "Yes, go, and say to this people,
*Matt 13:15 *Luke 8:10 'Listen carefully, but do not understand.
Rom 11:8 Watch closely, but learn nothing.'
6:10 Jer 5:21 10 Harden the hearts of these people.
*Mark 4:12 Plug their ears and shut their eyes.
*John 12:40 *Acts 28:26-27

6:1 King Uzziah died in 740 B.C.

▶ **GOD**

6:1-4 The throne of God. Can you imagine seeing a vision of God? Read 6:1-4 carefully. God gave Isaiah the words to describe something that can barely be put into words. As Isaiah brings us into God's royal throne room, it's apparent that He's the King—and we are not. This is how we also need to see God. He is not our "buddy" or a "grandfather in heaven." He's the King, and we dare not mock Him (Galatians 6:7). Meditate on the majestic description of God in this chapter, and give Him the honor He is due for being the King of all. (***See God****> God's Attributes> Self-Existent> The King is before and after everything,* TopicGuide page A17.)

6:1 God's throne room in heaven was the model for the Temple in Jerusalem, which was God's throne room on earth (Hebrews 8:5).

6:2-3 The Hebrew word *seraphim* means "fiery ones." These angelic beings continuously praised the holiness of the Lord. In Hebrew, emphasis is achieved by repetition, so the threefold chant of "holy, holy, holy" ascribes the highest holiness to God (Revelation 4:8).

▶ **GOD**

6:3 God is holy. The angels' repetition of "holy" in this verse underscores the importance of this attribute of God. What do they mean in saying that God is "holy"? They mean He is without any sin, without any defect, and without any unrighteousness. Not a drop. Not one wrong thought. Not one wrong action. This makes God different from anything in creation. If God is holy—the perfect One—shouldn't we give him the praise He deserves? This goes beyond simple songs and goes straight to the heart—God has set us aside as a holy people (1 Peter 2:9) for a holy God. Let us settle for nothing less than holy living for our holy God. (***See God****> God's Attributes> Holy> His holy presence rejects impurity,* TopicGuide page A16.)

6:4 The shaking of the earth and the presence of fire and smoke often accompanied the appearance of God on earth (compare Exodus 19:18-19; 1 Kings 19:11-13; Psalm 18:7-15; Ezekiel 20:47-48; Micah 1:3-4; Nahum 1:3-8).

6:5-7 "I am doomed" (literally "woe to me") is equivalent to the pronouncements of certain destruction issued against Judah in chapter 5. Isaiah's vision of God in His majestic holiness impressed upon him an overwhelming sense of his own sinfulness. Isaiah was then symbolically purified by fire and prepared to be a mouthpiece of the Lord among His people. The focus lies on the lips—the source of speech—because the prophet's role is primarily one of oral proclamation.

▶ **PURPOSE**

6:6 What angels do. On store shelves and in advertisements today, we see lots of angels. From little cupids to delicate waifs, these figures are merely figments of some artist's imagination. But this is not the way the Bible describes angels. Angels are powerful messengers of God not to be taken lightly (Psalms 78:49; 103:20). We know so little about angels, but this we do know—they delight in the salvation of sinners (Luke 15:7, 10), they delight in the worship of God (Isaiah 6; Revelation 7:11), and, as in this passage, they play some part in getting God's message out. Therefore, you can pray for God to send His angels to help you get the gospel message to as many people as possible. Thank God for the supernatural aid He sends through His angels. (***See Purpose****> God's Deeds> Manifestations> Use of angelic agents,* TopicGuide page A54.)

6:9-10 Isaiah received a sobering commission. He was to proclaim God's message to Judah knowing he would face a stubborn and rebellious people. These people would hear him without truly understanding or responding. Furthermore, Isaiah was to preach in such a way that actually fostered stubborn rejection. God was intent on purifying His people through judgment. (compare Matthew 13:13-15 and Romans 11:7-10).

That way, they will not see with their eyes,
nor hear with their ears,
nor understand with their hearts
and turn to Me for healing."*

11 Then I said, "Lord, how long will this go on?" 6:11 Lev 26:31 Mic 3:12
And He replied,

"Until their towns are empty,
their houses are deserted,
and the whole country is a wasteland;
12 until the LORD has sent everyone away, 6:12 Jer 4:29
and the entire land of Israel lies deserted.
13 If even a tenth—a remnant—survive, 6:13 Ezra 9:2 Job 14:7
it will be invaded again and burned.
But as a terebinth or oak tree leaves a stump when it is cut down,
so Israel's stump will be a holy seed."

A MESSAGE FOR AHAZ

7 When Ahaz, son of Jotham and grandson of Uzziah, was king of Judah, King Rezin of 7:1 2 Kgs 15:25, 37; 16:1
Syria* and Pekah son of Remaliah, the king of Israel, set out to attack Jerusalem.
However, they were unable to carry out their plan.
2 The news had come to the royal court of Judah: "Syria is allied with Israel* against us!" 7:2 Isa 7:13; 8:12
So the hearts of the king and his people trembled with fear, like trees shaking in a storm.
3 Then the LORD said to Isaiah, "Take your son Shear-jashub* and go out to meet King
Ahaz. You will find him at the end of the aqueduct that feeds water into the upper pool,
near the road leading to the field where cloth is washed.* 4 Tell him to stop worrying. Tell 7:4 Exod 14:13
him he doesn't need to fear the fierce anger of those two burned-out embers, King Rezin Isa 10:24; 30:15; 35:4
of Syria and Pekah son of Remaliah. 5 Yes, the kings of Syria and Israel are plotting against Lam 3:26
him, saying, 6 'We will attack Judah and capture it for ourselves. Then we will install the
son of Tabeel as Judah's king.' 7 But this is what the Sovereign LORD says: 7:7 Isa 8:10

"This invasion will never happen;
it will never take place;

6:9-10 Greek version reads *And He said, "Go and say to this people, / 'When you hear what I say, you will not understand. / When you see what I do, you will not comprehend.' / For the hearts of these people are hardened, / and their ears cannot hear, and they have closed their eyes— / so their eyes cannot see, / and their ears cannot hear, / and their hearts cannot understand, / and they cannot turn to Me and let Me heal them."* Compare Matt 13:14-15; Mark 4:12; Luke 8:10; Acts 28:26-27. 7:1 Hebrew *Aram;* also in 7:2, 4, 5, 8. 7:2 Hebrew *Ephraim,* referring to the northern kingdom of Israel; also in 7:5, 8, 9, 17. 7:3a *Shear-jashub* means "A remnant will return." 7:3b Or *bleached.*

7:1–39:8 Chapters 7–39 are concerned with the threat Assyria posed to Judah during Isaiah's lifetime. The section may be further divided into three parts: the threat of attack by Aram and Israel (chapters 7–12); God's response to the nations (chapters 13–27); and the invasion of Sennacherib (chapters 28–39).

7:1 The nations of Israel and Aram allied themselves against the looming Assyrian threat from the east. They invited Judah to join their coalition, but when Judah declined, they threatened military action against the nation (2 Kings 16:5-18; 2 Chronicles 28:16-21). These events took place between 736–734 BC.

7:3-4 As did the prophet Hosea, Isaiah gave his children names that carried prophetic significance. "Shear-jashub" means "a remnant will return." The name suggested both severe judgment and hope of restoration. By calling Rezin and Pekah "burned-out embers," Isaiah was signaling their imminent destruction.

▸ WORSHIP

7:3 God's message for us. In a general sense, every Christian functions as a prophet. When the prophets spoke, they carried God's message to the people who needed to hear it. Just as Isaiah had a message to give to a specific man—King Ahaz—God has given us a specific message to bring to the whole world—the good news that Jesus Christ has died for our sins and that we can be forgiven (Matthew 28:19-20). God wants you to warn people to flee the wrath of God and find safety—not in their good works, but in Christ alone (Galatians 6:12; Jude 1:21). The most important qualification for being used by God is not your résumé but His often-surprising calling. Is God calling you to be His messenger in your world? Can you help people in your world escape the judgment of the Almighty God? (***See Worship**> OT> Prophets> Prophets spoke to their times,* TopicGuide page A28.)

7:5-7 The plans of Pekah and Resin were set in direct opposition to the plans of the Lord. These foreign kings did not consider the will of the Sovereign Lord, whose purposes are always accomplished. Earthly powers cannot hope to challenge the will of God.

7:8 Isa 17:1-3

8 for Syria is no stronger than its capital, Damascus,
and Damascus is no stronger than its king, Rezin.
As for Israel, within sixty-five years
it will be crushed and completely destroyed.

7:9 2 Chr 20:20; Isa 30:12-14

9 Israel is no stronger than its capital, Samaria,
and Samaria is no stronger than its king, Pekah son of Remaliah.
Unless your faith is firm,
I cannot make you stand firm."

THE SIGN OF IMMANUEL

7:11 2 Kgs 19:29; Isa 37:30; 38:7-8

10 Later, the LORD sent this message to King Ahaz: 11 "Ask the LORD your God for a sign of
confirmation, Ahaz. Make it as difficult as you want—as high as heaven or as deep as the
place of the dead.*"
12 But the king refused. "No," he said, "I will not test the LORD like that."
13 Then Isaiah said, "Listen well, you royal family of David! Isn't it enough to exhaust human

7:14 Isa 8:8, 10; *Matt 1:23

patience? Must you exhaust the patience of my God as well? 14 All right then, the Lord Himself
will give you the sign. Look! The virgin* will conceive a Child! She will give birth to a Son and
will call Him Immanuel (which means 'God is with us'). 15 By the time this Child is old enough

7:15 Isa 8:4

to choose what is right and reject what is wrong, He will be eating yogurt* and honey. 16 For
before the Child is that old, the lands of the two kings you fear so much will both be deserted.

7:17 1 Kgs 12:16-17; Isa 10:5-6

17 "Then the LORD will bring things on you, your nation, and your family unlike anything
since Israel broke away from Judah. He will bring the king of Assyria upon you!"

7:18 Isa 5:26

18 In that day the LORD will whistle for the army of southern Egypt and for the army of As-
syria. They will swarm around you like flies and bees. 19 They will come in vast hordes and

7:19 Jer 16:16

settle in the fertile areas and also in the desolate valleys, caves, and thorny places. 20 In that
day the Lord will hire a "razor" from beyond the Euphrates River*—the king of Assyria—and

7:20 Isa 8:7; 10:5, 15; 24:1; Ezek 5:1-4

use it to shave off everything: your land, your crops, and your people.*
21 In that day a farmer will be fortunate to have a cow and two sheep or goats left.

7:21 Jer 39:10

22 Nevertheless, there will be enough milk for everyone because so few people will be left
in the land. They will eat their fill of yogurt and honey. 23 In that day the lush vineyards,
now worth 1,000 pieces of silver,* will become patches of briers and thorns. 24 The entire
land will become a vast expanse of briers and thorns, a hunting ground overrun by wild-
life. 25 No one will go to the fertile hillsides where the gardens once grew, for briers and
thorns will cover them. Cattle, sheep, and goats will graze there.

7:11 Hebrew *as deep as Sheol.* 7:14 Or *young woman.* 7:15 Or *curds;* also in 7:22. 7:20a Hebrew *the river.* 7:20b Hebrew *shave off the head, the hair of the legs, and the beard.* 7:23 Hebrew *1,000 shekels of silver,* about 25 pounds or 11.4 kilograms in weight.

7:8-9 Within Ahaz's lifetime the kingdom of Israel was destroyed by Assyria, and the people were carried away into captivity (722 BC, see 2 Kings 17).

7:10-12 The Lord offered to produce virtually any kind of sign to authenticate His message to Ahaz. Ahaz's refusal to accept the sign, while attempting to sound pious, was in fact motivated by a refusal to take God at His word. Ahaz preferred to trust in Assyria rather than the Lord. Isaiah's response to Ahaz in the following verses bears out this conclusion.

7:14 "Virgin" is used for the Hebrew word that typically refers to a woman of marriageable age who is, by implication, still in possession of her virginity. Of the seven occurrences of the word in the Old Testament, nowhere does it clearly refer to a young woman who is no longer a virgin. The Greek translation of the Old Testament, known as the Septuagint, likewise takes the word to mean a virgin. The name "Immanuel" means "God is with us" and promised God's presence among His people. The New Testament clearly identifies Jesus Christ as the ultimate fulfillment of Isaiah's sign (Matthew 1:23), but this does not rule out earlier fulfillments. Some suggest that Isaiah's child Maher-shalal-hash-baz (see 8:3) was the nearest fulfillment of the sign given to Ahaz. That means the birth of Isaiah's child was a foreshadowing of the birth of Jesus.

▸ GOD

7:14 God with us. "God is with us" is the message that is proclaimed each Christmas season. What more joyful promise can we claim than this? God didn't merely view our problems from the ivory tower of heaven. He chose to send His Son to a life of sorrow, pain, and humiliation among His people—all for the purpose of delivering us from our sin. Thank God for being here with us; sing joyfully of His fulfilled promises of nearness to us—even if it isn't the Christmas season! (***See God***> *God's Names*> *Son*> *Immanuel,* TopicGuide page A19.)

7:18-25 The advance of the Assyrian army would leave desolation and humiliation in its wake.

THE COMING ASSYRIAN INVASION

8 Then the LORD said to me, "Make a large signboard and clearly write this name on it:
Maher-shalal-hash-baz.*" 2I asked Uriah the priest and Zechariah son of Jeberekiah,
both known as honest men, to witness my doing this.
3Then I slept with my wife, and she became pregnant and gave birth to a son. And the
LORD said, "Call him Maher-shalal-hash-baz. 4For before this child is old enough to say
'Papa' or 'Mama,' the king of Assyria will carry away both the abundance of Damascus and
the riches of Samaria."
5Then the LORD spoke to me again and said, 6"My care for the people of Judah is like the
gently flowing waters of Shiloah, but they have rejected it. They are rejoicing over what
will happen to* King Rezin and King Pekah.* 7Therefore, the Lord will overwhelm them
with a mighty flood from the Euphrates River*—the king of Assyria and all his glory. This
flood will overflow all its channels 8and sweep into Judah until it is chin deep. It will spread
its wings, submerging your land from one end to the other, O Immanuel.

9 "Huddle together, you nations, and be terrified.
Listen, all you distant lands.
Prepare for battle, but you will be crushed!
Yes, prepare for battle, but you will be crushed!
10 Call your councils of war, but they will be worthless.
Develop your strategies, but they will not succeed.
For God is with us!*"

A CALL TO TRUST THE LORD

11 The LORD has given me a strong warning not to think like everyone else does. He said,

12 "Don't call everything a conspiracy, like they do,
and don't live in dread of what frightens them.
13 Make the LORD of Heaven's Armies holy in your life.
He is the One you should fear.
He is the One who should make you tremble.
14 He will keep you safe.
But to Israel and Judah
He will be a stone that makes people stumble,
a rock that makes them fall.
And for the people of Jerusalem
He will be a trap and a snare.
15 Many will stumble and fall,
never to rise again.
They will be snared and captured."

8:1 Isa 30:8; Hab 2:2
8:2 2 Kgs 16:10-11, 15-16
8:4 Isa 7:8-9, 16
8:6 Isa 7:1; 30:12
8:7 Isa 17:12-13; Amos 8:8; 9:5
8:8 Isa 7:14; 10:6; 30:28
8:9 Dan 2:34-35
8:11 Ezek 2:8; 3:14
8:12 Isa 7:2; *1 Pet 3:13-15
8:13 Num 20:12; Isa 5:16; 29:23
8:14 Isa 25:4; Ezek 11:16; Luke 2:34; *Rom 9:33; *1 Pet 2:8
8:15 Isa 28:13; Luke 20:18; Rom 9:32

8:1 *Maher-shalal-hash-baz* means "Swift to plunder and quick to carry away." 8:6a Or *They are rejoicing because of.* 8:6b Hebrew *and the son of Remaliah.* 8:7 Hebrew *the river.* 8:10 Hebrew *Immanuel!*

8:1 "Maher-shalal-hash-baz" means "swift to plunder and quick to carry away." The name anticipated the rapidity with which Israel and Aram would fall to the onslaught of the Assyrian army (see also 8:4).

8:3-4 Because this child functioned as a sign in much the same way as the child of 7:14-16, many believe that Isaiah's son is the immediate fulfillment of the Immanuel sign (see note at 7:14).

▸WORSHIP

8:11 Think differently. Not everything in this world is evil. There are many good pleasures, beautiful objects, and true ideas in God's world. But the Lord called Isaiah, in specific ways, to be different. He called Isaiah to not think like his apostate fellow citizens (8:11), to fear God more than people (8:13), and to trust God's prophetic Word (8:16-20). Rather than merely teaching separation from everything in the world, strive to live a vibrant, joyful life in the midst of God's creation (John 17:15; see also Colossians 1:17). (***See Worship****> NT> Our Role> Obedience> Believer not to be conformed to the world,* TopicGuide page A32.)

8:12-13 Isaiah confronted the king harshly with unpopular counsel, but he did so as the Lord's messenger. The Lord encouraged Isaiah to remain faithful in the face of threats and plots against him by the king and others in power.

8:16 Isa 50:4; Dan 12:4

16 Preserve the teaching of God;
  entrust His instructions to those who follow me.

8:17 Deut 31:17; Hab 2:3

17 I will wait for the LORD,
  who has turned away from the descendants of Jacob.
  I will put my hope in Him.

8:18 *Heb 2:13
8:19 Lev 20:6; 1 Sam 28:8; 2 Kgs 21:6
8:20 Mic 3:6; Luke 16:29
8:22 Jer 13:16; Amos 5:18, 20; Zeph 1:14-15

18 I and the children the LORD has given me serve as signs and warnings to Israel from
the LORD of Heaven's Armies who dwells in His Temple on Mount Zion.
19 Someone may say to you, "Let's ask the mediums and those who consult the spirits of
the dead. With their whisperings and mutterings, they will tell us what to do." But shouldn't
people ask God for guidance? Should the living seek guidance from the dead?
20 Look to God's instructions and teachings! People who contradict His word are com-
pletely in the dark. 21 They will go from one place to another, weary and hungry. And be-
cause they are hungry, they will rage and curse their king and their God. They will look up
to heaven 22 and down at the earth, but wherever they look, there will be trouble and an-
guish and dark despair. They will be thrown out into the darkness.

HOPE IN THE MESSIAH

9:1 2 Kgs 15:29; 2 Chr 16:4

9 1*Nevertheless, that time of darkness and despair will not go on forever. The land of Zebulun and Naphtali will be humbled, but there will be a time in the future when Galilee of the Gentiles, which lies along the road that runs between the Jordan and the sea, will be filled with glory.

9:2 *Matt 4:15-16

2*The people who walk in darkness
  will see a great light.
For those who live in a land of deep darkness,*
  a light will shine.

9:3 Isa 26:15; 35:10; 66:10

3 You will enlarge the nation of Israel,
  and its people will rejoice.
They will rejoice before You
  as people rejoice at the harvest
  and like warriors dividing the plunder.

9:4 Isa 49:26

4 For You will break the yoke of their slavery
  and lift the heavy burden from their shoulders.
You will break the oppressor's rod,
  just as You did when You destroyed the army
    of Midian.
5 The boots of the warrior
  and the uniforms bloodstained by war
will all be burned.
  They will be fuel for the fire.

9:1 Verse 9:1 is numbered 8:23 in Hebrew text. 9:2a Verses 9:2-21 are numbered 9:1-20 in Hebrew text. 9:2b Greek version reads *a land where death casts its shadow.* Compare Matt 4:16.

8:18 The names of Isaiah's children bore symbolic and prophetic weight for the people of Judah. See notes at 7:3-4 and 8:1.

8:19 Faced with the harsh realities of Isaiah's message, yet unwilling to repent and find forgiveness, the people of Judah turned to alternative and unlawful sources of comfort and guidance (see Deuteronomy 18:10-12). These mediums and psychics did not know the truth, however, because they did not know the will of God.

9:1-2 The territories of Zebulun and Naphtali in northern Israel suffered heavily during the Assyrian invasion. But the Lord promised a time of salvation and blessing, which he characterized as passing from darkness into light. This time of blessing would be marked by great joy (9:3) and peace (9:4-5) inaugurated by a Davidic king (9:6-7). The New Testament shows that Jesus Christ inaugurated this new age when He began His earthly ministry (Matthew 4:13-15).

[6] For a Child is born to us,
a Son is given to us.
The government will rest on His shoulders.
And He will be called:
Wonderful Counselor,* Mighty God,
Everlasting Father, Prince of Peace.
[7] His government and its peace
will never end.
He will rule with fairness and justice from the throne of His ancestor David
for all eternity.
The passionate commitment of the LORD of Heaven's Armies
will make this happen!

9:6 Deut 10:17 Neh 9:32 Isa 7:14; 26:3, 12 Matt 28:18 1 Cor 15:25

9:7 Dan 2:44 Luke 1:32-33

THE LORD'S ANGER AGAINST ISRAEL

[8] The Lord has spoken out against Jacob;
His judgment has fallen upon Israel.
[9] And the people of Israel* and Samaria,
who spoke with such pride and arrogance,
will soon know it.
[10] They said, "We will replace the broken bricks of our ruins
with finished stone,
and replant the felled sycamore-fig trees with cedars."

[11] But the LORD will bring Rezin's enemies against Israel
and stir up all their foes.
[12] The Syrians* from the east and the Philistines from the west
will bare their fangs and devour Israel.
But even then the LORD's anger will not be satisfied.
His fist is still poised to strike.

[13] For after all this punishment, the people will still not repent.
They will not seek the LORD of Heaven's Armies.
[14] Therefore, in a single day the LORD will destroy both the head and the tail,
the noble palm branch and the lowly reed.
[15] The leaders of Israel are the head,
and the lying prophets are the tail.
[16] For the leaders of the people have misled them.
They have led them down the path of destruction.

9:9 Isa 7:8-9

9:12 Ps 79:7

9:13 Jer 5:3 Hos 7:10

9:14 Isa 19:15 Rev 18:8

9:16 Matt 15:14

9:6 Or *Wonderful, Counselor.* 9:9 Hebrew *of Ephraim,* referring to the northern kingdom of Israel. 9:12 Hebrew *Arameans.*

9:6-7 The promises of a new age were intimately connected to the birth of an heir of David, who would firmly establish God's eternal kingdom. The titles given to this son of David follow a logical sequence from the planning of a battle to the securing of victory: "Wonderful Counselor" suggests a brilliant strategist; "Mighty God" is literally "God is a warrior" in the Hebrew text; "Everlasting Father" was a common royal title in the ancient Near East; and "Prince of Peace" suggests the kind of reign the Davidic king would enjoy. Isaiah's hope was realized in the birth of Jesus (Luke 1:30-33).

▸ GOD
9:6 God's names. How would Israel survive the onslaught of Assyria during Isaiah's time? Through a child. But not just any child: He would have every ability necessary to remove the gloom over the cursed northern kingdom—and the entire world (Genesis 3:15; Revelation 12:1-17). The titles in this verse are just the beginning—the kingly conqueror would grow in His authority and His zeal for God's glory (Isaiah 9:7). Every faithful king in David's line accomplished this to some extent, but the greatest fulfillment of this prophecy is in Jesus Christ. He is Israel's hope, and ours, too. (See Luke 1:31-32; also ***see God****> God's Names> God> The LORD is peace (YHWH Shalom),* TopicGuide page A18.)

9:8-13 The initial Assyrian invasion of Israel would not cure the nation of her pride and self-sufficiency. Israel would display defiance rather than humility. Israel's failure to repent and heed God's warning would result in further destruction from multiple directions. Israel's ally, Aram, would turn on them, and the Philistines, an age-old foe, would renew hostilities with them.

9:17 Amos 8:13; Matt 12:34
[17] That is why the Lord takes no pleasure in the
young men
and shows no mercy even to the widows
and orphans.
For they are all wicked hypocrites,
and they all speak foolishness.
But even then the LORD's anger will not be satisfied.
His fist is still poised to strike.

9:18 Mal 4:1
[18] This wickedness is like a brushfire.
It burns not only briers and thorns
but also sets the forests ablaze.
Its burning sends up clouds of smoke.

9:19 Joel 2:3; Mic 7:2, 6
[19] The land will be blackened
by the fury of the LORD of Heaven's Armies.
The people will be fuel for the fire,
and no one will spare even his own brother.

9:20 Isa 8:21-22; 49:26
[20] They will attack their neighbor on the right
but will still be hungry.
They will devour their neighbor on the left
but will not be satisfied.
In the end they will even eat their own children.*

9:21 Isa 5:25
[21] Manasseh will feed on Ephraim,
Ephraim will feed on Manasseh,
and both will devour Judah.
But even then the LORD's anger will not be satisfied.
His fist is still poised to strike.

10:1 Ps 94:20; Isa 59:14
10 [1] What sorrow awaits the unjust judges
and those who issue unfair laws.

10:2 Isa 1:23; 5:23
[2] They deprive the poor of justice
and deny the rights of the needy among My people.
They prey on widows
and take advantage of orphans.

10:3 Isa 13:6; Luke 19:43-44
[3] What will you do when I punish you,
when I send disaster upon you from a distant land?
To whom will you turn for help?
Where will your treasures be safe?

10:4 Isa 34:3; 66:16
[4] You will stumble along as prisoners
or lie among the dead.
But even then the LORD's anger will not be satisfied.
His fist is still poised to strike.

9:20 Or *eat their own arms.*

9:20-21 Because the tribes of Israel and Judah had rejected the God in whose worship they were bound together, they would suffer from internal hostilities and fight against each other.

10:1-4 Isaiah pronounced an oracle of certain destruction against Israel because of the rampant injustice that enveloped the nation. Those in power oppressed the weak and defenseless with impunity. God's coming judgment would render these same people helpless against the assault of Assyria's armies.

▶ GOD

10:1 Unjust judges. One of God's characteristics is that He loves justice. He notices when judges pass judgments that are unfair. God despises those actions that elevate the concerns of the rich or the powerful over the needs of the poor and the lowly. Don't be deceived—God is watching the way you handle yourself. If you are acting justly, He is pleased (Matthew 5:6; Hebrews 11:33). If you practice injustice, God will lovingly discipline you (Deuteronomy 16:20; Hebrews 12:5-6). Make sure you treat those under your authority honorably. (***See God****> God's Attributes> Just> God alone is the judge,* TopicGuide page A17.)

JUDGMENT AGAINST ASSYRIA

5 "What sorrow awaits Assyria, the rod of My anger.
I use it as a club to express My anger.
6 I am sending Assyria against a godless nation,
against a people with whom I am angry.
Assyria will plunder them,
trampling them like dirt beneath its feet.
7 But the king of Assyria will not understand that he is My tool;
his mind does not work that way.
His plan is simply to destroy,
to cut down nation after nation.
8 He will say,
'Each of my princes will soon be a king.
9 We destroyed Calno just as we did Carchemish.
Hamath fell before us as Arpad did.
And we destroyed Samaria just as we did Damascus.
10 Yes, we have finished off many a kingdom
whose gods were greater than those in Jerusalem and Samaria.
11 So we will defeat Jerusalem and her gods,
just as we destroyed Samaria with hers.'"

12 After the Lord has used the king of Assyria to accomplish His purposes on Mount Zion
and in Jerusalem, He will turn against the king of Assyria and punish him—for he is proud
and arrogant. 13 He boasts,

"By my own powerful arm I have done this.
With my own shrewd wisdom I planned it.
I have broken down the defenses of nations
and carried off their treasures.
I have knocked down their kings like a bull.
14 I have robbed their nests of riches
and gathered up kingdoms as a farmer gathers eggs.
No one can even flap a wing against me
or utter a peep of protest."

15 But can the ax boast greater power than the person who uses it?
Is the saw greater than the person who saws?
Can a rod strike unless a hand moves it?
Can a wooden cane walk by itself?
16 Therefore, the Lord, the LORD of Heaven's Armies,
will send a plague among Assyria's proud troops,
and a flaming fire will consume its glory.

10:5 Isa 13:5; Jer 51:20
10:6 Isa 5:25, 29; 9:17-19
10:7 Gen 50:20; Mic 4:11-12; Acts 2:23-24
10:9 2 Kgs 16:9; 2 Chr 35:20; Amos 6:2
10:10 2 Kgs 19:17-18
10:12 2 Kgs 19:31; Jer 50:18
10:13 2 Kgs 19:22-24; Isa 37:24-27; Ezek 28:4; Dan 4:30
10:15 Isa 10:5; 29:16; Jer 51:20; Rom 9:20-21

10:7-11 These verses illustrate the interrelationship of divine providence and human responsibility. The military campaigns the Assyrians undertook against Israel and Judah were motivated by their own avarice and cruelty, and so they were guilty before God for their aggression and arrogance. In God's wisdom, however, the wickedness of Assyria accomplished God's purposes. God's sovereignty does not overrule human responsibility, yet God is able to overrule human wickedness for His own ends (Romans 8:28).

10:15 The ax, the saw, the rod, and the cane were powerless to act on their own, and they could not take credit for their accomplishments. Likewise the proud Assyrians could not see that they were merely tools in the hands of the Lord.

▶ GOD

10:15 God is sovereign. In this chapter, Isaiah describes the power of God in controlling human affairs. Sometimes we make the mistake of thinking we can function without God. Even if we rebel against God, He is not rendered powerless. He is not wringing His hands or worrying when we sin. Even our free (yet foolish) rebellion fits into His plan. There is not one maverick molecule in the universe that God doesn't control. God directs all so that in the end all will glorify Him to the fullest. (***See God> God's Attributes> Sovereign> God controls nature for His purposes,*** TopicGuide page A17.)

10:16-19 The Assyrians actually succeeded in laying siege to Jerusalem; however, the Lord miraculously delivered the city by striking the Assyrian army with a mysterious plague (see 2 Kings 19; see also Isaiah 10:24-27).

10:17 Isa 27:4; 30:33; 31:9; 33:12; 37:23 Jer 4:4
17 The LORD, the Light of Israel, will be a fire;
the Holy One will be a flame.
He will devour the thorns and briers with fire,
burning up the enemy in a single night.
18 The LORD will consume Assyria's glory
like a fire consumes a forest in a fruitful land;
it will waste away like sick people in a plague.
10:19 Isa 21:17
19 Of all that glorious forest, only a few trees will survive—
so few that a child could count them!

HOPE FOR THE LORD'S PEOPLE

10:20 Isa 17:7-8
20 In that day the remnant left in Israel,
the survivors in the house of Jacob,
will no longer depend on allies
who seek to destroy them.
But they will faithfully trust the LORD,
the Holy One of Israel.
21 A remnant will return;*
yes, the remnant of Jacob will return to the Mighty God.
10:22 Isa 28:22 *Rom 9:27-28
22 But though the people of Israel are as numerous
as the sand of the seashore,
only a remnant of them will return.
The LORD has rightly decided to destroy His people.
23 Yes, the Lord, the LORD of Heaven's Armies,
has already decided to destroy the entire land.*

10:24 Exod 5:14-16
24 So this is what the Lord, the LORD of Heaven's Armies, says: "O My people in Zion, do
not be afraid of the Assyrians when they oppress you with rod and club as the Egyptians
10:25 Isa 17:14
did long ago. 25 In a little while My anger against you will end, and then My anger will rise
up to destroy them." 26 The LORD of Heaven's Armies will lash them with His whip, as He did
10:26 Exod 14:16, 27 Judg 7:25 Isa 37:36-38
when Gideon triumphed over the Midianites at the rock of Oreb, or when the LORD's staff
was raised to drown the Egyptian army in the sea.

10:27 Isa 14:25
27 In that day the LORD will end the bondage of His people.
He will break the yoke of slavery
and lift it from their shoulders.*
10:28 1 Sam 13:2, 5; 14:2
28 Look, the Assyrians are now at Aiath.
They are passing through Migron
and are storing their equipment at Micmash.
10:29 Josh 18:25; 21:17 1 Sam 10:26
29 They are crossing the pass
and are camping at Geba.
Fear strikes the town of Ramah.
All the people of Gibeah, the hometown of Saul,
are running for their lives.
10:30 Josh 21:18 1 Sam 25:44
30 Scream in terror,
you people of Gallim!

10:21 Hebrew *Shear-jashub;* see 7:3; 8:18. 10:22-23 Greek version reads *only a remnant of them will be saved. / For He will carry out His sentence quickly and with finality and righteousness; / for God will carry out His sentence upon all the world with finality.* Compare Rom 9:27-28. 10:27 As in Greek version; Hebrew reads *The yoke will be broken, / for you have grown so fat.*

10:28-34 Isaiah plotted the Assyrian invasion from north to south until they were within sight of Jerusalem. This marked the end of their advance (see note at 10:16-19; compare Micah 1:10-16).

Shout out a warning to Laishah.
Oh, poor Anathoth!
31 There go the people of Madmenah, all fleeing.
The citizens of Gebim are trying to hide.
32 The enemy stops at Nob for the rest of that day.
He shakes his fist at beautiful Mount Zion, the mountain of Jerusalem.
33 But look! The Lord, the LORD of Heaven's Armies,
will chop down the mighty tree of Assyria with great power!
He will cut down the proud.
That lofty tree will be brought down.
34 He will cut down the forest trees with an ax.
Lebanon will fall to the Mighty One.*

10:32 Isa 19:16 Zech 2:9
10:33 Isa 37:24 Ezek 31:2-3 Amos 2:9

A BRANCH FROM DAVID'S LINE

11 1 Out of the stump of David's family* will grow a shoot—
yes, a new Branch bearing fruit from the old root.
2 And the Spirit of the LORD will rest on Him—
the Spirit of wisdom and understanding,
the Spirit of counsel and might,
the Spirit of knowledge and the fear of the LORD.
3 He will delight in obeying the LORD.
He will not judge by appearance
nor make a decision based on hearsay.
4 He will give justice to the poor
and make fair decisions for the exploited.
The earth will shake at the force of His word,
and one breath from His mouth will destroy the wicked.
5 He will wear righteousness like a belt
and truth like an undergarment.
6 In that day the wolf and the lamb will live together;
the leopard will lie down with the baby goat.

11:1 Jer 23:5 Rev 5:5
11:2 Isa 61:1 Matt 3:16 John 1:32 Eph 1:17
11:3 John 2:24-25
11:4 Isa 30:28 2 Thes 2:8
11:6 Isa 65:25

10:34 Or *with an ax / as even the mighty trees of Lebanon fall.* 11:1 Hebrew *the stump of the line of Jesse.* Jesse was King David's father.

11:1 Isaiah compared the Davidic line to a tree that has been cut down to its stump as a result of the Lord's judgment. However, out of that stump would come a new Branch that would restore the Davidic monarchy. This expectation has been fulfilled in Jesus, who was a descendant of David (compare Revelation 5:5).

▸ GOD

11:1 The stump of David's family. Terrible tragedy can destroy families. Particularly in ancient times, war or famine could destroy entire generations or even entire tribes. David's descendants suffered greatly from the Assyrian and Babylonian invasions; they were left as lifeless and hopeless as a stump. But eventually God raised up Jesus, who was in the line of David (Matthew 1:1), from this seemingly ruined family. God is also able to raise up stable, godly leadership from your family, too. What steps do you need to take to clear the way for God to work in and through your family? How can you train your family to become humble leaders in the church and the world? (***See God****> God's Names> God> Deliverer/Savior,* TopicGuide page A18.)

11:2 The reign of the coming son of David would be ideal in every respect because He would be empowered by the Spirit of the Lord. Throughout the Old Testament, the Spirit of the Lord came upon Israel's political, military, and religious leaders in order to empower them for particular tasks (see Numbers 11:17, 25-26; Deuteronomy 34:9; Judges 3:10; 6:34; 1 Samuel 10:6; 2 Samuel 23:2). But the Spirit would uniquely rest on this descendant of David.

▸ WORSHIP

11:4 Jesus defends the poor and exploited. God's people have always known Him as a rescuer. God may work through kings and queens, but He takes special delight in lifting up the lowly (Deuteronomy 15:4-7; Psalm 34:18). Isaiah prophesied that the future Messiah would focus His efforts on the lowest in society—the poor, the sick, and the children (see Matthew 19:13-14; Luke 6:20; Matthew 4:23-25). God's ways have not changed—the church must pay special attention to the powerless in their community. Imitate Jesus, the Messiah, by helping to change the lives of the downtrodden around you. (***See Worship****> NT> Offerings> Contributions for the poor,* TopicGuide page A31.)

11:6-9 Isaiah beautifully describes the harmony and peace that would characterize the reign of the coming king. When

The calf and the yearling will be safe with the lion,
and a little child will lead them all.
7 The cow will graze near the bear.
The cub and the calf will lie down together.
The lion will eat hay like a cow.
8 The baby will play safely near the hole of a cobra.
Yes, a little child will put its hand in a nest of deadly snakes without harm.
9 Nothing will hurt or destroy in all My holy mountain,
for as the waters fill the sea,
so the earth will be filled with people who know the LORD.
10 In that day the heir to David's throne*
will be a banner of salvation to all the world.
The nations will rally to Him,
and the land where He lives will be a glorious place.*
11 In that day the Lord will reach out His hand a second time
to bring back the remnant of His people—
those who remain in Assyria and northern Egypt;
in southern Egypt, Ethiopia,* and Elam;
in Babylonia,* Hamath, and all the distant coastlands.
12 He will raise a flag among the nations
and assemble the exiles of Israel.
He will gather the scattered people of Judah
from the ends of the earth.

13 Then at last the jealousy between Israel* and Judah will end.
They will not be rivals anymore.
14 They will join forces to swoop down on Philistia to the west.
Together they will attack and plunder the nations to the east.
They will occupy the lands of Edom and Moab,
and Ammon will obey them.
15 The LORD will make a dry path through the gulf of the Red Sea.*
He will wave His hand over the Euphrates River,*
sending a mighty wind to divide it into seven streams
so it can easily be crossed on foot.
16 He will make a highway for the remnant of His people,
the remnant coming from Assyria,

11:9 Job 5:23; Isa 45:6; Ezek 34:25; Hos 2:18; Hab 2:14
11:10 Luke 2:32; John 3:14-15; *Rom 15:12
11:11 Isa 60:9; 66:19-20; Zech 10:10
11:12 Isa 11:10; Zeph 3:10
11:13 Jer 3:18; Ezek 37:16-17, 22
11:15 Isa 51:10
11:16 Exod 14:26-29; Isa 19:23

11:10a Hebrew *the root of Jesse.* 11:10b Greek version reads *In that day the heir to David's throne* [literally *the root of Jesse*] *will come, / and He will rule over the Gentiles. / They will place their hopes on Him.* Compare Rom 15:12. 11:11a Hebrew *in Pathros, Cush.* 11:11b Hebrew *in Shinar.* 11:13 Hebrew *Ephraim,* referring to the northern kingdom of Israel. 11:15a Hebrew *will destroy the tongue of the sea of Egypt.* 11:15b Hebrew *the river.*

the coming Davidic king reigns there will no longer be violence or strife in the created order. This promise is slowly working itself out in the diverse life of the church and awaits the return of Christ for its ultimate fulfillment.

▶ SPIRITUAL WARFARE

11:6 Nature will be at peace. Isaiah prophesied of a time when nature will be at peace. Right now, all of creation is burdened under the curse of sin (see Genesis 3:17-19). Death reigns everywhere because of sin, and that includes all plants and animals. They suffer because of our sinfulness. But in that future time, all creation will be at rest, for the Messiah will reign over the earth. What a day that will be! Are you excited about seeing the earth restored to its former glory? Praise Jesus that He will return and do away with the curse that Adam brought upon creation. (See Genesis 3:17-19; also ***see Spiritual Warfare****> Origin of Sin> Creation in Bondage> God Curses,* TopicGuide page A44.)

11:10 The hopes for restoration following God's judgment are also extended to the Gentiles. Banners were used in ancient warfare to communicate with and rally troops. The nations will rally around the Davidic king as armies around their banner. The inauguration of this hope can be seen through the influx of Gentiles into the church of Jesus Christ.

11:15-16 The Exodus from Egypt provided a model for God's future acts of salvation (see Exodus 14), and Isaiah points to it as a source of comfort and encouragement for God's people. Just as the Lord miraculously provided for Israel's escape from Egypt, He would orchestrate the deliverance of His people from Assyria (and later Babylon).

just as He did for Israel long ago
when they returned from Egypt.

SONGS OF PRAISE FOR SALVATION

12 [1] In that day you will sing:
"I will praise You, O LORD!
You were angry with me, but not any more.
Now You comfort me.
[2] See, God has come to save me.
I will trust in Him and not be afraid.
The LORD GOD is my strength and my song;
He has given me victory."
[3] With joy you will drink deeply
from the fountain of salvation!
[4] In that wonderful day you will sing:
"Thank the LORD! Praise His name!
Tell the nations what He has done.
Let them know how mighty He is!
[5] Sing to the LORD, for He has done wonderful things.
Make known His praise around the world.
[6] Let all the people of Jerusalem* shout His praise with joy!
For great is the Holy One of Israel who lives among you."

12:1 Isa 40:1
12:2 Ps 118:14; Isa 26:4
12:3 Jer 2:13; John 4:10; 7:37-38
12:4 Ps 145:4
12:5 Ps 98:1; Isa 44:23
12:6 Isa 54:1; Zeph 3:14, 15-17

A MESSAGE ABOUT BABYLON

13 Isaiah son of Amoz received this message concerning the destruction of Babylon:
[2] "Raise a signal flag on a bare hilltop.
Call up an army against Babylon.
Wave your hand to encourage them
as they march into the palaces of the high and mighty.
[3] I, the LORD, have dedicated these soldiers for this task.
Yes, I have called mighty warriors to express My anger,
and they will rejoice when I am exalted."

13:1 Jer 50:1-51
13:2 Isa 45:1-3
13:3 Joel 3:11

12:6 Hebrew *Zion.*

12:1-6 Isaiah ended his prophecies relating to the Assyrian crisis on a jubilant note. The prophet composed a song of praise that triumphantly celebrates God's salvation and proclaims the Lord's mercy and grace to all who hear.

12:1 This verse speaks of a day when God's people will return from their places of exile and the Kingdom of God will be restored (see note at 2:2). From the perspective of the New Testament, that era began with the first coming of Jesus Christ and will be consummated upon His return.

12:2 Fear of judgment would be replaced by hopeful confidence and trust in the Lord when He brought His people back from exile.

▸ADOPTION
12:5 Tell the whole world. Think of the best news you've ever heard—your surgery turned out great? You won the lottery? You found a lost child? You can hardly stop talking about this news. Those who experience God's deliverance and get a taste of His salvation are compelled to rejoice. Sharing our good news is both an act of praise directed toward God and an invitation for others to experience the goodness of the Lord. Join with all God's people and tell the whole world about how God delivered you from the chains of sin! (***See Adoption****> With Christ> Servants> Witness for Christ,* TopicGuide page A37.)

13:1–27:13 This is the second major section of the portion of Isaiah centered on the Assyrian crisis (chapters 7–39). The section itself may be divided in two parts: the first features a series of oracles directed at specific nations (13:1–23:18), and the second presents a more generalized description of the judgment God would exact upon the nations after delivering His people (24:1–27:13).

13:1–14:27 There are good reasons for believing this prophecy was in fact directed against the nation of Assyria rather than Babylon. First, the wider literary context is primarily concerned with Assyria rather than Babylon. Secondly, Assyria is explicitly mentioned in verses 14:24-27 without any indication that a new oracle has begun. Thirdly, the kings of Assyria took the title "king of Babylon."

13:3 The coalition of foreign armies envisioned here were the Lord's instruments of judgment against the Assyrians (see note at 13:1–14:27). Politics and warfare may appear as though people control them, but in reality God moves among the nations to accomplish His purposes (see note at 10:7-11).

13:4 Isa 5:30
[4] Hear the noise on the mountains!
Listen, as the vast armies march!
It is the noise and shouting of many nations.
The LORD of Heaven's Armies has called this army together.
13:5 Isa 5:26
[5] They come from distant countries,
from beyond the farthest horizons.
They are the LORD's weapons to carry out His anger.
With them He will destroy the whole land.

13:6 Isa 34:2, 8 Ezek 30:3 Amos 5:18
[6] Scream in terror, for the day of the LORD has arrived—
the time for the Almighty to destroy.
13:7 Ezek 21:7
[7] Every arm is paralyzed with fear.
Every heart melts,
13:8 Isa 21:3; 26:17
[8] and people are terrified.
Pangs of anguish grip them,
like those of a woman in labor.
They look helplessly at one another,
their faces aflame with fear.

13:9 Isa 66:15-16
[9] For see, the day of the LORD is coming—
the terrible day of His fury and fierce anger.
The land will be made desolate,
and all the sinners destroyed with it.
13:10 *Matt 24:29 *Mark 13:24-25
[10] The heavens will be black above them;
the stars will give no light.
The sun will be dark when it rises,
and the moon will provide no light.

13:11 Dan 5:22-23
[11] "I, the LORD, will punish the world for its evil
and the wicked for their sin.
I will crush the arrogance of the proud
and humble the pride of the mighty.
13:12 Isa 6:11-12
[12] I will make people scarcer than gold—
more rare than the fine gold of Ophir.
13:13 Hag 2:6
[13] For I will shake the heavens.
The earth will move from its place
when the LORD of Heaven's Armies displays His wrath
in the day of His fierce anger."

▸ WORSHIP

13:6 Fingers in our ears. Sometimes we like to be scared—at least when we have a little warning. Have you ever been so afraid that you screamed or ran away or jumped? Some people get so afraid that they retreat into another world, pretending as if whatever frightened them actually doesn't exist. This is at the heart of why unrepentant sinners deny God's existence (Romans 1:18-19)—they know they deserve God's wrath, and their fear of judgment, coupled with their determination not to repent, leaves them no other option than to pretend He's not there. Look reality in the face—do grave consequences face you or those around you? Do not pretend, do not ignore, but deal with your fear honestly. Do you fear discipline or punishment from God? Then make the changes you know will honor Him. (***See Worship****> OT> Reverence> Fear Him because of what He has done,* TopicGuide page A29.)

13:10, 13 The symbolic upheaval of the cosmic order is a typical way Scripture describes God's judgment (compare Joel 2:10, 31; Revelation 6:12-13).

▸ PURPOSE

13:13 Awaiting God's judgment. Picture two children—legs dangling from their chairs—waiting outside the principal's office to receive their discipline. They may be shivering, shaking, pale with perhaps a tear trickling down one of their cheeks. The fear we all have of punishment when we do evil is just a taste of the fear unsaved humanity will feel when it faces God's judgment (Revelation 20:11-15). We need to warn people about the coming judgment—and must not spare their feelings. Whatever negative feelings they may have now about the gospel is nothing compared to the fear of standing in the presence of a righteous God without Christ. Tell people the truth about God's fearsome judgment. (***See Purpose****> God's Deeds> Judgment> God promises judgment,* TopicGuide page A53.)

13:17 The Medes lived in the Zagros Mountains east of Assyria and played a significant role in the fall of Assyria.

14 Everyone in Babylon will run about like a hunted gazelle,
like sheep without a shepherd.
They will try to find their own people
and flee to their own land.
15 Anyone who is captured will be cut down—
run through with a sword.
16 Their little children will be dashed to death before their eyes.
Their homes will be sacked, and their wives will be raped.

17 "Look, I will stir up the Medes against Babylon.
They cannot be tempted by silver
or bribed with gold.
18 The attacking armies will shoot down the young men with arrows.
They will have no mercy on helpless babies
and will show no compassion for children."

19 Babylon, the most glorious of kingdoms,
the flower of Chaldean pride,
will be devastated like Sodom and Gomorrah
when God destroyed them.
20 Babylon will never be inhabited again.
It will remain empty for generation after generation.
Nomads will refuse to camp there,
and shepherds will not bed down their sheep.
21 Desert animals will move into the ruined city,
and the houses will be haunted by howling creatures.
Owls will live among the ruins,
and wild goats will go there to dance.
22 Hyenas will howl in its fortresses,
and jackals will make dens in its luxurious palaces.
Babylon's days are numbered;
its time of destruction will soon arrive.

A TAUNT FOR BABYLON'S KING

14 But the LORD will have mercy on the descendants of Jacob. He will choose Israel as
His special people once again. He will bring them back to settle once again in their
own land. And people from many different nations will come and join them there and
unite with the people of Israel.* 2 The nations of the world will help the LORD's people to re-
turn, and those who come to live in their land will serve them. Those who captured Israel
will themselves be captured, and Israel will rule over its enemies.

3 In that wonderful day when the LORD gives His people rest from sorrow and fear, from
slavery and chains, 4 you will taunt the king of Babylon. You will say,

"The mighty man has been destroyed.
Yes, your insolence* is ended.

13:14 1 Kgs 22:17; Matt 9:36
13:15 Jer 51:3-4
13:16 Ps 137:8-9; Hos 10:14
13:17 Jer 51:11
13:18 2 Chr 36:17
13:19 Gen 19:24; Rev 18:16-17, 19
13:20 Jer 51:37-43
13:21 Isa 34:11-15; Zeph 2:14
14:1 Ps 102:13; Isa 41:8-9; 49:13, 15; Zech 2:11-12
14:2 Isa 45:14; Dan 7:18, 27
14:3 Ezra 9:8-9; Jer 30:10
14:4 Hab 2:6

14:1 Hebrew *the house of Jacob.* The names "Jacob" and "Israel" are often interchanged throughout the Old Testament, referring sometimes to the individual patriarch and sometimes to the nation. 14:4 As in Dead Sea Scrolls; the meaning of the Masoretic Text is uncertain.

13:19 The allusion to infamous cities suggests both the level of wickedness that filled these foreign nations and the judgment that threatened to overwhelm them.

14:1-2 Isaiah described the restoration and renewal that would follow Israel's rescue from exile. This glorious age would be marked by the influx of Gentiles into the covenant community.

14:3-21 The fall of Babylon (or perhaps Assyria; see note at 13:1–14:27) would be the cause of great joy. The "taunt" of Babylon is best seen as a celebration of God's justice and the vindication of the righteous. Those who love righteousness rejoice when evil is overcome by the power of God.

[5] For the LORD has crushed your wicked power
and broken your evil rule.
14:6 Isa 47:6 [6] You struck the people with endless blows of rage
and held the nations in your angry grip
with unrelenting tyranny.
14:7 Ps 98:1-9 [7] But finally the earth is at rest and quiet.
Now it can sing again!
14:8 Isa 55:12 [8] Even the trees of the forest—
the cypress trees and the cedars of Lebanon—
sing out this joyous song:
'Since you have been cut down,
no one will come now to cut us down!'

[9] "In the place of the dead* there is excitement
over your arrival.
The spirits of world leaders and mighty kings long dead
stand up to see you.
14:10 Ezek 32:21 [10] With one voice they all cry out,
'Now you are as weak as we are!
14:11 Isa 5:14 [11] Your might and power were buried with you.*
The sound of the harp in your palace has ceased.
Now maggots are your sheet,
and worms your blanket.'

14:12 Luke 10:18 Rev 9:1 [12] "How you are fallen from heaven,
O shining star, son of the morning!
You have been thrown down to the earth,
you who destroyed the nations of the world.
14:13 Ezek 28:2 Matt 11:23 Luke 10:15 [13] For you said to yourself,
'I will ascend to heaven and set my throne
above God's stars.
I will preside on the mountain of the gods
far away in the north.*
14:14 2 Thes 2:4 [14] I will climb to the highest heavens
and be like the Most High.'
14:15 Matt 11:23 Luke 10:15 [15] Instead, you will be brought down to the place of the dead,
down to its lowest depths.
[16] Everyone there will stare at you and ask,
'Can this be the one who shook the earth
and made the kingdoms of the world tremble?
[17] Is this the one who destroyed the world
and made it into a wasteland?
Is this the king who demolished the world's greatest cities
and had no mercy on his prisoners?'

14:9 Hebrew *Sheol;* also in 14:15. **14:11** Hebrew *were brought down to Sheol.* **14:13** Or *on the heights of Zaphon.*

14:9-11 Isaiah sarcastically confronted the Assyrians with the perpetual enemy of all great people and empires—death and extinction. The Assyrian empire would soon crumble and would be no better off than all the nations they had taken such great pride in defeating.

14:12-15 Many Christians have understood this passage as a description of the fall of Satan. However, as the context makes clear, the passage refers to the kings of Assyria. The language also alludes to ancient Canaanite and Babylonian myths in which lesser gods attempt to usurp power from greater gods and fail. Isaiah employed these well-known myths to condemn Assyria for her hubris and arrogance. See Ezekiel 28.

18 "The kings of the nations lie in stately glory,
each in his own tomb,
19 but you will be thrown out of your grave
like a worthless branch.
Like a corpse trampled underfoot,
you will be dumped into a mass grave
with those killed in battle.
You will descend to the pit.
20 You will not be given a proper burial,
for you have destroyed your nation
and slaughtered your people.
The descendants of such an evil person
will never again receive honor.
21 Kill this man's children!
Let them die because of their father's sins!
They must not rise and conquer the earth,
filling the world with their cities."

22 This is what the LORD of Heaven's Armies says:
"I, Myself, have risen against Babylon!
I will destroy its children and its children's children,"
says the LORD.
23 "I will make Babylon a desolate place of owls,
filled with swamps and marshes.
I will sweep the land with the broom of destruction.
I, the LORD of Heaven's Armies, have spoken!"

14:19 Isa 5:25
14:20 Job 18:19; Ps 21:10
14:21 Exod 20:5; Isa 13:16
14:23 Isa 13:6; 34:11

A MESSAGE ABOUT ASSYRIA

24 The LORD of Heaven's Armies has sworn this oath:

"It will all happen as I have planned.
It will be as I have decided.
25 I will break the Assyrians when they are in Israel;
I will trample them on My mountains.
My people will no longer be their slaves
nor bow down under their heavy loads.
26 I have a plan for the whole earth,
a hand of judgment upon all the nations.
27 The LORD of Heaven's Armies has spoken—
who can change His plans?
When His hand is raised,
who can stop Him?"

14:24 Job 23:13; Isa 46:11
14:25 Isa 9:4; Nah 1:13
14:26 Isa 23:9
14:27 Exod 15:12; Isa 43:13; Dan 4:31, 35

A MESSAGE ABOUT PHILISTIA

28 This message came to me the year King Ahaz died:*

29 Do not rejoice, you Philistines,
that the rod that struck you is broken—
that the king who attacked you is dead.

14:28 2 Kgs 16:20

14:28 King Ahaz died in 715 B.C.

14:24-25 The prophecy now addresses itself explicitly to Assyria without the typical title that is used to transition from one nation to another (as in verse 14:28 or 15:1, for example), suggesting that Assyria, not Babylon, has been the real subject of this section.

14:28-32 The renewed Assyrian invasion from the north would prompt Philistia to send messengers to surrounding nations seeking to build a coalition against Assyria, but Jerusalem was instructed to rely on God alone for defense.

For from that snake a more poisonous snake will be born,
a fiery serpent to destroy you!

14:30 Isa 8:21; 11:4

30 I will feed the poor in My pasture;
the needy will lie down in peace.
But as for you, I will wipe you out with famine
and destroy the few who remain.

14:31 Jer 1:14

31 Wail at the gates! Weep in the cities!
Melt with fear, you Philistines!
A powerful army comes like smoke from the north.
Each soldier rushes forward eager to fight.

14:32 Ps 87:1, 5 Isa 25:4

32 What should we tell the Philistine messengers? Tell them,

"The LORD has built Jerusalem*;
its walls will give refuge to His oppressed people."

A MESSAGE ABOUT MOAB

15:1 Isa 11:4 Jer 48:1 Ezek 25:8-11

15 This message came to me concerning Moab:

In one night the town of Ar will be leveled,
and the city of Kir will be destroyed.

15:2 Jer 48:37

2 Your people will go to their temple in Dibon to mourn.
They will go to their sacred shrines to weep.
They will wail for the fate of Nebo and Medeba,
shaving their heads in sorrow and cutting off their beards.

15:3 Isa 22:4 Jer 48:38 Jon 3:6-8

3 They will wear burlap as they wander the streets.
From every home and public square will come the sound of wailing.
4 The people of Heshbon and Elealeh will cry out;
their voices will be heard as far away as Jahaz!
The bravest warriors of Moab will cry out in utter terror.
They will be helpless with fear.

15:5 Jer 48:5

5 My heart weeps for Moab.
Its people flee to Zoar and Eglath-shelishiyah.
Weeping, they climb the road to Luhith.
Their cries of distress can be heard all along the road to Horonaim.

14:32 Hebrew *Zion.*

▸ PURPOSE
14:30 God's punishment for his enemies. Because God is all-powerful, He controls nature and nations. Therefore, He can bring the powers of creation against His enemies—in this case, He used famine. But suffering isn't always a punishment from God. Those who seek after God will often suffer (Acts 14:22). Even so, you can trust that God will settle all accounts at the final judgment. Those who have sacrificed much for the Lord—and those who have not—will be rewarded with everything they deserve (Matthew 25). Prepare yourself and those you love for that awesome day. (***See Purpose****> God's Deeds> Judgment> Famine,* TopicGuide page A53.)

15:1–16:14 This prophecy was directed toward Moab, a nation east of Judah across the Dead Sea. Assyria destroyed Moab in approximately 715 BC.

15:2-4 In the wake of the Assyrian onslaught, the rites and rituals of mourning and grief would characterize Moabite society.

15:5 The Lord sounded a note of sorrow as He surveyed the suffering that would come upon Moab. The people of Moab were related to Israel through Abraham's nephew Lot (see Genesis 19:30-38).

▸ GOD
15:5 Tears of the heart. Often we don't think of God as having emotions like sorrow. Even happiness seems far away from the "unmoved mover" that most people imagine as their God. Yet the Bible ascribes all sorts of emotions to God. The difference is that God's tears are not from fear or surprise—God knows everything and fears nothing. And while we may take a perverse pleasure in the suffering of others, God takes no pleasure in the death of the wicked (Ezekiel 33:11). God feels pain when the creation He made is marred and destroyed, yet His pain is not related to loss—for who truly could take anything from God's hands? We can pray and know that God understands our emotional world and fully intends on maturing our emotions, behaviors, and thoughts until they conform to His own (Philippians 1:8; Revelation 2:9; Hebrews 2:17-18). (***See God****> God's Nature> Personality> Emotion> God can be moved to grief,* TopicGuide page A14.)

6 Even the waters of Nimrim are dried up!
The grassy banks are scorched.
The tender plants are gone;
nothing green remains.
7 The people grab their possessions
and carry them across the Ravine of Willows.
8 A cry of distress echoes through the land of Moab
from one end to the other—
from Eglaim to Beer-elim.
9 The stream near Dibon* runs red with blood,
but I am still not finished with Dibon!
Lions will hunt down the survivors—
both those who try to escape
and those who remain behind.

15:6 Jer 48:34; Joel 1:10-12

15:9 2 Kgs 17:25; Jer 50:17

16 1 Send lambs from Sela as tribute
to the ruler of the land.
Send them through the desert
to the mountain of beautiful Zion.
2 The women of Moab are left like homeless birds
at the shallow crossings of the Arnon River.
3 "Help us," they cry.
"Defend us against our enemies.
Protect us from their relentless attack.
Do not betray us now that we have escaped.
4 Let our refugees stay among you.
Hide them from our enemies until the terror is past."

When oppression and destruction have ended
and enemy raiders have disappeared,
5 then God will establish one of David's descendants as king.
He will rule with mercy and truth.
He will always do what is just
and be eager to do what is right.

6 We have heard about proud Moab—
about its pride and arrogance and rage.
But all that boasting has disappeared.
7 The entire land of Moab weeps.
Yes, everyone in Moab mourns
for the cakes of raisins from Kir-hareseth.
They are all gone now.

16:1 2 Kgs 3:4; 14:7; Isa 42:11

16:2 Num 21:13-14

16:4 Isa 9:4; 54:14

16:6 Jer 48:29; Zeph 2:8, 10

16:7 2 Kgs 3:25; Jer 48:31

15:9 As in Dead Sea Scrolls, some Greek manuscripts, and Latin Vulgate; Masoretic Text reads *Dimon;* also in 15:9b.

16:1-4 Lambs were the traditional form of Moabite tribute (2 Kings 3:4), suggesting Moab may have been willing to accept vassal status in exchange for shelter from the Assyrians.

▸ GOD

16:5 The Lord reigns. Let's be frank: it certainly doesn't look like Jesus is ruling the world, at least in the way we think about kings. Isaiah prophesied about the coming reign of King Jesus, joining the chorus of Old Testament believers (Jeremiah 23:5; 33:15) who looked for a Messiah-Priest to deliver them from their sins (Isaiah 53:4-6) and a Messiah-King to save them from every enemy (Isaiah 11:4; Psalm 110; Zechariah 9:9-10). Jesus certainly believed He was the one to fulfill those promises (Luke 4:21; Matthew 11:4-5). Those of Jesus' time wanted a king that would rule their world with an iron fist. But Jesus told them that His kingdom was, at that time, a spiritual one (John 6:66-69). Yes, King Jesus is in heaven, reigning. And yes, He is king here, too—but His reign is not easily seen outside the church. There will come a day when God will reveal the reign of His Son to all humanity (1 Timothy 6:15), and soon following, the entire universe will be revealed as being under Christ's authority (Revelation 12:10). (***See God*** *> God's Attributes> Eternal> The Son's reign will have no end,* TopicGuide page A15.)

16:8
Num 32:38
Isa 15:4
Jer 48:32

[8] The farms of Heshbon are abandoned;
the vineyards at Sibmah are deserted.
The rulers of the nations have broken down Moab—
that beautiful grapevine.
Its tendrils spread north as far as the town of Jazer
and trailed eastward into the wilderness.
Its shoots reached so far west
that they crossed over the Dead Sea.*

16:9
Jer 48:32

[9] So now I weep for Jazer and the vineyards of Sibmah;
My tears will flow for Heshbon and Elealeh.
There are no more shouts of joy
over your summer fruits and harvest.

16:10
Job 24:11
Isa 24:7-8
Jer 48:33
Amos 5:17

[10] Gone now is the gladness,
gone the joy of harvest.
There will be no singing in the vineyards,
no more happy shouts,
no treading of grapes in the winepresses.
I have ended all their harvest joys.

16:11
Isa 15:5; 63:15

[11] My heart's cry for Moab is like a lament on a harp.
I am filled with anguish for Kir-hareseth.*

16:12
1 Kgs 18:26-29
Jer 48:35

[12] The people of Moab will worship at their pagan shrines,
but it will do them no good.
They will cry to the gods in their temples,
but no one will be able to save them.

[13] The LORD has already said these things about Moab in the past. [14] But now the LORD
says, "Within three years, counting each day,* the glory of Moab will be ended. From its
great population, only a few of its people will be left alive."

A MESSAGE ABOUT DAMASCUS AND ISRAEL

17:1
Isa 10:9; 25:2

17 This message came to me concerning Damascus:

"Look, the city of Damascus will disappear!
It will become a heap of ruins.

17:2
Zeph 2:6

[2] The towns of Aroer will be deserted.
Flocks will graze in the streets and lie down undisturbed,
with no one to chase them away.

17:3
Isa 8:4
Hos 9:11

[3] The fortified towns of Israel* will also be destroyed,
and the royal power of Damascus will end.

16:8 Hebrew *the sea.* 16:11 Hebrew *Kir-heres,* a variant spelling of Kir-hareseth. 16:14 Hebrew *Within three years, as a servant bound by contract would count them.* 17:3a Hebrew *of Ephraim,* referring to the northern kingdom of Israel.

16:10-12 Wine often signifies blessing and prosperity. The devastation of Moab's vineyards suggests more than the loss of agricultural revenue—it suggests the loss of joy and happiness.

▸ WORSHIP
16:12 The futility of idols. Most people make decisions based on what they see. Because we cannot see God, we find it hard to believe in Him. We look around us and see all sorts of things that promise to make us successful, smarter, and more spiritual—but earthly things and mortal people can never save us. No matter how fervently we serve, no matter how we pay, earthly things cannot ultimately save. God alone is the only one able to deal with our sin and guilt. Make a commitment to ask God to help you trust in Him alone for your salvation, for your worth, and for your future. (***See Worship*> *OT*> *Reverence*> *Put away idols,* TopicGuide page A28.)

16:13-14 Prior warnings against Moab (perhaps the prophecies and laments of 15:1–16:12) had been issued. Their fulfillment was now imminent.

17:1-14 This prophecy was directed against Damascus, the capital of Aram (Syria). Damascus allied itself with Israel in a futile attempt to resist Assyrian power. They unsuccessfully attempted to draw Judah into their alliance (see Isaiah 7–8).

17:3 The fates of Israel and Aram were bound together because of their alliance against Assyria. Like the faded glory of Israel, the survivors of Aram would be scant.

All that remains of Syria*
will share the fate of Israel's departed glory,"
declares the LORD of Heaven's Armies.

4 "In that day Israel's* glory will grow dim;
its robust body will waste away.
5 The whole land will look like a grainfield
after the harvesters have gathered the grain.
It will be desolate,
like the fields in the valley of Rephaim after the harvest.
6 Only a few of its people will be left,
like stray olives left on a tree after the harvest.
Only two or three remain in the highest branches,
four or five scattered here and there on the limbs,"
declares the LORD, the God of Israel.

7 Then at last the people will look to their Creator
and turn their eyes to the Holy One of Israel.
8 They will no longer look to their idols for help
or worship what their own hands have made.
They will never again bow down to their Asherah poles
or worship at the pagan shrines they have built.
9 Their largest cities will be like a deserted forest,
like the land the Hivites and Amorites abandoned*
when the Israelites came here so long ago.
It will be utterly desolate.
10 Why? Because you have turned from the God who can save you.
You have forgotten the Rock who can hide you.
So you may plant the finest grapevines
and import the most expensive seedlings.
11 They may sprout on the day you set them out;
yes, they may blossom on the very morning you plant them,
but you will never pick any grapes from them.
Your only harvest will be a load of grief and unrelieved pain.

12 Listen! The armies of many nations
roar like the roaring of the sea.
Hear the thunder of the mighty forces
as they rush forward like thundering waves.

17:4 Isa 10:3, 16
17:5 Jer 51:33
17:6 Deut 4:27; Isa 24:13; 27:12
17:7 Isa 10:20; Hos 6:1
17:8 Exod 34:13; Isa 27:9; 30:22
17:10 Deut 32:4, 18, 30-31; Isa 30:29; 62:11
17:11 Hos 10:13
17:12 Jer 6:23

17:3b Hebrew *Aram.* 17:4 Hebrew *Jacob's.* See note on 14:1. 17:9 As in Greek version; Hebrew reads *like places of the wood and the highest bough.*

17:7-8 The judgment of God was intended to refine and purify Israel. First to go were the Asherah poles, dedicated to the worship of the Canaanite fertility goddess.

17:9-11 The prophet attributed the impending destruction of Israel to their wickedness and rejection of God. They relied on fortified cities rather than on the Lord, who is a rock of safety.

▶ GOD

17:10 Turning to the Rock. What is your greatest sin? Perhaps it's something you did once, or perhaps it's something you do every day. What about your nation? What's the worst harm your nation has ever done to its citizens, or to the innocent citizens of another nation? Among Israel's worst sins was turning away from God. Israel forgot how God had delivered His people from slavery in Egypt, how God had led them through the wilderness to the Promised Land, and how God had enabled them to defeat their enemies. It's encouraging to see how often God allowed them to face the consequences for their sin while offering hope on the other side of discipline. God will not allow sin to fester and linger in His people, but this does not mean He does not love His people—quite the opposite (1 Peter 4:17-19). Repent, and find out God's deep love for His people. (***See God****> God's Nature> Personality> Emotion> God is compassionate and loving,* TopicGuide page A14.)

17:12-14 The Assyrians assembled mighty armies composed of soldiers conscripted from subjugated nations. Their assault was aptly compared to the raging of the sea against the shore. However, the Lord was committed to the defense and vindication of His people.

17:13 Ps 1:4 Isa 29:5

[13] But though they thunder like breakers on a beach,
God will silence them, and they will run away.
They will flee like chaff scattered by the wind,
like a tumbleweed whirling before a storm.

17:14 2 Kgs 19:35 Isa 41:11-12

[14] In the evening Israel waits in terror,
but by dawn its enemies are dead.
This is the just reward of those who plunder us,
a fitting end for those who destroy us.

A MESSAGE ABOUT ETHIOPIA

18:1 Isa 20:3-5 Ezek 30:4, 6, 9 Zeph 2:12

18 [1] Listen, Ethiopia*—land of fluttering sails*
that lies at the headwaters of the Nile,

18:2 Exod 2:3 2 Chr 12:2-4 Isa 18:7

[2] that sends ambassadors
in swift boats down the river.

Go, swift messengers!
Take a message to a tall, smooth-skinned people,
who are feared far and wide
for their conquests and destruction,
and whose land is divided by rivers.

18:3 Ps 49:1 Mic 1:2

[3] All you people of the world,
everyone who lives on the earth—
when I raise my battle flag on the mountain, look!
When I blow the ram's horn, listen!
[4] For the LORD has told me this:
"I will watch quietly from My dwelling place—
as quietly as the heat rises on a summer day,
or as the morning dew forms during the harvest."

18:5 Isa 26:21 Ezek 17:6-10

[5] Even before you begin your attack,
while your plans are ripening like grapes,
the LORD will cut off your new growth with pruning shears.
He will snip off and discard your spreading branches.

18:6 Isa 56:9 Ezek 39:17-20

[6] Your mighty army will be left dead in the fields
for the mountain vultures and wild animals.
The vultures will tear at the corpses all summer.
The wild animals will gnaw at the bones all winter.

18:1a Hebrew *Cush.* 18:1b Or *land of many locusts;* Hebrew reads *land of whirring wings.*

▸ SPIRITUAL WARFARE

17:13 God's enemies never win. How much personal power do you wield? As people measure such things you may be quite commanding or relatively weak. But compare yourself to God—how do you measure up? He speaks—and a universe appears. He thinks—and it is done. His enemies only exist to fulfill their divinely ordained purpose—then they are defeated. If you are in a difficult situation, trust that God will not allow evil to exist in His universe one moment longer than necessary. He will defend and protect you in a way that honors His promises to you and glorifies His own name. (***See Spiritual Warfare****> Resisting Sin and Evil> Trusting God> God as Warrior> God's fight against the enemies of Israel,* TopicGuide page A46.)

18:1-7 This prophecy was directed against the nation of Ethiopia. The ancient land of Cush, or Ethiopia, was located south of Egypt. In Isaiah's day, Ethiopia and Egypt were closely associated, as they were allied against Assyria. After prophesying against Ethiopia in chapter 18, Isaiah would prophesy against Egypt in chapter 19, and then against both nations in chapter 20.

18:2 Contrary to Middle Eastern cultures, Egyptians and Ethiopians preferred a clean-shaven appearance.

▸ PURPOSE

18:4 God waits. Sometimes, it may seem as if God fails to execute His will on the earth. All over the world, people treat others inhumanely. Children are enslaved. The weak are robbed. The hungry are disregarded. The list goes on and on. Doesn't God see what's going on? Yes, God notes every injustice in the world. He is patiently waiting to act in the perfect time. We can be sure that God does take up the cause of the hurting and the sorrowful. If you get discouraged about what you see in the world, reread this verse. Keep in mind that God sees—and He will act. And when He does, all will know that it's been worth the wait. (***See Purpose****> God's Means> God's Sovereignty> God knows all,* TopicGuide page A52.)

7 At that time the LORD of Heaven's Armies will receive gifts
from this land divided by rivers,
from this tall, smooth-skinned people,
who are feared far and wide for their conquests and destruction.
They will bring the gifts to Jerusalem,*
where the LORD of Heaven's Armies dwells.

18:7 Zech 14:16-17

A MESSAGE ABOUT EGYPT

19 This message came to me concerning Egypt:

Look! The LORD is advancing against Egypt,
riding on a swift cloud.
The idols of Egypt tremble.
The hearts of the Egyptians melt with fear.

19:1 Josh 2:11; Ps 104:3; Jer 43:12; Matt 26:64

2 "I will make Egyptian fight against Egyptian—
brother against brother,
neighbor against neighbor,
city against city,
province against province.

19:2 Judg 7:22; Matt 10:21, 36

3 The Egyptians will lose heart,
and I will confuse their plans.
They will plead with their idols for wisdom
and call on spirits, mediums, and those who consult the spirits of the dead.

19:3 Isa 8:19

4 I will hand Egypt over
to a hard, cruel master.
A fierce king will rule them,"
says the Lord, the LORD of Heaven's Armies.

19:4 Isa 20:4; Ezek 29:19

5 The waters of the Nile will fail to rise and flood the fields.
The riverbed will be parched and dry.

19:5 Ezek 30:12

6 The canals of the Nile will dry up,
and the streams of Egypt will stink
with rotting reeds and rushes.

19:6 Exod 7:18

7 All the greenery along the riverbank
and all the crops along the river
will dry up and blow away.

19:7 Isa 23:3, 10

8 The fishermen will lament for lack of work.
Those who cast hooks into the Nile will groan,
and those who use nets will lose heart.
9 There will be no flax for the harvesters,
no thread for the weavers.

19:9 Prov 7:16

10 They will be in despair,
and all the workers will be sick at heart.

18:7 Hebrew *to Mount Zion.*

18:7 In the aftermath of the Assyrian invasion of northeastern Africa, the prophet foresaw a time when there would be people from Ethiopia among those who came to worship the Lord in His Temple at Jerusalem. This expectation is fulfilled by the inclusion of Gentiles into the people of God through the work of Christ (see especially the conversion of the Ethiopian eunuch in Acts 8:26-40).

19:1-25 The subject of this prophecy was the nation of Egypt. The prophet predicted the fall of Egypt to the Assyrian king Esarhaddon in 670 BC.

19:1 In the ancient Near East, clouds were frequently portrayed as the war chariots of the gods.

19:5-10 God's judgment against Egypt would also affect the realm of nature. Egypt was dependent on the Nile River for physical sustenance and commerce. Normally the Nile River flooded its banks each year, watering the land and depositing rich soil. Times of drought that lowered the level of the Nile and prevented these floods would have devastating effects that would be felt at all levels of Egyptian society.

19:11 [11] What fools are the officials of Zoan!
Gen 41:38-39 Their best counsel to the king of Egypt is stupid and wrong.
1 Kgs 4:30 Will they still boast to Pharaoh of their wisdom?
Acts 7:22 Will they dare brag about all their wise ancestors?
19:12 [12] Where are your wise counselors, Pharaoh?
Rom 9:17 Let them tell you what God plans,
what the LORD of Heaven's Armies is going to do to Egypt.
19:13 [13] The officials of Zoan are fools,
Jer 2:16 and the officials of Memphis* are deluded.
The leaders of the people
have led Egypt astray.
19:14 [14] The LORD has sent a spirit of foolishness on them,
Isa 3:12 so all their suggestions are wrong.
They cause Egypt to stagger
like a drunk in his vomit.
19:15 [15] There is nothing Egypt can do.
Isa 9:14-15 All are helpless—
the head and the tail,
19:16 the noble palm branch and the lowly reed.

Jer 51:30 [16]In that day the Egyptians will be as weak as women. They will cower in fear beneath
Heb 10:31 the upraised fist of the LORD of Heaven's Armies. [17]Just to speak the name of Israel will ter-
19:17 Dan 4:35 rorize them, for the LORD of Heaven's Armies has laid out His plans against them.
19:18 [18]In that day five of Egypt's cities will follow the LORD of Heaven's Armies. They will even
Isa 45:23; 65:16 begin to speak Hebrew, the language of Canaan. One of these cities will be Heliopolis, the
19:19 City of the Sun.*
Gen 28:18 [19]In that day there will be an altar to the LORD in the heart of Egypt, and there will be a
Josh 22:10, 26-27 monument to the LORD at its border. [20]It will be a sign and a witness that the LORD of
19:20 Isa 43:3, 11; 45:15, Heaven's Armies is worshiped in the land of Egypt. When the people cry to the LORD for
21; 49:25 help against those who oppress them, He will send them a savior who will rescue them.
19:21 [21]The LORD will make Himself known to the Egyptians. Yes, they will know the LORD and
Isa 56:7 will give their sacrifices and offerings to Him. They will make a vow to the LORD and will
19:22 Deut 32:39 keep it. [22]The LORD will strike Egypt, and then He will bring healing. For the Egyptians will
Isa 27:13; 45:14 turn to the LORD, and He will listen to their pleas and heal them.
Heb 12:11 [23]In that day Egypt and Assyria will be connected by a highway. The Egyptians and As-
19:23 syrians will move freely between their lands, and they will both worship God. [24]And Israel
Isa 11:16 will be their ally. The three will be together, and Israel will be a blessing to them. [25]For the
19:25 Hos 2:23

19:13 Hebrew *Noph.* 19:18 Or *will be the City of Destruction.*

19:11-15 The city of Zoan, otherwise known as Tanis, functioned as the Egyptian capital at the time.

19:17-25 In these verses, the prophet made astounding claims concerning the future of Egypt. He predicted the conversion of Egyptians to the worship of the Lord. The judgment that was about to fall upon Egypt would eventually produce a fear of the Lord among the Egyptians. Egypt and Assyria would band together with Israel and be welcomed into the covenant community. They too would be called the people of God. The fulfillment of these remarkable hopes began with small numbers of Egyptians joining exiled Israelites in worship, and it continued with greater intensity when the gospel broke through to the Gentiles following the death and resurrection of Christ. The final fulfillment of these hopes will come when people from all nations and languages gather to worship the God of Israel (Revelation 7:9).

▶ PURPOSE

19:22 God's ultimate purpose. Have you known people who experienced terrible times in their lives only to have those circumstances lead them to God? In this case, Isaiah sees that a terrible event in Egypt's history will cause that nation to come to God for healing. God can use suffering to break anyone's will. Of course, we'd rather have God change us through reading notes in a study Bible, but often that's not the way He works. He sovereignly orchestrates events and experiences to draw people to Himself. Trust God's perfect purpose in every circumstance. (***See Purpose***> *God's Deeds*> *Judgment*> *Plague upon Israel's enemies,* TopicGuide page A53; also ***see Worship***> *OT*> *Repentance*> *Nature*> *Repentance is characterized as turning from idols to the living God,* TopicGuide page A29.)

19:25 The way in which the Lord addressed the Egyptians and Assyrians signals their full participation in the covenant community (compare Exodus 19:5-6).

LORD of Heaven's Armies will say, "Blessed be Egypt, My people. Blessed be Assyria, the
land I have made. Blessed be Israel, My special possession!"

A MESSAGE ABOUT EGYPT AND ETHIOPIA

20 In the year when King Sargon of Assyria sent his commander in chief to capture
the Philistine city of Ashdod,* 2 the LORD told Isaiah son of Amoz, "Take off the
burlap you have been wearing, and remove your sandals." Isaiah did as he was told and
walked around naked and barefoot.

3 Then the LORD said, "My servant Isaiah has been walking around naked and barefoot
for the last three years. This is a sign—a symbol of the terrible troubles I will bring upon
Egypt and Ethiopia.* 4 For the king of Assyria will take away the Egyptians and Ethiopians*
as prisoners. He will make them walk naked and barefoot, both young and old, their but-
tocks bared, to the shame of Egypt. 5 Then the Philistines will be thrown into panic, for they
counted on the power of Ethiopia and boasted of their allies in Egypt! 6 They will say, 'If this
can happen to Egypt, what chance do we have? We were counting on Egypt to protect us
from the king of Assyria.' "

A MESSAGE ABOUT BABYLON

21 This message came to me concerning Babylon—the desert by the sea*:

Disaster is roaring down on you from the desert,
like a whirlwind sweeping in from the Negev.
2 I see a terrifying vision:
I see the betrayer betraying,
the destroyer destroying.
Go ahead, you Elamites and Medes,
attack and lay siege.
I will make an end
to all the groaning Babylon caused.
3 My stomach aches and burns with pain.
Sharp pangs of anguish are upon me,
like those of a woman in labor.
I grow faint when I hear what God is planning;
I am too afraid to look.
4 My mind reels and my heart races.
I longed for evening to come,
but now I am terrified of the dark.

5 Look! They are preparing a great feast.
They are spreading rugs for people to sit on.
Everyone is eating and drinking.
But quick! Grab your shields and prepare for battle.
You are being attacked!

20:1 1 Sam 5:1; 2 Kgs 18:17
20:2 1 Sam 19:24; Mic 1:8
20:3 Isa 8:18; 43:3
20:4 Isa 19:4; 47:2-3
20:5 Jer 9:23-24
20:6 Isa 10:3; 30:3-5, 7
21:1 Isa 13:20-22; Zech 9:14
21:2 Isa 33:1; Jer 49:34
21:3 Ps 48:6; 1 Thes 5:3
21:4 Deut 28:67
21:5 Jer 51:39, 57

20:1 Ashdod was captured by Assyria in 711 B.C. 20:3 Hebrew *Cush;* also in 20:5. 20:4 Hebrew *Cushites.* 21:1 Hebrew *concerning the desert by the sea.*

20:1-6 This prophecy concludes the oracles directed against Egypt and Ethiopia. While the subjects of the prophecy are Egypt and Ethiopia, the message is directed toward Judah.

20:2 The prophets were sometimes called upon to proclaim their message through symbolic actions and gestures (compare Jeremiah 13 and Ezekiel 5).

20:3-4 Isaiah's nakedness symbolized the wretched condition that awaited the Egyptians and Ethiopians, who would be led away captive following Assyria's conquest of their land.

20:5-6 This oracle's message to Judah was clear: The Philistines at Ashdod foolishly trusted in Egypt and Ethiopia to come to their aid against the Assyrians, but they were abandoned and destroyed. The Judeans were not to rely on these nations; they were to trust in the Lord alone.

6 Meanwhile, the Lord said to me,
"Put a watchman on the city wall.
Let him shout out what he sees.
21:7 Isa 21:9
7 He should look for chariots
drawn by pairs of horses,
and for riders on donkeys and camels.
Let the watchman be fully alert."

21:8 Hab 2:1
8 Then the watchman* called out,
"Day after day I have stood on the watchtower, my lord.
Night after night I have remained at my post.
21:9 Isa 46:1 Jer 50:2 Rev 14:8
9 Now at last—look!
Here comes a man in a chariot
with a pair of horses!"
Then the watchman said,
"Babylon is fallen, fallen!
All the idols of Babylon
lie broken on the ground!"
21:10 Jer 51:33
10 O my people, threshed and winnowed,
I have told you everything the LORD of Heaven's Armies has said,
everything the God of Israel has told me.

A MESSAGE ABOUT EDOM

21:11 Gen 32:3
11 This message came to me concerning Edom*:

21:8 As in Dead Sea Scrolls and Syriac version; Masoretic Text reads *a lion.* 21:11a Hebrew *Dumah,* which means "silence" or "stillness." It is a wordplay on the word *Edom.*

▸ GOD
20:6 It can happen to the best. It's hard to admit when we are wrong. It's even harder to be truly regretful for the mass chaos and confusion our sin often causes. Isaiah prophesied that Egypt and Ethiopia would be decimated by their enemies. But why? Because they would not repent and turn from their sin—they were rich, but they did not repent. They had great armies, but they did not repent. The Lord directed His judgment against them for disobeying His laws and for continuing to persecute God's people. As you look around you, do not fear—God is able to judge all, from the largest nation to the smallest town, for their corporate and individual sins against Him. Do not fret—God will deal with those who mock His Word. (***See God***> *Salvation> Father> Commands all to repent,* TopicGuide page A15.)

21:1-10 This prophecy was directed against the nation of Babylon. At the time, Babylon was a vassal of Assyria; however, the proud and ancient nation frequently attempted to re-establish its independence. Isaiah's prophecy was most likely directed at one such failed rebellion that was put down by Assyria in 689 BC. Babylon would eventually succeed in overthrowing the Assyrian empire (the Assyrian capital fell in 612 BC).

21:3-4 The prophet reacted with great horror to the revelation of Babylon's defeat. Isaiah's response may have been prompted by his awareness of Judah's temptation to trust in the strength of Babylon. If Judah allied itself with Babylon, it would no doubt meet the same fate (see Isaiah 39).

▸ MINISTRY
21:4 The role of a prophet. We get worried about the weather and concerned about our finances, but how often do we lay awake at night out of concern for someone's spiritual life? The fate of the nation of Israel so impacted Isaiah's mind that he couldn't sleep because of it. Today, people all around us are heading for God's judgment and need to be warned about their fate. That's why we must, in an outward, noticeable fashion, live for God. Doing good works to glorify God is a good start, but explaining why we do these good works is even better (Luke 14:34). Lay awake at night and think of ways to impact those around you. (***See Ministry***> *Transformation> Fill and Subdue> Being salt and light in the world,* TopicGuide page A56.)

▸ WORSHIP
21:5 The world is unaware. "Eat, drink, and be merry." How many people have you known with this basic attitude toward life? Such people don't want to recognize that God's judgment is coming (Luke 12:19), and they refuse to prepare for it. When you meet people who seem to have no concern regarding God's judgment, you must pray for a holy fear to come over them, for judgment is indeed coming. Pray that God will prick their consciences and make them sensitive to the gravity of their sin, for only then will they be ready to receive the good news of the gospel. (***See Worship***> *OT> Prophets> Prophets spoke to their times,* TopicGuide page A28.)

21:6-10 The lookout was posted to await the return of the victorious conquering army. When the army finally appeared, they triumphantly proclaimed the fall of Babylon. The Assyrians defeated the Babylonians in 689 BC.

21:11-12 This prophecy was addressed to the nation of Edom, which sought relief from the metaphorical darkness that had fallen on the nation as a result of Assyrian oppression. The prophet warned that while relief would be forthcoming, it would only be temporary. Following the fall of Assyria, Babylon would subjugate Edom.

Someone from Edom* keeps calling to me,
"Watchman, how much longer until morning?
When will the night be over?"
12 The watchman replies,
"Morning is coming, but night will soon return.
If you wish to ask again, then come back and ask."

A MESSAGE ABOUT ARABIA

13 This message came to me concerning Arabia:

21:13 Jer 49:28

O caravans from Dedan,
hide in the deserts of Arabia.
14 O people of Tema,
bring water to these thirsty people,
food to these weary refugees.

21:14 Gen 25:15

15 They have fled from the sword,
from the drawn sword,
from the bent bow
and the terrors of battle.

21:15 Isa 13:14-15

16 The Lord said to me, "Within a year, counting each day,* all the glory of Kedar will
come to an end. 17 Only a few of its courageous archers will survive. I, the LORD, the God of
Israel, have spoken!"

21:16 Ps 120:5; Isa 16:14

21:17 Isa 10:19

A MESSAGE ABOUT JERUSALEM

22 This message came to me concerning Jerusalem—the Valley of Vision*:

22:1 Jer 21:13; Joel 3:12, 14

What is happening?
Why is everyone running to the rooftops?
2 The whole city is in a terrible uproar.
What do I see in this reveling city?
Bodies are lying everywhere,
killed not in battle but by famine and disease.

22:2 Isa 23:7; Jer 14:18; Lam 2:20

3 All your leaders have fled.
They surrendered without resistance.
The people tried to slip away,
but they were captured, too.

22:3 Isa 21:15

4 That's why I said, "Leave me alone to weep;
do not try to comfort me.
Let me cry for my people
as I watch them being destroyed."

22:4 Jer 9:1

21:11b Hebrew *Seir*, another name for Edom. 21:16 Hebrew *Within a year, as a servant bound by contract would count it.* Some ancient manuscripts read *Within three years*, as in 16:14. 22:1 Hebrew *concerning the Valley of Vision.*

21:13-16 This prophecy was directed against the inhabitants of the region of Arabia. The wilderness of Arabia provided shelter for those who had fled from the Assyrians. Yet, even this barren region with but a few spots of life (such as Kedar), would be subject to Assyrian invasion.

22:1-14 This prophecy was directed toward Jerusalem on an occasion of deliverance from an imminent threat. The passage condemns a false sense of security that had overtaken the people.

22:1-4 Isaiah chastised the premature celebration of the people. They had gone to the rooftops to celebrate, but the prophet foresaw great sorrow coming upon the city. The conditions described by the prophet depict the suffering of a city under siege.

▸ ADOPTION
22:4 Isaiah's sorrow. They drive by you. They shop with you. They go to church with you. Look around you—odds are, you see someone who will face God's judgment. Isaiah wept for his people as he foresaw God's judgment. He cried for his people because he knew that they wouldn't listen. We can imitate the prophet's compassion by praying for friends and family members who do not believe in Jesus. Look around you—to whom can you tell the truth about God? Ask God for the vision to see those He is calling to Himself. (***See Adoption***> *With Christ*> *Servants*> *Witness for Christ,* TopicGuide page A37.)

22:5 Isa 37:3 Lam 2:2

[5] Oh, what a day of crushing defeat!
What a day of confusion and terror
brought by the Lord, the LORD of Heaven's Armies,
upon the Valley of Vision!
The walls of Jerusalem have been broken,
and cries of death echo from the mountainsides.

22:6 Isa 21:2

[6] Elamites are the archers,
with their chariots and charioteers.
The men of Kir hold up the shields.
[7] Chariots fill your beautiful valleys,
and charioteers storm your gates.

22:8 1 Kgs 7:2; 10:17

[8] Judah's defenses have been stripped away.
You run to the armory* for your weapons.
[9] You inspect the breaks in the walls of Jerusalem.*
You store up water in the lower pool.
[10] You survey the houses and tear some down
for stone to strengthen the walls.

22:11 2 Kgs 20:20; 25:4

[11] Between the city walls, you build a reservoir
for water from the old pool.
But you never ask for help from the One who did all this.
You never considered the One who planned this long ago.

22:12 Isa 32:11 Joel 1:13 Mic 1:16

[12] At that time the Lord, the LORD of Heaven's Armies,
called you to weep and mourn.
He told you to shave your heads in sorrow for your sins
and to wear clothes of burlap to show your remorse.

22:13 Isa 5:11, 22; 56:12 *1 Cor 15:32

[13] But instead, you dance and play;
you slaughter cattle and kill sheep.
You feast on meat and drink wine.
You say, "Let's feast and drink,
for tomorrow we die!"

22:14 Isa 65:7, 20

[14] The LORD of Heaven's Armies has revealed this to me: "Till the day you die, you will never be forgiven for this sin." That is the judgment of the Lord, the LORD of Heaven's Armies.

A MESSAGE FOR SHEBNA

[15] This is what the Lord, the LORD of Heaven's Armies, said to me: "Confront Shebna, the palace administrator, and give him this message:

22:8 Hebrew *to the House of the Forest;* see 1 Kgs 7:2-5. 22:9 Hebrew *the city of David.*

22:5-11 Isaiah described panic that would overtake the city in the face of the impending invasion and during the frantic efforts to prepare the city for the coming siege. Isaiah 22:9 probably refers to Hezekiah's impressive effort to keep the city's water supply flowing in the event of a siege (compare 2 Chronicles 32).

▸ SPIRITUAL WARFARE
22:12 Weep and mourn. We sometimes feel bad about how we have treated someone, yet we rarely have any intention of stopping our hurtful behavior. We may feel bad when we are caught in sin, but our sadness isn't derived from our sin, but from being caught. The Apostle Paul said, "For the kind of sorrow God wants us to experience leads us away from sin and results in salvation. There's no regret for that kind of sorrow. But worldly sorrow, which lacks repentance, results in spiritual death" (2 Corinthians 7:10). Repentance includes feeling true sorrow for what we have done. This sorrow, when combined with faith, will cause us to call to God for forgiveness, and He will help us avoid sin in the future. What sins grieve you? Repent right away. Your depressed feeling could be God's way of showing you that He wants you to repent. Listen to your feelings, especially when they direct you to God. (***See Spiritual Warfare***> *Resisting Sin and Evil> Embracing Christ> Repent of your sin,* TopicGuide page A46.)

22:15-25 Unlike the preceding prophecies, this one was addressed to an individual rather than a nation. Shebna was a high-ranking officer in the court of King Hezekiah, and he was intimately involved with the events surrounding the invasion of Sennacherib (2 Kings 18:18-37; 19:2).

16 "Who do you think you are,
and what are you doing here,
building a beautiful tomb for yourself—
a monument high up in the rock?
17 For the LORD is about to hurl you away, mighty man.
He is going to grab you,
18 crumple you into a ball,
and toss you away into a distant, barren land.
There you will die,
and your glorious chariots will be broken and useless.
You are a disgrace to your master!

19 "Yes, I will drive you out of office," says the LORD. "I will pull you down from your high
position. 20 And then I will call My servant Eliakim son of Hilkiah to replace you. 21 I will dress
him in your royal robes and will give him your title and your authority. And he will be a fa-
ther to the people of Jerusalem and Judah. 22 I will give him the key to the house of David—
the highest position in the royal court. When he opens doors, no one will be able to close
them; when he closes doors, no one will be able to open them. 23 He will bring honor to his
family name, for I will drive him firmly in place like a nail in the wall. 24 They will give him
great responsibility, and he will bring honor to even the lowliest members of his family.*"
25 But the LORD of Heaven's Armies also says: "The time will come when I will pull out the
nail that seemed so firm. It will come out and fall to the ground. Everything it supports will
fall with it. I, the LORD, have spoken!"

22:16 2 Chr 16:14; Matt 27:60
22:18 Job 18:18
22:19 Ezek 17:24
22:20 Isa 36:3
22:21 Gen 45:8
22:23 Job 36:7; Zech 10:4
22:25 Esth 9:24-25; Isa 46:11

A MESSAGE ABOUT TYRE

23 This message came to me concerning Tyre:

Weep, O ships of Tarshish,
for the harbor and houses of Tyre are gone!
The rumors you heard in Cyprus*
are all true.
2 Mourn in silence, you people of the coast
and you merchants of Sidon.
Your traders crossed the sea,
3 sailing over deep waters.

23:1 Josh 19:29; Ezek 26:1–28:19
23:2 Isa 47:5
23:3 Ezek 27:3-25

22:24 Hebrew *They will hang on him all the glory of his father's house: its offspring and offshoots, all its lesser vessels, from the bowls to all the jars.* 23:1 Hebrew *Kittim;* also in 23:12.

22:16-18 Shebna showed an example of the attitude condemned in the preceding prophecy against Jerusalem (see 22:12-14). He was self-absorbed, concerned only with his own glory and reputation. Archaeologists have uncovered Shebna's prominent tomb.

22:20-24 The image of keys suggests Eliakim's authority to grant access to the king and his affect-binding changes (compare Matthew 16:19 and Revelation 3:7). Unlike Shebna, Eliakim would exercise his office with a sincere concern for the people of Judah.

23:1-18 This prophecy concerned the city of Tyre, a coastal city well known for its commerce and trade. The Assyrians attacked the city in 732 BC.

23:1-3 Tyre and her merchant fleet acted as a conduit between Egypt and Sidon, a port city north of Tyre. Damage to Tyre would deliver a serious blow to the region's commerce.

23:1 Israel and Tyre shared a long-standing relationship dating back to the reign of Solomon (1 Kings 5:8-9). Tarshish is typically identified with a city in modern-day Spain on the opposite end of the Mediterranean Sea from Israel and Tyre.

▸ WORSHIP
23:3 Repentance of the rich. Why did Jesus say that it would be hard for the rich to enter heaven (Matthew 19:23)? It's not because they are spiritually any worse than the poor (Romans 3:23). But money can blind us to our spiritual needs. Having seemingly unlimited resources can make us sloppy in attitude and action (Luke 16:11). Ancient Tyre was like this, for the people of Tyre relied on their wealth rather than on God. But God said that Tyre would fall—not because of Tyre's riches—but because of Tyre's attitude. If you have great resources, remember that God wants your money and your heart. He wants you to realize that the abundant life (John 10:10) comes from Him alone, and that financial security is fleeting. Put your hope, your dreams, your security—everything—in His hands today. (***See Worship*** > *NT* > *Offerings* > *Be faithful with riches,* TopicGuide page A31.)

They brought you grain from Egypt*
and harvests from along the Nile.
You were the marketplace of the world.

23:4 Gen 10:15, 19 Jer 47:4
4 But now you are put to shame, city of Sidon,
for Tyre, the fortress of the sea, says,
"Now I am childless;
I have no sons or daughters."
5 When Egypt hears the news about Tyre,
there will be great sorrow.
6 Send word now to Tarshish!
Wail, you people who live in distant lands!

23:7 Isa 32:13
7 Is this silent ruin all that is left of your once joyous city?
What a long history was yours!
Think of all the colonists you sent to distant places.

8 Who has brought this disaster on Tyre,
that great creator of kingdoms?
Her traders were all princes,
her merchants were nobles.

23:9 Isa 5:13 Dan 4:37
9 The LORD of Heaven's Armies has done it
to destroy your pride
and bring low all earth's nobility.
10 Come, people of Tarshish,
sweep over the land like the flooding Nile,
for Tyre is defenseless.*

23:11 Isa 50:2 Zech 9:3-4
11 The LORD held out His hand over the sea
and shook the kingdoms of the earth.
He has spoken out against Phoenicia,*
ordering that her fortresses be destroyed.

23:12 Rev 18:22
12 He says, "Never again will you rejoice,
O daughter of Sidon, for you have been crushed.
Even if you flee to Cyprus,
you will find no rest."

23:13 Isa 13:21
13 Look at the land of Babylonia*—
the people of that land are gone!
The Assyrians have handed Babylon over
to the wild animals of the desert.
They have built siege ramps against its walls,
torn down its palaces,
and turned it to a heap of rubble.

14 Wail, O ships of Tarshish,
for your harbor is destroyed!

23:15 Jer 25:11
15 For seventy years, the length of a king's life, Tyre will be forgotten. But then the city
will come back to life as in the song about the prostitute:

23:3 Hebrew *from Shihor,* a branch of the Nile River. 23:10 The meaning of the Hebrew in this verse is uncertain. 23:11 Hebrew *Canaan.* 23:13 Or *Chaldea.*

23:8-9 Unlike the Assyrian empire, the kingdom of Tyre was built on commercial rather than military might. Yet, like the Assyrians, Tyre became arrogant and boastful, inciting God's displeasure.

23:15-18 Seventy years functioned as a standard period of time to fulfill divine judgment. It was a symbolic rather than a literal length of time (compare Jeremiah 25:11; 29:10; Daniel 9:2). Modern Tyre is located in southern Lebanon.

16 Take a harp and walk the streets,
you forgotten harlot.
Make sweet melody and sing your songs
so you will be remembered again.

17 Yes, after seventy years the LORD will revive Tyre. But she will be no different than she
was before. She will again be a prostitute to all kingdoms around the world. 18 But in the
end her profits will be given to the LORD. Her wealth will not be hoarded but will provide
good food and fine clothing for the LORD's priests.

23:18 Isa 60:5-9 Zech 14:20

DESTRUCTION OF THE EARTH

24 1 Look! The LORD is about to destroy the earth
and make it a vast wasteland.
He devastates the surface of the earth
and scatters the people.
2 Priests and laypeople,
servants and masters,
maids and mistresses,
buyers and sellers,
lenders and borrowers,
bankers and debtors—none will be spared.
3 The earth will be completely emptied and looted.
The LORD has spoken!

4 The earth mourns and dries up,
and the crops waste away and wither.
Even the greatest people on earth waste away.
5 The earth suffers for the sins of its people,
for they have twisted God's instructions,
violated His laws,
and broken His everlasting covenant.
6 Therefore, a curse consumes the earth.
Its people must pay the price for their sin.
They are destroyed by fire,
and only a few are left alive.
7 The grapevines waste away,
and there is no new wine.
All the merrymakers sigh and mourn.

24:5 Gen 3:17 Num 35:33-34

24:6 Zech 5:3-4

24:7 Joel 1:10, 12

▸ HOLINESS

23:17 The tragedy of Tyre. Consequences do not always turn us from sin. We've all paid a price for our moral weakness, yet this does not dissuade us from returning to the same thoughts, feelings and behavior that caused us so much pain. God pronounced judgment on Tyre, but God also admitted that the judgment would not have any effect. Tyre would survive the coming judgment and rebuild only to exhibit the same vices. Therefore, God said that the next punishment would be more severe. The New Testament tells us that God disciplines His children (Hebrews 12:5-11; Revelation 3:19). Examine your life for any sin that may lead to God's discipline. Repent of all known sin—every one—immediately. (***See Holiness*****>** *Submission> Delighting in God> Rejoicing in repentance,* TopicGuide page A40.)

24:1–27:13 These four chapters are often referred to as "Isaiah's Little Apocalypse." Here the prophet presents the Assyrian crisis as a time of cosmic and universal upheaval that will lead to renewal and blessing for God's people and the restoration of all creation.

▸ HOLINESS

24:2 No one will escape. The rich and powerful can often escape the consequences of their actions for a time. For example, the rich man can hire good lawyers to get him off in court. But this isn't true of God's judgment. No matter who you are, no matter what your reputation or wealth, you will stand naked before God. Like the destruction that Isaiah foretold here, nothing will be able to help you—not your church, not your career, not your friends. You alone will face God and His judgment. There is only one way to escape this judgment: by trusting in Christ to forgive your sins. Place your life—your sin, your joy, and your fears—in God's hands. (***See Holiness*****>** *God's Blessing> Obedience gives greater assurance of salvation,* TopicGuide page A42.)

24:4-6 Human sin carries devastating repercussions for the created order. From the time of Adam's rebellion in the garden (Genesis 3:17), the earth has been subjected to curse and futility (Romans 8:19-23).

24:8 Jer 16:9 [8] The cheerful sound of tambourines is stilled;
the happy cries of celebration are heard no more.
The melodious chords of the harp are silent.
24:9 Isa 5:11, 22 [9] Gone are the joys of wine and song;
alcoholic drink turns bitter in the mouth.
[10] The city writhes in chaos;
every home is locked to keep out intruders.
24:11 Isa 32:13 [11] Mobs gather in the streets, crying out for wine.
Joy has turned to gloom.
Gladness has been banished from the land.
24:12 Isa 45:2 [12] The city is left in ruins,
its gates battered down.
24:13 Isa 17:6 [13] Throughout the earth the story is the same—
only a remnant is left,
like the stray olives left on the tree
or the few grapes left on the vine after harvest.

24:14 Isa 12:6; 52:8 [14] But all who are left shout and sing for joy.
Those in the west praise the LORD's majesty.
24:15 Isa 42:4, 10, 12 [15] In eastern lands, give glory to the LORD.
In the lands beyond the sea, praise the name of the LORD, the God of Israel.
24:16 Isa 11:12; 28:5 [16] We hear songs of praise from the ends of the earth,
songs that give glory to the Righteous One!

But my heart is heavy with grief.
Weep for me, for I wither away.
Deceit still prevails,
and treachery is everywhere.
[17] Terror and traps and snares will be your lot,
you people of the earth.
24:18 Gen 7:10-12 Ps 46:2 [18] Those who flee in terror will fall into a trap,
and those who escape the trap will be caught in a snare.
Destruction falls like rain from the heavens;
the foundations of the earth shake.
24:19 Num 16:31-32 [19] The earth has broken up.
It has utterly collapsed;
it is violently shaken.
24:20 Isa 19:14; 43:27; 66:24 [20] The earth staggers like a drunk.
It trembles like a tent in a storm.
It falls and will not rise again,
for the guilt of its rebellion is very heavy.

24:21 Ps 76:12 [21] In that day the LORD will punish the gods in the heavens
and the proud rulers of the nations on earth.

24:10-13 The city described here is not one city, but urban life in general. The great cities, the pinnacles of human civilization, will fall into chaos.

▶ GOD

24:16 Sadness leading to joy. Some people believe Christians should always be happy. They walk through life with a smile pasted on their face, thinking this is obedience to the command to rejoice always (Philippians 4:4). But Isaiah's heart was heavy with grief over those who would suffer God's wrath. We rejoice with those who come to know Jesus as their Savior—but we also grieve over those who reject Him or have never heard the Good News. Don't flee from that healthy grief; when you feel it, let it lead you to prayer. Over time you will find that your love and concern for unbelievers will grow, and you will joyfully praise God for those who come to know Christ. (***See God*** *> God's Attributes> Merciful> Salvation and new life come through His mercy,* TopicGuide page A17.)

24:21-23 God's judgment will encompass both the physical and spiritual realms of life. On the great and final day of the Lord, all creation, visible and invisible, will be subject to Christ (Ephesians 1:21-22; 6:11-12; 2 Peter 2:4; Revelation 17–19). Echoes of this passage are heard in John's description of the new Jerusalem in Revelation 22:5.

[22] They will be rounded up and put in prison.
They will be shut up in prison
and will finally be punished.
[23] Then the glory of the moon will wane,
and the brightness of the sun will fade,
for the LORD of Heaven's Armies will rule on Mount Zion.
He will rule in great glory in Jerusalem,
in the sight of all the leaders of His people.

24:22 Isa 10:4
24:23 Mic 4:7 Heb 12:22 Rev 21:23

PRAISE FOR JUDGMENT AND SALVATION

25 [1] O LORD, I will honor and praise Your name,
for You are my God.
You do such wonderful things!
You planned them long ago,
and now You have accomplished them.
[2] You turn mighty cities into heaps of ruins.
Cities with strong walls are turned to rubble.
Beautiful palaces in distant lands disappear
and will never be rebuilt.
[3] Therefore, strong nations will declare Your glory;
ruthless nations will fear You.

[4] But You are a tower of refuge to the poor, O LORD,
a tower of refuge to the needy in distress.
You are a refuge from the storm
and a shelter from the heat.
For the oppressive acts of ruthless people
are like a storm beating against a wall,
[5] or like the relentless heat of the desert.
But You silence the roar of foreign nations.
As the shade of a cloud cools relentless heat,
so the boastful songs of ruthless people are stilled.

[6] In Jerusalem,* the LORD of Heaven's Armies
will spread a wonderful feast
for all the people of the world.
It will be a delicious banquet
with clear, well-aged wine and choice meat.
[7] There He will remove the cloud of gloom,
the shadow of death that hangs over the earth.

25:1 Exod 15:2 Ps 40:5 Eph 1:11
25:2 Isa 17:1
25:4 Isa 32:2
25:5 Jer 51:54-56
25:6 Isa 2:2-4

25:6 Hebrew *On this mountain;* also in 25:10.

▶ **GOD**

25:1 A promised future. Life can be tough. Suffering barges into our lives and, like an unwanted guest, it never leaves soon enough. But when Isaiah looked at the future—in which God promised joy, hope, and intimacy with His people—he felt confident (Isaiah 7:14; 49:4-5; 57:14-19). When judgment loomed and God's people seemed doomed, Isaiah looked at God's covenant promises and rejoiced at the inheritance that awaited His people (Isaiah 11:3-5). Rather than attempt to cope with or ignore the pain that comes from living in this world, accept it. Look at the death, the suffering—but then boldly look at the future. Keep them both before you and, like Isaiah, you'll be able to endure the present crisis and yet rejoice in God's incredible assurance of a future of intimacy with Him. (***See God****> God's Attributes> Eternal> The eternal God is the believers' source of security,* TopicGuide page A16.)

25:6-8 The restoration and renewal of God's people will usher in an era of universal peace and celebration. Death itself will be overcome, and all sorrow and pain will cease. The first coming of Christ secured these blessings for all of creation, and they will be fully realized when Christ returns (1 Corinthians 15:54-55; Revelation 7:17; 21:4).

25:8 Ps 69:9; Isa 65:19; *1 Cor 15:54-55; 1 Pet 4:14; Rev 21:4

8 He will swallow up death forever!*
The Sovereign LORD will wipe away all tears.
He will remove forever all insults and mockery
against His land and people.
The LORD has spoken!

25:9 Isa 30:18; 35:1-2, 10; 40:9

9 In that day the people will proclaim,
"This is our God!
We trusted in Him, and He saved us!
This is the LORD, in whom we trusted.
Let us rejoice in the salvation He brings!"
10 For the LORD's hand of blessing will rest on Jerusalem.
But Moab will be crushed.
It will be like straw trampled down and left to rot.

25:11 Isa 16:6

11 God will push down Moab's people
as a swimmer pushes down water with his hands.
He will end their pride
and all their evil works.

25:12 Isa 26:5

12 The high walls of Moab will be demolished.
They will be brought down to the ground,
down into the dust.

A SONG OF PRAISE TO THE LORD

26:1 Isa 12:1; 60:18

26 In that day, everyone in the land of Judah will sing this song:

Our city is strong!
We are surrounded by the walls of God's salvation.

26:2 Isa 45:25

2 Open the gates to all who are righteous;
allow the faithful to enter.

26:3 Isa 57:19

3 You will keep in perfect peace
all who trust in You,
all whose thoughts are fixed on You!

26:4 Isa 50:10

4 Trust in the LORD always,
for the LORD GOD is the eternal Rock.
5 He humbles the proud
and brings down the arrogant city.
He brings it down to the dust.

26:6 Isa 29:19

6 The poor and oppressed trample it underfoot,
and the needy walk all over it.

26:7 Ps 25:4-5; Isa 42:16

7 But for those who are righteous,
the way is not steep and rough.
You are a God who does what is right,
and You smooth out the path ahead of them.

26:8 Isa 12:4

8 LORD, we show our trust in You by obeying Your laws;
our heart's desire is to glorify Your name.

25:8 Greek version reads *Death is swallowed up in victory.* Compare 1 Cor 15:54.

25:10-12 In these verses, Moab is probably representative of God's enemies in general (compare Edom in 34:5-17). God's arrival will bring blessing to those who trusted in Him, but it will result in judgment for His enemies.

26:1-4 As opposed to the cities of wicked people that will fall into chaos on the day of God's judgment (see 24:10-13), the city of God, Jerusalem, will be safe and prosperous. The city will stand because the Lord is its foundation. Jerusalem will be a haven to all who trust in the Lord.

9 All night long I search for You;
in the morning I earnestly seek for God.
For only when You come to judge the earth
will people learn what is right.
10 Your kindness to the wicked
does not make them do good.
Although others do right, the wicked keep doing wrong
and take no notice of the LORD's majesty.
11 O LORD, they pay no attention to Your upraised fist.
Show them Your eagerness to defend Your people.
Then they will be ashamed.
Let Your fire consume Your enemies.

12 LORD, You will grant us peace;
all we have accomplished is really from You.
13 O LORD our God, others have ruled us,
but You alone are the One we worship.
14 Those we served before are dead and gone.
Their departed spirits will never return!
You attacked them and destroyed them,
and they are long forgotten.
15 O LORD, You have made our nation great;
yes, You have made us great.
You have extended our borders,
and we give You the glory!

16 LORD, in distress we searched for You.
We prayed beneath the burden of Your discipline.
17 Just as a pregnant woman
writhes and cries out in pain as she gives birth,
so were we in Your presence, LORD.
18 We, too, writhe in agony,
but nothing comes of our suffering.
We have not given salvation to the earth,
nor brought life into the world.
19 But those who die in the LORD will live;
their bodies will rise again!
Those who sleep in the earth
will rise up and sing for joy!
For Your life-giving light will fall like dew
on Your people in the place of the dead!

26:9 Pss 63:1; 77:2 Hos 5:15

26:10 Isa 22:12-13 John 5:37-38

26:11 Isa 10:17; 66:15, 24

26:13 Isa 2:8

26:15 Isa 54:2

26:16 Hos 5:15

26:17 John 16:21

26:18 Isa 33:11

26:19 Ezek 37:1-14 Dan 12:2 Eph 5:14

26:12-15 Isaiah anticipated the restoration of God's people. Foreign nations such as Assyria ruled over Judah for a time, but eventually God would deliver His people and usher in a time of renewed growth. This hope is fulfilled in the remarkable expansion of the church throughout the whole earth.

▸ SALVATION

26:12 Our good works come from God. "What a blessing I've been in others' lives!" "I was saved through the ministry of a friend." Have you ever said or thought such things? Such statements reveal a faulty understanding of our role in ministry. We do not produce spiritual growth in another person's life—only God does. Study Bibles don't do it. Churches don't do it. God deserves the credit for all that we do and experience. He predestines every good work (Ephesians 2:10), He empowers every good work (John 15:5), and He gets the glory for every good work (2 Corinthians 3:18). Don't be ungrateful to people, but ultimately give credit where credit is due. (***See Salvation*****>** *Receiving> Results> Works> Produced in us by God,* TopicGuide page A23.)

26:19 While God's judgment raged against Judah, it appeared as if the faithful had perished—but there was still hope. God would grant new life to His people; they would be raised from dust to life. From one perspective this hope anticipates the return of God's people from exile, but it also points to the hope of the resurrection secured by the work of Christ.

RESTORATION FOR ISRAEL

26:20 Ps 30:5 — 20 Go home, my people,
and lock your doors!
Hide yourselves for a little while
until the LORD's anger has passed.

26:21 Job 16:18 Mic 1:3 Jude 1:14 — 21 Look! The LORD is coming from heaven
to punish the people of the earth for their sins.
The earth will no longer hide those who have been killed.
They will be brought out for all to see.

27:1 Job 3:8 Ps 74:14 — **27** In that day the LORD will take His terrible, swift sword and punish Leviathan,*
the swiftly moving serpent, the coiling, writhing serpent. He will kill the dragon
of the sea.

27:2 Ps 80:8 — 2 "In that day,
sing about the fruitful vineyard.

27:3 John 10:28 — 3 I, the LORD, will watch over it,
watering it carefully.
Day and night I will watch so no one can harm it.

27:4 2 Sam 23:6 Isa 33:12 — 4 My anger will be gone.
If I find briers and thorns growing,
I will attack them;
I will burn them up—

27:5 Job 22:21 Isa 25:4 — 5 unless they turn to Me for help.
Let them make peace with Me;
yes, let them make peace with Me."

27:6 Isa 35:1-2; 37:31 — 6 The time is coming when Jacob's descendants will take root.
Israel will bud and blossom
and fill the whole earth with fruit!

27:7 Isa 10:12, 17 — 7 Has the LORD struck Israel
as He struck her enemies?

27:1 The identification of Leviathan is disputed, ranging from an earthly creature to a mythical sea monster in ancient literature.

▸ GOD

26:21 A timeless song of victory. Music, when added to biblical truth, expresses the deepest thoughts and feelings of our faith. Some of these songs are hymns and spiritual songs that, like a treasure chest of holy tradition, can be passed on to our children. But songs can also speak of the future, and in one such song, Isaiah prophesied about the joy God's people feel when He is victorious. In the past, present, and future, God's victories are worth celebrating. We unashamedly boast that our God is a warrior who makes His enemies tremble and will ultimately allow no criminal to go unpunished. When you are sad over the suffering and injustice of this present age, sing songs about the past, present and future victory of God over His enemies. (***See God****> God's Names> God> LORD of Heaven's Armies (YHWH Sabaoth; the warrior God),* TopicGuide page A18.)

27:1 In Canaanite mythology, the sea monster Leviathan embodied the forces of chaos, which the gods overcame as they brought order to creation. Isaiah used this familiar image to depict God's triumph over evil.

27:2-5 The metaphor of a vineyard was also employed in Isaiah 5:1-7. In chapter 5 the vineyard proved unfruitful, and the Lord allowed it to be overrun. This symbolized Israel's unfaithfulness and God's judgment. Here the vineyard is restored, and the Lord defends and cares for it once more.

27:6 Following their restoration, God's people would fulfill their purpose of spreading the kingdom of God throughout the earth.

▸ ADOPTION

27:7-9 Discipline versus destruction. Unlike the complete destruction that would come upon surrounding nations, Israel's punishment would be temporary. It was designed to restore the nation to faithfulness. This is the key difference between God's discipline of His people and God's judgment of sin in the world. Discipline is restorative, not punitive. It lasts until God's purpose is accomplished—our greater holiness and more passionate love for Him. When you suffer, always look for ways to turn it into a time of growth in your love for God and your hatred of sin. That will make the frequent painful situations in this world an opportunity instead of an obstacle. In this sense, you can "give thanks for everything" (Ephesians 5:20) because everything is an opportunity for God's glory and our good. (***See Adoption****> With Christ> Children of God> God disciplines His children,* TopicGuide page A36.)

Has He punished her
as He punished them?
8 No, but He exiled Israel to call her to account.
She was exiled from her land
as though blown away in a storm from the east.
9 The LORD did this to purge Israel's* wickedness,
to take away all her sin.
As a result, all the pagan altars will be crushed to dust.
No Asherah pole or pagan shrine will be left standing.
10 The fortified towns will be silent and empty,
the houses abandoned, the streets overgrown with weeds.
Calves will graze there,
chewing on twigs and branches.
11 The people are like the dead branches of a tree,
broken off and used for kindling beneath the cooking pots.
Israel is a foolish and stupid nation,
for its people have turned away from God.
Therefore, the One who made them
will show them no pity or mercy.

12 Yet the time will come when the LORD will gather them together like handpicked grain.
One by one He will gather them—from the Euphrates River* in the east to the Brook of
Egypt in the west. 13 In that day the great trumpet will sound. Many who were dying in ex-
ile in Assyria and Egypt will return to Jerusalem to worship the LORD on His holy mountain.

27:9 Isa 17:8; Dan 11:35
27:11 Deut 32:18, 28; Isa 43:1, 7
27:12 Deut 30:3-4; Isa 11:11
27:13 Zech 14:16; Matt 24:31; Rev 11:15

A MESSAGE ABOUT SAMARIA

28 1 What sorrow awaits the proud city of Samaria—
the glorious crown of the drunks of Israel.*
It sits at the head of a fertile valley,
but its glorious beauty will fade like a flower.
It is the pride of a people
brought down by wine.
2 For the Lord will send a mighty army against it.
Like a mighty hailstorm and a torrential rain,
they will burst upon it like a surging flood
and smash it to the ground.

28:2 Isa 8:7; 30:28; Nah 1:8

27:9 Hebrew *Jacob's.* See note on 14:1. 27:12 Hebrew *the river.* 28:1 Hebrew *What sorrow awaits the crowning glory of the drunks of Ephraim,* referring to Samaria, capital of the northern kingdom of Israel.

27:12-13 The prophet envisioned God gathering His people as a farmer gathers his crops at harvest time or as an army is mustered at the sound of a trumpet. The initial regrouping of God's people began when the exiles returned to Jerusalem following the Babylonian exile. The regrouping in its fullest sense commenced when Jesus called people to Himself, and they streamed into the church, which is an outpost of the heavenly Jerusalem (Galatians 4:26).

28:1–29:24 This passage opens the last part (28:1–39:8) of the first major section of Isaiah (1–39). The passage appears to address the years leading up to Sennacherib's invasion of Jerusalem (701 BC), which is the subject of chapters 36–37.

▸ SPIRITUAL WARFARE

28:1 Beware of drunkenness. Although Samaria and Israel didn't lack anything and their valleys were rich and productive, the people wasted their livelihood with excessive drinking. Ephesians 5:18 says, "Don't be drunk with wine, because that will ruin your life. Instead, be filled with the Holy Spirit." That's the choice we make when tempted to drink excessively or use any other drug that brings confusion and lack of self-control. Use alcohol carefully and enjoy its health benefits (1 Timothy 5:23) and emotional impact (Ecclesiastes 9:7; Judges 9:13) for God's glory. (***See Spiritual Warfare*** > *Resisting Sin and Evil* > *Resisting Temptation* > *What to Resist* > *We are to resist worldly influences,* TopicGuide page A45.)

28:1-13 Samaria was founded by the Israelite king Omri and functioned as the capital of the northern kingdom of Israel until the Assyrians destroyed it in 722 BC.

[3] The proud city of Samaria—
the glorious crown of the drunks of Israel*—
will be trampled beneath its enemies' feet.

28:4 Hos 9:10 Nah 3:12
[4] It sits at the head of a fertile valley,
but its glorious beauty will fade like a flower.
Whoever sees it will snatch it up,
as an early fig is quickly picked and eaten.

28:5 Isa 41:16; 62:3
[5] Then at last the LORD of Heaven's Armies
will Himself be Israel's glorious crown.
He will be the pride and joy
of the remnant of His people.

28:6 2 Chr 32:6-8 Isa 11:2; 25:4; 32:16
[6] He will give a longing for justice
to their judges.
He will give great courage
to their warriors who stand at the gates.

28:7 Hab 2:15-16
[7] Now, however, Israel is led by drunks
who reel with wine and stagger with alcohol.
The priests and prophets stagger with alcohol
and lose themselves in wine.
They reel when they see visions
and stagger as they render decisions.

28:8 Jer 48:26
[8] Their tables are covered with vomit;
filth is everywhere.

28:9 Heb 5:12-13
[9] "Who does the LORD think we are?" they ask.
"Why does He speak to us like this?
Are we little children,
just recently weaned?

28:10 Neh 9:30
[10] He tells us everything over and over—
one line at a time,
one line at a time,
a little here,
and a little there!"

28:11 Isa 33:19 *1 Cor 14:21
[11] So now God will have to speak to His people
through foreign oppressors who speak a strange language!

28:12 Jer 6:16 Matt 11:28-29
[12] God has told His people,
"Here is a place of rest;
let the weary rest here.
This is a place of quiet rest."
But they would not listen.

28:13 Matt 21:44
[13] So the LORD will spell out His message for them again,
one line at a time,
one line at a time,
a little here,
and a little there,

28:3 Hebrew *The crowning glory of the drunks of Ephraim;* see note on 28:1.

28:5-6 The restoration and renewal awaiting God's people following their time of judgment would be marked by justice and security provided by the Lord.

28:11-13 If Samaria's leaders would not heed the straightforward message of God through Isaiah, then they would be subjected to the invasions of foreigners whose language would be unintelligible. Samaria's refusal to acknowledge Isaiah's simple message of repentance confirmed the situation into which the prophet was commissioned in Isaiah 6:9-10.

so that they will stumble and fall.
They will be injured, trapped, and captured.

14 Therefore, listen to this message from the LORD,
you scoffing rulers in Jerusalem.
15 You boast, "We have struck a bargain to cheat death
and have made a deal to dodge the grave.*
The coming destruction can never touch us,
for we have built a strong refuge made of lies and deception."

16 Therefore, this is what the Sovereign LORD says:
"Look! I am placing a foundation stone in Jerusalem,*
a firm and tested stone.
It is a precious cornerstone that is safe to build on.
Whoever believes need never be shaken.*
17 I will test you with the measuring line of justice
and the plumb line of righteousness.
Since your refuge is made of lies,
a hailstorm will knock it down.
Since it is made of deception,
a flood will sweep it away.
18 I will cancel the bargain you made to cheat death,
and I will overturn your deal to dodge the grave.
When the terrible enemy sweeps through,
you will be trampled into the ground.
19 Again and again that flood will come,
morning after morning,
day and night,
until you are carried away."

This message will bring terror to your people.
20 The bed you have made is too short to lie on.
The blankets are too narrow to cover you.
21 The LORD will come as He did against the Philistines at Mount Perazim
and against the Amorites at Gibeon.
He will come to do a strange thing;
He will come to do an unusual deed:
22 For the Lord, the LORD of Heaven's Armies,
has plainly said that He is determined to crush the whole land.
So scoff no more,
or your punishment will be even greater.

23 Listen to me;
listen, and pay close attention.
24 Does a farmer always plow and never sow?
Is he forever cultivating the soil and never planting?

28:14 Isa 28:22
28:15 Isa 28:18
28:16 Ps 118:22; Matt 21:42; Acts 4:11; *Rom 9:33; 10:11; Eph 2:20; *1 Pet 2:6
28:17 Isa 61:8; Amos 7:7-9
28:18 Isa 28:15
28:19 Ps 88:15
28:21 2 Sam 5:20; Luke 19:41-44
28:22 Isa 10:22-23; 28:14

28:15 Hebrew *Sheol;* also in 28:18. 28:16a Hebrew *in Zion.* 28:16b Greek version reads *Look! I am placing a stone in the foundation of Jerusalem* [literally *Zion*], */ a precious cornerstone for its foundation, chosen for great honor. / Anyone who trusts in Him will never be disgraced.* Compare Rom 9:33; 1 Pet 2:6.

28:21-22 The Lord had defeated Israel's enemies in the past (2 Samuel 5:20; Joshua 10:11), but now He would strike down His own people in judgment.

28:23-29 Just as there is a certain logic to the way a farmer plows, plants, and harvests, so too was there a reason for the way God dealt with His people. In His wisdom, the Lord knows precisely how best to discipline His people and judge the nations.

25 Does he not finally plant his seeds—
black cumin, cumin, wheat, barley,
and emmer wheat—
each in its proper way,
and each in its proper place?
26 The farmer knows just what to do,
for God has given him understanding.
28:27 Amos 1:3 27 A heavy sledge is never used to thresh black cumin;
rather, it is beaten with a light stick.
A threshing wheel is never rolled on cumin;
instead, it is beaten lightly with a flail.
28 Grain for bread is easily crushed,
so he doesn't keep on pounding it.
He threshes it under the wheels of a cart,
but he doesn't pulverize it.
28:29 Rom 11:33 29 The LORD of Heaven's Armies is a wonderful teacher,
and He gives the farmer great wisdom.

A MESSAGE ABOUT JERUSALEM

29:1 2 Sam 5:9 **29** 1 "What sorrow awaits Ariel,* the City of David.
Year after year you celebrate your feasts.
29:2 Isa 3:26 2 Yet I will bring disaster upon you,
and there will be much weeping and sorrow.
For Jerusalem will become what her name Ariel means—
an altar covered with blood.
29:3 Lam 2:5; Luke 19:43-44 3 I will be your enemy,
surrounding Jerusalem and attacking its walls.
I will build siege towers
and destroy it.
29:4 Isa 8:19 4 Then deep from the earth you will speak;
from low in the dust your words will come.
Your voice will whisper from the ground
like a ghost conjured up from the grave.

29:5 Isa 17:13-14; 41:15-16; 1 Thes 5:3 5 "But suddenly, your ruthless enemies will be crushed
like the finest of dust.
Your many attackers will be driven away
like chaff before the wind.
Suddenly, in an instant,

29:1 *Ariel* sounds like a Hebrew term that means "hearth" or "altar."

▶ HOLINESS
28:29 God as a farmer. Any farmer knows that each crop must be treated differently. Each plant requires a certain type of soil, a specific amount of moisture, and a certain growing period. Therefore, the farmer adjusts his work to accommodate each type of crop. That's a picture of how God treats us—God makes us grow. And as we are watered, we mature, naturally bearing spiritual fruit. He knows exactly what you need to grow. Do not fret when difficult circumstances come. Such experiences stretch and bend us, making us stronger, more flexible, and more useful to Him. (See Ephesians 1:11; also ***see Holiness***> *God's Blessing*> *Obedience bears spiritual fruit,* TopicGuide page A42.)

29:1-4 The name Ariel, used to designate Jerusalem, sounds like the word for "altar" (see textual note at 29:1). Jerusalem, the place where God has set His altar, would nonetheless suffer God's judgment in the form of an invasion by a mighty army.

29:5-8 Amid dire warnings of judgment, Isaiah offered Jerusalem great hope. Just as quickly as Jerusalem was besieged, the city would be relieved. God would shatter the armies that had ravaged Judah. Jerusalem would not be utterly destroyed.

6 I, the LORD of Heaven's Armies, will act for you
with thunder and earthquake and great noise,
with whirlwind and storm and consuming fire.
7 All the nations fighting against Jerusalem*
will vanish like a dream!
Those who are attacking her walls
will vanish like a vision in the night.
8 A hungry person dreams of eating
but wakes up still hungry.
A thirsty person dreams of drinking
but is still faint from thirst when morning comes.
So it will be with your enemies,
with those who attack Mount Zion."

9 Are you amazed and incredulous?
Don't you believe it?
Then go ahead and be blind.
You are stupid, but not from wine!
You stagger, but not from liquor!
10 For the LORD has poured out on you a spirit of deep sleep.
He has closed the eyes of your prophets and visionaries.

11 All the future events in this vision are like a sealed book to them. When you give it to
those who can read, they will say, "We can't read it because it is sealed." 12 When you give
it to those who cannot read, they will say, "We don't know how to read."

13 And so the Lord says,
"These people say they are Mine.
They honor Me with their lips,
but their hearts are far from Me.
And their worship of Me
is nothing but man-made rules learned by rote.*
14 Because of this, I will once again astound these hypocrites
with amazing wonders.
The wisdom of the wise will pass away,
and the intelligence of the intelligent will disappear."

15 What sorrow awaits those who try to hide their plans from the LORD,
who do their evil deeds in the dark!

29:6 Matt 24:7; Mark 13:8; Luke 21:11; Rev 11:13, 19; 16:18
29:7 Zech 12:9
29:8 Isa 54:17
29:9 Isa 51:17
29:10 *Rom 11:8; 2 Thes 2:9-12
29:11 Dan 12:4; Matt 13:11
29:13 Ezek 33:31; *Mark 7:6-7
29:14 Isa 44:25; *1 Cor 1:19
29:15 Ps 10:11, 13; Isa 47:10

29:7 Hebrew *Ariel.* 29:13 Greek version reads *Their worship is a farce, / for they teach man-made ideas as commands from God.* Compare Mark 7:7.

▸ PURPOSE

29:6 God as an enemy. What would it be like to be an adversary of God? Most people never consider this fearful prospect. In this verse, God describes what He is like when He is enraged—a terrible storm, a consuming fire. What changes God's disposition toward you? The difference depends on your response to His Son, Jesus Christ. If you have accepted Jesus as your Lord and Savior, God is your friend. If you have rejected Jesus, God is your enemy. God has sent Christ to make peace with His enemies (Romans 5:1-2). Do not turn away from God's terms of surrender for you. (***See Purpose****> God's Deeds> Judgment> Plague upon Israel's enemies,* TopicGuide page A53.)

29:13 By Isaiah's time, Israelite religion had become mere formality. The people enjoyed the forms of worship without investing their hearts and minds. True religion joins the right forms of worship with sincerity and devotion. Jesus cited this passage in His condemnation of the Pharisees (Matthew 15:8-9).

▸ ADOPTION

29:13 Worshiping God with a sincere heart. God sees your heart. He can't be fooled—He knows if you are worshiping Him out of ritual or hypocrisy. The only worship He receives is that from a sincere love for Him and His Son, Jesus. If you are teaching Sunday school so you will look good to others, God will not honor your service. If you are singing in the choir because it is a tradition in your family, God will not honor that. Ask yourself, ask God—"What 'spiritual' things am I doing out of wrong motives?" Be prepared to receive any hard truths that God may show you about yourself and commit yourself to serving Him wholeheartedly. (***See Adoption****> Without Christ> Separated from God> Worship through lip service only,* TopicGuide page A36.)

29:15-16 God shapes and molds us as a potter fashions a pot. Paul used this passage in Romans 9:20-21 to challenge a person-centered view of religion.

"The LORD can't see us," they say.
"He doesn't know what's going on!"

29:16 Isa 45:9 Rom 9:20-21

16 How foolish can you be?
He is the Potter, and He is certainly greater than you, the clay!
Should the created thing say of the One who made it,
"He didn't make me"?
Does a jar ever say,
"The potter who made me is stupid"?

17 Soon—and it will not be very long—
the forests of Lebanon will become a fertile field,
and the fertile field will yield bountiful crops.

29:18 Isa 32:3

18 In that day the deaf will hear words read from a book,
and the blind will see through the gloom and darkness.

29:19 Isa 14:30, 32 Matt 5:5 Jas 2:5

19 The humble will be filled with fresh joy from the LORD.
The poor will rejoice in the Holy One of Israel.
20 The scoffer will be gone,
the arrogant will disappear,
and those who plot evil will be killed.

29:21 Amos 5:10, 12

21 Those who convict the innocent
by their false testimony will disappear.
A similar fate awaits those who use trickery to pervert justice
and who tell lies to destroy the innocent.

29:22 Isa 41:8

22 That is why the LORD, who redeemed Abraham, says to the people of Israel,*

"My people will no longer be ashamed
or turn pale with fear.
23 For when they see their many children
and all the blessings I have given them,
they will recognize the holiness of the Holy One of Israel.
They will stand in awe of the God of Jacob.

29:24 Isa 30:21; 41:20

24 Then the wayward will gain understanding,
and complainers will accept instruction.

JUDAH'S WORTHLESS TREATY WITH EGYPT

30:1 Isa 8:11-12

30 1 "What sorrow awaits My rebellious children,"
says the LORD.
"You make plans that are contrary to Mine.
You make alliances not directed by My Spirit,
thus piling up your sins.

29:22 Hebrew *of Jacob.* See note on 14:1.

▸ HOLINESS
29:16 Cursing the potter. Have you ever seen a child throw a temper tantrum? The child's raw emotion contrasted with his complete helplessness is a disturbing sight. Think of how we must appear to God when we literally or symbolically shake our fist at Him and say, "I want You to do what I want You to do!" God is not impressed by our emotions, our logic, or our excuses—it's simply not our place to instruct God. Make sure you're not trying to take the Potter's role in your life. Submit to God in every way and allow Him to guide your life completely. (***See Holiness***> *Submission*> *Trusting God*> *Obedience,* TopicGuide page A40.)

29:23 Under the Old Covenant, children and material prosperity were promised as blessings to those who were faithful to their covenant with the Lord (Deuteronomy 28:1-14).

30:1–32:20 In this section the prophet weaved together a series of warnings against reliance on Egypt for protection with admonitions to trust in God alone for deliverance.

30:1-5 Isaiah condemned in no uncertain terms Judah's alliance with Egypt. The alliance would prove futile and revealed a lack of trust in the Lord.

2 For without consulting Me,
you have gone down to Egypt for help.
You have put your trust in Pharaoh's protection.
You have tried to hide in his shade.
3 But by trusting Pharaoh, you will be humiliated,
and by depending on him, you will be disgraced.
4 For though his power extends to Zoan
and his officials have arrived in Hanes,
5 all who trust in him will be ashamed.
He will not help you.
Instead, he will disgrace you."

6 This message came to me concerning the animals in the Negev:

The caravan moves slowly
across the terrible desert to Egypt—
donkeys weighed down with riches
and camels loaded with treasure—
all to pay for Egypt's protection.
They travel through the wilderness,
a place of lionesses and lions,
a place where vipers and poisonous snakes live.
All this, and Egypt will give you nothing in return.
7 Egypt's promises are worthless!
Therefore, I call her Rahab—
the Harmless Dragon.*

A WARNING FOR REBELLIOUS JUDAH

8 Now go and write down these words.
Write them in a book.
They will stand until the end of time
as a witness
9 that these people are stubborn rebels
who refuse to pay attention to the LORD's instructions.
10 They tell the seers,
"Stop seeing visions!"
They tell the prophets,
"Don't tell us what is right.
Tell us nice things.
Tell us lies.

30:2 Isa 8:19; 31:1
30:3 Isa 36:6; Jer 42:18, 22
30:4 Isa 19:11
30:5 Isa 31:3; Jer 2:36
30:6 Deut 8:15
30:7 Isa 51:9
30:8 Isa 8:1
30:9 Isa 24:5; 28:15; 30:1
30:10 1 Kgs 22:8, 13; Jer 6:14; Ezek 13:7; Amos 2:12; 2 Tim 4:3-4

30:7 Hebrew *Rahab who sits still.* Rahab is the name of a mythical sea monster that represents chaos in ancient literature. The name is used here as a poetic name for Egypt.

▸ WORSHIP

30:2 Dangerous alliances. For Israel's leaders, it seemed like a good idea. Enemies were threatening their borders, so they decided to make an alliance with Egypt, their strong neighbor. But the problem was that the leaders didn't consult God, and then they didn't trust God's Word (Deuteronomy 7:2). They resorted to using their own common sense to find solutions to their dilemma. But before we criticize Israel's leaders too harshly, think of the times when you've done the same thing. We all have a tendency to act before we consult God, thinking that we know the best solution. Relying on God is the only solution that fits every problem. Seek God's will and harmonize your ideas with His perfect Word. (***See Worship****> NT> Our Role> Attitude> Trusting in the midst of trials,* TopicGuide page A31.)

30:6 Isaiah poignantly portrayed Judah's wealth slipping away on caravans to Egypt and all to no avail. Judah would pay Egypt immense amounts of money to secure aid against Assyria that would never materialize.

30:11 Job 21:14
[11] Forget all this gloom.
Get off your narrow path.
Stop telling us about your
'Holy One of Israel.'"

30:12 Isa 5:24; 59:13
[12] This is the reply of the Holy One of Israel:

"Because you despise what I tell you
and trust instead in oppression and lies,
30:13 Isa 26:21; 29:5
[13] calamity will come upon you suddenly—
like a bulging wall that bursts and falls.
In an instant it will collapse
and come crashing down.
30:14 Ps 2:9 Jer 19:10-11
[14] You will be smashed like a piece of pottery—
shattered so completely that
there won't be a piece big enough
to carry coals from a fireplace
or a little water from the well."

30:15 Isa 28:12; 32:17
[15] This is what the Sovereign LORD,
the Holy One of Israel, says:
"Only in returning to Me
and resting in Me will you be saved.
In quietness and confidence is your strength.
But you would have none of it.
30:16 Isa 31:1, 3
[16] You said, 'No, we will get our help from Egypt.
They will give us swift horses for riding into battle.'
But the only swiftness you are going to see
is the swiftness of your enemies chasing you!
30:17 Deut 28:25; 32:30
[17] One of them will chase a thousand of you.
Five of them will make all of you flee.
You will be left like a lonely flagpole on a hill
or a tattered banner on a distant mountaintop."

BLESSINGS FOR THE LORD'S PEOPLE

30:18 Isa 25:9 2 Pet 3:9, 15
[18] So the LORD must wait for you to come to Him
so He can show you His love and compassion.
For the LORD is a faithful God.
Blessed are those who wait for His help.

30:19 Isa 25:8; 65:24
[19] O people of Zion, who live in Jerusalem,
you will weep no more.
He will be gracious if you ask for help.
He will surely respond to the sound of your cries.
30:20 Ps 80:5
[20] Though the Lord gave you adversity for food
and suffering for drink,

30:15-17 Contrast with Leviticus 26:8, where God used similar language to promise Israel victory they proved obedient to His word.

▸ GOD

30:18 Turn back to God. Israel was a stubborn and rebellious nation. Time and time again, God pleaded with the Israelites to turn back to Him and enjoy His blessings. Instead, they continued on with their sin, thinking that its pleasures would endure. But their happiness only lasted for a short time, and their sin led them into captivity. Perhaps you have been far away from God for some time—certain sins have come between you and your heavenly Father. What is keeping you from Him? Remember that confessing your sins and living by faith will overcome any obstacle. He will never turn away a humbled sinner. (***See God***> *Relationship> Barriers> Unconfessed transgressions,* TopicGuide page A14.)

He will still be with you to teach you.
You will see your teacher with your own eyes.
21 Your own ears will hear Him.
Right behind you a voice will say,
"This is the way you should go,"
whether to the right or to the left.
22 Then you will destroy all your silver idols
and your precious gold images.
You will throw them out like filthy rags,
saying to them, "Good riddance!"

23 Then the LORD will bless you with rain at planting time. There will be wonderful har-
vests and plenty of pastureland for your livestock. 24 The oxen and donkeys that till the
ground will eat good grain, its chaff blown away by the wind. 25 In that day, when your en-
emies are slaughtered and the towers fall, there will be streams of water flowing down
every mountain and hill. 26 The moon will be as bright as the sun, and the sun will be seven
times brighter—like the light of seven days in one! So it will be when the LORD begins to
heal His people and cure the wounds He gave them.

27 Look! The LORD is coming from far away,
burning with anger,
surrounded by thick, rising smoke.
His lips are filled with fury;
His words consume like fire.
28 His hot breath pours out like a flood
up to the neck of His enemies.
He will sift out the proud nations for destruction.
He will bridle them and lead them away to ruin.

29 But the people of God will sing a song of joy,
like the songs at the holy festivals.
You will be filled with joy,
as when a flutist leads a group of pilgrims
to Jerusalem, the mountain of the LORD—
to the Rock of Israel.
30 And the LORD will make His majestic voice heard.
He will display the strength of His mighty arm.
It will descend with devouring flames,
with cloudbursts, thunderstorms, and huge hailstones.
31 At the LORD's command, the Assyrians will be shattered.
He will strike them down with His royal scepter.
32 And as the LORD strikes them with His rod of punishment,
His people will celebrate with tambourines and harps.
Lifting His mighty arm, He will fight the Assyrians.
33 Topheth—the place of burning—
has long been ready for the Assyrian king;
the pyre is piled high with wood.
The breath of the LORD, like fire from a volcano,
will set it ablaze.

30:21 Isa 35:8-9
30:22 Exod 32:2, 4
30:23 Ps 65:9-13
30:24 Matt 3:12
30:25 Isa 41:18
30:26 Isa 33:24; Hos 6:1-2; Rev 21:23; 22:5
30:27 Isa 66:15
30:28 2 Kgs 19:28; Isa 8:7-8; 2 Thes 2:8
30:31 Isa 31:8
30:32 1 Sam 18:6; Jer 31:4
30:33 Gen 19:24; Isa 34:9

30:27-28 Portrayals of God coming in judgment typically include elements of fire and smoke (see also 30:30). Compare Exodus 19:18 for similar imagery.

31:1-3 Isaiah pronounced judgment upon Judah because the nation relied on Egypt rather than the Lord. Throughout Israel's history, security and victory hinged not on force of arms

THE FUTILITY OF RELYING ON EGYPT

31:1 Ps 20:7 Isa 10:17 Hos 11:9 Hab 1:12

31 1 What sorrow awaits those who look to Egypt for help,
trusting their horses, chariots, and charioteers
and depending on the strength of human armies
instead of looking to the LORD,
the Holy One of Israel.

31:2 Num 23:19 Jer 44:29 Rom 16:27

2 In His wisdom, the LORD will send great disaster;
He will not change His mind.
He will rise against the wicked
and against their helpers.

31:3 Jer 15:6 Ezek 28:9

3 For these Egyptians are mere humans, not God!
Their horses are puny flesh, not mighty spirits!
When the LORD raises His fist against them,
those who help will stumble,
and those being helped will fall.
They will all fall down and die together.

31:4 Isa 42:13

4 But this is what the LORD has told me:

"When a strong young lion
stands growling over a sheep it has killed,
it is not frightened by the shouts and noise
of a whole crowd of shepherds.
In the same way, the LORD of Heaven's Armies
will come down and fight on Mount Zion.

31:5 Deut 32:11 Ps 91:4

5 The LORD of Heaven's Armies will hover over Jerusalem
and protect it like a bird protecting its nest.
He will defend and save the city;
He will pass over it and rescue it."

31:6 Isa 55:7 Jer 3:10, 14, 22 · 31:7 Isa 2:20

6 Though you are such wicked rebels, my people, come and return to the LORD. 7 I know
the glorious day will come when each of you will throw away the gold idols and silver im-
ages your sinful hands have made.

31:8 Isa 10:12; 14:2

8 "The Assyrians will be destroyed,
but not by the swords of men.
The sword of God will strike them,
and they will panic and flee.
The strong young Assyrians
will be taken away as captives.

31:9 Isa 13:2

9 Even the strongest will quake with terror,
and princes will flee when they see your battle flags,"

---

but on the strength of the Lord, who fought for His people. To depend on Egypt was to reject the Lord.

▶ HOLINESS
31:1 Self-reliance. Independence is a valued trait in our modern world. We've invented all kinds of machines to enable us to do things by ourselves, rather than looking to others for help. Our financial arrangements allow us to borrow money whenever we might need it. We can hire out for almost any service. But our spiritual lives should be different. God wanted Israel to rely on Him for sustenance, not Egypt or any other nation. God wants us to depend on His church, on our Christian friends, and most of all, on Him. If you are tempted to be self-reliant, submit yourself to God's will. Ask Him to give you a sense of your own weakness and His strength. (***See Holiness*** *> Law and Grace> Grace> Self-reliance,* TopicGuide page A41.)

31:4-5 The image of the lion is initially ambiguous. Is the Lord coming to defend or attack Jerusalem? Verse 5 clarifies that the Lord intends to protect, not harm, His people. Compare Deuteronomy 32:11.

31:8-9 Assyria would fall before the mighty power of God. The nation would be a victim of the same atrocities it perperated against other nations. The fire imagery recalls Isaiah 29:1-7.

says the LORD, whose fire burns in Zion,
whose flame blazes from Jerusalem.

ISRAEL'S ULTIMATE DELIVERANCE

32 1 Look, a righteous king is coming!
And honest princes will rule under him.
2 Each one will be like a shelter from the wind
and a refuge from the storm,
like streams of water in the desert
and the shadow of a great rock in a parched land.

3 Then everyone who has eyes will be able to see the truth,
and everyone who has ears will be able to hear it.
4 Even the hotheads will be full of sense and understanding.
Those who stammer will speak out plainly.
5 In that day ungodly fools will not be heroes.
Scoundrels will not be respected.
6 For fools speak foolishness
and make evil plans.
They practice ungodliness
and spread false teachings about the LORD.
They deprive the hungry of food
and give no water to the thirsty.
7 The smooth tricks of scoundrels are evil.
They plot crooked schemes.
They lie to convict the poor,
even when the cause of the poor is just.
8 But generous people plan to do what is generous,
and they stand firm in their generosity.

9 Listen, you women who lie around in ease.
Listen to me, you who are so smug.
10 In a short time—just a little more than a year—
you careless ones will suddenly begin to care.
For your fruit crops will fail,
and the harvest will never take place.
11 Tremble, you women of ease;
throw off your complacency.
Strip off your pretty clothes,
and put on burlap to show your grief.
12 Beat your breasts in sorrow for your bountiful farms
and your fruitful grapevines.

32:1 Jer 23:5; Ezek 37:24; Zech 9:9
32:2 Isa 25:4; 35:6
32:4 Isa 29:24
32:5 1 Sam 25:25
32:6 Isa 10:2; 59:7, 13
32:7 Isa 5:23; Jer 5:26-28; Mic 7:3
32:8 2 Cor 9:6-11
32:9 Isa 28:23; 47:8
32:10 Isa 5:5-6
32:11 Isa 22:12; 47:2

32:1-8 Isaiah revisited the promise of a coming king who would establish a kingdom of justice and righteousness (compare Isaiah 9:1-7; 11:1-9).

▸ SPIRITUAL WARFARE

32:2 One source. Think of your life on this earth as a walk through a desert. The sun beats down. The sand under your feet burns up. Your mouth is parched. All you can think of is an icy glass of pure water, but all you can see on the horizon are heat waves rising from the desert floor. There is only one thing—water—that can quench your thirst. Isaiah used this metaphor to explain that a day was coming when Israel would be rescued, and the source of their deliverance would be God. All of God's people long for a day of deliverance from sin and self and Satan (1 John 2:15-17; Galatians 5:16-17; 1 John 3:8). There is only one answer to the guilt of personal sin and the terror of evil—God's deliverance. Settle for nothing less than God's plan for your rescue. (***See Spiritual Warfare**> Resisting Sin and Evil> Embracing Christ> Entrust yourself to God's care,* TopicGuide page A45.)

32:9-14 The complacent women addressed by Isaiah exemplified the false security of Judah's inhabitants. They carried on with their lifestyle of luxury built upon injustice with no fear of God's judgment. However, God would soon strip away the sources of their prosperity.

32:13 13 For your land will be overgrown with thorns and briers.
Isa 5:5-6, 10, 17 Your joyful homes and happy towns will be gone.
32:14 14 The palace and the city will be deserted,
Isa 24:12 and busy towns will be empty.
Wild donkeys will frolic and flocks will graze
in the empty forts* and watchtowers
32:15 Ps 107:35 15 until at last the Spirit is poured out
Isa 11:2 on us from heaven.
Joel 2:28 Then the wilderness will become a fertile field,
and the fertile field will yield bountiful crops.

32:16 16 Justice will rule in the wilderness
Isa 33:5 and righteousness in the fertile field.
32:17 Isa 2:4 17 And this righteousness will bring peace.
Rom 14:17 Yes, it will bring quietness and confidence forever.
Jas 3:18 18 My people will live in safety, quietly at home.
32:18 They will be at rest.
Hos 2:18-23 19 Even if the forest should be destroyed
32:19 Isa 30:30 and the city torn down,
32:20 20 the LORD will greatly bless His people.
Isa 30:23 Wherever they plant seed, bountiful crops will spring up.
Their cattle and donkeys will graze freely.

A MESSAGE ABOUT ASSYRIA

33:1 Jer 25:12-14 **33** 1 What sorrow awaits you Assyrians, who have destroyed others*
Hab 2:8 but have never been destroyed yourselves.
You betray others,
but you have never been betrayed.
When you are done destroying,
you will be destroyed.
When you are done betraying,
you will be betrayed.
33:2 2 But LORD, be merciful to us,
Isa 25:9; 40:10 for we have waited for You.
Be our strong arm each day
and our salvation in times of trouble.
33:3 3 The enemy runs at the sound of Your voice.
Jer 25:30-31 When You stand up, the nations flee!
4 Just as caterpillars and locusts strip the fields and vines,
so the fallen army of Assyria will be stripped!

33:5 5 Though the LORD is very great and lives in heaven,
Ps 97:9 He will make Jerusalem* His home of justice and righteousness.

32:14 Hebrew *the Ophel.* 33:1 Hebrew *What sorrow awaits you, O destroyer.* The Hebrew text does not specifically name Assyria as the object of the prophecy in this chapter. 33:5 Hebrew *Zion;* also in 33:14.

32:15-17 The promised kingdom of righteousness would depend on the efficacy and power of God's Spirit (compare Isaiah 42:1; 61:1; Joel 2:28-29). The Spirit of God descended on Christ in order to empower Him during His earthly ministry (Luke 3:22). The Spirit is also poured out on the church as it continues the work of Christ on earth (Acts 2:38).

33:1-4 Isaiah pronounced judgment upon Assyria and prayed for Judah's salvation. When the Lord carried out His judgment against Assyria, the once powerful empire would be unable to stand.

33:5-6 The presence of God Himself would be the foundation of the promised kingdom of righteousness. The fear of the Lord, which is also the prerequisite of true wisdom (Proverbs 9:10), is key to rejoicing in the final victory of God.

6 In that day He will be your sure foundation,
providing a rich store of salvation, wisdom, and knowledge.
The fear of the LORD will be your treasure. 33:6 Ps 112:1-3 Isa 51:6

7 But now your brave warriors weep in public.
Your ambassadors of peace cry in bitter disappointment. 33:7 2 Kgs 18:18, 37
8 Your roads are deserted;
no one travels them anymore.
The Assyrians have broken their peace treaty
and care nothing for the promises they made before witnesses.*
They have no respect for anyone.
9 The land of Israel wilts in mourning. 33:9 Isa 10:34; 24:4; 35:2
Lebanon withers with shame.
The plain of Sharon is now a wilderness.
Bashan and Carmel have been plundered.

10 But the LORD says: "Now I will stand up. 33:10 Ps 12:5 Isa 2:19
Now I will show My power and might.
11 You Assyrians produce nothing but dry grass and stubble.
Your own breath will turn to fire and consume you.
12 Your people will be burned up completely, 33:12 2 Sam 23:6-7 Isa 10:17
like thornbushes cut down and tossed in a fire.
13 Listen to what I have done, you nations far away!
And you that are near, acknowledge My might!" 33:13 Isa 49:1

14 The sinners in Jerusalem shake with fear. 33:14 Isa 1:28; 30:27 Heb 12:29
Terror seizes the godless.
"Who can live with this devouring fire?" they cry.
"Who can survive this all-consuming fire?"
15 Those who are honest and fair, 33:15 Ps 24:3-4 Isa 58:6-11
who refuse to profit by fraud,
who stay far away from bribes,
who refuse to listen to those who plot murder,
who shut their eyes to all enticement to do wrong—
16 these are the ones who will dwell on high. 33:16 Isa 25:4; 49:10
The rocks of the mountains will be their fortress.
Food will be supplied to them,
and they will have water in abundance.

17 Your eyes will see the king in all his splendor, 33:17 Isa 6:5
and you will see a land that stretches into the distance.
18 You will think back to this time of terror, asking, 33:18 1 Cor 1:20
"Where are the Assyrian officers
who counted our towers?
Where are the bookkeepers
who recorded the plunder taken from our fallen city?"
19 You will no longer see these fierce, violent people 33:19 Deut 28:49-50
with their strange, unknown language.

33:8 As in Dead Sea Scrolls; Masoretic Text reads *care nothing for the cities.*

33:13-16 The presence of God in Jerusalem would be a blessing to the godly, but a threat to the wicked. Once again Isaiah spoke of a fire in the city, and here we learn that it was the fire of God's presence (compare Isaiah 29:1-2; 31:8-9). Only those faithful to the Lord are able to abide in God's presence in safety and joy (compare Psalms 15:2-5; 24:4). Ultimately it is only Christ who may enter God's presence by virtue of His own righteousness, but, through Christ, access has been secured for all who trust in Him (see Hebrews 4:14; 7:25).

33:20 Ps 46:5
20 Instead, you will see Zion as a place of holy festivals.
You will see Jerusalem, a city quiet and secure.
It will be like a tent whose ropes are taut
and whose stakes are firmly fixed.
33:21 Isa 48:18
21 The LORD will be our Mighty One.
He will be like a wide river of protection
that no enemy can cross,
that no enemy ship can sail upon.
33:22 Isa 49:25-26 Zech 9:9 Jas 4:12
22 For the LORD is our judge,
our lawgiver, and our king.
He will care for us and save us.
23 The enemies' sails hang loose
on broken masts with useless tackle.
Their treasure will be divided by the people of God.
Even the lame will take their share!
33:24 Mic 7:18-19 1 Jn 1:7-9
24 The people of Israel will no longer say,
"We are sick and helpless,"
for the LORD will forgive their sins.

A MESSAGE FOR THE NATIONS

34:1 Deut 32:1
34 1 Come here and listen, O nations of the earth.
Let the world and everything in it hear my words.
34:2 Isa 26:20-21
2 For the LORD is enraged against the nations.
His fury is against all their armies.
He will completely destroy* them,
dooming them to slaughter.
3 Their dead will be left unburied,
and the stench of rotting bodies will fill the land.
The mountains will flow with their blood.
34:4 Joel 2:31 *Matt 24:29 *Mark 13:24-25 2 Pet 3:10 Rev 6:12-14
4 The heavens above will melt away
and disappear like a rolled-up scroll.
The stars will fall from the sky
like withered leaves from a grapevine,
or shriveled figs from a fig tree.

34:2 The Hebrew term used here refers to the complete consecration of things or people to the LORD, either by destroying them or by giving them as an offering; similarly in 34:5.

33:20-22 The hope of these verses is realized in Christ, who is both King to His people and God among them. He will one day establish peace, justice, and prosperity in Jerusalem. Enemies would no longer threaten the city. His reign would perfectly embody the will of God. In fact, his reign is equated with the reign of God Himself. This hope is realized in Christ, who is both King to His people and God among them.

▸ GOD
33:22 God's titles reveal His nature. What is so important about these three titles of God: Lawgiver, Judge, and King? As Lawgiver, God sets up the rules by which we live. As Judge, He determines the penalty for disobeying these laws. And as King, He has the power to enforce the laws. Therefore, God perfectly gives, enacts, and enforces each moral law in the universe. But He also empowers us to live according to His rules—never forget, the King of Glory is also the King of Grace, and He has all the empowering grace you need to obey Him. (***See God***> *God's Names> God> Lawgiver,* TopicGuide page A18; also ***see God***> *God's Names> God> Judge,* TopicGuide page A18; also ***see God***> *God's Names> God> King,* TopicGuide page A18.)

34:1-17 In evocative and graphic language, Isaiah unfolded a cosmic vision of God's judgment. It is not only Assyria that would be judged; all of creation will be subject to God's justice. The scope of judgment envisioned by Isaiah will not be fully realized until the final judgment of God, but the destruction of nations like Assyria foreshadows God's ultimate judgment.

▸ WORSHIP
34:1 Listen to God. Can you imagine what this earth would be like if every nation listened—really listened—to God? We would have no more wars; injustice and cruelty would cease to exist. Crime would disappear. Nations would help each other, not fight for power. Of course, the nations of the world rarely listen to God. But we, the church, can. We can create pockets of "God-hearers" and thereby show the world the blessings of heeding God's voice. Pray that your church and your friendships are energized by a passion to hear and obey the voice of God. (***See Worship***> *OT> Prophets> Israel to listen and obey God's prophets,* TopicGuide page A28.)

[5] And when My sword has finished its work in the heavens,
it will fall upon Edom,
the nation I have marked for destruction.
[6] The sword of the LORD is drenched with blood
and covered with fat—
with the blood of lambs and goats,
with the fat of rams prepared for sacrifice.
Yes, the LORD will offer a sacrifice in the city of Bozrah.
He will make a mighty slaughter in Edom.
[7] Even men as strong as wild oxen will die—
the young men alongside the veterans.
The land will be soaked with blood
and the soil enriched with fat.

[8] For it is the day of the LORD's revenge,
the year when Edom will be paid back for all it did to Israel.*
[9] The streams of Edom will be filled with burning pitch,
and the ground will be covered with fire.
[10] This judgment on Edom will never end;
the smoke of its burning will rise forever.
The land will lie deserted from generation to generation.
No one will live there anymore.
[11] It will be haunted by the desert owl and the screech owl,
the great owl and the raven.*
For God will measure that land carefully;
He will measure it for chaos and destruction.
[12] It will be called the Land of Nothing,
and all its nobles will soon be gone.*
[13] Thorns will overrun its palaces;
nettles and thistles will grow in its forts.
The ruins will become a haunt for jackals
and a home for owls.
[14] Desert animals will mingle there with hyenas,
their howls filling the night.
Wild goats will bleat at one another among the ruins,
and night creatures* will come there to rest.
[15] There the owl will make her nest and lay her eggs.
She will hatch her young and cover them with her wings.
And the buzzards will come,
each one with its mate.

[16] Search the book of the LORD,
and see what He will do.
Not one of these birds and animals will be missing,
and none will lack a mate,

34:6 Isa 63:1
34:7 Ps 68:30
34:8 Isa 13:6; 63:4
34:9 Deut 29:23
34:10 Isa 1:31; Ezek 29:11; Mal 1:3-4; Rev 14:11; 19:3
34:11 Lam 2:8
34:13 Jer 9:11; 10:22
34:14 Isa 13:21
34:16 Isa 40:5
34:17 Jer 13:25

34:8 Hebrew *to Zion.* 34:11 The identification of some of these birds is uncertain. 34:12 The meaning of the Hebrew is uncertain. 34:14 Hebrew *Lilith,* possibly a reference to a mythical demon of the night.

34:5-15 It is likely that Edom here represents all ungodly nations. Compare Isaiah 25:10-12.

34:8 The sword of God's judgment is double-edged. By the same stroke the Lord will deliver His people from their oppression and judge their oppressors for their wickedness.

34:16-17 "The book of the Lord" (literally "scroll") symbolizes God's plan to establish justice and bless His people. The Spirit of God is responsible for bringing about God's will (see Isaiah 11:2; 32:15-17). Compare this scroll with the scrolls opened in Revelation (the first is in Revelation 5.

for the LORD has promised this.
His Spirit will make it all come true.
17 He has surveyed and divided the land
and deeded it over to those creatures.
They will possess it forever,
from generation to generation.

HOPE FOR RESTORATION

35:1 Isa 41:18-19; 51:3; 55:12-13

35 1 Even the wilderness and desert will be glad in those days.
The wasteland will rejoice and blossom with spring crocuses.

35:2 Isa 25:9; 60:13; 66:10, 14

2 Yes, there will be an abundance of flowers
and singing and joy!
The deserts will become as green as the mountains of Lebanon,
as lovely as Mount Carmel or the plain of Sharon.
There the LORD will display His glory,
the splendor of our God.

35:3 Job 4:3-4; Heb 12:12

3 With this news, strengthen those who have tired hands,
and encourage those who have weak knees.

35:4 Ps 145:19

4 Say to those with fearful hearts,
"Be strong, and do not fear,
for your God is coming to destroy your enemies.
He is coming to save you."

35:5 John 9:6-7

5 And when He comes, He will open the eyes of the blind
and unplug the ears of the deaf.

35:6 Luke 7:19-21; 11:14; John 7:38; Acts 3:7-8

6 The lame will leap like a deer,
and those who cannot speak will sing for joy!
Springs will gush forth in the wilderness,
and streams will water the wasteland.
7 The parched ground will become a pool,
and springs of water will satisfy the thirsty land.
Marsh grass and reeds and rushes will flourish
where desert jackals once lived.

35:8 Matt 7:13-14

8 And a great road will go through that once deserted land.
It will be named the Highway of Holiness.
Evil-minded people will never travel on it.
It will be only for those who walk in God's ways;
fools will never walk there.

35:9 Isa 51:10

9 Lions will not lurk along its course,
nor any other ferocious beasts.
There will be no other dangers.
Only the redeemed will walk on it.

▶ HOLINESS
35:2 Joy in discovering God. Isaiah described a time when everything on earth will celebrate the glory of God, including creation itself (see Romans 8:18-22). But we don't have to wait until that day to experience some of the joy of discovering God. We can read about Him in His Word and rejoice at all the things He has done for us. We can revel in creation and express the joy we feel in His creative works. We can praise Him for hearing our prayers. Joy isn't just for the future. Joy is for the here and now! (***See Holiness**> Submission> Delighting in God> Joy in discovering God,* TopicGuide page A40.)

35:3-4 God's reign will be a source of relief to the weak and feeble. According to the author of Hebrews, this strengthening of the weak takes place within the body of Christ, the church (Hebrews 12:12-13).

35:5-7 The coming Kingdom of God will conquer disease, pain, and sorrow. Healing will come to humanity and to the earth. The miracles of Christ were both the initial fulfillment of these hopes and the reason to hope for the ultimate fulfillment upon His return.

[10] Those who have been ransomed by the LORD will return. 35:10 Rev 21:4
They will enter Jerusalem* singing,
crowned with everlasting joy.
Sorrow and mourning will disappear,
and they will be filled with joy and gladness.

ASSYRIA INVADES JUDAH

36 In the fourteenth year of King Hezekiah's reign,* King Sennacherib of Assyria 36:1-22
came to attack the fortified towns of Judah and conquered them. [2]Then the king //2 Kgs 18:13-37
of Assyria sent his chief of staff* from Lachish with a huge army to confront King Hezekiah //2 Chr 32:9-19
in Jerusalem. The Assyrians took up a position beside the aqueduct that feeds water into
the upper pool, near the road leading to the field where cloth is washed.*

[3]These are the officials who went out to meet with them: Eliakim son of Hilkiah, the pal- 36:3
ace administrator; Shebna the court secretary; and Joah son of Asaph, the royal historian. Isa 22:15, 20

SENNACHERIB THREATENS JERUSALEM

[4]Then the Assyrian king's chief of staff told them to give this message to Hezekiah: 36:4 2 Kgs 18:19

"This is what the great king of Assyria says: What are you trusting in that makes you
so confident? [5]Do you think that mere words can substitute for military skill and 36:5 2 Kgs 18:7
strength? Who are you counting on, that you have rebelled against me? [6]On Egypt? 36:6 Ps 146:3
If you lean on Egypt, it will be like a reed that splinters beneath your weight and Ezek 29:6-7
pierces your hand. Pharaoh, the king of Egypt, is completely unreliable!

[7]"But perhaps you will say to me, 'We are trusting in the LORD our God!' But isn't 36:7
He the One who was insulted by Hezekiah? Didn't Hezekiah tear down His shrines Deut 12:2-5 2 Kgs 18:4-5
and altars and make everyone in Judah and Jerusalem worship only at the altar here
in Jerusalem?

[8]"I'll tell you what! Strike a bargain with my master, the king of Assyria. I will give
you 2,000 horses if you can find that many men to ride on them! [9]With your tiny 36:9 Isa 20:5
army, how can you think of challenging even the weakest contingent of my master's
troops, even with the help of Egypt's chariots and charioteers? [10]What's more, do you 36:10
think we have invaded your land without the LORD's direction? The LORD Himself told 1 Kgs 13:18
us, 'Attack this land and destroy it!'"

[11]Then Eliakim, Shebna, and Joah said to the Assyrian chief of staff, "Please speak to us 36:11
in Aramaic, for we understand it well. Don't speak in Hebrew,* for the people on the wall Ezra 4:7 Dan 2:4
will hear."

[12]But Sennacherib's chief of staff replied, "Do you think my master sent this message
only to you and your master? He wants all the people to hear it, for when we put this city

35:10 Hebrew *Zion.* 36:1 The fourteenth year of Hezekiah's reign was 701 B.C. 36:2a Or *the rabshakeh;* also in 36:4, 11, 12, 22. 36:2b Or *bleached.* 36:11 Hebrew *in the dialect of Judah;* also in 36:13.

36:1 Sennacherib's campaign included advances against Phoenicia, Philistine cities, Egypt, and Judah. The invasion is also recounted in 2 Kings 18:13–19:37.

36:4-10 The initial speech by Sennacherib's representative revolves around the theme of trust. This is a cunning piece of psychological warfare.

▸ HOLINESS
36:4 Who are you trusting? Have you ever been ridiculed for believing in God? The Assyrian commander confronted the people of Israel, taunting them for trusting in God. He said that they were foolish to put their confidence in a God that could never save them. Perhaps you have been taunted by someone—at work or school, online or in person—who felt that your faith in God was foolish. Did the confrontation threaten you? When you find yourself in a situation like this, remember what happened to the Assyrians. God defeated them, and Israel was not harmed. Use this story to help you trust in God in the face of ridicule for your faith. (See 2 Chronicles 32 and Isaiah 37; also ***see Holiness****> Submission> Trusting God> Overcoming,* TopicGuide page A40.)

36:7-11 The Assyrian commander wrongly assumed that Hezekiah's reforms (see 2 Kings 18:4) would have angered the God of Israel. But perhaps correctly, he assumed that many were angered by the removal of their shrines and idols. His continued speech is designed to splinter the unity of the city and is so effective that the leaders beg him to stop speaking in Hebrew.

under siege, they will suffer along with you. They will be so hungry and thirsty that they
will eat their own dung and drink their own urine."
36:13 2 Chr 32:18 13Then the chief of staff stood and shouted in Hebrew to the people on the wall, "Listen
to this message from the great king of Assyria! 14This is what the king says: Don't let Heze-
36:14 Isa 37:10 kiah deceive you. He will never be able to rescue you. 15Don't let him fool you into trust-
ing in the LORD by saying, 'The LORD will surely rescue us. This city will never fall into the
hands of the Assyrian king!'
36:16 Zech 3:10 16"Don't listen to Hezekiah! These are the terms the king of Assyria is offering: Make
peace with me—open the gates and come out. Then each of you can continue eating
from your own grapevine and fig tree and drinking from your own well. 17Then I will ar-
range to take you to another land like this one—a land of grain and new wine, bread and
vineyards.
36:19 2 Kgs 17:6 18"Don't let Hezekiah mislead you by saying, 'The LORD will rescue us!' Have the gods of
Isa 10:9-11; 37:11-13 any other nations ever saved their people from the king of Assyria? 19What happened to
Jer 49:23 the gods of Hamath and Arpad? And what about the gods of Sepharvaim? Did any god
36:20 1 Kgs 20:23, 28 rescue Samaria from my power? 20What god of any nation has ever been able to save
its people from my power? So what makes you think that the LORD can rescue Jerusalem
from me?"
21But the people were silent and did not utter a word because Hezekiah had com-
manded them, "Do not answer him."
22Then Eliakim son of Hilkiah, the palace administrator; Shebna the court secretary; and
Joah son of Asaph, the royal historian, went back to Hezekiah. They tore their clothes in
despair, and they went in to see the king and told him what the Assyrian chief of staff had
said.

HEZEKIAH SEEKS THE LORD'S HELP

37:1-13 //2 Kgs 19:1-13 **37** When King Hezekiah heard their report, he tore his clothes and put on burlap and
went into the Temple of the LORD. 2And he sent Eliakim the palace administrator,
Shebna the court secretary, and the leading priests, all dressed in burlap, to the prophet
37:3 Isa 22:5; 26:17-18 Isaiah son of Amoz. 3They told him, "This is what King Hezekiah says: Today is a day of
trouble, insults, and disgrace. It is like when a child is ready to be born, but the mother has
37:4 Isa 1:9; 10:20-22 no strength to deliver the baby. 4But perhaps the LORD your God has heard the Assyrian
chief of staff,* sent by the king to defy the living God, and will punish him for his words.
Oh, pray for those of us who are left!"

37:4 Or *the rabshakeh;* also in 37:8.

36:16-17 These words ironically echo the language of Deuteronomy (8:7-9; 30:15-20). The people of Jerusalem were in fact faced with a critical decision: Trust in their God, or trust in the Assyrian monarch. Both demanded ultimate allegiance, but only One possessed the right and power to demand such allegiance.

▶ HOLINESS
36:18 A test of faith. The battle lines were drawn. On one side stood the powerful King Sennacherib and his mighty army, who waited right outside Jerusalem's walls. Inside the walls, King Hezekiah stood with God. Sennacherib's chief of staff shouted, "Abandon your God. He can't help you!" Hezekiah told his people, "God will save you." In this case, the people listened to Hezekiah, and God did save the people through a miracle (2 Chronicles 32; Isaiah 37). In your life, influential voices may challenge your belief in God. Everyone faces the choice between faith in God's promises and faith in human threats. What will you do when confronted with this type of choice? (***See Holiness***> *Law and Grace> Law> Leaders and followers,* TopicGuide page A41.)

37:1-4 Hezekiah responded appropriately to the crisis by exhibiting humility and faith. He attired himself in clothing that reflected the perilous circumstances, and he sought help from God through the prophet Isaiah. He framed his petition in terms of Jerusalem's plight and God's own offended honor.

▶ WORSHIP
37:1 Repent and pray. When King Hezekiah faced an enemy that was much stronger than Israel, his reaction was to humble himself before God. He tore his clothes as a sign of his sorrow over his sins and he went to the Temple to pray (see Hezekiah's repentance in 2 Chronicles 32:26). In going to the Temple, he showed his desire to hear directly from God about his situation. Our actions are important, but God wants us to have holy reactions as well. As soon as we realize that we are in a difficult situation, our immediate response should be to confess our sins and seek God's wisdom. These two steps are our secret weapons to conquer our spiritual enemies. You are never stronger than when you repent and seek the Lord. (***See Worship***> *NT> Our Role> Mind and Heart> We are to have heaven's wisdom,* TopicGuide page A32.)

5After King Hezekiah's officials delivered the king's message to Isaiah, 6the prophet re- **37:6**
plied, "Say to your master, 'This is what the LORD says: Do not be disturbed by this blasphe- Isa 7:4; 35:4
mous speech against Me from the Assyrian king's messengers. 7Listen! I Myself will move
against him,* and the king will receive a message that he is needed at home. So he will re-
turn to his land, where I will have him killed with a sword.'"
8Meanwhile, the Assyrian chief of staff left Jerusalem and went to consult the king of As-
syria, who had left Lachish and was attacking Libnah.
9Soon afterward King Sennacherib received word that King Tirhakah of Ethiopia* was
leading an army to fight against him. Before leaving to meet the attack, he sent messen-
gers back to Hezekiah in Jerusalem with this message:

> 10"This message is for King Hezekiah of Judah. Don't let your God, in whom you trust,
> deceive you with promises that Jerusalem will not be captured by the king of Assyria.
> 11You know perfectly well what the kings of Assyria have done wherever they have **37:11**
> gone. They have completely destroyed everyone who stood in their way! Why should Isa 10:9-11
> you be any different? 12Have the gods of other nations rescued them—such nations as **37:12**
> Gozan, Haran, Rezeph, and the people of Eden who were in Tel-assar? My predecessors Gen 11:31; 2 Kgs 17:6
> destroyed them all! 13What happened to the king of Hamath and the king of Arpad? Acts 7:2
> What happened to the kings of Sepharvaim, Hena, and Ivvah?"

14After Hezekiah received the letter from the messengers and read it, he went up to the **37:14-20**
LORD's Temple and spread it out before the LORD. 15And Hezekiah prayed this prayer be- //2 Kgs 19:14-19
fore the LORD: 16"O LORD of Heaven's Armies, God of Israel, You are enthroned between **37:16** Exod 25:22
the mighty cherubim! You alone are God of all the kingdoms of the earth. You alone cre- Pss 80:1; 86:10
ated the heavens and the earth. 17Bend down, O LORD, and listen! Open Your eyes, O LORD, Jer 10:12
and see! Listen to Sennacherib's words of defiance against the living God.
18"It is true, LORD, that the kings of Assyria have destroyed all these nations. 19And they **37:18** 2 Kgs 15:29
have thrown the gods of these nations into the fire and burned them. But of course the As- 1 Chr 5:26
syrians could destroy them! They were not gods at all—only idols of wood and stone **37:19**
shaped by human hands. 20Now, O LORD our God, rescue us from his power; then all the Isa 17:8
kingdoms of the earth will know that You alone, O LORD, are God.*" **37:20** 1 Kgs 18:36-37

ISAIAH PREDICTS JUDAH'S DELIVERANCE

Isa 33:22; Ezek 36:23

21Then Isaiah son of Amoz sent this message to Hezekiah: "This is what the LORD, the God
of Israel, says: Because you prayed about King Sennacherib of Assyria, 22the LORD has spo- **37:22** Lam 2:13
ken this word against him: Zeph 3:14

37:7 Hebrew *I will put a spirit in him.* 37:9 Hebrew *of Cush.* 37:20 As in Dead Sea Scrolls (see also 2 Kgs 19:19); Masoretic Text reads *You alone are the LORD.*

37:5-7 The Lord's response evoked the holy war tradition of Israel. Faced with an overwhelming enemy, Judah was not to fear but to rely on God, who would fight for His people. Compare with Exodus 14:13-14; Joshua 1:8; 11:6.

▸ GOD

37:5-6 Sticks and stones. People seem extremely comfortable using God's name as a curse. We hear it on television, in the movies, and during conversations with unbelievers. It seems that many are anxious to defame the name of God or ridicule Him. These defamations rightly bother us emotionally, but they should not make us despair. Since Isaiah's time and before, people have said these things about God. The tirades don't bother Him. He knows what to do about these people and when to do it. If you are not in a position to defend God's holy name, trust that He is able to defend His honor. Keep blasphemy far from your lips and the lips of those under your care. (***See God**> God's Attributes> All-Powerful> No one can challenge what God does,* TopicGuide page A16.)

37:8-9 Libnah was located in Philistine territory about 15 miles southeast of Ashdod. Ethiopia (literally "Cush") is best associated with present-day Sudan. Tirhakah was not officially made king until shortly after the Sennacherib invasion, yet it was appropriate to refer to him as king since the readers would have known him as such. He later became Pharaoh in Egypt's twenty-fifth dynasty.

37:15-20 Hezekiah's remarkable prayer recalls the prayer of Solomon at the dedication of the Temple (1 Kings 8:23-53, especially verses 33-34). The prayer also ties into Isaiah's teachings on the character of God (Isaiah 42:8; 43:13; 44:6).

37:21-34 Isaiah's oracle is also found in 2 Kings 19:21-28. Sennacherib had railed against and mocked the God of Israel. He assumed divine prerogatives of blessing and cursing (Isaiah 36:16-17), and he addressed Hezekiah and Judah with claims of ultimate authority. Sennacherib's arrogance and disdain for the God of Israel would now lead to his own undoing.

"The virgin daughter of Zion
despises you and laughs at you.
The daughter of Jerusalem
shakes her head in derision as you flee.

37:23 Isa 5:15, 21 Ezek 39:7 Hab 1:12
23 "Whom have you been defying and ridiculing?
Against whom did you raise your voice?
At whom did you look with such haughty eyes?
It was the Holy One of Israel!

37:24 Isa 14:8
24 By your messengers you have defied the Lord.
You have said, 'With my many chariots
I have conquered the highest mountains—
yes, the remotest peaks of Lebanon.
I have cut down its tallest cedars
and its finest cypress trees.
I have reached its farthest heights
and explored its deepest forests.
25 I have dug wells in many foreign lands*
and refreshed myself with their water.
With the sole of my foot,
I stopped up all the rivers of Egypt!'

37:26 Isa 25:2 Acts 2:23; 4:27-28
26 "But have you not heard?
I decided this long ago.
Long ago I planned it,
and now I am making it happen.
I planned for you to crush fortified cities
into heaps of rubble.

37:27 Ps 129:6 Isa 40:7
27 That is why their people have so little power
and are so frightened and confused.
They are as weak as grass,
as easily trampled as tender green shoots.
They are like grass sprouting on a housetop,
scorched* before it can grow lush and tall.

37:28 Ps 139:1
28 "But I know you well—
where you stay
and when you come and go.
I know the way you have raged against Me.

37:29 Isa 30:28 Ezek 38:4
29 And because of your raging against Me
and your arrogance, which I have heard for Myself,
I will put My hook in your nose
and My bit in your mouth.
I will make you return
by the same road on which you came."

37:30 Lev 25:5, 11-12
30Then Isaiah said to Hezekiah, "Here is the proof that what I say is true:

"This year you will eat only what grows up by itself,
and next year you will eat what springs up from that.

37:25 As in Dead Sea Scrolls (see also 2 Kgs 19:24); Masoretic Text lacks *in many foreign lands.* 37:27 As in Dead Sea Scrolls and some Greek manuscripts (see also 2 Kgs 19:26); most Hebrew manuscripts read *like a terraced field.*

37:29 Assyrian art (see also 2 Chronicles 33:11) portrays Assyrians leading their vanquished foes into captivity like animals by hook and bit. In an instance of poetic justice, God seizes on this image to describe Assyria's coming retreat.

37:30-32 The second section of Isaiah's prophecy promised the king and his people recovery and healing. While initial conditions would be bleak, they would improve, and the remnant of Judah's population would take root and flourish.

But in the third year you will plant crops and harvest them;
you will tend vineyards and eat their fruit.
31 And you who are left in Judah,
who have escaped the ravages of the siege,
will put roots down in your own soil
and grow up and flourish.
32 For a remnant of My people will spread out from Jerusalem,
a group of survivors from Mount Zion.
The passionate commitment of the LORD of Heaven's Armies
will make this happen!

37:31 Isa 10:20; 27:6

37:32 //2 Kgs 19:31

33 "And this is what the LORD says about the king of Assyria:

"'His armies will not enter Jerusalem.
They will not even shoot an arrow at it.
They will not march outside its gates with their shields
nor build banks of earth against its walls.
34 The king will return to his own country
by the same road on which he came.
He will not enter this city,'
says the LORD.
35 'For My own honor and for the sake of My servant David,
I will defend this city and protect it.'"

37:35 2 Kgs 20:6 Isa 48:9, 11

36 That night the angel of the LORD went out to the Assyrian camp and killed 185,000 As-
syrian soldiers. When the surviving Assyrians* woke up the next morning, they found
corpses everywhere. 37 Then King Sennacherib of Assyria broke camp and returned to his
own land. He went home to his capital of Nineveh and stayed there.
38 One day while he was worshiping in the temple of his god Nisroch, his sons Adram-
melech and Sharezer killed him with their swords. They then escaped to the land of Ararat,
and another son, Esarhaddon, became the next king of Assyria.

37:36 //2 Kgs 19:35 Isa 10:12, 33-34

37:37 Gen 10:11 Jon 3:3 Zeph 2:13

37:38 Gen 8:4

HEZEKIAH'S SICKNESS AND RECOVERY

38 About that time Hezekiah became deathly ill, and the prophet Isaiah son of Amoz
went to visit him. He gave the king this message: "This is what the LORD says: 'Set
your affairs in order, for you are going to die. You will not recover from this illness.'"

38:1-8 //2 Kgs 20:1-11 2 Chr 32:24-26

37:36 Hebrew *When they.*

37:33-35 The final portion of Isaiah's oracle announced God's intention to defend Jerusalem for the sake of His own honor and His servant David.

37:36-38 The exact nature of the miraculous intervention is not specified. The Greek historian Herodotus and the Jewish historian Josephus both record Sennacherib's withdrawal under disastrous circumstances. In his own account, Sennacherib boasts of trapping Hezekiah in Jerusalem but says nothing of attacking the city. Other records are conspicuously silent on why the city was not taken. The Babylonian Chronicle records that, 20 years after the failed siege of Jerusalem in 681 BC, one of Sennacherib's sons murdered him while he was sacrificing to his god. He was not safe from the fulfillment of God's Word even in the temple of his god.

38:1-6 "About that time" is a phrase alerting the reader to generalized dates or rounded numbers. Hezekiah reigned for 29 years. Subtracting the 15 years granted at this juncture (38:6), the events described took place in or around Hezekiah's fourteenth year, the year of the invasion (36:1). A time shortly before the invasion seems most likely, given the presence of the substantial wealth in Judah's treasuries. Therefore, these events appear to have been arranged topically rather than chronologically, an occasional technique of ancient historians.

38:2-3 Hezekiah reacts to Isaiah's pronouncement with a desperate plea to God. God graciously responds by granting Hezekiah an additional 15 years of life. A prophet's words, although appearing irrevocable, were often intended to evoke a response of humble repentance and prayer that would then mitigate the announced judgment (compare Jonah 3:4, 10; 2 Chronicles 12:5, 7).

38:3 2When Hezekiah heard this, he turned his face to the wall and prayed to the LORD, 3"Re-
2 Kgs 18:5-6 member, O LORD, how I have always been faithful to You and have served You single-
Neh 13:14
Ps 6:6-8 mindedly, always doing what pleases You." Then he broke down and wept bitterly.
38:5 4Then this message came to Isaiah from the LORD: 5"Go back to Hezekiah and tell him,
2 Kgs 18:2, 13 'This is what the LORD, the God of your ancestor David, says: I have heard your prayer and
38:6 seen your tears. I will add fifteen years to your life, 6and I will rescue you and this city from
Isa 31:5 the king of Assyria. Yes, I will defend this city.
38:7 7" 'And this is the sign from the LORD to prove that He will do as He promised: 8I will
Isa 7:11, 14 cause the sun's shadow to move ten steps backward on the sundial* of Ahaz!' " So the
38:8
2 Kgs 20:9-11 shadow on the sundial moved backward ten steps.

HEZEKIAH'S POEM OF PRAISE

9When King Hezekiah was well again, he wrote this poem:

38:10 10 I said, "In the prime of my life,
Pss 102:24; 107:18 must I now enter the place of the dead?*
Am I to be robbed of the rest of my years?"
38:11 11 I said, "Never again will I see the LORD GOD
Ps 27:13 while still in the land of the living.
Never again will I see my friends
or be with those who live in this world.
38:12 12 My life has been blown away
Job 4:20
2 Cor 5:1 like a shepherd's tent in a storm.
It has been cut short,
as when a weaver cuts cloth from a loom.
Suddenly, my life was over.
38:13 13 I waited patiently all night,
Job 10:16 but I was torn apart as though by lions.
Suddenly, my life was over.
38:14 14 Delirious, I chattered like a swallow or a crane,
Job 7:11 and then I moaned like a mourning dove.
Ps 119:123
Ezek 7:16 My eyes grew tired of looking to heaven for help.
I am in trouble, Lord. Help me!"

15 But what could I say?
For He Himself sent this sickness.

38:8 Hebrew *the steps.* 38:10 Hebrew *enter the gates of Sheol?*

▶ GOD

38:3 God listens. When Hezekiah was struck down with a disease that appeared terminal, he immediately went to God with his problem. He knew that God was the ultimate healer. God listened when Hezekiah prayed and healed him. Hezekiah lived another 15 years. God also listens when you pray. If you are battling a serious illness today, take your situation to God in prayer. Tell Him what you are feeling. He may heal you of your disease, or He may give you the strength to endure your trial. Either outcome will be His perfect will for your life. Have confidence in God. He is the only One who can truly heal us. (***See God****> God's Names> God> The* LORD*, the healer (YHWH Rapha),* TopicGuide page A18.)

38:7-8 Signs were commonly granted in Isaiah's ministry to authenticate a prophetic word (Isaiah 7:11; 37:30). The use of a sundial (or similar structure—the Hebrew is unclear) may have symbolic weight. The shadow of death had crept up on Hezekiah, but God had "turned the clock back," as we might say today. Hezekiah's recovery mirrored the salvation of Jerusalem from the brink of destruction at the hands of Sennacherib.

38:9-20 Isaiah included a hymn of response composed by Hezekiah to commemorate his extraordinary healing. The hymn is not found in the parallel account of 2 Kings 18–20. The tone of the hymn moves from a lament over Hezekiah's illness (Isaiah 38:10-14) to a mixture of praise and thanksgiving prompted by the Lord's healing (38:15-20).

38:10-12 Hezekiah expressed all of the natural fears that those who face the prospect of an early death experience. At this point in the history of God's revelation, God's people had a limited knowledge of what would transpire after death. This limited knowledge caused God's people to value the present life as a time when they knew with certainty that they could praise God and experience His blessing.

Now I will walk humbly throughout my years
because of this anguish I have felt.
16 Lord, Your discipline is good,
for it leads to life and health.
You restore my health
and allow me to live!
17 Yes, this anguish was good for me,
for You have rescued me from death
and forgiven all my sins.
18 For the dead* cannot praise You;
they cannot raise their voices in praise.
Those who go down to the grave
can no longer hope in Your faithfulness.
19 Only the living can praise You as I do today.
Each generation tells of Your faithfulness to the next.
20 Think of it—the LORD is ready to heal me!
I will sing His praises with instruments
every day of my life
in the Temple of the LORD.

21 Isaiah had said to Hezekiah's servants, "Make an ointment from figs and spread it
over the boil, and Hezekiah will recover."
22 And Hezekiah had asked, "What sign will prove that I will go to the Temple of the LORD?"

38:16 Pss 39:13; 119:71, 75
38:17 Isa 43:25; Jer 31:34; Jon 2:6
38:18 Ps 6:5
38:19 Pss 78:5-7; 119:175
38:20 Pss 33:1-3; 116:17-19; 146:2
38:21 2 Kgs 20:7-8

ENVOYS FROM BABYLON

39 Soon after this, Merodach-baladan son of Baladan, king of Babylon, sent Heze-
kiah his best wishes and a gift. He had heard that Hezekiah had been very sick
and that he had recovered. 2 Hezekiah was delighted with the Babylonian envoys and
showed them everything in his treasure-houses—the silver, the gold, the spices, and the
aromatic oils. He also took them to see his armory and showed them everything in his
royal treasuries! There was nothing in his palace or kingdom that Hezekiah did not show
them.
3 Then Isaiah the prophet went to King Hezekiah and asked him, "What did those men
want? Where were they from?"
Hezekiah replied, "They came from the distant land of Babylon."
4 "What did they see in your palace?" asked Isaiah.

39:1-8 //2 Kgs 20:12-19
39:2 2 Kgs 18:15-16; 2 Chr 32:25, 31
39:3 Jer 5:15

38:18 Hebrew *Sheol*.

GOD
38:16 Hezekiah credits God. When Hezekiah was struck down with a terminal illness, he cried out to God for healing. God answered and healed Hezekiah. Immediately, Hezekiah thanked God for what He had done in his life. Often we fail to give God praise when He answers our prayers. We pray fervently when the problem looms in our life, but when God delivers us, we forget to go back to God and thank Him. To avoid this, make a prayer list of your requests to God. Then go back and thank Him for each answer. (***See God***> *God's Attributes> Faithful> God deserves thanks for His constant faithfulness,* TopicGuide page A16.)

38:18-19 Hezekiah was speaking here of praising God among the living (see textual note at 38:10). The dead are unable to speak God's praises.

38:21-22 It is unclear whether the ointment was applied for medicinal purposes or as a kind of sign. If applied for medicinal purposes, it does not invalidate God's promise of healing. God often works through secondary causes to bring about His desired purposes.

39:1 Merodach-baladan experienced a tumultuous career in Babylon. He was king from 720–709 BC. Then he was deposed by the Assyrians and found refuge in Elam. He enjoyed a brief resurgence in 703 BC, but was again defeated and exiled. A perpetual enemy of Assyria, Merodach-baladan sought to enlist Judah's aid in his struggle. His ostensible concern for Hezekiah's health was a thinly veiled excuse to pursue political goals.

39:2 Hezekiah was not merely providing an entertaining tour for his guests; he was consenting to an alliance with Babylon and demonstrating the resources at his disposal. Isaiah condemned this action in Isaiah 30–31. Relying on foreign allies suggested a failure to rely on God for Judah's security.

"They saw everything," Hezekiah replied. "I showed them everything I own—all my royal
treasuries."
39:5 1 Sam 15:16 5 Then Isaiah said to Hezekiah, "Listen to this message from the LORD of Heaven's Armies:
6 'The time is coming when everything in your palace—all the treasures stored up by your
39:6 2 Kgs 24:13 ancestors until now—will be carried off to Babylon. Nothing will be left,' says the LORD.
Jer 20:5 7 'Some of your very own sons will be taken away into exile. They will become eunuchs
39:7 Dan 1:2-7 who will serve in the palace of Babylon's king.'"
8 Then Hezekiah said to Isaiah, "This message you have given me from the LORD is good."
39:8 2 Chr 34:28 For the king was thinking, "At least there will be peace and security during my lifetime."

COMFORT FOR GOD'S PEOPLE

40:1 Isa 49:13 2 Cor 1:4

40 1 "Comfort, comfort My people,"
says your God.

40:2 Isa 53:5-6, 11 Zech 9:12

2 "Speak tenderly to Jerusalem.
Tell her that her sad days are gone
and her sins are pardoned.
Yes, the LORD has punished her twice over
for all her sins."

40:3 Mal 3:1 *Matt 3:3 *Mark 1:3 *Luke 3:4 *John 1:23

3 Listen! It's the voice of someone shouting,
"Clear the way through the wilderness
for the LORD!
Make a straight highway through the wasteland
for our God!

40:4 Ezek 17:24 *Luke 3:5

4 Fill in the valleys,
and level the mountains and hills.

39:5-7 Isaiah condemned Hezekiah's naive willingness to commit his wealth and resources to the Babylonians. These same Babylonians would return as enemies of Judah and remove all Judah's wealth and people. Within 100 years, the Babylonians successfully overthrew the Assyrians and established themselves as the leading power of the region. By 586 BC the Jerusalem Temple lay in ruins.

▶ GOD
39:6 Where is your pride? Why was God so angry with Hezekiah for showing the treasures of the Temple to the Babylonian envoys? Politically, his alliance with Babylon was forbidden (see Deuteronomy 7:2). Personally, he wasn't glorifying God; he was accepting God's glory for himself. We think that we deserve the credit for whatever good that comes to us. This is the pride that led even a mature man like Hezekiah to show the Babylonians all his "royal treasuries" (Isaiah 39:4). God wants us to realize that He is the source of all blessings and to have a humble attitude about them. Confess your pride to God and give Him the credit for all your blessings. (***See God*> *Relationship> Barriers> Pride,* TopicGuide page A14.)

39:8 The king's response revealed a profound selfishness. He callously accepted Isaiah's judgment, content that he would not live to see it.

40:1–66:24 Isaiah 40 begins the third major section of the book. Isaiah 1–5 introduced the major themes of the book. Isaiah 6–39 dealt principally with the threat posed by Assyria in Isaiah's own lifetime. In chapters 40–66, the prophet looked ahead to the time of Babylonian exile, offering hope for a glorious restoration for God's people. Like chapters 6–39, this section opens with a prophetic call (40:1-11). Along with the prophet's call, the major themes of chapters 40–66 include God's ability and intention to save His people, His instruments of salvation, and the necessity of repentance.

40:1-11 In Isaiah 6, the prophet received his initial call to office. This initial call involved proclaiming judgment. Here the prophet received a second call, this time to proclaim blessing and forgiveness. While the prophet's hesitation to the first call is understandable, his hesitation to the second call is somewhat surprising (40:6-9). The common thread, however, appears to be the perceived reluctance of the audience in either case to believe the message.

40:1-2 To speak "tenderly" literally means to speak "to the heart." The Lord was addressing the deepest, heartfelt longings of His people in exile.

▶ CHURCH
40:1 Words of peace. The first 39 chapters of Isaiah had been difficult for the original audience to read—the judgment of God upon Israel frightened them. Today, many believers are scarred and bleeding from the hardships of life. Paul writes, "[God] comforts us in all our troubles so that we can comfort others. When they are troubled, we will be able to give them the same comfort God has given us" (2 Corinthians 1:4). Much of this comfort can be given through the church and honest relationships. Look for ways that you can comfort those around you. Odds are, they need it. (***See Church*> *Role> Preach> Topics> Consolation and comfort,* TopicGuide page A50.)

40:3-5 The identity of the voice is unclear, but it announces a message of comfort: The Lord Himself will come to His people and lead them to salvation. Gospel writers see this passage as an anticipation of the ministry of John the Baptist, who prepared the people's hearts for the coming of Christ (Mark 1:1-4).

Straighten the curves,
and smooth out the rough places.
5 Then the glory of the LORD will be revealed,
and all people will see it together.
The LORD has spoken!"*

40:5 Hab 2:14 *Luke 3:6

6 A voice said, "Shout!"
I asked, "What should I shout?"

40:6 Job 14:2 1 Pet 1:24

"Shout that people are like the grass.
Their beauty fades as quickly
as the flowers in a field.
7 The grass withers and the flowers fade
beneath the breath of the LORD.
And so it is with people.
8 The grass withers and the flowers fade,
but the word of our God stands forever."

40:7 Jas 1:10-11 1 Pet 1:24

40:8 Matt 5:18 *1 Pet 1:25

9 O Zion, messenger of good news,
shout from the mountaintops!
Shout it louder, O Jerusalem.*
Shout, and do not be afraid.
Tell the towns of Judah,
"Your God is coming!"
10 Yes, the Sovereign LORD is coming in power.
He will rule with a powerful arm.
See, He brings His reward with Him as He comes.
11 He will feed His flock like a shepherd.
He will carry the lambs in His arms,
holding them close to His heart.
He will gently lead the mother sheep with their young.

40:10 Isa 59:16 Rev 22:12

40:11 Ezek 34:12-14, 23, 31 John 10:11, 14-16

THE LORD HAS NO EQUAL

12 Who else has held the oceans in his hand?
Who has measured off the heavens with his fingers?
Who else knows the weight of the earth
or has weighed the mountains and hills on a scale?

40:12 Isa 48:13

40:3-5 Greek version reads *He is a voice shouting in the wilderness, / "Prepare the way for the LORD's coming! / Clear a road for our God! / Fill in the valleys, / and level the mountains and hills. / And then the glory of the LORD will be revealed, / and all people will see the salvation sent from God. / The LORD has spoken!"* Compare Matt 3:3; Mark 1:3; Luke 3:4-6. **40:9** Or *O messenger of good news, shout to Zion from the mountaintops! Shout it louder to Jerusalem.*

40:9-11 Here Isaiah was instructed to boldly proclaim the Lord's message of comfort to the people of Judah. The "good news," from which we derive our word "gospel," is the glorious announcement of God's coming in power and blessing to heal His people and establish His kingdom. This expectation of universal restoration and renewal is ultimately fulfilled in the coming of Jesus.

40:12–44:23 Upon hearing Isaiah's message of comfort, many doubts and questions must have arisen in the hearts of the exiles. *Hasn't God abandoned us? Does He really intend to save us? Is God more powerful than Babylon and its gods?* Throughout this section Isaiah addressed many of those questions, especially those questions relating to God's power. The prophet affirmed in no uncertain terms God's absolute and unrivaled power, especially over the nations and their idols.

40:12-14 Through this series of rhetorical questions, the prophet established the incomprehensible scope of God's power and His immeasurable wisdom. The assumed reply to these questions is, of course, "no one." No one can claim to have ever instructed the Lord or given Him counsel.

IT'S TRUE—ABSOLUTE POWER CORRUPTS ABSOLUTELY—at least in most cases. But we can also find wonderful exceptions.

General George Washington is one example. At one point when the government of the United States of America was being formed, the colonists wanted to crown him king, but he declined. Instead, he helped the colonies form a republic. In 1789, he was elected the first President of the United States and remains one of the best examples of leadership to all who wish to work in civil service, for he used his power for the good of the people.

The Bible tells us that God uses His power for our benefit. He has our best interests in mind. God channels His power through us so that we can do more than we could ever do on our own. Ephesians 3:20 says, "Now all glory to God, who is able, through His mighty power at work within us, to accomplish infinitely more than we might ask or think." But God is more than just able—He is willing. Jesus stepped down from His heavenly throne, took on humanity, and lived among us for over thirty years, doing good and then dying on our behalf. He stepped out of heaven and into the mud and madness of this world to make peace between God and humanity. What other proof do we need? He is both willing and able to help those who call on Him (Luke 11:9).

What do you need help with today? Leading your family? Managing the challenges of a small business? Developing a ministry? Teaching children? God knows your need, and for His glory and your good He can energize your service to your family, the church, and the world.

13 Who is able to advise the Spirit of the LORD?*
Who knows enough to give Him advice or teach Him?
14 Has the LORD ever needed anyone's advice?
Does He need instruction about what is good?
Did someone teach Him what is right
or show Him the path of justice?

15 No, for all the nations of the world
are but a drop in the bucket.
They are nothing more
than dust on the scales.
He picks up the whole earth
as though it were a grain of sand.
16 All the wood in Lebanon's forests
and all Lebanon's animals would not be enough
to make a burnt offering worthy of our God.
17 The nations of the world are worth nothing to Him.
In His eyes they count for less than nothing—
mere emptiness and froth.

18 To whom can you compare God?
What image can you find to resemble Him?
19 Can He be compared to an idol formed in a mold,
overlaid with gold, and decorated with silver chains?
20 Or if people are too poor for that,
they might at least choose wood that won't decay
and a skilled craftsman
to carve an image that won't fall down!

21 Haven't you heard? Don't you understand?
Are you deaf to the words of God—
the words He gave before the world began?
Are you so ignorant?
22 God sits above the circle of the earth.
The people below seem like grasshoppers to Him!
He spreads out the heavens like a curtain
and makes His tent from them.
23 He judges the great people of the world
and brings them all to nothing.
24 They hardly get started, barely taking root,
when He blows on them and they wither.
The wind carries them off like chaff.

40:13 *Rom 11:34 *1 Cor 2:16
40:14 Col 2:3
40:15 Isa 17:13
40:17 Isa 29:7
40:18 Exod 8:10 Isa 46:5 Mic 7:18
40:19 Ps 115:4-8 Hab 2:18-19
40:20 Isa 46:7
40:21 Isa 51:13 Rom 1:19
40:22 Ps 104:2
40:23 Ps 107:40 Jer 25:18-27
40:24 Isa 17:13

40:13 Greek version reads *Who can know the LORD's thoughts?* Compare Rom 11:34; 1 Cor 2:16.

40:15-16 Lebanon was highly regarded for its abundant forests.

▸ PURPOSE
40:15 God is greater than His creation. A water drop is so small that when dropped into a full bucket, it disappears and cannot be distinguished from any other drop. A speck of dust is so light that it will not alter a normal household scale. That's how far God is above His creation—even all of it put together is as nothing before Him. The next time you hear ominous world news, remember that God is in charge. Some rulers may seem all-powerful and intent on unstoppable evil, but they are like an insect next to God. Put your trust in Him regarding your future. (***See Purpose****> God's Means> God's Sovereignty> God is King over every nation,* TopicGuide page A52.)

40:18-26 Another series of rhetorical questions establishes God's incomparable greatness.

▸ GOD
40:24 The fate of the powerful. Who do you consider one of the most powerful rulers in history? Joseph Stalin should probably be in this category. As dictator of the Soviet Union in the early 20th century, he had tremendous

25 "To whom will you compare Me?
Who is My equal?" asks the Holy One.

40:26 Ps 147:4; Isa 42:5

26 Look up into the heavens.
Who created all the stars?
He brings them out like an army, one after another,
calling each by its name.
Because of His great power and incomparable strength,
not a single one is missing.

40:27 Job 34:5-6; Isa 54:8

27 O Jacob, how can you say the LORD does not see your troubles?
O Israel, how can you say God ignores your rights?

40:28 Pss 90:2; 147:5; Rom 11:33

28 Have you never heard?
Have you never understood?
The LORD is the everlasting God,
the Creator of all the earth.
He never grows weak or weary.
No one can measure the depths of His understanding.

40:29 Jer 31:25

29 He gives power to the weak
and strength to the powerless.

40:30 Jer 9:21

30 Even youths will become weak and tired,
and young men will fall in exhaustion.

40:31 2 Cor 4:8-10, 16; Heb 12:3

31 But those who trust in the LORD will find new strength.
They will soar high on wings like eagles.
They will run and not grow weary.
They will walk and not faint.

GOD'S HELP FOR ISRAEL

41:1 Hab 2:20; Zech 2:13

41 1 "Listen in silence before Me, you lands beyond the sea.
Bring your strongest arguments.
Come now and speak.
The court is ready for your case.

41:2 2 Chr 36:23; Isa 46:11

2 "Who has stirred up this king from the east,
rightly calling him to God's service?
Who gives this man victory over many nations
and permits him to trample their kings underfoot?
With his sword, he reduces armies to dust.
With his bow, he scatters them like chaff before the wind.
3 He chases them away and goes on safely,
though he is walking over unfamiliar ground.

41:4 Isa 44:7; 48:12; Rev 1:8, 17-18; 22:13

4 Who has done such mighty deeds,
summoning each new generation from the beginning of time?

---

power. Yet what happened to him? On March 5, 1953, he died. What power does he have today? None. He lived for a few short decades and then he was gone. What about any other ruler? The same is true. None of them is able to wield his power for more than a few short years. How accurate the statement that when God blows His breath, "the wind carries them off like chaff." Because God is this powerful, we can trust Him with everything in our lives: the hopes we have, and our future. He is capable of keeping us in His presence forever. What do you find difficult to turn over to God? Memorize this verse to help you keep your confidence in Him. (***See God*> *God's Attributes> Sovereign> The powerful Creator reduces human rulers to nothing,* TopicGuide page A18.)

41:1 As if addressing lawyers in a courtroom, the Lord issued a series of questions to distant nations about His power to save His people. In the upcoming verses, the Lord will present irrefutable evidence before this court of His power and His intention to save His people.

41:2 The king from the east was Cyrus the Great. The Persian king solidified the Persian Empire through a series of sweeping campaigns throughout the Middle East. The Lord claimed Cyrus as His instrument for the execution of His plans.

It is I, the LORD, the First and the Last.
I alone am He."

5 The lands beyond the sea watch in fear.
Remote lands tremble and mobilize for war.
6 The idol makers encourage one another,
saying to each other, "Be strong!"
7 The carver encourages the goldsmith,
and the molder helps at the anvil.
"Good," they say. "It's coming along fine."
Carefully they join the parts together,
then fasten the thing in place so it won't fall over.

8 "But as for you, Israel My servant,
Jacob My chosen one,
descended from Abraham My friend,
9 I have called you back from the ends of the earth,
saying, 'You are My servant.'
For I have chosen you
and will not throw you away.
10 Don't be afraid, for I am with you.
Don't be discouraged, for I am your God.
I will strengthen you and help you.
I will hold you up with My victorious right hand.

11 "See, all your angry enemies lie there,
confused and humiliated.
Anyone who opposes you will die
and come to nothing.
12 You will look in vain
for those who tried to conquer you.
Those who attack you
will come to nothing.
13 For I hold you by your right hand—
I, the LORD your God.
And I say to you,
'Don't be afraid. I am here to help you.
14 Though you are a lowly worm, O Jacob,
don't be afraid, people of Israel, for I will help you.
I am the LORD, your Redeemer.
I am the Holy One of Israel.'
15 You will be a new threshing instrument
with many sharp teeth.
You will tear your enemies apart,
making chaff of mountains.
16 You will toss them into the air,
and the wind will blow them all away;
a whirlwind will scatter them.
Then you will rejoice in the LORD.
You will glory in the Holy One of Israel.

41:5 Josh 5:1; Ezek 26:15-16
41:6 Joel 3:9-11
41:8 Isa 51:2; Jas 2:23
41:9 Deut 7:6; Isa 11:11
41:10 Deut 31:6; Ps 89:13; Rom 8:31
41:11 Isa 29:5, 7-8
41:12 Job 20:7-9
41:13 Isa 45:1
41:14 Isa 43:14
41:15 Mic 4:13
41:16 Isa 35:10

41:7 Isaiah contains several stinging critiques of idolatry. It is the height of foolishness to trust in what human hands have made. These wobbly idols that cannot even stand on their own are a flimsy foundation on which to base one's hopes.

41:17 Isa 30:19; 42:16; 44:3
17 "When the poor and needy search for water and there is none,
and their tongues are parched from thirst,
then I, the LORD, will answer them.
I, the God of Israel, will never abandon them.
41:18 Ps 107:35 Isa 30:25
18 I will open up rivers for them on the high plateaus.
I will give them fountains of water in the valleys.
I will fill the desert with pools of water.
Rivers fed by springs will flow across the parched ground.
41:19 Isa 55:13
19 I will plant trees in the barren desert—
cedar, acacia, myrtle, olive, cypress, fir, and pine.
41:20 Job 12:7-9
20 I am doing this so all who see this miracle
will understand what it means—
that it is the LORD who has done this,
the Holy One of Israel who created it.

21 "Present the case for your idols,"
says the LORD.
"Let them show what they can do,"
says the King of Israel.*
41:22 Isa 43:9; 45:21
22 "Let them try to tell us what happened long ago
so that we may consider the evidence.
Or let them tell us what the future holds,
so we can know what's going to happen.
41:23 Jer 10:5 John 13:19
23 Yes, tell us what will occur in the days ahead.
Then we will know you are gods.
In fact, do anything—good or bad!
Do something that will amaze and frighten us.
41:24 1 Cor 8:4
24 But no! You are less than nothing and can do nothing at all.
Those who choose you pollute themselves.

41:25 Jer 50:3 Mic 7:10
25 "But I have stirred up a leader who will come from the north.
I have called him by name from the east.
I will give him victory over kings and princes.
He will trample them as a potter treads on clay.

41:26 Isa 44:7
26 "Who told you from the beginning
that this would happen?
Who predicted this,
making you admit that he was right?
No one said a word!

41:21 Hebrew *the King of Jacob.* See note on 14:1.

41:17-20 As elsewhere in Scripture, physical thirst becomes a metaphor for spiritual desire (see Psalm 42:1), and abundant water and vegetation are symbols of God's salvation.

41:21-24 Once again, the idols are subject to a scathing attack (see note at 41:7). The Lord challenged the idols to demonstrate their power, or even their mere existence, by making predictive prophecies or performing some mighty deed. The silence of the false gods betrayed their worthlessness.

▶ GOD

41:26 God's way always prevails. Some people see God as always worrying, always wringing His hands over the misbehavior of people on earth. But according to Isaiah, even when His people rebelled, they fulfilled His purpose. God never worries about whether or not His plans will be accomplished—He determines what will happen. He knows exactly what's going to happen and exactly how that will affect us. What does that leave for us? To do exactly what He said—repent, believe the gospel, and walk in the power of His Holy Spirit. (***See God**> God's Attributes> Sovereign> God has dominion over the affairs of people,* TopicGuide page A17.)

27 I was the first to tell Zion,
'Look! Help is on the way!'*
I will send Jerusalem a messenger with good news.
28 Not one of your idols told you this.
Not one gave any answer when I asked.
29 See, they are all foolish, worthless things.
All your idols are as empty as the wind.

41:27 Isa 40:9
41:28 Isa 63:5
41:29 Hab 2:18-19

THE LORD'S CHOSEN SERVANT

42 1 "Look at My Servant, whom I strengthen.
He is My Chosen One, who pleases Me.
I have put My Spirit upon Him.
He will bring justice to the nations.
2 He will not shout
or raise His voice in public.
3 He will not crush the weakest reed
or put out a flickering candle.
He will bring justice to all who have been wronged.
4 He will not falter or lose heart
until justice prevails throughout the earth.
Even distant lands beyond the sea will wait for His instruction.*"

5 God, the LORD, created the heavens and stretched them out.
He created the earth and everything in it.
He gives breath to everyone,
life to everyone who walks the earth.
And it is He who says,
6 "I, the LORD, have called you to demonstrate My righteousness.
I will take you by the hand and guard you,
and I will give you to My people, Israel,
as a symbol of My covenant with them.
And you will be a light to guide the nations.
7 You will open the eyes of the blind.
You will free the captives from prison,
releasing those who sit in dark dungeons.

8 "I am the LORD; that is My name!
I will not give My glory to anyone else,
nor share My praise with carved idols.

42:1-4 *Matt 12:18-21
42:1 Isa 11:2; 53:11 Matt 3:17; 12:18
42:3 Ps 72:2, 4
42:4 Isa 24:15; 66:19
42:5 Job 33:4 Ps 104:2 Isa 45:18 Acts 17:25
42:6 Jer 23:5-6 Luke 2:32
42:7 Isa 35:5; 61:1
42:8 Exod 3:15; 20:3-5

41:27 Or *'Look! They are coming home.'* 42:4 Greek version reads *And His name will be the hope of all the world.* Compare Matt 12:21.

42:1-4 This is the first of four servant songs. See also 49:1-7; 50:4-9; 52:13–53:12.

42:1 There is much debate about the identity of the servant. Elsewhere, the prophet Isaiah, David, and the nation of Israel are called servants of God (Isaiah 20:3; 37:35; 41:8-9). The New Testament identifies Jesus Christ as the Servant (Matthew 12:18-21; Acts 8:32-33).

42:5-7 Through the Lord's power the Servant would establish a new covenant with His people and lead the Gentiles to the truth. Jesus accomplished both of these hopes: He established a new and everlasting covenant through His death and resurrection (Hebrews 8:6-13), and entrance into this covenant was granted to all Gentiles. Blindness and captivity were literal realities for the exiles, and they also served as metaphors describing the spiritual darkness that had descended upon God's people.

▸ PURPOSE

42:5 God our King. Science often seems to give credit to someone other than God for the creation of the universe. Others dismiss God's role in the world by ascribing their blessings to "luck" or crediting their success to their personal efforts. Why do Christians think that way? Because our God is too small. We keep God safely at church, or only in our Bible study, and rarely recognize Him as the all-powerful King of our lives. Give Him the respect, honor, or even applause He is due. With God as your king, you'll see His kingdom in a whole new way. (***See Purpose**> God's Deeds> Special Acts> Creation,* TopicGuide page A52.)

42:9 Isa 48:3, 6
9 Everything I prophesied has come true,
and now I will prophesy again.
I will tell you the future before it happens."

A SONG OF PRAISE TO THE LORD

42:10 Ps 33:3
10 Sing a new song to the LORD!
Sing His praises from the ends of the earth!
Sing, all you who sail the seas,
all you who live in distant coastlands.
11 Join in the chorus, you desert towns;
let the villages of Kedar rejoice!
Let the people of Sela sing for joy;
shout praises from the mountaintops!
12 Let the whole world glorify the LORD;
let it sing His praise.
42:13 Isa 59:17; 66:14-16
13 The LORD will march forth like a mighty hero;
He will come out like a warrior, full of fury.
He will shout His battle cry
and crush all His enemies.

14 He will say, "I have long been silent;
yes, I have restrained Myself.
But now, like a woman in labor,
I will cry and groan and pant.
42:15 Ezek 38:19-20
15 I will level the mountains and hills
and blight all their greenery.
I will turn the rivers into dry land
and will dry up all the pools.
42:16 Ps 94:14 Isa 40:4 Luke 1:78-79 Eph 5:8
16 I will lead blind Israel down a new path,
guiding them along an unfamiliar way.
I will brighten the darkness before them
and smooth out the road ahead of them.
Yes, I will indeed do these things;
I will not forsake them.
42:17 Ps 97:7 Isa 44:9, 11
17 But those who trust in idols,
who say, 'You are our gods,'
will be turned away in shame.

ISRAEL'S FAILURE TO LISTEN AND SEE

42:18 Isa 35:5
18 "Listen, you who are deaf!
Look and see, you blind!
19 Who is as blind as My own people, My servant?
Who is as deaf as My messenger?
Who is as blind as My chosen people,
the servant of the LORD?

42:9 The fulfillment of previous prophecies regarding Damascus, Samaria, and Assyria, among others (chapters 14–23), vindicated the word and power of God. He alone is able to declare in advance what will take place and then make it a reality.

42:10-17 Peoples near and far are exhorted to praise the Lord with something "new." These "new songs" are typically associated with military triumph. See Judges 5 for an example.

42:18-25 The Lord here addressed Israel as His servant. As opposed to the Servant of the opening verses of the chapter, Israel was faithless and stubborn. As a result, the nation found itself in exile. Isaiah counseled Israel to recognize the work of God in their history and return to God in repentance.

20 You see and recognize what is right
but refuse to act on it.
You hear with your ears,
but you don't really listen."

42:20
Jer 6:10

21 Because He is righteous,
the LORD has exalted His glorious law.
22 But His own people have been robbed and plundered,
enslaved, imprisoned, and trapped.
They are fair game for anyone
and have no one to protect them,
no one to take them back home.

42:22
Isa 24:18

23 Who will hear these lessons from the past
and see the ruin that awaits you in the future?
24 Who allowed Israel to be robbed and hurt?
It was the LORD, against whom we sinned,
for the people would not walk in His path,
nor would they obey His law.
25 Therefore, He poured out His fury on them
and destroyed them in battle.
They were enveloped in flames,
but they still refused to understand.
They were consumed by fire,
but they did not learn their lesson.

42:24
Isa 48:18

42:25
Isa 5:25
Hos 7:9

THE SAVIOR OF ISRAEL

43 1 But now, O Jacob, listen to the LORD who created you.
O Israel, the One who formed you says,
"Do not be afraid, for I have ransomed you.
I have called you by name; you are Mine.
2 When you go through deep waters,
I will be with you.
When you go through rivers of difficulty,
you will not drown.
When you walk through the fire of oppression,
you will not be burned up;
the flames will not consume you.
3 For I am the LORD, your God,
the Holy One of Israel, your Savior.
I gave Egypt as a ransom for your freedom;
I gave Ethiopia* and Seba in your place.

43:1
Isa 44:2, 21-24; 45:3-4

43:2
Deut 31:6, 8
Dan 3:25, 27

43:3
Exod 20:2
Isa 43:11

43:3 Hebrew *Cush.*

43:1-4 The tone of the prophecy continued to be kindhearted. In tender, passionate words, the Lord promised to redeem His people. This redemption was not conditioned on any merit on the part of His people; it was entirely a work of grace.

▸ GOD
43:3 God is our Savior. It's an unavoidable fact: God kills people. Every day, some people die, others live, and all of it happens according to God's will. But these deaths are not random or senseless, for even death is an expression of God's love. Isaiah says that His people are singularly precious to Him, more beloved that any other, and His love has consequences. The greatest saving act that God did was to send His Son as a ransom for us, ransoming us from the slavery of sin (1 Timothy 2:5-6; Revelation 5:9). It's not so surprising that God caused the deaths of His enemies so that we could be saved. What is shocking is that God also caused the death of His Son for this same purpose. Trust in God alone to save you from your sins. He has paid the debt you could not afford. (***See God****> God's Names> God> Deliverer/Savior,* TopicGuide page A18.)

43:4 Isa 63:9

[4] Others were given in exchange for you.
I traded their lives for yours
because you are precious to Me.
You are honored, and I love you.

43:5 Isa 49:12 Jer 30:10-11

[5] "Do not be afraid, for I am with you.
I will gather you and your children from east and west.
43:6 Ps 107:3 2 Cor 6:17-18
[6] I will say to the north and south,
'Bring My sons and daughters back to Israel
from the distant corners of the earth.
43:7 Ps 100:3 Isa 46:13 Eph 2:10
[7] Bring all who claim Me as their God,
for I have made them for My glory.
It was I who created them.'"

43:8 Ezek 12:2

[8] Bring out the people who have eyes but are blind,
who have ears but are deaf.
43:9 Isa 41:22, 26
[9] Gather the nations together!
Assemble the peoples of the world!
Which of their idols has ever foretold such things?
Which can predict what will happen tomorrow?
Where are the witnesses of such predictions?
Who can verify that they spoke the truth?

[10] "But you are My witnesses, O Israel!" says the LORD.
"You are My servant.
You have been chosen to know Me, believe in Me,
and understand that I alone am God.
There is no other God—
there never has been, and there never will be.
43:11 Hos 13:4
[11] I, yes I, am the LORD,
and there is no other Savior.
43:12 Ps 81:9
[12] First I predicted your rescue,
then I saved you and proclaimed it to the world.
No foreign god has ever done this.
You are witnesses that I am the only God,"
says the LORD.
43:13 Job 9:12 Ps 90:2
[13] "From eternity to eternity I am God.
No one can snatch anyone out of My hand.
No one can undo what I have done."

THE LORD'S PROMISE OF VICTORY

43:14 Isa 41:14

[14] This is what the LORD says—your Redeemer, the Holy One of Israel:

"For your sakes I will send an army against Babylon,
forcing the Babylonians* to flee in those ships they are so proud of.

43:14 Or *Chaldeans.*

43:5-7 The Lord's regathering of His people who had been dispersed throughout the earth is a part of His original plan to create a people who would glorify Him.

▸ PURPOSE
43:7 For His glory. Why did God create you? Why did He take the time to form you as a unique individual? Isaiah tells us that we were created to give glory to God. We cannot do that unless we submit ourselves to Him and live in His will. The beginning of our act of praise to God is to claim Him as our Lord and Savior. Then, because He created us, we must serve Him. We must be willing to do things His way and to have a heart of love as He does. Are you glorifying God with your life? Is there any area of your life that you have not fully turned over to Him? Fulfill the purpose for which you were created and submit every portion of your life to God. (***See Purpose****> God's Deeds> Special Acts> Creation,* TopicGuide page A52.)

15 I am the LORD, your Holy One,
Israel's Creator and King.
16 I am the LORD, who opened a way through the waters,
making a dry path through the sea.
17 I called forth the mighty army of Egypt
with all its chariots and horses.
I drew them beneath the waves, and they drowned,
their lives snuffed out like a smoldering candlewick.

18 "But forget all that—
it is nothing compared to what I am going to do.
19 For I am about to do something new.
See, I have already begun! Do you not see it?
I will make a pathway through the wilderness.
I will create rivers in the dry wasteland.
20 The wild animals in the fields will thank Me,
the jackals and owls, too,
for giving them water in the desert.
Yes, I will make rivers in the dry wasteland
so My chosen people can be refreshed.
21 I have made Israel for Myself,
and they will someday honor Me before
the whole world.

22 "But, dear family of Jacob, you refuse to ask for My help.
You have grown tired of Me, O Israel!
23 You have not brought Me sheep or goats for burnt offerings.
You have not honored Me with sacrifices,
though I have not burdened and wearied you
with requests for grain offerings and frankincense.
24 You have not brought Me fragrant calamus
or pleased Me with the fat from sacrifices.
Instead, you have burdened Me with your sins
and wearied Me with your faults.

25 "I—yes, I alone—will blot out your sins for My own sake
and will never think of them again.
26 Let us review the situation together,
and you can present your case to prove your innocence.
27 From the very beginning, your first ancestor sinned
against Me;
all your leaders broke My laws.
28 That is why I have disgraced your priests;
I have decreed complete destruction* for Jacob
and shame for Israel.

43:15 Isa 44:6
43:16 Exod 14:21-22 Josh 3:15-16 Ps 77:19
43:17 Ps 76:5-6
43:18 Jer 16:14
43:19 Deut 8:15 2 Cor 5:17 Rev 21:5
43:20 Isa 41:17-18 2 Pet 2:9
43:21 Ps 102:18
43:22 Mic 6:3
43:23 Exod 30:34 Mal 1:6-8
43:24 Jer 6:20 Mal 2:17
43:25 Isa 55:7 Jer 31:34 Ezek 36:22
43:26 Isa 1:18; 43:9
43:28 Lam 2:2, 6 Ezek 5:15

43:28 The Hebrew term used here refers to the complete consecration of things or people to the LORD, either by destroying them or by giving them as an offering.

43:18-21 Having just called His people to remember the greatest act of salvation in their history, the Exodus from Egypt, the Lord here told them to forget it. They were to forget it because what God would now do to rescue His people would make the Exodus pale by comparison! Israel's redemption would be accompanied by a renewal of the whole created order.

43:22-28 Despite the multitude of Israel's sins, the Lord was prepared to forgive and cleanse His people. God's requirements were not unreasonable, yet Israel failed to obey the Lord.

44:1 Jer 30:10

44

[1] "But now, listen to Me, Jacob My servant,
Israel My chosen one.

44:2 Deut 32:15

[2] The LORD who made you and helps you says:
Do not be afraid, O Jacob, My servant,
O dear Israel,* My chosen one.

44:3 Isa 61:9 Joel 2:28

[3] For I will pour out water to quench your thirst
and to irrigate your parched fields.
And I will pour out My Spirit on your descendants,
and My blessing on your children.
[4] They will thrive like watered grass,
like willows on a riverbank.
[5] Some will proudly claim, 'I belong to the LORD.'
Others will say, 'I am a descendant of Jacob.'
Some will write the LORD's name on their hands
and will take the name of Israel as their own."

THE FOOLISHNESS OF IDOLS

44:6 Isa 41:21; 45:5-6, 21 Rev 1:8, 17

[6] This is what the LORD says—Israel's King and Redeemer, the LORD of Heaven's Armies:

"I am the First and the Last;
there is no other God.

44:7 Isa 41:22

[7] Who is like Me?
Let him step forward and prove to you his power.
Let him do as I have done since ancient times
when I established a people and explained its future.

44:8 Deut 4:35, 39 Isa 30:29

[8] Do not tremble; do not be afraid.
Did I not proclaim My purposes for you long ago?
You are My witnesses—is there any other God?
No! There is no other Rock—not one!"

44:9 Ps 97:7

[9] How foolish are those who manufacture idols.
These prized objects are really worthless.
The people who worship idols don't know this,
so they are all put to shame.

44:10 Jer 10:5 Hab 2:18 Acts 19:26

[10] Who but a fool would make his own god—
an idol that cannot help him one bit?
[11] All who worship idols will be disgraced
along with all these craftsmen—mere humans—
who claim they can make a god.

44:2 Hebrew *Jeshurun,* a term of endearment for Israel.

44:1-5 The Lord once more assured His people that He intended to save and restore them. God bound Himself to Israel long ago and He would not abandon them. The abundance of personal pronouns conveyed the intimate nature of God's relationship with His people. In the restoration, God would pour out abundant blessings upon His people, not the least of which would be the gift of His Spirit. Then His people would respond in faith and love; they would readily and proudly identify themselves with the Lord their God.

44:6-20 This passage is an extended critique of idolatry. The principle element of the prophet's condemnation of idolatry is the foolishness of worshiping something people have made with their own hands. Isaiah repeatedly pointed out the absurdity and tragic irony of worshiping material that is otherwise used to make a tool or start a fire, rather than worshiping the God who created human beings.

▸ GOD

44:6 God 2.0. If we could design our own god, it would not be like the God spoken of in the Scriptures. Most would prefer a god that answers every prayer positively, or a god that goes along with our cultural values, or a god that will welcome us to heaven no matter what. God's message to the ancient Israelites who struggled with this was, in essence, "Go ahead! Find a new god! See where it gets you!" It may have chaffed them to hear that this untamable God was their king, but it would be much worse if He were not. Seek to have an accurate view of God from nature and His Word, and get rid of the false ideas about God that clutter and confuse. (***See God****> God's Names> God> King,* TopicGuide page A18.)

They may all stand together,
but they will stand in terror and shame.

12 The blacksmith stands at his forge to make a sharp tool,
pounding and shaping it with all his might.
His work makes him hungry and weak.
It makes him thirsty and faint.
13 Then the wood-carver measures a block of wood
and draws a pattern on it.
He works with chisel and plane
and carves it into a human figure.
He gives it human beauty
and puts it in a little shrine.
14 He cuts down cedars;
he selects the cypress and the oak;
he plants the pine in the forest
to be nourished by the rain.
15 Then he uses part of the wood to make a fire.
With it he warms himself and bakes his bread.
Then—yes, it's true—he takes the rest of it
and makes himself a god to worship!
He makes an idol
and bows down in front of it!
16 He burns part of the tree to roast his meat
and to keep himself warm.
He says, "Ah, that fire feels good."
17 Then he takes what's left
and makes his god: a carved idol!
He falls down in front of it,
worshiping and praying to it.
"Rescue me!" he says.
"You are my god!"

18 Such stupidity and ignorance!
Their eyes are closed, and they cannot see.
Their minds are shut, and they cannot think.
19 The person who made the idol never stops to reflect,
"Why, it's just a block of wood!
I burned half of it for heat
and used it to bake my bread and roast my meat.
How can the rest of it be a god?
Should I bow down to worship a piece of wood?"
20 The poor, deluded fool feeds on ashes.
He trusts something that can't help him at all.

44:12 Isa 40:19; 41:7
44:13 Ps 115:5-7; Isa 41:7
44:15 2 Chr 25:14
44:17 1 Kgs 18:26, 28; Isa 45:20
44:18 Ps 81:12; Isa 6:9-10; 29:10; Jer 10:8, 14
44:19 Deut 27:15
44:20 Ps 102:9; Hos 4:12

44:13 The humanity that was made in God's image now attempts to make God in humanity's image. Idolatry wrongly elevates people to the place of God.

▶ SPIRITUAL WARFARE

44:20 The fool worships idols. In many societies, people worship idols of their own making. In the West, we may think we are beyond such "primitive" and "foolish" actions, yet we also worship gods of our own making. We worship possessions—cars, homes, lake retreats, or art pieces. We worship money—how much we can put in the bank, the size of our investments, or our buying power. Or we worship our work—the title we have, the degrees we have behind our name, or the position we have acquired. All these are idols of our own making. By worshiping them, we are just as foolish as people who worship statues. Examine your life to see if you have any idols—anything that you have made a greater priority than God in your life. (***See Spiritual Warfare*****>** *Originator of Sin> Satan's Strategies> Disguise himself,* TopicGuide page A45.)

Yet he cannot bring himself to ask,
"Is this idol that I'm holding in my hand a lie?"

RESTORATION FOR JERUSALEM

44:21 Isa 44:1-2; 46:8; 49:15

21 "Pay attention, O Jacob,
for you are My servant, O Israel.
I, the LORD, made you,
and I will not forget you.

44:22 Ps 51:1, 9 Isa 55:7 Acts 3:19 1 Pet 1:18-19

22 I have swept away your sins like a cloud.
I have scattered your offenses like the morning mist.
Oh, return to Me,
for I have paid the price to set you free."

44:23 Pss 69:34; 98:7-8

23 Sing, O heavens, for the LORD has done this wondrous thing.
Shout for joy, O depths of the earth!
Break into song,
O mountains and forests and every tree!
For the LORD has redeemed Jacob
and is glorified in Israel.

44:24 Isa 40:22

24 This is what the LORD says—
your Redeemer and Creator:
"I am the LORD, who made all things.
I alone stretched out the heavens.
Who was with Me
when I made the earth?

44:25 1 Cor 1:20, 27

25 I expose the false prophets as liars
and make fools of fortune-tellers.
I cause the wise to give bad advice,
thus proving them to be fools.

44:26 Jer 32:15, 44

26 But I carry out the predictions of My prophets!
By them I say to Jerusalem, 'People will live here again,'
and to the towns of Judah, 'You will be rebuilt;
I will restore all your ruins!'

44:27 Isa 50:2

27 When I speak to the rivers and say, 'Dry up!'
they will be dry.

44:28 2 Chr 36:22-23 Isa 14:32

28 When I say of Cyrus, 'He is My shepherd,'
he will certainly do as I say.
He will command, 'Rebuild Jerusalem';
he will say, 'Restore the Temple.'"

CYRUS, THE LORD'S CHOSEN ONE

45:1 Ps 73:23 Jer 51:11, 20, 24

45 1 This is what the LORD says to Cyrus, His anointed one,
whose right hand He will empower.
Before him, mighty kings will be paralyzed with fear.

44:22 God's grace precedes Israel's response. God's people are free to return to Him because He has already purchased their freedom.

44:28 Following his defeat of Babylon, the Persian ruler Cyrus allowed the Jewish exiles to go free and issued a decree calling for the rebuilding of the Temple in Jerusalem (compare 2 Chronicles 36:22-23 and Ezra 1:1-4). The prophecy is remarkable on two counts: It is unusually precise in calling Cyrus by name and controversial in designating a Gentile king by the royal title "shepherd."

45:1-4 It must have shocked Isaiah's audience to hear a Gentile king referred to as the Lord's "anointed." The title is elsewhere reserved for priests (Leviticus 16:32), kings (1 Samuel 2:10, 35; Psalm 18:50), the Messiah to come from David's line (Psalm 2:2), and all Israel (Habakkuk 3:13). This title does not mean Cyrus was a believer, but Cyrus was an instrument in God's hands through which He brought about the salvation of His people.

Their fortress gates will be opened,
never to shut again.
2 This is what the LORD says:

"I will go before you, Cyrus,
and level the mountains.*
I will smash down gates of bronze
and cut through bars of iron.
3 And I will give you treasures hidden in the darkness—
secret riches.
I will do this so you may know that I am the LORD,
the God of Israel, the One who calls you by name.

4 "And why have I called you for this work?
Why did I call you by name when you did not know Me?
It is for the sake of Jacob My servant,
Israel My chosen one.
5 I am the LORD;
there is no other God.
I have equipped you for battle,
though you don't even know Me,
6 so all the world from east to west
will know there is no other God.
I am the LORD, and there is no other.
7 I create the light and make the darkness.
I send good times and bad times.
I, the LORD, am the One who does these things.

8 "Open up, O heavens,
and pour out your righteousness.
Let the earth open wide
so salvation and righteousness can sprout up together.
I, the LORD, created them.

9 "What sorrow awaits those who argue with their Creator.
Does a clay pot argue with its maker?
Does the clay dispute with the one who shapes it, saying,
'Stop, you're doing it wrong!'
Does the pot exclaim,
'How clumsy can you be?'

45:2 Ps 107:16; Isa 40:4; Jer 51:30
45:3 Isa 49:1
45:4 Isa 43:1; Acts 17:23
45:5 Ps 18:39; Isa 44:8
45:6 Mal 1:11
45:7 Ps 104:20; Amos 3:6
45:8 Pss 72:6; 85:11; Isa 61:11
45:9 Rom 9:20-21

45:2 As in Dead Sea Scrolls and Greek version; Masoretic Text reads *the swellings.*

▸ PURPOSE
45:3 God's power over history. Human history can feel a bit out of control sometimes. People in large, powerful nations with plenty of resources may feel as though things are pretty predictable, but in many places life is much less certain. One big storm, one enraged politician, one errant bullet and the true weakness of humanity is exposed. But even in the midst of crises, we know that God establishes leaders, and God removes them. God uses human choice to fulfill His master plan for the universe. In this case, God used the army of Cyrus to help the nation of Israel. With God, we can be sure that everything we experience is part of His ultimate plan. Imagine how bold you can be in your faith, knowing that God is in control of the results! You can use God's Word without hesitation, knowing it will not fail to impact your life and those around you (Isaiah 55:11). (See Romans 8:28; also ***see Purpose***> *God's Means*> *God's Sovereignty*> *God decrees all,* TopicGuide page A52.)

45:5-8 The Lord emphatically affirmed His role as Creator of all things; He is absolutely sovereign over His creation. He is the source of all blessing and judgment; He brings both prosperity and calamity. The heavens and the earth are at His command, and if He has decreed salvation for His people, it will be so. The recurrent phrase "I am the LORD" or "I, the LORD" uses the divine name revealed to Moses in Exodus 3:14. The name reminded the exiles that the God who set their ancestors free from the power of Egypt was able now to set them free from Babylon.

45:9-13 Anticipating a critical response to His choice of Cyrus, the Lord reminded His people that He was their Creator and reserved the right to deliver them by whatever means He saw fit.

10 How terrible it would be if a newborn baby said to its father,
'Why was I born?'
or if it said to its mother,
'Why did you make me this way?'"

11 This is what the LORD says—
the Holy One of Israel and your Creator:
"Do you question what I do for My children?
Do you give Me orders about the work of My hands?
12 I am the One who made the earth
and created people to live on it.
With My hands I stretched out the heavens.
All the stars are at My command.
13 I will raise up Cyrus to fulfill My righteous purpose,
and I will guide his actions.
He will restore My city and free My captive people—
without seeking a reward!
I, the LORD of Heaven's Armies, have spoken!"

45:12 Neh 9:6; Jer 27:5
45:13 2 Chr 36:22-23; Isa 52:3

FUTURE CONVERSION OF GENTILES

14 This is what the LORD says:

"You will rule the Egyptians,
the Ethiopians,* and the Sabeans.

45:14 Isa 14:1-2; 49:23; 1 Cor 14:25

45:14 Hebrew *Cushites.*

▸ GOD
45:11-13 Cyrus does not rule. Politics, even in democratic nations, seems chaotic. The "good guys" don't always win. And those who do win do not always rule justly. But even this arena is under God's rule. Isaiah knew that Cyrus would be raised up, not by accident nor by his own choice—God would raise him up and use him as He saw fit. This regal Persian emperor, like the earth and the stars, existed and came forth at the command of God alone. If God is that involved in politics, then why shouldn't you follow His lead? Exercise your rights as a citizen and pray that God will use your vote to change His world for the better. (***See God****> God's Attributes> Sovereign> He raises and removes rulers,* TopicGuide page A17.)

45:14 The nations would in time be subject to God's people because they would recognize the presence of God among them. While the final fulfillment of such hope is still to come, we see partial fulfillment in the vast array of peoples that have accepted Christ as their Messiah and worship the God of Israel as their God.

BECAUSE GOD IS
ABSOLUTE TRUTH

I will believe what He says and live accordingly.

I, the LORD, speak only what is true and declare only what is right.

ISAIAH 45:19

FOR THE NEXT *GOD IS ABSOLUTE TRUTH* FEATURE SEE PAGE 1930.

They will come to you with all their merchandise,
and it will all be yours.
They will follow you as prisoners in chains.
They will fall to their knees in front of you and say,
'God is with you, and He is the only God.
There is no other.'"

15 Truly, O God of Israel, our Savior,
You work in mysterious ways.
16 All craftsmen who make idols will be humiliated.
They will all be disgraced together.
17 But the LORD will save the people of Israel
with eternal salvation.
Throughout everlasting ages,
they will never again be humiliated and disgraced.

18 For the LORD is God,
and He created the heavens and earth
and put everything in place.
He made the world to be lived in,
not to be a place of empty chaos.
"I am the LORD," He says,
"and there is no other.
19 I publicly proclaim bold promises.
I do not whisper obscurities in some dark corner.
I would not have told the people of Israel* to seek Me
if I could not be found.
I, the LORD, speak only what is true
and declare only what is right.

20 "Gather together and come,
you fugitives from surrounding nations.
What fools they are who carry around their wooden idols
and pray to gods that cannot save!
21 Consult together, argue your case.
Get together and decide what to say.
Who made these things known so long ago?
What idol ever told you they would happen?
Was it not I, the LORD?
For there is no other God but Me,
a righteous God and Savior.
There is none but Me.
22 Let all the world look to Me for salvation!
For I am God; there is no other.

45:16 Isa 44:11
45:17 Isa 51:6; Rom 11:26
45:18 Gen 1:2, 26; Ps 115:16; Isa 42:5
45:19 2 Chr 15:2; Isa 43:12; Jer 29:13-14
45:20 Isa 44:18-19; 46:6-7; Jer 10:5
45:21 Isa 43:3, 11; 44:7; Mark 12:32
45:22 Num 21:8-9; Isa 52:10; Mic 7:7

45:19 Hebrew *of Jacob.* See note on 14:1.

45:18-23 Isaiah revisited two recurring themes in this passage: God's power as Creator and His superiority to the idols of the nations. The exiles doubted God's promises of restoration made through the prophet Isaiah, so he repeated this subject matter.

▶ PURPOSE
45:18 A world of beauty. What if one morning the sun failed to come up? Or the rains ceased to fall? Even in a world cursed by sin, we see a world of beauty and order. We don't have to strive to make the sun appear each day or struggle to make it rain. This is because, in the beginning, God didn't create a chaotic, disordered world (Genesis 1:31). Even sin can't take away the imprint of His truth, goodness, and beauty in the universe. Thank God for the natural beauty He has created. Do whatever you can to make God's world more beautiful, orderly, and just. Look forward to the day when all of creation will be restored to its original perfection (Romans 8:22). (***See Purpose***> *God's Purpose*> *The heavens tell of His greatness,* TopicGuide page A52.)

45:23 *Rom 14:11 Phil 2:10-11 23 I have sworn by My own name;
I have spoken the truth,
and I will never go back on My word:
Every knee will bend to Me,
and every tongue will confess allegiance to Me.*"
24 The people will declare,
"The LORD is the source of all my righteousness and strength."
And all who were angry with Him
will come to Him and be ashamed.
45:25 Isa 53:11 25 In the LORD all the generations of Israel will be justified,
and in Him they will boast.

BABYLON'S FALSE GODS

46:1 Isa 21:9 Jer 50:2; 51:44 **46** 1 Bel and Nebo, the gods of Babylon,
bow as they are lowered to the ground.
They are being hauled away on ox carts.
The poor beasts stagger under the weight.
46:2 Jer 43:12-13 2 Both the idols and their owners are bowed down.
The gods cannot protect the people,
and the people cannot protect the gods.
They go off into captivity together.

46:3 Isa 10:21-22 3 "Listen to Me, descendants of Jacob,
all you who remain in Israel.
I have cared for you since you were born.
Yes, I carried you before you were born.
46:4 Ps 71:18 4 I will be your God throughout your lifetime—
until your hair is white with age.
I made you, and I will care for you.
I will carry you along and save you.

46:5 Isa 40:18, 25 5 "To whom will you compare Me?
Who is My equal?
46:6 Isa 44:12-17 6 Some people pour out their silver and gold
and hire a craftsman to make a god from it.
Then they bow down and worship it!
46:7 Isa 40:20 Jer 10:5 7 They carry it around on their shoulders,
and when they set it down, it stays there.
It can't even move!
And when someone prays to it, there is no answer.
It can't rescue anyone from trouble.

8 "Do not forget this! Keep it in mind!
Remember this, you guilty ones.

45:23 Hebrew *will confess;* Greek version reads *will confess and give praise to God.* Compare Rom 14:11.

46:1-2 Bel is a word meaning "lord" in reference to Marduk the chief god of Babylon. Nebo was the son of Marduk.

▶ GOD

46:5 God is greater than all. Many people learn to distrust authority. But John the Baptist said of Jesus, "He has come from above and is greater than anyone else. We are of the earth, and we speak of earthly things, but he has come from heaven and is greater than anyone else" (John 3:31). Humbly acknowledging God's sovereignty changes our perspective. Slowly but surely, we can learn to trust authority, because God is in charge. We can bravely obey, knowing that God is able to sustain and protect us in every circumstance. In the same way, do not misuse the power and influence God has given you, but help others around you to trust and appreciate authority. (***See God> God's Nature> Personality> Will> He accomplishes His purposes and good pleasure,*** TopicGuide page A14.)

46:8-13 Here the Lord made striking claims of sovereignty over human history, and it is this trait that distinguishes Him from the false gods.

9 Remember the things I have done in the past.
For I alone am God!
I am God, and there is none like Me.
10 Only I can tell you the future
before it even happens.
Everything I plan will come to pass,
for I do whatever I wish.
11 I will call a swift bird of prey from the east—
a leader from a distant land to come and do My bidding.
I have said what I would do,
and I will do it.

12 "Listen to Me, you stubborn people
who are so far from doing right.
13 For I am ready to set things right,
not in the distant future, but right now!
I am ready to save Jerusalem*
and show My glory to Israel.

46:10 Isa 41:26-27; 42:9 Acts 5:39

46:11 Num 23:19

46:12 Zech 7:11-12

46:13 Isa 51:5; 61:3

PREDICTION OF BABYLON'S FALL

47 1 "Come down, virgin daughter of Babylon, and sit in the dust.
For your days of sitting on a throne have ended.
O daughter of Babylonia,* never again will you be
the lovely princess, tender and delicate.
2 Take heavy millstones and grind flour.
Remove your veil, and strip off your robe.
Expose yourself to public view.
3 You will be naked and burdened with shame.
I will take vengeance against you without pity."

4 Our Redeemer, whose name is the LORD of Heaven's Armies,
is the Holy One of Israel.

5 "O beautiful Babylon, sit now in darkness and silence.
Never again will you be known as the queen of kingdoms.
6 For I was angry with My chosen people
and punished them by letting them fall into your hands.
But you, Babylon, showed them no mercy.
You oppressed even the elderly.
7 You said, 'I will reign forever as queen of the world!'
You did not reflect on your actions
or think about their consequences.

8 "Listen to this, you pleasure-loving kingdom,
living at ease and feeling secure.

47:1 Jer 48:18

47:2 Gen 24:65 1 Cor 11:5

47:3 Isa 63:4

47:5 Lam 2:10 Dan 2:37

47:6 Deut 28:50 Zech 1:15

47:7 Rev 18:7

47:8 Isa 22:13; 32:9, 11 Rev 18:7

46:13 Hebrew *Zion.* 47:1 Or *Chaldea;* also in 47:5.

46:11 The bird of prey from the east is Cyrus, who has already been mentioned by name (see 44:28).

47:1-3 The city of Babylon is personified as a young woman of great wealth and prestige. The great woman, however, would be humbled. These verses assume the tone of mourning, but only sarcastically; they are a taunt.

47:4-7 Although the Babylonians served God's purposes in judging His own people, they were nonetheless held responsible for her cruelty and arrogance. God is free to use people's sin to accomplish His purposes, but this never absolves people from their responsibility for acts they committed under no compulsion (compare Genesis 50:20 and Acts 4:23-28).

47:8-11 Babylon embodied the presumptuous self-reliance that is at the heart of human sinfulness. It is easy to see why Babylon came to be a symbol for sinful humanity in its opposition to God.

You say, 'I am the only one, and there is no other.
  I will never be a widow or lose my children.'

47:9 Isa 13:16; 1 Thes 5:2-3; Rev 18:8, 10, 23

9 Well, both these things will come upon you in a moment:
  widowhood and the loss of your children.
Yes, these calamities will come upon you,
  despite all your witchcraft and magic.

47:10 Ps 52:7; Isa 5:21; Ezek 8:12

10 "You felt secure in your wickedness.
  'No one sees me,' you said.
But your 'wisdom' and 'knowledge' have led you astray,
  and you said, 'I am the only one, and there is no other.'

47:11 Jer 51:8, 43

11 So disaster will overtake you,
  and you won't be able to charm it away.
Calamity will fall upon you,
  and you won't be able to buy your way out.
A catastrophe will strike you suddenly,
  one for which you are not prepared.

12 "Now use your magical charms!
  Use the spells you have worked at all these years!
Maybe they will do you some good.
  Maybe they can make someone afraid of you.

47:13 Isa 8:19

13 All the advice you receive has made you tired.
  Where are all your astrologers,
those stargazers who make predictions each month?
  Let them stand up and save you from what the future holds.

47:14 Jer 51:30, 32, 58; Nah 1:10

14 But they are like straw burning in a fire;
  they cannot save themselves from the flame.
You will get no help from them at all;
  their hearth is no place to sit for warmth.

47:15 Rev 18:11

15 And all your friends,
  those with whom you've done business since childhood,
will go their own ways,
  turning a deaf ear to your cries.

GOD'S STUBBORN PEOPLE

48:1 Isa 45:23

48 1 "Listen to Me, O family of Jacob,
  you who are called by the name of Israel
  and born into the family of Judah.
Listen, you who take oaths in the name of the LORD
  and call on the God of Israel.
You don't keep your promises,

▸ GOD

47:8 When luck runs out. We are generally unprepared for the tragedies of life. We don't know enough to foresee the disasters—large and small—that await us all. Isaiah told his people to expect political crisis and invasion, but their response was to find something other than God to deal with their anxiousness. They turned to pure fantasy to comfort them—luck and superstition. But this only made things worse. Not only did they seek their security in the unreal, but they also turned further away from God and His offer of grace. When the bottom falls out of your life, there is nothing left to do but look up—to God and His offer of grace. (***See God**> God's Nature> Personality> Will> No one obstructs God or can question His actions,* TopicGuide page A15.)

47:10 Babylon's wisdom and knowledge were intimately connected to the practices of divination and astrology.

47:12-14 Daniel 2 recounts a story that demonstrates the worthlessness of the professional diviners and astrologers in ancient Babylon.

48:1 In another courtroom scene (see Isaiah 1–5 for an extended example), Isaiah quickly identifies the crime, (48:1-2, 8), the criminals (48:1, 12), the injured party (48:1-2, 17), and the deserved sentence (48:9). Isaiah 48:12-22 details the sentence that most honors God (48:11).

2 even though you call yourself the holy city
and talk about depending on the God of Israel,
whose name is the LORD of Heaven's Armies.
3 Long ago I told you what was going to happen.
Then suddenly I took action,
and all My predictions came true.
4 For I know how stubborn and obstinate you are.
Your necks are as unbending as iron.
Your heads are as hard as bronze.
5 That is why I told you what would happen;
I told you beforehand what I was going to do.
Then you could never say, 'My idols did it.
My wooden image and metal god commanded it to happen!'
6 You have heard My predictions and seen them fulfilled,
but you refuse to admit it.
Now I will tell you new things,
secrets you have not yet heard.
7 They are brand new, not things from the past.
So you cannot say, 'We knew that all the time!'

8 "Yes, I will tell you of things that are entirely new,
things you never heard of before.
For I know so well what traitors you are.
You have been rebels from birth.
9 Yet for My own sake and for the honor of My name,
I will hold back My anger and not wipe you out.
10 I have refined you, but not as silver is refined.
Rather, I have refined you in the furnace of suffering.
11 I will rescue you for My sake—
yes, for My own sake!
I will not let My reputation be tarnished,
and I will not share My glory with idols!

FREEDOM FROM BABYLON

12 "Listen to Me, O family of Jacob,
Israel My chosen one!
I alone am God,
the First and the Last.
13 It was My hand that laid the foundations of the earth,
My right hand that spread out the heavens above.
When I call out the stars,
they all appear in order."

14 Have any of your idols ever told you this?
Come, all of you, and listen:
The LORD has chosen Cyrus as His ally.
He will use him to put an end to the empire of Babylon
and to destroy the Babylonian* armies.

15 "I have said it: I am calling Cyrus!
I will send him on this errand and will help him succeed.
16 Come closer, and listen to this.
From the beginning I have told you plainly what would happen."

48:2 Rom 2:17
48:3 Josh 21:45; Isa 42:9
48:4 Ezek 2:4
48:5 Jer 44:15-18
48:6 Isa 43:19
48:8 Deut 9:7, 24; Ps 58:3
48:9 Ps 103:8-10
48:10 1 Kgs 8:51; Ezek 22:18-22
48:11 Deut 32:26-27; Ps 106:8; Isa 42:8
48:12 Deut 32:39; Rev 1:17
48:13 Ps 102:25
48:14 Jer 50:21-29
48:15 Isa 41:2; 45:1-2
48:16 Isa 45:19

48:14 Or *Chaldean.*

And now the Sovereign LORD and His Spirit
have sent me with this message.

48:17 Ps 32:8 Isa 41:14

17 This is what the LORD says—
your Redeemer, the Holy One of Israel:
"I am the LORD your God,
who teaches you what is good for you
and leads you along the paths you should follow.

48:18 Deut 5:29; 32:29 Ps 119:165 Amos 5:24

18 Oh, that you had listened to My commands!
Then you would have had peace flowing like a gentle river
and righteousness rolling over you like waves in the sea.

48:19 Gen 22:17

19 Your descendants would have been like the sands along the seashore—
too many to count!
There would have been no need for your destruction,
or for cutting off your family name."

48:20 Isa 52:9 Jer 31:10-11

20 Yet even now, be free from your captivity!
Leave Babylon and the Babylonians.*
Sing out this message!
Shout it to the ends of the earth!
The LORD has redeemed His servants,
the people of Israel.*

48:21 Ps 78:15-16

21 They were not thirsty
when He led them through the desert.
He divided the rock,
and water gushed out for them to drink.
22 "But there is no peace for the wicked,"
says the LORD.

THE LORD'S SERVANT COMMISSIONED

49 1 Listen to me, all you in distant lands!
Pay attention, you who are far away!
The LORD called me before my birth;
from within the womb He called me by name.

49:2 Isa 51:16 Heb 4:12 Rev 1:16

2 He made my words of judgment as sharp as a sword.
He has hidden me in the shadow of His hand.
I am like a sharp arrow in His quiver.

48:20a Or *the Chaldeans.* 48:20b Hebrew *His servant, Jacob.* See note on 14:1.

48:18-19 Judah's violation of the terms of their covenant resulted in the promises of the Abrahamic covenant (Genesis 12:1-3; 15:5-6) being applied to a later generation. Today the increase of Abraham's descendants occurs primarily through the church spreading the gospel to every nation (Matthew 28:18-20).

48:20 God's rescue of His people would result in God's glory extended among the nations (Psalm 67).

▸ ADOPTION
48:22 No peace for the wicked. Have you ever ignored God's will for your life, closing your ears to His Word? The shocking truth behind this verse in Isaiah is that it was written to disobedient believers, not unbelievers. Isaiah said that God had been very clear with His people under the Old Covenant: If they listen to Him, they would live (Deuteronomy 28:1-14); if they ignored Him, they would perish (Deuteronomy 28:15-68). Similarly, under the New Covenant, God promises to convict us of our sin with His Spirit (John 16:8) and to discipline those who continue to ignore His voice (Hebrews 12:1-11). Do you lack peace? Take a moral survey of your life and repent of every sin you can find. Those who submit to the Prince of Peace will enjoy a peace the world may never know (John 14:27). (***See Adoption****> With Christ> Supernatural> A life of everlasting peace,* TopicGuide page A37.)

49:1-4 Once again we read a song about the Servant of the Lord (see notes at 42:1-4 and 42:1). Even before the Servant was born, the Lord called him to be His voice among the people. The Servant, however, here expressed frustration at the apparent futility of His work. Yet the Servant did not despair; instead He trusted God to accomplish His purpose. Christ, who ultimately embodied the Servant passages, proclaimed God's message among His people, but He was rejected by the very people He came to save.

3 He said to me, "You are My servant, Israel,
and you will bring Me glory."

4 I replied, "But my work seems so useless!
I have spent my strength for nothing and to no purpose.
Yet I leave it all in the LORD's hand;
I will trust God for my reward."

5 And now the LORD speaks— 49:5 Isa 12:2
the One who formed me in my mother's womb to be His servant,
who commissioned me to bring Israel back to Him.
The LORD has honored me,
and my God has given me strength.
6 He says, "You will do more than restore the people of Israel to Me. 49:6 Ps 37:28 Acts 13:47; 26:23
I will make you a light to the Gentiles,
and you will bring My salvation to the ends of the earth."

7 The LORD, the Redeemer 49:7 Ps 22:6-8 Isa 53:3
and Holy One of Israel,
says to the one who is despised and rejected by the nations,
to the one who is the servant of rulers:
"Kings will stand at attention when you pass by.
Princes will also bow low
because of the LORD, the faithful One,
the Holy One of Israel, who has chosen you."

PROMISES OF ISRAEL'S RESTORATION

8 This is what the LORD says: 49:8 Ps 69:13 Isa 44:26 2 Cor 6:2

"At just the right time, I will respond to you.*
On the day of salvation I will help you.
I will protect you and give you to the people
as My covenant with them.
Through you I will reestablish the land of Israel
and assign it to its own people again.
9 I will say to the prisoners, 'Come out in freedom,' 49:9 Isa 42:7 Luke 4:18
and to those in darkness, 'Come into the light.'
They will be My sheep, grazing in green pastures
and on hills that were previously bare.
10 They will neither hunger nor thirst. 49:10 Ps 23:2 Rev 7:16
The searing sun will not reach them anymore.
For the LORD in His mercy will lead them;
He will lead them beside cool waters.

49:8 Greek version reads *I heard you.* Compare 2 Cor 6:2.

49:6 The work of the Servant would not only restore Israel's relationship to their God, He would also draw Gentiles to the Lord. The truth of God would be spread throughout the earth as was intended from the beginning (Genesis 12:3; 22:18). The death and resurrection of Christ inaugurated the fulfillment of these hopes, which continues today through the evangelistic work of the church.

▸ ADOPTION

49:10 Our blessed future. Most children have all sorts of dreams about what they will do when they grow up. But at some point, many people become jaded by life's difficulties and stop dreaming big. Survival becomes the only goal. But God's people need to keep the larger perspective in view: One day we will enjoy the riches of heaven. We will live in God's presence, and He will provide for all our needs. What a blessed future that will be! Daily life can leave us hurting and sad, but set your mind on your blessed future. Rest in the unchanging promises of God, not the ever-changing circumstances of life. (***See Adoption> In Heaven> No hunger, thirst, or scorching heat,*** **TopicGuide page A38.**)

49:11 Isa 40:4 — 11 And I will make My mountains into level paths for them.
The highways will be raised above the valleys.
49:12 Isa 43:5-6 — 12 See, My people will return from far away,
from lands to the north and west,
and from as far south as Egypt.*"

49:13 Isa 54:1, 7-8, 10; Rev 12:12 — 13 Sing for joy, O heavens!
Rejoice, O earth!
Burst into song, O mountains!
For the LORD has comforted His people
and will have compassion on them in their suffering.

14 Yet Jerusalem* says, "The LORD has deserted us;
the Lord has forgotten us."

15 "Never! Can a mother forget her nursing child?
Can she feel no love for the child she has borne?
But even if that were possible,
I would not forget you!
49:16 Song 8:6; Isa 62:6 — 16 See, I have written your name on the palms of My hands.
Always in My mind is a picture of Jerusalem's walls in ruins.
17 Soon your descendants will come back,
and all who are trying to destroy you will go away.
49:18 Isa 45:23 — 18 Look around you and see,
for all your children will come back to you.
As surely as I live," says the LORD,
"they will be like jewels or bridal ornaments for you to display.

49:19 Isa 1:7; Zech 10:10 — 19 "Even the most desolate parts of your abandoned land
will soon be crowded with your people.
Your enemies who enslaved you
will be far away.
49:20 Isa 54:1-3 — 20 The generations born in exile will return and say,
'We need more room! It's crowded here!'
49:21 Lam 1:1 — 21 Then you will think to yourself,
'Who has given me all these descendants?
For most of my children were killed,
and the rest were carried away into exile.

49:12 As in Dead Sea Scrolls, which read *from the region of Aswan*, which is in southern Egypt. Masoretic Text reads *from the region of Sinim*. 49:14 Hebrew *Zion*.

49:14–50:3 The prophet anticipated that God's people in exile would respond to his message with skepticism and disbelief. In this passage he encouraged them by telling them that God had not abandoned them and that He would be true to His promises of salvation.

49:15-18 The Lord likened Himself to a loving mother who would never abandon her children. He ensured His people that they were constantly on His mind and heart. He would never forget them, and soon they would be set free to return home.

▶ ADOPTION
49:15 A God like a mother. In ancient Israel, everyone understood that sin doesn't change a mother's love for her child. And God swears that, like a mother never forgets her child, He will never forget us. No matter what a child may do, a mother will still cherish fond memories of how she held her child as a baby, how he smiled at her, and how she nursed him—and all is well. Even if it seems as if God does not hear your prayers, He is still there. Don't lose confidence in the fact that you are infinitely loved and cared for by God, who loves even His wayward children. (***See Adoption****> With Christ> United with Christ> Loved by God,* TopicGuide page A37.)

49:19-21 The Lord would not only return His people to their land, He would restore them in abundance. Their numbers would swell beyond the capacity of the land. While this did not happen when the first waves of exiles returned to the land, the spread of the gospel and growth of the church that was founded on the work of the Servant, Jesus Christ, exceeded all such expectations.

I was left here all alone.
Where did all these people come from?
Who bore these children?
Who raised them for me?'"

22 This is what the Sovereign LORD says:
"See, I will give a signal to the godless nations.
They will carry your little sons back to you in their arms;
they will bring your daughters on their shoulders.
23 Kings and queens will serve you
and care for all your needs.
They will bow to the earth before you
and lick the dust from your feet.
Then you will know that I am the LORD.
Those who trust in Me will never be put to shame."
24 Who can snatch the plunder of war from the hands of a warrior?
Who can demand that a tyrant* let his captives go?
25 But the LORD says,
"The captives of warriors will be released,
and the plunder of tyrants will be retrieved.
For I will fight those who fight you,
and I will save your children.
26 I will feed your enemies with their own flesh.
They will be drunk with rivers of their own blood.
All the world will know that I, the LORD,
am your Savior and your Redeemer,
the Mighty One of Israel.*"

49:22 Isa 11:10, 12; 14:2
49:23 Pss 25:3; 72:9 Isa 60:14, 16
49:25 Jer 50:33-34
49:26 Isa 14:4 Ezek 39:7

50 This is what the LORD says:

"Was your mother sent away because I divorced her?
Did I sell you as slaves to My creditors?
No, you were sold because of your sins.
And your mother, too, was taken because of your sins.
2 Why was no one there when I came?
Why didn't anyone answer when I called?
Is it because I have no power to rescue?
No, that is not the reason!
For I can speak to the sea and make it dry up!
I can turn rivers into deserts covered with dying fish.
3 I dress the skies in darkness,
covering them with clothes of mourning."

50:1 Deut 32:30 Isa 59:2 Jer 3:8
50:2 Gen 18:14 Exod 14:21 Josh 3:16
50:3 Rev 6:12

THE LORD'S OBEDIENT SERVANT

4 The Sovereign LORD has given me His words of wisdom,
so that I know how to comfort the weary.

50:4 Ps 5:3 Jer 31:25

49:24 As in Dead Sea Scrolls, Syriac version, and Latin Vulgate (also see 49:25); Masoretic Text reads *a righteous person.*
49:26 Hebrew *of Jacob.* See note on 14:1.

50:1-3 To be sold or divorced suggested a permanent rupture in God's relationship with Israel, who is envisioned as a slave and a wife. But God had done neither. Israel had been sent away because of her sin, but the rupture was temporary—God would redeem her.

50:4-11 In this third servant song, the Servant proclaimed His trust in God (see notes at 42:1-4 and 42:1). The Servant's mission would be difficult and discouraging. He would meet with bitter and violent opposition. Through it all, the Servant would rely on the Lord and find strength in Him. The Servant confided in God and relied upon His power to accomplish His purposes and vindicate His people.

Morning by morning He wakens me
and opens my understanding to His will.

50:5 Matt 26:39; John 8:29; 14:31; 15:10; Acts 26:19; Heb 5:8

5 The Sovereign LORD has spoken to me,
and I have listened.
I have not rebelled or turned away.
6 I offered my back to those who beat me
and my cheeks to those who pulled out my beard.

50:6 Matt 26:67; Mark 15:19; Luke 22:63

I did not hide my face
from mockery and spitting.

50:7 Ezek 3:8-9

7 Because the Sovereign LORD helps me,
I will not be disgraced.
Therefore, I have set my face like a stone,
determined to do His will.
And I know that I will not be put to shame.

50:8 Rom 8:33-34

8 He who gives me justice is near.
Who will dare to bring charges against me now?
Where are my accusers?
Let them appear!

50:9 Isa 54:17

9 See, the Sovereign LORD is on my side!
Who will declare me guilty?
All my enemies will be destroyed
like old clothes that have been eaten by moths!

50:10 Eph 5:8

10 Who among you fears the LORD
and obeys His servant?
If you are walking in darkness,
without a ray of light,
trust in the LORD
and rely on your God.

50:11 Isa 65:13-15

11 But watch out, you who live in your own light
and warm yourselves by your own fires.
This is the reward you will receive from Me:
You will soon fall down in great torment.

A CALL TO TRUST THE LORD

51:1 Gen 17:15-17

51 1 "Listen to Me, all who hope for deliverance—
all who seek the LORD!
Consider the rock from which you were cut,
the quarry from which you were mined.

51:2 Gen 12:1; Heb 11:11

2 Yes, think about Abraham, your ancestor,
and Sarah, who gave birth to your nation.

▸ WORSHIP

50:4 Listening to God. Each morning, Isaiah awoke with the desire to listen to what God had to say to him. What would our lives be like if we opened our eyes each morning desiring to listen to God and to obey His will? Plan to spend your first moments of the day with God. Begin a daily devotional plan tomorrow morning—not mechanically—but simply as a commitment to spend intimate time with God, just as you do with all those you love. (***See Worship****> OT> God's Supremacy> Required obedience in daily life and affairs,* TopicGuide page A26.)

50:6-7 These words are striking in their anticipation of the suffering Jesus would endure during His crucifixion (compare Matthew 27:26; Luke 9:51; John 19:1).

▸ HOLINESS

50:7 Telling the hard truth. It's not easy telling the truth. Isaiah's message was not well received by the people he served. Yet he continued speaking God's message, day in and day out. Why didn't he simply move or change his message? Why didn't he quit the ministry? Because he knew that God had called him to speak His words to these people. It was this conviction that rooted him to his unpopular message and his unfaithful flock. You may find God's message difficult at times—hard to say and hard to hear. Accept and honor God's Word by telling it and listening to it. (***See Holiness****> Disciplines> Of Engagement> Call to study,* TopicGuide page A42.)

Abraham was only one man when I called him.
But when I blessed him, he became a great nation."

3 The LORD will comfort Israel* again
and have pity on her ruins.
Her desert will blossom like Eden,
her barren wilderness like the garden of the LORD.
Joy and gladness will be found there.
Songs of thanksgiving will fill the air.

51:3
Gen 2:8
Isa 41:19

4 "Listen to Me, My people.
Hear Me, Israel,
for My law will be proclaimed,
and My justice will become a light to the nations.
5 My mercy and justice are coming soon.
My salvation is on the way.
My strong arm will bring justice to the nations.
All distant lands will look to Me
and wait in hope for My powerful arm.
6 Look up to the skies above,
and gaze down on the earth below.
For the skies will disappear like smoke,
and the earth will wear out like a piece of clothing.
The people of the earth will die like flies,
but My salvation lasts forever.
My righteous rule will never end!

51:4
Ps 78:1
Isa 42:4

51:5
Isa 46:13

51:6
Ps 102:25-26
Matt 24:35
2 Pet 3:10

7 "Listen to Me, you who know right from wrong,
you who cherish My law in your hearts.
Do not be afraid of people's scorn,
nor fear their insults.
8 For the moth will devour them as it devours clothing.
The worm will eat at them as it eats wool.
But My righteousness will last forever.
My salvation will continue from generation
to generation."

51:7
Ps 37:30-31
Matt 5:11
Acts 5:40-41

51:8
Isa 14:11

51:3 Hebrew *Zion;* also in 51:16.

51:3 Eden symbolized the fullness of God's blessing. Before humanity's rebellion, the Garden was a place of peace and abundance; God, humanity, and creation existed in perfect harmony. The hope of restoration envisioned the renewal of creation and the regaining of paradise lost. Not surprisingly, images of Eden reappear in John's depiction of heaven (Revelation 22:1-5).

▶ HOLINESS
51:4 Lawful world. Most of us value freedom more than law. We chafe under the rules we must follow in order to keep our jobs or to drive our vehicles safely—we don't even like to follow doctor's orders. Yet in God's kingdom, living under Christ's rule (and Christ's rules) is the means to experiencing freedom from debilitating sin (Romans 6:22). Instead of making excuses, use the Bible as your standard of behavior. When you read a commandment from God, don't see it as restrictive, but as a guide to loosing sin's chains. The freedom that comes from obedience to God's law is for the whole world to enjoy—tell them and show them the freedom Christ brings. (***See Holiness****> Law and Grace> Law> A window to view the world,* TopicGuide page A42.)

▶ GOD
51:7 Cherish God's law. How do we cherish God's law, especially since His law seems so hard to follow? First, we must love the One who gave the law because only then can we cherish what He has commanded. Ask God to give you a deeper trust and love for Him. Next, we must acknowledge that we cannot follow God's law by our own strength because we are sinful people. Ask for God's help through the power of His Holy Spirit to obey God's law. Then we can love God's law and begin to obey it. As we see how living up to God's standards enriches our lives, we will cherish His law even more and gain more motivation to repent and obey. (***See God****> God's Nature> Unique> He is the final lawgiver and judge,* TopicGuide page A15.)

51:9 Deut 4:34

9 Wake up, wake up, O LORD! Clothe Yourself with strength!
Flex Your mighty right arm!
Rouse Yourself as in the days of old
when You slew Egypt, the dragon of the Nile.*

51:10 Exod 14:21-22 Isa 63:11-12

10 Are You not the same today,
the One who dried up the sea,
making a path of escape through the depths
so that Your people could cross over?

51:11 Isa 61:7 Rev 7:17; 21:4; 22:3

11 Those who have been ransomed by the LORD will return.
They will enter Jerusalem* singing,
crowned with everlasting joy.
Sorrow and mourning will disappear,
and they will be filled with joy and gladness.

51:12 Ps 118:6 1 Pet 1:24

12 "I, yes I, am the One who comforts you.
So why are you afraid of mere humans,
who wither like the grass and disappear?

51:13 Deut 8:11 Job 9:8

13 Yet you have forgotten the LORD, your Creator,
the One who stretched out the sky like a canopy
and laid the foundations of the earth.
Will you remain in constant dread of human oppressors?
Will you continue to fear the anger of your enemies?
Where is their fury and anger now?
It is gone!

51:14 Isa 49:10

14 Soon all you captives will be released!
Imprisonment, starvation, and death will not be your fate!

51:15 Ps 107:25

15 For I am the LORD your God,
who stirs up the sea, causing its waves to roar.
My name is the LORD of Heaven's Armies.

51:16 Exod 33:22 Deut 18:18

16 And I have put My words in your mouth
and hidden you safely in My hand.
I stretched out* the sky like a canopy
and laid the foundations of the earth.
I am the One who says to Israel,
'You are My people!'"

51:17 Jer 25:15

17 Wake up, wake up, O Jerusalem!
You have drunk the cup of the LORD's fury.
You have drunk the cup of terror,
tipping out its last drops.

51:18 Ps 142:4

18 Not one of your children is left alive
to take your hand and guide you.
19 These two calamities have fallen on you:
desolation and destruction, famine and war.

51:9 Hebrew *You slew Rahab; You pierced the dragon.* Rahab is the name of a mythical sea monster that represents chaos in ancient literature. The name is used here as a poetic name for Egypt. 51:11 Hebrew *Zion.* 51:16 As in Syriac version (see also 51:13); Hebrew reads *planted.*

51:9-10 The prophet invoked the image of God as the Divine Warrior who fights for His people. The tradition arose from the Lord's victory over Egypt at the time of the Exodus (Exodus 15:3).

51:15 In the ancient world, the seas embodied the forces of evil and chaos, so God's control over the seas particularly expressed His power.

51:17 The cup is a frequent image of God's wrath (for example, Jeremiah 25:15-31; Ezekiel 23:31-34; Zechariah 12:2). The city of Jerusalem represented both those living in it and the exiles who looked to the city as their spiritual home.

And who is left to sympathize with you?
Who is left to comfort you?*
20 For your children have fainted and lie in the streets,
helpless as antelopes caught in a net.
The LORD has poured out His fury;
God has rebuked them.

21 But now listen to this, you afflicted ones
who sit in a drunken stupor,
though not from drinking wine.
22 This is what the Sovereign LORD,
your God and Defender, says:
"See, I have taken the terrible cup from your hands.
You will drink no more of My fury.
23 Instead, I will hand that cup to your tormentors,
those who said, 'We will trample you into the dust
and walk on your backs.'"

51:20 Isa 66:15; Jer 14:16
51:21 Isa 29:9
51:22 Jer 50:34
51:23 Jer 25:15-17, 26, 28

DELIVERANCE FOR JERUSALEM

52 1 Wake up, wake up, O Zion!
Clothe yourself with strength.
Put on your beautiful clothes, O holy city of Jerusalem,
for unclean and godless people will enter your gates no longer.
2 Rise from the dust, O Jerusalem.
Sit in a place of honor.
Remove the chains of slavery from your neck,
O captive daughter of Zion.
3 For this is what the LORD says:
"When I sold you into exile,
I received no payment.
Now I can redeem you
without having to pay for you."

4 This is what the Sovereign LORD says: "Long ago My people chose to live in Egypt. Now
they are oppressed by Assyria. 5 What is this?" asks the LORD. "Why are My people en-
slaved again? Those who rule them shout in exultation. My name is blasphemed all day
long.* 6 But I will reveal My name to My people, and they will come to know its power.
Then at last they will recognize that I am the One who speaks to them."

7 How beautiful on the mountains
are the feet of the messenger who brings good news,
the good news of peace and salvation,
the news that the God of Israel* reigns!

52:1 Exod 28:2, 40; Neh 11:1; Isa 48:2; 61:10; Rev 21:2, 27
52:3 Ps 44:12; Isa 63:4
52:5 Ezek 36:20, 23; *Rom 2:24
52:7 Ps 93:1; *Rom 10:15

51:19 As in Dead Sea Scrolls and Greek, Latin, and Syriac versions; Masoretic Text reads *How can I comfort you?* 52:5 Greek version reads *The Gentiles continually blaspheme My name because of you.* Compare Rom 2:24. 52:7 Hebrew *of Zion.*

52:4-6 At various times in history, Israel experienced captivity at the hands of the Egyptians, the Assyrians, and the Babylonians. Although God used these times of hardship to discipline His people, the nations acted against Israel without cause or provocation. God would judge each nation for their aggression and injustice.

52:7 The "good news" is the announcement of God's reign breaking forth into the world. It is this same message, this gospel, that Jesus proclaimed when He announced the appearance of God's kingdom (Matthew 4:17; Luke 4:43).

▶ ADOPTION

52:7 Beautiful feet. Perhaps when you look at your bare foot, you see something misshapen, wrinkled, or ugly. Oh, to have young, lovely feet again! But you can have beautiful feet—at least in their function. God doesn't look at our physical features, but at what we do with them. When we use our feet (or our mouth or hands or anything else) to spread the good news about Jesus Christ, they take on a new beauty. Our features become God's means to tell more people His good news. Use every part of your body to communicate the good news of Jesus Christ to those around you. (***See Adoption***> *With Christ*> *Servants*> *Witness for Christ,* TopicGuide page A37.)

52:8 Isa 62:6
[8] The watchmen shout and sing with joy,
for before their very eyes
they see the LORD returning to Jerusalem.*

52:9 Ps 98:4 Isa 61:4
[9] Let the ruins of Jerusalem break into joyful song,
for the LORD has comforted His people.
He has redeemed Jerusalem.

52:10 Ps 98:1-3 Luke 3:6
[10] The LORD has demonstrated His holy power
before the eyes of all the nations.
All the ends of the earth will see
the victory of our God.

52:11 Isa 1:16 *2 Cor 6:17 2 Tim 2:19
[11] Get out! Get out and leave your captivity,
where everything you touch is unclean.
Get out of there and purify yourselves,
you who carry home the sacred objects of the LORD.

52:12 Exod 12:11, 33; 14:19-20 Isa 26:7
[12] You will not leave in a hurry,
running for your lives.
For the LORD will go ahead of you;
yes, the God of Israel will protect you from behind.

THE LORD'S SUFFERING SERVANT

52:13 Phil 2:9
[13] See, My Servant will prosper;
He will be highly exalted.

52:14 Ps 22:6-7
[14] But many were amazed when they saw Him.*
His face was so disfigured He seemed hardly human,
and from His appearance, one would scarcely know He was a man.

52:15 *Rom 15:21
[15] And He will startle* many nations.
Kings will stand speechless in His presence.
For they will see what they had not been told;
they will understand what they had not heard about.*

53:1 *John 12:38 *Rom 10:16
53 [1] Who has believed our message?
To whom has the LORD revealed His powerful arm?

53:2 Isa 11:1
[2] My Servant grew up in the LORD's presence like a tender green shoot,
like a root in dry ground.
There was nothing beautiful or majestic about His appearance,
nothing to attract us to Him.

53:3 Ps 22:6 Luke 18:31-33 John 1:10-11
[3] He was despised and rejected—
a man of sorrows, acquainted with deepest grief.

52:8 Hebrew *to Zion.* 52:14 As in Syriac version; Hebrew reads *you.* 52:15a Or *cleanse.* 52:15b Greek version reads *Those who have never been told about Him will see, / and those who have never heard of Him will understand.* Compare Rom 15:21.

52:13–53:12 This is the fourth and final servant song and the most familiar (see notes at 42:1-4 and 42:1). It is also the Old Testament passage most frequently cited in the New Testament (for example, Matthew 8:17; 26:63, 67; Mark 9:12; 15:4-5; Luke 22:37; 23:33; John 12:38; Acts 3:13; 8:32-33). These New Testament passages clearly identify Jesus Christ in His suffering and exaltation as the fulfillment of Isaiah's Servant.

53:1-3 The Servant's humble origins, unimpressive appearance, and tragic life would make it difficult for some to believe that He was God's instrument of salvation.

▶ BIBLE
53:1 Old news, good news. While crucifixion may have originated as early as the seventh century BC, we have no evidence that the civilizations Isaiah was acquainted with practiced it. But God told Isaiah exactly what God's people should expect—that He would send a Savior who would be crucified for their sins. Isaiah accepted that message because it was completely consistent with what He knew about God from the Law of Moses and from his personal relationship with God. Thank God for His gift of salvation and His willingness to send special messengers to tell us the good news. He has prepared people in your path to accept God's message—tell them, and see an ancient story become good news once again. (***See Bible****> Unity> Authors> The fullness of salvation revealed to Old Testament prophets,* TopicGuide page A10.)

We turned our backs on Him and looked the other way.
He was despised, and we did not care.

4 Yet it was our weaknesses He carried;
it was our sorrows* that weighed Him down.
And we thought His troubles were a punishment from God,
a punishment for His own sins!
5 But He was pierced for our rebellion,
crushed for our sins.
He was beaten so we could be whole.
He was whipped so we could be healed.
6 All of us, like sheep, have strayed away.
We have left God's paths to follow our own.
Yet the LORD laid on Him
the sins of us all.

7 He was oppressed and treated harshly,
yet He never said a word.
He was led like a lamb to the slaughter.
And as a sheep is silent before the shearers,
He did not open His mouth.
8 Unjustly condemned,
He was led away.*
No one cared that He died without descendants,
that His life was cut short in midstream.*
But He was struck down
for the rebellion of My people.
9 He had done no wrong
and had never deceived anyone.
But He was buried like a criminal;
He was put in a rich man's grave.

10 But it was the LORD's good plan to crush Him
and cause Him grief.
Yet when His life is made an offering for sin,
He will have many descendants.
He will enjoy a long life,
and the LORD's good plan will prosper in His hands.
11 When He sees all that is accomplished by His anguish,
He will be satisfied.

53:4 *Matt 8:17; 1 Pet 2:24
53:5 Rom 4:25; 1 Cor 15:3; Heb 5:8; 9:28; 1 Pet 2:24-25
53:7 Matt 27:12-14; Luke 23:9
53:8 *Acts 8:32-33
53:9 Matt 27:57-60; *1 Pet 2:22; Rev 14:5
53:10 Ps 22:30; John 1:29
53:11 John 10:14-18; Rom 5:18-19

53:4 Or *Yet it was our sicknesses He carried; / it was our diseases.* 53:8a Greek version reads *He was humiliated and received no justice.* Compare Acts 8:33. 53:8b Or *As for His contemporaries, / who cared that His life was cut short in midstream?* Greek version reads *Who can speak of His descendants? / For His life was taken from the earth.* Compare Acts 8:33.

53:4-6 These verses beautifully express the substitutionary dimension of Christ's suffering. Christ suffered sorrow and violence in order for His people to enjoy peace with God. The Servant was sinless but took upon Himself the guilt of His people so that they could be set free from the guilt of their sins (see the apostle Paul's similar description in Romans 5).

53:10-12 The substitutionary suffering of Christ was no accident, nor was it a plan hatched by Jesus' followers after His death—it was the will of His Father. It was not God's plan for Christ to remain in humiliation—Christ's resurrection and ascension marked the first stages of His exaltation that will grow until His return, when all creation will acknowledge Him as King.

▸ BIBLE

53:10 God's plan to suffer. God planned for Christ's death thousands of years before it happened. In fact, God planned for our salvation before He created the world (Isaiah 46:9-10). He knew that Adam and Eve would sin. He knew that people would need redemption. He knew that His suffering Son would provide a way for the world to be at peace with Him and that this plan would demonstrate both justice and mercy (Romans 3:26). Suffering continues to be an important part of God's plan for our lives. Explore the Bible (Mark 10:38; 2 Corinthians 1:7; Ephesians 3:13; 1 Peter 2:21) and your own heart and find a willingness to suffer for God's glory and the good of those under your care. (***See Bible***> *Unity*> *Christ*> *Christ is the "suffering Servant,"* TopicGuide page A10.)

And because of His experience,
My righteous Servant will make it possible
for many to be counted righteous,
53:12 Matt 26:38-39, 42 *Mark 15:27 *Luke 22:37 2 Cor 5:21 Phil 2:9-11 1 Pet 2:24
for He will bear all their sins.
12 I will give Him the honors of a victorious soldier,
because He exposed Himself to death.
He was counted among the rebels.
He bore the sins of many and interceded for rebels.

FUTURE GLORY FOR JERUSALEM

54:1 Isa 62:4 *Gal 4:27

54 1 "Sing, O childless woman,
you who have never given birth!
Break into loud and joyful song, O Jerusalem,
you who have never been in labor.
For the desolate woman now has more children
than the woman who lives with her husband,"
says the LORD.
2 "Enlarge your house; build an addition.
Spread out your home, and spare no expense!
54:3 Gen 28:14 Isa 14:1-2
3 For you will soon be bursting at the seams.
Your descendants will occupy other nations
and resettle the ruined cities.

4 "Fear not; you will no longer live in shame.
Don't be afraid; there is no more disgrace for you.
You will no longer remember the shame of your youth
and the sorrows of widowhood.
54:5 Hos 2:19
5 For your Creator will be your husband;
the LORD of Heaven's Armies is His name!
He is your Redeemer, the Holy One of Israel,
the God of all the earth.
54:6 Isa 62:4
6 For the LORD has called you back from your grief—
as though you were a young wife abandoned by her husband,"
says your God.
54:7 Isa 11:12
7 "For a brief moment I abandoned you,
but with great compassion I will take you back.
54:8 Isa 49:10, 13; 60:10
8 In a burst of anger I turned My face away for a little while.
But with everlasting love I will have compassion on you,"
says the LORD, your Redeemer.
54:9 Gen 9:9-11 Ezek 39:29
9 "Just as I swore in the time of Noah
that I would never again let a flood cover the earth,
so now I swear
that I will never again be angry and punish you.

54:1-8 Jerusalem is portrayed as a woman who had been unfaithful in her youth and then appeared to suffer the grief of widowhood. But God, her husband, had not permanently cast her aside. He would redeem her and take her back as His wife; His compassion and love would remove all guilt and shame.

▸ GOD

54:5 God as a husband. In what way does your culture shape your ideas about God? Many ideas about God transcend culture, and the idea of God as a husband of the church is no exception (2 Corinthians 11:2; Revelation 21:2). In His role as husband, God provides for us, communicates with us, and protects us. What other ways do you see God as a husband to His people? Do you feel close enough to Him that you could talk to Him like a wife to her husband? Write down ways that a godly wife honors her husband. In which of those ways can you honor God? (***See God**> God's Names> God> Husband,* TopicGuide page A18.)

54:9-10 God's prophets announced the establishment of a new covenant following the Exile (see also Jeremiah 31:31; Ezekiel 37:26). This covenant, ultimately established by Christ (Hebrews 8), would be an eternal covenant that would never be severed.

10 For the mountains may move
and the hills disappear,
but even then My faithful love for you will remain.
My covenant of blessing will never be broken,"
says the LORD, who has mercy on you.

11 "O storm-battered city,
troubled and desolate!
I will rebuild you with precious jewels
and make your foundations from lapis lazuli.
12 I will make your towers of sparkling rubies,
your gates of shining gems,
and your walls of precious stones.
13 I will teach all your children,
and they will enjoy great peace.
14 You will be secure under a government that is just and fair.
Your enemies will stay far away.
You will live in peace,
and terror will not come near.
15 If any nation comes to fight you,
it is not because I sent them.
Whoever attacks you will go down in defeat.

16 "I have created the blacksmith
who fans the coals beneath the forge
and makes the weapons of destruction.
And I have created the armies that destroy.
17 But in that coming day
no weapon turned against you will succeed.
You will silence every voice
raised up to accuse you.
These benefits are enjoyed by the servants of the LORD;
their vindication will come from Me.
I, the LORD, have spoken!

54:10 2 Sam 23:5; Pss 89:34; 102:25-26
54:11 Isa 28:16
54:13 Isa 66:12; Jer 31:34; *John 6:45
54:14 Isa 9:4, 7
54:15 Isa 41:11-16
54:17 Isa 29:8

INVITATION TO THE LORD'S SALVATION

55 1 "Is anyone thirsty?
Come and drink—
even if you have no money!
Come, take your choice of wine or milk—
it's all free!

55:1 Ps 63:1; Lam 5:4; Matt 10:8; John 4:14; 7:37; Rev 3:18; 21:6; 22:17

54:11-17 Jerusalem suffered much through the ordeal of exile, but God promised her peace and justice. The prevalence of jewels symbolized the splendor and glory of the future city. The New Testament teaches us that the church is now the embodiment of the true Jerusalem, but the full enjoyment of these hopes is predicated on the return of Christ and the appearance of the new heaven and the new earth (Galatians 4:26; Hebrews 12:22; Revelation 21:19).

▸ SPIRITUAL WARFARE
54:16 God was not surprised. One reason news media exists is because we don't know the future. Without a book, a newspaper, or some type of communication, we don't even know the present or past if it takes place outside our personal lives. But God knows everything! God was not taken by surprise when Adam and Eve sinned. He has everything under control. He created the very creatures (angels, see Revelation 12:7-9) who turned on Him and brought evil into the world. We need not be surprised when we experience evil, either. We are neither good enough nor smart enough to avoid its chaotic impact on our lives. Expect the unexpected, prepare for temptation, and trust that God is watching over it all (2 Corinthians 1:8-10). (***See Spiritual Warfare****> God and Sin> Sin's Origin> Source of evil created by God,* TopicGuide page A45.)

55:1-2 Physical hunger and thirst serve as metaphors for spiritual longing. The Lord offers salvation to the poorest of people, reminding us that such salvation is entirely a work of God's grace.

55:2 Ps 22:26 Eccl 6:2 — 2 Why spend your money on food that does not give you strength?
Why pay for food that does you no good?
Listen to Me, and you will eat what is good.
You will enjoy the finest food.

55:3 *Acts 13:34 — 3 "Come to Me with your ears wide open.
Listen, and you will find life.
I will make an everlasting covenant with you.
I will give you all the unfailing love I promised to David.
4 See how I used him to display My power among the peoples.
I made him a leader among the nations.
55:5 Zech 8:22 — 5 You also will command nations you do not know,
and peoples unknown to you will come running to obey,
because I, the LORD your God,
the Holy One of Israel, have made you glorious."

55:6 Ps 32:6 2 Cor 6:1-2 — 6 Seek the LORD while you can find Him.
Call on Him now while He is near.
55:7 Isa 1:16; 44:22 — 7 Let the wicked change their ways
and banish the very thought of doing wrong.
Let them turn to the LORD that He may have mercy on them.
Yes, turn to our God, for He will forgive generously.

55:8 Isa 65:2 — 8 "My thoughts are nothing like your thoughts," says the LORD.
"And My ways are far beyond anything you could imagine.
55:9 Ps 103:11 — 9 For just as the heavens are higher than the earth,
so My ways are higher than your ways
and My thoughts higher than your thoughts.

55:10 2 Cor 9:10 — 10 "The rain and snow come down from the heavens
and stay on the ground to water the earth.
They cause the grain to grow,
producing seed for the farmer
and bread for the hungry.
55:11 Isa 46:10 — 11 It is the same with My word.
I send it out, and it always produces fruit.
It will accomplish all I want it to,
and it will prosper everywhere I send it.

55:3-5 God promised David an everlasting dominion over the people of God. Although David's immediate heirs were less than faithful to God, the promise is fulfilled in Christ, who, as a descendant of David, will rule over the people of God forever and extend the boundaries of God's kingdom to include Gentiles from every tribe and nation.

▶ BIBLE

55:7 Victory through surrender. From the beginning of time, God has continually called on people to repent. The first step we make that pleases God is to cry out for mercy and express our desire to stop rebelling against Him. Does repentance play a central part in your spiritual life? Does your wrongdoing grieve your heart? Or do you find it easy to ignore your own sin but very simple to discern others'? Focus on your sin, not everyone else's. Confess your sin—each one—and you will achieve victory through surrender (1 John 1:9). (***See Bible****> Uniqueness> Authoritative> Demands repentance,* TopicGuide page A10; also ***see Adoption****> Without Christ> Separated from God> Unrighteous,* TopicGuide page A36.)

▶ GOD

55:8 God's thoughts—our thoughts. Grace is an unspeakable insult to human pride. It says to us that we can't do it on our own, and that we deserve to die for our offenses against God—yet the gift of God is salvation through Christ. God's riches expose our poverty, our need, and our ignorance. In our worldly understanding, coming to God for salvation makes as much sense as a rat coming to a cat for salvation—but thank God for sending the Holy Spirit to lead us into the truth of salvation (John 14:17). God's plan of salvation may sound crazy (1 Corinthians 3:18-20), but it's the only way to Him. Humble yourself and pursue God's path—God's way. (***See God****> God's Nature> Personality> Intellect> God's thoughts surpass people's,* TopicGuide page A14.)

12 You will live in joy and peace.
The mountains and hills will burst into song,
and the trees of the field will clap their hands!
13 Where once there were thorns, cypress trees will grow.
Where nettles grew, myrtles will sprout up.
These events will bring great honor to the LORD's name;
they will be an everlasting sign of His power and love."

55:12 1 Chr 16:33 Jer 29:11
55:13 Jer 33:9

BLESSINGS FOR ALL NATIONS

56 This is what the LORD says:
"Be just and fair to all.
Do what is right and good,
for I am coming soon to rescue you
and to display My righteousness among you.
2 Blessed are all those
who are careful to do this.
Blessed are those who honor My Sabbath days of rest
and keep themselves from doing wrong.

3 "Don't let foreigners who commit themselves to the LORD say,
'The LORD will never let me be part of His people.'
And don't let the eunuchs say,
'I'm a dried-up tree with no children and no future.'
4 For this is what the LORD says:
I will bless those eunuchs
who keep My Sabbath days holy
and who choose to do what pleases Me
and commit their lives to Me.
5 I will give them—within the walls of My house—
a memorial and a name
far greater than sons and daughters could give.
For the name I give them is an everlasting one.
It will never disappear!

6 "I will also bless the foreigners who commit themselves to the LORD,
who serve Him and love His name,
who worship Him and do not desecrate the Sabbath day of rest,
and who hold fast to My covenant.

56:1 Ps 85:9 Isa 1:17
56:2 Exod 31:13-17 Ps 119:1-2 Ezek 20:12, 20
56:3 Acts 8:27, 37
56:5 Isa 2:2-3; 26:1; 62:2
56:6 Isa 60:10; 61:5

56:1–66:24 In this last major section of Isaiah, the prophet turns his attention against the sins of the community that would return from exile. The fullness of the restoration depended upon the sincere obedience and repentance of God's people. Enduring sin within the community would sabotage the glorious hopes of renewal and restoration.

56:1-2 The exercise of justice and the keeping of the Sabbath are central concerns throughout this section of Isaiah (56:4, 6; 58:13).

▸WORSHIP

56:2 One day of rest. Life has become so hectic that we go from one activity to another, barely having time to rest. One day can blur into the next. One reason why our lives seem so hectic is that we have abandoned God's principle of reserving one day of rest in which to honor God. The Old Testament people of God followed rules that ensured the Sabbath was a day of rest (Exodus 20:9). Do you need to revise your week so that you can honor God with one day? Try God's way of managing your time—work six days, and rest on His Sabbath (Acts 13:14; 16:13). (***See Worship***> *OT> Festivals> Sabbath,* TopicGuide page A26.)

56:3 The inclusion of Gentiles and eunuchs within the people of God is a recurring theme in Isaiah. The people of God throughout the Old Testament were for the most part defined ethnically—the descendants of Abraham. Yet, even the promises made to Abraham expressed the hope that God's people would one day bless every tribe and nation (Genesis 12:3; 22:18). The expansion of the church among the Gentiles accelerated the realization of this hope, which will be fulfilled in the multinational throng of worshipers before the throne of God as portrayed in John's vision (Revelation 7:9).

56:7 Isa 65:25 Mic 4:1-2 *Matt 21:13 *Mark 11:17 *Luke 19:46 Rom 12:1 Heb 13:15

[7] I will bring them to My holy mountain of Jerusalem
and will fill them with joy in My house of prayer.
I will accept their burnt offerings and sacrifices,
because My Temple will be called a house of prayer for all nations.

56:8 John 10:16

[8] For the Sovereign LORD,
who brings back the outcasts of Israel, says:
I will bring others, too,
besides My people Israel."

SINFUL LEADERS CONDEMNED

56:9 Jer 12:9

[9] Come, wild animals of the field!
Come, wild animals of the forest!
Come and devour My people!

56:10 Jer 14:13-14 Ezek 3:17

[10] For the leaders of My people—
the LORD's watchmen, His shepherds—
are blind and ignorant.
They are like silent watchdogs
that give no warning when danger comes.
They love to lie around, sleeping and dreaming.

56:11 Jer 22:17 Mic 3:5, 11

[11] Like greedy dogs, they are never satisfied.
They are ignorant shepherds,
all following their own path
and intent on personal gain.

56:12 Luke 12:19-20

[12] "Come," they say, "let's get some wine and have a party.
Let's all get drunk.
Then tomorrow we'll do it again
and have an even bigger party!"

57:1 2 Kgs 22:19-20 Ps 12:1

57

[1] Good people pass away;
the godly often die before their time.
But no one seems to care or wonder why.
No one seems to understand
that God is protecting them from the evil to come.
[2] For those who follow godly paths
will rest in peace when they die.

IDOLATROUS WORSHIP CONDEMNED

57:3 Matt 16:4

[3] "But you—come here, you witches' children,
you offspring of adulterers and prostitutes!

56:7 This verse was the basis of Jesus' critique of Temple worship in Matthew 21:13. God intends for all manner of men and women to worship Him and enjoy His blessing. Those who exclude others from the worship of God for reasons of race, color, socioeconomic standing, or other such prejudices strike against the very core of God's desire for humanity.

57:1 Death is never the worst that can happen to a righteous individual. Death, in fact, may be a blessing to God's people, sparing them from continued sorrow and pain in this life.

▸GOD
57:2 A peaceful death. Have you ever experienced the death of a close friend or relative? Was that person a Christian or not? Did the knowledge of that person's faith, or lack thereof, affect the grief you felt? God assures us that any person who follows Him does not need to fear death. Jesus has conquered the grave; therefore, we can claim this declaration: "But thank God! He gives us victory over sin and death through our Lord Jesus Christ" (1 Corinthians 15:57). Is this your hope? Are you trusting in Jesus to bring you through when your last days arrive? God waits to receive His precious people (Psalm 116:15); believers can rest assured that He will fulfill His promises to them (1 Corinthians 15:51-57). (See Job 19:25; also ***see God**> God's Attributes> All-Powerful> He has power over death,* TopicGuide page A15.)

4 Whom do you mock,
making faces and sticking out your tongues?
You children of sinners and liars!
5 You worship your idols with great passion
beneath the oaks and under every green tree.
You sacrifice your children down in the valleys,
among the jagged rocks in the cliffs.
6 Your gods are the smooth stones in the valleys.
You worship them with liquid offerings
and grain offerings.
They, not I, are your inheritance.
Do you think all this makes Me happy?
7 You have committed adultery on every high mountain.
There you have worshiped idols
and have been unfaithful to Me.
8 You have put pagan symbols
on your doorposts and behind your doors.
You have left Me
and climbed into bed with these detestable gods.
You have committed yourselves to them.
You love to look at their naked bodies.
9 You have given olive oil to Molech*
with many gifts of perfume.
You have traveled far,
even into the world of the dead,*
to find new gods to love.
10 You grew weary in your search,
but you never gave up.
Desire gave you renewed strength,
and you did not grow weary.

11 "Are you afraid of these idols?
Do they terrify you?
Is that why you have lied to Me
and forgotten Me and My words?
Is it because of My long silence
that you no longer fear Me?
12 Now I will expose your so-called good deeds.
None of them will help you.
13 Let's see if your idols can save you
when you cry to them for help.
Why, a puff of wind can knock them down!
If you just breathe on them, they fall over!
But whoever trusts in Me will inherit the land
and possess My holy mountain."

57:5 Ps 106:37-38; Jer 2:20; 7:31
57:6 Jer 7:18; Hab 2:19
57:7 Ezek 16:16, 28
57:8 Ezek 23:18
57:9 Ezek 23:16, 40
57:10 Jer 2:25
57:11 Ps 50:21; Prov 29:25; Jer 2:32
57:12 Mic 3:1-4
57:13 Ps 37:3, 9; Jer 30:14

57:9a Or *to the king.* 57:9b Hebrew *into Sheol.*

57:5 The worship of idols and false gods often took place underneath trees (Deuteronomy 12:2). Those who worshiped the god Molech sacrificed their children to him, which was considered the most wicked of pagan practices (Leviticus 20:1-5; Deuteronomy 18:10).

57:7-8 God was envisioned as Israel's faithful husband. Israel, however, had been an unfaithful wife who committed adultery by worshiping pagan idols.

GOD FORGIVES THE REPENTANT

57:14 Isa 62:10

14 God says, "Rebuild the road!
Clear away the rocks and stones
so My people can return from captivity."

57:15 Deut 33:27; Ps 34:18; Isa 66:1

15 The high and lofty One who lives in eternity,
the Holy One, says this:
"I live in the high and holy place
with those whose spirits are contrite and humble.
I restore the crushed spirit of the humble
and revive the courage of those with repentant hearts.

57:16 Mic 7:18

16 For I will not fight against you forever;
I will not always be angry.
If I were, all people would pass away—
all the souls I have made.

57:17 Isa 1:4

17 I was angry,
so I punished these greedy people.
I withdrew from them,
but they kept going on their own stubborn way.

57:18 Isa 53:5; 61:1-3

18 I have seen what they do,
but I will heal them anyway!
I will lead them.
I will comfort those who mourn,

57:19 Isa 26:12; Acts 2:39; Eph 2:17; Heb 13:15

19 bringing words of praise to their lips.
May they have abundant peace, both near and far,"
says the LORD, who heals them.

57:20 Job 18:5-14

20 "But those who still reject Me are like the restless sea,
which is never still
but continually churns up mud and dirt.

57:21 Isa 48:22

21 There is no peace for the wicked,"
says my God.

TRUE AND FALSE WORSHIP

58 1 "Shout with the voice of a trumpet blast.
Shout aloud! Don't be timid.
Tell my people Israel* of their sins!

58:2 Isa 29:13; Jer 7:9-10; Titus 1:16

2 Yet they act so pious!
They come to the Temple every day
and seem delighted to learn all about Me.

58:1 Hebrew *Jacob*. See note on 14:1.

57:15-21 The prophet contrasted those who humbly sought God's forgiveness with those who persisted in their sins. Those that came before God in repentance would find Him willing to forgive and bless them. Those who stubbornly rejected God's discipline and continued in their wickedness would never know peace.

58:1-5 Isaiah was to clearly confront the hypocrisy of the nation. The people engaged in all of the outward expressions of worship, but their hearts were far from God, and their society was plagued by exploitation and injustice. Yet despite their insincerity, the people expected God to bless them and hear their prayers. The prophet exposed the blatant contradiction between their religious observance and their sinful behavior. God is never pleased when we observe the forms of worship without purity of heart and true obedience.

▸ WORSHIP

58:2 One day a week? Wherever there are people, there are hypocrites. In Isaiah's time, many people acted religious but, frankly, couldn't care less about God. Today, God doesn't want "Sunday Christians." He wants us to follow Him every minute of every week. He sees your heart. Are you true to Him on Monday? Jesus is Lord on both Saturday night and Sunday morning. Give your heart to Him every moment. Flee from hypocrisy and embrace honesty—your interaction with God will move from a fickle affair to a devoted relationship (Luke 8:15; 1 Thessalonians 2:10). (***See Worship****> OT> God's Supremacy> Required a proper heart attitude,* TopicGuide page A27.)

They act like a righteous nation
that would never abandon the laws of its God.
They ask Me to take action on their behalf,
pretending they want to be near Me.
3 'We have fasted before You!' they say.
'Why aren't You impressed?
We have been very hard on ourselves,
and You don't even notice it!'

"I will tell you why!" I respond.
"It's because you are fasting to please yourselves.
Even while you fast,
you keep oppressing your workers.
4 What good is fasting
when you keep on fighting and quarreling?
This kind of fasting
will never get you anywhere with Me.
5 You humble yourselves
by going through the motions of penance,
bowing your heads
like reeds bending in the wind.
You dress in burlap
and cover yourselves with ashes.
Is this what you call fasting?
Do you really think this will please the LORD?

6 "No, this is the kind of fasting I want:
Free those who are wrongly imprisoned;
lighten the burden of those who work for you.
Let the oppressed go free,
and remove the chains that bind people.
7 Share your food with the hungry,
and give shelter to the homeless.
Give clothes to those who need them,
and do not hide from relatives who need your help.

8 "Then your salvation will come like the dawn,
and your wounds will quickly heal.
Your godliness will lead you forward,
and the glory of the LORD will protect you from behind.
9 Then when you call, the LORD will answer.
'Yes, I am here,' He will quickly reply.

"Remove the heavy yoke of oppression.
Stop pointing your finger and spreading vicious rumors!

58:3 Zech 7:5-6; Luke 18:9-12
58:4 1 Kgs 21:9-10
58:6 Neh 5:10-12
58:7 Deut 22:1-4; Ezek 18:7, 16; Matt 25:35; Luke 3:11; Heb 13:2
58:8 Ps 85:13; Jer 30:17

58:6-9 God called upon His people to stop oppressing the poor and to care for the needy. This was the kind of service that He desired. Fasting was meaningless if performed by those who on the same day took advantage of the less fortunate or failed to help those in need.

▶ MINISTRY
58:8 Shining mercy. When is the last time you have watched the sunrise? How do you feel as you stand and watch the dark blue change to shades of purple, then orange, then a blinding yellow? As the faint light becomes stronger, the world stirs. What a wonderful analogy to how believers become light to the world. Our mercy (58:6), selflessness (58:7), and truth-telling (58:9) shine like the early dawn in this darkened world. Bring light into a dark place through your radical obedience to God's commands. (***See Ministry**> Transformation> Fill and Subdue> Being salt and light in the world,* TopicGuide page A57.)

58:10 Deut 15:7 — 10 Feed the hungry,
and help those in trouble.
Then your light will shine out from the darkness,
and the darkness around you will be as bright as noon.

58:11 Ps 107:9; Song 4:15; John 4:14; 7:37-38 — 11 The LORD will guide you continually,
giving you water when you are dry
and restoring your strength.
You will be like a well-watered garden,
like an ever-flowing spring.

58:12 Ezek 36:10; Amos 9:11 — 12 Some of you will rebuild the deserted ruins of your cities.
Then you will be known as a rebuilder of walls
and a restorer of homes.

58:13 Ps 84:2, 10; Jer 17:21-27 — 13 "Keep the Sabbath day holy.
Don't pursue your own interests on that day,
but enjoy the Sabbath
and speak of it with delight as the LORD's holy day.
Honor the Sabbath in everything you do on that day,
and don't follow your own desires or talk idly.

58:14 Deut 32:13 — 14 Then the LORD will be your delight.
I will give you great honor
and satisfy you with the inheritance I promised to your ancestor Jacob.
I, the LORD, have spoken!"

WARNINGS AGAINST SIN

59:1 Jer 32:17 — **59** 1 Listen! The LORD's arm is not too weak to save you,
nor is His ear too deaf to hear you call.

59:2 Isa 1:15; Ezek 8:18 — 2 It's your sins that have cut you off from God.
Because of your sins, He has turned away
and will not listen anymore.

59:3 Jer 2:30, 34; Hos 4:2 — 3 Your hands are the hands of murderers,
and your fingers are filthy with sin.
Your lips are full of lies,
and your mouth spews corruption.

59:4 Ps 7:14 — 4 No one cares about being fair and honest.
The people's lawsuits are based on lies.
They conceive evil deeds
and then give birth to sin.

58:11-12 These verses make clear that these prophecies were directed to the community of exiles that would be set free and allowed to return to their land. Light and water were common yet evocative images of life and renewal closely linked to the Creation account (Genesis 1:1).

58:13-14 Observance of the Sabbath was a sign of God's relationship with His people (Exodus 31:13-17; Deuteronomy 5:4-5, 12-15; Ezekiel 20:20). In a hand-to-mouth agrarian society, it freed people to rest from their labors in order to worship God.

59:1-8 Isaiah redirected his audience's attention to their sinfulness. God would deliver them, but persistent sin would place them outside the covenant community (Deuteronomy 28:15-68). This catalogue is reminiscent of Paul's list of humanity's sins in Romans 3:10-19.

▶ MINISTRY
59:2-8 Sin and salvation. Have you sinned since you were saved? Then you face the same problem as these Israelites—what do we do with our continued tendency to sin? The language of this passage speaks of unrepentant sin and the danger of coming under God's promised discipline (Deuteronomy 28:15-68). Under the New Covenant, similar warnings exist to those who are in the church, yet continue to abide in sin rather than Christ (Hebrews 6:4-6; Matthew 25). Yes, Christians still sin. But our love affair with sin is now over (2 Corinthians 5:17). Make repentance and belief in the gospel your daily goal, and you will persevere unto the end (Revelation 3:10). (***See Ministry**> Great Commission> Reconcile> Necessary because there is enmity between God and humanity,* TopicGuide page A56.)

[5] They hatch deadly snakes
and weave spiders' webs.
Whoever falls into their webs will die,
and there's danger even in getting
near them.
[6] Their webs can't be made into clothing,
and nothing they do is productive.
All their activity is filled with sin,
and violence is their trademark.
[7] Their feet run to do evil,
and they rush to commit murder.
They think only about sinning.
Misery and destruction always follow them.
[8] They don't know where to find peace
or what it means to be just and good.
They have mapped out crooked roads,
and no one who follows them knows
a moment's peace.

[9] So there is no justice among us,
and we know nothing about right living.
We look for light but find only darkness.
We look for bright skies but walk in gloom.
[10] We grope like the blind along a wall,
feeling our way like people without eyes.
Even at brightest noontime,
we stumble as though it were dark.
Among the living,
we are like the dead.
[11] We growl like hungry bears;
we moan like mournful doves.
We look for justice, but it never comes.
We look for rescue, but it is far away from us.
[12] For our sins are piled up before God
and testify against us.
Yes, we know what sinners we are.
[13] We know we have rebelled and have denied the LORD.
We have turned our backs on our God.
We know how unfair and oppressive we have been,
carefully planning our deceitful lies.
[14] Our courts oppose the righteous,
and justice is nowhere to be found.
Truth stumbles in the streets,
and honesty has been outlawed.
[15] Yes, truth is gone,
and anyone who renounces evil is attacked.
The LORD looked and was displeased
to find there was no justice.

59:5 Job 8:14
59:6 Jer 6:7
59:7-8 Prov 1:16; Mark 7:21-22; *Rom 3:15-17
59:9 Isa 5:30
59:10 Deut 28:29; Lam 3:6
59:11 Ezek 7:16
59:12 Ezra 9:6; Hos 5:5
59:13 Matt 10:33; Titus 1:16
59:14 Hab 1:4
59:15 Isa 1:21-23; 5:23

59:14-15 The society had degenerated into a state of moral chaos; injustice prevailed, honesty was nonexistent, and those who sought to live righteously encountered violent opposition. Such circumstances deeply angered the Lord, who desired justice and truth from His people.

59:16 Ezek 22:30
16 He was amazed to see that no one intervened
to help the oppressed.
So He Himself stepped in to save them with His strong arm,
and His justice sustained Him.
59:17 Eph 6:14
17 He put on righteousness as His body armor
and placed the helmet of salvation on His head.
He clothed Himself with a robe of vengeance
and wrapped Himself in a cloak of divine passion.
18 He will repay His enemies for their evil deeds.
His fury will fall on His foes.
He will pay them back even to the ends of the earth.
59:19 Isa 30:28
19 In the west, people will respect the name of the LORD;
in the east, they will glorify Him.
For He will come like a raging flood tide
driven by the breath of the LORD.*

59:20 Ezek 18:30-31 Acts 2:38-39 *Rom 11:26-27
20 "The Redeemer will come to Jerusalem
to buy back those in Israel
who have turned from their sins,"*
says the LORD.

59:21 Isa 44:3 Jer 31:31-34
21 "And this is My covenant with them," says the LORD. "My Spirit will not leave them, and
neither will these words I have given you. They will be on your lips and on the lips of your
children and your children's children forever. I, the LORD, have spoken!

FUTURE GLORY FOR JERUSALEM

60:1 Eph 5:14
60 1 "Arise, Jerusalem! Let your light shine for all to see.
For the glory of the LORD rises to shine on you.
60:2 Col 1:13
2 Darkness as black as night covers all the nations of the earth,
but the glory of the LORD rises and appears over you.

59:19 Or *When the enemy comes like a raging flood tide, / the Spirit of the LORD will drive him back.* 59:20 Hebrew *The Redeemer will come to Zion / to buy back those in Jacob / who have turned from their sins.* Greek version reads *The One who rescues will come on behalf of Zion, / and He will turn Jacob away from ungodliness.* Compare Rom 11:26.

▸ BIBLE

59:16 Jesus reached down. In the Old Testament, there were no government or religious programs to help the poor. It was expected that each Israelite would help the poor in the community. When Jesus lived on earth, He exemplified the heart of God by healing the sick, comforting the lonely, and welcoming children. Jesus' life exemplified how God helps those who need it. His greatest act of compassion was to die for helpless sinners (Romans 5:8). This principle of compassion should encompass our lives. If Jesus died for the hopeless, we should serve the spiritually and physically poor and needy around us. Look around you—is there one person in your life you can help? Take some time and make a list of the people you can show mercy to over the next week. (***See Bible****> Unity> Salvation> Fulfilled in the Messiah,* TopicGuide page A11.)

59:16-19 Throughout Scripture, God is frequently portrayed as a warrior who fights on behalf of His people. The tradition appears to date back to the Exodus, when Moses spoke of God as a warrior fighting for His people at the Red Sea (Exodus 14:14; 15:3). The theme of warfare is continued in the New Testament, but it is spiritualized. The believer puts on the armor of God not to fight flesh and blood enemies, but to fight spiritual powers and forces of darkness through the power of Christ and the Spirit (Ephesians 6:14-17).

59:21 The restoration would bring about a new covenant order characterized by the outpouring of the Spirit (see note at 54:9-10; compare Jeremiah 31:31-34; Ezekiel 37:1-14; Joel 2:28).

60:1-3 The light of God's glory symbolizes the blessing of God's presence among His people. The contrast between the darkness blanketing the nations and the light shining on God's people is reminiscent of the Exodus, when darkness covered Egypt while Israel remained in the light (Exodus 10:21-26).

▸ MINISTRY

60:1 Shine your light. Isaiah called on God's people to be God's light for the nations. Jesus calls on us to do the same. He says, "Let your good deeds shine out for all to see, so that everyone will praise your heavenly Father" (Matthew 5:16). How can we do this? By sharing our faith in Christ with everyone we know. Jesus is the light; He is the One we reflect to the nations. If you are unsure how to share your faith, ask the Holy Spirit to lead you to someone who needs to know about Jesus Christ. Then follow His leading. (***See Ministry****> Transformation> Fill and Subdue> Being salt and light in the world,* TopicGuide page A57.)

3 All nations will come to your light;
mighty kings will come to see your radiance.

60:3
Isa 2:3

4 "Look and see, for everyone is coming home!
Your sons are coming from distant lands;
your little daughters will be carried home.
5 Your eyes will shine,
and your heart will thrill with joy,
for merchants from around the world will
come to you.
They will bring you the wealth of many lands.
6 Vast caravans of camels will converge on you,
the camels of Midian and Ephah.
The people of Sheba will bring gold and
frankincense
and will come worshiping the LORD.
7 The flocks of Kedar will be given to you,
and the rams of Nebaioth will be brought
for My altars.
I will accept their offerings,
and I will make My Temple glorious.

60:5
Ps 34:5
Isa 61:6

8 "And what do I see flying like clouds to Israel,
like doves to their nests?
9 They are ships from the ends of the earth,
from lands that trust in Me,
led by the great ships of Tarshish.
They are bringing the people of Israel home
from far away,
carrying their silver and gold.
They will honor the LORD your God,
the Holy One of Israel,
for He has filled you with splendor.

60:9-10
Ps 72:10
Isa 49:22-23

10 "Foreigners will come to rebuild your towns,
and their kings will serve you.
For though I have destroyed you in My anger,
I will now have mercy on you through My grace.
11 Your gates will stay open around the clock
to receive the wealth of many lands.
The kings of the world will be led as captives
in a victory procession.
12 For the nations that refuse to serve you
will be destroyed.

60:11
Isa 26:2

60:12
Zech 14:17

13 "The glory of Lebanon will be yours—
the forests of cypress, fir, and pine—
to beautify My sanctuary.
My Temple will be glorious!

60:4-14 The restoration of God's people would be accompanied by the submission of the nations to the people of God. The fulfillment of this hope began with the coming of Christ and the expansion of the church among the Gentiles. When Christ returns and every knee bows before Him, this expectation will be fully realized.

60:14 Isa 1:26; 14:1-2 Rev 3:9
14 The descendants of your tormentors
will come and bow before you.
Those who despised you
will kiss your feet.
They will call you the City of the LORD,
and Zion of the Holy One of Israel.

60:15 Isa 65:18 Jer 30:17-19
15 "Though you were once despised and hated,
with no one traveling through you,
I will make you beautiful forever,
a joy to all generations.
60:16 Isa 43:3, 11; 63:16
16 Powerful kings and mighty nations
will satisfy your every need,
as though you were a child
nursing at the breast of a queen.
You will know at last that I, the LORD,
am your Savior and your Redeemer,
the Mighty One of Israel.*
17 I will exchange your bronze for gold,
your iron for silver,
your wood for bronze,
and your stones for iron.
I will make peace your leader
and righteousness your ruler.
60:18 Isa 26:1
18 Violence will disappear from your land;
the desolation and destruction of war will end.
Salvation will surround you like city walls,
and praise will be on the lips of all
who enter there.

60:19 Isa 9:2 Zech 2:5 Rev 21:23; 22:5
19 "No longer will you need the sun to shine
by day,
nor the moon to give its light by night,
for the LORD your God will be your everlasting light,
and your God will be your glory.
60:20 Rev 21:4
20 Your sun will never set;
your moon will not go down.
For the LORD will be your everlasting light.
Your days of mourning will come to an end.
60:21 Ps 37:22 Isa 45:24-25
21 All your people will be righteous.
They will possess their land forever,
for I will plant them there with My own hands
in order to bring Myself glory.
60:22 Isa 51:2
22 The smallest family will become a thousand people,
and the tiniest group will become a mighty nation.
At the right time, I, the LORD, will make it happen."

60:16 Hebrew *of Jacob.* See note on 14:1.

60:18-22 These verses describe a remarkable hope of universal scope. The salvation that God held out for the exiles was not simply a return to their land; it encompassed the whole of creation. Not surprisingly, we hear of these ideal conditions of peace and blessing in John's descriptions of the new Jerusalem (Revelation 21:23; 22:5). This remarkable kingdom was postponed by the returning exiles because of their continued unfaithfulness.

GOOD NEWS FOR THE OPPRESSED

61 1 The Spirit of the Sovereign LORD is upon Me, **61:1-2**
for the LORD has anointed Me Isa 49:8-9
to bring good news to the poor. *Luke 4:18-19
He has sent Me to comfort the brokenhearted
and to proclaim that captives will be released
and prisoners will be freed.*
2 He has sent Me to tell those who mourn
that the time of the LORD's favor has come,*
and with it, the day of God's anger against their enemies.
3 To all who mourn in Israel,* **61:3**
He will give a crown of beauty for ashes, Ps 23:5
a joyous blessing instead of mourning, Jer 17:7-8
festive praise instead of despair.
In their righteousness, they will be like great oaks
that the LORD has planted for His own glory.

4 They will rebuild the ancient ruins, **61:4**
repairing cities destroyed long ago. Ezek 36:33
They will revive them, Amos 9:14
though they have been deserted for many generations.
5 Foreigners will be your servants. **61:5**
They will feed your flocks Isa 14:2
and plow your fields
and tend your vineyards.
6 You will be called priests of the LORD, **61:6**
ministers of our God. Isa 66:21
You will feed on the treasures of the nations
and boast in their riches.
7 Instead of shame and dishonor, **61:7**
you will enjoy a double share of honor. Zech 9:12

61:1 Greek version reads *and the blind will see.* Compare Luke 4:18. **61:2** Or *to proclaim the acceptable year of the LORD.* **61:3** Hebrew *in Zion.*

▸ MINISTRY

61:1 Setting the captives free. When you go shopping at the grocery store, what do you see in the people you meet? So many of them are prisoners in Satan's kingdom. They do not know our Jesus as their Savior, so they are burdened down with guilt and sinful habits they cannot break. They live in a cycle of despair and depression. We have the awesome responsibility of telling them how they can throw away their prison clothes and put on the robe of righteousness (Zechariah 3:4; Revelation 19:8). How can you help others learn about the freedom found in Christ? Isaiah knew the answer: Bring the good news of God's rescue to them. There is no substitute for telling people the message of the gospel—let nothing hinder you from giving it to those who need it. (***See Ministry****> Great Commission> Witness> Turn others from Satan to God,* TopicGuide page A56.)

61:1-2 The Spirit of God would empower the Servant to bring about the promises of salvation and blessing. This anointed one, or Messiah, would proclaim the good news of God. Jesus Christ claimed this remarkable passage as a prophecy of His mission (Luke 4:17-21). It is significant, however, that Christ stopped short of speaking of the "day of God's anger." That is reserved for His second coming when He will establish His kingdom and judge all humanity.

61:4-7 Isaiah reiterated the promises of God that he had faithfully proclaimed throughout the book. The restoration would bring unprecedented spiritual and physical blessing to God's people. Gentiles would acknowledge and submit to the God of Israel and become servants in the kingdom of God. Isaiah also announces the extension of priestly privileges to all of God's people (compare Exodus 19:6 and 1 Peter 2:9).

▸ MINISTRY

61:6 A minister of God. God has set aside some for full-time pastoral ministry. But we forget that even those of us with secular vocations are still full-time ministers in God's kingdom. First Peter 2:5 says, "You are living stones that God is building into His spiritual temple. What's more, you are His holy priests. Through the mediation of Jesus Christ, you offer spiritual sacrifices that please God." Being a priest is an active position. We cannot do a good job if all we do at church is sit in the pew. We are surrounded by a world that desperately needs what we have—the good news of Jesus Christ and a living example of a life changed by Christ. Prepare yourself through prayer each morning to serve as a minister for God in every place you go. (***See Ministry****> Transformation> Vocations> Minister,* TopicGuide page A57.)

You will possess a double portion of prosperity in your land,
and everlasting joy will be yours.

61:8 Gen 17:7 Isa 5:16 8 "For I, the LORD, love justice.
I hate robbery and wrongdoing.
I will faithfully reward My people for their suffering
and make an everlasting covenant with them.
61:9 Isa 44:3 9 Their descendants will be recognized
and honored among the nations.
Everyone will realize that they are a people
the LORD has blessed."

61:10 Isa 51:3; 52:1 10 I am overwhelmed with joy in the LORD my God!
For He has dressed me with the clothing of salvation
and draped me in a robe of righteousness.
I am like a bridegroom in his wedding suit
or a bride with her jewels.
11 The Sovereign LORD will show His justice to the nations of the world.
Everyone will praise Him!
His righteousness will be like a garden in early spring,
with plants springing up everywhere.

ISAIAH'S PRAYER FOR JERUSALEM

62:1 Isa 46:13 **62** 1 Because I love Zion,
I will not keep still.
Because my heart yearns for Jerusalem,
I cannot remain silent.
I will not stop praying for her
until her righteousness shines like the dawn,
and her salvation blazes like a burning torch.
62:2 Isa 56:5 2 The nations will see your righteousness.
World leaders will be blinded by your glory.
And you will be given a new name
62:3 Zech 9:16 1 Thes 2:19 by the LORD's own mouth.
3 The LORD will hold you in His hand for all to see—
62:4 Isa 54:6-7 Jer 32:41 Zeph 3:17-18 a splendid crown in the hand of God.
4 Never again will you be called "The Forsaken City"*
or "The Desolate Land."*

62:4a Hebrew *Azubah,* which means "forsaken." 62:4b Hebrew *Shemamah,* which means "desolate."

61:10-11 Here Jerusalem is personified as praising God with thanksgiving for salvation. New clothes signify the city's new status and honor. The intimate bond between God and His people is signified by the allusion to marriage, a metaphor that is used often in Scripture (compare Ephesians 5:25-33).

62:2-5 In ancient cultures, names were of great significance and were often seen as windows into the character of a person (compare Genesis 17:5; 32:28; Hosea 2:22-23; Revelation 2:17). When Jerusalem was subjected to destruction and its people exiled, the city was known as "The Desolate Land" and "The Forsaken City." However, when God restores His people, the city will once more be a place of blessing and beauty, which will be reflected in new names reflecting the city's new status.

▸ CHURCH

62:3 A crown in God's hand. Names mean something. Christians are called "salt" and "light" (Matthew 5:13-14), "Christ's ambassadors" (2 Corinthians 5:11-20), and other remarkable titles. Isaiah called believers a "splendid crown in the hand of God." In this case, God displays His people as a trophy or a prize won by His grace. His people have given their crowns to Him—He is their new King (Revelation 4:9-11)! It becomes a symbol of new identity as His "City" and "Bride" (62:4). How does that change your self-perception? Or your perception of other Christians around you? God has given you a new identity—live it! (***See Church***> *What> Many Titles> Crown in God's hand,* TopicGuide page A48.)

Your new name will be "The City of God's Delight"*
and "The Bride of God,"*
for the LORD delights in you
and will claim you as His bride.
5 Your children will commit themselves to you, O Jerusalem,
just as a young man commits himself to his bride.
Then God will rejoice over you
as a bridegroom rejoices over his bride.

6 O Jerusalem, I have posted watchmen on your walls;
they will pray day and night, continually.
Take no rest, all you who pray to the LORD.
7 Give the LORD no rest until He completes His work,
until He makes Jerusalem the pride of the earth.
8 The LORD has sworn to Jerusalem by His own strength:
"I will never again hand you over to your enemies.
Never again will foreign warriors come
and take away your grain and new wine.
9 You raised the grain, and you will eat it,
praising the LORD.
Within the courtyards of the Temple,
you yourselves will drink the wine you have pressed."

10 Go out through the gates!
Prepare the highway for My people to return!
Smooth out the road; pull out the boulders;
raise a flag for all the nations to see.
11 The LORD has sent this message to every land:
"Tell the people of Israel,*
'Look, your Savior is coming.
See, He brings His reward with Him as He comes.'"
12 They will be called "The Holy People"
and "The People Redeemed by the LORD."
And Jerusalem will be known as "The Desirable Place"
and "The City No Longer Forsaken."

62:5 Isa 65:19
62:6 Jer 14:21; Ezek 33:7
62:7 Luke 18:1-8
62:9 Isa 65:13, 21-23
62:10 Isa 11:10
62:11 Isa 49:6; Zech 9:9; *Matt 21:5; Rev 22:12
62:12 Deut 7:6; 1 Pet 2:9

JUDGMENT AGAINST THE LORD'S ENEMIES

63 1 Who is this who comes from Edom,
from the city of Bozrah,
with His clothing stained red?
Who is this in royal robes,
marching in His great strength?

63:1 Jer 49:13; Amos 1:12; Zeph 3:17

62:4c Hebrew *Hephzibah,* which means "My delight is in her." 62:4d Hebrew *Beulah,* which means "married."
62:11 Hebrew *Tell the daughter of Zion.*

62:7-8 Isaiah found no contradiction in praying for what God had promised. The Lord's sovereignty does not overrule human will and responsibility, but rather incorporates it.

62:9 The enjoyment of wine is often portrayed as a blessing of the new age brought about by God's salvation (Joel 2:24; Amos 9:13).

63:1-6 This passage is reminiscent of Isaiah 59:16-19. In the earlier passage, the Lord was depicted as a warrior arming himself for battle against the wicked on behalf of His people. Now we read of the Divine Warrior's return from battle. He is seen coming from Edom, which represents wicked and unrepentant nations (see note at 34:5-15). The winepress is a metaphor for the field of battle, and the crimson stains are stains of blood. The graphic imagery symbolizes God's judgment against the ungodly, which will be fully realized at Christ's return (see Revelation 19:15).

"It is I, the LORD, announcing your salvation!
It is I, the LORD, who has the power to save!"

63:2 Rev 19:13, 15
2 Why are Your clothes so red,
as if You have been treading out grapes?

63:3 Isa 22:5 Mic 7:10
3 "I have been treading the winepress alone;
no one was there to help Me.
In My anger I have trampled My enemies
as if they were grapes.
In My fury I have trampled My foes.
Their blood has stained My clothes.

63:4 Jer 51:6
4 For the time has come for Me to avenge My people,
to ransom them from their oppressors.

63:5 Isa 52:10; 59:16
5 I was amazed to see that no one intervened
to help the oppressed.
So I Myself stepped in to save them with My strong arm,
and My wrath sustained Me.
6 I crushed the nations in My anger
and made them stagger and fall to the ground,
spilling their blood upon the earth."

PRAISE FOR DELIVERANCE

63:7 1 Kgs 8:66 Pss 25:6-7; 86:5 Eph 2:4
7 I will tell of the LORD's unfailing love.
I will praise the LORD for all He has done.
I will rejoice in His great goodness to Israel,
which He has granted according to His mercy and love.

63:8 Exod 6:7
8 He said, "They are My very own people.
Surely they will not betray Me again."
And He became their Savior.

63:9 Exod 23:20-23 Judg 10:16
9 In all their suffering He also suffered,
and He personally* rescued them.
In His love and mercy He redeemed them.
He lifted them up and carried them
through all the years.

63:10 Ps 78:40 Acts 7:51 Eph 4:30
10 But they rebelled against Him
and grieved His Holy Spirit.
So He became their enemy
and fought against them.

63:9 Hebrew *and the angel of His presence.*

63:7–64:12 This section is a prayer of Isaiah that contains elements of praise, thanksgiving, repentance, and a cry for deliverance. Through this prayer, Isaiah modeled for the exiles the proper attitude of humble contrition that was required of them in order to enjoy the fullness of God's blessing.

▸ MINISTRY

63:7 Tell of the Lord's unfailing love. Part of mature worship is learning how to praise God for all that He has done. When we tell others about God, we can share how He has answered our prayers, provided for us, and comforted us. Most of all, we can explain how God has taken us from Satan's kingdom and into His own family. As His child, we are blessed with so many spiritual riches that we can't describe them all. Share with someone today about how God has turned your poverty into riches. (***See Ministry*****>** *Great Commission> Witness> Turn others from Satan to God,* TopicGuide page A56.)

63:9-10 This is a reference to Israel's suffering in Egypt and the Exodus (compare Acts 7:51; Ephesians 4:30).

[11] Then they remembered those days of old
when Moses led His people out of Egypt.
They cried out, "Where is the One who brought Israel through the sea,
with Moses as their shepherd?
Where is the One who sent His Holy Spirit
to be among His people?
[12] Where is the One whose power was displayed
when Moses lifted up his hand—
the One who divided the sea before them,
making Himself famous forever?
[13] Where is the One who led them through the bottom of the sea?
They were like fine stallions
racing through the desert, never stumbling.
[14] As with cattle going down into a peaceful valley,
the Spirit of the LORD gave them rest.
You led Your people, LORD,
and gained a magnificent reputation."

63:11 Num 11:17, 25, 29 Isa 51:9-10
63:12 Exod 6:6; 14:21-22
63:13 Jer 31:9
63:14 Josh 21:44

PRAYER FOR MERCY AND PARDON

[15] LORD, look down from heaven;
look from Your holy, glorious home, and see us.
Where is the passion and the might
You used to show on our behalf?
Where are Your mercy and compassion now?
[16] Surely You are still our Father!
Even if Abraham and Jacob* would disown us,
LORD, You would still be our Father.
You are our Redeemer from ages past.
[17] LORD, why have You allowed us to turn from Your path?
Why have You given us stubborn hearts so we no longer fear You?
Return and help us, for we are Your servants,
the tribes that are Your special possession.
[18] How briefly Your holy people possessed Your holy place,
and now our enemies have destroyed it.
[19] Sometimes it seems as though we never belonged to You,
as though we had never been known as Your people.

64

[1]*Oh, that You would burst from the heavens and come down!
How the mountains would quake in Your presence!
[2]*As fire causes wood to burn
and water to boil,

63:15 Ps 80:14
63:16 Isa 41:8 Jer 31:20
63:17 Num 10:36 Isa 29:13-14
63:18 Ps 74:3-7
63:19 Lam 3:43-45
64:1 Exod 19:18 Judg 5:5 Nah 1:5
64:2 Ps 99:1

63:16 Hebrew *Israel.* See note on 14:1. 64:1 Verse 64:1 is numbered 63:20 in Hebrew text. 64:2 Verses 64:2-12 are numbered 64:1-11 in Hebrew text.

63:11-14 The prophet offered a series of recollections from the Exodus and the wilderness wanderings. For the exiles, no event in Israelite history was more significant; the memory of the Exodus was at the heart of Israelite identity. It was in the Exodus that God demonstrated not only His great power but also His remarkable love and grace. Read about the Red Sea crossing in Exodus 14:21–15:21. References to the Spirit allude to Numbers 11:17, 25.

▸ PURPOSE
64:1 Isaiah's impatience. Even the prophet Isaiah became impatient at times. He wanted God to act—right then! That's a feeling we've all experienced. "Why doesn't God come right now and help me with my problem?" we ask. But God has His own timing. He knows exactly when and where He should act. We must place our trust in His master plan for our lives. He listens when we pray, and He acts when the time is right. Don't let your circumstances get in the way of your trust in Him. Trust Him in spite of your situation. He will work it out for your good in His own time. (***See Purpose*> *God's Means*> *God's Sovereignty*> *God has always had a plan,*** TopicGuide page A52.)

64:1-4 Isaiah's prayer invoked the memory of God's appearance at Mount Sinai and His deliverance of Israel from Egypt.

Your coming would make the nations tremble.
Then Your enemies would learn the reason for Your fame!

64:3 Pss 65:5; 66:5
[3] When You came down long ago,
You did awesome deeds beyond our highest expectations.
And oh, how the mountains quaked!

64:4 Isa 40:31 *1 Cor 2:9
[4] For since the world began,
no ear has heard,
and no eye has seen a God like You,
who works for those who wait for Him!
[5] You welcome those who gladly do good,
who follow godly ways.
But You have been very angry with us,
for we are not godly.
We are constant sinners;
how can people like us be saved?

64:6 Ps 90:5-6 Isa 1:30; 48:1
[6] We are all infected and impure with sin.
When we display our righteous deeds,
they are nothing but filthy rags.
Like autumn leaves, we wither and fall,
and our sins sweep us away like the wind.

64:7 Deut 31:18 Isa 1:15
[7] Yet no one calls on Your name
or pleads with You for mercy.
Therefore, You have turned away from us
and turned us over* to our sins.

64:8 Ps 100:3 Isa 45:9
[8] And yet, O LORD, You are our Father.
We are the clay, and You are the potter.
We all are formed by Your hand.

64:9 Mic 7:18
[9] Don't be so angry with us, LORD.
Please don't remember our sins forever.
Look at us, we pray,
and see that we are all Your people.
[10] Your holy cities are destroyed.
Zion is a wilderness;
yes, Jerusalem is a desolate ruin.

64:11 Ps 74:3-7
[11] The holy and beautiful Temple
where our ancestors praised You
has been burned down,
and all the things of beauty are destroyed.

64:12 Ps 83:1
[12] After all this, LORD, must You still refuse to help us?
Will You continue to be silent and punish us?

64:7 As in Greek, Syriac, and Aramaic versions; Hebrew reads *melted us.*

64:5b-9 Isaiah confessed his sins and the sins of the nation. Isaiah's words convey a deep awareness of human sinfulness. Sin infects the human soul so much that even apparent acts of goodness are stained. Given the depth of human sin and inability, it was only natural for Isaiah then to place his hope in God's sovereign grace. God is the potter who alone can fashion us into vessels that are pleasing to Him.

▸ SALVATION

64:6 A rampant infection. Hospital staff members take many precautions to avoid spreading infections. They change gloves whenever they move from one patient to another. They wash everything with special soap. They sterilize their instruments. Sin is like a virulent infection. It spreads everywhere, infecting every part of our lives. We need to take as many precautions to take care of our sin as the hospital staff does for infection. We need to read and study the Bible to recognize what sin is and to remind ourselves of God's standards. We need to confess sin as soon as we recognize its existence. We need to stay clear of situations that tempt us to sin. Begin cleaning up the sin in your life and keep it from spreading. (***See Salvation***> *Our Need*> *Sinful*> *Inability to save oneself,* TopicGuide page A22.)

JUDGMENT AND FINAL SALVATION

65 The LORD says,

"I was ready to respond, but no one asked for help.
I was ready to be found, but no one was looking for Me.
I said, 'Here I am, here I am!'
to a nation that did not call on My name.*
2 All day long I opened My arms to a rebellious people.*
But they follow their own evil paths
and their own crooked schemes.
3 All day long they insult Me to My face
by worshiping idols in their sacred gardens.
They burn incense on pagan altars.
4 At night they go out among the graves,
worshiping the dead.
They eat the flesh of pigs
and make stews with other forbidden foods.
5 Yet they say to each other,
'Don't come too close or you will defile me!
I am holier than you!'
These people are a stench in My nostrils,
an acrid smell that never goes away.

6 "Look, My decree is written out* in front of Me:
I will not stand silent;
I will repay them in full!
Yes, I will repay them—
7 both for their own sins
and for those of their ancestors,"
says the LORD.
"For they also burned incense on the mountains
and insulted Me on the hills.
I will pay them back in full!

8 "But I will not destroy them all,"
says the LORD.
"For just as good grapes are found among a cluster of bad ones
(and someone will say, 'Don't throw them all away—
some of those grapes are good!'),
so I will not destroy all Israel.
For I still have true servants there.

65:1-2 *Rom 10:20-21
65:3 Job 2:5
65:4 Lev 11:7
65:5 Matt 9:11 Luke 18:9-12
65:6 Ps 50:3, 21 Isa 42:14
65:7 Jer 13:25 Ezek 20:27-28 Hos 2:13

65:1 Or *to a nation that did not bear My name.* 65:1-2 Greek version reads *I was found by people who were not looking for Me. / I showed Myself to those who were not asking for Me. / All day long I opened My arms to them, / but they were disobedient and rebellious.* Compare Rom 10:20. 65:6 Or *their sins are written out;* Hebrew reads *it stands written.*

▸WORSHIP

65:1 People are seeking God. All over the world, people are seeking God and finding Him—from the deserts of Africa to the mountains of South America; on the prairies of North America and in the cities of Europe; from China to Brazil—wherever God's Word goes, people are coming to know Jesus Christ. It's the greatest movement in history, and it's the job that Jesus gave to us just before He went back to heaven. He is calling you to help bring others into His kingdom. Are you winning people to Christ, building up those who have just become Christians, or using your resources to enable others to do this work? (See Matthew 28:18-20; also ***see Worship****> OT> Prophets> Old Testament prophets witnessed to the future salvation in Christ,* TopicGuide page A28.)

65:2-5 God's own people, rather than remaining pure and holy, too often assimilated the religious practices of the pagan nations that surrounded them. Isaiah's regular mention of Israel's pagan behavior signals the grave spiritual danger of cultural assimilation.

65:9 Amos 9:11-15
9 I will preserve a remnant of the people of Israel*
and of Judah to possess My land.
Those I choose will inherit it,
and My servants will live there.

65:10 Josh 7:24 Isa 33:9
10 The plain of Sharon will again be filled with flocks
for My people who have searched for Me,
and the valley of Achor will be a place to pasture herds.

65:11 Isa 1:4, 28
11 "But because the rest of you have forsaken the LORD
and have forgotten His Temple,
and because you have prepared feasts to honor the god of Fate
and have offered mixed wine to the god of Destiny,

65:12 2 Chr 36:15-16 Prov 1:24
12 now I will 'destine' you for the sword.
All of you will bow down before the executioner.
For when I called, you did not answer.
When I spoke, you did not listen.
You deliberately sinned—before My very eyes—
and chose to do what you know I despise."

65:13 Isa 5:13
13 Therefore, this is what the Sovereign LORD says:
"My servants will eat,
but you will starve.
My servants will drink,
but you will be thirsty.
My servants will rejoice,
but you will be sad and ashamed.

65:14 Matt 8:12 Luke 13:28
14 My servants will sing for joy,
but you will cry in sorrow and despair.

65:15 Jer 24:9
15 Your name will be a curse word among My people,
for the Sovereign LORD will destroy you
and will call His true servants by another name.

65:16 Isa 45:23
16 All who invoke a blessing or take an oath
will do so by the God of truth.
For I will put aside My anger
and forget the evil of earlier days.

65:17 2 Cor 5:17 2 Pet 3:13
17 "Look! I am creating new heavens and a new earth,
and no one will even think about the old ones anymore.

65:18 Ps 98:1-9 Isa 35:10
18 Be glad; rejoice forever in My creation!
And look! I will create Jerusalem as a place of happiness.
Her people will be a source of joy.

65:9 Hebrew *remnant of Jacob.* See note on 14:1.

65:11-12 God made a play on words as He named one of their false gods, "Destiny," and then promised that those who worshiped it were destined for the sword.

▸ GOD

65:16 The God of truth. What would it be like if God were not the "God of truth"? We couldn't rely on what He said. He could change His mind whenever He felt like it, and our salvation would not be secure. We could not count on our heavenly home. We would be fearful in our prayers. Our lives would not be joyful. And these are just a few of the personal effects of worshiping a god who is untruthful. But our God is honest! Whatever He says is absolute truth. Praise God for His reliability. (***See God****> God's Attributes> True> He is "the God of truth,"* TopicGuide page A18.)

65:17-25 The prophet described the fullness of blessing that would accompany God's salvation. It was not merely a return to the land that was envisioned, but the restoration of the whole created order. God would not abandon His people or His creation. The fulfillment of these hopes was inaugurated at Christ's first advent, and it will be completed at Christ's return. The triumph of Christ will permanently eradicate all the effects of sin from God's good creation.

19 I will rejoice over Jerusalem
and delight in My people.
And the sound of weeping and crying
will be heard in it no more.

65:19 Jer 32:41; Rev 7:17

20 "No longer will babies die when only a few days old.
No longer will adults die before they have lived a full life.
No longer will people be considered old at one hundred!
Only the cursed will die that young!

65:20 Eccl 8:12-13

21 In those days people will live in the houses they build
and eat the fruit of their own vineyards.

65:21 Amos 9:14

22 Unlike the past, invaders will not take their houses
and confiscate their vineyards.
For My people will live as long as trees,
and My chosen ones will have time to enjoy their hard-won gains.
23 They will not work in vain,
and their children will not be doomed to misfortune.
For they are people blessed by the LORD,
and their children, too, will be blessed.

65:23 Isa 61:9

24 I will answer them before they even call to Me.
While they are still talking about their needs,
I will go ahead and answer their prayers!

65:24 Ps 91:15; Dan 10:12

25 The wolf and the lamb will feed together.
The lion will eat hay like a cow.
But the snakes will eat dust.
In those days no one will be hurt or destroyed on My holy mountain.
I, the LORD, have spoken!"

65:25 Gen 3:14; Isa 11:6-7, 9

66

This is what the LORD says:
"Heaven is My throne,
and the earth is My footstool.
Could you build Me a temple as good as that?
Could you build Me such a resting place?

66:1 Ps 11:4; Matt 5:34-35; John 4:20-21; *Acts 7:49-50

2 My hands have made both heaven and earth;
they and everything in them are Mine.*
I, the LORD, have spoken!

66:2 Ps 34:18; Matt 5:3-4; Luke 18:13-14

"I will bless those who have humble and contrite hearts,
who tremble at My word.
3 But those who choose their own ways—
delighting in their detestable sins—
will not have their offerings accepted.
When such people sacrifice a bull,
it is no more acceptable than a human sacrifice.
When they sacrifice a lamb,
it's as though they had sacrificed a dog!

66:2 As in Greek, Latin, and Syriac versions; Hebrew reads *these things are.*

66:1 In the new creation, all of heaven and earth will be God's Temple; the presence of God will permeate the whole universe. Because of this, an earthly Temple will no longer be necessary (see Revelation 21:22).

66:3-4 The Lord despises the religiosity of the unrepentant. Religious observance without sincerity of heart is the moral equivalent of paganism in God's eyes.

When they bring an offering of grain,
they might as well offer the blood of a pig.
When they burn frankincense,
it's as if they had blessed an idol.

66:4 Prov 1:31-32; 10:24 Jer 7:13, 30

[4] I will send them great trouble—
all the things they feared.
For when I called, they did not answer.
When I spoke, they did not listen.
They deliberately sinned before My very eyes
and chose to do what they know I despise."

66:5 Ps 38:20 Matt 5:10-12 Luke 13:17 John 9:34

[5] Hear this message from the LORD,
all you who tremble at His words:
"Your own people hate you
and throw you out for being loyal to My name.
'Let the LORD be honored!' they scoff.
'Be joyful in Him!'
But they will be put to shame.

66:6 Joel 3:7

[6] What is all the commotion in the city?
What is that terrible noise from the Temple?
It is the voice of the LORD
taking vengeance against His enemies.

[7] "Before the birth pains even begin,
Jerusalem gives birth to a son.
[8] Who has ever seen anything as strange as this?
Who ever heard of such a thing?
Has a nation ever been born in a single day?
Has a country ever come forth in a mere moment?
But by the time Jerusalem's* birth pains begin,
her children will be born.

66:9 Isa 37:3

[9] Would I ever bring this nation to the point of birth
and then not deliver it?" asks the LORD.
"No! I would never keep this nation from being born,"
says your God.

66:10 Ps 122:6 Rom 15:10

[10] "Rejoice with Jerusalem!
Be glad with her, all you who love her
and all you who mourn for her.
[11] Drink deeply of her glory
even as an infant drinks at its mother's comforting breasts."

66:12 Isa 60:5

[12] This is what the LORD says:
"I will give Jerusalem a river of peace and prosperity.
The wealth of the nations will flow to her.
Her children will be nursed at her breasts,
carried in her arms, and held on her lap.

66:13 2 Cor 1:4

[13] I will comfort you there in Jerusalem
as a mother comforts her child."

66:14 Prov 3:8 Zech 10:7

[14] When you see these things, your heart will rejoice.
You will flourish like the grass!

66:8 Hebrew *Zion's.*

66:7-9 The appearance of the new community of God's faithful would be so sudden that it is likened to a birth without pain. Jerusalem is personified as the mother of the new community; Paul applies this metaphor to the church (Galatians 4:26-28).

Everyone will see the LORD's hand of blessing on His servants—
and His anger against His enemies.
15 See, the LORD is coming with fire,
and His swift chariots roar like a whirlwind.
He will bring punishment with the fury of His anger
and the flaming fire of His hot rebuke.
16 The LORD will punish the world by fire
and by His sword.
He will judge the earth,
and many will be killed by Him.

17 "Those who 'consecrate' and 'purify' themselves in a sacred garden with its idol in the
center—feasting on pork and rats and other detestable meats—will come to a terrible end,"
says the LORD.
18 "I can see what they are doing, and I know what they are thinking. So I will gather all
nations and peoples together, and they will see My glory.
19 I will perform a sign among
them. And I will send those who survive to be messengers to the nations—to Tarshish, to
the Libyans* and Lydians* (who are famous as archers), to Tubal and Greece,* and to all the
lands beyond the sea that have not heard of My fame or seen My glory. There they will declare My glory to the nations.
20 They will bring the remnant of your people back from every
nation. They will bring them to My holy mountain in Jerusalem as an offering to the LORD.
They will ride on horses, in chariots and wagons, and on mules and camels," says the LORD.
21 "And I will appoint some of them to be My priests and Levites. I, the LORD, have spoken!

22 "As surely as My new heavens and earth will remain,
so will you always be My people,
with a name that will never disappear,"
says the LORD.
23 "All humanity will come to worship Me
from week to week
and from month to month.
24 And as they go out, they will see
the dead bodies of those who have rebelled against Me.
For the worms that devour them will never die,
and the fire that burns them will never go out.
All who pass by
will view them with utter horror."

66:16 Ezek 38:22

66:17 Lev 11:7

66:19 1 Chr 16:24; Isa 42:12

66:20 Isa 2:2-3; 43:5-6; 49:22; 52:11; 60:4

66:21 Isa 61:6; 1 Pet 2:5, 9

66:22 John 10:27-29; 2 Pet 3:13; Rev 21:1

66:23 Isa 27:13

66:24 Isa 1:31; Dan 12:2; *Mark 9:48

66:19a As in some Greek manuscripts, which read *Put* [that is, *Libya*]; Hebrew reads *Pul*. 66:19b Hebrew *Lud*. 66:19c Hebrew *Javan*.

▶ GOD

66:18 God blesses the whole world. As we listen to news about our surrounding world, the media often puts countries into categories like Muslim, Christian, or secular. America is often thought of as "Christian," Saudi Arabia as "Muslim," and France as "secular." But these divisions mean nothing to God, for His people are everywhere and His love extends beyond the borders of one nation or the other. Do not be distracted by national and religious labels—pray God's blessings on everyone and look forward to the day when all of God's people will be united in worship (Revelation 5:8-14). (***See God****> God's Nature> Personality> Emotion> God loves the whole world,* TopicGuide page A14.)

66:19-20 The sign mentioned here was God's imminent act of judgment upon the ungodly. Those who survived God's judgment would be the seed of a new community that would spread the truth of God throughout the nations. The Gentiles would in turn bring God's people back to their land.

66:22-24 The final words of Isaiah present a vision of God's consummated work of salvation. First, God's salvation would extend to the whole of creation; new heavens and a new earth would be established without sin or curse. Second, this new creation would be permanent. There would be no risk of a reversion into sin and death. Third, in the new creation, God's people would be comprised of both Jews and Gentiles; the redeemed would be a cross section of all humanity. Finally, the completion of God's salvation would also bring about the judgment of the wicked. The fulfillment of these expectations has already begun in the work of Christ and the life of the church, and it will be fully realized at Christ's glorious return.

JEREMIAH

PURPOSE

To warn the people of Judah and Jerusalem of the impending judgment of God because of their idolatry and their failure to walk in the stipulations of the Mosaic covenant.

It is tempting to survey the modern church scene and conclude that success in ministry is easy to come by: Just preach and they will come. Jeremiah, more than any other figure in the Old Testament, destroys that idea.

God called Jeremiah to the difficult task of warning the people of Judah—especially those in its capital city, Jerusalem—to turn away from their idolatry, apostasy, and moral degeneracy. Judah was at its lowest point spiritually, living on the verge of judgment. For four decades, Jeremiah took his message of warning to the people, only to be met with complete rejection. He was persecuted, ridiculed, imprisoned, and mocked. Because he was ministering to people who had rejected God's rule over their lives, he was rejected as well. Jeremiah became a picture of Jesus Christ's words to His disciples: "Everyone will hate you because you are My followers" (Luke 21:17).

DISCOVER GOD IN JEREMIAH

Jeremiah can be a discouraging book to read. Yet in the midst of spiritual darkness, God's attributes shine through:

God of Intimacy: Jeremiah had no problem discerning the call of God—the divine purpose—for his life. God told Jeremiah He had formed him in his mother's womb to be "My prophet to the nations" (Jeremiah 1:5). God had things to say to Judah and the surrounding nations, and Jeremiah was to be His mouthpiece. In spite of Jeremiah's protests (1:6), God touched his mouth and gave him the words he was to speak (1:9). But the horrifying message that Jeremiah was given (1:15-16) ensured that he would meet firm resistance, so God assured Jeremiah that He would be with him and would take care of him (1:17-19). God is an intimate God who is personally involved with all of those who serve Him—not just prophets and preachers. He was with Abraham (Genesis 12–17), Moses (Exodus 3–4), Joshua (Joshua 1), Paul (Acts 9), and many others. King David suggested that this intimacy is an abiding characteristic of God: He is with us wherever we go, shaping each of us in our mother's womb and laying out the path of our days before they ever come to pass (Psalm 139). God is "with us" more than just geographically; He is with us personally, working out His purpose for us.

God of Better Things: Even before the judgment of Judah, God stood ready to restore His people. One of His greatest promises to them was that He was going to do a new thing in their midst (Isaiah 42:9; 43:19). This new work is detailed in Jeremiah 31, where God says He will make a "new covenant" with His people (Jeremiah 31:31). This new covenant would complement and contrast with the older covenants that God's people had been under. God would continue to write His law on the minds and hearts of His people (compare Jeremiah 31:34 and Psalm 40:8), only to a greater degree. God would continue to send His Spirit to His people, only this time the Spirit would live in them (Acts 1:4-5, 8). Hebrews 8:6 reveals that Christ is the mediator of this new covenant, having fulfilled all the requirements of the laws of the first covenant (Matthew 5:17). Thus, our current reliance on the once-for-all sacrifice of Christ to satisfy the requirement for an atoning sacrifice for our sins is a change from the older covenants, which relied on regular sacrifices of animals. The book of Hebrews (particularly Hebrews 7–11) highlights the changes and similarities that make the New Covenant of Jeremiah 31 the very best it can be.

DISCOVERY VERSES

This is what the LORD says: "Stop at the crossroads and look around. Ask for the old, godly way, and walk in it. Travel its path, and you will find rest for your souls. But you reply, 'No, that's not the road we want!' "

(JEREMIAH 6:16)

This is what the LORD says: "Don't let the wise boast in their wisdom, or the powerful boast in their power, or the rich boast in their riches. But those who wish to boast should boast in this alone: that they truly know Me and understand that I am the LORD who demonstrates unfailing love and who brings justice and righteousness to the earth, and that I delight in these things. I, the LORD, have spoken!"

(JEREMIAH 9:23-24)

"For I know the plans I have for you," says the LORD. "They are plans for good and not for disaster, to give you a future and a hope."

(JEREMIAH 29:11)

GROWING THROUGH JEREMIAH

The faithfulness of Jeremiah is contrasted with the folly of the people of Judah, providing themes for disciples of Jesus:

Folly of Human Achievement: God told Jeremiah to indict Judah for its pride (9:23-24; 13:9). If it was easy for the people of Jeremiah's time to boast about their intelligence and accomplishments, how much easier is it today? Jeremiah would be dazzled by the technologies and "advancements" of our modern age. But he also would be dumbfounded that such advancements have blinded us to the truth that our trust must not be in human prowess. In an age when the wise boast in their wisdom, the strong in their strength, and the rich in their wealth (Jeremiah 9:23), the truly wise boast in only one thing: a knowledge of the Lord who is kind, just, and righteous (9:24). God has confounded the wise of this world by a seemingly foolish act: offering salvation through a crucified and risen Savior (1 Corinthians 1:18–2:10).

Folly of Trusting in Ourselves: Through Jeremiah, God says, "Cursed are those who put their trust in mere humans . . . but blessed are those who trust in the LORD and have made the LORD their hope and confidence" (17:5, 7). The problem with trusting in ourselves, Jeremiah says, is the human heart: It is "the most deceitful of all things and desperately wicked. Who really knows how bad it is?" (17:9). Disciples of Christ must cultivate faith in God to counter confidence in self.

Folly of Not Believing What God Says: God promised the people of Israel, in the early days of their nationhood, that if they did not allow the Promised Land to "rest" one year out of every seven, they would be taken off the land (Leviticus 26:34, 43). For nearly five centuries, the Israelites failed to cease their farming every seventh year, so they were taken into captivity for seventy years, just as Jeremiah prophesied (25:11-12; 2 Chronicles 36:21). God never says anything He doesn't mean, and He intends to see His word accomplished (Isaiah 55:10-11).

Folly of Fame and Fortune over Faithfulness: Jeremiah was one of the most persecuted of Old Testament prophets (Jeremiah 36–38). While we marvel at his fortitude and that of others (Hebrews 11), followers of Christ have been called to nothing less than a willingness to die for the gospel (Luke 14:27). Speaking the truth to troubled people will always test our ability to endure suffering. The apostle Paul made a painful promise to his disciple Timothy: "Everyone who wants to live a godly life in Christ Jesus will suffer persecution" (2 Timothy 3:12).

JEREMIAH FACTS

Author: Jeremiah. While the words of this book are Jeremiah's (1:1), they were written down by Baruch, Jeremiah's faithful friend and scribe, who recorded all of Jeremiah's prophecies (36:4).

Written to: Primarily to the people of Judah and the city of Jerusalem, though there are also prophetic condemnations of nine surrounding nations.

Date of writing: Sometime during Jeremiah's ministry, which spanned more than forty years (627 BC to a few years after the destruction of Jerusalem in 586 BC).

Setting: Jerusalem while it was being threatened by attacks from Assyria, Egypt, and Babylon; and Egypt, where Jeremiah ministered (and likely died) following the fall of Jerusalem.

OUTLINE

- **JEREMIAH 1:1–20:18**—Judgment on Judah
- **JEREMIAH 21:1–29:32**—Judgment by Babylon
- **JEREMIAH 30:1–33:26**—Hope for restoration
- **JEREMIAH 34:1–45:5**—The fall of Jerusalem
- **JEREMIAH 46:1–52:34**—Judgments on the nations

1:1 2 Chr 36:12, 21; Ezra 1:1
1:2 1 Kgs 13:2; 2 Kgs 21:24
1:3 2 Kgs 23:34
1:5 Ps 139:15-16; Isa 49:1, 5; Jer 25:15-26
1:6 Exod 4:10
1:7 Ezek 2:3-4
1:8 Jer 15:20; Ezek 2:6

1 These are the words of Jeremiah son of Hilkiah, one of the priests from the town of
Anathoth in the land of Benjamin. 2The LORD first gave messages to Jeremiah during
the thirteenth year of the reign of Josiah son of Amon, king of Judah.* 3The LORD's mes-
sages continued throughout the reign of King Jehoiakim, Josiah's son, until the eleventh
year of the reign of King Zedekiah, another of Josiah's sons. In August* of that eleventh
year the people of Jerusalem were taken away as captives.

JEREMIAH'S CALL AND FIRST VISIONS

4The LORD gave me this message:

5 "I knew you before I formed you in your mother's womb.
Before you were born I set you apart
and appointed you as My prophet to the nations."

6"O Sovereign LORD," I said, "I can't speak for You! I'm too young!"
7The LORD replied, "Don't say, 'I'm too young,' for you must go wherever I send you and
say whatever I tell you. 8And don't be afraid of the people, for I will be with you and will

1:2 The thirteenth year of Josiah's reign was 627 B.C. 1:3 Hebrew *In the fifth month,* of the ancient Hebrew lunar calendar. A number of events in Jeremiah can be cross-checked with dates in surviving Babylonian records and related accurately to our modern calendar. The fifth month in the eleventh year of Zedekiah's reign occurred within the months of August and September 586 B.C. Also see 52:12 and the note there.

1:1 Anathoth belonged to the Kohathite clan within the tribe of Levi (Joshua 21:10-19), indicating that Jeremiah was a Kohathite. The Kohathites were the priests responsible for the upkeep of the holy equipment in the Tabernacle and Temple (Numbers 3:27-31).

GOD

1:5 Knowing us prior to knowing Him. What are the earliest memories you have from childhood? Before you knew anything, God knew you. He knew you before you were even conceived! You are no accident. Like Jeremiah, your birth was ordained by God, who created you to do His will on earth (Psalm 139; Galatians 1:15). Let God's early care for you encourage you to obey Him with all your heart (Ephesians 2:10). The God who knew you first wants you to put Him first in everything you do. (***See God*****>** ***God's Attributes> All-Knowing> God misses nothing about us,*** **TopicGuide page A15.)**

1:5-10 By calling Jeremiah as His prophet, the Lord appointed Jeremiah to be His ambassador to Judah. He was vested with God's authority and would speak on His behalf, just as an earthly ambassador would do so on behalf of his king.

protect you. I, the LORD, have spoken!" 9Then the LORD reached out and touched my mouth 1:9 Exod 4:11-16 Deut 18:18
and said,

"Look, I have put My words in your mouth!
10 Today I appoint you to stand up 1:10 Isa 44:26-28 Jer 24:6; 31:28 2 Cor 10:4
against nations and kingdoms.
Some you must uproot and tear down,
destroy and overthrow.
Others you must build up
and plant."

11 Then the LORD said to me, "Look, Jeremiah! What do you see?" 1:11 Jer 24:3 Amos 7:8
And I replied, "I see a branch from an almond tree."
12And the LORD said, "That's right, and it means that I am watching,* and I will certainly
carry out all My plans." 1:12 Deut 32:35
13Then the LORD spoke to me again and asked, "What do you see now?" 1:13 Ezek 11:3, 7 Zech 4:2
And I replied, "I see a pot of boiling water, spilling from the north."
14"Yes," the LORD said, "for terror from the north will boil out on the people of this land.
15Listen! I am calling the armies of the kingdoms of the north to come to Jerusalem. I, the 1:14 Isa 41:25 Jer 4:6; 10:22
LORD, have spoken!

"They will set their thrones 1:15 Isa 22:7 Jer 9:11; 25:9
at the gates of the city.
They will attack its walls
and all the other towns of Judah.
16 I will pronounce judgment 1:16 Isa 2:8; 37:19 Jer 7:9; 10:3-5; 19:4
on My people for all their evil—
for deserting Me and burning incense to other gods.
Yes, they worship idols made with their own hands!

17 "Get up and prepare for action. 1:17 Ezek 2:6; 3:16-18
Go out and tell them everything I tell you to say.
Do not be afraid of them,
or I will make you look foolish in front of them.
18 For see, today I have made you strong
like a fortified city that cannot be captured,
like an iron pillar or a bronze wall.
You will stand against the whole land—
the kings, officials, priests, and people of Judah.
19 They will fight you, but they will fail. 1:19 Jer 1:8; 20:11
For I am with you, and I will take care of you.
I, the LORD, have spoken!"

1:12 The Hebrew word for "watching" *(shoqed)* sounds like the word for "almond tree" *(shaqed).*

1:11-12 The Hebrew name for the almond tree, *shaked,* signifies the speed or haste of the blossoms of the tree, which come before other trees—as early as late January. The farmer must be watching closely to see its advanced bloom. Jeremiah prophesied that God was like that farmer; He was watching carefully for the perfect moment to judge.

1:13-16 Invasion by a foreign power was a typical curse that God threatened against His people when they disobeyed (Leviticus 26:14-17, 25). Here, God called upon Babylon to invade Judah from the route of easiest access, which came from north of Judah.

▸ CHURCH

1:19 Special protection in special service. Christians have been given the special task of being salt and light in the world (Matthew 5:13-14). In this divinely appointed mission of advancing God's kingdom, we will often face resistance and persecution. Accomplishing God's will may cost a friendship or maybe even a job. There are risks in proclaiming God's truth to the world—but we must be willing to take them for the sake of the gospel. As with Jeremiah, God has promised to be with us every step of the way and to deliver us from our enemies (Matthew 1:21-23; 28:20). We have been given a special task and promised special protection. Don't be timid in carrying out your mission. (***See Church****> What> Many Titles> Sheep> The sheep trust the protection of the shepherd,* TopicGuide page A48.)

1:19 The phrase "I am with you" did not mean that God would be present with Jeremiah physically, but that God would be the warrior king, leading Jeremiah into battle.

THE LORD'S CASE AGAINST HIS PEOPLE

2:2 Isa 58:1 Jer 11:6 Ezek 16:8

2 The LORD gave me another message. He said, 2 "Go and shout this message to Jerusa-
lem. This is what the LORD says:

"I remember how eager you were to please Me
as a young bride long ago,
how you loved Me and followed Me
even through the barren wilderness.

2:3 Exod 19:5-6 Deut 7:6; 14:2 Isa 41:11 Jer 30:16

3 In those days Israel was holy to the LORD,
the first of His children.*
All who harmed His people were declared guilty,
and disaster fell on them.
I, the LORD, have spoken!"

2:5 2 Kgs 17:15 Jer 8:19 Mic 6:3

4 Listen to the word of the LORD, people of Jacob—all you families of Israel! 5 This is what
the LORD says:

"What did your ancestors find wrong with Me
that led them to stray so far from Me?
They worshiped worthless idols,
only to become worthless themselves.

2:6 Deut 8:15; 32:10

6 They did not ask, 'Where is the LORD
who brought us safely out of Egypt
and led us through the barren wilderness—
a land of deserts and pits,
a land of drought and death,
where no one lives or even travels?'

2:7 Deut 8:7-9; 11:10-12 Jer 3:2; 16:18

7 "And when I brought you into a fruitful land
to enjoy its bounty and goodness,
you defiled My land and
corrupted the possession I had promised you.

2:8 Jer 10:21; 23:13 Hab 2:18 Mal 2:6-7

8 The priests did not ask,
'Where is the LORD?'
Those who taught My word ignored Me,
the rulers turned against Me,
and the prophets spoke in the name of Baal,
wasting their time on worthless idols.

2:9 Ezek 20:35-36

9 Therefore, I will bring My case against you,"
says the LORD.
"I will even bring charges against your children's children
in the years to come.

2:3 Hebrew *the firstfruits of His harvest.*

2:2 Jeremiah was to deliver his message to Jerusalem because it was the capital city in which the king resided. It was to be understood that the message applied to the whole land over which the king ruled.

▸ GOD

2:3-8 Looking to the past for encouragement. Jeremiah, speaking for God, asked his audience a sarcastic question: "What did your ancestors find wrong with Me that led them to stray so far from Me?" He dared his audience to look into the past and find a single thing that God had done wrong. In the busyness of life, we become so preoccupied with our concerns that we ignore God's goodness in the past and neglect to focus on God's acts of salvation in our lives. The book of Psalms continually calls us to remember God's faithfulness in the past (see Psalms 78; 105; 106). These "Psalms of Remembrance" call us to worship God and inspire us to remain His followers. Make a list of the numerous ways God has demonstrated His faithfulness to you and make it your goal tomorrow to look for every way God is keeping His promises to you. (***See God****> God's Attributes> Faithful> His faithfulness endures,* TopicGuide page A16.)

2:9 God brought a lawsuit against His people in Jerusalem and throughout Judah. In times of blessing, God was the judge and advocate for His people. But because they had sinned so grievously, God had become their enemy. There was no judge or advocate left to defend them.

10 "Go west and look in the land of Cyprus*;
go east and search through the land of Kedar.
Has anyone ever heard of anything
as strange as this?
11 Has any nation ever traded its gods for new ones,
even though they are not gods at all?
Yet My people have exchanged their glorious God*
for worthless idols!
12 The heavens are shocked at such a thing
and shrink back in horror and dismay,"
says the LORD.
13 "For My people have done two evil things:
They have abandoned Me—
the fountain of living water.
And they have dug for themselves cracked cisterns
that can hold no water at all!

2:10 Ps 120:5; Isa 23:12; 37:19; Jer 49:28
2:11 106:20
2:13 Ps 36:9; Jer 17:13; John 4:14

THE RESULTS OF ISRAEL'S SIN

14 "Why has Israel become a slave?
Why has he been carried away as plunder?
15 Strong lions have roared against him,
and the land has been destroyed.
The towns are now in ruins,
and no one lives in them anymore.
16 Egyptians, marching from their cities of Memphis* and Tahpanhes,
have destroyed Israel's glory and power.
17 And you have brought this upon yourselves
by rebelling against the LORD your God,
even though He was leading you on the way!

18 "What have you gained by your alliances with Egypt
and your covenants with Assyria?
What good to you are the streams of the Nile*
or the waters of the Euphrates River?*
19 Your wickedness will bring its own punishment.
Your turning from Me will shame you.
You will see what an evil, bitter thing it is
to abandon the LORD your God and not to fear Him.
I, the Lord, the LORD of Heaven's Armies, have spoken!

20 "Long ago I broke the yoke that oppressed you
and tore away the chains of your slavery,

2:15 Jer 4:7
2:16 Jer 44:1; Hos 9:6
2:17 Deut 32:10; Jer 4:18
2:18 Josh 13:3; Isa 30:2
2:19 Ps 36:1; Isa 3:9; Jer 3:8; 5:24; Hos 11:7; Amos 8:10
2:20 Lev 26:13; Deut 12:2; Isa 57:5; Jer 3:2, 6; 17:2

2:10 Hebrew *Kittim.* 2:11 Hebrew *their glory.* 2:16 Hebrew *Noph.* 2:18a Hebrew *of Shihor,* a branch of the Nile River. 2:18b Hebrew *the river?*

2:10-13 Cyprus lay to the west and Kedar to the east. These metaphorically represented all the foreign nations familiar to Judah. Although the worthless gods of the foreign nations had failed to bless them, the foreigners remained faithful to their gods. In contrast, Judah betrayed the Lord, who had done wondrous things for them.

2:14-16 The Assyrians took the 10 northern tribes into captivity in 722 BC. By Jeremiah's time, Babylon and its territories had conquered Assyria. From 609 to 605 BC, Egypt and Babylon fought over the territory of the northern kingdom.

2:17 Despite the fact that God had "promised" the land of Israel to His people (Jeremiah 2:7), He later exiled them from the land because of their disobedience. The blessings that God had promised had been contingent upon the people's obedience (Jeremiah 18:1-10).

but still you said,
'I will not serve You.'
On every hill and under every green tree,
you have prostituted yourselves by bowing down to idols.

2:21 Exod 15:17 Ps 80:8 Isa 5:2, 4

21 But I was the One who planted you,
choosing a vine of the purest stock—the very best.
How did you grow into this corrupt wild vine?

2:22 Jer 4:14

22 No amount of soap or lye can make you clean.
I still see the stain of your guilt.
I, the Sovereign LORD, have spoken!

ISRAEL, AN UNFAITHFUL WIFE

2:23 Prov 30:12 Jer 7:31; 9:14

23 "You say, 'That's not true!
I haven't worshiped the images of Baal!'
But how can you say that?
Go and look in any valley in the land!
Face the awful sins you have done.
You are like a restless female camel
desperately searching for a mate.
24 You are like a wild donkey,
sniffing the wind at mating time.
Who can restrain her lust?
Those who desire her don't need to search,
for she goes running to them!

2:25 Deut 32:16 Jer 14:10; 18:12

25 When will you stop running?
When will you stop panting after other gods?
But you say, 'Save Your breath.
I'm in love with these foreign gods,
and I can't stop loving them now!'

2:26 Jer 48:27

26 "Israel is like a thief
who feels shame only when he gets caught.
They, their kings, officials, priests, and prophets—
all are alike in this.

2:27 Isa 26:16 Jer 18:17

27 To an image carved from a piece of wood they say,
'You are my father.'
To an idol chiseled from a block of stone they say,
'You are my mother.'
They turn their backs on Me,
but in times of trouble they cry out to Me,
'Come and save us!'

2:28 Deut 32:37 2 Kgs 17:30-31 Isa 45:20 Jer 11:12-13

28 But why not call on these gods you have made?
When trouble comes, let them save you if they can!
For you have as many gods
as there are towns in Judah.

2:29 Dan 9:11

29 Why do you accuse Me of doing wrong?
You are the ones who have rebelled,"
says the LORD.

2:30 Neh 9:26 Isa 1:5 Jer 5:3; 7:28; 26:20-24

30 "I have punished your children,
but they did not respond to My discipline.

2:23-25 The Bible commonly speaks of idolatry in terms of adultery (Jeremiah 3; Hosea 1–3). Here, God indicated His utter disgust with His people by comparing them not to human adulterers, but to animals in heat. Judah's idolatry had no semblance of dignity or reason.

You yourselves have killed your prophets
as a lion kills its prey.

31 "O My people, listen to the words of the LORD!
Have I been like a desert to Israel?
Have I been to them a land of darkness?
Why then do My people say, 'At last we are free from God!
We don't need Him anymore!'
32 Does a young woman forget her jewelry?
Does a bride hide her wedding dress?
Yet for years on end
My people have forgotten Me.

33 "How you plot and scheme to win your lovers.
Even an experienced prostitute could learn from you!
34 Your clothing is stained with the blood of the innocent and the poor,
though you didn't catch them breaking into your houses!
35 And yet you say,
'I have done nothing wrong.
Surely God isn't angry with me!'
But now I will punish you severely
because you claim you have not sinned.
36 First here, then there—
you flit from one ally to another asking for help.
But your new friends in Egypt will let you down,
just as Assyria did before.
37 In despair, you will be led into exile
with your hands on your heads,
for the LORD has rejected the nations you trust.
They will not help you at all.

2:31 Deut 32:15; Isa 45:19
2:32 Isa 17:10; Jer 3:21; Hos 8:14
2:34 2 Kgs 21:16; Jer 7:6; 19:4
2:35 Jer 25:31; 1 Jn 1:8, 10
2:36 2 Chr 28:16, 20-21; Hos 12:1; 1 Jn 1:8, 10
2:37 Jer 37:7-10

3 1 "If a man divorces a woman
and she goes and marries someone else,
he will not take her back again,
for that would surely corrupt the land.
But you have prostituted yourself with many lovers,
so why are you trying to come back to Me?"
says the LORD.
2 "Look at the shrines on every hilltop.
Is there any place you have not been defiled
by your adultery with other gods?
You sit like a prostitute beside the road waiting for a customer.
You sit alone like a nomad in the desert.
You have polluted the land with your prostitution
and your wickedness.
3 That's why even the spring rains have failed.
For you are a brazen prostitute and completely shameless.

3:1 Deut 24:4; Jer 4:1; Ezek 16:26, 28-29; Zech 1:3
3:2 Deut 12:2; Jer 2:7, 20; Ezek 16:25
3:3 Lev 26:19; Jer 6:15; 14:3-6

2:36-37 Rather than relying on the Lord for protection (Jeremiah 1:19), Judah had betrayed God by making treaties with powerful foreign countries. By associating these treaties with Judah's infidelity, Jeremiah indicated that the treaties were a type of religious idolatry (2:23-25; see also Exodus 34:15).

3:1-13, 20 Although the idolatrous worship of Israel and Judah often involved actual sexual activities (3:23; Deuteronomy 23:17), the focus of these verses is idolatry and not sexual sin. Marriage is used as a metaphor for God's relationship with Israel and Judah, so Israel's and Judah's idolatry is described as infidelity to God (Jeremiah 3:6, 13).

3:4 Ps 71:17 4 Yet you say to Me,
'Father, You have been my guide since my youth.
5 Surely You won't be angry forever!
Surely You can forget about it!'
So you talk,
but you keep on doing all the evil you can."

JUDAH FOLLOWS ISRAEL'S EXAMPLE

3:6 Jer 17:2 6During the reign of King Josiah, the LORD said to me, "Have you seen what fickle Israel has
Ezek 23:4-10 done? Like a wife who commits adultery, Israel has worshiped other gods on every hill and
under every green tree. 7I thought, 'After she has done all this, she will return to Me.' But
3:7 Ezek 16:47 she did not return, and her faithless sister Judah saw this. 8She saw that I divorced faithless
Israel because of her adultery. But that treacherous sister Judah had no fear, and now she,
3:8 Isa 50:1 too, has left Me and given herself to prostitution. 9Israel treated it all so lightly—she thought
Ezek 16:46-47; 23:11 nothing of committing adultery by worshiping idols made of wood and stone. So now the
3:9 land has been polluted. 10But despite all this, her faithless sister Judah has never sincerely
Isa 57:6 Jer 2:7, 27 returned to Me. She has only pretended to be sorry. I, the LORD, have spoken!"

HOPE FOR WAYWARD ISRAEL

3:11 11Then the LORD said to me, "Even faithless Israel is less guilty than treacherous Judah!
Ezek 16:51 12Therefore, go and give this message to Israel.* This is what the LORD says:

3:12 Ps 86:15 Jer 31:20; 33:26 "O Israel, My faithless people,
come home to Me again,
for I am merciful.
I will not be angry with you forever.
3:13 Deut 12:2; 30:1-3 Jer 14:20 13 Only acknowledge your guilt.
Admit that you rebelled against the LORD your God
and committed adultery against Him
by worshiping idols under every green tree.
Confess that you refused to listen to My voice.
I, the LORD, have spoken!

3:14 Jer 50:4-5 Hos 2:19 14 "Return home, you wayward children,"
says the LORD,
"for I am your master.
I will bring you back to the land of Israel*—
one from this town and two from that family—
from wherever you are scattered.

3:12 Hebrew *toward the north.* 3:14 Hebrew *to Zion.*

3:6-8 Judah, the southern kingdom, consisted of the tribes of Judah and Benjamin, which remained loyal to Judah. The remaining 10 tribes constituted the nation of Israel, the northern kingdom. Israel had been exiled from the Promised Land and sent into captivity by Assyria in 722 BC. Israel's exile should have taught Judah to remain faithful to the Lord, but Judah failed to learn from Israel's example.

▶ SPIRITUAL WARFARE
3:13-14 Loving discipline. In Jeremiah's time, God's punishment of Israel was not intended to be final. God's punishment of His people is never final. It is always part of a process of drawing us closer to Him. God wants His people to learn from their mistakes and repent. God disciplines believers in painful ways, but His discipline is ultimately motivated by love (Hebrews 12:5-11). If you have been under God's discipline, ask God to grant you a repentant heart. God is eager to bless us and to show us grace and mercy (Exodus 34:6), and He is faithful to forgive us when we repent (1 John 1:9). Turn away from sin and turn to God—you'll find a loving Father waiting for you. (***See Spiritual Warfare**> Resisting Sin and Evil> Consequences> Of Disobedience> Falling under discipline,* TopicGuide page A46.)

3:14-18 God offered to restore Israel and Judah to the Promised Land and to bless them exceedingly. Because Israel and Judah failed to repent, the restoration was not realized. In law and prophecy, God makes threats and promises knowing full well they will not be fulfilled due to the failure of His people. For another example, see the prophecy of Jonah to Nineveh and the repentance that forestalled God's judgment on them (Jonah 3:4, 10).

15 And I will give you shepherds after My own heart,
who will guide you with knowledge and understanding.

3:15 Jer 23:4; Acts 20:28

16 "And when your land is once more filled with people," says the LORD, "you will no lon-
ger wish for 'the good old days' when you possessed the Ark of the LORD's Covenant. You
will not miss those days or even remember them, and there will be no need to rebuild the
Ark. 17 In that day Jerusalem will be known as 'The Throne of the LORD.' All nations will
come there to honor the LORD. They will no longer stubbornly follow their own evil desires.
18 In those days the people of Judah and Israel will return together from exile in the north.
They will return to the land I gave their ancestors as an inheritance forever.

3:16 Isa 65:17
3:17 Jer 12:15-16; 16:19; 17:12; Ezek 43:7
3:18 Isa 11:13; 60:9; Jer 16:14-15; 31:8; 50:4-5; Hos 1:11; Amos 9:15

19 "I thought to Myself,
'I would love to treat you as My own children!'
I wanted nothing more than to give you this beautiful land—
the finest possession in the world.
I looked forward to your calling Me 'Father,'
and I wanted you never to turn from Me.
20 But you have been unfaithful to Me, you people of Israel!
You have been like a faithless wife who leaves her husband.
I, the LORD, have spoken."

3:19 Ps 16:6; Isa 63:16
3:20 Isa 48:8

21 Voices are heard high on the windswept mountains,
the weeping and pleading of Israel's people.
For they have chosen crooked paths
and have forgotten the LORD their God.

3:21 Isa 15:2; Jer 2:32

22 "My wayward children," says the LORD,
"come back to Me, and I will heal your wayward hearts."

"Yes, we're coming," the people reply,
"for You are the LORD our God.
23 Our worship of idols on the hills
and our religious orgies on the mountains
are a delusion.
Only in the LORD our God
will Israel ever find salvation.
24 From childhood we have watched
as everything our ancestors worked for—
their flocks and herds, their sons and daughters—
was squandered on a delusion.
25 Let us now lie down in shame
and cover ourselves with dishonor,
for we and our ancestors have sinned
against the LORD our God.
From our childhood to this day
we have never obeyed Him."

3:22 Hos 6:1; 14:4
3:23 Pss 3:8; 121:1-2; Jer 17:14
3:25 Ezra 9:7; Jer 22:21

4

1 "O Israel," says the LORD,
"if you wanted to return to Me, you could.
You could throw away your detestable idols
and stray away no more.

4:1 Jer 7:3, 7; 35:15; Joel 2:12

3:22-25 The response recorded here is part of the prophetic charge against Israel and Judah; it is the response God desired and required, not the response Israel and Judah actually offered.

4:2 Gen 22:18 Deut 10:20 Isa 65:16 Jer 9:24 1 Cor 1:31 Gal 3:8

2 Then when you swear by My name, saying,
'As surely as the LORD lives,'
you could do so
with truth, justice, and righteousness.
Then you would be a blessing to the nations of the world,
and all people would come and praise My name."

COMING JUDGMENT AGAINST JUDAH

4:3 Hos 10:12 Matt 13:7, 22

3 This is what the LORD says to the people of Judah and Jerusalem:

"Plow up the hard ground of your hearts!
Do not waste your good seed among thorns.

4:4 Deut 10:16 Isa 30:27 Jer 9:25-26; 21:12 Mark 9:43, 48 Rom 2:28-29

4 O people of Judah and Jerusalem,
surrender your pride and power.
Change your hearts before the LORD,*
or My anger will burn like an unquenchable fire
because of all your sins.

4:5 Josh 10:20 Jer 6:1 Hos 8:1

5 "Shout to Judah, and broadcast to Jerusalem!
Tell them to sound the alarm throughout the land:
'Run for your lives!
Flee to the fortified cities!'

4:6 Jer 1:14-15; 6:1, 22

6 Raise a signal flag as a warning for Jerusalem*:
'Flee now! Do not delay!'
For I am bringing terrible destruction upon you
from the north."

4:7 Isa 1:7; 6:11 Jer 2:15; 5:6; 25:9, 38

7 A lion stalks from its den,
a destroyer of nations.
It has left its lair and is headed your way.
It's going to devastate your land!
Your towns will lie in ruins,
with no one living in them anymore.

4:8 Isa 5:25; 10:4 Jer 30:24

8 So put on clothes of mourning
and weep with broken hearts,
for the fierce anger of the LORD
is still upon us.

4:4 Hebrew *Circumcise yourselves to the LORD, and take away the foreskins of your heart.* 4:6 Hebrew *Zion.*

▸ CHURCH

4:2 The church's responsibility to the world. Do you know someone who is always prepared? God has always had a plan to save sinners. But His plan doesn't happen by magic—the church is the caretaker of the gospel, and others cannot come to Christ unless they hear the message proclaimed by God's people (Romans 10:14-15). The Israelites of Jeremiah's time had failed in their calling to be the vehicle of blessing for other nations because of unrepentant sin. But God promises that the church will not fail. Even now, the church is assaulting the kingdom of darkness by spoiling its best efforts at evil and robbing it of its goods—the souls of men, women, and children (Matthew 16:18). The church is assured of the ultimate success of this mission: The gospel will be preached to all the nations (Matthew 24:14). (***See Church***> *Who> From Every Place and Age> Universal Church,* TopicGuide page A48.)

4:2 God's plan for Israel had always been to redeem the entire world through the faithfulness of His chosen people, bringing all nations to salvation (Genesis 12:3; 18:18; 22:18). From a human perspective, it might appear that Israel risked the salvation of the world by rebelling against God. But Jeremiah reminded Israel throughout his prophecies that though God ordains all, humans act freely within His plan. This truth underscores the importance of heeding God's warnings and commands.

4:3-14 The judgment against Judah and Jerusalem (Jeremiah 4:5-18, 23-31) could have been avoided if the people repented. The prophecy was not intended to reveal the unalterable future, but to motivate the people to change their behavior. Nevertheless, if they failed to repent, the judgment would come to pass as predicted.

4:6-7 The judgment contained in this prophecy was a Babylonian invasion. Although Babylon lay to the east, the easiest route by which Babylon could invade Judah lay to the north of Judah.

9 "In that day," says the LORD,
"the king and the officials will tremble in fear.
The priests will be struck with horror,
and the prophets will be appalled."

10 Then I said, "O Sovereign LORD,
the people have been deceived by what you said,
for you promised peace for Jerusalem.
But the sword is held at their throats!"

11 The time is coming when the LORD will say
to the people of Jerusalem,
"My dear people, a burning wind is blowing in from the desert,
and it's not a gentle breeze useful for winnowing grain.
12 It is a roaring blast sent by Me!
Now I will pronounce your destruction!"

13 Our enemy rushes down on us like storm clouds!
His chariots are like whirlwinds.
His horses are swifter than eagles.
How terrible it will be, for we are doomed!
14 O Jerusalem, cleanse your heart
that you may be saved.
How long will you harbor
your evil thoughts?
15 Your destruction has been announced
from Dan and the hill country of Ephraim.

16 "Warn the surrounding nations
and announce this to Jerusalem:
The enemy is coming from a distant land,
raising a battle cry against the towns of Judah.
17 They surround Jerusalem like watchmen around a field,
for My people have rebelled against Me,"
says the LORD.
18 "Your own actions have brought this upon you.
This punishment is bitter, piercing you to the heart!"

JEREMIAH WEEPS FOR HIS PEOPLE

19 My heart, my heart—I writhe in pain!
My heart pounds within me! I cannot be still.
For I have heard the blast of enemy trumpets
and the roar of their battle cries.
20 Waves of destruction roll over the land,
until it lies in complete desolation.
Suddenly my tents are destroyed;
in a moment my shelters are crushed.
21 How long must I see the battle flags
and hear the trumpets of war?

4:9 Jer 48:41
4:10 2 Thes 2:11
4:11 Jer 51:1; Ezek 17:10; Hos 13:15
4:13 Deut 28:49; Isa 66:15; Lam 4:19
4:14 Isa 1:16; Jer 13:27; Jas 4:8
4:15 Jer 6:19
4:16 Jer 5:15; Ezek 21:22
4:17 2 Kgs 25:1; Jer 5:23
4:18 Jer 2:17-19
4:19 Isa 21:3; 22:4; Hab 3:16
4:20 Jer 10:20; Ezek 7:26

4:9-10 The leaders of the nation were responsible to direct the people to the pure worship of the Lord, but they failed in their duty. But even though the people had been deceived into practicing idolatry, they would be judged for their sin. Their ignorance did not excuse their actions (1 Timothy 2:14).

4:15 These lands were part of the nation of Israel, not part of Judah. The announcement mentioned was not a contemporary prophecy; it was the actual exile of Israel that took place in 722 BC. Israel's exile served as a warning to Judah that they, too, would be exiled if they did not repent of their idolatry.

4:22 Jer 5:21; 10:8; 13:23 Rom 16:19

22 "My people are foolish
and do not know Me," says the LORD.
"They are stupid children
who have no understanding.
They are clever enough at doing wrong,
but they have no idea how to do right!"

JEREMIAH'S VISION OF COMING DISASTER

4:23 Isa 24:19
4:24 Isa 5:25 Ezek 38:20
4:25 Jer 9:10; 12:4 Zeph 1:3
4:26 Jer 9:10

23 I looked at the earth, and it was empty and formless.
I looked at the heavens, and there was no light.
24 I looked at the mountains and hills,
and they trembled and shook.
25 I looked, and all the people were gone.
All the birds of the sky had flown away.
26 I looked, and the fertile fields had become a wilderness.
The towns lay in ruins,
crushed by the LORD's fierce anger.

4:27 Jer 5:10, 18; 12:11-12; 30:11; 46:28
4:28 Num 23:19 Isa 5:30; 50:3 Jer 23:20; 30:24 Hos 4:3 Joel 2:30-31

27 This is what the LORD says:
"The whole land will be ruined,
but I will not destroy it completely.
28 The earth will mourn
and the heavens will be draped in black
because of My decree against My people.
I have made up My mind and will not change it."

4:29 Isa 2:19-21 Jer 16:16
4:30 2 Kgs 9:30 Jer 22:20, 22 Ezek 23:9-10, 22, 40

29 At the noise of charioteers and archers,
the people flee in terror.
They hide in the bushes
and run for the mountains.
All the towns have been abandoned—
not a person remains!
30 What are you doing,
you who have been plundered?
Why do you dress up in beautiful clothing
and put on gold jewelry?
Why do you brighten your eyes with mascara?
Your primping will do you no good!
The allies who were your lovers
despise you and seek to kill you.

4:31 Isa 1:15; 42:14 Jer 13:21 Lam 1:17

31 I hear a cry, like that of a woman in labor,
the groans of a woman giving birth to her first child.
It is beautiful Jerusalem*
gasping for breath and crying out,
"Help! I'm being murdered!"

4:31 Hebrew *the daughter of Zion.*

SPIRITUAL WARFARE

4:22 Sin creates ignorance. Jeremiah wept (4:19) over the sins of his nation because they had numbed themselves to the horrid truth—disaster was coming (4:27), and they would not be prepared. There would be no hope of effective retreat (4:29), no possibility of spending their way out of trouble (4:30), and no allies to save them. With the answer right in front of them—repentance—they would remain passive until they heard the armies marching upon their towns (4:29). It's no wonder that it takes a miracle to open sinners up to the gospel. As you share the gospel with unbelievers, pray that God's Spirit would take away the blinding nature of sin, open their eyes, and enable them to have faith in God's plan for their salvation. You can have amazing and persuasive arguments, but if the Holy Spirit is not at work, sin will win. (***See Spiritual Warfare****> Origin of Sin> Humanity's Fall> Spiritual> Spiritually blind,* TopicGuide page A44.)

THE SINS OF JUDAH

5 [1] "Run up and down every street in Jerusalem," says the LORD.
"Look high and low; search throughout the city!
If you can find even one just and honest person,
I will not destroy the city.
2 But even when they are under oath,
saying, 'As surely as the LORD lives,'
they are still telling lies!"

3 LORD, You are searching for honesty.
You struck Your people,
but they paid no attention.
You crushed them,
but they refused to be corrected.
They are determined, with faces set like stone;
they have refused to repent.

4 Then I said, "But what can we expect from the poor?
They are ignorant.
They don't know the ways of the LORD.
They don't understand God's laws.
5 So I will go and speak to their leaders.
Surely they know the ways of the LORD
and understand God's laws."
But the leaders, too, as one man,
had thrown off God's yoke
and broken His chains.
6 So now a lion from the forest will attack them;
a wolf from the desert will pounce on them.
A leopard will lurk near their towns,
tearing apart any who dare to venture out.
For their rebellion is great,
and their sins are many.

7 "How can I pardon you?
For even your children have turned from Me.
They have sworn by gods that are not gods at all!
I fed My people until they were full.
But they thanked Me by committing adultery
and lining up at the brothels.
8 They are well-fed, lusty stallions,
each neighing for his neighbor's wife.

5:1 Gen 18:26, 32; 2 Chr 16:9
5:2 Titus 1:16
5:3 Jer 7:26, 28; 8:5; 19:15; Ezek 3:8; Zeph 3:2
5:4 Isa 27:11; Jer 4:22; Hos 4:6
5:5 Jer 2:20; Mic 3:1
5:6 Jer 30:14-15; Hos 13:7; Hab 1:8
5:7 Deut 32:21; Josh 23:7; Jer 2:11; Zeph 1:5; Gal 4:8
5:8 Jer 13:27; 29:23; Ezek 22:11

5:1-2 The offer to save the city if one righteous person could be found recalls the bargain between God and Abraham regarding Sodom and Gomorrah (Genesis 18:17-33). At least one righteous person existed in Sodom and Gomorrah, namely Lot (2 Peter 2:7), but his presence was not enough to save the cities (Genesis 19:1-25). Jerusalem was worse than Sodom and Gomorrah because not even one righteous person could be found.

5:3 God's discipline of Judah was not a recent development. According to the terms of His covenant (Leviticus 26), God had been increasing Judah's discipline incrementally. As with all prior judgments, this one was intended to drive the people to repentance (Leviticus 26:18, 21, 23, 27), not to utterly destroy them (Leviticus 26:40-42).

▸ CHURCH
5:4 God's extra patience with the ignorant. In most legal systems, there is a basic rule: "Ignorance of the law is no excuse." God's view of the law, however, is slightly different: "Knowledge of the law brings greater guilt." God places greater accountability on those who are aware of His laws (Galatians 2:14; James 3:1), and the Bible often describes God as showing more patience toward people who are ignorant of His laws (Jonah 4:11; Deuteronomy 1:39). We should never treat sin lightly, but we need to learn from God's model for patience. Show kindness toward those who are ignorant of God's laws. Don't judge them (1 Corinthians 5:12-13), but love them and look for opportunities to tell them of God's gracious guidance. (***See Church****> Mission> Nurture> True teaching,* TopicGuide page A49.)

5:9 Jer 9:9

9 Should I not punish them for this?" says the LORD.
"Should I not avenge Myself against such a nation?

5:10 Jer 4:27

10 "Go down the rows of the vineyards and destroy the grapevines,
leaving a scattered few alive.
Strip the branches from the vines,
for these people do not belong to the LORD.

5:11 Jer 3:6-7

11 The people of Israel and Judah
are full of treachery against Me,"
says the LORD.

5:12 2 Chr 36:16; Jer 43:1-4

12 "They have lied about the LORD
and said, 'He won't bother us!
No disasters will come upon us.
There will be no war or famine.

5:13 Jer 14:13, 15

13 God's prophets are all windbags
who don't really speak for Him.
Let their predictions of disaster fall on themselves!'"

5:14 Jer 23:29

14 Therefore, this is what the LORD God of Heaven's Armies says:

"Because the people are talking like this,
My messages will flame out of your mouth
and burn the people like kindling wood.

5:15 Deut 28:49; Isa 5:26; 28:11

15 O Israel, I will bring a distant nation against you,"
says the LORD.
"It is a mighty nation,
an ancient nation,
a people whose language you do not know,
whose speech you cannot understand.

5:16 Isa 5:28; 13:18

16 Their weapons are deadly;
their warriors are mighty.

5:17 Lev 26:16; Deut 28:31, 33; Jer 8:16; Hos 8:14

17 They will devour the food of your harvest;
they will devour your sons and daughters.
They will devour your flocks and herds;
they will devour your grapes and figs.
And they will destroy your fortified towns,
which you think are so safe.

5:19 Deut 28:48; 29:24-26; 1 Kgs 9:8-9; Jer 16:10-13

18 "Yet even in those days I will not blot you out completely," says the LORD. 19 "And
when your people ask, 'Why did the LORD our God do all this to us?' you must reply, 'You
rejected Him and gave yourselves to foreign gods in your own land. Now you will serve
foreigners in a land that is not your own.'

A WARNING FOR GOD'S PEOPLE

20 "Make this announcement to Israel,*
and say this to Judah:

5:20 Hebrew *to the house of Jacob.* The names "Jacob" and "Israel" are often interchanged throughout the Old Testament, referring sometimes to the individual patriarch and sometimes to the nation.

5:10, 18 God's judgment on Judah would be extensive, but not complete. He would leave a remnant that He would later lead to repentance and from which He would rebuild the nation (Leviticus 26:40-42; Zechariah 8:6-12; Romans 11:5).

5:13 Many prophets claimed to speak on God's behalf, but God delegated authority only to those He personally called and commissioned, such as Jeremiah. Old and New Testament prophets did not merely speak a message from God to His people. They were personally commissioned by God to speak on His behalf, and their words were to be regarded as spoken by God himself. At this point in history, almost all the other prophets who claimed to speak for God were lying (5:31).

21 Listen, you foolish and senseless people,
with eyes that do not see
and ears that do not hear.
22 Have you no respect for Me?
Why don't you tremble in My presence?
I, the LORD, define the ocean's sandy shoreline
as an everlasting boundary that the waters cannot cross.
The waves may toss and roar,
but they can never pass the boundaries I set.
23 But My people have stubborn and rebellious hearts.
They have turned away and abandoned Me.
24 They do not say from the heart,
'Let us live in awe of the LORD our God,
for He gives us rain each spring and fall,
assuring us of a harvest when the time is right.'
25 Your wickedness has deprived you of these wonderful blessings.
Your sin has robbed you of all these good things.

26 "Among My people are wicked men
who lie in wait for victims like a hunter hiding in a blind.
They continually set traps
to catch people.
27 Like a cage filled with birds,
their homes are filled with evil plots.
And now they are great and rich.
28 They are fat and sleek,
and there is no limit to their wicked deeds.
They refuse to provide justice to orphans
and deny the rights of the poor.
29 Should I not punish them for this?" says the LORD.
"Should I not avenge Myself against such a nation?
30 A horrible and shocking thing
has happened in this land—
31 the prophets give false prophecies,
and the priests rule with an iron hand.
Worse yet, My people like it that way!
But what will you do when the end comes?

5:21 Isa 43:8; Ezek 12:2; Matt 13:15; Mark 8:18
5:22 Deut 28:58; Job 38:8-11; Pss 104:9; 119:120; Jer 2:19; 10:7
5:23 Ps 78:8; Jer 4:17
5:24 Gen 8:22; Ps 147:8; Joel 2:23; Matt 5:45
5:25 Jer 2:17; 4:18
5:26 Ps 10:9; Jer 18:22; Hab 1:15
5:28 Deut 32:15; Isa 1:23; Jer 7:6; 22:3; Zech 7:10
5:29 Mal 3:5
5:30 Jer 23:14; Hos 6:10
5:31 Jer 14:14; Ezek 13:6; Mic 2:11

JERUSALEM'S LAST WARNING

6 1 "Run for your lives, you people of Benjamin!
Get out of Jerusalem!
Sound the alarm in Tekoa!
Send up a signal at Beth-hakkerem!

6:1 Neh 3:14; Jer 1:14; 4:6

5:23-25 There is not a one-to-one correspondence between obedience and blessings, or between disobedience and curses (2 Samuel 12:22; Joel 2:14). Nevertheless, God does tend to bless people more frequently when they are obedient to Him (Genesis 4:7; Ephesians 6:2-3) and to punish them more frequently when they rebel against Him (Leviticus 26:14-39).

SALVATION
5:31 Willfully believing lies. We are most interested in listening to what we want to hear, rather than what we need to hear. Like the people of Jeremiah's day, we often enjoy listening to the lies of false prophets—preachers and teachers who avoid telling people the truth about their sin and its consequences. God's Word has the uncanny ability to diagnose our sinful condition, and it offers a remedy (Hebrews 4:12), but we must be willing to accept its message. When is the last time you allowed someone to tell you a hard truth about yourself? Make sure you are open to hearing what God is telling you through His true prophets. (***See Salvation***> *Receiving> Results> Works> Spring from a believing heart,* TopicGuide page A23.)

6:1 The invading Babylonians threatened even the holy city of Jerusalem. Jeremiah warned the people not to imagine that God's love for His city and Temple would stay His hand in the face of their disobedience (Jeremiah 7:4). Tekoa was the location of a fire signal that could be used to alert the countryside of danger.

A powerful army is coming from the north,
coming with disaster and destruction.

6:2 Deut 28:56; Jer 4:31
2 O Jerusalem,* you are My beautiful and delicate daughter—
but I will destroy you!

6:3 2 Kgs 25:1; Jer 4:17; 12:10; Luke 19:43
3 Enemies will surround you, like shepherds camped around the city.
Each chooses a place for his troops to devour.

6:4 Jer 6:23; 15:8
4 They shout, 'Prepare for battle!
Attack at noon!'
'No, it's too late; the day is fading,
and the evening shadows are falling.'

6:5 Isa 32:14; Jer 52:13
5 'Well then, let's attack at night
and destroy her palaces!'"

6:6 Deut 20:19-20; Jer 22:17; 32:24
6 This is what the LORD of Heaven's Armies says:
"Cut down the trees for battering rams.
Build siege ramps against the walls of Jerusalem.
This is the city to be punished,
for she is wicked through and through.

6:7 Jer 20:8; 30:12-13; Ezek 7:11, 23; Jas 3:10-12
7 She spouts evil like a fountain.
Her streets echo with the sounds of violence
and destruction.
I always see her sickness and sores.

6:8 Jer 7:28; 17:23; Ezek 23:18; Hos 9:12
8 Listen to this warning, Jerusalem,
or I will turn from you in disgust.
Listen, or I will turn you into a heap of ruins,
a land where no one lives."

6:9 Jer 8:3; 16:16; 49:9; Obad 1:5-6
9 This is what the LORD of Heaven's Armies says:
"Even the few who remain in Israel
will be picked over again,
as when a harvester checks each vine a second time
to pick the grapes that were missed."

ISRAEL'S CONSTANT REBELLION

6:10 Jer 7:26; 20:8; Acts 7:51
10 To whom can I give warning?
Who will listen when I speak?
Their ears are closed,
and they cannot hear.
They scorn the word of the LORD.
They don't want to listen at all.

6:11 Job 32:18-19; Jer 7:20; 9:21; 15:6; 20:9
11 So now I am filled with the LORD's fury.
Yes, I am tired of holding it in!

6:2 Hebrew *Daughter of Zion.*

6:2 Terms of endearment expressed God's love for Judah even as He spoke of punishment. This revealed His reluctance to punish Judah and His eagerness to forgive should Judah repent.

6:8 God's covenant with His people ensured that the nation would be punished if the people sinned (Leviticus 26:14-17) and that the punishments would increase if the people did not repent after being punished (Leviticus 26:18-28). The greatest punishment detailed was destruction in war followed by exile from the Promised Land (Leviticus 26:31-33).

▸ SALVATION

6:11-12 My sin affects my family. There is no doubt that certain sins have an immediate impact upon those around us, including our own family. For example, many parents indirectly train their children to be dishonest by their own deceptive practices. The Bible makes it clear that certain sins bear consequences upon our children and even upon our grandchildren (Exodus 20:4-6; 34:7). We must heed this warning of Scripture and live wisely, because our actions may impact more people than we think. (***See Salvation****> Our Need> Sinful> Influence of father,* TopicGuide page A22.)

"I will pour out My fury on children playing in the streets
and on gatherings of young men,
on husbands and wives
and on those who are old and gray.
12 Their homes will be turned over to their enemies, 6:12 Deut 28:30 Jer 8:10; 15:6; 38:22
as will their fields and their wives.
For I will raise My powerful fist
against the people of this land,"
says the LORD.
13 "From the least to the greatest, 6:13 Isa 56:11; 57:17 Jer 22:17 Mic 3:5, 11
their lives are ruled by greed.
From prophets to priests,
they are all frauds.
14 They offer superficial treatments 6:14 Jer 8:11-12 Ezek 13:10
for My people's mortal wound.
They give assurances of peace
when there is no peace.
15 Are they ashamed of their disgusting actions? 6:15 Jer 3:3; 8:12
Not at all—they don't even know how to blush!
Therefore, they will lie among the slaughtered.
They will be brought down when I punish them,"
says the LORD.

ISRAEL REJECTS THE LORD'S WAY

16 This is what the LORD says: 6:16 Jer 18:15; 31:21 Mal 4:4 *Matt 11:29
"Stop at the crossroads and look around.
Ask for the old, godly way, and walk in it.
Travel its path, and you will find rest for your souls.
But you reply, 'No, that's not the road we want!'
17 I posted watchmen over you who said, 6:17 Isa 21:11; 58:1 Jer 25:4 Ezek 3:17
'Listen for the sound of the alarm.'
But you replied,
'No! We won't pay attention!'

18 "Therefore, listen to this, all you nations.
Take note of My people's situation.
19 Listen, all the earth! 6:19 Isa 1:2 Jer 8:9
I will bring disaster on My people.
It is the fruit of their own schemes,
because they refuse to listen to Me.
They have rejected My word.
20 There's no use offering Me sweet frankincense from Sheba. 6:20 Pss 40:6; 50:7-9 Isa 1:11; 60:6; 66:3 Amos 5:21
Keep your fragrant calamus imported from distant lands!
I will not accept your burnt offerings.
Your sacrifices have no pleasing aroma for Me."

21 Therefore, this is what the LORD says: 6:21 Isa 8:14; 9:14-17 Jer 9:21-22; 13:16
"I will put obstacles in My people's path.
Fathers and sons will both fall over them.
Neighbors and friends will die together."

6:16 The destruction that Jeremiah prophesied was not unavoidable. Jeremiah was told to threaten Judah with coming destruction in order to persuade the people to repent of their sins. If Judah had repented, it is likely that God would have reduced or even eliminated the Babylonian threat (18:1-10; Joel 2:14; Jonah 3:9).

AN INVASION FROM THE NORTH

6:22 Jer 1:15; 10:22; 50:41-43

22 This is what the LORD says:
"Look! A great army coming from the north!
A great nation is rising against you from far-off lands.

6:23 Isa 5:30; Jer 4:29; 50:42

23 They are armed with bows and spears.
They are cruel and show no mercy.
They sound like a roaring sea
as they ride forward on horses.
They are coming in battle formation,
planning to destroy you, beautiful Jerusalem.*"

6:24 Isa 28:19; Jer 4:19-21

24 We have heard reports about the enemy,
and we wring our hands in fright.
Pangs of anguish have gripped us,
like those of a woman in labor.

6:25 Jer 12:12; 14:18

25 Don't go out to the fields!
Don't travel on the roads!
The enemy's sword is everywhere
and terrorizes us at every turn!

6:26 Jer 4:8; 25:34; Amos 8:10; Mic 1:10; Zech 12:10

26 Oh, My people, dress yourselves in burlap
and sit among the ashes.
Mourn and weep bitterly, as for the loss of an only son.
For suddenly the destroying armies will be upon you!

6:27 Jer 1:18; 15:20

27 "Jeremiah, I have made you a tester of metals,*
that you may determine the quality of My people.

6:28 Ezek 22:18

28 They are the worst kind of rebel,
full of slander.
They are as hard as bronze and iron,
and they lead others into corruption.

6:29 Jer 15:19

29 The bellows fiercely fan the flames
to burn out the corruption.
But it does not purify them,
for the wickedness remains.

6:30 Ps 119:119; Isa 1:22

30 I will label them 'Rejected Silver,'
for I, the LORD, am discarding them."

JEREMIAH SPEAKS AT THE TEMPLE

7:2 Jer 17:19
7:3 Jer 4:1; 18:11; 26:13

7 The LORD gave another message to Jeremiah. He said, 2 "Go to the entrance of the
LORD's Temple, and give this message to the people: 'O Judah, listen to this message
from the LORD! Listen to it, all of you who worship here! 3 This is what the LORD of Heaven's
Armies, the God of Israel, says:

6:23 Hebrew *daughter of Zion.* 6:27 As in Greek version; Hebrew reads *of metals in My people a fortress.*

▶ HOLINESS
6:27-30 Testing our mettle. God never intended life to be easy. Life in this world continually assaults our fragile egos, questions our simplistic assumptions, and tests the strength of our relationships. In Jeremiah's metallurgical example, God justified His rejection of unrepentant Israel because He had revealed their flaws through testing, but that's all He could find—impurities. No silver, no iron, no bronze—only dross remained after God tested them through the ministry of Jeremiah. When confronted with God's Word, how well do you pass the test? Does it reveal impurity, harshness, or someone in danger of being rejected? No matter what, your response should be the same: Take great delight in the Law of the Lord. Allow it to change your heart and mind (Psalm 119:121-128). (***See Holiness**> Law and Grace> Law> The moral law of God,* TopicGuide page A41.)

6:29-30 God's condemnation of Judah was stated in absolute terms (compare Jeremiah 5:1-2). This threat was hyperbolic, intended to frighten the people into repenting. In truth, if they did not repent, exile would refine them, as promised in the terms of God's agreement with the nation (Leviticus 26:43-45). Many would die, but a tiny remnant would be saved (compare Jeremiah 6:9).

"'Even now, if you quit your evil ways, I will let you stay in your own land. 4But don't be
fooled by those who promise you safety simply because the LORD's Temple is here. They
chant, "The LORD's Temple is here! The LORD's Temple is here!" 5But I will be merciful only
if you stop your evil thoughts and deeds and start treating each other with justice; 6only if
you stop exploiting foreigners, orphans, and widows; only if you stop your murdering;
and only if you stop harming yourselves by worshiping idols. 7Then I will let you stay in
this land that I gave to your ancestors to keep forever.

8"'Don't be fooled into thinking that you will never suffer because the Temple is here.
It's a lie! 9Do you really think you can steal, murder, commit adultery, lie, and burn in-
cense to Baal and all those other new gods of yours, 10and then come here and stand be-
fore Me in My Temple and chant, "We are safe!"—only to go right back to all those evils
again? 11Don't you yourselves admit that this Temple, which bears My name, has become
a den of thieves? Surely I see all the evil going on there. I, the LORD, have spoken!

12"'Go now to the place at Shiloh where I once put the Tabernacle that bore My name.
See what I did there because of all the wickedness of My people, the Israelites. 13While
you were doing these wicked things, says the LORD, I spoke to you about it repeatedly, but
you would not listen. I called out to you, but you refused to answer. 14So just as I de-
stroyed Shiloh, I will now destroy this Temple that bears My name, this Temple that you
trust in for help, this place that I gave to you and your ancestors. 15And I will send you out
of My sight into exile, just as I did your relatives, the people of Israel.*'

JUDAH'S PERSISTENT IDOLATRY

16"Pray no more for these people, Jeremiah. Do not weep or pray for them, and don't beg
Me to help them, for I will not listen to you. 17Don't you see what they are doing through-
out the towns of Judah and in the streets of Jerusalem? 18No wonder I am so angry! Watch
how the children gather wood and the fathers build sacrificial fires. See how the women
knead dough and make cakes to offer to the Queen of Heaven. And they pour out liquid
offerings to their other idol gods! 19Am I the One they are hurting?" asks the LORD. "Most of
all, they hurt themselves, to their own shame."

20So this is what the Sovereign LORD says: "I will pour out My terrible fury on this place. Its
people, animals, trees, and crops will be consumed by the unquenchable fire of My anger."

21This is what the LORD of Heaven's Armies, the God of Israel, says: "Take your burnt of-
ferings and your other sacrifices and eat them yourselves! 22When I led your ancestors out

7:4 Mic 3:11
7:5 Isa 1:19
7:6 Exod 22:21-24; Deut 6:14-15; 8:19
7:7 Deut 4:40
7:9 Exod 20:3
7:10 Ezek 23:39
7:11 Isa 56:7; Matt 21:13
7:12 Josh 18:1, 10
7:14 1 Kgs 9:7
7:15 2 Kgs 17:23
7:18 Deut 32:16
7:19 Job 35:6
7:21 Isa 1:11; Hos 8:13; Amos 5:21
7:22 1 Sam 15:22; Ps 51:16; Hos 6:6

7:15 Hebrew *of Ephraim,* referring to the northern kingdom of Israel.

7:5-6 Previously, God had accused the people primarily of idolatry and other sins directed against Him. Here He expanded the indictment to include sins against other Israelites and even Gentiles, especially those who had no legal advocates in Judah (orphans, widows, and foreigners).

7:8-11 The people wrongly believed that God would preserve at least His Temple, either because He had promised to do so (2 Chronicles 7:16) or for the sake of His holy name (Deuteronomy 12:5, 11, 21). God's promise to protect the Temple, however, was contingent upon the people's obedience (2 Chronicles 7:19-20). He was willing to endure the dishonor of His name for a time (Ezekiel 36:20-23).

7:12-14 The Ark of the Covenant had been residing in the Tabernacle at Shiloh when it was lost to the Philistines (1 Samuel 4). This loss had resulted in God's glory departing from Israel (1 Samuel 4:22), leaving the Israelites not only unprotected (Exodus 40:34-38) but also without hope in the salvation of God's kingdom (Exodus 33:14-16).

▸ GOD
7:14 Doomed to repeat history. Are you a good learner? All too often we repeat the mistakes of others and fail to learn from the consequences they have suffered. Scripture clearly shows us that generally our righteous choices bring blessings and our sinful choices bring curses. In this case, Jeremiah explained that God would destroy every religious institution in Israel and kick them out of the land—just as He had done in the past—if they would not heed His warnings. How is God warning you or your church today? Repent of all known sin and encourage those around you to do the same (1 John 1:9; Hosea 6:1-3). You can never go wrong with repentance. (***See God****> God's Attributes> Just> God rightly judges heart, mind, and deeds,* TopicGuide page A17.)

7:16 Here God instructed Jeremiah to refrain from interceding for the people, so that they would have no advocate. As a form of punishment or discipline, God sometimes removes from people the means through which grace might otherwise save them. Nevertheless, this prohibition was somewhat hyperbolic: The words Jeremiah was instructed to deliver to the people were a form of intercession on their behalf.

▸ WORSHIP
7:21-23 The nature of true obedience. Obedience involves more than compliance with the commandments of God—it involves our heart. Both the Old and New

7:23 of Egypt, it was not burnt offerings and sacrifices I wanted from them. [23]This is what I told
Exod 15:26; 19:5-6 Lev 26:12 them: 'Obey Me, and I will be your God, and you will be My people. Do everything as I say,
Deut 6:3 and all will be well!'
Isa 3:10 [24]"But My people would not listen to Me. They kept doing whatever they wanted, fol-
7:24 lowing the stubborn desires of their evil hearts. They went backward instead of forward.
Ps 81:11 Ezek 20:8, 13, 16, 21 [25]From the day your ancestors left Egypt until now, I have continued to send My servants,
7:26 the prophets—day in and day out. [26]But My people have not listened to Me or even tried
Jer 16:12; 17:23 to hear. They have been stubborn and sinful—even worse than their ancestors.
Matt 23:32 [27]"Tell them all this, but do not expect them to listen. Shout out your warnings, but do not
7:27 expect them to respond. [28]Say to them, 'This is the nation whose people will not obey the
Isa 65:12 Ezek 2:7 LORD their God and who refuse to be taught. Truth has vanished from among them; it is no
7:29 longer heard on their lips. [29]Shave your head in mourning, and weep alone on the moun-
Isa 15:2; 22:12 Mic 1:16 tains. For the LORD has rejected and forsaken this generation that has provoked His fury.'

THE VALLEY OF SLAUGHTER

7:30 [30]"The people of Judah have sinned before My very eyes," says the LORD. "They have set up
2 Kgs 21:4 Jer 32:34 their abominable idols right in the Temple that bears My name, defiling it. [31]They have built
7:31 2 Kgs 23:10 pagan shrines at Topheth, the garbage dump in the valley of Ben-Hinnom, and there they
Ps 106:38 burn their sons and daughters in the fire. I have never commanded such a horrible deed; it
never even crossed My mind to command such a thing! [32]So beware, for the time is com-
7:33 ing," says the LORD, "when that garbage dump will no longer be called Topheth or the valley
Deut 28:26 Ps 79:2 of Ben-Hinnom, but the Valley of Slaughter. They will bury the bodies in Topheth until there
is no more room for them. [33]The bodies of My people will be food for the vultures and wild
7:34 Isa 1:7; 24:7 animals, and no one will be left to scare them away. [34]I will put an end to the happy singing
and laughter in the streets of Jerusalem. The joyful voices of bridegrooms and brides will no
longer be heard in the towns of Judah. The land will lie in complete desolation.

8:1 **8** "In that day," says the LORD, "the enemy will break open the graves of the kings and
Ezek 6:5 officials of Judah, and the graves of the priests, prophets, and common people of Je-
8:2 rusalem. [2]They will spread out their bones on the ground before the sun, moon, and
2 Kgs 23:5 Zeph 1:5 stars—the gods My people have loved, served, and worshiped. Their bones will not be
Acts 7:42 gathered up again or buried but will be scattered on the ground like manure. [3]And the
8:3 Deut 30:1, 4 people of this evil nation who survive will wish to die rather than live where I will send
Rev 9:6 them. I, the LORD of Heaven's Armies, have spoken!

DECEPTION BY FALSE PROPHETS

[4]"Jeremiah, say to the people, 'This is what the LORD says:

"'When people fall down, don't they get up again?
When they discover they're on the wrong road, don't they turn back?

Testaments stress that the true nature of obedience is found in a heart that loves the Lord and is willing to submit to Him (Deuteronomy 6:5; Matthew 22:37). As Jeremiah noted, public displays of faith may be easily performed, but God knows our true motivation for obeying Him (Matthew 6:1). Ask God to give you a heart committed to obeying His commandments out of a love for Him. (***See Worship*****> *****OT> God's Supremacy> Required a proper heart attitude,*** TopicGuide page A27.)

7:27-28 Jeremiah's words of coming destruction would not have a positive effect of inspiring obedience, but this did not mean that Israel could not have avoided destruction if they repented (18:1-10). Whether the people obeyed or not, Jeremiah's words were still a means of revealing God's character and revealing the way God views human behavior.

7:34 Those who are about to fall under God's judgment are often oblivious to their doom, continuing on with life and the things that please them (Luke 17:26-30). There is probably an allusion here to the state of the world before the flood of Noah's day (Genesis 6:1-6; Matthew 24:38; Luke 17:27), implying that Judah's devastation would be as complete as the world's destruction at that time.

8:2 Disinterment and exposure of bones would dishonor the dead, thus adding insult to the injury threatened in Jeremiah 7:33. The bones would be exposed before the false gods Judah had served, proving that these false gods were powerless before the Lord.

8:4-7 The Lord's questions to Jeremiah were rhetorical. God's expression of surprise is intended to highlight the lack of common sense exhibited in Judah's rebellion.

5 Then why do these people stay on their self-destructive path?
Why do the people of Jerusalem refuse to turn back?
They cling tightly to their lies
and will not turn around.
6 I listen to their conversations
and don't hear a word of truth.
Is anyone sorry for doing wrong?
Does anyone say, "What a terrible thing I have done"?
No! All are running down the path of sin
as swiftly as a horse galloping into battle!
7 Even the stork that flies across the sky
knows the time of her migration,
as do the turtledove, the swallow, and the crane.*
They all return at the proper time each year.
But not My people!
They do not know the LORD's laws.
8 "'How can you say, "We are wise because we have the word
of the LORD,"
when your teachers have twisted it by writing lies?
9 These wise teachers will fall
into the trap of their own foolishness,
for they have rejected the word of the LORD.
Are they so wise after all?
10 I will give their wives to others
and their farms to strangers.
From the least to the greatest,
their lives are ruled by greed.
Yes, even My prophets and priests are like that.
They are all frauds.
11 They offer superficial treatments
for My people's mortal wound.
They give assurances of peace
when there is no peace.
12 Are they ashamed of these disgusting actions?
Not at all—they don't even know how to blush!

8:6 Job 39:21-25; Ps 14:2; Ezek 22:30; Mal 3:16; Rev 9:20
8:7 Prov 6:6-8; Song 2:12
8:8 Jer 4:22; Rom 1:22; 2:17
8:9 Jer 6:15; 1 Cor 1:27
8:10 Deut 28:30; Isa 56:11; Jer 6:12-13
8:11 Jer 6:14; 14:13-14; Lam 2:14; Ezek 13:10
8:12 Deut 32:35; Isa 3:9; 9:14; Zeph 3:5

8:7 The identification of some of these birds is uncertain.

▸ HOLINESS

8:8 Can I trust my pastor? Pastors and teachers can mislead people about God. Sometimes on purpose, sometimes not—but always with consequences. Getting the wrong directions from someone may send you driving in circles for hours, but getting wrong spiritual guidance may harm you for years. How can you know your teaching is true? By comparing it to God's Word. The teachers of Jeremiah's time taught only positive messages (8:11), but God's people needed to hear the truth about His promise to discipline them if they abandoned their covenant with Him (Deuteronomy 28:15-68; Leviticus 26:14-38). God's people cannot simply rely on books or teachers—we must read God's Word so we can discern between truth and error. Not only for your sake, but also for the sake of those around you—learn God's Word! (***See Holiness****> Disciplines> Of Engagement> Value of study,* TopicGuide page A42.)

8:8 Literally translated, "The lying pen of the scribes has made it into a lie." Scribes (sometimes translated "secretaries") were not responsible to interpret or teach the law until post-exilic times (Ezra 7:11). In Jeremiah's day, scribes primarily wrote and transcribed documents (Jeremiah 36:32). Teaching was the work of priests (Deuteronomy 33:10) and was done orally. Therefore, this verse could be understood to mean that the scribes had purposefully made inaccurate copies of the scrolls containing God's law. Because the people were taught from these corrupted scrolls, they believed lies rather than truth.

8:10 All the scriptural authorities in Judah were unfaithful to God and lied to the people about the Lord's word. The scribes were responsible to produce the texts of Scripture (Jeremiah 36:32). The priests were responsible for teaching God's requirements to the people (Deuteronomy 33:10). The prophets were responsible for teaching and holding God's people accountable to keeping His treaty according to the terms listed in Scripture. Since the scribes, priests, and prophets all acted deceitfully, the people did not know Scripture's true instructions.

Therefore, they will lie among the slaughtered.
They will be brought down when I punish them,
says the LORD.

8:13 Matt 21:19

13 I will surely consume them.
There will be no more harvests of figs and grapes.
Their fruit trees will all die.
Whatever I gave them will soon be gone.
I, the LORD, have spoken!'

8:14 Deut 29:18 Ps 69:21 Jer 3:25; 4:5; 9:15; 14:20 Matt 27:34

14 "Then the people will say,
'Why should we wait here to die?
Come, let's go to the fortified towns and die there.
For the LORD our God has decreed our destruction
and has given us a cup of poison to drink
because we sinned against the LORD.

8:15 Jer 14:19

15 We hoped for peace, but no peace came.
We hoped for a time of healing, but found only terror.

8:16 Judg 5:22

16 "The snorting of the enemies' warhorses can be heard
all the way from the land of Dan in the north!
The neighing of their stallions makes the whole land tremble.
They are coming to devour the land and everything in it—
cities and people alike.

8:17 Num 21:6 Deut 32:24 Ps 58:4-5

17 I will send these enemy troops among you
like poisonous snakes you cannot charm.
They will bite you, and you will die.
I, the Lord, have spoken!"

JEREMIAH WEEPS FOR SINFUL JUDAH

18 My grief is beyond healing;
my heart is broken.

8:19 Deut 32:21 Ps 31:6 Isa 13:4-5 Jer 4:16; 9:16

19 Listen to the weeping of my people;
it can be heard all across the land.
"Has the LORD abandoned Jerusalem?*" the people ask.
"Is her King no longer there?"
"Oh, why have they provoked My anger with their carved idols
and their worthless foreign gods?" says the LORD.

20 "The harvest is finished,
and the summer is gone," the people cry,
"yet we are not saved!"

8:21 Jer 4:19; 9:1; 14:17 Joel 2:6 Nah 2:10

21 I hurt with the hurt of my people.
I mourn and am overcome with grief.

8:19 Hebrew *Zion?*

▶ **BIBLE**

8:14 Giving up, not surrendering. Many have perished because of their determination that no matter what, they will not admit they are wrong. Back to the wall, down to their last dime, gas tank on empty—but everything is just fine! The people of Jeremiah's time, when faced with grave consequences for their sin, fled to their largest cities and hid in shame—but they would not repent. They were hiding in useless cities, and could sense the unstoppable armies coming closer—but they would not repent. You may know a non-Christian who, even though he understands that he will live in hell forever (Matthew 13:42, 50; 25:41-46; Mark 9:44-48; 2 Peter 2:9), still rejects the gospel. You may know others who are currently living in unrepentant sin—love them and let them know the truth from God's Word (Psalm 51:17). (***See Bible****> Unity> Kingdom of God> Repentance and faith embodies the kingdom,* TopicGuide page A11.)

8:18-21 Jeremiah interceded before God for the people of Jerusalem. Because they were so sinful and had no interest in repenting (8:12), he could present no case in their defense. Therefore, he simply wept, hoping his tears would speak where his words could not.

22 Is there no medicine in Gilead?
Is there no physician there?
Why is there no healing
for the wounds of my people?

8:22 Gen 37:25; Jer 14:19; 30:13; 46:11

9 1*If only my head were a pool of water
and my eyes a fountain of tears,
I would weep day and night
for all my people who have been slaughtered.
2*Oh, that I could go away and forget my people
and live in a travelers' shack in the desert.
For they are all adulterers—
a pack of treacherous liars.

9:1 Jer 8:18; 13:17

9:2 Pss 55:6-7; 120:5-6

JUDGMENT FOR DISOBEDIENCE

3 "My people bend their tongues like bows
to shoot out lies.
They refuse to stand up for the truth.
They only go from bad to worse.
They do not know Me,"
says the LORD.

9:3 Ps 64:3; Isa 59:4; Jer 9:8; Hos 4:1

4 "Beware of your neighbor!
Don't even trust your brother!
For brother takes advantage of brother,
and friend slanders friend.
5 They all fool and defraud each other;
no one tells the truth.
With practiced tongues they tell lies;
they wear themselves out with all their sinning.
6 They pile lie upon lie
and utterly refuse to acknowledge Me,"
says the LORD.

9:4 Gen 27:35; Prov 10:18; Jer 12:6

9:5 Mic 6:12

9:6 Jer 5:27; 11:10; 13:10; John 3:19-20

7 Therefore, this is what the LORD of Heaven's Armies says:
"See, I will melt them down in a crucible
and test them like metal.
What else can I do with My people?*
8 For their tongues shoot lies like poisoned arrows.
They speak friendly words to their neighbors
while scheming in their heart to kill them.
9 Should I not punish them for this?" says the LORD.
"Should I not avenge Myself against such a nation?"

9:7 Isa 1:25; Jer 6:27; Mal 3:3

9:8 Ps 28:3; Jer 5:26

9:9 Isa 1:24; Jer 5:9, 29

10 I will weep for the mountains
and wail for the wilderness pastures.

9:10 Jer 4:24-25; 12:4; Ezek 14:15; 29:11; 33:28; Hos 4:3

9:1 Verse 9:1 is numbered 8:23 in Hebrew text. 9:2 Verses 9:2-26 are numbered 9:1-25 in Hebrew text. 9:7 Hebrew *with the daughter of My people?* Greek version reads *with the evil daughter of My people?*

9:3-9 The Lord listed many sins that the people of Judah regularly committed against one another. Because the Lord is the great King over His people, His people are under His protection. Therefore, to sin against His people is also to sin against God and to invite His judgment (compare Matthew 25:45).

9:10-16 Jeremiah described what Judah would look like in the future if they failed to repent. The people would be exiled from the land, and the cities would become ghost towns and haunts for jackals. These were judgments mentioned in God's covenant with His people (Leviticus 26:22, 31-33).

For they are desolate and empty of life;
the lowing of cattle is heard no more;
the birds and wild animals have all fled.

9:11 Isa 25:2; 34:13 Jer 26:9

11 "I will make Jerusalem into a heap of ruins," says the LORD.
"It will be a place haunted by jackals.
The towns of Judah will be ghost towns,
with no one living in them."

9:12 Ps 107:43 Jer 23:10, 16 Hos 14:9
9:13 2 Chr 7:19-20 Ps 89:30 Jer 5:19; 22:9
9:14 Rom 1:21-24 1 Pet 1:18
9:15 Deut 29:18
9:16 Lev 26:33 Deut 28:64 Jer 13:24; 44:27 Ezek 5:2, 12

12 Who is wise enough to understand all this? Who has been instructed by the LORD and
can explain it to others? Why has the land been so ruined that no one dares to travel
through it?
13 The LORD replies, "This has happened because My people have abandoned My in-
structions; they have refused to obey what I said. 14 Instead, they have stubbornly fol-
lowed their own desires and worshiped the images of Baal, as their ancestors taught them.
15 So now, this is what the LORD of Heaven's Armies, the God of Israel, says: Look! I will feed
them with bitterness and give them poison to drink. 16 I will scatter them around the world,
in places they and their ancestors never heard of, and even there I will chase them with
the sword until I have destroyed them completely."

WEEPING IN JERUSALEM

9:17 Amos 5:16

17 This is what the LORD of Heaven's Armies says:
"Consider all this, and call for the mourners.
Send for the women who mourn at funerals.

9:18 Jer 14:17

18 Quick! Begin your weeping!
Let the tears flow from your eyes.

9:19 Deut 28:29 2 Chr 35:25 Jer 4:13; 7:15, 29; 15:1

19 Hear the people of Jerusalem* crying in despair,
'We are ruined! We are completely humiliated!
We must leave our land,
because our homes have been torn down.'"

20 Listen, you women, to the words of the LORD;
open your ears to what He has to say.
Teach your daughters to wail;
teach one another how to lament.

9:21 2 Chr 36:17 Jer 6:11; 18:21

21 For death has crept in through our windows
and has entered our mansions.
It has killed off the flower of our youth:
Children no longer play in the streets,
and young men no longer gather in the squares.

9:22 Ps 83:10 Isa 5:25 Jer 8:2; 16:4

22 This is what the LORD says:
"Bodies will be scattered across the fields like clumps of manure,
like bundles of grain after the harvest.
No one will be left to bury them."

9:19 Hebrew *Zion.*

9:17-19 It was very common for professional mourners to be hired for funerals. The Lord warned the people of Judah that their destruction was so imminent that it was time to hire these mourners.

9:20-22 The people had already suffered some punishments for their sin, confirming God's willingness to follow through with His threats. The punishments were intended to bring about the people's repentance. If they earnestly repented of their sin, God could spare them from the curses He had threatened (18:1-10).

23 This is what the LORD says:
"Don't let the wise boast in their wisdom,
or the powerful boast in their power,
or the rich boast in their riches.
24 But those who wish to boast
should boast in this alone:
that they truly know Me and understand that I am the LORD
who demonstrates unfailing love
and who brings justice and righteousness to the earth,
and that I delight in these things.
I, the LORD, have spoken!

25 "A time is coming," says the LORD, "when I will punish all those who are circumcised in
body but not in spirit—26 the Egyptians, Edomites, Ammonites, Moabites, the people who
live in the desert in remote places,* and yes, even the people of Judah. And like all these
pagan nations, the people of Israel also have uncircumcised hearts."

9:23 1 Kgs 20:10-11; Ps 49:6-9; Eccl 9:11; Ezek 28:3-7
9:24 Exod 34:6-7; Pss 36:5, 7; 44:8; Isa 10:8-12; 61:8; Mic 7:18; *1 Cor 1:31; 2 Cor 10:17; Gal 6:14
9:26 Lev 26:41; Jer 25:23; Ezek 44:7; Rom 2:28

IDOLATRY BRINGS DESTRUCTION

10 Hear the word that the LORD speaks to you, O Israel! 2 This is what the LORD says:

"Do not act like the other nations,
who try to read their future in the stars.
Do not be afraid of their predictions,
even though other nations are terrified by them.
3 Their ways are futile and foolish.
They cut down a tree, and a craftsman carves an idol.
4 They decorate it with gold and silver
and then fasten it securely with hammer and nails
so it won't fall over.
5 Their gods are like
helpless scarecrows in a cucumber field!

10:2 Lev 18:3; Isa 47:12-14
10:4 Isa 40:19; 41:7
10:5 Ps 115:5; Isa 41:23-24; 46:1, 7

9:26 Or *in the desert and clip the corners of their hair.*

▸ WORSHIP
9:25-26 Inside and Out. Many people confuse outward obedience with inner holiness. Jeremiah knew that the Israelites were indeed required to circumcise their males on the eighth day (Leviticus 12:3), but God's covenant with them not only required them to circumcise their bodies; they were also required to love God with their heart (Matthew 22:37). Like the people of Jeremiah's day, we often lapse into mere external obedience. A good example is how we give money to the church—perhaps we make a show out of giving a certain amount—but in our hearts, we hate giving money to charity. We begrudgingly think of the car we could be buying with our contributions (2 Corinthians 9:7). God looks at our exterior obedience, but He's more concerned with our interior life—our hope, our trust, our passion for Him. Focus on building your private love life with God, and let your outer obedience flow from an intimate relationship with Him. (***See Worship**> NT> Offerings> God loves a cheerful giver,* TopicGuide page A31.)

9:25 Circumcision was the sign of God's covenant with His people (Genesis 17:11). To be circumcised in spirit was to love and embrace God and His covenant (Deuteronomy 30:6), including its laws, blessings, and curses (Deuteronomy 30:19-20).

9:26 All people in all places are accountable to God both individually and corporately. Even if they have never been taught true worship of God, God will bring judgment against all idolaters and sinners (Romans 3:10-15).

10:2 The Lord forbade His people from participating in pagan religion and superstition, including astrology and the worship of heavenly bodies (compare Jeremiah 8:2).

▸ WORSHIP
10:2 Superstition about the heavens. Superstition dominates our society today. Some people read their horoscopes on a daily basis or consult Tarot cards in order to know what to expect next. Jeremiah warned the nation of Israel to be more concerned with their present actions than with the stars and various ways to predict the future. Jeremiah declared the movements of celestial bodies as a useless means for determining the future (Jeremiah 10:3). We, too, should listen to Jeremiah's words, commit to live righteously today, and learn to faithfully trust God for our future. What would it look like for you to put your hope in God and God alone? (***See Worship**> OT> God's Supremacy> Required obedience in daily life and affairs,* TopicGuide page A26.)

10:3-16 Jeremiah showed the stupidity of the idolatry that tempted the people of Judah. Idols are created by mere human beings and are completely impotent. By contrast, the Lord created human beings and everything else, and

They cannot speak,
and they need to be carried because they cannot walk.
Do not be afraid of such gods,
for they can neither harm you nor do you any good."

10:6 Deut 33:26; Pss 48:1; 96:4; Isa 12:6; Jer 10:16

6 LORD, there is no one like You!
For You are great, and Your name is full of power.
7 Who would not fear You, O King of nations?
That title belongs to You alone!

10:7 Ps 22:28; Dan 2:27-28; 1 Cor 1:19-20

Among all the wise people of the earth
and in all the kingdoms of the world,
there is no one like You.

10:8 Jer 4:22

8 People who worship idols are stupid and foolish.
The things they worship are made of wood!

10:9 Pss 72:10; 115:4; Isa 40:19; Dan 10:5

9 They bring beaten sheets of silver from Tarshish
and gold from Uphaz,
and they give these materials to skillful craftsmen
who make their idols.
Then they dress these gods in royal blue and purple robes
made by expert tailors.

10:10 Pss 10:16; 29:10; 76:7; Isa 65:16; Jer 50:46

10 But the LORD is the only true God.
He is the living God and the everlasting King!
The whole earth trembles at His anger.
The nations cannot stand up to His wrath.

10:11 Ps 96:5; Isa 2:18; Zeph 2:11

11 Say this to those who worship other gods: "Your so-called gods, who did not make the
heavens and earth, will vanish from the earth and from under the heavens."*

10:12 Job 9:8; 38:4-7; Pss 78:69; 148:4-5; Isa 40:22; 45:18; Jer 51:15

12 But God made the earth by His power,
and He preserves it by His wisdom.
With His own understanding
He stretched out the heavens.

10:13 Job 36:27-29; Pss 29:3-9; 135:7

13 When He speaks in the thunder,
the heavens roar with rain.
He causes the clouds to rise over the earth.
He sends the lightning with the rain
and releases the wind from His storehouses.

10:14 Jer 51:17

14 The whole human race is foolish and has no knowledge!
The craftsmen are disgraced by the idols they make,
for their carefully shaped works are a fraud.
These idols have no breath or power.

10:15 Isa 41:24; Jer 8:12; 14:22

15 Idols are worthless; they are ridiculous lies!
On the day of reckoning they will all be destroyed.

10:16 Deut 32:9; Isa 45:7; Jer 10:12; 31:35; 32:18; 51:19

16 But the God of Israel* is no idol!
He is the Creator of everything that exists,
including Israel, His own special possession.
The LORD of Heaven's Armies is His name!

10:11 The original text of this verse is in Aramaic. 10:16 Hebrew *the Portion of Jacob.* See note on 5:20.

His power is undeniable. In turning to idolatry, Judah had forgotten or ignored the Lord's power.

10:10 **One of the most common and prominent roles ascribed to God in Scripture is that of the everlasting King. In the context of the ancient world, this meant that He was the sovereign leader of a powerful nation that ruled over other nations and received tribute from them. The kings of Israel and Judah were among those who paid tribute to the Lord, mere servants of the everlasting King, whose kingdom included all of creation.**

THE COMING DESTRUCTION

17 Pack your bags and prepare to leave;
the siege is about to begin. 10:17 Ezek 12:3-12
18 For this is what the LORD says:
"Suddenly, I will fling out
all you who live in this land.
I will pour great troubles upon you,
and at last you will feel My anger." 10:18 1 Sam 25:29 Jer 14:17

19 My wound is severe,
and my grief is great.
My sickness is incurable,
but I must bear it. 10:19 Jer 4:31 Mic 7:9
20 My home is gone,
and no one is left to help me rebuild it.
My children have been taken away,
and I will never see them again. 10:20 Isa 51:18 Jer 4:20; 31:15 Lam 1:5; 2:4
21 The shepherds of my people have lost their senses.
They no longer seek wisdom from the LORD.
Therefore, they fail completely,
and their flocks are scattered. 10:21 Jer 23:2
22 Listen! Hear the terrifying roar of great armies
as they roll down from the north.
The towns of Judah will be destroyed
and become a haunt for jackals. 10:22 Jer 9:11; 49:33

JEREMIAH'S PRAYER

23 I know, LORD, that our lives are not our own.
We are not able to plan our own course. 10:23 Prov 20:24 Isa 26:7
24 So correct me, LORD, but please be gentle.
Do not correct me in anger, for I would die. 10:24 Ps 6:1
25 Pour out Your wrath on the nations that refuse to acknowledge You—
on the peoples that do not call upon Your name.
For they have devoured Your people Israel*;
they have devoured and consumed them,
making the land a desolate wilderness. 10:25 Ps 79:6 Jer 8:16; 50:7 Zeph 1:6; 3:8

JUDAH'S BROKEN COVENANT

11 The LORD gave another message to Jeremiah. He said, 2 "Remind the people of Ju-
dah and Jerusalem about the terms of My covenant with them. 3 Say to them, 'This 11:3 Deut 27:26 Gal 3:10

10:25 Hebrew *devoured Jacob.* See note on 5:20.

10:17-22 These words warn of the impending attack on Jerusalem by the Babylonian army and the subsequent exile of Judah's people. This prophecy may have been given shortly before this event as an urgent warning that the people should repent immediately. The "shepherds" are the priests, prophets, and other leaders who led the people into idolatry (5:5; 8:10).

▸HOLINESS
10:23 Luck or the Lord? Many non-Christians credit fate or luck as a major contributing factor in their personal success. The Christian, on the other hand, declares that God in His providence faithfully watches over His people every step of the way. God is actively participating in every event of your life in order to bring about His plans for you. We are not mere victims of impersonal forces, such as fate or natural selection; a very personal God is caring for us all the days of our lives (Philippians 4:19). Rejoice in the Lord. His love and care for you is no accident! (***See Holiness***> *Changed by God> God Provides> Extending grace to us,* TopicGuide page A41.)

10:24-25 Even though Jeremiah had not worshiped false gods or mistreated other people, he shared in Judah's corporate guilt. As a result, it was morally appropriate that he prayed for forgiveness. His prayer also served as a model of repentance for his audience.

11:2 Here Jeremiah made explicit what he had alluded to in prior chapters: Judah was in violation of the terms of God's

is what the LORD, the God of Israel, says: Cursed is anyone who does not obey the terms of
My covenant! 4For I said to your ancestors when I brought them out of the iron-smelting
furnace of Egypt, "If you obey Me and do whatever I command you, then you will be My
people, and I will be your God." 5I said this so I could keep My promise to your ancestors to
give you a land flowing with milk and honey—the land you live in today.'"

Then I replied, "Amen, LORD! May it be so."

6Then the LORD said, "Broadcast this message in the streets of Jerusalem. Go from town
to town throughout the land and say, 'Remember the ancient covenant, and do everything
it requires. 7For I solemnly warned your ancestors when I brought them out of Egypt, "Obey
Me!" I have repeated this warning over and over to this day, 8but your ancestors did not lis-
ten or even pay attention. Instead, they stubbornly followed their own evil desires. And be-
cause they refused to obey, I brought upon them all the curses described in this covenant.'"

9Again the LORD spoke to me and said, "I have discovered a conspiracy against Me
among the people of Judah and Jerusalem. 10They have returned to the sins of their fore-
fathers. They have refused to listen to Me and are worshiping other gods. Israel and Judah
have both broken the covenant I made with their ancestors. 11Therefore, this is what the
LORD says: I am going to bring calamity upon them, and they will not escape. Though they
beg for mercy, I will not listen to their cries. 12Then the people of Judah and Jerusalem will
pray to their idols and burn incense before them. But the idols will not save them when di-
saster strikes! 13Look now, people of Judah; you have as many gods as you have towns.
You have as many altars of shame—altars for burning incense to your god Baal—as there
are streets in Jerusalem.

14"Pray no more for these people, Jeremiah. Do not weep or pray for them, for I will not
listen to them when they cry out to Me in distress.

15"What right do My beloved people have to come to My Temple,
  when they have done so many immoral things?
Can their vows and sacrifices prevent their destruction?
  They actually rejoice in doing evil!

11:4 Exod 19:5; 24:3, 7 Deut 4:20 1 Kgs 8:51 Zech 8:8
11:5 Exod 13:5 Deut 7:12 Jer 32:22
11:6 Jer 3:12; 7:2
11:7 Exod 15:26 2 Chr 36:15
11:8 Lev 26:14-43 Ezek 20:8
11:9 Ezek 22:25
11:10 Deut 9:7 Judg 2:11-13 Ezek 16:59
11:11 Jer 6:19; 25:35
11:12 Deut 32:37 Jer 44:17
11:14 Ps 66:18 Hos 5:6

covenant, or treaty. As a prophet, Jeremiah was God's ambassador. When treaty violations occurred in the ancient world, it was common for the more powerful nation (in this case, God) to send an ambassador to the weaker nation (in this case, Judah) to remind them of their obligations under the treaty. This was a way to give the weaker nation the benefit of the doubt—perhaps they were not rebellious but had merely forgotten their obligations (compare 5:4-5).

11:3-5 The treaty, or covenant, between God and His people had always included conditions. If God's people were unfaithful, God would curse them; if they were faithful, He would bless them. In Jeremiah's day, many people of Judah had forgotten the stipulations of the treaty and assumed that God's blessings were unconditional (7:4, 8; 18:1-10). This reminder served as a warning for Judah to repent and to begin keeping the terms of the treaty once again.

11:6-8 A brief recapitulation of Israel's history demonstrated God's willingness to carry out covenant curses against His own people when they failed to keep the terms of their covenant with Him.

11:11 As the people of Judah continued in their gross idolatry and refusal to repent, God became more resolute about destroying them. Whereas He had previously offered to forgive them if they repented, here He no longer offered reprieve. His plans to punish them, however, was not absolute. True repentance might still have caused Him to relent (18:1-10), but the possibility had become more remote.

11:14 Previously, Jeremiah had been instructed not to intercede for Judah (7:16), but he interceded nonetheless (10:23-25). Jeremiah may not have sinned by doing this; God's instruction may have been designed to indicate the height of God's anger, with the specifics of ceasing to intercede overstated for effect. However, it is possible that Jeremiah sinned. In this case Jeremiah did not intercede for the people. Instead, he prayed against them after they plotted to kill him (11:19-20).

▸ GOD

11:15 Church is not enough. How can you go to church every Sunday and still end up in hell? A lack of faith—it voids any religious practices that you might perform (Romans 14:23; James 4:17). In Jeremiah's time, God said it this way: faithless, unrepentant people, even members of the covenant community, had no right to enter His Temple, no right to offer sacrifices, and no right to forgiveness. And it is still possible to enter such a situation under the New Covenant. Sins will not be forgiven if we fail to forgive others (Matthew 6:15), if we knowingly attribute the works of the Holy Spirit to Satan (Mark 3:28-29), and if we turn away from God after seeing for ourselves that He is real and that His promises are true (Hebrews 6:4-8). As in Jeremiah's time, these types of behavior reveal a heart that is far from God and has no interest in repentance. Make the measure of your spirituality not how often you go to church, but how often you repent and affirm the gospel. (***See God****> Relationship> Barriers> Disobedience,* TopicGuide page A14.)

16 I, the LORD, once called them a thriving olive tree,
beautiful to see and full of good fruit.
But now I have sent the fury of their enemies
to burn them with fire,
leaving them charred and broken.

17 "I, the LORD of Heaven's Armies, who planted this olive tree, have ordered it destroyed.
For the people of Israel and Judah have done evil, arousing My anger by burning incense
to Baal."

11:16 Pss 52:8; 83:2; Isa 27:11; Jer 21:14
11:17 Jer 2:21; 32:29

A PLOT AGAINST JEREMIAH

18 Then the LORD told me about the plots my enemies were making against me. 19 I was like
a lamb being led to the slaughter. I had no idea that they were planning to kill me! "Let's
destroy this man and all his words," they said. "Let's cut him down, so his name will be for-
gotten forever."

20 O LORD of Heaven's Armies,
You make righteous judgments,
and You examine the deepest thoughts and secrets.
Let me see your vengeance against them,
for I have committed my cause to You.

21 This is what the LORD says about the men of Anathoth who wanted me dead. They
had said, "We will kill you if you do not stop prophesying in the LORD's name." 22 So this is
what the LORD of Heaven's Armies says about them: "I will punish them! Their young men
will die in battle, and their boys and girls will starve to death. 23 Not one of these plotters
from Anathoth will survive, for I will bring disaster upon them when their time of punish-
ment comes."

11:18 1 Sam 23:11-12; 2 Kgs 6:9-10; Ezek 8:6
11:19 Pss 83:4; 109:13; Isa 53:7; Jer 18:18
11:20 Ps 7:9; Jer 17:10; 20:12
11:21 Jer 1:1; 12:5-6; 20:10; 26:8; 38:4
11:22 Jer 18:21; 21:14
11:23 Jer 6:9; 23:12; Hos 9:7; Mic 7:4

JEREMIAH QUESTIONS THE LORD'S JUSTICE

12 1 LORD, You always give me justice
when I bring a case before You.
So let me bring You this complaint:

12:1 Ezra 9:15; Job 13:3; Jer 5:27-28; 11:20; Hab 1:4

11:18-23 The Lord honored Jeremiah's prayer and agreed to kill all of those who threatened Jeremiah's life. This was in keeping with God's prior agreement with Jeremiah (1:17-19).

12:1-2 Jeremiah brought another lawsuit before God regarding the people of Judah, and again he petitioned for their destruction (12:3). This time Jeremiah did not limit his request to those who sought his life but extended it to all the wicked in the land.

BECAUSE GOD IS JUST

He will always treat me fairly.

You make righteous judgments,
and You examine the deepest thoughts and secrets.

JEREMIAH 11:20

FOR THE NEXT *GOD IS JUST* FEATURE SEE PAGE 1921.

Why are the wicked so prosperous?
Why are evil people so happy?

12:2 Isa 29:13; Ezek 17:5-10; 33:31; Titus 1:16

[2] You have planted them,
and they have taken root and prospered.
Your name is on their lips,
but You are far from their hearts.

12:3 Pss 7:9; 139:1-4; Jer 11:20

[3] But as for me, LORD, You know my heart.
You see me and test my thoughts.
Drag these people away like sheep to be butchered!
Set them aside to be slaughtered!

12:4 Jer 5:31; Hos 4:3; Joel 1:10-17

[4] How long must this land mourn?
Even the grass in the fields has withered.
The wild animals and birds have disappeared
because of the evil in the land.
For the people have said,
"The LORD doesn't see what's ahead for us!"

THE LORD'S REPLY TO JEREMIAH

12:5 Jer 50:44

[5] "If racing against mere men makes you tired,
how will you race against horses?
If you stumble and fall on open ground,
what will you do in the thickets near the Jordan?

12:6 Gen 37:4-11; Ps 69:8; Prov 26:25

[6] Even your brothers, members of your own family,
have turned against you.
They plot and raise complaints against you.
Do not trust them,
no matter how pleasantly they speak.

12:7 Jer 7:29; 11:15; Hos 11:1-4

[7] "I have abandoned My people, My special possession.
I have surrendered My dearest ones to their enemies.

12:8 Hos 9:15; Amos 6:8

[8] My chosen people have roared at Me like a lion of the forest,
so I have treated them with contempt.

12:9 2 Kgs 24:2; Isa 56:9; Jer 7:33; 15:3; 34:20

[9] My chosen people act like speckled vultures,*
but they themselves are surrounded by vultures.
Bring on the wild animals to pick their corpses clean!

12:10 Ps 80:8-16; Isa 5:1-7; Lam 1:10

[10] "Many rulers have ravaged My vineyard,
trampling down the vines
and turning all its beauty into a barren wilderness.

12:11 Jer 4:20, 27; 25:11

[11] They have made it an empty wasteland;
I hear its mournful cry.

12:9 Or *speckled hyenas.*

12:3 Jeremiah's request for justice was righteous, as was demonstrated by his invitation for God to examine him. He was not claiming that he was completely without sin (Psalm 130:3), but rather that he was bringing the case before God without treachery (Deuteronomy 19:18-19). The punishment he requested was fitting according to the terms of God's treaty with His people (Leviticus 26:27-39).

12:4, 11-14 Jeremiah notes that the Promised Land itself was suffering because of the people's wickedness. With God's blessing on the land, it provided abundant crops with little effort (Deuteronomy 8:7-10; 11:10-12) and was a place of safety (Deuteronomy 28:2-14). Under God's curse, however, the land suffered the reverse of these blessings (Deuteronomy 28:15-51).

12:7-9 These verses reveal glimpses of God's care for His people ("My chosen people," "My special possession," "My dearest ones") even amid expressions of anger. God was disgusted with His people's idolatry and treated them harshly in order to discipline them. God's terms of endearment offered hope to the faithful that He would not destroy them along with the wicked (Genesis 18:23-33; Jeremiah 5:1).

The whole land is desolate,
and no one even cares.
12 On all the bare hilltops,
destroying armies can be seen.
The sword of the LORD devours people
from one end of the nation to the other.
No one will escape!
13 My people have planted wheat
but are harvesting thorns.
They have worn themselves out,
but it has done them no good.
They will harvest a crop of shame
because of the fierce anger of the LORD."

12:12 Isa 34:6; Jer 47:6; Amos 9:4
12:13 Lev 26:16; Deut 28:38; Isa 55:2; Jer 4:26; 17:10; 25:37-38

A MESSAGE FOR ISRAEL'S NEIGHBORS

14 Now this is what the LORD says: "I will uproot from their land all the evil nations reaching
out for the possession I gave My people Israel. And I will uproot Judah from among them.
15 But afterward I will return and have compassion on all of them. I will bring them home to
their own lands again, each nation to its own possession. 16 And if these nations truly learn
the ways of My people, and if they learn to swear by My name, saying, 'As surely as the
LORD lives' (just as they taught My people to swear by the name of Baal), then they will be
given a place among My people. 17 But any nation who refuses to obey Me will be up-
rooted and destroyed. I, the LORD, have spoken!"

12:14 Zeph 2:8-10; Zech 2:8
12:15 Jer 49:6, 39
12:16 Josh 23:7
12:17 Ps 2:8-12

JEREMIAH'S LINEN LOINCLOTH

13 This is what the LORD said to me: "Go and buy a linen loincloth and put it on, but
do not wash it." 2 So I bought the loincloth as the LORD directed me, and I put it on.
3 Then the LORD gave me another message: 4 "Take the linen loincloth you are wearing,
and go to the Euphrates River.* Hide it there in a hole in the rocks." 5 So I went and hid it by
the Euphrates as the LORD had instructed me.
6 A long time afterward the LORD said to me, "Go back to the Euphrates and get the loin-
cloth I told you to hide there." 7 So I went to the Euphrates and dug it out of the hole where I
had hidden it. But now it was rotting and falling apart. The loincloth was good for nothing.
8 Then I received this message from the LORD: 9 "This is what the LORD says: This shows
how I will rot away the pride of Judah and Jerusalem. 10 These wicked people refuse to lis-
ten to Me. They stubbornly follow their own desires and worship other gods. Therefore,

13:1 Jer 13:11
13:2 Isa 20:2
13:4 Jer 51:63
13:5 Exod 39:42-43; 40:16
13:9 Lev 26:19
13:10 Jer 13:15-17

13:4 Hebrew *Perath;* also in 13:5, 6, 7.

PURPOSE

12:14 Mysterious justice. Have you ever sensed God working through an unbeliever in your life? Because Judah had sinned, God used foreign nations as a form of judgment upon His people in His land. But then God turned around and held these foreign invaders responsible for dealing harshly with His people (Joel 3:1-3). As difficult as this may be to comprehend from a human standpoint, God sovereignly controls everything that occurs in this world—yet it all happens freely. When Judas betrayed Christ, for instance, he was held accountable for his actions (Matthew 27:3-10; John 17:12; Acts 1:18). Yet because Judas betrayed Christ, we are able to experience salvation. Just because something appears to be evil does not mean God is not using it to accomplish good in your life. Look for God's hand in every circumstance. (***See Purpose*****> *God's Means> God's Sovereignty> God decrees all,* TopicGuide page A52.)

12:15-16 As He did throughout the Old Testament, here God extends the gospel to the Gentiles (Genesis 22:18; Psalm 72:17; Isaiah 42:6-7; 56:7-8). If they would convert to worship the Lord, the Gentile nations would be blessed along with Israel in the restoration after the Exile.

13:1-14 The symbolic action with the linen belt visually reinforced Jeremiah's message. Symbolic actions by prophets commonly indicated God's heightened intention to carry out His threat or offer. In this case, the prophetic action reinforced the finality of God's intention to destroy Judah.

13:1, 11 The loincloth was an undergarment and served as allusion to the intimacy shared by God and His people.

13:4-9 The belt's disintegration turned it into a filthy rag that no one would want to use as underwear. The image of wearing such a disgusting undergarment illustrated the revulsion God felt toward His idolatrous people.

13:11 Exod 19:5-6; Deut 32:10-11; Ps 81:11; Isa 43:21; Jer 7:24; 33:9
13:13 Pss 60:3; 75:8; Jer 25:27
13:14 Isa 27:11; Jer 6:21; 16:5; 19:9-11

they will become like this loincloth—good for nothing! 11 As a loincloth clings to a man's
waist, so I created Judah and Israel to cling to Me, says the LORD. They were to be My peo-
ple, My pride, My glory—an honor to My name. But they would not listen to Me.
12 "So tell them, 'This is what the LORD, the God of Israel, says: May all your jars be filled
with wine.' And they will reply, 'Of course! Jars are made to be filled with wine!'
13 "Then tell them, 'No, this is what the LORD means: I will fill everyone in this land with
drunkenness—from the king sitting on David's throne to the priests and the prophets, right
down to the common people of Jerusalem. 14 I will smash them against each other, even
parents against children, says the LORD. I will not let My pity or mercy or compassion keep
Me from destroying them.'"

A WARNING AGAINST PRIDE

13:15 Prov 16:5
13:16 Ps 96:8; Isa 5:30; 59:9; Amos 5:18
13:17 Jer 9:1; 23:1-2; Mal 2:2; Luke 19:41-42
13:18 2 Kgs 24:12, 15; 2 Chr 33:12, 19
13:20 Jer 1:15; 6:22; 13:17; 23:2

15 Listen and pay attention!
Do not be arrogant, for the LORD has spoken.
16 Give glory to the LORD your God
before it is too late.
Acknowledge Him before He brings darkness upon you,
causing you to stumble and fall on the darkening mountains.
For then, when you look for light,
you will find only terrible darkness and gloom.
17 And if you still refuse to listen,
I will weep alone because of your pride.
My eyes will overflow with tears,
because the LORD's flock will be led away into exile.

18 Say to the king and his mother,
"Come down from your thrones
and sit in the dust,
for your glorious crowns
will soon be snatched from your heads."
19 The towns of the Negev will close their gates,
and no one will be able to open them.
The people of Judah will be taken away as captives.
All will be carried into exile.

20 Open up your eyes and see
the armies marching down from the north!
Where is your flock—
your beautiful flock—
that He gave you to care for?

13:12 Because the people had forgotten that God's blessings were contingent upon their obedience (18:1-10), they expected God to bless them despite their unfaithfulness to Him.

13:15-19 Even though it would be hard to change God's mind (11:1-11), the threats Jeremiah delivered were not unavoidable. If the people repented earnestly and profusely, they might be spared.

13:18-23 As God's ambassadors, the prophets often directed their messages to the royal court. The king was responsible to care for the nation by ensuring that the people remained faithful to God, but he had failed in this duty, and his sin affected the whole nation (compare 15:4).

SPIRITUAL WARFARE

13:20 Facing reality. It is foolish to be so focused on the present that you fail to consider the consequences of your sins. Moses was a man who had all the pleasures of the Egyptian lifestyle at his disposal, but he chose to serve God rather than to enjoy those fleeting moments (Hebrews 11:25). The people of Jeremiah's time, however, refused to see the terrible judgment that was descending on them. Ask God to make you aware of any sin that might be bringing His judgment on you, and strive to keep your eyes fixed on the eternal prize of heaven. (***See Spiritual Warfare**> Origin of Sin> Humanity's Fall> Spiritual> Spiritually blind,* TopicGuide page A44.)

21 What will you say when the LORD takes the allies you have cultivated
and appoints them as your rulers?
Pangs of anguish will grip you,
like those of a woman in labor!
22 You may ask yourself,
"Why is all this happening to me?"
It is because of your many sins!
That is why you have been stripped
and raped by invading armies.
23 Can an Ethiopian* change the color of his skin?
Can a leopard take away its spots?
Neither can you start doing good,
for you have always done evil.

24 "I will scatter you like chaff
that is blown away by the desert winds.
25 This is your allotment,
the portion I have assigned to you,"
says the LORD,
"for you have forgotten Me,
putting your trust in false gods.
26 I Myself will strip you
and expose you to shame.
27 I have seen your adultery and lust,
and your disgusting idol worship out in the fields and on the hills.
What sorrow awaits you, Jerusalem!
How long before you are pure?"

13:21 Isa 13:8; Jer 4:31; 38:22
13:22 Jer 2:17-19; 9:2-9
13:23 Prov 27:22; Jer 4:22
13:24 Lev 26:33; Jer 9:16; 18:17; Ezek 5:2, 12
13:25 Ps 11:6; Jer 2:32; 3:21
13:26 Lam 1:8; Hos 2:10
13:27 Prov 1:22; Jer 2:20; 5:7-8; 11:15

JUDAH'S TERRIBLE DROUGHT

14 This message came to Jeremiah from the LORD, explaining why He was holding back the rain:

2 "Judah wilts;
commerce at the city gates grinds to a halt.
All the people sit on the ground in mourning,
and a great cry rises from Jerusalem.
3 The nobles send servants to get water,
but all the wells are dry.
The servants return with empty pitchers,
confused and desperate,
covering their heads in grief.
4 The ground is parched
and cracked for lack of rain.
The farmers are deeply troubled;
they, too, cover their heads.
5 Even the doe abandons her newborn fawn
because there is no grass in the field.

14:2 Isa 3:26; Jer 11:11; Zech 7:13
14:3 2 Sam 15:30; 1 Kgs 18:5; 2 Kgs 18:31
14:4 Joel 1:11, 19-20
14:5 Isa 15:6

13:23 Hebrew *a Cushite.*

14:1-6 In keeping with the terms of His treaty with His people, the Lord cursed the land with a drought in response to the people's sin (Deuteronomy 28:22-24). The precise time of this drought is not mentioned, though it may have occurred during Manasseh's reign (Jeremiah 15:4).

14:6 Job 39:5-6; Joel 1:18

6 The wild donkeys stand on the bare hills
panting like thirsty jackals.
They strain their eyes looking for grass,
but there is none to be found."

14:7 Isa 59:12; Hos 5:5

7 The people say, "Our wickedness has caught up with us, LORD,
but help us for the sake of Your own reputation.
We have turned away from You
and sinned against You again and again.

14:8 Ps 9:9; Isa 43:3; 63:8; Jer 17:13

8 O Hope of Israel, our Savior in times of trouble,
why are You like a stranger to us?
Why are You like a traveler passing through the land,
stopping only for the night?

14:9 Num 11:23; Ps 46:5; Isa 50:2; 63:19; Jer 8:19; 15:16

9 Are You also confused?
Is our champion helpless to save us?
You are right here among us, LORD.
We are known as Your people.
Please don't abandon us now!"

14:10 Ps 119:101; Jer 2:25; 6:20; 44:21-23; Hos 8:13

10 So this is what the LORD says to His people:
"You love to wander far from Me
and do not restrain yourselves.
Therefore, I will no longer accept you as My people.
Now I will remember all your wickedness
and will punish you for your sins."

THE LORD FORBIDS JEREMIAH TO INTERCEDE

14:11 Jer 7:16; 11:14
14:12 Isa 1:15; Jer 8:13
14:13 Jer 5:12; 6:14; 8:11; 23:17
14:14 Jer 5:31; 23:16, 25-26; 27:9-10
14:15 Ezek 14:10
14:16 Ps 79:2-3; Prov 1:31; Jer 7:33; 8:1-2; 13:22-25; 15:2-3

11 Then the LORD said to me, "Do not pray for these people anymore. 12 When they fast, I will pay no attention. When they present their burnt offerings and grain offerings to Me, I will not accept them. Instead, I will devour them with war, famine, and disease."

13 Then I said, "O Sovereign LORD, their prophets are telling them, 'All is well—no war or famine will come. The LORD will surely send you peace.' "

14 Then the LORD said, "These prophets are telling lies in My name. I did not send them or tell them to speak. I did not give them any messages. They prophesy of visions and revelations they have never seen or heard. They speak foolishness made up in their own lying hearts. 15 Therefore, this is what the LORD says: I will punish these lying prophets, for they have spoken in My name even though I never sent them. They say that no war or famine will come, but they themselves will die by war and famine! 16 As for the people to whom they prophesy—their bodies will be thrown out into the streets of Jerusalem, victims of famine and war. There will be no one left to bury them. Husbands, wives, sons, and daughters—all will be gone. For I will pour out their own wickedness on them. 17 Now, Jeremiah, say this to them:

14:17 Jer 8:21; 9:1; Lam 2:13

"Night and day my eyes overflow with tears.
I cannot stop weeping,

14:7-10 The Hebrew text does not directly identify the speaker; the words "The people say" are not present in the Hebrew text. It is possible that these words are Jeremiah's as he intercedes on behalf of the people (15:11). This is supported by the Lord's response (14:10) and by the people's refusal to turn back to God (15:7).

14:11 God instructed Jeremiah to stop interceding on behalf of the people. This prophecy was intended to shock Jeremiah's audience into recognizing the depth of their sin. God was no longer their protector (14:8); because they had betrayed Him, He had become their enemy.

▸ WORSHIP

14:12 Works without faith. "Faith without good deeds is useless" (James 2:20). But the reverse is also true: Good deeds without faith are useless. God required burnt and grain offerings from His people (Leviticus 1:3-17; 2:1-16), but His relationship with them was to be the basis for these offerings. God chose Israel to be His own people, and Israel was required to respond in faith and obedience to Him. They failed to respond to God inwardly. God requires not only our hands, but our hearts as well. Intimacy with God cannot be faked. Connect yourself to Him (John 15:5-8) and the good works will come without fail. (***See Worship****> NT> Our Role> Obedience> Show faith by our works,* TopicGuide page A32.)

for my virgin daughter—my precious people—
has been struck down
and lies mortally wounded.
18 If I go out into the fields,
I see the bodies of people slaughtered by the enemy.
If I walk the city streets,
I see people who have died of starvation.
The prophets and priests continue with their work,
but they don't know what they're doing."

14:18 Jer 6:25 Lam 1:20 Ezek 7:15

A PRAYER FOR HEALING

19 LORD, have You completely rejected Judah?
Do You really hate Jerusalem?*
Why have You wounded us past all hope of healing?
We hoped for peace, but no peace came.
We hoped for a time of healing, but found only terror.
20 LORD, we confess our wickedness
and that of our ancestors, too.
We all have sinned against You.
21 For the sake of Your reputation, LORD, do not abandon us.
Do not disgrace Your own glorious throne.
Please remember us,
and do not break Your covenant with us.

14:19 Job 30:26 Jer 8:15; 30:13 1 Thes 5:3

14:20 Ps 32:5 Jer 3:25

14:21 Ps 25:11 Jer 3:17; 14:7; 17:12

22 Can any of the worthless foreign gods send us rain?
Does it fall from the sky by itself?
No, You are the One, O LORD our God!
Only You can do such things.
So we will wait for You to help us.

14:22 1 Kgs 17:1 Isa 41:29 Jer 5:24; 10:3 Lam 3:26

JUDAH'S INEVITABLE DOOM

15 Then the LORD said to me, "Even if Moses and Samuel stood before Me pleading
for these people, I wouldn't help them. Away with them! Get them out of My sight!
2And if they say to you, 'But where can we go?' tell them, 'This is what the LORD says:

"'Those who are destined for death, to death;
those who are destined for war, to war;
those who are destined for famine, to famine;
those who are destined for captivity, to captivity.'

3"I will send four kinds of destroyers against them," says the LORD. "I will send the sword
to kill, the dogs to drag away, the vultures to devour, and the wild animals to finish up

15:1 Exod 32:11-14 1 Sam 7:9 Pss 99:6; 106:23 Jer 10:18; 52:3 Ezek 14:14, 20

15:2 Jer 14:12; 24:10; 43:11 Ezek 5:2, 12

15:3 Lev 26:16, 22, 25 Deut 28:26 Isa 18:6 Ezek 14:21

14:19 Hebrew *Zion?*

14:19-22 Despite the Lord's instruction not to intercede for the people (14:11), Jeremiah petitioned God to forgive them. He appealed again to God's character, and also to His covenant promises. Because the people did not share Jeremiah's sorrow over their sin, God did not forgive them (15:1).

15:1 These words imply that Moses and Samuel were even more highly favored by God than Jeremiah. Both Moses and Samuel were famous for interceding successfully on behalf of God's people (Exodus 32:11-14; 1 Samuel 7:9-10). Irregardless, Judah's sin had so far eclipsed the sins of prior generations that God was unwilling to change His mind regarding their punishment.

15:2-3 Death, war, famine, captivity, the sword, dogs, vultures, and wild animals were all established curses with which God had previously threatened His people. These curses would be put into effect if the people severely disobeyed the terms of God's treaty (Leviticus 26:14-33; Deuteronomy 28:25-26; 32:20-26).

15:4 2 Kgs 23:26-27; 24:3-4; Jer 24:9; 29:18 what is left. 4 Because of the wicked things Manasseh son of Hezekiah, king of Judah, did in
Jerusalem, I will make My people an object of horror to all the kingdoms of the earth.

15:5 Ps 69:20; Jer 13:14 5 "Who will feel sorry for you, Jerusalem?
Who will weep for you?
Who will even bother to ask how you are?
15:6 Jer 6:11, 19; 7:16, 24; Zeph 1:4 6 You have abandoned Me
and turned your back on Me,"
says the LORD.
"Therefore, I will raise My fist to destroy you.
I am tired of always giving you another chance.
15:7 Jer 18:21; 51:2; Hos 9:12-16 7 I will winnow you like grain at the gates of your cities
and take away the children you hold dear.
I will destroy My own people,
because they refuse to change their evil ways.
15:8 Isa 3:25-26; 4:1 8 There will be more widows
than the grains of sand on the seashore.
At noontime I will bring a destroyer
against the mothers of young men.
I will cause anguish and terror
to come upon them suddenly.
15:9 1 Sam 2:5; Isa 47:9; Amos 8:9 9 The mother of seven grows faint and gasps for breath;
her sun has gone down while it is still day.
She sits childless now,
disgraced and humiliated.
And I will hand over those who are left
to be killed by the enemy.
I, the LORD, have spoken!"

JEREMIAH'S COMPLAINT

15:10 Deut 23:19; Job 3:3; Jer 1:18-19; 20:7-8, 14 10 Then I said,

"What sorrow is mine, my mother.
Oh, that I had died at birth!
I am hated everywhere I go.
I am neither a lender who threatens to foreclose
nor a borrower who refuses to pay—
yet they all curse me."

15:11 Isa 41:10 11 The LORD replied,

"I will take care of you, Jeremiah.
Your enemies will ask you to plead on their behalf
in times of trouble and distress.

▸ SPIRITUAL WARFARE

15:6 Suffering for sin. God is exceptionally patient and longsuffering, especially when it comes to His people (Exodus 34:6-7). Nevertheless, God's patience is not inexhaustible. There comes a time when He begins to chastise us for our sins. If we are believers, He does this in love for the purpose of correcting us (Hebrews 12:5-11); if we are unbelievers, He rightly condemns us for our sin. In either case, as long as God does not kill us, His punishments present opportunities for us to repent and to receive forgiveness (Leviticus 26:14-45). Have you been suffering? Is it possible that God is chastising you for your sin? Is it possible that He is calling you to faith for the first time? If so, take advantage of the opportunity He has given you to receive His forgiveness and His blessings (Joel 2:12-14). (***See Spiritual Warfare***> *Resisting Sin and Evil> Consequences> Of Disobedience> Falling under discipline,* TopicGuide page A46.)

15:10 Despite the fact that Jeremiah interceded before God on behalf of the people of Judah, they hated him and rejected his prophecies. Jeremiah was so lonely and depressed that he despaired of his very life.

12 Can a man break a bar of iron from the north,
or a bar of bronze?
13 At no cost to them,
I will hand over your wealth and treasures
as plunder to your enemies,
for sin runs rampant in your land.
14 I will tell your enemies to take you
as captives to a foreign land.
For My anger blazes like a fire
that will burn forever.*"

15 Then I said,

"LORD, You know what's happening to me.
Please step in and help me. Punish my persecutors!
Please give me time; don't let me die young.
It's for Your sake that I am suffering.
16 When I discovered Your words, I devoured them.
They are my joy and my heart's delight,
for I bear Your name,
O LORD God of Heaven's Armies.
17 I never joined the people in their merry feasts.
I sat alone because Your hand was on me.
I was filled with indignation at their sins.
18 Why then does my suffering continue?
Why is my wound so incurable?
Your help seems as uncertain as a seasonal brook,
like a spring that has gone dry."

19 This is how the LORD responds:

"If you return to Me, I will restore you
so you can continue to serve Me.
If you speak good words rather than worthless ones,
you will be My spokesman.
You must influence them;
do not let them influence you!
20 They will fight against you like an attacking army,
but I will make you as secure as a fortified wall of bronze.
They will not conquer you,

15:12 Jer 28:14
15:13 Jer 17:3
15:14 Deut 28:64; Jer 16:13; 17:4
15:15 Ps 69:7-9; Jer 20:8
15:16 Job 23:12; Ps 119:103
15:17 Ps 102:7; 2 Cor 6:17
15:18 Jer 30:15
15:19 Ezek 44:23
15:20 Ps 46:7; Isa 41:10; Jer 1:8, 18-19; Ezek 3:9

15:14 As in some Hebrew manuscripts (see also 17:4); most Hebrew manuscripts read *will burn against you.*

15:15-17 Jeremiah ceased to intercede for the people and began to plead his own case, even asking God to punish those who opposed him. This should have shocked the people of Judah, who were used to Jeremiah interceding for them, and should have motivated them to repent of their sin in order to avoid the punishments Jeremiah requested.

▶ ADOPTION
15:15 Suffering for God. Sometimes our suffering is not the result of our sin, but the result of sin in the world and in others (Romans 12:14). Sometimes we are also called to suffer for the gospel, following the example of Jesus (1 Peter 2:19-23). When we suffer in this way, we bless the church (2 Corinthians 1:5-6; Philippians 1:29), we grow in God's grace (Romans 5:3-5; 8:17; Philippians 3:10; James 1:2-4), and we bear witness to the gospel (Galatians 6:17; 1 Peter 4:1-2). Are you suffering for your faith and your Lord? Look at your life—are you on the front lines of the Christian mission, or are you playing it safe? (***See Adoption***> *With Christ*> *Heirs of God*> *Receive inheritance through suffering,* TopicGuide page A36.)

15:18-21 Apparently Jeremiah overstepped his bounds by questioning God's good intentions toward him (compare 1:8, 19). God agreed to rescue Jeremiah and to retain him as a prophet on the condition that Jeremiah repent of this sin. Jeremiah's need for repentance and God's forgiveness served as a model for Judah to imitate.

for I am with you to protect and rescue you.
I, the LORD, have spoken!
15:21 Ps 37:40 — 21 Yes, I will certainly keep you safe from these wicked men.
Isa 49:26 — I will rescue you from their cruel hands."
Jer 39:11-12

JEREMIAH FORBIDDEN TO MARRY

16 The LORD gave me another message. He said, 2 "Do not get married or have children
16:3 — in this place. 3 For this is what the LORD says about the children born here in this city
Jer 15:8 — and about their mothers and fathers: 4 They will die from terrible diseases. No one will mourn
16:4 Pss 79:2; 83:10 — for them or bury them, and they will lie scattered on the ground like manure. They will die
Isa 18:6 — from war and famine, and their bodies will be food for the vultures and wild animals."
Jer 15:2-3; 34:20

JUDAH'S COMING PUNISHMENT

16:5 — 5 This is what the LORD says: "Do not go to funerals to mourn and show sympathy for these
Ps 25:6 Isa 27:11 — people, for I have removed My protection and peace from them. I have taken away My un-
Ezek 24:16-23 — failing love and My mercy. 6 Both the great and the lowly will die in this land. No one will
16:6 — bury them or mourn for them. Their friends will not cut themselves in sorrow or shave their
Deut 14:1 Ezek 9:6 — heads in sadness. 7 No one will offer a meal to comfort those who mourn for the dead—not
16:7 — even at the death of a mother or father. No one will send a cup of wine to console them.
Ezek 24:17 — 8 "And do not go to their feasts and parties. Do not eat and drink with them at all. 9 For
16:8 — this is what the LORD of Heaven's Armies, the God of Israel, says: In your own lifetime, be-
Eccl 7:2-4 — fore your very eyes, I will put an end to the happy singing and laughter in this land. The
16:9 — joyful voices of bridegrooms and brides will no longer be heard.
Hos 2:11 — 10 "When you tell the people all these things, they will ask, 'Why has the LORD decreed
16:10 — such terrible things against us? What have we done to deserve such treatment? What is
Deut 29:24-25 1 Kgs 9:8-9 — our sin against the LORD our God?'
16:11 — 11 "Then you will give them the LORD's reply: 'It is because your ancestors were unfaith-
Neh 9:26-29 — ful to Me. They worshiped other gods and served them. They abandoned Me and did not
1 Pet 4:3 — obey My word. 12 And you are even worse than your ancestors! You stubbornly follow
16:12 Mark 7:21 — your own evil desires and refuse to listen to Me. 13 So I will throw you out of this land and
16:13 — send you into a foreign land where you and your ancestors have never been. There you
Deut 4:26-27; 28:36 — can worship idols day and night—and I will grant you no favors!'

16:14
HOPE DESPITE THE DISASTER

Deut 15:15 — 14 "But the time is coming," says the LORD, "when people who are taking an oath will no
Isa 43:18-19 — longer say, 'As surely as the LORD lives, who rescued the people of Israel from the land of
16:16 — Egypt.' 15 Instead, they will say, 'As surely as the LORD lives, who brought the people of Isra-
Amos 4:2; 9:1-3 — el back to their own land from the land of the north and from all the countries to which He
Hab 1:14-15 — had exiled them.' For I will bring them back to this land that I gave their ancestors.
16:17 — 16 "But now I am sending for many fishermen who will catch them," says the LORD. "I
Luke 12:2 1 Cor 4:5 Heb :13 — am sending for hunters who will hunt them down in the mountains, hills, and caves. 17 I

16:1-4 The instruction to remain celibate was directed only to Jeremiah, not to the nation. Bearing children and being free from disease were great blessings God offered to the faithful people in the Promised Land (Deuteronomy 7:14-15). By contrast, childlessness and disease were curses on the unfaithful. Jeremiah's celibacy was not itself a curse; it was a sign to Judah of the curses that were about to fall on them. When prophets performed special actions like this, it demonstrated God's strong intention to carry out His words as stated. It also served as a warning to encourage Judah to repent and avoid the curse (Jeremiah 18:1-10).

16:5-7 As a second prophetic action confirming God's intentions, Jeremiah was not to attend funerals or offer sympathy to those who had lost loved ones. This was to demonstrate that God had withdrawn His own sympathy for them and that the nation would suffer many deaths and endure much loss if they failed to repent of their sin.

16:8-9 The third prophetic action Jeremiah was to take in order to confirm God's intentions was to abstain from celebrations. This symbolized the loss of happiness that the people would experience if they did not turn from their sin and seek God's forgiveness.

am watching them closely, and I see every sin. They cannot hope to hide from Me. [18]I
will double their punishment for all their sins, because they have defiled My land with
lifeless images of their detestable gods and have filled My territory with their evil
deeds."

16:18 Num 35:34 Jer 2:7; 3:9 Rev 18:6

JEREMIAH'S PRAYER OF CONFIDENCE

[19] LORD, You are my strength and fortress,
my refuge in the day of trouble!
Nations from around the world
will come to You and say,
"Our ancestors left us a foolish heritage,
for they worshiped worthless idols.
[20] Can people make their own gods?
These are not real gods at all!"
[21] The LORD says,
"Now I will show them My power;
now I will show them My might.
At last they will know and understand
that I am the LORD.

16:19 Ps 18:1-2 Isa 25:4 Jer 3:17; 4:2 Nah 1:7

16:20 Ps 115:4-8 Jer 5:7 Hos 8:4-6 Gal 4:8

16:21 Ps 83:18 Isa 43:3 Amos 5:8

JUDAH'S SIN AND PUNISHMENT

17 [1] "The sin of Judah
is inscribed with an iron chisel—
engraved with a diamond point on their stony hearts
and on the corners of their altars.
[2] Even their children go to worship
at their pagan altars and Asherah poles,
beneath every green tree
and on every high hill.
[3] So I will hand over My holy mountain—
along with all your wealth and treasures
and your pagan shrines—
as plunder to your enemies,
for sin runs rampant in your land.
[4] The wonderful possession I have reserved for you
will slip from your hands.

17:1 Job 19:24 Prov 3:3; 7:3 2 Cor 3:3

17:2 Exod 34:13 Jer 3:6

17:3 Isa 39:4-6 Jer 15:13; 20:5

17:4 Deut 28:48 Isa 5:25 Jer 7:20; 12:7; 15:14

▸ GOD

16:10-13 God's patience. How does God decide when to judge? In Jeremiah's day, God had already delayed His judgment for many generations. He had sent prophets like Jeremiah to His people on a regular basis to warn them of their sin through words and symbolic actions. The Judeans thought that because God allowed them economic success and personal happiness in the midst of their sin, He wouldn't condemn them—but they were wrong. Do not confuse a delay in God's discipline for approval of an unrepentant life. Judge your life and the lives around you by God's Word, not by apparent success. (***See God****> God's Attributes> Patient> God delays punishment as he awaits repentance*, TopicGuide page A17.)

16:16-18 The sinful people of Judah would have to endure many punishments before God would enable them to repent and be restored (see 2 Timothy 2:25).

16:19-21 God would make Himself known to the nations, and to His own people, by displaying His might as He disciplined His people. Through the disobedience of Judah (compare Romans 11:7-11), the Gentile nations would see the power of God and be moved to worship Him (Genesis 18:18).

17:2 Each of the places mentioned was a site for idolatrous pagan worship. Hills and trees were associated with the Canaanite gods. Asherah was the Canaanite goddess commonly associated with Baal, though she was originally the wife of the Canaanite god El. In addition to being a goddess of war and sex, she was considered to be a sacred prostitute. Canaanite worship involved both male and female temple prostitutes.

I will tell your enemies to take you
as captives to a foreign land.
For My anger blazes like a fire
that will burn forever."

WISDOM FROM THE LORD

17:5 Ps 146:3; 2 Chr 32:8; Isa 30:1; 31:3; Ezek 29:6-7
17:6 Deut 29:23; Jer 48:6
17:7 Pss 34:8; 40:4; 84:12; Prov 16:20
17:8 Pss 1:3; 92:12-14; Jer 14:1-6
17:9 Matt 13:15; Mark 2:17; 7:21-22; Rom 1:21; 7:11; Eph 4:22
17:10 1 Sam 16:7; Jer 11:20; Rom 8:27
17:12 Jer 14:21
17:13 Jer 14:8

5 This is what the LORD says:
"Cursed are those who put their trust in mere humans,
who rely on human strength
and turn their hearts away from the LORD.
6 They are like stunted shrubs in the desert,
with no hope for the future.
They will live in the barren wilderness,
in an uninhabited salty land.

7 "But blessed are those who trust in the LORD
and have made the LORD their hope and confidence.
8 They are like trees planted along a riverbank,
with roots that reach deep into the water.
Such trees are not bothered by the heat
or worried by long months of drought.
Their leaves stay green,
and they never stop producing fruit.

9 "The human heart is the most deceitful of all things,
and desperately wicked.
Who really knows how bad it is?
10 But I, the LORD, search all hearts
and examine secret motives.
I give all people their due rewards,
according to what their actions deserve."

JEREMIAH'S TRUST IN THE LORD

11 Like a partridge that hatches eggs she has not laid,
so are those who get their wealth by unjust means.
At midlife they will lose their riches;
in the end, they will become poor old fools.
12 But we worship at Your throne—
eternal, high, and glorious!
13 O LORD, the hope of Israel,
all who turn away from You will be disgraced.

▸ HOLINESS
17:5-10 Planted and producing. Christianity is not for lazy people. Jeremiah compared those who rely on themselves to shrubs in the desert with no future. Conversely, those who trust in God alone will be blessed and will thrive as trees firmly planted near abundant water (see also Psalm 1). Those trees produce fruit even in the midst of less than perfect circumstances. Humans are very capable of deceiving themselves and others into believing that when things are not optimal, we should stop working and stop producing. But God rewards us according to what we produce. If you want heavenly rewards, then God's Word says that you can't get them without producing fruit (1 Corinthians 3:13-15). (***See Holiness***> *God's Blessing> Obedience bears spiritual fruit,* TopicGuide page A42.)

17:9 Since humanity's fall into sin, the human heart has been entirely corrupted by sin to the degree that, apart from God's saving grace, people are incapable of pleasing God (Romans 8:5-8).

17:12 Because the Temple contained God's footstool (1 Chronicles 28:2), it was the symbol of His kingship over Judah and the location of His throne (Isaiah 6:1). It was the one location on earth where God regularly manifested His presence in a special and immediate way (Exodus 25:22).

They will be buried in the dust of the earth,
for they have abandoned the LORD, the fountain of living water.

14 O LORD, if You heal me, I will be truly healed;
if You save me, I will be truly saved.
My praises are for You alone!
15 People scoff at me and say,
"What is this 'message from the LORD' you talk about?
Why don't your predictions come true?"

16 LORD, I have not abandoned my job
as a shepherd for Your people.
I have not urged You to send disaster.
You have heard everything I've said.
17 LORD, don't terrorize me!
You alone are my hope in the day of disaster.
18 Bring shame and dismay on all who persecute me,
but don't let me experience shame and dismay.
Bring a day of terror on them.
Yes, bring double destruction upon them!

OBSERVING THE SABBATH

19 This is what the LORD said to me: "Go and stand in the gates of Jerusalem, first in the gate
where the king goes in and out, and then in each of the other gates. 20 Say to all the peo-
ple, 'Listen to this message from the LORD, you kings of Judah and all you people of Judah
and everyone living in Jerusalem. 21 This is what the LORD says: Listen to My warning! Stop
carrying on your trade at Jerusalem's gates on the Sabbath day. 22 Do not do your work on
the Sabbath, but make it a holy day. I gave this command to your ancestors, 23 but they did
not listen or obey. They stubbornly refused to pay attention or accept My discipline.

24 "'But if you obey Me, says the LORD, and do not carry on your trade at the gates or work
on the Sabbath day, and if you keep it holy, 25 then kings and their officials will go in and out
of these gates forever. There will always be a descendant of David sitting on the throne here
in Jerusalem. Kings and their officials will always ride in and out among the people of Judah
in chariots and on horses, and this city will remain forever. 26 And from all around Jerusalem,
from the towns of Judah and Benjamin, from the western foothills* and the hill country and
the Negev, the people will come with their burnt offerings and sacrifices. They will bring
their grain offerings, frankincense, and thanksgiving offerings to the LORD's Temple.

17:14 Deut 10:21 Ps 54:1 Jer 33:6
17:15 Isa 5:19 Amos 5:18
17:16 Jer 12:3
17:17 Jer 16:19 Nah 1:7
17:18 Ps 35:4, 26 Jer 20:11
17:20 Jer 19:3-4
17:21 Num 15:32-36 Neh 13:15-21 Mark 4:24 John 5:9-12
17:22 Exod 20:8; 31:13 Ezek 20:12
17:23 Jer 7:26; 19:15
17:24 Exod 15:26; 20:8-11 Deut 11:13 Ezek 20:20
17:25 2 Sam 7:16 Ps 132:13-14 Jer 22:4 Luke 1:32 Heb 12:2
17:26 Ps 107:22 Jer 33:11

17:26 Hebrew *the Shephelah.*

17:15 Jeremiah had been prophesying destruction for quite some time, but God had not yet brought ruin upon the people. This prophecy was probably delivered prior to the first military incursion by Babylon in 605 BC.

17:16-18 In the same breath that Jeremiah prayed for his persecutors' destruction, he protested that he had not asked God to send disaster. His meaning was that he had regularly interceded for the nation and had not prayed for their exile, even though he did pray against those specific people who persecuted him.

17:19-27 Despite the many warnings of destruction that Jeremiah issued to Judah and his prophetic actions and speeches confirming God's intentions, it was still true that God might relent and forgive Judah if the people repented. If they returned to God wholeheartedly and worshiped Him rightly, He would bless them instead of cursing them, establishing an unbroken line of Davidic kings on the throne of Judah and allowing the people to remain in the Promised Land forever. If they did not repent, God would bring to pass all the curses He had threatened.

WORSHIP

17:21-27 Not just like any other day. "How are you?" Answer: "I'm busy." How many people do you know who have exchanged a 5- or 6-day workweek for a 7-day workweek? In our obsession with getting things done, we often forget that God has ordered rest to be a regular part of our lives (Exodus 20:8-11). God wanted His people to set aside their regular business transactions for one day each week in order to worship Him in the Temple and trust in His provision. We, too, must learn the same lesson. With so many things to do in a week, allow a faithful keeping of the Sabbath to teach you that God controls everything in your life and that He should be worshiped. (***See Worship****> OT> Festivals> Sabbath,* TopicGuide page A26.)

17:27 Jer 39:8; Ezek 20:47; Amos 2:5
18:2 Jer 19:1-2
18:6 Isa 45:9; 64:8; Matt 20:15; Rom 9:20-21
18:7 Jer 1:10
18:8 Jer 7:3-7; Ezek 18:21; Jon 3:10
18:9 Jer 31:28; Amos 9:11-15
18:10 1 Sam 2:30; Jer 7:24-28; Ezek 33:18
18:11 2 Kgs 17:13; Isa 1:16-19; Jer 4:6; 11:11; Acts 26:20
18:12 Deut 29:19; Jer 2:25; 16:12
18:13 Jer 2:10-11; 23:14; Hos 6:10
18:15 Isa 62:10; 65:7; Jer 2:32; 6:16; 7:9; 44:17

27 "'But if you do not listen to Me and refuse to keep the Sabbath holy, and if on the Sab-
bath day you bring loads of merchandise through the gates of Jerusalem just as on other
days, then I will set fire to these gates. The fire will spread to the palaces, and no one will
be able to put out the roaring flames.'"

THE POTTER AND THE CLAY

18 The LORD gave another message to Jeremiah. He said, 2 "Go down to the potter's
shop, and I will speak to you there." 3 So I did as He told me and found the potter
working at his wheel. 4 But the jar he was making did not turn out as he had hoped, so he
crushed it into a lump of clay again and started over.
5 Then the LORD gave me this message: 6 "O Israel, can I not do to you as this potter has
done to his clay? As the clay is in the potter's hand, so are you in My hand. 7 If I announce
that a certain nation or kingdom is to be uprooted, torn down, and destroyed, 8 but then
that nation renounces its evil ways, I will not destroy it as I had planned. 9 And if I an-
nounce that I will plant and build up a certain nation or kingdom, 10 but then that nation
turns to evil and refuses to obey Me, I will not bless it as I said I would.
11 "Therefore, Jeremiah, go and warn all Judah and Jerusalem. Say to them, 'This is what
the LORD says: I am planning disaster for you instead of good. So turn from your evil ways,
each of you, and do what is right.'"
12 But the people replied, "Don't waste your breath. We will continue to live as we want
to, stubbornly following our own evil desires."
13 So this is what the LORD says:

"Has anyone ever heard of such a thing,
even among the pagan nations?
My virgin daughter Israel
has done something terrible!
14 Does the snow ever disappear from the mountaintops of Lebanon?
Do the cold streams flowing from those distant mountains ever run dry?
15 But My people are not so reliable, for they have deserted Me;
they burn incense to worthless idols.
They have stumbled off the ancient highways
and walk in muddy paths.

18:1 A prophet's claim to have received a message from God was equivalent to him claiming that he was God's chosen and authoritative representative. Jeremiah frequently reminded his audience of God's call on his life as he related God's messages to the people (compare 7:1; 11:1; 14:1; 21:1; 25:1; 26:1; 27:1). The people were so staunchly opposed to Jeremiah's messages that he constantly had to remind them of the authority behind his words.

18:2-6 The potter performed a symbolic act for Jeremiah. Such symbolic acts typically added emphasis to prophetic messages. Often, such as here, the interpretation of the act is not left to the reader's imagination but is made explicit in the text (compare 13:1-27; 19:1-15). In this case, the message was that God is always able to relent from punishment or withhold blessing, depending on the response of the people.

18:7-10 This passage clearly teaches that prophecy is fundamentally conditional. Even when a prophecy does not state a condition, conditions should be assumed. If the conditions are met, the prophecy may not come to pass as stated. If the conditions are not met, the prophecy may come to pass as stated. This is because prophecy, as well as foretelling the future, primarily functions to hold God's people accountable to their agreements or covenants with God. Therefore, just as God's treaties are conditional (Leviticus 26; Deuteronomy 28–30), prophecy is also conditional. When God's people obey His treaty faithfully, they have fulfilled the conditions for blessing; when they act unfaithfully, they have fulfilled the conditions for curses.

▶ PURPOSE

18:7-10 The purpose of prophecy. You are not alone in struggling to understand biblical prophecy. As God indicated to Jeremiah, He did not give prophecies merely for the purpose of revealing the future. In fact, the future He predicted was not even certain to come to pass. Rather, the Lord provided prophecies in order to motivate His people, both past and present, to repent of their sin and live faithfully and obediently before Him (Jeremiah 18:7-8, 11; Joel 2:14). As you read biblical prophecies, do not ask, "How will this passage be fulfilled in the future?" but rather, "What does this passage tell me about God and what He requires of me?" (***See Purpose****> God's Deeds> Judgment> Deliverance from judgment,* TopicGuide page A54.)

18:11-12 These words confirm that the purpose of prophecy is to inspire faithful living. God provided a warning of judgment and coupled it with an encouragement to repent. Judah's imagined response was that prophesying was useless because it would not motivate them to change their behavior.

16 Therefore, their land will become desolate,
  a monument to their stupidity.
All who pass by will be astonished
  and will shake their heads in amazement.
17 I will scatter My people before their enemies
  as the east wind scatters dust.
And in all their trouble I will turn My back on them
  and refuse to notice their distress."

A PLOT AGAINST JEREMIAH

18Then the people said, "Come on, let's plot a way to stop Jeremiah. We have plenty of
priests and wise men and prophets. We don't need him to teach the word and give us ad-
vice and prophecies. Let's spread rumors about him and ignore what he says."

19 LORD, hear me and help me!
  Listen to what my enemies are saying.
20 Should they repay evil for good?
  They have dug a pit to kill me,
though I pleaded for them
  and tried to protect them from Your anger.
21 So let their children starve!
  Let them die by the sword!
Let their wives become childless widows.
  Let their old men die in a plague,
  and let their young men be killed in battle!
22 Let screaming be heard from their homes
  as warriors come suddenly upon them.
For they have dug a pit for me
  and have hidden traps along my path.
23 LORD, You know all about their murderous plots against me.
  Don't forgive their crimes and blot out their sins.
Let them die before You.
  Deal with them in Your anger.

JEREMIAH'S SHATTERED JAR

19 This is what the LORD said to me: "Go and buy a clay jar. Then ask some of the
leaders of the people and of the priests to follow you. 2Go out through the Gate of
Broken Pots to the garbage dump in the valley of Ben-Hinnom, and give them this mes-
sage. 3Say to them, 'Listen to this message from the LORD, you kings of Judah and citizens
of Jerusalem! This is what the LORD of Heaven's Armies, the God of Israel, says: I will bring
a terrible disaster on this place, and the ears of those who hear about it will ring!
4" 'For Israel has forsaken Me and turned this valley into a place of wickedness. The peo-
ple burn incense to foreign gods—idols never before acknowledged by this generation, by

18:16 Jer 25:9; 48:27; 50:13 Ezek 33:28-29
18:17 Jer 13:24
18:18 Ps 52:2 Jer 2:8; 5:13; 8:8; 11:19; 18:11; 20:10 Mal 2:7
18:20 Pss 35:7; 57:6; 106:23 Jer 5:26
18:21 Ps 109:9-20 Jer 9:21; 11:22; 14:16
18:22 Ps 140:5 Jer 6:26
18:23 Jer 6:15, 21; 7:20; 17:4
19:1 Num 11:16
19:2 Josh 15:8 Jer 7:31
19:3 1 Sam 3:11
19:4 Deut 28:20 2 Kgs 21:6, 16 Isa 65:11 Jer 2:34; 7:6, 9; 11:13; 17:13 Dan 11:31

18:18-23 The people responded to Jeremiah's prophecies by rejecting his messages in favor of those of their idolatrous leaders. Although Jeremiah had previously interceded on behalf of the people, at this point he prayed that God would curse them according to the terms of the covenant (Leviticus 26; Deuteronomy 28–30). Even so, because his prayer was public and recorded in Scripture, it served as yet another warning to the rebellious people of Judah, offering them another opportunity to repent.

19:1-2, 10 Jeremiah was called to perform another prophetic action to emphasize God's intention to crush His people if they did not repent of their sin (compare 13:1-27; 18:1-6). The contrast between God's power over the hardened pot and over the soft clay (18:1-6) may have been intended to demonstrate His sovereign prerogative at every stage of His relationship with humanity.

19:3-4, 13 Jeremiah was to proclaim his message especially to the royal family and national leaders. As a prophet, Jeremiah was God's ambassador, or emissary, to Judah, serving as an official representative of God, the everlasting King, to Judah, His servant nation. Thus, it was appropriate that Jeremiah's comments be directed to the leadership of Judah.

their ancestors, or by the kings of Judah. And they have filled this place with the blood of
innocent children. [5]They have built pagan shrines to Baal, and there they burn their sons
as sacrifices to Baal. I have never commanded such a horrible deed; it never even crossed
My mind to command such a thing! [6]So beware, for the time is coming, says the LORD,
when this garbage dump will no longer be called Topheth or the valley of Ben-Hinnom,
but the Valley of Slaughter.

[7]"'For I will upset the careful plans of Judah and Jerusalem. I will allow the people to be
slaughtered by invading armies, and I will leave their dead bodies as food for the vultures
and wild animals. [8]I will reduce Jerusalem to ruins, making it a monument to their stupidity.
All who pass by will be astonished and will gasp at the destruction they see there. [9]I will see
to it that your enemies lay siege to the city until all the food is gone. Then those trapped in-
side will eat their own sons and daughters and friends. They will be driven to utter despair.'

[10]"As these men watch you, Jeremiah, smash the jar you brought. [11]Then say to them,
'This is what the LORD of Heaven's Armies says: As this jar lies shattered, so I will shatter
the people of Judah and Jerusalem beyond all hope of repair. They will bury the bodies
here in Topheth, the garbage dump, until there is no more room for them. [12]This is what I
will do to this place and its people, says the LORD. I will cause this city to become defiled
like Topheth. [13]Yes, all the houses in Jerusalem, including the palace of Judah's kings, will
become like Topheth—all the houses where you burned incense on the rooftops to your
star gods, and where liquid offerings were poured out to your idols.'"

[14]Then Jeremiah returned from Topheth, the garbage dump where he had delivered
this message, and he stopped in front of the Temple of the LORD. He said to the people
there, [15]"This is what the LORD of Heaven's Armies, the God of Israel, says: 'I will bring di-
saster upon this city and its surrounding towns as I promised, because you have stub-
bornly refused to listen to Me.'"

JEREMIAH AND PASHHUR

20 Now Pashhur son of Immer, the priest in charge of the Temple of the LORD, heard
what Jeremiah was prophesying. [2]So he arrested Jeremiah the prophet and had
him whipped and put in stocks at the Benjamin Gate of the LORD's Temple.

[3]The next day, when Pashhur finally released him, Jeremiah said, "Pashhur, the LORD has
changed your name. From now on you are to be called 'The Man Who Lives in Terror.'*

19:5 Lev 18:21; 2 Kgs 17:17; Ps 106:37-38; Jer 32:35
19:7 Pss 33:10-11; 79:2-3; Isa 28:17-18
19:8 1 Kgs 9:8; 2 Chr 7:21
19:9 Deut 28:53, 55; Ezek 5:10; Lam 4:10
19:10 Jer 19:1
19:11 Ps 2:9; Isa 30:14; Rev 2:27
19:13 Deut 4:19; 2 Kgs 17:16; Ezek 20:28; Zeph 1:5
19:14 Jer 26:2
19:15 Neh 9:17, 29; Ps 58:4
20:1 1 Chr 24:14; Ezra 2:37-38
20:2 1 Kgs 22:27; 2 Chr 16:10; 24:21; Job 13:27; Zech 14:10

20:3 Hebrew *Magor-missabib,* which means "surrounded by terror"; also in 20:10.

▸BIBLE

19:5, 9 Going too far. Can you image committing an act so sinful that God, who has literally "seen everything," would deem it as unthinkable? Well, that is exactly what God said about the practice of the people of Judah. The crimes of the people of Judah were, due to the fact that they knew better, high treason against God. The crimes were most despicable because they were committed against the weakest—children. Instead of bringing children into this world in order to instruct and nurture them (Deuteronomy 6:7; Ephesians 6:4), these parents used their children as instruments of pagan worship. Before you are quick to condemn these people, think of times in your own life when you have taken something holy and used it selfishly—even though you knew better. There's a lot of sin in our lives—follow God's instructions on how to free yourself from it (1 John 1:9; Romans 8:5-8). (***See Bible****> Unity> Kingdom of God> Repentance and faith embodies the kingdom,* TopicGuide page A11.)

19:5 God was appalled by the sacrifice of children to Baal and rejected any possibility that He approved of such an act in worship (compare Jeremiah 32:35). God did not oppose one human sacrifice, however. Redemption came through the sacrifice of Jesus Christ, who was fully human—and fully God (Hebrews 2:17). But God is particularly interested in protecting the helpless (Psalm 9:12), and He considers the children of His people to be His own children (Ezekiel 16:21).

19:14-15 Jeremiah prophesied that God's judgment would fall on the people of Judah because they had not repented after his earlier prophecies.

20:1-2 Because Jeremiah was God's authoritative emissary, to mistreat Jeremiah was to mistreat the Lord (Matthew 10:40-41; Luke 10:16). As a result, Pashhur evoked the Lord's anger for wrongly beating and imprisoning Jeremiah.

20:3 Changing Pashhur's name was both an exercise of authority over him and a symbolic action. As an act of authority, it indicated that even though Pashhur held enough authority within the religious institution to arrest Jeremiah, Jeremiah held higher authority over Pashhur as the Lord's emissary. This indicated that the people ought to listen to Jeremiah rather than Pashhur. As a symbolic action, Pashhur's new name warned of the judgment that would fall on Pashhur and all of Judah if they failed to repent.

4For this is what the LORD says: 'I will send terror upon you and all your friends, and you will
watch as they are slaughtered by the swords of the enemy. I will hand the people of Judah
over to the king of Babylon. He will take them captive to Babylon or run them through with
the sword. 5And I will let your enemies plunder Jerusalem. All the famed treasures of the
city—the precious jewels and gold and silver of your kings—will be carried off to Babylon.
6As for you, Pashhur, you and all your household will go as captives to Babylon. There you
will die and be buried, you and all your friends to whom you prophesied that everything
would be all right.'"

20:4 Jer 29:21; 39:6-7 Ezek 26:21
20:5 2 Kgs 20:17 2 Chr 36:10 Jer 15:13; 17:3; 27:21-22
20:6 Jer 14:14-15 Lam 2:14

JEREMIAH'S COMPLAINT

7 O LORD, You misled me,
and I allowed myself to be misled.
You are stronger than I am,
and You overpowered me.
Now I am mocked every day;
everyone laughs at me.
8 When I speak, the words burst out.
"Violence and destruction!" I shout.
So these messages from the LORD
have made me a household joke.
9 But if I say I'll never mention the LORD
or speak in His name,
His word burns in my heart like a fire.
It's like a fire in my bones!
I am worn out trying to hold it in!
I can't do it!
10 I have heard the many rumors about me.
They call me "The Man Who Lives in Terror."
They threaten, "If you say anything, we will report it."
Even my old friends are watching me,
waiting for a fatal slip.
"He will trap himself," they say,
"and then we will get our revenge on him."

11 But the LORD stands beside me like a great warrior.
Before Him my persecutors will stumble.
They cannot defeat me.

20:7 Ps 22:7 Lam 3:14 Ezek 3:14 Mic 3:8
20:8 2 Chr 36:16 Jer 6:10
20:9 Job 32:18-20 Ps 39:3 Jer 4:19 Acts 4:20
20:10 1 Kgs 19:2 Neh 6:6-13 Pss 31:13; 41:9 Jer 18:18
20:11 Deut 32:35-36 Jer 1:8; 15:20

20:6 Pashhur would be shown to be a false prophet when he and his friends were exiled. Moses taught that a prophet was false if his prophecies did not come true (Deuteronomy 18:20-22). Moses' teaching assumed that the prediction would fail to come true despite the fact that the conditions for fulfillment had been met.

20:7-10 God allowed the people to persecute Jeremiah despite the fact that God had said He would protect Jeremiah (1:8). This caused Jeremiah to lament his call as a prophet and to doubt God's good intentions toward him. God had not abandoned Jeremiah, however, nor had He permitted Jeremiah to be overcome. God enabled Jeremiah to endure mistreatment and punished Pashhur for his attacks on Jeremiah (20:3-4).

▶ BIBLE
20:8 Common sense. As we follow God's life guide, the Bible, we are sometimes led to decisions that are contrary to the expectations of society—and even our own. In Jeremiah's day, the Promised Land was the place of God's special presence and blessing. Nevertheless, when Babylon conquered the Promised Land, those who chose to stay in the besieged city were doomed—those who escaped lived. Later, those who chose to be dragged away into exile received God's greatest blessings, not those who remained in God's chosen land. Paul wrote in 1 Corinthians 1:18 that the message of the cross is foolish to those who are headed for destruction! But we who are being saved know it is the very power of God! Before you trust society and even your own fallible feelings, trust in God's Word to guide you through the day. (***See Bible***> *Power*> *Wisdom*> *Instruction through God's Word,* TopicGuide page A11.)

20:11-13 Jeremiah proclaimed words of hope, looking forward to God's salvation. Praise was a common element in Hebrew laments, typically offered in expectation of the salvation that God would ultimately bring.

They will fail and be thoroughly humiliated.
  Their dishonor will never be forgotten.

20:12 Pss 7:9; 17:3; 59:10; 62:8; 139:23 Jer 11:20; 17:10

12 O LORD of Heaven's Armies,
You test those who are righteous,
  and You examine the deepest thoughts and secrets.
Let me see Your vengeance against them,
  for I have committed my cause to You.

20:13 Pss 34:6; 69:33 Jer 15:21; 31:7

13 Sing to the LORD!
  Praise the LORD!
For though I was poor and needy,
  He rescued me from my oppressors.

20:14 Job 3:3-6

14 Yet I curse the day I was born!
  May no one celebrate the day of my birth.

20:15 Gen 21:6-7

15 I curse the messenger who told my father,
  "Good news—you have a son!"
16 Let him be destroyed like the cities of old
  that the LORD overthrew without mercy.
Terrify him all day long with battle shouts,

20:17 Job 3:10-11, 16; 10:18-19

17 because he did not kill me at birth.
Oh, that I had died in my mother's womb,
  that her body had been my grave!

20:18 Job 3:20; 14:1 Ps 102:3 Jer 15:10 1 Cor 4:9-13

18 Why was I ever born?
  My entire life has been filled
  with trouble, sorrow, and shame.

NO DELIVERANCE FROM BABYLON

21:1 2 Kgs 25:18-21 1 Chr 9:12 Jer 29:25, 29; 37:3

21:2 2 Kgs 25:1-2 Ps 44:1-4

21 The LORD spoke through Jeremiah when King Zedekiah sent Pashhur son of Mal-
kijah and Zephaniah son of Maaseiah, the priest, to speak with him. They begged
Jeremiah, 2 "Please speak to the LORD for us and ask Him to help us. King Nebuchadnezzar*
of Babylon is attacking Judah. Perhaps the LORD will be gracious and do a mighty miracle
as He has done in the past. Perhaps He will force Nebuchadnezzar to withdraw his armies."

21:2 Hebrew *Nebuchadrezzar,* a variant spelling of Nebuchadnezzar; also in 21:7.

▸ GOD

20:11-18 Mixed feelings. Jeremiah expressed conflicting feelings in this passage: hope in God (20:11-13) and utter despair (20:14-18). Most people can identify with this—we often feel a mix of contradictory ideas and emotions. In his mind, Jeremiah knew that God would take care of him, and that he would be vindicated and blessed in the end. But because he suffered so greatly in the meantime, Jeremiah was driven to depression. When hardship strikes, it is tempting to think that God has abandoned us, or to even curse our very existence (Job 3:1-3). In such times, it is important to know that God is still faithful and powerful, even if we feel like He is not. Memorize passages of Scripture such as Psalms 31:24; 33:18; and 43:5 to guide your prayers when you are troubled and confused. (***See God***> *God's Attributes> Faithful> God is faithful through calamity,* TopicGuide page A16.)

20:14-18 Jeremiah's regret over his life was intentionally overemphasized. Nevertheless, it stands in stark contrast to the hope he expressed in Jeremiah 20:11-13. Further, it implicitly rejects the prophetic call for which Jeremiah had been set aside before he was formed in the womb (1:5). Although Jeremiah's sentiments were likely sinful, it was right for him to confess his feelings honestly to God.

21:1-2 The leaders of Judah appealed to God for deliverance, but they failed to repent. They hoped for salvation from Babylon on the basis that God had done great things in the past. By this request, they demonstrated that they did not understand the nature of God's conditional agreement with His people, whereby He would bless them only when they were faithful to Him (18:1-10; see also Leviticus 26; Deuteronomy 28–30).

21:1 Zedekiah was the last king of Judah to rule in Jerusalem before the Babylonians under Nebuchadnezzar destroyed it in 586 BC. Zedekiah had been appointed to his kingship by Nebuchadnezzar and had taken an oath in the Lord's name to obey him, but then he rebelled against Nebuchadnezzar (2 Chronicles 36:10-13).

3 Jeremiah replied, "Go back to King Zedekiah and tell him, 4 'This is what the LORD, the
God of Israel, says: I will make your weapons useless against the king of Babylon and the
Babylonians* who are outside your walls attacking you. In fact, I will bring your enemies
right into the heart of this city. 5 I Myself will fight against you with a strong hand and a
powerful arm, for I am very angry. You have made Me furious! 6 I will send a terrible plague
upon this city, and both people and animals will die. 7 And after all that, says the LORD, I will
hand over King Zedekiah, his staff, and everyone else in the city who survives the disease,
war, and famine. I will hand them over to King Nebuchadnezzar of Babylon and to their
other enemies. He will slaughter them and show them no mercy, pity, or compassion.'
8 "Tell all the people, 'This is what the LORD says: Take your choice of life or death!
9 Everyone who stays in Jerusalem will die from war, famine, or disease, but those who go
out and surrender to the Babylonians will live. Their reward will be life! 10 For I have de-
cided to bring disaster and not good upon this city, says the LORD. It will be handed over to
the king of Babylon, and he will reduce it to ashes.'

JUDGMENT ON JUDAH'S KINGS

11 "Say to the royal family of Judah, 'Listen to this message from the LORD! 12 This is what
the LORD says to the dynasty of David:

"'Give justice each morning to the people you judge!
Help those who have been robbed;
rescue them from their oppressors.
Otherwise, My anger will burn like an unquenchable fire
because of all your sins.
13 I will personally fight against the people in Jerusalem,
that mighty fortress—
the people who boast, "No one can touch us here.
No one can break in here."
14 And I Myself will punish you for your sinfulness,
says the LORD.
I will light a fire in your forests
that will burn up everything around you.'"

A MESSAGE FOR JUDAH'S KINGS

22 This is what the LORD said to me: "Go over and speak directly to the king of Judah.
Say to him, 2 'Listen to this message from the LORD, you king of Judah, sitting on
David's throne. Let your attendants and your people listen, too. 3 This is what the LORD

21:4 Zech 14:2
21:5 Isa 5:25; 63:10; Jer 6:12
21:6 Jer 14:12; 32:24
21:7 2 Chr 36:17; Jer 13:14; Ezek 7:9; Hab 1:6-10
21:8 Deut 30:15, 19
21:9 Jer 38:2; 39:18
21:10 2 Chr 36:19
21:11 Jer 17:20
21:12 Isa 1:17; Jer 7:5, 20; 17:4; 22:3; Nah 1:6; Zech 7:9-10
21:13 2 Sam 5:6-7; Ps 125:2; Lam 4:12; Ezek 13:8; Obad 1:3-4
21:14 2 Chr 36:19; Jer 52:13
22:2 Isa 9:7; Luke 1:32
22:3 Exod 22:21-24; Ps 72:4; Jer 7:6; 19:4; 21:12; 22:17

21:4 Or *Chaldeans;* also in 21:9.

21:4-7 God had brought the Babylonians to Jerusalem specifically so that they might destroy the city. In this matter, Nebuchadnezzar was the Lord's chosen servant (25:9; 27:6). Far from being a challenge to God's authority, the Babylonian army was the instrument of His vengeance on His people.

21:11-12 Again, Jeremiah directed his threats toward the king of Judah (compare Jeremiah 13:18; 15:4; 17:19-22; 19:3-4, 13). One reason for the coming exile was that the kings of Judah had failed to rule righteously. It was their charge to lead God's people into fidelity to God and to enforce God's law (Psalm 89:20, 30-32), but instead they had perverted justice and encouraged idolatry.

21:13-14 The kings and inhabitants of Jerusalem wrongly thought that God would protect Jerusalem no matter what (Psalm 132:13-14). They had forgotten that God's blessings are conditional (Leviticus 26; Deuteronomy 28–30; Psalm 132:12). God Himself was willing to destroy Jerusalem if His people sinned greatly enough.

▸ SPIRITUAL WARFARE

21:13-14 Freedom to obey. Freedom in Christ means that we are free from the power of sin in order to serve God (Romans 6:14, 18; Galatians 5:1). This freedom should not be twisted to mean that we have a license to live as we please (Romans 6:1-2). The people of Jeremiah's time made this mistake regarding their position as God's chosen people. God repeatedly warned them that He would not hold back bringing judgment upon them for their sins. Likewise today, God warns believers of His discipline if they do not take their sin seriously (Romans 6:23). Pray for the Lord to keep you from this kind of presumption. (***See Spiritual Warfare****> Resisting Sin and Evil> Consequences> Of Disobedience> Falling under discipline,* TopicGuide page A46.)

22:1-4 The specific king is not identified. The reference may be to the house of David as a whole, since the preceding and following passages refer to several different kings of his line. If the people and the king would treat one another justly, God would protect them from foreign nations and prosper them.

says: Be fair-minded and just. Do what is right! Help those who have been robbed; rescue
them from their oppressors. Quit your evil deeds! Do not mistreat foreigners, orphans, and
22:4 Jer 17:25 widows. Stop murdering the innocent! 4 If you obey Me, there will always be a descendant
of David sitting on the throne here in Jerusalem. The king will ride through the palace
22:5 Amos 6:8 Heb 6:13 gates in chariots and on horses, with his parade of attendants and subjects. 5 But if you re-
fuse to pay attention to this warning, I swear by My own name, says the LORD, that this pal-
ace will become a pile of rubble.' "

A MESSAGE ABOUT THE PALACE

22:6 Isa 6:11 Jer 7:34 6 Now this is what the LORD says concerning Judah's royal palace:

"I love you as much as fruitful Gilead
and the green forests of Lebanon.
But I will turn you into a desert,
with no one living within your walls.
22:7 Isa 10:3-6, 33-34 Jer 4:6-7 7 I will call for wreckers,
who will bring out their tools to dismantle you.
They will tear out all your fine cedar beams
and throw them on the fire.

22:8 Deut 29:24-26 1 Kgs 9:8-9 2 Chr 7:20, 22 Jer 16:10 8 "People from many nations will pass by the ruins of this city and say to one another,
'Why did the LORD destroy such a great city?' 9 And the answer will be, 'Because they vio-
lated their covenant with the LORD their God by worshiping other gods.' "

22:9 2 Chr 34:25 Jer 11:3

A MESSAGE ABOUT JEHOAHAZ

10 Do not weep for the dead king or mourn his loss.
22:10 Jer 16:7; 44:14 Instead, weep for the captive king being led away!
For he will never return to see his native land again.

22:11 2 Kgs 23:30-34 11 For this is what the LORD says about Jehoahaz,* who succeeded his father, King Josiah,
22:12 2 Kgs 23:34 and was taken away as a captive: "He will never return. 12 He will die in a distant land and
will never again see his own country."

A MESSAGE ABOUT JEHOIAKIM

22:13 Jer 17:11 Hab 2:9 Jas 5:4 13 And the LORD says, "What sorrow awaits Jehoiakim,*
who builds his palace with forced labor.*

22:11 Hebrew *Shallum*, another name for Jehoahaz. 22:13a The brother and successor of the exiled Jehoahaz. See 22:18. 22:13b Hebrew *by unrighteousness*.

22:5 God swore that if the king and people were not faithful, He would send them into exile (Leviticus 26; 2 Kings 17:7-23). By this sworn statement, God obligated Himself to carry through with the threat. Whereas the people may have disregarded other warnings, this promise of destruction and exile demanded their attention—it was impossible that God would perpetually withhold judgment in light of His promise to punish them. Explicit promises constitute exceptions to the general rule that prophecy need not come to pass as stated (see Jeremiah 18:1-10).

▸ CHURCH
22:8 Put on display. Isn't it odd how the world pays special attention when a Christian is caught in a scandal? The people of Judah were warned that foreign nations would know the exact reason for their destruction. Jesus warns that, even today, the church is a city on a hill that cannot be hidden (Matthew 5:14). For better or for worse, we represent Him in this world. When Christians suffer or are charged with misbehavior, most unbelievers take the opportunity to lash out at God. We cannot avoid persecution—but God says we should not suffer for foolishness but for our faithfulness (1 Peter 2:20). Use the increased scrutiny of the world to your advantage—do great works of love and mercy and patience, against which there is no legitimate criticism possible (Galatians 5:22). (***See Church***> *What> Many Titles> The city of God*, TopicGuide page A48.)

22:10-12 Jehoahaz was deposed and taken into exile by Neco, king of Egypt. Neco appointed Jehoahaz's brother Jehoiakim to replace Jehoahaz as king. Josiah, the father of Jehoahaz and Jehoiakim had been a righteous king (2 Kings 23:25). Because of this, Josiah was blessed in life and in death and buried honorably (2 Kings 23:30). By contrast, his son Jehoahaz was evil and fell under God's curse. This passage was intended to teach the kings and the people of Judah to remain faithful to God and just in their actions in order to receive God's blessings, including the hope of restoration after exile.

He builds injustice into its walls,
for he makes his neighbors work for nothing.
He does not pay them for their labor.
14 He says, 'I will build a magnificent palace
with huge rooms and many windows.
I will panel it throughout with fragrant cedar
and paint it a lovely red.'
15 But a beautiful cedar palace does not make a great king!
Your father, Josiah, also had plenty to eat and drink.
But he was just and right in all his dealings.
That is why God blessed him.
16 He gave justice and help to the poor and needy,
and everything went well for him.
Isn't that what it means to know Me?"
says the LORD.
17 "But you! You have eyes only for greed and dishonesty!
You murder the innocent,
oppress the poor, and reign ruthlessly."

18Therefore, this is what the LORD says about Jehoiakim, son of King Josiah:

"The people will not mourn for him, crying to one another,
'Alas, my brother! Alas, my sister!'
His subjects will not mourn for him, crying,
'Alas, our master is dead! Alas, his splendor is gone!'
19 He will be buried like a dead donkey—
dragged out of Jerusalem and dumped
outside the gates!
20 Weep for your allies in Lebanon.
Shout for them in Bashan.
Search for them in the regions east of the river.*
See, they are all destroyed.
Not one is left to help you.
21 I warned you when you were prosperous,
but you replied, 'Don't bother me.'
You have been that way since childhood—
you simply will not obey Me!
22 And now the wind will blow away your allies.
All your friends will be taken away as captives.
Surely then you will see your wickedness and be ashamed.
23 It may be nice to live in a beautiful palace
paneled with wood from the cedars of Lebanon,
but soon you will groan with pangs of anguish—
anguish like that of a woman in labor.

22:14 Isa 5:8-9; Hab 1:4
22:15 2 Kgs 23:25; Jer 21:12; 42:6
22:16 Ps 72:1-4, 12-13; Jer 9:24
22:17 Jer 6:13; 8:10; Luke 12:15-20
22:18 1 Kgs 13:30
22:19 Jer 36:30
22:20 Deut 32:49
22:21 Jer 3:24-25; 13:10; 19:15; 32:30
22:22 Jer 20:11; 30:14
22:23 Jer 4:31

22:20 Or *in Abarim.*

▶ WORSHIP

22:15-16 More than evangelism. Some churches focus almost exclusively on social ministry and works of mercy. This should not be criticized—after all, Christ's ministry on earth involved much more than preaching and commanding people to repent and have faith (Matthew 11:4-6). Christ's mission was one of service in which He healed both the physical and spiritual needs of the people. God is calling us to do the same (John 20:21). Don't just meet the spiritual needs of people by sharing the gospel with them—find out if there is a way to meet their physical, social, or emotional needs. Minister to the whole person and you'll find a receptive ear for the whole gospel. (***See Worship****> NT> Sacrificial Living> Enables us to help meet other's needs,* TopicGuide page A34.)

A MESSAGE FOR JEHOIACHIN

22:24 Hag 2:23
22:25 2 Kgs 24:15-16 Jer 34:20

24“As surely as I live,” says the LORD, “I will abandon you, Jehoiachin* son of Jehoiakim,
king of Judah. Even if you were the signet ring on My right hand, I would pull you off. 25I
will hand you over to those who seek to kill you, those you so desperately fear—to King
Nebuchadnezzar* of Babylon and the mighty Babylonian* army. 26I will expel you and
your mother from this land, and you will die in a foreign country, not in your native land.
27You will never again return to the land you yearn for.

22:28 Hos 8:8
22:29 Jer 6:19 Mic 1:2
22:30 Matt 1:12

28 “Why is this man Jehoiachin like a discarded, broken jar?
  Why are he and his children to be exiled to a foreign land?
29 O earth, earth, earth!
  Listen to this message from the LORD!
30 This is what the LORD says:
‘Let the record show that this man Jehoiachin was childless.
  He is a failure,
for none of his children will succeed him on the throne of David
  to rule over Judah.’

THE RIGHTEOUS DESCENDANT

23:1 Isa 56:9-12 Jer 10:21; 50:6 Ezek 13:3; 34:1-2 Zech 11:17
23:2 Exod 32:34 Jer 44:22
23:3 Isa 11:11-16 Jer 31:7-8; 32:37
23:4 Jer 3:15; 31:10 John 6:39; 10:28 1 Pet 1:5
23:5 Isa 9:6-7; 11:1-5; 53:2 Jer 33:15-16 Zech 3:8; 6:12-13

23 “What sorrow awaits the leaders of My people—the shepherds of My sheep—for
they have destroyed and scattered the very ones they were expected to care for,”
says the LORD.
2Therefore, this is what the LORD, the God of Israel, says to these shepherds: “Instead of
caring for My flock and leading them to safety, you have deserted them and driven them
to destruction. Now I will pour out judgment on you for the evil you have done to them.
3But I will gather together the remnant of My flock from the countries where I have driven
them. I will bring them back to their own sheepfold, and they will be fruitful and increase
in number. 4Then I will appoint responsible shepherds who will care for them, and they
will never be afraid again. Not a single one will be lost or missing. I, the LORD, have spoken!

5 “For the time is coming,”
  says the LORD,

22:24 Hebrew *Coniah,* a variant spelling of Jehoiachin; also 22:28. 22:25a Hebrew *Nebuchadrezzar,* a variant spelling of Nebuchadnezzar. 22:25b Or *Chaldean.*

22:24-27 Jehoiachin replaced his father Jehoiakim as king when Jehoiakim was deposed and taken into captivity in Babylon. Because Jehoiachin was also evil, the Lord exiled him to Babylon as well. He was replaced by his uncle Zedekiah, Judah's last king before the fall of Jerusalem. As with the curse in Jeremiah 22:5, God swore that the curse on Jehoiachin would surely come to pass. Divine promises create an exception to the general rule that prophecy need not come to pass as stated (see 8:1-10).

22:30 The promised curse on Jehoiachin—removal from the throne—was extended to his immediate descendants. It is worth noting that Jesus Christ descended from Jehoiachin and traced His claim to David's throne specifically through Jehoiachin (Matthew 1:11-12), which shows us that this curse did not undermine God's promise of an unending dynasty to David. This curse also declared Jehoichim childless, though he in fact had 7 sons (1 Chronicles 3:17-18); but none of those sons would be an heir to the throne. As far as honor due to Jehoiachin's family, it would be as if he had never been king and had never had sons.

23:1-2 God was angry with the way the kings, prophets, priests, and other leaders had perverted justice and encouraged idolatry, thereby harming God's people. Because God cares so greatly for His people, He is exceedingly angry with anyone who hurts them—even if those who hurt them are also numbered among His special people (Matthew 18:6-7; 25:40-46).

23:3-6 The Lord planned to restore His chosen people to the Promised Land after their coming exile. This had always been His promised plan, according to the covenant He had made with Israel and Judah (Leviticus 26:40-45; Deuteronomy 30:1-10).

▶ GOD

23:5-6 Theocracy, not democracy. In the government of God, there is one official, and that person is Jesus Christ. Christ ascended to the throne as King because He inherited the throne from the Father, not because He was voted in by his followers (Matthew 28:18; Hebrews 1:2; Hebrews 2:8; Hebrews 3:6). God's kingdom is not a democracy, but a theocracy (ruled by God) in which the Lord of lords and King of kings reigns righteously over all of creation (1 Timothy 6:15; Revelation 17:14; Revelation 19:16). Show forth the lordship of Christ in your family, your job, and your civil responsibilities—over every inch of your world. (***See God> God's Names> God> King,*** TopicGuide page A18.)

"when I will raise up a righteous descendant*
from King David's line.
He will be a King who rules with wisdom.
He will do what is just and right throughout the land.
6 And this will be His name:
'The LORD Is Our Righteousness.'*
In that day Judah will be saved,
and Israel will live in safety.

7 "In that day," says the LORD, "when people are taking an oath, they will no longer say,
'As surely as the LORD lives, who rescued the people of Israel from the land of Egypt.'
8 Instead, they will say, 'As surely as the LORD lives, who brought the people of Israel back
to their own land from the land of the north and from all the countries to which He had ex-
iled them.' Then they will live in their own land."

23:6 Matt 1:21-23; Rom 3:21-22; 1 Cor 1:30

23:7 Isa 43:18-19; Jer 16:14-15

JUDGMENT ON FALSE PROPHETS

9 My heart is broken because of the false prophets,
and my bones tremble.
I stagger like a drunkard,
like someone overcome by wine,
because of the holy words
the LORD has spoken against them.
10 For the land is full of adultery,
and it lies under a curse.
The land itself is in mourning—
its wilderness pastures are dried up.
For they all do evil
and abuse what power they have.
11 "Even the priests and prophets
are ungodly, wicked men.
I have seen their despicable acts
right here in My own Temple,"
says the LORD.
12 "Therefore, the paths they take
will become slippery.
They will be chased through the dark,
and there they will fall.
For I will bring disaster upon them
at the time fixed for their punishment.
I, the LORD, have spoken!
13 "I saw that the prophets of Samaria were terribly evil,
for they prophesied in the name of Baal
and led My people of Israel into sin.

23:9 Hab 3:16

23:10 Ps 107:34; Jer 5:7-8; 9:10; 12:4; Hos 4:2-3

23:11 Jer 6:13; 7:9-10; 8:10

23:12 Ps 35:6; Isa 8:22; Jer 13:16; John 12:35

23:13 1 Kgs 18:18-21; Jer 2:8

23:5 Hebrew *a righteous branch.* 23:6 Hebrew *Yahweh Tsidqenu.*

23:7-8 The condition of Israel and Judah after their restoration would be far better than their conditions had ever been before—even under David and Solomon. Throughout the Old Testament, the greatest example of God's salvation to which the biblical writers appealed was the Exodus from Egypt. The prophesied restoration would exceed even this great work of God. As the New Testament reveals, this restoration was partially fulfilled in the first advent of Jesus Christ (Matthew 1:1) and will be finished at His second (Revelation 22:12).

23:9-32 Nearly all the prophets in Judah at this time were false. No doubt some probably believed themselves to be true prophets, just as false prophets of pagan religions often believe their own lies, but they were deluded. Jeremiah warned that no one should heed the prophets that opposed or contradicted him, or else they would fall under the same judgment as the false prophets.

23:14
Isa 1:9-10
Jer 5:30-31; 29:23
Ezek 13:22-23
Matt 11:24

14 But now I see that the prophets of Jerusalem are even worse!
They commit adultery and love dishonesty.
They encourage those who are doing evil
so that no one turns away from their sins.
These prophets are as wicked
as the people of Sodom and Gomorrah once were."

23:15
Deut 29:18
Jer 8:14; 9:15

15 Therefore, this is what the LORD of Heaven's Armies says concerning the prophets:

"I will feed them with bitterness
and give them poison to drink.
For it is because of Jerusalem's prophets
that wickedness has filled this land."

23:16
Jer 14:14
Ezek 13:2-3, 6
Matt 7:15
2 Cor 11:13-15
Gal 1:8-9
1 Jn 4:1

16 This is what the LORD of Heaven's Armies says to His people:

"Do not listen to these prophets when they prophesy to you,
filling you with futile hopes.
They are making up everything they say.
They do not speak for the LORD!

23:17
Jer 5:12; 8:11
Amos 9:10
Mic 2:11; 3:11

17 They keep saying to those who despise My word,
'Don't worry! The LORD says you will have peace!'
And to those who stubbornly follow their own desires,
they say, 'No harm will come your way!'

23:18
Job 15:8; 33:11

18 "Have any of these prophets been in the LORD's presence
to hear what He is really saying?
Has even one of them cared enough to listen?

23:19
Jer 30:23
Amos 1:14

19 Look! The LORD's anger bursts out like a storm,
a whirlwind that swirls down on the heads of the wicked.

23:20
Isa 55:11
Jer 30:24
Zech 1:5-6

20 The anger of the LORD will not diminish
until it has finished all He has planned.
In the days to come
you will understand all this very clearly.

23:21
Jer 14:14

21 "I have not sent these prophets,
yet they run around claiming to speak for Me.
I have given them no message,
yet they go on prophesying.

23:22
Jer 35:15
Zech 1:4
1 Thes 1:9-10

22 If they had stood before Me and listened to Me,
they would have spoken My words,
and they would have turned My people
from their evil ways and deeds.

23:23
Ps 139:1-10

23 Am I a God who is only close at hand?" says the LORD.
"No, I am far away at the same time.

23:24
Job 22:13-14
Ps 139:7-12
Isa 29:15-16

24 Can anyone hide from Me in a secret place?
Am I not everywhere in all the heavens and earth?"
says the LORD.

23:25
Jer 8:6; 29:8
23:26
1 Tim 4:1-2
23:27
Deut 13:1-3
Judg 3:7; 8:33-34

25 "I have heard these prophets say, 'Listen to the dream I had from God last night.' And
then they proceed to tell lies in My name. 26 How long will this go on? If they are prophets,
they are prophets of deceit, inventing everything they say. 27 By telling these false dreams,
they are trying to get My people to forget Me, just as their ancestors did by worshiping the
idols of Baal.

28 "Let these false prophets tell their dreams,
but let My true messengers faithfully proclaim My every word.
There is a difference between straw and grain!
29 Does not My word burn like fire?"
says the LORD.
"Is it not like a mighty hammer
that smashes a rock to pieces?

30 "Therefore," says the LORD, "I am against these prophets who steal messages from
each other and claim they are from Me. 31 I am against these smooth-tongued prophets
who say, 'This prophecy is from the LORD!' 32 I am against these false prophets. Their imagi-
nary dreams are flagrant lies that lead My people into sin. I did not send or appoint them,
and they have no message at all for My people. I, the LORD have spoken!

23:28 1 Cor 3:12-13
23:29 Jer 5:14; 20:9; 2 Cor 10:4-5
23:30 Ezek 13:8
23:32 Lam 2:14

FALSE PROPHECIES AND FALSE PROPHETS

33 "Suppose one of the people or one of the prophets or priests asks you, 'What prophecy
has the LORD burdened you with now?' You must reply, 'You are the burden!* The LORD
says He will abandon you!'
34 "If any prophet, priest, or anyone else says, 'I have a prophecy from the LORD,' I will
punish that person along with his entire family. 35 You should keep asking each other,
'What is the LORD's answer?' or 'What is the LORD saying?' 36 But stop using this phrase,
'prophecy from the LORD.' For people are using it to give authority to their own ideas, turn-
ing upside down the words of our God, the living God, the LORD of Heaven's Armies.
37 "This is what you should say to the prophets: 'What is the LORD's answer?' or 'What is
the LORD saying?' 38 But suppose they respond, 'This is a prophecy from the LORD!' Then you
should say, 'This is what the LORD says: Because you have used this phrase, "prophecy from
the LORD," even though I warned you not to use it, 39 I will forget you completely. I will expel
you from My presence, along with this city that I gave to you and your ancestors. 40 And I
will make you an object of ridicule, and your name will be infamous throughout the ages.'"

23:33 Jer 12:7; Nah 1:1; Hab 1:1; Zech 9:1
23:34 Lam 2:14; Zech 13:3
23:36 Jer 10:10; 2 Pet 3:16
23:39 Jer 7:14-15; Ezek 8:18
23:40 Jer 20:11; Ezek 5:14-15

GOOD AND BAD FIGS

24 After King Nebuchadnezzar* of Babylon exiled Jehoiachin* son of Jehoiakim,
king of Judah, to Babylon along with the officials of Judah and all the craftsmen

24:1 2 Kgs 24:10-16; 2 Chr 36:10; Jer 27:19-21; 29:1-2

23:33 As in Greek version and Latin Vulgate; Hebrew reads *What burden?* 24:1a Hebrew *Nebuchadrezzar,* a variant spelling of Nebuchadnezzar. 24:1b Hebrew *Jeconiah,* a variant spelling of Jehoiachin.

▸ WORSHIP

23:31-40 Modern day prophets. There should be a sharp distinction between the following: "I believe the Lord is leading me to say . . ." and "I have a prophecy from the Lord." In Jeremiah's time, so many people were claiming to have a message from God that it left the people utterly confused. Today, we have the same problem when people attempt to speak authoritatively as God's representatives. Jesus Christ is God's spokesman for the church as He is revealed in the Bible (Hebrews 1:1-3). God has given us pastors, teachers, and fellow Christians to help us understand the Scriptures, but not to deliver new authoritative messages from God. Help to explain God's Word, and depend on God's Spirit to empower you to apply God's Word accurately (John 16:13)—but don't add to it. (***See Worship****> OT> Prophets> Prophetic office of divine origin,* TopicGuide page A28.)

23:31-40 The false prophets had not received revelations from God, and they had not been commissioned as God's authoritative emissaries. Nevertheless, by using the formula "This prophecy is from the Lord," they claimed to speak with God's delegated authority. Those who lied about speaking on God's behalf in this manner were subject to the worst curses of God's treaty, such as exile from the Promised Land (Leviticus 26:31-34; Deuteronomy 28:36-37) and perpetual mockery among the nations.

24:1 This is one of the few prophecies in the book of Jeremiah that references a clear historical event. Jehoiachin was exiled in 597 BC. Since Zedekiah was still in Jerusalem (Jeremiah 24:8), this prophecy must have been given between 597 BC and 586 BC, before the fall of Jerusalem and the deportation of Zedekiah.

24:1 In ancient times, the most skilled and educated people of a conquered land were often carried away to serve in the conquering nation (compare Deuteronomy 21:10-11; Daniel 1:1-4).

24:1-10 In God's treaty with Israel and Judah, exile was a horrible curse (Leviticus 26:31-34; Deuteronomy 28:36-37). So it would have been natural for those in exile to think that God did not favor them, just as it would have been natural for those who remained in the Promised Land to believe that God was pleased with them. This prophecy explains that, contrary to expectations, those who were carried away into exile were blessed, and those who remained in the Promised Land were cursed.

and artisans, the LORD gave me this vision. I saw two baskets of figs placed in front of the LORD's Temple in Jerusalem. 2One basket was filled with fresh, ripe figs, while the other was filled with bad figs that were too rotten to eat.

3Then the LORD said to me, "What do you see, Jeremiah?"

I replied, "Figs, some very good and some very bad, too rotten to eat."

4Then the LORD gave me this message: 5"This is what the LORD, the God of Israel, says: The good figs represent the exiles I sent from Judah to the land of the Babylonians.* 6I will watch over and care for them, and I will bring them back here again. I will build them up and not tear them down. I will plant them and not uproot them. 7I will give them hearts that recognize Me as the LORD. They will be My people, and I will be their God, for they will return to Me wholeheartedly.

8"But the bad figs," the LORD said, "represent King Zedekiah of Judah, his officials, all the people left in Jerusalem, and those who live in Egypt. I will treat them like bad figs, too rotten to eat. 9I will make them an object of horror and a symbol of evil to every nation on earth. They will be disgraced and mocked, taunted and cursed, wherever I scatter them. 10And I will send war, famine, and disease until they have vanished from the land of Israel, which I gave to them and their ancestors."

24:2 Jer 29:17
24:5 Zech 13:9
24:6 Ezek 11:17
24:7 Zech 8:8; Heb 8:10
24:8 Ezek 12:13
24:9 1 Kgs 9:7; Ps 44:13-14; Isa 65:15
24:10 Isa 51:19; Jer 21:9; 27:8; Ezek 5:12-17

SEVENTY YEARS OF CAPTIVITY

25 This message for all the people of Judah came to Jeremiah from the LORD during the fourth year of Jehoiakim's reign over Judah.* This was the year when King Nebuchadnezzar* of Babylon began his reign.

2Jeremiah the prophet said to all the people in Judah and Jerusalem, 3"For the past twenty-three years—from the thirteenth year of the reign of Josiah son of Amon,* king of Judah, until now—the LORD has been giving me His messages. I have faithfully passed them on to you, but you have not listened.

4"Again and again the LORD has sent you His servants, the prophets, but you have not listened or even paid attention. 5Each time the message was this: 'Turn from the evil road you are traveling and from the evil things you are doing. Only then will I let you live in this land that the LORD gave to you and your ancestors forever. 6Do not provoke My anger by worshiping idols you made with your own hands. Then I will not harm you.'

25:2 Jer 1:2; 7:25-26; 11:7-8; 26:5; 36:2-3
25:3 2 Kgs 24:1-2; Jer 36:1; 46:2
25:5 Gen 17:8-10; Isa 55:6-7; Jer 4:1; 7:7; 35:15
25:6 Deut 6:14; 8:19; 2 Kgs 17:35

24:5 Or *Chaldeans.* 25:1a The fourth year of Jehoiakim's reign and the accession year of Nebuchadnezzar's reign was 605 B.C. 25:1b Hebrew *Nebuchadrezzar,* a variant spelling of Nebuchadnezzar; also in 25:9. 25:3 The thirteenth year of Josiah's reign was 627 B.C.

▸ ADOPTION

24:7 Heart transplant. Throughout the Old and New Testament, the message is the same concerning the heart: It is the source of both good and evil (Proverbs 4:23; Matthew 12:34-35; Mark 7:21-22). The Bible teaches us that prior to knowing Christ we had hearts made of stone (Ezekiel 11:19; Ezekiel 36:26). Our greatest need was for God to give us a new heart. The gospel does not seek to improve upon what already exists in us, but rather it seeks to recreate us into new beings (2 Corinthians 5:17). Ask God to change the hearts of those with whom you share the gospel so they can embrace His message with great joy. (***See Adoption****> With Christ> United with Christ> New heart,* TopicGuide page A37.)

24:8-10 Part of the reason that God had sent His favored people into exile was to protect them from the destruction that would rain upon those who remained in the Promised Land. The sinful leaders of Israel and many others who were grossly unfaithful would remain in Judah and experience the utter devastation God sent upon them. Those in captivity would enjoy the safety of serving in their captors' homes and would prosper (29:5-7).

▸ HOLINESS

24:8-10 Bad tree, bad fruit. Did you ever bite into a piece of fruit and then realize from the terrible taste that it was rotten? The fig was a very common fruit in Israel and Judah (1 Samuel 25:18), so Jeremiah's prophecy about bad figs was an effective image. God used Zedekiah and his followers' rebellion and disobedience as an example of what defines bad fruit. Avoid becoming classified as rotten by allowing yourself to be nourished by Christ (John 15). Stay rooted in God's Word and you'll have the nutrients to continue bearing fruit until the very end (Psalm 1). (***See Holiness****> God's Blessing> Obedience bears spiritual fruit,* TopicGuide page A42.)

25:3 Jeremiah's prophecies of judgment were not just occasional messages; he had been faithfully and consistently condemning the sin of the people for 23 years (1:2). Jeremiah's efforts, however, were unsuccessful in bringing about the people's repentance

7 “But you would not listen to Me,” says the LORD. “You made Me furious by worshiping
idols you made with your own hands, bringing on yourselves all the disasters you now suf-
fer. 8 And now the LORD of Heaven’s Armies says: Because you have not listened to Me, 9 I will
gather together all the armies of the north under King Nebuchadnezzar of Babylon, whom I
have appointed as My deputy. I will bring them all against this land and its people and
against the surrounding nations. I will completely destroy* you and make you an object of
horror and contempt and a ruin forever. 10 I will take away your happy singing and laughter.
The joyful voices of bridegrooms and brides will no longer be heard. Your millstones will fall
silent, and the lights in your homes will go out. 11 This entire land will become a desolate
wasteland. Israel and her neighboring lands will serve the king of Babylon for seventy years.

12 “Then, after the seventy years of captivity are over, I will punish the king of Babylon
and his people for their sins,” says the LORD. “I will make the country of the Babylonians* a
wasteland forever. 13 I will bring upon them all the terrors I have promised in this book—all
the penalties announced by Jeremiah against the nations. 14 Many nations and great kings
will enslave the Babylonians, just as they enslaved My people. I will punish them in pro-
portion to the suffering they cause My people.”

THE CUP OF THE LORD’S ANGER

15 This is what the LORD, the God of Israel, said to me: “Take from My hand this cup filled
to the brim with My anger, and make all the nations to whom I send you drink from it.
16 When they drink from it, they will stagger, crazed by the warfare I will send against
them.”

17 So I took the cup of anger from the LORD and made all the nations drink from it—every
nation to which the LORD sent me. 18 I went to Jerusalem and the other towns of Judah, and
their kings and officials drank from the cup. From that day until this, they have been a des-
olate ruin, an object of horror, contempt, and cursing. 19 I gave the cup to Pharaoh, king of
Egypt, his attendants, his officials, and all his people, 20 along with all the foreigners living
in that land. I also gave it to all the kings of the land of Uz and the kings of the Philistine cit-
ies of Ashkelon, Gaza, Ekron, and what remains of Ashdod. 21 Then I gave the cup to the
nations of Edom, Moab, and Ammon, 22 and the kings of Tyre and Sidon, and the kings of
the regions across the sea. 23 I gave it to Dedan, Tema, and Buz, and to the people who live
in distant places.* 24 I gave it to the kings of Arabia, the kings of the nomadic tribes of the

25:7 2 Kgs 17:17; 21:15 Jer 7:19; 32:30-33
25:10 Eccl 12:3-4 Isa 24:8-11 Jer 16:9 Ezek 26:13
25:11 Dan 9:2 Zech 7:5
25:12 Ezra 1:1 Isa 13:14 Jer 29:10; 50:1–51:64
25:13 Jer 36:4, 29, 32
25:14 Jer 27:7; 50:9
25:15 Jer 51:7
25:17 Jer 1:10
25:18 Isa 51:17
25:19 Jer 46:2-28
25:20 Job 1:1 Jer 47:1-7
25:21 Jer 48:1-47; 49:1-22 Amos 1:13-15; 2:1-3
25:22 Jer 47:4 Zech 9:2-4
25:23 Jer 49:7-8

25:9 The Hebrew term used here refers to the complete consecration of things or people to the LORD, either by destroying them or by giving them as an offering. 25:12 Or *Chaldeans*. 25:23 Or *who clip the corners of their hair*.

▸ GOD
25:9 God’s control over wicked rulers. Many nations in the world are ruled by decent people, others are ruled by less than decent people, and some nations are governed by chaotic despots. It would be easy for Christians under unpleasant circumstances to view these evil regimes as purest evil, controlled by Satan, and worthy of their hate. But this passage paints a unique picture of the relationship between pagan kings and God, with Nebuchadnezzar described as a deputy of God, God’s instrument for executing His will on earth. It makes for an uncomfortable mystery—how do we oppose unjust rulers without opposing God’s will? We should not tolerate oppressive rulers, but at the same time recognize that God mysteriously works through them for the advancement of His kingdom on earth (see Cyrus as God’s anointed in Isaiah 45:1). Yes, God controls and receives glory through all things! (***See God**> God’s Attributes> Sovereign> He raises and removes rulers,* TopicGuide page A17.)

25:11 God laid out His plan for the duration of the exile. This number 70 should not be interpreted literally, but rather should be seen as a number representing an extended period of time. In the ancient Near East, 70 years represented the lifespan of a king (Isaiah 23:15; see also Psalm 90:10). In Daniel 9, Daniel prayed for the exile to end, but God extended the period from 70 years to 490 years until the arrival of God’s Anointed One, Jesus Christ (Daniel 9:25).

▸ WORSHIP
25:15 Communion: a cup of wrath or a cup of blessing? The Bible typically describes God as holding two cups in His hands: a cup of wrath and a cup of blessing. The cup of His fury is poured out against unrepentant sinners (Psalm 75:8; Nahum 3:11); however, God extends a cup of salvation for all those who belong to Him (Psalms 16:5; 23:5; 116:13). In the sacrament of Communion, people partake of these cups. We, as believers, partake of God’s cup of blessing (1 Corinthians 10:16), which expresses God’s promise of a restored relationship through the death and resurrection of Christ Jesus. But the cup of Communion can also represent judgment for all those who partake of it unworthily—those who are outside of Christ (1 Corinthians 11:27-30). Let us approach God with a penitent and thankful heart as we partake of His fellowship in the Lord’s Supper. (***See Worship**> NT> Our Role> Mind and Heart> Lord’s Supper to be taken in a worthy manner,* TopicGuide page A32.)

25:25 desert, 25 and to the kings of Zimri, Elam, and Media. 26 And I gave it to the kings of the
Jer 49:34 northern countries, far and near, one after the other—all the kingdoms of the world. And fi-
25:26 nally, the king of Babylon* himself drank from the cup of the LORD's anger.
Jer 50:9; 51:41 27 Then the LORD said to me, "Now tell them, 'This is what the LORD of Heaven's Armies,
25:27 Ezek 21:4-5 the God of Israel, says: Drink from this cup of My anger. Get drunk and vomit; fall to rise
Hab 2:17 no more, for I am sending terrible wars against you.' 28 And if they refuse to accept the cup,
25:29 tell them, 'The LORD of Heaven's Armies says: You have no choice but to drink from it. 29 I
Prov 11:31 have begun to punish Jerusalem, the city that bears My name. Now should I let you go un-
1 Pet 4:17 punished? No, you will not escape disaster. I will call for war against all the nations of the
earth. I, the LORD of Heaven's Armies, have spoken!'

25:30 30 "Now prophesy all these things, and say to them,

Joel 2:11; 3:13
Amos 1:2 "'The LORD will roar against His own land
from His holy dwelling in heaven.
He will shout like those who tread grapes;
He will shout against everyone on earth.
25:31 31 His cry of judgment will reach the ends of the earth,
Isa 66:16 for the LORD will bring His case against all the nations.
Hos 4:1 He will judge all the people of the earth,
slaughtering the wicked with the sword.
I, the LORD, have spoken!'"

25:32 32 This is what the LORD of Heaven's Armies says:
Isa 30:30; 34:2-3 "Look! Disaster will fall upon nation after nation!
A great whirlwind of fury is rising
from the most distant corners of the earth!"

33 In that day those the LORD has slaughtered will fill the earth from one end to the other.
25:33 Isa 5:25 Jer 16:4 No one will mourn for them or gather up their bodies to bury them. They will be scattered
Ezek 39:4, 7 on the ground like manure.

25:34 34 Weep and moan, you evil shepherds!
Isa 34:7 Jer 50:27 Roll in the dust, you leaders of the flock!
The time of your slaughter has arrived;
you will fall and shatter like a fragile vase.
25:35 35 You will find no place to hide;
Jer 11:11 there will be no way to escape.
36 Listen to the frantic cries of the shepherds.
The leaders of the flock are wailing in despair,
for the LORD is ruining their pastures.
25:37 37 Peaceful meadows will be turned into a wasteland
Isa 27:11 by the LORD's fierce anger.
25:38 38 He has left His den like a strong lion seeking its prey,
Jer 4:7; 5:6 Hos 5:14; 13:7-8 and their land will be made desolate
by the sword of the enemy
and the LORD's fierce anger.

25:26 Hebrew *of Sheshach,* a code name for Babylon.

25:29 God's judgment began with His own house, Judah, but note that the reckoning also extended to include all of the nations of the world (25:18-26; 46–51).

25:32 God, who sovereignly rules over the whole world, was going to use the Babylonians to spread devastation to all nations. God's judgment is something to be feared. The fact that devastation had not yet reached Jerusalem was God's way of offering His people additional time to repent.

JEREMIAH'S ESCAPE FROM DEATH

26 This message came to Jeremiah from the LORD early in the reign of Jehoiakim
son of Josiah,* king of Judah. 2"This is what the LORD says: Stand in the courtyard
in front of the Temple of the LORD, and make an announcement to the people who have
come there to worship from all over Judah. Give them My entire message; include every
word. 3Perhaps they will listen and turn from their evil ways. Then I will change My mind
about the disaster I am ready to pour out on them because of their sins.
4"Say to them, 'This is what the LORD says: If you will not listen to Me and obey My word
I have given you, 5and if you will not listen to My servants, the prophets—for I sent them
again and again to warn you, but you would not listen to them—6then I will destroy this
Temple as I destroyed Shiloh, the place where the Tabernacle was located. And I will make
Jerusalem an object of cursing in every nation on earth.' "
7The priests, the prophets, and all the people listened to Jeremiah as he spoke in front
of the LORD'S Temple. 8But when Jeremiah had finished his message, saying everything
the LORD had told him to say, the priests and prophets and all the people at the Temple
mobbed him. "Kill him!" they shouted. 9"What right do you have to prophesy in the LORD'S
name that this Temple will be destroyed like Shiloh? What do you mean, saying that Jeru-
salem will be destroyed and left with no inhabitants?" And all the people threatened him
as he stood in front of the Temple.
10When the officials of Judah heard what was happening, they rushed over from the
palace and sat down at the New Gate of the Temple to hold court. 11The priests and proph-
ets presented their accusations to the officials and the people. "This man should die!" they
said. "You have heard with your own ears what a traitor he is, for he has prophesied
against this city."
12Then Jeremiah spoke to the officials and the people in his own defense. "The LORD
sent me to prophesy against this Temple and this city," he said. "The LORD gave me every
word that I have spoken. 13But if you stop your sinning and begin to obey the LORD your
God, He will change His mind about this disaster that He has announced against you. 14As
for me, I am in your hands—do with me as you think best. 15But if you kill me, rest assured
that you will be killing an innocent man! The responsibility for such a deed will lie on you,
on this city, and on every person living in it. For it is absolutely true that the LORD sent me
to speak every word you have heard."
16Then the officials and the people said to the priests and prophets, "This man does not
deserve the death sentence, for he has spoken to us in the name of the LORD our God."
17Then some of the wise old men stood and spoke to all the people assembled there.
18They said, "Remember when Micah of Moresheth prophesied during the reign of King
Hezekiah of Judah. He told the people of Judah,

26:2 Deut 4:2; Jer 7:2; 19:14; 42:4; Acts 20:20, 27
26:3 Isa 1:16-19; Jer 36:3-7
26:4 Lev 26:14; 1 Kgs 9:6; Isa 1:20; Jer 17:27; 22:5; 44:10, 23
26:5 Ezra 9:11; Jer 25:4
26:6 Ps 78:60-61; Jer 7:12, 14
26:7 Jer 5:31; Mic 3:11
26:8 Jer 11:19
26:10 Acts 21:31-32
26:11 Jer 18:23; 38:4; Matt 26:66; Acts 6:11-14
26:13 Jer 7:3, 5; 18:11
26:15 Num 35:33; Prov 6:16-17
26:16 Jer 36:19, 25; 38:7, 13; Acts 5:34-39; 23:9, 29; 25:25; 26:31
26:18 Mic 1:1; 3:12

26:1 The first year of Jehoiakim's reign was 608 B.C.

26:2 Jeremiah received a divine command to stand in the courtyard of the Temple and to speak all the words of God as He commanded. This incident is very similar to Jeremiah 7:1–8:3, except this chapter focuses more on the response of the people to the words of Jeremiah, rather than the actual words of Jeremiah.

26:6 Jeremiah again used Shiloh as an object lesson for the people gathered at the Temple of the Lord (Jeremiah 7:12, 14). The Tabernacle and the Ark of the Covenant were located at Shiloh during the early period of the judges (Joshua 18:1; 19:51). When the wife of Phinehas heard that the Philistines had captured the Ark, she named her child Ichabod because the glory of the Lord had departed from among His people (1 Samuel 4:21; Psalm 78:60-61). Jeremiah threatened the people of Jerusalem with the withdrawal of God's presence and the destruction of the Holy City.

▸ HOLINESS

26:8 Speaking the truth when it costs. Jeremiah had placed his life at risk by delivering a stern warning against the Lord's people. He was faithful to deliver the message and to not omit any of the words the Lord had commanded him to speak. As believers, we are called to proclaim the gospel to the world (John 20:21) and to display readiness in defending the faith (1 Peter 3:15). As we live out our calling, we should not be shocked that people will reject our message and us. Be prepared for anything to happen, but know that our duty is to speak the truth in love and that ultimately people are rejecting God, not you. (***See Holiness**> God's Blessing> Obedience leads to hardship and persecution,* TopicGuide page A42.)

▸ GOD

26:17-19 Looking to the past for guidance in the present. Everything in this world that you can see, touch, even

'This is what the LORD of Heaven's Armies says:
Mount Zion will be plowed like an open field;
Jerusalem will be reduced to ruins!
A thicket will grow on the heights
where the Temple now stands.'*

19 But did King Hezekiah and the people kill him for saying this? No, they turned from their
sins and worshiped the LORD. They begged Him for mercy. Then the LORD changed His
mind about the terrible disaster He had pronounced against them. So we are about to do
ourselves great harm."

20 At this time Uriah son of Shemaiah from Kiriath-jearim was also prophesying for the
LORD. And he predicted the same terrible disaster against the city and nation as Jeremiah
did. 21 When King Jehoiakim and the army officers and officials heard what he was saying,
the king sent someone to kill him. But Uriah heard about the plan and escaped in fear to
Egypt. 22 Then King Jehoiakim sent Elnathan son of Acbor to Egypt along with several
other men to capture Uriah. 23 They took him prisoner and brought him back to King Jehoi-
akim. The king then killed Uriah with a sword and had him buried in an unmarked grave.

24 Nevertheless, Ahikam son of Shaphan stood up for Jeremiah and persuaded the court
not to turn him over to the mob to be killed.

26:19 2 Chr 29:6-11; 32:26; Isa 37:1, 15-20
26:20 Josh 9:17; 1 Sam 6:21
26:21 1 Kgs 19:2-4; 2 Chr 16:10; Jer 36:26; Matt 10:23, 28
26:22 Jer 36:12
26:23 Jer 2:30
26:24 2 Kgs 22:12-14; Jer 1:18-19; 39:14; 40:5-6
27:2 Jer 28:10, 13; 30:8
27:3 Jer 25:21-22
27:5 Deut 9:29; Pss 115:15-16; 146:5-6; Acts 17:26
27:6 Ezek 29:18-20
27:7 Isa 14:4-6
27:8 Jer 24:10; 29:17; 42:15-16; Ezek 14:21; 17:19-21

JEREMIAH WEARS AN OX YOKE

27 This message came to Jeremiah from the LORD early in the reign of Zedekiah* son
of Josiah, king of Judah.

2 This is what the LORD said to me: "Make a yoke, and fasten it on your neck with leather
thongs. 3 Then send messages to the kings of Edom, Moab, Ammon, Tyre, and Sidon
through their ambassadors who have come to see King Zedekiah in Jerusalem. 4 Give them
this message for their masters: 'This is what the LORD of Heaven's Armies, the God of Israel,
says: 5 With My great strength and powerful arm I made the earth and all its people and
every animal. I can give these things of Mine to anyone I choose. 6 Now I will give your coun-
tries to King Nebuchadnezzar of Babylon, who is My servant. I have put everything, even the
wild animals, under his control. 7 All the nations will serve him, his son, and his grandson un-
til his time is up. Then many nations and great kings will conquer and rule over Babylon. 8 So

26:18 Mic 3:12. 27:1 As in some Hebrew manuscripts and Syriac version (see also 27:3, 12); most Hebrew manuscripts read *Jehoiakim.*

imagine—it changes. But God does not—He is immutable (1 Samuel 15:29). This is an odd thing, something to be puzzled over and wondered at as one would any description of God setting Himself apart from us. But even as a mystery, it is a source of encouragement for us today. The wise old men of Jeremiah's time knew that God would always respond to their genuine repentance. God hasn't changed—you can repent of your sin and find God's grace today. You can expect forgiveness when you repent. Take every sin you can think of and lay them before God. He'll know what to do—the same thing He's always done (Psalm 130:4; Luke 24:47). (***See God****> God's Attributes> Unchanging> God never changes,* TopicGuide page A18.)

26:17-23 Jehoiakim's response to the prophetic word from Uriah is contrasted with Hezekiah's response to Micah's prophecy. Hezekiah repented from sin when Micah told of the consequences the nation would endure for violating their covenant with God (Micah 3:12). Jehoiakim, on the other hand, not only rejected Uriah's call to repentance, but also killed him for declaring the Word of the Lord. Jehoiakim's execution of Uriah, an emissary of the Lord, dragged Judah deeper into sin.

26:24 Ahikam had served as an official in Josiah's court. He was a member of the envoy sent to Huldah to inquire about the Book of the Law (2 Kings 22:12-20). Nebuchadnezzer would later appoint Gedaliah, Ahikam's son, as governor of Judah after the exile (2 Kings 25:22; Jeremiah 39:14). Scripture portrays Ahikam as a supporter of the reforms instituted by Josiah and a much-needed ally to Jeremiah during this life-threatening circumstance.

27:2 God had decreed for the nations of the world, including Judah, to submit to Babylon for an appointed time. God told Jeremiah to place a yoke upon his neck to symbolize the slavery that the nations would endure under the Babylonian empire. This symbolic act is reminiscent of Jeremiah's actions in Jeremiah 13, in which he buried a loincloth of linen to communicate a message about God's intimacy with His people.

27:5 The phrase "great strength and powerful arm" was used to describe God's deliverance of His people from Egypt and their entrance into the Promise Land (Deuteronomy 9:29). Ironically, this same phrase was now utilized to depict God's great power turning against His people and all the nations of the world.

27:8-11 In God's case against the pagan nations, He created a conditional outcome based upon possible reactions to the Babylonian invasion. If a nation resisted the rule of the Babylonians, then God Himself would ensure victory for Babylon and the total destruction of the captured land. On the other hand, if a particular nation submitted to the king of Babylon, then God promised to preserve the people in the land.

you must submit to Babylon's king and serve him; put your neck under Babylon's yoke! I
will punish any nation that refuses to be his slave, says the LORD. I will send war, famine, and
disease upon that nation until Babylon has conquered it.
9“‘Do not listen to your false prophets, fortune-tellers, interpreters of dreams, mediums,
and sorcerers who say, “The king of Babylon will not conquer you.” 10They are all liars, and
their lies will lead to your being driven out of your land. I will drive you out and send you
far away to die. 11But the people of any nation that submits to the king of Babylon will be
allowed to stay in their own country to farm the land as usual. I, the LORD, have spoken!’”
12Then I repeated this same message to King Zedekiah of Judah. “If you want to live, sub-
mit to the yoke of the king of Babylon and his people. 13Why do you insist on dying—you
and your people? Why should you choose war, famine, and disease, which the LORD will
bring against every nation that refuses to submit to Babylon's king? 14Do not listen to the
false prophets who keep telling you, ‘The king of Babylon will not conquer you.’ They are
liars. 15This is what the LORD says: ‘I have not sent these prophets! They are telling you lies in
My name, so I will drive you from this land. You will all die—you and all these prophets, too.’”
16Then I spoke to the priests and the people and said, “This is what the LORD says: ‘Do
not listen to your prophets who claim that soon the gold articles taken from My Temple
will be returned from Babylon. It is all a lie! 17Do not listen to them. Surrender to the king
of Babylon, and you will live. Why should this whole city be destroyed? 18If they really are
prophets and speak the LORD'S messages, let them pray to the LORD of Heaven's Armies.
Let them pray that the articles remaining in the LORD'S Temple and in the king's palace and
in the palaces of Jerusalem will not be carried away to Babylon!’
19“For the LORD of Heaven's Armies has spoken about the pillars in front of the Temple,
the great bronze basin called the Sea, the water carts, and all the other ceremonial articles.
20King Nebuchadnezzar of Babylon left them here when he exiled Jehoiachin* son of Je-
hoiakim, king of Judah, to Babylon, along with all the other nobles of Judah and Jerusa-
lem. 21Yes, this is what the LORD of Heaven's Armies, the God of Israel, says about the
precious things still in the Temple and in the palace of Judah's king: 22‘They will all be car-
ried away to Babylon and will stay there until I send for them,’ says the LORD. ‘Then I will
bring them back to Jerusalem again.’”

JEREMIAH CONDEMNS HANANIAH

28 One day in late summer* of that same year—the fourth year of the reign of Zede-
kiah, king of Judah—Hananiah son of Azzur, a prophet from Gibeon, addressed

27:9 Exod 22:18 Deut 18:10 Isa 8:19 Mal 3:5
27:10 Jer 23:25
27:11 Jer 21:9; 38:2; 40:9-12; 42:10-11
27:13 Jer 38:23 Ezek 18:31
27:14 Ezek 13:22
27:15 2 Chr 25:16 Jer 23:21, 25; 29:9
27:16 2 Kgs 24:13 2 Chr 36:7, 10 Dan 1:2
27:18 1 Sam 7:8; 12:19, 23 1 Kgs 18:24
27:19 1 Kgs 7:15 2 Kgs 25:13, 17 Jer 52:17-23
27:20 2 Kgs 24:14-16
27:22 Ezra 5:13-15; 7:9 Jer 29:10; 32:5; 34:2-3
28:1 Jer 27:12

27:20 Hebrew *Jeconiah,* a variant spelling of Jehoiachin. 28:1 Hebrew *In the fifth month,* of the ancient Hebrew lunar calendar. The fifth month in the fourth year of Zedekiah's reign occurred within the months of August and September 593 B.C. Also see note on 1:3.

27:12 The oracle of judgment against the nations was repeated to Zedekiah, the king of Judah. Zedekiah was presented with a life-and-death situation, as were the pagan nations. God was making a clear statement: Babylon could not be and must not have been resisted. God had decreed for Nebuchadnezzar to be the ruling king over all the nations.

▶ BIBLE
27:14 Knowing whom to believe. We've all experienced it—hearing radically different versions of the same conversation, the same argument, or the same situation. When this happens, we may logically try to work it out, or we may speak to those with whom we disagree. But in matters concerning spiritual truths, the Word of God should operate as our ultimate standard for truth—not our own reasoning or the opinions of others (Hebrews 4:12-13; 2 Timothy 3:16-17). Certainly good logic and healthy relationships aid us in understanding God's Word, but too many people end up believing false doctrine because of poor reasoning and listening to untrustworthy people. In Jeremiah's day, false prophets kept the people's heads spinning—but the Word of God set them straight (Jeremiah 27:15). Allow God's Word to be your ultimate standard for truth. Compare every sermon (and study Bible note!) to God's perfect Word (Acts 17:10-11). (***See Bible****> Uniqueness> Flawless> Scripture is sure and convincing,* TopicGuide page A10.)

27:20-22 Jeremiah addressed the claims of the false teachers, who had ultimately attempted to accomplish two things. First, they wanted the people to believe that Jeremiah was not telling the truth concerning the mandated submission to the Babylonians (27:14). Second, they desired to create a false sense of hope concerning the length of their servitude to Babylon. Jeremiah countered the first claim by stating that the Lord was the one who declared his prophecies. Jeremiah diffused the optimistic outlook by stating that even the vessels left behind in the Temple would soon be carried away as well.

28:1-4 Though Hananiah's name means “the Lord is gracious,” he spread lies to the people of God. Hananiah appeared as the spokesperson for the group that supported the idea of a

me publicly in the Temple while all the priests and people listened. He said, 2“This is what
28:3 2 Chr 36:10 the LORD of Heaven's Armies, the God of Israel, says: ‘I will remove the yoke of the king of
Dan 1:2 Babylon from your necks. 3Within two years I will bring back all the Temple treasures that
28:4 King Nebuchadnezzar carried off to Babylon. 4And I will bring back Jehoiachin* son of Je-
2 Kgs 25:27 hoiakim, king of Judah, and all the other captives that were taken to Babylon. I will surely
28:7 break the yoke that the king of Babylon has put on your necks. I, the LORD, have spoken!’”
1 Kgs 22:28 5Jeremiah responded to Hananiah as they stood in front of all the priests and people at
28:8 1 Kgs 14:15; 17:1; the Temple. 6He said, “Amen! May your prophecies come true! I hope the LORD does every-
22:17 thing you say. I hope He does bring back from Babylon the treasures of this Temple and all
Isa 5:5-7 the captives. 7But listen now to the solemn words I speak to you in the presence of all these
Joel 1:20 Amos 1:2 people. 8The ancient prophets who preceded you and me spoke against many nations, al-
Nah 1:2 ways warning of war, disaster, and disease. 9So a prophet who predicts peace must show he
28:9 is right. Only when his predictions come true can we know that he is really from the LORD.”
Deut 18:22 10Then Hananiah the prophet took the yoke off Jeremiah's neck and broke it in pieces.
28:10 11And Hananiah said again to the crowd that had gathered, “This is what the LORD says:
Jer 27:2 ‘Just as this yoke has been broken, within two years I will break the yoke of oppression
28:12 from all the nations now subject to King Nebuchadnezzar of Babylon.’” With that, Jeremi-
Jer 1:2 ah left the Temple area.
28:13 Ps 107:16 12Soon after this confrontation with Hananiah, the LORD gave this message to Jeremiah:
28:14 13“Go and tell Hananiah, ‘This is what the LORD says: You have broken a wooden yoke, but
Deut 28:48 you have replaced it with a yoke of iron. 14The LORD of Heaven's Armies, the God of Israel,
Jer 25:11; 27:6, 8 says: I have put a yoke of iron on the necks of all these nations, forcing them into slavery
28:15 Lam 2:14 under King Nebuchadnezzar of Babylon. I have put everything, even the wild animals,
Ezek 13:2-3, 22; under his control.’”
22:28 15Then Jeremiah the prophet said to Hananiah, “Listen, Hananiah! The LORD has not
28:16 sent you, but the people believe your lies. 16Therefore, this is what the LORD says: ‘You
Deut 6:15; 13:5 1 Kgs 13:34 must die. Your life will end this very year because you have rebelled against the LORD.’”
17Two months later* the prophet Hananiah died.

28:4 Hebrew *Jeconiah,* a variant spelling of Jehoiachin. 28:17 Hebrew *In the seventh month of that same year.* See 28:1 and the note there.

short-term exile (27:16). Hananiah declared that within two years God would break the Babylonian yoke, return the missing articles of the Temple, and restore King Jehoiakim and the exiled people to Jerusalem.

28:6-8 To demonstrate his own personal preferences for Judah's future, Jeremiah affirmed his wishes that the prophecy of Hananiah would come true, but he had to confess that this prophecy was not in line with what the prophets before them had foretold.

▸ PURPOSE
28:8-9 Applying the truth versus speaking new truth. There is a difference between applying the Word of God to new circumstances and allowing new circumstances to change the Word of God. Because life is complex and circumstances change, we should continually seek ways to make the Bible meaningful and applicable to all of life's situations (1 Corinthians 9:19-23). But we are not at liberty to reshape the Bible by adding to or subtracting from the Scriptures (Deuteronomy 12:32). Allow God's Word to change what you say, what you do, and how you think—and not the other way around! (***See Purpose****> God's Means> Human Choice> Bringing our wills in subjection to God's will,* TopicGuide page A52.)

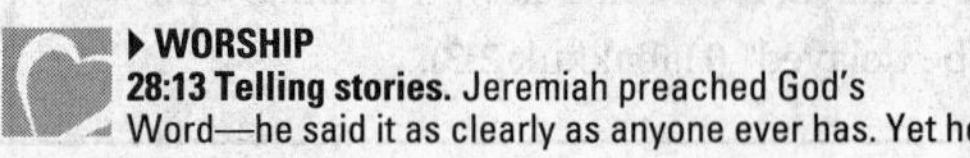

▸ WORSHIP
28:13 Telling stories. Jeremiah preached God's Word—he said it as clearly as anyone ever has. Yet he did not hesitate to tell stories, proverbs, and illustrations to make his points more memorable. Jesus used illustrations to communicate God's truth (Matthew 13:3; Matthew 20:1; Luke 18:2). Use an illustration today to help communicate God's truth with people you know—it might stimulate their interest to learn more about God. It might touch their emotions and their minds with God's truth. Learn to tell stories that help those under your care apply God's Word wisely. (***See Worship****> NT> Teaching and Preaching,* TopicGuide page A34.)

28:14 Hananiah may have been physically able to break the wooden yoke used by Jeremiah, but God warned that it had been replaced with one made of iron (15:12). This iron yoke symbolized the unbreakable dominion that Babylon would exercise over the nations, including Judah, and even over the beast of the fields.

28:15-17 The conflict between Jeremiah and Hananiah ended with an astonishing resolution. The phrase “you must die” may be translated as “be sent away.” Jeremiah declared that the prophet whom the Lord “has not sent” would “be sent away.” Jeremiah delivered a death sentence to Hananiah for his false prophecies (Deuteronomy 18:20). Hananiah died within two months (Jeremiah 28:17).

A LETTER TO THE EXILES

29 Jeremiah wrote a letter from Jerusalem to the elders, priests, prophets, and all the
people who had been exiled to Babylon by King Nebuchadnezzar. [2]This was af- **29:2**
ter King Jehoiachin,* the queen mother, the court officials, the other officials of Judah, and 2 Kgs 24:12
all the craftsmen and artisans had been deported from Jerusalem. [3]He sent the letter with Jer 22:24-28; 24:1
Elasah son of Shaphan and Gemariah son of Hilkiah when they went to Babylon as King
Zedekiah's ambassadors to Nebuchadnezzar. This is what Jeremiah's letter said:

[4]This is what the LORD of Heaven's Armies, the God of Israel, says to all the captives **29:4**
He has exiled to Babylon from Jerusalem: [5]"Build homes, and plan to stay. Plant Jer 24:5
gardens, and eat the food they produce. [6]Marry and have children. Then find **29:6**
spouses for them so that you may have many grandchildren. Multiply! Do not Jer 16:1-4

29:2 Hebrew *Jeconiah,* a variant spelling of Jehoiachin.

29:5-7 The Babylonian captivity was prophesied to last 70 years (see 25:11). When Jeremiah said that the exiled community should begin to build homes, plant gardens, and marry in Babylon, he was exhorting the people to settle down and plan to stay in exile a while. But Jeremiah went on to say that the exiles should pray for Judah and seek the prosperity of their captors. The people of God were to be concerned with and involved in the development of the Babylonian empire.

MY RESPONSE TO GOD

Worth the Wait

JEREMIAH 29:11-13

Does God's work in your world seem to go at a snail's pace? Do you feel frustrated that renewal in your nation, your neighborhood, your family–your own soul–takes too long? Imagine how God's ancient peoples felt.

After Nebuchadnezzar conquered Jerusalem (586 BC), the Judeans who were taken into captivity questioned whether God had abandoned them. They struggled to understand how God's promise could be true that a descendant of David would always rule as king in Jerusalem (2 Samuel 7:13; Psalm 132:11-12). They grappled with their future: How long would they live in exile? Should they attempt to keep the Mosaic Law or adopt the laws of the Babylonians and their gods?

In the midst of these difficult times, Jeremiah offered the people hope: God had plans for them–plans for good and not for disaster (Jeremiah 29:11). Through Jeremiah, God affirmed that He was still in control and still cared about His people. Years later, a group of exiles returned under the leadership of Zerubbabel and rebuilt the Temple (536 BC), with more returns and renewal in Jerusalem under the leadership of Ezra (445 BC). And 400 years after that, He fulfilled His promise of a king through Jesus, a descendant of David.

It only takes a moment for us to read that snippet–"400 years"–but it was ten generations for the Judeans. In this day of modern conveniences, we quickly grow weary praying for personal or societal circumstances. But God's people have always waited on Him (Job 24:1; Psalm 38:15; Romans 8:19). Modern Christians sometimes feel hopeless and abandoned–like the Judeans in captivity–but we can trust that God's plan, while taking an achingly long time to come to pass, is certain to succeed. As one of God's prophets said, "This vision is for a future time. It describes the end, and it will be fulfilled. If it seems slow in coming, wait patiently, for it will surely take place. It will not be delayed" (Habakkuk 2:3).

29:7 dwindle away! 7And work for the peace and prosperity of the city where I sent you
Ezra 6:10 into exile. Pray to the LORD for it, for its welfare will determine your welfare."
Dan 4:27 1 Tim 2:1-2 8This is what the LORD of Heaven's Armies, the God of Israel, says: "Do not let your
29:9 prophets and fortune-tellers who are with you in the land of Babylon trick you. Do
Jer 27:15; 29:31 not listen to their dreams, 9because they are telling you lies in My name. I have not
29:10 sent them," says the LORD.
2 Chr 36:21-23 Dan 9:2 10This is what the LORD says: "You will be in Babylon for seventy years. But then
Zeph 2:7 I will come and do for you all the good things I have promised, and I will bring you
Zech 7:5 home again. 11For I know the plans I have for you," says the LORD. "They are plans
29:11 Ps 40:5 for good and not for disaster, to give you a future and a hope. 12In those days when
Isa 40:9-11 you pray, I will listen. 13If you look for Me wholeheartedly, you will find Me. 14I will
29:12 be found by you," says the LORD. "I will end your captivity and restore your fortunes.
Ps 145:19 I will gather you out of the nations where I sent you and will bring you home again
Jer 33:3 to your own land."
29:13 Deut 4:29 15You claim that the LORD has raised up prophets for you in Babylon. 16But this is
1 Chr 22:19 what the LORD says about the king who sits on David's throne and all those still living
2 Chr 22:9 here in Jerusalem—your relatives who were not exiled to Babylon. 17This is what the
Jer 24:7 LORD of Heaven's Armies says: "I will send war, famine, and disease upon them and
29:14 Deut 30:1-10 make them like bad figs, too rotten to eat. 18Yes, I will pursue them with war, famine,
Isa 43:5-6 and disease, and I will scatter them around the world. In every nation where I send
29:18 them, I will make them an object of damnation, horror, contempt, and mockery.
Isa 65:15 Jer 25:9; 42:18 19For they refuse to listen to Me, though I have spoken to them repeatedly through
Lam 2:15-16 the prophets I sent. And you who are in exile have not listened either," says the LORD.
29:19 Jer 6:19; 26:5 20Therefore, listen to this message from the LORD, all you captives there in Babylon.
21This is what the LORD of Heaven's Armies, the God of Israel, says about your proph-
29:20 Ezek 11:9 ets—Ahab son of Kolaiah and Zedekiah son of Maaseiah—who are telling you lies in
My name: "I will turn them over to Nebuchadnezzar* for execution before your eyes.
29:21 Lam 2:14 22Their terrible fate will become proverbial, so that the Judean exiles will curse some-
one by saying, 'May the LORD make you like Zedekiah and Ahab, whom the king of
29:22 Isa 65:15 Babylon burned alive!' 23For these men have done terrible things among My people.
29:23 They have committed adultery with their neighbors' wives and have lied in My name,
2 Sam 13:12 Prov 5:21 saying things I did not command. I am a witness to this. I, the LORD, have spoken."

A MESSAGE FOR SHEMAIAH

29:25 24The LORD sent this message to Shemaiah the Nehelamite in Babylon: 25"This is what the
2 Kgs 25:18 LORD of Heaven's Armies, the God of Israel, says: You wrote a letter on your own authority

29:21 Hebrew *Nebuchadrezzar,* a variant spelling of Nebuchadnezzar.

29:8-9 The false prophets appear to have continued spreading lies and were now infiltrated among the exiled people. Jeremiah had already extensively addressed the issue of false prophets within Jerusalem (27:16-17), but here he countered the same activity occurring among those outside of Judah. It seems that these false prophets were promoting the same optimistic view of a short-term exile as espoused by Hananiah (28:3).

▸ GOD

29:11 Hope for the future. Have you ever put your hope in someone or something that let you down? Hope is one of the greatest gifts that God has given to His children (Romans 15:13)—the expectation or belief in something that is yet to come. The Bible's version is a hope that's grounded in what God has promised to do in the future. Our great expectations of God and His promises will always fall short of His grand plans (Romans 5:5) because He loves us—and just like us, God never wants to disappoint those He loves. Put your hope in God and be prepared for Him to go beyond everything you can hope and pray for (Ephesians 1:19-23). (***See God****> Salvation> Holy Spirit> Comforts,* TopicGuide page A15.)

29:17-18 The people of Judah who remained in Jerusalem incorrectly believed that God favored them and presumed that God's anger was limited to the exiled people. Jeremiah declared an oracle of curses upon those who remained in Jerusalem for their arrogance and unrepentant hearts. Jeremiah recited a phrase that summarized God's divine judgment: war, famine, and disease (Leviticus 26:14-33; Deuteronomy 28:25-26; 32:20-26; Jeremiah 21:7, 9; 27:8, 13).

29:24-28 Shemaiah, an exiled Judean in Babylon, had written a letter to the priests in Jerusalem to express his opposition to Jeremiah. Shemaiah believed Jeremiah to be on the side of the Babylonians and a traitor to the cause of Judah. He had expressed his frustration with Zephaniah the priest for failing to control Jeremiah.

to Zephaniah son of Maaseiah, the priest, and you sent copies to the other priests and peo-
ple in Jerusalem. You wrote to Zephaniah,

26 "The LORD has appointed you to replace Jehoiada as the priest in charge of the
house of the LORD. You are responsible to put into stocks and neck irons any crazy
man who claims to be a prophet. 27 So why have you done nothing to stop Jeremiah
from Anathoth, who pretends to be a prophet among you? 28 Jeremiah sent a letter
here to Babylon, predicting that our captivity will be a long one. He said, 'Build
homes, and plan to stay. Plant gardens, and eat the food they produce.'"

29 But when Zephaniah the priest received Shemaiah's letter, he took it to Jeremiah and
read it to him. 30 Then the LORD gave this message to Jeremiah: 31 "Send an open letter to
all the exiles in Babylon. Tell them, 'This is what the LORD says concerning Shemaiah the
Nehelamite: Since he has prophesied to you when I did not send him and has tricked you
into believing his lies, 32 I will punish him and his family. None of his descendants will see
the good things I will do for My people, for he has incited you to rebel against Me. I, the
LORD, have spoken!'"

29:26 Deut 13:1-5 Jer 20:1-2 Hos 9:7 Zech 13:1-5 John 10:20 Acts 16:24; 26:24-25 2 Cor 5:13

29:27 Jer 1:1

29:31 Jer 14:14-15; 28:15 Ezek 13:8, 16, 22-23

29:32 Deut 13:5 1 Sam 2:30-34 Jer 22:30; 28:16; 36:31

PROMISES OF DELIVERANCE

30 The LORD gave another message to Jeremiah. He said, 2 "This is what the LORD,
the God of Israel, says: Write down for the record everything I have said to you,
Jeremiah. 3 For the time is coming when I will restore the fortunes of My people of Israel
and Judah. I will bring them home to this land that I gave to their ancestors, and they will
possess it again. I, the LORD, have spoken!"

4 This is the message the LORD gave concerning Israel and Judah. 5 This is what the LORD
says:

"I hear cries of fear;
there is terror and no peace.
6 Now let Me ask you a question:
Do men give birth to babies?
Then why do they stand there, ashen-faced,
hands pressed against their sides
like a woman in labor?
7 In all history there has never been such a time of terror.
It will be a time of trouble for My people Israel.*
Yet in the end they will be saved!

30:2 Jer 25:13; 36:4, 28, 32 Hab 2:2

30:3 Ps 53:6 Jer 3:18; 16:15; 23:7-8; 29:10; 30:18; 36:4, 28 Ezek 20:42; 36:24 Zeph 3:20

30:5 Isa 5:30 Jer 6:25 Amos 5:16-18

30:6 Jer 4:31; 6:24; 22:23

30:7 Isa 2:12 Jer 2:27; 50:19 Lam 1:12 Dan 9:12 Joel 2:11

30:7 Hebrew *Jacob;* also in 30:10b, 18. See note on 5:20.

▸ HOLINESS

29:26 Expect to be called names. Have you ever been insulted for your beliefs? It is amazing the extreme lengths that nonbelievers will go to in order to insult or defame Christians. The world commonly hurls insults against us by branding us as "self-righteous" or "intolerant." In this verse, Shemaiah called Jeremiah a "crazy man." Rather than becoming angry with these people, we should be overjoyed to be counted among those who suffer for the cause of Christ (1 Peter 4:14). If you have never received an insult for following Christ, maybe you need to be a stronger witness for Him. (***See Holiness> God's Blessing> Obedience leads to hardship and persecution,*** TopicGuide page A42.)

29:29-32 Though there were many people who opposed Jeremiah, there were several individuals who appear to have supported him (26:24; 29:3). Zephaniah's willingness to show Shemaiah's letter to Jeremiah demonstrated his apparent support for Jeremiah.

30:1-3 Chapters 30–33 are often referred to as the "Book of Comfort" because of the message of hope contained within these chapters. Having refuted the lies of the false prophets about a short-term exile (27:12-17; 29:8-9), Jeremiah proceeded to offer a message of hope and reversal of fortune. It is important to note that Jeremiah's message of hope did not negate God's threatened judgment. The other prophets had not taken God's judgment seriously, but Jeremiah had persistently spoken against the sins of the people (Jeremiah 1–29).

30:7 A time of terror would fall upon the people of Israel. The day of God's judgment was commonly understood as God executing His final judgment upon His enemies and blessing His people. But this time of terror would not exclude the nation of Israel (Isaiah 2:12; Jeremiah 25:33; Lamentations 1:12; Ezekiel 30:3; Joel 1:15; Amos 5:18; Obadiah 1:15).

30:8 Isa 9:4 Ezek 34:27

[8] For in that day,"
says the LORD of Heaven's Armies,
"I will break the yoke from their necks
and snap their chains.
Foreigners will no longer be their masters.

30:9 Ezek 34:23-24; 37:24 Hos 3:5 Luke 1:69 Acts 2:30; 13:23-24

[9] For My people will serve the LORD their God
and their king descended from David—
the king I will raise up for them.

30:10 Isa 35:9; 43:5; 44:2 Jer 23:3; 29:14; 46:27-28 Mic 4:4

[10] "So do not be afraid, Jacob, My servant;
do not be dismayed, Israel,"
says the LORD.
"For I will bring you home again from distant lands,
and your children will return from their exile.
Israel will return to a life of peace and quiet,
and no one will terrorize them.

30:11 Jer 1:8, 19; 4:27; 5:10, 18; 10:24; 46:28

[11] For I am with you and will save you,"
says the LORD.
"I will completely destroy the nations where I have scattered you,
but I will not completely destroy you.
I will discipline you, but with justice;
I cannot let you go unpunished."

30:12 Jer 15:18

[12] This is what the LORD says:
"Your injury is incurable—
a terrible wound.

30:13 Jer 14:19; 46:11

[13] There is no one to help you
or to bind up your injury.
No medicine can heal you.

30:14 Jer 22:20, 22 Lam 1:2; 2:4-5

[14] All your lovers—your allies—have left you
and do not care about you anymore.
I have wounded you cruelly,
as though I were your enemy.
For your sins are many,
and your guilt is great.
[15] Why do you protest your punishment—
this wound that has no cure?
I have had to punish you
because your sins are many
and your guilt is great.

30:16 Isa 14:2 Jer 2:3; 10:25

[16] "But all who devour you will be devoured,
and all your enemies will be sent into exile.

30:8-9 On "that day," God's people would cease to be slaves of a foreign king and return as servants of the true King, the Lord. Hananiah had prophesied that God would break the yoke of Babylonian captivity, but he had incorrectly shortened the time of captivity from 70 years to 2 years (Jeremiah 28:11). Jeremiah confirmed that God indeed would liberate His people from Babylonian oppression, but only in His appointed time.

30:12-13 Jeremiah utilized a series of medical images to describe the state of Judah. The diagnosis for God's people was bleak and presented a hopeless condition for the nation. No medicine was available to heal the wound that God had dealt to His people.

▶ GOD

30:16-17 What motivates God to show compassion? Many Christians suffer with great remorse for the things they have done in their past. We must understand that God is neither anxiously waiting to zap us with lightning nor is He indifferent toward His own people (Isaiah 30:18). No, we serve a personal God who is the lover of our body and soul. He is determined—more determined than you are—to show His love to unlovely people like us (John 8:1-11). Do not back away from God's love, but embrace it, explore it—enjoy it! It's His gift to you (1 Corinthians 13:2). (***See God**> God's Nature> Personality> Emotion> God is compassionate and loving,* TopicGuide page A14.)

All who plunder you will be plundered,
and all who attack you will be attacked.
17 I will give you back your health
and heal your wounds," says the LORD.
"For you are called an outcast—
'Jerusalem* for whom no one cares.'"

18 This is what the LORD says:
"When I bring Israel home again from captivity
and restore their fortunes,
Jerusalem will be rebuilt on its ruins,
and the palace reconstructed as before.
19 There will be joy and songs of thanksgiving,
and I will multiply My people, not diminish them;
I will honor them, not despise them.
20 Their children will prosper as they did long ago.
I will establish them as a nation before Me,
and I will punish anyone who hurts them.
21 They will have their own ruler again,
and he will come from their own people.
I will invite him to approach Me," says the LORD,
"for who would dare to come unless invited?
22 You will be My people,
and I will be your God."

23 Look! The LORD's anger bursts out like a storm,
a driving wind that swirls down on the heads of the wicked.
24 The fierce anger of the LORD will not diminish
until it has finished all He has planned.
In the days to come
you will understand all this.

30:17 Ps 107:20 Isa 56:8 Jer 8:22; 33:6
30:18 1 Chr 29:1, 19 Pss 48:3; 122:7 Jer 31:38-40
30:19 Isa 12:1; 51:3; 55:5; 60:9 Jer 17:26; 33:11
30:20 Isa 54:14
30:21 Exod 3:5 Num 16:5
30:22 Exod 6:7 Jer 32:38 Hos 2:23 Zech 13:9
30:23 Jer 23:19-20
30:24 Jer 4:8; 23:20

HOPE FOR RESTORATION

31 "In that day," says the LORD, "I will be the God of all the families of Israel, and they
will be My people. 2 This is what the LORD says:

"Those who survive the coming destruction
will find blessings even in the barren land,
for I will give rest to the people of Israel."

3 Long ago the LORD said to Israel:
"I have loved you, My people, with an everlasting love.
With unfailing love I have drawn you to Myself.

31:1 Gen 17:7-8 Jer 30:22, 24 Rom 11:26-28
31:2 Exod 33:14 Josh 1:13
31:3 Deut 4:37; 7:8 Ps 25:6

30:17 Hebrew *Zion*.

30:22 The Promised Land represented a visible sign of God's favor on Israel. When God restored His people from exile, it would not simply be seen as a restoration to a geographical area, but also as a restoration of the people to their exclusive covenant relationship with their God (Exodus 6:7; Jeremiah 32:38; Ezekiel 36:28; Hosea 2:23; Zechariah 13:9).

▸ GOD
31:3-4 The basis for our relationship with God. Our relationship with God does not depend on our ability to obey His commandments—in fact, our inability to obey is one of the first truths about the gospel we must grasp to be saved. God's basis for continuing a relationship with you lies squarely on His everlasting love and unfailing love for you (Isaiah 30:18; Ephesians 2:8-10; 2 Thessalonians 3:5). The love the people of Israel had for God had not been everlasting, nor had their faithfulness been continuing. But God overrode their rebellion and continued to pursue them because of His covenant love. Praise the Lord today that His love is everlasting and never fails. Meditate on God's love for you as you seek to love others (Ephesians 1:4-6). (***See God*****>** *God's Attributes> Loving> Eternal plans are motivated by His love,* TopicGuide page A17.)

31:4 Isa 30:32; Jer 24:6; 33:7

4 I will rebuild you, My virgin Israel.
You will again be happy
and dance merrily with your tambourines.

31:5 Ps 107:37; Isa 65:21; Ezek 28:26

5 Again you will plant your vineyards on the mountains of Samaria
and eat from your own gardens there.
6 The day will come when watchmen will shout
from the hill country of Ephraim,
'Come, let us go up to Jerusalem*
to worship the LORD our God.'"

31:6 Isa 2:3; Mic 4:2

31:7 Pss 14:7; 28:9; Isa 37:31; 61:9; Jer 20:13; 23:3

7 Now this is what the LORD says:
"Sing with joy for Israel.*
Shout for the greatest of nations!
Shout out with praise and joy:
'Save your people, O LORD,
the remnant of Israel!'

31:8 Deut 30:4; Isa 40:11; 43:6; Ezek 34:16; Mic 4:6

8 For I will bring them from the north
and from the distant corners of the earth.
I will not forget the blind and lame,
the expectant mothers and women in labor.
A great company will return!

31:9 Isa 49:10; 63:13

9 Tears of joy will stream down their faces,
and I will lead them home with great care.
They will walk beside quiet streams
and on smooth paths where they will not stumble.
For I am Israel's father,
and Ephraim is My oldest child.

31:10 Isa 40:11; 66:19

10 "Listen to this message from the LORD,
you nations of the world;
proclaim it in distant coastlands:
The LORD, who scattered His people,
will gather them and watch over them
as a shepherd does his flock.

31:11 Isa 44:23; 48:20

11 For the LORD has redeemed Israel
from those too strong for them.

31:12 Isa 2:2; 35:10; 58:11; 60:20; 65:19; Hos 2:22; Joel 3:18; Mic 4:1; John 16:22

12 They will come home and sing songs of joy on the heights
of Jerusalem.
They will be radiant because of the LORD's good gifts—
the abundant crops of grain, new wine, and olive oil,
and the healthy flocks and herds.
Their life will be like a watered garden,
and all their sorrows will be gone.

31:13 Ps 30:11; Isa 51:11; 61:3; Zech 8:4-5

13 The young women will dance for joy,
and the men—old and young—will join in the celebration.
I will turn their mourning into joy.
I will comfort them and exchange their sorrow for rejoicing.

31:6 Hebrew *Zion;* also in 31:12. 31:7 Hebrew *Jacob;* also in 31:11. See note on 5:20.

31:10-11 The people of Israel were released from their captivity by One who is stronger than any nation. God previously displayed His power over the world by calling Nebuchadnezzar and the Babylonian army as instruments of judgment against His people and other nations (25:9; 27:6). God then declared that He would free His people by gathering them and redeeming them, thus showing Himself to be in total control of His people's destiny.

14 The priests will enjoy abundance,
and My people will feast on My good gifts.
I, the LORD, have spoken!" 31:14 Jer 50:19

RACHEL'S SADNESS TURNS TO JOY

15 This is what the LORD says: 31:15 Ps 77:2 Jer 10:20 *Matt 2:17-18

"A cry is heard in Ramah—
deep anguish and bitter weeping.
Rachel weeps for her children,
refusing to be comforted—
for her children are gone."

16 But now this is what the LORD says: 31:16 Isa 25:8; 30:19 Jer 30:3 Ezek 11:17
"Do not weep any longer,
for I will reward you," says the LORD.
"Your children will come back to you
from the distant land of the enemy.
17 There is hope for your future," says the LORD. 31:17 Jer 29:11
"Your children will come again to their own land.
18 I have heard Israel* saying, 31:18 Job 5:17 Pss 80:3, 7, 19; 94:12 Jer 17:14 Hos 4:16
'You disciplined me severely,
like a calf that needs training for the yoke.
Turn me again to You and restore me,
for You alone are the LORD my God.
19 I turned away from God, 31:19 Ezek 36:31 Luke 18:13
but then I was sorry.
I kicked myself for my stupidity!
I was thoroughly ashamed of all I did in my younger days.'

20 "Is not Israel still My son, 31:20 Isa 55:7 Hos 11:8; 14:4
My darling child?" says the LORD.
"I often have to punish him,
but I still love him.
That's why I long for him
and surely will have mercy on him.
21 Set up road signs; 31:21 Isa 48:20; 52:11
put up guideposts.
Mark well the path
by which you came.
Come back again, My virgin Israel;
return to your towns here.
22 How long will you wander,
My wayward daughter?
For the LORD will cause something new to happen—
Israel will embrace her God.*"

23 This is what the LORD of Heaven's Armies, the God of Israel, says: "When I bring them 31:23 Pss 48:1; 87:1 Isa 1:26
back from captivity, the people of Judah and its towns will again say, 'The LORD bless you,

31:18 Hebrew *Ephraim*, referring to the northern kingdom of Israel; also in 31:20. 31:22 Hebrew *a woman will court a suitor.*

31:15 Rachel was the wife of Jacob, the father of the 12 tribes of Israel. She was the mother of Joseph and Benjamin (Genesis 35:24). Jeremiah used the imagery of Rachel weeping over her children to express the grief suffered by the people of Israel and Judah. The New Testament utilizes this verse to describe the weeping and mourning experienced in Bethlehem when Herod ordered the slaughter of male infants in his attempt to murder Jesus (Matthew 2:18).

O righteous home, O holy mountain!' 24 Townspeople and farmers and shepherds alike will live together in peace and happiness. 25 For I have given rest to the weary and joy to the sorrowing."

26 At this, I woke up and looked around. My sleep had been very sweet.

27 "The day is coming," says the LORD, "when I will greatly increase the human population and the number of animals here in Israel and Judah. 28 In the past I deliberately uprooted and tore down this nation. I overthrew it, destroyed it, and brought disaster upon it. But in the future I will just as deliberately plant it and build it up. I, the LORD, have spoken!

29 "The people will no longer quote this proverb:

'The parents have eaten sour grapes,
    but their children's mouths pucker at the taste.'

30 All people will die for their own sins—those who eat the sour grapes will be the ones whose mouths will pucker.

31 "The day is coming," says the LORD, "when I will make a new covenant with the people of Israel and Judah. 32 This covenant will not be like the one I made with their ancestors when I took them by the hand and brought them out of the land of Egypt. They broke that covenant, though I loved them as a husband loves his wife," says the LORD.

33 "But this is the new covenant I will make with the people of Israel on that day," says the LORD. "I will put My instructions deep within them, and I will write them on their hearts. I will be their God, and they will be My people. 34 And they will not need to teach their neighbors, nor will they need to teach their relatives, saying, 'You should know the LORD.' For everyone, from the least to the greatest, will know Me already," says the LORD. "And I will forgive their wickedness, and I will never again remember their sins."

35 It is the LORD who provides the sun to light the day
    and the moon and stars to light the night,
    and who stirs the sea into roaring waves.
His name is the LORD of Heaven's Armies,
    and this is what He says:
36 "I am as likely to reject My people Israel
    as I am to abolish the laws of nature!"
37 This is what the LORD says:
"Just as the heavens cannot be measured
    and the foundations of the earth cannot be explored,
so I will not consider casting them away
    for the evil they have done.
    I, the LORD, have spoken!

38 "The day is coming," says the LORD, "when all Jerusalem will be rebuilt for Me, from the Tower of Hananel to the Corner Gate. 39 A measuring line will be stretched out over the

31:24 Ezek 36:10; Zech 8:4-8
31:25 John 4:14
31:26 Zech 4:1
31:27 Ezek 36:9-11; Hos 2:23
31:28 Dan 9:14
31:29 Lam 5:7; Ezek 18:2
31:30 Deut 24:16; Ezek 18:4, 20
31:31-34 *Heb 8:8-12
31:31 Luke 22:20; 1 Cor 11:25
31:32 Deut 1:31; 5:2-3; Isa 63:12
31:33 Heb 10:16
31:34 Isa 11:9; 43:25; Mic 7:18; Rom 11:27; 1 Thes 4:9; *Heb 10:17; 1 Jn 2:27
31:35 Gen 1:14-18; Pss 19:1-6; 136:7-9
31:36 Ps 89:36-37; Isa 54:9-10; Amos 9:8-9
31:37 Isa 40:12; Rom 11:2-5, 26-27
31:38 2 Chr 26:9; Neh 3:1; 12:39; Zech 14:10

31:31-33 God declares that He will establish a new covenant with Israel and Judah—all of the people of God. God's act of restoration should be seen as a renewal of His original covenant with the nation of Israel. God declared that He would once again possess the nation of Israel as His own people, just as He did in the time of the Exodus (Jeremiah 31:1; Exodus 6:7-8; Leviticus 26:12). Moses described a time when the people would be exiled from the Promised Land, but promised that the Lord would restore them to the land and renew His covenant with His people (Deuteronomy 30:1-10). This new covenant is ultimately fulfilled in the coming of Jesus Christ (Luke 22:20; 1 Corinthians 11:25; Hebrews 9:15).

31:34 The new covenant looks forward to a time when believers will no longer have to teach other people about the truth because everyone will know God (John 6:45; 1 John 5:20). This is the futuristic element of the new covenant. During Christ's second coming, the dead in Christ will be raised and the whole world will be made anew (1 Corinthians 15:50-58; Revelation 21:3-5).

hill of Gareb and across to Goah. 40And the entire area—including the graveyard and ash
dump in the valley, and all the fields out to the Kidron Valley on the east as far as the
Horse Gate—will be holy to the LORD. The city will never again be captured or destroyed."

JEREMIAH'S LAND PURCHASE

32 The following message came to Jeremiah from the LORD in the tenth year of the
reign of Zedekiah,* king of Judah. This was also the eighteenth year of the reign
of King Nebuchadnezzar.* 2Jerusalem was then under siege from the Babylonian army,
and Jeremiah was imprisoned in the courtyard of the guard in the royal palace. 3King Zed-
ekiah had put him there, asking why he kept giving this prophecy: "This is what the LORD
says: 'I am about to hand this city over to the king of Babylon, and he will take it. 4King
Zedekiah will be captured by the Babylonians* and taken to meet the king of Babylon face
to face. 5He will take Zedekiah to Babylon, and I will deal with him there,' says the LORD. 'If
you fight against the Babylonians, you will never succeed.'"

6At that time the LORD sent me a message. He said, 7"Your cousin Hanamel son of Shal-
lum will come and say to you, 'Buy my field at Anathoth. By law you have the right to buy
it before it is offered to anyone else.'"

8Then, just as the LORD had said He would, my cousin Hanamel came and visited me in
the prison. He said, "Please buy my field at Anathoth in the land of Benjamin. By law you
have the right to buy it before it is offered to anyone else, so buy it for yourself." Then I
knew that the message I had heard was from the LORD.

9So I bought the field at Anathoth, paying Hanamel seventeen pieces* of silver for it. 10I
signed and sealed the deed of purchase before witnesses, weighed out the silver, and paid
him. 11Then I took the sealed deed and an unsealed copy of the deed, which contained
the terms and conditions of the purchase, 12and I handed them to Baruch son of Neriah
and grandson of Mahseiah. I did all this in the presence of my cousin Hanamel, the wit-
nesses who had signed the deed, and all the men of Judah who were there in the court-
yard of the guardhouse.

13Then I said to Baruch as they all listened, 14"This is what the LORD of Heaven's Armies,
the God of Israel, says: 'Take both this sealed deed and the unsealed copy, and put them
into a pottery jar to preserve them for a long time.' 15For this is what the LORD of Heaven's
Armies, the God of Israel, says: 'Someday people will again own property here in this land
and will buy and sell houses and vineyards and fields.'"

JEREMIAH'S PRAYER

16Then after I had given the papers to Baruch, I prayed to the LORD:

> 17"O Sovereign LORD! You made the heavens and earth by your strong hand and
> powerful arm. Nothing is too hard for You! 18You show unfailing love to thousands,

32:1a The tenth year of Zedekiah's reign and the eighteenth year of Nebuchadnezzar's reign was 587 B.C. 32:1b Hebrew *Nebuchadrezzar,* a variant spelling of Nebuchadnezzar; also in 32:28. 32:4 Or *Chaldeans;* also in 32:5, 24, 25, 28, 29, 43. 32:9 Hebrew *17 shekels,* about 7 ounces or 194 grams in weight.

31:40 2 Kgs 23:6; Neh 3:28; Joel 3:17; Zech 14:20
32:1 2 Kgs 25:1-2; Jer 39:1-2
32:2 Neh 3:25
32:3 Jer 21:4-7; 26:8-9; 34:2-3
32:4 2 Kgs 25:4-7; Jer 37:17; 39:4-7
32:5 Ezek 12:12-13; 17:9-10, 15
32:7 Lev 25:25; Ruth 4:3-4
32:8 1 Sam 9:16-17; 10:3-7
32:9 Gen 23:16; Matt 27:9-10
32:10 Ruth 4:1, 9; Isa 8:1-2
32:15 Jer 30:18; 31:5, 12; Amos 9:14-15; Zech 3:10
32:16 Gen 32:9-12; Jer 12:1; Phil 4:6-7
32:17 Gen 18:14; 2 Kgs 19:15; Ps 102:25; Isa 40:26-29; Jer 27:5
32:18 Exod 34:6-7; Deut 7:9-10; 1 Kgs 16:1-3; Pss 50:1; 145:3; Jer 10:16; 20:11; 31:35; Matt 23:32-36

31:40 The Hinnom Valley was used as a dishonorable burial site and ash dump during Jeremiah's time. During the final restoration from exile, even the most impure and dishonorable regions of Jerusalem would be sanctified. God would no longer uproot or demolish His people; instead He would build up His holy city and plant His people within it (31:28; 42:10).

32:1-5 During the Babylonian siege of Jerusalem, King Zedekiah imprisoned Jeremiah in the courtyard of the guard in the royal palace. Zedekiah confronted Jeremiah for his prophecies of destruction and wanted to know why Jeremiah spoke such terrible things, but he lacked the faith to respond in repentance regarding the nation's sins.

32:8 Jeremiah's cousin, Hanamel, approached him concerning his familial privilege to buy a field in Anathoth, Jeremiah's hometown (Jeremiah 1:1). It is possible that Hanamel had to sell this land due to financial hardship and was now asking Jeremiah to buy back the property (see Leviticus 25:25-28). This act of buying back land was very important, because it ensured families their share in the inheritance of the Promised Land. Jeremiah's purchase of the field signified that God would one day restore the land to the exiled nation of Judah (Jeremiah 32:43).

32:16-25 Baruch assisted Jeremiah, primarily as a scribe (36:4). Once the field had been purchased and the documents were sealed, Jeremiah explained with his prayer the symbolism of the sale: God was not finished with His work in Israel.

32:19 Job 34:21 Ps 62:12 Isa 28:29 Matt 16:27 John 5:29
32:20 Pss 78:43; 105:27 Isa 63:12, 14 Dan 9:15
32:21 Deut 4:34; 26:8 1 Chr 17:21
32:22 Exod 13:5 Deut 1:8 Ps 105:9-11
32:23 Ezra 9:7 Pss 44:2-3; 78:54-55 Lam 1:18 Dan 9:11-12
32:24 Josh 23:15-16 Ezek 14:21 Zech 1:6
32:27 Num 16:22; 27:16 Matt 19:26
32:29 2 Chr 36:19
32:31 1 Kgs 11:7-8 2 Kgs 21:4-7, 15; 23:27; 24:3-4 Matt 23:37
32:32 Ezra 9:7 Isa 1:23
32:33 2 Chr 36:15-16
32:34 Ezek 8:5
32:35 Lev 18:21; 20:2-5 2 Chr 28:2-3; 33:6 Acts 7:43

but You also bring the consequences of one generation's sin upon the next. You are the great and powerful God, the LORD of Heaven's Armies. 19You have all wisdom and do great and mighty miracles. You see the conduct of all people, and You give them what they deserve. 20You performed miraculous signs and wonders in the land of Egypt—things still remembered to this day! And You have continued to do great miracles in Israel and all around the world. You have made Your name famous to this day.

21"You brought Israel out of Egypt with mighty signs and wonders, with a strong hand and powerful arm, and with overwhelming terror. 22You gave the people of Israel this land that You had promised their ancestors long before—a land flowing with milk and honey. 23Our ancestors came and conquered it and lived in it, but they refused to obey You or follow Your word. They have not done anything You comanded. That is why You have sent this terrible disaster upon them.

24"See how the siege ramps have been built against the city walls! Through war, famine, and disease, the city will be handed over to the Babylonians, who will conquer it. Everything has happened just as You said. 25And yet, O Sovereign LORD, You have told me to buy the field—paying good money for it before these witnesses—even though the city will soon be handed over to the Babylonians."

A PREDICTION OF JERUSALEM'S FALL

26Then this message came to Jeremiah from the LORD: 27"I am the LORD, the God of all the peoples of the world. Is anything too hard for Me? 28Therefore, this is what the LORD says: I will hand this city over to the Babylonians and to Nebuchadnezzar, king of Babylon, and he will capture it. 29The Babylonians outside the walls will come in and set fire to the city. They will burn down all these houses where the people provoked My anger by burning incense to Baal on the rooftops and by pouring out liquid offerings to other gods. 30Israel and Judah have done nothing but wrong since their earliest days. They have infuriated Me with all their evil deeds," says the LORD. 31"From the time this city was built until now, it has done nothing but anger Me, so I am determined to get rid of it.

32"The sins of Israel and Judah—the sins of the people of Jerusalem, the kings, the officials, the priests, and the prophets—have stirred up My anger. 33My people have turned their backs on Me and have refused to return. Even though I diligently taught them, they would not receive instruction or obey. 34They have set up their abominable idols right in My own Temple, defiling it. 35They have built pagan shrines to Baal in the valley of Ben-Hinnom, and there they sacrifice their sons and daughters to Molech. I have never commanded such a horrible deed; it never even crossed My mind to command such a thing. What an incredible evil, causing Judah to sin so greatly!

▸ GOD

32:17 Nothing is too difficult for God. God not only created the world, but through His power He sustains its very existence (Genesis 1:1; Hebrews 1:3). Jeremiah understood that the Lord is the great and powerful God (Jeremiah 32:18). Yet this all-powerful God knows every detail about your life, and there is no problem that He cannot fix, no prayer He cannot answer. Allow your thoughts and actions to reflect the fact that you serve a God who cannot be stopped. How would this look for you—would it mean putting away doubt? Or fleeing from the temptation of thinking that your sins are too big or awful for God to forgive? (***See God****> God's Attributes> All-Present> No task is too large or too difficult for Him,* TopicGuide page A16.)

32:23 God clearly taught Israel the consequences of refusing to keep their covenant with Him (Leviticus 26; 2 Kings 17:7-23; Deuteronomy 28).

32:26-31, 32-35 The imagery of God destroying His own prized creation (32:26-31) is mirrored with Israel's determination to destroy their creation—their children (32:35). Destruction of His creation due to extreme sin also hearkens back to God's demolition of the earth with a flood (Genesis 6:13) and His destruction of the cities of Sodom and Gomorrah (Genesis 19:24).

32:35 The people of Judah provoked God to anger by their idolatry and lack of repentance. When Jezebel married King Ahab, she promoted Baal worship in the northern kingdom of Israel (1 Kings 16:29-33; 18:20-40; 19:1-2). When the daughter of Jezebel, Athaliah, married King Jehoram, Baal worship infiltrated the southern kingdom of Judah (2 Kings 8:17-18, 24-26). The people of Judah then proceeded to worship the Ammonite god Molech by offering human sacrifices (see Leviticus 18:21).

A PROMISE OF RESTORATION

36"Now I want to say something more about this city. You have been saying, 'It will fall to
the king of Babylon through war, famine, and disease.' But this is what the LORD, the God of
Israel, says: 37I will certainly bring My people back again from all the countries where I will
scatter them in My fury. I will bring them back to this very city and let them live in peace
and safety. 38They will be My people, and I will be their God. 39And I will give them one
heart and one purpose: to worship Me forever, for their own good and for the good of all
their descendants. 40And I will make an everlasting covenant with them: I will never stop
doing good for them. I will put a desire in their hearts to worship Me, and they will never
leave Me. 41I will find joy doing good for them and will faithfully and wholeheartedly
replant them in this land.

42"This is what the LORD says: Just as I have brought all these calamities on them, so I
will do all the good I have promised them. 43Fields will again be bought and sold in this
land about which you now say, 'It has been ravaged by the Babylonians, a desolate land
where people and animals have all disappeared.' 44Yes, fields will once again be bought
and sold—deeds signed and sealed and witnessed—in the land of Benjamin and here in
Jerusalem, in the towns of Judah and in the hill country, in the foothills of Judah* and in
the Negev, too. For someday I will restore prosperity to them. I, the LORD, have spoken!"

PROMISES OF PEACE AND PROSPERITY

33 While Jeremiah was still confined in the courtyard of the guard, the LORD gave
him this second message: 2"This is what the LORD says—the LORD who made the
earth, who formed and established it, whose name is the LORD: 3Ask Me and I will tell you
remarkable secrets you do not know about things to come. 4For this is what the LORD, the
God of Israel, says: You have torn down the houses of this city and even the king's palace
to get materials to strengthen the walls against the siege ramps and swords of the enemy.
5You expect to fight the Babylonians,* but the men of this city are already as good as
dead, for I have determined to destroy them in My terrible anger. I have abandoned them
because of all their wickedness.

6"Nevertheless, the time will come when I will heal Jerusalem's wounds and give it pros-
perity and true peace. 7I will restore the fortunes of Judah and Israel and rebuild their
towns. 8I will cleanse them of their sins against Me and forgive all their sins of rebellion.
9Then this city will bring Me joy, glory, and honor before all the nations of the earth! The
people of the world will see all the good I do for My people, and they will tremble with awe
at the peace and prosperity I provide for them.

10"This is what the LORD says: You have said, 'This is a desolate land where people and
animals have all disappeared.' Yet in the empty streets of Jerusalem and Judah's other
towns, there will be heard once more 11the sounds of joy and laughter. The joyful voices

32:37 Deut 30:3 Isa 11:11-16 Ezek 11:17; 34:25, 28 Hos 1:11 Amos 9:14-15 Zech 14:11
32:38 *2 Cor 6:16
32:39 Deut 11:18-21 Ezek 37:25 John 17:21 Acts 4:32
32:40 Isa 55:3
32:41 Deut 30:9 Isa 65:19 Amos 9:15
32:42 Zech 8:14-15
32:43 Ezek 37:11-14
33:2 Exod 3:15; 15:3
33:3 Ps 50:15 Isa 48:6; 55:6-7
33:4 Isa 32:13-14
33:6 Isa 66:12
33:7 Ps 85:1 Amos 9:14-15
33:8 Ps 51:2 Heb 9:11-14
33:9 Ps 40:3 Isa 62:2, 4 Hos 3:5
33:10 Isa 35:10

32:44 Hebrew *the Shephelah.* 33:5 Or *Chaldeans.*

▸ GOD

32:40 An everlasting covenant. When we think of eternity, it can boggle the mind. This is not a bad thing—our minds should be puzzled with the greatness of God. The Scriptures also reveal something easier to understand—that eternity has a quality to it. That quality is a perfect relationship with God. Our connection with God can neither be broken nor amended. God is committed to us till the end—and that will never change. Thank God today for His unbreakable commitment to loving you—forever! (***See God****> God's Attributes> Good> God is good to His covenant people,* TopicGuide page A16.)

▸ WORSHIP

33:3 God enjoys hearing us pray. At times, many of us wonder if God listens to our prayers, much less if He's committed to providing an answer. This verse puts those questions to rest, for God is not only anxious to hear our requests, but also vows to answer them according to His will (also see Psalm 91:15). God may not always provide the answer we want when we want it (1 John 5:14-15), but that should not stop us from praying with hopeful expectation. Bring your requests confidently to God today. (***See Worship****> OT> Fasting and Prayer> Prayer> God vows to answer according to His will,* TopicGuide page A26.)

33:4-6 The phrase "I have abandoned" can also read "I will hide My face." In the Bible, when God's face was upon the nation of Israel it was a sign of God's favor, His presence, and His blessing (Numbers 6:25; Psalm 31:16). But if God's face was said to be hid from someone, it was a sign of abandonment (Deuteronomy 31:17-18; Psalm 27:9; 69:17; 143:7). In this chapter Jeremiah described the chaotic state of Jerusalem as a result of God hiding His face from His people.

of bridegrooms and brides will be heard again, along with the joyous songs of people
bringing thanksgiving offerings to the LORD. They will sing,

'Give thanks to the LORD of Heaven's Armies,
for the LORD is good.
His faithful love endures forever!'

33:12 Ezek 34:12-14 Zeph 2:6-7 For I will restore the prosperity of this land to what it was in the past, says the LORD.
12 "This is what the LORD of Heaven's Armies says: This land—though it is now desolate
33:13 Lev 27:32 Jer 17:26 Luke 15:4 and has no people and animals—will once more have pastures where shepherds can lead
their flocks. 13 Once again shepherds will count their flocks in the towns of the hill country,
the foothills of Judah,* the Negev, the land of Benjamin, the vicinity of Jerusalem, and all
the towns of Judah. I, the LORD, have spoken!
33:14 Hag 2:6-9 14 "The day will come, says the LORD, when I will do for Israel and Judah all the good
things I have promised them.

33:15 Ps 72:1-5 Isa 11:1-5 15 "In those days and at that time
I will raise up a righteous descendant* from King David's line.
He will do what is just and right throughout the land.
33:16 1 Cor 1:30 2 Cor 5:21 Phil 3:9 16 In that day Judah will be saved,
and Jerusalem will live in safety.
33:17 1 Kgs 2:4 Ps 89:29-37 And this will be its name:
'The LORD Is Our Righteousness.'*

17 For this is what the LORD says: David will have a descendant sitting on the throne of Isra-
33:18 Deut 18:1 Ezek 44:15 Heb 13:15 el forever. 18 And there will always be Levitical priests to offer burnt offerings and grain of-
ferings and sacrifices to Me."
19 Then this message came to Jeremiah from the LORD: 20 "This is what the LORD says: If
33:20 2 Sam 23:5 2 Chr 21:7 Ps 104:19-23 Isa 54:9 you can break My covenant with the day and the night so that one does not follow the
other, 21 only then will My covenant with My servant David be broken. Only then will he no
longer have a descendant to reign on his throne. The same is true for My covenant with
the Levitical priests who minister before Me. 22 And as the stars of the sky cannot be
33:22 Gen 22:17 counted and the sand on the seashore cannot be measured, so I will multiply the descen-
dants of My servant David and the Levites who minister before Me."
33:24 Neh 4:2-4 Ps 44:13-14 Isa 11:13 Jer 3:7-8, 10, 18 Ezek 36:2 23 The LORD gave another message to Jeremiah. He said, 24 "Have you noticed what peo-
ple are saying?—'The LORD chose Judah and Israel and then abandoned them!' They are
sneering and saying that Israel is not worthy to be counted as a nation. 25 But this is what
the LORD says: I would no more reject My people than I would change My laws that govern

33:25 Ps 74:16-17 33:13 Hebrew *the Shephelah.* 33:15 Hebrew *a righteous branch.* 33:16 Hebrew *Yahweh Tsidqenu.*

▸ HOLINESS

33:9 The impact of one life. We are called to be instruments of grace to those around us. If we are faithful servants of Christ, we should cause others to marvel at our commitment to Christ and God's forgiveness in our lives. It is impossible for us to make God more glorious, for He is an all-glorious God. But it is possible for us to help others esteem God more highly in their own lives. Take the time to cause God's glory to shine to those around you. Obey, love, risk, and rejoice—then you will see people respect God. (***See Holiness*> *God's Blessing*> *Obedience honors God,* TopicGuide page A42.)

33:15-16 The word "descendant" can also be translated as "branch" (see NLT textual note), which signifies new growth. God promised to send Judah a righteous ruler who would provide safety for His people. This prophecy is ultimately fulfilled in the person of Jesus Christ (2 Samuel 23:5; Ezekiel 29:21; Psalm 132:17; Zechariah 6:12).

33:20 The "covenant with the day and the night" may be a reference to God's covenant with creation when He made the lights to rule the day and the night (Genesis 1:16). God was saying that in the same way He permanently made the sun to rule over the day and the moon to rule over the evening, Israel will never cease from being God's people. This verse may also be a reference to God's covenant with Noah (Genesis 8:22).

33:22 God now linked His commitment to remain the God of Israel with His promises to Abraham (Genesis 15:5; 22:17). God promised Abraham that his descendants would be as innumerable as the stars in the sky and the sand on the seashore. God also specifically stated that He would preserve the office of king and priest. Christ fulfilled both the office of king and priest in one person (see Hebrews 7).

night and day, earth and sky. 26 I will never abandon the descendants of Jacob or David, My 33:26
servant, or change the plan that David's descendants will rule the descendants of Abraham, Hos 2:23
Isaac, and Jacob. Instead, I will restore them to their land and have mercy on them."

A WARNING FOR ZEDEKIAH

34 King Nebuchadnezzar of Babylon came with all the armies from the kingdoms he 34:1
ruled, and he fought against Jerusalem and the towns of Judah. At that time this 2 Kgs 25:1 Jer 1:15
message came to Jeremiah from the LORD: 2 "Go to King Zedekiah of Judah, and tell him, Dan 2:37-38
'This is what the LORD, the God of Israel, says: I am about to hand this city over to the king 34:2
of Babylon, and he will burn it down. 3 You will not escape his grasp but will be captured 2 Chr 36:11-12
and taken to meet the king of Babylon face to face. Then you will be exiled to Babylon. Jer 37:1-4
4 " 'But listen to this promise from the LORD, O Zedekiah, king of Judah. This is what the 34:3 2 Kgs 25:4-7
LORD says: You will not be killed in war 5 but will die peacefully. People will burn incense in Jer 21:7
your memory, just as they did for your ancestors, the kings who preceded you. They will 34:5
mourn for you, crying, "Alas, our master is dead!" This I have decreed, says the LORD.' " 2 Chr 16:14; 21:19
6 So Jeremiah the prophet delivered the message to King Zedekiah of Judah. 7 At this 34:7
time the Babylonian army was besieging Jerusalem, Lachish, and Azekah—the only forti- Josh 10:3, 10 2 Kgs 14:19
fied cities of Judah not yet captured. 2 Chr 11:5-10

FREEDOM FOR HEBREW SLAVES

8 This message came to Jeremiah from the LORD after King Zedekiah made a covenant with 34:8 Lev 25:39-46
the people, proclaiming freedom for the slaves. 9 He had ordered all the people to free Neh 5:1-13
their Hebrew slaves—both men and women. No one was to keep a fellow Judean in bond- 34:11
age. 10 The officials and all the people had obeyed the king's command, 11 but later they Hos 6:4
changed their minds. They took back the men and women they had freed, forcing them to 34:13 Deut 5:2-3, 27
be slaves again. Jer 31:32
12 So the LORD gave them this message through Jeremiah: 13 "This is what the LORD, the 34:14
God of Israel, says: I made a covenant with your ancestors long ago when I rescued them Exod 21:2 1 Kgs 9:22
from their slavery in Egypt. 14 I told them that every Hebrew slave must be freed after serv- 2 Kgs 17:13-14
ing six years. But your ancestors paid no attention to Me. 15 Recently you repented and did 34:15
what was right, following My command. You freed your slaves and made a solemn cov- Neh 10:29
enant with Me in the Temple that bears My name. 16 But now you have shrugged off your 34:16
oath and defiled My name by taking back the men and women you had freed, forcing Exod 20:7 1 Sam 15:11
them to be slaves once again. Ezek 18:24

33:26 At the conclusion of chapters 30–33, the Book of Comfort, God once again confirmed that His mercy would motivate Him to restore Judah to its original state. It is the Lord's compassion that prevents Him from eternally hiding His face from His people (compare Jeremiah 33:6).

34:4 The Lord not only prophesied concerning Zedekiah's capture, but also concerning the details of his death. It is important to note that this was a conditional prophecy, as is true for prophecy in general (18:5-11; 21:9; 22:4-5). God had already warned Zedekiah to submit to God's will by surrendering to Babylonian rule (27:12-15). If Zedekiah obeyed the Lord, he would die peacefully. But if he revolted against the Lord, he would suffer greatly. In the end, Zedekiah was captured, his eyes were plucked out after he witnessed the execution of his sons; then he was carried off into captivity (39:5-9; 52:11).

34:8 The treaty established between Zedekiah and the inhabitants of Judah was for the release of the slaves according to the law of God (Exodus 21:2; Deuteronomy 15:12; Jeremiah 34:14). This covenant appears to have been a move to spark reform among the people, just as in the days of Josiah (2 Kings 23:1-3).

34:11 Unfortunately, Zedekiah's attempted reform was short-lived. It is not certain how the slave masters were able to retrieve the freed slaves. Jeremiah's ministry was a plea for the people of God to turn from their sin and to return to God (3:14, 22; 4:1; 18:8; 26:3). But these verses show Judah's turning away in disobedience from the covenant they had made in the name of the Lord (34:16).

▸ SPIRITUAL WARFARE

34:16 Defiling God's name. The people of Judah had called on the name of the Lord to serve as a witness to their commitment to free the slaves according to God's Word. When they turned away from their promise to free the slaves, God held them in contempt for using His name in vain (Exodus 20:7-8). When we break our marriage vows and other promises made in God's name, we take His name in vain—it's a serious matter. Take care not to trivialize and blaspheme the names of God by phrases such as "Oh my God!" or casual versions such as "Geez." Flippant usages of God's names show a lack of respect of God. As believers in the Lord, we should use our words to reveal His glory, not diminish it. (***See Spiritual Warfare**> Originator of Sin> Satan's Goals> Tempt men to curse God's name,* TopicGuide page A45.)

34:17 Lev 26:34-35 [17]"Therefore, this is what the LORD says: Since you have not obeyed Me by setting your
Deut 28:25, 64 countrymen free, I will set you free to be destroyed by war, disease, and famine. You will
Matt 7:2 be an object of horror to all the nations of the earth. [18]Because you have broken the terms
34:18 of our covenant, I will cut you apart just as you cut apart the calf when you walked be-
Gen 15:10 tween its halves to solemnize your vows. [19]Yes, I will cut you apart, whether you are offi-
Hos 6:7 Mic 7:1-5 cials of Judah or Jerusalem, court officials, priests, or common people—for you have
34:20 broken your oath. [20]I will give you to your enemies, and they will kill you. Your bodies will
1 Sam 17:46 be food for the vultures and wild animals.
Jer 19:7 [21]"I will hand over King Zedekiah of Judah and his officials to the army of the king of
34:21 2 Kgs 25:18-21 Babylon. And although Babylon's king has left Jerusalem for a while, [22]I will call the Bab-
Ezek 17:16 ylonian armies back again. They will fight against this city and will capture it and burn it
down. I will see to it that all the towns of Judah are destroyed, with no one living there."

35:1 2 Kgs 23:34-36

THE FAITHFUL RECABITES

Dan 1:1 **35** This is the message the LORD gave Jeremiah when Jehoiakim son of Josiah was
35:2 1 Kgs 6:5-6, 8 king of Judah: [2]"Go to the settlement where the families of the Recabites live, and
1 Chr 2:55 invite them to the LORD's Temple. Take them into one of the inner rooms, and offer them
35:4 some wine."
1 Kgs 12:22 1 Chr 9:18 [3]So I went to see Jaazaniah son of Jeremiah and grandson of Habazziniah and all his
35:5 brothers and sons—representing all the Recabite families. [4]I took them to the Temple, and
Amos 2:12 we went into the room assigned to the sons of Hanan son of Igdaliah, a man of God. This
35:6 room was located next to the one used by the Temple officials, directly above the room of
Lev 10:9 2 Kgs 10:15, 23 Maaseiah son of Shallum, the Temple gatekeeper.
Luke 1:15 [5]I set cups and jugs of wine before them and invited them to have a drink, [6]but they re-
35:7 Exod 20:12 fused. "No," they said, "we don't drink wine, because our ancestor Jehonadab* son of Recab
Heb 11:9 gave us this command: 'You and your descendants must never drink wine. [7]And do not
build houses or plant crops or vineyards, but always live in tents. If you follow these com-
35:8 Col 3:20 mands, you will live long, good lives in the land.' [8]So we have obeyed him in all these things.
We have never had a drink of wine to this day, nor have our wives, our sons, or our daugh-
35:9 1 Tim 6:6 ters. [9]We haven't built houses or owned vineyards or farms or planted crops. [10]We have

35:6 Hebrew *Jonadab,* a variant spelling of Jehonadab; also in 35:10, 14, 16, 18, 19. See 2 Kgs 10:15.

34:17 Since the people of Judah had not lived up to their commitment to free the slaves, God would in turn set them "free" to suffer the brutality of war.

34:18 In Judah's covenant ceremony in verse 8, they took a calf and split it into two parts. The parties involved in the covenant then walked between the pieces as a symbolic act of the fate the offending party would suffer should the covenant be broken (compare Genesis 15:7-11, 17). God was now holding the people accountable to their agreement to free the slaves. For their violation, God would deliver them into the hands of their enemies to be devoured (Jeremiah 34:20).

35:2 The Recabites were a nomadic people who retreated to Jerusalem when the Babylonian army began seizing parts of Judah (Jeremiah 35:11). The Lord applauded the Recabites for being a model family of righteousness in their faithful observance of the instructions of their ancestor, Jehonadab. Jehonadab (or Jonadab) was the son of Recab, and is best known for assisting Jehu in his slaughter of Ahab's family and the worshipers of Baal (2 Kings 10:15-27).

▸ CHURCH

35:5 Convictions to the test. Regardless of how long we have been Christians, there are certain things that each of us refrains from participating in because of our convictions. The Word of God and our cultural upbringing often work together to shape our convictions. In the New Testament, some believers were convicted against eating meats and became vegetarians. But other believers saw nothing wrong with eating all kinds of foods. In this specific case, the apostle Paul neither attempted to impose vegetarianism on all believers, nor did he require the vegetarian to eat meat (Romans 14). We should be sensitive to the different convictions held by our fellow believers. We must be fully convinced in our own minds, and at the same time seek to live peaceably with all people (Romans 14:5, 19). (***See Church****> Role> Preach> Instructions> Use Caution> Conscience differences in eating and drinking,* TopicGuide page A50.)

35:6-7 The vows of the Recabites not only prohibited them from drinking wine, but also barred them from constructing and residing in stone houses and planting seeds and vineyards. The Recabites had faithfully observed Jehonadab's request for them to adopt a nomadic lifestyle and to refrain from certain activities.

lived in tents and have fully obeyed all the commands of Jehonadab, our ancestor. 11But
when King Nebuchadnezzar* of Babylon attacked this country, we were afraid of the Babylo-
nian and Syrian* armies. So we decided to move to Jerusalem. That is why we are here."
12Then the LORD gave this message to Jeremiah: 13"This is what the LORD of Heaven's
Armies, the God of Israel, says: Go and say to the people in Judah and Jerusalem, 'Come
and learn a lesson about how to obey Me. 14The Recabites do not drink wine to this day
because their ancestor Jehonadab told them not to. But I have spoken to you again and
again, and you refuse to obey Me. 15Time after time I sent you prophets, who told you,
"Turn from your wicked ways, and start doing things right. Stop worshiping other gods so
that you might live in peace here in the land I have given to you and your ancestors." But
you would not listen to Me or obey Me. 16The descendants of Jehonadab son of Recab
have obeyed their ancestor completely, but you have refused to listen to Me.'
17"Therefore, this is what the LORD God of Heaven's Armies, the God of Israel, says: 'Be-
cause you refuse to listen or answer when I call, I will send upon Judah and Jerusalem all
the disasters I have threatened.'"
18Then Jeremiah turned to the Recabites and said, "This is what the LORD of Heaven's Ar-
mies, the God of Israel, says: 'You have obeyed your ancestor Jehonadab in every respect,
following all his instructions.' 19Therefore, this is what the LORD of Heaven's Armies, the
God of Israel, says: 'Jehonadab son of Recab will always have descendants who serve Me.'"

BARUCH READS THE LORD'S MESSAGES

36 During the fourth year that Jehoiakim son of Josiah was king in Judah,* the LORD
gave this message to Jeremiah: 2"Get a scroll, and write down all My messages
against Israel, Judah, and the other nations. Begin with the first message back in the days
of Josiah, and write down every message, right up to the present time. 3Perhaps the peo-
ple of Judah will repent when they hear again all the terrible things I have planned for
them. Then I will be able to forgive their sins and wrongdoings."
4So Jeremiah sent for Baruch son of Neriah, and as Jeremiah dictated all the prophecies
that the LORD had given him, Baruch wrote them on a scroll. 5Then Jeremiah said to Bar-
uch, "I am a prisoner here and unable to go to the Temple. 6So you go to the Temple on
the next day of fasting, and read the messages from the LORD that I have had you write on

35:11 2 Kgs 24:1-2; Dan 1:1-2
35:13 Isa 28:9-12
35:14 2 Chr 36:15; Isa 30:9
35:15 Deut 6:14; Jer 29:19; Ezek 18:30-32; Acts 26:20
35:16 Mal 1:6
35:17 Prov 1:24-25; Mic 3:12; Luke 13:34-35; Rom 10:21
35:18 Exod 20:12; Eph 6:1-3
36:1 Jer 25:1-3; 45:1
36:2 Zech 5:1-2
36:3 Isa 55:7; Mark 4:12; Acts 3:19
36:4 Ezek 2:9
36:5 Jer 32:2
36:6 Zech 8:19

35:11a Hebrew *Nebuchadrezzar,* a variant spelling of Nebuchadnezzar. 35:11b Or *Chaldean and Aramean.* 36:1 The fourth year of Jehoiakim's reign was 605 B.C.

▸ HOLINESS

35:13 Learning your lesson. Some of us are a little slow—slow learners, slow to change, and slow to admit we are wrong. Others only have to suffer through one terrible experience in order to make lifestyle adjustments. The people of Judah were slow learners because in spite of the prophets God had sent to them, the multiple signs they had observed, and the righteous people placed among them, they persisted in their rebellion against God. God uses many different ways to get our attention—it would be wise for us to learn quickly. Think of several lessons you need to learn—and never unlearn—and take them to God. Ask Him to keep you from habitual sin (Romans 13:10-14). (***See Holiness****> Submission> Trusting God> Obedience,* TopicGuide page A40.)

35:15 "Turn" can also be read as "Each one turn." Jeremiah was sent to Judah to prophesy against sin. His work in Judah was not limited to evoking change from the high-ranking officials; God intended His message of judgment to generate a changed heart in every individual, regardless of societal rank or economic status.

35:19 The Lord blessed the Recabites for their obedience to their ancestor's instructions. The promise that God made to the Recabites bears similar language to the promise the Lord made with the house of David (1 Kings 2:4; 8:25; Jeremiah 33:17). Through the Recabites, God was teaching a lesson to Judah: Obedience would be rewarded with blessing, but disobedience would result in devastation.

36:1-8 This section gives a unique view into the process of how God's words were given to prophets and then were accepted as God's Word. God gave His message to Jeremiah. Jeremiah dictated that message to Baruch. Baruch wrote down the message and then read the message in the Temple as a message from God. At no point did God's message to Jeremiah cease to be His Word, though it went from person to person and from one medium to another.

36:4 The Lord told Jeremiah to write on a scroll all the messages that the Lord had given him over the years (36:2). Evidently, this was the first time Jeremiah was asked to do this. Jeremiah utilized a scribe named Baruch to write the actual book. This first scroll was not the final version of the book of Jeremiah, for there were many more events from his life and ministry that were yet to be recorded.

this scroll. Read them so the people who are there from all over Judah will hear them.
36:7 7 Perhaps even yet they will turn from their evil ways and ask the LORD's forgiveness before
1 Kgs 8:33 2 Kgs 22:13 it is too late. For the LORD has threatened them with His terrible anger."
Jer 26:3 8 Baruch did as Jeremiah told him and read these messages from the LORD to the people
at the Temple. 9 He did this on a day of sacred fasting held in late autumn,* during the fifth
year of the reign of Jehoiakim son of Josiah. People from all over Judah had come to Jeru-
36:10 salem to attend the services at the Temple on that day. 10 Baruch read Jeremiah's words on
Jer 26:10 the scroll to all the people. He stood in front of the Temple room of Gemariah, son of Sha-
phan the secretary. This room was just off the upper courtyard of the Temple, near the
New Gate entrance.
11 When Micaiah son of Gemariah and grandson of Shaphan heard the messages from
36:12 the LORD, 12 he went down to the secretary's room in the palace where the administrative
Jer 26:22 officials were meeting. Elishama the secretary was there, along with Delaiah son of She-
maiah, Elnathan son of Acbor, Gemariah son of Shaphan, Zedekiah son of Hananiah, and
36:13 all the other officials. 13 When Micaiah told them about the messages Baruch was reading
2 Kgs 22:9-10 to the people, 14 the officials sent Jehudi son of Nethaniah, grandson of Shelemiah and
great-grandson of Cushi, to ask Baruch to come and read the messages to them, too. So
Baruch took the scroll and went to them. 15 "Sit down and read the scroll to us," the officials
said, and Baruch did as they requested.
36:16 16 When they heard all the messages, they looked at one another in alarm. "We must
Amos 7:10-11 tell the king what we have heard," they said to Baruch. 17 "But first, tell us how you got
Acts 24:25 these messages. Did they come directly from Jeremiah?"
36:18 18 So Baruch explained, "Jeremiah dictated them, and I wrote them down in ink, word for
Jer 36:4 word, on this scroll."
36:19 19 "You and Jeremiah should both hide," the officials told Baruch. "Don't tell anyone
1 Kgs 17:3; 18:4 Jer 26:20-24 where you are!" 20 Then the officials left the scroll for safekeeping in the room of Elishama
the secretary and went to tell the king what had happened.

KING JEHOIAKIM BURNS THE SCROLL

36:21 2 Kgs 22:9-10 21 The king sent Jehudi to get the scroll. Jehudi brought it from Elishama's room and read it
Ezek 2:4-5 36:22 to the king as all his officials stood by. 22 It was late autumn, and the king was in a winter-
Amos 3:15 ized part of the palace, sitting in front of a fire to keep warm. 23 Each time Jehudi finished

36:23 Isa 5:18-19; 28:14, 22

36:9 Hebrew *in the ninth month,* of the ancient Hebrew lunar calendar (also in 36:22). The ninth month in the fifth year of Jehoiakim's reign occurred within the months of November and December 604 B.C. Also see note on 1:3.

▸ HOLINESS
36:4 The need for a written word. God, in His infinite wisdom, has chosen to preserve His divine Word in written form—and for this we are very thankful. Because God's Word has been written down, it has the ability to reach a wider audience than just the original listeners. God's message is one of salvation (36:7). Because God intends to spread His Word throughout the world, we should cultivate a love for the Bible and seek to share it with as many people as possible. Read it and share it—for through it God transforms lives (Romans 1:16). (***See Holiness****> Disciplines> Of Engagement> Call to Study,* TopicGuide page A42.)

36:8-20 After Baruch took the scroll to the Temple and read it aloud for the people, the officials of the Temple requested a private reading. When the officials confirmed that the words indeed came from Jeremiah, they were compelled to do two things: They ordered Baruch and Jeremiah to go into hiding for fear of Jehoiakim's response, and they provided an oral report to the king of what had transpired.

36:22-23 The chapter reaches its climax with Jehudi's reading of the scroll before King Jehoiakim. Winter was soon approaching in Jerusalem, and Jehoiakim sat by a fire while Jehudi read the scroll. Jehoiakim responded to the reading of the scroll by tearing each portion off and throwing it into the fire after it was read.

▸ WORSHIP
36:23 The proper response to God's Word. Have you ever wanted to throw your Bible across the room? We know we should treat God's Word with awe and respect, but sometimes we can become frustrated by what we find there. Jehoiakim experienced those same feelings, and this wicked king responded to God's Word with malice and proceeded to destroy it. He then ordered for Jeremiah and Baruch to be arrested (36:26). Thankfully, the Lord preserved the lives of these two men, but God would deal with Jehoiakim accordingly (36:30-31). But now, what about you? How do you respond to God's Word? Ignoring it is only slightly better than cutting it up—how can you best honor God's Word when you hear it? (***See Worship****> OT> Reverence> Leads to humility,* TopicGuide page A29.)

reading three or four columns, the king took a knife and cut off that section of the scroll. He then threw it into the fire, section by section, until the whole scroll was burned up. 24Neither the king nor his attendants showed any signs of fear or repentance at what they heard. 25Even when Elnathan, Delaiah, and Gemariah begged the king not to burn the scroll, he wouldn't listen.

26Then the king commanded his son Jerahmeel, Seraiah son of Azriel, and Shelemiah son of Abdeel to arrest Baruch and Jeremiah. But the LORD had hidden them.

JEREMIAH REWRITES THE SCROLL

27After the king had burned the scroll on which Baruch had written Jeremiah's words, the LORD gave Jeremiah another message. He said, 28"Get another scroll, and write everything again just as you did on the scroll King Jehoiakim burned. 29Then say to the king, 'This is what the LORD says: You burned the scroll because it said the king of Babylon would destroy this land and empty it of people and animals. 30Now this is what the LORD says about King Jehoiakim of Judah: He will have no heirs to sit on the throne of David. His dead body will be thrown out to lie unburied—exposed to the heat of the day and the frost of the night. 31I will punish him and his family and his attendants for their sins. I will pour out on them and on all the people of Jerusalem and Judah all the disasters I promised, for they would not listen to My warnings.'"

32So Jeremiah took another scroll and dictated again to his secretary, Baruch. He wrote everything that had been on the scroll King Jehoiakim had burned in the fire. Only this time he added much more!

ZEDEKIAH CALLS FOR JEREMIAH

37 Zedekiah son of Josiah succeeded Jehoiachin* son of Jehoiakim as the king of Judah. He was appointed by King Nebuchadnezzar* of Babylon. 2But neither King Zedekiah nor his attendants nor the people who were left in the land listened to what the LORD said through Jeremiah.

3Nevertheless, King Zedekiah sent Jehucal son of Shelemiah, and Zephaniah the priest, son of Maaseiah, to ask Jeremiah, "Please pray to the LORD our God for us." 4Jeremiah had not yet been imprisoned, so he could come and go among the people as he pleased.

5At this time the army of Pharaoh Hophra* of Egypt appeared at the southern border of Judah. When the Babylonian* army heard about it, they withdrew from their siege of Jerusalem.

6Then the LORD gave this message to Jeremiah: 7"This is what the LORD, the God of Israel, says: The king of Judah sent you to ask Me what is going to happen. Tell him, 'Pharaoh's army is about to return to Egypt, though he came here to help you. 8Then the Babylonians* will come back and capture this city and burn it to the ground.'

36:24 2 Kgs 19:1-2; Ps 36:1; Acts 5:34-39
36:26 1 Kgs 19:1-3, 10, 14; Jer 15:20-21
36:28 Jer 28:13-14; Zech 1:5-6
36:29 Deut 29:19; Isa 30:10-11; 45:9; Jer 25:8-11; 26:9
36:30 2 Kgs 24:12-15
36:31 Deut 28:15-19; Prov 29:1
36:32 Exod 34:1
37:1 2 Kgs 24:17; 1 Chr 3:15-16; 2 Chr 36:9-10; Jer 22:24, 28; Ezek 17:12-21
37:2 2 Kgs 24:18-20; 2 Chr 36:12; Prov 29:12
37:3 Jer 2:26-27; 21:1-2; 52:24
37:5 Ezek 17:15-16
37:7 Isa 30:1-3; 31:1-3; Jer 21:1-2; Ezek 17:17
37:8 Jer 34:22

37:1a Hebrew *Coniah,* a variant spelling of Jehoiachin. 37:1b Hebrew *Nebuchadrezzar,* a variant spelling of Nebuchadnezzar. 37:5a Hebrew *army of Pharaoh;* see 44:30. 37:5b Or *Chaldean;* also in 37:10, 11. 37:8 Or *Chaldeans;* also in 37:9, 13.

36:32 Jeremiah and Baruch wrote another scroll, according to the instructions from the Lord. This second writing was longer in length, and appears to have been an early version of the book of Jeremiah. But this second version was not yet the final copy of the book of Jeremiah (see note at Jeremiah 36:4).

▶ WORSHIP
37:2-3 Praying at the request of others. It is a great privilege to pray at someone's request and ask God to bring comfort or resolution to a specific crisis (Galatians 6:2). It is our Christian duty to make ourselves available to those who need our help—even an unfaithful man like Zedekiah. Often, there is nothing we can physically do for the person, but we can always go to our knees and ask God to intervene. Count it a privilege and a duty to pray for others, and then do it joyfully and immediately. (***See Worship****> OT> Fasting and Prayer> Prayer> At others' request,* TopicGuide page A26.)

37:7 God answered Zedekiah's prayer request by stating that the Egyptian army had only brought temporary relief. God said that the Egyptians would return home, and the Babylonian army would make its final run against Jerusalem. The Lord had now removed any sense of hope that either Zedekiah or the people had mustered. It seems that Judah had been counting on the Egyptians as their ally when the Assyrians had previously threatened to attack (2 Kings 18:21).

9 "This is what the LORD says: Do not fool yourselves into thinking that the Babylonians
are gone for good. They aren't! 10 Even if you were to destroy the entire Babylonian army,
leaving only a handful of wounded survivors, they would still stagger from their tents and
burn this city to the ground!"

JEREMIAH IS IMPRISONED

11 When the Babylonian army left Jerusalem because of Pharaoh's approaching army, 12 Jer-
emiah started to leave the city on his way to the territory of Benjamin, to claim his share of
the property among his relatives there.* 13 But as he was walking through the Benjamin Gate,
a sentry arrested him and said, "You are defecting to the Babylonians!" The sentry making
the arrest was Irijah son of Shelemiah, grandson of Hananiah.

14 "That's not true!" Jeremiah protested. "I had no intention of doing any such thing." But
Irijah wouldn't listen, and he took Jeremiah before the officials. 15 They were furious with
Jeremiah and had him flogged and imprisoned in the house of Jonathan the secretary.
Jonathan's house had been converted into a prison. 16 Jeremiah was put into a dungeon
cell, where he remained for many days.

17 Later King Zedekiah secretly requested that Jeremiah come to the palace, where the
king asked him, "Do you have any messages from the LORD?"

"Yes, I do!" said Jeremiah. "You will be defeated by the king of Babylon."

18 Then Jeremiah asked the king, "What crime have I committed? What have I done
against you, your attendants, or the people that I should be imprisoned like this? 19 Where
are your prophets now who told you the king of Babylon would not attack you or this
land? 20 Listen, my lord the king, I beg you. Don't send me back to the dungeon in the
house of Jonathan the secretary, for I will die there."

21 So King Zedekiah commanded that Jeremiah not be returned to the dungeon. In-
stead, he was imprisoned in the courtyard of the guard in the royal palace. The king also
commanded that Jeremiah be given a loaf of fresh bread every day as long as there was
any left in the city. So Jeremiah was put in the palace prison.

JEREMIAH IN A CISTERN

38 Now Shephatiah son of Mattan, Gedaliah son of Pashhur, Jehucal* son of Shelemi-
ah, and Pashhur son of Malkijah heard what Jeremiah had been telling the peo-
ple. He had been saying, 2 "This is what the LORD says: 'Everyone who stays in Jerusalem

37:9 Jer 29:8; Obad 1:3; Eph 5:6
37:10 Lev 26:36-38; Isa 30:17; Joel 2:11
37:12 Jer 32:8
37:13 Jer 18:18; 20:10; Zech 14:10; Acts 24:5-9, 13
37:14 Ps 27:12; Jer 40:4-6; Matt 5:11-12
37:15 Jer 18:23; 38:6; Matt 21:35; Acts 5:18; Heb 11:36
37:17 Jer 21:7; 38:14-16, 24-27; Ezek 12:12-13; 17:19-21
37:18 1 Sam 24:9; 26:18; John 10:32; Acts 25:8, 10-11
37:19 Deut 32:37-38
37:20 Jer 38:26
37:21 Job 5:20; Ps 33:18-19; Isa 33:16; Jer 52:6
38:1 Jer 21:8
38:2 Jer 21:9; 42:17

37:12 Hebrew *to separate from there in the midst of the people.* 38:1 Hebrew *Jucal,* a variant spelling of Jehucal; see 37:3.

37:10 Right before King David captured the city of Jerusalem, the Jebusites taunted David by claiming Jerusalem to be invincible and capable of being protected by the lame and the blind (2 Samuel 5:6-7). On this occasion, God states that even if the people of Judah could destroy their enemy, the wounded Babylonian soldiers would still be able to rise from their tents and overthrow the city. God sovereignly controlled the fate of the city of Jerusalem regardless of the size and condition of the army within its city limits, or the strength of any army attempting to overthrow it.

37:13-16 On Jeremiah's way to claim his share of a property in the town of Benjamin, Irijah, the captain of the guard, arrested him. Irijah accused Jeremiah of being a traitor and had him beaten and then placed in a dungeon. It is difficult to ascertain the connection between this account of Jeremiah's attempt to claim property and his encounter with Hanamel, who advised him of property he had the right to purchase (32:7). Here, Jeremiah is not yet in prison when he proceeds to purchase the land. But when Hanamel approached Jeremiah, he was already under arrest (32:2).

▸ HOLINESS

37:17 Seeking more words from God. God often reveals His will to us quite clearly—but we don't want to do it. So we delay through procrastination or even something sounding spiritual. Perhaps we want to talk to a certain person and get more counsel. Or perhaps we suddenly decide to pray about the matter for a week or so. The Lord had already revealed His will to King Zedekiah; the king simply failed to obey (37:2). There are many instances in Scripture where people are rebuked for failing to apply God's Word (Matthew 16:3; Matthew 22:29; Luke 24:25; John 5:39; Romans 15:4). Pray today for the Spirit to apply God's already-revealed Word to your life—it's likely to be all that you need. (***See Holiness***> *Submission> Trusting God>* ***Obedience,*** TopicGuide page A40.)

37:20-21 Jeremiah feared that if he were returned to the house of Jonathan he would die (37:15-16). Though Zedekiah failed to listen to Jeremiah's prophecies, he showed compassion toward the prophet. Zedekiah placed Jeremiah in a less stringent prison and allowed him to be fed a loaf of bread as long as the supply lasted. It appears as though Zedekiah was drawn to Jeremiah but lacked the determination to change his behavior.

will die from war, famine, or disease, but those who surrender to the Babylonians* will live.
Their reward will be life. They will live!' 3The LORD also says: 'The city of Jerusalem will cer-
tainly be handed over to the army of the king of Babylon, who will capture it.'"
4So these officials went to the king and said, "Sir, this man must die! That kind of talk
will undermine the morale of the few fighting men we have left, as well as that of all the
people. This man is a traitor!"
5King Zedekiah agreed. "All right," he said. "Do as you like. I can't stop you."
6So the officials took Jeremiah from his cell and lowered him by ropes into an empty cis-
tern in the prison yard. It belonged to Malkijah, a member of the royal family. There was
no water in the cistern, but there was a thick layer of mud at the bottom, and Jeremiah
sank down into it.
7But Ebed-melech the Ethiopian,* an important court official, heard that Jeremiah was in
the cistern. At that time the king was holding court at the Benjamin Gate, 8so Ebed-melech
rushed from the palace to speak with him. 9"My lord the king," he said, "these men have
done a very evil thing in putting Jeremiah the prophet into the cistern. He will soon die of
hunger, for almost all the bread in the city is gone."
10So the king told Ebed-melech, "Take thirty of my men with you, and pull Jeremiah out
of the cistern before he dies."
11So Ebed-melech took the men with him and went to a room in the palace beneath the
treasury, where he found some old rags and discarded clothing. He carried these to the
cistern and lowered them to Jeremiah on a rope. 12Ebed-melech called down to Jeremiah,
"Put these rags under your armpits to protect you from the ropes." Then when Jeremiah
was ready, 13they pulled him out. So Jeremiah was returned to the courtyard of the
guard—the palace prison—where he remained.

ZEDEKIAH QUESTIONS JEREMIAH

14One day King Zedekiah sent for Jeremiah and had him brought to the third entrance of
the LORD's Temple. "I want to ask you something," the king said. "And don't try to hide the
truth."
15Jeremiah said, "If I tell you the truth, you will kill me. And if I give you advice, you
won't listen to me anyway."
16So King Zedekiah secretly promised him, "As surely as the LORD our Creator lives, I will
not kill you or hand you over to the men who want you dead."
17Then Jeremiah said to Zedekiah, "This is what the LORD God of Heaven's Armies, the
God of Israel, says: 'If you surrender to the Babylonian officers, you and your family will
live, and the city will not be burned down. 18But if you refuse to surrender, you will not es-
cape! This city will be handed over to the Babylonians, and they will burn it to the ground.'"

38:3 Jer 21:10; 32:3-5
38:4 1 Kgs 18:17-18; Jer 26:11; Amos 7:10; Acts 16:20-21
38:5 2 Sam 3:39
38:6 Pss 40:2; 69:1-2, 14; Jer 37:15-16; Zech 9:11; Acts 16:24
38:9 Jer 37:21; 52:6
38:13 Jer 37:21; 39:14-15
38:14 1 Kgs 22:16; Jer 21:1-2; 37:17
38:15 Luke 22:67-68
38:16 Isa 42:5; Jer 37:17
38:17 2 Kgs 25:27-30; Ps 80:7, 14; Jer 21:8-10; 27:12, 17
38:18 2 Kgs 25:4-10; Jer 27:8; 37:8

38:2 Or *Chaldeans;* also in 38:18, 19, 23. 38:7 Hebrew *the Cushite.*

38:6 When the truth was revealed to King Jehoiakim, he destroyed the Word of God by putting the scroll into a fire (36:23). When the officials heard the Word of God, they sought to murder its spokesperson. The fact that Jeremiah was lowered into a cistern filled with mud would later symbolize Zedekiah's doom for not adhering to the Word of God (38:22). Ancient cisterns of this type were usually a hole in the ground with a small, watertight limestone cave beneath it. Rainwater would be drained into the hole, but dirt and sand would travel along with the water, creating a layer of sludge at the bottom.

38:7-13 The Ethiopian Ebed-melech, whose name means "servant of the king," wisely rescued Jeremiah from likely death. What the kings and priests of Israel would not do, foreigners would accomplish. This continues the theme in Jeremiah of foreigners carrying out God's will.

▸ ADOPTION

38:16 Lip service rather than heart service. It appears that religious talk was just lip service for Zedekiah. If this king truly believed the Lord as his Creator, he would have surrendered to the will of God. Many people have the tendency to say phrases such as "God bless you" without really taking to heart what they are saying (Matthew 15:7-9). Do we really pray for the person when we say we will? Has "God bless you" simply become a mundane formula? Let's pay attention to the things that we say to others and ensure that they come from a heart that believes and will act upon what we have said. Do not assume that everyone who uses Jesus' name is truly following Him (Matthew 7:21). (***See Adoption***> *Without Christ> Separated from God> Worship through lip service only,* TopicGuide page A36.)

19"But I am afraid to surrender," the king said, "for the Babylonians may hand me over
to the Judeans who have defected to them. And who knows what they will do to me!"
20Jeremiah replied, "You won't be handed over to them if you choose to obey the LORD.
Your life will be spared, and all will go well for you. 21But if you refuse to surrender, this is
what the LORD has revealed to me: 22All the women left in your palace will be brought out
and given to the officers of the Babylonian army. Then the women will taunt you, saying,

'What fine friends you have!
They have betrayed and misled you.
When your feet sank in the mud,
they left you to your fate!'

23All your wives and children will be led out to the Babylonians, and you will not escape.
You will be seized by the king of Babylon, and this city will be burned down."
24Then Zedekiah said to Jeremiah, "Don't tell anyone you told me this, or you will die!
25My officials may hear that I spoke to you, and they may say, 'Tell us what you and the
king were talking about. If you don't tell us, we will kill you.' 26If this happens, just tell them
you begged me not to send you back to Jonathan's dungeon, for fear you would die there."
27Sure enough, it wasn't long before the king's officials came to Jeremiah and asked
him why the king had called for him. But Jeremiah followed the king's instructions, and
they left without finding out the truth. No one had overheard the conversation between
Jeremiah and the king. 28And Jeremiah remained a prisoner in the courtyard of the guard
until the day Jerusalem was captured.

THE FALL OF JERUSALEM

39 In January* of the ninth year of King Zedekiah's reign, King Nebuchadnezzar*
came with his army to besiege Jerusalem. 2Two and a half years later, on July 18*
in the eleventh year of Zedekiah's reign, the Babylonians broke through the wall, and the
city fell. 3All the officers of the Babylonian army came in and sat in triumph at the Middle
Gate: Nergal-sharezer of Samgar, and Nebo-sarsekim,* a chief officer, and Nergal-sharezer,
the king's adviser, and all the other officers.
4When King Zedekiah and all the soldiers saw that the Babylonians had broken into the

38:19 Isa 51:12-13; 57:11; Jer 39:9; John 12:42
38:20 Isa 55:3; Jer 7:23; 11:4, 8; 26:13
38:22 Jer 6:12; 8:10; 43:6
38:23 2 Kgs 25:7; Jer 39:6; 41:10
38:26 Jer 37:15-16, 20
38:27 1 Sam 10:15-16; 16:2-5
38:28 Ps 23:4; Jer 37:20-21; 39:13-14
39:1 2 Kgs 25:1-12
39:2 2 Kgs 25:4; Jer 52:7
39:3 Jer 21:3-4
39:4 2 Kgs 25:4; Isa 30:15-16; Jer 52:7; Amos 2:14

39:1a Hebrew *in the tenth month,* of the ancient Hebrew lunar calendar. A number of events in Jeremiah can be cross-checked with dates in surviving Babylonian records and related accurately to our modern calendar. This event occurred on January 15, 588 B.C.; see 52:4a and the note there. 39:1b Hebrew *Nebuchadrezzar,* a variant spelling of Nebuchadnezzar; also in 39:11. 39:2 Hebrew *On the ninth day of the fourth month.* This day was July 18, 586 B.C.; also see note on 39:1a. 39:3 Or *Nergal-sharezer, Samgar-nebo, Sarsekim.*

38:19-20 In their secret council, Zedekiah revealed to Jeremiah that he believed himself to be in a no-win situation. If he surrendered to King Nebuchadnezzar, he feared that those who have already escaped to Babylon would seek to kill him. But if he remained in Jerusalem and continued to defend the city, then he would come under the judgment of God. What Zedekiah failed to acknowledge was that the Word of the Lord promised a safe passage should the king surrender. There should not have been a dilemma for the king.

38:24 Zedekiah must have feared the response from his officials concerning the Babylonians. Instead of acting on Jeremiah's words, Zedekiah acted as if the conversation never happened between them and told Jeremiah to do the same.

38:28 Because King Zedekiah was reluctant to act in submission to God's will, Jeremiah spent his final days imprisoned until the Babylonian siege was completed. Hope now appeared to have completely dissipated for Jerusalem.

39:1 Alas, all the words that the prophet Jeremiah had spoken concerning the fall of Jerusalem were realized beginning in the ninth year of Zedekiah's reign (approximately 587–586 BC). This siege should not simply be understood as the destruction of Jerusalem, but also as a description of the demise of Jeremiah's persecutors. With the fall of Jerusalem, God had sentenced His people with the ultimate covenant curse of disobedience—expulsion from the Promised Land (Leviticus 26:33; Deuteronomy 28:64).

▶ BIBLE

39:4 No hope apart from God's truth. Too many people live their lives like Zedekiah, hoping for security apart from obeying God. God's message to us should function as a lamp and a light to illuminate our lives, for without God's Word we walk in darkness and are destined to stumble through life (Psalm 119:105). Zedekiah was in a hopeless situation—surrounded by one of the world's most powerful armies—and when offered hope, he instead allowed fear to govern his response. Because he ignored God's message to him, his family died before his eyes. God has no "Ten Suggestions"—God commands us to obey Him, and the consequences for not heeding His Word can be awful. No matter the situation, obey God. (***See Bible*** *> Power> Wisdom> The beginning of wisdom is obedience to Scripture,* TopicGuide page A11.)

city, they fled. They waited for nightfall and then slipped through the gate between the
two walls behind the king's garden and headed toward the Jordan Valley.*
5But the Babylonian* troops chased the king and caught him on the plains of Jericho.
They took him to King Nebuchadnezzar of Babylon, who was at Riblah in the land of
Hamath. There the king of Babylon pronounced judgment upon Zedekiah. 6He made Zed-
ekiah watch as they slaughtered his sons and all the nobles of Judah. 7Then they gouged
out Zedekiah's eyes, bound him in bronze chains, and led him away to Babylon.
8Meanwhile, the Babylonians burned Jerusalem, including the palace, and tore down
the walls of the city. 9Then Nebuzaradan, the captain of the guard, sent to Babylon the rest
of the people who remained in the city as well as those who had defected to him. 10But
Nebuzaradan left a few of the poorest people in Judah, and he assigned them vineyards
and fields to care for.

JEREMIAH REMAINS IN JUDAH

11King Nebuchadnezzar had told Nebuzaradan, the captain of the guard, to find Jeremiah.
12"See that he isn't hurt," he said. "Look after him well, and give him anything he wants."
13So Nebuzaradan, the captain of the guard; Nebushazban, a chief officer; Nergal-
sharezer, the king's adviser; and the other officers of Babylon's king 14sent messengers to
bring Jeremiah out of the prison. They put him under the care of Gedaliah son of Ahikam
and grandson of Shaphan, who took him back to his home. So Jeremiah stayed in Judah
among his own people.
15The LORD had given the following message to Jeremiah while he was still in prison:
16"Say to Ebed-melech the Ethiopian,* 'This is what the LORD of Heaven's Armies, the God
of Israel, says: I will do to this city everything I have threatened. I will send disaster, not
prosperity. You will see its destruction, 17but I will rescue you from those you fear so much.
18Because you trusted Me, I will give you your life as a reward. I will rescue you and keep
you safe. I, the LORD, have spoken!' "

40 The LORD gave a message to Jeremiah after Nebuzaradan, the captain of the guard,
had released him at Ramah. He had found Jeremiah bound in chains among all the
other captives of Jerusalem and Judah who were being sent to exile in Babylon.
2The captain of the guard called for Jeremiah and said, "The LORD your God has brought
this disaster on this land, 3just as He said He would. For these people have sinned against

39:4 Hebrew *the Arabah.* 39:5 Or *Chaldean;* similarly in 39:8. 39:16 Hebrew *the Cushite.*

39:5 Jer 32:4-5; 52:8-9; Lam 4:20
39:6 Jer 24:8-10; 34:18-21; 52:10
39:7 2 Kgs 25:7; Jer 52:11; Ezek 12:13
39:8 2 Kgs 25:9-10; Neh 1:3
39:9 2 Kgs 25:11, 20; Jer 52:12-16, 26
39:10 2 Kgs 25:12
39:11 Job 5:15-16; Jer 1:8; 15:20-21
39:12 1 Pet 3:13
39:14 2 Kgs 22:12, 14; Jer 26:24; 40:1-6
39:16 Jer 21:10; Zech 1:6
39:17 Pss 41:1-2; 50:14-15
39:18 Ps 34:22; Jer 17:7-8; Rom 10:11
40:1 Eph 6:20
40:2 Deut 29:24-28; Jer 22:8-9; 50:7
40:3 Dan 9:11

39:5-7 Because Zedekiah did not submit as the Lord had instructed, he suffered a tragic fate (39:6-7)—witnessing the execution of his sons and his noblemen before being blinded and led away to Babylon in chains. No doubt Zedekiah would have even preferred death over his sufferings.

39:10 A reversal of fortunes took place in Judah: the poor, who had nothing, inherited the wealth of those who were forced to leave behind their many possessions. It is possible that the Babylonians used this tactic to stir up envy among those who were captured and exiled.

39:11 At the hands of his own people, Jeremiah was imprisoned, beaten, and thrust into near-death experiences (37:15), but in the hands of the enemy he was treated graciously. King Nebuchadnezzar himself ordered that Jeremiah be treated kindly and returned to his own homeland (see note at 40:1).

▸ ADOPTION
39:16-17 Who belongs to God's family? It is a common misconception to believe that in the Old Testament only Israelites belonged to the family of God. Ebed-melech, an Ethiopian, trusted in God's message, and the Lord delivered him from his enemies. The ultimate standard for belonging to God has never been determined by one's physical relationship to Abraham, but by one's spiritual relationship to God (Romans 4:9-25; Galatians 3:7-9). Are there people you know of different races or cultures with whom you fear sharing the gospel? Know that God will call people from all over the world to His side (Revelation 14:6), so we can tell the gospel to everyone without fear. (***See Adoption****> With Christ> Heirs of God> Inheritance shared by Jews and Gentiles alike,* TopicGuide page A36.)

40:1 Jeremiah was transferred in chains to Ramah from Jerusalem, where he had been imprisoned in the courtyard of the guard (38:28). Ramah was located just a few miles north of Jerusalem and appears to have been a clearinghouse for the Babylonians to export the people of Judah to Babylon. Since King Nebuchadnezzar had not intended for Jeremiah to be treated as a prisoner of war (39:11-14), Nebuzaradan, the commander, stepped in to ensure Jeremiah was treated fairly.

▸ GOD
40:2 Truth from an unexpected source. All truth is God's truth—God can speak to us anywhere through anyone. Nebuzaradan, the commander of the imperial

40:4 the LORD and disobeyed Him. That is why it happened. 4But I am going to take off your
Gen 20:15 chains and let you go. If you want to come with me to Babylon, you are welcome. I will see
Jer 39:11, 12 that you are well cared for. But if you don't want to come, you may stay here. The whole
40:5 land is before you—go wherever you like. 5If you decide to stay, then return to Gedaliah son
2 Kgs 25:23 of Ahikam and grandson of Shaphan. He has been appointed governor of Judah by the king
of Babylon. Stay there with the people he rules. But it's up to you; go wherever you like."
Then Nebuzaradan, the captain of the guard, gave Jeremiah some food and money and
40:6 let him go. 6So Jeremiah returned to Gedaliah son of Ahikam at Mizpah, and he lived in Ju-
Jer 39:14 dah with the few who were still left in the land.

GEDALIAH GOVERNS IN JUDAH

40:7 7The leaders of the Judean guerrilla bands in the countryside heard that the king of Bab-
2 Kgs 25:23-24 ylon had appointed Gedaliah son of Ahikam as governor over the poor people who were
Jer 39:10; 52:16 left behind in Judah—the men, women, and children who hadn't been exiled to Babylon.
40:8 8So they went to see Gedaliah at Mizpah. These included: Ishmael son of Nethaniah, Joha-
Jer 41:1 nan and Jonathan sons of Kareah, Seraiah son of Tanhumeth, the sons of Ephai the Ne-
tophathite, Jezaniah son of the Maacathite, and all their men.
40:9 2 Kgs 25:24 9Gedaliah vowed to them that the Babylonians* meant them no harm. "Don't be afraid
Jer 27:11 to serve them. Live in the land and serve the king of Babylon, and all will go well for you,"
40:10 he promised. 10"As for me, I will stay at Mizpah to represent you before the Babylonians
Jer 35:19; 39:10 who come to meet with us. Settle in the towns you have taken, and live off the land. Har-
vest the grapes and summer fruits and olives, and store them away."
40:11 11When the Judeans in Moab, Ammon, Edom, and the other nearby countries heard
1 Sam 11:1 that the king of Babylon had left a few people in Judah and that Gedaliah was the gover-
Isa 11:14; 16:4-5 nor, 12they began to return to Judah from the places to which they had fled. They stopped
40:12 Jer 43:5 at Mizpah to meet with Gedaliah and then went into the Judean countryside to gather a
great harvest of grapes and other crops.

A PLOT AGAINST GEDALIAH

40:13 13Soon after this, Johanan son of Kareah and the other guerrilla leaders came to Gedaliah
Jer 25:21; 41:10 at Mizpah. 14They said to him, "Did you know that Baalis, king of Ammon, has sent Ishma-
el son of Nethaniah to assassinate you?" But Gedaliah refused to believe them.
40:15 15Later Johanan had a private conference with Gedaliah and volunteered to kill Ishmael
1 Sam 26:8 2 Sam 21:17 secretly. "Why should we let him come and murder you?" Johanan asked. "What will hap-
Jer 42:1-2 pen then to the Judeans who have returned? Why should the few of us who are still left be
scattered and lost?"

40:9 Or *Chaldeans;* also in 40:10.

Babylonian guard, said that God had sent disaster upon Jerusalem because of their sin and disobedience to God; we should sit back and marvel at the testimony of this outsider who knew God's will better than most in Jerusalem. It is impossible for us to know what motivated this commander to speak (Matthew 27:54; Mark 15:39; Luke 23:47), but one thing is clear: We should not be quick to dismiss the words of others simply because we believe that we know more than they do—perhaps they know much more than we do, even about the Bible! Be prepared for God to speak to us through unlikely sources. Do not dismiss truth simply because of its apparent source. (***See God**> God's Attributes> True> God's truth is everlasting,* TopicGuide page A18.)

40:5 The prophet Jeremiah was given the option to choose where he wanted to live. Remember that Jeremiah was sorely mistreated during the years he ministered among his own people (37:13-16), but here the Babylonians treated him with great care. Jeremiah is not only given food but also was given some money and his freedom (37:21).

40:9 After the Babylonians removed Zedekiah from his position as king of Judah (39:5-7), Nebuchadnezzar appointed Gedaliah as governor over the land in Judah. Gedaliah's primary concern was to restore stability and peace to the land by encouraging submission to the Babylonian rule.

40:11 The news of a newly appointed governor and of a remnant remaining in Judah sent many former residents, who were scattered abroad, pouring back into Judah. The list of those who returned to Judah includes several army officers and their men in the countryside (40:7).

40:13-16 Not all who returned to the land of Judah when Gedaliah was appointed governor intended to gather a great harvest for food (40:12). Ishmael had the ulterior motive of assassinating the governor. Johanan alerted Gedaliah of the plot and even offered to kill Ishmael himself. But the governor refused to believe Johanan's news of a rumored assassination attempt.

16But Gedaliah said to Johanan, "I forbid you to do any such thing, for you are lying
about Ishmael."

40:16 Matt 10:16

THE MURDER OF GEDALIAH

41 But in midautumn,* Ishmael son of Nethaniah and grandson of Elishama, who
was a member of the royal family and had been one of the king's high officials,
went to Mizpah with ten men to meet Gedaliah. While they were eating together, 2Ishmael
and his ten men suddenly jumped up, drew their swords, and killed Gedaliah, whom the
king of Babylon had appointed governor. 3Ishmael also killed all the Judeans and the Bab-
ylonian* soldiers who were with Gedaliah at Mizpah.

4The next day, before anyone had heard about Gedaliah's murder, 5eighty men arrived
from Shechem, Shiloh, and Samaria to worship at the Temple of the LORD. They had
shaved off their beards, torn their clothes, and cut themselves, and had brought along
grain offerings and frankincense. 6Ishmael left Mizpah to meet them, weeping as he went.
When he reached them, he said, "Oh, come and see what has happened to Gedaliah!"

7But as soon as they were all inside the town, Ishmael and his men killed all but ten of
them and threw their bodies into a cistern. 8The other ten had talked Ishmael into letting
them go by promising to bring him their stores of wheat, barley, olive oil, and honey that
they had hidden away. 9The cistern where Ishmael dumped the bodies of the men he
murdered was the large one dug by King Asa when he fortified Mizpah to protect himself
against King Baasha of Israel. Ishmael son of Nethaniah filled it with corpses.

10Then Ishmael made captives of the king's daughters and the other people who had
been left under Gedaliah's care in Mizpah by Nebuzaradan, the captain of the guard.
Taking them with him, he started back toward the land of Ammon.

11But when Johanan son of Kareah and the other guerrilla leaders heard about Ishma-
el's crimes, 12they took all their men and set out to stop him. They caught up with him at
the large pool near Gibeon. 13The people Ishmael had captured shouted for joy when they
saw Johanan and the other guerrilla leaders. 14And all the captives from Mizpah escaped
and began to help Johanan. 15Meanwhile, Ishmael and eight of his men escaped from Jo-
hanan into the land of Ammon.

16Then Johanan son of Kareah and the other guerrilla leaders took all the people they
had rescued in Gibeon—the soldiers, women, children, and court officials* whom Ishmael

41:1 2 Kgs 25:25 Jer 39:14; 40:5-8, 13-14
41:2 2 Sam 3:27; 20:8-10 Pss 41:9; 109:5 John 13:18
41:5 Deut 14:1 Josh 18:1 1 Kgs 16:24 Ps 78:60 Jer 16:6
41:6 Jer 50:4
41:7 Isa 59:7 Ezek 22:27; 33:24, 26
41:9 1 Sam 13:6 1 Kgs 15:17-22 2 Chr 16:1-6 Heb 11:37-38
41:10 Jer 40:11-12; 43:6
41:11 Jer 40:7-8, 13-16
41:12 2 Sam 2:13
41:15 Prov 28:17
41:16 Jer 42:8, 14; 43:4-7
41:17 2 Sam 19:37-38

41:1 Hebrew *in the seventh month,* of the ancient Hebrew lunar calendar. This month occurred within the months of October and November 586 B.C.; also see note on 39:1a. 41:3 Or *Chaldean.* 41:16 Or *eunuchs.*

41:1-2 Ironically, after Johanan warned the governor of a plan to kill him (40:13-16), Gedaliah proceeded to have a meal with Ishmael and his men. The crime committed against the hospitable governor doesn't appear to have been significant, but the guerrilla leaders were concerned about Babylon, who had appointed Gedaliah to his position (41:18).

41:4-9 Ishmael's violent outburst now led him to take the lives of 70 innocent pilgrims, who seemed to have intended to mourn the destruction of Jerusalem. He allowed 10 of the 80 to live because they disclosed the location of hidden food. This provides a glimpse into Ishmael's greedy and wicked heart.

▸ SPIRITUAL WARFARE

41:6 Manipulating your emotions to deceive others. Do you know someone who can turn on the charm? Someone who has the ability to manipulate people with words, a smile, or both? If you are attractive, it's tempting to manipulate others for personal gain. Ishmael deceived the mourners by appearing to become just like them in order to lead them into a deathtrap. This kind of manipulation should be considered a form of lying (Proverbs 12:22). When we practice similar kinds of deceptions, we identify ourselves with Satan, who not only deceived Eve, but also is in the business of deceiving the whole world (1 Timothy 2:14; Revelation 12:9). Be transparent and speak truthfully. (***See Spiritual Warfare****> Originator of Sin> Satan's Character> Deceitful,* TopicGuide page A44.)

41:10 Ishmael moved from killing people to taking hostages. He and his followers decided to take refuge with the king of Ammon, who had originally sent him on his mission of destruction (40:14).

▸ ADOPTION

41:13 What causes you to shout for joy? The Scriptures mention several things that cause people to experience joy: a sensible son (Proverbs 10:1; 15:20; 27:11), an encouraging word (Proverbs 12:25), an opportunity to worship (Psalm 122:1), and righteous leaders (Proverbs 29:2). The greatest reason for joy given in the Scriptures, however, is the Lord's salvation (2 Chronicles 20:27; Psalms 5:11; 9:2-3; 16:9). Just as Johanan rescued the people of God from Ishmael, God delivered us from the grip of Satan and this world. Be overjoyed today with the salvation God has offered to us in Jesus Christ (Hebrews 9:28). (***See Adoption****> With Christ> Supernatural> A life of infinite joy,* TopicGuide page A37.)

had captured after he killed Gedaliah. 17They took them all to the village of Geruth-
kimham near Bethlehem, where they prepared to leave for Egypt. 18They were afraid of
what the Babylonians* would do when they heard that Ishmael had killed Gedaliah, the
governor appointed by the Babylonian king.

WARNING TO STAY IN JUDAH

42 Then all the guerrilla leaders, including Johanan son of Kareah and Jezaniah* son
of Hoshaiah, and all the people, from the least to the greatest, approached 2Jere-
miah the prophet. They said, "Please pray to the LORD your God for us. As you can see, we
are only a tiny remnant compared to what we were before. 3Pray that the LORD your God
will show us what to do and where to go."

4"All right," Jeremiah replied. "I will pray to the LORD your God, as you have asked, and I
will tell you everything He says. I will hide nothing from you."

5Then they said to Jeremiah, "May the LORD your God be a faithful witness against us if
we refuse to obey whatever He tells us to do! 6Whether we like it or not, we will obey the
LORD our God to whom we are sending you with our plea. For if we obey Him, everything
will turn out well for us."

7Ten days later the LORD gave His reply to Jeremiah. 8So he called for Johanan son of
Kareah and the other guerrilla leaders, and for all the people, from the least to the great-
est. 9He said to them, "You sent me to the LORD, the God of Israel, with your request, and
this is His reply: 10'Stay here in this land. If you do, I will build you up and not tear you
down; I will plant you and not uproot you. For I am sorry about all the punishment I have
had to bring upon you. 11Do not fear the king of Babylon anymore,' says the LORD. 'For I
am with you and will save you and rescue you from his power. 12I will be merciful to you
by making him kind, so he will let you stay here in your land.'

13"But if you refuse to obey the LORD your God, and if you say, 'We will not stay here;
14instead, we will go to Egypt where we will be free from war, the call to arms, and hunger,'
15then hear the LORD's message to the remnant of Judah. This is what the LORD of Heaven's
Armies, the God of Israel, says: 'If you are determined to go to Egypt and live there, 16the
very war and famine you fear will catch up to you, and you will die there. 17That is the fate

41:18 Isa 57:11; Luke 12:4-5
42:2 Deut 28:62; Isa 1:9; Acts 8:24
42:3 Ps 86:11; Prov 3:6; Mic 4:2
42:4 Ps 40:10
42:5 Mic 1:2
42:6 Exod 24:7; Deut 5:29; Jer 7:23
42:7 Ps 27:14
42:9 2 Kgs 22:15
42:10 Hos 11:8; Joel 2:13; Jon 3:10; 4:2
42:11 Ps 46:7, 11; Isa 43:5; Rom 8:31
42:12 Ps 106:45-46; Prov 16:7

41:18 Or *Chaldeans.* 42:1 Greek version reads *Azariah;* compare 43:2.

41:17 Ishmael's rampage had left Mizpah abandoned. Johanan and the people prepared to head to Egypt to escape the feared Babylonian reprisal.

42:1-2 Those who remained with Johanan after the ordeal with Ishmael now approached Jeremiah for instructions on what they should do next. The text emphasizes that the entire group was present with Jeremiah and that there were only a few remaining in Judah.

▸ WORSHIP

42:3 The specifics of God's will. Countless Christians worry about "finding" the will of God and staying in it. The Scriptures instruct us that instead of fretting we should seek the Lord in prayer (Philippians 4:6). There is a danger of becoming overly anxious about what we should do next, for it devalues God's promise to work through prayer, the Bible, and His Spirit. Much can be learned from Johanan and his company, because they recognized that their only chance of knowing what to do next would come through prayer. Do you have a big decision to make? Pray confidently for God's wisdom, for He has promised to provide it when you need it (James 1:5). (***See Worship****> NT> Our Role> Mind and Heart> We are to have heaven's wisdom,* TopicGuide page A32.)

42:5 Johanan and the people willingly called on God to hold them responsible to obey His instructions.

42:7-8 The time for uncertainty was now over for Johanan and his group. After 10 days had passed, Jeremiah emerged from private prayer with God to call the entire assembly together in order to hear the instructions from the Lord.

▸ GOD

42:10 God has feelings. God is not eager to punish, so it causes Him intense grief to bring judgment upon His own people (Joel 2:13-14). It is a good thing to be continually reminded that God, in both the Old and the New Testament, is full of compassion and mercy (Jeremiah 42:12), for He longs for His people to obey His word. God is not out to get you. If you are living in sin today, please know that God longs for you to find rest in His forgiving arms. Turn from your sin and go to God while you still can. (***See God****> God's Nature> Personality> Emotion> God is compassionate and loving,* TopicGuide page A14.)

42:13 If these remaining people disobeyed God's word and sought refuge in Egypt, the Lord would ensure that not one of them would survive or escape His wrath. Those who do not have faith or do not obey God will not escape God's wrath (Leviticus 26; Deuteronomy 28; Hebrews 11:6; Acts 17:30).

awaiting every one of you who insists on going to live in Egypt. Yes, you will die from war,
famine, and disease. None of you will escape the disaster I will bring upon you there.’
18 “This is what the LORD of Heaven’s Armies, the God of Israel, says: ‘Just as My anger
and fury have been poured out on the people of Jerusalem, so they will be poured out on
you when you enter Egypt. You will be an object of damnation, horror, cursing, and mock-
ery. And you will never see your homeland again.’
19 “Listen, you remnant of Judah. The LORD has told you: ‘Do not go to Egypt!’ Don’t for-
get this warning I have given you today. 20 For you were not being honest when you sent
me to pray to the LORD your God for you. You said, ‘Just tell us what the LORD our God says,
and we will do it!’ 21 And today I have told you exactly what He said, but you will not obey
the LORD your God any better now than you have in the past. 22 So you can be sure that
you will die from war, famine, and disease in Egypt, where you insist on going.”

JEREMIAH TAKEN TO EGYPT

43 When Jeremiah had finished giving this message from the LORD their God to all
the people, 2 Azariah son of Hoshaiah and Johanan son of Kareah and all the
other proud men said to Jeremiah, “You lie! The LORD our God hasn’t forbidden us to go to
Egypt! 3 Baruch son of Neriah has convinced you to say this, because he wants us to stay
here and be killed by the Babylonians* or be carried off into exile.”
4 So Johanan and the other guerrilla leaders and all the people refused to obey the
LORD’s command to stay in Judah. 5 Johanan and the other leaders took with them all the
people who had returned from the nearby countries to which they had fled. 6 In the crowd
were men, women, and children, the king’s daughters, and all those whom Nebuzaradan,
the captain of the guard, had left with Gedaliah. The prophet Jeremiah and Baruch were
also included. 7 The people refused to obey the voice of the LORD and went to Egypt, going
as far as the city of Tahpanhes.
8 Then at Tahpanhes, the LORD gave another message to Jeremiah. He said, 9 “While the
people of Judah are watching, take some large rocks and bury them under the pavement
stones at the entrance of Pharaoh’s palace here in Tahpanhes. 10 Then say to the people of
Judah, ‘This is what the LORD of Heaven’s Armies, the God of Israel, says: I will certainly
bring My servant Nebuchadnezzar,* king of Babylon, here to Egypt. I will set his throne
over these stones that I have hidden. He will spread his royal canopy over them. 11 And
when he comes, he will destroy the land of Egypt. He will bring death to those destined for
death, captivity to those destined for captivity, and war to those destined for war. 12 He will

42:18 2 Chr 36:16-19; Jer 29:18-19; 39:1-9
42:19 Deut 17:16; Ezek 2:5
42:20 Ezek 14:3
42:21 Deut 11:26; Ezek 2:7
42:22 Jer 43:11; Hos 9:6
43:2 2 Chr 36:13; Jer 5:12-13; 38:4; 42:5
43:3 Jer 36:4, 10, 32
43:4 Jer 42:5-6, 10-12
43:5 Jer 40:11-12
43:6 Jer 40:7
43:8 Jer 44:1; 46:14; Ezek 30:18
43:10 Jer 25:8-9, 11; 27:6; 46:13
43:11 Isa 19:1-25; Ezek 29:19-20
43:12 Jer 46:25; Ezek 30:13

43:3 Or *Chaldeans.* 43:10 Hebrew *Nebuchadrezzar,* a variant spelling of Nebuchadnezzar.

▸ BIBLE

43:2-3 Changing the subject. One way unbelievers will attempt to deflect a conversation away from the gospel is to attack the Bible. The text describes Johanan and his men as proud because they refused to believe the words of Jeremiah, instead blaming Baruch, Jeremiah’s secretary, with inventing the message from God. Sinners will seek to discredit the Word by claiming it to be full of errors. Be aware of this sinful tendency when sharing the gospel with unbelievers. Patiently show them the strengths of the Bible, including its perfections and remarkable accuracy. Challenge them to find a single error in its pages. Then rely on God’s Word to meet their every objection. (***See Bible****> Uniqueness> Flawless> Scripture is sure and convincing,* TopicGuide page A10.)

43:4 Johanan and his company had appeared extremely eager to obey the Lord whether He instructed them to stay in Judah or permitted them to flee to Egypt (42:1-5). But when the Lord revealed His will for them to stay in Judah, the entire party reacted against God’s Word and chose instead to go to Egypt.

▸ HOLINESS

43:6 Influence of a leader. It’s hard to know how many people you influence in a given week, but it’s probably more than you think. Our influence has the power to draw people closer to or farther away from God. Just meditate on the power of influence the kings in Judah had over their people in the books of 1 and 2 Kings. King Josiah brought great reform among the people of God (2 Kings 23:1-28), but King Manasseh was accused of leading the people to commit sin against God (2 Kings 21:16). Strive to be the kind of person that leads people to God, not away from Him. (***See Holiness****> Law and Grace> Law> Leaders and followers,* TopicGuide page A41.)

43:6-8 In terms of geography, Tahpanhes would have been the first significant town the traveling company came to on their way from Judah to Egypt. Jeremiah now found himself in Egypt in the midst of the traveling company who had disobeyed the Word of the Lord. The Bible does not clearly state it, but it appears that Johanan and his men forced Jeremiah to go into exile in Egypt.

set fire to the temples of Egypt's gods; he will burn the temples and carry the idols away as
plunder. He will pick clean the land of Egypt as a shepherd picks fleas from his cloak. And
he himself will leave unharmed. [13]He will break down the sacred pillars standing in the
temple of the sun* in Egypt, and he will burn down the temples of Egypt's gods.'"

JUDGMENT FOR IDOLATRY

44 This is the message Jeremiah received concerning the Judeans living in northern
Egypt in the cities of Migdol, Tahpanhes, and Memphis,* and in southern Egypt* as
well: [2]"This is what the LORD of Heaven's Armies, the God of Israel, says: You saw the ca-
lamity I brought on Jerusalem and all the towns of Judah. They now lie deserted and in ru-
ins. [3]They provoked My anger with all their wickedness. They burned incense and
worshiped other gods—gods that neither they nor you nor any of your ancestors had ever
even known.

[4]"Again and again I sent My servants, the prophets, to plead with them, 'Don't do these
horrible things that I hate so much.' [5]But My people would not listen or turn back from
their wicked ways. They kept on burning incense to these gods. [6]And so My fury boiled
over and fell like fire on the towns of Judah and into the streets of Jerusalem, and they are
still a desolate ruin today.

[7]"And now the LORD God of Heaven's Armies, the God of Israel, asks you: Why are you
destroying yourselves? For not one of you will survive—not a man, woman, or child
among you who has come here from Judah, not even the babies in your arms. [8]Why pro-
voke My anger by burning incense to the idols you have made here in Egypt? You will
only destroy yourselves and make yourselves an object of cursing and mockery for all the
nations of the earth. [9]Have you forgotten the sins of your ancestors, the sins of the kings
and queens of Judah, and the sins you and your wives committed in Judah and Jerusa-
lem? [10]To this very hour you have shown no remorse or reverence. No one has chosen to
follow My word and the decrees I gave to you and your ancestors before you.

[11]"Therefore, this is what the LORD of Heaven's Armies, the God of Israel, says: I am de-
termined to destroy every one of you! [12]I will take this remnant of Judah—those who were
determined to come here and live in Egypt—and I will consume them. They will fall here in
Egypt, killed by war and famine. All will die, from the least to the greatest. They will be an
object of damnation, horror, cursing, and mockery. [13]I will punish them in Egypt just as I
punished them in Jerusalem, by war, famine, and disease. [14]Of that remnant who fled to
Egypt, hoping someday to return to Judah, there will be no survivors. Even though they
long to return home, only a handful will do so."

44:1 Isa 19:13; Jer 43:7; 46:14
44:2 Isa 6:11; Mic 3:12
44:3 Deut 13:6; 32:17; Jer 32:30-32
44:4 Jer 32:34-35; 35:15; Ezek 8:10; Zech 7:7
44:6 Isa 51:17-20; Jer 7:17, 34
44:7 Jer 9:21; Ezek 33:11
44:8 1 Kgs 9:7-8; 2 Kgs 17:15-17; 2 Chr 7:19-20; Jer 11:12, 17; 1 Cor 10:21-22
44:10 Jer 6:15; 8:12
44:11 Lev 26:17; Jer 21:10; Amos 9:4
44:12 Isa 65:15; Jer 42:15-18, 22
44:14 Isa 10:20; Rom 9:27

43:13 Or *in Heliopolis*. 44:1a Hebrew *Noph*. 44:1b Hebrew *in Pathros*.

43:9 The Lord instructed Jeremiah to perform another symbolic act of judgment against the people of God (13:1, 12; 19:1; 27:2). He told him to bury large stones under the entrance to Pharaoh's palace. God wanted to make sure that this act was not done in private but in the open air so that all could see.

43:11-13 There would be no escaping God's judgment, for the prophesied battle that would occur in Egypt would claim only the lives of those who had been predetermined to be punished by death.

44:1 Jeremiah's ministry as a prophet continued with the people of God even after the fall of Jerusalem (Jeremiah 39), and even though he was now in Egypt. This new prophecy was addressed to the people of Judah who lived in Egypt, namely those who accompanied Johanan (Jeremiah 42).

44:2-6 In preparation for the charges the Lord would bring against the exiled people of Judah in Egypt, God rehearsed the fate of the inhabitants of Judah for the idolatrous worship and detestable practices they performed to provoke His anger (19:4).

44:7-8 Now the Lord turned His attention toward exposing the sinful practices of God's people living in Egypt. Though these people had exchanged their place of residency from Judah to Egypt, they had not reformed from their practice of idolatrous worship (44:2-6).

44:14 Even though God prophesied to bring His fury against the people of Judah in Egypt, He continued to extend the promise of restoration (Jeremiah 31:29-35). God was intent on fulfilling His promise for a new covenant and here alluded to an exodus from Egypt for a handful of people.

15 Then all the women present and all the men who knew that their wives had burned incense to idols—a great crowd of all the Judeans living in northern Egypt and southern Egypt*—answered Jeremiah, 16 "We will not listen to your messages from the LORD! 17 We will do whatever we want. We will burn incense and pour out liquid offerings to the Queen of Heaven just as much as we like—just as we, and our ancestors, and our kings and officials have always done in the towns of Judah and in the streets of Jerusalem. For in those days we had plenty to eat, and we were well off and had no troubles! 18 But ever since we quit burning incense to the Queen of Heaven and stopped worshiping her with liquid offerings, we have been in great trouble and have been dying from war and famine."

19 "Besides," the women added, "do you suppose that we were burning incense and pouring out liquid offerings to the Queen of Heaven, and making cakes marked with her image, without our husbands knowing it and helping us? Of course not!"

20 Then Jeremiah said to all of them, men and women alike, who had given him that answer, 21 "Do you think the LORD did not know that you and your ancestors, your kings and officials, and all the people were burning incense to idols in the towns of Judah and in the streets of Jerusalem? 22 It was because the LORD could no longer bear all the disgusting things you were doing that He made your land an object of cursing—a desolate ruin without inhabitants—as it is today. 23 All these terrible things happened to you because you have burned incense to idols and sinned against the LORD. You have refused to obey Him and have not followed His instructions, His decrees, and His laws."

24 Then Jeremiah said to them all, including the women, "Listen to this message from the LORD, all you citizens of Judah who live in Egypt. 25 This is what the LORD of Heaven's Armies, the God of Israel, says: 'You and your wives have said, "We will keep our promises to burn incense and pour out liquid offerings to the Queen of Heaven," and you have proved by your actions that you meant it. So go ahead and carry out your promises and vows to her!'

26 "But listen to this message from the LORD, all you Judeans now living in Egypt: 'I have sworn by My great name,' says the LORD, 'that My name will no longer be spoken by any of the Judeans in the land of Egypt. None of you may invoke My name or use this oath: "As surely as the Sovereign LORD lives." 27 For I will watch over you to bring you disaster and not good. Everyone from Judah who is now living in Egypt will suffer war and famine until all of you are dead. 28 Only a small number will escape death and return to Judah from Egypt. Then all those who came to Egypt will find out whose words are true—Mine or theirs!

29 "'And this is the proof I give you,' says the LORD, 'that all I have threatened will happen to you and that I will punish you here.' 30 This is what the LORD says: 'I will turn Pharaoh

44:15 Jer 5:1-5
44:17 Exod 16:3; 2 Kgs 17:16; Jer 7:18; Hos 2:5-9; Phil 3:19
44:18 Num 11:5-6; Mal 3:13-15
44:19 Num 30:6-7
44:21 Jer 11:13; 14:10; Ezek 8:10-11; 16:24; Hos 7:2
44:22 Isa 7:13
44:23 1 Kgs 9:9; Jer 7:13-15; 40:3; Dan 9:11-12
44:25 Ezek 20:39; Jas 1:13-15
44:26 Gen 22:16; Deut 32:40; Ps 50:16-17; Heb 6:13, 18
44:28 Isa 14:27; 46:9-10; Zech 1:5-6
44:29 Isa 40:8; Matt 24:15-16, 32
44:30 2 Kgs 25:4-7; Ezek 29:3

44:15 Hebrew *in Egypt, in Pathros.*

▸ BIBLE

44:15-19 Let's make a deal! Spouses make deals with each other all the time—"I'll let you be overweight if you'll let me be lazy" is a popular one. In this case, these Jewish husbands in Egypt did not prevent their wives from worshiping other gods. They knew when they married them that these outspoken unbelieving women would do exactly as they pleased, so the men didn't even try to stop them from worshiping idols. Today, both spouses have important roles to fulfill to ensure that the family is in line with God's plan (Ephesians 5:22-31; Colossians 3:18-21; 1 Peter 3:1-8). Work toward having a successful marriage by looking out for one another's spiritual well-being. Don't make any deals you are likely to regret. (***See Bible***> *Unity> Creation> Creation and marriage,* TopicGuide page A10.)

44:17-18 There was a disturbing spiritual descent occurring among this exiled community in Egypt. The community went from displaying eagerness to obey the word of the Lord (42:6) to rebelling against the Lord's command (43:4) to now foolishly claiming that their blessings resulted from their worship of the Queen of Heaven, the supreme female Egyptian deity of that time.

▸ GOD

44:18 Counterfeit idols. Idolatry was the core problem of this exiled community—and it's no different now. This group duped themselves into thinking that the "Queen of Heaven" was the source of all their blessings. We regularly fall into the sin of idolatry when we pursue "counterfeit gods"—money, relationships, prestige—which appear to offer bigger and better rewards than the true God. Such false gods tempt us with the lie that they can provide lasting happiness and security. Our true purpose for living is Christ; everything else is just a counterfeit promise that will eventually lead to a dead end (Philippians 1:21; Colossians 3:4). Keep yourself and your family from idols of the heart that so easily take us away from loving and obeying Christ (1 John 5:21). (***See God***> *God's Nature> Alive> God lives; idols don't,* TopicGuide page A14.)

44:25 The Lord sarcastically encouraged the people to fulfill their vows to the Queen of Heaven.

44:30 God's dealings with humanity extended beyond Israel's boundaries. The Lord would use the Babylonians in order to

Hophra, king of Egypt, over to his enemies who want to kill him, just as I turned King Zedekiah of Judah over to King Nebuchadnezzar* of Babylon.'"

A MESSAGE FOR BARUCH

45 The prophet Jeremiah gave a message to Baruch son of Neriah in the fourth year
45:3 of the reign of Jehoiakim son of Josiah,* after Baruch had written down everything
Ps 6:6 Jeremiah had dictated to him. He said, 2"This is what the LORD, the God of Israel, says to you,
2 Cor 4:1, 16 Gal 6:9 Baruch: 3You have said, 'I am overwhelmed with trouble! Haven't I had enough pain al-
45:4 ready? And now the LORD has added more! I am worn out from sighing and can find no rest.'
Jer 18:7-10 4"Baruch, this is what the LORD says: 'I will destroy this nation that I built. I will uproot
45:5 what I planted. 5Are you seeking great things for yourself? Don't do it! I will bring great di-
Isa 66:16 saster upon all these people; but I will give you your life as a reward wherever you go. I,
Matt 6:25, 31-32 Rom 12:16 the LORD, have spoken!'"

MESSAGES FOR THE NATIONS

46:1 **46** The following messages were given to Jeremiah the prophet from the LORD con-
Jer 1:10 Ezek 29-32 cerning foreign nations.

MESSAGES ABOUT EGYPT

2This message concerning Egypt was given in the fourth year of the reign of Jehoiakim
46:2 2 Kgs 23:29 son of Josiah, the king of Judah, on the occasion of the battle of Carchemish* when Pha-
2 Chr 35:20 raoh Neco, king of Egypt, and his army were defeated beside the Euphrates River by King
Nebuchadnezzar* of Babylon.

46:3 3 "Prepare your shields,
Joel 3:9 and advance into battle!
46:4 4 Harness the horses,
Ezek 21:9-11 and mount the stallions.
Take your positions.
Put on your helmets.
Sharpen your spears,
and prepare your armor.
46:5 5 But what do I see?
Isa 42:17 Jer 6:25; 49:29 The Egyptian army flees in terror.
Ezek 39:18

44:30 Hebrew *Nebuchadrezzar,* a variant spelling of Nebuchadnezzar. 45:1 The fourth year of Jehoiakim's reign was 605 B.C. 46:2a This event occurred in 605 B.C., during the fourth year of Jehoiakim's reign (according to the calendar system in which the new year begins in the spring). 46:2b Hebrew *Nebuchadrezzar,* a variant spelling of Nebuchadnezzar; also in 46:13, 26.

defeat Pharaoh Hophra, just as He had dealt with King Zedekiah. God may have been judging Egypt for its role in influencing Judah to revolt against the Lord (37:5)

45:1 The date provided in this chapter ("the fourth year of the reign of Jehoiakim") places these events during the time when Baruch, the secretary of Jeremiah, wrote down all the words on the scroll dictated to him by Jeremiah (36:4).

▸ WORSHIP

45:3 Grief upon grief. Have you ever felt as if everything was working against you? Tragedy or major disappointments have a way of leaving us with a sense of being abandoned by God. Baruch lamented the fact that rather than getting better, his pain and sorrows were multiplying. When we go through difficult times, we must remember that our prayers of lament should include some form of trust in God, for in His time our heavenly Father has promised to turn our mourning into dancing (Psalm 30:11). (***See Worship****> OT> Posture> Dancing> Mourning turned to dancing,* TopicGuide page A28.)

45:5 God reprimanded Baruch and then offered him a word of encouragement. Though God warned him against seeking greatness for himself, He promised Baruch that his life would be spared in the midst of the Babylonian conquest.

46:1 Most of the book of Jeremiah concerns God's judgment against unbelieving Judah, but now the attention turns toward foreign nations. Jeremiah continued the task as God's emissary and fulfilled his role as a prophet against nations and kingdoms (1:10).

46:2 Egypt seems to be the first nation in the line of God's judgment because of the unauthorized alliance that Judah formed with them and their influence regarding Judah's corruption (2 Kings 18:21; Jeremiah 37:7; 44:1-30).

The bravest of its fighting men run
without a backward glance.
They are terrorized at every turn,"
says the LORD.

6 "The swiftest runners cannot flee;
the mightiest warriors cannot escape.
By the Euphrates River to the north,
they stumble and fall.

7 "Who is this, rising like the Nile at floodtime,
overflowing all the land?
8 It is the Egyptian army,
overflowing all the land,
boasting that it will cover the earth like a flood,
destroying cities and their people.
9 Charge, you horses and chariots;
attack, you mighty warriors of Egypt!
Come, all you allies from Ethiopia, Libya, and Lydia*
who are skilled with the shield and bow!
10 For this is the day of the Lord, the LORD of Heaven's Armies,
a day of vengeance on His enemies.
The sword will devour until it is satisfied,
yes, until it is drunk with your blood!
The Lord, the LORD of Heaven's Armies, will receive a sacrifice today
in the north country beside the Euphrates River.

11 "Go up to Gilead to get medicine,
O virgin daughter of Egypt!
But your many treatments
will bring you no healing.
12 The nations have heard of your shame.
The earth is filled with your cries of despair.
Your mightiest warriors will run into each other
and fall down together."

13 Then the LORD gave the prophet Jeremiah this message about King Nebuchadnezzar's
plans to attack Egypt.

14 "Shout it out in Egypt!
Publish it in the cities of Migdol, Memphis,* and Tahpanhes!
Mobilize for battle,
for the sword will devour everyone around you.
15 Why have your warriors fallen?
They cannot stand, for the LORD has knocked them down.
16 They stumble and fall over each other
and say among themselves,
'Come, let's go back to our people,
to the land of our birth.
Let's get away from the sword of the enemy!'

46:6 Isa 30:16; Dan 11:18
46:7 Jer 47:2
46:8 Isa 10:13; 37:24
46:9 Nah 2:4; 3:9
46:10 Isa 31:8; 34:6; Zeph 1:7
46:11 Jer 8:22; 30:13; Ezek 30:21-26; Nah 3:19
46:12 Jer 2:36; Nah 3:8-10
46:13 Isa 19:1; Jer 43:10-11
46:14 Jer 44:1; Nah 2:13
46:15 Pss 18:39; 68:1-2
46:16 Lev 26:36-37; Jer 51:9

46:9 Hebrew *from Cush, Put, and Lud.* 46:14 Hebrew *Noph;* also in 46:19.

46:15 In the battle between the warriors of Egypt and God, only one would remain standing. The word "warriors" may be translated as "mighty ones," and may also serve as a reference to Apis, a sacred bull in the pagan worship of Egypt. The Mighty One of Israel would defeat the mighty ones of Egypt (Genesis 49:24; Isaiah 1:24; 49:26; 60:16; Psalm 132:2, 5).

46:17
1 Kgs 20:10-11
Isa 19:11-16

17 There they will say,
'Pharaoh, the king of Egypt, is a loudmouth
who missed his opportunity!'

46:18
1 Kgs 18:42
Ps 89:12
Jer 48:15

18 "As surely as I live," says the King,
whose name is the LORD of Heaven's Armies,
"one is coming against Egypt
who is as tall as Mount Tabor,
or as Mount Carmel by the sea!

46:19
Isa 20:4
Ezek 30:13

19 Pack up! Get ready to leave for exile,
you citizens of Egypt!
The city of Memphis will be destroyed,
without a single inhabitant.
20 Egypt is as sleek as a beautiful young cow,
but a horsefly from the north is on its way!
21 Egypt's mercenaries have become like fattened calves.
They, too, will turn and run,
for it is a day of great disaster for Egypt,
a time of great punishment.
22 Egypt flees, silent as a serpent gliding away.
The invading army marches in;
they come against her with axes like woodsmen.
23 They will cut down her people like trees," says the LORD,
"for they are more numerous than locusts.
24 Egypt will be humiliated;
she will be handed over to people from the north."

46:25
Isa 20:5-6
Jer 43:12-13
Ezek 30:13-16

46:26
Jer 44:30
Ezek 29:8-14; 32:11

25 The LORD of Heaven's Armies, the God of Israel, says: "I will punish Amon, the god of
Thebes,* and all the other gods of Egypt. I will punish its rulers and Pharaoh, too, and all
who trust in him. 26 I will hand them over to those who want them killed—to King Nebu-
chadnezzar of Babylon and his army. But afterward the land will recover from the ravages
of war. I, the LORD, have spoken!

46:27
Isa 41:13-14
Jer 23:3-4; 30:10-11; 50:19

27 "But do not be afraid, Jacob, My servant;
do not be dismayed, Israel.
For I will bring you home again from distant lands,
and your children will return from their exile.
Israel* will return to a life of peace and quiet,
and no one will terrorize them.

46:28
Ps 46:7
Isa 43:2
Jer 10:24
Amos 9:8-9

28 Do not be afraid, Jacob, My servant,
for I am with you," says the LORD.

46:25 Hebrew *of No.* 46:27 Hebrew *Jacob.* See note on 5:20.

46:20 The horsefly would serve a greater purpose than simply being a nuisance, for it would cause the Egyptians to flee for their lives (46:21). The horsefly most likely referred to Nebuchadnezzar (43:10; 46:26).

46:25 God's judgment would visit not only the political figures and their gods in Egypt, but also anyone who put their trust in them. This may be an allusion to those who had escaped from Judah against the will of God and began to practice idolatry in Egypt (44:15-18).

▸ MINISTRY
46:26 Healing of the nations. God's plan of restoration is not limited to a specific people group, but includes all of creation. In these oracles of judgment upon the foreign nations, God included a message of restoration (Jeremiah 48:47; 49:6, 39). God has never been concerned just about the land of Israel, but He has always exhibited a global perspective in His plan for redemption (Genesis 12:3; Psalm 67:4; Hebrews 11:31; Revelation 14:6). This makes foreign missions a necessary, joyful part of our personal outreach—are you gifted to go and tell the gospel to people around the world, or are you gifted to support missionaries through prayer and finances? Whichever is your gift (perhaps both!), do whatever you can to help the gospel go out to hurting people around the world (Revelation 22:2). (***See Ministry***> *Great Commission> Witness> Locally, regionally, worldwide,* TopicGuide page A56.)

"I will completely destroy the nations to which I have exiled you,
but I will not completely destroy you.
I will discipline you, but with justice;
I cannot let you go unpunished."

A MESSAGE ABOUT PHILISTIA

47 This is the LORD's message to the prophet Jeremiah concerning the Philistines of
Gaza, before it was captured by the Egyptian army. 2This is what the LORD says:

"A flood is coming from the north
to overflow the land.
It will destroy the land and everything in it—
cities and people alike.
People will scream in terror,
and everyone in the land will wail.
3 Hear the clatter of stallions' hooves
and the rumble of wheels as the chariots rush by.
Terrified fathers run madly,
without a backward glance at their helpless children.

4 "The time has come for the Philistines to be destroyed,
along with their allies from Tyre and Sidon.
Yes, the LORD is destroying the remnant of the Philistines,
those colonists from the island of Crete.*
5 Gaza will be humiliated, its head shaved bald;
Ashkelon will lie silent.
You remnant from the Mediterranean coast,*
how long will you lament and mourn?
6 "Now, O sword of the LORD,
when will you be at rest again?
Go back into your sheath;
rest and be still.

7 "But how can it be still
when the LORD has sent it on a mission?
For the city of Ashkelon
and the people living along the sea
must be destroyed."

47:1 Jer 25:17, 20; Amos 1:6; Zeph 2:4
47:2 Isa 14:31
47:3 Jer 8:16
47:4 Gen 10:13-14; Isa 14:31; 23:5; Amos 9:7
47:5 Jer 25:19-20; Amos 1:7-8; Zeph 2:4, 7; Zech 9:5
47:6 Jer 12:12
47:7 Ezek 14:17; Mic 6:9

47:4 Hebrew *from Caphtor.* 47:5 Hebrew *the plain.*

47:1 The oracle against the Philistines opened by describing an imminent attack upon their land by the Egyptians. But the focus of this prophecy centered not on Egypt but on the enemy who would attack from the north (27:6-7).

47:2 Water was often used as a symbol for chaos in the ancient Near East. God utilized the imagery of rising waters to depict the utter chaos the Philistines would soon endure.

47:3 The panic would become so great among the Philistines that they would abandon their parental duties, leaving their children behind as they attempted to save their own lives.

47:6-7 The metaphor of flooding waters that has dominated the oracle thus far now changes to describe the disaster as a sword.

▶ GOD

47:7 God's sword. A murderer is convicted and sits on death row. He waits while appeals come and go until gradually it become clear to him—he's not getting out. Time passes and then the next fact sinks in—he's going to die. Can he escape? No. As surely as the sun rises and sets, one day soon he knows he will die. This is exactly how it is for those who fail to repent of their sins and believe the gospel—they are under a death sentence. Just as surely as the city of Ashkelon was under God's wrath, and just as surely as any criminal, those who fail to cling to Jesus as the way, the truth, and the life will perish without peace with God (John 14:6). Pray that God would send His Holy Spirit to convict those with whom you share the gospel, so they might know safety from God's sword. (***See God****> Salvation> Holy Spirit> Convicts of sin,* TopicGuide page A15.)

A MESSAGE ABOUT MOAB

48:1 Num 32:37-38 Jer 48:22-23 Ezek 25:9-10
48 This message was given concerning Moab. This is what the LORD of Heaven's Armies, the God of Israel, says:

"What sorrow awaits the city of Nebo;
it will soon lie in ruins.
The city of Kiriathaim will be humiliated and captured;
the fortress will be humiliated and broken down.
48:2 Isa 15:4-5; 16:13-14
2 No one will ever brag about Moab again,
for in Heshbon there is a plot to destroy her.
'Come,' they say, 'we will cut her off from being a nation.'
The town of Madmen,* too, will be silenced;
the sword will follow you there.
3 Listen to the cries from Horonaim,
cries of devastation and great destruction.
4 All Moab is destroyed.
Her little ones will cry out.*
48:5 Isa 15:5
5 Her refugees weep bitterly,
climbing the slope to Luhith.
They cry out in terror,
descending the slope to Horonaim.
6 Flee for your lives!
Hide* in the wilderness!
48:7 Num 21:29 Jer 9:23
7 Because you have trusted in your wealth and skill,
you will be taken captive.
Your god Chemosh, with his priests and officials,
will be hauled off to distant lands!

48:8 Josh 13:10, 17, 21
8 "All the towns will be destroyed,
and no one will escape—
either on the plateaus or in the valleys,
for the LORD has spoken.
48:9 Isa 16:2
9 Oh, that Moab had wings
so she could fly away,*
for her towns will be left empty,
with no one living in them.
48:10 1 Kgs 20:42 Jer 47:6-7
10 Cursed are those who refuse to do the LORD's work,
who hold back their swords from shedding blood!

48:2 *Madmen* sounds like the Hebrew word for "silence"; it should not be confused with the English word *madmen.*
48:4 Greek version reads *Her cries are heard as far away as Zoar.* 48:6 Or *Hide like a wild donkey;* or *Hide like a juniper shrub;* or *Be like* [the town of] *Aroer.* The meaning of the Hebrew is uncertain. 48:9 Or *Put salt on Moab, / for she will be laid waste.*

48:1-47 This chapter provides the most extensive oracle concerning the nation of Moab in Scripture (see also Isaiah 15–16; Amos 2:1-3; Ezekiel 25:8-11; Zephaniah 2:8-11). Moab's relationship with Judah varied throughout Bible times. When Babylon conducted raids against Judah, Moab was counted among a group of nations that assisted Babylon (2 Kings 24:1-2). Moab would later provide support in Judah's rebellion against Babylon (Jeremiah 27:1-11).

▸ BIBLE
48:7 Misplaced trust. The people of Moab were destined for destruction because of their misplaced trust in their own abilities and in their national god, Chemosh (Jeremiah 17:5-8). The Bible repeatedly connects idolatry with reliance on wealth and skill, for trust in one's own wealth or ability is a form of idolatry (Matthew 6:24). God demands that our allegiance be placed solely in Him and that we reject anything that would interfere or compete with our loyalty to Him (Deuteronomy 6:4-5). Do you have a Chemosh in your life, drawing away your allegiance to the Lord? Maybe it's a relationship, a job, or a sinful habit. Ask the Lord to forgive you of your misplaced trust and renew your commitment to Him. (***See Bible> Uniqueness> Authoritative> Demands exclusive allegiance,*** **TopicGuide page A10.)**

48:8 The one who would act as God's agent in destroying Moab is not clearly stated, but it appears to refer to King Nebuchadnezzar (27:6).

11 "From his earliest history, Moab has lived in peace,
never going into exile.
He is like wine that has been allowed to settle.
He has not been poured from flask to flask,
and he is now fragrant and smooth.
12 But the time is coming soon," says the LORD,
"when I will send men to pour him from his jar.
They will pour him out,
then shatter the jar!
13 At last Moab will be ashamed of his idol Chemosh,
as the people of Israel were ashamed of their gold calf at Bethel.*
14 "You used to boast, 'We are heroes,
mighty men of war.'
15 But now Moab and his towns will be destroyed.
His most promising youth are doomed to slaughter,"
says the King, whose name is the LORD of Heaven's Armies.
16 "Destruction is coming fast for Moab;
calamity threatens ominously.
17 You friends of Moab,
weep for him and cry!
See how the strong scepter is broken,
how the beautiful staff is shattered!

18 "Come down from your glory
and sit in the dust, you people of Dibon,
for those who destroy Moab will shatter Dibon, too.
They will tear down all your towers.
19 You people of Aroer,
stand beside the road and watch.
Shout to those who flee from Moab,
'What has happened there?'

20 "And the reply comes back,
'Moab lies in ruins, disgraced;
weep and wail!
Tell it by the banks of the Arnon River:
Moab has been destroyed!'
21 Judgment has been poured out on the towns of the plateau—
on Holon and Jahaz* and Mephaath,
22 on Dibon and Nebo and Beth-diblathaim,
23 on Kiriathaim and Beth-gamul and Beth-meon,
24 on Kerioth and Bozrah—
all the towns of Moab, far and near.
25 "The strength of Moab has ended.
His arm has been broken," says the LORD.

48:11 Zeph 1:12; Zech 1:15
48:13 1 Kgs 12:29; Isa 45:16; Hos 10:6
48:14 Ps 33:16-17; Isa 10:13-16
48:15 Jer 46:18; 50:27
48:16 Isa 13:22
48:17 Isa 14:5
48:18 Josh 13:9, 17; Isa 47:1
48:19 Josh 12:2
48:20 Num 21:13; Isa 16:7
48:21 Josh 13:18; Isa 15:4
48:23 Josh 13:19
48:24 Amos 2:2
48:25 Pss 10:15; 75:10; Zech 1:19-21

48:13 Hebrew *ashamed when they trusted in Bethel.* 48:21 Hebrew *Jahzah*, a variant spelling of Jahaz.

48:11 The association of Moab with wine and drunkenness in this chapter reminded the audience that the Moabites began when a wine-filled Lot was seduced by his daughters (Genesis 19:30-38).

48:17-20 An imaginary conversation happens at the crossroads between Moab and her neighbors as she reports her losses. In the time of the judges, King Eglon of Moab ruled Israel (Judges 3), but due to his obesity, he was easily killed by a Hebrew assassin named Ehud.

48:25 Because the "arm" in the ancient world was a symbol for strength, it is here a metaphor for expressing annihilation (Psalm 10:15; Ezekiel 30:21-22, 24-25).

48:26 [26] "Let him stagger and fall like a drunkard,
Jer 25:15, 27 for he has rebelled against the LORD.
Moab will wallow in his own vomit,
ridiculed by all.
48:27 [27] Did you not ridicule the people of Israel?
Lam 2:15-17 Were they caught in the company of thieves
Zeph 2:8 that you should despise them as you do?

48:28 [28] "You people of Moab,
Ps 55:6 flee from your towns and live in the caves.
Song 2:14
Isa 2:19 Hide like doves that nest
in the clefts of the rocks.
48:29 [29] We have all heard of the pride of Moab,
Ps 138:6 for his pride is very great.
Isa 16:6
Zeph 2:8 We know of his lofty pride,
his arrogance, and his haughty heart.
[30] I know about his insolence,"
says the LORD,
"but his boasts are empty—
as empty as his deeds.
48:31 [31] So now I wail for Moab;
Isa 15:5; 16:7, 11 yes, I will mourn for Moab.
My heart is broken for the men of Kir-hareseth.*

48:32 [32] "You people of Sibmah, rich in vineyards,
Isa 16:8-9 I will weep for you even more than I did for Jazer.
Your spreading vines once reached as far as the Dead Sea,*
but the destroyer has stripped you bare!
He has harvested your grapes and summer fruits.
48:33 [33] Joy and gladness are gone from fruitful Moab.
Isa 16:10 The presses yield no wine.
No one treads the grapes with shouts of joy.
There is shouting, yes, but not of joy.

[34] "Instead, their awful cries of terror can be heard from Heshbon clear across to Elealeh
48:34 Gen 13:10 and Jahaz; from Zoar all the way to Horonaim and Eglath-shelishiyah. Even the waters of
Isa 15:4-6 Nimrim are dried up now.
48:35 [35] "I will put an end to Moab," says the LORD, "for the people offer sacrifices at the pagan
Isa 15:2 shrines and burn incense to their false gods. [36] My heart moans like a flute for Moab and
48:36 Kir-hareseth, for all their wealth has disappeared. [37] The people shave their heads and
Isa 16:11 beards in mourning. They slash their hands and put on clothes made of burlap. [38] There is
48:37 Isa 15:2-3 crying and sorrow in every Moabite home and on every street. For I have smashed Moab
48:38 like an old, unwanted jar. [39] How it is shattered! Hear the wailing! See the shame of Moab!
Jer 25:34 It has become an object of ridicule, an example of ruin to all its neighbors."

48:31 Hebrew *Kir-heres,* a variant spelling of Kir-hareseth; also in 48:36. 48:32 Hebrew *the sea of Jazer.*

48:26 A previous description in Jeremiah portrayed the Lord as extending a cup of wrath to Judah and foreign nations, including Moab (25:21). No military army would get credit for Moab's destruction; rather, the Lord Himself would execute divine judgment.

48:31 Kir-hareseth is modern Kerak, located east of the Dead Sea. See also Isaiah 16:7, 11.

48:39 Moab's destruction would be thorough—the people's national pride, their warrior spirit, and their cities would be destroyed. Even those who fled would find themselves running into a raging fire (48:45).

40This is what the LORD says:

"Look! The enemy swoops down like an eagle,
spreading his wings over Moab.
41 Its cities will fall,
and its strongholds will be seized.
Even the mightiest warriors will be in anguish
like a woman in labor.
42 Moab will no longer be a nation,
for it has boasted against the LORD.

43 "Terror and traps and snares will be your lot,
O Moab," says the LORD.
44 "Those who flee in terror will fall into a trap,
and those who escape the trap will step into a snare.
I will see to it that you do not get away,
for the time of your judgment has come,"
says the LORD.
45 "The people flee as far as Heshbon
but are unable to go on.
For a fire comes from Heshbon,
King Sihon's ancient home,
to devour the entire land
with all its rebellious people.

46 "O Moab, they weep for you!
The people of the god Chemosh are destroyed!
Your sons and your daughters
have been taken away as captives.
47 But I will restore the fortunes of Moab
in days to come.
I, the LORD, have spoken!"

This is the end of Jeremiah's prophecy concerning Moab.

48:40 Jer 49:22
48:41 Jer 30:6; 49:22
48:42 Ps 83:4; Jer 48:26
48:43 Isa 24:17; Lam 3:47
48:44 1 Kgs 19:17; Amos 5:19
48:45 Num 21:28-29; Ps 135:10-11
48:46 Num 21:29
48:47 Jer 12:17; 49:39

A MESSAGE ABOUT AMMON

49 This message was given concerning the Ammonites. This is what the LORD says:

"Are there no descendants of Israel
to inherit the land of Gad?

49:1 Ezek 25:2; Amos 1:13

48:46 The destruction of the worshipers of Chemosh meant the end of that false god's negative influence on the region. The children, who might have carried on the pagan worship, would be taken away (as was Daniel; see Daniel 1–2).

49:1-6 Ammon was one of the fiercest enemies of Judah. The Ammonites assisted the Babylonians in raids against Judah (2 Kings 24:2). Though it appeared that by conquering Gad the Ammonites had the upper hand against God's people, God prophesied judgment against them for their arrogance and idolatry. At the conclusion of this oracle of destruction, God promised to restore the Ammonites' land (see note at Jeremiah 46:26).

▸ WORSHIP
49:1-2 When other religions appear to gain ground. It may seem as though other religions are becoming more popular than Christianity. It has undoubtedly been true that throughout history, Christianity has steadily grown into a world religion, but Islam in particular is growing more quickly. This might be an unsettling reality for many Christians in light of God's promise to have a prevailing church (Isaiah 54:17; Matthew 16:18; Hebrews 12:28; Revelation 11:15). When the Ammonites gained control over Israel's territory of Gad, the people of Judah must have experienced a similar struggle. In the ancient world, military victories were considered a sign that the victorious army's god was greater than the god of the defeated army (Jeremiah 48:46). This oracle of judgment helps us to see that even though God's people have experienced setbacks in the past, God is not concerned. This, too, is a part of His plan. Pray that God's promise of a victorious church would become a reality in your part of the world today. (*See **Worship**> NT> Church Government> Jesus, the "cornerstone" of the church,* TopicGuide page A30.)

Why are you, who worship Molech,*
living in its towns?
49:2 2 Sam 11:1 Isa 14:2 Ezek 21:28
2 In the days to come," says the LORD,
"I will sound the battle cry against your city of Rabbah.
It will become a desolate heap of ruins,
and the neighboring towns will be burned.
Then Israel will take back the land
you took from her," says the LORD.

49:3 Josh 7:2-5; 8:1-29 Jer 48:2, 7
3 "Cry out, O Heshbon,
for the town of Ai is destroyed.
Weep, O people of Rabbah!
Put on your clothes of mourning.
Weep and wail, hiding in the hedges,
for your god Molech, with his priests and officials,
will be hauled off to distant lands.
49:4 Ps 62:10-11 Ezek 28:4-5 1 Tim 6:17
4 You are proud of your fertile valleys,
but they will soon be ruined.
You trusted in your wealth,
you rebellious daughter,
and thought no one could ever harm you.
49:5 Jer 16:16 Lam 4:15
5 But look! I will bring terror upon you,"
says the Lord, the LORD of Heaven's Armies.
"Your neighbors will chase you from your land,
and no one will help your exiles as they flee.
49:6 Jer 48:47; 49:39
6 But I will restore the fortunes of the Ammonites
in days to come.
I, the LORD, have spoken."

MESSAGES ABOUT EDOM

49:7 Gen 36:11, 15 Isa 34:5-6 Amos 1:12
7 This message was given concerning Edom. This is what the LORD of Heaven's Armies
says:

"Is there no wisdom in Teman?
Is no one left to give wise counsel?
49:8 Isa 21:13 Jer 25:23
8 Turn and flee!
Hide in deep caves, you people of Dedan!
For when I bring disaster on Edom,*
I will punish you, too!
49:9 Obad 1:5
9 Those who harvest grapes
always leave a few for the poor.
If thieves came at night,
they would not take everything.
10 But I will strip bare the land of Edom,
and there will be no place left to hide.

49:1 Hebrew *Malcam,* a variant spelling of Molech; also in 49:3. 49:8 Hebrew *Esau;* also in 49:10.

49:7-22 The rivalry between Judah and Edom had its roots in the conflict between Jacob and Esau (Genesis 25:25-26). Jacob was the father of the 12 tribes of Israel, and Esau was the forefather of the Edomites. These people groups experienced many struggles throughout their histories (Numbers 20:14-21; Judges 11:17-18; 2 Kings 14:7-10; Obadiah 1:1-21). God declared through His oracle of judgment that He would strip Edom bare and make the nation drink His cup of wrath. Because of their pride, the Edomites thought themselves to be exalted like an eagle. God would put them down by bringing an eagle, or an invading army, to swoop down upon them.

Its children, its brothers, and its neighbors
will all be destroyed,
and Edom itself will be no more.
11 But I will protect the orphans who remain among you.
Your widows, too, can depend on Me for help."

49:11 Ps 68:5 Zech 7:10

12And this is what the LORD says: "If the innocent must suffer, how much more must you!
You will not go unpunished! You must drink this cup of judgment! 13For I have sworn by
My own name," says the LORD, "that Bozrah will become an object of horror and a heap of
ruins; it will be mocked and cursed. All its towns and villages will be desolate forever."

49:12 Jer 25:15, 28-29 1 Pet 4:17

49:13 Isa 34:6, 9-15

14 I have heard a message from the LORD
that an ambassador was sent to the nations to say,
"Form a coalition against Edom,
and prepare for battle!"

49:14 Jer 50:14

15 The LORD says to Edom,
"I will cut you down to size among the nations.
You will be despised by all.
16 You have been deceived
by the fear you inspire in others
and by your own pride.
You live in a rock fortress
and control the mountain heights.
But even if you make your nest among the peaks with the eagles,
I will bring you crashing down,"
says the LORD.

49:15 Obad 1:1-4 Luke 1:51

49:16 Isa 14:13-15 Amos 9:2

17 "Edom will be an object of horror.
All who pass by will be appalled
and will gasp at the destruction they see there.
18 It will be like the destruction of Sodom and Gomorrah
and their neighboring towns," says the LORD.
"No one will live there;
no one will inhabit it.
19 I will come like a lion from the thickets of the Jordan,
leaping on the sheep in the pasture.
I will chase Edom from its land,
and I will appoint the leader of My choice.
For who is like Me, and who can challenge Me?
What ruler can oppose My will?"

49:17 Jer 51:37 Ezek 35:7

49:18 Gen 19:24-25 Deut 29:23 Amos 4:11

49:19 Isa 46:9 Jer 50:44

20 Listen to the LORD's plans against Edom
and the people of Teman.

49:20 Isa 14:24, 27 Jer 50:45 Mal 1:4-5

49:11 The weakest and smallest of the Edomites were instructed to hide in the narrow recesses of the deepest caves in the red mountains of Edom.

49:16 The modern site of the ancient rock fortress of Edom is called Petra. It is found in Jordan about 60 miles north of the Gulf of Aqaba.

▸PURPOSE

49:20 Submitting against their will. God is intent on both blessing and judging the world. The Lord's blessing is extended to those who humbly rely on Jesus Christ for their salvation, but His judgment is reserved for those who deny His Lordship in their lives (John 3:16-21). God's plan is definite and unchangeable, but its recipients may ignore or deny its truthfulness. Refusing to believe these promises of blessing and judgment will one day catch up with unbelievers, for God has guaranteed that one day all will recognize Jesus as Lord, whether in judgment or salvation (Romans 14:11). Take the time to pray that the Holy Spirit will change the hearts of those who are without Christ. (***See Purpose****> God's Means> Human Choice> Bringing our wills in subjection to God's will,* TopicGuide page A52.)

Even the little children will be dragged off like sheep,
and their homes will be destroyed.

49:21 Jer 50:46; Ezek 26:15, 18

21 The earth will shake with the noise of Edom's fall,
and its cry of despair will be heard all the way to the Red Sea.*

49:22 Isa 13:8; Jer 48:40-41

22 Look! The enemy swoops down like an eagle,
spreading his wings over Bozrah.
Even the mightiest warriors will be in anguish
like a woman in labor.

A MESSAGE ABOUT DAMASCUS

49:23 Exod 15:15; Isa 10:9; 57:20; Jer 39:5; Amos 6:2; Nah 2:10

23 This message was given concerning Damascus. This is what the LORD says:

"The towns of Hamath and Arpad are struck with fear,
for they have heard the news of their destruction.
Their hearts are troubled
like a wild sea in a raging storm.
24 Damascus has become feeble,
and all her people turn to flee.
Fear, anguish, and pain have gripped her
as they grip a woman in labor.

49:25 Jer 51:41

25 That famous city, a city of joy,
will be forsaken!

49:26 Jer 50:30

26 Her young men will fall in the streets and die.
Her soldiers will all be killed,"
says the LORD of Heaven's Armies.

49:27 1 Kgs 15:18-20; Amos 1:3-5

27 "And I will set fire to the walls of Damascus
that will burn up the palaces of Ben-hadad."

A MESSAGE ABOUT KEDAR AND HAZOR

49:28 Isa 21:16-17

28 This message was given concerning Kedar and the kingdoms of Hazor, which were attacked by King Nebuchadnezzar* of Babylon. This is what the LORD says:

"Advance against Kedar!
Destroy the warriors from the East!

49:29 Jer 46:5

29 Their flocks and tents will be captured,
and their household goods and camels will be taken away.
Everywhere shouts of panic will be heard:
'We are terrorized at every turn!'

49:30 Jer 25:8-9, 24; 27:6

30 Run for your lives," says the LORD.
"Hide yourselves in deep caves, you people of Hazor,
for King Nebuchadnezzar of Babylon has plotted against you
and is preparing to destroy you.

49:31 Judg 18:7; Isa 47:8

31 "Go up and attack that complacent nation,"
says the LORD.
"Its people live alone in the desert
without walls or gates.

49:21 Hebrew *sea of reeds.* 49:28 Hebrew *Nebuchadrezzar,* a variant spelling of Nebuchadnezzar; also in 49:30.

49:23-27 Damascus, the capital of Aram, is mentioned alongside the other nations as a recipient of the judgment of God. God does not list the sins of this nation, but rather emphasizes His sovereign control over this foreign country. The terrified response of Damascus was compared to a woman in labor (49:24).

49:28-33 The people of Kedar resided in the Arabian Desert and were known for tending camels, goats, and sheep (Genesis 25:13; Ezekiel 27:21). God directed the Babylonians to bring disaster to this land, though He did not provide the reason for this pronouncement.

32 Their camels and other livestock will all be yours.
I will scatter to the winds these people
who live in remote places.*
I will bring calamity upon them
from every direction," says the LORD.
33 "Hazor will be inhabited by jackals,
and it will be desolate forever.
No one will live there;
no one will inhabit it."

49:32 Jer 9:25-26; 25:23 Ezek 12:14-15

49:33 Isa 13:20-22 Zeph 2:9, 13-15

A MESSAGE ABOUT ELAM

34This message concerning Elam came to the prophet Jeremiah from the LORD at the begin-
ning of the reign of King Zedekiah of Judah. 35This is what the LORD of Heaven's Armies says:

"I will destroy the archers of Elam—
the best of their forces.
36 I will bring enemies from all directions,
and I will scatter the people of Elam to the four winds.
They will be exiled to countries around the world.
37 I Myself will go with Elam's enemies to shatter it.
In My fierce anger, I will bring great disaster
upon the people of Elam," says the LORD.
"Their enemies will chase them with the sword
until I have destroyed them completely.
38 I will set My throne in Elam," says the LORD,
"and I will destroy its king and officials.
39 But I will restore the fortunes of Elam
in days to come.
I, the LORD, have spoken!"

49:34 Gen 10:22 2 Kgs 24:17-18 Isa 11:11 Dan 8:2

49:35 Isa 22:6 Jer 51:56

49:36 Ezek 5:10 Rev 7:1

49:37 Jer 6:19; 30:24

49:39 Jer 48:47

A MESSAGE ABOUT BABYLON

50 The LORD gave Jeremiah the prophet this message concerning Babylon and the
land of the Babylonians.* 2This is what the LORD says:

"Tell the whole world,
and keep nothing back.
Raise a signal flag
to tell everyone that Babylon will fall!
Her images and idols* will be shattered.
Her gods Bel and Marduk will be utterly disgraced.

50:1 Isa 13:1 Rev 14:8

50:2 Isa 46:1 Jer 51:31

49:32 Or *who clip the corners of their hair.* 50:1 Or *Chaldeans;* also in 50:8, 25, 35, 45. 50:2 The Hebrew term (literally *round things*) probably alludes to dung.

49:34-39 The land of Elam, inhabited by a people known for their skill with the bow (49:35), was located to the east of Judah, near the modern Persian Gulf. However, one could not travel directly across the desert to reach it; it was necessary to follow a route that led northeast to the Euphrates and then down to Elam. Like the swirling sands of the nearby desert, the people of Elam would be blown away, yet restored to some degree at a later date.

50:1–51:64 Even though Babylon had been God's instrument of judgment against Judah and many other nations (27:6-7), God would now call them to account for their sins and bring His justice to bear upon their land and people. Just as God had raised Nebuchadnezzar and his army to defeat Judah, He would also raise an even stronger army to defeat the Babylonians. The judgment of Babylon in this oracle is linked together with the promised restoration of the nation of Israel (Jeremiah 30–33).

▸ PURPOSE

50:1 God's sovereignty and human responsibility. How could God use the Babylonians as agents of destruction (Jeremiah 20:5; 32:3, 24, 36) but then hold them accountable for their devastation against God's people? This mode of operation is confirmed in other places in Scripture, such as with Joseph's brothers, the Assyrians, and Judas (Genesis 50:20; Proverbs 16:4-5; Isaiah 10:5-15; Luke 22:22). God sovereignly controlled the

50:3 Zeph 1:3

[3] For a nation will attack her from the north
and bring such destruction that no one will live there again.
Everything will be gone;
both people and animals will flee.

HOPE FOR ISRAEL AND JUDAH

50:4 Ezra 3:12-13 Isa 11:12-13 Jer 31:9 Hos 1:11

[4] "In those coming days,"
says the LORD,
"the people of Israel will return home
together with the people of Judah.
They will come weeping
and seeking the LORD their God.

50:5 Isa 55:3 Jer 6:16; 32:40

[5] They will ask the way to Jerusalem*
and will start back home again.
They will bind themselves to the LORD
with an eternal covenant that will never be forgotten.

50:6 Isa 53:6 Jer 13:16 Ezek 34:15-16 Matt 9:36

[6] "My people have been lost sheep.
Their shepherds have led them astray
and turned them loose in the mountains.
They have lost their way
and can't remember how to get back to the sheepfold.

50:7 Jer 17:13

[7] All who found them devoured them.
Their enemies said,
'We did nothing wrong in attacking them,
for they sinned against the LORD,
their true place of rest,
and the hope of their ancestors.'

50:8 Jer 51:6 Rev 18:4

[8] "But now, flee from Babylon!
Leave the land of the Babylonians.
Like male goats at the head of the flock,
lead My people home again.
[9] For I am raising up an army
of great nations from the north.
They will join forces to attack Babylon,
and she will be captured.
The enemies' arrows will go straight to the mark;
they will not miss!

50:10 Jer 51:24, 35

[10] Babylonia* will be looted
until the attackers are glutted with loot.
I, the LORD, have spoken!

50:5 Hebrew *Zion;* also in 50:28. 50:10 Or *Chaldea.*

actions of each of these parties, including Babylon, by foreordaining what they would do. But because humanity is created in the image of God (Genesis 1:27-28), we are responsible to live according to God's standard of holiness (Leviticus 19:2; Matthew 5:48; 1 Peter 1:15-16). Because humanity is created free (Psalm 119:113; Joshua 24:15), we freely choose the good and evil that God has foreordained. It is a profound mystery how God is sovereign and humans remain responsible, but they are not contradictory. Worship God for His mysterious ways (1 Corinthians 2:7; Isaiah 55:6-9). (***See Purpose****> God's Means> God's Sovereignty> God decrees all,* TopicGuide page A52.)

50:4-7 After the Lord's initial message of judgment upon Babylon, the prophecy shifted to focus on the restoration of God's people. God promised that after the exile both Judah and Israel would dwell in His everlasting covenant. The people of God would return to the Promised Land and seek the Lord (Jeremiah 30–33).

50:9 Earlier Babylon was depicted as the conquering northern army, but now God would raise up another army from the north in order to bring judgment against Babylon (see note at Jeremiah 1:13-16).

BABYLON'S SURE FALL

11 "You rejoice and are glad,
you who plundered My chosen people.
You frisk about like a calf in a meadow
and neigh like a stallion.
12 But your homeland* will be overwhelmed
with shame and disgrace.
You will become the least of nations—
a wilderness, a dry and desolate land.
13 Because of the LORD's anger,
Babylon will become a deserted wasteland.
All who pass by will be horrified
and will gasp at the destruction they see there.

14 "Yes, prepare to attack Babylon,
all you surrounding nations.
Let your archers shoot at her; spare no arrows.
For she has sinned against the LORD.
15 Shout war cries against her from every side.
Look! She surrenders!
Her walls have fallen.
It is the LORD's vengeance,
so take vengeance on her.
Do to her as she has done to others!
16 Take from Babylon all those who plant crops;
send all the harvesters away.
Because of the sword of the enemy,
everyone will run away and rush back to their own lands.

HOPE FOR GOD'S PEOPLE

17 "The Israelites are like sheep
that have been scattered by lions.
First the king of Assyria ate them up.
Then King Nebuchadnezzar* of Babylon cracked their bones."
18 Therefore, this is what the LORD of Heaven's Armies,
the God of Israel, says:
"Now I will punish the king of Babylon and his land,
just as I punished the king of Assyria.
19 And I will bring Israel home again to its own land,
to feed in the fields of Carmel and Bashan,
and to be satisfied once more
in the hill country of Ephraim and Gilead.
20 In those days," says the LORD,
"no sin will be found in Israel or in Judah,
for I will forgive the remnant I preserve.

50:11 Jer 12:14; 46:20
50:12 Jer 22:6
50:13 Jer 18:16
50:14 Hab 2:8, 17
50:15 Ps 137:8
50:16 Jer 46:16
50:17 2 Kgs 18:9-13; 24:1, 10-12; Jer 4:7
50:18 Isa 10:12; Nah 1:1; 3:7, 18-19
50:19 Jer 31:10
50:20 Jer 31:34; Mic 7:19

50:12 Hebrew *your mother.* 50:17 Hebrew *Nebuchadrezzar,* a variant spelling of Nebuchadnezzar.

▸ GOD

50:20 Total salvation. Sin is everywhere—all around us, inside us, in our words and thoughts and emotions. Can you imagine the day when sin will no longer be present in your life? Probably not. But while our current struggle with sin is only temporary, it is a very real struggle (Romans 7:14-25; Ephesians 6:10-18). We must not fool ourselves into thinking that the fight is over, but we must strive in the power of the Spirit every day to defeat sin's power in our lives. We look forward to a day when this promise of victory for the people of God will be realized in our lives, but until then we must not tire in our war against sin (Romans 6:10-13). Continue your battle by not resisting the sanctifying power of the Holy Spirit (Ephesians 4:30). (***See God****> God's Attributes> Forgiving> God's forgiveness clears one's record,* TopicGuide page A16.)

THE LORD'S JUDGMENT ON BABYLON

50:21 Ezek 23:23
21 “Go up, My warriors, against the land of Merathaim
and against the people of Pekod.
Pursue, kill, and completely destroy* them,
as I have commanded you,” says the LORD.

50:22 Jer 4:19-21
22 “Let the battle cry be heard in the land,
a shout of great destruction.

50:23 Jer 51:20-24
23 Babylon, the mightiest hammer in all the earth,
lies broken and shattered.
Babylon is desolate among the nations!

50:24 Job 9:4; 40:2, 9; Jer 48:43
24 Listen, Babylon, for I have set a trap for you.
You are caught, for you have fought against the LORD.

50:25 Isa 13:4-5
25 The LORD has opened His armory
and brought out weapons to vent His fury.
The terror that falls upon the Babylonians
will be the work of the Sovereign LORD of Heaven's Armies.

50:26 Isa 14:23
26 Yes, come against her from distant lands.
Break open her granaries.
Crush her walls and houses into heaps of rubble.
Destroy her completely, and leave nothing!

50:27 Ps 37:13; Ezek 7:7
27 Destroy even her young bulls—
it will be terrible for them, too!
Slaughter them all!
For Babylon's day of reckoning has come.

50:28 Ps 149:6-9; Isa 48:20; Lam 1:10
28 Listen to the people who have escaped from Babylon,
as they tell in Jerusalem
how the LORD our God has taken vengeance
against those who destroyed His Temple.

50:29 Exod 10:3; Ps 137:8
29 “Send out a call for archers to come to Babylon.
Surround the city so none can escape.
Do to her as she has done to others,
for she has defied the LORD, the Holy One of Israel.

50:30 Jer 18:21
30 Her young men will fall in the streets and die.
Her soldiers will all be killed,”
says the LORD.

50:31 Nah 2:13
31 “See, I am your enemy, you arrogant people,”
says the Lord, the LORD of Heaven's Armies.
“Your day of reckoning has arrived—
the day when I will punish you.

50:32 Isa 10:12-15; Jer 21:14
32 O land of arrogance, you will stumble and fall,
and no one will raise you up.
For I will light a fire in the cities of Babylon
that will burn up everything around them.”

50:33 Isa 14:17; 58:6
33 This is what the LORD of Heaven's Armies says:
“The people of Israel and Judah have been wronged.
Their captors hold them and refuse to let them go.

50:21 The Hebrew term used here refers to the complete consecration of things or people to the LORD, either by destroying them or by giving them as an offering.

50:29-31 Just as Moab and Edom were condemned for their arrogance, Babylon was charged on the same count (48:29; 49:16). Because of their sin, God would repay their injustice with His justice, and they would receive judgment proportionate to the destruction they had executed.

34 But the One who redeems them is strong.
His name is the LORD of Heaven's Armies.
He will defend them
and give them rest again in Israel.
But for the people of Babylon
there will be no rest!

35 "The sword of destruction will strike the Babylonians,"
says the LORD.
"It will strike the people of Babylon—
her officials and wise men, too.
36 The sword will strike her wise counselors,
and they will become fools.
The sword will strike her mightiest warriors,
and panic will seize them.
37 The sword will strike her horses and chariots
and her allies from other lands,
and they will all become like women.
The sword will strike her treasures,
and they all will be plundered.
38 The sword will even strike her water supply,
causing it to dry up.
And why? Because the whole land is filled with idols,
and the people are madly in love with them.

39 "Soon Babylon will be inhabited by desert animals and hyenas.
It will be a home for owls.
Never again will people live there;
it will lie desolate forever.
40 I will destroy it as I* destroyed Sodom and Gomorrah
and their neighboring towns," says the LORD.
"No one will live there;
no one will inhabit it.

41 "Look! A great army is coming from the north.
A great nation and many kings
are rising against you from far-off lands.
42 They are armed with bows and spears.
They are cruel and show no mercy.
As they ride forward on horses,
they sound like a roaring sea.
They are coming in battle formation,
planning to destroy you, Babylon.
43 The king of Babylon has heard reports about the enemy,
and he is weak with fright.
Pangs of anguish have gripped him,
like those of a woman in labor.

50:34 Isa 14:3-7; 43:14 Mic 7:9

50:35 Jer 47:6 Dan 5:1-2, 7-8

50:36 Isa 44:25

50:37 Ps 20:7-8 Jer 25:19-20; 48:41

50:39 Isa 13:20

50:40 Gen 19:24-25 Luke 17:28-30 2 Pet 2:6 Jude 1:7

50:41 Isa 13:2-5

50:42 Isa 13:17-18 Hab 1:8

50:43 Jer 30:6

50:40 Hebrew *as God.*

50:38 The destruction of Babylon extended to a curse on the land itself, as it would no longer yield its most valuable of natural resources—water. This would have reminded the original audience of the first curse upon the land given in Genesis 3:17-19.

50:39-40 Deserted by AD 800 , Babylon lay under the desert sands until the late 1800s, when archaeologists rediscovered the site. The site was open to only limited archeological study until the 1990s, when Iraq attempted to create a tourist industry there. A few buildings and people exist there today (51:63-64).

50:44 Num 16:5 Job 41:10 Isa 46:9

44 "I will come like a lion from the thickets of the Jordan,
leaping on the sheep in the pasture.
I will chase Babylon from its land,
and I will appoint the leader of My choice.
For who is like Me, and who can challenge Me?
What ruler can oppose My will?"

45 Listen to the LORD's plans against Babylon
and the land of the Babylonians.
Even the little children will be dragged off like sheep,
and their homes will be destroyed.

50:46 Jer 10:10 Ezek 26:18

46 The earth will shake with the shout, "Babylon has been taken!"
and its cry of despair will be heard around the world.

51:1 Jer 4:11-12

51

1 This is what the LORD says:
"I will stir up a destroyer against Babylon
and the people of Babylonia.*

51:2 Jer 15:7 Matt 3:12

2 Foreigners will come and winnow her,
blowing her away as chaff.
They will come from every side
to rise against her in her day of trouble.

51:3 Jer 46:4

3 Don't let the archers put on their armor
or draw their bows.
Don't spare even her best soldiers!
Let her army be completely destroyed.*
4 They will fall dead in the land of the Babylonians,*
slashed to death in her streets.

51:5 Isa 54:7-8 Jer 33:24-26

5 For the LORD of Heaven's Armies
has not abandoned Israel and Judah.
He is still their God,
even though their land was filled with sin
against the Holy One of Israel."

51:6 Num 16:26 Rev 18:4

6 Flee from Babylon! Save yourselves!
Don't get trapped in her punishment!
It is the LORD's time for vengeance;
He will repay her in full.

51:7 Jer 25:15 Rev 14:8-10; 18:3

7 Babylon has been a gold cup in the LORD's hands,
a cup that made the whole earth drunk.
The nations drank Babylon's wine,
and it drove them all mad.

51:1 Hebrew *of Leb-kamai,* a code name for Babylonia. 51:3 The Hebrew term used here refers to the complete consecration of things or people to the LORD, either by destroying them or by giving them as an offering. 51:4 Or *Chaldeans;* also in 51:54.

50:44 Israel sits on a land bridge between Asia, Europe and Africa. It shares the plants and animals of all three continents. Lions roamed Israel until the 1200s, when they were hunted to extinction during the Crusades.

▶ **GOD**

51:5 Not forsaken. God has committed to never abandon His people, even if His people are not living the way they know they should (1 Samuel 12:22; 1 Kings 6:13; Psalm 94:14; Isaiah 44:21). God judged Israel, but He did not entirely forsake them (Isaiah 54:7). We can expect God's discipline in our lives when we disobey Him, and we can also expect God's loyalty to supersede our effort to live in a God-honoring way. God's loyalty emboldens us to risk, to rest, and to explore every aspect of the world and the Word, knowing that no matter where we go, we won't change God's basic commitment to us. Stop worrying—just walk by faith and, even in the dark valleys, know that God will not forsake you. (***See God****> God's Attributes> Faithful> His faithfulness endures,* TopicGuide page A16.)

51:7-8 Jeremiah used sarcasm, asking if what befell Babylon could be healed with medicine. The city's medical technology was useless against this ailment of the soul.

8 But suddenly Babylon, too, has fallen.
Weep for her.
Give her medicine.
Perhaps she can yet be healed.
9 We would have helped her if we could,
but nothing can save her now. **51:9** Jer 46:16
Let her go; abandon her.
Return now to your own land.
For her punishment reaches to the heavens;
it is so great it cannot be measured.
10 The LORD has vindicated us. **51:10** Isa 40:2
Come, let us announce in Jerusalem*
everything the LORD our God has done. Mic 7:9

11 Sharpen the arrows! **51:11** Joel 3:9-10
Lift up the shields!*
For the LORD has inspired the kings of the Medes
to march against Babylon and destroy her.
This is His vengeance against those
who desecrated His Temple.
12 Raise the battle flag against Babylon! **51:12** Jer 4:28
Reinforce the guard and station the watchmen.
Prepare an ambush,
for the LORD will fulfill all His plans against Babylon.
13 You are a city by a great river, **51:13** Hab 2:9-11
a great center of commerce,
but your end has come.
The thread of your life is cut.
14 The LORD of Heaven's Armies has taken this vow **51:14** Nah 3:15
and has sworn to it by His own name:
"Your cities will be filled with enemies,
like fields swarming with locusts,
and they will shout in triumph over you."

A HYMN OF PRAISE TO THE LORD

15 The LORD made the earth by His power,
and He preserves it by His wisdom. **51:15** Ps 146:5-6
With His own understanding Jer 10:12-16
He stretched out the heavens. Rom 1:20
16 When He speaks in the thunder,
the heavens are filled with water. **51:16** Job 37:2-5 Pss 18:13; 135:7 Jon 1:4

51:10 Hebrew *Zion;* also in 51:24. **51:11** Greek version reads *Fill up the quivers.*

51:11 God used the Babylonians to stir up the Medes to battle (Jeremiah 51:28). The Medes were closely linked to the Persians, and are commonly referred to in Scripture alongside each other (Esther 1:19; Daniel 8:20). The Persians and the Medes defeated the Babylonians to become the most powerful kingdom in the world (Isaiah 13:17; Daniel 5:28).

▸ WORSHIP

51:15 Creator and King. If you listen to popular songs, watch movies, or read new books, you'll hear a lot about God. Much of this discussion, however, describes a God who reflects our culture, rather than rules over it. But God is a King who demands our allegiance and obedience (see Deuteronomy 6:4-9). He is also the Creator of the world, and it is with this authority that He called the Babylonians to account for their deeds. Today, we need God as our King, for we need His royal protection. We also need to recognize God as our Creator to give a foundation for all God's redemptive acts. Seek out both these attributes of God in Scripture and ask God to reveal Himself to you through His Word. (***See Worship****> NT> Reverence> We fear Jesus, eternal creator and judge of mankind,* TopicGuide page A32.)

He causes the clouds to rise over the earth.
He sends the lightning with the rain
and releases the wind from His storehouses.

51:17 Isa 44:18-20 Hab 2:18-19
17 The whole human race is foolish and has no knowledge!
The craftsmen are disgraced by the idols they make,
for their carefully shaped works are a fraud.
These idols have no breath or power.
18 Idols are worthless; they are ridiculous lies!
On the day of reckoning they will all be destroyed.
51:19 Jer 10:16
19 But the God of Israel* is no idol!
He is the Creator of everything that exists,
including His people, His own special possession.
The LORD of Heaven's Armies is His name!

BABYLON'S GREAT PUNISHMENT

51:20 Mic 4:12-13
20 "You* are My battle-ax and sword,"
says the LORD.
"With you I will shatter nations
and destroy many kingdoms.
51:21 Exod 15:1
21 With you I will shatter armies—
destroying the horse and rider,
the chariot and charioteer.
51:22 Isa 13:15-16, 18
22 With you I will shatter men and women,
old people and children,
young men and maidens.
23 With you I will shatter shepherds and flocks,
farmers and oxen,
captains and officers.

24 "I will repay Babylon
and the people of Babylonia*
for all the wrong they have done
to My people in Jerusalem," says the LORD.
51:25 Rev 8:8
25 "Look, O mighty mountain, destroyer of the earth!
I am your enemy," says the LORD.
"I will raise My fist against you,
to knock you down from the heights.
When I am finished,
you will be nothing but a heap of burnt rubble.
51:26 Isa 13:19-22
26 You will be desolate forever.
Even your stones will never again be used for building.
You will be completely wiped out,"
says the LORD.

51:19 Hebrew *the Portion of Jacob.* See note on 5:20. 51:20 Possibly Cyrus, whom God used to conquer Babylon. Compare Isa 44:28; 45:1. 51:24 Or *Chaldea;* also in 51:35.

51:20-34 Following a hymn of praise to the Creator, Jeremiah returned to the theme of the destruction of Babylon. By worshiping God as the Creator, Jeremiah was effectively forming an answer to anyone who might have objected to the way God was treating Babylon. After all, if God created them, He could do with them what He pleased (Romans 9:14-29).

51:20-23 The Lord utilized parallel and opposite ideas to communicate totality: "horse and rider," "chariot and charioteer," "men and women," "old people and children," "young men and maidens," "shepherds and flocks," "farmers and oxen," "captains and officers." The purpose in using this kind of speech was to communicate that everything in Babylon would be destroyed.

27 Raise a signal flag to the nations.
Sound the battle cry!
Mobilize them all against Babylon.
Prepare them to fight against her!
Bring out the armies of Ararat, Minni, and Ashkenaz.
Appoint a commander,
and bring a multitude of horses like swarming locusts!
28 Bring against her the armies of the nations—
led by the kings of the Medes
and all their captains and officers.

29 The earth trembles and writhes in pain,
for everything the LORD has planned against Babylon stands unchanged.
Babylon will be left desolate without a single inhabitant.
30 Her mightiest warriors no longer fight.
They stay in their barracks, their courage gone.
They have become like women.
The invaders have burned the houses
and broken down the city gates.
31 The news is passed from one runner to the next
as the messengers hurry to tell the king
that his city has been captured.
32 All the escape routes are blocked.
The marshes have been set aflame,
and the army is in a panic.

33 This is what the LORD of Heaven's Armies,
the God of Israel, says:
"Babylon is like wheat on a threshing floor,
about to be trampled.
In just a little while
her harvest will begin."

34 "King Nebuchadnezzar* of Babylon has eaten and crushed us
and drained us of strength.
He has swallowed us like a great monster
and filled his belly with our riches.
He has thrown us out of our own country.
35 Make Babylon suffer as she made us suffer,"
say the people of Zion.
"Make the people of Babylonia pay for spilling our blood,"
says Jerusalem.

THE LORD'S VENGEANCE ON BABYLON

36 This is what the LORD says to Jerusalem:

"I will be your lawyer to plead your case,
and I will avenge you.

51:27 Gen 8:4; 10:3 2 Kgs 19:37 Isa 13:2-5

51:29 Jer 10:10 Amos 8:8

51:30 Ps 76:5 Isa 13:7-8; 45:1

51:33 Isa 21:10 Joel 3:13

51:34 Job 20:15 Ps 137:8 Isa 24:1-3

51:35 Ps 137:8

51:36 Ps 140:12 Rom 12:19

51:34 Hebrew *Nebuchadrezzar,* a variant spelling of Nebuchadnezzar.

51:27-28 "Ararat, Minni, and Ashkenaz" were located in modern central Iran and were under the dominion of the Medes in the alliance against Babylon. Scholars differ on whether this Ararat is connected to the location of the Mount Ararat upon which Noah's ark settled (Genesis 8:4), but it is very likely the same area mentioned in Isaiah 37:38.

51:31-32 Ancient reconnaissance consisted of small patrols reporting to an outpost. That outpost would send out messengers to report anything noteworthy back to the commander. In this case, the message was one of total defeat.

I will dry up her river,
as well as her springs,
37 and Babylon will become a heap of ruins,
haunted by jackals.
She will be an object of horror and contempt,
a place where no one lives.
38 Her people will roar together like strong lions.
They will growl like lion cubs.
51:39 Ps 76:5 Jer 25:27
39 And while they lie inflamed with all their wine,
I will prepare a different kind of feast
for them.
I will make them drink until they fall asleep,
and they will never wake up again,"
says the LORD.
40 "I will bring them down
like lambs to the slaughter,
like rams and goats to be sacrificed.

41 "How Babylon* is fallen—
great Babylon, praised throughout the earth!
Now she has become an object of horror
among the nations.
51:42 Dan 9:26
42 The sea has risen over Babylon;
she is covered by its crashing waves.
51:43 Isa 13:20
43 Her cities now lie in ruins;
she is a dry wasteland
where no one lives or even passes by.
51:44 Ezra 1:7 Isa 2:2
44 And I will punish Bel, the god of Babylon,
and make him vomit up all he has eaten.
The nations will no longer come and worship him.
The wall of Babylon has fallen!

A MESSAGE FOR THE EXILES

51:45 Gen 19:12-16 Isa 48:20 Acts 2:40
45 "Come out, My people, flee from Babylon.
Save yourselves! Run from the LORD's fierce anger.
46 But do not panic; don't be afraid
51:46 Isa 19:2
when you hear the first rumor of approaching
forces.
For rumors will keep coming year by year.
Violence will erupt in the land
as the leaders fight against each other.
51:47 Isa 21:9; 46:1-2
47 For the time is surely coming
when I will punish this great city and all her idols.

51:41 Hebrew *Sheshach,* a code name for Babylon.

51:41-44 Isaiah 14 and Revelation 14 use similar imagery. John referenced these verses in Revelation 14:8 to speak of the destruction of all empires that are at odds with God and His people.

51:42 In ancient Babylon, people believed that the great sea monster that dominated the sea with chaos had to be subjected before creation could occur (Psalms 74:13; 89:10; Isaiah 51:9). Destruction by elemental forces would cause those in Babylon to, in context of their own mythology, understand that their city would be taken back to the chaotic time before creation. Water did not literally cover it in its destruction any more than fire rained down from heaven on it (Jeremiah 32:26-35). Both are references to the elemental forces that their gods claimed to have mastered—these were being turned against them as the God of Israel showed His dominance of their pantheon.

Her whole land will be disgraced,
and her dead will lie in the streets.
48 Then the heavens and earth will rejoice,
for out of the north will come destroying armies
against Babylon," says the LORD. 51:48 Isa 44:23 Rev 18:20
49 "Just as Babylon killed the people of Israel
and others throughout the world,
so must her people be killed.
50 Get out, all you who have escaped the sword!
Do not stand and watch—flee while you can!
Remember the LORD, though you are in a far-off land,
and think about your home in Jerusalem."

51 "We are ashamed," the people say. 51:51 Lam 1:10
"We are insulted and disgraced
because the LORD's Temple
has been defiled by foreigners."

52 "Yes," says the LORD, "but the time is coming
when I will destroy Babylon's idols.
The groans of her wounded people
will be heard throughout the land.
53 Though Babylon reaches as high as the heavens 51:53
and makes her fortifications incredibly strong, Job 20:6-7
I will still send enemies to plunder her.
I, the LORD, have spoken!

BABYLON'S COMPLETE DESTRUCTION

54 "Listen! Hear the cry of Babylon,
the sound of great destruction from the land
of the Babylonians.
55 For the LORD is destroying Babylon. 51:55
He will silence her loud voice. Ps 69:2
Waves of enemies pound against her;
the noise of battle rings through the city.
56 Destroying armies come against Babylon. 51:56
Her mighty men are captured, Pss 76:3; 94:1-2
and their weapons break in their hands.
For the LORD is a God who gives just punishment;
He always repays in full.
57 I will make her officials and wise men drunk, 51:57
along with her captains, officers, and warriors. Ps 76:5-6
They will fall asleep
and never wake up again!"
says the King, whose name is
the LORD of Heaven's Armies.

58 This is what the LORD of Heaven's Armies says: 51:58
"The thick walls of Babylon will be leveled Hab 2:13
to the ground,
and her massive gates will be burned.
The builders from many lands have worked in vain,
for their work will be destroyed by fire!"

JEREMIAH'S MESSAGE SENT TO BABYLON

59The prophet Jeremiah gave this message to Seraiah son of Neriah and grandson of
Mahseiah, a staff officer, when Seraiah went to Babylon with King Zedekiah of Judah. This
was during the fourth year of Zedekiah's reign.* 60Jeremiah had recorded on a scroll all
the terrible disasters that would soon come upon Babylon—all the words written here.
61He said to Seraiah, "When you get to Babylon, read aloud everything on this scroll.
51:62 62Then say, 'LORD, you have said that you will destroy Babylon so that neither people nor
Isa 13:19-22 animals will remain here. She will lie empty and abandoned forever.' 63When you have
Ezek 35:9 finished reading the scroll, tie it to a stone and throw it into the Euphrates River. 64Then
51:63 Rev 18:21 say, 'In this same way Babylon and her people will sink, never again to rise, because of the
51:64 disasters I will bring upon her.'"
Nah 1:8-9 This is the end of Jeremiah's messages.

THE FALL OF JERUSALEM

52:1 **52** Zedekiah was twenty-one years old when he became king, and he reigned in Je-
2 Kgs 8:22; 24:18-20 rusalem eleven years. His mother was Hamutal, the daughter of Jeremiah from
52:2 Libnah. 2But Zedekiah did what was evil in the LORD's sight, just as Jehoiakim had done.
Jer 36:30-31 3These things happened because of the LORD's anger against the people of Jerusalem and
52:3 Judah, until He finally banished them from His presence and sent them into exile.
2 Chr 36:13 Zedekiah rebelled against the king of Babylon. 4So on January 15,* during the ninth
52:4 2 Kgs 25:1-7 year of Zedekiah's reign, King Nebuchadnezzar* of Babylon led his entire army against Je-
Jer 39:1 rusalem. They surrounded the city and built siege ramps against its walls. 5Jerusalem was
kept under siege until the eleventh year of King Zedekiah's reign.
52:6 6By July 18 in the eleventh year of Zedekiah's reign,* the famine in the city had become
Jer 38:9 very severe, and the last of the food was entirely gone. 7Then a section of the city wall was
52:7 broken down, and all the soldiers fled. Since the city was surrounded by the Babylonians,*
Jer 39:2, 4-7 they waited for nightfall. Then they slipped through the gate between the two walls be-
hind the king's garden and headed toward the Jordan Valley.*
52:8 8But the Babylonian troops chased King Zedekiah and caught him on the plains of
Jer 21:7; 38:23 Jericho, for his men had all deserted him and scattered. 9They took him to the king of Bab-
52:9 ylon at Riblah in the land of Hamath. There the king of Babylon pronounced judgment
2 Kgs 25:6
Jer 39:5

51:59 The fourth year of Zedekiah's reign was 593 B.C. **52:4a** Hebrew *on the tenth day of the tenth month,* of the ancient Hebrew lunar calendar. A number of events in Jeremiah can be cross-checked with dates in surviving Babylonian records and related accurately to our modern calendar. This day was January 15, 588 B.C. **52:4b** Hebrew *Nebuchadrezzar,* a variant spelling of Nebuchadnezzar; also in 52:12, 28, 29, 30. **52:6** Hebrew *By the ninth day of the fourth month* [in the eleventh year of Zedekiah's reign]. This day was July 18, 586 B.C.; also see note on 52:4a. **52:7a** Or *the Chaldeans;* similarly in 52:8, 17. **52:7b** Hebrew *the Arabah.*

51:59-64 Baruch delivered the oracle against the people of Judah, and here his brother Seraiah (32:12) delivered a prophecy of judgment against the Babylonians. These brothers represented the two different views the people of Judah were to hold toward the Babylonians. Baruch showed that Babylon was the agent of God to whom the people of Judah were to submit (Jeremiah 36). Seraiah underscored the message that God would restore His people from Babylonian oppression and bring judgment against the Babylonians (Jeremiah 50–51).

▸ SPIRITUAL WARFARE

52:2-3 Three steps toward destruction. Motivational speakers will often promise an improved quality of life to the individual who adopts their steps for success. The example of Zedekiah, on the other hand, offers a three-step continuum toward destruction. First, Zedekiah did evil in the eyes of the Lord. Second, Zedekiah's evil provoked the Lord to anger. Third, the Lord's anger led Him to exile His people. King Zedekiah was unwilling to turn from His sin of rebellion and submit to the Lord's will for his life. Take three steps away from the calamity of sin by repenting of your sins (Jeremiah 36:3; Matthew 4:17), believing the gospel (John 3:16; Romans 5:6-11), and living a new life (Galatians 5:16; Colossians 3:11). It will be the best three steps you've ever taken. (***See Spiritual Warfare**> Originator of Sin> Satan's Domain> Doomed to destruction,* TopicGuide page A44.)

52:9-11 This section recounts the horror Zedekiah endured at the hands of his enemies when the Babylonians captured him. Although it is not specifically mentioned here, the truly awful aspect of this story lies not in the harm done to Zedekiah and his supporters, but in Zedekiah's rebellion against God (52:2). Jeremiah offered Zedekiah an opportunity that would have spared his life, and the lives of those in Jerusalem, but Zedekiah chose not to submit to the Lord.

upon Zedekiah. 10He made Zedekiah watch as they slaughtered his sons and all the 52:10
other officials of Judah. 11Then they gouged out Zedekiah's eyes, bound him in bronze Jer 39:6
chains, and led him away to Babylon. Zedekiah remained there in prison until the day of 52:11
his death. Ezek 12:13

THE TEMPLE DESTROYED

12On August 17 of that year,* which was the nineteenth year of King Nebuchadnezzar's 52:12
reign, Nebuzaradan, the captain of the guard and an official of the Babylonian king, ar- 2 Kgs 25:8-21
rived in Jerusalem. 13He burned down the Temple of the LORD, the royal palace, and all the 52:13
houses of Jerusalem. He destroyed all the important buildings* in the city. 14Then he su- 2 Chr 36:19 Ps 74:6-8
pervised the entire Babylonian* army as they tore down the walls of Jerusalem on every Jer 39:8
side. 15Nebuzaradan, the captain of the guard, then took as exiles some of the poorest of 52:14
the people, the rest of the people who remained in the city, the defectors who had de- 2 Kgs 25:10
clared their allegiance to the king of Babylon, and the rest of the craftsmen. 16But Nebu-
zaradan allowed some of the poorest people to stay behind in Judah to care for the
vineyards and fields.

17The Babylonians broke up the bronze pillars in front of the LORD's Temple, the bronze 52:17
water carts, and the great bronze basin called the Sea, and they carried all the bronze 1 Kgs 7:15-36
away to Babylon. 18They also took all the ash buckets, shovels, lamp snuffers, basins, 52:18
dishes, and all the other bronze articles used for making sacrifices at the Temple. 19Nebu- 1 Kgs 7:45
zaradan, the captain of the guard, also took the small bowls, incense burners, basins, pots, 52:19 1 Kgs 7:50
lampstands, dishes, bowls used for liquid offerings, and all the other articles made of pure
gold or silver.

20The weight of the bronze from the two pillars, the Sea with the twelve bronze oxen be- 52:20
neath it, and the water carts was too great to be measured. These things had been made 1 Kgs 7:47
for the LORD's Temple in the days of King Solomon. 21Each of the pillars was 27 feet tall
and 18 feet in circumference.* They were hollow, with walls 3 inches thick.* 22The bronze 52:22
capital on top of each pillar was 7½ feet* high and was decorated with a network of 1 Kgs 7:20, 42
bronze pomegranates all the way around. 23There were 96 pomegranates on the sides,
and a total of 100 on the network around the top.

24Nebuzaradan, the captain of the guard, took with him as prisoners Seraiah the high 52:24
priest, Zephaniah the priest of the second rank, and the three chief gatekeepers. 25And 2 Kgs 25:18
from among the people still hiding in the city, he took an officer who had been in charge Ezra 7:1
of the Judean army; seven of the king's personal advisers; the army commander's chief
secretary, who was in charge of recruitment; and sixty other citizens. 26Nebuzaradan, the
captain of the guard, took them all to the king of Babylon at Riblah. 27And there at Riblah, 52:27
in the land of Hamath, the king of Babylon had them all put to death. So the people of Ju- Jer 13:19
dah were sent into exile from their land. Mic 4:10

28The number of captives taken to Babylon in the seventh year of Nebuchadnezzar's 52:28
reign* was 3,023. 29Then in Nebuchadnezzar's eighteenth year* he took 832 more. 30In 2 Kgs 24:2-3, 12-16

52:12 Hebrew *On the tenth day of the fifth month,* of the ancient Hebrew lunar calendar. This day was August 17, 586 B.C.; also see note on 52:4a. 52:13 Or *destroyed the houses of all the important people.* 52:14 Or *Chaldean.* 52:21a Hebrew *18 cubits* [8.1 meters] *tall and 12 cubits* [5.4 meters] *in circumference.* 52:21b Hebrew *4 fingers thick* [8 centimeters]. 52:22 Hebrew *5 cubits* [2.3 meters]. 52:28 This exile in the seventh year of Nebuchadnezzar's reign occurred in 597 B.C. 52:29 This exile in the eighteenth year of Nebuchadnezzar's reign occurred in 586 B.C.

52:13, 17-23 Although the burning of the city of Jerusalem was horrific, even more appalling was the destruction of the Temple of the Lord and the looting of the articles of worship. God had chosen to dwell among His people in Jerusalem, the great city of David, and had made His presence known in the Temple built by Solomon (1 Kings 8:10-11). The Temple symbolized God's commitment to be with His people, but in its burning, the prophecies of Moses were realized (Deuteronomy 31:17).

52:24 The Babylonians arrested and put to death both those who fled from Jerusalem and key officials who tried to defend Jerusalem against the Babylonian attack.

Nebuchadnezzar's twenty-third year* he sent Nebuzaradan, the captain of the guard, who
took 745 more—a total of 4,600 captives in all.

HOPE FOR ISRAEL'S ROYAL LINE

52:31 [31]In the thirty-seventh year of the exile of King Jehoiachin of Judah, Evil-merodach as-
2 Kgs 25:27-30 cended to the Babylonian throne. He was kind to* Jehoiachin and released him from
Ps 3:3 prison on March 31 of that year.* [32]He spoke kindly to Jehoiachin and gave him a higher
52:33 place than all the other exiled kings in Babylon. [33]He supplied Jehoiachin with new clothes
2 Sam 9:7, 13 to replace his prison garb and allowed him to dine in the king's presence for the rest of his
life. [34]So the Babylonian king gave him a regular food allowance as long as he lived. This
continued until the day of his death.

52:30 This exile in the twenty-third year of Nebuchadnezzar's reign occurred in 581 B.C. **52:31a** Hebrew *He raised the head of.* **52:31b** Hebrew *on the twenty-fifth day of the twelfth month,* of the ancient lunar Hebrew calendar. This day was March 31, 561 B.C.; also see note on 52:4a.

52:31-34 In an unexpected turn of events, the new king of Babylon, Evil-Merodach, showed compassion toward King Jehoiachin. Nothing in these verses indicates why the king of Babylon was prompted to be kind toward Jehoiachin, but this event seems to indicate that hope was still alive for the people of God. A future time of rebuilding was in store for Judah (Jeremiah 1:10; 30–33; see also note at 22:30).

▸ SALVATION

52:33 Salvation from the prison of sin. Prisoners are frequently incarcerated because they lack the willingness to change their behavior. Sin has the same effect—it holds us captive and then neutralizes our strength to overcome its power (Genesis 6:5; Jeremiah 17:9; Romans 3:10-11; Ephesians 2:1-3). Just as Jehoiachin could not liberate himself from prison and needed the king of Babylon to restore him to favor, so do we require an outside authority in order to reverse sin's curse upon us. How can God do it? The Father planned for salvation to take place (Acts 2:23), Jesus accomplished salvation by dying and being resurrected (Galatians 1:3-4), and the Holy Spirit applies salvation to our lives (Titus 3:5). Are you seeking to save yourself? Turn to God, who alone can remove the shackles that restrict you from living righteously. (***See Salvation****> Our Need> Corrupt> Bondage of the will in life's decisions,* TopicGuide page A22.)

LAMENTATIONS

PURPOSE

To explore the excruciating pain of God's people as they witnessed the destruction of Jerusalem and waited for the fulfillment of God's promises.

Though the Bible's primary message is the gospel of salvation, which is good news, some of the Bible contains bad news. Lamentations contains five of the saddest chapters in the Bible.

Lamentations is the continuation of the book of Jeremiah, which foretold of Jerusalem's impending destruction. Lamentations details the grief that followed this sad event. The book consists of five dirges in which the author eulogizes the once-glorious city of God. This dark hour of Israel's history glittered with a few promises that conveyed that not all was lost. Lamentations is a book for those in mourning and offers hope for a brighter morning to come.

DISCOVER GOD IN LAMENTATIONS

In this short book of the Old Testament, there are two aspects of God's actions that are highlighted:

A God Who Weeps: Jeremiah is called the "weeping prophet" because of the agony he expressed in this book. Like Jeremiah, Jesus wept over Jerusalem six centuries later (Matthew 23:37, 38). Jesus experienced a range of emotions similar to our own—including grief (Isaiah 53:3; Mark 14:34). Christians who feel deep emotions like sadness and loneliness and rejection (Lamentations 2:15-16; 3:14, 30) are experiencing normal emotions, ones with which Christ is acquainted. We see other negative emotions attributed to God in Lamentations, particularly anger in chapter 2.

A God Who Disciplines: God always keeps His promises. "The faithful love of the LORD never ends! His mercies never cease. Great is His faithfulness; His mercies begin afresh each morning" (Lamentations 3:22-23). But under the Old Covenant, He promised to discipline Israel as a nation for their refusal to keep their covenant promises to Him (Leviticus 26; Deuteronomy 28). Thus while holding out the hope found in repentance, God demonstrated His displeasure at Israel: "The LORD in His anger has cast a dark shadow over beautiful Jerusalem" (Lamentations 2:1). This anger was not spontaneous or uncontrolled—it was designed to promote repentance. God allows pain and suffering to enter the lives of the obedient and disobedient—see the pain that visited faithful Jeremiah. But the goal is always the same—to promote holiness and dependence on Him (Hosea 12:6).

GROWING THROUGH LAMENTATIONS

This brief book reveals many themes consistent with Christian discipleship:

Waiting on the Lord: Sometimes we find ourselves suffering, waiting, or struggling—and we can't figure out why. Jeremiah did nothing himself to bring about the suffering of the city, yet he was engulfed by it along with those who were responsible. But the prophet's confidence in God was not shaken. The Lord was his inheritance (3:24)—not the city, not Judah, not wealth or property that was lost, but the Lord. Therefore, he would wait: "The LORD is good to those who depend on Him, to those who search for Him. So it is good to wait quietly for salvation from the LORD" (3:25-26). Sometimes, we can't "fix" the situation we're in. But being certain of our inheritance gives us the ability to wait in peace (Isaiah 40:31).

All Is Never Lost: When Jerusalem was destroyed, many Israelites were killed or taken captive to Babylon. Yet Jeremiah wrote that Judah had been kept from complete destruction (3:22, see textual note). Even when death and destruction are all around, with God, all is never lost. Even though some lives were lost in Jerusalem, the purposes and plans of God—based on promises made to Abraham and David—would continue on. Even if our physical life on this earth ends unexpectedly and dramatically, when we know God, all is not lost. God is at work fulfilling His glory and His divine purpose for those who love Him (Romans 8:28).

DISCOVERY VERSES

The faithful love of the LORD never ends! His mercies never cease. Great is His faithfulness; His mercies begin afresh each morning.
(LAMENTATIONS 3:22-23)

But LORD, You remain the same forever! Your throne continues from generation to generation.
(LAMENTATIONS 5:19)

LAMENTATIONS FACTS

Author: Jeremiah is not named as the author, but a number of Jewish sources, as well as the Greek version of the Old Testament, name him as the author.

Written to: The devastated nation of Judah.

Date of writing: Jerusalem fell to Babylon in 586 BC, and Jeremiah probably wrote Lamentations before he was deported to Egypt as a prisoner of Judah's former rulers (Jeremiah 43).

Setting: Jerusalem.

OUTLINE

- **LAMENTATIONS 1**—Jerusalem Is Deserted and Forsaken
- **LAMENTATIONS 2**—Judgment and Repentance
- **LAMENTATIONS 3**—Lament and Hope
- **LAMENTATIONS 4**—Jerusalem Past and Present
- **LAMENTATIONS 5**—Prayer for Mercy

1:1 Isa 22:2 Jer 40:9

1 * 1 Jerusalem, once so full of people,
is now deserted.
She who was once great among the nations
now sits alone like a widow.
Once the queen of all the earth,
she is now a slave.

1:2 Job 19:13-14 Pss 6:6; 77:2-6 Jer 2:25; 22:20-22 Mic 7:5

2 She sobs through the night;
tears stream down her cheeks.
Among all her lovers,
there is no one left to comfort her.
All her friends have betrayed her
and become her enemies.

1:3 Lev 26:39 Deut 28:64-67 2 Kgs 25:4-5

3 Judah has been led away into captivity,
oppressed with cruel slavery.
She lives among foreign nations
and has no place of rest.
Her enemies have chased her down,
and she has nowhere to turn.

1:4 Jer 9:11; 10:22 Lam 2:6-7 Joel 1:8-13

4 The roads to Jerusalem* are in mourning,
for crowds no longer come to celebrate the festivals.
The city gates are silent,
her priests groan,
her young women are crying—
how bitter is her fate!

1:5 Ps 90:7-8 Ezek 8:17-18; 9:9-10

5 Her oppressors have become her masters,
and her enemies prosper,
for the LORD has punished Jerusalem
for her many sins.
Her children have been captured
and taken away to distant lands.

1:6 Jer 13:18

6 All the majesty of beautiful Jerusalem*
has been stripped away.
Her princes are like starving deer
searching for pasture.
They are too weak to run
from the pursuing enemy.

1 Each of the first four chapters of this book is an acrostic, laid out in the order of the Hebrew alphabet. The first word of each verse begins with a successive Hebrew letter. Chapters 1, 2, and 4 have one verse for each of the 22 Hebrew letters. Chapter 3 contains 22 stanzas of three verses each. Though chapter 5 has 22 verses, it is not an acrostic. **1:4** Hebrew *Zion;* also in 1:17. **1:6** Hebrew *of the daughter of Zion.*

1:1 In the Hebrew text of Lamentations, the book opens with the word "How." Asking "how deserted lies the city" communicates the shock that the once-great city of God had lost its citizens, its influence over other nations, and its own freedom. The word "how" also appears as the first word in the Hebrew text of Lamentations 2:1 and 4:1.

1:3 The event that caused Judah's suffering was the destruction of the city by the Babylonians and the exile of the people (Jeremiah 39:8-10). The phrase "no place of rest" recalls the dove sent out by Noah in the ark (Genesis 8:9). Like the dove, Judah searches for a place of stability and safekeeping.

1:4 The word translated "Jerusalem" here is literally "Zion" (see NLT textual note). The term "Zion" has a broad meaning in Scripture, referring to the heavenly city of God (Hebrews 12:22), the city of David (2 Samuel 5:6-9), the Temple in Jerusalem (Micah 3:12), and more generally the city of Jerusalem (Psalm 128:5). Figuratively, Zion represents the dwelling of God.

7 In the midst of her sadness and wandering,
  Jerusalem remembers her ancient splendor.
But now she has fallen to her enemy,
  and there is no one to help her.
Her enemy struck her down
  and laughed as she fell.

1:7 Jer 37:7 Lam 4:17

8 Jerusalem has sinned greatly,
  so she has been tossed away like a filthy rag.
All who once honored her now despise her,
  for they have seen her stripped naked and humiliated.
All she can do is groan
  and hide her face.

1:8 Isa 59:2-13

9 She defiled herself with immorality
  and gave no thought to her future.
Now she lies in the gutter
  with no one to lift her out.
"LORD, see my misery," she cries.
  "The enemy has triumphed."

1:9 Ps 74:23 Eccl 4:1 Isa 3:8 Jer 13:17-18 Ezek 24:13

10 The enemy has plundered her completely,
  taking every precious thing she owns.
She has seen foreigners violate her sacred Temple,
  the place the LORD had forbidden them to enter.

1:10 Ps 74:4-8 Isa 64:10-11 Jer 51:51

11 Her people groan as they search for bread.
  They have sold their treasures for food to stay alive.
"O LORD, look," she mourns,
  "and see how I am despised.

1:11 1 Sam 30:12

12 "Does it mean nothing to you, all you who pass by?
  Look around and see if there is any suffering like mine,
which the LORD brought on me
  when He erupted in fierce anger.

1:12 Isa 13:13 Jer 4:8; 18:16; 48:27

13 "He has sent fire from heaven that burns in my bones.
  He has placed a trap in my path and turned me back.
He has left me devastated,
  racked with sickness all day long.

1:13 Job 19:6; 30:30 Ps 22:14 Jer 44:6 Hab 3:16

14 "He wove my sins into ropes
  to hitch me to a yoke of captivity.
The Lord sapped my strength and turned me over to my enemies;
  I am helpless in their hands.

1:14 Prov 5:22 Isa 47:6 Jer 28:13-14; 32:3, 5 Ezek 25:4, 7

▸ **WORSHIP**

1:8 Does God punish me every time I sin? Do you fear committing a sin that deserves the brunt of God's justice? Many believers live in terror that they are one sin away from committing high treason against God. It's true that sin is serious business, but God is merciful (Psalm 103:8; 2 Peter 3:9) and has provided a way out of the mire of sin. Have you asked for God's forgiveness by confessing and forsaking your sin (Proverbs 28:13)? Perhaps you have, but your feelings still don't change—you still feel nervous and frightened. Stop—God hears the prayer of the penitent. Confess your sin and trust that Jesus' death is finally and fully satisfying to God (1 John 1:9). (***See Worship****> OT> Repentance> Nature> Obedience leads to blessing, failure to repent leads to curses,* TopicGuide page A29.)

1:10 Jerusalem's most treasured possessions were located within the Temple of God (Isaiah 64:11; 1 Kings 6:21-35). It was humiliating enough for God's people to lose their property and be exiled, but it was much worse for them to have the enemies of the Lord loot and destroy their central place of worship, for God prohibited foreigners from entering His Temple (Deuteronomy 23:3).

1:15
Isa 41:2
Jer 13:24; 37:10

15 "The Lord has treated my mighty men
with contempt.
At His command a great army has come
to crush my young warriors.
The Lord has trampled His beloved city*
like grapes are trampled in a winepress.

1:16
Ps 69:20
Eccl 4:1
Lam 1:2

16 "For all these things I weep;
tears flow down my cheeks.
No one is here to comfort me;
any who might encourage me are far away.
My children have no future,
for the enemy has conquered us."

1:17
2 Kgs 24:2-4
Isa 1:15
Jer 4:31

17 Jerusalem reaches out for help,
but no one comforts her.
Regarding His people Israel,*
the LORD has said,
"Let their neighbors be their enemies!
Let them be thrown away like a filthy rag!"

1:18
Deut 28:32, 41
1 Sam 12:14-15
Ps 119:75
Jer 12:1

18 "The LORD is right," Jerusalem says,
"for I rebelled against Him.
Listen, people everywhere;
look upon my anguish and despair,
for my sons and daughters
have been taken captive to distant lands.

1:19
Job 19:13-19
Jer 14:15
Lam 1:2; 2:20

19 "I begged my allies for help,
but they betrayed me.
My priests and leaders
starved to death in the city,
even as they searched for food
to save their lives.

1:20
Isa 16:11
Jer 4:19

20 "LORD, see my anguish!
My heart is broken
and my soul despairs,
for I have rebelled against You.
In the streets the sword kills,
and at home there is only death.

1:21
Ps 35:15
Isa 14:5-6; 47:6
Jer 30:16

21 "Others heard my groans,
but no one turned to comfort me.
When my enemies heard about my troubles,
they were happy to see what You had done.
Oh, bring the day You promised,
when they will suffer as I have suffered.

1:15 Hebrew *the virgin daughter of Judah*. 1:17 Hebrew *Jacob*. The names "Jacob" and "Israel" are often interchanged throughout the Old Testament, referring sometimes to the individual patriarch and sometimes to the nation.

1:19 The text could also be translated, "I called to my lovers." Judah had previously relied on the Egyptians to help them defend against an Assyrian attack (2 Kings 18:21), but the Egyptians never came to their aid. When the Babylonians attacked the city, Judah was left all alone. The prophets brought charges against Edom, the descendants of Esau, for failing to help Jerusalem in her time of need (Obadiah 1:11-12; Lamentations 4:21-22).

22 "Look at all their evil deeds, LORD.
Punish them,
as You have punished me
for all my sins.
My groans are many,
and I am sick at heart."

1:22 Neh 4:4-5; Ps 137:7-8

GOD'S ANGER AT SIN

2 1 The Lord in His anger
has cast a dark shadow over beautiful Jerusalem.*
The fairest of Israel's cities lies in the dust,
thrown down from the heights of heaven.
In His day of great anger,
the Lord has shown no mercy even to His Temple.*

2:1 Pss 99:5; 132:7; Isa 64:11; Ezek 28:14-16

2 Without mercy the Lord has destroyed
every home in Israel.*
In His anger He has broken down
the fortress walls of beautiful Jerusalem.*
He has brought them to the ground,
dishonoring the kingdom and its rulers.

2:2 Pss 21:9; 89:39-40; Lam 3:43

3 All the strength of Israel
vanishes beneath His fierce anger.
The Lord has withdrawn His protection
as the enemy attacks.
He consumes the whole land of Israel
like a raging fire.

2:3 Ps 75:5, 10; Isa 42:25; Jer 21:14

4 He bends His bow against His people,
as though He were their enemy.
His strength is used against them
to kill their finest youth.
His fury is poured out like fire
on beautiful Jerusalem.*

2:4 Job 6:4; 16:13; Jer 7:20; Lam 3:12-13

5 Yes, the Lord has vanquished Israel
like an enemy.

2:5 Jer 52:13; Lam 2:2

2:1a Hebrew *the daughter of Zion;* also in 2:8, 10, 18. 2:1b Hebrew *His footstool.* 2:2a Hebrew *Jacob;* also in 2:3b. See note on 1:17. 2:2b Hebrew *the daughter of Judah;* also in 2:5. 2:4 Hebrew *on the tent of the daughter of Zion.*

▸ SPIRITUAL WARFARE

1:22 Do Christians have enemies? When Jesus taught the disciples to pray in Matthew 6:10, He said, "May Your Kingdom come soon." By praying for the expansion of the Kingdom of God, you are also praying for the destruction of kingdoms opposed to God—those belonging to Satan and his followers. God's power may come upon His enemies in the form of the regenerating work of the Holy Spirit, or it may come through the execution of God's judgment upon their lives. Yes, Christians have enemies, for if Jesus had enemies, so will we (Matthew 24:9; 1 John 3:13). But we pray for God to show His power in their lives (Matthew 5:44), and we let God decide exactly how to do that. (***See Spiritual Warfare***> *Originator of Sin> Satan's Domain> Doomed to destruction,* TopicGuide page A44.)

2:1 A "dark shadow" figuratively means that Jerusalem was being placed under a cloud of God's anger. Since the Jews relied on rainwater to nourish their land and crops, a cloud formation in the sky brought hopeful expectations of God's blessing of rain (Deuteronomy 11:10-17). In contrast, this cloud formation over Jerusalem was not a picture of divine blessing, but of divine wrath.

2:4 The phrase "beautiful Jerusalem" is literally "daughter of Zion" in Hebrew. The grief over Jerusalem's exile was described in terms of a father-daughter relationship. The writer was describing God as an enemy of his own daughter, which was an intentionally shocking image.

He has destroyed her palaces
and demolished her fortresses.
He has brought unending sorrow and tears
upon beautiful Jerusalem.

2:6 Lam 1:4; Zeph 3:18

6 He has broken down His Temple
as though it were merely a garden shelter.
The LORD has blotted out all memory
of the holy festivals and Sabbath days.
Kings and priests fall together
before His fierce anger.

2:7 Ps 74:3-8; Isa 64:11; Ezek 7:20-22

7 The Lord has rejected His own altar;
He despises His own sanctuary.
He has given Jerusalem's palaces
to her enemies.
They shout in the LORD's Temple
as though it were a day of celebration.

2:8 2 Kgs 21:13; Isa 34:11; Amos 7:7-9

8 The LORD was determined
to destroy the walls of beautiful Jerusalem.
He made careful plans for their destruction,
then did what He had planned.
Therefore, the ramparts and walls
have fallen down before Him.

2:9 Neh 1:3; Jer 14:14; 23:16

9 Jerusalem's gates have sunk into the ground.
He has smashed their locks and bars.
Her kings and princes have been exiled to distant lands;
her law has ceased to exist.
Her prophets receive
no more visions from the LORD.

2:10 Job 2:13; Isa 3:26; Amos 8:3; Jon 3:6-8

10 The leaders of beautiful Jerusalem
sit on the ground in silence.
They are clothed in burlap
and throw dust on their heads.
The young women of Jerusalem
hang their heads in shame.

2:11 Jer 4:19; Lam 2:19

11 I have cried until the tears no longer come;
my heart is broken.
My spirit is poured out in agony
as I see the desperate plight of my people.
Little children and tiny babies
are fainting and dying in the streets.

2:12 Job 30:16; Ps 42:4

12 They cry out to their mothers,
"We need food and drink!"
Their lives ebb away in the streets
like the life of a warrior wounded in battle.

2:10 People of biblical times expressed grief by wearing burlap (Numbers 14:6; 2 Samuel 1:11; Isaiah 37:2; Ezra 9:3). Sackcloth is a coarse material, woven from flax, which was often used to make grain sacks. Wearing sackcloth was an external sign of an internal distress.

2:11 The awful images of defeat were still fresh in the mind of the author of Lamentations. He not only expressed sorrow for the condition of the entire nation, but also for the destruction of his people, including children and infants.

They gasp for life
as they collapse in their mothers' arms.

13 What can I say about you?
Who has ever seen such sorrow?
O daughter of Jerusalem,
to what can I compare your anguish?
O virgin daughter of Zion,
how can I comfort you?
For your wound is as deep as the sea.
Who can heal you?

2:13
Lam 1:12

14 Your prophets have said
so many foolish things, false to the core.
They did not save you from exile
by pointing out your sins.
Instead, they painted false pictures,
filling you with false hope.

2:14
Ezek 22:25, 28; 23:36
Mic 3:8

15 All who pass by jeer at you.
They scoff and insult beautiful Jerusalem,* saying,
"Is this the city called 'Most Beautiful in All the World'
and 'Joy of All the Earth'?"

2:15
Job 27:23
Pss 48:2; 50:2
Jer 18:16

16 All your enemies mock you.
They scoff and snarl and say,
"We have destroyed her at last!
We have long waited for this day,
and it is finally here!"

2:16
Pss 22:13; 56:2
Lam 3:46
Obad 1:12-15

17 But it is the LORD who did just as He planned.
He has fulfilled the promises of disaster
He made long ago.
He has destroyed Jerusalem without mercy.
He has caused her enemies to gloat over her
and has given them power over her.

2:17
Deut 28:43-44
Ps 89:42
Lam 1:5

18 Cry aloud* before the Lord,
O walls of beautiful Jerusalem!
Let your tears flow like a river
day and night.
Give yourselves no rest;
give your eyes no relief.

2:18
Ps 119:145
Lam 2:8
Hos 7:14
Hab 2:11

19 Rise during the night and cry out.
Pour out your hearts like water to the Lord.
Lift up your hands to Him in prayer,
pleading for your children,

2:19
1 Sam 1:15
Ps 42:3-4
Isa 51:20

2:15 Hebrew *the daughter of Jerusalem.* 2:18 Hebrew *Their heart cried.*

▸ GOD
2:17 Can God hold a grudge against me? It can be frightening and encouraging—God has guaranteed judgment against those who defy His commandments (Deuteronomy 28:15). God has also promised forgiveness to those who turn from their wickedness in repentance and faith (Jeremiah 18:8). Jerusalem did not turn from sin; therefore, God brought judgment upon them. But for those who repent, He has promised to completely remove their sins (Jeremiah 31:34). There are many legitimate reasons to fear God, but once you honestly repent, never give it a second thought—God certainly will not (Hebrews 8:12). If God chooses to not bring up your former sins, then why should you? (***See God****> God's Attributes> Faithful> God forgives the repentant,* TopicGuide page A16.)

for in every street
they are faint with hunger.

2:20 Exod 32:11 Deut 9:26 Ps 78:64 Jer 23:11-12 Lam 4:13, 16

20 "O LORD, think about this!
Should You treat Your own people this way?
Should mothers eat their own children,
those they once bounced on their knees?
Should priests and prophets be killed
within the Lord's Temple?

2:21 2 Chr 36:17 Jer 6:11 Zech 11:6

21 "See them lying in the streets—
young and old,
boys and girls,
killed by the swords of the enemy.
You have killed them in Your anger,
slaughtering them without mercy.

2:22 Ps 31:13 Isa 24:17-18 Jer 16:2-4

22 "You have invited terrors from all around,
as though You were calling them to a day of feasting.
In the day of the LORD's anger,
no one has escaped or survived.
The enemy has killed all the children
whom I carried and raised."

HOPE IN THE LORD'S FAITHFULNESS

3 1 I am the one who has seen the afflictions
that come from the rod of the LORD's anger.

3:2 Isa 59:9 Jer 4:23

2 He has led me into darkness,
shutting out all light.

3:3 Ps 38:2 Isa 5:25

3 He has turned His hand against me
again and again, all day long.

3:4 Pss 31:9-10; 38:2-8 Jer 50:17

4 He has made my skin and flesh grow old.
He has broken my bones.

3:5 Job 19:8

5 He has besieged and surrounded me
with anguish and distress.

3:6 Pss 88:5-6; 143:3

6 He has buried me in a dark place,
like those long dead.

3:7 Job 3:23 Jer 40:4

7 He has walled me in, and I cannot escape.
He has bound me in heavy chains.

▸ GOD

2:20 Is it right to question God? God controls all things in the universe; from Him come both calamities and good things (Lamentations 3:38). It is easy to rejoice in the midst of God's blessings, but often we struggle to accept His will when it includes disaster. The speaker in Lamentations demonstrated discouragement, but at the same time, he maintained his confidence in God (Lamentations 3:21-22). Expressing your pain to God must be done in the context of a faithful trust in the sovereign plan of God, a hopeful expectation that God will provide deliverance, and a genuine love of a merciful and compassionate God. Express your pain to a sovereign and compassionate God today. (***See God****> God's Nature> Personality> Emotion> God is compassionate and loving,* TopicGuide page A14.)

2:22 The prophet Zephaniah prophesied of a coming "day of the LORD's anger" when judgment would befall Judah and all the inhabitants of Jerusalem for their idolatrous worship and evil ways (Zephaniah 1:4-18). The day of the LORD had now come in the form of the Babylonian siege.

3:2 Jeremiah had prophesied that God would bring darkness on the land if Judah would not give glory to God (Jeremiah 13:16). Darkness represented a return to the original state of creation (Genesis 1:2), meaning God was threatening to cause the land to become formless and empty—a return to a chaotic state (Jeremiah 4:23).

3:7 While the rest of the population easily ignored their precarious situation, Jeremiah could not. He poured out his feelings about God's wrath on Israel (3:1-19) and Israel's anger at his message (3:14) in a way that was designed to shock the original audience into rethinking their own apathy.

8 And though I cry and shout,
He has shut out my prayers.
9 He has blocked my way with a high stone wall;
He has made my road crooked.

10 He has hidden like a bear or a lion,
waiting to attack me.
11 He has dragged me off the path and torn me in pieces,
leaving me helpless and devastated.
12 He has drawn His bow
and made me the target for His arrows.

13 He shot His arrows
deep into my heart.
14 My own people laugh at me.
All day long they sing their mocking songs.
15 He has filled me with bitterness
and given me a bitter cup of sorrow to drink.

16 He has made me chew on gravel.
He has rolled me in the dust.
17 Peace has been stripped away,
and I have forgotten what prosperity is.
18 I cry out, "My splendor is gone!
Everything I had hoped for from the LORD is lost!"

19 The thought of my suffering and homelessness
is bitter beyond words.*
20 I will never forget this awful time,
as I grieve over my loss.
21 Yet I still dare to hope
when I remember this:

22 The faithful love of the LORD never ends!*
His mercies never cease.
23 Great is His faithfulness;
His mercies begin afresh each morning.
24 I say to myself, "The LORD is my inheritance;
therefore, I will hope in Him!"

25 The LORD is good to those who depend on Him,
to those who search for Him.

3:8 Job 30:20; Ps 22:2
3:9 Isa 63:17; Hos 2:6
3:10 Job 10:16
3:11 Job 16:12-13; Hos 6:1
3:12 Ps 7:12-13
3:14 Ps 22:6-7; Lam 3:63
3:15 Jer 9:15
3:16 Ps 3:7; Prov 20:17
3:17 Jer 12:12
3:18 Job 17:15; Ezek 37:11
3:19 Lam 3:5, 15
3:20 Pss 42:5-6, 11; 43:5
3:21 Ps 130:7
3:22 Ps 78:38; Jer 3:12; Mal 3:6
3:24 Ps 73:26
3:25 Isa 25:9; 26:9

3:19 Or *is wormwood and gall.* 3:22 As in Syriac version; Hebrew reads *of the LORD keeps us from destruction.*

3:20 Jeremiah's emotional scars probably never went away completely, but his hope in God's abundant mercies gave him strength to persevere.

3:21 In spite of the personal anguish expressed by the writer, he still held out hope for the future. His hope was grounded in his understanding of the character of God (Lamentations 3:22-23). God promised to restore Judah from her captivity (Jeremiah 29:10-14). The author found consolation in God's faithful love for His people (Lamentations 3:22-27).

▸ GOD
3:22-23 Is God's love present in times of great difficulty? Even though Judah's situation had drastically changed from success to defeat, the author of Lamentations still described God's love as steadfast. When crisis comes into our lives, we often feel as though God has forgotten us—or worse, we believe God no longer loves us. But, like the writer of Lamentations, we need to recognize that God still loves us even during our times of pain and loneliness. If you are enduring a difficult time, find encouragement in this passage and in the loving, steadfast character of God. (***See God> God's Attributes> All-Present> God's continual presence brings contentment,*** TopicGuide page A16.)

3:24 "Inheritance" is a term commonly applied to the distribution of the various portions of the Promised Land to the tribes (Numbers 26:53 and following). The writer rejoiced that though the land promises may have been rescinded due to disobedience (Leviticus 26; Deuteronomy 28), Israel's greatest treasure is God Himself (Deuteronomy 32:9; Psalm 16:5).

3:26 Ps 37:7

26 So it is good to wait quietly
for salvation from the LORD.

27 And it is good for people to submit at an early age
to the yoke of His discipline:

3:28 Jer 15:17

28 Let them sit alone in silence
beneath the LORD's demands.

3:29 Job 16:15; 40:4

29 Let them lie face down in the dust,
for there may be hope at last.

3:30 Job 16:10; Isa 50:6; Matt 5:39

30 Let them turn the other cheek to those who strike them
and accept the insults of their enemies.

3:31 Ps 94:14; Isa 54:7-10

31 For no one is abandoned
by the Lord forever.

3:32 Pss 78:38; 106:43-45; Hos 11:8

32 Though He brings grief, He also shows compassion
because of the greatness of His unfailing love.

33 For He does not enjoy hurting people
or causing them sorrow.

34 If people crush underfoot
all the prisoners of the land,

3:35 Prov 17:15

35 if they deprive others of their rights
in defiance of the Most High,

3:36 Jer 22:3; Hab 1:13

36 if they twist justice in the courts—
doesn't the Lord see all these things?

3:37 Ps 33:9-11

37 Who can command things to happen
without the Lord's permission?

3:38 Job 2:10; Jer 32:42

38 Does not the Most High
send both calamity and good?

3:39 Mic 7:9; Heb 12:5-6

39 Then why should we, mere humans, complain
when we are punished for our sins?

3:40 Pss 119:59; 139:23-24; 2 Cor 13:5

40 Instead, let us test and examine our ways.
Let us turn back to the LORD.

3:40-41 The first person plural pronoun is utilized multiple times in these two verses ("Let us"). The speaker was urging the people of Judah to join him in repentance and confession before the Lord. He hoped that the Lord would relent from His anger and forgive the nation for their sin.

BECAUSE GOD IS FAITHFUL

I will trust Him to always keep His promises.

The faithful love of the LORD never ends! His mercies never cease.
Great is His faithfulness; His mercies begin afresh each morning.

LAMENTATIONS 3:22-23

FOR THE NEXT *GOD IS FAITHFUL* FEATURE SEE PAGE 2072.

41 Let us lift our hearts and hands
to God in heaven and say,
42 "We have sinned and rebelled,
and You have not forgiven us.

43 "You have engulfed us with Your anger, chased us down,
and slaughtered us without mercy.
44 You have hidden Yourself in a cloud
so our prayers cannot reach You.
45 You have discarded us as refuse and garbage
among the nations.

46 "All our enemies
have spoken out against us.
47 We are filled with fear,
for we are trapped, devastated, and ruined."
48 Tears stream from my eyes
because of the destruction of my people!

49 My tears flow endlessly;
they will not stop
50 until the LORD looks down
from heaven and sees.
51 My heart is breaking
over the fate of all the women of Jerusalem.

52 My enemies, whom I have never harmed,
hunted me down like a bird.
53 They threw me into a pit
and dropped stones on me.
54 The water rose over my head,
and I cried out, "This is the end!"

55 But I called on Your name, LORD,
from deep within the pit.
56 You heard me when I cried, "Listen to my pleading!
Hear my cry for help!"
57 Yes, You came when I called;
You told me, "Do not fear."

58 Lord, You are my lawyer! Plead my case!
For You have redeemed my life.
59 You have seen the wrong they have done to me, LORD.
Be my judge, and prove me right.
60 You have seen the vengeful plots
my enemies have laid against me.

3:41 Pss 25:1; 141:2
3:42 Neh 9:26 Jer 14:20
3:43 Lam 2:21
3:44 Lam 3:8
3:45 1 Cor 4:13
3:46 Lam 2:16
3:47 Isa 24:17-18 Jer 48:43-44
3:49 Ps 77:2
3:50 Isa 63:15
3:52 1 Sam 26:20 Pss 11:1; 35:7
3:53 Jer 37:16
3:54 Jon 2:3-5 Ps 69:2
3:56 Job 34:28 Pss 55:1; 116:12
3:57 Isa 41:10-14
3:58 Ps 34:22 Jer 50:34; 51:36
3:59 Pss 26:1; 43:1

3:55 Instead of giving up hope in his darkest moment, the prophet prayed to God from within the "pit." This may have referred to something from the prophet's actual personal experience (Jeremiah 38:6), or it may have been a symbolic reference to death (Psalm 88:6).

▸ WORSHIP
3:57 How does God answer my prayers? How many situations in your life have desperately needed God's deliverance? The writer of Lamentations found an answer to his prayers in God's presence. The Bible assures us that when we draw close to God, He draws close to us (James 4:8). God's presence in difficult times assures us of victory against our foes (Genesis 15:1; Jeremiah 30:10). Jesus knew His followers would face a myriad of challenges, so He promised them, "I am with you always, even to the end of the age" (Matthew 28:20). When we pray to God, there is nothing more precious or powerful that He can give us than Himself. (***See Worship****> OT> Fasting and Prayer> Prayer> God does not always say yes,* TopicGuide page A26.)

3:61 Lam 5:1
[61] LORD, You have heard the vile names they call me.
You know all about the plans they have made.
3:62 Pss 59:7; 140:3 Ezek 36:3
[62] My enemies whisper and mutter
as they plot against me all day long.
3:63 Lam 3:14
[63] Look at them! Whether they sit or stand,
I am the object of their mocking songs.

3:64 Ps 28:4 Jer 51:24
[64] Pay them back, LORD,
for all the evil they have done.
3:65 Deut 2:30 Isa 6:10
[65] Give them hard and stubborn hearts,
and then let Your curse fall on them!
[66] Chase them down in Your anger,
destroying them beneath the LORD's heavens.

GOD'S ANGER SATISFIED

4:1 2 Kgs 25:9-10
4 [1] How the gold has lost its luster!
Even the finest gold has become dull.
The sacred gemstones
lie scattered in the streets!

4:2 Isa 30:14 Jer 19:1, 11
[2] See how the precious children of Jerusalem,*
worth their weight in fine gold,
are now treated like pots of clay
made by a common potter.

4:3 Job 39:14-16 Lam 2:12
[3] Even the jackals feed their young,
but not my people Israel.
They ignore their children's cries,
like ostriches in the desert.

4:4 Jer 14:3
[4] The parched tongues of their little ones
stick to the roofs of their mouths in thirst.
The children cry for bread,
but no one has any to give them.

4:5 Jer 6:2 Amos 6:3-7
[5] The people who once ate the richest foods
now beg in the streets for anything they can get.
Those who once wore the finest clothes
now search the garbage dumps for food.

4:6 Gen 19:25 Jer 20:16 Ezek 16:48
[6] The guilt* of my people
is greater than that of Sodom,
where utter disaster struck in a moment
and no hand offered help.

4:7 Ps 51:7
[7] Our princes once glowed with health—
brighter than snow, whiter than milk.
Their faces were as ruddy as rubies,
their appearance like fine jewels.*

4:2 Hebrew *precious sons of Zion.* 4:6 Or *punishment.* 4:7 Hebrew *like lapis lazuli.*

4:3 Ancient Near East writers often depicted the jackal as wandering among the ruins of desolate cities (Lamentations 5:18). The ostrich was considered a careless, unwise, and harsh mother (Job 39:14-18). These two animals symbolized the wandering and careless people of Israel.

4:6 The word "guilt" may also be translated "punishment for iniquity." The author may have been saying that the destruction of Judah was worse than that of Sodom. God destroyed Sodom instantly, but He destroyed Jerusalem over a period of time. This allowed for repentance but lengthened the punishment.

8 But now their faces are blacker than soot.
No one recognizes them in the streets.
Their skin sticks to their bones;
it is as dry and hard as wood.

9 Those killed by the sword are better off
than those who die of hunger.
Starving, they waste away
for lack of food from the fields.

10 Tenderhearted women
have cooked their own children.
They have eaten them
to survive the siege.

11 But now the anger of the LORD is satisfied.
His fierce anger has been poured out.
He started a fire in Jerusalem*
that burned the city to its foundations.

12 Not a king in all the earth—
no one in all the world—
would have believed that an enemy
could march through the gates of Jerusalem.

13 Yet it happened because of the sins of her prophets
and the sins of her priests,
who defiled the city
by shedding innocent blood.

14 They wandered blindly
through the streets,
so defiled by blood
that no one dared touch them.

15 "Get away!" the people shouted at them.
"You're defiled! Don't touch us!"
So they fled to distant lands
and wandered among foreign nations,
but none would let them stay.

16 The LORD Himself has scattered them,
and He no longer helps them.
People show no respect for the priests
and no longer honor the leaders.

4:8 Ps 102:5; Lam 5:10
4:9 Lev 26:39
4:10 Deut 28:53-55; 2 Kgs 6:26-30; Lam 2:20
4:11 Deut 32:22
4:12 Jer 21:13
4:13 Jer 2:30; 26:8-9; Ezek 22:26
4:14 Deut 28:28-29; Isa 29:10; 56:10; 59:9-10
4:15 Lev 13:45-46; Jer 45:5
4:16 Isa 9:14-16; Jer 52:24-27

4:11 Hebrew *in Zion.*

▶ SPIRITUAL WARFARE
4:9 What does God think about suicide? In the Bible, there are five instances of suicide and nothing positive is recorded concerning these events. Instead, the life of each of these men is assessed in a critical way (1 Samuel 31:3-13; 2 Samuel 17:23; 1 Kings 16:18-19; Matthew 27:3-5). Finally, God condemns the unlawful taking of life (Exodus 20:13), even our own. It is our God-given duty to prevent murder or suicide, and also to protect and promote life whenever and wherever possible. You may struggle with thoughts of hurting yourself, but it's never God's will for you to take your life. Only God has the authority to do that. (***See Spiritual Warfare****> Resisting Sin and Evil> Consequences> Of Disobedience> Death,* TopicGuide page A46.)

4:12 It was the Lord who had protected Judah from the attacks of her enemies. The world and all of its kings had come to presume that Jerusalem was impenetrable. The Assyrians had previously failed to successfully attack Jerusalem (2 Kings 19). But now it was God Himself who had destroyed the city (Lamentations 4:11).

4:15 A tragic state of uncleanness had permeated Jerusalem. It was as if lepers had filled the city streets with their presence (Leviticus 13:45). The uncleanness drove all of the priests and prophets away (Lamentations 4:13-16).

4:17 Jer 37:7; Lam 1:7; Ezek 29:16

[17] We looked in vain for our allies
to come and save us,
but we were looking to nations
that could not help us.

4:18 Jer 5:31; 16:16; Amos 8:2

[18] We couldn't go into the streets
without danger to our lives.
Our end was near; our days were numbered.
We were doomed!

4:19 Deut 28:49; Isa 5:26-28; Jer 4:13; Hab 1:8

[19] Our enemies were swifter than eagles in flight.
If we fled to the mountains, they found us.
If we hid in the wilderness,
they were waiting for us there.

4:20 Jer 39:5; Ezek 12:12-13

[20] Our king—the LORD's anointed, the very life of our nation—
was caught in their snares.
We had thought that His shadow
would protect us against any nation on earth!

4:21 Isa 34:7; Amos 1:11; Obad 1:16

[21] Are you rejoicing in the land of Uz,
O people of Edom?
But you, too, must drink from the cup of the LORD's anger.
You, too, will be stripped naked in your drunkenness.

4:22 Isa 40:2; Jer 49:10

[22] O beautiful Jerusalem,* your punishment will end;
you will soon return from exile.
But Edom, your punishment is just beginning;
soon your many sins will be exposed.

PRAYER FOR RESTORATION

5:1 Ps 44:13-16

5 [1] LORD, remember what has happened to us.
See how we have been disgraced!

5:2 Isa 1:7; Hos 8:7-8; Zeph 1:13

[2] Our inheritance has been turned over to strangers,
our homes to foreigners.
[3] We are orphaned and fatherless.
Our mothers are widowed.

5:3 Exod 22:24; Jer 15:8; 18:21

[4] We have to pay for water to drink,
and even firewood is expensive.

5:4 Isa 3:1

4:22 Hebrew *O daughter of Zion.*

4:20 Nebuchadnezzar, king of Babylon, appointed the Israelite Zedekiah as king over Jerusalem. When Zedekiah rebelled against Nebuchadnezzar, the Babylonians responded by murdering his sons and sending him to Babylon (2 Kings 24:17–25:7). Zedekiah was considered the very "life of [the] nation," not because he merited the honor, but because the Lord had appointed him as leader of His people.

▸ CHURCH
4:22 Will there always be suffering in the world? Tragedy has touched us all. We must not allow ourselves to become so overburdened with grief that we neglect the promises of God. God promised Judah that a time of restoration would follow the period of devastation (Jeremiah 33). We must view our suffering as only temporary, and we should be encouraged by God's promise of restoration in this world or in the world to come (Jeremiah 29:11). In this lies the hope of every Christian—it will get better! (***See Church****> Who> From Every People> Those who are tempted to apostasy by suffering,* TopicGuide page A48.)

▸ SALVATION
5:1 Does God forget? When the Bible speaks of God remembering, it does not imply that He can forget things. Remembering is connected to God's covenant with His people (Genesis 9:15-16; Exodus 6:5; Jeremiah 14:21). The writer was begging God to fulfill His covenant promises. When God "forgot" (Lamentations 5:20) He is temporarily delaying His promises. As a believer, find comfort in an all-knowing God, who never forgets our misery. He will never forget you or His promises to you. (***See Salvation****> Receiving> Results> Works> God remembers them,* TopicGuide page A23.)

5 Those who pursue us are at our heels;
we are exhausted but are given no rest.
6 We submitted to Egypt and Assyria
to get enough food to survive.
7 Our ancestors sinned, but they have died—
and we are suffering the punishment they deserved!
8 Slaves have now become our masters;
there is no one left to rescue us.
9 We hunt for food at the risk of our lives,
for violence rules the countryside.
10 The famine has blackened our skin
as though baked in an oven.
11 Our enemies rape the women in Jerusalem*
and the young girls in all the towns of Judah.
12 Our princes are being hanged by their thumbs,
and our elders are treated with contempt.
13 Young men are led away to work at millstones,
and boys stagger under heavy loads of wood.
14 The elders no longer sit in the city gates;
the young men no longer dance and sing.
15 Joy has left our hearts;
our dancing has turned to mourning.
16 The garlands have* fallen from our heads.
Weep for us because we have sinned.
17 Our hearts are sick and weary,
and our eyes grow dim with tears.
18 For Jerusalem* is empty and desolate,
a place haunted by jackals.
19 But LORD, You remain the same forever!
Your throne continues from generation to generation.
20 Why do You continue to forget us?
Why have You abandoned us for so long?
21 Restore us, O LORD, and bring us back to You again!
Give us back the joys we once had!
22 Or have You utterly rejected us?
Are You angry with us still?

5:11 Hebrew *in Zion.* 5:16 Or *The crown has.* 5:18 Hebrew *Mount Zion.*

5:6 Hos 9:3
5:7 Jer 14:20; 16:12
5:8 Neh 5:15; Ps 7:2; Zech 11:6
5:9 Jer 40:9-12
5:10 Job 30:30; Lam 4:8
5:11 Isa 13:16; Zech 14:2
5:12 Isa 47:6; Lam 4:16
5:13 Jer 7:18
5:14 Isa 24:8; Jer 7:34
5:15 Jer 25:10; Amos 8:10
5:16 Job 19:9; Ps 89:39
5:17 Job 17:7; Ps 6:7; Isa 1:5; Lam 2:11
5:19 Pss 45:6; 102:12
5:20 Pss 13:1; 44:24
5:21 Ps 80:3; Isa 60:20-22; Jer 31:18
5:22 Ps 60:1; Isa 64:9

5:5 The people of Judah could find no rest from their affliction (1:3). There was no end in sight from persecution.

5:11 The parallelism intensifies from the first to the second comparisons. "Women" represent a more general term, while "young girls" are indicative of women of marriageable age. The atrocity of rape was not simply happening within Jerusalem but had also spread throughout the towns of Judah, a sign that the entire nation was in chaos.

5:15 The joy of the whole earth was Zion, the city of the great King (Psalm 48:2), but Jerusalem experienced a total reversal of its glorious condition. All joy had ceased in Jerusalem, and all exaltation had turned to mourning.

5:19 The writer recognized that with the Temple of the Lord in ruins, which many saw as the throne of God (Zechariah 6:13), the people would wonder whether God actually reigned on earth any longer. The author therefore testified to the eternal kingship of God (compare 2 Peter 1:11).

▸ SALVATION
5:21 Can I be totally restored after sin? We often think that we are unworthy to be reconciled with God after we have sinned against Him. How could God simply forgive us—with no strings attached? But the author, by faith, asked for things to be as they once were. By faith, we can experience the power and reality of total forgiveness from God. That doesn't mean there will be no earthly consequences for our sin—sin may disqualify us from marriage (1 Corinthians 7:11) or church office (1 Timothy 3:1-7), among other penalties assigned by the state (Romans 13:4). But by faith, we can trust in the perfect sacrifice of Christ on our behalf and know that God is not angry with us any more. (***See Salvation**> Receiving> Results> Sanctification,* TopicGuide page A23.)

EZEKIEL

PURPOSE

To proclaim God's judgment upon Israel and other nations and to announce future salvation for God's people.

Ezekiel's prophecy is not easy to understand, but it is compelling. It's hard to lazily drift over spectacular creatures and fiery wheels (chapter 1), the valley of dry bones (chapter 37), and a Temple that covers the whole land of Israel (chapters 40–48).

Ezekiel was a priest (1:3) whose service at the Temple in Jerusalem should have begun at age thirty. But when his time came, instead of serving in the glorious Temple, he was living in Babylon, a worldwide center of idolatry seven hundred miles away from Jerusalem's ruins. Instead of pursuing his priestly duties, Ezekiel was called by God to be a prophet.

Ezekiel's fellow deportees and those remaining in Jerusalem believed the Exile would end soon. False prophets encouraged this wrong belief (Ezekiel 13). They wrongly taught that since God loved Israel and Jerusalem, He would not allow the destruction of the nation to continue. Ezekiel had the unenviable position of explaining that it would not only continue, but that a much worse fate awaited Jerusalem (Ezekiel 8–11) before it would get better (Ezekiel 33–48).

DISCOVER GOD IN EZEKIEL

Ezekiel filled his autobiographical prophecy with many manifestations of God's attributes:

The Transcendence of God: God revealed Himself to Ezekiel through intermediaries such as angels (Ezekiel 8; 40–48) and a vision of "the glory of the LORD" (1:28) though not quite God Himself. God remained concealed, described in only the most fantastic, poetic language; He was surrounded in such splendor that Ezekiel wished to avert his eyes from the overwhelming view.

The Holiness of God: Sin is an affront to God, especially when it is committed by His covenant community (Ezekiel 2–24). God will judge the nations (Ezekiel 25–32), but He will reserve His greatest criticisms and gravest warnings for those who have sworn allegiance to Him (Leviticus 26; Deuteronomy 28). Because of His holiness, God's glory was forced to depart from the defiled Temple in Jerusalem (Ezekiel 9:3; 10:4, 18-19; 11:22-23), but His moral holiness also required that He send a Savior to truly rescue His people from sin (Galatians 1:4).

The Gracious and Merciful God: Ezekiel consoled the exiled Jews by pointing them to a time when God would restore those who repented (Ezekiel 3:19, 21; 33:12). He would be their true Shepherd; in contrast to the evil spiritual shepherds who fed on their fear (Ezekiel 34:1-10), God would guide them into a place of peace and restoration. Instead of confusing them, He would send a faithful watchman, warning them of the consequences of their crimes against the covenant (Ezekiel 3:16-17).

GROWING THROUGH EZEKIEL

Much of the content of the book of Ezekiel seems far removed from the daily life of a follower of Jesus. Nonetheless, there are themes throughout to stimulate spiritual growth:

Necessity of the Spirit: Jeremiah gave some of the first details of the new covenant God would make with His people (Jeremiah 31:31-37; Hebrews 8). But Ezekiel detailed the most significant difference between this new covenant and the old covenant: the increased power of the indwelling presence of the Holy Spirit (Ezekiel 36:27). This dynamic work of the Holy Spirit described by Ezekiel gave hope to struggling exiles who had been unable to follow the ways and will of God (Romans 8:9). For all who trust in Christ, God gives His Spirit as a guarantee that He will complete their salvation (2 Corinthians 1:22; 5:5), for the Holy Spirit helps the believer grow in Christlikeness. However, just as the sins of Judah caused the glory of God to depart, a Christian's sin can quench the fire of the Holy Spirit (1 Thessalonians 5:19). The Spirit's work of sanctification can, at great spiritual cost, be resisted (Ephesians 4:30).

DISCOVERY VERSES

As surely as I live, says the Sovereign LORD, I take no pleasure in the death of wicked people. I only want them to turn from their wicked ways so they can live. Turn! Turn from your wickedness, O people of Israel! Why should you die? (EZEKIEL 33:11)

And I will give you a new heart, and I will put a new spirit in you. I will take out your stony, stubborn heart and give you a tender, responsive heart. (EZEKIEL 36:26)

Accountability for Sin: A mistaken assumption in Israel was that righteousness could be "inherited" from one's righteous father, lessening the need for personal accountability before God. In Ezekiel 18, that notion is put to rest: "The person who sins is the one who will die" (18:4, 20). For those depending on tradition and family ties for their hope before God, Ezekiel gave a warning: The righteousness of other family members does not cover a person's sin. People live, die, and are judged individually, not corporately (Hebrews 9:27).

Renewed Worship: The book of Ezekiel ends with a highly detailed blueprint of a new Temple. It was architecturally very difficult to replicate, but the design still said two things: First, the future of God's people would be one of renewed, reformed worship. Worship would be central, not an afterthought, to God's work of fulfilling His promises to Abraham, Isaac, and Jacob and restoring Israel's fortunes. Second, the new Temple foreshadowed the return of God's glory to dwell among humanity. This would happen as Jesus Christ came to Israel and people beheld His glory, the splendor of God Himself (John 1:14).

EZEKIEL FACTS

Author: Ezekiel, a priest turned prophet who received his prophecies while living among the Jewish exiles in Babylon (Ezekiel 1:1-3).

Written to: The community of exiled Jews who had been taken captive to Babylon before and after the fall of Jerusalem.

Date of writing: Babylon's assault against Jerusalem occurred in three stages from 605–586 BC. Ezekiel was taken to Babylon in the second phase, along with about ten thousand other Jewish captives. Ezekiel prophesied in Babylon for about twenty years, from 590–570 BC.

Setting: The book of Ezekiel was written in Babylon, but the scope of the prophecy extended from Babylon to Judah and the surrounding nations.

OUTLINE

- **EZEKIEL 1:1–24:27**—Judgment on Judah and Jerusalem
- **EZEKIEL 25:1–32:32**—Judgment on the Nations
- **EZEKIEL 33:1–48:35**—Restoration of Judah and Jerusalem

A VISION OF LIVING BEINGS

1 On July 31* of my thirtieth year,* while I was with the Judean exiles beside the Kebar
River in Babylon, the heavens were opened and I saw visions of God. 2 This happened
during the fifth year of King Jehoiachin's captivity. 3 (The LORD gave this message to Ezekiel
son of Buzi, a priest, beside the Kebar River in the land of the Babylonians,* and he felt the
hand of the LORD take hold of him.)

4 As I looked, I saw a great storm coming from the north, driving before it a huge cloud
that flashed with lightning and shone with brilliant light. There was fire inside the cloud,
and in the middle of the fire glowed something like gleaming amber.* 5 From the center of
the cloud came four living beings that looked human, 6 except that each had four faces
and four wings. 7 Their legs were straight, and their feet had hooves like those of a calf and
shone like burnished bronze. 8 Under each of their four wings I could see human hands. So
each of the four beings had four faces and four wings. 9 The wings of each living being
touched the wings of the beings beside it. Each one moved straight forward in any direc-
tion without turning around.

10 Each had a human face in the front, the face of a lion on the right side, the face of an
ox on the left side, and the face of an eagle at the back. 11 Each had two pairs of out-
stretched wings—one pair stretched out to touch the wings of the living beings on either
side of it, and the other pair covered its body. 12 They went in whatever direction the spirit
chose, and they moved straight forward in any direction without turning around.

13 The living beings looked like bright coals of fire or brilliant torches, and lightning

1:1 Num 12:6 Isa 1:1 Dan 8:1-2 Matt 3:16 Luke 3:21 Acts 7:56 Rev 4:1; 19:11
1:2 2 Kgs 24:12
1:3 2 Kgs 3:15
1:4 Isa 21:1 Jer 23:19
1:5 Rev 4:6-8
1:7 Dan 10:6 Rev 1:15; 2:18
1:10 Ezek 10:14 Rev 4:7
1:11 Isa 6:2 Ezek 10:16, 19
1:13 Ps 104:4 Rev 4:5

1:1a Hebrew *On the fifth day of the fourth month,* of the ancient Hebrew lunar calendar. A number of dates in Ezekiel can be cross-checked with dates in surviving Babylonian records and related accurately to our modern calendar. This event occurred on July 31, 593 B.C. 1:1b Or *in the thirtieth year.* 1:3 Or *Chaldeans.* 1:4 Or *like burnished metal;* also in 1:27.

1:1 The prophet Ezekiel provided numerous dates for the various prophecies in his book (see notes at 3:16-21; 8:1–13:23; 20:1-4; 24:1-2; 26:1; 29:1; 31:1; 32:1; 33:21; 40:1). Most of his prophecies are arranged in chronological order throughout the book (26:1 and 29:17 being the only exceptions). "My thirtieth year" is literally translated "in the thirtieth year." The Kebar River was a canal connected to the Euphrates River for irrigation, which indicates that Ezekiel was already in Babylon at the time his ministry began. The phrase "visions of God" does not mean that Ezekiel saw God every time God spoke to him, but rather that the visions recorded in his book came from God.

1:2 King Jehoiachin's captivity began in 597 BC when Nebuchadnezzar deposed him and imprisoned him in Babylon. This was the year of the second wave of Babylonian captivity. The phrase "during the fifth year" implies a date of 593 BC, which was a strategic time for Ezekiel to begin his prophetic ministry—after the first two waves of captivity and before the last two. A large part of Ezekiel's message instructed God's people to stop listening to the false prophets, who claimed the captivity would end soon and Jerusalem would never fall. Jeremiah also tried to correct such false hopes. Ezekiel's message was that the worst was yet to come for Judah, but that God would remain faithful to His chosen people and would restore them in His own time and way.

1:3 The phrase "the LORD gave this message" is literally translated "the word of the LORD came," an expression Ezekiel used fifty times to introduce the messages God revealed to him. The phrase "the hand of the LORD" (or "take hold of") (see also 3:14, 22; 8:1; 33:22; 37:1; 40:1) shows God's sovereign control over Ezekiel's life.

1:4 In Ezekiel's initial vision he saw "a great storm" that included "a huge cloud" with "lightning" and "brilliant light." Scripture often describes God's presence, power, and judgment using imagery drawn from nature (Exodus 3:2-4; 40:34-35; Numbers 16:31-33; Job 38:1; Psalm 29:3; Matthew 27:45, 51; Revelation 1:16; 16:17-21). That this vision occurred in Babylon indicated that God's power was not limited to the land of Israel—a fundamental truth for both those still in Judah and those in captivity in Babylon.

1:5-14 The "four living beings" were cherubim (10:4-22) with four faces fixed in each of the four directions, illustrating God's omnipotence. The lightning in their midst symbolized God's control over the powers of nature, while the human and animal characteristics of the angels symbolized God's authority over the animal kingdom.

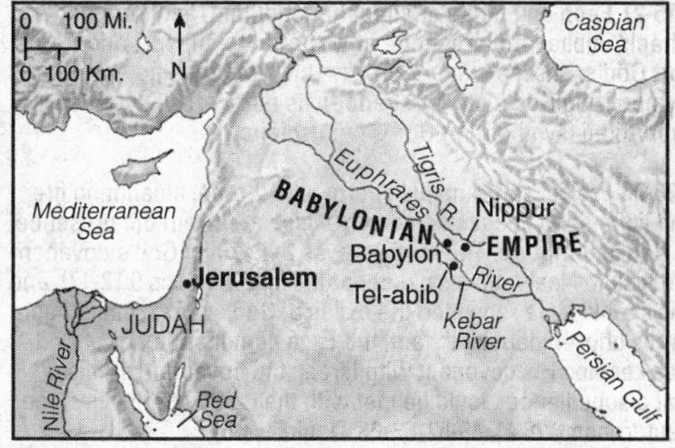

EXILE IN BABYLON
Ezekiel worked for God right where he was—among the exiles in various colonies near the Kebar River in Babylonia. Jerusalem and its Temple lay over 500 miles away, but Ezekiel helped the people understand that, although they were far from home, they did not need to be far from God.

seemed to flash back and forth among them. 14And the living beings darted to and fro like
flashes of lightning.
15As I looked at these beings, I saw four wheels touching the ground beside them, one
wheel belonging to each. 16The wheels sparkled as if made of beryl. All four wheels
looked alike and were made the same; each wheel had a second wheel turning crosswise
within it. 17The beings could move in any of the four directions they faced, without turning
as they moved. 18The rims of the four wheels were tall and frightening, and they were cov-
ered with eyes all around.
19When the living beings moved, the wheels moved with them. When they flew up-
ward, the wheels went up, too. 20The spirit of the living beings was in the wheels. So wher-
ever the spirit went, the wheels and the living beings also went. 21When the beings
moved, the wheels moved. When the beings stopped, the wheels stopped. When the be-
ings flew upward, the wheels rose up, for the spirit of the living beings was in the wheels.
22Spread out above them was a surface like the sky, glittering like crystal. 23Beneath this
surface the wings of each living being stretched out to touch the others' wings, and each
had two wings covering its body. 24As they flew, their wings sounded to me like waves
crashing against the shore or like the voice of the Almighty* or like the shouting of a
mighty army. When they stopped, they let down their wings. 25As they stood with wings
lowered, a voice spoke from beyond the crystal surface above them.
26Above this surface was something that looked like a throne made of blue lapis lazuli.
And on this throne high above was a figure whose appearance resembled a man. 27From
what appeared to be His waist up, He looked like gleaming amber, flickering like a fire.
And from His waist down, He looked like a burning flame, shining with splendor. 28All
around Him was a glowing halo, like a rainbow shining in the clouds on a rainy day. This is
what the glory of the LORD looked like to me. When I saw it, I fell face down on the ground,
and I heard someone's voice speaking to me.

1:14 Matt 24:27
1:16 Ezek 10:9-13
1:17 Ezek 1:12
1:18 Ezek 10:9-13; Rev 4:6, 8
1:19 Ezek 10:16-17, 19
1:21 Ezek 10:17
1:22 Ezek 10:1
1:24 2 Kgs 7:6; Ezek 10:5; 43:2; Dan 10:6; Rev 1:15; 19:6
1:26 Exod 24:10; Isa 6:1; 54:11; Ezek 10:1; Rev 1:13
1:27 Ezek 3:23
1:28 Rev 1:17; 4:3; 10:1

EZEKIEL'S CALL AND COMMISSION

2 "Stand up, son of man," said the voice. "I want to speak with you." 2The Spirit came
into me as He spoke, and He set me on my feet. I listened carefully to His words.
3"Son of man," He said, "I am sending you to the nation of Israel, a rebellious nation that
has rebelled against Me. They and their ancestors have been rebelling against Me to this
very day. 4They are a stubborn and hard-hearted people. But I am sending you to say to

2:2 Dan 8:18
2:3 1 Sam 8:7-8; Jer 3:25; Dan 9:5-13
2:4 Isa 48:4; Jer 5:3

1:24 Hebrew *Shaddai.*

1:15-21 Each angel had a wheel beneath him, and together the wheels implied the presence of a chariot to support and transport God's "throne" (see 1:26). The chariot could go anywhere (symbolizing God's omnipresence); its numerous "eyes" saw everything (symbolizing God's omniscience).

1:25-28 Ezekiel saw a manlike form on a throne, emanating fire and light—two images commonly associated with the presence of God in Scripture. The rainbow was the sign of God's covenant promise to Noah and his descendants (see Genesis 9:12-17), and this should have reminded the exiles of God's promises to them as His chosen people. In fact, the Exile demonstrated that God was keeping His covenant with Israel; the covenant promised that disobedience would be met with the curse of captivity (see Deuteronomy 28:41, 49-52, 63-68; Daniel 9:4-6).

▶ WORSHIP

1:28 Hit the dirt. "The Man upstairs," "Somebody up there likes me," "the Big Guy"—many such flippant expressions are references to God. Others are more crass, using God's name as a punctuation mark for profanity. Paul described such people aptly in Romans 3:18: "They have no fear of God at all." Ezekiel, however, took a humble posture when he was given this amazing glimpse of God's majesty. It was fitting for Ezekiel to fall flat on the ground in reverent worship. It is still fitting. Bow before your God. (***See Worship****> OT> Reverence> Let the earth fear God,* TopicGuide page A29.)

2:1 God calls Ezekiel "son of man" 93 times in the book, an expression that emphasizes his humanity. He was the created; God is the Creator. As God's creation, Ezekiel was totally dependent on God.

2:3 God called Ezekiel to be a prophet to His people at a time when Israel was "rebelling against [God]" (see note at 1:2; compare Ezekiel's call to Isaiah 6:1-13; Jeremiah 1:4-19; Hosea 1:2). God also referred to Israel as "a stubborn and hard-hearted people" (2:4).

2:4 The Hebrew title *Adonai Yahweh,* here translated "Sovereign LORD," emphasizes lordship and sovereignty. This expression occurs 315 times in the Old Testament, 217 of them in Ezekiel.

2:5 Matt 10:12-15 Acts 13:46 them, 'This is what the Sovereign LORD says!' 5And whether they listen or refuse to listen—
for remember, they are rebels—at least they will know they have had a prophet among
them.
2:6 2 Sam 23:6-7 Isa 51:12 Jer 1:8 Mic 7:4 6"Son of man, do not fear them or their words. Don't be afraid even though their threats
surround you like nettles and briers and stinging scorpions. Do not be dismayed by their
dark scowls, even though they are rebels. 7You must give them My messages whether
they listen or not. But they won't listen, for they are completely rebellious! 8Son of man,
2:8 Jer 15:16 Rev 10:9 listen to what I say to you. Do not join them in their rebellion. Open your mouth, and eat
what I give you."
2:9 Jer 36:2 Rev 5:1-5; 10:8-11 9Then I looked and saw a hand reaching out to me. It held a scroll, 10which He unrolled.
And I saw that both sides were covered with funeral songs, words of sorrow, and pro-
nouncements of doom.

3 The voice said to me, "Son of man, eat what I am giving you—eat this scroll! Then go
3:2 Jer 25:17 and give its message to the people of Israel." 2So I opened my mouth, and He fed me
3:3 Jer 6:11; 15:16 Rev 10:9-10 the scroll. 3"Fill your stomach with this," He said. And when I ate it, it tasted as sweet as
honey in my mouth.
4Then He said, "Son of man, go to the people of Israel and give them My messages. 5I
3:5 Jon 1:2; 3:2-4 Acts 26:17-18 am not sending you to a foreign people whose language you cannot understand. 6No, I
am not sending you to people with strange and difficult speech. If I did, they would listen!
3:7 Ezek 2:4 John 15:20 7But the people of Israel won't listen to you any more than they listen to Me! For the whole
lot of them are hard-hearted and stubborn. 8But look, I have made you as obstinate and
hard-hearted as they are. 9I have made your forehead as hard as the hardest rock! So
3:8 Jer 1:18 don't be afraid of them or fear their angry looks, even though they are rebels."

▸ MINISTRY
2:4-7 I'm not listening! Perhaps you have observed children singing or shouting very loud whenever they do not want to hear what is being said. Sometimes they cover their ears and shout, "I'm not listening!" Though this behavior may cease, the attitude can continue into teen years and adulthood, especially when it comes to hearing that we are sinful. By nature we have an inner rebellion that refuses to hear God's call to repentance (John 3:19-20). The people of Ezekiel's day had just such an attitude about their sin, but God told Ezekiel to deliver His message anyway. Like Ezekiel, we are instructed to call people to repentance, and we may encounter stiff resistance. But we cannot always wait for the "right time" to speak to people about their sin, because a favorable time may never come. Ask God to give you the courage to deliver His message of repentance to others, and leave the results to God. (***See Ministry****> Great Commission> Witness> Barriers> People don't want to hear the truth,* TopicGuide page A56.)

2:5-8 Like many of God's servants both before and after him, Ezekiel was called to deliver God's "messages" to His rebellious people, "whether they listen or not" (2:7). The tragedy was that Israel refused to listen to Ezekiel and suffered even more for it.

▸ GOD
2:8–3:4 Eat My words! Ezekiel was put on a special diet that was necessary for his task: God told him to eat His words. This was a strange command to say the least, but one that clearly indicated that Ezekiel was not to deliver his own ideas. Ezekiel's audience would have understood that this meant that Ezekiel was empowered and filled with God's Word—whatever came from Ezekiel's ministry was directly from God. Learn God's Word so that when you speak, people know you are primarily guided by God's Word, not your own experiences or imagination. (***See God****> God's Attributes> True> God's words are faithful and true,* TopicGuide page A18.)

2:9-10 The scroll that Ezekiel ate contained a message symbolizing death and destruction. This message would be the primary content of his prophetic ministry.

▸ WORSHIP
2:9 Sticks and stones. How often have you heard children chant, "Sticks and stones may break my bones but names will never hurt me"? Of course, we all know this is not true. Sometimes calling people names—or even casting a disapproving look—can deeply hurt others. Ezekiel was destined for some nasty looks. If looks could kill, he would have died many times! But he was instructed not to fear his enemies. How could he carry out such a command? Fear of people is conquered when you fear God even more. It is likely that you too will face intimidating scowls and verbal abuse when you speak out for Christ, but fear God more than mere people, and continue to speak! (***See Worship****> OT> Reverence> God delivers those who fear Him,* TopicGuide page A29.)

3:1-3 This is the first of many strange things God required of Ezekiel. He ate the scroll and found it to be "sweet as honey" (compare Revelation 10:9-11). Although the message was bitter, the scroll had a sweet taste because it was God's Word (compare Psalm 119:103).

3:4-9 Once again God warned Ezekiel that Israel was wicked and would not listen to his message (see notes at 2:3 and 2:5-8).

10 Then He added, "Son of man, let all My words sink deep into your own heart first. Lis-
ten to them carefully for yourself. 11 Then go to your people in exile and say to them, 'This
is what the Sovereign LORD says!' Do this whether they listen to you or not."
12 Then the Spirit lifted me up, and I heard a loud rumbling sound behind me. (May the
glory of the LORD be praised in His place!)* 13 It was the sound of the wings of the living be-
ings as they brushed against each other and the rumbling of their wheels beneath them.
14 The Spirit lifted me up and took me away. I went in bitterness and turmoil, but the
LORD's hold on me was strong. 15 Then I came to the colony of Judean exiles in Tel-abib,
beside the Kebar River. I was overwhelmed and sat among them for seven days.

A WATCHMAN FOR ISRAEL

16 After seven days the LORD gave me a message. He said, 17 "Son of man, I have appointed
you as a watchman for Israel. Whenever you receive a message from Me, warn people im-
mediately. 18 If I warn the wicked, saying, 'You are under the penalty of death,' but you fail
to deliver the warning, they will die in their sins. And I will hold you responsible for their
deaths. 19 If you warn them and they refuse to repent and keep on sinning, they will die in
their sins. But you will have saved yourself because you obeyed Me.
20 "If righteous people turn away from their righteous behavior and ignore the obstacles
I put in their way, they will die. And if you do not warn them, they will die in their sins.
None of their righteous acts will be remembered, and I will hold you responsible for their
deaths. 21 But if you warn righteous people not to sin and they listen to you and do not sin,
they will live, and you will have saved yourself, too."
22 Then the LORD took hold of me and said, "Get up and go out into the valley, and I will
speak to you there." 23 So I got up and went, and there I saw the glory of the LORD, just as I
had seen in my first vision by the Kebar River. And I fell face down on the ground.
24 Then the Spirit came into me and set me on my feet. He spoke to me and said, "Go to
your house and shut yourself in. 25 There, son of man, you will be tied with ropes so you
cannot go out among the people. 26 And I will make your tongue stick to the roof of your

3:10 Job 22:22
3:12 Acts 2:2; 8:39
3:13 2 Sam 5:24
3:15 Job 2:13
3:17 Isa 52:8; 58:1; 62:6; Jer 6:17; Ezek 33:7-9
3:18 Ezek 33:6, 8
3:19 2 Kgs 17:13-14; Acts 18:6
3:20 Jer 6:21; Zeph 1:6
3:21 Acts 20:31
3:22 Acts 9:6
3:23 Ezek 1:1, 28; Acts 7:55
3:26 Luke 1:20, 22

3:12 A possible reading for this verse is *Then the Spirit lifted me up, and as the glory of the LORD rose from its place, I heard a loud rumbling sound behind me.*

3:10 Every prophet, preacher, and teacher should do what God called Ezekiel to do: Let God's Word "sink deep into [his] own heart first." God's messengers must apply God's message to their own lives before delivering it to others.

▶ ADOPTION
3:10-11 A message for you. How often do you hear a sermon and think, "That is just what *they* need to hear. I hope *they* are listening!" It is easy to listen for someone else. But we see in this passage that Ezekiel was to listen with his ears and receive with his heart first, and then he was to deliver God's message to others. It is more difficult to discipline ourselves to first consider what personal applications we need to make. Ask God to help you hear what He is saying to you and apply it to your life. Then the message God gives you for others will flow out of your life, not just your mouth. (***See Adoption****> With Christ> Supernatural> Quick to listen,* TopicGuide page A37.)

3:12 God's Spirit lifted Ezekiel up so he could go and deliver his message to Israel. It is possible that Ezekiel was not actually physically transported; this could have been a vision in which Ezekiel was transported wherever the Spirit took him.

3:13 The sounds of the wings of the living beings and their wheels indicated that the chariot of God's presence was moving to take Ezekiel to the proper place to deliver the Lord's message.

3:14-15 Ezekiel had mixed emotions about his task, but the Lord strengthened him to carry it out (compare Jonah 1:1-3). The Spirit took him first to some exiles in Tel-abib. No such place exists in Babylon today, though the name is used for one of modern Israel's principal cities, Tel-Aviv. The ancient city of Tel-abib was near the Kebar River (see Ezekiel 1:1). Ezekiel silently observed the exiles' situation for seven days and was "overwhelmed" by what he saw (compare Job 2:13).

3:16-21 Ezekiel said nothing during the seven days (see note at 3:14-15), but after it was over the Lord gave him a message to deliver to Israel (see notes at 1:1 and 2:1). This happened just a week after Ezekiel's call in 593 BC (see note at 1:2). God appointed Ezekiel as a "watchman" to Israel. A city's watchman would find a high vantage point (such as a tower, a city wall, or a mountain peak) from which to look out for an attacking enemy, and he would warn the city upon sighting such an enemy. The watchman would be held responsible for the city's losses of life and property if he failed in his duty.

3:22-23 The Lord appeared once again to Ezekiel (see 1:3-28), who again was so overwhelmed by the experience that he "fell face down on the ground"—though no details are given about this event. The Hebrew word for "glory" (*kabod*) occurs 24 times in Ezekiel and, as elsewhere in the Old Testament, refers to the manifested presence of God (see Exodus 40:34-38; Isaiah 6:1-3).

3:27 mouth so that you will be speechless and unable to rebuke them, for they are rebels. 27But
Ezek 33:22 when I give you a message, I will loosen your tongue and let you speak. Then you will say
to them, 'This is what the Sovereign LORD says!' Those who choose to listen will listen, but
those who refuse will refuse, for they are rebels.

A SIGN OF THE COMING SIEGE

4:1 Isa 20:2 4 "And now, son of man, take a large clay brick and set it down in front of you. Then
Jer 13:1; 19:1 draw a map of the city of Jerusalem on it. 2Show the city under siege. Build a wall
4:3 around it so no one can escape. Set up the enemy camp, and surround the city with siege
Isa 8:18; 20:3 ramps and battering rams. 3Then take an iron griddle and place it between you and the
Jer 39:1-2 city. Turn toward the city and demonstrate how harsh the siege will be against Jerusalem.
4:4 This will be a warning to the people of Israel.
Lev 10:17 Num 18:1 4"Now lie on your left side and place the sins of Israel on yourself. You are to bear their
4:5 sins for the number of days you lie there on your side. 5I am requiring you to bear Israel's
Num 14:34 sins for 390 days—one day for each year of their sin. 6After that, turn over and lie on your
4:6 right side for 40 days—one day for each year of Judah's sin.
Dan 9:24-26 7"Meanwhile, keep staring at the siege of Jerusalem. Lie there with your arm bared and
Rev 11:2-3 prophesy her destruction. 8I will tie you up with ropes so you won't be able to turn from
side to side until the days of your siege have been completed.
4:9 Exod 9:32 9"Now go and get some wheat, barley, beans, lentils, millet, and emmer wheat, and mix
Isa 28:25 them together in a storage jar. Use them to make bread for yourself during the 390 days
4:12 you will be lying on your side. 10Ration this out to yourself, eight ounces* of food for each
Isa 36:12 day, and eat it at set times. 11Then measure out a jar* of water for each day, and drink it at
set times. 12Prepare and eat this food as you would barley cakes. While all the people are
watching, bake it over a fire using dried human dung as fuel and then eat the bread."
4:13 13Then the LORD said, "This is how Israel will eat defiled bread in the Gentile lands to which
Dan 1:8 I will banish them!"
Hos 9:3 14Then I said, "O Sovereign LORD, must I be defiled by using human dung? For I have
4:14 Lev 17:15; 22:8 never been defiled before. From the time I was a child until now I have never eaten any
Deut 14:3-5 animal that died of sickness or was killed by other animals. I have never eaten any meat
Acts 10:14 forbidden by the law."
4:16 15"All right," the LORD said. "You may bake your bread with cow dung instead of human
Lev 26:26 Isa 3:1 dung." 16Then He told me, "Son of man, I will make food very scarce in Jerusalem. It will be
Lam 5:4 weighed out with great care and eaten fearfully. The water will be rationed out drop by

4:10 Hebrew *20 shekels* [228 grams]. 4:11 Hebrew *1/6 of a hin* [about 1 pint or 0.6 liters].

4:1 Chapters 4–24 contain a series of judgments against Judah and Jerusalem. The messages in chapters 4–7 were not primarily verbal prophecies; Ezekiel enacted various symbolic actions that provided the people with visual illustrations of what would happen to them if they did not repent.

4:1-8 Ezekiel's first symbolic action recollected Nebuchadnezzar's siege of Jerusalem in 597 BC, the year Ezekiel was taken captive to Babylon. God's judgment on His people for their apostasy underscores the dangers of walking away from God.

4:9-17 In Ezekiel's second symbolic action, God called on him to bake bread over human dung and eat it during the 390 days he had to lie on his side (4:9-12; see note at 4:1-8). When Ezekiel objected to using human dung because he had always followed God's dietary laws (4:14; see Leviticus 11; compare Acts 10:9-16), God mercifully allowed him to use cow dung instead (4:15). This graphically depicted the defilement of God's people in foreign lands, where they would eat unclean food (4:13; compare Daniel 1:8-16).

▸ MINISTRY

4:10-17 Comfort zone. What task could God ask you to do that would make you the most uncomfortable? Sometimes Christians allow their fears to keep them from doing what God desires. Some people are terrified of speaking in public. Others are very uncomfortable around other ethnic groups. But God didn't allow Ezekiel's discomfort to excuse him from what he needed to do. God told him to bake barley cakes using human dung as fuel, which would have caused him to become ritually defiled. When Ezekiel expressed his reluctance to do so, God acquiesced in part to his concerns, but He still required him to burn dung to prepare his meal. God knows our weaknesses and is willing to make accommodations for them, but He never excuses us from obedience, even if it means making us uncomfortable. Ask God to help you obey His commands even when it pushes you outside your comfort zone. (***See Ministry**> Great Commission> Risk> Stepping outside of your "comfort zone,"* TopicGuide page A56.)

drop, and the people will drink it with dismay. 17 Lacking food and water, people will look
at one another in terror, and they will waste away under their punishment.

A SIGN OF THE COMING JUDGMENT

5 "Son of man, take a sharp sword and use it as a razor to shave your head and beard.
Use a scale to weigh the hair into three equal parts. 2 Place a third of it at the center of
your map of Jerusalem. After acting out the siege, burn it there. Scatter another third
across your map and chop it with a sword. Scatter the last third to the wind, for I will scatter
My people with the sword. 3 Keep just a bit of the hair and tie it up in your robe. 4 Then take
some of these hairs out and throw them into the fire, burning them up. A fire will then
spread from this remnant and destroy all of Israel.

5 "This is what the Sovereign LORD says: This is an illustration of what will happen to Je-
rusalem. I placed her at the center of the nations, 6 but she has rebelled against My regula-
tions and decrees and has been even more wicked than the surrounding nations. She has
refused to obey the regulations and decrees I gave her to follow.

7 "Therefore, this is what the Sovereign LORD says: You people have behaved worse than
your neighbors and have refused to obey My decrees and regulations. You have not even
lived up to the standards of the nations around you. 8 Therefore, I Myself, the Sovereign
LORD, am now your enemy. I will punish you publicly while all the nations watch. 9 Because
of your detestable idols, I will punish you like I have never punished anyone before or
ever will again. 10 Parents will eat their own children, and children will eat their parents. I
will punish you and scatter to the winds the few who survive.

11 "As surely as I live, says the Sovereign LORD, I will cut you off completely. I will show
you no pity at all because you have defiled My Temple with your vile images and detest-
able sins. 12 A third of your people will die in the city from disease and famine. A third of
them will be slaughtered by the enemy outside the city walls. And I will scatter a third to
the winds, chasing them with My sword. 13 Then at last My anger will be spent, and I will be
satisfied. And when My fury against them has subsided, all Israel will know that I, the LORD,
have spoken to them in My jealous anger.

14 "So I will turn you into a ruin, a mockery in the eyes of the surrounding nations and to
all who pass by. 15 You will become an object of mockery and taunting and horror. You will
be a warning to all the nations around you. They will see what happens when the LORD
punishes a nation in anger and rebukes it, says the LORD.

16 "I will shower you with the deadly arrows of famine to destroy you. The famine will

4:17 Lev 26:39
5:1 Lev 21:5; Isa 7:20; Dan 5:27
5:2 Lev 26:33; Jer 39:1-2
5:5 Jer 6:6; Lam 1:1
5:8 Jer 24:9; Zech 14:2
5:9 Dan 9:12; Matt 24:21
5:10 Lev 26:29; Ps 44:11; Jer 19:9; Amos 9:9; Zech 2:6; 7:14
5:12 Jer 15:2; 44:27; Amos 9:9; Zech 2:6
5:13 Isa 1:24; 59:17; Lam 4:11
5:15 Isa 66:15-16; Jer 22:8-9; 1 Cor 10:11
5:16 Deut 32:23-24

5:1-4 In Ezekiel's third symbolic action, God told him to shave his head and beard and to disperse the cuttings of hair in several ways. God told him to use a sword—not a razor—to shave, since the sword was an instrument of warfare, and God had become Israel's "enemy" (5:8). The law forbade a priest to shave (Leviticus 21:5) due to its association with pagan rituals, so this was particularly serious for Ezekiel, a priest, and would have graphically illustrated to the people how grievous their sins were. Shaving the head also signified humiliation (2 Samuel 10:4-5) or mourning (Isaiah 15:2).

5:2-12 The removal and dispersal of Ezekiel's hair anticipated the destruction of Jerusalem and the Temple in 587/586 BC. The removal of the hair from Ezekiel's head prefigures the Babylonian army's removal of Israel from the land. The destruction of the hair in three ways refers to the three ways God's people would suffer at the hands of the Babylonians: death from disease and famine in the city; death by the sword after the Babylonian soldiers conquered the city; and exile to a foreign land. The phrase "just a bit of the hair" signified the godly remnant that would survive to rebuild the nation after God's punishment was over.

5:13 God's people needed to know that the Babylonian captivity did not mean that God did not care about them or was powerless to stop their exile. God made it clear that He punished them because of His "jealous anger," which was provoked by their idolatry (see also 5:14-17).

▸ HOLINESS

5:13 Fight or surrender. There is an old saying in the African-American church: "Your arms are too short to box with God." No one with any sense should want to oppose God—yet we do it all the time. When Israel continued in sinful rebellion, God became her opponent so that the nations would be warned not to provoke Him. The city of Jerusalem would soon be made a pile of rubble as a demonstration of God's great might. As long as we remain in our sin, we are choosing to oppose God. Ask God to help you see areas of your life where you are choosing to be God's enemy, and repent of these sins. Surrender now. Know the victory that comes through surrender to God. (***See Holiness***> *Submission> Yielding to Spirit> Surrender your heart,* TopicGuide page A41; also ***see God***> *God's Names> Son> Friend of sinners,* TopicGuide page A18.)

become more and more severe until every crumb of food is gone. 17And along with the famine, wild animals will attack you and rob you of your children. Disease and war will stalk your land, and I will bring the sword of the enemy against you. I, the LORD, have spoken!"

5:17 Ezek 14:21

JUDGMENT AGAINST ISRAEL'S MOUNTAINS

6 Again a message came to me from the LORD: 2"Son of man, turn and face the mountains of Israel and prophesy against them. 3Proclaim this message from the Sovereign LORD against the mountains of Israel. This is what the Sovereign LORD says to the mountains and hills and to the ravines and valleys: I am about to bring war upon you, and I will smash your pagan shrines. 4All your altars will be demolished, and your places of worship will be destroyed. I will kill your people in front of your idols.* 5I will lay your corpses in front of your idols and scatter your bones around your altars. 6Wherever you live there will be desolation, and I will destroy your pagan shrines. Your altars will be demolished, your idols will be smashed, your places of worship will be torn down, and all the religious objects you have made will be destroyed. 7The place will be littered with corpses, and you will know that I alone am the LORD.

8"But I will let a few of My people escape destruction, and they will be scattered among the nations of the world. 9Then when they are exiled among the nations, they will remember Me. They will recognize how hurt I am by their unfaithful hearts and lustful eyes that long for their idols. Then at last they will hate themselves for all their detestable sins. 10They will know that I alone am the LORD and that I was serious when I said I would bring this calamity on them.

11"This is what the Sovereign LORD says: Clap your hands in horror, and stamp your feet. Cry out because of all the detestable sins the people of Israel have committed. Now they are going to die from war and famine and disease. 12Disease will strike down those who are far away in exile. War will destroy those who are nearby. And anyone who survives will be killed by famine. So at last I will spend My fury on them. 13They will know that I am the LORD when their dead lie scattered among their idols and altars on every hill and mountain and under every green tree and every great shade tree—the places where they offered sacrifices to their idols. 14I will crush them and make their cities desolate from the wilderness in the south to Riblah* in the north. Then they will know that I am the LORD."

6:2 Ezek 36:1
6:4 Lev 26:30; 2 Chr 14:5; Isa 27:9; Ezek 6:6
6:6 Zech 13:2
6:8 Isa 6:13; Jer 44:14, 28; Ezek 7:16; 14:22
6:9 Deut 30:2; Job 42:6; Ps 78:40; Isa 7:13; 43:24; Ezek 20:43; Hos 11:8
6:11 Ezek 5:12; 7:15; 9:4; 25:6
6:12 Lam 4:11-12; Ezek 5:13; Dan 9:7
6:13 1 Kgs 14:23; 2 Kgs 16:4; Isa 57:5-7; Ezek 20:27-28; Hos 4:13
6:14 Isa 5:25; Ezek 14:13

6:4 The Hebrew term (literally *round things*) probably alludes to dung; also in 6:5, 6, 9, 13. 6:14 As in some Hebrew manuscripts; most Hebrew manuscripts read *Diblah.*

6:1-6 In Ezekiel's fourth symbolic action, God told him to prophesy to the mountains, which personified the people of Israel themselves. The mountains would be overrun by enemy soldiers; pagan shrines and idols would be destroyed; and numerous people of Israel would be killed in front of them.

6:7 The phrase "you will know that I alone am the LORD" indicates that God's actions against Israel were both judicial and redemptive. The people of Israel needed to know that "the LORD" was more powerful than the false gods they worshiped, so that they would again worship Him alone.

6:8-10 God promised to preserve "a few of My people," but they would have to endure exile "among the nations of the world." The 70 years of captivity would cause them to "remember" that He alone is "the LORD." Idolatry had plagued the people of Israel for centuries, but after the captivity this particular sin was practically nonexistent. None of the post-exilic prophets addressed idolatry.

▸ PURPOSE

6:9 Clear judgment. It is very common for people to take tests to help them discover their strengths and weaknesses. Imagine your surprise if you took such a test and were informed that your weaknesses were unfaithfulness, lust, and wickedness! Yet these were the test results God's people received in Ezekiel's day. Human assessment tests can be wrong, but God's evaluation is always correct. Ezekiel told the people that a time would come when they would hate the wicked things they had done. Unfortunately, they would have to endure judgment and exile before they came to this proper self-assessment. Ask God to give you a proper self-assessment so that you can make any necessary changes before God steps in to get your attention. (***See Purpose***> *God's Deeds> Judgment> God promises judgment,* TopicGuide page A53.)

THE COMING OF THE END

7 Then this message came to me from the LORD: [2] "Son of man, this is what the Sovereign LORD says to Israel:

"The end is here!
Wherever you look—
east, west, north, or south—
your land is finished.
[3] No hope remains,
for I will unleash My anger against you.
I will call you to account
for all your detestable sins.
[4] I will turn My eyes away and show no pity.
I will repay you for all your detestable sins.
Then you will know that I am the LORD.

[5] "This is what the Sovereign LORD says:
Disaster after disaster
is coming your way!
[6] The end has come.
It has finally arrived.
Your final doom is waiting!
[7] O people of Israel, the day of your destruction is dawning.
The time has come; the day of trouble is near.
Shouts of anguish will be heard on the mountains,
not shouts of joy.
[8] Soon I will pour out My fury on you
and unleash My anger against you.
I will call you to account
for all your detestable sins.
[9] I will turn My eyes away and show no pity.
I will repay you for all your detestable sins.
Then you will know that it is I, the LORD,
who is striking the blow.

[10] "The day of judgment is here;
your destruction awaits!
The people's wickedness and pride
have blossomed to full flower.
[11] Their violence has grown into a rod
that will beat them for their wickedness.
None of these proud and wicked people will survive.
All their wealth and prestige will be swept away.
[12] Yes, the time has come;
the day is here!
Buyers should not rejoice over bargains,
nor sellers grieve over losses,
for all of them will fall
under My terrible anger.

7:2 Ezek 11:13; Amos 8:2, 10
7:4 Ezek 6:7; 11:21; 22:31; Hos 9:7
7:5 2 Kgs 21:12-13; Nah 1:9
7:7 Isa 22:5; Ezek 12:23-25, 28
7:8 Isa 42:25; Ezek 9:8; 14:19; 33:20; 36:19; Nah 1:6
7:10 Ps 89:32; Isa 10:5
7:12 Isa 5:13-14; Ezek 6:11-12; 1 Cor 7:29-31; Jas 5:8-9

7:1-27 Ezekiel's message in this chapter is a summary of the messages in the four symbolic actions in chapters 4–6. It begins and ends as many other prophecies in Ezekiel—an announcement of the source and a closing statement of the goal of the prophecy. This literary bracketing also appears in 6:1-14.

13 Even if the merchants survive,
they will never return to their business.
For what God has said applies to everyone—
it will not be changed!
Not one person whose life is twisted by sin
will ever recover.

THE DESOLATION OF ISRAEL

14 "The trumpet calls Israel's army to mobilize,
but no one listens,
for My fury is against them all.
15 There is war outside the city
and disease and famine within.
Those outside the city walls
will be killed by enemy swords.
Those inside the city
will die of famine and disease.
16 The survivors who escape to the mountains
will moan like doves, weeping for their sins.
17 Their hands will hang limp,
their knees will be weak as water.
18 They will dress themselves in burlap;
horror and shame will cover them.
They will shave their heads
in sorrow and remorse.

19 "They will throw their money in the streets,
tossing it out like worthless trash.
Their silver and gold won't save them
on that day of the LORD's anger.
It will neither satisfy nor feed them,
for their greed can only trip them up.
20 They were proud of their beautiful jewelry
and used it to make detestable idols and vile images.
Therefore, I will make all their wealth
disgusting to them.
21 I will give it as plunder to foreigners,
to the most wicked of nations,
and they will defile it.
22 I will turn My eyes from them
as these robbers invade and defile My treasured land.

7:14 Num 10:9; Jer 4:5
7:15 Jer 14:18; Ezek 6:11-12; 12:16
7:16 Isa 38:14; 59:11; Ezek 6:8; 14:22; Nah 2:7
7:17 Job 21:6; Isa 13:7; Ezek 21:7; 22:14; Heb 12:12
7:18 Isa 15:3; Ezek 27:31; Amos 8:10
7:19 Prov 11:4; Isa 2:20
7:20 Isa 30:22
7:21 2 Kgs 24:13; Ps 74:2-8
7:22 Jer 18:17; Ezek 39:23-24

7:14-27 The Lord provided some details about the awful punishment Israel was about to endure, and then He ended the message by repeating the main purpose of Israel's suffering—so they would "know that I am the LORD." These words end the first collection of Ezekiel's sermons and are repeated for emphasis at 12:16, 20 and again at 13:23, thereby closing the second major collection of Ezekiel's messages.

▸ WORSHIP

7:22 Profaning our holy places. Most people, both spiritual and unspiritual, have special places or things they do not want destroyed. The Jews of Ezekiel's time believed that because God had chosen Jerusalem as His dwelling place, and had supernaturally defended Jerusalem before (Isaiah 36–37; 2 Kings 18–19; 2 Chronicles 32), that He would never let the city be destroyed. But Jeremiah warned those in Jerusalem not to trust in the existence of the Temple as a guarantee of their own safety (Jeremiah 7:1-15; 26:1-19). God told His people repeatedly that He would not overlook their conduct simply to save a building or a city. Today, God will not overlook sin simply to save a church, a denomination, or a nation. A holy God hates sin and will, in the end, destroy everything that promotes it (Numbers 16:26; Isaiah 1:28). Do not get in God's way as He continues His holy war against sin. (***See Worship***> *OT> Place> Temple> Set apart from sin*, TopicGuide page A28.)

23 "Prepare chains for My people,
for the land is bloodied by terrible crimes.
Jerusalem is filled with violence.
24 I will bring the most ruthless of nations
to occupy their homes.
I will break down their proud fortresses
and defile their sanctuaries.
25 Terror and trembling will overcome My people.
They will look for peace but not find it.
26 Calamity will follow calamity;
rumor will follow rumor.
They will look in vain
for a vision from the prophets.
They will receive no teaching from the priests
and no counsel from the leaders.
27 The king and the prince will stand helpless,
weeping in despair,
and the people's hands
will tremble with fear.
I will bring on them
the evil they have done to others,
and they will receive the punishment
they so richly deserve.
Then they will know that I am the LORD."

IDOLATRY IN THE TEMPLE

8 Then on September 17,* during the sixth year of King Jehoiachin's captivity, while the
leaders of Judah were in my home, the Sovereign LORD took hold of me. 2I saw a fig-
ure that appeared to be a man. From what appeared to be His waist down, He looked like a
burning flame. From the waist up He looked like gleaming amber.* 3He reached out what
seemed to be a hand and took me by the hair. Then the Spirit lifted me up into the sky and
transported me to Jerusalem in a vision from God. I was taken to the north gate of the inner
courtyard of the Temple, where there is a large idol that has made the LORD very jealous.
4Suddenly, the glory of the God of Israel was there, just as I had seen it before in the valley.
5Then the LORD said to me, "Son of man, look toward the north." So I looked, and there
to the north, beside the entrance to the gate near the altar, stood the idol that had made
the LORD so jealous.
6"Son of man," He said, "do you see what they are doing? Do you see the detestable sins
the people of Israel are committing to drive Me from My Temple? But come, and you will
see even more detestable sins than these!" 7Then He brought me to the door of the Tem-

7:23 Jer 27:2; Ezek 8:17; 9:9; Hos 4:2
7:24 2 Chr 7:20; Ezek 21:31; 28:7; 33:28
7:25 Ezek 13:10, 16
7:26 Ps 74:9; Isa 47:11; Jer 4:20; 18:18; 37:17; Ezek 21:7; 22:26; Mic 3:6
7:27 Ps 35:26; Ezek 26:16
8:2 Ezek 1:4, 27-28
8:3 Ezek 3:12; 11:1; Dan 5:5
8:4 Ezek 1:27-28
8:5 Ps 78:58; Jer 3:2; 7:30; 32:34; Ezek 8:3; Zech 5:5
8:6 2 Kgs 23:4-5; Ezek 5:11; 8:9, 17

8:1 Hebrew *on the fifth day of the sixth month,* of the ancient Hebrew lunar calendar. This event occurred on September 17, 592 B.C.; also see note on 1:1. 8:2 Or *like burnished metal.*

8:1–13:23 The sixth year of King Jehoiachin's captivity was the year 592 BC—fourteen months after the prophecies in chapters 1–7 (see notes at 1:1 and 1:2). As in chapters 1–7, this series of visions begins with a heavenly figure revealing himself to Ezekiel and then continues with several judgments against Israel that include symbolic actions by Ezekiel. These visions occurred while Ezekiel was hosting "the leaders of Judah" (8:1).

8:2-4 In this vision, God appeared from the "waist down" as "a burning flame" and "from the waist up" as "gleaming amber" (see Ezekiel 1:26-27). Both spoke of the fiery judgments to come on Israel and Jerusalem. Ezekiel had an out-of-the-body experience as God's Spirit transported him to Jerusalem to observe what was occurring at the Temple. As a priest (see 1:3), Ezekiel would have been greatly concerned that the priests performed their duties as the law of Moses prescribed. God's glory was still there, despite Israel's wickedness.

8:5-6 Ezekiel saw an idol at "the entrance to the gate near the altar". The false god was set up near the sanctuary of the Temple, where the Lord alone was to be worshiped. This idol may have been the one erected by Manasseh (see 2 Chronicles 33:7, 15), for the Hebrew word is the same in both places and occurs elsewhere only in Deuteronomy 4:16-18. God then took Ezekiel to a place where "even more detestable sins" were occurring.

8:8 ple courtyard, where I could see a hole in the wall. 8He said to me, "Now, son of man, dig
Isa 29:15 into the wall." So I dug into the wall and found a hidden doorway.
8:10 9"Go in," He said, "and see the wicked and detestable sins they are committing in there!"
Exod 20:4 10So I went in and saw the walls engraved with all kinds of crawling animals and detest-
8:11 Num 11:16, 25; able creatures. I also saw the various idols* worshiped by the people of Israel. 11Seventy
16:17, 35 leaders of Israel were standing there with Jaazaniah son of Shaphan in the center. Each of
Jer 19:1 Luke 10:1 them held an incense burner, from which a cloud of incense rose above their heads.
12Then the LORD said to me, "Son of man, have you seen what the leaders of Israel are
8:14 Ezek 44:4; 46:9 doing with their idols in dark rooms? They are saying, 'The LORD doesn't see us; He has de-
8:16 serted our land!'" 13Then the LORD added, "Come, and I will show you even more detest-
Deut 4:19; 17:3 able sins than these!"
2 Chr 29:6 14He brought me to the north gate of the LORD's Temple, and some women were sitting
Job 31:26-28 Jer 2:27; 44:17 there, weeping for the god Tammuz. 15"Have you seen this?" He asked. "But I will show
Ezek 23:39 you even more detestable sins than these!"
8:17 16Then He brought me into the inner courtyard of the LORD's Temple. At the entrance to
Jer 7:18-19 Ezek 7:10-11, 23; 9:9; the sanctuary, between the entry room and the bronze altar, there were about twenty-five
16:26 men with their backs to the sanctuary of the LORD. They were facing east, bowing low to
Amos 3:10 Mic 2:2 the ground, worshiping the sun!
8:18 17"Have you seen this, son of man?" He asked. "Is it nothing to the people of Judah that
Isa 1:15 they commit these detestable sins, leading the whole nation into violence, thumbing their
Jer 11:11 noses at Me, and provoking My anger? 18Therefore, I will respond in fury. I will neither pity
Mic 3:4 Zech 7:13 nor spare them. And though they cry for mercy, I will not listen."

THE SLAUGHTER OF IDOLATERS

9:2 Ezek 10:2 **9** Then the LORD thundered, "Bring on the men appointed to punish the city! Tell them
to bring their weapons with them!" 2Six men soon appeared from the upper gate that

8:10 The Hebrew term (literally *round things*) probably alludes to dung.

▸ **GOD**

8:12 Eyes wide open. Sometimes the simple understanding of a child can be humorous, such as a little girl who covers her eyes with her hands and proclaims, "You can't see me!" She imagines that her inability to see must mean everyone else is also unable to see her. It is just as silly for people to imagine that God is unaware of their activities simply because they are not aware of Him. This verse reveals that God knew all about the sinful activities that were going on in the secret places in Jerusalem. There is no place God cannot see. There is no wall that can limit His gaze. He sees it all, and He knows everything you do, even in your most secret moments. Work to become intentionally transparent and completely honest in your relationship with God. (***See God****> God's Attributes> All-Knowing> One cannot hide from God,* TopicGuide page A15.)

8:14-15 At another section of the Temple Ezekiel saw women "weeping for the god Tammuz." The worship of this pagan god dates back to 3000 BC but is mentioned only here in Scripture. Tammuz was the god of vegetation whose female counterpart was Ishtar. But the Lord warned Ezekiel that He would show him even more "detestable sins" than these (see note at 8:16-18).

▸ **WORSHIP**

8:16 Change your focus. Imagine yourself attending a birthday party where everyone ignores the person that is supposed to be the center of attention. Instead of bringing a cake to him, everyone else receives a cake and blows out the candles. Instead of everyone giving him the most attention, everyone focuses on others in the room and acts as if he is not present. Ezekiel envisioned God's people in God's Temple, but they weren't focused on God. Rather, they had their backs turned toward Him and were hailing His creation instead. We shudder at this perversion of worship, but how often have you sat in church and thought about almost anything but God? Make every effort to center your worship on God and Him alone. Look for ways you subtly push God out of your life and diligently work to keep Him first. (***See Worship****> OT> God's Supremacy> Was God-centered (not worshiper-centered),* TopicGuide page A27.)

8:16-18 Israel's final sin that the Lord showed Ezekiel occurred in the inner Temple area, where 25 men with their backs toward the Temple were worshiping the sun. Either they were priests of God who were committing idolatry, or they were not priests and should not have been in that part of the Temple. Either way, these men had turned their backs on the worship of Yahweh and replaced Him with a false god, so He would "respond in fury." The god of the sun went by different names in ancient cultures, but Ra (Egypt), Tammuz (Sumerian and Babylon), Baal (Canaan), and Apollo (Greece and Rome) were the most common ones.

9:1-4 This chapter describes the Lord's response to the great sins Ezekiel had just seen (chapter 8). Six angelic guards of the city of Jerusalem, each holding "a deadly weapon," were called into the Lord's presence. God's glory moved from above the cherubim to the threshold of the Temple in preparation for its imminent departure (chapter 10). God then told the six guards to put a mark on the faithful in the city who were grieved by Israel's great sins. The mark signified ownership and protection (compare Genesis 4:15; Exodus 28:38; Revelation 13:16-18; 14:1).

faces north, each carrying a deadly weapon in his hand. With them was a man dressed in
linen, who carried a writer's case at his side. They all went into the Temple courtyard and
stood beside the bronze altar.
3 Then the glory of the God of Israel rose up from between the cherubim, where it had
rested, and moved to the entrance of the Temple. And the LORD called to the man dressed
in linen who was carrying the writer's case. 4 He said to him, "Walk through the streets of
Jerusalem and put a mark on the foreheads of all who weep and sigh because of the de-
testable sins being committed in their city."
5 Then I heard the LORD say to the other men, "Follow him through the city and kill every-
one whose forehead is not marked. Show no mercy; have no pity! 6 Kill them all—old and
young, girls and women and little children. But do not touch anyone with the mark. Begin
right here at the Temple." So they began by killing the seventy leaders.
7 "Defile the Temple!" the LORD commanded. "Fill its courtyards with corpses. Go!" So
they went and began killing throughout the city.
8 While they were out killing, I was all alone. I fell face down on the ground and cried
out, "O Sovereign LORD! Will Your fury against Jerusalem wipe out everyone left in Israel?"
9 Then He said to me, "The sins of the people of Israel and Judah are very, very great.
The entire land is full of murder; the city is filled with injustice. They are saying, 'The LORD
doesn't see it! The LORD has abandoned the land!' 10 So I will not spare them or have any
pity on them. I will fully repay them for all they have done."
11 Then the man in linen clothing, who carried the writer's case, reported back and said,
"I have done as You commanded."

9:3
Ezek 10:4; 11:22-23

9:4
Exod 12:7, 13
Ps 119:53, 136
Jer 13:17
2 Cor 1:22
2 Tim 2:19
Rev 7:2-3

9:6
2 Chr 36:17
Ezek 5:11; 8:11-12
Rev 9:4

9:8
1 Chr 21:16
Ezek 11:13
Amos 7:2-6

9:9
2 Kgs 21:16
Pss 10:11; 94:7
Isa 29:15
Ezek 7:23; 8:12; 22:2-3, 29
Mic 3:1-3; 7:3

9:10
Isa 65:6
Ezek 7:4; 8:18; 11:21; 24:14
Hos 9:7

THE LORD'S GLORY LEAVES THE TEMPLE

10 In my vision I saw what appeared to be a throne of blue lapis lazuli above the crys-
tal surface over the heads of the cherubim. 2 Then the LORD spoke to the man in
linen clothing and said, "Go between the whirling wheels beneath the cherubim, and take
a handful of burning coals and scatter them over the city." He did this as I watched.
3 The cherubim were standing at the south end of the Temple when the man went in,
and the cloud of glory filled the inner courtyard. 4 Then the glory of the LORD rose up from
above the cherubim and went over to the door of the Temple. The Temple was filled with
this cloud of glory, and the courtyard glowed brightly with the glory of the LORD. 5 The
moving wings of the cherubim sounded like the voice of God Almighty* and could be
heard even in the outer courtyard.
6 The LORD said to the man in linen clothing, "Go between the cherubim and take some

10:1
Exod 24:10
Ezek 1:22, 26
Rev 4:2-3

10:2
Ps 18:10-13
Isa 6:6
Rev 8:5

10:4
Exod 40:34-35
Isa 6:1-4

10:5
Job 40:9
Ezek 1:24
Rev 10:3

10:5 Hebrew *El-Shaddai.*

▶ GOD

9:4 Marked by God. How would you feel if someone suddenly approached you and wrote his name on your forehead with a permanent marker? Or tattooed it on your arm? In this passage, "a man dressed in linen" put a mark on those who were grieving their personal and national detachment from God. Ephesians 1:13 says that whenever we trust in Jesus, God identifies us as His own by marking us. The original language literally says that He has "sealed" us, much as an official document is sealed with wax or clay. Make no mistake, "the LORD knows those who are His" (2 Timothy 2:19). He has sealed His people with His Spirit. If you have trusted Jesus as your Savior, rejoice—God has specially marked you as His own. Live worthy of His mark. (***See God****> Salvation> Holy Spirit> Sealed by the Holy Spirit,* TopicGuide page A15.)

9:5-8 God told the six guards to kill all those without the mark on their foreheads without regard for age or gender (see note at 9:1-4). In Ezekiel's vision the guards symbolically carried out what the Babylonian army would do at a later date. As the destruction was occurring, Ezekiel feared that the Lord's "fury" would leave no survivors in Israel. The Lord didn't address Ezekiel's fear until he repeated it later (see note at 11:13-21).

10:1-5 God's glory was once again being escorted by the four living beings (see note at 1:5-14), and in this chapter they are called "cherubim" (see also 9:3). God's glory moved to the door of the Temple, where the Temple courtyard glowed brightly (10:4; compare Exodus 40:34-35).

10:6-17 In Ezekiel 1, God manifested Himself as arriving for Ezekiel's ordination. With similar fanfare, God's chariot/throne and His accompanying heavenly hosts symbolically departed the Temple.

burning coals from between the wheels." So the man went in and stood beside one of the
wheels. 7 Then one of the cherubim reached out his hand and took some live coals from
the fire burning among them. He put the coals into the hands of the man in linen clothing,
and the man took them and went out. 8 (All the cherubim had what looked like human
10:9 hands under their wings.)
Ezek 1:16-17 9 I looked, and each of the four cherubim had a wheel beside him, and the wheels spar-
10:11 kled like beryl. 10 All four wheels looked alike and were made the same; each wheel had a
Ezek 1:17 second wheel turning crosswise within it. 11 The cherubim could move in any of the four
10:12 Ezek 1:18 directions they faced, without turning as they moved. They went straight in the direction
Rev 4:6, 8 they faced, never turning aside. 12 Both the cherubim and the wheels were covered with
10:14 eyes. The cherubim had eyes all over their bodies, including their hands, their backs, and
1 Kgs 7:27-30, 36 Ezek 1:6, 10; 10:21 their wings. 13 I heard someone refer to the wheels as "the whirling wheels." 14 Each of the
Rev 4:7 four cherubim had four faces: the first was the face of an ox,* the second was a human
10:15 face, the third was the face of a lion, and the fourth was the face of an eagle.
Ezek 1:3-6, 19-21 15 Then the cherubim rose upward. These were the same living beings I had seen beside
10:17 the Kebar River. 16 When the cherubim moved, the wheels moved with them. When they
Ezek 1:12 lifted their wings to fly, the wheels stayed beside them. 17 When the cherubim stopped, the
10:18 wheels stopped. When they flew upward, the wheels rose up, for the spirit of the living be-
Ps 18:10 ings was in the wheels.
10:19 Ezek 1:22 18 Then the glory of the LORD moved out from the door of the Temple and hovered
10:20 above the cherubim. 19 And as I watched, the cherubim flew with their wheels to the east
Ezek 1:5, 26; 10:15 gate of the LORD's Temple. And the glory of the God of Israel hovered above them.
10:21 20 These were the same living beings I had seen beneath the God of Israel when I was by
Ezek 1:6, 8; 10:14; the Kebar River. I knew they were cherubim, 21 for each had four faces and four wings and
41:18-20 what looked like human hands under their wings. 22 And their faces were just like the faces of
10:22 Ezek 1:10, 12 the beings I had seen at the Kebar, and they traveled straight ahead, just as the others had.

JUDGMENT ON ISRAEL'S LEADERS

11:1 **11** Then the Spirit lifted me and brought me to the east gateway of the LORD's Temple,
Ezek 8:3; 43:5 where I saw twenty-five prominent men of the city. Among them were Jaazaniah
11:2 Isa 30:1 son of Azzur and Pelatiah son of Benaiah, who were leaders among the people.
Mic 2:1 2 The Spirit said to me, "Son of man, these are the men who are planning evil and giving

10:14 Hebrew *the face of a cherub;* compare 1:10.

10:18-19 God's glory moved from the door of the Temple to the east gate of the Temple, moving farther and farther away from its original dwelling place in the Most Holy Place.

▸ BIBLE
10:20 Interpreting the unclear. Ezekiel saw images that seemed just as fantastic to him as they do to us. He repeated himself here (compare 10:15), perhaps to make sure we understand and reaffirm that this was indeed what he saw—perhaps as much for his own benefit as for ours. The central message of this amazing vision is clear: God's blessings and protection were leaving Israel as a judgment against them and as a warning to the surrounding nations. While many things in the visions and prophecies of the Bible can be confusing, we can keep the central message in place by referring to the clearer passages surrounding them. Use the obvious texts to interpret or explain the less obvious, and never use the mysterious texts to interpret the plain. (***See Bible***> *Power> Equip> Provides insight,* TopicGuide page A11.)

11:1-12 The Lord promised Ezekiel that the 25 idolaters he saw earlier (see 8:16) would be judged for leading the people astray.

▸ SPIRITUAL WARFARE
11:2 False prophets. Terrible sins abound in this world—murder, rape, torture—and we are right to be angered by them. But among the worst sins in the world is one that causes few people to become upset: telling lies about God. God told Ezekiel that He would utterly destroy those who intentionally spoke false words about Him. To demonstrate that He meant what He said, God killed one of the false prophets on the spot (11:13). When you hear people telling lies about God and His Word, do not ignore them—they are committing a grave error. Pray for them and those who might be led astray by them. Like Ezekiel, warn them and others about the danger of promoting false doctrine (Jude 1:12-16). (***See Spiritual Warfare***> *Originator of Sin> Satan's Strategies> Demons> Demons sow false doctrine,* TopicGuide page A45.)

wicked counsel in this city. [3]They say to the people, 'Is it not a good time to build houses?
This city is like an iron pot. We are safe inside it like meat in a pot.*' [4]Therefore, son of
man, prophesy against them loudly and clearly."
[5]Then the Spirit of the LORD came upon me, and He told me to say, "This is what the
LORD says to the people of Israel: I know what you are saying, for I know every thought
that comes into your minds. [6]You have murdered many in this city and filled its streets
with the dead.
[7]"Therefore, this is what the Sovereign LORD says: This city is an iron pot all right, but the
pieces of meat are the victims of your injustice. As for you, I will soon drag you from this pot.
[8]I will bring on you the sword of war you so greatly fear, says the Sovereign LORD. [9]I will
drive you out of Jerusalem and hand you over to foreigners, who will carry out My judg-
ments against you. [10]You will be slaughtered all the way to the borders of Israel. I will exe-
cute judgment on you, and you will know that I am the LORD. [11]No, this city will not be an
iron pot for you, and you will not be like meat safe inside it. I will judge you even to the bor-
ders of Israel, [12]and you will know that I am the LORD. For you have refused to obey My de-
crees and regulations; instead, you have copied the standards of the nations around you."
[13]While I was still prophesying, Pelatiah son of Benaiah suddenly died. Then I fell face
down on the ground and cried out, "O Sovereign LORD, are You going to kill everyone in
Israel?"

HOPE FOR EXILED ISRAEL

[14]Then this message came to me from the LORD: [15]"Son of man, the people still left in Jeru-
salem are talking about you and your relatives and all the people of Israel who are in ex-
ile. They are saying, 'Those people are far away from the LORD, so now He has given their
land to us!'
[16]"Therefore, tell the exiles, 'This is what the Sovereign LORD says: Although I have scat-
tered you in the countries of the world, I will be a sanctuary to you during your time in ex-
ile. [17]I, the Sovereign LORD, will gather you back from the nations where you have been
scattered, and I will give you the land of Israel once again.'

11:3 Jer 1:13; Ezek 24:3, 6; 2 Pet 3:4
11:4 Ezek 3:4, 17
11:5 Jer 11:20; 17:10
11:6 Isa 1:15; Ezek 7:23; 22:2-6, 9, 12, 27; Matt 23:35
11:7 2 Kgs 25:18-22; Jer 52:24-27
11:9 Deut 28:36, 49-50; Ps 106:41
11:10 Num 34:8-9; Josh 13:5
11:12 Ezek 8:10, 14, 16; 18:8-9
11:13 Ezek 9:8
11:15 Ezek 33:24
11:16 Jer 29:7, 11
11:17 Isa 11:11-16; Jer 24:5-6

11:3 Hebrew *This city is the pot, and we are the meat.*

11:13-21 Again Ezekiel asked if the Lord would "kill everyone in Israel" (see note at 9:5-8), and this time the Lord responded that He would preserve a faithful remnant from those scattered among the nations.

BECAUSE GOD KNOWS EVERYTHING

I will go to Him with all my questions and concerns.

I know every thought that comes into your minds.

EZEKIEL 11:5

FOR THE NEXT *GOD KNOWS EVERYTHING* FEATURE SEE PAGE 1585.

18 “When the people return to their homeland, they will remove every trace of their vile images and detestable idols. 19 And I will give them singleness of heart and put a new spirit within them. I will take away their stony, stubborn heart and give them a tender, responsive heart,* 20 so they will obey My decrees and regulations. Then they will truly be My people, and I will be their God. 21 But as for those who long for vile images and detestable idols, I will repay them fully for their sins. I, the Sovereign LORD, have spoken!”

THE LORD'S GLORY LEAVES JERUSALEM

22 Then the cherubim lifted their wings and rose into the air with their wheels beside them, and the glory of the God of Israel hovered above them. 23 Then the glory of the LORD went up from the city and stopped above the mountain to the east.

24 Afterward the Spirit of God carried me back again to Babylonia,* to the people in exile there. And so ended the vision of my visit to Jerusalem. 25 And I told the exiles everything the LORD had shown me.

SIGNS OF THE COMING EXILE

12 Again a message came to me from the LORD: 2 “Son of man, you live among rebels who have eyes but refuse to see. They have ears but refuse to hear. For they are a rebellious people.

3 “So now, son of man, pretend you are being sent into exile. Pack the few items an exile could carry, and leave your home to go somewhere else. Do this right in front of the people so they can see you. For perhaps they will pay attention to this, even though they are such rebels. 4 Bring your baggage outside during the day so they can watch you. Then in the evening, as they are watching, leave your house as captives do when they begin a long march to distant lands. 5 Dig a hole through the wall while they are watching and go out through it. 6 As they watch, lift your pack to your shoulders and walk away into the night. Cover your face so you cannot see the land you are leaving. For I have made you a sign for the people of Israel.”

7 So I did as I was told. In broad daylight I brought my pack outside, filled with the things I might carry into exile. Then in the evening while the people looked on, I dug through the wall with my hands and went out into the night with my pack on my shoulder.

8 The next morning this message came to me from the LORD: 9 “Son of man, these rebels, the people of Israel, have asked you what all this means. 10 Say to them, ‘This is what the

11:18 Ezek 5:11; 37:23
11:19 Jer 24:7; 32:39; Ezek 36:26; Zech 7:12; 2 Cor 3:3
11:20 Ezek 36:27
11:21 Jer 16:18
11:23 Zech 14:4
11:24 Ezek 8:3; 37:1
12:2 Isa 6:9-10; Jer 5:21; Ezek 2:6-8; Matt 13:13-14; John 9:39-41
12:3 Jer 26:3; 36:3, 7; Luke 20:13; 2 Tim 2:25
12:4 2 Kgs 25:4; Jer 39:4; 52:7
12:6 Isa 8:18
12:10 2 Kgs 9:25; Isa 13:1; Mal 1:1

11:19 Hebrew *a heart of flesh.* 11:24 Or *Chaldea.*

▸ GOD

11:19 A new heart. Is it a spiritual advantage to be born a Jew? Or to be born of any other race? The apostle Paul's surprising answer is, “Yes, there are great benefits” to being a Jew (Romans 3:2). Some people groups have the Bible or an abundance of godly churches, while others do not. But this does not mean that Jews or any other race are more or less in need of Jesus Christ to be their Savior. Ezekiel knew God's people needed a “heart transplant”—God's gift of spiritual life—before they would be pleasing to Him (Ephesians 2:1-3). Just being Jewish was not enough. For God's people today, we need to realize that just being an American or belonging to a particular denomination or other affiliation is not enough—we must be born again. Pray for God to reveal to you your spiritual pride and ask Him to give you a new heart that pleases Him. (***See God****> Relationship> God Enables> Relationship with God requires a right heart,* TopicGuide page A14.)

11:22-23 The cherubim escorted God's glory away from the Temple and the city of Jerusalem and stopped above “the mountain to the east” (probably the Mount of Olives). The Lord was no longer dwelling in a special way in the midst of His people as He had for over eight centuries—since the time Moses and the Israelites built the Tabernacle, and God's glory filled it (Exodus 40:34-38).

12:1-2 The Lord called His people “rebels”; they still wouldn't listen even though they had suffered two waves of captivity already (see note at 1:2) and their kings were just vassals for King Nebuchadnezzar. The leaders continued to ignore God's warnings through His prophets (Jeremiah and Ezekiel in particular).

12:3-16 This passage contains another of Ezekiel's symbolic actions (see notes at 4:1 and 4:1-8). The Lord told the prophet to demonstrate for the people of Israel what going into exile would be like. He did this by carrying a few possessions in a bag, digging through a wall (as if to escape enemy soldiers), and walking into the night. When the people wanted to know what his actions meant, he was told to tell them that exile to Babylon awaited them all, including King Zedekiah who would “leave Jerusalem at night through a hole in the wall” (12:12). The record of this fulfilled prophecy is found in Jeremiah 39:4 and 2 Kings 25:4.

Sovereign LORD says: These actions contain a message for King Zedekiah in Jerusalem*
and for all the people of Israel.' 11Explain that your actions are a sign to show what will
soon happen to them, for they will be driven into exile as captives.
12"Even Zedekiah will leave Jerusalem at night through a hole in the wall, taking only
what he can carry with him. He will cover his face, and his eyes will not see the land he is
leaving. 13Then I will throw My net over him and capture him in My snare. I will bring him
to Babylon, the land of the Babylonians,* though he will never see it, and he will die there.
14I will scatter his servants and warriors to the four winds and send the sword after them.
15And when I scatter them among the nations, they will know that I am the LORD. 16But I
will spare a few of them from death by war, famine, or disease, so they can confess all
their detestable sins to their captors. Then they will know that I am the LORD."
17Then this message came to me from the LORD: 18"Son of man, tremble as you eat your
food. Shake with fear as you drink your water. 19Tell the people, 'This is what the Sover-
eign LORD says concerning those living in Israel and Jerusalem: They will eat their food
with trembling and sip their water in despair, for their land will be stripped bare because of
their violence. 20The cities will be destroyed and the farmland made desolate. Then you
will know that I am the LORD.' "

A NEW PROVERB FOR ISRAEL

21Again a message came to me from the LORD: 22"Son of man, you've heard that proverb
they quote in Israel: 'Time passes, and prophecies come to nothing.' 23Tell the people,
'This is what the Sovereign LORD says: I will put an end to this proverb, and you will soon
stop quoting it.' Now give them this new proverb to replace the old one: 'The time has
come for every prophecy to be fulfilled!'
24"There will be no more false visions and flattering predictions in Israel. 25For I am the
LORD! If I say it, it will happen. There will be no more delays, you rebels of Israel. I will fulfill
My threat of destruction in your own lifetime. I, the Sovereign LORD, have spoken!"
26Then this message came to me from the LORD: 27"Son of man, the people of Israel are
saying, 'He's talking about the distant future. His visions won't come true for a long, long
time.' 28Therefore, tell them, 'This is what the Sovereign LORD says: No more delay! I will
now do everything I have threatened. I, the Sovereign LORD, have spoken!' "

JUDGMENT AGAINST FALSE PROPHETS

13 Then this message came to me from the LORD: 2"Son of man, prophesy against
the false prophets of Israel who are inventing their own prophecies. Say to them,
'Listen to the word of the LORD. 3This is what the Sovereign LORD says: What sorrow awaits
the false prophets who are following their own imaginations and have seen nothing at all!'
4"O people of Israel, these prophets of yours are like jackals digging in the ruins. 5They
have done nothing to repair the breaks in the walls around the nation. They have not

12:11 Jer 15:2; 52:15, 28-30
12:12 2 Kgs 25:4; Jer 39:4; 52:7
12:13 Isa 24:17; Jer 39:7; 52:11; Hos 7:12
12:16 Jer 22:8-9
12:18 Ezek 4:16
12:19 Isa 6:11; Zech 7:14
12:20 Isa 7:23-24; Jer 25:9; Ezek 5:14; 36:3; Dan 9:17
12:22 Jer 5:12; Amos 6:3; 2 Pet 3:3-4
12:23 Joel 2:11; Zeph 1:14
12:24 Jer 14:13-16; Zech 13:2-4
12:25 Num 14:28-34; Hab 1:5
12:27 Dan 10:14
13:2 Isa 9:15; 56:9-12; Jer 37:19
13:3 Jer 23:28-32; Lam 2:14
13:5 Ps 106:23; Isa 58:12

12:10 Hebrew *the prince in Jerusalem;* similarly in 12:12. 12:13 Or *Chaldeans.*

12:17-20 In this brief symbolic action Ezekiel was to "tremble" as he ate his food and drank his water in order to demonstrate what the people of Israel would do in the aftermath of the Exile.

▸ BIBLE
12:22 Proverbial truth. Some truth is only designed to be useful in certain situations. That doesn't mean it isn't true—but it does have a specific application. The quoted proverb is true—time reveals some prophets to be false ones. But time also reveals the integrity of other prophets—it took 700 years for some of Isaiah's prophecies to come to fruition. The guidance offered in Scripture is not equally helpful in every situation (compare Proverbs 26:4, 5). But it is all without error. Learn as much truth as possible so you will be more able to dispense the right truth at the right time. Prayerfully seek to apply God's Word rightly. (***See Bible> Uniqueness> Authoritative> Demonstrates credibility,*** TopicGuide page A10.)

13:1-7 False prophets made up prophecies from "their own imaginations," but they would be destroyed by the army of Babylon—the very nation they predicted would not harm them. Jeremiah also denounced the false prophets (Jeremiah 14:14; 23:9-40). These false prophets only harmed the people with their messages.

helped it to stand firm in battle on the day of the LORD. [6]Instead, they have told lies and
13:6 made false predictions. They say, 'This message is from the LORD,' even though the LORD
Jer 28:15; 29:8 never sent them. And yet they expect Him to fulfill their prophecies! [7]Can your visions be
anything but false if you claim, 'This message is from the LORD,' when I have not even spo-
ken to you?
[8]"Therefore, this is what the Sovereign LORD says: Because what you say is false and
13:8 your visions are a lie, I will stand against you, says the Sovereign LORD. [9]I will raise My fist
Nah 2:13 against all the prophets who see false visions and make lying predictions, and they will be
13:9 Ezra 2:59-63 banished from the community of Israel. I will blot their names from Israel's record books,
Ps 69:28 and they will never again set foot in their own land. Then you will know that I am the Sov-
Jer 20:3-6 Dan 12:1 ereign LORD.
13:10 [10]"This will happen because these evil prophets deceive My people by saying, 'All is
Jer 8:11; 50:6 peaceful' when there is no peace at all! It's as if the people have built a flimsy wall, and
these prophets are trying to reinforce it by covering it with whitewash! [11]Tell these white-
washers that their wall will soon fall down. A heavy rainstorm will undermine it; great hail-
stones and mighty winds will knock it down. [12]And when the wall falls, the people will cry
out, 'What happened to your whitewash?'
[13]"Therefore, this is what the Sovereign LORD says: I will sweep away your whitewashed
13:13 Exod 9:24-25 wall with a storm of indignation, with a great flood of anger, and with hailstones of fury.
Ps 18:12-13 Rev 11:19; 16:21 [14]I will break down your wall right to its foundation, and when it falls, it will crush you.
13:14 Then you will know that I am the LORD. [15]At last My anger against the wall and those who
Mic 1:6 covered it with whitewash will be satisfied. Then I will say to you: 'The wall and those who
13:16 whitewashed it are both gone. [16]They were lying prophets who claimed peace would
Isa 57:21 come to Jerusalem when there was no peace. I, the Sovereign LORD, have spoken!'

JUDGMENT AGAINST FALSE WOMEN PROPHETS

13:17 Judg 4:4 [17]"Now, son of man, speak out against the women who prophesy from their own imagina-
2 Kgs 22:14 tions. [18]This is what the Sovereign LORD says: What sorrow awaits you women who are en-
Luke 2:36 snaring the souls of My people, young and old alike. You tie magic charms on their wrists
Acts 21:9 Rev 2:20 and furnish them with magic veils. Do you think you can trap others without bringing de-
13:18 struction on yourselves? [19]You bring shame on Me among My people for a few handfuls
2 Pet 2:14 of barley or a piece of bread. By lying to My people who love to listen to lies, you kill those
13:19 who should not die, and you promise life to those who should not live.
Prov 28:21 Jer 23:14, 17 [20]"This is what the Sovereign LORD says: I am against all your magic charms, which you
Mic 3:5 use to ensnare My people like birds. I will tear them from your arms, setting My people
13:21 free like birds set free from a cage. [21]I will tear off the magic veils and save My people
Pss 91:3; 124:7 from your grasp. They will no longer be your victims. Then you will know that I am the
13:22 LORD. [22]You have discouraged the righteous with your lies, but I didn't want them to be
Amos 5:12 2 Pet 2:18-19 sad. And you have encouraged the wicked by promising them life, even though they con-
13:23 tinue in their sins. [23]Because of all this, you will no longer talk of seeing visions that you
Mic 3:6 never saw, nor will you make predictions. For I will rescue My people from your grasp.
Zech 13:3 Then you will know that I am the LORD."

13:8-16 One of the Lord's judgments against the false prophets was that they would never see the land of Israel again, meaning they would die in exile. Along with death, their family name would be removed from the records of Israel, which meant that they would never return to reclaim their ancestral lands.

▶ HOLINESS

13:18-19 Harmful charms. Good luck charms, lucky numbers—some consider these to be harmless fun. In Ezekiel's day, a group of witches ensnared God's people with the lie that their charms could help them avoid God's judgment. This lie didn't keep them safe—the very opposite was true. It kept them in danger, trusting in demonic powers and trinkets to save them rather than repenting and pleading for God's mercy. There is no magic way to escape God's justice—only belief in the gospel will save us from His wrath. Rid your home, your church, and your life of anything to do with the occult. (***See Holiness***> *Disciplines*> *Of Abstinence*> *Resisting worldly influences,* TopicGuide page A42.)

THE IDOLATRY OF ISRAEL'S LEADERS

14 Then some of the leaders of Israel visited me, and while they were sitting with me,
2this message came to me from the LORD: 3"Son of man, these leaders have set up
idols* in their hearts. They have embraced things that will make them fall into sin. Why
should I listen to their requests? 4Tell them, 'This is what the Sovereign LORD says: The
people of Israel have set up idols in their hearts and fallen into sin, and then they go to a
prophet asking for a message. So I, the LORD, will give them the kind of answer their great
idolatry deserves. 5I will do this to capture the minds and hearts of all My people who
have turned from Me to worship their detestable idols.'

6"Therefore, tell the people of Israel, 'This is what the Sovereign LORD says: Repent and
turn away from your idols, and stop all your detestable sins. 7I, the LORD, will answer all
those, both Israelites and foreigners, who reject Me and set up idols in their hearts and so
fall into sin, and who then come to a prophet asking for My advice. 8I will turn against such
people and make a terrible example of them, eliminating them from among My people.
Then you will know that I am the LORD.

9"'And if a prophet is deceived into giving a message, it is because I, the LORD, have de-
ceived that prophet. I will lift My fist against such prophets and cut them off from the com-
munity of Israel. 10False prophets and those who seek their guidance will all be punished
for their sins. 11In this way, the people of Israel will learn not to stray from Me, polluting
themselves with sin. They will be My people, and I will be their God. I, the Sovereign LORD,
have spoken!'"

THE CERTAINTY OF THE LORD'S JUDGMENT

12Then this message came to me from the LORD: 13"Son of man, suppose the people of
a country were to sin against Me, and I lifted My fist to crush them, cutting off their food

14:1 2 Kgs 6:32
14:3 Isa 1:15
14:4 1 Kgs 21:20-24; 2 Kgs 1:16; Isa 66:4
14:5 Jer 2:11; Hos 10:2; Zech 7:12
14:6 1 Sam 7:3; Neh 1:9; Isa 30:22; 55:6-7
14:7 Exod 12:48; 20:10
14:8 Isa 65:15
14:9 Jer 6:14-15
14:11 Ezek 11:20; 44:10, 15
14:13 Ezek 15:8; 20:27

14:3 The Hebrew term (literally *round things*) probably alludes to dung; also in 14:4, 5, 6, 7.

▸ WORSHIP

14:3 Idols in the heart. Do you know what being a hypocrite is? An example is a person who appears to live as a Christian to outside observers, yet rejects God in his or her heart. Like these leaders in Israel, such people may even have religious or civil authority, yet that is no guarantee of true piety in their hearts. God's Word is clear—mere external righteousness is not sufficient to please God. God promises to destroy all those who reject His sovereignty in their hearts (14:8). In a heart filled with repentance, there is no room for idols. Repent of all you know of that keeps you from making God first in your heart—and when you are through, ask God to show you more. (***See Worship****> OT> Repentance> Nature> Repentance is characterized as turning from idols to the living God,* TopicGuide page A29.)

14:12-20 The Lord threatened sinful people with four judgments: famine, wild animals, war, and disease. All four had already fallen on Israel through the Babylonians, and it would happen again soon.

BECAUSE GOD IS HOLY

I will devote myself to him in purity, worship and service.

Repent and turn away from your idols.

EZEKIEL 14:6

FOR THE NEXT *GOD IS HOLY* FEATURE SEE PAGE 2237.

14:14 Gen 6:8 supply and sending a famine to destroy both people and animals. [14]Even if Noah, Daniel,
Job 1:1, 5 and Job were there, their righteousness would save no one but themselves, says the Sov-
Dan 10:11 ereign LORD.
Heb 11:7 [15]"Or suppose I were to send wild animals to invade the country, kill the people, and
14:16 make the land too desolate and dangerous to pass through. [16]As surely as I live, says the
Gen 19:29 Sovereign LORD, even if those three men were there, they wouldn't be able to save their
own sons or daughters. They alone would be saved, but the land would be made desolate.
14:17 [17]"Or suppose I were to bring war against the land, and I sent enemy armies to destroy
Ezek 5:12; 21:3-4; 25:13 both people and animals. [18]As surely as I live, says the Sovereign LORD, even if those three
Zeph 1:3 men were there, they wouldn't be able to save their own sons or daughters. They alone
would be saved.
14:19 [19]"Or suppose I were to pour out My fury by sending an epidemic into the land, and the
Jer 14:12 Ezek 5:12 disease killed people and animals alike. [20]As surely as I live, says the Sovereign LORD,
even if Noah, Daniel, and Job were there, they wouldn't be able to save their own sons or
daughters. They alone would be saved by their righteousness.
14:21 [21]"Now this is what the Sovereign LORD says: How terrible it will be when all four of
Amos 4:6-10 Rev 6:4-8 these dreadful punishments fall upon Jerusalem—war, famine, wild animals, and dis-
14:22 ease—destroying all her people and animals. [22]Yet there will be survivors, and they will
Ezek 36:20 come here to join you as exiles in Babylon. You will see with your own eyes how wicked
14:23 they are, and then you will feel better about what I have done to Jerusalem. [23]When you
Jer 22:8-9 meet them and see their behavior, you will understand that these things are not being
done to Israel without cause. I, the Sovereign LORD, have spoken!"

JERUSALEM—A USELESS VINE

15:2 **15** Then this message came to me from the LORD: [2]"Son of man, how does a grape-
Ps 80:8-16 Isa 5:1-7 vine compare to a tree? Is a vine's wood as useful as the wood of a tree? [3]Can its
Hos 10:1 wood be used for making things, like pegs to hang up pots and pans? [4]No, it can only be
John 15:1-6 used for fuel, and even as fuel, it burns too quickly. [5]Vines are useless both before and af-
15:4 Isa 27:11 ter being put into the fire!
Heb 6:8 [6]"And this is what the Sovereign LORD says: The people of Jerusalem are like grapevines
15:7 growing among the trees of the forest. Since they are useless, I have thrown them on the
Lev 26:17 fire to be burned. [7]And I will see to it that if they escape from one fire, they will fall into an-
1 Kgs 19:17 Isa 24:18 other. When I turn against them, you will know that I am the LORD. [8]And I will make the
Amos 5:19; 9:1-4 land desolate because My people have been unfaithful to Me. I, the Sovereign LORD, have
spoken!"

14:14 Noah, Daniel, and Job (see subsequent references to them in 14:16, 18, 20) were cited as examples of extremely faithful people whose personal righteousness was beyond question. However, in this dire situation, even Noah, Daniel, or Job couldn't have saved anyone but himself.

14:19 The judgment of deadly disease is mentioned in Deuteronomy 28 and Leviticus 26 as one of many consequences upon individual Israelites and their nation if they failed to stay faithful to their covenant with God.

14:21-23 The Lord promised, despite the wickedness of His people, that some would survive the punishments to come (see note at 11:13-21).

15:1-8 In this brief chapter the Lord compared Jerusalem to a useless vine. A vine is of no use for making things (15:2-3) and of little use as fuel for a fire (15:4-5). Similarly, Jerusalem was useless, so the Lord would see to it that the city would be burned up "because My people have been unfaithful" (15:8). Israel's purpose was to promote and spread the worship of the Lord throughout the world (Psalm 67:4), but the people's idolatry had rendered them useless.

▶ HOLINESS

15:8 Holy torment. No one in the world is as miserable as a rebellious Christian. Such a person brings upon himself the pain of damaged relationships and punishment for sin, and can even bring consequences to those around him as well. But thankfully Christians have the Holy Spirit to convict them of sin in order to bring about repentance (Galatians 5:16-25; John 15:26). As ancient Israel learned under the Old Covenant, when we break our promises to God, He will go to extreme measures to bring us back to Himself. In what area are you resisting God? Do not resist Him a moment longer (Ephesians 4:30), for you will grow more and more enslaved to the sin you are harboring (Hebrews 3:13). (***See Holiness> Disciplines> Of Abstinence> Resisting sinful urges,*** TopicGuide page A42.)

JERUSALEM—AN UNFAITHFUL WIFE

16 Then another message came to me from the LORD: 2"Son of man, confront Jerusa-
lem with her detestable sins. 3Give her this message from the Sovereign LORD:
You are nothing but a Canaanite! Your father was an Amorite and your mother a Hittite.
4On the day you were born, no one cared about you. Your umbilical cord was not cut, and
you were never washed, rubbed with salt, and wrapped in cloth. 5No one had the slightest
interest in you; no one pitied you or cared for you. On the day you were born, you were
unwanted, dumped in a field and left to die.

6"But I came by and saw you there, helplessly kicking about in your own blood. As you
lay there, I said, 'Live!' 7And I helped you to thrive like a plant in the field. You grew up and
became a beautiful jewel. Your breasts became full, and your body hair grew, but you
were still naked. 8And when I passed by again, I saw that you were old enough for love. So
I wrapped My cloak around you to cover your nakedness and declared My marriage vows.
I made a covenant with you, says the Sovereign LORD, and you became Mine.

9"Then I bathed you and washed off your blood, and I rubbed fragrant oils into your
skin. 10I gave you expensive clothing of fine linen and silk, beautifully embroidered, and
sandals made of fine goatskin leather. 11I gave you lovely jewelry, bracelets, beautiful
necklaces, 12a ring for your nose, earrings for your ears, and a lovely crown for your head.
13And so you were adorned with gold and silver. Your clothes were made of fine linen and
were beautifully embroidered. You ate the finest foods—choice flour, honey, and olive
oil—and became more beautiful than ever. You looked like a queen, and so you were!
14Your fame soon spread throughout the world because of your beauty. I dressed you in
My splendor and perfected your beauty, says the Sovereign LORD.

15"But you thought your fame and beauty were your own. So you gave yourself as a
prostitute to every man who came along. Your beauty was theirs for the asking. 16You
used the lovely things I gave you to make shrines for idols, where you played the prosti-
tute. Unbelievable! How could such a thing ever happen? 17You took the very jewels and
gold and silver ornaments I had given you and made statues of men and worshiped them.
This is adultery against Me! 18You used the beautifully embroidered clothes I gave you to
dress your idols. Then you used My special oil and My incense to worship them. 19Imag-
ine it! You set before them as a sacrifice the choice flour, olive oil, and honey I had given
you, says the Sovereign LORD.

20"Then you took your sons and daughters—the children you had borne to Me—and
sacrificed them to your gods. Was your prostitution not enough? 21Must you also slaugh-

16:2 Isa 58:1; Hos 8:1
16:4 Hos 2:3
16:5 Deut 32:10
16:7 Exod 1:7
16:8 Gen 22:16-18; Exod 19:5; 24:7-8; Ruth 3:9; Jer 2:2; Hos 2:18-20
16:11 Gen 24:22, 47; Isa 3:18-19
16:12 Jer 13:18
16:13 Deut 32:13-14; Ps 45:13-14
16:14 1 Kgs 10:1, 24; Ps 50:2; Lam 2:15
16:15 Isa 57:8; Jer 2:20; Ezek 27:3
16:19 Hos 2:8
16:20 Exod 13:2, 12; Ps 106:37-38; Jer 7:31
16:21 2 Kgs 17:17; Jer 19:5

16:1-63 This chapter contains the longest prophetic message in the book of Ezekiel. It is an allegory about the Lord and His relationship to Jerusalem, who proved to be an unfaithful wife and eventually became a prostitute. This harsh truth about unfaithful Jerusalem is reminiscent of the story of Hosea and his wife Gomer (Hosea 1–3).

16:1-14 The Lord denounced unfaithful Jerusalem, whom He calls a "Canaanite," referring to the pagans who lived in the Promised Land before Israelites conquered the land. Jerusalem was depicted as an orphan girl that no one wanted, yet the Lord nurtured and protected her, turning her into a queen.

▸ HOLINESS
16:5 Helpless without God. What would it be like to be cut off from God, without Christ as our Lord and Savior? The Bible compares it to being dead (Ephesians 2:1-2), sick (Mark 2:17), or separated from God (2 Samuel 14:14; Colossians 1:21). All these descriptions point to our complete inability to make things right with God on our own. God's gracious care for the baby by the roadside is another metaphor for the predicament in which God finds us prior to salvation. He saves us and clothes us with every imaginable spiritual blessing (Ephesians 1:3), yet, just like ancient Israel, we long for others to meet our needs. We use the gifts God gave us as a means to win favor with the world. The answer to our wanderlust is the same as the one given to Jerusalem—think about how He saved you when you were utterly helpless (16:22). Remember from where God has brought you, and consider His promises of future grace for those who persevere (Romans 8:17-18, 23; Ephesians 4:4). (***See Holiness> Changed by God> God Provides> Extending grace to us,*** TopicGuide page A41.)

16:15-34 In this second section of the allegory, the Lord declared that the orphan He nurtured into a queen became a prostitute. Hebrew terms related to prostitution occur 10 times in these verses and throughout the book of Ezekiel. The "lovers" of unfaithful Israel included the Egyptians, the Philistines, the Assyrians, and the Babylonians (16:26-29). Prostitution is a common metaphor describing Jerusalem's unfaithfulness to the Lord through idolatry (see also Isaiah 1:21; Jeremiah 2:20; Hosea 4:12).

16:20 Abortion was unknown in ancient Jerusalem, but infanticide is recorded during times of war (Isaiah 9:20; Lamentations 2:20) and in the worship of Adrammelech and Anammelech (Leviticus 18:21; 2 Kings 17:31).

ter My children by sacrificing them to idols? 22 In all your years of adultery and detestable
sin, you have not once remembered the days long ago when you lay naked in a field,
kicking about in your own blood.
23 "What sorrow awaits you, says the Sovereign LORD. In addition to all your other wick-
edness, 24 you built a pagan shrine and put altars to idols in every town square. 25 On every
street corner you defiled your beauty, offering your body to every passerby in an endless
stream of prostitution. 26 Then you added lustful Egypt to your lovers, provoking My anger
with your increasing promiscuity. 27 That is why I struck you with My fist and reduced your
boundaries. I handed you over to your enemies, the Philistines, and even they were
shocked by your lewd conduct. 28 You have prostituted yourself with the Assyrians, too. It
seems you can never find enough new lovers! And after your prostitution there, you still
were not satisfied. 29 You added to your lovers by embracing Babylonia,* the land of mer-
chants, but you still weren't satisfied.
30 "What a sick heart you have, says the Sovereign LORD, to do such things as these, act-
ing like a shameless prostitute. 31 You build your pagan shrines on every street corner and
your altars to idols in every square. In fact, you have been worse than a prostitute, so eager
for sin that you have not even demanded payment. 32 Yes, you are an adulterous wife who
takes in strangers instead of her own husband. 33 Prostitutes charge for their services—but
not you! You give gifts to your lovers, bribing them to come and have sex with you. 34 So
you are the opposite of other prostitutes. You pay your lovers instead of their paying you!

JUDGMENT ON JERUSALEM'S PROSTITUTION

35 "Therefore, you prostitute, listen to this message from the LORD! 36 This is what the Sover-
eign LORD says: Because you have poured out your lust and exposed yourself in prostitu-
tion to all your lovers, and because you have worshiped detestable idols,* and because
you have slaughtered your children as sacrifices to your gods, 37 this is what I am going to
do. I will gather together all your allies—the lovers with whom you have sinned, both
those you loved and those you hated—and I will strip you naked in front of them so they
can stare at you. 38 I will punish you for your murder and adultery. I will cover you with
blood in My jealous fury. 39 Then I will give you to these many nations who are your lov-
ers, and they will destroy you. They will knock down your pagan shrines and the altars to
your idols. They will strip you and take your beautiful jewels, leaving you stark naked.
40 They will band together in a mob to stone you and cut you up with swords. 41 They will
burn your homes and punish you in front of many women. I will stop your prostitution and
end your payments to your many lovers.
42 "Then at last My fury against you will be spent, and My jealous anger will subside. I
will be calm and will not be angry with you anymore. 43 But first, because you have not re-
membered your youth but have angered Me by doing all these evil things, I will fully re-
pay you for all of your sins, says the Sovereign LORD. For you have added lewd acts to all
your detestable sins. 44 Everyone who makes up proverbs will say of you, 'Like mother, like

16:24 Ps 78:58; Isa 57:5-7
16:25 Prov 9:14
16:26 Jer 7:18-19
16:27 Isa 9:12
16:28 2 Kgs 16:7-18; 2 Chr 28:16-23
16:30 Prov 9:13; Isa 3:9; Rev 17:1-6
16:31 Isa 52:3
16:33 Hos 8:9-10; Joel 3:3; Luke 15:30
16:36 Jer 19:5; Ezek 20:31; 23:37
16:37 Isa 47:3; Nah 3:5-6
16:38 Ps 79:3, 5; Jer 18:21; Zeph 1:17; Rev 16:6
16:41 2 Kgs 25:9
16:42 2 Sam 24:25; Isa 40:1-2; 54:9-10
16:43 Ps 78:42; Isa 63:10

16:29 Or *Chaldea*. **16:36** The Hebrew term (literally *round things*) probably alludes to dung.

16:30-34 While prostitution is viewed as a victimless crime in many societies, the seriousness of the sin is hinted at as it is compared to spiritual prostitution—idol worship. The book of Proverbs compares the temptations of foolishness to the temptations of a sly prostitute (Proverbs 5:3-17).

16:35-43 In the third section of the allegory, the Lord declared that He would force Jerusalem's "lovers" to turn against her and turn her into a prisoner, referring to the Babylonian captivity. The humiliation of Jerusalem the prostitute foreshadowed the destruction of the land of Judah, of Jerusalem, and of the Temple in the third wave of the Babylonian captivity (see note at 1:2).

16:44-52 In the fourth section of the allegory, the Lord described Jerusalem the prostitute as a relative of numerous other pagan nations or cities that did not acknowledge that the Lord is the one true God, such as the Hittites and the Amorites and Samaria and Sodom. Jerusalem's sins were even worse than those of these pagans, because Jerusalem had known the Lord but turned against Him.

daughter.' 45For your mother loathed her husband and her children, and so do you. And
you are exactly like your sisters, for they despised their husbands and their children. Truly
your mother was a Hittite and your father an Amorite.
46"Your older sister was Samaria, who lived with her daughters in the north. Your youn-
ger sister was Sodom, who lived with her daughters in the south. 47But you have not
merely sinned as they did. You quickly surpassed them in corruption. 48As surely as I live,
says the Sovereign LORD, Sodom and her daughters were never as wicked as you and your
daughters. 49Sodom's sins were pride, gluttony, and laziness, while the poor and needy
suffered outside her door. 50She was proud and committed detestable sins, so I wiped her
out, as you have seen.*
51"Even Samaria did not commit half your sins. You have done far more detestable
things than your sisters ever did. They seem righteous compared to you. 52Shame on you!
Your sins are so terrible that you make your sisters seem righteous, even virtuous.
53"But someday I will restore the fortunes of Sodom and Samaria, and I will restore
you, too. 54Then you will be truly ashamed of everything you have done, for your sins
make them feel good in comparison. 55Yes, your sisters, Sodom and Samaria, and all
their people will be restored, and at that time you also will be restored. 56In your proud
days you held Sodom in contempt. 57But now your greater wickedness has been ex-
posed to all the world, and you are the one who is scorned—by Edom* and all her neigh-
bors and by Philistia. 58This is your punishment for all your lewdness and detestable sins,
says the LORD.
59"Now this is what the Sovereign LORD says: I will give you what you deserve, for you
have taken your solemn vows lightly by breaking your covenant. 60Yet I will remember
the covenant I made with you when you were young, and I will establish an everlasting
covenant with you. 61Then you will remember with shame all the evil you have done. I
will make your sisters, Samaria and Sodom, to be your daughters, even though they are
not part of our covenant. 62And I will reaffirm My covenant with you, and you will know
that I am the LORD. 63You will remember your sins and cover your mouth in silent shame
when I forgive you of all that you have done. I, the Sovereign LORD, have spoken!"

A STORY OF TWO EAGLES

17 Then this message came to me from the LORD: 2"Son of man, give this riddle,
and tell this story to the people of Israel. 3Give them this message from the Sover-
eign LORD:

16:45 Isa 1:4
16:46 Gen 13:11-13; Jer 3:8-11
16:48 Matt 11:23-24
16:49 Gen 13:10; Ps 138:6; Isa 22:13; Luke 12:16-20
16:50 Gen 19:24-25
16:51 Jer 3:8-11; Matt 12:41-42
16:53 Isa 19:24-25
16:54 Jer 2:26
16:57 2 Kgs 16:5-7; Hos 2:10; 7:1
16:59 Isa 24:5
16:60 Jer 32:40
16:62 Jer 24:7
16:63 Ps 39:9; Dan 9:7-8; Rom 3:19
17:2 Ezek 20:49; 24:3
17:3 Jer 22:23; 48:40; Dan 4:22

16:50 As in a few Hebrew manuscripts and Greek version; Masoretic Text reads *as I have seen.* 16:57 Many ancient manuscripts read *Aram.*

16:53-58 In the fifth section of the allegory, the Lord explained that the orphaned prisoner-prostitute would repent and come back to Him—but not until her punishment was complete. Restoration after judgment was a common theme in the prophets' messages to Israel and Judah.

16:59-63 In the sixth section of the allegory, the Lord said that He would cleanse and restore His unfaithful wife Jerusalem after she repented. She broke the marriage covenant (an allusion to the covenant at Sinai), but the Lord would make "an everlasting covenant" with her, one that could not be broken. This is the new covenant of Jeremiah 31:31-34 (see also Hebrews 8:7-13 and Luke 22:20).

▸ ADOPTION
16:61 A glimmer of hope. Amidst the dark, foreboding condemnation of Jerusalem in this chapter, a promise of future grace still glimmers. This promise was not just for the people of Jerusalem but also for the entire world. The everlasting covenant that would arise from the Old Covenant would extend even to those who previously opposed God and His people. This everlasting covenant, far from doing away with the older covenant, reaffirms the past and brings people from every nation and language into communion with God (Acts 10:35; Revelation 7:9). By announcing this New Covenant for the whole world, God wanted to draw Israel to Himself (Acts 2; Romans 10:19). Let us rejoice that God has made a way for people everywhere to know Him through Jesus Christ. (***See Adoption*****>** *With Christ***>** *Heirs of God***>** *Inheritance shared by Jews and Gentiles alike,* TopicGuide page A36.)

17:1-10 These verses contain an allegory in which Israel was compared to a cedar tree and a vine (see note at 15:1-8). A great eagle cut off the top of the tree, but then a new seed sprouted a vine that grew toward the eagle. The second vine then inappropriately turned toward the second eagle instead of the one who planted it—then the vine withers away. The allegory is explained in 17:11-21.

"A great eagle with broad wings and long feathers,
covered with many-colored plumage,
came to Lebanon.
He seized the top of a cedar tree
4 and plucked off its highest branch.
He carried it away to a city filled with merchants.
He planted it in a city of traders.
17:5 Deut 8:7-9 Isa 44:4
5 He also took a seedling from the land
and planted it in fertile soil.
He placed it beside a broad river,
where it could grow like a willow tree.
6 It took root there and
grew into a low, spreading vine.
Its branches turned up toward the eagle,
and its roots grew down into the ground.
It produced strong branches
and put out shoots.
17:7 Ezek 31:4
7 But then another great eagle came
with broad wings and full plumage.
So the vine now sent its roots and branches
toward him for water,
8 even though it was already planted in good soil
and had plenty of water
so it could grow into a splendid vine
and produce rich leaves and luscious fruit.

9 "So now the Sovereign LORD asks:
Will this vine grow and prosper?
No! I will pull it up, roots and all!
I will cut off its fruit
and let its leaves wither and die.
I will pull it up easily
without a strong arm or a large army.
17:10 Ezek 19:12-14 Hos 13:15
10 But when the vine is transplanted,
will it thrive?
No, it will wither away
when the east wind blows against it.
It will die in the same good soil
where it had grown so well."

THE RIDDLE EXPLAINED

11 Then this message came to me from the LORD: 12 "Say to these rebels of Israel: Don't
you understand the meaning of this riddle of the eagles? The king of Babylon came to
17:13 2 Kgs 24:15-17 2 Chr 36:13
Jerusalem, took away her king and princes, and brought them to Babylon. 13 He made a
treaty with a member of the royal family and forced him to take an oath of loyalty. He

17:11-21 One way to view this section is that the great eagle is the king of Babylon, Nebuchadnezzar, who cut off the top of the tree, King Jehoiachin. This occurred at the second wave of the captivity when Nebuchadnezzar deposed Jehoiachin and took him captive to Babylon. The vine is Zedekiah, Jehoiachin's uncle, whom Nebuchadnezzar appointed in the former king's place. Zedekiah made a treaty with Pharaoh Hophra, the second great eagle, to overthrow Nebuchadnezzar, but the alliance failed, and Zedekiah was taken to Babylon, symbolized by the death of the vine. There are several similar interpretations, all highlighting the theme of the disloyalty of God's people and the discipline that would follow.

also exiled Israel's most influential leaders, [14]so Israel would not become strong again
and revolt. Only by keeping her treaty with Babylon could Israel survive.
[15]"Nevertheless, this man of Israel's royal family rebelled against Babylon, sending am-
bassadors to Egypt to request a great army and many horses. Can Israel break her sworn
treaties like that and get away with it? [16]No! For as surely as I live, says the Sovereign LORD,
the king of Israel will die in Babylon, the land of the king who put him in power and whose
treaty he disregarded and broke. [17]Pharaoh and all his mighty army will fail to help Israel
when the king of Babylon lays siege to Jerusalem again and destroys many lives. [18]For the
king of Israel disregarded his treaty and broke it after swearing to obey; therefore, he will
not escape.
[19]"So this is what the Sovereign LORD says: As surely as I live, I will punish him for break-
ing My covenant and disregarding the solemn oath he made in My name. [20]I will throw My
net over him and capture him in My snare. I will bring him to Babylon and put him on trial
for this treason against Me. [21]And all his best warriors* will be killed in battle, and those who
survive will be scattered to the four winds. Then you will know that I, the LORD, have spoken.
[22]"This is what the Sovereign LORD says: I will take a branch from the top of a tall cedar,
and I will plant it on the top of Israel's highest mountain. [23]It will become a majestic cedar,
sending forth its branches and producing seed. Birds of every sort will nest in it, finding
shelter in the shade of its branches. [24]And all the trees will know that it is I, the LORD, who
cuts the tall tree down and makes the short tree grow tall. It is I who makes the green tree
wither and gives the dead tree new life. I, the LORD, have spoken, and I will do what I said!"

THE JUSTICE OF A RIGHTEOUS GOD

18 Then another message came to me from the LORD: [2]"Why do you quote this prov-
erb concerning the land of Israel: 'The parents have eaten sour grapes, but their
children's mouths pucker at the taste'? [3]As surely as I live, says the Sovereign LORD, you
will not quote this proverb anymore in Israel. [4]For all people are Mine to judge—both par-
ents and children alike. And this is My rule: The person who sins is the one who will die.
[5]"Suppose a certain man is righteous and does what is just and right. [6]He does not feast
in the mountains before Israel's idols* or worship them. He does not commit adultery or
have intercourse with a woman during her menstrual period. [7]He is a merciful creditor, not

17:14 Jer 27:12-17; 38:17
17:15 2 Kgs 24:20; 2 Chr 36:13
17:16 Jer 52:11
17:17 Isa 36:6; Jer 37:7
17:18 1 Chr 29:24
17:20 Ezek 12:13; 20:36; 32:3
17:21 2 Kgs 25:5, 11; Amos 9:1-10
17:22 Pss 72:16; 80:15; Ezek 20:40; Zech 3:8; 4:12-14
17:24 Ps 96:12; Isa 55:12; Amos 9:11
18:2 Jer 31:29; Lam 5:7
18:4 Num 16:22; 27:16; Isa 42:5; 57:16; Zech 12:1; Rom 6:23
18:6 Deut 4:19
18:7 Lev 19:13; Matt 25:35-40; Luke 3:11

17:21 Or *his fleeing warriors.* The meaning of the Hebrew is uncertain. 18:6 The Hebrew term (literally *round things*) probably alludes to dung; also in 18:12, 15.

17:22-24 This prophecy returned to the imagery in 17:1-10 to express Israel's messianic hope. Only "the Sovereign LORD" could raise up "a tender green shoot" (see Isaiah 53:2) and plant it "on the top of Israel's highest mountain." Judah's monarchy ended with King Zedekiah's deportation to Babylon, but Jesus Christ—King David's greatest Son—would restore the monarchy and reign forever (Romans 1:3).

18:1-4 This prophecy is introduced by the "sour grapes" proverb in 18:2. As in chapter 12, Ezekiel used a contemporary proverb to highlight a new way of living among God's people. The people of Israel were trying to pass the blame for their captivity to their parents (18:4), which gave them reason to believe their captivity might be brief. But the Lord reassured them that He judges the individual according to the stipulations of the covenant. This principle of the righteous gaining life and the wicked receiving death goes back as far as the covenant God made with Adam and Eve (Genesis 2:16-17).

▸ WORSHIP

18:2 Taking responsibility. Do you have a quick temper? It's because your father yelled at you. Are you too critical of others? It's because your mother made you clean up your room. It sounds humorous, but it's not unusual to hear people blaming their parents for whatever problems they have. The people of Israel were blaming the Exile on their parents in an attempt to shirk their own responsibility for their situation. But God made it clear—His punishment was falling on them because of *their* behavior, and no one else's. Instead of blaming others, take responsibility for your actions, your character flaws, and your moral weaknesses. Give up the "blame game" and repent of your own sins. (***See Worship**> OT> Repentance> Examples> Exiles called to covenant renewal,* TopicGuide page A29.)

18:5-22 Three scenes (18:5-9, 10-13, 14-18) depict situations where the justice of God was illustrated with the goal (18:19-22) of demonstrating that while the Exile was not the fault of a single generation, the judgment of God never falls on one person or one family or one generation unfairly.

18:6 The law forbade sexual intercourse during a woman's menstrual period (Ezekiel 22:10; Leviticus 15:16-33; 18:19).

18:8 Exod 22:25 Lev 25:36 Deut 23:19 Zech 8:16
18:9 Hab 2:4 Rom 1:17
18:12 2 Kgs 21:11 Isa 59:6-7 Amos 4:1
18:13 Ezek 33:4-5
18:14 2 Chr 29:6-10; 34:21
18:16 Job 31:16 Ps 41:1
18:19 Exod 20:5 Zech 1:3-6
18:20 Deut 24:16 Matt 16:27 Rom 2:6-9
18:21 Ezek 33:12, 19
18:22 Ps 18:20-24 Ezek 33:16 Mic 7:19
18:23 Ps 147:11 Ezek 33:11 2 Pet 3:9
18:24 1 Sam 15:11 Prov 21:16 Ezek 33:18 Gal 3:3-4
18:25 Gen 18:25 Deut 32:4 Ezek 33:17, 20 Zeph 3:5 Mal 3:13-15
18:30 Ezek 14:6; 33:11 Hos 12:6

keeping the items given as security by poor debtors. He does not rob the poor but instead
gives food to the hungry and provides clothes for the needy. 8He grants loans without in-
terest, stays away from injustice, is honest and fair when judging others, 9and faithfully
obeys My decrees and regulations. Anyone who does these things is just and will surely
live, says the Sovereign LORD.

10"But suppose that man has a son who grows up to be a robber or murderer and re-
fuses to do what is right. 11And that son does all the evil things his father would never do—
he worships idols on the mountains, commits adultery, 12oppresses the poor and helpless,
steals from debtors by refusing to let them redeem their security, worships idols, commits
detestable sins, 13and lends money at excessive interest. Should such a sinful person live?
No! He must die and must take full blame.

14"But suppose that sinful son, in turn, has a son who sees his father's wickedness and
decides against that kind of life. 15This son refuses to worship idols on the mountains and
does not commit adultery. 16He does not exploit the poor, but instead is fair to debtors
and does not rob them. He gives food to the hungry and provides clothes for the needy.
17He helps the poor, does not lend money at interest, and obeys all My regulations and
decrees. Such a person will not die because of his father's sins; he will surely live. 18But
the father will die for his many sins—for being cruel, robbing people, and doing what was
clearly wrong among his people.

19"'What?' you ask. 'Doesn't the child pay for the parent's sins?' No! For if the child does
what is just and right and keeps My decrees, that child will surely live. 20The person who
sins is the one who will die. The child will not be punished for the parent's sins, and the
parent will not be punished for the child's sins. Righteous people will be rewarded for their
own righteous behavior, and wicked people will be punished for their own wickedness.
21But if wicked people turn away from all their sins and begin to obey My decrees and do
what is just and right, they will surely live and not die. 22All their past sins will be forgotten,
and they will live because of the righteous things they have done.

23"Do you think that I like to see wicked people die? says the Sovereign LORD. Of course
not! I want them to turn from their wicked ways and live. 24However, if righteous people
turn from their righteous behavior and start doing sinful things and act like other sinners,
should they be allowed to live? No, of course not! All their righteous acts will be forgotten,
and they will die for their sins.

25"Yet you say, 'The Lord isn't doing what's right!' Listen to Me, O people of Israel. Am I
the One not doing what's right, or is it you? 26When righteous people turn from their righ-
teous behavior and start doing sinful things, they will die for it. Yes, they will die because
of their sinful deeds. 27And if wicked people turn from their wickedness, obey the law, and
do what is just and right, they will save their lives. 28They will live because they thought it
over and decided to turn from their sins. Such people will not die. 29And yet the people of
Israel keep saying, 'The Lord isn't doing what's right!' O people of Israel, it is you who are
not doing what's right, not I.

30"Therefore, I will judge each of you, O people of Israel, according to your actions, says

---

18:10, 14 Having a righteous kinsman did not mean the unrighteous members of the family would escape punishment for their sin. (Deuteronomy 24:16; 2 Kings 14:6).

18:23-24 God's desire is for the wicked to turn from sin and live, not die. He cannot be received as Savior without also being accepted as Lord.

▶ SPIRITUAL WARFARE
18:23 God is not pleased. Some people envision God as cackling with almost sinister glee as His enemies are cast into hell. But God's repeated call for people to repent of their sins indicates that God desires their repentance, even though He knows that many will not. In fact, when God determines not to receive repentance, it is rare and explicitly noted (for instance, Isaiah 6:10). God wants us to be prepared to share the gospel message so when we meet those whom God has prepared to hear it, we can easily share it. The angels rejoice at the salvation of rebels. Nothing pleases God more than to change rebels into worshipers (Luke 15). (***See Spiritual Warfare*> *Resisting Sin and Evil*> *Consequences*> *Of Disobedience*> *Displeases God,* TopicGuide page A46.)

18:30-32 The Lord once again reminded the people of Israel that He would judge them according to their own wickedness and that He wanted them to turn from their wickedness and live.

the Sovereign LORD. Repent, and turn from your sins. Don't let them destroy you! 31 Put all
your rebellion behind you, and find yourselves a new heart and a new spirit. For why
should you die, O people of Israel? 32 I don't want you to die, says the Sovereign LORD. Turn
back and live!

18:31 Ps 51:10; Isa 1:16-17; 55:7; Acts 3:19

A FUNERAL SONG FOR ISRAEL'S KINGS

19 1 "Sing this funeral song for the princes of Israel:

19:1 2 Kgs 25:5-7

2 "What is your mother?
 A lioness among lions!
She lay down among the young lions
 and reared her cubs.
3 She raised one of her cubs
 to become a strong young lion.
He learned to hunt and devour prey,
 and he became a man-eater.

19:3 2 Kgs 23:31-34

4 Then the nations heard about him,
 and he was trapped in their pit.
They led him away with hooks
 to the land of Egypt.

19:4 2 Chr 36:4

5 "When the lioness saw
 that her hopes for him were gone,
she took another of her cubs
 and taught him to be a strong young lion.
6 He prowled among the other lions
 and stood out among them in his strength.
He learned to hunt and devour prey,
 and he, too, became a man-eater.

19:6 2 Kgs 24:9

7 He demolished fortresses*
 and destroyed their towns and cities.
Their farms were desolated,
 and their crops were destroyed.
The land and its people trembled in fear
 when they heard him roar.
8 Then the armies of the nations attacked him,
 surrounding him from every direction.
They threw a net over him
 and captured him in their pit.
9 With hooks, they dragged him into a cage
 and brought him before the king of Babylon.
They held him in captivity,
 so his voice could never again be heard
 on the mountains of Israel.

19:9 2 Kgs 24:15; 2 Chr 36:6

19:7 As in Greek version; Hebrew reads *He knew widows.*

19:1 This verse introduces a "funeral song" or lament for Judah's kings or "princes". The funeral song actually has two parts: one for King Jehoahaz and King Jehoiachin (see note at 19:2-9) and another for King Zedekiah (see note at 19:10-14).

19:2-9 The lion is the typical image used for the Davidic kings from the tribe of Judah (see Genesis 49:9-10). One of the lion cubs is Jehoahaz, a son of Josiah, who reigned only three months before being deposed and deported to Egypt by Pharaoh Neco (19:3-4; see 2 Chronicles 36:1-4). Jehoahaz was succeeded by Jehoiakim and then Jehoiachin, the second lion cub, who was deposed and deported to Babylon by Nebuchadnezzar (19:5-9; see 2 Chronicles 36:5-10).

19:10 Ps 80:8-11

10 "Your mother was like a vine
planted by the water's edge.
It had lush, green foliage
because of the abundant water.
11 Its branches became strong—
strong enough to be a ruler's scepter.
It grew very tall,
towering above all others.
It stood out because of its height
and its many lush branches.

19:12 Jer 31:28; Ezek 17:10; 28:17; Hos 13:15; John 15:6

12 But the vine was uprooted in fury
and thrown down to the ground.
The desert wind dried up its fruit
and tore off its strong branches,
so that it withered
and was destroyed by fire.

19:13 2 Kgs 24:12-16; Hos 2:3

13 Now the vine is transplanted to the wilderness,
where the ground is hard and dry.
14 A fire has burst out from its branches
and devoured its fruit.
Its remaining limbs are not
strong enough to be a ruler's scepter.

"This is a funeral song, and it will be used in a funeral."

THE REBELLION OF ISRAEL

20:1 Ezek 8:1, 11-12; 20:4 Ezek 16:2; 22:2; 20:5 Exod 6:2-3, 7; Deut 7:6; 14:2; Ezek 6:2-9; 20:6 Exod 33:3; Ps 48:2; Jer 33:24

20 On August 14,* during the seventh year of King Jehoiachin's captivity, some of
the leaders of Israel came to request a message from the LORD. They sat down in
front of me to wait for his reply. 2 Then this message came to me from the LORD: 3 "Son of
man, tell the leaders of Israel, 'This is what the Sovereign LORD says: How dare you come to
ask Me for a message? As surely as I live, says the Sovereign LORD, I will tell you nothing!'
4 "Son of man, bring charges against them and condemn them. Make them realize how
detestable the sins of their ancestors really were. 5 Give them this message from the Sover-
eign LORD: When I chose Israel—when I revealed Myself to the descendants of Jacob in
Egypt—I took a solemn oath that I, the LORD, would be their God. 6 I took a solemn oath that

20:1 Hebrew *In the fifth month, on the tenth day,* of the ancient Hebrew lunar calendar. This day was August 14, 591 B.C.; also see note on 1:1.

19:10-14 Nebuchadnezzar appointed Zedekiah, another son of Josiah, to replace Jehoachin as king. His reign lasted eleven years (597–586 BC) ending when the Babylonians destroyed Jerusalem and the Temple (see 2 Chronicles 36:11-21). The fall of Zedekiah ended the Davidic monarchy, indicated by the fact that none of the remaining limbs were "strong enough to be a ruler's scepter" (19:14).

▶ SPIRITUAL WARFARE

19:14 Sad songs. Throughout the centuries, God's people have often expressed their grief through music and song, and even God Himself has included sorrowful lyrics in His Word. Music can be used to celebrate a saint's entrance into heaven, giving expression to the odd mixture of sadness and joy that accompanies the death of a loved one, or it can be used to bemoan a dreadful fate, such as the fall of Jerusalem (see Lamentations). Do not gloss over the darkest images of evil and pain in the Bible, because God has put all things in His Word for our benefit. Allow yourself to be moved and taught by the pain and grief of these words. (See Psalms 13 and 88; also ***see Spiritual Warfare****> Resisting Sin and Evil> Consequences> Of Disobedience> Displeases God,* TopicGuide page A46.)

20:1-4 This message occurred on "August 14" (literally "in the fifth month, on the tenth day") in the year 591 BC, "the seventh year of King Jehoiachin's captivity." This means that the fall of Jerusalem was only five years away. Ezekiel was approached by "some of the leaders of Israel" who wanted to hear from the Lord about a certain matter, but the Lord refused to answer them. The rest of the chapter shows that God's only message for Israel's leaders was impending judgment because Israel was emulating the loathsome actions of their ancestors.

20:5-9 When the Lord rescued the Israelites from Egypt, He commanded them to forsake all foreign gods and idols and to worship Him alone. The Israelites continued to worship idols and other gods, yet God remained faithful to them to honor His name.

day that I would bring them out of Egypt to a land I had discovered and explored for
them—a good land, a land flowing with milk and honey, the best of all lands anywhere.
7Then I said to them, 'Each of you, get rid of the vile images you are so obsessed with. Do
not defile yourselves with the idols* of Egypt, for I am the LORD your God.'
8"But they rebelled against Me and would not listen. They did not get rid of the vile im-
ages they were obsessed with, or forsake the idols of Egypt. Then I threatened to pour out
My fury on them to satisfy My anger while they were still in Egypt. 9But I didn't do it, for I
acted to protect the honor of My name. I would not allow shame to be brought on My
name among the surrounding nations who saw Me reveal Myself by bringing the Israelites
out of Egypt. 10So I brought them out of Egypt and led them into the wilderness. 11There I
gave them My decrees and regulations so they could find life by keeping them. 12And I
gave them My Sabbath days of rest as a sign between them and Me. It was to remind them
that I am the LORD, who had set them apart to be holy.
13"But the people of Israel rebelled against Me, and they refused to obey My decrees there
in the wilderness. They wouldn't obey My regulations even though obedience would have
given them life. They also violated My Sabbath days. So I threatened to pour out My fury on
them, and I made plans to utterly consume them in the wilderness. 14But again I held back in
order to protect the honor of My name before the nations who had seen My power in bring-
ing Israel out of Egypt. 15But I took a solemn oath against them in the wilderness. I swore I
would not bring them into the land I had given them, a land flowing with milk and honey,
the most beautiful place on earth. 16For they had rejected My regulations, refused to follow
My decrees, and violated My Sabbath days. Their hearts were given to their idols. 17Never-
theless, I took pity on them and held back from destroying them in the wilderness.
18"Then I warned their children not to follow in their parents' footsteps, defiling them-
selves with their idols. 19'I am the LORD your God,' I told them. 'Follow My decrees, pay at-
tention to My regulations, 20and keep My Sabbath days holy, for they are a sign to remind
you that I am the LORD your God.'
21"But their children, too, rebelled against Me. They refused to keep My decrees and fol-
low My regulations, even though obedience would have given them life. And they also vi-
olated My Sabbath days. So again I threatened to pour out My fury on them in the
wilderness. 22Nevertheless, I withdrew My judgment against them to protect the honor of
My name before the nations that had seen My power in bringing them out of Egypt. 23But I
took a solemn oath against them in the wilderness. I swore I would scatter them among all
the nations 24because they did not obey My regulations. They scorned My decrees by vio-
lating My Sabbath days and longing for the idols of their ancestors. 25I gave them over to
worthless decrees and regulations that would not lead to life. 26I let them pollute them-
selves* with the very gifts I had given them, and I allowed them to give their firstborn chil-

20:7 Exod 20:2; Deut 29:16-18
20:8 Isa 63:10
20:9 Exod 32:11-14; Num 14:13
20:11 Exod 20:1-23; Lev 18:5
20:12 Exod 31:13, 17; Ezek 20:20
20:13 Num 14:11, 22; Isa 56:6
20:15 Ps 95:11
20:16 Ezek 11:21; 14:3-7
20:17 Jer 4:27; 5:18
20:18 Deut 4:3-4
20:19 Exod 6:7; 20:2; Deut 5:32
20:21 Num 25:1-3
20:22 Job 13:21; Ps 78:38; Isa 48:9-11
20:23 Deut 28:64-68; Jer 15:4
20:24 Ezek 6:9
20:25 Ps 81:12; Rom 1:21-25, 28; 2 Thes 2:9-11
20:26 Ezek 6:7; 20:30; Rom 11:8

20:7 The Hebrew term (literally *round things*) probably alludes to dung; also in 20:8, 16, 18, 24, 31, 39. 20:25-26 Or *I gave them worthless decrees and regulations. . . . I polluted them.*

20:10-26 The Lord led the Israelites into the wilderness, where they continued to rebel against Him. They failed to keep His laws, particularly the Sabbath law. Six times in these verses the Lord referred to the Sabbath days He had given them to keep but which they had violated. The Sabbath was not only a reminder to Israel that the Lord is the Creator God (Genesis 1:1–2:3); it was also the sign of the covenant at Mount Sinai (Exodus 31:12-18).

20:21 Ezekiel highlighted the violation of the Sabbath (20:12, 13, 19, 21, 24) as he elaborated on Israel's failure to obey God's law (20:13, 16). Isaiah connected Sabbath keeping as a priority among the ceremonial laws (Isaiah 56:1-10), as did God with its inclusion and extensive discussion in the Ten Commandments (Exodus 20:8-11).

▸ HOLINESS

20:26 A dying society. Culture—the set of distinctive material, intellectual, social, and spiritual values that make up a civilization—is a gift from God. Culture provides traditions, beliefs, and perspectives that help bind people together, but it also can bring negative influences. Israel's culture had become filled with "worthless decrees and regulations" (20:25) and God allowed them to continue their downward spiral. Their culture devolved to the point where it became acceptable to throw away their own children (20:31), one of God's greatest gifts to any civilization (Psalm 127:3). Treasure the gifts God has given you through your culture, but beware of the "worthless decrees and regulations" that destroy the abundant life that God desires to give people. (***See Holiness****> Submission> Yielding to Spirit> Resist the world's influence,* TopicGuide page A41.)

dren as offerings to their gods—so I might devastate them and remind them that I alone am the LORD.

JUDGMENT AND RESTORATION

27 "Therefore, son of man, give the people of Israel this message from the Sovereign LORD: Your ancestors continued to blaspheme and betray Me, 28 for when I brought them into the land I had promised them, they offered sacrifices on every high hill and under every green tree they saw! They roused My fury as they offered up sacrifices to their gods. They brought their perfumes and incense and poured out their liquid offerings to them. 29 I said to them, 'What is this high place where you are going?' (This kind of pagan shrine has been called Bamah—'high place'—ever since.)

30 "Therefore, give the people of Israel this message from the Sovereign LORD: Do you plan to pollute yourselves just as your ancestors did? Do you intend to keep prostituting yourselves by worshiping vile images? 31 For when you offer gifts to them and give your little children to be burned as sacrifices,* you continue to pollute yourselves with idols to this day. Should I allow you to ask for a message from Me, O people of Israel? As surely as I live, says the Sovereign LORD, I will tell you nothing.

32 "You say, 'We want to be like the nations all around us, who serve idols of wood and stone.' But what you have in mind will never happen. 33 As surely as I live, says the Sovereign LORD, I will rule over you with an iron fist in great anger and with awesome power. 34 And in anger I will reach out with My strong hand and powerful arm, and I will bring you back* from the lands where you are scattered. 35 I will bring you into the wilderness of the nations, and there I will judge you face to face. 36 I will judge you there just as I did your ancestors in the wilderness after bringing them out of Egypt, says the Sovereign LORD. 37 I will examine you carefully and hold you to the terms of the covenant. 38 I will purge you of all those who rebel and revolt against Me. I will bring them out of the countries where they are in exile, but they will never enter the land of Israel. Then you will know that I am the LORD.

39 "As for you, O people of Israel, this is what the Sovereign LORD says: Go right ahead and worship your idols, but sooner or later you will obey Me and will stop bringing shame on My holy name by worshiping idols. 40 For on My holy mountain, the great mountain of Israel, says the Sovereign LORD, the people of Israel will someday worship Me, and I will accept them. There I will require that you bring Me all your offerings and choice gifts and sacrifices. 41 When I bring you home from exile, you will be like a pleasing sacrifice to Me. And I will display My holiness through you as all the nations watch. 42 Then when I have brought you home to the land I promised with a solemn oath to give to your ancestors, you will know that I am the LORD. 43 You will look back on all the ways you defiled yourselves and will hate yourselves because of the evil you have done. 44 You will know that I am the LORD, O people of Israel, when I have honored My name by treating you mercifully in spite of your wickedness. I, the Sovereign LORD, have spoken!"

20:30 Judg 2:19
20:31 Ps 106:37-39; Jer 7:31; Ezek 16:20
20:32 Jer 2:25; 44:17; Ezek 16:20
20:34 Jer 42:18; 44:6; Lam 2:4; *2 Cor 6:17
20:36 Deut 32:10; 1 Cor 10:5-10
20:38 Ps 95:11; Ezek 34:17-22; Amos 9:9-10; Heb 4:3
20:39 Isa 1:12-15; Jer 44:25-26; Ezek 23:38-39
20:40 Isa 56:7; 60:7; Ezek 43:12, 27
20:41 Isa 27:12-13
20:43 Zech 12:10-14

20:31 Or *and make your little children pass through the fire.* 20:34 Greek version reads *I will welcome you.* Compare 2 Cor 6:17.

20:27-44 The years of the monarchy, both in Israel and in Judah, were marked by kings who allowed or even promoted idolatry (20:27-29). The Lord condemned Israel for imitating the pagan worship of the surrounding nations and following the idolatrous example of their ancestors (20:30-32). Israel would go into exile for polluting the Lord's "holy name" (20:39) and His "holy mountain" (20:40). Those who returned from the Exile would know that He is the Lord, who treated them mercifully despite their wickedness (20:44).

▸ CHURCH

20:37 Keeping our covenant. The word "covenant" often accompanies any discussion of our relationship with God, both in the Old Testament (Genesis 12:1-3, for instance) and in the New (Matthew 26:28; Acts 3:25; Hebrews 8:6, among others). In the Bible, a covenant is a series of God-initiated promises and requirements, often sealed and symbolized in blood sacrifice. By Ezekiel's time, Israel had rejected the promises and responsibilities of an intimate relationship with God, but God threatened to continue to hold them accountable to the terms of the covenant. We give honor to Christ's ultimate sacrifice when we satisfy the requirements of the New Covenant—believing the gospel and repenting of our sins. Thank God for sending Christ to be the perfect, once-for-all sacrifice so we could have a new covenant with God. (***See Church***> *What*> *Many Titles*> *Priests*> *Our high privilege is to be in covenant with God,* TopicGuide page A48.)

JUDGMENT AGAINST THE NEGEV

45*Then this message came to me from the LORD: 46"Son of man, turn and face the south*
and speak out against it; prophesy against the brushlands of the Negev. 47Tell the south-
ern wilderness, 'This is what the Sovereign LORD says: Hear the word of the LORD! I will set
you on fire, and every tree, both green and dry, will be burned. The terrible flames will not
be quenched and will scorch everything from south to north. 48And everyone in the world
will see that I, the LORD, have set this fire. It will not be put out.'"
49Then I said, "O Sovereign LORD, they are saying of me, 'He only talks in riddles!'"

THE LORD'S SWORD OF JUDGMENT

21 1*Then this message came to me from the LORD: 2"Son of man, turn and face Jeru-
salem and prophesy against Israel and her sanctuaries. 3Tell her, 'This is what the
LORD says: I am your enemy, O Israel, and I am about to unsheath My sword to destroy
your people—the righteous and the wicked alike. 4Yes, I will cut off both the righteous and
the wicked! I will draw My sword against everyone in the land from south to north. 5Every-
one in the world will know that I am the LORD. My sword is in My hand, and it will not re-
turn to its sheath until its work is finished.'
6"Son of man, groan before the people! Groan before them with bitter anguish and a
broken heart. 7When they ask why you are groaning, tell them, 'I groan because of the ter-
rifying news I have heard. When it comes true, the boldest heart will melt with fear; all
strength will disappear. Every spirit will faint; strong knees will become as weak as water.
And the Sovereign LORD says: It is coming! It's on its way!'"
8Then the LORD said to me, 9"Son of man, give the people this message from the LORD:

"A sword, a sword
  is being sharpened and polished.
10 It is sharpened for terrible slaughter
  and polished to flash like lightning!
Now will you laugh?
  Those far stronger than you have fallen beneath its power!*
11 Yes, the sword is now being sharpened and polished;
  it is being prepared for the executioner.

12 "Son of man, cry out and wail;
  pound your thighs in anguish,
for that sword will slaughter My people and their leaders—
  everyone will die!
13 It will put them all to the test.
  What chance do they have?*
  says the Sovereign LORD.

20:46 Jer 13:19
20:47 Isa 9:18
20:48 Jer 7:20; 17:27
20:49 Matt 13:12-13; John 16:25
21:2 Ezek 20:46
21:3 Isa 57:1; Jer 21:13; Ezek 5:8; Nah 2:13; 3:5
21:4 Jer 12:12; Ezek 7:2; 20:47
21:5 1 Sam 3:12; Nah 1:9
21:7 Isa 13:7; Ezek 7:26
21:9 Deut 32:41
21:10 Isa 34:5-6
21:12 Joel 1:13

20:45 Verses 20:45-49 are numbered 21:1-5 in Hebrew text. 20:46 Hebrew *toward Teman.* 21:1 Verses 21:1-32 are numbered 21:6-37 in Hebrew text. 21:10 The meaning of the Hebrew is uncertain. 21:13 The meaning of the Hebrew is uncertain.

20:45-49 In symbolic language Ezekiel told Israel that the Negev (the wilderness in the southern part of Judah) would be destroyed by fire. This referred to the destruction of Judah and Jerusalem by the Babylonian armies just five years later (see note on 20:1-4). The people of Israel complained that Ezekiel "only talks in riddles," so the Lord responded with a rather straightforward description of the destruction (chapter 21).

21:3 The word "sword" occurs ten times in this chapter and is used in anticipation of the destruction of Judah and Jerusalem (see note at 20:45-49). The sword belonged to the Lord and Nebuchadnezzar, the Lord's instrument of judgment on Judah. Judah's wickedness caused the Lord Himself to become the nation's "enemy."

21:10-11 Numerous other nations much stronger than Judah had succumbed to the might of Babylon, and Judah would fall too. "The executioner" was Nebuchadnezzar.

21:14
Lev 26:21, 24
14 "Son of man, prophesy to them
and clap your hands.
Then take the sword and brandish it twice,
even three times,
to symbolize the great massacre,
the great massacre facing them on every side.
21:15
Josh 2:11
2 Sam 17:10
Jer 17:27
15 Let their hearts melt with terror,
for the sword glitters at every gate.
It flashes like lightning
and is polished for slaughter!
16 O sword, slash to the right,
then slash to the left,
wherever you will,
wherever you want.
21:17
Ezek 5:13
17 I, too, will clap My hands,
and I will satisfy My fury.
I, the LORD, have spoken!"

OMENS FOR BABYLON'S KING

21:19 Deut 3:11 Amos 1:14
18 Then this message came to me from the LORD: 19 "Son of man, make a map and trace two
routes on it for the sword of Babylon's king to follow. Put a signpost on the road that
21:20 Jer 49:2 Ezek 25:5 Amos 1:14
comes out of Babylon where the road forks into two—20 one road going to Ammon and its
capital, Rabbah, and the other to Judah and fortified Jerusalem. 21 The king of Babylon
now stands at the fork, uncertain whether to attack Jerusalem or Rabbah. He calls his ma-
21:21 Num 23:23 Prov 16:33
gicians to look for omens. They cast lots by shaking arrows from the quiver. They inspect
the livers of animal sacrifices. 22 The omen in his right hand says, 'Jerusalem!' With batter-
ing rams his soldiers will go against the gates, shouting for the kill. They will put up siege
21:22 Ezek 4:2; 26:9
towers and build ramps against the walls. 23 The people of Jerusalem will think it is a false
omen, because of their treaty with the Babylonians. But the king of Babylon will remind
21:23 Ezek 17:16-18; 29:16
the people of their rebellion. Then he will attack and capture them.

24 "Therefore, this is what the Sovereign LORD says: Again and again you remind Me of
your sin and your guilt. You don't even try to hide it! In everything you do, your sins are
obvious for all to see. So now the time of your punishment has come!

21:25 Ps 37:13 Ezek 7:2-7
25 "O you corrupt and wicked prince of Israel, your final day of reckoning is here! 26 This
is what the Sovereign LORD says:

21:26 Ps 75:7 Jer 13:18 Ezek 16:12; 17:24
"Take off your jeweled crown,
for the old order changes.
Now the lowly will be exalted,
and the mighty will be brought down.

▶ GOD

21:14 Judgment and hope. Ezekiel's ministry was not only terrifying, but it was impossible to ignore—it was filled with clapping hands, flashing swords, and shouted messages of doom. The image of God clapping His hands in approval of the massacre was unspeakably troubling for a people who believed that God would save them no matter what (Jeremiah 7:4-8). Many people today believe that if God is a God of love, He will never let anyone suffer judgment for sin. But God has made it clear that He will judge sin (Romans 2:5; Revelation 18:5, 8), and, like Ezekiel, we must break the bad news to them. Yet we must also tell them God's message of hope in Jesus Christ. As God shows you people who need to be warned of the consequences of sin, be sure to carry out your responsibility. (***See God*** *> Salvation> Son> Removes God's wrath,* TopicGuide page A15.)

21:18-23 Nebuchadnezzar would use divination, casting lots, and "the livers of animal sacrifices" to determine what the Lord had already decided: He would lead his armies to attack and destroy Judah and Jerusalem (in place of Ammon, 21:20). The Lord had decided to use the Babylonians as His instrument of judgment against Judah, though Nebuchadnezzar thought it was his idea to capture them (compare Daniel 1:1-2).

21:25-27 Zedekiah was the "corrupt and wicked prince of Israel" who would lose his "jeweled crown" and be "brought down." Israel's monarchy would end with Zedekiah's deportation to Babylon in 586 BC (see 2 Kings 25:7), and it would not be restored until the coming of Jesus Christ, "the One . . . who has the right to judge."

27 Destruction! Destruction!
I will surely destroy the kingdom.
And it will not be restored until the One appears
who has the right to judge it.
Then I will hand it over to Him.

21:27 Ps 2:6; Jer 23:5-6; Ezek 34:24; 37:24; Hag 2:21-22

A MESSAGE FOR THE AMMONITES

28 "And now, son of man, prophesy concerning the Ammonites and their mockery. Give them this message from the Sovereign LORD:

21:28 Isa 31:8; Jer 12:12; Zeph 2:8-10

"A sword, a sword
is drawn for your slaughter.
It is polished to destroy,
flashing like lightning!
29 Your prophets have given false visions,
and your fortune-tellers have told lies.
The sword will fall on the necks of the wicked
for whom the day of final reckoning has come.

21:29 Jer 27:9; Ezek 13:6-9

30 "Now return the sword to its sheath,
for in your own country,
the land of your birth,
I will pass judgment upon you.
31 I will pour out My fury on you
and blow on you with the fire of My anger.
I will hand you over to cruel men
who are skilled in destruction.
32 You will be fuel for the fire,
and your blood will be spilled in your own land.
You will be utterly wiped out,
your memory lost to history,
for I, the LORD, have spoken!"

21:30 Jer 47:6-7; Ezek 25:5

21:31 Ps 18:15; Nah 1:6; Hab 1:6, 10

21:32 Ezek 25:10; Mal 4:1

THE SINS OF JERUSALEM

22 Now this message came to me from the LORD: 2 "Son of man, are you ready to
judge Jerusalem? Are you ready to judge this city of murderers? Publicly de-
nounce her detestable sins, 3 and give her this message from the Sovereign LORD: O city of
murderers, doomed and damned—city of idols,* filthy and foul—4 you are guilty because
of the blood you have shed. You are defiled because of the idols you have made. Your
day of destruction has come! You have reached the end of your years. I will make you an
object of mockery throughout the world. 5 O infamous city, filled with confusion, you will
be mocked by people far and near.

22:3 Ezek 23:37, 45; Zeph 3:3

22:4 2 Kgs 21:16; Ps 44:13-14; Ezek 5:14-15

22:3 The Hebrew term (literally *round things*) probably alludes to dung; also in 22:4.

22:1-16 Ezekiel's next three oracles listed the sins that Judah had committed to show that God's judgments on His people were justified. The sins most often mentioned involved bloodshed, which highlighted both moral and religious crimes.

▸ CHURCH

22:2 Are you ready? The Lord's questions were a challenge to Ezekiel, but they are also a challenge to us. God wanted Ezekiel to be fully in agreement with His message of doom to the holy city. Look at your church—are there things there that you need to bring to someone's attention? Injustice? False doctrine? Immorality? Is there an established process for addressing any obvious sin in your church? God commands churches to remove unrepentant sinners from their midst (1 Corinthians 5:4-5). If you see grave error, humbly and lovingly speak up (Acts 20:20; Ephesians 4:15)! (***See Church****> Role> Church Government> Local> To spiritually lead,* TopicGuide page A49.)

22:5-11 Ezekiel 22:5 explained the reactions of those surrounding Jerusalem to the chaos therein. Ezekiel 22:6-11 is a detailed explanation of the societal collapse.

6"Every leader in Israel who lives within your walls is bent on murder. 7Fathers and mothers are treated with contempt. Foreigners are forced to pay for protection. Orphans and widows are wronged and oppressed among you. 8You despise My holy things and violate My Sabbath days of rest. 9People accuse others falsely and send them to their death. You are filled with idol worshipers and people who do obscene things. 10Men sleep with their fathers' wives and have intercourse with women who are menstruating. 11Within your walls live men who commit adultery with their neighbors' wives, who defile their daughters-in-law, or who rape their own sisters. 12There are hired murderers, loan racketeers, and extortioners everywhere. They never even think of Me and My commands, says the Sovereign LORD.

13"But now I clap My hands in indignation over your dishonest gain and bloodshed. 14How strong and courageous will you be in My day of reckoning? I, the LORD, have spoken, and I will do what I said. 15I will scatter you among the nations and purge you of your wickedness. 16And when I have been dishonored among the nations because of you,* you will know that I am the LORD."

THE LORD'S REFINING FURNACE

17Then this message came to me from the LORD: 18"Son of man, the people of Israel are the worthless slag that remains after silver is smelted. They are the dross that is left over—a useless mixture of copper, tin, iron, and lead. 19So tell them, 'This is what the Sovereign LORD says: Because you are all worthless slag, I will bring you to My crucible in Jerusalem. 20Just as copper, iron, lead, and tin are melted down in a furnace, I will melt you down in the heat of My fury. 21I will gather you together and blow the fire of My anger upon you, 22and you will melt like silver in fierce heat. Then you will know that I, the LORD, have poured out My fury on you.'"

THE SINS OF ISRAEL'S LEADERS

23Again a message came to me from the LORD: 24"Son of man, give the people of Israel this message: In the day of My indignation, you will be like a polluted land, a land without rain. 25Your princes* plot conspiracies just as lions stalk their prey. They devour innocent people, seizing treasures and extorting wealth. They make many widows in the land. 26Your priests have violated My instructions and defiled My holy things. They make no distinction between what is holy and what is not. And they do not teach My people the difference between what is ceremonially clean and unclean. They disregard My Sabbath days so that I am dishonored among them. 27Your leaders are like wolves who tear apart their victims. They actually destroy people's lives for money! 28And your prophets cover up for them by announcing false visions and making lying predictions. They say, 'My message is from the Sovereign LORD,' when the LORD hasn't spoken a single word to them. 29Even common people oppress the poor, rob the needy, and deprive foreigners of justice.

30"I looked for someone who might rebuild the wall of righteousness that guards the

22:6 Isa 1:23
22:7 Exod 22:22; 23:9 Prov 22:22-23
22:10 Lev 18:8, 19
22:11 Lev 18:15 2 Sam 13:14
22:12 Lev 19:13; 25:36 Deut 27:25 Ps 106:21 Mic 7:2-3
22:13 Prov 28:8 Isa 33:15 Amos 2:6-8
22:15 Deut 4:27 Zech 7:14
22:18 Ps 119:119 Prov 17:3 Isa 1:22; 48:10 Jer 6:28
22:22 Ezek 20:8, 33 Hos 5:10
22:25 Jer 2:34; 15:8 Hos 6:9
22:26 Lev 10:10 1 Sam 2:12-17 Hag 2:11-14
22:28 Jer 23:25-32
22:29 Exod 23:9 Isa 5:7 Amos 3:10 Jas 5:4
22:30 Ps 106:23 Jer 5:1

22:16 Or *when you have been dishonored among the nations.* 22:25 As in Greek version; Hebrew reads *prophets.*

22:13 The phrase "clap My hands in indignation" communicates God calling attention to the sins of His people, fulfilling the prophecy of Jerusalem's inhabitants being mocked by the Gentiles (22:5).

22:15 Ezekiel reminded the Israelites that the impending Babylonian captivity would be the fulfillment of the Lord's determination to keep His part of the covenant. The Lord told Israel in the covenant at Mount Sinai that He would send them into exile for disobedience to the conditions of the covenant, and this exile would be the final stage of a series of judgments against them (see Deuteronomy 28:64-65).

22:23-24 Israel's condition would worsen until they became completely useless to anyone. While dissimilar, a polluted land and a waterless desert are equally without sustenance.

22:25-29 The Lord rebuked four groups of leaders for failing Him and His people: the princes, the priests, the government leaders, and the false prophets. Those who had authority abused those who did not. But the people themselves were also guilty of grievous sins. Society was thoroughly corrupt.

land. I searched for someone to stand in the gap in the wall so I wouldn't have to destroy
the land, but I found no one. 31 So now I will pour out My fury on them, consuming them
with the fire of My anger. I will heap on their heads the full penalty for all their sins. I, the
Sovereign LORD, have spoken!"

THE ADULTERY OF TWO SISTERS

23 This message came to me from the LORD: 2 "Son of man, once there were two sis-
ters who were daughters of the same mother. 3 They became prostitutes in Egypt.
Even as young girls, they allowed men to fondle their breasts. 4 The older girl was named
Oholah, and her sister was Oholibah. I married them, and they bore Me sons and daughters.
I am speaking of Samaria and Jerusalem, for Oholah is Samaria and Oholibah is Jerusalem.
5 "Then Oholah lusted after other lovers instead of Me, and she gave her love to the As-
syrian officers. 6 They were all attractive young men, captains and commanders dressed in
handsome blue, charioteers driving their horses. 7 And so she prostituted herself with the
most desirable men of Assyria, worshiping their idols* and defiling herself. 8 For when she
left Egypt, she did not leave her spirit of prostitution behind. She was still as lewd as in her
youth, when the Egyptians slept with her, fondled her breasts, and used her as a prostitute.
9 "And so I handed her over to her Assyrian lovers, whom she desired so much. 10 They
stripped her, took away her children as their slaves, and then killed her. After she received
her punishment, her reputation was known to every woman in the land.
11 "Yet even though Oholibah saw what had happened to Oholah, her sister, she fol-
lowed right in her footsteps. And she was even more depraved, abandoning herself to her
lust and prostitution. 12 She fawned over all the Assyrian officers—those captains and com-
manders in handsome uniforms, those charioteers driving their horses—all of them attrac-
tive young men. 13 I saw the way she was going, defiling herself just like her older sister.
14 "Then she carried her prostitution even further. She fell in love with pictures that were
painted on a wall—pictures of Babylonian* military officers, outfitted in striking red uni-
forms. 15 Handsome belts encircled their waists, and flowing turbans crowned their heads.
They were dressed like chariot officers from the land of Babylonia.* 16 When she saw these

22:31 Isa 10:5; Rom 2:8-9
23:2 Jer 3:7-10; Ezek 16:46
23:5 Ezek 16:28; Hos 8:9-10
23:6 Ezek 23:12, 23
23:7 Hos 5:3; 6:10
23:8 Exod 32:4; 1 Kgs 12:28; 2 Kgs 17:16
23:9-10 Ezek 16:37
23:11 Jer 3:8-11
23:12 2 Kgs 16:7
23:14 Ezek 8:10; 16:29
23:16 Matt 5:28

23:7 The Hebrew term (literally *round things*) probably alludes to dung; also in 23:30, 37, 39, 49. 23:14 Or *Chaldean.* 23:15 Or *Chaldea;* also in 23:16.

▸ CHURCH
22:30 Pastor-protector. God looks for people who stand up for His values and His people. Jesus Christ leads the church (Ephesians 5:23), but He also appoints leaders to guide God's people (Ephesians 4:11-13). These leaders are critical to the health of God's people as they preach and teach and train them to live righteously. Leaders in the home and church stand in the gap, protecting God's people from the harm of sin. Ask God to make you this kind of protector of those God has entrusted to your care. (***See Church***> *Role*> *Church Offices*> *Pastor-Teachers,* TopicGuide page A49.)

23:1-4 This chapter contains an allegory of two sisters representing the northern kingdom of Israel, with its capital in Samaria, and the southern kingdom of Judah, with its capital in Jerusalem. The sisters' common origin in Egypt spoke of their unity as Israelites before the Exodus. The imagery of prostitution refers to the idolatrous practices they learned in Egypt and carried with them everywhere they went (23:49). Israel was the older sister, since it was the first to fall into perpetual idolatry at the time of Jeroboam I (1 Kings 12:25-33). Israel was given the nickname Oholah (meaning "her own tent") since they invented their own pagan centers of worship. Judah is the younger sister; her nickname Oholibah (meaning "my tent is in her") was given because the Lord's true dwelling place was in her capital city of Jerusalem. The Lord's marriage to the two sisters is reminiscent of Ezekiel 16 (see note at 16:1-63) and Hosea 1–3.

▸ SALVATION
23:3 Calling sin by name. This chapter contains graphic and disturbing imagery. Ezekiel did not hesitate to shock his audience with images of lewd and grotesque behavior. While we may instinctively recoil at such language, we need to recognize that the Lord was simply describing Israel and Judah's sin as it really was—disgusting. We often try to minimize the offensiveness of our sin by calling it a disease or an addiction, and soon we are no longer ashamed, even convincing ourselves that we are not even responsible for our sin. But sometimes the beginning of freedom from sin is naming it—calling it exactly what it is. What ugliness needs to be removed from your life? (***See Salvation***> *Our Need*> *Sinful*> *Depraved,* TopicGuide page A22.)

23:5-10 The unfaithfulness of Oholah (Israel) to the Lord refers to the nation's idolatry and other grievous sins. The Lord rejected Israel because the nation followed after Assyria rather than Him, and this brought about Israel's exile to Assyria in 722 BC.

23:11-21 Despite what happened to her sister Oholah, Oholibah (Judah) was even more unfaithful. Judah aligned herself with Assyria and then Babylon both politically and spiritually.

23:14-17 Oholibah engaged in similar political/religious prostitution as her sister, but both her heart and her body became involved in the actions. But the feelings of love for those she pursued were not worthy of her, so she rejected them.

paintings, she longed to give herself to them, so she sent messengers to Babylonia to in-
23:17 vite them to come to her. 17 So they came and committed adultery with her, defiling her in
2 Kgs 24:17 the bed of love. After being defiled, however, she rejected them in disgust.
18 "In the same way, I became disgusted with Oholibah and rejected her, just as I had re-
jected her sister, because she flaunted herself before them and gave herself to satisfy their
lusts. 19 Yet she turned to even greater prostitution, remembering her youth when she was
23:20 a prostitute in Egypt. 20 She lusted after lovers with genitals as large as a donkey's and
Ezek 17:15 23:21 emissions like those of a horse. 21 And so, Oholibah, you relived your former days as a
Jer 3:9 young girl in Egypt, when you first allowed your breasts to be fondled.

THE LORD'S JUDGMENT OF OHOLIBAH

22 "Therefore, Oholibah, this is what the Sovereign LORD says: I will send your lovers
against you from every direction—those very nations from which you turned away in dis-
23:23 Gen 25:18 gust. 23 For the Babylonians will come with all the Chaldeans from Pekod and Shoa and
2 Kgs 20:14-17; 24:2 Koa. And all the Assyrians will come with them—handsome young captains, commanders,
Job 1:17 chariot officers, and other high-ranking officers, all riding their horses. 24 They will all come
Jer 50:21 Ezek 21:19 against you from the north* with chariots, wagons, and a great army prepared for attack.
They will take up positions on every side, surrounding you with men armed with shields
23:24 Jer 39:5-6 and helmets. And I will hand you over to them for punishment so they can do with you as
23:25 they please. 25 I will turn My jealous anger against you, and they will deal harshly with
Ezek 8:17-18; 23:47 you. They will cut off your nose and ears, and any survivors will then be slaughtered by
Zeph 1:18 the sword. Your children will be taken away as captives, and everything that is left will be
23:26 Ezek 16:39 burned. 26 They will strip you of your beautiful clothes and jewels. 27 In this way, I will put a
stop to the lewdness and prostitution you brought from Egypt. You will never again cast
23:27 Ezek 16:41 longing eyes on those things or fondly remember your time in Egypt.
23:28 28 "For this is what the Sovereign LORD says: I will surely hand you over to your enemies,
Jer 21:7-10 Ezek 16:37 to those you loathe, those you rejected. 29 They will treat you with hatred and rob you of
all you own, leaving you stark naked. The shame of your prostitution will be exposed to
23:29 Deut 28:48 all the world. 30 You brought all this on yourself by prostituting yourself to other nations,
23:30 defiling yourself with all their idols. 31 Because you have followed in your sister's footsteps,
Ezek 6:9 I will force you to drink the same cup of terror she drank.
23:31 2 Kgs 21:13 32 "Yes, this is what the Sovereign LORD says:

23:32 Ps 60:3 "You will drink from your sister's cup of terror,
Ezek 5:14-15 a cup that is large and deep.
It is filled to the brim
with scorn and derision.
23:33 33 Drunkenness and anguish will fill you,
Jer 25:15 for your cup is filled to the brim with distress and desolation,
the same cup your sister Samaria drank.
23:34 34 You will drain that cup of terror
Ps 75:8 Isa 51:17 to the very bottom.
Then you will smash it to pieces
and beat your breast in anguish.
I, the Sovereign LORD, have spoken!

23:24 As in Greek version; the meaning of the Hebrew is uncertain.

23:22-35 Judah's unfaithfulness to the Lord would end because the nation would no longer exist after it had been taken captive to Babylon. Thus, Oholah could no longer prostitute herself to Assyria, Babylon, Egypt, and her other lovers. The bluntness of the language here and the severity of the punishments show how seriously the Lord takes the first and second commandments (see Exodus 20:3-6).

23:32 God's judgment of Oholibah would not only be as terrible as her sins, but the punishment would be as public as her brazen crimes against God (Luke 12:3).

35 "And because you have forgotten Me and turned your back on Me, this is what the Sov-
ereign LORD says: You must bear the consequences of all your lewdness and prostitution."

THE LORD'S JUDGMENT ON BOTH SISTERS

36 The LORD said to me, "Son of man, you must accuse Oholah and Oholibah of all their de-
testable sins. 37 They have committed both adultery and murder—adultery by worshiping
idols and murder by burning as sacrifices the children they bore to Me. 38 Furthermore,
they have defiled My Temple and violated My Sabbath day! 39 On the very day that they
sacrificed their children to their idols, they boldly came into My Temple to worship! They
came in and defiled My house.

40 "You sisters sent messengers to distant lands to get men. Then when they arrived,
you bathed yourselves, painted your eyelids, and put on your finest jewels for them.
41 You sat with them on a beautifully embroidered couch and put My incense and My spe-
cial oil on a table that was spread before you. 42 From your room came the sound of many
men carousing. They were lustful men and drunkards* from the wilderness, who put
bracelets on your wrists and beautiful crowns on your heads. 43 Then I said, 'If they really
want to have sex with old worn-out prostitutes like these, let them!' 44 And that is what they
did. They had sex with Oholah and Oholibah, these shameless prostitutes. 45 But righteous
people will judge these sister cities for what they really are—adulterers and murderers.

46 "Now this is what the Sovereign LORD says: Bring an army against them and hand
them over to be terrorized and plundered. 47 For their enemies will stone them and kill
them with swords. They will butcher their sons and daughters and burn their homes. 48 In
this way, I will put an end to lewdness and idolatry in the land, and My judgment will be a
warning to others not to follow their wicked example. 49 You will be fully repaid for all your
prostitution—your worship of idols. Yes, you will suffer the full penalty. Then you will
know that I am the Sovereign LORD."

THE SIGN OF THE COOKING POT

24 On January 15,* during the ninth year of King Jehoiachin's captivity, this mes-
sage came to me from the LORD: 2 "Son of man, write down today's date, because
on this very day the king of Babylon is beginning his attack against Jerusalem. 3 Then give
these rebels an illustration with this message from the Sovereign LORD:

"Put a pot on the fire,
  and pour in some water.
4 Fill it with choice pieces of meat—
  the rump and the shoulder
  and all the most tender cuts.

23:35 1 Kgs 14:9; Neh 9:26; Hos 13:6
23:36 Isa 58:1; Jer 1:10
23:38 2 Kgs 21:4, 7; Jer 17:27
23:39 Jer 7:9-11
23:40 2 Kgs 9:30; Ezek 16:13-16
23:41 Esth 1:6; Jer 44:17
23:42 Gen 24:30; Jer 51:7; Ezek 16:11-12, 49; Amos 6:3-6
23:45 Ezek 16:38
23:46 Jer 15:4; 24:9; 29:18; Ezek 16:38
23:47 Jer 39:8
23:49 Isa 59:18; Ezek 9:10
24:2 2 Kgs 25:1; Jer 39:1; 52:4
24:3 Jer 1:13-14
24:4 Mic 3:2-3

23:42 Or *Sabeans.* 24:1 Hebrew *On the tenth day of the tenth month,* of the ancient Hebrew lunar calendar. This event occurred on January 15, 588 B.C.; also see note on 1:1.

▸ SPIRITUAL WARFARE

23:46-48 Judgment and consequences. Ezekiel's allegory directly connected Israel's punishment with her idolatry. She prostituted herself to the Assyrians, Babylonians, and Egyptians, and it was these same nations that then brought destruction and exile to Israel. Scripture often speaks of God's judgment in this way. God's punishment for sin is often to allow the natural consequences of our sin to take their self-destructive course in our lives (compare Romans 1:24). In a world ordered by a wise and just Creator, rejecting the Creator's moral order is a dangerous and fatal path to choose. Our sin is guaranteed to have terrible impact, and that may be on us, or it may be on someone around us caught in the current of our unbelief. Repent, and help others to repent of their sin. There is no situation that cannot be improved by repentance. (***See Spiritual Warfare****> Resisting Sin and Evil> Consequences> Of Disobedience> God may allow consequences to run their course,* TopicGuide page A46.)

24:1-2 This prophecy occurred "on January 15" (literally "on the tenth day of the tenth month") of the year 588 BC ("the ninth year of King Jehoiachin's captivity"), the day Nebuchadnezzar began his attack against Jerusalem. The siege on the city lasted two years and resulted in the destruction of the city and the Temple.

24:3-14 The illustration of the boiling pot was yet another warning of Judah's impending judgment. Twice the Lord declared that Jerusalem was "the city of murderers" (24:6, 9) and would thus suffer horrible bloodshed herself. Two other sins were specifically mentioned: "lewdness" (sexual immorality) and "idolatry"—the sin that had plagued the people of Israel since the days of their slavery in Egypt.

24:5 Jer 52:10, 24-27
5 Use only the best sheep from the flock,
and heap fuel on the fire beneath the pot.
Bring the pot to a boil,
and cook the bones along with the meat.

24:6 2 Kgs 24:3-4 Nah 3:1
6 "Now this is what the Sovereign LORD says:
What sorrow awaits Jerusalem,
the city of murderers!
She is a cooking pot
whose corruption can't be cleaned out.
Take the meat out in random order,
for no piece is better than another.

24:7 Lev 17:13 Deut 12:16
7 For the blood of her murders
is splashed on the rocks.
It isn't even spilled on the ground,
where the dust could cover it!

24:8 Isa 26:21
8 So I will splash her blood on a rock
for all to see,
an expression of My anger
and vengeance against her.

24:9 Hab 2:12
9 "This is what the Sovereign LORD says:
What sorrow awaits Jerusalem,
the city of murderers!
I Myself will pile up the fuel beneath her.
10 Yes, heap on the wood!
Let the fire roar to make the pot boil.
Cook the meat with many spices,
and afterward burn the bones.

24:11 Mal 4:1
11 Now set the empty pot on the coals.
Heat it red hot!
Burn away the filth and corruption.
12 But it's hopeless;
the corruption can't be cleaned out.
So throw it into the fire.

24:13 Ezek 8:18
13 Your impurity is your lewdness
and the corruption of your idolatry.
I tried to cleanse you,
but you refused.
So now you will remain in your filth
until My fury against you has been satisfied.

24:14 Ps 33:9 Isa 55:11
14 "I, the LORD, have spoken! The time has come, and I won't hold back. I will not change
My mind, and I will have no pity on you. You will be judged on the basis of all your wicked
actions, says the Sovereign LORD."

▸ PURPOSE

24:14 The end of mercy. Our modern sensibilities find it hard to believe that a time may come when God is unwilling to continue in mercy. For generations, Jerusalem had been warned of God's displeasure and His intention to punish the city. Jerusalem failed to heed these warnings, and now God's wrath was imminent and certain. The flood in Noah's time and the death of Christ were two other such instances when God was determined to unleash His unmitigated wrath. In all of these cases, however, the end of mercy also opened a new era of grace; the darkest hour signaled the approaching dawn. The Bible speaks so much of judgment—why do we avoid discussing it with those who need to hear? Warn all those who are lingering in a life of sin that they may yet avoid God's coming wrath if they repent and believe the gospel. (***See Purpose**> God's Deeds> Judgment,* TopicGuide page A53.)

THE DEATH OF EZEKIEL'S WIFE

15 Then this message came to me from the LORD: 16 "Son of man, with one blow I will take
away your dearest treasure. Yet you must not show any sorrow at her death. Do not weep;
let there be no tears. 17 Groan silently, but let there be no wailing at her grave. Do not un-
cover your head or take off your sandals. Do not perform the usual rituals of mourning or
accept any food brought to you by consoling friends."

18 So I proclaimed this to the people the next morning, and in the evening my wife died.
The next morning I did everything I had been told to do. 19 Then the people asked, "What
does all this mean? What are you trying to tell us?"

20 So I said to them, "A message came to me from the LORD, 21 and I was told to give this
message to the people of Israel. This is what the Sovereign LORD says: I will defile My Tem-
ple, the source of your security and pride, the place your heart delights in. Your sons and
daughters whom you left behind in Judea will be slaughtered by the sword. 22 Then you will
do as Ezekiel has done. You will not mourn in public or console yourselves by eating the
food brought by friends. 23 Your heads will remain covered, and your sandals will not be
taken off. You will not mourn or weep, but you will waste away because of your sins. You
will mourn privately for all the evil you have done. 24 Ezekiel is an example for you; you will
do just as he has done. And when that time comes, you will know that I am the LORD."

25 Then the LORD said to me, "Son of man, on the day I take away their stronghold—their
joy and glory, their heart's desire, their dearest treasure—I will also take away their sons
and daughters. 26 And on that day a survivor from Jerusalem will come to you in Babylon
and tell you what has happened. 27 And when he arrives, your voice will suddenly return
so you can talk to him, and you will be a symbol for these people. Then they will know
that I am the LORD."

A MESSAGE FOR AMMON

25 Then this message came to me from the LORD: 2 "Son of man, turn and face the
land of Ammon and prophesy against its people. 3 Give the Ammonites this mes-

24:16 Job 23:2; Song 7:10; Jer 13:17; 16:5; 22:10
24:17 Lev 21:10-12; 2 Sam 15:30; Jer 16:7
24:21 Ps 27:4; Jer 16:11; Ezek 23:47
24:23 Job 27:15; Ps 78:64
24:24 Ezek 4:3; Luke 11:29-30
24:25 Pss 48:2; 122:1-9; Jer 7:4; 11:22
24:26 1 Sam 4:12; Job 1:15-19; Ezek 33:21-22
24:27 Ezek 3:26; 33:22
25:2 Amos 1:13; Zeph 2:9
25:3 Ps 70:2-3; Ezek 21:28; 26:2; 36:2

24:15-19 The method the Lord used to convey His message to Israel on this occasion had to be the most personally devastating to Ezekiel. The Lord told Ezekiel that He would take away his "dearest treasure," but he would not be allowed to show any sorrow (24:16) or publicly mourn his loss. He could only groan silently (24:17). After Ezekiel told the people what the Lord said, his wife died. The people recognized that this was another cryptic message from the Lord, but they didn't understand it, so they asked Ezekiel to explain it.

JUDAH'S ENEMIES
Ammon, Moab, Edom, and Philistia, although once united with Judah against Babylon, had abandoned Judah and rejoiced to see its ruin. But these nations were as sinful as Judah and would also feel the sting of God's judgment.

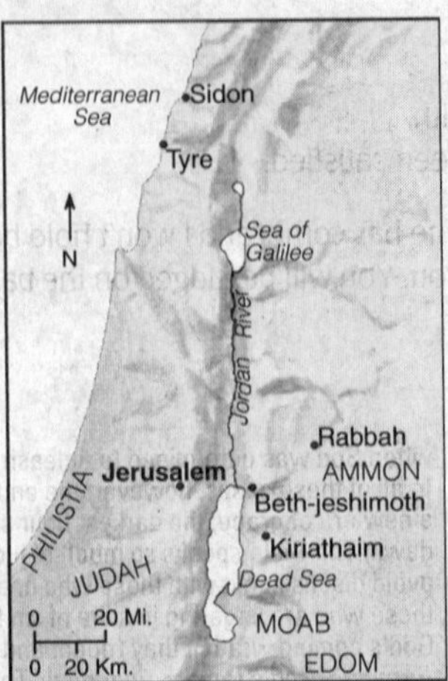

24:20-27 The fulfillment of the cryptic message given in 24:15-19 would occur in two ways. First, the Lord would desecrate His Temple—Judah's "joy and glory," their "heart's desire," and their "dearest treasure" (24:25)—by bringing in the Babylonian army to destroy it. Second, the people of Judah would lose their own sons and daughters to either death or captivity. Despite the loss of such dear treasures, none were to mourn their losses. It appears that their loss would not be on display because, in this situation, their emotional reaction to tragedy was not nearly as important as the message of judgment from God. In God's economy, grief over one's sin should take priority over that of the death of a loved one (2 Corinthians 12:21).

25:1 This verse introduces a transition from the use of several symbolic actions (see note at 4:1) and allegories in chapters 4–24 to more direct prophetic denunciations of Judah's enemies in chapters 25–32 (compare Isaiah 13–28; Jeremiah 46–51; Amos 1:3–2:3; Obadiah; Nahum). These judgment prophecies against Judah's wicked neighbors separate Ezekiel's denunciation of Judah's sins (chapters 4–24) from the promise of Judah's future restoration in chapters 33–48. The two common themes in these prophecies are: (1) each nation either contributed to Judah's downfall or rejoiced when it happened and thus deserved to be judged for their treatment of God's people; and (2) each nation was puffed up with pride and reveled in idolatrous practices.

25:2-7 Although the Ammonites were relatives of the Israelites (see Genesis 11:27; 19:34-36, 38), they often opposed God's people (Deuteronomy 23:3-4; Judges 3:13; 1 Samuel 11:1-3; 2 Samuel 10:1-14) and were known for their idolatry and other vices (1 Kings 11:7, 33; Amos 1:13; Zephaniah 2:9-10). The Lord's judgment on them would be so complete that they

25:4 Deut 28:33, 51; Judg 6:3, 33
25:5 2 Sam 12:26; Jer 49:2; Zeph 2:14-15
25:6 Zeph 2:8, 10; Obad 1:12
25:7 Amos 1:14-15
25:8 Isa 15:1; Jer 48:1; Amos 2:1
25:9 Num 32:37-38; 33:49; Josh 13:17-20; 1 Chr 5:8; Jer 48:23
25:13 Gen 36:34; Jer 49:7; Mal 1:3-4
25:14 Nah 1:2-4; Heb 10:30-31
25:15 Isa 14:29-31; Joel 3:4; Amos 1:6-8; Zeph 2:4-7; Zech 9:5-8
25:16 1 Sam 30:14; Jer 47:4

sage from the Sovereign LORD: Hear the word of the Sovereign LORD! Because you cheered
when My Temple was defiled, mocked Israel in her desolation, and laughed at Judah as
she went away into exile, 4 I will allow nomads from the eastern deserts to overrun your
country. They will set up their camps among you and pitch their tents on your land. They
will harvest all your fruit and drink the milk from your livestock. 5 And I will turn the city of
Rabbah into a pasture for camels, and all the land of the Ammonites into a resting place
for sheep and goats. Then you will know that I am the LORD.
6 "This is what the Sovereign LORD says: Because you clapped and danced and cheered
with glee at the destruction of My people, 7 I will raise My fist of judgment against you. I
will give you as plunder to many nations. I will cut you off from being a nation and destroy
you completely. Then you will know that I am the LORD.

A MESSAGE FOR MOAB

8 "This is what the Sovereign LORD says: Because the people of Moab have said that Judah
is just like all the other nations, 9 I will open up their eastern flank and wipe out their glori-
ous frontier towns—Beth-jeshimoth, Baal-meon, and Kiriathaim. 10 And I will hand Moab
over to nomads from the eastern deserts, just as I handed over Ammon. Yes, the Ammon-
ites will no longer be counted among the nations. 11 In the same way, I will bring My judg-
ment down on the Moabites. Then they will know that I am the LORD.

A MESSAGE FOR EDOM

12 "This is what the Sovereign LORD says: The people of Edom have sinned greatly by
avenging themselves against the people of Judah. 13 Therefore, says the Sovereign LORD, I
will raise My fist of judgment against Edom. I will wipe out its people and animals with the
sword. I will make a wasteland of everything from Teman to Dedan. 14 I will accomplish
this by the hand of My people of Israel. They will carry out My vengeance with anger, and
Edom will know that this vengeance is from Me. I, the Sovereign LORD, have spoken!

A MESSAGE FOR PHILISTIA

15 "This is what the Sovereign LORD says: The people of Philistia have acted against Judah
out of bitter revenge and long-standing contempt. 16 Therefore, this is what the Sovereign

---

would no longer be a nation. The Ammonites, like the Israelites, were overrun by the Babylonians and taken into exile. Their land has been occupied by Arab peoples ("nomads from the eastern deserts," 25:4) ever since.

25:8-11 The Moabites, also relatives of the Israelites (see Genesis 11:27; 19:30-33, 37), were the first to introduce Israel to the worship of the Canaanite god Baal (Numbers 21:1–25:5; 31:16), a sin that plagued Israel for centuries thereafter. Ironically, the Moabites—like their cousins the Ammonites—fought with the Babylonians against Israel; Jeremiah 27:3) but then were themselves overrun by Nebuchadnezzar's army and taken into exile. They, too, ceased to exist as a nation and were replaced by Arab peoples ("nomads from the eastern deserts," 25:10).

▶ PURPOSE
25:12 Vengeance belongs to the Lord. The small book of Obadiah describes a time when Edom took advantage of Judah by invading the land shortly after Judah had suffered a military defeat (Obadiah 1:11-14). Ezekiel explained that they were motivated out of a desire for vengeance. Vengeful attacks upon the weak do not comply with God's standards of justice. We, too, may be tempted to take advantage of those who have dealt unjustly with us in the past, but we must remember Christ's command to love even our enemy and place our confidence in God's ability to vindicate His people (Matthew 5:44; Romans 12:19). Deal with the weak and helpless as you would wish to be dealt with if you were in the same situation (Luke 6:31). (***See Purpose**> God's Deeds> Judgment> God promises judgment,* TopicGuide page A53.)

25:12-14 Edom (meaning "red,") was another name for Esau, Jacob's twin brother (Genesis 25:25-26), and thus the Edomites were not only the descendants of Esau but also relatives of Moab and Ammon. Esau lost both his blessing and his birthright to Jacob (Israel; see Genesis 25:27-34; 27:1-41), and the early animosity between the two brothers continued in their offspring. The Edomites were also idolatrous (2 Chronicles 25:14, 20) and deserving of God's judgment. Edom ceased to be a nation when Israel itself defeated the Edomites in the second century BC, making them "a wasteland . . . from Teman to Dedan" (that is, from the northernmost city to the southernmost).

25:15-17 Philistia was the homeland of a powerful, warrior nation whose chief god was Dagon (Judges 16:23; 1 Samuel 5:1-7). The Philistines harassed Israel especially during the time of the judges (Judges 3:31; 10:7; 13–16; 1 Samuel 4–5) and during Saul's reign (1 Samuel 13–14; 17), but they ceased to be a major threat after David's decisive victory over them (2 Samuel 5:17-25).

LORD says: I will raise My fist of judgment against the land of the Philistines. I will wipe out
the Kerethites and utterly destroy the people who live by the sea. 17I will execute terrible
vengeance against them to punish them for what they have done. And when I have in-
flicted My revenge, they will know that I am the LORD."

A MESSAGE FOR TYRE

26 On February 3, during the twelfth year of King Jehoiachin's captivity,* this mes-
sage came to me from the LORD: 2"Son of man, Tyre has rejoiced over the fall of
Jerusalem, saying, 'Ha! She who was the gateway to the rich trade routes to the east has
been broken, and I am the heir! Because she has been made desolate, I will become
wealthy!'
3"Therefore, this is what the Sovereign LORD says: I am your enemy, O Tyre, and I will
bring many nations against you, like the waves of the sea crashing against your shoreline.
4They will destroy the walls of Tyre and tear down its towers. I will scrape away its soil and
make it a bare rock! 5It will be just a rock in the sea, a place for fishermen to spread their
nets, for I have spoken, says the Sovereign LORD. Tyre will become the prey of many na-
tions, 6and its mainland villages will be destroyed by the sword. Then they will know that I
am the LORD.
7"This is what the Sovereign LORD says: From the north I will bring King Nebuchadnez-
zar* of Babylon against Tyre. He is king of kings and brings his horses, chariots, chari-
oteers, and great army. 8First he will destroy your mainland villages. Then he will attack
you by building a siege wall, constructing a ramp, and raising a roof of shields against you.
9He will pound your walls with battering rams and demolish your towers with sledgeham-
mers. 10The hooves of his horses will choke the city with dust, and the noise of the chari-
oteers and chariot wheels will shake your walls as they storm through your broken gates.
11His horsemen will trample through every street in the city. They will butcher your peo-
ple, and your strong pillars will topple.
12"They will plunder all your riches and merchandise and break down your walls. They
will destroy your lovely homes and dump your stones and timbers and even your dust
into the sea. 13I will stop the music of your songs. No more will the sound of harps be
heard among your people. 14I will make your island a bare rock, a place for fishermen to
spread their nets. You will never be rebuilt, for I, the LORD, have spoken. Yes, the Sovereign
LORD has spoken!

25:17 Ps 9:16
26:2 2 Sam 5:11; Isa 23:1; Jer 25:22
26:3 Jer 50:42; 51:42
26:4 Isa 23:11; Amos 1:10
26:7 Dan 2:37, 47; Nah 2:3-4
26:8 Jer 6:6; 32:24; 52:4
26:10 Jer 39:3
26:11 Isa 5:28; 26:5; Hab 1:8
26:12 2 Chr 32:27; Isa 23:8, 18; Amos 5:11
26:13 Isa 24:8-9; Amos 6:5; Rev 18:22-23
26:14 Deut 13:16; Job 12:14; Isa 14:27; Mal 1:4

26:1 Hebrew *In the eleventh year, on the first day of the month,* of the ancient Hebrew lunar calendar year. Since an element is missing in the date formula here, scholars have reconstructed this probable reading: *In the eleventh [month of the twelfth] year, on the first day of the month.* This reading would put this message on February 3, 585 B.C.; also see note on 1:1. 26:7 Hebrew *Nebuchadrezzar,* a variant spelling of Nebuchadnezzar.

26:1 "During the twelfth year" indicates that the fourth wave of the Babylonian captivity, and the destruction of Jerusalem and the Temple, were less than a year away (see note at 1:2).

26:2-3 Tyre was a chief city of Phoenicia and was located partly on the mainland coast and partly on an island fortress in the Mediterranean. It was strategically important for maritime shipping and trade. The people of Tyre prided themselves on the beauty, safety, and great wealth of their city. Tyre rejoiced when Jerusalem fell to the Babylonians because Judah's defeat would allow the city to prosper even more as they sought control over lucrative trade routes around the Mediterranean Sea.

▶ CHURCH
26:2 Opportunity for encouragement. There are two types of people in this world: those who feel pity when someone else fails, and those who see opportunity. Rather than work hard to improve themselves, these people grow through the failure of others. Though they may not succeed in tearing others down, they rejoice when someone else does the deed for them. This was how the leaders of Tyre acted toward Israel. And it's how many people act in the world and the church. When leaders fail in the church, many people, rather than stooping to pick them up, seek to replace them. The lust after power can blind us to the love God wants us to show for our neighbor. When you see weakness in others, see it as an opportunity to show them the love and mercy of God. (***See Church***> *Role*> *Church Community*> *Encouraging one another,* TopicGuide page A49.)

26:4-14 Nebuchadnezzar's army besieged Tyre for about thirteen years (587–574 BC), but he was never able to conquer the city completely. This was left for Alexander the Great about 240 years later (332 BC), and his conquest made the city a "bare rock" that was nothing but "a place for fishermen to spread their nets" (compare 26:19-21). The city was rebuilt and became powerful and influential once more by New Testament times.

THE EFFECT OF TYRE'S DESTRUCTION

26:15 Jer 49:21 15 "This is what the Sovereign LORD says to Tyre: The whole coastline will tremble at the
sound of your fall, as the screams of the wounded echo in the continuing slaughter. 16 All
26:16 Ps 35:26 the seaport rulers will step down from their thrones and take off their royal robes and
Jon 3:6 beautiful clothing. They will sit on the ground trembling with horror at your destruction.
26:17 Isa 14:12 17 Then they will wail for you, singing this funeral song:

Jer 48:39; 50:23 "O famous island city,
once ruler of the sea,
how you have been destroyed!
Your people, with their naval power,
once spread fear around the world.
26:18 18 Now the coastlands tremble at your fall.
Isa 23:5-7, 10-15 The islands are dismayed as you disappear.

26:19 Isa 8:7-8 19 "This is what the Sovereign LORD says: I will make Tyre an uninhabited ruin, like many
26:20 others. I will bury you beneath the terrible waves of enemy attack. Great seas will swallow
Ps 88:6 you. 20 I will send you to the pit to join those who descended there long ago. Your city will
Jon 2:2, 6 Zech 2:8 lie in ruins, buried beneath the earth, like those in the pit who have entered the world of
the dead. You will have no place of respect here in the land of the living. 21 I will bring you
26:21 Ezek 27:36 to a terrible end, and you will exist no more. You will be looked for, but you will never
again be found. I, the Sovereign LORD, have spoken!"

THE END OF TYRE'S GLORY

27:2 Jer 7:20; 9:10, 17-20 **27** Then this message came to me from the LORD: 2 "Son of man, sing a funeral song
for Tyre, 3 that mighty gateway to the sea, the trading center of the world. Give
Tyre this message from the Sovereign LORD:

"You boasted, O Tyre,
'My beauty is perfect!'
4 You extended your boundaries into the sea.
Your builders made your beauty perfect.
27:5 5 You were like a great ship
Deut 3:9 Song 4:8 built of the finest cypress from Senir.*
They took a cedar from Lebanon
to make a mast for you.
6 They carved your oars
27:6 Num 21:33 from the oaks of Bashan.
Jer 22:20 Zech 11:2 Your deck of pine from the coasts of Cyprus*
was inlaid with ivory.

27:5 Or *Hermon.* 27:6 Hebrew *Kittim.*

26:15-18 Tyre's neighbors and customers would be astonished and saddened at the city's destruction because their own safety and wealth could also come to a sudden end.

27:3-9 These verses describe the economic power and extensive influence of Tyre, sources of great pride to the people of the city. The Lord warns that pride comes before a fall (Proverbs 16:18). Like Tyre, Jerusalem was described as having perfect beauty before the city fell to the Babylonians (see Lamentations 2:15).

▸ GOD

27:3 The source of beauty. Human beings are instinctively attracted by beauty. We are drawn to beauty in people, in nature, in art, and in life itself. There is nothing wrong with appreciating and creating splendor (Psalm 50:2; 1 Peter 3:4), for it is all a reflection of God's own glory and beauty (1 Chronicles 16:27). Ultimately beauty points us to the source of all that is attractive—our glorious God (Psalm 96:6; 1 Corinthians 15:40-42). Our sinfulness, unfortunately, causes us to fall in love with beauty rather than the Source (Genesis 2:9; 3:6). Whenever we are attracted to lovely people or things, we should thank God for sharing a portion of His glory with this world. One day, He will grant His church an even greater share of His splendor (Revelation 21:2). Prepare yourself and those around you for that day. (***See God**> God's Attributes> Good> All good comes from God,* TopicGuide page A16.)

7 Your sails were made of Egypt's finest linen,
and they flew as a banner above you.
You stood beneath blue and purple awnings
made bright with dyes from the coasts of Elishah.
8 Your oarsmen came from Sidon and Arvad;
your helmsmen were skilled men from Tyre itself.
9 Wise old craftsmen from Gebal did the caulking.
Ships from every land came with goods to barter for your trade.

10 "Men from distant Persia, Lydia, and Libya* served in your great army. They hung
their shields and helmets on your walls, giving you great honor. 11 Men from Arvad and
Helech stood on your walls. Your towers were manned by men from Gammad. Their
shields hung on your walls, completing your beauty.
12 "Tarshish sent merchants to buy your wares in exchange for silver, iron, tin, and lead.
13 Merchants from Greece,* Tubal, and Meshech brought slaves and articles of bronze to
trade with you.
14 "From Togarmah came riding horses, chariot horses, and mules, all in exchange for
your goods. 15 Merchants came to you from Dedan.* Numerous coastlands were your cap-
tive markets; they brought payment in ivory tusks and ebony wood.
16 "Syria* sent merchants to buy your rich variety of goods. They traded turquoise, pur-
ple dyes, embroidery, fine linen, and jewelry of coral and rubies. 17 Judah and Israel traded
for your wares, offering wheat from Minnith, figs,* honey, olive oil, and balm.
18 "Damascus sent merchants to buy your rich variety of goods, bringing wine from Hel-
bon and white wool from Zahar. 19 Greeks from Uzal* came to trade for your merchandise.
Wrought iron, cassia, and fragrant calamus were bartered for your wares.
20 "Dedan sent merchants to trade their expensive saddle blankets with you. 21 The Ara-
bians and the princes of Kedar sent merchants to trade lambs and rams and male goats in
exchange for your goods. 22 The merchants of Sheba and Raamah came with all kinds of
spices, jewels, and gold in exchange for your wares.
23 "Haran, Canneh, Eden, Sheba, Asshur, and Kilmad came with their merchandise, too.
24 They brought choice fabrics to trade—blue cloth, embroidery, and multicolored carpets
rolled up and bound with cords. 25 The ships of Tarshish were your ocean caravans. Your
island warehouse was filled to the brim!

THE DESTRUCTION OF TYRE

26 "But look! Your oarsmen
have taken you into stormy seas!
A mighty eastern gale
has wrecked you in the heart of the sea!
27 Everything is lost—
your riches and wares,
your sailors and pilots,
your ship builders, merchants, and warriors.
On the day of your ruin,
everyone on board sinks into the depths of the sea.

27:7 Exod 25:4; Prov 7:16; Jer 10:9
27:8 Gen 10:18; 1 Kgs 9:27; 1 Chr 1:16
27:9 1 Kgs 5:18
27:10 Ezek 38:5
27:13 Gen 10:2-3; Isa 66:19; Ezek 38:2; Joel 3:3; Rev 18:13
27:15 Rev 18:12
27:16 Ezek 16:13, 18
27:17 Judg 11:33
27:18 Gen 14:15; Ezek 47:16-18
27:21 Isa 21:13; 60:7
27:22 Gen 10:7; 43:11; 1 Kgs 10:2; Isa 60:6; Ezek 38:13
27:23 2 Kgs 19:12; Isa 37:12; Amos 1:5; 6:2
27:26 Ps 48:7

27:10 Hebrew *Paras, Lud, and Put.* 27:13 Hebrew *Javan.* 27:15 Greek version reads *Rhodes.* 27:16 Hebrew *Aram;* some manuscripts read *Edom.* 27:17 The meaning of the Hebrew is uncertain. 27:19 Hebrew *Vedan and Javan from Uzal.* The meaning of the Hebrew is uncertain.

27:10-24 The geographical extent of Tyre's economic influence is clearly detailed in these verses. Tyre was the ancient equivalent of the New York Stock Exchange. Over 20 nations and almost 40 products were mentioned in connection with Tyre's economic and trade relations.

28 Your cities by the sea tremble
as your pilots cry out in terror.

27:29 Rev 18:17-19

29 All the oarsmen abandon their ships;
the sailors and pilots on shore come to stand on the beach.

27:30 1 Sam 4:12; 2 Sam 1:2; Jon 3:6; Rev 18:19

30 They cry aloud over you
and weep bitterly.
They throw dust on their heads
and roll in ashes.

27:31 Isa 16:9; 22:12; Ezek 7:18; 29:18

31 They shave their heads in grief for you
and dress themselves in burlap.
They weep for you with bitter anguish
and deep mourning.

27:32 Rev 18:18

32 As they wail and mourn over you,
they sing this sad funeral song:
'Was there ever such a city as Tyre,
now silent at the bottom of the sea?
33 The merchandise you traded
satisfied the desires of many nations.
Kings at the ends of the earth
were enriched by your trade.

27:34 Zech 9:3-4

34 Now you are a wrecked ship,
broken at the bottom of the sea.
All your merchandise and crew
have gone down with you.
35 All who live along the coastlands
are appalled at your terrible fate.
Their kings are filled with horror
and look on with twisted faces.

27:36 Ps 37:10, 36; Jer 49:17; Zeph 2:15

36 The merchants among the nations
shake their heads at the sight of you,*
for you have come to a horrible end
and will exist no more.'"

A MESSAGE FOR TYRE'S KING

28:2 Ps 82:6-7; 2 Thes 2:4

28 Then this message came to me from the LORD: 2"Son of man, give the prince of
Tyre this message from the Sovereign LORD:

"In your great pride you claim, 'I am a god!
I sit on a divine throne in the heart of the sea.'
But you are only a man and not a god,
though you boast that you are a god.

27:36 Hebrew *hiss at you.*

28:1-10 Here the Lord's judgment against Tyre was directed specifically at the king. King Ethbaal II of Tyre (585–573 BC) reigned during most of the Babylonian siege of the city (see note at 26:4-14). The king was rebuked twice for his pride in his wisdom and wealth, and both of these blessings would be lost when the Lord brought "the terror of the nations" (28:7) against them in judgment.

▸ SPIRITUAL WARFARE

28:2 Never alone. From the beginning we have been confronted with the temptation to be like God (Genesis 3:4-5). Surprisingly, the preposterous nature of the temptation has never dulled its appeal to humanity—no matter how self-destructive the sin, it still appeals to us. From the tower of Babel to the king of Tyre and beyond, we have continually tried to claim the privileges of God. Why? We desire complete independence and self-determination, making ourselves the sole authority in our lives. But such a quest is futile; we were never made to be able to function alone. God created us for both divine and human companionship (Genesis 2:7, 18). The Christian life is not one of solitude but rather of submission to a very present God and fellowship with God's people. (***See Spiritual Warfare****> Origin of Sin> Humanity's Fall> Spiritual> Separated from God,* TopicGuide page A44.)

3 You regard yourself as wiser than Daniel
and think no secret is hidden from you.
4 With your wisdom and understanding you have amassed great wealth—
gold and silver for your treasuries.
5 Yes, your wisdom has made you very rich,
and your riches have made you very proud.

6 "Therefore, this is what the Sovereign LORD says:
Because you think you are as wise as a god,
7 I will now bring against you a foreign army,
the terror of the nations.
They will draw their swords against your marvelous wisdom
and defile your splendor!
8 They will bring you down to the pit,
and you will die in the heart of the sea,
pierced with many wounds.
9 Will you then boast, 'I am a god!'
to those who kill you?
To them you will be no god
but merely a man!
10 You will die like an outcast*
at the hands of foreigners.
I, the Sovereign LORD, have spoken!"

11 Then this further message came to me from the LORD: 12 "Son of man, sing this funeral
song for the king of Tyre. Give him this message from the Sovereign LORD:

"You were the model of perfection,
full of wisdom and exquisite in beauty.
13 You were in Eden,
the garden of God.
Your clothing was adorned with every precious stone*—
red carnelian, pale-green peridot, white moonstone,
blue-green beryl, onyx, green jasper,
blue lapis lazuli, turquoise, and emerald—
all beautifully crafted for you
and set in the finest gold.
They were given to you
on the day you were created.
14 I ordained and anointed you
as the mighty angelic guardian.*
You had access to the holy mountain of God
and walked among the stones of fire.

15 "You were blameless in all you did
from the day you were created
until the day evil was found in you.

28:3 Dan 1:20
28:4 Zech 9:2-4
28:5 Job 31:24-25; Ps 52:7; Hos 12:7-8; 13:6
28:6 Exod 9:17
28:7 Dan 7:7; Hab 1:6-8
28:8 Ezek 27:26-27, 34
28:10 1 Sam 17:26, 36; Ezek 31:18
28:12 Ezek 27:2
28:13 Gen 2:8; Exod 28:17-20; 39:10-21; Isa 51:3; 54:11-12
28:14 Exod 25:17-20; Ezek 20:40
28:15 Isa 14:12

28:10 Hebrew *will die the death of the uncircumcised.* 28:13 The identification of some of these gemstones is uncertain.
28:14 Hebrew *guardian cherub;* similarly in 28:16.

28:11-19 This passage parallels Isaiah 14:12-17, which addresses the king of Babylon. This passage describes the unseen power behind the king of Tyre—Satan himself. Satan—and not the king of Tyre—seemed to be in view as seen in the following descriptions: He was "the model of perfection, full of wisdom and exquisite in beauty" (28:12); he was "in Eden, the garden of God" (28:13); he had "access to the holy mountain of God" (28:14); he was "blameless" until "evil was found" in him (28:15); and he was "banished" from "the mountain of God" (28:16).

28:16 Ezek 8:17 Hab 2:8, 17

[16] Your rich commerce led you to violence,
and you sinned.
So I banished you in disgrace
from the mountain of God.
I expelled you, O mighty guardian,
from your place among the stones of fire.

28:17 Isa 19:11

[17] Your heart was filled with pride
because of all your beauty.
Your wisdom was corrupted
by your love of splendor.
So I threw you to the ground
and exposed you to the curious gaze of kings.

28:18 Amos 1:9-10 Mal 4:3

[18] You defiled your sanctuaries
with your many sins and your dishonest trade.
So I brought fire out from within you,
and it consumed you.
I reduced you to ashes on the ground
in the sight of all who were watching.

28:19 Jer 51:64

[19] All who knew you are appalled at your fate.
You have come to a terrible end,
and you will exist no more."

A MESSAGE FOR SIDON

28:21 Gen 10:15-19 Isa 23:2-4, 12

[20]Then another message came to me from the LORD: [21]"Son of man, turn and face the city
of Sidon and prophesy against it. [22]Give the people of Sidon this message from the Sover-
eign LORD:

"I am your enemy, O Sidon,
and I will reveal My glory by what I do to you.
When I bring judgment against you
and reveal My holiness among you,
everyone watching will know
that I am the LORD.

28:23 Jer 51:52 Ezek 38:22

[23] I will send a plague against you,
and blood will be spilled in your streets.
The attack will come from every direction,
and your people will lie slaughtered within your walls.
Then everyone will know
that I am the LORD.

28:24 Num 33:55 Josh 23:13 Isa 55:13

[24] No longer will Israel's scornful neighbors
prick and tear at her like briers and thorns.
For then they will know
that I am the Sovereign LORD.

28:25 Ps 106:47 Isa 11:12-13 Jer 23:8

RESTORATION FOR ISRAEL

[25]"This is what the Sovereign LORD says: The people of Israel will again live in their own

28:20-24 Sidon was a sister city of Tyre. Both were located along the coast of Phoenicia. Sidon was only 23 miles north of Tyre and was much more exposed to enemy armies. Israel's king Ahab married the wicked Jezebel, who was the daughter of the king of Sidon (Ethbaal I; see 1 Kings 16:31-34). Jezebel reinstated the worship of Baal in Israel, which was partly responsible for the nation's downfall. The Lord declared that everyone would witness the destruction of Sidon and the demise of its people.

28:25-26 This promise of Judah's future restoration was set in the midst of God's judgment of Judah's enemies; this emphasized that the Lord would vindicate Himself through His chosen people. Although He had to punish His people with exile, He would also bring them back to their land. These two verses anticipate the fuller explanation of Judah's future restoration in chapters 33–48.

land, the land I gave My servant Jacob. For I will gather them from the distant lands where
I have scattered them. I will reveal to the nations of the world My holiness among My peo-
ple. 26They will live safely in Israel and build homes and plant vineyards. And when I pun- **28:26** Jer 32:15, 43-44 Amos 9:13-14
ish the neighboring nations that treated them with contempt, they will know that I am the
LORD their God."

A MESSAGE FOR EGYPT

29 On January 7,* during the tenth year of King Jehoiachin's captivity, this message
came to me from the LORD: 2"Son of man, turn and face Egypt and prophesy **29:2** Isa 19:1-17 Jer 46:2-25
against Pharaoh the king and all the people of Egypt. 3Give them this message from the
Sovereign LORD: **29:3** Isa 27:1

"I am your enemy, O Pharaoh, king of Egypt—
you great monster, lurking in the streams of the Nile.
For you have said, 'The Nile River is mine;
I made it for myself.'
4 I will put hooks in your jaws **29:4** 2 Kgs 19:28 Isa 37:29 Ezek 38:4
and drag you out on the land
with fish sticking to your scales.
5 I will leave you and all your fish **29:5** Jer 7:33; 34:20
stranded in the wilderness to die.
You will lie unburied on the open ground,
for I have given you as food to the wild animals and birds.
6 All the people of Egypt will know that I am the LORD, **29:6** Isa 36:6
for to Israel you were just a staff made of reeds.
7 When Israel leaned on you, **29:7** Jer 37:5-11 Ezek 17:15-17
you splintered and broke
and stabbed her in the armpit.
When she put her weight on you, you gave way,
and her back was thrown out of joint.

29:1 Hebrew *On the twelfth day of the tenth month,* of the ancient Hebrew lunar calendar. This event occurred on January 7, 587 B.C.; also see note on 1:1.

▸ HOLINESS
28:26 Facing the world's contempt. It is not uncommon for the enemies of God to rejoice when His people experience distress or misery. Throughout history the world has heaped scorn and disdain upon God's people. In the face of such opposition, however, we have been called to show both patience and love. But God has also promised us that our suffering will not go on forever. One day our cries of "How long?" will be answered, and God will avenge His people (Revelation 6:9-11). When confronted with the scorn of the world, remember that such suffering cannot compare with the glories and riches that await God's persevering people (Romans 8:18). (***See Holiness****> Changed by God> God provides> Temporal misery,* TopicGuide page A41.)

29:1 "On January 7" is literally "on the twelfth day of the tenth month." This prophecy against Egypt occurred "during the tenth year of King Jehoiachin's captivity," two years earlier than the dated message beginning in 26:1. The reason this prophecy is out of chronological sequence is unclear.

29:2 The Lord's judgment against Egypt is by far the most extensive in Ezekiel and continues through the end of chapter 32. Egypt had enslaved the Israelites for centuries prior to the Exodus and had promoted idolatry, including the deification of its Pharaohs. Egypt continued to be a world power throughout most of Israel's history, and Israel was often tempted to lean on Egypt for protection.

29:3 The pride of Pharaoh and the Egyptians can be seen in the claim that not only did Pharaoh own the Nile, but he also "made" it. Such arrogance would not go ignored or unpunished by the Lord, the Creator of all the earth.

▸ GOD
29:6-7 God is sovereign. In times of need we look for help from those who are stronger than we are. Judah saw in Egypt a strong nation that could offer help in times of war. But Judah ignored the strength of God, perhaps because the strength of God required faith to see it. The people of Judah soon discovered that their trust in Egypt was misplaced. Egypt had neither the will nor the power to help Judah. God, however, is both able and willing to help His people. When we find ourselves in deep need, it is often our impulse to seek help first from friends, family, doctors, or material resources. It is not wrong to seek help from these sources, but we must always recognize that God is ultimately our source of strength and help. (***See God****> God's Attributes> Sovereign> He is the only Sovereign,* TopicGuide page A17.)

29:6-9 Israel often looked to Egypt for aid against other enemies, but Egypt turned out to be a weak ally. Egypt was a frail "reed" that crumpled under pressure (compare 2 Kings 18:21), and it would become a desolate wasteland and be taken into captivity. Egypt too would know that the Lord, Israel's God, was the only God.

8 “Therefore, this is what the Sovereign LORD says: I will bring an army against you, O Egypt, and destroy both people and animals. 9 The land of Egypt will become a desolate wasteland, and the Egyptians will know that I am the LORD.

“Because you said, ‘The Nile River is mine; I made it,’ 10 I am now the enemy of both you and your river. I will make the land of Egypt a totally desolate wasteland, from Migdol to Aswan, as far south as the border of Ethiopia.* 11 For forty years not a soul will pass that way, neither people nor animals. It will be completely uninhabited. 12 I will make Egypt desolate, and it will be surrounded by other desolate nations. Its cities will be empty and desolate for forty years, surrounded by other ruined cities. I will scatter the Egyptians to distant lands.

13 “But this is what the Sovereign LORD also says: At the end of the forty years I will bring the Egyptians home again from the nations to which they have been scattered. 14 I will restore the prosperity of Egypt and bring its people back to the land of Pathros in southern Egypt from which they came. But Egypt will remain an unimportant, minor kingdom. 15 It will be the lowliest of all the nations, never again great enough to rise above its neighbors.

16 “Then Israel will no longer be tempted to trust in Egypt for help. Egypt’s shattered condition will remind Israel of how sinful she was to trust Egypt in earlier days. Then Israel will know that I am the Sovereign LORD.”

NEBUCHADNEZZAR TO CONQUER EGYPT

17 On April 26, the first day of the new year,* during the twenty-seventh year of King Jehoiachin’s captivity, this message came to me from the LORD: 18 “Son of man, the army of King Nebuchadnezzar* of Babylon fought so hard against Tyre that the warriors’ heads were rubbed bare and their shoulders were raw and blistered. Yet Nebuchadnezzar and his army won no plunder to compensate them for all their work. 19 Therefore, this is what the Sovereign LORD says: I will give the land of Egypt to Nebuchadnezzar, king of Babylon. He will carry off its wealth, plundering everything it has so he can pay his army. 20 Yes, I have given him the land of Egypt as a reward for his work, says the Sovereign LORD, because he was working for Me when he destroyed Tyre.

21 “And the day will come when I will cause the ancient glory of Israel to revive,* and then, Ezekiel, your words will be respected. Then they will know that I am the LORD.”

A SAD DAY FOR EGYPT

30 This is another message that came to me from the LORD: 2 “Son of man, prophesy and give this message from the Sovereign LORD:

“Weep and wail
  for that day,
3 for the terrible day is almost here—
  the day of the LORD!

29:9 Prov 18:12; 29:23
29:11 Jer 43:11-12
29:12 Jer 25:15-19; 27:6-11
29:13 Isa 19:22; Jer 46:26
29:14 Isa 11:11; Jer 44:1
29:15 Dan 11:42-43; Nah 3:8-9; Zech 10:11
29:16 Isa 30:1-3; 64:9; Hos 5:13; 8:13; 9:9
29:17 Ezek 24:1; 30:20
29:18 Jer 25:9; 27:6; Ezek 26:7-12
29:19 Jer 43:10-13; Ezek 30:10-12
29:20 Isa 10:6-7; 45:1-3
29:21 1 Sam 2:10; Pss 92:10; 132:17; Amos 3:7-8; Luke 21:15
30:2 Isa 13:6; 65:14; Joel 1:5, 11, 13, 15

29:10 Hebrew *from Migdol to Syene as far as the border of Cush.* 29:17 Hebrew *On the first day of the first month,* of the ancient Hebrew lunar calendar. This event occurred on April 26, 571 B.C.; also see note on 1:1. 29:18 Hebrew *Nebuchadrezzar,* a variant spelling of Nebuchadnezzar; also in 29:19. 29:21 Hebrew *I will cause a horn to sprout for the house of Israel.*

29:10-16 Egypt had promised to assist Judah against the Babylonians, but they failed to do so. Egypt would experience the same devastation at the hands of the Babylonians that Judah did (29:19) and would become desolate for 40 years, perhaps a reflection of Israel’s years of wandering in the wilderness. Egypt would be restored to its land after 40 years but would never be the world power it had been in its past.

▶ GOD
30:3 A day of despair. Judgment is understandably an uncomfortable topic even for Christians. Yet as we read Scripture we are constantly confronted with threats of God’s just wrath. Here Ezekiel warned Egypt of the coming “day of the LORD.” Several prophets referred to this day as a time of destruction and despair when God would pour out His sudden and overwhelming judgment upon His enemies. This judgment against Egypt and other nations, including His own people, foreshadowed the great and final “day of the LORD” when He will destroy all opposition to His reign and establish a kingdom of peace throughout all creation. While it will be a day of despair for the enemies of God, it will be a day of great rejoicing for God’s people. Praise God that He will one day vindicate His people and bring peace to the earth. (***See God***> *God’s Attributes*> *Just*> *God judges all people with justice,* TopicGuide page A16.)

It is a day of clouds and gloom,
a day of despair for the nations.
4 A sword will come against Egypt,
and those who are slaughtered will cover the ground.
Its wealth will be carried away
and its foundations destroyed.
The land of Ethiopia* will be ravished.
5 Ethiopia, Libya, Lydia, all Arabia,*
and all their other allies
will be destroyed in that war.

6 "For this is what the LORD says:
All of Egypt's allies will fall,
and the pride of her power will end.
From Migdol to Aswan*
they will be slaughtered by the sword,
says the Sovereign LORD.
7 Egypt will be desolate,
surrounded by desolate nations,
and its cities will be in ruins,
surrounded by other ruined cities.
8 And the people of Egypt will know that I am the LORD
when I have set Egypt on fire
and destroyed all their allies.
9 At that time I will send swift messengers in ships
to terrify the complacent Ethiopians.
Great panic will come upon them
on that day of Egypt's certain destruction.
Watch for it!
It is sure to come!

10 "For this is what the Sovereign LORD says:
By the power of King Nebuchadnezzar* of Babylon,
I will destroy the hordes of Egypt.
11 He and his armies—the most ruthless of all—
will be sent to demolish the land.
They will make war against Egypt
until slaughtered Egyptians cover the ground.
12 I will dry up the Nile River
and sell the land to wicked men.
I will destroy the land of Egypt and everything in it
by the hands of foreigners.
I, the LORD, have spoken!

13 "This is what the Sovereign LORD says:
I will smash the idols* of Egypt
and the images at Memphis.*

30:5 Jer 25:20, 24
30:6 Isa 20:3-6
30:8 Ps 58:11; Amos 1:4, 7, 10-14
30:9 Isa 18:1-2; Ezek 32:9-10; 38:11
30:12 Ezek 29:3, 9
30:13 Isa 2:18; Jer 44:1; 46:14

30:4 Hebrew *Cush;* similarly in 30:9. 30:5 Hebrew *Cush, Put, Lud, all Arabia, Cub. Cub* is otherwise unknown and may be another spelling for *Lub* (Libya). 30:6 Hebrew *to Syene.* 30:10 Hebrew *Nebuchadrezzar,* a variant spelling of Nebuchadnezzar. 30:13a The Hebrew term (literally *round things*) probably alludes to dung. 30:13b Hebrew *Noph;* also in 30:16.

30:4-6 Not only would Egypt face God's judgment, but so also would all the nations that helped Egypt attain and sustain its power in the ancient world.

30:13 "The Sovereign LORD" promised to "smash the idols of Egypt," the place where Israel first learned idolatrous practices. Over 1,200 gods existed in ancient Egypt at one time or another, making that nation a prime target for God's hatred of idolatry.

There will be no rulers left in Egypt;
terror will sweep the land.
30:14 Ps 78:12, 43 Isa 19:11, 13
14 I will destroy southern Egypt,*
set fire to Zoan,
and bring judgment against Thebes.*
15 I will pour out My fury on Pelusium,*
the strongest fortress of Egypt,
and I will stamp out
the hordes of Thebes.
16 Yes, I will set fire to all Egypt!
Pelusium will be racked with pain;
Thebes will be torn apart;
Memphis will live in constant terror.
30:17 Gen 41:45
17 The young men of Heliopolis and Bubastis*
will die in battle,
and the women* will be taken away as slaves.
30:18 Lev 26:13 Jer 43:8-13
18 When I come to break the proud strength of Egypt,
it will be a dark day for Tahpanhes, too.
A dark cloud will cover Tahpanhes,
and its daughters will be led away as captives.
30:19 Ps 9:16 Ezek 5:8, 15
19 And so I will greatly punish Egypt,
and they will know that I am the LORD."

THE BROKEN ARMS OF PHARAOH

30:20 Ezek 26:1
20 On April 29,* during the eleventh year of King Jehoiachin's captivity, this message came
to me from the LORD: 21 "Son of man, I have broken the arm of Pharaoh, the king of Egypt.
30:21 Pss 10:15; 37:17 Jer 30:13; 46:11
His arm has not been put in a cast so that it may heal. Neither has it been bound up with a
splint to make it strong enough to hold a sword. 22 Therefore, this is what the Sovereign
30:22 2 Kgs 24:7 Jer 37:7; 46:1-12, 21-25
LORD says: I am the enemy of Pharaoh, the king of Egypt! I will break both of his arms—the
good arm along with the broken one—and I will make his sword clatter to the ground. 23 I
will scatter the Egyptians to many lands throughout the world. 24 I will strengthen the arms
30:24 Isa 45:1, 5 Zeph 2:12 Zech 10:12
of Babylon's king and put My sword in his hand. But I will break the arms of Pharaoh, king
of Egypt, and he will lie there mortally wounded, groaning in pain. 25 I will strengthen the
arms of the king of Babylon, while the arms of Pharaoh fall useless to his sides. And when I
30:25 Josh 8:18 1 Chr 21:16 Isa 5:25
put My sword in the hand of Babylon's king and he brings it against the land of Egypt,
Egypt will know that I am the LORD. 26 I will scatter the Egyptians among the nations, dis-
persing them throughout the earth. Then they will know that I am the LORD."

30:14a Hebrew *Pathros.* **30:14b** Hebrew *No;* also in 30:15, 16. **30:15** Hebrew *Sin;* also in 30:16. **30:17a** Hebrew *of Awen and Pi-beseth.* **30:17b** Or *and her cities.* **30:20** Hebrew *On the seventh day of the first month,* of the ancient Hebrew lunar calendar. This event occurred on April 29, 587 B.C.; also see note on 1:1.

▸ GOD

30:18 Opposing pride. What breeds pride in your life? In many, personal strength or power tends to reveal pride. In some, power feeds the desire to be independent of God. In others, strength feeds the desire to rule over others. The more self-sufficient we think ourselves to be, the less we imagine we need God (1 John 2:16). We must be very careful to guard against pride by remembering that everything we have is from God. Are you wise? That's from God (1 Kings 10:24; James 3:17). Are you rich? He gives and takes away wealth (Genesis 31:16; Job 1:21-22). Pride and the temptations to pride are everywhere—there are no simple answers to it. But when we submit to the Holy Spirit, allowing Him to control our lives (Galatians 5:24-25), He will produce the antidote to pride—the fruit of the Spirit (Galatians 5:22-23). Keep following the Holy Spirit's leading and you will walk away from the temptations of pride. (***See God****> Relationship> Barriers> Pride,* TopicGuide page A14.)

30:25-26 The fall of Egypt to the Babylonians in exactly the way the Lord said it would occur would cause even the Egyptians to acknowledge that the Lord, the God of Israel, is the only true God (see also 30:19).

EGYPT COMPARED TO FALLEN ASSYRIA

31 On June 21,* during the eleventh year of King Jehoiachin's captivity, this message came to me from the LORD: 2"Son of man, give this message to Pharaoh, king of Egypt, and all his hordes:

31:2 Nah 3:8-9

"To whom would you compare your greatness?
3 You are like mighty Assyria,
which was once like a cedar of Lebanon,
with beautiful branches that cast deep forest shade
and with its top high among the clouds.
4 Deep springs watered it
and helped it to grow tall and luxuriant.
The water flowed around it like a river,
streaming to all the trees nearby.
5 This great tree towered high,
higher than all the other trees around it.
It prospered and grew long thick branches
because of all the water at its roots.
6 The birds nested in its branches,
and in its shade all the wild animals gave birth.
All the great nations of the world
lived in its shadow.
7 It was strong and beautiful,
with wide-spreading branches,
for its roots went deep
into abundant water.
8 No other cedar in the garden of God
could rival it.
No cypress had branches to equal it;
no plane tree had boughs to compare.
No tree in the garden of God
came close to it in beauty.
9 Because I made this tree so beautiful,
and gave it such magnificent foliage,
it was the envy of all the other trees of Eden,
the garden of God.

31:4 Ezek 17:5, 8 Rev 17:1, 15

31:5 Ps 1:3

31:6 Ezek 17:23 Dan 4:12, 21 Matt 13:32

31:8 Gen 2:8-9; 13:10 Ps 80:10 Isa 51:3

10"Therefore, this is what the Sovereign LORD says: Because Egypt* became proud and arrogant, and because it set itself so high above the others, with its top reaching to the

31:10 2 Chr 32:25 Isa 14:13-14 Dan 5:20

31:1 Hebrew *On the first day of the third month,* of the ancient Hebrew lunar calendar. This event occurred on June 21, 587 B.C.; also see note on 1:1. 31:10 Hebrew *you.*

31:1 "On June 21" is literally "on the first day of the third month." This prophecy was given in 587 BC, "during the eleventh year of King Jehoiachin's captivity," which placed it just 2 months after the preceding oracle (30:20). Ezekiel's prophecy continued to focus on the Lord's judgment of Egypt as in chapters 29–30.

31:2-3 Egypt was compared to Assyria in its greatness. Assyria succeeded Egypt as the dominant world power in the tenth century BC, but God judged both of them for their cruelty to Israel and other nations and for their great pride.

31:3-9 A tree was a common metaphor for a king or a kingdom in the ancient Near East. Assyria was like a "great tree" (31:5) that towered above all the others and provided sustenance for everything around it. The symbolism referred to the extent of the Assyrian Empire and was similar to Nebuchadnezzar's dream in Daniel 4:10-17. Like the king of Tyre in Ezekiel 28, the tree was given greater significance by associating it with the earliest of great trees in Eden (Genesis 2:9).

31:10-17 The Assyrians were "proud and arrogant" because of their great conquests. But the Lord judged Assyria for its pride and handed it over to a mighty nation that destroyed it (see 31:11)—a reference to the fall of Nineveh, the capital city of the Assyrian Empire, to the Babylonians in 612 BC.

31:11 Deut 18:12 Dan 5:18-19 Nah 3:18 31:12 Dan 4:14

clouds, 11 I will hand it over to a mighty nation that will destroy it as its wickedness de-
serves. I have already discarded it. 12 A foreign army—the terror of the nations—has cut it
down and left it fallen on the ground. Its branches are scattered across the mountains and
valleys and ravines of the land. All those who lived in its shadow have gone away and left
it lying there.

31:13 Isa 18:6 Rev 19:17-18 31:14 Num 16:30-33 Ps 63:9 Jon 2:2, 6 Eph 4:9

13 "The birds roost on its fallen trunk,
 and the wild animals lie among its branches.
14 Let the tree of no other nation
 proudly exult in its own prosperity,
though it be higher than the clouds
 and it be watered from the depths.
For all are doomed to die,
 to go down to the depths of the earth.
They will land in the pit
 along with everyone else on earth.

31:15 Nah 2:8-10 31:16 Isa 14:8 Hag 2:7 31:17 Ps 9:17 Dan 4:11-12 31:18 Ps 52:7 Jer 9:25-26 Matt 13:19

15 "This is what the Sovereign LORD says: When Assyria went down to the grave,* I made
the deep springs mourn. I stopped its rivers and dried up its abundant water. I clothed Leb-
anon in black and caused the trees of the field to wilt. 16 I made the nations shake with fear
at the sound of its fall, for I sent it down to the grave with all the others who descend to
the pit. And all the other proud trees of Eden, the most beautiful and the best of Lebanon,
the ones whose roots went deep into the water, took comfort to find it there with them in
the depths of the earth. 17 Its allies, too, were all destroyed and had passed away. They
had gone down to the grave—all those nations that had lived in its shade.
18 "O Egypt, to which of the trees of Eden will you compare your strength and glory?
You, too, will be brought down to the depths with all these other nations. You will lie there
among the outcasts* who have died by the sword. This will be the fate of Pharaoh and all
his hordes. I, the Sovereign LORD, have spoken!"

A WARNING FOR PHARAOH

32:2 Jer 46:7-8 Nah 2:11-13

32 On March 3,* during the twelfth year of King Jehoiachin's captivity, this message
came to me from the LORD: 2 "Son of man, mourn for Pharaoh, king of Egypt, and
give him this message:

32:3 Ezek 12:13

"You think of yourself as a strong young lion among the nations,
 but you are really just a sea monster,
heaving around in your own rivers,
 stirring up mud with your feet.
3 Therefore, this is what the Sovereign LORD says:
I will send many people
 to catch you in My net
 and haul you out of the water.

31:15 Hebrew *to Sheol;* also in 31:16, 17. 31:18 Hebrew *among the uncircumcised.* 32:1 Hebrew *On the first day of the twelfth month,* of the ancient Hebrew lunar calendar. This event occurred on March 3, 585 B.C.; also see note on 1:1.

31:18 Although Egypt was not the dominant world power in Ezekiel's time, it still had great influence and was sought after for alliances by many nations. Egypt's final collapse to the Babylonians ended their status as a world power (see note at 29:10-16).

32:1-16 "On March 3" is literally "on the first day of the twelfth month." This prophecy was given in 585 BC. Ezekiel's lament for Pharaoh demonstrated that God does not take pleasure in the death of the wicked (Ezekiel 33:11).

32:2-8 Ancient kings often compared themselves and their kingdoms to lions, and Pharaoh was no different. But the Lord's perspective was that Egypt was nothing more than "a sea monster" (compare 29:3) that moved about in "rivers" and stirred up mud (32:2). Ezekiel took elements of the mythology of the ancient Near East and turned them against Egypt (29:3-5) and would do it again against other nations (38:18-23).

4 I will leave you stranded on the land to die.
All the birds of the heavens will land on you,
and the wild animals of the whole earth
will gorge themselves on you.
5 I will scatter your flesh on the hills
and fill the valleys with your bones.
6 I will drench the earth with your gushing blood
all the way to the mountains,
filling the ravines to the brim.
7 When I blot you out,
I will veil the heavens and darken the stars.
I will cover the sun with a cloud,
and the moon will not give you its light.
8 I will darken the bright stars overhead
and cover your land in darkness.
I, the Sovereign LORD, have spoken!

9 "I will disturb many hearts when I bring news of your downfall to distant nations you
have never seen. 10 Yes, I will shock many lands, and their kings will be terrified at your
fate. They will shudder in fear for their lives as I brandish My sword before them on the
day of your fall. 11 For this is what the Sovereign LORD says:

"The sword of the king of Babylon
will come against you.
12 I will destroy your hordes with the swords of mighty warriors—
the terror of the nations.
They will shatter the pride of Egypt,
and all its hordes will be destroyed.
13 I will destroy all your flocks and herds
that graze beside the streams.
Never again will people or animals
muddy those waters with their feet.
14 Then I will let the waters of Egypt become calm again,
and they will flow as smoothly as olive oil,
says the Sovereign LORD.
15 And when I destroy Egypt
and strip you of everything you own
and strike down all your people,
then you will know that I am the LORD.
16 Yes, this is the funeral song
they will sing for Egypt.

32:4 Jer 8:2
32:6 Exod 7:17; Isa 34:3, 7; Rev 14:20
32:7 Prov 13:9; Amos 8:9
32:8 Gen 1:14
32:9 Exod 15:14-16; Rev 18:10-15
32:10 Ezek 26:16; 27:35
32:11 Jer 46:26
32:12 Ezek 28:7
32:15 Exod 7:5; 14:4, 18; Ps 83:17-18
32:16 2 Sam 3:33-34; 2 Chr 35:25; Jer 9:17

32:9-16 The imagery of the sea monster was dropped here in favor of more straightforward language about the defeat and destruction of Egypt at the hands of the Babylonians, who would act as the "sword" of the Lord. This would cause everyone to know that "the Sovereign LORD" had judged Egypt.

▶ PURPOSE

32:15 Judgments from the Lord? Whenever disaster strikes, some are quick to claim that this is God's judgment on one sin or the other. Since God controls all things (Job 37:15; Daniel 5:23), then disaster is certainly from Him just as much as blessing. When God unleashed his fearsome judgments upon the Egyptians, Ezekiel announced to the world that the terrible power of the Lord was at work—but with a message. If disaster had struck them without Ezekiel's prophecy to make the reason clear, it would have been just another tragedy to them. But through the Lord's mighty acts of judgment and Ezekiel's prophecy, it would become apparent to the Egyptians (and the world) that the God of Israel was the only true God and ruler of creation. God does still use disaster and difficulty to judge the world, for all things happen for His renown (Revelation 4:11). But do we know specifically what message accompanies each catastrophe? Not unless God's Word makes it clear. Do not be quick to assign one message or the other to a certain calamity unless you have the authority of God's Word behind you. (***See Purpose****> God's Deeds> Judgment> Plague upon Israel's enemies,* TopicGuide page A53.)

Let all the nations mourn.
  Let them mourn for Egypt and its hordes.
  I, the Sovereign LORD, have spoken!"

EGYPT FALLS INTO THE PIT

17 On March 17,* during the twelfth year, another message came to me from the LORD:
32:18 18 "Son of man, weep for the hordes of Egypt and for the other mighty nations.* For I will
Jer 1:10 send them down to the world below in company with those who descend to the pit. 19 Say
Hos 6:5 to them,

32:19 Jer 9:25-26

'O Egypt, are you lovelier than the other nations?
  No! So go down to the pit and lie there among the outcasts.*'

32:20 20 The Egyptians will fall with the many who have died by the sword, for the sword is
Ps 28:3 drawn against them. Egypt and its hordes will be dragged away to their judgment. 21 Down
32:21 in the grave* mighty leaders will mockingly welcome Egypt and its allies, saying, 'They
Isa 14:9-12 Luke 16:23-24 have come down; they lie among the outcasts, hordes slaughtered by the sword.'
22 "Assyria lies there surrounded by the graves of its army, those who were slaughtered
32:23 by the sword. 23 Their graves are in the depths of the pit, and they are surrounded by their
Isa 14:15 allies. They struck terror in the hearts of people everywhere, but now they have been
slaughtered by the sword.
32:24 24 "Elam lies there surrounded by the graves of all its hordes, those who were slaugh-
Gen 10:22 tered by the sword. They struck terror in the hearts of people everywhere, but now they
Job 28:13 have descended as outcasts to the world below. Now they lie in the pit and share the
Ps 52:5 Jer 49:34-39 shame of those who have gone before them. 25 They have a resting place among the
32:25 slaughtered, surrounded by the graves of all their hordes. Yes, they terrorized the nations
Ps 139:8 while they lived, but now they lie in shame with others in the pit, all of them outcasts,
slaughtered by the sword.
32:26 26 "Meshech and Tubal are there, surrounded by the graves of all their hordes. They
Gen 10:2 Isa 66:19 once struck terror in the hearts of people everywhere. But now they are outcasts, all
slaughtered by the sword. 27 They are not buried in honor like their fallen heroes, who
32:27 Prov 14:32 went down to the grave* with their weapons—their shields covering their bodies* and their
swords beneath their heads. Their guilt rests upon them because they brought terror to
everyone while they were still alive.
28 "You too, Egypt, will lie crushed and broken among the outcasts, all slaughtered by
the sword.

32:17 Hebrew *On the fifteenth day of the month,* presumably in the twelfth month of the ancient Hebrew lunar calendar (see 32:1). This would put this message at the end of King Jehoiachin's twelfth year of captivity, on March 17, 585 B.C.; also see note on 1:1. Greek version reads *On the fifteenth day of the first month,* which would put this message on April 27, 586 B.C., at the beginning of Jehoiachin's twelfth year. 32:18 The meaning of the Hebrew is uncertain. 32:19 Hebrew *the uncircumcised;* also in 32:21, 24, 25, 26, 28, 29, 30, 32. 32:21 Hebrew *in Sheol.* 32:27a Hebrew *to Sheol.* 32:27b The meaning of the Hebrew is uncertain.

32:18-32 In this final prophecy of Egypt's doom, the Lord indicated that Egypt's attempt to defeat the Babylonians would be just as futile as that of the other nations who had already fallen to them. These nations were depicted as lying in graves awaiting Egypt's arrival. Assyria fell to Babylon in 612 BC. Elam, which was east of Babylon, fell in 650 BC. Edom became a puppet state of the Babylonians shortly after Nebuchadnezzar came to power in 605 BC.

▶ GOD
32:18 Loving our enemies. Up until this point, much of Ezekiel's prophecies had centered on the theme of judgment. The prophet clearly and evocatively pronounced the certainty and fury of God's judgment. But now he was instructed to weep for those upon whom God's judgment would soon fall. Elsewhere in Ezekiel we are reminded that God takes no pleasure in the death of the wicked (18:23). There is a fine line between rejoicing over God's triumph and gloating over the punishment of the wicked. If we love our unbelieving neighbors, even if they are our enemies, we will have heavy hearts when we consider their destiny. Such sorrow should prompt us to be faithful messengers of God's gospel of forgiveness. (***See God> God's Attributes> Loving> To love enemies and the wicked is to be like God,*** TopicGuide page A17.)

32:28-29 The prophet uses the image of a slashing sword to represent generic military action 27 times in Ezekiel. See Ezekiel 5:2; 21:29; 38:21 for examples.

29 "Edom is there with its kings and princes. Mighty as they were, they also lie among
those slaughtered by the sword, with the outcasts who have gone down to the pit.
30 "All the princes of the north and the Sidonians are there with others who have died.
Once a terror, they have been put to shame. They lie there as outcasts with others who were
slaughtered by the sword. They share the shame of all who have descended to the pit.
31 "When Pharaoh and his entire army arrive, he will take comfort that he is not alone in
having his hordes killed, says the Sovereign LORD. 32 Although I have caused his terror to
fall upon all the living, Pharaoh and his hordes will lie there among the outcasts who were
slaughtered by the sword. I, the Sovereign LORD, have spoken!"

EZEKIEL AS ISRAEL'S WATCHMAN

33 Once again a message came to me from the LORD: 2 "Son of man, give your peo-
ple this message: 'When I bring an army against a country, the people of that
land choose one of their own to be a watchman. 3 When the watchman sees the enemy
coming, he sounds the alarm to warn the people. 4 Then if those who hear the alarm refuse
to take action, it is their own fault if they die. 5 They heard the alarm but ignored it, so the
responsibility is theirs. If they had listened to the warning, they could have saved their
lives. 6 But if the watchman sees the enemy coming and doesn't sound the alarm to warn
the people, he is responsible for their captivity. They will die in their sins, but I will hold the
watchman responsible for their deaths.'
7 "Now, son of man, I am making you a watchman for the people of Israel. Therefore, lis-
ten to what I say and warn them for Me. 8 If I announce that some wicked people are sure
to die and you fail to tell them to change their ways, then they will die in their sins, and I
will hold you responsible for their deaths. 9 But if you warn them to repent and they don't
repent, they will die in their sins, but you will have saved yourself.

THE WATCHMAN'S MESSAGE

10 "Son of man, give the people of Israel this message: You are saying, 'Our sins are heavy
upon us; we are wasting away! How can we survive?' 11 As surely as I live, says the Sover-
eign LORD, I take no pleasure in the death of wicked people. I only want them to turn from
their wicked ways so they can live. Turn! Turn from your wickedness, O people of Israel!
Why should you die?
12 "Son of man, give your people this message: The righteous behavior of righteous peo-
ple will not save them if they turn to sin, nor will the wicked behavior of wicked people de-
stroy them if they repent and turn from their sins. 13 When I tell righteous people that they
will live, but then they sin, expecting their past righteousness to save them, then none of
their righteous acts will be remembered. I will destroy them for their sins. 14 And suppose I
tell some wicked people that they will surely die, but then they turn from their sins and do
what is just and right. 15 For instance, they might give back a debtor's security, return what

32:29 Isa 34:5-15; Jer 49:7-22; Ezek 25:13
32:30 Jer 1:15; 25:26; Ezek 28:21-23; 38:15
33:2 2 Sam 18:24-25; 2 Kgs 9:17; Jer 12:12
33:4 Jer 6:17; Zech 1:4; Acts 18:6
33:5 Exod 9:19-21, 25; Ps 95:7; Heb 11:7
33:6 Isa 56:10
33:7 Isa 62:6-7; Jer 26:2; Acts 5:20
33:10 Lev 26:39; Isa 49:14
33:11 Hos 11:8; Acts 3:19; 1 Tim 2:4; 2 Pet 3:9
33:13 Heb 10:38; 2 Pet 2:20-21
33:14 Isa 55:7; Hos 14:1, 4; Mic 6:8
33:15 Lev 6:4-5; Num 5:6-8; Luke 19:8

33:1 This verse marks the transition to the last section of the book (chapters 33–48). In contrast to the Lord's judgments against Judah (chapters 4–24) and against numerous wicked nations (chapters 25–32), the Lord's messages in the rest of the book speak of hope, restoration, covenant, and the Messiah. The Lord would restore Israel, but He would do so in His own time and way. The Exile was a covenant curse on Israel for disobedience to the Lord (see Deuteronomy 28:36-37, 49-57, 63-68), but Israel's return and restoration would be a covenant blessing, the Lord's "covenant of peace" (see Ezekiel 34:25) that Israel did not earn or deserve.

▸ ADOPTION
33:7 The task of a watchman. The Lord appointed Ezekiel as the watchman of Israel. A watchman warned of impending trouble—Ezekiel's duty as a watchman was to warn the people of the trouble that would come without heartfelt repentance. Paul understood that God's people are to warn others of the dangers of unrepentant sin (2 Corinthians 13:2; 2 Thessalonians 3:15). We who know the reality of judgment and the hope of forgiveness are commissioned to warn those outside of Christ of their fate if they refuse to repent. Have we acted as faithful watchmen to those in our community? In our church? Let us pray for the strength and courage to fulfill our calling as modern watchmen. (***See Adoption> With Christ> Servants> Witness for Christ,*** TopicGuide page A37.)

33:10-11 Though God is just (33:20), He is no cosmic sadist who enjoys pain and suffering, even that of His enemies.

they have stolen, and obey My life-giving laws, no longer doing what is evil. If they do this,
then they will surely live and not die. 16None of their past sins will be brought up again, for
they have done what is just and right, and they will surely live.
17"Your people are saying, 'The Lord isn't doing what's right,' but it is they who are not
doing what's right. 18For again I say, when righteous people turn away from their righ-
teous behavior and turn to evil, they will die. 19But if wicked people turn from their wick-
edness and do what is just and right, they will live. 20O people of Israel, you are saying,
'The Lord isn't doing what's right.' But I judge each of you according to your deeds."

EXPLANATION OF JERUSALEM'S FALL

21On January 8,* during the twelfth year of our captivity, a survivor from Jerusalem came
to me and said, "The city has fallen!" 22The previous evening the LORD had taken hold of
me and given me back my voice. So I was able to speak when this man arrived the next
morning.
23Then this message came to me from the LORD: 24"Son of man, the scattered remnants
of Judah living among the ruined cities keep saying, 'Abraham was only one man, yet he
gained possession of the entire land. We are many; surely the land has been given to us as
a possession.' 25So tell these people, 'This is what the Sovereign LORD says: You eat meat
with blood in it, you worship idols,* and you murder the innocent. Do you really think the
land should be yours? 26Murderers! Idolaters! Adulterers! Should the land belong to you?'
27"Say to them, 'This is what the Sovereign LORD says: As surely as I live, those living in the
ruins will die by the sword. And I will send wild animals to eat those living in the open fields.
Those hiding in the forts and caves will die of disease. 28I will completely destroy the land
and demolish her pride. Her arrogant power will come to an end. The mountains of Israel
will be so desolate that no one will even travel through them. 29When I have completely de-
stroyed the land because of their detestable sins, then they will know that I am the LORD.'
30"Son of man, your people talk about you in their houses and whisper about you at the
doors. They say to each other, 'Come on, let's go hear the prophet tell us what the LORD is
saying!' 31So My people come pretending to be sincere and sit before you. They listen to
your words, but they have no intention of doing what you say. Their mouths are full of lust-
ful words, and their hearts seek only after money. 32You are very entertaining to them, like
someone who sings love songs with a beautiful voice or plays fine music on an instrument.
They hear what you say, but they don't act on it! 33But when all these terrible things happen
to them—as they certainly will—then they will know a prophet has been among them."

33:16 Isa 1:18; 43:25 Ezek 18:22
33:17 Ezek 18:24-29
33:21 Jer 39:1-2 Ezek 24:1-2, 26
33:22 Ezek 3:26-27; 24:27 Luke 1:64
33:24 Isa 51:1-2 Jer 39:10 Acts 7:5 Rom 4:12-13
33:25 Lev 17:10-14 Deut 12:16, 23 Jer 7:9-10
33:26 Mic 2:1-2 Zeph 3:3
33:27 Isa 2:19 Jer 15:2-4 Ezek 5:12-14
33:28 Jer 44:22 Ezek 6:14; 36:34
33:29 Isa 29:13; 58:2 Ezek 23:33, 35
33:30 Ezek 14:3
33:31 Ps 78:36-37 Isa 29:13 Matt 13:22 Luke 12:15 1 Jn 3:18
33:32 Mark 6:20

33:21 Hebrew *On the fifth day of the tenth month,* of the ancient Hebrew lunar calendar. This event occurred on January 8, 585 B.C.; also see note on 1:1. 33:25 The Hebrew term (literally *round things*) probably alludes to dung.

▸ SALVATION
33:20 Sin and repentance. Ultimately, each individual must stand alone before God and answer to Him. It won't be the fault of our church, our government, or our parents. We will all be held responsible for our thoughts, words, and deeds (Revelation 2:23). No one else can repent for us, and no one else can trust in the work of Christ on our behalf. If we have repented and received Christ's forgiveness, then we will be received into glorious, eternal fellowship with God (1 John 2:25). Those who have not turned from their sins, however, will remain guilty and unable to join God's perfected people in heaven (Hebrews 3:1; 6:19; 12:23). No more excuses for you or anyone else—now is the right time to get right with God (2 Corinthians 6:2). (***See Salvation**> Receiving> How> Repent of/turn from sin,* TopicGuide page A22.)

33:21 "On January 8" is literally "on the fifth day of the tenth month." The year was 585 BC, "the twelfth year of our captivity," which for Ezekiel began in 597 BC (see note at 1:2). Ezekiel's prophecies about the fall of Jerusalem to the Babylonians were now a reality: "The city has fallen!" Jerusalem had been destroyed several months earlier, and the news had just reached Babylon where Ezekiel lived. The Lord's prophecies about Israel's restoration in chapters 33–39 came to Ezekiel at the lowest point in Israel's history. The Lord's prophecies in chapters 40–48 came to Ezekiel 14 years later (see note at 40:1).

33:22-26 The people of Judah thought that since they were so numerous they deserved the Promised Land. But the Lord said they had committed murder, idolatry, and adultery, and thus they did not deserve the land. The Israelites had emulated the evil practices of the Canaanites, whom they were supposed to have driven out of the land (see Deuteronomy 7:1-5).

33:27-33 The Lord indicated that the devastation of the land of Israel had not ended. Even after the fall of Jerusalem, the Babylonians would continue to ravage the land until it was "desolate" (33:28). The people of Judah had paid no attention to Ezekiel's prophecies of judgment, but when everything happened just as he said, they would know that Ezekiel was truly a prophet of the Lord (33:33).

THE SHEPHERDS OF ISRAEL

34 Then this message came to me from the LORD: 2"Son of man, prophesy against
the shepherds, the leaders of Israel. Give them this message from the Sovereign
LORD: What sorrow awaits you shepherds who feed yourselves instead of your flocks.
Shouldn't shepherds feed their sheep? 3You drink the milk, wear the wool, and butcher
the best animals, but you let your flocks starve. 4You have not taken care of the weak. You
have not tended the sick or bound up the injured. You have not gone looking for those
who have wandered away and are lost. Instead, you have ruled them with harshness and
cruelty. 5So My sheep have been scattered without a shepherd, and they are easy prey for
any wild animal. 6They have wandered through all the mountains and all the hills, across
the face of the earth, yet no one has gone to search for them.

7"Therefore, you shepherds, hear the word of the LORD: 8As surely as I live, says the Sov-
ereign LORD, you abandoned My flock and left them to be attacked by every wild animal.
And though you were My shepherds, you didn't search for My sheep when they were lost.
You took care of yourselves and left the sheep to starve. 9Therefore, you shepherds, hear
the word of the LORD. 10This is what the Sovereign LORD says: I now consider these shep-
herds My enemies, and I will hold them responsible for what has happened to My flock.
I will take away their right to feed the flock, and I will stop them from feeding themselves. I
will rescue My flock from their mouths; the sheep will no longer be their prey.

34:2 Jer 10:21; 23:1 Mic 3:1-3 John 10:11; 21:15-17
34:3 Isa 56:11 Ezek 22:27 Zech 11:5, 16
34:4 Zech 11:15-16 Matt 9:36; 18:12-13 1 Pet 5:3
34:5 Jer 10:21; 23:2
34:6 Ps 142:4 1 Pet 2:25
34:8 Acts 20:29

34:1-10 Ezekiel condemned "the leaders of Israel" for being false shepherds. This passage is similar to chapter 22, where Ezekiel compared Israel's leaders to "lions" (22:25) and "wolves" (22:27). The Lord said these false shepherds were His "enemies" (34:10) and promised to remove them as leaders and to take care of the sheep of Israel Himself.

▶ CHURCH
34:2 The shepherds of God's people. What is the biggest responsibility you have in your life? Those who are leaders among the people of God bear an enormous responsibility—they are entrusted with the care of God's treasured possession, the church. The leaders in Ezekiel's day had forfeited their responsibility and forsaken the care of God's people. The Lord strongly condemned these shepherds for their dereliction of duty, and they would be punished in due time. Likewise those who rule and care for God's people in the church today must care for the souls of God's people and never use their position for personal gain. The people of God, likewise, must recognize the seriousness of their leaders' call and grant them due respect and honor (1 Peter 5:1-5). Help your leaders do the best job possible as they care for God's people. (***See Church***> *Role*> *Church Offices*> *Pastor-Teachers,* TopicGuide page A49.)

MY RESPONSE TO GOD

The Good Shepherd

EZEKIEL 34

"The LORD is my shepherd" (Psalm 23:1). This is one of the best known and most comforting passages in all of Scripture. Why does the knowledge that God is our Shepherd offer so much assurance? It comforts us because we know God is the Good Shepherd (John 10:11, 14). Unlike others in authority, He leads us flawlessly. Many leaders do not care for us when we are weak, sick, or lost (Ezekiel 34:4, 6), or they harm or mistreat us to get what they want (Ezekiel 34:21). But God our Good Shepherd will never treat us carelessly or callously.

It may sound trite, but it's true–when you are lost, look to the Lord for guidance. When in danger, trust that He will rescue you. When wounded, know that He heals. When weak, be assured that He will provide strength. When hungry, find comfort in knowing that He will feed you. Our time on earth may be filled with trials and troubles, but our Good Shepherd will ultimately lead His people into eternal peace and rest.

34:11 THE GOOD SHEPHERD

John 10:16 11 "For this is what the Sovereign LORD says: I Myself will search and find My sheep. 12 I will
34:12 be like a shepherd looking for his scattered flock. I will find My sheep and rescue them
Jer 23:3; 31:10 Joel 2:2 from all the places where they were scattered on that dark and cloudy day. 13 I will bring
Luke 19:10 them back home to their own land of Israel from among the peoples and nations. I will
34:14 feed them on the mountains of Israel and by the rivers and in all the places where people
Ps 23:2 live. 14 Yes, I will give them good pastureland on the high hills of Israel. There they will lie
John 10:9 down in pleasant places and feed in the lush pastures of the hills. 15 I Myself will tend My
34:16 Isa 10:16; 49:26 sheep and give them a place to lie down in peace, says the Sovereign LORD. 16 I will search
34:17 for My lost ones who strayed away, and I will bring them safely home again. I will ban-
Zech 10:3 dage the injured and strengthen the weak. But I will destroy those who are fat and power-
Mal 4:1 ful. I will feed them, yes—feed them justice!
Matt 25:32 17 "And as for you, My flock, this is what the Sovereign LORD says to His people: I will
34:18 Num 16:9, 13 judge between one animal of the flock and another, separating the sheep from the goats.
2 Sam 7:19 18 Isn't it enough for you to keep the best of the pastures for yourselves? Must you also
34:21 trample down the rest? Isn't it enough for you to drink clear water for yourselves? Must
Deut 33:17 Dan 8:4 you also muddy the rest with your feet? 19 Why must My flock eat what you have trampled
Luke 13:14-16 down and drink water you have fouled?
34:22 20 "Therefore, this is what the Sovereign LORD says: I will surely judge between the fat
Ps 72:12-14 sheep and the scrawny sheep. 21 For you fat sheep pushed and butted and crowded My
34:23 sick and hungry flock until you scattered them to distant lands. 22 So I will rescue My flock,
Isa 40:11 and they will no longer be abused. I will judge between one animal of the flock and an-
Jer 23:4-6; 30:9 John 10:11 other. 23 And I will set over them one shepherd, My servant David. He will feed them and
Heb 13:20 be a shepherd to them. 24 And I, the LORD, will be their God, and My servant David will be a
34:24 Jer 30:9 prince among My people. I, the LORD, have spoken!

34:25 Isa 11:6-9 THE LORD'S COVENANT OF PEACE

Jer 33:16 25 "I will make a covenant of peace with My people and drive away the dangerous animals
34:26 from the land. Then they will be able to camp safely in the wildest places and sleep in the
Gen 12:2 woods without fear. 26 I will bless My people and their homes around My holy hill. And in
Deut 28:12 Isa 32:15; 44:3 the proper season I will send the showers they need. There will be showers of blessing.
34:27 27 The orchards and fields of My people will yield bumper crops, and everyone will live in
Lev 26:13 safety. When I have broken their chains of slavery and rescued them from those who en-
Ps 85:12 Isa 52:2-3 slaved them, then they will know that I am the LORD. 28 They will no longer be prey for

34:11-16 The Lord said that He would be "like a shepherd looking for His scattered flock." The people of Israel were scattered among many nations (Egypt, Assyria, and Babylon in particular), but the Lord promised to bring them back to the land and care for them. Jesus called Himself "the good shepherd", who would die for His sheep and gather all of them together as "one flock with one shepherd" (John 10: 11,16). Jesus the Shepherd is the fulfillment of the Lord's promises in Ezekiel 34:11-24.

34:17 Not everyone who claims to belong to the Lord really does, so the Lord will judge all people, "separating the sheep from the goats." Jesus used this same imagery in reference to His role as judge. Jesus will fulfill this prophecy at the judgment referred to in Matthew 25:31-46.

34:23-24 These words were spoken about 400 years after David's time. David was the shepherd who became Israel's greatest king, and he declared that the Lord was his shepherd (Psalm 23:1). David was caretaker of Israel, and the Lord was the Shepherd over all. The people of Ezekiel's day, knowing that David was no longer alive, might have recognized this as referring to the coming Messiah (see also 37:24). Jesus Christ, the descendent of King David, is the "David" who will one day rule side-by-side with the Lord over all Israel (see also Revelation 21:22; 22:1).

▶ HOLINESS
34:25-31 The peaceful Shepherd. It's never easy to bring peace to well-established enemies. When the Shepherd-King came to deliver God's people, He continued the development of God's rich promises to His people by making a new covenant. Jesus Christ, the Good Shepherd (see Hebrews 8:7-13), has gathered God's sheep and brought them to God (Psalm 95:7; John 10:1-16). Because of unity with Christ (Romans 7:4; Galatians 3:27), they have already begun to enjoy the best blessings of God. A day will come when we fully partake of every blessing that God has given Christ (Ephesians 1:3). In that day we will fully grasp the peace that Christ has made between God and His people as we see the perfect peace that exists between God and His redeemed. (***See Holiness**> Changed by God> The Son Purchases> Jesus' peacemaking with God,* TopicGuide page A41.)

other nations, and wild animals will no longer devour them. They will live in safety, and
no one will frighten them.
29 "And I will make their land famous for its crops, so My people will never again suffer
from famines or the insults of foreign nations. 30 In this way, they will know that I, the LORD
their God, am with them. And they will know that they, the people of Israel, are My people,
says the Sovereign LORD. 31 You are My flock, the sheep of My pasture. You are My people,
and I am your God. I, the Sovereign LORD, have spoken!"

A MESSAGE FOR EDOM

35 Again a message came to me from the LORD: 2 "Son of man, turn and face Mount
Seir, and prophesy against its people. 3 Give them this message from the Sover-
eign LORD:

"I am your enemy, O Mount Seir,
and I will raise My fist against you
to destroy you completely.
4 I will demolish your cities
and make you desolate.
Then you will know that I am the LORD.

5 "Your eternal hatred for the people of Israel led you to butcher them when they were
helpless, when I had already punished them for all their sins. 6 As surely as I live, says the
Sovereign LORD, since you show no distaste for blood, I will give you a bloodbath of your
own. Your turn has come! 7 I will make Mount Seir utterly desolate, killing off all who try to
escape and any who return. 8 I will fill your mountains with the dead. Your hills, your val-
leys, and your ravines will be filled with people slaughtered by the sword. 9 I will make you
desolate forever. Your cities will never be rebuilt. Then you will know that I am the LORD.
10 "For you said, 'The lands of Israel and Judah will be ours. We will take possession of
them. What do we care that the LORD is there!' 11 Therefore, as surely as I live, says the Sover-
eign LORD, I will pay back your angry deeds with My own. I will punish you for all your acts of
anger, envy, and hatred. And I will make Myself known to Israel* by what I do to you. 12 Then
you will know that I, the LORD, have heard every contemptuous word you spoke against the
mountains of Israel. For you said, 'They are desolate; they have been given to us as food to
eat!' 13 In saying that, you boasted proudly against Me, and I have heard it all!
14 "This is what the Sovereign LORD says: The whole world will rejoice when I make you
desolate. 15 You rejoiced at the desolation of Israel's territory. Now I will rejoice at yours!
You will be wiped out, you people of Mount Seir and all who live in Edom! Then you will
know that I am the LORD.

34:30 Ps 46:7, 11; Ezek 36:28; 37:27
34:31 Mic 7:14; John 10:11
35:2 Gen 36:6-8
35:5 Ezek 7:2; 21:25, 29; 25:12; Obad 1:10
35:7 Ezek 25:13
35:8 Isa 34:5-6; Ezek 31:12; 32:4-5
35:9 Jer 49:13; Ezek 25:13
35:10 Ps 48:1-3; Ezek 36:2, 5
35:11 Pss 9:16; 137:7; Ezek 25:14; Amos 1:11
35:12 Jer 50:7; Ezek 36:2
35:13 Isa 10:13-14; Ezek 36:3; Dan 11:36
35:14 Isa 44:23; 49:13; Jer 51:48
35:15 Isa 34:5-6; Lam 4:21; Obad 1:12, 15

35:11 Hebrew *to them;* Greek version reads *to you.*

35:3-9 The Lord described the coming judgment and destruction of Mount Seir (Edom), which was executed partially by the Babylonians but ultimately by Israel in the second century BC (see note at 25:12-14).

35:10-15 Two reasons were given for the Lord's judgment of Edom. First, the Edomites took advantage of Judah's struggles against Babylon and claimed some of Judah's land as their own (see also 36:5), particularly in the southern area. Second, Edom "rejoiced" when Judah was overrun by the Babylonians (see note at 25:1).

▶ GOD

35:11 I will bring honor to My name. When we look at the defects that are found in legal systems, we see that, humanly speaking, justice is difficult. Sometimes the guilty are found innocent. Occasionally, the innocent are punished. The victims of crime go without vindication. God's judgment is perfect—but even though ideal, it sometimes bothers us. Hell is troubling. The punishments God hands out to places like Edom seem very rough. We agree that evil must be punished, but it's difficult to imagine how it is an avenue God uses to bring renown to Himself. Yet, God affirmed that through His judgment on Edom, He would bring honor to His name. His grace and mercy to His redeemed gives Him glory, and His justice and wrath against unrepentant sinners brings Him glory as well. Both acts reveal a holy God who will act consistently with His nature. Even though some aspects and actions of God make us uncomfortable, they glorify God just the same. Increase your love for God by taking a close look at every part of His character and deciding to give Him the honor He is due. (***See God**> God's Attributes> Holy> God guards his holy reputation,* TopicGuide page A16.)

RESTORATION FOR ISRAEL

36 "Son of man, prophesy to Israel's mountains. Give them this message: O moun-
tains of Israel, hear the word of the LORD! 2This is what the Sovereign LORD says:
Your enemies have taunted you, saying, 'Aha! Now the ancient heights belong to us!'
3Therefore, son of man, give the mountains of Israel this message from the Sovereign
LORD: Your enemies have attacked you from all directions, making you the property of
many nations and the object of much mocking and slander. 4Therefore, O mountains of Is-
rael, hear the word of the Sovereign LORD. He speaks to the hills and mountains, ravines
and valleys, and to ruined wastes and long-deserted cities that have been destroyed and
mocked by the surrounding nations. 5This is what the Sovereign LORD says: My jealous an-
ger burns against these nations, especially Edom, because they have shown utter con-
tempt for Me by gleefully taking My land for themselves as plunder.

6"Therefore, prophesy to the hills and mountains, the ravines and valleys of Israel. This
is what the Sovereign LORD says: I am furious that you have suffered shame before the sur-
rounding nations. 7Therefore, this is what the Sovereign LORD says: I have taken a solemn
oath that those nations will soon have their own shame to endure.

8"But the mountains of Israel will produce heavy crops of fruit for My people—for they
will be coming home again soon! 9See, I care about you, and I will pay attention to you.
Your ground will be plowed and your crops planted. 10I will greatly increase the popula-
tion of Israel, and the ruined cities will be rebuilt and filled with people. 11I will increase
not only the people, but also your animals. O mountains of Israel, I will bring people to live
on you once again. I will make you even more prosperous than you were before. Then
you will know that I am the LORD. 12I will cause My people to walk on you once again, and
you will be their territory. You will never again rob them of their children.

13"This is what the Sovereign LORD says: The other nations taunt you, saying, 'Israel is a
land that devours its own people and robs them of their children!' 14But you will never
again devour your people or rob them of their children, says the Sovereign LORD. 15I will
not let you hear those other nations insult you, and you will no longer be mocked by
them. You will not be a land that causes its nation to fall, says the Sovereign LORD."

16Then this further message came to me from the LORD: 17"Son of man, when the people
of Israel were living in their own land, they defiled it by the evil way they lived. To Me their
conduct was as unclean as a woman's menstrual cloth. 18They polluted the land with mur-
der and the worship of idols,* so I poured out My fury on them. 19I scattered them to many
lands to punish them for the evil way they had lived. 20But when they were scattered
among the nations, they brought shame on My holy name. For the nations said, 'These
are the people of the LORD, but He couldn't keep them safe in His own land!' 21Then I was
concerned for My holy name, on which My people brought shame among the nations.

36:2 Deut 32:13; Ps 78:69; Isa 58:14; Hab 3:19
36:3 Jer 2:15; 51:34
36:4 Deut 11:11; Ps 79:4; Jer 48:27
36:5 Isa 66:15-16; Jer 50:11; Mic 7:8
36:6 Ps 123:4
36:8 Isa 27:6
36:9 Lev 26:9
36:10 Isa 27:6; 49:17-22; Jer 31:27-28
36:11 Jer 30:18
36:13 Num 13:32
36:15 Isa 54:4; Jer 18:15
36:18 2 Chr 34:21, 25; Lam 2:4; 4:11
36:19 Deut 28:64; Amos 9:9; Rom 2:6
36:20 Isa 52:5; Ezek 12:16; *Rom 2:24
36:21 Ps 74:18; Isa 48:9; Ezek 20:44

36:18 The Hebrew term (literally *round things*) probably alludes to dung; also in 36:25.

36:1-7 The Lord addressed "Israel's mountains" as these places were strategic military positions sought by Israel's enemies. The mountains also held pagan holy places "high on the mountains" (Deuteronomy 12:2), which He also may have been referencing here. The Lord called the land of Israel "My land" to remind everyone who the ultimate owner really is (see also Micah 1:3).

36:8-15 The Lord promised to restore Israel in such a way that the land would produce an abundance of crops. The people would become numerous and rebuild their cities, their livestock would increase greatly, and Israel would never again be an object of scorn by foreign nations (see also 36:28-38). All of these were the Lord's way of reversing the suffering the people of Israel endured during their time of subservience to foreign nations and their exile to Babylon.

36:13-14 The Hebrew word for "devour" in these verses is the same as in Numbers 13:32, where the spies Joshua sent to survey the land described it as a land that would "devour anyone who goes to live there." Here God challenges a similar taunt that other nations were saying against Israel.

36:20-24 The Exile caused the reputation of the Lord (Yahweh, Israel's God) to be questioned. Israel's harsh treatment at the hands of so many evil enemy nations made these pagan peoples think their gods were more powerful than Israel's God. The main reason that the Lord would restore Israel was so His holy name would no longer be dishonored. The restoration would show the nations who the Lord is.

22"Therefore, give the people of Israel this message from the Sovereign LORD: I am
bringing you back, but not because you deserve it. I am doing it to protect My holy name,
on which you brought shame while you were scattered among the nations. 23I will show
how holy My great name is—the name on which you brought shame among the nations.
And when I reveal My holiness through you before their very eyes, says the Sovereign
LORD, then the nations will know that I am the LORD. 24For I will gather you up from all the
nations and bring you home again to your land.
25"Then I will sprinkle clean water on you, and you will be clean. Your filth will be
washed away, and you will no longer worship idols. 26And I will give you a new heart, and
I will put a new spirit in you. I will take out your stony, stubborn heart and give you a ten-
der, responsive heart.* 27And I will put My Spirit in you so that you will follow My decrees
and be careful to obey My regulations.
28"And you will live in Israel, the land I gave your ancestors long ago. You will be My
people, and I will be your God. 29I will cleanse you of your filthy behavior. I will give you
good crops of grain, and I will send no more famines on the land. 30I will give you great
harvests from your fruit trees and fields, and never again will the surrounding nations be
able to scoff at your land for its famines. 31 Then you will remember your past sins and de-
spise yourselves for all the detestable things you did. 32But remember, says the Sovereign
LORD, I am not doing this because you deserve it. O My people of Israel, you should be ut-
terly ashamed of all you have done!
33"This is what the Sovereign LORD says: When I cleanse you from your sins, I will repop-
ulate your cities, and the ruins will be rebuilt. 34The fields that used to lie empty and deso-
late in plain view of everyone will again be farmed. 35And when I bring you back, people
will say, 'This former wasteland is now like the Garden of Eden! The abandoned and ru-
ined cities now have strong walls and are filled with people!' 36Then the surrounding na-
tions that survive will know that I, the LORD, have rebuilt the ruins and replanted the
wasteland. For I, the LORD, have spoken, and I will do what I say.
37"This is what the Sovereign LORD says: I am ready to hear Israel's prayers and to in-
crease their numbers like a flock. 38They will be as numerous as the sacred flocks that fill
Jerusalem's streets at the time of her festivals. The ruined cities will be crowded with peo-
ple once more, and everyone will know that I am the LORD."

A VALLEY OF DRY BONES

37 The LORD took hold of me, and I was carried away by the Spirit of the LORD to a
valley filled with bones. 2He led me all around among the bones that covered the
valley floor. They were scattered everywhere across the ground and were completely dried
out. 3Then He asked me, "Son of man, can these bones become living people again?"
"O Sovereign LORD," I replied, "You alone know the answer to that."

36:22 Deut 9:5-7; Ps 106:8
36:23 Ps 126:2
36:24 Isa 43:5-6
36:25 Zech 13:1; John 3:5; Titus 3:5-6; Heb 10:22
36:26 Ps 51:10; 2 Cor 5:17
36:27 Isa 59:21; Ezek 37:14
36:28 Jer 30:22
36:29 Ezek 34:27-29; Hos 2:21-23
36:30 Lev 26:4
36:32 Deut 9:5
36:33 Isa 58:12; Zech 8:7-8
36:35 Isa 51:3
36:36 Hos 14:4-7
36:38 1 Kgs 8:63; 2 Chr 35:7-9
37:1 Jer 7:32–8:2; Acts 8:39
37:3 Deut 32:29; 1 Sam 2:6; Isa 26:19

36:26 Hebrew *a heart of flesh.*

36:25-27 When the Lord would restore the people of Israel to their land, He would do so by making the nation completely different from what they were. Jesus used this passage as background for His description of the new birth, particularly "born of water and the Spirit" (John 3:5).

▸ HOLINESS
36:26-27 God's Spirit in you. Even in the Old Testament, people could not be saved without the Holy Spirit dwelling within them. Similarly, just as the Holy Spirit must change us before He dwells in us (John 3:5-6), He had to give new hearts to the people of Israel and Judah. And it was these new hearts that enabled them to love and obey Him (Deuteronomy 30:6). In the same way, it is only through the Holy Spirit living within us (Philippians 2:13), and the new hearts that He has given us (Acts 16:14), that we can keep God's commandments (John 14:15). The next time you are struggling with sin, rely on the power of the Spirit who indwells you to overcome it. He is there—depend on Him. (***See Holiness***> *Changed by God*> *The Spirit Enables*> *Regenerates believers,* TopicGuide page A41.)

37:1-10 This vision began with an out-of-body experience. "The Spirit of the LORD" took Ezekiel's spirit "to a valley filled with bones." The Lord then told Ezekiel that these bones would live again because He would breathe life into them. After the bones were reassembled into human form, the Lord breathed life into all of them so that they stood on their feet as "a great army." This apocalyptic vision expressed the same truth as the restoration passage in 36:25-27: The Lord will regenerate His people so that they can live again and enjoy His eternal blessings.

37:4 Isa 42:18
37:5 Ps 104:29-30; John 20:22; Eph 2:5; Rev 11:11
37:6 Joel 2:27; 3:17
37:7 Jer 13:5-7
37:9 Ps 104:30; Hos 13:14
37:10 Jer 30:19; Rev 11:11
37:11 Ps 141:7; Isa 49:14
37:12 Deut 32:39; Isa 26:19; Ezek 36:24; Hos 13:14; Amos 9:14-15
37:14 Ezek 11:19; 36:27; Joel 2:28-29
37:16 1 Kgs 12:16-20; 2 Chr 10:17-19
37:17 Isa 11:13; 50:4; Hos 1:11
37:18 Ezek 20:49; 24:19
37:21 Isa 43:5-6; Ezek 39:27
37:22 Isa 11:13; Jer 50:4; Ezek 34:13-14; Hos 1:11

[4]Then He said to me, "Speak a prophetic message to these bones and say, 'Dry bones, listen to the word of the LORD! [5]This is what the Sovereign LORD says: Look! I am going to put breath into you and make you live again! [6]I will put flesh and muscles on you and cover you with skin. I will put breath into you, and you will come to life. Then you will know that I am the LORD.'"

[7]So I spoke this message, just as He told me. Suddenly as I spoke, there was a rattling noise all across the valley. The bones of each body came together and attached themselves as complete skeletons. [8]Then as I watched, muscles and flesh formed over the bones. Then skin formed to cover their bodies, but they still had no breath in them.

[9]Then He said to me, "Speak a prophetic message to the winds, son of man. Speak a prophetic message and say, 'This is what the Sovereign LORD says: Come, O breath, from the four winds! Breathe into these dead bodies so they may live again.'"

[10]So I spoke the message as He commanded me, and breath came into their bodies. They all came to life and stood up on their feet—a great army.

[11]Then He said to me, "Son of man, these bones represent the people of Israel. They are saying, 'We have become old, dry bones—all hope is gone. Our nation is finished.' [12]Therefore, prophesy to them and say, 'This is what the Sovereign LORD says: O My people, I will open your graves of exile and cause you to rise again. Then I will bring you back to the land of Israel. [13]When this happens, O My people, you will know that I am the LORD. [14]I will put My Spirit in you, and you will live again and return home to your own land. Then you will know that I, the LORD, have spoken, and I have done what I said. Yes, the LORD has spoken!'"

REUNION OF ISRAEL AND JUDAH

[15]Again a message came to me from the LORD: [16]"Son of man, take a piece of wood and carve on it these words: 'This represents Judah and its allied tribes.' Then take another piece and carve these words on it: 'This represents Ephraim and the northern tribes of Israel.'* [17]Now hold them together in your hand as if they were one piece of wood. [18]When your people ask you what your actions mean, [19]say to them, 'This is what the Sovereign LORD says: I will take Ephraim and the northern tribes and join them to Judah. I will make them one piece of wood in My hand.'

[20]"Then hold out the pieces of wood you have inscribed, so the people can see them. [21]And give them this message from the Sovereign LORD: I will gather the people of Israel from among the nations. I will bring them home to their own land from the places where they have been scattered. [22]I will unify them into one nation on the mountains of Israel. One king will rule them all; no longer will they be divided into two nations or into two

37:16 Hebrew *This is Ephraim's wood, representing Joseph and all the house of Israel.*

37:11-14 The Lord interpreted Ezekiel's vision in 37:1-10. The people of Israel in exile were "old, dry bones," but one day the Lord would open the "graves of exile" and cause Israel to rise again so they could return to the land of Israel. The Lord reaffirmed that the Spirit would dwell in His people, as well as the reason for His actions on Israel's behalf: "Then you will know that I, the LORD, have spoken, and I have done what I said." This theme recurs throughout the book of Ezekiel.

▶ ADOPTION

37:12 New lives, new bodies. Ezekiel used the image of resurrected bodies to teach Judah about the restoration of God's people to the Promised Land. But the message doesn't stop there—God isn't satisfied with mere political restoration. Our restoration to the new Jerusalem (Revelation 21:1-5) will not be complete until our bodies are resurrected (Romans 8:23; 1 Corinthians 15:42), too. Heaven is not our final destination—we will spend eternity in new bodies on the new earth (2 Peter 3:13). We will never get sick, and we will never grow old. No one will be crippled. No one will be blind. Everyone's body will be perfect. No matter what physical infirmity you have now, one day it will be gone. Give thanks to God for this coming blessing, and take comfort in this great hope. (***See Adoption****> With Christ> Supernatural> Raised from the dead,* TopicGuide page A37.)

37:15-28 Ezekiel took two sticks to represent Judah and Israel and joined them together. This action meant that the Lord would unify them as one nation when He restored His people under one king and "one shepherd," referred to as "David" (37:24-25). Many of the Lord's numerous promises about the restoration of Israel did not occur when the people returned from the Exile to the land of Israel around 535 BC (see Ezra 1–2). These promises await fulfillment at the return of Christ, when God's faithful people will relate to God through an everlasting "covenant of peace" (37:26).

kingdoms. 23They will never again pollute themselves with their idols* and vile images
and rebellion, for I will save them from their sinful backsliding. I will cleanse them. Then
they will truly be My people, and I will be their God.
24"My servant David will be their king, and they will have only one shepherd. They will
obey My regulations and be careful to keep My decrees. 25They will live in the land I gave
My servant Jacob, the land where their ancestors lived. They and their children and their
grandchildren after them will live there forever, generation after generation. And My ser-
vant David will be their prince forever. 26And I will make a covenant of peace with them,
an everlasting covenant. I will give them their land and increase their numbers,* and I will
put My Temple among them forever. 27I will make My home among them. I will be their
God, and they will be My people. 28And when My Temple is among them forever, the na-
tions will know that I am the LORD, who makes Israel holy."

37:24 Jer 30:21 Hos 3:5
37:25 Isa 11:1
37:26 Jer 30:19 Heb 13:20
37:27 Lev 26:11 *2 Cor 6:16
37:28 Exod 31:13 Zeph 3:15

A MESSAGE FOR GOG

38 This is another message that came to me from the LORD: 2"Son of man, turn and
face Gog of the land of Magog, the prince who rules over the nations of Meshech
and Tubal, and prophesy against him. 3Give him this message from the Sovereign LORD:
Gog, I am your enemy! 4I will turn you around and put hooks in your jaws to lead you out
with your whole army—your horses and charioteers in full armor and a great horde armed
with shields and swords. 5Persia, Ethiopia, and Libya* will join you, too, with all their weap-
ons. 6Gomer and all its armies will also join you, along with the armies of Beth-togarmah
from the distant north, and many others.
7"Get ready; be prepared! Keep all the armies around you mobilized, and take com-
mand of them. 8A long time from now you will be called into action. In the distant future
you will swoop down on the land of Israel, which will be enjoying peace after recovering
from war and after its people have returned from many lands to the mountains of Israel.
9You and all your allies—a vast and awesome army—will roll down on them like a storm
and cover the land like a cloud.
10"This is what the Sovereign LORD says: At that time evil thoughts will come to your
mind, and you will devise a wicked scheme. 11You will say, 'Israel is an unprotected land
filled with unwalled villages! I will march against her and destroy these people who live
in such confidence! 12I will go to those formerly desolate cities that are now filled with
people who have returned from exile in many nations. I will capture vast amounts of
plunder, for the people are rich with livestock and other possessions now. They think the
whole world revolves around them!' 13But Sheba and Dedan and the merchants of Tar-
shish will ask, 'Do you really think the armies you have gathered can rob them of silver

38:2 Rev 20:8-9
38:4 Isa 43:17 Ezek 39:2 Dan 11:40
38:5 Gen 10:6-7 Ezek 27:10; 30:4-5
38:6 Gen 10:2-3 Ezek 27:14
38:8 Isa 11:11
38:9 Isa 5:28 Jer 4:13 Joel 2:2
38:10 Ps 36:4 Mic 2:1
38:11 Isa 37:24-25 Zech 2:4-5
38:12 Isa 10:6
38:13 Isa 10:5-7

37:23 The Hebrew term (literally *round things*) probably alludes to dung. 37:26 Hebrew reads *I will give them and increase their numbers;* Greek version omits the entire phrase. 38:5 Hebrew *Paras, Cush, and Put.*

▸ GOD

37:23 God's relentless pursuit. In Ezekiel's day, God's people had turned from the pure worship of the Lord and were worshiping false gods. But even though they were sinning grossly against Him, God was still committed to them (Genesis 17:7), and He chose to save them. God is still committed to people today. Even when we were covered in our sins and rebellion against God, not interested in repenting or in worshiping Him, God drew us to Himself, and He became our God, and we became truly His. Are you praying for someone to be saved? Do you have a family member or friend who hates God and His gospel? Don't give up hope! God can change anyone's heart! (***See God****> Salvation> Father> Draws the unbeliever,* TopicGuide page A15.)

38:1-2 The Lord's last message of judgment in Ezekiel was against "Gog of the land of Magog." This message falls into seven sections, each one being introduced with a word of judgment from "the Sovereign LORD." Gog was likely a cryptic way for Ezekiel to refer to the king of Babylon with Magog being Babylon itself, the only major enemy of Israel not mentioned in the earlier judgments (Ezekiel 25–32). It is not clear, however, which Babylonian king was intended.

38:3-9 The Lord declared Himself the "enemy" of Gog and revealed His plan to destroy him. At a time when Israel would be at "peace" in the land, Gog and his allies (38:5-6) would invade Israel with a massive army. Israel was invaded numerous times after this prophecy was given, but the deliverance described in the rest of this passage did not occur during any of them.

38:10-13 Tyrant kings of the past were always on the lookout for weak nations to invade and conquer, and Gog was no different. Gog would think that Israel was unprotected and ready to be conquered and plundered. Some nations would object, but apparently they would do nothing to help Israel.

and gold? Do you think you can drive away their livestock and seize their goods and carry off plunder?'

14"Therefore, son of man, prophesy against Gog. Give him this message from the Sovereign LORD: When My people are living in peace in their land, then you will rouse yourself.* 15You will come from your homeland in the distant north with your vast cavalry and your mighty army, 16and you will attack My people Israel, covering their land like a cloud. At that time in the distant future, I will bring you against My land as everyone watches, and My holiness will be displayed by what happens to you, Gog. Then all the nations will know that I am the LORD.

17"This is what the Sovereign LORD asks: Are you the one I was talking about long ago, when I announced through Israel's prophets that in the future I would bring you against My people? 18But this is what the Sovereign LORD says: When Gog invades the land of Israel, My fury will boil over! 19In My jealousy and blazing anger, I promise a mighty shaking in the land of Israel on that day. 20All living things—the fish in the sea, the birds of the sky, the animals of the field, the small animals that scurry along the ground, and all the people on earth—will quake in terror at My presence. Mountains will be thrown down; cliffs will crumble; walls will fall to the earth. 21I will summon the sword against you on all the hills of Israel, says the Sovereign LORD. Your men will turn their swords against each other. 22I will punish you and your armies with disease and bloodshed; I will send torrential rain, hailstones, fire, and burning sulfur! 23In this way, I will show My greatness and holiness, and I will make Myself known to all the nations of the world. Then they will know that I am the LORD.

THE SLAUGHTER OF GOG'S HORDES

39 "Son of man, prophesy against Gog. Give him this message from the Sovereign LORD: I am your enemy, O Gog, ruler of the nations of Meshech and Tubal. 2I will turn you around and drive you toward the mountains of Israel, bringing you from the distant north. 3I will knock the bow from your left hand and the arrows from your right hand, and I will leave you helpless. 4You and your army and your allies will all die on the mountains. I will feed you to the vultures and wild animals. 5You will fall in the open fields, for I have spoken, says the Sovereign LORD. 6And I will rain down fire on Magog and on all your allies who live safely on the coasts. Then they will know that I am the LORD.

7"In this way, I will make known My holy name among My people of Israel. I will not let anyone bring shame on it. And the nations, too, will know that I am the LORD, the Holy One

38:14 Jer 23:5-6; Zech 2:5, 8
38:17 Isa 5:26-30; 34:1-6
38:18 Ps 18:7-8
38:19 Joel 3:16; Hag 2:6-7; Heb 12:26-29
38:20 Jer 4:24; Nah 1:5-6; Zech 14:4-5
38:21 Judg 7:22; 2 Chr 20:23; Hag 2:22
38:22 Ps 11:6; Zech 14:12-15; Rev 16:21
38:23 Ps 9:16
39:1 Ezek 38:2-4
39:3 Pss 46:9; 76:3; Jer 21:4-5; Hos 1:5
39:4 Isa 14:24-25
39:6 Jer 25:22; Amos 1:4-7; Nah 1:6
39:7 Exod 20:7

38:14 As in Greek version; Hebrew reads *then you will know.*

▸ SPIRITUAL WARFARE

38:16 God's victory has already begun. Ezekiel portrayed a future situation after God had restored His people to the Promised Land. Israel would live in peace, needing neither army nor weapons (Isaiah 2:4). Eventually, however, all the enemies that had tormented Israel and Judah in Ezekiel's day would advance against them once again—but it would be a trap! This time, God Himself would meet Israel's enemies in battle—His people wouldn't even have to lift a finger. This same restoration has already begun for us. Jesus defeated our enemies at the cross (Colossians 2:15), and a day is coming when He will completely destroy them (Romans 16:20). So take heart! Our salvation has begun, and because it has begun, we should have great confidence that Jesus will complete what He has started (Philippians 1:6). (***See Spiritual Warfare****> Originator of Sin> Satan's Domain> Doomed to destruction,* TopicGuide page A44.)

38:17-23 Gog and his armies would invade Israel, but this would result in their own destruction because of the Lord's awesome display of power on Israel's behalf. In this sense, they spoke to the ultimate destruction of all those who oppose God's people. The identities of Gog and the land he ruled, Magog, are often tied to Babylon, but there is no evidence to make a strong case. However, Meshech and Tubal (39:1) are confirmed from multiple secular sources as tribes that dwelt in Anatolia (near modern Turkey) between the twelfth and eighth centuries BC.

39:1-16 The Lord's destruction of Gog's armies would be so complete and devastating that Israel would enjoy the plunder for seven years (39:9) and would bury the dead for seven months (39:12) to cleanse the land of defilement by pagan invaders. These numbers represented complete victory for God's people and complete destruction of the enemy.

▸ GOD

39:7 God's holy name. When God says that His name is holy, what does He mean? Should we avoid using the words "God" or "Lord"? Or only say them in prayer or worship? God's name represents God Himself. To keep God's name holy is to revere God Himself. It is to speak about God in ways that honor Him—and not in ways that slander Him. It is to live righteously and honorably so that others will think, "Their God must be an awesome God!" Remember that your life is a witness to the world about the character of your God. So, live righteously, so that you bring honor to Him and keep His name holy. (***See God****> God's Names> God> Holy One of Israel,* TopicGuide page A18.)

of Israel. 8That day of judgment will come, says the Sovereign LORD. Everything will hap-
pen just as I have declared it.
9"Then the people in the towns of Israel will go out and pick up your small and large
shields, bows and arrows, javelins and spears, and they will use them for fuel. There will be
enough to last them seven years! 10They won't need to cut wood from the fields or forests, for
these weapons will give them all the fuel they need. They will plunder those who planned to
plunder them, and they will rob those who planned to rob them, says the Sovereign LORD.
11"And I will make a vast graveyard for Gog and his hordes in the Valley of the Trav-
elers, east of the Dead Sea.* It will block the way of those who travel there, and they will
change the name of the place to the Valley of Gog's Hordes. 12It will take seven months for
the people of Israel to bury the bodies and cleanse the land. 13Everyone in Israel will help,
for it will be a glorious victory for Israel when I demonstrate My glory on that day, says the
Sovereign LORD.
14"After seven months, teams of men will be appointed to search the land for skeletons
to bury, so the land will be made clean again. 15Whenever bones are found, a marker will
be set up so the burial crews will take them to be buried in the Valley of Gog's Hordes.
16(There will be a town there named Hamonah, which means 'horde.') And so the land will
finally be cleansed.
17"And now, son of man, this is what the Sovereign LORD says: Call all the birds and wild
animals. Say to them: Gather together for My great sacrificial feast. Come from far and
near to the mountains of Israel, and there eat flesh and drink blood! 18Eat the flesh of
mighty men and drink the blood of princes as though they were rams, lambs, goats, and
bulls—all fattened animals from Bashan! 19Gorge yourselves with flesh until you are glut-
ted; drink blood until you are drunk. This is the sacrificial feast I have prepared for you.
20Feast at My banquet table—feast on horses and charioteers, on mighty men and all kinds
of valiant warriors, says the Sovereign LORD.
21"In this way, I will demonstrate My glory to the nations. Everyone will see the punish-
ment I have inflicted on them and the power of My fist when I strike. 22And from that time
on the people of Israel will know that I am the LORD their God. 23The nations will then
know why Israel was sent away to exile—it was punishment for sin, for they were unfaith-
ful to their God. Therefore, I turned away from them and let their enemies destroy them.
24I turned My face away and punished them because of their defilement and their sins.

RESTORATION FOR GOD'S PEOPLE

25"So now, this is what the Sovereign LORD says: I will end the captivity of My people*; I will
have mercy on all Israel, for I jealously guard My holy reputation! 26They will accept re-
sponsibility for their past shame and unfaithfulness after they come home to live in peace
in their own land, with no one to bother them. 27When I bring them home from the lands
of their enemies, I will display My holiness among them for all the nations to see. 28Then
My people will know that I am the LORD their God, because I sent them away to exile and
brought them home again. I will leave none of My people behind. 29And I will never again
turn My face from them, for I will pour out My Spirit upon the people of Israel. I, the Sover-
eign LORD, have spoken!"

39:9 Ps 46:9
39:10 Isa 14:2; Mic 5:8; Hab 2:8
39:13 Jer 33:9; Ezek 28:22; Zeph 3:19-20
39:17 Isa 34:6-7; Jer 46:10; Zeph 1:7; Rev 19:17-18
39:18 Deut 32:14; Ps 22:12; Jer 51:40; Amos 4:1
39:20 Ps 76:5-6; Ezek 38:4; Hag 2:22; Rev 19:18
39:21 Exod 9:16; Ezek 38:16, 23
39:23 Isa 59:2; Ezek 39:29; 36:18-19
39:24 2 Kgs 17:7; Jer 2:17, 19; 4:18; Ezek 36:19
39:25 Jer 33:7; Ezek 34:13; 36:10; Hos 1:11
39:26 Ezek 34:25-28; Mic 4:4
39:27 Ezek 28:25-26; 37:21
39:29 Isa 32:15; Ezek 36:27; 37:14; Joel 2:28-29; Acts 2:17

39:11 Hebrew *the sea.* 39:25 Hebrew *of Jacob.*

39:17-24 Carnivorous birds and animals were invited to feast on "horses and charioteers, on mighty men and all kinds of valiant warriors" who were killed during their invasion of Israel. Revelation 19:17-18 uses similar imagery to describe Christ's defeat of the beast (Antichrist) and his armies.

39:25-29 Many of the themes related to the Lord's restoration of Israel are repeated in this closing section, which also serves to prepare the reader for the vision of the new Temple and Israel's return to the land (chapters 40–48). The Babylonian captivity would end with repentant Israel's return to the land "to live in peace in their own land, with no one to bother them" (39:26). The historical records of Ezra and Nehemiah indicate that this was not the case for those who returned to the land in 535 BC, so the fulfillment of this passage awaits another day in the future (see all notes on chapters 36–37). On that day, the Lord will pour out His Spirit on the people of Israel (see 36:26-27).

40:1 2 Kgs 25:1-7 Jer 39:1-9
40:2 Ps 48:2 Ezek 20:40 Mic 4:1 Rev 21:10
40:3 Dan 10:5-6 Zech 2:1-2 Rev 11:1; 21:15
40:4 Jer 26:2 Ezek 43:10; 44:5 Acts 20:27
40:5 Ezek 42:20
40:6 Ezek 8:16; 11:1; 43:1
40:7 1 Kgs 6:5-10 2 Chr 31:11 Jer 35:4 Ezek 40:29, 33, 36

THE NEW TEMPLE AREA

40 On April 28,* during the twenty-fifth year of our captivity—fourteen years after the fall of Jerusalem—the LORD took hold of me. [2]In a vision from God He took me to the land of Israel and set me down on a very high mountain. From there I could see toward the south what appeared to be a city. [3]As He brought me nearer, I saw a man whose face shone like bronze standing beside a gateway entrance. He was holding in his hand a linen measuring cord and a measuring rod.

[4]He said to me, "Son of man, watch and listen. Pay close attention to everything I show you. You have been brought here so I can show you many things. Then you will return to the people of Israel and tell them everything you have seen."

THE EAST GATEWAY

[5]I could see a wall completely surrounding the Temple area. The man took a measuring rod that was 10½ feet* long and measured the wall, and the wall was 10½ feet* thick and 10½ feet high.

[6]Then he went over to the eastern gateway. He climbed the steps and measured the threshold of the gateway; it was 10½ feet front to back.* [7]There were guard alcoves on each side built into the gateway passage. Each of these alcoves was 10½ feet square, with a distance between them of 8¾ feet* along the passage wall. The gateway's inner threshold, which led to the entry room at the inner end of the gateway passage, was 10½ feet front to back. [8]He also measured the entry room of the gateway.* [9]It was 14 feet* across, with supporting columns 3½ feet* thick. This entry room was at the inner end of the gateway structure, facing toward the Temple.

[10]There were three guard alcoves on each side of the gateway passage. Each had the same measurements, and the dividing walls separating them were also identical. [11]The man measured the gateway entrance, which was 17½ feet* wide at the opening and 22¾ feet* wide in the gateway passage. [12]In front of each of the guard alcoves was a 21-inch* curb. The alcoves themselves were 10½ feet* on each side.

40:1 Hebrew *At the beginning of the year, on the tenth day of the month,* of the ancient Hebrew lunar calendar. This event occurred on April 28, 573 B.C.; also see note on 1:1. **40:5a** Hebrew *6 long cubits* [3.2 meters], *each being a cubit* [18 inches or 45 centimeters] *and a handbreadth* [3 inches or 8 centimeters] *in length.* **40:5b** Hebrew *1 rod* [3.2 meters]; also in 40:5c, 7. **40:6** As in Greek version, which reads *1 rod* [3.2 meters] *deep;* Hebrew reads *1 rod deep, and 1 threshold, 1 rod deep.* **40:7** Hebrew *5 cubits* [2.7 meters]; also in 40:48. **40:8** Many Hebrew manuscripts add *which faced inward toward the Temple; it was 1 rod* [10.5 feet or 3.2 meters] *deep.* [9]*Then he measured the entry room of the gateway.* **40:9a** Hebrew *8 cubits* [4.2 meters]. **40:9b** Hebrew *2 cubits* [1.1 meters]. **40:11a** Hebrew *10 cubits* [5.3 meters]. **40:11b** Hebrew *13 cubits* [6.9 meters]. **40:12a** Hebrew *1 cubit* [53 centimeters]. **40:12b** Hebrew *6 cubits* [3.2 meters].

40:1 "On April 28" is literally "at the beginning of the year, on the tenth day of the month." This vision occurred in the year 573 BC, "during the twenty-fifth year of our captivity—fourteen years after the fall of Jerusalem." This is the last date given in the book of Ezekiel. The end of the captivity was still 38 years away, and the people in exile knew that everything Ezekiel had said about their sins and the Babylonian captivity was true. But this latest message from God would give them hope for the future.

40:2 Ezekiel had another out-of-body experience (see note at 37:1-10), and though he was physically still in Babylon, the Lord transported him "in a vision" (see also 1:1; 8:2-4) to "the land of Israel."

40:3-4 After arriving in the land by way of a vision, Ezekiel saw "a man whose face shone like bronze" who would be his guide and interpreter. Angels often have the face of a man (Genesis 18:1-16); but in this case, the supernatural setting and glowing bronze face (similar to the bronze feet of the angels in Ezekiel 1:7) left little doubt that this vision guide was a supernatural being.

40:5-49 The new Temple is the focus of 40:5–42:20. A sanctuary, a special place for the Lord (Yahweh) to dwell among His people, was a major aspect of Israel's covenant relationship with Him. The Tabernacle was the first sanctuary (see Exodus 25–40) and became the prototype for Solomon's Temple (1 Kings 5–8). The Babylonians destroyed Solomon's Temple in 586 BC. The Temple built by Zerubbabel and the postexilic remnant (see Ezra 1–6) in 515 BC was desecrated by Antiochus IV in 165 BC. Herod the Great greatly expanded and improved this Temple, but the Roman army destroyed it in AD 70. The Temple in Ezekiel's vision was an ideal Temple that could have been built if the postexilic remnant had been faithful to the Lord. Because they faltered, the Temple they built was not even as grand as Solomon's (Ezra 3:12).

40:6 The architecture of the Temple was less a blueprint for a building and more a theological statement. As one drew near the Temple, steps led to a raised platform that served as the outer court. More steps led to a yet higher platform—an inner court (40:34, 37). Another flight of stairs led to the Temple building (40:49; 41:8). The changes in elevation and proximity to the inner sanctuary communicated a greater sanctity.

13Then he measured the entire width of the gateway, measuring the distance between
the back walls of facing guard alcoves; this distance was 43¾ feet.* 14He measured the di-
viding walls all along the inside of the gateway up to the entry room of the gateway; this
distance was 105 feet.* 15The full length of the gateway passage was 87½ feet* from one
end to the other. 16There were recessed windows that narrowed inward through the walls
of the guard alcoves and their dividing walls. There were also windows in the entry room.
The surfaces of the dividing walls were decorated with carved palm trees.

THE OUTER COURTYARD

17Then the man brought me through the gateway into the outer courtyard of the Temple.
A stone pavement ran along the walls of the courtyard, and thirty rooms were built against
the walls, opening onto the pavement. 18This pavement flanked the gates and extended
out from the walls into the courtyard the same distance as the gateway entrance. This was
the lower pavement. 19Then the man measured across the Temple's outer courtyard be-
tween the outer and inner gateways; the distance was 175 feet.*

THE NORTH GATEWAY

20The man measured the gateway on the north just like the one on the east. 21Here, too,
there were three guard alcoves on each side, with dividing walls and an entry room. All
the measurements matched those of the east gateway. The gateway passage was 87½
feet long and 43¾ feet wide between the back walls of facing guard alcoves. 22The win-
dows, the entry room, and the palm tree decorations were identical to those in the east
gateway. There were seven steps leading up to the gateway entrance, and the entry room
was at the inner end of the gateway passage. 23Here on the north side, just as on the east,
there was another gateway leading to the Temple's inner courtyard directly opposite this
outer gateway. The distance between the two gateways was 175 feet.

THE SOUTH GATEWAY

24Then the man took me around to the south gateway and measured its various parts, and
they were exactly the same as in the others. 25It had windows along the walls as the others
did, and there was an entry room where the gateway passage opened into the outer court-
yard. And like the others, the gateway passage was 87½ feet long and 43¾ feet wide be-
tween the back walls of facing guard alcoves. 26This gateway also had a stairway of seven
steps leading up to it, and an entry room at the inner end, and palm tree decorations along
the dividing walls. 27And here again, directly opposite the outer gateway, was another gate-
way that led into the inner courtyard. The distance between the two gateways was 175 feet.

GATEWAYS TO THE INNER COURTYARD

28Then the man took me to the south gateway leading into the inner courtyard. He mea-
sured it, and it had the same measurements as the other gateways. 29Its guard alcoves,
dividing walls, and entry room were the same size as those in the others. It also had win-
dows along its walls and in the entry room. And like the others, the gateway passage was

40:14 Exod 27:9; 1 Chr 28:6; Ps 100:4; Isa 62:9; Ezek 42:1
40:16 1 Kgs 6:4; Ezek 41:26; 1 Cor 13:12
40:17 1 Chr 9:26; 2 Chr 31:11; Ezek 46:21; Rev 11:2
40:22 1 Kgs 6:29-35; 7:36; 2 Chr 3:5; Rev 7:9
40:23 Exod 27:9-18; 38:9-12
40:24 Ezek 46:9

40:13 Hebrew *25 cubits* [13.3 meters]; also in 40:21, 25, 29, 30, 33, 36. 40:14 Hebrew *60 cubits* [31.8 meters]. The meaning of the Hebrew in this verse is uncertain. 40:15 Hebrew *50 cubits* [26.5 meters]; also in 40:21, 25, 29, 33, 36. 40:19 Hebrew *100 cubits* [53 meters]; also in 40:23, 27, 47.

40:16 The palm trees mentioned here are also in 40:22, 31, 34, 37. The major design element in Israel's ancient sanctuaries was botanical; varieties of trees and plants covered the holy area (Exodus 25:34; 37:19; 1 Kings 6:18, 29, 32, 35). The sanctuaries of Israel intended to set before Israel the goal of once again dwelling in God's first garden, the Garden of Eden.

40:17 Common worshipers used the outer court, but only priests and Levites entered the inner court. The text does not specify the use of the 30 rooms (41:6) surrounding the perimeter of the outer court, but Jeremiah 35:2 hints that they were used as reception areas.

40:28 A wall separated the inner court from the outer one. A trio of gates, a design used throughout the Holy City (see for instance, Ezekiel 48:31), allowed passage between them.

87½ feet long and 43¾ feet wide. 30(The entry rooms of the gateways leading into the inner courtyard were 14 feet* across and 43¾ feet wide.) 31The entry room to the south gateway faced into the outer courtyard. It had palm tree decorations on its columns, and there were eight steps leading to its entrance.

32Then he took me to the east gateway leading to the inner courtyard. He measured it, and it had the same measurements as the other gateways. 33Its guard alcoves, dividing walls, and entry room were the same size as those of the others, and there were windows along the walls and in the entry room. The gateway passage measured 87½ feet long and 43¾ feet wide. 34Its entry room faced into the outer courtyard. It had palm tree decorations on its columns, and there were eight steps leading to its entrance.

40:35 Ezek 44:4; 47:2

35Then he took me around to the north gateway leading to the inner courtyard. He measured it, and it had the same measurements as the other gateways. 36The guard alcoves, dividing walls, and entry room of this gateway had the same measurements as in the others and the same window arrangements. The gateway passage measured 87½ feet long and 43¾ feet wide. 37Its entry room faced into the outer courtyard, and it had palm tree decorations on the columns. There were eight steps leading to its entrance.

ROOMS FOR PREPARING SACRIFICES

40:38 1 Kgs 6:8; 1 Chr 28:12; 2 Chr 4:6; Neh 13:5, 9; Ezek 41:10; 42:13
40:39 Lev 1:2-17; 4:2-3; 5:6; 6:6; 7:1-2; Ezek 46:2
40:42 Exod 20:25

38A door led from the entry room of one of the inner gateways into a side room, where the meat for sacrifices was washed. 39On each side of this entry room were two tables, where the sacrificial animals were slaughtered for the burnt offerings, sin offerings, and guilt offerings. 40Outside the entry room, on each side of the stairs going up to the north entrance, were two more tables. 41So there were eight tables in all—four inside and four outside—where the sacrifices were cut up and prepared. 42There were also four tables of finished stone for preparation of the burnt offerings, each 31½ inches square and 21 inches high.* On these tables were placed the butchering knives and other implements for slaughtering the sacrificial animals. 43There were hooks, each 3 inches* long, fastened to the foyer walls. The sacrificial meat was laid on the tables.

ROOMS FOR THE PRIESTS

40:44 1 Chr 6:31-32; 16:41-43; 25:1-7
40:45 Lev 8:35; 1 Chr 9:23
40:46 1 Kgs 2:35; Ezek 43:19; 48:11

44Inside the inner courtyard were two rooms,* one beside the north gateway, facing south, and the other beside the south* gateway, facing north. 45And the man said to me, "The room beside the north inner gate is for the priests who supervise the Temple maintenance. 46The room beside the south inner gate is for the priests in charge of the altar—the descendants of Zadok—for they alone of all the Levites may approach the LORD to minister to Him."

40:30 As in 40:9, which reads *8 cubits* [14 feet or 4.2 meters]; here the Hebrew reads *5 cubits* [8¾ feet or 2.7 meters]. Some Hebrew manuscripts and the Greek version omit this entire verse. 40:42 Hebrew *1½ cubits* [80 centimeters] *long and 1½ cubits wide and 1 cubit* [53 centimeters] *high.* 40:43 Hebrew *a handbreadth* [8 centimeters]. 40:44a As in Greek version; Hebrew reads *rooms for singers.* 40:44b As in Greek version; Hebrew reads *east.*

40:38 The slaughter of animals occurred in the gateways to the inner court where the altar (43:13-27) was located. The portions were washed (Leviticus 1:9; 2 Chronicles 4:6) as one would wash something about to be cooked for a meal, hanging them on hooks (40:43) to wait their turn on the altar.

▶ WORSHIP

40:38-43 One sacrifice, good for all time. Before Jesus came to earth, God instituted a complex sacrificial system to foreshadow Christ's death on the cross. These sacrifices atoned for sin (Leviticus 1:4; 4:20-35; 5:6-18) not on the basis of the deaths of the animals (Hebrews 10:4-6), but on the basis of the then-future death of Jesus (John 1:29). As worshipers looked to God in faith, God reckoned Christ's merit to them, and thereby counted them as righteous and forgiven in His sight (Genesis 15:6). And the same is true today. We can be forgiven and counted righteous only on the basis of Christ's atonement (John 14:6), which is obtained by faith (Galatians 3:24). If you truly trust in Christ for your forgiveness and righteousness, then God has saved you—rejoice and be thankful! But if you haven't trusted in Christ, you are still in your sin, so repent and give your life to God. Today can be the day of your salvation (2 Corinthians 6:2). (***See Worship****> OT> Place> Tabernacle> Christ fulfills the Old Testament sacrificial system,* TopicGuide page A27.)

40:45-46 Rooms for the priests were inside the inner court, next to the gateway on the north and south. The northern room was for the priests officiating at the altar. The southern room was for the priests involved in other duties in the Temple.

THE INNER COURTYARD AND TEMPLE

[47]Then the man measured the inner courtyard, and it was a square, 175 feet wide and 175 feet across. The altar stood in the courtyard in front of the Temple. [48]Then he brought me to the entry room of the Temple. He measured the walls on either side of the opening to the entry room, and they were 8¾ feet thick. The entrance itself was 24½ feet* wide, and the walls on each side of the entrance were an additional 5¼ feet* long. [49]The entry room was 35 feet* wide and 21 feet* deep. There were ten steps leading up to it, with a column on each side.

41 After that, the man brought me into the sanctuary of the Temple. He measured the walls on either side of its doorway, and they were 10½ feet* thick. [2]The doorway was 17½ feet* wide, and the walls on each side of it were 8¾ feet* long. The sanctuary itself was 70 feet long and 35 feet wide.*

[3]Then he went beyond the sanctuary into the inner room. He measured the walls on either side of its entrance, and they were 3½ feet* thick. The entrance was 10½ feet wide, and the walls on each side of the entrance were 12¼ feet* long. [4]The inner room of the sanctuary was 35 feet* long and 35 feet wide. "This," he told me, "is the Most Holy Place."

[5]Then he measured the wall of the Temple, and it was 10½ feet thick. There was a row of rooms along the outside wall; each room was 7 feet* wide. [6]These side rooms were built in three levels, one above the other, with thirty rooms on each level. The supports for these side rooms rested on exterior ledges on the Temple wall; they did not extend into the wall. [7]Each level was wider than the one below it, corresponding to the narrowing of the Temple wall as it rose higher. A stairway led up from the bottom level through the middle level to the top level.

[8]I saw that the Temple was built on a terrace, which provided a foundation for the side rooms. This terrace was 10½ feet* high. [9]The outer wall of the Temple's side rooms was 8¾ feet thick. This left an open area between these side rooms [10]and the row of rooms along the outer wall of the inner courtyard. This open area was 35 feet wide, and it went all the way around the Temple. [11]Two doors opened from the side rooms into the terrace yard, which was 8¾ feet wide. One door faced north and the other south.

40:48 1 Kgs 6:3
40:49 Jer 52:17-23; Rev 3:12
41:1 Ezek 40:2-3, 17
41:2 1 Kgs 6:2, 17; 2 Chr 3:3
41:4 Exod 26:33-34; 1 Kgs 6:20; 2 Chr 3:8; Heb 9:3-8
41:5 1 Kgs 6:5
41:6 1 Kgs 6:6, 10
41:7 1 Kgs 6:8
41:8 Ezek 40:5
41:10 Ezek 40:17

40:48a Hebrew *14 cubits* [7.4 meters]. **40:48b** Hebrew *3 cubits* [1.6 meters]. **40:49a** Hebrew *20 cubits* [10.6 meters]. **40:49b** As in Greek version, which reads *12 cubits* [21 feet or 6.4 meters]; Hebrew reads *11 cubits* [19¼ feet or 5.8 meters]. **41:1** Hebrew *6 cubits* [3.2 meters]; also in 41:3, 5. **41:2a** Hebrew *10 cubits* [5.3 meters]. **41:2b** Hebrew *5 cubits* [2.7 meters]; also in 41:9, 11. **41:2c** Hebrew *40 cubits* [21.2 meters] *long and 20 cubits* [10.6 meters] *wide.* **41:3a** Hebrew *2 cubits* [1.1 meters]. **41:3b** Hebrew *7 cubits* [3.7 meters]. **41:4** Hebrew *20 cubits* [10.6 meters]; also in 41:4b, 10. **41:5** Hebrew *4 cubits* [2.1 meters]. **41:8** Hebrew *1 rod, 6 cubits* [3.2 meters].

41:1-12 Both Moses' Tabernacle and Solomon's Temple had an outer sanctuary called the Holy Place and an inner sanctuary called the Most Holy Place or the Holy of Holies. Ezekiel's angelic guide took him to both of these places and measured their entrances and columns (41:1-4). After the angel measured the wall again (41:5; see 40:5), he showed Ezekiel various rooms, terraces, and buildings connected to the Temple (41:6-12). Many of these features had counterparts in Solomon's Temple.

41:3 The measurements of the Temple (40:1–42:20) and the measurements of the land of Israel (47:13–48:35) form literary bookends for this last section of Ezekiel, with the center of this final section being the measurements of a holy section of land in the middle of Israel (45:1-12). The whole book of Ezekiel shows a careful organization, communicating that God had a well-ordered plan for restoring Israel and for proper worship of Himself.

▸ WORSHIP
41:4 The final Temple. Ezekiel greatly encouraged the exilic community by explaining God's offer to rebuild the Temple that the Babylonians had destroyed. After all, the Temple was where God manifested His presence with His people (2 Chronicles 6:41), especially in the Most Holy Place (Exodus 25:22). Christians, however, have no need of a Temple (John 4:21-24), just as we will not need one when Christ returns (Revelation 21:22), because we are already seated with Christ in heaven at the Father's right hand (Ephesians 1:20; 2:6). We have no need of a special place on earth to draw near to Him. This good news means that all believers have the same direct access to God's presence, which used to belong to the high priest alone. The next time you pray, remember that you are in God's immediate presence and that He listens carefully to your prayers (2 Chronicles 6:14-42). (***See Worship***> *OT> Place> Temple,* TopicGuide page A27.)

41:13-26 These verses give the dimensions of the Holy Place, the Most Holy Place, the courtyards, the walls, and various carvings. Only one piece of furniture was mentioned in this Temple: "an altar" that was actually "the table that stands in the LORD's presence" (41:22). This altar was likely not for sacrifices or incense, but corresponds to the table of the Bread of the Presence in the Tabernacle (Exodus 25:23-30). The presence of cherubim also corresponds to elements for the Tabernacle (Exodus 25:17-22; 26:1, 31).

41:12 Ezek 42:1; Rev 21:27; 22:14-15
41:13 Ezek 40:47
41:15 Ezek 42:1, 10, 13
41:16 1 Kgs 6:4, 15
41:18 1 Kgs 6:29; 7:36; 2 Chr 3:5; Ezek 10:18
41:19 Ezek 1:10; 10:14
41:22 Exod 30:1-3, 8; Ezek 44:16; Mal 1:7, 12; Rev 8:3
41:23 1 Kgs 6:31-35
41:24 1 Kgs 6:34
41:26 Ezek 40:7-12
42:1 Ezek 40:2-3, 17; 41:9, 12-15
42:2 Ezek 41:13
42:3 Ezek 40:17; 41:10

[12]A large building stood on the west, facing the Temple courtyard. It was 122½ feet wide and 157½ feet long, and its walls were 8¾ feet* thick. [13]Then the man measured the Temple, and it was 175 feet* long. The courtyard around the building, including its walls, was an additional 175 feet in length. [14]The inner courtyard to the east of the Temple was also 175 feet wide. [15]The building to the west, including its two walls, was also 175 feet wide.

The sanctuary, the inner room, and the entry room of the Temple [16]were all paneled with wood, as were the frames of the recessed windows. The inner walls of the Temple were paneled with wood above and below the windows. [17]The space above the door leading into the inner room, and its walls inside and out, were also paneled. [18]All the walls were decorated with carvings of cherubim, each with two faces, and there was a carving of a palm tree between each of the cherubim. [19]One face—that of a man—looked toward the palm tree on one side. The other face—that of a young lion—looked toward the palm tree on the other side. The figures were carved all along the inside of the Temple, [20]from the floor to the top of the walls, including the outer wall of the sanctuary.

[21]There were square columns at the entrance to the sanctuary, and the ones at the entrance of the Most Holy Place were similar. [22]There was an altar made of wood, 5¼ feet high and 3½ feet across.* Its corners, base, and sides were all made of wood. "This," the man told me, "is the table that stands in the LORD's presence."

[23]Both the sanctuary and the Most Holy Place had double doorways, [24]each with two swinging doors. [25]The doors leading into the sanctuary were decorated with carved cherubim and palm trees, just as on the walls. And there was a wooden roof at the front of the entry room to the Temple. [26]On both sides of the entry room were recessed windows decorated with carved palm trees. The side rooms along the outside wall also had roofs.

ROOMS FOR THE PRIESTS

42 Then the man led me out of the Temple courtyard by way of the north gateway. We entered the outer courtyard and came to a group of rooms against the north wall of the inner courtyard. [2]This structure, whose entrance opened toward the north, was 175 feet long and 87½ feet wide.* [3]One block of rooms overlooked the 35-foot* width of

41:12 Hebrew *70 cubits* [37.1 meters] *wide and 90 cubits* [47.7 meters] *long, and its walls were 5 cubits* [2.7 meters] *thick.* 41:13 Hebrew *100 cubits* [53 meters]; also in 41:13b, 14, 15. 41:22 Hebrew *3 cubits* [1.6 meters] *high and 2 cubits* [1.1 meters] *across.* 42:2 Hebrew *100 cubits* [53 meters] *long and 50 cubits* [26.5 meters] *wide.* 42:3 Hebrew *20 cubits* [10.6 meters].

▶ WORSHIP

41:18-19 Images in worship. God forbids certain uses of images in worship (Exodus 20:4-5), but He does not forbid all uses of images. The Tabernacle (Exodus 26:1, 31) and Solomon's Temple (1 Kings 7:25, 29, 36) both contained many images of created beings, and even the Ark of the Covenant had two cherubim on it (Exodus 25:18-22). In the same way, many churches have paintings, stained-glass windows, and crosses. But God always objects to images when they are used in idolatrous ways and worshiped as gods (Exodus 20:5; Deuteronomy 5:9). Even otherwise good images, such as the snake Moses made (Numbers 21:8), are forbidden when they are misused in this way (2 Kings 18:4). Are there images in your church? You should feel free to appreciate them if they add to the church's beauty and help you remember God. But you should never regard them as a means of gaining influence or favor with God. (***See Worship****> OT> Prohibitions> Wrong Objects> Images,* TopicGuide page A28.)

42:1-14 The angel led Ezekiel from the Temple courtyard to "a group of rooms" to the north. These rooms overlooked the Temple area, and another block of rooms were on the south side of the Temple. The angel guide explained that these structures were "holy" and would be used "to store the . . . sacred offerings" (42:13). The priests would also have special garments to wear when offering sacrifices (42:14; compare Exodus 28).

▶ SPIRITUAL WARFARE

42:1 Fighting beside the angels. In Scripture, angels are sometimes portrayed as being indistinguishable from human beings (Genesis 18:2; Joshua 5:13). They can walk among us and not be recognized as supernatural beings (Genesis 19:1-8). In this section, Ezekiel was led around by a being identified as a "man" in the NLT, but one whose features and activities lead most to believe he was a supernatural being (see note at Ezekiel 40:3-4). The author of Hebrews encouraged all Christians to show great hospitality to all, for a stranger might actually be one of God's heavenly angels (Hebrews 13:2). As the uncertainty to the identity of Ezekiel's guide shows us, the spiritual world is real, and it is not entirely distinct from our world. Angels and demons surround us, waging war against one another, and we are not immune from their influence (2 Corinthians 10:3-5). Don't be fooled into thinking that spiritual warfare is mere superstition; rather, be on guard (Ephesians 6:18). As demonic forces attempt to ruin God's people, defend the kingdom of God (Romans 14:17; Revelation 12:10-11). Stand on the side of the angels and do battle as the Lord has given you strength. (***See Spiritual Warfare****> Resisting Sin and Evil> Standing Firm> Empowered to do spiritual warfare,* TopicGuide page A46.)

the inner courtyard. Another block of rooms looked out onto the pavement of the outer
courtyard. The two blocks were built three levels high and stood across from each other.
[4]Between the two blocks of rooms ran a walkway 17½ feet* wide. It extended the entire
175 feet* of the complex, and all the doors faced north. [5]Each of the two upper levels of
rooms was narrower than the one beneath it because the upper levels had to allow space
for walkways in front of them. [6]Since there were three levels and they did not have sup-
porting columns as in the courtyards, each of the upper levels was set back from the level
beneath it. [7]There was an outer wall that separated the rooms from the outer courtyard; it
was 87½ feet* long. [8]This wall added length to the outer block of rooms, which extended
for only 87½ feet, while the inner block—the rooms toward the Temple—extended for
175 feet. [9]There was an eastern entrance from the outer courtyard to these rooms.
[10]On the south* side of the Temple there were two blocks of rooms just south of the in-
ner courtyard between the Temple and the outer courtyard. These rooms were arranged
just like the rooms on the north. [11]There was a walkway between the two blocks of rooms
just like the complex on the north side of the Temple. This complex of rooms was the
same length and width as the other one, and it had the same entrances and doors. The di-
mensions of each were identical. [12]So there was an entrance in the wall facing the doors
of the inner block of rooms, and another on the east at the end of the interior walkway.
[13]Then the man told me, "These rooms that overlook the Temple from the north and
south are holy. Here the priests who offer sacrifices to the LORD will eat the most holy offer-
ings. And because these rooms are holy, they will be used to store the sacred offerings—
the grain offerings, sin offerings, and guilt offerings. [14]When the priests leave the sanctu-
ary, they must not go directly to the outer courtyard. They must first take off the clothes
they wore while ministering, because these clothes are holy. They must put on other
clothes before entering the parts of the building complex open to the public."
[15]When the man had finished measuring the inside of the Temple area, he led me out
through the east gateway to measure the entire perimeter. [16]He measured the east side
with his measuring rod, and it was 875 feet long.* [17]Then he measured the north side, and
it was also 875 feet. [18]The south side was also 875 feet, [19]and the west side was also
875 feet. [20]So the area was 875 feet on each side with a wall all around it to separate what
was holy from what was common.

THE LORD'S GLORY RETURNS

43 After this, the man brought me back around to the east gateway. [2]Suddenly, the
glory of the God of Israel appeared from the east. The sound of His coming was

42:4 Ezek 46:19
42:6 Ezek 41:6
42:7 Ezek 41:13-14
42:9 Ezek 44:5; 46:19
42:13 Lev 6:25, 29; 7:6; 10:13-17; Num 18:9-10
42:14 Exod 29:4-9; Isa 61:10; Zech 3:4-5
42:15 Ezek 43:1
42:16 Ezek 40:3, 5
43:1 Ezek 10:19; 40:6; 44:1; 46:1
43:2 Isa 6:3; Ezek 10:4, 18-19; 11:23; Rev 1:15; 18:1

42:4a Hebrew *10 cubits* [5.3 meters]. 42:4b Hebrew *100 cubits* [53 meters]; also in 42:8. 42:7 Hebrew *50 cubits* [26.5 meters]; also in 42:8. 42:10 As in Greek version; Hebrew reads *east.* 42:16 As in 45:2 and in Greek version at 42:17, which reads *500 cubits* [265 meters]; Hebrew reads *500 rods* [5,250 feet or 1,590 meters]; similarly in 42:17, 18, 19, 20.

▸ WORSHIP

42:13 Eating the most holy offerings. Why did God allow the priests to eat of His holy sacrifices? Doesn't that sound dangerous—taking what was offered to God? One reason God asked for sacrifices was to feed His priests. The priests received a share of most sacrifices and offerings that were brought to the Temple (Exodus 29:28; Leviticus 6:17-18). Two points flow from this: First, this was a means of sustenance for them, since the priests and other Levites were given no land to farm (Joshua 18:7; Ezekiel 44:28-29). God's ministers deserve to be paid for their work (1 Corinthians 9:10). Second, we are commanded to eat of the Lord's Supper. We do so as an act of worship, recalling the holy sacrifice made by Christ for us. As we spiritually partake of His body and blood (1 Corinthians 11:23-26), we are spiritually nourished. Like the Levites, there is no place else we can go for the spiritual food we need—it is found with God alone. Honor Christ's sacrifice by gratefully partaking of the Lord's Supper whenever it is offered. (***See Worship****> OT> Offerings> Blood sacrifices> Burnt Offering,* TopicGuide page A27.)

42:20 The five hundred cubits mentioned (see NLT textual note) consisted of the length of the outer north gateway (50), plus the length of the outer court (100), plus the length of the inner north gateway (50), plus the lengths across the inner court (100), the opposite (south) inner gateway (50), the opposite side of the outer court (100), and the opposite outer (south) gateway (50). This was intended to give a sense of perfection and order to those imagining this Temple. God had a perfect plan for reinstituting proper worship of Himself. Future Jews believed that these blueprints for the Temple were more figurative and not true architectural directions, so the Temple in Jerusalem in Jesus' time was built along the lines of Solomon's Temple, and not the one discussed in this vision.

43:1-27 In Ezekiel's first vision he saw the glory of the Lord coming from a storm out of the north (1:4-28). Then the glory moved from the Temple area to the east gate (10:4, 18-19), then to the Mount of Olives (11:22-25), and finally it disap-

like the roar of rushing waters, and the whole landscape shone with His glory. [3]This vision was just like the others I had seen, first by the Kebar River and then when He came to destroy Jerusalem. I fell face down on the ground. [4]And the glory of the LORD came into the Temple through the east gateway.

[5]Then the Spirit took me up and brought me into the inner courtyard, and the glory of the LORD filled the Temple. [6]And I heard someone speaking to me from within the Temple, while the man who had been measuring stood beside me. [7]The LORD said to me, "Son of man, this is the place of My throne and the place where I will rest My feet. I will live here forever among the people of Israel. They and their kings will not defile My holy name any longer by their adulterous worship of other gods or by honoring the relics of their kings who have died. [8]They put their idol altars right next to Mine with only a wall between them and Me. They defiled My holy name by such detestable sin, so I consumed them in My anger. [9]Now let them stop worshiping other gods and honoring the relics of their kings, and I will live among them forever.

[10]"Son of man, describe to the people of Israel the Temple I have shown you, so they will be ashamed of all their sins. Let them study its plan, [11]and they will be ashamed* of what they have done. Describe to them all the specifications of the Temple—including its entrances and exits—and everything else about it. Tell them about its decrees and laws. Write down all these specifications and decrees as they watch so they will be sure to remember and follow them. [12]And this is the basic law of the Temple: absolute holiness! The entire top of the mountain where the Temple is built is holy. Yes, this is the basic law of the Temple.

THE ALTAR

[13]"These are the measurements of the altar*: There is a gutter all around the altar 21 inches deep and 21 inches wide,* with a curb 9 inches* wide around its edge. And this is the height* of the altar: [14]From the gutter the altar rises 3½ feet* to a lower ledge that surrounds the altar and is 21 inches* wide. From the lower ledge the altar rises 7 feet* to the upper ledge that is also 21 inches wide. [15]The top of the altar, the hearth, rises another 7 feet higher, with a horn rising up from each of the four corners. [16]The top of the altar is

43:3 Jer 1:10; Ezek 3:23
43:4 Ezek 44:2
43:5 1 Kgs 8:10-11; 2 Cor 12:2-4
43:6 Ezek 1:26; 40:3
43:7 Lev 26:30; Ps 47:8; Jer 16:18; Ezek 6:5; 37:26-28
43:8 Ezek 8:3
43:9 Ezek 18:30, 31
43:10 Ezek 40:4
43:11 Ezek 11:20; 12:3; 36:27; 44:5
43:12 Ezek 40:2
43:13 Exod 27:1-8; 2 Chr 4:1
43:14 Ezek 45:19
43:15 Exod 27:2; Lev 9:9; 1 Kgs 1:49-50; Ps 118:27
43:16 Exod 27:1

43:11 As in Greek version; Hebrew reads *if they are ashamed.* 43:13a Hebrew *measurements of the altar in long cubits, each being a cubit* [18 inches or 45 centimeters] *and a handbreadth* [3 inches or 8 centimeters] *in length.* 43:13b Hebrew *a cubit* [53 centimeters] *deep and a cubit wide.* 43:13c Hebrew *1 span* [23 centimeters]. 43:13d As in Greek version; Hebrew reads *base.* 43:14a Hebrew *2 cubits* [1.1 meters]. 43:14b Hebrew *1 cubit* [53 centimeters]; also in 43:14d. 43:14c Hebrew *4 cubits* [2.1 meters]; also in 43:15.

peared completely. In this vision, it returned in a greater way than before. This hope of God's glory returning to the Temple was fulfilled in an even greater manner than expected when Jesus made His dwelling among people, and His glory was revealed (John 1:14). He was the radiance of God's glory, the exact representation of His being (Hebrews 1:3).

▸ CHURCH
43:2-5 The glory of the Lord. In his earlier ministry, Ezekiel had seen the glory of the Lord depart from the Temple (Ezekiel 11:23)—a tragic loss for Israel (Exodus 33:15-16; 1 Samuel 4:21-22). Subsequently, the Temple itself was destroyed. But here, the Lord indicated that if the people would repent, He would return to Israel in all His glory, rebuilding His Temple and dwelling there in the midst of His people (Ezekiel 43:9-11). Of course, God's restored presence alone would have been enough to encourage His people, but He even promised to protect and bless them. For those of us who trust in Christ, God's blessing and protection cover us at all times, and His glory now resides in us, the church, who are His new temple (Ephesians 2:20-22). Such a great gift from God should fill us with gratitude and make us desire to obey Him. (***See Church***> *What> Many Titles> Cornerstone/Holy Temple,* TopicGuide page A48.)

▸ GOD
43:12 Absolute holiness. Worship, Ezekiel says, is about holiness. But what is holiness? In Scripture, holiness simply means "separateness." Things that are holy to God are set aside for special use in God's service. For example, when God insisted that His Temple be treated as holy, He meant, among other things, that worshipers were not to bring foreign idols into His presence (Ezekiel 43:8-9). In fact, the first commandment, "You must not have any other god but Me" (Exodus 20:3), might be more literally translated, "There shall not be for you other gods in My presence." Worshipers of the Lord are also required to exalt the one true God as special, which is why we set aside a special holy day each week to worship Him (Exodus 20:8). And more than this, those who worship God must pursue righteousness in everything because we are always in His immediate presence (Romans 12:1; Ephesians 5:27; Colossians 1:22). (***See God***> *God's Attributes> Holy> His holiness demands exclusive worship,* TopicGuide page A16.)

43:13-27 These verses describe the regulations for the consecration of the altar and its use, which preceded the regular offerings (43:18-26). This roughly mirrored the seven-day dedication of Solomon's Temple (2 Chronicles 7:8-9). The eighth day (43:27) begins regular sacrifices.

square, measuring 21 feet by 21 feet.* 17The upper ledge also forms a square, measuring
24½ feet by 24½ feet,* with a 21-inch gutter and a 10½-inch curb* all around the edge.
There are steps going up the east side of the altar."
18Then He said to me, "Son of man, this is what the Sovereign LORD says: These will be
the regulations for the burning of offerings and the sprinkling of blood when the altar is
built. 19At that time, the Levitical priests of the family of Zadok, who minister before Me,
are to be given a young bull for a sin offering, says the Sovereign LORD. 20You will take
some of its blood and smear it on the four horns of the altar, the four corners of the upper
ledge, and the curb that runs around that ledge. This will cleanse and make atonement for
the altar. 21Then take the young bull for the sin offering and burn it at the appointed place
outside the Temple area.
22"On the second day, sacrifice as a sin offering a young male goat that has no physical
defects. Then cleanse and make atonement for the altar again, just as you did with the
young bull. 23When you have finished the cleansing ceremony, offer another young bull
that has no defects and a perfect ram from the flock. 24You are to present them to the LORD,
and the priests are to sprinkle salt on them and offer them as a burnt offering to the LORD.
25"Every day for seven days a male goat, a young bull, and a ram from the flock will be
sacrificed as a sin offering. None of these animals may have physical defects of any kind.
26Do this each day for seven days to cleanse and make atonement for the altar, thus set-
ting it apart for holy use. 27On the eighth day, and on each day afterward, the priests will
sacrifice on the altar the burnt offerings and peace offerings of the people. Then I will ac-
cept you. I, the Sovereign LORD, have spoken!"

THE PRINCE, LEVITES, AND PRIESTS

44 Then the man brought me back to the east gateway in the outer wall of the Tem-
ple area, but it was closed. 2And the LORD said to me, "This gate must remain
closed; it will never again be opened. No one will ever open it and pass through, for the
LORD, the God of Israel, has entered here. Therefore, it must always remain shut. 3Only the
prince himself may sit inside this gateway to feast in the LORD'S presence. But he may
come and go only through the entry room of the gateway."
4Then the man brought me through the north gateway to the front of the Temple. I
looked and saw that the glory of the LORD filled the Temple of the LORD, and I fell face
down on the ground.
5And the LORD said to me, "Son of man, take careful notice. Use your eyes and ears, and
listen to everything I tell you about the regulations concerning the LORD'S Temple. Take
careful note of the procedures for using the Temple's entrances and exits. 6And give these
rebels, the people of Israel, this message from the Sovereign LORD: O people of Israel,
enough of your detestable sins! 7You have brought uncircumcised foreigners into My

43:17 Exod 20:26
43:18 Exod 40:29; Lev 1:5, 11; Ezek 2:1; Heb 9:21-22
43:19 1 Kgs 2:35; Heb 7:27
43:20 Lev 8:15; 9:9
43:21 Exod 29:14; Lev 4:11-12; Heb 13:11
43:23 Exod 29:1
43:24 Lev 2:13; Num 18:19; Mark 9:49-50; Col 4:6
43:25 Exod 29:35-37; Lev 8:33, 35
43:27 Lev 3:1; 9:1; 17:5
44:1 Ezek 40:6
44:3 Gen 31:54; Exod 24:9-11; Zech 6:12-13
44:4 Ezek 1:28; 3:23
44:5 Deut 12:32; 32:46
44:6 1 Pet 4:3
44:7 Gen 17:14; Exod 12:43-49; Lev 22:25; 26:41; Jer 4:4; 9:26

43:16 Hebrew *12 cubits* [6.4 meters] *long and 12 cubits wide.* **43:17a** Hebrew *14 cubits* [7.4 meters] *long and 14 cubits wide.*
43:17b Hebrew *a gutter of 1 cubit* [53 centimeters] *and a curb of ½ a cubit* [27 centimeters].

43:18-27 These verses describe the altar. It was built as a series of platforms, like an ancient ziggurat. Biblical scholars and ancient rabbis have often been puzzled by the altar's design, because it seems to contradict God's command against building altars with steps (Exodus 20:24-26). This tension is resolved by not viewing the design of the Temple in Ezekiel's visions as building plans, but as using architecture to teach about the nature of restored worship in Israel.

43:21 The author of Hebrews referenced this "outside" offering as one aspect of Christ's sacrificial offering of Himself (Hebrews 13:11-13; see also Exodus 29:14; Leviticus 4:12, 21; 8:17; 9:11; 16:27).

44:3 The guide showed Ezekiel a royal officer, a "prince" who would rule in restored Israel. This may have been the same kingly office spoken of in Ezekiel 37:24 or it may have been a more figurative title given to all future leaders, in which case their role in Israel might be addressed.

▸ WORSHIP
44:7 A heart for God. God requires His people to love Him—especially those that serve as His ministers. In Ezekiel's vision, the Lord was disgusted by the appointment of unbelieving ministers. It is important to notice that His criticism here was leveled against Israel for appointing these unbelievers, rather than against the unbelievers themselves. In the same way, God holds His church accountable to appoint believing ministers and pastors that love God with all their heart. Next time your church is looking for a pastor, remember that his love for the Lord is just as important as any of his other qualifications

44:8 Num 18:7
44:9 Joel 3:17; Zech 14:21
44:10 Num 18:23; 2 Kgs 23:8-9
44:11 Num 3:5-37; 4:1-33; 16:8-9; 18:2, 6; 1 Chr 26:1; 2 Chr 29:34
44:12 2 Kgs 16:10-16; Hos 4:6; 5:1
44:13 Num 18:3; 2 Kgs 23:9
44:14 Num 18:4, 6; 1 Chr 23:28, 32
44:15 Num 18:7; Jer 33:18-22
44:17 Exod 39:27-29
44:18 Exod 28:40, 42
44:19 Lev 16:23-24
44:20 Lev 21:5; Num 6:5
44:21 Lev 10:8-9
44:22 Lev 21:7, 13-15
44:23 Lev 10:10; Deut 33:10; Hos 4:6; Mal 2:6

sanctuary—people who have no heart for God. In this way, you defiled My Temple even as you offered Me My food, the fat and blood of sacrifices. In addition to all your other detestable sins, you have broken My covenant. [8]Instead of safeguarding My sacred rituals, you have hired foreigners to take charge of My sanctuary.

[9]"So this is what the Sovereign LORD says: No foreigners, including those who live among the people of Israel, will enter My sanctuary if they have not been circumcised and have not surrendered themselves to the LORD. [10]And the men of the tribe of Levi who abandoned Me when Israel strayed away from Me to worship idols* must bear the consequences of their unfaithfulness. [11]They may still be Temple guards and gatekeepers, and they may slaughter the animals brought for burnt offerings and be present to help the people. [12]But they encouraged My people to worship idols, causing Israel to fall into deep sin. So I have taken a solemn oath that they must bear the consequences for their sins, says the Sovereign LORD. [13]They may not approach Me to minister as priests. They may not touch any of My holy things or the holy offerings, for they must bear the shame of all the detestable sins they have committed. [14]They are to serve as the Temple caretakers, taking charge of the maintenance work and performing general duties.

[15]"However, the Levitical priests of the family of Zadok continued to minister faithfully in the Temple when Israel abandoned Me for idols. These men will serve as My ministers. They will stand in My presence and offer the fat and blood of the sacrifices, says the Sovereign LORD. [16]They alone will enter My sanctuary and approach My table to serve Me. They will fulfill all My requirements.

[17]"When they enter the gateway to the inner courtyard, they must wear only linen clothing. They must wear no wool while on duty in the inner courtyard or in the Temple itself. [18]They must wear linen turbans and linen undergarments. They must not wear anything that would cause them to perspire. [19]When they return to the outer courtyard where the people are, they must take off the clothes they wear while ministering to Me. They must leave them in the sacred rooms and put on other clothes so they do not endanger anyone by transmitting holiness to them through this clothing.

[20]"They must neither shave their heads nor let their hair grow too long. Instead, they must trim it regularly. [21]The priests must not drink wine before entering the inner courtyard. [22]They may choose their wives only from among the virgins of Israel or the widows of the priests. They may not marry other widows or divorced women. [23]They will teach My people the difference between what is holy and what is common, what is ceremonially clean and unclean.

44:10 The Hebrew term (literally *round things*) probably alludes to dung; also in 44:12.

(Ezekiel 34:2-8). And remember that loving the Lord from the heart is your greatest responsibility, too (Matthew 22:36-38). (***See Worship****> OT> Priesthood> Duties> Only Aaron and his descendants could serve as priests,* TopicGuide page A28; also ***see Worship****> NT> Our Role> Holiness> Two great commandments,* TopicGuide page A32.)

44:10-14 Though foreigners had served in the Temple in the past (for example, the Carite guards (2 Kings 11:4), they would no longer be allowed to enter into this idealized future Temple. The tasks they had performed properly belonged to the Levites (Numbers 1:50-53; 3:6, 8, 28-32). Priestly families had engaged in idolatry earlier (Ezekiel 8:6), so they would serve with the other Levites by being confined to more menial tasks. The priesthood would be restricted to the descendants of Zadok (44:15; 40:45-46).

▸ MINISTRY
44:19-25 Holy witnesses. The regulations Ezekiel listed for the priests were above and beyond the regulations given to the nation at large (Exodus 28). These special rules marked the priests as God's holy servants. The New Testament also teaches that the leaders and teachers of God's people are held to a higher standard than the rest of the church (1 Timothy 3:2; James 3:1). But it also teaches that each one of us must be holy, just as the priests were called to be holy in Ezekiel's vision (1 Peter 2:5-9). All God's people serve as symbols of God's holiness to our world. And because we belong to Him, He holds us to a higher standard (Luke 12:48). The world is watching the way you live (1 Peter 3:16). It is watching your attitudes, your behaviors, and your lifestyle, and it is learning about your God by observing you. Live a pure life, one that presents a worthy testimony to your holy Lord. This may be the best evangelism you can ever perform. (***See Ministry****> Great Commission> Make Disciples> Disciples are not just followers, but also witnesses,* TopicGuide page A56.)

24 “They will serve as judges to resolve any disagreements among My people. Their de-
cisions must be based on My regulations. And the priests themselves must obey My in-
structions and decrees at all the sacred festivals, and see to it that the Sabbaths are set
apart as holy days.
25 “A priest must not defile himself by being in the presence of a dead person unless it is
his father, mother, child, brother, or unmarried sister. In such cases it is permitted. 26 Even
then, he can return to his Temple duties only after being ceremonially cleansed and then
waiting for seven days. 27 The first day he returns to work and enters the inner courtyard
and the sanctuary, he must offer a sin offering for himself, says the Sovereign LORD.
28 “The priests will not have any property or possession of land, for I alone am their spe-
cial possession. 29 Their food will come from the gifts and sacrifices brought to the Temple
by the people—the grain offerings, the sin offerings, and the guilt offerings. Whatever any-
one sets apart* for the LORD will belong to the priests. 30 The first of the ripe fruits and all the
gifts brought to the LORD will go to the priests. The first samples of each grain harvest and
the first of your flour must also be given to the priests so the LORD will bless your homes.
31 The priests may not eat meat from any bird or animal that dies a natural death or that
dies after being attacked by another animal.

DIVISION OF THE LAND

45 “When you divide the land among the tribes of Israel, you must set aside a section
for the LORD as his holy portion. This piece of land will be 8⅓ miles long and 6⅔
miles wide.* The entire area will be holy. 2 A section of this land, measuring 875 feet by
875 feet,* will be set aside for the Temple. An additional strip of land 87½ feet* wide is to be
left empty all around it. 3 Within the larger sacred area, measure out a portion of land 8⅓
miles long and 3⅓ miles wide.* Within it the sanctuary of the Most Holy Place will be lo-
cated. 4 This area will be holy, set aside for the priests who minister to the LORD in the sanctu-
ary. They will use it for their homes, and My Temple will be located within it. 5 The strip of
sacred land next to it, also 8⅓ miles long and 3⅓ miles wide, will be a living area for the Le-
vites who work at the Temple. It will be their possession and a place for their towns.*
6 “Adjacent to the larger sacred area will be a section of land 8⅓ miles long and 1⅔
miles wide.* This will be set aside for a city where anyone in Israel can live.
7 “Two special sections of land will be set apart for the prince. One section will share a
border with the east side of the sacred lands and city, and the second section will share a
border on the west side. Then the far eastern and western borders of the prince’s lands will
line up with the eastern and western boundaries of the tribal areas. 8 These sections of land
will be the prince’s allotment. Then My princes will no longer oppress and rob My people;
they will assign the rest of the land to the people, giving an allotment to each tribe.

44:24 Deut 17:8-9; 21:5; 2 Chr 19:8-10; Ezek 20:12, 20
44:25 Lev 21:1-3
44:26 Num 19:13-19
44:27 Num 6:9-11
44:28 Num 18:20; Deut 10:9; Josh 13:33
44:29 Lev 27:21, 28; Num 18:9, 14-15; Josh 13:14
44:30 Num 15:20; 18:12; 2 Chr 31:4-6, 10; Neh 10:35-37; Mal 3:10
44:31 Lev 22:8; Deut 14:21; Ezek 4:14
45:1 Josh 13:7; 14:2; Ps 16:5-6; Ezek 47:21; 48:8-9
45:2 Ezek 42:16-20
45:3 Ezek 48:10
45:4 Num 16:5; Ezek 40:45; 44:13-14; 48:10-11
45:5 Ezek 48:12-14
45:6 Ezek 48:15-16
45:7 Ezek 46:16-18; 48:21-22
45:8 Josh 11:23; Isa 11:3-5; Jer 23:5-6; Ezek 22:27; 46:18

44:29 The Hebrew term used here refers to the complete consecration of things or people to the LORD, either by destroying them or by giving them as an offering. 45:1 Reflecting the Greek version, which reads *25,000 cubits* [13.3 kilometers] *long and 20,000 cubits* [10.6 kilometers] *wide;* Hebrew reads *25,000 cubits long and 10,000 cubits* [3⅓ miles or 5.3 kilometers] wide. Compare 45:3, 5; 48:9. 45:2a Hebrew *500 cubits* [265 meters] *by 500 cubits, a square.* 45:2b Hebrew *50 cubits* [26.5 meters]. 45:3 Hebrew *25,000 cubits* [13.3 kilometers] *long and 10,000 cubits* [5.3 kilometers] *wide;* also in 45:5. 45:5 As in Greek version; Hebrew reads *They will have as their possession 20 rooms.* 45:6 Hebrew *25,000 cubits* [13.3 kilometers] *long and 5,000 cubits* [2.65 kilometers] *wide.*

45:1-8 Four special areas of land were designated: for the Temple (45:1-3); for the priests and Levites who ministered in the Temple (45:4-5); for a special city only for Israelites (45:6); and for the home of the prince (45:7-8), who will receive a special tax to meet his needs (see 45:13-17). These laws about honesty (45:9-12) were directed to those who acted as royal judges or kings in this vision of restored worship and a restored Israel.

▸ MINISTRY

45:8-9 Leading disciples. In this vision, the princes of Israel had abused their power, using it to steal the ancestral land of those under their influence. This was a terrible sin, since some of the greatest blessings God had promised were tied to these family inheritances. Sadly, leaders in the church sometimes take advantage of their people, using guilt or lies or poor theology to line their own pockets (1 Timothy 6:5). God will judge these leaders severely (1 Timothy 6:9-10), for He is especially protective of weak and abused believers (Exodus 22:22-24; Psalm 9:9; James 2:1-13). Never provoke God’s wrath by exploiting His beloved children. (***See Ministry****> Great Commission> Make Disciples> Disciples function under God’s authority,* TopicGuide page A56.)

RULES FOR THE PRINCES

9 "For this is what the Sovereign LORD says: Enough, you princes of Israel! Stop your violence and oppression and do what is just and right. Quit robbing and cheating My people out of their land. Stop expelling them from their homes, says the Sovereign LORD. 10 Use only honest weights and scales and honest measures, both dry and liquid.* 11 The homer* will be your standard unit for measuring volume. The ephah and the bath* will each measure one-tenth of a homer. 12 The standard unit for weight will be the silver shekel.* One shekel will consist of twenty gerahs, and sixty shekels will be equal to one mina.*

SPECIAL OFFERINGS AND CELEBRATIONS

13 "You must give this tax to the prince: one bushel of wheat or barley for every 60* you harvest, 14 one percent of your olive oil,* 15 and one sheep or goat for every 200 in your flocks in Israel. These will be the grain offerings, burnt offerings, and peace offerings that will make atonement for the people who bring them, says the Sovereign LORD. 16 All the people of Israel must join in bringing these offerings to the prince. 17 The prince will be required to provide offerings that are given at the religious festivals, the new moon celebrations, the Sabbath days, and all other similar occasions. He will provide the sin offerings, burnt offerings, grain offerings, liquid offerings, and peace offerings to purify the people of Israel, making them right with the LORD.*

18 "This is what the Sovereign LORD says: In early spring, on the first day of each new year,* sacrifice a young bull with no defects to purify the Temple. 19 The priest will take blood from this sin offering and put it on the doorposts of the Temple, the four corners of the upper ledge of the altar, and the gateposts at the entrance to the inner courtyard. 20 Do this also on the seventh day of the new year for anyone who has sinned through error or ignorance. In this way, you will purify* the Temple.

21 "On the fourteenth day of the first month,* you must celebrate the Passover. This festival will last for seven days. The bread you eat during that time must be made without yeast. 22 On the day of Passover the prince will provide a young bull as a sin offering for himself and the people of Israel. 23 On each of the seven days of the feast he will prepare a burnt offering to the LORD, consisting of seven young bulls and seven rams without defects. A male goat will also be given each day for a sin offering. 24 The prince will provide a basket of flour as a grain offering and a gallon of olive oil* with each young bull and ram.

25 "During the seven days of the Festival of Shelters, which occurs every year in early autumn,* the prince will provide these same sacrifices for the sin offering, the burnt offering, and the grain offering, along with the required olive oil.

46 "This is what the Sovereign LORD says: The east gateway of the inner courtyard will be closed during the six workdays each week, but it will be open on Sabbath days and the days of new moon celebrations. 2 The prince will enter the entry room of the gateway from the outside. Then he will stand by the gatepost while the priest offers his burnt offering and peace offering. He will bow down in worship inside the gateway passage

45:9 Neh 5:1-5; Jer 6:7; 22:3; Zech 8:16
45:10 Lev 19:35-36; Deut 25:13-15; Prov 11:1; 16:11; Mic 6:10-11
45:12 Exod 30:13; Lev 27:25; Num 3:47
45:15 Lev 1:4; 6:30
45:17 Lev 23:1-44; 1 Kgs 8:62-64; 2 Chr 31:3; Ezek 46:4-12
45:18 Exod 12:2; Lev 16:16, 20; 22:20; Heb 9:14
45:19 Lev 16:18-20; Ezek 43:20
45:20 Lev 4:27; Ps 19:12
45:21 Exod 12:18; Lev 23:5-8; Num 9:2-3; 28:16-17
45:22 Lev 4:14
45:23 Lev 23:8; Num 28:16-25; Job 42:8
45:24 Num 28:12-15; Ezek 46:5-7
45:25 Lev 23:33-36; Num 29:12-38
46:1 Exod 20:9-10; Isa 66:23; Ezek 44:1-2
46:2 Ezek 44:3

45:10 Hebrew *use honest scales, an honest ephah, and an honest bath.* **45:11a** The *homer* measures about 40 gallons or 182 liters. **45:11b** The *ephah* is a dry measure; the *bath* is a liquid measure. **45:12a** The *shekel* weighs about 0.4 ounces or 11 grams. **45:12b** Elsewhere the *mina* is equated to 50 shekels. **45:13** Hebrew *1/6 of an ephah from each homer of wheat and 1/6 of an ephah from each homer of barley.* **45:14** Hebrew *the portion of oil, measured by the bath, is 1/10 of a bath from each cor, which consists of 10 baths or 1 homer, for 10 baths are equivalent to a homer.* **45:17** Or *to make atonement for the people of Israel.* **45:18** Hebrew *On the first day of the first month,* of the Hebrew calendar. This day in the ancient Hebrew lunar calendar occurred in March or April. **45:20** Or *will make atonement for.* **45:21** This day in the ancient Hebrew lunar calendar occurred in late March, April, or early May. **45:24** Hebrew *an ephah* [20 quarts or 22 liters] *of flour . . . and a hin* [3.8 liters] *of olive oil.* **45:25** Hebrew *the festival which begins on the fifteenth day of the seventh month* (see Lev 23:34). This day in the ancient Hebrew lunar calendar occurred in late September, October, or early November.

45:21-25 Celebrating the Passover would be renewed, as would the Festival of Shelters (also called Booths or Tabernacles), to remind the Israelites of their deliverance from Egypt (see Leviticus 23:33-43).

and then go back out the way he came. The gateway will not be closed until evening. [3]The
common people will bow down and worship the LORD in front of this gateway on Sabbath
days and the days of new moon celebrations.
[4]"Each Sabbath day the prince will present to the LORD a burnt offering of six lambs and
one ram, all with no defects. [5]He will present a grain offering of a basket of choice flour to
go with the ram and whatever amount of flour he chooses to go with each lamb, and he is
to offer one gallon of olive oil* for each basket of flour. [6]At the new moon celebrations, he
will bring one young bull, six lambs, and one ram, all with no defects. [7]With the young bull
he must bring a basket of choice flour for a grain offering. With the ram he must bring an-
other basket of flour. And with each lamb he is to bring whatever amount of flour he
chooses to give. With each basket of flour he must offer one gallon of olive oil.
[8]"The prince must enter the gateway through the entry room, and he must leave the
same way. [9]But when the people come in through the north gateway to worship the LORD
during the religious festivals, they must leave by the south gateway. And those who en-
tered through the south gateway must leave by the north gateway. They must never leave
by the same gateway they came in, but must always use the opposite gateway. [10]The
prince will enter and leave with the people on these occasions.
[11]"So at the special feasts and sacred festivals, the grain offering will be a basket of choice
flour with each young bull, another basket of flour with each ram, and as much flour as the
prince chooses to give with each lamb. Give one gallon of olive oil with each basket of flour.
[12]When the prince offers a voluntary burnt offering or peace offering to the LORD, the east
gateway to the inner courtyard will be opened for him, and he will offer his sacrifices as he
does on Sabbath days. Then he will leave, and the gateway will be shut behind him.
[13]"Each morning you must sacrifice a one-year-old lamb with no defects as a burnt of-
fering to the LORD. [14]With the lamb, a grain offering must also be given to the LORD—about
three quarts of flour with a third of a gallon of olive oil* to moisten the choice flour. This
will be a permanent law for you. [15]The lamb, the grain offering, and the olive oil must be
given as a daily sacrifice every morning without fail.
[16]"This is what the Sovereign LORD says: If the prince gives a gift of land to one of his
sons as his inheritance, it will belong to him and his descendants forever. [17]But if the
prince gives a gift of land from his inheritance to one of his servants, the servant may keep
it only until the Year of Jubilee, which comes every fiftieth year.* At that time the land will

46:3 Luke 1:10
46:4 Ezek 45:17
46:5 Ezek 45:24
46:7 Deut 16:17
46:8 Ezek 44:1-3
46:9 Ps 84:7
46:10 2 Chr 6:3; 7:4 Ps 42:4
46:11 Ezek 45:17
46:12 Lev 23:38 2 Chr 29:31 Ezek 44:3; 45:17
46:13 Exod 29:38 Num 28:3-4 Isa 50:4
46:14 Exod 29:42 Num 28:5-6
46:15 Exod 29:42 Num 28:6
46:16 2 Chr 21:3
46:17 Lev 25:10

46:5 Hebrew *an ephah* [20 quarts or 22 liters] *of choice flour . . . a hin* [3.8 liters] *of olive oil;* similarly in 46:7, 11. **46:14** Hebrew *⅙ of an ephah* [3.7 liters] *of flour with ⅓ of a hin* [1.3 liters] *of olive oil.* **46:17** Hebrew *until the Year of Release;* see Lev 25:8-17.

46:4 The Sabbath burnt offerings designated here differed from the instructions given in Numbers 28:9, where only two lambs were required. The practices of first-century priests followed the Numbers 28 pattern, showing that they understood the instructions given here to be more illustrative of the rich, effusive worship in the renewed Israel, and not literal commands.

▸ WORSHIP

46:12 Voluntary offerings. The Old Testament required many different offerings, tithes, and taxes, which could, in some years, amount to far more than ten percent of an individual's income—totaling perhaps as much as thirty percent. On top of this, God provided regulations for voluntary offerings, which people could bring for a variety of reasons, such as to give thanks, or to celebrate, or in conjunction with a vow. Taken as a whole, this system encouraged God's people to be quite generous with their money. But of course, it was often the case that the priests and the laypeople were greedy, not even wanting to give what was required to God, much less voluntary offerings (Malachi 3:8-10). Be faithful to God in your giving. And if He has blessed you with an abundance, or if you are particularly thankful for some way He has blessed you, or if you take a special vow, consider giving even more to Him as a voluntary offering. (***See Worship****> OT> Offerings> Other Sacrifices> Tithing,* TopicGuide page A27.)

▸ ADOPTION

46:16-18 Heirs and rulers. In Israel, land was extremely important. Land rights for Jewish tribes and families were permanent from the time they conquered the Promised Land (Leviticus 25:23-25). This mirrored the permanence of God's salvation of Israel from Egypt. Similarly, Ezekiel's affirmation of the permanence of hereditary land rights illustrated the permanence of the restoration God offered to Israel during the Babylonian captivity. Unfortunately the land was taken by foreign powers. Using similar language, Christ said that believers have a permanent inheritance in the kingdom of God (Matthew 25:34) that can never be taken away (Luke 12:33). Our Promised Land is the whole world (Romans 4:13), which we will rule over (2 Timothy 2:12) when Jesus returns and renews the creation (Revelation 21:1-5). What does this mean to us? It means this is God's world, and He's given the entire planet to us to renew and restore to His ideal (Genesis 1:27-31; Matthew 28:18-20). (***See Adoption****> With Christ> Heirs of God> We shall reign with Him,* TopicGuide page A36.)

return to the prince. But when the prince gives gifts to his sons, those gifts will be perma-
46:18 Ezek 45:8 Mic 2:1-2 nent. 18 And the prince may never take anyone's property by force. If he gives property to
his sons, it must be from his own land, for I do not want any of My people unjustly evicted
from their property."

THE TEMPLE KITCHENS

19 In my vision, the man brought me through the entrance beside the gateway and led me
to the sacred rooms assigned to the priests, which faced toward the north. He showed me
46:20 Lev 2:4-7 2 Chr 35:13 a place at the extreme west end of these rooms. 20 He explained, "This is where the priests
will cook the meat from the guilt offerings and sin offerings and bake the flour from the
grain offerings into bread. They will do it here to avoid carrying the sacrifices through the
outer courtyard and endangering the people by transmitting holiness to them."

21 Then he brought me back to the outer courtyard and led me to each of its four corners.
In each corner I saw an enclosure. 22 Each of these enclosures was 70 feet long and 52½
feet wide,* surrounded by walls. 23 Along the inside of these walls was a ledge of stone with
fireplaces under the ledge all the way around. 24 The man said to me, "These are the kitch-
ens to be used by the Temple assistants to boil the sacrifices offered by the people."

THE RIVER OF HEALING

47:1 Ps 46:4 Joel 2:13 Zech 13:1 Rev 22:1, 17

47 In my vision, the man brought me back to the entrance of the Temple. There I
saw a stream flowing east from beneath the door of the Temple and passing to
the right of the altar on its south side. 2 The man brought me outside the wall through the
47:5 Isa 11:9 Hab 2:14 north gateway and led me around to the eastern entrance. There I could see the water
flowing out through the south side of the east gateway.

3 Measuring as he went, he took me along the stream for 1,750 feet* and then led me
47:7 Isa 60:21; 61:3 Rev 22:2 across. The water was up to my ankles. 4 He measured off another 1,750 feet and led me
across again. This time the water was up to my knees. After another 1,750 feet, it was up
47:8 Deut 3:17 Isa 35:6-7; 41:17-19; 44:3 to my waist. 5 Then he measured another 1,750 feet, and the river was too deep to walk
across. It was deep enough to swim in, but too deep to walk through.

6 He asked me, "Have you been watching, son of man?" Then he led me back along the
47:9 Isa 12:3 John 4:14; 7:37-38 Rev 21:6 riverbank. 7 When I returned, I was surprised by the sight of many trees growing on both
sides of the river. 8 Then he said to me, "This river flows east through the desert into the
valley of the Dead Sea.* The waters of this stream will make the salty waters of the Dead
47:10 Num 34:6 2 Chr 20:2 Ps 104:25 Ezek 26:5; 48:28 Matt 13:47 Luke 5:5-9 Sea fresh and pure. 9 There will be swarms of living things wherever the water of this river
flows. Fish will abound in the Dead Sea, for its waters will become fresh. Life will flourish
wherever this water flows. 10 Fishermen will stand along the shores of the Dead Sea. All the
way from En-gedi to En-eglaim, the shores will be covered with nets drying in the sun. Fish
of every kind will fill the Dead Sea, just as they fill the Mediterranean.* 11 But the marshes

46:22 Hebrew *40 cubits* [21.2 meters] *long and 30 cubits* [15.9 meters] *wide.* **47:3** Hebrew *1,000 cubits* [530 meters]; also in 47:4, 5. **47:8** Hebrew *the sea.* **47:10** Hebrew *the great sea;* also in 47:15, 17, 19, 20.

46:20 Old Covenant worship combined prayer and sacrifice with a communal meal. The regulations here specified where and how the Levites would serve the sacrificial meals to the worshipers. New Covenant worship also includes a meal celebrating the once-for-all sacrifice of Jesus Christ (1 Corinthians 11:17-33).

47:1-12 Ezekiel watched as a stream turned into a river flowing eastward from the entrance to the Temple. It cleansed the Dead Sea and populated it with marine life that was good for food. Trees grew on each side of the river, providing fruit for food and leaves for healing. This river was reminiscent of the four rivers flowing from Eden (Genesis 2:10-14) and anticipated the river flowing from God's throne in the new heaven and earth (Revelation 22:1-2).

▸ GOD

47:2-9 Living water. Ezekiel described life-giving, fresh water, suitable for drinking and for irrigation, flowing from the Temple. This miraculous water would cure all ailments and turn saltwater into fresh. In the New Testament, Jesus indicated that Ezekiel's vision would ultimately be fulfilled by the Holy Spirit (John 7:38-39), who gives life to our own spirits (John 3:6; 6:63) and will resurrect our bodies on the last day (Romans 8:9-11). This should inspire us to turn to the Spirit for all His life-giving blessings. We cannot expect to have the cure within ourselves for the sin and sickness that we encounter in this world. Only the Holy Spirit can cleanse us and prepare us for serving Him here and worshiping Him in heaven (Titus 3:6). (***See God***> *Salvation> Holy Spirit> Provides new life,* TopicGuide page A15.)

and swamps will not be purified; they will still be salty. 12 Fruit trees of all kinds will grow
along both sides of the river. The leaves of these trees will never turn brown and fall, and
there will always be fruit on their branches. There will be a new crop every month, for they
are watered by the river flowing from the Temple. The fruit will be for food and the leaves
for healing."

BOUNDARIES FOR THE LAND

13 This is what the Sovereign LORD says: "Divide the land in this way for the twelve tribes of
Israel: The descendants of Joseph will be given two shares of land.* 14 Otherwise each tribe
will receive an equal share. I took a solemn oath and swore that I would give this land to
your ancestors, and it will now come to you as your possession.

15 "These are the boundaries of the land: The northern border will run from the
Mediterranean toward Hethlon, then on through Lebo-hamath to Zedad; 16 then it will
run to Berothah and Sibraim, which are on the border between Damascus and
Hamath, and finally to Hazer-hatticon, on the border of Hauran. 17 So the northern
border will run from the Mediterranean to Hazar-enan, on the border between
Hamath to the north and Damascus to the south.

18 "The eastern border starts at a point between Hauran and Damascus and runs
south along the Jordan River between Israel and Gilead, past the Dead Sea* and as
far south as Tamar.* This will be the eastern border.

19 "The southern border will go west from Tamar to the waters of Meribah at Ka-
desh* and then follow the course of the Brook of Egypt to the Mediterranean. This
will be the southern border.

20 "On the west side, the Mediterranean itself will be your border from the southern
border to the point where the northern border begins, opposite Lebo-hamath.

21 "Divide the land within these boundaries among the tribes of Israel. 22 Distribute the land
as an allotment for yourselves and for the foreigners who have joined you and are raising
their families among you. They will be like native-born Israelites to you and will receive an
allotment among the tribes. 23 These foreigners are to be given land within the territory of
the tribe with whom they now live. I, the Sovereign LORD, have spoken!

DIVISION OF THE LAND

48 "Here is the list of the tribes of Israel and the territory each is to receive. The terri-
tory of Dan is in the extreme north. Its boundary line follows the Hethlon road to
Lebo-hamath and then runs on to Hazar-enan on the border of Damascus, with Hamath to
the north. Dan's territory extends all the way across the land of Israel from east to west.

47:12 Gen 2:9; Ps 1:3; Jer 17:8; Rev 22:2
47:13 Gen 48:5; Num 34:1-13; 1 Chr 5:1; Ezek 48:4-5
47:14 Gen 12:7; Deut 1:8; Ezek 20:5-6
47:15 Num 34:7-9; Ezek 48:1
47:16 Num 13:21; 1 Kgs 8:65
47:17 Num 34:9; Ezek 48:1
47:18 Gen 13:10-11; Num 34:10-12
47:19 Num 34:3-5; Deut 32:51; Isa 27:12
47:20 Num 34:6
47:22 Isa 14:1; 56:6-7; Acts 11:18; Rom 10:12; Eph 2:12-14; Col 3:11
48:1 Exod 1:1; Josh 19:40-48

47:13 It was important to retain twelve portions of land. Since Levi had no portion, the descendants of Joseph's sons, Ephraim and Manasseh, received land as two tribes. 47:18a Hebrew *the eastern sea.* 47:18b As in Greek version; Hebrew reads *you will measure.* 47:19 Hebrew *waters of Meribath-kadesh.*

47:13–48:29 The land allotments for the 12 tribes of Israel given here correspond in principle to the division of the land after the conquest under Joshua (see Joshua 13–21). But in Ezekiel's description, the land would be portioned quite differently—in horizontal stripes. Each tribe would be positioned either above or below the others, with its territory extending from the eastern to the western borders of the Promised Land. There would be some movement from north to south as well, Zebulun, Issachar, and Gad would be south of Jerusalem.

▸ ADOPTION
47:22-23 Jews and Gentiles united. In the restored kingdom, Gentiles would be heirs along with Israel in the Promised Land, even gaining a permanent inheritance of real estate. This was a radical change from the original distribution of the land, in which only the Israelites received portions. Ezekiel's vision corresponded to the promise to Abraham that all nations would be blessed through his son Isaac (Genesis 22:18) and to Isaiah's visions of the future (Isaiah 56:3-8). But this promise was never realized in the Old Testament. Instead, it is being fulfilled in Christ, who has abolished the distinctions between Jewish and Gentile believers (Ephesians 2:11-22), giving us all a share of His own inheritance (Galatians 3:27-29). This racial reconciliation between Jews and Gentiles in Christ should not only give us joy, but also cause us to see every believer as united in Christ and inspire us to work toward the social reconciliation of all races in the church. (***See Adoption****> With Christ> Heirs of God> Inheritance shared by Jews and Gentiles alike,* TopicGuide page A36.)

2"Asher's territory lies south of Dan's and also extends from east to west. 3Naphtali's
land lies south of Asher's, also extending from east to west. 4Then comes Manasseh south
of Naphtali, and its territory also extends from east to west. 5South of Manasseh is Ephra-
im, 6and then Reuben, 7and then Judah, all of whose boundaries extend from east to west.
8"South of Judah is the land set aside for a special purpose. It will be 8⅓ miles* wide and
will extend as far east and west as the tribal territories, with the Temple at the center.
9"The area set aside for the LORD's Temple will be 8⅓ miles long and 6⅔ miles wide.*
10For the priests there will be a strip of land measuring 8⅓ miles long by 3⅓ miles wide,*
with the LORD's Temple at the center. 11This area is set aside for the ordained priests, the
descendants of Zadok who served Me faithfully and did not go astray with the people of
Israel and the rest of the Levites. 12It will be their special portion when the land is distrib-
uted, the most sacred land of all. Next to the priests' territory will lie the land where the
other Levites will live.

13"The land allotted to the Levites will be the same size and shape as that belonging to
the priests—8⅓ miles long and 3⅓ miles wide. Together these portions of land will mea-
sure 8⅓ miles long by 6⅔ miles wide.* 14None of this special land may ever be sold or
traded or used by others, for it belongs to the LORD; it is set apart as holy.

15"An additional strip of land 8⅓ miles long by 1⅔ miles wide,* south of the sacred
Temple area, will be allotted for public use—homes, pasturelands, and common lands,
with a city at the center. 16The city will measure 1½ miles* on each side—north, south,
east, and west. 17Open lands will surround the city for 150 yards* in every direction.
18Outside the city there will be a farming area that stretches 3⅓ miles to the east and 3⅓
miles to the west* along the border of the sacred area. This farmland will produce food for
the people working in the city. 19Those who come from the various tribes to work in the
city may farm it. 20This entire area—including the sacred lands and the city—is a square
that measures 8⅓ miles* on each side.

21"The areas that remain, to the east and to the west of the sacred lands and the city,
will belong to the prince. Each of these areas will be 8⅓ miles wide, extending in opposite
directions to the eastern and western borders of Israel, with the sacred lands and the sanc-
tuary of the Temple in the center. 22So the prince's land will include everything between
the territories allotted to Judah and Benjamin, except for the areas set aside for the sacred
lands and the city.

23"These are the territories allotted to the rest of the tribes. Benjamin's territory lies just
south of the prince's lands, and it extends across the entire land of Israel from east to west.
24South of Benjamin's territory lies that of Simeon, also extending across the land from east
to west. 25Next is the territory of Issachar with the same eastern and western boundaries.

26"Then comes the territory of Zebulun, which also extends across the land from east to
west. 27The territory of Gad is just south of Zebulun with the same borders to the east and

48:2 Gen 30:12-13 Josh 19:24-31
48:3 Gen 30:7-8 Josh 19:32-39
48:4 Gen 30:22-24; 41:51; 48:5, 14-20 Josh 13:29-31; 17:1-11
48:5 Josh 16:5-10; 17:8-10, 14-18
48:6 Josh 13:15-21
48:7 Josh 15:1-63
48:8 Ezek 45:1-6 Rev 21:3, 22
48:10 Ezek 44:28; 45:4
48:11 Ezek 44:10-15
48:14 Lev 25:32-34
48:15 Ezek 42:20; 45:6
48:16 Rev 21:16
48:21 Ezek 34:24; 45:7
48:23 Gen 35:16-19 Josh 18:21-28
48:24 Gen 29:33; 49:5-7 Josh 19:1-9
48:25 Gen 30:14-18 Josh 19:17-23
48:26 Gen 30:19-20 Josh 19:10-16
48:27 Gen 30:10-11 Josh 13:24-28 Ezek 47:19-20

48:8 Hebrew *25,000 cubits* [13.3 kilometers]. **48:9** Reflecting one Greek manuscript and the Greek reading in 45:1: *25,000 cubits* [13.3 kilometers] *long and 20,000 cubits* [10.6 kilometers] *wide;* Hebrew reads *25,000 cubits long and 10,000 cubits* [3⅓ *miles or 5.3 kilometers] wide.* Similarly in 48:13b. Compare 45:1-5; 48:10-13. **48:10** Hebrew *25,000 cubits* [13.3 kilometers] *long by 10,000 cubits* [5.3 kilometers] *wide;* also in 48:13a. **48:13** See note on 48:9. **48:15** Hebrew *25,000 cubits* [13.3 kilometers] *long by 5,000 cubits* [2.65 kilometers] *wide.* **48:16** Hebrew *4,500 cubits* [2.4 kilometers]; also in 48:30, 32, 33, 34. **48:17** Hebrew *250 cubits* [133 meters]. **48:18** Hebrew *10,000 cubits* [5.3 kilometers] *to the east and 10,000 cubits to the west.* **48:20** Hebrew *25,000 cubits* [13.3 kilometers]; also in 48:21.

48:4-5 The tribe of Joseph received a double portion, which was divided between the descendants of Joseph's sons, Ephraim and Manasseh. The double portion traditionally went to the oldest son (Deuteronomy 21:17), but this birthright could be transferred voluntarily (Genesis 25:33) or revoked. In the idealized land allotment of Ezekiel, the boundaries changed, but even in the ideal world Joseph's sons, Ephraim and Manasseh, kept his double portion, which had been taken from the unworthy firstborn, Reuben (1 Chronicles 5:1).

48:8-22 The book of Ezekiel describes the nature of the restored Israel by carefully unfolding the new Temple (Ezekiel 40–42), the new land (Ezekiel 47–48), and then a special, central portion of land reexamined here (see also Ezekiel 45:1-8). In particular, it focuses on the southern strip of land that would have the holy Temple upon it (48:8). This would be the "prince's land" (48:22), so it has royal connotations as well as religious. These two concepts were never far separated in ancient Israel.

west. 28The southern border of Gad runs from Tamar to the waters of Meribah at Kadesh*
and then follows the Brook of Egypt to the Mediterranean.*
29"These are the allotments that will be set aside for each tribe's exclusive possession. I,
the Sovereign LORD, have spoken!

48:28 Num 34:6
48:29 Ezek 47:13-23

THE GATES OF THE CITY

30"These will be the exits to the city: On the north wall, which is 1½ miles long, 31there will
be three gates, each one named after a tribe of Israel. The first will be named for Reuben,
the second for Judah, and the third for Levi. 32On the east wall, also 1½ miles long, the
gates will be named for Joseph, Benjamin, and Dan. 33The south wall, also 1½ miles long,
will have gates named for Simeon, Issachar, and Zebulun. 34And on the west wall, also 1½
miles long, the gates will be named for Gad, Asher, and Naphtali.
35"The distance around the entire city will be 6 miles.* And from that day the name of
the city will be 'The LORD Is There.'*"

48:31 Rev 21:12-13
48:35 Isa 12:6; 24:23; Jer 3:17; 23:6; 33:16; Joel 3:21; Zech 2:10; Rev 21:3; 22:3

48:28a Hebrew *waters of Meribah-kadesh.* 48:28b Hebrew *the great sea.* 48:35a Hebrew *18,000 cubits* [9.6 kilometers].
48:35b Hebrew *Yahweh Shammah.*

48:30-35 The city of God's dwelling was not named, but it must have been Jerusalem, the city where God's Temple was (48:22). Before the conquest of the land under Joshua, the twelve tribes camped around the four sides of the Tabernacle, three on each side (see Numbers 2). The New Jerusalem will have three gates on each of the four walls around the city named after the twelve tribes (see also Revelation 21:12-13). Ezekiel ends with a wonderful promise for God's people regarding His eternal presence with them: The city will be named "The LORD Is There."

▸ MINISTRY

48:35 The LORD Is There. The great hope of ancient Israel was that God would dwell in their midst as their king, protecting them from their enemies, blessing them with health and good crops, and dwelling with them in fellowship (Exodus 33:15-17). Through Christ, we are counted as being perfectly faithful to God, so that every blessing that the Lord ever offered, both to Abraham (Galatians 3:9-14) and to his descendants are now being realized in us (Ephesians 1:3-14), including the promise to be present with us (Matthew 28:20). We are the temple that God dwells in (1 Corinthians 3:16; Ephesians 2:20-22)—the Lord is *here*! In Christ, you have inherited, and will receive in full, the world (Romans 4:13; 2 Peter 3:13; Revelation 1:5-6). But not the sinful world—a world with God in our midst (Revelation 21:2). This is the fulfillment of the vision of renewed worship that Ezekiel foretold. We await that day and cry, "Come, Lord Jesus! Come in Your fullness!" (Revelation 22:20). (***See Ministry***> *Great Commission> Make Disciples> Disciples enjoy God's presence,* TopicGuide page A56.)

DANIEL

PURPOSE

To declare the sovereignty of God over all world rulers and kingdoms as an encouragement to Jewish exiles in Babylon and those returning to Israel.

One theme dominates the book of Daniel: kingdoms. Through Daniel's personal experiences in the royal court of Babylon and through his visions, God taught His people vital lessons about human and divine kingdoms.

As a young man, Daniel was part of a group of Israelites exiled to Babylon from Jerusalem in 605 BC. He quickly rose through the ranks (along with his friends Shadrach, Meshach, and Abednego) as a wise and trusted counselor to the royal court. God revealed to Daniel sweeping vistas of present and future events related to Babylon and kingdoms that would follow. But the most far-reaching of Daniel's visions concerned the ultimate establishment of the Kingdom of God—a kingdom that would have no end.

DISCOVER GOD IN DANIEL

Daniel is a book that reveals the "size" of God: He is bigger in every way than all the rulers who might challenge His authority. The attributes of God revealed in Daniel confirm this:

Omniscience: The king of Babylon had a dream he could not understand, so he called in his wise men to tell him its meaning. But the king required the wise men to prove their supernatural ability by revealing not just the meaning of the dream but the dream itself. The wise men protested that no one could know another person's dream, but the king stood firm. When the wise men failed the king's test, Daniel asked for permission to try, and "that night the secret was revealed to Daniel in a vision" (Daniel 2:19). With gratitude, Daniel praised God for His omniscience—His knowledge of everything: "He reveals deep and mysterious things and knows what lies hidden in darkness, though He is surrounded by light" (2:22). God's all-knowing nature is both a warning and a comfort: We cannot hide things from God, but we can take comfort in that fact, because He knows everything (Acts 5:1-11).

Sovereignty: Since the Creation, a drama has been played out on the stage of world history. The script was written beforehand, but the drama's protagonist (God) and antagonist (Satan) continue to play out every scene. At stake is world dominion, now and for eternity. At present, Satan is allowed to empower earthly rulers to contest the purposes of God (1 John 5:19). But the prophecies of Daniel reveal clearly that all human kingdoms are only temporary and that God is sovereignly working through the events of world history to confound the efforts of His enemies, whether natural or supernatural. The kingdoms of this world will one day cease to exist, and God's kingdom will be established forever (Daniel 2:44; 4:17; 7:27). Amid the clash of earthly kingdoms, it is comforting to know that every moment brings us closer to the day when God's kingdom will be established forever.

Warrior: After the Hebrews passed safely through the Red Sea and the waters covered over the Egyptian armies, Moses and his sister Miriam sang a song of triumph: "The Lord is a warrior; Yahweh is His name!" (Exodus 15:3). This warrior side of God's character is revealed dramatically again in Daniel 10. Daniel had been praying about something for three weeks. When an angel finally arrived to deliver the answer to his prayer, the angel's explanation for his delayed arrival was astounding: He had been engaged in spiritual warfare with a demonic power in the heavenly realms (10:12-13). Only with the assistance of Michael, the archangel, did he break free to attend to Daniel's prayer. God is a warrior, employing His heavenly hosts whenever and wherever needed to bring victory and success to His people (Psalm 103:20-21; Hebrews 1:14).

DISCOVERY VERSES

Praise the name of God forever and ever, for He has all wisdom and power. He controls the course of world events; He removes kings and sets up other kings. He gives wisdom to the wise and knowledge to the scholars. He reveals deep and mysterious things and knows what lies hidden in darkness, though He is surrounded by light. (DANIEL 2:20-22)

As my vision continued that night, I saw someone like a son of man coming with the clouds of heaven. He approached the Ancient One and was led into His presence. He was given authority, honor, and sovereignty over all the nations of the world, so that people of every race and nation and language would obey Him. His rule is eternal—it will never end. His kingdom will never be destroyed. (DANIEL 7:13-14)

GROWING THROUGH DANIEL

Daniel and his three friends displayed great characteristics of faith during their days in Babylon:

Courage: When Daniel's enemies leveled trumped-up charges of treason against him, Daniel did not grovel or defend himself before the king. He was thrown into a den of lions to be devoured, but his courage and faith sustained him (Daniel 6). Courage is a mark of those who trust in One they know to be greater than any danger.

Obedience: Daniel's three friends were charged with disobeying a royal decree to bow to an image of the king. But Shadrach, Meshach, and Abednego knew that the worship of an idol was forbidden by the stipulations of God's covenant with Israel (Exodus 20:5). When the king threatened to have Daniel's friends thrown into a blazing furnace if they would not comply with his command, they replied that while God might or might not rescue them from the furnace, they would choose death over disobedience (Daniel 3:16-18). Whenever human laws violate God's laws, the disciple of Christ must always choose obedience, no matter what consequences this choice may bring (Acts 4:19-20; 5:29).

Spiritual Discipline: Daniel was a godly young man living in an ungodly environment. Three times a day, Daniel prayed facing west, toward Jerusalem (see 2 Chronicles 6:38-39). In a moment of crisis, his enemies found him praying, not worrying (6:10-11). In the midst of a foreign nation, surrounded by unbelievers, Daniel deepened his intimacy with God through regular prayer.

DANIEL FACTS

Author: Daniel is addressed as the recipient of the prophecies in 12:4, and he related his activities in the first person beginning in 7:2 (see also 9:2; 10:2). Jesus Christ also referred to this book as having been written by Daniel (Matthew 24:15, quoting Daniel 9:27; 11:31; 12:11).

Written to: Daniel's prophecies were delivered to the pagan kings of Babylon and Persia, but his overall message was for the exiled Jewish community.

Date of writing: Daniel finished his work by 530 BC.

Setting: The prophecies of Daniel were delivered in Mesopotamia (modern Iraq), where Daniel was in service to Babylon and, later, the Medo-Persian Empire.

OUTLINE

- **DANIEL 1:1–6:28**—Daniel's Experiences in Exile
- **DANIEL 7:1–12:13**—Daniel's Visions in Exile

DANIEL IN NEBUCHADNEZZAR'S COURT

1:1 2 Kgs 24:1; 2 Chr 36:6
1 During the third year of King Jehoiakim's reign in Judah,* King Nebuchadnezzar of
Babylon came to Jerusalem and besieged it. 2The LORD gave him victory over King
1:2 Isa 11:11; Jer 27:19-20; Zech 5:5-11
Jehoiakim of Judah and permitted him to take some of the sacred objects from the Temple
of God. So Nebuchadnezzar took them back to the land of Babylonia* and placed them in
the treasure-house of his god.

1:3 Isa 39:7
3Then the king ordered Ashpenaz, his chief of staff, to bring to the palace some of the
young men of Judah's royal family and other noble families, who had been brought to
Babylon as captives. 4"Select only strong, healthy, and good-looking young men," he said.
"Make sure they are well versed in every branch of learning, are gifted with knowledge
and good judgment, and are suited to serve in the royal palace. Train these young men in
1:5 Dan 1:8, 19
the language and literature of Babylon.*" 5The king assigned them a daily ration of food
and wine from his own kitchens. They were to be trained for three years, and then they
would enter the royal service.

1:6 Ezek 14:14, 20; 28:3; Matt 24:15
6Daniel, Hananiah, Mishael, and Azariah were four of the young men chosen, all from
the tribe of Judah. 7The chief of staff renamed them with these Babylonian names:

1:7 Dan 2:49; 3:12-30; 4:8; 5:12
Daniel was called Belteshazzar.
Hananiah was called Shadrach.
Mishael was called Meshach.
Azariah was called Abednego.

1:1 This event occurred in 605 B.C., during the third year of Jehoiakim's reign (according to the calendar system in which the new year begins in the spring). 1:2 Hebrew *the land of Shinar.* 1:4 Or *of the Chaldeans.*

1:1 The story of Daniel begins in the waning years of the Judean monarchy. Josiah was killed attempting to intervene in the battle of Carchemish. The kings who succeeded him were all puppet kings under either the Egyptians or the Babylonians. The events described in these verses are difficult to correlate with other extant biblical and extrabiblical data with any certainty. Yet, it seems that in 605 BC, Judah, along with other smaller states in the region, became vassals of Babylon. Nominal tokens of submission were exacted such as the taking of captives and temple vessels. This began the three years of submission related in 2 Kings 24:1.

1:2 Daniel states that the Lord "gave" King Nebuchadnezzar victory over King Jehoiakim. This word "gave" occurs in three places in chapter 1 (see also 1:9, 17). The implication is that God Himself delivered Jerusalem to Nebuchadnezzar, affirming that, despite appearances to the contrary, God was still in control. If God was the One who gave Jerusalem to Babylon, then God could deliver Jerusalem from Babylon. The eyes of faith recognize that even though Nebuchadnezzar had put the articles of the Temple in his treasury and attributed the victory to his gods, it was actually the God of Israel who had allowed him to succeed.

TAKEN TO BABYLON
Daniel, as a captive of Babylonian soldiers, faced a long and difficult march to a new land. The 500-mile trek, under harsh conditions, certainly tested his faith in God.

▸ BIBLE

1:3-7 Worldly influences. Daniel and his three friends were in a tough spot. The Babylonian king had ordered these promising young men to be thoroughly trained in Babylonian culture and religion. Even their names were changed to show submission to Babylonian gods. The goal of all this was to foster conformity in the bright young leaders in Israel, starting with small acts of compliance and eventually leading to complete assimilation. Small compromises often seem insignificant at first, but they pile up and eventually lead to a life that is indistinguishable from that of a non-Christian (Revelation 3:15-18). Jesus does not want you to "copy the behavior and customs of this world" (Romans 12:2) but rather to be in the world—but not of it (John 17:15); to be "as shrewd as snakes and harmless as doves" (Matthew 10:16). Ask Jesus to help you resist conformity with the sinful world so that He can use you to bring the world into conformity with His purposes (Matthew 5:13-16). (***See Bible***> *Power> Worldview> Discernment against worldly philosophy*, TopicGuide page A12.)

1:4-5 The expanding Babylonian Empire required a bureaucratic infrastructure that was too vast to be handled by the Babylonian population alone, so qualified exiles from subdued nations were trained and called on to fill necessary roles.

8But Daniel was determined not to defile himself by eating the food and wine given to
them by the king. He asked the chief of staff for permission not to eat these unacceptable
foods. 9Now God had given the chief of staff both respect and affection for Daniel. 10But he
responded, "I am afraid of my lord the king, who has ordered that you eat this food and
wine. If you become pale and thin compared to the other youths your age, I am afraid the
king will have me beheaded."
11Daniel spoke with the attendant who had been appointed by the chief of staff to look af-
ter Daniel, Hananiah, Mishael, and Azariah. 12"Please test us for ten days on a diet of vegeta-
bles and water," Daniel said. 13"At the end of the ten days, see how we look compared to the
other young men who are eating the king's food. Then make your decision in light of what
you see." 14The attendant agreed to Daniel's suggestion and tested them for ten days.
15At the end of the ten days, Daniel and his three friends looked healthier and better nour-
ished than the young men who had been eating the food assigned by the king. 16So after that,
the attendant fed them only vegetables instead of the food and wine provided for the others.
17God gave these four young men an unusual aptitude for understanding every aspect
of literature and wisdom. And God gave Daniel the special ability to interpret the mean-
ings of visions and dreams.
18When the training period ordered by the king was completed, the chief of staff
brought all the young men to King Nebuchadnezzar. 19The king talked with them, and no
one impressed him as much as Daniel, Hananiah, Mishael, and Azariah. So they entered
the royal service. 20Whenever the king consulted them in any matter requiring wisdom
and balanced judgment, he found them ten times more capable than any of the magicians
and enchanters in his entire kingdom.
21Daniel remained in the royal service until the first year of the reign of King Cyrus.*

NEBUCHADNEZZAR'S DREAM

2 One night during the second year of his reign,* Nebuchadnezzar had such disturbing
dreams that he couldn't sleep. 2He called in his magicians, enchanters, sorcerers, and

1:8 Lev 11:47; Deut 32:38; Ezek 4:13-14; Hos 9:3
1:9 Ps 106:46; Prov 16:7
1:12 Dan 1:16
1:15 Exod 23:25; Prov 10:22
1:16 Dan 1:12
1:17 1 Kgs 3:12, 28; Job 32:8; Dan 1:20; 2:19; 7:1; 8:1
1:19 Gen 41:46; Jer 15:1; Dan 1:5
1:20 Num 14:22; Isa 19:3; Dan 1:17; 2:2, 27-28; 4:18; 5:7
1:21 Dan 6:28; 10:1
2:1 Gen 40:5-8; 41:1, 8; Esth 6:1; Job 33:15-17; Dan 6:18

1:21 Cyrus began his reign (over Babylon) in 539 B.C. 2:1 The second year of Nebuchadnezzar's reign was 603 B.C.

1:8 Sometimes it is assumed that Daniel was attempting to uphold Levitical dietary standards by abstaining from the king's food. However, there is nothing in the dietary law that prohibits the consumption of wine for anyone except a Nazirite. Furthermore, later in the book it is implied that Daniel had no problem consuming these foods (10:2-3). It is likely that Daniel was seeking to protect his identity and strengthen his faith by abstaining from certain foods.

▶ GOD

1:17-20 God on stage. Imagine you are in Jerusalem. You hear Jesus teaching the crowds. You see Him doing miracles. Would you ever dream of jumping in and trying to upstage Him? The idea seems ludicrous. Yet we do something like this whenever we boast in the gifts we have received. Whenever you attempt to seek full credit for something you've done and make no effort to redirect the honor to God, you act as if you deserve all the praise. It is not wrong to thank others for their words of kindness, but it is another thing altogether to gloat as if you are something great (Acts 12:22-23). "If everything you have is from God, why boast as though it were not a gift?" (1 Corinthians 4:7). (***See God****> God's Names> Holy Spirit> Gives gifts,* TopicGuide page A19.)

1:21 The opening verse of this chapter referenced Nebuchadnezzar's capture of Jerusalem, and here we read that Daniel remained in the royal service until the reign of Cyrus, the king of Persia who eventually defeated Babylon. The implicit message is that Daniel, the servant of God, outlasted even Babylon, and God is greater than any human kingdom. This provided hope for those living in exile in Babylon.

▶ WORSHIP

2:1-3 Prophetic dreams. There are people housed in mental institutions who believe they receive direct messages from God. Others lie about hearing messages from God. Others have religious experiences that make it seem to them as though God is communicating with them. In this story, however, Nebuchadnezzar received a legitimate message from God through a dream. Later, Daniel also received a message from God in a dream: the interpretation of the king's dream (2:19). Does this mean that we should understand all our dreams to be messages from God? No. Some passages of Scripture, like this one, are descriptive, showing us accurate history but without implying that we should attempt to recreate that history in our lives. When you read passages like this, look for other passages that give explicit teaching about the topic, and always interpret your religious experiences with Scripture, not the other way around. (***See Worship****> OT> Prophets> Test of the prophet,* TopicGuide page A28.)

2:2 Dreams, particularly those of leaders, carried great significance in the ancient world. The king's anxiety may have been aroused because he was unable to remember the contents of the dream; to have forgotten a dream was considered a bad omen.

ACCOMPLISH IT ALL

AS A YOUNG MAN, Chet was a salesman and a coach. At the time, he wasn't interested in spiritual matters; instead he threw himself into his other activities. But God had other plans. Chet became a Christian and quickly sensed a call into pastoral ministry. Many years later, Chet looked back on his early life and realized that the Lord had been preparing him for the ministry through his various activities. God was always at work, giving him the people skills that helped him tremendously in his pastoral position.

A young woman, Jennifer, felt led to homeschool her children because the local schools were substandard. Year after year, she faithfully taught her children. One year her church launched an after-school program to tutor elementary age children while presenting the gospel. Since she knew the subject areas all the way through those grade levels, she jumped into the program with both feet. What God had led her to do at home provided her with the experience she needed to begin a vital new ministry in her community.

Young Daniel, serving in a foreign court, wanted to serve God in his new surroundings, but how? God was faithful and gave him the opportunity to serve Him. And He can do it for you, too. Paul writes, "Now you have every spiritual gift you need as you eagerly wait for the return of our Lord Jesus Christ. He will keep you strong to the end. . . . God will do this, for He is faithful to do what He says" (1 Corinthians 1:7-9).

Do you feel as if you might fall short of the tasks God has called you to? How can you be so sure that God will equip you to do what He asks of you? First Peter 4:19 assures, "Keep on doing what is right, and trust your lives to the God who created you, for He will never fail you."

What is it that God has asked you to do in this time and place? Do your knees quake whenever you think about sharing your faith? Has God called you to participate in a ministry that is more difficult than anything you have ever done before? Think about what God asked of His Son, Jesus. He endured the humiliation of the cross for our sakes. God the Father provided Jesus with everything necessary to accomplish the task completely. God will help you in the same way. He is faithful to keep His promises. Step out in faith and accomplish whatever He has asked you to do.

astrologers,* and he demanded that they tell him what he had dreamed. As they stood
before the king, 3he said, "I have had a dream that deeply troubles me, and I must know
what it means."
4Then the astrologers answered the king in Aramaic,* "Long live the king! Tell us the
dream, and we will tell you what it means."
5But the king said to the astrologers, "I am serious about this. If you don't tell me what
my dream was and what it means, you will be torn limb from limb, and your houses will be
turned into heaps of rubble! 6But if you tell me what I dreamed and what the dream means,
I will give you many wonderful gifts and honors. Just tell me the dream and what it means!"
7They said again, "Please, Your Majesty. Tell us the dream, and we will tell you what it
means."
8The king replied, "I know what you are doing! You're stalling for time because you
know I am serious when I say, 9'If you don't tell me the dream, you are doomed.' So you
have conspired to tell me lies, hoping I will change my mind. But tell me the dream, and
then I'll know that you can tell me what it means."
10The astrologers replied to the king, "No one on earth can tell the king his dream! And
no king, however great and powerful, has ever asked such a thing of any magician, en-
chanter, or astrologer! 11The king's demand is impossible. No one except the gods can tell
you your dream, and they do not live here among people."
12The king was furious when he heard this, and he ordered that all the wise men of Bab-
ylon be executed. 13And because of the king's decree, men were sent to find and kill Dan-
iel and his friends.
14When Arioch, the commander of the king's guard, came to kill them, Daniel handled
the situation with wisdom and discretion. 15He asked Arioch, "Why has the king issued
such a harsh decree?" So Arioch told him all that had happened. 16Daniel went at once to
see the king and requested more time to tell the king what the dream meant.
17Then Daniel went home and told his friends Hananiah, Mishael, and Azariah what
had happened. 18He urged them to ask the God of heaven to show them His mercy by tell-
ing them the secret, so they would not be executed along with the other wise men of Bab-
ylon. 19That night the secret was revealed to Daniel in a vision. Then Daniel praised the
God of heaven. 20He said,

"Praise the name of God forever and ever,
for He has all wisdom and power.
21 He controls the course of world events;
He removes kings and sets up other kings.
He gives wisdom to the wise
and knowledge to the scholars.

2:4 Ezra 4:7; Isa 36:11; Dan 3:9; 5:10
2:5 Ezra 6:11; Dan 2:12; 3:29
2:6 Dan 2:48; 5:7, 16, 29
2:9 Esth 4:11; Isa 41:22-24
2:10 Dan 2:27
2:11 Gen 41:39; Exod 29:45; Isa 57:15; Dan 5:11
2:12 Ps 76:10; Dan 2:5; 3:13
2:13 Dan 1:19-20
2:14 Dan 2:24
2:18 Gen 18:28; Isa 37:4; Jer 33:3; Ezek 36:27; Dan 2:23
2:19 Num 12:6; 2 Kgs 6:8-12; Job 33:15-16; Dan 7:2, 7
2:20 1 Chr 29:11-12; Job 12:13; Pss 103:1-2; 113:2; Dan 2:21-23
2:21 1 Kgs 3:9-10; 4:29; Job 12:18-19; Ps 75:6-7; Dan 7:25; Jas 1:5

2:2 Or *Chaldeans;* also in 2:4, 5, 10. 2:4 The original text from this point through chapter 7 is in Aramaic.

2:3-10 There were three exchanges between the king and the diviners that became increasingly intense. The king's anger grew, as did the fear of the diviners as they began to realize what the king was asking. If the king truly remembered his dream, then his actions reflected an attempt to test the worthiness of the diviners. The portrayal of the king may be the most important feature of the exchange: He was unstable, insecure, and irrational.

▸ WORSHIP

2:18-23 Focusing on God. What comes to mind when you receive something you have hoped for? Daniel knew that God is merciful, so he sought and obtained mercy from Him. In response, Daniel praised God by reviewing His nature and deeds. Daniel was not informing God of things He didn't know. Rather, he was worshiping God by speaking the truth about Him in praise. Reviewing the truth about God brings Him glory, for it openly acknowledges that He is the One who is great, not us. Your worship should proclaim the reasons God is glorious and worthy of praise. Glorifying Him is the reason you exist (1 Corinthians 10:31). As you experience and learn of God's great deeds toward His people, recall these things in your worship and give Him praise. (***See Worship****> OT> God's Supremacy> Was God-centered,* TopicGuide page A27.)

2:20-23 Although the content of the dream is as yet unknown to the reader, the prayer foreshadows the main thrust of the dream: The dream will speak of the rise and fall of empires. Daniel acknowledged that God stood behind these developments. Power and wisdom resided not with a great king or powerful magicians, but with the God of a small band of exiles.

22 He reveals deep and mysterious things
and knows what lies hidden in darkness,
though He is surrounded by light.
23 I thank and praise You, God of my ancestors,
for You have given me wisdom and strength.
You have told me what we asked of You
and revealed to us what the king demanded."

DANIEL INTERPRETS THE DREAM

24 Then Daniel went in to see Arioch, whom the king had ordered to execute the wise men of Babylon. Daniel said to him, "Don't kill the wise men. Take me to the king, and I will tell him the meaning of his dream."

25 Arioch quickly took Daniel to the king and said, "I have found one of the captives from Judah who will tell the king the meaning of his dream!"

26 The king said to Daniel (also known as Belteshazzar), "Is this true? Can you tell me what my dream was and what it means?"

27 Daniel replied, "There are no wise men, enchanters, magicians, or fortune-tellers who can reveal the king's secret. 28 But there is a God in heaven who reveals secrets, and He has shown King Nebuchadnezzar what will happen in the future. Now I will tell you your dream and the visions you saw as you lay on your bed.

29 "While Your Majesty was sleeping, you dreamed about coming events. He who reveals secrets has shown you what is going to happen. 30 And it is not because I am wiser than anyone else that I know the secret of your dream, but because God wants you to understand what was in your heart.

31 "In your vision, Your Majesty, you saw standing before you a huge, shining statue of a man. It was a frightening sight. 32 The head of the statue was made of fine gold. Its chest and arms were silver, its belly and thighs were bronze, 33 its legs were iron, and its feet were a combination of iron and baked clay. 34 As you watched, a rock was cut from a mountain,

2:22 Job 12:22; 26:6 Ps 139:12 Isa 45:7 Jer 23:24 Dan 2:19, 28 Jas 1:17 1 Jn 1:5
2:23 Gen 31:42 Dan 2:21
2:24 Dan 2:12-13 Acts 27:24
2:25 Gen 41:14 Dan 1:6; 5:13; 6:13
2:27 Dan 2:2, 10-11; 5:7-8
2:28 Gen 40:8; 41:16 Dan 2:22, 45
2:30 Gen 41:16 Ps 139:2 Isa 43:3 Dan 1:17
2:31 Hab 1:7
2:34 Dan 8:25 Zech 4:6

2:24 At a time when most wise men were fleeing Babylon, Daniel took counsel with Arioch, charged with killing the now-worthless wise men of the king. This wise alliance with a pagan mirrors Daniel's conversation with a royal official in 1:11 and prepares counter-examples for the exiles' later refusal to cooperate with Nebuchadnezzar (3:16-18).

2:29-30 Daniel displayed spiritual maturity and diplomatic skills by simultaneously honoring the king ("Your Majesty"), exalting God ("He who reveals secrets"), and humbling himself ("not because I am wiser").

BECAUSE GOD KNOWS EVERYTHING

I will go to Him with all my questions and concerns.

He controls the course of world events;
He removes kings and sets up other kings.
He gives wisdom to the wise and knowledge to the scholars.

DANIEL 2:21

FOR THE NEXT *GOD KNOWS EVERYTHING* FEATURE SEE PAGE 1762.

but not by human hands. It struck the feet of iron and clay, smashing them to bits. 35The whole statue was crushed into small pieces of iron, clay, bronze, silver, and gold. Then the wind blew them away without a trace, like chaff on a threshing floor. But the rock that knocked the statue down became a great mountain that covered the whole earth.

36"That was the dream. Now we will tell the king what it means. 37Your Majesty, you are the greatest of kings. The God of heaven has given you sovereignty, power, strength, and honor. 38He has made you the ruler over all the inhabited world and has put even the wild animals and birds under your control. You are the head of gold.

39"But after your kingdom comes to an end, another kingdom, inferior to yours, will rise to take your place. After that kingdom has fallen, yet a third kingdom, represented by bronze, will rise to rule the world. 40Following that kingdom, there will be a fourth one, as strong as iron. That kingdom will smash and crush all previous empires, just as iron smashes and crushes everything it strikes. 41The feet and toes you saw were a combination of iron and baked clay, showing that this kingdom will be divided. Like iron mixed with clay, it will have some of the strength of iron. 42But while some parts of it will be as strong as iron, other parts will be as weak as clay. 43This mixture of iron and clay also shows that these kingdoms will try to strengthen themselves by forming alliances with each other through intermarriage. But they will not hold together, just as iron and clay do not mix.

44"During the reigns of those kings, the God of heaven will set up a kingdom that will never be destroyed or conquered. It will crush all these kingdoms into nothingness, and it will stand forever. 45That is the meaning of the rock cut from the mountain, though not by human hands, that crushed to pieces the statue of iron, bronze, clay, silver, and gold. The great God was showing the king what will happen in the future. The dream is true, and its meaning is certain."

NEBUCHADNEZZAR REWARDS DANIEL

46Then King Nebuchadnezzar threw himself down before Daniel and worshiped him, and he commanded his people to offer sacrifices and burn sweet incense before him. 47The king said to Daniel, "Truly, your God is the greatest of gods, the Lord over kings, a revealer of mysteries, for you have been able to reveal this secret."

48Then the king appointed Daniel to a high position and gave him many valuable gifts. He made Daniel ruler over the whole province of Babylon, as well as chief over all his wise men. 49At Daniel's request, the king appointed Shadrach, Meshach, and Abednego to be in charge of all the affairs of the province of Babylon, while Daniel remained in the king's court.

NEBUCHADNEZZAR'S GOLD STATUE

3 King Nebuchadnezzar made a gold statue ninety feet tall and nine feet wide* and set it up on the plain of Dura in the province of Babylon. 2Then he sent messages to the high officers, officials, governors, advisers, treasurers, judges, magistrates, and all the pro-

3:1 Aramaic *60 cubits* [27 meters] *tall and 6 cubits* [2.7 meters] *wide.*

2:35 Pss 1:4; 37:10 Isa 17:13 Hos 13:3

2:37 Isa 10:8; 47:5 Jer 27:6-7 Ezek 26:7 Hos 8:10

2:38 Ps 50:10

2:40 Dan 7:7, 23

2:44 Pss 2:9; 145:13 Isa 9:6-7; 60:12 Ezek 37:25 Mic 4:7

2:45 Gen 41:28, 32 Deut 10:17 2 Sam 7:22 Dan 2:29 Rev 22:6

2:46 Lev 26:31 Dan 3:5, 7 Acts 10:25; 14:13 Rev 19:10; 22:8

2:47 Deut 10:17 Dan 3:15; 4:25 Amos 3:7

2:48 Gen 41:39-43 Dan 2:6; 3:1, 12, 30; 5:16

2:49 Esth 2:19, 21 Dan 3:12-30 Amos 5:15

3:1 Isa 46:6 Jer 16:20 Dan 2:31 Hab 2:19

3:2 Dan 3:3, 27; 6:1-7

2:36-45 There have been various attempts to understand the four kingdoms of Nebuchadnezzar's dream. The most common view throughout the history of Jewish and Christian interpretation has seen the metals as kingdoms and identified them with the Babylonian, Medo-Persian, Greek, and Roman empires. A second view believes the Babylonian, Median, Persian, and Greek empires are represented. Though neither view is conclusive, the main point is clear and undisputed: Earthly kingdoms come and go, rise and fall; but the Kingdom of God will endure forever.

2:46 Jewish and Christian interpreters have noted the irregularity of Daniel receiving worship without protest, especially since the Bible commands us to worship God alone (Deuteronomy 10:20; Isaiah 26:13). However, it was not unusual for an ambassador of a deity or king to be accorded with the honors due his master. Daniel may have been receiving the offering and incense on behalf of his God. The pagan king was not humbling himself before Daniel, but before the power of the God of Israel.

3:1 The statue, or image, links chapter 3 with the preceding chapter. Perhaps we are to imagine that the image in Nebuchadnezzar's dream had inspired him to construct the present image. He may have been seeking to counter the predicted fall of his kingdom by establishing a statue to memorialize his reign forever.

3:4 Isa 40:9; 58:1 Dan 3:7; 4:1; 6:25 Rev 18:2
3:5 Dan 3:7, 10
3:6 Jer 29:22 Dan 3:11, 15, 21; 6:7 Matt 13:42 Rev 9:2; 14:11
3:8 Ezra 4:12-16 Esth 3:8-9
3:10 Dan 6:12
3:13 Dan 2:12; 3:19
3:14 Isa 46:1 Dan 3:1; 4:8
3:15 Exod 5:2 Isa 36:18-20 Jer 50:2 Dan 2:47
3:16 Dan 1:7; 3:12
3:17 1 Sam 17:37 Ps 27:1-2 Isa 26:3-4 Jer 1:8
3:18 Josh 24:15 1 Kgs 19:14 Dan 3:28

vincial officials to come to the dedication of the statue he had set up. 3 So all these officials*
came and stood before the statue King Nebuchadnezzar had set up.
4 Then a herald shouted out, "People of all races and nations and languages, listen to the
king's command! 5 When you hear the sound of the horn, flute, zither, lyre, harp, pipes, and
other musical instruments,* bow to the ground to worship King Nebuchadnezzar's gold
statue. 6 Anyone who refuses to obey will immediately be thrown into a blazing furnace."
7 So at the sound of the musical instruments,* all the people, whatever their race or na-
tion or language, bowed to the ground and worshiped the gold statue that King Nebu-
chadnezzar had set up.
8 But some of the astrologers* went to the king and informed on the Jews. 9 They said to
King Nebuchadnezzar, "Long live the king! 10 You issued a decree requiring all the people
to bow down and worship the gold statue when they hear the sound of the horn, flute,
zither, lyre, harp, pipes, and other musical instruments. 11 That decree also states that
those who refuse to obey must be thrown into a blazing furnace. 12 But there are some
Jews—Shadrach, Meshach, and Abednego—whom you have put in charge of the province
of Babylon. They pay no attention to you, Your Majesty. They refuse to serve your gods
and do not worship the gold statue you have set up."
13 Then Nebuchadnezzar flew into a rage and ordered that Shadrach, Meshach, and
Abednego be brought before him. When they were brought in, 14 Nebuchadnezzar said to
them, "Is it true, Shadrach, Meshach, and Abednego, that you refuse to serve my gods or
to worship the gold statue I have set up? 15 I will give you one more chance to bow down
and worship the statue I have made when you hear the sound of the musical instruments.*
But if you refuse, you will be thrown immediately into the blazing furnace. And then what
god will be able to rescue you from my power?"
16 Shadrach, Meshach, and Abednego replied, "O Nebuchadnezzar, we do not need to
defend ourselves before you. 17 If we are thrown into the blazing furnace, the God whom
we serve is able to save us. He will rescue us from your power, Your Majesty. 18 But even if
He doesn't, we want to make it clear to you, Your Majesty, that we will never serve your
gods or worship the gold statue you have set up."

THE BLAZING FURNACE

3:19 Lev 26:18-28

19 Nebuchadnezzar was so furious with Shadrach, Meshach, and Abednego that his face
became distorted with rage. He commanded that the furnace be heated seven times hot-
ter than usual. 20 Then he ordered some of the strongest men of his army to bind Shadrach,

3:3 Aramaic *the high officers, officials, governors, advisers, treasurers, judges, magistrates, and all the provincial officials.* 3:5 The identification of some of these musical instruments is uncertain. 3:7 Aramaic *the horn, flute, zither, lyre, harp, and other musical instruments.* 3:8 Aramaic *Chaldeans.* 3:15 Aramaic *the horn, flute, zither, lyre, harp, pipes, and other musical instruments.*

▸ HOLINESS
3:5-12 God above all. When is it appropriate to refuse an order of someone in authority over you? Daniel's friends defied the king, but they didn't defy their King. They were "willing to die rather than serve or worship any god except their own God" (3:28). Similarly, the Jewish authorities ordered Peter and John to stop preaching in the name of Jesus, but they replied, "Do you think God wants us to obey you rather than Him? We cannot stop telling about everything we have seen and heard" (Acts 4:19-20). Nebuchadnezzar's order would have forced these men to disobey God's order, and God outranked the king of Babylon. Jesus made this promise: "Everyone who acknowledges Me publicly here on earth, I will also acknowledge before My Father in heaven" (Matthew 10:32). When the earthly rulers forbid what God commands or command what God forbids, He frees us to disobey those in authority (Exodus 1:15-21; Acts 5:29; Romans 13:1-7).

(***See Holiness**> Maturing> Imitating God> His commands,* TopicGuide page A40.)

3:8-12 It appears that in the large gathering before the image, the refusal of the Jews to bow would have gone unnoticed by the king were it not for some of the officials who came forward to accuse them. It seems that in this case the officials were motivated by ethnic or religious prejudice; whereas in Daniel 6, they appear to have been motivated by professional envy.

3:16-18 The men were not certain that God would deliver them. But their resolve to follow God did not depend on the certainty of deliverance but rather on the strength of their conviction. This gives the story a priceless realism that has spoken deeply to Jews and Christians for generations, for most have perished in similar situations.

Meshach, and Abednego and throw them into the blazing furnace. 21 So they tied them up and threw them into the furnace, fully dressed in their pants, turbans, robes, and other garments. 22 And because the king, in his anger, had demanded such a hot fire in the furnace, the flames killed the soldiers as they threw the three men in. 23 So Shadrach, Meshach, and Abednego, securely tied, fell into the roaring flames.

24 But suddenly, Nebuchadnezzar jumped up in amazement and exclaimed to his advisers, "Didn't we tie up three men and throw them into the furnace?"

"Yes, Your Majesty, we certainly did," they replied.

25 "Look!" Nebuchadnezzar shouted. "I see four men, unbound, walking around in the fire unharmed! And the fourth looks like a god*!"

26 Then Nebuchadnezzar came as close as he could to the door of the flaming furnace and shouted: "Shadrach, Meshach, and Abednego, servants of the Most High God, come out! Come here!"

So Shadrach, Meshach, and Abednego stepped out of the fire. 27 Then the high officers, officials, governors, and advisers crowded around them and saw that the fire had not touched them. Not a hair on their heads was singed, and their clothing was not scorched. They didn't even smell of smoke!

28 Then Nebuchadnezzar said, "Praise to the God of Shadrach, Meshach, and Abednego! He sent His angel to rescue His servants who trusted in Him. They defied the king's command and were willing to die rather than serve or worship any god except their own God. 29 Therefore, I make this decree: If any people, whatever their race or nation or language, speak a word against the God of Shadrach, Meshach, and Abednego, they will be torn limb from limb, and their houses will be turned into heaps of rubble. There is no other god who can rescue like this!"

30 Then the king promoted Shadrach, Meshach, and Abednego to even higher positions in the province of Babylon.

NEBUCHADNEZZAR'S DREAM ABOUT A TREE

4 1*King Nebuchadnezzar sent this message to the people of every race and nation and language throughout the world:

"Peace and prosperity to you!

2 "I want you all to know about the miraculous signs and wonders the Most High God has performed for me.

3:22 Dan 2:15
3:25 Ps 91:3-9; Isa 43:2; Jer 1:8, 19
3:26 Deut 4:20; 1 Kgs 8:51; Dan 3:17; 4:2
3:27 Isa 43:2; Dan 3:2; Heb 11:34
3:28 Ps 34:7-8; Isa 37:36; Dan 3:25; 6:22; Acts 5:19; 12:7
3:29 Ezra 6:11; Dan 3:12, 15
3:30 Dan 2:49; 3:12
4:1 Dan 6:25
4:2 Dan 3:26; 4:17, 24-25, 34

3:25 Aramaic *like a son of the gods.* 4:1 Verses 4:1-3 are numbered 3:31-33 in Aramaic text.

3:24-25 The king was amazed to see four, rather than three, individuals in the furnace and proclaimed that the fourth person looked like a god. Some have taken this to be an appearance of Christ, but another possibility is that it was an angel. It is noteworthy that the Babylonians didn't associate this with Marduk or any other Babylonian god associated with fire—they knew the God of the Jews had saved the exiles, not their own gods.

3:26-30 At the start of the chapter, the officials assembled to look in awe at the statue the king had built; at the end of the chapter they assembled to look in awe at God's work of deliverance. Likewise, at the start of the chapter the king issued a decree requiring the worship of the image he had made, but at the end of the chapter he issued a decree forbidding slander of the God of Israel. These kinds of reversals are common throughout Scripture; they illustrate that God is not limited by human power, position, or pronouncement (Exodus 8:8-10; Joshua 4:24; Matthew 2:13-18).

▸ GOD
3:29 Eternal Savior. As He did with Shadrach, Meshach, and Abednego, God has the power to save all of His people from death in the flames—but He often doesn't. Instead He often allows His people to demonstrate their love for Him by giving up their lives. But God still saves them from a much greater danger—eternal hell. God's people may suffer here on earth, but they will never suffer again! God's Son showed His power to save us from hell when He rose from the dead. If you have trusted God with your future, then you can be certain that you will be delivered by "our great God and Savior, Jesus Christ" (Titus 2:13). (***See God**> God's Names> God> Deliverer/Savior,* TopicGuide page A18.)

4:1 The perspective from which this story is recounted is rather unusual. Nebuchadnezzar himself serves as the narrator, and his words are presented in the form of a royal encyclical. The addressees of the letter are not simply the inhabitants of Babylon, but people of "every race and nation and language throughout the world." This universal scope serves to frame the chapter in terms of the relationship between human and divine power, with Nebuchadnezzar representing all earthly power.

3 How great are His signs,
 how powerful His wonders!
His kingdom will last forever,
 His rule through all generations.

4*"I, Nebuchadnezzar, was living in my palace in comfort and prosperity. 5But one night I had a dream that frightened me; I saw visions that terrified me as I lay in my bed. 6So I issued an order calling in all the wise men of Babylon, so they could tell me what my dream meant. 7When all the magicians, enchanters, astrologers,* and fortune-tellers came in, I told them the dream, but they could not tell me what it meant. 8At last Daniel came in before me, and I told him the dream. (He was named Belteshazzar after my god, and the spirit of the holy gods is in him.)

9"I said to him, 'Belteshazzar, chief of the magicians, I know that the spirit of the holy gods is in you and that no mystery is too great for you to solve. Now tell me what my dream means.

10"'While I was lying in my bed, this is what I dreamed. I saw a large tree in the middle of the earth. 11The tree grew very tall and strong, reaching high into the heavens for all the world to see. 12It had fresh green leaves, and it was loaded with fruit for all to eat. Wild animals lived in its shade, and birds nested in its branches. All the world was fed from this tree.

13"'Then as I lay there dreaming, I saw a messenger,* a holy one, coming down from heaven. 14The messenger shouted,

"Cut down the tree and lop off its branches!
 Shake off its leaves and scatter its fruit!
Chase the wild animals from its shade
 and the birds from its branches.
15 But leave the stump and the roots in the ground,
 bound with a band of iron and bronze
 and surrounded by tender grass.
Now let him be drenched with the dew of heaven,
 and let him live with the wild animals among the plants of the field.
16 For seven periods of time,
 let him have the mind of a wild animal
 instead of the mind of a human.
17 For this has been decreed by the messengers*;
 it is commanded by the holy ones,
so that everyone may know
 that the Most High rules over the kingdoms of the world.
He gives them to anyone He chooses—
 even to the lowliest of people."

18"'Belteshazzar, that was the dream that I, King Nebuchadnezzar, had. Now tell me what it means, for none of the wise men of my kingdom can do so. But you can tell me because the spirit of the holy gods is in you.'

4:3 Deut 4:34; Ps 77:19; Isa 25:1; Dan 2:44; 4:34; 6:26
4:4 Ps 30:6; Isa 47:7-8
4:5 Dan 4:10, 13
4:6 Gen 41:8; Dan 2:2
4:7 Isa 44:25; Jer 27:9-10; Dan 2:7
4:8 Dan 1:7; 4:9, 18
4:9 Gen 41:38; Ezek 28:3; Dan 1:20; 2:4-5, 47-48; 4:8; 5:11
4:10 Ezek 31:3-4
4:12 Jer 27:6-7; Ezek 31:7; Matt 13:32; Luke 13:19
4:13 Deut 33:2; Ps 89:7; Dan 8:13
4:14 Jer 51:5-6; Ezek 31:10-14; Matt 3:10; 7:19; Rev 10:3; 18:2
4:15 Job 14:7-9
4:16 Dan 7:25
4:17 1 Sam 2:8; Ps 9:16; Dan 4:25; 11:21
4:18 Gen 41:8; 1 Kgs 14:2-3; Dan 4:7; 5:8

4:4 Verses 4:4-37 are numbered 4:1-34 in Aramaic text. 4:7 Or *Chaldeans.* 4:13 Aramaic *a watcher;* also in 4:23. 4:17 Aramaic *the watchers.*

4:4-7 As in chapter 2, the king had a dream that he sought to understand, but his sages disappointed him, being unable to interpret the dream (even though this time the king revealed what happened in his dream). It may have been that the sages were unwilling to confront the king with what they surmised to be a sign of an obviously negative fate for the king.

4:10-12 In many cultures, a fruitful, protective tree symbolizes the life-giving quality of the earth. Often in ancient art, a sacred tree at the center of the earth served as a symbolic link between heaven and earth. In this case the king himself was personified as that tree.

4:14-17, 33 There is a progression in the way the king's judgment is described: In 4:15 the king is with the beasts; in 4:16 the king undergoes a psychological transformation; and finally in 4:33 the king experiences physical transformation.

DANIEL EXPLAINS THE DREAM

19"Upon hearing this, Daniel (also known as Belteshazzar) was overcome for a time,
frightened by the meaning of the dream. Then the king said to him, 'Belteshazzar,
don't be alarmed by the dream and what it means.'
"Belteshazzar replied, 'I wish the events foreshadowed in this dream would happen
to your enemies, my lord, and not to you! 20The tree you saw was growing very tall
and strong, reaching high into the heavens for all the world to see. 21It had fresh green
leaves and was loaded with fruit for all to eat. Wild animals lived in its shade, and birds
nested in its branches. 22That tree, Your Majesty, is you. For you have grown strong
and great; your greatness reaches up to heaven, and your rule to the ends of the earth.
23"'Then you saw a messenger, a holy one, coming down from heaven and saying,
"Cut down the tree and destroy it. But leave the stump and the roots in the ground,
bound with a band of iron and bronze and surrounded by tender grass. Let him be
drenched with the dew of heaven. Let him live with the animals of the field for seven
periods of time."
24"'This is what the dream means, Your Majesty, and what the Most High has
declared will happen to my lord the king. 25You will be driven from human society,
and you will live in the fields with the wild animals. You will eat grass like a cow, and
you will be drenched with the dew of heaven. Seven periods of time will pass while
you live this way, until you learn that the Most High rules over the kingdoms of the
world and gives them to anyone He chooses. 26But the stump and roots of the tree
were left in the ground. This means that you will receive your kingdom back again
when you have learned that heaven rules.
27"'King Nebuchadnezzar, please accept my advice. Stop sinning and do what is
right. Break from your wicked past and be merciful to the poor. Perhaps then you will
continue to prosper.'

THE DREAM'S FULFILLMENT

28"But all these things did happen to King Nebuchadnezzar. 29Twelve months later he
was taking a walk on the flat roof of the royal palace in Babylon. 30As he looked out
across the city, he said, 'Look at this great city of Babylon! By my own mighty power,
I have built this beautiful city as my royal residence to display my majestic splendor.'
31"While these words were still in his mouth, a voice called down from heaven,
'O King Nebuchadnezzar, this message is for you! You are no longer ruler of this
kingdom. 32You will be driven from human society. You will live in the fields with the
wild animals, and you will eat grass like a cow. Seven periods of time will pass while
you live this way, until you learn that the Most High rules over the kingdoms of the
world and gives them to anyone He chooses.'
33"That same hour the judgment was fulfilled, and Nebuchadnezzar was driven
from human society. He ate grass like a cow, and he was drenched with the dew of

4:19 1 Sam 3:17; 2 Sam 18:32; Dan 7:15, 28; 8:27
4:22 2 Sam 12:7; Jer 27:6-7; Dan 2:37-38
4:24 Job 40:11-12; Ps 107:40
4:25 Ps 75:7; Jer 27:5; Dan 4:17, 33; 5:21
4:26 Dan 4:31
4:27 Gen 41:33-37; 1 Kgs 21:29; Ps 41:1-3; Prov 28:13; Isa 55:6-7; Ezek 18:21-22; Jon 3:9
4:28 Num 23:19; Zech 1:6
4:29 2 Pet 3:9
4:30 Hab 2:4
4:33 Dan 4:25; 5:21

4:19-27 According to Daniel, the tree represented the king himself; the greatness of the tree was reflective of Nebuchadnezzar's own greatness. This judgment would be lifted only when the king acknowledged that the Most High is sovereign over all nations.

4:25 Jeremiah 27:5-6 and Daniel 2:37-38 speak of Nebuchadnezzar's dominion over the beasts of the field. God's judgment led to an ironic reversal of this status.

▸ GOD
4:30 Purging pride. Nebuchadnezzar's statements represent one of the greatest obstacles to obtaining grace—our selfish pride. He was obsessed with what he had built with his "own mighty power" to demonstrate his "majestic splendor." But the Bible makes it clear that "the LORD detests the proud; they will surely be punished" (Proverbs 16:5). By his own power, Nebuchadnezzar couldn't see himself rightly, and neither can we. Ask God to show you where you are prideful, and look in His Word to find the prescription that He offers (Matthew 20:28; 1 Corinthians 13:4; 1 Peter 5:5). (***See God**> Relationship> Barriers> Pride,* TopicGuide page A14.)

4:33 Based on the Bible's description of Nebuchadnezzar's condition here, some scholars have suggested that he was experiencing *zooanthropy*—the belief that one is an animal. Others have understood this description metaphorically, speculating that it conveys the effects of being isolated from society due to mental instability. Either way, Nebuchadnezzar,

heaven. He lived this way until his hair was as long as eagles' feathers and his nails
were like birds' claws.

NEBUCHADNEZZAR PRAISES GOD

4:34 Ps 102:24; Jer 10:10; Dan 4:2; 5:18, 21; Rev 4:10; 10:6

34"After this time had passed, I, Nebuchadnezzar, looked up to heaven. My sanity
returned, and I praised and worshiped the Most High and honored the One who lives
forever.

His rule is everlasting,
 and His kingdom is eternal.

4:35 Job 42:2; Ps 135:6; Isa 40:17; 43:13; 45:9; Dan 6:27; Rom 9:20

35 All the people of the earth
 are nothing compared to Him.
He does as He pleases
 among the angels of heaven
 and among the people of the earth.
No one can stop Him or say to Him,
 'What do you mean by doing these things?'

4:36 2 Chr 33:12-13; Prov 22:4; Dan 2:31

36"When my sanity returned to me, so did my honor and glory and kingdom. My
advisers and nobles sought me out, and I was restored as head of my kingdom, with
even greater honor than before.

4:37 Exod 18:11; Ps 33:4-5; Matt 23:12

37"Now I, Nebuchadnezzar, praise and glorify and honor the King of heaven. All
His acts are just and true, and He is able to humble the proud."

THE WRITING ON THE WALL

5:1 Esth 1:3; Isa 22:12-14 **5:2** 2 Kgs 24:13; Ezra 1:7-11; Dan 1:2 **5:4** Rev 9:20

5 Many years later King Belshazzar gave a great feast for 1,000 of his nobles, and he
drank wine with them. 2While Belshazzar was drinking the wine, he gave orders to
bring in the gold and silver cups that his predecessor,* Nebuchadnezzar, had taken from
the Temple in Jerusalem. He wanted to drink from them with his nobles, his wives, and his
concubines. 3So they brought these gold cups taken from the Temple, the house of God in
Jerusalem, and the king and his nobles, his wives, and his concubines drank from them.
4While they drank from them they praised their idols made of gold, silver, bronze, iron,
wood, and stone.

5:2 Aramaic *father;* also in 5:11, 13, 18.

---

who considered himself the founder of Babylon, had now been driven out of the city and into the chaos of the wilderness. His humiliation was complete.

4:34-37 The central issue of this chapter is made explicit in 4:37 when the king acknowledged that God is sovereign.

▸ GOD
4:35 Broken pride. God had determined to humble Nebuchadnezzar, and nothing could stop His plans, for this is the same God who merely spoke, and all of creation came into existence (Genesis 1). God can easily make a power-crazed man even crazier. After Nebuchadnezzar grazed like a cow for a while, he didn't have any more illusions—he knew God was powerful, not him. Unfortunately, many people live under the illusion that they are invincible. Pray that God will do whatever it takes to get them (or even you!) to acknowledge that He is the only One with the power to do as He pleases. Humble yourself and stay that way, or God guarantees that you will face His loving discipline (Luke 1:51; 14:11). (***See God****> Relationship> Barriers> Pride,* TopicGuide page A14.)

5:1 Belshazzar was the son of Nabonidus, the last official king of Babylon. While Nabonidus spent time away from Babylon, possibly up to 10 years, Belshazzar ruled in his place.

5:1-4 It is important to realize that this feast took place as an enemy army waited just outside the gates of the city (5:30-31). From one perspective this reinforces the king's hubris and his incompetence—at the edge of disaster the king wined and dined. The feast may also have been a political rally—a gathering meant to raise support for the king in the face of the impending battle.

▸ SALVATION
5:2-4 Saved from hate. It is appalling to imagine Belshazzar's lips drinking from God's holy cups while praising idols. Yet it is equally staggering to remember that, prior to salvation, we all taunted God with our sinful words, thoughts, and actions. But God still loved us and gave His Son to die in our place even while we were His enemies (Romans 5:6-10). He paid our debt and then pursued us even while we hated Him. Why? So He could give us "the privilege of repenting of [our] sins and receiving eternal life" (Acts 11:18). He did all this while we were sitting with Belshazzar. Marvel at this great love that pursued you until you were transformed into God's friend. (***See Salvation****> Our need> Sinful> Depraved,* TopicGuide page A22.)

5 Suddenly, they saw the fingers of a human hand writing on the plaster wall of the
king's palace, near the lampstand. The king himself saw the hand as it wrote, 6 and his face
turned pale with fright. His knees knocked together in fear and his legs gave way beneath
him.

7 The king shouted for the enchanters, astrologers,* and fortune-tellers to be brought be-
fore him. He said to these wise men of Babylon, "Whoever can read this writing and tell
me what it means will be dressed in purple robes of royal honor and will have a gold chain
placed around his neck. He will become the third highest ruler in the kingdom!"

8 But when all the king's wise men had come in, none of them could read the writing or
tell him what it meant. 9 So the king grew even more alarmed, and his face turned pale. His
nobles, too, were shaken.

10 But when the queen mother heard what was happening, she hurried to the banquet
hall. She said to Belshazzar, "Long live the king! Don't be so pale and frightened. 11 There is a
man in your kingdom who has within him the spirit of the holy gods. During Nebuchadnez-
zar's reign, this man was found to have insight, understanding, and wisdom like that of the
gods. Your predecessor, the king—your predecessor King Nebuchadnezzar—made him chief
over all the magicians, enchanters, astrologers, and fortune-tellers of Babylon. 12 This man
Daniel, whom the king named Belteshazzar, has exceptional ability and is filled with divine
knowledge and understanding. He can interpret dreams, explain riddles, and solve difficult
problems. Call for Daniel, and he will tell you what the writing means."

DANIEL EXPLAINS THE WRITING

13 So Daniel was brought in before the king. The king asked him, "Are you Daniel, one of
the exiles brought from Judah by my predecessor, King Nebuchadnezzar? 14 I have heard
that you have the spirit of the gods within you and that you are filled with insight, under-
standing, and wisdom. 15 My wise men and enchanters have tried to read the words on the
wall and tell me their meaning, but they cannot do it. 16 I am told that you can give inter-
pretations and solve difficult problems. If you can read these words and tell me their
meaning, you will be clothed in purple robes of royal honor, and you will have a gold
chain placed around your neck. You will become the third highest ruler in the kingdom."

17 Daniel answered the king, "Keep your gifts or give them to someone else, but I will tell
you what the writing means. 18 Your Majesty, the Most High God gave sovereignty, majes-
ty, glory, and honor to your predecessor, Nebuchadnezzar. 19 He made him so great that
people of all races and nations and languages trembled before him in fear. He killed those
he wanted to kill and spared those he wanted to spare. He honored those he wanted to
honor and disgraced those he wanted to disgrace. 20 But when his heart and mind were
puffed up with arrogance, he was brought down from his royal throne and stripped of his
glory. 21 He was driven from human society. He was given the mind of a wild animal, and
he lived among the wild donkeys. He ate grass like a cow, and he was drenched with the
dew of heaven, until he learned that the Most High God rules over the kingdoms of the
world and appoints anyone He desires to rule over them.

5:7 Or *Chaldeans;* also in 5:11.

5:6 Ps 69:23; Ezek 7:17; 21:7; Dan 7:28; Nah 2:10
5:7 Gen 41:42-44; Isa 44:25; 47:13; Ezek 16:11; Dan 5:11, 16, 29; 6:2-3
5:9 Job 18:11-14; Isa 21:2-4; Jer 6:24; Dan 5:6
5:10 Dan 3:9; 6:6
5:11 Gen 41:11-15; Dan 2:47; 4:8-9; 5:14
5:12 Dan 4:18
5:13 Dan 1:1; 2:25
5:15 Isa 47:12; Dan 5:8
5:16 Gen 40:8
5:17 2 Kgs 5:16
5:18 Jer 25:5-7; Dan 2:37; 4:2, 17; 5:21
5:19 Prov 16:14; Dan 2:12; 3:6; 11:3
5:20 Exod 9:17; Isa 14:13-15; Jer 13:18; Dan 4:30; Luke 18:14
5:21 Exod 9:14-16; Ps 83:17-18; Ezek 17:24

5:5-6 Belshazzar saw a disembodied hand that wrote a message on a wall. His fearful reaction was described rather graphically. The phrase "his legs gave way" is an attempt to render the literal phrase, "the knots of his loins were loosened." The Hebrew likely infers that he fouled his clothing in some manner.

▸ CHURCH
5:17 Ministering for God. Even Christian ministry can become all about the money. There is nothing in Scripture that prohibits Christian workers from receiving gifts or pay for their work (see Daniel 2:48), but there is always a danger that God's messengers may become so obsessed with material goods that they begin working only for the money (Titus 1:11). Daniel was not preoccupied with the question, "What's in it for me?" He perceived that Belshazzar's motives were not right, so he made it clear that he did not use God's gift in order to be paid. Ask God to keep your ministry motives pure so that material gain will never distract you. Pray that you will be so obsessed with God that personal gain never has any sway over your decisions. (***See Church**> Role> Glorify God> As a motive toward obedience,* TopicGuide page A49.)

22"You are his successor,* O Belshazzar, and you knew all this, yet you have not hum-
bled yourself. 23For you have proudly defied the Lord of heaven and have had these cups
from His Temple brought before you. You and your nobles and your wives and concu-
bines have been drinking wine from them while praising gods of silver, gold, bronze, iron,
wood, and stone—gods that neither see nor hear nor know anything at all. But you have
not honored the God who gives you the breath of life and controls your destiny! 24So God
has sent this hand to write this message.

25"This is the message that was written: MENE, MENE, TEKEL, and PARSIN. 26This is what
these words mean:

Mene means 'numbered'—God has numbered the days of your reign and has brought it to an end.

27 *Tekel* means 'weighed'—you have been weighed on the balances and have not measured up.

28 *Parsin** means 'divided'—your kingdom has been divided and given to the Medes and Persians."

29Then at Belshazzar's command, Daniel was dressed in purple robes, a gold chain was
hung around his neck, and he was proclaimed the third highest ruler in the kingdom.
30That very night Belshazzar, the Babylonian* king, was killed.*
31*And Darius the Mede took over the kingdom at the age of sixty-two.

DANIEL IN THE LIONS' DEN

6 1*Darius the Mede decided to divide the kingdom into 120 provinces, and he ap-
pointed a high officer to rule over each province. 2The king also chose Daniel and two
others as administrators to supervise the high officers and protect the king's interests. 3Dan-
iel soon proved himself more capable than all the other administrators and high officers. Be-
cause of Daniel's great ability, the king made plans to place him over the entire empire.

4Then the other administrators and high officers began searching for some fault in the
way Daniel was handling government affairs, but they couldn't find anything to criticize or
condemn. He was faithful, always responsible, and completely trustworthy. 5So they con-
cluded, "Our only chance of finding grounds for accusing Daniel will be in connection with
the rules of his religion."

6So the administrators and high officers went to the king and said, "Long live King Darius!

5:22 Exod 10:3; 2 Chr 33:23; 36:12
5:23 2 Kgs 14:10; Job 3:14; 12:10; Jer 10:23; 50:29; Dan 5:3-4; Hab 2:18-19
5:26 Isa 13:6, 17; Jer 50:41-43
5:27 Job 31:6; Ps 62:9
5:28 Isa 21:2; 45:1-2; Dan 5:31; 6:28
5:30 Isa 21:4-9; Jer 51:11, 31, 39, 57
5:31 Dan 6:1; 9:1
6:1 Esth 1:1
6:2 Ezra 4:22; Esth 7:4; Dan 2:48-49; 5:16, 29
6:3 Gen 41:40; Dan 5:12
6:4 Gen 43:18; Luke 23:14-15; Phil 2:15
6:5 Acts 24:13-16
6:6 Neh 2:3

5:22 Aramaic *son.* 5:28 Aramaic *Peres,* the singular of *Parsin.* 5:30a Or *Chaldean.* 5:30b The Persians and Medes conquered Babylon in October 539 B.C. 5:31 Verse 5:31 is numbered 6:1 in Aramaic text. 6:1 Verses 6:1-28 are numbered 6:2-29 in Aramaic text.

5:25-28 The words *mene, tekel,* and *parsin* are three different nouns representing units of money: mina, shekel, and a half. Daniel, however, interpreted them as verbal forms, giving the sense of "numbered, weighed, and divided." It became clear that a time had been appointed for the king to be judged and punished.

5:30-31 The identity of Darius the Mede is much disputed. His name does not appear outside the book of Daniel. Some have believed Darius to be a throne name for Gubaru, governor of Babylon known from Akkadian texts. Others associate Darius with Cyrus the Great. It was not uncommon for a king to assume different names for different nations he ruled.

6:1-2 Chapter 6 opens with Daniel serving in the Persian Empire, which had conquered the Babylonian Empire. The empire underwent political reorganization (6:1), but God's continued blessing of Daniel's work caused friction with his peers.

6:3-5 Unlike chapter 3 where motivation to persecute God's people apparently arose from ethnic or religious reasons, here the officials seemed to be acting on the basis of professional envy. Their plan shows that the officials must have been confident that Daniel would never waver in his prayers.

▸ BIBLE

6:6 A perfect trap. Satan is no fool. He knows how to cause trouble. Daniel wanted to live out his vibrant faith before Darius and his court—but these advisers found a way to make that illegal. That put Daniel in a bind—if he lived out his faith without compromise, then he would surely perish (6:7). And if he compromised, he might not have died, but he would have ceased to show forth an intimate relationship with God. It was a "lose-lose" situation—until God intervened. You may feel as if you are in a bind, a no-win situation, with no good options. But God made a way for Daniel to keep his integrity and complete his mission—He can do it for you, too. Don't believe the lie that you have no options—obedience and trusting God is always your best choice. (***See Bible> Unity> God's Message> Devotion to God,*** TopicGuide page A11.)

7We are all in agreement—we administrators, officials, high officers, advisers, and gover-
nors—that the king should make a law that will be strictly enforced. Give orders that for the
next thirty days any person who prays to anyone, divine or human—except to you, Your
Majesty—will be thrown into the den of lions. 8And now, Your Majesty, issue and sign this
law so it cannot be changed, an official law of the Medes and Persians that cannot be re-
voked." 9So King Darius signed the law.
10But when Daniel learned that the law had been signed, he went home and knelt down
as usual in his upstairs room, with its windows open toward Jerusalem. He prayed three
times a day, just as he had always done, giving thanks to his God. 11Then the officials
went together to Daniel's house and found him praying and asking for God's help. 12So
they went straight to the king and reminded him about his law. "Did you not sign a law
that for the next thirty days any person who prays to anyone, divine or human—except to
you, Your Majesty—will be thrown into the den of lions?"
"Yes," the king replied, "that decision stands; it is an official law of the Medes and Per-
sians that cannot be revoked."
13Then they told the king, "That man Daniel, one of the captives from Judah, is ignoring
you and your law. He still prays to his God three times a day."
14Hearing this, the king was deeply troubled, and he tried to think of a way to save Dan-
iel. He spent the rest of the day looking for a way to get Daniel out of this predicament.
15In the evening the men went together to the king and said, "Your Majesty, you know
that according to the law of the Medes and the Persians, no law that the king signs can be
changed."
16So at last the king gave orders for Daniel to be arrested and thrown into the den of
lions. The king said to him, "May your God, whom you serve so faithfully, rescue you."
17A stone was brought and placed over the mouth of the den. The king sealed the stone
with his own royal seal and the seals of his nobles, so that no one could rescue Daniel.
18Then the king returned to his palace and spent the night fasting. He refused his usual en-
tertainment and couldn't sleep at all that night.
19Very early the next morning, the king got up and hurried out to the lions' den. 20When
he got there, he called out in anguish, "Daniel, servant of the living God! Was your God,
whom you serve so faithfully, able to rescue you from the lions?"
21Daniel answered, "Long live the king! 22My God sent His angel to shut the lions'
mouths so that they would not hurt me, for I have been found innocent in His sight. And I
have not wronged you, Your Majesty."
23The king was overjoyed and ordered that Daniel be lifted from the den. Not a scratch
was found on him, for he had trusted in his God.
24Then the king gave orders to arrest the men who had maliciously accused Daniel. He

6:8 Esth 1:19; 3:12 · Isa 10:1 · Matt 24:35
6:10 1 Kgs 8:48-49 · Pss 34:1; 95:6 · 1 Thes 5:17-18
6:12 Esth 1:19 · Acts 16:19-21
6:13 Esth 3:8 · Dan 3:12 · Acts 5:29
6:15 Esth 8:8 · Ps 94:20-21
6:16 Job 5:19 · Ps 37:39-40 · Jer 38:5
6:17 Lam 3:53 · Matt 27:66
6:18 2 Sam 12:16-17 · Esth 6:1 · Rev 18:22
6:20 Jer 32:17 · Hos 12:6
6:22 Ps 91:11-13 · Acts 12:11 · 2 Tim 4:17 · Heb 11:33
6:23 Ps 118:8 · Isa 26:3
6:24 Deut 19:18-19 · 2 Kgs 14:6

6:10 The book of Daniel taught exiles how to live out their faith in another land. Through this story, the author shows that prayer is a religious practice that is essential and cannot be compromised. Prayer is mentioned 12 other times in Daniel, with the theme of prayer culminating in Daniel 10:12.

6:13-18 The king was a reluctant executioner trapped by his own decree. His distress probably resulted from the realization that he had been manipulated by his officials, and he would now lose a trusted and competent adviser. Darius expressed his desire that Daniel be saved by his God and then spent an anxious night of self-denial awaiting the outcome of Daniel's stay in the den.

▸ GOD

6:17 Opposing God's power. God's prophet was trapped. Lions were everywhere, a large stone was rolled over the pit, and then darkness fell. The king's seal meant no one could possibly get inside to help Daniel, right? But behind the scenes, "the One who rules in heaven laughs" at the futile efforts of those who oppose Him (Psalm 2:4). Later, another ruler named Pilate placed his seal upon a large stone as an assurance that nothing would happen to the dead body inside. But no stone or seal could keep God from raising His Son (Matthew 27:62–28:4). We can trust that God is never hindered from accomplishing His will to deliver His people. Walk forward in faith and trust God to rescue you from Satan's schemes. And don't be afraid to chuckle—God certainly does—at the useless attempts of Satan to stop God from accomplishing His great purpose. (***See God***> *God's Attributes> All-Powerful> His resurrection power is immeasurably great,* TopicGuide page A16.)

6:26-27 The king's decree took the form of an encyclical issued throughout the land, a 1600-mile route completed in a week. The Persian messengers mounted appropriate animals for the terrain (usually horses) to circulate such legal notices, and they were noted by the Greek historian Herodotus as men

had them thrown into the lions' den, along with their wives and children. The lions leaped
on them and tore them apart before they even hit the floor of the den.
6:25 Ezra 1:1-2; Esth 3:12; 8:9; Hos 1:10; 1 Pet 1:2
25 Then King Darius sent this message to the people of every race and nation and lan-
guage throughout the world:

"Peace and prosperity to you!

6:26 Ps 93:1-2
26 "I decree that everyone throughout my kingdom should tremble with fear before
the God of Daniel.

6:27 Dan 4:3

For He is the living God,
  and He will endure forever.
His kingdom will never be destroyed,
  and His rule will never end.
27 He rescues and saves His people;
  He performs miraculous signs and wonders
  in the heavens and on earth.
He has rescued Daniel
  from the power of the lions."

28 So Daniel prospered during the reign of Darius and the reign of Cyrus the Persian.*

DANIEL'S VISION OF FOUR BEASTS

7:1 Job 33:14-16; Dan 2:1, 26-28; 4:5-9; Jer 36:4; Joel 2:28

7 Earlier, during the first year of King Belshazzar's reign in Babylon,* Daniel had a
dream and saw visions as he lay in his bed. He wrote down the dream, and this is
what he saw.
7:2 Rev 7:1
2 In my vision that night, I, Daniel, saw a great storm churning the surface of a great sea,
with strong winds blowing from every direction. 3 Then four huge beasts came up out of
7:3 Rev 13:1
the water, each different from the others.
4 The first beast was like a lion with eagles' wings. As I watched, its wings were pulled off,
and it was left standing with its two hind feet on the ground, like a human being. And it
was given a human mind.
5 Then I saw a second beast, and it looked like a bear. It was rearing up on one side, and
it had three ribs in its mouth between its teeth. And I heard a voice saying to it, "Get up!
Devour the flesh of many people!"
6 Then the third of these strange beasts appeared, and it looked like a leopard. It had
four bird's wings on its back, and it had four heads. Great authority was given to this beast.
7:7 Rev 12:3; 13:1
7 Then in my vision that night, I saw a fourth beast—terrifying, dreadful, and very strong.
It devoured and crushed its victims with huge iron teeth and trampled their remains be-
neath its feet. It was different from any of the other beasts, and it had ten horns.
8 As I was looking at the horns, suddenly another small horn appeared among them.
Three of the first horns were torn out by the roots to make room for it. This little horn had
eyes like human eyes and a mouth that was boasting arrogantly.

7:9 Ezek 1:13; 10:2, 6; Mark 9:3; Rev 1:14

9 I watched as thrones were put in place
  and the Ancient One* sat down to judge.

6:28 Or *of Darius, that is, the reign of Cyrus the Persian.* **7:1** The first year of Belshazzar's reign (who was co-regent with his father, Nabonidus) was 556 B.C. (or perhaps as late as 553 B.C.). **7:9** Aramaic *an Ancient of Days;* also in 7:13, 22.

who "will not be hindered, either by snow or rain or heat or by the darkness of night."

7:2 **Daniel had the vision reported here during the first year of Belshazzar's reign. The writer of Daniel placed these visions after the history of Daniel's life so the reader would know that God had successfully spoken through Daniel before.**

7:9-10 **The motifs surrounding Daniel's throne vision—such as thrones, fire, wheels, attendants, and books—all feature prominently in both the Old Testament and New Testament. Compare Isaiah 6; 1 Kings 22:19-22; Ezekiel 1; and Revelation 4. The imagery is clearly symbolic, but it's difficult to know exactly what it is intended to represent. For instance, the "fire" mentioned here could have multiple connotations, but majesty and judgment appear to be prominent.**

His clothing was as white as snow,
His hair like purest wool.
He sat on a fiery throne
with wheels of blazing fire,
10 and a river of fire was pouring out,
flowing from His presence.
Millions of angels ministered to Him;
many millions stood to attend Him.
Then the court began its session,
and the books were opened.

11 I continued to watch because I could hear the little horn's boastful speech. I kept watch-
ing until the fourth beast was killed and its body was destroyed by fire. 12 The other three
beasts had their authority taken from them, but they were allowed to live a while longer.*
13 As my vision continued that night, I saw someone like a son of man* coming with the
clouds of heaven. He approached the Ancient One and was led into His presence. 14 He
was given authority, honor, and sovereignty over all the nations of the world, so that peo-
ple of every race and nation and language would obey Him. His rule is eternal—it will
never end. His kingdom will never be destroyed.

THE VISION IS EXPLAINED

15 I, Daniel, was troubled by all I had seen, and my visions terrified me. 16 So I approached
one of those standing beside the throne and asked him what it all meant. He explained it
to me like this: 17 "These four huge beasts represent four kingdoms that will arise from the
earth. 18 But in the end, the holy people of the Most High will be given the kingdom, and
they will rule forever and ever."
19 Then I wanted to know the true meaning of the fourth beast, the one so different from
the others and so terrifying. It had devoured and crushed its victims with iron teeth and
bronze claws, trampling their remains beneath its feet. 20 I also asked about the ten horns
on the fourth beast's head and the little horn that came up afterward and destroyed three
of the other horns. This horn had seemed greater than the others, and it had human eyes
and a mouth that was boasting arrogantly. 21 As I watched, this horn was waging war
against God's holy people and was defeating them, 22 until the Ancient One—the Most
High—came and judged in favor of His holy people. Then the time arrived for the holy
people to take over the kingdom.
23 Then he said to me, "This fourth beast is the fourth world power that will rule the
earth. It will be different from all the others. It will devour the whole world, trampling and
crushing everything in its path. 24 Its ten horns are ten kings who will rule that empire.
Then another king will arise, different from the other ten, who will subdue three of them.
25 He will defy the Most High and oppress the holy people of the Most High. He will try to
change their sacred festivals and laws, and they will be placed under his control for a time,
times, and half a time.
26 "But then the court will pass judgment, and all his power will be taken away and com-

7:10 Pss 50:3; 97:3 Isa 30:27 Dan 7:22, 26; 12:1 Rev 5:11; 20:11-15

7:11 Rev 19:20; 20:10

7:13 *Matt 26:64 *Mark 13:26 *Luke 21:27 Rev 1:13; 14:14

7:14 Pss 2:6-8; 72:17; 102:22 Dan 7:27 Eph 1:20-22 Heb 12:28 Rev 1:6

7:15 Dan 4:19; 7:28

7:16 Dan 8:13-16; 10:5-6, 11-12 Zech 1:8-11 Rev 5:5; 7:13-14

7:18 Isa 60:12-14 Dan 7:22, 25, 27 Rev 2:26-27; 20:4

7:21 Rev 13:7

7:22 Dan 7:10 1 Cor 6:2-3

7:24 Rev 17:12

7:25 Dan 4:2; 11:36; 12:7 Rev 12:14; 13:6-7; 18:24

7:26 Rev 17:14; 19:2

7:12 Aramaic *for a season and a time.* 7:13 Or *like a Son of Man.*

7:13 The phrase "like a man" or "like a son of man" can refer to any individual human being, as it does throughout Ezekiel. The traditional Christian understanding has been that the "son of man" is Jesus, following the lead of the Gospels where "Son of Man" becomes Jesus' preferred self-designation.

7:19-22 If we identify the fourth kingdom as Greece, then the little horn of the fourth beast in chapter 7 is equivalent to the little horn in chapter 8. Scholars agree that the little horn refers to Antiochus Epiphanes, the Greek ruler who oppressed the Jewish people during the second century BC.

7:23-25 The small horn is accused of three deeds, which can reasonably be made to correspond to the Jewish experience during the reign of Antiochus: blasphemy, persecution of faithful Jews, and forbidding the keeping of Sabbath and other feast days.

pletely destroyed. 27 Then the sovereignty, power, and greatness of all the kingdoms under heaven will be given to the holy people of the Most High. His kingdom will last forever, and all rulers will serve and obey Him."

28 That was the end of the vision. I, Daniel, was terrified by my thoughts and my face was pale with fear, but I kept these things to myself.

DANIEL'S VISION OF A RAM AND GOAT

8 1* During the third year of King Belshazzar's reign, I, Daniel, saw another vision, following the one that had already appeared to me. 2 In this vision I was at the fortress of Susa, in the province of Elam, standing beside the Ulai River.*

3 As I looked up, I saw a ram with two long horns standing beside the river.* One of the horns was longer than the other, even though it had grown later than the other one. 4 The ram butted everything out of his way to the west, to the north, and to the south, and no one could stand against him or help his victims. He did as he pleased and became very great.

5 While I was watching, suddenly a male goat appeared from the west, crossing the land so swiftly that he didn't even touch the ground. This goat, which had one very large horn between its eyes, 6 headed toward the two-horned ram that I had seen standing beside the river, rushing at him in a rage. 7 The goat charged furiously at the ram and struck him, breaking off both his horns. Now the ram was helpless, and the goat knocked him down and trampled him. No one could rescue the ram from the goat's power.

8 The goat became very powerful. But at the height of his power, his large horn was broken off. In the large horn's place grew four prominent horns pointing in the four directions of the earth. 9 Then from one of the prominent horns came a small horn whose power grew very great. It extended toward the south and the east and toward the glorious land of Israel. 10 Its power reached to the heavens, where it attacked the heavenly army, throwing some of the heavenly beings and some of the stars to the ground and trampling them. 11 It even challenged the Commander of heaven's army by canceling the daily sacrifices offered to Him and by destroying His Temple. 12 The army of heaven was restrained from responding to this rebellion. So the daily sacrifice was halted, and truth was overthrown. The horn succeeded in everything it did.*

13 Then I heard two holy ones talking to each other. One of them asked, "How long will the events of this vision last? How long will the rebellion that causes desecration stop the daily sacrifices? How long will the Temple and heaven's army be trampled on?"

14 The other replied, "It will take 2,300 evenings and mornings; then the Temple will be made right again."

GABRIEL EXPLAINS THE VISION

15 As I, Daniel, was trying to understand the meaning of this vision, someone who looked

7:27 Pss 2:6-12; 22:27; 86:9; 145:13 Isa 60:12 Dan 2:44; 4:34; 7:14, 18, 22 Luke 1:33 Rev 11:1, 5; 20:4
8:2 Gen 10:22; 14:1 Esth 1:2 Isa 11:11 Jer 25:25 Dan 7:2, 15
8:3 Dan 8:20
8:4 Deut 33:17 1 Kgs 22:11 Ezek 34:21
8:5 Dan 8:8, 21; 11:3
8:8 2 Chr 26:16 Dan 5:20; 7:2; 8:22 Rev 7:1
8:9 Dan 8:23; 11:16, 41
8:10 Jer 48:26, 42 Dan 7:7; 8:7; 11:31 Rev 12:4
8:11 Ezek 46:14 Dan 11:31, 36-37; 12:11
8:12 Isa 59:14
8:13 Pss 74:10; 79:5 Dan 4:13, 23; 12:6, 8 Luke 10:22; 21:24 Heb 10:29 Rev 6:10; 11:2
8:14 Dan 7:25; 12:7, 11 Rev 11:2-3; 12:14; 13:5
8:15 Dan 7:13; 10:16, 18

8:1 The original text from this point through chapter 12 is in Hebrew. See note at 2:4. 8:2 Or *the Ulai Gate;* also in 8:16. 8:3 Or *the gate;* also in 8:6. 8:11-12 The meaning of the Hebrew for these verses is uncertain.

▶ GOD

7:28 Experiencing God. Have you ever had an experience that left you shaken? A car accident, surprising news, or a bad dream? Daniel had a spiritual experience that left him upset—what did it all mean? Was it all from God, or from his imagination? Though his first thought was to keep the vision to himself, he eventually wrote all his prophecies down. But his initial instinct was correct—it is not wise to immediately share the stories of our most intimate moments with God. Our deepest religious experiences are not fodder for casual conversation, any more than our most intimate experiences with our spouse or friends are (Luke 2:19). Ask God to give you the wisdom to know when to speak about Him and when to be silent. (***See God****> Relationship> God Enables> Relationship with God requires a right heart,* TopicGuide page A14.)

8:1-2 This chronological notice sets the reception of the dream in the reign of Belshazzar, who was the subject of chapter 5. Belshazzar foreshadows the "little horn" through his blasphemous arrogance. Daniel's vision transports him to the city of Susa in the province of Elam on the Ulai River.

8:10-12 The power of the small horn reached beyond human dimensions. It grew until it reached into the heavens and entered into a conflict with the heavenly army. Surprisingly, the text reports that the small horn achieved a certain degree of success. Then the horn challenged the "Commander of heaven's army." These incursions against heaven appear to be equated with the desecration of the Temple and the halting of the worship of God's people.

like a man stood in front of me. 16And I heard a human voice calling out from the Ulai
River, "Gabriel, tell this man the meaning of his vision."
17As Gabriel approached the place where I was standing, I became so terrified that I fell
with my face to the ground. "Son of man," he said, "you must understand that the events
you have seen in your vision relate to the time of the end."
18While he was speaking, I fainted and lay there with my face to the ground. But Gabriel
roused me with a touch and helped me to my feet.
19Then he said, "I am here to tell you what will happen later in the time of wrath. What
you have seen pertains to the very end of time. 20The two-horned ram represents the
kings of Media and Persia. 21The shaggy male goat represents the king of Greece,* and
the large horn between his eyes represents the first king of the Greek Empire. 22The four
prominent horns that replaced the one large horn show that the Greek Empire will break
into four kingdoms, but none as great as the first.
23"At the end of their rule, when their sin is at its height, a fierce king, a master of in-
trigue, will rise to power. 24He will become very strong, but not by his own power. He will
cause a shocking amount of destruction and succeed in everything he does. He will de-
stroy powerful leaders and devastate the holy people. 25He will be a master of deception
and will become arrogant; he will destroy many without warning. He will even take on the
Prince of princes in battle, but he will be broken, though not by human power.
26"This vision about the 2,300 evenings and mornings* is true. But none of these things
will happen for a long time, so keep this vision a secret."
27Then I, Daniel, was overcome and lay sick for several days. Afterward I got up and per-
formed my duties for the king, but I was greatly troubled by the vision and could not
understand it.

DANIEL'S PRAYER FOR HIS PEOPLE

9 It was the first year of the reign of Darius the Mede, the son of Ahasuerus, who be-
came king of the Babylonians.* 2During the first year of his reign, I, Daniel, learned
from reading the word of the LORD, as revealed to Jeremiah the prophet, that Jerusalem

8:16 Dan 9:21; Luke 1:19, 26
8:17 Ezek 1:28; 6:2; 44:4; Dan 2:46; 8:19; 11:35, 40; Rev 1:17
8:18 Ezek 2:2; Dan 10:9-10, 16, 18; Luke 9:32
8:19 Dan 8:15-17
8:24 Dan 8:11-13; 11:36; 12:7; Rev 13:3-9; 16:6; 17:12-17
8:25 Job 34:20; Dan 2:34, 45
8:27 Dan 7:28; 8:17; Hab 3:16
9:1 Dan 5:31; 11:1
9:2 2 Chr 36:21; Ezra 1:1; Jer 25:11; 29:10; Zech 7:5

8:21 Hebrew *of Javan.* 8:26 Hebrew *about the evenings and mornings;* compare 8:14. 9:1 Or *the Chaldeans.*

8:19 The vision is said to pertain "to the very end of time." But what is the end in view? It cannot be the end in the sense of the second coming of Christ, because the events described appear to be fulfilled in the second century BC. The "end of time" is most likely that time when the prophecy at hand has been fulfilled.

8:20-22 The two-horned ram represents the Medo-Persian Empire. Media, the smaller horn, rose to prominence first, but was soon eclipsed by the larger Persian Empire under Cyrus the Great. From the perspective of Babylon, it advanced west, north, and south (8:4). The goat represents the Greek Empire. The large single horn is Alexander the Great, who conquered much of the known world, including Persia. At the height of his power, however, Alexander died at the age of 33 in 323 BC. His empire was then divided among his four generals, hence the four horns that arise here.

8:23-25 The little horn that arises is almost universally acknowledged to be Antiochus IV Epiphanes. His evil rule negatively affected almost every part of Jewish culture. Historically Antiochus's hostility toward the Jews was grounded in his aggressive policies of Hellenization, or the conversion of other cultures to the Greek worldview and way of life.

▸ CHURCH
8:27 Sympathy pains. When a woman is enduring labor pains, her husband is often at her side grimacing with each contraction. A caring husband doesn't literally feel the severity of the pain, but sympathizes with his wife's agony. This is similar to what Daniel felt when he heard of the hardship that was going to come upon Israel (8:9). It affected him so deeply that he became ill. Paul knew what it was like to feel this emotional link with God's people: "Who is weak without my feeling that weakness? Who is led astray, and I do not burn with anger?" (2 Corinthians 11:28-29). Daniel and Paul felt such pain because they cared so much (Daniel 10:2). Ask God to give you such a concern for His church that you understand His command: "Be happy with those who are happy, and weep with those who weep" (Romans 12:15). (***See Church***> *What> Supernatural Body> Care given to the weakest (yet most necessary) parts,* TopicGuide page A48.)

9:1 Darius's identity in history is much debated (see note at Daniel 5:30-31). The original audience of Daniel's prophecy knew who Darius and his father were, just as the audience of Isaiah knew the kings by which he dated his prophecies (Isaiah 6:1).

9:2 Daniel was said to understand from reading Jeremiah (most likely from 25:11-12 and 29:10) that Jerusalem was to "lie desolate for seventy years." The letter to the exiles in which Jeremiah's reference to the 70 years is found was written after the deportation in 597–596 BC. The first year of Darius's reign was 538 BC. This gives only a time span of 58 or 59 years. What caught Daniel's interest was that although 70 years had not passed so far, Babylon had fallen. For Daniel and Jeremiah, the fall of Babylon hearkened the restoration of Israel.

must lie desolate for seventy years.* 3So I turned to the LORD God and pleaded with Him in
prayer and fasting. I also wore rough burlap and sprinkled myself with ashes.
4I prayed to the LORD my God and confessed:

"O Lord, You are a great and awesome God! You always fulfill Your covenant and
keep Your promises of unfailing love to those who love You and obey Your
commands. 5But we have sinned and done wrong. We have rebelled against You
and scorned Your commands and regulations. 6We have refused to listen to Your
servants the prophets, who spoke on Your authority to our kings and princes and
ancestors and to all the people of the land.

7"Lord, You are in the right; but as You see, our faces are covered with shame. This
is true of all of us, including the people of Judah and Jerusalem and all Israel, scattered
near and far, wherever You have driven us because of our disloyalty to You. 8O LORD,
we and our kings, princes, and ancestors are covered with shame because we have
sinned against You. 9But the Lord our God is merciful and forgiving, even though we
have rebelled against Him. 10We have not obeyed the LORD our God, for we have not
followed the instructions He gave us through His servants the prophets. 11All Israel has
disobeyed Your instruction and turned away, refusing to listen to Your voice.

"So now the solemn curses and judgments written in the Law of Moses, the servant
of God, have been poured down on us because of our sin. 12You have kept Your
word and done to us and our rulers exactly as You warned. Never has there been
such a disaster as happened in Jerusalem. 13Every curse written against us in the Law
of Moses has come true. Yet we have refused to seek mercy from the LORD our God
by turning from our sins and recognizing His truth. 14Therefore, the LORD has brought
upon us the disaster He prepared. The LORD our God was right to do all of these
things, for we did not obey Him.

15"O Lord our God, You brought lasting honor to Your name by rescuing Your
people from Egypt in a great display of power. But we have sinned and are full of
wickedness. 16In view of all Your faithful mercies, Lord, please turn Your furious anger
away from Your city Jerusalem, Your holy mountain. All the neighboring nations
mock Jerusalem and Your people because of our sins and the sins of our ancestors.

17"O our God, hear Your servant's prayer! Listen as I plead. For Your own sake,
Lord, smile again on Your desolate sanctuary.

18"O my God, lean down and listen to me. Open Your eyes and see our despair.
See how Your city—the city that bears Your name—lies in ruins. We make this plea,
not because we deserve help, but because of Your mercy.

19"O Lord, hear. O Lord, forgive. O Lord, listen and act! For Your own sake, do not
delay, O my God, for Your people and Your city bear Your name."

GABRIEL'S MESSAGE ABOUT THE ANOINTED ONE

20I went on praying and confessing my sin and the sin of my people, pleading with the
LORD my God for Jerusalem, His holy mountain. 21As I was praying, Gabriel, whom I had

9:2 See Jer 25:11-12; 29:10.

9:4 Deut 7:9, 21; Neh 9:32
9:5 Isa 53:6; Lam 1:18, 20
9:6 2 Chr 36:16; Jer 44:4-5, 21
9:7 Ezra 9:6-7; Jer 2:26-27; 3:25; 23:6; 33:16
9:10 2 Kgs 17:13-15; 18:12
9:11 Isa 1:2-4; Jer 8:5-10
9:12 Isa 44:26; Jer 44:2-6; Ezek 5:9; Zech 1:6
9:13 Lev 26:14-45; Deut 28:15-68; Isa 9:13; Jer 2:30; 5:3
9:14 Jer 31:28; 44:27
9:15 Deut 5:15; Neh 9:10; Jer 32:20
9:16 Ezek 5:14; Dan 9:20; Joel 3:17; Zech 8:3
9:17 Num 6:24-26; Lam 5:18
9:18 Ps 80:14; Isa 37:17; Jer 7:12; 36:7
9:20 Isa 6:5; 58:9
9:21 Exod 29:39; 1 Kgs 18:36; Ezra 9:4

▸ BIBLE
9:2 Trusting the Word. What did Daniel read while in Babylon? It is interesting to see that the prophet Daniel was reading the writings of another prophet, Jeremiah. Daniel recognized that Jeremiah's prophecies had unique authority from God since they were the "word of the LORD." New Testament writers also recognized the authority of the writings of the other apostles. Paul quoted both Deuteronomy and Luke's Gospel in the same verse, calling them "Scripture" (1 Timothy 5:18-19), and Peter also referred to Paul's writings as Scripture (2 Peter 3:15-16). You are privileged to be reading a Bible that contains all of these writings. Thank God for giving you a Bible so you can meditate on the same words that were studied by the apostles and prophets. (***See Bible***> *Uniqueness*> *Authoritative*> *Demonstrates credibility,* TopicGuide page A10.)

9:11-14 Daniel and the other prophets served as covenant lawyers, pointing out the breach of contract (Leviticus 26, Deuteronomy 28) between Israel and God. In this case, Daniel was the attorney accusing Israel yet pleading with the judge (9:17) for mercy. For another example of prophets as attorneys, see Isaiah 1–5.

seen in the earlier vision, came swiftly to me at the time of the evening sacrifice. 22He ex-
plained to me, "Daniel, I have come here to give you insight and understanding. 23The
moment you began praying, a command was given. And now I am here to tell you what it
was, for you are very precious to God. Listen carefully so that you can understand the
meaning of your vision.

24"A period of seventy sets of seven* has been decreed for your people and your holy city
to finish their rebellion, to put an end to their sin, to atone for their guilt, to bring in ever-
lasting righteousness, to confirm the prophetic vision, and to anoint the Most Holy Place.*
25Now listen and understand! Seven sets of seven plus sixty-two sets of seven* will pass from
the time the command is given to rebuild Jerusalem until a ruler—the Anointed One*—
comes. Jerusalem will be rebuilt with streets and strong defenses,* despite the perilous times.

26"After this period of sixty-two sets of seven,* the Anointed One will be killed, appearing
to have accomplished nothing, and a ruler will arise whose armies will destroy the city and
the Temple. The end will come with a flood, and war and its miseries are decreed from that
time to the very end. 27The ruler will make a treaty with the people for a period of one set
of seven,* but after half this time, he will put an end to the sacrifices and offerings. And as a
climax to all his terrible deeds,* he will set up a sacrilegious object that causes desecration,*
until the fate decreed for this defiler is finally poured out on him."

DANIEL'S VISION OF A MESSENGER

10 In the third year of the reign of King Cyrus of Persia,* Daniel (also known as Belte-
shazzar) had another vision. He understood that the vision concerned events cer-
tain to happen in the future—times of war and great hardship.

2When this vision came to me, I, Daniel, had been in mourning for three whole weeks.
3All that time I had eaten no rich food. No meat or wine crossed my lips, and I used no fra-
grant lotions until those three weeks had passed.

4On April 23,* as I was standing on the bank of the great Tigris River, 5I looked up and
saw a man dressed in linen clothing, with a belt of pure gold around his waist. 6His body
looked like a precious gem. His face flashed like lightning, and his eyes flamed like
torches. His arms and feet shone like polished bronze, and his voice roared like a vast mul-
titude of people.

7Only I, Daniel, saw this vision. The men with me saw nothing, but they were suddenly
terrified and ran away to hide. 8So I was left there all alone to see this amazing vision. My
strength left me, my face grew deathly pale, and I felt very weak. 9Then I heard the man
speak, and when I heard the sound of his voice, I fainted and lay there with my face to the
ground.

9:22 Zech 1:9, 14
9:23 Matt 24:15
9:24 Lev 25:8; Num 14:34; 2 Chr 29:24; Isa 51:6, 8; 53:10; Rom 3:21; 5:10
9:25 Ezra 4:24; 6:1-15; Neh 2:1-8; 3:1; Isa 9:6; John 1:41; 4:25
9:26 Isa 53:8; Nah 1:8; Matt 24:2; Mark 9:12; 13:2; Luke 19:43-44; 24:26
9:27 Isa 10:23; 28:22; Dan 11:31; *Matt 24:15; *Mark 13:14; *Luke 21:20
10:1 Dan 1:17, 21; 2:21; 6:28
10:2 Ezra 9:4-5; Neh 1:4
10:4 Ezek 1:3
10:5 Jer 10:9; Ezek 9:2; Rev 1:13; 15:6
10:6 Rev 1:14-15; 2:18
10:7 2 Kgs 6:17; Ezek 12:18; Acts 9:7
10:8 Gen 32:24; Dan 7:28; 8:27; Hab 3:16
10:9 Gen 15:12

9:24a Hebrew *seventy sevens.* **9:24b** Or *the Most Holy One.* **9:25a** Hebrew *Seven sevens plus sixty-two sevens.* **9:25b** Or *an anointed one;* similarly in 9:26. Hebrew reads *a messiah.* **9:25c** Or *and a moat,* or *and trenches.* **9:26** Hebrew *After sixty-two sevens.* **9:27a** Hebrew *for one seven.* **9:27b** Hebrew *And on the wing of abominations;* the meaning of the Hebrew is uncertain. **9:27c** Hebrew *an abomination of desolation.* **10:1** The third year of Cyrus's reign was 536 B.C. **10:4** Hebrew *On the twenty-fourth day of the first month,* of the ancient Hebrew lunar calendar. This date in the book of Daniel can be cross-checked with dates in surviving Persian records and can be related accurately to our modern calendar. This event occurred on April 23, 536 B.C.

9:25-27 For Daniel, the end of Babylon signified the beginning of the next stage of the coming Kingdom of God. He knew Jeremiah's prophecy that Babylon's power would extend no more than 70 years (Jeremiah 25:11-12). But after Babylon fell, there would be another period characterized by the passing of "sevens." These "sevens" not only represent a significant length of time but, according to this passage, significant events as well. The actions described in 9:26-27 seem to fit most naturally with the atrocities of Antiochus against Jerusalem.

10:1 The revelation came to Daniel in the third year of Cyrus the Great, king of Persia (536/535 BC). By this time, the first wave of Jewish exiles had already been allowed to return to their homeland.

10:2-3 Daniel was engaged in a number of ascetic practices associated with mourning. The fragrant oils were most likely used to keep the skin moist in the dry heat.

10:5-6 This description of the angel closely resembles Ezekiel's vision in Ezekiel 1 and the vision of Christ in Revelation 1. Linen was the traditional clothing for priests (Leviticus 6:10).

10 Just then a hand touched me and lifted me, still trembling, to my hands and knees.
11 And the man said to me, "Daniel, you are very precious to God, so listen carefully to
what I have to say to you. Stand up, for I have been sent to you." When he said this to me, I
stood up, still trembling.
12 Then he said, "Don't be afraid, Daniel. Since the first day you began to pray for under-
standing and to humble yourself before your God, your request has been heard in heaven. I
have come in answer to your prayer. 13 But for twenty-one days the spirit prince* of the king-
dom of Persia blocked my way. Then Michael, one of the archangels,* came to help me, and
I left him there with the spirit prince of the kingdom of Persia.* 14 Now I am here to explain
what will happen to your people in the future, for this vision concerns a time yet to come."
15 While he was speaking to me, I looked down at the ground, unable to say a word.
16 Then the one who looked like a man* touched my lips, and I opened my mouth and began
to speak. I said to the one standing in front of me, "I am filled with anguish because of the vi-
sion I have seen, my lord, and I am very weak. 17 How can someone like me, your servant,
talk to you, my lord? My strength is gone, and I can hardly breathe."
18 Then the one who looked like a man touched me again, and I felt my strength return-
ing. 19 "Don't be afraid," he said, "for you are very precious to God. Peace! Be encouraged!
Be strong!"
As he spoke these words to me, I suddenly felt stronger and said to him, "Please speak
to me, my lord, for you have strengthened me."
20 He replied, "Do you know why I have come? Soon I must return to fight against the
spirit prince of the kingdom of Persia, and after that the spirit prince of the kingdom of
Greece* will come. 21 Meanwhile, I will tell you what is written in the Book of Truth. (No one
helps me against these spirit princes except Michael, your spirit prince.* 11:1 I have been
standing beside Michael* to support and strengthen him since the first year of the reign of
Darius the Mede.)

KINGS OF THE SOUTH AND NORTH

11 2 "Now then, I will reveal the truth to you. Three more Persian kings will reign, to be
succeeded by a fourth, far richer than the others. He will use his wealth to stir up
everyone to fight against the kingdom of Greece.*
3 "Then a mighty king will rise to power who will rule with great authority and accomplish

10:10 Jer 1:9
10:11 Job 4:14-15; Ezek 2:1; Dan 8:16-17
10:13 Jude 1:9; Rev 12:7
10:14 Dan 2:28; 8:26; 12:4, 9
10:15 Ezek 24:27; Luke 1:20
10:16 Jer 1:9; Dan 7:15; 8:15
10:17 Exod 24:10-11; Isa 6:1-5
10:18 Isa 35:3-4
10:19 Josh 1:6-9; Judg 6:23; Isa 35:4; 43:1
10:20 Dan 8:21; 11:2
10:21 Dan 12:1, 4
11:1 Dan 5:31; 9:1
11:2 Dan 8:21, 26; 10:1, 20-21
11:3 Dan 5:19; 8:4-5, 21; 11:16, 36

10:13a Hebrew *the prince;* also in 10:13c, 20. 10:13b Hebrew *the chief princes.* 10:13c As in one Greek version; Hebrew reads *and I was left there with the kings of Persia.* The meaning of the Hebrew is uncertain. 10:16 As in most manuscripts of the Masoretic Text; one manuscript of the Masoretic Text and one Greek version read *Then something that looked like a human hand.* 10:20 Hebrew *of Javan.* 10:21 Hebrew *against these except Michael, your prince.* 11:1 Hebrew *him.* 11:2 Hebrew *of Javan.*

10:12-14 This passage reveals the cosmic struggle behind the earthly struggle of God's people. It speaks of conflicts in the heavenly realm that affect the course of history on earth. Here the "spirit prince of the kingdom of Persia," a demonic being connected to the fate of the nation, opposed the messenger sent to Daniel. Perhaps the delivery of the message might have insured or accelerated the dissolution of the Persian Empire. Here Michael is named for the first time in the Old Testament; he is called one of the archangels and is linked with the people of God. See also Daniel 12:1.

▸ SPIRITUAL WARFARE

10:12-14 Angels in a holy war. God gives us weapons to use in spiritual warfare, but sometimes He calls in additional support—angels to hinder Satan's attacks on His holy soldiers. Here a heavenly visitor told Daniel about a battle that had taken place for 21 days and about the assistance the less-ranked angel received from the archangel Michael. Angels are very powerful (and unusual; see Ezekiel 1:5-12; Isaiah 6:2-4), and those that serve God use their power to restrain evil and to help us. But they are not ours to command—nowhere in Scripture do we see people praying for their help or asking God to send them. God alone decides when and where they will serve. Thank God for His sovereign assignment of His angels in the right place, at the right time. (***See Spiritual Warfare***> *Resisting Sin and Evil*> *Resisting Temptation*> *How to Resist*> *By the help of angels,* TopicGuide page A45.)

10:15-17 Like the prophet Isaiah (Isaiah 6:7), Daniel's lips were touched to symbolize his preparation for prophetic ministry.

10:20–11:1 The language and circumstances of this chapter are extremely unusual, but the final message of the angel is found here: God would wage war against Persia and then Greece. These are represented by evil "spirit princes" or demons, because their intention against God's people would be the destruction of their spiritual identity.

11:2-20 Scholars consider the events detailed in this prophecy to span the time of Daniel to the time of Antiochus Epiphanes, between 300–100 BC.

everything he sets out to do. [4]But at the height of his power, his kingdom will be broken
apart and divided into four parts. It will not be ruled by the king's descendants, nor will the
kingdom hold the authority it once had. For his empire will be uprooted and given to others.
[5]"The king of the south will increase in power, but one of his own officials will become
more powerful than he and will rule his kingdom with great strength.
[6]"Some years later an alliance will be formed between the king of the north and the
king of the south. The daughter of the king of the south will be given in marriage to the
king of the north to secure the alliance, but she will lose her influence over him, and so will
her father. She will be abandoned along with her supporters. [7]But when one of her rela-
tives* becomes king of the south, he will raise an army and enter the fortress of the king of
the north and defeat him. [8]When he returns to Egypt, he will carry back their idols with
him, along with priceless articles of gold and silver. For some years afterward he will leave
the king of the north alone.
[9]"Later the king of the north will invade the realm of the king of the south but will soon
return to his own land. [10]However, the sons of the king of the north will assemble a mighty
army that will advance like a flood and carry the battle as far as the enemy's fortress.
[11]"Then, in a rage, the king of the south will rally against the vast forces assembled by
the king of the north and will defeat them. [12]After the enemy army is swept away, the king
of the south will be filled with pride and will execute many thousands of his enemies. But
his success will be short lived.
[13]"A few years later the king of the north will return with a fully equipped army far
greater than before. [14]At that time there will be a general uprising against the king of the
south. Violent men among your own people will join them in fulfillment of this vision, but
they will not succeed. [15]Then the king of the north will come and lay siege to a fortified
city and capture it. The best troops of the south will not be able to stand in the face of the
onslaught.
[16]"The king of the north will march onward unopposed; none will be able to stop him.
He will pause in the glorious land of Israel,* intent on destroying it. [17]He will make plans to
come with the might of his entire kingdom and will form an alliance with the king of the
south. He will give him a daughter in marriage in order to overthrow the kingdom from
within, but his plan will fail.
[18]"After this, he will turn his attention to the coastland and conquer many cities. But a
commander from another land will put an end to his insolence and cause him to retreat in
shame. [19]He will take refuge in his own fortresses but will stumble and fall and be seen no
more.
[20]"His successor will send out a tax collector to maintain the royal splendor. But after a
very brief reign, he will die, though not from anger or in battle.
[21]"The next to come to power will be a despicable man who is not in line for royal suc-
cession. He will slip in when least expected and take over the kingdom by flattery and in-
trigue. [22]Before him great armies will be swept away, including a covenant prince. [23]With
deceitful promises, he will make various alliances. He will become strong despite having
only a handful of followers. [24]Without warning he will enter the richest areas of the land.
Then he will distribute among his followers the plunder and wealth of the rich—something
his predecessors had never done. He will plot the overthrow of strongholds, but this will
last for only a short while.
[25]"Then he will stir up his courage and raise a great army against the king of the south.
The king of the south will go to battle with a mighty army, but to no avail, for there will be

11:4 Jer 49:36; Ezek 37:9; Dan 7:2; 8:8; Zech 2:6; Rev 7:1
11:5 Dan 11:9, 11, 14, 25, 40
11:6 Dan 11:7, 13, 15, 40
11:7 Dan 11:19, 38-39
11:8 Isa 37:19; 46:1-2; Jer 43:12-13
11:10 Isa 8:8; Jer 46:7-8; 51:42; Dan 11:26, 40
11:13 Dan 4:16; 12:7
11:15 Jer 6:6; Ezek 4:2; 17:17
11:16 Josh 1:5; Dan 5:19; 8:9; 11:3, 36, 41
11:17 2 Kgs 12:17; Ezek 4:3, 7
11:18 Gen 10:5; Isa 66:19; Zeph 2:11
11:19 Pss 27:2; 37:36; Jer 46:6; Ezek 26:21
11:20 Isa 60:17
11:24 Num 13:20; Neh 9:25; Ezek 34:14

11:7 Hebrew *a branch from her roots.* 11:16 Hebrew *the glorious land.*

11:16 The "glorious land" refers to the Promised Land of Israel.

11:21-24 The remainder of the chapter focuses on the reign of Antiochus IV Epiphanes, who persecuted the Jewish community and vandalized the Temple.

plots against him. 26His own household will cause his downfall. His army will be swept
away, and many will be killed. 27Seeking nothing but each other's harm, these kings will
plot against each other at the conference table, attempting to deceive each other. But it
will make no difference, for the end will come at the appointed time.

28"The king of the north will then return home with great riches. On the way he will set
himself against the people of the holy covenant, doing much damage before continuing
his journey.

29"Then at the appointed time he will once again invade the south, but this time the re-
sult will be different. 30For warships from western coastlands* will scare him off, and he will
withdraw and return home. But he will vent his anger against the people of the holy cov-
enant and reward those who forsake the covenant.

31"His army will take over the Temple fortress, pollute the sanctuary, put a stop to the
daily sacrifices, and set up the sacrilegious object that causes desecration.* 32He will flatter
and win over those who have violated the covenant. But the people who know their God
will be strong and will resist him.

33"Wise leaders will give instruction to many, but these teachers will die by fire and
sword, or they will be jailed and robbed. 34During these persecutions, little help will arrive,
and many who join them will not be sincere. 35And some of the wise will fall victim to per-
secution. In this way, they will be refined and cleansed and made pure until the time of the
end, for the appointed time is still to come.

36"The king will do as he pleases, exalting himself and claiming to be greater than every
god, even blaspheming the God of gods. He will succeed, but only until the time of wrath
is completed. For what has been determined will surely take place. 37He will have no re-
spect for the gods of his ancestors, or for the god loved by women, or for any other god,
for he will boast that he is greater than them all. 38Instead of these, he will worship the god
of fortresses—a god his ancestors never knew—and lavish on him gold, silver, precious
stones, and expensive gifts. 39Claiming this foreign god's help, he will attack the strongest
fortresses. He will honor those who submit to him, appointing them to positions of author-
ity and dividing the land among them as their reward.*

40"Then at the time of the end, the king of the south will attack the king of the north.
The king of the north will storm out with chariots, charioteers, and a vast navy. He will in-
vade various lands and sweep through them like a flood. 41He will enter the glorious land
of Israel,* and many nations will fall, but Moab, Edom, and the best part of Ammon will es-
cape. 42He will conquer many countries, and even Egypt will not escape. 43He will gain
control over the gold, silver, and treasures of Egypt, and the Libyans and Ethiopians* will
be his servants.

44"But then news from the east and the north will alarm him, and he will set out in great
anger to destroy and obliterate many. 45He will stop between the glorious holy mountain

11:27 Pss 52:1; 64:6 Jer 9:3-5 Dan 11:35, 40 Hab 2:3 Acts 17:31
11:30 Gen 10:4 Num 24:24 Jer 2:10
11:31 Dan 8:11-13; 9:27; 12:11 Matt 24:15 Mark 13:14
11:32 Mic 5:7-9 Zech 9:13-16; 10:3-6
11:33 Matt 24:9 John 16:2 Heb 11:36-38
11:34 Matt 7:15 Rom 16:18
11:35 Deut 8:16 Prov 17:3 Dan 12:10 Zech 13:9 John 15:2
11:36 Deut 10:17 Ps 136:2 Isa 10:25; 14:13; 26:20 Dan 2:47; 5:20; 7:8, 11; 8:11; 9:27; 11:3 2 Thes 2:4 Rev 13:5-6
11:40 Isa 5:28 Jer 4:13
11:41 Jer 48:47; 49:6
11:43 2 Chr 12:3 Ezek 30:4-5 Nah 3:9
11:45 Isa 65:25; 66:20 Dan 9:16, 20

11:30 Hebrew *from Kittim.* 11:31 Hebrew *the abomination of desolation.* 11:39 Or *at a price.* 11:41 Hebrew *the glorious land.* 11:43 Hebrew *Cushites.*

11:31-35 Antiochus IV violently persecuted the Jewish people. The height of his atrocities against the Temple and its worship came in December 168 BC. The apocryphal books of 1 and 2 Maccabees record these tragic events. Many faithful Jews resisted the persecutions of Antiochus to the point of death. Eventually, a priest named Matthias and his sons began a resistance movement that overthrew the oppressive regime and restored the Temple and its worship in 165 BC.

▸ WORSHIP
11:31 Future knowledge. Each year modern fortune-tellers and astrologers give their predictions about world events and, year after year, even their general predictions are proven wrong. Yet many continue to be intrigued with the idea that someone might know the future. God's Word demonstrates knowledge of the future, such as this detailed message He sent to Daniel. God gives us the promise that nothing in the future "will ever be able to separate us from the love of God that is revealed in Christ Jesus our Lord" (Romans 8:38-39). Isn't that enough to know? Let this truth eliminate any anxiety you might have about future events. (***See Worship> OT> Prophets> Old Testament prophets witnessed to the future salvation in Christ,*** TopicGuide page A28.)

11:36–12:3 It is possible that these prophecies are about the last Antichrist and the end of history, but it is not obvious from the text. It is best to remain flexible about the interpretation of these verses. The general idea is straightforward: The people of God will ultimately triumph over the forces of evil that attack them.

and the sea and will pitch his royal tents. But while he is there, his time will suddenly run
out, and no one will help him.

THE TIME OF THE END

12 "At that time Michael, the archangel* who stands guard over your nation, will
arise. Then there will be a time of anguish greater than any since nations first
came into existence. But at that time every one of your people whose name is written in
the book will be rescued. 2Many of those whose bodies lie dead and buried will rise up,
some to everlasting life and some to shame and everlasting disgrace. 3Those who are
wise will shine as bright as the sky, and those who lead many to righteousness will shine
like the stars forever. 4But you, Daniel, keep this prophecy a secret; seal up the book until
the time of the end, when many will rush here and there, and knowledge will increase."
5Then I, Daniel, looked and saw two others standing on opposite banks of the river.
6One of them asked the man dressed in linen, who was now standing above the river,
"How long will it be until these shocking events are over?"
7The man dressed in linen, who was standing above the river, raised both his hands to-
ward heaven and took a solemn oath by the One who lives forever, saying, "It will go on
for a time, times, and half a time. When the shattering of the holy people has finally come
to an end, all these things will have happened."
8I heard what he said, but I did not understand what he meant. So I asked, "How will all
this finally end, my lord?"
9But he said, "Go now, Daniel, for what I have said is kept secret and sealed until the
time of the end. 10Many will be purified, cleansed, and refined by these trials. But the
wicked will continue in their wickedness, and none of them will understand. Only those
who are wise will know what it means.
11"From the time the daily sacrifice is stopped and the sacrilegious object that causes
desecration* is set up to be worshiped, there will be 1,290 days. 12And blessed are those
who wait and remain until the end of the 1,335 days!
13"As for you, go your way until the end. You will rest, and then at the end of the days,
you will rise again to receive the inheritance set aside for you."

12:1 Jer 30:7; Ezek 5:9; Dan 7:10; 9:12; 10:21; 12:4; Matt 24:21; Rev 16:18
12:2 Isa 26:19; Ezek 37:12-14; Matt 25:46; John 5:28-29
12:3 Isa 53:11; John 5:35
12:4 Isa 8:16; 11:9; Rev 22:10
12:6 Ezek 9:2; Zech 1:12-13; Matt 24:3
12:7 Ezek 20:5; Luke 21:24; Rev 10:5-7; 12:14
12:10 Isa 32:6-7; Hos 14:9; Rev 11:2; 12:6; 13:5
12:11 Dan 9:27; 11:31; Matt 24:15
12:12 Isa 30:18
12:13 Ps 16:5; Rev 14:13

12:1 Hebrew *the great prince.* 12:11 Hebrew *the abomination of desolation.*

12:2 This verse is one of the few unambiguous references in the Old Testament to the bodily resurrection of the dead (see also Job 19:25-26; Isaiah 26:19; Ezekiel 37:11-12).

12:5-13 Once again the exact meaning of the angel's words in this passage is difficult to understand, not only for Daniel, but also for us. The general idea, however, seems to be that God's people will continue to be persecuted by the wicked until the time appointed by God.

12:7 The "time, times, and half a time" is enigmatic and intentionally unclear, showing that the timing of God's great acts are not easily pinned down. This continues Daniel's theme of trust in a sovereign God. Shadrach, Meshach, and Abednego did not know when and how or even if God would rescue them; but they trusted that God would sustain them through times of persecution that are entirely under His control (3:16-18).

▸ HOLINESS

12:10 Maturity through suffering. Some believe that the key to developing personal maturity is suffering. Others counter this by noting that there are many miserable, bitter people who suffer and only grow more miserable. Daniel was told that the wicked do not benefit from suffering. They only continue in their wickedness. On the other hand, Daniel was also told that some will endure the same suffering and the result will be that they are purified, cleansed, and refined. They will prove James right when he said suffering produces character in the Christian (James 1:2-4). What is the difference? God promises believers that He will use all things to promote their faith and maturity (Romans 8:28). God begins a work of maturity in believers at the very first step of their spiritual journey, and He will not let anything stop Him from completing it (Philippians 1:6). Work with God as He shapes you into the person you were intended to be (Ephesians 4:30). (***See Holiness**> Submission> Identifying with Christ> Suffering with Him,* TopicGuide page A40.)

HOSEA

PURPOSE

To warn Israel of the judgment of God and reassure them of the hope of restoration if they repented.

If there is a heartrending story in the Old Testament, it is Hosea. In obedience to God's command, this prophet married—and loved—a prostitute. Later, when she returned to her adulterous ways, Hosea bought her out of slavery for himself.

Hosea was called by God to prophesy against Israel (the ten northern tribes, referred to by Hosea as "Ephraim") in the days of its spiritual prostitution before the people were carried into captivity by Assyria. Part of Hosea's calling included the difficult task of loving an unfaithful wife in order to demonstrate God's love for His people Israel. Hosea's love for his wife, Gomer, showed that God's love for His bride, Israel, was constant and unshakeable despite all the nation's unfaithfulness.

DISCOVER GOD IN HOSEA

Hosea reveals many facets of the love of God:

Loyal Love: Many Bible students are familiar with the Greek word for "unconditional love," *agape*. Fewer are familiar with the corresponding Hebrew word in the Old Testament: *hesed*. God's love for Israel in the Old Testament was nothing if not loyal. The promises made to Abraham, Isaac, Jacob, and David, which were confirmed again and again by the prophets, leave no doubt that God's covenant people forever will be "His most precious possession" (Zechariah 2:8). God freely declared that He is as likely to do away with the laws of nature as to break His covenant of love (*hesed*) with Israel (Jeremiah 31:35-36). Hosea's loyal love for his wife, Gomer, is a picture of God's loyal love for Israel. Hosea declared: "I will make you My wife forever, showing you righteousness and justice, unfailing love [*hesed*] and compassion" (Hosea 2:19). The apostle Paul confirmed God's continuing loyalty to His people in the New Testament when he stated that "nothing in all creation will ever be able to separate us from the love [*agape*] of God" (Romans 8:39).

Pursuing Love: Human beings do not have the innate capacity to pursue forever the object of their love when there is no response. But God's love does just that; nothing will keep Him from pursuing the object of His love—His people. God told Hosea to pursue Gomer, to go into the marketplace of sin where she had willingly gone and purchase her back (Hosea 3:1-3). In the same way, God said He would "win [Israel] back once again" (Hosea 2:14). God's love never fails (1 Corinthians 13:7), and all who are called by His name should reflect this same tireless love for others by the power of the Holy Spirit.

GROWING THROUGH HOSEA

Hosea emphasizes several spiritual traits to emulate:

Faithfulness: Spiritual unfaithfulness is compared to adultery in Hosea (2:4-6; 4:15; 5:4). The abandonment of one's relationship to God in the pursuit of other gods is equated with leaving one's marriage and becoming an adulterer (Revelation 17:5). While followers of Christ may rarely face the temptation to worship pagan idols, there are plenty of other opportunities for unfaithfulness. Greed and materialism are two sins that Paul equated with idolatry, following Jesus' grave warning about serving "God and money" (Matthew 6:24).

Forgiveness: The old saying "To err is human, to forgive divine" is exactly right. Forgiveness is a divine characteristic, but one that is to be emulated by those who follow God. Hosea's forgiveness of Gomer's blatant adultery demonstrated this unrelenting divine love, which God has shown to all who follow Him. Ephesians 4:32 connects divine and human forgiveness in no uncertain terms: "Instead, be kind to each other, tenderhearted, forgiving one another, just as God through Christ has forgiven you." To the same degree that God has forgiven us, we ought to show forgiveness to those who wrong us. This proves that the grace of God is working in us (Matthew 6:15).

DISCOVERY VERSES

I will make you My wife forever, showing you righteousness and justice, unfailing love and compassion. I will be faithful to you and make you Mine, and you will finally know Me as the LORD. (HOSEA 2:19-20)

Oh, that we might know the LORD! Let us press on to know Him. He will respond to us as surely as the arrival of dawn or the coming of rains in early spring. (HOSEA 6:3)

HOSEA FACTS

Author: Hosea (1:1).

Written to: The northern kingdom of Israel (or "Ephraim," the name of one of the key tribes that constituted the kingdom of Israel), especially its leaders (5:1).

Date of writing: Hosea prophesied over a period of four decades, covering the reigns of several kings (1:1; approximately 760–720 BC).

Setting: The exact setting of Hosea's prophecy is unknown; he prophesied in the region of the tribe of Ephraim (13:1, 12, 15).

OUTLINE

- **HOSEA 1:1–3:5**—Lessons on Restoration from Hosea's Life
- **HOSEA 4:1–14:9**—Lessons on Restoration from Hosea's Prophecies

1:1
2 Kgs 15:32-38; 16:2-20; 18:1-8
2 Chr 26:1-23; 27:1-9; 28:1-27; 29:1-32
Mic 1:1

1 The LORD gave this message to Hosea son of Beeri during the years when Uzziah, Jotham, Ahaz, and Hezekiah were kings of Judah, and Jeroboam son of Jehoash* was king of Israel.

HOSEA'S WIFE AND CHILDREN

1:2
Jer 3:1
Hos 2:5; 3:1

2 When the LORD first began speaking to Israel through Hosea, He said to him, "Go and marry a prostitute,* so that some of her children will be conceived in prostitution. This will illustrate how Israel has acted like a prostitute by turning against the LORD and worshiping other gods."

1:4
2 Kgs 10:1-36

3 So Hosea married Gomer, the daughter of Diblaim, and she became pregnant and gave Hosea a son. 4 And the LORD said, "Name the child Jezreel, for I am about to punish King Jehu's dynasty to avenge the murders he committed at Jezreel. In fact, I will bring an end to Israel's independence. 5 I will break its military power in the Jezreel Valley."

1:7
Ps 44:3-7
Isa 30:18

6 Soon Gomer became pregnant again and gave birth to a daughter. And the LORD said to Hosea, "Name your daughter Lo-ruhamah—'Not loved'—for I will no longer show love to the people of Israel or forgive them. 7 But I will show love to the people of Judah. I will free them from their enemies—not with weapons and armies or horses and charioteers, but by My power as the LORD their God."

1:9
*1 Pet 2:10

8 After Gomer had weaned Lo-ruhamah, she again became pregnant and gave birth to a second son. 9 And the LORD said, "Name him Lo-ammi—'Not My people'—for Israel is not My people, and I am not their God.

1:10
Gen 22:17; 32:12
Isa 63:16; 64:8
Jer 33:22
*Rom 9:26

1:11
Isa 11:12
Jer 30:21
Ezek 37:21-24
Hos 3:5

10* "Yet the time will come when Israel's people will be like the sands of the seashore—too many to count! Then, at the place where they were told, 'You are not My people,' it will be said, 'You are children of the living God.' 11 Then the people of Judah and Israel will unite together. They will choose one leader for themselves, and they will return from exile together. What a day that will be—the day of Jezreel*—when God will again plant His people in His land.

2:1* "In that day you will call your brothers Ammi—'My people.' And you will call your sisters Ruhamah—'The ones I love.'

CHARGES AGAINST AN UNFAITHFUL WIFE

2:2
Isa 50:1
Hos 4:5

2 2 "But now bring charges against Israel—your mother—
for she is no longer My wife,
and I am no longer her husband.

1:1 Hebrew *Joash,* a variant spelling of Jehoash. 1:2 Or *a promiscuous woman.* 1:10 Verses 1:10-11 are numbered 2:1-2 in Hebrew text. 1:11 *Jezreel* means "God plants." 2:1 Verses 2:1-23 are numbered 2:3-25 in Hebrew text.

▸ GOD

1:2 Living illustration. "Go and marry a prostitute? Are you sure, Lord?" Many have struggled with the notion that God would have ordered Hosea to marry a woman who was already promiscuous, and some scholars have proposed that Gomer may have initially been chaste when she married Hosea and only later became a prostitute. But it is very possible that "marry a prostitute" means just that. This confusing command was designed to shock Israel into understanding that the nation was acting like Gomer (see Ezekiel 16 for similar imagery) by selling herself like a prostitute to other gods. How is God revealing your sin to you? Be aware that God is busy teaching us through everyday circumstances. (***See God****> Relationship> God's Desire> God pursues a relationship,* TopicGuide page A14.)

1:4 Hosea's wife Gomer gave birth to Jezreel, the first of three children. As with Hosea and Gomer's marriage, each child's name conveyed a message from God to Israel.

1:8-9 Gomer's third child's name carried a terrible message. "Not My people" signified a break in Israel's covenant with God (Exodus 6:7). God had always identified Himself in a unique way with Israel, but now He denied that He was their God and that they were His people (Amos 9:7).

2:1 After the Lord changed the significance of Jezreel's name from judgment to blessing, He also changed "not My people" to "My people" and "not loved" to "the ones I love." The naming of Gomer's children foretold of national judgment, and their renaming offered hope for the future restoration of Israel.

Tell her to remove the prostitute's makeup from her face
and the clothing that exposes her breasts.
3 Otherwise, I will strip her as naked
as she was on the day she was born.
I will leave her to die of thirst,
as in a dry and barren wilderness.
4 And I will not love her children,
for they were conceived in prostitution.
5 Their mother is a shameless prostitute
and became pregnant in a shameful way.
She said, 'I'll run after other lovers
and sell myself to them for food and water,
for clothing of wool and linen,
and for olive oil and drinks.'

6 "For this reason I will fence her in with thornbushes.
I will block her path with a wall
to make her lose her way.

2:3 Isa 20:2-3; 32:13-14 Jer 14:3 Ezek 16:7, 22 Hos 13:15

2:5 Jer 2:25; 3:1-2 Ezek 23:16-17, 40-45

2:6 Job 19:8

2:2-4 As an angry spouse would disown illegitimate children, God was pictured disowning all the people of Israel.

2:3 Ezekiel 16:8-13 portrayed God taking Israel from shameful nakedness and graciously clothing her just as a man would adorn his bride. This verse presents the opposite: God would strip His wife naked and cast her away with nothing. Israel would be publicly humiliated (Hosea 2:10) and left to die when God brought judgment.

▸ GOD
2:6-8 The jealous God. In an age when we can order a custom car, tailored clothing, and food cooked exactly as we like, it's tempting to think that we can mix-and-match beliefs from different religions and make one that works for us. But this is not an option for those who love God. Hosea shows that God is like a jealous husband who truly loves his bride. Imagine how jealous a groom would be if his new wife began flirting with other men even before the wedding reception was over! Christians do the same thing when they dabble with other religions or give priority to anything over Jesus Christ. The One who loves you enough to die for you will not share your affections with another. He is jealous for you. Respond to God's unwavering love for you by giving Him the exclusive devotion He deserves. (***See God****> God's Nature> Personality> Emotion> God jealously desires exclusive worship,* TopicGuide page A14.)

MY RESPONSE TO GOD

The Scandalous Love of God

HOSEA 1–3

What must have gone through Hosea's mind when God told him to marry a prostitute? We can only wonder.

The prophet Hosea followed God's instructions and married Gomer. Not surprisingly, she was unfaithful to him and soon left him for another lover. Yet under God's instruction, Hosea sought her out and brought her home. Why would God ask Hosea to do such a thing?

Hosea's relationship with unfaithful Gomer is a living picture of God's relationship with unfaithful Israel. Just as Gomer left her husband, Hosea, to become intimate with other men, many in Israel had strayed from God and prostituted themselves to false religions. As Gomer's life spiraled out of control, she ended up in slavery. But Hosea bought her back (3:2), foreshadowing how God would send His only Son to redeem us from our slavery to sin and death.

Hosea's faithfulness to Gomer is a picture of God's faithfulness to us. He loves us. He refuses to give up on us (Luke 15). He takes the initiative to seek us out when we wander away. Hosea's story shows the extraordinary effort God takes to bring unfaithful covenant people back into His family.

2:7 Jer 2:2; 3:1 Ezek 23:4 Hos 5:13

[7] When she runs after her lovers,
she won't be able to catch them.
She will search for them
but not find them.
Then she will think,
'I might as well return to my husband,
for I was better off with him than I am now.'

2:8 Ezek 16:18 Hos 8:4

[8] She doesn't realize it was I who gave her everything she has—
the grain, the new wine, the olive oil;
I even gave her silver and gold.
But she gave all My gifts to Baal.

[9] "But now I will take back the ripened grain and new wine
I generously provided each harvest season.
I will take away the wool and linen clothing
I gave her to cover her nakedness.

2:10 Ezek 16:37 Hos 8:7

[10] I will strip her naked in public,
while all her lovers look on.
No one will be able
to rescue her from My hands.

2:11 Isa 1:13-14 Jer 7:34; 16:9

[11] I will put an end to her annual festivals,
her new moon celebrations, and her Sabbath days—
all her appointed festivals.

2:12 Jer 5:17; 8:13

[12] I will destroy her grapevines and fig trees,
things she claims her lovers gave her.
I will let them grow into tangled thickets,
where only wild animals will eat the fruit.

2:13 Jer 7:9 Ezek 23:40-42 Hos 4:13; 11:2

[13] I will punish her for all those times
when she burned incense to her images of Baal,
when she put on her earrings and jewels
and went out to look for her lovers
but forgot all about Me,"
says the LORD.

THE LORD'S LOVE FOR UNFAITHFUL ISRAEL

2:14 Ezek 20:33-38

[14] "But then I will win her back once again.
I will lead her into the desert
and speak tenderly to her there.

2:15 Josh 7:26 Jer 2:1-3 Ezek 16:8, 22

[15] I will return her vineyards to her
and transform the Valley of Trouble* into a gateway of hope.
She will give herself to Me there,
as she did long ago when she was young,
when I freed her from her captivity in Egypt.

2:16 Isa 54:5 Hos 2:7

[16] When that day comes," says the LORD,
"you will call Me 'my husband'
instead of 'my master.'*

2:15 Hebrew *valley of Achor.* 2:16 Hebrew *'my baal.'*

2:15 The mention of vineyards recalls the bounty in the Promised Land and the huge cluster of grapes carried by the spies (Numbers 13:23). God would take them through testing in order to bring them to blessing. The reference to the Valley of Trouble (literally "Achor") recalls the days of Joshua when Achan sinned and the nation was judged (Joshua 7:26). The Valley of Trouble (representing judgment and exile) would be transformed into a gateway of hope. Judgment would rekindle the love Israel had when she was young.

[17] O Israel, I will wipe the many names of Baal from your lips,
and you will never mention them again.
[18] On that day I will make a covenant
with all the wild animals and the birds of the sky
and the animals that scurry along the ground
so they will not harm you.
I will remove all weapons of war from the land,
all swords and bows,
so you can live unafraid
in peace and safety.
[19] I will make you My wife forever,
showing you righteousness and justice,
unfailing love and compassion.
[20] I will be faithful to you and make you Mine,
and you will finally know Me as the LORD.

[21] "In that day, I will answer,"
says the LORD.
"I will answer the sky as it pleads for clouds.
And the sky will answer the earth with rain.
[22] Then the earth will answer the thirsty cries
of the grain, the grapevines, and the olive trees.
And they in turn will answer,
'Jezreel'—'God plants!'
[23] At that time I will plant a crop of Israelites
and raise them for Myself.
I will show love
to those I called 'Not loved.'*
And to those I called 'Not My people,'*
I will say, 'Now you are My people.'
And they will reply, 'You are our God!'"

2:18 Lev 26:5-6; Job 5:23; Isa 2:4; Ezek 34:25; 39:1-10
2:20 Jer 31:34; Hos 6:6; 13:4
2:21 Zech 8:12
2:22 Jer 31:27-28; Joel 2:19
2:23 Hos 1:6, 9; *Rom 9:25; *1 Pet 2:10

HOSEA'S WIFE IS REDEEMED

3 Then the LORD said to me, "Go and love your wife again, even though she* commits adultery with another lover. This will illustrate that the LORD still loves Israel, even though the people have turned to other gods and love to worship them.*"

[2] So I bought her back for fifteen pieces of silver* and five bushels of barley and a measure of wine.* [3] Then I said to her, "You must live in my house for many days and stop your prostitution. During this time, you will not have sexual relations with anyone, not even with me.*"

3:2 Ruth 4:10

2:23a Hebrew *Lo-ruhamah;* see 1:6. 2:23b Hebrew *Lo-ammi;* see 1:9. 3:1a Or *Go and love a woman who.* 3:1b Hebrew *love their raisin cakes.* 3:2a Hebrew *15 shekels of silver,* about 6 ounces or 171 grams in weight. 3:2b As in Greek version, which reads *a homer of barley and a measure of wine;* Hebrew reads *a homer* [5 bushels or 182 liters] *of barley and a lethech* [2.5 bushels or 91 liters] *of barley.* 3:3 Or *and I will live with you.*

2:18 Glorious images of peace and security were laid before Hosea's audience to make them ache for restoration with God. One day all of nature and all the nations will be at peace. At that time, the imminent curses (see Deuteronomy 28) will be transformed into blessings.

▸ GOD
3:1 The persistent lover. Hosea presents God as a lover who won't take no for an answer. He is persistent to pursue His beloved even when she seems unlovable. But why? In Deuteronomy 7:7-8, Moses told Israel, "The LORD did not set His heart on you and choose you because you were more numerous than other nations, for you were the smallest of all nations! Rather, it was simply that the LORD loves you, and He was keeping the oath He had sworn to your ancestors." The Lord loves you like this simply because He has chosen to do so! Jesus said this glorious pursuit was at the heart of His mission, "The Son of Man came to seek and save those who are lost" (Luke 19:10). If you are a Christian, marvel that God pursued you when you were still a sinner (Romans 5:8) and that your lack of loveliness will never stop His persistent pursuit (Romans 8:35-39). Revel in His affection! (***See God****>* *God's Nature> Personality> Relationships> God wants a relationship with His people,* TopicGuide page A14.)

3:4 Judg 17:6 [4]This shows that Israel will go a long time without a king or prince, and without sacri-
fices, sacred pillars, priests,* or even idols! [5]But afterward the people will return and de-
3:5 Jer 50:4-5 Ezek 34:24 vote themselves to the LORD their God and to David's descendant, their king.* In the last
days, they will tremble in awe of the LORD and of His goodness.

THE LORD'S CASE AGAINST ISRAEL

4:1 Isa 59:4 Jer 7:28 Hos 12:2 Mic 6:2

4 [1] Hear the word of the LORD, O people of Israel!
The LORD has brought charges against you, saying:
"There is no faithfulness, no kindness,
no knowledge of God in your land.

4:2 Hos 6:8-9; 7:1-4; 10:4

[2] You make vows and break them;
you kill and steal and commit adultery.
There is violence everywhere—
one murder after another.

4:3 Isa 24:4; 33:9 Zeph 1:3

[3] That is why your land is in mourning,
and everyone is wasting away.
Even the wild animals, the birds of the sky,
and the fish of the sea are disappearing.

4:4 Deut 17:12 Ezek 3:26 Amos 5:10, 13

[4] "Don't point your finger at someone else
and try to pass the blame!
My complaint, you priests,
is with you.*

4:5 Ezek 14:3, 7 Hos 5:5

[5] So you will stumble in broad daylight,
and your false prophets will fall with you in the night.
And I will destroy Israel, your mother.

4:6 Hos 4:14 Zech 11:8-9, 15-17 Mal 2:7-8

[6] My people are being destroyed
because they don't know Me.
Since you priests refuse to know Me,
I refuse to recognize you as My priests.
Since you have forgotten the laws of your God,
I will forget to bless your children.

4:7 Hos 10:1; 13:6 Hab 2:16

[7] The more priests there are,
the more they sin against Me.
They have exchanged the glory of God
for the shame of idols.*

3:4 Hebrew *ephod,* the vest worn by the priest. **3:5** Hebrew *to David their king.* **4:4** Hebrew *Your people are like those with a complaint against the priests.* **4:7** As in Syriac version and an ancient Hebrew tradition; Masoretic Text reads *I will turn their glory into shame.*

3:3-4 Although Gomer had been saved from utter ruin and was back at home under Hosea's care, they were not intimately joined for many days. Why this arrangement? Like Gomer, Israel would also be spared utter ruin after exile. Yet, while in exile, Israel would not enjoy God's presence in the same way as before.

4:1-2 The subject matter abruptly switches from the hope of blessings in the last days to the horror of the present lawsuit against Israel. It is likely that this is the beginning of a separate set of prophecies, perhaps delivered later in Hosea's ministry. The setting is a courtroom where the prosecutor is piling up charges before God the judge.

▶ BIBLE
4:5-9 Instructed by the Word. Why should we care about teaching the word of God? In the Old Testament, the priests from the tribe of Levi were given a responsibility as leaders to teach the word of God (Deuteronomy 31:11; 33:10). But the priests in Judah were not teaching or living by God's word. As a result, the wrong people were in the wrong places doing wrong things. In the New Testament, God commands His leaders to "preach the word of God" and to "patiently correct, rebuke, and encourage your people with good teaching" (2 Timothy 4:2). You should care about the teaching of the word because God demands that those who lead His church be "able to teach" (1 Timothy 3:2). Ask God to make you value the teaching of His word, and then seek Him to give you leaders who will boldly preach and teach His word. (***See Bible*> *Power*> *Wisdom*> *Instruction leads to wisdom,* TopicGuide page A11.)

8 "When the people bring their sin offerings, the priests get fed.
So the priests are glad when the people sin!
9 'And what the priests do, the people also do.'
So now I will punish both priests and people
for their wicked deeds.
10 They will eat and still be hungry.
They will play the prostitute and gain nothing from it,
for they have deserted the LORD
11 to worship other gods.

"Wine has robbed My people
of their understanding.
12 They ask a piece of wood for advice!
They think a stick can tell them the future!
Longing after idols
has made them foolish.
They have played the prostitute,
serving other gods and deserting their God.
13 They offer sacrifices to idols on the mountaintops.
They go up into the hills to burn incense
in the pleasant shade of oaks, poplars, and terebinth trees.

"That is why your daughters turn to prostitution,
and your daughters-in-law commit adultery.
14 But why should I punish them
for their prostitution and adultery?
For your men are doing the same thing,
sinning with whores and shrine prostitutes.
O foolish people! You refuse to understand,
so you will be destroyed.

15 "Though you, Israel, are a prostitute,
may Judah avoid such guilt.
Do not join the false worship at Gilgal or Beth-aven,*
even though they take oaths there in the LORD's name.
16 Israel is stubborn,
like a stubborn heifer.
So should the LORD feed her
like a lamb in a lush pasture?
17 Leave Israel* alone,
because she is married to idolatry.
18 When the rulers of Israel finish their drinking,
off they go to find some prostitutes.
They love shame more than honor.*

4:9 Isa 24:2; Jer 5:31
4:11 Isa 5:12; 28:7
4:12 Jer 2:27
4:13 Jer 2:20; 3:6; Ezek 6:13; Hos 2:13; 11:2
4:14 Deut 23:17
4:16 Isa 5:17; 7:25
4:17 Ps 81:12

4:15 *Beth-aven* means "house of wickedness"; it is being used as another name for Bethel, which means "house of God."
4:17 Hebrew *Ephraim,* referring to the northern kingdom of Israel. 4:18 As in Greek version; the meaning of the Hebrew is uncertain.

4:8 A similar abuse is recorded in 1 Samuel 2 when Eli's sons were abusing their position as priests to rob the people. God rebuked Eli, saying, "You and they have become fat from the best offerings of My people Israel!" (1 Samuel 2:29). Paul likewise warned about leaders who would use their position for material gain (Titus 1:11) and rebuked the Corinthians for letting sinful leaders exploit them (2 Corinthians 11:19).

SALVATION

4:18-19 Jesus the shame bearer. Imagine if the worst sins you ever committed were publicly announced for all to hear. Would it make you consider changing your identity and moving to another country? Hosea told Israel's leaders that God would soon judge them for their shameful behavior. In the New Testament, both Jesus and Paul likewise warned

4:19 Hos 12:1; 13:15

19 So a mighty wind will sweep them away.
Their sacrifices to idols will bring them shame.

THE FAILURE OF ISRAEL'S LEADERS

5 1 "Hear this, you priests.
Pay attention, you leaders of Israel.
Listen, you members of the royal family.
Judgment has been handed down against you.
For you have led the people into a snare
by worshiping the idols at Mizpah and Tabor.
2 You have dug a deep pit to trap them at Acacia Grove.*
But I will settle with you for what you have done.

5:3 Amos 5:12

3 I know what you are like, O Ephraim.
You cannot hide yourself from Me, O Israel.
You have left Me as a prostitute leaves her husband;
you are utterly defiled.

5:4 Hos 4:6, 14

4 Your deeds won't let you return to your God.
You are a prostitute through and through,
and you do not know the LORD.

5:5 2 Kgs 17:19-20; Ezek 23:31-35

5 "The arrogance of Israel testifies against her;
Israel and Ephraim will stumble under their load of guilt.
Judah, too, will fall with them.

5:6 Isa 1:15; Ezek 8:6; Mic 6:6-7

6 When they come with their flocks and herds
to offer sacrifices to the LORD,
they will not find Him,
because He has withdrawn from them.

5:7 Hos 2:4

7 They have betrayed the honor of the LORD,
bearing children that are not His.
Now their false religion will devour them
along with their wealth.*

8 "Sound the alarm in Gibeah!
Blow the trumpet in Ramah!
Raise the battle cry in Beth-aven*!
Lead on into battle, O warriors of Benjamin!

5:2 Hebrew *at Shittim.* The meaning of the Hebrew for this sentence is uncertain. 5:7 The meaning of the Hebrew is uncertain. 5:8 *Beth-aven* means "house of wickedness"; it is being used as another name for Bethel, which means "house of God."

of a day when all that is hidden will be brought to light and judged (Mark 4:22; Romans 2:16). We all have done shameful things, so what hope do we have on such a day? The Scriptures tell us that the judgment for all of our shameful deeds was placed on Jesus as He hung naked on a cross for all to see (2 Corinthians 5:21; Hebrews 12:2). He was publicly shamed so that we would never be. If you have trusted Christ, rejoice that you have been freed from the fear of the day of God's judgment. (***See Salvation****> Jesus' Work> Crucifixion> Jesus bore our sins,* TopicGuide page A22.)

▸HOLINESS

5:4 Changing inside. Have you ever noticed how patterns of sin can become so powerful that they begin to define a person? In Matthew 15:19-20, Jesus tells us the source of our problem: "For from the heart come evil thoughts." James was aware of this powerful force within. He called it the "evil desires at war within you" (James 4:1). Notice the seriousness of this bondage: Israel's wicked hearts would not let them return to the Lord. They were, as Hosea said, prostitutes "through and through." What they needed is what we all need—a Savior who can change our hearts! Jesus gives us victory over the power of sin by placing the Holy Spirit inside us (Romans 6). We can now be internally motivated to "turn from godless living and sinful pleasures" (Titus 2:12). If you are a Christian, God has given you His Spirit so you can desire and do something besides sin. Cooperate with Him as He leads you to personal righteousness. (***See Holiness****> Changed by God> The Spirit Enables> Indwells believers,* TopicGuide page A41.)

5:7 The phrase "bearing children that are not His" recalls the children Gomer bore as a result of her sexual immorality. Those children were not Hosea's, just as Israel's idolatrous deeds were not born from their union with God.

5:8-9 Hosea used the warning signals of war to mock Israel. They could raise the battle cry and blow the horn in every town in the nearby territory of Benjamin, but it would be to no avail.

9 One thing is certain, Israel*:
On your day of punishment,
you will become a heap of rubble.

10 "The leaders of Judah have become like thieves.*
So I will pour My anger on them like a waterfall.
11 The people of Israel will be crushed and broken
by My judgment
because they are determined to worship idols.*
12 I will destroy Israel as a moth consumes wool.
I will make Judah as weak as rotten wood.

13 "When Israel and Judah saw how sick they were,
Israel turned to Assyria—
to the great king there—
but he could neither help nor cure them.
14 I will be like a lion to Israel,
like a strong young lion to Judah.
I will tear them to pieces!
I will carry them off,
and no one will be left to rescue them.
15 Then I will return to My place
until they admit their guilt and turn to Me.
For as soon as trouble comes,
they will earnestly search for Me."

5:9 Isa 28:1-4; 37:3 Hos 9:11-17

5:10 Deut 27:17 Pss 32:6; 93:3-4 Ezek 7:8

5:12 Ps 39:11 Isa 51:8

5:13 Jer 30:12

5:14 Pss 7:2; 50:22 Hos 13:7

5:15 Isa 64:7-9 Jer 2:27

A CALL TO REPENTANCE

6 1 "Come, let us return to the LORD.
He has torn us to pieces;
now He will heal us.
He has injured us;
now He will bandage our wounds.
2 In just a short time He will restore us,
so that we may live in His presence.
3 Oh, that we might know the LORD!
Let us press on to know Him.
He will respond to us as surely as the arrival
of dawn
or the coming of rains in early spring."

6:1 Isa 30:26 Jer 50:4 Hos 14:4 Zeph 2:1-3

6:2 Ps 30:5

6:3 Isa 2:3 Joel 2:23 Mic 4:2

5:9 Hebrew *Ephraim*, referring to the northern kingdom of Israel; also in 5:11, 12, 13, 14. 5:10 Hebrew *like those who move a boundary marker.* 5:11 Or *determined to follow human commands.* The meaning of the Hebrew is uncertain.

5:10 A boundary marker (see NLT textual note) was a rock that indicated where one property ended and another began. Deuteronomy 19:14 expressly said moving such a landmark was forbidden. Hosea included this charge lest Judah imagine her sneaky deceit went unnoticed.

▶ SPIRITUAL WARFARE

5:15 Blessed adversity. Why would a loving God send hardship into the life of His people? When bad things happen to Christians, often they get mad at God and do not learn from the pain. Hebrews 12:6 says that "the LORD disciplines those He loves, and He punishes each one He accepts as His child." James adds that trials produce virtues we couldn't gain otherwise (James 1:2-4). In these verses God explained that He would bring adversity to Israel in order to cause His people to admit their guilt and look to Him for help. If hard times make us repentant, humble, and ready to seek God, we should call them blessed adversities! Admit to God any wrong perspectives you've had regarding hardships He has allowed in your life; ask Him to help you not to despise trouble, but to see it as part of His plan for His people. (***See Spiritual Warfare*** *> Resisting Sin and Evil> Trusting God> Faithful Soldiers> Endure hardship,* TopicGuide page A46.)

6:4 Ps 78:34-37 Hos 13:3
4 "O Israel* and Judah,
what should I do with you?" asks the LORD.
"For your love vanishes like the morning mist
and disappears like dew in the sunlight.
6:5 Heb 4:12
5 I sent My prophets to cut you to pieces—
to slaughter you with My words,
with judgments as inescapable as light.
6:6 *Matt 9:13; 12:7
6 I want you to show love,*
not offer sacrifices.
I want you to know Me*
more than I want burnt offerings.
7 But like Adam,* you broke My covenant
and betrayed My trust.

8 "Gilead is a city of sinners,
tracked with footprints of blood.
6:9 Jer 7:9 Ezek 22:9 Hos 4:2
9 Priests form bands of robbers,
waiting in ambush for their victims.
They murder travelers along the road to Shechem
and practice every kind of sin.
10 Yes, I have seen something horrible in Ephraim and Israel:
My people are defiled by prostituting themselves with other gods!

6:11 Jer 51:33 Joel 3:13
11 "O Judah, a harvest of punishment is also waiting for you,
though I wanted to restore the fortunes of My people.

ISRAEL'S LOVE FOR WICKEDNESS

7:1 Ezek 24:13 Hos 7:13
7 1 "I want to heal Israel,* but its sins are too great.
Samaria is filled with liars.
Thieves are on the inside
and bandits on the outside!
7:2 Jer 2:19 Hos 8:13
2 Its people don't realize
that I am watching them.
Their sinful deeds are all around them,
and I see them all.

7:3 Hos 7:5 Mic 7:3
3 "The people entertain the king with their wickedness,
and the princes laugh at their lies.
7:4 Jer 9:2; 23:10
4 They are all adulterers,
always aflame with lust.

6:4 Hebrew *Ephraim,* referring to the northern kingdom of Israel. 6:6a Greek version reads *to show mercy.* Compare Matt 9:13; 12:7. 6:6b Hebrew *to know God.* 6:7 Or *But at Adam.* 7:1 Hebrew *Ephraim,* referring to the northern kingdom of Israel; also in 7:8, 11.

6:4-5 God grieved over the lack of substance in Israel's love—it hardly lasted a moment. They hadn't properly responded to the warnings of the prophets that had cut like a sword. Jesus ironically repeated this theme when He noted that Israel had "murdered the prophets" (Matthew 23:31) instead of responding in repentance to their deadly prophetic warnings.

6:7-10 Instead of returning (6:1) and pressing on to know God (6:3) and being merciful (6:6), Israel heaped sin upon sin. This list describes various sinful practices throughout Israel. They were covenant breakers, murderers, robbers, religious hypocrites, and idolaters. God's impending judgment was entirely just.

6:7 "Adam" may be a reference to an unidentified city or region (much as Gilead, Shechem, and Ephraim in 6:8-10) or it may be a reference to the first man. The first man did violate the terms established by God in the Garden of Eden (Genesis 2:17; 3:6). Israel had been given everything, but like Adam, the people quickly fell into the deepest of sins.

7:3 God commanded Israel's king to read the law daily that he might fear God (Deuteronomy 17:19). Instead, the kings did not delight in God's law but in the wickedness of the people. The officials God placed in authority to restrain evil were actually promoting it.

They are like an oven that is kept hot
while the baker is kneading the dough.
5 On royal holidays, the princes get drunk with wine,
carousing with those who mock them.
6 Their hearts are like an oven
blazing with intrigue.
Their plot smolders* through the night,
and in the morning it breaks out like a raging fire.
7 Burning like an oven,
they consume their leaders.
They kill their kings one after another,
and no one cries to Me for help.

8 "The people of Israel mingle with godless foreigners,
making themselves as worthless as a half-baked cake!
9 Worshiping foreign gods has sapped their strength,
but they don't even know it.
Their hair is gray,
but they don't realize they're old and weak.
10 Their arrogance testifies against them,
yet they don't return to the LORD their God
or even try to find Him.

11 "The people of Israel have become like silly, witless doves,
first calling to Egypt, then flying to Assyria for help.
12 But as they fly about,
I will throw My net over them
and bring them down like a bird from the sky.
I will punish them for all the evil they do.*

13 "What sorrow awaits those who have deserted Me!
Let them die, for they have rebelled against Me.
I wanted to redeem them,
but they have told lies about Me.
14 They do not cry out to Me with sincere hearts.
Instead, they sit on their couches and wail.
They cut themselves,* begging foreign gods for grain and new wine,
and they turn away from Me.
15 I trained them and made them strong,
yet now they plot evil against Me.
16 They look everywhere except to the Most High.
They are as useless as a crooked bow.

7:5 Isa 28:1
7:7 Isa 64:7
7:9 Isa 1:7
7:10 Hos 5:5
7:11 Hos 12:1
7:12 Ezek 12:13
7:13 Matt 23:37
7:14 Amos 2:8
7:15 Nah 1:9
7:16 Ps 78:57; Ezek 23:32; Hos 9:3, 6

7:6 Hebrew *Their baker sleeps.* 7:12 Hebrew *I will punish them because of what was reported against them in the assembly.*
7:14 As in Greek version; Hebrew reads *They gather together.*

7:6-7 Whereas sexual immorality was compared to a blazing oven in 7:4, now the burning passion refers to an insatiable desire to devise a way to overthrow the king. The fire is pictured as raging and ready to consume at a moment's notice. This passion consumed four kings in Israel in the last 30 years of the nation's existence. Yet even when such chaos reigned, the people were hard-hearted and did not call on the Lord.

▸ HOLINESS
7:14-16 Fruitless tears. Hosea pictured the people of Israel wailing on their couches, but feeling bad about consequences received for sin is not repentance (2 Corinthians 7:10). A child may cry buckets of tears when being disciplined, yet have no genuine remorse for what he or she did. The people of Israel hated the consequences for sin, but they didn't hate sin itself. David recognized this as he cried out in true repentance, "Against You, and You alone, have I sinned; I have done what is evil in Your sight" (Psalm 51:4). When we admit our offenses against God, our tears will produce something much better than red eyes: forgiveness and restoration (1 John 1:9). Ask God for a hatred of sin that is far greater than a hatred of the consequences of sin. (***See Holiness****> Changed by God> God Provides> Conviction of sin,* TopicGuide page A41.)

Their leaders will be killed by their enemies
because of their insolence toward Me.
Then the people of Egypt
will laugh at them.

ISRAEL HARVESTS THE WHIRLWIND

8:1 Hab 1:8
8 [1] "Sound the alarm!
The enemy descends like an eagle on the people of the LORD,
for they have broken My covenant
and revolted against My law.
[2] Now Israel pleads with Me,
'Help us, for You are our God!'
[3] But it is too late.
The people of Israel have rejected what is good,
and now their enemies will chase after them.
8:4 Hos 2:8; 13:10
[4] The people have appointed kings without My consent,
and princes without My knowledge.
By making idols for themselves from their silver and gold,
they have brought about their own destruction.

8:5 Jer 13:27
[5] "O Samaria, I reject this calf—
this idol you have made.
My fury burns against you.
How long will you be incapable of innocence?
8:6 Hos 13:2
[6] This calf you worship, O Israel,
was crafted by your own hands!
It is not God!
Therefore, it must be smashed to bits.

8:7 Isa 66:15 Nah 1:3
[7] "They have planted the wind
and will harvest the whirlwind.
The stalks of grain wither
and produce nothing to eat.
And even if there is any grain,
foreigners will eat it.
8:8 Jer 51:34
[8] The people of Israel have been swallowed up;
they lie among the nations like an old discarded pot.
8:9 Jer 2:24 Ezek 16:33
[9] Like a wild donkey looking for a mate,
they have gone up to Assyria.

▸ SALVATION

8:1-2 Fruitless confession. Are those who claim to be Christians truly saved if they continue to live contrary to God's commandments? Hosea saw Israel crying out, "You are our God!" when the nation faced judgment. But the nation had broken God's covenant with them and revolted against His law. Such people are only fooling themselves. Jesus said, "Not everyone who calls out to Me, 'Lord! Lord!' will enter the Kingdom of Heaven. Only those who actually do the will of My Father in heaven will enter" (Matthew 7:21). Genuine faith will produce genuine fruit, a life marked by obedience. Pray that the belief in your heart, the confession of your mouth, and the obedience in your life will all declare the same thing: "Jesus is Lord!" (***See Salvation***> *Receiving*> *Results*> *Bear fruit of the Spirit,* TopicGuide page A23.)

8:7 Israel had "planted the wind" by turning from God and paying Assyria for security (8:9). Israel would "harvest the whirlwind" of judgment from God at the hands of the armies of Assyria (8:9-10). The foreigners who would eat what little grain the Israelites produced were the very nation the Israelites had relied on instead of God.

8:8 God had treated Israel as a special treasure (Micah 7:14). However, Israel had become as useless as an old pot because it had consorted with foreign nations. In ancient times, the ordinary citizen's pots were used until completely broken, then thrown away.

The people of Israel* have sold themselves—
sold themselves to many lovers.
10 But though they have sold themselves to many allies,
I will now gather them together for judgment.
Then they will writhe
under the burden of the great king.

11 "Israel has built many altars to take away sin,
but these very altars became places for sinning!
12 Even though I gave them all My laws,
they act as if those laws don't apply to them.
13 The people of Israel love their rituals of sacrifice,
but to Me their sacrifices are all meaningless.
I will hold My people accountable for their sins,
and I will punish them.
They will return to Egypt.
14 Israel has forgotten its Maker and built great palaces,
and Judah has fortified its cities.
Therefore, I will send down fire on their cities
and will burn up their fortresses."

8:10 Jer 42:2; Ezek 16:37; Hos 10:10
8:13 Hos 7:2; 1 Cor 4:5
8:14 Jer 17:27; Hos 2:13; 4:6; 13:6

HOSEA ANNOUNCES ISRAEL'S PUNISHMENT

9 1 O people of Israel,
do not rejoice as other nations do.
For you have been unfaithful to your God,
hiring yourselves out like prostitutes,
worshiping other gods on every threshing floor.
2 So now your harvests will be too small to feed you.
There will be no grapes for making new wine.
3 You may no longer stay here in the LORD's land.
Instead, you will return to Egypt,
and in Assyria you will eat food
that is ceremonially unclean.
4 There you will make no offerings of wine to the LORD.
None of your sacrifices there will please Him.
They will be unclean, like food touched by a person
in mourning.
All who present such sacrifices will be defiled.
They may eat this food themselves,
but they may not offer it to the LORD.
5 What then will you do on festival days?
How will you observe the LORD's festivals?
6 Even if you escape destruction from Assyria,
Egypt will conquer you, and Memphis* will bury you.

9:1 Isa 22:12-13
9:2 Hos 2:9
9:3 Ezek 4:13
9:4 Exod 29:40; Hag 2:14
9:5 Hos 2:11; Joel 1:13
9:6 Isa 5:6; 7:23; Hos 10:8

8:9 Hebrew *Ephraim*, referring to the northern kingdom of Israel; also in 8:11. 9:6 Memphis was the capital of northern Egypt.

8:9-10 As in Jeremiah 2:24, Israel was compared to a wild donkey alone in the wilderness. Wherever the people had gone searching for aid from their allies, God found them and gathered them together for judgment. Instead of lightening the load, Assyria would become an oppressive burden.

9:4 The phrase "food touched by a person in mourning" refers to God's restriction for anyone who came into contact either with a dead body or the home in which the person died (Numbers 5:2; 19:14). Such people were considered unclean for seven days and could not come to worship God. Israel would be continually unclean in the defiled land of Assyria.

Nettles will take over your treasures of silver;
 thistles will invade your ruined homes.

9:7 Isa 10:3 Jer 10:15; 29:26 Lam 2:14 Ezek 7:2-7; 13:3, 10

7 The time of Israel's punishment has come;
 the day of payment is here.
 Soon Israel will know this all too well.
Because of your great sin and hostility,
 you say, "The prophets are crazy
 and the inspired men are fools!"
8 The prophet is a watchman over Israel* for my God,
 yet traps are laid for him wherever he goes.
 He faces hostility even in the house of God.

9:9 Isa 31:6 Hos 7:2; 8:13

9 The things my people do are as depraved
 as what they did in Gibeah long ago.
God will not forget.
 He will surely punish them for their sins.

9:10 Num 25:1-9

10 The LORD says, "O Israel, when I first found you,
 it was like finding fresh grapes in the desert.
When I saw your ancestors,
 it was like seeing the first ripe figs of the season.
But then they deserted Me for Baal-peor,
 giving themselves to that shameful idol.
Soon they became vile,
 as vile as the god they worshiped.

9:11 Hos 4:7

11 The glory of Israel will fly away like a bird,
 for your children will not be born
or grow in the womb
 or even be conceived.

9:12 Hos 7:13

12 Even if you do have children who grow up,
 I will take them from you.
It will be a terrible day when I turn away
 and leave you alone.
13 I have watched Israel become as beautiful as Tyre.
 But now Israel will bring out her children for slaughter."

14 O LORD, what should I request for Your people?
 I will ask for wombs that don't give birth
 and breasts that give no milk.

9:15 Isa 1:23 Hos 7:2; 12:2 Amos 4:4; 5:5

15 The LORD says, "All their wickedness began at Gilgal;
 there I began to hate them.

9:8 Hebrew *Ephraim,* referring to the northern kingdom of Israel; also in 9:11, 13, 16.

▶ CHURCH

9:7 The unpopular truth. It is unlikely that Hosea was invited to many parties. His immoral wife and illegitimate children were quite a scandal! But even more, at any minute God could tell him to rebuke those around him! In Hosea's day, society had become so steeped in sin that genuine prophets were treated as crazy people, not honored mouthpieces of God. But the Bible declares, "To one who listens, valid criticism is like a gold earring or other gold jewelry" (Proverbs 17:10; 25:12). Second Timothy 4:3 warns about a time when people will not tolerate what the Bible says about them and will "look for teachers who will tell them whatever their itching ears want to hear." Perhaps we would be better off if people like Hosea attended our parties! Ask God for an ability to love and fully receive everything He has to say, even if that means rebuke! (***See Church****> Role> Preach> Instructions> Tell the whole truth,* TopicGuide page A50.)

9:9 Judges 19 describes the rape, murder, and brutal dismembering of a concubine, all of which occurred at Gibeah. This event was so gruesome that people said, "Such a horrible crime has not been committed in all the time since Israel left Egypt" (Judges 19:30). It was just that bad in Hosea's day.

I will drive them from My land
because of their evil actions.
I will love them no more
because all their leaders are rebels.
16 The people of Israel are struck down.
Their roots are dried up,
and they will bear no more fruit.
And if they give birth,
I will slaughter their beloved children."

17 My God will reject the people of Israel
because they will not listen or obey.
They will be wanderers,
homeless among the nations.

9:16 Ezek 24:21

THE LORD'S JUDGMENT AGAINST ISRAEL

10 1 How prosperous Israel is—
a luxuriant vine loaded with fruit.
But the richer the people get,
the more pagan altars they build.
The more bountiful their harvests,
the more beautiful their sacred pillars.
2 The hearts of the people are fickle;
they are guilty and must be punished.
The LORD will break down their altars
and smash their sacred pillars.
3 Then they will say, "We have no king
because we didn't fear the LORD.
But even if we had a king,
what could he do for us anyway?"
4 They spout empty words
and make covenants they don't intend to keep.
So injustice springs up among them
like poisonous weeds in a farmer's field.

5 The people of Samaria tremble in fear
for what might happen to their calf idol at Beth-aven.*

10:1 1 Kgs 14:23 Isa 5:1-7 Ezek 15:1-5 Hos 8:11; 12:11

10:2 1 Kgs 18:21 Hos 10:8 Mic 5:13 Zeph 1:5

10:4 Ps 12:4 Hos 4:2

10:5 Hos 8:5

10:5a *Beth-aven* means "house of wickedness"; it is being used as another name for Bethel, which means "house of God."

9:17 When Assyria invaded and Samaria fell in 722 BC, the nation of Israel went into captivity and was never restored. Second Kings 17:22-23 ends the account of the history of Israel with these chilling words: "They did not turn from these sins [of idolatry] until the LORD finally swept them away from His presence, just as all His prophets had warned. So Israel was exiled from their land to Assyria, where they remain to this day."

▸ SALVATION
10:1-2 The heart of the problem. Is poverty the root of wickedness? Deuteronomy 6:11-12 warned Israel: "When you have eaten your fill in this land, be careful not to forget the LORD." God knows that people are sinful and have a tendency to forget Him even when He has provided abundantly for them. This is what happened to the people in Hosea's day. Their increased prosperity resulted only in increased wickedness. While the Bible is clear that the rich should be eager to help the poor (Galatians 2:10), we should not be fooled into thinking that people's spiritual well-being can be improved merely by changing their level of prosperity. Such a change in a person's heart can only come from Jesus Christ. Ask God to show you how you can help people gain the true riches found in Jesus Christ. (***See Salvation**> Our Need> Corrupt> Tendency toward sinfulness,* TopicGuide page A22.)

10:5-7 Hosea mocked the nation's silly allegiance to the calf idol—they trembled and mourned over its impending demise. And why all the emotion? Couldn't their god take care of itself? No, the calf's lifeless form would be carried away into Assyria to be given to their king as a gift, just as Israel's king would also be removed.

The people mourn and the priests wail,
because its glory will be stripped away.*

10:6 Hos 10:5

6 This idol will be carted away to Assyria,
a gift to the great king there.
Ephraim will be ridiculed and Israel will be shamed,
because its people have trusted in this idol.
7 Samaria and its king will be cut off;
they will float away like driftwood on an ocean wave.

10:8 Hos 5:8; 9:6; 10:5 *Luke 23:30 Rev 6:16

8 And the pagan shrines of Aven,* the place of Israel's sin,
will crumble.
Thorns and thistles will grow up around their altars.
They will beg the mountains, "Bury us!"
and plead with the hills, "Fall on us!"

9 The LORD says, "O Israel, ever since Gibeah,
there has been only sin and more sin!
You have made no progress whatsoever.
Was it not right that the wicked men of Gibeah
were attacked?

10:10 Ezek 5:13

10 Now whenever it fits My plan,
I will attack you, too.
I will call out the armies of the nations
to punish you for your multiplied sins.

10:11 Jer 28:14

11 "Israel* is like a trained heifer treading out the grain—
an easy job she loves.
But I will put a heavy yoke on her tender neck.
I will force Judah to pull the plow
and Israel* to break up the hard ground.

10:12 Prov 11:18 Isa 45:8

12 I said, 'Plant the good seeds of righteousness,
and you will harvest a crop of love.
Plow up the hard ground of your hearts,
for now is the time to seek the LORD,
that He may come
and shower righteousness upon you.'

10:13 Ps 33:16 Gal 6:7-8

13 "But you have cultivated wickedness
and harvested a thriving crop of sins.
You have eaten the fruit of lies—
trusting in your military might,
believing that great armies
could make your nation safe.

10:5b Or *because it will be taken away into exile.* 10:8 *Aven* is a reference to Beth-aven; see 10:5a and the note there. 10:11a Hebrew *Ephraim,* referring to the northern kingdom of Israel. 10:11b Hebrew *Jacob.* The names "Jacob" and "Israel" are often interchanged throughout the Old Testament, referring sometimes to the individual patriarch and sometimes to the nation.

10:8 Hosea warned that when the horrible day of judgment comes, people will wish for death. Jesus used this image from Hosea on the way to the cross (see Luke 23:28-31) to predict that Israel would endure a terrible judgment for killing Him. Hosea's prophecy was fulfilled in the siege on Samaria in 722 BC, and Jesus' prophecy was fulfilled when Jerusalem was destroyed by Rome in AD 70. Another day of judgment from "the wrath of the Lamb" is pictured in Revelation 6:16. On that day, people will cry these same words as they try to hide from Jesus.

10:11 In Hosea 4:16, Israel's stubbornness was compared to a stubborn heifer. Now, Israel was called a trained heifer, which pictures a content life under a kind master. But change was coming. Labor under the oppressor's yoke would be hard, as it was in Egypt (Exodus 1:11; 5:9). Jesus used this imagery when He promised to remove people's heavy burdens and replace them with His easy yoke (Matthew 11:28-30).

14 Now the terrors of war
will rise among your people.
All your fortifications will fall,
just as when Shalman destroyed Beth-arbel.
Even mothers and children
were dashed to death there.
15 You will share that fate, Bethel,
because of your great wickedness.
When the day of judgment dawns,
the king of Israel will be completely destroyed.

10:14 2 Kgs 17:3

THE LORD'S LOVE FOR ISRAEL

11 1 "When Israel was a child, I loved him,
and I called My son out of Egypt.
2 But the more I* called to him,
the farther he moved from Me,
offering sacrifices to the images of Baal
and burning incense to idols.
3 I Myself taught Israel* how to walk,
leading him along by the hand.
But he doesn't know or even care
that it was I who took care of him.
4 I led Israel along
with My ropes of kindness and love.
I lifted the yoke from his neck,
and I Myself stooped to feed him.

5 "But since My people refuse to return to Me,
they will return to Egypt
and will be forced to serve Assyria.
6 War will swirl through their cities;
their enemies will crash through their gates.
They will destroy them,
trapping them in their own evil plans.
7 For My people are determined to desert Me.
They call Me the Most High,
but they don't truly honor Me.

11:1 Exod 4:22 Hos 2:15; 12:9, 13; 13:4 Matt 2:15

11:2 Judg 10:6 2 Kgs 17:13-15 Isa 65:7 Jer 18:15 Hos 2:13; 13:1-2

11:3 Deut 1:31 Jer 30:17

11:4 Exod 16:32 Ps 78:25 Jer 31:2-3

11:6 Hos 13:16

11:7 Jer 8:5

11:2 As in Greek version; Hebrew reads *they*. 11:3 Hebrew *Ephraim*, referring to the northern kingdom of Israel; also in 11:8, 9, 12.

10:14-15 The phrase "when Shalman destroyed Beth-arbel" refers to a gruesome battle familiar to Hosea's audience but unknown to modern history. Beth-arbel is likely in the region of Gilead, east of the Jordan River.

▶ BIBLE
11:1 Who is the son? When Matthew quoted this verse in his Gospel (Matthew 2:14-15) did he fail to properly apply Hosea's teaching? God refers to Israel as His son here, but Matthew applied this verse to Jesus Christ. How can both interpretations be correct? God designated Israel as His son (Exodus 4:22), but because of sin, Israel never fulfilled the requirements of this title (see Hosea 11:2). God's Son, Jesus, came as an Israelite and fulfilled the law that the son, Israel, never did (Galatians 4:4-5). Matthew understood this and appropriately quoted Hosea regarding this particular event. Because Jesus fulfilled Israel's tasks as the sinless obedient Son, those who place their trust in Him become God's people (1 Peter 2:9-10). Worship Jesus the Son for fulfilling all that Israel—and we—could never fulfill. (***See Bible**> Unity> OT Points to NT> Fulfillment of Old Testament prophecy in the New Testament,* TopicGuide page A11.)

11:5-6 God's deliverance and tender care for Israel is contrasted with the insanity of Israel's refusal to return to Him. If God's people would not willingly submit to the rule of such a loving father, then a tyrant, the king of Assyria, would rule them. Instead of tender compassion, they would experience the horrors of war.

11:8 Gen 14:8 Deut 29:23 Hos 6:4; 7:1
8 "Oh, how can I give you up, Israel?
How can I let you go?
How can I destroy you like Admah
or demolish you like Zeboiim?
My heart is torn within Me,
and My compassion overflows.
11:9 Deut 13:17 Isa 5:24; 12:6; 41:14 Jer 26:3
9 No, I will not unleash My fierce anger.
I will not completely destroy Israel,
for I am God and not a mere mortal.
I am the Holy One living among you,
and I will not come to destroy.
11:10 Isa 31:4; 66:2, 5 Hos 3:5; 6:1-3 Joel 3:16 Amos 1:2; 3:4
10 For someday the people will follow Me.
I, the LORD, will roar like a lion.
And when I roar,
My people will return trembling from the west.
11:11 Isa 11:11; 60:8 Ezek 28:25-26 Hos 7:11
11 Like a flock of birds, they will come from Egypt.
Trembling like doves, they will return from Assyria.
And I will bring them home again,"
says the LORD.

CHARGES AGAINST ISRAEL AND JUDAH

12*Israel surrounds Me with lies and deceit,
but Judah still obeys God
and is faithful to the Holy One.*

12:1 Gen 41:6 Jer 22:22 Ezek 17:10
12 1*The people of Israel* feed on the wind;
they chase after the east wind all day long.
They pile up lies and violence;
they are making an alliance with Assyria
while sending olive oil to buy support from Egypt.
12:2 Hos 4:1 Mic 6:2
2 Now the LORD is bringing charges against Judah.
He is about to punish Jacob* for all his deceitful ways,
and pay him back for all he has done.
12:3 Gen 25:26
3 Even in the womb,
Jacob struggled with his brother;
when he became a man,
he even fought with God.

11:12a Verse 11:12 is numbered 12:1 in Hebrew text. **11:12b** Or *and Judah is unruly against God, the faithful Holy One.* The meaning of the Hebrew is uncertain. **12:1a** Verses 12:1-14 are numbered 12:2-15 in Hebrew text. **12:1b** Hebrew *Ephraim,* referring to the northern kingdom of Israel; also in 12:8, 14. **12:2** *Jacob* sounds like the Hebrew word for "deceiver."

11:8 Lest someone imagine that God was cold and indifferent about the punishment that was to come on his son, Hosea presented God as a father bursting forth with emotion. A caring father cannot flippantly hand his child over to destruction even if the father knows it is deserved. Hosea was urging the people of Israel to see that God's affection for them was more intense than that of any earthly father.

11:10 A future time of restoration was envisioned after captivity, thus it is clear that the compassion of 11:8-9 does not utterly eliminate judgment. Note the difference in demeanor after the Exile: God's people would follow Him instead of going their own way, and they would tremble before Him rather than arrogantly defy Him. The lion's roar represented power that would shake the nations into releasing God's people (Haggai 2:21-23).

12:1 Ecclesiastes often uses the phrase "meaningless—like chasing the wind" to illustrate utter futility (Ecclesiastes 1:14; 2:17). To "feed on" or "chase after" wind is to do something that is not worthwhile, and to do it "all day long" is the height of folly. Israel's deceitful nature is seen in her desire to make futile alliances with Egypt and Assyria to avoid siege.

4 Yes, he wrestled with the Angel and won.
He wept and pleaded for a blessing from Him.
There at Bethel he met God face to face,
and God spoke to him*—
5 the LORD God of Heaven's Armies,
the LORD is His name!
6 So now, come back to your God.
Act with love and justice,
and always depend on Him.

7 But no, the people are like crafty merchants
selling from dishonest scales—
they love to cheat.
8 Israel boasts, "I am rich!
I've made a fortune all by myself!
No one has caught me cheating!
My record is spotless!"

9 "But I am the LORD your God,
who rescued you from slavery in Egypt.
And I will make you live in tents again,
as you do each year at the Festival of Shelters.*
10 I sent My prophets to warn you
with many visions and parables."

11 But the people of Gilead are worthless
because of their idol worship.
And in Gilgal, too, they sacrifice bulls;
their altars are lined up like the heaps of stone
along the edges of a plowed field.
12 Jacob fled to the land of Aram,
and there he* earned a wife by tending sheep.
13 Then by a prophet
the LORD brought Jacob's descendants* out of Egypt;
and by that prophet
they were protected.
14 But the people of Israel
have bitterly provoked the LORD,
so their Lord will now sentence them to death
in payment for their sins.

12:4 Gen 28:13-19; 32:24-30; 35:10-15
12:5 Exod 3:15
12:6 Mic 7:7
12:7 Prov 11:1; Amos 8:5; Mic 6:11
12:8 Hos 13:6; Rev 3:17
12:9 Lev 23:42
12:10 2 Kgs 17:13; Ezek 17:2; 20:49
12:12 Gen 28:5; 29:20
12:13 Exod 14:19-22; Isa 63:11-12
12:14 2 Kgs 17:7-18; Ezek 18:10-13

12:4 As in Greek and Syriac versions; Hebrew reads *to us.* 12:9 Hebrew *as in the days of your appointed feast.* 12:12 Hebrew *Israel.* See note on 10:11b. 12:13 Hebrew *brought Israel.* See note on 10:11b.

12:4 The first half of this verse recalls Genesis 32:22-30, when Jacob wrestled with the angel, pleading earnestly for a blessing prior to the meeting with his brother Esau. In this encounter the angel changed Jacob's name from "heel grabber" to *Israel*, "one who struggles with God" (see Genesis 32:28 and text note). The second half of the verse refers to Genesis 35:9-15, when God appeared to Jacob at Bethel and restated his name change and the blessing He had promised to Abraham and Isaac. This history would have been especially relevant to the audience in Israel, since they had turned Bethel into an idolatrous shrine.

12:12-13 God provided a wife for Jacob even when he was running from his brother because of his deception (Genesis 27:42-44). Later God provided for Jacob's descendents by sending Moses, a prophet, to guide and protect them. These examples show that God had been consistently faithful to provide, even when Jacob was unfaithful. The reference to Moses as a prophet also recalls the prophetic warnings in Hosea 12:10 and explains Hosea's role, one more prophetic voice.

THE LORD'S ANGER AGAINST ISRAEL

13:1 Hos 2:8-17
13 1 When the tribe of Ephraim spoke,
the people shook with fear,
for that tribe was important in Israel.
But the people of Ephraim sinned by worshiping Baal
and thus sealed their destruction.

13:2 Isa 44:17-20; 46:6 Jer 10:2-5 Hos 8:6
2 Now they continue to sin by making silver idols,
images shaped skillfully with human hands.
"Sacrifice to these," they cry,
"and kiss the calf idols!"

13:3 Ps 68:2 Isa 17:13 Dan 2:35 Hos 6:4
3 Therefore, they will disappear like the morning mist,
like dew in the morning sun,
like chaff blown by the wind,
like smoke from a chimney.

13:4 Exod 20:2-3 Isa 43:11; 45:21-22
4 "I have been the LORD your God
ever since I brought you out of Egypt.
You must acknowledge no God but Me,
for there is no other savior.

13:5 Deut 2:7; 8:15; 32:10
5 I took care of you in the wilderness,
in that dry and thirsty land.

13:6 Hos 2:13; 4:6; 8:14
6 But when you had eaten and were satisfied,
you became proud and forgot Me.
7 So now I will attack you like a lion,
like a leopard that lurks along the road.

13:8 Ps 50:22
8 Like a bear whose cubs have been taken away,
I will tear out your heart.
I will devour you like a hungry lioness
and mangle you like a wild animal.

9 "You are about to be destroyed, O Israel—
yes, by Me, your only helper.

13:10 2 Kgs 17:4 Hos 8:4
10 Now where is* your king?
Let him save you!
Where are all the leaders of the land,
the king and the officials you demanded of Me?

13:11 1 Sam 8:7 1 Kgs 14:7-10 Hos 10:7
11 In My anger I gave you kings,
and in My fury I took them away.

13:10 As in Greek and Syriac versions and Latin Vulgate; Hebrew reads *I will be.*

▸ WORSHIP
13:1-3 Oh, to be influential! Why is power so alluring? Ephraim was blessed with an influential role among the Israelite tribes, just as Jacob had indicated when he blessed Joseph's sons (Genesis 48). But Ephraim failed in its leadership role by worshiping Baal. Great power must be accompanied by great responsibility if we are to avoid certain destruction. For this reason, the Bible makes it clear that leaders in the church are to be evaluated primarily on the basis of character (1 Timothy 3:1-12; Titus 1:6-9). Furthermore, James 3:1 warns that those who desire to teach in the church "will be judged more strictly." If God has placed you in a position of influence, pray that He will help you to remain faithful to Him in all things, so that you can use your power to further His kingdom, not your own selfish interests. (***See Worship****> OT> God's Supremacy> Required a proper heart attitude,* TopicGuide page A27.)

13:7-9 Hosea again applies the teaching of Moses in Deuteronomy 8:19: "But I assure you of this: If you ever forget the LORD your God and follow other gods, worshiping and bowing down to them, you will certainly be destroyed." God had warned His people through Moses (Hosea 12:13) and many other prophets (12:10), and now Hosea's voice is the exclamation point at the end of a long prophetic sentence: Beware, Israel. God will tear you apart and devour you like the wildest beast imaginable!

[12] "Ephraim's guilt has been collected,
and his sin has been stored up for punishment.
[13] Pain has come to the people
like the pain of childbirth,
but they are like a child
who resists being born.
The moment of birth has arrived,
but they stay in the womb!

[14] "Should I ransom them from the grave*?
Should I redeem them from death?
O death, bring on your terrors!
O grave, bring on your plagues!*
For I will not take pity on them.
[15] Ephraim was the most fruitful of all his brothers,
but the east wind—a blast from the LORD—
will arise in the desert.
All their flowing springs will run dry,
and all their wells will disappear.
Every precious thing they own
will be plundered and carried away.
[16] The people of Samaria
must bear the consequences of their guilt
because they rebelled against their God.
They will be killed by an invading army,
their little ones dashed to death against the ground,
their pregnant women ripped open by swords."

13:12 Deut 32:34-35; Rom 2:5
13:13 Mic 4:9-10
13:14 Isa 25:8; Ezek 37:12-13; 1 Cor 15:55; Phil 3:21
13:15 Jer 51:36; Hos 10:1
13:16 2 Kgs 15:16

HEALING FOR THE REPENTANT

14 [1] Return, O Israel, to the LORD your God,
for your sins have brought you down.
[2] Bring your confessions, and return to the LORD.
Say to Him,
"Forgive all our sins and graciously receive us,
so that we may offer You our praises.

14:2 Mic 7:18-19; Heb 13:15

13:14a Hebrew *Sheol;* also in 13:14b. **13:14b** Greek version reads *O death, where is your punishment? / O grave* [Hades], *where is your sting?* Compare 1 Cor 15:55.

13:12 The theme of God keeping a record of sin is prevalent in Hosea (7:2; 9:9), and it continues into the New Testament (Romans 2:5). Here we see an image of a storage room filled with a collection of sins, past and present.

▸ ADOPTION
13:14 Victory over death's terror. The Bible clearly states that we all deserve death for our sins—not just Israel in Hosea's time, but everyone. This includes both physical death and eternal separation from God's blessings (Genesis 2:17). But the good news is that Jesus took God's curse for all believers on the cross (Galatians 3:13) so that death and hell would not be our destination. When He rose from the dead on the third day it was "the first of a great harvest of all who have died" (1 Corinthians 15:20). Paul took this passage from Hosea and joyfully proclaimed that the answer for the terror of death is Jesus Christ: "Death is swallowed up in victory. O death, where is your victory? O death, where is your sting?" (1 Corinthians 15:54-55). If Jesus does not return in your lifetime, your body will die. But since Christ has risen, so will you! Heartily praise Jesus for removing the terror of death by bearing your curse and triumphing over death. (***See Adoption> Without Christ> Separated from God> Facing second death,*** TopicGuide page A36.)

14:1 As the threat of God coming as a lion in Hosea 5:14 led into a plea for the people to return to the Lord in 6:1, the prophet now moves from his most graphic representations of Assyrian brutality (13:7-9, 16) to another urgent plea for the people to return to the Lord. Returning has been a theme throughout Hosea (2:7; 3:5; 5:4; 7:10; 11:10). After all of the judgment described in the book, this section rises in intensity like one who is pleading (in Hebrew, "return" occurs in reference to Israel three more times in this last chapter: 14:1, 2, 7). A proper turnaround must begin with a clear statement of the problem—sin.

14:3 Pss 10:14; 68:5 Mic 5:10

[3] Assyria cannot save us,
nor can our warhorses.
Never again will we say to the idols we have made,
'You are our gods.'
No, in You alone
do the orphans find mercy."

14:4 Isa 57:18 Zeph 3:17

[4] The LORD says,
"Then I will heal you of your faithlessness;
My love will know no bounds,
for My anger will be gone forever.

14:5 Song 2:1 Matt 6:28

[5] I will be to Israel
like a refreshing dew from heaven.
Israel will blossom like the lily;
it will send roots deep into the soil
like the cedars in Lebanon.

14:6 Ps 52:8 Jer 11:16

[6] Its branches will spread out like beautiful olive trees,
as fragrant as the cedars of Lebanon.

14:7 Ps 91:1-4

[7] My people will again live under My shade.
They will flourish like grain and blossom like grapevines.
They will be as fragrant as the wines of Lebanon.

14:8 Isa 41:19 Hos 14:3

[8] "O Israel,* stay away from idols!
I am the One who answers your prayers and cares for you.
I am like a tree that is always green;
all your fruit comes from Me."

14:9 Ps 107:43 Isa 1:28; 26:7 Jer 9:12

[9] Let those who are wise understand these things.
Let those with discernment listen carefully.
The paths of the LORD are true and right,
and righteous people live by walking in them.
But in those paths sinners stumble and fall.

14:8 Hebrew *Ephraim,* referring to the northern kingdom of Israel.

14:4 In her sinful rebellion, Israel is pictured as one who is sick (5:13; Revelation 3:17-18) and unloved (Hosea 1:6; 9:15). If Israel would stop turning to other sources for help, God would turn to heal and love them. This message of hope would encourage the remnant in captivity.

▸ PURPOSE

14:9 Only two options. Have you ever wondered why the Bible so often presents all decisions in terms of two paths? Why aren't there more alternatives? Hosea's audience could go forward in only one of two ways. One way was to go the way of the righteous, who return to God and find life in His path. Another was to go the way of unrepentant sinners and stumble on the path (Hosea 4:5; 5:5). Jesus spoke of these same choices in life and warned that the two options will have radically different outcomes: eternal punishment or eternal life (Matthew 25:46). The Bible regularly gives two options because there is a right and a wrong answer to moral situations. Ask God for wisdom as you make choices every day—choices between good and evil. (***See Purpose***> *God's Means> Human Choice> God's view,* TopicGuide page A52.)

JOEL

PURPOSE

To warn the people of Judah to repent before they experienced the full force of God's judgment.

As Jesus hung on the cross, He used what little breath remained to cry out, "Father, forgive them, for they don't know what they are doing" (Luke 23:34). Sin often blinds us to God's hand in the events around us. The prophet Joel saw a devastating calamity on the horizon, and warned sin-blinded Judah: "The day of the LORD is near, the day when destruction comes from the Almighty. How terrible that day will be!" (Joel 1:15).

The central figure of judgment in Joel was a plague of locusts. Every person would have recognized the swarm of mad grasshoppers, remembering the stories of how God plagued their enemies in Egypt with them. They would have also remembered God's solemn curse, which they probably doubted would ever happen: "A foreign nation you have never heard about will eat the crops you worked so hard to grow. You will suffer under constant oppression and harsh treatment. You will plant much but harvest little, for locusts will eat your crops." (Deuteronomy 28:33, 38). Joel would call God's people back to the curse of the swarming insects to remind them that this was a covenant sanction, as when so many died at Peor for worshiping Baal and others died fleeing the little town of Ai. Israel was not facing a human enemy it could outwit or destroy. Israel was facing the Almighty God.

DISCOVER GOD IN JOEL

Joel presented a dramatic picture of destruction and judgment, yet the seeking and saving attributes of God are clearly seen:

Restorer: God said to Israel, "I will give you back what you lost to the swarming locusts, the hopping locusts, the stripping locusts, and the cutting locusts. It was I who sent this great destroying army against you" (Joel 2:25; see 2:21-27). If God causes devastation, He can certainly reverse its effects. Regardless of the realm—nature, finances, relationships, or spirituality—the God of miracles can cause the desert to bloom overnight. The God who restores can overcome years of neglect and destruction. But, as we see in Joel, those who wish God's blessings must repent, and not merely internally or mentally—they must show a real change in behavior (1:13-14; 2:15-17).

Savior: The "day of the LORD" is a prominent theme in Joel, as in other Old Testament prophetic books. Joel was speaking of a time of divine judgment to come in the near future, but the term *Day of the Lord* is used in the New Testament to refer to a time of judgment that will occur when God will settle all accounts with His covenant people and the nations. When that day comes, God's judgment will be poured out, but His people will be saved. For this reason, the apostle Peter used Joel's words (Joel 2:28-32; see Acts 2:17-21) at Pentecost to urge the people to turn to Christ, for "everyone who calls on the name of the LORD will be saved" (Acts 2:21; see Joel 2:32). The apostle Paul also quoted Joel when he told the Roman Christians the same thing: Everyone who calls on the name of the Lord will be saved (Romans 10:13). Likewise, Paul and Silas told a Gentile jailer in Philippi to believe in (call on) the Lord Jesus Christ in order to be saved (Acts 16:31). God is a saving God.

GROWING THROUGH JOEL

In calling people to turn from sin, Joel addressed numerous aspects of living the godly life:

Repentance: Repentance involves a change of one's mind concerning God, which leads to a change of direction in one's life. No one can come under the lordship of Jesus Christ without repentance. While repentance ultimately may involve "tearing" away some of the outward aspects of one's life, it begins with the tearing of the heart (Joel 2:13). When the heart is broken over sin, external changes in behavior follow.

Warnings: Joel's prophecy was written to warn the people of Judah about the coming Day of the Lord, using the destruction of the locust plague as an illustration. The book of Proverbs says the person who ignores warnings is foolish (Proverbs 9:7-8); such a person will call out in the day of trouble and receive no answer. Warnings about the coming Day of the Lord should not be ignored, because the final day of judgment will arrive when we least expect it (Matthew 25:1-30). The only preparation possible is a life of faith and repentance.

Discernment: Spiritual discernment is the ability to look beneath the surface of events or words and understand their spiritual implications. There were spiritual implications in the plague of locusts that struck Judah, but Joel was afraid that the people were too spiritually dull to understand the signs of the times. Jesus Christ accused Jewish leaders in His day of the same lack of discernment: "You know how to interpret the weather signs in the sky, but you don't know how to interpret the signs of the times!" (Matthew 16:3). Jesus revealed many other signs that would occur at the end of the age (Matthew 24), and the discerning disciple will look for them. Signs provided but ignored are of no benefit.

DISCOVERY VERSES

The day of the LORD is near, the day when destruction comes from the Almighty. How terrible that day will be! (JOEL 1:15)

"Don't tear your clothing in your grief, but tear your hearts instead." Return to the LORD your God, for He is merciful and compassionate, slow to get angry and filled with unfailing love. He is eager to relent and not punish. (JOEL 2:13)

JOEL FACTS

Author: Joel (1:1). He is not mentioned elsewhere in Scripture (except in a reference in Acts 2:16).

Written to: Given his references to the southern tribes and the capital city of Jerusalem (2:32; 3:1, 6, 8, 16-20), Joel appears to have been writing to the inhabitants of Judah.

Date of writing: There are no time indicators in the book of Joel. An affinity with the book of Amos and the prominence of nations such as Philistia, Egypt, and Edom (3:4, 19) may indicate a date in the late ninth century BC.

Setting: The southern kingdom of Judah and its capital, Jerusalem.

OUTLINE

- **JOEL 1:1–2:17**—The Need for Repentance
- **JOEL 2:18–3:21**—The Fruit of Repentance

1:1 Jer 1:2 Acts 2:16

1 The LORD gave this message to Joel son of Pethuel.

MOURNING OVER THE LOCUST PLAGUE

1:2 Jer 30:7 Joel 2:2, 16

2 Hear this, you leaders of the people.
Listen, all who live in the land.
In all your history,
has anything like this happened before?

1:3 Exod 10:2

3 Tell your children about it in the years to come,
and let your children tell their children.
Pass the story down from generation to generation.

1:4 Deut 28:38-39 Isa 33:4 Joel 2:25 Nah 3:15-16

4 After the cutting locusts finished eating the crops,
the swarming locusts took what was left!
After them came the hopping locusts,
and then the stripping locusts,* too!

1:5 Joel 3:3

5 Wake up, you drunkards, and weep!
Wail, all you wine-drinkers!
All the grapes are ruined,
and all your sweet wine is gone.

1:6 Joel 2:2, 11 Rev 9:8

6 A vast army of locusts* has invaded My land,
a terrible army too numerous to count.
Its teeth are like lions' teeth,
its fangs like those of a lioness.

1:7 Isa 5:6 Amos 4:9

7 It has destroyed My grapevines
and ruined My fig trees,
stripping their bark and destroying it,
leaving the branches white and bare.

8 Weep like a bride dressed in black,
mourning the death of her husband.

1:9 Joel 1:13; 2:14

9 For there is no grain or wine
to offer at the Temple of the LORD.
So the priests are in mourning.
The ministers of the LORD are weeping.

1:10 Isa 24:4, 7

10 The fields are ruined,
the land is stripped bare.

1:4 The precise identification of the four kinds of locusts mentioned here is uncertain. 1:6 Hebrew *A nation.*

1:1 Joel's father is mentioned here, as is common in other prophetic books of the Bible (Jeremiah 1:1; Ezekiel 1:3; Hosea 1:1; Jonah 1:1; Zephaniah 1:1; Zechariah 1:1). This not only identified the prophets' general location and family relations, but it also confirmed that they were not foreigners, and therefore were not predicting the downfall of Israel for political gain.

▸ WORSHIP

1:3 Telling the truth to our children. Some people believe that they shouldn't teach their children anything about God—children should form their own religious beliefs. But no one takes that route when teaching children math or teaching them not to play with fire—why avoid teaching children religious truth? The Bible says parents have the responsibility of guiding their children away from the moral evils in the world (Proverbs 22:6). This involves protecting them from evil and helping them to learn the truth about God's blessings and judgments (Deuteronomy 6:7; Joshua 4:6-7; Psalm 78:3-8). If you are a parent (or want to be one), commit to lovingly telling your children about the joys of following God and the consequences of turning away from Him. (***See Worship***> *OT> Teaching and Preaching> Primary religious responsibility of the family to their children was education,* TopicGuide page A29.)

1:4 By the time of Joel's prophecy, Judah had already experienced a devastating locust plague. Four different uses of the Hebrew word for "locust" exist in this verse that may indicate different stages of development for the locust. This repetition of "locust" emphasizes the widespread destruction they inflicted upon the land. Locusts are among the instruments God historically used for punishment (Exodus 10:12-15).

The grain is destroyed,
the grapes have shriveled,
and the olive oil is gone.

11 Despair, all you farmers!
Wail, all you vine growers!
Weep, because the wheat and barley—
all the crops of the field—are ruined.
12 The grapevines have dried up,
and the fig trees have withered.
The pomegranate trees, palm trees, and apple trees—
all the fruit trees—have dried up.
And the people's joy has dried up with them.

13 Dress yourselves in burlap and weep, you priests!
Wail, you who serve before the altar!
Come, spend the night in burlap,
you ministers of my God.
For there is no grain or wine
to offer at the Temple of your God.
14 Announce a time of fasting;
call the people together for a solemn meeting.
Bring the leaders
and all the people of the land
into the Temple of the LORD your God,
and cry out to Him there.
15 The day of the LORD is near,
the day when destruction comes from the Almighty.
How terrible that day will be!

16 Our food disappears before our very eyes.
No joyful celebrations are held in the house of our God.
17 The seeds die in the parched ground,
and the grain crops fail.
The barns stand empty,
and granaries are abandoned.
18 How the animals moan with hunger!
The herds of cattle wander about confused,
because they have no pasture.
The flocks of sheep and goats bleat in misery.

19 LORD, help us!
The fire has consumed the wilderness pastures,
and flames have burned up all the trees.
20 Even the wild animals cry out to you
because the streams have dried up,
and fire has consumed the wilderness pastures.

1:11 Amos 5:16
1:12 Song 2:3; Hab 3:17-18; Hag 2:19
1:13 1 Kgs 21:27; Jer 4:8
1:14 Jon 3:8
1:15 Isa 13:9; Jer 30:7; Ezek 7:2-13; Joel 2:1
1:16 Isa 3:7; Amos 4:6-7
1:17 Isa 17:10-11
1:19 Pss 50:15; 91:15; Mic 7:7
1:20 1 Kgs 17:7; 18:5; Ps 104:21; Joel 1:18

1:13-14 The prophet Joel provided specific instructions to the priest. These ministers were to lead the nation of Judah into a time of mourning, fasting, and repenting.

▸ HOLINESS
1:19 Praying through suffering. When tragedy strikes, we often find ourselves wondering if God is truly in control of our circumstances, and that can lead us to drift away from Him. The prophet Joel understood that although God had permitted Israel's suffering, He alone could restore all things to their rightful place. We should not run away from God in times of trial; but, through prayer, we can earnestly seek Him who alone can deliver us. Do not flee from God during a crisis, but run to Him and find help. (***See Holiness> Submission> Identifying with Christ> Suffering with Him,*** TopicGuide page A40.)

LOCUSTS INVADE LIKE AN ARMY

2:1 Joel 1:15; 2:11, 15, 31; 3:14 Zeph 1:16

2 [1] Sound the alarm in Jerusalem*!
Raise the battle cry on My holy mountain!
Let everyone tremble in fear
because the day of the LORD is upon us.

2:2 Dan 9:12 Joel 1:2, 6; 2:5, 10-11, 31

[2] It is a day of darkness and gloom,
a day of thick clouds and deep blackness.
Suddenly, like dawn spreading across the mountains,
a great and mighty army appears.
Nothing like it has been seen before
or will ever be seen again.

2:3 Gen 2:8 Ps 105:34-35 Isa 51:3

[3] Fire burns in front of them,
and flames follow after them.
Ahead of them the land lies
as beautiful as the Garden of Eden.
Behind them is nothing but desolation;
not one thing escapes.

2:4 Rev 9:7

[4] They look like horses;
they charge forward like warhorses.*

2:5 Isa 5:24; 30:30 Rev 9:9

[5] Look at them as they leap along the mountaintops.
Listen to the noise they make—like the rumbling of chariots,
like the roar of fire sweeping across a field of stubble,
or like a mighty army moving into battle.

2:6 Isa 13:8 Jer 30:6

[6] Fear grips all the people;
every face grows pale with terror.

2:7 Isa 5:26-29

[7] The attackers march like warriors
and scale city walls like soldiers.
Straight forward they march,
never breaking rank.
[8] They never jostle each other;
each moves in exactly the right position.
They break through defenses
without missing a step.

2:9 Exod 10:6 Jer 9:21 John 10:1

[9] They swarm over the city
and run along its walls.
They enter all the houses,
climbing like thieves through the windows.

2:10 Ps 18:7 Isa 13:10 Joel 2:31; 3:15 Nah 1:5 Matt 24:29; 27:51 *Mark 13:24-25

[10] The earth quakes as they advance,
and the heavens tremble.
The sun and moon grow dark,
and the stars no longer shine.

2:11 Ps 46:6 Joel 2:1; 3:16

[11] The LORD is at the head of the column.
He leads them with a shout.
This is His mighty army,
and they follow His orders.
The day of the LORD is an awesome, terrible thing.
Who can possibly survive?

2:1 Hebrew *Zion;* also in 2:15, 23. 2:4 Or *like charioteers.*

2:1-10 Joel announced that the coming day of judgment would fall on Judah, including the city of Jerusalem. The blowing of the trumpet was not a rally cry to arms, but an alarm signaling the fall of Judah to a ravaging pagan army sent by God.

A CALL TO REPENTANCE

12 That is why the LORD says,
"Turn to Me now, while there is time.
Give Me your hearts.
Come with fasting, weeping, and mourning.
13 Don't tear your clothing in your grief,
but tear your hearts instead."
Return to the LORD your God,
for He is merciful and compassionate,
slow to get angry and filled with unfailing love.
He is eager to relent and not punish.
14 Who knows? Perhaps He will give you a reprieve,
sending you a blessing instead of this curse.
Perhaps you will be able to offer grain and wine
to the LORD your God as before.

15 Blow the ram's horn in Jerusalem!
Announce a time of fasting;
call the people together
for a solemn meeting.
16 Gather all the people—
the elders, the children, and even the babies.
Call the bridegroom from his quarters
and the bride from her private room.
17 Let the priests, who minister in the LORD's presence,
stand and weep between the entry room to the Temple and the altar.
Let them pray, "Spare Your people, LORD!
Don't let Your special possession become an object of mockery.
Don't let them become a joke for unbelieving foreigners who say,
'Has the God of Israel left them?'"

THE LORD'S PROMISE OF RESTORATION

18 Then the LORD will pity His people
and jealously guard the honor of His land.
19 The LORD will reply,
"Look! I am sending you grain and new wine and olive oil,
enough to satisfy your needs.
You will no longer be an object of mockery
among the surrounding nations.
20 I will drive away these armies from the north.
I will send them into the parched wastelands.
Those in the front will be driven into the Dead Sea,
and those at the rear into the Mediterranean.*

2:12 Deut 4:29-30
2:13 Exod 34:6; Amos 7:2-6
2:14 Hag 2:19
2:15 Num 10:3; Joel 2:1
2:17 Pss 44:13; 79:10; Isa 37:20
2:18 Isa 60:10; Zech 1:14
2:19 Ezek 34:29; 36:15; Hos 2:21-22
2:20 Deut 11:24; Jer 1:14-15; Zech 14:8

2:20 Hebrew *into the eastern sea, . . . into the western sea.*

▸ WORSHIP

2:12-13 Does God use fear to motivate me? God wanted the people of Judah to repent of their evil ways. He warned them that the locust and the drought were only precursors to a greater judgment that was approaching. God's purpose for us is not simply that we fear His judgments, though He clearly still uses punishment to motivate us to obedience (Luke 12:5; Acts 5:11). God desires instead for all to approach Him with repentant hearts. He wants repentance to flow from an intimate relationship with Him, and that means love mingled with fear—reverence—is an excellent motivator for repentance. Turn to Him today—He will always receive your humble repentance (2 Corinthians 7:10). (***See Worship****> OT> Reverence> God shows mercy to those who fear Him,* TopicGuide page A29.)

2:19 The prophecy of destruction in 2:1-10 depended on Judah's response to Joel's warning. If the people followed Joel's instructions and turned from their sin, the Lord pledged to restore their land and to bless them.

The stench of their rotting bodies will rise over
the land."

Surely the LORD has done great things!
21 Don't be afraid, My people.
Be glad now and rejoice,
for the LORD has done great things.

2:22 Ps 65:12-13
22 Don't be afraid, you animals of the field,
for the wilderness pastures will soon be green.
The trees will again be filled with fruit;
fig trees and grapevines will be loaded down once more.

2:23 Ps 149:2 Hos 6:3 Zech 10:1
23 Rejoice, you people of Jerusalem!
Rejoice in the LORD your God!
For the rain He sends demonstrates His faithfulness.
Once more the autumn rains will come,
as well as the rains of spring.
24 The threshing floors will again be piled high with grain,
and the presses will overflow with new wine and olive oil.

25 The LORD says, "I will give you back what you lost
to the swarming locusts, the hopping locusts,
the stripping locusts, and the cutting locusts.*
It was I who sent this great destroying army against you.

2:26 Ps 67:5-7 Isa 45:17
26 Once again you will have all the food you want,
and you will praise the LORD your God,
who does these miracles for you.
Never again will My people be disgraced.

2:27 Lev 26:11-12 Isa 45:5-6, 18 Joel 3:17, 21
27 Then you will know that I am among My people Israel,
that I am the LORD your God, and there is no other.
Never again will My people be disgraced.

THE LORD'S PROMISE OF HIS SPIRIT

2:28-32 *Acts 2:17-21
28*"Then, after doing all those things,
I will pour out My Spirit upon all people.
Your sons and daughters will prophesy.
Your old men will dream dreams,
and your young men will see visions.

2:29 1 Cor 12:13 Gal 3:28
29 In those days I will pour out My Spirit
even on servants—men and women alike.

2:25 The precise identification of the four kinds of locusts mentioned here is uncertain. 2:28 Verses 2:28-32 are numbered 3:1-5 in Hebrew text.

2:23 The rainy season for Israel typically lasts for seven months, between October and April. The bulk of the rain occurs between December and February. But here the Lord extended His blessing of abundant rain to include the early and latter months of the rainy season. God promised to rain down abundant blessing as He reigned over His people in Judah.

▸ GOD
2:27 Getting our attention. The world we live in provides difficulties—and God knows it and allows it for good reason. Tragedy frequently causes us to see the brokenness of our lives. Difficult times can shred flimsy faith and false ideas about God, showing our need to trust in His truth. God's ultimate desire for you is not that you would wait for calamity to strike before you repent, but rather that you would heed His warnings of potential consequences for sin and that you would turn in repentance toward Him. Do not wait for pain to point out sin in your life—pursue purity today. (***See God**> Relationship> God's Desire> God pursues a relationship,* TopicGuide page A14.)

2:28-29 God's promise of blessing shifts from pouring out rain upon His people and giving them a great harvest to pouring out His Spirit upon His people and watching them experience a spiritual harvest. This experience of the full bounty of the Holy Spirit coming to God's people would not be fulfilled until Pentecost (Acts 2:17-21).

30 And I will cause wonders in the heavens and on the earth—
blood and fire and columns of smoke.
31 The sun will become dark,
and the moon will turn blood red
before that great and terrible* day of the LORD arrives.
32 But everyone who calls on the name of the LORD
will be saved,
for some on Mount Zion in Jerusalem will escape,
just as the LORD has said.
These will be among the survivors
whom the LORD has called.

2:30-31 Joel 2:1, 10; 3:15 Matt 24:29 Mark 13:24-25

2:32 Isa 4:2 *Rom 10:13

JUDGMENT AGAINST ENEMY NATIONS

3 1*"At the time of those events," says the LORD,
"when I restore the prosperity of Judah and Jerusalem,
2 I will gather the armies of the world
into the valley of Jehoshaphat.*
There I will judge them
for harming My people, My special possession,
for scattering My people among the nations,
and for dividing up My land.
3 They threw dice* to decide which of My people
would be their slaves.
They traded boys to obtain prostitutes
and sold girls for enough wine to get drunk.

3:2 Isa 66:16, 18 Ezek 36:1-5 Joel 3:12, 14

3:3 Obad 1:11 Nah 3:10

4"What do you have against Me, Tyre and Sidon and you cities of Philistia? Are you try-
ing to take revenge on Me? If you are, then watch out! I will strike swiftly and pay you back
for everything you have done. 5You have taken My silver and gold and all My precious
treasures, and have carried them off to your pagan temples. 6You have sold the people of
Judah and Jerusalem to the Greeks,* so they could take them far from their homeland.
7"But I will bring them back from all the places to which you sold them, and I will pay
you back for everything you have done. 8I will sell your sons and daughters to the people
of Judah, and they will sell them to the people of Arabia,* a nation far away. I, the LORD,
have spoken!"

3:4 Ezek 25:15-17; 26:1-3

3:5 2 Kgs 12:18 2 Chr 21:16-17

3:7 Isa 43:5-6 Jer 23:8

9 Say to the nations far and wide:
"Get ready for war!
Call out your best warriors.
Let all your fighting men advance for the attack.
10 Hammer your plowshares into swords
and your pruning hooks into spears.
Train even your weaklings to be warriors.
11 Come quickly, all you nations everywhere.
Gather together in the valley."

And now, O LORD, call out your warriors!

3:9 Isa 34:1 Jer 46:3; 51:27 Zech 14:2-3

3:10 Isa 2:4 Mic 4:3

2:31 Greek version reads *glorious.* 3:1 Verses 3:1-21 are numbered 4:1-21 in Hebrew text. 3:2 *Jehoshaphat* means "the LORD judges." 3:3 Hebrew *They cast lots.* 3:6 Hebrew *to the peoples of Javan.* 3:8 Hebrew *to the Sabeans.*

3:2 *Jehoshaphat* literally means "the LORD judges." Joel 3:14 calls this valley the "valley of decision."

3:9 The Lord asked the nations to prepare for battle even though He had already determined that they would lose (Joel 3:2, 19) and had sealed their humiliation.

3:12 Ps 76:8-9 Isa 3:13 Joel 3:2, 14

12 "Let the nations be called to arms.
Let them march to the valley of Jehoshaphat.
There I, the LORD, will sit
to pronounce judgment on them all.

3:13 Hos 6:11 Matt 13:39 Mark 4:29 Rev 14:15-19

13 Swing the sickle,
for the harvest is ripe.*
Come, tread the grapes,
for the winepress is full.
The storage vats are overflowing
with the wickedness of these people."

3:14 Isa 34:2-8 Joel 2:1; 3:2, 12

14 Thousands upon thousands are waiting in the valley of decision.
There the day of the LORD will soon arrive.

3:15 Joel 2:10, 31

15 The sun and moon will grow dark,
and the stars will no longer shine.

3:16 Hos 11:10 Amos 1:2

16 The LORD's voice will roar from Zion
and thunder from Jerusalem,
and the heavens and the earth will shake.
But the LORD will be a refuge for His people,
a strong fortress for the people of Israel.

BLESSINGS FOR GOD'S PEOPLE

3:17 Isa 11:9 Ezek 20:40

17 "Then you will know that I, the LORD your God,
live in Zion, My holy mountain.
Jerusalem will be holy forever,
and foreign armies will never conquer her again.

3:18 Exod 3:8 Amos 9:13

18 In that day the mountains will drip with sweet wine,
and the hills will flow with milk.
Water will fill the streambeds of Judah,
and a fountain will burst forth from the LORD's Temple,
watering the arid valley of acacias.*

3:19 Amos 1:11 Obad 1:10

19 But Egypt will become a wasteland
and Edom will become a wilderness,
because they attacked the people of Judah
and killed innocent people in their land.

3:20 Ezek 37:25 Amos 9:15

20 "But Judah will be filled with people forever,
and Jerusalem will endure through all generations.

3:21 Isa 4:4 Ezek 36:25, 29

21 I will pardon My people's crimes,
which I have not yet pardoned;
and I, the LORD, will make My home
in Jerusalem* with My people."

3:13 Greek version reads *for the harvest time has come.* Compare Mark 4:29. **3:18** Hebrew *valley of Shittim.* **3:21** Hebrew *Zion.*

▸ GOD

3:16 God's plan: rescue and wrath. In the same motion, God often achieves very different results. Noah and his family were spared when God judged the world through the Flood (Genesis 6–7). The nation of Israel was protected during the Passover (Exodus 12), while Egypt suffered harsh loss. In the final day of the LORD that will be executed by Jesus Christ, the world will experience judgment, but the people of God will be rescued (Matthew 24:37-44). None of these groups were spared from all discomfort or trouble, but each one saw God miraculously intervene. From what do you need to be rescued? God has a plan, in His own time, to save you. Trust Him and keep looking for the means of rescue He provides. (***See God***> *God's Attributes> Sovereign> He has a plan for his people and will carry it out,* TopicGuide page A17.)

3:19 Because the nations of Egypt and Edom had shed the blood of God's people, God would now turn both of these nations into a desolate wasteland (1 Kings 14:25-26; Isaiah 19:1-15; Lamentations 4:21; Obadiah 1:9-14).

AMOS

PURPOSE

To rouse the people of Israel from their complacency and false sense of security and warn them of coming judgment.

The concept of "tough love" has gained popularity in contemporary counseling circles. This approach affirms the benefit of firmness and directness when gentler methods fail. Amos could be called the "tough-love prophet" of the Old Testament.

In the eighth century BC, things seemed to be booming in the northern tribes of Israel: The nation was politically stable, the economy was doing well, and the future looked positive. These favorable conditions created a false sense of security and independence, and religion in Israel was reduced to mere formality—ritual devoid of true spirituality. In fact, pagan idolatry had replaced the worship of the one true God. Sin was rampant in the nation, and the powerful took advantage of the weak. In God's sight, the nation was ripe for discipline. Into this setting God sent Amos—a blunt-talking farmer who told it like it was (bad) and like it was about to become (worse). Amos offered fewer words of consolation to Israel than any other prophet, but enough to let them know there was still hope to be found by trusting in God (9:11-15).

DISCOVER GOD IN AMOS

It is tempting to re-create God in our own image, giving Him the personality *we* imagine He should have. Our preference is usually something along the lines of "meek and mild." Amos, however, did not tone down the wrathful aspect of God's nature, but instead presented the boldness and bluntness of God's justice and judgment:

God of Heaven's Armies: Amos refers to God as "the LORD God of Heaven's Armies" at least nine times (see, for example, 3:13; 4:13; 5:14). There is no mistaking Amos's (God's) intended meaning: God had armies, both heavenly (angels) and earthly (the Assyrians), who stood ready to do His bidding. By speaking in such a bold way about God to those who supposedly were His people, Amos intended to give the Israelites a wake-up call. "The God of armies" was a title generally reserved as a threat when speaking to God's enemies—but that is exactly what God's own people had become. God does not change sides for anyone. All who oppose Him must be prepared to bear the brunt of His might in one form or another.

Directness: Many who read Matthew 23 in the New Testament are shocked by Jesus' blunt language with the Pharisees. Several times He called them hypocrites, as well as blind guides, blind fools, snakes, and sons of vipers. But Amos shows that Jesus was not the first to use strong and direct language in addressing sinners: "Listen to me, you fat cows living in Samaria, you women who oppress the poor and crush the needy, and who are always calling to your husbands, 'Bring us another drink!' " (4:1). The cows of Samaria were a pampered breed in Canaan, given the best of everything—and Amos compared the wealthy women of Samaria to these bovine behemoths. God said the day was coming when they would be led away with hooks in their noses (4:2). Archaeologists have found Assyrian engravings showing prisoners being led by ropes attached to hooks in their noses or lips. God doesn't speak this bluntly often, but when He does, we should listen.

GROWING THROUGH AMOS

A warning and an exhortation surface in Amos as themes for followers of Christ:

Complacency: Amos decried Israel's spiritual complacency by declaring, "What sorrow awaits you who lounge in luxury in Jerusalem, and you who feel secure in Samaria!" (6:1). Spiritual complacency comes when we think we have already arrived at our spiritual destination. The writer of the New Testament book of Hebrews issued Amos-like warnings to those who might grow complacent in their place of spiritual privilege: "Be careful then, dear brothers and sisters. Make sure that your own hearts are not evil and unbelieving, turning you away from the living God" (Hebrews 3:12). Complacency is the poisonous fruit of self-righteousness.

Calling: Amos was up-front about his prophetic role: "I'm not a professional prophet, and I was never trained to be one. I'm just a shepherd, and I take care of sycamore-fig trees. But the LORD called me away from my flock and told me, 'Go and prophesy to My people in Israel' " (7:14-15). Amos was not the first person plucked from obscurity by God and given an important task—think of Abraham, Moses, David, many of the prophets, Mary, John the Baptist, and Paul. In many cases, commoners seem to be God's first choice. But the most important thing about being used by God is not one's résumé but one's response to God's calling.

DISCOVERY VERSES

For the LORD is the one who shaped the mountains, stirs up the winds, and reveals His thoughts to mankind. He turns the light of dawn into darkness and treads on the heights of the earth. The LORD God of Heaven's Armies is His name! (AMOS 4:13)

In that day I will restore the fallen house of David. I will repair its damaged walls. From the ruins I will rebuild it and restore its former glory. (AMOS 9:11)

AMOS FACTS

Author: Amos (1:1). Amos is mentioned nowhere else in the Old Testament. A shepherd and grower of figs (7:14), Amos lived in Judah but was sent by God to prophesy against the northern tribes of Israel.

Written to: The leaders and people of the morally and spiritually corrupt nation of Israel.

Date of writing: Around 760 BC.

Setting: The main location in Amos seems to be Samaria, the capital of Israel.

OUTLINE

- **AMOS 1:1–2:16**—Judgment on the Nations
- **AMOS 3:1–9:10**—Judgment on Israel
- **AMOS 9:11-15**—Hope for Restoration

1:1 2 Sam 14:2; 2 Kgs 14:23-29; Zech 14:5
1:2 Isa 42:13; Jer 12:4; 14:2; 25:30; Joel 1:18-19; 3:16

1 This message was given to Amos, a shepherd from the town of Tekoa in Judah. He
received this message in visions two years before the earthquake, when Uzziah was
king of Judah and Jeroboam II, the son of Jehoash,* was king of Israel.
2 This is what he saw and heard:

"The LORD's voice will roar from Zion
and thunder from Jerusalem!
The lush pastures of the shepherds will dry up;
the grass on Mount Carmel will wither and die."

GOD'S JUDGMENT ON ISRAEL'S NEIGHBORS

1:3 Isa 8:4; Amos 2:1, 4, 6

3 This is what the LORD says:

"The people of Damascus have sinned again and again,*
and I will not let them go unpunished!
They beat down My people in Gilead
as grain is threshed with iron sledges.

1:4 1 Kgs 20:1; 2 Kgs 6:24

4 So I will send down fire on King Hazael's palace,
and the fortresses of King Ben-hadad will be destroyed.
5 I will break down the gates of Damascus
and slaughter the people in the valley of Aven.
I will destroy the ruler in Beth-eden,
and the people of Aram will go as captives to Kir,"
says the LORD.

1:6 1 Sam 6:17; Jer 47:1, 5; Ezek 35:5; Amos 1:9, 11; Obad 1:11

6 This is what the LORD says:

"The people of Gaza have sinned again and again,
and I will not let them go unpunished!

1:1 Hebrew *Joash,* a variant spelling of Jehoash. 1:3 Hebrew *have committed three sins, even four;* also in 1:6, 9, 11, 13.

1:1 Amos was called to prophesy to the northern kingdom of Israel in the midst of a time of great prosperity during Uzziah's reign in Judah and Jeroboam II's reign in Israel (2 Kings 14:25-28; 15:1; 2 Chronicles 26:10-11) These prophecies were given two years before a memorable earthquake. Zechariah, who prophesied centuries later, recalled the people fleeing during this event (Zechariah 14:5).

▶ WORSHIP
1:2 The roaring God. What makes you afraid? A shepherd watching sheep in the dark wilderness would surely experience uncontrollable trembling whenever a lion's roar invaded the silence. Amos may have experienced this fear, since he frequently utilized the words *lion* and *roar.* He used the image of a lion's ferocious roar to illustrate what it is like to hear God's voice as He booms forth with threats of judgment. Amos again pictured God as a roaring lion in 3:8, and urged Israel to tremble in fear. Sometimes it is right to fear God (Isaiah 66:2), as God does not make idle threats. As you read Amos, pray for those around you who show disdain at God's threats of wrath. Look at your own life and make certain you are safe from the wrath of God through a living faith in Jesus Christ. (***See Worship****> OT> Reverence> God delivers those who fear Him,* TopicGuide page A29.)

1:3-5 The announcement of judgment upon one of Israel's enemies, the nation of Aram (Damascus is the capital city), is the first in a series of eight judgments upon eight different nations (Amos 1:3–2:16). Each new section begins with words indicating the divine authority of the message: "This is what the LORD says"; each section also repeats the phrase "for three sins . . . even for four," denoting the repeated nature of the infractions (the NLT translates this phrase "have sinned again and again"; see textual note at 1:3). Another feature of each section is the repeated assurance that God "will not let them go unpunished."

1:3 Amos condemned the people of Aram for their brutal treatment of God's people in Gilead, likening it to threshing wheat with an iron sledge (Isaiah 41:15). Such sledges were designed to break up the heads of harvested grain. God declared that He would respond in like manner by breaking down the gates of their capital city, Damascus (Amos 1:5).

▶ GOD
1:4-5 God behind the scenes. Does God use the nations to carry out His plans? Throughout the book of Amos, God is not even slightly embarrassed to claim full responsibility for the judgments that would come upon these nations, even though that judgment usually would come through the power of a foreign army. God emphatically states "I will" in each of the eight judgment speeches, leaving no question regarding who was ultimately responsible. God is the King of kings, and He wields nation against nation as a warrior wields a sword. Within a generation of Amos's prophecies, God used Assyria's armies to accomplish His purposes, just as He later used Babylon, Greece, Persia, and Rome. Worship our God, who still works behind the scenes to cause nations to carry out His judgments on earth. (***See God****> God's Attributes> Sovereign> God has dominion over the affairs of people,* TopicGuide page A17.)

They sent whole villages into exile,
selling them as slaves to Edom.
7 So I will send down fire on the walls of Gaza,
and all its fortresses will be destroyed.
8 I will slaughter the people of Ashdod
and destroy the king of Ashkelon.
Then I will turn to attack Ekron,
and the few Philistines still left will be killed,"
says the Sovereign LORD.

1:8
Isa 14:29-31
Jer 47:1-7
Ezek 25:16
Zeph 2:4-7
Zech 9:6

9 This is what the LORD says:

"The people of Tyre have sinned again and again,
and I will not let them go unpunished!
They broke their treaty of brotherhood with Israel,
selling whole villages as slaves to Edom.
10 So I will send down fire on the walls of Tyre,
and all its fortresses will be destroyed."

1:9
1 Kgs 5:1; 9:11-14
Isa 23:1-18

11 This is what the LORD says:

"The people of Edom have sinned again and again,
and I will not let them go unpunished!
They chased down their relatives, the Israelites, with swords,
showing them no mercy.
In their rage, they slashed them continually
and were unrelenting in their anger.
12 So I will send down fire on Teman,
and the fortresses of Bozrah will be destroyed."

1:11
Num 20:14-21
Isa 34:5-6; 63:1-3
Jer 49:7-22
Ezek 25:12-14
Obad 1:10-12
Mic 7:18

1:12
Jer 49:7, 20
Obad 1:9

13 This is what the LORD says:

"The people of Ammon have sinned again and again,
and I will not let them go unpunished!
When they attacked Gilead to extend their borders,
they ripped open pregnant women with their swords.
14 So I will send down fire on the walls of Rabbah,
and all its fortresses will be destroyed.
The battle will come upon them with shouts,
like a whirlwind in a mighty storm.
15 And their king* and his princes will go into exile together,"
says the LORD.

1:13
2 Kgs 15:16
Jer 49:1-6
Ezek 25:2-7
Hos 13:16

1:14
Jer 49:2
Amos 2:2

1:15
Jer 49:3

2

This is what the LORD says:

"The people of Moab have sinned again and again,*
and I will not let them go unpunished!

2:1
Isa 15:1-9; 16:1-14
Jer 48:1-7
Zech 2:8-9

1:15 Hebrew *malcam,* possibly referring to their god Molech. 2:1 Hebrew *have committed three sins, even four;* also in 2:4, 6.

▸ GOD

1:8 Human life isn't disposable. Have you ever wondered what God thinks about the terrible ways people harm and destroy other people? God declared His impending judgment on several nations for treating human life as if it did not matter. Aram viciously pummeled people. Philistia and Tyre mercilessly sold people into slavery. Edom used swords on people with unbridled fury. Ammon ripped open pregnant women. Moab desecrated a king's dead body. Each indictment highlights that God not only notices these atrocities but also is moved to anger because of them. Humans are unique in all of creation because they are made in God's own image (Genesis 1:27), so God is angered at such acts of disrespect toward humanity. Praise God for His concern for people and for the assurance that He will carry out perfect justice. (***See God****> God's Nature> Personality> Rebellion rightly angers God,* TopicGuide page A14.)

They desecrated the bones of Edom's king,
burning them to ashes.
2:2 Jer 48:24, 41, 45
2 So I will send down fire on the land of Moab,
and all the fortresses in Kerioth will be destroyed.
The people will fall in the noise of battle,
as the warriors shout and the ram's horn sounds.
2:3 Isa 40:23
3 And I will destroy their king
and slaughter all their princes,"
says the LORD.

GOD'S JUDGMENT ON JUDAH AND ISRAEL

2:4 Judg 2:17-20; 2 Kgs 17:19; Amos 3:2
4 This is what the LORD says:

"The people of Judah have sinned again and again,
and I will not let them go unpunished!
They have rejected the instruction of the LORD,
refusing to obey His decrees.
They have been led astray by the same lies
that deceived their ancestors.
2:5 Jer 17:27; Hos 8:14
5 So I will send down fire on Judah,
and all the fortresses of Jerusalem will be destroyed."

2:6 2 Kgs 18:12; Joel 3:3, 6; Amos 5:11; 8:4-6
6 This is what the LORD says:

"The people of Israel have sinned again and again,
and I will not let them go unpunished!
They sell honorable people for silver
and poor people for a pair of sandals.
2:7 Hos 4:14; Amos 5:12; 8:4
7 They trample helpless people in the dust
and shove the oppressed out of the way.
Both father and son sleep with the same woman,
corrupting My holy name.
2:8 Exod 22:26; Amos 4:1; 6:6
8 At their religious festivals,
they lounge in clothing their debtors put up as security.
In the house of their god,
they drink wine bought with unjust fines.

2:9 Ezek 17:9; Mal 4:1
9 "But as My people watched,
I destroyed the Amorites,

2:2 The desecration of the tomb of Edom's king and the burning of his bones served no military purpose. How could it? The king was already dead. Rather, Moab purposefully denigrated the body of the king, similar to the way the Philistines beheaded Saul and displayed his corpse on a wall (1 Samuel 31:9-10). God would judge them for their complete disrespect for human dignity.

2:4-5 Amos focused on Judah's condemnation in part because of the clear teaching that the southern kingdom had received. Other nations did not have the Temple of God or the law of God, but Judah could not make excuses based on ignorance (Romans 2:12). Jesus taught that much is required from those to whom much is given, and much more is required from those to whom much more is given (Luke 12:47-48).

2:6-16 This section of judgment is four times longer than any of the prior declarations of judgment. The length and specific content reveal that Amos declared the judgments on the other nations with the purpose of setting up this main point: Israel, like the other nations, was overdue for judgment from God.

▸ WORSHIP
2:6 Humble enough to see. Israel would likely have applauded all of the preceding indictments, even against their own brothers in Judah. But now the lion turned his attention and roared at them. Amos declared that Israel could not boast in moral superiority, since they were flagrantly sinning against the God who redeemed them out of slavery in Egypt and gave them numerous privileges (Amos 2:9-11). Like Judah, Israel had been given much, but they only became arrogant, especially in matters of religion (Amos 2:8; 4:5; 5:7; 5:21; 6:8). Jesus taught us to remove the log out of our own eye prior to evaluating problems with the eyesight of other people (Matthew 7:5). Ask God to remove any sense of arrogant self-righteousness within you and to instill in you a heart of humble obedience. (***See Worship**> OT> Reverence> Leads to humility*, TopicGuide page A29.)

though they were as tall as cedars
and as strong as oaks.
I destroyed the fruit on their branches
and dug out their roots.
10 It was I who rescued you from Egypt
and led you through the desert for forty years,
so you could possess the land of the Amorites.
11 I chose some of your sons to be prophets
and others to be Nazirites.
Can you deny this, My people of Israel?"
asks the LORD.
12 "But you caused the Nazirites to sin by making them drink wine,
and you commanded the prophets, 'Shut up!'
13 "So I will make you groan
like a wagon loaded down with sheaves of grain.
14 Your fastest runners will not get away.
The strongest among you will become weak.
Even mighty warriors will be unable to save themselves.
15 The archers will not stand their ground.
The swiftest runners won't be fast enough to escape.
Even those riding horses won't be able to save themselves.
16 On that day the most courageous of your fighting men
will drop their weapons and run for their lives,"
says the LORD.

2:10 Exod 3:8; 12:51 Deut 2:7; 8:2-4
2:11 Num 6:2-3 Jer 7:25
2:12 Isa 30:10 Jer 11:21 Amos 7:13, 16
2:14 Ps 33:16 Isa 30:16-17 Jer 9:23
2:15 Isa 31:3 Jer 51:56 Ezek 39:3
2:16 Judg 4:15-16

3 Listen to this message that the LORD has spoken against you, O people of Israel and Judah—against the entire family I rescued from Egypt:

2 "From among all the families on the earth,
I have been intimate with you alone.
That is why I must punish you
for all your sins."

3:1 Jer 8:3; 13:11
3:2 Exod 19:5-6 Deut 7:6 Ezek 20:36-38 Rom 2:9

WITNESSES AGAINST GUILTY ISRAEL

3 Can two people walk together
without agreeing on the direction?
4 Does a lion ever roar in a thicket
without first finding a victim?
Does a young lion growl in its den
without first catching its prey?
5 Does a bird ever get caught in a trap
that has no bait?
Does a trap spring shut
when there's nothing to catch?
6 When the ram's horn blows a warning,
shouldn't the people be alarmed?
Does disaster come to a city
unless the LORD has planned it?

3:3 Gen 5:22; 6:9 Lev 26:23-24
3:4 Ps 104:21 Hos 11:10
3:6 Isa 14:24-27 Jer 6:1 Hos 5:8

3:3-8 These many questions have one common feature: a clear cause-and-effect relationship. The questions progress from general observations of nature to Amos's central point: if the Lord had declared judgment on Israel, then their only acceptable response could be one of fear and repentance.

3:7 Gen 18:17 Dan 9:22-27 John 15:15

7 Indeed, the Sovereign LORD never does anything
until He reveals His plans to His servants the prophets.

3:8 Jer 20:9 Acts 4:20

8 The lion has roared—
so who isn't frightened?
The Sovereign LORD has spoken—
so who can refuse to proclaim His message?

3:9 Amos 8:6

9 Announce this to the leaders of Philistia*
and to the great ones of Egypt:
"Take your seats now on the hills around Samaria,
and witness the chaos and oppression in Israel."

3:10 Ps 14:4 Jer 4:22 Amos 5:7; 6:12 Hab 2:8-11 Zeph 1:9 Zech 5:3-4

10 "My people have forgotten how to do right,"
says the LORD.
"Their fortresses are filled with wealth
taken by theft and violence.

3:11 Amos 6:14

11 Therefore," says the Sovereign LORD,
"an enemy is coming!
He will surround them and shatter their defenses.
Then he will plunder all their fortresses."

3:12 1 Sam 17:34-37

12 This is what the LORD says:

"A shepherd who tries to rescue a sheep from
a lion's mouth
will recover only two legs or a piece of an ear.
So it will be for the Israelites in Samaria lying on
luxurious beds,
and for the people of Damascus reclining on couches.*

3:13 Ezek 2:7

13 "Now listen to this, and announce it throughout all Israel,*" says the Lord, the LORD
God of Heaven's Armies.

3:14 Amos 4:4; 5:5-6; 7:10, 13

14 "On the very day I punish Israel for its sins,
I will destroy the pagan altars at Bethel.
The horns of the altar will be cut off
and fall to the ground.

3:15 Judg 3:20 1 Kgs 22:39 Jer 36:22

15 And I will destroy the beautiful homes of the wealthy—
their winter mansions and their summer houses, too—
all their palaces filled with ivory,"
says the LORD.

3:9 Hebrew *Ashdod.* 3:12 Or *So it will be when the Israelites in Samaria are rescued / with only a broken bed and a tattered pillow.* 3:13 Hebrew *the house of Jacob.* The names "Jacob" and "Israel" are often interchanged throughout the Old Testament, referring sometimes to the individual patriarch and sometimes to the nation.

3:7-8 Amos declared: "The lion has roared!" In case there was any question who was doing the roaring, Amos clearly stated that the Sovereign Lord had spoken. In this artful manner, Amos justified his role and appropriate reaction and called his audience to likewise react appropriately to the voice of the Lord by trembling in fear.

3:10-11 One of Amos's central concerns was the poor and the oppressed (see 5:11-12; 8:5-6). Ignoring God's commandments had become such an embedded pattern in the Israelites' lives that they had forgotten how to act righteously. Against God's specific instructions, the rich were robbing and depriving their own brothers to increase their wealth. This was a consistent problem in Israel's history; see Nehemiah 5:3-13 for a post-exilic example of the oppression of the poor and God's condemnation of such behavior.

3:12 Amos used another lion image when he spoke of retrieving only a portion of a sheep mauled by a lion. Likewise, when God's lion-like judgment would bite down upon Israel, they also would be shattered and tattered.

ISRAEL'S FAILURE TO LEARN

4 [1] Listen to me, you fat cows*
living in Samaria,
you women who oppress the poor
and crush the needy,
and who are always calling to your husbands,
"Bring us another drink!"
[2] The Sovereign LORD has sworn this by His holiness:
"The time will come when you will be led away
with hooks in your noses.
Every last one of you will be dragged away
like a fish on a hook!
[3] You will be led out through the ruins of the wall;
you will be thrown from your fortresses,*"
says the LORD.

[4] "Go ahead and offer sacrifices to the idols at Bethel.
Keep on disobeying at Gilgal.
Offer sacrifices each morning,
and bring your tithes every three days.
[5] Present your bread made with yeast
as an offering of thanksgiving.
Then give your extra voluntary offerings
so you can brag about it everywhere!
This is the kind of thing you Israelites love to do,"
says the Sovereign LORD.

[6] "I brought hunger to every city
and famine to every town.
But still you would not return to Me,"
says the LORD.

[7] "I kept the rain from falling
when your crops needed it the most.
I sent rain on one town
but withheld it from another.
Rain fell on one field,
while another field withered away.
[8] People staggered from town to town looking for water,
but there was never enough.
But still you would not return to Me,"
says the LORD.

4:1 Ps 22:12; Amos 2:8; 3:9; 5:11; 6:11
4:2 Isa 37:29; Jer 16:16; Ezek 29:4; 38:4
4:3 Ezek 12:5, 12
4:5 Lev 7:13; 22:18-21; Hos 9:1, 10
4:6 Isa 3:1; Jer 14:18; Hag 2:17
4:7 1 Kgs 8:35-36; Zech 14:17
4:8 1 Kgs 18:5; Jer 14:3-4; Ezek 4:16; Mic 6:14; Hag 1:6

4:1 Hebrew *you cows of Bashan.* 4:3 Or *thrown out toward Harmon,* possibly a reference to Mount Hermon.

4:1 The cows of Bashan were well fed due to the location of their pasturelands in the most fertile part of Gilead. Psalm 22:12 mentions the strength of these cows, and Ezekiel 39:18 refers to their fatness.

4:2-3 Samaria fell under the siege of Assyria's armies in 722 BC, less than 50 years after Amos delivered this prophecy.

4:4-5 Bethel was a city with an unauthorized worship center established by Jeroboam. Gilgal was another city in Israel that had subsequently been established as a religious shrine where sacrifices were offered (see Hosea 4:15; 12:11). With biting irony, Amos urged the people to rush to these places but not to worship—rather to sin. The flurry of activity at these places (daily sacrifices, frequent tithes, extra offerings) only heaped up guilt before God (Romans 2:5), especially since they boasted as if they were righteous.

4:6-12 These verses summarize the curses for disobeying God's commands that are enumerated in Deuteronomy 28:15-68. Amos scanned the past and recalled that Israel experienced these curses many times, just as God had promised. Because all these past revelations of judgment had failed to evoke a proper response, Israel had to prepare to meet the intensified wrath of God (Isaiah 9:13-17).

4:9 Deut 28:22 Joel 2:25

9 "I struck your farms and vineyards with blight and mildew.
Locusts devoured all your fig and olive trees.
But still you would not return to Me,"
says the LORD.

4:10 Exod 9:3-6 Lev 26:25 Isa 9:13 Jer 11:22; 18:21 Amos 8:3

10 "I sent plagues on you
like the plagues I sent on Egypt long ago.
I killed your young men in war
and led all your horses away.*
The stench of death filled the air!
But still you would not return to Me,"
says the LORD.

4:11 Gen 19:24-25 Jer 23:14

11 "I destroyed some of your cities,
as I destroyed* Sodom and Gomorrah.
Those of you who survived
were like charred sticks pulled from a fire.
But still you would not return to Me,"
says the LORD.

12 "Therefore, I will bring upon you all the disasters I have announced.
Prepare to meet your God in judgment, you people of Israel!"

4:13 Job 38:4-11 Pss 135:7; 139:2 Dan 2:28, 30 Amos 5:8; 8:9

13 For the LORD is the One who shaped the mountains,
stirs up the winds, and reveals His thoughts to mankind.
He turns the light of dawn into darkness
and treads on the heights of the earth.
The LORD God of Heaven's Armies is His name!

A CALL TO REPENTANCE

5:1 Jer 9:10 Ezek 19:1, 14

5 Listen, you people of Israel! Listen to this funeral song I am singing:

5:2 Isa 51:18 Jer 14:17; 50:32 Amos 8:14

2 "The virgin Israel has fallen,
never to rise again!
She lies abandoned on the ground,
with no one to help her up."

3 The Sovereign LORD says:

"When a city sends a thousand men to battle,
only a hundred will return.

4:10 Or *and slaughtered your captured horses.* 4:11 Hebrew *as when God destroyed.*

▸ PURPOSE

4:12-13 A dangerous God. Why is it that many people assume that meeting God will be pleasant for everyone? It is clear that Amos did not believe this. Amos urged his audience to realize that they were not facing angry men but rather an angry God as their opponent. He shapes mountains, stirs winds, turns light to darkness, and treads mountains under His feet. Only a fool would not seek terms of peace ahead of time. Don't be a fool. If you have not made peace with this awesome God by fleeing from sin and trusting in Jesus, consider the earth-shaking nature of what lies ahead. Count the cost today. Run to Jesus and avoid meeting God unprepared. (***See Purpose****> God's Deeds> Judgment> Mountains quake/earthquake,* TopicGuide page A53.)

5:1 Funeral songs were designed to aid the audience in the process of mourning over the loss of a loved one (see David's funeral song for Saul and Jonathan in 2 Samuel 1:17-27). Amos was so sure of the coming judgment that he sang of Israel's death as if it had already occurred. See also Ezekiel's funeral song for Tyre prior to its demise in Ezekiel 27.

5:3 It is hard to conceive the depth of grief that would sweep over a community if 9 out of every 10 of their enlisted children perished during a war. It is no wonder Amos was singing sad songs. However, in all of the sadness there was perhaps a glimmer of hope: One soldier in 10 might return—the devastation would not be complete. This may be the first hint in Amos that there could be hope in the future, salvation for a remnant (developed more fully in Amos 9:8-15). In a book dark with despair, even a brief ray of light glows like the sun.

When a town sends a hundred,
only ten will come back alive."

4Now this is what the LORD says to the family of Israel:

5:4 Deut 4:29; 32:46-47

"Come back to Me and live!
5 Don't worship at the pagan altars at Bethel;
don't go to the shrines at Gilgal or Beersheba.
For the people of Gilgal will be dragged off into exile,
and the people of Bethel will be reduced to nothing."
6 Come back to the LORD and live!
Otherwise, He will roar through Israel* like a fire,
devouring you completely.
Your gods in Bethel
won't be able to quench the flames.
7 You twist justice, making it a bitter pill for the oppressed.
You treat the righteous like dirt.

5:6 Deut 4:24

5:7 Amos 2:3; 5:12; 6:12

8 It is the LORD who created the stars,
the Pleiades and Orion.
He turns darkness into morning
and day into night.
He draws up water from the oceans
and pours it down as rain on the land.
The LORD is His name!
9 With blinding speed and power He destroys the strong,
crushing all their defenses.

5:8 Job 9:9; 12:22; 37:13; 38:31-34 Amos 9:6

5:9 Amos 2:14 Mic 5:11

10 How you hate honest judges!
How you despise people who tell the truth!
11 You trample the poor,
stealing their grain through taxes and unfair rent.
Therefore, though you build beautiful stone houses,
you will never live in them.
Though you plant lush vineyards,
you will never drink wine from them.
12 For I know the vast number of your sins
and the depth of your rebellions.
You oppress good people by taking bribes
and deprive the poor of justice in the courts.
13 So those who are smart keep their mouths shut,
for it is an evil time.

5:10 Amos 5:15

5:11 Isa 59:15 Mic 6:15

5:12 Isa 1:23 Amos 2:6

5:6 Hebrew *the house of Joseph.*

▸ WORSHIP

5:4-6 The only God. Are there many paths to God? Is God pleased with sincere religious effort, even if it is misguided? God clearly states that the only hope is to seek Him and live. Seek *Him*, not merely religious activity or external morality. Israel was certainly religious, worshiping in Bethel and Gilgal and even crossing the border into Judah to worship at Beersheba. People still run from place to place like this, seeking a religious experience. But all the sincerity in the world will not help if a person is sincerely wrong. God alone must be worshiped, and He must be worshiped His way (Exodus 20:3-4). God has now revealed Himself to us in His Son (Hebrews 1:1-3). Jesus is *the* way, not one option among many (John 14:6), and God raised Him from the dead to prove it (Acts 2:32). All other paths lead away from God. Seek God in the one way He commands, through Jesus the Savior, and live. (***See Worship****> OT> God's Supremacy> God alone was to be worshiped—no one else,* TopicGuide page A26.)

5:8-9 This is the second of three unique interjections from the prophet (note the similar language in 4:13 and 9:5-6). Each one boldly declares the awesome majesty of God, who created and commands all things. This message appears in the middle of a list of Israel's infractions, almost as if Amos was unable to hold it back.

5:14 Mic 3:11 [14] Do what is good and run from evil
so that you may live!
Then the LORD God of Heaven's Armies will be your helper,
just as you have claimed.
5:15 Ps 97:10 Joel 2:14 Rom 12:9 [15] Hate evil and love what is good;
turn your courts into true halls of justice.
Perhaps even yet the LORD God of Heaven's Armies
will have mercy on the remnant of His people.*

5:16 Amos 8:3, 10 Joel 1:8, 11 [16]Therefore, this is what the Lord, the LORD God of Heaven's Armies, says:

"There will be crying in all the public squares
and mourning in every street.
Call for the farmers to weep with you,
and summon professional mourners to wail.
5:17 Isa 16:10 [17] There will be wailing in every vineyard,
for I will destroy them all,"
says the LORD.

WARNING OF COMING JUDGMENT

5:18 Isa 5:30 Jer 30:7 Joel 1:15; 2:1, 31 [18] What sorrow awaits you who say,
"If only the day of the LORD were here!"
You have no idea what you are wishing for.
That day will bring darkness, not light.
5:19 Job 20:24 [19] In that day you will be like a man who runs from a lion—
only to meet a bear.
Escaping from the bear, he leans his hand against a wall in his house—
and he's bitten by a snake.
5:20 Isa 13:10 [20] Yes, the day of the LORD will be dark and hopeless,
without a ray of joy or hope.

5:21 Lev 26:31 Isa 1:11-16 Jer 14:12 Hos 5:6 [21] "I hate all your show and pretense—
the hypocrisy of your religious festivals and solemn assemblies.
[22] I will not accept your burnt offerings and grain offerings.
I won't even notice all your choice peace offerings.
5:22 Isa 66:3 [23] Away with your noisy hymns of praise!
I will not listen to the music of your harps.
5:24 Jer 22:3 Mic 6:8 [24] Instead, I want to see a mighty flood of justice,
an endless river of righteous living.

[25]"Was it to Me you were bringing sacrifices and offerings during the forty years in the
wilderness, Israel? [26]No, you served your pagan gods—Sakkuth your king god and Kaiwan

5:15 Hebrew *the remnant of Joseph.*

5:15 Amos held out a glimmer of hope that "perhaps" the Lord would show some form of mercy (this was based on God's frequent mercy that reduced the severity of judgment He had announced if the people responded in repentance; see Jeremiah 18:1-10). God relented when Nineveh repented (Jonah 4:1-3; Luke 11:32). However, the next two verses show that Amos did not expect repentance to surface.

▶ WORSHIP

5:23-24 Everyday worship. Is the Sabbath worship in your church perfect? If you made a list of the ways it could be improved, it is unlikely that Amos's criticisms would make it on your list. Just as Isaiah criticized Israel's practice of fasting when they ignored social concern and action (Isaiah 58), Amos condemned Israel's worship when they ignored justice and righteous living. Face it—Sabbath worship can compound the sin of the previous week if we simply go through the motions of church without repenting of our sin. A worshiping heart will demonstrate itself outside the four walls of a church building with compassion for the poor and mercy on the sinful. Congregations that refuse to repent and live righteously in the community will never make a joyful noise to the Lord—just noise. Make sure your everyday life makes your worship more acceptable to God. (***See Worship****> OT> God's Supremacy> Required obedience in daily life and affairs,* TopicGuide page A26.)

your star god—the images you made for yourselves. 27So I will send you into exile, to a
land east of Damascus,*" says the LORD, whose name is the God of Heaven's Armies.

6 1 What sorrow awaits you who lounge in luxury in Jerusalem,*
and you who feel secure in Samaria!
You are famous and popular in Israel,
and people go to you for help.
2 But go over to Calneh
and see what happened there.
Then go to the great city of Hamath
and down to the Philistine city of Gath.
You are no better than they were,
and look at how they were destroyed.
3 You push away every thought of coming disaster,
but your actions only bring the day of judgment closer.
4 How terrible for you who sprawl on ivory beds
and lounge on your couches,
eating the meat of tender lambs from the flock
and of choice calves fattened in the stall.
5 You sing trivial songs to the sound of the harp
and fancy yourselves to be great musicians like David.
6 You drink wine by the bowlful
and perfume yourselves with fragrant lotions.
You care nothing about the ruin of your nation.*
7 Therefore, you will be the first to be led away as captives.
Suddenly, all your parties will end.

8The Sovereign LORD has sworn by His own name, and this is what He, the LORD God of
Heaven's Armies, says:

"I despise the arrogance of Israel,*
and I hate their fortresses.
I will give this city
and everything in it to their enemies."

(9If there are ten men left in one house, they will all die. 10And when a relative who is re-
sponsible to dispose of the dead* goes into the house to carry out the bodies, he will ask
the last survivor, "Is anyone else with you?" When the person begins to swear, "No, by . . . ,"
he will interrupt and say, "Stop! Don't even mention the name of the LORD.")

6:1 Exod 19:5; Isa 32:9-11
6:2 Gen 10:10; 1 Sam 17:23; 2 Kgs 18:34; 2 Chr 26:6; Isa 10:9
6:3 Amos 9:10
6:4 Ezek 34:2-3
6:5 1 Chr 15:16; 23:5; Isa 5:12
6:8 Lev 26:30
6:9 Amos 5:3
6:10 1 Sam 31:12; Amos 5:13; 8:3

5:26-27 Greek version reads *No, you carried your pagan gods—the shrine of Molech, the star of your god Rephan, and the images you made for yourselves. So I will send you into exile, to a land east of Damascus.* Compare Acts 7:43. 6:1 Hebrew *in Zion.* 6:6 Hebrew *of Joseph.* 6:8 Hebrew *Jacob.* See note on 3:13. 6:10 Or *to burn the dead.* The meaning of the Hebrew is uncertain.

6:1 Jerusalem (literally Zion), the mountain capital of Judah, and Samaria (literally Mount Samaria), the mountain capital of Israel, looked down on their neighbors from their raised sites. Their comfortable and seemingly secure life had caused them to become complacent, but big changes were coming.

HOLINESS

6:4-6 Spiritual matters. During the holidays it becomes especially evident that we are obsessed with possessions. Amos's audience was obsessed with material goods, but they were poor in the way God measures wealth. In Luke 12:16-21, Jesus told the story of a rich man who prospered and spent all his energy seeking more money. Unexpectedly, God brought his life to an end, and all that the man had accumulated was of no use to him. Jesus' point: One day your life will come to an end. On that day, assets will not matter. If we are not rich in the things of God (Romans 11:33; 2 Corinthians 6:10; 8:9), we will lose everything that matters—our immortal soul. Are you as concerned as Amos that your friends and family be spared this same fate? Commit to spending more time building up your spiritual life and less time building up your earthly one. (***See Holiness*> *Disciplines*> *Of Abstinence*> *Stewardship,* TopicGuide page A42.)

6:9-10 These verses stand in vivid contrast to the life of ease portrayed in 6:4-6. Luxurious leisure is replaced with trembling in the shadows. There is but one survivor. Ten men in the home have been killed. When someone comes to assist with the disposal of the bodies, the fearful person begs for silence lest God will return. The days of distraction are coming to an end.

11 When the LORD gives the command,
homes both great and small will be smashed to pieces.
12 Can horses gallop over boulders?
Can oxen be used to plow them?
But that's how foolish you are when you turn justice into poison
and the sweet fruit of righteousness into bitterness.
13 And you brag about your conquest of Lo-debar.*
You boast, "Didn't we take Karnaim* by our own strength?"
14 "O people of Israel, I am about to bring an enemy nation against you,"
says the LORD God of Heaven's Armies.
"They will oppress you throughout your land—
from Lebo-hamath in the north
to the Arabah Valley in the south."

6:11 Amos 3:15
6:12 Hos 10:4; Amos 5:7, 11-12
6:14 Num 34:7-8; 2 Kgs 14:25; Jer 5:15

A VISION OF LOCUSTS

7 The Sovereign LORD showed me a vision. I saw Him preparing to send a vast swarm of locusts over the land. This was after the king's share had been harvested from the fields
and as the main crop was coming up. 2In my vision the locusts ate every green plant in sight.
Then I said, "O Sovereign LORD, please forgive us or we will not survive, for Israel* is so small."
3So the LORD relented from this plan. "I will not do it," He said.

A VISION OF FIRE

4Then the Sovereign LORD showed me another vision. I saw Him preparing to punish His people with a great fire. The fire had burned up the depths of the sea and was devouring the entire land. 5Then I said, "O Sovereign LORD, please stop or we will not survive, for Israel is so small."
6Then the LORD relented from this plan, too. "I will not do that either," said the Sovereign LORD.

7:1 Exod 10:12-16; Nah 3:15-17
7:2 Exod 10:15; Isa 37:4; Jer 14:7; 42:2; Ezek 9:8; 11:13
7:3 Deut 32:36; Jer 26:19; Hos 11:8
7:4 Isa 66:15-16; Amos 2:5
7:6 Amos 7:3

A VISION OF A PLUMB LINE

7Then He showed me another vision. I saw the Lord standing beside a wall that had been

6:13a *Lo-debar* means "nothing." 6:13b *Karnaim* means "horns," a term that symbolizes strength. 7:2 Hebrew *Jacob;* also in 7:5. See note on 3:13.

6:14 The people of Israel acted as if God didn't exist, boasting about their strength and their accomplishments. In reply, God promised to utilize His strength to accomplish His desire—their overthrow. And He would use the most humiliating tool possible to eliminate their arrogant national pride—a pagan enemy nation, Assyria.

7:1–9:4 The introduction to Amos states that the book is a record of the visions he received (1:1). This section of the book describes five specific pictures the Lord showed Amos. Each vision relates to the impending overthrow of Israel by Assyria.

7:1-3 In this first vision, God showed Amos a familiar image that every farmer would dread: a devouring plague of locusts (Joel 1:4 uses this same image). God inflicted Egypt with just such a plague (Exodus 10:12-15), and now Israel was being threatened with similar judgment—a promised curse for their disobedience (Deuteronomy 28:18, 38). A society that relied upon the harvest for food would be ravaged by widespread starvation. Amos pleaded for mercy, and God relented.

▸ MINISTRY
7:2 A God who listens. Do you ever wonder if your prayers actually accomplish anything? Centuries before Amos, Abraham dialogued with God on behalf of Sodom and Gomorrah until God agreed to spare the city if only 10 righteous people could be found (Genesis 18:22-32). Moses is also frequently pictured in prayer, begging God for mercy when Israel deserved judgment (Exodus 32:11-14). Here Amos pleaded to God on Israel's behalf, and God relented. James 5:17 encourages us to pray, saying that "Elijah was as human as we are," yet God listened to him and withheld rain because of his prayers. God still listens to His people when they pray—and He acts. Pray to the Father and ask Him to show mercy to people you know. (***See Ministry****> Great Commission> Make Disciples> Disciples pray,* TopicGuide page A56.)

7:4-6 Amos's first vision was of locusts invading the land. In the second vision, God showed him a fire that had already vaporized the sea and was heading toward the land. Amos again pleaded, and God again relented.

7:7-9 The third and fourth visions are pictures that need interpretation to be understood (see Jeremiah 1:11-19 and Revelation 17 for similar visions). A plumb line would be hung straight alongside a wall to make sure it was perfectly straight. God's law judged Israel in the way a plumb line judges a crooked wall, and their errant ways became obvious. The wall had to be destroyed and rebuilt.

built using a plumb line. He was using a plumb line to see if it was still straight. 8And the
LORD said to me, "Amos, what do you see?"
I answered, "A plumb line."
And the Lord replied, "I will test My people with this plumb line. I will no longer ignore
all their sins. 9The pagan shrines of your ancestors* will be ruined, and the temples of Isra-
el will be destroyed; I will bring the dynasty of King Jeroboam to a sudden end."

AMOS AND AMAZIAH

10Then Amaziah, the priest of Bethel, sent a message to Jeroboam, king of Israel: "Amos is
hatching a plot against you right here on your very doorstep! What he is saying is intolera-
ble. 11He is saying, 'Jeroboam will soon be killed, and the people of Israel will be sent
away into exile.'"
12Then Amaziah sent orders to Amos: "Get out of here, you prophet! Go on back to the
land of Judah, and earn your living by prophesying there! 13Don't bother us with your
prophecies here in Bethel. This is the king's sanctuary and the national place of worship!"
14But Amos replied, "I'm not a professional prophet, and I was never trained to be one.*
I'm just a shepherd, and I take care of sycamore-fig trees. 15But the LORD called me away
from my flock and told me, 'Go and prophesy to My people in Israel.' 16Now then, listen to
this message from the LORD:

"You say,
'Don't prophesy against Israel.
Stop preaching against my people.*'
17 But this is what the LORD says:
'Your wife will become a prostitute in this city,
and your sons and daughters will be killed.
Your land will be divided up,
and you yourself will die in a foreign land.
And the people of Israel will certainly become
captives in exile,
far from their homeland.'"

A VISION OF RIPE FRUIT

8 Then the Sovereign LORD showed me another vision. In it I saw a basket filled with
ripe fruit. 2"What do you see, Amos?" He asked.
I replied, "A basket full of ripe fruit."
Then the LORD said, "Like this fruit, Israel is ripe for punishment! I will not delay their
punishment again. 3In that day the singing in the Temple will turn to wailing. Dead bodies
will be scattered everywhere. They will be carried out of the city in silence. I, the Sovereign
LORD, have spoken!"

4 Listen to this, you who rob the poor
and trample down the needy!
5 You can't wait for the Sabbath day to be over
and the religious festivals to end
so you can get back to cheating the helpless.

7:8 Isa 28:17; 34:11 Amos 8:2
7:9 2 Kgs 15:8-10
7:10 1 Kgs 12:31-32 2 Kgs 14:23-24
7:12 1 Sam 9:9
7:13 1 Kgs 12:29, 32; 13:1 Amos 2:12 Acts 4:17-18
7:14 1 Kgs 20:35 2 Kgs 2:3-7; 4:38
7:15 Jer 1:7 Ezek 2:3-4
7:16 Amos 7:13 Mic 2:6
7:17 Jer 14:16; 20:6 Hos 4:13-14
8:2 Jer 24:1-3 Amos 7:8
8:3 Hos 10:5-6 Amos 5:23
8:4 Amos 2:6-7; 5:11
8:5 Neh 13:15-21 Hos 12:7

7:9 Hebrew *of Isaac.* 7:14 Or *I'm not a prophet nor the son of a prophet.* 7:16 Hebrew *against the house of Isaac.*

8:1-3 Like a basket full of ripe fruit, Israel was ripe for punishment.

8:5 Isaiah 58:13 says that God's people should consider the Sabbath a delight, not a burden. Instead of delighting in a day of rest, Israel despised the Sabbath rest. They wanted to hurry back to work so they could get richer by taking advantage of the poor.

You measure out grain with dishonest measures
and cheat the buyer with dishonest scales.*
6 And you mix the grain you sell
with chaff swept from the floor.
Then you enslave poor people
for one piece of silver or a pair of sandals.

8:7 Deut 33:26-29; Pss 10:11; 47:4; 68:34; Hos 7:2; 8:13

7 Now the LORD has sworn this oath
by His own name, the Pride of Israel*:
"I will never forget
the wicked things you have done!

8:8 Pss 18:7; 114:3-7; Jer 46:8; Amos 9:5

8 The earth will tremble for your deeds,
and everyone will mourn.
The ground will rise like the Nile River at floodtime;
it will heave up, then sink again.

8:9 Amos 4:13; 5:8; Mic 3:6; Matt 27:45; Mark 15:33; Luke 23:44-45

9 "In that day," says the Sovereign LORD,
"I will make the sun go down at noon
and darken the earth while it is still day.

8:10 Isa 15:2-3; Ezek 7:18; Amos 5:23; 6:4-7

10 I will turn your celebrations into times of mourning
and your singing into weeping.
You will wear funeral clothes
and shave your heads to show your sorrow—
as if your only son had died.
How very bitter that day will be!

11 "The time is surely coming," says the Sovereign LORD,
"when I will send a famine on the land—
not a famine of bread or water
but of hearing the words of the LORD.

8:12 Ezek 20:3, 31

12 People will stagger from sea to sea
and wander from border to border*
searching for the word of the LORD,
but they will not find it.

8:13 Isa 41:17; Lam 1:18; 2:21; Hos 2:3

13 Beautiful girls and strong young men
will grow faint in that day,
thirsting for the LORD's word.

8:14 1 Kgs 12:28-29

14 And those who swear by the shameful idols of Samaria—
who take oaths in the name of the god of Dan
and make vows in the name of the god of Beersheba*—
they will all fall down,
never to rise again."

8:5 Hebrew *You make the ephah* [a unit for measuring grain] *small and the shekel* [a unit of weight] *great, and you deal falsely by using deceitful balances.* 8:7 Hebrew *the pride of Jacob.* See note on 3:13. 8:12 Hebrew *from north to east.* 8:14 Hebrew *the way of Beersheba.*

▶ SALVATION

8:7 The forgetful God? Does God ever forget? God declared to Amos's audience: "I will never forget the wicked things you have done!" But one of the great promises in the Bible seems to say the opposite: "And I will forgive their wickedness, and I will never again remember their sins" (Jeremiah 31:34). How can one verse say God will not forget, while another says He will forget? Since Jesus took the place of believers on the cross, God does not punish them for those sins. He will not "remember" those sins when the final judgment comes. God does not literally forget them like we forget where we put our keys. He still knows every single sin you have done. Yet, unlike with Amos's audience, God mercifully chooses "not to remember" the sins of His people anymore. Rejoice to know that God does not hold against you the sin you wish you could forget. (***See Salvation***> *Receiving> Results> Works> God remembers them,* TopicGuide page A23.)

A VISION OF GOD AT THE ALTAR

9 Then I saw a vision of the Lord standing beside the altar. He said,

"Strike the tops of the Temple columns,
so that the foundation will shake.
Bring down the roof
on the heads of the people below.
I will kill with the sword those who survive.
No one will escape!

2 "Even if they dig down to the place of the dead,*
I will reach down and pull them up.
Even if they climb up into the heavens,
I will bring them down.
3 Even if they hide at the very top of Mount Carmel,
I will search them out and capture them.
Even if they hide at the bottom of the ocean,
I will send the sea serpent after them to bite them.
4 Even if their enemies drive them into exile,
I will command the sword to kill them there.
I am determined to bring disaster upon them
and not to help them."

5 The Lord, the LORD of Heaven's Armies,
touches the land and it melts,
and all its people mourn.
The ground rises like the Nile River at floodtime,
and then it sinks again.
6 The LORD's home reaches up to the heavens,
while its foundation is on the earth.
He draws up water from the oceans
and pours it down as rain on the land.
The LORD is His name!

7 "Are you Israelites more important to Me
than the Ethiopians?*" asks the LORD.
"I brought Israel out of Egypt,
but I also brought the Philistines from Crete*
and led the Arameans out of Kir.

8 "I, the Sovereign LORD,
am watching this sinful nation of Israel.
I will destroy it
from the face of the earth.
But I will never completely destroy the family of Israel,*"
says the LORD.
9 "For I will give the command
and will shake Israel along with the other nations

9:1 Zeph 2:14
9:2 Ps 139:7-10
9:3 Job 34:22; Ps 139:9-11; Isa 27:1; Jer 16:16
9:4 Lev 26:33; Jer 44:11
9:5 Ps 46:2, 6; Isa 64:1
9:6 Ps 104:3, 6, 13
9:7 2 Chr 14:9, 12; Isa 20:4-5; 43:3
9:8 Jer 5:10; Joel 2:32; Amos 7:17
9:9 Isa 30:28

9:2 Hebrew *to Sheol.* 9:7a Hebrew *the Cushites?* 9:7b Hebrew *Caphtor.* 9:8 Hebrew *the house of Jacob.* See note on 3:13.

9:1-4 The fifth vision expanded on the third and fourth visions, showing that the judgment of Israel would be horrible and widespread. God ordered the Temple columns to be struck, causing massive casualties. Anyone fortunate to escape would only run until they were killed in battle. With this threat, there was no opportunity for Amos to intercede (as in the first and second visions). There was no dialogue (as in the third and fourth visions). Wherever fleeing Israelites would go to evade God, He would find them.

as grain is shaken in a sieve,
yet not one true kernel will be lost.
10 But all the sinners will die by the sword—
all those who say, 'Nothing bad will happen to us.'

A PROMISE OF RESTORATION

9:11 Isa 16:5; 63:11
11 "In that day I will restore the fallen house* of David.
I will repair its damaged walls.
From the ruins I will rebuild it
and restore its former glory.
12 And Israel will possess what is left of Edom
and all the nations I have called to be Mine.*"
The LORD has spoken,
and He will do these things.

9:13 Lev 26:5 Joel 3:18, 20
13 "The time will come," says the LORD,
"when the grain and grapes will grow faster
than they can be harvested.
Then the terraced vineyards on the hills of Israel
will drip with sweet wine!
9:14 Isa 61:4 Jer 30:18; 31:28
14 I will bring My exiled people of Israel
back from distant lands,
and they will rebuild their ruined cities
and live in them again.
They will plant vineyards and gardens;
they will eat their crops and drink their wine.
9:15 Ezek 34:28
15 I will firmly plant them there
in their own land.
They will never again be uprooted
from the land I have given them,"
says the LORD your God.

9:11a Or *kingdom;* Hebrew reads *tent.* 9:11b-12 Greek version reads *and restore its former glory, / so that the rest of humanity, including the Gentiles— / all those I have called to be Mine—might seek Me.* Compare Acts 15:16-17.

9:11 The restoration and salvation of the remnant was linked with the kingdom of David. Amos rejected Israel's line of kings. Israel's only hope for the future lay in the royal line of David, who was from Judah. It was no accident, therefore, that the first words of Matthew's Gospel state, "This is a record of the ancestors of Jesus the Messiah, a descendant of David." The restoration of David's kingdom began when Jesus came proclaiming the kingdom (Matthew 4:23).

▸ CHURCH

9:12 Accepting everyone. In the early church, the leaders met in Jerusalem to discuss whether Gentiles should be fully accepted along with Jews (Acts 15:1-21). James, the leader of the church in Jerusalem, quoting Amos 9:11-12, noted that the prophets predicted a time when Gentiles that have been called by the Lord would be brought into the restored kingdom of David. Paul, a delegate at this meeting, later summarized what Amos foresaw: "Both Gentiles and Jews who believe the Good News share equally in the riches inherited by God's children" (Ephesians 3:6). God intends our churches to reflect the rich diversity of our communities. What sort of people are in your neighborhood? Are they welcome in your church? Do your best to make sure your church is a reflection of the multi-national ideal we see in Scripture (Revelation 7:9). (***See Church****> Who> From Every Place and Age> Local Church,* TopicGuide page A48.)

9:13-14 Amos again used familiar agricultural images to express the hope of future restoration, which would reverse the earlier curses. These offers of blessing were intended to motivate Israel toward repentance and faithfulness after exile. Such restoration promises are ultimately fulfilled in the renewed earth that Christians will enjoy forever (Revelation 21:1; 22:1-2; Romans 8:19-21).

9:15 The Lord will reverse the curse of destruction from the face of the land (9:8). A glorious picture of blessing was laid before those who would be scattered among the nations: God will plant them once again in the land, and they will never be uprooted. Paul widened the promise, showing that all of Abraham's children by faith (Jews and Gentiles) will eternally inherit not just that land but also the whole earth (Romans 4:13).

OBADIAH

PURPOSE

To condemn Edom for its arrogance and pride and to assure Israel of its future restoration.

Feuds occur in the best of families, and Isaac's family was no exception. But while Isaac's two sons, Jacob and Esau, appeared to have settled their feud (see Genesis 27 and 33), Esau's descendants never got the message.

Jacob's twelve sons fathered the twelve tribes from which the entire nation of Israel descended. Esau's descendants became the Edomites, occupying land south of the Dead Sea. The Edomites were often a thorn in Israel's side, taking every opportunity to antagonize them. They lived a haughty and proud existence in their mountain strongholds, feeling free to behave without accountability toward Israel and fearing no retribution. Edom's failure to help the Israelites during their wilderness wanderings (Numbers 20:14-21) apparently had been forgiven. Much later during Obadiah's time, however, an enemy had invaded Jerusalem, and Edom failed to give aid. For this act of complicity God brought Edom to the bar of justice and found the nation guilty (1:10-14).

DISCOVER GOD IN OBADIAH

One primary attribute of God stands out in this brief book:

Vengeance: It may seem less offensive to use the word *punishment* for this characteristic of God, but that is due to a faulty understanding of vengeance. We usually think of vengeance as being retaliation and self-motivated. We see it as a means of payback—an eye for an eye. But we are not able to perfectly judge when and how vengeance should be given out. For that reason, God tells us not to seek vengeance on our own but to leave all vengeance to Him (Romans 12:19), for He is the perfect Judge. He will take vengeance at the proper time on those who deserve it (Deuteronomy 32:35, 41, 43). Edom's time was up, as Obadiah clearly prophesied (1:10). The Edomites began to deteriorate as a nation in the latter part of the Old Testament period and vanished from historical records by the time the Romans destroyed Jerusalem in AD 70. Vengeance on God's part is not self-serving, but justice serving. Because He is a God of righteousness, justice will be served in His vengeance.

GROWING THROUGH OBADIAH

The single-chapter book of Obadiah brims with themes for the follower of Jesus:

Brotherly Love: The world says that "blood is thicker than water," meaning family ties are stronger than other ties. But in Jacob and Esau's case, that wasn't true—the Edomites did not come to the aid of their relatives the Israelites in their hour of need. The truth is "a real friend sticks closer than a brother" (Proverbs 18:24). True Old Testament brotherhood was based on covenant commitment (1 Samuel 18:1-4)—a oneness the New Testament calls *koinonia* (fellowship; commonness). Esau's descendants didn't have a covenant commitment to Jacob's descendants, and it cost them dearly in the end. This principle of covenant commitment is the reason Jesus said that the members of His family are those who do the will of God (Luke 8:21). To give a biblical twist to the age-old saying, "the Spirit is thicker than blood."

DISCOVERY VERSES

You should not have gloated when they exiled your relatives to distant lands. You should not have rejoiced when the people of Judah suffered such misfortune. You should not have spoken arrogantly in that terrible time of trouble.

(OBADIAH 1:12)

Those who have been rescued will go up to Mount Zion in Jerusalem to rule over the mountains of Edom. And the LORD Himself will be king!"

(OBADIAH 1:21)

Weep with Those Who Weep: When the Edomites saw Judah being attacked by its enemies, they gloated and even looted their cousins' ransacked houses in Jerusalem (1:13). The apostle Paul, however, said that love "does not rejoice about injustice," regardless of where it occurs (1 Corinthians 13:6). He also said that we reveal true compassion and love when we weep with those who weep (Romans 12:15). Even if the Edomites couldn't take up the sword to defend their relatives, their eyes should have been filled with tears of shared sorrow.

Retaliate with Love: Unjust treatment often leads to the temptation for retaliation and vengeance. But the Christian is to leave all vengeance in the hands of He who judges justly (Romans 12:19). Paul quoted Proverbs 20:25 when he said, "Instead, 'If your enemies are hungry, feed them. If they are thirsty, give them something to drink. In doing this, you will heap burning coals of shame on their heads.' Don't let evil conquer you, but conquer evil by doing good" (Romans 12:20-21). Jacob had treated Edom's ancestor, Esau, unjustly. If Edom had spent the ensuing years repaying Israel with love and kindness, however, it might still be around today.

OBADIAH FACTS

Author: Obadiah (1:1). While a number of Obadiahs are mentioned in the Old Testament, none can be identified as this author with certainty. Nothing is known of Obadiah's background or call to the prophetic ministry.

Written to: Israel and the nation of Edom, who were the descendants of Jacob's twin brother, Esau (Genesis 25:19-34).

Date of writing: The date cannot be set with certainty, but many scholars accept the middle of the ninth century BC.

Setting: Edom and Jerusalem.

OUTLINE

- **OBADIAH 1:1-16**—Judgment on Edom
- **OBADIAH 1:17-21**—Restoration of Israel

This is the vision that the Sovereign LORD revealed to Obadiah concerning the land of Edom.

EDOM'S JUDGMENT ANNOUNCED

1:1 Isa 34:5-15; 63:1-6 Jer 49:7-22 Ps 137:7 Ezek 25:12-14 Joel 3:19 Amos 1:11-12

We have heard a message from the LORD
that an ambassador was sent to the nations to say,
"Get ready, everyone!
Let's assemble our armies and attack Edom!"

1:2 Num 24:15-19

2 The LORD says to Edom,
"I will cut you down to size among the nations;
you will be greatly despised.

1:3 Isa 16:6 Jer 49:15-16 Rev 18:7

3 You have been deceived by your own pride
because you live in a rock fortress
and make your home high in the mountains.
'Who can ever reach us way up here?'
you ask boastfully.

1:4 Job 39:26-30 Isa 14:12-15

4 But even if you soar as high as eagles
and build your nest among the stars,
I will bring you crashing down,"
says the LORD.

5 "If thieves came at night and robbed you
(what a disaster awaits you!),
they would not take everything.
Those who harvest grapes
always leave a few for the poor.
But your enemies will wipe you out completely!

1:5-6 Jer 49:9-10

6 Every nook and cranny of Edom*
will be searched and looted.
Every treasure will be found and taken.

1:7 Isa 19:11-14 Jer 30:14

7 "All your allies will turn against you.
They will help to chase you from your land.
They will promise you peace
while plotting to deceive and destroy you.
Your trusted friends will set traps for you,
and you won't even know about it.

1:8 Job 5:12-14 Isa 19:3, 13-14; 29:14

8 At that time not a single wise person
will be left in the whole land of Edom,"
says the LORD.
"For on the mountains of Edom
I will destroy everyone who has understanding.

6 Hebrew *Esau;* also in 8b, 9, 18, 19, 21.

1:1 The Hebrew word translated "vision" is not limited to a visual image. It could have been an auditory message, a dream, or any variety of means through which God gave Obadiah His word. Obadiah confirmed that what looked to the Edomites like a human plot against them was actually a plan orchestrated by God (1:2).

1:2-21 The rest of Obadiah is a speech of judgment (1:2-16) and hope (1:17-21).

1:3 An almost impregnable fortress city named Sela (or "rock") towered over the mountainous terrain of Edom. The topography of the area and of Sela in particular contributed to the illusion of safety the Edomites enjoyed. The Greeks would later name the city Petra. Both names mean "rock."

[9] The mightiest warriors of Teman
will be terrified,
and everyone on the mountains of Edom
will be cut down in the slaughter.

1:9
Jer 49:20-22
Amos 1:12

REASONS FOR EDOM'S PUNISHMENT

[10] "Because of the violence you did
to your close relatives in Israel,*
you will be filled with shame
and destroyed forever.
[11] When they were invaded,
you stood aloof, refusing to help them.
Foreign invaders carried off their wealth
and cast lots to divide up Jerusalem,
but you acted like one of Israel's enemies.

1:10
Ezek 25:12-14

1:11
Ps 137:7
Joel 3:3
Nah 3:10

[12] "You should not have gloated
when they exiled your relatives to distant lands.
You should not have rejoiced
when the people of Judah suffered such misfortune.
You should not have spoken arrogantly
in that terrible time of trouble.
[13] You should not have plundered the land of Israel
when they were suffering such calamity.
You should not have gloated over their destruction
when they were suffering such calamity.
You should not have seized their wealth
when they were suffering such calamity.
[14] You should not have stood at the crossroads,
killing those who tried to escape.
You should not have captured the survivors
and handed them over in their terrible time of trouble.

1:12
Ezek 35:15
Mic 4:11

1:13
Ezek 35:5

EDOM DESTROYED, ISRAEL RESTORED

[15] "The day is near when I, the LORD,
will judge all godless nations!
As you have done to Israel,
so it will be done to you.
All your evil deeds
will fall back on your own heads.
[16] Just as you swallowed up My people
on My holy mountain,

1:15
Jer 50:29
Ezek 30:3
Joel 1:15
Hab 2:8

1:16
Jer 25:15; 49:12

10 Hebrew *your brother Jacob.* The names "Jacob" and "Israel" are often interchanged throughout the Old Testament, referring sometimes to the individual patriarch and sometimes to the nation.

1:10-11 The reasons for Edom's punishment were their brutality and lack of sympathy for their Israelite cousins.

▶ WORSHIP

1:14 Kindness to enemies. Have you ever wished your enemies would go away—forever? Perhaps you've daydreamed about the exact nature of their defeat, about the arguments you would win against them, or about their humiliation—or perhaps even about their death. Judah had every reason to feel this way about Edom. This distant cousin took advantage of Judah in their hour of need, and instead of helping Judah, Edom looted homes and killed refugees or turned them over to Judah's foes. You may have rationalized all sorts of "justice" you want to do to someone who has hurt you or someone you love. But Christ has another way. Jesus forgave those who killed Him (Luke 23:34). And He died for His enemies (Romans 5:10). Revisit your plans for your enemies and carefully consider whether your plans are part of God's will—or yours. (***See Worship****> NT> Prayer> Instructions> Pray for enemies,* TopicGuide page A33.)

so you and the surrounding nations
will swallow the punishment I pour out on you.
Yes, all you nations will drink and stagger
and disappear from history.

1:17 Isa 14:1-3 Amos 9:11-15

17 "But Jerusalem* will become a refuge for those who escape;
it will be a holy place.
And the people of Israel* will come back
to reclaim their inheritance.

1:18 Zech 12:6

18 The people of Israel will be a raging fire,
and Edom a field of dry stubble.
The descendants of Joseph will be a flame
roaring across the field, devouring everything.
There will be no survivors in Edom.
I, the LORD, have spoken!

1:19 Jer 31:5; 32:44

19 "Then My people living in the Negev
will occupy the mountains of Edom.
Those living in the foothills of Judah*
will possess the Philistine plains
and take over the fields of Ephraim and Samaria.
And the people of Benjamin
will occupy the land of Gilead.

1:20 1 Kgs 17:9

20 The exiles of Israel will return to their land
and occupy the Phoenician coast as far north as Zarephath.
The captives from Jerusalem exiled in the north*
will return home and resettle the towns of the Negev.

1:21 Ps 22:28 Zech 14:9 Rev 11:15; 19:6

21 Those who have been rescued* will go up to* Mount Zion in Jerusalem
to rule over the mountains of Edom.
And the LORD Himself will be king!"

17a Hebrew *Mount Zion.* **17b** Hebrew *house of Jacob;* also in 18. See note on 10. **19** Hebrew *the Shephelah.* **20** Hebrew *in Sepharad.* **21a** As in Greek and Syriac versions; Hebrew reads *Rescuers.* **21b** Or *from.*

1:17-18 In contrast to Edom's doom, Israel's future is victory. This victory was partially fulfilled in Christ's first advent and will be fully completed upon His triumphal return (1:21; 1 Timothy 6:15; Revelation 12:10).

JONAH

PURPOSE

To tell the people of Israel that the Lord desires to save people from among the Gentiles.

The book of Jonah is unique among the Minor Prophets in that it uses a story rather than an oracle to communicate God's message—the message that the future holds great hope for the Gentiles.

The story itself is simple—God told Jonah to warn the immense, evil city of Nineveh that He would soon destroy them. Jonah refused and ran away, but God convinced him to go nonetheless. Surprisingly, Nineveh repented, but rebellious Jonah hadn't learned his lesson, so he sat outside the city, still not grasping why God would enable Gentiles to repent and thereby avoid destruction.

But the events in the story and the questions it raises are as shocking and sensational as being swallowed alive by a giant fish: Why did Jonah run? Why did God tell a fish to swallow Jonah? Did God change His mind about destroying Nineveh, or was it His plan all along to save them? These questions, like the story itself, run through the mind of young and old readers long after the story is over.

DISCOVER GOD IN JONAH

Jonah, though comprising only forty-eight verses, contains significant theological content. It reveals critical aspects of God's character.

Sovereign Creator: Jonah's misunderstanding of God's goal of worldwide worship is first addressed in chapter 1, in which God reminded Jonah that He is sovereign over the heavens and earth and all the forces and animals that inhabit it. God designated nature to achieve His ends with the prophet first with a storm and a great fish. In a finale of natural forces, God created a vine and leaf, then a worm to devour them. A scorching wind followed, causing Jonah and the reader to deal more honestly with their objections to God extending His grace to the so-called "unworthy."

Merciful: Romans 9 tells us that God shows mercy to whomever He decides. Too often we automatically exclude some people even from the possibility of God's redeeming love. But the book of Jonah teaches that God extends His mercy far beyond what Israel would have thought possible. The people of Nineveh were famous for their wickedness and ruthlessness toward those they conquered. But God's mercy changed hearts and brought widespread repentance and belief even among those who were foreigners and enemies of the covenant God of Israel.

GROWING THROUGH JONAH

Two important themes in Jonah apply to believers of all ages:

Obedience and Ideas: The book of Jonah shows the connection between the prophet's bad ideas and his poor choices. When called to go to Nineveh, he went—in the other direction. After God providentially guided (practically forced!) Jonah to obey, the prophet chose to be angry when God displayed mercy to sinners. His disobedient actions flowed from his hatred of Gentiles (Jonah 4:2). His sinful anger came directly from his belief that God's love was misplaced on anyone but the Jews.

Repentance: Jonah reminds us that God calls all people everywhere to repent and believe in His promises. Repentance, as is so clearly shown in this book, is the act of humbling ourselves before God, turning from our wicked ways, and trusting in the kindness and forgiveness of the King of the Universe. Too often Christians live as if repentance is a one-time act at the moment of salvation. But the Scriptures call believers to repent whenever they rebel against God. While the work of Christ is sure and permanent for those who trust in Him, the Christian life is one of continual repentance and trusting in God's mercy. Jonah believed God, but needed to repent of his rebellion (in chapters 1 and 2) and of his anger (in chapter 4).

DISCOVERY VERSES

I will offer sacrifices to You with songs of praise, and I will fulfill all my vows. For my salvation comes from the LORD alone. (JONAH 2:9)

When God saw what they had done and how they had put a stop to their evil ways, He changed His mind and did not carry out the destruction He had threatened. (JONAH 3:10)

I knew that You are a merciful and compassionate God, slow to get angry and filled with unfailing love. (JONAH 4:2)

JONAH FACTS

Author: Unknown. The book of 2 Kings speaks of Jonah as a prophet to the northern kingdom (2 Kings 14:25-28), and the best assumption is that this same Jonah is portrayed here.

Written to: Israel (under King Jeroboam II).

Date of writing: Though the book of Jonah is difficult to date precisely, if the book recounts the actions of the same Jonah that is mentioned in 2 Kings 14:25-28, then the book would have been written after that time (eighth century BC) but before the sacking of Nineveh in 612 BC by the Medes.

Setting: Beginning in Israel, the setting moves to the Mediterranean Sea, and then to present-day Iraq, the location of Nineveh in the Assyrian Empire.

OUTLINE

- **JONAH 1:1-16**—Jonah Runs from the Lord
- **JONAH 1:17–2:10**—Jonah and the Great Fish
- **JONAH 3:1-10**—Jonah Goes to Nineveh
- **JONAH 4:1-11**—Jonah's Anger at the Lord's Mercy

1:1
2 Kgs 14:25
Matt 12:39-41; 16:4
Luke 11:29-30, 32
1:2
2 Kgs 19:36
Ezra 9:6
Isa 58:1
Jer 1:7-10
Hos 7:2
Jon 3:3
1:3
Gen 3:8; 4:16
2 Chr 2:16; 9:21
Ps 139:7
Isa 23:6
Acts 9:36
1:5
1 Kgs 18:26
Acts 27:18-19, 38
1:6
Ps 107:28-29
Jon 3:8-9
1:7
Josh 7:14, 18-19
1 Sam 14:41-42
1:8
Gen 47:3
1:9
Gen 1:9
Ezra 1:2; 5:11
Neh 1:4; 9:6
1:12
John 11:50
1:15
Ps 89:9
Mark 4:41

JONAH RUNS FROM THE LORD

1 The LORD gave this message to Jonah son of Amittai: 2"Get up and go to the great city
of Nineveh. Announce My judgment against it because I have seen how wicked its
people are."
3But Jonah got up and went in the opposite direction to get away from the LORD. He
went down to the port of Joppa, where he found a ship leaving for Tarshish. He bought a
ticket and went on board, hoping to escape from the LORD by sailing to Tarshish.
4But the LORD hurled a powerful wind over the sea, causing a violent storm that threat-
ened to break the ship apart. 5Fearing for their lives, the desperate sailors shouted to their
gods for help and threw the cargo overboard to lighten the ship.
But all this time Jonah was sound asleep down in the hold. 6So the captain went down
after him. "How can you sleep at a time like this?" he shouted. "Get up and pray to your
god! Maybe He will pay attention to us and spare our lives."
7Then the crew cast lots to see which of them had offended the gods and caused the ter-
rible storm. When they did this, the lots identified Jonah as the culprit. 8"Why has this aw-
ful storm come down on us?" they demanded. "Who are you? What is your line of work?
What country are you from? What is your nationality?"
9Jonah answered, "I am a Hebrew, and I worship the LORD, the God of heaven, who
made the sea and the land."
10The sailors were terrified when they heard this, for he had already told them he was run-
ning away from the LORD. "Oh, why did you do it?" they groaned. 11And since the storm was
getting worse all the time, they asked him, "What should we do to you to stop this storm?"
12"Throw me into the sea," Jonah said, "and it will become calm again. I know that this
terrible storm is all my fault."
13Instead, the sailors rowed even harder to get the ship to the land. But the stormy sea was
too violent for them, and they couldn't make it. 14Then they cried out to the LORD, Jonah's
God. "O LORD," they pleaded, "don't make us die for this man's sin. And don't hold us responsi-
ble for his death. O LORD, You have sent this storm upon him for Your own good reasons."
15Then the sailors picked Jonah up and threw him into the raging sea, and the storm

---

1:2 Nineveh was an ancient city even in Jonah's day, mentioned first in Genesis 10:11-12. It was a royal residence for emperors of the Assyrian Empire. Its ruins are located today along the Tigris River in Iraq near the city of Mosul. Assyria brutally conquered much of the ancient Near East and finally toppled the northern kingdom of Israel in 722 BC, at least one generation prior to the ministry of Jonah (2 Kings 14:25).

1:3 Tarshish has traditionally been associated with a land far west of the Middle East. Scholars often plot the city on the southern coast of Spain because ancient Greek literature mentions the city of Tartessos on the Spanish coast. It is also mentioned in 1 Kings 22:48 (see textual note) and in Ezekiel 27:12.

▸ SPIRITUAL WARFARE

1:3 Running away. Have you ever gone in the opposite direction from what you knew for certain God intended for you? Jonah did just that. The Hebrew text says that he went "down" to Joppa, "down" into the hold of the ship, and eventually was tossed "down" into the sea (2:3). Jonah's downward movement is a literary picture of spiritual descent that results from disobedience and rebellion. Rebellion against God is never a virtue (Jude 1:15), no matter how we attempt to excuse it. Determine to move up toward God, not down away from Him. (***See Spiritual Warfare**> Resisting Sin and Evil> Resisting Temptation> What to Resist> We are to resist sinful urges,* TopicGuide page A45.)

1:7 Casting lots was a common way of discerning direction in the ancient world when common wisdom did not yield a solution to a problem. Even ancient Israel used lots in certain circumstances (for instance, in determining the scapegoat in Leviticus 16:8-10 and during the distribution of tribal lands in Numbers 26:55 and Joshua 14:2). But Proverbs 16:33 reminds those who trust God that He is sovereign even over such "chance" instruments as lots.

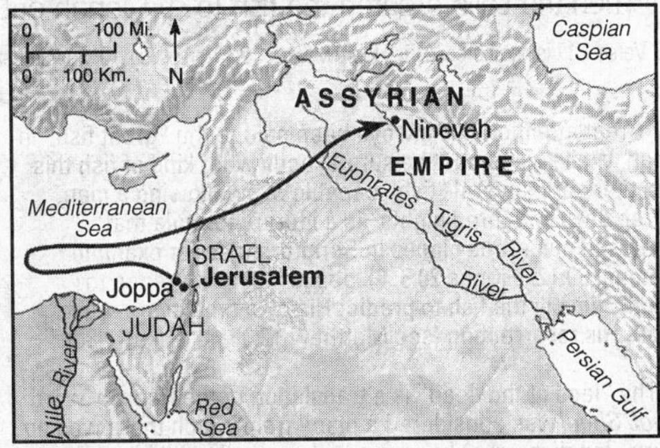

JONAH'S ROUNDABOUT JOURNEY
God told Jonah to go to Nineveh, the capital of the Assyrian Empire. Many of Jonah's countrymen had experienced the atrocities of these fierce people. The last place Jonah wanted to go was on a missionary trip to Nineveh! So he went in the opposite direction. He boarded a ship in Joppa that was headed for Tarshish. But Jonah could not run from God.

stopped at once! [16]The sailors were awestruck by the LORD's great power, and they offered
Him a sacrifice and vowed to serve Him.
[17]*Now the LORD had arranged for a great fish to swallow Jonah. And Jonah was inside
the fish for three days and three nights.

JONAH'S PRAYER

2 [1]*Then Jonah prayed to the LORD his God from inside the fish. [2]He said,

"I cried out to the LORD in my great trouble,
  and He answered me.
I called to You from the land of the dead,*
  and LORD, You heard me!
[3] You threw me into the ocean depths,
  and I sank down to the heart of the sea.
The mighty waters engulfed me;
  I was buried beneath Your wild and stormy waves.
[4] Then I said, 'O LORD, You have driven me from Your presence.
  Yet I will look once more toward Your holy Temple.'
[5] "I sank beneath the waves,
  and the waters closed over me.
  Seaweed wrapped itself around my head.
[6] I sank down to the very roots of the mountains.
  I was imprisoned in the earth,
  whose gates lock shut forever.
But You, O LORD my God,
  snatched me from the jaws of death!
[7] As my life was slipping away,
  I remembered the LORD.
And my earnest prayer went out to You
  in Your holy Temple.
[8] Those who worship false gods
  turn their backs on all God's mercies.
[9] But I will offer sacrifices to You with songs of praise,
  and I will fulfill all my vows.
  For my salvation comes from the LORD alone."

[10]Then the LORD ordered the fish to spit Jonah out onto the beach.

1:16 Ps 66:13-14
1:17 Matt 12:40; 16:4
2:1 Ps 130:1
2:2 Pss 18:4-6; 22:24
2:3 Ps 42:7
2:4 1 Kgs 8:38; Pss 5:7; 31:22
2:5 Ps 69:1; Lam 3:54
2:6 Pss 16:10; 30:3; Isa 38:17; 40:12
2:7 2 Chr 30:27; Pss 18:6; 77:10-11; 142:3
2:9 Pss 3:8; 50:14; 68:20; Hos 14:2

1:17 Verse 1:17 is numbered 2:1 in Hebrew text. **2:1** Verses 2:1-10 are numbered 2:2-11 in Hebrew text. **2:2** Hebrew *from Sheol.*

1:17 Great attention has always been paid to the "great fish" in Jonah. While we cannot be sure exactly what kind of fish this was, there are several "fish" capable of swallowing a man. "Three days and three nights" is a literary formula that appears in numerous places in Scripture (see for example 1 Samuel 30:12; 2 Kings 20:5, 8). Jesus made reference to Jonah's time in the fish to predict His own time in the grave before His resurrection (see Matthew 12:39-40; Luke 11:30).

2:2 The "land of the dead" is a translation of the Hebrew word *Sheol. Sheol* was considered a place from which there was no return. Jonah may not have seen what swallowed him, but regardless, he had no realistic expectation of return to the realm of life.

2:3, 6 Again the downward motif is important to see in these verses. The metaphor here says that Jonah had descended as far as possible.

▸ PURPOSE

2:6 A reversal of fortune. In the Hebrew text, Jonah's prayer (2:2-9) is in a poetic form much like a psalm. The first half acknowledges the prophet's precarious state, going from bad to worse to worst. Then, in the middle of verse 6, there is a divine reversal. "But You, O LORD my God," begins the rebirth of faith, trust, and obedience. These verses are like a sketch of our lives. It may seem at times as though we are descending down a path from which there is no hope of rescue, but with God all things are possible. He can redeem any situation if we turn to Him in repentance and submission. Call out to God for His divine reversal in your darkest hour. (***See Purpose*** > *God's Deeds*> *Judgment*> *Deliverance from judgment,* TopicGuide page A54.)

▸ SALVATION

2:9 Salvation from God alone. This confession of Jonah summarizes vast portions of both Old Testament and New Testament belief. Moses and the prophets reminded Israel to not trust in idols, foreign gods, or the strength of mere humans. Jesus told His followers that our human effort accom-

JONAH GOES TO NINEVEH

3:2 **3** Then the LORD spoke to Jonah a second time: 2“Get up and go to the great city of Nin-
Jer 1:17 eveh, and deliver the message I have given you.”
Ezek 2:7 3This time Jonah obeyed the LORD’s command and went to Nineveh, a city so large that
3:3 it took three days to see it all.* 4On the day Jonah entered the city, he shouted to the
Jon 1:2; 4:11 crowds: “Forty days from now Nineveh will be destroyed!” 5The people of Nineveh be-
3:4 Matt 12:41 lieved God’s message, and from the greatest to the least, they declared a fast and put on
Luke 11:32 burlap to show their sorrow.
6When the king of Nineveh heard what Jonah was saying, he stepped down from his
throne and took off his royal robes. He dressed himself in burlap and sat on a heap of
3:7 ashes. 7Then the king and his nobles sent this decree throughout the city:

2 Chr 20:3 “No one, not even the animals from your herds and flocks, may eat or drink anything
3:8 Ps 130:1-2 at all. 8People and animals alike must wear garments of mourning, and everyone
Jon 1:6, 14 must pray earnestly to God. They must turn from their evil ways and stop all their
3:9 Joel 2:14 violence. 9Who can tell? Perhaps even yet God will change His mind and hold back
His fierce anger from destroying us.”

3:10 Jer 18:8 10When God saw what they had done and how they had put a stop to their evil ways, He
Amos 7:3, 6 changed His mind and did not carry out the destruction He had threatened.

JONAH’S ANGER AT THE LORD’S MERCY

4:2 **4** This change of plans greatly upset Jonah, and he became very angry. 2So he com-
Exod 34:6 Ps 86:5 plained to the LORD about it: “Didn’t I say before I left home that You would do this,
Joel 2:13 LORD? That is why I ran away to Tarshish! I knew that You are a merciful and compassion-
ate God, slow to get angry and filled with unfailing love. You are eager to turn back from
4:3 1 Kgs 19:4 destroying people. 3Just kill me now, LORD! I’d rather be dead than alive if what I predicted
Job 6:8-9 will not happen.”
4The LORD replied, “Is it right for you to be angry about this?”
5Then Jonah went out to the east side of the city and made a shelter to sit under as he
waited to see what would happen to the city. 6And the LORD God arranged for a leafy plant

3:3 Hebrew *a great city to God, of three days’ journey.*

plishes nothing (John 6:63). And Paul declared that grace alone makes dead souls alive (Ephesians 2:1, 5). Are you trusting in your own efforts to be good enough to earn salvation? Repent of such effort. Trust in Christ’s goodness rather than your own. Rest in His grace rather than in any self-perceived righteousness of your own. (***See Salvation****> Our Need> Sinful> Dead in sin (first and second deaths),* TopicGuide page A22.)

3:3 Nineveh was a large city, especially for its day. The ruins are located in two massive mounds on either side of the Khosr River. The city’s ruins stretch almost two kilometers along the river and about 600 meters back from the river. It extends over 1,850 acres in size, compared to the 13 acres of Jerusalem in the time of David.

3:6 The king of Nineveh took four actions that testified to his outward repentance: He stepped down from the throne, took off his royal robe (both actions symbolically relinquished his power and authority), put on burlap, and sat in ashes (both actions identified him with the lowly and the contrite).

▸ WORSHIP
3:8-9 Change your ways. A wise leader doesn’t simply guide the behaviors of his subjects, but he also pays attention to their hearts and attitudes. Even this pagan king understood this—he acknowledged that such outward acts of social goodness were no guarantee that God would bless people. People look at the outward appearance, but God looks at the heart. We can do good things for the wrong reasons and God knows. Examine your heart today and ask if your outward actions are a true reflection of your heart. Encourage those under your care to love God outwardly and inwardly. (***See Worship****> OT> Reverence> Awe of God means obeying His commandments,* TopicGuide page A28.)

4:2 Jonah’s words reveal his motivations—Jonah had no desire for God’s mercy to extend to the Assyrian people. He believed the Assyrians were too wicked to deserve God’s grace, but he also likely desired to preserve Israel’s exclusive hold on God’s mercy and blessing.

▸ HOLINESS
4:4 Resisting God. When we are angry, we have great difficulty listening, especially to critiques of our own behavior. Jonah would not listen to God’s question of rebuke and correction. Instead, he continued to justify his attitude. When you sense God is asking you such corrective questions through the Scriptures and His Holy Spirit, do not persist in self-righteousness. Instead, repent of your hard heart, trust God’s good intentions for you, and turn from your sin. (***See Holiness****> Submission> Yielding to Spirit> Do not attempt to stop the Spirit’s work,* TopicGuide page A40.)

4:6-8 In these verses, the quiet, providential hand of God moved to teach Jonah that He is concerned for all people. Jonah’s lack of concern for Nineveh looked petty compared to his concern for the plant and his own comfort.

to grow there, and soon it spread its broad leaves over Jonah's head, shading him from
the sun. This eased his discomfort, and Jonah was very grateful for the plant.
7But God also arranged for a worm! The next morning at dawn the worm ate through
the stem of the plant so that it withered away. 8And as the sun grew hot, God arranged for
a scorching east wind to blow on Jonah. The sun beat down on his head until he grew faint
and wished to die. "Death is certainly better than living like this!" he exclaimed.
9Then God said to Jonah, "Is it right for you to be angry because the plant died?"
"Yes," Jonah retorted, "even angry enough to die!"
10Then the LORD said, "You feel sorry about the plant, though you did nothing to put it
there. It came quickly and died quickly. 11But Nineveh has more than 120,000 people liv-
ing in spiritual darkness,* not to mention all the animals. Shouldn't I feel sorry for such a
great city?"

4:7 Joel 1:12
4:8 Isa 49:10; Ezek 19:12; Hos 13:15
4:11 Jon 1:2; 3:2; 3:10

4:11 Hebrew *people who don't know their right hand from their left.*

▸ HOLINESS
4:10-11 Misguided pity. Jonah had his priorities mixed up on a colossal scale. He pitied a plant, and yet he felt no compassion toward the multitudes of lost men, women, and children of Nineveh. Do you have your priorities in such an order that they glorify God? Ask God to help you examine your priorities. Consider whether you are concerned too much about insignificant things and not enough about eternal things. (***See Holiness***> *Changed by God*> *God provides*> *Directing us,* TopicGuide page A41.)

MY RESPONSE TO GOD

Reaching out to Everyone

JONAH 4:2

Almost everyone knows the story of Jonah—how a big fish swallowed the prophet and after three days spit him out onto dry land. Many also know that this happened because Jonah was running away from God.

But fewer know why Jonah fled God's call to go to Nineveh, one of the most important cities in Assyria, and tell people there to repent (Jonah 1:2). He didn't run away because he felt inadequate to be a missionary or because he was afraid of leaving his home. Jonah resisted God's call because he was a racist—he wanted all of the Assyrians to die and suffer eternal punishment with no opportunity to hear the good news of a sovereign, merciful God (Jonah 4:2). His prejudice sent him on a foolish game of hide-and-seek from the Almighty God—and you can guess who won.

It is true that the Assyrian Empire was an aggressive and oppressive political regime. It is true that their people had different cultural and moral standards. Their generals were guilty of some of the most heinous war atrocities that can be imagined. But with all that being true, God still had a plan to offer them the opportunity to repent—no society is too degraded to be redeemed by God. No sinner is too bad to be made good by God's grace.

Racism is unbiblical for two reasons. First, we all come from the same parents—Adam and Eve—who were made in God's image (Genesis 1:25-26). As God's image-bearers, all people are worthy of our respect. Second, racism is forbidden because in Christ, God has destroyed the barriers that divide races (Ephesians 2:14). We must share the gospel with people from every tribe and nation because God's goal is to create a body of worshipers from all over the world (Revelation 7:9-10). Racism has no place in the hearts of those who love the gospel and believe in God's worldwide vision for His church.

MICAH

PURPOSE

To expose the sins of Judah and Israel, announce God's judgment, and promise hope to those who repented.

From the traditional Christmas story, most people know that Jesus Christ was born in Bethlehem. But did you know that this birthplace was identified hundreds of years before the event by the prophet Micah?

Micah's prophetic words follow the familiar pattern of all the prophets: condemnation and consolation. In his prophecies about God's future consolation for the nation—following a judgment to cleanse the people of their sins—Micah foretold the coming of One who would "stand to lead His flock with the LORD's strength, in the majesty of the name of the LORD His God. Then His people will live there undisturbed, for He will be highly honored around the world. And He will be the source of peace" (5:4-5). That One, of course, is Jesus Christ, the centerpiece of Micah's prophecy. The glory of this coming One, however, was balanced by the ills He came to set right, as Micah spared nothing and no one in describing the reasons for God's judgment against Judah and Israel.

DISCOVER GOD IN MICAH

Certain attributes of God are clearly seen in Micah's prophecies of condemnation and consolation:

Prophecy: Micah's ministry included both *forthtelling* (speaking about the present) and *foretelling* (speaking about the future). Micah's pinpointing of the birthplace of Christ (Micah 5:2; Matthew 2:6) was one of the most startling of Old Testament prophecies. Micah said His origins would be "from the distant past," which could only be a reference to the divine origins of the Messiah, whom other prophets had also foretold. When Christ did appear, His eternal past was confirmed on more than a few occasions (John 1:2; 8:58; 17:5, 24). Christ manifested prophecy as a characteristic of God in His own trifold ministry of Prophet, Priest, and King. And this attribute was self-evident in the Old Testament as God spoke through His human messengers about things that consistently came to pass. We can have security in knowing that God knows every detail of the future.

Pardon: Perhaps the most profound attribute of God—one that sets Him apart from the gods of every other religion—is His response to human sin: He pardons it. Pardoning sin is not the same as excusing sin or ignoring it. Pardon means that the guilty go free on the basis of a debt having been paid in the eyes of an authority. Micah prophesied that the day would come when God would restore a repentant remnant of Israel to covenant blessing after having pardoned the people's sin: "Once again You will have compassion on us. You will trample our sins under Your feet and throw them into the depths of the ocean!" (7:19). But the pardon for their sins required a payment—and Jesus paid it all. God could look into the future, accept that Jesus would die for those sins (Revelation 13:8), and then pardon His people in light of that sure sacrifice.

Peace: A statue in the north garden of the United Nations headquarters in New York City shows a man beating a sword into a plow—a symbol of turning from war to peace. Commendably, this image is adapted from Micah 4:3: "The Lord ... will settle disputes between strong nations far away. They will hammer their swords into plowshares and their spears into pruning hooks. Nation will no longer fight against nation, nor train for war anymore." However, no sinful human being can bring true peace. Only when the God of peace reigns over all the earth will there be true peace. Micah was prophesying that a day of universal peace would come when God would rule over all human affairs. Because God *is* peace, peace will come when His presence rules over all.

DISCOVERY VERSES

But you, O Bethlehem Ephrathah, are only a small village among all the people of Judah. Yet a ruler of Israel will come from you, One whose origins are from the distant past.

(MICAH 5:2)

No, O people, the LORD has told you what is good, and this is what He requires of you: to do what is right, to love mercy, and to walk humbly with your God.

(MICAH 6:8)

GROWING THROUGH MICAH

From a godly Old Testament prophet come spiritual themes for the follower of Christ:

Confronting Sin: Few people like confrontation, but for an Old Testament prophet like Micah, it was part of the job description. Micah's self-evaluation contains the key to carrying out his calling: the leading of the Spirit. He said, "I am filled with power—with the Spirit of the Lord. I am filled with justice and strength to boldly declare Israel's sin and rebellion" (3:8). Mere confrontation does not accomplish the purposes of God; it must arise from the leading of God's Spirit. Let the Spirit guide you as to the proper time and method for challenging sin.

Practicing the Future: The prophet anticipated that the Messiah would turn the values of this world upside down. The lame, the outcast, and the grieving would be invited into God's presence (Micah 4:6). Jesus echoed this as He said His followers should invite "the poor, the crippled, the lame, and the blind" instead of the rich when hosting a dinner (Luke 14:13). As we walk in Christ's steps, we will lift up the weak and the helpless. God's people will minister to the very young and very old, valuing those people whom society casts aside.

Faith and Works: Throughout Scripture, God condemns those who profess to follow Him yet have no deeds to match. Micah also denounced this hypocrisy, emphasizing that doing right, loving mercy, and walking humbly are the things that truly please God (Micah 6:8). The apostle James put it even more simply: "Faith is dead without good works" (James 2:26).

MICAH FACTS

Author: Micah (1:1). This prophet was from the town of Moresheth in Judah (1:1, 14), but little else is known of his background. Like Amos, he was from a rural background, an outsider to the royal and priestly culture of Jerusalem.

Written to: Judah is the primary subject of Micah's prophecy, though he also addresses Israel.

Date of writing: Micah prophesied during the reigns of three kings of Judah (1:1); his ministry spanned about fifty years (739–686 BC). Because the third of those kings, Hezekiah (715–686 BC), brought about significant reforms in Judah, Micah's ministry may have ended early in Hezekiah's reign.

Setting: Micah addresses the capital cities of both Samaria and Judah, but he primarily focuses on Jerusalem, Judah's capital city.

OUTLINE

- **MICAH 1:1–2:13**—Judgment and Deliverance of a Remnant of Judah and Israel
- **MICAH 3:1–5:15**—Judgment and Deliverance of Judah and Jerusalem's Leaders
- **MICAH 6:1–7:20**—Judgment and Deliverance of a Remnant of Judah and Jerusalem

1:1 **1** The LORD gave this message to Micah of Moresheth during the years when Jotham,
1 Chr 3:12-13 Ahaz, and Hezekiah were kings of Judah. The visions he saw concerned both Samar-
Jer 26:18 ia and Jerusalem.

GRIEF OVER SAMARIA AND JERUSALEM

1:2 [2] Attention! Let all the people of the world listen!
Ps 50:7 Let the earth and everything in it hear.
Jer 6:19 The Sovereign LORD is making accusations against you;
the LORD speaks from His holy Temple.

1:3 [3] Look! The LORD is coming!
Isa 26:21 He leaves His throne in heaven
Amos 4:13 and tramples the heights of the earth.

1:4 [4] The mountains melt beneath His feet
Ps 97:5 and flow into the valleys
Isa 64:1-2 like wax in a fire,
Nah 1:5 like water pouring down a hill.

1:5 [5] And why is this happening?
2 Chr 34:3-4 Because of the rebellion of Israel*—
Amos 8:14 yes, the sins of the whole nation.
Who is to blame for Israel's rebellion?
Samaria, its capital city!
Where is the center of idolatry in Judah?
In Jerusalem, its capital!

1:6 [6] "So I, the LORD, will make the city of Samaria
Jer 31:5 a heap of ruins.
Ezek 13:14 Her streets will be plowed up
for planting vineyards.
I will roll the stones of her walls into the valley below,
exposing her foundations.

1:7 [7] All her carved images will be smashed.
Deut 9:21; 23:18 All her sacred treasures will be burned.
2 Chr 34:7 These things were bought with the money
earned by her prostitution,
and they will now be carried away
to pay prostitutes elsewhere."

1:5 Hebrew *Jacob;* also in 1:5b. The names "Jacob" and "Israel" are often interchanged throughout the Old Testament, referring sometimes to the individual patriarch and sometimes to the nation.

1:2-3 The interjections "Attention!" and "Look!" alert the reader to the urgency of the situation—judgment was coming soon on Samaria and the rest of the northern kingdom of Israel.

1:5 Samaria, the capital city of Israel, and Jerusalem, the capital city of Judah, were condemned as centers of idolatry when they should have been worship centers of the true God (Micah 3:9-12).

8 Therefore, I will mourn and lament.
I will walk around barefoot and naked.
I will howl like a jackal
and moan like an owl.
9 For my people's wound
is too deep to heal.
It has reached into Judah,
even to the gates of Jerusalem.

10 Don't tell our enemies in Gath*;
don't weep at all.
You people in Beth-leaphrah,*
roll in the dust to show your despair.
11 You people in Shaphir,*
go as captives into exile—naked and ashamed.
The people of Zaanan*
dare not come outside their walls.
The people of Beth-ezel* mourn,
for their house has no support.
12 The people of Maroth* anxiously wait for relief,
but only bitterness awaits them
as the LORD's judgment reaches
even to the gates of Jerusalem.
13 Harness your chariot horses and flee,
you people of Lachish.*
You were the first city in Judah
to follow Israel in her rebellion,
and you led Jerusalem* into sin.
14 Send farewell gifts to Moresheth-gath*;
there is no hope of saving it.
The town of Aczib*
has deceived the kings of Israel.
15 O people of Mareshah,*
I will bring a conqueror to capture your town.
And the leaders* of Israel
will go to Adullam.

16 Oh, people of Judah, shave your heads in sorrow,
for the children you love will be snatched away.
Make yourselves as bald as a vulture,
for your little ones will be exiled to distant lands.

1:8 Isa 13:21-22; 20:2-4
1:9 Jer 30:11-15; Mic 1:12
1:11 Ezek 23:29
1:12 Job 30:26; Isa 59:9-11; Jer 8:15; 14:19
1:13 Josh 10:3
1:14 Josh 15:44
1:15 Josh 12:15; 15:35, 44
1:16 Isa 22:12

1:10a *Gath* sounds like the Hebrew term for "tell." 1:10b *Beth-leaphrah* means "house of dust." 1:11a *Shaphir* means "pleasant." 1:11b *Zaanan* sounds like the Hebrew term for "come out." 1:11c *Beth-ezel* means "adjoining house." 1:12 *Maroth* sounds like the Hebrew term for "bitter." 1:13a *Lachish* sounds like the Hebrew term for "team of horses." 1:13b Hebrew *the daughter of Zion.* 1:14a *Moresheth* sounds like the Hebrew term for "gift" or "dowry." 1:14b *Aczib* means "deception." 1:15a *Mareshah* sounds like the Hebrew term for "conqueror." 1:15b Hebrew *the glory.*

▸ WORSHIP

1:8 Humble confrontation. Is it wrong to point out faults in others? Micah faithfully communicated God's message, but he also agonized over his message of God's impending judgment. It should never bring joy to a Christian to deal with other believers in wrongdoing. We should agonize over the sins of fellow Christians and humbly seek to restore them to God in a spirit of meekness (Galatians 6:1; James 5:19-20). If telling people they are wrong brings satisfaction to your life, you must repent of your sin and seek forgiveness from God. (***See Worship****> OT> Reverence> Revere God in the assembly,* TopicGuide page A29.)

1:10 Micah expressed lament over Gath, which was the first in a series of 12 cities that would experience the judgment of the Lord (Micah 1:10-15). Each saying or message about the town is matched to the city name (see NLT textual note).

JUDGMENT AGAINST WEALTHY OPPRESSORS

2:1 Prov 3:29-30 Isa 32:7 Hos 7:6-7

2 [1] What sorrow awaits you who lie awake at night,
thinking up evil plans.
You rise at dawn and hurry to carry them out,
simply because you have the power to do so.

2:2 Isa 5:8

[2] When you want a piece of land,
you find a way to seize it.
When you want someone's house,
you take it by fraud and violence.
You cheat a man of his property,
stealing his family's inheritance.

2:3 Isa 2:11-12 Jer 18:11

[3] But this is what the LORD says:
"I will reward your evil with evil;
you won't be able to pull your neck out of the noose.
You will no longer walk around proudly,
for it will be a terrible time."

2:4 Jer 6:12; 8:10 Hab 2:6

[4] In that day your enemies will make fun of you
by singing this song of despair about you:
"We are finished,
completely ruined!
God has confiscated our land,
taking it from us.
He has given our fields
to those who betrayed us.*"

2:5 Deut 32:8 Josh 18:4, 10

[5] Others will set your boundaries then,
and the LORD's people will have no say
in how the land is divided.

TRUE AND FALSE PROPHETS

2:6 Isa 30:10 Amos 2:12

[6] "Don't say such things,"
the people respond.*
"Don't prophesy like that.
Such disasters will never come our way!"

2:7 Pss 15:1-2; 84:11 Jer 15:16

[7] Should you talk that way, O family of Israel?*
Will the LORD's Spirit have patience with such behavior?
If you would do what is right,
you would find My words comforting.

2:8 Jer 12:8 Mic 3:2-3; 7:2-3

[8] Yet to this very hour
My people rise against Me like an enemy!

2:4 Or *to those who took us captive.* 2:6 Or *the prophets respond;* Hebrew reads *they prophesy.* 2:7 Hebrew *O house of Jacob?* See note on 1:5a.

▸ WORSHIP

2:1 Business before God. Have you ever been treated unjustly by an employer or a business? If you have the chance, let them know that God is taking note—He does not approve of those who take advantage of others. These landowners in Micah's time were judged because they had abused their authority in order to satisfy their covetous appetites. It is tempting for anyone in authority to take advantage of other people for their own gain. We must remember that we all answer to a God who holds us accountable for our dealings with those who work for us and those with whom we do business. Ask God to help you to deal justly with your clients and business associates. (***See Holiness****> OT> God's Supremacy> Required obedience in daily life and affairs,* TopicGuide page A26.)

2:6 The prophecy suddenly changes to a discussion of the way Israel responded to Nahum's message. It was the faithless response to the prophecy as much as the initial disobedience that sealed Israel's doom.

You steal the shirts right off the backs
of those who trusted you,
making them as ragged as men
returning from battle.
9 You have evicted women from their pleasant homes
and forever stripped their children of all that God would give them.
10 Up! Begone!
This is no longer your land and home,
for you have filled it with sin
and ruined it completely.

11 Suppose a prophet full of lies would say to you,
"I'll preach to you the joys of wine and alcohol!"
That's just the kind of prophet you would like!

2:9 Jer 10:20
2:10 Lev 18:24-28 Deut 12:9 Ps 106:38
2:11 Jer 5:31 Mic 3:5, 11

HOPE FOR RESTORATION

12 "Someday, O Israel, I will gather you;
I will gather the remnant who are left.
I will bring you together again like sheep in a pen,
like a flock in its pasture.
Yes, your land will again
be filled with noisy crowds!
13 Your leader will break out
and lead you out of exile,
out through the gates of the enemy cities,
back to your own land.
Your king will lead you;
the LORD Himself will guide you."

2:12 Isa 11:11 Mic 4:7; 5:7; 7:18

JUDGMENT AGAINST ISRAEL'S LEADERS

3 1 I said, "Listen, you leaders of Israel!
You are supposed to know right from wrong,
2 but you are the very ones
who hate good and love evil.
You skin My people alive
and tear the flesh from their bones.
3 Yes, you eat My people's flesh,
strip off their skin,
and break their bones.
You chop them up
like meat for the cooking pot.
4 Then you beg the LORD for help in times of trouble!
Do you really expect Him to answer?
After all the evil you have done,
He won't even look at you!"

3:1 Jer 5:5
3:2 Ezek 22:27
3:3 Ps 14:4 Ezek 11:7 Zeph 3:3
3:4 Deut 31:17 Ps 18:41 Prov 1:28 Isa 1:15; 59:2 Mic 7:13

2:12 In both the Old Testament and the New Testament, God is described as guiding His people as a shepherd guides his sheep (Psalm 23; Jeremiah 23:3; 31:10; Luke 15:1-7; John 10). Here Jerusalem is compared to a sheepfold where the people of God will once again be reunited into the presence of God in order to celebrate His goodness (Jeremiah 31:7-9).

▶ HOLINESS
3:2 Excuses, excuses. Most of us admit we are sinners, but we almost always have a list of reasons for our crimes against God and humanity. Our reasons may be so convincing that we feel able to reverse the moral order and call evil good and good evil (Romans 12:9). Let's stop excusing our sinful actions, stop coping with sinful habits, and begin confessing our wrongdoing. Then we can experience the power of God unleashed through repentance. God promises that when we confess our sin and, by faith, turn from evil to good, we will see change (1 John 1:8-9). Repent or make excuses—it's your choice. (***See Holiness****> Submission> Yielding to Spirit> Resist fleshly empowerment,* TopicGuide page A41.)

3:5 Jer 6:14; 14:14-15
5 This is what the LORD says:
"You false prophets are leading My people astray!
You promise peace for those who give you food,
but you declare war on those who refuse to feed you.
3:6 Isa 8:20-22; 29:10; 59:10 Amos 8:9-10
6 Now the night will close around you,
cutting off all your visions.
Darkness will cover you,
putting an end to your predictions.
The sun will set for you prophets,
and your day will come to an end.
3:7 Isa 44:25 Zech 13:4
7 Then you seers will be put to shame,
and you fortune-tellers will be disgraced.
And you will cover your faces
because there is no answer from God."

3:8 Isa 58:1; 61:1-2
8 But as for me, I am filled with power—
with the Spirit of the LORD.
I am filled with justice and strength
to boldly declare Israel's sin and rebellion.
3:9 Isa 1:23
9 Listen to me, you leaders of Israel!
You hate justice and twist all that is right.
3:10 Jer 22:13-17 Ezek 22:25-28 Hab 2:9-12
10 You are building Jerusalem
on a foundation of murder and corruption.
11 You rulers make decisions based on bribes;
3:11 Isa 48:2 Hos 4:18
you priests teach God's laws only for a price;
you prophets won't prophesy unless you are paid.
Yet all of you claim to depend on the LORD.
"No harm can come to us," you say,
"for the LORD is here among us."
3:12 Jer 9:11; 26:18
12 Because of you, Mount Zion will be plowed like an open field;
Jerusalem will be reduced to ruins!
A thicket will grow on the heights
where the Temple now stands.

THE LORD'S FUTURE REIGN

4:1 Pss 22:27; 86:9 Jer 3:17
4 1 In the last days, the mountain of the LORD's house
will be the highest of all—
the most important place on earth.
It will be raised above the other hills,
and people from all over the world will stream there to worship.
4:2 Ps 25:8-12 Isa 2:3; 4:3; 42:1-4 Jer 31:6 Zech 14:8-9
2 People from many nations will come and say,
"Come, let us go up to the mountain of the LORD,
to the house of Jacob's God.

3:5 In Micah's day, good news often came attached with a price tag. The prophets told the people what they wanted to hear as long as the people met the needs of the prophets. The false prophets gave unwarranted hope to the people (2:6), and here promised peace when war was around the corner.

3:11 Three branches of leadership in Jerusalem had succumbed to greed. Judges were influenced by bribes, and priests and prophets did their jobs only when paid.

4:1 Jerusalem would soon be annihilated and its people exiled (Micah 2:12), but the Lord promised salvation in the last days (2:12). "In the last days" could refer to the general future or to the coming of the Messiah. Even though the Babylonians would lead Jerusalem into captivity, restoration was promised to Jerusalem in the near future (Jeremiah 25:11-12). The New Testament speaks of Jesus inaugurating the last days (Hebrews 1:1-3), the church as living in the last days (Acts 2:17), and the last days as something that is yet to come (2 Timothy 3:1; 2 Peter 3:3).

There He will teach us His ways,
and we will walk in His paths."
For the LORD's teaching will go out from Zion;
His word will go out from Jerusalem.
3 The LORD will mediate between peoples
and will settle disputes between strong nations
far away.
They will hammer their swords into plowshares
and their spears into pruning hooks.
Nation will no longer fight against nation,
nor train for war anymore.
4 Everyone will live in peace and prosperity,
enjoying their own grapevines and fig trees,
for there will be nothing to fear.
The LORD of Heaven's Armies
has made this promise!
5 Though the nations around us follow their idols,
we will follow the LORD our God forever and ever.

4:3 Isa 11:3-5

4:4 Lev 26:6; Isa 40:5

4:5 2 Kgs 17:29, 34; Zech 3:10; 10:12

ISRAEL'S RETURN FROM EXILE

6 "In that coming day," says the LORD,
"I will gather together those who are lame,
those who have been exiles,
and those whom I have filled with grief.
7 Those who are weak will survive as a remnant;
those who were exiles will become a strong nation.
Then I, the LORD, will rule from Jerusalem*
as their king forever."
8 As for you, Jerusalem,
the citadel of God's people,*
your royal might and power
will come back to you again.
The kingship will be restored
to My precious Jerusalem.

9 But why are you now screaming in terror?
Have you no king to lead you?
Have your wise people all died?
Pain has gripped you like a woman in childbirth.

4:6 Zeph 3:19

4:7 Isa 9:6-7; 24:23

4:8 Ps 48:12; Isa 1:26; Zech 9:10

4:9 Jer 8:19

4:7 Hebrew *Mount Zion.* 4:8 Hebrew *As for you, Migdal-eder, / the Ophel of the daughter of Zion.*

▸ MINISTRY

4:5 Faith in an unbelieving world. If you work or live with people who are not Christians, you know firsthand the difficulty of keeping the faith in a world full of unbelief. We must resolve as the faithful did in Micah's time to remain true in our worship of God—no matter what. We have been called to be light to those who live in darkness (Matthew 5:13-16) and there is nothing in this world that should be able to darken our witness. Because Christ Himself said He was the light of the world (John 8:12), He empowers us to live out our Christian faith in spite of the challenges we face in our workplace or residence. Commit to a humble reliance on Christ for the power to remain faithful while living among the faithless. (***See Ministry***> *Transformation> Fill and Subdue> Being salt and light in the world,* TopicGuide page A57.)

4:7 Greed had corrupted the positions of authority held by the rulers, priests, and prophets, but God determined to set things in order by taking on Himself the role of King. This promise would find its fulfillment in the person of Christ, who would bear the government upon His shoulders (Isaiah 9:6). Christ's kingship is everlasting (Luke 1:33), ruled by righteousness (Hebrews 1:8), welcoming to the saints (2 Peter 1:10-11), and joyous for the world (Revelation 19:6-7).

4:10 / 2 Kgs 20:18 / Isa 48:20 / Hos 2:14 / Mic 7:8-12

10 Writhe and groan like a woman in labor,
you people of Jerusalem,*
for now you must leave this city
to live in the open country.
You will soon be sent in exile
to distant Babylon.
But the LORD will rescue you there;
He will redeem you from the grip of your enemies.

4:11 / Isa 5:25-30

11 Now many nations have gathered against you.
"Let her be desecrated," they say.
"Let us see the destruction of Jerusalem.*"

4:12 / Ps 147:19-20 / Isa 55:8

12 But they do not know the LORD's thoughts
or understand His plan.
These nations don't know
that He is gathering them together
to be beaten and trampled
like sheaves of grain on a threshing floor.

4:13 / Isa 41:15-16; 60:9

13 "Rise up and crush the nations, O Jerusalem!"*
says the LORD.
"For I will give you iron horns and bronze hooves,
so you can trample many nations to pieces.
You will present their stolen riches to the LORD,
their wealth to the LORD of all the earth."

5:1 / Job 16:10 / Lam 3:30

5

1*Mobilize! Marshal your troops!
The enemy is laying siege to Jerusalem.
They will strike Israel's leader
in the face with a rod.

A RULER FROM BETHLEHEM

5:2 / Ps 102:25 / Jer 30:21 / Zech 9:9 / *Matt 2:6 / John 1:1-2; 7:42

2* But you, O Bethlehem Ephrathah,
are only a small village among all the people of Judah.
Yet a ruler of Israel will come from you,
One whose origins are from the distant past.

5:3 / Isa 10:20-22 / Hos 11:8 / Mic 4:10; 5:7-8; 7:13

3 The people of Israel will be abandoned to their enemies
until the woman in labor gives birth.
Then at last His fellow countrymen
will return from exile to their own land.

5:4 / Isa 9:6; 52:10 / Mic 7:14

4 And He will stand to lead His flock with the LORD's strength,
in the majesty of the name of the LORD His God.

4:10 Hebrew *O daughter of Zion.* 4:11 Hebrew *of Zion.* 4:13 Hebrew *"Rise up and thresh, O daughter of Zion."*
5:1 Verse 5:1 is numbered 4:14 in Hebrew text. 5:2 Verses 5:2-15 are numbered 5:1-14 in Hebrew text.

4:10 Labor pains are excruciating, but a life is born when the labor ends. The Babylonians would invade Jerusalem and turn it into a heap of rubble causing the Jews great hardship (2 Kings 25). God, however, promised to one day redeem His people from the grip of their enemies and give them new life.

5:2 Micah's prophecy included a promise not only of a remnant people (Micah 2:12-13) but also of a king who would arise from among the people. Jesus Christ, as the son of David, fulfilled this prophecy. He was born in Bethlehem (Matthew 2:6), yet He also existed from eternity (Colossians 1:17).

5:4 The prophet continued to speak of the Messiah by explaining the nature and scope of His kingship. The prophecy describes the Messiah leading the people as a shepherd does his sheep (Luke 15:1-7; John 10) and being clothed in the strength and majesty of God (Psalms 93:1). His reign would include not only the nation of Israel but also the entire world (Matthew 28:18-20; Romans 14:11).

Then His people will live there undisturbed,
for He will be highly honored around the world.
5 And He will be the source of peace.

When the Assyrians invade our land
and break through our defenses,
we will appoint seven rulers to watch over us,
eight princes to lead us.
6 They will rule Assyria with drawn swords
and enter the gates of the land of Nimrod.
He will rescue us from the Assyrians
when they pour over the borders to invade our land.

THE REMNANT PURIFIED

7 Then the remnant left in Israel*
will take their place among the nations.
They will be like dew sent by the LORD
or like rain falling on the grass,
which no one can hold back
and no one can restrain.
8 The remnant left in Israel
will take their place among the nations.
They will be like a lion among the animals of the forest,
like a strong young lion among flocks of sheep and goats,
pouncing and tearing as they go
with no rescuer in sight.
9 The people of Israel will stand up to their foes,
and all their enemies will be wiped out.

10 "In that day," says the LORD,
"I will slaughter your horses
and destroy your chariots.
11 I will tear down your walls
and demolish your defenses.
12 I will put an end to all witchcraft,
and there will be no more fortune-tellers.
13 I will destroy all your idols and sacred pillars,
so you will never again worship the work of your own hands.
14 I will abolish your idol shrines with their Asherah poles
and destroy your pagan cities.

5:5 Isa 8:7-8
5:6 Gen 10:8-11; Isa 37:36-37; Nah 2:11-13
5:7 Deut 32:2; Ps 72:6
5:8 Gen 49:9; Ps 50:22; Zech 10:5
5:9 Ps 10:12
5:10 Hos 14:3; Zech 9:10
5:11 Isa 2:12-17; Hos 10:14; Amos 5:9
5:12 Deut 18:10-12
5:13 Isa 2:8, 18-19
5:14 Exod 34:13

5:7 Hebrew *in Jacob;* also in 5:8. See note on 1:5a.

▸ GOD

5:5 Bringing Peace. What sort of peace does Christ offer His people? Some define peace as the absence of war and hostilities or the presence of an agreement to end hostilities between two parties. This prophecy looks forward to the day when the world will respect Israel's sovereignty and no longer threaten it, and when any who do invade Israel will be destroyed (5:6). Today, Christ's peace is found in the absence of strife between His people and God (Romans 5:1-10) and in the presence of His Holy Spirit, leading to personal serenity (Romans 8:6; Galatians 5:22). It's true that Christ's reconciling peace can resolve personal struggles, but the resolution of all hostilities is not a present but a future reality (Matthew 6:34; Romans 2:9). Jesus Christ can bring calm assurance into your life that goes beyond your current circumstances (John 14:27). Receive His gift of peace today. (***See God*** > *Salvation* > *Son* > *Reconciles us to God,* TopicGuide page A15.)

5:14 Asherah was one of the chief deities in the Canaanite religion. As a Canaanite goddess, Asherah was believed to be the wife of El and the mother of Baal. When Elijah was on Mount Carmel, he summoned not only the 450 prophets of Baal, but also 400 prophets of Asherah (1 Kings 18:19). The "Asherah poles" were a regular fixture of pagan worship, existing since before the time of Moses (Deuteronomy 7:5; 16:21) as symbols of fertility.

5:15 Ps 149:7 Isa 1:24; 65:12

[15] I will pour out My vengeance
on all the nations that refuse to obey Me."

THE LORD'S CASE AGAINST ISRAEL

6 Listen to what the LORD is saying:

"Stand up and state your case against Me.
Let the mountains and hills be called to witness your complaints.

6:2 Hos 4:1; 12:2

[2] And now, O mountains,
listen to the LORD's complaint!
He has a case against His people.
He will bring charges against Israel.

6:3 Jer 2:5, 31

[3] "O My people, what have I done to you?
What have I done to make you tired of Me?
Answer Me!

6:4 Exod 20:1-2 Ps 77:20

[4] For I brought you out of Egypt
and redeemed you from slavery.
I sent Moses, Aaron, and Miriam to help you.

6:5 Num 22:5-6; 25:1 Josh 5:9-10

[5] Don't you remember, My people,
how King Balak of Moab tried to have you cursed
and how Balaam son of Beor blessed you instead?
And remember your journey from Acacia Grove* to Gilgal,
when I, the LORD, did everything I could
to teach you about My faithfulness."

6:6 Pss 40:6-8; 51:16-17

[6] What can we bring to the LORD?
What kind of offerings should we give Him?
Should we bow before God
with offerings of yearling calves?

6:7 Lev 18:21; 20:1-5 Ps 50:9 Isa 40:16

[7] Should we offer Him thousands of rams
and ten thousand rivers of olive oil?
Should we sacrifice our firstborn children
to pay for our sins?

6:8 Deut 10:12-13 Isa 57:15

[8] No, O people, the LORD has told you what is good,
and this is what He requires of you:
to do what is right, to love mercy,
and to walk humbly with your God.

6:5 Hebrew *Shittim.*

6:1-2 The chapter opens with a scene of a courtroom. In Micah 6:1, God was the defendant, but then in 6:2, He was the plaintiff. He continued to act as the plaintiff as He brought charges against the accused, Israel. The mountains and the foundations of the earth were called to be witnesses (Deuteronomy 4:26). The prophet Hosea portrayed a similar scene in his writings (Hosea 4:1–5:15).

▸ GOD

6:6-8 Religion without relationship. How many times have you prayed before a meal without paying attention to the words you've spoken? Or sang a hymn in church while thinking of something else? It's easy to become accustomed to the routines of the Christian life. We may speak certain ways, listen to certain music, and pray before we eat, but go through a whole day without truly depending on God, repenting of our sin, and worshiping Him. We must guard against our tendency to go through the motions without experiencing an intimate relationship with God. Micah's audience wanted to find the right religious ceremony to make their nation right with God, but that would never work. Knowing God requires more than external obedience or religious habits (though obedience certainly is required). Any religion can offer ritual—only Christianity offers a real relationship with the God who created the universe. Walk humbly with Him. (***See God**> Relationship> God Enables> Relationship with God requires a right heart,* TopicGuide page A14.)

ISRAEL'S GUILT AND PUNISHMENT

9 Fear the LORD if you are wise!
His voice calls to everyone in Jerusalem:
"The armies of destruction are coming;
the LORD is sending them.*
10 What shall I say about the homes of the wicked
filled with treasures gained by cheating?
What about the disgusting practice
of measuring out grain with dishonest measures?*
11 How can I tolerate your merchants
who use dishonest scales and weights?
12 The rich among you have become wealthy
through extortion and violence.
Your citizens are so used to lying
that their tongues can no longer tell the truth.

13 "Therefore, I will wound you!
I will bring you to ruin for all your sins.
14 You will eat but never have enough.
Your hunger pangs and emptiness will remain.
And though you try to save your money,
it will come to nothing in the end.
You will save a little,
but I will give it to those who conquer you.
15 You will plant crops
but not harvest them.
You will press your olives
but not get enough oil to anoint yourselves.
You will trample the grapes
but get no juice to make your wine.
16 You keep only the laws of evil King Omri;
you follow only the example of wicked King Ahab!
Therefore, I will make an example of you,
bringing you to complete ruin.
You will be treated with contempt,
mocked by all who see you."

MISERY TURNED TO HOPE

7 1 How miserable I am!
I feel like the fruit picker after the harvest
who can find nothing to eat.

6:10 Jer 5:26-27; Amos 3:10; 8:5
6:12 Isa 3:8
6:13 Isa 1:5-7; 6:11
6:14 Lev 26:26; Isa 9:20; 30:6
6:15 Deut 28:38-40; Jer 12:13; Amos 5:11; Zeph 1:13
6:16 1 Kgs 16:25, 29-33; Jer 7:24; 18:15-16; 25:9
7:1 Isa 28:4; Hos 9:10

6:9 Hebrew *"Listen to the rod. / Who appointed it?"* 6:10 Hebrew *of using the short ephah?* The ephah was a unit for measuring grain.

▸ GOD

6:10-12 Beneficial justice. We have a tendency to think that God winks at sin—after all, we sin and are not struck down. Others appear to sin more than we do and seem to suffer no immediate punishment. The Scriptures remind us that nothing is hidden from God (Proverbs 15:3). Judah was filled with dishonest practices, and God took note. Micah's exhortations serve as reminders that God doesn't—He cannot—overlook sin. God has promised to hear our prayers of confession and show great mercy toward us because of Christ's redemptive work (Ephesians 2:4-7; 1 Peter 3:12). Do not be fooled—God sees your every step. Because of that, Jesus died for every sin. You can bring every sin you find in your life to God—He'll know what to do with it. (***See God> God's Attributes> Just> The righteous God justifies those who believe in Jesus,*** TopicGuide page A17.)

6:16 Omri and Ahab were both wicked kings in Israel's history. Omri became king of Israel only after he led an assault on the city of Tirzah in order to murder King Zimri. Omri exceeded all preceding kings in wicked deeds (1 Kings 16:15-28). King Ahab, the son of Omri, reintroduced Baal worship, and was considered even worse than his father (1 Kings 16:29-33).

7:1 Micah's audience knew the disappointment of either planting and yet having nothing at harvesttime or of attempting to

Not a cluster of grapes or a single early fig
can be found to satisfy my hunger.
7:2 Isa 57:1; 59:7 Jer 5:26 Hos 5:1
2 The godly people have all disappeared;
not one honest person is left on the earth.
They are all murderers,
setting traps even for their own brothers.
7:3 Prov 4:16-17 Mic 3:11
3 Both their hands are equally skilled at doing evil!
Officials and judges alike demand bribes.
The people with influence get what they want,
and together they scheme to twist justice.
7:4 Isa 10:3; 22:5 Ezek 2:6 Nah 1:10
4 Even the best of them is like a brier;
the most honest is as dangerous as a hedge
of thorns.
But your judgment day is coming swiftly now.
Your time of punishment is here, a time of confusion.
7:5 Jer 9:4-5
5 Don't trust anyone—
not your best friend or even your wife!
7:6 *Matt 10:35-36 *Luke 12:53
6 For the son despises his father.
The daughter defies her mother.
The daughter-in-law defies her mother-in-law.
Your enemies are right in your own household!

7:7 Pss 4:3; 130:5
7 As for me, I look to the LORD for help.
I wait confidently for God to save me,
and my God will certainly hear me.
7:8 Prov 24:15-16 Isa 9:2 Amos 9:11
8 Do not gloat over me, my enemies!
For though I fall, I will rise again.
Though I sit in darkness,
the LORD will be my light.
7:9 Ps 37:6 Jer 50:34
9 I will be patient as the LORD punishes me,
for I have sinned against Him.
But after that, He will take up my case
and give me justice for all I have suffered from
my enemies.
The LORD will bring me into the light,
and I will see His righteousness.
7:10 Isa 51:23 Zech 10:5
10 Then my enemies will see that the LORD is on my side.
They will be ashamed that they taunted me, saying,
"So where is the LORD—
that God of yours?"
With my own eyes I will see their downfall;
they will be trampled like mud in the streets.

7:11 Amos 9:11
11 In that day, Israel, your cities will be rebuilt,
and your borders will be extended.

glean from the leftover crops, yet finding nothing left (Ruth 2:2-3).

7:5 In a time when multiple generations commonly lived and slept together in small homes, familial tension and distrust served as a poignant warning of the difficult days to come.

7:11 It was God's intention for Israel to extend its borders to the size God described (Joshua 13–21), but the influence of Israel would go much further, even to the fulfillment of God's promise to Abraham that he would be a father of many nations (Genesis 17:5; Romans 4:17). In the New Testament, God's command to extend the borders of His holy people comes by way of evangelism (Matthew 28:18-20).

12 People from many lands will come and honor you—
from Assyria all the way to the towns of Egypt,
from Egypt all the way to the Euphrates River,*
and from distant seas and mountains.
13 But the land* will become empty and desolate
because of the wickedness of those who live there.

7:12
Isa 11:16; 19:23-25

7:13
Isa 3:10-11
Mic 6:13

THE LORD'S COMPASSION ON ISRAEL

14 O LORD, protect Your people with Your shepherd's staff;
lead Your flock, Your special possession.
Though they live alone in a thicket
on the heights of Mount Carmel,*
let them graze in the fertile pastures of Bashan and Gilead
as they did long ago.

7:14
Amos 9:11

15 "Yes," says the LORD,
"I will do mighty miracles for you,
like those I did when I rescued you
from slavery in Egypt."

7:15
Exod 3:20

16 All the nations of the world will stand amazed
at what the LORD will do for you.
They will be embarrassed
at their feeble power.
They will cover their mouths in silent awe,
deaf to everything around them.
17 Like snakes crawling from their holes,
they will come out to meet the LORD our God.
They will fear Him greatly,
trembling in terror at His presence.

7:16
Mic 3:7

7:17
Gen 3:14
Pss 9:20; 72:9

18 Where is another God like You,
who pardons the guilt of the remnant,
overlooking the sins of His special people?
You will not stay angry with Your people forever,
because You delight in showing unfailing love.
19 Once again You will have compassion on us.
You will trample our sins under Your feet
and throw them into the depths of the ocean!
20 You will show us Your faithfulness and unfailing love
as You promised to our ancestors Abraham and Jacob long ago.

7:18
Exod 34:9
Num 14:18-19
Jer 4:2; 32:41

7:19
Isa 43:25
Jer 50:20

7:20
Gen 24:27; 32:9-10
Deut 7:8, 12
Luke 1:72

7:12 Hebrew *the river.* 7:13 Or *earth.* 7:14 Or *surrounded by a fruitful land.*

7:12-13 The Lord's earlier prophecy now specifically identifies Assyria and Egypt as two of the nations that will gather together in Jerusalem to worship the living God (Micah 4:2). Though Assyria and Egypt are mentioned, Micah also emphasized that the entire world will one day acknowledge God as their King.

▸ GOD

7:18-20 A good God. Have you ever wondered why God works with sinful, fallible humans? God would have been justified in utterly destroying Israel on many occasions, but as Moses pointed out, it would not have been consistent with God's character (Exodus 32:10-13). What is consistent with His character is His delight in showing forgiveness, compassion, and unfailing love to His people. God's first impulse toward His sinful people is not wrath or discipline, but grace and faithfulness. We can always come to God and find Him delighting in our repentance (Luke 15). (***See God**> God's Attributes> Forgiving> God is ready to forgive,* TopicGuide page A16.)

NAHUM

PURPOSE

To declare God's forthcoming judgment upon the nation of Assyria so that Judah would be comforted.

God's messages do not have to be boring. In one sense, Nahum's message is not any different from the other prophets—judgment comes to those who do not repent. But his brevity and style set him apart as an important messenger for God. Within a span of forty-seven verses, he uses almost every literary form known to ancient writers—metaphor, simile, synecdoche, woe, satire, dirge, various parallel structures, partial acrostic, alliteration, and assonance—all within a vivid prose. Nahum shows that God's people can use art and skill in communicating God's truths to our families and to the nations.

About one hundred years earlier, Jonah preached to Nineveh. God's judgment on Assyria was delayed due to their repentance (760 BC), but the reforms did not last. In Nahum's day, things were much as they had been before Jonah preached. Assyria continued to gain notoriety for the way it used brutality in warfare to shock its enemies into submission, and Nineveh returned to its murderous and evil ways. In short, Nineveh and Assyria were ripe for the judgment of God. The judgment prophesied by Nahum occurred in 612 BC, when the Babylonian Empire conquered and destroyed Assyria (Ezekiel 32:22-23). Though Assyria had conquered the northern kingdom of Israel in 722 BC and harassed the southern kingdom of Judah, Nahum delivered the consoling word to Judah that Assyria would afflict them no more (1:12).

DISCOVER GOD IN NAHUM

Nahum dramatically displays several attributes of God:

Sovereign Warrior: God may have waited over one hundred years, but the Warrior God would now take revenge on His foes. They would not escape, nor would they have any chance at victory (1:3-6). But God's vengeance was not haphazard—His faithful people would be protected (1:7, 15) as He swept His foes away like pebbles in an overwhelming flood.

Involved in History: God does not simply sit in heaven resting and pondering. He is involved in the arena of history. God's involvement in creation was not an abstraction to Nahum, for he worshiped a God who brings nations into being—and destroys them (1:2; 2:13). History is neither under human control nor satanic direction nor random selection. It is under the control of God alone (1:14).

GROWING THROUGH NAHUM

The book of Nahum suggests themes appropriate for the follower of Christ:

A Majority with God: Martyrs through the centuries have demonstrated that obeying the call of God takes courage. Though Nahum was not martyred in his ministry, it would not have been easy for him to prophesy against Nineveh, center of the most powerful and influential culture of his time. The apostle Peter, on the other hand, denied allegiance to Jesus when confronted by a mere servant girl (Matthew 26:69-75)—though once he was filled with the Spirit at Pentecost, Peter became characterized by great courage (Acts 4–5). One is never alone when called by God, regardless of appearances. With God, numbers do not make the majority.

Dangers of National Sin: Throughout the Bible, God deals with people both as individuals and as groups. He blesses individuals and their families (such as Abraham; Genesis 12–17), and He curses individuals and their families (Genesis 9:25; Galatians 1:8). In this case, God condemns an entire nation because that nation turned away from His offer of repentance through Jonah. God can and will deal strongly with nations who turn away from His blessings and promote the violence and destruction and arrogance embodied by the capitol of the Assyrian Empire (Jude 1:5; Revelation 11:18).

DISCOVERY VERSES

The LORD is good, a strong refuge when trouble comes. He is close to those who trust in Him. (NAHUM 1:7)

Even though the destroyer has destroyed Judah, the LORD will restore its honor. Israel's vine has been stripped of branches, but He will restore its splendor. (NAHUM 2:2)

NAHUM FACTS

Author: Nahum (1:1). Nothing is known of Nahum except his place of origin, Elkosh. The town of Capernaum, or the "Village of Nahum," is located on the Sea of Galilee and may have a historical connection to him. Elkosh could be a forgotten name for that area.

Written to: Assyria, but it was intended to bring comfort to the people of Judah.

Date of writing: Nahum refers to the destruction of the Egyptian city of Thebes (3:8-10; 663 BC) as a past event and the destruction of Nineveh (612 BC) as a future event. Therefore, the book was written between these dates.

Setting: Nahum wrote in Judah about Nineveh.

OUTLINE

- **NAHUM 1:1-8**—God's Anger against Nineveh
- **NAHUM 1:9–2:10**—God's Judgment on Nineveh
- **NAHUM 2:11–3:19**—God's Mockery of Nineveh

1:1 Isa 13:1; Zeph 2:13

1 This message concerning Nineveh came as a vision to Nahum, who lived in Elkosh.

THE LORD'S ANGER AGAINST NINEVEH

1:2 Exod 20:5; Deut 4:24; 32:35; Ps 94:1

2 The LORD is a jealous God,
filled with vengeance and rage.
He takes revenge on all who oppose Him
and continues to rage against His enemies!

1:3 Exod 34:5-7; Pss 50:3; 104:3

3 The LORD is slow to get angry, but His power is great,
and He never lets the guilty go unpunished.
He displays His power in the whirlwind and the storm.
The billowing clouds are the dust beneath His feet.

1:4 Isa 33:9; Matt 8:26

4 At His command the oceans dry up,
and the rivers disappear.
The lush pastures of Bashan and Carmel fade,
and the green forests of Lebanon wither.

1:5 Exod 19:19; 2 Sam 22:8-9; Mic 1:4

5 In His presence the mountains quake,
and the hills melt away;
the earth trembles,
and its people are destroyed.

1:6 1 Kgs 19:11; Jer 10:10; Mal 3:2

6 Who can stand before His fierce anger?
Who can survive His burning fury?
His rage blazes forth like fire,
and the mountains crumble to dust in His presence.

1:7 1 Chr 16:34; Pss 25:8; 100:5

7 The LORD is good,
a strong refuge when trouble comes.
He is close to those who trust in Him.

1:8 Isa 8:7

8 But He will sweep away His enemies
in an overwhelming flood.
He will pursue His foes
into the darkness of night.

1:9 Pss 2:1-4; 21:11

9 Why are you scheming against the LORD?
He will destroy you with one blow;
He won't need to strike twice!

1:10 Isa 9:18; Mal 4:1

10 His enemies, tangled like thornbushes
and staggering like drunks,
will be burned up like dry stubble in a field.

1:1 The word "message" can also mean "oracle." In Scripture, an oracle denotes a God-given message of judgment upon a foreign nation (Isaiah 13:1; 15:1; 17:1; 19:1). The prophet Nahum received an oracle from the Lord against Nineveh, one of the capital cities of Assyria (Jonah 3:6-10; Zephaniah 2:13-15). Assyria toppled the northern kingdom of Israel in 722 BC, thus Nahum's prophecy came after that time, but before the prophesied fall of Nineveh in 612 BC.

▶ GOD

1:2 A jealous God. Isn't jealousy a sin? The Bible does speak of jealousy negatively (Acts 7:9; 17:5; 1 Corinthians 13:4), but the use of the word is not sinful when applied to God. When the Scriptures speak of God's jealousy, it means that He does not tolerate challengers to His covenant with Israel (Numbers 25:11; Deuteronomy 6:15; Isaiah 59:17; Ezekiel 5:13; 38:18-19). God is zealous for His people's loyalty (Zechariah 1:14), and any threat to His relationship with them is met with His jealousy, vengeance, and wrath. We should not be apologetic about saying God desires to be exclusively worshiped; instead, we can demonstrate that God is concerned with preserving our devotion to Him because anything else is irrational and sinful (Exodus 20:3-6; Deuteronomy 6:4), destructive to our hearts and minds (Romans 1:23-32). (***See God***> *God's Nature> Unique> There is none like Him,* TopicGuide page A15.)

1:4 Bashan was located northeast of the Sea of Galilee. Its territory extended from the foot of Mount Hermon to the Yarmuk River (Deuteronomy 32:14). Mount Carmel was a mountainous ridge located in the northwest section of Israel; it formed the southwest border of the Jezreel Valley. Lebanon was another mountain range in the north near Tyre and Sidon. These mountain ranges represented regions of beauty and fertility. Bashan was known for its luscious pastures, which fed fat, healthy cattle (Ezekiel 39:18).

11 Who is this wicked counselor of yours
who plots evil against the LORD?

12 This is what the LORD says:
"Though the Assyrians have many allies,
they will be destroyed and disappear.
O My people, I have punished you before,
but I will not punish you again.
13 Now I will break the yoke of bondage from your neck
and tear off the chains of Assyrian oppression."

1:13 Isa 9:4 Jer 2:20

14 And this is what the LORD says concerning the Assyrians in Nineveh:
"You will have no more children to carry on your name.
I will destroy all the idols in the temples of your gods.
I am preparing a grave for you
because you are despicable!"

1:14 Nah 3:4-6

15*Look! A messenger is coming over the mountains with good news!
He is bringing a message of peace.
Celebrate your festivals, O people of Judah,
and fulfill all your vows,
for your wicked enemies will never invade your land again.
They will be completely destroyed!

1:15 Isa 29:7-8; 40:9; 52:7 Rom 10:15

THE FALL OF NINEVEH

2 1*Your enemy is coming to crush you, Nineveh.
Man the ramparts! Watch the roads!
Prepare your defenses! Call out your forces!

2 Even though the destroyer has destroyed Judah,
the LORD will restore its honor.
Israel's vine has been stripped of branches,
but He will restore its splendor.

2:2 Isa 60:15 Ezek 37:21-23

3 Shields flash red in the sunlight!
See the scarlet uniforms of the valiant troops!
Watch as their glittering chariots move into position,
with a forest of spears waving above them.
4 The chariots race recklessly along the streets
and rush wildly through the squares.

2:3 Ezek 23:14-15

2:4 Jer 4:13 Nah 3:2

1:15 Verse 1:15 is numbered 2:1 in Hebrew text. 2:1 Verses 2:1-13 are numbered 2:2-14 in Hebrew text.

1:11 The "wicked counselor" of Nineveh may refer to Sennacherib, who sent threatening messages to Jerusalem concerning a planned attack if the people of Israel did not submit to him (2 Kings 18–19). Some recent scholars have suggested that the "counselor" may refer to Belial, a demon comparable to Satan or an Assyrian god. This wicked counselor who leads the people to doom stands in contrast with the messenger who brings good news for God's people (Nahum 1:15).

2:3 Nahum provided a description of the army's dress and strategy. In 612 BC the Babylonians joined forces with the Medes and led an assault against Nineveh. The color "red" may have been a reference to the field dress of the Babylonian army, or it may have symbolized the bloodshed that would soon occur.

▸ HOLINESS

2:4 Strategic temptation. Does it feel like you have people running races around you? When temptation attacks our lives, it may take the form of an impossible project, an aggressive coworker, an irrational family member, or any number of other situations—but they all represent opportunities to sin. The situation appeared chaotic in Nineveh, but the Babylonians destroyed Nineveh with a well-organized strategy. We must not be deceived into thinking that all temptations arise at random—each temptation may be part of a well-thought-out plan of Satan to distract us from our God-given responsibilities. Be on the alert (1 Peter 5:8)! Always be on the lookout for a way of escape from the traps Satan may lay in our path. (***See Holiness****> Disciplines> Of Abstinence> Resisting Satan's schemes,* TopicGuide page A42.)

They flash like firelight
and move as swiftly as lightning.
2:5 Jer 46:12 5 The king shouts to his officers;
they stumble in their haste,
rushing to the walls to set up their defenses.
6 The river gates have been torn open!
The palace is about to collapse!
2:7 Isa 32:12; 59:11 7 Nineveh's exile has been decreed,
and all the servant girls mourn its capture.
They moan like doves
and beat their breasts in sorrow.
2:8 Jer 46:5 8 Nineveh is like a leaking water reservoir!
The people are slipping away.
"Stop, stop!" someone shouts,
but no one even looks back.
9 Loot the silver!
Plunder the gold!
There's no end to Nineveh's treasures—
its vast, uncounted wealth.
2:10 Josh 2:11 10 Soon the city is plundered, empty, and ruined.
Hearts melt and knees shake.
The people stand aghast,
their faces pale and trembling.

2:11 Isa 5:29 11 Where now is that great Nineveh,
that den filled with young lions?
It was a place where people—like lions
and their cubs—
walked freely and without fear.
12 The lion tore up meat for his cubs
and strangled prey for his mate.
He filled his den with prey,
his caverns with his plunder.

2:13 Ps 46:8-9 13 "I am your enemy!"
says the LORD of Heaven's Armies.
"Your chariots will soon go up in smoke.
Your young men* will be killed in battle.
Never again will you plunder conquered nations.
The voices of your proud messengers will be heard no more."

2:13 Hebrew *young lions.*

2:11-12 The lion was the dominant symbol of Assyria in the ancient Near East. When Assyria seized and captured other nations, it acted as a lion tearing and strangling its prey in order to feed her cubs. This oracle taunted the Assyrians because their power and ferociousness were useless against their approaching enemies.

▶ GOD
2:13 A Warrior on our side. When something frightens us, we want to run, especially if it's something we don't understand, like spiritual warfare. We'd rather just retreat and let someone else handle it. But the Bible teaches us to take courage—not in our own human abilities, but in God's promise of victory and of His presence (Joshua 1:5). Our Christian life is bombarded with assaults, and we must continually remind ourselves of God's promises. He fights on behalf of His people (Exodus 15:3; Joshua 23:10; Romans 8:31). Fear not, for the Warrior is on your side, and He prepares you for battle against even those things you cannot see (Ephesians 6:10-20). Stand firm against the devil, knowing God stands with you (James 4:7). (***See God****> God's Names> God> LORD of Heaven's Armies,* TopicGuide page A18.)

THE LORD'S JUDGMENT AGAINST NINEVEH

3 [1] What sorrow awaits Nineveh,
the city of murder and lies!
She is crammed with wealth
and is never without victims.
[2] Hear the crack of whips,
the rumble of wheels!
Horses' hooves pound,
and chariots clatter wildly.
[3] See the flashing swords and glittering spears
as the charioteers charge past!
There are countless casualties,
heaps of bodies—
so many bodies that
people stumble over them.
[4] All this because Nineveh,
the beautiful and faithless city,
mistress of deadly charms,
enticed the nations with her beauty.
She taught them all her magic,
enchanting people everywhere.

[5] "I am your enemy!"
says the LORD of Heaven's Armies.
"And now I will lift your skirts
and show all the earth your nakedness and shame.
[6] I will cover you with filth
and show the world how vile you really are.
[7] All who see you will shrink back and say,
'Nineveh lies in ruins.
Where are the mourners?'
Does anyone regret your destruction?"

[8] Are you any better than the city of Thebes,*
situated on the Nile River, surrounded by water?
She was protected by the river on all sides,
walled in by water.
[9] Ethiopia* and the land of Egypt
gave unlimited assistance.
The nations of Put and Libya
were among her allies.
[10] Yet Thebes fell,
and her people were led away as captives.
Her babies were dashed to death
against the stones of the streets.

3:1 Ezek 24:6-9
3:2 Nah 2:3-4
3:3 Isa 34:13
3:4 Isa 47:9; Rev 17:1-6; 18:2-3
3:5 Isa 47:3
3:6 Job 9:31; Isa 14:16
3:7 Isa 51:19; Jer 15:5
3:8 Isa 19:6-8; Jer 46:25; Ezek 30:14-16
3:9 Isa 20:5-6; Jer 46:9
3:10 2 Kgs 8:12; Ps 137:9; Hos 13:16

3:8 Hebrew *No-amon;* also in 3:10. 3:9 Hebrew *Cush.*

3:4-5 God promised to destroy Nineveh for her cruelty and deceitfulness (Nahum 3:1). Because of her trickery and seductiveness, Nineveh was likened to a prostitute. The Lord would treat her as ancient societies treated prostitutes caught in the act of adultery—He would expose her deeds to the world (Isaiah 47:1-3).

3:8 Thebes was the capital city of Egypt for much of its history. Many historians consider it to be the first monumental city in human civilization. Thebes's prominence was renowned during Nahum's time, and many were shocked by her destruction at the hands of the Assyrians in 663 BC. The Lord used Thebes as an example of what He would do to the great city of Nineveh.

Soldiers threw dice* to get Egyptian officers as servants.
All their leaders were bound in chains.

3:11 Isa 49:26 Jer 25:15-27
11 And you, Nineveh, will also stagger like a drunkard.
You will hide for fear of the attacking enemy.
12 All your fortresses will fall.
They will be devoured like the ripe figs
that fall into the mouths
of those who shake the trees.

3:13 Isa 19:16 Jer 50:37; 51:30
13 Your troops will be as weak
and helpless as women.
The gates of your land will be opened wide to the enemy
and set on fire and burned.

3:14 2 Chr 32:3-4 Nah 2:1
14 Get ready for the siege!
Store up water!
Strengthen the defenses!
Go into the pits to trample clay,
and pack it into molds,
making bricks to repair the walls.

3:15 Isa 66:15-16 Joel 1:4
15 But the fire will devour you;
the sword will cut you down.
The enemy will consume you like locusts,
devouring everything they see.
There will be no escape,
even if you multiply like swarming locusts.
16 Your merchants have multiplied
until they outnumber the stars.
But like a swarm of locusts,
they strip the land and fly away.
17 Your guards* and officials are also like swarming locusts
that crowd together in the hedges on a cold day.
But like locusts that fly away when the sun comes up,
all of them will fly away and disappear.

3:18 1 Kgs 22:17 Ps 76:5-6 Isa 56:10 Jer 50:18
18 Your shepherds are asleep, O Assyrian king;
your princes lie dead in the dust.
Your people are scattered across the mountains
with no one to gather them together.

3:19 Jer 30:13 Lam 2:15 Mic 1:9
19 There is no healing for your wound;
your injury is fatal.
All who hear of your destruction
will clap their hands for joy.
Where can anyone be found
who has not suffered from your continual cruelty?

3:10 Hebrew *They cast lots.* 3:17 Or *princes.*

3:14 The Lord had announced to Nineveh that an enemy was approaching, and He sarcastically called for the city to make preparations, knowing that the city would be destroyed (Nahum 2:1).

3:19 Since there were none who had been untouched by the cruelty of the Assyrians, there were none who would grieve at their destruction.

HABAKKUK

PURPOSE

To reflect on the apparent triumph of evil in light of God's sovereignty.

The prophet Habakkuk echoed the question of Psalm 73, where Asaph wondered about God's seeming indifference to the problem of evil: Why do the wicked seem to prosper and the righteous suffer?

Habakkuk asked God two questions. First, why was God allowing wickedness and sin to go unanswered within the nation of Judah? God replied that He was raising up the nation of Babylon to chasten Judah. While that answered Habakkuk's question, it raised an issue that seemed even more troubling: How could God use a wicked nation like Babylon to judge a less-wicked one like Judah? Through his struggles with this question, Habakkuk learned to rest in the judgments of God—to live by faith instead of by reason (2:4). His beautiful confession (chapter 3) is a testament of praise to the One he learned to trust even when he couldn't get a satisfying answer to his questions.

DISCOVER GOD IN HABAKKUK

Theologians use the term *theodicy* to describe the book of Habakkuk: a justification of God's goodness and justice in the face of evil. Two of God's attributes help to explain the need for a theodicy:

Inscrutableness: This long word means that God is beyond finding out. To put it in the words of Isaiah 55:8-9, "'My thoughts are nothing like your thoughts,' says the LORD. 'And My ways are far beyond anything you could imagine. For just as the heavens are higher than the earth, so My ways are higher than your ways and My thoughts higher than your thoughts.'" In understanding God, we are often like the woman who reached out for healing by touching the hem of Jesus Christ's robe (Matthew 9:20). She understood little of the deep essence of the person of Christ; indeed, she could reach Him only at the outer fringes of His being. But that was enough. And the mysteries of God became enough for Habakkuk. To paraphrase the prophet, "Though I don't understand what I see, I will trust Him" (Habakkuk 3:17-18). Because many of the answers to our questions about God are unreachable by us at present, we must learn to live by faith.

Timelessness: Habakkuk's first question for God was, "How long, O LORD?" (1:2). It was a question dictated by Habakkuk's impatience over the passing of time. But God is not bound by the constraints of time as we are. God accommodated Habakkuk with His answer, saying that He would do something about the problem of wickedness in Judah during Habakkuk's lifetime. But with regard to Habakkuk's second question—Why would God use wicked Babylon to judge Judah?—God showed Habakkuk His own perspective on time: The future is as good as done in the present. He told Habakkuk to record Babylon's coming judgment and send the report throughout the land—before it happened (2:3). Babylon fell more than sixty years after Habakkuk was given the revelation of its judgment by God, but it did fall. The more we learn to trust God, the less we will be constrained by our earthly understanding of time.

GROWING THROUGH HABAKKUK

Habakkuk was a man with legitimate questions for God, yet he learned to live free from being crippled by his concerns—a worthy goal of the disciple of Christ.

DISCOVERY VERSES

The LORD replied, "Look around at the nations; look and be amazed! For I am doing something in your own day, something you wouldn't believe even if someone told you about it. I am raising up the Babylonians." (HABAKKUK 1:5-6)

Look at the proud! They trust in themselves, and their lives are crooked. But the righteous will live by their faithfulness to God. (HABAKKUK 2:4)

I have heard all about you, LORD. I am filled with awe by Your amazing works. In this time of our deep need, help us again as You did in years gone by. And in Your anger, remember Your mercy. (HABAKKUK 3:2)

Living in Peace: God doesn't mind questions—even difficult, edgy ones like Habakkuk's. In fact, we are told by Paul to do just what Habakkuk did: bring our questions and requests directly to God (Philippians 4:6; see also Hebrews 4:16). When we do, the result will be the same as Habakkuk's: "Then you will experience God's peace, which exceeds anything we can understand" (Philippians 4:7; see Habakkuk 3:17-18). Living in peace is not about having the answers; it is about committing the questions to the One who does.

Living with Strength: Anxiety, worry, and consternation can literally sap one's strength. When David was in turmoil over hidden sin in his life, his "body wasted away" and he "groaned all day long." His strength "evaporated like water in the summer heat" (Psalm 32:3-4). When Habakkuk had concerns, he took them straight to God, got His answers, and then declared: "The Sovereign LORD is my strength! He makes me as surefooted as a deer, able to tread upon the heights" (3:19). Don't ignore Habakkuk's lessons on faith and try to conquer mountains in your own strength; place your trust in God and experience His strength.

HABAKKUK FACTS

Author: Habakkuk (1:1; 3:1). He is mentioned nowhere else in the Old Testament, and virtually nothing is known of his background.

Written to: The people of Judah, the southern kingdom.

Date of writing: There are no specific time references in the book, but a likely date for Habakkuk's writing is during the reign of the wicked King Jehoiakim of Judah, prior to the beginning of the Babylonian invasions of Judah in 605 BC.

Setting: Habakkuk wrote and prophesied in Judah, but his comments arose out of the rising military situation coming from Babylon.

OUTLINE

- **HABAKKUK 1:1-11**—Habakkuk's First Complaint and God's Answer
- **HABAKKUK 1:12–2:20**—Habakkuk's Second Complaint and God's Answer
- **HABAKKUK 3:1-10**—Habakkuk's Prayer of Trust

1:1 Isa 13:1; Nah 1:1

1 This is the message that the prophet Habakkuk received in a vision.

HABAKKUK'S COMPLAINT

1:2 Pss 13:1-4; 22:1-2; Jer 14:9

2 How long, O LORD, must I call for help?
But You do not listen!
"Violence is everywhere!" I cry,
but You do not come to save.

1:3 Ps 55:9-11; Jer 20:8

3 Must I forever see these evil deeds?
Why must I watch all this misery?
Wherever I look,
I see destruction and violence.
I am surrounded by people
who love to argue and fight.

1:4 Pss 22:12; 119:126; Isa 5:20

4 The law has become paralyzed,
and there is no justice in the courts.
The wicked far outnumber the righteous,
so that justice has become perverted.

THE LORD'S REPLY

1:5 Isa 29:9; *Acts 13:41

5 The LORD replied,

"Look around at the nations;
look and be amazed!*
For I am doing something in your own day,
something you wouldn't believe
even if someone told you about it.

1:6 Deut 28:49-50; 2 Kgs 24:2

6 I am raising up the Babylonians,*
a cruel and violent people.
They will march across the world
and conquer other lands.

1:7 Jer 39:5-9

7 They are notorious for their cruelty
and do whatever they like.

1:8 Jer 4:13

8 Their horses are swifter than cheetahs*
and fiercer than wolves at dusk.
Their charioteers charge from far away.
Like eagles, they swoop down to devour their prey.

9 "On they come, all bent on violence.
Their hordes advance like a desert wind,
sweeping captives ahead of them like sand.

1:10 2 Kgs 25:6-7; 2 Chr 36:6; Jer 32:24; 33:4-5; Ezek 26:7-11

10 They scoff at kings and princes
and scorn all their fortresses.

1:5 Greek version reads *Look you mockers; / look and be amazed and die.* Compare Acts 13:41. 1:6 Or *Chaldeans.* 1:8 Or *leopards.*

▸ WORSHIP

1:2 Complaining prayers. Habakkuk complained that God seemed unconcerned about the pervasive wickedness in Judah. "O LORD, how long will this go on?" is a familiar refrain in the Scriptures (Psalm 13; 89:46-51). Such a lament is not mere self-absorbed grumbling, however. Rather, by bringing our questions and disappointments to God, we are seeking Him honestly and passionately. We can imitate Habakkuk's actions because Jesus has given us the privilege to "come boldly to the throne of our gracious God. There we will receive His mercy, and we will find grace to help us when we need it most" (Hebrews 4:16). Pray boldly in Jesus' name! (***See Worship****> OT> Reverence> God shows mercy to those who fear Him,* TopicGuide page A29.)

1:5 Habakkuk's complaints of unresponsiveness lead God to declare that He was doing something very great in Habakkuk's time.

1:8 The invading Babylonian armies would be swift, vicious, and devouring. Fearsome beasts are used elsewhere in Scripture to graphically portray coming judgment (Hosea 13:7-8).

They simply pile ramps of earth
against their walls and capture them!
11 They sweep past like the wind 1:11
and are gone. Jer 4:11-12
But they are deeply guilty,
for their own strength is their god."

HABAKKUK'S SECOND COMPLAINT

12 O LORD my God, my Holy One, You who are eternal— 1:12
surely You do not plan to wipe us out? Deut 32:4, 30-31
O LORD, our Rock, You have sent these Babylonians to correct us,
to punish us for our many sins.
13 But You are pure and cannot stand the sight of evil. 1:13
Will You wink at their treachery? Ps 50:21
Should You be silent while the wicked 1 Pet 1:15-16
swallow up people more righteous than they?
14 Are we only fish to be caught and killed?
Are we only sea creatures that have no leader?
15 Must we be strung up on their hooks 1:15
and caught in their nets while they rejoice and celebrate? Jer 16:16
16 Then they will worship their nets 1:16
and burn incense in front of them. Jer 44:17-18
"These nets are the gods who have made us rich!"
they will claim.
17 Will You let them get away with this forever? 1:17
Will they succeed forever in their heartless conquests? Isa 14:6

2 1 I will climb up to my watchtower 2:1
and stand at my guardpost. Pss 5:3; 85:8
There I will wait to see what the LORD says Isa 21:8
and how He* will answer my complaint.

THE LORD'S SECOND REPLY

2 Then the LORD said to me,

"Write My answer plainly on tablets, 2:2 Deut 27:8 Isa 8:1
so that a runner can carry the correct message to others. Rev 1:19
3 This vision is for a future time. 2:3
It describes the end, and it will be fulfilled. Dan 8:17-19; 9:24-27; 10:1, 14
If it seems slow in coming, wait patiently, *Heb 10:37
for it will surely take place.
It will not be delayed.

2:1 As in Syriac version; Hebrew reads *I*.

▸ HOLINESS

1:13 Truth from a surprising source. How can God use ungodly nations to accomplish His goals? This was Habakkuk's complaint against God. Yet, as Peter declared, this was the same situation with Jesus' crucifixion: "[God's] prearranged plan was carried out when Jesus was betrayed. With the help of lawless Gentiles, you nailed Him to a cross and killed Him" (Acts 2:23). Perhaps a non-Christian in authority over you has been trying to help you—but you won't listen because he is not a Christian. Make it your goal to care less about who is teaching you and more about whether their words are true or not. Listen for God's truth from every source. (***See Holiness***> *Law and Grace*> *Grace*> *True teaching,* TopicGuide page A42.)

1:14-16 Habakkuk reflected on the attitudes and actions of a nation like Babylon using images from fishing. Like a fisherman who draws up helpless fish with a hook or a net, the Babylonians would rejoice over the results of their conquest (for the use of the net as a symbol of judgment, see Ezekiel 32:3). Then, as a fisherman would boast of his own ability, they would "worship their nets" for providing so bountifully, indicating their self-sufficiency and pride.

2:4 Pss 10:4; 49:16-20 Prov 3:6; 16:3 *Rom 1:17 *Gal 3:11 *Heb 10:38

4 "Look at the proud!
They trust in themselves, and their lives are crooked.
But the righteous will live by their faithfulness to God.*
5 Wealth* is treacherous,
and the arrogant are never at rest.
They open their mouths as wide as the grave,*
and like death, they are never satisfied.
In their greed they have gathered up many nations
and swallowed many peoples.

2:6 Isa 14:4-5, 10 Jer 50:13, 34-35 Hab 2:9, 12, 15, 19

6 "But soon their captives will taunt them.
They will mock them, saying,
'What sorrow awaits you thieves!
Now you will get what you deserve!
You've become rich by extortion,
but how much longer can this go on?'

2:7 Prov 29:1

7 Suddenly, your debtors will take action.
They will turn on you and take all you have,
while you stand trembling and helpless.

2:8 Isa 33:1 Zech 2:8-9

8 Because you have plundered many nations;
now all the survivors will plunder you.
You committed murder throughout the countryside
and filled the towns with violence.

2:9 Jer 22:13

9 "What sorrow awaits you who build big houses
with money gained dishonestly!
You believe your wealth will buy security,
putting your family's nest beyond the reach of danger.
10 But by the murders you committed,
you have shamed your name and forfeited your lives.

2:11 Josh 24:27 Luke 19:40

11 The very stones in the walls cry out against you,
and the beams in the ceilings echo the complaint.

2:12 Mic 3:10 Hab 2:9, 15, 19

12 "What sorrow awaits you who build cities
with money gained through murder and corruption!

2:13 Isa 50:11

13 Has not the LORD of Heaven's Armies promised
that the wealth of nations will turn to ashes?
They work so hard,
but all in vain!

2:14 Pss 22:27; 86:9 Isa 11:9 Zech 14:9

14 For as the waters fill the sea,
the earth will be filled with an awareness
of the glory of the LORD.

2:3b-4 Greek version reads *If the vision is delayed, wait patiently, / for it will surely come and not delay. /[4]I will take no pleasure in anyone who turns away. / But the righteous person will live by My faith.* Compare Rom 1:17; Gal 3:11; Heb 10:37-38. 2:5a As in Dead Sea Scroll 1QpHab; other Hebrew manuscripts read *Wine.* 2:5b Hebrew *as Sheol.*

▶ **BIBLE**

2:4 Saved by faith. Have you ever wondered where the New Testament writers got their ideas about justification by faith? Paul said that the gospel message he proclaimed came "by direct revelation from Jesus Christ" (Galatians 1:12)—but later he quoted Habakkuk 2:4 (Galatians 3:11). Jesus had revealed to Paul that no one is justified before God by the law; instead, "the righteous person will live by [God's] faith" (2:4, see textual note). The Old Testament's teaching of justification by faith became Paul's message as well. Commit yourself to the Bible's unified message: People are only declared to be right in God's sight if they have faith. (***See Bible**> Unity> Salvation> Old Testament and New Testament teach salvation by faith,* TopicGuide page A11.)

2:6 The first "woe" of five (translated here as "What sorrow awaits you thieves" was uttered in this taunt. Babylon's cursed state was part of the promise that would be "slow in coming" (2:3), but Habakkuk saw that punishment would ultimately come.

15 "What sorrow awaits you who make your neighbors drunk!
You force your cup on them
so you can gloat over their shameful nakedness.
16 But soon it will be your turn to be disgraced.
Come, drink and be exposed!
Drink from the cup of the LORD's judgment,
and all your glory will be turned to shame.
17 You cut down the forests of Lebanon.
Now you will be cut down.
You destroyed the wild animals,
so now their terror will be yours.
You committed murder throughout the countryside
and filled the towns with violence.

18 "What good is an idol carved by man,
or a cast image that deceives you?
How foolish to trust in your own creation—
a god that can't even talk!
19 What sorrow awaits you who say to wooden idols,
'Wake up and save us!'
To speechless stone images you say,
'Rise up and teach us!'
Can an idol tell you what to do?
They may be overlaid with gold and silver,
but they are lifeless inside.
20 But the LORD is in His holy Temple.
Let all the earth be silent before Him."

2:15 Hos 7:5
2:16 Jer 25:15-16
2:17 Jer 51:35
2:18 Isa 42:17; Jer 2:27-28; 50:2
2:19 1 Kgs 18:26-29; Jer 10:4-5
2:20 Zeph 1:7; Zech 2:13

HABAKKUK'S PRAYER

3 This prayer was sung by the prophet Habakkuk*:
2 I have heard all about You, LORD.
I am filled with awe by Your amazing works.
In this time of our deep need,
help us again as You did in years gone by.
And in Your anger,
remember Your mercy.

3 I see God moving across the deserts from Edom,*
the Holy One coming from Mount Paran.*

3:2 Pss 78:38-39; 85:6; Isa 54:8; Jer 10:7
3:3 Deut 5:24; Pss 48:10; 113:4; 148:13

3:1 Hebrew adds *according to shigionoth*, probably indicating the musical setting for the prayer. 3:3a Hebrew *Teman*.
3:3b Hebrew adds *selah;* also in 3:9, 13. The meaning of this Hebrew term is uncertain; it is probably a musical or literary term.

▸ GOD

2:16 The cup of God's wrath. What did Habakkuk mean by "the cup of the LORD's judgment"? Habakkuk's metaphor imagined God's judgment as an intoxicating wine. God would force His enemies to consume His wrath, and they would stagger under its power. Consider this: When Jesus was intensely praying just prior to the crucifixion, He said, "My Father! If this cup cannot be taken away unless I drink it, Your will be done" (Matthew 26:42). On the cross, "God made Christ, who never sinned, to be the offering for our sin" (2 Corinthians 5:21). Jesus took the cup of judgment you deserve and drank every drop on the cross. When you take the Lord's Supper and drink the cup, remember that this cup signifies the great blessing (Psalm 16:5; Luke 22:20) of being united to Christ, who drank from the cup of wrath offered Him by the Father. (***See God****> Salvation> Son> Removes God's wrath,* TopicGuide page A15.)

2:20 In contrast to the idols of the nations, who cannot do or say anything, Judah's God is alive and enthroned in His holy Temple (Psalm 11:4). The order for the earth to be silent was likely an indication that judgment was coming, as in Zechariah 2:13: "Be silent before the LORD, all humanity, for He is springing into action from His holy dwelling." When God issues His judgments, there is no place for debate (Romans 3:19).

3:1 The remainder of the book is a prayer that is structured like a song. It begins with a designation (the Hebrew adds "according to *shigionoth*"; see NLT textual note), which likely refers to some form of musical meter. The section ends with instructions about the performance of the song (3:19), and the term *selah* appears three times in the text (see NLT textual note at 3:3). The way these ancient songs were to be performed is not altogether clear, but the markings are common features within ancient Hebrew songs.

His brilliant splendor fills the heavens,
and the earth is filled with His praise.

3:4 Job 26:14 Pss 18:12; 104:1

4 His coming is as brilliant as the sunrise.
Rays of light flash from His hands,
where His awesome power is hidden.

3:5 Exod 12:29-30 Deut 32:24-25

5 Pestilence marches before Him;
plague follows close behind.
6 When He stops, the earth shakes.
When He looks, the nations tremble.
He shatters the everlasting mountains
and levels the eternal hills.
He is the Eternal One!

3:7 Exod 15:14

7 I see the people of Cushan in distress,
and the nation of Midian trembling in terror.

3:8 Exod 7:19-20

8 Was it in anger, LORD, that You struck the rivers
and parted the sea?
Were You displeased with them?
No, You were sending your chariots of salvation!
9 You brandished Your bow
and Your quiver of arrows.
You split open the earth with flowing rivers.

3:10 Ps 93:3

10 The mountains watched and trembled.
Onward swept the raging waters.
The mighty deep cried out,
lifting its hands to the LORD.
11 The sun and moon stood still in the sky
as Your brilliant arrows flew
and Your glittering spear flashed.

3:12 Isa 41:15

12 You marched across the land in anger
and trampled the nations in Your fury.

3:13 Ps 110:6

13 You went out to rescue Your chosen people,
to save Your anointed ones.
You crushed the heads of the wicked
and stripped their bones from head to toe.

3:14 Judg 7:22 Dan 11:40

14 With his own weapons,
You destroyed the chief of those
who rushed out like a whirlwind,
thinking Israel would be easy prey.

3:15 Hab 3:8

15 You trampled the sea with Your horses,
and the mighty waters piled high.
16 I trembled inside when I heard this;
my lips quivered with fear.

3:6-11 The reader is alerted to the shift from more literal to more artistic language when mountains are pictured as watching and water is pictured as "lifting its hands" (3:10). Such descriptions were meant to stir the imagination, not to be scientific descriptions. The book of Revelation is also packed with songs and poetic images taken from the prophetic writings of the Old Testament (for instance, Revelation 6:12-14; 14:16).

▶ WORSHIP

3:16 Falling down. Have you ever wondered what it might be like to directly encounter God? The Scriptures record a number of occasions in which people have been given glimpses of God's glory (Daniel 10:8-9; Isaiah 6:5; Ezekiel 1:28–2:2; 3:15). Habakkuk was praying while reflecting on God's past dealings and got caught up in a revelation of His majesty. His strength gave way and he trembled in fear. His knees refused to hold him upright. It is no wonder that John tells us, "I fell at His feet as if I were dead" when he saw Jesus in just a portion of His glory (Revelation 1:17). Don't be afraid to fall down in worship before this strength-sapping God and cry "Holy, holy, holy!" (Revelation 4:8). Know that one day, you will directly encounter God, and He will give you the strength to stand in His presence (Colossians 1:22). (***See Worship****> OT> Place> Temple> The Lord's glory comes down,* TopicGuide page A27.)

My legs gave way beneath me,*
and I shook in terror.
I will wait quietly for the coming day
when disaster will strike the people who invade us.
17 Even though the fig trees have no blossoms,
and there are no grapes on the vines;
even though the olive crop fails,
and the fields lie empty and barren;
even though the flocks die in the fields,
and the cattle barns are empty,
18 yet I will rejoice in the LORD!
I will be joyful in the God of my salvation!
19 The Sovereign LORD is my strength!
He makes me as surefooted as a deer,*
able to tread upon the heights.

(For the choir director: This prayer is to be accompanied by stringed instruments.)

3:17 Jer 5:17 Joel 1:10-12 Amos 4:9

3:18 Ps 97:12 Isa 12:2 Luke 1:47 Phil 4:4

3:19 Pss 18:13; 46:1-5

3:16 Hebrew *Decay entered my bones.* 3:19 Or *He gives me the speed of a deer.*

▸ GOD

3:19 No more questions. Life is mysterious. We often have more questions than answers. As if that weren't enough, God is mysterious—Psalm 145:3 says, "No one can measure his greatness." Habakkuk didn't get everything figured out, but he comprehended that the Lord rules over every situation. He can raise up a foreign army to discipline His own people. So what did Habakkuk do? He considered God's greatness and broke forth in praise. You can know this with certainty: "God causes everything to work together for the good of those who love God" (Romans 8:28). "Everything" includes the confusing situations in your life. You know enough to praise your mysterious God in every circumstance with humility and awe! (***See God****> God's Names> Holy Spirit> Revealer,* TopicGuide page A19.)

MY RESPONSE TO GOD

From Complaints to Confidence

HABAKKUK 3:16-19

The prophet Habakkuk complained to God about the injustice he witnessed in Judah. When God told Habakkuk that He was going to send the Babylonian army to punish Judah, Habakkuk trembled in fear. The Babylonians were more evil than the people of Judah; how could a just God use the evil Babylonians to punish His people?

Despite the imminent attack, Habakkuk found confidence in God. His questioning turned into a statement of faith. Habakkuk's emotions moved from anxiety to peaceful expectation (3:16) as he considered God's sovereign oversight of all events. As long as God was in control, Habakkuk could wait patiently for Him to solve the problem of injustice. And even when crops failed and flocks of animals died (3:17), Habakkuk would still worship God and rejoiced in His salvation (3:18). Habakkuk lived by faith, trusting in God's promise of salvation to those who believe.

Like Habakkuk, we witness things in our society that don't seem right and wonder why God doesn't just step in and correct injustice now. We can follow Habakkuk's example of trusting that God is in control and believing that He will solve injustice as He sees fit.

ZEPHANIAH

PURPOSE

To announce and explain the coming Day of the Lord to the people of God.

When will God act? Why does He take so long to bless, to judge, to heal, and to change us? He's God—so why should He wait for a certain "Day of the Lord" to fix things? Questions like these have always puzzled God's people, but the principles in Zephaniah give us some answers.

Zephaniah prophesied during the reign of the godly King Josiah of Judah (640–609 BC). Josiah introduced a number of reforms in Judah, but the nation had been led for fifty-five years by two of its most evil kings, Manasseh and Amon, and the people had followed their wickedness. As a result, Zephaniah brought the dual message of the prophets: judgment followed by salvation and restoration.

The focus of Zephaniah's message was the coming Day of the Lord, when Judah and the wicked nations that surrounded it would be judged. After that judgment, however, Judah would be restored to favor and blessing from the Lord. Just as some aspects of the judgment could be affected by repentance (2:1-3), some aspects of the restoration could be mitigated by faithlessness (Leviticus 26; Deuteronomy 28). But in the end, God would make certain that His holy people and His holy places were saved from their enemies and their own sin (Zephaniah 3:9-20).

DISCOVER GOD IN ZEPHANIAH

Zephaniah reveals two of the most profound attributes of God: His supremacy and His sovereign decree.

Supreme: The most profound and yet most simple statement in Scripture about God is one He made about Himself. God introduced Himself to Moses by saying, " 'I AM' " (Exodus 3:14). In the Ten Commandments He expanded that statement: "I am the LORD your God. . . . You must not have any other god but Me' " (Exodus 20:2-3). Centuries later, the Son of God used the phrase "I am" to describe Himself on a number of occasions: "'I am the bread of life'" (John 6:35); "'the light of the world'" (John 8:12); "'the gate'" (John 10:7); "'the good shepherd'" (John 10:11); "'the resurrection and the life'" (John 11:25); "'the way, the truth, and the life'" (John 14:6); "'the true grapevine'" (John 15:1). So when personified Nineveh boasted, "I am, and beside me there is none" (Zephaniah 2:15, literally translated), this was a direct challenge to the supremacy of the God of Israel, whose throne was in Jerusalem. Because of its arrogance, Nineveh became "an utter ruin, a haven for wild animals" (Zephaniah 2:15). God *is*—and He will allow no others to take His place.

Sovereign Decree: God has a plan. In spite of sin among the nations, sin among His people, sin from the political or religious leadership—God would accomplish His goals of rescuing

His people and defeating His enemies (Zephaniah 3:9-20). Within that overall plan, there is freedom to either heed or ignore His will. But that does not impact God's overall plan (Matthew 26:39-42). But in Zephaniah, the Day of the Lord does not depend on anything but God's promises and God's eternal plan (Deuteronomy 29:29).

GROWING THROUGH ZEPHANIAH

A warning and a promise from Zephaniah become themes for the follower of Christ:

DISCOVERY VERSES

Stand in silence in the presence of the Sovereign LORD, for the awesome day of the LORD's judgment is near. (ZEPHANIAH 1:7)

Seek the LORD, all who are humble, and follow His commands. Seek to do what is right and to live humbly. Perhaps even yet the LORD will protect you—protect you from His anger on that day of destruction. (ZEPHANIAH 2:3)

For the LORD your God is living among you. He is a mighty savior. He will take delight in you with gladness. With His love, He will calm all your fears. He will rejoice over you with joyful songs. (ZEPHANIAH 3:17)

Complacency: Some things in life move slowly: time, growth, decay—and complacency. Part of Zephaniah's warning to Jerusalem was to "those who sit complacent in their sins. They think the LORD will do nothing to them" (1:12). The apostle Peter dealt with people who were equally indifferent about their sin. They thought God would never bother to deal with them (2 Peter 3:3-4). Christians today should not think they are immune to the subtle encroachment of complacency. God is clear that He will discipline His people when they sin (1 Corinthians 6:9; Galatians 6:7; James 1:15), just as He warned the people of Judah that they would be chastised for their sin.

Right Living: Just as there is loving reconciliation between a parent and a child who has been disciplined, so Zephaniah promised restoration to Judah (Zephaniah 3:14, 20). The result of all discipline is "a peaceful harvest of right living for those who are trained in this way" (Hebrews 12:11). The chastening of the Lord leads to right living, but it is far better to live right in the first place and avoid His discipline altogether.

ZEPHANIAH FACTS

Author: Zephaniah (1:1). Little is known of Zephaniah except that he was a fourth-generation descendant of the godly king Hezekiah. His royal lineage probably indicates a high social standing in Jerusalem.

Written to: The leaders and people of Judah.

Date of writing: Zephaniah prophesied during the reign of Josiah (1:1); specifically, he prophesied before Josiah's reforms, which narrows the window even more to between 640–630 BC.

Setting: Jerusalem.

OUTLINE

- **ZEPHANIAH 1:1-18**—God Promises to Send Judgment
- **ZEPHANIAH 2:1-3**—God Offers Hope for Restoration
- **ZEPHANIAH 2:4–3:8**—God Promises to Send Judgment
- **ZEPHANIAH 3:9-20**—God Offers Hope for Restoration

1:1 2 Kgs 22:1–23:28 2 Chr 34:1–35:26

1 The LORD gave this message to Zephaniah when Josiah son of Amon was king of Judah. Zephaniah was the son of Cushi, son of Gedaliah, son of Amariah, son of Hezekiah.

COMING JUDGMENT AGAINST JUDAH

1:2 Isa 6:11
2 "I will sweep away everything
from the face of the earth," says the LORD.
1:3 Isa 6:11-12 Jer 4:25; 9:10
3 "I will sweep away people and animals alike.
I will sweep away the birds of the sky and the fish
in the sea.
I will reduce the wicked to heaps of rubble,*
and I will wipe humanity from the face of the earth,"
says the LORD.
1:4 2 Kgs 23:4-7
4 "I will crush Judah and Jerusalem with My fist
and destroy every last trace of their Baal worship.
I will put an end to all the idolatrous priests,
so that even the memory of them will disappear.
1:5 1 Kgs 11:33
5 For they go up to their roofs
and bow down to the sun, moon, and stars.
They claim to follow the LORD,
but then they worship Molech,* too.
1:6 Isa 1:4; 9:13
6 And I will destroy those who used to worship Me
but now no longer do.
They no longer ask for the LORD's guidance
or seek My blessings."

1:7 Isa 34:6 Hab 2:20 Zech 2:13
7 Stand in silence in the presence of the Sovereign LORD,
for the awesome day of the LORD's judgment is near.
The LORD has prepared His people for a great slaughter
and has chosen their executioners.*
1:8 Isa 24:21-23
8 "On that day of judgment,"
says the LORD,
"I will punish the leaders and princes of Judah
and all those following pagan customs.
1:9 Amos 3:10
9 Yes, I will punish those who participate in pagan worship ceremonies,
and those who fill their masters' houses with violence
and deceit.

1:3 The meaning of the Hebrew is uncertain. 1:5 Hebrew *Malcam,* a variant spelling of Molech; or it could possibly mean *their king.* 1:7 Hebrew *has prepared a sacrifice and sanctified His guests.*

1:1 A revival took place in Judah after the Book of the Law was recovered from the Temple. When King Josiah realized that Judah was living in disobedience to God's law, he implemented sweeping reforms by cutting down, removing, and destroying all idolatrous worship (2 Kings 22:1–23:14).

1:2-3 God speaks directly to His audience through the prophet Zephaniah. He warns the entire world that His judgment is coming, and it will include both humans and animals. This language echoes the ancient story of the Flood in Genesis (Genesis 6:7).

▸ GOD

1:5 Knowing the future. Is there anything wrong with dabbling in astrology? People regularly turn to other religions and practices, contrary to Scripture, in order to find meaning and direction for their lives. While it is not necessarily sinful to wonder about what lies ahead for us, Scripture makes it clear that we should never consult anyone but the Lord and His Word for special insight into the future (Deuteronomy 4:19; 17:2-5; Isaiah 47:10-14). We must encourage those involved in astrology to look beyond the stars and to see the Creator of the stars, for He alone gives true illumination for today and for what lies ahead (Psalm 27:1). (***See God***> *God's Attributes> Sovereign> God controls time and seasons,* TopicGuide page A18.)

1:7 The "day of the LORD's judgment," also referred to as "that day," is a dominant theme in the prophetic books of the Bible (Isaiah 2:12; Jeremiah 25:33; Lamentations 1:12; Ezekiel 30:3; Joel 1:15; Amos 5:18; Obadiah 1:15). It refers to the time when God's final judgment will be poured out upon the nations for their unbelief and wicked practices (Zephaniah 1:1-18).

10 "On that day," says the LORD,
"a cry of alarm will come from the Fish Gate
and echo throughout the New Quarter of the city.*
And a great crash will sound from the hills.
11 Wail in sorrow, all you who live in the market area,
for all the merchants and traders will be destroyed.

12 "I will search with lanterns in Jerusalem's darkest corners
to punish those who sit complacent in their sins.
They think the LORD will do nothing to them,
either good or bad.
13 So their property will be plundered,
their homes will be ransacked.
They will build new homes
but never live in them.
They will plant vineyards
but never drink wine from them.

14 "That terrible day of the LORD is near.
Swiftly it comes—
a day of bitter tears,
a day when even strong men will cry out.
15 It will be a day when the LORD's anger is poured out—
a day of terrible distress and anguish,
a day of ruin and desolation,
a day of darkness and gloom,
a day of clouds and blackness,
16 a day of trumpet calls and battle cries.
Down go the walled cities
and the strongest battlements!

17 "Because you have sinned against the LORD,
I will make you grope around like the blind.
Your blood will be poured into the dust,
and your bodies will lie rotting on the ground."
18 Your silver and gold will not save you
on that day of the LORD's anger.
For the whole land will be devoured
by the fire of His jealousy.
He will make a terrifying end
of all the people on earth.*

1:10 2 Chr 33:14 Neh 3:3; 12:39
1:12 Jer 16:16-17 Amos 6:1
1:13 Deut 28:30 Amos 5:11
1:14 Ezek 7:16-18
1:15 Isa 22:5 Joel 2:2
1:16 Isa 2:12-15 Jer 4:19
1:17 Deut 28:28-29 Pss 79:3; 83:10 Isa 59:10 Jer 8:2; 9:22
1:18 Zeph 3:8

A CALL TO REPENTANCE

2 1 Gather together—yes, gather together,
you shameless nation.

2:1 2 Chr 20:4 Jer 3:3; 6:15 Joel 1:14

1:10 Or *the Second Quarter,* a newer section of Jerusalem. Hebrew reads *the Mishneh.* 1:18 Or *the people living in the land.*

1:10-12 The Lord is pictured here as searching through various sections of the city in order to execute His judgment. God's judgment would affect all sectors of society, both inside Jerusalem and in the surrounding area.

▸ GOD
1:12 Getting away with it. Many people incorrectly perceive God as indifferent toward the things of the world. With this kind of thinking, He becomes, as in the day of Zephaniah, a God who is feeble. Don't think you can sin and get away with it! God's apparent inactivity among the wicked should not be mistaken as a sign that He is uninterested or powerless. The Bible tells us that God delays judgment upon unbelievers because He is patient and merciful (2 Peter 3:9). Warn your unbelieving friends and relatives of God's impending judgment, and encourage them to repent of their sins and ask for His forgiveness. (***See God**> God's Attributes> Merciful> God is merciful to sinners,* TopicGuide page A17.)

2:2 Zeph 1:18

2 Gather before judgment begins,
before your time to repent is blown away like chaff.
Act now, before the fierce fury of the LORD falls
and the terrible day of the LORD's anger begins.

2:3 Ps 57:1 Amos 5:6, 14-15

3 Seek the LORD, all who are humble,
and follow His commands.
Seek to do what is right
and to live humbly.
Perhaps even yet the LORD will protect you—
protect you from His anger on that day of destruction.

JUDGMENT AGAINST PHILISTIA

2:4 Amos 1:6-8 Zech 9:5

4 Gaza and Ashkelon will be abandoned,
Ashdod and Ekron torn down.

2:5 Isa 14:29, 31

5 And what sorrow awaits you Philistines*
who live along the coast and in the land of Canaan,
for this judgment is against you, too!
The LORD will destroy you
until not one of you is left.
6 The Philistine coast will become a wilderness pasture,
a place of shepherd camps
and enclosures for sheep and goats.

2:7 Isa 32:14 Zeph 3:20

7 The remnant of the tribe of Judah will pasture there.
They will rest at night in the abandoned houses in Ashkelon.
For the LORD their God will visit His people in kindness
and restore their prosperity again.

JUDGMENT AGAINST MOAB AND AMMON

2:8 Ezek 25:3, 8

8 "I have heard the taunts of the Moabites
and the insults of the Ammonites,
mocking My people
and invading their borders.

2:9 Isa 11:14; 15:1-9

9 Now, as surely as I live,"
says the LORD of Heaven's Armies, the God of Israel,
"Moab and Ammon will be destroyed—
destroyed as completely as Sodom and Gomorrah.
Their land will become a place of stinging nettles,
salt pits, and eternal desolation.

2:5 Hebrew *Kerethites.*

2:3 The Lord had previously condemned His people for not seeking Him (Zephaniah 1:6), but here He offers mercy to those who would repent of their sin and follow His commands. "Perhaps" refers to an imminent threat of invasion. God's promise of forgiveness and eternal salvation is certain (Isaiah 55:6-7; Romans 10:9).

2:4-5 The first in a series of four oracles against foreign nations was directed to the coastland region of Philistia. The other oracles were directed at Moab and Ammon (2:8-9), Ethiopia and Cush (2:12), and Assyria (2:13). God threatened to eliminate all of them for their unbelief.

▸ ADOPTION
2:7 Loss and gain. God's judgment against the Philistines was that their enemies, the Judeans, would walk through the formerly impregnable city gates of their capital and live there in peace. Their shame would become Judah's gain. All believers should be encouraged to know that the Lord cares for us and promises to restore all that we have lost or suffered on account of our Christian witness (Matthew 5:11-12). Some of this restoration may come from unexpected sources—even unbelievers—for God owns everything (Psalm 50:10). God may see fit to wait and reward those who have sacrificed much for His kingdom in heaven (1 Corinthians 3:14). We can take comfort in God's promise to reward those who seek Him (Hebrews 11:6). Do not fear sacrifice for God, for when done in faith, it is an investment in your spiritual riches. (***See Adoption***> *In Heaven*> *Future full of spiritual riches,* TopicGuide page A38.)

The remnant of My people will plunder them
and take their land."

10 They will receive the wages of their pride,
for they have scoffed at the people of the LORD of Heaven's Armies.
11 The LORD will terrify them
as He destroys all the gods in the land.
Then nations around the world will worship the LORD,
each in their own land.

2:10 Isa 16:6-10; Jer 48:28-31; Zeph 2:8
2:11 Joel 2:11; Zeph 1:4; 3:4

JUDGMENT AGAINST ETHIOPIA AND ASSYRIA

12 "You Ethiopians* will also be slaughtered
by my sword," says the LORD.

2:12 Isa 20:3-4

13 And the LORD will strike the lands of the north with His fist,
destroying the land of Assyria.
He will make its great capital, Nineveh, a desolate wasteland,
parched like a desert.
14 The proud city will become a pasture for flocks and herds,
and all sorts of wild animals will settle there.
The desert owl and screech owl will roost on its ruined columns,
their calls echoing through the gaping windows.
Rubble will block all the doorways,
and the cedar paneling will be exposed to the weather.
15 This is the boisterous city,
once so secure.
"I am the greatest!" it boasted.
"No other city can compare with me!"
But now, look how it has become an utter ruin,
a haven for wild animals.
Everyone passing by will laugh in derision
and shake a defiant fist.

2:13 Nah 3:7
2:14 Isa 34:11
2:15 1 Kgs 9:7-8; Isa 22:2-7; 32:14; 47:8

JERUSALEM'S REBELLION AND REDEMPTION

3 1 What sorrow awaits rebellious, polluted Jerusalem,
the city of violence and crime!
2 No one can tell it anything;
it refuses all correction.
It does not trust in the LORD
or draw near to its God.
3 Its leaders are like roaring lions
hunting for their victims.
Its judges are like ravenous wolves at evening time,
who by dawn have left no trace of their prey.
4 Its prophets are arrogant liars seeking their own gain.
Its priests defile the Temple by disobeying God's instructions.
5 But the LORD is still there in the city,
and He does no wrong.

3:1 Jer 6:6
3:2 Ps 78:22; Jer 5:3
3:3 Ezek 22:6-12
3:4 Ezek 22:26; Mal 2:7-9
3:5 Jer 3:3

2:12 Hebrew *Cushites.*

3:2 Jerusalem's sin was more scandalous than that of the other nations because God had revealed His will to the city in special ways.

3:6-7 God summarized His case against Jerusalem. God reminded Jerusalem how He had debilitated other enemies (Amos 2:9; Micah 6:5). He had called His people to worship and

Day by day He hands down justice,
and He does not fail.
But the wicked know no shame.

3:6 Zeph 2:5
[6] "I have wiped out many nations,
devastating their fortress walls and towers.
Their streets are now deserted;
their cities lie in silent ruin.
There are no survivors—
none at all.

3:7 Hos 9:9
[7] I thought, 'surely they will have reverence for Me now!
Surely they will listen to My warnings.
Then I won't need to strike again,
destroying their homes.'
But no, they get up early
to continue their evil deeds.

3:8 Ps 27:14 Ezek 38:14-23 Zeph 1:18
[8] Therefore, be patient," says the LORD.
"Soon I will stand and accuse these evil nations.
For I have decided to gather the kingdoms of the earth
and pour out My fiercest anger and fury on them.
All the earth will be devoured
by the fire of My jealousy.

3:9 Ps 22:27
[9] "Then I will purify the speech of all people,
so that everyone can worship the LORD together.

3:10 Ps 68:31 Isa 60:7
[10] My scattered people who live beyond the rivers
of Ethiopia*
will come to present their offerings.

3:11 Isa 11:9
[11] On that day you will no longer need to be ashamed,
for you will no longer be rebels against Me.
I will remove all proud and arrogant people from
among you.
There will be no more haughtiness on My holy mountain.

3:12 Nah 1:7
[12] Those who are left will be the lowly and humble,
for it is they who trust in the name of the LORD.

3:13 Hos 2:18 Mic 4:7 Rev 14:5
[13] The remnant of Israel will do no wrong;
they will never tell lies or deceive one another.
They will eat and sleep in safety,
and no one will make them afraid."

[14] Sing, O daughter of Zion;
shout aloud, O Israel!
Be glad and rejoice with all your heart,
O daughter of Jerusalem!

3:15 Isa 33:22 Ezek 37:26-28 Zech 8:3
[15] For the LORD will remove His hand of judgment
and will disperse the armies of your enemy.
And the LORD Himself, the King of Israel,
will live among you!

3:10 Hebrew *Cush.*

revere Him and obey His instructions so that He would not have to punish them. But the people of Jerusalem failed to heed the Lord's instructions.

3:13 The Babylonians would besiege and capture Jerusalem, but God promised to return the faithful remnant to their land (2 Kings 25:27-30; Lamentations 4:22; Micah 4:10).

At last your troubles will be over,
and you will never again fear disaster.
16 On that day the announcement to Jerusalem will be,
"Cheer up, Zion! Don't be afraid!
17 For the LORD your God is living among you.
He is a mighty savior.
He will take delight in you with gladness.
With His love, He will calm all your fears.*
He will rejoice over you with joyful songs."

18 "I will gather you who mourn for the appointed festivals;
you will be disgraced no more.*
19 And I will deal severely with all who have oppressed you.
I will save the weak and helpless ones;
I will bring together
those who were chased away.
I will give glory and fame to My former exiles,
wherever they have been mocked and shamed.
20 On that day I will gather you together
and bring you home again.
I will give you a good name, a name of distinction,
among all the nations of the earth,
as I restore your fortunes before their very eyes.
I, the LORD, have spoken!"

3:16 Isa 35:3-4 Heb 12:12-13
3:17 Isa 62:5; 63:1
3:19 Isa 60:14 Ezek 34:16
3:20 Isa 56:5; 66:22 Ezek 37:12 Zeph 2:7

3:17 Or *He will be silent in His love.* Greek and Syriac versions read *He will renew you with His love.* 3:18 The meaning of the Hebrew for this verse is uncertain.

▸ HOLINESS

3:16-17 Delighted, not indifferent. God is not neutral in His dealings towards you. Don't picture God as impersonally weighing evidence for or against you. Nor should you see Him with lighting bolts in His hands ready to zap you when you sin. The Bible is full of examples of God blessing His people because of His great delight in them (Numbers 14:8; Deuteronomy 30:9; Psalm 147:11; Isaiah 65:19; Jeremiah 32:41). Cheer up! Yes, life can be terribly difficult, but what is a brief time of suffering here compared to an eternity with God who "rejoices over you with joyful songs"? God truly loves you and looks forward to the day when He will lavish you with every spiritual blessing (Ephesians 1:3). Set your mind on the day when you will fully delight in God and He will fully delight in you. (***See Holiness**> Submission> Delighting in God> Gladness in God,* TopicGuide page A40.)

HAGGAI

PURPOSE

To call on God's people to make the Temple their top priority and finish the rebuilding. Haggai declared that they could not expect God's blessing without making Him their top priority.

Procrastination. Lethargy. Apathy. Don't we all face temptations like these? The Jews who were allowed to return from Babylon to Jerusalem were no different.

When King Cyrus of Persia released fifty thousand Jews to return from exile to Jerusalem, the foundation for the Temple was completed within two years. Then some of their neighbors began to oppose the rebuilding project, fearing the reestablishment of a strong Jewish state. Intimidated, distracted, and apathetic toward the task, the people stopped work on God's house and began attending to their own houses and affairs. A prophet named Haggai (along with Zechariah) was called by God to spur the people to action once again. The second Temple was finally dedicated twenty years after construction had begun (Ezra 6:15-18).

DISCOVER GOD IN HAGGAI

Haggai pointed out important aspects of God's character that should make an impact on the life of His people:

God of Cause and Effect: If there was a "formula" in the Old Testament for maintaining a relationship with God, it was this: "If you will . . . then I will. . . ." The Ten Commandments constituted the core of the moral and spiritual law of Israel. God basically said, *"If* you keep these commandments, *then* I will bless you. You will be blessed and will be a blessing to others." This was cause and effect (obedience and blessing) theology (see Deuteronomy 28). The generation returning from captivity had to relearn this lesson. Twice in chapter 1, Haggai tells the people to "Look at what's happening to you!" (1:5, 7). Things weren't going very well because the people were ignoring God (see Haggai 1:6-11). Later, Jesus Christ taught His own disciples: "But *if* you remain in Me . . . [*then*] you may ask for anything you want, and it will be granted!" (John 15:7). Resistance to the idea of cause and effect with God dissolves when we realize how quickly obedience brings His blessing.

Grace: Except for laying the foundation of the second Temple, the returned exiles from Babylon had lived self-centered lives. This was evidenced by the poor harvests during those days (Haggai 2:15-17). The harvest in Israel was one of the chief manifestations of God's blessing, which was dependent upon the people's faithfulness (see Isaiah 5). Yet even then, God showed His grace to His people. Because of their response to the message of Haggai, God said, "From this day onward I will bless you" (2:19). When God determines to bless His people, He will not be thwarted.

GROWING THROUGH HAGGAI

The Jews who returned struggled with faithfulness, making them living lessons for disciples of Jesus:

Priorities: The people in Jerusalem offered a weak rationale for their failure to complete the Temple: "The time has not yet come" (Haggai 1:2). God's reply through Haggai was incisive: "Why are you living in luxurious houses while My house lies in ruins?" (1:4). The simple fact was that the people had put a higher priority on what was easier. Building a house for God meant sacrifice, opposition from pagan neighbors, and hard work. Their priorities were out of line, and the lack of blessings in their lives showed it.

Faith that Works: The apostle James is most famous in the Bible for insisting on a lively faith that gives birth to good deeds (James 2:14, 18, 20-26). Haggai was a man of true faith, so he could say, "Be strong. . . . Be strong. . . . Be strong. . . . And now get to work" (Haggai 2:4). If being "strong" is about passionate belief, then "work" must be deeds. The Temple was not going to get built by faith alone, and neither would it be built appropriately by deeds alone. Our sanctification is about maintaining an intimate relationship with God that empowers the good works that naturally flow from a passionate faith.

Eliminate the Yeast: Haggai took the priests through a refresher course in the rules of contact: If a consecrated item touches another item, the second item does not become consecrated. But if an unclean, defiled item touches another item the second item becomes defiled. Because the Jews were being disobedient and unfaithful, they were defiling everything they touched (Haggai 2:10-14). Sin is like a little yeast that spreads through the whole batch of dough: It takes only one wrong person in a group to infect all the others (see Galatians 5:9).

DISCOVERY VERSES

Then the LORD sent this message through the prophet Haggai: "Why are you living in luxurious houses while My house lies in ruins?"

(HAGGAI 1:3-4)

But now the LORD says: Be strong, Zerubbabel. Be strong, Jeshua son of Jehozadak, the high priest. Be strong, all you people still left in the land. And now get to work, for I am with you, says the LORD of Heaven's Armies.

(HAGGAI 2:4-5)

HAGGAI FACTS

Author: Haggai (1:1). He is not mentioned in the Old Testament except in this book (nine times) and twice in Ezra (5:1; 6:14). Haggai returned from Babylon with the group led by Zerubbabel in 538 BC. He might have been taken to Babylon as a child in the deportation of 586 BC. Then it is possible that he remembered the glory of Solomon's Temple (2:3). If that were the case, he would have been sixty to eighty years old at the time of his ministry.

Written to: Haggai's prophecy is consistently addressed to Zerubbabel and Jeshua (1:1), as well as to the remnant of the returned exiles (1:12, 14; 2:2)

Date of writing: 520 BC (1:1).

Setting: Jerusalem.

OUTLINE

- **HAGGAI 1:1-15**—God Calls His People to Rebuild the Temple
- **HAGGAI 2:1-9**—God Promises a More Glorious Temple
- **HAGGAI 2:10-19**—God Promises Blessings for His Faithful People
- **HAGGAI 2:20-23**—God Promises Victory over His Enemies

A CALL TO REBUILD THE TEMPLE

1 On August 29* of the second year of King Darius's reign, the LORD gave a message
through the prophet Haggai to Zerubbabel son of Shealtiel, governor of Judah, and
to Jeshua* son of Jehozadak, the high priest.
2"This is what the LORD of Heaven's Armies says: The people are saying, 'The time has
not yet come to rebuild the house of the LORD.'"
3Then the LORD sent this message through the prophet Haggai: 4"Why are you living in
luxurious houses while My house lies in ruins? 5This is what the LORD of Heaven's Armies
says: Look at what's happening to you! 6You have planted much but harvest little. You eat
but are not satisfied. You drink but are still thirsty. You put on clothes but cannot keep
warm. Your wages disappear as though you were putting them in pockets filled with
holes!
7"This is what the LORD of Heaven's Armies says: Look at what's happening to you!
8Now go up into the hills, bring down timber, and rebuild My house. Then I will take plea-
sure in it and be honored, says the LORD. 9You hoped for rich harvests, but they were poor.
And when you brought your harvest home, I blew it away. Why? Because My house lies in
ruins, says the LORD of Heaven's Armies, while all of you are busy building your own fine
houses. 10It's because of you that the heavens withhold the dew and the earth produces
no crops. 11I have called for a drought on your fields and hills—a drought to wither the
grain and grapes and olive trees and all your other crops, a drought to starve you and your
livestock and to ruin everything you have worked so hard to get."

OBEDIENCE TO GOD'S CALL

12Then Zerubbabel son of Shealtiel, and Jeshua son of Jehozadak, the high priest, and the
whole remnant of God's people began to obey the message from the LORD their God.
When they heard the words of the prophet Haggai, whom the LORD their God had sent, the
people feared the LORD. 13Then Haggai, the LORD's messenger, gave the people this mes-
sage from the LORD: "I am with you, says the LORD!"
14So the LORD sparked the enthusiasm of Zerubbabel son of Shealtiel, governor of Ju-
dah, and the enthusiasm of Jeshua son of Jehozadak, the high priest, and the enthusiasm
of the whole remnant of God's people. They began to work on the house of their God, the
LORD of Heaven's Armies, 15on September 21* of the second year of King Darius's reign.

1:1 Ezra 2:2; 3:8; 5:1-2; 6:6-14; Zech 6:11
1:4 Hag 1:9
1:6 Hag 1:9; 2:16
1:8 Ezra 3:7-13; Ps 132:13-14; Hag 2:7, 9
1:9 Isa 40:7; Hag 1:4
1:10 Deut 28:24; 1 Kgs 8:35-36; 17:1; Joel 1:18-20
1:11 Deut 28:22-24
1:12 Ps 112:1; Isa 50:10; Hag 1:1
1:13 Mal 2:7; 3:1
1:14-15 Ezra 5:2; Neh 4:6; Hag 1:1

1:1a Hebrew *On the first day of the sixth month,* of the ancient Hebrew lunar calendar. A number of dates in Haggai can be cross-checked with dates in surviving Persian records and related accurately to our modern calendar. This event occurred on August 29, 520 B.C. 1:1b Hebrew *Joshua,* a variant spelling of Jeshua; also in 1:12, 14. 1:15 Hebrew *on the twenty-fourth day of the sixth month,* of the ancient Hebrew lunar calendar. This event occurred on September 21, 520 B.C.; also see note on 1:1a.

▶ CHURCH

1:2 Building the church community. Since God is not calling you to dedicate your life to rebuilding a physical building in Jerusalem, should you just ignore the entire book of Haggai? Of course not; a closer reading reveals that we actually have the same task as Haggai. First, we must understand that rebuilding the Temple was primary on God's agenda at that point in history because the structure was the only acceptable place to offer sacrifices and worship to God, and represented God's presence on the earth. However, when Jesus Christ came, He fulfilled the purposes of the Temple. The old rituals were "never able to provide perfect cleansing for those who came to worship"; but Jesus forgave our sins, leaving "no need to offer any more sacrifices" (Hebrews 10:1, 18). Whereas the Old Testament saint would cry out, "I love your sanctuary, LORD, the place where Your glorious presence dwells" (Psalm 26:8), the New Testament experience is that "we are carefully joined together in Him." (see Ephesians 2:21-22). In principle, we should labor for the building up of the body of Christ just as the saints in the time of Haggai worked to build up the Temple. For God's glory, build up your church. (***See Church**> Mission> Nurture> Fostering Community,* TopicGuide page A49.)

1:4 The true priorities of the people of Haggai's day were revealed by the grandness of their homes and the sad state of the Temple.

1:14 The renewed enthusiasm mentioned here came from the Holy Spirit (Haggai 2:5; Zechariah 4:6).

1:15 After God gave His message to Haggai, just over three weeks lapsed before the Judeans began to rebuild the Temple. It is likely that this amount of time was needed to arrange for materials and a labor force.

THE NEW TEMPLE'S DIMINISHED SPLENDOR

2 Then on October 17 of that same year,* the LORD sent another message through the
prophet Haggai. 2 “Say this to Zerubbabel son of Shealtiel, governor of Judah, and to
Jeshua* son of Jehozadak, the high priest, and to the remnant of God's people there in the
land: 3 ‘Does anyone remember this house—this Temple—in its former splendor? How, in
comparison, does it look to you now? It must seem like nothing at all! 4 But now the LORD
says: Be strong, Zerubbabel. Be strong, Jeshua son of Jehozadak, the high priest. Be
strong, all you people still left in the land. And now get to work, for I am with you, says the
LORD of Heaven's Armies. 5 My Spirit remains among you, just as I promised when you
came out of Egypt. So do not be afraid.'
6 “For this is what the LORD of Heaven's Armies says: In just a little while I will again shake
the heavens and the earth, the oceans and the dry land. 7 I will shake all the nations, and
the treasures of all the nations will be brought to this Temple. I will fill this place with glory,
says the LORD of Heaven's Armies. 8 The silver is Mine, and the gold is Mine, says the LORD
of Heaven's Armies. 9 The future glory of this Temple will be greater than its past glory,
says the LORD of Heaven's Armies. And in this place I will bring peace. I, the LORD of
Heaven's Armies, have spoken!”

2:3 Ezra 3:12
2:4 Deut 31:23; Acts 7:9; Eph 6:10-12
2:5 Exod 29:45-46; Neh 9:10; Isa 63:11, 14
2:6 Ezek 38:19; *Heb 12:26
2:7 1 Kgs 8:11; Isa 60:4-9

BLESSINGS PROMISED FOR OBEDIENCE

10 On December 18* of the second year of King Darius's reign, the LORD sent this message
to the prophet Haggai: 11 “This is what the LORD of Heaven's Armies says. Ask the priests
this question about the law: 12 ‘If one of you is carrying some meat from a holy sacrifice in
his robes and his robe happens to brush against some bread or stew, wine or olive oil, or
any other kind of food, will it also become holy?'”
The priests replied, “No.”
13 Then Haggai asked, “If someone becomes ceremonially unclean by touching a dead
person and then touches any of these foods, will the food be defiled?”
And the priests answered, “Yes.”

2:10 Hag 1:15
2:12 Exod 29:37; Ezek 44:19; Matt 23:19
2:13 Num 19:11-12, 22

2:1 Hebrew *on the twenty-first day of the seventh month,* of the ancient Hebrew lunar calendar. This event (in the second year of Darius's reign) occurred on October 17, 520 B.C.; also see note on 1:1a. 2:2 Hebrew *Joshua,* a variant spelling of Jeshua; also in 2:4. 2:10 Hebrew *On the twenty-fourth day of the ninth month,* of the ancient Hebrew lunar calendar (similarly in 2:18). This event occurred on December 18, 520 B.C.; also see note on 1:1a.

2:1 The work on the Temple had been in progress for almost a month when the Lord spoke to Haggai. It is possible that the magnitude of the task was beginning to overwhelm the workers, so this prophecy would have provided needed encouragement.

2:3 Ezra 3:12 records the loud weeping of the older generation when the new Temple's foundation was initially set in place. About 16 years after that initial effort, repairs finally had resumed. After a month of labor, the Temple continued to be unimpressive. The Temple built by Solomon was a massive facility with ornate decorations inside and out (2 Chronicles 3–4).

2:4 Three words of encouragement were pronounced: one to Zerubbabel (confirming God's recognition of him), one to Jeshua (confirming the same), and one to the assembly. Haggai's encouragement was similar to that given to Israel's troops whenever they went into battle: "Do not lose heart or panic or tremble before them. For the LORD your God is going with you!" (Deuteronomy 20:3-4).

▶ BIBLE
2:4-5 Listening to the Word. Do you spend more time listening to yourself and your own judgments or to the truth of God's Word? Even as Christians, we should trust the advice of God's Word more than our own understanding. What would Haggai's audience have concluded if they only listened to themselves? They had many good reasons to be fearful and hopeless, like the 10 spies who brought a bad report from the Promised Land (Numbers 13:31-33). The task was enormous. They were few. They were weak. Their resources were inadequate. If they chose to speak of their own assessment of the situation instead of God's promises, they certainly weren't going to "encourage each other with these words" (1 Thessalonians 4:13-18). God's people will never accomplish anything if they just focus on the negatives. Preach the Word to yourself and to others, and listen to yourself whine and complain a lot less. (***See Bible> Power> Wisdom> Instruction through God's Word,*** TopicGuide page A11.)

2:8 Where could the people get enough resources to build a Temple? Haggai issued this reminder: God owns everything (Psalm 50:10). The nations are His servants. God was assuring His people that He is able to shake His own resources out of the pockets of the nations (compare Zechariah 14:14; Revelation 21:26).

2:14 14Then Haggai responded, "That is how it is with this people and this nation, says the
Prov 15:8 LORD. Everything they do and everything they offer is defiled by their sin. 15Look at what
Isa 1:11-15 was happening to you before you began to lay the foundation of the LORD's Temple.
2:15 Ezra 3:10; 4:24 16When you hoped for a twenty-bushel crop, you harvested only ten. When you expected
Hag 1:5 to draw fifty gallons from the winepress, you found only twenty. 17I sent blight and mil-
2:16 dew and hail to destroy everything you worked so hard to produce. Even so, you refused
Hag 1:9 to return to Me, says the LORD.
2:18 18"Think about this eighteenth day of December, the day* when the foundation of the
Hag 2:10 LORD's Temple was laid. Think carefully. 19I am giving you a promise now while the seed is
still in the barn.* You have not yet harvested your grain, and your grapevines, fig trees,
pomegranates, and olive trees have not yet produced their crops. But from this day on-
ward I will bless you."

PROMISES FOR ZERUBBABEL

2:21 20On that same day, December 18,* the LORD sent this second message to Haggai: 21"Tell
Hag 2:6 Heb 12:26 Zerubbabel, the governor of Judah, that I am about to shake the heavens and the earth. 22I
2:22 will overthrow royal thrones and destroy the power of foreign kingdoms. I will overturn
Mic 5:10 their chariots and riders. The horses will fall, and their riders will kill each other.
23"But when this happens, says the LORD of Heaven's Armies, I will honor you, Zerubba-
bel son of Shealtiel, My servant. I will make you like a signet ring on My finger, says the
LORD, for I have chosen you. I, the LORD of Heaven's Armies, have spoken!"

2:18 Or *On this eighteenth day of December, think about the day.* 2:19 Hebrew *Is the seed yet in the barn?* 2:20 Hebrew *On the twenty-fourth day of the [ninth] month;* see note on 2:10.

2:20-21 God had a special word of encouragement for Zerubbabel. In this time when Israel was returning to the land and experiencing an accompanying spiritual renewal, Zerubbabel represented the nation's hope for the Christ that was to come from David's line. Though Persia only recognized Zerubbabel as a governor, his lineage held the hope for the future King.

2:23 A signet ring bore the mark of its owner and was used to authenticate official documents. It was a symbol of personal authority. God is the owner of this symbolic ring He wears, named for king Zerubbabel, and He will not take it off. Jeremiah gave the opposite news to Jehoiakim, whom God swore would be rejected even if he were God's own signet ring (Jeremiah 22:24).

ZECHARIAH

PURPOSE

To reassure and encourage the restored Jewish community as the second Temple was completed.

Of the sixteen prophetic books of the Old Testament, four are referred to as the Major Prophets (Isaiah, Jeremiah, Ezekiel, and Daniel) and twelve as the Minor Prophets (Hosea through Malachi). The Major/Minor categories are not based on content—all the books are equally important—but primarily on length. Zechariah is sometimes called the "major minor prophet" because his is the longest of the twelve shorter books and contains important references to the coming Messiah.

Zechariah ministered alongside Haggai in the community of returned Jews who were rebuilding the Temple under Zerubbabel. Whereas Haggai's message was primarily one of exhortation ("get the Temple built . . ."), Zechariah's was one of explanation and encouragement ("get the Temple built *because* . . ."). The Temple was needed as a centerpiece for the restored people of Israel in anticipation of the glorious rule and reign of the coming Messiah. Zechariah's message was delivered through a series of eight visions (1:7–6:8), four sermons (chapters 7–8), and two apocalyptic oracles (chapters 9–14).

DISCOVER GOD IN ZECHARIAH

Zechariah's prophetic visions and oracles are among the most complex in the Old Testament. But in the midst of them, God's attributes are plainly revealed:

Compassionate: Everything God commands His people to do is a reflection of His own character; He never asks us to do something He has not done Himself. We are to love because He is love. We are to be generous because He is generous. And we are to display mercy and kindness because He is merciful and kind (Zechariah 7:9). During the reconstruction of the Temple, Jews came from Bethel to inquire of the priests and prophets whether they should continue their regular fasts that commemorated the anniversary of Jerusalem's destruction. Zechariah responded by saying that instead of fasting the people should act like God: "Judge fairly, and show mercy and kindness to one another. Do not oppress widows, orphans, foreigners, and the poor. And do not scheme against each other" (7:9-10). Any religious act that is not grounded in God's attributes becomes a selfish act, not a godly one.

Rejoicing: Though many see God as eternally somber, the truth is that the God of the Bible is always ready to celebrate. He is constantly looking for those who are doing good in order that He might bless them and celebrate them (2 Chronicles 16:9; Zechariah 4:10). One of the reasons Zechariah encouraged the Jews to rebuild the Temple in Jerusalem was that it might once again become the center of celebration in the nation—and the world: "The traditional fasts and times of mourning you have kept . . . are now ended. They will become festivals of joy and celebration for the people of Judah" (8:19). He went on to say that one day people from all over the world would come to Jerusalem seeking the Lord and asking for His blessing (see 8:20-21). They would come to celebrate the Lord and His blessings! God loves to celebrate, and He delights in seeing mourning turned to joy (Esther 9:22; Psalm 30:11; Isaiah 35:10; 51:11; 61:3; Jeremiah 31:13).

DISCOVERY VERSES

So the angel said to the others standing there, "Take off his filthy clothes." And turning to Jeshua he said, "See, I have taken away your sins, and now I am giving you these fine new clothes."

(ZECHARIAH 3:4)

Then he said to me, "This is what the LORD says to Zerubbabel: It is not by force nor by strength, but by My Spirit, says the LORD of Heaven's Armies."

(ZECHARIAH 4:6)

Then I will pour out a spirit of grace and prayer on the family of David and on the people of Jerusalem. They will look on Me whom they have pierced and mourn for Him as for an only son. They will grieve bitterly for Him as for a firstborn son who has died.

(ZECHARIAH 12:10)

Protecting: In one of Zechariah's eight visions (1:7–6:8), he saw a man about to measure the width and length of Jerusalem (2:1-13). An angel told him to stop because the Lord would soon bless the city with such an overflow of people and livestock that the walls would be rendered useless. The Lord said that instead of a wall for protection, "I, Myself, will be a protective wall of fire around Jerusalem. . . . And I will be the glory inside the city!" (2:5). The Lord also said, "Anyone who harms you harms My most precious possession" (2:8). God is a protector, and all who live in covenant with Him share the benefit of that attribute (Psalm 91).

GROWING THROUGH ZECHARIAH

Within Zechariah's prophecies, two lessons for followers of Christ appear:

Christlikeness: A profound prediction occurs in Zechariah 8:23: "In those days ten men from different nations and languages of the world will clutch at the sleeve of one Jew. And they will say, 'Please let us walk with you, for we have heard that God is with you.'" Nothing is as strong a tool for evangelism—for leading others to God—than a life that reflects God's presence. People followed Jesus Christ because they, like Nicodemus, were convinced that God was with Him: "We all know that God has sent You to teach us. Your miraculous signs are evidence that God is with You" (John 3:2). When people see Christ in the lives of His followers, they will follow those disciples to God.

Exchanging the Good for the Best: A group from Bethel (ten miles north of Jerusalem) came to visit the work site of the Temple with a question for the religious professionals there: Should they continue fasting as they had done since the destruction of the first Temple seventy years before, or could they now stop (7:2-3)? Zechariah answered their question with one from God: "Was it really for Me that you were fasting?" He was concerned that they were fasting (and raising the question) with selfish motives (7:4-7). Zechariah said that God had never commanded them to fast, and in the meantime, they had ignored the weightier matters of justice to the weak and loving their neighbors (7:10). Let us fast and pray and read the Word as often as we can, but never let those practices crowd out the most important practices of all—loving God and loving our neighbor as ourselves.

ZECHARIAH FACTS

Author: Zechariah (1:1). Descended from a priestly line, Zechariah was born in Babylon during the Exile and returned to Jerusalem with his grandfather Iddo (Nehemiah 12:4) under Zerubbabel's leadership.

Written to: The community of returned Jews that were charged with rebuilding the Temple in Jerusalem.

Date of Writing: The same as Haggai, around 520 BC.

Setting: Jerusalem, following the first return of the Jews from Babylon in 538 BC.

OUTLINE

▸ **ZECHARIAH 1:1-6**—Zechariah's First Message

1:1 Ezra 4:24; 5:1; Neh 12:4, 16
1:2 2 Chr 36:16
1:3 Isa 31:6; Mal 3:7
1:4 2 Chr 24:19; 29:6-10; 36:15; Jer 6:17; 11:6-8
1:5 John 8:52
1:6 Jer 12:16-17; Lam 2:17
1:8 Neh 8:15; Isa 41:19; 55:13; Zech 6:2-3; Rev 6:4
1:9 Zech 2:3
1:11 Isa 14:7
1:12 Ps 74:10; Isa 64:9-12; Jer 25:11-12; Dan 9:2

A CALL TO RETURN TO THE LORD

1 In November* of the second year of King Darius's reign, the LORD gave this message
to the prophet Zechariah son of Berekiah and grandson of Iddo:
2 "I, the LORD, was very angry with your ancestors. 3 Therefore, say to the people, 'This is
what the LORD of Heaven's Armies says: Return to Me, and I will return to you, says the
LORD of Heaven's Armies.' 4 Don't be like your ancestors who would not listen or pay atten-
tion when the earlier prophets said to them, 'This is what the LORD of Heaven's Armies
says: Turn from your evil ways, and stop all your evil practices.'
5 "Where are your ancestors now? They and the prophets are long dead. 6 But every-
thing I said through My servants the prophets happened to your ancestors, just as I said.
As a result, they repented and said, 'We have received what we deserved from the LORD of
Heaven's Armies. He has done what He said He would do.' "

A MAN AMONG THE MYRTLE TREES

7 Three months later, on February 15,* the LORD sent another message to the prophet Zech-
ariah son of Berekiah and grandson of Iddo.
8 In a vision during the night, I saw a man sitting on a red horse that was standing among
some myrtle trees in a small valley. Behind him were riders on red, brown, and white
horses. 9 I asked the angel who was talking with me, "My lord, what do these horses mean?"
"I will show you," the angel replied.
10 The rider standing among the myrtle trees then explained, "They are the ones the
LORD has sent out to patrol the earth."
11 Then the other riders reported to the angel of the LORD, who was standing among the
myrtle trees, "We have been patrolling the earth, and the whole earth is at peace."
12 Upon hearing this, the angel of the LORD prayed this prayer: "O LORD of Heaven's Ar-
mies, for seventy years now You have been angry with Jerusalem and the towns of Judah.

1:1 Hebrew *In the eighth month.* A number of dates in Zechariah can be cross-checked with dates in surviving Persian records and related accurately to our modern calendar. This month of the ancient Hebrew lunar calendar occurred within the months of October and November 520 B.C. 1:7 Hebrew *On the twenty-fourth day of the eleventh month, the month of Shebat, in the second year of Darius.* This event occurred on February 15, 519 B.C.; also see note on 1:1.

1:1 Zechariah and Haggai both ministered to the people who returned to Jerusalem after being in exile (compare Ezra 5:1). Zechariah's first recorded prophecy came in 520 BC, just two months after Haggai began to address the returnees about rebuilding the Temple (compare Haggai 1:1). It is likely that Zechariah's grandfather Iddo was one of the priests listed in Nehemiah 12:4, which would make Zechariah both a priest and a prophet.

1:7 Five months after the Temple project was formally initiated (Haggai 1:14-15), Zechariah received another word from the Lord.

1:8-17 This vision is the first of eight. Zechariah saw angelic messengers who assured him of God's rule over the world's powers and His continuing compassion for Jerusalem. Prophets frequently received symbolic pictures or visions of heavenly realities from God in order to communicate His messages (compare Amos 7:1-9; Ezekiel 1; Revelation 4–5). John was shown a similar vision of four colored horses in Revelation 6:1-8. John's vision seemed to attach some significance to the colors of the horses; Zechariah's vision does not appear to do so.

▸ GOD

1:12 How long? What do God's angels and the saints in heaven talk about? In reference to the returned exiles, the angel in this verse asked God, "How long until You again show mercy to them?" First Peter 1:12 tells us the angels are very interested in the way God works out His plans for His people: "Even the angels are eagerly watching these things happen." Likewise, Christians who were killed for the sake of the gospel are pictured as crying out in heaven, "How long before You judge the people who belong to this world and avenge our blood for what they have done to us?" (Revelation 6:10). One reason Jesus came to earth is because He cares when you cry "How long?" Rest in the assurance that your Savior will not stop working for your benefit until "He humbles all His enemies beneath His feet" (1 Corinthians 15:25). (***See God**> God's Attributes> Patient> Believers can appeal to their patient God,* TopicGuide page A17.)

How long until You again show mercy to them?" 13And the LORD spoke kind and comfort- 1:13
ing words to the angel who talked with me. Isa 40:1-2 Zech 4:1
14Then the angel said to me, "Shout this message for all to hear: 'This is what the LORD of
Heaven's Armies says: My love for Jerusalem and Mount Zion is passionate and strong. 15But I 1:14 Zech 1:17; 8:2
am very angry with the other nations that are now enjoying peace and security. I was only a 1:15
little angry with My people, but the nations inflicted harm on them far beyond My intentions. Ps 123:4
16"'Therefore, this is what the LORD says: I have returned to show mercy to Jerusalem. Amos 1:11
My Temple will be rebuilt, says the LORD of Heaven's Armies, and measurements will be 1:16 Ezra 6:14-15
taken for the reconstruction of Jerusalem.*' Isa 54:8-10
17"Say this also: 'This is what the LORD of Heaven's Armies says: The towns of Israel will Zech 2:10
again overflow with prosperity, and the LORD will again comfort Zion and choose Jerusa- 1:17
lem as His own.'" Isa 44:26; 51:3

FOUR HORNS AND FOUR BLACKSMITHS

18*Then I looked up and saw four animal horns. 19"What are these?" I asked the angel who 1:19
was talking with me. 1 Kgs 22:11
He replied, "These horns represent the nations that scattered Judah, Israel, and Jerusalem."
20Then the LORD showed me four blacksmiths. 21"What are these men coming to do?" I 1:20
asked. Isa 44:12; 54:16
The angel replied, "These four horns—these nations—scattered and humbled Judah. 1:21 Ps 75:10
Now these blacksmiths have come to terrify those nations and throw them down and de- Zech 1:18-19
stroy them."

FUTURE PROSPERITY OF JERUSALEM

2 1*When I looked again, I saw a man with a measuring line in his hand. 2"Where are 2:1
you going?" I asked. Ezek 40:3-5
He replied, "I am going to measure Jerusalem, to see how wide and how long it is." 2:2
3Then the angel who was with me went to meet a second angel who was coming to- Jer 31:39 Rev 21:15-17
ward him. 4The other angel said, "Hurry, and say to that young man, 'Jerusalem will some-
day be so full of people and livestock that there won't be room enough for everyone!
Many will live outside the city walls. 5Then I, Myself, will be a protective wall of fire around 2:5
Jerusalem, says the LORD. And I will be the glory inside the city!'" Zech 2:10-11

THE EXILES ARE CALLED HOME

6The LORD says, "Come away! Flee from Babylon in the land of the north, for I have scat- 2:6
tered you to the four winds. 7Come away, people of Zion, you who are exiled in Babylon!" Isa 48:20 Jer 3:18; 31:10
8After a period of glory, the LORD of Heaven's Armies sent me* against the nations who 2:8
plundered you. For He said, "Anyone who harms you harms My most precious posses- Deut 32:10
sion.* 9I will raise My fist to crush them, and their own slaves will plunder them." Then you Isa 60:7-14
will know that the LORD of Heaven's Armies has sent me. 2:9
10The LORD says, "Shout and rejoice, O beautiful Jerusalem,* for I am coming to live Isa 14:2 2:10
among you. 11Many nations will join themselves to the LORD on that day, and they, too, Zech 9:9

1:16 Hebrew *and the measuring line will be stretched out over Jerusalem.* 1:18 Verses 1:18-21 are numbered 2:1-4 in Hebrew text. 2:1 Verses 2:1-13 are numbered 2:5-17 in Hebrew text. 2:8a The meaning of the Hebrew is uncertain. 2:8b Hebrew *Anyone who touches you touches the pupil of His eye.* 2:10 Hebrew *O daughter of Zion.* 2:11 Mic 4:2

1:18-21 These verses record Zechariah's second vision. He received a vision of four horns and four blacksmiths. The horns represented nations through which God inflicted judgment on His people. The role of the blacksmiths was to "destroy" those nations. The powerful LORD of Hosts would surely judge the nations that oppressed His people.

2:1-13 In his third vision, Zechariah saw an angel with a measuring line who intended to measure the dimensions of Jerusalem. He was told that the city would grow beyond expectations and will even include the nations, because God would prosper and protect it.

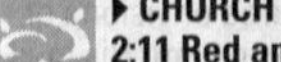

▸ CHURCH

2:11 Red and yellow, black and white. God promised Abraham that his descendant would be a blessing to all the nations (Genesis 12:3; Galatians 3:16). The Gentile nations receive all the blessings of Abraham "because of their

2:12 will be My people. I will live among you, and you will know that the LORD of Heaven's Ar-
Deut 32:9 mies sent me to you. [12]The land of Judah will be the LORD's special possession in the holy
2:13 Ps 78:65-66 land, and He will once again choose Jerusalem to be His own city. [13]Be silent before the
Hab 2:20 LORD, all humanity, for He is springing into action from His holy dwelling."
Zeph 1:7

3:1 **CLEANSING FOR THE HIGH PRIEST**

Ezra 5:2 Job 1:6-12 **3** Then the angel showed me Jeshua* the high priest standing before the angel of the
Ps 109:6 LORD. The Accuser, Satan,* was there at the angel's right hand, making accusations
Hag 1:1 against Jeshua. [2]And the LORD said to Satan, "I, the LORD, reject your accusations, Satan.
Zech 6:11 Yes, the LORD, who has chosen Jerusalem, rebukes you. This man is like a burning stick
3:2 that has been snatched from the fire."
2 Chr 6:6 Amos 4:11 [3]Jeshua's clothing was filthy as he stood there before the angel. [4]So the angel said to
Zech 2:12 the others standing there, "Take off his filthy clothes." And turning to Jeshua he said, "See,
Jude 1:23 I have taken away your sins, and now I am giving you these fine new clothes."
3:3 Ezra 9:15 [5]Then I said, "They should also place a clean turban on his head." So they put a clean
3:4 priestly turban on his head and dressed him in new clothes while the angel of the LORD
Isa 43:25; 61:10 stood by.
Zech 3:9 [6]Then the angel of the LORD spoke very solemnly to Jeshua and said, [7]"This is what the
3:7 1 Kgs 3:14 LORD of Heaven's Armies says: If you follow My ways and carefully serve Me, then you will
Isa 62:9 be given authority over My Temple and its courtyards. I will let you walk among these oth-
3:8 ers standing here.
Isa 4:2; 8:18; 11:1; [8]"Listen to Me, O Jeshua the high priest, and all you other priests. You are symbols of
53:2 things to come. Soon I am going to bring My servant, the Branch. [9]Now look at the jewel I
Jer 33:15 Ezek 12:11 have set before Jeshua, a single stone with seven facets.* I will engrave an inscription on it,
Zech 6:12 says the LORD of Heaven's Armies, and I will remove the sins of this land in a single day.

3:9 Jer 31:34 Zech 4:10

3:1a Hebrew *Joshua,* a variant spelling of Jeshua; also in 3:3, 4, 6, 8, 9. 3:1b Hebrew *The satan;* similarly in 3:2.
3:9 Hebrew *seven eyes.*

faith" (Galatians 3:8-9). The multitude of people Zechariah saw filling Jerusalem (Zechariah 2:4) included other nations, a common image in the books of the prophets (see Isaiah 56:6-8; 66:19-21). Amos looked forward to this day of blessing when the restored kingdom of David would include all the nations God calls to be His own (Amos 9:11-12; Acts 15:13-19). Paul knew this had happened when Jesus "united Jews and Gentiles into one people when, in His own body on the cross, He broke down the wall of hostility that separated us" (Ephesians 2:14). It's always been God's plan that there will be a multiethnic crowd in heaven (Revelation 5:9). Don't let bigotry or racism or a lack of comfort with those different from you spoil your participation in God's ideal—a church and a heaven filled with people of every kind. (***See Church****> Who> From Every Place and Age> Church in the future,* TopicGuide page A48.)

2:12 Zechariah looked forward to the day when God's promises regarding the land would be reinstated and the people would claim the inheritance He promised to Abraham (Genesis 15:18-20). Paul expanded the land promises to encompass the entire world in Romans 4:13.

3:1-10 In his fourth vision, Zechariah watched as the angel of the Lord called for people to remove the high priest's filthy clothing and to dress him in beautiful adornment. The high priest, Jeshua, represents a cleansed priesthood and a people that are graciously covered and made acceptable before God. Christ is revealed here as the Lord who cleanses our sins and covers us in His robe of righteousness.

3:1 Jeshua was the high priest who helped re-establish the priesthood in Jerusalem after the Exile. His name is prominent in Haggai's prophecies alongside that of Zerubbabel, the representative of David's kingly line (see Haggai 1:1; see also Ezra 5:2). Zechariah observed an interaction between two heavenly figures: the adversary, Satan, who was accusing Jeshua, and the angel of the LORD, who was defending him. Satan, whose name means "accuser," is identified elsewhere as "the one who accuses [our brothers and sisters] before our God day and night" (Revelation 12:10; see also Job 1:6-12).

▸ BIBLE

3:1 Who is this angel of the Lord? There are mysteries in this world. The Bible, rather than clearing them up, often adds to the list of things we do not understand. For instance, who is this "angel of the LORD"? Some believe he is just a unique angelic spokesman, while many others think the evidence indicates that he is the eternal Son of God before He came to earth as Jesus (in Zechariah 3:2, he is called "the LORD"). He speaks for God (Genesis 22:12; 31:11-13; Zechariah 3:6-7), yet he is also a distinct personality (Zechariah 1:12). Here in Zechariah, he acts like the Son of God when he defends God's people when Satan accuses them (3:2) and provides for the removal of sins (3:4). If this is the Son, he is no created angel (Hebrews 1:4); he is the divine Creator (Hebrews 1:8-12). Still confused? Then approach God with humility, acknowledging to Him that there are some things in His Word that you do not understand. (***See Bible****> Unity> Kingdom of God> Kingdom is a mystery,* TopicGuide page A11.)

3:8 The angel spoke of a coming servant who was also called the Branch. The title *servant* recalls the suffering one who would bring redemption (Isaiah 53:4-11), and the title *Branch* recalls the expected King sprouting up from David's line (Isaiah 11:1).

10 "And on that day, says the LORD of Heaven's Armies, each of you will invite your
neighbor to sit with you peacefully under your own grapevine and fig tree."

A LAMPSTAND AND TWO OLIVE TREES

4 Then the angel who had been talking with me returned and woke me, as though I
had been asleep. 2 "What do you see now?" he asked.
I answered, "I see a solid gold lampstand with a bowl of oil on top of it. Around the bowl
are seven lamps, each having seven spouts with wicks. 3 And I see two olive trees, one on
each side of the bowl." 4 Then I asked the angel, "What are these, my lord? What do they
mean?"
5 "Don't you know?" the angel asked.
"No, my lord," I replied.
6 Then he said to me, "This is what the LORD says to Zerubbabel: It is not by force nor by
strength, but by My Spirit, says the LORD of Heaven's Armies. 7 Nothing, not even a mighty
mountain, will stand in Zerubbabel's way; it will become a level plain before him! And
when Zerubbabel sets the final stone of the Temple in place, the people will shout: 'May
God bless it! May God bless it!'*"
8 Then another message came to me from the LORD: 9 "Zerubbabel is the one who laid
the foundation of this Temple, and he will complete it. Then you will know that the LORD of
Heaven's Armies has sent me. 10 Do not despise these small beginnings, for the LORD re-
joices to see the work begin, to see the plumb line in Zerubbabel's hand."
(The seven lamps* represent the eyes of the LORD that search all around the world.)
11 Then I asked the angel, "What are these two olive trees on each side of the lampstand,
12 and what are the two olive branches that pour out golden oil through two gold tubes?"
13 "Don't you know?" he asked.
"No, my lord," I replied.
14 Then he said to me, "They represent the two heavenly beings who stand in the court
of the Lord of all the earth."

A FLYING SCROLL

5 I looked up again and saw a scroll flying through the air.
2 "What do you see?" the angel asked.
"I see a flying scroll," I replied. "It appears to be about 30 feet long and 15 feet wide."*

3:10 1 Kgs 4:25; Mic 4:4
4:1 Zech 1:9
4:2 Exod 25:31, 37; Rev 4:5
4:3 Zech 4:11-12, 14; Rev 11:4
4:5 Zech 1:9
4:6 Isa 11:2-4; Hos 1:7; Hag 2:4-5; Eph 6:17
4:7 Ezra 3:11-13; Jer 51:25
4:9 Ezra 3:8-10; 5:16; Zech 6:12-15
4:10 Amos 7:2, 7-8; Hag 2:3; Zech 3:9; Rev 1:12
4:14 Exod 29:7; Isa 61:1-3; Dan 9:24-26; Mic 4:13; Zech 3:1-7; Rev 11:4
5:1 Jer 36:1-6; Ezek 2:9-10

4:7 Hebrew *'Grace, grace to it.'* 4:10 Or *The seven facets* (see 3:9); Hebrew reads *These seven.* 5:2 Hebrew *20 cubits* [9 meters] *long and 10 cubits* [4.5 meters] *wide.*

4:1-14 In his fifth vision, Zechariah was shown an image of two trees that supplied oil to seven burning lamps. The fact that Zechariah was awakened here indicates an apparent gap in time between the reception of the first four visions and the second four.

4:6-7 Zechariah's audience would have known that the task of keeping the ornate lamps with 49 wicks continually burning was far too great for just two olive trees (Zechariah 4:2-3). The power source for those two multi-flamed lamps would be the same as the source for Zerubbabel's and Jeshua's—God Himself. Haggai also directed these two anointed leaders to God's Spirit (Haggai 2:4-5) for the power to complete their task.

▸ GOD
4:14 Anointed in power. The oil in the vision speaks of an anointing or empowering from the Holy Spirit. Jeshua and Zerubbabel were unique conduits of God's power for the task at hand. In Israel, the high priest and the king were both anointed with oil (Exodus 29:7; 1 Kings 1:39). Why should we care about these anointed offices? Because they culminate in Jesus, the only King who is also a Priest (Psalm 110). The term *Messiah* (usually rendered *Christ* in the New Testament) means "the anointed one." This title is only fitting for Jesus, since "God gives Him the Spirit without limit" (John 3:34). The exciting truth is that God has always planned that His people would be filled to the brim with His Spirit (Numbers 11:29; Joel 2:28-32). Ask God to show you the full power of His Holy Spirit who indwells you (Acts 13:52; 1 Corinthians 6:19). Rely on Him, and do not resist His guidance (Ephesians 4:30). (***See God*** *> God's Names> Holy Spirit> Empowers,* TopicGuide page A19.)

5:1-4 In his sixth vision, Zechariah was shown a huge scroll with indictments written on both sides against the wicked. This scroll was massive, possibly so that all may read its contents or so that it could contain the list of all the infractions against God's law. The dimensions indicate that the scroll was unrolled so its judgments could be announced. The vision demonstrated that God was planning to purge the land and destroy all lawbreakers.

5:3 [3]Then he said to me, "This scroll contains the curse that is going out over the entire
Exod 20:15 Jer 26:6 land. One side of the scroll says that those who steal will be banished from the land; the
Mal 3:8-9 other side says that those who swear falsely will be banished from the land. [4]And this is
5:4 what the LORD of Heaven's Armies says: I am sending this curse into the house of every
Lev 14:34-45 thief and into the house of everyone who swears falsely using My name. And My curse
Jer 2:26 will remain in that house and completely destroy it—even its timbers and stones."
Hos 4:2-3
Hab 2:9-11
Mal 3:5

A WOMAN IN A BASKET

5:5 [5]Then the angel who was talking with me came forward and said, "Look up and see what's
Zech 1:9 coming."
5:6 [6]"What is it?" I asked.
Lev 19:36 He replied, "It is a basket for measuring grain,* and it's filled with the sins* of everyone
Amos 8:5 throughout the land."
[7]Then the heavy lead cover was lifted off the basket, and there was a woman sitting in-
5:8 side it. [8]The angel said, "The woman's name is Wickedness," and he pushed her back into
Hos 12:7 the basket and closed the heavy lid again.
Mic 6:11 [9]Then I looked up and saw two women flying toward us, gliding on the wind. They had
wings like a stork, and they picked up the basket and flew into the sky.
[10]"Where are they taking the basket?" I asked the angel.
5:11 [11]He replied, "To the land of Babylonia,* where they will build a temple for the basket.
Gen 10:10 And when the temple is ready, they will set the basket there on its pedestal."
Isa 11:11
Dan 1:2

FOUR CHARIOTS

6:1 **6** Then I looked up again and saw four chariots coming from between two bronze
Zech 1:18; 6:5 mountains. [2]The first chariot was pulled by red horses, the second by black horses,
6:2 Rev 6:4-5 [3]the third by white horses, and the fourth by powerful dappled-gray horses. [4]"And what
6:3 are these, my lord?" I asked the angel who was talking with me.
Rev 6:2 [5]The angel replied, "These are the four spirits* of heaven who stand before the Lord of
6:5 all the earth. They are going out to do His work. [6]The chariot with black horses is going
Jer 49:36 north, the chariot with white horses is going west,* and the chariot with dappled-gray
Ezek 37:9 Dan 7:2 horses is going south."
Rev 7:1 [7]The powerful horses were eager to set out to patrol the earth. And the LORD said, "Go
6:6 and patrol the earth!" So they left at once on their patrol.
Ezek 1:4
Dan 11:5-6, 9, 40

5:6a Hebrew *an ephah* [20 quarts or 22 liters]; also in 5:7, 8, 9, 10, 11. 5:6b As in Greek version; Hebrew reads *the appearance.* 5:11 Hebrew *the land of Shinar.* 6:5 Or *the four winds.* 6:6 Hebrew *is going after them.*

5:5-11 In his seventh vision, Zechariah saw a woman being taken away in a basket to the land of Babylonia. God showed that He would take the initiative to remove wickedness from the land. The basket was an *ephah*, which would hold only about five gallons, a space too small for a child, let alone the woman named "Wickedness." When Wickedness tried to escape, she was not allowed to get out of the basket, demonstrating that God was in control of the removal of wickedness.

▸ ADOPTION
5:9 Take it away! Can this odd picture of a stork-like creature carrying a basket have anything to do with your life? Absolutely! In this unusual imagery, God is once again pictured as the One who takes the initiative to remove our wickedness, just as He did with Jeshua (Zechariah 3:3-4). The same removal was pictured yearly when the high priest would lay his hands on the scapegoat, confess the nation's sins, and send the goat away into the wilderness (Leviticus 16:21). Jesus fulfilled this ceremony when "the LORD laid on Him the sins of us all" (Isaiah 53:6). Jesus has fulfilled every foreshadowing of sin's removal by bearing the penalty for sin upon Himself. Praise God that your sins are gone forever! (***See Adoption*** *> With Christ> Redemption> Forgiveness of sins,* TopicGuide page A37.)

6:1-8 In his eighth vision, Zechariah saw four chariots with colored horses going throughout the earth to do God's bidding. Revelation 6:1-8 uses similar imagery, but John assigns specific judgments to each colored horse. The colors may be part of the symbolism here, but that is not clarified. What is evident is that God is controlling the affairs of the nations and one day will judge everyone that oppresses His people.

8Then the LORD summoned me and said, "Look, those who went north have vented the
anger of My Spirit* there in the land of the north."

6:8 Jer 1:14-15; Ezek 5:13; Zech 1:15

THE CROWNING OF JESHUA

9Then I received another message from the LORD: 10"Heldai, Tobijah, and Jedaiah will
bring gifts of silver and gold from the Jews exiled in Babylon. As soon as they arrive, meet
them at the home of Josiah son of Zephaniah. 11Accept their gifts, and make a crown* from
the silver and gold. Then put the crown on the head of Jeshua* son of Jehozadak, the high
priest. 12Tell him, 'This is what the LORD of Heaven's Armies says: Here is the man called
the Branch. He will branch out from where He is and build the Temple of the LORD. 13Yes,
He will build the Temple of the LORD. Then He will receive royal honor and will rule as king
from His throne. He will also serve as priest from His throne,* and there will be perfect har-
mony between His two roles.'
14"The crown will be a memorial in the Temple of the LORD to honor those who gave it—
Heldai,* Tobijah, Jedaiah, and Josiah* son of Zephaniah."
15People will come from distant lands to rebuild the Temple of the LORD. And when this
happens, you will know that my messages have been from the LORD of Heaven's Armies.
All this will happen if you carefully obey what the LORD your God says.

6:9 Zech 1:1; 7:1; 8:1
6:10 Ezra 7:14-16; 8:26-30
6:12 Isa 4:2-3; 11:1; Jer 23:5-6; Zech 3:8; 4:6-9
6:13 Ps 110:4; Isa 9:6; 11:10
6:15 Isa 56:6-8; 60:10; Zech 3:7

A CALL TO JUSTICE AND MERCY

7 On December 7* of the fourth year of King Darius's reign, another message came to
Zechariah from the LORD. 2The people of Bethel had sent Sharezer and Regemme-
lech,* along with their attendants, to seek the LORD's favor. 3They were to ask this question
of theprophets and the priests at the Temple of the LORD of Heaven's Armies: "Should we
continue to mourn and fast each summer on the anniversary of the Temple's destruction,*
as we have done for so many years?"
4The LORD of Heaven's Armies sent me this message in reply: 5"Say to all your people
and your priests, 'During these seventy years of exile, when you fasted and mourned in
the summer and in early autumn,* was it really for Me that you were fasting? 6And even

7:2 Zech 8:21
7:3 Ezra 3:10-12
7:5 Isa 58:5; Zech 1:12; Matt 5:16; 6:2, 5, 16; 23:5

6:8 Hebrew *have given My Spirit rest.* **6:11a** As in Greek and Syriac versions; Hebrew reads *crowns.* **6:11b** Hebrew *Joshua,* a variant spelling of Jeshua. **6:13** Or *There will be a priest by His throne.* **6:14a** As in Syriac version (compare 6:10); Hebrew reads *Helem.* **6:14b** As in Syriac version (compare 6:10); Hebrew reads *Hen.* **7:1** Hebrew *On the fourth day of the ninth month, the month of Kislev,* of the ancient Hebrew lunar calendar. This event occurred on December 7, 518 B.C.; also see note on 1:1. **7:2** Or *Bethel-sharezer had sent Regemmelech.* **7:3** Hebrew *mourn and fast in the fifth month.* The Temple had been destroyed in the fifth month of the ancient Hebrew lunar calendar (August 586 B.C.); see 2 Kgs 25:8. **7:5** Hebrew *fasted and mourned in the fifth and seventh months.* The fifth month of the ancient Hebrew lunar calendar usually occurs within the months of July and August. The seventh month usually occurs within the months of September and October; both the Day of Atonement and the Festival of Shelters were celebrated in the seventh month.

▸ PURPOSE

6:8 Babylon has fallen. Babylon has long represented the power of wickedness in the world. In the book of Revelation, John portrayed evil the same way, using Babylon as the symbol for hatred against God and His people (Revelation 17). In his vision, an angel announced, "Babylon is fallen—that great city is fallen!" (Revelation 18:2), and a vast crowd in heaven responded to the good news, shouting "Praise the LORD!" (Revelation 19:1). Our God is Lord of all the earth; evil will not have the last word, just as the Exile in Babylon was not the last word. When oppressors are judged and God's anger at sin has been fully vented, "there will be no more death or sorrow or crying or pain" (Revelation 21:4). Yearn for that day. Cry out on behalf of all God's people, "Come, Lord Jesus!" (Revelation 22:20). (***See Purpose****> God's Deeds> Judgment> Babylon destroyed,* TopicGuide page A54.)

6:9-13 Zechariah's first four visions culminated in the revelation that Jeshua was symbolic of Jesus, the Servant/Branch who would come and remove all sin in a single day (3:8-10). In 4:1, Zechariah was startled awake to receive a second set of four visions. They culminate here with a vision of the same person, Jesus the Priest/King. In this section, Zechariah was instructed to carry out a symbolic ceremony in which he crowned Jeshua and prophesied about the Branch.

6:13 The ministry of Jeshua foreshadowed the royal rule (Colossians 1:15-20) and priesthood of Christ (Hebrews 9).

7:1 Almost two years had passed since Zechariah received the night visions described in chapters 1–6.

7:2-3 Bethel was an idolatrous center in Israel prior to the Assyrian exile (2 Kings 23:15; Amos 5:5). Jeroboam set up a calf idol there as an alternative worship center to Jerusalem, the worship site ordained by God (1 Kings 12:26-30). The fact that the residents of Bethel were seeking direction from the approved priests and prophets in Jerusalem initially appears to be a positive sign.

now in your holy festivals, aren't you eating and drinking just to please yourselves? [7]Isn't this the same message the LORD proclaimed through the prophets in years past when Jerusalem and the towns of Judah were bustling with people, and the Negev and the foothills of Judah* were well populated?' "

[8]Then this message came to Zechariah from the LORD: [9]"This is what the LORD of Heaven's Armies says: Judge fairly, and show mercy and kindness to one another. [10]Do not oppress widows, orphans, foreigners, and the poor. And do not scheme against each other.

[11]"Your ancestors refused to listen to this message. They stubbornly turned away and put their fingers in their ears to keep from hearing. [12]They made their hearts as hard as stone, so they could not hear the instructions or the messages that the LORD of Heaven's Armies had sent them by His Spirit through the earlier prophets. That is why the LORD of Heaven's Armies was so angry with them.

[13]"Since they refused to listen when I called to them, I would not listen when they called to Me, says the LORD of Heaven's Armies. [14]As with a whirlwind, I scattered them among the distant nations, where they lived as strangers. Their land became so desolate that no one even traveled through it. They turned their pleasant land into a desert."

PROMISED BLESSINGS FOR JERUSALEM

8 Then another message came to me from the LORD of Heaven's Armies: [2]"This is what the LORD of Heaven's Armies says: My love for Mount Zion is passionate and strong; I am consumed with passion for Jerusalem!

[3]"And now the LORD says: I am returning to Mount Zion, and I will live in Jerusalem. Then Jerusalem will be called the Faithful City; the mountain of the LORD of Heaven's Armies will be called the Holy Mountain.

[4]"This is what the LORD of Heaven's Armies says: Once again old men and women will walk Jerusalem's streets with their canes and will sit together in the city squares. [5]And the streets of the city will be filled with boys and girls at play.

[6]"This is what the LORD of Heaven's Armies says: All this may seem impossible to you now, a small remnant of God's people. But is it impossible for Me? says the LORD of Heaven's Armies.

[7]"This is what the LORD of Heaven's Armies says: You can be sure that I will rescue My people from the east and from the west. [8]I will bring them home again to live safely in Jerusalem. They will be My people, and I will be faithful and just toward them as their God.

[9]"This is what the LORD of Heaven's Armies says: Be strong and finish the task! Ever since the laying of the foundation of the Temple of the LORD of Heaven's Armies, you have

7:7 Jer 17:26; 22:21; Zech 1:4
7:9 Mic 6:8
7:10 Exod 22:22; Deut 24:14-18; Prov 22:22-23
7:11 Ps 58:4-5; Jer 8:5; Acts 7:57
7:12 Neh 9:30; Jer 17:1; Ezek 3:9; Dan 9:11-12
7:13 Prov 1:24-28; Isa 1:15
7:14 Deut 28:64; Jer 12:10; 23:19; 44:6
8:3 Zech 2:10
8:4 Isa 65:20-22
8:5 Jer 30:19-20
8:6 Ps 118:23; Jer 32:17, 27
8:7 Ps 107:2-3; Isa 11:11; 43:5; Amos 9:14-15
8:8 Ezek 37:28; Zech 2:11; 10:10
8:9 Ezra 5:1; 6:14; Hag 2:4

7:7 Hebrew *the Shephelah.*

▸ BIBLE

7:12 God's mouthpieces. Who is the source of the message that was delivered by the prophets? The Bible clearly proclaims that the warnings of the prophets were not religious ravings; Zechariah says these were the words of the LORD Almighty. As 2 Timothy 3:16 states, "All Scripture is inspired by God" (*inspired* literally means "breathed out"). This is why Hebrews 10:15 reads, "the Holy Spirit also testifies," when referring to the words of Jeremiah. Yet Israel ignored God's mouthpieces, and that, Zechariah said, "is why the LORD ... was so angry with them." We must take seriously what is in the Bible (Isaiah 66:2). It's not enough to read it, or study it, or teach it to others—we must respond to it by faith. (***See Bible***> *Uniqueness> Inspired> Divinely inspired,* TopicGuide page A10.)

▸ WORSHIP

8:3-23 Blessings, anyone? Because God lavishes blessings on His people with such abandon, we find it hard to believe passages like these mean what they say. Here, Zechariah repeated part of the covenant contract given to Israel that pertains to blessing (see Leviticus 26), laying before the audience a picture of the ideal blessed state (Deuteronomy 28:1-14). What is the message? Seize these wonderful blessings by faithful obedience (see 3:6-7; 6:15). Did Israel seize these blessings? Rarely ever. But God had a plan to bless not only Israel, but also the nations—and so He sent Christ (Galatians 3:13-14). Jesus fulfilled the Old Covenant and established the New Covenant, making a way for people all over the world to experience the blessings of being right with God through faith and repentance. In principle, every blessing in this passage belongs to those who approach God by faith today. Read and marvel at the vast spiritual riches God has given those who trust in Christ. (***See Worship***> *OT> Repentance> Nature> Obedience leads to blessing, failure to repent leads to curses,* TopicGuide page A29.)

heard what the prophets have been saying about completing the building. 10 Before the
work on the Temple began, there were no jobs and no money to hire people or animals.
No traveler was safe from the enemy, for there were enemies on all sides. I had turned
everyone against each other.
11 "But now I will not treat the remnant of My people as I treated them before, says the
LORD of Heaven's Armies. 12 For I am planting seeds of peace and prosperity among you.
The grapevines will be heavy with fruit. The earth will produce its crops, and the heavens
will release the dew. Once more I will cause the remnant in Judah and Israel to inherit
these blessings. 13 Among the other nations, Judah and Israel became symbols of a cursed
nation. But no longer! Now I will rescue you and make you both a symbol and a source of
blessing. So don't be afraid. Be strong, and get on with rebuilding the Temple!
14 "For this is what the LORD of Heaven's Armies says: I was determined to punish you
when your ancestors angered Me, and I did not change My mind, says the LORD of
Heaven's Armies. 15 But now I am determined to bless Jerusalem and the people of Judah.
So don't be afraid. 16 But this is what you must do: Tell the truth to each other. Render ver-

8:10 Isa 19:2; Amos 3:6; 9:4; Hag 1:6-11; 2:16-19
8:11 Isa 12:1
8:12 Gen 27:28
8:13 Ps 72:17; Jer 29:18; Dan 9:11; Zech 14:11
8:14 Jer 4:28; 29:11-14; Ezek 24:14
8:16 *Eph 4:25

8:10-12 In Haggai 1:9, God took credit for Israel's lack of prosperity prior to the initiation of the Temple project, saying, "I blew it away." Here God takes credit for Israel's past lack of security, saying, "I had turned everyone against each other" (Zechariah 8:10). The threatened curses had become reality because of the people's disobedience. The words "But now" (8:11) indicate a shift from the days of meager returns and insecurity. In contrast with the curse of desolation (7:14), the blessing of the covenant included bountiful harvests (Leviticus 26:3-5), which harkened back to an overturning of the curse on the ground (Genesis 3:17-18) and looked forward to the complete removal of the curse from all of creation (Romans 8:20-22).

MY RESPONSE TO GOD

God's Work First

ZECHARIAH 8:9

Working to build God's kingdom is rarely on the top of our to-do list. We may say God is our first priority, but our actions tell us otherwise. Watching television, shopping, or putting in too many hours at work often take precedence over playing with our children, caring for the poor, or serving God's people.

The tendency to prioritize our own work ahead of God's work is not a new problem. About 2,500 years ago, some Judeans returned to Jerusalem after forty-eight years of exile, and they began to rebuild the Temple—but after a few years they stopped without completing the task. Instead, they worked to make houses for themselves (Haggai 1:4, 9). The prophets Haggai and Zechariah urged the people to make God's work their top priority. "Now go up into the hills, bring down timber, and rebuild My house," the Lord said through Haggai (Haggai 1:8). And through Zechariah He commanded, "Be strong and finish the task! Ever since the laying of the foundation of the Temple of the LORD of Heaven's Armies, you have heard what the prophets have been saying about completing the building" (Zechariah 8:9).

The prophets call us from the distant past with a timely message: Make worshiping God, loving your family, and doing effective ministry your top priorities. At the end of your life, you will never wish you'd spent more time at work. No one ever said on their deathbed that they wish they'd spent more time cleaning the kitchen or playing video games. Make your life matter by putting God's work first.

8:17 Zech 5:3-4; 7:10 Mal 3:5 · 8:19 Isa 12:1 Zech 7:3-5; 8:16 Luke 1:74-75 · 8:20 Zech 2:11; 14:16 · 8:22 Isa 49:6, 22-23 60:3-12 · 8:23 Isa 45:14; 60:14

dicts in your courts that are just and that lead to peace. [17]Don't scheme against each
other. Stop your love of telling lies that you swear are the truth. I hate all these things, says
the LORD."

[18]Here is another message that came to me from the LORD of Heaven's Armies. [19]"This is
what the LORD of Heaven's Armies says: The traditional fasts and times of mourning you
have kept in early summer, midsummer, autumn, and winter* are now ended. They will
become festivals of joy and celebration for the people of Judah. So love truth and peace.

[20]"This is what the LORD of Heaven's Armies says: People from nations and cities around
the world will travel to Jerusalem. [21]The people of one city will say to the people of an-
other, 'Come with us to Jerusalem to ask the LORD to bless us. Let's worship the LORD of
Heaven's Armies. I'm determined to go.' [22]Many peoples and powerful nations will come
to Jerusalem to seek the LORD of Heaven's Armies and to ask for His blessing.

[23]"This is what the LORD of Heaven's Armies says: In those days ten men from different
nations and languages of the world will clutch at the sleeve of one Jew. And they will say,
'Please let us walk with you, for we have heard that God is with you.'"

JUDGMENT AGAINST ISRAEL'S ENEMIES

9:1 Amos 1:3-5 · 9:2 Jer 49:23 Ezek 28:3-5 · 9:3 Josh 19:29 · 9:4 Isa 23:1-7 Ezek 27:32; 28:16, 18

9 This is the message* from the LORD against the land of Aram* and the city of Damas-
cus, for the eyes of humanity, including all the tribes of Israel, are on the LORD.

[2] Doom is certain for Hamath,
near Damascus,
and for the cities of Tyre and Sidon,
though they are so clever.
[3] Tyre has built a strong fortress
and has made silver and gold
as plentiful as dust in the streets!
[4] But now the Lord will strip away Tyre's possessions
and hurl its fortifications into the sea,
and it will be burned to the ground.
[5] The city of Ashkelon will see Tyre fall
and will be filled with fear.
Gaza will shake with terror,
as will Ekron, for their hopes will be dashed.
Gaza's king will be killed,
and Ashkelon will be deserted.
[6] Foreigners will occupy the city of Ashdod.
I will destroy the pride of the Philistines.

8:19 Hebrew *in the fourth, fifth, seventh, and tenth months.* The fourth month of the ancient Hebrew lunar calendar usually occurs within the months of June and July. The fifth month usually occurs within the months of July and August. The seventh month usually occurs within the months of September and October. The tenth month usually occurs within the months of December and January. 9:1a Hebrew *An Oracle: The message.* 9:1b Hebrew *land of Hadrach.*

8:20-22 The previous vision of an expanding city (1:17) filled with foreigners who were joined to the Lord (2:11) now reappears. The transformation from fasting to festivity (8:19) would testify that a great God lived in Jerusalem. Hostility between the nations would be replaced by a united resolve to seek the Lord at His Temple (Isaiah 2:2-5). This state of affairs would fulfill God's original intention that Abraham's descendants should be a blessing to the nations (Zechariah 8:13; Genesis 12:3).

9:1-8 The prophets often announced a future time of blessing for God's people alongside a promise of judgment for the nations that despised God. They warned that the people of the nations that did not join themselves to the great crowd going to Jerusalem to worship would endure judgment from an angry God. Many scholars believe these judgments upon the nations were at least partially fulfilled by Alexander the Great in his conquests in the ancient Near East in 333–332 BC.

9:3-4 Tyre was a seemingly impregnable island fortress, but Isaiah prophesied that God would demolish the city to show His contempt for all human pride (Isaiah 23:9). Alexander the Great humbled the people of Tyre in 332 BC when he destroyed the part of the city that was on the mainland, built a walkway to the island from the debris, and captured the fortress.

7 I will grab the bloody meat from their mouths
and snatch the detestable sacrifices from their teeth.
Then the surviving Philistines will worship our God
and become like a clan in Judah.*
The Philistines of Ekron will join My people,
as the ancient Jebusites once did.
8 I will guard My Temple
and protect it from invading armies.
I am watching closely to ensure
that no more foreign oppressors overrun My people's land.

9:8
Isa 52:1; 54:14

ZION'S COMING KING

9 Rejoice, O people of Zion!*
Shout in triumph, O people of Jerusalem!
Look, your King is coming to you.
He is righteous and victorious,*
yet He is humble, riding on a donkey—
riding on a donkey's colt.
10 I will remove the battle chariots from Israel*
and the warhorses from Jerusalem.
I will destroy all the weapons used in battle,
and your King will bring peace to the nations.
His realm will stretch from sea to sea
and from the Euphrates River* to the ends of the earth.*
11 Because of the covenant I made with you,
sealed with blood,
I will free your prisoners
from death in a waterless dungeon.
12 Come back to the place of safety,
all you prisoners who still have hope!
I promise this very day
that I will repay two blessings for each of your troubles.
13 Judah is My bow,
and Israel is My arrow.
Jerusalem* is My sword,
and like a warrior, I will brandish it against the Greeks.*

14 The LORD will appear above His people;
His arrows will fly like lightning!
The Sovereign LORD will sound the ram's horn
and attack like a whirlwind from the southern desert.

9:9
Ps 97:6-8
Isa 9:6-7; 57:15
Jer 23:5-6
Zech 2:10
*Matt 21:5
*John 12:15

9:10
Ps 72:17
Isa 57:18-19
Mic 4:2-10; 5:4

9:11
Exod 24:8
Heb 10:29

9:12
Isa 61:7
Joel 3:16

9:13
Ps 45:3
Jer 51:20
Joel 3:6-8

9:14
Ps 18:14
Isa 27:13; 31:5

9:7 Hebrew *and will become a leader in Judah.* 9:9a Hebrew *O daughter of Zion!* 9:9b Hebrew *and is being vindicated.* 9:10a Hebrew *Ephraim,* referring to the northern kingdom of Israel; also in 9:13. 9:10b Hebrew *the river.* 9:10c Or *the end of the land.* 9:13a Hebrew *Zion.* 9:13b Hebrew *the sons of Javan.*

▶ GOD

9:9 Unusual ruler, unusual rule. When Jesus rode into Jerusalem on the traditional Israelite mount of a king, a sure-footed donkey, He caused a great stir among those who were familiar with Zechariah's prophecy (Luke 19:28-45). The crowds immediately identified Jesus as the promised Messiah who would rescue them from their troubles (Zechariah 9:16). And that's exactly what happened—but not as they expected. The real rescue of God's people as promised by Zechariah continues even today, with Jesus ruling and reigning from heaven, overseeing the continued salvation of His people (Revelation 7:10) and the utter defeat of His enemies (Revelation 19:1-3). Don't grow weary waiting for God's complete victory. Don't put your hope in political victories as the key to advancing the Kingdom, as those in Jesus' time did (Luke 19:41-44; 2 Corinthians 10:4). Instead, put your trust in your King and the spiritual weapons He has ordained to accomplish His victory (2 Corinthians 10:3-5; Ephesians 6:12). (***See God****> God's Names> Son> King,* TopicGuide page A19.)

9:15 Zech 12:6
15 The LORD of Heaven's Armies will protect His people,
and they will defeat their enemies by hurling great stones.
They will shout in battle as though drunk with wine.
They will be filled with blood like a bowl,
drenched with blood like the corners of the altar.
9:16 Isa 62:3
16 On that day the LORD their God will rescue His people,
just as a shepherd rescues his sheep.
They will sparkle in His land
like jewels in a crown.
17 How wonderful and beautiful they will be!
The young men will thrive on abundant grain,
and the young women will flourish on new wine.

THE LORD WILL RESTORE HIS PEOPLE

10:1 Jer 10:13 Hos 6:3 Joel 2:23-24
10 1 Ask the LORD for rain in the spring,
for He makes the storm clouds.
And He will send showers of rain
so every field becomes a lush pasture.
10:2 Ezek 34:5, 8 Mic 3:6-11 Matt 9:36 Mark 6:34
2 Household gods give worthless advice,
fortune-tellers predict only lies,
and interpreters of dreams pronounce
falsehoods that give no comfort.
So My people are wandering like lost sheep;
they are attacked because they have no shepherd.

10:3 Ezek 34:2, 7, 12
3 "My anger burns against your shepherds,
and I will punish these leaders.*
For the LORD of Heaven's Armies has arrived
to look after Judah, His flock.
He will make them strong and glorious,
like a proud warhorse in battle.
4 From Judah will come the cornerstone,
the tent peg,
the bow for battle,
and all the rulers.
10:5 2 Sam 22:43
5 They will be like mighty warriors in battle,
trampling their enemies in the mud under their feet.
Since the LORD is with them as they fight,
they will overthrow even the enemy's horsemen.
10:6 Isa 54:8
6 "I will strengthen Judah and save Israel*;
I will restore them because of My compassion.
It will be as though I had never rejected them,
for I am the LORD their God, who will hear their cries.

10:3 Or *these male goats.* 10:6 Hebrew *save the house of Joseph.*

▶ HOLINESS

10:1-3 Directions, please. Where do you get guidance when your life doesn't seem to be going in the right direction? In this text, seeking direction from God is contrasted with seeking direction from idols and fortune-tellers. Idols are mocked in Scripture as powerless human creations (see Isaiah 44:13). Jeremiah also bluntly called fortune-tellers "liars" (Jeremiah 27:9-10; compare Micah 3:7). Confused Christians may wander to fortune-tellers, horoscopes, or New Age spirit guides, practices forbidden by God (Deuteronomy 18:10-14; 2 Chronicles 33:5-6), while looking for God's guidance—but it's right in front of them (Psalm 119:105). God also promises that His Spirit will guide us (John 14:17), and the encouraging counsel of godly people plays a part as well (Hebrews 10:24-25). Seeking occult assistance is a sure way to get lost—and stay that way. (***See Holiness****> Changed by God> God Provides> Directing us,* TopicGuide page A41.)

7 The people of Israel* will become like mighty warriors,
and their hearts will be made happy as if by wine.
Their children, too, will see it and be glad;
their hearts will rejoice in the LORD.
8 When I whistle to them, they will come running,
for I have redeemed them.
From the few who are left,
they will grow as numerous as they were before.
9 Though I have scattered them like seeds among the nations,
they will still remember Me in distant lands.
They and their children will survive
and return again to Israel.
10 I will bring them back from Egypt
and gather them from Assyria.
I will resettle them in Gilead and Lebanon
until there is no more room for them all.
11 They will pass safely through the sea of distress,*
for the waves of the sea will be held back,
and the waters of the Nile will dry up.
The pride of Assyria will be crushed,
and the rule of Egypt will end.
12 By My power* I will make My people strong,
and by My authority they will go wherever they wish.
I, the LORD, have spoken!"

10:8 Isa 5:26; 7:18-19 Jer 33:22 Ezek 36:11
10:9 1 Kgs 8:47-48 Ezek 6:9
10:10 Isa 11:11-16; 49:19-21
10:11 Isa 19:5-7 Ezek 30:13 Zeph 2:13
10:12 Mic 4:5

11 1 Open your doors, Lebanon,
so that fire may devour your cedar forests.
2 Weep, you cypress trees, for all the ruined cedars;
the most majestic ones have fallen.
Weep, you oaks of Bashan,
for the thick forests have been cut down.
3 Listen to the wailing of the shepherds,
for their rich pastures are destroyed.
Hear the young lions roaring,
for their thickets in the Jordan Valley are ruined.

11:3 Jer 2:15; 25:34-36; 50:44

THE GOOD AND EVIL SHEPHERDS

4This is what the LORD my God says: "Go and care for the flock that is intended for slaugh-
ter. 5The buyers slaughter their sheep without remorse. The sellers say, 'Praise the LORD!
Now I'm rich!' Even the shepherds have no compassion for them. 6Likewise, I will no lon-
ger have pity on the people of the land," says the LORD. "I will let them fall into each other's

11:5 Jer 50:7 Ezek 34:2-6 Hos 12:8 1 Tim 6:9
11:6 Isa 9:19-21 Jer 13:14 Zech 8:10; 14:13

10:7 Hebrew *of Ephraim.* 10:11 Or *the sea of Egypt,* referring to the Red Sea. 10:12 Hebrew *In the LORD.*

▸ SALVATION

10:8-10 Redeemed by God. What does it mean to be redeemed? In our text, God says He will call His people out of the nations and prosper them, having redeemed them, or paid the price required to get them out of slavery. All such images look forward to the cross, where God "purchased our freedom with the blood of His Son" (Ephesians 1:7). This high price was paid before you ever desired to be purchased: "God showed His great love for us by sending Christ to die for us while we were still sinners" (Romans 5:8). Praise God for buying you with the costly blood of Jesus and changing you from a slave to sin to a child of God (Galatians 3–4). (***See Salvation***> *Receiving*> *When*> *Redeemed/rescued/ransomed,* TopicGuide page A22.)

11:1-3 Three images were used to illustrate the judgment that was to come. The greatest trees in all the nations were destroyed; the shepherds mourned their lowly state; and the young lions roared over the destruction of their habitat. The shepherds may have been the leaders of the haughty nations in 10:11 or the leaders of Israel who were addressed in the subsequent verses.

hands and into the hands of their king. They will turn the land into a wilderness, and I will
not rescue them."
11:7 Pss 90:17; 133:1 Ezek 37:16-23 [7]So I cared for the flock intended for slaughter—the flock that was oppressed. Then I
took two shepherd's staffs and named one Favor and the other Union. [8]I got rid of their
three evil shepherds in a single month.
11:8 Hos 5:7 But I became impatient with these sheep, and they hated me, too. [9]So I told them, "I
11:9 Ps 69:22-28 Jer 15:2-3 won't be your shepherd any longer. If you die, you die. If you are killed, you are killed.
And let those who remain devour each other!"
11:10 Jer 14:21 [10]Then I took my staff called Favor and cut it in two, showing that I had revoked the cov-
enant I had made with all the nations. [11]That was the end of my covenant with them. The
suffering flock was watching me, and they knew that the LORD was speaking through my
actions.
11:12-13 *Matt 27:9-10 Acts 1:18-19 [12]And I said to them, "If you like, give me my wages, whatever I am worth; but only if
you want to." So they counted out for my wages thirty pieces of silver.
[13]And the LORD said to me, "Throw it to the potter*"—this magnificent sum at which they
valued me! So I took the thirty coins and threw them to the potter in the Temple of the LORD.
11:14 Zech 11:6 [14]Then I took my other staff, Union, and cut it in two, showing that the bond of unity be-
tween Judah and Israel was broken.
11:15 Zech 11:17 [15]Then the LORD said to me, "Go again and play the part of a worthless shepherd. [16]This
illustrates how I will give this nation a shepherd who will not care for those who are dying,
11:16 Jer 23:2, 22 Ezek 34:2-6 nor look after the young,* nor heal the injured, nor feed the healthy. Instead, this shepherd
will eat the meat of the fattest sheep and tear off their hooves.

11:17 Zech 10:2; 11:15 [17]"What sorrow awaits this worthless shepherd
who abandons the flock!
The sword will cut his arm
and pierce his right eye.
His arm will become useless,
and his right eye completely blind."

FUTURE DELIVERANCE FOR JERUSALEM

12:1 Job 26:7 Jer 51:15 Heb 1:10-12 **12** This* message concerning the fate of Israel came from the LORD: "This message is
from the LORD, who stretched out the heavens, laid the foundations of the earth,

11:13 Syriac version reads *into the treasury;* also in 11:13b. Compare Matt 27:6-10. 11:16 Or *the scattered.* 12:1 Hebrew *An Oracle: This.*

11:4-17 Zechariah was told to portray a shepherd as an object lesson for the people. Public demonstrations, like miniature stage productions, were one means God used to communicate through the prophets (see also Isaiah 20:2-4; Jeremiah 32:6-15; Ezekiel 4:1-8; Hosea 1–3).

11:10-11 Part of Zechariah's prophecy involved two shepherd's staffs. The meaning of "Favor," the first staff, is that the people had rejected the shepherd, thus God's goodwill toward Israel had ended. Now God's protection, the "wall of fire" that surrounded Jerusalem (2:5), would be removed. The shattered second staff, "Union," reminded them that in more than a political sense, Judah and Israel were divided.

▸ SPIRITUAL WARFARE

11:17 Certain doom. God's acts of judgment throughout history make one thing clear—God is not opposed to punishing the guilty. In past history, God threatened judgment on Israel (see Hosea 9:17) and then on Judah (see Jeremiah 21:3-7). Israel's leaders ordered the murder of their own Messiah (Acts 3:14-15) and continued to persecute the apostles and the early church (Acts 9:1; 1 Thessalonians 2:14-16). In response, God was true to His word. He brought horrible devastation from the Romans, and the second Temple was demolished in AD 70. In the future, God "has set a day for judging the world" (Acts 17:31) and on that day He "will bring our darkest secrets to light and will reveal our private motives" (1 Corinthians 4:5). God will keep His promise to judge sin—He's already proven that. Prepare today for that certain appointment. Do your best to prepare those around you for that day. (***See Spiritual Warfare**> Originator of Sin> Satan's Domain> Doomed to destruction,* TopicGuide page A44.)

12:1–14:21 The final three chapters of Zechariah are comprised of a series of messages that present ideal images of blessings for the people of God and curses upon their enemies. Once again, the central figure who brings the blessing of forgiveness and restoration is the Good Shepherd who receives God's judgment (13:7) by being pierced for His people (12:10). These pictures foreshadow Christ's return and the culmination of history. It is not clear what immediate situation Zechariah referred to by "that day" (12:4, 6; 13:1, 2, 4; 14:4, 6, 8, 20). Thus, it is difficult to understand how Zechariah's original audience would have understood the original "day" Zechariah had in mind.

and formed the human spirit. 2I will make Jerusalem like an intoxicating drink that makes
the nearby nations stagger when they send their armies to besiege Jerusalem and Judah.
3On that day I will make Jerusalem an immovable rock. All the nations will gather against
it to try to move it, but they will only hurt themselves.
4"On that day," says the LORD, "I will cause every horse to panic and every rider to lose
his nerve. I will watch over the people of Judah, but I will blind all the horses of their ene-
mies. 5And the clans of Judah will say to themselves, 'The people of Jerusalem have found
strength in the LORD of Heaven's Armies, their God.'
6"On that day I will make the clans of Judah like a flame that sets a woodpile ablaze or
like a burning torch among sheaves of grain. They will burn up all the neighboring nations
right and left, while the people living in Jerusalem remain secure.
7"The LORD will give victory to the rest of Judah first, before Jerusalem, so that the peo-
ple of Jerusalem and the royal line of David will not have greater honor than the rest of Ju-
dah. 8On that day the LORD will defend the people of Jerusalem; the weakest among them
will be as mighty as King David! And the royal descendants will be like God, like the angel
of the LORD who goes before them! 9For on that day I will begin to destroy all the nations
that come against Jerusalem.
10"Then I will pour out a spirit* of grace and prayer on the family of David and on the
people of Jerusalem. They will look on Me whom they have pierced and mourn for Him as
for an only son. They will grieve bitterly for Him as for a firstborn son who has died. 11The
sorrow and mourning in Jerusalem on that day will be like the great mourning for Hadad-
rimmon in the valley of Megiddo.
12"All Israel will mourn, each clan by itself, and with the husbands separate from their
wives. The clan of David will mourn alone, as will the clan of Nathan, 13the clan of Levi,
and the clan of Shimei. 14Each of the surviving clans from Judah will mourn separately,
and with the husbands separate from their wives.

A FOUNTAIN OF CLEANSING

13 "On that day a fountain will be opened for the dynasty of David and for the peo-
ple of Jerusalem, a fountain to cleanse them from all their sins and impurity.
2"And on that day," says the LORD of Heaven's Armies, "I will erase idol worship through-
out the land, so that even the names of the idols will be forgotten. I will remove from the
land both the false prophets and the spirit of impurity that came with them. 3If anyone
continues to prophesy, his own father and mother will tell him, 'You must die, for you
have prophesied lies in the name of the LORD.' And as he prophesies, his own father and
mother will stab him.
4"On that day people will be ashamed to claim the prophetic gift. No one will pretend
to be a prophet by wearing prophet's clothes. 5He will say, 'I'm no prophet; I'm a farmer. I

12:2 Ps 75:8; Isa 51:17, 22-23
12:3 Dan 2:34-35, 44-45; Matt 21:44
12:6 Isa 10:16-18; Obad 1:18
12:7 Amos 9:11
12:8 Exod 14:19; Lev 26:8; Ps 82:6; Mic 7:8; Zech 9:14-15
12:10 Joel 2:28-29; John 19:34-37; Rev 1:7
12:11 Matt 24:30
13:1 Num 19:9-22; Ps 51:2, 7
13:2 Exod 23:13; 1 Kgs 22:22
13:3 Deut 13:6-11; Jer 23:25
13:4 2 Kgs 1:8; Mic 3:6-7; Matt 3:4
13:5 Amos 7:14

12:10 Or *the Spirit*.

12:11 "Hadad-rimmon" combines the names of two ancient storm deities. They shared worship space with Anat, the deceased consort of Baal, in a temple located near Megiddo. Canaanite fertility rituals required periodic mourning, and it is to these rituals that Zechariah referred, comparing their mourning to the grief in Jerusalem.

▶ GOD

13:2 Get rid of it! Genuine revival is like thoroughly cleaning a house. Cleaning a house involves removing junk that has accumulated over the years, and genuine revival involves removing all spiritual filth that has crept into our lives. Zechariah described a removal by God that would be so thorough that the names of the former idols would be forgotten. The false prophets who influenced the people toward evil would also be cast out. You cannot truly clean your house and keep all the junk you have accumulated, and neither can you turn to God while clinging to unholy idols or sinful associations. What's in your house? What idols are you depending on to save you? What relationships are hindering your relationship with God? Ask God to help you identify these so that anything that displeases Him can be removed. (***See God**> Salvation> Son> Sanctifies and cleanses the church*, TopicGuide page A15.)

13:5-6 When the Lord erased idolatry from the land, false prophets would be ashamed to admit that they had practiced such deceit, and would deny their involvement with it. They would lie about how they acquired the scars that distinguished them as prophets. These scars were likely from self-abusive activities that were common in pagan rituals (see 1 Kings 18:28).

began working for a farmer as a boy.' 6And if someone asks, 'Then what about those
wounds on your chest?*' he will say, 'I was wounded at my friends' house!'

THE SCATTERING OF THE SHEEP

13:7 Isa 40:11; 53:4-5, 10 *Matt 26:31 *Mark 14:27

7 "Awake, O sword, against My shepherd,
the man who is My partner,"
says the LORD of Heaven's Armies.
"Strike down the shepherd,
and the sheep will be scattered,
and I will turn against the lambs.

13:8 Zech 11:6-9

8 Two-thirds of the people in the land
will be cut off and die," says the LORD.
"But one-third will be left in the land.

13:9 Isa 48:10 Hos 2:23 Zech 12:10

9 I will bring that group through the fire
and make them pure.
I will refine them like silver
and purify them like gold.
They will call on My name,
and I will answer them.
I will say, 'These are My people,'
and they will say, 'The LORD is our God.'"

THE LORD WILL RULE THE EARTH

14:1 Mal 4:1

14 Watch, for the day of the LORD is coming when your possessions will be plundered
right in front of you! 2I will gather all the nations to fight against Jerusalem. The
city will be taken, the houses looted, and the women raped. Half the population will be
taken into captivity, and the rest will be left among the ruins of the city.

14:4 Ezek 11:23 Mic 1:3-4 Zech 4:7

3Then the LORD will go out to fight against those nations, as He has fought in times past.
4On that day His feet will stand on the Mount of Olives, east of Jerusalem. And the Mount of
Olives will split apart, making a wide valley running from east to west. Half the mountain

14:5 Isa 29:6 Matt 16:27; 25:31 Jude 1:14

will move toward the north and half toward the south. 5You will flee through this valley, for
it will reach across to Azal.* Yes, you will flee as you did from the earthquake in the days of
King Uzziah of Judah. Then the LORD my God will come, and all His holy ones with Him.*

14:6 Acts 2:16, 20

14:7 Rev 21:23-25; 22:5

6On that day the sources of light will no longer shine,* 7yet there will be continuous day!
Only the LORD knows how this could happen. There will be no normal day and night, for at
evening time it will still be light.

13:6 Hebrew *wounds between your hands?* 14:5a The meaning of the Hebrew is uncertain. 14:5b As in Greek version; Hebrew reads *with you.* 14:6 Hebrew *there will be no light, no cold or frost.* The meaning of the Hebrew is uncertain.

▸ GOD

13:7 God orders Jesus' death. Who was responsible for Christ's death? Would you be surprised to discover it is God? This startling point is clearly expressed when Zechariah presented God ordering that a sword be used to strike His own Good Shepherd. Isaiah 53:10 expresses the same point: "But it was the LORD's good plan to crush Him and cause Him grief." But why would God strike the only person who ever pleased Him? Because He loves sinners. The Father made His sinless Son the object of His judgment (2 Corinthians 5:21), and our Good Shepherd took this judgment willingly. You deserved the sword from God for your rebellion. In love, God provided a substitute for you. Why? So He could spare you. Marvel at such love (Ephesians 3:18-19), and do not hesitate to share it with others. (***See God****> Salvation> Father> Made Christ to be sin for us,* TopicGuide page A15.)

14:1-21 In this last series of images, Zechariah described "the day of the LORD," a time of ultimate blessing for God's people and ultimate judgment on God's enemies. Such images are common whenever the prophets describe "that day." These blessings and curses were fulfilled at various times in history, but ultimately they will be fulfilled when Jesus returns. The New Testament writers (especially John in Revelation) describe Jesus' second coming with imagery drawn from Zechariah and the other prophets.

14:4-5 Zechariah described God's coming by saying His "feet" will touch the Mount of Olives in Jerusalem. God's coming will split the earth, making a way of escape for His persecuted flock. Earth-shaking images were often used to communicate the awesome power of God when He comes in judgment (see Psalm 18:7-12; Isaiah 29:5-7). This scene is similar to the imagery of Revelation 16:17-21, which describes God judging His enemies through an earthquake that splits the great city.

8 On that day life-giving waters will flow out from Jerusalem, half toward the Dead Sea
and half toward the Mediterranean,* flowing continuously in both summer and winter.
9 And the LORD will be king over all the earth. On that day there will be one LORD—His
name alone will be worshiped.
10 All the land from Geba, north of Judah, to Rimmon, south of Jerusalem, will become
one vast plain. But Jerusalem will be raised up in its original place and will be inhabited all
the way from the Benjamin Gate over to the site of the old gate, then to the Corner Gate,
and from the Tower of Hananel to the king's winepresses. 11 And Jerusalem will be filled,
safe at last, never again to be cursed and destroyed.
12 And the LORD will send a plague on all the nations that fought against Jerusalem. Their
people will become like walking corpses, their flesh rotting away. Their eyes will rot in
their sockets, and their tongues will rot in their mouths. 13 On that day they will be terrified,
stricken by the LORD with great panic. They will fight their neighbors hand to hand. 14 Ju-
dah, too, will be fighting at Jerusalem. The wealth of all the neighboring nations will be
captured—great quantities of gold and silver and fine clothing. 15 This same plague will
strike the horses, mules, camels, donkeys, and all the other animals in the enemy camps.
16 In the end, the enemies of Jerusalem who survive the plague will go up to Jerusalem
each year to worship the King, the LORD of Heaven's Armies, and to celebrate the Festival
of Shelters. 17 Any nation in the world that refuses to come to Jerusalem to worship the
King, the LORD of Heaven's Armies, will have no rain. 18 If the people of Egypt refuse to at-
tend the festival, the LORD will punish them with the same plague that He sends on the
other nations who refuse to go. 19 Egypt and the other nations will all be punished if they
don't go to celebrate the Festival of Shelters.
20 On that day even the harness bells of the horses will be inscribed with these words:
HOLY TO THE LORD. And the cooking pots in the Temple of the LORD will be as sacred as the
basins used beside the altar. 21 In fact, every cooking pot in Jerusalem and Judah will be
holy to the LORD of Heaven's Armies. All who come to worship will be free to use any of
these pots to boil their sacrifices. And on that day there will no longer be traders* in the
Temple of the LORD of Heaven's Armies.

14:8 Ezek 47:1-12; John 7:37-38; Rev 22:1-2
14:9 Deut 6:4; Ps 47:7; Zech 9:9
14:10 2 Kgs 14:13
14:11 Ps 48:8; Rev 22:3
14:14 Zech 12:2
14:16 Isa 60:6-9; 66:18-21
14:20 Exod 39:30; Ezek 46:20
14:21 Neh 8:10; Rom 14:6-7; 1 Cor 10:31

14:8 Hebrew *half toward the eastern sea and half toward the western sea.* 14:21 Hebrew *Canaanites.*

▶ GOD

14:8 Life-giving waters. Like a modern work of art, Joel 3:18 unexpectedly envisioned a life-giving fountain bursting out of the Temple and causing flowers to bloom in desert regions. Later, Jesus said He was the temple (John 2:19-22), and He boldly stood in Jerusalem and echoed Zechariah by claiming to be the source of life-giving water (John 7:37-38). In heaven there is no Temple, for "the Lord God Almighty and the Lamb are its temple" (Revelation 21:22). But the metaphor continues with a river of water flowing freely from the throne of God and of the Lamb (Revelation 22:1). The principle remains the same through each passage—God has provided the means for our spiritual renewal and life. The Old Covenant saints saw this primarily coming from the Temple, but Jesus sharpened the focus to Himself. If you are thirsty, struggling, and feeling weak from your war with the world and your own sin, then stay close to Jesus. He is the source of spiritual life for all who believe. (***See God**> God's Names> Son> The Life,* TopicGuide page A18.)

14:12-16 "That day" would be characterized by the judgment of God's enemies as well as blessing for His people. God's enemies would be plagued severely and baffled into fighting one another. Meanwhile, God's people would be united and victorious, plundering their enemies. Zechariah's words assured his audience that oppressing nations would be judged fully and finally someday. Even better, any people from the nations who survived the plague would be transformed from enemies into worshipers of God, as illustrated by their participation in the Festival of Shelters.

14:20-21 "HOLY TO THE LORD" was the inscription on the high priest's turban, an indication that he was uniquely set apart to serve a holy God (Exodus 28:36). In the day of the LORD, the most common items in society—a harness bell or a cooking pot—would be equally set apart to God, eliminating the distinction between "sacred" and "secular." This picture anticipates the way the new Jerusalem will be permeated with light from God and the Lamb (Revelation 21:23), making everything and everyone "HOLY TO THE LORD."

MALACHI

PURPOSE

To warn Judah, particularly the priests,
of the dangers of continually ignoring the law of Moses.

For hundreds of years God spoke to His people through His servants the prophets, but with the words of Malachi that period came to an end. After Malachi's voice, the next words Israel heard from God came four hundred years later through John the Baptist: "Repent of your sins and turn to God, for the Kingdom of Heaven is near" (Matthew 3:2).

Despite the prophetic ministries of Haggai and Zechariah and the leadership of Zerubbabel, Ezra, and Nehemiah, the returned exiles quickly fell back into the sinful patterns of their ancestors. They rebuilt the Temple and the walls around Jerusalem, but those physical restorations were not matched by spiritual renewal in their lives. Jews intermarried with their pagan neighbors; priests failed to handle the finances of the Temple; and many others abused the poor, worshiped idols, and adopted the same sinful lifestyles that sent them into captivity in the first place. Malachi's message served as God's last word to Israel. After this, Israel waited for the "messenger" (Malachi 3:1-2; 4:5-6) who would tell them the next step in God's solution for the problem of a sinful human race.

DISCOVER GOD IN MALACHI

At a time when it would have been easy for God to wash His hands of a faithless people, His attributes of constancy, love, and justice remained clear:

Divine Constancy: We can imagine how we would have felt at this point in dealing with God's chosen people: exasperated! After 1,600 years of dealing with Abraham's family, this is what it had come to—a morally and physically scattered people disappearing into the sands of Israel. It is amazing to find God uttering these words through Malachi: "I am the Lord, and I do not change. That is why you descendants of Jacob are not already destroyed. Ever since the days of your ancestors, you have scorned My decrees and failed to obey them. Now return to Me, and I will return to you" (3:6-7). One of the most reassuring aspects of the character of God is that He never changes, which means He never goes back on His word. He said through Jeremiah that Israel would never cease to exist before Him (Jeremiah 31:36). If He completely destroyed them, it would be a violation of His own character. Once God has made a promise to His people (for example, that He will never fail nor abandon us; see Deuteronomy 31:8; Hebrews 13:5), that promise will never be revoked.

Chosen Love: The Jews' circumstances caused them to doubt God's love. They wondered: Why hasn't the glory of the Lord filled the Temple we rebuilt? Where is God's blessing on our land and crops? How can God say He loves us, given our circumstances? When the prophets told the people of God's love, they responded, "Really? How [has He] loved us?" (1:2).

Malachi reminded them that God had loved their ancestor Jacob and rejected Jacob's twin brother, Esau (1:2-3). That love was a choice God made (Romans 9:10-16). Their circumstances were not a measure of God's love for them—His feelings toward His faithful people were settled.

Perfect Justice: When others seem more evil than we are or when those who have done us harm go unpunished, we wonder, *where is God's justice?* That is what the Jews of Malachi's day wondered (2:17). Malachi assured them that justice was coming, but he warned them that they might not like the results, because it would come first to Israel (3:1-5). God would appear with the heat of a blazing fire and the sting of strong soap to cleanse His people from sin and make Israel "holy and without fault" (Ephesians 5:27). If we demand God's justice, we should be prepared for it to fall on everyone—including ourselves.

DISCOVERY VERSES

"But My name is honored by people of other nations from morning till night. All around the world they offer sweet incense and pure offerings in honor of My name. For My name is great among the nations," says the LORD of Heaven's Armies. (MALACHI 1:11)

"Look! I am sending My messenger, and he will prepare the way before Me. Then the Lord you are seeking will suddenly come to His Temple. The messenger of the covenant, whom you look for so eagerly, is surely coming," says the LORD of Heaven's Armies. (MALACHI 3:1)

But for you who fear My name, the Sun of Righteousness will rise with healing in His wings. And you will go free, leaping with joy like calves let out to pasture. (MALACHI 4:2)

GROWING THROUGH MALACHI

Malachi touches on a number of practical themes important to the follower of Christ:

Give God the Best: The half-hearted spiritual attitudes of the Jews who returned were nowhere more evident than in what they gave to God. The law required that their sacrifices and offerings to Him be the first and best of what they gained. Instead, they brought blind, crippled, and diseased animals from their flocks to offer to Him—gifts that would be unacceptable even to a human authority (1:6-9). Our time, our efforts—everything we give to God should be our very best.

Don't Be a Stumbling Block: Throughout Scripture, God reserves harsh words for leaders who cause less mature believers to stumble and sin (Malachi 2:1, 7-9; Romans 14). Leaders are appointed by God to show others the ways of wisdom and righteousness, not the ways of sin and immorality. Because everyone functions as a leader at some point in life, Malachi's words to the priests are applicable to everyone. Be a positive influencer of those under your authority—God holds accountable those who harm the ones under their care (Matthew 18:6).

Let God Prove Himself: Malachi challenged the laypeople and priests of Israel to become the solution to their own problem. Because the people had stopped bringing their tithes and priests had mismanaged the portions that were delivered, God had stopped His blessings (3:8-12). Giving faithfully and freely and deeply of our resources frees us from the chains of materialism and puts us in a position of depending on God to meet our needs.

MALACHI FACTS

Author: Malachi (1:1). This prophet is not mentioned anywhere else in the Old Testament.

Written to: The community of Jews who returned to Judah after living in exile in Babylon.

Date of writing: Because the sins Malachi addressed are similar to issues addressed by Nehemiah, the two were likely contemporaries. Malachi possibly ministered in the period between Nehemiah's first and second visits to Jerusalem, approximately 432–425 BC.

Setting: Jerusalem and the surrounding region of Israel.

OUTLINE

▸ **MALACHI 1:1-5**—God's Love for Israel

▸ **MALACHI 1:6–2:16**—Israel's Unfaithfulness

▸ **MALACHI 2:17–4:6**—God's Judgment

1 This is the message* that the LORD gave to Israel through the prophet Malachi.*

THE LORD'S LOVE FOR ISRAEL

1:2-3 *Rom 9:13 2 "I have always loved you," says the LORD.
But you retort, "Really? How have You loved us?"
And the LORD replies, "This is how I showed My love for you: I loved your ancestor Ja-
cob, 3 but I rejected his brother, Esau, and devastated his hill country. I turned Esau's inheri-
tance into a desert for jackals."
1:4 Isa 9:10 4 Esau's descendants in Edom may say, "We have been shattered, but we will rebuild the
ruins."
But the LORD of Heaven's Armies replies, "They may try to rebuild, but I will demolish them
again. Their country will be known as 'The Land of Wickedness,' and their people will be
1:5 Pss 35:27; 48:1 called 'The People with Whom the LORD Is Forever Angry.' 5 When you see the destruction for
yourselves, you will say, 'Truly, the LORD's greatness reaches far beyond Israel's borders!'"

UNWORTHY SACRIFICES

1:6 Exod 20:12 Deut 31:12 Isa 1:2 6 The LORD of Heaven's Armies says to the priests: "A son honors his father, and a servant
respects his master. If I am your father and master, where are the honor and respect I de-
serve? You have shown contempt for My name!
"But you ask, 'How have we ever shown contempt for Your name?'
7 "You have shown contempt by offering defiled sacrifices on My altar.
1:7 Lev 21:6-8 "Then you ask, 'How have we defiled the sacrifices?*'
1:8 Lev 1:3 Deut 15:21 "You defile them by saying the altar of the LORD deserves no respect. 8 When you give
blind animals as sacrifices, isn't that wrong? And isn't it wrong to offer animals that are
crippled and diseased? Try giving gifts like that to your governor, and see how pleased he
is!" says the LORD of Heaven's Armies.
1:9 Lev 23:33-44 Ps 51:17 9 "Go ahead, beg God to be merciful to you! But when you bring that kind of offering,
why should He show you any favor at all?" asks the LORD of Heaven's Armies.

1:1a Hebrew *An Oracle: The message.* 1:1b *Malachi* means "my messenger." 1:7 As in Greek version; Hebrew reads *defiled You?*

1:1 During the fifth century BC, God sent the struggling Jewish community in Judah leaders like Ezra and Nehemiah to aid them in restoring Jerusalem and their own broken spirits. The message of the book of Malachi addresses the same problems of this period. The form of the book is mostly that of a debate. For example, Malachi 1:2-5 shows a dispute between God and Israel about whether God really loves Israel.

1:2-4 The origin of the conflict between Jacob and Esau is recorded in Genesis 27–28. While Jacob and Esau eventually reconciled (see Genesis 33:4), their descendants were often in conflict. Edom was the nation that descended from Esau. It was located in the mountainous region southeast of the Dead Sea. Because Edom took advantage of Israel when other nations attacked God's people, God promised to destroy Edom totally (see the book of Obadiah).

▸ WORSHIP
1:6 Don't ignore Him. Cultures all over the world honor their ancestors, their scientists, and their artists—but not the One who created everything, including truth and beauty. This is the situation that existed in Malachi's day. In this passage, God began a second round of dialogue with Israel, and He pointed out that though fathers and masters were honored, He was not. Even though He was Israel's true Father and true Master (see Psalm 123:2), it was as if He didn't even exist. Even in the midst of obeying God's commands, you may lose sight of who is behind it all. Repent of your wandering away and return to intimacy with Him (Luke 10:38-42). (***See Worship****> OT> Reverence> Let the earth fear God,* TopicGuide page A29.)

1:8 God's regulations for sacrifices called for animals that were perfect (see Leviticus 22:17-25), but many of the animals the Israelites were bringing were blind, diseased, or lame. Such sacrifices were not really sacrifices at all, since they were of little use anyway. God sarcastically asked whether people would be so bold as to insult their Persian governor by offering him such animals. The obvious answer was no.

10“How I wish one of you would shut the Temple doors so that these worthless sacrifices 1:10
could not be offered! I am not pleased with you,” says the LORD of Heaven’s Armies, “and I Isa 1:13
will not accept your offerings. 11But My name is honored* by people of other nations from Jer 14:12
morning till night. All around the world they offer* sweet incense and pure offerings in honor 1:11 Ps 113:3
of My name. For My name is great among the nations,” says the LORD of Heaven’s Armies. Isa 60:6-7
12“But you dishonor My name with your actions. By bringing contemptible food, you
are saying it’s all right to defile the Lord’s table. 13You say, ‘It’s too hard to serve the LORD,’ 1:13
and you turn up your noses at My commands,” says the LORD of Heaven’s Armies. “Think Isa 43:22-24
of it! Animals that are stolen and crippled and sick are being presented as offerings!
Should I accept from you such offerings as these?” asks the LORD.
14“Cursed is the cheat who promises to give a fine ram from his flock but then sacrifices 1:14
a defective one to the Lord. For I am a great king,” says the LORD of Heaven’s Armies, “and Exod 12:5 Lev 22:18-21
My name is feared among the nations! Ps 72:8-11

A WARNING TO THE PRIESTS

2 “Listen, you priests—this command is for you! 2Listen to Me and make up your minds
to honor My name,” says the LORD of Heaven’s Armies, “or I will bring a terrible curse
against you. I will curse even the blessings you receive. Indeed, I have already cursed
them, because you have not taken My warning to heart. 3I will punish your descendants
and splatter your faces with the manure from your festival sacrifices, and I will throw you 2:4
on the manure pile. 4Then at last you will know it was I who sent you this warning so that Num 3:12
My covenant with the Levites can continue,” says the LORD of Heaven’s Armies. 2:5 Num 25:12
5“The purpose of My covenant with the Levites was to bring life and peace, and that is
what I gave them. This required reverence from them, and they greatly revered Me and 2:6
stood in awe of My name. 6They passed on to the people the truth of the instructions they Deut 33:10
received from Me. They did not lie or cheat; they walked with Me, living good and righ- 2:7
teous lives, and they turned many from lives of sin. Lev 10:11 Num 27:21
7“The words of a priest’s lips should preserve knowledge of God, and people should go Deut 17:8-11
to him for instruction, for the priest is the messenger of the LORD of Heaven’s Armies. 8But 2:8
you priests have left God’s paths. Your instructions have caused many to stumble into sin. Neh 13:29 Isa 9:16
You have corrupted the covenant I made with the Levites,” says the LORD of Heaven’s Ar- Ezek 44:10
mies. 9“So I have made you despised and humiliated in the eyes of all the people. For you 2:9
have not obeyed Me but have shown favoritism in the way you carry out My instructions.” Deut 1:17 1 Sam 2:30

A CALL TO FAITHFULNESS 2:10

10Are we not all children of the same Father? Are we not all created by the same God? Exod 19:5 Josh 24:3
Then why do we betray each other, violating the covenant of our ancestors? Jer 31:9
11Judah has been unfaithful, and a detestable thing has been done in Israel and in Jeru- 2:11
salem. The men of Judah have defiled the LORD’s beloved sanctuary by marrying women Ezra 9:1-2 Jer 3:7-9

1:11a Or *will be honored.* 1:11b Or *will offer.*

▸ PURPOSE

1:14 God is a Great King. Is God being egotistical by commanding people to glorify and worship Him? This would be wrong if God were just another person. But God is not like us. He is the King of the entire universe, which He created. If you were approaching the leader of your country, how would you react? Now imagine approaching the Ruler of not just the entire earth but also the entire universe! It is therefore appropriate and good to show deepest respect to God as the great King of everyone and everything. (***See Purpose****> God’s Means> God’s Sovereignty> God is King over every nation,* TopicGuide page A52.)

2:1-2 God then focused His warnings on the priests of Israel. God holds those who lead and teach His people to a higher standard (see James 3:1) because of their additional knowledge and responsibilities. God said He had been working against these priests, trying to get their attention, yet the priests had not repented or given Him the honor He deserved. Malachi 2:10-16 shows that the priests’ unfaithfulness had infected the whole nation.

2:4-8 No passage in the Old Testament records the details of the covenant between the Lord and the tribe of Levi. Numerous passages make clear, however, that the Levites were specially set apart for the Lord’s service. Jeremiah 33:21 and Nehemiah 13:29 also reference the Lord’s covenant with Levi.

2:11 Intermarriage with foreign women was a continual temptation and common sin for the Israelites. The problem was not racial. For example, according to Joshua 6:25, Rahab the Canaanite prostitute became part of the Israelite community, and Matthew 1:5 indicates she was part of the genealogy of

who worship idols. 12May the LORD cut off from the nation of Israel* every last man who
has done this and yet brings an offering to the LORD of Heaven's Armies.
13Here is another thing you do. You cover the LORD's altar with tears, weeping and
groaning because He pays no attention to your offerings and doesn't accept them with
2:14 pleasure. 14You cry out, "Why doesn't the LORD accept my worship?" I'll tell you why! Be-
Prov 5:18 cause the LORD witnessed the vows you and your wife made when you were young. But
you have been unfaithful to her, though she remained your faithful partner, the wife of
your marriage vows.
2:15 15Didn't the LORD make you one with your wife? In body and spirit you are His.* And
Gen 2:24 Matt 19:4-6 what does He want? Godly children from your union. So guard your heart; remain loyal to
1 Cor 7:10, 14 the wife of your youth. 16"For I hate divorce!" says the LORD, the God of Israel. "To divorce
2:16 your wife is to overwhelm her with cruelty,*" says the LORD of Heaven's Armies. "So guard
Matt 5:31; 19:6-8 Mark 10:4-5 your heart; do not be unfaithful to your wife."
17You have wearied the LORD with your words.
2:17 Isa 5:20; 43:22, 24 "How have we wearied Him?" you ask.
Zeph 1:12 You have wearied Him by saying that all who do evil are good in the LORD's sight, and
He is pleased with them. You have wearied Him by asking, "Where is the God of justice?"

THE COMING DAY OF JUDGMENT

3:1 *Matt 11:10 3 "Look! I am sending My messenger, and he will prepare the way before Me. Then
*Mark 1:2 *Luke 7:27 the Lord you are seeking will suddenly come to His Temple. The messenger of the

2:12 Hebrew *from the tents of Jacob.* The names "Jacob" and "Israel" are often interchanged throughout the Old Testament, referring sometimes to the individual patriarch and sometimes to the nation. 2:15 Or *Didn't the one LORD make us and preserve our life and breath?* or *Didn't the one LORD make her, both flesh and spirit?* The meaning of the Hebrew is uncertain. 2:16 Hebrew *to cover one's garment with violence.*

Jesus. Instead, the problem was that foreign women worshiped idols and led their husbands away from worship of the Lord, the only true God. Ezra worked to stamp out this practice after the exiles returned from Babylon (Ezra 9–10), but the people's repentance was short-lived, and by the time of Malachi's writing, the practice had returned.

▸ HOLINESS

2:12 Holy heart. Growing in grace takes more than a religious ritual, whether it be a ritual from the Old Testament, or regular church attendance, or Bible study, or fasting and prayer. Many men of Israel had married foreign women and tolerated their idolatry, yet these men apparently continued to bring offerings to the Lord, as if there was nothing wrong in their families. But God said that their hypocritical offerings did not make them holy in His sight. Are there areas in your life where you are ignoring God's clear command? Do not think that going to church, giving an offering, or saying a prayer smoothes over your actions. God calls you to give yourself completely to Him. Make Him Lord of your entire life; do not hold any area back. (***See Holiness***> *Submission*> *Yielding to spirit*> *Present yourselves holy,* TopicGuide page A41.)

2:15-16 God clearly reaffirmed what marriage is: a man and a woman becoming one. God hates divorce. When we marry, we are to remain faithful to our spouse and are only released from our covenant in cases of sexual immorality (Matthew 19:9) or abandonment (1 Corinthians 7:15).

▸ BIBLE

2:16 Building Relationships. Disobedience to God leads to broken relationships. For the Israelites, it led to broken relationships with each other (marital divorce) and with God (spiritual divorce). Ephesians 5:21-33 indicates that marriage is a picture of our relationship with God. How does your relationship with God reflect on your marriage or your closest relationships? Both positively and negatively, do you treat God the way you treat those you love the deepest? Good relationships must be guarded and nurtured with time, effort, and, most of all, love. Guard your marriage with God with the same vigor (if not more) that you guard your human relationships with. (***See Bible***> *Unity*> *Doctrines*> *Principles of marriage,* TopicGuide page A10.)

▸ BIBLE

3:1-5 The Word that exposes. You may attempt to casually peruse the Bible or read it at random, but this is as wise as playing with a sharp knife. You must be careful when you open up the Bible—it's not what you expect. Hebrews 4:12 explains that the written Word does what the messenger of the covenant in Malachi's prophecy would do—reveal our sin. "For the word of God is alive and powerful. It is sharper than the sharpest two-edged sword, cutting between soul and spirit, between joint and marrow. It exposes our innermost thoughts and desires." Do we treat the Bible casually, perusing it at random? Do we treat the Bible like a textbook, good for studying to pass the occasional spiritual quiz, but for little else? How does the way you treat the Bible reveal your spiritual condition? (***See Bible***> *Power*> *Equip*> *Sword of the Spirit,* TopicGuide page A11.)

3:1 In the ancient Near East, before a king entered a city, a messenger would arrive to announce the king's arrival and prepare the city for the king's entrance. A close reading of this verse shows that the "messenger" in the first sentence and the "messenger of the covenant" in the third sentence are not the same person. The first messenger will prepare the way for the second. Matthew 11:10 tells us that John the Baptist was the messenger preparing the way for Jesus. Malachi 3:2-4 indicates that the "messenger of the covenant" will purify the nation, judge it, and bring a spiritual reformation. These roles go beyond the activity of John the Baptist and were achieved by the work of Jesus, the Messiah.

covenant, whom you look for so eagerly, is surely coming," says the LORD of Heaven's
Armies.
2"But who will be able to endure it when He comes? Who will be able to stand and face
Him when He appears? For He will be like a blazing fire that refines metal, or like a strong
soap that bleaches clothes. 3He will sit like a refiner of silver, burning away the dross. He
will purify the Levites, refining them like gold and silver, so that they may once again offer
acceptable sacrifices to the LORD. 4Then once more the LORD will accept the offerings
brought to Him by the people of Judah and Jerusalem, as He did in the past.
5"At that time I will put you on trial. I am eager to witness against all sorcerers and adul-
terers and liars. I will speak against those who cheat employees of their wages, who op-
press widows and orphans, or who deprive the foreigners living among you of justice, for
these people do not fear Me," says the LORD of Heaven's Armies.

3:2 Ezek 22:14; Matt 3:10-12; Rev 6:16-17
3:3 Dan 12:10
3:4 2 Chr 7:3; Ps 51:19
3:5 Exod 22:22; Jer 7:9-10; Jas 5:4

A CALL TO REPENTANCE

6"I am the LORD, and I do not change. That is why you descendants of Jacob are not already
destroyed. 7Ever since the days of your ancestors, you have scorned My decrees and failed
to obey them. Now return to Me, and I will return to you," says the LORD of Heaven's Armies.
"But you ask, 'How can we return when we have never gone away?'
8"Should people cheat God? Yet you have cheated Me!
"But you ask, 'What do You mean? When did we ever cheat You?'
"You have cheated Me of the tithes and offerings due to Me. 9You are under a curse, for
your whole nation has been cheating Me. 10Bring all the tithes into the storehouse so there
will be enough food in My Temple. If you do," says the LORD of Heaven's Armies, "I will
open the windows of heaven for you. I will pour out a blessing so great you won't have
enough room to take it in! Try it! Put Me to the test! 11Your crops will be abundant, for I will
guard them from insects and disease.* Your grapes will not fall from the vine before they
are ripe," says the LORD of Heaven's Armies. 12"Then all nations will call you blessed, for
your land will be such a delight," says the LORD of Heaven's Armies.
13"You have said terrible things about Me," says the LORD.
"But you say, 'What do You mean? What have we said against You?'
14"You have said, 'What's the use of serving God? What have we gained by obeying His
commands or by trying to show the LORD of Heaven's Armies that we are sorry for our
sins? 15From now on we will call the arrogant blessed. For those who do evil get rich, and
those who dare God to punish them suffer no harm.'"

3:7 Zech 1:3
3:8 Neh 13:11
3:12 Deut 28:3-12; Isa 61:9; 62:4
3:14-15 Ps 73:13

THE LORD'S PROMISE OF MERCY

16Then those who feared the LORD spoke with each other, and the LORD listened to what

3:16 Ps 56:8

3:11 Hebrew *from the devourer.*

3:2-3 Refining is the process of purifying metal after it has been mined.

▶ GOD

3:6 God does not change. As we get older, our bodies change. Our minds change. Our relationships change. It is difficult for us to understand that a being like God never changes. If God changed as we do, He would most certainly change His mind about having mercy on sinners like Israel and like us. Do you sometimes feel that you have done something so terrible that God could never possibly forgive you? The greatest proof that God's love for you will never end is that He never began to love you—He has always done so (1 Chronicles 16:34; Lamentations 3:22-23; Romans 8:35-39). God does not change (Hebrews 1:10-12), nor does His love for you change. (***See God> God's Attributes> Unchanging> His love is never-ending,*** TopicGuide page A17.)

3:8 A tithe is an offering of one tenth of a portion. Israelites in the Old Testament were commanded to give ten percent of their harvest crops to the Levites (Leviticus 27:30-34), which was a gracious requirement from the God who created the entire earth and owns everything in it (Psalm 50:10-11). There was a second tithe prescribed in Deuteronomy 14:25-26 to fund the journey to and from the yearly feast in Jerusalem. There was a third tithe mentioned in Deuteronomy 26:12-13 where in the third year of the seven-year cycle, a tithe was given to support the Levites, widows, and orphans. In this case, the priests were failing to pass on a portion of the first tithe to the Levites (Numbers 18:20-32), and thus were accused of robbing God.

3:16-18 There were some Israelites who did fear the Lord and followed Him with their hearts. They were no doubt wondering if they would be punished along with the wicked. God assured them that they would be spared because of their faith even as their nation was judged. God emphasized the same point in Ezekiel 18:1-32.

HAVE YOU EVER EXPERIENCED AN EARTHQUAKE? The feeling is quite unnerving. Suddenly, the earth—the very foundation that you have walked on and counted on—is unstable and unreliable. The walls shake; the furniture trembles. Is the roof going to collapse? You cannot find anything on which to steady yourself. Even if you haven't personally experienced an earthquake, you have probably seen broadcasts of the devastation an earthquake can cause. Victims' faces express their anxiety, fear, and sorrow.

People who do not trust in God live in a world that is constantly shifting. Nothing they believe or count on is reliable. Their perspectives on morals and the future change rapidly, tethered to their flittering feelings and changing circumstances. But those who trust in God stand on firm ground, because He is unchanging. We can rely on Him to be "the same yesterday, today, and forever" (Hebrews 13:8). James writes, "Whatever is good and perfect comes down to us from God our Father, who created all the lights in the heavens. He never changes or casts a shifting shadow" (James 1:17).

Because God never changes, our future is eternal and secure. We can claim the promises in His book and rest in them. The following are some of the ways God's unchanging nature gives us confidence about the future:

- *Stability.* God's character is always the same, so we don't need to fear that He will change His mind about what He says.
- *Eternal significance.* Everything God has said about us remains true—forever!
- *Unwavering guidance.* We can depend on God's leading in our lives as we trust and obey Him.
- *Timeless truth.* God's words are valid forever, a sure foundation for our lives.

Have you put your trust in God and His unchanging nature? Are you resting in Him? Remember the words of Philippians 1:6, "I am certain that God, who began the good work within you, will continue His work until it is finally finished on the day when Christ Jesus returns." Because God never changes, He will never change His mind or leave unfinished what He has started.

they said. In His presence, a scroll of remembrance was written to record the names of
those who feared Him and always thought about the honor of His name.
17 "They will be My people," says the LORD of Heaven's Armies. "On the day when I act in
judgment, they will be My own special treasure. I will spare them as a father spares an
obedient child. 18 Then you will again see the difference between the righteous and the
wicked, between those who serve God and those who do not."

THE COMING DAY OF JUDGMENT

4 1* The LORD of Heaven's Armies says, "The day of judgment is coming, burning like a
furnace. On that day the arrogant and the wicked will be burned up like straw. They
will be consumed—roots, branches, and all.
2 "But for you who fear My name, the Sun of Righteousness will rise with healing in His
wings.* And you will go free, leaping with joy like calves let out to pasture. 3 On the day
when I act, you will tread upon the wicked as if they were dust under your feet," says the
LORD of Heaven's Armies.
4 "Remember to obey the Law of Moses, My servant—all the decrees and regulations that
I gave him on Mount Sinai* for all Israel.
5 "Look, I am sending you the prophet Elijah before the great and dreadful day of the
LORD arrives. 6 His preaching will turn the hearts of fathers to their children, and the hearts
of children to their fathers. Otherwise I will come and strike the land with a curse."

4:1 Verses 4:1-6 are numbered 3:19-24 in Hebrew text. 4:2 Or *the sun of righteousness will rise with healing in its wings.* 4:4 Hebrew *Horeb*, another name for Sinai.

3:17 Neh 13:22; 1 Pet 2:9
3:18 Ps 58:11
4:1 Isa 5:24; Mal 3:2
4:2 Isa 30:26; 35:6
4:3 Mic 7:10
4:4 Deut 4:1
4:5 Matt 11:14; Mark 9:11-13; Luke 1:17; John 1:21
4:6 Isa 11:4; Luke 1:17; Rev 19:15

▸ GOD

4:1-3 The day of judgment is coming. Do you look around at the wicked people who prosper in this world and wonder whether you are fooling yourself to follow Jesus? Malachi lived at a time when it was hard to believe that God was ever going to judge evil. Many therefore questioned whether God was truly powerful and able to act. Many wondered whether faith in God's judgment of evil was simply an idealistic dream. But look at God's Word—at the many times God pointedly judged those who refused to repent (Genesis 6:5-8; Genesis 19:16, 24; Daniel 5:22-31; and many more). Nevertheless, it can be wearisome to wait on God's perfect timing. Ask God to help you leave judgment in His hands until Christ returns (Acts 17:31). (***See God**> God's Attributes> Just> A day is fixed for His righteous judgment of the world,* TopicGuide page A16.)

4:4-5 Moses and Elijah are often mentioned together as a summary of the Old Testament. Moses represents the law of God, which underpinned all of Israelite life, and Elijah represents the prophetic tradition, which called the Israelites to faithfulness to the law. The mention of the law and the prophets provides a fitting ending not only to Malachi's book but also to all 12 of the Minor Prophets and issues a call to faithfulness for all who follow God.

4:5-6 Elijah was God's major prophet during the evil reign of Ahab, king of the northern kingdom of Israel (see 1 Kings 17). The promise of Elijah in this verse is clearly connected to the first messenger in Malachi 3:1, because both verses begin with the phrase "'Look, I am sending . . .'" Malachi 4:6 indicates that the work of this second Elijah would be to focus on bringing the people to repentance. Since Elijah did not die (2 Kings 2:11), some people read 4:5 as an indication that Elijah himself was to return bodily. In Matthew 11:14, however, Jesus says that John the Baptist fulfilled this prophecy not because he was literally Elijah (see John 1:21) but because he preached with the same spirit and power as Elijah did (see Luke 1:17).

BECAUSE GOD
NEVER CHANGES

My future is secure and eternal.

I am the LORD, and I do not change.

MALACHI 3:6

FOR THE NEXT *GOD NEVER CHANGES* FEATURE SEE PAGE 2126.

NEW TESTAMENT

KEY PLACES IN MATTHEW

The broken lines (—·—) indicate modern boundaries.

Jesus' earthly story begins in the town of Bethlehem in the Roman province of Judea (2:1). A threat to kill the infant king led Joseph to take his family to Egypt (2:14). When they returned, God led them to settle in Nazareth in Galilee (2:22, 23). At about age 30, Jesus was baptized in the Jordan River and was tempted by Satan in the Judean wilderness (3:13; 4:1). Jesus set up his base of operations in Capernaum (4:12, 13) and from there ministered throughout Israel, telling parables, teaching about the Kingdom, and healing the sick. He traveled to the region of the Gadarenes around Gadara and healed two demon-possessed men (8:28ff); fed over 5,000 people with five loaves and two fish on the shores of Galilee near Bethsaida (14:15ff); healed the sick in Gennesaret (14:34ff); ministered to the Gentiles in Tyre and Sidon (15:21ff); visited Caesarea Philippi, where Peter declared Him to be the Messiah (16:13ff); and taught in Perea, east of the Jordan (19:1). As He set out on His last visit to Jerusalem, He told the disciples what would happen to Him there (20:17ff). He spent some time in Jericho (20:29) and then stayed in Bethany at night as He went back and forth to Jerusalem during His last week (21:17ff). In Jerusalem He would be crucified, but He would rise again.

PURPOSE

To present Jesus as the deliverer–the Messianic King–that God promised and the Old Testament Scriptures foretold.

Matthew knew that the world was in trouble—people in his day knew things weren't quite right. They were longing for God to appear and bring some change to the trouble they faced under the oppression of a foreign power that had subjugated the whole known world.

God had promised the people of Israel that He would bring them a Deliverer/King who ultimately would lead them into a wonderful realm of peace and blessing. The entire world would experience transformation through His coming. This Deliverer would be called the *Messiah*—a Hebrew word that means "anointed one." To speak of someone being anointed is to note that that person has been particularly blessed by God for a particular task. Jesus is that Messiah. (The Greek word for "anointed one" is *Christ*, another title for Jesus.)

Matthew's purpose is to demonstrate that Jesus is that Messiah and to display what changes will follow in the world in the wake of His coming. Jesus came from the right family line to fulfill the promise of the Messiah (1:1-17). He was born where the prophets said the Messiah would be born (2:5-6). Throughout this Gospel, Matthew makes clear that Jesus fulfilled the promises of the Old Testament regarding the coming Messiah (for example, see 4:13-16; 11:10-15; 12:15-21; 21:1-5; 26:31-32, 52-54; 27:9). And Jesus' miracles are presented as evidence that God's Kingdom has broken into the world through Jesus in a unique and powerful way (8:14-17; 12:28).

The change that was to come in the world is found in Jesus' own words, which make up over sixty percent of Matthew's Gospel. In the numerous recorded sermons of Jesus found in Matthew (5:1–7:28; 10:5-42; 23:1-39; 24:1–25:46), we can hear Jesus explain the kind of life His entrance into the world would usher in.

Matthew closes his account of Jesus' inaugural mission with Jesus' commission—given to His followers—to extend His presence, influence, and power throughout the whole world (28:16-20). Jesus is indeed the deliverer, the Savior, and the Messiah for all people everywhere.

DISCOVER GOD IN MATTHEW

We can grow in our understanding of God's priorities, passions, and character as we watch the life and ministry of Jesus, the Messiah, God's promised deliverer unfold. Jesus came to live out His Father's plan and to reveal the Father to us.

Promise Keeper: Right from the start, Matthew reminds us that Jesus' life and ministry were nothing less than the fulfillment of what God had promised long before (for example, see 1:22; 2:5; 3:3). Throughout his Gospel, Matthew affirms time and again that Jesus is the demonstration of God's faithfulness to His Word.

Ever-present God: One of the first prophecies that Matthew cites affirmed that Jesus would be called *Immanuel*, a Hebrew name that means "God is with us" (1:22-23). This theme of God's presence among His people surfaces often throughout the book (for example, 5:3-10; 6:6, 8), and Jesus' acts of deliverance from oppression signify the reality of this truth (12:28).

Loving Father: In the many teachings of Jesus that Matthew records, Jesus typically referred to God as "Father" and pictured Him as One who cares for those who choose to become disciples (for example, see 6:28-34; 7:7-11). Jesus also taught His disciples to pray by addressing God as "Father" (6:9), which conveys a sense of tenderness and closeness.

GROWING THROUGH MATTHEW

Matthew's Gospel provides ample insights for the follower of Jesus through both His life and His words.

The Values of the Kingdom: In what is called the Sermon on the Mount (chapters 5–7), Jesus explained what really matters in His Kingdom. These words are not a how-to guide for getting into heaven, but a description of the kind of attitude that should be found among those who seek to live under Jesus' influence and rule.

The Servants of the Kingdom: When Jesus sent out His twelve closest followers for the first time (chapter 10), He detailed how they were to serve God and people. Because Jesus had come to bring a new kind of life, the twelve were to go out spreading that kind of life. They were to live as extensions of Jesus' own ministry in every community they visited.

The Growth of the Kingdom: In chapter 13, Jesus told a number of parables that explained how His Kingdom would move throughout the earth. A few of the parables pictured the variety of responses people would have toward His message—some would receive Jesus and His message and some would not (13:1-23, 36-43). But in spite of the mixed response, Jesus made it clear that His Kingdom would ultimately reign victorious (13:24-33, 47-50).

The Priorities of the Kingdom: In a series of short messages (chapters 18–19), Matthew records Jesus' words regarding what needs to be foremost in the mind and heart of every one of His followers. Living out the kind of life Jesus intends for His followers will require humility (18:1-10), a heart ready to forgive others (18:21-35), and a willingness to live for the values of Jesus' Kingdom above all else (19:16-30).

The Future of the Kingdom: Although Jesus inaugurated the "breaking in" of God's Kingdom into this world, Jesus told His friends and followers that the full realization of Kingdom life was still in the future (chapters 24–25). Even though Jesus didn't tell them all the details, it is clear from what He said that there is hardship ahead for those who seek to follow Him—but that trouble will ultimately give way to a glorious victory for Jesus and those who believe in Him.

DISCOVERY VERSES

But Jesus said, "Let the children come to Me. Don't stop them! For the Kingdom of Heaven belongs to those who are like these children."
(MATTHEW 19:14)

Jesus traveled through all the towns and villages of that area, teaching in the synagogues and announcing the Good News about the Kingdom. And He healed every kind of disease and illness. When He saw the crowds, He had compassion on them because they were confused and helpless, like sheep without a shepherd.
(MATTHEW 9:35-36)

A sign was fastened to the cross above Jesus' head, announcing the charge against Him. It read: "This is Jesus, the King of the Jews." (MATTHEW 27:37)

MATTHEW FACTS

Author: Matthew. No evidence or tradition argues otherwise. (Papias, an earlier church father who lived c. AD 60–130, made a widely known reference to the writings of Matthew.) The author of this Gospel demonstrates a familiarity with the money and taxes of the day (17:24, 27; 18:24; 25:15-30), which adds support to his identity as Matthew (also called Levi son of Alphaeus; see Mark 2:14).

Written to: Matthew clearly was interested in the fulfillment of the Old Testament Scriptures as has already been noted; there are more direct references and allusions to the Old

Testament in Matthew than in the other Gospels. Matthew also gives indication that his readers were familiar with Jewish practices of the day (see, for example, 12:9-10; 15:1-2). These observations, supported by some references from early church history, suggest that Matthew was writing primarily to a Jewish audience.

Date of writing: Matthew noted that the guards' story of what happened at the empty tomb of Jesus is one "they still tell . . . today" (28:15), suggesting that some time had passed since the events of the resurrection. Matthew made no reference, however, to the destruction of the Temple in Jerusalem (AD 70), which would have been very significant to his Jewish readers. Thus, Matthew probably wrote his account sometime between the mid-50s and the mid-60s.

Setting: Since Jesus spent all of His earthly life in and around the land of Palestine, Matthew's Gospel is set in Palestine and the neighboring areas.

OUTLINE

▸ **MATTHEW 1:1–4:11**—Presentation of Jesus as the Messiah

▸ **MATTHEW 4:12–11:30**—Proclamation of Jesus the Messiah

▸ **MATTHEW 12:1–20:28**—Progressive Rejection of Jesus as the Messiah

▸ **MATTHEW 20:29–28:20**—Jesus' Death and Resurrection the Fulfillment of Old Testament Messianic Prophecies

THE ANCESTORS OF JESUS THE MESSIAH

1:1-17 //Luke 3:23-38
1:1 Gen 22:18; 1 Chr 17:11
1:2 Gen 21:3, 12; 25:26; 29:35; 1 Chr 1:34
1:3 Gen 38:29-30; Ruth 4:12, 18-19; 1 Chr 2:4-5, 9

1 This is a record of the ancestors of Jesus the Messiah, a descendant of David* and of Abraham:

2 Abraham was the father of Isaac.
Isaac was the father of Jacob.
Jacob was the father of Judah and his brothers.
3 Judah was the father of Perez and Zerah (whose mother was Tamar).
Perez was the father of Hezron.
Hezron was the father of Ram.*
4 Ram was the father of Amminadab.

1:1 Greek *Jesus the Messiah, son of David.* 1:3 Greek *Aram,* a variant spelling of Ram; also in 1:4. See 1 Chr 2:9-10.

1:1 Matthew was a Jewish author writing for readers who were concerned about the Jewish faith and history. He began his account of the good news about Jesus by providing a genealogy that shows readers: (1) Jesus is a true Jew, descended from Abraham; (2) Jesus has a claim to the Jewish throne because He descended from David; and (3) Jesus is the promised Messiah, a title that refers to a promised Deliverer who would come from God and establish God's Kingdom on earth.

▸ **BIBLE**
1:1-16 God's covenant with Abraham. God doesn't make small promises. He made a covenant with Abraham (Genesis 12:1-9) promising to bless Abraham's descendants, and ultimately all the peoples of the world. In Galatians 3:16, Paul emphasized that this promise was to be fulfilled through a single descendant of Abraham. That person is Jesus Christ. He blesses all those who look to God and place their faith in Him to provide a Savior (Galatians 3:29). Look to God for salvation, for He is just as faithful to fulfill His marvelous promises today as He was with Abraham. (***See Bible***> *Unity> Christ> Christ in the promise to Abraham,* TopicGuide page A10.)

1:2-17 Matthew's genealogy may not include all those in Jesus' lineage. Matthew was selective in highlighting key people in the genealogy in order to underscore Jesus' royal heritage. Matthew arranged the names in three groups of fourteen, which was the number assigned to David's name by Hebrew scholars who practiced *gematria.* Gematria consists of two main practices: the assignment of numbers to Hebrew letters and words, and the study of the meaning of those numbers. Gematria predates Kaballa and should not be confused with this mystical sect of Judaism.

1:3-6 Uncharacteristic of genealogies of the day, Matthew's genealogy noted four women: Tamar, Rahab, Ruth, and Bathsheba. These women played significant roles in the life of the nation of Israel—and were celebrated in the Old Testament for their actions—yet their highest honor is their mention here as a significant part of Jesus' lineage.

Amminadab was the father of Nahshon.
Nahshon was the father of Salmon.
5 Salmon was the father of Boaz (whose mother was Rahab).
Boaz was the father of Obed (whose mother was Ruth).
Obed was the father of Jesse.

1:4-5 Ruth 4:13, 17-22; 1 Chr 2:10-12, 15; Heb 11:31

6 Jesse was the father of King David.
David was the father of Solomon (whose mother was Bathsheba, the widow of Uriah).
7 Solomon was the father of Rehoboam.
Rehoboam was the father of Abijah.
Abijah was the father of Asa.*
8 Asa was the father of Jehoshaphat.
Jehoshaphat was the father of Jehoram.*
Jehoram was the father* of Uzziah.
9 Uzziah was the father of Jotham.
Jotham was the father of Ahaz.
Ahaz was the father of Hezekiah.
10 Hezekiah was the father of Manasseh.
Manasseh was the father of Amon.*
Amon was the father of Josiah.

1:6 Ruth 4:17, 22; 2 Sam 12:24; 1 Chr 2:13-15

1:7-10 1 Chr 3:10-14

11 Josiah was the father of Jehoiachin* and his brothers (born at the time of the exile to Babylon).
12 After the Babylonian exile:
Jehoiachin was the father of Shealtiel.
Shealtiel was the father of Zerubbabel.
13 Zerubbabel was the father of Abiud.
Abiud was the father of Eliakim.
Eliakim was the father of Azor.
14 Azor was the father of Zadok.
Zadok was the father of Akim.
Akim was the father of Eliud.
15 Eliud was the father of Eleazar.
Eleazar was the father of Matthan.
Matthan was the father of Jacob.
16 Jacob was the father of Joseph, the husband of Mary.
Mary gave birth to Jesus, who is called the Messiah.

1:11 2 Kgs 24:14-16; 1 Chr 3:15-16; Jer 27:20; Dan 1:1-2

1:12 1 Chr 3:17, 19; Ezra 3:2

1:16 Matt 27:17, 22; Luke 2:11

17 All those listed above include fourteen generations from Abraham to David, fourteen from David to the Babylonian exile, and fourteen from the Babylonian exile to the Messiah.

THE BIRTH OF JESUS THE MESSIAH

18 This is how Jesus the Messiah was born. His mother, Mary, was engaged to be married to Joseph. But before the marriage took place, while she was still a virgin, she became pregnant through the power of the Holy Spirit. 19 Joseph, her fiancé, was a good man and did not want to disgrace her publicly, so he decided to break the engagement* quietly.

20 As he considered this, an angel of the Lord appeared to him in a dream. "Joseph, son of David," the angel said, "do not be afraid to take Mary as your wife. For the child within

1:18-25 //Luke 2:1-7

1:18 Luke 1:27, 35; Gal 4:4

1:19 Deut 24:1

1:20 Luke 1:35

1:7 Greek *Asaph*, a variant spelling of Asa; also in 1:8. See 1 Chr 3:10. 1:8a Greek *Joram*, a variant spelling of Jehoram; also in 1:8b. See 1 Kgs 22:50 and note at 1 Chr 3:11. 1:8b Or *ancestor;* also in 1:11. 1:10 Greek *Amos*, a variant spelling of Amon; also in 1:10b. See 1 Chr 3:14. 1:11 Greek *Jeconiah*, a variant spelling of Jehoiachin; also in 1:12. See 2 Kgs 24:6 and note at 1 Chr 3:16. 1:19 Greek *to divorce her.*

1:16 Matthew comments carefully about Jesus' relationship to Joseph and Mary, anticipating what he will reveal about Jesus' unique birth. In 1:18 Matthew reveals that Mary "became pregnant through the power of the Holy Spirit."

1:21 Luke 1:31; 2:11, 21 Acts 5:31; 13:23 Heb 7:25
1:23 *Isa 7:14; 8:8, 10 John 1:14 1 Tim 3:16
1:25 Luke 1:31
2:1 Luke 1:5; 2:4-7
2:2 Num 24:17 Jer 23:5 Matt 2:9 Rev 22:16

her was conceived by the Holy Spirit. 21And she will have a son, and you are to name Him
Jesus,* for He will save His people from their sins."
22All of this occurred to fulfill the Lord's message through His prophet:

23 "Look! The virgin will conceive a child!
She will give birth to a son,
and they will call Him Immanuel,*
which means 'God is with us.'"

24When Joseph woke up, he did as the angel of the Lord commanded and took Mary as
his wife. 25But he did not have sexual relations with her until her son was born. And Joseph named Him Jesus.

VISITORS FROM THE EAST

2 Jesus was born in Bethlehem in Judea, during the reign of King Herod. About that
time some wise men* from eastern lands arrived in Jerusalem, asking, 2"Where is the
newborn king of the Jews? We saw His star as it rose,* and we have come to worship Him."
3King Herod was deeply disturbed when he heard this, as was everyone in Jerusalem.
4He called a meeting of the leading priests and teachers of religious law and asked,
"Where is the Messiah supposed to be born?"

1:21 *Jesus* means "The LORD saves." 1:23 Isa 7:14; 8:8, 10 (Greek version). 2:1 Or *royal astrologers;* Greek reads *magi;* also in 2:7, 16. 2:2 Or *star in the east.*

▸ GOD
1:21-23 "God is with us." The God we worship is not some distant, uninvolved deity who is unconcerned about our lives and what is happening in our world. Our God is not only aware of what is occurring on this planet, but He is also willing and able to intervene on our behalf. How do we know this? In an incredible act of grace, God came in the person of the Son and took on human flesh in order to live among us and rescue us from our sin. Look around you—can you see how God is with you? Or do you find it hard to see His work? Ask God to help you see Him working in your life and your world. (***See God***> *God's Names> Son> Immanuel,* TopicGuide page A19.)

1:23 This is the first of many Old Testament quotes that Matthew offers as he presents Jesus as the Messiah, the promised Deliverer that the nation of Israel was looking for. This quote comes from Isaiah 7:14, part of a passage in which the prophet spoke about God's plans for the nation's future.

2:1-2 The wise men who came looking for the newborn Jewish king would have likely been counselors and advisers of the royal courts in lands to the east of Israel. Such men would have studied both religious texts and natural signs in a desire to discern what was going on in the world. They had seen a unique star in the sky that suggested to them that Israel was to have a new king.

▸ WORSHIP
2:1-11 The wise men worshiped the Christ child. How seriously do you take your worship? How much do you let your hunger for worship influence your life? Consider the wise men mentioned in these verses. They must have journeyed for months and faced untold hardships. They sacrificed the comforts their position afforded and risked their lives at the hands of bandits and, not the least, King Herod. And what was their goal? Simply to worship Jesus. Are you easily dissuaded from finding a good church or a quiet moment to worship God? It's always worth the effort to find a way to worship Jesus the King. (***See Worship***> *NT> Christ's Supremacy> Jesus is God with us,* TopicGuide page A29.)

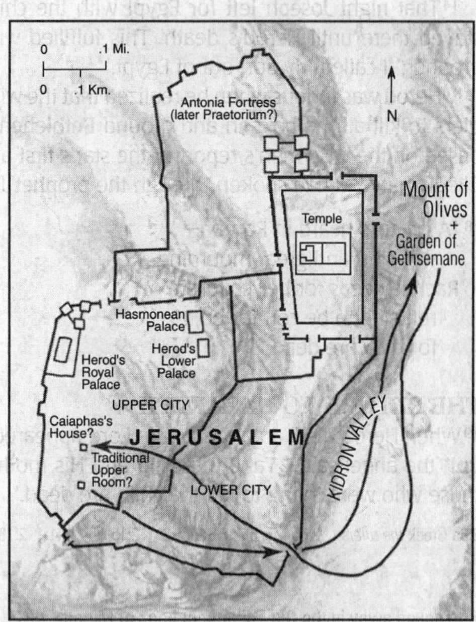

THE PASSOVER MEAL AND GETHSEMANE
Jesus, who would soon be the final Passover Lamb, ate the traditional Passover meal with His disciples in the upper room of a house in Jerusalem. During the meal they partook of the bread and wine, which would be the elements of future Communion celebrations, and then went out to the Garden of Gethsemane on the Mount of Olives.

5 "In Bethlehem in Judea," they said, "for this is what the prophet wrote: 2:5 John 7:42

6 'And you, O Bethlehem in the land of Judah, 2:6
are not least among the ruling cities* of Judah, *Mic 5:2
for a ruler will come from you
who will be the shepherd for My people Israel.'*"

7 Then Herod called for a private meeting with the wise men, and he learned from them
the time when the star first appeared. 8 Then he told them, "Go to Bethlehem and search
carefully for the child. And when you find Him, come back and tell me so that I can go and
worship Him, too!"

9 After this interview the wise men went their way. And the star they had seen in the east 2:9
guided them to Bethlehem. It went ahead of them and stopped over the place where the Matt 2:2
child was. 10 When they saw the star, they were filled with joy! 11 They entered the house 2:11
and saw the child with His mother, Mary, and they bowed down and worshiped Him. Then Ps 72:10
they opened their treasure chests and gave Him gifts of gold, frankincense, and myrrh. Isa 60:6

12 When it was time to leave, they returned to their own country by another route, for 2:12
God had warned them in a dream not to return to Herod. Matt 2:22

THE ESCAPE TO EGYPT

13 After the wise men were gone, an angel of the Lord appeared to Joseph in a dream. "Get 2:13
up! Flee to Egypt with the child and His mother," the angel said. "Stay there until I tell you Matt 1:20; 2:19
to return, because Herod is going to search for the child to kill Him."

14 That night Joseph left for Egypt with the child and Mary, His mother, 15 and they 2:15
stayed there until Herod's death. This fulfilled what the Lord had spoken through the *Hos 11:1
prophet: "I called My Son out of Egypt."*

16 Herod was furious when he realized that the wise men had outwitted him. He sent sol-
diers to kill all the boys in and around Bethlehem who were two years old and under,
based on the wise men's report of the star's first appearance. 17 Herod's brutal action ful-
filled what God had spoken through the prophet Jeremiah:

18 "A cry was heard in Ramah— 2:18
weeping and great mourning. *Jer 31:15
Rachel weeps for her children,
refusing to be comforted,
for they are dead."*

THE RETURN TO NAZARETH

19 When Herod died, an angel of the Lord appeared in a dream to Joseph in Egypt. 20 "Get 2:19
up!" the angel said. "Take the child and His mother back to the land of Israel, because Matt 1:20; 2:12
those who were trying to kill the child are dead." 2:20 Exod 4:19

2:6a Greek *the rulers.* 2:6b Mic 5:2; 2 Sam 5:2. 2:15 Hos 11:1. 2:18 Jer 31:15.

2:6 Tucked away in the Old Testament book of Micah was a prophecy about a future ruler of Israel (Micah 5:2). This prophecy came some 700 years before the birth of Jesus.

2:12 Though some readers may be troubled by the notion that wise men sought signs in the heavens and other forms of divination to learn of the birth of Jesus, Matthew makes it clear that God Himself was revealing important truths to these men.

2:13 To escape King Herod, who had been appointed by the Romans over the land of Israel, Joseph fled with his family to Egypt. At this time there were a considerable number of Jewish residents in the land of Egypt who had moved there either voluntarily or by force during prior international conflicts.

2:15 This reference is from the Old Testament prophet Hosea (11:1). The prophecy appears to have held two meanings: One regarding the nation of Israel (which was "called" out of Egypt during the time of the Exodus), and the other regarding Jesus, the Messiah and Son of God. Many Old Testament prophecies contain similarly layered meanings.

2:22 Matt 2:12 — 21 So Joseph got up and returned to the land of Israel with Jesus and His mother. 22 But
when he learned that the new ruler of Judea was Herod's son Archelaus, he was afraid to
2:23 Judg 13:5, 7 — go there. Then, after being warned in a dream, he left for the region of Galilee. 23 So the
Luke 2:39 — family went and lived in a town called Nazareth. This fulfilled what the prophets had said:
John 1:45-46; Acts 4:10; 24:5 — "He will be called a Nazarene."

JOHN THE BAPTIST PREPARES THE WAY

3:1-12 //Mark 1:1-8 //Luke 3:1-18 //John 1:19-28

3 In those days John the Baptist came to the Judean wilderness and began preaching.
His message was, 2 "Repent of your sins and turn to God, for the Kingdom of Heaven
is near.*" 3 The prophet Isaiah was speaking about John when he said,

3:4 Lev 11:22 — "He is a voice shouting in the wilderness,
2 Kgs 1:8 — 'Prepare the way for the LORD's coming!
Clear the road for Him!'"*

3:7 Matt 12:34; 23:33; Rom 5:9 — 4 John's clothes were woven from coarse camel hair, and he wore a leather belt around
1 Thes 1:10 — his waist. For food he ate locusts and wild honey. 5 People from Jerusalem and from all of
3:8 Acts 26:20 — Judea and all over the Jordan Valley went out to see and hear John. 6 And when they con-
fessed their sins, he baptized them in the Jordan River.
3:9 — 7 But when he saw many Pharisees and Sadducees coming to watch him baptize,* he de-
John 8:33, 37, 39 — nounced them. "You brood of snakes!" he exclaimed. "Who warned you to flee God's
Acts 13:26; Rom 4:12 — coming wrath? 8 Prove by the way you live that you have repented of your sins and turned
3:10 — to God. 9 Don't just say to each other, 'We're safe, for we are descendants of Abraham.'
Matt 7:19; Luke 13:7 — That means nothing, for I tell you, God can create children of Abraham from these very
John 15:6 — stones. 10 Even now the ax of God's judgment is poised, ready to sever the roots of the

3:2 Or *has come,* or *is coming soon.* 3:3 Isa 40:3 (Greek version). 3:7 Or *coming to be baptized.*

2:22 When Herod died, Rome divided the land he ruled among three of his sons. Archelaus ruled in the south (including the region around Jerusalem), Antipas governed the area around the Sea of Galilee (where Nazareth was) and along the eastern bank of the Jordan River, and Philip presided over the lands north and east of the Sea of Galilee (a predominantly Gentile area). Antipas was the youngest of the three, and although he ended up being a troubling ruler in his own right, Archelaus might well have seemed like a greater threat to the safety of Joseph and his young family as they returned to the land of Israel.

3:3 The Old Testament prophet Isaiah ministered during a time when God's judgment had fallen on Israel because of sin. But in chapter 40 of his book, the prophet brought a word of comfort from God. God promised one day to restore the nation and bring blessing. The quote Matthew used came from this section, where God promised to come to His people once more (Isaiah 40:3).

▸ GOD

3:3-11 Spiritual blessing in Christ. John the Baptist declared that he was preparing the way for "the LORD's coming." By quoting Isaiah 40:3, he was announcing the arrival of God Incarnate on the scene. And what would God do when He arrived? From John's vantage point, one of God's most significant deeds would be to pour out the Holy Spirit on the people of God, much as John immersed people in water. The followers of Jesus were to be "Spirit-powered" people. Such an outpouring may take many different forms—some rather surprising—but the Spirit's presence in our lives will always bring about change in our character (Galatians 5:16-26). Today, display the promise of the Spirit by bearing the fruit of the Spirit—godly character. (***See God***> *Salvation*> *Son*> *Baptizes with the Holy Spirit,* TopicGuide page A15.)

3:6 The word *baptize* means "to dip" or "to immerse." The Jews of John's time used baptism to signify one's change of heart toward God. Gentiles who had converted to Judaism were baptized as a picture of their cleansing before God.

3:7 There were a number of religious factions in Israel during this time. Matthew mentions two here: the Pharisees, who were teachers of the Scriptures and tended to be religiously and politically conservative; and the Sadducees, who were primarily made up of the aristocracy and the priests who served in the Temple. The Sadducees tended to be more liberal in both their religious and political views.

3:7-12 Matthew noted earlier that John the Baptist was fulfilling a prophecy of consolation from Isaiah (Matthew 3:3). John spoke of the "coming One"; however, his message included judgment as well as comfort. The coming of the Kingdom of God in the person of the Messiah would create trouble for some in the nation.

▸ HOLINESS

3:9 A right heart. Many people seem to think that they are at peace with God simply because of their upbringing. The misguided idea is that if you are from the "right group," God must automatically accept you. But that's just not true. John the Baptist pointed this out to the religious people of his day. They thought that being descendants of Abraham was all that was needed to settle their accounts with God. John said no, Jesus said no (Luke 13:1-3), and Paul said no (Romans 2:29). With God, the matter of the heart is always the heart of the matter. (***See Holiness***> *Submission*> *Yielding to Spirit*> *Surrender your heart,* TopicGuide page A41.)

trees. Yes, every tree that does not produce good fruit will be chopped down and thrown
into the fire.
11"I baptize with* water those who repent of their sins and turn to God. But someone is
coming soon who is greater than I am—so much greater that I'm not worthy even to be His
slave and carry His sandals. He will baptize you with the Holy Spirit and with fire.* 12He is
ready to separate the chaff from the wheat with His winnowing fork. Then He will clean up
the threshing area, gathering the wheat into His barn but burning the chaff with never-
ending fire."

3:11 John 1:26-27, 31, 33 Acts 1:5; 2:3-4; 13:24; 19:4
3:12 Matt 13:30

THE BAPTISM OF JESUS

13Then Jesus went from Galilee to the Jordan River to be baptized by John. 14But John
tried to talk Him out of it. "I am the one who needs to be baptized by You," he said, "so why
are You coming to me?"
15But Jesus said, "It should be done, for we must carry out all that God requires.*" So
John agreed to baptize Him.
16After His baptism, as Jesus came up out of the water, the heavens were opened* and
He saw the Spirit of God descending like a dove and settling on Him. 17And a voice from
heaven said, "This is My dearly loved Son, who brings Me great joy."

3:13-17 Mark 1:9-11 Luke 3:21-22 John 1:31-34
3:16 Isa 11:2
3:17 Gen 22:2 Ps 2:7 Isa 42:1 Matt 12:18; 17:5 Mark 9:7 Luke 9:35

THE TEMPTATION OF JESUS

4 Then Jesus was led by the Spirit into the wilderness to be tempted there by the devil.
2For forty days and forty nights He fasted and became very hungry.
3During that time the devil* came and said to Him, "If You are the Son of God, tell these
stones to become loaves of bread."
4But Jesus told him, "No! The Scriptures say,

'People do not live by bread alone,
but by every word that comes from the mouth of God.'*"

5Then the devil took Him to the holy city, Jerusalem, to the highest point of the Temple,
6and said, "If You are the Son of God, jump off! For the Scriptures say,

4:1-11 //Mark 1:12-13 //Luke 4:1-13
4:1 Gen 3:1-7 1 Thes 3:5
4:2 Exod 34:28 1 Kgs 19:8
4:4 *Deut 8:3
4:6 *Ps 91:11-12

3:11a Or *in.* 3:11b Or *in the Holy Spirit and in fire.* 3:15 Or *for we must fulfill all righteousness.* 3:16 Some manuscripts read *opened to Him.* 4:3 Greek *the tempter.* 4:4 Deut 8:3.

3:13 Jesus came from Galilee in the north to be baptized by John, who was ministering in the south. Jesus had grown up in Nazareth in the region of Galilee (see 2:22-23), and apparently He was still living there at this time.

3:15 John's baptism symbolized the washing and renewing that comes from the repentance from sin. When Jesus came to be baptized, John recognized that there was no reason for Jesus to undergo such a ritual, since Jesus was sinless. Jesus, however, submitted to John's "ministry of preparation"—not because He needed to be cleansed or to repent of sin, but because in doing so Jesus demonstrated He was prepared to fulfill all of God's righteous commands, even those that seemed unsuitable for Him, such as His death on the cross.

▸ SPIRITUAL WARFARE
4:1-17 Facing the foe. If you were about to face an enemy in a duel, it would be crucial that you were acquainted with and adequately trained in the use of the weapons at hand. Jesus sets before all His followers the model for how we, too, can fight the enemy of our souls. Scripture is the weapon; Jesus quoted and applied it. Unless we, too, are well acquainted with this spiritual weapon, we might find ourselves in trouble when spiritual battles rage around us. Are you ready to do battle, or are you unsure that there even is a battle around you? Read the Bible and you'll discover God has equipped you to fight—not with guns and such things—but with prayer and His Word (Ephesians 6:12-13; 1 Timothy 1:18). (***See Spiritual Warfare****> Resisting Sin and Evil> Resisting Temptation> How to Resist> By Scripture,* TopicGuide page A45.)

4:3 The devil is a spiritual being who constantly seeks to deceive God's people. He is not God's equal, but is a created angel who has turned against his Creator in rebellion (John 8:44; 13:2; Revelation 12:9).

4:3-11 The devil asked whether Jesus was the "Son of God." Clearly, the devil understood this title to denote divine authority and power, which would mean that Jesus ought to be able to perform certain deeds. The expression speaks of someone who is in a familial relationship with God and who possesses deity Himself (John 1:49; 10:36; 19:7 Romans 1:4). This expression is not found anywhere else except Genesis 6:2-4 (see note at Genesis 6).

'He will order His angels to protect you.
And they will hold you up with their hands
so you won't even hurt your foot on a stone.'*"

4:7 7 Jesus responded, "The Scriptures also say, 'You must not test the LORD your God.'*"
*Deut 6:16 8 Next the devil took Him to the peak of a very high mountain and showed Him all the
kingdoms of the world and their glory. 9 "I will give it all to You," he said, "if You will kneel
down and worship me."
4:10 10 "Get out of here, Satan," Jesus told him. "For the Scriptures say,
*Deut 6:13

'You must worship the LORD your God
and serve only Him.'*"

4:11 11 Then the devil went away, and angels came and took care of Jesus.
Luke 22:43
Heb 1:14
Jas 4:7

THE MINISTRY OF JESUS BEGINS

4:12-17 12 When Jesus heard that John had been arrested, He left Judea and returned to Galilee.
//Mark 1:14-15 13 He went first to Nazareth, then left there and moved to Capernaum, beside the Sea of
//Luke 4:14-15 Galilee, in the region of Zebulun and Naphtali. 14 This fulfilled what God said through the
prophet Isaiah:

4:15-16 15 "In the land of Zebulun and of Naphtali,
*Isa 9:1-2; 42:6-7 beside the sea, beyond the Jordan River,
Luke 2:32 in Galilee where so many Gentiles live,
16 the people who sat in darkness
have seen a great light.
And for those who lived in the land where death casts its shadow,
a light has shined."*

4:17 17 From then on Jesus began to preach, "Repent of your sins and turn to God, for the
Matt 3:2; 10:7 Kingdom of Heaven is near."*

THE FIRST DISCIPLES

4:18-22 18 One day as Jesus was walking along the shore of the Sea of Galilee, He saw two broth-
//Mark 1:16-20 ers—Simon, also called Peter, and Andrew—throwing a net into the water, for they fished
//Luke 5:1-11 for a living. 19 Jesus called out to them, "Come, follow Me, and I will show you how to fish
4:19 for people!" 20 And they left their nets at once and followed Him.
Matt 16:17-18
John 1:42 21 A little farther up the shore He saw two other brothers, James and John, sitting in a
4:20 boat with their father, Zebedee, repairing their nets. And He called them to come, too.
Mark 10:28 22 They immediately followed Him, leaving the boat and their father behind.
Luke 18:28

4:6 Ps 91:11-12. **4:7** Deut 6:16. **4:10** Deut 6:13. **4:15-16** Isa 9:1-2 (Greek version). **4:17** Or *has come,* or *is coming soon.*

4:12 Jesus returned to Galilee and began His ministry after John was arrested. With John's ministry forcibly brought to an end, the time of preparation was over, and Jesus—the One John foretold would follow him—could now begin His ministry.

4:14-16 Again, Matthew connects the good news about Jesus to Old Testament prophecy and quotes from the prophet Isaiah (9:1-2). The "land of Zebulun and of Naphtali . . . in Galilee" refers to regions of Israel that were settled by the descendants of Jacob's sons Zebulun and Naphtali.

▸ MINISTRY

4:18-22 Ordinary qualifications. Who is qualified for ministry? Does it take a college education, a seminary degree, or a special pedigree? The first few whom Jesus called to join in this work may shed some light on the qualifications. They were common laborers—fishermen and tax collectors. They were deeply involved in the normal life of business, family, and friends. They had received no special training—though they soon did receive the most extraordinary on-the-job training in history. Plain, ordinary people were the folks Jesus identified as perfect for ministry. Jesus will enlist you, too. Do you feel unqualified? Good, for that's part of what He requires (Luke 17:10). Humbly offer yourself to Christ and see how He uses you! (***See Ministry****> Great Commission> Make Disciples> Disciples strategically use knowledge, skills, and abilities,* TopicGuide page A56.)

CROWDS FOLLOW JESUS

23 Jesus traveled throughout the region of Galilee, teaching in the synagogues and an-
nouncing the Good News about the Kingdom. And He healed every kind of disease and
illness. 24 News about Him spread as far as Syria, and people soon began bringing to Him
all who were sick. And whatever their sickness or disease, or if they were demon pos-
sessed or epileptic or paralyzed—He healed them all. 25 Large crowds followed Him wher-
ever He went—people from Galilee, the Ten Towns,* Jerusalem, from all over Judea, and
from east of the Jordan River.

4:23-25 //Luke 6:17-19
4:23 Matt 9:35 Mark 1:39 Luke 4:15

THE SERMON ON THE MOUNT

5 One day as He saw the crowds gathering, Jesus went up on the mountainside and sat
down. His disciples gathered around Him, 2 and He began to teach them.

5:1 Luke 6:12 John 6:3

THE BEATITUDES

3 "God blesses those who are poor and realize their need for Him,*
for the Kingdom of Heaven is theirs.
4 God blesses those who mourn,
for they will be comforted.
5 God blesses those who are humble,
for they will inherit the whole earth.

5:3-12 //Luke 6:20-23
5:3 Isa 57:15 Matt 25:34
5:4 Isa 61:2-3
5:5 Ps 37:11 Rom 4:13

4:25 Greek *Decapolis.* 5:3 Greek *poor in spirit.*

4:23 Synagogues were meeting places and worship centers developed after the Jews were scattered by the Assyrians (722 BC) and Babylonians (586 BC). In the absence of accessibility to the Temple, many cities had built synagogues, and Jesus initially focused His ministry in those centers of Jewish life.

4:23-25 As with the other Gospel writers, Matthew could not record for us all that Jesus said and did. Instead, Matthew simply summarized Jesus' early days of ministry.

▸ HOLINESS
5:2-11 Citizens of the Kingdom. In many businesses, communities, and settings, you can tell who the "important" people are. They stand out; they make themselves known. Even in the Kingdom of God, there are "stand-out" people. The only difference is that what characterizes citizens of Jesus' Kingdom is entirely opposite of what characterizes those who see themselves as important in the world. Gentleness, humility, mercy, peacemaking—those are the characteristics that measure the truly blessed in Jesus' eyes. Do you want to be blessed by God and treated as an important citizen of His Kingdom? Start with a commitment to holiness and the availability to serve. If you want to be blessed, roll up your sleeves and prepare to get your hands dirty. (***See Holiness> Disciplines> Of Engagement> Service,*** TopicGuide page A42.)

5:3 "Those who are poor and realize their need for Him" is the translation of a Greek phrase that literally means "poor in spirit." This means recognizing one's own spiritual bankruptcy before God and, thus, admitting one's need.

BECAUSE GOD IS MERCIFUL

He forgives me of my sins when I sincerely confess them.

God blesses those who are merciful, for they will be shown mercy.

MATTHEW 5:7

FOR THE NEXT *GOD IS MERCIFUL* FEATURE SEE PAGE 2125.

5:6 Isa 55:1-2
5:7 Matt 18:33; Jas 2:13
5:8 Ps 24:3-4
5:9 Heb 12:14; Jas 3:18
5:10 2 Tim 2:12; 1 Pet 3:14
5:11 Matt 10:22; 1 Pet 4:14
5:12 Acts 7:52; Heb 11:32-38; Jas 5:10
5:13 Mark 9:50; Luke 14:34-35
5:14 John 8:12; 9:5; Phil 2:15
5:15 Mark 4:21; Luke 8:16; 11:33
5:16 Eph 5:8-9; 1 Pet 2:12
5:17 Rom 3:31
5:18 Luke 16:17; 21:33
5:19 Jas 2:10
5:21 Matt 19:18; Mark 10:19; Luke 18:20; Rom 13:9; Jas 2:11
5:22 Eph 4:26; Jas 1:19-20; 1 Jn 3:15

6 God blesses those who hunger and thirst for justice,*
for they will be satisfied.
7 God blesses those who are merciful,
for they will be shown mercy.
8 God blesses those whose hearts are pure,
for they will see God.
9 God blesses those who work for peace,
for they will be called the children of God.
10 God blesses those who are persecuted for doing right,
for the Kingdom of Heaven is theirs.

11 "God blesses you when people mock you and persecute you and lie about you* and
say all sorts of evil things against you because you are My followers. 12 Be happy about it!
Be very glad! For a great reward awaits you in heaven. And remember, the ancient proph-
ets were persecuted in the same way.

TEACHING ABOUT SALT AND LIGHT

13 "You are the salt of the earth. But what good is salt if it has lost its flavor? Can you make
it salty again? It will be thrown out and trampled underfoot as worthless.

14 "You are the light of the world—like a city on a hilltop that cannot be hidden. 15 No one
lights a lamp and then puts it under a basket. Instead, a lamp is placed on a stand, where it
gives light to everyone in the house. 16 In the same way, let your good deeds shine out for
all to see, so that everyone will praise your heavenly Father.

TEACHING ABOUT THE LAW

17 "Don't misunderstand why I have come. I did not come to abolish the law of Moses or
the writings of the prophets. No, I came to accomplish their purpose. 18 I tell you the truth,
until heaven and earth disappear, not even the smallest detail of God's law will disappear
until its purpose is achieved. 19 So if you ignore the least commandment and teach others
to do the same, you will be called the least in the Kingdom of Heaven. But anyone who
obeys God's laws and teaches them will be called great in the Kingdom of Heaven.

20 "But I warn you—unless your righteousness is better than the righteousness of the
teachers of religious law and the Pharisees, you will never enter the Kingdom of Heaven!

TEACHING ABOUT ANGER

21 "You have heard that our ancestors were told, 'You must not murder. If you commit
murder, you are subject to judgment.'* 22 But I say, if you are even angry with someone,*
you are subject to judgment! If you call someone an idiot,* you are in danger of being
brought before the court. And if you curse someone,* you are in danger of the fires of hell.*

23 "So if you are presenting a sacrifice* at the altar in the Temple and you suddenly
remember that someone has something against you, 24 leave your sacrifice there at the
altar. Go and be reconciled to that person. Then come and offer your sacrifice to God.

5:6 Or *for righteousness.* 5:11 Some manuscripts omit *and lie about you.* 5:21 Exod 20:13; Deut 5:17. 5:22a Some manuscripts add *without cause.* 5:22b Greek uses an Aramaic term of contempt: *If you say to your brother, 'Raca.'* 5:22c Greek *if you say, 'You fool.'* 5:22d Greek *Gehenna;* also in 5:29, 30. 5:23 Greek *gift;* also in 5:24.

5:13 Common salt had a variety of purposes in Jesus' day. Typically, it served to flavor and preserve certain foods. Unlike the pure salt that is widely available today, its "saltiness" could leach out and lose its flavor. Then the salt would be thrown into the road, where it would retard the growth of weeds.

5:17 In Jesus' time, the Old Testament was often referred to as the Law, the Writings, and the Prophets, or sometimes simply the Law and the Prophets. Jesus' reference here was a way of referring to the entire Old Testament.

5:21, 27, 31, 33, 38, 43 When Jesus referred to a "law" or a "commandment," He was referencing a law from one of the first five books of the Old Testament. These books contained the bulk of the law, which detailed how God's people should live as His covenant people. Jesus was not disregarding the law itself, but the truncated or limited interpretation of the law promoted by the religious leaders of that day.

25 "When you are on the way to court with your adversary, settle your differences
quickly. Otherwise, your accuser may hand you over to the judge, who will hand you over
to an officer, and you will be thrown into prison. 26 And if that happens, you surely won't
be free again until you have paid the last penny.*

TEACHING ABOUT ADULTERY

27 "You have heard the commandment that says, 'You must not commit adultery.'* 28 But I
say, anyone who even looks at a woman with lust has already committed adultery with
her in his heart. 29 So if your eye—even your good eye*—causes you to lust, gouge it out
and throw it away. It is better for you to lose one part of your body than for your whole
body to be thrown into hell. 30 And if your hand—even your stronger hand*—causes you to
sin, cut it off and throw it away. It is better for you to lose one part of your body than for
your whole body to be thrown into hell.

TEACHING ABOUT DIVORCE

31 "You have heard the law that says, 'A man can divorce his wife by merely giving her a
written notice of divorce.'* 32 But I say that a man who divorces his wife, unless she has
been unfaithful, causes her to commit adultery. And anyone who marries a divorced
woman also commits adultery.

TEACHING ABOUT VOWS

33 "You have also heard that our ancestors were told, 'You must not break your vows; you
must carry out the vows you make to the LORD.'* 34 But I say, do not make any vows! Do
not say, 'By heaven!' because heaven is God's throne. 35 And do not say, 'By the earth!' be-
cause the earth is His footstool. And do not say, 'By Jerusalem!' for Jerusalem is the city of
the great King. 36 Do not even say, 'By my head!' for you can't turn one hair white or black.
37 Just say a simple, 'Yes, I will,' or 'No, I won't.' Anything beyond this is from the evil one.

TEACHING ABOUT REVENGE

38 "You have heard the law that says the punishment must match the injury: 'An eye for an
eye, and a tooth for a tooth.'* 39 But I say, do not resist an evil person! If someone slaps you on
the right cheek, offer the other cheek also. 40 If you are sued in court and your shirt is taken
from you, give your coat, too. 41 If a soldier demands that you carry his gear for a mile,* carry it
two miles. 42 Give to those who ask, and don't turn away from those who want to borrow.

TEACHING ABOUT LOVE FOR ENEMIES

43 "You have heard the law that says, 'Love your neighbor'* and hate your enemy. 44 But
I say, love your enemies!* Pray for those who persecute you! 45 In that way, you will be

5:25-26 Matt 18:34-35; Luke 12:58-59
5:27 Matt 19:18; Mark 10:19; Luke 18:20; Rom 13:9; Jas 2:11
5:29-30 Matt 18:8-9; Mark 9:43-47
5:31 Matt 19:7; Mark 10:4
5:32 1 Cor 7:10-11
5:33 Lev 19:12; Num 30:2; Deut 23:21
5:34 Isa 66:1; Matt 23:22; Jas 5:12
5:37 Jas 5:12
5:38-48 //Luke 6:27-35
5:39 Rom 12:17; 1 Cor 6:7; 1 Pet 3:9
5:43 Matt 19:19; 22:39; Mark 12:31; Luke 10:27; Rom 13:9; Gal 5:14; Jas 2:8
5:44 Exod 23:4-5; Prov 25:21; Luke 23:34; Acts 7:60; Rom 12:14, 20; 1 Cor 4:12

5:26 Greek *the last kodrantes* [i.e., quadrans]. 5:27 Exod 20:14; Deut 5:18. 5:29 Greek *your right eye.* 5:30 Greek *your right hand.* 5:31 Deut 24:1. 5:33 Num 30:2. 5:38 Greek *the law that says: 'An eye for an eye and a tooth for a tooth.'* Exod 21:24; Lev 24:20; Deut 19:21. 5:41 Greek *milion* [4,854 feet or 1,478 meters]. 5:43 Lev 19:18. 5:44 Some manuscripts add *Bless those who curse you. Do good to those who hate you.* Compare Luke 6:27-28.

5:29-30 Jesus chose the eradication of the most vital senses—touch and sight—to illustrate that God's judgment is much worse than the remarkable suffering that can accompany the fight against sin and temptation.

5:34 This was not a universal prohibition, since Jesus Himself took an oath before the high priest (Matthew 26:63). Paul also swore with God as his witness (Romans 1:9). Jesus teaches here that all those who live in the Kingdom should speak as if every word is under oath.

5:41 The Romans ruled Israel in Jesus' day, and a Roman soldier could order anyone nearby to help him carry his gear for one *milion* (just short of a modern mile).

▸ HOLINESS

5:44-48 Showing God's love. Members of the same family typically bear a family resemblance. Often you can discern who belongs to a certain family by similarities in physical appearance, speech, conduct, or preferences of food or clothing. Jesus used the concept of family likeness to show how His followers were to love others. As children of God, we are called to resemble Him in the way we selflessly love others. Is your affection manipulative or overly sensual? Does it draw people closer to honesty or holiness? Does it draw people to God? Imitate your Father in heaven and give your love freely to those around you. (***See Holiness> Maturing> Imitating God> His likeness,*** TopicGuide page A40.)

acting as true children of your Father in heaven. For He gives His sunlight to both the evil
and the good, and He sends rain on the just and the unjust alike. 46If you love only those
who love you, what reward is there for that? Even corrupt tax collectors do that much. 47If
you are kind only to your friends,* how are you different from anyone else? Even pagans
do that. 48But you are to be perfect, even as your Father in heaven is perfect.

TEACHING ABOUT GIVING TO THE NEEDY

6 "Watch out! Don't do your good deeds publicly, to be admired by others, for you will
lose the reward from your Father in heaven. 2When you give to someone in need,
don't do as the hypocrites do—blowing trumpets in the synagogues and streets to call at-
tention to their acts of charity! I tell you the truth, they have received all the reward they
will ever get. 3But when you give to someone in need, don't let your left hand know what
your right hand is doing. 4Give your gifts in private, and your Father, who sees everything,
will reward you.

TEACHING ABOUT PRAYER AND FASTING

5"When you pray, don't be like the hypocrites who love to pray publicly on street corners
and in the synagogues where everyone can see them. I tell you the truth, that is all the re-
ward they will ever get. 6But when you pray, go away by yourself, shut the door behind you,
and pray to your Father in private. Then your Father, who sees everything, will reward you.
7"When you pray, don't babble on and on as people of other religions do. They think their
prayers are answered merely by repeating their words again and again. 8Don't be like them,
for your Father knows exactly what you need even before you ask Him! 9Pray like this:

Our Father in heaven,
  may Your name be kept holy.
10 May Your Kingdom come soon.
May Your will be done on earth,
  as it is in heaven.
11 Give us today the food we need,*
12 and forgive us our sins,
  as we have forgiven those who sin against us.
13 And don't let us yield to temptation,*
  but rescue us from the evil one.*

5:48 Lev 19:2; Deut 18:13; Luke 6:36; 1 Pet 1:16
6:1-2 Matt 23:5
6:4 Matt 6:6, 18
6:5 Matt 6:16; 23:5; Luke 18:10-14
6:6 2 Kgs 4:33; Isa 26:20
6:7 Eccl 5:1-2
6:8 Matt 6:32; Luke 12:30
6:9-13 //Luke 11:2-4
6:9 1 Pet 1:17
6:10 Matt 26:39, 42; Luke 22:42
6:11 Prov 30:8; John 6:32
6:13 Luke 22:40, 46; John 17:15; 2 Thes 3:3; 2 Tim 4:18

5:47 Greek *your brothers.* 6:11 Or *Give us today our food for the day;* or *Give us today our food for tomorrow.* 6:13a Or *And keep us from being tested.* 6:13b Or *from evil.* Some manuscripts add *For Yours is the kingdom and the power and the glory forever. Amen.*

5:48 Jesus was not insisting that His followers live in a kind of sinless perfection identical to the holiness of God. When He spoke of being perfect, He was using a word that means "complete" or "mature." Imitating the Pharisees was aiming too low—they weren't good enough.

6:6 The expression Jesus used for shutting the door conveys the sense of not just closing but securing the door. The idea was to pray in complete privacy. This isn't to say that people should never pray with others, but rather that prayer should be offered with the proper motive.

6:7 The uncommon word *babble* refers to stuttering or indistinct speech. A picture of this kind of praying can be seen in 1 Kings 18:26, where we read that the prophets of Baal continually repeated the phrase "O Baal, answer us!" from morning until evening.

6:9 Although there are a few references in the Old Testament to God as Father (see Psalm 103:13; Isaiah 63:16), we fully receive the freedom to address the most holy God in terms of such intimacy in this model prayer.

▸ WORSHIP

6:9-13 The Jesus prayer. There must have been something very impressive about Jesus' prayers. There is no record of His closest friends asking Him to teach them to walk on water, raise the dead, or multiply bread and fish; but they do ask Him to teach them to pray. In a simple and short model prayer, Jesus offered some profound insights into how every friend of God can and should approach Him in prayer: 1) Speak to God intimately and openly in (6:9); 2) Affirm your desire to see His will done (6:10); 3) Appreciate the blessings that come your way daily (6:11); 4) Realize that your access to God is rooted in the grace and forgiveness extended to you (6:12); 5) Flee from temptation, but rely on God for your ultimate victory over sin. (***See Worship***> *NT> Prayer> Examples> Jesus> The Lord's Prayer,* TopicGuide page A33.)

14 "If you forgive those who sin against you, your heavenly Father will forgive you. 15 But
if you refuse to forgive others, your Father will not forgive your sins.
16 "And when you fast, don't make it obvious, as the hypocrites do, for they try to look
miserable and disheveled so people will admire them for their fasting. I tell you the truth,
that is the only reward they will ever get. 17 But when you fast, comb your hair and wash
your face. 18 Then no one will notice that you are fasting, except your Father, who knows
what you do in private. And your Father, who sees everything, will reward you.

TEACHING ABOUT MONEY AND POSSESSIONS

19 "Don't store up treasures here on earth, where moths eat them and rust destroys them,
and where thieves break in and steal. 20 Store your treasures in heaven, where moths and
rust cannot destroy, and thieves do not break in and steal. 21 Wherever your treasure is,
there the desires of your heart will also be.
22 "Your eye is a lamp that provides light for your body. When your eye is good, your
whole body is filled with light. 23 But when your eye is bad, your whole body is filled with
darkness. And if the light you think you have is actually darkness, how deep that darkness is!
24 "No one can serve two masters. For you will hate one and love the other; you will be
devoted to one and despise the other. You cannot serve both God and money.
25 "That is why I tell you not to worry about everyday life—whether you have enough
food and drink, or enough clothes to wear. Isn't life more than food, and your body more
than clothing? 26 Look at the birds. They don't plant or harvest or store food in barns, for
your heavenly Father feeds them. And aren't you far more valuable to Him than they are?
27 Can all your worries add a single moment to your life?
28 "And why worry about your clothing? Look at the lilies of the field and how they grow.
They don't work or make their clothing, 29 yet Solomon in all his glory was not dressed as
beautifully as they are. 30 And if God cares so wonderfully for wildflowers that are here to-
day and thrown into the fire tomorrow, He will certainly care for you. Why do you have so
little faith?
31 "So don't worry about these things, saying, 'What will we eat? What will we drink?
What will we wear?' 32 These things dominate the thoughts of unbelievers, but your heav-
enly Father already knows all your needs. 33 Seek the Kingdom of God* above all else, and
live righteously, and He will give you everything you need.
34 "So don't worry about tomorrow, for tomorrow will bring its own worries. Today's
trouble is enough for today.

DO NOT JUDGE OTHERS

7 "Do not judge others, and you will not be judged. 2 For you will be treated as you treat
others.* The standard you use in judging is the standard by which you will be judged.*
3 "And why worry about a speck in your friend's eye* when you have a log in your own?

6:33 Some manuscripts do not include *of God.* 7:2a Or *For God will judge you as you judge others.* 7:2b Or *The measure you give will be the measure you get back.* 7:3 Greek *your brother's eye;* also in 7:5.

6:14 Mark 11:25; Eph 4:32; Col 3:13
6:15 Matt 18:35
6:16 Isa 58:5
6:19-21 //Luke 12:33-34
6:19 Prov 23:4; Jas 5:2-3
6:20 Matt 19:21; Mark 10:21; Luke 18:22; 1 Tim 6:19
6:22-23 //Luke 11:34-36
6:23 Matt 20:15; Mark 7:22
6:24 //Luke 16:13
6:25-34 //Luke 12:22-31
6:25 Phil 4:6; 1 Tim 6:6, 8; 1 Pet 5:7
6:26 Job 38:41
6:30 Matt 8:26; 14:31; 16:8
6:32 Matt 6:8; Luke 12:30
6:33 Ps 37:4, 25; Mark 10:29, 30
7:1-2 //Luke 6:37-42; Rom 2:1-3; 14:4; 1 Cor 4:5; 5:12; Jas 4:11-12

▸ SALVATION

6:24 Just one Master. How often have you seen someone driving erratically or especially slowly and then realized that it was because they were talking on a cell phone? No matter how hard we try, some things require too much of our attention to allow us to do other things at the same time. When Jesus spoke of the impossibility of serving "two masters," He was addressing something similar. He was talking about the danger of assuming you can live for two mastering passions or two over-arching life goals. It's not just hard to juggle God and money; Jesus says that it is impossible. For a follower of Jesus, this brings clarity to life—either we are receiving sustenance from Him as the center of our lives or we're not. Which is it for you? Which master do you truly depend upon? (***See Salvation***> *Receiving*> *When*> *New master,* TopicGuide page A22.)

6:29 Solomon was David's son and successor as king in Israel (2 Chronicles 9:13-28). He was a wise and wealthy ruler who was arrayed in the finest of garments.

7:3 Here we see evidence of Jesus' sense of humor. By using hyperbole (an exaggerated statement to illustrate a point), Jesus conveyed His message in a powerful and engaging way.

4 How can you think of saying to your friend,* 'Let me help you get rid of that speck in your
eye,' when you can't see past the log in your own eye? 5 Hypocrite! First get rid of the log in
your own eye; then you will see well enough to deal with the speck in your friend's eye.
6 "Don't waste what is holy on people who are unholy.* Don't throw your pearls to pigs!
They will trample the pearls, then turn and attack you.

7:7-11 //Luke 11:9-13
7:7 Matt 21:22; Mark 11:24; Luke 11:9-13; John 14:13-14; 15:7; 16:23-24; Jas 1:5-6; 1 Jn 3:21-22; 5:14-15
7:11 Jas 1:17

EFFECTIVE PRAYER

7 "Keep on asking, and you will receive what you ask for. Keep on seeking, and you will
find. Keep on knocking, and the door will be opened to you. 8 For everyone who asks, re-
ceives. Everyone who seeks, finds. And to everyone who knocks, the door will be opened.
9 "You parents—if your children ask for a loaf of bread, do you give them a stone in-
stead? 10 Or if they ask for a fish, do you give them a snake? Of course not! 11 So if you sin-
ful people know how to give good gifts to your children, how much more will your
heavenly Father give good gifts to those who ask Him.

7:12 Luke 6:31; Rom 13:8-10; Gal 5:14

THE GOLDEN RULE

12 "Do to others whatever you would like them to do to you. This is the essence of all that is
taught in the law and the prophets.

7:13 //Luke 13:24
7:14 John 14:6; Acts 14:22

THE NARROW GATE

13 "You can enter God's Kingdom only through the narrow gate. The highway to hell* is
broad, and its gate is wide for the many who choose that way. 14 But the gateway to life is
very narrow and the road is difficult, and only a few ever find it.

7:15 Jer 23:16; Matt 24:11, 24; Luke 6:26; Acts 20:29; Rom 16:17; 2 Pet 2:1; 1 Jn 4:1
7:16-20 Matt 12:33; //Luke 6:43-44
7:21-23 //Luke 13:25-27

THE TREE AND ITS FRUIT

15 "Beware of false prophets who come disguised as harmless sheep but are really vicious
wolves. 16 You can identify them by their fruit, that is, by the way they act. Can you pick
grapes from thornbushes, or figs from thistles? 17 A good tree produces good fruit, and a
bad tree produces bad fruit. 18 A good tree can't produce bad fruit, and a bad tree can't pro-
duce good fruit. 19 So every tree that does not produce good fruit is chopped down and
thrown into the fire. 20 Yes, just as you can identify a tree by its fruit, so you can identify
people by their actions.

7:21 Luke 6:46; Jas 1:22
7:22 Acts 19:13-15

TRUE DISCIPLES

21 "Not everyone who calls out to Me, 'Lord! Lord!' will enter the Kingdom of Heaven. Only
those who actually do the will of My Father in heaven will enter. 22 On judgment day many

7:4 Greek *your brother.* **7:6** Greek *Don't give the sacred to dogs.* **7:13** Greek *The road that leads to destruction.*

▸ WORSHIP

7:7-11 Devoted to prayer. Prayer is a bit mysterious. It's not easy to understand how God hears our prayers and why He values them, yet God wants us to be in constant and regular communication with Him. In these few words, Jesus highlighted one of the most important facets of prayer: persistence. When we are persistent in talking with God about what is on our heart and consistent in expressing our desires to Him, we are admitting by that very process that He is the One we trust, the One we look to, the only One we can ultimately depend on. Show a life of dependence on God by devoting yourself to public and private prayer. (***See Worship***> *NT> Prayer> Instructions> Devote yourselves to prayer,* TopicGuide page A33.)

7:13 Jesus did not actually use the word "hell" (see NLT textual note), although the idea is possibly implied in His statement. Jesus was warning listeners against the seductive, easy life of sin (Psalm 1:6).

▸ CHURCH

7:21-23 Knowing Christ. Sadly, some people act as if Jesus simply wants to see a bunch of people "doing stuff" for Him. It is true that those Jesus invites into life are also called to work for His Kingdom, but His central concern for His followers is that they know Him. Jesus drew a sharp contrast between "religious people" and those who actually have eternal life. Religious people merely do things—even some impressive things. Those who truly have eternal life are those who know Jesus personally. Religion isn't a bad thing. Churches and songs and various programs can be very good. But at the center of it all must be a healthy and personal relationship with Christ. (***See Church***> *Who> From Every People> Those who know much of God,* TopicGuide page A48.)

will say to Me, 'Lord! Lord! We prophesied in Your name and cast out demons in Your
name and performed many miracles in Your name.' 23But I will reply, 'I never knew you.
Get away from Me, you who break God's laws.'

BUILDING ON A SOLID FOUNDATION

24"Anyone who listens to My teaching and follows it is wise, like a person who builds a
house on solid rock. 25Though the rain comes in torrents and the floodwaters rise and the
winds beat against that house, it won't collapse because it is built on bedrock. 26But any-
one who hears My teaching and doesn't obey it is foolish, like a person who builds a
house on sand. 27When the rains and floods come and the winds beat against that house,
it will collapse with a mighty crash."

28When Jesus had finished saying these things, the crowds were amazed at His teach-
ing, 29for He taught with real authority—quite unlike their teachers of religious law.

7:23 Matt 25:12, 41; Luke 13:25-27
7:24-27 //Luke 6:47-49
7:24 2 Tim 2:19; Jas 1:22
7:26 Jas 1:23
7:27 Ezek 13:10-12
7:28 Matt 13:54; Mark 1:22; 6:2; Luke 4:32; John 7:46

MY RESPONSE TO GOD

Trouble in the Church

MATTHEW 18:15-20

Loving parents discipline their children because they want them to grow up to be strong, wise, and mature. God also disciplines His children because He loves them and wants them to be holy (Hebrews 12:11; 1 Peter 1:15-16). God commands the church to participate in His work by practicing another kind of discipline—confronting and correcting serious sin (1 Corinthians 5:12-13; 2 Corinthians 2:6).

What are the effects of church discipline?

- It protects the church's purity (1 Corinthians 5:7).
- It corrects, restores, and strengthens repentant sinners (Matthew 18:15; Galatians 6:1-2; James 5:20).
- It produces strong, healthy faith (Titus 1:13).
- It limits the influence of false teachers (Titus 1:10-11).
- It sets an example to the rest of the body (1 Timothy 5:20).

Some churches miss out on these wonderful blessings of discipline because they think it's just not nice to confront sin. But in trying to be nice, they end up seriously harming all the members of the church. Other churches become too judgmental; they focus solely on disciplining sinners and show no interest in restoring broken sinners. This attitude, too, is ultimately damaging to the whole church.

God calls the church to consistently and gently confront and correct serious sin. We find the principles for this in Matthew 18:15-19, where Christ's instructions are to go to a friend in private and point out the offense. If that isn't effective, we are to take others with and do it again. If the offender refuses to listen to your pleas, then take your evidence to the church. If the person repents, then you have won that person back. But if not, the church should no longer treat the sinner as a Christian—but only as long as the person lives in unrepentant sin. When sinners repent, welcome them back (2 Corinthians 2:5-11). This is how God calls us to deal with trouble in the church.

JESUS HEALS A MAN WITH LEPROSY

8:1-4 **8** Large crowds followed Jesus as He came down the mountainside. [2]Suddenly, a man
//Mark 1:40-44 with leprosy approached Him and knelt before Him. "Lord," the man said, "if You are
//Luke 5:12-14 willing, You can heal me and make me clean."
[3]Jesus reached out and touched him. "I am willing," He said. "Be healed!" And instantly
8:4 the leprosy disappeared. [4]Then Jesus said to him, "Don't tell anyone about this. Instead,
Lev 14:1-32 go to the priest and let him examine you. Take along the offering required in the law of
Moses for those who have been healed of leprosy.* This will be a public testimony that
you have been cleansed."

THE FAITH OF A ROMAN OFFICER

8:5-13 [5]When Jesus returned to Capernaum, a Roman officer* came and pleaded with Him,
//Luke 7:1-10 [6]"Lord, my young servant* lies in bed, paralyzed and in terrible pain."
8:5-7 [7]Jesus said, "I will come and heal him."
John 4:43-54 [8]But the officer said, "Lord, I am not worthy to have You come into my home. Just say
8:8 Ps 107:20 the word from where You are, and my servant will be healed. [9]I know this because I am
under the authority of my superior officers, and I have authority over my soldiers. I only
need to say, 'Go,' and they go, or 'Come,' and they come. And if I say to my slaves, 'Do
this,' they do it."
8:10-12 [10]When Jesus heard this, He was amazed. Turning to those who were following Him, He
Ps 107:3 Matt 13:41-42; 21:43 said, "I tell you the truth, I haven't seen faith like this in all Israel! [11]And I tell you this, that
//Luke 13:28-29 many Gentiles will come from all over the world—from east and west—and sit down with
Acts 10:45; 11:18; 14:27 Abraham, Isaac, and Jacob at the feast in the Kingdom of Heaven. [12]But many Israelites—
Eph 3:6 those for whom the Kingdom was prepared—will be thrown into outer darkness, where
there will be weeping and gnashing of teeth."
8:13 [13]Then Jesus said to the Roman officer, "Go back home. Because you believed, it has
Matt 9:29; 15:28 John 4:50-51 happened." And the young servant was healed that same hour.

JESUS HEALS MANY PEOPLE

8:14-16 [14]When Jesus arrived at Peter's house, Peter's mother-in-law was sick in bed with a high
//Mark 1:29-34 fever. [15]But when Jesus touched her hand, the fever left her. Then she got up and pre-
//Luke 4:38-41 pared a meal for Him.
[16]That evening many demon-possessed people were brought to Jesus. He cast out the
8:17 evil spirits with a simple command, and He healed all the sick. [17]This fulfilled the word of
*Isa 53:4 the Lord through the prophet Isaiah, who said,

"He took our sicknesses
and removed our diseases."*

THE COST OF FOLLOWING JESUS

[18]When Jesus saw the crowd around Him, He instructed His disciples to cross to the other
side of the lake.

8:4 See Lev 14:2-32. 8:5 Greek *a centurion;* similarly in 8:8, 13. 8:6 Or *child;* also in 8:13. 8:17 Isa 53:4.

8:2-4 It would have been quite unusual for someone with leprosy to be found in the midst of a crowd. Such people were considered not only sick but also religiously and ceremonially unclean, and were not permitted to have normal social contact with others (Leviticus 13:3, 44-46; 22:4-7). By having the man present himself to the priest to be examined, Jesus was following God's commands regarding the reinstatement of former lepers to the community.

▸ SPIRITUAL WARFARE

8:5-13 Trusting Jesus. The Roman officer's words and actions provide a perfect model for us. The officer came to Jesus because he knew that Jesus could meet his need. The officer was honest and straightforward with Jesus about his need. The officer was willing to trust Jesus to meet his need with a simple word. The officer needed nothing more. Do you have this much faith in Jesus to meet your needs? Entrust yourself to God's care and you'll soon find new opportunities to trust Him. (***See Spiritual Warfare*****>** *Resisting Sin and Evil> Embracing Christ> Entrust yourself to God's care,* TopicGuide page A45.)

8:17 Even prior to Jesus' atonement for sin, He fulfilled Isaiah's prophecies (see Isaiah 53) about the Messiah's healing ministry.

[19]Then one of the teachers of religious law said to Him, "Teacher, I will follow You wher- 8:19-22 //Luke 9:57-62
ever You go."
[20]But Jesus replied, "Foxes have dens to live in, and birds have nests, but the Son of
Man* has no place even to lay His head." 8:22 Matt 9:9 Mark 2:14 Luke 9:59 John 1:43; 21:19
[21]Another of His disciples said, "Lord, first let me return home and bury my father."
[22]But Jesus told him, "Follow Me now. Let the spiritually dead bury their own dead.*"

JESUS CALMS THE STORM

[23]Then Jesus got into the boat and started across the lake with His disciples. [24]Suddenly, a 8:23-27 //Mark 4:36-41 //Luke 8:22-25
fierce storm struck the lake, with waves breaking into the boat. But Jesus was sleeping.
[25]The disciples went and woke Him up, shouting, "Lord, save us! We're going to drown!"
[26]Jesus responded, "Why are you afraid? You have so little faith!" Then He got up and 8:26 Pss 89:10; 107:25-32 Matt 6:30
rebuked the wind and waves, and suddenly there was a great calm.
[27]The disciples were amazed. "Who is this man?" they asked. "Even the winds and
waves obey Him!"

JESUS HEALS TWO DEMON-POSSESSED MEN

[28]When Jesus arrived on the other side of the lake, in the region of the Gadarenes,* two 8:28-34 //Mark 5:1-17 //Luke 8:26-37
men who were possessed by demons met Him. They lived in a cemetery and were so vio-
lent that no one could go through that area.
[29]They began screaming at Him, "Why are You interfering with us, Son of God? Have 8:29 Mark 1:24 Luke 4:34 2 Pet 2:4
You come here to torture us before God's appointed time?"
[30]There happened to be a large herd of pigs feeding in the distance. [31]So the demons
begged, "If You cast us out, send us into that herd of pigs."
[32]"All right, go!" Jesus commanded them. So the demons came out of the men and en-
tered the pigs, and the whole herd plunged down the steep hillside into the lake and
drowned in the water.
[33]The herdsmen fled to the nearby town, telling everyone what happened to the
demon-possessed men. [34]Then the entire town came out to meet Jesus, but they begged 8:34 Acts 16:39
Him to go away and leave them alone.

JESUS HEALS A PARALYZED MAN

9 Jesus climbed into a boat and went back across the lake to His own town. [2]Some 9:1-8 //Mark 2:3-12 //Luke 5:18-26
people brought to Him a paralyzed man on a mat. Seeing their faith, Jesus said to the
paralyzed man, "Be encouraged, My child! Your sins are forgiven."

8:20 "Son of Man" is a title Jesus used for Himself. **8:22** Greek *Let the dead bury their own dead.* **8:28** Other manuscripts read *Gerasenes;* still others read *Gergesenes.* Compare Mark 5:1; Luke 8:26.

8:21 It is doubtful that the disciple here was saying that his father had just died and he simply wanted to participate in the funeral. Instead, he was probably saying that he wanted to refrain from following Jesus wholeheartedly until his father passed away and he was able to collect his inheritance.

▸ GOD
8:23-27 Controlling the elements. Jesus does not show off. Whether in the stories of the Gospels or the story of our own life, Jesus—God in the flesh—merely responds to our needs and displays the power and majesty intrinsic to His nature. Such was the case when He stilled the storm that threatened the lives of His disciples. When Jesus spoke to wind and waves and demons and sickness, they all obeyed Him. The disciples rightly asked in amazement, "Who is this Man?" What is the right answer? Make sure you know it. Make certain you stay in humble submission to the One to whom all creation bows low. (*See God> God's Attributes> Sovereign> God controls nature for His purposes,* TopicGuide page A17.)

8:28-32 Although demons are spiritual beings without physical bodies, they appear to desire bodies (human or even animal) in which to dwell. We see no evidence in Scripture of demons inhabiting inanimate objects.

▸ GOD
9:2 Our greatest need. When Jesus announced that the sins of the paralyzed man were forgiven, many thoughts probably stirred in the minds of those nearby. The religious leaders raised a question about whether Jesus had the right to do such a thing. The friends of the paralyzed man may have wondered how Jesus could have overlooked the man's more obvious need. But we can be sure of one thing—Jesus addressed the man's deepest need. We often come to Jesus with dire physical problems, and He doesn't overlook those. But He also doesn't overlook our most critical need of all—the need to receive forgiveness for our sins. Repent regularly and find Jesus there to meet your greatest need. (*See God> Salvation> Son> Forgives sins,* TopicGuide page A15.)

9:3 [3]But some of the teachers of religious law said to themselves, "That's blasphemy! Does
Matt 26:65 John 10:33 He think He's God?"
9:4 [4]Jesus knew* what they were thinking, so He asked them, "Why do you have such evil
Matt 12:25 thoughts in your hearts? [5] Is it easier to say 'Your sins are forgiven,' or 'Stand up and walk'?
Luke 6:8; 9:47; 11:17 [6] So I will prove to you that the Son of Man* has the authority on earth to forgive sins." Then
9:6-8 Jesus turned to the paralyzed man and said, "Stand up, pick up your mat, and go home!"
Matt 15:31 Luke 7:16 [7]And the man jumped up and went home! [8]Fear swept through the crowd as they saw
Acts 9:33-35 this happen. And they praised God for sending a man with such great authority.*

JESUS CALLS MATTHEW

9:9-13 [9]As Jesus was walking along, He saw a man named Matthew sitting at his tax collector's
//Mark 2:14-17 //Luke 5:27-32 booth. "Follow Me and be My disciple," Jesus said to him. So Matthew got up and followed
Him.

[10]Later, Matthew invited Jesus and His disciples to his home as dinner guests, along
9:11 with many tax collectors and other disreputable sinners. [11]But when the Pharisees saw
Matt 11:19 Luke 5:30; 15:1-2; 19:7 this, they asked His disciples, "Why does your teacher eat with such scum?*"
[12]When Jesus heard this, He said, "Healthy people don't need a doctor—sick people do."
9:13 [13]Then He added, "Now go and learn the meaning of this Scripture: 'I want you to show
Hos 6:6 Mic 6:6-8 mercy, not offer sacrifices.' For I have come to call not those who think they are righteous,
Matt 12:7 Luke 19:10 1 Tim 1:15 but those who know they are sinners."

A DISCUSSION ABOUT FASTING

9:14-17 [14]One day the disciples of John the Baptist came to Jesus and asked Him, "Why don't Your
//Mark 2:18-22 //Luke 5:33-39 disciples fast* like we do and the Pharisees do?"
9:15 [15]Jesus replied, "Do wedding guests mourn while celebrating with the groom? Of course
John 3:29 not. But someday the groom will be taken away from them, and then they will fast.
[16] "Besides, who would patch old clothing with new cloth? For the new patch would
shrink and rip away from the old cloth, leaving an even bigger tear than before.
[17] "And no one puts new wine into old wineskins. For the old skins would burst from the
pressure, spilling the wine and ruining the skins. New wine is stored in new wineskins so
that both are preserved."

JESUS HEALS IN RESPONSE TO FAITH

9:18-26 [18]As Jesus was saying this, the leader of a synagogue came and knelt before Him. "My
//Mark 5:22-43 //Luke 8:41-56 daughter has just died," he said, "but You can bring her back to life again if You just come
and lay Your hand on her."
[19]So Jesus and His disciples got up and went with him. [20]Just then a woman who had
suffered for twelve years with constant bleeding came up behind Him. She touched the
fringe of His robe, [21]for she thought, "If I can just touch His robe, I will be healed."
9:22 [22]Jesus turned around, and when He saw her He said, "Daughter, be encouraged! Your
Matt 9:29 Mark 10:52 faith has made you well." And the woman was healed at that moment.
Luke 7:50; 17:19 Acts 3:16

9:4 Some manuscripts read *saw*. 9:6 "Son of Man" is a title Jesus used for Himself. 9:8 Greek *for giving such authority to human beings.* 9:11 Greek *with tax collectors and sinners?* 9:13 Hos 6:6 (Greek version). 9:14 Some manuscripts read *fast often.*

9:7-8 The crowd was awestruck that God had authorized Jesus to work among them this way. This led to God-centered worship. Jesus' now-undeniable healing ministry increased faith in His authority to forgive the sins of those who admitted their need (9:12).

9:11 Tax collectors were Jewish men who cooperated with the oppressive Roman Empire to gather taxes from their own people. They were hated by their fellow Jews, who identified them as sinners.

9:15-17 Jesus' three short parables illustrated the same basic point: Jesus' teaching was incompatible with the established religious system. He was not intent on destroying the Old Covenant, but He would establish a newer, modified one (Jeremiah 31:31-33; Luke 22:20; 2 Corinthians 3).

23When Jesus arrived at the official's home, He saw the noisy crowd and heard the fu-
neral music. 24"Get out!" He told them. "The girl isn't dead; she's only asleep." But the
crowd laughed at Him. 25After the crowd was put outside, however, Jesus went in and took
the girl by the hand, and she stood up! 26The report of this miracle swept through the en-
tire countryside.

JESUS HEALS THE BLIND

27After Jesus left the girl's home, two blind men followed along behind Him, shouting,
"Son of David, have mercy on us!"
28They went right into the house where He was staying, and Jesus asked them, "Do you
believe I can make you see?"
"Yes, Lord," they told Him, "we do."
29Then He touched their eyes and said, "Because of your faith, it will happen." 30Then
their eyes were opened, and they could see! Jesus sternly warned them, "Don't tell any-
one about this." 31But instead, they went out and spread His fame all over the region.
32When they left, a demon-possessed man who couldn't speak was brought to Jesus.
33So Jesus cast out the demon, and then the man began to speak. The crowds were
amazed. "Nothing like this has ever happened in Israel!" they exclaimed.
34But the Pharisees said, "He can cast out demons because He is empowered by the
prince of demons."

THE NEED FOR WORKERS

35Jesus traveled through all the towns and villages of that area, teaching in the syna-
gogues and announcing the Good News about the Kingdom. And He healed every kind of
disease and illness. 36When He saw the crowds, He had compassion on them because
they were confused and helpless, like sheep without a shepherd. 37He said to His disciples,
"The harvest is great, but the workers are few. 38So pray to the Lord who is in charge of the
harvest; ask Him to send more workers into His fields."

JESUS SENDS OUT THE TWELVE APOSTLES

10 Jesus called His twelve disciples together and gave them authority to cast out evil*
spirits and to heal every kind of disease and illness. 2Here are the names of the
twelve apostles:

first, Simon (also called Peter),
then Andrew (Peter's brother),
James (son of Zebedee),
John (James's brother),
3 Philip,
Bartholomew,
Thomas,

9:23 2 Chr 35:25; Jer 9:17-18
9:24 John 11:11-13
9:27 Matt 20:29-31; Mark 10:47
9:30 Mark 7:36
9:31 Mark 7:36
9:32-33 Matt 12:22; Mark 7:32, 35; 9:17, 25; Luke 11:14
9:34 Matt 12:24; Mark 3:22; Luke 11:15
9:35 Matt 4:23
9:36 *Num 27:17; 1 Kgs 22:17; *2 Chr 18:16; Ezek 34:5; *Zech 10:2; Mark 6:34
9:37-38 Luke 10:2; John 4:35
10:2-4 //Mark 3:13-19; //Luke 6:12-16; John 1:40-49; Acts 1:13

10:1 Greek *unclean.*

9:30-31 It may seem strange that Jesus would instruct someone who had been healed *not* to tell anyone about it. This concurs with other decisions Christ made early in His ministry intentionally to forestall a full comprehension of His purposes (Mark 1:44; 5:43; 7:36). At this stage of His ministry, the attention may have resulted in larger crowds (Mark 1:41-45; 3:9-10) demanding more healings, and His ministry was primarily one of preaching, not healing (Luke 4:42-43).

▸ MINISTRY
9:35-38 Workers for the fields. When Jesus, God-in-the-flesh, walked the streets of Palestine, He chose not to do everything Himself, but also to work through others. Jesus told His followers that they should pray that the Father would raise up others who could join in the work of spreading the Kingdom. What a profound exhortation is wrapped up in Jesus' model here! If He saw the need to pray for others to join Him in the work, how can we fail to see that we, on our own, are not adequate for what lies ahead? Let's neither overestimate our own significance in the work of God nor undervalue the need to pray for more workers in His fields. (***See Ministry*****>** *Great Commission> Description> People are invited to Christ,* TopicGuide page A56.)

Matthew (the tax collector),
James (son of Alphaeus),
Thaddaeus,*
4 Simon (the zealot*),
Judas Iscariot (who later betrayed Him).

5 Jesus sent out the twelve apostles with these instructions: "Don't go to the Gentiles or
the Samaritans, 6 but only to the people of Israel—God's lost sheep. 7 Go and announce to
them that the Kingdom of Heaven is near.* 8 Heal the sick, raise the dead, cure those with
leprosy, and cast out demons. Give as freely as you have received!
9 "Don't take any money in your money belts—no gold, silver, or even copper coins.
10 Don't carry a traveler's bag with a change of clothes and sandals or even a walking stick.
Don't hesitate to accept hospitality, because those who work deserve to be fed.
11 "Whenever you enter a city or village, search for a worthy person and stay in his
home until you leave town. 12 When you enter the home, give it your blessing. 13 If it turns
out to be a worthy home, let your blessing stand; if it is not, take back the blessing. 14 If any
household or town refuses to welcome you or listen to your message, shake its dust from
your feet as you leave. 15 I tell you the truth, the wicked cities of Sodom and Gomorrah will
be better off than such a town on the judgment day.
16 "Look, I am sending you out as sheep among wolves. So be as shrewd as snakes and
harmless as doves. 17 But beware! For you will be handed over to the courts and will be
flogged with whips in the synagogues. 18 You will stand trial before governors and kings
because you are My followers. But this will be your opportunity to tell the rulers and other
unbelievers about Me.* 19 When you are arrested, don't worry about how to respond or
what to say. God will give you the right words at the right time. 20 For it is not you who will
be speaking—it will be the Spirit of your Father speaking through you.
21 "A brother will betray his brother to death, a father will betray his own child, and chil-
dren will rebel against their parents and cause them to be killed. 22 And all nations will
hate you because you are My followers.* But everyone who endures to the end will be
saved. 23 When you are persecuted in one town, flee to the next. I tell you the truth, the
Son of Man* will return before you have reached all the towns of Israel.
24 "Students* are not greater than their teacher, and slaves are not greater than their

10:4 Matt 26:25; 27:3 Mark 14:44 John 6:64; 12:4; 13:2, 26-27
10:5 2 Kgs 17:24 John 4:9
10:6 Jer 50:6 Matt 15:24
10:7 Matt 3:2; 4:17
10:9-10 1 Cor 9:14 1 Tim 5:18
10:15 Gen 18:20–19:29 Matt 11:23-24 2 Pet 2:6 Jude 1:7
10:16 Luke 10:3 Acts 20:29
10:17 Acts 5:40; 22:19; 26:11
10:18 Acts 25:24-26
10:19-20 Luke 12:11-12 Acts 4:8
10:21 Mic 7:6
10:22 John 15:21
10:24 John 13:16; 15:20

10:3 Other manuscripts read *Lebbaeus;* still others read *Lebbaeus who is called Thaddaeus.* 10:4 Greek *the Cananean,* an Aramaic term for Jewish nationalists. 10:7 Or *has come,* or *is coming soon.* 10:18 Or *But this will be your testimony against the rulers and other unbelievers.* 10:22 Greek *on account of My name.* 10:23 "Son of Man" is a title Jesus used for Himself. 10:24 Or *Disciples.*

10:5-7 Jesus' initial commission to His followers was to go "only to the people of Israel" and not focus on the Gentiles (non-Jewish people) or the Samaritans (a people of mixed heritage, partly Jewish and partly Gentile). The scope of ministry for Jesus' disciples would broaden later to include all peoples.

▸ MINISTRY
10:5-15 Taking risks for Christ. What does Jesus need you to bring along in order to be effective in the ministry He is carrying out in the world? His departing instructions to the twelve disciples are rich with insight. The disciples were not to rely on their own resources and planning but instead had to step out into the unknown and take risks. But in doing this, they had the opportunity for the Spirit to work in and through them as they served as extensions of Jesus' own ministry. Although these guidelines don't apply to us in exactly the same way, they certainly point us in the right direction as we think about what we need to "bring along" as we seek to be involved in the spreading of the Kingdom. (***See Ministry**> Great Commission> Risk> Stepping outside of your "comfort zone,"* TopicGuide page A56.)

10:7-8 As the followers of Jesus went out with the proclamation, "The Kingdom of Heaven is near," they were also to minister to the needs of those they met. Thus, in word and in deed, they were extensions of Jesus' own ministry.

10:15 Sodom and Gomorrah were cities mentioned in Genesis 18–19. Sodom was the city in which Abraham's nephew Lot settled (Genesis 13). Ultimately it came under the judgment of God (along with Gomorrah) for its gross immorality. The Old Testament often mentions these cities as examples of wickedness punished by God.

10:23 There has been much debate and discussion about what Jesus meant when He said, "I tell you the truth, the Son of Man will return before you have reached all the towns of Israel." Some believe that this is in reference to Jesus meeting up with the twelve after their current mission. Others see it as a reference to His coming in judgment to destroy Jerusalem in AD 70. It is more likely, however, that this refers to His Second Coming, and the point is simply this: There will always be work for Jesus' followers to do before His return.

master. 25 Students are to be like their teacher, and slaves are to be like their master. And
since I, the master of the household, have been called the prince of demons,* the mem-
bers of My household will be called by even worse names!

26 "But don't be afraid of those who threaten you. For the time is coming when every-
thing that is covered will be revealed, and all that is secret will be made known to all.
27 What I tell you now in the darkness, shout abroad when daybreak comes. What I whis-
per in your ear, shout from the housetops for all to hear!

28 "Don't be afraid of those who want to kill your body; they cannot touch your soul.
Fear only God, who can destroy both soul and body in hell.* 29 What is the price of two
sparrows—one copper coin*? But not a single sparrow can fall to the ground without your
Father knowing it. 30 And the very hairs on your head are all numbered. 31 So don't be
afraid; you are more valuable to God than a whole flock of sparrows.

32 "Everyone who acknowledges Me publicly here on earth, I will also acknowledge be-
fore My Father in heaven. 33 But everyone who denies Me here on earth, I will also deny
before My Father in heaven.

34 "Don't imagine that I came to bring peace to the earth! I came not to bring peace, but
a sword.

35 'I have come to set a man against his father,
a daughter against her mother,
and a daughter-in-law against her mother-in-law.
36 Your enemies will be right in your own household!'*

37 "If you love your father or mother more than you love Me, you are not worthy of
being Mine; or if you love your son or daughter more than Me, you are not worthy of be-
ing Mine. 38 If you refuse to take up your cross and follow Me, you are not worthy of being

10:25 Greek *Beelzeboul;* other manuscripts read *Beezeboul;* Latin version reads *Beelzebub.* 10:28 Greek *Gehenna.*
10:29 Greek *one assarion* [i.e., one "as," a Roman coin equal to 1/16 of a denarius]. 10:35-36 Mic 7:6.

10:26-33 //Luke 12:2-9
10:26 Mark 4:22
10:28 Isa 8:12-13; Heb 10:31
10:29 Luke 12:6
10:30 1 Sam 14:45; 2 Sam 14:11; Luke 21:18; Acts 27:34
10:31 Matt 6:26; 12:12
10:32 Rom 10:9; Rev 3:5
10:33 Mark 8:38; Luke 9:26; 2 Tim 2:12
10:34-36 //Luke 12:51-53
10:35-36 *Mic 7:6
10:37 Luke 14:26
10:38 Matt 16:24; Mark 8:34; Luke 9:23; 14:27

▸ CHURCH
10:28-30 Under Jesus' care. It's hard to give yourself to meaningful service in the Kingdom if you are afraid of what it might cost you. If you are concerned about whether your life is at risk as you step outside of your comfort zone, you won't be able to minister freely. Jesus' words to His followers are just what we need to hear if we are going to be free to extend ourselves in spite of the perceived risks. He tells us that the Father watches over us in tangible, practical, and intimate ways. We are safe in His care! (***See Church****> What> Supernatural Body> Relationship> Treasured by Christ,* TopicGuide page A48.)

10:38-39 In Jesus' day, those who were sentenced to die under Roman law generally carried their cross to their place of execution. Someone carrying a cross was a "walking dead." His life, as he knew it, was over. Jesus inferred that following Him was a journey marked by suffering and signaled an end to a life dominated by sin.

BECAUSE GOD KNOWS EVERYTHING

I will go to Him with all my questions and concerns.

The very hairs on your head are all numbered.

MATTHEW 10:30

FOR THE NEXT *GOD KNOWS EVERYTHING* FEATURE SEE PAGE 2044.

Mine. 39If you cling to your life, you will lose it; but if you give up your life for Me, you will
find it.
40"Anyone who receives you receives Me, and anyone who receives Me receives the Fa-
ther who sent Me. 41If you receive a prophet as one who speaks for God,* you will be given
the same reward as a prophet. And if you receive righteous people because of their righ-
teousness, you will be given a reward like theirs. 42And if you give even a cup of cold wa-
ter to one of the least of My followers, you will surely be rewarded."

JESUS AND JOHN THE BAPTIST

11 When Jesus had finished giving these instructions to His twelve disciples, He went
out to teach and preach in towns throughout the region.
2John the Baptist, who was in prison, heard about all the things the Messiah was doing.
So he sent his disciples to ask Jesus, 3"Are You the Messiah we've been expecting,* or
should we keep looking for someone else?"
4Jesus told them, "Go back to John and tell him what you have heard and seen—5the
blind see, the lame walk, the lepers are cured, the deaf hear, the dead are raised to life,
and the Good News is being preached to the poor. 6And tell him, 'God blesses those who
do not turn away because of Me.*'"
7As John's disciples were leaving, Jesus began talking about him to the crowds. "What
kind of man did you go into the wilderness to see? Was he a weak reed, swayed by every
breath of wind? 8Or were you expecting to see a man dressed in expensive clothes? No,
people with expensive clothes live in palaces. 9Were you looking for a prophet? Yes, and
he is more than a prophet. 10John is the man to whom the Scriptures refer when they say,

'Look, I am sending My messenger ahead of You,
and he will prepare Your way before You.'*

11"I tell you the truth, of all who have ever lived, none is greater than John the Baptist.
Yet even the least person in the Kingdom of Heaven is greater than he is! 12And from the
time John the Baptist began preaching until now, the Kingdom of Heaven has been force-
fully advancing,* and violent people are attacking it. 13For before John came, all the
prophets and the law of Moses looked forward to this present time. 14And if you are will-
ing to accept what I say, he is Elijah, the one the prophets said would come.* 15Anyone
with ears to hear should listen and understand!
16"To what can I compare this generation? It is like children playing a game in the public
square. They complain to their friends,
17'We played wedding songs,
and you didn't dance,

10:39 Matt 16:25; Mark 8:35; Luke 9:24; 17:33; John 12:25
10:40 John 12:44; 13:20
10:41 1 Kgs 17:9-24; 2 Kgs 4:8-37
11:2-19 //Luke 7:18-35
11:3 Mal 3:1
11:5 Isa 35:4-6; 42:7, 18; 61:1; Luke 4:18-19
11:6 Matt 13:57
11:7 Matt 3:5
11:9 Matt 14:5; 21:26; Luke 1:76
11:10 Exod 23:20; *Mal 3:1; Mark 1:2; Luke 7:27
11:12-13 Luke 16:16
11:14 Mal 4:5; Matt 17:10-13; Mark 9:11-13; Luke 1:17; John 1:21
11:15 Matt 13:9, 43; Mark 4:9, 23; Luke 8:8; 14:35; Rev 2:7

10:41 Greek *receive a prophet in the name of a prophet.* 11:3 Greek *Are You the One who is coming?* 11:6 Or *who are not offended by Me.* 11:10 Mal 3:1. 11:12 Or *the Kingdom of Heaven has suffered from violence.* 11:14 See Mal 4:5.

11:1-6 Given the expectations of people in John the Baptist's day, his question makes sense. Many Jews were hoping that God would send a military deliverer; Jesus clearly wasn't that kind of Messiah. Jesus' answer, however, confirmed His understanding of His role. (See Isaiah 35:5; 61:1)

▸ GOD
11:2-6 Jesus' ministry. Apparently, John the Baptist had grown discouraged while sitting in prison. He began to wonder whether Jesus was, in fact, the promised Deliverer he had been awaiting. So he sent a messenger to Jesus with a question, and although the answer may not have been what John had anticipated, it was the answer he needed to hear. We often come to Jesus with certain expectations about how He should carry out His calling as Messiah; we expect Him to do things the way we think He should! But Jesus was clear; He knew what His calling was. As Messiah, He came to meet needs, to care for those who are hurting, and to proclaim the Good News that the Kingdom of God is present. We must be careful to not be offended by Jesus' ministry but to join with Him in it. (***See God**> Salvation> Son> Came to save what was lost,* TopicGuide page A15.)

11:10-15 In Malachi 4:5, God promised to send Elijah before the end times. The Jewish people anticipated a restoration of Elijah's ministry before the coming of the Messiah. According to Jesus, although John the Baptist was not a reincarnation of Elijah, he fulfilled the promise of a prophet like Elijah coming to prepare the way for the Messiah.

so we played funeral songs,
and you didn't mourn.'

18 For John didn't spend his time eating and drinking, and you say, 'He's possessed by a
demon.' 19 The Son of Man,* on the other hand, feasts and drinks, and you say, 'He's a
glutton and a drunkard, and a friend of tax collectors and other sinners!' But wisdom is
shown to be right by its results."

11:18 Matt 3:4; Luke 1:15
11:19 Matt 9:11, 14

JUDGMENT FOR THE UNBELIEVERS

20 Then Jesus began to denounce the towns where He had done so many of His miracles,
because they hadn't repented of their sins and turned to God. 21 "What sorrow awaits you,
Korazin and Bethsaida! For if the miracles I did in you had been done in wicked Tyre and
Sidon, their people would have repented of their sins long ago, clothing themselves in
burlap and throwing ashes on their heads to show their remorse. 22 I tell you, Tyre and Si-
don will be better off on judgment day than you.
23 "And you people of Capernaum, will you be honored in heaven? No, you will go down
to the place of the dead.* For if the miracles I did for you had been done in wicked Sodom,
it would still be here today. 24 I tell you, even Sodom will be better off on judgment day
than you."

11:20-24 //Luke 10:13-15
11:21-22 Isa 23:1-8; Ezek 26–28; Joel 3:4-8; Amos 1:9-10; Zech 9:2-4; Matt 10:15
11:23 *Isa 14:13, 15

JESUS' PRAYER OF THANKSGIVING

25 At that time Jesus prayed this prayer: "O Father, Lord of heaven and earth, thank You for
hiding these things from those who think themselves wise and clever, and for revealing
them to the childlike. 26 Yes, Father, it pleased You to do it this way!
27 "My Father has entrusted everything to Me. No one truly knows the Son except the
Father, and no one truly knows the Father except the Son and those to whom the Son
chooses to reveal Him."
28 Then Jesus said, "Come to Me, all of you who are weary and carry heavy burdens, and
I will give you rest. 29 Take My yoke upon you. Let Me teach you, because I am humble
and gentle at heart, and you will find rest for your souls. 30 For My yoke is easy to bear, and
the burden I give you is light."

11:25-27 //Luke 10:21-22; Eph 1:17-18
11:27 Matt 28:18; John 3:35; 10:15; 17:2, 25-26
11:29 *Jer 6:16
11:30 1 Jn 5:3

A DISCUSSION ABOUT THE SABBATH

12 At about that time Jesus was walking through some grainfields on the Sabbath.
His disciples were hungry, so they began breaking off some heads of grain and
eating them. 2 But some Pharisees saw them do it and protested, "Look, Your disciples are
breaking the law by harvesting grain on the Sabbath."

12:1-8 //Mark 2:23-28; //Luke 6:1-5
12:2 Exod 20:10; Deut 5:14; Luke 13:14; 14:3; John 5:10; 7:23; 9:16

11:19 "Son of Man" is a title Jesus used for Himself. 11:23 Greek *to Hades.*

11:21-24 Jesus named two Gentile cities, Tyre and Sidon, considered unclean and wicked by His audience. Those cities would have repented if they had witnessed what had been happening through His ministry in the unrepentant Jewish cities of Korazin and Bethsaida. In the same way Jesus compared Sodom, an Old Testament example of societal wickedness, to the lack of repentance in Capernaum.

▸ SALVATION
11:25-26 God causes responses to the gospel. We are to be involved in the intentional, international spreading of the Good News about Jesus' salvation. Jesus enlists all His followers in the ongoing extension of His ministry of inviting people into true life. But does the effectiveness of our efforts rest on our ability to draw people to Jesus? Not at all. Jesus' prayer makes it clear that understanding the truth about the Good News is more than just getting the facts straight. Real response to the Good News is a work that the Father does in the hearts of people. Stay focused on your part in God's plan to send the gospel to every land, and trust God for the results. (***See Salvation***> *Receiving*> *How*> *Respond to God's call/invitation to salvation,* TopicGuide page A22.)

12:1-2 One of the Ten Commandments handed down by God to the people of Israel through Moses was to "observe the Sabbath" (Exodus 20:8-11). The Jewish teachers of the law in Jesus' day had developed very strict rules about what this commandment meant, believing if they surrounded the commandments with sub-commandments, they could reduce the number of sins against God. In this passage, Jesus pointed out that having more rules does not produce more righteousness. Paul continues that theme in Romans 3–4.

12:3 1 Sam 21:1-6 3Jesus said to them, "Haven't you read in the Scriptures what David did when he and his
companions were hungry? 4He went into the house of God, and he and his companions
12:4 Lev 24:5-9 broke the law by eating the sacred loaves of bread that only the priests are allowed to eat.
5And haven't you read in the law of Moses that the priests on duty in the Temple may
12:5 Num 28:9-10 work on the Sabbath? 6I tell you, there is One here who is even greater than the Temple!
7But you would not have condemned My innocent disciples if you knew the meaning of
12:6 Matt 12:41-42 Luke 11:31-32 this Scripture: 'I want you to show mercy, not offer sacrifices.'* 8For the Son of Man* is
Lord, even over the Sabbath!"

12:7 *Hos 6:6 Mic 6:6-8 Matt 9:13

JESUS HEALS ON THE SABBATH

9Then Jesus went over to their synagogue, 10where He noticed a man with a deformed
12:9-14 //Mark 3:1-6 //Luke 6:6-11 hand. The Pharisees asked Jesus, "Does the law permit a person to work by healing on
the Sabbath?" (They were hoping He would say yes, so they could bring charges against
12:10 Luke 13:14; 14:3 John 9:16 Him.)
11And He answered, "If you had a sheep that fell into a well on the Sabbath, wouldn't
you work to pull it out? Of course you would. 12And how much more valuable is a person
12:11 Luke 14:5 than a sheep! Yes, the law permits a person to do good on the Sabbath."
13Then He said to the man, "Hold out your hand." So the man held out his hand, and it
12:12 Matt 6:26; 10:31 was restored, just like the other one! 14Then the Pharisees called a meeting to plot how to
kill Jesus.

JESUS, GOD'S CHOSEN SERVANT

12:15 //Mark 3:7-12 //Luke 6:17-19 15But Jesus knew what they were planning. So He left that area, and many people fol-
lowed Him. He healed all the sick among them, 16but He warned them not to reveal who
He was. 17This fulfilled the prophecy of Isaiah concerning Him:

12:18-21 *Isa 42:1-4 18"Look at My Servant, whom I have chosen.
He is My Beloved, who pleases Me.
I will put My Spirit upon Him,
and He will proclaim justice to the nations.
19He will not fight or shout
or raise His voice in public.
20He will not crush the weakest reed
or put out a flickering candle.
Finally He will cause justice to be victorious.
21And His name will be the hope
of all the world."*

12:7 Hos 6:6 (Greek version). 12:8 "Son of Man" is a title Jesus used for Himself. 12:18-21 Isa 42:1-4 (Greek version for 42:4).

12:3-8 Jesus appealed to a favorite son of the nation of Israel, King David, to illustrate that keeping rigid extrapolations of the Law in the face of genuine need does not honor God (see 1 Samuel 21:1-6).

▶ADOPTION

12:13 Full healing. A bone breaks. The doctor sets it, and later the cast or brace is removed. But while the bone may have healed, there's a problem. The limb has been immobile for a while and the patient must work hard to get his strength back. One aspect of Jesus' supernatural power is that the people He healed did not require physical therapy or any further treatment—they were ready to go. His healing immediately restored complete functionality. In the spiritual realm, Jesus changes people into new persons with new life (2 Corinthians 5:17). There is no room for a gray area, where people are half Christians. Jesus changes us—once and for all—into a new creation. Make sure that people know—and that you believe—that Jesus is not offering a modest spiritual upgrade—He's doing a brand new thing in the life of all who embrace Christ. (***See Adoption*****>** *With Christ> Supernatural> All things are new,* TopicGuide page A37.)

12:18-21 This quotation from Isaiah demonstrates Matthew's understanding that Jesus fulfilled this Old Testament prophecy through His bearing of the Spirit (see also Matthew 3:16), His preaching ministry (Matthew 5:1; Luke 4:18), His humility (see also Matthew 11:29; 21:5), His mercy (Matthew 9:29-33; 20:30), and the worldwide scope of His ministry (see also Matthew 28:18-20).

JESUS AND THE PRINCE OF DEMONS

22Then a demon-possessed man, who was blind and couldn't speak, was brought to Jesus.
He healed the man so that he could both speak and see. 23The crowd was amazed and
asked, "Could it be that Jesus is the Son of David, the Messiah?"
24But when the Pharisees heard about the miracle, they said, "No wonder He can cast
out demons. He gets His power from Satan,* the prince of demons."
25Jesus knew their thoughts and replied, "Any kingdom divided by civil war is doomed.
A town or family splintered by feuding will fall apart. 26And if Satan is casting out Satan, he
is divided and fighting against himself. His own kingdom will not survive. 27And if I am
empowered by Satan, what about your own exorcists? They cast out demons, too, so they
will condemn you for what you have said. 28But if I am casting out demons by the Spirit of
God, then the Kingdom of God has arrived among you. 29For who is powerful enough to
enter the house of a strong man like Satan and plunder his goods? Only someone even
stronger—someone who could tie him up and then plunder his house.
30"Anyone who isn't with Me opposes Me, and anyone who isn't working with Me is ac-
tually working against Me.
31"So I tell you, every sin and blasphemy can be forgiven—except blasphemy against
the Holy Spirit, which will never be forgiven. 32Anyone who speaks against the Son of Man
can be forgiven, but anyone who speaks against the Holy Spirit will never be forgiven, ei-
ther in this world or in the world to come.
33"A tree is identified by its fruit. If a tree is good, its fruit will be good. If a tree is bad, its
fruit will be bad. 34You brood of snakes! How could evil men like you speak what is good
and right? For whatever is in your heart determines what you say. 35A good person pro-
duces good things from the treasury of a good heart, and an evil person produces evil
things from the treasury of an evil heart. 36And I tell you this, you must give an account on
judgment day for every idle word you speak. 37The words you say will either acquit you or
condemn you."

THE SIGN OF JONAH

38One day some teachers of religious law and Pharisees came to Jesus and said, "Teacher,
we want You to show us a miraculous sign to prove Your authority."
39But Jesus replied, "Only an evil, adulterous generation would demand a miraculous
sign; but the only sign I will give them is the sign of the prophet Jonah. 40For as Jonah was
in the belly of the great fish for three days and three nights, so will the Son of Man be in
the heart of the earth for three days and three nights.

12:22-32 //Mark 3:20-30 //Luke 11:14-23
12:22-23 Matt 9:32-33
12:24 Matt 9:34
12:25 Matt 9:4
12:27 Matt 9:34 Acts 19:13
12:28 Acts 10:38
12:30 Mark 9:40 Luke 9:50
12:31-32 Mark 3:28-30 Luke 12:10
12:33 Matt 7:16-20 Luke 6:43-45
12:34 Matt 3:7; 23:33
12:38 Matt 16:1 Mark 8:11-12 Luke 11:16 John 2:18; 6:30 1 Cor 1:22
12:38-42 Matt 16:4 //Luke 11:29-32
12:40 Jon 1:17

12:24 Greek *Beelzeboul;* also in 12:27. Other manuscripts read *Beezeboul;* Latin version reads *Beelzebub.*

12:22-32 Jesus had told John earlier that His ministry was confirmed by the fact that the blind were regaining their sight and other miracles of healing were taking place (11:4-6). Such works were clear indicators that Jesus might well be the promised Messiah. Due to the undeniable fact of Jesus' miracles, the envious religious leaders could do nothing but spread lies about Jesus being a servant of Satan (12:24). Jesus answered their preposterous charge (12:25-29) and warned them of the danger of continuing to lie about Jesus' Spirit-empowered works (12:32).

▸ ADOPTION
12:33-37 The root of the fruit. In Jesus' interactions with the religious people of His day, we glimpse His desires for all people. Jesus is not interested merely in altering behavior. He does not want people simply to say and do the right things. He wants to create new hearts, with good deeds and repentance bursting forth from them. Like a tree that bears fruit consistent with its nature, so people bear fruit consistent with who—and what—they are. Jesus changes people, and we will certainly bear the fruit of that change in our passions and behaviors. Do not delude yourself into thinking that someone who perpetually lives like the devil can enjoy all the blessings of God, including heaven. Our words and deeds will reveal the foundation of our lives. What do your words and deeds say about the source of your spiritual life? (***See Adoption**> With Christ> Servants> Appointed to bear fruit,* TopicGuide page A37.)

12:38-41 Jesus had been doing many signs (see 11:4; 12:22-23), but the religious leaders were still not persuaded of Jesus' true identity due to their evil nature (12:34-37). Even the requests for more proofs of His power were rooted in their evil nature (12:39). The "three days and three nights" phrase (12:40) is a figurative expression meaning "three days." It is not in conflict with Luke 24:46 or 1 Corinthians 15:4 which state that Jesus was raised "on the third day."

12:41 Jon 1:2; 3:5 · 12:42 1 Kgs 10:1-10; 2 Chr 9:1-12; Matt 12:6 · 12:43-45 //Luke 11:24-26 · 12:45 2 Pet 2:20

41"The people of Nineveh will stand up against this generation on judgment day and condemn it, for they repented of their sins at the preaching of Jonah. Now someone greater than Jonah is here—but you refuse to repent. 42The queen of Sheba* will also stand up against this generation on judgment day and condemn it, for she came from a distant land to hear the wisdom of Solomon. Now someone greater than Solomon is here—but you refuse to listen.

43"When an evil* spirit leaves a person, it goes into the desert, seeking rest but finding none. 44Then it says, 'I will return to the person I came from.' So it returns and finds its former home empty, swept, and in order. 45Then the spirit finds seven other spirits more evil than itself, and they all enter the person and live there. And so that person is worse off than before. That will be the experience of this evil generation."

12:46-50 //Mark 3:31-35; //Luke 8:19-21 · 12:46 Mark 6:3; John 2:12; 7:3-5; Acts 1:14 · 12:50 John 15:14

THE TRUE FAMILY OF JESUS

46As Jesus was speaking to the crowd, His mother and brothers stood outside, asking to speak to Him. 47Someone told Jesus, "Your mother and Your brothers are outside, and they want to speak to You."*

48Jesus asked, "Who is My mother? Who are My brothers?" 49Then He pointed to His disciples and said, "Look, these are My mother and brothers. 50Anyone who does the will of My Father in heaven is My brother and sister and mother!"

13:1-15 //Mark 4:1-12; //Luke 8:4-10 · 13:9 Matt 11:15; 13:43 · 13:11 Matt 11:25; 16:17; 1 Cor 2:10, 14; Col 1:27; 1 Jn 2:20, 27 · 13:12 Matt 25:29; Mark 4:25; Luke 19:26

PARABLE OF THE FARMER SCATTERING SEED

13 Later that same day Jesus left the house and sat beside the lake. 2A large crowd soon gathered around Him, so He got into a boat. Then He sat there and taught as the people stood on the shore. 3He told many stories in the form of parables, such as this one:

"Listen! A farmer went out to plant some seeds. 4As he scattered them across his field, some seeds fell on a footpath, and the birds came and ate them. 5Other seeds fell on shallow soil with underlying rock. The seeds sprouted quickly because the soil was shallow. 6But the plants soon wilted under the hot sun, and since they didn't have deep roots, they died. 7Other seeds fell among thorns that grew up and choked out the tender plants. 8Still other seeds fell on fertile soil, and they produced a crop that was thirty, sixty, and even a hundred times as much as had been planted! 9Anyone with ears to hear should listen and understand."

10His disciples came and asked Him, "Why do You use parables when You talk to the people?"

11He replied, "You are permitted to understand the secrets* of the Kingdom of Heaven, but others are not. 12To those who listen to My teaching, more understanding will be given, and they will have an abundance of knowledge. But for those who are not listening,

12:42 Greek *The queen of the south.* **12:43** Greek *unclean.* **12:47** Some manuscripts do not include verse 47. Compare Mark 3:32 and Luke 8:20. **13:11** Greek *the mysteries.*

12:42 According to 1 Kings 10:1-10, the queen of Sheba came to learn from Solomon because of his great wisdom. Jesus chastised the religious leaders because though He was greater than Solomon, they wouldn't listen to Him.

12:46-50 Jesus had half-brothers, making it most likely that Mary and Joseph had other children. However, since Joseph is gone from the scene, he may have been older when he married Mary. It is possible some or all of these half-brothers were from a previous marriage of Joseph. Regardless, Jesus asserts that those who do the will of God are His closest relatives.

13:1-58 This chapter gives several parables, or brief illustrations, about the nature of the Kingdom. An unusual arrangement of the positive and the negative (what it is not) teachings about the Kingdom can make this a puzzling chapter to read. It may be helpful to read the positive (13:3-9, 18-23, 31-35, 44-46) and then the negative sections (13:10-17, 24-30, 36-43, 47-50).

13:10-15 Jesus quoted Isaiah 6:9-10 to explain His teaching. He wasn't saying that He taught in parables *so that* the people would not understand. He was referring to what God had told Isaiah at the beginning of Isaiah's ministry: In spite of the fact that Isaiah had a word from God, the people would not listen or understand. The same was true of Jesus' earthly ministry.

even what little understanding they have will be taken away from them. 13 That is why I
use these parables,

> For they look, but they don't really see.
> They hear, but they don't really listen or understand.

14 This fulfills the prophecy of Isaiah that says,

> 'When you hear what I say,
> you will not understand.
> When you see what I do,
> you will not comprehend.
> 15 For the hearts of these people are hardened,
> and their ears cannot hear,
> and they have closed their eyes—
> so their eyes cannot see,
> and their ears cannot hear,
> and their hearts cannot understand,
> and they cannot turn to Me
> and let Me heal them.'*

16 "But blessed are your eyes, because they see; and your ears, because they hear. 17 I
tell you the truth, many prophets and righteous people longed to see what you see, but
they didn't see it. And they longed to hear what you hear, but they didn't hear it.
18 "Now listen to the explanation of the parable about the farmer planting seeds: 19 The
seed that fell on the footpath represents those who hear the message about the Kingdom
and don't understand it. Then the evil one comes and snatches away the seed that was
planted in their hearts. 20 The seed on the rocky soil represents those who hear the mes-
sage and immediately receive it with joy. 21 But since they don't have deep roots, they
don't last long. They fall away as soon as they have problems or are persecuted for believ-
ing God's word. 22 The seed that fell among the thorns represents those who hear God's
word, but all too quickly the message is crowded out by the worries of this life and the lure
of wealth, so no fruit is produced. 23 The seed that fell on good soil represents those who
truly hear and understand God's word and produce a harvest of thirty, sixty, or even a
hundred times as much as had been planted!"

PARABLE OF THE WHEAT AND WEEDS

24 Here is another story Jesus told: "The Kingdom of Heaven is like a farmer who planted
good seed in his field. 25 But that night as the workers slept, his enemy came and planted
weeds among the wheat, then slipped away. 26 When the crop began to grow and produce
grain, the weeds also grew.

13:13 Jer 5:21
13:14-15 *Isa 6:9-10
13:16-17 //Luke 10:23-24
13:17 John 8:56; Heb 11:13; 1 Pet 1:10-12
13:18-23 //Mark 4:13-20; //Luke 8:11-15
13:22 Matt 19:23; Luke 12:16-21; 1 Tim 6:9-10, 17
13:24 Mark 4:26-29

13:14-15 Isa 6:9-10 (Greek version).

13:16-23 This inerrant interpretation of the parable is extremely valuable, for it gives the reader Jesus' own principles for interpreting the other 39 parables of Christ found throughout the Gospels. This interpretation shows that some people may appear to be Christians for a period of time, but in the end, only those who bear fruit who are true believers. (This echoes Jesus' earlier comments in Matthew 12:33.)

▸ SPIRITUAL WARFARE
13:19 The thief of sermons. Satan, the murderous deceiver of the world, is no stranger to the church. Jesus made it clear that Satan is a sermon-snatcher, stealing the impact and meaning of God's preached Word away from the hearts of those who hear. Powerless to defeat God's Word, Satan fans the flames of human unbelief and doubt so that God's message has as little effect as possible on those who hear it. When you find excuses for not studying the Bible regularly, do you blame it on something benign? When you become drowsy at the mere mention of the word "sermon," does that strike you as a coincidence? Satan and his demons are busy turning people away from God's Word, and we must take up the weapons of spiritual warfare (2 Corinthians 10:3-4; 1 Corinthians 16:13; Philippians 1:30; Ephesians 6:13-18) and fight for God's Word to have an active part in our lives every day. (***See Spiritual Warfare***> *Originator of Sin> Satan's Goals> Keep men from faith in God,* TopicGuide page A45.)

13:24-30 This illustration about the Kingdom presupposes that the reader understands that the "Kingdom of Heaven" has

27“The farmer’s workers went to him and said, ‘Sir, the field where you planted that
good seed is full of weeds! Where did they come from?’
28“ ‘An enemy has done this!’ the farmer exclaimed.
“ ‘Should we pull out the weeds?’ they asked.
13:30 29“ ‘No,’ he replied, ‘you’ll uproot the wheat if you do. 30Let both grow together until the
Matt 3:12 harvest. Then I will tell the harvesters to sort out the weeds, tie them into bundles, and
burn them, and to put the wheat in the barn.’ ”

PARABLE OF THE MUSTARD SEED

13:31-32 31Here is another illustration Jesus used: “The Kingdom of Heaven is like a mustard seed
//Mark 4:30-32 //Luke 13:18-19 planted in a field. 32It is the smallest of all seeds, but it becomes the largest of garden
13:32 plants; it grows into a tree, and birds come and make nests in its branches.”

Ps 104:12 Ezek 17:23; 31:6 Dan 4:12, 21

PARABLE OF THE YEAST

13:33 33Jesus also used this illustration: “The Kingdom of Heaven is like the yeast a woman used
Luke 13:20-21 1 Cor 5:6 in making bread. Even though she put only a little yeast in three measures of flour, it per-
Gal 5:9 meated every part of the dough.”
13:34 34Jesus always used stories and illustrations like these when speaking to the crowds. In
John 16:25 fact, He never spoke to them without using such parables. 35This fulfilled what God had
13:35 spoken through the prophet:
*Ps 78:2

“I will speak to you in parables.
I will explain things hidden since the creation of the world.*”

PARABLE OF THE WHEAT AND WEEDS EXPLAINED

13:36 36Then, leaving the crowds outside, Jesus went into the house. His disciples said, “Please
Matt 15:15 explain to us the story of the weeds in the field.”
13:38 37Jesus replied, “The Son of Man* is the farmer who plants the good seed. 38The field is
John 8:44 1 Jn 3:10 the world, and the good seed represents the people of the Kingdom. The weeds are
13:39 the people who belong to the evil one. 39The enemy who planted the weeds among
Joel 3:13 the wheat is the devil. The harvest is the end of the world,* and the harvesters are the
Rev 14:15 angels.
13:41 40“Just as the weeds are sorted out and burned in the fire, so it will be at the end of the
Matt 24:31 Mark 13:27 world. 41The Son of Man will send His angels, and they will remove from His Kingdom
13:42 everything that causes sin and all who do evil. 42And the angels will throw them into the fi-
Matt 8:12; 13:50; 22:13; 24:51; 25:30 ery furnace, where there will be weeping and gnashing of teeth. 43Then the righteous will
Luke 13:28 shine like the sun in their Father’s Kingdom. Anyone with ears to hear should listen and
13:43 understand!
Dan 12:3

13:35 Some manuscripts do not include *of the world.* Ps 78:2. 13:37 “Son of Man” is a title Jesus used for Himself. 13:39 Or *the age;* also in 13:40, 49.

both a “now” and a “not yet” aspect. Broadly, the Kingdom is everywhere that God sovereignly reigns—all creation is His (Psalms 47:1-9; 83:18; Daniel 4:25-26). God has always ruled from heaven over all the earth (Matthew 5:34; Ephesians 1:20; Hebrews 12:2; Revelation 7:15). But all people and institutions on earth do not yet recognize God’s authority. The Bible teaches that a day will come when God’s rule will be acknowledged everywhere and all creation will submit to Him in voluntary obedience (1 Chronicles 16:31; Psalm 97:1-2). The beginning of Christ’s ministry marked the beginning of the end for all rebellion against God (Matthew 3:2, 4:17; Mark 1:15). In these parables, Jesus makes it clear that good and evil will coexist in this final stage of the Kingdom until a day of final judgment (Malachi 4; 1 Corinthians 15:50-58; Revelation 11:15).

13:31-32 Jesus was not making a scientific assertion about the size of the mustard seed compared to all other seeds that might be known throughout the world (or throughout the ages). He was using what was familiar to His hearers. For them, the mustard seed was the smallest of common seeds. The small size implied that God’s manifest rule begins in a small way, almost unnoticeably, but then becomes powerful and plainly visible.

PARABLES OF THE HIDDEN TREASURE AND THE PEARL

44"The Kingdom of Heaven is like a treasure that a man discovered hidden in a field. In his ex-
citement, he hid it again and sold everything he owned to get enough money to buy the field.
45"Again, the Kingdom of Heaven is like a merchant on the lookout for choice pearls.
46When he discovered a pearl of great value, he sold everything he owned and bought it!

PARABLE OF THE FISHING NET

47"Again, the Kingdom of Heaven is like a fishing net that was thrown into the water and
caught fish of every kind. 48When the net was full, they dragged it up onto the shore, sat
down, and sorted the good fish into crates, but threw the bad ones away. 49That is the way
it will be at the end of the world. The angels will come and separate the wicked people
from the righteous, 50throwing the wicked into the fiery furnace, where there will be weep-
ing and gnashing of teeth. 51Do you understand all these things?"

"Yes," they said, "we do."

52Then He added, "Every teacher of religious law who becomes a disciple in the King-
dom of Heaven is like a homeowner who brings from his storeroom new gems of truth as
well as old."

JESUS REJECTED AT NAZARETH

53When Jesus had finished telling these stories and illustrations, He left that part of the
country. 54He returned to Nazareth, His hometown. When He taught there in the syna-
gogue, everyone was amazed and said, "Where does He get this wisdom and the power to
do miracles?" 55Then they scoffed, "He's just the carpenter's son, and we know Mary, His
mother, and His brothers—James, Joseph,* Simon, and Judas. 56All His sisters live right
here among us. Where did He learn all these things?" 57And they were deeply offended
and refused to believe in Him.

Then Jesus told them, "A prophet is honored everywhere except in his own hometown and
among his own family." 58And so He did only a few miracles there because of their unbelief.

THE DEATH OF JOHN THE BAPTIST

14 When Herod Antipas, the ruler of Galilee,* heard about Jesus, 2he said to his ad-
visers, "This must be John the Baptist raised from the dead! That is why He can do
such miracles."

3For Herod had arrested and imprisoned John as a favor to his wife Herodias (the former
wife of Herod's brother Philip). 4John had been telling Herod, "It is against God's law for

13:44 Phil 3:7-8
13:47 Matt 22:10
13:50 Matt 8:12; 13:42; 22:13; 24:51; 25:30 Luke 13:28
13:53-58 //Mark 6:1-6 //Luke 4:16-30
13:53 Matt 7:28
13:54 John 7:15
13:55 Matt 12:46 Luke 3:23 John 6:42
13:57 Luke 4:24 John 4:44
14:1-12 //Mark 6:14-29 //Luke 9:7-9
14:3 Luke 3:19-20
14:4 Lev 18:16; 20:21

13:55 Other manuscripts read *Joses;* still others read *John.* 14:1 Greek *Herod the tetrarch.* Herod Antipas was a son of King Herod and was ruler over Galilee.

▸ ADOPTION
13:44 Rejoicing in our greatest treasure. What motivates a follower of Jesus in the life of discipleship? Duty? Obligation? Although those may occasionally stir the heart, this parable reveals what ought to be the core of our motivation: passionate love! When we discover the treasures that are to be found as we serve in God's Kingdom, everything else pales in comparison. The pursuit of God's Kingdom-ideals is not a matter of "what I ought to do" as much as "what I long to do," because passionate love becomes the foundation of everything we say and do (1 Corinthians 13:1-3). The Christian life is a delightful discovery of who loves us and how our loving God wants us to live and act. Make certain that holy passion for God and those around you is the central motivation for everything you do. (***See Adoption****> With Christ> Supernatural> A life of infinite joy,* TopicGuide page A37.)

13:53-58 As noted earlier (12:46-49), Jesus likely had half brothers. Here the crowd implied that His father had been a well-known builder in Nazareth, His family was well-known, and that His sisters as well as His mother and brothers continued to reside there.

14:1 The Greek literally reads "Herod the tetrarch." This meant that he ruled one-fourth of the domain of Herod the Great, his father. Herod the tetrarch (or Herod Antipas, as he was known) ruled Galilee, the region of Nazareth, Jesus' hometown.

14:3 Herodias, granddaughter of Herod the Great, daughter of Aristobulus, had been married to her uncle Herod Philip (another son of Herod the Great). She divorced him to marry another uncle, Herod Antipas, after he had divorced his wife. Thus, Herod Antipas married his brother's ex-wife as well as his own niece.

SHOULD CHRISTIANS BE TRYING to take over the world? Should churches be advocating certain political positions? What role does Jesus want Christians to have in society? All these questions are answered in principle when we understand what the Kingdom of God is.

First, the Bible plainly says what the Kingdom is not. Paul said, "The Kingdom of God is not a matter of what we eat or drink, but of living a life of goodness and peace and joy in the Holy Spirit" (Romans 14:17). It is not a set of behaviors such as the music we listen to or the clothes we wear.

It's also not a geographic place. Jesus said to the questioning Pharisee, Nicodemus, "Unless you are born again, you cannot see the Kingdom of God" and "No one can enter the Kingdom of God without being born of water and the Spirit" (John 3:3, 5). Entering the Kingdom of God does not involve a geographic journey, but a spiritual one initiated by God.

The Kingdom is not a peripheral or secondary matter, either. Jesus calls us to "seek the Kingdom of God above all else" (Matthew 6:33). The wealthy who make money their first order of business can never enter the Kingdom (Matthew 19:24), while prostitutes who repent and make the Kingdom a priority will easily enter it.

But what is the Kingdom? The illustrations of the Kingdom in Matthew 13 presuppose that the reader understands that the "Kingdom of Heaven" or "Kingdom of God" has both broad and narrow aspects. Broadly, the Kingdom is every place over which God sovereignly reigns—and so all creation is part of His Kingdom (Psalm 47:1-9; 83:18; Daniel 4:25-26). God has always ruled from heaven over all the earth (Matthew 5:34; Ephesians 1:20; Hebrews 12:2; Revelation 7:15). But more narrowly, many people and institutions on earth do not yet recognize God's authority. The Bible attests that there will come a day when people everywhere will acknowledge God's and all creation will submit to Him in voluntary obedience; just such a state now exists in heaven (1 Chronicles 16:31; Psalm 97:1-2). The ministry of Christ provides the process or means by which God has chosen to ensure the world's recognition of His rule. The beginning of His ministry marked the beginning of the end for all rebellion against God (Matthew 3:2, 4:17; Mark 1:15). Jesus made it clear that good and bad will coexist in this final stage of the Kingdom until a day of final judgment (Malachi 4; Matthew 25:33; 1 Corinthians 15:50-58; Revelation 11:15).

There is more to the Kingdom than converting people to Christ. The Good News empowers believers to exhibit a positive, transforming way of life in the culture in which God has placed us. The Gospel is about redeeming the entire universe (Isaiah 65:17; 66:22; Romans 8:19-22; Revelation 21:1-5): more and more people enjoying the grace of God found in the gospel, more and more people entering into God's kingdom, and more people obeying His will. As Jesus prayed, "May Your kingdom come soon. May Your will be done on earth, as it is in heaven" (Matthew 6:10).

you to marry her." [5]Herod wanted to kill John, but he was afraid of a riot, because all the 14:5
people believed John was a prophet. Matt 11:9; 21:26
[6]But at a birthday party for Herod, Herodias's daughter performed a dance that greatly
pleased him, [7]so he promised with a vow to give her anything she wanted. [8]At her
mother's urging, the girl said, "I want the head of John the Baptist on a tray!" [9]Then the king
regretted what he had said; but because of the vow he had made in front of his guests, he
issued the necessary orders. [10]So John was beheaded in the prison, [11]and his head was 14:10
brought on a tray and given to the girl, who took it to her mother. [12]Later, John's disciples Matt 17:12
came for his body and buried it. Then they went and told Jesus what had happened. 14:12 Acts 8:2

JESUS FEEDS FIVE THOUSAND

[13]As soon as Jesus heard the news, He left in a boat to a remote area to be alone. But the 14:13-21
crowds heard where He was headed and followed on foot from many towns. [14]Jesus saw //Mark 6:32-44 //Luke 9:10-17
the huge crowd as He stepped from the boat, and He had compassion on them and healed //John 6:1-13
their sick. 14:14
[15]That evening the disciples came to Him and said, "This is a remote place, and it's al- Matt 9:36 Mark 1:41
ready getting late. Send the crowds away so they can go to the villages and buy food for Heb 2:17-18; 4:15;
themselves." 5:1-3
[16]But Jesus said, "That isn't necessary—you feed them." 14:16-20
[17]"But we have only five loaves of bread and two fish!" they answered. 2 Kgs 4:42-44
[18]"Bring them here," He said. [19]Then He told the people to sit down on the grass. Jesus 14:19-22 Matt 15:35-39
took the five loaves and two fish, looked up toward heaven, and blessed them. Then, Mark 8:6-10
breaking the loaves into pieces, He gave the bread to the disciples, who distributed it to
the people. [20]They all ate as much as they wanted, and afterward, the disciples picked up
twelve baskets of leftovers. [21]About 5,000 men were fed that day, in addition to all the
women and children!

JESUS WALKS ON WATER

[22]Immediately after this, Jesus insisted that His disciples get back into the boat and cross 14:22-33 //Mark 6:45-52
to the other side of the lake, while He sent the people home. [23]After sending them home, //John 6:15-21
He went up into the hills by Himself to pray. Night fell while He was there alone. 14:23
[24]Meanwhile, the disciples were in trouble far away from land, for a strong wind had Luke 9:28
risen, and they were fighting heavy waves. [25]About three o'clock in the morning* Jesus
came toward them, walking on the water. [26]When the disciples saw Him walking on the 14:26
water, they were terrified. In their fear, they cried out, "It's a ghost!" Luke 24:37
[27]But Jesus spoke to them at once. "Don't be afraid," He said. "Take courage. I am here!*"
[28]Then Peter called to Him, "Lord, if it's really You, tell me to come to You, walking on
the water."
[29]"Yes, come," Jesus said.

14:25 Greek *In the fourth watch of the night.* 14:27 Or *The 'I Am' is here;* Greek reads *I am.* See Exod 3:14.

14:15 The disciples' reference to the place being remote doesn't mean that they were in the desert, but only that they were in a relatively uninhabited place. The people would have had to travel some distance to find a place to buy food.

▸ WORSHIP

14:16-19 Attempting the impossible. When Jesus asked His followers to feed the multitude, they responded the way most people would likely have responded in the same situation: "Impossible!" They looked at the need and at their resources, and then concluded that it couldn't be done. But Jesus never issues a futile or idle instruction. When He said that He wanted the disciples to feed the crowd, He meant it. And that is exactly what happened. Although Jesus participated in meeting the need, the disciples were indeed the ones who distributed the food to those who were hungry. *They* fed the crowd—with Jesus' help. Jesus often calls His followers to do what may seem impossible, but with His help we will in fact be able to do all that He tells us to do. (***See Worship*** > *NT* > *Sacrificial Living* > *Enables us to help meet others' needs,* TopicGuide page A34.)

▸ CHURCH

14:28-31 Taking risks. Did Peter fail when he tried to walk on water? He started out walking on the water, but then, apparently because of his lack of faith, he began to sink. But Peter *did* walk on water! He is one of only two people who have ever done that. That certainly doesn't seem like failure. Sure, he wasn't as successful as Jesus. But Peter was willing, and he took a risk at Jesus' invitation. And Jesus was there all the time to ensure that Peter wouldn't go under. Peter had the opportunity

So Peter went over the side of the boat and walked on the water toward Jesus. 30But
when he saw the strong* wind and the waves, he was terrified and began to sink. "Save
me, Lord!" he shouted.
31Jesus immediately reached out and grabbed him. "You have so little faith," Jesus said.
"Why did you doubt Me?"
32When they climbed back into the boat, the wind stopped. 33Then the disciples wor-
shiped Him. "You really are the Son of God!" they exclaimed.
34After they had crossed the lake, they landed at Gennesaret. 35When the people recog-
nized Jesus, the news of His arrival spread quickly throughout the whole area, and soon
people were bringing all their sick to be healed. 36They begged Him to let the sick touch at
least the fringe of His robe, and all who touched Him were healed.

JESUS TEACHES ABOUT INNER PURITY

15 Some Pharisees and teachers of religious law now arrived from Jerusalem to see
Jesus. They asked Him, 2"Why do Your disciples disobey our age-old tradition?
For they ignore our tradition of ceremonial hand washing before they eat."
3Jesus replied, "And why do you, by your traditions, violate the direct commandments
of God? 4For instance, God says, 'Honor your father and mother,'* and 'Anyone who
speaks disrespectfully of father or mother must be put to death.'* 5But you say it is all right
for people to say to their parents, 'Sorry, I can't help you. For I have vowed to give to God
what I would have given to you.' 6In this way, you say they don't need to honor their par-
ents.* And so you cancel the word of God for the sake of your own tradition. 7You hypo-
crites! Isaiah was right when he prophesied about you, for he wrote,

8 'These people honor Me with their lips,
but their hearts are far from Me.
9 Their worship is a farce,
for they teach man-made ideas as commands from God.'*"

10Then Jesus called to the crowd to come and hear. "Listen," He said, "and try to under-
stand. 11It's not what goes into your mouth that defiles you; you are defiled by the words
that come out of your mouth."
12Then the disciples came to Him and asked, "Do You realize You offended the Phari-
sees by what You just said?"

14:31 Matt 6:30
14:33 Ps 2:7; Matt 16:16; 26:63; 27:54; Mark 1:1; Luke 22:70; John 1:49; 6:69; Rom 1:4
14:34-36 //Mark 6:53-56
14:36 Matt 9:20-21
15:1-20 //Mark 7:1-23
15:2 Luke 11:38
15:4 *Exod 20:12; 21:17; *Lev 20:9; *Deut 5:16; Matt 19:19; Mark 10:19; Luke 18:20; Eph 6:2
15:8-9 *Isa 29:13
15:9 Col 2:20-22
15:11 Matt 12:34; Acts 10:14-15

14:30 Some manuscripts do not include *strong*. **15:4a** Exod 20:12; Deut 5:16. **15:4b** Exod 21:17 (Greek version); Lev 20:9 (Greek version). **15:6** Greek *their father;* other manuscripts read *their father or their mother.* **15:8-9** Isa 29:13 (Greek version).

to walk on water and experience Jesus' saving power. That would be one experience of discipleship he would never forget. And all he had to do was get out of the boat when Jesus invited him. Step quickly when you sense Jesus inviting you to take risks for Him. (***See Church****> What> Many Titles> Sheep> The sheep trust the protection of the shepherd,* TopicGuide page A48.)

14:31 The word translated "doubt" literally means "to be pulled in two directions."

14:33 A faithful Jew worshiped God alone (Deuteronomy 6:4; 10:20; 13:4; Joshua 22:22; 24:18, 24). Although the disciples might not have yet fully understood who Jesus was, their worship tells us they saw Him as God.

15:2 Though not specifically required by the Old Testament law, the religious leaders had come to see ceremonial hand washing as a symbolic religious act that they performed with great attention to detail. Jesus ignored this practice and thereby showed His authority over the Jewish religious leaders and His desire to reject unhelpful human traditions.

15:7-9 Jesus' concern was that the religious leaders emphasized their particular traditions and overlooked what God stressed. As a result, thinking themselves spiritual, they allowed their religious traditions to override other God-given commandments.

▶ GOD

15:12-14 No more Mr. Nice Guy. Some people seem to think Jesus did everything He could to placate people—a real "Mr. Nice Guy." But that's just not true. Although Jesus never purposefully went out of His way to offend, when Kingdom values and priorities came into conflict with the way people wanted to live, offense was inevitable. In such cases, Jesus made no apologies. When the religious leaders were offended by something He said, He simply affirmed that whatever the Father had not planted would be pulled up by the roots. Jesus has some tough things to say about unbiblical human traditions. Do some of those apply to you? Be ready to receive tough questions and tough answers from God's Word. God's goal is to cleanse your life of sin (Philippians 1:6). (***See God****> God's Attributes> True> God's words are true and completely righteous,* TopicGuide page A18.)

13 Jesus replied, "Every plant not planted by My heavenly Father will be uprooted, 14 so
ignore them. They are blind guides leading the blind, and if one blind person guides an-
other, they will both fall into a ditch."
15 Then Peter said to Jesus, "Explain to us the parable that says people aren't defiled by
what they eat."
16 "Don't you understand yet?" Jesus asked. 17 "Anything you eat passes through the
stomach and then goes into the sewer. 18 But the words you speak come from the heart—
that's what defiles you. 19 For from the heart come evil thoughts, murder, adultery, all sex-
ual immorality, theft, lying, and slander. 20 These are what defile you. Eating with un-
washed hands will never defile you."

THE FAITH OF A GENTILE WOMAN

21 Then Jesus left Galilee and went north to the region of Tyre and Sidon. 22 A Gentile*
woman who lived there came to Him, pleading, "Have mercy on me, O Lord, Son of David!
For my daughter is possessed by a demon that torments her severely."
23 But Jesus gave her no reply, not even a word. Then His disciples urged Him to send
her away. "Tell her to go away," they said. "She is bothering us with all her begging."
24 Then Jesus said to the woman, "I was sent only to help God's lost sheep—the people of
Israel."
25 But she came and worshiped Him, pleading again, "Lord, help me!"
26 Jesus responded, "It isn't right to take food from the children and throw it to the dogs."
27 She replied, "That's true, Lord, but even dogs are allowed to eat the scraps that fall be-
neath their masters' table."
28 "Dear woman," Jesus said to her, "your faith is great. Your request is granted." And her
daughter was instantly healed.

JESUS HEALS MANY PEOPLE

29 Jesus returned to the Sea of Galilee and climbed a hill and sat down. 30 A vast crowd
brought to Him people who were lame, blind, crippled, those who couldn't speak, and
many others. They laid them before Jesus, and He healed them all. 31 The crowd was
amazed! Those who hadn't been able to speak were talking, the crippled were made well,
the lame were walking, and the blind could see again! And they praised the God of Israel.

JESUS FEEDS FOUR THOUSAND

32 Then Jesus called His disciples and told them, "I feel sorry for these people. They have
been here with Me for three days, and they have nothing left to eat. I don't want to send
them away hungry, or they will faint along the way."

15:13 Isa 60:21; 61:3 John 15:2 1 Cor 3:9
15:14 Matt 23:16, 24 Luke 6:39 Rom 2:19
15:18 Matt 12:34 Jas 3:6
15:19 Rom 1:29-31 1 Cor 5:10-11; 6:9-10 Gal 5:19-21
15:21-28 //Mark 7:24-30
15:24 Matt 10:6 Rom 15:8
15:25 Matt 8:2
15:28 Matt 8:10
15:29-31 //Mark 7:31-37
15:30 Isa 35:5-6 Matt 4:23; 11:5 Luke 7:22
15:32-39 //Mark 8:1-10
15:32 Matt 9:36

15:22 Greek *Canaanite*.

15:16-20 The religious leaders in Jesus' day believed *external* things rendered someone unclean and unacceptable before God, so they followed many regulations to keep from becoming defiled. But Jesus made it clear that externals aren't the problem—what comes out of the mouth shows what's in the heart, and the heart is what is unclean.

15:21-28 Matthew identified this woman as a Gentile (literally, "Canaanite") from "the region of Tyre and Sidon." This meant the Jews considered her unclean and untouchable. Jesus asked a piercing question to determine her trust, and then complimented her faith and healed her daughter. Jesus' treatment of her indicates that He didn't see her as unworthy of receiving God's grace.

▸ HOLINESS
15:21-28 Mighty Faith. When you approach God with a need, how committed are you to getting what you ask of Him? Do you approach Him as one option among many? What if things don't immediately turn in the direction you desire—will you consider other options? In His encounter with a Gentile woman whose daughter was in great need, Jesus found someone with a singular faith. What made her faith so noteworthy? Perhaps just these things: She admitted she needed help, she saw Him as her only option, and even when things didn't initially look like they were going the way she wanted, she would not back away (Luke 18:1-8). Her eyes were on Jesus, and she would not go away, no matter what. That is what great faith has always looked like. Stay focused on Jesus as your only hope. (***See Holiness> Submission> Trusting God> Faithfulness,*** TopicGuide page A41.)

15:26-27 Jesus' words to the woman sound harsh to modern ears. In speaking this way, He affirmed the primacy of His call to minister to the children (of Israel). Even while He referred to woman in the same way Jews typically referred to Gentiles ("dogs"), the Gentile woman demonstrated faith in Christ—something many Jews were slow to do (15:7-9). The passage intentionally begs the question that if "the dogs" even recognized Jesus' authority, what did that say about Jews?

15:33 33 The disciples replied, “Where would we get enough food here in the wilderness for
Mark 6:37 such a huge crowd?”
John 6:5 34 Jesus asked, “How much bread do you have?”
15:34-37 Matt 14:17-20 They replied, “Seven loaves, and a few small fish.”
Mark 6:38-43 35 So Jesus told all the people to sit down on the ground. 36 Then He took the seven
Luke 9:13-17 John 6:9-13 loaves and the fish, thanked God for them, and broke them into pieces. He gave them to
the disciples, who distributed the food to the crowd.
15:37 37 They all ate as much as they wanted. Afterward, the disciples picked up seven large
Matt 16:10 baskets of leftover food. 38 There were 4,000 men who were fed that day, in addition to all
15:38 the women and children. 39 Then Jesus sent the people home, and He got into a boat and
Matt 14:21 Mark 6:44 crossed over to the region of Magadan.

LEADERS DEMAND A MIRACULOUS SIGN

16:1-12 //Mark 8:11-21 **16** One day the Pharisees and Sadducees came to test Jesus, demanding that He
show them a miraculous sign from heaven to prove His authority.
16:1 Matt 12:38 2 He replied, “You know the saying, ‘Red sky at night means fair weather tomorrow; 3 red
Luke 11:16 sky in the morning means foul weather all day.’ You know how to interpret the weather
John 6:30 1 Cor 1:22 signs in the sky, but you don’t know how to interpret the signs of the times!* 4 Only an evil,
adulterous generation would demand a miraculous sign, but the only sign I will give them
16:2-3 Luke 12:54-56 is the sign of the prophet Jonah.*” Then Jesus left them and went away.

16:4 Matt 12:39

YEAST OF THE PHARISEES AND SADDUCEES

Luke 11:29 5 Later, after they crossed to the other side of the lake, the disciples discovered they had
16:6 Luke 12:1 forgotten to bring any bread. 6 “Watch out!” Jesus warned them. “Beware of the yeast of
the Pharisees and Sadducees.”
7 At this they began to argue with each other because they hadn’t brought any bread.
16:9 Matt 14:14-21 8 Jesus knew what they were saying, so He said, “You have so little faith! Why are you ar-
Mark 6:34-44 guing with each other about having no bread? 9 Don’t you understand even yet? Don’t
Luke 9:11-17 John 6:1-13 you remember the 5,000 I fed with five loaves, and the baskets of leftovers you picked
up? 10 Or the 4,000 I fed with seven loaves, and the large baskets of leftovers you picked
16:10 Matt 15:32-38 up? 11 Why can’t you understand that I’m not talking about bread? So again I say, ‘Be-
Mark 8:1-9 ware of the yeast of the Pharisees and Sadducees.’”
16:11 Luke 12:1 12 Then at last they understood that He wasn’t speaking about the yeast in bread, but
about the deceptive teaching of the Pharisees and Sadducees.

PETER’S DECLARATION ABOUT JESUS

16:13-20 //Mark 8:27-30 13 When Jesus came to the region of Caesarea Philippi, He asked His disciples, “Who do
//Luke 9:18-21 people say that the Son of Man is?”*

16:2-3 Several manuscripts do not include any of the words in 16:2-3 after *He replied.* 16:4 Greek *the sign of Jonah.*
16:13 “Son of Man” is a title Jesus used for Himself.

16:6 Jesus used yeast throughout His teachings as an illustration of hypocrisy (Mark 8:14-15; Luke 12:1). As yeast creates a fermentation process that spreads throughout a loaf of bread, so hypocrisy causes changes among God’s people. Paul later used the metaphor to refer to false teachers and their doctrine (Galatians 5:9).

▶ GOD

16:8-11 Basis of a relationship. Relationships are rooted in something—it could be shared interests, physical attraction, or even a fear of loneliness. Throughout the Gospels, we see that a relationship with Jesus is rooted in faith. Even when He walked the streets of Palestine during His life on earth, He longed for people to place their trust in Him and to rely on Him. But that didn’t (and still doesn’t) happen automatically. Just as love grows over time, so does faith. Jesus hinted at one of the factors that helps faith to grow—remembering what He has done for us. Reflecting on what He has already done invigorates our confidence in His ability and renews our faith in Him. (***See God***> *Relationship> God’s Desire> God pursues a relationship,* TopicGuide page A14.)

16:13-17 Jesus’ question brings to the surface the various ways people thought of “the Son of Man.” But while people may deduce certain things about Jesus from His actions, only a supernatural act of God can reveal Jesus in an accurate and saving way (16:17).

[14]"Well," they replied, "some say John the Baptist, some say Elijah, and others say Jeremiah or one of the other prophets."
[15]Then He asked them, "But who do you say I am?"
[16]Simon Peter answered, "You are the Messiah,* the Son of the living God."
[17]Jesus replied, "You are blessed, Simon son of John,* because My Father in heaven has revealed this to you. You did not learn this from any human being. [18]Now I say to you that you are Peter (which means 'rock'),* and upon this rock I will build My church, and all the powers of hell* will not conquer it. [19]And I will give you the keys of the Kingdom of Heaven. Whatever you forbid* on earth will be forbidden in heaven, and whatever you permit* on earth will be permitted in heaven."
[20]Then He sternly warned the disciples not to tell anyone that He was the Messiah.

16:16 Matt 1:16; 14:33 Mark 14:61 John 1:34, 49; 6:69; 11:27; 20:31
16:17 Gal 1:16
16:18 John 1:42 1 Cor 3:11 Eph 2:20-22; 4:15-16 1 Pet 2:4-5
16:19 Matt 18:18 John 20:23

JESUS PREDICTS HIS DEATH

[21]From then on Jesus* began to tell His disciples plainly that it was necessary for Him to go to Jerusalem, and that He would suffer many terrible things at the hands of the elders, the leading priests, and the teachers of religious law. He would be killed, but on the third day He would be raised from the dead.
[22]But Peter took Him aside and began to reprimand Him* for saying such things. "Heaven forbid, Lord," he said. "This will never happen to You!"
[23]Jesus turned to Peter and said, "Get away from Me, Satan! You are a dangerous trap to Me. You are seeing things merely from a human point of view, not from God's."
[24]Then Jesus said to His disciples, "If any of you wants to be My follower, you must turn from your selfish ways, take up your cross, and follow Me. [25]If you try to hang on to your

16:21-28 //Mark 8:31–9:1 //Luke 9:21-27
16:21 John 2:19 1 Cor 15:3-4
16:23 Matt 4:10
16:24 Matt 10:38 Luke 14:27
16:25 Matt 10:39 Luke 17:33 John 12:25

16:16 Or *the Christ. Messiah* (a Hebrew term) and *Christ* (a Greek term) both mean "the anointed one." 16:17 Greek *Simon bar-Jonah;* see John 1:42; 21:15-17. 16:18a Greek *that you are Peter.* 16:18b Greek *and the gates of Hades.* 16:19a Or *bind,* or *lock.* 16:19b Or *loose,* or *open.* 16:21 Some manuscripts read *Jesus the Messiah.* 16:22 Or *began to correct Him.*

▶ **CHURCH**
16:15-18 Confessing the truth. What makes the church what it is? Rules and bylaws? Denominational affiliation? Jesus didn't build a building and endow a fund or start a denomination—He invited people to know Him. Peter saw this; that is why He confessed that Jesus was "the Messiah, the son of the living God." It is that confession—the confident belief in Jesus as Lord—that is the foundation for the church Jesus seeks to build. Christian maturity means many things, but it starts and continues with a God-inspired declaration of Christ as Savior. Make sure you, your family, and your church stay Christ centered as you live and articulate your beliefs. (***See Church****> What> Supernatural Body> Under Christ,* TopicGuide page A48.)

16:16 Peter's confession underscores a key point that Matthew has made eight times since the opening chapters of his Gospel until now: Jesus is the Messiah (Matthew 1:1; 2:4; 11:2, 3; 12:23; 16; 17:1-13; 18). Matthew identified Jesus as the Messiah a total of 22 times in his Gospel.

16:18 Peter's name (a nickname given to him by Jesus) means "rock." There is some question about what Jesus means when He speaks of building His church upon "this rock." Some understand Jesus to be saying that Peter will be the foundation of the new assembly of followers of Jesus. This is at least partially true as Peter was the one Jesus used to launch His church at Pentecost (Acts 2). Others understand Jesus to be referring to the confession that Peter had just made (16:16).

16:20 The people still did not understand the implications of Jesus' ministry as the Messiah, and so He didn't want His disciples declaring what they had begun to comprehend; such a declaration would only lead to confusion.

▶ **GOD**
16:21 The unexpected Messiah. As Jesus journeyed with His followers in the first half of His earthly ministry, they finally began to understand who He was. They came to recognize that He was the Messiah—the promised Deliverer and Ruler spoken of in the Old Testament Scriptures. At that point, Jesus offered them an entirely new perspective: Yes, He was the Messiah; but, no, He was not the kind of Messiah they had been expecting. He told them that He would be put to death and that He would rise from the dead. Even with hints of this from Isaiah 53, they still could not imagine how this could be true. How do you respond when God's Word contradicts your understanding of who He is? Flush out false images and ideas about God from your mind by prayerfully and diligently studying God's Word. (***See God****> God's Names> Son> Messiah/Christ,* TopicGuide page A19.)

16:21-23 Although Peter had rightly come to understand that Jesus was the Messiah, he still did not understand Jesus' mission. Jesus' strong response to Peter's correction shows that Peter had a sinful motive for keeping Jesus from harm, a motive rooted in human weakness rather than holy wisdom.

▶ **HOLINESS**
16:25 The way down is the way up. The Christian life doesn't always seem entirely logical—it sometimes embraces paradox. Jesus identified one such oddity as He pointed out that those who lived self-protective lives would in the end lose everything worth having. There are other inversions of this type in Scripture, such as James's and Peter's warnings that only the humble will be exalted (James 4:10; 1 Peter 5:6) and Paul's discovery of God's glory in human frailty (2 Corinthians 12:10). Jesus' own self-sacrifice, from

16:26 life, you will lose it. But if you give up your life for My sake, you will save it. 26 And what do
Ps 49:7-9 you benefit if you gain the whole world but lose your own soul?* Is anything worth more
Matt 4:8-9 16:27 than your soul? 27 For the Son of Man will come with His angels in the glory of His Father
Prov 24:12 and will judge all people according to their deeds. 28 And I tell you the truth, some stand-
Matt 25:31 Rev 22:12 ing here right now will not die before they see the Son of Man coming in His Kingdom."

17:1-13
THE TRANSFIGURATION

//Mark 9:2-13 //Luke 9:28-36 **17** Six days later Jesus took Peter and the two brothers, James and John, and led
17:2 them up a high mountain to be alone. 2As the men watched, Jesus' appearance
2 Pet 1:16-18 was transformed so that His face shone like the sun, and His clothes became as white as
light. 3 Suddenly, Moses and Elijah appeared and began talking with Jesus.
4Peter exclaimed, "Lord, it's wonderful for us to be here! If You want, I'll make three shel-
ters as memorials*—one for You, one for Moses, and one for Elijah."
17:5 Ps 2:7 5But even as he spoke, a bright cloud overshadowed them, and a voice from the cloud
Matt 3:17; 12:18 said, "This is My dearly loved Son, who brings Me great joy. Listen to Him." 6The disciples
Mark 1:11 were terrified and fell face down on the ground.
Luke 3:22 7Then Jesus came over and touched them. "Get up," He said. "Don't be afraid." 8And
2 Pet 1:17 when they looked up, Moses and Elijah were gone, and they saw only Jesus.
9As they went back down the mountain, Jesus commanded them, "Don't tell anyone
what you have seen until the Son of Man* has been raised from the dead."
17:10-13 10Then His disciples asked Him, "Why do the teachers of religious law insist that Elijah
//Mark 9:11-13 must return before the Messiah comes?*"
17:10-11 Mal 4:5-6 11Jesus replied, "Elijah is indeed coming first to get everything ready. 12 But I tell you, Eli-
Luke 1:16-17 jah has already come, but he wasn't recognized, and they chose to abuse him. And in the
17:12 same way they will also make the Son of Man suffer." 13 Then the disciples realized He was
Matt 11:14 talking about John the Baptist.

JESUS HEALS A DEMON-POSSESSED BOY

17:14-21 14At the foot of the mountain, a large crowd was waiting for them. A man came and knelt
//Mark 9:14-29 before Jesus and said, 15 "Lord, have mercy on my son. He has seizures and suffers terribly.
//Luke 9:37-43 He often falls into the fire or into the water. 16So I brought him to Your disciples, but they
couldn't heal him."

16:26 Or *your self?* also in 16:26b. 17:4 Greek *three tabernacles.* 17:9 "Son of Man" is a title Jesus used for Himself.
17:10 Greek *that Elijah must come first?*

which all spiritual life springs, is the perfect example. Jesus was about to show in one awful and bloody illustration exactly what shouldering one's cross means (16:24). But it is only through the cross that one gains the crown. We cannot hope to understand what it means to be a Christian without understanding the life of service and sacrifice that Jesus promised those who follow Him. Come, follow Jesus. Come and die—and you will find true life. (***See Holiness***> *Submission> Identifying with Christ> Suffering with Him,* TopicGuide page A40.)

17:3-5 Jewish expectations about the future included the possibility that both Moses and Elijah would reappear on the earth. To Jews, these men embodied the law and the prophets. Seeing Jesus with them at once would have both informed and confused them as to whether Jesus was equal to or above these men, so God clarified this with a supernatural message that removed all doubt (17:5).

▸ BIBLE

17:6 A second opinion. One afternoon, on a high mountain, Jesus pulled back the curtain and let Peter, James, and John glimpse who He was. It's odd that this led to confusion and fear, not clarity. It took God's words from heaven (17:5) and the touch of Jesus (17:7) for them to understand and recover from this supernatural experience. You may have unusual experiences with God—it's not unheard of to be deeply impacted physically and emotionally by extended prayer, fasting, and worship. It's important to judge these experiences by the same pattern we see in this story: by the light of God's Word. Let His Word interpret your experiences rather than the other way around. (***See Bible***> *Power> Equip> Catalyst for faith,* TopicGuide page A11.)

17:10 On the basis of Malachi 4:5, the Jewish religious teachers held that Elijah would return to the earth prior to the coming of the Messiah and the expected end of the ages.

17:11-13 Jesus was not saying that John the Baptist was a reincarnation of Elijah. (John himself denied that in John 1:21.) The disciples understood that Jesus meant that John carried out a ministry like Elijah's and fulfilled the promises of Malachi 4:5.

17:16 The people expected that the disciples might well have been able to carry out the same kind of ministry they had seen from Jesus. This likely occurred after Jesus sent out the 72 disciples, who reported success in casting out demons in Jesus' name (Luke 10:17).

17 Jesus said, "You faithless and corrupt people! How long must I be with you? How long
must I put up with you? Bring the boy here to Me." 18 Then Jesus rebuked the demon in the
boy, and it left him. From that moment the boy was well.
19 Afterward the disciples asked Jesus privately, "Why couldn't we cast out that demon?"
20 "You don't have enough faith," Jesus told them. "I tell you the truth, if you had faith
even as small as a mustard seed, you could say to this mountain, 'Move from here to
there,' and it would move. Nothing would be impossible.*"

17:17 Deut 32:5, 20
17:18 Matt 8:13; 9:22; 15:28
17:20 Matt 21:21; Mark 11:23; Luke 17:6; 1 Cor 13:2

JESUS AGAIN PREDICTS HIS DEATH

22 After they gathered again in Galilee, Jesus told them, "The Son of Man is going to be be-
trayed into the hands of His enemies. 23 He will be killed, but on the third day He will be
raised from the dead." And the disciples were filled with grief.

17:22-23 //Mark 9:30-32; //Luke 9:43-45

PAYMENT OF THE TEMPLE TAX

24 On their arrival in Capernaum, the collectors of the Temple tax* came to Peter and asked
him, "Doesn't your teacher pay the Temple tax?"
25 "Yes, He does," Peter replied. Then he went into the house.
But before he had a chance to speak, Jesus asked him, "What do you think, Peter?* Do
kings tax their own people or the people they have conquered?*"
26 "They tax the people they have conquered," Peter replied.
"Well, then," Jesus said, "the citizens are free! 27 However, we don't want to offend them,
so go down to the lake and throw in a line. Open the mouth of the first fish you catch, and
you will find a large silver coin.* Take it and pay the tax for both of us."

17:24 Exod 30:13
17:25 Matt 22:17-22; Rom 13:7

THE GREATEST IN THE KINGDOM

18 About that time the disciples came to Jesus and asked, "Who is greatest in the
Kingdom of Heaven?"
2 Jesus called a little child to Him and put the child among them. 3 Then He said, "I tell
you the truth, unless you turn from your sins and become like little children, you will never
get into the Kingdom of Heaven. 4 So anyone who becomes as humble as this little child is
the greatest in the Kingdom of Heaven.
5 "And anyone who welcomes a little child like this on My behalf* is welcoming Me.
6 But if you cause one of these little ones who trusts in Me to fall into sin, it would be
better for you to have a large millstone tied around your neck and be drowned in the
depths of the sea.
7 "What sorrow awaits the world, because it tempts people to sin. Temptations are inevi-

18:3 Matt 19:14; Mark 10:15; Luke 18:17; 1 Pet 2:2
18:4 Matt 20:26-27; Mark 10:43-44; Luke 22:26
18:5 Matt 10:40; Luke 10:16; John 13:20
18:6-9 1 Cor 8:12-13

17:20 Some manuscripts add verse 21, *But this kind of demon won't leave except by prayer and fasting.* Compare Mark 9:29. 17:24 Greek *the two-drachma [tax]*; also in 17:24b. See Exod 30:13-16; Neh 10:32-33. 17:25a Greek *Simon?* 17:25b Greek *their sons or others?* 17:27 Greek *a stater* [a Greek coin equivalent to four drachmas]. 18:5 Greek *in My name.*

17:20-21 The statement that the disciples did not have "enough faith" doesn't mean that faith can be calculated or measured. Their lack of faith had more to do with their failure to use their faith rather than the size of faith. Paul later taught that there is a special gift that enables some of God's people to have more effectiveness in praying for miracles of this type (1 Corinthians 12:28-30).

17:24-27 The Temple tax was a payment made by every Jewish man twenty years of age and older (Exodus 30:11-16). The monies were used for the maintenance of the Temple in Jerusalem. Jesus didn't see this tax as obligatory for Him, but out of deference to the leaders, He made a way for Peter to pay the amount for both of them through an astounding miracle.

▸ PURPOSE

17:27 Jesus provides for His people. When you first read the account of Jesus providing for the tax money expected of Him through a miraculous surprise in the mouth of a fish, it might seem like a capricious act. Was Jesus just entertaining Peter with a miracle? Certainly not. Although this miraculous answer to a practical need was not a promise that Jesus will do the same for all of His followers whenever taxes are due, it is another glimpse into the character of Jesus. Even practical matters like taxes are of concern to Him, and it is not beyond Him to meet such needs in miraculous ways. (***See Purpose*****>** *God's Deeds> Special Acts> Miracles> Jesus> Tax money provided,* TopicGuide page A53.)

18:8-9 Matt 5:29-30
18:10 Acts 12:15; Heb 1:14
18:12-14 //Luke 15:3-7
18:15 Lev 19:17; Luke 17:3; Gal 6:1; Jas 5:19-20
18:16 *Deut 19:15; John 8:17; 2 Cor 13:1; 1 Tim 5:19
18:17 Rom 16:17; 1 Cor 6:1-6
18:18 Matt 16:19; John 20:23
18:19 Matt 7:7; 21:22; Mark 11:24; John 15:7; 16:23; Jas 1:5; 1 Jn 3:22; 5:14-15
18:20 Matt 28:20; John 14:23
18:21-22 Luke 17:3-4

table, but what sorrow awaits the person who does the tempting. 8So if your hand or foot
causes you to sin, cut it off and throw it away. It's better to enter eternal life with only one
hand or one foot than to be thrown into eternal fire with both of your hands and feet. 9And
if your eye causes you to sin, gouge it out and throw it away. It's better to enter eternal life
with only one eye than to have two eyes and be thrown into the fire of hell.*

10"Beware that you don't look down on any of these little ones. For I tell you that in
heaven their angels are always in the presence of My heavenly Father.*

PARABLE OF THE LOST SHEEP

12"If a man has a hundred sheep and one of them wanders away, what will he do? Won't
he leave the ninety-nine others on the hills and go out to search for the one that is lost?
13And if he finds it, I tell you the truth, he will rejoice over it more than over the ninety-nine
that didn't wander away! 14In the same way, it is not My heavenly Father's will that even
one of these little ones should perish.

CORRECTING ANOTHER BELIEVER

15"If another believer* sins against you,* go privately and point out the offense. If the other
person listens and confesses it, you have won that person back. 16But if you are unsuc-
cessful, take one or two others with you and go back again, so that everything you say
may be confirmed by two or three witnesses. 17If the person still refuses to listen, take
your case to the church. Then if he or she won't accept the church's decision, treat that per-
son as a pagan or a corrupt tax collector.

18"I tell you the truth, whatever you forbid* on earth will be forbidden in heaven, and
whatever you permit* on earth will be permitted in heaven.

19"I also tell you this: If two of you agree here on earth concerning anything you ask, My
Father in heaven will do it for you. 20For where two or three gather together as My follow-
ers,* I am there among them."

PARABLE OF THE UNFORGIVING DEBTOR

21Then Peter came to Him and asked, "Lord, how often should I forgive someone* who
sins against me? Seven times?"

18:9 Greek *the Gehenna of fire.* **18:10** Some manuscripts add verse 11, *And the Son of Man came to save those who are lost.* Compare Luke 19:10. **18:15a** Greek *If your brother.* **18:15b** Some manuscripts do not include *against you.* **18:18a** Or *bind,* or *lock.* **18:18b** Or *loose,* or *open.* **18:20** Greek *gather together in My name.* **18:21** Greek *my brother.*

18:8-9 Jesus was using hyperbole to underscore the serious nature of sin. He was not advocating self-mutilation as a remedy for sin. He knows it is possible to sin in the heart (see Matthew 5:28) even without having the physical wherewithal to carry out a sinful action.

▸ GOD

18:12-14 Seek to save the lost. Why does God reach into our world and rescue sinners? Why does God pursue those who are alienated from Him? In this short parable, Jesus provides insight into what moves the heart of God to act on our behalf: joy! The shepherd goes after that which is lost and does so for the joy of finding what He longs to have. How do your pursuits reveal what you long to have? Let your life be marked by a passionate pursuit of what makes God rejoice. (***See God**> Relationship> God's Desire> God pursues a relationship,* TopicGuide page A14.)

▸ CHURCH

18:15-18 Purity and community. Jesus was intent on establishing a community of followers who would give themselves to holy life and joyful ministry (Acts 1–2). But He was aware of the challenges that any gathering of sinful people would face. One problem that must be addressed is how to deal with public sin within the community of faith. It can't be overlooked; that would be denying the essential holiness that should characterize the church. Yet simply driving out the offender would be inconsistent with our commitment to community and heartfelt fellowship. To deal with public, unrepentant sin, Jesus outlined a step-by-step plan that affirms both the holiness and unity of the church. As you deal with sin among your circle of friends and in your church, strike a balance between unity and holiness, and welcome the repentant back into fellowship as soon as possible (Luke 15; 2 Corinthians 2:5-11). (***See Church**> Role> Conflict> Restoration,* TopicGuide page A49.)

18:20 This verse isn't saying that Jesus isn't present with each of His individual followers. It underscores that when the collective body of His followers acts in His name, their unity of mind and purpose manifests His presence (John 17:20-23).

18:21-22 Peter thought he was being generous, since the religious leaders of the day taught that one only needed to forgive an offense three times. Jesus' shocking reply was not intended to give Peter a specific number of times to forgive. It was a proverbial number suggesting an unlimited number of times. See Genesis 4:24 for another example of this expression.

22“No, not seven times,” Jesus replied, “but seventy times seven!*

23“Therefore, the Kingdom of Heaven can be compared to a king who decided to bring his accounts up to date with servants who had borrowed money from him. 24In the process, one of his debtors was brought in who owed him millions of dollars.* 25He couldn't pay, so his master ordered that he be sold—along with his wife, his children, and everything he owned—to pay the debt.

26“But the man fell down before his master and begged him, ‘Please, be patient with me, and I will pay it all.’ 27Then his master was filled with pity for him, and he released him and forgave his debt.

28“But when the man left the king, he went to a fellow servant who owed him a few thousand dollars.* He grabbed him by the throat and demanded instant payment.

29“His fellow servant fell down before him and begged for a little more time. ‘Be patient with me, and I will pay it,’ he pleaded. 30But his creditor wouldn't wait. He had the man arrested and put in prison until the debt could be paid in full.

31“When some of the other servants saw this, they were very upset. They went to the king and told him everything that had happened. 32Then the king called in the man he had forgiven and said, ‘You evil servant! I forgave you that tremendous debt because you pleaded with me. 33Shouldn't you have mercy on your fellow servant, just as I had mercy on you?’ 34Then the angry king sent the man to prison to be tortured until he had paid his entire debt.

35“That's what My heavenly Father will do to you if you refuse to forgive your brothers and sisters* from your heart.”

DISCUSSION ABOUT DIVORCE AND MARRIAGE

19 When Jesus had finished saying these things, He left Galilee and went down to the region of Judea east of the Jordan River. 2Large crowds followed Him there, and He healed their sick.

3Some Pharisees came and tried to trap Him with this question: “Should a man be allowed to divorce his wife for just any reason?”

4“Haven't you read the Scriptures?” Jesus replied. “They record that from the beginning ‘God made them male and female.’* 5And He said, ‘This explains why a man leaves his father and mother and is joined to his wife, and the two are united into one.’* 6Since they are no longer two but one, let no one split apart what God has joined together.”

7“Then why did Moses say in the law that a man could give his wife a written notice of divorce and send her away?”* they asked.

8Jesus replied, “Moses permitted divorce only as a concession to your hard hearts, but it

18:23 Matt 25:19
18:25 Lev 25:39; 2 Kgs 4:1; Neh 5:5
18:27 Luke 7:42
18:34 Matt 5:25-26; Luke 12:58-59
18:35 Matt 6:15; Mark 11:25; Eph 4:32; Col 3:13
19:1-9 //Mark 10:1-12
19:2 Matt 4:23
19:3 Matt 5:31
19:4 *Gen 1:27; 5:2
19:5 *Gen 2:24; 1 Cor 6:16; Eph 5:31
19:7 *Deut 24:1; Matt 5:31

18:22 Or *seventy-seven times.* 18:24 Greek *10,000 talents* [375 tons or 340 metric tons of silver]. 18:28 Greek *100 denarii.* A denarius was equivalent to a laborer's full day's wage. 18:35 Greek *your brother.* 19:4 Gen 1:27; 5:2. 19:5 Gen 2:24. 19:7 See Deut 24:1.

▸ WORSHIP

18:23-35 Believers are forgivers. Sometime or another, someone will offend you. He or she will do something to hurt you or someone you love. What are you going to do about it? You can take revenge. You can pretend it didn't happen but inwardly be consumed with anger. But holding a grudge harms only you—as someone once said, “It's like drinking poison and hoping someone else dies.” An unwillingness to forgive keeps you in the grip of the original offense. Breaking free from past sin against you begins with forgiveness. As a Christian, you have tasted true forgiveness, so you are able to forgive (Matthew 6:12-15; Colossians 1:14). Being a mature Christian means you are more and more willing to do so (Colossians 3:13; Ephesians 4:31-32). Show true maturity by freely forgiving those who harm you. (***See Worship****> NT> Fellowship> Preserving> Forgive one another,* TopicGuide page A31.)

19:3 The trap laid for Jesus was rooted in two schools of thought among the Jewish leaders of the day. Both sides drew their views from Deuteronomy 24:1. Rabbi Shammai argued that the only grounds for divorce was adultery, while Rabbi Hillel insisted that almost any offense justified divorce. The Jewish leaders hoped to trap Jesus by forcing Him to come down on one side of the debate or the other, thereby alienating some of the Jewish leadership. Jesus avoided directly answering their question but implied that His position was narrower than Rabbi Hillel's.

▸ BIBLE

19:8 Marriage is forever. How many people do you know who have been divorced? When you consider how many people experience divorce and how much pain they suffer, it's impossible to discuss the topic impersonally. Yet that's

19:9 Matt 5:32 was not what God had originally intended. [9]And I tell you this, whoever divorces his wife
and marries someone else commits adultery—unless his wife has been unfaithful.*"
Luke 16:18 1 Cor 7:10-11 [10]Jesus' disciples then said to Him, "If this is the case, it is better not to marry!"
19:11 1 Cor 7:7-9, 17 [11]"Not everyone can accept this statement," Jesus said. "Only those whom God helps.
[12]Some are born as eunuchs, some have been made eunuchs by others, and some choose
19:12 1 Cor 7:32, 34 not to marry* for the sake of the Kingdom of Heaven. Let anyone accept this who can."

JESUS BLESSES THE CHILDREN

19:13-15 //Mark 10:13-16 //Luke 18:15-17 [13]One day some parents brought their children to Jesus so He could lay His hands on them
and pray for them. But the disciples scolded the parents for bothering Him.
19:14 Matt 18:2-3 [14]But Jesus said, "Let the children come to Me. Don't stop them! For the Kingdom of
Heaven belongs to those who are like these children." [15]And He placed His hands on their
19:16-30 //Mark 10:17-31 //Luke 18:18-30 heads and blessed them before He left.

THE RICH MAN

19:16 Matt 19:29 Luke 10:25 [16]Someone came to Jesus with this question: "Teacher,* what good deed must I do to have
eternal life?"
19:17 Lev 18:5 [17]"Why ask Me about what is good?" Jesus replied. "There is only One who is good. But
to answer your question—if you want to receive eternal life, keep* the commandments."
Luke 10:28 [18]"Which ones?" the man asked.
19:19 Exod 20:12 And Jesus replied: "'You must not murder. You must not commit adultery. You must not
Deut 5:16 steal. You must not testify falsely. [19]Honor your father and mother. Love your neighbor as
Matt 5:43-44; 22:39 yourself.'*"
Luke 10:27 Rom 13:9 [20]"I've obeyed all these commandments," the young man replied. "What else must I do?"
[21]Jesus told him, "If you want to be perfect, go and sell all your possessions and give the
19:21 Acts 2:45; 4:34-37 money to the poor, and you will have treasure in heaven. Then come, follow Me."
19:23 [22]But when the young man heard this, he went away sad, for he had many possessions.
Matt 13:22 1 Tim 6:9-10 [23]Then Jesus said to His disciples, "I tell you the truth, it is very hard for a rich person to

19:9 Some manuscripts add *And anyone who marries a divorced woman commits adultery.* Compare Matt 5:32. 19:12 Greek *and some make themselves eunuchs.* 19:16 Some manuscripts read *Good Teacher.* 19:17 Some manuscripts read *continue to keep.* 19:18-19 Exod 20:12-16; Deut 5:16-20; Lev 19:18.

how the religious leaders of Jesus' day seemed to approach it. They didn't seem to be concerned with people—divorce was a topic of theology, a way to trap Jesus. When Jesus spoke of divorce (see Matthew 5:31-32), He thought of the damage sin does to families, and He recommended God's best plan for a situation in which a spouse breaks the marriage covenant. As He did this, He affirmed two truths that we must hold in tension: God intended marriage to be permanent *and* God permitted divorce when immorality broke the marriage covenant (Matthew 5:32). Notice that the Bible never commands divorce—but it's an option for those who have been sexually betrayed by their spouses. Let the Scriptures—not situations—shape your views on divorce. Prayerfully receive the guidelines of Scripture on how to build a holy, lasting marriage (Ephesians 5:21-33). (***See Bible****> Unity> Doctrines> Principles of marriage,* TopicGuide page A10.)

19:11 Jesus said that refraining from marriage is only possible (literally translated) "for those to whom it is given." That is, the ability to remain happily unmarried is a gift from God (1 Corinthians 7:7).

19:13-15 To Jesus, children were a blessing, not a bother. He used the faithful parents and their children as an illustration of how the Kingdom of Heaven is advanced when godly families bring their children to Him.

19:16-22 This young man, though he was rich, sensed he lacked something—eternal life. But when Jesus explained the cost—that he had to submit every part of his life to God's will—he walked away. This caused a discussion among Jesus' disciples about money and the spiritual difficulties for those with many resources (19:23-27).

▸ WORSHIP

19:21 The greatest treasure. Jesus was not giving the rich young man a formula for absolute holiness. The word *perfect* can convey a variety of ideas according to its context. In this case, the sense of the word is "mature." Jesus was helping the young man understand what a developed faith would look like. Jesus knew that the young man's attachment to all his possessions was keeping him from advancing spiritually. His instructions are not His command to everyone; they are tailor-made for this young man, who prized his things more than he did Jesus. What is keeping you from advancing in your spiritual life? Target that weakness. Pray, read Scripture, and repent until it is no longer a barrier between you and God. (***See Worship****> NT> Offerings> Lay up treasures in heaven,* TopicGuide page A31.)

19:23-25 Because most Jews interpreted material wealth as a sign of blessing from God, Jesus was giving a startling word in saying that "it is very hard" for someone with wealth to get into the Kingdom of God. But Jesus made it clear that *no one* gets in without God making it happen.

enter the Kingdom of Heaven. 24I'll say it again—it is easier for a camel to go through the
eye of a needle than for a rich person to enter the Kingdom of God!"
25The disciples were astounded. "Then who in the world can be saved?" they asked.
26Jesus looked at them intently and said, "Humanly speaking, it is impossible. But with
God everything is possible."
27Then Peter said to Him, "We've given up everything to follow You. What will we get?"
28Jesus replied, "I assure you that when the world is made new* and the Son of Man* sits
upon His glorious throne, you who have been My followers will also sit on twelve thrones,
judging the twelve tribes of Israel. 29And everyone who has given up houses or brothers or
sisters or father or mother or children or property, for My sake, will receive a hundred times
as much in return and will inherit eternal life. 30But many who are the greatest now will be
least important then, and those who seem least important now will be the greatest then.*

PARABLE OF THE VINEYARD WORKERS

20 "For the Kingdom of Heaven is like the landowner who went out early one morn-
ing to hire workers for his vineyard. 2He agreed to pay the normal daily wage*
and sent them out to work.
3"At nine o'clock in the morning he was passing through the marketplace and saw some
people standing around doing nothing. 4So he hired them, telling them he would pay
them whatever was right at the end of the day. 5So they went to work in the vineyard. At
noon and again at three o'clock he did the same thing.
6"At five o'clock that afternoon he was in town again and saw some more people stand-
ing around. He asked them, 'Why haven't you been working today?'
7"They replied, 'Because no one hired us.'
"The landowner told them, 'Then go out and join the others in my vineyard.'
8"That evening he told the foreman to call the workers in and pay them, beginning with
the last workers first. 9When those hired at five o'clock were paid, each received a full
day's wage. 10When those hired first came to get their pay, they assumed they would re-
ceive more. But they, too, were paid a day's wage. 11When they received their pay, they
protested to the owner, 12'Those people worked only one hour, and yet you've paid them
just as much as you paid us who worked all day in the scorching heat.'
13"He answered one of them, 'Friend, I haven't been unfair! Didn't you agree to work all
day for the usual wage? 14Take your money and go. I wanted to pay this last worker the
same as you. 15Is it against the law for me to do what I want with my money? Should you
be jealous because I am kind to others?'
16"So those who are last now will be first then, and those who are first will be last."

19:26 Gen 18:14; Job 42:2; Jer 32:17; Zech 8:6
19:27 Matt 4:19
19:28 Luke 22:28-30; Rev 3:21
19:30 Matt 20:16; Mark 10:31; Luke 13:30
20:1 Matt 21:28, 33
20:8 Lev 19:13; Deut 24:15
20:15 Deut 15:9
20:16 Matt 19:30; Mark 10:31; Luke 13:30

19:28a Or *in the regeneration.* 19:28b "Son of Man" is a title Jesus used for Himself. 19:30 Greek *But many who are first will be last; and the last, first.* 20:2 Greek *a denarius,* the payment for a full day's labor; similarly in 20:9, 10, 13.

▸ HOLINESS

19:26 Salvation is God's gift. Like many people today, Jesus' disciples mistakenly believed that material blessing was a sign of God's special favor. If someone had been blessed with material wealth or worldly status, it was assumed that he or she enjoyed a particularly close relationship with God. But Jesus dismissed such thinking, causing His puzzled disciples to wonder: "Who in the world can be saved?" Jesus' answer was that nothing about us makes us fit for eternal life; eternal life is a gift God bestows regardless of our worldly status or wealth. Trust in nothing but Christ and His righteousness to make you fit for heaven (Romans 5:17-18). (***See Holiness**> Law and Grace> Grace> The gift of grace,* TopicGuide page A42.)

19:27-30 Jesus repeated His previous message about the paradoxical values of the Kingdom (see Matthew 16:25), but one thing is not backwards—God's people will be rewarded for their labors (1 Corinthians 3:13-14).

20:1-16 Jesus further compares the paradoxical values of the Kingdom to benefits bestowed on workers who had served from the beginning matching the benefits of those hired later. Gentiles who would soon be pouring into the church enjoy the same salvation as the Jews. More generally, this parable shows that God is a debtor to no one and rewards all people according to how He sees fit.

▸ HOLINESS

20:15 Is God fair? In this short parable, Jesus illustrated a critical facet of the gospel—and one that causes many to stumble. Is it fair that the same eternal life

JESUS AGAIN PREDICTS HIS DEATH

20:17-19 //Mark 10:32-34 //Luke 18:31-34
20:18-19 Matt 16:21; 17:22-23 Luke 9:22 Acts 2:23

17 As Jesus was going up to Jerusalem, He took the twelve disciples aside privately and told them what was going to happen to Him. 18 "Listen," He said, "we're going up to Jerusalem, where the Son of Man* will be betrayed to the leading priests and the teachers of religious law. They will sentence Him to die. 19 Then they will hand Him over to the Romans* to be mocked, flogged with a whip, and crucified. But on the third day He will be raised from the dead."

JESUS TEACHES ABOUT SERVING OTHERS

20:20-28 //Mark 10:35-45
20:21 Matt 19:28

20 Then the mother of James and John, the sons of Zebedee, came to Jesus with her sons. She knelt respectfully to ask a favor. 21 "What is your request?" He asked.

She replied, "In Your Kingdom, please let my two sons sit in places of honor next to You, one on Your right and the other on Your left."

20:22 Matt 26:39, 42 Mark 14:36 Luke 22:42 John 18:11

22 But Jesus answered by saying to them, "You don't know what you are asking! Are you able to drink from the bitter cup of suffering I am about to drink?"

"Oh yes," they replied, "we are able!"

20:23 Acts 12:2 Rev 1:9

23 Jesus told them, "You will indeed drink from My bitter cup. But I have no right to say who will sit on My right or My left. My Father has prepared those places for the ones He has chosen."

20:24-28 //Luke 22:24-27
20:26 Matt 23:11 Mark 9:35 Luke 9:48
20:28 Isa 53:10 Phil 2:7 1 Tim 2:6 1 Pet 1:18-19

24 When the ten other disciples heard what James and John had asked, they were indignant. 25 But Jesus called them together and said, "You know that the rulers in this world lord it over their people, and officials flaunt their authority over those under them. 26 But among you it will be different. Whoever wants to be a leader among you must be your servant, 27 and whoever wants to be first among you must become your slave. 28 For even the Son of Man came not to be served but to serve others and to give His life as a ransom for many."

JESUS HEALS TWO BLIND MEN

20:29-34 //Mark 10:46-52 //Luke 18:35-43

29 As Jesus and the disciples left the town of Jericho, a large crowd followed behind. 30 Two blind men were sitting beside the road. When they heard that Jesus was coming that way, they began shouting, "Lord, Son of David, have mercy on us!"

31 "Be quiet!" the crowd yelled at them.

But they only shouted louder, "Lord, Son of David, have mercy on us!"

32 When Jesus heard them, He stopped and called, "What do you want Me to do for you?"

33 "Lord," they said, "we want to see!" 34 Jesus felt sorry for them and touched their eyes. Instantly they could see! Then they followed Him.

20:18 "Son of Man" is a title Jesus used for Himself. 20:19 Greek *the Gentiles.*

---

is given to those who make a deathbed repentance and those who have followed God for a lifetime? God is indeed fair, but His fairness may not match our understanding of what is fair (Romans 9:12-18). The truth is, *none* of us deserve His glorious and generous grace. The undeserved promises of God that appear in this world of sin are to be delighted in, not argued with or over-analyzed. Look for God's grace and rejoice in it where it can be found. (***See Holiness****> Changed by God> God Provides> Extending grace to us,* TopicGuide page A41.)

20:21-22 Although the mother of James and John raised the subject of the seats of honor with Jesus, His reply and the response from the brothers make it clear that their mother wasn't asking in their absence.

20:22-23 It is unlikely that James and John fully understood what lay ahead for them. James became the first martyr (Acts 12:2), and John was exiled beause of his faith in Jesus (Revelation 1:9).

▸ ADOPTION

20:26-27 Leadership in the Kingdom. It's no surprise that Jesus had a very different theory of leadership than most. Rather than looking to powerful figures, He illustrated leadership through servants, slaves, and those who give up their lives. How would this look if you applied it in your family, on your job, or at your church? Perhaps you'll be honored for your efforts, but perhaps not. That is not your concern. Concern yourself with pleasing God and pursuing His kind of greatness by His methods. Then you will be great in His eyes. (***See Adoption****> With Christ> Servants> Created to do good works,* TopicGuide page A37.)

20:28 Jesus not only highlighted His own life as an example of a servant leader, but He also demonstrated commitment to His principles in the best way possible—by surrendering His life on the cross (1 Corinthians 2:2; Galatians 3:13). This act of service stands as a central symbol of the Christian faith (Galatians 6:14).

JESUS' TRIUMPHANT ENTRY

21 As Jesus and the disciples approached Jerusalem, they came to the town of Beth-
phage on the Mount of Olives. Jesus sent two of them on ahead. 2"Go into the vil-
lage over there," He said. "As soon as you enter it, you will see a donkey tied there, with its
colt beside it. Untie them and bring them to Me. 3If anyone asks what you are doing, just
say, 'The Lord needs them,' and he will immediately let you take them."
4This took place to fulfill the prophecy that said,

5 "Tell the people of Israel,*
'Look, your King is coming to you.
He is humble, riding on a donkey—
riding on a donkey's colt.'"*

6The two disciples did as Jesus commanded. 7They brought the donkey and the colt to
Him and threw their garments over the colt, and He sat on it.*
8Most of the crowd spread their garments on the road ahead of Him, and others cut
branches from the trees and spread them on the road. 9Jesus was in the center of the pro-
cession, and the people all around Him were shouting,

"Praise God* for the Son of David!
Blessings on the One who comes in the name of the LORD!
Praise God in highest heaven!"*

10The entire city of Jerusalem was in an uproar as He entered. "Who is this?" they asked.
11And the crowds replied, "It's Jesus, the prophet from Nazareth in Galilee."

JESUS CLEARS THE TEMPLE

12Jesus entered the Temple and began to drive out all the people buying and selling ani-
mals for sacrifice. He knocked over the tables of the money changers and the chairs of
those selling doves. 13He said to them, "The Scriptures declare, 'My Temple will be called a
house of prayer,' but you have turned it into a den of thieves!"*
14The blind and the lame came to Him in the Temple, and He healed them. 15The lead-
ing priests and the teachers of religious law saw these wonderful miracles and heard even
the children in the Temple shouting, "Praise God for the Son of David."
But the leaders were indignant. 16They asked Jesus, "Do You hear what these children
are saying?"

21:1-9 //Mark 11:1-10 //Luke 19:28-38 //John 12:12-19
21:5 *Isa 62:11 *Zech 9:9
21:9 *Pss 118:25-26; 148:1 Luke 13:35
21:11 Luke 7:16, 39 John 1:21, 25; 6:14; 7:40; 9:17
21:12-17 //Mark 11:15-19 //Luke 19:45-48 //John 2:13-22
21:13 *Isa 56:7 *Jer 7:11
21:14 Isa 35:5-6
21:15 Matt 21:9
21:16 *Ps 8:2

21:5a Greek *Tell the daughter of Zion.* Isa 62:11. 21:5b Zech 9:9. 21:7 Greek *over them, and He sat on them.* 21:9a Greek *Hosanna,* an exclamation of praise that literally means "save now"; also in 21:9b, 15. 21:9b Pss 118:25-26; 148:1. 21:13 Isa 56:7; Jer 7:11.

▸ SPIRITUAL WARFARE

21:1-3 Obedience in the gray. It undoubtedly appeared to be a peculiar set of instructions—find a particular donkey and his colt and untie them. If anyone asks about taking (stealing?) the donkeys, tell that person, "The Lord" needs them. Do you think *you* would have carried out those instructions as two of Jesus' disciples did? Wouldn't you have felt a little uncomfortable not obtaining permission *before* you began untying them? In this case, the purpose was to fulfill prophecy (Zechariah 9:9). But did the disciples know that? This little episode in the life of Jesus reminds us that we must follow Jesus' instructions—even those that may seem counterintuitive at first (Matthew 20:16; Mark 9:35; Revelation 22:13). We do not know exactly what God is trying to accomplish when He asks us to do things that often seem difficult. But be sure that your obedience will do more in this world than you can ever imagine, and it will lay up great rewards in the next (Jeremiah 17:10; Hebrews 11:6). (***See Spiritual Warfare****> Resisting Sin and Evil> Consequences> Of Obedience> Pleases God,* TopicGuide page A46.)

21:4-5 This prophecy is drawn from both Isaiah 62:11 and Zechariah 9:9. It was common practice among the religious teachers of the day to join two or more passages together, as long as they were referring to the same matter.

21:9 Although they probably did not fully understand the ramifications of what they were announcing, the crowd surrounding Jesus was celebrating Him, identifying Him as the promised Messiah. The words they were shouting came from Psalm 118:26, part of one of the songs sung by pilgrims en route to Jerusalem for an upcoming religious festival.

21:10-13 "Uproar," the word Matthew used to describe the effect of Jesus' arrival on the city, conveys the idea of being shaken, as if by an earthquake. Jesus' shaking of Jerusalem foreshadowed the violent method He would use to teach God's desire that the Temple would be a place of holy worship, not heartless commerce.

"Yes," Jesus replied. "Haven't you ever read the Scriptures? For they say, 'You have
21:17 taught children and infants to give You praise.'*" 17Then He returned to Bethany, where
Mark 11:1 He stayed overnight.
John 11:1, 18; 12:1

JESUS CURSES THE FIG TREE

21:18-22 18In the morning, as Jesus was returning to Jerusalem, He was hungry, 19and He noticed a
//Mark 11:12-14, fig tree beside the road. He went over to see if there were any figs, but there were only
20-24 leaves. Then He said to it, "May you never bear fruit again!" And immediately the fig tree
withered up.
20The disciples were amazed when they saw this and asked, "How did the fig tree wither
21:21 so quickly?"
Matt 17:20 21Then Jesus told them, "I tell you the truth, if you have faith and don't doubt, you can
Luke 17:6 1 Cor 13:2 do things like this and much more. You can even say to this mountain, 'May you be lifted
Jas 1:6 up and thrown into the sea,' and it will happen. 22You can pray for anything, and if you
21:22 have faith, you will receive it."
Matt 7:7-11
John 14:13-14

THE AUTHORITY OF JESUS CHALLENGED

21:23-27 //Mark 11:27-33 23When Jesus returned to the Temple and began teaching, the leading priests and elders
//Luke 20:1-8 came up to Him. They demanded, "By what authority are You doing all these things? Who
21:23 gave You the right?"
Acts 4:7 24"I'll tell you by what authority I do these things if you answer one question," Jesus re-
plied. 25"Did John's authority to baptize come from heaven, or was it merely human?"
They talked it over among themselves. "If we say it was from heaven, He will ask us why
21:26 we didn't believe John. 26But if we say it was merely human, we'll be mobbed because the
Matt 11:9 people believe John was a prophet." 27So they finally replied, "We don't know."
And Jesus responded, "Then I won't tell you by what authority I do these things.

PARABLE OF THE TWO SONS

21:28 28"But what do you think about this? A man with two sons told the older boy, 'Son, go out
Luke 15:11 and work in the vineyard today.' 29The son answered, 'No, I won't go,' but later he
changed his mind and went anyway. 30Then the father told the other son, 'You go,' and he
said, 'Yes, sir, I will.' But he didn't go.
31"Which of the two obeyed his father?"
They replied, "The first."*

21:16 Ps 8:2. 21:29-31 Other manuscripts read *"The second."* In still other manuscripts the first son says "Yes" but does nothing, the second son says "No" but then repents and goes, and the answer to Jesus' question is that the second son obeyed his father.

21:19 The kind of fig trees growing around the city in Jesus' day should have had some "early" figs along with the foliage. Jesus' pronouncement on the fig tree was not a capricious act; He passed an appropriate judgment on something that appeared to be living but was actually ineffective and fruitless.

▸ WORSHIP
21:21-22 Praying according to God's will. When Jesus spoke to His followers about the power of prayer, He was not telling them that if they only believed something, they could make it happen. Jesus isn't a proponent of mind over matter or a champion of the power of positive thinking. Faith is rooted in a radical dependence upon God. When you are walking with Him, dependent on Him, and following His lead, then what you ask for in prayer will happen. But it's not because you have such power; it's because you are walking in step with the One who has all power. When your prayers are according to His will, they cannot fail, for His will cannot be stopped by anyone. (***See Worship***> *NT> Prayer> Instructions> Pray with humility,* TopicGuide page A33.)

▸ CHURCH
21:28-31 The repentant son. Disobedience is not always immediately evident. In Jesus' parable of the two sons, the father never discovered what the reader knows—both sons were foolish, but there was hope for one of them. Jesus knew that the coming mass inclusion of Gentiles into the church would cause upheaval, so He included parables like this to help the early church understand that the initial refusal of the Gentile world to join in worship of God would not continue. It has always been God's plan to include people from around the world in the growing Kingdom, so the church should fearlessly reach out to people of all kinds and colors. Remember this story when you talk with people who are initially resistant to the gospel—it may be God's plan to draw them to Himself sooner than you think! (***See Church***> *Who> From Every People> Gentile converts,* TopicGuide page A48.)

Then Jesus explained His meaning: "I tell you the truth, corrupt tax collectors and prosti-
tutes will get into the Kingdom of God before you do. 32For John the Baptist came and 21:32 Matt 3:1-12
showed you the right way to live, but you didn't believe him, while tax collectors and pros- Luke 3:12-13;
titutes did. And even when you saw this happening, you refused to believe him and repent 7:29-30
of your sins. 21:33-46 //Mark 12:1-12 //Luke 20:9-19

PARABLE OF THE EVIL FARMERS

33"Now listen to another story. A certain landowner planted a vineyard, built a wall around 21:33 Isa 5:1-2
it, dug a pit for pressing out the grape juice, and built a lookout tower. Then he leased the
vineyard to tenant farmers and moved to another country. 34At the time of the grape har-
vest, he sent his servants to collect his share of the crop. 35But the farmers grabbed his ser- 21:35 Matt 23:34, 37
vants, beat one, killed one, and stoned another. 36So the landowner sent a larger group of
his servants to collect for him, but the results were the same.
37"Finally, the owner sent his son, thinking, 'Surely they will respect my son.'
38"But when the tenant farmers saw his son coming, they said to one another, 'Here
comes the heir to this estate. Come on, let's kill him and get the estate for ourselves!' 39So
they grabbed him, dragged him out of the vineyard, and murdered him.
40"When the owner of the vineyard returns," Jesus asked, "what do you think he will do
to those farmers?"
41The religious leaders replied, "He will put the wicked men to a horrible death and 21:41 Matt 8:11-12
lease the vineyard to others who will give him his share of the crop after each harvest." Luke 21:24
42Then Jesus asked them, "Didn't you ever read this in the Scriptures? Acts 13:46

'The stone that the builders rejected 21:42 *Ps 118:22-23
has now become the cornerstone. Isa 28:16
This is the LORD's doing, Acts 4:11 Eph 2:20
and it is wonderful to see.'* 1 Pet 2:6-7

43I tell you, the Kingdom of God will be taken away from you and given to a nation that
will produce the proper fruit. 44Anyone who stumbles over that stone will be broken to 21:44 Isa 8:14-15
pieces, and it will crush anyone it falls on.*" Dan 2:34-35, 44-45
45When the leading priests and Pharisees heard this parable, they realized He was tell-
ing the story against them—they were the wicked farmers. 46They wanted to arrest Him, 21:46 Matt 21:26
but they were afraid of the crowds, who considered Jesus to be a prophet.

PARABLE OF THE GREAT FEAST

22 Jesus also told them other parables. He said, 2"The Kingdom of Heaven can be il- 22:1-10
lustrated by the story of a king who prepared a great wedding feast for his son. //Luke 14:15-24
3When the banquet was ready, he sent his servants to notify those who were invited. But 22:3
they all refused to come! Matt 21:34

21:42 Ps 118:22-23. 21:44 This verse is omitted in some early manuscripts. Compare Luke 20:18.

22:1-14 Different cultures have different traditions associated with marriage. In Jesus' day, wedding festivities could last as long as a week. Typically, guests would be invited twice; once so they could make plans for the upcoming event, and again when the feast was ready. The servants who went "to notify those who were invited" were literally "calling those who had already been called" to attend.

▸ ADOPTION

22:1-14 Glorious feast—rejected. God provided food for Adam and Eve in the Garden of Eden (Genesis 2:9; 3:6)—but they rejected it. God provided food for His people wandering in the desert (Numbers 21:5; Deuteronomy 8:16)—but they rejected it. So it's not unexpected that Jesus would use the image of great provision rejected to illustrate God's gracious invitation to join in the Kingdom. In this case, many of God's covenant people, the Jews, rejected the grand banquet of grace spread by Christ. God's response was to reject those who reject His Son and welcome people all over the world to the delights of His Son (Matthew 26:26-28; John 4:13-15). Today, the very people we think should be enjoying Christ—the religious, the people like us—often reject Him. And those whom we might never imagine embracing Christ show a deep hunger for Him. Don't be surprised at who accepts and who rejects the gospel—simply tell the truth about the rich feast of the gospel and see who is hungry for more. (***See Adoption*> *With Christ*> *Heirs of God*> *Inheritance reserved in heaven,* TopicGuide page A36.)

22:4 4"So he sent other servants to tell them, 'The feast has been prepared. The bulls and fat-
Matt 21:36 tened cattle have been killed, and everything is ready. Come to the banquet!' 5But the
22:6 guests he had invited ignored them and went their own way, one to his farm, another to
Matt 21:35 his business. 6Others seized his messengers and insulted them and killed them.
22:7 Luke 19:27 7"The king was furious, and he sent out his army to destroy the murderers and burn
22:8 their town. 8And he said to his servants, 'The wedding feast is ready, and the guests I in-
Acts 13:46 vited aren't worthy of the honor. 9Now go out to the street corners and invite everyone
22:10 you see.' 10So the servants brought in everyone they could find, good and bad alike, and
Matt 13:47-48 the banquet hall was filled with guests.
11"But when the king came in to meet the guests, he noticed a man who wasn't wearing
22:12 the proper clothes for a wedding. 12'Friend,' he asked, 'how is it that you are here without
Matt 20:13; 26:50 wedding clothes?' But the man had no reply. 13Then the king said to his aides, 'Bind his
22:13 Matt 8:12; 25:30 hands and feet and throw him into the outer darkness, where there will be weeping and
22:14 gnashing of teeth.'
2 Pet 1:10 Rev 17:14 14"For many are called, but few are chosen."

TAXES FOR CAESAR

22:15-22 15Then the Pharisees met together to plot how to trap Jesus into saying something for
//Mark 12:13-17 which He could be arrested. 16They sent some of their disciples, along with the supporters
//Luke 20:20-26 of Herod, to meet with Him. "Teacher," they said, "we know how honest You are. You
22:17 teach the way of God truthfully. You are impartial and don't play favorites. 17Now tell us
Matt 17:25 what You think about this: Is it right to pay taxes to Caesar or not?"
18But Jesus knew their evil motives. "You hypocrites!" He said. "Why are you trying to
trap Me? 19Here, show Me the coin used for the tax." When they handed Him a Roman
coin,* 20He asked, "Whose picture and title are stamped on it?"
22:21 21"Caesar's," they replied.
Rom 13:7 "Well, then," He said, "give to Caesar what belongs to Caesar, and give to God what
22:23-33 belongs to God."
//Mark 12:18-27 //Luke 20:27-40 22His reply amazed them, and they went away.

DISCUSSION ABOUT RESURRECTION

22:23 Acts 23:8 23That same day Jesus was approached by some Sadducees—religious leaders who say
1 Cor 15:12 there is no resurrection from the dead. They posed this question: 24"Teacher, Moses said,
22:24 'If a man dies without children, his brother should marry the widow and have a child who
Deut 25:5-6 will carry on the brother's name.' 25Well, suppose there were seven brothers. The oldest
one married and then died without children, so his brother married the widow. 26But the
second brother also died, and the third brother married her. This continued with all seven
of them. 27Last of all, the woman also died. 28So tell us, whose wife will she be in the resur-
22:29 rection? For all seven were married to her."
John 20:9 29Jesus replied, "Your mistake is that you don't know the Scriptures, and you don't

22:19 Greek *a denarius.* 22:24 Deut 25:5-6.

22:14 The entire covenant community of Israel was called to repentance (Ezekiel 14:6; Hosea 14:1), but few were chosen to come to the fullest expression of their Judaism—faith in Christ as their Messiah (Romans 5:1-6).

22:18 The word *hypocrite* originally meant "actor," meaning that Jesus was accusing the Pharisees of being insincere or deceitful in their questioning of Him.

22:19-20 The tax was a tribute paid, per person, to the Roman government using money coined by Rome. The coins had the figure of Caesar, the emperor, on them, as well as an inscription of the emperor's name.

▸ BIBLE

22:29 Knowing the Author. Even people who know a lot about the Scriptures can be quite ignorant when it comes to truly *knowing* the Scriptures. Some religious leaders confronted Jesus, seeking to trap Him in a theological dilemma. His reply indicated that they were ignorant of two basic things: They didn't really know the Scriptures (they only quoted sections without real understanding), and they didn't really know the God of the Scriptures. It's not enough to know the stories of the Bible. We must come to grips with the truths we find there and come to know the Author of those truths. (***See Bible***> *Uniqueness> Inspired> A record of God's own words,* TopicGuide page A10.)

know the power of God. [30] For when the dead rise, they will neither marry nor be given in
marriage. In this respect they will be like the angels in heaven.
[31] "But now, as to whether there will be a resurrection of the dead—haven't you ever
read about this in the Scriptures? Long after Abraham, Isaac, and Jacob had died, God
said,* [32] 'I am the God of Abraham, the God of Isaac, and the God of Jacob.'* So He is the
God of the living, not the dead."
[33] When the crowds heard Him, they were astounded at His teaching.

22:32 Acts 7:32
22:33 Matt 7:28; 13:54 Mark 11:18

THE MOST IMPORTANT COMMANDMENT

[34] But when the Pharisees heard that He had silenced the Sadducees with His reply, they
met together to question Him again. [35] One of them, an expert in religious law, tried to trap
Him with this question: [36] "Teacher, which is the most important commandment in the law
of Moses?"
[37] Jesus replied, "'You must love the LORD your God with all your heart, all your soul, and
all your mind.'* [38] This is the first and greatest commandment. [39] A second is equally im-
portant: 'Love your neighbor as yourself.'* [40] The entire law and all the demands of the
prophets are based on these two commandments."

22:34-40 //Mark 12:28-34 //Luke 10:25-28
22:35 Luke 10:25
22:39 Matt 5:43; 19:19 Mark 12:31 Luke 10:27 Rom 13:9 Gal 5:14 Jas 2:8
22:40 Matt 7:12 Luke 10:25-28 Rom 13:10

WHOSE SON IS THE MESSIAH?

[41] Then, surrounded by the Pharisees, Jesus asked them a question: [42] "What do you think
about the Messiah? Whose son is He?"
They replied, "He is the son of David."
[43] Jesus responded, "Then why does David, speaking under the inspiration of the Spirit,
call the Messiah 'my Lord'? For David said,

[44] 'The LORD said to my Lord,
Sit in the place of honor at My right hand
until I humble Your enemies beneath Your feet.'*

[45] Since David called the Messiah 'my Lord,' how can the Messiah be his son?"
[46] No one could answer Him. And after that, no one dared to ask Him any more questions.

22:41-46 //Mark 12:35-37 //Luke 20:41-44
22:43 2 Sam 23:2 Acts 2:30 2 Pet 1:20-21
22:44 Acts 2:34-35 Heb 1:13
22:46 Mark 12:34 Luke 20:40

JESUS CRITICIZES THE RELIGIOUS LEADERS

23 Then Jesus said to the crowds and to His disciples, [2] "The teachers of religious law
and the Pharisees are the official interpreters of the law of Moses.* [3] So practice
and obey whatever they tell you, but don't follow their example. For they don't practice
what they teach. [4] They crush people with unbearable religious demands and never lift a
finger to ease the burden.

23:2 Ezra 7:6, 25 Neh 8:1-4
23:4 Luke 11:46 Acts 15:20 Gal 6:13

22:31 Greek *read about this? God said.* 22:32 Exod 3:6. 22:37 Deut 6:5. 22:39 Lev 19:18. 22:44 Ps 110:1. 23:2 Greek *and the Pharisees sit in the seat of Moses.*

22:35-36 Apparently, the religious leader asked this question about the greatest commandment hoping that Jesus would affirm one religious party's "favorite" commandment and put Himself at odds with those who had a different "favorite."

22:37-40 The Ten Commandments are a helpful summary of the law given to God's people through Moses (Exodus 20:1-17). Jesus' summary is even more concise, yet just like the Ten Commandments (see division at Exodus 20:12), it still reflects God's expectations for us—to love Him and to love those around us.

22:40 Jews in Jesus' day often spoke of the Old Testament under the two headings of "the Law" and "the Prophets."

22:41-46 The dilemma for the religious leaders here was that they were thinking of the Messiah ("the son of David") as a descendant of David who was, in some sense, inferior to David, the great king of Israel. Jesus' question to them raised the issue of whether they had rightly understood who the Messiah was to be.

23:2 When Jesus spoke of the religious leaders as "the official interpreters of the law of Moses," He confirmed that this was exactly the service that they should have provided. But these leaders were also burdening people with traditions and requirements that were never prescribed by God's law, and the people were unable to bear this weight (Galatians 1:14; 2:11-14).

23:5 Exod 13:9 Num 15:37-40 Deut 6:8 Matt 6:1-2
23:6 Luke 14:7
23:9 Mal 1:6
23:11 Matt 20:26-27 Mark 9:35; 10:43-45 Luke 9:48; 22:26
23:12 Job 22:29 Prov 29:23 Ezek 21:26 Luke 14:11; 18:14
23:13 Luke 11:52
23:16 Isa 9:16 Matt 5:33-35; 15:14 Rom 2:19
23:19 Exod 29:37
23:21 1 Kgs 8:13 Ps 26:8
23:22 Ps 11:4 Isa 66:1 Matt 5:34 Acts 7:49
23:23 Lev 27:30 Hos 6:6 Mic 6:8 Zech 7:9 Luke 11:42
23:24 Matt 23:16

5 "Everything they do is for show. On their arms they wear extra wide prayer boxes with Scripture verses inside, and they wear robes with extra long tassels.* 6 And they love to sit at the head table at banquets and in the seats of honor in the synagogues. 7 They love to receive respectful greetings as they walk in the marketplaces, and to be called 'Rabbi.'*

8 "Don't let anyone call you 'Rabbi,' for you have only one teacher, and all of you are equal as brothers and sisters.* 9 And don't address anyone here on earth as 'Father,' for only God in heaven is your spiritual Father. 10 And don't let anyone call you 'Teacher,' for you have only one teacher, the Messiah. 11 The greatest among you must be a servant. 12 But those who exalt themselves will be humbled, and those who humble themselves will be exalted.

13 "What sorrow awaits you teachers of religious law and you Pharisees. Hypocrites! For you shut the door of the Kingdom of Heaven in people's faces. You won't go in yourselves, and you don't let others enter either.*

15 "What sorrow awaits you teachers of religious law and you Pharisees. Hypocrites! For you cross land and sea to make one convert, and then you turn that person into twice the child of hell* you yourselves are!

16 "Blind guides! What sorrow awaits you! For you say that it means nothing to swear 'by God's Temple,' but that it is binding to swear 'by the gold in the Temple.' 17 Blind fools! Which is more important—the gold or the Temple that makes the gold sacred? 18 And you say that to swear 'by the altar' is not binding, but to swear 'by the gifts on the altar' is binding. 19 How blind! For which is more important—the gift on the altar or the altar that makes the gift sacred? 20 When you swear 'by the altar,' you are swearing by it and by everything on it. 21 And when you swear 'by the Temple,' you are swearing by it and by God, who lives in it. 22 And when you swear 'by heaven,' you are swearing by the throne of God and by God, who sits on the throne.

23 "What sorrow awaits you teachers of religious law and you Pharisees. Hypocrites! For you are careful to tithe even the tiniest income from your herb gardens,* but you ignore the more important aspects of the law—justice, mercy, and faith. You should tithe, yes, but do not neglect the more important things. 24 Blind guides! You strain your water so you won't accidentally swallow a gnat, but you swallow a camel!*

23:5 Greek *They enlarge their phylacteries and lengthen their tassels.* 23:7 *Rabbi,* from Aramaic, means "master" or "teacher." 23:8 Greek *brothers.* 23:13 Some manuscripts add verse 14, *What sorrow awaits you teachers of religious law and you Pharisees. Hypocrites! You shamelessly cheat widows out of their property and then pretend to be pious by making long prayers in public. Because of this, you will be severely punished.* Compare Mark 12:40 and Luke 20:47. 23:15 Greek *of Gehenna;* also in 23:33. 23:23 Greek *tithe the mint, the dill, and the cumin.* 23:24 See Lev 11:4, 23, where gnats and camels are both forbidden as food.

23:5 The "prayer boxes" (called *phylacteries*) Jesus referred to were part of the custom of the day with pious Jews. Following Deuteronomy 6:8, they would take small rolls of parchment and tie them in boxes to their hands. Those who thought themselves to be especially "holy" would wear very large and noticeable prayer boxes.

▸GOD

23:5-7 Holiness on parade. We all like to be liked. We know certain people whose approval we crave above others'. In Jesus' day, many religious people performed their pious activities for an audience. The problem, however, is that whenever people practice religion for the approval of others, they aren't living holy lives. They are living for human approval, which is the cheapest of rewards. Pleasing God is truly all that matters (Deuteronomy 13:18; Hebrews 13:16-20). (***See God> God's Attributes> All-Knowing> God sees it all,*** TopicGuide page A15.)

23:8-10 In the context of warning religious leaders against misusing their authority, Jesus warned His followers not to assume elevated names in order to create a religious elite. While God gives different roles to His people (1 Corinthians 12:27-28; Ephesians 4:11), all are equal in Christ (Romans 6:3; Galatians 3:28).

23:23 The Old Testament had a provision for giving a tenth of agricultural produce to the Levites, who then distributed it as needed with one tenth of that sum going to the Temple (Leviticus 27:30; Numbers 18:20-32). Jesus pointed out that although the religious leaders were attentive to tithing from even their herb gardens (see NLT textual note), they often overlooked the major issues.

23:24 Both the gnat and the camel were animals that were considered to be ceremonially unclean. Jesus used this humorous image to show again how the religious leaders paid such great attention to small matters so as not to make themselves "unholy," yet they overlooked truly significant issues.

25“What sorrow awaits you teachers of religious law and you Pharisees. Hypocrites! For
you are so careful to clean the outside of the cup and the dish, but inside you are filthy—
full of greed and self-indulgence! 26You blind Pharisee! First wash the inside of the cup
and the dish,* and then the outside will become clean, too.
27“What sorrow awaits you teachers of religious law and you Pharisees. Hypocrites! For
you are like whitewashed tombs—beautiful on the outside but filled on the inside with
dead people’s bones and all sorts of impurity. 28Outwardly you look like righteous people,
but inwardly your hearts are filled with hypocrisy and lawlessness.
29“What sorrow awaits you teachers of religious law and you Pharisees. Hypocrites! For
you build tombs for the prophets your ancestors killed, and you decorate the monuments
of the godly people your ancestors destroyed. 30Then you say, ‘If we had lived in the days
of our ancestors, we would never have joined them in killing the prophets.’
31“But in saying that, you testify against yourselves that you are indeed the descen-
dants of those who murdered the prophets. 32Go ahead and finish what your ancestors
started. 33Snakes! Sons of vipers! How will you escape the judgment of hell?
34“Therefore, I am sending you prophets and wise men and teachers of religious law.
But you will kill some by crucifixion, and you will flog others with whips in your syna-
gogues, chasing them from city to city. 35As a result, you will be held responsible for the
murder of all godly people of all time—from the murder of righteous Abel to the murder of
Zechariah son of Barachiah, whom you killed in the Temple between the sanctuary and
the altar. 36I tell you the truth, this judgment will fall on this very generation.

JESUS GRIEVES OVER JERUSALEM

37“O Jerusalem, Jerusalem, the city that kills the prophets and stones God’s messengers!
How often I have wanted to gather your children together as a hen protects her chicks be-
neath her wings, but you wouldn’t let Me. 38And now, look, your house is abandoned and
desolate.* 39For I tell you this, you will never see Me again until you say, ‘Blessings on the
One who comes in the name of the LORD!’*”

JESUS FORETELLS THE FUTURE

24 As Jesus was leaving the Temple grounds, His disciples pointed out to Him the
various Temple buildings. 2But He responded, “Do you see all these buildings? I
tell you the truth, they will be completely demolished. Not one stone will be left on top of
another!”
3Later, Jesus sat on the Mount of Olives. His disciples came to Him privately and said,

23:25 Mark 7:4
23:27 Luke 11:44; Acts 23:3
23:28 Luke 16:15
23:31 Acts 7:52
23:33 Matt 3:7; 12:34; Luke 3:7
23:34 Matt 10:23; Acts 7:52; 22:19; 2 Cor 11:23-25; 1 Thes 2:15
23:35 Gen 4:8; 2 Chr 24:20-21; Zech 1:1; Heb 11:4
23:37-39 //Luke 13:34-35
23:38 1 Kgs 9:7-8; Jer 12:7; 22:5; Ezek 10:4, 18-19
23:39 *Ps 118:26; Matt 21:9; Mark 11:10; Luke 19:38
24:1-35 //Mark 13:1-31; //Luke 21:5-36
24:2 Luke 19:44
24:3 Matt 13:39; 28:20; Luke 17:30

23:26 Some manuscripts do not include *and the dish.* 23:38 Some manuscripts do not include *and desolate.* 23:39 Ps 118:26.

▸ HOLINESS
23:25-26 Holiness starts in the heart. People use many standards to measure themselves. Most everyone wants to look attractive or powerful—and to appear humble and sincere at the same time. Often these outward appearances are wrongly used to measure spiritual vitality. True spirituality is not about how things look on the outside. True spirituality, true holiness, is about the inside—what’s in the heart (Acts 15:9; Hebrews 10:22). As you cultivate the spiritual growth of those under your care, make sure you do not focus on mere externals but focus primarily on things that will affect the heart, the attitude, and the spirit—the internal world. If that can be surrendered to God, then the outer behavior will follow. (***See Holiness****> Submission> Yielding to Spirit> Surrender your heart,* TopicGuide page A41.)

23:27 The Old Testament taught that those who were in direct contact with dead bodies or objects connected to those dead bodies were unclean for 7 days (Numbers 19:11-22). In an effort to guard against this defilement, Jews of Jesus’ time went further by also claiming that touching a tombstone or the exterior of a tomb made one defiled for a certain period of time. Tombs were coated with whitewash (a simple paint traditionally made from lime, chalk, and hot water) to beautify them. The comparison Jesus made to the religious leaders is chilling—like the tombs, they were clean on the outside, but inside they were filled with decaying flesh that truly defiled people.

24:1-3 After Jesus’ startling words about the future destruction of the Temple in Jerusalem, the disciples came to Him with two specific questions: 1) When would the destruction of the Temple take place? 2) What would be the signs of His return? Jesus’ reply is called “The Olivet Discourse,” and condensed versions of it appear in Luke 21 and Mark 13.

"Tell us, when will all this happen? What sign will signal Your return and the end of the
world?*"
4 Jesus told them, "Don't let anyone mislead you, 5 for many will come in My name,
claiming, 'I am the Messiah.' They will deceive many. 6 And you will hear of wars and
threats of wars, but don't panic. Yes, these things must take place, but the end won't follow
immediately. 7 Nation will go to war against nation, and kingdom against kingdom. There
will be famines and earthquakes in many parts of the world. 8 But all this is only the first of
the birth pains, with more to come.
9 "Then you will be arrested, persecuted, and killed. You will be hated all over the world
because you are My followers.* 10 And many will turn away from Me and betray and hate
each other. 11 And many false prophets will appear and will deceive many people. 12 Sin
will be rampant everywhere, and the love of many will grow cold. 13 But the one who en-
dures to the end will be saved. 14 And the Good News about the Kingdom will be preached
throughout the whole world, so that all nations* will hear it; and then the end will come.
15 "The day is coming when you will see what Daniel the prophet spoke about—the sac-
rilegious object that causes desecration* standing in the Holy Place." (Reader, pay atten-
tion!) 16 "Then those in Judea must flee to the hills. 17 A person out on the deck of a roof
must not go down into the house to pack. 18 A person out in the field must not return even
to get a coat. 19 How terrible it will be for pregnant women and for nursing mothers in
those days. 20 And pray that your flight will not be in winter or on the Sabbath. 21 For there
will be greater anguish than at any time since the world began. And it will never be so
great again. 22 In fact, unless that time of calamity is shortened, not a single person will sur-
vive. But it will be shortened for the sake of God's chosen ones.
23 "Then if anyone tells you, 'Look, here is the Messiah,' or 'There he is,' don't believe it.
24 For false messiahs and false prophets will rise up and perform great signs and wonders
so as to deceive, if possible, even God's chosen ones. 25 See, I have warned you about this
ahead of time.
26 "So if someone tells you, 'Look, the Messiah is out in the desert,' don't bother to go and
look. Or, 'Look, he is hiding here,' don't believe it! 27 For as the lightning flashes in the east
and shines to the west, so it will be when the Son of Man* comes. 28 Just as the gathering of
vultures shows there is a carcass nearby, so these signs indicate that the end is near.*

24:4 Mark 13:5
24:5 Matt 24:11, 23-24; John 5:43; 1 Jn 2:18
24:6 Dan 2:28-29
24:7 Isa 19:2
24:9-14 Matt 10:17-22
24:9 John 16:2
24:11 Matt 24:5, 24
24:14 Matt 28:19; Rev 3:10; 16:14
24:15 Dan 9:27; 11:31; 12:11
24:17 Luke 17:31
24:21 Dan 12:1; Joel 2:2; Rev 3:10; 7:14
24:23-24 Luke 17:21-23; 2 Thes 2:9-10; 1 Jn 4:1-3; Rev 13:13-14
24:26-27 Luke 17:23-24
24:28 Luke 17:37; Rev 19:17

24:3 Or *the age?* 24:9 Greek *on account of My name.* 24:14 Or *all peoples.* 24:15 Greek *the abomination of desolation.* See Dan 9:27; 11:31; 12:11. 24:27 "Son of Man" is a title Jesus used for Himself. 24:28 Greek *Wherever the carcass is, the vultures gather.*

▶ BIBLE
24:4-6 Final instructions. Jesus had been talking about His future return and had told His followers about some of the things that lay ahead. His comments made them curious, and they asked for more details about what "the end" would be like. Jesus repeatedly stressed two dangers: spiritual deception (24:4-8) and persecution (24:9-22). Since Jesus' words were spoken, Satan has used these twin terrors to break down the resolve of God's people and raise havoc in the church. Chaos on an international scale remains high (24:7), but through it all, God's people have been instructed in only a few things—don't panic (24:6), endure to the very end (24:13), and preach the gospel to the whole world (24:14). (***See Bible****> Power> Convict> Cuts through deception,* TopicGuide page A11.)

▶ CHURCH
24:14 God's Kingdom is spreading. It began on a strip of land along the eastern shore of the Mediterranean Sea. From there it spread north around the sea and into the heart of the Roman world. And it has since been gradually permeating all the nations, peoples, cultures, and countries of the world. Jesus' followers are involved in taking the Good News of His Kingdom to all peoples everywhere. It has always been God's desire (Psalm 67:4), and He will see it accomplished before He returns. How can you be more involved in bringing the gospel to the nations? Find more ways to participate in this great privilege. (***See Church****> Mission> Establish> The gospel of Christ is Kingdom-oriented,* TopicGuide page A49.)

24:15 The reference to "the sacrilegious object" came from prophecies in the book of Daniel about what would happen in the "last days" (Daniel 9:27; 11:31; 12:11). Wherever religious sacrilege has taken place, God's people have wondered if this was the fulfillment of this prophecy. But "the sacrilegious object" should likely be read more literally as the "abomination that causes desolation." The abominable siege of Jerusalem resulted in its being left desolate (Jeremiah 12:7; 22:5). This corresponds to Jesus' teaching in Luke 21:20 and with Daniel 8:13, wherein scriptures predict that rebelliousness of God's covenant people resulted in the desolation of the Temple. According to Jesus' prelude to the Olivet Discourse, in some sense the desolation of Jerusalem had already begun (23:38) due to apostasy.

[29] "Immediately after the anguish of those days,

the sun will be darkened,
  the moon will give no light,
the stars will fall from the sky,
  and the powers in the heavens will be shaken.*

[30] And then at last, the sign that the Son of Man is coming will appear in the heavens, and
there will be deep mourning among all the peoples of the earth. And they will see the Son
of Man coming on the clouds of heaven with power and great glory.* [31] And He will send
out His angels with the mighty blast of a trumpet, and they will gather His chosen ones
from all over the world*—from the farthest ends of the earth and heaven.

[32] "Now learn a lesson from the fig tree. When its branches bud and its leaves begin to
sprout, you know that summer is near. [33] In the same way, when you see all these things,
you can know His return is very near, right at the door. [34] I tell you the truth, this genera-
tion* will not pass from the scene until all these things take place. [35] Heaven and earth will
disappear, but My words will never disappear.

[36] "However, no one knows the day or hour when these things will happen, not even the
angels in heaven or the Son Himself.* Only the Father knows.

[37] "When the Son of Man returns, it will be like it was in Noah's day. [38] In those days be-
fore the flood, the people were enjoying banquets and parties and weddings right up to the
time Noah entered his boat. [39] People didn't realize what was going to happen until the
flood came and swept them all away. That is the way it will be when the Son of Man comes.

[40] "Two men will be working together in the field; one will be taken, the other left. [41] Two
women will be grinding flour at the mill; one will be taken, the other left.

[42] "So you, too, must keep watch! For you don't know what day your Lord is coming.
[43] Understand this: If a homeowner knew exactly when a burglar was coming, he would
keep watch and not permit his house to be broken into. [44] You also must be ready all the
time, for the Son of Man will come when least expected.

[45] "A faithful, sensible servant is one to whom the master can give the responsibility of
managing his other household servants and feeding them. [46] If the master returns and
finds that the servant has done a good job, there will be a reward. [47] I tell you the truth, the
master will put that servant in charge of all he owns. [48] But what if the servant is evil and

24:29 Isa 13:10; 34:4 Ezek 32:7 Joel 2:10, 31; 3:15 Rev 6:12-13
24:30 *Dan 7:13 Zech 12:10-14 Rev 1:7
24:31 1 Cor 15:52 1 Thes 4:16 Rev 8:2; 11:15
24:33 Jas 5:9
24:34 Matt 16:28
24:35 Matt 5:18 Luke 16:17
24:36 Acts 1:7 1 Thes 5:1-2
24:37-39 Gen 6:9–7:24 //Luke 17:26-27
24:40-41 Luke 17:34-35
24:42 Matt 25:13 Luke 12:40 1 Thes 5:6 Rev 3:3; 16:15
24:45-51 //Luke 12:41-48

24:29 See Isa 13:10; 34:4; Joel 2:10. **24:30** See Dan 7:13. **24:31** Greek *from the four winds.* **24:34** Or *this age,* or *this nation.* **24:36** Some manuscripts do not include *or the Son Himself.*

▸ WORSHIP

24:30-31 Jesus will return. When the head of state enters a hall for an official function, everyone knows it. Attention is drawn to him as he takes his proper seat; his presence is announced, and all in attendance are aware that the business at hand can now begin. That is what it will be like when Jesus returns. Whether every person on the planet will see it or not is beside the point—no one will mistake this person for another charlatan (24:24, 27). Everyone who sees His arrival will know that life on earth will be forever altered. In that moment, our faith will instantly be converted to sight (John 20:24-28), for everything we have believed about Jesus will be finally and completely demonstrated as true. Get ready for that day as if it were tomorrow. (***See Worship****> NT> Christ's Kingship> Jesus shall return as King and Judge,* TopicGuide page A30.)

24:33-34 Jesus' assertion that "this generation will not pass from the scene until all these things take place" has been understood and interpreted in myriad ways, each with their own strengths and weaknesses. "This generation" could mean "this race" or "this kind of people," but it is more likely to mean the people who were alive when Jesus spoke. "All these things" refers to all the birth pangs (24:8) and signs that would lead up to the greatest birth pang of all—the siege and fall of Jerusalem, which happened in AD 70. But an unknown length of time follows the trials Jesus mentioned and His return (Matthew 24:36-44), so we continue to wait for His coming.

24:36 In the humility of His incarnation (John 1:1), the Son of God laid aside some exercise of His divine knowledge. Jesus affirmed that there was at least one thing that the Father knew that He Himself did not know. Even with His knowledge of Scripture and full understanding of everything He had just said, He did not know the date of His return.

24:45 With this parable and the several illustrations from 24:36-50, Jesus gave the key points of His largest and most complex parables upcoming in 25:1-13, 14-30. The point of all these verses is that with the intentional uncertainty of Jesus' time of judgment, it is absolutely critical to maintain vigilance and discipline. This was particularly focused on Jews who had waited for a Messiah to come, yet were now turning away from Him.

thinks, 'My master won't be back for a while,' 49and he begins beating the other servants,
partying, and getting drunk? 50The master will return unannounced and unexpected,
24:51 51and he will cut the servant to pieces and assign him a place with the hypocrites. In that
Matt 8:12; 25:30 place there will be weeping and gnashing of teeth.

PARABLE OF THE TEN BRIDESMAIDS

25:1 **25** "Then the Kingdom of Heaven will be like ten bridesmaids* who took their lamps
Luke 12:35-38 and went to meet the bridegroom. 2Five of them were foolish, and five were
wise. 3The five who were foolish didn't take enough olive oil for their lamps, 4but the
25:5 other five were wise enough to take along extra oil. 5When the bridegroom was delayed,
1 Thes 5:6 they all became drowsy and fell asleep.
25:8 6"At midnight they were roused by the shout, 'Look, the bridegroom is coming! Come
Luke 12:35-40 out and meet him!'
7"All the bridesmaids got up and prepared their lamps. 8Then the five foolish ones
asked the others, 'Please give us some of your oil because our lamps are going out.'
9"But the others replied, 'We don't have enough for all of us. Go to a shop and buy some
for yourselves.'
25:10 Luke 13:24-25 10"But while they were gone to buy oil, the bridegroom came. Then those who were
Rev 19:9 ready went in with him to the marriage feast, and the door was locked. 11Later, when the
other five bridesmaids returned, they stood outside, calling, 'Lord! Lord! Open the door
for us!'
12"But he called back, 'Believe me, I don't know you!'
25:13 Matt 24:42, 44 13"So you, too, must keep watch! For you do not know the day or hour of My return.
Mark 13:35
Luke 12:40

PARABLE OF THE THREE SERVANTS

25:14-30 14"Again, the Kingdom of Heaven can be illustrated by the story of a man going on a long
//Luke 19:11-27 trip. He called together his servants and entrusted his money to them while he was gone.
25:15 Matt 18:24-25 15He gave five bags of silver* to one, two bags of silver to another, and one bag of silver to
Rom 12:3, 6 the last—dividing it in proportion to their abilities. He then left on his trip.
16"The servant who received the five bags of silver began to invest the money and
earned five more. 17The servant with two bags of silver also went to work and earned two
more. 18But the servant who received the one bag of silver dug a hole in the ground and
hid the master's money.
25:19 19"After a long time their master returned from his trip and called them to give an ac-
Matt 18:23 count of how they had used his money. 20The servant to whom he had entrusted the five
bags of silver came forward with five more and said, 'Master, you gave me five bags of sil-
ver to invest, and I have earned five more.'

25:1 Or *virgins;* also in 25:7, 11. 25:15 Greek *talents;* also throughout the story. A talent is equal to 75 pounds or 34 kilograms.

25:1-13 In Bible times, the bride and groom did not make their way individually to a common place for the wedding. Instead, the bridegroom would journey to the home of the bride and escort her, in grand style, back to his home for the wedding festivities.

▸ CHURCH
25:1-13 Get ready! You have been invited! A celebration has been planned. It will be a wonderful and joyful gathering. What should you do to prepare as the time for the celebration draws near? What plans should you alter? What details should you attend to? Would it not be reasonable to be at least as attentive and prepared as we anticipate the arrival of our Lord and Savior, who might return when we least expect Him? We make plans when we are invited to earthly affairs, but what preparations should we make to ready ourselves for meeting Jesus? Make sure you and those who are under your care are prepared for that remarkable day. (***See Church****> What> Many Titles> Bride> Who joyfully awaits the wedding day,* TopicGuide page A48.)

▸ HOLINESS
25:14-30 Faithful to the Master. It is easy to compare ourselves to others. We look at what we are doing in Jesus' Kingdom, and we notice what others are doing as well. We compare effort, impact, results, and perceived significance. But in this parable, Jesus shows us that ministry is not evaluated on the basis of results—notice the obedient servants had vastly different results from one another. He looks for faithfulness. Leave the results up to Him and spread the good news of the gospel wherever you can. (***See Holiness****> Submission> Trusting God> Faithfulness,* TopicGuide page A41.)

21 "The master was full of praise. 'Well done, my good and faithful servant. You have
been faithful in handling this small amount, so now I will give you many more responsibil-
ities. Let's celebrate together!'*
22 "The servant who had received the two bags of silver came forward and said, 'Master,
you gave me two bags of silver to invest, and I have earned two more.'
23 "The master said, 'Well done, my good and faithful servant. You have been faithful in
handling this small amount, so now I will give you many more responsibilities. Let's cele-
brate together!'
24 "Then the servant with the one bag of silver came and said, 'Master, I knew you were a
harsh man, harvesting crops you didn't plant and gathering crops you didn't cultivate. 25 I
was afraid I would lose your money, so I hid it in the earth. Look, here is your money back.'
26 "But the master replied, 'You wicked and lazy servant! If you knew I harvested crops I
didn't plant and gathered crops I didn't cultivate, 27 why didn't you deposit my money in
the bank? At least I could have gotten some interest on it.'
28 "Then he ordered, 'Take the money from this servant, and give it to the one with the
ten bags of silver. 29 To those who use well what they are given, even more will be given,
and they will have an abundance. But from those who do nothing, even what little they
have will be taken away. 30 Now throw this useless servant into outer darkness, where
there will be weeping and gnashing of teeth.'

THE FINAL JUDGMENT

31 "But when the Son of Man* comes in His glory, and all the angels with Him, then He will
sit upon His glorious throne. 32 All the nations* will be gathered in His presence, and He will
separate the people as a shepherd separates the sheep from the goats. 33 He will place the
sheep at His right hand and the goats at His left.
34 "Then the King will say to those on His right, 'Come, you who are blessed by My Fa-
ther, inherit the Kingdom prepared for you from the creation of the world. 35 For I was hun-
gry, and you fed Me. I was thirsty, and you gave Me a drink. I was a stranger, and you
invited Me into your home. 36 I was naked, and you gave Me clothing. I was sick, and you
cared for Me. I was in prison, and you visited Me.'
37 "Then these righteous ones will reply, 'Lord, when did we ever see You hungry and
feed You? Or thirsty and give You something to drink? 38 Or a stranger and show You hos-
pitality? Or naked and give You clothing? 39 When did we ever see You sick or in prison
and visit You?'
40 "And the King will say, 'I tell you the truth, when you did it to one of the least of these
My brothers and sisters,* you were doing it to Me!'
41 "Then the King will turn to those on the left and say, 'Away with you, you cursed ones,
into the eternal fire prepared for the devil and his demons.* 42 For I was hungry, and you

25:21 Matt 24:45-46; Luke 16:10
25:29 Matt 13:12; Mark 4:25; Luke 8:18
25:30 Matt 8:12; Luke 13:28
25:31 Deut 33:2; Dan 7:13; Zech 14:5; Matt 19:28; Acts 1:11; 1 Thes 4:16; 2 Thes 1:7; Rev 20:11
25:32 Ezek 34:17, 20; Rev 20:12
25:33 Luke 12:32
25:34 Luke 22:30; 1 Cor 15:50; Gal 5:21
25:35-36 Job 31:32; Isa 58:7; Heb 13:3; Jas 2:15-16
25:40 Prov 19:17; Matt 10:40, 42
25:41 Matt 7:23; Mark 9:48; 2 Pet 2:4; Jude 1:7; Rev 20:10

25:21 Greek *Enter into the joy of your master* [or *your Lord*]; also in 25:23. **25:31** "Son of Man" is a title Jesus used for Himself. **25:32** Or *peoples.* **25:40** Greek *My brothers.* **25:41** Greek *his angels.*

25:18 Jesus described the servant who hid his master's money as fearful, wicked, and lazy (25:25-26). Generally speaking, this describes all those who steal from their employers, but it is a particularly pointed warning for those who sin against God.

25:31-32 Jesus' description here of His own return and rule is reminiscent of Daniel's vision of the judgment that would come in the last days (see Daniel 7:13-14).

▸ WORSHIP

25:31-46 Being Jesus. Jesus' commission to His followers is quite clear: We are to "make disciples" of all people (28:19-20). We are to address their spiritual needs. But as primary as that call is, we cannot overlook what else is on Jesus' heart—that we show love for others by meeting their physical needs, just as if it were Jesus we were helping. We cannot minister simply to people's spiritual needs; our call is to minister to others regarding *all* their needs. Look around you, your community, and your neighborhood—what do people need that you are strategically placed to provide? Look into their eyes and see Jesus—then ask yourself how much you can do to help. (***See Worship***> *NT> Sacrificial Living> Enables us to help meet others' needs,* TopicGuide page A34.)

didn't feed Me. I was thirsty, and you didn't give Me a drink. 43 I was a stranger, and you
didn't invite Me into your home. I was naked, and you didn't give Me clothing. I was sick
and in prison, and you didn't visit Me.'

44 "Then they will reply, 'Lord, when did we ever see You hungry or thirsty or a stranger
or naked or sick or in prison, and not help You?'

25:45 Prov 14:31; 17:5

45 "And He will answer, 'I tell you the truth, when you refused to help the least of these
My brothers and sisters, you were refusing to help Me.'

25:46 Dan 12:2; John 3:15, 36; 5:29; Acts 13:46-48; Rom 2:7-8; Gal 6:8

46 "And they will go away into eternal punishment, but the righteous will go into eternal
life."

THE PLOT TO KILL JESUS

26:1-5 //Mark 14:1-2; //Luke 22:1-2; John 11:45-53

26:2 Exod 12:1-27; Matt 20:18-19; 27:26; Mark 15:15; Luke 24:7, 20; John 19:16

26:3 Ps 2:2; John 11:47-53; Acts 4:6

26 When Jesus had finished saying all these things, He said to His disciples, 2 "As
you know, Passover begins in two days, and the Son of Man* will be handed over
to be crucified."

3 At that same time the leading priests and elders were meeting at the residence of Caia-
phas, the high priest, 4 plotting how to capture Jesus secretly and kill Him. 5 "But not during
the Passover celebration," they agreed, "or the people may riot."

JESUS ANOINTED AT BETHANY

26:6-13 //Mark 14:3-9; //John 12:1-8

26:11 Deut 15:11

6 Meanwhile, Jesus was in Bethany at the home of Simon, a man who had previously had
leprosy. 7 While He was eating,* a woman came in with a beautiful alabaster jar of expen-
sive perfume and poured it over His head.

8 The disciples were indignant when they saw this. "What a waste!" they said. 9 "It could
have been sold for a high price and the money given to the poor."

10 But Jesus, aware of this, replied, "Why criticize this woman for doing such a good
thing to Me? 11 You will always have the poor among you, but you will not always have
Me. 12 She has poured this perfume on Me to prepare My body for burial. 13 I tell you the
truth, wherever the Good News is preached throughout the world, this woman's deed will
be remembered and discussed."

JUDAS AGREES TO BETRAY JESUS

26:14-16 //Mark 14:10-11; //Luke 22:3-6; John 11:57

26:15 Exod 21:32; Zech 11:12

14 Then Judas Iscariot, one of the twelve disciples, went to the leading priests 15 and asked,
"How much will you pay me to betray Jesus to you?" And they gave him thirty pieces of sil-
ver. 16 From that time on, Judas began looking for an opportunity to betray Jesus.

THE LAST SUPPER

26:17-30 //Mark 14:12-26; //Luke 22:7-14, 22-23; //John 13:21-30

26:17 Exod 12:18-20; Deut 16:5-8

17 On the first day of the Festival of Unleavened Bread, the disciples came to Jesus and
asked, "Where do You want us to prepare the Passover meal for You?"

18 "As you go into the city," He told them, "you will see a certain man. Tell him, 'The
Teacher says: My time has come, and I will eat the Passover meal with My disciples at your
house.'" 19 So the disciples did as Jesus told them and prepared the Passover meal there.

26:2 "Son of Man" is a title Jesus used for Himself. 26:7 Or *reclining.*

26:1-2 The Passover feast began a weeklong celebration known as the Festival of Unleavened Bread that commemorated the deliverance of God's people from their bondage in Egypt (Exodus 12:1-20).

▶ WORSHIP

26:6-13 We give our best. What would you sacrifice to let Jesus know of your love for Him? How would you express yourself in worship even if others might notice? In these verses a woman came before Jesus and poured out her love for Him in an extravagant way. Some people present were concerned. Wasn't that a waste? Wasn't that too much? Jesus didn't think so. Pour yourself out in worship—give every drop of yourself to Jesus. (***See Worship***> *NT> Our Role> Mind and Heart> Fervent in Spirit,* TopicGuide page A32.)

26:17-19 The Passover meal was to be celebrated as a family in a home. Those who had traveled to Jerusalem to celebrate the feast would either join with their extended families in the city or find an available room in which they could enjoy the meal.

20When it was evening, Jesus sat down at the table* with the twelve disciples.* 21While
they were eating, He said, "I tell you the truth, one of you will betray Me."

22Greatly distressed, each one asked in turn, "Am I the one, Lord?"

23He replied, "One of you who has just eaten from this bowl with Me will betray Me. 24For
the Son of Man must die, as the Scriptures declared long ago. But how terrible it will be for
the one who betrays Him. It would be far better for that man if he had never been born!"

25Judas, the one who would betray Him, also asked, "Rabbi, am I the one?"

And Jesus told Him, "You have said it."

26As they were eating, Jesus took some bread and blessed it. Then He broke it in pieces
and gave it to the disciples, saying, "Take this and eat it, for this is My body."

27And He took a cup of wine and gave thanks to God for it. He gave it to them and said,
"Each of you drink from it, 28for this is My blood, which confirms the covenant* between
God and His people. It is poured out as a sacrifice to forgive the sins of many. 29Mark My
words—I will not drink wine again until the day I drink it new with you in My Father's
Kingdom."

30Then they sang a hymn and went out to the Mount of Olives.

JESUS PREDICTS PETER'S DENIAL

31On the way, Jesus told them, "Tonight all of you will desert Me. For the Scriptures say,

'God will strike* the Shepherd,
and the sheep of the flock will be scattered.'

26:23 Ps 41:9
26:24 Ps 22:7-8, 16-18; Isa 53:8-9; Luke 24:25-27, 46; 1 Pet 1:10-11
26:28 Exod 24:8; Jer 31:31; Zech 9:11; Heb 9:20
26:29 Acts 10:41
26:30 Pss 113–118
26:31-35 //Mark 14:27-31; //Luke 22:31-34; //John 13:36-38
26:31 *Zech 13:7; John 16:32

26:20a Or *Jesus reclined.* 26:20b Some manuscripts read *the Twelve.* 26:28 Some manuscripts read *the new covenant.* 26:31 Greek *I will strike.* Zech 13:7.

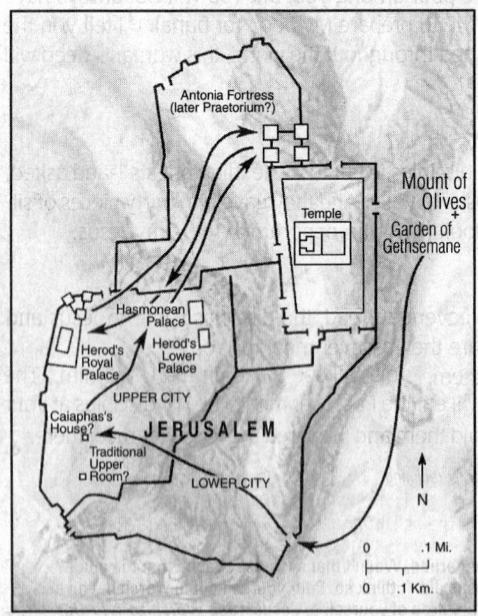

JESUS' TRIAL
After Judas singled Jesus out for arrest, the mob took Jesus first to Caiaphas, the high priest. This trial, a mockery of justice, ended at daybreak with their decision to kill Him; but the Jews needed Rome's permission for the death sentence. Jesus was taken to Pilate (who was probably in the Praetorium), then to Herod (Luke 23:5–12), and back to Pilate, who sentenced Him to die.

26:26-30 The Passover meal included very specific items of food that represented and reminded the Jewish people of God's deliverance so many years earlier. Jesus explained the New Covenant in the context of the Passover feast to bridge the connection between the Old and New Covenant. In that setting His words and actions would have had a tremendous impact on those seated with Him but an even greater significance after His death and resurrection.

▸ SALVATION
26:26-28 True sacrifice. The foundations of the Lord's Supper go all the way back to the Garden of Eden, when God provided food and clothing for Adam and Eve. But we directly trace it back to the time of Moses. Fourteen hundred years before Christ's birth, God's people were enslaved, trapped in Egypt. But God heard their cries and made a way for them to escape. To commemorate their rescue, God directed them to partake of the Passover. Through instituting the Lord's Supper in the context of the Passover, Jesus framed His sacrifice as a form of rescue, of redemption from slavery and from the wrath of God and the penalty of sin. Each time you partake of the Lord's Supper, think back to the Passover and forward to the great feast we will share with God's people in heaven (Matthew 8:11; 22:2; John 6:53-58). (***See Salvation**> Jesus' Work> Crucifixion> One sacrifice good for all time*, TopicGuide page A22.)

26:31-35 Jesus understood prophecy well enough to know that all His disciples would desert Him. Peter fell asleep when he should have been watching and praying (26:40), but it wasn't until the middle of the night that he fully revealed his weakness (26:74).

32But after I have been raised from the dead, I will go ahead of you to Galilee and meet
you there."
33Peter declared, "Even if everyone else deserts You, I will never desert You."
34Jesus replied, "I tell you the truth, Peter—this very night, before the rooster crows, you
will deny three times that you even know Me."
35"No!" Peter insisted. "Even if I have to die with You, I will never deny You!" And all the
other disciples vowed the same.

JESUS PRAYS IN GETHSEMANE

36Then Jesus went with them to the olive grove called Gethsemane, and He said, "Sit here
while I go over there to pray." 37He took Peter and Zebedee's two sons, James and John,
and He became anguished and distressed. 38He told them, "My soul is crushed with grief
to the point of death. Stay here and keep watch with Me."
39He went on a little farther and bowed with His face to the ground, praying, "My Father!
If it is possible, let this cup of suffering be taken away from Me. Yet I want Your will to be
done, not Mine."
40Then He returned to the disciples and found them asleep. He said to Peter, "Couldn't
you watch with Me even one hour? 41Keep watch and pray, so that you will not give in to
temptation. For the spirit is willing, but the body is weak!"
42Then Jesus left them a second time and prayed, "My Father! If this cup cannot be
taken away* unless I drink it, Your will be done." 43When He returned to them again, He
found them sleeping, for they couldn't keep their eyes open.
44So He went to pray a third time, saying the same things again. 45Then He came to the dis-
ciples and said, "Go ahead and sleep. Have your rest. But look—the time has come. The Son of
Man is betrayed into the hands of sinners. 46Up, let's be going. Look, My betrayer is here!"

JESUS IS BETRAYED AND ARRESTED

47And even as Jesus said this, Judas, one of the twelve disciples, arrived with a crowd of
men armed with swords and clubs. They had been sent by the leading priests and elders
of the people. 48The traitor, Judas, had given them a prearranged signal: "You will know
which one to arrest when I greet Him with a kiss." 49So Judas came straight to Jesus.
"Greetings, Rabbi!" he exclaimed and gave Him the kiss.
50Jesus said, "My friend, go ahead and do what you have come for."
Then the others grabbed Jesus and arrested Him. 51But one of the men with Jesus
pulled out his sword and struck the high priest's slave, slashing off his ear.
52"Put away your sword," Jesus told him. "Those who use the sword will die by the
sword. 53Don't you realize that I could ask My Father for thousands* of angels to protect
us, and He would send them instantly? 54But if I did, how would the Scriptures be fulfilled
that describe what must happen now?"
55Then Jesus said to the crowd, "Am I some dangerous revolutionary, that you come
with swords and clubs to arrest Me? Why didn't you arrest Me in the Temple? I was there
teaching every day. 56But this is all happening to fulfill the words of the prophets as re-
corded in the Scriptures." At that point, all the disciples deserted Him and fled.

26:32 Matt 28:7
26:34 Matt 26:69-75; Mark 14:66-72; Luke 22:56-62; John 18:25-27
26:35 John 13:37
26:36-46 //Mark 14:32-42; //Luke 22:40-46
26:36 John 18:1
26:38 *Pss 42:6; 43:5; John 12:27
26:39 Matt 20:22; John 5:30; 6:38; Heb 5:7-8
26:41 Matt 6:13
26:45 John 12:23-27; 13:1; 17:1
26:47-56 //Mark 14:43-50; //Luke 22:47-53; //John 18:3-11
26:53 2 Kgs 6:16-17; Ps 91:11; Dan 7:10
26:54 Ps 22:7-8, 16-18; Isa 53:8-9; Luke 24:25-27, 46; 1 Pet 1:10-11
26:55 Mark 12:35; Luke 21:37; John 7:14, 28; 18:20
26:56 Isa 53:7; Zech 13:7; Matt 26:31

26:42 Greek *If this cannot pass.* 26:53 Greek *twelve legions.*

26:36-46 Jesus faced His most distressing hours with prayer, but not the prayers the reader might expect of God in human flesh (John 1:1). Though Jesus was fully God, He was fully human, and it was during this time that He seemed most human and frail, displaying deep emotion (26:38), falling to the ground in mental anguish (26:39), and praying for relief from suffering. He also displayed the need for companionship (26:40) during this heartbreakingly painful time, but there was no one who could help Him. Jesus had to bear the burden of His sacrifice alone.

26:51 John 18:10 reveals that the man Peter struck was named "Malchus," the servant of the high priest. Legends about his conversion and ministry circulated in the early church, but no historical basis for these stories has been found.

JESUS BEFORE THE COUNCIL

57Then the people who had arrested Jesus led Him to the home of Caiaphas, the high
priest, where the teachers of religious law and the elders had gathered. 58Meanwhile, Pe-
ter followed Him at a distance and came to the high priest's courtyard. He went in and sat
with the guards and waited to see how it would all end.
59Inside, the leading priests and the entire high council* were trying to find witnesses
who would lie about Jesus, so they could put Him to death. 60But even though they found
many who agreed to give false witness, they could not use anyone's testimony. Finally,
two men came forward 61who declared, "This man said, 'I am able to destroy the Temple
of God and rebuild it in three days.'"
62Then the high priest stood up and said to Jesus, "Well, aren't You going to answer
these charges? What do You have to say for Yourself?" 63But Jesus remained silent. Then
the high priest said to Him, "I demand in the name of the living God—tell us if You are the
Messiah, the Son of God."
64Jesus replied, "You have said it. And in the future you will see the Son of Man seated
in the place of power at God's right hand* and coming on the clouds of heaven."*
65Then the high priest tore his clothing to show his horror and said, "Blasphemy! Why
do we need other witnesses? You have all heard His blasphemy. 66What is your verdict?"
"Guilty!" they shouted. "He deserves to die!"
67Then they began to spit in Jesus' face and beat Him with their fists. And some slapped
Him, 68jeering, "Prophesy to us, You Messiah! Who hit You that time?"

PETER DENIES JESUS

69Meanwhile, Peter was sitting outside in the courtyard. A servant girl came over and said
to him, "You were one of those with Jesus the Galilean."
70But Peter denied it in front of everyone. "I don't know what you're talking about," he
said.
71Later, out by the gate, another servant girl noticed him and said to those standing
around, "This man was with Jesus of Nazareth.*"
72Again Peter denied it, this time with an oath. "I don't even know the man," he said.
73A little later some of the other bystanders came over to Peter and said, "You must be
one of them; we can tell by your Galilean accent."
74Peter swore, "A curse on me if I'm lying—I don't know the man!" And immediately the
rooster crowed.
75Suddenly, Jesus' words flashed through Peter's mind: "Before the rooster crows, you
will deny three times that you even know Me." And he went away, weeping bitterly.

26:57-68 //Mark 14:53-65 //Luke 22:54-55, 63-71 //John 18:13-14, 19-24
26:58 Mark 14:66 Luke 22:55 John 18:15
26:60 Deut 19:15 Ps 27:12
26:61 Matt 27:40 John 2:19 Acts 6:14
26:63 Matt 16:16-18
26:64 Ps 110:1 *Dan 7:13 Matt 24:30 Rev 1:7
26:65-66 Lev 24:16 John 19:7
26:67 Isa 50:6; 53:5
26:69-75 //Mark 14:66-72 //Luke 22:55-62 //John 18:16-18, 25-27
26:75 Matt 26:34 Mark 14:30 Luke 22:34 John 13:38

26:59 Greek *the Sanhedrin.* 26:64a Greek *seated at the right hand of the power.* See Ps 110:1. 26:64b See Dan 7:13.
26:71 Or *Jesus the Nazarene.*

26:59 The "high council" was called the *Sanhedrin.* It was a group of 71 ruling Jewish men who had been granted authority by Rome to administrate Jewish religious affairs. The Sanhedrin consisted of the high priest, the elders (priests and wealthy laypeople), and the scribes (professional lawyers trained in Old Testament, theology, and jurisprudence). They figured prominently in the Gospels and again in the book of Acts (Acts 4:6; 5:21, 24-26; 22:5). Their power seems limited at some points (John 18:31) and rashly brandished at other times (Acts 7:54-60).

26:60-61 According to Old Testament law, judicial cases required more than one witness to corroborate any accusation against the defendant (Deuteronomy 17:6; 19:15).

▸GOD

26:69-75 Peter's sin paid for by Christ. There is no way around it—Peter took a huge step back in his relationship with Jesus when he denied to several witnesses that he even knew Jesus. We can rationalize what happened by talking about the pressure he was facing or by exploring the turmoil in his mind and heart as the One he had come to love and trust was hauled away to be put to death. But in the end Peter denied Jesus. But here's the good news: Jesus knew what would happen, and it didn't make Him reject Peter. That doesn't diminish the seriousness of what Peter did; it only means that what Peter did wasn't enough to ruin the relationship Jesus wanted with him. You have sinned—but have you ruined your relationship with Jesus? Peter would say no (John 21:15-17; 2 Peter 3:9). (***See God**> Relationship> God Enables> God accepts us through Christ,* TopicGuide page A14.)

27:1-2 **JUDAS HANGS HIMSELF**

Mark 15:1 **27** Very early in the morning the leading priests and the elders met again to lay
Luke 23:1-2 John 18:28 plans for putting Jesus to death. 2Then they bound Him, led Him away, and took
27:3 Him to Pilate, the Roman governor.
Matt 26:14-15 3When Judas, who had betrayed Him, realized that Jesus had been condemned to die,
he was filled with remorse. So he took the thirty pieces of silver back to the leading priests
and the elders. 4"I have sinned," he declared, "for I have betrayed an innocent man."
27:5-10 "What do we care?" they retorted. "That's your problem."
Acts 1:18-19 5Then Judas threw the silver coins down in the Temple and went out and hanged himself.
6The leading priests picked up the coins. "It wouldn't be right to put this money in the Tem-
ple treasury," they said, "since it was payment for murder."* 7After some discussion they finally
27:9-10 decided to buy the potter's field, and they made it into a cemetery for foreigners. 8That is why
*Jer 32:6-9 the field is still called the Field of Blood. 9This fulfilled the prophecy of Jeremiah that says,
*Zech 11:12-13
"They took* the thirty pieces of silver—
the price at which he was valued by the people of Israel,
10 and purchased the potter's field,
as the LORD directed."*

JESUS' TRIAL BEFORE PILATE

27:11-14 11Now Jesus was standing before Pilate, the Roman governor. "Are You the king of the
//Mark 15:2-5 Jews?" the governor asked Him.
//Luke 23:3-5 Jesus replied, "You have said it."
//John 18:33-38 12But when the leading priests and the elders made their accusations against Him, Jesus
27:12 Isa 53:7 remained silent. 13"Don't You hear all these charges they are bringing against You?" Pilate
Matt 26:63 demanded. 14But Jesus made no response to any of the charges, much to the governor's
John 19:9 1 Pet 2:22 surprise.
27:14 15Now it was the governor's custom each year during the Passover celebration to re-
Mark 14:61 lease one prisoner to the crowd—anyone they wanted. 16This year there was a notorious
27:15-26 prisoner, a man named Barabbas.* 17As the crowds gathered before Pilate's house that
//Mark 15:6-15 morning, he asked them, "Which one do you want me to release to you—Barabbas, or
//Luke 23:13-25 //John 18:39–19:16 Jesus who is called the Messiah?" 18(He knew very well that the religious leaders had ar-
rested Jesus out of envy.)
19Just then, as Pilate was sitting on the judgment seat, his wife sent him this message:
27:19 Job 33:14-16 "Leave that innocent man alone. I suffered through a terrible nightmare about Him last night."
27:20 20Meanwhile, the leading priests and the elders persuaded the crowd to ask for Barab-
Acts 3:14 bas to be released and for Jesus to be put to death. 21So the governor asked again, "Which
of these two do you want me to release to you?"
The crowd shouted back, "Barabbas!"
27:22 22Pilate responded, "Then what should I do with Jesus who is called the Messiah?"
Matt 1:16 They shouted back, "Crucify Him!"

27:6 Greek *since it is the price for blood.* 27:9 Or *I took.* 27:9-10 Greek *as the LORD directed me.* Zech 11:12-13; Jer 32:6-9.
27:16 Some manuscripts read *Jesus Barabbas;* also in 27:17.

27:1 The high council had limited governing authority when it came to Jewish affairs. History shows that the Romans retained the power to take a life on some occasions but clearly didn't in others (Acts 7:54-60). Thus, the religious leaders needed a delicate way to make certain they could carry out their desire to put Jesus to death. This was one reason for the civil trial of Jesus.

27:6 No Mosaic law prohibited accepting money rooted in illegal activities, but this was another traditional law put into place to guard Moses' laws from being broken. The priests believed that Judas, by His betrayal, bore the greatest responsibility for killing Jesus, thus they could not accept the silver into the Temple treasury.

27:19 Matthew records that Pilate's wife, known in history as Claudia Procula, was warned in a dream not to harm Jesus. This ironic detail is included by Matthew to further illustrate that if a non-Christian Roman woman could have mercy on Jesus, then surely His own people should have treated Him with respect.

23"Why?" Pilate demanded. "What crime has He committed?"
But the mob roared even louder, "Crucify Him!"
24Pilate saw that he wasn't getting anywhere and that a riot was developing. So he sent
for a bowl of water and washed his hands before the crowd, saying, "I am innocent of this
man's blood. The responsibility is yours!"
25And all the people yelled back, "We will take responsibility for His death—we and our
children!"*
26So Pilate released Barabbas to them. He ordered Jesus flogged with a lead-tipped
whip, then turned Him over to the Roman soldiers to be crucified.

THE SOLDIERS MOCK JESUS

27Some of the governor's soldiers took Jesus into their headquarters* and called out the
entire regiment. 28They stripped Him and put a scarlet robe on Him. 29They wove thorn
branches into a crown and put it on His head, and they placed a reed stick in His right hand
as a scepter. Then they knelt before Him in mockery and taunted, "Hail! King of the Jews!"
30And they spit on Him and grabbed the stick and struck Him on the head with it. 31When
they were finally tired of mocking Him, they took off the robe and put His own clothes on
Him again. Then they led Him away to be crucified.

THE CRUCIFIXION

32Along the way, they came across a man named Simon, who was from Cyrene,* and the
soldiers forced him to carry Jesus' cross. 33And they went out to a place called Golgotha
(which means "Place of the Skull"). 34The soldiers gave Him wine mixed with bitter gall, but
when He had tasted it, He refused to drink it.
35After they had nailed Him to the cross, the soldiers gambled for His clothes by throw-
ing dice.* 36Then they sat around and kept guard as He hung there. 37A sign was fastened
to the cross above Jesus' head, announcing the charge against Him. It read: "This is Jesus,
the King of the Jews." 38Two revolutionaries* were crucified with Him, one on His right and
one on His left.
39The people passing by shouted abuse, shaking their heads in mockery. 40"Look at
You now!" they yelled at Him. "You said You were going to destroy the Temple and re-
build it in three days. Well then, if You are the Son of God, save Yourself and come down
from the cross!"
41The leading priests, the teachers of religious law, and the elders also mocked Jesus.
42"He saved others," they scoffed, "but He can't save Himself! So He is the King of Israel, is
He? Let Him come down from the cross right now, and we will believe in Him! 43He
trusted God, so let God rescue Him now if He wants Him! For He said, 'I am the Son of

27:24 Deut 21:5-9; Ps 26:6
27:25 Acts 5:28
27:26 Isa 53:5; John 19:1
27:27-31 //Mark 15:16-20; John 18:28, 33; 19:2-3
27:29 Ps 22:8; Isa 53:3; John 19:2-3
27:30 Isa 50:6
27:31 Isa 53:7
27:32-44 //Mark 15:21-32; //Luke 23:26-43; //John 19:17-24
27:34 Ps 69:21
27:35 *Ps 22:18
27:38 Isa 53:12
27:39 Pss 22:7; 109:25; Lam 2:15
27:40 Matt 26:61; John 2:19-20

27:25 Greek *"His blood be on us and on our children."* 27:27 Or *into the Praetorium.* 27:32 *Cyrene* was a city in northern Africa. 27:35 Greek *by casting lots.* A few late manuscripts add *This fulfilled the word of the prophet: "They divided My garments among themselves and cast lots for My robe."* See Ps 22:18. 27:38 Or *criminals;* also in 27:44.

27:32-33 Crucifixion was a public punishment. Typically, the Roman government executed those accused of capital crimes in full view of the populace in order to deter others from committing the same crimes.

▸ WORSHIP
27:34 Facing death. One might overlook Matthew's comment about the "drink" offered to Jesus as He hung on the cross: spiced wine ("bitter gall"). The spiced wine given to those being crucified was intended to dull their senses; it was a drug to enable them to die more quickly—and quietly. But Jesus refused it (Luke 22:18). Jesus offered His life; it wasn't taken from Him. He faced death, embraced it, and conquered it. And He did it for you. As you struggle with the difficulties of living a mature Christian life, as you fight temptation, remember—Jesus died for you. That is all that matters. (***See Worship****> NT> Christ's Supremacy> Christ willingly provided a sacrifice,* TopicGuide page A29.)

27:37 Since crucifixion was a public form of execution, the charge against the person being executed typically was posted on the cross for all to see.

▸ MINISTRY
27:43, 63 The hardest heart. As a follower of Jesus, you will have the opportunity to share with others the Good News that is found in Him. As you share, you will undoubtedly encounter people who refuse to listen. But notice something about those who gathered around the cross—even Jesus' enemies: Perhaps they remembered some of what He had said and

God.' " 44Even the revolutionaries who were crucified with Him ridiculed Him in the
same way.

27:45-56 //Mark 15:33-41
THE DEATH OF JESUS
//Luke 23:44-49 45At noon, darkness fell across the whole land until three o'clock. 46At about three o'clock,
//John 19:28-37 Jesus called out with a loud voice, *"Eli, Eli,* lema sabachthani?"* which means "My God, My
27:45 God, why have You abandoned Me?"*
Amos 8:9 47Some of the bystanders misunderstood and thought He was calling for the prophet
27:46 *Ps 22:1 Elijah. 48One of them ran and filled a sponge with sour wine, holding it up to Him on a reed
stick so He could drink. 49But the rest said, "Wait! Let's see whether Elijah comes to save
27:48 Ps 69:21 Him."*
John 19:29-30 50Then Jesus shouted out again, and He released His spirit. 51At that moment the curtain
27:51 in the sanctuary of the Temple was torn in two, from top to bottom. The earth shook, rocks
Exod 26:31-33 split apart, 52and tombs opened. The bodies of many godly men and women who had
Heb 10:19-20 died were raised from the dead. 53They left the cemetery after Jesus' resurrection, went
27:52 Ezek 37:12 into the holy city of Jerusalem, and appeared to many people.
54The Roman officer* and the other soldiers at the crucifixion were terrified by the earth-
27:55-56 quake and all that had happened. They said, "This man truly was the Son of God!"
Luke 8:2-3 55And many women who had come from Galilee with Jesus to care for Him were watch-
ing from a distance. 56Among them were Mary Magdalene, Mary (the mother of James
and Joseph), and the mother of James and John, the sons of Zebedee.

27:46a Some manuscripts read *Eloi, Eloi.* **27:46b** Ps 22:1. **27:49** Some manuscripts add *And another took a spear and pierced His side, and out flowed water and blood.* Compare John 19:34. **27:54** Greek *The centurion.*

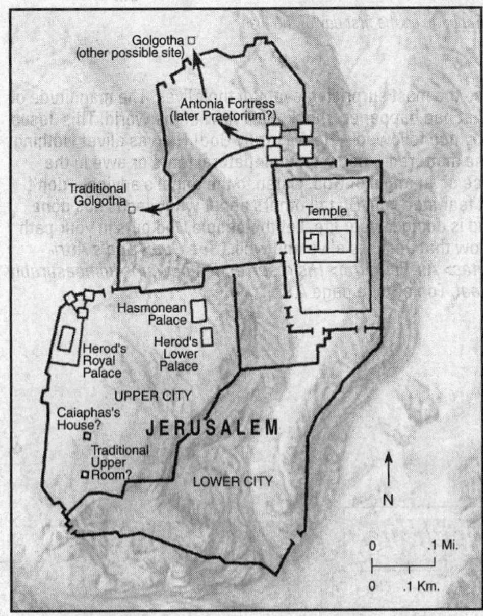

THE WAY OF THE CROSS
The Roman soldiers took Jesus into their headquarters at the Praetorium and mocked Him, dressing Him in a scarlet robe and a crown of thorns. They then led Him to the crucifixion site outside the city. He was so weakened by His beatings that He could not carry His cross, and a man from Cyrene was forced to carry it to Golgotha.

taught, perhaps not. Even so one of them was led to proclaim: "Truly, this was the Son of God!" (27:54). As you talk with those who are seemingly resistant to the gospel, keep in mind that your words may still have an impact sometime later. Speak boldly, knowing that God can change anyone—after all, He changed you! (***See Ministry****> Great Commission> Witness> Barriers> People don't want to hear the truth,* TopicGuide page A56.)

27:46-49 In His anguish, Jesus cried out words from Psalm 22:1.The words were apparently in Aramaic, a dialect of Hebrew widely spoken in the land of Israel at the time. Not everyone who was watching Jesus' execution spoke fluent Aramaic, and some apparently misunderstood what Jesus had said.

27:51 The Temple in Jerusalem was the center of the sacrificial system for the Jewish people. There they offered sacrifices to "cover" their sins and find acceptance before God. Inside the Temple was a room called "the Most Holy Place," which represented the very presence of God. That area was separated from the rest of the Temple by a very special curtain. Only the high priest could go into the Most Holy Place, and then only in a prescribed way at set times. Thus, the tearing of the curtain symbolized the fulfillment of the Old Covenant and the new access that God's people had to Him (Hebrews 4:16).

27:55 Some people who were eyewitnesses to Jesus' death and burial (27:61) were also eyewitnesses to His resurrection (see Matthew 28:1).

THE BURIAL OF JESUS

57As evening approached, Joseph, a rich man from Arimathea who had become a follower
of Jesus, 58went to Pilate and asked for Jesus' body. And Pilate issued an order to release it
to Him. 59Joseph took the body and wrapped it in a long sheet of clean linen cloth. 60He
placed it in his own new tomb, which had been carved out of the rock. Then he rolled a
great stone across the entrance and left. 61 Both Mary Magdalene and the other Mary were
sitting across from the tomb and watching.

THE GUARD AT THE TOMB

62The next day, on the Sabbath,* the leading priests and Pharisees went to see Pilate. 63They
told him, "Sir, we remember what that deceiver once said while He was still alive: 'After three
days I will rise from the dead.' 64So we request that you seal the tomb until the third day. This
will prevent His disciples from coming and stealing His body and then telling everyone He
was raised from the dead! If that happens, we'll be worse off than we were at first."

65Pilate replied, "Take guards and secure it the best you can." 66So they sealed the tomb
and posted guards to protect it.

THE RESURRECTION

28 Early on Sunday morning,* as the new day was dawning, Mary Magdalene and
the other Mary went out to visit the tomb.

2Suddenly there was a great earthquake! For an angel of the Lord came down from
heaven, rolled aside the stone, and sat on it. 3His face shone like lightning, and his cloth-
ing was as white as snow. 4The guards shook with fear when they saw him, and they fell
into a dead faint.

5Then the angel spoke to the women. "Don't be afraid!" he said. "I know you are looking
for Jesus, who was crucified. 6He isn't here! He is risen from the dead, just as He said would

27:57-61 //Mark 15:42-47 //Luke 23:50-56 //John 19:38-42

27:61 Matt 27:56; 28:1 Mark 15:40, 47; 16:1 Luke 24:10 John 19:25

27:63 Matt 12:40; 16:21; 17:23; 20:19 Mark 8:31; 9:31; 10:34 Luke 9:22; 18:33

27:64 Matt 28:13

27:66 Dan 6:17

28:1-8 //Mark 16:1-11 //Luke 24:1-11 //John 20:1-10

28:6 Matt 12:40; 16:21; 17:23; 20:19 Mark 8:31; 9:31; 10:34 Luke 9:22; 18:33; 24:7

27:62 Or *On the next day, which is after the Preparation.* 28:1 Greek *After the Sabbath, on the first day of the week.*

27:57-61 Joseph was a godly Jew and an elder member of the Sanhedrin. As he gave Jesus his expensive, hand-carved tomb, he fulfilled the prophecy in Isaiah 53:9.

▸ GOD

28:5, 10 Fear and joy. It's only natural that Jesus' resurrection gave His disciples great joy. But notice that the angel had to remind the women who were the first to encounter the good news of the resurrection, "Don't be afraid." Jesus' resurrection may have been joyful, but it was also the most surprising event of their lives. The magnitude of what had happened shook their view of the world. This Jesus they had followed—He was truly God! He was alive! Nothing else mattered—not even their natural fears or awe in the face of an angel of God. Listen to the angel's advice—don't let fear stop you. Go tell others about what Jesus has done and is doing in your life. Let the people God puts in your path know that Jesus is alive and well. (***See God**> God's Attributes> All-Powerful> His resurrection power is immeasurably great,* TopicGuide page A16.)

BECAUSE GOD IS EVER-PRESENT

He is always with me.

I am with you always, even to the end of the age.

MATTHEW 28:20

FOR THE NEXT *GOD IS EVER-PRESENT* FEATURE SEE PAGE 2062.

28:7 Matt 26:32; Mark 14:28; 16:7
28:10 John 20:17; Rom 8:29; Heb 2:11-13, 17
28:13 Matt 27:64
28:16-20 //Luke 24:36-49; //John 20:19-23
28:16 Matt 26:32; 28:7-10
28:18 Dan 7:13-14; John 3:35; 13:3; 17:2; Eph 1:20-22; Phil 2:9-10
28:19 Luke 24:47; Acts 1:8; 2:38
28:20 Matt 18:20; John 14:23

happen. Come, see where His body was lying. 7And now, go quickly and tell His disciples
that He has risen from the dead, and He is going ahead of you to Galilee. You will see Him
there. Remember what I have told you."
8The women ran quickly from the tomb. They were very frightened but also filled with
great joy, and they rushed to give the disciples the angel's message. 9And as they went,
Jesus met them and greeted them. And they ran to Him, grasped His feet, and worshiped
Him. 10Then Jesus said to them, "Don't be afraid! Go tell My brothers to leave for Galilee,
and they will see Me there."

THE REPORT OF THE GUARD

11As the women were on their way, some of the guards went into the city and told the
leading priests what had happened. 12A meeting with the elders was called, and they de-
cided to give the soldiers a large bribe. 13They told the soldiers, "You must say, 'Jesus' dis-
ciples came during the night while we were sleeping, and they stole His body.' 14If the
governor hears about it, we'll stand up for you so you won't get in trouble." 15So the
guards accepted the bribe and said what they were told to say. Their story spread widely
among the Jews, and they still tell it today.

THE GREAT COMMISSION

16Then the eleven disciples left for Galilee, going to the mountain where Jesus had told
them to go. 17When they saw Him, they worshiped Him—but some of them doubted!
18Jesus came and told His disciples, "I have been given all authority in heaven and on
earth. 19Therefore, go and make disciples of all the nations,* baptizing them in the name
of the Father and the Son and the Holy Spirit. 20Teach these new disciples to obey all the
commands I have given you. And be sure of this: I am with you always, even to the end of
the age."

28:19 Or *all peoples.*

28:11-15 It appears that those guarding the tomb were Roman soldiers (27:65-66). If these guards had fallen asleep on their watch, they could have been put to death. The religious leaders offered to "stand up" for them if they got into trouble by fabricating a story about the disciples stealing Jesus' body while they slept. This further demonstrated the intertwining of the Romans and the religious leaders of that time.

▸ WORSHIP

28:17 Stirred to worship. What makes you want to worship? One marvelous picture of worship is found in Isaiah 6. When Isaiah "saw the Lord," he worshiped. In this vision he caught a glimpse of the glory of God. Likewise, after the resurrection, Jesus' disciples "saw Him, [and] they worshiped Him." Seeing Jesus was enough to draw them to heartfelt worship. Through the words of Scripture, through reflecting on the gospel, through the eyes of faith that can see the grace of God at work—in all these ways, seek to get your eyes on God. If you do, you will catch a glimpse of His glory. With your family, in private, and with all God's people on Sunday, give God full-hearted worship. (***See Worship**> NT> Reverence> God demands our undivided reverence,* TopicGuide page A32.)

▸ ADOPTION

28:18-20 Representing Jesus. So, what's next? After Jesus defeated death and returned to life in a supernatural form, what else was left for Him? He had a message for His disciples and He has a message for us—tell the world! Jesus came to earth for a reason—to die in the place of sinful people so they could be forgiven and be brought into union with His holy Father. Can you help spread that message? How can you be a more effective ambassador for Christ? Every person has a group of people to whom they are specially prepared and equipped to testify. Pray and ask God to reveal those whom He has prepared for hearing the gospel from you. Then: "Tell them!" (***See Adoption**> With Christ> Servants> Ambassadors for Christ,* TopicGuide page A37.)

KEY PLACES IN MARK

The broken lines (—·—) indicate modern boundaries.

Of the four Gospels, Mark's narrative is the most chronological—that is, most of the stories are positioned in the order they actually occurred. Though the shortest of the four, the Gospel of Mark contains the most events; it is action-packed. Most of this action centers in Galilee, where Jesus began His ministry. Capernaum served as His base of operation (1:21; 2:1; 9:33), from which He would go out to cities like Bethsaida, where He healed a blind man (8:22ff); Gennesaret, where He performed many healings (6:53ff); Tyre and Sidon (to the far north), where He healed many, drove out demons, and met the woman from Syrian Phoenicia (3:8; 7:24ff); and Caesarea Philippi, where Peter declared Him to be the Messiah (8:27ff). After His ministry in Galilee and the surrounding regions, Jesus headed for Jerusalem (10:1). Before going there, Jesus told His disciples three times that he would be crucified there and then come back to life (8:31; 9:31; 10:33, 34).

MARK

PURPOSE

To introduce us to Jesus, the Son of God incarnate, who came into our world to serve those in need.

If God came to earth, what would He do? We discover the answer in Mark's Gospel: He would come to serve.

Mark contributes to the Gospels' rich portrait of Jesus by focusing on His character and role as a servant (10:43-45). Unlike the other three Gospels, which include many of Jesus' teachings in their accounts, Mark highlights how Jesus served multitudes by meeting needs, how He served His disciples by giving them an entirely new experience of life, and how He served the whole world by offering Himself as a sacrifice for sin. It may sound surprising to think of Jesus, God-come-to-earth, as a servant, but this perspective is not foreign to the Scriptures.

The prophet Isaiah declared that God is different from the idols of the world because He is the One who "works for those who wait for Him!" (Isaiah 64:4). Many of the psalms picture God as the One who helps or aids those in need (for example, see Psalms 70:1-5; 121:1-8). God, in fact, identifies Himself as the "helper" of Israel (Hosea 13:9).

This is the picture of God that Mark reveals through the actions of Jesus: Jesus tenderly cared for a woman with a flow of blood (5:24-34); He gave personal attention to a deaf man who had a speech impediment (7:31-37). He fed those who were hungry (6:35-44); and He protected His followers from the accusations of the religious leaders (2:23-28). The Son of Man came "not to be served but to serve others" (Mark 10:45).

DISCOVER GOD IN MARK

Mark does not give us the noble genealogies of Jesus found in Matthew and Luke, nor does he tell us of Jesus' preincarnate glory as John does. Mark introduces us to Jesus by telling us what He did—His focus is on Jesus' actions, through which we can discover the character of God as revealed in Jesus.

Servant: In the polytheistic understanding of the Roman world, the gods often competed with each other for the attention and affection of worshipers. These gods, however, merely reflected the sinful character of those who imagined them and were often portrayed as selfish despots. When the living God came to earth in the form of a man, He showed Himself to be quite different from the gods of human imagination. Mark shows clearly how God, in Jesus, came to serve (10:45). Repeatedly, Mark relates accounts of Jesus ministering to the needs of others, whether their need was spiritual, emotional, or material.

Power: Mark highlights the power that flowed through the life and ministry of Jesus. Jesus is One who served in power, whether by teaching with a power that amazed (1:21-22), delivering those who were oppressed by demons (5:1-20), exercising control over nature (4:35-41), or meeting other specific needs (8:1-10). But this display of power was not like fireworks in the sky or the roaring of a storm. in each occasion when Jesus evidenced the power of God, it was power leveraged in serving. Jesus explained this principle when talking about those who wield power in the world (10:42-44); they use their power for selfish ends, but it wasn't to be that way for Him or for those who chose to follow Him.

GROWING THROUGH MARK

Followers of Jesus today can learn from Mark how Jesus served and trained His followers:

The call: Jesus was not an aloof, far-off leader, merely dictating to His followers what needed to be done. He invited His followers to walk with Him so that He could then send them to serve others in a similar fashion (1:17; 3:13-15; 6:7-12). Although Jesus did have a more intimate relationship with the twelve, He invited all who heard His voice to a life of discipleship and ministry (3:31-35; 8:34-37; 9:38-40). And as Jesus' followers go out into the known world, He continues to affirm this call, working alongside all those who believe (16:15-20).

The tasks: Jesus' training did not come in lecture format only; some of His more powerful teaching came through the assignments He gave His followers. For example, when Jesus called His followers to feed the multitude, His disciples were supposed to learn something from the experience (6:52; 8:18-21). They were to learn by doing, not merely by listening (6:7-13). Ultimately, His call to them, and all who would follow, is not merely to learn about what it means to follow Him but to actively carry that out (16:15-20).

The model: Servanthood is at the heart of Jesus' Kingdom; He taught about it and invited His disciples to embrace such a lifestyle (9:35; 10:42-44). He offered His own life as an example of servanthood (10:45).

DISCOVERY VERSES

Later on, after John was arrested, Jesus went into Galilee where He preached God's Good News. "The time promised by God has come at last!" He announced. "The Kingdom of God is near! Repent of your sins and believe the Good News!"

(MARK 1:14-15)

Whoever wants to be a leader among you must be your servant, and whoever wants to be first among you must be the slave of everyone else. For even the Son of Man came not to be served but to serve others and to give His life as a ransom for many.

(MARK 10:43-45)

MARK FACTS

Author: Mark has been identified as the author of this Gospel. The early church fathers—Papias, Irenaeus, Origen, and Clement of Alexandria—affirmed Mark's authorship. Even though Mark was not an eyewitness himself (although some do think that the young man mentioned in 14:51-52 may have been Mark), he likely compiled his account of Jesus' time on earth from the teachings of the apostle Peter (according to Papias as mentioned earlier). Acts 12:12 informs us that Mark's mother's home was used as a meeting place for the church in Jerusalem. From Colossians 4:10, we learn that Mark was related to Barnabas, the missionary and companion of Paul. Mark clearly enjoyed a close friendship with Peter (1 Peter 5:13). The words of that great apostle are what flavor Mark's Gospel. Peter's influence is evident in the descriptions of the healing of Peter's mother-in-law (1:30-31) and the account of Peter's denial (14:66-71).

Written to: In a number of places, Mark translates Hebrew or Aramaic phrases for his readers (for example, see 3:17; 5:41; 15:22). He also explains Jewish customs (as in 7:3-4). Something that is not evident in most translations are Mark's "Latinisms," stylistic usage that would have been familiar to those for whom Hebrew was not the native tongue. Also, Mark seems to be far less concerned with demonstrating Jesus' fulfillment of Jewish Old Testament prophecies than the other Gospel writers. These observations, along with the insight from the early church fathers that Mark wrote his Gospel from the teachings of Peter while Peter was in Rome, lead to the reasonable conclusion that Mark was writing for a non-Jewish population within the Roman empire.

Date of writing: There are no decisive indicators pointing to precisely when Mark wrote his Gospel, but some estimate is possible. If it is true that Mark based his Gospel on the teachings of Peter and wrote it when Peter was in Rome, we can assume that the Gospel was probably not written before AD 57. It is inconceivable that Paul, who wrote to the church in Rome AD 57, would not have mentioned Peter if he had been there at that time. Since Mark included no references to the destruction of the Temple in Jerusalem (AD 70), he likely wrote before that very significant event. Thus, it is possible that he penned his account between AD 57 and 65.

Setting: As with all the Gospels, Mark's account covers the life and ministry of Jesus throughout the land of Palestine. He also ministered for a short while in the region referred to as the "Ten Towns" (the "Decapolis"; 5:20 and 7:31) and in Tyre (7:24) and Sidon (7:31), which were predominantly Gentile regions.

OUTLINE

- **MARK 1:1–8:26**—Jesus' Ministry of Serving
- **MARK 8:27–10:52**—Jesus' Teachings about Serving
- **MARK 11:1–15:47**—Jesus' Life Given as a Ransom for Others
- **MARK 16:1-20**—Jesus' Ministry of Service Extended to His Followers

JOHN THE BAPTIST PREPARES THE WAY

1:1 Matt 1:1 John 1:34 1 Jn 4:15

1 This is the Good News about Jesus the Messiah, the Son of God.* It began [2]just as the
prophet Isaiah had written:

1:2-8 //Matt 3:1-11 //Luke 3:1-16 //John 1:19-28

1:2-3 John 1:23

"Look, I am sending My messenger ahead of You,
and he will prepare Your way.*
[3] He is a voice shouting in the wilderness,
'Prepare the way for the LORD's coming!
Clear the road for Him!'*"

1:4 Acts 13:24; 19:4

[4]This messenger was John the Baptist. He was in the wilderness and preached that people
should be baptized to show that they had repented of their sins and turned to God to be

1:6 Lev 11:22 2 Kgs 1:8 Zech 13:4

forgiven. [5]All of Judea, including all the people of Jerusalem, went out to see and hear
John. And when they confessed their sins, he baptized them in the Jordan River. [6]His
clothes were woven from coarse camel hair, and he wore a leather belt around his waist.
For food he ate locusts and wild honey.

1:7 Acts 13:25

[7]John announced: "Someone is coming soon who is greater than I am—so much greater

1:8 Joel 2:28 Acts 2:4; 10:45; 11:16

that I'm not even worthy to stoop down like a slave and untie the straps of His sandals. [8]I
baptize you with* water, but He will baptize you with the Holy Spirit!"

1:9-11 //Matt 3:13-17 //Luke 3:21-22

THE BAPTISM AND TEMPTATION OF JESUS

[9]One day Jesus came from Nazareth in Galilee, and John baptized Him in the Jordan River.

1:11 Matt 12:18 Mark 9:7 Luke 9:35

[10]As Jesus came up out of the water, He saw the heavens splitting apart and the Holy Spirit
descending on Him* like a dove. [11]And a voice from heaven said, "You are My dearly
loved Son, and You bring Me great joy."

1:1 Some manuscripts do not include *the Son of God.* 1:2 Mal 3:1. 1:3 Isa 40:3 (Greek version). 1:8 Or *in;* also in 1:8b. 1:10 Or *toward Him,* or *into Him.*

1:1 The word *Messiah* is the English transliteration of a Hebrew word that means "the anointed one." God had promised through the Old Testament prophets to send an anointed Deliverer who would establish His Kingdom on earth (see, for example, Daniel 9:24-27 and Acts 4:26-28). This "anointing" meant the Deliverer would bear the special empowerment of the Holy Spirit reserved for select kings, prophets, and priests of the Old Covenant.

1:6 John's peculiar style of dress and diet would have reminded the people in his day of a prophet of old who had spoken to the people of Israel (see 2 Kings 1:7-9).

12 The Spirit then compelled Jesus to go into the wilderness, 13 where He was tempted by
Satan for forty days. He was out among the wild animals, and angels took care of Him.
14 Later on, after John was arrested, Jesus went into Galilee, where He preached God's
Good News.* 15 "The time promised by God has come at last!" He announced. "The King-
dom of God is near! Repent of your sins and believe the Good News!"

1:14-15 Luke 5:1-11; John 1:35-42
1:14 Mark 6:17-18
1:15 Gal 4:4; Eph 1:10

THE FIRST DISCIPLES

16 One day as Jesus was walking along the shore of the Sea of Galilee, He saw Simon* and

1:14 Some manuscripts read *the Good News of the Kingdom of God.* 1:16 *Simon* is called "Peter" in 3:16 and thereafter.

▸ MINISTRY
1:15 The gospel and the Kingdom. What is your response to Jesus' Good News? Some people think Jesus wants them to be religious—going to church or praying more or reading the Bible regularly—and though these are good habits to have, there is a deeper response to which we are called. Jesus linked the Good News to acceptance of the presence, power, and rule of God. This acceptance goes much deeper than committing to a new Bible reading plan—it allows you to participate in a revolution against the forces that seek to ruin your life and your world. Have you joined the revolution? (***See Ministry****> Transformation> Fill and Subdue> Influencing every sphere of life,* TopicGuide page A57.)

▸ CHURCH
1:16-18 Pursuing Christ. What were Simon and Andrew getting themselves into? They didn't know, and frankly neither did we when we first started following Jesus.

MY RESPONSE TO GOD

One God, Three Persons

MARK 1:9-11

Christians worship God alone–period. We do not worship many gods, but one God (Deuteronomy 6:4; Mark 12:32; Romans 3:30). But believers also historically believe in the Trinity, God in three persons. How can this be reconciled?

Starting with the first few verses of Genesis, Scripture reveals the reality of the Trinity. There we find references to God and the Spirit of God–a strong hint of plurality within God's singular nature. John 1:1 reveals that Christ was also present: "In the beginning the Word already existed. The Word was with God, and the Word was God." Although these passages don't use the technical language of the creeds and confessions, they show that God is one being with three persons. To illustrate this, He patterned humanity after Himself–one race with a plurality of genders, and nationalities (Genesis 1:27; 10:20).

We also see all three persons of the Trinity at Jesus' baptism (Mark 1:9-11). The Father acknowledged the Son, and the Spirit descended on Him. Christ commanded that our baptism be like His–in the name of the Father and the Son and the Holy Spirit (Matthew 28:19). Both Christ's baptism and ours testify to the doctrine of the Trinity.

But how can three equal and unlimited persons share in the full properties of a single being? By illustration, we may consider a title to a house. There is a type of ownership in which every owner of the house individually owns the whole house, not just part of it. It might seem from one perspective that more than one house is owned, but in fact there is only one house. Such ownership would be similar to the Trinity, in which there are three persons who all share one essence–God.

While it is a mystery exactly how God can be one and yet exist as three eternal and separate persons, this truth is revealed in Scripture. The God Christians confess and worship is, in the words of hymn writer Reginald Heber, "God in three persons, blessed Trinity." Let us honor and marvel at every person of the Trinity.

1:16-20 //Matt 4:18-22 //Luke 5:1-11 his brother Andrew throwing a net into the water, for they fished for a living. 17Jesus called
out to them, "Come, follow Me, and I will show you how to fish for people!" 18And they left
their nets at once and followed Him.

1:19 Matt 10:2 Mark 3:17; 10:35 Luke 5:10 19A little farther up the shore Jesus saw Zebedee's sons, James and John, in a boat re-
pairing their nets. 20He called them at once, and they also followed Him, leaving their fa-
ther, Zebedee, in the boat with the hired men.

JESUS CASTS OUT AN EVIL SPIRIT

1:21-28 //Luke 4:31-41 21Jesus and His companions went to the town of Capernaum. When the Sabbath day
came, He went into the synagogue and began to teach. 22The people were amazed at His
1:22 Matt 7:28-29 teaching, for He taught with real authority—quite unlike the teachers of religious law.
23Suddenly, a man in the synagogue who was possessed by an evil* spirit began shout-
1:24 Matt 8:29 ing, 24"Why are You interfering with us, Jesus of Nazareth? Have You come to destroy us? I
John 6:69 know who You are—the Holy One sent from God!"
1:26 25Jesus cut him short. "Be quiet! Come out of the man," He ordered. 26At that, the evil
Mark 9:20 spirit screamed, threw the man into a convulsion, and then came out of him.
27Amazement gripped the audience, and they began to discuss what had happened. "What
sort of new teaching is this?" they asked excitedly. "It has such authority! Even evil spirits obey
1:28 Mark 9:26 His orders!" 28The news about Jesus spread quickly throughout the entire region of Galilee.

JESUS HEALS MANY PEOPLE

1:29-34 29After Jesus left the synagogue with James and John, they went to Simon and Andrew's
//Matt 8:14-17 home. 30Now Simon's mother-in-law was sick in bed with a high fever. They told Jesus
//Luke 4:38-41 about her right away. 31So He went to her bedside, took her by the hand, and helped her
sit up. Then the fever left her, and she prepared a meal for them.
32That evening after sunset, many sick and demon-possessed people were brought to

1:23 Greek *unclean;* also in 1:26, 27.

But when Jesus invited them to spend their lives with Him—which was the idea "following" conveyed—they took Him up on the offer. It's a decision we all must make. Will we live empty, hurried lives that focus on following our lists, or will we intentionally and intimately follow Jesus? (***See Church**> Who> From Every People> Those who know much of God,* TopicGuide page A48.)

1:21-22 Jesus did not teach like other teachers of religious law, who typically taught by quoting what other teachers had said. Jesus taught with real authority.

▸ PURPOSE

1:29-31 Not like the others. Simon and Andrew had been with Jesus only for a short while. They had heard Him teach, and they were impressed. But when Jesus delivered a man afflicted by a demonic spirit, they were astonished. That was enough to nudge them to make a request of Jesus that they would never have made of another rabbi: would He come and heal Simon's ailing mother-in-law? Have you seen enough of Jesus to sense that you can bring your needs and the needs of those around you to Him? Keep reading, keep praying, and you'll find new faith in this man, Jesus Christ. (***See Purpose**> God's Deeds> Special Acts> Miracles> Jesus> Peter's mother-in-law healed,* TopicGuide page A53.)

1:32 Jesus had healed Simon's mother-in-law after the Sabbath service. Faithful Jews were careful not to work on the Sabbath, which began at sundown on Friday and ended at sundown on Saturday. Carrying the sick and afflicted through the streets of the city was classified as work, so only after the sun had set would people have begun to bring the infirm to Jesus.

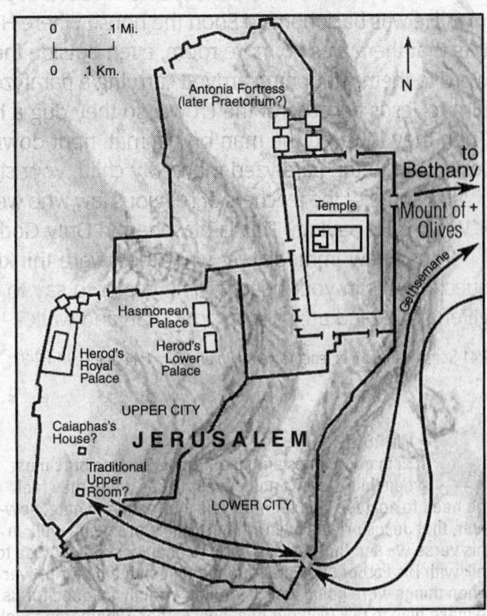

UPPER ROOM AND GETHSEMANE

Jesus and the disciples ate the traditional Passover meal in an upper room in the city and then went to the Mount of Olives into a garden called Gethsemane. In the cool of the evening, Jesus prayed for strength to face the trial and suffering ahead.

Jesus. 33 The whole town gathered at the door to watch. 34 So Jesus healed many people 1:34
who were sick with various diseases, and He cast out many demons. But because the de- Mark 3:12
mons knew who He was, He did not allow them to speak.

JESUS PREACHES IN GALILEE

35 Before daybreak the next morning, Jesus got up and went out to an isolated place to 1:35-39
pray. 36 Later Simon and the others went out to find Him. 37 When they found Him, they //Luke 4:42-44
said, "Everyone is looking for You." 1:38
38 But Jesus replied, "We must go on to other towns as well, and I will preach to them, Isa 61:1
too. That is why I came." 39 So He traveled throughout the region of Galilee, preaching in 1:39
the synagogues and casting out demons. Matt 4:23; 9:35

JESUS HEALS A MAN WITH LEPROSY

40 A man with leprosy came and knelt in front of Jesus, begging to be healed. "If You are
willing, You can heal me and make me clean," he said. 1:40-45 //Matt 8:2-4
41 Moved with compassion,* Jesus reached out and touched him. "I am willing," He said. //Luke 5:12-16
"Be healed!" 42 Instantly the leprosy disappeared, and the man was healed. 43 Then Jesus
sent him on his way with a stern warning: 44 "Don't tell anyone about this. Instead, go to 1:44
the priest and let him examine you. Take along the offering required in the law of Moses Lev 14:1-32
for those who have been healed of leprosy.* This will be a public testimony that you have
been cleansed."
45 But the man went and spread the word, proclaiming to everyone what had happened.
As a result, large crowds soon surrounded Jesus, and He couldn't publicly enter a town
anywhere. He had to stay out in the secluded places, but people from everywhere kept
coming to Him.

JESUS HEALS A PARALYZED MAN

2 When Jesus returned to Capernaum several days later, the news spread quickly that 2:1-12
He was back home. 2 Soon the house where He was staying was so packed with visi- //Matt 9:1-8
tors that there was no more room, even outside the door. While He was preaching God's //Luke 5:18-26
word to them, 3 four men arrived carrying a paralyzed man on a mat. 4 They couldn't bring 2:2 Eph 2:17
him to Jesus because of the crowd, so they dug a hole through the roof above His head. Heb 2:3
Then they lowered the man on his mat, right down in front of Jesus. 5 Seeing their faith, 2:5
Jesus said to the paralyzed man, "My child, your sins are forgiven." Luke 7:48
6 But some of the teachers of religious law who were sitting there thought to themselves, 2:7
7 "What is He saying? This is blasphemy! Only God can forgive sins!" Ps 130:3-4 Isa 43:25
8 Jesus knew immediately what they were thinking, so He asked them, "Why do you 2:8
question this in your hearts? 9 Is it easier to say to the paralyzed man 'Your sins are for- Matt 16:8
given,' or 'Stand up, pick up your mat, and walk'? 10 So I will prove to you that the Son of

1:41 Some manuscripts read *Moved with anger.* 1:44 See Lev 14:2-32.

▸ WORSHIP

1:35 In good times and bad. People tend to pray most when things aren't going well. That's when they feel the need to come to God for help. It is interesting to note, however, that Jesus prayed even when things were going well. In this verse we see that He rose early to find an isolated place to talk with His Father. If Jesus sought out such a time for prayer when things were going well, it would certainly be good for us to make time to talk with our heavenly Father, whether in tough times or in good times. (***See Worship****> NT> Prayer> Instructions> Pray without ceasing,* TopicGuide page A33.)

1:40-44 Lepers were considered not just sick but "unclean." That meant they were not permitted to live in the village, could not spend time with friends and family, and could not participate in worship alongside the people of Israel. Jesus' grace and power not only restored the man to health, but also made the lesions on his skin go away. He could then present himself as "clean" to the priests, who had the authority to permit the man to return to normal life in the community.

2:6-7 When the religious leaders discussed among themselves why Jesus was speaking about forgiving sins, they were raising a legitimate issue. Only God could do that. If this man, Jesus, was saying He could forgive sins, then He was saying He carried the authority of God.

Man* has the authority on earth to forgive sins." Then Jesus turned to the paralyzed man
and said, [11]"Stand up, pick up your mat, and go home!"
2:12 [12]And the man jumped up, grabbed his mat, and walked out through the stunned on-
Matt 9:33 lookers. They were all amazed and praised God, exclaiming, "We've never seen anything
like this before!"

JESUS CALLS LEVI (MATTHEW)

2:13-17 [13]Then Jesus went out to the lakeshore again and taught the crowds that were coming to
//Matt 9:9-13 Him. [14]As He walked along, He saw Levi son of Alphaeus sitting at his tax collector's booth.
//Luke 5:27-32 "Follow Me and be My disciple," Jesus said to him. So Levi got up and followed Him.
2:14 John 1:43 [15]Later, Levi invited Jesus and His disciples to his home as dinner guests, along with
many tax collectors and other disreputable sinners. (There were many people of this kind
among Jesus' followers.) [16]But when the teachers of religious law who were Pharisees*
saw Him eating with tax collectors and other sinners, they asked His disciples, "Why does
He eat with such scum?*"
2:17 [17]When Jesus heard this, He told them, "Healthy people don't need a doctor—sick peo-
Luke 19:10 ple do. I have come to call not those who think they are righteous, but those who know
1 Tim 1:15 they are sinners."

A DISCUSSION ABOUT FASTING

2:18-22 [18]Once when John's disciples and the Pharisees were fasting, some people came to Jesus
//Matt 9:14-17 and asked, "Why don't Your disciples fast like John's disciples and the Pharisees do?"
//Luke 5:33-38 [19]Jesus replied, "Do wedding guests fast while celebrating with the groom? Of course
2:19 John 3:29 not. They can't fast while the groom is with them. [20]But someday the groom will be taken
Rev 19:7 away from them, and then they will fast.
2:20 [21]"Besides, who would patch old clothing with new cloth? For the new patch would
Luke 17:22 shrink and rip away from the old cloth, leaving an even bigger tear than before.
2:22 [22]"And no one puts new wine into old wineskins. For the wine would burst the wine-
Gal 3:1-3 skins, and the wine and the skins would both be lost. New wine calls for new wineskins."
2:23-28
//Matt 12:1-8

//Luke 6:1-5

A DISCUSSION ABOUT THE SABBATH

2:23 [23]One Sabbath day as Jesus was walking through some grainfields, His disciples began
Deut 23:25

2:10 "Son of Man" is a title Jesus used for Himself. 2:16a Greek *the scribes of the Pharisees.* 2:16b Greek *with tax collectors and sinners?*

▸ MINISTRY

2:13-17 In and out. In most societies, there are those who are "in" and those who are not. It's fairly easy to distinguish between these two groups by watching how we respond to them. Do you meet their eyes as you walk by, or look away? Do you speak to them, or ignore them? Jesus, however, does not treat people as we do. In His day, tax collectors ranked among the lowest in Jewish society—they were Jews who collected fees and taxes levied by the Roman government. Other Jews despised tax collectors for working for their oppressors, but Jesus invited one of them to be one of His closest disciples. Jesus welcomes any and all who are willing to follow Him. How about you? Can you be more open to having significant conversations and interactions with those outside your social circle? (***See Ministry****> Great Commission> Description> People are invited to Christ,* TopicGuide page A56.)

2:14-16 The Roman government used local citizens to collect taxes from their own people. The religious leaders regularly linked such people with "sinners."

2:19 In Jesus' day, wedding celebrations often lasted several days. As long as the bridegroom was there, the celebrating would continue.

▸ WORSHIP

2:21-22 Not another patch. When Jesus first began His ministry of teaching and healing, He stirred up controversy. He wasn't necessarily seeking to cause trouble, but the Kingdom that He called His followers to join naturally clashed with life as usual. Through two short parables, Jesus drove home the point that we cannot simply "patch" His ways into our way of life. Every part of our culture, our vocations, and our private lives is touched by the new life that Jesus offers. Submit to Him, and look for (and participate in!) the changes that He brings to every area of life. (***See Worship****> NT> Christ's Kingship> Kingdom of God> New cloth and old garment,* TopicGuide page A30.)

2:22 In Jesus' day, wine was made by putting fresh grape juice into a bag made from tanned goatskin that was then sewn closed. As the juice fermented into wine, gases were released, stretching the wineskin. A stretched wineskin could be used to hold wine that had already been fermented, but fresh juice could not be put in a used wineskin, because there would be no more "stretch" left in the skin.

breaking off heads of grain to eat. 24But the Pharisees said to Jesus, "Look, why are they
breaking the law by harvesting grain on the Sabbath?"
25Jesus said to them, "Haven't you ever read in the Scriptures what David did when he
and his companions were hungry? 26He went into the house of God (during the days when
Abiathar was high priest) and broke the law by eating the sacred loaves of bread that only
the priests are allowed to eat. He also gave some to his companions."
27Then Jesus said to them, "The Sabbath was made to meet the needs of people, and
not people to meet the requirements of the Sabbath. 28So the Son of Man is Lord, even
over the Sabbath!"

2:25-26 1 Sam 21:1-7
2:27 Exod 23:12; Deut 5:14; John 7:21-24

JESUS HEALS ON THE SABBATH

3 Jesus went into the synagogue again and noticed a man with a deformed hand.
2Since it was the Sabbath, Jesus' enemies watched Him closely. If He healed the
man's hand, they planned to accuse Him of working on the Sabbath.
3Jesus said to the man with the deformed hand, "Come and stand in front of everyone."
4Then He turned to His critics and asked, "Does the law permit good deeds on the Sabbath,
or is it a day for doing evil? Is this a day to save life or to destroy it?" But they wouldn't
answer Him.
5He looked around at them angrily and was deeply saddened by their hard hearts. Then
He said to the man, "Hold out your hand." So the man held out his hand, and it was re-
stored! 6At once the Pharisees went away and met with the supporters of Herod to plot
how to kill Jesus.

3:1-6 //Matt 12:9-14; //Luke 6:6-11
3:5 Mark 6:52; 8:17
3:6 Matt 22:15-16; Mark 12:13

CROWDS FOLLOW JESUS

7Jesus went out to the lake with His disciples, and a large crowd followed Him. They came
from all over Galilee, Judea, 8Jerusalem, Idumea, from east of the Jordan River, and even
from as far north as Tyre and Sidon. The news about His miracles had spread far and wide,
and vast numbers of people came to see Him.
9Jesus instructed His disciples to have a boat ready so the crowd would not crush Him.
10He had healed many people that day, so all the sick people eagerly pushed forward to
touch Him. 11And whenever those possessed by evil* spirits caught sight of Him, the spirits
would throw them to the ground in front of Him shrieking, "You are the Son of God!" 12But
Jesus sternly commanded the spirits not to reveal who He was.

3:7-12 //Matt 12:15-16; //Luke 6:17-19
3:7-8 Matt 4:25
3:10 Mark 4:1
3:11-12 Mark 1:24-25, 34; Luke 4:41; Acts 16:16-17

JESUS CHOOSES THE TWELVE APOSTLES

13Afterward Jesus went up on a mountain and called out the ones He wanted to go with

3:13-19 //Matt 10:1-4; //Luke 6:12-16

3:11 Greek *unclean;* also in 3:30.

2:25-28 The Old Testament required people to rest on the Sabbath (see Exodus 20:8-11). The religious leaders had defined, in very specific terms, what qualified as rest and what they considered work. They interpreted the disciples' actions as "harvesting," which was not permitted on the Sabbath. But as Lord of the Sabbath (2:28), Jesus was uniquely qualified to restore proper Sabbath observance.

2:25-28 During Old Testament times, fresh loaves of bread were placed "before the LORD" in the Tabernacle. Later they were removed and given to the priests to eat. The fact that God did not condemn David's actions indicated that ceremonial laws did not take precedence over genuine needs (see 1 Samuel 21:1-6).

▶ HOLINESS
3:1-5 Always reforming. Does the church need to make changes in its beliefs and practice? Who makes those changes, and how do we know whether those changes are legitimate? People in Jesus' time faced the same challenges. To illustrate His authority to make needed changes to the Sabbath observance of His time, Jesus demonstrated His mercy and power by healing a man with a deformity. Jesus then set Himself to the business of restoring the Sabbath to what God designed it to be. Take the words and principles of the Bible and ask God to help you reform your religious practices so that they become bridges, rather than roadblocks, to trusting Him more and more. (***See Holiness*****>** *Submission> Trusting God> Obedience,* TopicGuide page A40.)

3:7-8 Mark tells us that people were coming to see Jesus from all over the Roman province of Palestine (which included Galilee and Judea) and even from beyond that province (including the Gentile regions of Tyre and Sidon and the eastern side of the Jordan). Jesus' influence was spreading beyond the immediate vicinity of His hometown.

Him. And they came to Him. 14 Then He appointed twelve of them and called them His
apostles.* They were to accompany Him, and He would send them out to preach, 15 giving
them authority to cast out demons. 16 These are the twelve He chose:

Simon (whom He named Peter),
17 James and John (the sons of Zebedee, but Jesus nicknamed them "Sons of Thunder"*),
18 Andrew,
Philip,
Bartholomew,
Matthew,
Thomas,
James (son of Alphaeus),
Thaddaeus,
Simon (the zealot*),
19 Judas Iscariot (who later betrayed Him).

JESUS AND THE PRINCE OF DEMONS

20 One time Jesus entered a house, and the crowds began to gather again. Soon He and His
disciples couldn't even find time to eat. 21 When His family heard what was happening,
they tried to take Him away. "He's out of His mind," they said.
22 But the teachers of religious law who had arrived from Jerusalem said, "He's possessed
by Satan,* the prince of demons. That's where He gets the power to cast out demons."
23 Jesus called them over and responded with an illustration. "How can Satan cast out
Satan?" He asked. 24 "A kingdom divided by civil war will collapse. 25 Similarly, a family
splintered by feuding will fall apart. 26 And if Satan is divided and fights against himself,
how can he stand? He would never survive. 27 Let Me illustrate this further. Who is power-
ful enough to enter the house of a strong man like Satan and plunder his goods? Only
someone even stronger—someone who could tie him up and then plunder his house.
28 "I tell you the truth, all sin and blasphemy can be forgiven, 29 but anyone who blas-
phemes the Holy Spirit will never be forgiven. This is a sin with eternal consequences."
30 He told them this because they were saying, "He's possessed by an evil spirit."

THE TRUE FAMILY OF JESUS

31 Then Jesus' mother and brothers came to see Him. They stood outside and sent word

3:14 Mark 6:30
3:16 Matt 16:17-18; John 1:42
3:17 Luke 9:54
3:20-30 //Matt 12:22-32; //Luke 11:14-23
3:22 John 7:20; 8:48, 52; 10:20
3:27 Isa 49:24-25
3:28-30 //Matt 12:31-33; Luke 12:10; 1 Jn 5:16
3:31-35 //Matt 12:46-50; //Luke 8:19-21
3:31 Mark 6:3; John 7:3-5

3:14 Some manuscripts do not include *and called them His apostles.* 3:17 Greek *whom He named Boanerges, which means Sons of Thunder.* 3:18 Greek *the Cananean,* an Aramaic term for Jewish nationalists. 3:22 Greek *Beelzeboul;* other manuscripts read *Beezeboul;* Latin version reads *Beelzebub.*

3:14 Clearly, Jesus' group of disciples was growing (see 3:7-8). As His ministry continued to expand, He selected twelve individuals from among this group to work, live, and serve with Him in a particularly intense and personal way.

3:21 Jesus' selection of twelve apostles prompted the thought that He was "out of His mind." The nation of Israel traced its history to the twelve sons of Jacob, and the descendants of those sons became the twelve tribes of Israel. When Jesus selected twelve special followers, it is likely that His family believed He was attempting to start a new Israel.

▸ SPIRITUAL WARFARE

3:23-27 Jesus is a warrior. Jesus came into the world with the stated agenda to destroy Satan and his works. When He announced the arrival of the Kingdom of God, He was declaring war on the kingdom of Satan. Matthew 12:22-30 makes it clear that when Jesus demonstrated His power over demons, He proved that His Kingdom was among the Israelites (Matthew 12:28). By removing demons, Jesus and His disciples struck a grave blow to Satan's ability to harm people. As Jesus explained, He came to overthrow the "strong man" (Satan) who had troubled, afflicted, and held captive the souls of men and women. Does Jesus bear swords or bombs in His battle? No. And neither should we, for the battle we join is one of prayer and holy living, and we seek to defeat our enemy by helping to liberate those within his grasp. Are you in the fight? (***See Spiritual Warfare****> Originator of Sin> Satan's Domain> Doomed to destruction,* TopicGuide page A44.)

3:28-29 Although it is hard to say conclusively what this "unforgivable" sin is, a few things can be noted. These religious leaders were intentionally seeking to undermine Jesus' Spirit-empowered ministry—and His accompanying Satan-binding signs (3:22). This sin of intentionally attributing the work of the Holy Spirit to demons demonstrated the work of a degenerate heart that would not seek forgiveness from God.

3:31-32 Although some Christians believe that Jesus was an only child and that Mary never had any other children after His birth, this passage and others throughout the Gospels suggest otherwise. James, Joseph, Simon, and Judas are mentioned as the brothers of Jesus. See Matthew 13:55; Mark 6:3; Luke 2:7 (noting the "first child" phrase); 8:19-21.

for Him to come out and talk with them. 32There was a crowd sitting around Jesus, and
someone said, "Your mother and Your brothers* are outside asking for You."
33Jesus replied, "Who is My mother? Who are My brothers?" 34Then He looked at those
around Him and said, "Look, these are My mother and brothers. 35Anyone who does
God's will is My brother and sister and mother."

PARABLE OF THE FARMER SCATTERING SEED

4 Once again Jesus began teaching by the lakeshore. A very large crowd soon gath-
ered around Him, so He got into a boat. Then He sat in the boat while all the people
remained on the shore. 2He taught them by telling many stories in the form of parables,
such as this one:
3"Listen! A farmer went out to plant some seed. 4As he scattered it across his field, some
of the seed fell on a footpath, and the birds came and ate it. 5Other seed fell on shallow
soil with underlying rock. The seed sprouted quickly because the soil was shallow. 6But
the plant soon wilted under the hot sun, and since it didn't have deep roots, it died. 7Other
seed fell among thorns that grew up and choked out the tender plants so they produced
no grain. 8Still other seeds fell on fertile soil, and they sprouted, grew, and produced a
crop that was thirty, sixty, and even a hundred times as much as had been planted!" 9Then
He said, "Anyone with ears to hear should listen and understand."
10Later, when Jesus was alone with the twelve disciples and with the others who were
gathered around, they asked Him what the parables meant.
11He replied, "You are permitted to understand the secret* of the Kingdom of God. But I
use parables for everything I say to outsiders, 12so that the Scriptures might be fulfilled:

'When they see what I do,
they will learn nothing.
When they hear what I say,
they will not understand.
Otherwise, they will turn to Me
and be forgiven.'*"

13Then Jesus said to them, "If you can't understand the meaning of this parable, how
will you understand all the other parables? 14The farmer plants seed by taking God's word
to others. 15The seed that fell on the footpath represents those who hear the message,
only to have Satan come at once and take it away. 16The seed on the rocky soil represents
those who hear the message and immediately receive it with joy. 17But since they don't
have deep roots, they don't last long. They fall away as soon as they have problems or are
persecuted for believing God's word. 18The seed that fell among the thorns represents
others who hear God's word, 19but all too quickly the message is crowded out by the

3:34 John 20:17; Rom 8:29; Heb 2:11
3:35 Matt 7:21
4:1-9 //Matt 13:1-23; //Luke 8:4-8
4:2 Mark 4:33-34
4:9 Matt 11:15; Mark 4:23
4:10-12 //Matt 13:10-17; //Luke 8:9-10
4:12 *Isa 6:9-10; John 12:39-40; Acts 28:26-27
4:13-20 //Matt 13:18-23; //Luke 8:11-15
4:14 Eph 3:8; Jas 1:18; 1 Pet 1:23-25
4:15 2 Cor 4:4; 1 Pet 5:8
4:19 1 Tim 6:9-10, 17; 1 Jn 2:15-17

3:32 Some manuscripts add *and sisters.* 4:11 Greek *mystery.* 4:12 Isa 6:9-10 (Greek version).

▸ SALVATION

4:1-11 Paying attention. Although they were not fully aware of it, the disciples had been given the "secret of the Kingdom of God." These "secrets" were the messages that Jesus gave especially to His disciples. In this context, Jesus had told a parable about various kinds of soils. Some soil received the seed, and the seed took root and sprouted. The simple point of the parable is clear: Listen! (4:12, 22-25) Truly listening to God is not easy—even Jesus' disciples struggled to do it well. Today we have God's Word and the promised ministry of the Spirit to help us understand it (Psalm 143:10; Luke 12:12; John 14:26; 1 John 2:27). But this doesn't happen without our active attention to God's Word and the Spirit's direction. Listen! (Matthew 7:24; 11:15) (***See Salvation****> Receiving> How> Respond to God's call/invitation to salvation,* TopicGuide page A22.)

4:12 In quoting Isaiah 6:9-10, Jesus seemed to have been saying that He taught in parables so that people wouldn't understand. Jesus purposely obscured His message, because a key part of His ministry included making it clear who truly believed and who didn't.

4:15 Satan was regularly present in Jesus' stories and ministry. Here he is portrayed as distracting those who hear the gospel from following through with its implications. Other Scriptures show us how Satan tempted Eve (Genesis 3:1-19) and Jesus (Luke 4:2-13). He often disguises himself so it is difficult to know when he or his minions are at work (2 Corinthians 2:11; 11:14). But in every situation, by God's power, we can resist Satan's influence (Matthew 4:1-11; 2 Corinthians 2:11; 10:3-6; Ephesians 4:26-27; James 4:7; 1 Peter 5:8-9).

worries of this life, the lure of wealth, and the desire for other things, so no fruit is pro-
duced. 20And the seed that fell on good soil represents those who hear and accept God's
word and produce a harvest of thirty, sixty, or even a hundred times as much as had
been planted!"

PARABLE OF THE LAMP

4:21-25 Matt 5:15 //Luke 8:16-18 **4:22** Matt 10:26 Luke 12:2 **4:23** Matt 11:15; 13:43 **4:25** Matt 13:12; 25:29 Luke 19:26

21 Then Jesus asked them, "Would anyone light a lamp and then put it under a basket or
under a bed? Of course not! A lamp is placed on a stand, where its light will shine. 22For
everything that is hidden will eventually be brought into the open, and every secret will be
brought to light. 23Anyone with ears to hear should listen and understand."
24Then He added, "Pay close attention to what you hear. The closer you listen, the more
understanding you will be given*—and you will receive even more. 25To those who listen
to My teaching, more understanding will be given. But for those who are not listening,
even what little understanding they have will be taken away from them."

PARABLE OF THE GROWING SEED

4:26-27 1 Cor 3:6-7 **4:28-29** Matt 9:37-38 Rev 14:15

26Jesus also said, "The Kingdom of God is like a farmer who scatters seed on the ground.
27Night and day, while he's asleep or awake, the seed sprouts and grows, but he does not
understand how it happens. 28The earth produces the crops on its own. First a leaf blade
pushes through, then the heads of wheat are formed, and finally the grain ripens. 29And as
soon as the grain is ready, the farmer comes and harvests it with a sickle, for the harvest
time has come."

PARABLE OF THE MUSTARD SEED

4:30-32 //Matt 13:31-32 //Luke 13:18-19 **4:32** Ezek 17:23; 31:6 Dan 4:12, 21 **4:33** Matt 13:34-35 **4:34** John 16:25

30Jesus said, "How can I describe the Kingdom of God? What story should I use to illustrate
it? 31It is like a mustard seed planted in the ground. It is the smallest of all seeds, 32but it
becomes the largest of all garden plants; it grows long branches, and birds can make nests
in its shade."
33Jesus used many similar stories and illustrations to teach the people as much as they
could understand. 34In fact, in His public ministry He never taught without using parables;
but afterward, when He was alone with His disciples, He explained everything to them.

JESUS CALMS THE STORM

4:35-41 //Matt 8:23-27 //Luke 8:22-25

35As evening came, Jesus said to His disciples, "Let's cross to the other side of the lake."
36So they took Jesus in the boat and started out, leaving the crowds behind (although
other boats followed). 37But soon a fierce storm came up. High waves were breaking into
the boat, and it began to fill with water.
38Jesus was sleeping at the back of the boat with His head on a cushion. The disciples
woke Him up, shouting, "Teacher, don't You care that we're going to drown?"

4:24 Or *The measure you give will be the measure you get back.*

4:28-29 Jesus used agrarian illustrations to help His audience understand the principles of His teachings (4:33). These illustrations obscure His mission to the unbelievers and powerfully communicate His core values and principles to those of faith (4:12).

4:35-41 Because of the hills surrounding the Sea of Galilee and the moisture sweeping in from the Mediterranean, dangerous storms could arise quickly.

▶ SPIRITUAL WARFARE

4:35-41 Jesus looks for faith. Faith is easy to maintain in church, but how does your faith manifest itself in the awful storms of life? Jesus' disciples saw Him performing miracles, so they mentally knew what He could do. But would Jesus use His power to save them? Or would He sleep and perish along with the crew? After Jesus calmed the storm, He gently rebuked the disciples, questioning whether they had much faith. Neither in their panicked waking of Jesus nor in their question, "Don't You care?" did they demonstrate faith. We may sound or act very spiritual when times are easy, but when the storms of life start to blow, faith and doubt are revealed. Studying God's Word is an excellent catalyst for faith (Romans 10:17), so spend serious time in His Word. (***See Spiritual Warfare****> Resisting Sin and Evil> Embracing Christ> Entrust yourself to God's care,* TopicGuide page A45.)

39When Jesus woke up, He rebuked the wind and said to the waves, "Silence! Be still!" Suddenly the wind stopped, and there was a great calm. 40Then He asked them, "Why are you afraid? Do you still have no faith?"

4:39 Pss 65:8; 107:25-32

41The disciples were absolutely terrified. "Who is this man?" they asked each other. "Even the wind and waves obey Him!"

4:41 Ps 33:8-9

JESUS HEALS A DEMON-POSSESSED MAN

5 So they arrived at the other side of the lake, in the region of the Gerasenes.* 2When Jesus climbed out of the boat, a man possessed by an evil* spirit came out from a cemetery to meet Him. 3This man lived among the burial caves and could no longer be restrained, even with a chain. 4Whenever he was put into chains and shackles—as he often was—he snapped the chains from his wrists and smashed the shackles. No one was strong enough to subdue him. 5Day and night he wandered among the burial caves and in the hills, howling and cutting himself with sharp stones.

5:1-20 //Matt 8:28-34 //Luke 8:26-39

6When Jesus was still some distance away, the man saw Him, ran to meet Him, and bowed low before Him. 7With a shriek, he screamed, "Why are You interfering with me, Jesus, Son of the Most High God? In the name of God, I beg You, don't torture me!" 8For Jesus had already said to the spirit, "Come out of the man, you evil spirit."

5:7-8 Acts 16:17

9Then Jesus demanded, "What is your name?"

And he replied, "My name is Legion, because there are many of us inside this man." 10Then the evil spirits begged Him again and again not to send them to some distant place.

11There happened to be a large herd of pigs feeding on the hillside nearby. 12"Send us into those pigs," the spirits begged. "Let us enter them."

13So Jesus gave them permission. The evil spirits came out of the man and entered the pigs, and the entire herd of 2,000 pigs plunged down the steep hillside into the lake and drowned in the water.

14The herdsmen fled to the nearby town and the surrounding countryside, spreading the news as they ran. People rushed out to see what had happened. 15A crowd soon gathered around Jesus, and they saw the man who had been possessed by the legion of demons. He was sitting there fully clothed and perfectly sane, and they were all afraid. 16Then those who had seen what happened told the others about the demon-possessed man and the pigs. 17And the crowd began pleading with Jesus to go away and leave them alone.

5:15 Matt 4:24

18As Jesus was getting into the boat, the man who had been demon possessed begged to go with Him. 19But Jesus said, "No, go home to your family, and tell them everything the Lord has done for you and how merciful He has been." 20So the man started off to visit the Ten Towns* of that region and began to proclaim the great things Jesus had done for him; and everyone was amazed at what he told them.

5:18 Ps 116:12

5:20 Ps 116:16; Isa 63:7; 1 Tim 1:13-14

5:1 Other manuscripts read *Gadarenes;* still others read *Gergesenes.* See Matt 8:28; Luke 8:26. 5:2 Greek *unclean;* also in 5:8, 13. 5:20 Greek *Decapolis.*

5:1 The land of the Gerasenes was on the eastern side of the Sea of Galilee. It was less heavily Jewish than most other parts of the land where Jesus spent His years of ministry. Notice that when this encounter was over, the man went to visit "the Ten Towns" or Decapolis (5:20), a region of predominantly Gentile towns.

5:2-7 This account shows the evil spirit making itself known through destructive behavior, supernatural power and strength, and supernatural insight. These indicators are also found in other encounters with demons in Scripture (Matthew 8:28-32; 15:22; 17:14-18). Jesus' method of dealing with demons involved simple commands (Matthew 17:18; Mark 1:34) by His own authority, a method He passed on to His disciples (Mark 3:15); this technique was used successfully by other believers as well (Mark 9:38).

5:9 *Legion* referred to a group of four to six thousand Roman soldiers. This man was under the influence of a large number of demons—a fact that was corroborated by the self-destructive act of the large herd of pigs later in the account.

5:16-17 The crowd grew concerned that Jesus' ministry would lead to more losses of livestock, so they begged Jesus to go away. The people were more concerned with their purses than with other people.

JESUS HEALS IN RESPONSE TO FAITH

5:21-43 21 Jesus got into the boat again and went back to the other side of the lake, where a large
//Matt 9:18-26 //Luke 8:40-56 crowd gathered around Him on the shore. 22 Then a leader of the local synagogue, whose
5:23 Matt 8:3 name was Jairus, arrived. When he saw Jesus, he fell at His feet, 23 pleading fervently with
Mark 6:5; 7:32; Him. "My little daughter is dying," he said. "Please come and lay Your hands on her; heal
8:23, 25 her so she can live."
Luke 4:40; 13:13 Acts 9:12, 17; 28:8 24 Jesus went with him, and all the people followed, crowding around Him. 25 A woman in
5:25 the crowd had suffered for twelve years with constant bleeding. 26 She had suffered a great
Lev 15:25-30 deal from many doctors, and over the years she had spent everything she had to pay them,
but she had gotten no better. In fact, she had gotten worse. 27 She had heard about Jesus, so
5:27 she came up behind Him through the crowd and touched His robe. 28 For she thought to
Mark 3:10 herself, "If I can just touch His robe, I will be healed." 29 Immediately the bleeding stopped,
Acts 19:11-12 and she could feel in her body that she had been healed of her terrible condition.
5:30 30 Jesus realized at once that healing power had gone out from Him, so He turned
Luke 6:19 around in the crowd and asked, "Who touched My robe?"
31 His disciples said to Him, "Look at this crowd pressing around You. How can You ask,
'Who touched Me?' "
32 But He kept on looking around to see who had done it. 33 Then the frightened woman,
trembling at the realization of what had happened to her, came and fell to her knees in
5:34 front of Him and told Him what she had done. 34 And He said to her, "Daughter, your faith
Mark 10:52 has made you well. Go in peace. Your suffering is over."
Luke 7:50; 17:19; 18:42 35 While He was still speaking to her, messengers arrived from the home of Jairus, the
Acts 14:9 leader of the synagogue. They told him, "Your daughter is dead. There's no use troubling
the Teacher now."
5:36 36 But Jesus overheard* them and said to Jairus, "Don't be afraid. Just have faith."
John 11:25-40 37 Then Jesus stopped the crowd and wouldn't let anyone go with Him except Peter,
James, and John (the brother of James). 38 When they came to the home of the synagogue
5:39 leader, Jesus saw much commotion and weeping and wailing. 39 He went inside and
John 11:11 asked, "Why all this commotion and weeping? The child isn't dead; she's only asleep."
5:40 40 The crowd laughed at Him. But He made them all leave, and He took the girl's father
Acts 9:40 and mother and His three disciples into the room where the girl was lying. 41 Holding her
5:41-42 Luke 7:14

5:36 Or *ignored.*

5:24-26 This woman's physical ailment was not her only problem. Her constant hemorrhaging also rendered her "unclean"—meaning she would have been cut off from normal social and family interactions.

▶ GOD

5:25-34 Spiritual relationships. It is easy to see people simply in terms of their most obvious problems or needs—a deformed limb, an orphaned child, a sick woman. But Jesus saw more; He saw the whole person. When a woman with a hemorrhage touched Jesus and was healed, she knew it, and so did Jesus. Why, then, did He stop and call for her? Didn't Jesus remember that a little girl's life was hanging in the balance as He delayed? Jesus wasn't wasting time; He took time to talk to and listen to this woman, who had been an outcast because of her affliction. Express your faith through your relationships and you'll see God at work in more lives than just your own. (***See God***> *Relationship> God Enables> God interacts with people,* TopicGuide page A14.)

5:34, 36 Both Jairus and the woman with the hemorrhage needed the same thing: faith. Jesus told the woman, "Your faith has made you well." And Jesus told Jairus not to be afraid but "Just have faith." Jesus was inviting others to a confident reliance in Himself.

▶ ADOPTION

5:35-43 Dealing with problems by faith. Jesus never promised anyone that if they followed Him or asked Him for help that their life would be problem-free. Even those who enjoy an intimate relationship with Jesus may face heartache and problems. Some believe that dealing with life's challenges by faith means inaction, but Jairus demonstrated his faith by action—he went to Jesus (5:22, 23) and humbled himself before Him. As you look to Christ for help in your struggles, do not forget the example of Jairus, whose belief in Christ meant an active pursuit of a solution. (***See Adoption***> *With Christ> Redemption> Promise of rescue from trouble,* TopicGuide page A37.)

5:38-40 The crowd gathered around Jairus' house likely included a number of "professional mourners." Funeral minstrels performed their duties as the first part of the Jewish mourning ceremony. Their dirges consisted of choral or antiphonal song accompanied by hand clapping. Even a poor man was expected to hire a minimum of two flute players and one professional mourner, so it is probable that a synagogue ruler would be expected to do more. Jesus' remark that the little girl was "only asleep" brought ridicule from these professionals, in stark contrast to the respectful manner in which Jairus dealt with Christ.

hand, He said to her, *"Talitha koum,"* which means "Little girl, get up!" [42]And the girl, who
was twelve years old, immediately stood up and walked around! They were overwhelmed
and totally amazed. [43]Jesus gave them strict orders not to tell anyone what had happened,
and then He told them to give her something to eat.

JESUS REJECTED AT NAZARETH

6 Jesus left that part of the country and returned with His disciples to Nazareth, His
hometown. [2]The next Sabbath He began teaching in the synagogue, and many who
heard Him were amazed. They asked, "Where did He get all this wisdom and the power to
perform such miracles?" [3]Then they scoffed, "He's just a carpenter, the son of Mary* and
the brother of James, Joseph,* Judas, and Simon. And His sisters live right here among us."
They were deeply offended and refused to believe in Him.
[4]Then Jesus told them, "A prophet is honored everywhere except in his own hometown
and among his relatives and his own family." [5]And because of their unbelief, He couldn't
do any miracles among them except to place His hands on a few sick people and heal
them. [6]And He was amazed at their unbelief.

JESUS SENDS OUT THE TWELVE DISCIPLES

Then Jesus went from village to village, teaching the people. [7]And He called His twelve
disciples together and began sending them out two by two, giving them authority to cast
out evil* spirits. [8]He told them to take nothing for their journey except a walking stick—no
food, no traveler's bag, no money.* [9]He allowed them to wear sandals but not to take a
change of clothes.
[10]"Wherever you go," He said, "stay in the same house until you leave town. [11]But if any
place refuses to welcome you or listen to you, shake its dust from your feet as you leave to
show that you have abandoned those people to their fate."
[12]So the disciples went out, telling everyone they met to repent of their sins and turn to
God. [13]And they cast out many demons and healed many sick people, anointing them
with olive oil.

THE DEATH OF JOHN THE BAPTIST

[14]Herod Antipas, the king, soon heard about Jesus, because everyone was talking about
Him. Some were saying,* "This must be John the Baptist raised from the dead. That is why
He can do such miracles." [15]Others said, "He's the prophet Elijah." Still others said, "He's a
prophet like the other great prophets of the past."

5:43 Matt 8:4; Mark 1:44; 7:36
6:1-6 //Matt 13:53-58; //Luke 4:16-30
6:2 John 7:15
6:3 John 6:42
6:4 John 4:44
6:5 Matt 9:18
6:7-13 //Matt 10:1, 5-15; //Luke 9:1-6
6:7 Luke 10:1
6:8-9 Luke 10:4
6:10 Luke 10:7
6:11 Luke 10:11; Acts 13:51
6:13 Luke 10:34; Jas 5:14
6:14-29 //Matt 14:1-12; //Luke 9:7-9
6:15 Matt 16:14

6:3a Some manuscripts read *He's just the son of the carpenter and of Mary.* 6:3b Most manuscripts read *Joses;* see Matt 13:55. 6:7 Greek *unclean.* 6:8 Greek *no copper coins in their money belts.* 6:14 Some manuscripts read *He was saying.*

6:1-2 When Jesus returned to Nazareth and taught in a synagogue, the people "were amazed." The word carries the sense of being struck with a blow. These citizens from His hometown had a difficult time accepting that Jesus, who grew up on their streets, was teaching, healing, and delivering people from demonic oppression.

▸ HOLINESS

6:6-13 Walk the talk. Jesus knew that simply telling someone how to live could only teach so much—so He added life experience to His disciples' education. Their mission was twofold—teaching and healing as Jesus had demonstrated. Their mission was short-term—they brought very few supplies and were dependent on the local population for support. This accomplished another goal—it forced them to come back to Jesus regularly for food and shelter when their mission in a town was over. Jesus knows that we cannot easily duplicate His ministry. Though we'll be rejected and will experience the pain of persecution, we must remember to follow His instructions for ministry and seek intimacy with Him. (***See Holiness**> Submission> Trusting God> Obedience,* TopicGuide page A40.)

6:7-13 In Mark 3:14, we read about Jesus choosing His twelve closest followers, whom He would teach and send out to do His work. Here we see the beginnings of their ministry. Mark 6:13 notes that the disciples anointed the sick with oil, a practice that was generally reserved for consecrating prophets, priests, and kings (Exodus 29:7; 1 Kings 19:16; 2 Kings 9:6). Jesus' followers would continue to connect prayers for healing with anointing with oil (James 5:14), showing that under the New Covenant even the sick are prepared for holy ministry (1 Peter 2:9).

6:15 Many Jews—in Jesus' day and even now—believed that Elijah would return to the earth prior to the establishment of the Messiah's rule (see Malachi 3:1; 4:5-6). Elijah's ministry included powerful preaching and miracles, which explains the comparison of Jesus to Elijah.

16 When Herod heard about Jesus, he said, "John, the man I beheaded, has come back from the dead."

6:17-18 Lev 18:15-16; 20:21 Luke 3:19-20

17 For Herod had sent soldiers to arrest and imprison John as a favor to Herodias. She had been his brother Philip's wife, but Herod had married her. 18 John had been telling Herod, "It is against God's law for you to marry your brother's wife." 19 So Herodias bore a grudge against John and wanted to kill him. But without Herod's approval she was powerless, 20 for Herod respected John; and knowing that he was a good and holy man, he protected him. Herod was greatly disturbed whenever he talked with John, but even so, he liked to listen to him.

21 Herodias's chance finally came on Herod's birthday. He gave a party for his high government officials, army officers, and the leading citizens of Galilee. 22 Then his daughter, also named Herodias,* came in and performed a dance that greatly pleased Herod and his guests. "Ask me for anything you like," the king said to the girl, "and I will give it to you."

6:23 Esth 5:3-6; 7:2

23 He even vowed, "I will give you whatever you ask, up to half my kingdom!"

24 She went out and asked her mother, "What should I ask for?"

Her mother told her, "Ask for the head of John the Baptist!"

25 So the girl hurried back to the king and told him, "I want the head of John the Baptist, right now, on a tray!"

26 Then the king deeply regretted what he had said; but because of the vows he had made in front of his guests, he couldn't refuse her. 27 So he immediately sent an executioner to the prison to cut off John's head and bring it to him. The soldier beheaded John in the prison, 28 brought his head on a tray, and gave it to the girl, who took it to her mother. 29 When John's disciples heard what had happened, they came to get his body and buried it in a tomb.

JESUS FEEDS FIVE THOUSAND

6:30 Luke 9:10; 10:17

30 The apostles returned to Jesus from their ministry tour and told Him all they had done and taught. 31 Then Jesus said, "Let's go off by ourselves to a quiet place and rest awhile."

6:31 Mark 3:20

He said this because there were so many people coming and going that Jesus and His apostles didn't even have time to eat.

6:32-44 //Matt 14:13-21 //Luke 9:10-17 //John 6:5-13

32 So they left by boat for a quiet place, where they could be alone. 33 But many people recognized them and saw them leaving, and people from many towns ran ahead along the shore and got there ahead of them. 34 Jesus saw the huge crowd as He stepped from the boat, and He had compassion on them because they were like sheep without a shepherd. So He began teaching them many things.

6:34 *Num 27:17 *1 Kgs 22:17 *2 Chr 18:16 *Zech 10:2 Matt 9:36

35 Late in the afternoon His disciples came to Him and said, "This is a remote place, and it's already getting late. 36 Send the crowds away so they can go to the nearby farms and villages and buy something to eat."

6:37 2 Kgs 4:42-44 Matt 15:33 Mark 8:4

37 But Jesus said, "You feed them."

"With what?" they asked. "We'd have to work for months to earn enough money* to buy food for all these people!"

6:38 Matt 15:34 Mark 8:5

38 "How much bread do you have?" He asked. "Go and find out."

They came back and reported, "We have five loaves of bread and two fish."

39 Then Jesus told the disciples to have the people sit down in groups on the green grass. 40 So they sat down in groups of fifty or a hundred.

6:22 Some manuscripts read *the daughter of Herodias herself.* **6:37** Greek *It would take 200 denarii.* A denarius was equivalent to a laborer's full day's wage.

▸ PURPOSE

6:30-44 The impossible need. How big would our need have to be before we would conclude that Jesus couldn't address it? Here the disciples sat with 5,000 men (not counting the women and children) to listen to Jesus teach. As the day wore on, it became evident that the people were more interested in listening to Jesus than finding food for themselves. So Jesus asked the disciples to help meet the need. They thought it was impossible—but as they followed His directions, the need was met and everyone was amazed. Do you give God opportunities to do amazing things in your life? Live by faith and look out—God can do anything! (***See Purpose**> God's Deeds> Special Acts> Miracles> Jesus> Feeding the 5,000,* TopicGuide page A53.)

41Jesus took the five loaves and two fish, looked up toward heaven, and blessed them. **6:41**
Then, breaking the loaves into pieces, He kept giving the bread to the disciples so they Matt 14:19
could distribute it to the people. He also divided the fish for everyone to share. 42They all
ate as much as they wanted, 43and afterward, the disciples picked up twelve baskets of
leftover bread and fish. 44A total of 5,000 men and their families were fed from those
loaves!

JESUS WALKS ON WATER

45Immediately after this, Jesus insisted that His disciples get back into the boat and head **6:45-52**
across the lake to Bethsaida, while He sent the people home. 46After telling everyone //Matt 14:22-33
good-bye, He went up into the hills by Himself to pray. //John 6:16-21
47Late that night, the disciples were in their boat in the middle of the lake, and Jesus was
alone on land. 48He saw that they were in serious trouble, rowing hard and struggling
against the wind and waves. About three o'clock in the morning* Jesus came toward them,
walking on the water. He intended to go past them, 49but when they saw Him walking on
the water, they cried out in terror, thinking He was a ghost. 50They were all terrified when
they saw Him.
But Jesus spoke to them at once. "Don't be afraid," He said. "Take courage! I am here!*"
51Then He climbed into the boat, and the wind stopped. They were totally amazed, 52for **6:52**
they still didn't understand the significance of the miracle of the loaves. Their hearts were Mark 8:17-21
too hard to take it in.
53After they had crossed the lake, they landed at Gennesaret. They brought the boat to **6:53-56**
shore 54and climbed out. The people recognized Jesus at once, 55and they ran throughout //Matt 14:34-36
the whole area, carrying sick people on mats to wherever they heard He was. 56Wherever **6:56**
He went—in villages, cities, or the countryside—they brought the sick out to the market- Matt 9:20
places. They begged Him to let the sick touch at least the fringe of His robe, and all who Mark 5:27
touched Him were healed. Luke 8:44

JESUS TEACHES ABOUT INNER PURITY

7 One day some Pharisees and teachers of religious law arrived from Jerusalem to see **7:1-23**
Jesus. 2They noticed that some of His disciples failed to follow the Jewish ritual of //Matt 15:1-20
hand washing before eating. 3(The Jews, especially the Pharisees, do not eat until they **7:2**
have poured water over their cupped hands,* as required by their ancient traditions. Luke 11:38
4Similarly, they don't eat anything from the market until they immerse their hands* in wa- Acts 10:14, 28
ter. This is but one of many traditions they have clung to—such as their ceremonial wash- **7:3**
ing of cups, pitchers, and kettles.*) Gal 1:14
Col 2:8

6:48 Greek *About the fourth watch of the night.* 6:50 Or *The 'I AM' is here;* Greek reads *I am.* See Exod 3:14. 7:3 Greek *have washed with the fist.* 7:4a Some manuscripts read *sprinkle themselves.* 7:4b Some manuscripts add *and dining couches.*

7:4
Matt 23:25
Luke 11:39

6:45, 53 Jesus made His disciples go ahead of Him to Bethsaida, a city on the northeast side of the Sea of Galilee. But Mark tells us that they arrived at Gennesaret, which is on the Gentile-populated northwest side of the Sea of Galilee, a fair distance from their designated destination. They didn't reach the place Jesus had told them to go.

▸ GOD
6:52 Don't miss the wonders. What can keep you from seeing and appreciating the mighty works that God does in and through your life? The disciples apparently missed something here. When Jesus came walking on the water, they were afraid. They did not need to fear, but they had missed "the significance of the miracle of the loaves" because their hearts were hard. The same thing can happen to us. If our hearts are hardened by problems like unconfessed sin (Hebrews 3:13), we will be unable to understand what God is trying to teach us. Don't miss God's messages to you because of a hardened heart. (***See God****> Relationship> Barriers> Hardened heart,* TopicGuide page A14.)

7:3-4 Because he explained this Jewish practice, it is clear that Mark's primary audience was non-Jewish people.

7:3-9 The Scriptures do not specifically command this particular practice of washing; only washing of illness-defiled clothing is mentioned (Leviticus 13:6, 34; 14:8). Over the years, Jews embraced a large collection of oral traditions; as a result, Jewish leaders in Jesus' day considered many practices and rituals equal to the law though they were only tradition. Jesus never condemned tradition in general, except when tradition was treated as equal to the Mosaic law, or when it hindered people from serving God (Matthew 15:6; see also Galatians 1:14; Colossians 2:6-8).

5So the Pharisees and teachers of religious law asked Him, "Why don't Your disciples fol-
low our age-old tradition? They eat without first performing the hand-washing ceremony."
7:6-7 6Jesus replied, "You hypocrites! Isaiah was right when he prophesied about you, for he
*Isa 29:13 Col 2:22 wrote,

'These people honor Me with their lips,
but their hearts are far from Me.
7 Their worship is a farce,
for they teach man-made ideas as commands from God.'*

8For you ignore God's law and substitute your own tradition."
7:9 9Then He said, "You skillfully sidestep God's law in order to hold on to your own tradi-
Isa 24:4-5 tion. 10For instance, Moses gave you this law from God: 'Honor your father and mother,'*
7:10 and 'Anyone who speaks disrespectfully of father or mother must be put to death.'* 11But
*Exod 20:12; 21:17 *Lev 20:9 you say it is all right for people to say to their parents, 'Sorry, I can't help you. For I have
Deut 5:16 1 Tim 5:8 vowed to give to God what I would have given to you.' 12In this way, you let them disre-
gard their needy parents. 13And so you cancel the word of God in order to hand down
your own tradition. And this is only one example among many others."
14Then Jesus called to the crowd to come and hear. "All of you listen," He said, "and try
7:15 to understand. 15It's not what goes into your body that defiles you; you are defiled by
1 Cor 8:8 1 Tim 4:4 what comes from your heart.*"
17Then Jesus went into a house to get away from the crowd, and His disciples asked
7:17 Mark 9:28 Him what He meant by the parable He had just used. 18"Don't you understand either?" He
asked. "Can't you see that the food you put into your body cannot defile you? 19Food
7:19 Acts 10:15; 11:9 doesn't go into your heart, but only passes through the stomach and then goes into the
Rom 14:1-12 Col 2:16 sewer." (By saying this, He declared that every kind of food is acceptable in God's eyes.)
1 Tim 4:3-5 20And then He added, "It is what comes from inside that defiles you. 21For from within,
7:21-22 out of a person's heart, come evil thoughts, sexual immorality, theft, murder, 22adultery,
Rom 1:29-31 Gal 5:19-21 greed, wickedness, deceit, lustful desires, envy, slander, pride, and foolishness. 23All these
Titus 1:15 vile things come from within; they are what defile you."

THE FAITH OF A GENTILE WOMAN

7:24-30 24Then Jesus left Galilee and went north to the region of Tyre.* He didn't want anyone to
//Matt 15:21-28 know which house He was staying in, but He couldn't keep it a secret. 25Right away a
woman who had heard about Him came and fell at His feet. Her little girl was possessed by
an evil* spirit, 26and she begged Him to cast out the demon from her daughter.

7:7 Isa 29:13 (Greek version). 7:10a Exod 20:12; Deut 5:16. 7:10b Exod 21:17 (Greek version); Lev 20:9 (Greek version). 7:11 Greek *'What I would have given to you is Corban' (that is, a gift).* 7:15 Some manuscripts add verse 16, *Anyone with ears to hear should listen and understand.* Compare 4:9, 23. 7:24 Some manuscripts add *and Sidon.* 7:25 Greek *unclean.*

▸ WORSHIP

7:6-13 The heart of worship. What makes worship truly worship? The songs? The eloquent prayers? The powerful message? The sacrificial giving? It is possible to do all of these things in a highly religious way and still not worship, according to Jesus. True worship must be from the heart, not merely an external or intellectual exercise. But it's not entirely without external acts, either. Worship is an intentional act of bringing honor to God that flows from an attitude of submission to His authority and awe at His majesty. True worship springs up from the depths of our souls and flows out in a vibrant and expressive manner that bears witness to the greatness of God. Let the ends of the earth be inspired by your worship and respond in kind (Psalm 97:1). (***See Worship***> *NT> Our Role> Mind and Heart> Heart-felt worship,* TopicGuide page A32.)

7:24 The region of Tyre was located near the northern border of Israel. It was predominantly Gentile, and the Syrian Phoenician woman who came to Jesus there was a Gentile (7:26).

▸ SALVATION

7:24-30 We respond to Jesus in faith. At first reading, it seems as if Jesus was not interested at all in helping this woman with her need. But in reality Jesus was simply affirming His call and purpose. When the woman responded by affirming that "even the dogs . . . are allowed to eat the scraps," she was making a profound statement of faith. In effect she was saying, "Yes, Jesus, I recognize that You have Your call and purpose, but whatever crumbs You choose to brush off in my direction will be more than enough for me." Are you willing to demonstrate this same faith in Jesus? (***See Salvation***> *Receiving> How> Faith in Christ,* TopicGuide page A22.)

Since she was a Gentile, born in Syrian Phoenicia, 27Jesus told her, "First I should feed the children—My own family, the Jews.* It isn't right to take food from the children and throw it to the dogs."

28She replied, "That's true, Lord, but even the dogs under the table are allowed to eat the scraps from the children's plates."

29"Good answer!" He said. "Now go home, for the demon has left your daughter." 30And when she arrived home, she found her little girl lying quietly in bed, and the demon was gone.

JESUS HEALS A DEAF MAN

31Jesus left Tyre and went up to Sidon before going back to the Sea of Galilee and the region of the Ten Towns.* 32A deaf man with a speech impediment was brought to Him, and the people begged Jesus to lay His hands on the man to heal him.

33Jesus led him away from the crowd so they could be alone. He put His fingers into the man's ears. Then, spitting on His own fingers, He touched the man's tongue. 34Looking up to heaven, He sighed and said, *"Ephphatha,"* which means, "Be opened!" 35Instantly the man could hear perfectly, and his tongue was freed so he could speak plainly!

36Jesus told the crowd not to tell anyone, but the more He told them not to, the more they spread the news. 37They were completely amazed and said again and again, "Everything He does is wonderful. He even makes the deaf to hear and gives speech to those who cannot speak."

JESUS FEEDS FOUR THOUSAND

8 About this time another large crowd had gathered, and the people ran out of food again. Jesus called His disciples and told them, 2"I feel sorry for these people. They have been here with Me for three days, and they have nothing left to eat. 3If I send them home hungry, they will faint along the way. For some of them have come a long distance."

4His disciples replied, "How are we supposed to find enough food to feed them out here in the wilderness?"

5Jesus asked, "How much bread do you have?"

"Seven loaves," they replied.

6So Jesus told all the people to sit down on the ground. Then He took the seven loaves, thanked God for them, and broke them into pieces. He gave them to His disciples, who distributed the bread to the crowd. 7A few small fish were found, too, so Jesus also blessed these and told the disciples to distribute them.

8They ate as much as they wanted. Afterward, the disciples picked up seven large baskets of leftover food. 9There were about 4,000 people in the crowd that day, and Jesus sent them home after they had eaten. 10Immediately after this, He got into a boat with His disciples and crossed over to the region of Dalmanutha.

7:31-37 //Matt 15:29-31
7:33 Mark 8:23; John 9:6
7:34 Matt 14:19; Mark 6:41; John 11:41; 17:1
7:36 Matt 8:4
7:37 Isa 35:5-6
8:1-10 //Matt 15:32-39; Mark 6:32-44
8:2 Matt 9:36
8:4 Num 11:21-22; 2 Kgs 4:42-43
8:7 Matt 14:19
8:10 Matt 15:39

7:27 Greek *Let the children eat first.* 7:31 Greek *Decapolis.*

7:27 The Jews in Jesus' day referred to the Gentiles as "dogs"; they considered the Gentiles to be cut off from the people of God. Jesus seemed to speak intentionally in this common, offensive manner to test the faith of the woman. The fact that He healed her daughter, however, indicates that He loved her and validated her genuine faith, thus challenging the wrong beliefs of that day.

7:31 Jesus returned to the area of the Ten Towns near the place where He had delivered the man living in the tombs from the many demons who had tormented him. Jesus had sent the man into the Gentile-populated Decapolis region to tell everyone the great things Jesus had done for him (5:19-20). Apparently the man proceeded to do that very thing, for when Jesus returned to the area a crowd showed up (7:32-33), seeking His help.

▸ GOD

8:1-9 Merciful Savior. This is the second time Mark recorded that Jesus fed a multitude using only the most meager of resources. Many would see what Jesus did here and conclude that God's power was working in and through Him—and that would be a reasonable conclusion. But don't miss the other thing Mark told us: *why* Jesus did these miracles. In both cases, Jesus saw a need and responded. He felt compassion for the hungry people. He immediately set in motion events that would feed the people. We worry about our gifts to the needy being misused—perhaps we worry too much. Compassion sometimes means giving and letting God worry about the precise outcome of our generosity. (***See God****> God's Nature> Personality> Emotion> God is compassionate and loving,* TopicGuide page A14.)

PHARISEES DEMAND A MIRACULOUS SIGN

8:11-21 //Matt 16:1-12 Luke 11:16, 29 John 6:30

11 When the Pharisees heard that Jesus had arrived, they came and started to argue with Him. Testing Him, they demanded that He show them a miraculous sign from heaven to prove His authority.

12 When He heard this, He sighed deeply in His spirit and said, "Why do these people keep demanding a miraculous sign? I tell you the truth, I will not give this generation any such sign." 13 So He got back into the boat and left them, and He crossed to the other side of the lake.

YEAST OF THE PHARISEES AND HEROD

8:15 Luke 12:1

14 But the disciples had forgotten to bring any food. They had only one loaf of bread with them in the boat. 15 As they were crossing the lake, Jesus warned them, "Watch out! Beware of the yeast of the Pharisees and of Herod."

8:17 Isa 6:9-10 Mark 6:52 · 8:18 *Jer 5:21 Ezek 12:2 Matt 13:13 · 8:19 Mark 6:41-44 Luke 9:17 John 6:13 · 8:20 Matt 15:37

16 At this they began to argue with each other because they hadn't brought any bread. 17 Jesus knew what they were saying, so He said, "Why are you arguing about having no bread? Don't you know or understand even yet? Are your hearts too hard to take it in? 18 'You have eyes—can't you see? You have ears—can't you hear?'* Don't you remember anything at all? 19 When I fed the 5,000 with five loaves of bread, how many baskets of leftovers did you pick up afterward?"

"Twelve," they said.

20 "And when I fed the 4,000 with seven loaves, how many large baskets of leftovers did you pick up?"

"Seven," they said.

21 "Don't you understand yet?" He asked them.

JESUS HEALS A BLIND MAN

8:23 Mark 7:33 John 9:6 · 8:26 Matt 8:4

22 When they arrived at Bethsaida, some people brought a blind man to Jesus, and they begged Him to touch the man and heal him. 23 Jesus took the blind man by the hand and led him out of the village. Then, spitting on the man's eyes, He laid His hands on him and asked, "Can you see anything now?"

24 The man looked around. "Yes," he said, "I see people, but I can't see them very clearly. They look like trees walking around."

25 Then Jesus placed His hands on the man's eyes again, and his eyes were opened. His sight was completely restored, and he could see everything clearly. 26 Jesus sent him away, saying, "Don't go back into the village on your way home."

PETER'S DECLARATION ABOUT JESUS

8:27-30 //Matt 16:13-20 //Luke 9:18-21 John 6:67-71 · 8:28 Matt 14:2 · 8:29 Matt 16:20 Luke 9:20 John 6:69; 11:27

27 Jesus and His disciples left Galilee and went up to the villages near Caesarea Philippi. As they were walking along, He asked them, "Who do people say I am?"

28 "Well," they replied, "some say John the Baptist, some say Elijah, and others say You are one of the other prophets."

29 Then He asked them, "But who do you say I am?"

Peter replied, "You are the Messiah.*"

30 But Jesus warned them not to tell anyone about Him.

8:18 Jer 5:21. 8:29 Or *the Christ. Messiah* (a Hebrew term) and *Christ* (a Greek term) both mean "the anointed one."

8:11 When the religious leaders asked Jesus for a "sign from heaven," they likely weren't asking Jesus simply to do a miracle—they had seen those before. They wanted Him to do a particular kind of miracle, perhaps some kind of display from the sky, like Elijah's or David's fire from heaven (1 Kings 18:36-38; 2 Kings 1:10; 1 Chronicles 21:26).

8:15 When Jesus cautioned the disciples about the "yeast of the Pharisees and of Herod," He wasn't making a reference to their baking habits—although the disciples' thoughts turned to bread. He was cautioning them about the false teachings of both the religious and the political rulers of the day (Matthew 16:6-12).

JESUS PREDICTS HIS DEATH

31 Then Jesus began to tell them that the Son of Man* must suffer many terrible things and
be rejected by the elders, the leading priests, and the teachers of religious law. He would
be killed, but three days later He would rise from the dead. 32 As He talked about this
openly with His disciples, Peter took Him aside and began to reprimand Him for saying
such things.*

33 Jesus turned around and looked at His disciples, then reprimanded Peter. "Get away
from Me, Satan!" He said. "You are seeing things merely from a human point of view, not
from God's."

34 Then, calling the crowd to join His disciples, He said, "If any of you wants to be My fol-
lower, you must turn from your selfish ways, take up your cross, and follow Me. 35 If you try
to hang on to your life, you will lose it. But if you give up your life for My sake and for the
sake of the Good News, you will save it. 36 And what do you benefit if you gain the whole
world but lose your own soul?* 37 Is anything worth more than your soul? 38 If anyone is
ashamed of Me and My message in these adulterous and sinful days, the Son of Man will
be ashamed of that person when He returns in the glory of His Father with the holy angels."

8:31–9:1 //Matt 16:21-28 //Luke 9:21-27
8:34 Matt 10:38 Luke 14:27
8:35 Matt 10:39 Luke 17:33 John 12:25
8:38 Matt 10:33 Luke 12:9

9 Jesus went on to say, "I tell you the truth, some standing here right now will not die
before they see the Kingdom of God arrive in great power!"

THE TRANSFIGURATION

2 Six days later Jesus took Peter, James, and John, and led them up a high mountain to be
alone. As the men watched, Jesus' appearance was transformed, 3 and His clothes became
dazzling white, far whiter than any earthly bleach could ever make them. 4 Then Elijah and
Moses appeared and began talking with Jesus.

5 Peter exclaimed, "Rabbi, it's wonderful for us to be here! Let's make three shelters as
memorials*—one for You, one for Moses, and one for Elijah." 6 He said this because he
didn't really know what else to say, for they were all terrified.

7 Then a cloud overshadowed them, and a voice from the cloud said, "This is My dearly
loved Son. Listen to Him." 8 Suddenly, when they looked around, Moses and Elijah were
gone, and they saw only Jesus with them.

9:2-10 //Matt 17:1-9 //Luke 9:28-36 2 Pet 1:17-18
9:3 Dan 7:9 Matt 28:3
9:7 Exod 40:34 Deut 18:15 Heb 1:2; 2:3; 12:25

8:31 "Son of Man" is a title Jesus used for Himself. 8:32 Or *began to correct Him.* 8:36 Or *your self?* also in 8:37.
9:5 Greek *three tabernacles.*

8:31 The Old Testament used the phrase *son of man* to speak about those who represented God, like Ezekiel (see Ezekiel 2:1, 3, 6, 8) or Daniel (see Daniel 8:17). But the title was also used to refer to the One who would come from God as the promised Deliverer (as in Daniel 7:13 and Psalm 80:17). Jesus used the title to refer to Himself: He is the One who represents God because He is the Messiah, the promised Deliverer.

8:33 Jesus was not identifying Peter as Satan. Because Peter was "seeing things merely from a human point of view" and was attempting to persuade Jesus not to die for His people, Peter was acting as an agent to accomplish Satan's purposes.

8:34 The expression "take up your cross" has slipped into the common language of many cultures. People use it to refer to doing something hard or enduring some great difficulty. But when Jesus spoke of taking up a cross, He was referring to a form of execution. To follow Jesus, the disciples' way of life would have to come to an end—and not without pain.

▸ HOLINESS
8:34-35 Following His agenda. Jesus saves, but He also rules. Our experience of release from the power and penalty of sin can never be separated from embracing Jesus Christ as our Master and taking the road He walked. This means giving up the right to hang on to our life, just as Jesus gave up the right to hang on to His. The people who follow Him must give up their agenda for their life and embrace His. To put it simply, new life can be experienced fully only on Jesus' terms. In God's Kingdom, surrender and service lead to victory and the right to rule (Mark 9:33-35; Matthew 18:1-4; Luke 9:46-48; John 13:1-17). In God's world, you cannot be exalted unless you humble yourself. (***See Holiness***> *Submission*> *Yielding to Spirit*> *Surrender your heart,* TopicGuide page A41.)

▸ WORSHIP
9:2-8 Pray with your ears open. How much sense would it make for a passenger boarding a plane to advise the pilot on the best way to handle the aircraft? Yet this is exactly what we do with Jesus, and Peter did the same thing (8:32). Often our prayers are little more than telling Jesus what we think is best. That is why the Father's counsel to the disciples here is so important: "This is my dearly loved Son. Listen to Him." When was the last time you really listened for the voice of the Son in your time of prayer? Take time to wait, listen, and faithfully respond to the revealing power of the Spirit. (***See Worship***> *NT*> *Prayer*> *Instructions*> *Pray believing,* TopicGuide page A33.)

9As they went back down the mountain, He told them not to tell anyone what they had
seen until the Son of Man* had risen from the dead. 10So they kept it to themselves, but
they often asked each other what He meant by "rising from the dead."
9:11-13 11Then they asked Him, "Why do the teachers of religious law insist that Elijah must re-
//Matt 17:10-12 turn before the Messiah comes?*"
12Jesus responded, "Elijah is indeed coming first to get everything ready. Yet why do the
Scriptures say that the Son of Man must suffer greatly and be treated with utter contempt?
9:13 13But I tell you, Elijah has already come, and they chose to abuse him, just as the Scrip-
Ps 22:6-7; Isa 50:6; 53:3 tures predicted."
Matt 11:14

JESUS HEALS A DEMON-POSSESSED BOY

9:14-29 14When they returned to the other disciples, they saw a large crowd surrounding them,
//Matt 17:14-21 and some teachers of religious law were arguing with them. 15When the crowd saw Jesus,
//Luke 9:37-42 they were overwhelmed with awe, and they ran to greet Him.
16"What is all this arguing about?" Jesus asked.
17One of the men in the crowd spoke up and said, "Teacher, I brought my son so You
could heal him. He is possessed by an evil spirit that won't let him talk. 18And whenever
this spirit seizes him, it throws him violently to the ground. Then he foams at the mouth
and grinds his teeth and becomes rigid.* So I asked Your disciples to cast out the evil spirit,
but they couldn't do it."
19Jesus said to them,* "You faithless people! How long must I be with you? How long
must I put up with you? Bring the boy to Me."
9:20 20So they brought the boy. But when the evil spirit saw Jesus, it threw the child into a
Mark 1:26 violent convulsion, and he fell to the ground, writhing and foaming at the mouth.
21"How long has this been happening?" Jesus asked the boy's father.
He replied, "Since he was a little boy. 22The spirit often throws him into the fire or into
water, trying to kill him. Have mercy on us and help us, if You can."
9:23 23"What do you mean, 'If I can'?" Jesus asked. "Anything is possible if a person believes."
Matt 21:21; Mark 11:23-24 24The father instantly cried out, "I do believe, but help me overcome my unbelief!"
Luke 17:6 25When Jesus saw that the crowd of onlookers was growing, He rebuked the evil* spirit.
John 11:40; Acts 14:9 "Listen, you spirit that makes this boy unable to hear and speak," He said. "I command you
to come out of this child and never enter him again!"
9:24 Luke 17:5 26Then the spirit screamed and threw the boy into another violent convulsion and left
9:25 him. The boy appeared to be dead. A murmur ran through the crowd as people said, "He's
Acts 10:38 dead." 27But Jesus took him by the hand and helped him to his feet, and he stood up.
9:26 28Afterward, when Jesus was alone in the house with His disciples, they asked Him,
Mark 1:26 "Why couldn't we cast out that evil spirit?"
9:27 Matt 8:15 29Jesus replied, "This kind can be cast out only by prayer.*"

9:9 "Son of Man" is a title Jesus used for Himself. 9:11 Greek *that Elijah must come first?* 9:18 Or *becomes weak.* 9:19 Or *said to His disciples.* 9:25 Greek *unclean.* 9:29 Some manuscripts read *by prayer and fasting.*

9:11-13 Both the disciples and Jesus believed that Elijah would return before the Messiah came to rule in Israel (see note on 6:15). It is clear from other Gospels that Jesus had John the Baptist in mind (see Matthew 11:12-14). Jesus was not saying, however, that John was Elijah come back to life; rather, John fulfilled Elijah's role and possessed "the spirit and power of Elijah" (Luke 1:17).

9:14-29 From these verses it is clear that the healing of satanic oppression and illness requires faith (9:23-24; James 5:15)—faith that was not present in the disciples nor the possessed boy's father. Jesus directed them to build their faith through prayer, though faith may also be increased through exposure to godly preaching and Scripture (Romans 10:17) and obedience (1 Timothy 3:13).

▸ GOD

9:29 God strengthens. Sometimes as we seek to live out the Christian faith, we face a significant challenge and conclude that the task before us is impossible. More than one Christian has ended up saying, "Well, maybe Jesus could have handled this, but I can't." Take courage. Jesus never calls you to do something without offering to empower you to do the work. Perhaps the task requires you to *pray* for the need confronting you; the disciples received this word after failing to deliver a young boy from affliction: "This kind can be cast out only by prayer." Don't depend on your own resources; use the spiritual tools God provides to do His work (Ephesians 6:10-20). (***See God****> Salvation> Holy Spirit> Strengthens us,* TopicGuide page A15.)

JESUS AGAIN PREDICTS HIS DEATH

[30]Leaving that region, they traveled through Galilee. Jesus didn't want anyone to know He
was there, [31]for He wanted to spend more time with His disciples and teach them. He said
to them, "The Son of Man is going to be betrayed into the hands of His enemies. He will be
killed, but three days later He will rise from the dead." [32]They didn't understand what He
was saying, however, and they were afraid to ask Him what He meant.

9:30-32 //Matt 17:22-23 //Luke 9:43-45
9:31 Matt 16:21 Mark 8:31 Luke 9:22

THE GREATEST IN THE KINGDOM

[33]After they arrived at Capernaum and settled in a house, Jesus asked His disciples, "What
were you discussing out on the road?" [34]But they didn't answer, because they had been ar-
guing about which of them was the greatest. [35]He sat down, called the twelve disciples
over to Him, and said, "Whoever wants to be first must take last place and be the servant
of everyone else."

[36]Then He put a little child among them. Taking the child in His arms, He said to them,
[37]"Anyone who welcomes a little child like this on My behalf* welcomes Me, and anyone
who welcomes Me welcomes not only Me but also My Father who sent Me."

9:33-37 //Matt 18:1-5 //Luke 9:46-48
9:35 Matt 20:27
9:37 Matt 10:40 Luke 10:16 John 13:20

USING THE NAME OF JESUS

[38]John said to Jesus, "Teacher, we saw someone using Your name to cast out demons, but
we told him to stop because he wasn't in our group."

[39]"Don't stop him!" Jesus said. "No one who performs a miracle in My name will soon be
able to speak evil of Me. [40]Anyone who is not against us is for us. [41]If anyone gives you
even a cup of water because you belong to the Messiah, I tell you the truth, that person
will surely be rewarded.

[42]"But if you cause one of these little ones who trusts in Me to fall into sin, it would be
better for you to be thrown into the sea with a large millstone hung around your neck. [43]If
your hand causes you to sin, cut it off. It's better to enter eternal life with only one hand
than to go into the unquenchable fires of hell* with two hands.* [45]If your foot causes you
to sin, cut it off. It's better to enter eternal life with only one foot than to be thrown into hell
with two feet.* [47]And if your eye causes you to sin, gouge it out. It's better to enter the
Kingdom of God with only one eye than to have two eyes and be thrown into hell,
[48]'where the maggots never die and the fire never goes out.'*

[49]"For everyone will be tested with fire.* [50]Salt is good for seasoning. But if it loses its fla-
vor, how do you make it salty again? You must have the qualities of salt among your-
selves and live in peace with each other."

9:38-41 Num 11:26-29 //Luke 9:49-50
9:39 1 Cor 12:3
9:40 Matt 12:30 Luke 11:23
9:42-48 //Matt 18:6-9 //Luke 17:1-2
9:43 Matt 5:30; 18:8
9:47 Matt 5:29
9:48 2 Thes 1:9
9:50 Matt 5:13 Luke 14:34 Rom 12:18 Col 4:6

DISCUSSION ABOUT DIVORCE AND MARRIAGE

10 Then Jesus left Capernaum and went down to the region of Judea and into the
area east of the Jordan River. Once again crowds gathered around Him, and as
usual He was teaching them.

10:1-12 //Matt 19:1-12

9:37 Greek *in My name.* 9:43a Greek *Gehenna;* also in 9:45, 47. 9:43b Some manuscripts add verse 44, *'where the maggots never die and the fire never goes out.'* See 9:48. 9:45 Some manuscripts add verse 46, *'where the maggots never die and the fire never goes out.'* See 9:48. 9:48 Isa 66:24. 9:49 Greek *salted with fire;* other manuscripts add *and every sacrifice will be salted with salt.*

9:36-37 Although children in Jesus' day might have received love from their parents, they were considered to be relatively worthless in society. Anyone who "welcomes a little child" would have been embracing someone who couldn't do anything for you, someone from whom you couldn't get anything to benefit yourself.

9:42-48 Jesus was not suggesting that physically assaulting one's own body is the real solution to sin. He was using hyperbole—a powerful and over-extended image to drive home a point. Jesus doesn't want any of His followers to overlook the seriousness of sin.

9:50 Salt has always been used to flavor and preserve food. In the Old Testament, salt was also used in certain ceremonies (Leviticus 2:13) to remind God's people of their promises to Him. Elisha used salt to miraculously purify a water supply (2 Kings 2:21). Jesus referenced salt here to emphasize the need for believers to remain holy; by compromising, they would cease to further the Kingdom of God by positively influencing society.

2 Some Pharisees came and tried to trap Him with this question: "Should a man be al-
lowed to divorce his wife?"
3 Jesus answered them with a question: "What did Moses say in the law about divorce?"
10:4 4 "Well, he permitted it," they replied. "He said a man can give his wife a written notice of
Deut 24:1-3 divorce and send her away."
10:6 5 But Jesus responded, "He wrote this commandment only as a concession to your hard
Gen 1:27; 5:2 hearts. 6 But 'God made them male and female' from the beginning of creation. 7 'This ex-
10:7-8 *Gen 2:24 plains why a man leaves his father and mother and is joined to his wife,* 8 and the two are
1 Cor 6:16 united into one.'* Since they are no longer two but one, 9 let no one split apart what God
Eph 5:31 has joined together."
10 Later, when He was alone with His disciples in the house, they brought up the subject
10:11 again. 11 He told them, "Whoever divorces his wife and marries someone else commits
Matt 5:32 adultery against her. 12 And if a woman divorces her husband and marries someone else,
Luke 16:18 1 Cor 7:10-11 she commits adultery."

JESUS BLESSES THE CHILDREN

10:13-16 13 One day some parents brought their children to Jesus so He could touch and bless them.
//Matt 19:13-15 //Luke 18:15-17 But the disciples scolded the parents for bothering Him.
14 When Jesus saw what was happening, He was angry with His disciples. He said to
them, "Let the children come to Me. Don't stop them! For the Kingdom of God belongs to
10:15 those who are like these children. 15 I tell you the truth, anyone who doesn't receive the
Matt 18:3 Kingdom of God like a child will never enter it." 16 Then He took the children in His arms
10:16 Mark 9:36 and placed His hands on their heads and blessed them.

THE RICH MAN

10:17-31 17 As Jesus was starting out on His way to Jerusalem, a man came running up to Him, knelt
//Matt 19:16-30 //Luke 18:18-30 down, and asked, "Good Teacher, what must I do to inherit eternal life?"
18 "Why do you call Me good?" Jesus asked. "Only God is truly good. 19 But to answer
10:19 *Exod 20:12-16 your question, you know the commandments: 'You must not murder. You must not com-
*Deut 5:16-20 mit adultery. You must not steal. You must not testify falsely. You must not cheat anyone.
Rom 13:9 Honor your father and mother.'*"
20 "Teacher," the man replied, "I've obeyed all these commandments since I was young."
10:21 21 Looking at the man, Jesus felt genuine love for him. "There is still one thing you
Matt 6:19-20 haven't done," He told him. "Go and sell all your possessions and give the money to the
Luke 12:33 poor, and you will have treasure in heaven. Then come, follow Me."
Acts 2:44-45

10:4 See Deut 24:1. **10:6** Gen 1:27; 5:2. **10:7** Some manuscripts do not include *and is joined to his wife.* **10:7-8** Gen 2:24. **10:19** Exod 20:12-16; Deut 5:16-20.

10:2 In the Old Testament (Deuteronomy 24:1-4), God made provision through Moses for a man to divorce his wife. By Jesus' time, some had turned this provision into a license for a man to instantly divorce his wife for any reason, while others required that more stringent guidelines be followed. By asking this question, the leaders were hoping to catch Jesus on the horns of a dilemma. If He affirmed that a man should be able to divorce his wife, then they could criticize Him for undermining marriage, but if He rejected this idea, they could accuse Him of opposing the Old Testament law.

10:7-9 Jesus here made a key point about marriage: God designed it to be an exclusive relationship between a man and a woman. Jesus affirmed the Genesis account of Creation as He described God's intentions for marriage.

10:17-18 When Jesus affirmed that "only God is truly good," He was gently probing an issue with which the man was struggling. Clearly the man thought he "measured up" pretty well to what "good" looks like. Jesus wanted him to see that God's character, not human behavior, provides the standard for what is "good."

▸ GOD

10:17-21 God defines. In the world in which we live, it seems as if everyone has a unique standard for what is "right" or "good." Everyone's measuring stick seems to be different. Even in Jesus' day, some thought they knew how to measure what was good, and they often used themselves as the standard. Jesus made it clear when He was speaking to a young rich man that God is *the* standard for what is good. Look to Him and His Word, not to your friends or your leaders or anyone else as the final arbiter of good and evil. (***See God*> *God's Attributes> Holy> His holiness is the standard for believers' behavior,* TopicGuide page A16.)

22At this the man's face fell, and he went away sad, for he had many possessions.
23Jesus looked around and said to His disciples, "How hard it is for the rich to enter the
Kingdom of God!" 24This amazed them. But Jesus said again, "Dear children, it is very 10:24
hard* to enter the Kingdom of God. 25In fact, it is easier for a camel to go through the eye Matt 7:13-14
of a needle than for a rich person to enter the Kingdom of God!" John 3:5
26The disciples were astounded. "Then who in the world can be saved?" they asked.
27Jesus looked at them intently and said, "Humanly speaking, it is impossible. But not 10:27
with God. Everything is possible with God." Gen 18:14
28Then Peter began to speak up. "We've given up everything to follow You," he said. Job 42:2 Mark 14:36
29"Yes," Jesus replied, "and I assure you that everyone who has given up house or 10:28
brothers or sisters or mother or father or children or property, for My sake and for the Mark 1:18
Good News, 30will receive now in return a hundred times as many houses, brothers, sis- 10:30
ters, mothers, children, and property—along with persecution. And in the world to come 2 Tim 3:12
that person will have eternal life. 31But many who are the greatest now will be least impor- 10:31
tant then, and those who seem least important now will be the greatest then.*" Matt 20:16 Luke 13:30

JESUS AGAIN PREDICTS HIS DEATH

32They were now on the way up to Jerusalem, and Jesus was walking ahead of them. The 10:32-34
disciples were filled with awe, and the people following behind were overwhelmed with //Matt 20:17-19
fear. Taking the twelve disciples aside, Jesus once more began to describe everything that //Luke 18:31-34
was about to happen to Him. 33"Listen," He said, "we're going up to Jerusalem, where the 10:33 Matt 16:21; 17:22-23
Son of Man* will be betrayed to the leading priests and the teachers of religious law. They Mark 8:31; 9:31
will sentence Him to die and hand Him over to the Romans.* 34They will mock Him, spit on Luke 24:7
Him, flog Him with a whip, and kill Him, but after three days He will rise again." 10:34 Isa 50:6

JESUS TEACHES ABOUT SERVING OTHERS

35Then James and John, the sons of Zebedee, came over and spoke to Him. "Teacher," 10:35-45
they said, "we want You to do us a favor." //Matt 20:20-28
36"What is your request?" He asked.
37They replied, "When You sit on Your glorious throne, we want to sit in places of honor
next to You, one on Your right and the other on Your left."
38But Jesus said to them, "You don't know what you are asking! Are you able to drink 10:38
from the bitter cup of suffering I am about to drink? Are you able to be baptized with the Luke 12:50
baptism of suffering I must be baptized with?" John 18:11
39"Oh yes," they replied, "we are able!" 10:39
Then Jesus told them, "You will indeed drink from My bitter cup and be baptized with Acts 12:2
My baptism of suffering. 40But I have no right to say who will sit on My right or My left. Rev 1:9
God has prepared those places for the ones He has chosen."
41When the ten other disciples heard what James and John had asked, they were indig-

10:24 Some manuscripts read *very hard for those who trust in riches.* 10:31 Greek *But many who are first will be last; and the last, first.* 10:33a "Son of Man" is a title Jesus used for Himself. 10:33b Greek *the Gentiles.*

10:23-27 The disciples, like many in their day, thought that rich people must be close to God because they enjoyed the "blessing" of wealth. Jesus contradicted their assumption by declaring that riches are a hindrance, not an advantage, to entering the Kingdom of God. Since the disciples were all richer than the very poor, they immediately grew worried, but Jesus reassured them that "Everything is possible with God."

10:28-31 Peter believed that he and the other disciples had already given up all that mattered—family and property (10:29). Jesus explained that whatever is given up for God's sake will not go unrewarded (1 Corinthians 3:12-14; Hebrews 11:6).

10:37 In ancient times, the seat immediately to the right of a ruler was considered the place of greatest honor. Second to it was the seat on the left side of the ruler (1 Kings 2:19 and Psalm 110:1).

▸ HOLINESS

10:41-45 Significance through servanthood. What does it take to really make an impact for the Kingdom? How can a disciple live in such a way to make his or her life truly count? There is one simple secret: Serve others. Mark repeats this point throughout his Gospel to make sure this counter-intuitive concept is clear to his readers. Ask God to help you to grasp fully what it means to be a servant-leader in His Kingdom. (***See Holiness****> Disciplines> Of Engagement> Service,* TopicGuide page A42.)

10:42 nant. 42 So Jesus called them together and said, "You know that the rulers in this world lord it
Luke 22:25-27 over their people, and officials flaunt their authority over those under them. 43 But among you
1 Pet 5:3 it will be different. Whoever wants to be a leader among you must be your servant, 44 and
10:43-44 Matt 23:11 whoever wants to be first among you must be the slave of everyone else. 45 For even the Son
Mark 9:35 Luke 22:26 of Man came not to be served but to serve others and to give His life as a ransom for many."

JESUS HEALS BLIND BARTIMAEUS

46 Then they reached Jericho, and as Jesus and His disciples left town, a large crowd fol-
10:45 Matt 20:28 lowed Him. A blind beggar named Bartimaeus (son of Timaeus) was sitting beside the
John 13:14 road. 47 When Bartimaeus heard that Jesus of Nazareth was nearby, he began to shout,
Phil 2:7 1 Tim 2:5-6 "Jesus, Son of David, have mercy on me!"
Titus 2:14 48 "Be quiet!" many of the people yelled at him.
10:46-52 //Matt 20:29-34 But he only shouted louder, "Son of David, have mercy on me!"
//Luke 18:35-43 49 When Jesus heard him, He stopped and said, "Tell him to come here."
So they called the blind man. "Cheer up," they said. "Come on, He's calling you!" 50 Barti-
10:47 Isa 11:1 maeus threw aside his coat, jumped up, and came to Jesus.
Jer 23:5-6 51 "What do you want Me to do for you?" Jesus asked.
Matt 9:27; 15:22 "My rabbi,*" the blind man said, "I want to see!"
52 And Jesus said to him, "Go, for your faith has healed you." Instantly the man could see,
10:52 Matt 9:22 and he followed Jesus down the road.*

Mark 5:34 Luke 7:50; 8:48;

JESUS' TRIUMPHANT ENTRY

17:19 **11** As Jesus and His disciples approached Jerusalem, they came to the towns of Beth-
11:1-10 phage and Bethany on the Mount of Olives. Jesus sent two of them on ahead. 2 "Go
//Matt 21:1-9 //Luke 19:28-38 into that village over there," He told them. "As soon as you enter it, you will see a young
//John 12:12-19 donkey tied there that no one has ever ridden. Untie it and bring it here. 3 If anyone asks,
11:2 'What are you doing?' just say, 'The Lord needs it and will return it soon.'"
1 Sam 6:7 Zech 9:9 4 The two disciples left and found the colt standing in the street, tied outside the front
door. 5 As they were untying it, some bystanders demanded, "What are you doing, untying
that colt?" 6 They said what Jesus had told them to say, and they were permitted to take it.
7 Then they brought the colt to Jesus and threw their garments over it, and He sat on it.
8 Many in the crowd spread their garments on the road ahead of Him, and others spread
leafy branches they had cut in the fields. 9 Jesus was in the center of the procession, and
11:9-10 the people all around Him were shouting,

Pss 118:25-26; 148:1 "Praise God!
Blessings on the One who comes in the name of the LORD!
10 Blessings on the coming Kingdom of our ancestor David!
Praise God in highest heaven!"*

10:51 Greek uses the Hebrew term *Rabboni*. 10:52 Or *on the way*. 11:9 Greek *Hosanna*, an exclamation of praise that literally means "save now"; also in 11:10. 11:9-10 Pss 118:25-26; 148:1.

10:45 Jesus spoke of giving His life "as a ransom." This means He thought about His death in terms of purchasing slaves out of slavery. Although not fully explained in this one verse, Jesus was saying that He was going to substitute His life for the lives of others so that they could have freedom.

▶ BIBLE
10:46-52 The God who serves. In His encounter with Bartimaeus, Jesus offered a shocking, common invitation: "What do you want Me to do for you?" Jesus Christ, Lord of the Universe, honored the role of servant by performing it. This is not what we expect—how could the Lord of the Universe ever offer to provide for us? Never think that you are above humbly helping those around you. If the role of servant wasn't beneath Christ, it's certainly not beneath you. (***See Bible****> Unity> Christ> Christ is the "suffering servant,"* TopicGuide page A10.)

11:2-7 In ancient times, when a king entered a city as a conqueror, he typically would ride in on his war steed. In ancient Israel, if the king was coming in peace, he would choose a donkey or a colt. Jesus came to bring peace in a way that was foretold by the prophet Zechariah nearly five hundred years earlier (see Zechariah 9:9).

11:9-10 As Jewish pilgrims made their way to Jerusalem, they sang Psalms 120–134. The words the crowd shouted upon Jesus' entrance came from Psalm 118, which ends with words that speak about entering the Temple for worship (Psalm 118:19).

11 So Jesus came to Jerusalem and went into the Temple. After looking around carefully 11:11
at everything, He left because it was late in the afternoon. Then He returned to Bethany Matt 21:10, 17
with the twelve disciples.

JESUS CURSES THE FIG TREE

12 The next morning as they were leaving Bethany, Jesus was hungry. 13 He noticed a fig 11:12-14
tree in full leaf a little way off, so He went over to see if He could find any figs. But there //Matt 21:18-19
were only leaves because it was too early in the season for fruit. 14 Then Jesus said to the
tree, "May no one ever eat your fruit again!" And the disciples heard Him say it.

JESUS CLEARS THE TEMPLE

15 When they arrived back in Jerusalem, Jesus entered the Temple and began to drive out 11:15-19
the people buying and selling animals for sacrifices. He knocked over the tables of the //Matt 21:12-17
money changers and the chairs of those selling doves, 16 and He stopped everyone from us- //Luke 19:45-48 //John 2:13-22
ing the Temple as a marketplace.* 17 He said to them, "The Scriptures declare, 'My Temple 11:17
will be called a house of prayer for all nations,' but you have turned it into a den of thieves.'"* *Isa 56:7 *Jer 7:11
18 When the leading priests and teachers of religious law heard what Jesus had done, 11:18
they began planning how to kill Him. But they were afraid of Him because the people were Matt 21:46
so amazed at His teaching. Mark 12:12
19 That evening Jesus and the disciples left* the city. Luke 20:19
20 The next morning as they passed by the fig tree He had cursed, the disciples noticed it 11:20-25
had withered from the roots up. 21 Peter remembered what Jesus had said to the tree on the //Matt 21:20-22
previous day and exclaimed, "Look, Rabbi! The fig tree You cursed has withered and died!" 11:22
22 Then Jesus said to the disciples, "Have faith in God. 23 I tell you the truth, you can say Matt 17:20
to this mountain, 'May you be lifted up and thrown into the sea,' and it will happen. But Luke 17:6
you must really believe it will happen and have no doubt in your heart. 24 I tell you, you 11:24
can pray for anything, and if you believe that you've received it, it will be yours. 25 But Matt 7:7
when you are praying, first forgive anyone you are holding a grudge against, so that your 11:25
Father in heaven will forgive your sins, too.*" Matt 5:23; 6:14

THE AUTHORITY OF JESUS CHALLENGED

27 Again they entered Jerusalem. As Jesus was walking through the Temple area, the lead- 11:27-33
ing priests, the teachers of religious law, and the elders came up to Him. 28 They de- //Matt 21:23-27 //Luke 20:1-8
manded, "By what authority are You doing all these things? Who gave You the right to do
them?"

11:16 Or *from carrying merchandise through the Temple.* 11:17 Isa 56:7; Jer 7:11. 11:19 Greek *they left;* other manuscripts read *He left.* 11:25 Some manuscripts add verse 26, *But if you refuse to forgive, your Father in heaven will not forgive your sins.* Compare Matt 6:15.

11:13 The fig trees that grew near Bethany had small, edible buds. These buds typically appeared before the full fruit of the season. This tree had none, which indicated that it would not have had any fruit later. It was alive, but it wasn't going to bear fruit. Jesus' cursing of the tree was a dramatic parable, picturing what He found when He turned His attention to the Temple—the appearance of life, but no spiritual fruit.

11:17 Jesus was quoting Isaiah 56:7 and Jeremiah 7:11. Both passages make reference to God's desire for appropriate worship from those who draw near to Him.

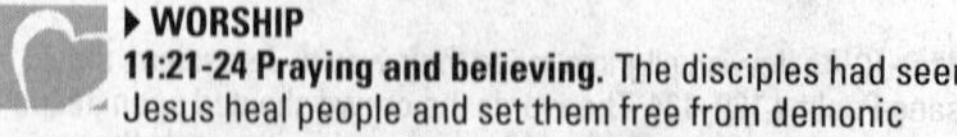

▶ WORSHIP

11:21-24 Praying and believing. The disciples had seen Jesus heal people and set them free from demonic oppression—but killing trees? This was not the sort of miracle they were accustomed to. He used their surprise to teach them that if by faith they asked God to act, then they would see dramatic answers (11:21-23). This wasn't an invitation to pray silly or sinful prayers; Jesus only asked for the things He knew were in the Father's will. But we can be sure that whenever we pray according to the will of God, the answers *will* happen. (***See Worship****> NT> Prayer> Instructions> Prayer certainty,* TopicGuide page A33.)

11:27-32 Religious leaders challenged Jesus' cleansing of the Temple (11:15-18). They believed He would answer that it was from God, and they could then claim that only the crazy (John 10:20) or demon-controlled (Matthew 12:24) would attack the Temple. But Jesus avoided the question, citing their inability to speak clearly of John's source of authority.

29“I’ll tell you by what authority I do these things if you answer one question,” Jesus
replied. 30“Did John’s authority to baptize come from heaven, or was it merely human?
Answer Me!”

31 They talked it over among themselves. “If we say it was from heaven, He will ask why
11:32 we didn’t believe John. 32But do we dare say it was merely human?” For they were afraid
Matt 14:5; 21:46 of what the people would do, because everyone believed that John was a prophet. 33So
they finally replied, “We don’t know.”

And Jesus responded, “Then I won’t tell you by what authority I do these things.”

PARABLE OF THE EVIL FARMERS

12:1-12 **12** Then Jesus began teaching them with stories: “A man planted a vineyard. He built
//Matt 21:33-46 a wall around it, dug a pit for pressing out the grape juice, and built a lookout
//Luke 20:9-19 tower. Then he leased the vineyard to tenant farmers and moved to another country. 2At
12:1 Isa 5:1-2 the time of the grape harvest, he sent one of his servants to collect his share of the crop.
3But the farmers grabbed the servant, beat him up, and sent him back empty-handed. 4The
12:5 owner then sent another servant, but they insulted him and beat him over the head. 5The
2 Chr 24:21; 36:15-16 next servant he sent was killed. Others he sent were either beaten or killed, 6until there was
Neh 9:26 only one left—his son whom he loved dearly. The owner finally sent him, thinking, ‘Surely
Matt 23:34-37 Acts 7:52 they will respect my son.’

1 Thes 2:15 7“But the tenant farmers said to one another, ‘Here comes the heir to this estate. Let’s
12:6 Rom 8:3 kill him and get the estate for ourselves!’ 8So they grabbed him and murdered him and
Gal 4:4 threw his body out of the vineyard.

12:8 9“What do you suppose the owner of the vineyard will do?” Jesus asked. “I’ll tell you—
Heb 13:12 he will come and kill those farmers and lease the vineyard to others. 10Didn’t you ever
12:10-11 read this in the Scriptures?

*Ps 118:22-23 Acts 4:11 ‘The stone that the builders rejected
Rom 9:33 has now become the cornerstone.
Eph 2:20 1 Pet 2:5-7 11 This is the LORD’s doing,
and it is wonderful to see.’*”

12:12 12The religious leaders* wanted to arrest Jesus because they realized He was telling the
Mark 11:18 story against them—they were the wicked farmers. But they were afraid of the crowd, so
they left Him and went away.

TAXES FOR CAESAR

12:13-17 13Later the leaders sent some Pharisees and supporters of Herod to trap Jesus into saying
//Matt 22:15-22 something for which He could be arrested. 14“Teacher,” they said, “we know how honest You
//Luke 20:20-26 are. You are impartial and don’t play favorites. You teach the way of God truthfully. Now tell
us—is it right to pay taxes to Caesar or not? 15Should we pay them, or shouldn’t we?”

12:10-11 Ps 118:22-23. 12:12 Greek *They.*

12:1-12 The imagery of a wine-making operation would have been familiar to Jesus’ audience, as the countryside was dotted with similar vineyards with walls made from stones cleared from the fields, and low towers to guard against animals and thieves. In this story, tenant farmers treated their employer badly, just as the religious leaders had insulted and ignored God and His representatives. God’s solution would be to destroy those who had harmed His Son.

12:10 Jesus was quoting from Psalm 118:22-23. This passage would have been on the minds of the people at this time because it was from the section of the Psalms sung by the Jewish pilgrims while making their way to Jerusalem for the Passover celebration. The word *cornerstone* refers to a particular stone fit into either the corner of a building or as the capstone of an arch. In either case, such a stone served as a critical piece of the building.

12:13 The Pharisees were religiously conservative and resistant to Roman rule in Israel. The supporters of Herod (a group called the Herodians) embraced Rome’s appointed king, Herod, and sought to work cooperatively with Rome. Jesus had caused tension among groups at both ends of the political spectrum.

Jesus saw through their hypocrisy and said, "Why are you trying to trap Me? Show Me a
Roman coin,* and I'll tell you." 16When they handed it to Him, He asked, "Whose picture
and title are stamped on it?"

"Caesar's," they replied.

17"Well, then," Jesus said, "give to Caesar what belongs to Caesar, and give to God what
belongs to God."

His reply completely amazed them.

12:17 Rom 13:7

DISCUSSION ABOUT RESURRECTION

18Then Jesus was approached by some Sadducees—religious leaders who say there is no
resurrection from the dead. They posed this question: 19"Teacher, Moses gave us a law that
if a man dies, leaving a wife without children, his brother should marry the widow and have
a child who will carry on the brother's name.* 20Well, suppose there were seven brothers.
The oldest one married and then died without children. 21So the second brother married the
widow, but he also died without children. Then the third brother married her. 22This contin-
ued with all seven of them, and still there were no children. Last of all, the woman also died.
23So tell us, whose wife will she be in the resurrection? For all seven were married to her."

24Jesus replied, "Your mistake is that you don't know the Scriptures, and you don't
know the power of God. 25For when the dead rise, they will neither marry nor be given in
marriage. In this respect they will be like the angels in heaven.

26"But now, as to whether the dead will be raised—haven't you ever read about this in
the writings of Moses, in the story of the burning bush? Long after Abraham, Isaac, and Ja-
cob had died, God said to Moses,* 'I am the God of Abraham, the God of Isaac, and the God
of Jacob.'* 27So He is the God of the living, not the dead. You have made a serious error."

12:18-27 //Matt 22:23-33 //Luke 20:27-38 Acts 23:8 1 Cor 15:12

12:19 *Gen 38:8 *Deut 25:5

12:25 1 Cor 15:42, 49, 52

12:27 Matt 22:32 Luke 20:38

THE MOST IMPORTANT COMMANDMENT

28One of the teachers of religious law was standing there listening to the debate. He real-
ized that Jesus had answered well, so he asked, "Of all the commandments, which is the
most important?"

29Jesus replied, "The most important commandment is this: 'Listen, O Israel! The LORD
our God is the one and only LORD. 30And you must love the LORD your God with all your
heart, all your soul, all your mind, and all your strength.'* 31The second is equally impor-
tant: 'Love your neighbor as yourself.'* No other commandment is greater than these."

32The teacher of religious law replied, "Well said, Teacher. You have spoken the truth
by saying that there is only one God and no other. 33And I know it is important to love Him
with all my heart and all my understanding and all my strength, and to love my neighbor

12:28-34 //Matt 22:34-40 //Luke 10:25-28

12:29-30 Luke 10:27

12:31 Rom 13:9 Gal 5:14 Jas 2:8

12:32 1 Cor 8:4-6

12:33 Mic 6:6-8

12:15 Greek *a denarius.* 12:19 See Deut 25:5-6. 12:26a Greek *in the story of the bush? God said to him.* 12:26b Exod 3:6. 12:29-30 Deut 6:4-5. 12:31 Lev 19:18.

12:16-17 A typical coin in circulation under Rome in that day would have borne the image of the Roman emperor and an inscription of his name and title. In answering their question in this manner, Jesus implicitly reminded them that human beings bear the image of God and thus belong to Him (Genesis 1:26).

12:18 For the most part, the Sadducees were made up of the Jewish aristocracy, who tended to favor cooperation with Rome. They shared some of the religious convictions of the Pharisees but differed on many other issues. They did not believe in the supernatural, including demons, angels, or a future resurrection.

12:19-23 The Sadducees' question was rooted in Deuteronomy 25:5-10. That passage laid out instructions for the perpetuation of a family line and the passing on of family property if an Israelite man died without a male heir. The Sadducees had constructed a trick question—one that they didn't really care to have answered—because they didn't believe that there would be a physical resurrection. They were simply trying to cause Jesus to stumble over a difficult case.

12:26 Jesus referred to Exodus 3:6. The Scriptures in Jesus' day hadn't yet been divided up into chapters and verses, so He referred to "the writings of Moses, in the story of the burning bush." Moses was the primary author of the first five books of the Old Testament.

12:26-27 Jesus' point was that Abraham, Isaac, and Jacob were not dead but still alive and in the presence of God.

12:29-30 Jesus quoted Deuteronomy 6:4-5, which formed part of a very common confession of faith that faithful Jews repeated daily.

12:34 Matt 22:46; Luke 20:40

as myself. This is more important than to offer all of the burnt offerings and sacrifices required in the law."

34Realizing how much the man understood, Jesus said to him, "You are not far from the Kingdom of God." And after that, no one dared to ask Him any more questions.

WHOSE SON IS THE MESSIAH?

12:35-37 //Matt 22:41-46; //Luke 20:41-44 — 12:36 2 Sam 23:2; *Ps 110:1

35Later, as Jesus was teaching the people in the Temple, He asked, "Why do the teachers of religious law claim that the Messiah is the son of David? 36For David himself, speaking under the inspiration of the Holy Spirit, said,

'The LORD said to my Lord,
Sit in the place of honor at My right hand
until I humble Your enemies beneath Your feet.'*

12:37 Rom 1:3; 9:5; Rev 22:16

37Since David himself called the Messiah 'my Lord,' how can the Messiah be his son?" The large crowd listened to Him with great delight.

12:38-40 //Matt 23:1-36; //Luke 11:37-52; 20:45-47 — 12:39 Luke 11:43

38Jesus also taught: "Beware of these teachers of religious law! For they like to parade around in flowing robes and receive respectful greetings as they walk in the marketplaces. 39And how they love the seats of honor in the synagogues and the head table at banquets. 40Yet they shamelessly cheat widows out of their property and then pretend to be pious by making long prayers in public. Because of this, they will be more severely punished."

THE WIDOW'S OFFERING

12:41-44 //Luke 21:1-4 — 12:41 2 Kgs 12:9; John 8:20 — 12:43-44 2 Cor 8:12

41Jesus sat down near the collection box in the Temple and watched as the crowds dropped in their money. Many rich people put in large amounts. 42Then a poor widow came and dropped in two small coins.*

43Jesus called His disciples to Him and said, "I tell you the truth, this poor widow has given more than all the others who are making contributions. 44For they gave a tiny part of their surplus, but she, poor as she is, has given everything she had to live on."

JESUS FORETELLS THE FUTURE

13:1-31 //Matt 24:1-35; //Luke 21:5-36 — 13:2 Luke 19:44

13 As Jesus was leaving the Temple that day, one of His disciples said, "Teacher, look at these magnificent buildings! Look at the impressive stones in the walls."

2Jesus replied, "Yes, look at these great buildings. But they will be completely demolished. Not one stone will be left on top of another!"

3Later, Jesus sat on the Mount of Olives across the valley from the Temple. Peter, James, John, and Andrew came to Him privately and asked Him, 4"Tell us, when will all this happen? What sign will show us that these things are about to be fulfilled?"

12:36 Ps 110:1. 12:42 Greek *two lepta, which is a kodrantes* [i.e., a quadrans].

12:35-37 Most Jews believed that the Messiah was to be David's son (a descendant of David; see Isaiah 9:7 and Luke 1:32). By asking this question (referring to Psalm 110:1, widely held to be about the Messiah), Jesus was stirring His hearers to think more deeply about the identity of the Messiah.

12:41-42 The receptacles for offerings in the Temple were in a public area. It was possible to make quite a show of giving one's offering—something that "many rich people" apparently did. The widow put in "two small coins." That was equivalent to what a day laborer would make for about 15 minutes of work. It was hardly a great sum, but for the widow it was a sacrificial gift of worship.

▸WORSHIP
12:41-44 Giving from the heart. Even a child can bring a tear to the eye of his mother with the simplest of heartfelt gifts. Likewise, God is not impressed with how much we might give; what matters to Him is the heart that is behind the gift. That is the reason that Jesus could say that the woman who gave what appeared to be the smallest actually gave the most. She gave sacrificially from the heart. Find ways to give that count in God's eyes (1 Corinthians 3:12-15). (***See Worship****> NT> Sacrificial Living> More blessed to give than to receive,* TopicGuide page A34.)

13:3-4 Like many of the Jewish people of the day, the followers of Jesus were anticipating the culmination of God's plan for His people and the end of the age. As they sat overlooking the Temple, the disciples asked Jesus when the destruction of the Temple would take place, since that would signal the beginning of the end. Jesus' discussion of this topic is also found summarized in Luke 21 and Matthew 24.

5 Jesus replied, "Don't let anyone mislead you, 6 for many will come in My name, claim-
ing, 'I am the Messiah.'* They will deceive many. 7 And you will hear of wars and threats of
wars, but don't panic. Yes, these things must take place, but the end won't follow immedi-
ately. 8 Nation will go to war against nation, and kingdom against kingdom. There will be
earthquakes in many parts of the world, as well as famines. But this is only the first of the
birth pains, with more to come.

9 "When these things begin to happen, watch out! You will be handed over to the local
councils and beaten in the synagogues. You will stand trial before governors and kings be-
cause you are My followers. But this will be your opportunity to tell them about Me.* 10 For
the Good News must first be preached to all nations.* 11 But when you are arrested and
stand trial, don't worry in advance about what to say. Just say what God tells you at that
time, for it is not you who will be speaking, but the Holy Spirit.

12 "A brother will betray his brother to death, a father will betray his own child, and chil-
dren will rebel against their parents and cause them to be killed. 13 And everyone will hate
you because you are My followers.* But the one who endures to the end will be saved.

14 "The day is coming when you will see the sacrilegious object that causes desecration*
standing where he* should not be." **(Reader, pay attention!)** "Then those in Judea must flee
to the hills. 15 A person out on the deck of a roof must not go down into the house to pack.
16 A person out in the field must not return even to get a coat. 17 How terrible it will be for
pregnant women and for nursing mothers in those days. 18 And pray that your flight will
not be in winter. 19 For there will be greater anguish in those days than at any time since
God created the world. And it will never be so great again. 20 In fact, unless the Lord short-
ens that time of calamity, not a single person will survive. But for the sake of His chosen
ones He has shortened those days.

21 "Then if anyone tells you, 'Look, here is the Messiah,' or 'There he is,' don't believe it.
22 For false messiahs and false prophets will rise up and perform signs and wonders so as
to deceive, if possible, even God's chosen ones. 23 Watch out! I have warned you about
this ahead of time!

24 "At that time, after the anguish of those days,

the sun will be darkened,
  the moon will give no light,
25 the stars will fall from the sky,
  and the powers in the heavens will be shaken.*

13:5 2 Thes 2:3, 10-12; 1 Tim 4:1; 2 Tim 3:13; 1 Jn 4:6
13:6 John 5:43
13:8 2 Chr 15:6; Isa 19:2
13:9-12 //Matt 10:17-22; //Luke 21:12-16
13:10 Rom 10:18
13:11 Matt 10:19-20; Luke 12:11-12
13:12 Mic 7:6
13:13 Matt 10:22; John 15:18-21
13:14 Matt 24:15; 2 Thes 2:3
13:17 Luke 23:29
13:19 Dan 9:26; 12:1; Joel 2:2; Rev 7:14
13:21 Luke 17:23
13:22 Deut 13:1-3; 2 Thes 2:9-10; Rev 13:13
13:23 2 Pet 3:17
13:24-25 Ezek 32:7-8; Rev 6:12-14; 8:12

13:6 Greek *claiming, 'I am.'* 13:9 Or *But this will be your testimony against them.* 13:10 Or *all peoples.* 13:13 Greek *on account of My name.* 13:14a Greek *the abomination of desolation.* See Dan 9:27; 11:31; 12:11. 13:14b Or *it.* 13:24-25 See Isa 13:10; 34:4; Joel 2:10.

▸ HOLINESS

13:9-13 Obedience may bring persecution. The followers of Jesus are on the winning side. The Bible makes the end of history clear: Jesus will return to earth in victory (Matthew 12:20; 1 John 5:4; Revelation 19:1-3, 11-21). But until that time, there will be trouble. As Jesus detailed what life would be like on earth before His return, He told us the truth: We may well face serious persecution. In fact, if we don't, we may be doing something wrong. Be faithful enough to be persecuted for who you are and what you believe (2 Timothy 3:12; 1 Peter 3:17; 4:19). (***See Holiness****> God's Blessing> Obedience leads to hardship and persecution,* TopicGuide page A42.)

13:14 The reference to "the sacrilegious object" came from Daniel's message about what would happen in the "last days" (Daniel 9:27; 11:31; 12:11). In AD 70, the Roman siege of Jerusalem left the city desolate (Jeremiah 12:7; 22:5), and this is likely what was in view. This corresponds to Jesus' teaching in Luke 21:20 and to Daniel 8:13, where the rebelliousness of God's covenant people resulted in the desolation of Jerusalem and the Temple. The destruction of the Temple would end the sacrificial system that was commanded under the Old Covenant and fulfilled by Jesus Christ (Hebrews 10:1-18).

▸ WORSHIP

13:18 Pray big. With all sorts of daily problems swirling about them, Jesus told His followers that they should pray about the details of His coming. This might seem like an odd comment—how can prayer affect when or how Jesus returns? Apparently, our prayers make a difference—even in the nature of His return! God weaves answers to our prayers into His master plan. As you pray, thank God for responding to the requests that we bring to Him. Repent of your lack of prayer and ask God to help you participate in His plan for this world through faithful, bold prayer. (***See Worship****> NT> Prayer> Instructions> Pray concerning the end times,* TopicGuide page A33.)

13:23-27 Jesus spoke of the end of the age by summarizing what the prophets pictured would happen when the Messiah came to earth in power (see Isaiah 13:10; 34:4; Joel 2:10).

13:26 *Dan 7:13 Matt 16:27 Rev 1:7
13:27 Deut 30:4 Zech 2:6
13:31 Matt 5:18 Luke 16:17
13:32 Acts 1:7
13:33-37 Matt 25:13-14 Luke 12:35-40 Rom 13:11 Eph 6:17-18 Col 4:2 1 Thes 5:6

26 Then everyone will see the Son of Man* coming on the clouds with great power and
glory.* 27 And He will send out His angels to gather His chosen ones from all over the
world*—from the farthest ends of the earth and heaven.

28 "Now learn a lesson from the fig tree. When its branches bud and its leaves begin to
sprout, you know that summer is near. 29 In the same way, when you see all these things
taking place, you can know that His return is very near, right at the door. 30 I tell you the
truth, this generation* will not pass from the scene before all these things take place.
31 Heaven and earth will disappear, but My words will never disappear.

32 "However, no one knows the day or hour when these things will happen, not even the
angels in heaven or the Son Himself. Only the Father knows. 33 And since you don't know
when that time will come, be on guard! Stay alert*!

34 "The coming of the Son of Man can be illustrated by the story of a man going on a
long trip. When he left home, he gave each of his slaves instructions about the work they
were to do, and he told the gatekeeper to watch for his return. 35 You, too, must keep
watch! For you don't know when the master of the household will return—in the evening,
at midnight, before dawn, or at daybreak. 36 Don't let him find you sleeping when he ar-
rives without warning. 37 I say to you what I say to everyone: Watch for him!"

JESUS ANOINTED AT BETHANY

14:1-2 //Matt 26:1-5 //Luke 22:1-2 John 11:55-57
14:3-9 //Matt 26:6-13 //John 12:1-8
14:3 Luke 7:37-38
14:7 Deut 15:11
14:8 John 19:40

14 It was now two days before Passover and the Festival of Unleavened Bread. The
leading priests and the teachers of religious law were still looking for an opportu-
nity to capture Jesus secretly and kill Him. 2 "But not during the Passover celebration," they
agreed, "or the people may riot."

3 Meanwhile, Jesus was in Bethany at the home of Simon, a man who had previously
had leprosy. While He was eating,* a woman came in with a beautiful alabaster jar of ex-
pensive perfume made from essence of nard. She broke open the jar and poured the per-
fume over His head.

4 Some of those at the table were indignant. "Why waste such expensive perfume?" they
asked. 5 "It could have been sold for a year's wages* and the money given to the poor!" So
they scolded her harshly.

6 But Jesus replied, "Leave her alone. Why criticize her for doing such a good thing to Me?
7 You will always have the poor among you, and you can help them whenever you want to.
But you will not always have Me. 8 She has done what she could and has anointed My body
for burial ahead of time. 9 I tell you the truth, wherever the Good News is preached through-
out the world, this woman's deed will be remembered and discussed."

JUDAS AGREES TO BETRAY JESUS

14:10-11 //Matt 26:14-16 //Luke 22:3-6

10 Then Judas Iscariot, one of the twelve disciples, went to the leading priests to arrange
to betray Jesus to them. 11 They were delighted when they heard why he had come, and

13:26a "Son of Man" is a title Jesus used for Himself. 13:26b See Dan 7:13. 13:27 Greek *from the four winds.* 13:30 Or *this age,* or *this nation.* 13:33 Some manuscripts add *and pray.* 14:3 Or *reclining.* 14:5 Greek *for 300 denarii.* A denarius was equivalent to a laborer's full day's wage.

13:32 As startling as it may be, Jesus declared that in His incarnation (the time when He came to earth and took on human flesh) there were some things He didn't know.

▸ WORSHIP

14:3-9 Enthusiastic worship. For many followers of Jesus, the experience of worship is formal, predictable, and frankly uninspiring. But it doesn't have to be that way. Here we see a true worshiper—she blessed Jesus by lavishly pouring out great amounts of perfume and anointing His head with it. Jesus received her ministry to Him and promised those watching that her deed would be remembered everywhere the gospel went. Follow her example of enthusiasm, extravagance, and expressiveness; let your heart move you to adoration of Jesus. (***See Worship***> *NT> Our Role> Mind and Heart> Fervent in Spirit,* TopicGuide page A32.)

14:10-11 Jesus' enemies enlisted Judas to betray Him into their hands, but not because they did not know where He was. Jesus often appeared in public, even showing up at the Temple after arriving in Jerusalem. Fearing that a riot would break out if they arrested Him in the Temple, they needed Judas to signal to them the most opportune time to take Jesus quietly.

they promised to give him money. So he began looking for an opportunity to betray
Jesus.

THE LAST SUPPER

[12]On the first day of the Festival of Unleavened Bread, when the Passover lamb is sacri-
ficed, Jesus' disciples asked Him, "Where do You want us to go to prepare the Passover
meal for You?"
[13]So Jesus sent two of them into Jerusalem with these instructions: "As you go into the
city, a man carrying a pitcher of water will meet you. Follow him. [14]At the house he en-
ters, say to the owner, 'The Teacher asks: Where is the guest room where I can eat the
Passover meal with My disciples?' [15]He will take you upstairs to a large room that is al-
ready set up. That is where you should prepare our meal." [16]So the two disciples went
into the city and found everything just as Jesus had said, and they prepared the Passover
meal there.
[17]In the evening Jesus arrived with the twelve disciples.* [18]As they were at the table*
eating, Jesus said, "I tell you the truth, one of you eating with Me here will betray Me."
[19]Greatly distressed, each one asked in turn, "Am I the one?"
[20]He replied, "It is one of you twelve who is eating from this bowl with Me. [21]For the Son
of Man* must die, as the Scriptures declared long ago. But how terrible it will be for the one
who betrays Him. It would be far better for that man if he had never been born!"
[22]As they were eating, Jesus took some bread and blessed it. Then He broke it in pieces
and gave it to the disciples, saying, "Take it, for this is My body."
[23]And He took a cup of wine and gave thanks to God for it. He gave it to them, and they
all drank from it. [24]And He said to them, "This is My blood, which confirms the covenant*
between God and His people. It is poured out as a sacrifice for many. [25]I tell you the truth,
I will not drink wine again until the day I drink it new in the Kingdom of God."
[26]Then they sang a hymn and went out to the Mount of Olives.

14:12-26 //Matt 26:17-25 //Luke 22:7-14, 21-23 //John 13:21-30
14:12 Exod 12:14-21 Deut 16:1-4 1 Cor 5:7-8
14:14 Exod 12:8 Lev 23:5
14:18 *Ps 41:9
14:21 Ps 22:1-21 Isa 53:3-8
14:22-25 //Matt 26:26-29 //Luke 22:15-20 //1 Cor 11:23-25
14:23 1 Cor 10:16

JESUS PREDICTS PETER'S DENIAL

[27]On the way, Jesus told them, "All of you will desert Me. For the Scriptures say,

'God will strike* the Shepherd,
  and the sheep will be scattered.'

[28]But after I am raised from the dead, I will go ahead of you to Galilee and meet you there."
[29]Peter said to Him, "Even if everyone else deserts You, I never will."
[30]Jesus replied, "I tell you the truth, Peter—this very night, before the rooster crows
twice, you will deny three times that you even know Me."

14:27-31 //Matt 26:31-35 //Luke 22:31-34 //John 13:36-38
14:27 *Zech 13:7
14:28 Mark 16:7

14:17 Greek *the Twelve.* 14:18 Or *As they reclined.* 14:21 "Son of Man" is a title Jesus used for Himself. 14:24 Some manuscripts read *the new covenant.* 14:27 Greek *I will strike.* Zech 13:7.

14:12 Every Jewish family was required to celebrate the Passover, a special memorial meal. Those who had traveled to Jerusalem to celebrate would either join with relatives and friends who lived in Jerusalem, or they would rent a room in which to celebrate.

14:21 Throughout the Gospels it is clear that Jesus' death was not an accident. Jesus declared that He came to give His life as a ransom for others (10:45), and here He made it clear that God Himself ordained Jesus' death.

▸ SALVATION
14:22-25 Jesus died for His followers. In Jesus' final meal with His closest followers, He made the core of His ministry clear. He shared some bread and passed a cup to them and affirmed that He was going to give His life in exchange for theirs. This is the heart of God's offer of salvation: Jesus died in our place; He suffered for us. This is the basis for this new covenant, an eternal agreement that gives all who believe in Jesus a right standing with God. Constantly remembering Jesus' death for you may seem morbid. But when you grasp that He died for you, the uneasiness you feel should turn to gratitude. Be grateful for what Christ our King was willing to suffer to defeat sin once and for all. (***See Salvation**> Jesus' Work> Crucifixion> Died for us,* TopicGuide page A22.)

14:23-24 The covenant that God established with the people of Israel when He delivered them from their bondage in Egypt formed the heart of the Passover celebration that Jesus and His followers enjoyed here. The blood of a lamb inaugurated that covenant (Exodus 12:23). Likewise, Jesus inaugurated a new covenant for His followers through His blood.

31 "No!" Peter declared emphatically. "Even if I have to die with You, I will never deny
You!" And all the others vowed the same.

JESUS PRAYS IN GETHSEMANE

14:32-42 //Matt 26:36-46 //Luke 22:39-46 John 18:1
14:33 Matt 17:1 Mark 9:2 Luke 9:28
14:34 *Pss 42:6; 43:5 John 12:27
14:36 Matt 20:22 John 5:30; 6:38; 18:11 Rom 8:15 Gal 4:6
14:38 Rom 7:22-23

32 They went to the olive grove called Gethsemane, and Jesus said, "Sit here while I go and
pray." 33 He took Peter, James, and John with Him, and He became deeply troubled and
distressed. 34 He told them, "My soul is crushed with grief to the point of death. Stay here
and keep watch with Me."
35 He went on a little farther and fell to the ground. He prayed that, if it were possible, the
awful hour awaiting Him might pass Him by. 36 "Abba, Father,"* He cried out, "everything is
possible for You. Please take this cup of suffering away from Me. Yet I want Your will to be
done, not Mine."
37 Then He returned and found the disciples asleep. He said to Peter, "Simon, are you
asleep? Couldn't you watch with Me even one hour? 38 Keep watch and pray, so that you
will not give in to temptation. For the spirit is willing, but the body is weak."
39 Then Jesus left them again and prayed the same prayer as before. 40 When He re-
turned to them again, He found them sleeping, for they couldn't keep their eyes open.
And they didn't know what to say.
41 When He returned to them the third time, He said, "Go ahead and sleep. Have your
rest. But no—the time has come. The Son of Man is betrayed into the hands of sinners.
42 Up, let's be going. Look, My betrayer is here!"

JESUS IS BETRAYED AND ARRESTED

14:43-50 //Matt 26:47-56 //Luke 22:47-53 //John 18:3-12
14:47 John 18:10
14:49 Isa 53:7-9 Luke 24:44
14:50 Ps 88:8 John 16:32

43 And immediately, even as Jesus said this, Judas, one of the twelve disciples, arrived with
a crowd of men armed with swords and clubs. They had been sent by the leading priests,
the teachers of religious law, and the elders. 44 The traitor, Judas, had given them a prear-
ranged signal: "You will know which one to arrest when I greet Him with a kiss. Then you
can take Him away under guard." 45 As soon as they arrived, Judas walked up to Jesus.
"Rabbi!" he exclaimed, and gave Him the kiss.
46 Then the others grabbed Jesus and arrested Him. 47 But one of the men with Jesus
pulled out his sword and struck the high priest's slave, slashing off his ear.
48 Jesus asked them, "Am I some dangerous revolutionary, that you come with swords
and clubs to arrest Me? 49 Why didn't you arrest Me in the Temple? I was there among you
teaching every day. But these things are happening to fulfill what the Scriptures say about
Me."
50 Then all His disciples deserted Him and ran away. 51 One young man following behind
was clothed only in a long linen shirt. When the mob tried to grab him, 52 he slipped out of
his shirt and ran away naked.

JESUS BEFORE THE COUNCIL

14:53-65 //Matt 26:57-68 //Luke 22:54-55, 63-71 //John 18:12-14, 19-24
14:54 Matt 26:3 John 18:18

53 They took Jesus to the high priest's home where the leading priests, the elders, and the
teachers of religious law had gathered. 54 Meanwhile, Peter followed Him at a distance and
went right into the high priest's courtyard. There he sat with the guards, warming himself
by the fire.

14:36 *Abba* is an Aramaic term for "father."

14:36 The word *Abba* in Aramaic (the common street-language spoken in Israel during Jesus' day) could arguably be translated as "Daddy." It is a term of intimate relationship.

14:43-52 Judas led the Roman soldiers and Jewish fighters directly to Jesus' place of prayer. He knew Jesus well enough to know exactly where He would be at this time of night. The kiss he delivered was an ordinary greeting of that day among friends.

14:51-52 Mark, the author of this Gospel, might be the young man who followed Jesus and fled the scene during His arrest.

55 Inside, the leading priests and the entire high council* were trying to find evidence
against Jesus, so they could put Him to death. But they couldn't find any. 56 Many false wit-
nesses spoke against Him, but they contradicted each other. 57 Finally, some men stood up
and gave this false testimony: 58 "We heard Him say, 'I will destroy this Temple made with
human hands, and in three days I will build another, made without human hands.'" 59 But
even then they didn't get their stories straight!
60 Then the high priest stood up before the others and asked Jesus, "Well, aren't You go-
ing to answer these charges? What do You have to say for Yourself?" 61 But Jesus was si-
lent and made no reply. Then the high priest asked Him, "Are You the Messiah, the Son of
the Blessed One?"
62 Jesus said, "I AM.* And you will see the Son of Man seated in the place of power at
God's right hand* and coming on the clouds of heaven.*"
63 Then the high priest tore his clothing to show his horror and said, "Why do we need
other witnesses? 64 You have all heard His blasphemy. What is your verdict?"
"Guilty!" they all cried. "He deserves to die!"
65 Then some of them began to spit at Him, and they blindfolded Him and beat Him with
their fists. "Prophesy to us," they jeered. And the guards slapped Him as they took Him
away.

PETER DENIES JESUS

66 Meanwhile, Peter was in the courtyard below. One of the servant girls who worked for
the high priest came by 67 and noticed Peter warming himself at the fire. She looked at him
closely and said, "You were one of those with Jesus of Nazareth.*"

14:56 Ps 35:11 Prov 6:16-19; 19:5
14:58 Mark 15:29 John 2:19
14:61 Isa 53:7 1 Pet 2:23
14:62 Matt 16:27; 24:30 Mark 8:38; 13:26 Acts 1:11 1 Thes 4:16 2 Thes 1:7 Rev 1:7; 22:20
14:63 Lev 10:6; 21:10 Num 14:6
14:64 Lev 24:16 John 19:7
14:65 Isa 50:6; 53:5
14:66-72 //Matt 26:69-75 //Luke 22:56-62 //John 18:15-18.

14:55 Greek *the Sanhedrin.* 14:62a Or *The 'I AM' is here;* or *I am the LORD.* See Exod 3:14. 14:62b Greek *at the right hand of the power.* See Ps 110:1. 14:62c See Dan 7:13. 14:67 Or *Jesus the Nazarene.*

14:55 The "high council" or Sanhedrin was a panel of seventy Jewish leaders to whom Rome had granted governing authority. They were allowed to adjudicate certain affairs pertaining to the life and laws of the Jewish people, but they did not always have the power to take a life. History records that the governing Romans granted and removed that authority as they pleased. The Sanhedrin exercised its power very carefully in this case, while with Stephen they passed judgment quickly and without any permission from the Romans (Acts 7).

▸ HOLINESS
14:66-72 Jesus' followers must be loyal. After three years of following Jesus and learning from Him, Peter had truly come to love Him. But in a moment of desperation, Peter denied even knowing Jesus. We shouldn't dismiss Peter's actions as those of a madman or a traitor, for we do the same thing when, either in word or deed, we deny that we are one of Jesus' followers. Peter was deeply stirred by his denial; he broke down and wept. Though Jesus knew of Peter's betrayal, He wasn't about to give up on him. The same is true for us as well. Jesus is more loyal to us than we can ever be to Him. When you discover you have betrayed Jesus with your sin, go to Him and find immediate forgiveness and restoration. (***See Holiness> Submission> Trusting God> Faithfulness,*** TopicGuide page A41.)

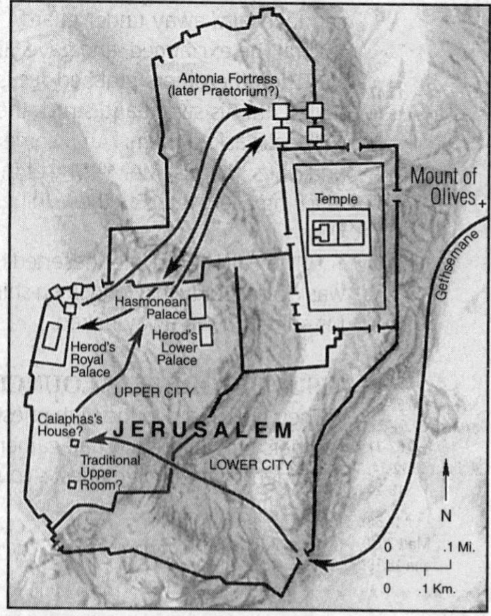

JESUS' TRIAL
From Gethsemane, Jesus' trial began at the home of Caiaphas, the high priest. Jesus was then taken to Pilate, the Roman governor. Luke records that Pilate sent Him to Herod, who was in Jerusalem—presumably in one of his two palaces (Luke 23:5-12). Herod sent Him back to Pilate, who handed Jesus over to be crucified.

[68]But Peter denied it. "I don't know what you're talking about," he said, and he went out
into the entryway. Just then, a rooster crowed.*
[69]When the servant girl saw him standing there, she began telling the others, "This man
14:70 is definitely one of them!" [70]But Peter denied it again.
Acts 2:7 A little later some of the other bystanders confronted Peter and said, "You must be one
of them, because you are a Galilean."
[71]Peter swore, "A curse on me if I'm lying—I don't know this man you're talking about!"
14:72 [72]And immediately the rooster crowed the second time.
Mark 14:30 Suddenly, Jesus' words flashed through Peter's mind: "Before the rooster crows twice,
you will deny three times that you even know Me." And he broke down and wept.

JESUS' TRIAL BEFORE PILATE

15:1 **15** Very early in the morning the leading priests, the elders, and the teachers of reli-
Matt 27:1 gious law—the entire high council*—met to discuss their next step. They bound
Luke 23:1
John 18:28 Jesus, led Him away, and took Him to Pilate, the Roman governor.
[2]Pilate asked Jesus, "Are You the king of the Jews?"
15:2-15
//Matt 27:11-14 Jesus replied, "You have said it."
//Luke 23:2-3, 18-25 [3]Then the leading priests kept accusing Him of many crimes, [4]and Pilate asked Him,
//John 18:29–19:6 "Aren't You going to answer them? What about all these charges they are bringing against
15:5 You?" [5]But Jesus said nothing, much to Pilate's surprise.
Isa 53:7
Mark 14:60-61 [6]Now it was the governor's custom each year during the Passover celebration to release
Luke 23:9 one prisoner—anyone the people requested. [7]One of the prisoners at that time was Barab-
bas, a revolutionary who had committed murder in an uprising. [8]The crowd went to Pilate
and asked him to release a prisoner as usual.
[9]"Would you like me to release to you this 'King of the Jews'?" Pilate asked. [10](For he real-
15:11 ized by now that the leading priests had arrested Jesus out of envy.) [11]But at this point the
Acts 3:14 leading priests stirred up the crowd to demand the release of Barabbas instead of Jesus. [12]Pi-
late asked them, "Then what should I do with this man you call the king of the Jews?"
[13]They shouted back, "Crucify Him!"
[14]"Why?" Pilate demanded. "What crime has He committed?"
But the mob roared even louder, "Crucify Him!"
15:15 [15]So to pacify the crowd, Pilate released Barabbas to them. He ordered Jesus flogged
Isa 53:6 with a lead-tipped whip, then turned Him over to the Roman soldiers to be crucified.

THE SOLDIERS MOCK JESUS

15:16-20 [16]The soldiers took Jesus into the courtyard of the governor's headquarters (called the
//Matt 27:27-31 Praetorium) and called out the entire regiment. [17]They dressed Him in a purple robe, and
//John 19:2-3 they wove thorn branches into a crown and put it on His head. [18]Then they saluted Him
and taunted, "Hail! King of the Jews!" [19]And they struck Him on the head with a reed stick,
spit on Him, and dropped to their knees in mock worship. [20]When they were finally tired of
mocking Him, they took off the purple robe and put His own clothes on Him again. Then
they led Him away to be crucified.

14:68 Some manuscripts do not include *Just then, a rooster crowed.* 15:1 Greek *the Sanhedrin;* also in 15:43.

14:70 Matthew notes that Peter's accent betrayed his Galilean heritage (Matthew 26:73).

15:1 The "high council" of the Jews could not simply have Jesus killed—this would have caused riots and disturbances (Matthew 14:5; 26:5; Mark 11:32; 14:2). Thus, after reaching their verdict, the leaders took Jesus to Pilate, the leading Roman authority for the region. This would both distribute the blame for Jesus' death to the Romans and show deference to Pilate.

15:10 Pilate realized that this was no simple legal case, but that the Jewish leaders had brought him a competing religious authority, one that they envied and wished dead. He would have dismissed the case at this point, but the priests had directed the crowds to threaten violence if Pilate released Jesus.

15:15 Pilate had previously been in trouble with the Roman emperor for allowing unrest in Israel under his rule, so the volatility of the crowd demanding Jesus' crucifixion gave him pause. He gave in, hoping to calm them down and secure his own position of authority by strengthening his alliance with the Jewish religious leadership.

THE CRUCIFIXION

21A passerby named Simon, who was from Cyrene,* was coming in from the countryside
just then, and the soldiers forced him to carry Jesus' cross. (Simon was the father of Alex-
ander and Rufus.) 22And they brought Jesus to a place called Golgotha (which means
"Place of the Skull"). 23They offered Him wine drugged with myrrh, but He refused it.
24Then the soldiers nailed Him to the cross. They divided His clothes and threw dice* to
decide who would get each piece. 25It was nine o'clock in the morning when they crucified
Him. 26A sign was fastened to the cross, announcing the charge against Him. It read, "The
King of the Jews." 27Two revolutionaries* were crucified with Him, one on His right and
one on His left.*
29The people passing by shouted abuse, shaking their heads in mockery. "Ha! Look at
You now!" they yelled at Him. "You said You were going to destroy the Temple and re-
build it in three days. 30Well then, save Yourself and come down from the cross!"
31The leading priests and teachers of religious law also mocked Jesus. "He saved oth-
ers," they scoffed, "but He can't save Himself! 32Let this Messiah, this King of Israel, come
down from the cross so we can see it and believe Him!" Even the men who were crucified
with Jesus ridiculed Him.

15:21-32 //Matt 27:32-44 //Luke 23:26-43 //John 19:17-27
15:23 Ps 69:21
15:24 *Ps 22:18
15:25 John 19:14
15:29 Pss 22:7; 109:2 Mark 14:58 John 2:19
15:32 Zeph 3:15

THE DEATH OF JESUS

33At noon, darkness fell across the whole land until three o'clock. 34Then at three o'clock
Jesus called out with a loud voice, *"Eloi, Eloi, lema sabachthani?"* which means "My God,
My God, why have You abandoned Me?"*
35Some of the bystanders misunderstood and thought He was calling for the prophet
Elijah. 36One of them ran and filled a sponge with sour wine, holding it up to Him on a
reed stick so He could drink. "Wait!" he said. "Let's see whether Elijah comes to take Him
down!"
37Then Jesus uttered another loud cry and breathed His last. 38And the curtain in the
sanctuary of the Temple was torn in two, from top to bottom.
39When the Roman officer* who stood facing Him* saw how He had died, he exclaimed,
"This man truly was the Son of God!"
40Some women were there, watching from a distance, including Mary Magdalene, Mary
(the mother of James the younger and of Joseph*), and Salome. 41They had been follow-
ers of Jesus and had cared for Him while He was in Galilee. Many other women who had
come with Him to Jerusalem were also there.

15:33-41 //Matt 27:45-56 //Luke 23:44-49 //John 19:28-30
15:34 *Ps 22:1
15:36 Ps 69:21
15:38 Exod 26:31-33 Heb 10:19-20
15:40-41 Luke 8:2-3

15:21 *Cyrene* was a city in northern Africa. **15:24** Greek *cast lots.* See Ps 22:18. **15:27a** Or *Two criminals.* **15:27b** Some manuscripts add verse 28, *And the Scripture was fulfilled that said, "He was counted among those who were rebels."* See Isa 53:12; also compare Luke 22:37. **15:34** Ps 22:1. **15:39a** Greek *the centurion;* similarly in 15:44, 45. **15:39b** Some manuscripts add *heard His cry and.* **15:40** Greek *Joses;* also in 15:47. See Matt 27:56.

15:22-28 Crucifixion was a common form of execution under the Roman government. As was typically the case, Jesus was crucified in a place where passersby would be able to see Him die and read the charges posted above His head.

15:34-35 Jesus cried out from the cross in Aramaic, a dialect of Hebrew spoken in Israel at the time. Some apparently misunderstood what He was saying. His cry echoed a prayer of David found in Psalm 22:1 and is an accurate, though partial expression of the consequences He faced by becoming the offering for sin (2 Corinthians 5:21).

▸ GOD
15:37-39 Life and death. Jesus' whole life led up to His death—every moment of every day seemed to be focused on the moment He would breathe His last breath on the cross. So it is not unexpected that the moment of His death would bring dramatic signs of a new day of salvation: A Roman guard at the foot of the cross declared, "This man truly was the Son of God!" We, too, should be drawn to worship Jesus as we stand at the foot of the cross and reflect on Jesus' death. Look at how it reveals His plan to give new access to God to people from every nation and tongue—this Man truly was the Son of God! (*See **God**> God's Names> Son> Son of God,* TopicGuide page A19.)

15:38 In the Temple, a massive curtain separated the Most Holy Place from the Holy Place. The high priest entered the Most Holy Place only once a year with the blood of sacrificed animals to atone for the sins of the people. Thus, the curtain represented the separation that existed between God and His people because of their sin. The tearing of the curtain represented the new access that all people have to God through Christ.

15:42-47 THE BURIAL OF JESUS

//Matt 27:57-61 [42]This all happened on Friday, the day of preparation,* the day before the Sabbath. As eve-
//Luke 23:50-56 ning approached, [43]Joseph of Arimathea took a risk and went to Pilate and asked for Jesus'
//John 19:38-42 15:43 body. (Joseph was an honored member of the high council, and he was waiting for the King-
Luke 2:25, 38 dom of God to come.) [44]Pilate couldn't believe that Jesus was already dead, so he called for
the Roman officer and asked if He had died yet. [45]The officer confirmed that Jesus was
15:46 dead, so Pilate told Joseph he could have the body. [46]Joseph bought a long sheet of linen
Acts 13:29 cloth. Then he took Jesus' body down from the cross, wrapped it in the cloth, and laid it in a
tomb that had been carved out of the rock. Then he rolled a stone in front of the entrance.
[47]Mary Magdalene and Mary the mother of Joseph saw where Jesus' body was laid.

16:1-8 THE RESURRECTION

//Matt 28:1-8 **16** Saturday evening, when the Sabbath ended, Mary Magdalene, Mary the mother
//Luke 24:1-10 //John 20:1-8 of James, and Salome went out and purchased burial spices so they could anoint
16:1 Jesus' body. [2]Very early on Sunday morning,* just at sunrise, they went to the tomb. [3]On
Luke 23:56 the way they were asking each other, "Who will roll away the stone for us from the en-
John 19:39-40 trance to the tomb?" [4]But as they arrived, they looked up and saw that the stone, which
16:3 Mark 15:46 was very large, had already been rolled aside.
16:5 [5]When they entered the tomb, they saw a young man clothed in a white robe sitting on the
John 20:12 right side. The women were shocked, [6]but the angel said, "Don't be alarmed. You are looking
Acts 1:10; 10:30 for Jesus of Nazareth,* who was crucified. He isn't here! He is risen from the dead! Look, this is
16:6 where they laid His body. [7]Now go and tell His disciples, including Peter, that Jesus is going
Acts 2:23-32 Rom 1:3-4 ahead of you to Galilee. You will see Him there, just as He told you before He died."
1 Cor 15:4-12, 20 [8]The women fled from the tomb, trembling and bewildered, and they said nothing to
Rev 1:18 16:7 anyone because they were too frightened.*

Matt 26:32 Mark 14:28 John 21:1

15:42 Greek *It was the day of preparation.* 16:2 Greek *on the first day of the week;* also in 16:9. 16:6 Or *Jesus the Nazarene.*
16:8 The most reliable early manuscripts of the Gospel of Mark end at verse 8. Other manuscripts include various endings to the Gospel. A few include both the "shorter ending" and the "longer ending." The majority of manuscripts include the "longer ending" immediately after verse 8.

16:1 It was improper to leave a body on the cross during the Sabbath. Although Joseph of Arimathea had taken Jesus' body down and laid it in a tomb, the body had not been fully prepared for burial. Thus, as soon as the Sabbath was over, two of Jesus' followers returned to the tomb to finish the burial procedure.

▸ GOD
16:7 Love overcomes betrayal. The resurrection of Jesus was such resounding good news! Jesus, the one they loved so dearly was no longer dead but alive forever! The angel told the women to go and share that news. But what about Peter, who had made such grand promises, only to deny Jesus when times got rough? The angel specifically told the women to go and tell "His disciples, including Peter," that Jesus was going to meet them in Galilee. Jesus' love was enough for Peter's denial and for you. If Jesus could forgive Peter, He can certainly forgive you for your sins against Him. Go to Him and receive forgiveness (2 Timothy 2:10-13; 1 John 1:9). (***See God**> God's Attributes> Loving> God loves His people, even when they are faithless,* TopicGuide page A17.)

16:8 If the text of Mark ends with this verse (as some scholars believe it does), then the puzzled fear of the women stands in testimony even more than their words could—Jesus was gone! And rather than spreading their confusion, they kept their experience and feelings to themselves. Their actions directly contradicted the persistent rumors that Jesus' disappearance was part of a coordinated plan (Matthew 28:13-15); in fact, His resurrection was a surprise that very few had truly expected.

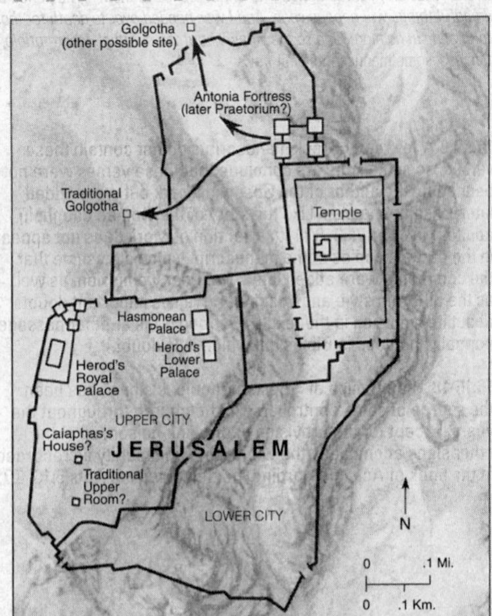

JESUS' ROUTE TO GOLGOTHA
After being sentenced by Pilate, Jesus was taken from the praetorium to Golgotha, a place outside the city, for crucifixion.

[Shorter Ending of Mark]

Then they briefly reported all this to Peter and his companions. Afterward Jesus Himself sent them out from east to west with the sacred and unfailing message of salvation that gives eternal life. Amen.

[Longer Ending of Mark]

9After Jesus rose from the dead early on Sunday morning, the first person who saw Him
was Mary Magdalene, the woman from whom He had cast out seven demons. 10She went
to the disciples, who were grieving and weeping, and told them what had happened. 11But
when she told them that Jesus was alive and she had seen Him, they didn't believe her.

12Afterward He appeared in a different form to two of His followers who were walking
from Jerusalem into the country. 13They rushed back to tell the others, but no one believed them.

14Still later He appeared to the eleven disciples as they were eating together. He rebuked them for their stubborn unbelief because they refused to believe those who had seen Him after He had been raised from the dead.*

15And then He told them, "Go into all the world and preach the Good News to everyone.
16Anyone who believes and is baptized will be saved. But anyone who refuses to believe
will be condemned. 17These miraculous signs will accompany those who believe: They
will cast out demons in My name, and they will speak in new languages.* 18They will be
able to handle snakes with safety, and if they drink anything poisonous, it won't hurt them. They will be able to place their hands on the sick, and they will be healed."

19When the Lord Jesus had finished talking with them, He was taken up into heaven
and sat down in the place of honor at God's right hand. 20And the disciples went everywhere and preached, and the Lord worked through them, confirming what they said by many miraculous signs.

16:9-11 Matt 28:1-10; John 20:11-18
16:12-13 Luke 24:13-35
16:14-18 Matt 28:16-20; Luke 24:36-49; John 20:19-23; Acts 1:6-8
16:15 Col 1:23
16:16 Acts 2:38; 16:31, 33
16:17 Acts 2:4, 11; 8:7; 10:46; 16:18; 19:6
16:18 Luke 10:19; Acts 28:3-6
16:19-20 Luke 24:50-53; Acts 1:9-11
16:19 Ps 110:1; Rom 8:34; Col 3:1

16:14 Some early manuscripts add: *And they excused themselves, saying, "This age of lawlessness and unbelief is under Satan, who does not permit God's truth and power to conquer the evil [unclean] spirits. Therefore, reveal Your justice now." This is what they said to Christ. And Christ replied to them, "The period of years of Satan's power has been fulfilled, but other dreadful things will happen soon. And I was handed over to death for those who have sinned, so that they may return to the truth and sin no more, and so they may inherit the spiritual, incorruptible, and righteous glory in heaven."* 16:17 Or *new tongues;* some manuscripts omit *new.*

16:9-20 A few early Greek manuscripts do not contain these verses, so some scholars conclude that these verses were not penned by the author of the Gospel of Mark but were added later by someone else. Like the story of the woman caught in adultery in John 7:53–8:11, this section of Mark does not appear in the earliest copies of the manuscript, so most assume that the comments were added later. Their early omission, as well as the different style and vocabulary, raises important doubts about its inclusion in the text. (First John 5:7 is another passage normally included in Bibles but which is in doubt.)

16:15-18 The promise of "these miraculous signs" has been the source of some controversy in the church throughout the years. Except for the provision of drinking poison, all of the other signs accompany the witnessing community as recorded in the book of Acts. (Regarding the demonic, see Acts 5:16; 8:7; regarding new languages, see Acts 2:3, 4; 10:46; for an example of safety in the face of serpents, note Acts 28:3-6; and for the ministry of healing, see Acts 4:30; 5:16; 8:7.)

▸ ADOPTION

16:15-20 Jesus works through His followers. Ultimately, Jesus intended His followers to go out into the world to carry out the very kind of ministry that He Himself had undertaken. They were to teach about the Kingdom, meet the needs of others, and invite people into a life of fellowship with God. It seems like a nearly unreachable calling. How can people like us live out the life and ministry of Jesus? There is only one way: We must invite and allow Jesus to work in and through us, confirming His ministry through us as only He can. (***See Adoption**> With Christ> Supernatural> Christ lives through believers,* TopicGuide page A37.)

LUKE

PURPOSE

To present Jesus to the world beyond the Jewish community as the One who has come to rescue all who are lost.

What would you do if you lost something precious to you? Would you start looking for it? Would you go out of your way to find it? If it were precious enough, would you even pay something to get it back? This is a key theme in Luke's recounting of the life and ministry of Jesus: He came from God "to seek and save those who are lost" (19:10).

By highlighting a number of Jesus' parables that are not found in the other Gospels, Luke underscores Jesus' mission of rescuing those who are lost. For example, when asked about why He was on such a relentless pursuit of those whom the religious leaders of the day preferred to shun, Jesus answered by telling of a prodigal son (15:11-32). Jesus' point was that those He spent time with are those whom the Father truly loved. The seriousness of Jesus' mission becomes apparent in His parable of a rich man in hell (16:19-31). Eternity hangs in the balance, so Jesus' mission to rescue those who are lost is critical.

DISCOVER GOD IN LUKE

Luke helps us see all three persons of the Godhead at work in the Incarnation. Luke wove his account together in a way that allows us to see not only Jesus, who is the Son of Man; but also the Father, who sent the Son of Man into the world; and the Spirit who empowered Jesus.

The Father, who sent the Son of Man: Throughout Luke's account, we catch glimpses of the Father. Jesus was clearly aware of His relationship with the Father (2:49), and the Father spoke audibly to Him at His baptism (3:21-22). But perhaps even more telling was the way Jesus spoke of the Father: telling others about the Father, explaining what He is like (6:35-36; 10:21-22; 12:30-31), and teaching His followers to pray to God as Father (11:2-4). Many of Jesus' parables in Luke give us insight into God's character as our Father (for example, see 11:5-13; 15:11-32).

The Spirit, who empowers the Son of Man: The Spirit's role in the life and ministry of Jesus is a significant theme in Luke's Gospel. The Spirit empowered Jesus (3:22; 4:14), led Him (4:1), and authenticated what Jesus did (4:18). The Spirit's presence and power were not only felt in the lives of others through Jesus (4:14, 18) but also in Jesus Himself (10:21).

Jesus, who is the Son of Man: Repeatedly, Luke records Jesus referring to Himself as the Son of Man. Jesus regularly identified Himself with this title (5:24; 6:5; 7:34; 9:26), and He revealed His self-understanding of this role when He declared, "The Son of Man came to seek and save those who are lost" (19:10). Jesus received this mission from His heavenly Father, and He carried it out in the power of the Spirit (2:49; 10:21-22; 4:14-21).

GROWING THROUGH LUKE

Jesus was "on a mission from God." As we have noted, He was seeking those who were lost and bringing them life—and He is still doing this today. One of the ways any follower of Jesus can grow is to get on board with what Jesus is doing—to join Him in His mission (10:1-17; 24:45-49). As you move through Luke, you will better understand and learn how to participate with Jesus in His mission. Pay attention to:

The Prophecies Fulfilled: The Old Testament prophets foretold Jesus' ministry (2:25-33). If you are going to partner with Jesus in His ministry, you will need to understand that He came to bring salvation to all peoples everywhere.

The Purpose Given: Jesus understood that the heart of His ministry lay in the purpose that the Holy Spirit had given Him (4:14-19). As you pursue the life of a follower of Jesus you will need to rely on the presence and power of the Spirit, as Jesus did.

The Ministry Described: To confirm that He was the fulfillment of God's promises, Jesus described the kind of ministry He had undertaken—the same kind that He continues today through His followers (7:21-23).

The Tasks Assigned: Although Jesus' twelve disciples (later called apostles) had a distinctive role in carrying out and extending the ministry of Jesus, it is important to recognize that He delegated others to participate as well (9:1-6; 10:1-12). His commission to present-day believers is quite similar, and all His followers are empowered to join in what He is doing.

The Parables Told: Jesus told parables that illustrated His own mission and call (15:1-32). When confronted with a challenge to the kind of ministry He was carrying out, Jesus told three related parables: the story of the lost sheep, the story of the lost coin, and the story of the lost son. Taken together, these three parables underscore the heart of the ministry Jesus has undertaken—and invites His followers to join.

The Purpose Stated: As Jesus ministered to an outcast from Jewish society, He offered a simple yet profound summation of what He had come to do: seek and save the lost (19:10). Those who partner with Jesus must give themselves to that same mission.

DISCOVERY VERSES

And so I tell you, keep on asking, and you will receive what you ask for. Keep on seeking, and you will find. Keep on knocking, and the door will be opened to you. For everyone who asks, receives. Everyone who seeks, finds. And to everyone who knocks, the door will be opened. (LUKE 11:9-10)

The Son of Man came to seek and save those who are lost. (LUKE 19:10)

He isn't here! He is risen from the dead! Remember what He told you back in Galilee, that the Son of Man must be betrayed into the hands of sinful men and be crucified, and that He would rise again on the third day. (LUKE 24:6-7)

LUKE FACTS

Author: The opening verses in the Gospel of Luke and the book of Acts, reveal that both books were written by the same person (Luke) and initially were intended for the same person, a man named Theophilus (Luke 1:1-4; Acts 1:1-5). The book of Acts and other New Testament writings give further clues to the author's identity. In a number of passages in Acts the author includes himself in the narrative, mentioning what "we" did (Acts 16:1-17; 20:5–21:18; 27:1–28:16). Comparing this information with Paul's comments about his traveling companions makes it apparent that Luke (mentioned three times by Paul in Colossians 4:14; 2 Timothy 4:11; and Philemon 1:24) is the one who penned both this Gospel and the book of Acts. Luke's authorship of this Gospel was also widely accepted in the early church. Luke was most likely a Gentile and a physician (see Colossians 4:14). Although apparently not an eyewitness to the events he wrote about, Luke prepared a careful account, no doubt drawing on the input of the apostles he came to know and the teaching of the eminent apostle Paul.

Written to: Of all the Gospels, Luke's alone has a clearly identified recipient, a man named Theophilus (Luke 1:1-4; Acts 1:1-5). The title used by Luke to address Theophilus ("most honorable") was one typically used to refer to an individual of some high rank in the Roman government. (Paul used a similar title to address Festus, governor of Judea, and Felix, also a governor of Judea; Acts 23:26; 24:2-3; 26:25.) We cannot be certain of Theophilus's nationality, but since Luke did not give much attention to substantiating Jesus' Messianic "credentials," it could well be that Theophilus was a Gentile.

Date of writing: Recognizing the association that exists between this Gospel and Acts, we can derive a date for Luke from Acts. The book of Acts concludes with Paul still in prison (during the early 60s), and there is no mention of the destruction of Jerusalem, which occurred in AD 70. This would suggest that Luke wrote Acts sometime around the mid-60s to 70. Since Acts is the second volume that Luke wrote, we can reasonably conclude that this Gospel must have been written sometime prior to the mid-60s. Luke utilized written accounts of those who were eyewitnesses of the life and ministry of Jesus (Luke 1:1-4), and some time undoubtedly lapsed between Jesus' ascension and the writing of the Gospel, but we cannot determine with certainty the length of this lapse; the best we can say is that Luke was written some time after AD 30.

Setting: Luke traces the life and ministry of Jesus throughout the land of Palestine, which included the Roman provinces of Galilee (4:31), Samaria (17:11), and Judea (4:44).

OUTLINE

- **LUKE 1:1–4:13**—The Son of God Enters the World as the Son of Man
- **LUKE 4:12–9:50**—The Son of Man Begins Ministry of Seeking and Saving the Lost
- **LUKE 9:51–19:27**—The Son of Man Explains What He Is Doing and Why
- **LUKE 19:28–24:53**—The Death and Resurrection of the Son of Man

INTRODUCTION

1:1-2 **1** Many people have set out to write accounts about the events that have been fulfilled
John 15:27 among us. [2]They used the eyewitness reports circulating among us from the early
Acts 1:21-22 Heb 2:3 disciples.* [3]Having carefully investigated everything from the beginning, I also have de-
2 Pet 1:16 cided to write a careful account for you, most honorable Theophilus, [4]so you can be cer-
1 Jn 1:1-4 tain of the truth of everything you were taught.

1:3 Acts 1:1

THE BIRTH OF JOHN THE BAPTIST FORETOLD

1:5 [5]When Herod was king of Judea, there was a Jewish priest named Zechariah. He was a
1 Chr 24:10 member of the priestly order of Abijah, and his wife, Elizabeth, was also from the priestly
2 Chr 31:2 Matt 2:1 line of Aaron. [6]Zechariah and Elizabeth were righteous in God's eyes, careful to obey all of
1:8 the Lord's commandments and regulations. [7]They had no children because Elizabeth was
1 Chr 24:19 unable to conceive, and they were both very old.
2 Chr 8:14 [8]One day Zechariah was serving God in the Temple, for his order was on duty that
1:9 Exod 30:7 week. [9]As was the custom of the priests, he was chosen by lot to enter the sanctuary of the

1:2 Greek *from those who from the beginning were servants of the word.*

1:1 Some scholars believe that "many people" may refer to Matthew's and Mark's Gospels, while others believe they refer to some other sources now lost. In any case, Luke was aware of other efforts to provide written records of the life and ministry of Jesus.

1:3 Both the Gospel of Luke and the book of Acts are addressed to Theophilus. Although this name could be translated as "lover of God" (meaning Luke could be speaking to a generic God lover), it is most likely the name of a ranking government official, as indicated by the title "most honorable." Similar titles are found in Acts 23:26; 24:2-3.

1:3 Although Luke wrote a "careful account," we should not conclude that he wrote everything that could be written about Jesus' life and ministry (see John 20:30-31; 21:25). The expression speaks of an orderly recounting of what he had found to be true and what he believed would be necessary to establish the veracity of Jesus' claims.

1:8 The priests of Israel served in the Temple in Jerusalem in a variety of capacities. They had a rotating schedule. There were 24 groups of priests, and each group served for eight days, twice a year.

1:9 Zechariah's opportunity to serve in the sanctuary and burn incense was a rare opportunity that fell to him through the casting of lots. It was a high honor to undertake this service.

KEY PLACES IN LUKE

The broken lines (—·—·) indicate modern boundaries.

Luke begins his account in the Temple in Jerusalem, giving us the background for the birth of John the Baptist, then moves on to the town of Nazareth and the story of Mary, chosen to be Jesus' mother (1:26ff). As a result of Caesar's call for a census, Mary and Joseph had to travel to Bethlehem, where Jesus was born in fulfillment of prophecy (2:1ff). Jesus grew up in Nazareth and began His earthly ministry by being baptized by John (3:21, 22) and tempted by Satan (4:1ff). Much of His ministry focused on Galilee: He set up His "home" in Capernaum (4:31ff), and from there He taught throughout the region (8:1ff). Later He visited Gerasa (also called Gadara), where He healed a demon-possessed man (8:36ff). He fed more than 5,000 people with one lunch on the shores of the Sea of Galilee near Bethsaida (9:10ff). Jesus always traveled to Jerusalem for the major festivals, and He enjoyed visiting friends in nearby Bethany (10:38ff). He healed 10 men with leprosy on the border between Galilee and Samaria (17:11) and helped a dishonest tax collector in Jericho turn his life around (19:1ff). The little villages of Bethphage and Bethany on the Mount of Olives were Jesus' resting places during His last days on earth. He was crucified outside Jerusalem's walls, but He would rise again. Two of Jesus' followers walking on the road leading to Emmaus were among the first to see the resurrected Christ (24:13ff).

Lord and burn incense. 10While the incense was being burned, a great crowd stood out-
side, praying.
11While Zechariah was in the sanctuary, an angel of the Lord appeared to him, standing
to the right of the incense altar. 12Zechariah was shaken and overwhelmed with fear when
he saw him. 13But the angel said, "Don't be afraid, Zechariah! God has heard your prayer.
Your wife, Elizabeth, will give you a son, and you are to name him John. 14You will have
great joy and gladness, and many will rejoice at his birth, 15for he will be great in the eyes
of the Lord. He must never touch wine or other alcoholic drinks. He will be filled with the
Holy Spirit, even before his birth.* 16And he will turn many Israelites to the Lord their God.
17He will be a man with the spirit and power of Elijah. He will prepare the people for the
coming of the Lord. He will turn the hearts of the fathers to their children,* and he will
cause those who are rebellious to accept the wisdom of the godly."
18Zechariah said to the angel, "How can I be sure this will happen? I'm an old man now,
and my wife is also well along in years."
19Then the angel said, "I am Gabriel! I stand in the very presence of God. It was He who
sent me to bring you this good news! 20But now, since you didn't believe what I said, you
will be silent and unable to speak until the child is born. For my words will certainly be ful-
filled at the proper time."
21Meanwhile, the people were waiting for Zechariah to come out of the sanctuary, won-
dering why he was taking so long. 22When he finally did come out, he couldn't speak to
them. Then they realized from his gestures and his silence that he must have seen a vision
in the sanctuary.
23When Zechariah's week of service in the Temple was over, he returned home. 24Soon
afterward his wife, Elizabeth, became pregnant and went into seclusion for five months.
25"How kind the Lord is!" she exclaimed. "He has taken away my disgrace of having no
children."

THE BIRTH OF JESUS FORETOLD

26In the sixth month of Elizabeth's pregnancy, God sent the angel Gabriel to Nazareth, a
village in Galilee, 27to a virgin named Mary. She was engaged to be married to a man
named Joseph, a descendant of King David. 28Gabriel appeared to her and said, "Greet-
ings, favored woman! The Lord is with you!*"
29Confused and disturbed, Mary tried to think what the angel could mean. 30"Don't be
afraid, Mary," the angel told her, "for you have found favor with God! 31You will conceive
and give birth to a son, and you will name Him Jesus. 32He will be very great and will be
called the Son of the Most High. The Lord God will give Him the throne of His ancestor Da-
vid. 33And He will reign over Israel* forever; His Kingdom will never end!"
34Mary asked the angel, "But how can this happen? I am a virgin."
35The angel replied, "The Holy Spirit will come upon you, and the power of the Most
High will overshadow you. So the baby to be born will be holy, and He will be called the
Son of God. 36What's more, your relative Elizabeth has become pregnant in her old age!

1:13 Luke 1:30, 60
1:15 Num 6:3; Judg 13:4; Jer 1:5; Matt 11:11
1:16 Mal 4:5-6
1:17 Mal 4:5; Matt 17:11-13
1:18 Gen 18:11
1:19 Dan 8:16; 9:21
1:20 Ezek 3:26
1:25 Gen 30:23; Isa 4:1
1:26 Matt 2:23
1:27 Matt 1:16, 18; Luke 2:5
1:31 Isa 7:14; Matt 1:21-23
1:32 2 Sam 7:12-16; Isa 9:6-7; 16:5; Jer 23:5; Phil 2:10; 1 Tim 6:15
1:33 Ps 89:3-4; Isa 9:7; Jer 33:17; Dan 2:44; 7:14, 27; Heb 1:8
1:35 Matt 1:20; Mark 1:1; John 1:34; 20:31; Rom 1:4

1:15 Or *even from birth.* 1:17 See Mal 4:5-6. 1:28 Some manuscripts add *Blessed are you among women.* 1:33 Greek *over the house of Jacob.*

1:13 The angel of the Lord informed Zechariah that his promised son's name should be *John*, which means "God is gracious." It was a fitting name for a son given to this priest and his wife in their old age.

1:17 John would grow up to fulfill Old Testament promises about the return of a prophet like Elijah of old. (See Isaiah 40:1-11 and Malachi 3:1-5.) John was not a reincarnation of Elijah (as he himself confirmed later; see John 1:21), but he was to carry on a ministry like Elijah's (Matthew 17:12; Mark 9:12).

1:27 In the days of Mary and Joseph, engagement was a very serious matter. It typically lasted about a year and was as binding as marriage. Unfaithfulness was considered adultery and was punishable by death.

1:28 Mary was favored due to God's sovereign choice to allow her to receive God Incarnate into her womb. God's favor also rested on the apostles (Acts 4:33), Moses (Acts 7:10), and Paul (1 Corinthians 3:10; 15:10).

People used to say she was barren, but she's now in her sixth month. 37 For nothing is im- 1:37
possible with God.*" Gen 18:14
38 Mary responded, "I am the Lord's servant. May everything you have said about me
come true." And then the angel left her.

MARY VISITS ELIZABETH

39 A few days later Mary hurried to the hill country of Judea, to the town 40 where Zechariah 1:41
lived. She entered the house and greeted Elizabeth. 41 At the sound of Mary's greeting, Eliz- Gen 25:22
abeth's child leaped within her, and Elizabeth was filled with the Holy Spirit. Luke 1:15
42 Elizabeth gave a glad cry and exclaimed to Mary, "God has blessed you above all 1:42
women, and your child is blessed. 43 Why am I so honored, that the mother of my Lord Judg 5:24
should visit me? 44 When I heard your greeting, the baby in my womb jumped for joy. 1:43 Luke 2:11
45 You are blessed because you believed that the Lord would do what He said."

THE MAGNIFICAT: MARY'S SONG OF PRAISE

46 Mary responded, 1:46-55 1 Sam 2:1-10 Ps 34:2-3

"Oh, how my soul praises the Lord.
47 How my spirit rejoices in God my Savior! 1:47 1 Tim 1:1; 2:3 Titus 1:3; 2:10; 3:4
48 For He took notice of His lowly servant girl,
and from now on all generations will call me blessed. 1:48 1 Sam 1:11
49 For the Mighty One is holy,
and He has done great things for me. 1:49 Ps 111:9
50 He shows mercy from generation to generation
to all who fear Him. 1:50 Ps 103:13, 17
51 His mighty arm has done tremendous things!
He has scattered the proud and haughty ones. 1:51 2 Sam 22:28 Ps 89:10
52 He has brought down princes from their thrones
and exalted the humble. 1:52 Job 5:12; 12:19
53 He has filled the hungry with good things
and sent the rich away with empty hands. 1:53 1 Sam 2:5 Ps 107:9
54 He has helped His servant Israel
and remembered to be merciful. 1:54 Ps 98:3 Isa 41:8
55 For He made this promise to our ancestors,
to Abraham and his children forever." 1:55

56 Mary stayed with Elizabeth about three months and then went back to her own home. Gen 17:7; 22:17

THE BIRTH OF JOHN THE BAPTIST

57 When it was time for Elizabeth's baby to be born, she gave birth to a son. 58 And when
her neighbors and relatives heard that the Lord had been very merciful to her, everyone
rejoiced with her.

1:37 Some manuscripts read *For the word of God will never fail.*

▸ HOLINESS

1:38 Submitting to God's will. What would you do if the Lord spoke to you and told you that He was going to step into your life and turn your world upside down? How would you respond if He suddenly gave you responsibilities you weren't prepared to handle? That is what happened to Mary. Not yet married, this young girl learned not only that she would miraculously become pregnant, but also that something unimaginable was going to happen through that child. She replied the way any growing disciple should: "I am the Lord's servant. May everything you have said about me come true." Mature believers model this sort of faithful flexibility. Do you see it in those you count as mature? Try measuring maturity in believers by their humble, submissive attitude to God. Are you mature? (***See Holiness**> Submission> Yielding to Spirit> Accept the unexpected,* TopicGuide page A41.)

1:39-45 Elizabeth and her child testified to the supernatural nature of Mary's pregnancy. By the Holy Spirit, Elizabeth pronounced a blessing upon Mary and Jesus.

1:46-55 Mary modeled her song of praise after Hannah's prayer (1 Samuel 2:1-10). Both mothers understood that their children were a blessing from God and a sign of His mercy toward His people.

1:59 Gen 17:12; Lev 12:3; Luke 2:21; Phil 3:5

59 When the baby was eight days old, they all came for the circumcision ceremony.
They wanted to name him Zechariah, after his father. 60 But Elizabeth said, "No! His name
is John!"
61 "What?" they exclaimed. "There is no one in all your family by that name." 62 So they
used gestures to ask the baby's father what he wanted to name him. 63 He motioned for a
writing tablet, and to everyone's surprise he wrote, "His name is John." 64 Instantly Zechari-
ah could speak again, and he began praising God.

1:66 Luke 2:19; Acts 11:21

65 Awe fell upon the whole neighborhood, and the news of what had happened spread
throughout the Judean hills. 66 Everyone who heard about it reflected on these events and
asked, "What will this child turn out to be?" For the hand of the Lord was surely upon him
in a special way.

ZECHARIAH'S PROPHECY

1:67 Joel 2:28

67 Then his father, Zechariah, was filled with the Holy Spirit and gave this prophecy:

1:68 Pss 41:13; 72:18; 106:48; 111:9

68 "Praise the Lord, the God of Israel,
because He has visited and redeemed His people.

1:69 1 Sam 2:1-10; Pss 18:2; 132:17; Ezek 29:21

69 He has sent us a mighty Savior*
from the royal line of His servant David,
70 just as He promised
through His holy prophets long ago.

1:70 Jer 23:5; Acts 3:21; Rom 1:2-4

71 Now we will be saved from our enemies
and from all who hate us.
72 He has been merciful to our ancestors
by remembering His sacred covenant—

1:71 Ps 106:10

1:72-73 Pss 105:8-9; 106:45-46

73 the covenant He swore with an oath
to our ancestor Abraham.
74 We have been rescued from our enemies
so we can serve God without fear,

1:73-74 Gen 22:16-18

75 in holiness and righteousness
for as long as we live.

1:75 Eph 4:24

1:76 Isa 40:3; Mal 3:1

76 "And you, my little son,
will be called the prophet of the Most High,
because you will prepare the way for the Lord.

1:77 Jer 31:34

77 You will tell His people how to find salvation
through forgiveness of their sins.

1:78 Mal 4:2

78 Because of God's tender mercy,
the morning light from heaven is about to break upon us,*

1:79 Isa 9:2; 58:8; 60:1-2; Matt 4:16

79 to give light to those who sit in darkness and in the shadow of death,
and to guide us to the path of peace."

1:80 Luke 2:40, 52

80 John grew up and became strong in spirit. And he lived in the wilderness until he be-
gan his public ministry to Israel.

1:69 Greek *has raised up a horn of salvation for us.* 1:78 Or *the Morning Light from Heaven is about to visit us.*

1:59 God required Abraham and all his male descendants to be circumcised as a sign of God's covenantal agreement with them (Genesis 17:12).

▸ GOD

1:68-79 Delivering on time. Zechariah's prophetic song, delivered at the birth of his son John, was filled with the promises of God. Did those promises take time? Yes. Does God still take more time than we'd like to demonstrate His faithfulness? Yes. But when His blessings come, they come at just the right time (Isaiah 60:22; Matthew 10:19; Ephesians 1:10; 1 Timothy 6:15; Titus 1:3). We cannot see the bigger picture of everything God is accomplishing when He keeps His Word—we see only how it affects us. Trust that when God keeps His promises, He times them perfectly for His maximum glory and our maximum good. (***See God****> God's Attributes> Faithful> God deserves thanks for His constant faithfulness,* TopicGuide page A16.)

THE BIRTH OF JESUS

2 At that time the Roman emperor, Augustus, decreed that a census should be taken 2:1-7
throughout the Roman Empire. 2(This was the first census taken when Quirinius was //Matt 1:18-25
governor of Syria.) 3All returned to their own ancestral towns to register for this census. 2:5
4And because Joseph was a descendant of King David, he had to go to Bethlehem in Ju- Luke 1:27
dea, David's ancient home. He traveled there from the village of Nazareth in Galilee. 5He 2:6 Matt 1:25
took with him Mary, his fiancée, who was now obviously pregnant. Gal 4:4
6And while they were there, the time came for her baby to be born. 7She gave birth to 2:9
her first child, a son. She wrapped Him snugly in strips of cloth and laid Him in a manger, Acts 5:19
because there was no lodging available for them. 2:11 John 4:42; 20:31

THE SHEPHERDS AND ANGELS

8That night there were shepherds staying in the fields nearby, guarding their flocks of
sheep. 9Suddenly, an angel of the Lord appeared among them, and the radiance of the
Lord's glory surrounded them. They were terrified, 10but the angel reassured them. "Don't
be afraid!" he said. "I bring you good news that will bring great joy to all people. 11The Sav-
ior—yes, the Messiah, the Lord—has been born today in Bethlehem, the city of David!
12And you will recognize Him by this sign: You will find a baby wrapped snugly in strips of
cloth, lying in a manger."
13Suddenly, the angel was joined by a vast host of others—the armies of heaven—prais- 2:13
ing God and saying, Ps 103:20 Rev 5:11

14 "Glory to God in highest heaven,
and peace on earth to those with whom God is pleased." 2:14 Isa 57:19

15When the angels had returned to heaven, the shepherds said to each other, "Let's go Luke 19:38
to Bethlehem! Let's see this thing that has happened, which the Lord has told us about."
16They hurried to the village and found Mary and Joseph. And there was the baby, lying
in the manger. 17After seeing Him, the shepherds told everyone what had happened and 2:17
what the angel had said to them about this child. 18All who heard the shepherds' story Luke 2:10-12
were astonished, 19but Mary kept all these things in her heart and thought about them 2:19
often. 20The shepherds went back to their flocks, glorifying and praising God for all they Luke 2:51
had heard and seen. It was just as the angel had told them.

JESUS IS PRESENTED IN THE TEMPLE

21Eight days later, when the baby was circumcised, He was named Jesus, the name given 2:21 Gen 17:12
Him by the angel even before He was conceived. Lev 12:3 Matt 1:21

▸GOD

2:1-20 Coming down. It was the most amazing and revolutionary thing that would ever happen on earth—God was going to visit in human form. In Old Testament days, God sometimes revealed Himself to people (Exodus 3:4-6; 19:16–20:21; 40:34; Isaiah 6:1-10). The power of the glory of God often startled those who witnessed such revelations. But notice how He chose to come to earth in the New Testament: born of humble parents in a nondescript village, taking His first breath in a stable. God-made-flesh drank milk from His mother's breast, played in the mud, and then, when everything was ready, revealed Himself as the Messiah. The incarnation reveals that God's plan all along has been intimate fellowship with His people. Do not be satisfied with anything less than an active, open relationship with Christ. (***See God****> God's Names> Son> Incarnation,* TopicGuide page A19.)

2:3 Apparently the census was taken based on family descent. Thus, returning "to their own ancestral towns" did not necessitate returning to the town in which one was born, but to the town that was the root of one's family line or tribe. Historians have not yet identified the Roman records related to this census.

2:7 Snugly wrapping the newborn in criss-crossed strips of cloth was a common practice to keep the child warm.

2:11 The angels use a variety of words to describe the newborn child. First, *Savior*—a Roman term that often referred to an emperor who delivered his people from oppression and harm. Savior was also very popular in the Old Testament (see, for example, 2 Samuel 22:2-3; Psalm 18:2; Isaiah 43:3-11). Next, *Messiah*—a reference to the Old Testament promises of a God-given leader and deliverer, translated "Anointed One" in Daniel 9:25-26; Psalm 2:2; 132:17. Finally, *Lord*—a title meaning "master" or "ruler", used of God from the very beginning of the Hebrew Bible (150 times in Genesis alone; see, for example, Genesis 2:4-22).

2:22 [22]Then it was time for their purification offering, as required by the law of Moses after
Lev 12:2-6 the birth of a child; so His parents took Him to Jerusalem to present Him to the Lord. [23]The
2:23 *Exod 13:2, 12, 15 law of the Lord says, "If a woman's first child is a boy, he must be dedicated to the LORD."*
2:24 [24]So they offered the sacrifice required in the law of the Lord—"either a pair of turtledoves
Lev 5:11; 12:8 or two young pigeons."

THE PROPHECY OF SIMEON

2:25 [25]At that time there was a man in Jerusalem named Simeon. He was righteous and devout
*Isa 40:1; 49:13 and was eagerly waiting for the Messiah to come and rescue Israel. The Holy Spirit was
2:26 Ps 89:48 upon him [26]and had revealed to him that he would not die until he had seen the Lord's
John 8:51 Messiah. [27]That day the Spirit led him to the Temple. So when Mary and Joseph came to
Heb 11:5 present the baby Jesus to the Lord as the law required, [28]Simeon was there. He took the
child in his arms and praised God, saying,

[29] "Sovereign Lord, now let Your servant die in peace,
as You have promised.
2:30-31 [30] I have seen Your salvation,
Isa 40:5; 52:10 [31] which You have prepared for all people.
Acts 4:12 [32] He is a light to reveal God to the nations,
2:32 Isa 42:6-7; 46:13; and He is the glory of Your people Israel!"

49:6 [33]Jesus' parents were amazed at what was being said about Him. [34]Then Simeon
2:34 Isa 8:14 blessed them, and he said to Mary, the baby's mother, "This child is destined to cause
1 Cor 1:23 many in Israel to fall, but He will be a joy to many others. He has been sent as a sign from
1 Pet 2:7-8 God, but many will oppose Him. [35]As a result, the deepest thoughts of many hearts will be
revealed. And a sword will pierce your very soul."

THE PROPHECY OF ANNA

[36]Anna, a prophet, was also there in the Temple. She was the daughter of Phanuel from the
tribe of Asher, and she was very old. Her husband died when they had been married only
2:37 1 Tim 5:5 seven years. [37]Then she lived as a widow to the age of eighty-four.* She never left the Tem-
2:38 ple but stayed there day and night, worshiping God with fasting and prayer. [38]She came
Isa 52:9 along just as Simeon was talking with Mary and Joseph, and she began praising God.
Luke 1:68; 24:21 She talked about the child to everyone who had been waiting expectantly for God to rescue
2:39 Matt 2:23 Jerusalem.
2:40 [39]When Jesus' parents had fulfilled all the requirements of the law of the Lord, they re-
Luke 1:80 turned home to Nazareth in Galilee. [40]There the child grew up healthy and strong. He was
filled with wisdom, and God's favor was on Him.

2:23 Exod 13:2. **2:24** Lev 12:8. **2:37** Or *She had been a widow for eighty-four years.*

2:22 Old Testament law held that a woman was ceremonially unclean for a period of time after the birth of a child. She had to go through a rite that would render her ceremonially clean, at the end of which the couple would make an offering to the Lord (Leviticus 12).

▸ GOD
2:26-35 God speaks to His friends. Both Simeon and Anna walked with God. They could sense that God was up to something in the world and that the right time had come. God didn't keep His friends Simeon and Anna in the dark. Through the Spirit, God spoke to them and used them to confirm that He was keeping His promises to Israel and the world by sending a Savior. By soaking ourselves in the Word and heeding the guidance of the Spirit, we can become more sensitive to God's promptings. As you read God's Word and pray to Him, let the Holy Spirit reveal truth to you about God's work in your world. (***See God****> God's Names> Holy Spirit> Speaks,* TopicGuide page A19.)

2:29 The opening words to Simeon's song signaled that his purpose in life had been to see God's promises of a Messiah fulfilled in his lifetime.

2:34-35 Jesus' life purpose was more complex than Simeon's. Jesus' life would create tensions—He would be rejected, opposed, bring joy, and reveal secret fears.

JESUS SPEAKS WITH THE TEACHERS

41 Every year Jesus' parents went to Jerusalem for the Passover festival. 42 When Jesus was
twelve years old, they attended the festival as usual. 43 After the celebration was over, they
started home to Nazareth, but Jesus stayed behind in Jerusalem. His parents didn't miss
Him at first, 44 because they assumed He was among the other travelers. But when He didn't
show up that evening, they started looking for Him among their relatives and friends.

45 When they couldn't find Him, they went back to Jerusalem to search for Him there.
46 Three days later they finally discovered Him in the Temple, sitting among the religious
teachers, listening to them and asking questions. 47 All who heard Him were amazed at His
understanding and His answers.

48 His parents didn't know what to think. "Son," His mother said to Him, "why have You
done this to us? Your father and I have been frantic, searching for You everywhere."

49 "But why did you need to search?" He asked. "Didn't you know that I must be in My
Father's house?"* 50 But they didn't understand what He meant.

51 Then He returned to Nazareth with them and was obedient to them. And His mother
stored all these things in her heart.

52 Jesus grew in wisdom and in stature and in favor with God and all the people.

JOHN THE BAPTIST PREPARES THE WAY

3 It was now the fifteenth year of the reign of Tiberius, the Roman emperor. Pontius Pi-
late was governor over Judea; Herod Antipas was ruler* over Galilee; his brother Philip
was ruler* over Iturea and Traconitis; Lysanias was ruler over Abilene. 2 Annas and Caia-
phas were the high priests. At this time a message from God came to John son of Zechari-
ah, who was living in the wilderness. 3 Then John went from place to place on both sides of
the Jordan River, preaching that people should be baptized to show that they had repented
of their sins and turned to God to be forgiven. 4 Isaiah had spoken of John when he said,

"He is a voice shouting in the wilderness,
'Prepare the way for the LORD's coming!
  Clear the road for Him!
5 The valleys will be filled,
  and the mountains and hills made level.
The curves will be straightened,
  and the rough places made smooth.
6 And then all people will see
  the salvation sent from God.'"*

7 When the crowds came to John for baptism, he said, "You brood of snakes! Who
warned you to flee God's coming wrath? 8 Prove by the way you live that you have re-
pented of your sins and turned to God. Don't just say to each other, 'We're safe, for we are

2:41 Exod 12:24-27; Deut 16:1-8
2:47 Matt 7:28; John 7:15
2:48 Luke 3:23; 4:22
2:49 John 2:16
2:50 Mark 9:32
2:51 Luke 2:19
2:52 1 Sam 2:26; Prov 3:4; Luke 1:80
3:1-16 //Matt 3:1-12; //Mark 1:2-8; //John 1:19-28
3:2 Luke 1:80
3:3 Acts 13:24; 19:4
3:4-6 *Isa 40:3-5
3:6 Luke 2:30-31; Acts 28:28; Titus 2:11
3:7 Matt 12:34; 23:33
3:8 John 8:33, 37, 39; Acts 3:25

2:49 Or *"Didn't you realize that I should be involved with My Father's affairs?"* 3:1a Greek *Herod was tetrarch.* Herod Antipas was a son of King Herod. 3:1b Greek *tetrarch;* also in 3:1c. 3:4-6 Isa 40:3-5 (Greek version).

2:41-52 Luke uses verse 40 to transition from Jesus' birth to an event that mirrored the tensions prophesied by Simeon. Jesus' simple commitment to spending time at the Temple revealed His glory to the teachers (2:47) and to Mary (2:51), but it also caused pain and frustration for His parents (2:48).

3:3 John's baptism was similar to the purification baptisms that rabbis applied to converts. In this case, those baptized were announcing their preparation for and intention to follow a future rabbi—the Messiah.

▸ MINISTRY

3:7 When time is running out. Most people like to be nice. They want to be liked by as many people as possible. But being nice isn't everything. John the Baptist shows that there is a time and a place for announcing the worst possible scenario and not caring one bit what people think. John skipped the funny illustrations and went right to the central problem—sin. His love for people and his sense that they must immediately prepare themselves for Christ's coming suspended ordinary courtesy—he just told it like it was. When you meet someone, don't necessarily wait to start a relationship before speaking the truth. That's not always best. Sometimes you must simply take a deep breath and tell that person about how God saved you. When time is running out, tell the truth and stop worrying so much about your popularity. John the Baptist certainly didn't. (***See Ministry***> *Great Commission> Witness> Having a bold witness,* TopicGuide page A56.)

3:9 descendants of Abraham.' That means nothing, for I tell you, God can create children of
Matt 7:19 Abraham from these very stones. 9 Even now the ax of God's judgment is poised, ready to
John 15:6 sever the roots of the trees. Yes, every tree that does not produce good fruit will be
chopped down and thrown into the fire."
10 The crowds asked, "What should we do?"
3:11 Jas 2:15 11 John replied, "If you have two shirts, give one to the poor. If you have food, share it
1 Jn 3:17 with those who are hungry."
3:12 12 Even corrupt tax collectors came to be baptized and asked, "Teacher, what should
Luke 7:29 we do?"
3:13 13 He replied, "Collect no more taxes than the government requires."
Luke 19:8 14 "What should we do?" asked some soldiers.
3:14 Exod 23:1 John replied, "Don't extort money or make false accusations. And be content with your
Lev 19:11 pay."
3:16 15 Everyone was expecting the Messiah to come soon, and they were eager to know
Mark 1:4 whether John might be the Messiah. 16 John answered their questions by saying, "I baptize
John 1:26-27, 33 Acts 1:5; 2:3; 11:16; you with* water; but someone is coming soon who is greater than I am—so much greater
13:25; 19:4 that I'm not even worthy to be His slave and untie the straps of His sandals. He will baptize
3:17 you with the Holy Spirit and with fire.* 17 He is ready to separate the chaff from the wheat
Matt 13:30 with His winnowing fork. Then He will clean up the threshing area, gathering the wheat
into His barn but burning the chaff with never-ending fire." 18 John used many such warn-
ings as he announced the Good News to the people.
3:19-20 19 John also publicly criticized Herod Antipas, the ruler of Galilee,* for marrying Hero-
Matt 14:3 Mark 6:17 dias, his brother's wife, and for many other wrongs he had done. 20 So Herod put John in
prison, adding this sin to his many others.

THE BAPTISM OF JESUS

3:21-22 //Matt 3:13-17 21 One day when the crowds were being baptized, Jesus Himself was baptized. As He was
//Mark 1:9-11 praying, the heavens opened, 22 and the Holy Spirit, in bodily form, descended on Him like
John 1:29-34 a dove. And a voice from heaven said, "You are My dearly loved Son, and You bring Me
3:22 Gen 22:2 great joy.*"

Ps 2:7 Isa 42:1

THE ANCESTORS OF JESUS

Matt 12:18; 17:5 Mark 9:7 23 Jesus was about thirty years old when He began His public ministry.
Luke 9:35 Jesus was known as the son of Joseph.
2 Pet 1:17 3:23-38 Joseph was the son of Heli.
//Matt 1:1-17 24 Heli was the son of Matthat.
3:23 Matthat was the son of Levi.
Luke 4:22 Levi was the son of Melki.
John 6:42

3:16a Or *in.* 3:16b Or *in the Holy Spirit and in fire.* 3:19 Greek *Herod the tetrarch.* 3:22 Some manuscripts read *My Son, and today I have become Your Father.*

SALVATION

3:21-22 God revealed. To us in His Word, and in Jesus' baptism God revealed Himself so that those there and those who read this passage would know that Jesus Christ was the One about whom John the Baptist had been speaking—the Lord made flesh (3:4). If Jesus was and is the Messiah, then the world and everyone in it (including you) has the responsibility to respond in love and trust God's command to receive the ministry and authority of His Son. (***See Salvation****> Receiving> How> Respond to God's call/invitation to salvation,* TopicGuide page A22.)

3:23 Luke revealed to us that Jesus was born to Mary through a miracle of God (1:26-38). He carefully noted that Jesus "was known as the son of Joseph."

3:23-38 The genealogies in Matthew and Luke are not identical, but are complementary. Each is true, but each is a partial summary of Jesus' ancestry. Matthew listed Abraham and David as the primary ancestors, emphasizing that Jesus fulfilled the promises of the Abrahamic Covenant (Genesis 12:1-3; 15:1-5) and was the climax of David's royal heritage (2 Samuel 7; 1 Chronicles 17:11-14; Romans 1:3). Luke traced Jesus' lineage beginning with Adam, showing Jesus as the fulfillment of God's promises to him and to all humanity (Genesis 3:15). Since Luke was a Gentile, this point would have been especially important to him.

Melki was the son of Jannai.
Jannai was the son of Joseph.
25 Joseph was the son of Mattathias.
Mattathias was the son of Amos.
Amos was the son of Nahum.
Nahum was the son of Esli.
Esli was the son of Naggai.
26 Naggai was the son of Maath.
Maath was the son of Mattathias.
Mattathias was the son of Semein.
Semein was the son of Josech.
Josech was the son of Joda.
27 Joda was the son of Joanan.
Joanan was the son of Rhesa.
Rhesa was the son of Zerubbabel.
Zerubbabel was the son of Shealtiel.
Shealtiel was the son of Neri.
28 Neri was the son of Melki.
Melki was the son of Addi.
Addi was the son of Cosam.
Cosam was the son of Elmadam.
Elmadam was the son of Er.
29 Er was the son of Joshua.
Joshua was the son of Eliezer.
Eliezer was the son of Jorim.
Jorim was the son of Matthat.
Matthat was the son of Levi.
30 Levi was the son of Simeon.
Simeon was the son of Judah.
Judah was the son of Joseph.
Joseph was the son of Jonam.
Jonam was the son of Eliakim.
31 Eliakim was the son of Melea.
Melea was the son of Menna.
Menna was the son of Mattatha.
Mattatha was the son of Nathan.
Nathan was the son of David.
32 David was the son of Jesse.
Jesse was the son of Obed.
Obed was the son of Boaz.
Boaz was the son of Salmon.*
Salmon was the son of Nahshon.
33 Nahshon was the son of Amminadab.
Amminadab was the son of Admin.
Admin was the son of Arni.*
Arni was the son of Hezron.
Hezron was the son of Perez.
Perez was the son of Judah.
34 Judah was the son of Jacob.
Jacob was the son of Isaac.

3:27
1 Chr 3:17
Ezra 3:2

3:31-33
Ruth 4:18-22
1 Sam 16:1, 13
2 Sam 5:14
1 Chr 2:9-12; 3:5

3:34-36
Gen 11:10-26
1 Chr 1:24-27

3:32 Greek *Sala,* a variant spelling of Salmon; also in 3:32b. See Ruth 4:22. 3:33 Some manuscripts read *Amminadab was the son of Aram. Arni* and *Aram* are alternate spellings of Ram. See 1 Chr 2:9-10.

Isaac was the son of Abraham.
Abraham was the son of Terah.
Terah was the son of Nahor.
35 Nahor was the son of Serug.
Serug was the son of Reu.
Reu was the son of Peleg.
Peleg was the son of Eber.
Eber was the son of Shelah.
3:36-38 Gen 4:25–5:32 1 Chr 1:1-4
36 Shelah was the son of Cainan.
Cainan was the son of Arphaxad.
Arphaxad was the son of Shem.
Shem was the son of Noah.
Noah was the son of Lamech.
37 Lamech was the son of Methuselah.
Methuselah was the son of Enoch.
Enoch was the son of Jared.
Jared was the son of Mahalalel.
Mahalalel was the son of Kenan.
3:38 Gen 1:26-27; 2:7; 5:1-2
38 Kenan was the son of Enosh.*
Enosh was the son of Seth.
Seth was the son of Adam.
Adam was the son of God.

THE TEMPTATION OF JESUS

4:1-13 //Matt 4:1-11 //Mark 1:12-13 John 3:34

4 Then Jesus, full of the Holy Spirit, returned from the Jordan River. He was led by the
Spirit in the wilderness,* 2 where He was tempted by the devil for forty days. Jesus ate
nothing all that time and became very hungry.

4:1 Isa 11:2; 61:1

3 Then the devil said to Him, "If You are the Son of God, tell this stone to become a loaf
of bread."

4:2 Exod 34:28 1 Kgs 19:8 Heb 4:15

4 But Jesus told him, "No! The Scriptures say, 'People do not live by bread alone.'*"
5 Then the devil took Him up and revealed to Him all the kingdoms of the world in a mo-
ment of time. 6 "I will give You the glory of these kingdoms and authority over them," the
devil said, "because they are mine to give to anyone I please. 7 I will give it all to You if You
will worship me."

4:4 *Deut 8:3

4:6 Matt 28:18 John 12:31; 14:30 1 Jn 5:19 Rev 13:2

8 Jesus replied, "The Scriptures say,

'You must worship the LORD your God
and serve only Him.'*"

4:8 *Deut 6:13; 10:20

9 Then the devil took Him to Jerusalem, to the highest point of the Temple, and said, "If
You are the Son of God, jump off! 10 For the Scriptures say,

4:10-11 *Ps 91:11-12

'He will order His angels to protect and guard You.
11 And they will hold You up with their hands
so You won't even hurt Your foot on a stone.'*"

3:38 Greek *Enos*, a variant spelling of Enosh; also in 3:38b. See Gen 5:6. 4:1 Some manuscripts read *into the wilderness.* 4:4 Deut 8:3. 4:8 Deut 6:13. 4:10-11 Ps 91:11-12.

▸ HOLINESS

4:1-14 Temptation in God's plan. Jesus knew that temptation had a place in the plan of God, for He was led by the Spirit to face powerful temptations from Satan. Temptation is also in God's plan for us—but so is our victory over it. God has granted us His Word and His Spirit to prepare us to escape Satan's traps; by escaping these traps, we will have learned anew the importance of relying on the Word and following the leadership of the Spirit. Join Jesus in asking God to help us avoid temptation, and, if we must face it, that He would deliver us from the "evil one" (Matthew 6:9-13). (**See Holiness**> *Changed by God> God Provides> Chastening us,* TopicGuide page A41.)

4:2 The word *devil* refers to an accuser or slanderer (see Job 1:6-12; 2:1-7; and Zechariah 3:1-2.)

[12]Jesus responded, "The Scriptures also say, 'You must not test the LORD your God.'*" 4:12 *Deut 6:16
[13]When the devil had finished tempting Jesus, he left Him until the next opportunity came. 4:13 Heb 4:15

JESUS REJECTED AT NAZARETH

[14]Then Jesus returned to Galilee, filled with the Holy Spirit's power. Reports about Him 4:14-15 //Matt 4:12-17 //Mark 1:14-15 John 4:43-45
spread quickly through the whole region. [15]He taught regularly in their synagogues and
was praised by everyone.
[16]When He came to the village of Nazareth, His boyhood home, He went as usual to the 4:16-30 //Matt 13:53-58 //Mark 6:1-6
synagogue on the Sabbath and stood up to read the Scriptures. [17]The scroll of Isaiah the
prophet was handed to Him. He unrolled the scroll and found the place where this was
written:

[18] "The Spirit of the LORD is upon Me, 4:18-19 *Isa 61:1-2
for He has anointed Me to bring Good News to the poor.

4:12 Deut 6:16.

4:16-21 It was common for the Jewish men of the community to take turns reading from and explaining the Scriptures during worship services in the synagogue. Jesus performed this service just as all Jewish men did. As Jesus sat down, the group expected Him to expound upon the passage, but instead He declared that the prophetic passage He read came true as He was reading it. God's Spirit truly rested on Jesus Christ, and His mission would lead to freedom for all who believe His message (Romans 3:24).

▸ MINISTRY

4:18-19 Good News for bad people. Christians commonly speak of sharing the Good News with others. In fact, the word *gospel* is derived from the term *good news.* But just what is at the heart of this Good News that we share? One way to summarize it is found here—a new day has dawned, and new life has begun for those who trust in Christ as their Messiah. Our message of the gospel will be longer or shorter according to the situation or person we are sharing with, but it certainly should never contradict Jesus' core message: The gospel is good news for hurting people. (***See Ministry***> *Great Commission> Description,* TopicGuide page A56.)

MY RESPONSE TO GOD

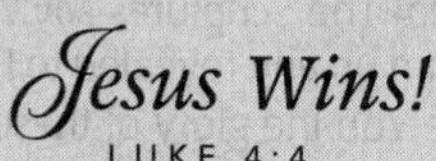

Jesus Wins!

LUKE 4:4

You can rejoice. Even when you as an individual and the church as a whole seem to be weak and ineffective in stopping Satan and the evil in this world, the fact remains that Jesus has promised us a share in His victory over all evil.

We learn of this promise first in the Garden of Eden. God promised that a son of Adam and Eve would be injured by the serpent (Genesis 3:15) but would in turn crush the serpent's head. Isaiah foretold this same event when he described how the Suffering Servant would be wounded (Isaiah 53) but would save God's people from sin.

In the New Testament we read how Satan confronted Jesus, hoping that, just as Adam and Eve fell, Jesus would fall to temptation. But Jesus never fell (Luke 4:1-13). He stood up to each temptation with the Word of God, and He did not stumble as Adam and Eve had (Romans 5:12-18). Even when the power of death seemed to defeat Him on the cross, Jesus rose to victory over sin, Satan, and suffering. And while all of those enemies still exist today, they are in full retreat before Jesus and His faithful army, the church. Jesus' foes await a certain future of complete defeat when Jesus returns in all His glory.

Praise God for protecting His people from Satan and empowering them through the Holy Spirit to march on to complete victory through Jesus Christ our Lord!

He has sent Me to proclaim that captives will be released,
that the blind will see,
that the oppressed will be set free,
19 and that the time of the LORD's favor has come.*"

20He rolled up the scroll, handed it back to the attendant, and sat down. All eyes in the synagogue looked at Him intently. 21Then He began to speak to them. "The Scripture you've just heard has been fulfilled this very day!"

22Everyone spoke well of Him and was amazed by the gracious words that came from His lips. "How can this be?" they asked. "Isn't this Joseph's son?"

23Then He said, "You will undoubtedly quote Me this proverb: 'Physician, heal yourself'—meaning, 'Do miracles here in Your hometown like those You did in Capernaum.' 24But I tell you the truth, no prophet is accepted in His own hometown.

25"Certainly there were many needy widows in Israel in Elijah's time, when the heavens were closed for three and a half years, and a severe famine devastated the land. 26Yet Elijah was not sent to any of them. He was sent instead to a foreigner—a widow of Zarephath in the land of Sidon. 27And there were many lepers in Israel in the time of the prophet Elisha, but the only one healed was Naaman, a Syrian."

28When they heard this, the people in the synagogue were furious. 29Jumping up, they mobbed Him and forced Him to the edge of the hill on which the town was built. They intended to push Him over the cliff, 30but He passed right through the crowd and went on His way.

JESUS CASTS OUT A DEMON

31Then Jesus went to Capernaum, a town in Galilee, and taught there in the synagogue every Sabbath day. 32There, too, the people were amazed at His teaching, for He spoke with authority.

33Once when He was in the synagogue, a man possessed by a demon—an evil* spirit—began shouting at Jesus, 34"Go away! Why are You interfering with us, Jesus of Nazareth? Have You come to destroy us? I know who You are—the Holy One sent from God!"

35Jesus cut him short. "Be quiet! Come out of the man," He ordered. At that, the demon threw the man to the floor as the crowd watched; then it came out of him without hurting him further.

36Amazed, the people exclaimed, "What authority and power this man's words possess! Even evil spirits obey Him, and they flee at His command!" 37The news about Jesus spread through every village in the entire region.

JESUS HEALS MANY PEOPLE

38After leaving the synagogue that day, Jesus went to Simon's home, where He found Simon's mother-in-law very sick with a high fever. "Please heal her," everyone begged. 39Standing at her bedside, He rebuked the fever, and it left her. And she got up at once and prepared a meal for them.

4:19 Lev 25:8-10; 2 Cor 6:2
4:22 Luke 2:47; John 6:42; 7:15
4:23 Matt 4:13; 11:23; Mark 1:21-28; 2:1-12
4:24 Matt 13:57; Mark 6:4; John 4:44
4:25-26 1 Kgs 17:1-9; 18:1; Jas 5:17
4:27 2 Kgs 5:1-14
4:29 Num 15:35; Acts 7:58; Heb 13:12
4:30 John 8:59
4:31-37 //Mark 1:23-28
4:31 Matt 4:13-16; John 2:12
4:32 Matt 7:28-29; John 7:46
4:34 Luke 4:41; John 6:69
4:35 Luke 4:39-41
4:38-41 //Matt 8:14-17; //Mark 1:29-34

4:18-19 Or *and to proclaim the acceptable year of the LORD.* Isa 61:1-2 (Greek version); 58:6. 4:33 Greek *unclean;* also in 4:36.

4:23-27 Jesus pointed out that Elijah left Israel to live with a widow in the Gentile region of Sidon, and that the only recorded healing of a leper in the time of the prophet Elisha was performed on a Gentile. Jesus made these comments to explain His refusal to perform miracles and signs in His hometown of Nazareth.

4:33 The sense of the word translated "possessed" is not that the demon owned the man he was afflicting but that the man *had* a demon (perhaps in the sense of how we might speak of someone having a disease).

4:37 The expression Luke used to describe the spread of the news about Jesus carries the idea of the resounding reply of an echo. The reports about Jesus kept echoing throughout the region.

4:39 The word and touch of Jesus completely restored Peter's mother-in-law, enabling her to rise and immediately prepare a meal for her guests.

[40]As the sun went down that evening, people throughout the village brought sick family 4:40-41
members to Jesus. No matter what their diseases were, the touch of His hand healed every Matt 8:16-17
one. [41]Many were possessed by demons; and the demons came out at His command, Mark 1:32-34
shouting, "You are the Son of God!" But because they knew He was the Messiah, He re- 4:41
buked them and refused to let them speak. Mark 3:11

JESUS CONTINUES TO PREACH

[42]Early the next morning Jesus went out to an isolated place. The crowds searched every-
where for Him, and when they finally found Him, they begged Him not to leave them. 4:42-44 Matt 4:23
[43]But He replied, "I must preach the Good News of the Kingdom of God in other towns, too, //Mark 1:35-39
because that is why I was sent." [44]So He continued to travel around, preaching in syna- 4:43
gogues throughout Judea.* Luke 8:1

4:44 Matt 4:23 Mark 1:39

THE FIRST DISCIPLES

5 One day as Jesus was preaching on the shore of the Sea of Galilee,* great crowds 5:1-11
pressed in on Him to listen to the word of God. [2]He noticed two empty boats at the //Matt 4:18-22
water's edge, for the fishermen had left them and were washing their nets. [3]Stepping into //Mark 1:16-20
one of the boats, Jesus asked Simon,* its owner, to push it out into the water. So He sat in
the boat and taught the crowds from there.
[4]When He had finished speaking, He said to Simon, "Now go out where it is deeper, and 5:4
let down your nets to catch some fish." John 21:6
[5]"Master," Simon replied, "we worked hard all last night and didn't catch a thing. But if 5:5 John 21:3
You say so, I'll let the nets down again." [6]And this time their nets were so full of fish they
began to tear! [7]A shout for help brought their partners in the other boat, and soon both 5:6 John 21:11
boats were filled with fish and on the verge of sinking.
[8]When Simon Peter realized what had happened, he fell to his knees before Jesus and 5:8
said, "Oh, Lord, please leave me—I'm too much of a sinner to be around You." [9]For he was Gen 18:27
awestruck by the number of fish they had caught, as were the others with him. [10]His part- Job 42:5-6
ners, James and John, the sons of Zebedee, were also amazed.
Jesus replied to Simon, "Don't be afraid! From now on you'll be fishing for people!"
[11]And as soon as they landed, they left everything and followed Jesus. 5:11 Matt 19:27

JESUS HEALS A MAN WITH LEPROSY

[12]In one of the villages, Jesus met a man with an advanced case of leprosy. When the man 5:12-14
saw Jesus, he bowed with his face to the ground, begging to be healed. "Lord," he said, "if //Matt 8:2-4
You are willing, You can heal me and make me clean." //Mark 1:40-44

4:44 Some manuscripts read *Galilee.* 5:1 Greek *Lake Gennesaret,* another name for the Sea of Galilee. 5:3 *Simon* is called "Peter" in 6:14 and thereafter.

4:44 Jesus initially carried out His ministry in the synagogues in Galilee and Judea. This was a reasonable place to begin because faithful Jews would gather every Sabbath in their neighborhood synagogues. These were the center of Jewish life in every town.

5:1-3 With a large crowd pressing in on Him, Jesus asked Simon to take Him out in a boat a short way from the shore. This way, Jesus' voice, naturally amplified by the water, would carry more easily to the people as they sat on the shore.

▸ PURPOSE

5:1-11 Jesus' miracles meet needs. Jesus did not just randomly do "God stuff." When He responded to a situation in a miraculous and powerful way, there was a reason. Why this miracle of fish, of all things? Why for Simon Peter? It wasn't just to convince Peter that Jesus was God in the flesh—Peter didn't understand that until much later (see Matthew 16:15-17). Peter apparently had a family business; he was a fisherman and was married. Jesus was about to call him to leave the fishing for at least a while. But before the call, Jesus met the financial need to take care of his family. His mercy upon Peter and his family shined through this miracle. Make sure your words and actions reveal the same sort of mercy and compassion for the needs of God's people. (***See Purpose****> God's Deeds> Special Acts> Miracles> Jesus> First miraculous catch of fish,* TopicGuide page A53.)

5:5 In Jesus' day, fishermen would go out at night with large nets and let them down in the dark water, often hanging a lantern off the side of the boat to attract bait fish into the area, which would then attract even larger fish into the net. During the day, the fish would have been able to see and avoid the nets; so this kind of fishing wouldn't typically be done during the day. This would account for Simon's reluctance to let down his nets in the daylight, as Jesus had commanded.

13 Jesus reached out and touched him. "I am willing," He said. "Be healed!" And instantly
5:14 the leprosy disappeared. 14 Then Jesus instructed him not to tell anyone what had hap-
Lev 14:2-32 pened. He said, "Go to the priest and let him examine you. Take along the offering re-
quired in the law of Moses for those who have been healed of leprosy.* This will be a
public testimony that you have been cleansed."

5:15 15 But despite Jesus' instructions, the report of His power spread even faster, and vast
Matt 9:26 crowds came to hear Him preach and to be healed of their diseases. 16 But Jesus often
withdrew to the wilderness for prayer.

JESUS HEALS A PARALYZED MAN

5:17-26 17 One day while Jesus was teaching, some Pharisees and teachers of religious law were
//Matt 9:1-8 sitting nearby. (It seemed that these men showed up from every village in all Galilee and
//Mark 2:1-12 Judea, as well as from Jerusalem.) And the Lord's healing power was strongly with Jesus.

18 Some men came carrying a paralyzed man on a sleeping mat. They tried to take him
inside to Jesus, 19 but they couldn't reach Him because of the crowd. So they went up to the
roof and took off some tiles. Then they lowered the sick man on his mat down into the
5:20 crowd, right in front of Jesus. 20 Seeing their faith, Jesus said to the man, "Young man, your
Luke 7:48 sins are forgiven."

5:21 21 But the Pharisees and teachers of religious law said to themselves, "Who does He
Isa 43:25; 55:7 Luke 7:49 think He is? That's blasphemy! Only God can forgive sins!"

5:22 22 Jesus knew what they were thinking, so He asked them, "Why do you question this in
Luke 6:8; 9:47 your hearts? 23 Is it easier to say 'Your sins are forgiven,' or 'Stand up and walk'? 24 So I will
5:24-25 prove to you that the Son of Man* has the authority on earth to forgive sins." Then Jesus
John 5:8-9 turned to the paralyzed man and said, "Stand up, pick up your mat, and go home!"

25 And immediately, as everyone watched, the man jumped up, picked up his mat, and
went home praising God. 26 Everyone was gripped with great wonder and awe, and they
praised God, exclaiming, "We have seen amazing things today!"

JESUS CALLS LEVI (MATTHEW)

5:27-32 27 Later, as Jesus left the town, He saw a tax collector named Levi sitting at his tax collec-
//Matt 9:9-13 tor's booth. "Follow Me and be My disciple," Jesus said to him. 28 So Levi got up, left every-
//Mark 2:13-17 thing, and followed Him.

5:29-30 29 Later, Levi held a banquet in his home with Jesus as the guest of honor. Many of Levi's
Luke 15:1-2 fellow tax collectors and other guests also ate with them. 30 But the Pharisees and their
teachers of religious law complained bitterly to Jesus' disciples, "Why do you eat and
drink with such scum?*"

5:14 See Lev 14:2-32. 5:24 "Son of Man" is a title Jesus used for Himself. 5:30 Greek *with tax collectors and sinners?*

5:14 It might seem that the disappearance of the leprosy was all the proof the man needed that he was healed. However, since leprosy also made a person ceremonially unclean, he still would need a priest to pronounce him clean in order for the Jewish community to welcome him back.

▸ GOD

5:17-26 First things first. The friends of the paralyzed man knew what they wanted—they longed for Jesus to heal their desperately ill friend. They went to extreme lengths to get the bedridden man into the presence of Jesus. And what was the first thing Jesus did? He spoke to the man about His sin. Can you imagine how the man's friends must have talking among themselves? "What's this? We brought him to be healed!" But thankfully, in His wisdom Jesus did what was most important first. That's how Jesus wants us to do things, too. Don't be distracted by the apparent crisis, but look deeper and see the real needs God can meet among His people. (***See God****> God's Names> Son> Healer*, TopicGuide page A19.)

5:18-19 Houses in that day typically had an external set of stairs that led to a flat portion of the roof. Not being able to get in to see Jesus, the friends of the paralyzed man decided to make an alternate opening in order to get their friend into Jesus' presence.

5:21-23 To commit blasphemy was to speak contemptuously or disparagingly about God—to insult Him by word or deed. When Jesus spoke to the paralyzed man and forgave his sins, He clearly carried out the role of God. If He hadn't had the right to do that, He would have insulted God.

5:30 The religious leaders of the day (and most Jews in general) despised tax collectors, who typically were Jewish men who worked for Rome to gather taxes from their fellow Jews. Tax collectors were considered one of the lowest classes in society.

31 Jesus answered them, "Healthy people don't need a doctor—sick people do. 32 I have
come to call not those who think they are righteous, but those who know they are sinners
and need to repent."

A DISCUSSION ABOUT FASTING

33 One day some people said to Jesus, "John the Baptist's disciples fast and pray regularly, and
so do the disciples of the Pharisees. Why are Your disciples always eating and drinking?"
34 Jesus responded, "Do wedding guests fast while celebrating with the groom? Of course
not. 35 But someday the groom will be taken away from them, and then they will fast."
36 Then Jesus gave them this illustration: "No one tears a piece of cloth from a new gar-
ment and uses it to patch an old garment. For then the new garment would be ruined, and
the new patch wouldn't even match the old garment.
37 "And no one puts new wine into old wineskins. For the new wine would burst the
wineskins, spilling the wine and ruining the skins. 38 New wine must be stored in new
wineskins. 39 But no one who drinks the old wine seems to want the new wine. 'The old is
just fine,' they say."

5:33-39 //Matt 9:14-17 //Mark 2:18-22
5:34 John 3:29
5:35 Luke 9:22; 17:22

A DISCUSSION ABOUT THE SABBATH

6 One Sabbath day as Jesus was walking through some grainfields, His disciples broke
off heads of grain, rubbed off the husks in their hands, and ate the grain. 2 But some
Pharisees said, "Why are You breaking the law by harvesting grain on the Sabbath?"
3 Jesus replied, "Haven't you read in the Scriptures what David did when he and his com-
panions were hungry? 4 He went into the house of God and broke the law by eating the sa-
cred loaves of bread that only the priests can eat. He also gave some to his companions."
5 And Jesus added, "The Son of Man* is Lord, even over the Sabbath."

JESUS HEALS ON THE SABBATH

6 On another Sabbath day, a man with a deformed right hand was in the synagogue
while Jesus was teaching. 7 The teachers of religious law and the Pharisees watched

6:1-5 //Matt 12:1-8 //Mark 2:23-28
6:1 Deut 23:25
6:2 John 5:10
6:3-4 1 Sam 21:6
6:4 Lev 24:5-9
6:7 Luke 14:1

6:5 "Son of Man" is a title Jesus used for Himself.

▸ **GOD**

5:31-32 The hidden illness. We all know people who didn't know they were ill but suddenly discovered that they were close to death's door. At first they might have denied the results of the test, and then grown angry at the doctors. But until they accepted that they were ill and needed help, there was little chance that they would get better. That is similar to the way some people respond to the gospel. The commands of God and our own consciences reveal that our souls are sick with sin—but what will we do? Ignore it? Rail against God? We must submit to His diagnosis and solution—the forgiveness that comes through Jesus Christ. Jesus stands ready to heal the spiritually ill. If you know someone who is struggling with the gospel, make certain he understands the often-hidden symptoms of unrepentant sin in his life. And be committed to finding the sin in your life, too. (***See God**> Relationship> Barriers> Unconfessed transgressions,* TopicGuide page A14.)

6:1-2 One of the requirements of the Old Testament law was for the seventh day, the Sabbath, to be set aside as a day of rest (Exodus 20:8-11; Deuteronomy 5:12-15). No work was to be done on the Sabbath, but religious leaders had broadened God's command, defining work as even plucking seeds from plants for a quick snack. These and other traditional commands cut people off from God, but Jesus made it clear that the commands of Moses were intended to help God's people, not starve them.

▸ **WORSHIP**

6:1-5 Who is Lord of your Sabbath? The Sabbath was a fundamental sign of the covenant that existed between God and His people (Exodus 31:16-17). In order to ensure that people kept the Sabbath holy, the religious leaders had established a number of rules about what could and could not be done on the Sabbath. However, all the rules obscured the real purpose of the Sabbath. Jesus sought to set things right, and He began to do that by making the amazing claim that He, Himself, was the real Master of the Sabbath. Make Jesus—not your own recreation or your job or anything else—Master of your Sabbath. (***See Worship**> NT> Our Role> Obedience> Called to keep a Sabbath,* TopicGuide page A32.)

6:3-5 First Samuel 21:1-6 records that David and his men ate bread that was supposed to be served only to the priests at the Tabernacle. Technically, David disobeyed the law of Moses; however, there was no other food available, and the men were hungry. God did not rebuke David for this act, although He did rebuke him at other times. Jesus referred to this story to imply that there were appropriate situations in which the ceremonial laws of the Old Testament could be broken.

6:6-11 According to the religious leaders of Jesus' day, saving a life was a recognized exception to the prohibitions against working on the Sabbath. But they insisted that people should refrain from doing anything that could be put off until after the Sabbath. Thus, Jesus' healing of this man (since it was not a matter of life or death) was seen as a violation of the Sabbath rules.

6:8 Luke 5:22; 9:47 Jesus closely. If He healed the man's hand, they planned to accuse Him of working on
the Sabbath.
8 But Jesus knew their thoughts. He said to the man with the deformed hand, "Come and
stand in front of everyone." So the man came forward. 9 Then Jesus said to His critics, "I
have a question for you. Does the law permit good deeds on the Sabbath, or is it a day for
doing evil? Is this a day to save life or to destroy it?"
10 He looked around at them one by one and then said to the man, "Hold out your
hand." So the man held out his hand, and it was restored! 11 At this, the enemies of Jesus
were wild with rage and began to discuss what to do with Him.

JESUS CHOOSES THE TWELVE APOSTLES

6:12-16 //Matt 10:2-4 //Mark 3:13-19 12 One day soon afterward Jesus went up on a mountain to pray, and He prayed to God all
night. 13 At daybreak He called together all of His disciples and chose twelve of them to be
6:13 John 6:70 apostles. Here are their names:

6:14-15 Acts 1:13 14 Simon (whom He named Peter),
Andrew (Peter's brother),
James,
John,
Philip,
Bartholomew,
15 Matthew,
Thomas,
James (son of Alphaeus),
Simon (who was called the zealot),
16 Judas (son of James),
Judas Iscariot (who later betrayed Him).

CROWDS FOLLOW JESUS

6:17-19 //Matt 4:23-25 17 When they came down from the mountain, the disciples stood with Jesus on a large,
level area, surrounded by many of His followers and by the crowds. There were people
from all over Judea and from Jerusalem and from as far north as the seacoasts of Tyre and
Sidon. 18 They had come to hear Him and to be healed of their diseases; and those trou-
6:19 Matt 9:20 Mark 5:30 bled by evil* spirits were healed. 19 Everyone tried to touch Him, because healing power
went out from Him, and He healed everyone.

THE BEATITUDES

6:20-23 //Matt 5:1-12 20 Then Jesus turned to His disciples and said,

"God blesses you who are poor,
for the Kingdom of God is yours.

6:18 Greek *unclean.*

▸ WORSHIP
6:12 Prayer priority. How much do you need prayer? How important is it to you? Do you depend on it, or can you just as easily skip it? Apparently Jesus couldn't go without prayer. That is an astounding observation. Jesus, God the Son, took time to pray. In this verse, we see Him spending time with His heavenly Father—all night! The next morning, Jesus took action on a major initiative and appointed the Twelve to be with Him. It seemed that He did not want to make such an important decision without spending significant time about it in prayer. What about you? (***See Worship****> NT> Prayer> Examples> Jesus> Christ prayed as a regular practice,* TopicGuide page A33.)

6:17-26 Luke summarized the Beatitudes slightly different than Matthew (see Matthew 5). It is likely that both accounts are summaries of sermons Jesus gave on several occasions. These teachings highlight what Christ values in His Kingdom. They also address the problems that New Testament believers would face as they spread the gospel throughout the world (6:22-26).

21 God blesses you who are hungry now,
for you will be satisfied.
God blesses you who weep now,
for in due time you will laugh.

22 What blessings await you when people hate you and exclude you and mock you and
curse you as evil because you follow the Son of Man. 23 When that happens, be happy!
Yes, leap for joy! For a great reward awaits you in heaven. And remember, their ancestors
treated the ancient prophets that same way.

SORROWS FORETOLD

24 "What sorrow awaits you who are rich,
for you have your only happiness now.
25 What sorrow awaits you who are fat and prosperous now,
for a time of awful hunger awaits you.
What sorrow awaits you who laugh now,
for your laughing will turn to mourning and sorrow.
26 What sorrow awaits you who are praised by the crowds,
for their ancestors also praised false prophets.

LOVE FOR ENEMIES

27 "But to you who are willing to listen, I say, love your enemies! Do good to those who
hate you. 28 Bless those who curse you. Pray for those who hurt you. 29 If someone slaps
you on one cheek, offer the other cheek also. If someone demands your coat, offer your
shirt also. 30 Give to anyone who asks; and when things are taken away from you, don't try
to get them back. 31 Do to others as you would like them to do to you.
32 "If you love only those who love you, why should you get credit for that? Even sinners
love those who love them! 33 And if you do good only to those who do good to you, why
should you get credit? Even sinners do that much! 34 And if you lend money only to those
who can repay you, why should you get credit? Even sinners will lend to other sinners for
a full return.
35 "Love your enemies! Do good to them. Lend to them without expecting to be repaid.
Then your reward from heaven will be very great, and you will truly be acting as children
of the Most High, for He is kind to those who are unthankful and wicked. 36 You must be
compassionate, just as your Father is compassionate.

DO NOT JUDGE OTHERS

37 "Do not judge others, and you will not be judged. Do not condemn others, or it will all
come back against you. Forgive others, and you will be forgiven. 38 Give, and you will re-
ceive. Your gift will return to you in full—pressed down, shaken together to make room for
more, running over, and poured into your lap. The amount you give will determine the
amount you get back.*"
39 Then Jesus gave the following illustration: "Can one blind person lead another? Won't
they both fall into a ditch? 40 Students* are not greater than their teacher. But the student
who is fully trained will become like the teacher.

6:21 Isa 55:1; 61:3; Rev 7:16-17
6:22 John 15:19; 16:2; 1 Pet 4:14
6:23 2 Chr 36:16; Acts 5:41; 7:52; Jas 1:2
6:24 Jas 5:1
6:25 Isa 5:22; 65:13
6:26 Jas 4:4
6:27-35 //Matt 5:38-48
6:27 Prov 25:21; Rom 12:20
6:28 Rom 12:14
6:30 Deut 15:7-8, 10
6:31 Matt 7:12
6:33-35 Lev 25:35-36
6:36 Matt 5:48
6:37-42 //Matt 7:1-5
6:38 Ps 79:12; Mark 4:24
6:39 Matt 15:14
6:40 Matt 10:24-25; John 13:16; 15:20

6:38 Or *The measure you give will be the measure you get back.* 6:40 Or *Disciples.*

▸ SALVATION

6:35-36 Come into His family. Jesus invites everyone, young and old, into the life that He shares with the Father. This life is at the heart of the salvation He offers—but what is this life? It's relational—a new connection with God. We are to relate to others the way God does—we are supposed to bear a family resemblance to our Father and to our elder brother, Jesus. Even when we don't speak the gospel directly, people should be able to see a difference in us. They should learn about God's character by watching our character. Our words and actions can welcome people into the family of God, or they can scare them away. Which do yours do? (***See Salvation***> *Receiving> When> Member of God's family,* TopicGuide page A23.)

41 “And why worry about a speck in your friend's eye* when you have a log in your own?
42 How can you think of saying, ‘Friend,* let me help you get rid of that speck in your eye,’
when you can't see past the log in your own eye? Hypocrite! First get rid of the log in your
own eye; then you will see well enough to deal with the speck in your friend's eye.

THE TREE AND ITS FRUIT

6:43-45 43 “A good tree can't produce bad fruit, and a bad tree can't produce good fruit. 44 A tree is
//Matt 7:17-20; identified by its fruit. Figs are never gathered from thornbushes, and grapes are not picked
12:34-35 from bramble bushes. 45 A good person produces good things from the treasury of a good
6:44 Matt 12:33 heart, and an evil person produces evil things from the treasury of an evil heart. What you
say flows from what is in your heart.

BUILDING ON A SOLID FOUNDATION

6:46 46 “So why do you keep calling Me ‘Lord, Lord!’ when you don't do what I say? 47 I will show
Mal 1:6 you what it's like when someone comes to Me, listens to My teaching, and then follows it.
Matt 7:21 48 It is like a person building a house who digs deep and lays the foundation on solid rock.
6:47-49 When the floodwaters rise and break against that house, it stands firm because it is well
//Matt 7:24-27 built. 49 But anyone who hears and doesn't obey is like a person who builds a house with-
out a foundation. When the floods sweep down against that house, it will collapse into a
heap of ruins.”

THE FAITH OF A ROMAN OFFICER

7:1-10 **7** When Jesus had finished saying all this to the people, He returned to Capernaum. 2 At
//Matt 8:5-13 //John 4:43-54 that time the highly valued slave of a Roman officer* was sick and near death. 3 When
7:2 the officer heard about Jesus, he sent some respected Jewish elders to ask Him to come
John 4:47 and heal his slave. 4 So they earnestly begged Jesus to help the man. “If anyone deserves
7:5 Your help, he does,” they said, 5 “for he loves the Jewish people and even built a syna-
Acts 10:2 gogue for us.”

6 So Jesus went with them. But just before they arrived at the house, the officer sent
some friends to say, “Lord, don't trouble Yourself by coming to my home, for I am not wor-
7:7 thy of such an honor. 7 I am not even worthy to come and meet You. Just say the word
Ps 107:20 from where You are, and my servant will be healed. 8 I know this because I am under the
authority of my superior officers, and I have authority over my soldiers. I only need to say,
‘Go,’ and they go, or ‘Come,’ and they come. And if I say to my slaves, ‘Do this,’ they do it.”

9 When Jesus heard this, He was amazed. Turning to the crowd that was following Him,
He said, “I tell you, I haven't seen faith like this in all Israel!” 10 And when the officer's
friends returned to his house, they found the slave completely healed.

6:41 Greek *your brother's eye;* also in 6:42. 6:42 Greek *Brother.* 7:2 Greek *a centurion;* similarly in 7:6.

▸ BIBLE
6:46-49 Foundational words. Most people are ready to admit that Jesus was like no other man. Most will acknowledge that His teaching was without equal. But once we recognize that Jesus is without comparison, how should we respond to Him? Some think that it's enough merely to acknowledge His superiority. But Jesus tells us that we need to take His words as the *only* true basis for life. Anything else will result in a life without a real foundation. (***See Bible****> Power> Equip> Sustains our lives,* TopicGuide page A11.)

▸ SALVATION
7:1-10 Faith is believing. What comes to mind when you think of faith? Some see it as “believing something to be true when you know it's not true.” That's not biblical faith; that's foolishness. Some act as if faith is working up a kind of courage to face something hard. That's not biblical faith; that's simply strength of will. Jesus commended the faith of the Roman officer; He said that the man's faith was without comparison. And all the man did was to say that he would take Jesus at His word. That's the heart of real faith. Don't complicate your faith in God—just believe Him and live knowing that what He says is true. (***See Salvation****> Receiving> How> Faith in Christ,* TopicGuide page A22.)

7:2 The word translated in the NLT as “Roman officer” is literally translated “centurion.” A centurion commanded a company of 50 to 100 men.

7:9 The Roman officer was likely a God-fearer, or a Gentile who had converted to Judaism without submitting to circumcision. This, combined with his generosity, would explain his great respect among the Jews, who were usually distrustful of Roman military leaders.

JESUS RAISES A WIDOW'S SON

11 Soon afterward Jesus went with His disciples to the village of Nain, and a large crowd
followed Him. 12 A funeral procession was coming out as He approached the village gate.
The young man who had died was a widow's only son, and a large crowd from the village
was with her. 13 When the Lord saw her, His heart overflowed with compassion. "Don't
cry!" He said. 14 Then He walked over to the coffin and touched it, and the bearers stopped.
"Young man," He said, "I tell you, get up." 15 Then the dead boy sat up and began to talk!
And Jesus gave him back to his mother.

16 Great fear swept the crowd, and they praised God, saying, "A mighty prophet has risen
among us," and "God has visited His people today." 17 And the news about Jesus spread
throughout Judea and the surrounding countryside.

JESUS AND JOHN THE BAPTIST

18 The disciples of John the Baptist told John about everything Jesus was doing. So John
called for two of his disciples, 19 and he sent them to the Lord to ask Him, "Are You the
Messiah we've been expecting,* or should we keep looking for someone else?"

20 John's two disciples found Jesus and said to Him, "John the Baptist sent us to ask, 'Are
You the Messiah we've been expecting, or should we keep looking for someone else?' "

21 At that very time, Jesus cured many people of their diseases, illnesses, and evil spirits,
and He restored sight to many who were blind. 22 Then He told John's disciples, "Go back to
John and tell him what you have seen and heard—the blind see, the lame walk, the lepers
are cured, the deaf hear, the dead are raised to life, and the Good News is being preached
to the poor. 23 And tell him, 'God blesses those who do not turn away because of Me.'"*

24 After John's disciples left, Jesus began talking about him to the crowds. "What kind of
man did you go into the wilderness to see? Was he a weak reed, swayed by every breath
of wind? 25 Or were you expecting to see a man dressed in expensive clothes? No, people
who wear beautiful clothes and live in luxury are found in palaces. 26 Were you looking for
a prophet? Yes, and he is more than a prophet. 27 John is the man to whom the Scriptures
refer when they say,

> 'Look, I am sending My messenger ahead of You,
> and he will prepare Your way before You.'*

28 I tell you, of all who have ever lived, none is greater than John. Yet even the least person
in the Kingdom of God is greater than he is!"

29 When they heard this, all the people—even the tax collectors—agreed that God's way
was right,* for they had been baptized by John. 30 But the Pharisees and experts in religious
law rejected God's plan for them, for they had refused John's baptism.

7:11-16 1 Kgs 17:17-24; 2 Kgs 4:32-37; Mark 5:21-24, 35-43; John 11:1-44
7:12 Luke 8:42; 9:38
7:13 Luke 8:52
7:14 Luke 8:54; John 11:43; Acts 9:40
7:16 Luke 1:65-68
7:17 Matt 9:26
7:18-35 //Matt 11:2-19
7:19 Mal 3:1-3
7:22 *Isa 29:18-19; 35:5-6; 42:18; 61:1; Luke 4:18
7:26 Luke 1:76
7:27 *Exod 23:20; *Mal 3:1
7:28 Luke 1:15
7:29-30 Matt 21:32; Luke 3:7, 12

7:19 Greek *Are You the One who is coming?* Also in 7:20. **7:23** Or *who are not offended by Me.* **7:27** Mal 3:1. **7:29** Or *praised God for His justice.*

7:18-19 Like many others in his day, John the Baptist had certain expectations about what would happen when the promised Messiah arrived. Apparently, Jesus was not doing all that John thought the Messiah would do, so John sent word from prison to Jesus to ask whether He was, in fact, the One they had all been awaiting.

▸ GOD
7:21-23 The unexpected Messiah. Many of the Jews in Jesus' day saw the Messiah as fundamentally a political deliverer. Because Jesus didn't seem to fit that image, questions were raised about whether He was, in fact, the Messiah. Even John the Baptist wrestled with that question. But Jesus answered John in a clear way. He is the Messiah because the presence and the power of the Kingdom of God came into our world through Him. He is the Messiah because He fulfilled the prophecies like no one else could. But as with John, Jesus doesn't deliver us from trouble the way we may have expected. We tend to think that if we trust Jesus, we won't ever face any struggles. But Jesus is a surprising Savior who rescues us in His own way, in His own timing. Trust Him to rescue you at just the right time. (***See God****> God's Names> Son> Messiah/Christ,* TopicGuide page A19.)

7:27-28 Jesus continued to rely upon the witness of John the Baptist. John was greatest among the old covenant ministers and had the clearest understanding of who Jesus was and what His plans were. But after Christ's ministry was complete, even the least mature believer would have knowledge and supernatural gifting that would surpass John's.

31 "To what can I compare the people of this generation?" Jesus asked. "How can I de-
scribe them? 32 They are like children playing a game in the public square. They complain
to their friends,

'We played wedding songs,
and you didn't dance,
so we played funeral songs,
and you didn't weep.'

7:33 33 For John the Baptist didn't spend his time eating bread or drinking wine, and you say,
Luke 1:15 'He's possessed by a demon.' 34 The Son of Man,* on the other hand, feasts and drinks, and
you say, 'He's a glutton and a drunkard, and a friend of tax collectors and other sinners!'
7:35 35 But wisdom is shown to be right by the lives of those who follow it.*"
1 Cor 1:24

JESUS ANOINTED BY A SINFUL WOMAN

7:36-50
Matt 26:6-13 36 One of the Pharisees asked Jesus to have dinner with him, so Jesus went to his home
Mark 14:3-9 and sat down to eat.* 37 When a certain immoral woman from that city heard He was eat-
John 12:1-8 ing there, she brought a beautiful alabaster jar filled with expensive perfume. 38 Then she
7:37 knelt behind Him at His feet, weeping. Her tears fell on His feet, and she wiped them off
Luke 8:2 with her hair. Then she kept kissing His feet and putting perfume on them.
7:39 39 When the Pharisee who had invited Him saw this, he said to himself, "If this man were
Matt 21:11 a prophet, He would know what kind of woman is touching Him. She's a sinner!"
40 Then Jesus answered his thoughts. "Simon," He said to the Pharisee, "I have some-
thing to say to you."
"Go ahead, Teacher," Simon replied.
41 Then Jesus told him this story: "A man loaned money to two people—500 pieces of
7:42 silver* to one and 50 pieces to the other. 42 But neither of them could repay him, so he
Matt 18:27 kindly forgave them both, canceling their debts. Who do you suppose loved him more af-
Col 2:13 ter that?"
7:44
Gen 18:4 43 Simon answered, "I suppose the one for whom he canceled the larger debt."
1 Tim 5:10 "That's right," Jesus said. 44 Then He turned to the woman and said to Simon, "Look at
7:45 this woman kneeling here. When I entered your home, you didn't offer Me water to wash
Rom 16:16 the dust from My feet, but she has washed them with her tears and wiped them with her
1 Cor 16:20
2 Cor 13:12 hair. 45 You didn't greet Me with a kiss, but from the time I first came in, she has not
1 Thes 5:26 stopped kissing My feet. 46 You neglected the courtesy of olive oil to anoint My head, but
1 Pet 5:14 she has anointed My feet with rare perfume.
7:46
2 Sam 12:20 47 "I tell you, her sins—and they are many—have been forgiven, so she has shown Me
Ps 23:5

7:34 "Son of Man" is a title Jesus used for Himself. 7:35 Or *But wisdom is justified by all her children.* 7:36 Or *and reclined.*
7:41 Greek *500 denarii.* A denarius was equivalent to a laborer's full day's wage.

▸ **GOD**

7:36-50 The spark of worship. If you have ever held a baby in your arms, you have probably had the pleasure of watching her look up at you and smile. Your response is almost automatic: You smile back and hold her close. No one has to tell you to do that; the response flows naturally. Worship should come that naturally to us. It should rise from our hearts. But what prompts our hearts to worship? Many things might, but this encounter between Jesus and one sinful woman points us to a key issue: Receiving forgiveness naturally gives rise to loving worship. Drink deeply of God's forgiveness, and you will find your heart overflowing in loving worship. (***See God**> God's Attributes> Forgiving> Those forgiven much will love much,* TopicGuide page A16.)

7:37 Judging by the way Luke described this woman, it is clear that she was well known to be sexually immoral. Thus, her sensual offering of perfume and wiping Jesus' feet with her hair was all the more unnerving to those attending the dinner.

7:38 In Jesus' culture, when guests came to eat, they would remove their sandals and recline on one side with their feet extending outward.

7:39 Simon, a religious leader who had hosted the party, assumed that if Jesus were indeed a prophet, He would have immediately recognized the character of the woman at His feet and would have resisted and rebuked her.

7:44 Simon apparently had neglected some common expressions of hospitality when Jesus arrived to dine at his house. Jesus highlighted the woman's attention and devotion in contrast to his neglect.

much love. But a person who is forgiven little shows only little love." 48 Then Jesus said to the woman, "Your sins are forgiven."

49 The men at the table said among themselves, "Who is this man, that He goes around forgiving sins?"

50 And Jesus said to the woman, "Your faith has saved you; go in peace."

7:48-49 Luke 5:20-21
7:50 Matt 9:22

WOMEN WHO FOLLOWED JESUS

8 Soon afterward Jesus began a tour of the nearby towns and villages, preaching and announcing the Good News about the Kingdom of God. He took His twelve disciples with Him, 2 along with some women who had been cured of evil spirits and diseases. Among them were Mary Magdalene, from whom He had cast out seven demons; 3 Joanna, the wife of Chuza, Herod's business manager; Susanna; and many others who were contributing their own resources to support Jesus and His disciples.

8:1 Matt 4:23
8:2 Matt 27:55-56 Mark 15:40-41 Luke 23:49
8:3 Matt 14:1

PARABLE OF THE FARMER SCATTERING SEED

4 One day Jesus told a story in the form of a parable to a large crowd that had gathered from many towns to hear Him: 5 "A farmer went out to plant his seed. As he scattered it across his field, some seed fell on a footpath, where it was stepped on, and the birds ate it. 6 Other seed fell among rocks. It began to grow, but the plant soon wilted and died for lack of moisture. 7 Other seed fell among thorns that grew up with it and choked out the tender plants. 8 Still other seed fell on fertile soil. This seed grew and produced a crop that was a hundred times as much as had been planted!" When He had said this, He called out, "Anyone with ears to hear should listen and understand."

9 His disciples asked Him what this parable meant. 10 He replied, "You are permitted to understand the secrets* of the Kingdom of God. But I use parables to teach the others so that the Scriptures might be fulfilled:

'When they look, they won't really see.
When they hear, they won't understand.'*

11 "This is the meaning of the parable: The seed is God's word. 12 The seeds that fell on the footpath represent those who hear the message, only to have the devil come and take it away from their hearts and prevent them from believing and being saved. 13 The seeds on the rocky soil represent those who hear the message and receive it with joy. But since they don't have deep roots, they believe for a while, then they fall away when they face temptation. 14 The seeds that fell among the thorns represent those who hear the message, but all too quickly the message is crowded out by the cares and riches and pleasures of this life. And so they never grow into maturity. 15 And the seeds that fell on the good soil represent honest, good-hearted people who hear God's word, cling to it, and patiently produce a huge harvest.

8:4-15 //Matt 13:1-23 //Mark 4:1-20
8:10 *Isa 6:9-10
8:11 1 Pet 1:23
8:12 1 Cor 1:21
8:14 Matt 19:23 1 Tim 6:9, 10 2 Tim 4:10
8:16-18 //Mark 4:21-25

PARABLE OF THE LAMP

16 "No one lights a lamp and then covers it with a bowl or hides it under a bed. A lamp is placed on a stand, where its light can be seen by all who enter the house. 17 For all that is

8:16 Matt 5:15 Luke 11:33 Phil 2:15-16
8:17 Matt 10:26 Luke 12:2

8:10a Greek *mysteries*. 8:10b Isa 6:9 (Greek version).

8:2 Mary's name indicates that she was from Magdala, which was possibly on the northwest shore of the Sea of Galilee. Her devotion to Jesus was evident in that she was one of the few who remained at the foot of the cross when Jesus later suffered and died (Matthew 27:56; John 19:25), and she was one of the first to see Jesus after He had risen (John 20:1-2, 11-18). The Gospel writers, unlike their contemporaries, included women prominently in their historical records.

8:9-10 Jesus was not intentionally obscuring the truth from His hearers (see 8:16-18). His quote from Isaiah 6:9 was more of an observation than a purpose statement. Jesus continued to teach—and use parables—in spite of the fact that many did not understand Him.

secret will eventually be brought into the open, and everything that is concealed will be
brought to light and made known to all.
8:18 18"So pay attention to how you hear. To those who listen to My teaching, more under-
Matt 25:29 standing will be given. But for those who are not listening, even what they think they
Luke 19:26 understand will be taken away from them."

THE TRUE FAMILY OF JESUS

8:19-21 19Then Jesus' mother and brothers came to see Him, but they couldn't get to Him because
//Matt 12:46-50 of the crowd. 20Someone told Jesus, "Your mother and Your brothers are outside, and they
//Mark 3:31-35 want to see You."
21Jesus replied, "My mother and My brothers are all those who hear God's word and
obey it."

JESUS CALMS THE STORM

8:22-25 22One day Jesus said to His disciples, "Let's cross to the other side of the lake." So they got
//Matt 8:23-27 into a boat and started out. 23As they sailed across, Jesus settled down for a nap. But soon
//Mark 4:35-41 a fierce storm came down on the lake. The boat was filling with water, and they were in
real danger.
24The disciples went and woke Him up, shouting, "Master, Master, we're going to drown!"
When Jesus woke up, He rebuked the wind and the raging waves. Suddenly the storm
stopped and all was calm. 25Then He asked them, "Where is your faith?"
The disciples were terrified and amazed. "Who is this man?" they asked each other.
"When He gives a command, even the wind and waves obey Him!"

JESUS HEALS A DEMON-POSSESSED MAN

8:26-39 26So they arrived in the region of the Gerasenes,* across the lake from Galilee. 27As Jesus
//Matt 8:28-34 was climbing out of the boat, a man who was possessed by demons came out to meet Him.
//Mark 5:1-20 For a long time he had been homeless and naked, living in a cemetery outside the town.
28As soon as he saw Jesus, he shrieked and fell down in front of Him. Then he screamed,
8:28 Matt 8:29 "Why are You interfering with me, Jesus, Son of the Most High God? Please, I beg You,
Mark 1:23-24 don't torture me!" 29For Jesus had already commanded the evil* spirit to come out of him.
This spirit had often taken control of the man. Even when he was placed under guard and
put in chains and shackles, he simply broke them and rushed out into the wilderness,
completely under the demon's power.
30Jesus demanded, "What is your name?"
8:31 "Legion," he replied, for he was filled with many demons. 31The demons kept begging
Rev 9:1-2, 11; 20:3 Jesus not to send them into the bottomless pit.*

8:26 Other manuscripts read *Gadarenes;* still others read *Gergesenes;* also in 8:37. See Matt 8:28; Mark 5:1. 8:29 Greek *unclean.* 8:31 Or *the abyss,* or *the underworld.*

▸ BIBLE

8:18 Listening. How often do you hear the words someone says, but you don't understand them? Frankly, you weren't paying attention. Treating others this way causes our relationships to suffer because they know we place the television, a song, a book we might be reading or whatever distracts us ahead of them. Treating Jesus this way is even more serious. Our neglect of His Word and His direction takes not listening to another level—to the level of rebellion. We are the losers if we don't pay close attention to everything He tells us. (***See Bible****> Power> Wisdom> Instruction leads to wisdom,* TopicGuide page A11.)

8:19-21 Although no mention is made of any brothers and sisters in the accounts of Jesus' early years, verses such as these suggest that Mary had other children after Jesus (Matthew 13:55; 27:56; Mark 3:31; 6:3; Acts 1:14; Galatians 1:19). The absence of any reference to Joseph, Mary's husband, has led some to suggest that Joseph may have died by this time in Jesus' ministry.

8:23-24 Because of the geography surrounding the Sea of Galilee and the strong, humid winds blowing in from the Mediterranean Sea, it was not unusual for storms to show up rather unexpectedly. This storm must have been particularly fierce to cause experienced fishermen such as Peter, James, and John to voice concern that they might die (5:3-10).

8:30 A full Roman legion typically had more than 6,000 men. It is not certain whether this man was under the influence of that many demons, but it is clear that he was filled with many of them.

32There happened to be a large herd of pigs feeding on the hillside nearby, and the de-
mons begged Him to let them enter into the pigs.
So Jesus gave them permission. 33Then the demons came out of the man and entered
the pigs, and the entire herd plunged down the steep hillside into the lake and drowned.
34When the herdsmen saw it, they fled to the nearby town and the surrounding country-
side, spreading the news as they ran. 35People rushed out to see what had happened. A
crowd soon gathered around Jesus, and they saw the man who had been freed from the
demons. He was sitting at Jesus' feet, fully clothed and perfectly sane, and they were all
afraid. 36Then those who had seen what happened told the others how the demon-
possessed man had been healed. 37And all the people in the region of the Gerasenes 8:37
begged Jesus to go away and leave them alone, for a great wave of fear swept over them. Acts 16:39
So Jesus returned to the boat and left, crossing back to the other side of the lake. 38The
man who had been freed from the demons begged to go with Him. But Jesus sent him
home, saying, 39"No, go back to your family, and tell them everything God has done for
you." So he went all through the town proclaiming the great things Jesus had done for him.

JESUS HEALS IN RESPONSE TO FAITH

40On the other side of the lake the crowds welcomed Jesus, because they had been wait- 8:40-56
ing for Him. 41Then a man named Jairus, a leader of the local synagogue, came and fell at //Matt 9:18-26 //Mark 5:21-43
Jesus' feet, pleading with Him to come home with him. 42His only daughter,* who was 8:43
about twelve years old, was dying. Lev 15:25-30
As Jesus went with him, He was surrounded by the crowds. 43A woman in the crowd had
suffered for twelve years with constant bleeding,* and she could find no cure. 44Coming up
behind Jesus, she touched the fringe of His robe. Immediately, the bleeding stopped.
45"Who touched Me?" Jesus asked.
Everyone denied it, and Peter said, "Master, this whole crowd is pressing up against You."
46But Jesus said, "Someone deliberately touched Me, for I felt healing power go out 8:46
from Me." 47When the woman realized that she could not stay hidden, she began to trem- Luke 5:17; 6:19
ble and fell to her knees in front of Him. The whole crowd heard her explain why she had
touched Him and that she had been immediately healed. 48"Daughter," He said to her, 8:48
"your faith has made you well. Go in peace." Matt 9:22
49While He was still speaking to her, a messenger arrived from the home of Jairus, the Mark 5:34 Luke 7:50; 17:19;
leader of the synagogue. He told him, "Your daughter is dead. There's no use troubling 18:42
the Teacher now."
50But when Jesus heard what had happened, He said to Jairus, "Don't be afraid. Just
have faith, and she will be healed."
51When they arrived at the house, Jesus wouldn't let anyone go in with Him except Pe-

8:42 Or *His only child, a daughter.* 8:43 Some manuscripts add *having spent everything she had on doctors.*

8:43-48 This woman's condition would have rendered her not just chronically ill but also ceremonially unclean (see Leviticus 15:25). She not only suffered physically—she was also cut off from all normal Jewish life.

▸ ADOPTION

8:43-48 Listening, waiting, watching. Sometimes people who need help are easy to spot, but others quietly suffer, pretending everything is fine. Look at Jesus and His encounter with the ill woman: He sensed her needs even as she attempted to hide them. Look around you—there are people pretending they are fine, yet they are lost and hurting. Learn to sense their hurt and show those quietly suffering that there is hope and healing in a real relationship with Christ. (***See Adoption****> With Christ> Supernatural> Quick to listen,* TopicGuide page A37.)

▸ HOLINESS

8:49-56 Trusting in the dark times. Jesus is trustworthy. Yet even those who know this sometimes struggle with His timing, His judgment, and His handling of what they have entrusted to Him. Jairus came to Jesus because his daughter was sick, and Jesus agreed to go to his home to heal her. But Jesus delayed His journey to the sick girl's side, and word came that she had died. If you were Jairus, what would you have done in that situation? Weep? Reprimand Jesus for not coming through? Undoubtedly all that and more went through Jairus's mind and heart. You can be assured that you will face dark times when you will wonder where Jesus is and what's taking Him so long to answer your prayers. Heed Jesus' advice to Jairus: "Don't be afraid. Just have faith" (8:50). (***See Holiness****> Submission> Trusting God> Faithfulness,* TopicGuide page A41.)

8:52 ter, John, James, and the little girl's father and mother. 52 The house was filled with people
Luke 7:13 weeping and wailing, but He said, "Stop the weeping! She isn't dead; she's only asleep."
8:54 53 But the crowd laughed at Him because they all knew she had died. 54 Then Jesus took
Luke 7:14 her by the hand and said in a loud voice, "My child, get up!" 55 And at that moment her life*
8:56 Matt 8:4 returned, and she immediately stood up! Then Jesus told them to give her something to
Mark 7:36 eat. 56 Her parents were overwhelmed, but Jesus insisted that they not tell anyone what
Luke 5:14 had happened.

JESUS SENDS OUT THE TWELVE DISCIPLES

9:1-6 **9** One day Jesus called together His twelve disciples* and gave them power and au-
//Matt 10:5-15 thority to cast out all demons and to heal all diseases. 2 Then He sent them out to tell
//Mark 6:7-13 9:3 everyone about the Kingdom of God and to heal the sick. 3 "Take nothing for your jour-
Luke 10:4; 22:35 ney," He instructed them. "Don't take a walking stick, a traveler's bag, food, money,* or
9:4 even a change of clothes. 4 Wherever you go, stay in the same house until you leave town.
Luke 10:5-7 5 And if a town refuses to welcome you, shake its dust from your feet as you leave to show
9:5 that you have abandoned those people to their fate."
Luke 10:10-11 Acts 13:51 6 So they began their circuit of the villages, preaching the Good News and healing the sick.

HEROD'S CONFUSION

9:7-9 7 When Herod Antipas, the ruler of Galilee,* heard about everything Jesus was doing, he
//Matt 14:1-12 was puzzled. Some were saying that John the Baptist had been raised from the dead.
//Mark 6:14-29 8 Others thought Jesus was Elijah or one of the other prophets risen from the dead.
9:8 Matt 11:14 9 "I beheaded John," Herod said, "so who is this man about whom I hear such stories?"
9:9 Luke 23:8 And he kept trying to see Him.

JESUS FEEDS FIVE THOUSAND

9:10-17 10 When the apostles returned, they told Jesus everything they had done. Then He slipped
//Matt 14:13-21 quietly away with them toward the town of Bethsaida. 11 But the crowds found out where
//Mark 6:30-44 //John 6:1-14 He was going, and they followed Him. He welcomed them and taught them about the
Kingdom of God, and He healed those who were sick.
12 Late in the afternoon the twelve disciples came to Him and said, "Send the crowds
away to the nearby villages and farms, so they can find food and lodging for the night.
There is nothing to eat here in this remote place."

8:55 Or *her spirit.* 9:1 Greek *the Twelve;* other manuscripts read *the twelve apostles.* 9:3 Or *silver coins.* 9:7 Greek *Herod the tetrarch.* Herod Antipas was a son of King Herod and was ruler over Galilee.

▸ MINISTRY

9:1-6 Word and deed. As important as it was for Jesus to declare the Good News, He also ministered in the power of the Spirit to the wounded, the sick, and the broken. When Jesus sent His 12 disciples out to minister and begin the work of the Kingdom, their commission was twofold: proclaim the Good News and meet needs. Our commission is no different. We are to proclaim the Good News in both word and deed (Acts 6:1-3; 20:35; Galatians 2:10; 5:13; Hebrews 6:10). Help people discover God's love for them and the church's love for the world by helping the poor and needy in your community. (***See Ministry**> Great Commission> Witness> Witness in word and deed,* TopicGuide page A56.)

9:5 "[T]o show that you have abandoned those people to their fate" is a strong statement. Jesus commanded the 12 disciples to curse those who did not receive their ministry.

9:7-9 Herod had been somewhat impressed with John the Baptist, but he ultimately had John imprisoned (Luke 3:19-20) and later beheaded (Matthew 14:3-12). He apparently saw some similarities between the ministries of Jesus and John.

▸ PURPOSE

9:10-17 Participating in a miracle. It was an amazing miracle—thousands fed with a negligible amount of food. In all the amazement, however, it is easy to overlook the disciples' role in the miracle. They had just come back from their own ministry experience, which had stretched their faith. They had stepped out in boldness to minister to others, and God had met their needs through the generosity of His people (9:4). As they regrouped with Jesus, all they saw was the crowd—and Jesus said, "You feed them" (9:13). He wanted to feed the hungry, but He also wanted to grow His disciples' faith. When they faltered Jesus graciously helped them, but true to Jesus' words, His disciples fed the crowd their supper—and cleaned up afterward! Jesus allows us, even with our imperfect faith, the honor of serving with Him. Look for ways to participate in His works of grace in this world. (***See Purpose**> God's Deeds> Miracles> Jesus> Feeding the 5,000,* TopicGuide page A53.)

13But Jesus said, "You feed them."

"But we have only five loaves of bread and two fish," they answered. "Or are You expecting us to go and buy enough food for this whole crowd?" 14For there were about 5,000 men there.

Jesus replied, "Tell them to sit down in groups of about fifty each." 15So the people all sat down. 16Jesus took the five loaves and two fish, looked up toward heaven, and blessed them. Then, breaking the loaves into pieces, He kept giving the bread and fish to the disciples so they could distribute it to the people. 17They all ate as much as they wanted, and afterward, the disciples picked up twelve baskets of leftovers!

9:17 2 Kgs 4:44

PETER'S DECLARATION ABOUT JESUS

18One day Jesus left the crowds to pray alone. Only His disciples were with Him, and He asked them, "Who do people say I am?"

19"Well," they replied, "some say John the Baptist, some say Elijah, and others say You are one of the other ancient prophets risen from the dead."

20Then He asked them, "But who do you say I am?"

Peter replied, "You are the Messiah* sent from God!"

9:18-20 //Matt 16:13-20 //Mark 8:27-30
9:19 Luke 9:7-8
9:20 John 6:68-69

JESUS PREDICTS HIS DEATH

21Jesus warned His disciples not to tell anyone who He was. 22"The Son of Man* must suffer many terrible things," He said. "He will be rejected by the elders, the leading priests, and the teachers of religious law. He will be killed, but on the third day He will be raised from the dead."

23Then He said to the crowd, "If any of you wants to be My follower, you must turn from your selfish ways, take up your cross daily, and follow Me. 24If you try to hang on to your life, you will lose it. But if you give up your life for My sake, you will save it. 25And what do you benefit if you gain the whole world but are yourself lost or destroyed? 26If anyone is ashamed of Me and My message, the Son of Man will be ashamed of that person when He returns in His glory and in the glory of the Father and the holy angels. 27I tell you the truth, some standing here right now will not die before they see the Kingdom of God."

9:21-27 //Matt 16:21-28 //Mark 8:31–9:1
9:23 Matt 10:38 Luke 14:27
9:24 Matt 10:39 Luke 17:33 John 12:25
9:26 Matt 10:33 Luke 12:9 2 Tim 2:12

THE TRANSFIGURATION

28About eight days later Jesus took Peter, John, and James up on a mountain to pray. 29And as He was praying, the appearance of His face was transformed, and His clothes became dazzling white. 30Suddenly, two men, Moses and Elijah, appeared and began talking with Jesus. 31They were glorious to see. And they were speaking about His exodus from this world, which was about to be fulfilled in Jerusalem.

9:28-36 //Matt 17:1-13 //Mark 9:2-10
9:31-32 2 Pet 1:15-16

9:20 Or *the Christ. Messiah* (a Hebrew term) and *Christ* (a Greek term) both mean "the anointed one." 9:22 "Son of Man" is a title Jesus used for Himself.

9:16 It is interesting to note where this miracle occurred. Luke tells us that Jesus broke the bread and "kept giving the bread and fish to the disciples." This miracle of multiplying apparently happened in Jesus' very hands.

9:20 Although Peter did acknowledge that Jesus was the Messiah (the promised deliverer from God spoken of in the Old Testament prophecies), it is not clear whether Peter really understood the full ramifications of his confession.

9:21 It was not out of shame that Jesus instructed His followers not to tell about His identity as the Messiah. The people of Israel had their own ideas about what the Messiah should do, and it's possible that Jesus wanted to avoid stirring up those expectations.

9:27 Suggestions for what Jesus meant by "before they see the Kingdom of God" include the Transfiguration (9:28), Resurrection (Luke 24:1-12) and Ascension (Acts 1:1-12), Pentecost (Acts 2), the destruction of Jerusalem in AD 70, and His triumphant Second Coming. All of these events spoke of various aspects of Jesus' present and coming Kingdom. (See the article on the Kingdom of God on page 1771.)

9:28-36 The continued revelation of who Jesus is to the future leaders of the church moved from the comparatively pedestrian miracle of feeding people to a dazzling supernatural display unlike anything ever seen. The disciples failed to understand the significance of the situation, and planned to set up mini-tabernacles for those present. But God the Father made it clear: Worship Christ, not Moses and Elijah.

32Peter and the others had fallen asleep. When they woke up, they saw Jesus' glory and
the two men standing with Him. 33As Moses and Elijah were starting to leave, Peter, not
even knowing what he was saying, blurted out, "Master, it's wonderful for us to be here!
Let's make three shelters as memorials*—one for You, one for Moses, and one for Elijah."
34But even as he was saying this, a cloud overshadowed them, and terror gripped them as
the cloud covered them.

9:35 Deut 18:15; Ps 2:7; Isa 42:1; Matt 3:17; 2 Pet 1:17

35Then a voice from the cloud said, "This is My Son, My Chosen One.* Listen to Him."
36When the voice finished, Jesus was there alone. They didn't tell anyone at that time
what they had seen.

9:37-43a //Matt 17:14-21; //Mark 9:14-29

9:38 Luke 7:12

JESUS HEALS A DEMON-POSSESSED BOY

37The next day, after they had come down the mountain, a large crowd met Jesus. 38A
man in the crowd called out to Him, "Teacher, I beg You to look at my son, my only child.
39An evil spirit keeps seizing him, making him scream. It throws him into convulsions so
that he foams at the mouth. It batters him and hardly ever leaves him alone. 40I begged
Your disciples to cast out the spirit, but they couldn't do it."

41Jesus said, "You faithless and corrupt people! How long must I be with you and put up
with you?" Then He said to the man, "Bring your son here."

42As the boy came forward, the demon knocked him to the ground and threw him into a vi-
olent convulsion. But Jesus rebuked the evil* spirit and healed the boy. Then He gave him
back to his father. 43Awe gripped the people as they saw this majestic display of God's power.

9:43b-45 //Matt 17:22-23; //Mark 9:30-32; 2 Pet 1:16

9:44 Luke 18:32

9:45 Mark 9:32; Luke 18:34

JESUS AGAIN PREDICTS HIS DEATH

While everyone was marveling at everything He was doing, Jesus said to His disciples,
44"Listen to Me and remember what I say. The Son of Man is going to be betrayed into the
hands of His enemies." 45But they didn't know what He meant. Its significance was hidden
from them, so they couldn't understand it, and they were afraid to ask Him about it.

9:46-48 //Matt 18:1-5; //Mark 9:33-37

9:47 Matt 9:4

9:48 Matt 10:40; Luke 10:16

THE GREATEST IN THE KINGDOM

46Then His disciples began arguing about which of them was the greatest. 47But Jesus knew
their thoughts, so He brought a little child to His side. 48Then He said to them, "Anyone who
welcomes a little child like this on My behalf* welcomes Me, and anyone who welcomes Me
also welcomes My Father who sent Me. Whoever is the least among you is the greatest."

9:49-50 //Mark 9:38-40

9:50 Matt 12:30; Luke 11:23

USING THE NAME OF JESUS

49John said to Jesus, "Master, we saw someone using Your name to cast out demons, but
we told him to stop because he isn't in our group."

50But Jesus said, "Don't stop him! Anyone who is not against you is for you."

9:51 Mark 16:19; Luke 13:22; 17:11; 18:31; 19:28

9:54 2 Kgs 1:10, 12

OPPOSITION FROM SAMARITANS

51As the time drew near for Him to ascend to heaven, Jesus resolutely set out for Jerusa-
lem. 52He sent messengers ahead to a Samaritan village to prepare for His arrival. 53But
the people of the village did not welcome Jesus because He was on His way to Jerusalem.
54When James and John saw this, they said to Jesus, "Lord, should we call down fire from
heaven to burn them up*?" 55But Jesus turned and rebuked them.* 56So they went on to
another village.

9:33 Greek *three tabernacles.* **9:35** Some manuscripts read *This is My dearly loved Son.* **9:42** Greek *unclean.* **9:48** Greek *in My name.* **9:54** Some manuscripts add *as Elijah did.* **9:55** Some manuscripts add an expanded conclusion to verse 55 and an additional sentence in verse 56: *And He said, "You don't realize what your hearts are like. 56For the Son of Man has not come to destroy people's lives, but to save them."*

9:44 Jesus' words to His followers meant literally to let what He was saying about His approaching death "sink into their ears."

THE COST OF FOLLOWING JESUS

[57]As they were walking along, someone said to Jesus, "I will follow You wherever You go." 9:57-62
[58]But Jesus replied, "Foxes have dens to live in, and birds have nests, but the Son of Man //Matt 8:19-22
has no place even to lay His head."
[59]He said to another person, "Come, follow Me."
The man agreed, but he said, "Lord, first let me return home and bury my father."
[60]But Jesus told him, "Let the spiritually dead bury their own dead!* Your duty is to go 9:60
and preach about the Kingdom of God." Matt 3:2
[61]Another said, "Yes, Lord, I will follow You, but first let me say good-bye to my family." 9:61
[62]But Jesus told him, "Anyone who puts a hand to the plow and then looks back is not fit 1 Kgs 19:20
for the Kingdom of God." 9:62 Phil 3:13

JESUS SENDS OUT HIS DISCIPLES

10 The Lord now chose seventy-two* other disciples and sent them ahead in pairs to 10:1
all the towns and places He planned to visit. [2]These were His instructions to them: Mark 6:7
"The harvest is great, but the workers are few. So pray to the Lord who is in charge of the 10:2
harvest; ask Him to send more workers into His fields. [3]Now go, and remember that I am Matt 9:37-38
sending you out as lambs among wolves. [4]Don't take any money with you, nor a trav- John 4:35
eler's bag, nor an extra pair of sandals. And don't stop to greet anyone on the road. 10:3 Matt 10:16
[5]"Whenever you enter someone's home, first say, 'May God's peace be on this house.' 10:4
[6]If those who live there are peaceful, the blessing will stand; if they are not, the blessing 2 Kgs 4:29
will return to you. [7]Don't move around from home to home. Stay in one place, eating and Luke 9:3
drinking what they provide. Don't hesitate to accept hospitality, because those who work 10:7
deserve their pay. 1 Cor 9:6-14 1 Tim 5:18
[8]"If you enter a town and it welcomes you, eat whatever is set before you. [9]Heal the sick, 10:9
and tell them, 'The Kingdom of God is near you now.' [10]But if a town refuses to welcome you, Matt 3:2

9:60 Greek *Let the dead bury their own dead.* 10:1 Some manuscripts read *seventy;* also in 10:17.

▸ WORSHIP
9:57-62 A life of adventure. Anyone is welcome to join the journey of following Jesus. But as Jesus has shown us, not everyone is ready to submit to His Lordship. Many want the crown, but not many want the cross. A disciple must have a singular focus. A God-centered lifestyle is not easy, but it is required for all who call Jesus their Lord. In this passage, the numerous excuses people gave for not following Jesus may sound strange to us, but what excuses do you hear in your own heart for not submitting to Jesus' claims on your thoughts, feelings, and behaviors? List them on a piece of paper and ask God to help you repent of your sin and eliminate those excuses from your life. Return to that list and mark them off as God gives you victory over them. (***See Worship***> *NT> Sacrificial Living> Counting the cost of following Jesus,* TopicGuide page A34.)

9:59-60 Jesus' words here were not as harsh as they may first seem. Most likely the man's father had not yet died, and the man was pleading to refrain from following until he had settled all his other relationships. Thus, this man's concern was similar to the one mentioned in 9:61.

9:62 A farmer couldn't plow a straight row except by looking ahead. Looking back for even a quick glance could cause the plow to veer to the side. It also raised the risk of ruining the plow by running it into a rock in the ground.

10:1-12 Having first commissioned the 12 disciples, now Jesus expanded His scope of ministry to His other close followers. The smaller ministry team and this larger one shared the same principles of simplicity and humble dependence on God and His people for their food and shelter.

▸ WORSHIP
10:2 Prayer fuels ministry. Every friend and follower of Jesus talks to Him. But often we make prayer the period at the end of the sentence. That is, we begin with a plan, a strategy, our ideas, and our goals. Then, after we have laid everything out as we would like to see it, we ask for God's help. But the model here is different. Jesus' way of doing ministry began in prayer, because Jesus knew that all significant ministry is really the work of the Father. Before you make your plans, set the entire situation before Him in prayer. (***See Worship***> *NT> Prayer> Instructions> Sanctify all things with prayer,* TopicGuide page A33.)

▸ MINISTRY
10:3-12 Proclaim the Kingdom. As Jesus carried out the work of the Kingdom, it is clear that He included two major categories of ministry: proclamation and demonstration. That is, Jesus taught, and He also met real needs in amazing ways. When He sent His disciples out to share in His ministry, they did the same things. As the ministry of Jesus grew, He sent out 70 others, as recorded here, and their commission was the same. They were to go into the world proclaiming the Good News of the presence of the Kingdom of God and bring the blessings of that Kingdom into the lives of those they met. Jesus invites all His followers into the same kind of life and ministry (Acts 6:1-3; 20:35; Galatians 2:10; 5:13; Hebrews 6:10). (***See Ministry***> *Great Commission> Witness> Witness in word and deed,* TopicGuide page A56.)

go out into its streets and say, 11 'We wipe even the dust of your town from our feet to show
10:12 Gen 19:24-25 that we have abandoned you to your fate. And know this—the Kingdom of God is near!' 12 I as-
Matt 10:15 sure you, even wicked Sodom will be better off than such a town on judgment day.
10:13-16 13 "What sorrow awaits you, Korazin and Bethsaida! For if the miracles I did in you had
//Matt 11:20-24 been done in wicked Tyre and Sidon, their people would have repented of their sins long
10:14 ago, clothing themselves in burlap and throwing ashes on their heads to show their remorse.
Isa 23 14 Yes, Tyre and Sidon will be better off on judgment day than you. 15 And you people of Ca-
Ezek 26–28 pernaum, will you be honored in heaven? No, you will go down to the place of the dead.*"
10:15 *Isa 14:13, 15 16 Then He said to the disciples, "Anyone who accepts your message is also accepting
10:16 Me. And anyone who rejects you is rejecting Me. And anyone who rejects Me is rejecting
Matt 10:40 God, who sent Me."
John 5:23 17 When the seventy-two disciples returned, they joyfully reported to Him, "Lord, even
1 Thes 4:8 the demons obey us when we use Your name!"
10:18 18 "Yes," He told them, "I saw Satan fall from heaven like lightning! 19 Look, I have given
John 12:31 Rev 12:8-9 you authority over all the power of the enemy, and you can walk among snakes and scor-
10:19 pions and crush them. Nothing will injure you. 20 But don't rejoice because evil spirits obey
Acts 28:3-5 you; rejoice because your names are registered in heaven."

10:20 Exod 32:32

JESUS' PRAYER OF THANKSGIVING

Isa 4:3 Phil 4:3 21 At that same time Jesus was filled with the joy of the Holy Spirit, and He said, "O Father,
Rev 3:5 Lord of heaven and earth, thank You for hiding these things from those who think them-
10:21-24 //Matt 11:25-27 selves wise and clever, and for revealing them to the childlike. Yes, Father, it pleased You
to do it this way.
10:22 Matt 28:18 22 "My Father has entrusted everything to Me. No one truly knows the Son except the Fa-
John 1:18; 3:35 ther, and no one truly knows the Father except the Son and those to whom the Son
10:23-24 chooses to reveal Him."
//Matt 13:16-17 23 Then when they were alone, He turned to the disciples and said, "Blessed are the eyes
10:24 that see what you have seen. 24 I tell you, many prophets and kings longed to see what you
1 Pet 1:10-14 see, but they didn't see it. And they longed to hear what you hear, but they didn't hear it."

THE MOST IMPORTANT COMMANDMENT

10:25-28 25 One day an expert in religious law stood up to test Jesus by asking Him this question:
//Matt 22:34-40 //Mark 12:28-31 "Teacher, what should I do to inherit eternal life?"
10:27 26 Jesus replied, "What does the law of Moses say? How do you read it?"
*Lev 19:18 27 The man answered, " 'You must love the LORD your God with all your heart, all your
Deut 6:5 soul, all your strength, and all your mind.' And, 'Love your neighbor as yourself.' "
10:28 28 "Right!" Jesus told him. "Do this and you will live!"
Lev 18:5 Rom 10:5 29 The man wanted to justify his actions, so he asked Jesus, "And who is my neighbor?"

10:15 Greek *to Hades.* 10:27 Deut 6:5; Lev 19:18.

10:13-14 The cities of Tyre and Sidon were on the coast of the Mediterranean Sea north of the region of Galilee. In Old Testament times, they had come under God's judgment because of their corrupt ways. (See Isaiah 23:1; Jeremiah 25:15-22; and Ezekiel 26–28.) Bethsaida was on the Sea of Galilee and was the hometown of Philip, Andrew, and Peter. Bethsaida, Korazin, and Capernaum formed a triangle of the most frequent ministry locations for Jesus and His followers. Judgment would be worse for those cities in proportion to the repeated exposure they had to the gospel and the person of Jesus.

10:13 Burlap had a number of uses and was worn as a sign of penitence by those who were mourning or beseeching God's favor. Similarly, covering oneself with ashes was a sign of voluntary humiliation.

▸ HOLINESS

10:21-22 True change. Perhaps you have been blessed to see irreligious people come to find life in God, those who are friends and followers of Jesus begin to live in a fresh dimension of vitality and power, or religious people move from checking off a list of morals to a real relationship with the living God. What causes such remarkable and awesome changes? A good strategic plan? An effective outreach program? Some compelling literature? A great message? Although God may be pleased to use such things, Jesus' prayer here pulls our focus back to the main reason that people experience true life change: God reveals Himself to them. Although we may participate in what God does, He is the One who brings about the heart change we long to see—in ourselves and in others. (***See Holiness****> Changed by God> God Provides> By His Word,* TopicGuide page A41.)

PARABLE OF THE GOOD SAMARITAN

30 Jesus replied with a story: "A Jewish man was traveling on a trip from Jerusalem to Jeri-
cho, and he was attacked by bandits. They stripped him of his clothes, beat him up, and
left him half dead beside the road.
31 "By chance a priest came along. But when he saw the man lying there, he crossed to **10:31**
the other side of the road and passed him by. 32 A Temple assistant* walked over and Lev 21:1-3
looked at him lying there, but he also passed by on the other side.
33 "Then a despised Samaritan came along, and when he saw the man, he felt compas-
sion for him. 34 Going over to him, the Samaritan soothed his wounds with olive oil and
wine and bandaged them. Then he put the man on his own donkey and took him to an
inn, where he took care of him. 35 The next day he handed the innkeeper two silver coins,*
telling him, 'Take care of this man. If his bill runs higher than this, I'll pay you the next time
I'm here.'
36 "Now which of these three would you say was a neighbor to the man who was at-
tacked by bandits?" Jesus asked.
37 The man replied, "The one who showed him mercy."
Then Jesus said, "Yes, now go and do the same."

JESUS VISITS MARTHA AND MARY

38 As Jesus and the disciples continued on their way to Jerusalem, they came to a certain **10:38**
village where a woman named Martha welcomed Him into her home. 39 Her sister, Mary, John 11:1; 12:2-3
sat at the Lord's feet, listening to what He taught. 40 But Martha was distracted by the big
dinner she was preparing. She came to Jesus and said, "Lord, doesn't it seem unfair to You
that my sister just sits here while I do all the work? Tell her to come and help me."
41 But the Lord said to her, "My dear Martha, you are worried and upset over all these **10:41**
details! 42 There is only one thing worth being concerned about. Mary has discovered it, Matt 6:25-34
and it will not be taken away from her." Luke 12:11, 22

10:42 Ps 27:4 Phil 3:13-14

TEACHING ABOUT PRAYER

11 Once Jesus was in a certain place praying. As He finished, one of His disciples **11:1**
came to Him and said, "Lord, teach us to pray, just as John taught his disciples." Luke 3:21
2 Jesus said, "This is how you should pray:* **11:2-4** //Matt 6:9-13

10:32 Greek *A Levite.* 10:35 Greek *two denarii.* A denarius was equivalent to a laborer's full day's wage. 11:2 Some manuscripts add additional phrases from the Lord's Prayer as it reads in Matt 6:9-13.

10:30-37 Jesus' parable of the "Good Samaritan" is very well known, even among those who don't really know Jesus; yet many miss the power of the story. When Jesus first used this illustration, Jews hated the Samaritans; Samaritans were not considered true heirs to the promises of Israel. Most Jews had absolutely no dealings with Samaritans (John 4:9, 20, 22).

▸ ADOPTION

10:30-37 Service, please. Most people don't mind serving others from time to time. If it is convenient, if it fits into the schedule for the day, if the one in need is part of our circle of friends, or if the kindness is reciprocated—any of those things can create an environment that makes serving rather easy. But what if the service is inconvenient, an interruption, costly in time and resources, without chance of reciprocation, or, above all, rendered to someone to whom we would not normally give the time of day? Jesus reminds us in the Parable of the Good Samaritan that the latter kind of service best characterizes those who belong to the Kingdom. (***See Adoption****> With Christ> Supernatural> Freedom from selfishness,* TopicGuide page A37.)

▸ BIBLE

10:38-42 Giving our attention. Sometimes Jesus said things that are hard to believe. For example, He essentially said to Martha: The only thing worth being concerned about is giving attention to Me! What about the practical needs that require attention? What about paying bills, preparing meals, spending time with our kids, washing cars, mowing the lawn? If we gave all our attention to being with Jesus, who would do those other things? But this line of questioning betrays our misunderstanding that we are more concerned about the important things of life than Jesus is. He won't let anything that is important be left undone if we are willing to do the one thing He deems important: Give Him our attention. (***See Bible****> Unity> Kingdom of God> Seeking the kingdom is highest priority,* TopicGuide page A11.)

11:2 The idea of speaking to or about God as "Father" is not altogether absent from the Old Testament (see Psalm 103:13 and Isaiah 63:16). However, addressing God as Father in prayer was almost unknown until Jesus' ministry (John 5:17, 43; 6:32; 8:18-19, 38, 49).

"Father, may Your name be kept holy.
May Your Kingdom come soon.
3 Give us each day the food we need,*
11:4 4 and forgive us our sins,
Matt 18:35 as we forgive those who sin against us.
Mark 11:25 And don't let us yield to temptation.*"

5 Then, teaching them more about prayer, He used this story: "Suppose you went to a
friend's house at midnight, wanting to borrow three loaves of bread. You say to him, 6 'A
11:7 friend of mine has just arrived for a visit, and I have nothing for him to eat.' 7 And suppose
Matt 26:10 he calls out from his bedroom, 'Don't bother me. The door is locked for the night, and my
Luke 18:5 Gal 6:17 family and I are all in bed. I can't help you.' 8 But I tell you this—though he won't do it for
11:8 friendship's sake, if you keep knocking long enough, he will get up and give you whatever
Luke 18:1-6 you need because of your shameless persistence.*
11:9-13 //Matt 7:7-11 9 "And so I tell you, keep on asking, and you will receive what you ask for. Keep on seek-
ing, and you will find. Keep on knocking, and the door will be opened to you. 10 For every-
one who asks, receives. Everyone who seeks, finds. And to everyone who knocks, the
door will be opened.
11 "You fathers—if your children ask* for a fish, do you give them a snake instead? 12 Or if
11:13 they ask for an egg, do you give them a scorpion? Of course not! 13 So if you sinful people
Jas 1:17 know how to give good gifts to your children, how much more will your heavenly Father
give the Holy Spirit to those who ask Him."

JESUS AND THE PRINCE OF DEMONS

11:14-23 14 One day Jesus cast out a demon from a man who couldn't speak, and when the demon
//Matt 12:22-32 was gone, the man began to speak. The crowds were amazed, 15 but some of them said,
//Mark 3:20-30 "No wonder He can cast out demons. He gets His power from Satan,* the prince of de-
11:15 Matt 9:34 mons." 16 Others, trying to test Jesus, demanded that He show them a miraculous sign
11:16 from heaven to prove His authority.
Matt 12:38; 16:1 17 He knew their thoughts, so He said, "Any kingdom divided by civil war is doomed. A
11:17 family splintered by feuding will fall apart. 18 You say I am empowered by Satan. But if Satan
Matt 9:4

11:3 Or *Give us each day our food for the day;* or *Give us each day our food for tomorrow.* 11:4 Or *And keep us from being tested.* 11:8 Or *in order to avoid shame,* or *so his reputation won't be damaged.* 11:11 Some manuscripts add *for bread, do you give them a stone? Or [if they ask].* 11:15 Greek *Beelzeboul;* also in 11:18, 19. Other manuscripts read *Beezeboul;* Latin version reads *Beelzebub.*

▸ WORSHIP

11:2-4 A disciple's prayer. Although commonly referred to as the "Lord's Prayer," the model found here is really more of a disciple's prayer—a prayer for Jesus' followers. Jesus may have prayed these things, but He was offering His followers a template for praying. His intention was not that we merely repeat these words, but that we pray along these lines. Specifically: 1) Make the will of God your highest priority; 2) trust in His daily provision; 3) forgive others as God has forgiven you; and 4) flee temptation. Let these themes permeate your daily prayer life. (***See Worship****> NT> Prayer> Examples> Jesus> The Lord's Prayer,* TopicGuide page A33.)

▸ WORSHIP

11:5-13 Persistent prayers. No one in his right mind would want to be guilty of pestering God—or would he? Jesus' advice on prayer seems more aggressive than many of us might imagine. In these short parables, Jesus tells us that, on our end, persistence counts. Not because our persistence allows us to prevail over God and He merely capitulates to our demands, but because our persistence demonstrates that we are depending on no one else. We are saying that God alone is the One we rely on to meet our need. That is the posture of faith. That kind of praying makes a difference. (***See Worship****> NT> Prayer> Instructions> Persevere in prayer,* TopicGuide page A33.)

11:15 The religious leaders literally accused Jesus of being in league with "Beelzeboul" (or, alternatively, Beelzebub), which originally was an alternate name of the pagan deity, Baal (2 Kings 1:2-3, 6, 16). The Jews came to associate this name with Satan.

▸ SPIRITUAL WARFARE

11:17-22 Outmatched foe. As we listen to people share about the problems they face every day or hear the news of what is going on around the world, it is hard to deny that there is some power at work corrupting, destroying, and ruining what is good. The Bible identifies that power with a fallen angel—Satan. Knowing that there is a powerful supernatural enemy who opposes the things of God and the people of God could leave us with a bleak outlook on life. But Jesus makes it clear that God is greater, and that we are safe in His hands. Do not cower before your evil foe, but do not pretend he's not dangerous, either (Psalm 22:13; 1 Peter 5:8). (***See Spiritual Warfare****> Originator of Sin> Satan's Domain> Doomed to destruction,* TopicGuide page A44.)

is divided and fighting against himself, how can his kingdom survive? [19]And if I am empow-
ered by Satan, what about your own exorcists? They cast out demons, too, so they will con-
demn you for what you have said. [20]But if I am casting out demons by the power of God,* **11:20**
then the Kingdom of God has arrived among you. [21]For when a strong man like Satan is Exod 8:19
fully armed and guards his palace, his possessions are safe—[22]until someone even stronger **11:22** Isa 49:24; 53:12
attacks and overpowers him, strips him of his weapons, and carries off his belongings.
[23]"Anyone who isn't with Me opposes Me, and anyone who isn't working with Me is ac-
tually working against Me.
[24]"When an evil* spirit leaves a person, it goes into the desert, searching for rest. But **11:24-26**
when it finds none, it says, 'I will return to the person I came from.' [25]So it returns and finds //Matt 12:43-45
that its former home is all swept and in order. [26]Then the spirit finds seven other spirits
more evil than itself, and they all enter the person and live there. And so that person is
worse off than before."
[27]As He was speaking, a woman in the crowd called out, "God bless Your mother—the **11:27**
womb from which You came, and the breasts that nursed You!" Luke 1:28, 42, 48
[28]Jesus replied, "But even more blessed are all who hear the word of God and put it into **11:28** Luke 6:47; 8:21
practice."

THE SIGN OF JONAH

[29]As the crowd pressed in on Jesus, He said, "This evil generation keeps asking Me to **11:29-32**
show them a miraculous sign. But the only sign I will give them is the sign of Jonah. //Matt 12:38-42 1 Cor 1:22
[30]What happened to him was a sign to the people of Nineveh that God had sent him. **11:30**
What happens to the Son of Man* will be a sign to these people that He was sent by God. Jon 1:17; 2:10
[31]"The queen of Sheba* will stand up against this generation on judgment day and con- **11:31**
demn it, for she came from a distant land to hear the wisdom of Solomon. Now someone 1 Kgs 10:1-10
greater than Solomon is here—but you refuse to listen. [32]The people of Nineveh will also 2 Chr 9:1-12
stand up against this generation on judgment day and condemn it, for they repented of **11:32**
their sins at the preaching of Jonah. Now someone greater than Jonah is here—but you re- Jon 3:5, 8, 10
fuse to repent.

RECEIVING THE LIGHT

[33]"No one lights a lamp and then hides it or puts it under a basket.* Instead, a lamp is **11:33** Matt 5:15
placed on a stand, where its light can be seen by all who enter the house. Luke 8:16
[34]"Your eye is a lamp that provides light for your body. When your eye is good, your **11:34-36**
whole body is filled with light. But when it is bad, your body is filled with darkness. [35]Make //Matt 6:22-23
sure that the light you think you have is not actually darkness. [36]If you are filled with light,
with no dark corners, then your whole life will be radiant, as though a floodlight were fill-
ing you with light."

JESUS CRITICIZES THE RELIGIOUS LEADERS

11:37-54 //Matt 23:1-36 //Mark 12:38-40 //Luke 20:45-47

[37]As Jesus was speaking, one of the Pharisees invited Him home for a meal. So He went in **11:38**
and took His place at the table.* [38]His host was amazed to see that He sat down to eat with- Mark 7:3-4

11:20 Greek *by the finger of God.* 11:24 Greek *unclean.* 11:30 "Son of Man" is a title Jesus used for Himself. 11:31 Greek *The queen of the south.* 11:33 Some manuscripts omit *or puts it under a basket.* 11:37 Or *and reclined.*

11:24 Although Jesus did not reveal a fully developed demonology, He did indicate that demons are actual spiritual beings intent on inhabiting and disrupting the lives of people.

11:31 First Kings 10:1-10 tells of the queen of Sheba's visit of King Solomon. She recognized his great wisdom and sought to learn from him, unlike the religious leaders of Jesus' day, who, though they were confronted with someone much wiser than Solomon, remained resistant.

11:32 Nineveh was a corrupt and pagan city that was visited by the Old Testament prophet Jonah. When Jonah preached, the people of the city repented; however they ultimately turned back to their evil ways and judgment came shortly after the prophet Nahum's oracle against the nation.

11:37-40 The religious leaders at this time were careful to maintain ceremonial cleanliness by avoiding contact with anything not considered holy and by practicing various ritual washings.

11:39 Matt 23:25 Mark 7:20-23
11:41 Luke 12:33
11:42 Lev 27:30 Matt 23:23
11:43 Matt 23:6-7 Mark 12:38-39
11:44 Matt 23:27-28
11:46 Matt 23:4
11:47 Matt 23:29-32
11:48 Acts 7:51-53; 8:1
11:49-51 Matt 23:34-36 1 Cor 1:24, 30
11:51 Gen 4:8 2 Chr 24:20-21
11:52 Matt 23:13
11:54 Luke 20:20

out first performing the hand-washing ceremony required by Jewish custom. 39 Then the Lord said to him, "You Pharisees are so careful to clean the outside of the cup and the dish, but inside you are filthy—full of greed and wickedness! 40 Fools! Didn't God make the inside as well as the outside? 41 So clean the inside by giving gifts to the poor, and you will be clean all over.

42 "What sorrow awaits you Pharisees! For you are careful to tithe even the tiniest income from your herb gardens,* but you ignore justice and the love of God. You should tithe, yes, but do not neglect the more important things.

43 "What sorrow awaits you Pharisees! For you love to sit in the seats of honor in the synagogues and receive respectful greetings as you walk in the marketplaces. 44 Yes, what sorrow awaits you! For you are like hidden graves in a field. People walk over them without knowing the corruption they are stepping on."

45 "Teacher," said an expert in religious law, "you have insulted us, too, in what you just said."

46 "Yes," said Jesus, "what sorrow also awaits you experts in religious law! For you crush people with unbearable religious demands, and you never lift a finger to ease the burden. 47 What sorrow awaits you! For you build monuments for the prophets your own ancestors killed long ago. 48 But in fact, you stand as witnesses who agree with what your ancestors did. They killed the prophets, and you join in their crime by building the monuments! 49 This is what God in His wisdom said about you:* 'I will send prophets and apostles to them, but they will kill some and persecute the others.'

50 "As a result, this generation will be held responsible for the murder of all God's prophets from the creation of the world—51 from the murder of Abel to the murder of Zechariah, who was killed between the altar and the sanctuary. Yes, it will certainly be charged against this generation.

52 "What sorrow awaits you experts in religious law! For you remove the key to knowledge from the people. You don't enter the Kingdom yourselves, and you prevent others from entering."

53 As Jesus was leaving, the teachers of religious law and the Pharisees became hostile and tried to provoke Him with many questions. 54 They wanted to trap Him into saying something they could use against Him.

12:1 Matt 16:6, 11-12
12:2-9 //Matt 10:26-33
12:2 Mark 4:22
12:4 John 15:14-15
12:5 Heb 10:31

A WARNING AGAINST HYPOCRISY

12 Meanwhile, the crowds grew until thousands were milling about and stepping on each other. Jesus turned first to His disciples and warned them, "Beware of the yeast of the Pharisees—their hypocrisy. 2 The time is coming when everything that is covered up will be revealed, and all that is secret will be made known to all. 3 Whatever you have said in the dark will be heard in the light, and what you have whispered behind closed doors will be shouted from the housetops for all to hear!

4 "Dear friends, don't be afraid of those who want to kill your body; they cannot do any more to you after that. 5 But I'll tell you whom to fear. Fear God, who has the power to kill you and then throw you into hell.* Yes, He's the One to fear.

11:42 Greek *tithe the mint, the rue, and every herb.* 11:49 Greek *Therefore, the wisdom of God said.* 12:5 Greek *Gehenna.*

11:44 Contact with a dead human body would render someone ceremonially unclean for a period of seven days (Numbers 19:11), but the Jewish leaders had extended this rule to graves as well. For this reason, tombs were rinsed with a mixture of water, lime, and chalk. However, when the white calcite wore off, a person could become "unclean" by inadvertently stepping on a poorly marked tomb, mistaking it for an ordinary rock or marker.

12:1 In preparation for the Jewish feast of Passover, a faithful Jew would clean his house of all yeast (Exodus 12:19-20) to remind himself of the speedy fashion in which God rescued His people from Egypt. Yeast was also forbidden in many of the sacrifices offered by the Israelites, and this led to its association with corruption (Leviticus 2:4-5; Numbers 6:14-15). Jesus implied with His illustration that the Jewish leaders, due to unrepentant hypocrisy, made themselves and those around them unclean before God.

6 "What is the price of five sparrows—two copper coins*? Yet God does not forget a single one of them. 7 And the very hairs on your head are all numbered. So don't be afraid; you are more valuable to God than a whole flock of sparrows.

8 "I tell you the truth, everyone who acknowledges Me publicly here on earth, the Son of Man* will also acknowledge in the presence of God's angels. 9 But anyone who denies Me here on earth will be denied before God's angels. 10 Anyone who speaks against the Son of Man can be forgiven, but anyone who blasphemes the Holy Spirit will not be forgiven.

11 "And when you are brought to trial in the synagogues and before rulers and authorities, don't worry about how to defend yourself or what to say, 12 for the Holy Spirit will teach you at that time what needs to be said."

PARABLE OF THE RICH FOOL

13 Then someone called from the crowd, "Teacher, please tell my brother to divide our father's estate with me."

14 Jesus replied, "Friend, who made Me a judge over you to decide such things as that?" 15 Then He said, "Beware! Guard against every kind of greed. Life is not measured by how much you own."

16 Then He told them a story: "A rich man had a fertile farm that produced fine crops. 17 He said to himself, 'What should I do? I don't have room for all my crops.' 18 Then he said, 'I know! I'll tear down my barns and build bigger ones. Then I'll have room enough to store all my wheat and other goods. 19 And I'll sit back and say to myself, "My friend, you have enough stored away for years to come. Now take it easy! Eat, drink, and be merry!"'

20 "But God said to him, 'You fool! You will die this very night. Then who will get everything you worked for?'

21 "Yes, a person is a fool to store up earthly wealth but not have a rich relationship with God."

TEACHING ABOUT MONEY AND POSSESSIONS

22 Then, turning to His disciples, Jesus said, "That is why I tell you not to worry about everyday life—whether you have enough food to eat or enough clothes to wear. 23 For life is more than food, and your body more than clothing. 24 Look at the ravens. They don't plant or harvest or store food in barns, for God feeds them. And you are far more valuable to Him than any birds! 25 Can all your worries add a single moment to your life? 26 And if worry can't accomplish a little thing like that, what's the use of worrying over bigger things?

27 "Look at the lilies and how they grow. They don't work or make their clothing, yet Solomon in all his glory was not dressed as beautifully as they are. 28 And if God cares so wonderfully for flowers that are here today and thrown into the fire tomorrow, He will certainly care for you. Why do you have so little faith?

12:8 Luke 15:10 Rev 3:5
12:9 Mark 8:38 Luke 9:26 2 Tim 2:12
12:10 Matt 12:31-32 Mark 3:28-29 1 Jn 5:16
12:11-12 Matt 10:19-20 Mark 13:11 Luke 21:12-15
12:14 Exod 2:14 Acts 7:27, 35
12:15 Job 20:20; 31:24 Ps 62:10 1 Tim 6:9-10
12:19 Prov 27:1 1 Cor 15:32 Jas 5:1-5
12:20 Job 27:8 Ps 39:6-7
12:22-31 //Matt 6:25-34
12:24 Job 38:41 Ps 147:9
12:27 1 Kgs 10:1-10

12:6 Greek *two assaria* [Roman coins equal to 1/16 of a denarius]. 12:8 "Son of Man" is a title Jesus used for Himself.

▸ HOLINESS
12:11-12 Words for the timid. Any time you begin to share the Good News that is found in life with Jesus, you are at risk. Someone may misunderstand you or even attack you personally for speaking up. With such potential risks, it might seem safer just to say nothing. But that is not an option. Those who know Jesus have the privilege and responsibility of sharing the Good News about Him. Jesus told His friends that when they had to defend themselves for following Him, the Spirit would give them all they needed to say. So, rest easy. You are not sharing the Good News on your own. The Spirit is there, and He is sufficient for whatever risks you might face. (***See Holiness***> *Changed by God> God Provides> Provides words to say,* TopicGuide page A41.)

▸ ADOPTION
12:22-33 Delivered from worry. Jesus made a seemingly simple and clear statement: Do not worry about the "stuff" of life. He was not saying that we should live irresponsibly, but He was telling all who followed Him that they should not be overtaken with concern about such things. But how do we live this out in a world where bills need to be paid, kids need to be cared for, and work needs to be done? How can we be free from worrying about such things? By trusting in God, who provides for all of life. When we rest in this truth, worry melts away. (***See Adoption***> *With Christ> Supernatural> Freedom from worry,* TopicGuide page A37.)

12:27 Solomon was the wealthiest king of Israel (1 Kings 10:14-29; 1 Chronicles 29:25).

[29] "And don't be concerned about what to eat and what to drink. Don't worry about such
12:30 Matt 6:8 things. [30] These things dominate the thoughts of unbelievers all over the world, but your
Father already knows your needs. [31] Seek the Kingdom of God above all else, and He will
give you everything you need.
12:32 Luke 22:29 [32] "So don't be afraid, little flock. For it gives your Father great happiness to give you the
Kingdom.
12:33 Matt 19:21 Acts 2:45 [33] "Sell your possessions and give to those in need. This will store up treasure for you in
heaven! And the purses of heaven never get old or develop holes. Your treasure will be
safe; no thief can steal it and no moth can destroy it. [34] Wherever your treasure is, there
the desires of your heart will also be.

BE READY FOR THE LORD'S COMING

12:35-36 Matt 25:1-13 Mark 13:33-37 [35] "Be dressed for service and keep your lamps burning, [36] as though you were waiting for
your master to return from the wedding feast. Then you will be ready to open the door
12:35 *Exod 12:11 and let him in the moment he arrives and knocks. [37] The servants who are ready and wait-
ing for his return will be rewarded. I tell you the truth, he himself will seat them, put on an
12:37 Luke 17:7-8 John 13:4 apron, and serve them as they sit and eat! [38] He may come in the middle of the night or
just before dawn.* But whenever he comes, he will reward the servants who are ready.
12:39-46 //Matt 24:43-51 [39] "Understand this: If a homeowner knew exactly when a burglar was coming, he
would not permit his house to be broken into. [40] You also must be ready all the time, for
12:39 1 Thes 5:2 Rev 16:15 the Son of Man will come when least expected."
[41] Peter asked, "Lord, is that illustration just for us or for everyone?"
12:40 Mark 13:33 [42] And the Lord replied, "A faithful, sensible servant is one to whom the master can give
the responsibility of managing his other household servants and feeding them. [43] If the
master returns and finds that the servant has done a good job, there will be a reward. [44] I
tell you the truth, the master will put that servant in charge of all he owns. [45] But what if the
servant thinks, 'My master won't be back for a while,' and he begins beating the other ser-
vants, partying, and getting drunk? [46] The master will return unannounced and unex-
pected, and he will cut the servant in pieces and banish him with the unfaithful.
12:47 Deut 25:2 Jas 4:17 [47] "And a servant who knows what the master wants, but isn't prepared and doesn't
carry out those instructions, will be severely punished. [48] But someone who does not
12:48 Lev 5:17 Num 15:27-30 know, and then does something wrong, will be punished only lightly. When someone has
been given much, much will be required in return; and when someone has been entrusted
with much, even more will be required.

JESUS CAUSES DIVISION

12:50 Mark 10:38-39 [49] "I have come to set the world on fire, and I wish it were already burning! [50] I have a terri-
ble baptism of suffering ahead of Me, and I am under a heavy burden until it is accom-
12:51-53 //Matt 10:34-36 plished. [51] Do you think I have come to bring peace to the earth? No, I have come to divide
people against each other! [52] From now on families will be split apart, three in favor of Me,
and two against—or two in favor and three against.
12:53 *Mic 7:6 [53] 'Father will be divided against son
and son against father;
mother against daughter
and daughter against mother;

12:38 Greek *in the second or third watch.*

12:35-48 As in Matthew 25, Jesus taught the importance of persevering in our faith and maintaining diligence in our spiritual journey.

12:48 In God's judgment, some sins are more severe than others (John 19:11). Yet each sin breaks God's law and must be punished (James 2:10). Just as sins are not all alike, situations are not all alike. Jesus consistently taught that those who sin knowingly are guiltier than those who sin in ignorance (John 9:41).

and mother-in-law against daughter-in-law
and daughter-in-law against mother-in-law.'*"

[54]Then Jesus turned to the crowd and said, "When you see clouds beginning to form in 12:54-56
the west, you say, 'Here comes a shower.' And you are right. [55]When the south wind blows, Matt 16:2-3
you say, 'Today will be a scorcher.' And it is. [56]You fools! You know how to interpret the 12:58-59
weather signs of the earth and sky, but you don't know how to interpret the present times. Matt 5:25-26
[57]"Why can't you decide for yourselves what is right? [58]When you are on the way to
court with your accuser, try to settle the matter before you get there. Otherwise, your ac-
cuser may drag you before the judge, who will hand you over to an officer, who will throw
you into prison. [59]And if that happens, you won't be free again until you have paid the
very last penny.*"

A CALL TO REPENTANCE

13 About this time Jesus was informed that Pilate had murdered some people from
Galilee as they were offering sacrifices at the Temple. [2]"Do you think those Galile- 13:2
ans were worse sinners than all the other people from Galilee?" Jesus asked. "Is that why John 9:2-3
they suffered? [3]Not at all! And you will perish, too, unless you repent of your sins and turn 13:3
to God. [4]And what about the eighteen people who died when the tower in Siloam fell on Ps 7:12
them? Were they the worst sinners in Jerusalem? [5]No, and I tell you again that unless you 13:4 John 9:7, 11
repent, you will perish, too." 13:5 Ps 7:12

PARABLE OF THE BARREN FIG TREE

[6]Then Jesus told this story: "A man planted a fig tree in his garden and came again and 13:6 Isa 5:2
again to see if there was any fruit on it, but he was always disappointed. [7]Finally, he said Matt 21:19 Mark 11:12-14
to his gardener, 'I've waited three years, and there hasn't been a single fig! Cut it down. It's 13:7
just taking up space in the garden.' Hab 3:17
[8]"The gardener answered, 'Sir, give it one more chance. Leave it another year, and I'll Matt 3:10
give it special attention and plenty of fertilizer. [9]If we get figs next year, fine. If not, then 13:8
you can cut it down.'" 2 Pet 3:9, 15

JESUS HEALS ON THE SABBATH

[10]One Sabbath day as Jesus was teaching in a synagogue, [11]He saw a woman who had 13:10
been crippled by an evil spirit. She had been bent double for eighteen years and was un- Matt 4:23
able to stand up straight. [12]When Jesus saw her, He called her over and said, "Dear woman, 13:13
you are healed of your sickness!" [13]Then He touched her, and instantly she could stand Mark 5:23
straight. How she praised God! 13:14
[14]But the leader in charge of the synagogue was indignant that Jesus had healed her on Exod 20:9-10 Deut 5:13-14
the Sabbath day. "There are six days of the week for working," he said to the crowd. Matt 12:10 Mark 3:2
"Come on those days to be healed, not on the Sabbath." Luke 6:7
[15]But the Lord replied, "You hypocrites! Each of you works on the Sabbath day! Don't John 5:16
you untie your ox or your donkey from its stall on the Sabbath and lead it out for water? 13:15
[16]This dear woman, a daughter of Abraham, has been held in bondage by Satan for eigh- Luke 14:5
teen years. Isn't it right that she be released, even on the Sabbath?" 13:16
[17]This shamed His enemies, but all the people rejoiced at the wonderful things He did. Luke 19:9

12:53 Mic 7:6. 12:59 Greek *last lepton* [the smallest Jewish coin].

13:1-2 Although there is no historical record of this event in the administration of Pontius Pilate outside this Gospel account, the event itself is consistent with what we know about Pilate. Literally, Luke said that Pilate "mixed their blood with their sacrifices."

13:2-5 In Jesus' day, people believed such calamities were divine acts of judgment. Jesus insisted that not just a few, but all are equally worthy of God's judgment (Romans 3:9-23).

13:10-17 As indicated by the comments of the synagogue leader, many of the religious leaders considered healing to be a kind of work. Therefore, they deemed it unlawful to heal on the Sabbath.

PARABLE OF THE MUSTARD SEED

13:18-21 //Matt 13:31-33 //Mark 4:30-32

18Then Jesus said, "What is the Kingdom of God like? How can I illustrate it? 19It is like a
tiny mustard seed that a man planted in a garden; it grows and becomes a tree, and the
birds make nests in its branches."

PARABLE OF THE YEAST

20He also asked, "What else is the Kingdom of God like? 21It is like the yeast a woman
used in making bread. Even though she put only a little yeast in three measures of flour, it
permeated every part of the dough."

THE NARROW DOOR

22Jesus went through the towns and villages, teaching as He went, always pressing on to-
ward Jerusalem. 23Someone asked Him, "Lord, will only a few be saved?"

13:24 //Matt 7:13; Mark 10:25; 1 Tim 6:12
13:25 //Matt 7:21-23; Matt 25:10-11
13:27 *Ps 6:8; Matt 25:12
13:28-29 //Matt 8:10-11
13:29 Ps 107:3; Isa 43:5; 49:12; 59:19; Rev 14:15; 21:13; 22:16
13:30 Matt 19:30; 20:16; Mark 10:31

He replied, 24"Work hard to enter the narrow door to God's Kingdom, for many will try
to enter but will fail. 25When the master of the house has locked the door, it will be too
late. You will stand outside knocking and pleading, 'Lord, open the door for us!' But He will
reply, 'I don't know you or where you come from.' 26Then you will say, 'But we ate and
drank with You, and You taught in our streets.' 27And He will reply, 'I tell you, I don't know
you or where you come from. Get away from Me, all you who do evil.'

28"There will be weeping and gnashing of teeth, for you will see Abraham, Isaac, Jacob,
and all the prophets in the Kingdom of God, but you will be thrown out. 29And people will
come from all over the world—from east and west, north and south—to take their places in
the Kingdom of God. 30And note this: Some who seem least important now will be the
greatest then, and some who are the greatest now will be least important then.*"

JESUS GRIEVES OVER JERUSALEM

13:33 Matt 16:21

31At that time some Pharisees said to Him, "Get away from here if You want to live! Herod
Antipas wants to kill You!"

32Jesus replied, "Go tell that fox that I will keep on casting out demons and healing peo-
ple today and tomorrow; and the third day I will accomplish My purpose. 33Yes, today,
tomorrow, and the next day I must proceed on My way. For it wouldn't do for a prophet of
God to be killed except in Jerusalem!

13:30 Greek *Some are last who will be first, and some are first who will be last.*

▶ SPIRITUAL WARFARE

13:16 The devil in our details. Why do bad things happen to good people? People have asked this question for centuries. There are no simple answers, but there *are* hints of answers. When Jesus healed a woman suffering from a deformity, He described her as being "held in bondage by Satan." Does this mean all physical afflictions are demonic in origin? No, it is clear from the rest of this Gospel that not all trouble has its roots in Satan's activity. But some things do. That means we need to be discerning and ask the Lord to show us how to address traumas appropriately in our lives and the lives of others. (***See Spiritual Warfare****> Originator of sin> Satan's Influence> He distresses them,* TopicGuide page A44.)

13:20-21 As noted earlier (12:1), the Bible often cites yeast as a symbol of sin and corruption. But here, Jesus used the image in a positive way. Just as a little leaven is enough to permeate a whole loaf of bread and make the dough rise, so the small beginnings of the Good News of the Kingdom would ultimately have great influence.

▶ HOLINESS

13:22-27 Surrender to victory. Wherever you go in the world, you will find "religious" people. They do good things: they bow in worship; they make sacrifices; they read religious books; and they try to win others to their way of life. All this they do in the hope of gaining God's favor. The sad news is that no amount of good deeds will ever win God over—our acts can never gain us acceptance by God or forgiveness for our past sins. The Good News is that there is a better way to find this acceptance and forgiveness: Surrender your life to God (2 Chronicles 30:8; Psalm 2:12; James 4:7; 1 Peter 5:6). This is the beginning, middle, and end of our contribution to our spiritual lives—continual and deepened surrender. Surrender your thoughts, emotions, your actions—everything. Combine that with faith in Christ's sacrifice for us (Galatians 5:1, 8, 13) and you'll know the freedom that comes from the surrendered life (Romans 6:15). (***See Holiness****> Submission> Yielding to Spirit> Surrender your heart,* TopicGuide page A41.)

13:31 This is the Herod who beheaded John. He was also the son of Herod the Great, who had sought to have Jesus killed as an infant.

34 "O Jerusalem, Jerusalem, the city that kills the prophets and stones God's messengers! **13:34-35**
How often I have wanted to gather your children together as a hen protects her chicks be- //Matt 23:37-39
neath her wings, but you wouldn't let Me. 35 And now, look, your house is abandoned. And Luke 19:41-44
you will never see Me again until you say, 'Blessings on the One who comes in the name **13:35** *Ps 118:26
of the LORD!'*" Jer 12:7; 22:5 Luke 19:38

JESUS HEALS ON THE SABBATH

14 One Sabbath day Jesus went to eat dinner in the home of a leader of the Phari- **14:1**
sees, and the people were watching Him closely. 2 There was a man there whose Luke 7:36; 11:37
arms and legs were swollen.* 3 Jesus asked the Pharisees and experts in religious law, "Is it **14:3**
permitted in the law to heal people on the Sabbath day, or not?" 4 When they refused to Luke 6:9
answer, Jesus touched the sick man and healed him and sent him away. 5 Then He turned **14:5**
to them and said, "Which of you doesn't work on the Sabbath? If your son* or your cow Matt 12:11
falls into a pit, don't you rush to get him out?" 6 Again they could not answer.

JESUS TEACHES ABOUT HUMILITY

7 When Jesus noticed that all who had come to the dinner were trying to sit in the seats of **14:7**
honor near the head of the table, He gave them this advice: 8 "When you are invited to a wed- Matt 23:6
ding feast, don't sit in the seat of honor. What if someone who is more distinguished than you **14:8-11** Prov 25:6-7
has also been invited? 9 The host will come and say, 'Give this person your seat.' Then you will
be embarrassed, and you will have to take whatever seat is left at the foot of the table!
10 "Instead, take the lowest place at the foot of the table. Then when your host sees you,
he will come and say, 'Friend, we have a better place for you!' Then you will be honored in **14:11**
front of all the other guests. 11 For those who exalt themselves will be humbled, and those Matt 23:12
who humble themselves will be exalted." Luke 18:14
12 Then He turned to His host. "When you put on a luncheon or a banquet," He said,
"don't invite your friends, brothers, relatives, and rich neighbors. For they will invite you
back, and that will be your only reward. 13 Instead, invite the poor, the crippled, the lame,
and the blind. 14 Then at the resurrection of the righteous, God will reward you for inviting **14:14**
those who could not repay you." Acts 24:15

PARABLE OF THE GREAT FEAST

15 Hearing this, a man sitting at the table with Jesus exclaimed, "What a blessing it will be
to attend a banquet* in the Kingdom of God!"
16 Jesus replied with this story: "A man prepared a great feast and sent out many invita- **14:16-24**
tions. 17 When the banquet was ready, he sent his servant to tell the guests, 'Come, the //Matt 22:1-10
banquet is ready.' 18 But they all began making excuses. One said, 'I have just bought a
field and must inspect it. Please excuse me.' 19 Another said, 'I have just bought five pairs
of oxen, and I want to try them out. Please excuse me.' 20 Another said, 'I now have a wife, **14:20**
so I can't come.' Deut 24:5
21 "The servant returned and told his master what they had said. His master was furious 1 Cor 7:33
and said, 'Go quickly into the streets and alleys of the town and invite the poor, the crip-
pled, the blind, and the lame.' 22 After the servant had done this, he reported, 'There is still

13:35 Ps 118:26. 14:2 Or *who had dropsy.* 14:5 Some manuscripts read *donkey.* 14:15 Greek *to eat bread.*

▸ ADOPTION

14:7-11 Special—but not worthy. It is incredible that Jesus freely invites us into a relationship with the holy God. Because of what Jesus has done (and in spite of what we have done), we are invited to intimacy with the Almighty. In one sense, that makes us special. But be careful: It's a short trip from realizing how special we are as the objects of God's love and mercy to thinking we are important in our own right. In this parable, Jesus cautioned against such thinking, reminding us that humility is the right attitude of heart when we are invited to feast at the King's table. (***See Adoption****> With Christ> Redemption> Humble self-estimation,* TopicGuide page A37.)

14:15-24 It was common practice in Jesus' day to first send out an invitation for a celebration or feast, and then, when all the preparations had been finished, to send out a second invitation to let the guests know it was time to attend.

room for more.' 23 So his master said, 'Go out into the country lanes and behind the
14:24 Matt 21:43 hedges and urge anyone you find to come, so that the house will be full. 24 For none of
Acts 13:46 those I first invited will get even the smallest taste of my banquet.'"

THE COST OF BEING A DISCIPLE

14:26-27 25 A large crowd was following Jesus. He turned around and said to them, 26 "If you want to
//Matt 10:37-38 be My disciple, you must hate everyone else by comparison—your father and mother, wife
14:26 and children, brothers and sisters—yes, even your own life. Otherwise, you cannot be My
Deut 33:9 disciple. 27 And if you do not carry your own cross and follow Me, you cannot be My disciple.
Matt 16:24 Mark 8:34 28 "But don't begin until you count the cost. For who would begin construction of a build-
Luke 9:23; 18:29 ing without first calculating the cost to see if there is enough money to finish it? 29 Other-
John 12:25 wise, you might complete only the foundation before running out of money, and then
14:27 Matt 10:38; 16:24 everyone would laugh at you. 30 They would say, 'There's the person who started that
Mark 8:34 Luke 9:23 building and couldn't afford to finish it!'
31 "Or what king would go to war against another king without first sitting down with his
counselors to discuss whether his army of 10,000 could defeat the 20,000 soldiers
14:33 marching against him? 32 And if he can't, he will send a delegation to discuss terms of
Phil 3:7-8 peace while the enemy is still far away. 33 So you cannot become My disciple without giv-
14:34 Matt 5:13 ing up everything you own.
Mark 9:50 34 "Salt is good for seasoning. But if it loses its flavor, how do you make it salty again?
14:35 35 Flavorless salt is good neither for the soil nor for the manure pile. It is thrown away. Any-
Matt 11:15 one with ears to hear should listen and understand!"

PARABLE OF THE LOST SHEEP

15:1 Matt 9:11 **15** Tax collectors and other notorious sinners often came to listen to Jesus teach.
Luke 5:29 2 This made the Pharisees and teachers of religious law complain that He was as-
Gal 2:12 sociating with such sinful people—even eating with them!
15:2 3 So Jesus told them this story: 4 "If a man has a hundred sheep and one of them gets
Luke 5:30 lost, what will he do? Won't he leave the ninety-nine others in the wilderness and go to
15:4-7 search for the one that is lost until he finds it? 5 And when he has found it, he will joyfully
//Matt 18:12-14 carry it home on his shoulders. 6 When he arrives, he will call together his friends and
neighbors, saying, 'Rejoice with me because I have found my lost sheep.' 7 In the same
way, there is more joy in heaven over one lost sinner who repents and returns to God than
over ninety-nine others who are righteous and haven't strayed away!

▸ HOLINESS

14:25-27 Hollow man. "Get your heart in the game!" the coach screamed at the lumbering basketball player. It's painful to watch a performer who looks bored, distracted, and disengaged from what he's doing. That was Jesus' concern as He spoke to His followers about living as true disciples. He had seen the impact of hypocrisy on God's people and He knew He could not build a church of hollow men and women, externally religious but internally rebellious. When you fail to perform in a way that honors God, search out your inner motivations—why did you fail? What was wrong with your heart? Let Him fill you with the faith, hope, and love that energize your life for Him (1 Corinthians 13:1-13). (***See Holiness****> Submission> Identifying with Christ> Living a gospel-centered life,* TopicGuide page A40.)

▸ WORSHIP

14:27-32 Consider the cost. What will it mean for you to follow Jesus as one of His disciples? What does your future hold if you decide to live "all out" for Him? Jesus put it in a simple yet provocative way: You will have to "carry your own cross" to follow. That means your life, as you know it, will come to end. Your life will be given over to another. If that is true, you will have to ask yourself, "Am I willing to trade life on my terms for life on Jesus' terms?" Jesus invites you to trade life on your terms for the life He offers. It's a trade well worth the cost. (***See Worship****> NT> Sacrificial Living> Counting the cost of following Jesus,* TopicGuide page A34.)

14:27 Death by crucifixion was a common form of capital punishment by the Romans of Jesus' time. A condemned person was forced to carry his cross to the place of execution so that all could see the humiliating end that came to those who broke Rome's laws.

14:34 Technically, it is impossible for salt (as it is known today) to lose its saltiness. But what was used as salt in Jesus' day was not pure salt, and it was possible for the actual salt of the mixture to be leached out, leaving behind only the useless leftover material.

15:1-2 Jesus' enemies and friends were puzzled at God's seeking love for sinners. These three stories explain God's delight at finding and rescuing the helpless.

PARABLE OF THE LOST COIN

8 "Or suppose a woman has ten silver coins* and loses one. Won't she light a lamp and sweep the entire house and search carefully until she finds it? 9 And when she finds it, she will call in her friends and neighbors and say, 'Rejoice with me because I have found my lost coin.' 10 In the same way, there is joy in the presence of God's angels when even one sinner repents."

PARABLE OF THE LOST SON

11 To illustrate the point further, Jesus told them this story: "A man had two sons. 12 The younger son told his father, 'I want my share of your estate now before you die.' So his father agreed to divide his wealth between his sons.

13 "A few days later this younger son packed all his belongings and moved to a distant land, and there he wasted all his money in wild living. 14 About the time his money ran out, a great famine swept over the land, and he began to starve. 15 He persuaded a local farmer to hire him, and the man sent him into his fields to feed the pigs. 16 The young man became so hungry that even the pods he was feeding the pigs looked good to him. But no one gave him anything.

17 "When he finally came to his senses, he said to himself, 'At home even the hired servants have food enough to spare, and here I am dying of hunger! 18 I will go home to my father and say, "Father, I have sinned against both heaven and you, 19 and I am no longer worthy of being called your son. Please take me on as a hired servant."'

20 "So he returned home to his father. And while he was still a long way off, his father saw him coming. Filled with love and compassion, he ran to his son, embraced him, and kissed him. 21 His son said to him, 'Father, I have sinned against both heaven and you, and I am no longer worthy of being called your son.*'

22 "But his father said to the servants, 'Quick! Bring the finest robe in the house and put it on him. Get a ring for his finger and sandals for his feet. 23 And kill the calf we have been fattening. We must celebrate with a feast, 24 for this son of mine was dead and has now returned to life. He was lost, but now he is found.' So the party began.

25 "Meanwhile, the older son was in the fields working. When he returned home, he heard music and dancing in the house, 26 and he asked one of the servants what was going on. 27 'Your brother is back,' he was told, 'and your father has killed the fattened calf. We are celebrating because of his safe return.'

28 "The older brother was angry and wouldn't go in. His father came out and begged him, 29 but he replied, 'All these years I've slaved for you and never once refused to do a single thing you told me to. And in all that time you never gave me even one young goat for a feast with my friends. 30 Yet when this son of yours comes back after squandering your money on prostitutes, you celebrate by killing the fattened calf!'

15:12 Deut 21:17

15:18 Ps 51:4

15:20 Gen 45:14-15; 46:29

15:22 Gen 41:42; Zech 3:4; Rev 6:11

15:24 Eph 2:1, 5; 5:14

15:8 Greek *ten drachmas.* A drachma was the equivalent of a full day's wage. 15:21 Some manuscripts add *Please take me on as a hired servant.*

15:11-12 Jesus' description of the young son in this parable likely came as a great shock to His audience. For a son to ask for his inheritance before the death of his father would be tantamount to saying, "I wish you were dead!"

▸ ADOPTION

15:11-32 The gracious Father. We do not merit God's shocking, seeking love. In the first parable, the wet, smelly sheep did not deserve rescue. In the second case, the coin could not bid the woman to seek for it. The rebellious son, though he was a miserable sinner, planned a repentance speech—but only got halfway through it before the father smothered him in kisses, pronounced him forgiven, showered him with gifts, and planned a big party! If God is gracious to no-account sheep, immobile coins, and rebellious children, how gracious will He be to His beloved children who truly repent? Jesus is ready to forgive you today. Turn to Him and enjoy His gracious gift of forgiveness. (*See Adoption> With Christ> Children of God> Loved by the Father,* TopicGuide page A36.)

15:15-16 To the Jews, pigs were ceremonially unclean. The young man's job would have been tremendously offensive to Jews.

15:25-31 The scene shifted from the reunited father and son to the elder son, who, despite his loyalty, was filled with bitterness. This portion of the parable returned to Jesus' theme of the dangers of hypocrisy—in this case, external obedience to God, but internal hatred of His grace.

15:31 31 “His father said to him, ‘Look, dear son, you have always stayed by me, and every-
Prov 29:3 thing I have is yours. 32 We had to celebrate this happy day. For your brother was dead and
John 17:10, 24 has come back to life! He was lost, but now he is found!’ ”

PARABLE OF THE SHREWD MANAGER

16:1 **16** Jesus told this story to His disciples: “There was a certain rich man who had a
Luke 15:13, 30 manager handling his affairs. One day a report came that the manager was wast-
ing his employer’s money. 2 So the employer called him in and said, ‘What’s this I hear
about you? Get your report in order, because you are going to be fired.’
3 “The manager thought to himself, ‘Now what? My boss has fired me. I don’t have the
strength to dig ditches, and I’m too proud to beg. 4 Ah, I know how to ensure that I’ll have
plenty of friends who will give me a home when I am fired.’
5 “So he invited each person who owed money to his employer to come and discuss the
situation. He asked the first one, ‘How much do you owe him?’ 6 The man replied, ‘I owe
him 800 gallons of olive oil.’ So the manager told him, ‘Take the bill and quickly change it
to 400 gallons.*’
7 “ ‘And how much do you owe my employer?’ he asked the next man. ‘I owe him 1,000
bushels of wheat,’ was the reply. ‘Here,’ the manager said, ‘take the bill and change it to
800 bushels.*’
16:8 8 “The rich man had to admire the dishonest rascal for being so shrewd. And it is true
John 12:36 that the children of this world are more shrewd in dealing with the world around them
Eph 5:8; 1 Thes 5:5 than are the children of the light. 9 Here’s the lesson: Use your worldly resources to benefit
16:10-12 others and make friends. Then, when your earthly possessions are gone, they will wel-
Matt 25:20-30 come you to an eternal home.*
Luke 19:17-26 10 “If you are faithful in little things, you will be faithful in large ones. But if you are dishonest
16:13 in little things, you won’t be honest with greater responsibilities. 11 And if you are untrust-
Matt 6:24 worthy about worldly wealth, who will trust you with the true riches of heaven? 12 And if you
16:14; Luke 23:35 are not faithful with other people’s things, why should you be trusted with things of your own?
1 Tim 3:3 13 “No one can serve two masters. For you will hate one and love the other; you will be
16:15 devoted to one and despise the other. You cannot serve both God and money.”
Prov 24:12; Matt 23:28 14 The Pharisees, who dearly loved their money, heard all this and scoffed at Him.
Luke 8:9-14 15 Then He said to them, “You like to appear righteous in public, but God knows your
16:16 hearts. What this world honors is detestable in the sight of God.
Matt 11:12-13 16 “Until John the Baptist, the law of Moses and the messages of the prophets were your
16:17 guides. But now the Good News of the Kingdom of God is preached, and everyone is ea-
Matt 5:18 ger to get in.* 17 But that doesn’t mean that the law has lost its force. It is easier for heaven
16:18; Matt 5:32; 19:9 and earth to disappear than for the smallest point of God’s law to be overturned.
Mark 10:11-12 18 “For example, a man who divorces his wife and marries someone else commits adul-
1 Cor 7:10-11 tery. And anyone who marries a woman divorced from her husband commits adultery.”

16:6 Greek *100 baths . . . 50 [baths].* 16:7 Greek *100 korous . . . 80 [korous].* 16:9 Or *you will be welcomed into eternal homes.* 16:16 Or *everyone is urged to enter in.*

16:1 Jesus’ stories usually don’t include characters of mixed morals—but the story of the seeking Father (15:11-31) and this parable of the crafty steward included people who did both good and evil. Jesus used them to make spiritual points.

16:8 To be shrewd is to recognize how to make the most of a situation. The employer did not praise the manager for being dishonest or for looking out only for himself; the commendation was for his shrewdness.

16:13 The word translated “money” here does not refer only to cash or other mediums of exchange. It means wealth in all its forms, which people might depend upon instead of God.

▸ GOD

16:13 One master. Just watch a child standing before a selection of candy after he has been told he can have something. Perhaps he ends up just looking . . . and looking. Maybe you see him reach for one thing, only to pull his hand back and start for another. What is the problem? Does the child not like candy? Certainly not! The problem is that the child likes all kinds of candy! It’s hard to choose one thing when your appetites and tastes draw you to many things. Every follower of Jesus faces the same challenge. Jesus puts it succinctly: You cannot divide your loyalties. You can have only one prevailing passion, only one master. (***See God****> God’s Nature> Unique> He alone is God, the only sovereign,* TopicGuide page A15.)

PARABLE OF THE RICH MAN AND LAZARUS

19 Jesus said, "There was a certain rich man who was splendidly clothed in purple and fine
linen and who lived each day in luxury. 20 At his gate lay a poor man named Lazarus who
was covered with sores. 21 As Lazarus lay there longing for scraps from the rich man's ta-
ble, the dogs would come and lick his open sores.

22 "Finally, the poor man died and was carried by the angels to be with Abraham.* The 16:22
rich man also died and was buried, 23 and his soul went to the place of the dead.* There, in Matt 8:11
torment, he saw Abraham in the far distance with Lazarus at his side.

24 "The rich man shouted, 'Father Abraham, have some pity! Send Lazarus over here to 16:24
dip the tip of his finger in water and cool my tongue. I am in anguish in these flames.' Luke 3:8

25 "But Abraham said to him, 'Son, remember that during your lifetime you had every- 16:25
thing you wanted, and Lazarus had nothing. So now he is here being comforted, and you Luke 6:24
are in anguish. 26 And besides, there is a great chasm separating us. No one can cross over
to you from here, and no one can cross over to us from there.'

27 "Then the rich man said, 'Please, Father Abraham, at least send him to my father's
home. 28 For I have five brothers, and I want him to warn them so they don't end up in this 16:28
place of torment.' Acts 18:5

29 "But Abraham said, 'Moses and the prophets have warned them. Your brothers can 16:29
read what they wrote.' Luke 24:27, 44

30 "The rich man replied, 'No, Father Abraham! But if someone is sent to them from the John 1:45; 5:45-47
dead, then they will repent of their sins and turn to God.' Acts 15:21

31 "But Abraham said, 'If they won't listen to Moses and the prophets, they won't listen 16:31 //Matt 6:24
even if someone rises from the dead.'" John 11:44-48

TEACHINGS ABOUT FORGIVENESS AND FAITH

17 One day Jesus said to His disciples, "There will always be temptations to sin, but 17:1-3
what sorrow awaits the person who does the tempting! 2 It would be better to be //Matt 18:7
thrown into the sea with a millstone hung around your neck than to cause one of these lit- //Mark 9:42
tle ones to fall into sin. 3 So watch yourselves! 17:3

"If another believer* sins, rebuke that person; then if there is repentance, forgive. 4 Even Matt 18:15
if that person wrongs you seven times a day and each time turns again and asks forgive-
ness, you must forgive."

5 The apostles said to the Lord, "Show us how to increase our faith." 17:5 Mark 9:24

6 The Lord answered, "If you had faith even as small as a mustard seed, you could say to 17:6
this mulberry tree, 'May you be uprooted and thrown into the sea,' and it would obey you! Matt 17:20; 21:21

7 "When a servant comes in from plowing or taking care of sheep, does his master say,

16:22 Greek *into Abraham's bosom.* 16:23 Greek *to Hades.* 17:3 Greek *If your brother.*

▶ BIBLE

16:19-31 The way to life. In the story of the rich man and Lazarus, Jesus spoke of life after death. The rich man was suffering; he realized that he did not embrace the life that God had offered him. But no messenger was sent to his family—his opportunity to help them spiritually was over. Does that mean God had no interest in reaching them? Absolutely not. It means that He had already done what was needed to reach them—God gave His Word, the Scriptures. Every person can find within God's word what he or she needs to know to embrace the life God offers to all. Be sure to let those in your family know the facts about heaven, hell, and the way to eternal life. Then stand back and pray. (***See Bible****> Uniqueness> Authoritative> All-sufficient,* TopicGuide page A10.)

16:29-31 Many readers question whether this is a fictional parable or a factual one. This appears to be a story rooted in Jewish folk belief, but as the story of the thieving manager earlier in the chapter was not a study in business management, so this parable was not an instruction in the mechanics of the afterlife.

17:2 A millstone, a large, heavy stone with a hole through the middle, was used for grinding grain.

17:5-10 While speaking on the topic of faith, Jesus explained that even the smallest application of faith in God can change the world. He used the mulberry tree as an example, because the religious teachers of the day often used that tree as an illustration of stability, believing that the deep roots of the bush would enable it to remain in the earth many years.

'Come in and eat with me'? 8 No, he says, 'Prepare my meal, put on your apron, and serve
me while I eat. Then you can eat later.' 9 And does the master thank the servant for doing
17:10 what he was told to do? Of course not. 10 In the same way, when you obey Me you should
1 Cor 9:16 say, 'We are unworthy servants who have simply done our duty.'"

TEN HEALED OF LEPROSY

17:11 Luke 9:51-52; 13:22 11 As Jesus continued on toward Jerusalem, He reached the border between Galilee and
17:12 Samaria. 12 As He entered a village there, ten lepers stood at a distance, 13 crying out,
Lev 13:46 "Jesus, Master, have mercy on us!"
17:14 14 He looked at them and said, "Go show yourselves to the priests."* And as they went,
Lev 14:2-3 they were cleansed of their leprosy.
Luke 5:14 15 One of them, when he saw that he was healed, came back to Jesus, shouting, "Praise
17:16 God!" 16 He fell to the ground at Jesus' feet, thanking Him for what He had done. This man
Matt 10:5 was a Samaritan.
17 Jesus asked, "Didn't I heal ten men? Where are the other nine? 18 Has no one returned
17:19 to give glory to God except this foreigner?" 19 And Jesus said to the man, "Stand up and go.
Matt 9:22 Your faith has healed you.*"
Luke 7:50; 18:42

THE COMING OF THE KINGDOM

17:20 20 One day the Pharisees asked Jesus, "When will the Kingdom of God come?"
John 3:3; 18:36 Jesus replied, "The Kingdom of God can't be detected by visible signs.* 21 You won't be
able to say, 'Here it is!' or 'It's over there!' For the Kingdom of God is already among
17:23 you.*"
Mark 13:21 22 Then He said to His disciples, "The time is coming when you will long to see the day
Luke 17:21; 21:8 when the Son of Man returns,* but you won't see it. 23 People will tell you, 'Look, there is
17:24 the Son of Man,' or 'Here he is,' but don't go out and follow them. 24 For as the lightning
1 Tim 6:15
17:25 flashes and lights up the sky from one end to the other, so it will be on the day when the
Matt 16:21 Son of Man comes. 25 But first the Son of Man must suffer terribly* and be rejected by this
Mark 8:31
Luke 9:22 generation.

17:14 See Lev 14:2-32. 17:19 Or *Your faith has saved you.* 17:20 Or *by your speculations.* 17:21 Or *is within you,* or *is in your grasp.* 17:22 Or *long for even one day with the Son of Man.* "Son of Man" is a title Jesus used for Himself. 17:25 Or *suffer many things.*

▶ CHURCH
17:11-19 Helping the helpless. Many of us may not know people afflicted with leprosy, but we certainly know social outcasts. Perhaps because of mental illness or social ineptitude, some people just don't fit into society. The lepers of Jesus' day were forbidden to come near others due to fear of contamination, as well as religious restrictions (Leviticus 13). Jesus did not ignore their needs—in fact, He rejoiced to heal people just like this (Matthew 11:5). There are some people you struggle to minister to—or perhaps even to be around. Those are the very people whom God wants you to love—for your sake and theirs. Reach out to those who are unable to help themselves and you'll participate in Christ's ministry to the "least of these" (Matthew 25:40, 45). (***See Church*****>** *Who***>** *From Every People***>** *The "least of these,"* TopicGuide page A48.)

17:12 According to Jewish law (Leviticus 13:45-46), those afflicted with leprosy were ceremonially unclean and were supposed to have no contact with healthy people. Thus, when these lepers heard that Jesus was near, they still remained some distance away.

17:14 The priests were the only ones who could officially pronounce someone clean from leprosy (Leviticus 13).

▶ CHURCH
17:20-37 Jesus embodies God's Kingdom. Because we don't always see things from Jesus' perspective, we can often come away from the Scriptures a bit disoriented. For example, in this passage, Jesus spoke of the coming of the Kingdom of God. Other passages make it clear that the return of Jesus will be accompanied by catastrophic changes and events (Matthew 24:4-14; Mark 13:8-9). Jesus also said the Kingdom of God will come without visible signs. How can both be true? The resolution lies in understanding that the presence of the Kingdom is found in the person of Jesus. As He was speaking, the Kingdom was present, within reach. Even now, all who choose to follow Him enter that Kingdom. But there is still coming a full and future manifestation of the Kingdom at His return. The Kingdom *is* present now . . . and will be present in a fuller way when He returns. Keep building the Church, establishing God's rightful rule over your family, your business—everything you touch—and you'll see the presence of the Kingdom now. (***See Church*****>** *Mission***>** *Establish***>** *The Kingdom is both now and not yet,* TopicGuide page A49.)

26 "When the Son of Man returns, it will be like it was in Noah's day. 27 In those days, the
people enjoyed banquets and parties and weddings right up to the time Noah entered his
boat and the flood came and destroyed them all.

28 "And the world will be as it was in the days of Lot. People went about their daily busi-
ness—eating and drinking, buying and selling, farming and building—29 until the morning
Lot left Sodom. Then fire and burning sulfur rained down from heaven and destroyed
them all. 30 Yes, it will be 'business as usual' right up to the day when the Son of Man is re-
vealed. 31 On that day a person out on the deck of a roof must not go down into the house
to pack. A person out in the field must not return home. 32 Remember what happened to
Lot's wife! 33 If you cling to your life, you will lose it, and if you let your life go, you will save
it. 34 That night two people will be asleep in one bed; one will be taken, the other left.
35 Two women will be grinding flour together at the mill; one will be taken, the other left.*"

37 "Where will this happen, Lord?"* the disciples asked.

Jesus replied, "Just as the gathering of vultures shows there is a carcass nearby, so these
signs indicate that the end is near."*

17:26-27 //Matt 24:37-39
17:28 Gen 19:1-28
17:30 2 Thes 1:7
17:31 Matt 24:17-18; Mark 13:15-16
17:33 Matt 10:39; 16:25; Mark 8:35; Luke 9:24; John 12:25
17:35 Matt 24:41
17:37 Matt 24:28

PARABLE OF THE PERSISTENT WIDOW

18 One day Jesus told His disciples a story to show that they should always pray and
never give up. 2 "There was a judge in a certain city," He said, "who neither feared
God nor cared about people. 3 A widow of that city came to him repeatedly, saying, 'Give
me justice in this dispute with my enemy.' 4 The judge ignored her for a while, but finally
he said to himself, 'I don't fear God or care about people, 5 but this woman is driving me
crazy. I'm going to see that she gets justice, because she is wearing me out with her con-
stant requests!' "

6 Then the Lord said, "Learn a lesson from this unjust judge. 7 Even he rendered a just de-
cision in the end. So don't you think God will surely give justice to His chosen people who
cry out to Him day and night? Will He keep putting them off? 8 I tell you, He will grant jus-
tice to them quickly! But when the Son of Man* returns, how many will He find on the
earth who have faith?"

18:1 Rom 12:12; Col 4:2; 1 Thes 5:17
18:5 Luke 11:7-8
18:7 Rev 6:10
18:8 1 Tim 4:1

PARABLE OF THE PHARISEE AND TAX COLLECTOR

9 Then Jesus told this story to some who had great confidence in their own righteousness
and scorned everyone else: 10 "Two men went to the Temple to pray. One was a Pharisee,

17:35 Some manuscripts add verse 36, *Two men will be working in the field; one will be taken, the other left.* Compare Matt 24:40. 17:37a Greek *"Where, Lord?"* 17:37b Greek *"Wherever the carcass is, the vultures gather."* 18:8 "Son of Man" is a title Jesus used for Himself.

17:26-27 God told Noah that a flood was coming upon the whole earth as judgment against wickedness and sin (Genesis 6–7). Although the people living at the time heard the message of coming judgment and could see Noah building a large boat as instructed by God, they ignored the message.

17:28-29 The day God brought judgment on the sinful people of Sodom was just like every other day—with the exception that God had sent His angels to the city to remove Lot and his family (Genesis 19:1-29). Life continued as normal until fire fell from heaven.

17:32 When Lot and his family were told to flee the destruction of Sodom, they were warned not to look back at the place they were leaving (Genesis 19:17). Lot's wife did not take the warning seriously, and she turned into a pillar of salt (Genesis 19:26).

18:9-14 The Pharisees were a political/religious party who held conservative interpretations of the Old Testament and who also revered the oral traditions of their teachers. The Bible generally refers to the leaders of the Pharisees when it uses the term *Pharisees.* Tax collectors were Jewish men who had agreed to collect taxes from their own people for the benefit of the Roman government, which ruled Israel in Jesus' day. Jews despised tax collectors for assisting their oppressors.

▸ GOD

18:9-14 Honest before God. Typically a person wants to make a good impression on the first day of work or when meeting someone admired from afar. We naturally think that if people like us, we'll get something from them that we value. But such thinking actually hinders our relationship with God. God already knows what we are really like, inside and out. So when we come into His presence trying to manipulate Him (as the Pharisee in Jesus' story), He's not impressed (Psalm 18:27; Luke 14:11). The right way to approach God is simply to receive His grace with humility and gratitude and be honest about who you are before Him (Psalm 17:1; 25:21; Luke 8:15). (***See God****> Relationship> Barriers> Pride,* TopicGuide page A14.)

18:11 and the other was a despised tax collector. 11 The Pharisee stood by himself and prayed
Matt 6:5 this prayer*: 'I thank You, God, that I am not a sinner like everyone else. For I don't cheat, I
18:12 don't sin, and I don't commit adultery. I'm certainly not like that tax collector! 12 I fast twice
Matt 23:23 a week, and I give You a tenth of my income.'
13 "But the tax collector stood at a distance and dared not even lift his eyes to heaven as
he prayed. Instead, he beat his chest in sorrow, saying, 'O God, be merciful to me, for I am
18:14 Matt 23:12 a sinner.' 14 I tell you, this sinner, not the Pharisee, returned home justified before God. For
Luke 14:11 those who exalt themselves will be humbled, and those who humble themselves will
be exalted."

JESUS BLESSES THE CHILDREN

18:15-17 //Matt 19:13-15 15 One day some parents brought their little children to Jesus so He could touch and bless
//Mark 10:13-16 them. But when the disciples saw this, they scolded the parents for bothering Him.
16 Then Jesus called for the children and said to the disciples, "Let the children come to
Me. Don't stop them! For the Kingdom of God belongs to those who are like these chil-
18:17 dren. 17 I tell you the truth, anyone who doesn't receive the Kingdom of God like a child
Matt 18:3 will never enter it."

THE RICH MAN

18:18-30 //Matt 19:16-30 18 Once a religious leader asked Jesus this question: "Good Teacher, what should I do to
//Mark 10:17-31 inherit eternal life?"
18:20 19 "Why do you call Me good?" Jesus asked him. "Only God is truly good. 20 But to an-
*Exod 20:13-16 swer your question, you know the commandments: 'You must not commit adultery. You
*Deut 5:17-20 must not murder. You must not steal. You must not testify falsely. Honor your father and
mother.'*"
21 The man replied, "I've obeyed all these commandments since I was young."
18:22 22 When Jesus heard his answer, He said, "There is still one thing you haven't done. Sell
Matt 6:20 all your possessions and give the money to the poor, and you will have treasure in
heaven. Then come, follow Me."
23 But when the man heard this he became very sad, for he was very rich.
24 When Jesus saw this,* He said, "How hard it is for the rich to enter the Kingdom of God!

18:11 Some manuscripts read *stood and prayed this prayer to himself.* 18:20 Exod 20:12-16; Deut 5:16-20. 18:24 Some manuscripts read *When Jesus saw how sad the man was.*

▸ ADOPTION

18:15-17 Nothing is free. Perhaps you have heard the slightly cynical voice of the world-weary: "There is no such thing as a free lunch." "Nothing is free." "If it looks like it's too good to be true, it probably is!" It is fascinating that you won't hear such things from children. When you offer something for free to a child, he typically accepts the offer. When you surprise a young one with something that seems too good to be true, she embraces it as not only true but as something especially for her. That is the kind of attitude that Jesus commends. That is the heart of true faith. Receiving the offer of life means receiving an offer that seems too good to be true—but it is true! (***See Adoption****> With Christ> Children of God> God gives good things to His children,* TopicGuide page A36.)

18:19-21 When Jesus replied to the young man's question, He initially cited only a few of the Ten Commandments—the section of the Old Testament writings considered the "core" of what God desired for His people (Exodus 20:12-16 and Deuteronomy 5:16-20). At first, Jesus avoided the other commandments that actually addressed this young man's basic problem.

▸ SALVATION

18:24-27 Saving ourselves. Have you ever tried to push a car while sitting in it? It's not very effective, and perhaps even impossible. Yet people try a similar trick when they attempt to save themselves from the consequences of their sin. Our good works may be commendable and our convictions sound, but we still cannot save ourselves. The message of the New Testament is that there is salvation through faith in Christ's works alone (Galatians 5:11). Faith in our own efforts (Galatians 3:3) to accomplish salvation is counter to the message of Christ: "The Spirit alone gives eternal life. Human effort accomplishes nothing" (John 6:63). Put no confidence in your efforts to make yourself better. Instead, put your confidence in Christ's work on the cross and in His continued prayers on your behalf (Romans 8:34; Hebrews 4:14; 7:25; 9:24). Then, you will be ready to work and serve in God's Kingdom (Philippians 2:12; 2 Peter 3:14). (***See Salvation****> Our Need> Sinful> Inability to save oneself,* TopicGuide page A22.)

25In fact, it is easier for a camel to go through the eye of a needle than for a rich person to
enter the Kingdom of God!"
26Those who heard this said, "Then who in the world can be saved?"
27He replied, "What is impossible for people is possible with God."
28Peter said, "We've left our homes to follow You."
29"Yes," Jesus replied, "and I assure you that everyone who has given up house or wife
or brothers or parents or children, for the sake of the Kingdom of God, 30will be repaid
many times over in this life, and will have eternal life in the world to come."

JESUS AGAIN PREDICTS HIS DEATH

31Taking the twelve disciples aside, Jesus said, "Listen, we're going up to Jerusalem,
where all the predictions of the prophets concerning the Son of Man will come true. 32He
will be handed over to the Romans,* and He will be mocked, treated shamefully, and spit
upon. 33They will flog Him with a whip and kill Him, but on the third day He will rise
again."
34But they didn't understand any of this. The significance of His words was hidden from
them, and they failed to grasp what He was talking about.

JESUS HEALS A BLIND BEGGAR

35As Jesus approached Jericho, a blind beggar was sitting beside the road. 36When he
heard the noise of a crowd going past, he asked what was happening. 37They told him
that Jesus the Nazarene* was going by. 38So he began shouting, "Jesus, Son of David, have
mercy on me!"
39"Be quiet!" the people in front yelled at him.
But he only shouted louder, "Son of David, have mercy on me!"
40When Jesus heard him, He stopped and ordered that the man be brought to Him. As
the man came near, Jesus asked him, 41"What do you want Me to do for you?"
"Lord," he said, "I want to see!"
42And Jesus said, "All right, receive your sight! Your faith has healed you." 43Instantly the
man could see, and he followed Jesus, praising God. And all who saw it praised God, too.

JESUS AND ZACCHAEUS

19 Jesus entered Jericho and made His way through the town. 2There was a man
there named Zacchaeus. He was the chief tax collector in the region, and he had
become very rich. 3He tried to get a look at Jesus, but he was too short to see over the
crowd. 4So he ran ahead and climbed a sycamore-fig tree beside the road, for Jesus was
going to pass that way.

18:28 Matt 4:19
18:31-34 //Matt 20:17-19 //Mark 10:32-34
18:31 Ps 22 Isa 53 Luke 9:51; 24:25-27, 44
18:32 Matt 16:21 Luke 9:22, 44
18:35-43 //Matt 20:29-34 //Mark 10:46-52
18:38 Matt 9:27
18:41 Mark 10:36
18:42 Matt 9:22 Luke 7:50; 17:19
18:43 Luke 19:37
19:1 Luke 18:35
19:4 1 Kgs 10:27 1 Chr 27:28

18:32 Greek *the Gentiles.* 18:37 Or *Jesus of Nazareth.*

18:25 In speaking of a camel going through the eye of a needle, Jesus showed His sense of humor, even though the issue He was addressing was deadly serious. Jesus' difficult image shows the impossibility of using any status or possession to attain heaven—in fact, depending on such things makes the journey impossible. His disciples partially understood the lesson and despaired, thinking that possessions of any sort might keep them from heaven (18:26). But this is not what Jesus said. They did not grasp His point at that time (18:34).

18:38 By addressing Jesus with the respectful title "Son of David," the blind man showed that he recognized that Jesus was the rightful heir to David's throne. Luke used irony to make his point—even the blind man could see that Jesus was the rightful heir to the promises given to David (Matthew 9:27; 12:23; 15:22; Luke 20:41).

▶ WORSHIP
18:40-42 A flaming faith. Watch Jesus in these passages. See Him reach out to people. Does He look like someone who is hesitant to meet the needs of His people? Does He refuse to help the hurting, or grow weary with the constant requests for healing and salvation? No. And as always, Jesus looks for more than an opportunity for mercy—He wants to fan the flames of faith, too. So when a blind man was brought to Jesus, He asked him a puzzling question: "What do you want Me to do for you?" Wasn't it obvious? Was Jesus the One who was blind to the man's need? Jesus was doing more than healing a body—He was healing a soul. When you pray for healing in yourself and others, come to Christ boldly—but be prepared. Jesus will also use our needs as a means to build our faith, so you may get more than you bargained for. (***See Worship****> NT> Prayer> Instructions> Pray believing,* TopicGuide page A33.)

5When Jesus came by, He looked up at Zacchaeus and called him by name. "Zacchaeus!" He said. "Quick, come down! I must be a guest in your home today."

6Zacchaeus quickly climbed down and took Jesus to his house in great excitement and joy. 7But the people were displeased. "He has gone to be the guest of a notorious sinner," they grumbled.

8Meanwhile, Zacchaeus stood before the Lord and said, "I will give half my wealth to the poor, Lord, and if I have cheated people on their taxes, I will give them back four times as much!"

9Jesus responded, "Salvation has come to this home today, for this man has shown himself to be a true son of Abraham. 10For the Son of Man* came to seek and save those who are lost."

PARABLE OF THE TEN SERVANTS

11The crowd was listening to everything Jesus said. And because He was nearing Jerusalem, He told them a story to correct the impression that the Kingdom of God would begin right away. 12He said, "A nobleman was called away to a distant empire to be crowned king and then return. 13Before he left, he called together ten of his servants and divided among them ten pounds of silver,* saying, 'Invest this for me while I am gone.' 14But his people hated him and sent a delegation after him to say, 'We do not want him to be our king.'

15"After he was crowned king, he returned and called in the servants to whom he had given the money. He wanted to find out what their profits were. 16The first servant reported, 'Master, I invested your money and made ten times the original amount!'

17" 'Well done!' the king exclaimed. 'You are a good servant. You have been faithful with the little I entrusted to you, so you will be governor of ten cities as your reward.'

18"The next servant reported, 'Master, I invested your money and made five times the original amount.'

19" 'Well done!' the king said. 'You will be governor over five cities.'

20"But the third servant brought back only the original amount of money and said, 'Master, I hid your money and kept it safe. 21I was afraid because you are a hard man to deal with, taking what isn't yours and harvesting crops you didn't plant.'

22" 'You wicked servant!' the king roared. 'Your own words condemn you. If you knew that I'm a hard man who takes what isn't mine and harvests crops I didn't plant, 23why didn't you deposit my money in the bank? At least I could have gotten some interest on it.'

24"Then, turning to the others standing nearby, the king ordered, 'Take the money from this servant, and give it to the one who has ten pounds.'

25" 'But, master,' they said, 'he already has ten pounds!'

26" 'Yes,' the king replied, 'and to those who use well what they are given, even more will be given. But from those who do nothing, even what little they have will be taken away. 27And as for these enemies of mine who didn't want me to be their king—bring them in and execute them right here in front of me.' "

JESUS' TRIUMPHANT ENTRY

28After telling this story, Jesus went on toward Jerusalem, walking ahead of His disciples. 29As He came to the towns of Bethphage and Bethany on the Mount of Olives, He sent two

19:7 Matt 9:11; Luke 5:30; 15:2
19:8 Exod 22:1; Num 5:7; Luke 3:12-13
19:9 Matt 9:13; Acts 16:31-34; 1 Tim 1:15
19:10 Ezek 34:12, 16; John 3:17
19:11-27 //Matt 25:14-30
19:11 Acts 1:6
19:12 Mark 13:34
19:17 Luke 16:10
19:22 Job 15:6; Matt 12:37
19:26 Matt 13:12; Mark 4:25; Luke 8:18
19:27 Luke 19:14
19:28-38 //Matt 21:1-11; //Mark 11:1-11; //John 12:12-19

19:10 "Son of Man" is a title Jesus used for Himself. 19:13 Greek *ten minas;* one mina was worth about three months' wages.

19:7 As noted previously (18:9-14), the majority of the Jewish people looked down on tax collectors. Zacchaeus, a tax collector, bore the description of "notorious sinner."

▸ GOD
19:10 Rescue the lost. How would you sum up the life and ministry of Jesus? How do you think most people see Him? A great teacher? A prophet? A moral leader? A miracle worker? A holy man? Most of those pictures of Jesus have some element of truth to them. But how did Jesus see Himself? He summed up His life and ministry by saying that He came to seek and save those who are lost. Above all else, Jesus is the Savior. Let your relationship with Him be marked by that divine summary as you depend on Him for salvation from sin, Satan, and self. Rest and rely on Him alone as your sole source of favor with God (2 Timothy 2:1). (***See God***> *Salvation> Son> Came to save what was lost,* TopicGuide page A15.)

disciples ahead. 30"Go into that village over there," He told them. "As you enter it, you will
see a young donkey tied there that no one has ever ridden. Untie it and bring it here. 31If
anyone asks, 'Why are you untying that colt?' just say, 'The Lord needs it.'"

32So they went and found the colt, just as Jesus had said. 33And sure enough, as they
were untying it, the owners asked them, "Why are you untying that colt?"

34And the disciples simply replied, "The Lord needs it." 35So they brought the colt to
Jesus and threw their garments over it for Him to ride on.

36As He rode along, the crowds spread out their garments on the road ahead of Him.
37When He reached the place where the road started down the Mount of Olives, all of His
followers began to shout and sing as they walked along, praising God for all the wonderful
miracles they had seen.

38 "Blessings on the King who comes in the name of the LORD!
Peace in heaven, and glory in highest heaven!"*

39But some of the Pharisees among the crowd said, "Teacher, rebuke Your followers for
saying things like that!"

40He replied, "If they kept quiet, the stones along the road would burst into cheers!"

JESUS WEEPS OVER JERUSALEM

41But as He came closer to Jerusalem and saw the city ahead, He began to weep. 42"How I
wish today that you of all people would understand the way to peace. But now it is too
late, and peace is hidden from your eyes. 43Before long your enemies will build ramparts
against your walls and encircle you and close in on you from every side. 44They will crush
you into the ground, and your children with you. Your enemies will not leave a single
stone in place, because you did not accept your opportunity for salvation."

JESUS CLEARS THE TEMPLE

45Then Jesus entered the Temple and began to drive out the people selling animals for
sacrifices. 46He said to them, "The Scriptures declare, 'My Temple will be a house of
prayer,' but you have turned it into a den of thieves."*

47After that, He taught daily in the Temple, but the leading priests, the teachers of reli-
gious law, and the other leaders of the people began planning how to kill Him. 48But they
could think of nothing, because all the people hung on every word He said.

THE AUTHORITY OF JESUS CHALLENGED

20 One day as Jesus was teaching the people and preaching the Good News in the
Temple, the leading priests, the teachers of religious law, and the elders came up
to Him. 2They demanded, "By what authority are You doing all these things? Who gave
You the right?"

3"Let Me ask you a question first," He replied. 4"Did John's authority to baptize come
from heaven, or was it merely human?"

19:36 2 Kgs 9:13
19:38 *Pss 118:25-26; 148:1; Luke 2:14; 13:35
19:40 Hab 2:11
19:41 Luke 13:34-35; John 11:35
19:43 Isa 29:3; Jer 6:6; Ezek 4:2; Luke 21:20
19:44 Ps 137:9; Luke 21:6
19:45-48 //Matt 21:12-17; //Mark 11:15-19; //John 2:13-22
19:46 *Isa 56:7; *Jer 7:11
19:47 Matt 26:55; Luke 21:37; 22:53; John 18:20
20:1-8 //Matt 21:23-27; //Mark 11:27-33
20:2 John 2:18; Acts 4:7; 7:27
20:4 Mark 1:4

19:38 Pss 118:26; 148:1. 19:46 Isa 56:7; Jer 7:11.

19:36-38 With Passover drawing near, many pilgrims had journeyed to Jerusalem for the festival. As they traveled into the city, they sang the Psalms of Ascent (Psalm 120–134). When Jesus came, these pilgrims celebrated His arrival, expressing their longings and hopes for the coming of God's promised Messiah.

19:45-46 The Temple was to be a place of worship, and part of this worship involved offering animal sacrifices. In the Temple grounds that were designated as worship areas for Gentiles, the religious leaders had set up booths to inspect and sell animals for sacrifice, often charging the people who had come for worship more than was necessary. Thus, what should have been a place of prayer for all nations had become a place for swindling others out of money. As Jesus cleared the Temple, He quoted from Isaiah 56:7 and Jeremiah 7:11.

20:1-8 Religious leaders sought to challenge Jesus' act of cleansing the Temple (Luke 19:45-48). They probably believed He would answer that His authority came from God. They could then claim that only the crazy (John 10:20) or demon-controlled (Matthew 12:24) would attack the Temple. But Jesus thwarted their rhetorical trap, citing their inability to speak clearly of John's source of authority.

5They talked it over among themselves. "If we say it was from heaven, He will ask why we
20:6 didn't believe John. 6But if we say it was merely human, the people will stone us because
Luke 7:29 they are convinced John was a prophet." 7So they finally replied that they didn't know.
8And Jesus responded, "Then I won't tell you by what authority I do these things."

PARABLE OF THE EVIL FARMERS

20:9-19 9Now Jesus turned to the people again and told them this story: "A man planted a vineyard,
Isa 5:1-7 leased it to tenant farmers, and moved to another country to live for several years. 10At
//Matt 21:33-46
//Mark 12:1-12 the time of the grape harvest, he sent one of his servants to collect his share of the crop. But
20:10-12 the farmers attacked the servant, beat him up, and sent him back empty-handed. 11So the
2 Chr 36:15-16 owner sent another servant, but they also insulted him, beat him up, and sent him away
empty-handed. 12A third man was sent, and they wounded him and chased him away.
13"'What will I do?' the owner asked himself. 'I know! I'll send my cherished son. Surely
they will respect him.'
20:14 14"But when the tenant farmers saw his son, they said to each other, 'Here comes the
Heb 1:2 heir to this estate. Let's kill him and get the estate for ourselves!' 15So they dragged him
out of the vineyard and murdered him.
"What do you suppose the owner of the vineyard will do to them?" Jesus asked. 16"I'll
tell you—he will come and kill those farmers and lease the vineyard to others."
"How terrible that such a thing should ever happen," His listeners protested.
20:17 17Jesus looked at them and said, "Then what does this Scripture mean?

*Ps 118:22 'The stone that the builders rejected
Acts 4:11 has now become the cornerstone.'*

20:18 18Everyone who stumbles over that stone will be broken to pieces, and it will crush any-
Isa 8:14-15 one it falls on."
Dan 2:34-35 19The teachers of religious law and the leading priests wanted to arrest Jesus immedi-
ately because they realized He was telling the story against them—they were the wicked
farmers. But they were afraid of the people's reaction.

TAXES FOR CAESAR

20:20-26 20Watching for their opportunity, the leaders sent spies pretending to be honest men.
//Matt 22:15-22
//Mark 12:13-17 They tried to get Jesus to say something that could be reported to the Roman governor so

20:17 Ps 118:22.

20:9-19 Immediately following His counterattack on the hypocritical religious leadership, Jesus told a story designed to humble them even further. The priests and teachers realized the story was about their rejection of God and His appointed Messiah, but they were powerless to harm Jesus due to the favor of the people.

▶ SALVATION
20:17-18 Tripped up. Human wisdom doesn't know exactly how to handle Jesus and His sacrifice for sin. We want to make Him a great teacher—but One that was wrong when He said He was the only way to the Father (John 14:6). We want to make Him a nice religious fellow, but in truth He hated religion that didn't honor Him and His Father. He promised to crush anyone who falls under His judgment. That's not the nice, sweet, tame Jesus that most people want to have as their friend. But He cannot be tamed. He will not settle for anything less than a repentant, broken heart that cries out to Him for salvation. The only way not to stumble over Jesus is to bow down to Him. (***See Salvation**> Receiving> How> Repent of/turn from sin,* TopicGuide page A22.)

20:20 Rome had granted governing authority to the Sanhedrin in exchange for their cooperation in maintaining order in the land. They were allowed to adjudicate certain affairs pertaining to the life and laws of the Jewish people, but they did not always have the power to take life. History records that the governing Romans granted and removed that authority as they pleased. The Sanhedrin exercised its power very carefully in this case, while with Stephen they passed judgment quickly and without any permission from the Romans (Acts 7).

▶ PURPOSE
20:20-26 One King to rule them all. In an amazing display of tolerance, large predatory fish allow small "cleaner fish" to swim around with them. At times, they even let the little cleaner fish swim into their mouths and eat away any debris found lodged there. It would be nothing for the large fish to swallow the little ones whole, but they allow them to remain. Keep that picture in mind as you think about the kingdoms of this world. God is sovereign over all; He is the one true King. But He tolerates a lot of little kings . . . for a time. Because He permits their continuance, we must grant them appropriate honor. But in all we do, we cannot lose sight of the One who deserves our ultimate allegiance. Stay focused on your one true King. (***See Purpose**> God's Means> God's Sovereignty> God is King over every nation,* TopicGuide page A52.)

he would arrest Jesus. 21"Teacher," they said, "we know that You speak and teach what is
right and are not influenced by what others think. You teach the way of God truthfully.
22Now tell us—is it right for us to pay taxes to Caesar or not?"

23He saw through their trickery and said, 24"Show Me a Roman coin.* Whose picture and
title are stamped on it?"

"Caesar's," they replied.

25"Well then," He said, "give to Caesar what belongs to Caesar, and give to God what be-
longs to God."

26So they failed to trap Him by what He said in front of the people. Instead, they were
amazed by His answer, and they became silent.

20:25 Luke 23:2 Rom 13:6-7

DISCUSSION ABOUT RESURRECTION

27Then Jesus was approached by some Sadducees—religious leaders who say there is no
resurrection from the dead. 28They posed this question: "Teacher, Moses gave us a law
that if a man dies, leaving a wife but no children, his brother should marry the widow and
have a child who will carry on the brother's name.* 29Well, suppose there were seven
brothers. The oldest one married and then died without children. 30So the second brother
married the widow, but he also died. 31Then the third brother married her. This continued
with all seven of them, who died without children. 32Finally, the woman also died. 33So tell
us, whose wife will she be in the resurrection? For all seven were married to her!"

34Jesus replied, "Marriage is for people here on earth. 35But in the age to come, those
worthy of being raised from the dead will neither marry nor be given in marriage. 36And
they will never die again. In this respect they will be like angels. They are children of God
and children of the resurrection.

37"But now, as to whether the dead will be raised—even Moses proved this when he
wrote about the burning bush. Long after Abraham, Isaac, and Jacob had died, he referred
to the Lord* as 'the God of Abraham, the God of Isaac, and the God of Jacob.'* 38So He is
the God of the living, not the dead, for they are all alive to Him."

39"Well said, Teacher!" remarked some of the teachers of religious law who were stand-
ing there. 40And then no one dared to ask Him any more questions.

20:27-40 //Matt 22:23-33 //Mark 12:18-27
20:27 Acts 23:8
20:28 *Deut 25:5
20:36 John 1:12 Gal 4:5-7 1 Jn 3:1-2
20:37 *Exod 3:6

WHOSE SON IS THE MESSIAH?

41Then Jesus presented them with a question. "Why is it," He asked, "that the Messiah is
said to be the son of David? 42For David himself wrote in the book of Psalms:

20:41-44 //Matt 22:41-46 //Mark 12:35-37
20:42-43 *Ps 110:1

20:24 Greek *a denarius.* 20:28 See Deut 25:5-6. 20:37a Greek *when he wrote about the bush. He referred to the Lord.* 20:37b Exod 3:6.

20:22-25 Some Jews wanted to rise up in armed rebellion against the oppressive Roman government; others sought accommodation. Each faction tended to dislike the other. If the Jewish authorities could have forced Jesus to "take sides," they might have been able to undermine His popular appeal. The issue of taxes was clearly a major concern for both factions.

20:24-25 A typical coin in circulation under Rome in that day would have borne the image of the Roman emperor and an inscription of his name and title. In answering their question in this manner, Jesus reminded them that human beings bear the image of God, and thus we belong to Him (Genesis 1:26).

20:27 There were two notable religious factions in Israel at the time: the Sadducees and the Pharisees. The Pharisees were more conservative in their views, both religiously and politically. The Sadducees were at the other end of the spectrum. In addition to a more lenient view of standards of holy living, the Sadducees denied the existence of angelic beings and discounted any future resurrection, while the Pharisees affirmed both.

20:27-40 The Sadducees wanted Jesus' ministry to fail, so they attempted to trick Him into an unwise answer on a hot theological debate of their day—the resurrection. Jesus responded by critiquing their illustration (20:34) and strongly siding with the Pharisees, who were likely the ones who offered favorable comments (20:39). But Jesus' sharp answer quieted the Sadducees, who realized that Jesus' answers only curried more favor.

20:41-46 David was considered Israel's greatest king. Under David's leadership, the nation flourished. God made a covenant with David and promised that one of his descendants would one day sit on an eternal throne, extending David's reign forever (2 Samuel 7:26; 22:51; 1 Kings 9:5). That coming descendant was understood to be the Messiah. Jesus was not only David's promised offspring; He is also David's Lord and God.

20:42-43 Jesus quoted from Psalm 110:1, a song of praise to the king.

'The LORD said to my Lord,
Sit in the place of honor at My right hand
43 until I humble Your enemies,
making them a footstool under Your feet.'*

44 Since David called the Messiah 'Lord,' how can the Messiah be his son?"
20:45-47 45 Then, with the crowds listening, He turned to His disciples and said, 46 "Beware of
//Matt 23:1-36 these teachers of religious law! For they like to parade around in flowing robes and love to
//Mark 12:38-40 receive respectful greetings as they walk in the marketplaces. And how they love the seats
//Luke 11:37-54 of honor in the synagogues and the head table at banquets. 47 Yet they shamelessly cheat
widows out of their property and then pretend to be pious by making long prayers in pub-
lic. Because of this, they will be severely punished."

THE WIDOW'S OFFERING

21:1-4 **21** While Jesus was in the Temple, He watched the rich people dropping their gifts in
//Mark 12:41-44 the collection box. 2 Then a poor widow came by and dropped in two small coins.*
3 "I tell you the truth," Jesus said, "this poor widow has given more than all the rest of
them. 4 For they have given a tiny part of their surplus, but she, poor as she is, has given
everything she has."

JESUS FORETELLS THE FUTURE

21:5-36 5 Some of His disciples began talking about the majestic stonework of the Temple and the
//Matt 24:1-35 memorial decorations on the walls. But Jesus said, 6 "The time is coming when all these
//Mark 13:1-31 things will be completely demolished. Not one stone will be left on top of another!"
21:6 Luke 19:44 7 "Teacher," they asked, "when will all this happen? What sign will show us that these
things are about to take place?"
21:8 8 He replied, "Don't let anyone mislead you, for many will come in My name, claiming, 'I
Luke 17:23 am the Messiah,'* and saying, 'The time has come!' But don't believe them. 9 And when
you hear of wars and insurrections, don't panic. Yes, these things must take place first, but
21:10 the end won't follow immediately." 10 Then He added, "Nation will go to war against na-
2 Chr 15:6 tion, and kingdom against kingdom. 11 There will be great earthquakes, and there will be
Isa 19:2 famines and plagues in many lands, and there will be terrifying things and great miracu-
lous signs from heaven.
21:12 12 "But before all this occurs, there will be a time of great persecution. You will be dragged
Acts 12:4 into synagogues and prisons, and you will stand trial before kings and governors because

20:42-43 Ps 110:1. 21:2 Greek *two lepta* [the smallest of Jewish coins]. 21:8 Greek *claiming, 'I am.'*

21:1-4 In the Temple there were receptacles in which people could place their monetary offerings. Often, those who were wealthy made a show of their giving. In that setting, Jesus called attention to a poor widow who put in only two small coins—less then a common laborer would have made for an hour's work.

▸ GOD
21:1-4 What does God need? What can you give someone who has everything? What kind of gift do you give to one who appears to have no needs or unfulfilled desires? What amount of money could we ever give God that would matter? Some people (like some of the religious leaders of Jesus' day) think that God is impressed with the amount of a gift. But that doesn't impress God; He doesn't need our money. He wants our hearts—and everything else in our lives—laid before Him to do with what He will. True worshipers come to God humbly, and the amounts of their gifts are of much less consequence than the surrender of their souls (Romans 12:1-2). Lavish God with your gifts to Him. (***See God***> *God's Attributes> Self-existent> We have nothing materially that God needs or wants,* TopicGuide page A17.)

21:7-24 The Old Testament prophets spoke of a future day of judgment on Israel and on the world. It would be a time of great trouble on the earth, and was sometimes referred to as the "day of the Lord." As Jesus described what would happen in the future just prior to His return, He was describing the very things the Old Testament prophets associated with that future day of judgment. (See Joel 1:15–2:17; 3:14-21; Amos 5:18-20; Zechariah 12:9; Malachi 4:1-5.) The tension in this passage surrounds whether Jesus was foretelling events that would occur sooner or later—but since Jesus spoke of those standing around Him possibly being deceived (21:8), at least some portion of this chapter occurred in the coming years. The conquering of Jerusalem (21:24) certainly referred to the Roman Empire's destruction of the Temple and the city in AD 70, roughly 40 years later.

you are My followers. 13But this will be your opportunity to tell them about Me.* 14So don't
worry in advance about how to answer the charges against you, 15for I will give you the
right words and such wisdom that none of your opponents will be able to reply or refute
you! 16Even those closest to you—your parents, brothers, relatives, and friends—will betray
you. They will even kill some of you. 17And everyone will hate you because you are My fol-
lowers.* 18But not a hair of your head will perish! 19By standing firm, you will win your souls.
20"And when you see Jerusalem surrounded by armies, then you will know that the time
of its destruction has arrived. 21Then those in Judea must flee to the hills. Those in Jerusa-
lem must get out, and those out in the country should not return to the city. 22For those will
be days of God's vengeance, and the prophetic words of the Scriptures will be fulfilled.
23How terrible it will be for pregnant women and for nursing mothers in those days. For
there will be disaster in the land and great anger against this people. 24They will be killed
by the sword or sent away as captives to all the nations of the world. And Jerusalem will be
trampled down by the Gentiles until the period of the Gentiles comes to an end.
25"And there will be strange signs in the sun, moon, and stars. And here on earth the na-
tions will be in turmoil, perplexed by the roaring seas and strange tides. 26People will be ter-
rified at what they see coming upon the earth, for the powers in the heavens will be shaken.
27Then everyone will see the Son of Man* coming on a cloud with power and great glory.*
28So when all these things begin to happen, stand and look up, for your salvation is near!"
29Then He gave them this illustration: "Notice the fig tree, or any other tree. 30When the
leaves come out, you know without being told that summer is near. 31In the same way,
when you see all these things taking place, you can know that the Kingdom of God is near.
32I tell you the truth, this generation will not pass from the scene until all these things have
taken place. 33Heaven and earth will disappear, but My words will never disappear.
34"Watch out! Don't let your hearts be dulled by carousing and drunkenness, and by the
worries of this life. Don't let that day catch you unaware, 35like a trap. For that day will
come upon everyone living on the earth. 36Keep alert at all times. And pray that you might
be strong enough to escape these coming horrors and stand before the Son of Man."
37Every day Jesus went to the Temple to teach, and each evening He returned to spend
the night on the Mount of Olives. 38The crowds gathered at the Temple early each morn-
ing to hear Him.

JUDAS AGREES TO BETRAY JESUS

22 The Festival of Unleavened Bread, which is also called Passover, was approach-
ing. 2The leading priests and teachers of religious law were plotting how to kill
Jesus, but they were afraid of the people's reaction.
3Then Satan entered into Judas Iscariot, who was one of the twelve disciples, 4and he
went to the leading priests and captains of the Temple guard to discuss the best way to be-

21:13 Phil 1:12
21:14 Luke 12:11-12
21:15 Acts 6:10
21:18 Matt 10:30
21:22 Deut 32:35; Dan 9:24-27; Hos 9:7
21:23 1 Cor 7:26, 28
21:24 Isa 5:5; 63:18; Dan 8:13; 2 Pet 3:10, 12; Rev 11:2
21:26 *Isa 34:4
21:27 *Dan 7:13; Matt 26:64; Rev 1:7; 14:14
21:33 Isa 40:6-8; Matt 5:18
21:34 Matt 24:48-50; Rom 13:13; 1 Thes 5:3
21:36 Mark 13:33
21:37 Luke 19:47; 22:39; John 8:1-2
22:1-2 //Matt 26:1-5; //Mark 14:1-2
22:3-6 //Matt 26:14-16; //Mark 14:10-11
22:3 John 13:2, 27; Acts 1:17

21:13 Or *This will be your testimony against them.* 21:17 Greek *on account of My name.* 21:27a "Son of Man" is a title Jesus used for Himself. 21:27b See Dan 7:13.

21:13 Trouble for the church will always provide us with the opportunity to be made holy (Daniel 11:35; 2 Corinthians 12:10) and to bear witness to God's love and power (2 Thessalonians 1:3-4).

21:24 The "period of the Gentiles" may refer to the time when Rome triumphed over Israel or the time when the gospel would be preached to the Gentiles (Acts 15:7; Galatians 2:2, 14; Ephesians 3:6).

21:25-34 This section is puzzling because of its mysterious topic as well as the timing of these events. Some of these details seem to have occurred sooner (21:31), others have been happening throughout history (21:25-26), and still others have not yet occurred (21:27). Luke summarizes what our response should be to Jesus' messages about the end times: Keep alert (21:36).

21:37 This verse indicates that Jesus repeated many of His teachings, and Luke summarized them for us here. It also signals that Jesus' primary teaching ministry was over and His passion (His death and resurrection) was about to begin.

22:1-2 With the celebration of the Festival of Unleavened Bread and Passover, throngs of pilgrims came to Jerusalem. Many of them had enthusiastically welcomed Jesus into the city when He arrived (19:36-40), so those plotting Jesus' murder had to be cautious, not wanting to stir up the crowd that embraced Jesus so favorably.

22:5 tray Jesus to them. 5They were delighted, and they promised to give him money. 6So he
Zech 11:12 agreed and began looking for an opportunity to betray Jesus so they could arrest Him
1 Tim 6:10 when the crowds weren't around.

THE LAST SUPPER

22:7-13 //Matt 26:17-20 7Now the Festival of Unleavened Bread arrived, when the Passover lamb is sacrificed.
//Mark 14:12-16 8Jesus sent Peter and John ahead and said, "Go and prepare the Passover meal, so we can
22:8 eat it together."
Exod 12:8-11 9"Where do You want us to prepare it?" they asked Him.
22:10 10He replied, "As soon as you enter Jerusalem, a man carrying a pitcher of water will
1 Sam 10:2-7 meet you. Follow him. At the house he enters, 11say to the owner, 'The Teacher asks:
Where is the guest room where I can eat the Passover meal with My disciples?' 12He will
take you upstairs to a large room that is already set up. That is where you should prepare
our meal." 13They went off to the city and found everything just as Jesus had said, and
they prepared the Passover meal there.
22:15-20 14When the time came, Jesus and the apostles sat down together at the table.* 15Jesus
//Matt 26:26-29 //Mark 14:22-25 said, "I have been very eager to eat this Passover meal with you before My suffering be-
//1 Cor 11:23-26 gins. 16For I tell you now that I won't eat this meal again until its meaning is fulfilled in the
22:16 Kingdom of God."
Luke 14:15 17Then He took a cup of wine and gave thanks to God for it. Then He said, "Take this
22:19 and share it among yourselves. 18For I will not drink wine again until the Kingdom of God
Luke 24:30 Acts 27:35 has come."
22:20 19He took some bread and gave thanks to God for it. Then He broke it in pieces and gave
Exod 24:8 it to the disciples, saying, "This is My body, which is given for you. Do this to remember Me."
Jer 31:31-34 Heb 9:15-18 20After supper He took another cup of wine and said, "This cup is the new covenant be-
22:21-23 tween God and His people—an agreement confirmed with My blood, which is poured out
//Matt 26:21-25 as a sacrifice for you.*
//Mark 14:18-21 21"But here at this table, sitting among us as a friend, is the man who will betray Me.
//John 13:21-26 22For it has been determined that the Son of Man* must die. But what sorrow awaits the
22:21 Ps 41:9 one who betrays Him." 23The disciples began to ask each other which of them would ever
John 13:21 do such a thing.
22:22 24Then they began to argue among themselves about who would be the greatest
Acts 2:23; 4:28 among them. 25Jesus told them, "In this world the kings and great men lord it over their

22:24-27 //Matt 20:24-28

22:14 Or *reclined together.* 22:19-20 Some manuscripts omit 22:19b-20, *which is given for you . . . which is poured out as a sacrifice for you.* 22:22 "Son of Man" is a title Jesus used for Himself.

22:7-8 The Passover was a celebration that commemorated the deliverance of the nation of Israel from bondage in Egypt (as explained in Exodus 12:1-20). This annual feast was linked to the very identity of Israel as a nation, and it included a memorial meal and the sacrifice of one special lamb for each family. As visitors in the city, Jesus and His followers had to find a place to celebrate the feast together.

▸ ADOPTION
22:14-30 A foretaste of glory. An appetizer is served before the main course of a meal to whet your appetite—to give you a foretaste of what is to come. It is part of the meal, but not the whole meal. It stirs your hunger but does not fully satisfy it. When Jesus broke bread and shared a cup of wine with His dearest friends at the Last Supper, He was offering them an appetizer. He was inviting them into life in the Kingdom. He was instructing them that the foundation for Kingdom life was His own death, burial, and resurrection. But He was also reminding them that this was only a foretaste of the wonders and joy yet awaiting them (Romans 8:23). As believers, we are enjoying the appetizer of a forever feast with Jesus (Revelation 19:7-9). (***See Adoption****> With Christ> Supernatural> A life of infinite joy,* TopicGuide page A37.)

22:19 The Passover meal was a God-ordained means of recalling God's work in delivering the people of Israel from their oppressors in Egypt and bringing them into a new covenantal relationship with Himself (Exodus 12:1-20). Therefore, it was incredibly significant for Jesus to alter the Passover celebration by calling His followers to remember *Him.*

22:20 The Passover celebration reminded the people of Israel that God had chosen to identify Himself with them. God had made a covenant—an agreement—with the nation after He led them out of Egypt. For Jesus to inaugurate a "new covenant" in the midst of the Passover meal signified a radical new understanding of what God was doing. A number of Old Testaments prophets foretold how God would establish a "new covenant" with His people. (See, for example, Jeremiah 31:31-34 and Ezekiel 11:19-20.)

people, yet they are called 'friends of the people.' 26But among you it will be different.
Those who are the greatest among you should take the lowest rank, and the leader
should be like a servant. 27Who is more important, the one who sits at the table or the one
who serves? The one who sits at the table, of course. But not here! For I am among you as
one who serves.
28"You have stayed with Me in My time of trial. 29And just as My Father has granted Me
a Kingdom, I now grant you the right 30to eat and drink at My table in My Kingdom. And
you will sit on thrones, judging the twelve tribes of Israel.

JESUS PREDICTS PETER'S DENIAL

31"Simon, Simon, Satan has asked to sift each of you like wheat. 32But I have pleaded in
prayer for you, Simon, that your faith should not fail. So when you have repented and
turned to Me again, strengthen your brothers."
33Peter said, "Lord, I am ready to go to prison with You, and even to die with You."
34But Jesus said, "Peter, let Me tell you something. Before the rooster crows tomorrow
morning, you will deny three times that you even know Me."

22:26 Matt 23:11 Mark 9:35 1 Pet 5:5
22:27 John 13:4-16
22:28-30 //Matt 19:28
22:31-34 //Matt 26:31-35 //Mark 14:27-31 //John 13:36-38
22:31 Job 1:6-12 Amos 9:9
22:32 John 17:9, 15; 21:15
22:33 John 11:16

▸ WORSHIP
22:31-32 Praying for you. Jesus and His friends were sharing an intimate meal together. He had spoken of His impending death; sorrow filled the air. He told them that they were all going to betray Him—even Peter, who thought himself so brave. Jesus knew Peter's weaknesses; He knew that Peter, too, would stumble. After telling Peter this, Jesus added that He had prayed for Peter. What great news! Jesus, knowing our weaknesses and foreseeing all our stumbles, still loves us and prays for us (Romans 8:34; Hebrews 7:25). Jesus is praying for you, and His Father perfectly hears and answers His prayers (Hebrews 9:24). This means that your life is a reflection of Jesus' prayers for you. Let this truth impact the way you view your life and circumstances. (***See Worship****> NT> Prayer> Instructions> Christ intercedes for us,* TopicGuide page A32.)

MY RESPONSE TO GOD

Spiritual Breathing

LUKE 22:32

We often find ourselves struggling with heated outbursts and filthy language–and that's just on the drive to work! The rest of the day can often reveal the very worst in us. But God has not left us to wrestle with our sin alone; He has given us the pattern of repenting and believing–like inhaling and exhaling–to energize us to live the Christian life.

One of the keys to experiencing the joy of effective repentance is spiritual breathing. Just as physical breathing detoxifies our inner organs, spiritual breathing detoxifies our spirits. It is God's way of teaching us to live lives of repentance.

Physical breathing has two parts: exhaling impure air and inhaling pure air. Spiritual breathing also has two parts. As the Holy Spirit uses God's Word to make us aware of a thought, emotion, or behavior that displeases God, we need to "exhale," to confess the impurity of our sin to God. Confession means agreeing with God that we have sinned and that we need to change (Hosea 6:1; Luke 24:47). That's the first part.

The second part of spiritual breathing is "inhaling"–praying a prayer of submission to God's will as defined by the Bible. Through this simple (but not easy!) prayer, we willingly surrender to the Holy Spirit's cleansing work in our lives (Ephesians 4:29-30). Spiritual breathing is as ordinary and necessary as physical breathing–it's God's way for us to surrender to His will.

(22:35 Matt 10:9-10; Luke 9:3) 35 Then Jesus asked them, "When I sent you out to preach the Good News and you did
not have money, a traveler's bag, or extra clothing, did you need anything?"
"No," they replied.
36 "But now," He said, "take your money and a traveler's bag. And if you don't have a
(22:37 *Isa 53:12; Mark 15:28) sword, sell your cloak and buy one! 37 For the time has come for this prophecy about Me to
be fulfilled: 'He was counted among the rebels.'* Yes, everything written about Me by the
prophets will come true."
38 "Look, Lord," they replied, "we have two swords among us."
"That's enough," He said.

JESUS PRAYS ON THE MOUNT OF OLIVES

(22:39-46 //Matt 26:36-46; //Mark 14:32-42) 39 Then, accompanied by the disciples, Jesus left the upstairs room and went as usual to
the Mount of Olives. 40 There He told them, "Pray that you will not give in to temptation."
(22:40 Matt 6:13) 41 He walked away, about a stone's throw, and knelt down and prayed, 42 "Father, if You
are willing, please take this cup of suffering away from Me. Yet I want Your will to be done,
not Mine." 43 Then an angel from heaven appeared and strengthened Him. 44 He prayed
more fervently, and He was in such agony of spirit that His sweat fell to the ground like
great drops of blood.*
45 At last He stood up again and returned to the disciples, only to find them asleep, ex-
hausted from grief. 46 "Why are you sleeping?" He asked them. "Get up and pray, so that
you will not give in to temptation."

JESUS IS BETRAYED AND ARRESTED

(22:47-53 //Matt 26:47-56; //Mark 14:43-49; //John 18:3-11) 47 But even as Jesus said this, a crowd approached, led by Judas, one of the twelve disci-
ples. Judas walked over to Jesus to greet Him with a kiss. 48 But Jesus said, "Judas, would
you betray the Son of Man with a kiss?"
49 When the other disciples saw what was about to happen, they exclaimed, "Lord,
should we fight? We brought the swords!" 50 And one of them struck at the high priest's
slave, slashing off his right ear.
51 But Jesus said, "No more of this." And He touched the man's ear and healed him.
52 Then Jesus spoke to the leading priests, the captains of the Temple guard, and the el-
ders who had come for Him. "Am I some dangerous revolutionary," He asked, "that you
come with swords and clubs to arrest Me? 53 Why didn't you arrest Me in the Temple? I was
(22:53 Luke 19:47; John 7:30) there every day. But this is your moment, the time when the power of darkness reigns."

PETER DENIES JESUS

(22:54-62 //Matt 26:57-58, 69-75; //Mark 14:53-54, 66-72; //John 18:12-18, 25-27) 54 So they arrested Him and led Him to the high priest's home. And Peter followed at a dis-
tance. 55 The guards lit a fire in the middle of the courtyard and sat around it, and Peter
joined them there. 56 A servant girl noticed him in the firelight and began staring at him.
Finally she said, "This man was one of Jesus' followers!"

22:37 Isa 53:12. 22:43-44 Verses 43 and 44 are not included in many ancient manuscripts.

22:37 Jesus referred to Isaiah 53:12. Isaiah 53 is perhaps the clearest statement of the substitutionary atonement of Christ in the Old Testament.

▸ SPIRITUAL WARFARE

22:39-40 Resist temptation through prayer. Often it takes painful consequences to teach children to obey. You can warn a child not to touch a flame because it will burn him, but curiosity often gets the best of him, and he ends up with a painful burn on his finger. Sadly, many adult followers of Jesus tend to learn things the same way. We still play around with sin, not trusting God's warnings against it. We play with temptation like a child playing with fire. But we don't have to continue learning only by painful consequences. Pray for help to avoid temptation, to back away from it, and to experience victory over it. Keep your distance from sin through prayer, and you won't get burned. (***See Spiritual Warfare**> Resisting Sin and Evil> Resisting Temptation> How to Resist> By the help of God*, TopicGuide page A45.)

22:39-46 Jesus' passion began as He cried out to God over His struggles with the deep suffering that loomed before Him. He took His closest friends with Him on this first part of His journey to the cross, but they immediately fell asleep. Jesus had to walk this path alone.

57 But Peter denied it. "Woman," he said, "I don't even know him!"
58 After a while someone else looked at him and said, "You must be one of them!"
"No, man, I'm not!" Peter retorted.
59 About an hour later someone else insisted, "This must be one of them, because he is a
Galilean, too."
60 But Peter said, "Man, I don't know what you are talking about." And immediately,
while he was still speaking, the rooster crowed.
61 At that moment the Lord turned and looked at Peter. Suddenly, the Lord's words 22:61
flashed through Peter's mind: "Before the rooster crows tomorrow morning, you will deny Luke 7:13
three times that you even know Me." 62 And Peter left the courtyard, weeping bitterly.
63 The guards in charge of Jesus began mocking and beating Him. 64 They blindfolded 22:63-65
Him and said, "Prophesy to us! Who hit You that time?" 65 And they hurled all sorts of terri- //Matt 26:67-68
ble insults at Him. //Mark 14:65

JESUS BEFORE THE COUNCIL

66 At daybreak all the elders of the people assembled, including the leading priests and the 22:66-71
teachers of religious law. Jesus was led before this high council,* 67 and they said, "Tell us, //Matt 26:63-66; 27:1
are You the Messiah?" //Mark 14:61-64; 15:1
But He replied, "If I tell you, you won't believe Me. 68 And if I ask you a question, you //John 18:19-24
won't answer. 69 But from now on the Son of Man will be seated in the place of power at 22:69
God's right hand.*" Ps 110:1 Dan 7:13 Acts 7:56
70 They all shouted, "So, are You claiming to be the Son of God?"
And He replied, "You say that I am." 22:70
71 "Why do we need other witnesses?" they said. "We ourselves heard Him say it." Matt 4:3

JESUS' TRIAL BEFORE PILATE

23 Then the entire council took Jesus to Pilate, the Roman governor. 2 They began to 23:1-5
state their case: "This man has been leading our people astray by telling them not //Matt 27:1-2, 11-14 //Mark 15:2-5
to pay their taxes to the Roman government and by claiming He is the Messiah, a king." //John 18:29-38
3 So Pilate asked Him, "Are You the king of the Jews?" 23:2
Jesus replied, "You have said it." John 19:12
4 Pilate turned to the leading priests and to the crowd and said, "I find nothing wrong 23:4
with this man!" 1 Tim 6:13
5 Then they became insistent. "But He is causing riots by His teaching wherever He
goes—all over Judea, from Galilee to Jerusalem!"
6 "Oh, is He a Galilean?" Pilate asked. 7 When they said that He was, Pilate sent Him to
Herod Antipas, because Galilee was under Herod's jurisdiction, and Herod happened to be
in Jerusalem at the time.
8 Herod was delighted at the opportunity to see Jesus, because he had heard about Him and 23:8
had been hoping for a long time to see Him perform a miracle. 9 He asked Jesus question after Luke 9:9
question, but Jesus refused to answer. 10 Meanwhile, the leading priests and the teachers of re- 23:9
ligious law stood there shouting their accusations. 11 Then Herod and his soldiers began John 19:9
mocking and ridiculing Jesus. Finally, they put a royal robe on Him and sent Him back to Pi-
late. 12 (Herod and Pilate, who had been enemies before, became friends that day.) 23:12 Acts 4:27

22:66 Greek *before their Sanhedrin.* 22:69 See Ps 110:1.

23:1-2 The charges raised against Jesus before the Roman governor Pilate were not the same ones that the Jewish ruling council brought against Jesus. The religious leaders felt that Jesus' self-identification as the Son of God was somehow blasphemous, but that charge would not have concerned the Roman ruler. Thus, when Jesus was brought before Pilate, they brought other charges in the hope of getting Jesus convicted of a crime worthy of death in the eyes of Rome.

23:6-7 The land of Israel was divided among several Roman rulers at the time. Pilate ruled in the southern area in and around Jerusalem. Herod Antipas ruled the northern area of Galilee, where Jesus was originally from, as well as a strip of territory east of the Jordan River. Thus Pilate thought he could rid himself of the Jewish leaders' request by sending Jesus to Herod, who "happened to be in Jerusalem at the time."

23:13-25 13 Then Pilate called together the leading priests and other religious leaders, along with the
//Matt 27:15-26 //Mark 15:6-15 people, 14 and he announced his verdict. "You brought this man to me, accusing Him of lead-
//John 18:39–19:16 ing a revolt. I have examined Him thoroughly on this point in your presence and find Him in-
23:16 nocent. 15 Herod came to the same conclusion and sent Him back to us. Nothing this man has
John 19:1 done calls for the death penalty. 16 So I will have Him flogged, and then I will release Him."*
Acts 16:37 18 Then a mighty roar rose from the crowd, and with one voice they shouted, "Kill Him,
23:18 and release Barabbas to us!" 19 (Barabbas was in prison for taking part in an insurrection in
Acts 3:13-14 Jerusalem against the government, and for murder.) 20 Pilate argued with them, because
he wanted to release Jesus. 21 But they kept shouting, "Crucify Him! Crucify Him!"
22 For the third time he demanded, "Why? What crime has He committed? I have found no
reason to sentence Him to death. So I will have Him flogged, and then I will release Him."
23 But the mob shouted louder and louder, demanding that Jesus be crucified, and their
voices prevailed. 24 So Pilate sentenced Jesus to die as they demanded. 25 As they had re-
quested, he released Barabbas, the man in prison for insurrection and murder. But he
turned Jesus over to them to do as they wished.

THE CRUCIFIXION

23:26 26 As they led Jesus away, a man named Simon, who was from Cyrene,* happened to be
Matt 27:32 coming in from the countryside. The soldiers seized him and put the cross on him and
Mark 15:21 John 19:17 made him carry it behind Jesus. 27 A large crowd trailed behind, including many grief-
23:29 stricken women. 28 But Jesus turned and said to them, "Daughters of Jerusalem, don't
Luke 21:23 weep for Me, but weep for yourselves and for your children. 29 For the days are coming
23:30 when they will say, 'Fortunate indeed are the women who are childless, the wombs that
Isa 2:19 have not borne a child and the breasts that have never nursed.' 30 People will beg the
Hos 10:8 Rev 6:16 mountains, 'Fall on us,' and plead with the hills, 'Bury us.' 31 For if these things are done
23:32 when the tree is green, what will happen when it is dry?*"
Isa 53:12 32 Two others, both criminals, were led out to be executed with Him. 33 When they came
Matt 27:38 Mark 15:27 to a place called The Skull,* they nailed Him to the cross. And the criminals were also cruci-
John 19:18 fied—one on His right and one on His left.
23:33-43 34 Jesus said, "Father, forgive them, for they don't know what they are doing."* And the
//Matt 27:33-44 //Mark 15:22-32 soldiers gambled for His clothes by throwing dice.*
//John 19:17-24

23:16 Some manuscripts add verse 17, *Now it was necessary for him to release one prisoner to them during the Passover celebration.* Compare Matt 27:15; Mark 15:6; John 18:39. 23:26 *Cyrene* was a city in northern Africa. 23:30 Hos 10:8. 23:31 Or *If these things are done to Me, the living tree, what will happen to you, the dry tree?* 23:33 Sometimes rendered *Calvary,* which comes from the Latin word for "skull." 23:34a This sentence is not included in many ancient manuscripts. 23:34b Greek *by casting lots.* See Ps 22:18.

23:16 Flogging was a form of punishment in which a prisoner was severely beaten by a whip that had pieces of bone or metal imbedded in the ends of the whipcords. It was often intended to weaken a victim for execution. Those subjected to a Roman flogging were beaten to the very point of death. Jewish law (Deuteronomy 25:2-3) dictated never using more than 40 lashes, but there is no reason to think the Romans paid any attention to such Jewish laws.

▶ GOD

23:33-49 Loss of life. It is a difficult picture to imagine. They flogged Jesus, beating Him to within moments of death. They painfully pierced His scalp with a crown of thorns. They nailed Him to a cross, and He endured excruciating agony as He was forced to push against the nails in His feet for every breath. Jesus loved us enough to endure all this torture and the sufferings of three days of death so He could save sinners (1 Timothy 1:15). There was no other way to save us except through the life, death, and resurrection of Jesus Christ. Trust nothing else to save you except the bloody death of Jesus Christ on your behalf. (***See God****> God's Attributes> Loving> God loved the world enough to send His Son to die,* TopicGuide page A17.)

▶ GOD

23:35-37 Jesus must die. To many people, Jesus' death on the cross just doesn't make sense. They think that if God was really at work in the life of Jesus, He shouldn't have had to die. Some of those who stood by watching Jesus die held this view. They called for Him to rescue Himself from death. What all these critics of the cross fail to understand is that if they had their way, there would be no way. That is, if Jesus had saved Himself from death, we would all be left to face eternal death for our sin. The death of Jesus does make sense—but only when we look at it from God's point of view. How do you view Jesus' death? Jesus saw it as a nonnegotiable symbol for how we are to live the Christian life (Matthew 10:38; 16:24; Luke 14:27). Seek to live a life that is modeled on Jesus' willing, sacrificial life and death. (***See God****> God's Attributes> Loving> God loved the world enough to send His Son to die,* TopicGuide page A17.)

23:38 Roman executioners typically displayed the charges of the condemned person above his head.

35The crowd watched and the leaders scoffed. "He saved others," they said, "let Him 23:35
save Himself if He is really God's Messiah, the Chosen One." 36The soldiers mocked Him, Ps 22:17
too, by offering Him a drink of sour wine. 37They called out to Him, "If You are the King of 23:36
the Jews, save Yourself!" 38A sign was fastened to the cross above Him with these words: Pss 22:7; 69:21
"This is the King of the Jews." Matt 27:48
39One of the criminals hanging beside Him scoffed, "So You're the Messiah, are You?
Prove it by saving Yourself—and us, too, while You're at it!"
40But the other criminal protested, "Don't you fear God even when you have been sen-
tenced to die? 41We deserve to die for our crimes, but this man hasn't done anything
wrong." 42Then he said, "Jesus, remember me when You come into Your Kingdom."
43And Jesus replied, "I assure you, today you will be with Me in paradise." 23:43
2 Cor 12:3-4
Rev 2:7

THE DEATH OF JESUS

44By this time it was noon, and darkness fell across the whole land until three o'clock. 23:44-49
45The light from the sun was gone. And suddenly, the curtain in the sanctuary of the Tem- //Matt 27:45-56
ple was torn down the middle. 46Then Jesus shouted, "Father, I entrust My spirit into Your //Mark 15:33-41
hands!"* And with those words He breathed His last. //John 19:28-30
47When the Roman officer* overseeing the execution saw what had happened, he wor- 23:45
shiped God and said, "Surely this man was innocent.*" 48And when all the crowd that came Exod 26:31-33 Heb 9:3, 8; 10:19-20
to see the crucifixion saw what had happened, they went home in deep sorrow.* 49But 23:46
Jesus' friends, including the women who had followed Him from Galilee, stood at a dis- *Ps 31:5
tance watching. 23:48
Luke 18:13
23:49
Ps 38:11

THE BURIAL OF JESUS

50Now there was a good and righteous man named Joseph. He was a member of the Jew- 23:50-56
ish high council, 51but he had not agreed with the decision and actions of the other reli- //Matt 27:57-61 //Mark 15:42-47
gious leaders. He was from the town of Arimathea in Judea, and he was waiting for the //John 19:38-42
Kingdom of God to come. 52He went to Pilate and asked for Jesus' body. 53Then he took 23:53
the body down from the cross and wrapped it in a long sheet of linen cloth and laid it in a Luke 19:30
new tomb that had been carved out of rock. 54This was done late on Friday afternoon, the
day of preparation,* as the Sabbath was about to begin.
55As His body was taken away, the women from Galilee followed and saw the tomb 23:55
where His body was placed. 56Then they went home and prepared spices and ointments Luke 8:2; 23:49
to anoint His body. But by the time they were finished the Sabbath had begun, so they 23:56
rested as required by the law. Exod 12:16; 20:10
Lev 23:8

THE RESURRECTION

24:1-10

24 But very early on Sunday morning* the women went to the tomb, taking the //Matt 28:1-8
spices they had prepared. 2They found that the stone had been rolled away from //Mark 16:1-11 //John 20:1-8

23:46 Ps 31:5. 23:47a Greek *the centurion.* 23:47b Or *righteous.* 23:48 Greek *went home beating their breasts.* 24:1
23:54 Greek *It was the day of preparation.* 24:1 Greek *But on the first day of the week, very early in the morning.* John 20:19
1 Cor 16:2

23:45 In the Temple, a massive curtain separated the Most Holy Place from the Holy Place. The high priest entered the Most Holy Place only once a year with the blood of sacrificed animals to atone for the sins of the people. Thus, the curtain represented the separation that existed between God and His people because of their sin. The tearing of the curtain represented the new access that all people have to God through Christ.

23:50-56 The Sabbath, a day of worship for the Jews, began at sundown on Friday. Joseph wanted to make the initial preparations for Jesus' burial before sundown because no work was allowed on the Sabbath day (23:56).

24:1 It is likely that the women had earlier prepared what was needed to complete Jesus' burial, planning to return after the Sabbath so they could participate in Sabbath worship without being defiled (Numbers 19:11).

▸ SALVATION
24:1-12 Slow to believe. People might think that those who lived in Jesus' day were more gullible than

the entrance. [3]So they went in, but they didn't find the body of the Lord Jesus. [4]As they
stood there puzzled, two men suddenly appeared to them, clothed in dazzling robes.
[5]The women were terrified and bowed with their faces to the ground. Then the men
asked, "Why are you looking among the dead for someone who is alive? [6]He isn't here!
He is risen from the dead! Remember what He told you back in Galilee, [7]that the Son of
Man* must be betrayed into the hands of sinful men and be crucified, and that He would
rise again on the third day."
[8]Then they remembered that He had said this. [9]So they rushed back from the tomb to tell
His eleven disciples—and everyone else—what had happened. [10]It was Mary Magdalene, Jo-
anna, Mary the mother of James, and several other women who told the apostles what had
happened. [11]But the story sounded like nonsense to the men, so they didn't believe it.
[12]However, Peter jumped up and ran to the tomb to look. Stooping, he peered in and saw
the empty linen wrappings; then he went home again, wondering what had happened.

THE WALK TO EMMAUS

[13]That same day two of Jesus' followers were walking to the village of Emmaus, seven
miles* from Jerusalem. [14]As they walked along they were talking about everything that
had happened. [15]As they talked and discussed these things, Jesus Himself suddenly came
and began walking with them. [16]But God kept them from recognizing Him.
[17]He asked them, "What are you discussing so intently as you walk along?"
They stopped short, sadness written across their faces. [18]Then one of them, Cleopas, re-
plied, "You must be the only person in Jerusalem who hasn't heard about all the things
that have happened there the last few days."
[19]"What things?" Jesus asked.

24:3 Mark 16:19; Acts 1:21; 4:33
24:4 Acts 1:10
24:6 Matt 16:21; Luke 9:22
24:8 John 2:22
24:10 Matt 27:56; Luke 8:1-3
24:11 Mark 16:11
24:12 John 20:3-7
24:13-15 Mark 16:12-13
24:15 Matt 18:20
24:16 John 20:14; 21:4
24:18 John 19:25

24:7 "Son of Man" is a title Jesus used for Himself. 24:13 Greek *60 stadia* [11.1 kilometers].

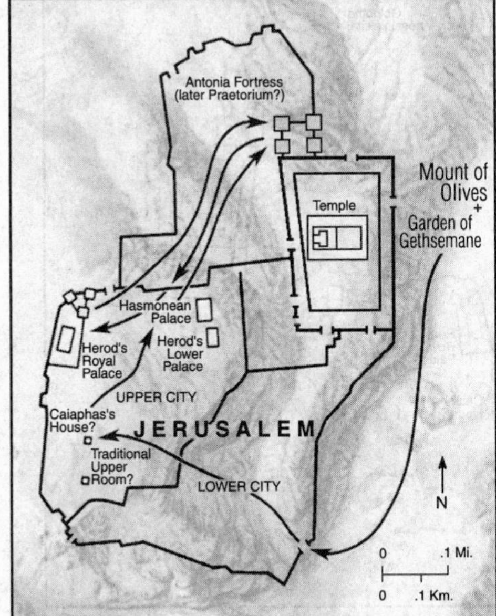

JESUS' TRIAL
Taken from Gethsemane, Jesus first appeared before the Jewish high council, which had convened at daybreak at Caiaphas's house. From there He went to Pilate, the Roman governor; then to Herod, tetrarch of Galilee, who was visiting in Jerusalem; and back to Pilate, who, in desperation, sentenced Jesus to die.

people are today. But notice how Luke described the reaction of Jesus' followers on the morning of the Resurrection. They were "puzzled" (24:4); "the story sounded like nonsense" to many of them (24:11); they didn't believe that Jesus was alive at first (24:11); and Peter left "wondering what had happened" (24:12). They had just witnessed the execution of the One they believed to be the Messiah. If He were alive, it would have been the best news ever. But they were certainly not gullible about it. And neither are we. The Resurrection isn't just a nice story; it is earth-shattering truth—even if, when we first hear the news, we find it hard to believe! (***See Salvation****> Jesus' Work> Resurrection> Appeared to apostles,* TopicGuide page A22.)

24:4-5 Although Luke described those who spoke to the women in the tomb as "two men," they were clearly more than that. The women were terrified at their appearance, and the men had supernatural insight into what had happened to the body of Jesus.

24:8 Jesus had plainly stated these things, as Luke recorded in 9:22 and 18:32-33.

24:9 Jesus had selected 12 disciples, but the number was now 11, since Judas Iscariot had betrayed Jesus and then killed himself (Luke 22:47-48; see also Matthew 27:1-5).

24:13-34 Jesus' postresurrection visit with His people gives insights into how He intended His people to explain His person and ministry. In this situation, Jesus quizzed them as to what they knew about Him, and then, starting in the Old Testament, He explained all that it said about Him (24:27). Only afterward did Jesus reveal Himself to them (24:30-31).

"The things that happened to Jesus, the man from Nazareth," they said. "He was a
prophet who did powerful miracles, and He was a mighty teacher in the eyes of God and
all the people. 20But our leading priests and other religious leaders handed Him over to be
condemned to death, and they crucified Him. 21We had hoped He was the Messiah who
had come to rescue Israel. This all happened three days ago.
22"Then some women from our group of His followers were at His tomb early this morn-
ing, and they came back with an amazing report. 23They said His body was missing, and
they had seen angels who told them Jesus is alive! 24Some of our men ran out to see, and
sure enough, His body was gone, just as the women had said."
25Then Jesus said to them, "You foolish people! You find it so hard to believe all that the
prophets wrote in the Scriptures. 26 Wasn't it clearly predicted that the Messiah would have
to suffer all these things before entering His glory?" 27Then Jesus took them through the
writings of Moses and all the prophets, explaining from all the Scriptures the things con-
cerning Himself.
28By this time they were nearing Emmaus and the end of their journey. Jesus acted as if
He were going on, 29but they begged Him, "Stay the night with us, since it is getting late."
So He went home with them. 30As they sat down to eat,* He took the bread and blessed it.
Then He broke it and gave it to them. 31Suddenly, their eyes were opened, and they rec-
ognized Him. And at that moment He disappeared!
32They said to each other, "Didn't our hearts burn within us as He talked with us on the
road and explained the Scriptures to us?" 33And within the hour they were on their way
back to Jerusalem. There they found the eleven disciples and the others who had gath-
ered with them, 34who said, "The Lord has really risen! He appeared to Peter.*"

24:20 Luke 23:13
24:21 Luke 1:68; Acts 1:6
24:22-23 Matt 28:1-8; Mark 16:1-8
24:26 Matt 26:24; Luke 24:7, 44; John 12:23-24; 13:31-32; Acts 17:3; Heb 2:10; 5:5
24:27 Gen 3:15; Num 21:8-9; 24:17; Deut 18:15, 18; Isa 4:2; 7:14; 9:1-2, 6-7; Ezek 34:23-24; 37:24-25
24:34 1 Cor 15:5

24:30 Or *As they reclined.* 24:34 Greek *Simon.*

▸ BIBLE

24:24-26, 44-46 All about Him. The Bible as we know it today is divided into two parts. The first part is the Old Testament, which have been the Scriptures of the Jewish people from the time of ancient Israel to the present day. The second part is the New Testament, which is a collection of inspired writings collected during the formative years of the church. Some mistakenly think of the two as separate works. You may even hear people talk about the "God of the Old Testament" in contrast to the "God of the New Testament." All such thinking is misguided. When Jesus explained His suffering, death, and resurrection, He turned to the Old Testament. The Bible is one book focused on one overarching idea: God is restoring people to a relationship with Himself through the sacrifice of His Son. (***See Bible****> Unity> OT Points to NT> Christ in the Old Testament revealed in the New Testament,* TopicGuide page A11.)

24:26 A number of passages speak of the suffering of the Messiah. One notable example is Isaiah 53. Philip the Evangelist taught about Jesus from that Old Testament passage in Acts 8:29-34 (see also Luke 24:44-47).

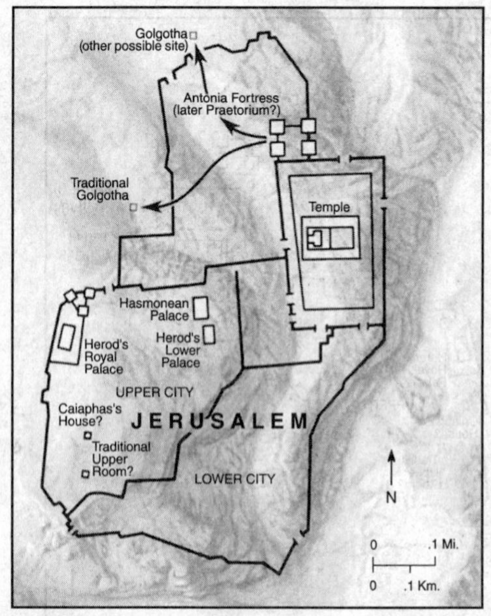

JESUS LED AWAY TO DIE
As Jesus was led away through the streets of Jerusalem, He could no longer carry His cross, and Simon of Cyrene was given the burden. Jesus was crucified, along with common criminals, on a hill outside Jerusalem.

JESUS APPEARS TO THE DISCIPLES

35 Then the two from Emmaus told their story of how Jesus had appeared to them as they
were walking along the road, and how they had recognized Him as He was breaking the
24:36-49 bread. 36 And just as they were telling about it, Jesus Himself was suddenly standing there
//Matt 28:16-20 //John 20:19-23 among them. "Peace be with you," He said. 37 But the whole group was startled and fright-
ened, thinking they were seeing a ghost!

38 "Why are you frightened?" He asked. "Why are your hearts filled with doubt? 39 Look
at My hands. Look at My feet. You can see that it's really Me. Touch Me and make sure
that I am not a ghost, because ghosts don't have bodies, as you see that I do." 40 As He
spoke, He showed them His hands and His feet.

41 Still they stood there in disbelief, filled with joy and wonder. Then He asked them, "Do
you have anything here to eat?" 42 They gave Him a piece of broiled fish, 43 and He ate it as
they watched.

24:44 44 Then He said, "When I was with you before, I told you that everything written about
Luke 24:27 Me in the law of Moses and the prophets and in the Psalms must be fulfilled." 45 Then He
opened their minds to understand the Scriptures. 46 And He said, "Yes, it was written long
24:47 ago that the Messiah would suffer and die and rise from the dead on the third day. 47 It was
Acts 2:38; 10:43; 13:38; 26:18 also written that this message would be proclaimed in the authority of His name to all the
24:48 nations,* beginning in Jerusalem: 'There is forgiveness of sins for all who repent.' 48 You
John 15:27 are witnesses of all these things.

24:49 49 "And now I will send the Holy Spirit, just as My Father promised. But stay here in the
Acts 2:1-4 city until the Holy Spirit comes and fills you with power from heaven."

THE ASCENSION

24:50-53 50 Then Jesus led them to Bethany, and lifting His hands to heaven, He blessed them.
Mark 16:19 Acts 1:4-14 51 While He was blessing them, He left them and was taken up to heaven.* 52 So they wor-
24:53 shiped Him and then returned to Jerusalem filled with great joy. 53 And they spent all of
Acts 2:46; 3:1; 5:42 their time in the Temple, praising God.

24:47 Or *all peoples.* 24:51 Some manuscripts do not include *and was taken up to heaven.*

24:35-49 Jesus' postresurrection appearances clearly demonstrated that Jesus was a real person, not a ghost or rumor. He visited with His friends, ate fish (24:42), and completed His teaching ministry (24:44-48), leaving the rest up to the ministry of the Holy Spirit (24:49).

▸ MINISTRY
24:46-49 Connected to power. Jesus died and conquered death and sin. Jesus rose from the dead and freely extends life to all people. He commissioned the handful of believers: Go and tell this Good News to people everywhere. He told them to wait until the Spirit came to empower them. From the opening chapters of the book of Acts, we know that these first followers had a unique encounter with the Spirit at Pentecost. The Spirit came, and He hasn't left. So disciples today don't need to wait before they go out. We are to share the Good News in the power of the Spirit. (***See Ministry****> Great Commission> Witness> Witness in the power of the Holy Spirit,* TopicGuide page A56.)

24:49 John the Baptist was the first to mention this promise, with the Spirit-baptism of Christ foreshadowing our own (Luke 3:16).

KEY PLACES IN JOHN

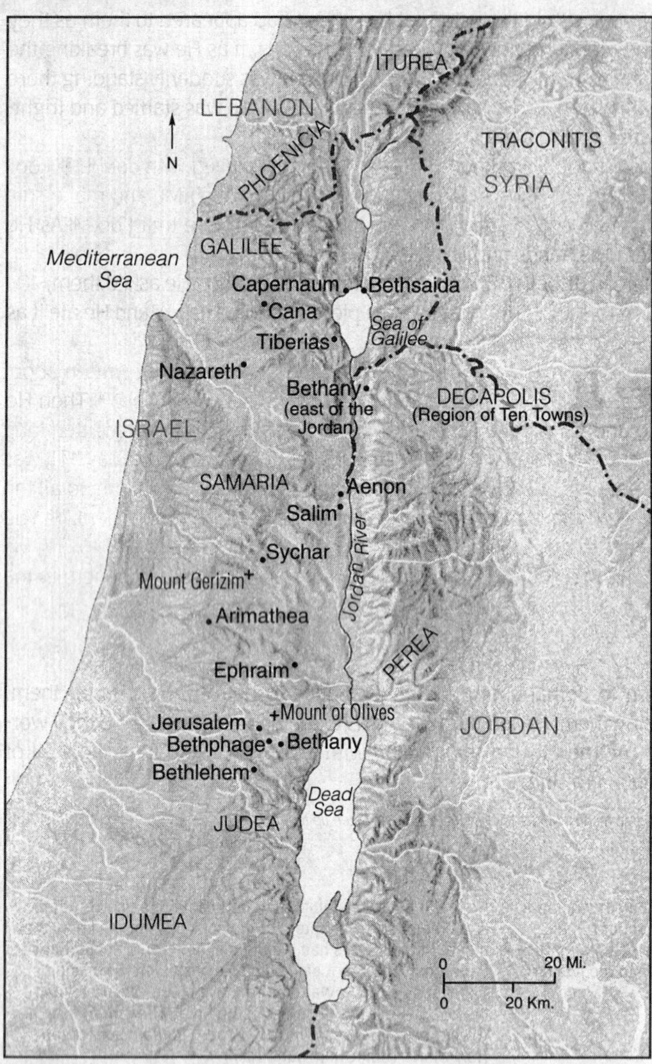

The broken lines (—·—·) indicate modern boundaries.

John's story begins as John the Baptist ministers near Bethany east of the Jordan (1:28ff). Jesus also begins His ministry, talking to some of the men who would later become His 12 disciples. Jesus' ministry in Galilee began with a visit to a wedding in Cana (2:1ff). Then He went to Capernaum, which became His new home (2:12). He journeyed to Jerusalem for the special festivals (2:13) and there met with Nicodemus, a religious leader (3:1ff). When Jesus left Judea, He traveled through Samaria and ministered to the Samaritans (4:1ff). Jesus did miracles in Galilee (4:46ff) and in Judea and Jerusalem (5:1ff). We follow Him as He fed 5,000 near Bethsaida beside the Sea of Galilee (Sea of Tiberias) (6:1ff), walked on the water to His frightened disciples (6:16ff), preached through Galilee (7:1), returned to Jerusalem (7:2ff), preached beyond the Jordan in Perea (10:40), raised Lazarus from the dead in Bethany (11:1ff), and finally entered Jerusalem for the last time to celebrate the Passover with His disciples and give them key teachings about what was to come and how they should act. His last hours before His crucifixion were spent in the city (13:1ff), in a grove of olive trees (the Garden of Gethsemane) (18:1ff), and finally in various buildings in Jerusalem during his trial (18:12ff). He would be crucified, but He would rise again as He had promised.

JOHN

PURPOSE

To teach readers that an intimate relationship with Jesus, the Son of God, is the key to life.

John writes history with a purpose—to invite people to an intimate, trusting relationship with Jesus Christ, the miracle-working Son of God. We know this because John made it clear: "The disciples saw Jesus do many other miraculous signs in addition to the ones recorded in this book. But these are written so that you may continue to believe that Jesus is the Messiah, the Son of God, and that by believing in Him you will have life by the power of His name" (John 20:30-31). John's unique portrait of Jesus completes God's message from the four Gospels concerning the amazing gift of Jesus Christ and the offer He makes to the world.

It's important to recognize that for John, faith or belief goes beyond an affirmation of truth. To believe in Jesus or put your faith in Him means to trust Him. The woman at the Samaritan well found her soul thirst quenched as she came to trust Jesus (4:1-42). A woman who was caught in sin found a life she could only have imagined as she experienced forgiveness through faith (8:1-11). And Thomas, often considered a doubter, ended up making a profound confession of his trust and reliance on Jesus (20:24-29). John presents portraits of these and many others to draw us each into a deep and abiding dependence on Jesus.

DISCOVER GOD IN JOHN

John shows us a side of Jesus that we see only glimmers of in the other three Gospels. In the unified portrait of Jesus provided by the four evangelists, John gives us a taste of the divinity of our great Savior. Jesus is:

The Word of God: John tells us that this Word of God is none other than Jesus. This means that Jesus reveals to us what we need to know of God (1:18).

The Lamb of God: When Jesus first came on the scene, the one called John the Baptist declared that He was the Lamb of God (1:36). This means that Jesus is the One who addresses the problem of sin in our lives.

The Gift of God: In an encounter with a woman at a well, Jesus identified Himself as the gift of God, the One who can give thirsty souls what they long for (4:10).

The Son of God: Throughout this Gospel, Jesus is referred to as the Son of God. He bears a "family resemblance" to His heavenly Father and shares His Father's same nature and character.

The Revealer of God: Toward the end of His earthly ministry Jesus told His friends and followers, "Anyone who has seen Me has seen the Father" (14:9). Jesus is the One who fully reveals to us what God is like.

Taken all together, these descriptions of Jesus let us know that the One we encounter in the pages of the Gospels is none other than God Himself, clothed in human flesh. To know this Jesus, is to know God.

DISCOVERY VERSES

In the beginning the Word already existed. The Word was with God, and the Word was God. He existed in the beginning with God. God created everything through Him, and nothing was created except through Him. The Word gave life to everything that was created, and His life brought light to everyone. The light shines in the darkness, and the darkness can never extinguish it. (JOHN 1:1-5)

The Word became human and made His home among us. He was full of unfailing love and faithfulness. And we have seen His glory, the glory of the Father's one and only Son. (JOHN 1:14-15)

For God loved the world so much that He gave His one and only Son, so that everyone who believes in Him will not perish but have eternal life. (JOHN 3:16-17)

I give them eternal life, and they will never perish. No one can snatch them away from Me, for My Father has given them to Me, and He is more powerful than anyone else. No one can snatch them from the Father's hand. The Father and I are one. (JOHN 10:28-30)

GROWING THROUGH JOHN

Growing to be a friend and follower of Jesus is what being a disciple is all about. Thinking rightly about Jesus and your relationship with Him is essential to that life as a disciple. John's Gospel is of great help in that regard, because we get glimpses into Jesus' own self-understanding and what that means for those who are His friends. These moments of self-disclosure can become avenues for growing in your faith and dependence on Jesus. You can learn about Jesus as He speaks of Himself as:

The Bread of Life (6:35): Bread is a metaphor for what sustains us in our daily life; without basics like bread, we couldn't live. And that was Jesus' point. For real life—the kind of life God wants for us—Jesus is the one essential. Look to Him to satisfy your soul.

The Light of the World (8:12): The only way to see things plainly is to have enough light. In the darkness, it is almost impossible to see. Jesus boldly declared that He is the light we need for life. Let Him guide you and light your way.

The Good Shepherd (10:11): Life is full of challenges and dangers. What can keep us safe? Jesus used the illustration of a good shepherd to speak of His own care for His friends and followers. He will do everything necessary to keep and guard us—He even died so that we can have life. Is your life in His care?

The Resurrection and the Life (11:25): In whom can you trust when you are facing life's biggest challenges? It would be best to put your confidence in One who can truly handle all that comes your way. In the account of the raising of Lazarus, we learn that Jesus has power over life and death by word and by deed.

The Way, the Truth, and the Life (14:6): Life presents us many options, but Jesus is much more than one option among many. In fact, Jesus is more than just the One who *points to* truth and life—He *is* the way, the truth, and the life. We find meaning, purpose, and direction for our lives in and through Him.

The True Grapevine (15:1): How, then, are we to experience this life Jesus wants for those who follow Him? It is all about "remaining" in Him. Jesus pictured this when He spoke of Himself as the "true grapevine" and His disciples as "branches." Abiding in relationship with Jesus—like a branch clinging to the vine—is the real secret to the life of a disciple.

JOHN FACTS

Author: John was one of two brothers, sons of Zebedee; he came from a family of fishermen (Mark 1:20; John 21:2). He is never mentioned by name in the Gospel he penned, but he left hints identifying himself as the author (13:23; 20:2; 21:20). John's intimacy with Jesus gives this Gospel tender insight into relationship with Jesus.

Written to: John wrote a Gospel that completed and augmented the previous Gospels. His audience was the first-century believer, who likely faced persecution and rival worldviews as Christianity spread throughout the world.

Date of writing: There are not many indicators as to when John composed his account of Jesus' life. It was likely written before his epistles (1, 2, & 3 John) and before the book of Revelation. Although it might have been written as late as circa AD 90, the most likely date was before the fall of Jerusalem in AD 70, in light of the lack of references to that cataclysmic event. This places the writing of this Gospel sometime between AD 60 and AD 70.

Setting: More than any other Gospel, the book of John pays attention to the geography of Israel. Rather than moving chronologically, often John moved the narrative from place to place, highlighting events that occurred in each location. Geography is more a means of arranging material in the book of John than in any other book in the New Testament.

OUTLINE

- **JOHN 1:1-51**—The Incarnation and Introduction of God the Son
- **JOHN 2:1–12:50**—Christ's Public Ministry: Signs and Revelations
- **JOHN 13:1–17:26**—Christ's Farewell Discourses
- **JOHN 18:1–20:10**—Christ's Crucifixion and Resurrection
- **JOHN 20:11–21:25**—Christ's Post-resurrection Appearances

PROLOGUE: CHRIST, THE ETERNAL WORD

1:1 **1** 1 In the beginning the Word already existed.
Gen 1:1 The Word was with God,
Phil 2:6 1 Jn 5:20 and the Word was God.
2 He existed in the beginning with God.
1:3 1 Cor 8:6 3 God created everything through Him,
Col 1:16-17 and nothing was created except through Him.
Heb 1:2 4 The Word gave life to everything that was created,*
1:4 John 3:15-16, 36; and His life brought light to everyone.
6:35, 48; 8:12; 11:25; 14:6 5 The light shines in the darkness,
1 Jn 5:12, 20 and the darkness can never extinguish it.*

1:5 John 3:19; 9:5 6 God sent a man, John the Baptist,* 7 to tell about the light so that everyone might be-
lieve because of his testimony. 8 John himself was not the light; he was simply a witness to
1:7 John 5:33 tell about the light. 9 The One who is the true light, who gives light to everyone, was com-
1:9 ing into the world.
1 Jn 2:8 10 He came into the very world He created, but the world didn't recognize Him. 11 He

1:3-4 Or *and nothing that was created was created except through Him. The Word gave life to everything.* 1:5 Or *and the darkness has not understood it.* 1:6 Greek *a man named John.*

1:1-18 These verses provide the reader with a behind-the-scenes introduction. This is similar to the introduction to Job, which reveals what took place in a heavenly court session between God and Satan (Job 1:6–2:6). Job never knew about the meeting, nor did the other characters. But the reader is made aware, which greatly helps the book to make sense. Likewise, John's introduction provides special insight into the unique character of Jesus, giving the reader greater knowledge than most of the characters who interacted with Jesus.

1:1 "In the beginning" is the same phrase that describes the start of creation in Genesis 1:1. John's Gospel will describe a new beginning, one that is greater than the original creation. Gentile philosophers of John's time understood "the Word" as the divine source that brings order to everything. John added to this that the Word did not have a beginning like a created thing. He (the Word) is a person who is distinct from the Father, yet He is also fully God just like the Father. The rest of the account tells about this mysterious Word.

1:2-3 The Bible says that everything comes from one source, the God of Israel, who is the Lord (Psalm 148). John declares that the Word is the Creator (see also Colossians 1:15-17 and Hebrews 1:1-3). John shows that the one Lord includes three persons that can be distinguished from one another: the Father, the Word (the Son, 1:14), and the Spirit.

came to His own people, and even they rejected Him. 12But to all who believed Him and
accepted Him, He gave the right to become children of God. 13They are reborn—not with a
physical birth resulting from human passion or plan, but a birth that comes from God.
14So the Word became human* and made His home among us. He was full of unfailing
love and faithfulness.* And we have seen His glory, the glory of the Father's one and only Son.
15John testified about Him when He shouted to the crowds, "This is the One I was talk-
ing about when I said, 'Someone is coming after me who is far greater than I am, for He ex-
isted long before me.'"
16From His abundance we have all received one gracious blessing after another.* 17For
the law was given through Moses, but God's unfailing love and faithfulness came through
Jesus Christ. 18No one has ever seen God. But the unique One, who is Himself God,* is near
to the Father's heart. He has revealed God to us.

1:12 Rom 8:15-16, 29; 1 Jn 3:1, 23
1:14 Rom 1:3; 8:3; Gal 4:4; Phil 2:6-8; Col 2:9; Heb 2:14; 1 Jn 1:1; 4:2-3
1:17 Exod 31:18; 34:28; John 7:19
1:18 Exod 33:20; Col 1:15

1:14a Greek *became flesh.* **1:14b** Or *grace and truth;* also in 1:17. **1:16** Or *received the grace of Christ rather than the grace of the law;* Greek reads *received grace upon grace.* **1:18** Some manuscripts read *But the one and only Son.*

1:12-13 There were some people that were not hostile to the light; instead they believed and received Jesus. Their membership in God's family has nothing to do with human desire or power but is a result of being born with new life from the Spirit (3:3-6). Every genuine child of God believes in Jesus and has the Spirit within.

1:14 John clarified that the Word he described is the Son of the Father, a prevalent theme in this Gospel (for example, 8:28-42). The words "one and only Son" mean that this person is the "unique, one-of-a-kind Son" (just as Isaac was Abraham's only son even though he also had Ishmael; see Hebrews 11:17). This Son is unique in that He never had a beginning, unlike every other son. Instead, He has always been the Son of His Father (1:1). When the divine Son came from heaven He truly became human (except He isn't sinful; 2 Corinthians 5:21). He is at the same time both God and man. No one else is anything like Him. The writer of this Gospel attests that he has personally seen this Son and knows He is beyond human ability to ever fully comprehend.

▸ SALVATION

1:14 God next door. Can you imagine what it must have been like to live next door to Jesus? If you lived in Nazareth during those years, would you have recognized Him as the Son of God? What an astounding fact—God lived among us! Even more amazing is the fact that God lives *within* us through His Holy Spirit. Paul writes, "The Spirit of God, who raised Jesus from the dead, lives in you" (Romans 8:11). What could be more intimate than this relationship, which God shares with all believers? We have more access to Him than if He lived next door. Do you talk to God regularly? Do your actions reflect the intimacy of God's Spirit living in you? Seek intimacy with Him, since He has drawn near to you. (***See Salvation****> Jesus' Work> Crucifixion> The Word dwelt among us,* TopicGuide page A22.)

MY RESPONSE TO GOD

God Talk

JOHN 1

Words are powerful. We can use words to communicate complex ideas and strong emotions, influencing the way our listeners think or feel. But while human language has limited power, God's words always accomplish what He desires. When He created the world, He used words to call all things into existence from nothing (Genesis 1:3-26).

God has chosen words as a way to communicate about Himself. Even with the limits of human language, God also wants us to use words to tell others about Him so they can come to believe (Romans 10:14). Just as the apostles testified about what they had seen Jesus do when He walked on earth, so we can testify about how Jesus has changed our lives (1 John 1:1-2). Combining that honest testimony with rational explanation for our hope in Christ will give us powerful words that the Spirit may use to lead others to Christ (John 17:20; 1 Peter 3:15).

Let us give great attention to the words we speak about God, knowing that they are powerful and that we owe it to God to speak accurately of Him and His will for humanity.

THE TESTIMONY OF JOHN THE BAPTIST

1:19-28 //Matt 3:1-12 //Mark 1:2-8 //Luke 3:1-16
1:20 Luke 3:15 John 3:28
1:21 Deut 18:15 Mal 4:5 Matt 11:14
1:23 *Isa 40:3
1:26 Mal 3:1 Matt 3:11 Mark 1:8 Luke 3:16
1:27 Mark 1:7 John 1:15 Acts 13:25
1:29 Isa 53:7 1 Cor 5:7 1 Pet 1:19
1:30 John 1:15, 27
1:32 Matt 3:16 Mark 1:10 Luke 3:22
1:33 Luke 3:16 Acts 1:5
1:34 John 1:49; 10:36; 11:27; 20:30-31

19 This was John's testimony when the Jewish leaders sent priests and Temple assistants* from
Jerusalem to ask John, "Who are you?" 20 He came right out and said, "I am not the Messiah."
21 "Well then, who are you?" they asked. "Are you Elijah?"
"No," he replied.
"Are you the Prophet we are expecting?"*
"No."
22 "Then who are you? We need an answer for those who sent us. What do you have to
say about yourself?"
23 John replied in the words of the prophet Isaiah:

"I am a voice shouting in the wilderness,
'Clear the way for the LORD's coming!'"*

24 Then the Pharisees who had been sent 25 asked him, "If you aren't the Messiah or Eli-
jah or the Prophet, what right do you have to baptize?"
26 John told them, "I baptize with* water, but right here in the crowd is Someone you do
not recognize. 27 Though His ministry follows mine, I'm not even worthy to be His slave
and untie the straps of His sandal."
28 This encounter took place in Bethany, an area east of the Jordan River, where John
was baptizing.

JESUS, THE LAMB OF GOD

29 The next day John saw Jesus coming toward him and said, "Look! The Lamb of God who
takes away the sin of the world! 30 He is the One I was talking about when I said, 'A man is
coming after me who is far greater than I am, for He existed long before me.' 31 I did not
recognize Him as the Messiah, but I have been baptizing with water so that He might be re-
vealed to Israel."
32 Then John testified, "I saw the Holy Spirit descending like a dove from heaven and
resting upon Him. 33 I didn't know He was the One, but when God sent me to baptize with
water, He told me, 'The One on whom you see the Spirit descend and rest is the One who
will baptize with the Holy Spirit.' 34 I saw this happen to Jesus, so I testify that He is the Cho-
sen One of God."*

1:19 Greek *and Levites.* 1:21 Greek *Are you the Prophet?* See Deut 18:15, 18; Mal 4:5-6. 1:23 Isa 40:3. 1:26 Or *in;* also in 1:31, 33. 1:34 Some manuscripts read *the Son of God.*

1:19-25 In Jesus' day, the Jewish leadership consisted of the priests, Temple assistants, and Pharisees. They inquired about the identity of this unusual wilderness preacher, John the Baptist. He occasionally directed his message of repentance and the need for baptism toward them, a clear challenge to their authority (Matthew 3:7-10). Their direct questions would intensify into interrogations in Jesus' ministry (for example, John 8:13-59; 10:19-31; 18:19-24), and they would end in angry shouts demanding Jesus' crucifixion (19:6-8).

1:20-21 *Messiah* means "anointed one" and was a title for the expected deliverer from the line of Judah (Jeremiah 30:9). Moses said a special prophet like him would come in the future (Deuteronomy 18:15; see also John 6:14), and Malachi prophesied about a person like Elijah who would precede the coming of the Lord to change people's hearts (Malachi 4:5). John the Baptist firmly denied that he was the Messiah or Elijah (although Christ confirmed in Matthew 11:14 that John's Elijah-like ministry fulfilled this expectancy; see also Luke 1:17).

1:29 John is the only Gospel writer who called Jesus the Lamb. This title for Jesus was a favorite of John's; he used it over 35 times in Revelation alone. This particular name sets the stage for John's presentation of Jesus as God's sacrifice, the Lamb sent from heaven to die in our place (see John 19:36, which refers to the sacrifice of the Passover lamb in Exodus 12:46).

▶ BIBLE

1:29 The sacrificial lamb. When we read this verse and think about lambs, our thoughts generally turn to pictures of a cute, woolly creature romping over a lush field. But the Jews of Jesus' day would have visualized a very different image. Every year, they saw many lambs slaughtered in the Temple as a symbol of the need for blood to be shed for their sins. When John the Baptist called Jesus the Lamb of God, he was referring to this bloody sacrifice in the Temple. Isaiah prophesied of the Messiah, "He was led like a lamb to the slaughter" (Isaiah 53:7). We deserve to be slaughtered for our sins, but Jesus Christ took that penalty, bearing the wrath of God for us. Live by faith in Christ's surrender to the curse of the cross and you'll find forgiveness easier to give and to receive (Romans 1:16-17). (***See Bible***> *Unity> OT Types> Lamb,* TopicGuide page A11.)

THE FIRST DISCIPLES

35The following day John was again standing with two of his disciples. 36As Jesus walked
by, John looked at Him and declared, "Look! There is the Lamb of God!" 37When John's
two disciples heard this, they followed Jesus.
38Jesus looked around and saw them following. "What do you want?" He asked them.
They replied, "Rabbi" (which means "Teacher"), "where are You staying?"
39"Come and see," He said. It was about four o'clock in the afternoon when they went with
Him to the place where He was staying, and they remained with Him the rest of the day.
40Andrew, Simon Peter's brother, was one of these men who heard what John said and
then followed Jesus. 41Andrew went to find his brother, Simon, and told him, "We have
found the Messiah" (which means "Christ"*).
42Then Andrew brought Simon to meet Jesus. Looking intently at Simon, Jesus said,
"Your name is Simon, son of John—but you will be called Cephas" (which means "Peter"*).
43The next day Jesus decided to go to Galilee. He found Philip and said to him, "Come,
follow Me." 44Philip was from Bethsaida, Andrew and Peter's hometown.
45Philip went to look for Nathanael and told him, "We have found the very person
Moses* and the prophets wrote about! His name is Jesus, the son of Joseph from Nazareth."
46"Nazareth!" exclaimed Nathanael. "Can anything good come from Nazareth?"
"Come and see for yourself," Philip replied.
47As they approached, Jesus said, "Now here is a genuine son of Israel—a man of com-
plete integrity."
48"How do You know about me?" Nathanael asked.
Jesus replied, "I could see you under the fig tree before Philip found you."
49Then Nathanael exclaimed, "Rabbi, You are the Son of God—the King of Israel!"
50Jesus asked him, "Do you believe this just because I told you I had seen you under the
fig tree? You will see greater things than this." 51Then He said, "I tell you the truth, you will
all see heaven open and the angels of God going up and down on the Son of Man, the
One who is the stairway between heaven and earth.*"

THE WEDDING AT CANA

2 The next day* there was a wedding celebration in the village of Cana in Galilee.
Jesus' mother was there, 2and Jesus and His disciples were also invited to the cele-
bration. 3The wine supply ran out during the festivities, so Jesus' mother told Him, "They
have no more wine."
4"Dear woman, that's not our problem," Jesus replied. "My time has not yet come."
5But His mother told the servants, "Do whatever He tells you."
6Standing nearby were six stone water jars, used for Jewish ceremonial washing. Each

1:40 Matt 4:18-22; Mark 1:16; Luke 5:2-11
1:41 Ps 2:2; John 4:25
1:42 Matt 16:18; 1 Cor 15:5; 1 Pet 2:5
1:43 John 6:5-6; 12:20-22
1:45 Gen 3:15; Num 21:8-9; 24:17; Deut 18:15, 18; Isa 4:2; 7:14; 9:1-2, 6-7; 11:1-10; 22:22-24; 32:1-4; 35:5-6; 40:3-11; 42:1-9; 49:1-10; 52:10, 13; 53:1-12; 61:1-2; Jer 23:5-6; 30:9; Ezek 34:23-24; 37:24-25
1:49 2 Sam 7:14; Ps 2:2; John 1:34; 20:31
1:51 Gen 28:12
2:1 John 1:35, 43
2:4 John 7:30; 8:20
2:6 Mark 7:3-4; John 3:25

1:41 *Messiah* (a Hebrew term) and *Christ* (a Greek term) both mean "the anointed one." 1:42 The names *Cephas* (from Aramaic) and *Peter* (from Greek) both mean "rock." 1:45 Greek *Moses in the law.* 1:51 Greek *going up and down on the Son of Man;* see Gen 28:10-17. "Son of Man" is a title Jesus used for Himself. 2:1 Greek *On the third day,* see 1:35, 43.

1:45-46 Joseph and his family fled for safety from Bethlehem to Egypt. They later settled in Nazareth, a town in Galilee, where Jesus was raised (Matthew 2:13, 19-23). The religious leaders in Jerusalem were skeptical about people from this outer region since they often mixed with foreigners in marriage and religion. This negative conception of Galilee surfaced again later in Jesus' ministry (7:52).

1:51 Throughout his ministry, Jesus explained how He was the fulfillment of many Old Testament images (see also 2:19-22; 6:32-35). Here Jesus referred to Jacob's dream of a ladder that extended from earth to heaven (see NLT textual note). Jesus is the link between heaven and earth, the only way that people on earth will go to heaven (14:6). Jesus spoke of His firsthand knowledge of heaven and His impending return there (6:33, 62; 8:38; 16:5). Jesus is both human and God, a perfect mediator to unite people to God once again (1 Timothy 2:5).

2:1-12 Jesus performed His first sign at a wedding in Cana by turning water into wine. In Jewish culture, an overabundance of wine was a symbol of blessing from God (Genesis 49:11; Deuteronomy 33:28). This miracle showed that the promised age of blessing had come in Jesus.

2:1-2 Wedding feasts in biblical times could involve many people and extend for several days after the formal ceremony.

could hold twenty to thirty gallons.* 7Jesus told the servants, "Fill the jars with water."
When the jars had been filled, 8He said, "Now dip some out, and take it to the master of
ceremonies." So the servants followed His instructions.
2:9 John 4:46 9When the master of ceremonies tasted the water that was now wine, not knowing
where it had come from (though, of course, the servants knew), he called the bridegroom
over. 10"A host always serves the best wine first," he said. "Then, when everyone has had a
lot to drink, he brings out the less expensive wine. But you have kept the best until now!"
2:11 John 2:23; 3:2; 4:54; 6:14; 11:47; 12:37 11This miraculous sign at Cana in Galilee was the first time Jesus revealed His glory. And
His disciples believed in Him.
2:12 Matt 12:46-50 12After the wedding He went to Capernaum for a few days with His mother, His brothers,
and His disciples.

JESUS CLEARS THE TEMPLE

2:13-22 //Matt 21:12-17 //Mark 11:15-19 //Luke 19:45-48 13It was nearly time for the Jewish Passover celebration, so Jesus went to Jerusalem. 14In
the Temple area He saw merchants selling cattle, sheep, and doves for sacrifices; He also
saw dealers at tables exchanging foreign money. 15Jesus made a whip from some ropes
2:13 Deut 16:1-6 John 6:4; 11:55 and chased them all out of the Temple. He drove out the sheep and cattle, scattered the
money changers' coins over the floor, and turned over their tables. 16Then, going over to
2:16 Luke 2:49 the people who sold doves, He told them, "Get these things out of here. Stop turning My
Father's house into a marketplace!"
2:17 *Ps 69:9 17Then His disciples remembered this prophecy from the Scriptures: "Passion for God's
house will consume Me."*

2:6 Greek *2 or 3 measures* [75 to 113 liters]. 2:17 Or *"Concern for God's house will be My undoing."* Ps 69:9.

▸ GOD

2:7 Showing His glory. When did Jesus first reveal His glory to you? Were you in church, with a friend, or in private worship? The first sign Jesus gave of His deity may seem to us highly unspiritual—He made wine! And not just any wine, but one so good that it put all the other vintages to shame. But Jesus is like that—He reveals Himself in small ways. To the faithless eye, He seems ordinary, but to those with eyes of faith, He is extraordinary. Jesus' disciples didn't just appreciate the good wine; they believed in Jesus through this miracle (2:11). Do you have eyes of faith, looking for what Jesus is doing around you? Obey Jesus and look with eyes of faith for His works, and He will give you even deeper faith in Him. (***See God**> God's Attributes> Loving> God loves those who love His Son (and obey Him),* TopicGuide page A17.)

2:11 John referred to this as a sign (his favorite word for Jesus' miracles), which produced belief within the hearts of Jesus' disciples. This miracle signified that Jesus was the expected Messiah who replaced the ceremonial washing of John's baptism (John 1:26) with the long-awaited abundant wine of His Kingdom (see Isaiah 25:6; Jeremiah 31:12; Amos 9:13). The bounty Christ brings appears again in the statements about the living water (4:13-14; 7:37-39) and the feeding of the 5,000 (6:1-13, 35). The wine served in the Lord's Supper looks forward to the celebration believers will enjoy when Jesus comes again (Luke 22:18-22).

2:13 Passover was an annual celebration of Israel's deliverance from Egyptian bondage (Exodus 12). Jewish feasts are prominent in John's Gospel: an unspecified feast in 5:1, the Festival of Shelters in 7:2, the Festival of Dedication (or Hanukkah) in 10:22, and three Passovers (see also 6:4; 13:1 and 18:28).

2:14-15 God hates all sin, but occasionally the Scriptures state some things God especially hates (Proverbs 6:16-19; Zechariah 8:17; Malachi 2:16). Jesus' unusually harsh action shows that He especially hated the presence of the merchants and money changers in the Temple area. This event appears to have been early in Christ's public ministry. Apparently there was another action much like this that occurred late in His ministry (Matthew 21:12-13; Mark 11:15-17; Luke 19:45-46).

2:16-17 John recalled Jesus saying "My Father" more than any other Gospel writer. The fury of the Son was aroused because of the desecration of His Father's house. The disciples saw this as a fulfillment of Psalm 69:9, which recounts the feelings of a righteous person who personally shares God's emotions. No one could more adequately represent the Father's passions than Jesus, since He "expresses the very character of God" (Hebrews 1:3).

▸ WORSHIP

2:17 A passion for God's house. It is easy to be very critical of the church. We manifest this attitude through our conversations about church leaders, through our tendency to change churches often, through miserly financial support for ministers, and through a variety of other negative actions. Jesus certainly held strong opinions about His Father's house. Without being "anti-church" or "anti-established religion," He was critical of the sinful religious practices of His day, and He expressed this in His anger at the desecration of the Temple. How would you describe your desire for the purity of the church? Would passion be an accurate definition—or do you just ignore the church? We should pine for the holy fellowship of other believers. We should ache to hear God's Word preached with courage. We should long to worship God through biblical, relevant, and God-centered music. Focus your passion for the purity of the church into good works, good worship, and regular prayer for your pastor. (***See Worship**> NT> Our Role> Mind and Heart> Fervent in spirit,* TopicGuide page A32.)

18 But the Jewish leaders demanded, "What are You doing? If God gave You authority to
do this, show us a miraculous sign to prove it."
19 "All right," Jesus replied. "Destroy this temple, and in three days I will raise it up."
20 "What!" they exclaimed. "It has taken forty-six years to build this Temple, and You can
rebuild it in three days?" 21 But when Jesus said "this temple," He meant His own body.
22 After He was raised from the dead, His disciples remembered He had said this, and they
believed both the Scriptures and what Jesus had said.

JESUS AND NICODEMUS

23 Because of the miraculous signs Jesus did in Jerusalem at the Passover celebration,
many began to trust in Him. 24 But Jesus didn't trust them, because He knew human na-
ture. 25 No one needed to tell Him what mankind is really like.

3 There was a man named Nicodemus, a Jewish religious leader who was a Pharisee.
2 After dark one evening, he came to speak with Jesus. "Rabbi," he said, "we all know
that God has sent You to teach us. Your miraculous signs are evidence that God is with
You."
3 Jesus replied, "I tell you the truth, unless you are born again,* you cannot see the King-
dom of God."
4 "What do You mean?" exclaimed Nicodemus. "How can an old man go back into his
mother's womb and be born again?"
5 Jesus replied, "I assure you, no one can enter the Kingdom of God without being born
of water and the Spirit.* 6 Humans can reproduce only human life, but the Holy Spirit gives
birth to spiritual life.* 7 So don't be surprised when I say, 'You* must be born again.' 8 The
wind blows wherever it wants. Just as you can hear the wind but can't tell where it comes
from or where it is going, so you can't explain how people are born of the Spirit."
9 "How are these things possible?" Nicodemus asked.
10 Jesus replied, "You are a respected Jewish teacher, and yet you don't understand
these things? 11 I assure you, We tell you what We know and have seen, and yet you won't
believe Our testimony. 12 But if you don't believe Me when I tell you about earthly things,
how can you possibly believe if I tell you about heavenly things? 13 No one has ever gone

2:19 Matt 26:61; 27:40 Mark 14:58 Acts 6:14
2:21 John 10:38; 14:2, 10; 17:21 1 Cor 3:16; 6:19
2:22 Luke 24:6-8 John 12:16; 14:26
2:23 John 7:31; 11:47-48
3:1-2 John 7:50; 19:39
3:2 Matt 22:16 Acts 2:22; 10:38
3:3 John 1:13
3:5 Ezek 36:26-27 Titus 3:5 2 Pet 1:11
3:6 John 1:13 Rom 8:15-16 1 Cor 15:50 Gal 4:6
3:8 Eccl 11:5
3:13 John 6:38, 42 Eph 4:8-10

3:3 Or *born from above;* also in 3:7. 3:5 Or *and spirit.* The Greek word for *Spirit* can also be translated *wind;* see 3:8. 3:6 Greek *what is born of the Spirit is spirit.* 3:7 The Greek word for *you* is plural; also in 3:12.

2:23-24 John describes the superficial faith of those who saw the signs and were convinced that Jesus was special but failed to establish a trusting commitment to Him. John 6:14 shows us how the crowd saw the feeding of the 5,000 and professed belief that Jesus was the expected Prophet. Yet after they found Him and heard Him teach, "many of His disciples turned away and deserted Him" (John 6:66; compare Luke 8:13). John wanted his audience to trade the superficial faith that is based on signs, for the wholehearted trust of a true disciple. Such disciples do not turn away from Jesus.

3:3 Jesus demonstrated that He didn't need anyone to tell Him about human nature as He moved directly to the spiritual issue that needed to be addressed (2:25). Nicodemus needed to know about a new birth from the Spirit. Without it, he could not perceive God's Kingdom or understand who Jesus was.

3:5 "Water and the Spirit" has numerous possibilities of interpretation. It may contrast natural birth and spiritual birth (1:13). Or it may refer to moving beyond the external water baptism of John the Baptist, which prepared God's people for the powerful Spirit baptism that Christ alone can give (1:26, 33). It may just be two ways of referring to the Spirit, since the Bible uses such language to describe the Spirit's cleansing (Ezekiel 36:25-27; Titus 3:5). The Greek and Hebrew words for Spirit are the same as the word for wind ("water and wind"), which is the metaphor used in 3:8.

▶ BIBLE

3:5 The entrance to the Kingdom. A popular view of heaven pictures the entrance as a locked gate located in the clouds. Saint Peter stands next to the entrance, checking the names of those who want to enter into heaven. But we see nothing in the Bible that confirms this religious rumor. The only way to find assurance of our place in heaven is through new birth—a spiritual birth. Saint Peter won't get us into heaven, and neither will our own good works. But our bad deeds—our sin—will prevent us from entering heaven. Our only hope is to be born again—by God's Spirit. Our own works can never reverse the curse on all sinners—we need Jesus Christ to send His Spirit to change us (1 Samuel 10:6; Luke 1:17; Romans 2:29). Flee from religious fables and follow God's instructions on how to be right with Him. (***See Bible***> *Unity> Kingdom of God> New birth supplies entrance to the Kingdom,* TopicGuide page A11.)

GOD AS A FATHER

WHEN YOU THINK ABOUT GOD as your heavenly Father, what sort of picture does that evoke in your mind? Do you see a kindly old man with spectacles who pats you on the back and says, "There, there"? Or do you see an angry madman with clenched fists, waiting for you to make a mistake? Sometimes our personal picture of our God has little resemblance to the God described in the Bible.

"Father" is one of God's favorite self-designations. Malachi 2:10 gives the breadth of God's fatherhood to the Israelites: "Are we not all children of the same Father? Are we not all created by the same God?" God names Himself as our Father because He has created us (Deuteronomy 32:6).

Because God cares about His people, He defends us like a father protects his children. Psalm 68:5 says, "Father to the fatherless, defender of widows—this is God, whose dwelling is holy." God is involved in our lives: "The LORD corrects those He loves, just as a father corrects a child in whom he delights" (Proverbs 3:12). God gives us great promises about His role as our Father. Psalm 27:10 says, "Even if my father and mother abandon me, the LORD will hold me close."

The New Testament reveals more qualities of God's fatherhood. Jesus says to those who believe in Him, "The Father Himself loves you dearly because you love Me and believe that I came from God" (John 16:27). Matthew 7:11 tells us that God gives us good gifts as a father showers good things on his children. First Peter 1:17 says that our Father has no favorites. He treats us all with His tender loving care. He also rewards His children when they obey Him.

Are you getting a better idea of the implications of God being your Father? No matter what our circumstances are, we can be sure that God will walk with us through each trial and difficulty. God takes an interest in every part of His children's lives. He sees us when we obey and when we disobey His Word. He disciplines us when we are going in the wrong direction. He comforts us when we are bereft. Those who know Him as Father will find Him a faithful one.

to heaven and returned. But the Son of Man* has come down from heaven. 14And as
Moses lifted up the bronze snake on a pole in the wilderness, so the Son of Man must be
lifted up, 15so that everyone who believes in Him will have eternal life.*
16"For God loved the world so much that He gave His one and only Son, so that every-
one who believes in Him will not perish but have eternal life. 17God sent His Son into the
world not to judge the world, but to save the world through Him.
18"There is no judgment against anyone who believes in Him. But anyone who does not
believe in Him has already been judged for not believing in God's one and only Son.
19And the judgment is based on this fact: God's light came into the world, but people
loved the darkness more than the light, for their actions were evil. 20All who do evil hate
the light and refuse to go near it for fear their sins will be exposed. 21But those who do
what is right come to the light so others can see that they are doing what God wants.*"

JOHN THE BAPTIST EXALTS JESUS

22Then Jesus and His disciples left Jerusalem and went into the Judean countryside. Jesus
spent some time with them there, baptizing people.
23At this time John the Baptist was baptizing at Aenon, near Salim, because there was
plenty of water there; and people kept coming to him for baptism. 24(This was before John
was thrown into prison.) 25A debate broke out between John's disciples and a certain Jew*
over ceremonial cleansing. 26So John's disciples came to him and said, "Rabbi, the man
you met on the other side of the Jordan River, the One you identified as the Messiah, is
also baptizing people. And everybody is going to Him instead of coming to us."
27John replied, "No one can receive anything unless God gives it from heaven. 28You
yourselves know how plainly I told you, 'I am not the Messiah. I am only here to prepare
the way for Him.' 29It is the bridegroom who marries the bride, and the best man is simply
glad to stand with him and hear his vows. Therefore, I am filled with joy at His success.
30He must become greater and greater, and I must become less and less.
31"He has come from above and is greater than anyone else. We are of the earth, and
we speak of earthly things, but He has come from heaven and is greater than anyone
else.* 32He testifies about what He has seen and heard, but how few believe what He tells
them! 33Anyone who accepts His testimony can affirm that God is true. 34For He is sent by
God. He speaks God's words, for God gives Him the Spirit without limit. 35The Father loves
His Son and has put everything into His hands. 36And anyone who believes in God's Son

3:14 Num 21:8-9; John 8:28; 12:32
3:15 John 20:31; 1 Jn 5:11-12
3:16 Rom 5:8; 8:32; 1 Jn 4:9-10; 5:13
3:20 Eph 5:11-13
3:21 1 Jn 1:6
3:24 Matt 4:12
3:26 John 1:7, 34
3:27 John 19:11; 1 Cor 4:7; Heb 5:4
3:28 Mal 3:1; John 1:20, 23
3:29 Matt 9:15; 2 Cor 11:2; Rev 21:9
3:31 1 Jn 4:5
3:33 1 Jn 5:10
3:35 Matt 28:18; John 5:20; 10:17; 15:9; 17:23
3:36 John 3:16; 1 Jn 5:12-13

3:13 Some manuscripts add *who lives in heaven.* "Son of Man" is a title Jesus used for Himself. 3:15 Or *everyone who believes will have eternal life in Him.* 3:21 Or *can see God at work in what He is doing.* 3:25 Some manuscripts read *some Jews.* 3:31 Some manuscripts omit *and is greater than anyone else.*

3:14-15 Jesus referred to an incident recounted in Numbers 21:4-9 that Nicodemus would have known. God used poisonous snakes to curse the Israelites for their grumbling. God mercifully instructed Moses to construct a replica of a snake and place it atop a pole so that those who had been bitten could look at it and live. Jesus used this picture to predict His death on the cross. He would be lifted up like this as He paid the price for sinners. All who look to Him in faith will receive eternal life, just as those who looked upon the serpent were given physical life.

3:16 The Father gave His only Son when He sent Him from heaven to earth to be lifted up on the cross (3:13-14). This is why Jesus is called "the Lamb of God who takes away the sin of the world!" (1:29). God sent His Son to be sacrificed in our place because He truly loves sinners (Romans 5:6-8).

▸ GOD

3:16-18 Does God hate me? If you are convinced that God hates you, it will be hard for you to trust Him with your life. But the Bible teaches that God loves you and has a wonderful plan for your life. The goal of God's redemptive plan wasn't to express His anger at the world but to express His intent to save. God already knows who will reject His Son, and their punishment has already been established, but there will be no eternal judgment for those who believe; Christ has suffered our punishment for us. Jesus gave everything so you could know God's saving love. Live in freedom, not fear. (***See God****> Relationship> God's Desire> God loves and wants to be loved,* TopicGuide page A14.)

3:18 The need for salvation through Jesus is universal. Those who have not expressed faith in Christ are living dangerously every day because they are condemned already (Romans 1:20; 3:9, 23).

3:26 John's disciples apparently were concerned that Jesus' rising popularity would eclipse that of their teacher.

has eternal life. Anyone who doesn't obey the Son will never experience eternal life but
remains under God's angry judgment."

JESUS AND THE SAMARITAN WOMAN

4 Jesus* knew the Pharisees had heard that He was baptizing and making more disci-
ples than John 2(though Jesus Himself didn't baptize them—His disciples did). 3So He
left Judea and returned to Galilee.
4He had to go through Samaria on the way. 5Eventually He came to the Samaritan vil-
lage of Sychar, near the field that Jacob gave to his son Joseph. 6Jacob's well was there;
and Jesus, tired from the long walk, sat wearily beside the well about noontime. 7Soon a
Samaritan woman came to draw water, and Jesus said to her, "Please give Me a drink."
8He was alone at the time because His disciples had gone into the village to buy some
food.
9The woman was surprised, for Jews refuse to have anything to do with Samaritans.*
She said to Jesus, "You are a Jew, and I am a Samaritan woman. Why are You asking me
for a drink?"
10Jesus replied, "If you only knew the gift God has for you and who you are speaking to,
you would ask Me, and I would give you living water."
11"But sir, You don't have a rope or a bucket," she said, "and this well is very deep.
Where would You get this living water? 12And besides, do You think You're greater than
our ancestor Jacob, who gave us this well? How can You offer better water than he and his
sons and his animals enjoyed?"
13Jesus replied, "Anyone who drinks this water will soon become thirsty again. 14But
those who drink the water I give will never be thirsty again. It becomes a fresh, bubbling
spring within them, giving them eternal life."
15"Please, sir," the woman said, "give me this water! Then I'll never be thirsty again, and
I won't have to come here to get water."
16"Go and get your husband," Jesus told her.
17"I don't have a husband," the woman replied.
Jesus said, "You're right! You don't have a husband—18for you have had five husbands,
and you aren't even married to the man you're living with now. You certainly spoke the
truth!"
19"Sir," the woman said, "You must be a prophet. 20So tell me, why is it that you Jews in-
sist that Jerusalem is the only place of worship, while we Samaritans claim it is here at
Mount Gerizim,* where our ancestors worshiped?"

4:1 John 3:22, 26
4:4 Matt 10:5; Luke 9:52
4:5-6 Gen 33:19; 48:22; Josh 24:32
4:7 Gen 24:17; 1 Kgs 17:10
4:9 Ezra 4:1-3; 9–10; Matt 10:5; Luke 9:52-53; John 8:48; Acts 10:48
4:10 Isa 12:3; 44:3; Jer 2:13; 17:13; John 7:37-39; 1 Cor 12:13; Rev 7:17; 21:6; 22:17
4:14 John 6:35; 7:38
4:15 John 6:34
4:19 Matt 21:46; John 7:40; 9:17
4:20 Deut 11:29; 12:5-14; Josh 8:33

4:1 Some manuscripts read *The Lord.* 4:9 Some manuscripts omit this sentence. 4:20 Greek *on this mountain.*

▸ GOD
4:4 Out of His way. In some sense, Jesus' entire ministry was a journey in which He went out of His way to show His love to us. In this case, He made a point to travel through the region of Samaria. Jews of that time typically avoided walking through Samaria, because most Jews hated the Samaritans, and the Samaritans returned the favor. Jesus didn't let those barriers of hate hinder Him. He knew about this woman who needed His truth. In the same way, Jesus went out of His way—to the cross—so that you could know God's truth about salvation. What will you do with Jesus' message of love and salvation today? Believe it? Tell others about it? (***See God> Salvation> Son> Came to save what was lost,*** TopicGuide page A15.)

4:6 Jesus experienced fatigue just like every other person. When the Word became human (1:14), He didn't merely take on a man's appearance; His humanity was real in every way.

4:11 Just as Nicodemus revealed his earthly thinking when Jesus told him about being born again (3:4), the woman could think only in earthly terms about water. It is ironic that she was questioning the One who turned water into wine (2:6-11) about how He could get living water.

4:16-18 Jesus' request quickly moved this woman from the superficial to the substantial (as He did with Nicodemus in 3:3). Jesus demonstrated that He was the Son of God by revealing facts about her life with His supernatural knowledge (as He did with Nathaniel in 1:48).

4:20 Part of the tension between Jews and Samaritans (4:9) was a dispute over the proper place of worship. The Samaritans established an alternative worship site on Mount Gerizim, a location rich in heritage (Deuteronomy 11:29; 27:12; Joshua 8:33; Judges 9:7). God specified Jerusalem, however, as the only proper place to offer sacrifices (2 Chronicles 7:12).

21 Jesus replied, "Believe Me, dear woman, the time is coming when it will no longer matter whether you worship the Father on this mountain or in Jerusalem. 22 You Samaritans know very little about the One you worship, while we Jews know all about Him, for salvation comes through the Jews. 23 But the time is coming—indeed it's here now—when true worshipers will worship the Father in spirit and in truth. The Father is looking for those who will worship Him that way. 24 For God is Spirit, so those who worship Him must worship in spirit and in truth."

25 The woman said, "I know the Messiah is coming—the One who is called Christ. When He comes, He will explain everything to us."

26 Then Jesus told her, "I AM the Messiah!"*

27 Just then His disciples came back. They were shocked to find Him talking to a woman, but none of them had the nerve to ask, "What do You want with her?" or "Why are You talking to her?" 28 The woman left her water jar beside the well and ran back to the village, telling everyone, 29 "Come and see a man who told me everything I ever did! Could He possibly be the Messiah?" 30 So the people came streaming from the village to see Him.

31 Meanwhile, the disciples were urging Jesus, "Rabbi, eat something."

32 But Jesus replied, "I have a kind of food you know nothing about."

33 "Did someone bring Him food while we were gone?" the disciples asked each other.

34 Then Jesus explained: "My nourishment comes from doing the will of God, who sent Me, and from finishing His work. 35 You know the saying, 'Four months between planting and harvest.' But I say, wake up and look around. The fields are already ripe* for harvest. 36 The harvesters are paid good wages, and the fruit they harvest is people brought to eternal life. What joy awaits both the planter and the harvester alike! 37 You know the saying, 'One plants and another harvests.' And it's true. 38 I sent you to harvest where you didn't plant; others had already done the work, and now you will get to gather the harvest."

MANY SAMARITANS BELIEVE

39 Many Samaritans from the village believed in Jesus because the woman had said, "He told me everything I ever did!" 40 When they came out to see Him, they begged Him to stay in their village. So He stayed for two days, 41 long enough for many more to hear His message and believe. 42 Then they said to the woman, "Now we believe, not just because of what you told us, but because we have heard Him ourselves. Now we know that He is indeed the Savior of the world."

4:21 Mal 1:11; 1 Tim 2:8
4:22 2 Kgs 17:28-41; Isa 2:3; Rom 3:1-2; 9:4-5
4:23-24 2 Cor 3:17-18; Phil 3:3
4:25 Deut 18:15
4:26 Mark 14:61-62; John 9:37
4:29 Matt 9:37; John 7:26
4:34 John 5:30, 36; 6:38; 17:4
4:35 Matt 9:37; Luke 10:2
4:37 Job 31:8; Mic 6:15
4:42 Luke 2:11; 1 Jn 4:14

4:26 Or *"The 'I AM' is here"*; or *"I am the LORD"*; Greek reads *"I am, the One speaking to you."* See Exod 3:14. 4:35 Greek *white.*

4:22 God blessed the Jews with the Scriptures and the promise that salvation through the Messiah would come through them (Romans 3:2; 9:4-5).

4:23 The word "spirit" may refer to the unseen inner part of humans, or it may refer to the Holy Spirit. If the human spirit is intended, then the emphasis is on worship that is internal rather than external. This concurs with Jesus' point that the external rituals of Temple worship in Jerusalem would soon disappear (4:21). If the Holy Spirit is intended, then the emphasis is on the Spirit's presence inside believers, which characterizes worship in the new age (Philippians 3:3). The Father actively pursues sincere worshipers who will praise His Son in the power of the Spirit.

4:24 This verse may be saying that God's nature is spiritual, meaning He is invisible and not composed of created matter (1 Timothy 1:17). God's spiritual nature cannot be contained, thus Solomon said, "Not even the highest heavens can contain Him! So who am I to consider building a Temple for Him?" (2 Chronicles 2:6). Since God is Spirit, He is above limitations of space and can be in more than one place at any given time. Alternatively, this verse could be stating that God is the Spirit, emphasizing that the Holy Spirit's presence with us is God with us, and now the Holy Spirit actively manifests Himself in the life of every believer (Acts 2).

4:25-26 Jesus' identity, as understood by the woman, had progressively moved from Jew to prophet to Messiah. The woman was privileged to hear Jesus make such an open identification, for He often avoided the title Messiah because of the political misconceptions of the Jews (see Mark 8:29-30; Luke 4:41). In Samaria, however, He was far away from the tension with the Jewish leaders and could speak freely.

▸ HOLINESS

4:34 Energized by work. Do you feel tired? Are you always busy? Do you wonder if you'll ever finish your endless projects? We all have met people who live to work; perhaps you yourself are such a person. But God wants more to overflow from our lives than what we produce through our vocations. Even though Jesus was busy with traveling and eating and other pedestrian activities of the first century, He said He existed to do God's will. Obeying God through serving others is much more satisfying than anything else we can do, and it's the only work we can do on earth that is guaranteed to fill us up, not drain us. Be filled with the joy that comes from committing to do the will of God. (***See Holiness**> Disciplines> Of Engagement> Service,* TopicGuide page A42.)

JESUS HEALS AN OFFICIAL'S SON

4:43-54 [43]At the end of the two days, Jesus went on to Galilee. [44]He Himself had said that a
//Matt 8:5-13 prophet is not honored in his own hometown. [45]Yet the Galileans welcomed Him, for they
//Luke 7:1-10 had been in Jerusalem at the Passover celebration and had seen everything He did there.
4:44 Matt 13:57 [46]As He traveled through Galilee, He came to Cana, where He had turned the water into
Luke 4:24 wine. There was a government official in nearby Capernaum whose son was very sick.
4:45 [47]When he heard that Jesus had come from Judea to Galilee, he went and begged Jesus to
John 2:23 come to Capernaum to heal his son, who was about to die.
4:46 [48]Jesus asked, "Will you never believe in Me unless you see miraculous signs and
John 2:1-11 wonders?"
4:48 1 Cor 1:22 [49]The official pleaded, "Lord, please come now before my little boy dies."
4:50 [50]Then Jesus told him, "Go back home. Your son will live!" And the man believed what
Matt 8:13 Jesus said and started home.
Mark 7:29 [51]While the man was on his way, some of his servants met him with the news that his
son was alive and well. [52]He asked them when the boy had begun to get better, and they
4:53 replied, "Yesterday afternoon at one o'clock his fever suddenly disappeared!" [53]Then the
Acts 11:14; 16:14-15 father realized that that was the very time Jesus had told him, "Your son will live." And he
4:54 and his entire household believed in Jesus. [54]This was the second miraculous sign Jesus
John 2:11 did in Galilee after coming from Judea.

JESUS HEALS A LAME MAN

5:1 **5** Afterward Jesus returned to Jerusalem for one of the Jewish holy days. [2]Inside the
Lev 23:1-2 Deut 16:1 city, near the Sheep Gate, was the pool of Bethesda,* with five covered porches.
John 2:13 [3]Crowds of sick people—blind, lame, or paralyzed—lay on the porches.* [5]One of the men
5:2 lying there had been sick for thirty-eight years. [6]When Jesus saw him and knew he had
Neh 3:1; 12:39 been ill for a long time, He asked him, "Would you like to get well?"
5:8 [7]"I can't, sir," the sick man said, "for I have no one to put me into the pool when the wa-
Matt 9:6 Mark 2:11 ter bubbles up. Someone else always gets there ahead of me."
Luke 5:24 [8]Jesus told him, "Stand up, pick up your mat, and walk!"
[9]Instantly, the man was healed! He rolled up his sleeping mat and began walking! But
5:10 this miracle happened on the Sabbath, [10]so the Jewish leaders objected. They said to the
Neh 13:15-20 man who was cured, "You can't work on the Sabbath! The law doesn't allow you to carry
Jer 17:21 Matt 12:2 that sleeping mat!"

5:2 Other manuscripts read *Beth-zatha;* still others read *Bethsaida.* 5:3 Some manuscripts add an expanded conclusion to verse 3 and all of verse 4: *waiting for a certain movement of the water, [4]for an angel of the Lord came from time to time and stirred up the water. And the first person to step in after the water was stirred was healed of whatever disease he had.*

4:43-54 The sign-seeking crowd in Galilee and an official seeking healing provided an opportunity for Jesus to address superficial faith. In contrast to the reactionary "faith" of the Galileans that was sparked by the sight of Jesus' miracles and quickly faded, the official demonstrated a genuine, deep faith when Jesus pronounced the healing of his son. The resulting salvation of his family is recounted here to motivate other households to respond with similar faith.

4:53-54 This second sign resulted in widespread expressions of faith. We see a pattern of entire households coming to faith during the early church's ministry (see Acts 11:14-17; 16:14-15, 31-34; 18:8).

5:1-30 The healing of a man on the Sabbath raised questions about Jesus' authority and provided a setting for Him to explain the special union He has with the Father. By recording this foundational teaching about Jesus, John hoped to help his readers place their faith in Jesus the Messiah, the Son of God (20:31).

5:1 Jesus' return to Jerusalem would be marked by an increase in opposition from the Jewish leaders. Such opposition is prominent in this chapter and would increase throughout His ministry.

▸ WORSHIP

5:10 Against the rules. Can you picture those dour-faced religious leaders watching Jesus heal a lame man? They certainly didn't participate in the joy of that holy moment. And they surely didn't accept the significance of the sign—it proved that Jesus was the Son of God. They missed the meaning of the event because they were wrapped up in their own rules—the keeping of the Sabbath had become more important than the welfare of God's people. But before you wag your finger at these religious leaders, how many times have you let your personal rules impede someone's welfare? How often have you let your rules keep you from rejoicing with God's people? Don't fall into the trap that ensnared the religious leaders: Love people more than policy. (***See Worship****> NT> Fellowship> Nature> God lives in us as we love each other,* TopicGuide page A31.)

[11]But he replied, "The man who healed me told me, 'Pick up your mat and walk.'"

[12]"Who said such a thing as that?" they demanded.

[13]The man didn't know, for Jesus had disappeared into the crowd. [14]But afterward Jesus found him in the Temple and told him, "Now you are well; so stop sinning, or something even worse may happen to you." [15]Then the man went and told the Jewish leaders that it was Jesus who had healed him.

JESUS CLAIMS TO BE THE SON OF GOD

[16]So the Jewish leaders began harassing* Jesus for breaking the Sabbath rules. [17]But Jesus replied, "My Father is always working, and so am I." [18]So the Jewish leaders tried all the harder to find a way to kill Him. For He not only broke the Sabbath, He called God His Father, thereby making Himself equal with God.

[19]So Jesus explained, "I tell you the truth, the Son can do nothing by Himself. He does only what He sees the Father doing. Whatever the Father does, the Son also does. [20]For the Father loves the Son and shows Him everything He is doing. In fact, the Father will show Him how to do even greater works than healing this man. Then you will truly be astonished. [21]For just as the Father gives life to those He raises from the dead, so the Son gives life to anyone He wants. [22]In addition, the Father judges no one. Instead, He has given the Son absolute authority to judge, [23]so that everyone will honor the Son, just as they honor the Father. Anyone who does not honor the Son is certainly not honoring the Father who sent Him.

[24]"I tell you the truth, those who listen to My message and believe in God who sent Me have eternal life. They will never be condemned for their sins, but they have already passed from death into life.

[25]"And I assure you that the time is coming, indeed it's here now, when the dead will hear My voice—the voice of the Son of God. And those who listen will live. [26]The Father has life in Himself, and He has granted that same life-giving power to His Son. [27]And He has given Him authority to judge everyone because He is the Son of Man.* [28]Don't be so surprised! Indeed, the time is coming when all the dead in their graves will hear the voice

5:14 John 8:11
5:17 John 9:4; 14:10
5:18 John 1:1, 18; 10:30, 33; 20:28 Phil 2:6 Titus 2:13 2 Pet 1:1 1 Jn 5:21
5:19 John 8:28; 12:49; 14:10
5:21 John 11:25
5:22 John 3:17; 5:27
5:23 1 Jn 2:23
5:24 John 3:15; 20:30-31 1 Jn 3:14; 5:13
5:25 John 4:21; 6:63, 68
5:26 John 1:4; 6:57 1 Jn 5:11-12
5:27 John 9:39 Acts 10:42; 17:31

5:16 Or *persecuting.* **5:27** "Son of Man" is a title Jesus used for Himself.

5:14 Jesus did not say the man's sin caused the illness. Sometimes illness is directly linked to a particular sin (2 Chronicles 26:19-20; 1 Corinthians 11:30) and sometimes it is not (John 9:3). The main point is that 38 years of illness is nothing compared to coming before God on the day of judgment, since He can "destroy both soul and body in hell" (Matthew 10:28). Our sin problem is our main problem.

5:18 The Jewish leaders understood what it meant for Jesus to call God "My Father" and to assert that His work completely coincided with the Father's. This was, in their eyes, unforgivable blasphemy and the reason for the rapid move from persecution (5:16) to a desire for murder. On two other occasions, Jesus made similar claims and elicited the same response (8:58-59; 10:30-31). Eventually the leaders would devise a specific plan to carry out their intentions (11:53).

5:22 The Son's primary emphasis in coming to earth was not judgment but salvation (3:17). However, all people will ultimately face the Son as their judge (2 Corinthians 5:10). Jesus is the Lamb on the throne (Revelation 5:6) who performs both roles: Savior and Judge.

▸ADOPTION
5:24 Eternal life. How long is eternal life? That is a question that we cannot answer, because finite people cannot measure eternity. But it's clear that it involves an infinite quantity of time and an infinite high quality of life. God gives us eternal life because we are united to Christ—Christ has the life "in Himself" (5:26). But how do we get this incredible gift? Part of the answer appeared earlier in John's Gospel—it is a free gift of God (John 3:16). But it is not separate from a healthy response of obedience (5:29). Receive Christ's gift, and then live an obedient life. This will reveal that you are already participating in the blessings of eternal life. (***See Adoption****> With Christ> Heirs of God> Endowed with eternal life,* TopicGuide page A36.)

5:25-26 The life that will be given to believers on the day of resurrection (1 Corinthians 15:52) is already present because Jesus *is* "the resurrection and the life" (11:25). Believers are already receiving a life that will continue forever. Jesus can impart life to others because life is in Him (1:4), just as it is in the Father.

5:27 In the book of Daniel, the prophet was shown a vision of a "son of man" who approached the Ancient One and "was given authority, honor, and sovereignty over all the nations of the world" (Daniel 7:13-14). "Son of Man" is the title Jesus used most when referring to Himself, probably because it both acknowledged His status as ruler over nations and emphasized His solidarity with the human race. Had Jesus used the title "Messiah," the Jews would have likely misunderstood His identity.

of God's Son, 29 and they will rise again. Those who have done good will rise to experience eternal life, and those who have continued in evil will rise to experience judgment. 30 I can do nothing on My own. I judge as God tells Me. Therefore, My judgment is just, because I carry out the will of the One who sent Me, not My own will.

WITNESSES TO JESUS

31 "If I were to testify on My own behalf, My testimony would not be valid. 32 But Someone else is also testifying about Me, and I assure you that everything He says about Me is true. 33 In fact, you sent investigators to listen to John the Baptist, and his testimony about Me was true. 34 Of course, I have no need of human witnesses, but I say these things so you might be saved. 35 John was like a burning and shining lamp, and you were excited for a while about his message. 36 But I have a greater witness than John—My teachings and My miracles. The Father gave Me these works to accomplish, and they prove that He sent Me. 37 And the Father who sent Me has testified about Me Himself. You have never heard His voice or seen Him face to face, 38 and you do not have His message in your hearts, because you do not believe Me—the One He sent to you.

39 "You search the Scriptures because you think they give you eternal life. But the Scriptures point to Me! 40 Yet you refuse to come to Me to receive this life.

41 "Your approval means nothing to Me, 42 because I know you don't have God's love within you. 43 For I have come to you in My Father's name, and you have rejected Me. Yet if others come in their own name, you gladly welcome them. 44 No wonder you can't believe! For you gladly honor each other, but you don't care about the honor that comes from the One who alone is God.*

5:29 Dan 12:2; Matt 25:46; Acts 24:15
5:30 John 5:19; 6:38
5:31 John 8:13-14
5:32 John 8:18
5:36 John 10:25, 38; 14:11; 15:24; 1 Jn 5:9
5:37 Deut 4:12; John 1:18; 8:18; 1 Tim 1:17
5:38 1 Jn 2:14
5:39 Luke 24:27, 44; Acts 13:27; Rom 2:17-20
5:41 John 12:43

5:44 Some manuscripts read *from the only One.*

5:29 Christ's authority (5:27) extends to the distant future, when He will judge the hearts and deeds of all humanity. This judgment includes works (Romans 2:6-10; Revelation 20:12-13) because they reveal the presence or absence of saving faith (Ephesians 2:10; James 2:14-17).

5:31-47 John was interested in presenting witnesses to validate Jesus' claim to be the divine Son of God. Jesus stated that John the Baptist, His own works, the Father, the Scriptures, and Moses all validated His claims. John wanted his readers to consider these testimonies and respond with faith.

5:31 Jesus showed that His claims were even supported under the law of Moses, which required two or three witnesses in court (Deuteronomy 19:15).

5:33-47 Jesus summoned five witnesses to testify on His behalf. The Jewish leaders first sent messengers to John the Baptist, who testified that Jesus was the Lamb of God, who takes away the sin of the world (1:19-35). The second witness was the works of Jesus (NLT translates "works" as "My teachings and My miracles")—Jesus did "miraculous signs among them that no one else could do" (see also 15:24), which testified to His unique power. The Father was the third witness (5:37-38), followed by the Scriptures (5:39-40) and Moses (5:45-47).

BECAUSE GOD IS JUST

He will always treat me fairly.

Those who have done good will rise to experience eternal life, and those who have continued in evil will rise to experience judgment.

JOHN 5:29

FOR THE NEXT *GOD IS JUST* FEATURE SEE PAGE 2026.

45 "Yet it isn't I who will accuse you before the Father. Moses will accuse you! Yes,
Moses, in whom you put your hopes. 46 If you really believed Moses, you would believe
Me, because he wrote about Me. 47 But since you don't believe what he wrote, how will
you believe what I say?"

5:46 Gen 3:15; Deut 18:15, 18; Luke 24:27, 44; Acts 26:22-23

JESUS FEEDS FIVE THOUSAND

6 After this, Jesus crossed over to the far side of the Sea of Galilee, also known as the
Sea of Tiberias. 2 A huge crowd kept following Him wherever He went, because they
saw His miraculous signs as He healed the sick. 3 Then Jesus climbed a hill and sat down
with His disciples around Him. 4 (It was nearly time for the Jewish Passover celebration.)
5 Jesus soon saw a huge crowd of people coming to look for Him. Turning to Philip, He
asked, "Where can we buy bread to feed all these people?" 6 He was testing Philip, for
He already knew what He was going to do.
7 Philip replied, "Even if we worked for months, we wouldn't have enough money* to
feed them!"
8 Then Andrew, Simon Peter's brother, spoke up. 9 "There's a young boy here with five
barley loaves and two fish. But what good is that with this huge crowd?"
10 "Tell everyone to sit down," Jesus said. So they all sat down on the grassy slopes. (The
men alone numbered about 5,000.) 11 Then Jesus took the loaves, gave thanks to God,
and distributed them to the people. Afterward He did the same with the fish. And they all
ate as much as they wanted. 12 After everyone was full, Jesus told His disciples, "Now
gather the leftovers, so that nothing is wasted." 13 So they picked up the pieces and filled
twelve baskets with scraps left by the people who had eaten from the five barley loaves.
14 When the people saw Him* do this miraculous sign, they exclaimed, "Surely, He is the
Prophet we have been expecting!"* 15 When Jesus saw that they were ready to force Him
to be their king, He slipped away into the hills by Himself.

6:1-13 //Matt 14:13-21; //Mark 6:32-44; //Luke 9:10-17
6:4 John 11:55
6:5 John 1:43
6:8 John 1:40
6:9 2 Kgs 4:43; John 21:9, 13
6:14 Deut 18:15, 18; Acts 3:22; 7:37

JESUS WALKS ON WATER

16 That evening Jesus' disciples went down to the shore to wait for Him. 17 But as dark-
ness fell and Jesus still hadn't come back, they got into the boat and headed across the
lake toward Capernaum. 18 Soon a gale swept down upon them, and the sea grew very

6:16-23 //Matt 14:23-33; //Mark 6:47-51

6:7 Greek *Two hundred denarii would not be enough.* A denarius was equivalent to a laborer's full day's wage. 6:14a Some manuscripts read *Jesus.* 6:14b See Deut 18:15, 18; Mal 4:5-6.

6:1-15 All four Gospels contain an account of Jesus' miraculous feeding of 5,000 people (compare Matthew 14:15-21; Mark 6:35-44; Luke 9:12-17). Unlike John, the other Gospels contain much information about Jesus' ministry and teaching in the region of Galilee. John seems to have been aware of these accounts and intentionally added descriptive information, filled in gaps, and made theological comments that enhance the readers' understanding about Jesus as the Messiah, the Son of God (20:31).

6:4 John's unique mention of the Passover represents his interest in the Jewish feasts (see note at 2:13). It also brings to mind Israel's exodus from Egypt and wilderness wandering, a subject that dominates the later part of the chapter (6:31-58).

6:11 John uniquely specified that the crowd received "as much as they wanted," a fact that emphasized that the supply was abundant (like the abundant wine at Cana in 2:6-10, and the abundant spring in 4:14). This was not a small snack. Everyone ate until they were completely satisfied, symbolic of the new age of blessing that dawned with the coming of the Messiah.

▸ WORSHIP

6:11 Jesus' prayer of thanksgiving. Jesus depended on His heavenly Father—for everything. He gave thanks for everything. Here we see Him blessing the food in prayer before anyone ate—yet we don't sense that it was out of obligation or habit, but sincere thanksgiving. In a similar way, we give thanks to God for our meals because He has provided our food and enables us to enjoy it. This prayer is a discipline we can build within our families and in our personal lives. No matter how humble or lavish the blessing, God deserves constant and unfeigned praise for His gifts to us (Romans 14:6; Ephesians 5:20). (***See Worship****> NT> Prayer> Examples> Jesus> Christ prayed as a regular practice,* TopicGuide page A33.)

6:15 Other Gospels tell this story, but only John mentioned the crowd's desire to make Jesus their king by force. They knew that Moses delivered Israel from Egypt, so they thought this prophet would be a good candidate to deliver them from their Roman oppressors. Jesus truly is the Prophet and the King (Revelation 19:16), but He is not the sort of ruler that the people of His day desired (see 18:33-37). When Jesus came to earth the first time, He delivered people from sin, not from other people.

6:19 rough. 19They had rowed three or four miles* when suddenly they saw Jesus walking on
Job 9:8 the water toward the boat. They were terrified, 20but He called out to them, "Don't be
6:20 afraid. I am here!*" 21Then they were eager to let Him in the boat, and immediately they
Matt 14:27 arrived at their destination!

JESUS, THE BREAD OF LIFE

22The next day the crowd that had stayed on the far shore saw that the disciples had taken
6:23 the only boat, and they realized Jesus had not gone with them. 23Several boats from Tibe-
John 6:11 rias landed near the place where the Lord had blessed the bread and the people had
eaten. 24So when the crowd saw that neither Jesus nor His disciples were there, they got
into the boats and went across to Capernaum to look for Him. 25They found Him on the
6:27 other side of the lake and asked, "Rabbi, when did You get here?"
Matt 3:17; 17:5 Mark 1:11; 9:7 26Jesus replied, "I tell you the truth, you want to be with Me because I fed you, not be-
Luke 3:22 cause you understood the miraculous signs. 27But don't be so concerned about perishable
John 1:33; 4:14; 6:50-51, 54, 58 things like food. Spend your energy seeking the eternal life that the Son of Man* can give
Acts 2:22 you. For God the Father has given Me the seal of His approval."
Rom 6:23 28They replied, "We want to perform God's works, too. What should we do?"
6:29 29Jesus told them, "This is the only work God wants from you: Believe in the One He has
1 Jn 3:23 sent."
6:31 Exod 16:15 30They answered, "Show us a miraculous sign if You want us to believe in You. What
Num 11:7-9 can You do? 31After all, our ancestors ate manna while they journeyed through the wilder-
Neh 9:15 ness! The Scriptures say, 'Moses gave them bread from heaven to eat.'*"
6:35 John 4:14; 6:48; 32Jesus said, "I tell you the truth, Moses didn't give you bread from heaven. My Father
7:37-38 did. And now He offers you the true bread from heaven. 33The true bread of God is the
6:37 One who comes down from heaven and gives life to the world."
John 10:28-29; 34"Sir," they said, "give us that bread every day."
17:2, 24 35Jesus replied, "I am the bread of life. Whoever comes to Me will never be hungry
6:38 John 4:34; 5:30 again. Whoever believes in Me will never be thirsty. 36But you haven't believed in Me
6:39 even though you have seen Me. 37However, those the Father has given Me will come to
John 10:28-29; Me, and I will never reject them. 38For I have come down from heaven to do the will of
17:12; 18:9 God who sent Me, not to do My own will. 39And this is the will of God, that I should not
6:40 lose even one of all those He has given Me, but that I should raise them up at the last day.
John 12:45 40For it is My Father's will that all who see His Son and believe in Him should have eternal
6:41 life. I will raise them up at the last day."
John 6:33, 35, 51, 58 41Then the people* began to murmur in disagreement because He had said, "I am the
6:42 bread that came down from heaven." 42They said, "Isn't this Jesus, the son of Joseph? We
Luke 4:22 John 7:27-28 know His father and mother. How can He say, 'I came down from heaven'?"

6:19 Greek *25 or 30 stadia* [4.6 or 5.5 kilometers]. 6:20 Or *The 'I Am' is here;* Greek reads *I am.* See Exod 3:14. 6:27 "Son of Man" is a title Jesus used for Himself. 6:31 Exod 16:4; Ps 78:24. 6:41 Greek *Jewish people;* also in 6:52.

6:21 As soon as Jesus entered the boat, the difficulty with the weather completely ceased (Matthew 14:32). Jesus' presence transformed the chaos of the deep, a trait that the Bible says belongs to the Lord alone (Psalms 65:5-7; 89:9). John is the only Gospel writer who notes that as soon as Jesus entered the boat they reached their destination "immediately," probably a reference to another miracle.

6:22-24 Unaware that Jesus had walked across the sea to join the disciples, the crowds that sought to make Him king began to assemble again. Their intense search for Jesus ended on the west bank of the Sea of Galilee in Capernaum, a place where Jesus had stayed and performed much ministry (John 2:12; Mark 1:21; 2:1; Luke 7:1).

6:27 The people had labored to cross the sea in order to eat perishable food. However, they had not exerted themselves in the least to seek eternal life from Jesus. Their priorities were upside-down (as were the disciples' values in 4:31-34).

6:35 Jesus does not only distributed physical bread that gives life, He *is* the Bread of Life. He alone fulfills the deepest longings of the human heart (pictured as hunger and thirst) for all that believe. This is the second of nine "I AM" statements, a unique emphasis in John's Gospel. Jesus is also revealed as the Messiah (4:26), the Light of the World (8:12), the "I AM" (8:58), the Gate (10:7), the Good Shepherd (10:11), the Resurrection and the Life (11:25), the Way, the Truth, and the Life (14:6), and the True Grapevine (15:1).

43But Jesus replied, "Stop complaining about what I said. 44For no one can come to Me
unless the Father who sent Me draws them to Me, and at the last day I will raise them up.
45As it is written in the Scriptures,* 'They will all be taught by God.' Everyone who listens to
the Father and learns from Him comes to Me. 46(Not that anyone has ever seen the Father;
only I, who was sent from God, have seen Him.)
47"I tell you the truth, anyone who believes has eternal life. 48Yes, I am the bread of life!
49Your ancestors ate manna in the wilderness, but they all died. 50Anyone who eats the
bread from heaven, however, will never die. 51I am the living bread that came down from
heaven. Anyone who eats this bread will live forever; and this bread, which I will offer so
the world may live, is My flesh."
52Then the people began arguing with each other about what He meant. "How can this
man give us His flesh to eat?" they asked.
53So Jesus said again, "I tell you the truth, unless you eat the flesh of the Son of Man and
drink His blood, you cannot have eternal life within you. 54But anyone who eats My flesh
and drinks My blood has eternal life, and I will raise that person at the last day. 55For My
flesh is true food, and My blood is true drink. 56Anyone who eats My flesh and drinks My
blood remains in Me, and I in him. 57I live because of the living Father who sent Me; in the
same way, anyone who feeds on Me will live because of Me. 58I am the true bread that
came down from heaven. Anyone who eats this bread will not die as your ancestors did
(even though they ate the manna) but will live forever."
59He said these things while He was teaching in the synagogue in Capernaum.

MANY DISCIPLES DESERT JESUS

60Many of His disciples said, "This is very hard to understand. How can anyone accept it?"
61Jesus was aware that His disciples were complaining, so He said to them, "Does this
offend you? 62Then what will you think if you see the Son of Man ascend to heaven
again? 63The Spirit alone gives eternal life. Human effort accomplishes nothing. And the
very words I have spoken to you are spirit and life. 64But some of you do not believe Me."
(For Jesus knew from the beginning which ones didn't believe, and He knew who would

6:44 Jer 31:3; John 6:65; 12:32
6:45 *Isa 54:13; Jer 31:33-34; 1 Thes 4:9; Heb 8:10-11
6:46 John 1:18; 5:37; 7:29
6:47 John 3:15-16, 36
6:51 John 10:10-11; Heb 10:10
6:54 John 6:39-40, 44
6:56 John 14:20; 15:4-7; 17:21-23; 1 Jn 2:24; 3:24
6:57 John 5:26
6:62 John 3:13; 17:5; Acts 1:9-11; Eph 4:8
6:63 John 3:34; Rom 8:2; 1 Cor 15:45; 2 Cor 3:6; 1 Pet 3:18
6:64 John 13:11

6:45 Greek *in the prophets.* Isa 54:13.

▸ MINISTRY
6:44 God draws them to Jesus. The Father has drawn every person who has come to Him and received Jesus Christ as Savior. The Holy Spirit convicts those who are spiritually dead, making them aware of their sins. This is the beginning of the process to eternal life. None of us would have come to God if He hadn't searched for us first. Romans 3:11 says, "No one is seeking God." Even when you were oblivious to God, He was drawing you to His side. Pray that God will draw your friends and loved ones to Him also. (***See Ministry****> Great Commission> Make Disciples> Prayers> That God would draw them,* TopicGuide page A56.)

6:49-50 Manna could not have been the true bread from heaven because everyone that ate it still died. The benefits of manna were temporary. Everyone who feeds by faith upon Jesus, the Bread of Life, will have a life that lasts forever (11:25).

▸ BIBLE
6:49 Lessons from manna. When the nation of Israel crossed the Red Sea, what lay before them were miles and miles of desert. How could this young nation of adults, children, and livestock survive? God provided manna from heaven. Each morning it rained down on the desert floor, and the people gathered it. That's a wonderful picture of what Jesus has done for us. As the Bread of Life, He is the only thing standing between eternal death and us. As we partake of His life, we receive eternal life. Then Jesus nourishes our souls. His Word is the manna we feast on every morning. Praise God that He has given us the Bread of Life! Demonstrate your dependence on Christ today by reading His Word, praying, and doing acts of mercy rather than attending to your ordinary comforts. (***See Bible****> Unity> OT Types> Manna,* TopicGuide page A11.)

6:53 A comparison with John 6:35 shows that eating and drinking symbolize coming to Christ in faith. Believers take Jesus into their inner being, just as food and drink are taken into their bodies. "Flesh" and "blood" especially refer to Christ's death, so eating and drinking means feasting on Jesus who is "the Lamb of God who takes away the sin of the world" (1:29).

6:56-57 Jesus referred to the divine gift of manna in the wilderness (Exodus 16:32) and used it as an illustration of giving Himself as sustaining spiritual food to God's people. Partaking of the bread and wine of the Lord's Supper is a picture of faith that assists us to understand our continuing need to feed on Christ by faith (1 Corinthians 10:16; see also John 15:4).

6:60-65 Jesus' previous teaching that His own body sustains the faithful offended many of His disciples. Many left, and those that remained questioned whether this teaching would prevent others from following Him. Jesus answered this objection by pointing out that inoffensive teaching is not the key to drawing people to Himself. Rather, the Holy Spirit sovereignly draws them (see Galatians 3:3; Revelation 22:17).

6::69 betray Him.) 65 Then He said, "That is why I said that people can't come to Me unless the
Matt 16:16 Father gives them to Me."
Mark 1:24; 8:29
Luke 9:20 66 At this point many of His disciples turned away and deserted Him. 67 Then Jesus
1 Jn 2:20 turned to the Twelve and asked, "Are you also going to leave?"
68 Simon Peter replied, "Lord, to whom would we go? You have the words that give eter-
nal life. 69 We believe, and we know You are the Holy One of God.*"
6:70-71 70 Then Jesus said, "I chose the twelve of you, but one is a devil." 71 He was speaking of
Matt 10:4; 26:14
John 13:27 Judas, son of Simon Iscariot, one of the Twelve, who would later betray Him.

JESUS AND HIS BROTHERS

7:1 **7** After this, Jesus traveled around Galilee. He wanted to stay out of Judea, where the
John 5:18; 7:19; Jewish leaders were plotting His death. 2 But soon it was time for the Jewish Festival of
8:37, 40 Shelters, 3 and Jesus' brothers said to Him, "Leave here and go to Judea, where Your fol-
7:2
Lev 23:34 lowers can see Your miracles! 4 You can't become famous if You hide like this! If You can
Deut 16:16 do such wonderful things, show Yourself to the world!" 5 For even His brothers didn't be-
7:3 lieve in Him.
Matt 12:46
6 Jesus replied, "Now is not the right time for Me to go, but you can go anytime. 7 The
7:6
John 2:4; 7:30; 8:20 world can't hate you, but it does hate Me because I accuse it of doing evil. 8 You go on. I'm
7:7 not going* to this festival, because My time has not yet come." 9 After saying these things,
John 15:18 Jesus remained in Galilee.

JESUS TEACHES OPENLY AT THE TEMPLE

10 But after His brothers left for the festival, Jesus also went, though secretly, staying out of
7:11
John 11:56 public view. 11 The Jewish leaders tried to find Him at the festival and kept asking if any-
7:12 one had seen Him. 12 There was a lot of grumbling about Him among the crowds. Some ar-
John 7:40-43 gued, "He's a good man," but others said, "He's nothing but a fraud who deceives the
7:13 people." 13 But no one had the courage to speak favorably about Him in public, for they
John 9:22-23 were afraid of getting in trouble with the Jewish leaders.
7:15 14 Then, midway through the festival, Jesus went up to the Temple and began to teach.
Matt 13:54
Luke 2:47 15 The people* were surprised when they heard Him. "How does He know so much when
Acts 4:13 He hasn't been trained?" they asked.
7:16 16 So Jesus told them, "My message is not My own; it comes from God who sent Me.
John 8:28; 12:49;
14:10 17 Anyone who wants to do the will of God will know whether My teaching is from God or

6:69 Other manuscripts read *You are the Christ, the Holy One of God;* still others read *You are the Christ, the Son of God;* and still others read *You are the Christ, the Son of the living God.* 7:8 Some manuscripts read *not yet going.* 7:15 Greek *Jewish people.*

6:70-71 Even though Judas continued as one of the twelve disciples, he did not fool Jesus (compare 6:64-65). Jesus chose Judas knowing he would betray Him. He repeated this fact to His disciples just prior to Judas' betrayal so that when it happened they would believe that He was the Messiah (13:19).

7:1 From the amount of time between Passover in John 6:4 to the Festival of Shelters in 7:2, we may estimate that Jesus spent about six months in Galilee avoiding the threat to His life in Judea.

7:2 Those who attended the Festival of Shelters stayed in temporary huts to acknowledge the wilderness wandering of their ancient ancestors. A daily ritual that involved pouring out water helped the Israelites remember the provision of water in the desert (Numbers 20:2-13). They also observed a solemn lamp-lighting ceremony, recalling the light from the pillar of fire that accompanied Israel at night (Exodus 13:21-22).

7:10 The timing and secret manner of Jesus' visit followed His Father's agenda, which in many ways opposed the agenda of His brothers (see 7:4-5).

▶ GOD

7:12 Who is Jesus? Everyone seems to have an opinion about who Jesus is: "He was a great teacher, but just a man." "He never existed; He's a myth." "He was man who stirred up riots and had a band of followers, but He's not alive today." The people who were present with Jesus had different opinions, too. But make no mistake: Jesus clearly claimed that He was the Son of God, the Savior of the world (Matthew 26:63-64). Find someone today who needs to hear about God's Son and tell that person what Jesus clearly said about who He is. (***See God****> God's Names> Son> Son of God,* TopicGuide page A19.)

7:15-18 Jesus' teaching was not derived from human teachers but from God the Father, who sent Him. This claim is similar to that in 5:19, where Jesus said that He "does only what He sees the Father doing."

is merely My own. 18 Those who speak for themselves want glory only for themselves, but
a person who seeks to honor the one who sent him speaks truth, not lies. 19 Moses gave
you the law, but none of you obeys it! In fact, you are trying to kill Me."
20 The crowd replied, "You're demon possessed! Who's trying to kill You?"
21 Jesus replied, "I did one miracle on the Sabbath, and you were amazed. 22 But you
work on the Sabbath, too, when you obey Moses' law of circumcision. (Actually, this tradi-
tion of circumcision began with the patriarchs, long before the law of Moses.) 23 For if the
correct time for circumcising your son falls on the Sabbath, you go ahead and do it so as
not to break the law of Moses. So why should you be angry with Me for healing a man on
the Sabbath? 24 Look beneath the surface so you can judge correctly."

IS JESUS THE MESSIAH?

25 Some of the people who lived in Jerusalem started to ask each other, "Isn't this the man
they are trying to kill? 26 But here He is, speaking in public, and they say nothing to Him.
Could our leaders possibly believe that He is the Messiah? 27 But how could He be? For we
know where this man comes from. When the Messiah comes, He will simply appear; no
one will know where He comes from."
28 While Jesus was teaching in the Temple, He called out, "Yes, you know Me, and you
know where I come from. But I'm not here on My own. The One who sent Me is true, and
you don't know Him. 29 But I know Him because I come from Him, and He sent Me to you."
30 Then the leaders tried to arrest Him; but no one laid a hand on Him, because His time*
had not yet come.
31 Many among the crowds at the Temple believed in Him. "After all," they said, "would
you expect the Messiah to do more miraculous signs than this man has done?"
32 When the Pharisees heard that the crowds were whispering such things, they and the
leading priests sent Temple guards to arrest Jesus. 33 But Jesus told them, "I will be with
you only a little longer. Then I will return to the One who sent Me. 34 You will search for Me
but not find Me. And you cannot go where I am going."
35 The Jewish leaders were puzzled by this statement. "Where is He planning to go?"
they asked. "Is He thinking of leaving the country and going to the Jews in other lands?*
Maybe He will even teach the Greeks! 36 What does He mean when He says, 'You will
search for Me but not find Me,' and 'You cannot go where I am going'?"

JESUS PROMISES LIVING WATER

37 On the last day, the climax of the festival, Jesus stood and shouted to the crowds, "Anyone
who is thirsty may come to Me! 38 Anyone who believes in Me may come and drink! For the

7:18 John 5:41, 44; 8:50, 54
7:19 John 1:17; 7:1, 25; 8:37-40
7:20 John 8:48, 52; 10:20
7:21-22 Gen 17:10-13; Lev 12:3
7:23 John 5:8-10, 16; Acts 7:8
7:24 Isa 11:3-4; John 8:15
7:27 John 9:29
7:28-29 John 8:26, 55; 17:25
7:30 John 8:20
7:31 John 2:23; 8:30; 10:42; 11:45; 12:11, 42
7:33 John 13:33; 16:5, 10, 16-18
7:34 John 8:21; 13:33
7:37 Isa 55:1; John 4:10, 14; 6:35; Rev 22:17
7:38 Prov 18:4; Isa 58:11; Ezek 47:1-10; Joel 3:18

7:30 Greek *His hour.* 7:35 Or *the Jews who live among the Greeks?*

7:22-24 Jesus revealed the double standard of the crowd. If someone broke the Sabbath to do a higher good (circumcising a child on the proper day) it was appropriate, but when Jesus did something even better on the Sabbath (making someone completely well) He was condemned. Jesus called for a proper evaluation of the facts, implying that the people were so intent on murdering Him that they were blind to the truth.

7:30 The leaders sought to arrest Jesus because He claimed to have intimate knowledge of God the Father (John 5:18). But God rules over all the details of life (Proverbs 16:33; 21:1) and would not allow Jesus to be seized before the proper time (John 7:6).

7:37 During the Festival of Shelters, a golden pitcher was filled with water and carried through Jerusalem daily while the crowd rejoiced with music and dance. The water was poured out on the altar in the Temple, likely symbolizing God's past provision of water in the desert and His present provision of water for the nation's crops. Jesus boldly stood in the Temple area at the climax of the festivities and proclaimed that He was the One who could fulfill the deepest thirst within. He supplies living water.

▸ WORSHIP
7:38 Springs of living water. One of the most glorious sights in the desert is a spring of water. Wherever water is found, it turns the soil green with lush vegetation. The air feels cooler, and the sun feels less oppressive. Jesus described believers as springs of living water—cool, flowing, and clean. No matter how barren life is around us, within us we have the source of lush spiritual growth. As we tell others about the eternal life we have with Jesus, we share that water with others. If living water is flowing out of you, people will know it and will want to know where it comes from. What will you say? Tell them what Jesus has done in your life and how they can know Him, too. Give them the chance to know God intimately and to overflow with His living water. (***See***

Scriptures declare, 'Rivers of living water will flow from his heart.'"* 39(When He said "living
water," He was speaking of the Spirit, who would be given to everyone believing in Him. But
the Spirit had not yet been given,* because Jesus had not yet entered into His glory.)

DIVISION AND UNBELIEF

40When the crowds heard Him say this, some of them declared, "Surely this man is the
Prophet we've been expecting."* 41Others said, "He is the Messiah." Still others said, "But
He can't be! Will the Messiah come from Galilee? 42For the Scriptures clearly state that the
Messiah will be born of the royal line of David, in Bethlehem, the village where King David
was born."* 43So the crowd was divided about Him. 44Some even wanted Him arrested, but
no one laid a hand on Him.

45When the Temple guards returned without having arrested Jesus, the leading priests
and Pharisees demanded, "Why didn't you bring Him in?"

46"We have never heard anyone speak like this!" the guards responded.

47"Have you been led astray, too?" the Pharisees mocked. 48"Is there a single one of us
rulers or Pharisees who believes in Him? 49This foolish crowd follows Him, but they are ig-
norant of the law. God's curse is on them!"

50Then Nicodemus, the leader who had met with Jesus earlier, spoke up. 51"Is it legal to
convict a man before he is given a hearing?" he asked.

52They replied, "Are you from Galilee, too? Search the Scriptures and see for yourself—
no prophet ever comes* from Galilee!"

[*The most ancient Greek manuscripts do not include John 7:53–8:11.*]

53Then the meeting broke up, and everybody went home.

A WOMAN CAUGHT IN ADULTERY

8 Jesus returned to the Mount of Olives, 2but early the next morning He was back
again at the Temple. A crowd soon gathered, and He sat down and taught them. 3As
He was speaking, the teachers of religious law and the Pharisees brought a woman who
had been caught in the act of adultery. They put her in front of the crowd.

4"Teacher," they said to Jesus, "this woman was caught in the act of adultery. 5The law
of Moses says to stone her. What do You say?"

6They were trying to trap Him into saying something they could use against Him, but
Jesus stooped down and wrote in the dust with His finger. 7They kept demanding an an-
swer, so He stood up again and said, "All right, but let the one who has never sinned throw
the first stone!" 8Then He stooped down again and wrote in the dust.

7:37-38 Or *"Let anyone who is thirsty come to Me and drink. 38For the Scriptures declare, 'Rivers of living water will flow from the heart of anyone who believes in Me.'"* **7:39** Some manuscripts read *But as yet there was no Spirit.* Still others read *But as yet there was no Holy Spirit.* **7:40** See Deut 18:15, 18; Mal 4:5-6. **7:42** See Mic 5:2. **7:52** Some manuscripts read *the prophet does not come.*

7:39 John 14:17-18; 16:7; 20:22 Rom 8:9 1 Cor 15:45 2 Cor 3:17
7:40 Deut 18:15 John 6:14
7:41 John 1:46
7:42 2 Sam 7:12 Ps 89:3-4 Mic 5:2 Matt 1:1; 2:5-10 Luke 2:4
7:43 John 9:16; 10:19
7:46 Matt 7:28
7:48 John 12:42
7:51 Deut 1:16
7:52 Isa 9:1-2 Matt 4:14-16 John 1:46
8:2 Matt 26:55
8:5 Lev 20:10 Deut 22:22-24 Job 31:11
8:6 Matt 22:15
8:7 Deut 17:7

Worship*> NT> Cleansing> Drinking from Christ produces living water,* TopicGuide page A30.)

7:39 John 14:17 states that the disciples had known the presence of the Spirit, but they would come to know Him more intimately because He would live inside them. After Jesus paid for sin on the cross, was resurrected, and ascended into heaven to be enthroned, a new era began (14:26). This explains why Jesus said, "It is best for you that I go away, because if I don't, the Advocate won't come" (16:7).

7:52 The Pharisees' slanderous association of Nicodemus with Galilee was intended to silence his reasonable statement. Their assertion was false—Jonah and Nahum likely came from Galilee.

7:53–8:11 Many scholars understand this section to be a later addition to John's Gospel. Many of the best Greek manuscripts do not have this material, and other manuscripts have this section in different locations in the book. It even appears attached to Luke's Gospel in one source. These facts make some people unsure about whether it should be in the Bible, even though it may be a genuine story about the life of Christ. The flow of John's account continues very naturally at 8:12, so it is possible that John did not intend this material to be placed in this location in his Gospel. In any case, we can appreciate this story of God's grace to a helpless sinner, and then move on to the rest of the book of John for more careful study.

9 When the accusers heard this, they slipped away one by one, beginning with the old-
est, until only Jesus was left in the middle of the crowd with the woman. 10 Then Jesus
stood up again and said to the woman, "Where are your accusers? Didn't even one of
them condemn you?"
11 "No, Lord," she said.
And Jesus said, "Neither do I. Go and sin no more."

8:11 John 5:14

JESUS, THE LIGHT OF THE WORLD

12 Jesus spoke to the people once more and said, "I am the light of the world. If you follow
Me, you won't have to walk in darkness, because you will have the light that leads to life."
13 The Pharisees replied, "You are making those claims about Yourself! Such testimony
is not valid."
14 Jesus told them, "These claims are valid even though I make them about Myself. For I
know where I came from and where I am going, but you don't know this about Me. 15 You
judge Me by human standards, but I do not judge anyone. 16 And if I did, My judgment
would be correct in every respect because I am not alone. The Father* who sent Me is with
Me. 17 Your own law says that if two people agree about something, their witness is ac-
cepted as fact.* 18 I am one witness, and My Father who sent Me is the other."
19 "Where is Your father?" they asked.
Jesus answered, "Since you don't know who I am, you don't know who My Father is. If
you knew Me, you would also know My Father." 20 Jesus made these statements while He
was teaching in the section of the Temple known as the Treasury. But He was not arrested,
because His time* had not yet come.

8:12 Isa 9:1-2; John 1:4-5, 9; 3:19; 9:5; 12:35-36, 46; 2 Cor 4:6
8:14 John 7:28; 9:29
8:16 John 5:30
8:17-18 Deut 17:6; 19:15; John 5:37; 1 Jn 5:7-9
8:19 John 14:7, 9
8:20 Mark 12:41; John 7:30

THE UNBELIEVING PEOPLE WARNED

21 Later Jesus said to them again, "I am going away. You will search for Me but will die in
your sin. You cannot come where I am going."
22 The people* asked, "Is He planning to commit suicide? What does He mean, 'You can-
not come where I am going'?"
23 Jesus continued, "You are from below; I am from above. You belong to this world; I do
not. 24 That is why I said that you will die in your sins; for unless you believe that I AM who I
claim to be,* you will die in your sins."

8:21 John 7:34, 36; 13:33
8:22 John 7:35
8:23 John 3:31; 17:14
8:24 Exod 3:14-15; John 4:26; 8:28, 58; 13:19

8:16 Some manuscripts read *The One.* 8:17 See Deut 19:15. 8:20 Greek *His hour.* 8:22 Greek *Jewish people;* also in 8:31, 48, 52, 57. 8:24 Greek *unless you believe that I am.* See Exod 3:14.

GOD

8:11 The mercy of Jesus. What tenderness Jesus displayed when He spoke to this sinful woman! She was defenseless before the religious rulers. She had committed a terrible sin, but Jesus put His finger on a bigger truth: We are all guilty of sin and deserve God's judgment. Haste to judge and punish was never intended in the law of Moses. Jesus was the only person in the crowd who had the authority to condemn her instantly—but He chose not to do so. Instead, He had mercy on her. He offers this same mercy to you. Humble yourself, accept His mercy, and receive eternal life. No matter what the condemning voices say, Jesus stands ready to forgive. Are you ready to receive His forgiveness? (***See God****> God's Attributes> Merciful> God is merciful to sinners,* TopicGuide page A17.)

8:12 The lighting ceremony at the Festival of Shelters provides the background for this "I AM" saying of Jesus. Each night worshipers filled the entire Temple area with light from torches and lamps, chasing away the shadows and allowing extended hours of celebration (see note at 7:2). In this setting, Jesus claimed to be the true light from heaven (Psalm 36:9) that dispels the confusing darkness of sin and illuminates the path to life (John 1:5-9).

8:15 Elsewhere Jesus made it clear that He does judge people (John 9:39). Later writers interpreted this as a future judgment (Acts 10:42). Jesus here meant that He does not judge anyone in the fallible way that people judge. He never evaluates things on the basis of external appearances (John 2:24-25; 1 Samuel 16:7). But when He did judge (Matthew 16:6), He did so in word only and did not yet carry out God's full justice against the guilty. That will occur in the final judgment (Matthew 25:31-46).

8:19 This question about His earthly father shows "they still didn't understand that He was talking about His Father" (8:27). It also introduces a lengthy dialogue contrasting Jesus' relationship with His Father to their relationship with Abraham (8:33-40), God (8:41-42), and the devil (8:44). The Pharisees couldn't grasp Jesus' unique identification with His Father (neither could His own disciples; 14:8-9).

8:21 Their unbelief showed their opposition to Jesus, thus they would "die in [their] sin." Those who die apart from Jesus' forgiveness are excluded from heaven (Revelation 21:8; 22:15). Once a person dies in sin, there is no opportunity for remedy (Matthew 25:10-11; Luke 16:26).

[25] "Who are You?" they demanded.

Jesus replied, "The One I have always claimed to be.* [26] I have much to say about you and much to condemn, but I won't. For I say only what I have heard from the One who sent Me, and He is completely truthful." [27] But they still didn't understand that He was talking about His Father.

[28] So Jesus said, "When you have lifted up the Son of Man on the cross, then you will understand that I AM He.* I do nothing on My own but say only what the Father taught Me. [29] And the One who sent Me is with Me—He has not deserted Me. For I always do what pleases Him." [30] Then many who heard Him say these things believed in Him.

JESUS AND ABRAHAM

[31] Jesus said to the people who believed in Him, "You are truly My disciples if you remain faithful to My teachings. [32] And you will know the truth, and the truth will set you free."

[33] "But we are descendants of Abraham," they said. "We have never been slaves to anyone. What do You mean, 'You will be set free'?"

[34] Jesus replied, "I tell you the truth, everyone who sins is a slave of sin. [35] A slave is not a permanent member of the family, but a son is part of the family forever. [36] So if the Son sets you free, you are truly free. [37] Yes, I realize that you are descendants of Abraham. And yet some of you are trying to kill Me because there's no room in your hearts for My message. [38] I am telling you what I saw when I was with My Father. But you are following the advice of your father."

[39] "Our father is Abraham!" they declared.

"No," Jesus replied, "for if you were really the children of Abraham, you would follow his example.* [40] Instead, you are trying to kill Me because I told you the truth, which I heard from God. Abraham never did such a thing. [41] No, you are imitating your real father."

They replied, "We aren't illegitimate children! God Himself is our true Father."

[42] Jesus told them, "If God were your Father, you would love Me, because I have come to you from God. I am not here on My own, but He sent Me. [43] Why can't you understand what I am saying? It's because you can't even hear Me! [44] For you are the children of your father the devil, and you love to do the evil things he does. He was a murderer from the beginning. He has always hated the truth, because there is no truth in him. When he lies, it is consistent with his character; for he is a liar and the father of lies. [45] So when I tell the truth, you just naturally don't believe Me! [46] Which of you can truthfully accuse Me of sin? And since I

8:28 John 3:14; 5:19; 8:24; 12:32
8:29 John 4:34; 6:38; 8:16; 14:10; 16:32
8:31 John 15:7; 2 Jn 1:9
8:32 Rom 8:2; 2 Cor 3:17; Gal 5:1, 13
8:33 Matt 3:9; Luke 3:8
8:34 Rom 6:16, 20; 2 Pet 2:19
8:35 Gen 21:10; Gal 4:30
8:39 Matt 3:9; John 8:33; Gal 3:7, 14, 29
8:41 Deut 32:6; Isa 63:16; 64:8; Mal 1:6
8:42 1 Jn 5:1
8:44 Gen 3:4; 4:9; 1 Jn 3:8
8:45 John 18:37

8:25 Or *Why do I speak to you at all?* 8:28 Greek *When you have lifted up the Son of Man, then you will know that I am.* "Son of Man" is a title Jesus used for Himself. 8:39 Some manuscripts read *if you are really the children of Abraham, follow his example.*

8:28 Jesus' identity would be proven when He was "lifted up" ("on the cross" is added by NLT; see textual note). Jesus may have been referring to being lifted up on the cross (like the serpent on the pole in 3:14) or to being lifted up to an exalted place. Possibly He intended a play on words, as if to say, "When you lift Me up on the cross I will then be lifted as Savior, and then lifted up to My rightful place of glory in heaven" (12:32). One day everyone will know the proper identity of the exalted Son of Man (see Daniel 7:13-14; Philippians 2:10-11).

▸ GOD

8:32 Are you free? People all over the world want to be free. They groan under the hands of cruel dictators and corrupt governments. Yet political freedom is not the ultimate freedom. Only God can give freedom that dictators or governments cannot take away. Many who live in freedom are still chained by sin, unable to do what's good and right. They destroy their own lives with bad habits and sinful actions. Greed, lust, envy, and pride win the day. Yet many who live under harsh political conditions experience God's freedom. They know the power of God to break the chains of sin. Be free! Turn your life over to Christ and obey God's Word. (***See God****> God's Attributes> True> True freedom comes from abiding in God's truth,* TopicGuide page A18.)

8:38-40 These Jews claimed Abraham as their father (the one whom God called His friend, Isaiah 41:8), and yet they themselves were not friends of God. Abraham received messengers from God and honored them (Genesis 18:1-8), but the Jews refused to receive the words of the very Son of God. Abraham killed a calf to feed the God-sent messengers (Genesis 18:7), but the Jews wanted to kill God's unique Messenger (Matthew 21:38).

8:44-45 The Jews lied about their spiritual heritage (8:39) and relationship with God (8:41), and they wanted to kill Jesus (see 8:59). This revealed that their father was not who they claimed, for they were acting like the ultimate liar and murderer, the devil. He hates the truth; thus it was not surprising to Jesus that the devil's children did not believe His words.

am telling you the truth, why don't you believe Me? 47 Anyone who belongs to God listens gladly to the words of God. But you don't listen because you don't belong to God."

48 The people retorted, "You Samaritan devil! Didn't we say all along that You were possessed by a demon?"

49 "No," Jesus said, "I have no demon in Me. For I honor My Father—and you dishonor Me. 50 And though I have no wish to glorify Myself, God is going to glorify Me. He is the true judge. 51 I tell you the truth, anyone who obeys My teaching will never die!"

52 The people said, "Now we know You are possessed by a demon. Even Abraham and the prophets died, but You say, 'Anyone who obeys My teaching will never die!' 53 Are You greater than our father Abraham? He died, and so did the prophets. Who do You think You are?"

54 Jesus answered, "If I want glory for Myself, it doesn't count. But it is My Father who will glorify Me. You say, 'He is our God,'* 55 but you don't even know Him. I know Him. If I said otherwise, I would be as great a liar as you! But I do know Him and obey Him. 56 Your father Abraham rejoiced as he looked forward to My coming. He saw it and was glad."

57 The people said, "You aren't even fifty years old. How can You say You have seen Abraham?*"

58 Jesus answered, "I tell you the truth, before Abraham was even born, I Am!*" 59 At that point they picked up stones to throw at Him. But Jesus was hidden from them and left the Temple.

JESUS HEALS A MAN BORN BLIND

9 As Jesus was walking along, He saw a man who had been blind from birth. 2 "Rabbi," His disciples asked Him, "why was this man born blind? Was it because of his own sins or his parents' sins?"

8:47 1 Jn 4:6
8:50 John 5:41
8:51 John 5:24; 11:25-26
8:53 John 4:12
8:54 John 16:14; 17:5
8:55 John 7:28-29; 15:10
8:56 Gen 18:18; 22:17-18; Matt 13:17; Heb 11:13
8:58 Exod 3:14; Isa 43:10, 13; John 1:1; 8:24, 28
9:2 Exod 20:5; Ezek 18:20; Luke 13:2; John 9:34

8:54 Some manuscripts read *your God.* 8:57 Some manuscripts read *How can You say Abraham has seen You?* 8:58 Or *before Abraham was even born, I have always been alive;* Greek reads *before Abraham was, I am.* See Exod 3:14.

8:48-49 Jesus' true assertion about the devil being the father of His accusers evoked their false slander. They resorted to calling Him names, revealing their hatred. This pattern of false accusation ultimately manifested itself in the worst dishonor of all, the crucifixion (19:6-7, 15-16).

8:58-59 Jesus did not merely claim that He existed before Abraham. He claimed that He is the Lord, who has eternally existed (John 1:1; also see the eternal "I Am" statements in Isaiah 41:4; 43:13). Jesus repeatedly claimed to be the God of the Jewish leaders, and they tried to kill Him for this because they believed He was lying and thereby blaspheming the name of the Lord (Luke 4:17-30; John 5:18; 10:31; see also Leviticus 24:16). However, it was not Jesus' time to die, so He hid Himself and departed.

9:1-41 The story about the healing of a man who was born blind demonstrates the contrast between blindness and sight, both physical and spiritual. The man who was healed received much more than physical sight. As the story progressed, he gradually saw more and more about Jesus until he expressed faith and worshiped Him. In contrast, the Jewish leaders claimed to have spiritual sight, but their hostility and slander toward Jesus showed they were the ones who were truly blind.

BECAUSE GOD IS ABSOLUTE TRUTH

I will believe what He says and live accordingly.

You are truly My disciples if you remain faithful to My teachings. And you will know the truth, and the truth will set you free.

JOHN 8:31-32

FOR THE NEXT *GOD IS ABSOLUTE TRUTH* FEATURE SEE PAGE 1942.

9:3 3 "It was not because of his sins or his parents' sins," Jesus answered. "This happened so
John 11:4 the power of God could be seen in him. 4 We must quickly carry out the tasks assigned us
9:4 John 5:17; 11:9; by the One who sent us.* The night is coming, and then no one can work. 5 But while I am
12:35 here in the world, I am the light of the world."
9:5 6 Then He spit on the ground, made mud with the saliva, and spread the mud over the
Isa 49:6 blind man's eyes. 7 He told him, "Go wash yourself in the pool of Siloam" (Siloam means
John 1:4-5, 9; 8:12; 12:46 "sent"). So the man went and washed and came back seeing!
9:6 8 His neighbors and others who knew him as a blind beggar asked each other, "Isn't this
Mark 8:23 the man who used to sit and beg?" 9 Some said he was, and others said, "No, he just looks
9:7 like him!"
2 Kgs 5:10 But the beggar kept saying, "Yes, I am the same one!"
Isa 35:5 10 They asked, "Who healed you? What happened?"
9:8 11 He told them, "The man they call Jesus made mud and spread it over my eyes and told
Acts 3:10 me, 'Go to the pool of Siloam and wash yourself.' So I went and washed, and now I can see!"
12 "Where is He now?" they asked.
"I don't know," he replied.
9:14 13 Then they took the man who had been blind to the Pharisees, 14 because it was on the
Luke 13:14 John 5:9 Sabbath that Jesus had made the mud and healed him. 15 The Pharisees asked the man all
about it. So he told them, "He put the mud over my eyes, and when I washed it away, I
could see!"
9:16 16 Some of the Pharisees said, "This man Jesus is not from God, for He is working on the
John 3:2; 7:43 Sabbath." Others said, "But how could an ordinary sinner do such miraculous signs?" So
there was a deep division of opinion among them.
9:17 17 Then the Pharisees again questioned the man who had been blind and demanded,
Matt 21:11 "What's your opinion about this man who healed you?"
The man replied, "I think He must be a prophet."
18 The Jewish leaders still refused to believe the man had been blind and could now see,
so they called in his parents. 19 They asked them, "Is this your son? Was he born blind? If
so, how can he now see?"
20 His parents replied, "We know this is our son and that he was born blind, 21 but we
9:22 don't know how he can see or who healed him. Ask him. He is old enough to speak for
Luke 6:22 himself." 22 His parents said this because they were afraid of the Jewish leaders, who had
John 7:13; 12:42; 16:2; 19:38 announced that anyone saying Jesus was the Messiah would be expelled from the syna-
Acts 5:13 gogue. 23 That's why they said, "He is old enough. Ask him."

9:4 Other manuscripts read *I must quickly carry out the tasks assigned Me by the One who sent Me;* still others read *We must quickly carry out the tasks assigned us by the One who sent Me.*

9:3 Jesus challenged the assumption that suffering is always directly linked to particular sins. He showed that another possibility exists and that it applies in this case: Suffering can be a part of God's plan to show His power and bring Himself glory. God can demonstrate His power through healing (as in this case) or through sustaining someone in the midst of suffering (2 Corinthians 12:8-10).

GOD

9:5 The light of the world. How is Jesus the light of the world? In Isaiah 49:6, God says of His Messiah, "You will do more than restore the people of Israel to Me. I will make You a light to the Gentiles, and You will bring My salvation to the ends of the earth." In John 1:5, 9, John writes, "The light shines in the darkness" and "the One who is the true light, who gives light to everyone, was coming into the world." Jesus is the way for Jews as well as Gentiles to find safety and find God. Today, Jesus still shows people how to find peace with God. Show people Jesus, and watch Him direct them to His Father. (***See God> God's Names> Son> Light of the world,*** TopicGuide page A19.)

9:5 Jesus demonstrated that He is the light of the world by giving a blind man physical sight, just as He demonstrated that He is the Resurrection and the Life by raising Lazarus from the dead (John 11).

9:15-16 Some of the Pharisees were so opposed to Jesus that they tried to charge Him with breaking the Sabbath for making mud to apply to the blind man's eyes. Overlooking the amazing miracle, they arrogantly proclaimed that Jesus could not be from God. Others were amazed at the miracle and wondered how a sinner could do such a thing. Jesus' amazing works forced people to make a decision about Him.

9:22-23 In such a highly religious society, to be cast out of the synagogue meant an end to all relationships a person previously enjoyed. Anyone who professed that Jesus was the Messiah could be sure that such persecution would come (Matthew 10:17; 2 Timothy 3:12). John knew that many people folded under such pressure (John 12:42-43), so he wanted his readers to count the cost realistically (Luke 14:28-33) and then proclaim Christ with boldness (Acts 4:18-20).

24 So for the second time they called in the man who had been blind and told him, "God
should get the glory for this,* because we know this man Jesus is a sinner."
25 "I don't know whether He is a sinner," the man replied. "But I know this: I was blind,
and now I can see!"
26 "But what did He do?" they asked. "How did He heal you?"
27 "Look!" the man exclaimed. "I told you once. Didn't you listen? Why do you want to
hear it again? Do you want to become His disciples, too?"
28 Then they cursed him and said, "You are His disciple, but we are disciples of Moses!
29 We know God spoke to Moses, but we don't even know where this man comes from."
30 "Why, that's very strange!" the man replied. "He healed my eyes, and yet you don't
know where He comes from? 31 We know that God doesn't listen to sinners, but He is
ready to hear those who worship Him and do His will. 32 Ever since the world began, no
one has been able to open the eyes of someone born blind. 33 If this man were not from
God, He couldn't have done it."
34 "You were born a total sinner!" they answered. "Are you trying to teach us?" And they
threw him out of the synagogue.

SPIRITUAL BLINDNESS

35 When Jesus heard what had happened, He found the man and asked, "Do you believe
in the Son of Man?*"
36 The man answered, "Who is He, sir? I want to believe in Him."
37 "You have seen Him," Jesus said, "and He is speaking to you!"
38 "Yes, Lord, I believe!" the man said. And he worshiped Jesus.
39 Then Jesus told him,* "I entered this world to render judgment—to give sight to the
blind and to show those who think they see* that they are blind."
40 Some Pharisees who were standing nearby heard Him and asked, "Are You saying
we're blind?"
41 "If you were blind, you wouldn't be guilty," Jesus replied. "But you remain guilty be-
cause you claim you can see.

THE GOOD SHEPHERD AND HIS SHEEP

10 1 "I tell you the truth, anyone who sneaks over the wall of a sheepfold, rather than
going through the gate, must surely be a thief and a robber! 2 But the one who en-
ters through the gate is the shepherd of the sheep. 3 The gatekeeper opens the gate for
him, and the sheep recognize his voice and come to him. He calls his own sheep by name

9:24 Josh 7:19
9:28 John 5:45
9:29 John 8:14
9:31 Job 27:8-9; Pss 34:15; 66:18; 145:19; Prov 15:29; Isa 1:15; Jer 11:11; 14:12; Mic 3:4; Zech 7:13
9:33 John 3:2
9:34 John 9:2
9:37 John 4:26
9:39 Luke 4:18
9:40 Rom 2:19
9:41 John 15:22
10:2 Acts 20:28

9:24 Or *Give glory to God, not to Jesus;* Greek reads *Give glory to God.* 9:35 Some manuscripts read *the Son of God?* "Son of Man" is a title Jesus used for Himself. 9:38-39a Some manuscripts do not include *"Yes, Lord, I believe!" the man said. And he worshiped Jesus. Then Jesus told him.* 9:39b Greek *those who see.*

9:34 The Pharisees clung to the cultural assumption that God had cursed those born handicapped because of the sin of their parents (9:1-2). Because a descendant of Aaron with a physical deformity was limited in his service in the Temple (Leviticus 21:16-23), the Pharisees concluded that all who suffer deformities are cursed and should be kept away from the Temple, only having access to the synagogue (Mark 3:1; Luke 6:6).

▸ WORSHIP

9:37-38 Worship the Son. What are the earliest things you remember seeing as a child? The blind man's first sight was the face of his Savior. His response was appropriate (compare 12:1-8; 20:28) and anticipated the worship of God's sin-healed people in heaven (Revelation 5:8-14). Like all of God's people, the beggar received more than physical sight; he could now see the Kingdom of God (3:3) and offer proper worship to the King. His understanding had progressed from Jesus being a mysterious man, to a prophet, to the Son of Man who is worthy of faith and worship. Have your ideas and feelings about Jesus progressed from when you first heard of Him? Make sure your understanding and love of Him deepens and matures as He continues to manifest Himself in your life. (***See Worship***> *NT> Christ's Supremacy> Jesus is worshiped by the blind man,* TopicGuide page A29.)

9:40-41 Jesus pointed out that spiritual blindness is much worse than physical blindness. A doctor cannot bring healing to patients that refuse services, but Jesus gives sight to those who admit their spiritual blindness (Matthew 9:11-13).

10:1-21 Jesus used the imagery of shepherding to illustrate His sacrificial love and care for His people. The shepherd that wants only the best for the sheep, even if it means giving His life in their place, is worthy of complete trust.

and leads them out. 4After he has gathered his own flock, he walks ahead of them, and
they follow him because they know his voice. 5They won't follow a stranger; they will run
from him because they don't know his voice."
6Those who heard Jesus use this illustration didn't understand what He meant, 7so He
explained it to them: "I tell you the truth, I am the gate for the sheep. 8All who came before
Me* were thieves and robbers. But the true sheep did not listen to them. 9Yes, I am the
gate. Those who come in through Me will be saved.* They will come and go freely and will
find good pastures. 10The thief's purpose is to steal and kill and destroy. My purpose is to
give them a rich and satisfying life.
11"I am the good shepherd. The good shepherd sacrifices His life for the sheep. 12A
hired hand will run when he sees a wolf coming. He will abandon the sheep because they
don't belong to him and he isn't their shepherd. And so the wolf attacks them and scatters
the flock. 13The hired hand runs away because he's working only for the money and
doesn't really care about the sheep.
14"I am the good shepherd; I know My own sheep, and they know Me, 15just as My Fa-
ther knows Me and I know the Father. So I sacrifice My life for the sheep. 16I have other
sheep, too, that are not in this sheepfold. I must bring them also. They will listen to My
voice, and there will be one flock with one shepherd.
17"The Father loves Me because I sacrifice My life so I may take it back again. 18No one
can take My life from Me. I sacrifice it voluntarily. For I have the authority to lay it down
when I want to and also to take it up again. For this is what My Father has commanded."
19When He said these things, the people* were again divided in their opinions about
Him. 20Some said, "He's demon possessed and out of His mind. Why listen to a man like
that?" 21Others said, "This doesn't sound like a man possessed by a demon! Can a demon
open the eyes of the blind?"

JESUS CLAIMS TO BE THE SON OF GOD

22It was now winter, and Jesus was in Jerusalem at the time of Hanukkah, the Festival of
Dedication. 23He was in the Temple, walking through the section known as Solomon's

10:7 John 14:6
10:8 Jer 23:1-2; Ezek 34:2-3
10:9 Ps 118:20; John 14:6
10:10 John 5:40; Acts 20:29; 2 Pet 2:1
10:11 Isa 40:11; Ezek 34:11-16, 23; Heb 13:20; 1 Pet 2:25; 1 Jn 3:16; Rev 7:17
10:14 2 Tim 2:19
10:15 Matt 11:27
10:16 Isa 56:8; Ezek 37:24; John 11:52; Eph 2:14-18
10:17-18 Phil 2:8-9; Heb 5:8; 7:16
10:23 Acts 3:11; 5:12

10:8 Some manuscripts do not include *before Me.* 10:9 Or *will find safety.* 10:19 Greek *Jewish people;* also in 10:24, 31.

10:7 Just as a sheepfold had only one point of entry, anyone that enters into the secure place for the people of God must go through Jesus. He may have been referring to the way a shepherd would place his own body in the opening as a human gate to the sheepfold. Jesus is the one way into the sheepfold and He protects all those inside.

▸ CHURCH
10:14 I'm a sheep? You may not think it's too wonderful to be compared to a sheep—most don't smell very good. But with Christ as our shepherd, it's an honor to be called His sheep. In New Testament times, a shepherd knew all of his sheep intimately, cared for their every need, and even slept beside them to make sure they were protected. That's how intimately Jesus knows us (10:5). Jesus protects us from our enemies—Satan and his forces (10:15). A shepherd will also lead his sheep to green pastures so that they can be sustained during difficult times. Jesus guides us to an abundant life (10:10). The next time you face a challenge (such as waking up tomorrow morning!), picture Jesus as your Shepherd and trust Him to guide and protect you. (***See Church****> What> Many Titles> Sheep,* TopicGuide page A48.)

10:16 The phrase "other sheep" refers to the Gentiles (Isaiah 56:6-8; Ephesians 3:6). After Jesus' death and resurrection, the good news went out into the world, and Christ's sheep among the Gentiles responded to the Good Shepherd's voice: "All who were chosen for eternal life became believers" (Acts 13:48).

10:18 Jesus' life was not taken, as if the cross was a horrible tragedy that should have been avoided. Rather, His death was according to God's eternal will and plan because He loves sinners (Acts 4:28; John 3:16). Jesus had the power to avoid His death (Matthew 26:53; John 18:6), but He accomplished the Father's plan willingly and in full obedience (Philippians 2:8). He willingly laid His life down because He loves His church (John 10:18; Ephesians 3:18-19; 5:25).

10:22-42 The people's questions provided Jesus an opportunity to explain that His work was in unity with the Father's work. Because of this unity, both Father and Son work together to securely hold everyone who believed in Him. Jesus' claims caused a violent reaction among the people, and Jesus showed the unreasonable nature of their response by referring to the signs He had performed.

10:22 Hanukkah (or the Festival of Dedication) was a yearly event celebrating the dedication of the Temple after Antiochus IV Epiphanes defiled it in 167 BC. The revolt under the leadership of Judas Maccabeus was the most recent deliverance in the history of the Jews. It was not one of the feasts God commanded but was popular among the people since they longed for a similar deliverance from Rome.

Colonnade. 24The people surrounded Him and asked, "How long are You going to keep
us in suspense? If You are the Messiah, tell us plainly."
25Jesus replied, "I have already told you, and you don't believe Me. The proof is the
work I do in My Father's name. 26 But you don't believe Me because you are not My sheep.
27 My sheep listen to My voice; I know them, and they follow Me. 28 I give them eternal life,
and they will never perish. No one can snatch them away from Me, 29 for My Father has
given them to Me, and He is more powerful than anyone else.* No one can snatch them
from the Father's hand. 30 The Father and I are one."
31 Once again the people picked up stones to kill Him. 32Jesus said, "At My Father's direc-
tion I have done many good works. For which one are you going to stone Me?"
33They replied, "We're stoning you not for any good work, but for blasphemy! You, a
mere man, claim to be God."
34Jesus replied, "It is written in your own Scriptures* that God said to certain leaders of
the people, 'I say, you are gods!'* 35 And you know that the Scriptures cannot be altered. So
if those people who received God's message were called 'gods,' 36 why do you call it blas-
phemy when I say, 'I am the Son of God'? After all, the Father set Me apart and sent Me into
the world. 37 Don't believe Me unless I carry out My Father's work. 38 But if I do His work, be-
lieve in the evidence of the miraculous works I have done, even if you don't believe Me.
Then you will know and understand that the Father is in Me, and I am in the Father."
39 Once again they tried to arrest Him, but He got away and left them. 40He went beyond
the Jordan River near the place where John was first baptizing and stayed there awhile.
41And many followed Him. "John didn't perform miraculous signs," they remarked to one
another, "but everything he said about this man has come true." 42And many who were
there believed in Jesus.

THE RAISING OF LAZARUS

11 A man named Lazarus was sick. He lived in Bethany with his sisters, Mary and
Martha. 2This is the Mary who later poured the expensive perfume on the Lord's
feet and wiped them with her hair.* Her brother, Lazarus, was sick. 3 So the two sisters sent
a message to Jesus telling Him, "Lord, Your dear friend is very sick."
4But when Jesus heard about it He said, "Lazarus's sickness will not end in death. No, it
happened for the glory of God so that the Son of God will receive glory from this." 5 So al-
though Jesus loved Martha, Mary, and Lazarus, 6He stayed where He was for the next two
days. 7Finally, He said to His disciples, "Let's go back to Judea."

10:24 Luke 22:67
10:25 John 5:36; 10:38; 14:11
10:26 John 8:47
10:28 John 6:37, 39; 17:12
10:29 John 14:28; 17:2, 6, 24
10:30 John 1:1; 10:38; 14:8-11; 17:21-24
10:33 Lev 24:16; Matt 26:63-66; John 1:1, 18; 5:18; 20:28; Rom 9:5; Phil 2:6; Titus 2:13; 2 Pet 1:1; 1 Jn 5:20
10:36 John 5:17-20
10:42 John 2:23; 7:31; 8:30; 11:45; 12:11, 42
11:1 Matt 21:17; Luke 10:38
11:2 John 12:3
11:4 John 9:3

10:29 Other manuscripts read *for what My Father has given Me is more powerful than anything;* still others read *for regarding that which My Father has given Me, He is greater than all.* 10:34a Greek *your own law.* 10:34b Ps 82:6. 11:2 This incident is recorded in chapter 12.

10:31 When Jesus claimed to be "I AM" in 8:58, the Jews knew He was claiming to be more than a messenger from God (see also 5:18)—He was claiming to be the God of Israel! They grabbed stones then, and now they grabbed stones once again. The Jews thought that anyone who dared to utter such words should die, and they were right—except, of course, if that person were Jesus, who really was God.

10:38 Jesus continued the theme from the beginning of His discussion (10:25) and urged the Jews to consider at least the obvious witness that His miracles provided. Others had found this evidence compelling (3:2; 9:16; 10:21). Jesus was saying, "Even if you don't trust My own testimony about Myself, the miracles I have performed provide enough evidence to show that I am indeed the Messiah."

10:40-42 Jesus left the center of opposition and settled near the Jordan where John the Baptist had prepared the way. In contrast to the unbelief in Jerusalem (10:26), some saw the evidence of Jesus' miracles and responded in faith. John wanted his readers to hear their testimony and do likewise (20:29-31).

11:1-44 The death of Lazarus provided the setting in which Jesus explained what it means to believe in Him and have eternal life. He proclaimed Himself to be the Resurrection and the Life and then demonstrated it by raising Lazarus from the dead. This amazing miracle increased the tension among the Jewish leadership in Jerusalem.

11:1 Bethany was less than two miles from Jerusalem (11:18), the place of the greatest hostility against Jesus. The mention of this region would remind readers of past interactions that culminated in attempts to kill Jesus (11:16; 8:59; 10:31).

11:4 Jesus had taught His disciples that a certain man's blindness was not the result of someone's sin, but that God's power might be publicly displayed (9:3). Likewise, Lazarus' sickness would also glorify God, who is Life Himself. Honoring God the Son always brings honor to His Father (5:23).

11:8 John 8:59; 10:31
11:9 John 9:4
11:10 John 12:35
11:11 Dan 12:2; Matt 9:24; 27:52; Mark 5:39; Luke 8:52; Acts 7:60; 1 Cor 11:30
11:16 Matt 10:3; John 14:5; 20:24-28; 21:2; Acts 1:3
11:17 John 11:39
11:20 Luke 10:38-42
11:22 John 16:30
11:23-24 Dan 12:2; John 5:28-29; Acts 24:15; Phil 3:21; 1 Thes 4:14
11:25 John 1:4; 3:36; 5:21; 6:39-40; 14:6; Col 1:18; 3:4; 1 Jn 1:1-2; 5:10-11; Rev 1:17-18
11:26 John 8:51
11:27 Matt 16:16; John 6:14

8But His disciples objected. "Rabbi," they said, "only a few days ago the people* in Judea
were trying to stone You. Are You going there again?"
9Jesus replied, "There are twelve hours of daylight every day. During the day people
can walk safely. They can see because they have the light of this world. 10 But at night
there is danger of stumbling because they have no light." 11 Then He said, "Our friend Laz-
arus has fallen asleep, but now I will go and wake him up."
12The disciples said, "Lord, if he is sleeping, he will soon get better!" 13They thought
Jesus meant Lazarus was simply sleeping, but Jesus meant Lazarus had died.
14So He told them plainly, "Lazarus is dead. 15 And for your sakes, I'm glad I wasn't
there, for now you will really believe. Come, let's go see him."
16Thomas, nicknamed the Twin,* said to his fellow disciples, "Let's go, too—and die with
Jesus."
17When Jesus arrived at Bethany, He was told that Lazarus had already been in his
grave for four days. 18Bethany was only a few miles* down the road from Jerusalem, 19and
many of the people had come to console Martha and Mary in their loss. 20When Martha
got word that Jesus was coming, she went to meet Him. But Mary stayed in the house.
21 Martha said to Jesus, "Lord, if only You had been here, my brother would not have died.
22But even now I know that God will give You whatever You ask."
23Jesus told her, "Your brother will rise again."
24"Yes," Martha said, "he will rise when everyone else rises, at the last day."
25Jesus told her, "I am the resurrection and the life.* Anyone who believes in Me will live,
even after dying. 26 Everyone who lives in Me and believes in Me will never ever die. Do
you believe this, Martha?"
27"Yes, Lord," she told Him. "I have always believed You are the Messiah, the Son of
God, the One who has come into the world from God." 28Then she returned to Mary. She
called Mary aside from the mourners and told her, "The Teacher is here and wants to see
you." 29So Mary immediately went to Him.
30Jesus had stayed outside the village, at the place where Martha met Him. 31 When the
people who were at the house consoling Mary saw her leave so hastily, they assumed she
was going to Lazarus's grave to weep. So they followed her there. 32When Mary arrived
and saw Jesus, she fell at His feet and said, "Lord, if only You had been here, my brother
would not have died."

11:8 Greek *Jewish people;* also in 11:19, 31, 33, 36, 45, 54. 11:16 Greek *Thomas, who was called Didymus.* 11:18 Greek *was about 15 stadia* [about 2.8 kilometers]. 11:25 Some manuscripts do not include *and the life.*

11:15 Jesus' purpose for delaying the visit becomes clear. He was aware that Lazarus had died and that God was setting the stage for a demonstration that would produce faith. This aligned perfectly with John's own purpose for writing this book (20:31).

11:21-24 Martha's words seem to have come from a combination of confusion and faith. She had faith that Jesus could have healed Lazarus if He had arrived earlier, but it appeared that she actually did not believe anything significant would be done for him at this point. Martha claimed to know that the Father would give the Son whatever He asked, but her conception of what this might be was still limited. (Others' claims to knowledge are found in 3:2; 4:25; 6:42; 7:27; 8:52; 9:24.) Martha correctly affirmed that Lazarus' body would one day be raised from the dead, but she did not realize that the One who would raise the dead on the last day was standing before her now and might have plans for the present (5:25-29).

▸ GOD
11:25 Alive again! Do you have a Christian loved one who has passed on to the life beyond? Do you worry about where that person is right now and if you will really see him or her again? The future resurrection of the body and eternal life in the age to come are found in Jesus alone. Believers will continue to die until then, but one day Jesus will raise us from death, just as He Himself triumphed over the grave (1 Corinthians 15:54-55). When Jesus rose from the dead, He became "the first of a great harvest of all who have died" (1 Corinthians 15:20). We will never endure the shame and deprivation of hell. Take hold of that promise and trust Jesus for your future and the well-being of your Christian loved one. (***See God**> God's Names> Son> The Resurrection,* TopicGuide page A19.)

11:26 Because Jesus is the source of resurrection and life, those who believe in Him already have received eternal life. It is a present possession (5:24). If their bodies cease functioning, the life they have in Jesus does not. In this sense, believers cannot die, because the moment their souls departs from their bodies they are immediately present with the Savior, and He is the source of eternal life (Luke 20:37-38; 2 Corinthians 5:8).

[33]When Jesus saw her weeping and saw the other people wailing with her, a deep
anger welled up within Him,* and He was deeply troubled. [34]"Where have you put him?"
He asked them.
They told Him, "Lord, come and see." [35]Then Jesus wept. [36]The people who were stand- 11:35
ing nearby said, "See how much He loved him!" [37]But some said, "This man healed a blind Luke 19:41
man. Couldn't He have kept Lazarus from dying?" 11:37
[38]Jesus was still angry as He arrived at the tomb, a cave with a stone rolled across its en- John 9:6-7
trance. [39]"Roll the stone aside," Jesus told them. 11:39 John 11:17
But Martha, the dead man's sister, protested, "Lord, he has been dead for four days. The
smell will be terrible."
[40]Jesus responded, "Didn't I tell you that you would see God's glory if you believe?"
[41]So they rolled the stone aside. Then Jesus looked up to heaven and said, "Father, thank 11:41
You for hearing Me. [42]You always hear Me, but I said it out loud for the sake of all these Matt 11:25
people standing here, so that they will believe You sent Me." [43]Then Jesus shouted, "Laza- 11:42 John 12:30
rus, come out!" [44]And the dead man came out, his hands and feet bound in graveclothes, 11:43
his face wrapped in a headcloth. Jesus told them, "Unwrap him and let him go!" Luke 7:14

THE PLOT TO KILL JESUS

[45]Many of the people who were with Mary believed in Jesus when they saw this happen.
[46]But some went to the Pharisees and told them what Jesus had done. [47]Then the leading 11:47
priests and Pharisees called the high council* together. "What are we going to do?" they Matt 26:3-5
asked each other. "This man certainly performs many miraculous signs. [48]If we allow Him 11:49
to go on like this, soon everyone will believe in Him. Then the Roman army will come and Matt 26:3
destroy both our Temple* and our nation." 11:50 John 18:13-14
[49]Caiaphas, who was high priest at that time,* said, "You don't know what you're talking 11:51
about! [50]You don't realize that it's better for you that one man should die for the people Exod 28:30
than for the whole nation to be destroyed." Num 27:21
[51]He did not say this on his own; as high priest at that time he was led to prophesy that 11:52 Isa 49:6
Jesus would die for the entire nation. [52]And not only for that nation, but to bring together John 10:16
and unite all the children of God scattered around the world. 1 Jn 2:2
[53]So from that time on, the Jewish leaders began to plot Jesus' death. [54]As a result, Jesus 11:53 Matt 26:4

11:33 Or *He was angry in His spirit.* 11:47 Greek *the Sanhedrin.* 11:48 Or *our position;* Greek reads *our place.* 11:49 Greek *that year;* also in 11:51.

11:33 When the Resurrection and the Life came into the vicinity of death and human wailing, He was deeply stirred. This agitated response may have been directed at sin, which causes death (Romans 6:23), or at the crowd that was faithless and full of sorrow "like people who have no hope" (1 Thessalonians 4:13).

▸ GOD

11:35 When God weeps. Why did Jesus weep when He came to Lazarus's tomb? His tears show how much He cared for His friends. Obviously, Jesus knew that He was about to raise Lazarus from the dead. Jesus knows everything in the past, present, and future, so Jesus also knew about the pain Lazarus and his two sisters experienced. This story shows us that Jesus is not a passive observer of our pain. He knows your every thought and sees every tear (Psalm 56:8). Go to Jesus when your heart hurts. Tell Him all about your pain and know that He shares it with you. (***See God****> God's Nature> Personality> Emotion> God can be moved to grief,* TopicGuide page A14.)

11:44 Lazarus emerged from the tomb and proved that Jesus' words to Martha were true (11:25-26). This scene provided a miniature picture of a greater resurrection that will occur in the future (5:28) when Jesus speaks and the perishable, earthly bodies of all believers will immediately be transformed into heavenly bodies (1 Corinthians 15:53). It also confirmed that Jesus' words presently impart eternal life to everyone that believes. (Similarly healing a paralyzed man demonstrated His power to forgive in Matthew 9:6).

11:50-51 Caiaphas said much more than he had intended. He certainly wasn't preaching the necessity of Jesus' death as the Lamb of God in the place of the perishing. Rather, he merely sought to convince the leaders to kill one man in order to avoid an uprising that would invite Rome to kill the whole nation. John wanted his readers to see the irony in the high priest's unconscious prophecy.

11:52 John had already shown that Jesus had "other sheep, too, that are not in this sheepfold" (10:16). Jesus would die for "all who have been called by the Lord our God" (Acts 2:39). Later some Greeks sought Jesus (12:20-21), indicating that the time of gathering from all the nations had come. Many from all over the world would be drawn to Him as He was lifted up on the cross (12:32).

stopped His public ministry among the people and left Jerusalem. He went to a place near
the wilderness, to the village of Ephraim, and stayed there with His disciples.
11:55 55 It was now almost time for the Jewish Passover celebration, and many people from all
Exod 12:13 2 Chr 30:17-19 over the country arrived in Jerusalem several days early so they could go through the pu-
Matt 26:1-2 Mark 14:1 rification ceremony before Passover began. 56 They kept looking for Jesus, but as they
stood around in the Temple, they said to each other, "What do you think? He won't come
for Passover, will He?" 57 Meanwhile, the leading priests and Pharisees had publicly or-
dered that anyone seeing Jesus must report it immediately so they could arrest Him.

12:1-8 //Matt 26:6-13 //Mark 14:3-9

JESUS ANOINTED AT BETHANY

12 Six days before the Passover celebration began, Jesus arrived in Bethany, the
12:1 home of Lazarus—the man He had raised from the dead. 2 A dinner was prepared
John 11:1 in Jesus' honor. Martha served, and Lazarus was among those who ate* with Him. 3 Then
12:2 Mary took a twelve-ounce jar* of expensive perfume made from essence of nard, and
Luke 10:38-42 she anointed Jesus' feet with it, wiping His feet with her hair. The house was filled with
12:3 the fragrance.
Luke 7:37-38 4 But Judas Iscariot, the disciple who would soon betray Him, said, 5 "That perfume was
12:4 John 6:71 worth a year's wages.* It should have been sold and the money given to the poor." 6 Not
12:6 that he cared for the poor—he was a thief, and since he was in charge of the disciples'
John 13:29 money, he often stole some for himself.
12:7 7 Jesus replied, "Leave her alone. She did this in preparation for My burial. 8 You will al-
John 19:40 ways have the poor among you, but you will not always have Me."
12:8 9 When all the people* heard of Jesus' arrival, they flocked to see Him and also to see
Deut 15:11 Lazarus, the man Jesus had raised from the dead. 10 Then the leading priests decided to kill
12:10 Luke 16:31 Lazarus, too, 11 for it was because of him that many of the people had deserted them* and
believed in Jesus.

12:12-19 //Matt 21:1-11 //Mark 11:1-11 //Luke 19:28-38

JESUS' TRIUMPHANT ENTRY

12 The next day, the news that Jesus was on the way to Jerusalem swept through the city. A
12:13 Lev 23:40 large crowd of Passover visitors 13 took palm branches and went down the road to meet
*Ps 118:25-26 Zeph 3:15 Him. They shouted,

12:2 Or *who reclined.* 12:3 Greek *took 1 litra* [327 grams]. 12:5 Greek *worth 300 denarii.* A denarius was equivalent to a laborer's full day's wage. 12:9 Greek *Jewish people;* also in 12:11. 12:11 Or *had deserted their traditions;* Greek reads *had deserted.*

11:55 Caiaphas's previous "prophecy" about Jesus as a substitute (11:50) and the mention of Passover foreshadowed the cross. Jesus is the Passover Lamb (1 Corinthians 5:7) whose blood would be shed to keep His people from perishing (John 3:16). As thousands of lambs were being brought to Jerusalem to be killed for the annual Passover festival (see Exodus 12:1-14), the Lamb of God awaited His hour (12:23) to be slain for the sins of the world (1:29; 10:18).

12:1-8 Mary anointed Jesus with expensive perfume as an act of heartfelt devotion. Mary presents a picture of affectionate faith in Jesus—a sharp contrast to Judas's miserly unbelief.

12:4-5 John recalled Judas's actions with the benefit of hindsight and labeled him "the disciple who would soon betray Him." In 6:71 the Gospel writer recorded that Judas did just that. Judas had considered Mary's extravagant gift to Jesus a waste.

12:8 Using the money for the poor would be advisable in other settings at other times, but Mary understood the privilege of the Savior's presence with them. Her lavish act was appropriate, for Jesus would not be with them for much longer (13:33; 16:7).

▸ MINISTRY

12:10 Expect resistance. After Lazarus was raised from the dead, the religious rulers plotted to kill him and destroy the evidence of Jesus' deity. Imagine the foolishness of that plot—Lazarus had already been raised from the dead once—why not again? But the religious rulers couldn't stand the testimony that Lazarus gave about the power of Jesus. Don't be surprised if a similar experience happens to you. Satan is an unrelenting enemy. He doesn't like the testimony to Jesus' power that your life provides. When God is visibly working in your life, expect an attack from Satan. But also know that God will be with you. If you are His, every moment of your life is a sermon, bearing witness that Jesus is the Son of God. (***See Ministry*****>** *Great Commission> Make Disciples> Disciples are not just followers, but also witnesses,* TopicGuide page A56.)

12:12-13 The crowd in Jerusalem went out in celebration while waving palm branches, like a public welcoming committee ushering a royal visitor into the city (Revelation 7:9). Their praise of Jesus as "the One who comes in the name of the Lord" came from Psalm 118, a text that references the rejected stone that becomes the cornerstone. (Jesus applied Psalm 118:22 to Himself in Matthew 21:42; also see Acts 4:11; 1 Peter 2:7.)

"Praise God!*
Blessings on the One who comes in the name of the LORD!
Hail to the King of Israel!"*

14 Jesus found a young donkey and rode on it, fulfilling the prophecy that said:
15 "Don't be afraid, people of Jerusalem.*
Look, your King is coming,
riding on a donkey's colt."*

16 His disciples didn't understand at the time that this was a fulfillment of prophecy. But
after Jesus entered into His glory, they remembered what had happened and realized that
these things had been written about Him.
17 Many in the crowd had seen Jesus call Lazarus from the tomb, raising Him from the
dead, and they were telling others* about it. 18 That was the reason so many went out to
meet Him—because they had heard about this miraculous sign. 19 Then the Pharisees said
to each other, "There's nothing we can do. Look, everyone* has gone after Him!"

JESUS PREDICTS HIS DEATH

20 Some Greeks who had come to Jerusalem for the Passover celebration 21 paid a visit to
Philip, who was from Bethsaida in Galilee. They said, "Sir, we want to meet Jesus." 22 Philip
told Andrew about it, and they went together to ask Jesus.
23 Jesus replied, "Now the time has come for the Son of Man* to enter into His glory. 24 I
tell you the truth, unless a kernel of wheat is planted in the soil and dies, it remains alone.
But its death will produce many new kernels—a plentiful harvest of new lives. 25 Those
who love their life in this world will lose it. Those who care nothing for their life in this
world will keep it for eternity. 26 Anyone who wants to be My disciple must follow Me, be-
cause My servants must be where I am. And the Father will honor anyone who serves Me.
27 "Now My soul is deeply troubled. Should I pray, 'Father, save Me from this hour'? But
this is the very reason I came! 28 Father, bring glory to Your name."
Then a voice spoke from heaven, saying, "I have already brought glory to My name,
and I will do so again." 29 When the crowd heard the voice, some thought it was thunder,
while others declared an angel had spoken to Him.
30 Then Jesus told them, "The voice was for your benefit, not Mine. 31 The time for judg-
ing this world has come, when Satan, the ruler of this world, will be cast out. 32 And when I
am lifted up from the earth, I will draw everyone to Myself." 33 He said this to indicate how
He was going to die.
34 The crowd responded, "We understood from Scripture* that the Messiah would live
forever. How can You say the Son of Man will die? Just who is this Son of Man, anyway?"
35 Jesus replied, "My light will shine for you just a little longer. Walk in the light while you

12:15 Isa 35:4; *Zech 9:9
12:16 John 2:22; 7:39
12:17 John 11:43-44
12:18 John 12:11; 19:37
12:21 John 1:43-44
12:23 John 13:32; 17:1
12:24 1 Cor 15:36
12:25 Matt 10:39; Luke 9:24; 17:33
12:26 John 14:3; 17:24
12:27 Ps 6:3; Matt 26:38; Mark 14:34
12:28 Matt 3:17; 17:5; Mark 1:11; 9:7; Luke 3:22; 9:35; 2 Pet 1:17-18
12:31 John 14:30; 16:11; Eph 2:2
12:32 John 3:14; 6:44
12:34 Pss 89:4, 36; 110:4; Isa 9:7; Ezek 37:25; Dan 7:14
12:35 John 8:12; 9:4; 12:46

12:13a Greek *Hosanna,* an exclamation of praise adapted from a Hebrew expression that means "save now." 12:13b Ps 118:25-26; Zeph 3:15. 12:15a Greek *daughter of Zion.* 12:15b Zech 9:9. 12:17 Greek *were testifying.* 12:19 Greek *the world.* 12:23 "Son of Man" is a title Jesus used for Himself. 12:34 Greek *from the law.*

12:19 The religious leaders' desperation increased as they saw Jesus drawing more followers to Himself (John 4:1). This is another way that John demonstrated the mounting tension between the Pharisees and Jesus (John 7:32; 11:46).

12:23-26 In Christ's life and the lives of His followers, great renown and honor was found in self-sacrifice and suffering. Rewards from God are obtained through humbly following Christ's path to redemptive suffering, not through obtaining power or prestige (2 Corinthians 1:7).

12:28 The Father spoke audibly at the beginning of Jesus' ministry when Jesus was baptized and again when Jesus was transfigured (Luke 3:22; 9:35). In both instances the Father commended the Son. Here also at the end of Jesus' ministry the Father extolled the Son for bringing glory to Him thus far, and stated that He would receive glorify again in the hour of the crucifixion.

12:31 Since there is no other way to the Father, Jesus' death would bring judgment to an unbelieving world that rejected Him (14:6). The preaching of the crucified Savior was like an offensive odor to them (2 Corinthians 2:15-16), revealing that the wrath of God remained upon them (3:36). The prince of this world, the devil (14:30; 16:11), would also be cast out (Revelation 12:9) despite his most violent assaults upon Jesus.

can, so the darkness will not overtake you. Those who walk in the darkness cannot see
12:36 John 8:59 where they are going. 36 Put your trust in the light while there is still time; then you will be-
Eph 5:8 come children of the light."
1 Thes 5:5 After saying these things, Jesus went away and was hidden from them.

THE UNBELIEF OF THE PEOPLE

37 But despite all the miraculous signs Jesus had done, most of the people still did not be-
12:38 *Isa 53:1 lieve in Him. 38 This is exactly what Isaiah the prophet had predicted:

Rom 10:16 "LORD, who has believed our message?
To whom has the LORD revealed His powerful arm?"*

39 But the people couldn't believe, for as Isaiah also said,

12:40 40 "The Lord has blinded their eyes
*Isa 6:10 and hardened their hearts—
Matt 13:14 so that their eyes cannot see,
and their hearts cannot understand,
and they cannot turn to Me
and have Me heal them."*

12:41 41 Isaiah was referring to Jesus when he said this, because he saw the future and spoke of
Isa 6:1 the Messiah's glory. 42 Many people did believe in Him, however, including some of the
12:42 Jewish leaders. But they wouldn't admit it for fear that the Pharisees would expel them
John 7:13, 48; 9:22-23; 12:11 from the synagogue. 43 For they loved human praise more than the praise of God.
12:43 44 Jesus shouted to the crowds, "If you trust Me, you are trusting not only Me, but also
John 5:44 God who sent Me. 45 For when you see Me, you are seeing the One who sent Me. 46 I have
12:45 come as a light to shine in this dark world, so that all who put their trust in Me will no longer
John 14:9 remain in the dark. 47 I will not judge those who hear Me but don't obey Me, for I have come
12:46 to save the world and not to judge it. 48 But all who reject Me and My message will be
John 1:4; 3:19; 8:12; 9:5 judged on the day of judgment by the truth I have spoken. 49 I don't speak on My own au-
12:47 thority. The Father who sent Me has commanded Me what to say and how to say it. 50 And I
John 3:17; 8:15 know His commands lead to eternal life; so I say whatever the Father tells Me to say."

JESUS WASHES HIS DISCIPLES' FEET

13:1 John 16:28; 17:1 **13** Before the Passover celebration, Jesus knew that His hour had come to leave this
13:2 world and return to His Father. He had loved His disciples during His ministry on
Luke 22:3 earth, and now He loved them to the very end.* 2 It was time for supper, and the devil had
John 6:70-71

12:38 Isa 53:1. 12:40 Isa 6:10. 13:1 Or *He showed them the full extent of His love.*

▸ SPIRITUAL WARFARE

12:36 The time is coming! Corrupt people triumph. Evil spreads like a contagious disease. Horrible acts are broadcast worldwide, and then copycat crimes occur in many places. Events in the world sometimes make it look as if Satan is winning. But a day is coming when Satan will be judged. He will pay for the harm he has inflicted upon the earth. Then he will be assigned to an eternal punishment that, to one degree or another, awaits all who defy God (Revelation 19:20; 20:10, 14-15). His judgment is sure! Do not cower before Satan and his minions, but stand firm, knowing he is a doomed foe. (***See Spiritual Warfare**> Originator of Sin> Satan's Domain> Doomed to destruction,* TopicGuide page A44.)

12:39-40 John quoted Isaiah 6:10 to show that the Israelites were unable to see, understand, or turn because the Lord hadn't enabled them (see 6:44, 65). Paul quoted the Old Testament to make the same point about Israel: "God has put them into a deep sleep. To this day He has shut their eyes so they do not see, and closed their ears so they do not hear" (Romans 11:8).

12:47-48 Although the Son of Man has been given authority to judge on the last day (5:27), Jesus' primary emphasis in His earthly ministry was not to condemn the world, but to save it (3:17). However, those who reject Christ will not escape His words but will be judged by His truth at the final judgment at the end of time.

13:1-20 The account of Jesus' washing the disciple's feet on the night of the Last Supper is unique to John's Gospel. This action showed Jesus' loving service to His disciples and symbolized the highest service He would soon render on the cross.

13:1 The Passover sacrifice and the Exodus were about to be fulfilled in Christ's death and in the deliverance His people would receive from their sin (see note at 11:55).

already prompted Judas,* son of Simon Iscariot, to betray Jesus. 3Jesus knew that the Fa-
ther had given Him authority over everything and that He had come from God and would
return to God. 4So He got up from the table, took off His robe, wrapped a towel around His
waist, 5and poured water into a basin. Then He began to wash the disciples' feet, drying
them with the towel He had around Him.
6When Jesus came to Simon Peter, Peter said to Him, "Lord, are You going to wash my
feet?"
7Jesus replied, "You don't understand now what I am doing, but someday you will."
8"No," Peter protested, "You will never ever wash my feet!"
Jesus replied, "Unless I wash you, you won't belong to Me."
9Simon Peter exclaimed, "Then wash my hands and head as well, Lord, not just my feet!"
10Jesus replied, "A person who has bathed all over does not need to wash, except for the
feet,* to be entirely clean. And you disciples are clean, but not all of you." 11For Jesus knew
who would betray Him. That is what He meant when He said, "Not all of you are clean."
12After washing their feet, He put on His robe again and sat down and asked, "Do you
understand what I was doing? 13You call Me 'Teacher' and 'Lord,' and you are right, be-
cause that's what I am. 14And since I, your Lord and Teacher, have washed your feet, you
ought to wash each other's feet. 15I have given you an example to follow. Do as I have
done to you. 16I tell you the truth, slaves are not greater than their master. Nor is the mes-
senger more important than the One who sends the message. 17Now that you know these
things, God will bless you for doing them.

JESUS PREDICTS HIS BETRAYAL

18"I am not saying these things to all of you; I know the ones I have chosen. But this fulfills
the Scripture that says, 'The one who eats My food has turned against Me.'* 19I tell you this
beforehand, so that when it happens you will believe that I AM the Messiah.* 20I tell you
the truth, anyone who welcomes My messenger is welcoming Me, and anyone who wel-
comes Me is welcoming the Father who sent Me."
21Now Jesus was deeply troubled,* and He exclaimed, "I tell you the truth, one of you
will betray Me!"

13:4 Luke 12:37; 22:27
13:5 Luke 7:44; John 12:3
13:8 Ezek 36:25; 1 Cor 6:11; Eph 5:26; Titus 3:5
13:10 John 15:3
13:11 John 6:64, 70-71; 13:2
13:13 1 Cor 12:3
13:14 Luke 22:27; 1 Tim 5:10; 1 Pet 5:5
13:15 Phil 2:5-7; 1 Pet 5:3-5; 1 Jn 2:6; 3:16
13:17 Jas 1:25
13:18 *Ps 41:9
13:20 Matt 10:40; Luke 10:16
13:21-30 //Matt 26:21-25; //Mark 14:18-21; //Luke 22:21-23

13:2 Or *the devil had already intended for Judas.* 13:10 Some manuscripts do not include *except for the feet.* 13:18 Ps 41:9. 13:19 Or *that the 'I AM' has come;* or *that I am the LORD;* Greek reads *that I am.* See Exod 3:14. 13:21 Greek *was troubled in His spirit.*

▶ WORSHIP
13:3-5 Cleansing the sole. Walking around in dust, mud, and garbage all day could create some very smelly feet. So when guests entered a home, a household servant would welcome them by washing their feet. As a demonstration of humility and service, Jesus, God the Son, "took the humble position of a slave" (Philippians 2:6-7) and washed His disciples' feet. Then He instructed His disciples to wash each other's feet as well (13:14-15), meaning that they should humbly serve each other. Look around you and see how you can serve God's people, for when we learn to serve well, we become more like our Lord. (***See Worship***> *NT> Fellowship> Preserving> Serve one another,* TopicGuide page A31.)

13:10-11 Even though Judas was washed on the outside along with the other disciples, he was unclean on the inside because of unbelief. No one needed to tell Jesus about Judas's true nature (2:24-25). He knew the sheep the Father had given to Him (10:27-29).

▶ BIBLE
13:13 Jesus is Lord. Jesus knew who He was. But do we? As Christians we often use the word "Lord" when naming Jesus, but do we think of what that title means? Lord means absolute master. In the first century, the ordinary servant obeyed his lord's commands without objection. The servant addressed his lord with complete respect. Servants made no peep if they were asked to do something that seemed beneath them. When you address Jesus as Lord—whether in prayer or in speech—make it a reminder of the place of honor Jesus has in your life. Find ways to honor Christ as Lord in your education, vocation, and communication. (***See Bible***> *Unity> Christ> Christ is the "LORD,"* TopicGuide page A10.)

13:18 Jesus had personally selected all of the disciples, even Judas. But He knew that Judas had not been selected to receive eternal life (5:21; 6:39, 70-71; 17:12) and that He would eventually betray Him in fulfillment of the Scriptures. Regardless of his close proximity to Jesus, Judas's true nature was revealed when he turned against Jesus as an enemy.

13:21 The betrayal by someone so close and the horrible crucifixion that would result from this betrayal deeply troubled Jesus. His emotions evidenced His full humanity (see note at 11:35).

13:23 22The disciples looked at each other, wondering whom He could mean. 23The disciple
John 19:26 Jesus loved was sitting next to Jesus at the table.* 24Simon Peter motioned to him to ask,
13:25 John 21:20 "Who's He talking about?" 25So that disciple leaned over to Jesus and asked, "Lord, who
is it?"
26Jesus responded, "It is the one to whom I give the bread I dip in the bowl." And when
13:27 Luke 22:3 He had dipped it, He gave it to Judas, son of Simon Iscariot. 27When Judas had eaten the
John 13:2 bread, Satan entered into him. Then Jesus told him, "Hurry and do what you're going to
13:29 do." 28None of the others at the table knew what Jesus meant. 29Since Judas was their trea-
John 12:6 surer, some thought Jesus was telling him to go and pay for the food or to give some
13:30 Luke 22:53 money to the poor. 30So Judas left at once, going out into the night.

JESUS PREDICTS PETER'S DENIAL

13:31-32 John 12:23; 17:1, 5 31As soon as Judas left the room, Jesus said, "The time has come for the Son of Man* to en-
13:33 ter into His glory, and God will be glorified because of Him. 32And since God receives glory
John 7:33-34; 8:21 because of the Son,* He will soon give glory to the Son. 33Dear children, I will be with you
13:34 Lev 19:18 only a little longer. And as I told the Jewish leaders, you will search for Me, but you can't
Eph 5:2 come where I am going. 34So now I am giving you a new commandment: Love each other.
1 Thes 4:9 1 Pet 1:22 Just as I have loved you, you should love each other. 35Your love for one another will
1 Jn 2:8; 3:23; 4:10-11 prove to the world that you are My disciples."
36Simon Peter asked, "Lord, where are You going?"
13:35 And Jesus replied, "You can't go with Me now, but you will follow Me later."
1 Jn 3:14; 4:20 37"But why can't I come now, Lord?" he asked. "I'm ready to die for You."
13:36 John 21:18 38Jesus answered, "Die for Me? I tell you the truth, Peter—before the rooster crows to-
2 Pet 1:14 morrow morning, you will deny three times that you even know Me.

JESUS, THE WAY TO THE FATHER

14:2 Ps 90:1 **14** "Don't let your hearts be troubled. Trust in God, and trust also in Me. 2There is
John 2:16, 19-21; 14:6 more than enough room in My Father's home.* If this were not so, would I have
told you that I am going to prepare a place for you?* 3When everything is ready, I will
14:3 John 14:10-11, come and get you, so that you will always be with Me where I am. 4And you know the way
18-20; 16:16-22; to where I am going."
17:21-24 5"No, we don't know, Lord," Thomas said. "We have no idea where You are going, so
how can we know the way?"

13:23 Greek *was reclining on Jesus' bosom.* The "disciple Jesus loved" was probably John. 13:31 "Son of Man" is a title Jesus used for Himself. 13:32 Some manuscripts omit *And since God receives glory because of the Son.* 14:2a Or *There are many rooms in My Father's house.* 14:2b Or *If this were not so, I would have told you that I am going to prepare a place for you.* Some manuscripts read *If this were not so, I would have told you. I am going to prepare a place for you.*

13:27 Satan entered Judas even before the bread from Jesus' hand disappeared from the betrayer's mouth. Jesus referred to the devil as "a murderer from the beginning" (8:44); so it is fitting that he would enter Judas at this decisive moment to set in motion the events culminating in Jesus' crucifixion. But Satan was not truly in control of these events, for it was Jesus that sent Judas out quickly to perform his role. Jesus was squarely facing the horror of the coming hour (Isaiah 50:6-7).

13:37-38 Peter didn't know that following Jesus truly would eventually cost him his life. He boldly stated his willingness to die for Jesus, but this assertion proved false three times before the next sunrise (18:15-27). After this humbling experience and restoration by Jesus (21:15-17), Peter would later be filled with the Holy Spirit to preach the gospel with boldness (Acts 2–3).

14:1–17:26 These words of Jesus on the night before His betrayal appear only in John's Gospel. The other accounts highlight Jesus' words when instituting the Lord's Supper, but John omitted this material and focused on the words of comfort Jesus spoke to His disciples.

14:2 Jesus described Heaven as a huge house with more than enough space for all who believe in Him. The residence belongs to Jesus' Father, and because of Jesus' obedience to death He has complete authority to assign the rooms. The disciples should have found comfort in knowing that Jesus was going to prepare rooms for them to live there with Him.

[6]Jesus told him, "I am the way, the truth, and the life. No one can come to the Father ex-
cept through Me. [7]If you had really known Me, you would know who My Father is.* From
now on, you do know Him and have seen Him!"
[8]Philip said, "Lord, show us the Father, and we will be satisfied."
[9]Jesus replied, "Have I been with you all this time, Philip, and yet you still don't know
who I am? Anyone who has seen Me has seen the Father! So why are you asking Me to
show Him to you? [10]Don't you believe that I am in the Father and the Father is in Me? The
words I speak are not My own, but My Father who lives in Me does His work through Me.
[11]Just believe that I am in the Father and the Father is in Me. Or at least believe because of
the work you have seen Me do.
[12]"I tell you the truth, anyone who believes in Me will do the same works I have done,
and even greater works, because I am going to be with the Father. [13]You can ask for any-
thing in My name, and I will do it, so that the Son can bring glory to the Father. [14]Yes, ask
Me for anything in My name, and I will do it!

14:6 John 1:4, 14, 16; 8:32; 10:10; 11:25; Rom 5:2; Eph 2:18; Heb 10:20; 1 Jn 5:20
14:7 John 6:46; 8:19; 1 Jn 2:13
14:9 John 1:14, 18; 12:45; 2 Cor 4:4; Col 1:15; Heb 1:3
14:10 John 5:19; 10:38; 17:11, 21-24

JESUS PROMISES THE HOLY SPIRIT

[15]"If you love Me, obey* My commandments. [16]And I will ask the Father, and He will give

14:16 John 14:26; 15:26

14:7 Some manuscripts read *If you have really known Me, you will know who My Father is.* 14:15 Other manuscripts read *you will obey;* still others read *you should obey.*

14:6 Jesus answered Thomas's question in an unexpected way by declaring that He is the only way anyone can come to the Father (Acts 4:12). Jesus' famous answer to Thomas's short sighted question showed that He understood His role as the way for sinners to approach the Father (John 10:9), as the foundation and fulfillment of all truths about God (8:32), and as the source of life to all who believe (1:4).

14:8-10 The Son is a distinct person, but He is fully divine exactly as the Father is (1:1). To encounter Jesus is not to encounter only part of God, nor is His revelation of God lacking in any way. Jesus is all the revelation of God that humans will ever need. The intimate interaction between the Father and Son is never interrupted, thus Jesus' words and works portray His Father perfectly. Paul stated it this way in Colossians 1:15: "Christ is the visible image of the invisible God."

▸ SALVATION
14:13 In Jesus' name. Many say the phrase "In Jesus' name" at the end of prayers, but what does it mean? Is it a magic formula to get whatever we wish? First, it means we pray with Christ's authority, not our own. We do not approach God in our own strength or based on our reputation, but on the reputation of our Master. Second, it means making our requests according to Christ's will, not our own (1 John 5:14-15). Finally, we pray and work in Jesus' name because everything we do and say centers on our Lord and Master, and every answer of prayer comes from the Father to bring glory to His Son (John 17:1). When you pray, do so with the intent of truly praying "in Jesus' name." (***See Salvation***> *Receiving> Results> Works> To be done in Jesus' name,* TopicGuide page A23.)

14:16-18 Though Jesus was leaving, He was not abandoning them like orphans. He would send the Spirit to make His home within each believer (14:23). Just as Jesus had spoken of the unity between Father and Son (14:9-10), now this unity would extend to the person of the Holy Spirit as well.

BECAUSE GOD IS
ABSOLUTE TRUTH

I will believe what He says and live accordingly.

Jesus told him, "I am the way, the truth, and the life."

JOHN 14:6

FOR THE NEXT *GOD IS ABSOLUTE TRUTH* FEATURE SEE PAGE 1947.

14:17 Rom 8:15-16; 1 Jn 3:24 | 14:20 John 10:38; 15:4-5; 16:16, 23; 17:21-24 | 14:21 John 15:10; 16:27; 1 Jn 2:5; 2 Jn 1:6 | 14:22 Luke 6:16; Acts 10:41 | 14:23 Prov 8:17; Ps 91:1; John 15:10; Eph 3:17; 1 Jn 4:16; 5:3; Rev 3:20; 21:3 | 14:24 John 7:16; 14:10 | 14:26 John 1:33; 15:26; 16:7; 20:22; 1 Jn 2:20, 27 | 14:27 John 16:33; 20:19; Phil 4:7; Col 3:15

you another Advocate,* who will never leave you. 17 He is the Holy Spirit, who leads into all
truth. The world cannot receive Him, because it isn't looking for Him and doesn't recognize
Him. But you know Him, because He lives with you now and later will be in you.* 18 No, I will
not abandon you as orphans—I will come to you. 19 Soon the world will no longer see Me,
but you will see Me. Since I live, you also will live. 20 When I am raised to life again, you will
know that I am in My Father, and you are in Me, and I am in you. 21 Those who accept My
commandments and obey them are the ones who love Me. And because they love Me, My
Father will love them. And I will love them and reveal Myself to each of them."
22 Judas (not Judas Iscariot, but the other disciple with that name) said to Him, "Lord, why
are You going to reveal Yourself only to us and not to the world at large?"
23 Jesus replied, "All who love Me will do what I say. My Father will love them, and We
will come and make Our home with each of them. 24 Anyone who doesn't love Me will not
obey Me. And remember, My words are not My own. What I am telling you is from the Father
who sent Me. 25 I am telling you these things now while I am still with you. 26 But when
the Father sends the Advocate as My representative—that is, the Holy Spirit—He will teach
you everything and will remind you of everything I have told you.
27 "I am leaving you with a gift—peace of mind and heart. And the peace I give is a gift
the world cannot give. So don't be troubled or afraid. 28 Remember what I told you: I am
going away, but I will come back to you again. If you really loved Me, you would be happy
that I am going to the Father, who is greater than I am. 29 I have told you these things before
they happen so that when they do happen, you will believe.
30 "I don't have much more time to talk to you, because the ruler of this world approaches.
He has no power over Me, 31 but I will do what the Father requires of Me, so that
the world will know that I love the Father. Come, let's be going.

JESUS, THE TRUE VINE

15:1 Ps 80:8-11; Isa 5:1-7 | 15:3 Eph 5:26

15 "I am the true grapevine, and My Father is the gardener. 2 He cuts off every branch
of Mine that doesn't produce fruit, and He prunes the branches that do bear fruit so
they will produce even more. 3 You have already been pruned and purified by the message

14:16 Or *Comforter,* or *Encourager,* or *Counselor.* Greek reads *Paraclete;* also in 14:26. 14:17 Some manuscripts read *and is in you.*

▸ ADOPTION

14:27 "Have a good day!" In social situations, we wish each other all sorts of blessings that we barely mean—"Have a good day!" is common. But Jesus meant what He said. He didn't speak simply to fulfill a social expectation or to fill an awkward moment. His words carried weight. So when He communicates and imparts peace, we must take it seriously—particularly since Jesus is the Prince of Peace (Isaiah 9:6). This peace He delivers doesn't refer to life without conflict or struggle. Instead, it first means that our souls will live in peace, rather than in strife, with God (Romans 5:1-2). Second, it means that our inner worlds ("mind and heart," 14:27) are not torn apart by the tension between heavenly and earthly realities, between Jesus' death on the cross and His heavenly reign, and between our own earthly struggles and our victory in Christ. Live in light of the peace that God gives His people through Jesus Christ. (***See Adoption****> With Christ> Supernatural> A life of everlasting peace,* TopicGuide page A37.)

14:28 The Father and Son are both equally God, yet the Father has a greater role as the sender, whereas the Son has taken the lesser role as the servant who is sent (Isaiah 53). Jesus was about to complete His lowly role by giving His "life as a ransom for many" on the cross (Mark 10:45). Then God elevated Him to the highest place as King of kings (Philippians 2:9-11). Jesus was telling the disciples that they should rejoice to see His work as a servant conclude (19:30) and His reign in heaven begin.

14:30 Jesus wanted His disciples to know that the hours of struggle that would culminate in the cross would involve a real battle with personal evil. But the devil did not have the authority to force Jesus to the cross, for he had no claims against the perfect Lamb of God (8:46; 1 Peter 1:19; Revelation 12:10).

▸ GOD

15:1 The gardener. If you've ever watched an experienced gardener trim a bush, you'll see an artist in action. He snips away the wild or dead sections and shapes the limbs to form a beautiful ornament. In the agrarian culture of Jesus' time, the vine was a familiar symbol of blessing in Israel's culture—a golden vine even adorned the entry to the Temple. Israel itself is pictured as a vine owned by God (Psalm 80:8-16; Isaiah 5:1-7; Jeremiah 2:21). The privilege of being connected to Jesus Christ, the true Vine, is both a symbol of the great blessing of union with Christ and a symbol of our responsibility to bear fruit. Do whatever you can to enhance the natural fruit bearing of those united to Christ. (***See God****> God's Names> Father> Gardener,* TopicGuide page A18.)

15:2 Branches that do not bear fruit refer to the superficially religious (see notes at 2:23-24; 4:43-54). These people display their lack of real faith when they do not obey Christ's words (12:47) or who fail to "remain" in Jesus by faith (see 6:54-56). Their lack of fruit shows they are not connected to the Vine (8:31).

I have given you. 4 Remain in Me, and I will remain in you. For a branch cannot produce
fruit if it is severed from the vine, and you cannot be fruitful unless you remain in Me.
5 "Yes, I am the vine; you are the branches. Those who remain in Me, and I in them, will
produce much fruit. For apart from Me you can do nothing. 6 Anyone who does not remain
in Me is thrown away like a useless branch and withers. Such branches are gathered into a
pile to be burned. 7 But if you remain in Me and My words remain in you, you may ask for
anything you want, and it will be granted! 8 When you produce much fruit, you are My true
disciples. This brings great glory to My Father.
9 "I have loved you even as the Father has loved Me. Remain in My love. 10 When you
obey My commandments, you remain in My love, just as I obey My Father's command-
ments and remain in His love. 11 I have told you these things so that you will be filled with
My joy. Yes, your joy will overflow! 12 This is My commandment: Love each other in the
same way I have loved you. 13 There is no greater love than to lay down one's life for one's
friends. 14 You are My friends if you do what I command. 15 I no longer call you slaves, be-
cause a master doesn't confide in His slaves. Now you are My friends, since I have told you
everything the Father told Me. 16 You didn't choose Me. I chose you. I appointed you to go
and produce lasting fruit, so that the Father will give you whatever you ask for, using My
name. 17 This is My command: Love each other.

15:4 John 6:56
15:6 Matt 3:10; 7:19; 13:42
15:8 Matt 5:16
15:9 John 3:35
15:10 John 14:15
15:11 John 17:13; 1 Jn 1:4
15:12 John 13:34
15:13 John 10:11; Rom 5:6-8
15:16 Rom 1:13; Phil 1:22

15:6 Ezekiel used the imagery of a vine that is tossed out as "useless," and to be burned" when he described God's judgment on His unfaithful people (Ezekiel 15:6-8). Those who say they believe (Matthew 7:22; John 8:30) and then demonstrate their falsehood in fruitless lives (Matthew 25:41-46; John 8:59) will be thrown into a place with others that are unbelieving—into the flames (Revelation 21:8).

15:10-11 Jesus did not strain to obey His Father, as if it were pure drudgery. Rather, doing His will brought Him more delight than anything else does (4:34). Jesus' joyous obedience to the Father that He loves is our perfect model (14:31). When we obey Jesus in this manner, we bask in His love and enjoy "a rich and satisfying life" (10:10).

15:16 Lest there be any pride on the disciples' part, Jesus reminded them that He initiated their relationship (13:18). He chose them and appointed them to their great calling as His followers. After the resurrection, Jesus commissioned His friends and specially set them apart so they might declare God's gospel of forgiveness for sins (20:21-23). Their message is still bearing "lasting fruit" all over the world.

MY RESPONSE TO GOD

Abiding and Obeying

JOHN 15:1

"Sucker shoots" is, by design, not a complimentary designation. Gardeners often find such shoots growing on plants, sucking nutrients away from the healthy branches on a vine, and creating knots of fibers where debris collects. A good gardener cuts away these shoots so that the branches can stay healthy and produce fruit.

Jesus explained that we are like branches and God is like a good gardener. He prunes away anything distracting or detrimental, cleaning us up so that we can produce the fruit of Christlikeness (John 15:1-2). God wants us to depend on Christ alone for our sustenance. Jesus said, "Remain in Me, and I will remain in you. For a branch cannot produce fruit if it is severed from the vine, and you cannot be fruitful unless you remain in Me" (John 15:4).

There are many ways to know whether we are abiding in Christ. John 15 identifies one sign to look for–obedience. Jesus said, "When you obey My commandments, you remain in My love, just as I obey My Father's commandments and remain in His love" (John 15:10). To remain obedient to God's commands is a sure sign that His love sustains us.

15:19 John 17:14; 1 Jn 4:5
15:21 Matt 5:11; 1 Pet 4:14
15:22 John 9:41
15:24 John 5:36; 9:41
15:26 John 14:17; 1 Jn 5:7
15:27 John 21:24; 1 Jn 1:2; 4:14
16:2 John 9:22
16:3 John 15:21
16:4 John 13:19
16:5 John 7:33; 13:36
16:7 John 14:26; 15:26
16:9 John 15:22
16:10 Acts 3:14; 7:52; Rom 1:17; 1 Pet 3:18
16:11 John 12:31

THE WORLD'S HATRED

18 "If the world hates you, remember that it hated Me first. 19 The world would love you as one of its own if you belonged to it, but you are no longer part of the world. I chose you to come out of the world, so it hates you. 20 Do you remember what I told you? 'A slave is not greater than the master.' Since they persecuted Me, naturally they will persecute you. And if they had listened to Me, they would listen to you. 21 They will do all this to you because of Me, for they have rejected the One who sent Me. 22 They would not be guilty if I had not come and spoken to them. But now they have no excuse for their sin. 23 Anyone who hates Me also hates My Father. 24 If I hadn't done such miraculous signs among them that no one else could do, they would not be guilty. But as it is, they have seen everything I did, yet they still hate Me and My Father. 25 This fulfills what is written in their Scriptures*: 'They hated Me without cause.'

26 "But I will send you the Advocate*—the Spirit of truth. He will come to you from the Father and will testify all about Me. 27 And you must also testify about Me because you have been with Me from the beginning of My ministry.

16 "I have told you these things so that you won't abandon your faith. 2 For you will be expelled from the synagogues, and the time is coming when those who kill you will think they are doing a holy service for God. 3 This is because they have never known the Father or Me. 4 Yes, I'm telling you these things now, so that when they happen, you will remember My warning. I didn't tell you earlier because I was going to be with you for a while longer.

THE WORK OF THE HOLY SPIRIT

5 "But now I am going away to the One who sent Me, and not one of you is asking where I am going. 6 Instead, you grieve because of what I've told you. 7 But in fact, it is best for you that I go away, because if I don't, the Advocate* won't come. If I do go away, then I will send Him to you. 8 And when He comes, He will convict the world of its sin, and of God's righteousness, and of the coming judgment. 9 The world's sin is that it refuses to believe in Me. 10 Righteousness is available because I go to the Father, and you will see Me no more. 11 Judgment will come because the ruler of this world has already been judged.

15:25 Greek *in their law.* Pss 35:19; 69:4. 15:26 Or *Comforter,* or *Encourager,* or *Counselor.* Greek reads *Paraclete.* 16:7 Or *Comforter,* or *Encourager,* or *Counselor.* Greek reads *Paraclete.*

15:21 The world despised the prophets God sent, and now His Son was on earth, they would kill Him (Mark 12:7-8). Jesus told His disciples that mistreatment from the world put them in good company. But believers that suffer because of their identification with Jesus are always richly rewarded (Hebrews 11:6, 35-40), therefore they can leap for joy in the midst of difficulty (Luke 6:23).

▸ GOD
15:26 Sending the Holy Spirit. Even among the nicest of folks, disagreements eventually spring up. That's why John took various opportunities throughout his book to illustrate the perfect agreement that exists between all persons of the Trinity. The Trinity describes God's existence as one being in three persons (Matthew 3:16, 17; Mark 1:10, 11; Luke 3:21, 22; John. 1:32-34). Jesus reminded His followers that the Spirit would come in a special way in the future, and rather than acting on His own, He would do the will of the Father, just as Christ had done. The Father loves the Son, the Son loves the Father, and both of them send the Holy Spirit to bring harmony and unity to the church (Philippians 2:1). Cooperate with the Holy Spirit (Ephesians 4:30) and show forth the mystery of the unity of the Godhead to a watching world. (***See God****> God's Names> Son> Sends the Holy Spirit,* TopicGuide page A19.)

▸ WORSHIP
16:2 Attacked for God? Religious people can be most cruel. They are often at their worst when they think they are doing God's will. Those who tortured Jesus "thought His troubles were a punishment from God" (Isaiah 53:4). Jesus' disciples were identified with Him, so they become targets for that same cruelty (John 17:14). Many people inside and outside the church imagine that attacking professing believers for one reason or another serves God, but it serves no one but themselves (Acts 7:54-58; 14:19; 21:27-32; 23:10-12). Do you ever face persecution in the church or the world? Perhaps you are not being enough like Jesus to become a target for persecution. By God's grace, live a life so much like Christ's that you taste the same sort of troubles that He experienced—and then experience His glorious rescue. (***See Worship****> NT> Teaching and Preaching> Persecution for preaching the Word,* TopicGuide page A34.)

16:7 For Jesus to "go away" back to heaven, He first had to go to the cross to provide for humanity's greatest need—forgiveness of sins. After Jesus was raised and then ascended back to heaven, the Spirit would come to remind the disciples of Jesus' teaching (14:26) and make them powerful witnesses (15:27).

12 "There is so much more I want to tell you, but you can't bear it now. 13 When the Spirit
of truth comes, He will guide you into all truth. He will not speak on His own but will tell
you what He has heard. He will tell you about the future. 14 He will bring Me glory by tell-
ing you whatever He receives from Me. 15 All that belongs to the Father is Mine; this is why
I said, 'The Spirit will tell you whatever He receives from Me.'

SADNESS WILL BE TURNED TO JOY

16 "In a little while you won't see Me anymore. But a little while after that, you will see Me
again."

17 Some of the disciples asked each other, "What does He mean when He says, 'In a little
while you won't see Me, but then you will see Me,' and 'I am going to the Father'? 18 And
what does He mean by 'a little while'? We don't understand."

19 Jesus realized they wanted to ask Him about it, so He said, "Are you asking yourselves
what I meant? I said in a little while you won't see Me, but a little while after that you will
see Me again. 20 I tell you the truth, you will weep and mourn over what is going to happen
to Me, but the world will rejoice. You will grieve, but your grief will suddenly turn to won-
derful joy. 21 It will be like a woman suffering the pains of labor. When her child is born, her
anguish gives way to joy because she has brought a new baby into the world. 22 So you
have sorrow now, but I will see you again; then you will rejoice, and no one can rob you of
that joy. 23 At that time you won't need to ask Me for anything. I tell you the truth, you will
ask the Father directly, and He will grant your request because you use My name. 24 You
haven't done this before. Ask, using My name, and you will receive, and you will have
abundant joy.

25 "I have spoken of these matters in figures of speech, but soon I will stop speaking figu-
ratively and will tell you plainly all about the Father. 26 Then you will ask in My name. I'm
not saying I will ask the Father on your behalf, 27 for the Father Himself loves you dearly
because you love Me and believe that I came from God.* 28 Yes, I came from the Father
into the world, and now I will leave the world and return to the Father."

29 Then His disciples said, "At last You are speaking plainly and not figuratively. 30 Now
we understand that You know everything, and there's no need to question You. From this
we believe that You came from God."

31 Jesus asked, "Do you finally believe? 32 But the time is coming—indeed it's here now—
when you will be scattered, each one going his own way, leaving Me alone. Yet I am not
alone because the Father is with Me. 33 I have told you all this so that you may have peace
in Me. Here on earth you will have many trials and sorrows. But take heart, because I have
overcome the world."

16:13 John 14:17, 26
16:15 John 17:10
16:16 John 14:18-24
16:20 Mark 16:10; Luke 23:27; John 20:20
16:21 Isa 13:8; 21:3; 26:17; Acts 13:33; Col 1:18
16:22 Isa 66:14; John 20:20
16:23 John 14:20; 16:26
16:24 John 15:11
16:25 Ps 78:2; John 10:6
16:27 John 8:42; 14:21; 17:8
16:28 John 13:3
16:32 Zech 13:7; Matt 26:31; John 8:29
16:33 John 14:27; Rom 5:1; 8:37; 1 Jn 5:4

16:27 Some manuscripts read *from the Father.*

▸ GOD

16:13 Finding truth. Do you despair over finding out what's really true? Contradictory ideas, conflicting studies, opinions, and stories bombard us every day. One study says that children are not harmed by divorce. Another study says that they are. Whom do we believe? How can we sort through it all to uncover the core principles of life? Jesus promises that the Holy Spirit will guide us into all truth. By reading God's Word and asking the Holy Spirit to reveal God's truth to you, you can find the truth you need for your life. Compare everything you hear and see to God's revealed will in His Word. (***See God**> God's Attributes> True> His Spirit guides believers into all truth,* TopicGuide page A18.)

16:13-15 The Spirit does not act independently of the Son, just as the Son acts in harmony with the Father (5:19-20; 8:28; 10:30). The Spirit glorified the Son by teaching the disciples what the Son had given the Spirit to say. Each person of the Trinity has a distinct role, yet each is God (John 1:1; Acts 5:3-4). The Bible repeatedly shows that within the one God there are three distinct persons (Matthew 28:19; Mark 1:10-11; 2 Corinthians 13:14).

16:25 Jesus has veiled His language because His disciples were unable to bear the full truth at that time (16:12). He had spoken this way about His crucifixion (3:14; 8:28; 12:23, 32), His resurrection (2:19-22; 16:16), His ascension (7:33-34; 16:7), the coming of the Spirit (7:37-39), and His return (14:3).

16:30-32 Jesus just told His disciples they would need to wait for a future time for clarity (16:25), but the disciples claimed to have it already. Jesus' response shows that their lofty view of their own knowledge and faith would soon be severely tested. Jesus had already told Peter that he would deny Him (13:38), and now He revealed that they all would abandon Him and scatter in His hour of need (Mark 14:50-52).

THE PRAYER OF JESUS

17:1 John 13:31
17:2 Matt 28:18; John 6:37, 39
17:3 Phil 3:8; 1 Jn 5:20
17:5 John 1:1-2; 17:24; Phil 2:6
17:8 John 13:3; 16:30
17:9 1 Jn 5:19
17:11 Gal 3:28
17:12 John 6:39
17:13 John 7:33; 15:11

17 After saying all these things, Jesus looked up to heaven and said, "Father, the hour
has come. Glorify Your Son so He can give glory back to You. 2 For You have given
Him authority over everyone. He gives eternal life to each one You have given Him. 3 And
this is the way to have eternal life—to know You, the only true God, and Jesus Christ, the
One You sent to earth. 4 I brought glory to You here on earth by completing the work You
gave Me to do. 5 Now, Father, bring Me into the glory We shared before the world began.

6 "I have revealed You* to the ones You gave Me from this world. They were always
Yours. You gave them to Me, and they have kept Your word. 7 Now they know that every-
thing I have is a gift from You, 8 for I have passed on to them the message You gave Me.
They accepted it and know that I came from You, and they believe You sent Me.

9 "My prayer is not for the world, but for those You have given Me, because they belong
to You. 10 All who are Mine belong to You, and You have given them to Me, so they bring
Me glory. 11 Now I am departing from the world; they are staying in this world, but I am
coming to You. Holy Father, You have given Me Your name;* now protect them by the
power of Your name so that they will be united just as We are. 12 During My time here, I
protected them by the power of the name You gave Me.* I guarded them so that not one
was lost, except the one headed for destruction, as the Scriptures foretold.

13 "Now I am coming to You. I told them many things while I was with them in this world so
they would be filled with My joy. 14 I have given them Your word. And the world hates them

17:6 Greek *have revealed Your name;* also in 17:26. 17:11 Some manuscripts read *You have given Me these [disciples].*
17:12 Some manuscripts read *I protected those You gave Me, by the power of Your name.*

17:2 Before the world was ever created, the Son was given a mission of salvation with the authority to carry it out (John 10:18; 1 Peter 1:20). The Father would gather His people (John 10:16, 29; Ephesians 1:4) and giving them to His Son so they might have eternal life (John 6:37; 5:24-26) by His death in their place (John 10:15). Jesus rehearsed aloud the plan that brought Him to this crucial time in His ministry—perhaps the most crucial time in all of history (John 13:3).

▸ GOD

17:3 Ask the expert. If your car is acting up, do you take it to a hospital for repair? If your pacemaker begins malfunctioning, do you bring it to your auto mechanic? Absolutely not! But so many people consult everyone but the One who created them regarding life's most important questions. We often turn to movies, books, or the Internet. But Jesus makes it clear: To discover God and know His Son personally is the path to eternal life. Mark your progress in your spiritual journey by how intimately you know Christ. Make it your goal to know Jesus more and you'll discover the riches that Christ has for those who love Him (17:6). (***See God***> *God's Attributes*> *True*> *Eternal life is knowing the only true God,* TopicGuide page A18.)

17:14-16 Since Jesus chose His disciples out of the world and gave them the Father's word, the world and the devil hated their new identity and message (15:19-21). In His victory over death and sin Jesus defeated the devil (John 12:31; Revelation 12:9) and made a public mockery of the demons (Colossians 2:15). But the devil will still angrily torment Christ's followers as he approaches final destruction (Revelation 20:10). Jesus' disciples are to be witnesses in the world (15:27), so He prays for their protection from the evil one (Matthew 6:13).

BECAUSE GOD IS ABSOLUTE TRUTH

I will believe what He says and live accordingly.

When the Spirit of truth comes, He will guide you into all truth.

JOHN 16:13

FOR THE NEXT *GOD IS ABSOLUTE TRUTH* FEATURE SEE PAGE 2207.

because they do not belong to the world, just as I do not belong to the world. 15 I'm not ask-
ing You to take them out of the world, but to keep them safe from the evil one. 16 They do not
belong to this world any more than I do. 17 Make them holy by Your truth; teach them Your
word, which is truth. 18 Just as You sent Me into the world, I am sending them into the world.
19 And I give Myself as a holy sacrifice for them so they can be made holy by Your truth.
20 "I am praying not only for these disciples but also for all who will ever believe in Me

17:15 1 Jn 5:18
17:18 John 20:21
17:19 Heb 2:11

17:20 Jesus' prayer now extended to future concerns as He considered the disciples' mission. As they remained in Him, their mission would bear much fruit (John 15:8; Acts 2:41; 4:4). In Revelation 7:9, John received a vision of the fruit of the disciples' ministry: "I saw a vast crowd, too great to count, from every nation and tribe and people and language, standing in front of the throne and before the Lamb."

▸ WORSHIP
17:20 Jesus prayed for you! When we are at our spiritual best, we are sensitive to the needs of others. We pray easily and frequently. But when we are stressed out, we can hardly think about anyone but ourselves. When Jesus was in the Garden of Gethsemane, He prepared Himself for His destiny—death on a cross. At this most stressful moment, He prayed for you! He already had you in mind. He prayed that all His followers would be united as one and would spread His message to others. Jesus always has you on His mind. Thank Him for His intimate attention to you. (***See Worship****> NT> Prayer> Examples> Jesus> Christ's prayer in the Garden of Gethsemane,* TopicGuide page A33.)

MY RESPONSE TO GOD

One Prayer, Many Divisions

JOHN 17:21

If God answers anyone's prayers, He certainly answers the prayers of His Son, Jesus. That's why we must carefully look at Jesus' final prayer for His church more carefully, for it appears as if the very opposite to His request has occurred.

Jesus prayed that His people would share the same unity that He and His heavenly Father share: "I pray that they will all be one, just as You and I are one–as You are in Me, Father, and I am in You. And may they be in Us so that the world will believe You sent Me" (John 17:21). But look around us–church buildings side by side, denominations by the thousands, and churches splitting over major–and minor–disagreements.

This reality doesn't mean that denominations in the church are necessarily sinful. As Paul said, "Of course, there must be divisions among you so that you who have God's approval will be recognized!" (1 Corinthians 11:19). But the existence of divisions does mean that a major portion of the church's mission on earth–to manifest the unity of the Godhead–is an uphill battle. The continued partitioning of God's people means that Jesus' prayer isn't answered–or does it?

The book of Ephesians answers this puzzling question. Ephesians 4:3 is a command: "Make every effort to keep yourselves united in the Spirit, binding yourselves together with peace." Clearly God wants us to strive to manifest solidarity through peaceful interactions with each other. But 4:4 speaks of the answer to Christ's prayer–"For there is one body and one Spirit, just as you have been called to one glorious hope for the future." So God's people have been made one, in answer to Christ's prayer–but we need to learn to manifest it to the watching world.

The functional and spiritual chaos in the church sends mixed messages to a world that needs to hear Jesus' prayer loud and clear–the unified God has made a unified people. Remember that as you seek peaceful solutions to conflicts with believers.

17:21 through their message. 21 I pray that they will all be one, just as You and I are one—as You
John 10:38 are in Me, Father, and I am in You. And may they be in Us so that the world will believe
Gal 3:28 You sent Me.
17:22 John 17:11 22 "I have given them the glory You gave Me, so they may be one as We are one. 23 I am
17:24 in them and You are in Me. May they experience such perfect unity that the world will
John 1:14; 12:26 know that You sent Me and that You love them as much as You love Me. 24 Father, I want
17:25 these whom You have given Me to be with Me where I am. Then they can see all the glory
Matt 11:27 You gave Me because You loved Me even before the world began!
17:26 25 "O righteous Father, the world doesn't know You, but I do; and these disciples know
John 15:9 You sent Me. 26 I have revealed You to them, and I will continue to do so. Then Your love
for Me will be in them, and I will be in them."

JESUS IS BETRAYED AND ARRESTED

18:1 **18** After saying these things, Jesus crossed the Kidron Valley with His disciples and
2 Sam 15:23 entered a grove of olive trees. 2 Judas, the betrayer, knew this place, because
Matt 26:36 Mark 14:32 Jesus had often gone there with His disciples. 3 The leading priests and Pharisees had
18:3-11 given Judas a contingent of Roman soldiers and Temple guards to accompany him. Now
//Matt 26:47-56 //Mark 14:43-50 with blazing torches, lanterns, and weapons, they arrived at the olive grove.
//Luke 22:47-53 4 Jesus fully realized all that was going to happen to Him, so He stepped forward to meet
18:3 them. "Who are you looking for?" He asked.
John 7:32, 45 5 "Jesus the Nazarene,"* they replied.
18:4 "I AM He,"* Jesus said. (Judas, who betrayed Him, was standing with them.) 6 As Jesus
John 6:64 said "I AM He," they all drew back and fell to the ground! 7 Once more He asked them,
"Who are you looking for?"

18:5a Or *Jesus of Nazareth;* also in 18:7. 18:5b Or *"The 'I AM' is here";* or *"I am the LORD";* Greek reads *I am;* also in 18:6, 8. See Exod 3:14.

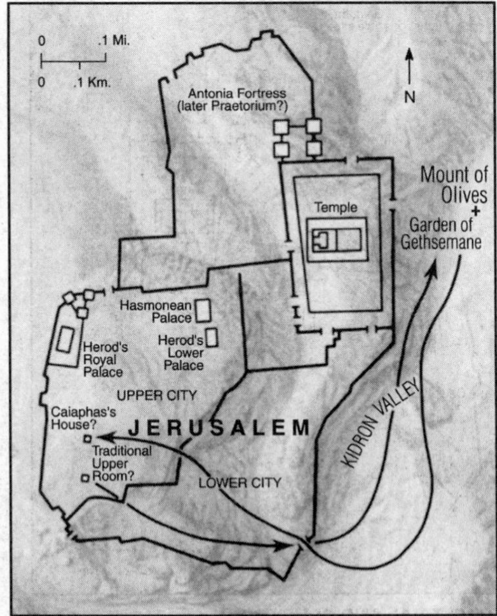

BETRAYAL IN THE GARDEN
After eating the Passover meal in the upper room, Jesus and His disciples went to Gethsemane, where Judas led the Temple guard to arrest Jesus. Jesus was then taken to Caiaphas's house for His first of many trials.

17:24 Jesus' glory is partially visible in this life by all believers (2 Corinthians 3:18), but our vision of His glory will be greatest when He comes again (1 John 3:2). Jesus concluded His prayer where He began—speaking of coming for His own to bring them to their designated rooms in His Father's house (14:1-3). Believers are not bothersome intruders in heaven. Rather, when they occupy their assigned places and behold the Son's glory, it will be just what the Father and Son have always desired.

18:1 John omitted the agonizing session of prayer in the grove of olive trees (the Garden of Gethsemane) that is recorded in the other three Gospel accounts (Matthew 26:36-46; Mark 14:32-42; Luke 22:40-46). However he did use similar language as the other Gospels regarding this event when he described Jesus as being "deeply troubled" about His approaching death on the cross (12:27). Also in John 18:11 Jesus spoke of the crucifixion as "the cup of suffering the Father has given Me."

18:5-6 Jesus merely uttered "I AM He" (see NLT textual note, see also 8:58 and 13:19 and textual notes) and the entire armed mob stumbled backward to the ground (see 7:46 for another testimony to the power of His words). John alone recorded this detail, showing that Jesus had the power to avoid arrest if He chose to use it (see also Matthew 26:53).

And again they replied, "Jesus the Nazarene."
[8]"I told you that I AM He," Jesus said. "And since I am the One you want, let these others
go." [9]He did this to fulfill His own statement: "I did not lose a single one of those You have 18:9 John 6:39; 17:12
given Me."*
[10]Then Simon Peter drew a sword and slashed off the right ear of Malchus, the high 18:10 Luke 22:36, 38
priest's slave. [11]But Jesus said to Peter, "Put your sword back into its sheath. Shall I not 18:11 Matt 20:22; 26:39 Mark 10:38; 14:36 Luke 22:42
drink from the cup of suffering the Father has given Me?"

JESUS AT THE HIGH PRIEST'S HOUSE

[12]So the soldiers, their commanding officer, and the Temple guards arrested Jesus and 18:12-14 //Matt 26:57-58 //Mark 14:53-54 //Luke 22:54
tied Him up. [13]First they took Him to Annas, the father-in-law of Caiaphas, the high priest 18:13 Luke 3:2 John 18:24
at that time.* [14]Caiaphas was the one who had told the other Jewish leaders, "It's better 18:14 John 11:49-51
that one man should die for the people."

PETER'S FIRST DENIAL

[15]Simon Peter followed Jesus, as did another of the disciples. That other disciple was ac-
quainted with the high priest, so he was allowed to enter the high priest's courtyard with 18:16-18 //Matt 26:69-70 //Mark 14:66-68 //Luke 22:55-57
Jesus. [16]Peter had to stay outside the gate. Then the disciple who knew the high priest
spoke to the woman watching at the gate, and she let Peter in. [17]The woman asked Peter,
"You're not one of that man's disciples, are you?"
"No," he said, "I am not."
[18]Because it was cold, the household servants and the guards had made a charcoal fire. 18:18 Mark 14:54, 67
They stood around it, warming themselves, and Peter stood with them, warming himself.

18:9 See John 6:39 and 17:12. 18:13 Greek *that year.*

▸ PURPOSE

18:10 Spiritual reactions. We may criticize Peter for reacting rashly when he cut off Malchus's ear. Yet we often react the same way when we face adversity—we strike out. But our first impulse in that type of conflict should be to open our eyes, look around, and pray. If Peter had remembered Christ's words, he would have realized that Jesus was letting events play out for a reason: our salvation (Matthew 16:21; 20:18). Jesus knew He had to endure the cross. God has a purpose in our sufferings, too. It may not be His will for us to fight against every offense, answering every show of force with equal force. By remembering Christ's Words, you can be prepared to act instead of simply react. (***See Purpose****> God's Deeds> Special Acts> Miracles> Jesus> Malchus's ear restored,* TopicGuide page A53; also ***see Church****> Role> Conflict> Preventative teaching,* TopicGuide page A49.)

18:24 Caiaphas was the high priest at this time, also serving as president of the Sanhedrin. His long tenure (AD 18–36) demonstrated his political skills as he placated both Jewish religious authorities and Roman civil ones. Both he and Pilate were relieved of their responsibilities during the same year. Archaeologists discovered his ossuary (the urn containing his remains) in a small tomb in 1990.

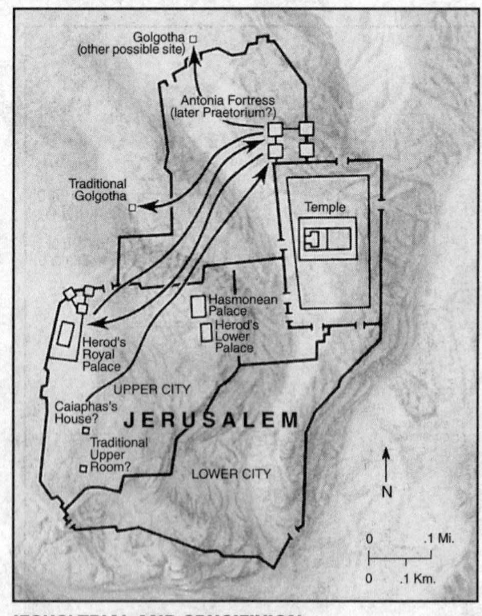

JESUS' TRIAL AND CRUCIFIXION
Jesus was taken from trial before the Jewish high council to trial before the Roman governor, Pilate, in Pilate's palace. Pilate sent Him to Herod (Luke 23:5-12), but Herod just returned Jesus to Pilate. Responding to threats from the mob, Pilate finally turned Jesus over to be crucified.

THE HIGH PRIEST QUESTIONS JESUS

18:19-24 //Matt 26:59-68 //Mark 14:55-65 //Luke 22:63-71; 18:20 Matt 26:55, John 7:26; 18:22 John 19:3; 18:23 Matt 5:39, Acts 23:2-5; 18:24 Matt 26:3

19 Inside, the high priest began asking Jesus about His followers and what He had been
teaching them. 20 Jesus replied, "Everyone knows what I teach. I have preached regularly in
the synagogues and the Temple, where the people* gather. I have not spoken in secret.
21 Why are you asking Me this question? Ask those who heard Me. They know what I said."
22 Then one of the Temple guards standing nearby slapped Jesus across the face. "Is that
the way to answer the high priest?" he demanded.
23 Jesus replied, "If I said anything wrong, you must prove it. But if I'm speaking the truth,
why are you beating Me?"
24 Then Annas bound Jesus and sent Him to Caiaphas, the high priest.

PETER'S SECOND AND THIRD DENIALS

18:25-27 //Matt 26:71-75 //Mark 14:69-72 //Luke 22:58-62; 18:27 John 13:38

25 Meanwhile, as Simon Peter was standing by the fire warming himself, they asked him
again, "You're not one of His disciples, are you?"
He denied it, saying, "No, I am not."
26 But one of the household slaves of the high priest, a relative of the man whose ear Pe-
ter had cut off, asked, "Didn't I see you out there in the olive grove with Jesus?" 27 Again Pe-
ter denied it. And immediately a rooster crowed.

JESUS' TRIAL BEFORE PILATE

18:28-38 //Matt 27:1-2, 11-14 //Mark 15:1-5 //Luke 23:1-5; 18:32 Matt 20:19, John 12:32; 18:33 Luke 23:3, John 19:9; 18:36 Matt 26:53, Luke 17:21, John 6:15; 18:37 John 8:47, 1 Jn 4:6

28 Jesus' trial before Caiaphas ended in the early hours of the morning. Then He was taken
to the headquarters of the Roman governor.* His accusers didn't go inside because it
would defile them, and they wouldn't be allowed to celebrate the Passover. 29 So Pilate,
the governor, went out to them and asked, "What is your charge against this man?"
30 "We wouldn't have handed Him over to you if He weren't a criminal!" they retorted.
31 "Then take Him away and judge Him by your own law," Pilate told them.
"Only the Romans are permitted to execute someone," the Jewish leaders replied.
32 (This fulfilled Jesus' prediction about the way He would die.*)
33 Then Pilate went back into his headquarters and called for Jesus to be brought to him.
"Are You the king of the Jews?" he asked Him.
34 Jesus replied, "Is this your own question, or did others tell you about Me?"
35 "Am I a Jew?" Pilate retorted. "Your own people and their leading priests brought You
to me for trial. Why? What have You done?"
36 Jesus answered, "My Kingdom is not an earthly kingdom. If it were, My followers
would fight to keep Me from being handed over to the Jewish leaders. But My Kingdom is
not of this world."
37 Pilate said, "So You are a king?"
Jesus responded, "You say I am a king. Actually, I was born and came into the world to
testify to the truth. All who love the truth recognize that what I say is true."

18:20 Greek *Jewish people;* also in 18:38. 18:28 Greek *to the Praetorium;* also in 18:33. 18:32 See John 12:32-33.

18:27 Peter had barely uttered his third denial when he heard the rooster crow. Morning had come and Jesus' words had proven true (13:38). The other Gospels mention Peter's recollection of Jesus' words and his tears of remorse (Matthew 26:75; Mark 14:72; Luke 22:61-62), but John leaves his readers silently imagining the sinking feeling that followed the rooster's crowing.

18:28 The Jewish leaders wanted to avoid defilement so they could participate in the rest of the religious celebration. (Passover festivities continued for seven days after the lamb was killed for the Passover meal.) They obsessed about external cleanliness, but they were unconcerned about the moral filth of killing an innocent man.

18:31-32 The Jewish leaders' statement was only a half-truth, because they practiced capital punishment in religious courts (John 8:1-11; Acts 7:54-59). Deferring to the Roman authorities was part of the Jewish leaders' plan to avoid culpability before the general public while having Jesus killed.

18:37 Jesus had already stated what His Kingdom was not (18:36), and now He implied what it was: God's righteous reign in the earth, mediated by His Son, Jesus Christ. The Kingdom of God begins in the hearts of the redeemed who receive His truth (Colossians 1:13) and moves outward (Mark 12:33-35). Though it has implications for politics (Romans 13:1-5), the Kingdom of God is not preeminently political (18:36). The Kingdom of God is wherever Christ's gospel brings repentance and submission.

38"What is truth?" Pilate asked. Then he went out again to the people and told them, "He
is not guilty of any crime. 39But you have a custom of asking me to release one prisoner **18:39–19:5**
each year at Passover. Would you like me to release this 'King of the Jews'?" //Matt 27:15-31 //Mark 15:6-20
40But they shouted back, "No! Not this man. We want Barabbas!" (Barabbas was a //Luke 23:13-25
revolutionary.)

JESUS SENTENCED TO DEATH

19 Then Pilate had Jesus flogged with a lead-tipped whip. 2The soldiers wove a **19:1**
crown of thorns and put it on His head, and they put a purple robe on Him. 3"Hail! Isa 50:6; 53:5
King of the Jews!" they mocked, as they slapped Him across the face. **19:3**
4Pilate went outside again and said to the people, "I am going to bring Him out to you John 18:22
now, but understand clearly that I find Him not guilty." 5Then Jesus came out wearing the **19:4**
crown of thorns and the purple robe. And Pilate said, "Look, here is the man!" Luke 23:4 John 18:38
6When they saw Him, the leading priests and Temple guards began shouting, "Crucify **19:6**
Him! Crucify Him!" John 18:31
"Take Him yourselves and crucify Him," Pilate said. "I find Him not guilty."
7The Jewish leaders replied, "By our law He ought to die because He called Himself the **19:7**
Son of God." Lev 24:16 Matt 26:63-66
8When Pilate heard this, He was more frightened than ever. 9He took Jesus back into the
headquarters* again and asked Him, "Where are You from?" But Jesus gave no answer.
10"Why don't You talk to me?" Pilate demanded. "Don't You realize that I have the power
to release You or crucify You?"
11Then Jesus said, "You would have no power over Me at all unless it were given to you **19:11**
from above. So the one who handed Me over to you has the greater sin." Rom 13:1
12Then Pilate tried to release Him, but the Jewish leaders shouted, "If you release this man, **19:12**
you are no 'friend of Caesar.'* Anyone who declares himself a king is a rebel against Caesar." Luke 23:2 Acts 17:7
13When they said this, Pilate brought Jesus out to them again. Then Pilate sat down on **19:13**
the judgment seat on the platform that is called the Stone Pavement (in Hebrew, *Gabba-* Matt 27:19
tha). 14It was now about noon on the day of preparation for the Passover. And Pilate said
to the people,* "Look, here is your king!"

19:9 Greek *the Praetorium.* 19:12 "Friend of Caesar" is a technical term that refers to an ally of the emperor. 19:14 Greek *Jewish people;* also in 19:20.

▸ WORSHIP

18:40 Anyone but Jesus! Many people and organizations want to get rid of God. Some people try to banish His name from public discourse just so they won't be reminded of Him and His claims. But how sweet His name is to those who love Him! To believers, His name sounds like a song. The apostle Paul said that he used to scoff at the name of Jesus (1 Timothy 1:13) and that this was evidence of his unbelief and ignorance. No matter what language you speak, cherish His name in that language. Use it honorably and be patient with those who ignorantly attempt to take God out of the public square. As you live a joyful, productive, and thoroughly Christian life, you will demonstrate the folly of trying to remove Jesus from the world. (***See Worship****> NT> Christ's Supremacy> Christ's name commands reverence,* TopicGuide page A30.)

19:1 This was likely the first of two floggings, the latter occurring when the proceedings with Pilate had finished (Matthew 27:26; Mark 15:15). Pilate thought Jesus was innocent (18:38) and his motive for this flogging is clear: "I will have Him flogged, and then I will release Him" (Luke 23:16).

▸ HOLINESS

19:3 The humiliation of Jesus. What's your most embarrassing moment? Did anything good come of it? The prophet Isaiah foretold Jesus' humiliation: "I offered My back to those who beat Me and My cheeks to those who pulled out My beard. I did not hide My face from mockery and spitting" (Isaiah 50:6). Jesus not only endured physical pain, but also degradation—for our sakes. You can't spiritually save anyone through your pain, but how you bear up under humiliation can give honor to God and help others know Him better. If Jesus bore His suffering with patience (1 Peter 2:21-23), then so can you. Pray that God would use your suffering and tragedies to draw others closer to Him. (***See Holiness****> Submission> Identifying with Christ> Suffering with Him,* TopicGuide page A40.)

19:7 The Jews had previously objected when Jesus called Himself the Son of God because it was a claim to deity (5:18; 10:33, 36), and God's law prohibited blasphemy. However, Jesus told them, "the Scriptures point to Me!" (5:39). The leaders claimed that the law they received from Moses condemned Jesus (Leviticus 24:16), but actually it verifies that He is the Son of God (5:46).

19:14 The day of preparation likely referred to the day before the Sabbath in Passover week. John seems to be saying that morning was already passing and there was but a short time left before Sabbath (a point that is significant later; see 19:31). Mark 15:25 states, "It was nine o'clock in the morning when they crucified Him" (the third hour), while this verse reads

15 "Away with Him," they yelled. "Away with Him! Crucify Him!"
"What? Crucify your king?" Pilate asked.
"We have no king but Caesar," the leading priests shouted back.
16 Then Pilate turned Jesus over to them to be crucified.

THE CRUCIFIXION

19:16-27 So they took Jesus away. 17 Carrying the cross by Himself, He went to the place called Place
//Matt 27:32-44 of the Skull (in Hebrew, *Golgotha*). 18 There they nailed Him to the cross. Two others were
//Mark 15:21-32 crucified with Him, one on either side, with Jesus between them. 19 And Pilate posted a sign
//Luke 23:26-43 over Him that read, "Jesus of Nazareth,* the King of the Jews." 20 The place where Jesus was
crucified was near the city, and the sign was written in Hebrew, Latin, and Greek, so that
many people could read it.
21 Then the leading priests objected and said to Pilate, "Change it from 'The King of the
Jews' to 'He said, I am King of the Jews.'"
22 Pilate replied, "No, what I have written, I have written."
23 When the soldiers had crucified Jesus, they divided His clothes among the four of
them. They also took His robe, but it was seamless, woven in one piece from top to bot-
19:24 tom. 24 So they said, "Rather than tearing it apart, let's throw dice* for it." This fulfilled the
*Ps 22:18 Scripture that says, "They divided My garments among themselves and threw dice for My
clothing."* So that is what they did.
19:25 25 Standing near the cross were Jesus' mother, and His mother's sister, Mary (the wife of
Matt 27:55-56 Clopas), and Mary Magdalene. 26 When Jesus saw His mother standing there beside the
Mark 15:40-41 disciple He loved, He said to her, "Dear woman, here is your son." 27 And He said to this dis-
Luke 8:2; 23:49 ciple, "Here is your mother." And from then on this disciple took her into his home.
19:26 John 2:4; 13:23; 20:2; 21:7, 20

THE DEATH OF JESUS

19:28-37 28 Jesus knew that His mission was now finished, and to fulfill Scripture He said, "I am
//Matt 27:45-56 thirsty."* 29 A jar of sour wine was sitting there, so they soaked a sponge in it, put it on a
//Mark 15:33-41 hyssop branch, and held it up to His lips. 30 When Jesus had tasted it, He said, "It is fin-
//Luke 23:44-49 ished!" Then He bowed His head and released His spirit.
19:28 *Pss 22:15; 69:21
31 It was the day of preparation, and the Jewish leaders didn't want the bodies hanging
19:30 Job 19:26-27 there the next day, which was the Sabbath (and a very special Sabbath, because it was the
Passover). So they asked Pilate to hasten their deaths by ordering that their legs be bro-
19:31 Deut 21:22-23 ken. Then their bodies could be taken down. 32 So the soldiers came and broke the legs of

19:19 Or *Jesus the Nazarene.* **19:24a** Greek *cast lots.* **19:24b** Ps 22:18. **19:28** See Pss 22:15; 69:21.

that it was "about noon" (the sixth hour). It is possible that Mark's time reference encompassed all of the events that took place throughout that morning, whereas John referred only to the conclusion of the trial just prior to the actual crucifixion.

19:15 The Jewish leaders' admission of allegiance to Caesar was a major concession. This public statement of loyalty was the only currency the Jewish leaders had to offer Pilate in exchange for crucifying Jesus.

19:17-42 John recorded the crucifixion of Israel's true King and emphasized His obedience to the Father in every detail until He had completely finished the work. In His agony, Jesus still cared toward His mother, showing that He is both the perfect earthly son and the heavenly Son. His death fulfilled Scripture in every respect. After Jesus' death, two men honored Him in burial as the time of His humiliation had passed.

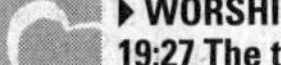

▸ WORSHIP

19:27 The tender King. Even in Jesus' most trying hour, He still attended to the needs of those under His care. As the oldest son in His family, He was responsible for His mother. He made sure that she had someone to care for her. When we go through trials and pain, we usually think only about ourselves. But in Jesus, we see the example of how to endure with sensitivity to both others' needs as well as your own. If you are in the midst of a time of adversity, ask Jesus to help you see the needs of others around you. Pay special attention to the elderly in your family and honor them by making sure they are cared for during difficult times (Ephesians 6:2-3). (***See Worship***> *NT> Our Role> Obedience> Do not neglect doing good,* TopicGuide page A32.)

19:30 Jesus completed everything the Father sent Him to accomplish (17:4). He lived without sin and died in perfect obedience to the Father's will, paying the entire price that sinners deserved to pay. "It is finished" is not a statement of defeat but of victory. As He bowed His head to die, He was sure that salvation had been accomplished for all believers.

19:32 Breaking the crucified person's legs prevented him from being able to push himself up to take a breath. This accelerated the execution by causing the victim to die of suffocation.

the two men crucified with Jesus. 33But when they came to Jesus, they saw that He was al-
ready dead, so they didn't break His legs. 34One of the soldiers, however, pierced His side
with a spear, and immediately blood and water flowed out. 35(This report is from an eye-
witness giving an accurate account. He speaks the truth so that you also can believe.*)
36These things happened in fulfillment of the Scriptures that say, "Not one of His bones
will be broken,"* 37and "They will look on the One they pierced."*

THE BURIAL OF JESUS

38Afterward Joseph of Arimathea, who had been a secret disciple of Jesus (because he
feared the Jewish leaders), asked Pilate for permission to take down Jesus' body. When Pi-
late gave permission, Joseph came and took the body away. 39With him came Nicode-
mus, the man who had come to Jesus at night. He brought seventy-five pounds* of
perfumed ointment made from myrrh and aloes. 40Following Jewish burial custom, they
wrapped Jesus' body with the spices in long sheets of linen cloth. 41The place of crucifix-
ion was near a garden, where there was a new tomb, never used before. 42And so, be-
cause it was the day of preparation for the Jewish Passover* and since the tomb was close
at hand, they laid Jesus there.

THE RESURRECTION

20 Early on Sunday morning,* while it was still dark, Mary Magdalene came to the
tomb and found that the stone had been rolled away from the entrance. 2She ran
and found Simon Peter and the other disciple, the one whom Jesus loved. She said, "They
have taken the Lord's body out of the tomb, and we don't know where they have put Him!"
3Peter and the other disciple started out for the tomb. 4They were both running, but the
other disciple outran Peter and reached the tomb first. 5He stooped and looked in and saw
the linen wrappings lying there, but he didn't go in. 6Then Simon Peter arrived and went
inside. He also noticed the linen wrappings lying there, 7while the cloth that had covered
Jesus' head was folded up and lying apart from the other wrappings. 8Then the disciple
who had reached the tomb first also went in, and he saw and believed—9for until then
they still hadn't understood the Scriptures that said Jesus must rise from the dead. 10Then
they went home.

JESUS APPEARS TO MARY MAGDALENE

11Mary was standing outside the tomb crying, and as she wept, she stooped and looked
in. 12She saw two white-robed angels, one sitting at the head and the other at the foot of

19:35 John 20:30-31; 21:24 1 Jn 1:1
19:36 *Exod 12:46 Num 9:12 *Ps 34:20
19:37 *Zech 12:10 Rev 1:7
19:38-42 //Matt 27:57-61 //Mark 15:42-47 //Luke 23:50-56
19:39 John 3:1-2; 7:50
19:40 Luke 24:12 John 20:5-7
20:1-8 //Matt 28:1-8 //Mark 16:1-8 //Luke 24:1-12
20:2 John 13:23
20:3 Luke 24:12
20:5 John 19:40
20:7 John 11:44
20:9 John 2:22
20:11-18 Mark 16:9-11
20:12 Mark 16:5 Luke 24:4

19:35 Some manuscripts read *can continue to believe.* **19:36** Exod 12:46; Num 9:12; Ps 34:20. **19:37** Zech 12:10. **19:39** Greek *100 litras* [32.7 kilograms]. **19:42** Greek *because of the Jewish day of preparation.* **20:1** Greek *On the first day of the week.*

20:1-31 John presented the Resurrection with a special emphasis on eyewitness testimony. He told of the firsthand observations of the grave clothing in the empty tomb, and he also recorded Jesus' personal interactions with Mary, the disciples, and Thomas. John's account shows that Jesus' resurrection is a fact and that it is appropriate to confess Jesus as Lord and God.

▶ SALVATION

20:1 An unlikely participant. Of all the people who knew Jesus, whom would you predict would first see Him after He was resurrected? Mary Magdalene would probably not be at the top of your list—she's been a minor player in the narrative so far. But her qualification for seeing the Lord makes perfect sense—she loved Jesus! Although the disciples ran away, she followed her Lord to the cross and stayed with His body until it was buried. She was so devoted that she went to the tomb as soon as the Sabbath was over. Holy love goes beyond circumstances and translates into real action on behalf of the beloved. When is the last time you did something simply because you loved Jesus? Show your love for Christ with action. (***See Salvation**> Receiving> Results> Works> Expression of gratitude,* TopicGuide page A23.)

20:7 The emphasis on the exact state of the wrappings and folded cloth shows that this was eyewitness testimony. John reported specific details so his readers could know that their faith is based on fact, not fantasy (21:24).

20:8-9 The unnamed "disciple" mentioned here appears to be John's favorite self-designation (see also John 14:22; 18:15; 20:2-4). The orderly appearance of the tomb testified against Mary's assumption, since no one would have removed the 75 pounds of spices and wrappings prior to stealing the body. The scene was significant enough to cause him to believe that something supernatural had occurred, even though he still hadn't fully comprehended the Resurrection or the Scriptures (1 Corinthians 15:4).

the place where the body of Jesus had been lying. 13“Dear woman, why are you crying?”
the angels asked her.
“Because they have taken away my Lord,” she replied, “and I don’t know where they
have put Him.”

20:14 Mark 16:9; Luke 24:16; John 21:4
20:17 Matt 28:10; John 16:28; Rom 8:29; Col 1:18; Heb 2:11

14She turned to leave and saw Someone standing there. It was Jesus, but she didn’t recog-
nize Him. 15“Dear woman, why are you crying?” Jesus asked her. “Who are you looking for?”
She thought He was the gardener. “Sir,” she said, “if You have taken Him away, tell me
where You have put Him, and I will go and get Him.”
16“Mary!” Jesus said.
She turned to Him and cried out, “Rabboni!” (which is Hebrew for “Teacher”).
17“Don’t cling to Me,” Jesus said, “for I haven’t yet ascended to the Father. But go find
My brothers and tell them, ‘I am ascending to My Father and your Father, to My God and
your God.’ ”
18Mary Magdalene found the disciples and told them, “I have seen the Lord!” Then she
gave them His message.

20:19-23 //Matt 28:16-20; //Luke 24:36-49
20:20 John 16:20-22; 19:34
20:21 Matt 28:19; John 17:18
20:22 John 7:37-39; 14:16-18, 26

JESUS APPEARS TO HIS DISCIPLES

19That Sunday evening* the disciples were meeting behind locked doors because they
were afraid of the Jewish leaders. Suddenly, Jesus was standing there among them!
“Peace be with you,” He said. 20As He spoke, He showed them the wounds in His hands
and His side. They were filled with joy when they saw the Lord! 21Again He said, “Peace be
with you. As the Father has sent Me, so I am sending you.” 22Then He breathed on them
and said, “Receive the Holy Spirit. 23If you forgive anyone’s sins, they are forgiven. If you
do not forgive them, they are not forgiven.”

20:24 John 11:16
20:28 John 1:1, 18; 10:30; 14:9; Phil 2:6; Col 2:9; Titus 2:13; 2 Pet 1:1; 1 Jn 5:20
20:29 1 Pet 1:8

JESUS APPEARS TO THOMAS

24One of the twelve disciples, Thomas (nicknamed the Twin),* was not with the others
when Jesus came. 25They told him, “We have seen the Lord!”
But he replied, “I won’t believe it unless I see the nail wounds in His hands, put my fin-
gers into them, and place my hand into the wound in His side.”
26Eight days later the disciples were together again, and this time Thomas was with them.
The doors were locked; but suddenly, as before, Jesus was standing among them. “Peace be
with you,” He said. 27Then He said to Thomas, “Put your finger here, and look at My hands.
Put your hand into the wound in My side. Don’t be faithless any longer. Believe!”
28“My Lord and my God!” Thomas exclaimed.
29Then Jesus told him, “You believe because you have seen Me. Blessed are those who
believe without seeing Me.”

20:19 Greek *In the evening of that day, the first day of the week.* 20:24 Greek *Thomas, who was called Didymus.*

20:19-26 Jesus’ appearance in the secured room (see also 20:26) indicated something miraculous about the new mode of existence He enjoyed in a resurrected body (1 Corinthians 15:44). Jesus’ risen body was not totally new. It was a wonderful transformation of His former body. The marks from the crucifixion in His hands and side were clearly visible, proving that His body wasn’t an illusion. John wanted his readers to know that Jesus had indeed died (19:33-35) and that He was raised to life again (20:5-8). Jesus’ closest friends verified this fact when He appeared to them (20:27).

20:21-22 Jesus commissioned His disciples as “sent ones,” just as Jesus had been the Father’s “sent One.” Jesus commissioned them by He breathing on them and giving them the Holy Spirit to set them apart for the task (just as the Spirit uniquely set Jesus apart for His task, 1:32-34). “Spirit” and “breath” are the same word in both Greek and Hebrew, thus explaining Christ’s usage of the symbol of breathing to represent His gift of the Spirit.

▸ WORSHIP

20:28 Thomas believes. We all have doubt. Perhaps that’s why John made the point to include this in his Gospel—everyone can identify with the story of Thomas’s unbelief. Everyone, no matter how mature, occasionally thinks, “I wonder if this God-stuff is true.” When Thomas first heard of Jesus’ resurrection, he required tangible evidence before he would believe. But once he saw Jesus, he worshiped Him as Lord and God. Like Thomas, we wait, wondering about the future, and a day is coming when as plain as day, He will arrive. Look forward to that day of clarity, when our doubt will be washed away by the manifest presence of Jesus Christ. (***See Worship***> *NT> Christ’s Supremacy> Thomas worships Jesus alone as God,* TopicGuide page A30.)

PURPOSE OF THE BOOK

30The disciples saw Jesus do many other miraculous signs in addition to the ones re- 20:30
corded in this book. 31But these are written so that you may continue to believe* that Jesus John 21:25
is the Messiah, the Son of God, and that by believing in Him you will have life by the 20:31
power of His name. John 3:15; 19:35; 1 Jn 5:13

EPILOGUE: JESUS APPEARS TO SEVEN DISCIPLES 21:2

21 Later, Jesus appeared again to the disciples beside the Sea of Galilee.* This is how it John 1:45-51; 11:16; 20:24
happened. 2Several of the disciples were there—Simon Peter, Thomas (nicknamed
the Twin),* Nathanael from Cana in Galilee, the sons of Zebedee, and two other disciples.
3Simon Peter said, "I'm going fishing." 21:3
"We'll come, too," they all said. So they went out in the boat, but they caught nothing all Luke 5:5
night.
4At dawn Jesus was standing on the beach, but the disciples couldn't see who He was. 21:4
5He called out, "Fellows,* have you caught any fish?" Luke 24:16; John 20:14
"No," they replied.
6Then He said, "Throw out your net on the right-hand side of the boat, and you'll get 21:6
some!" So they did, and they couldn't haul in the net because there were so many fish in it. Luke 5:4-7
7Then the disciple Jesus loved said to Peter, "It's the Lord!" When Simon Peter heard that 21:7
it was the Lord, he put on his tunic (for he had stripped for work), jumped into the water, John 13:23
and headed to shore. 8The others stayed with the boat and pulled the loaded net to the
shore, for they were only about a hundred yards* from shore. 9When they got there, they 21:9
found breakfast waiting for them—fish cooking over a charcoal fire, and some bread. John 18:18
10"Bring some of the fish you've just caught," Jesus said. 11So Simon Peter went aboard
and dragged the net to the shore. There were 153 large fish, and yet the net hadn't torn.
12"Now come and have some breakfast!" Jesus said. None of the disciples dared to ask
Him, "Who are You?" They knew it was the Lord. 13Then Jesus served them the bread and
the fish. 14This was the third time Jesus had appeared to His disciples since He had been 21:14
raised from the dead. John 20:19, 26

20:31 Some manuscripts read *that you may believe.* 21:1 Greek *Sea of Tiberias,* another name for the Sea of Galilee. 21:2 Greek *Thomas, who was called Didymus.* 21:5 Greek *Children.* 21:8 Greek *200 cubits* [90 meters].

20:30 John stated that he was selective about the things he recorded in his account. Jesus performed so many other signs (see note at 2:11) that one volume couldn't contain them all (21:25).

21:1-25 John's final resurrection account clarified the disciples' mission. Jesus revealed Himself to His disciples by repeating a miracle they had experienced when He first called them to follow Him. The intimate setting of breakfast with friends was a demonstration that Jesus' resurrected body was real, not imaginary. It was also an ideal setting in which Jesus could restore and reinstate His friend Peter after his three denials.

21:3 The disciples were not yet fulfilling Jesus' commission to be His witnesses (15:25-26) even though He had set them apart as His representatives (20:21-23). It appears that they had simply returned to the comfort and familiarity of their former trade.

▸ PURPOSE

21:6 Full nets. Most people don't find God when they are fishing. But early in Jesus' ministry, He performed the same miracle before Simon Peter that He later performed after His resurrection. Jesus said then, "Don't be afraid! From now on you'll be fishing for people! (Luke 5:10). That was when Peter left everything and followed Jesus. It was not a coincidence that Jesus once again performed the miracle of the full nets during the last days of His ministry. He was reminding Peter of the great mission for His church: fishing for people. Are you fishing for people? Are you catching any fish? Take advantage of opportunities that God sends your way to share what He has done in your life. (***See Purpose****> God's Deeds> Special Acts> Miracles> Jesus> Second miraculous catch of fish,* TopicGuide page A53.)

21:12 Jesus once again served His friends as He did when He washed their feet, but this time Peter did not object (compare 13:2-8). Jesus had spoken of a future day when the master would reward His faithful followers by seating them, and then He would "put on an apron, and serve them" as they sat and ate (Luke 12:35-37).

21:13 The Gospel accounts of Jesus' postresurrection appearances are very tactile, emphasizing how real Christ was. On the road to Emmaus, Jesus met two of His followers and "took the bread and blessed it. Then He broke it and gave it to them" (Luke 24:30). When He first appeared to the gathered disciples, He encouraged them to touch Him, saying, "I am not a ghost, because ghosts don't have bodies, as you see that I do" (Luke 24:39); then He ate some fish before their eyes (Luke 24:43). Here He served a meal to His friends. John was emphasizing that Jesus' body was not imaginary.

21:15 15After breakfast Jesus asked Simon Peter, "Simon son of John, do you love Me more
Matt 26:33 than these?*"
"Yes, Lord," Peter replied, "You know I love You."
"Then feed My lambs," Jesus told him.
21:16 16Jesus repeated the question: "Simon son of John, do you love Me?"
Acts 20:28 "Yes, Lord," Peter said, "You know I love You."
Heb 13:20-21
1 Pet 5:2-3 "Then take care of My sheep," Jesus said.
21:17 17A third time He asked him, "Simon son of John, do you love Me?"
John 13:38; 16:30 Peter was hurt that Jesus asked the question a third time. He said, "Lord, You know
everything. You know that I love You."
Jesus said, "Then feed My sheep.
18"I tell you the truth, when you were young, you were able to do as you liked; you
dressed yourself and went wherever you wanted to go. But when you are old, you will
stretch out your hands, and others* will dress you and take you where you don't want to
21:19 go." 19Jesus said this to let him know by what kind of death he would glorify God. Then
John 13:36
2 Pet 1:14 Jesus told him, "Follow Me."
20Peter turned around and saw behind them the disciple Jesus loved—the one who had
21:20
John 13:23, 25 leaned over to Jesus during supper and asked, "Lord, who will betray You?" 21Peter asked
Jesus, "What about him, Lord?"
21:22 22Jesus replied, "If I want him to remain alive until I return, what is that to you? As for you,
Matt 16:27 follow Me." 23So the rumor spread among the community of believers* that this disciple
wouldn't die. But that isn't what Jesus said at all. He only said, "If I want him to remain alive
21:24 until I return, what is that to you?"
John 15:27; 19:35
1 Jn 1:1-3 24This disciple is the one who testifies to these events and has recorded them here. And
3 Jn 1:12 we know that his account of these things is accurate.
21:25 25Jesus also did many other things. If they were all written down, I suppose the whole
John 20:30 world could not contain the books that would be written.

21:15 Or *more than these others do?* 21:18 Some manuscripts read *and another one.* 21:23 Greek *the brothers.*

21:15-17 Peter had claimed to love Jesus so much that he would die for Him (13:37), but Jesus knew him better and predicted his three denials. Now Jesus asked about his love three times, once for each denial. After each affirmation, Jesus kindly recommissioned Peter, telling him to care for His people like a good shepherd—like his Master (10:11-18).

21:25 By modern standards, relatively little is known about Jesus' life. His birth is covered quite closely, as is His childhood interaction with religious leaders, but then nothing is recorded about Jesus' life from age 12 (Luke 2:41-51) to 30. The Gospel writers each had their own purposes for recounting the story of Jesus, and John consciously edited his story to show people that Jesus was the Son of God (John 20:31).

KEY PLACES IN ACTS

Modern names and boundaries are shown in gray.

The apostle Paul, whose missionary journeys fill much of this book, traveled tremendous distances as he tirelessly spread the gospel across much of the Roman Empire. His combined trips, by land and sea, equal more than 13,000 air miles.

1 Judea Jesus ascended to heaven from the Mount of Olives, outside Jerusalem, and his followers returned to the city to await the infilling of the Holy Spirit, which occurred at Pentecost. Peter gave a powerful sermon that was heard by Jews from across the empire. The Jerusalem church grew, but Stephen was martyred for his faith by Jewish leaders who did not believe in Jesus (1:1–7:60).

2 Samaria After Stephen's death, persecution of Christians intensified, but it caused the believers to leave Jerusalem and spread the gospel to other cities in the empire. Philip took the gospel into Samaria, and even to a man from Ethiopia (8:1-40).

3 Syria Paul (Saul) began his story as a persecutor of Christians, only to be met by Jesus himself on the road to Damascus. He became a believer, but his new faith caused opposition, so he returned to Tarsus, his home, for safety. Barnabas sought out Paul in Tarsus and brought him to the church in Antioch of Syria, where they worked together. Meanwhile, Peter had received a vision that led him to Caesarea, where he presented the gospel to a Gentile family, who became believers (9:1–12:25).

4 Cyprus and Galatia Paul and Barnabas were dedicated by the church in Antioch of Syria for God's work of spreading the gospel to other cities. They set off on their first missionary journey through Cyprus and Galatia (13:1–14:28).

5 Jerusalem Controversy between Jewish Christians and Gentile Christians over the matter of keeping the law led to a special council, with delegates from the churches in Antioch and Jerusalem meeting in Jerusalem. Together, they resolved the conflict and the news was taken back to Antioch (15:1-35).

6 Macedonia Barnabas traveled to Cyprus while Paul took a second missionary journey. He revisited the churches in Galatia and headed toward Ephesus, but the Holy Spirit said no. So he turned north toward Bithynia and Pontus but again was told not to go. He then received the "Macedonian call," and followed the Spirit's direction into the cities of Macedonia (15:36–17:14).

7 Achaia Paul traveled from Macedonia to Athens and Corinth in Achaia, then traveled by ship to Ephesus before returning to Caesarea, Jerusalem, and finally back to Antioch (17:15–18:22).

8 Ephesus Paul's third missionary journey took him back through Cilicia and Galatia, this time straight to Ephesus in Asia. He visited other cities in Asia before going back to Macedonia and Achaia. He returned to Jerusalem by ship, despite his knowledge that arrest awaited him there (18:23–23:30).

9 Caesarea Paul was arrested in Jerusalem and taken to Antipatris, then on to Caesarea under Roman guard. Paul always took advantage of any opportunity to share the gospel, and he did so before many Gentile leaders. Because Paul appealed his case to Caesar, he began the long journey to Rome (23:31–26:32).

10 Rome After storms, layovers in Crete, and shipwreck on the island of Malta, Paul arrived in Sicily and finally in Italy, where he traveled by land, under guard, to his long-awaited destination: Rome, the capital of the empire (27:1–28:31).

PURPOSE

To demonstrate how the ministry of Jesus continued to spread into the whole world through the lives of His followers by the power of the Holy Spirit.

The Gospels end on a glorious note: Jesus conquered death and the grave! He rose from the dead! His friends and followers saw Him, ate with Him, and talked with Him. He was alive! Soon after His resurrection, however, Jesus ascended into heaven—He physically left the earth (Acts 1:9). What would happen to those He left behind? With their leader gone, would Christianity fade away? Luke's account in Acts answers that question.

Jesus' life and ministry didn't end with the Gospels. He continues to extend His work, His teachings, and His personal ministry through those who have come to know and love Him. Peter, one of the first to follow Jesus, became a leading figure in the new community that grew out of the ministry of Jesus. In the early chapters of Acts (1–12) we see him head out into Jerusalem and beyond to carry on the work of his Savior. Philip was one of those who came to believe in the Jesus that Peter spoke about so freely. Philip's ministry started with tending tables for the needy (6:1-5), but quickly developed into something more than he could have ever imagined (chapters 8–12). Saul, a Jewish leader who persecuted Christians, met the risen Jesus and was forever changed. In the last half of Acts (13–28), Luke recorded how the Spirit used Saul, then called Paul (Acts 13:9), to take the message and ministry of Jesus to the far regions of the known world.

DISCOVER GOD IN ACTS

Although the book of Acts is often referred to as the "Acts of the Apostles," it perhaps could more rightly be referred to as the "Acts of the Holy Spirit." Though the apostles (key leaders in the early church) play a significant role in the book, the central figure really is the Holy Spirit:

The Empowering Spirit: In the first chapter, Jesus tells His followers that when the Spirit comes upon them, they will receive power (1:8). This concept of the Spirit empowering believers to live the Christian life permeates Acts. Whether serving the needs of others (6:1-5), sharing the Good News with boldness (8:26-40), or even facing terrible persecution (7:55-60), believers do everything through the power of the Holy Spirit.

The Guiding Spirit: How are Christians to know what God wants of them? How is a church to know what course of action to pursue? From Acts it is clear that the Spirit guides the followers of Jesus in big and little ways. For some, it may be a nudge or a sense of direction (15:28; 16:6-8); for others it may be a clear "word from the Lord" (9:10-16; 10:19; 13:1-3). The people of God are led by the Spirit of God to spread the Good News about Jesus.

The Ever-present Spirit: Throughout Acts it is evident that wherever the followers of Jesus are the Spirit is there, wherever the Good News is declared the Spirit is working; whenever lives undergo a change the Spirit is the agent of change. For the early church, the Spirit was an ever-present help.

GROWING THROUGH ACTS

One of the ways to grow through Acts is to watch where the Spirit goes—to follow the geographical spread of the Good News as recorded by Luke. The Spirit draws and leads the people of God to move from their places of comfort into new territory, taking the Good News to those who have not heard. We can imitate the Spirit's three-stage approach to spreading the Good News:

To Those in Jerusalem (Acts 2–4). In the early chapters of Acts, the followers of Jesus tell their message to those nearest to them. Is it harder or easier to share the news with those most like you? You will find that those you know best might respond to the Good News about Jesus warmly (2:41-42), but they might also find reason to resist what you have to say (4:13-20). In either case, we will need Spirit-empowered boldness (4:29-31).

To Those on the Fringes of Jewish Society (Acts 8–12). Moving out of your comfort zone is a challenge. How do you take those first steps to reach out to others with the Good News about Jesus? You'll find the Spirit opening up opportunities (8:29-40), and as you follow His lead you will come across those who are already hungry to hear the Good News (10:34-48).

To the Whole Known World (Acts 13–21). It can be challenging to find a way to break new ground in reaching our world with the gospel, but as we see in Acts, the Holy Spirit paves the way, appointing those who will go (13:1-4), empowering those who are sharing and speaking (13:9; 19:6), and providing direction along the way (16:6-10; 20:23). A constant, conscious dependence on the Spirit of God is the surest way to participate in Jesus' ongoing ministry to the world.

DISCOVERY VERSES

But you will receive power when the Holy Spirit comes upon you. And you will be My witnesses, telling people about Me everywhere—in Jerusalem, throughout Judea, in Samaria, and to the ends of the earth. (ACTS 1:8)

People of Israel, listen! God publicly endorsed Jesus the Nazarene by doing powerful miracles, wonders, and signs through Him, as you well know. (ACTS 2:22)

Brothers, listen! We are here to proclaim that through this man Jesus there is forgiveness for your sins. (ACTS 13:38)

ACTS FACTS

Author: The opening verses of both Luke and Acts make it clear they were written by the same person (Luke 1:1-4; Acts 1:1-2). In several passages in Acts, the author refers to Paul and his companions as "we" (16:10-17; 20:5–21:18; 27:1–28:16), suggesting that the author himself was among them. Other books mention Luke as an associate of Paul (Colossians 4:14; 2 Timothy 4:11; Philemon 1:24). As a close friend of Paul, Luke writes about the early life of the church from a unique vantage point.

Written to: In the opening verses of this Gospel and Acts, Luke notes that he is writing to Theophilus, who apparently held some sort of official Roman position. The title used by Luke to address Theophilus ("most honorable") typically referred to an individual of high rank in the Roman government. Paul used it to address Festus, governor of Judea, and Felix, also a governor of Judea (translated "most excellent" in Acts 23:26; 24:2-3; 26:25).

Date of writing: We know from the historical resources available to us that Paul was martyred between AD 59 and 62, that a fierce persecution against Christians began under the Roman emperor Nero in AD 64, and that the city of Jerusalem was destroyed in AD 70. Since none of these very significant facts are mentioned by Luke and he ends his Gospel with Paul in prison in Rome (Acts 28), many scholars believe that Luke compiled Acts in its final form prior to Paul's death. This book dates at or before AD 62.

Setting: Acts is a geographically oriented book; following the outline of Acts 1:8, Luke leads us from the city of Jerusalem in the land of Palestine throughout the area in and around the Mediterranean Sea. It takes us through Syria, Asia Minor, the islands of Cyprus and Malta, and ultimately to Rome, where the narrative ends with Paul in prison.

OUTLINE

- **ACTS 1:1–2:47**—The Spirit empowers the followers of Jesus.
- **ACTS 3:1–8:4**—The Spirit guides the followers of Jesus.
- **ACTS 8:5–12:25**—The Spirit leads the followers of Jesus to spread the Good News.
- **ACTS 13:1–21:16**—The Spirit leads Paul, Barnabas, and Silas to take the Good News throughout the known world.
- **ACTS 21:17–28:31**—The Spirit sustains and keeps Paul through his prison ordeal.

THE PROMISE OF THE HOLY SPIRIT

1:1 **1** In my first book* I told you, Theophilus, about everything Jesus began to do and
Luke 1:3 teach 2 until the day He was taken up to heaven after giving His chosen apostles fur-
1:2 Matt 28:19-20 ther instructions through the Holy Spirit. 3 During the forty days after His crucifixion, He ap-
Luke 24:49-51 peared to the apostles from time to time, and He proved to them in many ways that He
1:3 was actually alive. And He talked to them about the Kingdom of God.
Luke 24:33-36 4 Once when He was eating with them, He commanded them, "Do not leave Jerusalem
John 20:19, 26; 21:1, 14 until the Father sends you the gift He promised, as I told you before. 5 John baptized with*
1:4 water, but in just a few days you will be baptized with the Holy Spirit."
Luke 24:49 John 14:16-17, 26 Acts 2:33

THE ASCENSION OF JESUS

6 So when the apostles were with Jesus, they kept asking Him, "Lord, has the time come for
1:5 Luke 3:16 You to free Israel and restore our kingdom?"
7 He replied, "The Father alone has the authority to set those dates and times, and they
1:7 Matt 24:36 are not for you to know. 8 But you will receive power when the Holy Spirit comes upon
1 Thes 5:1-2 you. And you will be My witnesses, telling people about Me everywhere—in Jerusalem,
1:8 Luke 24:48 throughout Judea, in Samaria, and to the ends of the earth."
John 15:27

1:1 The reference is to the Gospel of Luke. 1:5 Or *in;* also in 1:5b.

1:1-3 Continuing the narrative he began in his Gospel, Luke addressed this account to Theophilus, whose name means "lover of God" or "loved of God" (Luke 1:3). The book begins by summarizing Jesus' earthly ministry. Luke's purpose is to show how God has worked to establish His Kingdom anew in the world through the person and work of Jesus Christ.

1:4-5 God's plan from the beginning was to apply the salvation accomplished by Christ through the power of the Holy Spirit. God was about to fulfill His promise to Abraham and his descendants to make them a blessing to the nations (Acts 3:25; Galatians 3:14) by empowering the apostles' ministry through His Spirit and deploying them throughout the world (Luke 24:49; John 14:16-17, 26; John 15:26-27; 16:7-14).

1:6-8 Jesus deemed the disciples' question about restoring the kingdom of Israel as irrelevant to the task at hand. Christ, in His human nature, did not appear to possess such knowledge prior to the crucifixion, resurrection, and ascension (Mark 13:32); such knowledge was reserved for the Father alone. Christ redirected His disciples' attention to the broader concept of the expansion of God's Kingdom through the power of the Holy Spirit. The Kingdom of God was to spread according to a specific strategy, which also forms the basic layout of the book of Acts: in Jerusalem (Acts 3:1–8:1), throughout Judea, in Samaria (8:1–12:25), and to the ends of the earth (13:1–28:31).

MINISTRY

1:8 The plan. Do you ever wish you could be part of some earthshaking event? If you are a follower of Christ, you are! The moment in history recorded here is the beginning of the most powerful spiritual movement in history. Because the Holy Spirit is the power behind the movement, it cannot fail. This movement grows by repeating two steps: Begin in your own community, and reach out to form new communities of faithful believers. It's simple, but it's not easy—that's why God has given us His Spirit to empower this mission. If you struggle with evangelism, submit to the empowering Holy Spirit, and you'll find the strength to fulfill your part of God's plan. (***See Ministry**> Great Commission> Witness> Locally, regionally, worldwide,* TopicGuide page A56.)

9 After saying this, He was taken up into a cloud while they were watching, and 1:9
they could no longer see Him. 10 As they strained to see Him rising into heaven, two white- Mark 16:19
robed men suddenly stood among them. 11 "Men of Galilee," they said, "why are you 1:11
standing here staring into heaven? Jesus has been taken from you into heaven, but some- Rev 1:7
day He will return from heaven in the same way you saw Him go!"

MATTHIAS REPLACES JUDAS

12 Then the apostles returned to Jerusalem from the Mount of Olives, a distance of half a mile.* 1:12
13 When they arrived, they went to the upstairs room of the house where they were staying. Luke 24:50, 52
Here are the names of those who were present: Peter, John, James, Andrew, Philip, 1:13
Thomas, Bartholomew, Matthew, James (son of Alphaeus), Simon (the Zealot), and Judas Matt 10:2-4 Mark 3:16-19
(son of James). 14 They all met together and were constantly united in prayer, along with Luke 6:14-16
Mary the mother of Jesus, several other women, and the brothers of Jesus. 1:14
15 During this time, when about 120 believers* were together in one place, Peter stood up Acts 2:42
and addressed them. 16 "Brothers," He said, "the Scriptures had to be fulfilled concerning Ju- 1:16
das, who guided those who arrested Jesus. This was predicted long ago by the Holy Spirit, Ps 41:9
speaking through King David. 17 Judas was one of us and shared in the ministry with us." 1:17 John 6:70-71
18 (Judas had bought a field with the money he received for his treachery. Falling Acts 1:24-25
headfirst there, his body split open, spilling out all his intestines. 19 The news of his death 1:18 Matt 27:3-8

1:12 Greek *a Sabbath day's journey.* 1:15 Greek *brothers.*

▸ GOD

1:9 Not just another miracle. Life with Jesus meant excitement—healings, casting out demons, conquering death—but the jaw-dropping amazement of the moment when Jesus ascended into heaven left even the disciples breathless. His ascension wasn't just for show—this was the culmination of Jesus' ministry. He spent 40 days after His resurrection teaching and encouraging His disciples; now Jesus' ascension into heaven punctuated that teaching and demonstrated the Father's acceptance. Does the image of Jesus ascending to heaven fill you with awe and humility? Does it encourage you to embrace His teachings? When you struggle with Jesus' challenging teachings, remember that God affirmed every word Jesus said as true by His resurrection and ascension. (***See God***> *God's Names> Son> Ascension,* TopicGuide page A19.)

1:15-20 At this time, the number of apostles was down to eleven from twelve because Judas had defected from the ranks and committed suicide after he betrayed Jesus Christ (Matthew 27:5). It was extremely important for the apostles to total twelve, for they were God's judicial representatives of the nation of Israel, and symbolized a restored Israel (Luke 22:30).

MY RESPONSE TO GOD

Right Here, Right Now

ACTS 1

When we think about being involved in ministry or mission work, many of us picture ourselves in faraway places, perhaps at an orphanage or clinic in a country across the ocean. For many, such images can be overwhelming and scary. Although God does call some people to travel great distances to do His work, we must remember that there is also a reason why He has placed us right where we are. Your mission field includes those who are already around you.

Jesus instructed His disciples to start their ministry in Jerusalem–exactly where they were already spending most of their time (Acts 1:12). Then they were to spread their work to their larger region, and finally into the known world: "You will receive power when the Holy Spirit comes upon you. And you will be My witnesses, telling people about Me everywhere–in Jerusalem, throughout Judea, in Samaria, and to the ends of the earth" (Acts 1:8).

You are already a missionary–right here, right now.

spread to all the people of Jerusalem, and they gave the place the Aramaic name *Akel-*
dama, which means "Field of Blood.")
1:20 20 Peter continued, "This was written in the book of Psalms, where it says, 'Let his home
Pss 69:25; 109:8 become desolate, with no one living in it.' It also says, 'Let someone else take his position.'
1:21-22 21 "So now we must choose a replacement for Judas from among the men who were
Mark 1:9-11 with us the entire time we were traveling with the Lord Jesus—22 from the time He was bap-
tized by John until the day He was taken from us. Whoever is chosen will join us as a wit-
ness of Jesus' resurrection."
23 So they nominated two men: Joseph called Barsabbas (also known as Justus) and
1:24 Matthias. 24 Then they all prayed, "O Lord, You know every heart. Show us which of these
Acts 6:6 men You have chosen 25 as an apostle to replace Judas in this ministry, for he has deserted
1:26 us and gone where he belongs." 26 Then they cast lots, and Matthias was selected to be-
Prov 16:33 come an apostle with the other eleven.

THE HOLY SPIRIT COMES

2:1
Lev 23:15-21 **2** On the day of Pentecost* all the believers were meeting together in one place. 2 Sud-
Deut 16:9-11 denly, there was a sound from heaven like the roaring of a mighty windstorm, and it
Acts 1:14; 20:16 filled the house where they were sitting. 3 Then, what looked like flames or tongues of fire
2:2 appeared and settled on each of them. 4 And everyone present was filled with the Holy
Acts 4:31 Spirit and began speaking in other languages,* as the Holy Spirit gave them this ability.
2:4 Mark 16:17 5 At that time there were devout Jews from every nation living in Jerusalem. 6 When they
Acts 4:31; 10:44-46; heard the loud noise, everyone came running, and they were bewildered to hear their
19:6 1 Cor 12:10; 13:1 own languages being spoken by the believers.
2:7 7 They were completely amazed. "How can this be?" they exclaimed. "These people are all
Acts 1:11 from Galilee, 8 and yet we hear them speaking in our own native languages! 9 Here we are—
2:9 Parthians, Medes, Elamites, people from Mesopotamia, Judea, Cappadocia, Pontus, the
Acts 16:6; 19:10 province of Asia, 10 Phrygia, Pamphylia, Egypt, and the areas of Libya around Cyrene, visitors
1 Pet 1:1 from Rome 11 (both Jews and converts to Judaism), Cretans, and Arabs. And we all hear these
2:10 people speaking in our own languages about the wonderful things God has done!" 12 They
Matt 27:32 Acts 13:13; 16:6 stood there amazed and perplexed. "What can this mean?" they asked each other.
2:13 13 But others in the crowd ridiculed them, saying, "They're just drunk, that's all!"
1 Cor 14:23 Eph 5:18

PETER PREACHES TO THE CROWD

14 Then Peter stepped forward with the eleven other apostles and shouted to the crowd,
"Listen carefully, all of you, fellow Jews and residents of Jerusalem! Make no mistake

1:20 Pss 69:25; 109:8. **2:1** The Festival of Pentecost came 50 days after Passover (when Jesus was crucified). **2:4** Or *in other tongues.*

1:23-26 In the Old Testament, God sometimes used "sacred lots" to reveal His will (Proverbs 16:33 [dice]; Joshua 18:6; 1 Samuel 14:41-42; 1 Chronicles 26:13; Nahum 3:10). The selection of Matthias is the last instance in Scripture where believers use lots to divine the will of God (1:26). Hereafter, the people of God rely on the Holy Spirit and God's revealed Word for direction, precluding the need for the sacred lot (6:2-4).

2:1-4 The promised Holy Spirit of God arrived in dramatic fashion on the day of Pentecost, and His presence was manifested in three ways. First, He was in the windstorm, for His presence infuses life and generates new creations (Ezekiel 36:26-27; 37:9-10, 13-14; 2 Corinthians 5:17). Second, the Spirit appeared as tongues of fire, because He displays the holiness of God, who radiates light, justice, and purity (Deuteronomy 4:24; Matthew 3:11-12; Hebrews 12:29). Third, The Holy Spirit's presence empowered those who were present to speak in tongues, a gift that enabled the people to speak the wonders of God (Acts 10:46; 19:6; 1 Corinthians 12–14).

2:5-11 The curse God brought against humanity for their pride at the Tower of Babel was reversed at Pentecost, for instead of living in confusion the people of God were unified in their understanding of the power of the Spirit (Genesis 11:1-9). Babel had dispersed people in different directions throughout the world, but at Pentecost people were brought together from abroad in order to experience a supernatural harmony (Acts 2:9-11).

2:14-21 Since confusion had arisen as to the meaning of the signs witnessed, Peter addressed the crowd in an attempt to clarify the purpose for the Spirit's coming. Moses had earnestly desired a time when the Spirit would descend upon all people (Numbers 11:29), the prophet Joel had prophesied that the day would one day come (Joel 2:28-32), and the apostle Peter declared that the day had now arrived. God was transforming His people into a nation made of all who call upon the name of Jesus Christ as Savior.

about this. 15 These people are not drunk, as some of you are assuming. Nine o'clock in
the morning is much too early for that. 16 No, what you see was predicted long ago by the
prophet Joel:

17 'In the last days,' God says, 2:17-21
'I will pour out My Spirit upon all people. *Joel 2:28-32
Your sons and daughters will prophesy.
Your young men will see visions,
and your old men will dream dreams.
18 In those days I will pour out My Spirit 2:18
even on My servants—men and women alike— Num 11:29
and they will prophesy. 1 Cor 12:10
19 And I will cause wonders in the heavens above
and signs on the earth below—
blood and fire and clouds of smoke.
20 The sun will become dark, 2:20
and the moon will turn blood red Matt 24:29
before that great and glorious day of the LORD arrives.
21 But everyone who calls on the name of the LORD 2:21
will be saved.'* Rom 10:13

22 "People of Israel, listen! God publicly endorsed Jesus the Nazarene* by doing powerful 2:22 John 3:2
miracles, wonders, and signs through Him, as you well know. 23 But God knew what would
happen, and His prearranged plan was carried out when Jesus was betrayed. With the 2:23 1 Pet 1:20
help of lawless Gentiles, you nailed Him to a cross and killed Him. 24 But God released Him 2:24
from the horrors of death and raised Him back to life, for death could not keep Him in its Acts 3:15
grip. 25 King David said this about Him: 2:25-28 *Ps 16:8-11 Acts 13:30-35

'I see that the LORD is always with Me.
I will not be shaken, for He is right beside Me.
26 No wonder My heart is glad,
and My tongue shouts His praises!
My body rests in hope.
27 For You will not leave My soul among the dead*
or allow Your Holy One to rot in the grave.
28 You have shown Me the way of life,
and You will fill Me with the joy of Your presence.'* 2:29 1 Kgs 2:10

29 "Dear brothers, think about this! You can be sure that the patriarch David wasn't refer- Acts 13:36
ring to himself, for he died and was buried, and His tomb is still here among us. 30 But he 2:30
was a prophet, and he knew God had promised with an oath that one of David's own 2 Sam 7:12-14 *Pss 89:4; 132:11

2:17-21 Joel 2:28-32. 2:22 Or *Jesus of Nazareth.* 2:27 Greek *in Hades;* also in 2:31. 2:25-28 Ps 16:8-11 (Greek version).

2:17-20 The "last days" began with the fulfillment of Joel's prophecy (Joel 2:28-32) on Pentecost and will end with the return of Christ. The gift of prophecy manifested by people from many nations demonstrates the beginning of the last days. This phenomenon occurred throughout the history of the early church (1 Corinthians 14:1-5). The idea of God pouring out His Spirit is repeated throughout the Bible (Isaiah 32:15; 44:3), in Acts (10:45), and each time a person is converted (Titus 3:6).

▸ HOLINESS

2:18 Power for all. Not every Christian is wealthy or smart or physically attractive by the world's standards. In fact, relatively few may fit this profile (Matthew 19:23). But every believer shares in the power of the Holy Spirit; therefore, everyone in God's family is powerful. You will be able to do whatever God calls you to do because He gives you the power to accomplish the work. God's plan for the world includes you and your faithful obedience. Step out boldly when you work for God, assured that the Holy Spirit will empower you. Ask God to continue to fill and empower you to achieve the opportunities for service that He puts before you. (***See Holiness***> *Submission*> *Yielding to Spirit*> *Power of the Spirit is for all,* TopicGuide page A41.)

2:31 descendants would sit on His throne. 31David was looking into the future and speaking of
*Ps 16:10 the Messiah's resurrection. He was saying that God would not leave Him among the dead
2:33 or allow His body to rot in the grave.
John 14:26 Acts 1:4, 8 32"God raised Jesus from the dead, and we are all witnesses of this. 33Now He is exalted
Eph 4:8 to the place of highest honor in heaven, at God's right hand. And the Father, as He had
Phil 2:9 promised, gave Him the Holy Spirit to pour out upon us, just as you see and hear today.
2:34-35 *Ps 110:1 34For David himself never ascended into heaven, yet he said,

'The LORD said to my Lord,
"Sit in the place of honor at My right hand
35 until I humble Your enemies,
making them a footstool under Your feet."'*

2:36 36"So let everyone in Israel know for certain that God has made this Jesus, whom you
Acts 5:30-31 crucified, to be both Lord and Messiah!"
2:37 37Peter's words pierced their hearts, and they said to him and to the other apostles,
Acts 16:30 "Brothers, what should we do?"
2:38 Mark 16:16 38Peter replied, "Each of you must repent of your sins and turn to God, and be baptized
Acts 3:19; 8:12; in the name of Jesus Christ for the forgiveness of your sins. Then you will receive the gift
22:16 of the Holy Spirit. 39This promise is to you, and to your children, and even to the
2:39 Gentiles*—all who have been called by the Lord our God." 40Then Peter continued preach-
Isa 44:3; 57:19 Eph 2:13 ing for a long time, strongly urging all his listeners, "Save yourselves from this crooked
2:40 generation!"
Deut 32:5 41Those who believed what Peter said were baptized and added to the church that
Phil 2:15 day—about 3,000 in all.

THE BELIEVERS FORM A COMMUNITY

2:42 42All the believers devoted themselves to the apostles' teaching, and to fellowship, and to
Acts 20:7 sharing in meals (including the Lord's Supper*), and to prayer.
43A deep sense of awe came over them all, and the apostles performed many miracu-
2:44-45 lous signs and wonders. 44And all the believers met together in one place and shared
Acts 4:32-37 everything they had. 45They sold their property and possessions and shared the money
with those in need. 46They worshiped together at the Temple each day, met in homes for
2:47 the Lord's Supper, and shared their meals with great joy and generosity*—47all the while
Acts 4:4; 6:7 Rom 14:18 praising God and enjoying the goodwill of all the people. And each day the Lord added to
their fellowship those who were being saved.

2:34-35 Ps 110:1. 2:39 Or *and to people far in the future;* Greek reads *and to those far away.* 2:42 Greek *the breaking of bread;* also in 2:46. 2:46 Or *and sincere hearts.*

2:38 When the onlookers asked Peter how they should personally respond to the reality of Jesus' death, resurrection, and ascension, Peter declared that they must repent and be baptized. Repentance involves turning away from sin and is the appropriate response to God's revealed truth (Ezekiel 14:6; 33:11; Matthew 3:7-8; 4:17). Christ instituted baptism as an external means of confirming and clarifying the spiritual cleansing by the Spirit and acceptance into God's family (Matthew 28:18-20; Titus 3:5).

▸ WORSHIP
2:42 Partners in prayer. As someone once said, "God has no mute children." This is nowhere more evident than in the book of Acts. Throughout the book God's people gathered to pray (1:14; 4:24; 6:6; 7:59; 9:40; 10:9; 12:5, 12; 13:3; 14:23; 16:13, 25; 20:36; 21:5; 27:29). They realized that nothing could accomplish their goals for God like talking to God. Many of them had seen Jesus in the flesh, listened to His sermons, and watched Him perform miracles. Now that Jesus had gone back to heaven, his followers knew how important it was to keep communicating with God. Do you have this same devotion to prayer? How can you pray more and deeper? When you pray, know that you join God's people of every age in a fundamental act of devotion. (***See Worship****> NT> Prayer> Examples> Others> The first disciples devote themselves to prayer,* TopicGuide page A33.)

2:42-47 As the church began to grow, four marks distinguished God's worshiping community: devotion to the apostle's teaching, fellowship, sharing in meals, and prayer.

PETER HEALS A CRIPPLED BEGGAR

3 Peter and John went to the Temple one afternoon to take part in the three o'clock 3:1
prayer service. 2As they approached the Temple, a man lame from birth was being Acts 10:3, 9, 30
carried in. Each day he was put beside the Temple gate, the one called the Beautiful Gate, 3:2
so he could beg from the people going into the Temple. 3When he saw Peter and John Acts 14:8
about to enter, he asked them for some money.

4Peter and John looked at him intently, and Peter said, "Look at us!" 5The lame man looked 3:4
at them eagerly, expecting some money. 6But Peter said, "I don't have any silver or gold for Acts 13:9; 14:9
you. But I'll give you what I have. In the name of Jesus Christ the Nazarene,* get up and* walk!" 3:6
7Then Peter took the lame man by the right hand and helped him up. And as he did, the Acts 4:10
man's feet and ankles were instantly healed and strengthened. 8He jumped up, stood on 3:8
his feet, and began to walk! Then, walking, leaping, and praising God, he went into the John 5:14
Temple with them.

9All the people saw him walking and heard him praising God. 10When they realized he 3:9
was the lame beggar they had seen so often at the Beautiful Gate, they were absolutely Acts 4:16, 21
astounded! 11They all rushed out in amazement to Solomon's Colonnade, where the man 3:10
was holding tightly to Peter and John. John 9:8

3:11 John 10:23 Acts 5:12

PETER PREACHES IN THE TEMPLE

12Peter saw his opportunity and addressed the crowd. "People of Israel," he said, "what is
so surprising about this? And why stare at us as though we had made this man walk by our

3:6a Or *Jesus Christ of Nazareth.* 3:6b Some manuscripts omit *get up and.*

▸ WORSHIP

3:1 Praying together. Have you ever regarded the habit of praying before meals or other activities merely a boring ritual or an empty tradition? The early church certainly didn't. Right from the very beginning—at the first prayer service (1:14)—these men and women relied on prayer to accomplish God's will. They saw miracles happen. Praying with other believers is one of the joys of our faith and increases our intimacy with Jesus, for He says He will be with us in a special way when we pray together (Matthew 18:20). It is important that we join with others in prayer today. Does your church have a prayer service? Does your family pray together? Adjust your schedule and your attitude to make prayer a priority. (***See Worship***> *NT> Prayer> Examples> Others> The disciples pray in the Temple,* TopicGuide page A33.)

3:1-6 The Christian community had been witnessing the apostles perform a multitude of miracles in their times of fellowship (2:43), but the healing of the crippled beggar demonstrated God's working through the apostles in a public location. This healing "in the name of Jesus" was an expression of Jesus' authority over sickness. By associating this miracle with Jesus, the apostles also showed to whom believers should direct thanksgiving for this event (Romans 1:5).

3:12-16 Peter's healing of the lame man served as a precursor to the sermon he delivered to those gathered near the Temple. God empowered him to heal the man so that he could point the people to even greater healing: salvation in Christ Jesus. The prophets of the Old Testament commonly used signs as symbols of God's power to reveal God's message of judgment or salvation (Jeremiah 13:1; 19:1; 27:2; Ezekiel 4:1; 5:1).

BECAUSE
GOD IS RIGHTEOUS

I will live by His standards.

All the believers devoted themselves to the apostles' teaching, and to fellowship, and to sharing in meals (including the Lord's Supper), and to prayer.

ACTS 2:42

FOR THE NEXT *GOD IS RIGHTEOUS* FEATURE SEE PAGE 2241.

own power or godliness? 13For it is the God of Abraham, Isaac, and Jacob—the God of all
our ancestors—who has brought glory to His servant Jesus by doing this. This is the same
Jesus whom you handed over and rejected before Pilate, despite Pilate's decision to re-
lease Him. 14You rejected this holy, righteous One and instead demanded the release of a
murderer. 15You killed the Author of life, but God raised Him from the dead. And we are
witnesses of this fact!

16"Through faith in the name of Jesus, this man was healed—and you know how crip-
pled he was before. Faith in Jesus' name has healed him before your very eyes.

17"Friends,* I realize that what you and your leaders did to Jesus was done in ignorance.
18But God was fulfilling what all the prophets had foretold about the Messiah—that He must
suffer these things. 19Now repent of your sins and turn to God, so that your sins may be
wiped away. 20Then times of refreshment will come from the presence of the Lord, and He
will again send you Jesus, your appointed Messiah. 21For He must remain in heaven until
the time for the final restoration of all things, as God promised long ago through His holy
prophets. 22Moses said, 'The LORD your God will raise up for you a Prophet like me from
among your own people. Listen carefully to everything He tells you.'* 23Then Moses said,
'Anyone who will not listen to that Prophet will be completely cut off from God's people.'*

24"Starting with Samuel, every prophet spoke about what is happening today. 25You are
the children of those prophets, and you are included in the covenant God promised to
your ancestors. For God said to Abraham, 'Through your descendants* all the families on
earth will be blessed.' 26When God raised up His servant, Jesus, He sent Him first to you
people of Israel, to bless you by turning each of you back from your sinful ways."

3:13 *Exod 3:6, 15; Matt 22:32; Acts 5:30; 7:32
3:17 Luke 23:34; Acts 13:27; 1 Tim 1:13
3:18 Pss 22; 41:9; 69:4, 21; Isa 50:6; 53:4-11; Zech 12:10; 13:7; Luke 24:27, 44, 46
3:21 Luke 1:70
3:22 *Deut 18:15, 18; John 1:20-21; 7:40-41, 52
3:23 Lev 23:29; Deut 18:19
3:25 *Gen 22:18; 26:4; Rom 9:4-8
3:26 Acts 13:46; Rom 1:16

PETER AND JOHN BEFORE THE COUNCIL

4 While Peter and John were speaking to the people, they were confronted by the
priests, the captain of the Temple guard, and some of the Sadducees. 2These leaders
were very disturbed that Peter and John were teaching the people that through Jesus there
is a resurrection of the dead. 3They arrested them and, since it was already evening, put
them in jail until morning. 4But many of the people who heard their message believed it, so
the number of believers now totaled about 5,000 men, not counting women and children.*

4:1 Luke 22:4
4:3 Acts 5:18
4:4 Acts 4:21

3:17 Greek *Brothers.* 3:22 Deut 18:15. 3:23 Deut 18:19; Lev 23:29. 3:25 Greek *your seed;* see Gen 12:3; 22:18. 4:4 Greek *5,000 adult males.*

3:17-18 Christ's death was not an accidental killing, nor was it the result of an angry mob pressuring a helpless political leader. It was a necessary consequence of God's predetermined plan. The ignorant people of Jerusalem attempted to dispose of Jesus by murdering Him, but in so doing they actually accomplished God's plan for salvation (4:28).

▸MINISTRY

3:19 Pray for unbelievers. Right from the beginning of the church, Jesus has given His people instructions He wants us to heed. He commissions them to go out and tell people about Him (1:8). The believers in the first church obeyed Him by spreading the news about Jesus everywhere they went (Colossians 1:28). Here Peter urged his listeners to repent and turn away from their sins. One way we can help in this important responsibility of warning unbelievers of their sinful condition is to pray for them that they will repent. Do you have a list of people you pray for on a regular basis? How many of these are unbelievers? Ask God to grant them salvation (Psalm 14:7; Isaiah 62:1; 1 Timothy 2:1). (***See Ministry*** *> Great Commission> Make Disciples> Prayers> That they might turn from their sin,* TopicGuide page A56.)

3:19 The root of humanity's problem is a broken relationship with God. The only hope for reconciliation with God is through the gracious offer of salvation in Jesus Christ. Peter exhorted the people to receive the gift of salvation by simultaneously turning from their sin in repentance and turning to God in faith.

3:23-26 Peter coupled the promise of salvation with a stern warning for those who would rebel against the authoritative message first delivered by Moses and currently proclaimed in the last days. God will ultimately reject those who reject Christ, for He has made union in Christ the only standard for inclusion in or exclusion from His covenant family (Ephesians 2:19-22).

4:4 The ministry of Peter and John was not intended to generate followers of an anti-Jewish sect. Their objective was to point people to God in repentance and faith (2:38; 3:19; 11:21; 20:21). Many who heard Peter's sermon believed in Christ, but the religious leaders (some were Sadducees) did not believe in the resurrection (Mark 12:18-27; Luke 20:27-38; Acts 23:8), and they had Peter and John imprisoned for teaching that people would be resurrected through Christ.

5 The next day the council of all the rulers and elders and teachers of religious law met
in Jerusalem. 6 Annas the high priest was there, along with Caiaphas, John, Alexander, and
other relatives of the high priest. 7 They brought in the two disciples and demanded, "By
what power, or in whose name, have you done this?"
8 Then Peter, filled with the Holy Spirit, said to them, "Rulers and elders of our people,
9 are we being questioned today because we've done a good deed for a crippled man? Do
you want to know how he was healed? 10 Let me clearly state to all of you and to all the
people of Israel that he was healed by the powerful name of Jesus Christ the Nazarene,*
the man you crucified but whom God raised from the dead. 11 For Jesus is the one referred
to in the Scriptures, where it says,

'The stone that you builders rejected
has now become the cornerstone.'*

12 There is salvation in no one else! God has given no other name under heaven by which
we must be saved."
13 The members of the council were amazed when they saw the boldness of Peter and
John, for they could see that they were ordinary men with no special training in the Scrip-
tures. They also recognized them as men who had been with Jesus. 14 But since they could
see the man who had been healed standing right there among them, there was nothing
the council could say. 15 So they ordered Peter and John out of the council chamber* and
conferred among themselves.
16 "What should we do with these men?" they asked each other. "We can't deny that
they have performed a miraculous sign, and everybody in Jerusalem knows about it.
17 But to keep them from spreading their propaganda any further, we must warn them not
to speak to anyone in Jesus' name again." 18 So they called the apostles back in and com-
manded them never again to speak or teach in the name of Jesus.
19 But Peter and John replied, "Do you think God wants us to obey you rather than Him?
20 We cannot stop telling about everything we have seen and heard."
21 The council then threatened them further, but they finally let them go because they
didn't know how to punish them without starting a riot. For everyone was praising God 22 for
this miraculous sign—the healing of a man who had been lame for more than forty years.

4:6 Matt 26:3; Luke 3:2
4:7 Matt 21:23
4:10 Acts 2:24; 3:6
4:11 *Ps 118:22; Isa 28:16; Matt 21:42; 1 Pet 2:4, 7
4:12 Matt 1:21; Acts 10:43; 1 Tim 2:5
4:13 Matt 11:25
4:15 Acts 5:34-35
4:16 John 11:47; Acts 3:6-10
4:17-19 Acts 5:28-29
4:20 1 Jn 1:1, 3

THE BELIEVERS PRAY FOR COURAGE

23 As soon as they were freed, Peter and John returned to the other believers and told them
what the leading priests and elders had said. 24 When they heard the report, all the believ-
ers lifted their voices together in prayer to God: "O Sovereign Lord, Creator of heaven and
earth, the sea, and everything in them— 25 You spoke long ago by the Holy Spirit through
our ancestor David, Your servant, saying,

4:24 *Exod 20:11; *Ps 146:6
4:25-26 *Ps 2:1-2

4:10 Or *Jesus Christ of Nazareth.* 4:11 Ps 118:22. 4:15 Greek *the Sanhedrin.*

4:8-12 When Peter was brought before the council of the Sanhedrin, he defended himself by accusing the leaders of murdering the Jesus he was now preaching about (Luke 22:66). Peter illustrated his sermon by using the Old Testament to show that the rejection of Christ was part of God's plan (Psalm 118:22).

▸ GOD
4:12 Causing a commotion. Everywhere Peter and the disciples went they caused a stir—not because they were obnoxious or loud, but because they preached the message of Jesus Christ. The message itself caused a problem for some people. For the sake of the gospel, Peter was even put in prison. This would be just one of the many times Peter suffered for his Lord. He never gave up spreading the gospel because he knew that Jesus was the only bridge between God and man. Have you ever had the honor of suffering for the sake of the gospel? Ask God to give you Peter's wisdom and boldness in causing a holy commotion with the gospel. (***See God****> Salvation> Son> Only bridge between God and man,* TopicGuide page A15.)

4:19-20 The apostles were boldly committed to obeying their God-given task of proclaiming the gospel (Matthew 28:18-20). Nothing could stop them from spreading the Good News, not even the powerful religious leaders of their time. The apostles did not advocate an extreme form of resisting authority, but only when they were faced with a choice between obeying God and obeying people (see Romans 13:1-7).

'Why were the nations so angry?
Why did they waste their time with futile plans?
26 The kings of the earth prepared for battle;
the rulers gathered together
against the LORD
and against His Messiah.'*

4:27 27 "In fact, this has happened here in this very city! For Herod Antipas, Pontius Pilate
Isa 61:1 the governor, the Gentiles, and the people of Israel were all united against Jesus, Your
Acts 3:13 holy servant, whom You anointed. 28 But everything they did was determined before-
4:28 Acts 2:23 hand according to Your will. 29 And now, O Lord, hear their threats, and give us, Your ser-
4:29 vants, great boldness in preaching Your word. 30 Stretch out Your hand with healing
Eph 6:19 power; may miraculous signs and wonders be done through the name of Your holy ser-
4:30 vant Jesus."
Acts 5:12 31 After this prayer, the meeting place shook, and they were all filled with the Holy Spirit.
4:31 Acts 2:4; 16:26 Then they preached the word of God with boldness.

THE BELIEVERS SHARE THEIR POSSESSIONS

4:32 32 All the believers were united in heart and mind. And they felt that what they owned was
Acts 2:44 not their own, so they shared everything they had. 33 The apostles testified powerfully to
4:33-35 Acts 2:45-47 the resurrection of the Lord Jesus, and God's great blessing was upon them all. 34 There
were no needy people among them, because those who owned land or houses would sell
them 35 and bring the money to the apostles to give to those in need.
4:36 36 For instance, there was Joseph, the one the apostles nicknamed Barnabas (which
Acts 9:27; 11:19-30; 12:25; 13:2 means "Son of Encouragement"). He was from the tribe of Levi and came from the island
of Cyprus. 37 He sold a field he owned and brought the money to the apostles.

ANANIAS AND SAPPHIRA

5:2 **5** But there was a certain man named Ananias who, with his wife, Sapphira, sold some
Acts 4:34-35, 37 property. 2 He brought part of the money to the apostles, claiming it was the full
5:3 amount. With his wife's consent, he kept the rest.
Deut 23:21 John 13:2 3 Then Peter said, "Ananias, why have you let Satan fill your heart? You lied to the Holy

4:25-26 Or *His anointed one;* or *His Christ.* Ps 2:1-2.

4:29-31 The Sanhedrin intended to prevent the growth of the early church, but through God's grace, His people became even stronger through difficulties. Empowered by the Holy Spirit, these early Christians spoke the Word of God with great boldness.

4:32-37 The church continued to grow in unity under the ministry of the apostles and the direction of the Holy Spirit. Many Christians were moved by the needs of the poor, and they began selling their possessions and surrendering their goods to the oversight of the apostles. One individual in particular, Barnabas, is singled out for his generosity. Barnabas, along with the apostle Paul, would later play a significant role in the advancement of the gospel throughout the world (9:27; 11:23-24; 13:1-3).

▸ WORSHIP

4:34 Meeting needs. The first-century church was (and still is) an amazing group of people. They were a united bunch, caring for each other's needs. From the Day of Pentecost when the Holy Spirit came upon them, they were devoted to each other and to prayer (2:41-42). There were no denominations or divisions, for "all the believers were united in heart and mind" (4:32). Each person saw to the needs of his Christian brothers and sisters and to the apostles, who served them sacrificially. One of our purposes in God's Kingdom is to build up each other in the Lord (Ephesians 4:16). Are you doing your part to aid and comfort the body of Christ? Ask God what He would have you do to meet the needs of your Christian friends. (***See Worship****> NT> Sacrificial Living> Enables us to help meet others' needs,* TopicGuide page A34.)

5:1-10 Up to this point, the early church had only received attacks from external forces (4:3-22), but now Satan attempted to defeat the blossoming church with an internal attack. In contrast to Barnabas, the "Son of Encouragement" (4:36-37), Ananias and Sapphira's story brought fear to the early church. The sin of Ananias and Sapphira was not simply deceit, but also a failure to recognize that a Holy God and His Holy Spirit reside in the midst of the church of Jesus Christ. Their lack of integrity violated God's standard for truthfulness and put the testimony of the church at risk. God would not be mocked by fabricated acts of mercy (Matthew 6:1-4).

Spirit, and you kept some of the money for yourself. 4 The property was yours to sell or not
sell, as you wished. And after selling it, the money was also yours to give away. How could
you do a thing like this? You weren't lying to us but to God!"
5 As soon as Ananias heard these words, he fell to the floor and died. Everyone who
heard about it was terrified. 6 Then some young men got up, wrapped him in a sheet, and
took him out and buried him.
7 About three hours later his wife came in, not knowing what had happened. 8 Peter
asked her, "Was this the price you and your husband received for your land?"
"Yes," she replied, "that was the price."
9 And Peter said, "How could the two of you even think of conspiring to test the Spirit of
the Lord like this? The young men who buried your husband are just outside the door, and
they will carry you out, too."
10 Instantly, she fell to the floor and died. When the young men came in and saw that
she was dead, they carried her out and buried her beside her husband. 11 Great fear
gripped the entire church and everyone else who heard what had happened.

THE APOSTLES HEAL MANY

12 The apostles were performing many miraculous signs and wonders among the people.
And all the believers were meeting regularly at the Temple in the area known as Solo-
mon's Colonnade. 13 But no one else dared to join them, even though all the people had
high regard for them. 14 Yet more and more people believed and were brought to the
Lord—crowds of both men and women. 15 As a result of the apostles' work, sick people
were brought out into the streets on beds and mats so that Peter's shadow might fall
across some of them as he went by. 16 Crowds came from the villages around Jerusalem,
bringing their sick and those possessed by evil* spirits, and they were all healed.

THE APOSTLES MEET OPPOSITION

17 The high priest and his officials, who were Sadducees, were filled with jealousy. 18 They
arrested the apostles and put them in the public jail. 19 But an angel of the Lord came at
night, opened the gates of the jail, and brought them out. Then he told them, 20 "Go to the
Temple and give the people this message of life!"
21 So at daybreak the apostles entered the Temple, as they were told, and immediately
began teaching.
When the high priest and his officials arrived, they convened the high council*—the full
assembly of the elders of Israel. Then they sent for the apostles to be brought from the jail
for trial. 22 But when the Temple guards went to the jail, the men were gone. So they re-
turned to the council and reported, 23 "The jail was securely locked, with the guards stand-
ing outside, but when we opened the gates, no one was there!"
24 When the captain of the Temple guard and the leading priests heard this, they were

5:5 Acts 2:43
5:9 1 Cor 10:9
5:12 Mark 16:15-20; John 10:23; Acts 3:10; Heb 2:4
5:13 Acts 2:47
5:17 Acts 4:1, 2
5:18 Acts 4:3
5:19 Acts 12:7-10
5:20 John 6:63, 68
5:21 Acts 4:5-6
5:24 Acts 4:1

5:16 Greek *unclean.* 5:21 Greek *Sanhedrin;* also in 5:27, 41.

▸ SPIRITUAL WARFARE

5:4 Attacking the church. Why would God kill someone for lying about money? Did He do it because Ananias and Sapphira didn't give enough money to Him? No—their sin was their lie, not their lack of generosity. In telling this lie, they provided opportunity for the first internal attack of Satan, the father of all lies (John 8:44), upon the new covenant community. God demonstrated how He felt about those who would cause damage to His church and offense to His Spirit through lies—He destroyed them. Do you know people who use lies and deceit to tear apart the church? Pity them. It may look as if they are succeeding, but they are positioning themselves for judgment. Make certain that you never allow Satan to use you in his mission to destroy God's churches. (***See Spiritual Warfare****> Resisting Sin and Evil> Consequences> Of Disobedience> Death,* TopicGuide page A46.)

5:12-16 God's judgment against Ananias and Sapphira stands in contrast to the life-giving ministry He manifested through His faithful people. While God's judgment brought fear (5:11), His healing ministry attracted more and more people into the early church.

5:17-26 The jealous Sadducees imprisoned the apostles, but later that same evening an angel of the Lord miraculously released them so that they could return to the task of preaching the gospel. The religious leaders were unable to prevent the advancement of God's church (4:1-22).

5:26 perplexed, wondering where it would all end. [25]Then someone arrived with startling
Matt 14:5; 21:26 news: "The men you put in jail are standing in the Temple, teaching the people!"
5:28 Matt 23:35; 27:25 [26]The captain went with his Temple guards and arrested the apostles, but without vio-
Acts 2:23; 4:18; 7:52 lence, for they were afraid the people would stone them. [27]Then they brought the apostles
5:29 before the high council, where the high priest confronted them. [28]"Didn't we tell you never
Acts 4:19 again to teach in this man's name?" he demanded. "Instead, you have filled all Jerusalem
5:30 with your teaching about Him, and you want to make us responsible for His death!"
Acts 10:39 [29]But Peter and the apostles replied, "We must obey God rather than any human authority.
5:31 [30]The God of our ancestors raised Jesus from the dead after you killed Him by hanging Him
Acts 2:33 Heb 2:10 on a cross.* [31]Then God put Him in the place of honor at his right hand as Prince and Savior.
5:32 He did this so the people of Israel would repent of their sins and be forgiven. [32]We are wit-
Luke 24:28 John 15:26-27 nesses of these things and so is the Holy Spirit, who is given by God to those who obey Him."
[33]When they heard this, the high council was furious and decided to kill them. [34]But one
5:33 Acts 7:54 member, a Pharisee named Gamaliel, who was an expert in religious law and respected
5:34 by all the people, stood up and ordered that the men be sent outside the council chamber
Acts 22:3 for a while. [35]Then he said to his colleagues, "Men of Israel, take care what you are plan-
5:36 ning to do to these men! [36]Some time ago there was that fellow Theudas, who pretended
Acts 21:38 to be someone great. About 400 others joined him, but he was killed, and all his followers
5:37 went their various ways. The whole movement came to nothing. [37]After him, at the time of
Luke 2:1-2; 13:1-2 the census, there was Judas of Galilee. He got people to follow him, but he was killed, too,
5:39 and all his followers were scattered.
Prov 21:30 Isa 46:10 [38]"So my advice is, leave these men alone. Let them go. If they are planning and doing
5:40 these things merely on their own, it will soon be overthrown. [39]But if it is from God, you
Matt 10:17 will not be able to overthrow them. You may even find yourselves fighting against God!"
Mark 13:9 [40]The others accepted his advice. They called in the apostles and had them flogged.
5:41 Matt 5:10-12 Then they ordered them never again to speak in the name of Jesus, and they let them go.
John 15:21 [41]The apostles left the high council rejoicing that God had counted them worthy to suf-
1 Pet 4:13 fer disgrace for the name of Jesus.* [42]And every day, in the Temple and from house to
5:42 Acts 2:46 house, they continued to teach and preach this message: "Jesus is the Messiah."

SEVEN MEN CHOSEN TO SERVE

6:1 Acts 2:45; 4:35 **6** But as the believers* rapidly multiplied, there were rumblings of discontent. The
1 Tim 5:3 Greek-speaking believers complained about the Hebrew-speaking believers, saying
that their widows were being discriminated against in the daily distribution of food.

5:30 Greek *on a tree.* 5:41 Greek *for the name.* 6:1 Greek *disciples;* also in 6:2, 7.

▸ SPIRITUAL WARFARE

5:29 Obeying God instead of man. Almost everyone wants to be liked. We want the basic approval of those around us. The question is this—how far are we willing to go to get this commendation? Are we willing to violate our principles? Our consciences? God's Word? but Peter faced a clear-cut decision—either stop sharing the gospel to please the Jewish leaders or continue to obey the Great Commission of Jesus Christ (Matthew 28:18-20; see also Acts 1:8). His answer was simple: These leaders did not have the authority to forbid that which God had commanded, so he would obey God rather than people. How are you tempted to please people rather than God? Does your desire to be liked get in the way of your obedience? Don't strive for the approval of people around you—focus on pleasing God (Deuteronomy 13:18; Hebrews 11:5; 13:6) and do not allow the brief applause of humanity to distract you. (***See Spiritual Warfare***> *Resisting Sin and Evil> Embracing Christ> Obey His Word,* TopicGuide page A45.)

5:38-39 Gamaliel, a respected scholar of the time, who taught the apostle Paul (22:3), offered a cautionary word concerning the Sanhedrin's treatment of the apostles. If God was indeed behind the actions of the 12 apostles, then not even the most powerful religious leader could stop them.

5:40-42 For the apostles the cost of becoming followers of Christ and leaders of God's church entailed a commitment to remaining faithful to their divine calling in spite of arrests, gag orders, beatings, and trials suffered at the hands of angry mobs and religious leaders (Acts 4:3; 8:3; 9:1-2; 16:23; 18:12-17; 22:23–23:10). The church continued to thrive under persecution (see note at 4:29-31), and the apostles considered it a privilege to suffer for the cause of Christ.

6:1 God's primary purpose for the apostles was the advancement of the gospel beginning in Jerusalem and expanding onward to the ends of the earth (1:8). A problem arose concerning a perceived discrimination over the daily distribution of food. This controversy threatened to mire the apostles in a ministry that was not their God-given mandate to spread the gospel.

[2]So the Twelve called a meeting of all the believers. They said, "We apostles should
spend our time teaching the word of God, not running a food program. [3]And so, brothers, 6:3
select seven men who are well respected and are full of the Spirit and wisdom. We will 1 Tim 3:7-8
give them this responsibility. [4]Then we apostles can spend our time in prayer and teach- 6:4
ing the word." Acts 1:14
[5]Everyone liked this idea, and they chose the following: Stephen (a man full of faith and 6:5
the Holy Spirit), Philip, Procorus, Nicanor, Timon, Parmenas, and Nicolas of Antioch (an Acts 21:8

6:2-6 The Christian community did not confirm these seven men in the same manner as the apostles had appointed Matthias (see note at 1:23-26), but the Lord was no less involved in the decision-making process. These seven deacons, or servants, were selected based on internal characteristics, which the Holy Spirit alone could manifest within them (Acts 2:4; Galatians 5:16-23). Then the apostles laid hands on them and ordained them to office.

▸ WORSHIP

6:3 An office of mercy. The early church was not a chaotic mishmash of people doing whatever each person thought best. Instead, the first believers organized themselves so that everyone could serve God effectively and efficiently. Their commitment to mercy-sensitive ministry required the appointment of deacons to help care for the needs of the new believers and the surrounding community. These godly men were wise and respected (see 1 Timothy 3:8-13). Take every opportunity to honor the office of deacon, making sure deacons have the resources they need to serve God by providing for the widows, orphans, and destitute in and around your church. (***See Worship**> NT> Church Government> First appointment of deacons,* TopicGuide page A30.)

▸ WORSHIP

6:4 Devotion to prayer. As the early church began organizing itself to carry out the ministry that Jesus had given them, they kept prayer as one of their foremost activities. Many times in the book of Acts, we see believers turning to prayer (1:14; 2:42; 4:24). They prayed as the Holy Spirit moved, and many came to follow Jesus. They prayed when persecution came their way. They prayed for each other. They prayed for the leadership of the church. What examples they are to us! Commit yourself to being a person of prayer just as those first Christians were. (***See Worship**> NT> Prayer> Examples> Others> The first disciples devote themselves to prayer,* TopicGuide page A33.)

MY RESPONSE TO GOD

One People under God

ACTS 6:1

After Jesus' ascension (Acts 1), the church grew quickly by the power of the Holy Spirit. God changed and brought together thousands of unique people. But with all the new and diverse believers, wouldn't the church become fractured? Right from the outset, the church showed a profound, practical unity by meeting with one another, sharing their food and possessions, and continuing to welcome new members (Acts 2:42-44).

The unity of the newly formed church, however, did not mean complete agreement—Luke doesn't gloss over the conflict between Greek and Jewish groups in the early church (Acts 6:1). But the leaders called the church together, and the church picked seven mature men of mixed backgrounds to work together to solve the problems that had caused the crisis. The result: God's message spread to even more people (Acts 6:7) as people witnessed God at work among them, and this confirmed the authority of the apostles. God's promises to save people from all over the world were true (Genesis 12:2-3)!

When there is disunity in the church, look on it as an opportunity to see God prove that His words are true and that He will unify His people. Through that unity, the world will know that Jesus is real. As Jesus prayed, "I pray that they will all be one, just as You and I are One—as You are in Me, Father, and I am in You. And may they be in Us so that the world will believe You sent Me" (John 17:21).

6:6 earlier convert to the Jewish faith). 6These seven were presented to the apostles, who
Num 8:10 prayed for them as they laid their hands on them.
Acts 1:24; 13:3
1 Tim 4:14 7So God's message continued to spread. The number of believers greatly increased in
6:7 Jerusalem, and many of the Jewish priests were converted, too.
Acts 12:24; 19:20; 21:20

STEPHEN IS ARRESTED

8Stephen, a man full of God's grace and power, performed amazing miracles and signs
6:9 among the people. 9But one day some men from the Synagogue of Freed Slaves, as it was
Matt 27:32 called, started to debate with him. They were Jews from Cyrene, Alexandria, Cilicia, and
6:10 Luke 21:15 the province of Asia. 10None of them could stand against the wisdom and the Spirit with
6:11 which Stephen spoke.
Matt 26:59-61 11So they persuaded some men to lie about Stephen, saying, "We heard him blas-
pheme Moses, and even God." 12This roused the people, the elders, and the teachers of re-
ligious law. So they arrested Stephen and brought him before the high council.*
6:13 13The lying witnesses said, "This man is always speaking against the holy Temple and
Acts 7:48; 21:28 against the law of Moses. 14We have heard him say that this Jesus of Nazareth* will de-
6:14 John 2:19-21 stroy the Temple and change the customs Moses handed down to us."
Acts 21:21 15At this point everyone in the high council stared at Stephen, because his face became
as bright as an angel's.

STEPHEN ADDRESSES THE COUNCIL

7 Then the high priest asked Stephen, "Are these accusations true?"
7:2 2This was Stephen's reply: "Brothers and fathers, listen to me. Our glorious God
Gen 11:31–12:1; 15:7 Acts 22:1 appeared to our ancestor Abraham in Mesopotamia before he settled in Haran.* 3God told
7:3 him, 'Leave your native land and your relatives, and come into the land that I will show
Gen 12:1 you.' 4So Abraham left the land of the Chaldeans and lived in Haran until his father died.
7:4 Then God brought him here to the land where you now live.
Gen 12:5 5"But God gave him no inheritance here, not even one square foot of land. God did
Heb 11:8 promise, however, that eventually the whole land would belong to Abraham and his
7:5 Gen 12:7; 13:15; 15:2, 18; 17:8; 24:7

6:12 Greek *Sanhedrin;* also in 6:15. 6:14 Or *Jesus the Nazarene.* 7:2 *Mesopotamia* was the region now called Iraq. *Haran* was a city in what is now called Syria. 7:3 Gen 12:1.

6:7 The author provides the reader with a snapshot of the progress of the church (see also 13:49; 19:20). Even some of the priests, the very enemies of the church, began believing in Christ (4:5-7; 5:27). This explosive growth came on the heels of a disruption to community life, for the enemy was continually at work behind the scenes seeking ways to break up God's people (5:3). But God transformed persecutions into fuel for growth and expansion in the church.

6:8-14 Stephen was the most prominent individual among the seven chosen by the church, for he alone is specifically described as "full of faith and the Holy Spirit" (6:5), and "full of God's grace and power" (6:8). Stephen's witness was so powerful that none of his enemies could argue or stand against him, and so these evil men from several countries plotted to use false testimony to frame Stephen before the high council.

6:15 Instead of showing signs of fear or distress, Stephen's countenance became as the face of an angel, captivating the attention of members of the high council (Exodus 34:29-35; Ecclesiastes 8:1; Matthew 13:43). The Lord was with Stephen, and he would not back down from the attacks of the opposition (Acts 7).

7:1-48 In this speech, Stephen pointed out that Israel was consistently unfaithful to God, despite God's consistent covenant faithfulness to them. By this time in history, Israel's unfaithfulness to the covenant allowed the gospel to go forth to the Gentiles (1:8). Stephen's lengthy speech also has numerous points where numbers are rounded, events are summarized, and portions of history are condensed. These appear to present disagreements with numbers and locations in other passages and versions of Scripture (see notes following). This suggests that Luke accurately recorded the hasty defense of Stephen, who was delivering a sweeping view of Israel's relationship with God rather than giving a precise account of history.

▸ MINISTRY

7:2 Living openly. You may have never heard of any specific individual being persecuted for following Christ. But in 2005 alone, an estimated 200 million Christians around the world knew that if they were identified as Christians, they (or their families) would be fired, jailed, tortured, or killed. Stephen was involved enough in the early church (6:5) to know that following the gospel of Jesus Christ carried a price. Like Stephen, you live in a situation where you could face persecution for your beliefs. Or do you? If you are not facing persecution, why not? Is it because of your timidity, or something else? Live your faith in such a way that others can identify you as a Christian. (***See Ministry****> Great Commission> Witness> Witness in the power of the Holy Spirit,* TopicGuide page A56.)

descendants—even though he had no children yet. 6 God also told him that his descen-
dants would live in a foreign land, where they would be oppressed as slaves for
400 years. 7 'But I will punish the nation that enslaves them,' God said, 'and in the end
they will come out and worship Me here in this place.'*

8 "God also gave Abraham the covenant of circumcision at that time. So when Abraham
became the father of Isaac, he circumcised him on the eighth day. And the practice was
continued when Isaac became the father of Jacob, and when Jacob became the father of
the twelve patriarchs of the Israelite nation.

9 "These patriarchs were jealous of their brother Joseph, and they sold him to be a slave
in Egypt. But God was with him 10 and rescued him from all his troubles. And God gave him
favor before Pharaoh, king of Egypt. God also gave Joseph unusual wisdom, so that Pha-
raoh appointed him governor over all of Egypt and put him in charge of the palace.

11 "But a famine came upon Egypt and Canaan. There was great misery, and our ances-
tors ran out of food. 12 Jacob heard that there was still grain in Egypt, so he sent his sons—
our ancestors—to buy some. 13 The second time they went, Joseph revealed his identity to
his brothers,* and they were introduced to Pharaoh. 14 Then Joseph sent for his father, Ja-
cob, and all his relatives to come to Egypt, seventy-five persons in all. 15 So Jacob went to
Egypt. He died there, as did our ancestors. 16 Their bodies were taken to Shechem and bur-
ied in the tomb Abraham had bought for a certain price from Hamor's sons in Shechem.

17 "As the time drew near when God would fulfill His promise to Abraham, the number of
our people in Egypt greatly increased. 18 But then a new king came to the throne of Egypt
who knew nothing about Joseph. 19 This king exploited our people and oppressed them,
forcing parents to abandon their newborn babies so they would die.

20 "At that time Moses was born—a beautiful child in God's eyes. His parents cared for
him at home for three months. 21 When they had to abandon him, Pharaoh's daughter
adopted him and raised him as her own son. 22 Moses was taught all the wisdom of the
Egyptians, and he was powerful in both speech and action.

23 "One day when Moses was forty years old, he decided to visit his relatives, the people
of Israel. 24 He saw an Egyptian mistreating an Israelite. So Moses came to the man's de-
fense and avenged him, killing the Egyptian. 25 Moses assumed his fellow Israelites would
realize that God had sent him to rescue them, but they didn't.

26 "The next day he visited them again and saw two men of Israel fighting. He tried to be
a peacemaker. 'Men,' he said, 'you are brothers. Why are you fighting each other?'

27 "But the man in the wrong pushed Moses aside. 'Who made you a ruler and judge
over us?' he asked. 28 'Are you going to kill me as you killed that Egyptian yesterday?'
29 When Moses heard that, he fled the country and lived as a foreigner in the land of Midi-
an. There his two sons were born.

30 "Forty years later, in the desert near Mount Sinai, an angel appeared to Moses in the
flame of a burning bush. 31 When Moses saw it, he was amazed at the sight. As he went to
take a closer look, the voice of the LORD called out to him, 32 'I am the God of your ancestors—
the God of Abraham, Isaac, and Jacob.' Moses shook with terror and did not dare to look.

7:6 *Gen 15:13-14
7:7 Exod 3:12
7:8 Gen 17:10-14; 21:2-4; 25:26; 35:23-26
7:9 Gen 37:28; 39:2; Ps 105:17
7:10 Gen 41:37-43; Ps 105:21
7:11 Gen 41:54
7:12 Gen 42:1-2
7:13 Gen 45:1-4
7:14 Gen 45:9-10; 46:26-27; Deut 10:22
7:15 Gen 46:5-7; 49:33; Exod 1:6
7:16 Gen 23:16-20
7:17-18 *Exod 1:7-8; Ps 105:24
7:19 Exod 1:10-11, 22
7:20 Exod 2:2; Heb 11:23
7:21 Exod 2:3-10
7:22 1 Kgs 4:30; Isa 19:11
7:23-24 Exod 2:11-12
7:26-28 *Exod 2:13-14
7:29 Exod 2:15
7:30-31 Exod 3:1-4
7:32-34 *Exod 3:4-10

7:5-7 Gen 12:7; 15:13-14; Exod 3:12. 7:13 Other manuscripts read *Joseph was recognized by his brothers.*

7:6 Exodus 12:40 states that this period of time was 430 years, while the prophecy of Genesis 15:13 rounds it off to 400. Stephen's reference uses the more general number to refer to this span of time.

7:14 Exodus 1:5 refers to 70 direct descendants of Joseph, but the Dead Sea scrolls and the ancient Greek version of Exodus read 75. Throughout his speech, Stephen alludes to the Septuagint, the Greek version of the Old Testament in use during his time. The additional five descendants come from the Septuagint version of Genesis 46:20, which has a longer genealogy of Joseph, mentioning four grandsons and one great-grandson, for a total of five more descendants.

7:16 Stephen's summary of those "taken to Shechem" didn't include the entire group discussed here, especially all 75 of Joseph's descendants. The audience was familiar with the burial sites of the patriarchs, with the stories of Jacob buried in Hebron (Genesis 50:13) and Joseph buried at Shechem (Genesis 33:19; 50:25; Exodus 13:19; Joshua 24:32). His "all of them" was a brief, partial summary, showing the rush of the last words of Stephen.

33 "Then the LORD said to him, 'Take off your sandals, for you are standing on holy
ground. 34 I have certainly seen the oppression of My people in Egypt. I have heard their
groans and have come down to rescue them. Now go, for I am sending you back to
Egypt.'*

35 "So God sent back the same man His people had previously rejected when they de-
manded, 'Who made you a ruler and judge over us?' Through the angel who appeared to
him in the burning bush, God sent Moses to be their ruler and savior. 36 And by means of
many wonders and miraculous signs, He led them out of Egypt, through the Red Sea, and
through the wilderness for forty years.

37 "Moses himself told the people of Israel, 'God will raise up for you a Prophet like me
from among your own people.'* 38 Moses was with our ancestors, the assembly of God's
people in the wilderness, when the angel spoke to him at Mount Sinai. And there Moses
received life-giving words to pass on to us.*

39 "But our ancestors refused to listen to Moses. They rejected him and wanted to return
to Egypt. 40 They told Aaron, 'Make us some gods who can lead us, for we don't know what
has become of this Moses, who brought us out of Egypt.' 41 So they made an idol shaped
like a calf, and they sacrificed to it and celebrated over this thing they had made. 42 Then
God turned away from them and abandoned them to serve the stars of heaven as their
gods! In the book of the prophets it is written,

'Was it to Me you were bringing sacrifices and offerings
during those forty years in the wilderness, Israel?
43 No, you carried your pagan gods—
the shrine of Molech,
the star of your god Rephan,
and the images you made to worship them.
So I will send you into exile
as far away as Babylon.'*

44 "Our ancestors carried the Tabernacle* with them through the wilderness. It was con-
structed according to the plan God had shown to Moses. 45 Years later, when Joshua led
our ancestors in battle against the nations that God drove out of this land, the Taberna-
cle was taken with them into their new territory. And it stayed there until the time of King
David.

46 "David found favor with God and asked for the privilege of building a permanent
Temple for the God of Jacob.* 47 But it was Solomon who actually built it. 48 However, the
Most High doesn't live in temples made by human hands. As the prophet says,

49 'Heaven is My throne,
and the earth is My footstool.
Could you build Me a temple as good as that?'
asks the LORD.
'Could you build Me such a resting place?
50 Didn't My hands make both heaven and earth?'*

7:35 *Exod 2:14
7:36 Exod 7:3; 12:41
7:37 *Deut 18:15; Acts 3:22
7:38 Exod 19:1-6; Deut 32:45-47
7:39 Num 14:3
7:40 *Exod 32:1, 23
7:42-43 *Amos 5:25-27
7:44 Exod 25:9, 40; Heb 8:5
7:45 Josh 3:14-17; 18:1; 23:9; 2 Sam 7:2, 6
7:46 2 Sam 7:2-16; 1 Kgs 8:17; Ps 132:1-5
7:47 1 Kgs 6:1-38
7:48 2 Chr 2:6; Isa 57:15; Eph 2:22; 1 Pet 2:5
7:49-50 *Isa 66:1-2

7:31-34 Exod 3:5-10. **7:37** Deut 18:15. **7:38** Some manuscripts read *to you.* **7:42-43** Amos 5:25-27 (Greek version). **7:44** Greek *the tent of witness.* **7:46** Some manuscripts read *the house of Jacob.* **7:49-50** Isa 66:1-2.

7:38, 53 The reference to the angel who spoke to Moses on Mount Sinai (Exodus 20:1, 21) could be taken two ways. Stephen could mean that he believed God assumed the role or even manifested a physical form of an angelic messenger (Genesis 18:1-15; Joshua 5:14-15) when He spoke to Moses. It could also be a reference to God's habit of communicating through angels throughout history (Acts 7:53; Galatians 3:19; Hebrews 2:2).

7:48-50 Stephen's speech exposes the falsehood of the claim that God could be contained within the Israelite nation and Temple. Following Solomon's wisdom (1 Kings 8:22-30), he explains that the entire earth is subject to God's rule and presence, for God exists beyond the confines of a single nation and a single building.

[51]"You stubborn people! You are heathen* at heart and deaf to the truth. Must you for- 7:51 Exod 32:9; 33:3, 5
ever resist the Holy Spirit? That's what your ancestors did, and so do you! [52]Name one
prophet your ancestors didn't persecute! They even killed the ones who predicted the 7:52 Matt 23:30-34
coming of the Righteous One—the Messiah whom you betrayed and murdered. [53]You de- 7:53 Gal 3:19
liberately disobeyed God's law, even though you received it from the hands of angels."
[54]The Jewish leaders were infuriated by Stephen's accusation, and they shook their fists 7:55 Heb 1:3, 13
at him in rage.* [55]But Stephen, full of the Holy Spirit, gazed steadily into heaven and saw
the glory of God, and he saw Jesus standing in the place of honor at God's right hand. 7:56 Matt 3:16
[56]And he told them, "Look, I see the heavens opened and the Son of Man standing in the
place of honor at God's right hand!" 7:58 Lev 24:14-16 Deut 17:7
[57]Then they put their hands over their ears and began shouting. They rushed at him
[58]and dragged him out of the city and began to stone him. His accusers took off their coats 7:59 Ps 31:5 Luke 23:46
and laid them at the feet of a young man named Saul.*
[59]As they stoned him, Stephen prayed, "Lord Jesus, receive my spirit." [60]He fell to his 7:60 Luke 23:34
knees, shouting, "Lord, don't charge them with this sin!" And with that, he died.

8 Saul was one of the witnesses, and he agreed completely with the killing of Stephen.

PERSECUTION SCATTERS THE BELIEVERS

A great wave of persecution began that day, sweeping over the church in Jerusalem; and 8:1 Acts 7:58
all the believers except the apostles were scattered through the regions of Judea and

7:51 Greek *uncircumcised.* 7:54 Greek *they were grinding their teeth against him.* 7:58 *Saul* is later called Paul; see 13:9.

7:51-53 Stephen indicted the religious leaders of his day with the same sin of rebellion their ancestors had committed. Just as the Israelites of old had rejected Moses (7:35, 39) and the other prophets sent by God (2 Chronicles 35:21-22; 36:15-16), the Jews in Stephen's day had rejected Jesus Christ as the Messiah of God.

▸ GOD
7:51 Resisting the Holy Spirit. The Bible describes the human race with raw honesty. For instance, God makes it clear that for all our value and His general love for all humanity (John 3:16), our actions are often evil (Genesis 6:5; Proverbs 21:4; Romans 3:23). One of our evils is that we resist the work of the Holy Spirit (Ephesians 4:30; 1 Thessalonians 5:19). This offense carries grave consequences (Acts 5:3). But not all resist Him. At least one person who resisted the conviction of the Holy Spirit during the stoning of Stephen came to Christ later—the apostle Paul (initially called Saul; see 7:58). Stephen never saw the fruit of his preaching in Paul's life—he died after his message was completed. But Stephen knew and we know that God works in hearts (Acts 16:14) to bring people to Himself. God is not discouraged by those who resist Him—should we be? Keep creating opportunities for the Holy Spirit to manifest Himself in your life and in the lives of those around you. (***See God***> *God's Names> Holy Spirit> Comes Upon> Is resisted,* TopicGuide page A19.)

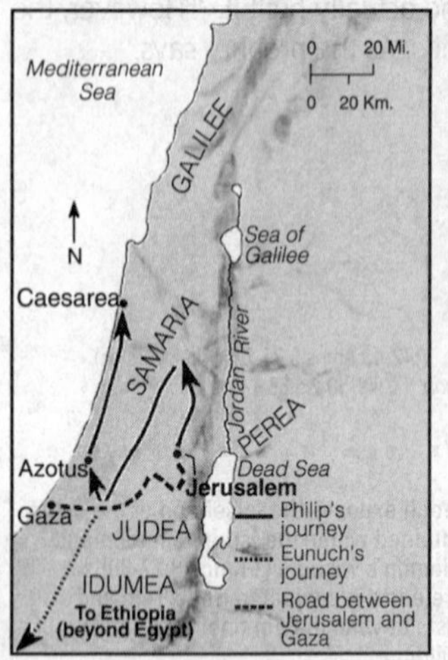

PHILIP'S MINISTRY
To escape persecution in Jerusalem, Philip fled to Samaria, where he continued preaching the gospel. While he was there, an angel commanded him to meet an Ethiopian official on the road between Jerusaem and Gaza. The man became a believer before continuing on to Ethiopia. Philip then went from Azotus to Caesarea.

7:54-58 The ministry of Jesus Christ for His people did not end after He ascended into heaven and took His place at the right of the Father. He continues to intercede on behalf of those who call Him Lord (Hebrews 2:12-18; 1 John 2:1). At the very instant the leaders became infuriated with Stephen, the heavens opened, and Christ appeared, showing that Christ was Stephen's defense attorney and advocate in the heavenly council.

7:57-60 Stephen would become the early church's first recorded martyr. As Stephen is dragged out of the city to be stoned, Luke introduces the reader to Saul, later called Paul (13:9). Paul would become the greatest missionary apostle for the church. Stephen's stoning evokes memories of the crucifixion of Jesus Christ (Luke 23:34, 46).

8:1-3 The external persecution against the church had now reached its climax in the book of Acts; all the believers in Jerusalem had fled for their lives outside the city, and only the apostles remained behind. But what the enemies meant for evil, God transformed for good by advancing the gospel into the surrounding towns and villages through the witness and testimonies of His faithful followers.

Samaria. 2(Some devout men came and buried Stephen with great mourning.) 3But Saul
was going everywhere to destroy the church. He went from house to house, dragging out
both men and women to throw them into prison.

PHILIP PREACHES IN SAMARIA

4But the believers who were scattered preached the Good News about Jesus wherever
they went. 5Philip, for example, went to the city of Samaria and told the people there
about the Messiah. 6Crowds listened intently to Philip because they were eager to hear his
message and see the miraculous signs he did. 7Many evil* spirits were cast out, screaming
as they left their victims. And many who had been paralyzed or lame were healed. 8So
there was great joy in that city.

9A man named Simon had been a sorcerer there for many years, amazing the people of
Samaria and claiming to be someone great. 10Everyone, from the least to the greatest,
often spoke of him as "the Great One—the Power of God." 11They listened closely to him
because for a long time he had astounded them with his magic.

12But now the people believed Philip's message of Good News concerning the Kingdom
of God and the name of Jesus Christ. As a result, many men and women were baptized.
13Then Simon himself believed and was baptized. He began following Philip wherever he
went, and he was amazed by the signs and great miracles Philip performed.

14When the apostles in Jerusalem heard that the people of Samaria had accepted God's
message, they sent Peter and John there. 15As soon as they arrived, they prayed for these
new believers to receive the Holy Spirit. 16The Holy Spirit had not yet come upon any of
them, for they had only been baptized in the name of the Lord Jesus. 17Then Peter and
John laid their hands upon these believers, and they received the Holy Spirit.

18When Simon saw that the Spirit was given when the apostles laid their hands on peo-
ple, he offered them money to buy this power. 19"Let me have this power, too," he ex-
claimed, "so that when I lay my hands on people, they will receive the Holy Spirit!"

20But Peter replied, "May your money be destroyed with you for thinking God's gift can
be bought! 21You can have no part in this, for your heart is not right with God. 22Repent of
your wickedness and pray to the Lord. Perhaps He will forgive your evil thoughts, 23for I
can see that you are full of bitter jealousy and are held captive by sin."

24"Pray to the Lord for me," Simon exclaimed, "that these terrible things you've said
won't happen to me!"

25After testifying and preaching the word of the Lord in Samaria, Peter and John re-
turned to Jerusalem. And they stopped in many Samaritan villages along the way to
preach the Good News.

8:7 Greek *unclean.*

8:3 Acts 9:1; 22:4; 26:9-11; 1 Cor 15:9; Gal 1:13
8:4 Acts 8:1; 11:19
8:5 Acts 6:5; 21:8
8:7 Matt 10:1; Mark 6:7; 16:17
8:9 Acts 5:36; 13:6
8:12 Acts 2:38
8:13 Acts 19:11
8:14 Acts 8:1
8:15 Acts 2:38; 19:2
8:16 Acts 10:44
8:17 Acts 6:6; 19:6
8:20 Matt 10:8; Acts 2:38
8:21 Ps 78:37
8:22 Acts 2:38
8:23 Deut 29:17-18; Isa 58:6
8:24 Exod 8:8; Num 21:7

8:4-8 Philip, one of the seven servants appointed to assist the apostles (6:5), brought the gospel to the people of Samaria. Philip's actions formed a bridge between the believers in Jerusalem and those who received the gospel in Samaria. Philip, who would later be recognized as "the Evangelist" (21:8), not only spread God's Kingdom up to Samaria (in fulfillment of the Lord's command in 1:8), but through his preaching also helped to tear down the wall of discrimination that existed between Jerusalem and Samaria (John 4:1-26). God's plan is for His family to be made up of people from every nation, language and ethnicity (Revelation 5:9).

8:9-25 Simon, a sorcerer or magician, captivated the attention of the Samaritans until the arrival of Philip. When Philip arrived, he performed miracles and preached the Good News of Jesus Christ. Though Simon was converted and baptized, time would tell that his conversion was based on a superficial acknowledgment of the gospel and that his true intentions were to gain spiritual gifts through money. A church leader of the second century, Irenaeus, explained that Simon would later become a proponent of the Gnostic heresy.

▸ WORSHIP

8:22 Power hungry. When the apostles went about spreading the gospel, they ran into all kinds of odd situations. In this case, Peter encountered a man who wanted to buy the power he saw Peter display. Peter sensed this was not said out of ignorance, so he rebuked him. Simon's sin was bitterness (8:23). His resentment at God for giving power to the unlearned apostles revealed itself when he attempted to bribe them. Power-hungry attitudes can spring up in places we don't expect. This interferes with God's work and with our spiritual growth. Repenting of such sins is difficult because it involves an admission of weakness—the very opposite of what the proud want to do. Truly listen to those who find fault with you. If they are right, repent and ask God for cleansing, and thank them for their ministry to you. (***See Worship**> NT> Our Role> Attitude> Willing to repent of bad attitude,* TopicGuide page A32.)

PHILIP AND THE ETHIOPIAN EUNUCH

26 As for Philip, an angel of the Lord said to him, "Go south* down the desert road that runs
from Jerusalem to Gaza." 27 So he started out, and he met the treasurer of Ethiopia, a eu-
nuch of great authority under the Kandake, the queen of Ethiopia. The eunuch had gone
to Jerusalem to worship, 28 and he was now returning. Seated in his carriage, he was read-
ing aloud from the book of the prophet Isaiah.
29 The Holy Spirit said to Philip, "Go over and walk along beside the carriage."
30 Philip ran over and heard the man reading from the prophet Isaiah. Philip asked, "Do
you understand what you are reading?"
31 The man replied, "How can I, unless someone instructs me?" And he urged Philip to
come up into the carriage and sit with him.
32 The passage of Scripture he had been reading was this:

"He was led like a sheep to the slaughter.
And as a lamb is silent before the shearers,
He did not open His mouth.
33 He was humiliated and received no justice.
Who can speak of His descendants?
For His life was taken from the earth."*

34 The eunuch asked Philip, "Tell me, was the prophet talking about himself or someone
else?" 35 So beginning with this same Scripture, Philip told him the Good News about Jesus.
36 As they rode along, they came to some water, and the eunuch said, "Look! There's
some water! Why can't I be baptized?"* 38 He ordered the carriage to stop, and they went
down into the water, and Philip baptized him.
39 When they came up out of the water, the Spirit of the Lord snatched Philip away. The
eunuch never saw him again but went on his way rejoicing. 40 Meanwhile, Philip found
himself farther north at the town of Azotus. He preached the Good News there and in
every town along the way until he came to Caesarea.

SAUL'S CONVERSION

9 Meanwhile, Saul was uttering threats with every breath and was eager to kill the
Lord's followers.* So he went to the high priest. 2 He requested letters addressed to
the synagogues in Damascus, asking for their cooperation in the arrest of any followers of
the Way he found there. He wanted to bring them—both men and women—back to Jerusa-
lem in chains.
3 As he was approaching Damascus on this mission, a light from heaven suddenly shone

8:26 Acts 5:19; 6:5
8:27 1 Kgs 8:41-43; Ps 68:31; Isa 56:3-5; Zeph 3:10
8:32-33 *Isa 53:7-8
8:35 Luke 24:27; Acts 18:28
8:36 Acts 10:47
8:39 1 Kgs 18:12; 2 Kgs 2:16; Ezek 3:12
9:1-29 //Acts 22:3-21; 26:9-18
9:1 Acts 8:3
9:2 Acts 9:14; 22:4
9:3 Acts 22:6-7; 26:12-13; 1 Cor 15:8

8:26 Or *Go at noon.* 8:32-33 Isa 53:7-8 (Greek version). 8:36 Some manuscripts add verse 37, *"You can," Philip answered, "if you believe with all your heart." And the eunuch replied, "I believe that Jesus Christ is the Son of God."* 9:1 Greek *disciples.*

8:26-29 Philip's supernatural journey from Samaria demonstrates that it was no accident that the early church broke through traditional walls of separation (see note at 8:4-8) between Jews and Gentiles—it was God's will. Here Philip shares the gospel with an Ethiopian eunuch, formally prohibited from entering into community with God's people (Deuteronomy 23:1).

8:30-40 The story of Philip and the Ethiopian eunuch begins on a desert road (8:26) but ends in the waters of baptism. What stood between the initial and the concluding interactions between these two men was the proclamation by Philip and the faith of the Ethiopian eunuch. Philip clarified that Isaiah taught that God had sent His Son as a Lamb to be slaughtered for the sins of His people. Philip then left the Ethiopian, transported supernaturally to Azotus, otherwise known as the ancient Philistine city Ashdod.

▸ MINISTRY

8:38 The role of baptism. Do you really have to be baptized? It may seem rather useless or even embarrassing to have water poured on you or to be dunked in it, but the New Testament church seemed to think it was very important (Romans 6:4; Ephesians 4:5). After hearing Philip teach from the Old Testament Scriptures, the eunuch believed that he should be immediately baptized (Acts 8:37). Baptism would serve as a sacrament or a holy sign pointing to the new spiritual reality the Holy Spirit had washed all of his sins away (Psalm 51:7; Titus 3:5). As we witness for Christ and see people enter into the Kingdom of God, we too can disciple them in their new faith, and part of discipleship is baptism. Do not ignore teaching this step of obedience to those who believe (Acts 2:38; 16:33). (***See Ministry*** *> Great Commission> Make Disciples> Disciple by baptizing,* TopicGuide page A56.)

down around him. [4]He fell to the ground and heard a voice saying to him, "Saul! Saul!
Why are you persecuting Me?"
9:5 Acts 5:39 [5]"Who are You, lord?" Saul asked.
And the voice replied, "I am Jesus, the one you are persecuting! [6]Now get up and go
into the city, and you will be told what you must do."
9:7 Dan 10:7 [7]The men with Saul stood speechless, for they heard the sound of someone's voice but
Acts 22:9; 26:14 saw no one! [8]Saul picked himself up off the ground, but when he opened his eyes he was
blind. So his companions led him by the hand to Damascus. [9]He remained there blind for
three days and did not eat or drink.
9:10 [10]Now there was a believer* in Damascus named Ananias. The Lord spoke to him in a
Acts 10:3; 11:5; 12:9; vision, calling, "Ananias!"
22:12 "Yes, Lord!" he replied.
9:11 [11]The Lord said, "Go over to Straight Street, to the house of Judas. When you get there,
Acts 21:39 ask for a man from Tarsus named Saul. He is praying to Me right now. [12]I have shown him
a vision of a man named Ananias coming in and laying hands on him so he can see again."
9:13 Acts 26:10 [13]"But Lord," exclaimed Ananias, "I've heard many people talk about the terrible things
9:15 this man has done to the believers* in Jerusalem! [14]And he is authorized by the leading
Acts 13:2 priests to arrest everyone who calls upon Your name."
Rom 1:1 Gal 1:15-16 [15]But the Lord said, "Go, for Saul is My chosen instrument to take My message to the
1 Tim 1:12 Gentiles and to kings, as well as to the people of Israel. [16]And I will show him how much
9:16 he must suffer for My name's sake."
Acts 20:23; 21:11 2 Cor 11:23-27 [17]So Ananias went and found Saul. He laid his hands on him and said, "Brother Saul, the
Lord Jesus, who appeared to you on the road, has sent me so that you might regain your
9:17 Acts 13:52; 22:12-13 sight and be filled with the Holy Spirit." [18]Instantly something like scales fell from Saul's
1 Cor 9:1; 15:8 eyes, and he regained his sight. Then he got up and was baptized. [19]Afterward he ate
9:19 some food and regained his strength.
Acts 26:20

9:10 Greek *disciple;* also in 9:26, 36. 9:13 Greek *God's holy people;* also in 9:32, 41.

9:4-6 The blinding light from heaven at midday brought Saul's actions into clear focus, for although Saul's intent in Damascus was to attack what he viewed as a renegade cult, he was actually assaulting the Lord Jesus Christ (Exodus 16:8; 1 Samuel 8:7; Luke 10:16). Through the conversion of Saul, God's grace conquered the heart of another enemy of God. This theme would be important throughout Saul's (soon to be Paul's) future ministry (Romans 5:1-2, 10-11).

9:10-16 When the Lord instructed Ananias to visit Saul, Ananias initially resisted because he had heard of Saul's previous actions against Christians. But the Lord put Ananias at ease by explaining God's master plan for Saul. Although Saul's intention was to persecute the church, God intended for Saul to be converted to Christ and to become God's chosen instrument to take the gospel to the ends of the earth (1:8).

▸ MINISTRY
9:15 Dangerous obedience. Can you see the dilemma that Ananias faced? God was asking him to contact the man who had been actively pursuing the death and imprisonment of Christians. To do what God asked was to put his life in danger. But look at what was at stake in Ananias's obedience. Saul (later called Paul) would become the one who carried the gospel to the ends of the known world. He wrote many books in the New Testament. God knew His plans for Saul—Ananias didn't. That's why it was so important for Ananias to obey God's call no matter what. Is God calling you to do something difficult? Take courage from this story and obey no matter what. (***See Ministry****> Great Commission> Risk> Stepping outside your "comfort zone,"* TopicGuide page A56.)

SYRIA
To Arabia
Mediterranean Sea
Damascus
Sea of Galilee
N
Jordan River
Jerusalem
Dead Sea
JUDEA
0 20 Mi.
0 20 Km.

SAUL TRAVELS TO DAMASCUS
Many Christians fled Jerusalem when persecution began after Stephen's death, seeking refuge in other cities and countries. Saul tracked them down, even traveling 150 miles to Damascus in Syria to bring Christians back in chains to Jerusalem. But as he neared the ancient city, he discovered that God had other plans for him (9:15).

SAUL IN DAMASCUS AND JERUSALEM

Saul stayed with the believers* in Damascus for a few days. [20]And immediately he began
preaching about Jesus in the synagogues, saying, "He is indeed the Son of God!"
[21]All who heard him were amazed. "Isn't this the same man who caused such devasta- **9:21**
tion among Jesus' followers in Jerusalem?" they asked. "And didn't he come here to arrest Acts 8:3
them and take them in chains to the leading priests?"
[22]Saul's preaching became more and more powerful, and the Jews in Damascus couldn't **9:22**
refute his proofs that Jesus was indeed the Messiah. [23]After a while some of the Jews plot- Acts 18:28
ted together to kill him. [24]They were watching for him day and night at the city gate so they **9:23** Acts 23:12
could murder him, but Saul was told about their plot. [25]So during the night, some of the **9:24**
other believers* lowered him in a large basket through an opening in the city wall. Acts 20:3; 23:16, 20
[26]When Saul arrived in Jerusalem, he tried to meet with the believers, but they were all 2 Cor 11:32
afraid of him. They did not believe he had truly become a believer! [27]Then Barnabas **9:25**
brought him to the apostles and told them how Saul had seen the Lord on the way to Da- 1 Sam 19:12 2 Cor 11:33
mascus and how the Lord had spoken to Saul. He also told them that Saul had preached **9:26**
boldly in the name of Jesus in Damascus. Acts 22:17
[28]So Saul stayed with the apostles and went all around Jerusalem with them, preaching Gal 1:17-18
boldly in the name of the Lord. [29]He debated with some Greek-speaking Jews, but they **9:27**
tried to murder him. [30]When the believers* heard about this, they took him down to Caes- Acts 4:36
area and sent him away to Tarsus, his hometown.
[31]The church then had peace throughout Judea, Galilee, and Samaria, and it became **9:31**
stronger as the believers lived in the fear of the Lord. And with the encouragement of the Acts 8:1
Holy Spirit, it also grew in numbers.

PETER HEALS AENEAS AND RAISES DORCAS

[32]Meanwhile, Peter traveled from place to place, and he came down to visit the believers **9:32**
in the town of Lydda. [33]There he met a man named Aeneas, who had been paralyzed and Acts 8:14

9:19 Greek *disciples;* also in 9:26, 38. **9:25** Greek *His disciples.* **9:30** Greek *brothers.*

CILICIA
Tarsus
Antioch
SYRIA
Mediterranean Sea
Damascus
Caesarea
From Arabia
Jerusalem
N
0 150 Mi.
0 150 Km.

SAUL'S RETURN TO TARSUS

At least three years elapsed between Acts 9:22 and 9:26. After time alone in Arabia (see Galatians 1:16-18), Saul (Paul) returned to Damascus and then to Jerusalem. The apostles were reluctant to believe that this former persecutor could have become one of them. Saul escaped to Caesarea, where he caught a ship and returned to Tarsus.

9:20-22 After Saul had physically recuperated from his encounter with the Lord, he immediately launched into his preaching ministry. The crowd was amazed, for the same man that had once persecuted the followers of Christ was now proving through his words that Jesus was the Son of God. As a preacher, Saul grew stronger and stronger after each sermon.

9:26-31 Jesus had instructed that the gospel should spread beginning from Jerusalem (Matthew 28:18-20), and now Saul brings the gospel to Jerusalem from another city, Damascus. God did not favor one geographical area over another, for the entire world had now become His mission field (Acts 7:49-50).

▸ WORSHIP

9:31 Fear and awe. What was the secret of the success of the early church? Part of it was their fear of God. It gave them boldness to challenge their enemies in a time of persecution and hardship. Having a fear of God enables us to put His honor first in our lives—above our reputations, our worldly desires, our limitations, and our fear of people. Fearing God means knowing what He can do and giving Him respect and honor. To develop a deeper fear of God, take time to meditate on His character and holiness. Look at the lives of those in the Bible who feared Him (Genesis 42:18; Nehemiah 7:2; Job 2:3; Acts 10:2, 22) and seek to emulate the boldness and holiness that flowed from their lives. (***See Worship****> NT> Reverence> Fear/awe was a mark of the Early Church,* TopicGuide page A32; also ***see God****> God's Attributes> Holy> God's holiness demands exclusive worship,* TopicGuide page A16.)

9:32-43 Peter continued his role as apostle by ministering to believers in the surrounding areas (8:14). On both of these occasions, Peter restored the believer to health through the power of Jesus Christ, not his own power. In the case of Aeneas, Peter spoke in the name of Jesus Christ (9:34). And in the case of Tabitha, Peter prayed for her healing (9:40).

9:34 bedridden for eight years. 34Peter said to him, "Aeneas, Jesus Christ heals you! Get up, and
Acts 3:6; 4:10 roll up your sleeping mat!" And he was healed instantly. 35Then the whole population of
9:35 Lydda and Sharon saw Aeneas walking around, and they turned to the Lord.
Acts 2:41 36There was a believer in Joppa named Tabitha (which in Greek is Dorcas*). She was al-
9:36 1 Tim 2:10 ways doing kind things for others and helping the poor. 37About this time she became ill
Titus 3:8 and died. Her body was washed for burial and laid in an upstairs room. 38But the believers
had heard that Peter was nearby at Lydda, so they sent two men to beg him, "Please come
as soon as possible!"
39So Peter returned with them; and as soon as he arrived, they took him to the upstairs
9:40 room. The room was filled with widows who were weeping and showing him the coats
1 Kgs 17:19-23 and other clothes Dorcas had made for them. 40But Peter asked them all to leave the
2 Kgs 4:32-36 room; then he knelt and prayed. Turning to the body he said, "Get up, Tabitha." And she
Matt 9:25 John 11:43 opened her eyes! When she saw Peter, she sat up! 41He gave her his hand and helped her
9:42 up. Then he called in the widows and all the believers, and he presented her to them alive.
Acts 2:41 42The news spread through the whole town, and many believed in the Lord. 43And Peter
9:43 Acts 10:6 stayed a long time in Joppa, living with Simon, a tanner of hides.

CORNELIUS CALLS FOR PETER

10:1-2 10 In Caesarea there lived a Roman army officer* named Cornelius, who was a cap-
Acts 8:40; 27:1, 3 tain of the Italian Regiment. 2He was a devout, God-fearing man, as was everyone
10:3 in his household. He gave generously to the poor and prayed regularly to God. 3One after-
Acts 3:1 noon about three o'clock, he had a vision in which he saw an angel of God coming toward
10:4 him. "Cornelius!" the angel said.
2 Chr 7:15 Rev 8:4 4Cornelius stared at him in terror. "What is it, sir?" he asked the angel.
10:6 And the angel replied, "Your prayers and gifts to the poor have been received by God as
Acts 9:43 an offering! 5Now send some men to Joppa, and summon a man named Simon Peter. 6He
is staying with Simon, a tanner who lives near the seashore."
7As soon as the angel was gone, Cornelius called two of his household servants and a
devout soldier, one of his personal attendants. 8He told them what had happened and
sent them off to Joppa.

PETER VISITS CORNELIUS

10:9-32 9The next day as Cornelius's messengers were nearing the town, Peter went up on the flat
//Acts 11:5-14 roof to pray. It was about noon, 10and he was hungry. But while a meal was being prepared,

9:36 The names *Tabitha* in Aramaic and *Dorcas* in Greek both mean "gazelle." 10:1 Greek *a centurion;* similarly in 10:22.

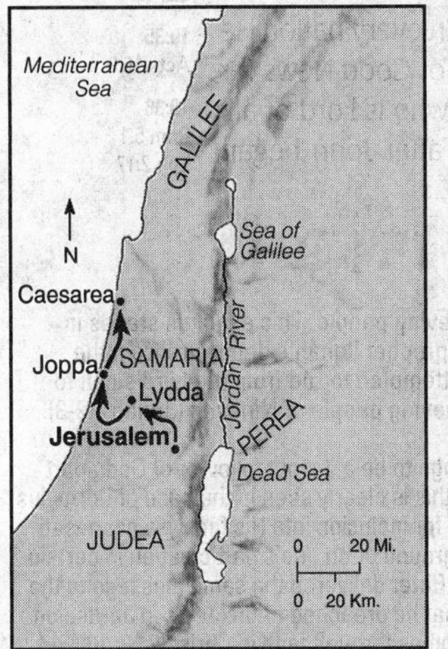

PETER'S MINISTRY
Peter traveled to the ancient crossroads town of Lydda, where he healed crippled Aeneas. The believers in Joppa, an old port city, sent for him after a wonderful woman died. Peter went and brought her back to life. While in Joppa, Peter had a vision that led him to take the gospel to Cornelius, a Gentile, in Caesarea.

10:1-6 Cornelius, a Roman officer of the Italian Regiment, was a devout, caring, and religious man. In the book of Acts, "God-fearing" people represent a special category of individuals who participated in Jewish synagogues but had not been fully converted to the Jewish religion (13:16, 26; 16:14; 17:4, 17; 18:7). God had compassion on Cornelius, and an angel instructed him to send for the apostle Peter in Joppa.

10:9-15 The day after Cornelius's encounter with an angel of God, the Lord appears to Peter with the purpose of removing the racial and spiritual barriers that existed in the apostle's mind. Through a vision of clean and unclean animals, God taught Peter that He did not show favoritism to any one particular nation, but that indeed He was the Lord of the entire world (Leviticus 11; also see notes at Acts 7:49-50 and 9:26-31).

he fell into a trance. 11He saw the sky open, and something like a large sheet was let down
by its four corners. 12In the sheet were all sorts of animals, reptiles, and birds. 13Then a voice
said to him, "Get up, Peter; kill and eat them."
14"No, Lord," Peter declared. "I have never eaten anything that our Jewish laws have de-
clared impure and unclean.*"
15But the voice spoke again: "Do not call something unclean if God has made it clean."
16The same vision was repeated three times. Then the sheet was suddenly pulled up to
heaven.
17Peter was very perplexed. What could the vision mean? Just then the men sent by Cor-
nelius found Simon's house. Standing outside the gate, 18they asked if a man named Si-
mon Peter was staying there.
19Meanwhile, as Peter was puzzling over the vision, the Holy Spirit said to him, "Three
men have come looking for you. 20Get up, go downstairs, and go with them without hesi-
tation. Don't worry, for I have sent them."
21So Peter went down and said, "I'm the man you are looking for. Why have you come?"
22They said, "We were sent by Cornelius, a Roman officer. He is a devout and God-fearing
man, well respected by all the Jews. A holy angel instructed him to summon you to his
house so that he can hear your message." 23So Peter invited the men to stay for the night.
The next day he went with them, accompanied by some of the brothers from Joppa.
24They arrived in Caesarea the following day. Cornelius was waiting for them and had
called together his relatives and close friends. 25As Peter entered his home, Cornelius fell at his
feet and worshiped him. 26But Peter pulled him up and said, "Stand up! I'm a human being
just like you!" 27So they talked together and went inside, where many others were assembled.
28Peter told them, "You know it is against our laws for a Jewish man to enter a Gentile
home like this or to associate with you. But God has shown me that I should no longer
think of anyone as impure or unclean. 29So I came without objection as soon as I was sent
for. Now tell me why you sent for me."
30Cornelius replied, "Four days ago I was praying in my house about this same time,
three o'clock in the afternoon. Suddenly, a man in dazzling clothes was standing in front
of me. 31He told me, 'Cornelius, your prayer has been heard, and your gifts to the poor
have been noticed by God! 32Now send messengers to Joppa, and summon a man named
Simon Peter. He is staying in the home of Simon, a tanner who lives near the seashore.'
33So I sent for you at once, and it was good of you to come. Now we are all here, waiting
before God to hear the message the Lord has given you."

THE GENTILES HEAR THE GOOD NEWS

34Then Peter replied, "I see very clearly that God shows no favoritism. 35In every nation He
accepts those who fear Him and do what is right. 36This is the message of Good News for
the people of Israel—that there is peace with God through Jesus Christ, who is Lord of all.
37You know what happened throughout Judea, beginning in Galilee, after John began

10:11 Ezek 1:1-3; Matt 3:16; Acts 7:56
10:14 Lev 11:1-47; Ezek 4:14
10:15 Matt 15:11; Rom 14:14, 17, 20; 1 Cor 10:25; 1 Tim 4:3-4; Titus 1:15
10:19 Acts 11:12; 13:2
10:20 Acts 15:7-9
10:22 Acts 10:2
10:23 Acts 10:45; 11:12
10:24 Acts 8:40
10:25-26 Acts 14:13-15; Rev 19:10; 22:9
10:28 John 4:9; Acts 11:3; 15:9
10:30-33 Acts 10:1-8
10:34 Deut 10:17; Rom 2:11; Col 3:25
10:35 Acts 15:9
10:36 Rom 5:1; Eph 2:17

10:14 Greek *anything common and unclean.*

10:19 One of the marks of the beginning of the last days (2:17-20) and this special outpouring of grace to the Gentiles was an increase in the gift of prophecy. Not only did Peter experience this, but so did Cornelius, in direct fulfillment of the prophecy in Joel 2:28-32.

10:24 Philip's ministry had led him to the city of Caesarea (8:40), but now Peter's experience with Cornelius in Caesarea would open the floodgates for the proclamation of the gospel to include all Gentile nations beyond the territories of Jerusalem, Judea, and Samaria (Acts 1:8; 9:31; 13:1-3). With the blessing of the Lord, Peter departed from Joppa in order to evangelize an unbelieving people. This example stands in stark contrast to the prophet Jonah's departure from the same city when he attempted to run from the Lord's call to minister to the unbelieving people of Nineveh (Jonah 1:2-3).

10:34-43 It is not enough to be a devout follower of God apart from knowing Christ; this is clearly seen in the case of Cornelius (10:2). God's standard for inclusion into His family is not based on one's ethnic background or on one's participation in certain rituals (10:15). In fact, Peter delivered the same message to the people in Caesarea that he preached to the Jews in Jerusalem: Forgiveness of sins comes through faith in Christ (2:38; 10:43).

10:38 Luke 4:18-19 preaching his message of baptism. [38]And you know that God anointed Jesus of Nazareth
with the Holy Spirit and with power. Then Jesus went around doing good and healing all
who were oppressed by the devil, for God was with Him.

10:39 [39]"And we apostles are witnesses of all He did throughout Judea and in Jerusalem. They
Luke 24:48 put Him to death by hanging Him on a cross,* [40]but God raised Him to life on the third day.
10:40-41 John 21:12-13 Then God allowed Him to appear, [41]not to the general public,* but to us whom God had
chosen in advance to be His witnesses. We were those who ate and drank with Him after
10:42 Matt 28:19 He rose from the dead. [42]And He ordered us to preach everywhere and to testify that Jesus
2 Cor 5:10 is the One appointed by God to be the Judge of all—the living and the dead. [43]He is the
10:43 One all the prophets testified about, saying that everyone who believes in Him will have
Isa 53:11 Jer 31:34 their sins forgiven through His name."

THE GENTILES RECEIVE THE HOLY SPIRIT

10:44 Acts 11:15; 15:8 [44]Even as Peter was saying these things, the Holy Spirit fell upon all who were listening to
10:46 the message. [45]The Jewish believers* who came with Peter were amazed that the gift of
Mark 16:17 the Holy Spirit had been poured out on the Gentiles, too. [46]For they heard them speaking
Acts 2:4; 19:6 in tongues and praising God.

10:47 Then Peter asked, [47]"Can anyone object to their being baptized, now that they have re-
Acts 8:36; 11:17 ceived the Holy Spirit just as we did?" [48]So he gave orders for them to be baptized in the
10:48 Acts 2:38; 19:5 name of Jesus Christ. Afterward Cornelius asked him to stay with them for several days.

PETER EXPLAINS HIS ACTIONS

11 Soon the news reached the apostles and other believers* in Judea that the Gentiles
had received the word of God. [2]But when Peter arrived back in Jerusalem, the Jew-
11:3 ish believers* criticized him. [3]"You entered the home of Gentiles* and even ate with them!"
Acts 10:28 Gal 2:12 they said.

11:5-14 [4]Then Peter told them exactly what had happened. [5]"I was in the town of Joppa," he
//Acts 10:9-32 said, "and while I was praying, I went into a trance and saw a vision. Something like a large
sheet was let down by its four corners from the sky. And it came right down to me. [6]When I
looked inside the sheet, I saw all sorts of small animals, wild animals, reptiles, and birds.
[7]And I heard a voice say, 'Get up, Peter; kill and eat them.'

[8]"'No, Lord,' I replied. 'I have never eaten anything that our Jewish laws have declared
impure or unclean.*'

[9]"But the voice from heaven spoke again: 'Do not call something unclean if God has
made it clean.' [10]This happened three times before the sheet and all it contained was
pulled back up to heaven.

[11]"Just then three men who had been sent from Caesarea arrived at the house where
11:12 Acts 10:23, 45 we were staying. [12]The Holy Spirit told me to go with them and not to worry that they

10:39 Greek *on a tree.* 10:41 Greek *the people.* 10:45 Greek *The faithful ones of the circumcision.* 11:1 Greek *brothers.* 11:2 Greek *those of the circumcision.* 11:3 Greek *of uncircumcised men.* 11:8 Greek *anything common or unclean.*

▶ SALVATION
10:43 An accepting God. You don't need to be smart, beautiful, athletic, or rich to be accepted by God. He welcomes people of any race or culture or background. He offers the one thing you can't give yourself—forgiveness through the sacrifice of Jesus Christ. This forgiveness is complete, lacking nothing. There is no sin so hideous that God won't forgive it. God has never met a sinner so depraved that He can't give him a new birth. Do you need God's forgiveness? Believing in God and repenting of your sins is what God requires. Let everyone know about the forgiveness God offers! (***See Salvation> Receiving> When> Forgiven,*** TopicGuide page A23.)

10:44-48 The experience at Pentecost and Samaria was relived now among the Gentiles gathered in Caesarea (2:2-4; 8:17). God interrupts Peter's sermon by sending down the Holy Spirit among the people. God used the Spirit to welcome these Gentile believers in a unique way as fellow citizens of His Kingdom.

11:1-4 Upon Peter's return to Jerusalem, he was confronted and criticized by the believing Jews who continued to live with a wall of separation between themselves and the Gentile world. Peter's explanation served as a defense for his fellowship with a Gentile and as an instruction to the community in Jerusalem that God's offer of salvation extended to include non-Jewish people.

11:8 Jewish dietary laws were and continue to be an important part of Judaism. Foods in accord with these ancient laws are termed *kosher* meaning they are ritually pure. Peter's remark relates to the dietary laws in Leviticus 11.

were Gentiles. These six brothers here accompanied me, and we soon entered the home of the man who had sent for us. 13He told us how an angel had appeared to him in his home and had told him, 'Send messengers to Joppa, and summon a man named Simon Peter. 14He will tell you how you and everyone in your household can be saved!'

15"As I began to speak," Peter continued, "the Holy Spirit fell on them, just as He fell on us at the beginning. 16Then I thought of the Lord's words when He said, 'John baptized with* water, but you will be baptized with the Holy Spirit.' 17And since God gave these Gentiles the same gift He gave us when we believed in the Lord Jesus Christ, who was I to stand in God's way?"

18When the others heard this, they stopped objecting and began praising God. They said, "We can see that God has also given the Gentiles the privilege of repenting of their sins and receiving eternal life."

THE CHURCH IN ANTIOCH OF SYRIA

19Meanwhile, the believers who had been scattered during the persecution after Stephen's death traveled as far as Phoenicia, Cyprus, and Antioch of Syria. They preached the word of God, but only to Jews. 20However, some of the believers who went to Antioch from Cyprus and Cyrene began preaching to the Gentiles* about the Lord Jesus. 21The power of the Lord was with them, and a large number of these Gentiles believed and turned to the Lord.

22When the church at Jerusalem heard what had happened, they sent Barnabas to Antioch. 23When he arrived and saw this evidence of God's blessing, he was filled with joy, and he encouraged the believers to stay true to the Lord. 24Barnabas was a good man, full of the Holy Spirit and strong in faith. And many people were brought to the Lord.

25Then Barnabas went on to Tarsus to look for Saul. 26When he found him, he brought him back to Antioch. Both of them stayed there with the church for a full year, teaching large crowds of people. (It was at Antioch that the believers* were first called Christians.)

27During this time some prophets traveled from Jerusalem to Antioch. 28One of them named Agabus stood up in one of the meetings and predicted by the Spirit that a great famine was coming upon the entire Roman world. (This was fulfilled during the reign of Claudius.) 29So the believers in Antioch decided to send relief to the brothers and sisters* in Judea, everyone giving as much as they could. 30This they did, entrusting their gifts to Barnabas and Saul to take to the elders of the church in Jerusalem.

11:13 Acts 10:30-32
11:14 Acts 10:22, 44; 16:31
11:15 Acts 2:4
11:16 Acts 1:5
11:17 Acts 10:47
11:18 Acts 13:48
11:19 Acts 8:1-4; 13:1; 14:25-27; 15:3
11:21 Luke 1:66 Acts 2:41
11:22 Acts 4:36
11:23 Acts 13:43; 14:26; 15:40; 20:24
11:24 Acts 2:41
11:25 *Acts 9:30
11:27 Acts 13:1; 15:32
11:28 Acts 21:10
11:29 Rom 15:26
11:30 Acts 12:25 1 Pet 5:1

11:16 Or *in;* also in 11:16b. 11:20 Greek *the Hellenists* (i.e., those who speak Greek); other manuscripts read *the Greeks.* 11:26 Greek *disciples;* also in 11:29. 11:29 Greek *the brothers.*

▸ HOLINESS
11:19 The truth about obedience to God. Perhaps you have heard Christians say that if you obey God, your life will be pleasant and prosperous. But consider the lives of the early Christians—they obeyed God and reaped persecution. God has a purpose for the persecution that He allows His people to experience. Often He uses it to disperse His people into new areas where people need to hear the gospel. If you live a peaceful, serene, trouble-free life, this may not be a sign of God's blessing—it may be a sign of your spiritual laziness! Hardships, persecutions, and trials are a normal part of the Christian life (14:22). Don't be surprised if your obedience to God leads to hardship. Rejoice in doing God's will through your difficult situation. (***See Holiness****> God's Blessing> Obedience leads to hardship and persecution,* TopicGuide page A42.)

11:19-21 God's sovereignty was evident even in the stoning of Stephen. Stephen's murder was instrumental in propelling believers out of Jerusalem and into neighboring cities so that the gospel could spread abroad (8:1). In the power of the Lord, believers in Antioch continued to preach God's message of salvation, and many were converted to Christ.

11:25-26 Here Barnabas encounters Paul for the second time (9:27), and in this occurrence he takes Paul to preach the gospel in Antioch. Previously, believers were referred to as those who belonged to "the Way" (9:2), but this is the first time in Scripture that followers of Christ are called "Christians."

11:27-30 When Agabus prophesied that a severe famine would affect the Roman world, the Christians in Antioch responded by organizing a collection for their fellow believers in Judea. Agabus later prophesied about Paul's capture (21:10-14), and Acts 21:30-33 records the fulfillment of this prophecy.

JAMES IS KILLED AND PETER IS IMPRISONED

12 About that time King Herod Agrippa* began to persecute some believers in the
12:2 Matt 4:21; 20:23 church. 2He had the apostle James (John's brother) killed with a sword. 3When Her-
Mark 10:39 od saw how much this pleased the Jewish people, he also arrested Peter. (This took place
12:3 during the Passover celebration.*) 4Then he imprisoned him, placing him under the guard
Exod 12:15; 23:15 of four squads of four soldiers each. Herod intended to bring Peter out for public trial after
12:4-10 Acts 5:18-25 the Passover. 5But while Peter was in prison, the church prayed very earnestly for him.

PETER'S MIRACULOUS ESCAPE FROM PRISON

12:5 Acts 1:14 Eph 6:18 6The night before Peter was to be placed on trial, he was asleep, fastened with two chains
12:7 between two soldiers. Others stood guard at the prison gate. 7Suddenly, there was a bright
Acts 5:19 light in the cell, and an angel of the Lord stood before Peter. The angel struck him on the
side to awaken him and said, "Quick! Get up!" And the chains fell off his wrists. 8Then the
angel told him, "Get dressed and put on your sandals." And he did. "Now put on your coat
and follow me," the angel ordered.
12:9 Acts 9:10 9So Peter left the cell, following the angel. But all the time he thought it was a vision. He
12:10 didn't realize it was actually happening. 10They passed the first and second guard posts and
Acts 5:19; 16:26 came to the iron gate leading to the city, and this opened for them all by itself. So they
passed through and started walking down the street, and then the angel suddenly left him.
12:11 Ps 34:7 11Peter finally came to his senses. "It's really true!" he said. "The Lord has sent His angel
Dan 3:28; 6:22 and saved me from Herod and from what the Jewish leaders* had planned to do to me!"
2 Pet 2:9 12When he realized this, he went to the home of Mary, the mother of John Mark, where
12:12 many were gathered for prayer. 13He knocked at the door in the gate, and a servant girl
Acts 12:25; 15:37 Col 4:10 named Rhoda came to open it. 14When she recognized Peter's voice, she was so over-
1 Pet 5:13 joyed that, instead of opening the door, she ran back inside and told everyone, "Peter is
12:15 standing at the door!"
Matt 18:10 15"You're out of your mind!" they said. When she insisted, they decided, "It must be his
angel."
16Meanwhile, Peter continued knocking. When they finally opened the door and saw
12:17 him, they were amazed. 17He motioned for them to quiet down and told them how the
Acts 15:13; 21:18 Lord had led him out of prison. "Tell James and the other brothers what happened," he
said. And then he went to another place.
18At dawn there was a great commotion among the soldiers about what had happened

12:1 Greek *Herod the king.* He was the nephew of Herod Antipas and a grandson of Herod the Great. 12:3 Greek *the days of unleavened bread.* 12:11 Or *the Jewish people.*

12:1-3 The church continued to suffer persecution at the hands of unbelieving religious and political leaders (4:1-3, 18; 5:17-40; 7:54–8:1). King Herod executed James, the second martyr in the Jerusalem church (Stephen was the first, see 7:54-59), and then he had Peter arrested. Becoming a Christian demanded a willingness to suffer persecution and a readiness to give up one's life (Luke 14:26-33).

▸ WORSHIP
12:5 The power of God. Once again, we see the first believers joining in prayer. This was their habit during hard times, in church meetings, and in the Temple. The verse makes it clear that the believers prayed "very earnestly," not halfheartedly, for Peter. Later Peter was miraculously released from prison, and the believers' response shows that they couldn't believe that their prayers had an answer so quickly! What responses have you seen in answer to your prayers? Take a few moments to think of some and write them down, and praise God for His amazing power. (***See Worship****> NT> Prayer> Examples> Others> Believers pray for Peter in prison,* TopicGuide page A33.)

12:5 Because the believers in the book of Acts depended upon God for victory, prayer played a dominant role in their lives (1:14; 2:42; 6:4). When Peter was imprisoned, the church responded by doing the only thing they could do at the time—they prayed earnestly.

12:6-10 Herod took every ordinary means to prevent Peter's escape. Luke's description shows that this was the Roman version of the highest security prison possible, with many layers of defenses to keep prisoners in and keep would-be rescuers out.

12:16-17 Although Peter was led out of a maximum-security prison in which iron gates were opened supernaturally (12:10), he was unable to enter his friend's house because a shut door kept him out. With this brief encounter, Luke demonstrates that it was not Peter's human stealth or lock-picking skills that freed him, but the power of God.

to Peter. 19Herod Agrippa ordered a thorough search for him. When he couldn't be found, **12:19**
Herod interrogated the guards and sentenced them to death. Afterward Herod left Judea Acts 8:40; 16:27
to stay in Caesarea for a while.

THE DEATH OF HEROD AGRIPPA

20Now Herod was very angry with the people of Tyre and Sidon. So they sent a delegation
to make peace with him because their cities were dependent upon Herod's country for **12:22** Ezek 28:2
food. The delegates won the support of Blastus, Herod's personal assistant, 21and an ap-
pointment with Herod was granted. When the day arrived, Herod put on his royal robes, **12:23** 1 Sam 25:38
sat on his throne, and made a speech to them. 22The people gave him a great ovation, 2 Sam 24:16-17 2 Kgs 19:35
shouting, "It's the voice of a god, not of a man!" Dan 5:20
23Instantly, an angel of the Lord struck Herod with a sickness, because he accepted the peo-
ple's worship instead of giving the glory to God. So he was consumed with worms and died. **12:24**
24Meanwhile, the word of God continued to spread, and there were many new believers. Acts 6:7; 19:20

12:19-23 At the beginning of this chapter, King Herod appears to control the fate of the Christians. Though there is a tendency to think that strong political figures have strong influence over human affairs, King Herod's control crumbled when one angel delivered Peter from imprisonment and another killed the king. God allowed Herod to persecute the church for a time, but He would not tolerate Herod accepting worship from his subjects.

▸ PURPOSE

12:23 Don't mess with God. Typically it's not very safe to mock or anger powerful people—and that includes God. He may act sooner (as in Herod's case) or later, but no one can mock God and get away with it. Angels protect the godly, but they bring judgment to the wicked (see Matthew 13:39-43). God's divine justice upon Christ at the cross demonstrates that God's judgment has deadly consequences, for Jesus took upon Himself the punishment that our sin deserved. Be very clear with those you talk to that those who do not repent of their sins face certain punishment (Matthew 25:46; Romans 5:10). (***See Purpose***> *God's Deeds> Manifestations> Use of angelic agents*, TopicGuide page A54.)

12:24 Nothing could stop the expansion of the Christian church, not even worldly kings who acted as though they were gods. In the midst of persecution and death, the church of God did not diminish, but rather continued to grow in numbers and prevail against opposition (Matthew 16:18).

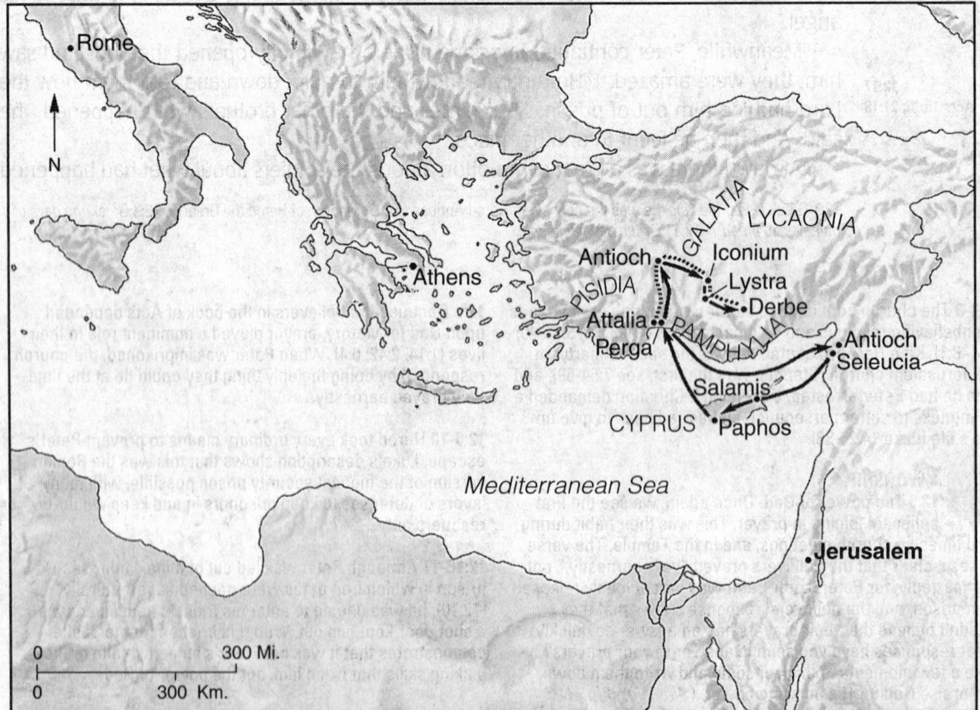

PAUL'S FIRST MISSIONARY JOURNEY (ACTS 13:1–14:28)

12:25 25When Barnabas and Saul had finished their mission to Jerusalem, they returned,* tak-
Acts 11:29-30 ing John Mark with them.

BARNABAS AND SAUL ARE COMMISSIONED

13:1 Acts 11:27 **13** Among the prophets and teachers of the church at Antioch of Syria were Barnabas,
Rom 16:21 Simeon (called "the black man"*), Lucius (from Cyrene), Manaen (the childhood
13:2 companion of King Herod Antipas*), and Saul. 2One day as these men were worshiping the
Acts 9:15 Lord and fasting, the Holy Spirit said, "Dedicate Barnabas and Saul for the special work to
Gal 1:15-16 which I have called them." 3So after more fasting and prayer, the men laid their hands on
13:3 Acts 6:6 them and sent them on their way.

PAUL'S FIRST MISSIONARY JOURNEY

4So Barnabas and Saul were sent out by the Holy Spirit. They went down to the seaport of
13:5 Seleucia and then sailed for the island of Cyprus. 5There, in the town of Salamis, they went
Acts 9:20; 12:12 to the Jewish synagogues and preached the word of God. John Mark went with them as
their assistant.
13:6 6Afterward they traveled from town to town across the entire island until finally they
Matt 7:15 Acts 8:9 reached Paphos, where they met a Jewish sorcerer, a false prophet named Bar-Jesus. 7He
had attached himself to the governor, Sergius Paulus, who was an intelligent man. The
governor invited Barnabas and Saul to visit him, for he wanted to hear the word of God.
13:8 8But Elymas, the sorcerer (as his name means in Greek), interfered and urged the governor
2 Tim 3:8 to pay no attention to what Barnabas and Saul said. He was trying to keep the governor
from believing.
13:9 9Saul, also known as Paul, was filled with the Holy Spirit, and he looked the sorcerer in
Acts 2:4 the eye. 10Then he said, "You son of the devil, full of every sort of deceit and fraud, and en-
13:10 emy of all that is good! Will you never stop perverting the true ways of the Lord? 11Watch
Hos 14:9 Matt 13:38 now, for the Lord has laid His hand of punishment upon you, and you will be struck blind.
John 8:44 You will not see the sunlight for some time." Instantly mist and darkness came over the
13:11 man's eyes, and he began groping around begging for someone to take his hand and
2 Kgs 6:18 Acts 9:8 lead him.
12When the governor saw what had happened, he became a believer, for he was aston-
ished at the teaching about the Lord.

12:25 Or *mission, they returned to Jerusalem.* Other manuscripts read *mission, they returned from Jerusalem;* still others read *mission, they returned from Jerusalem to Antioch.* 13:1a Greek *who was called Niger.* 13:1b Greek *Herod the tetrarch.*

13:1 God gifted His church with a leadership that was spiritually and culturally diverse. Prophets and teachers led the church at Antioch of Syria (1 Corinthians 12:28; Ephesians 4:11). The leaders of this church included men with various skin colors and from different countries and unique social standings.

▸ WORSHIP
13:3 Prayer with fasting. The early church had come a long way. The message of Jesus Christ was spreading widely from Jerusalem outward. Now the church at Antioch was preparing to send a team of missionaries. To prepare Saul and Barnabas for their mission, the believers prayed and fasted. Whenever we begin a new step in our ministry—whether for our church or our personal ministry—we should take time to pray about that first step. Bathing our actions with prayer will help us to see our mission God's way rather than our own way. As you pray, also consider observing a fast to help you focus on God's will for your mission. Fasting is not done to curry favor with God but to help us set our minds and hearts on Him. Use fasting to help you pray over difficult circumstances. (***See Worship****> NT> Prayer> Instructions> Pray with fasting,* TopicGuide page A33.)

13:2-4 God governs the affairs of His church by calling, appointing, and equipping His leaders. In this chapter, the Holy Spirit is credited with appointing Paul and Barnabas to become missionaries, sending them out to the task, and empowering their speech (13:9). Even though it was the leaders of the church in Antioch who prayed, fasted, and laid hands on Paul and Barnabas, the two men's actions were under the full control of the Holy Spirit.

13:6-11 A second encounter with a sorcerer is now described in the book of Acts (see 8:9-25). Bar-Jesus literally means "son of salvation," and Elymas means "the wise one." Bar-Jesus' wicked intent was apparent to Paul, for Paul confronted the man. Before Paul struck him with blindness, the apostle in essence renamed this magician from "son of salvation" to "son of the devil." Elymas claimed to be a wise person, but the Bible identifies him as a false prophet.

PAUL PREACHES IN ANTIOCH OF PISIDIA

[13]Paul and his companions then left Paphos by ship for Pamphylia, landing at the port town of Perga. There John Mark left them and returned to Jerusalem. [14]But Paul and Barnabas traveled inland to Antioch of Pisidia.*

On the Sabbath they went to the synagogue for the services. [15]After the usual readings from the books of Moses* and the prophets, those in charge of the service sent them this message: "Brothers, if you have any word of encouragement for the people, come and give it."

[16]So Paul stood, lifted his hand to quiet them, and started speaking. "Men of Israel," he said, "and you God-fearing Gentiles, listen to me.

[17]"The God of this nation of Israel chose our ancestors and made them multiply and grow strong during their stay in Egypt. Then with a powerful arm He led them out of their slavery. [18]He put up with them* through forty years of wandering in the wilderness. [19]Then He destroyed seven nations in Canaan and gave their land to Israel as an inheritance. [20]All this took about 450 years.

"After that, God gave them judges to rule until the time of Samuel the prophet. [21]Then the people begged for a king, and God gave them Saul son of Kish, a man of the tribe of Benjamin, who reigned for forty years. [22]But God removed Saul and replaced him with David, a man about whom God said, 'I have found David son of Jesse, a man after My own heart. He will do everything I want him to do.'*

[23]"And it is one of King David's descendants, Jesus, who is God's promised Savior of Israel! [24]Before He came, John the Baptist preached that all the people of Israel needed to repent of their sins and turn to God and be baptized. [25]As John was finishing his ministry he asked, 'Do you think I am the Messiah? No, I am not! But He is coming soon—and I'm not even worthy to be His slave and untie the sandals on His feet.'

[26]"Brothers—you sons of Abraham, and also you God-fearing Gentiles—this message of salvation has been sent to us! [27]The people in Jerusalem and their leaders did not recognize Jesus as the One the prophets had spoken about. Instead, they condemned Him, and in doing this they fulfilled the prophets' words that are read every Sabbath. [28]They found no legal reason to execute Him, but they asked Pilate to have Him killed anyway.

[29]"When they had done all that the prophecies said about Him, they took Him down from the cross* and placed Him in a tomb. [30]But God raised Him from the dead! [31]And over a period of many days He appeared to those who had gone with Him from Galilee to Jerusalem. They are now His witnesses to the people of Israel.

[32]"And now we are here to bring you this Good News. The promise was made to our

13:14 Acts 14:19, 21
13:17 Exod 6:6-7; Deut 7:6-8
13:18 Exod 16:35; Num 14:34
13:19 Deut 7:1
13:20 Judg 2:16; 1 Sam 3:20
13:21 1 Sam 8:5; 9:1-2; 10:21-24
13:22 1 Sam 13:14; 1 Sam 16:1, 13
13:23 2 Sam 7:12; Isa 11:1; Luke 2:11
13:24 Mark 1:4-5
13:25 Mark 1:7; John 1:20
13:27 Acts 3:17
13:28 Matt 27:22-23; Acts 3:14
13:29 Matt 27:59-60; Luke 23:52-53
13:30 Matt 28:6; Acts 2:24
13:31 Luke 24:48; Acts 1:11; 1 Cor 15:5
13:32 Rom 1:2-4

13:13-14 *Pamphylia* and *Pisidia* were districts in what is now Turkey. 13:15 Greek *from the law*. 13:18 Some manuscripts read *He cared for them;* compare Deut 1:31. 13:22 1 Sam 13:14. 13:29 Greek *from the tree*.

13:13 The departure of John Mark passes without comment by Luke, but this will later be a source of conflict between Paul and Barnabas (15:36-41).

13:16-42 This was not Paul's first sermon (13:5), but Luke used it as a sample of Paul's preaching to a mixture of Jews and Gentiles on his first missionary journey. Paul begins in the Old Testament, using it to prove that Jesus was the Messiah (13:23), just as was prophesied (13:29). God's resurrection of Jesus proved that He was God the Son (13:30, 33-34) and therefore had the authority to forgive sin (13:38-39).

13:20 Paul calls Samuel a prophet (as does 1 Samuel 3:20), but he also served as a priest (1 Samuel 2:18) and a judge (1 Samuel 7:6, 15). Focusing on Samuel's prophetic role highlights Luke's theme that a rise in prophetic activity signals a time of change in God's Kingdom (2:17-20; 10:19).

▸ CHURCH

13:32 Finding a crowd. Paul has now set out on his first missionary journey, one of several that he will make in his lifetime. In this first trip, he sets a pattern for evangelism that he will use in later trips: When he enters a new town or city, he immediately goes to the synagogue where many people gather and begins preaching the Good News. If Paul had not been so diligent in bringing the Good News of Jesus Christ to so many places, perhaps we would not have the privilege of knowing Jesus today. Where do your friends gather to talk? How can you interact with more people and create more opportunities to build redemptive relationships? Ask God to help you be a faithful witness for Him by creating more opportunities to meet people. (***See Church**> Role> Preach> Topics> Evangelize> Around the world,* TopicGuide page A50.)

13:33 ancestors, [33]and God has now fulfilled it for us, their descendants, by raising Jesus. This is
*Ps 2:7 Heb 1:5; 5:5 what the second psalm says about Jesus:

'You are My Son.
Today I have become Your Father.'*

13:34 *Isa 55:3 [34]For God had promised to raise Him from the dead, not leaving Him to rot in the grave.
He said, 'I will give You the sacred blessings I promised to David.'* [35]Another psalm ex-
13:35 *Ps 16:10 plains it more fully: 'You will not allow Your Holy One to rot in the grave.'* [36]This is not a
reference to David, for after David had done the will of God in his own generation, he died
13:36 1 Kgs 2:10 and was buried with his ancestors, and his body decayed. [37]No, it was a reference to
13:37 someone else—someone whom God raised and whose body did not decay.

Acts 2:24 [38]*"Brothers, listen! We are here to proclaim that through this Man Jesus there is forgive-
13:39 ness for your sins. [39]Everyone who believes in Him is declared right with God—something
Rom 3:28; 10:4 the law of Moses could never do. [40]Be careful! Don't let the prophets' words apply to you.
For they said,

[41] 'Look, you mockers,
13:41 *Hab 1:5 be amazed and die!
For I am doing something in your own day,
something you wouldn't believe
even if someone told you about it.'*"

[42]As Paul and Barnabas left the synagogue that day, the people begged them to speak
about these things again the next week. [43]Many Jews and devout converts to Judaism
followed Paul and Barnabas, and the two men urged them to continue to rely on the grace
of God.

PAUL TURNS TO THE GENTILES

[44]The following week almost the entire city turned out to hear them preach the word of
13:45 the Lord. [45]But when some of the Jews saw the crowds, they were jealous; so they slan-
Acts 8:6 1 Pet 4:4 dered Paul and argued against whatever he said.
Jude 1:10 [46]Then Paul and Barnabas spoke out boldly and declared, "It was necessary that we first
13:46 preach the word of God to you Jews. But since you have rejected it and judged yourselves
Acts 18:6 unworthy of eternal life, we will offer it to the Gentiles. [47]For the Lord gave us this com-
13:47 *Isa 49:6 mand when he said,

Luke 2:32 'I have made You a light to the Gentiles,
to bring salvation to the farthest corners of the earth.'*"

13:48 Rom 8:29-30 [48]When the Gentiles heard this, they were very glad and thanked the Lord for his mes-
Eph 1:4-5, 11 1 Pet 1:2 sage; and all who were chosen for eternal life became believers. [49]So the Lord's message
spread throughout that region.

13:51 Matt 10:14 [50]Then the Jews stirred up the influential religious women and the leaders of the city,
Mark 6:11 and they incited a mob against Paul and Barnabas and ran them out of town. [51]So they
Luke 9:5; 10:11 Acts 18:6 shook the dust from their feet as a sign of rejection and went to the town of Iconium.
13:52 1 Pet 1:8 [52]And the believers* were filled with joy and with the Holy Spirit.

13:33 Or *Today I reveal You as My Son.* Ps 2:7. 13:34 Isa 55:3. 13:35 Ps 16:10. 13:38 English translations divide verses 38 and 39 in various ways. 13:41 Hab 1:5 (Greek version). 13:47 Isa 49:6. 13:52 Greek *the disciples.*

13:42-43 Paul concluded his sermon with a message of danger for all who would ignore the message of forgiveness of sins and righteousness through faith in God's promises in Christ (13:38-42). This threat of judgment did not repel the audience but left many converts wanting to hear more from Paul and Barnabas.

13:48 Paul and Barnabas encountered opposition from a group of Jews who were jealous of how God was at work among the people (13:45; see also 5:17). Despite the Jews' attempt to create a distraction at the synagogue, God powerfully gave Paul the wisdom to regain control of the situation and to lead more people to Christ.

PAUL AND BARNABAS IN ICONIUM

14 The same thing happened in Iconium.* Paul and Barnabas went to the Jewish syn-
agogue and preached with such power that a great number of both Jews and
Greeks became believers. 2 Some of the Jews, however, spurned God's message and poi-
soned the minds of the Gentiles against Paul and Barnabas. 3 But the apostles stayed there
a long time, preaching boldly about the grace of the Lord. And the Lord proved their mes-
sage was true by giving them power to do miraculous signs and wonders. 4 But the people
of the town were divided in their opinion about them. Some sided with the Jews, and
some with the apostles.
5 Then a mob of Gentiles and Jews, along with their leaders, decided to attack and stone
them. 6 When the apostles learned of it, they fled to the region of Lycaonia—to the towns of
Lystra and Derbe and the surrounding area. 7 And there they preached the Good News.

PAUL AND BARNABAS IN LYSTRA AND DERBE

8 While they were at Lystra, Paul and Barnabas came upon a man with crippled feet. He had
been that way from birth, so he had never walked. He was sitting 9 and listening as Paul
preached. Looking straight at him, Paul realized he had faith to be healed. 10 So Paul called
to him in a loud voice, "Stand up!" And the man jumped to his feet and started walking.
11 When the crowd saw what Paul had done, they shouted in their local dialect, "These
men are gods in human form!" 12 They decided that Barnabas was the Greek god Zeus and
that Paul was Hermes, since he was the chief speaker. 13 Now the temple of Zeus was lo-
cated just outside the town. So the priest of the temple and the crowd brought bulls and
wreaths of flowers to the town gates, and they prepared to offer sacrifices to the apostles.
14 But when the apostles Barnabas and Paul heard what was happening, they tore their
clothing in dismay and ran out among the people, shouting, 15 "Friends,* why are you do-
ing this? We are merely human beings—just like you! We have come to bring you the
Good News that you should turn from these worthless things and turn to the living God,
who made heaven and earth, the sea, and everything in them. 16 In the past He permitted
all the nations to go their own ways, 17 but He never left them without evidence of Himself
and His goodness. For instance, He sends you rain and good crops and gives you food and
joyful hearts." 18 But even with these words, Paul and Barnabas could scarcely restrain the
people from sacrificing to them.
19 Then some Jews arrived from Antioch and Iconium and won the crowds to their side.
They stoned Paul and dragged him out of town, thinking he was dead. 20 But as the believ-
ers* gathered around him, he got up and went back into the town. The next day he left
with Barnabas for Derbe.

14:1 Acts 13:45
14:2 2 Tim 3:11
14:3 Heb 2:4
14:4 Acts 28:24
14:5 Acts 14:19; 20:3; 2 Tim 3:11
14:6 Matt 10:23
14:8 Acts 3:2
14:10 Acts 3:8
14:11 Acts 28:6
14:15 Exod 20:11; Ps 146:6; Matt 16:16; Acts 10:26; 1 Thes 1:9; Rev 14:7
14:16 Ps 81:12
14:17 Ps 147:8; Rom 1:20
14:19 Acts 13:45; 2 Cor 11:25; 2 Tim 3:11

14:1 *Iconium,* as well as *Lystra* and *Derbe* (14:6), were towns in what is now Turkey. 14:15 Greek *Men.* 14:20 Greek *disciples;* also in 14:22, 28.

14:4-5 God's message of salvation demands a response of repentance and faith (2:38; 3:19; 8:22; 17:30; 26:20). The counterresponse of unbelief may be obvious (14:5) or surprising (14:11-18).

14:11-13 Many in Lystra believed that Barnabas and Paul were the Greek gods Zeus and Hermes. In ancient Lystra, there was a legend concerning a visit that Zeus and Hermes once paid to the Phrygian hill country. These two gods came dressed as humans in search of hospitality, but only one elderly couple in the entire city welcomed them into their home. Zeus and Hermes blessed the couple by transforming their home into a temple and cursed the rest of the city by burning down all the surrounding homes.

14:14-17 In Lystra, Paul and Barnabas experienced their first encounter with a group outside of a synagogue setting (13:14; 14:1). Paul's approach with the people of Lystra was different from his approach with his other audiences, for they were ignorant concerning the true God of the Bible (compare 13:16). In this instance, Paul started with the story of Creation and taught that God, as their Creator, required repentance and faith.

▶ PURPOSE

14:14-18 Worshiping ministers. God has given His church remarkably gifted people, and we often make these people our leaders and give them the respect they deserve (1 Timothy 5:17-18). But some Christians place their leaders up too high, giving them more honor and glory than they deserve (1 Corinthians 1:11-13). If you allow your leaders to live in ways that do not honor God, then you are saying they are above God and His Word. Lovingly hold your leaders accountable to God's Word (1 Timothy 3:1-13), and do not give them the kind of adulation that is reserved for God alone. (***See Purpose***> *God's Deeds> Common Grace> On individuals,* TopicGuide page A54.)

PAUL AND BARNABAS RETURN TO ANTIOCH OF SYRIA

21 After preaching the Good News in Derbe and making many disciples, Paul and Barnabas
14:22 returned to Lystra, Iconium, and Antioch of Pisidia, 22 where they strengthened the believ-
2 Tim 3:12 ers. They encouraged them to continue in the faith, reminding them that we must suffer
many hardships to enter the Kingdom of God. 23 Paul and Barnabas also appointed elders
in every church. With prayer and fasting, they turned the elders over to the care of the
Lord, in whom they had put their trust. 24 Then they traveled back through Pisidia to Pam-
phylia. 25 They preached the word in Perga, then went down to Attalia.
14:26 26 Finally, they returned by ship to Antioch of Syria, where their journey had begun. The
Acts 13:1-3 believers there had entrusted them to the grace of God to do the work they had now com-
14:27 pleted. 27 Upon arriving in Antioch, they called the church together and reported every-
1 Cor 16:9 Col 4:3 thing God had done through them and how He had opened the door of faith to the
Rev 3:8 Gentiles, too. 28 And they stayed there with the believers for a long time.

THE COUNCIL AT JERUSALEM

15:1 Lev 12:3 Gal 5:2
15 While Paul and Barnabas were at Antioch of Syria, some men from Judea arrived
and began to teach the believers*: "Unless you are circumcised as required by the
15:2 law of Moses, you cannot be saved." 2 Paul and Barnabas disagreed with them, arguing ve-
Acts 11:30 Gal 2:1-10 hemently. Finally, the church decided to send Paul and Barnabas to Jerusalem, accompa-
15:3 nied by some local believers, to talk to the apostles and elders about this question. 3 The
Acts 11:19; 14:27 church sent the delegates to Jerusalem, and they stopped along the way in Phoenicia and
Samaria to visit the believers. They told them—much to everyone's joy—that the Gentiles,
too, were being converted.
4 When they arrived in Jerusalem, Barnabas and Paul were welcomed by the whole
church, including the apostles and elders. They reported everything God had done
15:5 through them. 5 But then some of the believers who belonged to the sect of the Pharisees
Acts 15:11 stood up and insisted, "The Gentile converts must be circumcised and required to follow
the law of Moses."
15:7-8 6 So the apostles and elders met together to resolve this issue. 7 At the meeting, after a
Acts 2:4; 10:44; 11:15 long discussion, Peter stood and addressed them as follows: "Brothers, you all know that
15:9 God chose me from among you some time ago to preach to the Gentiles so that they
Acts 10:43 could hear the Good News and believe. 8 God knows people's hearts, and He confirmed
Rom 10:12 that He accepts Gentiles by giving them the Holy Spirit, just as He did to us. 9 He made no

15:1 Greek *brothers;* also in 15:3, 23, 32, 33, 36, 40.

14:21-24 After having traveled as far as Derbe, Paul and Barnabas retraced their steps. Surprisingly, they returned to three towns that had previously persecuted them (13:50; 14:1-2, 19). They returned in order to strengthen the believers, encourage them to remain faithful, and to warn them of the suffering they would soon endure. Paul and Barnabas appointed elders to oversee the affairs of the church in their absence (1 Timothy 5:17-19; Titus 1:5; James 5:14).

▸ ADOPTION
14:22 The difficulties of Christianity. Paul and Barnabas traveled around Asia Minor, visiting newly formed churches and starting new ones. Knowing these little churches were small and weak, they sought to strengthen them. One of the encouragements they gave them was that to live faithfully in God's Kingdom means enduring great trouble. Later Paul would tell Timothy, "Everyone who wants to live a godly life in Christ Jesus will suffer persecution" (2 Timothy 3:12). Many Christians have a difficult time understanding and accepting the truth that persecution is a part of a faithful Christian life. They opt instead to see Christianity primarily as living morally and praying to God. Meditate on these passages and ask God to strengthen you to be ready to receive whatever trouble the gospel brings your way. (*See Adoption> With Christ> Children of God> Children share suffering and glory,* TopicGuide page A36.)

14:26-28 The Bible describes Paul and Barnabas as having been entrusted to the "grace of God." On this missionary journey they had been instruments used by God to lead unbelievers to Christ and to nurture Christians in their faith. Paul and Barnabas provided a glowing report to the leaders who had sent them off on their first missionary journey (13:1-3).

15:1 This group of adherents to the Mosaic law did not properly understand God's grace in salvation, nor did they have a proper understanding of the rite of circumcision in the Old Testament. God never intended for His people to obtain salvation through their own works. God granted forgiveness of sins through faith and repentance (Isaiah 30:15; Ephesians 2:8-9). God ultimately required that His people be spiritually circumcised, and physical circumcision under the Old Covenant served only as a sign of true faith (Deuteronomy 10:16; 30:6; Jeremiah 4:4; Ezekiel 18:31; Romans 2:28-29).

distinction between us and them, for He cleansed their hearts through faith. 10So why are
you now challenging God by burdening the Gentile believers* with a yoke that neither we
nor our ancestors were able to bear? 11We believe that we are all saved the same way, by
the undeserved grace of the Lord Jesus."

12Everyone listened quietly as Barnabas and Paul told about the miraculous signs and
wonders God had done through them among the Gentiles.

13When they had finished, James stood and said, "Brothers, listen to me. 14Peter* has told
you about the time God first visited the Gentiles to take from them a people for Himself.
15And this conversion of Gentiles is exactly what the prophets predicted. As it is written:

16 'Afterward I will return
and restore the fallen house* of David.
I will rebuild its ruins
and restore it,
17 so that the rest of humanity might seek the LORD,
including the Gentiles—
all those I have called to be Mine.
The LORD has spoken—
18 He who made these things known so long ago.'*

19"And so my judgment is that we should not make it difficult for the Gentiles who are
turning to God. 20Instead, we should write and tell them to abstain from eating food of-
fered to idols, from sexual immorality, from eating the meat of strangled animals, and
from consuming blood. 21For these laws of Moses have been preached in Jewish syna-
gogues in every city on every Sabbath for many generations."

THE LETTER FOR GENTILE BELIEVERS

22Then the apostles and elders together with the whole church in Jerusalem chose dele-
gates, and they sent them to Antioch of Syria with Paul and Barnabas to report on this de-
cision. The men chosen were two of the church leaders*—Judas (also called Barsabbas)
and Silas. 23This is the letter they took with them:

"This letter is from the apostles and elders, your brothers in Jerusalem. It is written to the Gentile believers in Antioch, Syria, and Cilicia. Greetings!

24"We understand that some men from here have troubled you and upset you with

15:10 Matt 23:4; Gal 5:1
15:11 Rom 3:24; Eph 2:5-8
15:12 Acts 14:27; 15:4
15:13 Acts 12:17
15:14 Acts 15:7-9
15:16-17 *Amos 9:11-12
15:18 Isa 45:21
15:20 Gen 9:4; Exod 20:3-4; Lev 3:17; Deut 12:16; 1 Cor 8:7; 10:7
15:21 Acts 13:15
15:22 Acts 15:27; 16:19; 1 Pet 5:12
15:24 Gal 1:7; 5:10

15:10 Greek *disciples.* 15:14 Greek *Symeon.* 15:16 Or *kingdom;* Greek reads *tent.* 15:16-18 Amos 9:11-12 (Greek version); Isa 45:21. 15:22 Greek *were leaders among the brothers.*

15:9 God determined that His family would be made up of believers who were of Jewish and non-Jewish descent (Galatians 3:28). These Jews failed to understand that the blood shed by Jesus Christ on the cross was sufficient for the forgiveness of all sins (Hebrews 9:11-28). Instead, false teachers thought that through the shedding of their own blood in the ceremony of circumcision they could obtain salvation.

▶ SPIRITUAL WARFARE
15:10 Checklist Christianity. What is the burden that Paul mentions here? It is the yoke of legalism—the temptation to load ourselves up with *dos* and *don'ts* that make rule keeping, not love for Christ, central for salvation and continued favor with God. It's not that God doesn't want us to obey His rules—quite the opposite is true (Colossians 2:6; 1 Thessalonians 4:8). Love for Christ, manifested in a life of repentance and belief, marks us most clearly as Christians. And as that love grows, we will want to satisfy God's wishes, even when they conflict with the demands of those around us. Examine your heart to determine your attitude toward God's rules—is love your motivation for obedience, or is your Christian obedience an attempt to earn His love? (***See Spiritual Warfare****> Resisting Sin and Evil> Putting On and Off> Taking Off> The yoke of legalism,* TopicGuide page A46.)

15:19-21 James the brother of Jesus (Matthew 13:55) recommended to the group that only certain prohibitions from the law of Moses continue to be required of the Gentile believers. It appears that many of these regulations were only temporary and served as a happy medium for the relationship between Jews and Gentiles. With the exception of abstaining from sexual immorality (1 Thessalonians 4:3), the Bible does not require the other practices in the later books of the Bible (Romans 14).

15:22-35 After the critical ruling by the Jerusalem Council, a binding letter was sent to the entire region (15:23). The letter carried the same authority as the leadership in Jerusalem, with its authenticity confirmed by Judas and Silas (15:40). Because of its importance, Luke includes this letter in its entirety.

their teaching, but we did not send them! 25 So we decided, having come to complete
agreement, to send you official representatives, along with our beloved Barnabas and
15:26 Paul, 26 who have risked their lives for the name of our Lord Jesus Christ. 27 We are
Acts 14:19 sending Judas and Silas to confirm what we have decided concerning your question.
1 Cor 15:30 28 "For it seemed good to the Holy Spirit and to us to lay no greater burden on you
than these few requirements: 29 You must abstain from eating food offered to idols,
15:29 from consuming blood or the meat of strangled animals, and from sexual immorality.
Gen 9:4
Lev 17:10-14 If you do this, you will do well. Farewell."

30 The messengers went at once to Antioch, where they called a general meeting of the
believers and delivered the letter. 31 And there was great joy throughout the church that
day as they read this encouraging message.
15:32 32 Then Judas and Silas, both being prophets, spoke at length to the believers, encourag-
Acts 11:27; 13:1 ing and strengthening their faith. 33 They stayed for a while, and then the believers sent
them back to the church in Jerusalem with a blessing of peace.* 35 Paul and Barnabas
stayed in Antioch. They and many others taught and preached the word of the Lord there.

PAUL AND BARNABAS SEPARATE

15:36
Acts 13:4, 13-14, 51; 36 After some time Paul said to Barnabas, "Let's go back and visit each city where we previ-
14:1, 6, 24-25 ously preached the word of the Lord, to see how the new believers are doing." 37 Barnabas
15:37 agreed and wanted to take along John Mark. 38 But Paul disagreed strongly, since John
Acts 12:12, 25 Mark had deserted them in Pamphylia and had not continued with them in their work.
15:38
Acts 13:13 15:33 Some manuscripts add verse 34, *But Silas decided to stay there.*

15:36-38 For their second missionary journey, Barnabas recommended that his cousin John Mark come along with him and Paul. Paul refused because John Mark had defected from the traveling group on their first journey (13:5, 13).

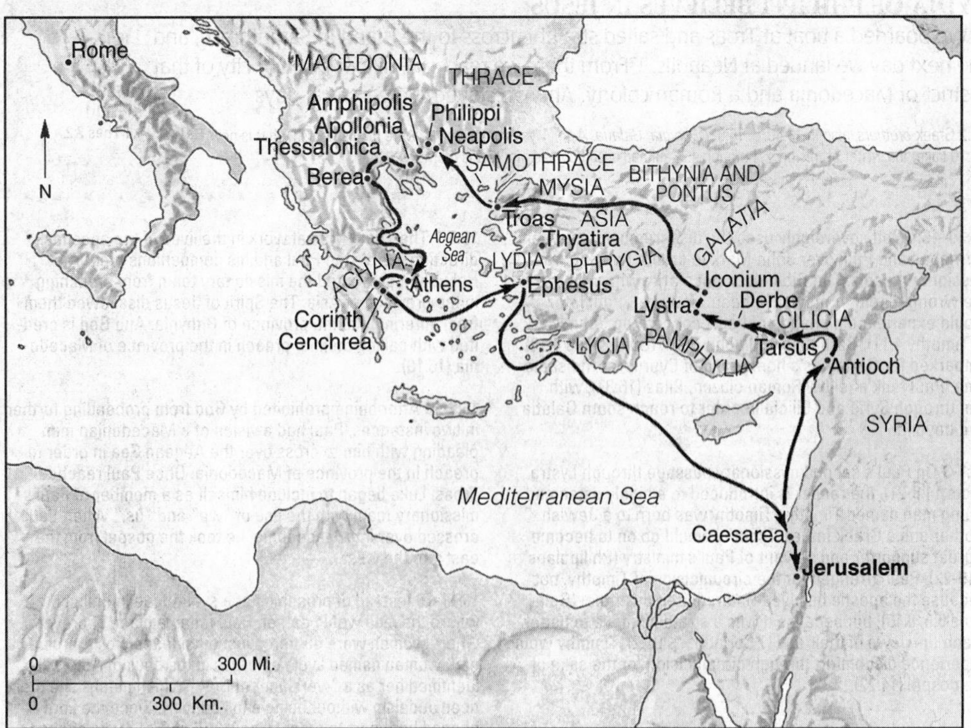

PAUL'S SECOND MISSIONARY JOURNEY (ACTS 15:36–18:22)

39Their disagreement was so sharp that they separated. Barnabas took John Mark with
him and sailed for Cyprus. 40Paul chose Silas, and as he left, the believers entrusted him to
the Lord's gracious care. 41Then he traveled throughout Syria and Cilicia, strengthening
the churches there.

PAUL'S SECOND MISSIONARY JOURNEY

16 Paul went first to Derbe and then to Lystra, where there was a young disci-
ple named Timothy. His mother was a Jewish believer, but his father was a
Greek. 2Timothy was well thought of by the believers* in Lystra and Iconium, 3so Paul
wanted him to join them on their journey. In deference to the Jews of the area, he ar-
ranged for Timothy to be circumcised before they left, for everyone knew that his father
was a Greek. 4Then they went from town to town, instructing the believers to follow the
decisions made by the apostles and elders in Jerusalem. 5So the churches were strength-
ened in their faith and grew larger every day.

16:1 Acts 14:6; Phil 2:19-22; 2 Tim 1:2, 5-6; 3:15
16:3 Gal 2:3-5
16:5 Acts 9:31

A CALL FROM MACEDONIA

6Next Paul and Silas traveled through the area of Phrygia and Galatia, because the Holy
Spirit had prevented them from preaching the word in the province of Asia at that time.
7Then coming to the borders of Mysia, they headed north for the province of Bithynia,* but
again the Spirit of Jesus did not allow them to go there. 8So instead, they went on through
Mysia to the seaport of Troas.

9That night Paul had a vision: A man from Macedonia in northern Greece was standing
there, pleading with him, "Come over to Macedonia and help us!" 10So we* decided to
leave for Macedonia at once, having concluded that God was calling us to preach the
Good News there.

16:7 Rom 8:9; Phil 1:19
16:8 2 Cor 2:12; 2 Tim 4:13
16:9 Rom 15:26

LYDIA OF PHILIPPI BELIEVES IN JESUS

11We boarded a boat at Troas and sailed straight across to the island of Samothrace, and
the next day we landed at Neapolis. 12From there we reached Philippi, a major city of that
district of Macedonia and a Roman colony. And we stayed there several days.

16:11 2 Cor 2:12
16:12 Phil 1:1; 1 Thes 2:2

16:2 Greek *brothers;* also in 16:40. 16:6-7 *Phrygia, Galatia, Asia, Mysia,* and *Bithynia* were all districts in what is now Turkey.
16:10 Luke, the writer of this book, here joined Paul and accompanied him on his journey.

15:39–16:1 God sovereignly used the disagreement between Barnabas and Paul over John Mark to create two separate missionary teams. The Bible does not clarify who was in the wrong—neither may have been. However, Paul later would experience a change of heart concerning John Mark (2 Timothy 4:11). Barnabas and John Mark (Colossians 4:10) embarked for Barnabas's home area of Cyprus; at the same time, Paul took a fellow Roman citizen, Silas (16:37), with him through Syria and Cilicia in order to reach south Galatia and beyond.

16:1-3 On Paul's second missionary passage through Lystra (Acts 14:8-21), the reader is introduced to a highly esteemed young man named Timothy. Timothy was born to a Jewish mother and a Greek father. Timothy would go on to become a great supporter and servant of Paul's ministry (Philippians 2:19-22). Paul arranged for the circumcision of Timothy, not because the apostle believed God required this ritual (Galatians 5:6; 6:15), but because it was a strategic move to better reach the Jews of their day (1 Corinthians 9:22). Timothy would experience discomfort through circumcision for the sake of the gospel (14:22).

16:6-7 The Trinity was at work in the lives of the apostles, directing every step Paul and his companions took. The Holy Spirit prevented the missionary team from preaching in the province of Asia. The Spirit of Jesus disallowed them from entering into the province of Bithynia. And God is credited with calling them to preach in the province of Macedonia (16:10).

16:8-10 After being prohibited by God from proceeding further in two instances, Paul had a vision of a Macedonian man pleading with him to cross over the Aegean Sea in order to preach in the province of Macedonia. Once Paul reached Troas, Luke began to include himself as a member of Paul's missionary team with the use of "we" and "us." When Paul crossed over into Macedonia, he took the gospel from the east into the west.

16:11-15 Instead of preaching at a synagogue in Philippi, where the men would gather, Paul found a place of prayer where women were gathered just outside the city. A prominent woman named Lydia emerges in the book of Acts. Luke identified her as a "worshiper of God," which means she practiced Judaism without being a full convert. Since the Lord opened her heart to receive the Word of God, Lydia opened her house to fellowship with Paul and his companions.

13On the Sabbath we went a little way outside the city to a riverbank, where we thought
people would be meeting for prayer, and we sat down to speak with some women who
16:14 had gathered there. 14One of them was Lydia from Thyatira, a merchant of expensive pur-
Rev 1:11; 2:18, 24 ple cloth, who worshiped God. As she listened to us, the Lord opened her heart, and she
accepted what Paul was saying. 15She was baptized along with other members of her
household, and she asked us to be her guests. "If you agree that I am a true believer in the
Lord," she said, "come and stay at my home." And she urged us until we agreed.

PAUL AND SILAS IN PRISON

16:16 16One day as we were going down to the place of prayer, we met a demon-possessed
Deut 18:10-11 1 Sam 28:3, 7 slave girl. She was a fortune-teller who earned a lot of money for her masters. 17She fol-
lowed Paul and the rest of us, shouting, "These men are servants of the Most High God,
and they have come to tell you how to be saved."
16:18 18This went on day after day until Paul got so exasperated that he turned and said to the
Mark 16:17 demon within her, "I command you in the name of Jesus Christ to come out of her." And
Acts 19:13 instantly it left her.
19Her masters' hopes of wealth were now shattered, so they grabbed Paul and Silas and
16:20 dragged them before the authorities at the marketplace. 20"The whole city is in an uproar
Acts 17:6 because of these Jews!" they shouted to the city officials. 21"They are teaching customs
16:21 Esth 3:8 that are illegal for us Romans to practice."
16:22 22A mob quickly formed against Paul and Silas, and the city officials ordered them
2 Cor 11:25 stripped and beaten with wooden rods. 23They were severely beaten, and then they were
1 Thes 2:2 thrown into prison. The jailer was ordered to make sure they didn't escape. 24So the jailer
put them into the inner dungeon and clamped their feet in the stocks.
16:25 25Around midnight Paul and Silas were praying and singing hymns to God, and the
Eph 5:19 other prisoners were listening. 26Suddenly, there was a massive earthquake, and the
16:26 prison was shaken to its foundations. All the doors immediately flew open, and the chains
Acts 5:19; 12:10 of every prisoner fell off! 27The jailer woke up to see the prison doors wide open. He as-
16:27 Acts 12:18-19 sumed the prisoners had escaped, so he drew his sword to kill himself. 28But Paul shouted
to him, "Stop! Don't kill yourself! We are all here!"
29The jailer called for lights and ran to the dungeon and fell down trembling before Paul
16:30 Acts 2:37 and Silas. 30Then he brought them out and asked, "Sirs, what must I do to be saved?"
16:31 31They replied, "Believe in the Lord Jesus and you will be saved, along with everyone in
John 3:15 your household." 32And they shared the word of the Lord with him and with all who lived
Acts 11:14 in his household. 33Even at that hour of the night, the jailer cared for them and washed
their wounds. Then he and everyone in his household were immediately baptized. 34He
brought them into his house and set a meal before them, and he and his entire household
rejoiced because they all believed in God.
35The next morning the city officials sent the police to tell the jailer, "Let those men go!"
36So the jailer told Paul, "The city officials have said you and Silas are free to leave. Go
in peace."

16:16-34 A demon possessed slave girl testified that Paul and Silas were servants of God. Paul sensed that this was not the kind of notoriety he wanted (Mark 1:34) and silenced her, but not before the demon was able to interrupt Paul's ministry (16:19). However, God turned this into an opportunity to spread the gospel (16:25-34).

▸ WORSHIP

16:25 The puzzle of prayer and praise. Christians act strangely sometimes. It's not natural to sing and pray after you've been severely beaten and unjustly thrown into prison. When every bone and muscle in your body aches, when you've just faced a crowd that wanted you dead, most people would expect you to cry and be depressed. But prayer and praise demonstrated that the Holy Spirit was working in Paul and Silas. With prayer and praise, God's Spirit revealed His grace and glory through them. The tragic circumstances were the dark background that highlighted their radiant witness for Christ. As trials begin to threaten your comfort or well-being, turn to prayer and praise to demonstrate and articulate your trust in God. (***See Worship***> *NT> Prayer> Examples> Others> Paul and Silas pray in prison,* TopicGuide page A33.)

37 But Paul replied, “They have publicly beaten us without a trial and put us in prison— 16:37
and we are Roman citizens. So now they want us to leave secretly? Certainly not! Let them Acts 22:25
come themselves to release us!”
38 When the police reported this, the city officials were alarmed to learn that Paul and Si- 16:38
las were Roman citizens. 39 So they came to the jail and apologized to them. Then they Acts 22:29
brought them out and begged them to leave the city. 40 When Paul and Silas left the prison, 16:39 Matt 8:34
they returned to the home of Lydia. There they met with the believers and encouraged
them once more. Then they left town. 16:40 Acts 16:14

PAUL PREACHES IN THESSALONICA

17 Paul and Silas then traveled through the towns of Amphipolis and Apollonia and 17:1-9
came to Thessalonica, where there was a Jewish synagogue. 2 As was Paul’s cus- 1 Thes 1:1; 2:1-2
tom, he went to the synagogue service, and for three Sabbaths in a row he used the Scrip- 2 Thes 1:1
tures to reason with the people. 3 He explained the prophecies and proved that the 17:2 Acts 9:20; 13:14;
Messiah must suffer and rise from the dead. He said, “This Jesus I’m telling you about is 17:10, 17
the Messiah.” 4 Some of the Jews who listened were persuaded and joined Paul and Silas, 17:3
along with many God-fearing Greek men and quite a few prominent women.* Luke 24:26 Acts 3:18; 9:22; 18:5
5 But some of the Jews were jealous, so they gathered some troublemakers from the 17:5
marketplace to form a mob and start a riot. They attacked the home of Jason, searching for Rom 16:21
Paul and Silas so they could drag them out to the crowd.* 6 Not finding them there, they 1 Thes 2:14
dragged out Jason and some of the other believers* instead and took them before the city 17:6
council. “Paul and Silas have caused trouble all over the world,” they shouted, “and now they Acts 16:20, 21
are here disturbing our city, too. 7 And Jason has welcomed them into his home. They are all 17:7
guilty of treason against Caesar, for they profess allegiance to another king, named Jesus.” Luke 23:2 John 19:12
8 The people of the city, as well as the city council, were thrown into turmoil by these
reports. 9 So the officials forced Jason and the other believers to post bond, and then they
released them.

PAUL AND SILAS IN BEREA

10 That very night the believers sent Paul and Silas to Berea. When they arrived there, they

17:4 Some manuscripts read *quite a few of the wives of the leading men.* 17:5 Or *the city council.* 17:6 Greek *brothers;* also in 17:10, 14.

▶ HOLINESS

16:34 A family affair. This verse shows us how important the family is to the spreading of the gospel. The family is the most effective place in which to train growing children in godly character. When parents love and serve God, they influence the entire household. The jailer changed the eternal destiny of his entire family by bringing Paul and Silas into his home. He spread his joy of discovering God to his family. You, too, can make your home the primary training ground for your children. Participate in a ministry as a family—whether going to serve at a homeless shelter, praying for your neighbors, or bringing meals to a sick friend. Read the Bible together and worship as a family unit. Study the Bible, talk about your sin and God’s grace, and discover God together. (***See Holiness***> *Submission*> *Learning God’s Word*> *Teaching your children,* TopicGuide page A40.)

17:1-2 Paul’s second stop in Macedonia, following his visit to Philippi, was the city of Thessalonica. As capital city of the province of Macedonia, Thessalonica was the largest and most flourishing city in the region. Although we read that Paul reasoned with the people for three consecutive Sabbaths in the synagogue, his ministry was not limited to three weeks. During his time in Thessalonica, Paul worked to raise support (1 Thessalonians 2:9) and received multiple gifts from the believers in Philippi (Philippians 4:16), implying that he spent a period of time in Thessalonica.

▶ WORSHIP

17:2 Worship regularly. How often do you go to church? It can be tempting to sleep in on Sundays, so Hebrews 10:25 says, “Let us not neglect our meeting together, as some people do, but encourage one another, especially now that the day of His return is drawing near.” Paul followed this principle by regularly going to the synagogue, where he studied the Scriptures with others. He also met with the believers for worship. We can always find fault with a church or find errors in the content of a sermon, but God doesn’t say to attend a perfect church—just to go to church. Find encouragement and accountability through regular attendance of your local church’s worship services. (***See Worship***> *NT*> *Our Role*> *Obedience*> *Called to keep a Sabbath,* TopicGuide page A32.)

17:4-9 In contrast to some of the Jews who came to faith in Christ, many other Jews grew jealous of what Paul and his companions were accomplishing for the cause of Christ (see also 5:17; 13:45). These jealous Jews rounded up a group of shady characters in order to accuse the missionary team of proclaiming that Jesus was a rival king to the emperor of Rome. The proclamation of the gospel of Christ in Thessalonica caused turmoil among the unbelieving people and city officials, for their unbelief blinded their ability to rightly judge the evidences presented to them.

17:11 went to the Jewish synagogue. [11]And the people of Berea were more open-minded than
John 5:39 those in Thessalonica, and they listened eagerly to Paul's message. They searched the
Scriptures day after day to see if Paul and Silas were teaching the truth. [12]As a result, many
Jews believed, as did many of the prominent Greek women and men.
17:13 [13]But when some Jews in Thessalonica learned that Paul was preaching the word of God
Acts 14:19 in Berea, they went there and stirred up trouble. [14]The believers acted at once, sending
17:14 Matt 10:23 Paul on to the coast, while Silas and Timothy remained behind. [15]Those escorting Paul
17:15 went with him all the way to Athens; then they returned to Berea with instructions for Silas
Acts 18:5 1 Thes 3:1 and Timothy to hurry and join him.

PAUL PREACHES IN ATHENS

[16]While Paul was waiting for them in Athens, he was deeply troubled by all the idols he saw
17:17 everywhere in the city. [17]He went to the synagogue to reason with the Jews and the God-
Acts 18:19 fearing Gentiles, and he spoke daily in the public square to all who happened to be there.
17:18 [18]He also had a debate with some of the Epicurean and Stoic philosophers. When he
1 Cor 1:22 told them about Jesus and His resurrection, they said, "What's this babbler trying to say
with these strange ideas he's picked up?" Others said, "He seems to be preaching about
some foreign gods."
[19]Then they took him to the high council of the city.* "Come and tell us about this new
teaching," they said. [20]"You are saying some rather strange things, and we want to know
what it's all about." [21](It should be explained that all the Athenians as well as the foreign-
ers in Athens seemed to spend all their time discussing the latest ideas.)
[22]So Paul, standing before the council,* addressed them as follows: "Men of Athens, I
17:23 notice that you are very religious in every way, [23]for as I was walking along I saw your
John 4:22 many shrines. And one of your altars had this inscription on it: 'To an Unknown God.' This
17:24 1 Kgs 8:27 God, whom you worship without knowing, is the One I'm telling you about.
Isa 42:5 [24]"He is the God who made the world and everything in it. Since He is Lord of heaven
Acts 7:48 and earth, He doesn't live in man-made temples, [25]and human hands can't serve His
17:25 needs—for He has no needs. He Himself gives life and breath to everything, and He satisfies
Ps 50:12 Isa 42:5 every need. [26]From one man* He created all the nations throughout the whole earth. He
decided beforehand when they should rise and fall, and He determined their boundaries.
17:26 Deut 32:8 [27]"His purpose was for the nations to seek after God and perhaps feel their way toward
17:27 Him and find Him—though He is not far from any one of us. [28]For in Him we live and move
Isa 55:6 and exist. As some of your* own poets have said, 'We are His offspring.' [29]And since this is
Jer 23:23-24 true, we shouldn't think of God as an idol designed by craftsmen from gold or silver or stone.
17:29 Isa 40:18-25 [30]"God overlooked people's ignorance about these things in earlier times, but now He

Rom 1:23 17:19 Or *the most learned society of philosophers in the city.* Greek reads *the Areopagus.* 17:22 Traditionally rendered
17:30 *standing in the middle of Mars Hill;* Greek reads *standing in the middle of the Areopagus.* 17:26 Greek *From one;* other
Acts 14:16 manuscripts read *From one blood.* 17:28 Some manuscripts read *our.*

17:10-15 During the night, the believers sent Paul and Silas about 40 miles west of Thessalonica to the city of Berea. Berea was not as prominent as the other major cities in the province of Macedonia, but these missionaries were surprised to discover that the Bereans were more open-minded than the residents of Thessalonica. The Bereans thoroughly examined the Scriptures to verify all that the apostles spoke.

17:18 Though the days of Socrates, Plato, and Aristotle were long gone, Athens remained a center for great philosophers in the days of Paul's ministry. Paul encountered the Epicureans and the Stoics during his visit there. The Epicureans were followers of the teachings of Epicurus (342–270 BC), who believed that maximizing pleasure was the most meaningful goal of life. They also thought that the Greek gods had reached such a high level of existence that they no longer cared for the concerns of men. The Stoics, whose founder was Zeno of Cyprus (334–262 BC), believed in a fatalistic world ruled by the impersonal force of natural law. Both of these groups lacked the proper knowledge of a loving God who is concerned with human affairs.

17:22-28 Paul was greatly disturbed with the idolatry that was widespread throughout the city of Athens (17:16). His response provides an excellent example of evangelism that is perceptive to the needs and culture of his audience yet straightforward in confronting people with the truth of the gospel. Ingeniously, Paul used their altar dedicated to an "Unknown God" in order to teach them about the true God. As he had done with the people of Lystra, Paul taught these pagans about God as Creator before teaching them about Jesus as Savior (14:15).

commands everyone everywhere to repent of their sins and turn to Him. 31 For He has set
a day for judging the world with justice by the Man He has appointed, and He proved to
everyone who this is by raising Him from the dead."

32 When they heard Paul speak about the resurrection of the dead, some laughed in
contempt, but others said, "We want to hear more about this later." 33 That ended Paul's
discussion with them, 34 but some joined him and became believers. Among them were
Dionysius, a member of the council,* a woman named Damaris, and others with them.

17:31 Ps 96:13; Acts 10:42

PAUL MEETS PRISCILLA AND AQUILA IN CORINTH

18 Then Paul left Athens and went to Corinth.* 2 There he became acquainted with a
Jew named Aquila, born in Pontus, who had recently arrived from Italy with his
wife, Priscilla. They had left Italy when Claudius Caesar deported all Jews from Rome.
3 Paul lived and worked with them, for they were tentmakers* just as he was.

18:2 Rom 16:3; 1 Cor 16:19
18:3 Acts 20:34; 1 Cor 4:12; 9:15

17:34 Greek *an Areopagite.* 18:1 *Athens* and *Corinth* were major cities in Achaia, the region in the southern portion of the Greek peninsula. 18:3 Or *leatherworkers.*

GOD

17:31 A day is coming. The day has been set. It is inevitable. No one will escape. That day is the one in which every person who has ever lived will face God's judgment. Then we will see for ourselves a demonstration of the purity of God's righteousness and the perfection of His justice. God's justice will be so perfect that no one will be able to answer back. But one man will have an answer—Jesus Christ will speak up for those who have trusted in His perfect sacrifice on that day. God proved this by raising Jesus from the dead, showing that everything He had said was true. This includes His promise to judge all humanity (John 9:39; Acts 10:42; Romans 2:16). Prepare yourself and those under your care for that day. (***See God****> God's Attributes> Just> A day is fixed for His righteous judgment of the world,* TopicGuide page A17.)

18:1-2 Paul left the intellectual city of Athens for the commercial city of Corinth. As the capital of the province of Achaia, Corinth was among the largest cities in the Roman Empire during the first century. Though Paul left Silas and Timothy in the region of Macedonia (17:14), the Lord blessed the apostle with the company of Aquila and Priscilla, fellow tentmakers or bivocational ministers in Corinth.

MY RESPONSE TO GOD

The Source of Our Significance

ACTS 17:27

If a child asked you, "Why did God make me?" what would you say? Did God make us because He was lonely and needed friends? Was it because He was bored? Or did He need us to do something that He could not do for himself?

If your God is the God of the Bible, then the answer is no to all three. The God revealed in Scripture is completely independent and self-sufficient (Isaiah 40:12-31). No one created God, but God created everything (Genesis 1). He doesn't need anything, but everything else needs Him (Psalm 50:12). We are dependent upon God for all our needs, but He doesn't depend on us–not for money, friendship, worship, or even our work for His kingdom (Psalm 50:9-12).

So how can we be significant to God if He is completely self-sufficient? God has chosen to lavish His love on all humanity, and particularly to His people (Psalm 37:28). God creating and treasuring the whole world (John 3:16), particularly His church (Ephesians 5:25), adds more value to our lives that we can ever add by our own achievement.

The value we have will never change because God's loving character will never change (Psalm 102:25-27; Hebrews 1:10-12). The apostle John made it clear when he said, "See how very much our Father loves us, for He calls us His children, and that is what we are!" (1 John 3:1)

4Each Sabbath found Paul at the synagogue, trying to convince the Jews and Greeks
18:5 Acts 17:3; 18:28 alike. 5And after Silas and Timothy came down from Macedonia, Paul spent all his time
18:6 preaching the word. He testified to the Jews that Jesus was the Messiah. 6But when they
Matt 10:14 opposed and insulted him, Paul shook the dust from his clothes and said, "Your blood is
Acts 13:45-46; 20:26 upon your own heads—I am innocent. From now on I will go preach to the Gentiles."
7Then he left and went to the home of Titius Justus, a Gentile who worshiped God and
18:8 lived next door to the synagogue. 8Crispus, the leader of the synagogue, and everyone in
1 Cor 1:14 his household believed in the Lord. Many others in Corinth also heard Paul, became believers, and were baptized.
18:9-10 Isa 41:10 9One night the Lord spoke to Paul in a vision and told him, "Don't be afraid! Speak out!
Jer 1:18 Don't be silent! 10For I am with you, and no one will attack and harm you, for many people
in this city belong to Me." 11So Paul stayed there for the next year and a half, teaching the
word of God.
12But when Gallio became governor of Achaia, some Jews rose up together against Paul
and brought him before the governor for judgment. 13They accused Paul of "persuading
people to worship God in ways that are contrary to our law."
14But just as Paul started to make his defense, Gallio turned to Paul's accusers and said,
"Listen, you Jews, if this were a case involving some wrongdoing or a serious crime, I
18:15 would have a reason to accept your case. 15But since it is merely a question of words and
John 18:31 names and your Jewish law, take care of it yourselves. I refuse to judge such matters."
16And he threw them out of the courtroom.
18:17 Acts 18:8 17The crowd* then grabbed Sosthenes, the leader of the synagogue, and beat him right
1 Cor 1:1 there in the courtroom. But Gallio paid no attention.

PAUL RETURNS TO ANTIOCH OF SYRIA

18:18 Num 6:18 18Paul stayed in Corinth for some time after that, then said good-bye to the brothers and sis-
Acts 21:24 ters* and went to nearby Cenchrea. There he shaved his head according to Jewish custom,
Rom 16:1 marking the end of a vow. Then he set sail for Syria, taking Priscilla and Aquila with him.
18:19 Eph 1:1 19They stopped first at the port of Ephesus, where Paul left the others behind. While he
Rev 1:11; 2:1

18:17 Greek *Everyone;* other manuscripts read *All the Greeks.* 18:18 Greek *brothers;* also in 18:27.

18:5-6 Silas and Timothy arrived with positive news about the faithful believers who were enduring persecution in Thessalonica (1 Thessalonians 3:6-10). But in Corinth, Paul shook the dust off his clothes, which symbolically expressed his release from any guilt before God concerning the unrepentant Jews there.

▸MINISTRY
18:8 Love Him or hate Him. Whenever Paul came to a new city, he typically went to the synagogue and preached about Jesus. His preaching resulted in two different reactions. The religious leaders either opposed him or they believed in Jesus. In Corinth, the leader of the synagogue believed in Jesus, along with his family and many other people of that city. When you witness for Jesus, don't be surprised when you experience very different reactions. Some people will reject your message, and perhaps even reject you! But it's not important what people think of you—it's important what people think of God. Are you afraid to share your faith in Christ because you are afraid what people may think of you? Set aside your pride and set Jesus before those God places in your path. (***See Ministry***> *Great Commission> Witness> Having a bold witness,* TopicGuide page A56.)

18:9-11 In the vision of the man of Macedonia, God directed Paul to leave Troas and to pursue new ministry opportunities in the province of Macedonia (16:8-10). Now, in this second vision, God instructed Paul to stay in Corinth, for God would protect him from harm and convert more souls through his ministry there.

18:12-16 Since Gallio ruled that Christians were a sect within the Jewish religion, the apostles were not to be held in contempt of Roman law. Roman law prohibited the practice of any religion not legally sanctioned by the Roman Empire, and Judaism was sanctioned at that time. The case brought before Gallio was extremely important to the survival of Christianity in the Roman world, for if he had ruled in favor of the Jewish protesters it may have spelled the end to the public proclamation of the gospel. Thankfully, God was in control of the entire hearing and ensured the survival of Christianity (Psalms 37:28; 97:10; 145:20).

18:18-23 Paul appears to have been participating in a Nazirite vow, by which a man made a promise to God to abstain from all intoxicating drinks, to let his hair grow, to abstain from entering any house polluted by having a dead body in it, or to attend any funeral (Numbers 6:1-21). This type of vow lasted various periods of time, including a lifetime (see Judges 13). Paul signaled the end of his vow by cutting his hair at Cenchrea (Acts 18:18), though he delayed some portion of the proper ceremonies until he reached Jerusalem (Acts 21:23-24). By keeping this vow, we see that while Paul viewed the law as fulfilled in Christ (Romans 10:4), this did not mean that it was unprofitable or forbidden to heed the instructions of the law in some cases.

was there, he went to the synagogue to reason with the Jews. [20]They asked him to stay
longer, but he declined. [21]As he left, however, he said, "I will come back later,* God will- **18:21** Jas 4:15
ing." Then he set sail from Ephesus. [22]The next stop was at the port of Caesarea. From **18:22** Acts 8:40; 11:19
there he went up and visited the church at Jerusalem* and then went back to Antioch.
[23]After spending some time in Antioch, Paul went back through Galatia and Phrygia, vis- **18:23** Acts 16:6
iting and strengthening all the believers.*

APOLLOS INSTRUCTED AT EPHESUS

[24]Meanwhile, a Jew named Apollos, an eloquent speaker who knew the Scriptures well, had **18:24** Acts 19:1; 1 Cor 1:12; 4:6; 16:12; Titus 3:13
arrived in Ephesus from Alexandria in Egypt. [25]He had been taught the way of the Lord, and
he taught others about Jesus with an enthusiastic spirit* and with accuracy. However, he
knew only about John's baptism. [26]When Priscilla and Aquila heard him preaching boldly in
the synagogue, they took him aside and explained the way of God even more accurately. **18:25** Acts 19:3
[27]Apollos had been thinking about going to Achaia, and the brothers and sisters in Eph- **18:27** 2 Cor 3:1
esus encouraged him to go. They wrote to the believers in Achaia, asking them to wel-
come him. When he arrived there, he proved to be of great benefit to those who, by God's
grace, had believed. [28]He refuted the Jews with powerful arguments in public debate. **18:28** Acts 9:22
Using the Scriptures, he explained to them that Jesus was the Messiah.

18:21 Some manuscripts read *"I must by all means be at Jerusalem for the upcoming festival, but I will come back later."* **18:22** Greek *the church.* **18:23** Greek *disciples;* also in 18:27. **18:25** Or *with enthusiasm in the Spirit.*

18:25-28 Momentarily, the writer of Acts diverts the reader's attention away from describing Paul's third missionary journey in order to focus on Apollos and his need for a fuller understanding of the Christian life. Apollos is a well-instructed man and aware of the ministry of Jesus Christ, but he lacked information concerning the pouring out of the Holy Spirit at Pentecost and in Samaria and Caesarea (2:1-4; 8:14-17; 10:44-46; 19:1-7).

PAUL'S THIRD MISSIONARY JOURNEY (ACTS 18:23–21:16)

PAUL'S THIRD MISSIONARY JOURNEY

19:1 Acts 18:24 **19** While Apollos was in Corinth, Paul traveled through the interior regions until he
19:2 reached Ephesus, on the coast, where he found several believers.* 2"Did you re-
John 7:39; 20:22 Acts 8:16 ceive the Holy Spirit when you believed?" he asked them.
"No," they replied, "we haven't even heard that there is a Holy Spirit."
19:3 Acts 18:25 3"Then what baptism did you experience?" he asked.
And they replied, "The baptism of John."
19:4 Mark 1:4 4Paul said, "John's baptism called for repentance from sin. But John himself told the peo-
19:5 ple to believe in the One who would come later, meaning Jesus."
Acts 8:12, 16; 10:48 5As soon as they heard this, they were baptized in the name of the Lord Jesus. 6Then
Gal 3:27 when Paul laid his hands on them, the Holy Spirit came on them, and they spoke in other
19:6 Acts 2:4; 10:44, 46 tongues and prophesied. 7There were about twelve men in all.

PAUL MINISTERS IN EPHESUS

19:8 Acts 28:23 8Then Paul went to the synagogue and preached boldly for the next three months, argu-
ing persuasively about the Kingdom of God. 9But some became stubborn, rejecting his
message and publicly speaking against the Way. So Paul left the synagogue and took the
19:10 Acts 20:31 believers with him. Then he held daily discussions at the lecture hall of Tyrannus. 10This
went on for the next two years, so that people throughout the province of Asia—both Jews
and Greeks—heard the word of the Lord.
19:11 Mark 16:20 11God gave Paul the power to perform unusual miracles. 12When handkerchiefs or
aprons that had merely touched his skin were placed on sick people, they were healed of
19:12 Acts 5:15-16 their diseases, and evil spirits were expelled.
19:13 Matt 12:27 13A group of Jews was traveling from town to town casting out evil spirits. They tried to
Mark 9:38 use the name of the Lord Jesus in their incantation, saying, "I command you in the name
Luke 9:49 of Jesus, whom Paul preaches, to come out!" 14Seven sons of Sceva, a leading priest, were
19:15 doing this. 15But one time when they tried it, the evil spirit replied, "I know Jesus, and I
Mark 1:24, 34 know Paul, but who are you?" 16Then the man with the evil spirit leaped on them, over-
Luke 4:34, 41 powered them, and attacked them with such violence that they fled from the house, na-
ked and battered.
19:17 Acts 5:5, 11 17The story of what happened spread quickly all through Ephesus, to Jews and Greeks
alike. A solemn fear descended on the city, and the name of the Lord Jesus was greatly
19:19 Deut 18:10-14 honored. 18Many who became believers confessed their sinful practices. 19A number of

19:1 Greek *disciples;* also in 19:9, 30.

19:1-7 When Paul arrived in Ephesus, he encountered some remaining disciples of John the Baptist who were likely Jewish. Like Apollos (18:25), these men were ignorant of the outpouring of the Spirit at Pentecost. John the Baptist's ministry was a baptism of repentance (Mark 1:4; Luke 3:3). Paul redirected their attention from these basic teachings to the teachings of Jesus Christ (19:4). After this, Pentecost was relived at Ephesus as the Holy Spirit descended upon the believers there, just as He had done previously (see 1:5; 10:44-48). This outpouring of the Spirit continued to confirm that the promises of God apply to people of all kinds throughout the whole world (1:8).

19:8-10 The book of Acts is concerned with communicating that the preaching of the gospel represents the Kingdom of God at work in the world (1:3; 8:12; 14:22; 20:25; 28:23, 31). When the people in the synagogue refused to listen to Paul's teachings concerning the Kingdom of God, the apostle moved on to the lecture hall of Tyrannus for two years. God used these two years at the hall to help propel the gospel throughout all of Asia, for many people came to hear Paul and returned to their hometowns with the message of salvation.

▸ BIBLE

19:13-20 Watch for imposters. Many claim to be God's representatives as they perform apparently pious deeds (Matthew 25:31-46). On the surface, the sons of Sceva seemed like Paul—they also cast out demons (16:18). But they were imposters. We have such people around us today. They are working outside the authority and power of God. Yet they can appear religious. John instructs us, "Dear friends, do not believe everyone who claims to speak by the Spirit. You must test them to see if the spirit they have comes from God" (1 John 4:1). And what is that test? John says that the false teachers could be tested by finding out what they believed about Jesus (1 John 4:2-3). If you have concerns about a certain teacher, find out specifically what they believe about Christ—and compare that to Scripture. That will go a long way toward eliminating any confusion about false ministers. (***See Bible****> Uniqueness> Authoritative> Demands exclusive allegiance,* TopicGuide page A10.)

19:13-20 The Jewish priest Sceva and his seven sons had a family business that included exorcism. They attempted to invoke the names of Paul and Jesus in their incantations, but an evil spirit exposed their falsehoods and assaulted them. The response was a humble fear and respect for the name of Jesus (19:17).

them who had been practicing sorcery brought their incantation books and burned them
at a public bonfire. The value of the books was several million dollars.* [20]So the message
about the Lord spread widely and had a powerful effect.
[21]Afterward Paul felt compelled by the Spirit* to go over to Macedonia and Achaia be-
fore going to Jerusalem. "And after that," he said, "I must go on to Rome!" [22]He sent his two
assistants, Timothy and Erastus, ahead to Macedonia while he stayed awhile longer in the
province of Asia.

THE RIOT IN EPHESUS

[23]About that time, serious trouble developed in Ephesus concerning the Way. [24]It began
with Demetrius, a silversmith who had a large business manufacturing silver shrines of the
Greek goddess Artemis.* He kept many craftsmen busy. [25]He called them together, along
with others employed in similar trades, and addressed them as follows:
"Gentlemen, you know that our wealth comes from this business. [26]But as you have
seen and heard, this man Paul has persuaded many people that handmade gods aren't
really gods at all. And he's done this not only here in Ephesus but throughout the entire
province! [27]Of course, I'm not just talking about the loss of public respect for our business.
I'm also concerned that the temple of the great goddess Artemis will lose its influence and
that Artemis—this magnificent goddess worshiped throughout the province of Asia and all
around the world—will be robbed of her great prestige!"
[28]At this their anger boiled, and they began shouting, "Great is Artemis of the Ephesi-
ans!" [29]Soon the whole city was filled with confusion. Everyone rushed to the amphithe-
ater, dragging along Gaius and Aristarchus, who were Paul's traveling companions from
Macedonia. [30]Paul wanted to go in, too, but the believers wouldn't let him. [31]Some of the
officials of the province, friends of Paul, also sent a message to him, begging him not to
risk his life by entering the amphitheater.
[32]Inside, the people were all shouting, some one thing and some another. Everything
was in confusion. In fact, most of them didn't even know why they were there. [33]The Jews
in the crowd pushed Alexander forward and told him to explain the situation. He mo-
tioned for silence and tried to speak. [34]But when the crowd realized he was a Jew, they
started shouting again and kept it up for two hours: "Great is Artemis of the Ephesians!
Great is Artemis of the Ephesians!"
[35]At last the mayor was able to quiet them down enough to speak. "Citizens of Ephesus,"
he said. "Everyone knows that Ephesus is the official guardian of the temple of the great
Artemis, whose image fell down to us from heaven. [36]Since this is an undeniable fact, you
should stay calm and not do anything rash. [37]You have brought these men here, but they
have stolen nothing from the temple and have not spoken against our goddess.

19:20 Acts 6:7; 12:24
19:21 Acts 23:11; Rom 15:25; 1 Cor 16:5
19:22 Rom 16:23; 2 Tim 4:20
19:23 2 Cor 1:8
19:24 Acts 16:16
19:26 Ps 115:4; Isa 44:10-20; Jer 10:3-5; Acts 17:29; 1 Cor 8:4
19:28 Acts 18:19
19:29 Acts 20:4; Rom 16:23; 1 Cor 1:14; Col 4:10; Phlm 1:24
19:32 Acts 21:34
19:33 1 Tim 1:20
19:37 Rom 2:22

19:19 Greek *50,000 pieces of silver,* each of which was the equivalent of a day's wage. 19:21 Or *decided in his spirit.*
19:24 *Artemis* is otherwise known as Diana.

▸ SALVATION

19:17-20 The gospel produces results. Upon conversion some people change like night and day—one moment they are filled with hate, the next they are filled with love. Others change more gradually. Still others have religious experiences but do not change at all. The new believers in Ephesus were like the former—they immediately rid themselves of the horrid, demonic books that had immersed them in the world of the occult. Sometimes even mature Christians need cleansing in their lives—stripping away possessions, ideas, or practices that have led them away from God. The work of the Holy Spirit will produce tangible, purifying results in your life. Do not struggle against His holy labors in your life (Ephesians 4:30). (***See Salvation****> Receiving> Results> New life,* TopicGuide page A23.)

19:23-27 The temple of Artemis in Ephesus was recognized as one of the Seven Wonders of the World. Since many worshipers came from all over the world to give offerings at the temple, it provided an abundant source of wealth for the city. Demetrius may have been the president of a silversmith guild in Ephesus. He managed to gain the support of the entire city of Ephesus for his cause by convincing fellow silversmiths of the danger Paul posed to their industry and to the honor of the goddess of the temple.

19:35-41 Previously, Gallio, the governor of Achaia, had provided protection for the Christians under Roman law (18:12-17), and now the mayor of Ephesus did the same. When the situation appeared to be getting out of control for those gathered in the theater, the mayor brought to the people's attention the proper legal procedures for handling these disputes. This action by the mayor diffused the tension that had been building for over two hours, and the assembled mob disbanded.

38"If Demetrius and the craftsmen have a case against them, the courts are in session
and the officials can hear the case at once. Let them make formal charges. 39And if there
are complaints about other matters, they can be settled in a legal assembly. 40I am afraid
we are in danger of being charged with rioting by the Roman government, since there is
no cause for all this commotion. And if Rome demands an explanation, we won't know
what to say." 41*Then he dismissed them, and they dispersed.

PAUL GOES TO MACEDONIA AND GREECE

20:1 Acts 16:9-10
20:3 Acts 9:23-24; 23:12; 2 Cor 11:26
20:4 Acts 16:1; 19:29; 21:29; Eph 6:21; 2 Tim 4:20; Titus 3:12
20:6 Acts 16:8, 10

20 When the uproar was over, Paul sent for the believers* and encouraged them.
Then he said good-bye and left for Macedonia. 2While there, he encouraged the
believers in all the towns he passed through. Then he traveled down to Greece, 3where he
stayed for three months. He was preparing to sail back to Syria when he discovered a plot
by some Jews against his life, so he decided to return through Macedonia.
4Several men were traveling with him. They were Sopater son of Pyrrhus from Berea;
Aristarchus and Secundus from Thessalonica; Gaius from Derbe; Timothy; and Tychicus
and Trophimus from the province of Asia. 5They went on ahead and waited for us at Tro-
as. 6After the Passover* ended, we boarded a ship at Philippi in Macedonia and five days
later joined them in Troas, where we stayed a week.

PAUL'S FINAL VISIT TO TROAS

20:7 Acts 2:42, 46; 1 Cor 16:2; Rev 1:10
20:10 1 Kgs 17:21; 2 Kgs 4:34; Matt 9:23-24

7On the first day of the week, we gathered with the local believers to share in the Lord's
Supper.* Paul was preaching to them, and since he was leaving the next day, he kept talk-
ing until midnight. 8The upstairs room where we met was lighted with many flickering
lamps. 9As Paul spoke on and on, a young man named Eutychus, sitting on the windowsill,
became very drowsy. Finally, he fell sound asleep and dropped three stories to his death
below. 10Paul went down, bent over him, and took him into his arms. "Don't worry," he
said, "he's alive!" 11Then they all went back upstairs, shared in the Lord's Supper,* and ate
together. Paul continued talking to them until dawn, and then he left. 12Meanwhile, the
young man was taken home unhurt, and everyone was greatly relieved.

PAUL MEETS THE EPHESIAN ELDERS

20:15 2 Tim 4:20

13Paul went by land to Assos, where he had arranged for us to join him, while we traveled
by ship. 14He joined us there, and we sailed together to Mitylene. 15The next day we
sailed past the island of Kios. The following day we crossed to the island of Samos, and* a
day later we arrived at Miletus.
16Paul had decided to sail on past Ephesus, for he didn't want to spend any more time in
the province of Asia. He was hurrying to get to Jerusalem, if possible, in time for the Festi-
val of Pentecost. 17But when we landed at Miletus, he sent a message to the elders of the
church at Ephesus, asking them to come and meet him.

19:41 Some translations include verse 41 as part of verse 40. 20:1 Greek *disciples.* 20:6 Greek *the days of unleavened bread.* 20:7 Greek *to break bread.* 20:11 Greek *broke the bread.* 20:15 Some manuscripts read *and having stayed at Trogyllium.*

20:7 The church in the city of Troas gathered for worship on the first day of the week in order to observe the Lord's Supper as commanded by Christ (Luke 22:14-20; 1 Corinthians 11:23-26). This passage marks the first explicit statement in Scripture that believers gathered to worship on the first day of the week (Revelation 1:10).

20:9-12 Paul's act of raising Eutychus from the dead is the final recorded resurrection in Scripture. This miracle bears much similarity to the resurrections performed by Elijah and Elisha (1 Kings 17:17-24; 2 Kings 4:32-37). Believers still await the final resurrection of the body in the second coming of Christ (1 Thessalonians 4:16).

20:16 At this point, Paul chose not to return to Ephesus in order to arrive at Jerusalem by Pentecost (19:21) and deliver the collection for the poor raised by the believers abroad (Romans 15:25-32; 1 Corinthians 16:1-4; 2 Corinthians 8–9).

20:17-35 Paul describes his behavior as a model of godly leadership for the elders (20:18-27, 33-35). He warns them to keep watch over themselves and their flock, for hypocrites and false teachers would infiltrate the Christian community from the outside and the inside (20:28-30). Finally, Paul entrusts the elders to the care and oversight of God and His Word (18:32), for these alone could bring to pass all that Paul asked of the elders.

18When they arrived he declared, "You know that from the day I set foot in the province
of Asia until now 19I have done the Lord's work humbly and with many tears. I have en-
dured the trials that came to me from the plots of the Jews. 20I never shrank back from tell-
ing you what you needed to hear, either publicly or in your homes. 21I have had one
message for Jews and Greeks alike—the necessity of repenting from sin and turning to
God, and of having faith in our Lord Jesus.

22"And now I am bound by the Spirit* to go to Jerusalem. I don't know what awaits me,
23except that the Holy Spirit tells me in city after city that jail and suffering lie ahead. 24But
my life is worth nothing to me unless I use it for finishing the work assigned me by the
Lord Jesus—the work of telling others the Good News about the wonderful grace of God.

25"And now I know that none of you to whom I have preached the Kingdom will ever
see me again. 26I declare today that I have been faithful. If anyone suffers eternal death,
it's not my fault,* 27for I didn't shrink from declaring all that God wants you to know.

28"So guard yourselves and God's people. Feed and shepherd God's flock—His church,
purchased with His own blood*—over which the Holy Spirit has appointed you as elders.*
29I know that false teachers, like vicious wolves, will come in among you after I leave, not
sparing the flock. 30Even some men from your own group will rise up and distort the truth
in order to draw a following. 31Watch out! Remember the three years I was with you—my
constant watch and care over you night and day, and my many tears for you.

32"And now I entrust you to God and the message of His grace that is able to build you
up and give you an inheritance with all those He has set apart for Himself.

33"I have never coveted anyone's silver or gold or fine clothes. 34You know that these
hands of mine have worked to supply my own needs and even the needs of those who
were with me. 35And I have been a constant example of how you can help those in need
by working hard. You should remember the words of the Lord Jesus: 'It is more blessed to
give than to receive.'"

36When he had finished speaking, he knelt and prayed with them. 37They all cried as
they embraced and kissed him good-bye. 38They were sad most of all because he had said
that they would never see him again. Then they escorted him down to the ship.

PAUL'S JOURNEY TO JERUSALEM

21 After saying farewell to the Ephesian elders, we sailed straight to the island of
Cos. The next day we reached Rhodes and then went to Patara. 2There we
boarded a ship sailing for Phoenicia. 3We sighted the island of Cyprus, passed it on
our left, and landed at the harbor of Tyre, in Syria, where the ship was to unload its cargo.

20:21 Acts 2:38; 26:18
20:24 Acts 21:13; 2 Tim 4:7
20:26 Acts 18:6
20:28 Ps 74:2; John 21:15-17; 1 Pet 5:2
20:29 Matt 7:15; John 10:12
20:30 1 Jn 2:19
20:31 Acts 19:10
20:32 Deut 33:3-4; Acts 26:18; Eph 1:18; Col 1:12; 3:24; 1 Pet 1:4
20:33 1 Sam 12:3; 1 Cor 9:11; 2 Cor 7:2; 11:9; 12:14-17
20:34 Acts 18:3; 1 Cor 4:12; 1 Thes 2:9
20:35 1 Thes 4:11
20:37 Rom 16:16
21:1 Acts 16:10

20:22 Or *by my spirit*, or *by an inner compulsion;* Greek reads *by the spirit.* 20:26 Greek *I am innocent of the blood of all.*
20:28a Or *with the blood of His own [Son].* 20:28b Greek *overseers.*

▸ MINISTRY

20:23 How can we measure up? As we compare our experiences to those of God's people in the Bible, we may often feel as though we are not measuring up. Does being holy mean we should get regular messages from God? Or having the spiritual adventures we see Paul and his friends experiencing in the book of Acts? In Galatians 5:25 Paul writes, "Since we are living by the Spirit, let us follow the Spirit's leading in every part of our lives." God may not tell you to do the exact same things as Paul did—He may not "tell" you anything—but that's not your concern. Follow God's Word and follow the guidance of the Holy Spirit—however it manifests itself—as He leads you into truth and obedience (John 14:17). (***See Ministry***> *Great Commission> Witness> Witness in the power of the Holy Spirit,* TopicGuide page A56.)

▸ WORSHIP

20:35 Truly giving. You're probably very familiar with Jesus' saying, "It is more blessed to give than to receive." Do you believe this? You can tell if you truly believe it by examining your giving practices. If someone flipped through your checkbook, would they notice patterns of giving? If someone followed you around for a few days, would they notice your generosity? Sometimes we give lip service to biblical principles, but we don't act on them. This is hypocrisy—nothing more, nothing less. Repent and you'll find great joy in sharing with others the blessings God has given you. (***See Worship***> *NT> Sacrificial Living> More blessed to give than to receive,* TopicGuide page A34.)

20:36-38 The elders of Ephesus no doubt understood that Paul himself had lived up to all that he had requested of them as leaders. In their final farewell, their deep love for the apostle is evident in the many tears they shed realizing that this would be their final encounter. The apostle Paul had given three years of his life in order to teach, shepherd, and protect the believers in the city of Ephesus. God had used Paul as an instrument for transforming the lives and practices of the people there.

21:4 4We went ashore, found the local believers,* and stayed with them a week. These be-
Acts 20:23; 21:11 lievers prophesied through the Holy Spirit that Paul should not go on to Jerusalem. 5When
21:5 we returned to the ship at the end of the week, the entire congregation, including women*
Acts 20:36 and children, left the city and came down to the shore with us. There we knelt, prayed,
6and said our farewells. Then we went aboard, and they returned home.

7The next stop after leaving Tyre was Ptolemais, where we greeted the brothers and sis-
21:8 Acts 6:5; 8:26, 40 ters* and stayed for one day. 8The next day we went on to Caesarea and stayed at the
Eph 4:11 home of Philip the Evangelist, one of the seven men who had been chosen to distribute
2 Tim 4:5 food. 9He had four unmarried daughters who had the gift of prophecy.

21:9 Joel 2:28 10Several days later a man named Agabus, who also had the gift of prophecy, arrived
Acts 2:17 from Judea. 11He came over, took Paul's belt, and bound his own feet and hands with it.
21:10 Then he said, "The Holy Spirit declares, 'So shall the owner of this belt be bound by the
Acts 11:28 Jewish leaders in Jerusalem and turned over to the Gentiles.'" 12When we heard this, we
21:11 and the local believers all begged Paul not to go on to Jerusalem.

Acts 20:23; 21:33 13But he said, "Why all this weeping? You are breaking my heart! I am ready not only to
21:13 be jailed at Jerusalem but even to die for the sake of the Lord Jesus." 14When it was clear
Acts 20:24 that we couldn't persuade him, we gave up and said, "The Lord's will be done."

21:14 Matt 26:39

PAUL ARRIVES AT JERUSALEM

15After this we packed our things and left for Jerusalem. 16Some believers from Caesarea
accompanied us, and they took us to the home of Mnason, a man originally from Cyprus
and one of the early believers. 17When we arrived, the brothers and sisters in Jerusalem
welcomed us warmly.

18The next day Paul went with us to meet with James, and all the elders of the Jerusalem
21:19 church were present. 19After greeting them, Paul gave a detailed account of the things God
Acts 15:12 had accomplished among the Gentiles through his ministry.

21:4 Greek *disciples;* also in 21:16. 21:5 Or *wives.* 21:7 Greek *brothers;* also in 21:17.

21:4 Luke frequently mentions that Paul and his friends had Holy Spirit-inspired insights about Paul's journey and the dangers he faced. The believers in Tyre desired for Paul not to go to Jerusalem, because the Spirit had made clear to them that he would suffer greatly there. Then Agabus visited, seeming to repeat the same warning as the others: Jerusalem held danger. All these messages were judged as being from the Spirit, but the response to them was different—Paul believed that in spite of the danger he must go to Jerusalem. His friends desired he should not. In the end, Paul's friends may have had a prayer similar to the Master's as He faced His own death: "I want Your will to be done, not Mine" (Mark 14:36).

▸ WORSHIP

21:5 Praying our pain. God's people have always gathered to pray (Acts 12:12; James 5:14). In this case, everyone participated—men, women, and children. They all felt sorrow and helplessness as they knew that Paul was going away to face grave danger in Jerusalem. Rather than lash out in anger at God for being unfair to Paul or criticizing Paul for going against their requests, they prayed. By laying their grief and hope before God, they could face any future that God had for them and their beloved leader. Rather than retreating from pain, bring it to God. Bathe every part of your life, especially the painful portions, in the prayers of the community of God's people. (***See Worship****> NT> Prayer> Examples> Others> The first disciples devote themselves to prayer,* TopicGuide page A33.)

21:8-9 Philip played a significant role in the spread of the gospel in the early part of the book of Acts (see note at 8:4-8). But now Luke reveals to the reader that his daughters also made contributions to the Kingdom of God. In the book of Acts, women have an important role in the life of the church. Women are among those gathered together in prayer before the day of Pentecost (1:14). The apostles react quickly to the neglected needs of the Grecian widows (6:1-7). The disciple Dorcas is commended for her good deeds and ministry to the poor (9:36-42). While in Philippi, Paul and his companions are welcomed into the house of Lydia (16:15). Priscilla and her husband accompanied Paul on his journey to Syria and helped Apollos gain a fuller understanding of the Scriptures (18:18, 26).

21:10-11 Fifteen years earlier, Agabus the prophet correctly foretold about a famine that would come upon the entire Roman Empire (11:27-28). At that time, the disciples determined to gather a collection to help the believers in Judea. Here, the prophet reemerges to take Paul's belt and act out what awaited him in Jerusalem (see also Isaiah 20:2; Jeremiah 13:4-11; 19:1-15; Ezekiel 4–5). This prophecy foreshadows what happens in Acts 21:30-35 and 28:17.

▸ SPIRITUAL WARFARE

21:19 Giving an account. Too many Christians live lonely lives, cut off from the church, from friends, and from accountability. Paul was an apostle—he didn't need the approval of anyone, did he? But as he went along from church to church, he gave an account of what he had done. As he did this, the believers prayed for him (21:5-6). The difficulties and victories of his life and ministry were an open book to his fellow believers, so they knew how to pray for him. How are you being accountable to others? Are you open to suggestions from them? Do they know enough about what you are facing each day to pray for you or warn you of spiritual danger? (***See Spiritual Warfare****> Resisting Sin and Evil> Resisting Temptation> How to Resist> By the help of our friends,* TopicGuide page A45.)

[20]After hearing this, they praised God. And then they said, "You know, dear brother, how many thousands of Jews have also believed, and they all follow the law of Moses very seriously. [21]But the Jewish believers here in Jerusalem have been told that you are teaching all the Jews who live among the Gentiles to turn their backs on the laws of Moses. They've heard that you teach them not to circumcise their children or follow other Jewish customs. [22]What should we do? They will certainly hear that you have come.

[23]"Here's what we want you to do. We have four men here who have completed their vow. [24]Go with them to the Temple and join them in the purification ceremony, paying for them to have their heads ritually shaved. Then everyone will know that the rumors are all false and that you yourself observe the Jewish laws.

[25]"As for the Gentile believers, they should do what we already told them in a letter: They should abstain from eating food offered to idols, from consuming blood or the meat of strangled animals, and from sexual immorality."

21:20 Acts 15:1, 5; Gal 3:10-11
21:21 Acts 16:3; Gal 2:3
21:23 Acts 18:18
21:24 Num 6:5, 13-20
21:25 Acts 15:19-29

PAUL IS ARRESTED

[26]So Paul went to the Temple the next day with the other men. They had already started the purification ritual, so he publicly announced the date when their vows would end and sacrifices would be offered for each of them.

[27]The seven days were almost ended when some Jews from the province of Asia saw Paul

21:26 Num 6:1-21; 1 Cor 9:20
21:27 Acts 24:18; 26:21

21:27-30 Paul continued to observe some aspects of the law of Moses, such as this purification vow (detailed in Numbers 6:9, 13-20), even into the latter portions of his ministry. His great respect for the law made the charge against him by the unruly Jews even more unbelievable. Trophimus, the one accused of trespassing in the Temple, was a believer from Ephesus, and one of Paul's traveling companions from Greece to Macedonia (Acts 20:4). Paul wrote in Ephesians 2:18-19 that there are no longer any barriers to Gentiles approaching God. The misunderstanding of the Jews may have been connected to this teaching.

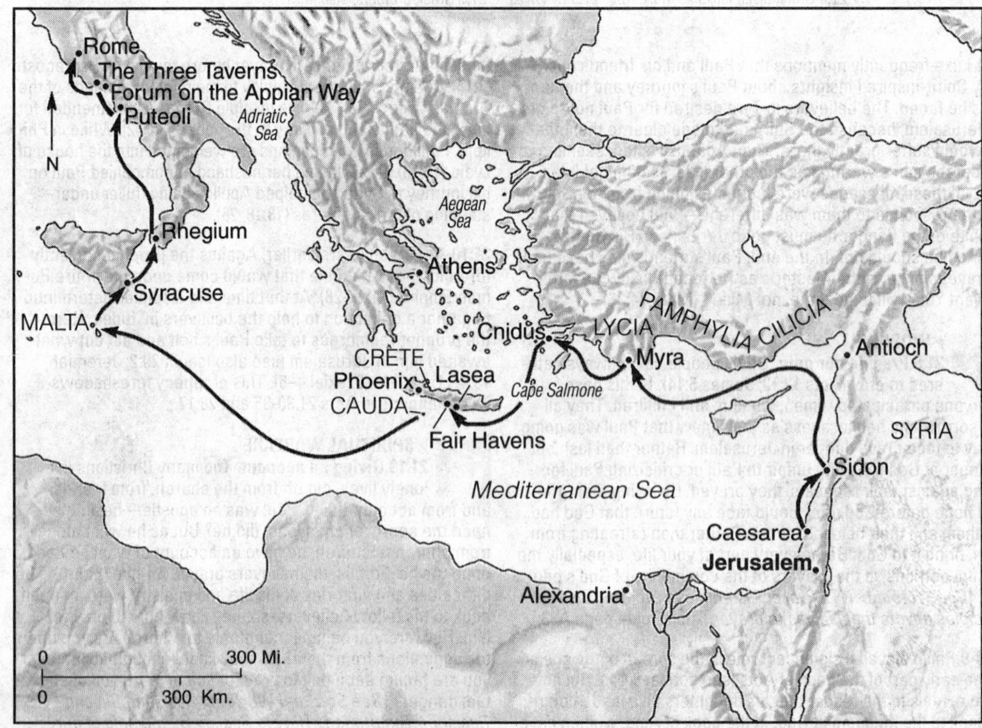

PAUL'S JOURNEY TO ROME (ACTS 21:17–28:31)

21:28 in the Temple and roused a mob against him. They grabbed him, [28]yelling, "Men of Israel,
Matt 24:15 help us! This is the man who preaches against our people everywhere and tells everybody to
Acts 6:13; 24:5-6 disobey the Jewish laws. He speaks against the Temple—and even defiles this holy place by
21:29 Acts 20:4 bringing in Gentiles.*" [29](For earlier that day they had seen him in the city with Trophimus, a
2 Tim 4:20 Gentile from Ephesus,* and they assumed Paul had taken him into the Temple.)
[30]The whole city was rocked by these accusations, and a great riot followed. Paul was
grabbed and dragged out of the Temple, and immediately the gates were closed behind
him. [31]As they were trying to kill him, word reached the commander of the Roman regi-
21:32 ment that all Jerusalem was in an uproar. [32]He immediately called out his soldiers and of-
Acts 23:27 ficers* and ran down among the crowd. When the mob saw the commander and the
troops coming, they stopped beating Paul.
21:33 [33]Then the commander arrested him and ordered him bound with two chains. He asked
Acts 20:23 the crowd who he was and what he had done. [34]Some shouted one thing and some an-
Eph 6:20 other. Since he couldn't find out the truth in all the uproar and confusion, he ordered that
Paul be taken to the fortress. [35]As Paul reached the stairs, the mob grew so violent the sol-
21:36 Luke 23:18 diers had to lift him to their shoulders to protect him. [36]And the crowd followed behind,
John 19:15 shouting, "Kill him, kill him!"
Acts 22:22

PAUL SPEAKS TO THE CROWD

[37]As Paul was about to be taken inside, he said to the commander, "May I have a word
with you?"
"Do you know Greek?" the commander asked, surprised. [38]"Aren't you the Egyptian
who led a rebellion some time ago and took 4,000 members of the Assassins out into the
desert?"
21:39 [39]"No," Paul replied, "I am a Jew and a citizen of Tarsus in Cilicia, which is an important
Acts 9:11; 22:3 city. Please, let me talk to these people." [40]The commander agreed, so Paul stood on the
21:40 stairs and motioned to the people to be quiet. Soon a deep silence enveloped the crowd,
Acts 26:14 and he addressed them in their own language, Aramaic.*

22:1 **22** "Brothers and esteemed fathers," Paul said, "listen to me as I offer my defense."
Acts 7:2 [2]When they heard him speaking in their own language,* the silence was even
22:3-21 greater.
//Acts 9:1-29; 26:9-18 [3]Then Paul said, "I am a Jew, born in Tarsus, a city in Cilicia, and I was brought up and
22:3 educated here in Jerusalem under Gamaliel. As his student, I was carefully trained in our
Acts 5:34-40 Jewish laws and customs. I became very zealous to honor God in everything I did, just like
Rom 10:2 all of you today. [4]And I persecuted the followers of the Way, hounding some to death, ar-
22:4 resting both men and women and throwing them in prison. [5]The high priest and the
Acts 8:3; 9:2 whole council of elders can testify that this is so. For I received letters from them to our
Jewish brothers in Damascus, authorizing me to bring the Christians from there to Jerusa-
lem, in chains, to be punished.

21:28 Greek *Greeks.* 21:29 Greek *Trophimus, the Ephesian.* 21:32 Greek *centurions.* 21:40 Or *Hebrew.* 22:2 Greek *in Aramaic,* or *in Hebrew.*

21:31-40 Once again, the Romans preserved the life of the apostle Paul (see note at 19:35-41). The commander of the Roman troops intervened on Paul's behalf by bringing an end to the beating the Jews were illegally rendering to the apostle. Paul's home city, Tarsus, was the capital city of Cilicia, a Roman province.

22:1-2 Paul now had the platform to share his story with the crowd gathered before him. He began by respectfully addressing the people in Aramaic as "brothers and fathers" (7:2). Aramaic was a common language spoken by the people living in Palestine during the first century. Jews of that time generally spoke Aramaic as their mother tongue, as Hebrew had slipped into disuse during the time of the Exile. Paul was making a gesture of goodwill by choosing to speak in the Jews' mother tongue rather than in Greek, the language of the hated Roman Empire.

22:4-6 Early Christians were often referred to as followers of the "Way" (9:2; 19:9, 23), and this appears to have been a legitimate designation before Roman officials (24:14, 22). The name may have originated from Jesus' own teaching when He taught, "I am the way, the truth, and the life" (John 14:6).

6 “As I was on the road, approaching Damascus about noon, a very bright light from heaven suddenly shone down around me. 7 I fell to the ground and heard a voice saying to me, ‘Saul, Saul, why are you persecuting Me?’

8 “ ‘Who are You, lord?’ I asked.

“And the voice replied, ‘I am Jesus the Nazarene,* the One you are persecuting.’ 9 The people with me saw the light but didn’t understand the voice speaking to me.

10 “I asked, ‘What should I do, Lord?’

“And the Lord told me, ‘Get up and go into Damascus, and there you will be told everything you are to do.’

11 “I was blinded by the intense light and had to be led by the hand to Damascus by my companions. 12 A man named Ananias lived there. He was a godly man, deeply devoted to the law, and well regarded by all the Jews of Damascus. 13 He came and stood beside me and said, ‘Brother Saul, regain your sight.’ And that very moment I could see him!

14 “Then he told me, ‘The God of our ancestors has chosen you to know His will and to see the Righteous One and hear Him speak. 15 For you are to be His witness, telling everyone what you have seen and heard. 16 What are you waiting for? Get up and be baptized. Have your sins washed away by calling on the name of the Lord.’

17 “After I returned to Jerusalem, I was praying in the Temple and fell into a trance. 18 I saw a vision of Jesus* saying to me, ‘Hurry! Leave Jerusalem, for the people here won’t accept your testimony about Me.’

19 “ ‘But Lord,’ I argued, ‘they certainly know that in every synagogue I imprisoned and beat those who believed in you. 20 And I was in complete agreement when Your witness Stephen was killed. I stood by and kept the coats they took off when they stoned him.’

21 “But the Lord said to me, ‘Go, for I will send you far away to the Gentiles!’ ”

22 The crowd listened until Paul said that word. Then they all began to shout, “Away with such a fellow! He isn’t fit to live!” 23 They yelled, threw off their coats, and tossed handfuls of dust into the air.

PAUL REVEALS HIS ROMAN CITIZENSHIP

24 The commander brought Paul inside and ordered him lashed with whips to make him confess his crime. He wanted to find out why the crowd had become so furious. 25 When they tied Paul down to lash him, Paul said to the officer* standing there, “Is it legal for you to whip a Roman citizen who hasn’t even been tried?”

26 When the officer heard this, he went to the commander and asked, “What are you doing? This man is a Roman citizen!”

27 So the commander went over and asked Paul, “Tell me, are you a Roman citizen?”

“Yes, I certainly am,” Paul replied.

22:6 Acts 9:2-8; 26:12-13
22:9 Acts 9:7; 26:13
22:11 Acts 9:8
22:12 Acts 9:17
22:14 Acts 3:13; 1 Cor 15:8
22:15 Acts 26:16
22:16 Acts 2:38; Rom 10:13; 1 Cor 6:11; Heb 10:22
22:19 Acts 8:3; 22:4-5; 26:9-11
22:20 Acts 7:57–8:1
22:21 Acts 9:15; 13:2; Rom 15:15-16
22:22 Acts 21:36; 25:24
22:25 Acts 16:37

22:8 Or *Jesus of Nazareth.* 22:18 Greek *Him.* 22:25 Greek *the centurion;* also in 22:26.

22:12-14 In Paul’s defense of his ministry, he explained that Ananias, a highly respected Jew, had been led by God to return his sight and to confirm his call into the ministry (see 9:10-19).

22:18 God often works out His purposes through human agents. Earlier, Luke explained that Paul had left Jerusalem because the believers had uncovered a plot to take Paul’s life and had secretly escorted him out of the city (9:28-30). In Paul’s attempt to explain the reasons for his departure, he revealed that he left Jerusalem because God had specifically directed him to do so.

▸ MINISTRY
22:21 Our call. A genuine call for help doesn’t come very often. A person may become panicked in a pool, or a nation will call up men to defend its borders. A call for help may go out in times of natural disaster such as a tsunami or hurricane. But Christ issued the greatest call of all—the Great Commission. And He is still calling today as He sends us into every corner of the world to witness for Him. That call is not an “if you’re not busy” command; it is given to us to obey right now (Matthew 28:18-20). How have you obeyed this call? God may or may not be asking you to serve in a foreign mission field, but if you look out your window, you can see the mission field in your neighborhood. Answer Christ’s call by sharing your faith where you live. (***See Ministry****> Great Commission> Witness> Christ issues the call of the gospel,* TopicGuide page A56.)

22:23-29 The legal process during first century Roman rule could be fair, but it could also be quite harsh, especially in this case as Paul was likely only guilty of disturbing the peace. It was unlawful for a Roman citizen, such as Paul, to be scourged prior to a trial hearing and sentencing (16:38), so even attempting to do so might have had serious consequences for the commanding officer.

28 “I am, too,” the commander muttered, “and it cost me plenty!”
Paul answered, “But I am a citizen by birth!”
29 The soldiers who were about to interrogate Paul quickly withdrew when they heard
he was a Roman citizen, and the commander was frightened because he had ordered him
bound and whipped.

22:29 Acts 16:38

PAUL BEFORE THE HIGH COUNCIL

30 The next day the commander ordered the leading priests into session with the Jewish
high council.* He wanted to find out what the trouble was all about, so he released Paul to
have him stand before them.

23 Gazing intently at the high council,* Paul began: “Brothers, I have always lived
before God with a clear conscience!”
2 Instantly Ananias the high priest commanded those close to Paul to slap him on the
mouth. 3 But Paul said to him, “God will slap you, you corrupt hypocrite!* What kind of
judge are you to break the law yourself by ordering me struck like that?”
4 Those standing near Paul said to him, “Do you dare to insult God’s high priest?”
5 “I’m sorry, brothers. I didn’t realize he was the high priest,” Paul replied, “for the Scrip-
tures say, ‘You must not speak evil of any of your rulers.’*”
6 Paul realized that some members of the high council were Sadducees and some were
Pharisees, so he shouted, “Brothers, I am a Pharisee, as were my ancestors! And I am on
trial because my hope is in the resurrection of the dead!”
7 This divided the council—the Pharisees against the Sadducees—8 for the Sadducees say
there is no resurrection or angels or spirits, but the Pharisees believe in all of these. 9 So
there was a great uproar. Some of the teachers of religious law who were Pharisees
jumped up and began to argue forcefully. “We see nothing wrong with him,” they
shouted. “Perhaps a spirit or an angel spoke to him.” 10 As the conflict grew more violent,

23:1 1 Cor 4:4; 2 Cor 1:12; 1 Tim 3:9; Heb 13:18; 1 Pet 3:16, 21
23:2 John 18:22; Acts 24:1
23:3 Lev 19:15; Ezek 13:10-15; John 7:51
23:5 *Exod 22:28
23:6 Acts 26:5; Phil 3:5
23:8 Matt 22:23; Mark 12:18; Luke 20:27

22:30 Greek *Sanhedrin.* 23:1 Greek *Sanhedrin;* also in 23:6, 15, 20, 28. 23:3 Greek *you whitewashed wall.* 23:5 Exod 22:28.

▸ GOD
22:30 A wise defense. There are dark places in this world, places where it appears as if God can hardly be present. One such place is where Christians are persecuted, where our beliefs are ridiculed and earthly lives are threatened. In these dark spaces, God asks us to be His witnesses. Paul had to stand before the Jewish high council. Although these were the religious leaders of Paul’s day, they were enemies of the gospel. Notice how Paul handled these troublemakers—he spoke forcefully and turned their bickering, faultfinding attitudes against them, leaving them arguing among themselves (23:1-11). What places or people in your world seem to oppose everything you believe? How do you handle those conflicts? Ask God to give you wisdom to be light in those dark places. (***See God****> Salvation> Holy Spirit> Those who walk in the Spirit are led by the Spirit,* TopicGuide page A15.)

▸ WORSHIP
23:1 Arguing with integrity. Paul wasted no time offering a defense for his teachings. He starts by testifying that he had always—even as a Pharisee—lived what he believed. Being sensitive to any accusation, the high priest took offense at Paul’s assertion, probably perceiving it as a backhanded attack upon the council—as if they were not acting in integrity. Paul’s testimony of integrity is where all believers must begin their defense against those who oppose us. How can we hope to prove God’s existence, show the truth of the gospel, or demonstrate any other facet of the Christian faith if our own lives testify against the same truths? Look carefully at your life—what portions clearly argue against something that you claim to believe? Repent and live a life that demonstrates what you believe is true. (***See Worship****> NT> Our Role> Obedience> Loving God means keeping His commandments,* TopicGuide page A32.)

23:6-8 Paul wisely used theological disagreements between the Pharisees and Sadducees to turn the discussion away from his trial and certain punishment. Paul’s continued identification with the Pharisees demonstrates that he did not believe that all Jewish religious leaders were by definition enemies of God. His own life showed that one could be a godly Jewish religious leader.

▸ GOD
23:10-11 God in charge. Paul knew he was in trouble when he had to rely on the conquerors of Israel, the Romans, to protect him from the Jewish leaders. Prison, even under protective custody, was extremely difficult. Paul knew that suffering lay ahead of him in Rome. Yet in all this, Jesus reassured him that He was still in control. It may look like others control your life. When your boss comes in and tells you that you are being laid off, do you still think God is in control? When you have to leave your home because your landlord has sold the property, do you still believe God is in charge? No matter what happens, be assured that God knows your future and is in charge. (***See God****> God’s Attributes> Sovereign> God has dominion over the affairs of people,* TopicGuide page A17.)

the commander was afraid they would tear Paul apart. So he ordered his soldiers to go
and rescue him by force and take him back to the fortress.
11 That night the Lord appeared to Paul and said, "Be encouraged, Paul. Just as you have 23:11
been a witness to Me here in Jerusalem, you must preach the Good News in Rome as well." Acts 18:9; 27:24; 28:23

THE PLAN TO KILL PAUL

12 The next morning a group of Jews* got together and bound themselves with an oath not 23:12 Acts 9:23
to eat or drink until they had killed Paul. 13 There were more than forty of them in the con-
spiracy. 14 They went to the leading priests and elders and told them, "We have bound 23:14-15
ourselves with an oath to eat nothing until we have killed Paul. 15 So you and the high Acts 25:3
council should ask the commander to bring Paul back to the council again. Pretend you
want to examine his case more fully. We will kill him on the way."
16 But Paul's nephew—his sister's son—heard of their plan and went to the fortress and 23:16
told Paul. 17 Paul called for one of the Roman officers* and said, "Take this young man to Acts 21:34
the commander. He has something important to tell him."
18 So the officer did, explaining, "Paul, the prisoner, called me over and asked me to
bring this young man to you because he has something to tell you."
19 The commander took his hand, led him aside, and asked, "What is it you want to tell
me?"
20 Paul's nephew told him, "Some Jews are going to ask you to bring Paul before the
high council tomorrow, pretending they want to get some more information. 21 But don't
do it! There are more than forty men hiding along the way ready to ambush him. They
have vowed not to eat or drink anything until they have killed him. They are ready now,
just waiting for your consent."
22 "Don't let anyone know you told me this," the commander warned the young man.

PAUL IS SENT TO CAESAREA

23 Then the commander called two of his officers and ordered, "Get 200 soldiers ready to 23:23
leave for Caesarea at nine o'clock tonight. Also take 200 spearmen and 70 mounted Acts 8:40
troops. 24 Provide horses for Paul to ride, and get him safely to Governor Felix." 25 Then he
wrote this letter to the governor:

26 "From Claudius Lysias, to his Excellency, Governor Felix: Greetings!
27 "This man was seized by some Jews, and they were about to kill him when 23:27
I arrived with the troops. When I learned that he was a Roman citizen, I removed Acts 21:30-33; 22:25-29
him to safety. 28 Then I took him to their high council to try to learn the basis of the 23:28
accusations against him. 29 I soon discovered the charge was something regarding Acts 22:30
their religious law—certainly nothing worthy of imprisonment or death. 30 But when 23:29
I was informed of a plot to kill him, I immediately sent him on to you. I have told his Acts 18:14-15; 25:18-19; 26:31; 28:18
accusers to bring their charges before you."

31 So that night, as ordered, the soldiers took Paul as far as Antipatris. 32 They returned to 23:30 Acts 24:19; 25:16
the fortress the next morning, while the mounted troops took him on to Caesarea. 33 When 23:33 Acts 8:40

23:12 Greek *the Jews*. 23:17 Greek *centurions;* also in 23:23.

23:12-15 When the enemies of Paul saw no quick legal remedy to get rid of the apostle, they plotted to do the job themselves by ambushing him on his next visit to the high council. The Jewish leaders agreed to assist the vigilantes in their plot for murder, demonstrating their thorough hypocrisy.

23:16 God exhorted Paul to take courage because He had promised the apostle safe passage to Rome (23:11). Providentially, God allowed Paul's nephew to uncover the plan to ambush the apostle. This is the only mention of Paul's relatives in Scripture.

23:24 The Roman emperor Claudius appointed Felix as governor over the region of Judea (AD 52–60). Historians characterize the rule of Felix as tyrannical and oppressive. He is recorded to have assassinated the high priest Jonathan with the help of a band of robbers. Later, Felix would hope for a bribe from Paul but kept him in prison for two years as a favor to the Jews (24:26-27).

they arrived in Caesarea, they presented Paul and the letter to Governor Felix. [34]He read it and then asked Paul what province he was from. "Cilicia," Paul answered.

[35]"I will hear your case myself when your accusers arrive," the governor told him. Then the governor ordered him kept in the prison at Herod's headquarters.*

PAUL APPEARS BEFORE FELIX

24 Five days later Ananias, the high priest, arrived with some of the Jewish elders and the lawyer* Tertullus, to present their case against Paul to the governor. [2]When Paul was called in, Tertullus presented the charges against Paul in the following address to the governor:

"Your Excellency, you have provided a long period of peace for us Jews and with foresight have enacted reforms for us. [3]For all of this we are very grateful to you. [4]But I don't want to bore you, so please give me your attention for only a moment. [5]We have found this man to be a troublemaker who is constantly stirring up riots among the Jews all over the world. He is a ringleader of the cult known as the Nazarenes. [6]Furthermore, he was trying to desecrate the Temple when we arrested him.* [8]You can find out the truth of our accusations by examining him yourself." [9]Then the other Jews chimed in, declaring that everything Tertullus said was true.

[10]The governor then motioned for Paul to speak. Paul said, "I know, sir, that you have been a judge of Jewish affairs for many years, so I gladly present my defense before you. [11]You can quickly discover that I arrived in Jerusalem no more than twelve days ago to worship at the Temple. [12]My accusers never found me arguing with anyone in the Temple, nor stirring up a riot in any synagogue or on the streets of the city. [13]These men cannot prove the things they accuse me of doing.

[14]"But I admit that I follow the Way, which they call a cult. I worship the God of our ancestors, and I firmly believe the Jewish law and everything written in the prophets. [15]I have the same hope in God that these men have, that He will raise both the righteous and the unrighteous. [16]Because of this, I always try to maintain a clear conscience before God and all people.

[17]"After several years away, I returned to Jerusalem with money to aid my people and to offer sacrifices to God. [18]My accusers saw me in the Temple as I was completing a purification ceremony. There was no crowd around me and no rioting. [19]But some Jews from

23:34 Acts 6:9; 21:39; 22:3
23:35 Acts 25:16
24:1 Acts 23:2, 24-30, 35
24:3 Acts 23:26; 26:25
24:5 Mark 1:24; Acts 16:20; 17:6; 24:14
24:6 Acts 21:28, 30
24:9 1 Thes 2:16
24:11 Acts 21:27
24:13 Acts 25:7
24:14 Acts 9:2; 26:22
24:15 Dan 12:2; Matt 22:31-32; John 5:28-29; Acts 23:6; 28:20
24:16 Acts 23:1
24:17 Acts 11:29-30; Rom 15:25-28; 1 Cor 16:1-4; 2 Cor 8:1-4; Gal 2:10
24:18 Acts 21:26-27

23:35 Greek *Herod's Praetorium.* 24:1 Greek *some elders and an orator.* 24:6 Some manuscripts add an expanded conclusion to verse 6, all of verse 7, and an additional phrase in verse 8: *We would have judged him by our law, [7]but Lysias, the commander of the garrison, came and violently took him away from us, [8]commanding his accusers to come before you.*

24:2-4 The prosecuting attorney in the case against Paul was Tertullus, who most likely practiced law regularly in the Roman court system. The introduction of Tertullus's speech is full of flattery and statements that did not reflect the Jewish sentiments concerning this murderous and oppressive governor (see note at 23:24).

24:2-8 Tertullus brought three charges against Paul: (1) Paul was a troublemaker. (2) He was a ringleader of a sect called the Nazarenes. (3) He was in the act of desecrating the Temple at the time he was apprehended. This is the only time in Scripture that Christians are referred to as a cult known as the Nazarenes. This designation may be traced to the fact that Jesus grew up in the city of Nazareth (Matthew 2:23), or it may be connected to the Nazirite vow Paul had taken earlier (Acts 21:26; Numbers 6:1-21). Regardless, this name continued to be used among Gnostic cults who produced writings under the title "The Gospel of the Nazarenes."

24:13-18 In comparison to Tertullus's introductory speech, Paul's defense did not begin with an insincere praise of the governor (24:2-4). Rather, Paul was polite in recognizing the tenure of Felix as governor and was thankful for the opportunity to make his defense. Paul responded to the three charges brought against him by making three claims: (1) He was not a troublemaker, for he arrived in Jerusalem only twelve days earlier, six of which were spent in custody. (2) He was indeed a disciple of the Way, but it is not a cult. (3) He did not desecrate the Temple but came to bring offerings for the poor and to present himself as ceremonially clean in the Temple.

▸ADOPTION

24:14 An open book. Paul was very open about his affiliation with Jesus Christ. In this situation, he might have fared better if he had just avoided mentioning his belief in Christ. In fact, he probably would have kept himself from going to jail. Jesus tells us, "Everyone who acknowledges Me publicly here on earth, I will also acknowledge before My Father in heaven" (Matthew 10:32). We all have times when linking ourselves with our Lord causes difficulty. During those times, ask God to give you the boldness to proclaim the name of Jesus. (***See Adoption****> With Christ> Servants> Witness for Christ,* TopicGuide page A37.)

the province of Asia were there—and they ought to be here to bring charges if they have
anything against me! 20Ask these men here what crime the Jewish high council* found me
guilty of, 21except for the one time I shouted out, 'I am on trial before you today because I
believe in the resurrection of the dead!'"

22At that point Felix, who was quite familiar with the Way, adjourned the hearing and
said, "Wait until Lysias, the garrison commander, arrives. Then I will decide the case." 23He
ordered an officer* to keep Paul in custody but to give him some freedom and allow his
friends to visit him and take care of his needs.

24A few days later Felix came back with his wife, Drusilla, who was Jewish. Sending for
Paul, they listened as he told them about faith in Christ Jesus. 25As he reasoned with them
about righteousness and self-control and the coming day of judgment, Felix became
frightened. "Go away for now," he replied. "When it is more convenient, I'll call for you
again." 26He also hoped that Paul would bribe him, so he sent for him quite often and
talked with him.

27After two years went by in this way, Felix was succeeded by Porcius Festus. And be-
cause Felix wanted to gain favor with the Jewish people, he left Paul in prison.

PAUL APPEARS BEFORE FESTUS

25 Three days after Festus arrived in Caesarea to take over his new responsibilities,
he left for Jerusalem, 2where the leading priests and other Jewish leaders met
with him and made their accusations against Paul. 3They asked Festus as a favor to trans-
fer Paul to Jerusalem (planning to ambush and kill him on the way). 4But Festus replied
that Paul was at Caesarea and he himself would be returning there soon. 5So he said,
"Those of you in authority can return with me. If Paul has done anything wrong, you can
make your accusations."

6About eight or ten days later Festus returned to Caesarea, and on the following day he
took his seat in court and ordered that Paul be brought in. 7When Paul arrived, the Jewish
leaders from Jerusalem gathered around and made many serious accusations they
couldn't prove.

8Paul denied the charges. "I am not guilty of any crime against the Jewish laws or the
Temple or the Roman government," he said.

9Then Festus, wanting to please the Jews, asked him, "Are you willing to go to Jerusa-
lem and stand trial before me there?"

10But Paul replied, "No! This is the official Roman court, so I ought to be tried right here.

24:21 Acts 23:6
24:23 Acts 27:3; 28:16, 30
24:25 Acts 10:42; Gal 5:23; 2 Pet 1:6
24:27 Acts 25:9, 14
25:1 Acts 24:27
25:2 Acts 24:1; 25:15
25:3 Acts 23:15
25:5 Acts 23:30
25:6 Acts 25:17
25:7 Acts 24:5-6, 13
25:8 Acts 6:13; 24:12; 28:17
25:9 Acts 24:27
25:10 Acts 25:21

24:20 Greek *Sanhedrin.* 24:23 Greek *a centurion.*

24:24 According to the Jewish historian Josephus, Drusilla left her husband, King Azizus of Emesa (modern-day Hims, Syria), so that she could marry Felix. Drusilla was the Jewish sister of Agrippa II, the appointed king of Chalcis (modern-day Qinnesrin, Syria) in AD 50.

24:25 Felix was both attracted to and terrorized by Paul's teachings about faith in Jesus Christ and the future judgment. He was familiar enough with Christianity to understand something about it (24:22), but his depraved heart kept him from repenting of his sin and turning to God in faith.

25:1-2 Porcius Festus succeeded Antonius Felix as governor of Judea (24:27). The historian Josephus considered Festus to have been wise and just in his rule over the province. In contrast to Felix, Festus from the outset attempted to reconcile the relationship between Rome and the Jews by visiting Jerusalem and meeting with religious leaders. Prudently, Festus was not so overly eager to please the Jews that he would not grant Paul a proper hearing. Unlike Felix, Festus did not delay dealing with the apostle Paul and agreed to reopen the case immediately upon his return to Caesarea.

▸ ADOPTION

25:2 A fierce opposition. There's a saying, "Time heals all wounds." But it's not always true. Paul had been in jail for more than two years, yet the religious leaders' hatred hadn't cooled one bit. Satan and his forces fanned the flames of their hate, hoping to defeat the new church, and he is doing the same thing today. Some people exhibit a deep hatred toward Christianity and would do anything to destroy it. But just like Paul, we can stand firm because we know whom we serve—the King of Kings. Paul wrote, "Overwhelming victory is ours through Christ" (Romans 8:37). When you hear of those who adamantly oppose God's people, do not cower. Do not think first of political or social solutions. Think of Christ's victory and pray like one whose victory is sure. (***See Adoption*****>** *With Christ> Supernatural> Victory over Satan,* TopicGuide page A37.)

25:11 You know very well I am not guilty of harming the Jews. 11 If I have done something wor-
Acts 26:32; 28:19 thy of death, I don't refuse to die. But if I am innocent, no one has a right to turn me over to
these men to kill me. I appeal to Caesar!"
12 Festus conferred with his advisers and then replied, "Very well! You have appealed to
Caesar, and to Caesar you will go!"
13 A few days later King Agrippa arrived with his sister, Bernice,* to pay their respects to
25:14 Festus. 14 During their stay of several days, Festus discussed Paul's case with the king. "There
Acts 24:27 is a prisoner here," he told him, "whose case was left for me by Felix. 15 When I was in Jerusa-
25:15 lem, the leading priests and Jewish elders pressed charges against him and asked me to
Acts 25:1-2 condemn him. 16 I pointed out to them that Roman law does not convict people without a
25:16 Acts 23:30 trial. They must be given an opportunity to confront their accusers and defend themselves.
17 "When his accusers came here for the trial, I didn't delay. I called the case the very
25:18-19 next day and ordered Paul brought in. 18 But the accusations made against him weren't
Acts 18:14-15; 23:29 any of the crimes I expected. 19 Instead, it was something about their religion and a dead
man named Jesus, who Paul insists is alive. 20 I was at a loss to know how to investigate
these things, so I asked him whether he would be willing to stand trial on these charges in
25:21 Jerusalem. 21 But Paul appealed to have his case decided by the emperor. So I ordered that
Acts 25:11-12 he be held in custody until I could arrange to send him to Caesar."
25:22 22 "I'd like to hear the man myself," Agrippa said.
Acts 9:15 And Festus replied, "You will—tomorrow!"

PAUL SPEAKS TO AGRIPPA

23 So the next day Agrippa and Bernice arrived at the auditorium with great pomp, accom-
panied by military officers and prominent men of the city. Festus ordered that Paul be
25:24 brought in. 24 Then Festus said, "King Agrippa and all who are here, this is the man whose
Acts 22:22 death is demanded by all the Jews, both here and in Jerusalem. 25 But in my opinion he
25:25 has done nothing deserving death. However, since he appealed his case to the emperor, I
Acts 23:9 have decided to send him to Rome.
26 "But what shall I write the emperor? For there is no clear charge against him. So I have
brought him before all of you, and especially you, King Agrippa, so that after we examine
him, I might have something to write. 27 For it makes no sense to send a prisoner to the
emperor without specifying the charges against him!"

25:13 Greek *Agrippa the king and Bernice arrived.*

25:11-12 Sensing that Festus might concede to the Jewish request to try Paul in Jerusalem, Paul appealed to Caesar. Roman citizens accused of a capital offense had the right to appeal their case to Rome. God was at work in the life of Paul, not only protecting him from the deathtrap the Jews had set for him upon his return to Jerusalem (25:3), but also ensuring that he would visit Rome as promised. God's working in this situation began at Paul's birth, which is when Paul inherited his Roman citizenship (22:28).

25:13 According to the Jewish historian Josephus, this was Herod Agrippa II, the brother of Bernice and Drusilla (see note at 24:24). His responsibilities focused on the Temple and included appointing a high priest and acting as guardian of the Temple treasury and distributor of the priestly vestments. Agrippa II married his sister Bernice.

▸ SALVATION

25:14 The witness spreads. The message about Jesus Christ and what He has done for us is so exciting that it spreads rapidly—it is truly Good News! Paul witnessed about Christ to Festus. Then Festus went and told King Agrippa what Paul had said. King Agrippa, his sister Bernice, and Festus all came to hear Paul's words. You'll be surprised at what will happen when you witness, too. People will be so intrigued about Jesus that they will spread the news to their friends. You don't know what happens to your words—God's words—and their effects. Be assured that God will use your obedience in sharing your faith in Christ. (***See Salvation*****>** *Receiving> Results> Expressed in obedience to Great Commission,* TopicGuide page A23.)

25:19 Because of Agrippa's familiarity with the Jewish religion (26:3; see note at 25:13), Festus explained to Agrippa that he was dumbfounded to understand what charges the Jews had against Paul. For Festus, the claim that a man named Jesus had once died but was now resurrected seemed too insignificant a claim to be tried by Roman leaders. Festus, in his unbelief, undervalued the significance of the gospel. In Christ alone is found forgiveness of sins and a promise of eternal life (Romans 6:22-23; Ephesians 1:7; Colossians 1:14).

25:26-27 Since Paul appealed to Caesar, Festus had to send him to Rome along with a letter of explanation. This letter was to contain a statement explaining the nature and history of the case. With the help of Agrippa, high-ranking officers, and the leading men of Caesarea, Festus hoped to obtain more information from Paul in order to provide Caesar with a reasonable explanation.

26 Then Agrippa said to Paul, "You may speak in your defense."
So Paul, gesturing with his hand, started his defense: 2"I am fortunate, King
Agrippa, that you are the one hearing my defense today against all these accusations
made by the Jewish leaders, 3for I know you are an expert on all Jewish customs and con-
troversies. Now please listen to me patiently!
4"As the Jewish leaders are well aware, I was given a thorough Jewish training from my
earliest childhood among my own people and in Jerusalem. 5If they would admit it, they
know that I have been a member of the Pharisees, the strictest sect of our religion. 6Now I
am on trial because of my hope in the fulfillment of God's promise made to our ancestors.
7In fact, that is why the twelve tribes of Israel zealously worship God night and day, and
they share the same hope I have. Yet, Your Majesty, they accuse me for having this hope!
8Why does it seem incredible to any of you that God can raise the dead?
9"I used to believe that I ought to do everything I could to oppose the very name of
Jesus the Nazarene.* 10Indeed, I did just that in Jerusalem. Authorized by the leading
priests, I caused many believers* there to be sent to prison. And I cast my vote against
them when they were condemned to death. 11Many times I had them punished in the syn-
agogues to get them to curse Jesus.* I was so violently opposed to them that I even chased
them down in foreign cities.
12"One day I was on such a mission to Damascus, armed with the authority and com-
mission of the leading priests. 13About noon, Your Majesty, as I was on the road, a light
from heaven brighter than the sun shone down on me and my companions. 14We all fell
down, and I heard a voice saying to me in Aramaic,* 'Saul, Saul, why are you persecuting
Me? It is useless for you to fight against My will.'*
15"'Who are You, lord?' I asked.
"And the Lord replied, 'I am Jesus, the One you are persecuting. 16Now get to your feet!
For I have appeared to you to appoint you as My servant and witness. You are to tell the
world what you have seen and what I will show you in the future. 17And I will rescue you
from both your own people and the Gentiles. Yes, I am sending you to the Gentiles 18to
open their eyes, so they may turn from darkness to light and from the power of Satan to
God. Then they will receive forgiveness for their sins and be given a place among God's
people, who are set apart by faith in Me.'
19"And so, King Agrippa, I obeyed that vision from heaven. 20I preached first to those in
Damascus, then in Jerusalem and throughout all Judea, and also to the Gentiles, that all
must repent of their sins and turn to God—and prove they have changed by the good
things they do. 21Some Jews arrested me in the Temple for preaching this, and they tried
to kill me. 22But God has protected me right up to this present time so I can testify to every-
one, from the least to the greatest. I teach nothing except what the prophets and Moses

26:4 Gal 1:13; Phil 3:5-6
26:6 Gen 3:15; 22:18; 26:4; Deut 18:15; Isa 7:14; 9:6-7; Jer 23:5-6; 33:14; Ezek 34:23; 37:24; Dan 9:24; Mal 3:1; 4:2; Acts 13:32; 23:6
26:7 Phil 3:11; 1 Thes 3:10
26:8 Dan 12:2; Acts 23:6
26:9 John 15:21; 16:2; 1 Tim 1:13
26:10 Acts 8:3; 22:4-5
26:12-18 //Acts 9:1-19; 22:6-16
26:14 Acts 9:7
26:16 Gal 1:12; Col 1:25; 1 Tim 1:12
26:17 Acts 13:46-48; 22:21; Rom 11:13; 15:16; Gal 1:15-16; 2:7-9; 1 Tim 2:7; 2 Tim 1:11
26:18 Isa 35:5; 42:7, 16; 61:1; Luke 1:77, 79; Eph 1:11; 5:8; Col 1:13; 1 Pet 2:9
26:20 Matt 3:8; Acts 9:19-29
26:22 Luke 24:27, 44

26:9 Or *Jesus of Nazareth.* 26:10 Greek *many of God's holy people.* 26:11 Greek *to blaspheme.* 26:14a Or *Hebrew.* 26:14b Greek *It is hard for you to kick against the oxgoads.*

26:6-8 In Paul's defense speech, he unquestionably connected the hope of Israel with the resurrection of Jesus Christ. Paul argued that Christianity is not a religion that broke away from Judaism but that Jesus Christ is the fulfillment of what was promised long ago to the Jews. God had sent His Son into the world in order to move His people into the next stage in the history of salvation.

26:14 The phrase "it is useless for you to fight against My will" can also be translated, "it is hard for you to kick against the ox goads." (Goads are sticks used for prodding animals.) This was a commonly used proverb among the Greeks to signify the futility of striving against fate or the will of the gods. Jesus used this phrase to mean that as useless as it was for an ox to kick against the goads of the plowman, it was pointless for Paul to continue working against Him and His people.

▸ MINISTRY
26:18 Great and small. Have you ever looked around you and felt very small? Insignificant? The universe is a big place, and God is even bigger. But consider how important you are to God. He has entrusted you with creation (Genesis 1:26-27) and with a vital mission (Matthew 28:18-20). What greater worth and work could we have been given? As you tell people about what God has done in your life, make sure they understand the grand design He has for them. Discover the joy of bringing someone from the emptiness of unbelief to the fullness of knowing God—and you—much better. (***See Ministry****> Great Commission> Witness> Turn others from Satan to God,* TopicGuide page A56.)

26:23 Isa 42:6; 49:6 Luke 24:46-47 Rom 1:3-4 1 Cor 15:20 Col 1:18 Rev 1:5 said would happen—23 that the Messiah would suffer and be the first to rise from the dead,
and in this way announce God's light to Jews and Gentiles alike."
24 Suddenly, Festus shouted, "Paul, you are insane. Too much study has made you crazy!"
25 But Paul replied, "I am not insane, Most Excellent Festus. What I am saying is the sober
truth. 26 And King Agrippa knows about these things. I speak boldly, for I am sure these
26:24 1 Cor 4:10 events are all familiar to him, for they were not done in a corner! 27 King Agrippa, do you
believe the prophets? I know you do—"
26:26 John 18:20 Acts 26:3 28 Agrippa interrupted him. "Do you think you can persuade me to become a Christian
so quickly?"*
29 Paul replied, "Whether quickly or not, I pray to God that both you and everyone here
in this audience might become the same as I am, except for these chains."
26:31 Acts 23:9, 29 30 Then the king, the governor, Bernice, and all the others stood and left. 31 As they went
out, they talked it over and agreed, "This man hasn't done anything to deserve death or
imprisonment."
26:32 Acts 25:11 32 And Agrippa said to Festus, "He could have been set free if he hadn't appealed to Caesar."

PAUL SAILS FOR ROME

27:1 Acts 25:12 27 When the time came, we set sail for Italy. Paul and several other prisoners were
placed in the custody of a Roman officer* named Julius, a captain of the Imperial
27:2 Acts 19:29; 20:4 Regiment. 2 Aristarchus, a Macedonian from Thessalonica, was also with us. We left on a
ship whose home port was Adramyttium on the northwest coast of the province of Asia;* it
was scheduled to make several stops at ports along the coast of the province.
3 The next day when we docked at Sidon, Julius was very kind to Paul and let him go
27:3 Matt 11:21 Acts 24:23; 27:43; 28:2, 16 ashore to visit with friends so they could provide for his needs. 4 Putting out to sea from
there, we encountered strong headwinds that made it difficult to keep the ship on course,
so we sailed north of Cyprus between the island and the mainland. 5 Keeping to the open
sea, we passed along the coast of Cilicia and Pamphylia, landing at Myra, in the province
27:6 Acts 28:11 of Lycia. 6 There the commanding officer found an Egyptian ship from Alexandria that was
bound for Italy, and he put us on board.
7 We had several days of slow sailing, and after great difficulty we finally neared Cnidus.
But the wind was against us, so we sailed across to Crete and along the sheltered coast of
the island, past the cape of Salmone. 8 We struggled along the coast with great difficulty
27:9 Lev 16:29-31 and finally arrived at Fair Havens, near the town of Lasea. 9 We had lost a lot of time. The
weather was becoming dangerous for sea travel because it was so late in the fall,* and
Paul spoke to the ship's officers about it.

26:28 Or *"A little more, and your arguments would make me a Christian."* 27:1 Greek *centurion;* similarly in 27:6, 11, 31, 43. 27:2 *Asia* was a Roman province in what is now western Turkey. 27:9 Greek *because the fast was now already gone by.* This fast was associated with the Day of Atonement (*Yom Kippur*), which occurred in late September or early October.

26:27-28 After Festus had interrupted Paul's speech by suggesting that the apostle was insane, Paul focused his attention on King Agrippa. Paul asked the king a direct question concerning his beliefs in the hope of Israel and the fulfillment of those promises in Jesus Christ. At this point, Agrippa was unwilling to respond. He intended only to assist Festus with preparing a letter of explanation to Caesar (25:26), not to debate an expert. Agrippa dodges Paul's question by responding with a question himself.

26:29 Paul used Agrippa's question to address the entire assembly. He expressed that his prayer to God was for the conversion of every single person gathered together in the room. Paul was taking advantage of every opportunity given to him by God to evangelize people for Jesus Christ.

27:1-3 Julius was a Roman centurion of the Imperial Regiment, an honorary title commonly given to auxiliary troops. Julius, a kind man, bore the responsibility of escorting Paul and other detainees in Palestine to Rome. The use of *we* indicates that Luke was aboard as well (see note at 16:8-10), and he may have been acting as the ship's doctor (Colossians 4:14).

27:5-6 The weather conditions had diverted the vessel carrying Paul to a safer route along the eastern Mediterranean coast until it landed in Myra, a city in the province of Lycia. Julius ordered that all those traveling with him be transferred onto a larger Alexandrian ship. Rome imported most of its grain from Egypt, and this ship from Alexandria appears to have been carrying a large shipment of grain on its way to the city of Rome (27:38).

27:9-10 The phrase "late in the fall" suggests that the time was near to observe a fast that occurred around the Day of Atonement in late September or early October. The stormy season in the Mediterranean Sea begins in early November, and most sailing ceases during the winter months. Concerned for the well-being of the travelers, Paul warned the sailors and Julius to stay put or suffer the dangers of perilous waters.

10"Men," he said, "I believe there is trouble ahead if we go on—shipwreck, loss of cargo,
and danger to our lives as well." 11But the officer in charge of the prisoners listened more
to the ship's captain and the owner than to Paul. 12And since Fair Havens was an exposed
harbor—a poor place to spend the winter—most of the crew wanted to go on to Phoenix,
farther up the coast of Crete, and spend the winter there. Phoenix was a good harbor with
only a southwest and northwest exposure.

THE STORM AT SEA

13When a light wind began blowing from the south, the sailors thought they could make
it. So they pulled up anchor and sailed close to the shore of Crete. 14But the weather 27:14
changed abruptly, and a wind of typhoon strength (called a "northeaster") burst across the Mark 4:37
island and blew us out to sea. 15The sailors couldn't turn the ship into the wind, so they
gave up and let it run before the gale.

16We sailed along the sheltered side of a small island named Cauda,* where with great
difficulty we hoisted aboard the lifeboat being towed behind us. 17Then the sailors bound
ropes around the hull of the ship to strengthen it. They were afraid of being driven across
to the sandbars of Syrtis off the African coast, so they lowered the sea anchor to slow the
ship and were driven before the wind.

18The next day, as gale-force winds continued to batter the ship, the crew began throw- 27:18
ing the cargo overboard. 19The following day they even took some of the ship's gear and Jon 1:5
threw it overboard. 20The terrible storm raged for many days, blotting out the sun and the
stars, until at last all hope was gone.

21No one had eaten for a long time. Finally, Paul called the crew together and said, 27:21
"Men, you should have listened to me in the first place and not left Crete. You would have Acts 27:10
avoided all this damage and loss. 22But take courage! None of you will lose your lives, 27:23
even though the ship will go down. 23For last night an angel of the God to whom I belong Acts 18:9; 23:11
and whom I serve stood beside me, 24and he said, 'Don't be afraid, Paul, for you will surely 2 Tim 4:17
stand trial before Caesar! What's more, God in His goodness has granted safety to every- 27:24 Acts 23:11
one sailing with you.' 25So take courage! For I believe God. It will be just as he said. 26But 27:25 Rom 4:20-21
we will be shipwrecked on an island." 27:26 Acts 28:1

THE SHIPWRECK

27About midnight on the fourteenth night of the storm, as we were being driven across the
Sea of Adria,* the sailors sensed land was near. 28They dropped a weighted line and found
that the water was 120 feet deep. But a little later they measured again and found it was only
90 feet deep.* 29At this rate they were afraid we would soon be driven against the rocks along
the shore, so they threw out four anchors from the back of the ship and prayed for daylight.

30Then the sailors tried to abandon the ship; they lowered the lifeboat as though they
were going to put out anchors from the front of the ship. 31But Paul said to the command-
ing officer and the soldiers, "You will all die unless the sailors stay aboard." 32So the sol-
diers cut the ropes to the lifeboat and let it drift away.

33Just as day was dawning, Paul urged everyone to eat. "You have been so worried that

27:16 Some manuscripts read *Clauda*. 27:27 The *Sea of Adria* includes the central portion of the Mediterranean. 27:28 Greek *20 fathoms . . . 15 fathoms* [37 meters . . . 27 meters].

27:22-26 Paul trusted God in every circumstance, even when he did not know exactly how things would turn out (20:22-23). But in this case, an angel of God had appeared to Paul in a vision speaking words of comfort and safety for all 276 people aboard the ship (27:37). Paul understood that the Lord was with him and that he served and belonged to the Lord; therefore, Paul could trust His every word.

27:27-32 The precision of these numbers enabled researchers to recover three of these anchors, with the fourth recovered in the form of modern diving weights, into which the anchor had been melted. Archaeological findings like these affirm the integrity of the Bible.

27:33-41 Among the hardened sailors, solders, and desperate criminals, there was despair and mutiny (27:30). However,

27:34 you haven't touched food for two weeks," he said. 34"Please eat something now for your
Matt 10:30 own good. For not a hair of your heads will perish." 35Then he took some bread, gave
Luke 12:7 27:35 thanks to God before them all, and broke off a piece and ate it. 36Then everyone was en-
Matt 14:19 couraged and began to eat—37all 276 of us who were on board. 38After eating, the crew
27:38 lightened the ship further by throwing the cargo of wheat overboard.
Jon 1:5 39When morning dawned, they didn't recognize the coastline, but they saw a bay with a
Acts 27:18 beach and wondered if they could get to shore by running the ship aground. 40So they cut
off the anchors and left them in the sea. Then they lowered the rudders, raised the foresail,
27:41 and headed toward shore. 41But they hit a shoal and ran the ship aground too soon. The
2 Cor 11:25 bow of the ship stuck fast, while the stern was repeatedly smashed by the force of the
waves and began to break apart.
42The soldiers wanted to kill the prisoners to make sure they didn't swim ashore and es-
27:43-44 cape. 43But the commanding officer wanted to spare Paul, so he didn't let them carry out
Acts 27:22, 24 their plan. Then he ordered all who could swim to jump overboard first and make for land.
44The others held onto planks or debris from the broken ship.* So everyone escaped safely
to shore.

PAUL ON THE ISLAND OF MALTA

28:1 Acts 27:26, 39 **28** Once we were safe on shore, we learned that we were on the island of Malta.
2The people of the island were very kind to us. It was cold and rainy, so they built
a fire on the shore to welcome us.
3As Paul gathered an armful of sticks and was laying them on the fire, a poisonous
28:4 snake, driven out by the heat, bit him on the hand. 4The people of the island saw it hang-
Luke 13:2, 4 ing from his hand and said to each other, "A murderer, no doubt! Though he escaped the
28:5 sea, justice will not permit him to live." 5But Paul shook off the snake into the fire and was
Mark 16:18 unharmed. 6The people waited for him to swell up or suddenly drop dead. But when they
Luke 10:19 had waited a long time and saw that he wasn't harmed, they changed their minds and de-
28:6 Acts 14:11 cided he was a god.
7Near the shore where we landed was an estate belonging to Publius, the chief official
28:8 of the island. He welcomed us and treated us kindly for three days. 8As it happened, Publi-
Jas 5:14-15 us's father was ill with fever and dysentery. Paul went in and prayed for him, and laying
his hands on him, he healed him. 9Then all the other sick people on the island came and
were healed. 10As a result we were showered with honors, and when the time came to sail,
people supplied us with everything we would need for the trip.

27:44 Or *or were helped by members of the ship's crew.*

Paul advised the Roman officers and encouraged the crew, for he knew that God had a plan to save everyone from the coming wreck.

27:42-44 Paul's presence was a blessing to all aboard the Alexandrian ship (compare Jonah 1). Though the soldiers plotted to execute all the prisoners, they were saved because of the compassion Julius had for Paul. God's promise was fulfilled, and not a single soul perished out on the sea.

▶ BIBLE
27:44 God's will never fails. Paul had prophesied that the trip he undertook would result in a shipwreck. But God also revealed to him that everyone would be saved (27:22-23). Everyone did survive the shipwreck—even though some didn't know how to swim (27:43). Paul's experience can encourage us to place our trust in God's Word. The promises He gives us He will fulfill. The future events He has revealed to us will come to pass. We can place our faith firmly in Him because what He says always comes true. What promise in the Scripture is most dear to you? Thank God that He will fulfill it. (***See Bible***> *Uniqueness> Inspired> His promises never fail,* TopicGuide page A10.)

28:1-6 If beatings, imprisonments, starvation, and shipwreck were not enough, now Luke records that a snake bit Paul. Modern Malta has no poisonous snakes, and perhaps ancient Malta had very few, making this event all the more unusual. Those with Paul concluded that Paul must have been a murderer whose god, having failed to kill him once, would try again. But when Paul suffered no effects of the bite, the group concluded that the apostle must have been a divine being (see also 14:11-20).

28:7-10 Some scholars have suggested that Publius's father suffered from Malta fever, known commonly as brucellosis. Brucellosis is an infectious disease that causes infertility, fever, and weakness. The large number of goats on the island likely transmitted the disease to the Maltans.

PAUL ARRIVES AT ROME

11 It was three months after the shipwreck that we set sail on another ship that had win- 28:11
tered at the island—an Alexandrian ship with the twin gods* as its figurehead. 12 Our first Acts 27:6
stop was Syracuse,* where we stayed three days. 13 From there we sailed across to Rhegi-
um.* A day later a south wind began blowing, so the following day we sailed up the coast
to Puteoli. 14 There we found some believers,* who invited us to spend a week with them.
And so we came to Rome.
15 The brothers and sisters* in Rome had heard we were coming, and they came to meet
us at the Forum* on the Appian Way. Others joined us at The Three Taverns.* When Paul
saw them, he was encouraged and thanked God.
16 When we arrived in Rome, Paul was permitted to have his own private lodging, 28:16
though he was guarded by a soldier. Acts 24:23; 27:3

PAUL PREACHES AT ROME UNDER GUARD

17 Three days after Paul's arrival, he called together the local Jewish leaders. He said to 28:17
them, "Brothers, I was arrested in Jerusalem and handed over to the Roman government, Acts 24:12-13; 25:8
even though I had done nothing against our people or the customs of our ancestors. 18 The 28:18
Romans tried me and wanted to release me, because they found no cause for the death Acts 23:29
sentence. 19 But when the Jewish leaders protested the decision, I felt it necessary to ap- 28:19
peal to Caesar, even though I had no desire to press charges against my own people. 20 I Acts 25:11
asked you to come here today so we could get acquainted and so I could explain to you 28:20 Acts 26:6
that I am bound with this chain because I believe that the hope of Israel—the Messiah—has 28:22
already come." Acts 24:14
21 They replied, "We have had no letters from Judea or reports against you from anyone
who has come here. 22 But we want to hear what you believe, for the only thing we know
about this movement is that it is denounced everywhere."
23 So a time was set, and on that day a large number of people came to Paul's lodging.
He explained and testified about the Kingdom of God and tried to persuade them about
Jesus from the Scriptures. Using the law of Moses and the books of the prophets, he spoke
to them from morning until evening. 24 Some were persuaded by the things he said, but 28:24
others did not believe. 25 And after they had argued back and forth among themselves, Acts 14:4
they left with this final word from Paul: "The Holy Spirit was right when he said to your an-
cestors through Isaiah the prophet,

26 'Go and say to this people: 28:26-27
When you hear what I say, *Isa 6:9-10
you will not understand. John 12:39-40
When you see what I do,
you will not comprehend.
27 For the hearts of these people are hardened,

28:11 The *twin gods* were the Roman gods Castor and Pollux. 28:12 *Syracuse* was on the island of Sicily. 28:13 *Rhegium* was on the southern tip of Italy. 28:14 Greek *brothers*. 28:15a Greek *brothers*. 28:15b *The Forum* was about 43 miles (70 kilometers) from Rome. 28:15c *The Three Taverns* was about 35 miles (57 kilometers) from Rome. 28:26-27 Isa 6:9-10 (Greek version).

28:11-16 The dangerous winter months were over, so Julius rounded up sailors and prisoners and set sail for Rome. The rest of the trip went smoothly, in contrast to almost every previous step.

28:17-24 Paul met with the Jewish leaders in Rome and began preaching to them, but in the end, the Gentiles were much more receptive to the gospel than Paul's brothers were (28:28).

Acts began with a series of Old Testament prophecies confirming God's desire that the gospel go to the Gentiles (2:17-36); it ends with a prophecy from Isaiah confirming the same (28:26-27).

28:24 Paul's responsibility was not to convert people to Christ but to faithfully proclaim the truth of Jesus Christ. He was set apart by God to be a missionary and to take the message of the gospel to the ends of the earth.

and their ears cannot hear,
and they have closed their eyes—
so their eyes cannot see,
and their ears cannot hear,
and their hearts cannot understand,
and they cannot turn to Me
and let Me heal them.'*

28:28 Pss 67:2; 98:3; Luke 3:6; Acts 13:46
28:30 Acts 28:16

28So I want you to know that this salvation from God has also been offered to the Gentiles,
and they will accept it."*
30For the next two years, Paul lived in Rome at his own expense.* He welcomed all who
visited him, 31boldly proclaiming the Kingdom of God and teaching about the Lord Jesus
Christ. And no one tried to stop him.

28:28 Some manuscripts add verse 29, *And when he had said these words, the Jews departed, greatly disagreeing with each other.* **28:30** Or *in his own rented quarters.*

28:28-30 The book of Acts has an unexpected ending. Luke does not conclude the book with Paul's trial but with the message that the Gentiles would accept the gospel and that Paul boldly and without hindrance proclaimed the Kingdom of God (see note at 19:8-10). The gospel began in Jerusalem and spread to the city of Rome, the very heart of the Roman Empire (1:8). Luke faithfully tracked the spread of the Kingdom of God to encourage believers that our role is to be servants of and witnesses for Jesus Christ (see note at 26:16).

▸ MINISTRY
28:31 Making disciples. The book of Acts ends the way it began: with a call to make disciples of Jesus Christ. Acts 1:8 gives us Christ's commission to go and be His witnesses everywhere starting in Jerusalem. Here Paul continues this mission, even though he was a prisoner in Rome. Through everything he suffered, he never stopped spreading the message of Jesus and building up the believers. That mission is ours also. The times we live in might be very different from Paul's day, but the message is the same. People's hearts are still darkened with sin. They still desperately need a Savior. You can be like those believers in Acts and help to make disciples. Just tell everyone who will listen about the love and forgiveness Jesus offers and teach those who respond to His love to live godly, fruitful lives. (***See Ministry***> *Great Commission*> *Make Disciples*> *Disciple by teaching,* TopicGuide page A56.)

ROMANS

PURPOSE

To explain how God makes sinful people righteous.

Every undertaking has certain "fundamentals." Whether you are learning to play soccer, trying to master your new computer, or attempting to manage your personal finances, there are certain key ideas and habits that you need to fully grasp. In the Christian life there are fundamentals as well—certain key concepts that every disciple must come to understand before faith growth is possible.

In anticipation of meeting the believers in Rome (15:24), Paul writes this letter to lay out the essentials of the Good News that is found in Jesus the Messiah, who fulfilled of all God's previous plans and promises. Specifically, Paul explains how God can make broken, sinful people holy, changing them by faith, through grace, so that they are in right standing with Him. Simply put, Paul's letter to the Romans is a guidebook to salvation.

DISCOVER GOD IN ROMANS

The key to understanding Paul's letter to the Romans is an understanding of the righteousness of God—that is, God's holy and uncompromising character and its implications for His relationship with people. As Paul discusses God's righteousness and how He draws people into right standing with Himself, we see some particular aspects of God's nature and character.

Righteous Judge: At issue in Romans is how people, who fall short of God's demands for them, can stand in right relationship before Him (3:3-8). Paul helps us understand that God is a righteous judge; He is just and fair and does what is right (3:23-26). The gospel is a just way to forgive sinners. God accepts the sacrifice of Christ on our behalf, and those who embrace this holy transaction—and the person of Jesus Christ—are saved.

Empowering Spirit: The kind of life God desires for His people is one of holiness and power. How can those who are "merely human" live this kind of life? Through the work of the Spirit of God. In Romans 8 we encounter the Holy Spirit, who inhabits and influences every Christian. Through the Spirit's work in us, we can live the way God desires, turning from sin to holy living and even praying effectively when we are at a loss as to how or what to pray.

Absolute Sovereign: What do you call someone who will always be in the right (3:4), who is always able to do what he says (4:21), who can and does work everything together for his own purposes (8:28), who is free to respond to people as he chooses (9:16-18), and who not only works all things for his own glory but upholds everything toward that end (11:36)? In Romans, God is portrayed as sovereign—He is the God who works all things according to the good pleasure of His own will.

GROWING THROUGH ROMANS

In a systematic way in his letter to the Romans, Paul weaves together his argument to show both the need all people have for God's work of grace and the incredible outcome of that work of grace in their lives. Understanding Paul's train of thought and his thinking about righteousness, or "right standing with God" will be of great value to any growing disciple.

Every Person's Need: Paul begins by laying out the case that everyone is in need of being made right with God (1:1–3:20). Because of sin, all humans are cut off from life with God. This should form the foundation for every disciple's understanding of his or her life with God—we come to Him because of our great need.

God's Gracious Solution: Paul then presented the Good News: God has made a way for anyone to be made right with Him in and through what Jesus has done (3:21–5:21). What each person desperately needs, God reveals in the gospel. Here is the real starting point for life as a disciple—new life through God's solution: His Son, Jesus Christ.

God's Wonderful Provision: Because God is not interested in just pardoning sinful people but making them positively holy in His sight, Paul next explains how God works in those who believe to produce in them character consistent with their right standing (chapters 6–8). Jesus' provision of righteousness results in a true and dramatic change in the life of everyone who believes.

God's Worldwide Plan: If God planned on sending the gospel to the nations through Paul's ministry, then a fundamental objection to this plan is that it appears as if He failed to convert the Jews through His message of hope—so why would this message work among the Gentiles? And was God simply abandoning the Jews? Romans 9–11 explains how God did not fail in His ongoing plan for the Jews and how the winning of the world of Gentiles would be helpful, not harmful, in bringing many Jews to God.

God's Intended Outcome: Paul is imminently practical; he always addresses how the Good News should make a difference in the lives of those who believe. Having laid out the work of God in His people, Paul lays out principles for living a life that is in line with a right standing with God (chapters 12–15).

DISCOVERY VERSES

For I am not ashamed of this Good News about Christ. It is the power of God at work, saving everyone who believes—the Jew first and also the Gentile. This Good News tells us how God makes us right in His sight. This is accomplished from start to finish by faith. As the Scriptures say, "It is through faith that a righteous person has life." (ROMANS 1:16-17)

But now God has shown us a way to be made right with Him without keeping the requirements of the law, as was promised in the writings of Moses and the prophets long ago. We are made right with God by placing our faith in Jesus Christ. And this is true for everyone who believes, no matter who we are. For everyone has sinned; we all fall short of God's glorious standard. Yet God, with undeserved kindness, declares that we are righteous. He did this through Christ Jesus when He freed us from the penalty for our sins. (ROMANS 3:21-24)

Therefore, since we have been made right in God's sight by faith, we have peace with God because of what Jesus Christ our Lord has done for us. (ROMANS 5:1)

ROMANS FACTS

Author: The beginning and the end of the book credit Paul as the writer of Romans (1:1; 15–16). As was common in his epistles (1 Corinthians 16:21; Galatians 6:11; Colossians 4:18; 2 Thessalonians 3:17; and Philemon 1:19), Paul dictated this letter (16:22) while someone else took down his words.

Written to: Paul had longed to visit the Roman church, since, as the Roman historian Suetonius confirms, a great number of Christians lived there as early as AD 49. Romans 1:13 signals that the church there was predominately Gentile, though many Jews belonged to the church there as well (Acts 2:10-11). Paul had not yet been to Rome, the capital city at the heart of the empire, but he longed to go (Romans 1:13).

Date of writing: Paul gives us some good indicators of the time he wrote this letter. He apparently wrote from Gaius' home in Corinth (16:23; compare this with 1 Corinthians 1:14). Apparently, he wrote this letter while staying for some months in Greece (Acts 20:2-6). This suggests that Paul wrote this letter near the end of his last missionary journey (Romans 15:19; compare Acts 18:23–21:14) around AD 57.

Setting: Paul likely wrote from Gaius' home in Corinth during the three months described in Acts 20:2-3. This is made more likely as he sends greetings to the Romans from those who lived in Corinth (Phoebe is mentioned in Romans 16:1-2; Gaius in 16:23 [see also 1 Corinthians 1:14]; Erastus in 16:23 [see also Acts 19:22; 2 Timothy 4:20]). This letter was written to Rome, the center of the vast Roman Empire.

OUTLINE

- **ROMANS 1:1–3:20**—Sin: Why We Need God's Righteousness
- **ROMANS 3:21–5:21**—Salvation: How God Provides This Righteousness
- **ROMANS 6:1–8:39**—Sanctification: God's Ongoing Work of Righteousness in Us
- **ROMANS 9:1–11:36**—Sovereignty: God's Freedom in Granting This Righteousness
- **ROMANS 12:1–16:27**—Service: Practical Expressions of Living Righteously

GREETINGS FROM PAUL

1:3 Matt 1:1; 22:42 Rom 9:5 2 Tim 2:8
1:4 Acts 13:33 Rom 8:11
1:5 Acts 9:15 Rom 16:26 Gal 1:16 Eph 3:8-9
1:7 1 Cor 1:2 2 Cor 1:1 Gal 1:3 Eph 1:1

1 This letter is from Paul, a slave of Christ Jesus, chosen by God to be an apostle and
sent out to preach His Good News. 2God promised this Good News long ago through
His prophets in the holy Scriptures. 3The Good News is about His Son. In His earthly life He
was born into King David's family line, 4and He was shown to be* the Son of God when He
was raised from the dead by the power of the Holy Spirit.* He is Jesus Christ our Lord.
5Through Christ, God has given us the privilege* and authority as apostles to tell Gentiles
everywhere what God has done for them, so that they will believe and obey Him, bringing
glory to His name.
6And you are included among those Gentiles who have been called to belong to Jesus
Christ. 7I am writing to all of you in Rome who are loved by God and are called to be His
own holy people.

May God our Father and the Lord Jesus Christ give you grace and peace.

GOD'S GOOD NEWS

1:8 Rom 16:19 1 Thes 1:8
1:9 Eph 1:16 Phil 1:8-9 1 Thes 2:5 2 Tim 1:3
1:10 Rom 15:23, 32
1:11 Rom 15:23
1:13 John 15:16 Rom 15:22

8Let me say first that I thank my God through Jesus Christ for all of you, because your faith
in Him is being talked about all over the world. 9God knows how often I pray for you. Day
and night I bring you and your needs in prayer to God, whom I serve with all my heart* by
spreading the Good News about His Son.
10One of the things I always pray for is the opportunity, God willing, to come at last to
see you. 11For I long to visit you so I can bring you some spiritual gift that will help you
grow strong in the Lord. 12When we get together, I want to encourage you in your faith,
but I also want to be encouraged by yours.
13I want you to know, dear brothers and sisters,* that I planned many times to visit you,
but I was prevented until now. I want to work among you and see spiritual fruit, just as I

1:4a Or *and was designated.* 1:4b Or *by the Spirit of holiness;* or *in the new realm of the Spirit.* 1:5 Or *the grace.* 1:9 Or *in my spirit.* 1:13 Greek *brothers.*

1:1-7 Paul's introduction to Romans falls into two parts. Verses 1-7 contain the typical introductory elements and brief theological truths that will be developed more thoroughly throughout the book. "Grace and peace" from God and Christ should be taken as more than just a standard phrase Paul puts in his letters. Grace is God's unearned favor that brings a person to faith in Christ, which brings peace between the believer and God. Paul reveals his belief in Jesus' deity by praying for both God the Father and the Lord Jesus Christ to bless the Roman believers.

1:8-15 This is the second part of Paul's introduction, discussing the intent of his ministry among the Romans and the rest of the world. Knowing the strategic importance of the city of Rome, and therefore of the church there, Paul sought to visit Rome as soon as possible. Paul's journey to Rome under Roman guard and his two-year imprisonment there were likely not what he had in mind when he wrote this letter (see Acts 27–28).

have seen among other Gentiles. 14 For I have a great sense of obligation to people in both
the civilized world and the rest of the world,* to the educated and uneducated alike. 15 So I
am eager to come to you in Rome, too, to preach the Good News.
16 For I am not ashamed of this Good News about Christ. It is the power of God at work,
saving everyone who believes—the Jew first and also the Gentile.* 17 This Good News tells
us how God makes us right in His sight. This is accomplished from start to finish by faith.
As the Scriptures say, "It is through faith that a righteous person has life."*

GOD'S ANGER AT SIN

18 But God shows His anger from heaven against all sinful, wicked people who suppress
the truth by their wickedness.* 19 They know the truth about God because He has made it
obvious to them. 20 For ever since the world was created, people have seen the earth and
sky. Through everything God made, they can clearly see His invisible qualities—His eter-
nal power and divine nature. So they have no excuse for not knowing God.
21 Yes, they knew God, but they wouldn't worship Him as God or even give Him thanks.
And they began to think up foolish ideas of what God was like. As a result, their minds

1:14 1 Cor 9:16
1:16 Acts 3:26; 1 Cor 1:18, 24
1:17 *Hab 2:4; Gal 3:11; Heb 10:38
1:18 Eph 5:6; Col 3:6
1:19 Acts 14:15-17; 17:24-28
1:20 Job 12:7-9; Ps 19:1
1:21 2 Kgs 17:15; Eph 4:17-18

1:14 Greek *to Greeks and barbarians.* 1:16 Greek *also the Greek.* 1:17 Or *"The righteous will live by faith."* Hab 2:4.
1:18 Or *who, by their wickedness, prevent the truth from being known.*

1:16-17 "I am not ashamed" is another way of saying "I am proud" (compare 1 Corinthians 1:31). Paul quotes Habakkuk 2:4 to support his insistence that a person can have a right relationship with God only by faith (see also Galatians 3:11 and Hebrews 10:38). The Greek literally reads, "The righteous person by faith will live." This quote provides a general outline of Romans 1–8. Chapters 1–4 explain how a sinner deserving God's judgment can be declared righteous before Him by faith ("the righteous person by faith"). Chapters 5–8 explain the nature of the life of faith ("will live").

1:18-23 The present tense of "God shows His anger" (literally, "the wrath of God is being revealed") indicates that God's anger continuously falls upon people who refuse to acknowledge "the truth" (1:18).

▶ **BIBLE**
1:19-22 No excuses. We may debate whether God's existence can be proven, but Paul explains in 1:19-20 that evidence of God's existence and power is found in nature. Paul says that only fools deny this truth. God has provided sufficient evidence of His existence through creation, so that those who deny His role as Creator are guilty of sin—they have "no excuse" for not seeing the evidence and drawing a proper conclusion. Keep this in mind as you share the gospel with unbelievers. Thank God for revealing His existence to them, and ask God to give you the wisdom to point out His signs and His power to those who do not believe. (***See Bible**> Unity> Creation,* TopicGuide page A10.)

THE GOSPEL GOES TO ROME
When Paul wrote his letter to the church in Rome, he had not yet been there, but he had taken the gospel "from Jerusalem all the way to Illyricum" (15:19). He planned to visit and preach in Rome one day and hoped to continue to take the gospel farther west—even to Spain.

1:22 became dark and confused. 22 Claiming to be wise, they instead became utter fools. 23 And
Jer 10:14 1 Cor 1:20 instead of worshiping the glorious, ever-living God, they worshiped idols made to look
1:23 like mere people and birds and animals and reptiles.
Deut 4:15-19 24 So God abandoned them to do whatever shameful things their hearts desired. As a re-
Ps 106:20 sult, they did vile and degrading things with each other's bodies. 25 They traded the truth
1:24 about God for a lie. So they worshiped and served the things God created instead of the Cre-
Acts 14:16 ator Himself, who is worthy of eternal praise! Amen. 26 That is why God abandoned them to
1:26 their shameful desires. Even the women turned against the natural way to have sex and in-
1 Thes 4:5 stead indulged in sex with each other. 27 And the men, instead of having normal sexual rela-
1:27 Lev 18:22; 20:13 tions with women, burned with lust for each other. Men did shameful things with other men,
1 Cor 6:9 and as a result of this sin, they suffered within themselves the penalty they deserved.
28 Since they thought it foolish to acknowledge God, He abandoned them to their foolish
thinking and let them do things that should never be done. 29 Their lives became full of
every kind of wickedness, sin, greed, hate, envy, murder, quarreling, deception, malicious
1:30 behavior, and gossip. 30 They are backstabbers, haters of God, insolent, proud, and boast-
2 Tim 3:2 ful. They invent new ways of sinning, and they disobey their parents. 31 They refuse to
1:31 understand, break their promises, are heartless, and have no mercy. 32 They know God's
2 Tim 3:3 justice requires that those who do these things deserve to die, yet they do them anyway.
1:32 Rom 6:23 Worse yet, they encourage others to do them, too.

GOD'S JUDGMENT OF SIN

2:1 **2** You may think you can condemn such people, but you are just as bad, and you have
Matt 7:1 no excuse! When you say they are wicked and should be punished, you are con-
demning yourself, for you who judge others do these very same things. 2 And we know
2:4 Rom 9:22 that God, in His justice, will punish anyone who does such things. 3 Since you judge others
2 Pet 3:9, 15 for doing these things, why do you think you can avoid God's judgment when you do the
2:5 same things? 4 Don't you see how wonderfully kind, tolerant, and patient God is with you?
Ps 110:5 Does this mean nothing to you? Can't you see that His kindness is intended to turn you
2:6 from your sin?
*Ps 62:12 5 But because you are stubborn and refuse to turn from your sin, you are storing up terri-
Matt 16:27 ble punishment for yourself. For a day of anger is coming, when God's righteous judgment
2:7 Matt 25:46 will be revealed. 6 He will judge everyone according to what they have done. 7 He will give
2 Tim 4:14 eternal life to those who keep on doing good, seeking after the glory and honor and

1:24-32 God often executes judgment by withholding His restraint on human sin, allowing people to give full expression to their evil desires. As a result people perverted sexuality and resorted to homosexual activities. They gave in to every form of wickedness as a result of their refusal to acknowledge God.

▸ GOD
1:26-27 Sexuality and unbelief. Unbelief—not homosexuality—is Paul's greatest concern for those living in Rome. It was certainly true that Greek and Roman culture allowed homosexuality and pederasty, considering it a natural activity. And Paul's audience certainly needed to understand that sin, sexual or not, comes quite naturally to us—but Paul wasn't delivering a lecture on sexual sin. His point was that unbelief has all sorts of behavioral, emotional, and intellectual consequences. As we leave the truths of God further behind, everything—even our most intimate relationships—grow more and more twisted. All things become a curse to those who turn their backs on the Creator and His truths. Yet God offers even the most sexually broken a fresh start through repentance and belief in His gospel. Tell that to everyone who needs to hear it—and don't forget to believe it for yourself. (***See God****> God's Attributes> Forgiving> God forgives those who repent,* TopicGuide page A16.)

▸ GOD
2:3 God will judge. Does the Bible send mixed messages about judging others? Some think so, reading passages like Matthew 7:1, which says, "Do not judge others, and you will not be judged." But 1 Corinthians 5:12 says, "It certainly is your responsibility to judge those inside the church who are sinning." So, do we judge or not? Some have been given the responsibility and authority to judge: The state rightly judges those who break the law of the land (Romans 13:1-5); the parent rightly judges and punishes a rebellious child (Proverbs 23:13); the leaders in a church rightly judge an unrepentant, sinful member (1 Corinthians 5:12). But those outside of our jurisdiction must be left to God (James 4:12). Trust that God will properly deal with others according to their standing with Christ (Revelation 6:10), and use your power to condemn very carefully. (***See God****> God's Attributes> Just> God judges all people with justice,* TopicGuide page A16.)

2:5-11 These verses explain that God's judgment is universal, that it will be "for the Jew first and also for the Gentile" (2:9) since God is impartial. God will give eternal life to those who do good but wrath to those who refuse to obey. Paul defines in later chapters that true goodness (2:10) depends on faith in Christ.

immortality that God offers. 8But He will pour out His anger and wrath on those who live for
themselves, who refuse to obey the truth and instead live lives of wickedness. 9There will
be trouble and calamity for everyone who keeps on doing what is evil—for the Jew first and
also for the Gentile.* 10But there will be glory and honor and peace from God for all who do
good—for the Jew first and also for the Gentile. 11For God does not show favoritism.
12When the Gentiles sin, they will be destroyed, even though they never had God's writ-
ten law. And the Jews, who do have God's law, will be judged by that law when they fail to
obey it. 13For merely listening to the law doesn't make us right with God. It is obeying the law
that makes us right in His sight. 14Even Gentiles, who do not have God's written law, show
that they know His law when they instinctively obey it, even without having heard it. 15They
demonstrate that God's law is written in their hearts, for their own conscience and thoughts
either accuse them or tell them they are doing right. 16And this is the message I proclaim—
that the day is coming when God, through Christ Jesus, will judge everyone's secret life.

THE JEWS AND THE LAW

17You who call yourselves Jews are relying on God's law, and you boast about your spe-
cial relationship with Him. 18You know what He wants; you know what is right because
you have been taught His law. 19You are convinced that you are a guide for the blind and
a light for people who are lost in darkness. 20You think you can instruct the ignorant and
teach children the ways of God. For you are certain that God's law gives you complete
knowledge and truth.
21Well then, if you teach others, why don't you teach yourself? You tell others not to
steal, but do you steal? 22You say it is wrong to commit adultery, but do you commit adul-
tery? You condemn idolatry, but do you use items stolen from pagan temples?* 23You are
so proud of knowing the law, but you dishonor God by breaking it. 24No wonder the Scrip-
tures say, "The Gentiles blaspheme the name of God because of you."*
25The Jewish ceremony of circumcision has value only if you obey God's law. But if you

2:8 2 Thes 2:12
2:11 Gal 2:6; Eph 6:9; Col 3:25
2:13 Matt 7:21; John 13:17; Jas 1:22-25
2:14 Acts 10:35
2:16 Acts 10:42; Rom 16:25; 2 Tim 2:8
2:17 Mic 3:11
2:20 2 Tim 3:5
2:21 Matt 23:3-4
2:24 *Isa 52:5; Ezek 36:20
2:25 Gal 5:3

2:9 Greek *also for the Greek;* also in 2:10. 2:22 Greek *do you steal from temples?* 2:24 Isa 52:5 (Greek version).

2:12-16 Since the Jews (formerly known as Israelites) received God's law at Mount Sinai, some assumed that they would never be the objects of God's judgment—despite the clear record of the Old Testament to the contrary (Leviticus 26:14-46; Deuteronomy 28:15-68). But Paul explains that the Gentiles could be judged without the law and that the Jews could be judged with the law.

2:17-24 Paul contrasts what the Jews know (2:17-20) with what they actually do (2:21-24). The Jews believe that the law gives them a special relationship with God and allows them to know the difference between right and wrong (vv. 17-18), which was true.

BECAUSE GOD IS JUST

He will always treat me fairly.

He will judge everyone according to what they have done. He will give eternal life to those who keep on doing good. . . . But He will pour out His anger and wrath on those who live for themselves.

ROMANS 2:6-8

FOR THE NEXT *GOD IS JUST* FEATURE SEE PAGE 2096.

don't obey God's law, you are no better off than an uncircumcised Gentile. 26 And if the
Gentiles obey God's law, won't God declare them to be His own people? 27 In fact,
uncircumcised Gentiles who keep God's law will condemn you Jews who are circumcised
and possess God's law but don't obey it.

28 For you are not a true Jew just because you were born of Jewish parents or because
you have gone through the ceremony of circumcision. 29 No, a true Jew is one whose heart
is right with God. And true circumcision is not merely obeying the letter of the law; rather,
it is a change of heart produced by God's Spirit. And a person with a changed heart seeks
praise* from God, not from people.

GOD REMAINS FAITHFUL

3 Then what's the advantage of being a Jew? Is there any value in the ceremony of cir-
cumcision? 2 Yes, there are great benefits! First of all, the Jews were entrusted with
the whole revelation of God.*

3 True, some of them were unfaithful; but just because they were unfaithful, does that
mean God will be unfaithful? 4 Of course not! Even if everyone else is a liar, God is true. As
the Scriptures say about Him,

"You will be proved right in what you say,
and You will win Your case in court."*

5 "But," some might say, "our sinfulness serves a good purpose, for it helps people see
how righteous God is. Isn't it unfair, then, for Him to punish us?" (This is merely a human
point of view.) 6 Of course not! If God were not entirely fair, how would He be qualified to
judge the world? 7 "But," someone might still argue, "how can God condemn me as a sin-
ner if my dishonesty highlights His truthfulness and brings Him more glory?" 8 And some
people even slander us by claiming that we say, "The more we sin, the better it is!" Those
who say such things deserve to be condemned.

ALL PEOPLE ARE SINNERS

9 Well then, should we conclude that we Jews are better than others? No, not at all, for we
have already shown that all people, whether Jews or Gentiles,* are under the power of sin.
10 As the Scriptures say,

2:28 Matt 3:9; John 8:39; Gal 6:15
2:29 Deut 30:6; John 5:44; Rom 7:6; 2 Cor 3:6; 10:18; Phil 3:3; Col 2:11; 1 Pet 3:4
3:2 Deut 4:7-8; Ps 147:19-20; Acts 7:38
3:4 *Ps 51:4
3:5 Rom 5:8
3:7 Rom 9:19
3:8 Rom 6:1
3:9 Rom 1:18–2:24
3:10-12 *Pss 14:1-3; 53:1-3

2:29 Or *receives praise.* 3:2 Greek *the oracles of God.* 3:4 Ps 51:4 (Greek version).

2:25-29 Paul introduces two important subjects here: circumcision (2:25-27) and what it means to be a Jew (2:28-29). He returns to both of these later in the book (circumcision, 4:10-12; being a Jew, 9:6-8). As a sign of the Old Covenant, circumcision did not guarantee a Jew's relationship with God any more than baptism does under the New Covenant. Christians are saved by Christ, not baptism (Titus 3:4-7; Romans 10:8-13).

▸ GOD
2:28-29 Jews need Jesus, too. Do you believe that those who practice other religions go to heaven? The Bible's answer is clear: Jesus alone provides the way to God (John 14:6). But what about the Jews? Surely their special place in God's plan means they can go to heaven, regardless of their accepting Christ or not, right? Wrong. While it is true that all true Jews go to heaven, here Paul defines a "true Jew" as one who is changed inside as well as outside. Paul's message in Romans 1–4—and our call to evangelize all the world—only makes sense if you accept Paul's statement that "everyone has sinned" (Romans 3:23). This "everyone" includes Jews. So share the gospel with your Jewish friends. Let them know that God has a plan for us to trust in the words and works of the greatest Jew of all time—Jesus the Messiah. (***See God> Salvation> Son> Only bridge between God and man,*** TopicGuide page A15.)

3:1-4 The main "advantage" of being Jewish was that God's revelation was given to the Jews, particularly the Old Testament. But the honor of receiving God's revelation came with the responsibility to obey it, which is where the Jews had failed miserably—as Paul would show in Romans 3:9-20.

3:5-8 Paul anticipated an objection to his argument about the disobedience of the Jews. He hears someone saying, "Our sinfulness serves a good purpose, for it helps people see how righteous God is." But God is also the holy Judge of the universe, and His justification of sinners is complementary—not contradictory—to His judgment of sinners. Paul develops these ideas later in the book, particularly at 3:19–4:25.

3:9-20 Paul's string of Old Testament quotations in 3:10-18 demonstrates that Jews were just as sinful as Gentiles. One of God's purposes in giving the Mosaic law was to show all people how guilty they are (3:19) by exposing how sinful they are (3:20). God never intended for the law to be a means of earning salvation. Only faith pleases God (see note at 14:23 and compare Hebrews 11:6).

"No one is righteous—
not even one.
11 No one is truly wise;
no one is seeking God.
12 All have turned away;
all have become useless.
No one does good,
not a single one."*
13 "Their talk is foul, like the stench from an open grave.
Their tongues are filled with lies."
"Snake venom drips from their lips."*
14 "Their mouths are full of cursing and bitterness."*
15 "They rush to commit murder.
16 Destruction and misery always follow them.
17 They don't know where to find peace."*
18 "They have no fear of God at all."*

19 Obviously, the law applies to those to whom it was given, for its purpose is to keep
people from having excuses, and to show that the entire world is guilty before God. 20 For
no one can ever be made right with God by doing what the law commands. The law sim-
ply shows us how sinful we are.

CHRIST TOOK OUR PUNISHMENT

21 But now God has shown us a way to be made right with Him without keeping the re-
quirements of the law, as was promised in the writings of Moses* and the prophets long
ago. 22 We are made right with God by placing our faith in Jesus Christ. And this is true for
everyone who believes, no matter who we are.
23 For everyone has sinned; we all fall short of God's glorious standard. 24 Yet God, with
undeserved kindness, declares that we are righteous. He did this through Christ Jesus
when He freed us from the penalty for our sins. 25 For God presented Jesus as the sacrifice
for sin. People are made right with God when they believe that Jesus sacrificed His life,
shedding His blood. This sacrifice shows that God was being fair when He held back and
did not punish those who sinned in times past, 26 for He was looking ahead and including

3:13 *Pss 5:9; 140:3
3:14 *Ps 10:7
3:15-17 *Isa 59:7-8
3:18 *Ps 36:1
3:19 Rom 2:12
3:20 Ps 143:2; Rom 4:15; 7:7; Gal 2:16; 3:11
3:21 Rom 1:2, 17; 9:30
3:22 Rom 4:11; 10:4, 12; Gal 2:16; Col 3:11
3:24 Eph 2:8; Heb 9:12
3:25 Lev 16:10; Heb 9:12-14; 1 Pet 1:19; 1 Jn 4:10

3:9 Greek *or Greeks.* 3:10-12 Pss 14:1-3; 53:1-3 (Greek version). 3:13 Pss 5:9 (Greek version); 140:3. 3:14 Ps 10:7 (Greek version). 3:15-17 Isa 59:7-8. 3:18 Ps 36:1. 3:21 Greek *in the law.*

▸ SALVATION
3:10-12 Complete sinners. Many people will admit that they are sinners—we all make mistakes—but few will admit that sin is so much a part of their being that they can never do anything good. Paul believed that both Jews and Gentiles were thoroughly tainted by sin. Body, soul, spirit, mind, emotions—all are touched by sin, though some aspects may be more marred than others (1:21). Because nothing good can come out of people, we can never perfectly obey the law. With a debt of sin and no ability to pay back that debt, it is hopeless to depend on ourselves to make things right with God. What are you relying on to make things right with God? Trust in God's gracious gift of Christ to change you into the person God wants you to be. (***See Salvation***> *Our Need> Sinful> Depraved,* TopicGuide page A22.)

▸ HOLINESS
3:20 The purpose of the law. Many people believe that in Old Testament times, people were saved through obedience to the law, while in the New Testament people are saved by grace through faith in Christ. According to Paul, the Jewish scholar and apostle, nothing could be further from the truth. The law does not justify, but terrify—the more we look at it, obey it, and understand it, "the law simply shows us how sinful we are" (Romans 3:20). We can use the law as a picture of God and His character (Exodus 3:15-16; Isaiah 33:22; Romans 7:2-9, 12), a window through which to view the world (Proverbs 3:31-32; Isaiah 51:4; Micah 4:2), and a mirror to view ourselves (1 Kings 9:4-9; Psalm 51:4; Matthew 5:17-19). But we cannot use it to gain salvation. This is not and never has been God's way. (***See Holiness***> *Law and Grace> Law> A mirror to view ourselves,* TopicGuide page A41.)

3:21-26 From 1:18–3:20, Paul explained the bad news of human sin and guilt and of divine judgment. The phrase "but now" (3:21) comes as a breath of fresh air as the apostle begins his explanation of the good news. The Greek word for "sin" (3:23) means "to miss the mark" and is drawn from the imagery of an archer shooting at a target but missing his mark. All are equally lost in God's sight since "everyone has sinned" and cannot match "God's glorious standard" (3:23). But God accepts both Jews and Gentiles fully and on an equal basis when they believe in Jesus.

VIRUS CONTROL

THE FIRST TIME GINA NOTICED something wrong with her computer, she shrugged it off. Her little cursor arrow began jumping around on her screen when she was not trying to move it. But then the problems became more troubling: Her computer turned itself off and restarted again—without her permission! Error messages popped up on the screen. Finally, her computer programs slowed to the point that she couldn't get her work done. She worked and worked on it, but failing to fix it, she took her laptop to a service technician. He performed diagnostic tests and found over 100 viruses. Her computer was totally infected and couldn't be cleaned up—it was beyond repair.

When Adam and Eve first sinned in the Garden of Eden, they infected the human race with sin (Romans 5:12). Since then, every person born on earth has been infected with the "sin virus," and we spread it on to others. Our nature (Psalm 51:5) and our actions are polluted with sin so that, left to ourselves, we have no hope of dealing with our sin problem.

In Romans 3, Paul reveals just how deep the problem of sin is. It impacts our morality, our minds, and our mouths. It fills our hearts with murderous thoughts and makes us miserable.

If we can't save ourselves, then God must act. His holy, perfect nature demands justice (Isaiah 5:16; Romans 2:2). He cannot allow the guilt and pollution of sin to spread unchecked. He must take action against that which distorts and destroys His creation. He must take action against that which breaks His laws—otherwise, He would be a negligent judge.

This is where the gospel starts to make sense. If we are still imagining we are only slightly bothered by sin and able to save ourselves, then we have no reason to trust in the gospel—we can just try harder and eventually save ourselves. But if we are spiritually dead (Ephesians 2:1) and unable to do anything to save ourselves (John 15:5), then no one but God Himself can help us. By substituting Jesus, the sinless Son of God, for us, God's justice is satisfied.

The problem of that awful soul-virus, the guilt and pollution of sin, is also solved because we are united to Christ (Galatians 3:26-28) and given access to all the blessings given to Him by the Father (John 1:16; Ephesians 3:6; Revelation 21:7)—including His perfect, righteous, holy standing before God. This is the message of Romans: The grave problem of life-sapping sin can only be solved by the death of Christ (Romans 5:15-21).

them in what He would do in this present time. God did this to demonstrate His righteous-
ness, for He Himself is fair and just, and He declares sinners to be right in His sight when
they believe in Jesus.
[27]Can we boast, then, that we have done anything to be accepted by God? No, because
our acquittal is not based on obeying the law. It is based on faith. [28]So we are made right
with God through faith and not by obeying the law.
[29]After all, is God the God of the Jews only? Isn't He also the God of the Gentiles? Of
course He is. [30]There is only one God, and He makes people right with Himself only by
faith, whether they are Jews or Gentiles.* [31]Well then, if we emphasize faith, does this
mean that we can forget about the law? Of course not! In fact, only when we have faith do
we truly fulfill the law.

3:27 Rom 2:17; 4:2; 1 Cor 1:29-31
3:28 Acts 13:39
3:29 Rom 10:12; Gal 3:28
3:31 Matt 5:17

THE FAITH OF ABRAHAM

4 Abraham was, humanly speaking, the founder of our Jewish nation. What did He dis-
cover about being made right with God? [2]If his good deeds had made him acceptable
to God, He would have had something to boast about. But that was not God's way. [3]For
the Scriptures tell us, "Abraham believed God, and God counted him as righteous because
of his faith."*
[4]When people work, their wages are not a gift, but something they have earned. [5]But
people are counted as righteous, not because of their work, but because of their faith in
God who forgives sinners. [6]David also spoke of this when he described the happiness of
those who are declared righteous without working for it:

[7] "Oh, what joy for those
whose disobedience is forgiven,
whose sins are put out of sight.
[8] Yes, what joy for those
whose record the LORD has cleared of sin."*

[9]Now, is this blessing only for the Jews, or is it also for uncircumcised Gentiles?* Well, we
have been saying that Abraham was counted as righteous by God because of his faith. [10]But
how did this happen? Was he counted as righteous only after he was circumcised, or was it
before he was circumcised? Clearly, God accepted Abraham before he was circumcised!

4:2 1 Cor 1:31
4:3 *Gen 15:6; Gal 3:6; Jas 2:23
4:4 Rom 11:6; Gal 2:16
4:7-8 *Ps 32:1-2; 2 Cor 5:19
4:9 Gen 15:6; Rom 3:30

3:30 Greek *whether they are circumcised or uncircumcised.* 4:3 Gen 15:6. 4:7-8 Ps 32:1-2 (Greek version). 4:9 Greek *is this blessing only for the circumcised, or is it also for the uncircumcised?*

3:27-31 Paul draws a logical conclusion from his discussion of sin and salvation thus far: A person cannot boast about gaining favor with God since he cannot do anything to earn it. Good deeds cannot save someone because sin pollutes all human activity—even our best works. Thus, salvation must be based on faith and not obedience to the law (3:28). Faith in Christ does not nullify the law, but fulfills it, as Paul's discussion in 4:1-8 explains.

4:1-3 Abraham was declared righteous without good works and before he was circumcised (see note at 4:9-12). The Jews acknowledge Abraham as a precedent for their relationship with God because he was "the founder of our Jewish nation" (4:1). Paul quotes Genesis 15:6 to show that Abraham's salvation was based not on good works but on the fact that he believed God (4:3). In 4:6-8, Paul uses another Old Testament saint, King David, as an example of salvation by faith.

4:4-8 Paul uses the workplace to make a point about works in 4:4. A person who has a job receives wages for his work, "not a gift" (literally "grace") from his employer.

▸ SALVATION

4:4-5 Earning salvation. Many people choose to rely on their own works, rather than God's grace, to obtain salvation. But there is one key problem with such self-reliance: unbelief in God's ordained means of salvation. The great tragedy of working for your salvation is that no one ever accomplishes it. Only Jesus can provide salvation, which is received by faith (Hebrews 10:39), through grace (Titus 2:11). Ironically, no one can offer anything to God in exchange for their salvation—except their wretched sin. Do you know people who try to make atonement for their own sin? Do you know people who refuse to trust God and trust instead in rituals or institutions for their salvation? Warn them away from such foolishness (Galatians 2:21). (***See Salvation****> Receiving> How> Faith in Christ,* TopicGuide page A22.)

4:9-12 Circumcision was such an important ritual in Jewish life that many Jews believed an uncircumcised man could never be saved (compare Acts 15:1). Circumcision was "a sign" (4:11; see Genesis 17:11) of Abraham's covenant with God. God physically marked him so he and the entire world could understand he was "the spiritual father" (4:12) of all believers, Jews and Gentiles.

11 Circumcision was a sign that Abraham already had faith and that God had already accepted him and declared him to be righteous—even before he was circumcised. So Abraham is the spiritual father of those who have faith but have not been circumcised. They are counted as righteous because of their faith. 12 And Abraham is also the spiritual father of those who have been circumcised, but only if they have the same kind of faith Abraham had before he was circumcised.

13 Clearly, God's promise to give the whole earth to Abraham and his descendants was based not on his obedience to God's law, but on a right relationship with God that comes by faith. 14 If God's promise is only for those who obey the law, then faith is not necessary and the promise is pointless. 15 For the law always brings punishment on those who try to obey it. (The only way to avoid breaking the law is to have no law to break!)

16 So the promise is received by faith. It is given as a free gift. And we are all certain to receive it, whether or not we live according to the law of Moses, if we have faith like Abraham's. For Abraham is the father of all who believe. 17 That is what the Scriptures mean when God told him, "I have made you the father of many nations."* This happened because Abraham believed in the God who brings the dead back to life and who creates new things out of nothing.

18 Even when there was no reason for hope, Abraham kept hoping—believing that he would become the father of many nations. For God had said to him, "That's how many descendants you will have!"* 19 And Abraham's faith did not weaken, even though, at about 100 years of age, he figured his body was as good as dead—and so was Sarah's womb. 20 Abraham never wavered in believing God's promise. In fact, his faith grew stronger, and in this he brought glory to God. 21 He was fully convinced that God is able to do whatever He promises. 22 And because of Abraham's faith, God counted him as righteous. 23 And when God counted him as righteous, it wasn't just for Abraham's benefit. It was recorded 24 for our benefit, too, assuring us that God will also count us as righteous if we believe in Him, the One who raised Jesus our Lord from the dead. 25 He was handed over to die because of our sins, and He was raised to life to make us right with God.

FAITH BRINGS JOY

5 Therefore, since we have been made right in God's sight by faith, we have peace with God because of what Jesus Christ our Lord has done for us. 2 Because of our faith,

4:11 Gen 17:10-11
4:13 Gen 18:18; 22:17-18; Gal 3:29
4:14 Gal 3:18
4:15 Rom 3:20; 7:12; 1 Cor 15:55-56; Gal 3:10
4:16 Gal 3:7
4:17 *Gen 17:5; Isa 48:13; John 5:21; 1 Cor 1:28
4:18 *Gen 15:5
4:19 Gen 17:17; 18:11; Heb 11:11
4:22 *Gen 15:6; Rom 4:3
4:24 1 Pet 1:21
4:25 Isa 53:4-5; Rom 8:30; 1 Cor 15:17; 2 Cor 5:15; 1 Pet 1:21
5:1 Rom 3:28
5:2 Eph 2:18; 3:12

4:17 Gen 17:5. **4:18** Gen 15:5.

4:13-17 God's promise to Abraham (Genesis 12:1-3) and His covenant with him (Genesis 15) were based on God's grace that Abraham received by faith (4:13). In a theme repeated throughout Paul's writings, law-based salvation nullifies faith and makes God's promise "pointless" (4:14).

▸ GOD
4:18-25 Maturing faith. The first steps of our spiritual walk can be shaky. Abraham laughed when God told him that he would have a child through the elderly Sarah (Genesis 17:17), but he still believed that God would make good on His promise of giving Abraham descendants as numerous as the stars. God provides His children with a faith that believes He can do anything (Ephesians 2:9-10), and this is the kind of faith that Abraham demonstrated. Don't let faltering first steps of faith convince you that your faith isn't real—keep trusting, keep loving, and keep marching forward, always trusting that the God who started your spiritual journey will be faithful to help you complete it (Philippians 1:6). (***See God****> God's Attributes> Faithful> God faithfully matures believers,* TopicGuide page A16.)

5:1-2 "Therefore" looks back to all that Paul has said in chapters 1–4 about salvation, which he summarizes here by saying, "we have been made right in God's sight by faith" (5:1). He now begins his discussion of the nature of the life of faith, showing that faith in Christ leads to a life characterized by peace (chapter 5), sanctification (chapter 6), freedom from the law (chapter 7), and the powerful indwelling of the Holy Spirit (chapter 8).

▸ GOD
5:1 Peace through faith. Ever since the first man, Adam, rebelled against God, all humanity has been at odds with Him (5:12). It is as if the head of our nation has declared war on another nation—even though we were not involved in the decision, we are nonetheless at war. But the removal of sin "by the death of His Son" (5:10) brought reconciliation to sinners who believe, resulting in "peace with God" (5:1). Sinners are no longer God's enemies, but are placed in His family as sons, a concept Paul develops in chapter 8. Do you feel at peace with God? Do you see that Jesus made a peace treaty between God and those who believe? Trust in God's Word and "rejoice" (5:3) in what Christ has done for those who believe. (***See God****> Salvation> Son> Reconciles us to God,* TopicGuide page A15.)

Christ has brought us into this place of undeserved privilege where we now stand, and we
confidently and joyfully look forward to sharing God's glory.
[3]We can rejoice, too, when we run into problems and trials, for we know that they help
us develop endurance. [4]And endurance develops strength of character, and character
strengthens our confident hope of salvation. [5]And this hope will not lead to disappoint-
ment. For we know how dearly God loves us, because He has given us the Holy Spirit to fill
our hearts with His love.
[6]When we were utterly helpless, Christ came at just the right time and died for us sin-
ners. [7]Now, most people would not be willing to die for an upright person, though some-
one might perhaps be willing to die for a person who is especially good. [8]But God showed
His great love for us by sending Christ to die for us while we were still sinners. [9]And since
we have been made right in God's sight by the blood of Christ, He will certainly save us
from God's condemnation. [10]For since our friendship with God was restored by the death
of His Son while we were still His enemies, we will certainly be saved through the life of
His Son. [11]So now we can rejoice in our wonderful new relationship with God because our
Lord Jesus Christ has made us friends of God.

5:3 Matt 5:12
5:5 2 Cor 1:22; Gal 4:6; Eph 1:13; Phil 1:20
5:6 Gal 4:4; Eph 5:2
5:8 John 3:16; 1 Jn 4:10
5:9 Rom 1:18; 2:5, 8
5:10 Rom 8:34; 2 Cor 5:18-19; Eph 2:3

5:3-5 The Christian life is marked by "problems and trials" (5:3), but this is by God's design to help believers grow and depend more on Him. Paul mentions the Holy Spirit infrequently early in Romans (1:4; 2:29; 5:5), anticipating a more extensive explanation of the Holy Spirit's role in the life of believers in chapter 8, in which the Spirit is mentioned 20 times.

5:6-11 Paul describes unbelievers in four ways in verses 6-10: "utterly helpless" and "sinners" (literally, "ungodly") in verse 6; "sinners" in verse 8; and "enemies" in verse 10. Such negative terms reinforce the truth that we are completely sinful and without hope of saving ourselves.

▶ ADOPTION

5:8-9 Measuring God's love. It's not unheard of for enemies to show respect for one another. But God's love goes far beyond anything we've ever imagined—He showed His love to His enemies by sending His own Son to die for them. That is love! This love, expressed through the shedding of the blood of Christ, saves believers from God's judgment (5:9). In Romans 1:18, God's wrath is a present reality; by Romans 2:5 it awaits a future time of judgment. Here Paul shows that Christ's death saves believers from both—God's wrath in the present and in the future. This is the measure of the love of God—Christ's outstretched arms on the cross. (***See Adoption***> *With Christ*> *United with Christ*> *Loved by God,* TopicGuide page A37.)

MY RESPONSE TO GOD

Peace with God

ROMANS 5

The minister's life crumbled around him. He lost his job, divorced his wife, and lived in shame. Before this happened, he had been known as a man of the Word, a man of prayer, a man who had unusual gifts and abilities to discern the will of God. He had led thousands of people to Christ. What happened?

The former minister sadly explained, "There is a saying, 'Sin will keep you from God's Word, or God's Word will keep you from sin.' I knew and believed that, but my life got so busy that I more and more ceased to depend on the Lord and His Word until finally there was little time for God at all. That is when I fell into sin."

That is how Adam and Eve fell–they stopped paying attention to God's instructions (Genesis 3:1-7). They pursued one moment of fruitless rebellion, but in exchange, they lost almost all the blessings God had given them. God was gracious to the minister who fell, He was gracious to Adam and Eve, and He can be gracious to you, too. But you must humble yourself before Him. You must offer God nothing but your sin, and accept from Him what you could never get on your own–peace with God through our Lord Jesus Christ (Romans 5:1-11).

5:12
ADAM AND CHRIST CONTRASTED

Gen 2:17; 3:19 12 When Adam sinned, sin entered the world. Adam's sin brought death, so death spread
Rom 6:23
1 Cor 15:21-22 to everyone, for everyone sinned. 13 Yes, people sinned even before the law was given.
5:13 But it was not counted as sin because there was not yet any law to break. 14 Still, everyone
Rom 4:15 died—from the time of Adam to the time of Moses—even those who did not disobey an ex-
5:14 plicit commandment of God, as Adam did. Now Adam is a symbol, a representation of
1 Cor 15:22, 45 Christ, who was yet to come. 15 But there is a great difference between Adam's sin and
God's gracious gift. For the sin of this one man, Adam, brought death to many. But even
greater is God's wonderful grace and His gift of forgiveness to many through this other
man, Jesus Christ. 16 And the result of God's gracious gift is very different from the result of
5:17 that one man's sin. For Adam's sin led to condemnation, but God's free gift leads to our be-
1 Cor 15:21 ing made right with God, even though we are guilty of many sins. 17 For the sin of this one
5:18 man, Adam, caused death to rule over many. But even greater is God's wonderful grace
Isa 53:11 and His gift of righteousness, for all who receive it will live in triumph over sin and death
1 Cor 15:22
5:19 through this one man, Jesus Christ.
Phil 2:8 18 Yes, Adam's one sin brings condemnation for everyone, but Christ's one act of righ-
5:20 teousness brings a right relationship with God and new life for everyone. 19 Because one
Rom 4:15; 7:8 person disobeyed God, many became sinners. But because one other person obeyed God,
Gal 3:19 many will be made righteous.
5:21
Rom 6:23 20 God's law was given so that all people could see how sinful they were. But as people
sinned more and more, God's wonderful grace became more abundant. 21 So just as sin
ruled over all people and brought them to death, now God's wonderful grace rules instead,
giving us right standing with God and resulting in eternal life through Jesus Christ our Lord.
6:1
Rom 3:5-8

6:2
SIN'S POWER IS BROKEN

Rom 8:13 **6** Well then, should we keep on sinning so that God can show us more and more of His
Col 2:20; 3:3 wonderful grace? 2 Of course not! Since we have died to sin, how can we continue to
6:3
Gal 3:27 live in it? 3 Or have you forgotten that when we were joined with Christ Jesus in baptism,
6:4 we joined Him in His death? 4 For we died and were buried with Christ by baptism. And just
Eph 4:22-24 as Christ was raised from the dead by the glorious power of the Father, now we also may
Col 2:12; 3:10 live new lives.

5:12-17 Paul traces every human sin ever committed in history back to Adam's one sin in the Garden of Eden (Genesis 3). Paul's teaching on original sin and corporate headship in these verses may be succinctly summarized as follows: A person isn't a sinner because he sins; he sins because he is a sinner, and he is a sinner because Adam sinned. Christ's death for sin reversed the death Adam's sin brought into the world, resulting in the provision of grace and a right relationship with God through faith in "one man, Jesus Christ" (5:17).

5:18-21 Paul's comparison of the effects of Adam's act of disobedience and Jesus' act of obedience is not intended to imply they are equal opposites. Just because all humanity (excepting Christ) is sinful and lost in Adam does not mean that all humanity is saved in Christ, for it is only those who fulfill the requirements of the gospel (1:16-17; 10:9-10) that receive Christ's benefits.

6:1–7:25 In chapters 6–7 Paul anticipates four questions that may arise about his teachings on salvation. The first question occurs in 6:1, and his answer comes in 6:2-14. Paul's statement in 6:14 about law and grace raises a second question in 6:15, which he answers in 6:16–7:6. Paul's teaching about the law in 7:4-6 raises a third question in 7:7a, which he answers in 7:7b-12. Finally, Paul's teaching about the law in 7:7b-12 raises a fourth question in 7:13a, which he answers in 7:13b-25. In response to all four questions, Paul immediately says, "Of course not!" (6:2, 15; 7:7, 13) before giving his full response.

▸ ADOPTION

6:3 Dying with Christ. Have you been baptized? Do you know it symbolizes that you died with Christ? But since you are obviously still alive and reading this note, that requires some explanation. Baptism demonstrates the spiritual unity we have with Christ (Galatians 3:27), and in that unity, we partake of all the blessings that belong to Jesus. He belongs to God's family—so do we (Galatians 3–4). Jesus is filled with the Holy Spirit (Luke 4:14)—so are we (Acts 2:4). If we are united to Christ, that means He not only died for us, but we also died with Him—so we will be resurrected from the dead; we will be given authority. What are the implications in your spiritual life if you have truly died with Christ? One of many is that we live as a creation reborn in God's eyes—that old life died with Christ and the new life has begun (2 Corinthians 5:17). Live the new life, and stay away from the old, decaying ways of the past. (***See Adoption*** *> With Christ> United with Christ> The exchanged life,* TopicGuide page A37.)

6:5-11 Believers are "united" with Christ in both His death and His resurrection, for His resurrection assures believers of their own resurrection as well (see 1 Corinthians 15:12-23).

[5]Since we have been united with Him in His death, we will also be raised to life as He was.
[6]We know that our old sinful selves were crucified with Christ so that sin might lose its
power in our lives. We are no longer slaves to sin. [7]For when we died with Christ we were set
free from the power of sin. [8]And since we died with Christ, we know we will also live with
Him. [9]We are sure of this because Christ was raised from the dead, and He will never die
again. Death no longer has any power over Him. [10]When He died, He died once to break the
power of sin. But now that He lives, He lives for the glory of God. [11]So you also should con-
sider yourselves to be dead to the power of sin and alive to God through Christ Jesus.
[12]Do not let sin control the way you live;* do not give in to sinful desires. [13]Do not let

6:5 Phil 3:10-11 Col 2:12; 3:1
6:6 Gal 2:20; 5:24 Col 2:12
6:7 1 Pet 4:1
6:10 Heb 7:27
6:11 Col 2:20; 3:3

6:12 Or *Do not let sin reign in your body, which is subject to death.*

▸ ADOPTION

6:11-14 Victory over sin. Have you ever tried to count how many times you sin each day? Try it—it's quite enlightening to do a moral inventory of your sinful thoughts, words, and deeds. The good news is that God empowers us to refuse to give in to temptation and sin—but the choice is ours to make. This is the reason Paul commands believers to stop letting sin control them. Even though Christ has died for their sins and they are dead to sin and no longer under its authority, believers can continue to live as if sin still controls them. Sins are committed in the body (see 1 Corinthians 6:12-20; 1 Thessalonians 4:3-4), so Paul calls on believers to take control of their bodies' activities by using them for God's glory instead of using them for "evil" (6:13). Do something very risky—ask God to reveal your sin to you. Then ask Him for the grace to sin less than you did the day before, and dedicate yourself to submitting to His sanctifying work in your life (Ephesians 4:30). (***See Adoption***> *With Christ*> *Supernatural*> *Dead to sin but alive to God,* TopicGuide page A37.)

6:12-14 Paul advises the Romans that putting themselves back under the authority of the Mosaic covenant will only lead to more sin. This happens because the law naturally reveals sin in the believer's heart (7:4-6), but it also makes more sin possible through giving greater knowledge of God and ourselves, and thus greater responsibility. Paul discusses the implications of this statement about law and grace starting with the question in 6:15 and continuing to the end of chapter 7.

MY RESPONSE TO GOD

Saved from What?

ROMANS 6–8

For a while, Adam and Eve lived in perfection, but they eventually succumbed to temptation and sinned against God (Genesis 3). We were designed to live in perfection, too (Luke 10:27; Romans 13:8), but we also have sinned and fallen short of God's standard (Romans 3:23).

Can we ever be restored to that perfection? By the grace of God, yes.

First, God saves us from the *penalty* of sin. Through the new birth (John 3), we are "made right with God through Christ" (2 Corinthians 5:21).

Second, God frees us from the *power* of sin. Our sinful nature still influences us, and we continue to commit many sins no matter how much we grow to hate it. Often we cry out in frustration with Paul, "Oh, what a miserable person I am! Who will free me from this life that is dominated by sin and death?" (Romans 7:24). Of course it is God who will save us. "Because you belong to Him, the power of the life-giving Spirit has freed you from the power of sin that leads to death" (Romans 8:2). The Holy Spirit sanctifies us, slowly freeing us from sin's hold on us (Romans 8:23).

Third, God will one day deliver us from the *presence* of sin. The process of sanctification is painful, but it is nothing compared to the perfection that awaits us! After we die, we will see Him as He really is, unstained by sin and sorrow and guilt, and "we will be like Him" (1 John 3:2). In that moment, we will be changed, for every curse of sin that has plagued us will flee before our loving Father's gaze.

6:13 Rom 12:1; 2 Cor 5:14
6:14 Rom 7:4, 6; 8:2, 12; Gal 5:18; 1 Jn 3:16
6:16 John 8:34; 2 Pet 2:19
6:17 2 Tim 1:13
6:18 John 8:32
6:21 Rom 7:5; 8:6, 13
6:22 John 8:32; Rom 8:2; 1 Cor 7:22; 1 Pet 1:9; 2:16
6:23 Matt 25:46; John 3:16; 17:2; Rom 5:21; Gal 6:8
7:2 1 Cor 7:39
7:3 Luke 16:18
7:4 Rom 6:6; 8:2; Gal 5:18; Col 2:14; 1 Pet 2:24
7:5 Rom 6:21; 8:8; Gal 5:19-21

any part of your body become an instrument of evil to serve sin. Instead, give yourselves
completely to God, for you were dead, but now you have new life. So use your whole
body as an instrument to do what is right for the glory of God. [14]Sin is no longer your mas-
ter, for you no longer live under the requirements of the law. Instead, you live under the
freedom of God's grace.

[15]Well then, since God's grace has set us free from the law, does that mean we can go
on sinning? Of course not! [16]Don't you realize that you become the slave of whatever you
choose to obey? You can be a slave to sin, which leads to death, or you can choose to
obey God, which leads to righteous living. [17]Thank God! Once you were slaves of sin, but
now you wholeheartedly obey this teaching we have given you. [18]Now you are free from
your slavery to sin, and you have become slaves to righteous living.

[19]Because of the weakness of your human nature, I am using the illustration of slavery
to help you understand all this. Previously, you let yourselves be slaves to impurity and
lawlessness, which led ever deeper into sin. Now you must give yourselves to be slaves to
righteous living so that you will become holy.

[20]When you were slaves to sin, you were free from the obligation to do right. [21]And
what was the result? You are now ashamed of the things you used to do, things that end in
eternal doom. [22]But now you are free from the power of sin and have become slaves of
God. Now you do those things that lead to holiness and result in eternal life. [23]For the
wages of sin is death, but the free gift of God is eternal life through Christ Jesus our Lord.

NO LONGER BOUND TO THE LAW

7 Now, dear brothers and sisters*—you who are familiar with the law—don't you know
that the law applies only while a person is living? [2]For example, when a woman mar-
ries, the law binds her to her husband as long as he is alive. But if he dies, the laws of mar-
riage no longer apply to her. [3]So while her husband is alive, she would be committing
adultery if she married another man. But if her husband dies, she is free from that law and
does not commit adultery when she remarries.

[4]So, my dear brothers and sisters, this is the point: You died to the power of the law when
you died with Christ. And now you are united with the One who was raised from the dead.
As a result, we can produce a harvest of good deeds for God. [5]When we were controlled by

7:1 Greek *brothers;* also in 7:4.

6:15-19 The question in 6:15 is similar to the one in 6:1, but the emphasis is different. Romans 6:1 asks whether believers should continue to sin to receive more of God's constant grace. Verse 15 asks whether believers may continue to sin since they do not relate to God by law but by grace. But the answer is the same: "Of course not!" In 6:19, Paul explains that he is using the analogy of slavery to simplify and illustrate the believer's relationship to sin and righteousness, but he also warns the reader not to press the analogy too far.

▸ADOPTION

6:19 Living free. The liberty to perform any and every act of sin and wickedness is often trumpeted as true liberty, but anyone who has ever sinned knows that's a lie. The truth is that slavery to sin is the most abusive form of slavery a person can experience, while freedom from sin is the most liberating freedom a person can enjoy. Before conversion, all are "slaves to impurity and lawlessness"; after conversion to Christ, we exchange masters and become "slaves to righteous living" (6:19), enabling us to enjoy to the fullest our relationship with God through Christ. Everyone is either a slave to sin or a slave to righteousness. Live in a manner consistent with your identity in Christ—as a slave to righteousness. (***See Adoption> With Christ> Supernatural> A life of liberating freedom,*** TopicGuide page A37.)

6:20-23 Paul previously used accounting terms to describe salvation (Romans 4:4-8), and in 6:23 he does the same to contrast the way we receive sin and eternal life. If someone could cash in the value of sin, the transaction would give him nothing but death. The price of eternal life was God's Son; the debt was paid in full, so the believer receives eternal life as a free gift by faith (see Ephesians 2:8-9).

7:1-6 Paul's answer to the question about sin that began in 6:1, then developed further in 6:15, is answered in these verses. Paul does not attempt to be thorough in his discussion of marriage and remarriage (as in 1 Corinthians 7); he simply uses marriage to make a point in his continuing discussion about the believer's relationship with the law.

7:4-5 The married woman is analogous to the believer, and the first husband is analogous to the law. Christ is the second husband. The death of the first husband means that the wife is dead to that relationship and free to marry another. Similarly, the believer's identity with Christ on the cross means that he has died to the law; that is, the law no longer has authority over him.

our old nature,* sinful desires were at work within us, and the law aroused these evil desires
that produced a harvest of sinful deeds, resulting in death. 6But now we have been released
from the law, for we died to it and are no longer captive to its power. Now we can serve God,
not in the old way of obeying the letter of the law, but in the new way of living in the Spirit.

GOD'S LAW REVEALS OUR SIN

7Well then, am I suggesting that the law of God is sinful? Of course not! In fact, it was the
law that showed me my sin. I would never have known that coveting is wrong if the law
had not said, "You must not covet."* 8But sin used this command to arouse all kinds of cov-
etous desires within me! If there were no law, sin would not have that power. 9At one time
I lived without understanding the law. But when I learned the command not to covet, for
instance, the power of sin came to life, 10and I died. So I discovered that the law's com-
mands, which were supposed to bring life, brought spiritual death instead. 11Sin took ad-
vantage of those commands and deceived me; it used the commands to kill me. 12But still,
the law itself is holy, and its commands are holy and right and good.
13But how can that be? Did the law, which is good, cause my death? Of course not! Sin
used what was good to bring about my condemnation to death. So we can see how terri-
ble sin really is. It uses God's good commands for its own evil purposes.

STRUGGLING WITH SIN

14So the trouble is not with the law, for it is spiritual and good. The trouble is with me, for I
am all too human, a slave to sin. 15I don't really understand myself, for I want to do what is
right, but I don't do it. Instead, I do what I hate. 16But if I know that what I am doing is
wrong, this shows that I agree that the law is good. 17So I am not the one doing wrong; it is
sin living in me that does it.
18And I know that nothing good lives in me, that is, in my sinful nature.* I want to do
what is right, but I can't. 19I want to do what is good, but I don't. I don't want to do what is
wrong, but I do it anyway. 20But if I do what I don't want to do, I am not really the one do-
ing wrong; it is sin living in me that does it.
21I have discovered this principle of life—that when I want to do what is right, I inevitably
do what is wrong. 22I love God's law with all my heart. 23But there is another power* within
me that is at war with my mind. This power makes me a slave to the sin that is still within
me. 24Oh, what a miserable person I am! Who will free me from this life that is dominated by
sin and death? 25Thank God! The answer is in Jesus Christ our Lord. So you see how it is: In
my mind I really want to obey God's law, but because of my sinful nature I am a slave to sin.

7:6 2 Cor 3:6; Gal 5:22; Phil 3:3
7:7 *Exod 20:17; *Deut 5:21; Rom 4:15
7:8 Rom 4:15
7:10 Lev 18:5; Rom 10:5; 2 Cor 3:7; Gal 3:12
7:11 Gen 3:13; Heb 3:13
7:12 1 Tim 1:8
7:14 1 Kgs 21:20-25; Rom 3:9; 6:6
7:15 Gal 5:17
7:18 Gen 6:5; 8:21; John 3:6; Rom 8:3
7:21 Rom 8:2
7:22 Pss 1:2; 40:8
7:23 Gal 5:17; Jas 4:1; 1 Pet 2:11
7:24 Rom 6:6; 8:2
7:25 Rom 6:16, 22; 1 Cor 15:57; 2 Cor 2:14

7:5 Greek *When we were in the flesh.* 7:7 Exod 20:17; Deut 5:21. 7:18 Greek *my flesh;* also in 7:25. 7:23 Greek *law;* also in 7:23b.

7:7-12 From verse 12 to the end of the chapter, Paul uses himself as a prototype regarding the struggle with the law, sin, and the Christian life. Despite the fact that the law is perfect (7:12), Paul realized that the law could never provide the spiritual life God wanted for him. He eventually understood the true purpose of the law—for Paul, "the power of sin came to life, and I died" (7:9-10).

7:13-20 Paul's comments in verses 7-12 raise a question about the law: "Did the law, which is good, cause my death?" The "death" is not a literal spiritual or physical death, but a decline in spiritual health or faith.

▸ HOLINESS
7:17-18 Wrestling with sin. Paul's struggle with sin sounds so much like our own—can someone as mature as Paul still experience so much conflict with sin? Clearly he can. Paul says that he knows the right things to do, but sin permeates everything—even his desire to not sin! Sin is organic, permeating Paul's body and desires and deeds (7:5). But it is also spiritual, described as a "sinful nature" (7:18, 25) that controls the mind (8:6). What hope do we have? Are we doomed to a life of wrestling with sin? Yes—but it's a fight that we will win. Christ guarantees the very best outcome we can hope for, for every struggle is a means of growth (5:3-5). God will use even our sin as a part of His magnificent plan to save us (8:1-4). Sin remains, but God's grace remains as well, freeing us from sin's slavery and leading us into more and more freedom. (***See Holiness****> Disciplines> Of Abstinence> Resisting sinful urges,* TopicGuide page A42.)

7:21-25 In dramatic and seemingly despairing language, Paul concludes his discussion of the law and the believer by continuing to use himself as a prototype. Paul's love for God's law did not provide the power he needed to keep it. Paul knew that sin remained in his body, and it would cause him to lose spiritual vitality and power in his Christian life. Attempting to keep the law caused this, and only Jesus Christ and the power of the Spirit could change such horrible defeat into victory, as Paul explains in chapter 8.

8:2 Rom 8:11 2 Cor 3:6 Gal 2:19; 5:1
8:3 Acts 13:38 2 Cor 5:21 Phil 2:7 Heb 2:14; 4:15
8:4 Gal 5:16, 25
8:6 Rom 6:23 Gal 6:8
8:9 John 14:17-18, 23 Gal 4:6 Phil 1:19 1 Pet 1:11
8:10 John 14:20; 15:5; 17:23, 26 2 Cor 13:5 Col 1:26-27
8:11 Rom 6:5 1 Cor 6:14; 15:45
8:13 Gal 6:8 Col 3:5
8:14 John 1:12 Gal 3:26 Rev 21:7
8:15 Gal 4:5-6
8:16 2 Cor 1:22 Eph 1:13
8:17 Gal 3:29; 4:7

LIFE IN THE SPIRIT

8 So now there is no condemnation for those who belong to Christ Jesus. 2And because
you belong to Him, the power* of the life-giving Spirit has freed you* from the power
of sin that leads to death. 3The law of Moses was unable to save us because of the weak-
ness of our sinful nature.* So God did what the law could not do. He sent His own Son in a
body like the bodies we sinners have. And in that body God declared an end to sin's con-
trol over us by giving His Son as a sacrifice for our sins. 4He did this so that the just require-
ment of the law would be fully satisfied for us, who no longer follow our sinful nature but
instead follow the Spirit.

5Those who are dominated by the sinful nature think about sinful things, but those who
are controlled by the Holy Spirit think about things that please the Spirit. 6So letting your
sinful nature control your mind leads to death. But letting the Spirit control your mind
leads to life and peace. 7For the sinful nature is always hostile to God. It never did obey
God's laws, and it never will. 8That's why those who are still under the control of their sin-
ful nature can never please God.

9But you are not controlled by your sinful nature. You are controlled by the Spirit if you
have the Spirit of God living in you. (And remember that those who do not have the Spirit
of Christ living in them do not belong to Him at all.) 10And Christ lives within you, so even
though your body will die because of sin, the Spirit gives you life* because you have been
made right with God. 11The Spirit of God, who raised Jesus from the dead, lives in you.
And just as God raised Christ Jesus from the dead, He will give life to your mortal bodies
by this same Spirit living within you.

12Therefore, dear brothers and sisters,* you have no obligation to do what your sinful
nature urges you to do. 13For if you live by its dictates, you will die. But if through the
power of the Spirit you put to death the deeds of your sinful nature,* you will live. 14For all
who are led by the Spirit of God are children* of God.

15So you have not received a spirit that makes you fearful slaves. Instead, you received
God's Spirit when He adopted you as His own children.* Now we call Him, "Abba, Father."*
16For His Spirit joins with our spirit to affirm that we are God's children. 17And since we are
His children, we are His heirs. In fact, together with Christ we are heirs of God's glory. But if
we are to share His glory, we must also share His suffering.

8:2a Greek *the law;* also in 8:2b. 8:2b Some manuscripts read *me.* 8:3 Greek *our flesh;* similarly in 8:4, 5, 6, 7, 8, 9, 12. 8:10 Or *your spirit is alive.* 8:12 Greek *brothers;* also in 8:29. 8:13 Greek *deeds of the body.* 8:14 Greek *sons;* also in 8:19. 8:15a Greek *you received a spirit of sonship.* 8:15b *Abba* is an Aramaic term for "father."

8:1-39 Romans 8 contains Paul's concluding argument on living by faith. This chapter has two major parts: Verses 1-17 explain how to live by faith in the power of the Spirit; verses 18-39 show that God's plan of salvation for His children cannot fail, since He has sovereignly predetermined our glorious future with Him. But our glorious future does not do away with pain; all God's people will suffer since they are united to His Son.

▸ SPIRITUAL WARFARE
8:1 Not guilty. What God says about believers is reality— anything different is a lie. God says that believers are not and will never be condemned. God has already meted out the punishment for your sin through the cross of Christ, and He has declared that you—His child—can never be under His condemnation. Therefore, never let anyone or anything make you think that God is mad at you. You will experience His loving discipline but never His condemnation. In 8:34 Paul asks who will condemn one of God's children. The answer is, "No one!" Certainly not God Himself, for He has said you are in a right relationship with Him. The next time you hear the voice of condemnation in your ears, shout triumphantly, "No condemnation!" (***See Spiritual Warfare***> *Resisting Sin and Evil*> *Putting On and Off*> *Taking Off*> *The yoke of legalism,* TopicGuide page A46.)

8:5-11 In these verses, Paul continues to contrast the physical side of our struggle with sin with the intervention of the Holy Spirit. The body and its desires act as the rudder for the unbeliever, while the Holy Spirit guides the believer. Paul's purpose in mentioning the resurrection at this point is to highlight that the same Spirit that will raise all believers from the dead for eternal life with the Lord is available to us now—just as surely as Jesus lives, we can live by faith and please God today.

8:12-17 Being placed under the law again condemns Christians, and they "will die" (8:13). Neither physical nor spiritual death is at stake; instead, Christians are in danger of sapping their own spiritual vitality. Paul is saying to believers who still want to live under the law, "You're killing yourselves!" But if they live by the power of the Spirit and refuse to put themselves back under the law, they will live; that is, they will experience true spiritual vitality.

THE FUTURE GLORY

[18]Yet what we suffer now is nothing compared to the glory He will reveal to us later. [19]For
all creation is waiting eagerly for that future day when God will reveal who His children
really are. [20]Against its will, all creation was subjected to God's curse. But with eager hope,
[21]the creation looks forward to the day when it will join God's children in glorious freedom
from death and decay. [22]For we know that all creation has been groaning as in the pains of
childbirth right up to the present time. [23]And we believers also groan, even though we
have the Holy Spirit within us as a foretaste of future glory, for we long for our bodies to be
released from sin and suffering. We, too, wait with eager hope for the day when God will
give us our full rights as His adopted children,* including the new bodies He has promised
us. [24]We were given this hope when we were saved. (If we already have something, we
don't need to hope* for it. [25]But if we look forward to something we don't yet have, we
must wait patiently and confidently.)

[26]And the Holy Spirit helps us in our weakness. For example, we don't know what God
wants us to pray for. But the Holy Spirit prays for us with groanings that cannot be ex-
pressed in words. [27]And the Father who knows all hearts knows what the Spirit is saying,
for the Spirit pleads for us believers* in harmony with God's own will. [28]And we know that
God causes everything to work together* for the good of those who love God and are
called according to His purpose for them. [29]For God knew His people in advance, and He
chose them to become like His Son, so that His Son would be the firstborn among many

8:19 2 Pet 3:13; 1 Jn 3:2
8:21 Acts 3:21; 2 Pet 3:13; Rev 21:1
8:23 2 Cor 1:22; 5:5; Phil 3:21
8:24 2 Cor 5:7; 1 Thes 5:8
8:26 John 14:16
8:27 1 Cor 4:5
8:28 Eph 1:11; 3:11; 2 Tim 1:9
8:29 Eph 1:5; Col 1:18; 2 Tim 2:19; Heb 1:6; 1 Pet 1:2

8:23 Greek *wait anxiously for sonship.* 8:24 Some manuscripts read *wait.* 8:27 Greek *for God's holy people.* 8:28 Some manuscripts read *And we know that everything works together.*

8:18-27 In these verses, Paul explains further how suffering relates to God's redemptive purposes (see "suffering" in 8:17 and "suffer" in 8:18; see "glory" in 8:18, 30). The mysterious "groanings" of the Holy Spirit are mentioned in 8:26, amplifying the moans of creation and of believers. Since the Spirit is deity, He needs no words, for God knows the intent of the Spirit (8:26-27; compare 1 John 5:14).

8:28-30 The sufferings endured by believers are neither in vain nor outside of God's sovereign control. In fact, everything that happens to believers serves a wonderful purpose. Paul uses five verbs in these verses to explain God's plan for His children from beginning to end—God "knew," "chose," "called," gave "right standing," and "gave them His glory." These provide partial answers to questions such as, "Why did God save me?" and, "How did I become a Christian?"

▸ SALVATION

8:29 Chipping away. A little boy watched a sculptor begin chiseling a large slab of marble. The little boy watched in wonder as the marble slab eventually took on the face of Abraham Lincoln. "How did you do that?" the boy asked in amazement. The sculptor said with a smile, "All I have to do is chip away everything that doesn't look like Lincoln." Pain, persecution, stress, misunderstandings, and financial problems are all indications of your Father's commitment to your growth. Your loving Father uses the struggles of this life to chip away at the flaws in your character so that the end product (you!) will look like His Son. Thank God, the Master Sculptor of your soul, for His work in your life and His dedication to a glorious future (8:30). (***See Salvation**> Receiving> Results> Sanctification (progressive aspect),* TopicGuide page A23.)

BECAUSE GOD IS SOVEREIGN

I will joyfully submit to His will.

God causes everything to work together for the good of those who love God and are called according to His purpose for them.

ROMANS 8:28

FOR THE NEXT *GOD IS SOVEREIGN* FEATURE SEE PAGE 2146.

brothers and sisters. [30]And having chosen them, He called them to come to Him. And having called them, He gave them right standing with Himself. And having given them right standing, He gave them His glory.

NOTHING CAN SEPARATE US FROM GOD'S LOVE

[31]What shall we say about such wonderful things as these? If God is for us, who can ever be against us? [32]Since He did not spare even His own Son but gave Him up for us all, won't He also give us everything else? [33]Who dares accuse us whom God has chosen for His own? No one—for God Himself has given us right standing with Himself. [34]Who then will condemn us? No one—for Christ Jesus died for us and was raised to life for us, and He is sitting in the place of honor at God's right hand, pleading for us.

[35]Can anything ever separate us from Christ's love? Does it mean He no longer loves us if we have trouble or calamity, or are persecuted, or hungry, or destitute, or in danger, or threatened with death? [36](As the Scriptures say, "For your sake we are killed every day; we are being slaughtered like sheep."*) [37]No, despite all these things, overwhelming victory is ours through Christ, who loved us.

[38]And I am convinced that nothing can ever separate us from God's love. Neither death nor life, neither angels nor demons,* neither our fears for today nor our worries about tomorrow—not even the powers of hell can separate us from God's love. [39]No power in the sky above or in the earth below—indeed, nothing in all creation will ever be able to separate us from the love of God that is revealed in Christ Jesus our Lord.

GOD'S SELECTION OF ISRAEL

9 With Christ as my witness, I speak with utter truthfulness. My conscience and the Holy Spirit confirm it. [2]My heart is filled with bitter sorrow and unending grief [3]for my people, my Jewish brothers and sisters.* I would be willing to be forever cursed—cut off from Christ!—if that would save them. [4]They are the people of Israel, chosen to be God's adopted children.* God revealed His glory to them. He made covenants with them and gave them His law. He gave them the privilege of worshiping Him and receiving His wonderful promises. [5]Abraham, Isaac, and Jacob are their ancestors, and Christ Himself was an

8:31 Ps 118:6
8:32 John 3:16; Rom 4:25; 5:8
8:33 Isa 50:8
8:34 Ps 110:1; 1 Jn 2:1
8:35 1 Cor 4:11; 2 Cor 11:26-27
8:36 *Ps 44:22
8:37 John 16:33; 1 Cor 15:57; 1 Jn 5:4
8:38 John 10:28; Col 3:3
8:39 Rom 5:3-8
9:1 1 Tim 2:7
9:3 Exod 32:32
9:4 Exod 4:22; Deut 4:13; 7:6; Eph 2:12
9:5 John 1:1, 18; Rom 1:3; Titus 2:13; 2 Pet 1:1; 1 Jn 5:20

8:36 Ps 44:22. 8:38 Greek *nor rulers.* 9:3 Greek *my brothers.* 9:4 Greek *chosen for sonship.*

8:31-39 Romans 8:31-35 contain a series of rhetorical questions that help Paul come to his conclusion in 8:37-39. Each question moves his argument forward and recalls previous themes developed in Romans. This section marks the climactic end of Paul's eight-chapter argument that the best hope for those who wish to serve God is to live by faith in His gracious promises.

▸ GOD
8:38-39 How secure are you? Hanging from the side of a mountain, the climber is only as secure as his equipment. This holds true in the spiritual realm as well. Who is responsible for your spiritual security? God is! And His strength is absolute. Your salvation is invulnerable—but not because of what you have done, can do, or will do. Paul explains in Romans 8 that eternal security is based on the power of God, His eternal purposes in salvation, Christ's death and resurrection, and the work of the Spirit in your life. All three Persons of the Trinity ensure your spiritual security—you do not. This is why Paul can say that nothing—whether past, present, or future, whether physical or metaphysical—can separate us from God's love in Christ. When all else fails around you, you can believe that God will accomplish His good purpose in you. (***See God****> God's Attributes> Eternal> The eternal God is the believer's source of security,* TopicGuide page A16.)

9:3 In Romans 9–11, Paul answers an unspoken but obvious objection to his message that salvation is received by grace through faith: what about the Jews? Since the blessings of the New Covenant would surpass all national boundaries (Romans 1:5, 16), would Israel be left behind? The message of salvation by grace through faith perhaps confused Gentile readers into thinking they were superior to the Jews in God's kingdom (Galatians 3:28). Paul's own grief (Romans 9:2-3) mixes with his wisdom, revealing profound hope for Jews and Gentiles alike.

▸ WORSHIP
9:5 Valuing tradition. God's people stand on God's Word—our faith and piety are directed by the Bible. But our understanding of the Bible is not limited to our own personal opinion. God has gifted us with valuable perspectives from saints who have gone before us as well. In this chapter, Paul encourages his readers to not ignore God's past dealings with Israel, but to reflect on them, using them to understand God's redemptive work among the Jews in the future. Trust God's Word above all, but do not ignore theology, history, or classic books of the Christian faith. By standing on the shoulders of giants who have gone before us, we may see God and His actions more clearly. (***See Worship****> OT> Reverence> For those who came before,* TopicGuide page A29.)

Israelite as far as His human nature is concerned. And He is God, the One who rules over
everything and is worthy of eternal praise! Amen.*
6Well then, has God failed to fulfill His promise to Israel? No, for not all who are born
into the nation of Israel are truly members of God's people! 7Being descendants of
Abraham doesn't make them truly Abraham's children. For the Scriptures say, "Isaac is the
son through whom your descendants will be counted,"* though Abraham had other
children, too. 8This means that Abraham's physical descendants are not necessarily
children of God. Only the children of the promise are considered to be Abraham's chil-
dren. 9For God had promised, "I will return about this time next year, and Sarah will have
a son."*
10This son was our ancestor Isaac. When he married Rebekah, she gave birth to twins.*
11But before they were born, before they had done anything good or bad, she received a
message from God. (This message shows that God chooses people according to His own
purposes; 12He calls people, but not according to their good or bad works.) She was told,
"Your older son will serve your younger son."* 13In the words of the Scriptures, "I loved Ja-
cob, but I rejected Esau."*
14Are we saying, then, that God was unfair? Of course not! 15For God said to Moses,

> "I will show mercy to anyone I choose,
> and I will show compassion to anyone I choose."*

16So it is God who decides to show mercy. We can neither choose it nor work for it.
17For the Scriptures say that God told Pharaoh, "I have appointed you for the very pur-
pose of displaying My power in you and to spread My fame throughout the earth."* 18So
you see, God chooses to show mercy to some, and He chooses to harden the hearts of oth-
ers so they refuse to listen.
19Well then, you might say, "Why does God blame people for not responding? Haven't
they simply done what He makes them do?"
20No, don't say that. Who are you, a mere human being, to argue with God? Should the
thing that was created say to the one who created it, "Why have you made me like this?"
21When a potter makes jars out of clay, doesn't He have a right to use the same lump of

9:6 Num 23:19 Rom 2:28 Gal 6:16
9:7 *Gen 21:12 Heb 11:18
9:8 Rom 8:14 Gal 3:16; 4:23
9:9 *Gen 18:10, 14
9:10 Gen 25:21
9:12 *Gen 25:23
9:13 *Mal 1:2-3
9:14 Deut 32:4
9:15 *Exod 33:19
9:16 Eph 2:8
9:17 *Exod 9:16
9:18 Exod 4:21; 14:4 Josh 11:20 Rom 11:25
9:20 Isa 29:16; 45:9
9:21 Jer 18:6 2 Tim 2:20

9:5 Or *May God, the One who rules over everything, be praised forever. Amen.* **9:7** Gen 21:12. **9:9** Gen 18:10, 14. **9:10** Greek *she conceived children through this one man.* **9:12** Gen 25:23. **9:13** Mal 1:2-3. **9:15** Exod 33:19. **9:17** Exod 9:16 (Greek version).

9:6-9 Paul rejects the idea that God's promises to Israel have failed, insisting that God's faithfulness to Abraham is shown in the holy distinction between his two sons, Ishmael and Isaac. See Genesis 18:1-15 and 21:1-7.

9:10-13 From the human point of view, Abraham and Isaac's children were joint heirs. With Isaac and Ishmael, as with Jacob and Esau, God's choice had nothing to do with anything they did or would do. But God's choice in both cases reversed the standard cultural practice of the firstborn receiving the greatest blessing, showing that it is God's choice, not cultural values, that determine whom God blesses. This addresses the questions Paul's readers may have had concerning whether Jews or Gentiles held an unequal place in God's kingdom based on the Jews being "firstborn."

▸ **PURPOSE**

9:14-15 The gospel will not fail. Paul is not especially patient with people who question God's character. When God's honor is at stake, he sees little value in continued dialogue. Paul will not allow God to be mocked in his presence. But after his rebuke (Romans 9:20), Paul makes it clear that it isn't in the mocker's best interests to persuade God to change His character—if it's not fair for God to condemn anyone, then it's not fair to save anyone, including mockers (9:23). The good news is that God has created men and women and children around the world to be receptive to the gospel (9:18). He will not allow His Word to be preached without effect (Isaiah 55:11), and He has always known that His plan (Matthew 28:18-20) would work—His people would be saved. With that in mind, we can boldly share the gospel, joyfully enduring persecution and having confidence that God has already prepared the means and the end of His redemption of lost humanity. (***See Purpose> God's Means> God's Sovereignty> God chooses some and leaves others in their rebellion,*** TopicGuide page A52.)

9:19-24 Paul refuses to provide an answer to those who would question God's fairness, but instead rebukes those who ask such questions because they are critical of the holy God and manifest a lack of faith. The closest he comes to an answer to the ungrateful question is in 9:23-24, where he points out that if the critic demands fairness, then it would be entirely fair to withhold the riches of glory from all. This returns the reader to the previous theme from chapters 2–4: All sinners deserve God's wrath; no sinner deserves God's grace—whether Jew or Gentile.

9:22 clay to make one jar for decoration and another to throw garbage into? [22]In the same way,
Jer 50:25 even though God has the right to show His anger and His power, He is very patient with
9:23 those on whom His anger falls, who are destined for destruction. [23]He does this to make
Rom 8:30 the riches of His glory shine even brighter on those to whom He shows mercy, who were
9:24 prepared in advance for glory. [24]And we are among those whom He selected, both from
Rom 3:29 the Jews and from the Gentiles.
9:25 *Hos 2:23 [25]Concerning the Gentiles, God says in the prophecy of Hosea,

"Those who were not My people,
I will now call My people.
And I will love those
whom I did not love before."*

9:26 *Hos 1:10 [26]And,

"Then, at the place where they were told,
'You are not My people,'
there they will be called
'children of the living God.'"*

9:27 [27]And concerning Israel, Isaiah the prophet cried out,
*Isa 10:22
*Hos 1:10 "Though the people of Israel are as numerous as the sand of the seashore,
only a remnant will be saved.
9:28 [28]For the LORD will carry out His sentence upon the earth
Isa 10:22-23; 28:22 quickly and with finality."

9:29 [29]And Isaiah said the same thing in another place:
*Isa 1:9

"If the LORD of Heaven's Armies
had not spared a few of our children,
we would have been wiped out like Sodom,
destroyed like Gomorrah."*

ISRAEL'S UNBELIEF

9:30 [30]What does all this mean? Even though the Gentiles were not trying to follow God's stan-
Gal 2:16 dards, they were made right with God. And it was by faith that this took place. [31]But the
Heb 11:7 people of Israel, who tried so hard to get right with God by keeping the law, never suc-
9:31 Isa 51:1 ceeded. [32]Why not? Because they were trying to get right with God by keeping the law* in-
Rom 10:2-3 stead of by trusting in Him. They stumbled over the great rock in their path. [33]God warned
Gal 5:4 them of this in the Scriptures when He said,
9:32
Isa 8:14 "I am placing a stone in Jerusalem* that makes people stumble,
9:33 a rock that makes them fall.
*Isa 28:16
Rom 10:11 But anyone who trusts in Him
1 Pet 2:6, 8 will never be disgraced."*

9:25 Hos 2:23. 9:26 Greek *sons of the living God.* Hos 1:10. 9:27-28 Isa 10:22-23 (Greek version). 9:29 Isa 1:9.
9:32 Greek *by works.* 9:33a Greek *in Zion.* 9:33b Isa 8:14; 28:16 (Greek version).

9:25-33 It is ironic that the Gentiles found God's salvation even though they were not looking for it, but the Jews rejected salvation while attempting to keep God's law. The Gentiles accepted God's righteousness by faith in Christ, but many Jews depended on works rather than faith for their salvation (1 Corinthians 1:23).

10 Dear brothers and sisters,* the longing of my heart and my prayer to God is for the
people of Israel to be saved. 2I know what enthusiasm they have for God, but it is 10:2
misdirected zeal. 3For they don't understand God's way of making people right with Him- Acts 22:3
self. Refusing to accept God's way, they cling to their own way of getting right with God by 10:3
trying to keep the law. 4For Christ has already accomplished the purpose for which the law Rom 9:31-32
was given.* As a result, all who believe in Him are made right with God. 10:4 Gal 3:24

SALVATION IS FOR EVERYONE

5For Moses writes that the law's way of making a person right with God requires obedience 10:5 Lev 18:5
to all of its commands.* 6But faith's way of getting right with God says, "Don't say in your Ezek 20:11, 13, 21
heart, 'Who will go up to heaven' (to bring Christ down to earth). 7And don't say, 'Who will Rom 7:10
go down to the place of the dead' (to bring Christ back to life again)." 8In fact, it says, 10:6-8 *Deut 30:12-14

"The message is very close at hand;
 it is on your lips and in your heart."*

And that message is the very message about faith that we preach: 9If you confess with 10:9
your mouth that Jesus is Lord and believe in your heart that God raised Him from the Matt 10:32
dead, you will be saved. 10For it is by believing in your heart that you are made right with 10:11
God, and it is by confessing with your mouth that you are saved. 11As the Scriptures tell us, *Isa 28:16
"Anyone who trusts in Him will never be disgraced."* 12Jew and Gentile* are the same in Rom 9:33
this respect. They have the same Lord, who gives generously to all who call on Him. 13For 10:12 Acts 15:9
"Everyone who calls on the name of the LORD will be saved."* Eph 2:4-7

14But how can they call on Him to save them unless they believe in Him? And how can 10:13
they believe in Him if they have never heard about Him? And how can they hear about *Joel 2:32
Him unless someone tells them? 15And how will anyone go and tell them without being Acts 2:21
sent? That is why the Scriptures say, "How beautiful are the feet of messengers who bring 10:15 *Isa 52:7
good news!"* *Nah 1:15

10:1 Greek *Brothers.* 10:4 Or *For Christ is the end of the law.* 10:5 See Lev 18:5. 10:6-8 Deut 30:12-14. 10:11 Isa 28:16 (Greek version). 10:12 Greek *and Greek.* 10:13 Joel 2:32. 10:15 Isa 52:7.

10:1 Paul loves the Jewish people because they are his kinsmen, and it pains him that the majority have not come to faith in Christ (9:3). So, in this chapter he persuades his Gentile readers in Rome to open their hearts to the Jews. The Roman church had once included many Jewish believers, but Claudius exiled them from Rome in AD 51. At the time Paul wrote to the Romans, the exile had been lifted, and many Jews were returning to Rome and being incorporated into the church. Paul wanted to ensure that the Gentile believers in Rome would share his love for them.

▸ BIBLE

10:2 Sincerely wrong. Paul understood something that many do not today—the truth of an idea has nothing to do with the sincerity or zeal of the person who expresses it. Paul was zealous in his practice of Judaism, but he later recognized that he was wrong (Philippians 3:6). Paul's former friends were passionate and devoted to their version of Judaism. But that didn't mean they were right—worse, it meant that they would be judged more harshly by God (Matthew 23:13-15), because in their zeal they misled more people with their lies about how people are made right with God. Look at what you believe—do you follow certain doctrines and practices because you are convinced they are taught in the Word, or because someone who seems sincere told you to believe it? Judge everything by God's Word, not by the fervor of the one who brings the message to you. (***See Bible***> *Power> Equip> Foundation for defending truth,* TopicGuide page A11.)

10:2-8 Paul quotes Deuteronomy 30:11-14 to show that salvation has always come through faith. This demonstrates that the Jews in Paul's day who sought salvation through works denied not only the teachings of Jesus but also the teachings of Moses, whom they believed would save them.

▸ SALVATION

10:9-10 Salvation for all! Few texts in the Bible are as misused as Romans 10:9-10. Some people seem to think that this text means that we can be saved by invoking Jesus' name—and if we do, He will automatically save us. But Paul isn't saying that at all. Paul is saying that, aside from all the differences in Jews and Gentiles, they both need their hearts changed in order to rightly confess Jesus as Lord. God's plan is that both groups go tell others about God's promises to all who believe (10:14). When you tell the gospel to others, make sure you are speaking from a changed heart with the goal of producing a changed heart in the other person. (***See Salvation***> *Receiving> Results> Works> Spring from a believing heart,* TopicGuide page A23.)

10:12-15 Just like the Gentiles, the Jewish people could not obtain salvation unless they heard and believed the gospel. In Isaiah 52:1-8, the prophet had foretold that a day would come when the Israelites would suffer for their disobedience. But he had also said that God would redeem them, and that their watchmen would proclaim the gospel or "good news" when God's redemption was manifested. Paul encourages his Gentiles readers to be the watchmen (Ezekiel 33:1-9) who proclaim this gospel to the Jews, bringing them to faith and salvation.

10:16 *Isa 53:1 John 12:38 Heb 4:2 · 10:17 Gal 3:2, 5 Col 3:16 · 10:18 *Ps 19:4 · 10:19 *Deut 32:21

16 But not everyone welcomes the Good News, for Isaiah the prophet said, "LORD, who
has believed our message?"* 17 So faith comes from hearing, that is, hearing the Good
News about Christ. 18 But I ask, have the people of Israel actually heard the message? Yes,
they have:

"The message has gone throughout the earth,
and the words to all the world."*

19 But I ask, did the people of Israel really understand? Yes, they did, for even in the time of
Moses, God said,

"I will rouse your jealousy through people who are not even a nation.
I will provoke your anger through the foolish Gentiles."*

10:20 *Isa 65:1 Rom 9:30

20 And later Isaiah spoke boldly for God, saying,

"I was found by people who were not looking for Me.
I showed Myself to those who were not asking for Me."*

10:21 *Isa 65:2

21 But regarding Israel, God said,

"All day long I opened My arms to them,
but they were disobedient and rebellious."*

11:1 Phil 3:5

GOD'S MERCY ON ISRAEL

11 I ask, then, has God rejected His own people, the nation of Israel? Of course not! I
myself am an Israelite, a descendant of Abraham and a member of the tribe of
Benjamin.

11:2 1 Sam 12:22 · 11:3 *1 Kgs 19:10, 14 · 11:4 *1 Kgs 19:18 · 11:5 Rom 9:27 · 11:6 Rom 4:4 · 11:7 Rom 9:31 · 11:8 *Deut 29:4 *Isa 29:10 Matt 13:14 John 12:40 Acts 28:26-27

2 No, God has not rejected His own people, whom He chose from the very beginning. Do
you realize what the Scriptures say about this? Elijah the prophet complained to God
about the people of Israel and said, 3 "LORD, they have killed Your prophets and torn down
Your altars. I am the only one left, and now they are trying to kill me, too."*
4 And do you remember God's reply? He said, "No, I have 7,000 others who have never
bowed down to Baal!"*
5 It is the same today, for a few of the people of Israel* have remained faithful because of
God's grace—His undeserved kindness in choosing them. 6 And since it is through God's
kindness, then it is not by their good works. For in that case, God's grace would not be
what it really is—free and undeserved.
7 So this is the situation: Most of the people of Israel have not found the favor of God
they are looking for so earnestly. A few have—the ones God has chosen—but the hearts of
the rest were hardened. 8 As the Scriptures say,

10:16 Isa 53:1. **10:18** Ps 19:4. **10:19** Deut 32:21. **10:20** Isa 65:1 (Greek version). **10:21** Isa 65:2 (Greek version).
11:3 1 Kgs 19:10, 14. **11:4** 1 Kgs 19:18. **11:5** Greek *for a remnant.*

10:16-21 How could the Gentiles bring the gospel to the Jews? After all, the Gentiles had learned the gospel from the Jews. Besides this, if people do not come to faith, it is because God has not chosen them (Romans 9:4-12). So why should the Gentiles evangelize the unbelieving Jews? The answer lies in 10:19, in the quote from Deuteronomy 32:21. God had punished the Jews for their unbelief. But for those God had chosen, unbelief was only temporary. The salvation of the Gentiles would be the means God used to provoke these chosen unbelievers to faith in Christ.

11:1-6 God's plan is for Jews and Gentiles alike to be united in Christ. But in Rome, the church consisted almost entirely of Gentiles. Moreover, the Jews as a whole had rejected Christ as their Messiah. This might have led some Roman believers to wrongly conclude that the church and the gospel were God's plan for the Gentiles alone. Paul called attention to himself and to other Jews as proof that the church and the gospel are the only plan of salvation for both Jews and Gentiles.

11:7-12 Here, Paul speaks of God's choice in a temporal sense. Some of the unbelieving Jews had been "chosen" by God for salvation, and God had made this choice before He created the world (Romans 9:28-30; Ephesians 1:4). Paul indicates that God has also chosen the precise time that each of these chosen people would come to faith. Some Jews were converted earlier, but others He chose not to bring to faith until the gospel had gone to the Gentiles. These were the Jews that Paul encourages his Gentile readers to evangelize and convert (Romans 10:14-15).

"God has put them into a deep sleep.
To this day He has shut their eyes so they do not see,
and closed their ears so they do not hear."*

9Likewise, David said, 11:9-10 *Ps 69:22-23

"Let their bountiful table become a snare,
a trap that makes them think all is well.
Let their blessings cause them to stumble,
and let them get what they deserve.
10 Let their eyes go blind so they cannot see,
and let their backs be bent forever."*

11Did God's people stumble and fall beyond recovery? Of course not! They were dis- 11:11
obedient, so God made salvation available to the Gentiles. But He wanted His own people Acts 13:46; 18:6
to become jealous and claim it for themselves. 12Now if the Gentiles were enriched be-
cause the people of Israel turned down God's offer of salvation, think how much greater a
blessing the world will share when they finally accept it.
13I am saying all this especially for you Gentiles. God has appointed me as the apostle to
the Gentiles. I stress this, 14for I want somehow to make the people of Israel jealous of 11:14
what you Gentiles have, so I might save some of them. 15For since their rejection meant 1 Cor 9:20
that God offered salvation to the rest of the world, their acceptance will be even more 2 Tim 1:9
wonderful. It will be life for those who were dead! 16And since Abraham and the other pa- 11:15
triarchs were holy, their descendants will also be holy—just as the entire batch of dough is Luke 15:24, 32 Rom 5:10
holy because the portion given as an offering is holy. For if the roots of the tree are holy, 11:17
the branches will be, too. Jer 11:16
17But some of these branches from Abraham's tree—some of the people of Israel—have Eph 2:11-16

11:8 Isa 29:10; Deut 29:4. 11:9-10 Ps 69:22-23 (Greek version).

11:13-14 Paul also hopes that when the unbelieving Jews see that God is saving and blessing the Gentiles, these Jews will become jealous and be provoked to faith in Christ. He hopes that this might happen as a direct result of his ministry, so that he can participate in saving his beloved kinsmen.

11:16-21 Paul uses the image of an olive tree to represent the physical children of Abraham, which contained the whole community of God's special people. Believing children remained in the tree and thrived, but unbelieving children of Abraham were broken off and discarded. In their place, God grafted in believing Gentiles. So the olive tree represents the entire community of God's people—which today is the visible church. In time, all the unbelievers will be purged from the tree, but for now many unbelievers remain (Matthew 13:24-30, 36-43).

BECAUSE GOD KNOWS EVERYTHING

I will go to Him with all my questions and concerns.

How great are God's riches and wisdom and knowledge!

ROMANS 11:33

FOR THE NEXT *GOD KNOWS EVERYTHING* FEATURE SEE PAGE 2258.

11:18 been broken off. And you Gentiles, who were branches from a wild olive tree, have been
John 4:22 grafted in. So now you also receive the blessing God has promised Abraham and his chil-
dren, sharing in the rich nourishment from the root of God's special olive tree. 18But you
must not brag about being grafted in to replace the branches that were broken off. You are
just a branch, not the root.
11:20 19"Well," you may say, "those branches were broken off to make room for me." 20Yes,
Rom 12:16 but remember—those branches were broken off because they didn't believe in Christ, and
11:22 John 15:2, 14 you are there because you do believe. So don't think highly of yourself, but fear what
Heb 3:14 could happen. 21For if God did not spare the original branches, He won't* spare you either.
11:23 22Notice how God is both kind and severe. He is severe toward those who disobeyed,
2 Cor 3:14-16 but kind to you if you continue to trust in His kindness. But if you stop trusting, you also
will be cut off. 23And if the people of Israel turn from their unbelief, they will be grafted in
again, for God has the power to graft them back into the tree. 24You, by nature, were a
branch cut from a wild olive tree. So if God was willing to do something contrary to nature
by grafting you into His cultivated tree, He will be far more eager to graft the original
branches back into the tree where they belong.

11:25 Luke 21:24 Rom 12:16

GOD'S MERCY IS FOR EVERYONE

25I want you to understand this mystery, dear brothers and sisters,* so that you will not
feel proud about yourselves. Some of the people of Israel have hard hearts, but this will
last only until the full number of Gentiles comes to Christ. 26And so all Israel will be saved.
As the Scriptures say,

11:26-27 Ps 14:7 "The One who rescues will come from Jerusalem,*
Isa 59:20-21 and He will turn Israel away from ungodliness.
Jer 31:31-34 27 And this is My covenant with them,
Heb 8:8; 10:16 that I will take away their sins."*

11:29 28Many of the people of Israel are now enemies of the Good News, and this benefits you
Heb 7:21 Gentiles. Yet they are still the people He loves because He chose their ancestors Abraham,
11:32 Gal 3:22 Isaac, and Jacob. 29For God's gifts and His call can never be withdrawn. 30Once, you
1 Tim 2:4 Gentiles were rebels against God, but when the people of Israel rebelled against Him, God
11:33 was merciful to you instead. 31Now they are the rebels, and God's mercy has come to you
Isa 45:15; 55:8 so that they, too, will share* in God's mercy. 32For God has imprisoned everyone in disobe-
dience so He could have mercy on everyone.
33Oh, how great are God's riches and wisdom and knowledge! How impossible it is for
us to understand His decisions and His ways!

11:21 Some manuscripts read *perhaps He won't.* 11:25 Greek *brothers.* 11:26a Greek *from Zion.* 11:26b Greek *Jacob.* 11:26-27 Isa 59:20-21; 27:9 (Greek version). 11:31 Other manuscripts read *will now share;* still others read *will someday share.*

11:22-24 The Jews who rejected Christ had been removed from the visible community of the people of God. But if they came to faith in Christ, they would have been grafted back into the church.

11:25-32 Paul returned to the idea that some of the Jews that God had chosen for salvation had not yet come to faith. God had allowed them to reject the gospel temporarily in order that the gospel might spread to the Gentiles. But once the Gentiles were solidly established, God would bring these chosen Jews to faith as well.

▸ GOD
11:33 Celebration of mystery. What moves you to worship and praise? After a discussion of some of the most debated topics in Christianity—election and the place of Jews in God's future plans—Paul is not moved to fatalism or gloom or a bold prediction of how and when everything will turn out; instead he suddenly bursts out into a hymn of wondering praise! Paul knows God, and he loves God, so mysteries and conundrums don't hinder his trust. When faced with profound truths about God and His creation that Paul admits he can't quite understand, He worships God for His rich wisdom that is so far beyond his own. Do you have questions about God? Do you struggle to understand His Word? Do not despair. Humble yourself before Him, asking Him to reveal His truth to you—and if He says, "Wait," then worship Him for His wisdom in showing you the truths you need when you need them. (***See God**> God's Attributes> All-knowing> God's unfathomable knowledge of His people,* TopicGuide page A15.)

34 For who can know the LORD's thoughts?
Who knows enough to give Him advice?*
35 And who has given Him so much
that He needs to pay it back?*

36 For everything comes from Him and exists by His power and is intended for His glory.
All glory to Him forever! Amen.

11:34 Job 15:8; 36:22 *Isa 40:13 Jer 23:18 1 Cor 2:16
11:35 Job 41:11
11:36 1 Cor 8:6

A LIVING SACRIFICE TO GOD

12 And so, dear brothers and sisters,* I plead with you to give your bodies to God be-
cause of all He has done for you. Let them be a living and holy sacrifice—the kind
He will find acceptable. This is truly the way to worship Him.* 2 Don't copy the behavior and
customs of this world, but let God transform you into a new person by changing the way
you think. Then you will learn to know God's will for you, which is good and pleasing and
perfect.

12:1 Rom 6:13 1 Pet 2:5
12:2 Gal 1:4 Eph 4:23 Col 3:10

11:34 Isa 40:13 (Greek version). 11:35 See Job 41:11. 12:1a Greek *brothers.* 12:1b Or *This is your spiritual worship;* or *This is your reasonable service.*

WORSHIP

12:1-2 An acceptable sacrifice. How do we become holy? Some read these verses and imagine that offering our bodies as living sacrifices is what makes us pleasing to God. But Paul has already made it clear that God has made us holy and pleasing to Himself through Christ, not through our works (Romans 5:1; 9:12; 11:6). This is the fundamental truth that keeps us from being conformed to the world—the gospel. So powerful is God's provision for us in Christ, so powerful is the life that is lived by faith alone (Romans 1:17; 3:28; 4:5) that Paul says if our minds grasp this new thought, then our lives will be transformed. Your faith-energized life will be an acceptable sacrifice—but not because you are inherently pleasing to Him. God accepts you on account of Christ and Christ alone. (***See Worship***> *NT> Christ's Supremacy> His sacrifice provides true cleansing from sin,* TopicGuide page A29.)

MY RESPONSE TO GOD

Every Part Appreciated

ROMANS 12:6

Imagine a jealous elbow. "I'm just not being appreciated!" says the jealous elbow, watching the hand and wrist get all the glory for playing the violin. So the elbow decides to refuse to do its job of bending the arm. No more music—now the whole body suffers (1 Corinthians 12:14-20).

Like this imaginary elbow, we may feel jealous of others' gifts and talents for ministry and withhold service in the church. Or perhaps we are like Moses, who felt inadequate to free the Israelites from Egyptian bondage as God had directed him. "Lord, please! Send someone else," Moses pleaded (Exodus 4:13). But God equipped him with the abilities—and the people—he needed. He used a runaway criminal who needed his brother as a spokesman to rescue His people from slavery.

God has given each of us different gifts (Romans 12:6) and has arranged us in His body, the church, just where He wants us to be (1 Corinthians 12:18). Spiritual gifts are not limited to those listed in Romans 12:6-8—these are representative of the variety of ways God has enabled you and those around you to live holy and happy lives. Use your gifts—whatever they are—as an act of worship to God and an act of service to Christ's body. By doing so, you will please God and enable those in your community to work as God intended.

3Because of the privilege and authority* God has given me, I give each of you this warn-
ing: Don't think you are better than you really are. Be honest in your evaluation of your-
selves, measuring yourselves by the faith God has given us.* 4Just as our bodies have
many parts and each part has a special function, 5so it is with Christ's body. We are many
parts of one body, and we all belong to each other.

6In His grace, God has given us different gifts for doing certain things well. So if God has
given you the ability to prophesy, speak out with as much faith as God has given you. 7If
your gift is serving others, serve them well. If you are a teacher, teach well. 8If your gift is to
encourage others, be encouraging. If it is giving, give generously. If God has given you
leadership ability, take the responsibility seriously. And if you have a gift for showing
kindness to others, do it gladly.

9Don't just pretend to love others. Really love them. Hate what is wrong. Hold tightly to
what is good. 10Love each other with genuine affection,* and take delight in honoring
each other. 11Never be lazy, but work hard and serve the Lord enthusiastically.* 12Rejoice
in our confident hope. Be patient in trouble, and keep on praying. 13When God's people
are in need, be ready to help them. Always be eager to practice hospitality.

14Bless those who persecute you. Don't curse them; pray that God will bless them. 15Be
happy with those who are happy, and weep with those who weep. 16Live in harmony with
each other. Don't be too proud to enjoy the company of ordinary people. And don't think
you know it all!

17Never pay back evil with more evil. Do things in such a way that everyone can see
you are honorable. 18Do all that you can to live in peace with everyone.

19Dear friends, never take revenge. Leave that to the righteous anger of God. For the
Scriptures say,

"I will take revenge;
I will pay them back,"*
says the LORD.

20Instead,

"If your enemies are hungry, feed them.
If they are thirsty, give them something to drink.
In doing this, you will heap
burning coals of shame on their heads."*

21Don't let evil conquer you, but conquer evil by doing good.

12:3 1 Cor 12:11; Eph 4:7
12:4 1 Cor 12:12
12:5 1 Cor 12:27; Eph 4:25
12:6-8 1 Cor 12:4-11; 1 Pet 4:10-11
12:9 Amos 5:15; 1 Tim 1:5
12:10 John 13:34; Phil 2:3; 1 Thes 4:9; 2 Pet 1:7
12:11 Acts 18:25; 20:19; Rev 3:15
12:12 Rom 5:2; Heb 10:32, 36
12:13 Heb 13:2
12:14 Matt 5:44
12:15 Job 30:25
12:16 Prov 3:7; Isa 5:21
12:17 Prov 3:4; 20:22; 1 Thes 5:15
12:19 *Deut 32:35
12:20 *Prov 25:21-22; Matt 5:44

12:3a Or *Because of the grace;* compare 1:5. 12:3b Or *by the faith God has given you;* or *by the standard of our God-given faith.* 12:10 Greek *with brotherly love.* 12:11 Or *but serve the Lord with a zealous spirit;* or *but let the Spirit excite you as you serve the Lord.* 12:19 Deut 32:35. 12:20 Prov 25:21-22.

12:3-5 Believers are mystically united both to Christ and to one another in Christ. Collectively, we are one. In typical fashion, Paul compared this union to the parts of a human body (1 Corinthians 12:12-30; Ephesians 4:12-16). No believer can meet all the needs of another, and all believers have needs that only others can fill. When believers live and minister in harmony with one another, the church's work thrives, and the needs of individual believers are met.

12:6-8 These spiritual gifts God gives are supernatural empowerments to accomplish tasks within the body of Christ. Some of them resemble natural talents and abilities, but when they are given as gifts, they flow from the Holy Spirit rather than from the individual. The list here, like the others in the New Testament (1 Corinthians 12:28-30; Ephesians 4:11), is representative rather than comprehensive. God may gift His people in any way He sees fit in order to build up the church.

12:9-14 Christians are called to love one another, to love their neighbors, and even to love their enemies. Here, Paul's exhortation to love is based primarily on the fact that we are united to one another in Christ (12:16). Believers love others in tangible, earnest ways because it benefits each other, the body of Christ.

12:17-21 In and of itself, vengeance is not evil. God Himself is vengeful, and His vengeance is an expression of His justice (Romans 12:19; see Psalm 94:1; compare Deuteronomy 32:35-43). But when we take vengeance into our own hands, we do not act with the righteousness of God (James 1:20), and we pervert the systems of justice that God has established, such as our earthly governments (Romans 13:1-5) and God's final judgment (John 5:29).

RESPECT FOR AUTHORITY

13 Everyone must submit to governing authorities. For all authority comes from God,
and those in positions of authority have been placed there by God. 2So anyone
who rebels against authority is rebelling against what God has instituted, and they will be
punished. 3For the authorities do not strike fear in people who are doing right, but in those
who are doing wrong. Would you like to live without fear of the authorities? Do what is
right, and they will honor you. 4The authorities are God's servants, sent for your good. But
if you are doing wrong, of course you should be afraid, for they have the power to punish
you. They are God's servants, sent for the very purpose of punishing those who do what is
wrong. 5So you must submit to them, not only to avoid punishment, but also to keep a
clear conscience.

6Pay your taxes, too, for these same reasons. For government workers need to be paid.
They are serving God in what they do. 7Give to everyone what you owe them: Pay your
taxes and government fees to those who collect them, and give respect and honor to
those who are in authority.

LOVE FULFILLS GOD'S REQUIREMENTS

8Owe nothing to anyone—except for your obligation to love one another. If you love your
neighbor, you will fulfill the requirements of God's law. 9For the commandments say, "You
must not commit adultery. You must not murder. You must not steal. You must not
covet."* These—and other such commandments—are summed up in this one command-
ment: "Love your neighbor as yourself."* 10Love does no wrong to others, so love fulfills
the requirements of God's law.

11This is all the more urgent, for you know how late it is; time is running out. Wake up,
for our salvation is nearer now than when we first believed. 12The night is almost gone;
the day of salvation will soon be here. So remove your dark deeds like dirty clothes, and
put on the shining armor of right living. 13Because we belong to the day, we must live de-
cent lives for all to see. Don't participate in the darkness of wild parties and drunkenness,

13:1 Dan 2:21 John 19:11 Titus 3:1
13:3 1 Pet 2:13-14
13:5 1 Pet 2:13
13:7 Matt 22:21 Mark 12:17 Luke 20:25
13:8 Matt 5:34 John 13:34
13:9 Exod 20:13-15, 17 *Lev 19:18 Deut 5:17-19, 21
13:10 Matt 22:39 John 13:34-35 Gal 5:13-14
13:11 1 Cor 7:29-31 1 Thes 5:5-6 Jas 5:8 1 Pet 4:7
13:12 Eph 5:11; 6:13 1 Thes 5:8
13:13 Luke 21:34 Eph 5:18

13:9a Exod 20:13-15, 17. **13:9b** Lev 19:18.

13:1-5 God delegates authority to human governments, obligating Christians to be lawful. Yet our obedience to the government is conditional. We must obey those laws that fulfill the role God has assigned to the government, namely enforcing true justice and encouraging true goodness. But when the government's laws directly conflict with God's commands, we must disobey the government (Acts 5:29).

▸ CHURCH

13:1 Christians and government. For 2,000 years, some Christians have appealed to the Bible in support of different political systems. But God's Word is not a book of political philosophy. It does not lay out the details for a Christian approach to science or economics, and it does not advocate any particular form of human government. It does, however, teach us that the government should be just and moral and that God will judge unrighteous nations (Obadiah 1:15). He even assigns spiritual powers to oversee and interact with human governments (1 Kings 22:20-22; Daniel 10:13-20; Revelation 16:14). So while we are free to participate in a variety of types of government, we must always do so with an understanding that human governments must submit to and uphold godly justice. Use your vote, your opinion, and your rights as a citizen to establish just rule in your local and national government. It is your duty. (***See Church**> Role> Church Government> Society> Church honors authority of government,* TopicGuide page A49.)

13:6-7 Like Jesus before him (Matthew 22:17-21), Paul teaches that Christians must pay their taxes. The government must use the taxes to fulfill its obligations before God. Although the Bible teaches that it is right to disobey those laws that are ungodly, it does not teach that Christians may withhold their taxes when the government's laws are evil. It is worth noting that the government to which Jesus and Paul referred was the Roman government—the very government that crucified Jesus.

13:8-10 Jesus taught that the commandments to love God and neighbor summarize all of God's laws (Matthew 22:36-40). Here, Paul affirms Jesus' teaching that when we truly act in a loving way, we always do what is right. The entire Old Testament was designed to teach God's people what it means to love God and to love our neighbors (2 Timothy 3:16-17). This means that if we fail to understand the meaning of God's laws, we also fail to understand the biblical meaning of "love." If we truly understand love as God does, we will be motivated to keep God's law rather than to ignore it (John 14:15).

13:11-12 Previously, Paul exhorted righteous living because it benefits believers through our union with Christ (Romans 12:9-14). Here, he provides additional motivation for believers to live godly lives: They may be meeting Jesus soon, either when He returns in triumph or when they perish under the sword of persecution. One way or another, the Lord's day of reckoning is drawing near, and Paul wants his readers to live a life motivated by love (13:8-10) with actions that are fitting for our relatively short time remaining.

14:1 or in sexual promiscuity and immoral living, or in quarreling and jealousy. [14]Instead,
1 Cor 9:22 clothe yourself with the presence of the Lord Jesus Christ. And don't let yourself think
14:2 1 Cor 10:25-27 about ways to indulge your evil desires.

14:3 **THE DANGER OF CRITICISM**

Col 2:16 **14** Accept other believers who are weak in faith, and don't argue with them about
14:4 what they think is right or wrong. [2]For instance, one person believes it's all right to
Matt 7:1 eat anything. But another believer with a sensitive conscience will eat only vegetables.
14:5 Gal 4:10 [3]Those who feel free to eat anything must not look down on those who don't. And those
14:6 who don't eat certain foods must not condemn those who do, for God has accepted them.
1 Cor 10:30 [4]Who are you to condemn someone else's servants? They are responsible to the Lord, so
14:7 let Him judge whether they are right or wrong. And with the Lord's help, they will do what
2 Cor 5:15 is right and will receive His approval.
Gal 2:20 [5]In the same way, some think one day is more holy than another day, while others think
14:8 every day is alike. You should each be fully convinced that whichever day you choose is ac-
Phil 1:20 1 Thes 5:10 ceptable. [6]Those who worship the Lord on a special day do it to honor Him. Those who eat
14:9 any kind of food do so to honor the Lord, since they give thanks to God before eating. And
Rev 1:18 those who refuse to eat certain foods also want to please the Lord and give thanks to God.
14:10 [7]For we don't live for ourselves or die for ourselves. [8]If we live, it's to honor the Lord. And if
Matt 25:31-32 Acts 17:31 we die, it's to honor the Lord. So whether we live or die, we belong to the Lord. [9]Christ died
2 Cor 5:10 and rose again for this very purpose—to be Lord both of the living and of the dead.
14:11 [10]So why do you condemn another believer*? Why do you look down on another believer?
*Isa 45:23; 49:18 Remember, we will all stand before the judgment seat of God. [11]For the Scriptures say,

"'As surely as I live,' says the LORD,
'every knee will bend to Me,
and every tongue will confess and give praise to God.*'"

14:10 Greek *your brother;* also in 14:10b, 13, 15, 21. 14:11 Or *confess allegiance to God.* Isa 49:18; 45:23 (Greek version).

13:14 This verse literally instructs believers to put on the Lord Jesus Christ as if He were clothing or armor. This continues the metaphor from 13:12-13, where Paul exhorted his readers to discard their soiled clothing of sin and wear the armor of God (see Ephesians 6:11-17). The image summarizes Paul's teaching in this chapter by instructing us to imitate Christ, especially with regard to His submission to the government (Luke 23:4), His reputation for good behavior (Luke 2:52), and His love for other people.

▶ ADOPTION

13:14 Time to change. Have you ever caught yourself setting aside time to sin? Maybe you arrange your schedule so that you'll run into someone who inspires your lust. Or perhaps you keep pornography hidden in your house—you know it is sinful, but you keep it just in case you change your mind about it one day. Paul encouraged believers not to look ahead to times when we might sin, and not to make it easy to take advantage of such times. As James taught, once we give over our minds to anticipating sin, we eventually act upon those sinful desires (James 1:15). Instead, we should clean house—figuratively and literally. Throw away the things that help you sin. Don't go to places where you expect to find strong temptations. Stop thinking about sin, and start thinking about the purity of life your Savior requires of you (Colossians 3:1-5). (***See Adoption****> With Christ> Redemption> Freedom from dependency and lust,* TopicGuide page A37.)

▶ CHURCH

14:1 Freedom and conscience. Sometimes one Christian thinks an action is acceptable to God, while another believes it is sinful. And believe it or not, sometimes they are both right. When our consciences are weak, we feel guilty about actions that are not actually sinful. And when we act against our consciences, we sin (Romans 14:14, 23). Our natural inclination might be to insist on our freedoms and compel weaker Christians to accept doctrines and practices they do not yet understand. But Paul's solution was different: Stronger Christians should not require weaker Christians to overcome their weaknesses in this area. And if their freedoms cause the weaker Christians to sin against their consciences, stronger Christians should even be willing to sacrifice their freedoms (compare 15:1). Which is more important to you, your freedoms or the well-being of your fellow Christians? (***See Church****> What> Supernatural Body> Care given to the weakest (yet most necessary) parts,* TopicGuide page A48.)

14:2-3 In the Old Testament, eating vegetables appears to have been a means of ensuring that dietary laws were not violated (Daniel 1:8-16). Old Testament dietary laws did not forbid the eating of meat, but they did restrict the types of meat that could be eaten (Leviticus 11:1-47). This may be what Paul had in mind, or he may have been referring to the practice of avoiding meat that had been sacrificed to idols (1 Corinthians 8:10-13).

14:5-6 Paul's mention that "one day is more holy than another day" is referring to the annual Jewish holidays, which were also known as Sabbaths (Leviticus 16:31; 23:27-32). The "special day" mentioned in 14:6 is likely a reference to a religious holiday given greater standing than the rest. If an attack upon the importance of the weekly Sabbath were in view here, it would have been simpler to say, "Some people believe that the Sabbath is holier than any other day, but I do not." Paul strongly affirmed a commitment to keeping the Sabbath both in practice (Acts 13:14; 17:2; 18:4) and in preaching (Acts 25:8).

12 Yes, each of us will give a personal account to God. 13 So let's stop condemning each
other. Decide instead to live in such a way that you will not cause another believer to
stumble and fall.
14 I know and am convinced on the authority of the Lord Jesus that no food, in and of it-
self, is wrong to eat. But if someone believes it is wrong, then for that person it is wrong.
15 And if another believer is distressed by what you eat, you are not acting in love if you
eat it. Don't let your eating ruin someone for whom Christ died. 16 Then you will not be
criticized for doing something you believe is good. 17 For the Kingdom of God is not a
matter of what we eat or drink, but of living a life of goodness and peace and joy in the
Holy Spirit. 18 If you serve Christ with this attitude, you will please God, and others will ap-
prove of you, too. 19 So then, let us aim for harmony in the church and try to build each
other up.
20 Don't tear apart the work of God over what you eat. Remember, all foods are accept-
able, but it is wrong to eat something if it makes another person stumble. 21 It is better not
to eat meat or drink wine or do anything else if it might cause another believer to stumble.
22 You may believe there's nothing wrong with what you are doing, but keep it between
yourself and God. Blessed are those who don't feel guilty for doing something they have
decided is right. 23 But if you have doubts about whether or not you should eat something,
you are sinning if you go ahead and do it. For you are not following your convictions. If
you do anything you believe is not right, you are sinning.

LIVING TO PLEASE OTHERS

15 We who are strong must be considerate of those who are sensitive about things
like this. We must not just please ourselves. 2 We should help others do what is
right and build them up in the Lord. 3 For even Christ didn't live to please Himself. As the
Scriptures say, "The insults of those who insult you, O God, have fallen on me."* 4 Such

15:3 Greek *who insult you have fallen on me.* Ps 69:9.

14:12 Gal 6:5
14:13 Matt 7:1; 2 Cor 6:3
14:14 Acts 10:15; 1 Cor 8:7
14:15 1 Cor 8:11-13
14:16 1 Cor 10:30; Titus 2:5
14:17 Rom 15:13; Gal 5:22
14:19 Rom 12:18; 15:2
14:20 Acts 10:15; 1 Cor 8:9-12
14:21 1 Cor 8:13
14:22 1 Jn 3:21
15:2 Rom 14:19; 1 Cor 9:19; 10:24; Gal 6:2
15:3 *Ps 69:9
15:4 Rom 4:23-24; 2 Tim 3:16

14:13 Some Christians are bound by their conscience not to participate in behaviors that mature Christians might rightly enjoy. Mature Christians must not condemn these who are weaker in faith but must receive them and nurture them. But this does not imply that we should never judge anyone for anything. On the contrary, there are many other cases in which Christians are required to issue condemnations (1 Corinthians 5:9-13).

14:21 Paul employs a technical term for food that accorded with Jewish dietary laws. This may imply that the weaker Christians felt free to eat only what the Old Testament had called "clean" (compare Leviticus 11:1-47). These dietary laws had originally functioned to set apart Israel as God's special people (Leviticus 11:44-45). With the inclusion of the Gentiles in God's holy nation (Deuteronomy 32:21; 1 Peter 2:9-10), the Old Testament forms of obedience to these laws became obsolete (Galatians 2:12-14). Christians are still to distinguish themselves from the rest of the world, but not through a special diet.

14:23 Even when our consciences may be misinformed, it is wrong to do what we believe to be evil because then we are not living by faith (1:17). The best solution in such cases is to read the Word and retrain the conscience to respond according to its clear teachings.

15:1-2 Once again, Paul emphasizes that it is far more important to build up the church than it is to exercise our freedoms (see Romans 14:1-23; compare 1 Corinthians 8:1-13). We should not partake in behaviors that result in others sinning against their conscience.

▸ CHURCH
15:1-7 You first! Even under the apostles' ministry, the church was frequently divided in sinful ways (1 Corinthians 1:10-12; Galatians 2:12-13). In the Roman church, Paul tried to cure the divisions between those whose theology was accurate and those whose theology needed improvement (Romans 14:1-23). In the modern church, thousands of denominations exist because of differences in theology, even in evangelical circles. And many of these divisions result from differences even less significant than the dietary practices Paul describes in Romans 14:1-23. As Paul teaches, the unity of the church is worth far more than getting our way on minor points of theology and preference. Don't insist on having things your way. Instead, insist on unity and peace, and do your part to bear with and build up others. (***See Church****> Mission> Nurture> Fostering Community,* TopicGuide page A49.)

15:3-4 Paul quotes Psalm 69:9 and indicates that it had been written, at least in part, for the benefit of the church. The New Testament regularly affirms that the Old Testament is neither irrelevant nor inapplicable to us. On the contrary, it is our rule of faith and life (2 Timothy 3:16-17). God intended it to apply to us just as certainly as it applied to its original readers (compare 1 Corinthians 9:9-11; 10:11). However, since Christ fulfilled the sacrificial system (Hebrews 8:8-13; 10:1-10), and some of the laws spe-

things were written in the Scriptures long ago to teach us. And the Scriptures give us hope
and encouragement as we wait patiently for God's promises to be fulfilled.
15:5 [5]May God, who gives this patience and encouragement, help you live in complete har-
1 Cor 1:10 mony with each other, as is fitting for followers of Christ Jesus. [6]Then all of you can join
2 Cor 1:3 together with one voice, giving praise and glory to God, the Father of our Lord Jesus
15:6 Rev 1:6 Christ.
[7]Therefore, accept each other just as Christ has accepted you so that God will be given
15:7 Rom 14:1 glory. [8]Remember that Christ came as a servant to the Jews* to show that God is true to the
15:8 promises He made to their ancestors. [9]He also came so that the Gentiles might give glory
Matt 15:24 Acts 3:25-26 to God for His mercies to them. That is what the psalmist meant when he wrote:

2 Cor 1:20 "For this, I will praise you among the Gentiles;
15:9 *2 Sam 22:50 I will sing praises to your name."*

*Ps 18:49 [10]And in another place it is written,

15:10 *Deut 32:43 "Rejoice with His people,
you Gentiles."*

[11]And yet again,

15:11 *Ps 117:1 "Praise the LORD, all you Gentiles.
Praise Him, all you people of the earth."*

15:12 [12]And in another place Isaiah said,

Isa 11:10 Rev 5:5; 22:16 "The heir to David's throne will come,
and He will rule over the Gentiles.
They will place their hope on Him."*

[13]I pray that God, the source of hope, will fill you completely with joy and peace be-
cause you trust in Him. Then you will overflow with confident hope through the power of
the Holy Spirit.

PAUL'S REASON FOR WRITING

15:14 [14]I am fully convinced, my dear brothers and sisters,* that you are full of goodness. You
2 Pet 1:12 know these things so well you can teach each other all about them. [15]Even so, I have been
15:15 Rom 1:5; 12:3 bold enough to write about some of these points, knowing that all you need is this re-
15:16 minder. For by God's grace, [16]I am a special messenger from Christ Jesus to you Gentiles. I
Phil 2:17 bring you the Good News so that I might present you as an acceptable offering to God,
15:17 made holy by the Holy Spirit. [17]So I have reason to be enthusiastic about all Christ Jesus
Phil 3:3 has done through me in my service to God. [18]Yet I dare not boast about anything except
15:18 Rom 1:5 what Christ has done through me, bringing the Gentiles to God by my message and by the

15:8 Greek *servant of circumcision.* 15:9 Ps 18:49. 15:10 Deut 32:43. 15:11 Ps 117:1. 15:12a Greek *The root of Jesse.* David was the son of Jesse. 15:12b Isa 11:10 (Greek version). 15:14 Greek *brothers;* also in 15:30.

cifically pointed to the governing of Israel (such as Deuteronomy 19:14; 27:17), and changes in culture have taken place (for instance, Deuteronomy 22:8), these applications are more general, though still binding to Christians today.

15:8-13 One of Paul's greatest concerns in this letter is to reconcile Jews and Gentiles in the church. In these verses, he indicates that he exhorted stronger Christians to accept weaker Christians specifically to smooth over problems between these two ethnic groups. His intention was to give each group good reason to value the other.

15:14-16 Paul indicates that in his prior discussion of stronger and weaker Christians (14:1–15:7), it was the Gentiles who were the stronger Christians and the Jews who were the weaker Christians. Historically, the Jews had planted the church in Rome, and the congregation had grown to include both Jews and Gentiles. But in AD 51, Claudius banished the Jews from that city. In the years since that time, the Gentile believers had grown greatly in the faith. By the time Paul wrote his letter to the Romans, the Jews were returning to the city. Apparently, many of these Jewish Christians in Rome were newer converts or simply had not had the opportunity for their faith to mature.

way I worked among them. 19 They were convinced by the power of miraculous signs and
wonders and by the power of God's Spirit.* In this way, I have fully presented the Good
News of Christ from Jerusalem all the way to Illyricum.*
20 My ambition has always been to preach the Good News where the name of Christ has
never been heard, rather than where a church has already been started by someone else.
21 I have been following the plan spoken of in the Scriptures, where it says,

"Those who have never been told about Him will see,
and those who have never heard of Him will understand."*

22 In fact, my visit to you has been delayed so long because I have been preaching in these
places.

PAUL'S TRAVEL PLANS

23 But now I have finished my work in these regions, and after all these long years of waiting,
I am eager to visit you. 24 I am planning to go to Spain, and when I do, I will stop off in Rome.
And after I have enjoyed your fellowship for a little while, you can provide for my journey.
25 But before I come, I must go to Jerusalem to take a gift to the believers* there. 26 For
you see, the believers in Macedonia and Achaia* have eagerly taken up an offering for the
poor among the believers in Jerusalem. 27 They were glad to do this because they feel they
owe a real debt to them. Since the Gentiles received the spiritual blessings of the Good
News from the believers in Jerusalem, they feel the least they can do in return is to help
them financially. 28 As soon as I have delivered this money and completed this good deed
of theirs, I will come to see you on my way to Spain. 29 And I am sure that when I come,
Christ will richly bless our time together.
30 Dear brothers and sisters, I urge you in the name of our Lord Jesus Christ to join in my
struggle by praying to God for me. Do this because of your love for me, given to you by
the Holy Spirit. 31 Pray that I will be rescued from those in Judea who refuse to obey God.
Pray also that the believers there will be willing to accept the donation* I am taking to Jeru-
salem. 32 Then, by the will of God, I will be able to come to you with a joyful heart, and we
will be an encouragement to each other.
33 And now may God, who gives us His peace, be with you all. Amen.*

PAUL GREETS HIS FRIENDS

16 I commend to you our sister Phoebe, who is a deacon in the church in Cen-
chrea. 2 Welcome her in the Lord as one who is worthy of honor among God's

15:19 Acts 19:11; 1 Cor 2:4; 1 Thes 1:5
15:20 Rom 1:15; 1 Cor 3:10; 2 Cor 10:13, 15
15:21 *Isa 52:15
15:22 Rom 1:10-13; 1 Thes 2:18
15:23 Acts 19:21; Rom 1:10-11
15:24 1 Cor 16:6
15:25 Acts 19:21; 20:22
15:26 1 Cor 16:1; 2 Cor 8:1; 9:2
15:27 1 Cor 9:11
15:29 Rom 1:10-11
15:30 2 Cor 1:11; Col 1:8; 4:12
15:31 2 Thes 3:2
15:32 Phlm 1:7
15:33 Rom 16:20; Heb 13:20
16:1 Acts 18:18
16:2 Phil 2:29

15:19a Other manuscripts read *the Spirit;* still others read *the Holy Spirit.* 15:19b *Illyricum* was a region northeast of Italy. 15:21 Isa 52:15 (Greek version). 15:25 Greek *God's holy people;* also in 15:26, 31. 15:26 *Macedonia* and *Achaia* were the northern and southern regions of Greece. 15:31 Greek *the ministry;* other manuscripts read *the gift.* 15:33 Some manuscripts omit *Amen.* One very early manuscript places 16:25-27 here.

WORSHIP

15:20-21 Play your part. What's your ambition in life? Paul's was to preach the gospel in new places. That's not the only valid way to spend your life, but it's not a bad one either. What aspect of building the Kingdom of God has the Lord laid on your heart? Has He given you a love for teaching? Or for caring for those in need? Or for evangelism? We each have our own gifts from God (1 Corinthians 12:7), and we each have our own calling. What is God's plan for you in His church? If you don't know, pray about it. Ask wise Christians and church leaders what they think your gifts are. Look for aspects of the Lord's work that you enjoy doing. And once you find your gifts and enjoyment, dedicate yourself to doing them. You and the church will both benefit, and the Lord will be pleased with your efforts. (***See Worship**> NT> Holy Spirit> The Church is one body with many members,* TopicGuide page A31.)

15:20-29 Paul's plan to use Rome as a base of operations for mission work in Spain was altered by his arrest in Jerusalem shortly after he delivered the offering mentioned here (Acts 21:33). His arrest began a two-year imprisonment in Caesarea Maritima on the coast of Samaria (Acts 24:27), followed by a two-year imprisonment in Rome (Acts 28:30). It is not known if the apostle ever made it to Spain.

16:1-2 The word "deacon" may simply indicate that Phoebe was a servant of the church, or it may designate the office of deacon. Similarly, Paul's high praise for her may simply be intended as an expression of appreciation and recommendation, or it may imply that Phoebe had a powerful and influential diaconal ministry. In its other uses in Romans, the Greek word here translated "deacon" identifies a servant who possesses some form of authority (13:4; 15:8).

people. Help her in whatever she needs, for she has been helpful to many, and especially
to me.
3Give my greetings to Priscilla and Aquila, my co-workers in the ministry of Christ Jesus.
4In fact, they once risked their lives for me. I am thankful to them, and so are all the Gentile
16:5 churches. 5Also give my greetings to the church that meets in their home.
1 Cor 16:15, 19; Col 4:15 Greet my dear friend Epenetus. He was the first person from the province of Asia to be-
Phlm 1:2 come a follower of Christ. 6Give my greetings to Mary, who has worked so hard for your
16:7 benefit. 7Greet Andronicus and Junia,* my fellow Jews,* who were in prison with me. They
Rom 16:11, 21 are highly respected among the apostles and became followers of Christ before I did.
Col 4:10; Phlm 1:23 8Greet Ampliatus, my dear friend in the Lord. 9Greet Urbanus, our co-worker in Christ, and
16:10 my dear friend Stachys.
Acts 11:14 10Greet Apelles, a good man whom Christ approves. And give my greetings to the be-
16:11 lievers from the household of Aristobulus. 11Greet Herodion, my fellow Jew.* Greet the
Rom 16:7, 21 Lord's people from the household of Narcissus. 12Give my greetings to Tryphena and Try-
phosa, the Lord's workers, and to dear Persis, who has worked so hard for the Lord.
16:13 13Greet Rufus, whom the Lord picked out to be His very own; and also his dear mother,
Mark 15:21 who has been a mother to me.
2 Jn 1:1; **16:16** 14Give my greetings to Asyncritus, Phlegon, Hermes, Patrobas, Hermas, and the broth-
1 Cor 16:20 ers and sisters* who meet with them. 15Give my greetings to Philologus, Julia, Nereus and
1 Thes 5:26 his sister, and to Olympas and all the believers* who meet with them. 16Greet each other
1 Pet 5:14 in Christian love.* All the churches of Christ send you their greetings.

16:17; 1 Cor 5:9, 11

PAUL'S FINAL INSTRUCTIONS

2 Thes 3:6 17And now I make one more appeal, my dear brothers and sisters. Watch out for people
2 Tim 3:5 who cause divisions and upset people's faith by teaching things contrary to what you have
Titus 3:10; 2 Jn 1:10 been taught. Stay away from them. 18Such people are not serving Christ our Lord; they are
16:18 serving their own personal interests. By smooth talk and glowing words they deceive in-
Phil 3:19 nocent people. 19But everyone knows that you are obedient to the Lord. This makes me
Col 2:4; 2 Pet 2:3 very happy. I want you to be wise in doing right and to stay innocent of any wrong. 20The
16:19 God of peace will soon crush Satan under your feet. May the grace of our Lord Jesus* be
Matt 10:16 with you.
16:20 21Timothy, my fellow worker, sends you his greetings, as do Lucius, Jason, and Sosipa-
Gen 3:15 ter, my fellow Jews.

16:21 Acts 13:1; 16:1; 17:5

16:7a *Junia* is a feminine name. Some late manuscripts accent the word so it reads *Junias*, a masculine name; still others read *Julia* (feminine). **16:7b** Or *compatriots;* also in 16:21. **16:11** Or *compatriot.* **16:14** Greek *brothers;* also in 16:17. **16:15** Greek *all of God's holy people.* **16:16** Greek *with a sacred kiss.* **16:20** Some manuscripts read *Lord Jesus Christ.*

16:6 Paul did not identify this Mary with any of the four mentioned in the Gospels (the mother of Jesus, the mother of James and John, the wife of Clopas, and Mary Magdalene). This Mary is otherwise unknown in Scripture.

16:7, 11 The word "apostle" simply means "one who is sent." Andronicus and Junia were not apostles in the same sense that Paul was an apostle. The term was descriptive not only to those who held the authoritative office of apostle (namely the original disciples, Matthias, and Paul), but also to messengers, such as Jesus (Hebrews 3:1) and Barnabas (Acts 13:4, 14). It is the latter sense that is meant here. Paul fought quite vigorously to defend his claim to apostleship (2 Corinthians 10–11).

▸ SPIRITUAL WARFARE
16:18-25 You've got to serve someone. No one is free. We are either enslaved to sin or enslaved to God (Romans 6:17-18). In a sense, we are slaves to both (Romans 7:25). We are influenced and even compelled by both our sinful natures (Romans 8:5-8; Galatians 5:17) and by God (Mark 1:12; Acts 20:22; Philippians 2:12-13). God is able to empower us through the Holy Spirit to resist sin and perform the good works that He has planned for us (Ephesians 2:10). Are you struggling with sin? Do you feel like you can't overcome it by yourself? Well, you can't. But God can overcome it, and He can strengthen you to stand firm against it. Acknowledge that He is your rightful master, pray for His help, and rely on His strength. (***See Spiritual Warfare*** > *Resisting Sin and Evil* > *Embracing Christ* > *Entrust yourself to God's care,* TopicGuide page A45.)

16:20 This verse recalls the first proclamation of the gospel: the prophecy that Eve's son would crush the head of the serpent (Genesis 3:15; compare Revelation 12:9; 20:2). Ultimately, Christ is the prophesied son who fulfills this prophecy. But one of the ways He does this is through His church (Matthew 16:18).

[22]I, Tertius, the one writing this letter for Paul, send my greetings, too, as one of the
Lord's followers.
[23]Gaius says hello to you. He is my host and also serves as host to the whole church.
Erastus, the city treasurer, sends you his greetings, and so does our brother Quartus.*
[25]Now all glory to God, who is able to make you strong, just as my Good News says.
This message about Jesus Christ has revealed His plan for you Gentiles, a plan kept secret
from the beginning of time. [26]But now as the prophets* foretold and as the eternal God
has commanded, this message is made known to all Gentiles everywhere, so that they too
might believe and obey Him. [27]All glory to the only wise God, through Jesus Christ, for-
ever. Amen.

16:25
1 Cor 2:1
Eph 1:9; 3:3-5
Col 1:26-27; 2:2
2 Tim 1:9-10
1 Pet 1:20

16:26
Rom 1:2, 5

16:27
Rom 11:36

16:23 Some manuscripts add verse 24, *May the grace of our Lord Jesus Christ be with you all. Amen.* Still others add this sentence after verse 27. 16:26 Greek *the prophetic writings.*

16:22 In this letter, Paul employed a secretary who wrote down the apostle's words. This was a common practice in the ancient world. Paul used secretaries on many occasions, sometimes adding a signature or final greeting in his own hand (see 1 Corinthians 16:21; Galatians 6:11; Colossians 4:18; 2 Thessalonians 3:17).

1 CORINTHIANS

PURPOSE

To call believers to wholehearted, holy living amidst division, disorder, and difficulty in the local church.

Sometimes people idealize life in the early church. As we look around and see problems in the church today and see believers who are not living holy lives, we often think, *If only things could be like they were in the early church. . . .* But such a wish is typically based on an unrealistic view of those early days.

Although the early church was often lively, vibrant, and growing, it was not without its challenges. The apostle Paul wrote 1 Corinthians to a church with both problems and questions. The problems included divided loyalties to different teachers in the church (chapter 3), immorality that the congregation tolerated (chapter 5), and ministry that was carried out in an uncaring way (chapters 12–14). The questions ranged from very pragmatic issues such as dealing with lawsuits (6:1-8) to more personal and complex issues surrounding marriage (chapter 7) to theological questions related to the future resurrection (chapter 15). As you get to know the Corinthians through this letter, you will come to see that many of the struggles that the church faces today are not significantly different from those faced by the early church.

DISCOVER GOD IN 1 CORINTHIANS

Because of Paul's practical bent in addressing issues in the Corinthian church, we don't get as much straightforward instruction about God as we do in some of his other letters. Though we have to look closely for fresh insights about God, He is always present in Paul's thinking, and careful attention teaches us the following:

Jesus, the Crucified Savior: The believers in Corinth had allowed themselves to become divided over which teacher they followed. Paul was appalled at this behavior, because for him there was only one rallying point for the church: Jesus Christ, the One who was crucified so that men and women could have life. In the first two chapters, Paul eloquently affirms the power of the message of the cross and how that humble, simple message of salvation in Jesus alone stands in contrast to the world's approach to power and salvation.

The Spirit, the Powerful Indweller: Some of the problems that the Corinthian believers faced were rooted in their misunderstanding of the Holy Spirit. Repeatedly in this letter, Paul calls their attention to the Spirit who lives inside each follower of Jesus (2:11-16; 3:16-17; 6:19-20; 12:7-11). Paul knew the presence of the Spirit in their lives should reveal supernatural character as well as special gifts.

The Father, the Jealous God: Challenges in the Corinthian church were drawing believers away from true, single-hearted devotion to God. Paul called them not to lose sight of the God who had made them His own and to devote themselves to Him completely. Paul reminded them that it was God the Father who brought them to faith (1:26-31) and that He was the One who brings growth in the church (3:1-9). Paul tells the believers that they live to glorify God (6:20; 8:6; 10:31).

GROWING THROUGH 1 CORINTHIANS

Paul wrote the letter of 1 Corinthians to address various concerns and questions from the church there, so it is arranged in a topical way. It is immediately applicable to any congregation struggling with similar issues. There are, however, some larger themes that run throughout the letter that can be of great help to any disciple seeking to grow, regardless of whether he or she is facing the particular issues being addressed by Paul.

The Cross of Christ: For Paul the message of the Cross is *the* message of the church (1:17–2:5). It is central to the worship of the community of faith (11:23-26), and it is joined together with the promise of the coming resurrection (15:12-28). Paul never tired of talking about Jesus' life, death, and resurrection.

The Power of the Spirit: Paul affirms that even the glorious good news about Jesus' death needs to be backed up by the power of the Spirit if that message is going to transform lives (2:4-5). The Spirit enables the believer to understand truth (2:12-16) and empowers the ongoing ministry of the community of believers (12:1-13).

A Holy and Transformed Life: Paul sees the Corinthians manifesting only some of the signs of the presence of the Spirit in their midst (1 Corinthians 14), but he fails to find them showing the character that marks God's people (1 Corinthians 5; 13). When reflecting on the immorality that is tolerated in the church (5:1-8; 6:12-20), he calls them to abandon sin and live as those who have truly been gripped by the Good News about Jesus through the Spirit. Paul's expectation is clear—all those who belong to Jesus ought to live in a loving and holy manner.

DISCOVERY VERSES

Run from sexual sin! No other sin so clearly affects the body as this one does. For sexual immorality is a sin against your own body. (1 CORINTHIANS 6:18)

There are different kinds of spiritual gifts, but the same Spirit is the source of them all. (1 CORINTHIANS 12:4)

If I could speak all the languages of earth and of angels, but didn't love others, I would only be a noisy gong or a clanging cymbal. (1 CORINTHIANS 13:1)

I passed on to you what was most important and what had also been passed on to me. Christ died for our sins, just as the Scriptures said. He was buried, and He was raised from the dead on the third day, just as the Scriptures said. (1 CORINTHIANS 15:3-4)

1 CORINTHIANS FACTS

Author: Paul identifies himself as the writer of this letter (1:1). Paul had spent extended time in Corinth, so he writes as one who was familiar to the Corinthian believers.

Written to: The church in Corinth was founded when Paul brought the gospel to them on one of his missionary journeys (Acts 18). Paul had to flee Philippi (Acts 16), Thessalonica, and Berea (Acts 17) because of persecution and trouble. When he arrived in Corinth, however, Jesus told Paul he would be safe staying there a while. Paul eventually stayed there three and a half years, working as a tentmaker to support himself while preaching and teaching (Acts 18).

Date of writing: In the closing chapter of the letter, Paul tells the Corinthians that he is writing from Ephesus and is intending to visit them after going through Macedonia (1 Corinthians 16:5-9). The book of Acts records that Paul stayed in Ephesus about three years (Acts 19), so this letter would have been written sometime near the end of his stay there. That would place it around AD 55.

Setting: Paul wrote from the city of Ephesus where he had been ministering for some three years, but the setting of the book is Corinth. This southern city was the largest of ancient Greece, five times the size of Athens and known for its raucous lifestyle.

OUTLINE

▸ **1 CORINTHIANS 1:1–6:20**—Problems in the church

1 CORINTHIANS 1:1–4:21*—Immature Divisions*

1 CORINTHIANS 5:1-13*—Immoral Behavior*

1 CORINTHIANS 6:1-20*—Inconsistent Decisions*

- ▸**1 CORINTHIANS 7:1–16:5**—Questions from the church
  - ***1 CORINTHIANS 7:1-40**—Marriage*
  - ***1 CORINTHIANS 8:1–11:1**—Questionable Practices*
  - ***1 CORINTHIANS 11:2-34**—Church Life*
  - ***1 CORINTHIANS 12:1–14:40**—Spiritual Gifts*
  - ***1 CORINTHIANS 15:1-58**—The Resurrection*
  - ***1 CORINTHIANS 16:1-4**—Finances*
- ▸**1 CORINTHIANS 16:5-24**—Greetings to the church

GREETINGS FROM PAUL

1:1 Acts 18:17; Rom 1:1
1 This letter is from Paul, chosen by the will of God to be an apostle of Christ Jesus, and
from our brother Sosthenes.

1:2 Rom 8:28; 10:12-13; 2 Tim 2:22
2I am writing to God's church in Corinth,* to you who have been called by God to be His
own holy people. He made you holy by means of Christ Jesus,* just as He did for all people
everywhere who call on the name of our Lord Jesus Christ, their Lord and ours.

1:3 Rom 1:7
3May God our Father and the Lord Jesus Christ give you grace and peace.

1:4 Rom 1:8

PAUL GIVES THANKS TO GOD

1:5 2 Cor 8:7; 9:11
4I always thank my God for you and for the gracious gifts He has given you, now that you
belong to Christ Jesus. 5Through Him, God has enriched your church in every way—with all

1:7 Rom 8:19, 23; Phil 3:20; 2 Thes 1:7; Titus 2:13; 2 Pet 3:12
of your eloquent words and all of your knowledge. 6This confirms that what I told you about
Christ is true. 7Now you have every spiritual gift you need as you eagerly wait for the return

1:2a *Corinth* was the capital city of Achaia, the southern region of the Greek peninsula. 1:2b Or *because you belong to Christ Jesus.*

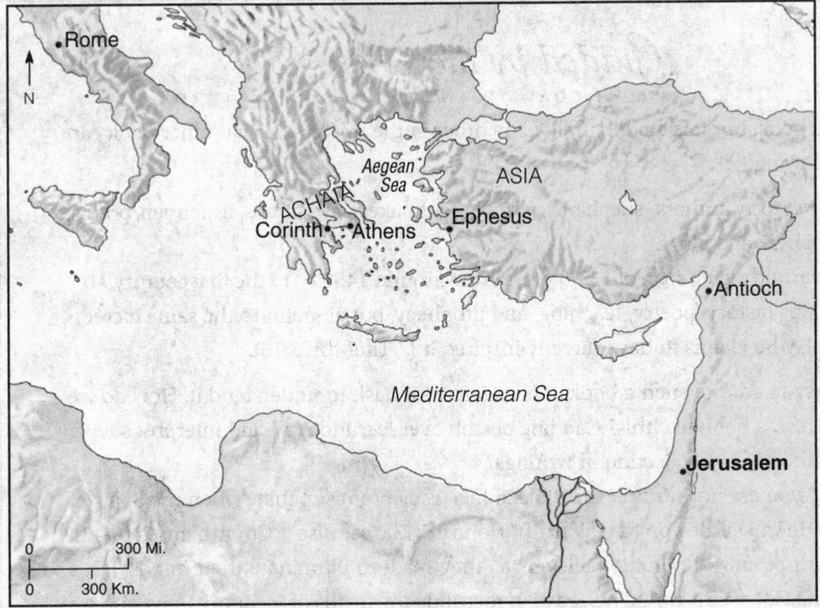

CORINTH AND EPHESUS
Paul wrote this letter to Corinth during his three-year visit in Ephesus on his third missionary journey. The two cities sat across from each other on the Aegean Sea—both were busy and important ports. Titus may have carried this letter from Ephesus to Corinth (2 Corinthians 12:18).

1:1 Sosthenes was Paul's companion at the time he composed this letter. There had been a synagogue leader in Corinth named Sosthenes who probably led the legal action against Paul in front of the Roman proconsul (see Acts 18:17). If this is the same Sosthenes, then he had later converted to Christianity and left Corinth to travel with Paul. Alternately, this could simply be another person named Sosthenes who was known to the Corinthian church.

of our Lord Jesus Christ. [8]He will keep you strong to the end so that you will be free from all
blame on the day when our Lord Jesus Christ returns. [9]God will do this, for He is faithful to
do what He says, and He has invited you into partnership with His Son, Jesus Christ our Lord.

1:8
Phil 1:6
1 Thes 3:13; 5:23
2 Thes 3:3

DIVISIONS IN THE CHURCH

[10]I appeal to you, dear brothers and sisters,* by the authority of our Lord Jesus Christ, to live in
harmony with each other. Let there be no divisions in the church. Rather, be of one mind,
united in thought and purpose. [11]For some members of Chloe's household have told me
about your quarrels, my dear brothers and sisters. [12]Some of you are saying, "I am a follower
of Paul." Others are saying, "I follow Apollos," or "I follow Peter,*" or "I follow only Christ."
[13]Has Christ been divided into factions? Was I, Paul, crucified for you? Were any of you
baptized in the name of Paul? Of course not! [14]I thank God that I did not baptize any of

1:10
Rom 15:5
1 Cor 11:18

1:12
John 1:42
Acts 18:24

1:13
Acts 2:38
Eph 4:5

1:14
Acts 18:8; 19:29
Rom 16:23

1:10 Greek *brothers;* also in 1:11, 26. 1:12 Greek *Cephas.*

▸ HOLINESS
1:10-17 Christ, the focus of the Christian. Paul is appalled at the Corinthian Christians' behavior because for him there is only one rallying point for the church: Jesus Christ, the One who was crucified so that men and women could have life. Christ alone is our Savior, and He alone is the focal point of the church. It is easy to meet an exciting leader or great teacher and be swept away by his or her influence and insight. But even if a pastor or Christian leader is speaking truth, we are to follow not that leader but Christ, who is speaking through him or her. Is your true allegiance to Jesus Christ or to a particular pastor or Christian leader? Do not lose your focus on Christ. (***See Holiness****> Submission> Identifying with Christ> Abiding in Christ,* TopicGuide page A40.)

1:11 Chloe was a woman whose household members (possibly slaves) informed Paul in Ephesus of arguments within the Corinthian church. It is not known whether Chloe lived in Corinth or Ephesus.

1:12 As mentioned in the introduction to this letter, Paul was the author of this letter. Apollos was an eloquent preacher at the time of Paul's missionary journeys (see Acts 18:24–19:1). Peter was a leader among Jesus' 12 disciples. The Corinthian Christians were lining up behind their favorite teacher and primarily considering themselves as followers of that teacher, not as part of the church as a whole. These factions within the church were divisive and argumentative.

MY RESPONSE TO GOD

Guided by the Spirit

1 CORINTHIANS 2

The Bible is a book, but it is a book unlike any other in the universe. What other book can claim the following:

- It has over forty authors–shepherds, farmers, tentmakers, physicians, fishermen, priests, philosophers, and kings.
- It was written over a span of 1,500 years, from around 1450 BC to the first century AD.
- It contains history, poetry, teaching, and prophecy, but all point to the same incredible God, who claims to have directly inspired it (2 Timothy 3:16).

While it is easy to admire such a book, it is a Herculean task to understand it. How do we even start to read a book like this? Can one person ever learn to read and interpret such a complicated and diverse collection of writings?

Fortunately you are not reading the Bible alone. Jesus promised that "when the Spirit of truth comes, He will guide you into all truth" (John 16:13a; see also 1 Corinthians 2:10-15). The Holy Spirit promises to guide believers as they read–to illuminate their minds. Jesus prayed that the Holy Spirit would be active in revealing the truths of Scripture to us, and we should expect Jesus' prayers to be answered. It is His promise and our heritage that the Holy Spirit teaches us through the Word (2 Corinthians 1:22; 1 John 2:27).

1:17 Matt 28:19; John 4:2; Acts 26:17; 2 Cor 10:10; 11:16
1:18 Rom 1:16; 2 Cor 2:15; 4:3
1:19 *Isa 29:14
1:20 Job 12:17; Isa 19:11-12; 44:25
1:21 Matt 11:25
1:22 Matt 12:38
1:24 Col 2:3
1:25 2 Cor 13:4
1:26 Matt 11:25; John 7:48; Jas 2:1-5
1:28 Rom 4:17
1:29 Eph 2:9
1:30 Jer 23:5-6; Rom 3:24; 2 Cor 5:21
1:31 *Jer 9:24; 2 Cor 10:17
2:2 Gal 6:14
2:3 2 Cor 10:1; Gal 4:13

you except Crispus and Gaius, 15 for now no one can say they were baptized in my name. 16 (Oh yes, I also baptized the household of Stephanas, but I don't remember baptizing anyone else.) 17 For Christ didn't send me to baptize, but to preach the Good News—and not with clever speech, for fear that the cross of Christ would lose its power.

THE WISDOM OF GOD

18 The message of the cross is foolish to those who are headed for destruction! But we who are being saved know it is the very power of God. 19 As the Scriptures say,

"I will destroy the wisdom of the wise
and discard the intelligence of the intelligent."*

20 So where does this leave the philosophers, the scholars, and the world's brilliant debaters? God has made the wisdom of this world look foolish. 21 Since God in His wisdom saw to it that the world would never know Him through human wisdom, He has used our foolish preaching to save those who believe. 22 It is foolish to the Jews, who ask for signs from heaven. And it is foolish to the Greeks, who seek human wisdom. 23 So when we preach that Christ was crucified, the Jews are offended and the Gentiles say it's all nonsense.

24 But to those called by God to salvation, both Jews and Gentiles,* Christ is the power of God and the wisdom of God. 25 This foolish plan of God is wiser than the wisest of human plans, and God's weakness is stronger than the greatest of human strength.

26 Remember, dear brothers and sisters, that few of you were wise in the world's eyes or powerful or wealthy* when God called you. 27 Instead, God chose things the world considers foolish in order to shame those who think they are wise. And He chose things that are powerless to shame those who are powerful. 28 God chose things despised by the world,* things counted as nothing at all, and used them to bring to nothing what the world considers important. 29 As a result, no one can ever boast in the presence of God.

30 God has united you with Christ Jesus. For our benefit God made Him to be wisdom itself. Christ made us right with God; He made us pure and holy, and He freed us from sin. 31 Therefore, as the Scriptures say, "If you want to boast, boast only about the LORD."*

PAUL'S MESSAGE OF WISDOM

2 When I first came to you, dear brothers and sisters,* I didn't use lofty words and impressive wisdom to tell you God's secret plan.* 2 For I decided that while I was with you I would forget everything except Jesus Christ, the One who was crucified. 3 I came to

1:19 Isa 29:14. 1:24 Greek *and Greeks.* 1:26 Or *high born.* 1:28 Or *God chose those who are low born.* 1:31 Jer 9:24.
2:1a Greek *brothers.* 2:1b Greek *God's mystery;* other manuscripts read *God's testimony.*

1:20-23 The "philosophers, the scholars, and the world's brilliant debaters" were three types of intellectual leaders in the ancient world. Together, they represent the pinnacle of human wisdom. The message of the gospel was foolishness to these intellectual leaders: They could not imagine a religion in which God Himself became human and even died. Paul, however, notes the extreme irony: These wisest of human beings were in fact foolish because they did not understand God's plan. True wisdom is found in God (1:21), even if it looks strange to human eyes.

1:26 Paul mentions three types of people who have influence in the world: the wise, the powerful, and the wealthy. Believers trying to spread the message of Jesus Christ would be tempted to target these three groups in order to gain prestige for the Christian message. And in fact, 1 Corinthians 4:8 indicates that the Corinthian Christians had become wealthy and powerful in a worldly sense. God, however, chooses the opposite evangelistic strategy. Verse 27 indicates that He chooses to spread the gospel through the people and things that the world thinks are unimportant.

▸ SPIRITUAL WARFARE

1:28 Resisting the world's "wisdom." Few people enjoy looking foolish in front of others. Because of this, believers are constantly tempted to try to make our beliefs more acceptable by the world's standards of wisdom. But we stand on the gospel that God gave us, even though it looks foolish to the world. Has a teacher, a professor, a colleague, or even a stranger ever ridiculed you for your beliefs? Have you compromised your beliefs when in public to look more wise or sophisticated? Do not aim to be wise in the world's eyes. Stand for the gospel even if it brings ridicule. (***See Spiritual Warfare*>** *Resisting Sin and Evil> Resisting Temptation> What to Resist> We are to resist worldly influences,* TopicGuide page A45.)

1:30-31 Paul reaffirms that Jesus Christ alone is the way to salvation. Jesus makes us "right with God" and "pure and holy." Paul also specifies how Jesus did this: by giving Himself to purchase our freedom. We are set free from sin by one thing only: Jesus giving up His own life for our sake. This removes any human right to be proud, because our salvation is a gift we have received, not something we have earned.

you in weakness—timid and trembling. 4And my message and my preaching were very plain. Rather than using clever and persuasive speeches, I relied only on the power of the Holy Spirit. 5I did this so you would trust not in human wisdom but in the power of God.

6Yet when I am among mature believers, I do speak with words of wisdom, but not the kind of wisdom that belongs to this world or to the rulers of this world, who are soon forgotten. 7No, the wisdom we speak of is the mystery of God*—His plan that was previously hidden, even though He made it for our ultimate glory before the world began. 8But the rulers of this world have not understood it; if they had, they would not have crucified our glorious Lord. 9That is what the Scriptures mean when they say,

"No eye has seen, no ear has heard,
  and no mind has imagined
what God has prepared
  for those who love Him."*

10But* it was to us that God revealed these things by His Spirit. For His Spirit searches out everything and shows us God's deep secrets. 11No one can know a person's thoughts except that person's own spirit, and no one can know God's thoughts except God's own Spirit. 12And we have received God's Spirit (not the world's spirit), so we can know the wonderful things God has freely given us.

13When we tell you these things, we do not use words that come from human wisdom. Instead, we speak words given to us by the Spirit, using the Spirit's words to explain spiritual truths.* 14But people who aren't spiritual* can't receive these truths from God's Spirit. It all sounds foolish to them and they can't understand it, for only those who are spiritual can understand what the Spirit means. 15Those who are spiritual can evaluate all things, but they themselves cannot be evaluated by others. 16For,

2:5 2 Cor 4:7; 6:7
2:6 Eph 4:13; Phil 3:15; Heb 5:14
2:7 Rom 16:25
2:8 Jas 2:1
2:9 *Isa 64:4; 65:17
2:10 Matt 11:25; 13:11; John 14:26; 15:26; 16:13-15; 1 Jn 2:27
2:11 Prov 20:27; Jer 17:9; Rom 11:33
2:12 John 16:13-15; Rom 8:15
2:13 2 Pet 1:20-21
2:14 John 8:47; 14:17; Jude 1:19
2:16 *Isa 40:13; Rom 11:34

2:7 Greek *But we speak God's wisdom in a mystery.* 2:9 Isa 64:4. 2:10 Some manuscripts read *For.* 2:13 Or *explaining spiritual truths in spiritual language,* or *explaining spiritual truths to spiritual people.* 2:14 Or *who don't have the Spirit;* or *who have only physical life.*

2:4 Paul purposely restrained himself when he shared the gospel with the Corinthians. We know from Acts 17:22-31 that Paul was capable of philosophical argumentation, but he chose not to use those skills in Corinth. Both 1 Corinthians 2:3 and 2 Corinthians 10:1 indicate that the Corinthians considered Paul a weak and timid speaker. Paul understood, though, that God works even through weak human messengers (2 Corinthians 12:10).

2:7 The "mystery of God" is simply the gospel: the "foolish" message (1:25) of the Messiah crucified on a cross, which Paul has been discussing. Christ's death and resurrection on the cross was not an afterthought or a mistake; it was God's plan from "before the world began." Yet until Christ came, this plan was secret; it was hidden from human understanding. The Greek word for "mystery" in this verse does not indicate something that can be unraveled or discovered but something no human mind could ever understand unless it is specially revealed. Verse 10 indicates that God has done precisely this for those who have received the Holy Spirit.

2:10-12 Paul's analogy has three points—only we know our deepest thoughts, and God alone knows His mind. But since God has given us His Spirit, who is Himself God, we can know the will of God.

▸ GOD

2:12 Who is the Holy Spirit? If you mention to most Christians that they have a "Spirit guide," they might look at you strangely. But Paul repeatedly calls the Corinthian Christians' attention to the Spirit, who indwells and directs them. From Paul's perspective, the Christian life is lived through the power of the Spirit, who is God Himself. Paul affirms that even the glorious Good News about Jesus' death needs to be backed up by the power of the Spirit if that word is going to transform lives (2:4-5). Further, the Christian's grasp of truth is realized not through being smarter than others or having a secret Bible-decoder, but through the illuminating Holy Spirit (2:12-16). When you read the Bible, does it seem hard to understand? The Spirit's role is to help you understand. Pray to God that you will be open to receiving the wisdom that is offered to you through the Holy Spirit. (***See God***> *Salvation> Holy Spirit> Helps us understand things of God,* TopicGuide page A15.)

2:14 Paul indicates that people who are not Christians are unable to understand the wisdom of God. The foolishness that Paul discusses in chapters 1 and 2 has at its root a moral cause: sin. Our sin does not merely harm others (though it almost always does); it also harms us by warping our understanding, making us unable to understand the things of God.

2:16 Paul quotes Isaiah 40:13, a verse from a section of Isaiah that emphasizes the complete superiority of God's wisdom over that of humanity. This highlights the remarkable truth that "we have the mind of Christ." Because the Holy Spirit dwells in Christians, the gap between our understanding and the wisdom of God is bridged. This does not mean that we can now "teach Him," but merely that we have now been privileged to understand His counsel.

"Who can know the LORD's thoughts?
Who knows enough to teach Him?"*

But we understand these things, for we have the mind of Christ.

PAUL AND APOLLOS, SERVANTS OF CHRIST

3 Dear brothers and sisters,* when I was with you I couldn't talk to you as I would to spiritual people.* I had to talk as though you belonged to this world or as though you were infants in the Christian life.* 2I had to feed you with milk, not with solid food, because you weren't ready for anything stronger. And you still aren't ready, 3for you are still controlled by your sinful nature. You are jealous of one another and quarrel with each other. Doesn't that prove you are controlled by your sinful nature? Aren't you living like people of the world? 4When one of you says, "I am a follower of Paul," and another says, "I follow Apollos," aren't you acting just like people of the world?

5After all, who is Apollos? Who is Paul? We are only God's servants through whom you believed the Good News. Each of us did the work the Lord gave us. 6I planted the seed in your hearts, and Apollos watered it, but it was God who made it grow. 7It's not important who does the planting, or who does the watering. What's important is that God makes the seed grow. 8The one who plants and the one who waters work together with the same purpose. And both will be rewarded for their own hard work. 9For we are both God's workers. And you are God's field. You are God's building.

10Because of God's grace to me, I have laid the foundation like an expert builder. Now others are building on it. But whoever is building on this foundation must be very careful. 11For no one can lay any foundation other than the one we already have—Jesus Christ.

12Anyone who builds on that foundation may use a variety of materials—gold, silver, jewels, wood, hay, or straw. 13But on the judgment day, fire will reveal what kind of work each builder has done. The fire will show if a person's work has any value. 14If the work survives, that builder will receive a reward. 15But if the work is burned up, the builder will

2:16 Isa 40:13 (Greek version). 3:1a Greek *Brothers.* 3:1b Or *to people who have the Spirit.* 3:1c Greek *in Christ.*

3:1 Gal 6:1; Eph 4:14
3:2 Heb 5:12-13; 1 Pet 2:2
3:3 Rom 13:13; 1 Cor 1:10-11; 11:18
3:4 1 Cor 1:12; Gal 5:20
3:5 Acts 18:24; Rom 12:3, 6; 2 Cor 6:4
3:6 Acts 18:4-11
3:8 Pss 18:20; 62:12
3:9 Isa 61:3; Eph 2:20-22; 1 Pet 2:5
3:10 Rom 15:20
3:11 Isa 28:16; Eph 2:20; 1 Pet 2:4-6
3:13 1 Cor 4:5; 2 Tim 1:12, 18; 4:8
3:15 Jude 1:23

WORSHIP

3:1-4 Christians are transformed people. Paul sees the Corinthians living as mere people; he calls them to a transformed life, living as those who have truly been gripped by the Good News about Jesus and the Spirit. Do you live by the power of the Spirit? Has your life changed as a result of knowing and following Jesus Christ? Make no mistake: A changed life does not earn you salvation. Instead, a changed life follows salvation; it is the *inevitable* result of being saved from sin. Take a hard look at yourself—has there been a life change? If not, consider carefully whether you have really understood the gospel (2 Peter 1:10). (***See Worship****> NT> Our Role> Holiness> Christian life means being transformed,* TopicGuide page A32.)

3:2 Paul is unable to speak to his friends in Corinth as he would to mature Christians. The chief indication that the Corinthian Christians are still spiritual babies is their jealousy and quarreling.

3:6 To explain the partnership between himself and Apollos, Paul uses an agrarian illustration, one that would be easily grasped in the ancient world.

3:10-12 When a house is built, the first step is to lay a foundation. Once the foundation is laid, the house must be built on top of that foundation, and it must conform to it. If the walls of the house are not properly supported by the foundation, they are subject to collapse, and the house will be liable to fall down during storms or to gradually break apart over time. Paul emphasizes that Jesus Christ is the foundation for Christian life and ministry, and like the house, we must build on Him alone and conform to Him.

3:13 A "judgment day" will come when Christians' lives and ministries will be tested by fire. "Fire" draws upon the imagery of a refining furnace. Refining is the process of purifying metal by heating it to very high temperatures. When metal ores are mined from the earth, they contain a mixture of the metal (whether it be gold, copper, iron, or another metal) and various impurities. In the process of refining, the ore is heated, and the impurities are separated from the pure metal, becoming dross. The dross either burns away or is removed by the refiner. What remains is metal that is pure and useful.

3:14-15 The "reward" that Christians will receive for good work is not salvation, because verse 15 indicates that even the Christian who builds poorly will be saved. There are other rewards, however, that Christians will receive from God for their work. Anyone who lives his or her life foolishly will lose this additional reward; this is a "great loss" and comparable to escaping from a house fire alive, but losing everything one owns.

suffer great loss. The builder will be saved, but like someone barely escaping through a
wall of flames.
[16]Don't you realize that all of you together are the temple of God and that the Spirit of
God lives in* you? [17]God will destroy anyone who destroys this temple. For God's temple
is holy, and you are that temple.
[18]Stop deceiving yourselves. If you think you are wise by this world's standards, you
need to become a fool to be truly wise. [19]For the wisdom of this world is foolishness to
God. As the Scriptures say,

"He traps the wise
in the snare of their own cleverness."*

[20]And again,

"The LORD knows the thoughts of the wise;
He knows they are worthless."*

[21]So don't boast about following a particular human leader. For everything belongs to
you—[22]whether Paul or Apollos or Peter,* or the world, or life and death, or the present
and the future. Everything belongs to you, [23]and you belong to Christ, and Christ belongs
to God.

3:16 Or *among.* 3:19 Job 5:13. 3:20 Ps 94:11. 3:22 Greek *Cephas.*

3:16 1 Cor 6:19; 2 Cor 6:16
3:17 Eph 2:21-22
3:18 Isa 5:21; 1 Cor 8:2; Gal 6:3
3:19 *Job 5:13; 1 Cor 1:20, 27
3:20 *Ps 94:11
3:21 Rom 8:32
3:22 Rom 8:38
3:23 1 Cor 11:3

3:16-17 In the New Covenant, we are God's temple (1 Corinthians 6:19). This is true of each Christian individually, but in the context of chapter 3, Paul uses this metaphor to refer to the church as a whole—all Christians. The threat that God will bring ruin on anyone who ruins His Temple was a rebuke to the Corinthian Christians, who were ruining the church there by their quarreling and divisiveness.

▶ ADOPTION
3:18 Foolish wisdom. What sorts of people are thought of as wise in the world? Do people think of you as wise? If they do, review why people think you are prudent—is it because you are extremely pragmatic, logical, and unflappable, or because you live your life based on the instructions from God's Word? To do so may not make you seem so wise. You may appear to be quite foolish. Are you willing to be scorned or looked down upon for the sake of the gospel? Take some time to think about it today, and ask God for His sort of wisdom—from His Word (James 1:5). (***See Adoption****> With Christ> Heirs of God> Spiritual blessing of wisdom,* TopicGuide page A36.)

3:19-20 Paul first quotes Job 5:13, a book that emphasizes the limits of human wisdom and understanding. He then quotes from Psalm 94:11, a psalm that emphasizes the foolishness of those who think God does not see or judge human actions. These Old Testament Scriptures reinforce Paul's argument about the limits of human knowledge and wisdom in the face of God's transcendent wisdom.

BECAUSE GOD IS EVER-PRESENT

He is always with me.

Don't you realize that all of you together are the temple of God
and that the Spirit of God lives in you?

1 CORINTHIANS 3:16

FOR THE NEXT *GOD IS EVER-PRESENT* FEATURE SEE PAGE 2220.

PAUL'S RELATIONSHIP WITH THE CORINTHIANS

4 So look at Apollos and me as mere servants of Christ who have been put in charge of explaining God's mysteries. [2]Now, a person who is put in charge as a manager must be faithful. [3]As for me, it matters very little how I might be evaluated by you or by any human authority. I don't even trust my own judgment on this point. [4]My conscience is clear, but that doesn't prove I'm right. It is the Lord Himself who will examine me and decide.

[5]So don't make judgments about anyone ahead of time—before the Lord returns. For He will bring our darkest secrets to light and will reveal our private motives. Then God will give to each one whatever praise is due.

[6]Dear brothers and sisters,* I have used Apollos and myself to illustrate what I've been saying. If you pay attention to what I have quoted from the Scriptures,* you won't be proud of one of your leaders at the expense of another. [7]For what gives you the right to make such a judgment? What do you have that God hasn't given you? And if everything you have is from God, why boast as though it were not a gift?

[8]You think you already have everything you need. You think you are already rich. You have begun to reign in God's kingdom without us! I wish you really were reigning already, for then we would be reigning with you. [9]Instead, I sometimes think God has put us apostles on display, like prisoners of war at the end of a victor's parade, condemned to die. We have become a spectacle to the entire world—to people and angels alike.

[10]Our dedication to Christ makes us look like fools, but you claim to be so wise in Christ! We are weak, but you are so powerful! You are honored, but we are ridiculed. [11]Even now we go hungry and thirsty, and we don't have enough clothes to keep warm. We are often beaten and have no home. [12]We work wearily with our own hands to earn our living. We bless those who curse us. We are patient with those who abuse us. [13]We appeal gently when evil things are said about us. Yet we are treated like the world's garbage, like everybody's trash—right up to the present moment.

4:6a Greek *Brothers.* 4:6b Or *If you learn not to go beyond "what is written."*

4:1 Rom 16:25; Titus 1:7
4:2 Luke 12:42
4:4 Ps 143:2
4:5 Matt 7:1; 2 Cor 5:10; Rev 20:12
4:7 John 3:27; Rom 12:3, 6
4:8 Rev 3:17, 21
4:9 Rom 8:36; Heb 10:33
4:10 1 Cor 1:18; 3:18; 2 Cor 11:19
4:11 Acts 23:2; Rom 8:35; 2 Cor 11:23-27
4:12 Matt 5:44; Acts 18:3; 1 Pet 3:9
4:13 Lam 3:45

4:1 See note on 2:7. "God's mysteries" refers to the gospel, which had been kept secret. Though God's redemptive plan existed from before time began, it was not revealed until God brought it about through history in the person of Jesus Christ.

▸ HOLINESS
4:2-4 God's Word trains the conscience. How do we know if we have been faithful? Paul was careful to say that neither the Corinthians' judgment of him nor the judgment of other people is a true indicator of faithfulness. Even more, Paul noted that having a clear conscience is no guarantee that we have been faithful. If you are a believer, your conscience, like the rest of you, is gradually being renewed in the image of God. That means it can be a good guide in decisions, and as you grow in God's grace it will become a better and better guide. But your conscience is not completely trustworthy. It can still mislead you and even lead you into sin. Therefore, do not simply ask, "Am I at peace with this decision?" That is good, but not enough. More importantly, search God's Word and ask, "Is it clear that God approves of this decision?" (***See Holiness***> *Submission> Learning God's Word> Renewing the mind,* TopicGuide page A40.)

4:5 Paul indicates that God's judgment will not simply be based on our actions, but also on our motives for our actions. An action that is nominally good but done for the wrong reasons (such as pride) will not count as righteousness in the day of judgment (see Matthew 7:15-23).

4:7 Paul emphasizes that all physical and spiritual riches are gifts from God. Such a view of life eliminates all boasting, because boasting is pride in our own power. If the Corinthian Christians would have truly understood how much they were indebted to God, then all their prideful quarrels would have quickly ended.

4:8-13 Paul is extremely sarcastic in these verses. He draws two pictures of the Christian life, one picture based on the apostles' lives and one picture based on the Corinthians' lives. He contrasts these pictures to show how far off track the Corinthian Christians' lives had become. The Corinthians considered themselves well fed, rich, wise, and powerful. The apostles, on the other hand, who brought the gospel to the Corinthians, were poor, mocked, hungry, thirsty, cold, and beaten. The Corinthians looked like kings and the apostles like prisoners of war.

▸ HOLINESS
4:8-14 Trials accompany the Christian life. Which of the two pictures Paul describes matches your life? Do you resemble Paul and the other apostles, or the Corinthians? If your life is merely one of ease and glory, then you need to listen to Paul's warning to the Corinthians. You will not necessarily be called to every hardship that faced the apostles, but Jesus does promise that His followers will experience persecution (John 15:20). If you have faced no hardships because of your faith, ask yourself whether you are pursuing an easy life or a godly life. (***See Holiness***> *God's Blessing> Obedience leads to hardship and persecution,* TopicGuide page A42.)

14 I am not writing these things to shame you, but to warn you as my beloved children.
15 For even if you had ten thousand others to teach you about Christ, you have only one
spiritual father. For I became your father in Christ Jesus when I preached the Good News to
you. 16 So I urge you to imitate me.
17 That's why I have sent Timothy, my beloved and faithful child in the Lord. He will re-
mind you of how I follow Christ Jesus, just as I teach in all the churches wherever I go.
18 Some of you have become arrogant, thinking I will not visit you again. 19 But I will
come—and soon—if the Lord lets me, and then I'll find out whether these arrogant people
just give pretentious speeches or whether they really have God's power. 20 For the King-
dom of God is not just a lot of talk; it is living by God's power. 21 Which do you choose?
Should I come with a rod to punish you, or should I come with love and a gentle spirit?

PAUL CONDEMNS SPIRITUAL PRIDE

5 I can hardly believe the report about the sexual immorality going on among you—
something that even pagans don't do. I am told that a man in your church is living in
sin with his stepmother.* 2 You are so proud of yourselves, but you should be mourning in
sorrow and shame. And you should remove this man from your fellowship.
3 Even though I am not with you in person, I am with you in the Spirit.* And as though I
were there, I have already passed judgment on this man 4 in the name of the Lord Jesus.
You must call a meeting of the church.* I will be present with you in spirit, and so will the
power of our Lord Jesus. 5 Then you must throw this man out and hand him over to Satan
so that his sinful nature will be destroyed* and he himself* will be saved on the day the
Lord* returns.

4:14 1 Cor 6:5; 15:34; 2 Cor 6:13
4:15 Gal 4:19
4:16 1 Cor 11:1; Phil 3:17; 1 Thes 1:6
4:17 Acts 16:1; 19:22; 1 Tim 1:2
4:19 Acts 18:21; 1 Cor 16:5; 2 Cor 1:15-16
4:20 1 Cor 2:4
4:21 2 Cor 1:23; 2:1
5:1 Lev 18:7-8; Deut 22:30; 27:20; Eph 5:3
5:3 Col 2:5
5:4 2 Thes 3:6
5:5 1 Tim 1:20

5:1 Greek *his father's wife.* 5:3 Or *in spirit.* 5:4 Or *In the name of the Lord Jesus, you must call a meeting of the church.* 5:5a Or *so that his body will be destroyed;* Greek reads *for the destruction of the flesh.* 5:5b Greek *and the spirit.* 5:5c Other manuscripts read *the Lord Jesus;* still others read *our Lord Jesus Christ.*

4:17 Timothy was a convert from Paul's ministry and one of Paul's regular companions. He first appears in the Bible in Acts 16:1-3 where Paul chose him to become his assistant on his second missionary journey. Paul sometimes left Timothy behind to continue his work, as in Berea (see Acts 17:14), and other times he sent Timothy ahead of himself, as to Macedonia (see Acts 19:22). Timothy is mentioned often in the Pauline letters, including 2 Corinthians, Philippians, Colossians, 1 and 2 Thessalonians, and Philemon. Paul put Timothy in charge of the church at Ephesus and wrote him two pastoral letters (1 and 2 Timothy) to help him perform that significant task.

4:18-21 Paul threatens to return to Corinth to discipline some of those who oppose him, just as a parent sometimes must discipline an obstinate child. Second Corinthians 10:1-2 indicates that some in the Corinthian church felt Paul would be too cowardly to give correction in person, and such thoughts likely already existed in the Corinthian church at the time Paul wrote 1 Corinthians. It appears that Paul did return to Corinth, and this is probably what 2 Corinthians 2:1 calls his "painful visit."

5:1 A man in the Corinthian church was having an affair with his stepmother, which Leviticus 18:8 explicitly condemns. Corinth was a port town notorious for its immorality, but this behavior would have been shockingly evil even by the lax moral standards of pagan Corinth.

▸ HOLINESS
5:1-2 Am I free to sin? In ancient Corinth, there were some who thought that because Jesus had forgiven them, it did not really matter how they lived. As a result, some were living seriously immoral lives. Paul corrects this misguided thinking in chapters 5 and 6. What about you? Have you used the grace of Christ as an excuse for immorality? Have you ever said, "Well, I can't judge them, they are under grace," as an excuse to not confront sin in others—or yourself? Far from being an excuse for immorality, the grace of Christ motivates us to holy living out of gratitude for what Jesus has done for us (see Romans 6:1-23). If you have been using grace as a cover for sin, you have been showing scorn for Jesus' sacrifice on the cross. Stop now and repent. (***See Holiness**> Law and Grace> Grace> Not an opportunity for the flesh,* TopicGuide page A42.)

5:2 The Corinthian Christians were proud of their tolerance of the immoral man's sin. The Bible does promote tolerance if it is defined as treating others (including those of other religions) with respect, just as you would like to be treated (Matthew 22:39). But tolerance should never be misconstrued to mean approval of sin, much less pride in the approval of sin, which was the behavior of the Corinthian church.

5:3-5 Paul tells the Corinthians to meet together and to cast the rebelliously unrepentant man out from their fellowship. The purpose of this church discipline is for restoration, not simple punishment. This man was to be cast out of the Corinthian fellowship not simply to destroy his sinful nature (his sinful tendencies), but because doing so would work for the salvation of his soul. Second Corinthians 2:5-11 indicates that this course of action worked—the man in question truly repented and returned to the church, at which point Paul instructed the church to forgive him.

5:4 Paul knows this process of discipline will be difficult for the Corinthian church, and he reminds them of the promise of Matthew 18:18-20—the power of Jesus Christ will be with them in a special way during this difficult meeting.

[6]Your boasting about this is terrible. Don't you realize that this sin is like a little yeast
that spreads through the whole batch of dough? [7]Get rid of the old "yeast" by removing
this wicked person from among you. Then you will be like a fresh batch of dough made
without yeast, which is what you really are. Christ, our Passover Lamb, has been sacrificed
for us.* [8]So let us celebrate the festival, not with the old bread* of wickedness and evil, but
with the new bread* of sincerity and truth.

[9]When I wrote to you before, I told you not to associate with people who indulge in sex-
ual sin. [10]But I wasn't talking about unbelievers who indulge in sexual sin, or are greedy,
or cheat people, or worship idols. You would have to leave this world to avoid people like
that. [11]I meant that you are not to associate with anyone who claims to be a believer* yet
indulges in sexual sin, or is greedy, or worships idols, or is abusive, or is a drunkard, or
cheats people. Don't even eat with such people.

[12]It isn't my responsibility to judge outsiders, but it certainly is your responsibility to
judge those inside the church who are sinning. [13]God will judge those on the outside; but
as the Scriptures say, "You must remove the evil person from among you."*

AVOIDING LAWSUITS WITH CHRISTIANS

6 When one of you has a dispute with another believer, how dare you file a lawsuit and
ask a secular court to decide the matter instead of taking it to other believers*! [2]Don't
you realize that someday we believers will judge the world? And since you are going to
judge the world, can't you decide even these little things among yourselves? [3]Don't you
realize that we will judge angels? So you should surely be able to resolve ordinary dis-
putes in this life. [4]If you have legal disputes about such matters, why go to outside judges
who are not respected by the church? [5]I am saying this to shame you. Isn't there anyone in
all the church who is wise enough to decide these issues? [6]But instead, one believer* sues
another—right in front of unbelievers!

[7]Even to have such lawsuits with one another is a defeat for you. Why not just accept
the injustice and leave it at that? Why not let yourselves be cheated? [8]Instead, you your-
selves are the ones who do wrong and cheat even your fellow believers.*

5:6 Matt 16:6, 12; Gal 5:9
5:7 Exod 12:3-6, 21; 13:7; Isa 53:7; 1 Pet 1:19; Rev 5:6
5:8 Exod 12:15-19; Deut 16:3
5:11 Rom 16:17; 2 Thes 3:6; 2 Jn 1:10
5:12 Mark 4:11
5:13 *Deut 17:7; 19:19; 21:21; 24:7
6:1 Matt 18:17
6:2 Dan 7:22; Luke 22:30; Rev 3:21
6:3 2 Pet 2:4; Jude 1:6
6:7 Matt 5:39; 1 Thes 5:15; 1 Pet 3:9
6:8 1 Thes 4:6

5:7 Greek *has been sacrificed.* 5:8a Greek *not with old leaven.* 5:8b Greek *but with unleavened [bread].* 5:11 Greek *a brother.* 5:13 Deut 17:7. 6:1 Greek *God's holy people;* also in 6:2. 6:6 Greek *one brother.* 6:8 Greek *even the brothers.*

5:7-8 Paul bolsters his argument for Christian purity by recalling the image of the Passover from Exodus 12:1-29. At the Passover, a lamb was sacrificed, and its blood was put on the doorposts and lintels of the Israelites' houses. That lamb's blood caused the plague of death that the Lord unleashed on the Egyptian firstborn to pass by the Israelites' homes, sparing their firstborn children from certain death. Paul indicates that Jesus is our Passover Lamb; His blood spares us from certain death. The Israelites remembered and celebrated Passover by eating bread made without yeast. Paul calls the Corinthians to celebrate Christ our Passover Lamb appropriately, with "new bread of sincerity and truth."

5:9 This verse indicates that the letter we call 1 Corinthians was not the first letter between Paul and the Corinthian church. Paul had written a previous letter to them that they had apparently misinterpreted. This previous letter dealt with similar issues, particularly how to deal with sexually immoral people who claimed to be part of the church, so Paul refers to it here.

▸ WORSHIP
5:9-13 A dual response to immorality. The Christian response to immorality is not as simple as you might think. Paul commands God's people to lovingly judge sin and sinners in their own midst but also to leave the judging of non-Christians up to God. Have you withdrawn from contact with non-Christians because you feel they are immoral? You need not do that. In fact, if possible, you should plan on ways to stay in regular contact with them. They need the very thing God has given you—His grace. On the other hand, have you tolerated unrepentant immorality among your friends who claim the name of Christ? Look around you and judge sin and sinners as God commands. (***See Worship**> NT> Fellowship> Preserving> Admonish one another,* TopicGuide page A31.)

5:12 The Bible says that overt and unrepentant disobedience can cause banishment from the community of faith (Genesis 3:23; Numbers 12:1-15; 2 Kings 23:27). The authority to pronounce such banishment is not given to any individual in the church; the local church as a whole body is charged with pronouncing judgment and forgiveness. Jesus lays out the process of such discipline in Matthew 18:15-20. In 2 Corinthians 2:5-11, Paul reminds the church to exercise this authority with compassion and to receive the guilty back into fellowship if they show the fruit of true repentance.

6:7 The root problem behind the lawsuits between the Corinthian believers was a focus on personal rights. The Corinthian Christians were looking out for themselves first. If they were wronged, their first instinct was to seek revenge in the most immediate way possible—through secular courts. Paul instead calls them to patiently work out the differences that arise between believers in the framework of the church.

9Don't you realize that those who do wrong will not inherit the Kingdom of God? Don't fool
yourselves. Those who indulge in sexual sin, or who worship idols, or commit adultery, or are
male prostitutes, or practice homosexuality, 10or are thieves, or greedy people, or drunkards,
or are abusive, or cheat people—none of these will inherit the Kingdom of God. 11Some of you
were once like that. But you were cleansed; you were made holy; you were made right with
God by calling on the name of the Lord Jesus Christ and by the Spirit of our God.

AVOIDING SEXUAL SIN

12You say, "I am allowed to do anything"—but not everything is good for you. And even
though "I am allowed to do anything," I must not become a slave to anything. 13You say,
"Food was made for the stomach, and the stomach for food." (This is true, though someday
God will do away with both of them.) But you can't say that our bodies were made for sexual
immorality. They were made for the Lord, and the Lord cares about our bodies. 14And God
will raise us from the dead by His power, just as He raised our Lord from the dead.
15Don't you realize that your bodies are actually parts of Christ? Should a man take his
body, which is part of Christ, and join it to a prostitute? Never! 16And don't you realize that if a
man joins himself to a prostitute, he becomes one body with her? For the Scriptures say, "The
two are united into one."* 17But the person who is joined to the Lord is one spirit with Him.
18Run from sexual sin! No other sin so clearly affects the body as this one does. For sexual
immorality is a sin against your own body. 19Don't you realize that your body is the temple
of the Holy Spirit, who lives in you and was given to you by God? You do not belong to your-
self, 20for God bought you with a high price. So you must honor God with your body.

INSTRUCTION ON MARRIAGE

7 Now regarding the questions you asked in your letter. Yes, it is good to live a celibate
life.* 2But because there is so much sexual immorality, each man should have his
own wife, and each woman should have her own husband.

6:9-10 Gal 5:19-21; Eph 5:5; Rev 22:15
6:11 Acts 22:16; Rom 8:30
6:13 Col 2:22; 1 Thes 4:3-5
6:14 Acts 2:24; Rom 6:5; 1 Cor 15:15, 20; Eph 1:19-20
6:16 *Gen 2:24; Matt 19:5
6:17 John 17:21-23; Rom 8:9-11, 16; 2 Cor 3:17; Gal 2:20
6:18 1 Thes 4:3-4
6:19 Rom 14:7-8; 1 Cor 3:16; 2 Cor 6:16
6:20 Phil 1:20; 1 Pet 1:18-19

6:16 Gen 2:24. 7:1 Greek *It is good for a man not to touch a woman.*

▸ ADOPTION

6:9-11 Heart checkup. Can an unrepentant thief, homosexual, or any other sinner who habitually and defiantly sins against God and man go to heaven? No. But Paul is clear that people just like this can be cleansed of these sins. All can receive salvation in Jesus Christ, and He promises to wash away all your sins when you repent and trust Him as Savior and Lord. If you have received salvation, do not let guilt rule you for having committed any of these sins; they are forgiven! But if some continue, unrepentant and defiant, in a lifestyle characterized by sin even after an apparent conversion, then they should have no assurance that their salvation experience was real. Take the warning passages like this seriously (see Hebrews 2:1-3; 3:8–4:2; 6:4-12 for more examples) and use them to help you examine your heart (2 Peter 1:10). (***See Adoption****> With Christ> United with Christ> New creation in Christ,* TopicGuide page A37.)

6:12-13 Paul is answering common sentiments or attitudes of the Corinthians that have justified their sin. He alternates back and forth between a Corinthian statement "you may say" and his rebuttal.

6:13-15 Contrary to those who say that Christianity is only about your spiritual life, Paul explicitly affirms that our physical bodies are good things—that God cares about our physical bodies and that He has an eternal plan that includes redeeming our physical bodies. Our bodies, not just our spirits, are considered "part of Christ" and will be saved and resurrected.

6:16-17 Paul grounds his argument for sexual purity in creation. Genesis 2:24 says that Adam and Eve became one flesh, setting the pattern for marriage, which is a monogamous commitment between a man and a woman. Paul magnifies the argument against a Christian visiting a prostitute by noting that Christians are united to Christ. Effectively then, a Christian visiting a prostitute (or engaging in any sexually immoral behavior) is dragging Christ into his or her sexual escapade. Paul means for this image to shock the Corinthians into seeing immorality as a God-dishonoring practice.

▸ BIBLE

6:14-20 Spiritual sex. The port town of Corinth, like many others in the ancient world, was a haven for vices. Prostitution was not only legal but encouraged. The temple of Aphrodite specialized in providing the finest sacred prostitutes for their worshipers. The association of sexual activity with worship was not a problem; for Paul, everything should be an act of worship—but toward God (Romans 12:1-2; 1 Corinthians 8:6; Ephesians 5:1). Sex is never merely physical; it is always emotional as well as spiritual. Do not rationalize illicit sexual activity by stating that it is merely physical—it's never that simple. Honor God with your body by using sex the way the Bible intended—as an act of worship to Him. (***See Bible****> Unity> Creation> Creation and marriage,* TopicGuide page A10.)

7:1 Paul now begins to answer some questions the Corinthian church had asked him in a previous letter. The first question was whether singleness (which would require celibacy for a Christian) was good. Paul makes it very clear that for those who have a gift from God that enables them to resist sexual sin while single, singleness is good. Likewise, Paul makes it clear that it is not wrong for Christians to marry, but that there might be certain times of crisis (7:28-29) where it is not wise.

7:3 [3]The husband should fulfill his wife's sexual needs, and the wife should fulfill her hus-
Exod 21:10 band's needs. [4]The wife gives authority over her body to her husband, and the husband
1 Pet 3:7 gives authority over his body to his wife.
[5]Do not deprive each other of sexual relations, unless you both agree to refrain from
7:5 1 Thes 3:5 sexual intimacy for a limited time so you can give yourselves more completely to prayer.
Afterward, you should come together again so that Satan won't be able to tempt you be-
7:6 2 Cor 8:8 cause of your lack of self-control. [6]I say this as a concession, not as a command. [7]But I
7:7 wish everyone were single, just as I am. But God gives to some the gift of marriage, and to
Matt 19:11-12 others the gift of singleness.
1 Cor 9:5; 12:11 [8]So I say to those who aren't married and to widows—it's better to stay unmarried, just
7:9 1 Tim 5:14 as I am. [9]But if they can't control themselves, they should go ahead and marry. It's better
7:10 to marry than to burn with lust.
Mal 2:14-16 [10]But for those who are married, I have a command that comes not from me, but from
Matt 5:32; 19:9 the Lord.* A wife must not leave her husband. [11]But if she does leave him, let her remain
Mark 10:10-12 Luke 16:18 single or else be reconciled to him. And the husband must not leave his wife.
[12]Now, I will speak to the rest of you, though I do not have a direct command from the
Lord. If a Christian man* has a wife who is not a believer and she is willing to continue liv-
ing with him, he must not leave her. [13]And if a Christian woman has a husband who is
7:14 not a believer and he is willing to continue living with her, she must not leave him. [14]For
Mal 2:15 the Christian wife brings holiness to her marriage, and the Christian husband* brings ho-
liness to his marriage. Otherwise, your children would not be holy, but now they are
7:15 holy. [15](But if the husband or wife who isn't a believer insists on leaving, let them go. In
Rom 14:19 such cases the Christian husband or wife* is no longer bound to the other, for God has
7:16 called you* to live in peace.) [16]Don't you wives realize that your husbands might be
Rom 11:14 1 Pet 3:1 saved because of you? And don't you husbands realize that your wives might be saved
because of you?
7:17 [17]Each of you should continue to live in whatever situation the Lord has placed you,
1 Cor 4:17; 14:33 and remain as you were when God first called you. This is my rule for all the churches.
7:18 Acts 15:1-19 [18]For instance, a man who was circumcised before he became a believer should not try to
Gal 5:2 reverse it. And the man who was uncircumcised when he became a believer should not be
7:19 circumcised now. [19]For it makes no difference whether or not a man has been circum-
Rom 2:25-27 cised. The important thing is to keep God's commandments.
Gal 5:6; 6:15 [20]Yes, each of you should remain as you were when God called you. [21]Are you a slave?
Col 3:11 7:22 Don't let that worry you—but if you get a chance to be free, take it. [22]And remember, if you
John 8:36 were a slave when the Lord called you, you are now free in the Lord. And if you were free
Eph 6:6 when the Lord called you, you are now a slave of Christ. [23]God paid a high price for you, so
1 Pet 2:16 don't be enslaved by the world.* [24]Each of you, dear brothers and sisters,* should remain
7:23 1 Cor 6:20 1 Pet 1:18 as you were when God first called you.

7:10 See Matt 5:32; 19:9; Mark 10:11-12; Luke 16:18. 7:12 Greek *a brother.* 7:14 Greek *the brother.* 7:15a Greek *the brother or sister.* 7:15b Some manuscripts read *us.* 7:23 Greek *don't become slaves of people.* 7:24 Greek *brothers;* also in 7:29.

7:10-11 Paul makes it clear that when we marry, we are to remain faithfully married to our spouse except in cases of adultery (Matthew 19:9) or abandonment (see note at 7:14). Divorce is never taken lightly in the Bible (see Malachi 2:15-16).

7:10-12 When Paul says he has a command that comes "not from me, but from the Lord," he does not imply that the remainder of his letter is not authoritative. Instead, he is indicating that the command he gives simply repeats Jesus' words (Mark 10:11-12). On the other hand, the situation he addresses—a marriage in which only one person is a believer—is one that Jesus did not specifically address during His earthly ministry. Paul therefore gives his own inspired judgment as to how to address the specific situation in Corinth. Paul's letter is still Scripture and is still authoritative because of his apostleship.

7:14 As the church grew, whole families often became Christians at once (see, for example, Acts 16:31-34). However, sometimes only a portion of the family converted—one spouse, but not the other. Paul counsels the couple to remain married unless his or her spouse leaves. In another situation, Ezra commanded the immediate separation of couples who had spiritually-mixed marriages (Ezra 10:11), so Paul's advice (1 Corinthians 7:12) to remain married should not be construed as license or advice to pursue marriage to an unbeliever.

25 Now regarding your question about the young women who are not yet married. I do 7:25
not have a command from the Lord for them. But the Lord in His mercy has given me wis- 2 Cor 4:1
dom that can be trusted, and I will share it with you. 26 Because of the present crisis,* I think 1 Tim 1:12-13
it is best to remain as you are. 27 If you have a wife, do not seek to end the marriage. If you
do not have a wife, do not seek to get married. 28 But if you do get married, it is not a sin.
And if a young woman gets married, it is not a sin. However, those who get married at this
time will have troubles, and I am trying to spare you those problems.
29 But let me say this, dear brothers and sisters: The time that remains is very short. So 7:29
from now on, those with wives should not focus only on their marriage. 30 Those who Rom 13:11
weep or who rejoice or who buy things should not be absorbed by their weeping or their
joy or their possessions. 31 Those who use the things of the world should not become at- 7:31
tached to them. For this world as we know it will soon pass away. 1 Jn 2:17
32 I want you to be free from the concerns of this life. An unmarried man can spend his
time doing the Lord's work and thinking how to please Him. 33 But a married man has to
think about his earthly responsibilities and how to please his wife. 34 His interests are di- 7:34
vided. In the same way, a woman who is no longer married or has never been married can 1 Tim 5:5
be devoted to the Lord and holy in body and in spirit. But a married woman has to think
about her earthly responsibilities and how to please her husband. 35 I am saying this for
your benefit, not to place restrictions on you. I want you to do whatever will help you serve
the Lord best, with as few distractions as possible.
36 But if a man thinks that he's treating his fiancée improperly and will inevitably give in
to his passion, let him marry her as he wishes. It is not a sin. 37 But if he has decided firmly
not to marry and there is no urgency and he can control his passion, he does well not to
marry. 38 So the person who marries his fiancée does well, and the person who doesn't 7:38
marry does even better. Heb 13:4
39 A wife is bound to her husband as long as he lives. If her husband dies, she is free to 7:39
marry anyone she wishes, but only if he loves the Lord.* 40 But in my opinion it would be better Rom 7:2
for her to stay single, and I think I am giving you counsel from God's Spirit when I say this. 2 Cor 6:14

7:40
1 Cor 7:6, 25

FOOD SACRIFICED TO IDOLS

8 Now regarding your question about food that has been offered to idols. Yes, we 8:1
know that "we all have knowledge" about this issue. But while knowledge makes us Acts 15:20, 29
feel important, it is love that strengthens the church. 2 Anyone who claims to know all the 8:2

1 Cor 3:18; 13:8-9
Gal 6:3

7:26 Or *the pressures of life.* 7:39 Greek *but only in the Lord.*

7:26 Scholars hold three different positions regarding the identification of the "present crisis" to which Paul refers. One position holds that he refers to great woes that will come immediately before the return of Christ, which Paul believed was coming very soon. This is unlikely, because Paul specifically refers to the crisis as present, not future. The second position holds that he refers to the tribulations and troubles that face all Christians as the time that remains is "very short" (see 7:29-31). The third position is that Paul refers to a specific crisis that the Corinthian Christians were enduring at the time he wrote. Given that Paul elsewhere affirms marriage without qualifications (see Ephesians 5:23-33 and 1 Timothy 5:14), the third option is most likely correct—that the present crisis was in some way particular to the Corinthian church and that a temporary moratorium on marriages was wise.

▸ BIBLE
7:32-38 Singles only. Do you, or did you, feel satisfied with being single? Christian singleness has a very specific purpose: It is to be a means of serving the Lord more effectively and wholeheartedly. For however long someone is single, it is an opportunity to focus more time and devotion directly on the Lord. Getting married is clearly not wrong, and if you want to marry, Paul approves (7:36). But in searching for marriage, be aware that it can become a distraction to your spiritual walk. Search for someone who will encourage you spiritually, not someone who will distract you and pull you away from the Lord. (***See Bible**> Unity> God's Message> Devotion to God,* TopicGuide page A11.)

7:39 Paul is writing to Christian widows, and he indicates that remarriage is acceptable, but only to another Christian (see 2 Corinthians 6:14). This principle applies not only to Christian widows, but also to all single Christians. In 7:14, Paul indicates that a Christian should remain married to a nonbeliever whom he or she had married before becoming a Christian.

▸ WORSHIP
8:1-3 Knowing God versus knowing about God. The Corinthians were smart. They knew more than most about God and spirituality. So why did Paul rebuke them? In verse 2, he notes that the main result of their knowledge was to make themselves feel important—this doesn't build up the church. Have you been blessed to know a lot about God,

8:3 answers doesn't really know very much. 3But the person who loves God is the one whom
Gal 4:9 God recognizes.*
8:4 4So, what about eating meat that has been offered to idols? Well, we all know that an
Deut 4:35, 39; 6:4 1 Cor 10:19 idol is not really a god and that there is only one God. 5There may be so-called gods both
8:6 in heaven and on earth, and some people actually worship many gods and many lords.
John 1:3 6But we know that there is only one God, the Father, who created everything, and we live
Acts 17:28 1 Cor 12:5 for Him. And there is only one Lord, Jesus Christ, through whom God made everything
Eph 4:5-6 and through whom we have been given life.
Col 1:16 7However, not all believers know this. Some are accustomed to thinking of idols as be-
8:7 ing real, so when they eat food that has been offered to idols, they think of it as the wor-
Rom 14:14 ship of real gods, and their weak consciences are violated. 8It's true that we can't win
8:8 Rom 14:17 God's approval by what we eat. We don't lose anything if we don't eat it, and we don't
gain anything if we do.
8:9 Rom 14:1, 13, 21 9But you must be careful so that your freedom does not cause others with a weaker
2 Cor 6:3 Gal 5:13 conscience to stumble. 10For if others see you—with your "superior knowledge"—eating in
the temple of an idol, won't they be encouraged to violate their conscience by eating food
8:11 Rom 14:15, 20 that has been offered to an idol? 11So because of your superior knowledge, a weak be-
8:12 liever* for whom Christ died will be destroyed. 12And when you sin against other believ-
Matt 18:6 ers* by encouraging them to do something they believe is wrong, you are sinning against
8:13 Christ. 13So if what I eat causes another believer to sin, I will never eat meat again as long
Rom 14:21 as I live—for I don't want to cause another believer to stumble.

PAUL GIVES UP HIS RIGHTS

9:1 Acts 9:3; 18:9 1 Tim 2:7 **9** Am I not as free as anyone else? Am I not an apostle? Haven't I seen Jesus our Lord
2 Tim 1:11 with my own eyes? Isn't it because of my work that you belong to the Lord? 2Even if

8:3 Some manuscripts read *the person who loves has full knowledge.* 8:11 Greek *brother;* also in 8:13. 8:12 Greek *brothers.*

either because of your schooling or by studying on your own? That is a gift, but be careful it does not make you prideful. Unless your knowledge about God makes you love Him more, you do not "really know very much" (8:2). Do not let yourself stop at knowing about God; make sure your knowledge brings you to love Him. (***See Worship****> OT> Reverence> The beginning of knowledge,* TopicGuide page A29.)

8:4 Almost all meat sold in Corinth had been part of a sacrifice in worship of an idol. After the rituals and sacrifice were complete, excess meat from the animal sacrifice would be sold in the marketplace or served to paying customers in the temple (similar to a restaurant, not as an explicit part of the idol feast). For the Corinthian Christians, this created a dilemma: When buying meat, were they betraying God by indirectly participating in the worship of idols? Paul answers with a theological truth—that idols are simply phonies and that there is only one true God. This means that the meat itself is not tainted; Christians can buy it and eat it without worry.

8:7 A Christian with a "weak conscience" in this passage does not indicate someone with a lack of devotion or holiness. Instead, a "weak conscience" is Paul's term to indicate someone who has not mentally grasped the freedom that comes from the truth that only the Lord is the true God (8:4). "Weak" believers in this sense are often some of the most devoted people to God and to His Law; they simply have a tendency to underappreciate their Christian freedom.

8:9 The specific result of the Corinthian Christians' freedom is that they may eat meat from the marketplace or temples without concerning themselves about its origin. Paul warns them, however, that Christian freedom must be used with love for a weaker brother or sister in Christ.

▸ ADOPTION

8:9-13 Love guides freedom. Most people have no moral problem with eating meat, but what about drinking alcohol? Or many other "gray areas" of the Christian experience that believers have different opinions on? Paul's main concern here is not who's right or wrong, but who should be humble and serve others. Paul's major concern is that the believers who had stronger consciences were overindulging their Christian freedom and therefore harming others. If there is such a risk, Paul radically states, "I will never eat meat again as long as I live." Know that you have Christian liberty, but use it carefully, to build up, not damage, other Christians. If someone has a weak conscience, abstain from behavior that might offend. Are you willing to deny yourself as radically as Paul was? (***See Adoption****> With Christ> Supernatural> A life of liberating freedom,* TopicGuide page A37.)

8:11 This principle regarding the responsibilities of the strong believer is also stated in Romans 14:23. If a strong believer causes a weaker believer to stumble, the strong believer has led the weaker one into sin.

8:12-13 The principle of showing deference toward the weak does not mean the scruples of the most fragile believer should rule a church. The mature, not the immature, set the tone for the community (1 Corinthians 11:1-2; Philippians 3:17; Hebrews 5:12).

9:1-3 Some in the Corinthian church were questioning Paul's apostleship and authority. Against that accusation, Paul levels four rhetorical questions, each of which demands a yes answer. Any one of these questions would be sufficient to prove Paul's authority, but the combination of all four makes an overwhelming case.

others think I am not an apostle, I certainly am to you. You yourselves are proof that I am
the Lord's apostle.
3This is my answer to those who question my authority.* 4Don't we have the right to live
in your homes and share your meals? 5Don't we have the right to bring a Christian wife
with us as the other apostles and the Lord's brothers do, and as Peter* does? 6Or is it only
Barnabas and I who have to work to support ourselves?
7What soldier has to pay his own expenses? What farmer plants a vineyard and doesn't
have the right to eat some of its fruit? What shepherd cares for a flock of sheep and isn't al-
lowed to drink some of the milk? 8Am I expressing merely a human opinion, or does the
law say the same thing? 9For the law of Moses says, "You must not muzzle an ox to keep it
from eating as it treads out the grain."* Was God thinking only about oxen when He said
this? 10Wasn't He actually speaking to us? Yes, it was written for us, so that the one who
plows and the one who threshes the grain might both expect a share of the harvest.
11Since we have planted spiritual seed among you, aren't we entitled to a harvest of
physical food and drink? 12If you support others who preach to you, shouldn't we have an
even greater right to be supported? But we have never used this right. We would rather
put up with anything than be an obstacle to the Good News about Christ.
13Don't you realize that those who work in the temple get their meals from the offerings
brought to the temple? And those who serve at the altar get a share of the sacrificial offer-
ings. 14In the same way, the Lord ordered that those who preach the Good News should
be supported by those who benefit from it. 15Yet I have never used any of these rights.
And I am not writing this to suggest that I want to start now. In fact, I would rather die than
lose my right to boast about preaching without charge. 16Yet preaching the Good News is
not something I can boast about. I am compelled by God to do it. How terrible for me if I
didn't preach the Good News!
17If I were doing this on my own initiative, I would deserve payment. But I have no
choice, for God has given me this sacred trust. 18What then is my pay? It is the opportunity
to preach the Good News without charging anyone. That's why I never demand my rights
when I preach the Good News.
19Even though I am a free man with no master, I have become a slave to all people to
bring many to Christ. 20When I was with the Jews, I lived like a Jew to bring the Jews to Christ.
When I was with those who follow the Jewish law, I too lived under that law. Even though I

9:3 Greek *those who examine me.* 9:5 Greek *Cephas.* 9:9 Deut 25:4.

9:4 Luke 10:8
9:5 Matt 8:14; 12:46
9:6 2 Thes 3:8-9
9:7 Deut 20:6; Prov 27:18; 2 Tim 2:4
9:9 1 Tim 5:18
9:10 2 Tim 2:6
9:12 2 Cor 6:3; 11:7-12
9:13 Lev 6:16, 26; Num 18:8, 31
9:14 Matt 10:10; Gal 6:6; 1 Tim 5:18
9:15 Acts 18:3; 2 Cor 11:9-10
9:16 Acts 9:15; Rom 1:14
9:17 Gal 2:7; Eph 3:1-8; Phil 1:16, 17; Col 1:25
9:18 2 Cor 11:7; 12:13
9:19 Gal 5:13
9:20 Acts 16:3; 21:20-26; Rom 11:14

9:4-9 Paul makes four arguments that he has a right to material support from the congregations he serves. First, he asks two more rhetorical questions that demand the answer yes. Second, he highlights the fact that he asks no more than any other disciples, such as the brothers of Jesus and Peter. Third, he makes three analogies to soldiers, farmers, and shepherds—all of whom are paid for their labors. Finally, he appeals to the Scriptures, quoting Deuteronomy 25:4, which he indicates applies not simply to oxen, but also to human laborers for the gospel.

9:6 Barnabas was an early convert to Christianity in Jerusalem. He was selected by the apostles as Paul's companion for missionary work, specifically to help the growing church in Antioch of Syria (see Acts 11:19-26). He recruited Paul to help in that work, where they remained for a year. Barnabas and Paul were then commissioned to preach beyond the boundaries of Antioch (see Acts 13:2-3).

▸WORSHIP

9:10-12 Money and ministers. Why in the world does Paul compare ministers to farm animals? His illustration from the Old Testament is designed to establish empathy for poor ministers. He argues from the lesser to the greater—if you feed your poor farm animals that work hard, then you should give resources to your hard-working pastor. Are you supporting those who work to bring you the gospel? Has your church or fellowship made certain they are paid enough to be able to do their work without distraction? Are you personally contributing to their support? Even if you have limited financial resources, give faithful prayer and encouragement to those who labor on your behalf in the local church. (***See Worship***> *NT> Sacrificial Living> Sacrificial giving helps to support full-time workers,* TopicGuide page A34.)

9:15-23 Immediately after asserting his right to financial support from the Corinthian church, Paul states that he will not use that right. Paul denies himself for the sake of ministry in two ways. First, he does not accept a wage for his preaching, even though he has a clear right to do so (9:15-19). Second, he often chooses to live in a lifestyle he does not prefer for the sake of reaching others (9:20-23). When Paul is among Jews, he submits himself to their lifestyle, even though he is theologically free from the ceremonial laws. When he is with the oppressed, he willingly shares in their oppression, because taking the gospel to people is his overriding goal.

9:21 Rom 2:12, 14
9:22 Rom 11:14; 2 Cor 11:29
9:24 Phil 3:14; 2 Tim 4:7; Heb 12:1
9:25 2 Tim 2:5; 4:8; Jas 1:12
10:1 Exod 13:21-22
10:3 Exod 16:4, 35; Deut 8:3
10:4 Exod 17:6; Num 20:11; John 6:31-58; 7:37; Rev 22:17
10:5 Num 14:16, 23; Heb 3:17; Jude 1:5
10:6 Num 11:4, 34
10:7 Exod 32:4-19
10:9 Exod 17:2; Num 21:5-6
10:10 Num 14:2, 36

am not subject to the law, I did this so I could bring to Christ those who are under the law.
21 When I am with the Gentiles who do not follow the Jewish law,* I too live apart from that
law so I can bring them to Christ. But I do not ignore the law of God; I obey the law of Christ.
22 When I am with those who are weak, I share their weakness, for I want to bring the
weak to Christ. Yes, I try to find common ground with everyone, doing everything I can to
save some. 23 I do everything to spread the Good News and share in its blessings.
24 Don't you realize that in a race everyone runs, but only one person gets the prize? So
run to win! 25 All athletes are disciplined in their training. They do it to win a prize that will
fade away, but we do it for an eternal prize. 26 So I run with purpose in every step. I am not
just shadowboxing. 27 I discipline my body like an athlete, training it to do what it should.
Otherwise, I fear that after preaching to others I myself might be disqualified.

LESSONS FROM ISRAEL'S IDOLATRY

10 I don't want you to forget, dear brothers and sisters,* about our ancestors in the
wilderness long ago. All of them were guided by a cloud that moved ahead of
them, and all of them walked through the sea on dry ground. 2 In the cloud and in the sea,
all of them were baptized as followers of Moses. 3 All of them ate the same spiritual food,
4 and all of them drank the same spiritual water. For they drank from the spiritual rock that
traveled with them, and that rock was Christ. 5 Yet God was not pleased with most of them,
and their bodies were scattered in the wilderness.
6 These things happened as a warning to us, so that we would not crave evil things as they
did, 7 or worship idols as some of them did. As the Scriptures say, "The people celebrated
with feasting and drinking, and they indulged in pagan revelry."* 8 And we must not engage
in sexual immorality as some of them did, causing 23,000 of them to die in one day.
9 Nor should we put Christ* to the test, as some of them did and then died from snake-
bites. 10 And don't grumble as some of them did, and then were destroyed by the angel of

9:21 Greek *those without the law.* 10:1 Greek *brothers.* 10:7 Exod 32:6. 10:9 Some manuscripts read *the Lord.*

▶ SPIRITUAL WARFARE

9:23 Denying ourselves for the gospel. Are you willing, like Paul, to deny yourself for the sake of sharing the gospel? Are you willing to give until it hurts? Are you willing to live in places or ways you do not naturally enjoy in order to reach people who have not heard about Christ? You reach people with the gospel by going where they are and living with them. Ultimately, this is not merely Paul's example, but the example of Jesus Himself, who, being God, became man, giving up the pleasure of heavenly glory to walk on this earth and then die on a cross—all to save sinners (see Philippians 2:5-8). Will you follow Paul as he followed Jesus? (***See Spiritual Warfare****> Resisting Sin and Evil> Trusting God> Faithful Soldiers> Deny self,* TopicGuide page A46.)

9:24-27 Paul explains his point by comparing spiritual disciplines to the regimens of a runner and a boxer. Success in each sport requires tremendous training and discipline. If people will train and discipline themselves that much for an earthly prize, Paul asks, should Christians not have even more discipline, since our prize is eternal? Paul encourages the Corinthians who have received grace to be active, not passive, in applying that grace in their lives.

9:27 The Greek text of this verse literally says, "I beat my body." At some times in history, Christians have interpreted this as a command for self-flagellation. That interpretation, however, misses the context of the phrase—the athletic metaphor Paul is developing. Paul's point is to emphasize the strict training of an athlete and to encourage the Corinthians to be equally serious in their spiritual disciplines.

10:1-4 Paul refers to several different events during Israel's Exodus from Egypt, including God's provision of a cloud to lead them (Exodus 13:21-22), the crossing of the Red Sea (Exodus 14), God's provision of water (Exodus 15:22-27), and God's provision of manna and meat (Exodus 16:1-21). By referring to these various portions of Exodus, Paul calls the Corinthians' attention to the entire Exodus experience of Israel. By saying that the Israelites were "baptized" in verse 2, Paul shows the Corinthians that there are strong similarities and connections between their experience and that of Old Testament Israel.

10:4 Paul refers to the times that God brought water from the rock at Massah and Meribah for the Israelites to drink (see Exodus 17:1-7 and Numbers 20:8-13). The Israelites did not carry a physical rock with them during the Exodus and the time in the desert; instead, God brought water in various ways to sustain the Israelites in the barren desert (see also Exodus 15:22-27). Paul's point is that the ultimate provider of sustenance for the Israelites was not a physical rock, but God Himself. Hence Paul says, "That rock was Christ," because God traveling with them ultimately was the source of the water they needed to live.

10:5-11 Paul continues referring to events from the Exodus, applying them to the Corinthians as a warning. Verse 7 refers to Israel's sin in creating and worshiping the gold calf (see Exodus 32:1-10). Verse 8 refers to the Israelites' idolatry with Baal of Peor (see Numbers 25:1-9). Verse 9 refers to the people's complaints against Moses and the Lord, which led to a plague of poisonous snakes (see Numbers 21:5-6), and verse 10 refers to the people's grumbling against the Lord, which led to a plague of death (see Numbers 16:41-50).

death. 11 These things happened to them as examples for us. They were written down to
warn us who live at the end of the age.
12 If you think you are standing strong, be careful not to fall. 13 The temptations in your
life are no different from what others experience. And God is faithful. He will not allow the
temptation to be more than you can stand. When you are tempted, He will show you a
way out so that you can endure.
14 So, my dear friends, flee from the worship of idols. 15 You are reasonable people. De-
cide for yourselves if what I am saying is true. 16 When we bless the cup at the Lord's Table,
aren't we sharing in the blood of Christ? And when we break the bread, aren't we sharing
in the body of Christ? 17 And though we are many, we all eat from one loaf of bread, show-
ing that we are one body. 18 Think about the people of Israel. Weren't they united by eat-
ing the sacrifices at the altar?
19 What am I trying to say? Am I saying that food offered to idols has some significance,
or that idols are real gods? 20 No, not at all. I am saying that these sacrifices are offered to
demons, not to God. And I don't want you to participate with demons. 21 You cannot drink

10:12 Rom 11:20
10:13 2 Pet 2:9
10:14 1 Jn 5:21
10:16 Matt 26:26-28; Acts 2:42
10:17 Eph 4:16
10:18 Lev 7:6, 14-15
10:20 Deut 32:17; Rev 9:20
10:21 2 Cor 6:15-16

▶ **BIBLE**

10:11 Forgetful and rebellious. Does it amaze you how often the people of Israel turned away from God, who had just saved them from slavery in Egypt and demonstrated His power with the ten plagues? Do the Israelites seem unbelievably forgetful? Yet we are just as forgetful: God has saved us from sin and repeatedly cared and provided for us, but we regularly turn away from Him, too. Israel's rebellion is not recorded to make us feel proud, but to give us insight into our own rebellion. According to 10:11, these events were written down to warn us, showing us not just what the Israelites did, but also what we ourselves do. Look closely in the mirror of the Old Testament—what do you see about God and yourself? (***See Bible****> Power> Wisdom> Guidance for life,* TopicGuide page A11.)

10:15-20 Paul compares the Christian sacrament of communion with pagan idol feasts. Both create unity between the worshiper and that which is worshiped. Communion shows that Christians share the body of Jesus Christ. Idol feasts, on the other hand, create a spiritual unity with false gods, which have demonic influence behind them. The two are incompatible.

▶ **GOD**

10:21-22 God requires total allegiance. God demands total allegiance; He will not allow you to combine your worship of Him with worship of other gods. This message is profoundly unpopular in today's world, but the Christian message is exclusive—we are to worship God alone. Do you pray to and worship many different gods "just to be safe?" This does not make you safe; instead it offends the only true God. Do you borrow and combine elements of several religions into a mix that makes you feel spiritual? You are actually creating an unstable compound, one in which your preferences are the most important element. Doing so is an assertion of independence from God and rebellion against Him, not a means of following Him. We are to follow the God who made us, and we must allow Him to determine the way we do so. Leave all other gods behind and follow only the God of the Bible. (***See God****> God's Nature> Personality> Emotion> God jealously desires exclusive worship,* TopicGuide page A14.)

BECAUSE GOD IS FAITHFUL

I will trust Him to always keep His promises.

The temptations in your life are no different from what others experience. And God is faithful. He will not allow the temptation to be more than you can stand. When you are tempted, He will show you a way out so that you can endure.

1 CORINTHIANS 10:13

FOR THE NEXT *GOD IS FAITHFUL* FEATURE SEE PAGE 2181.

from the cup of the Lord and from the cup of demons, too. You cannot eat at the Lord's Table and at the table of demons, too. 22 What? Do we dare to rouse the Lord's jealousy? Do you think we are stronger than He is?

23 You say, "I am allowed to do anything"*—but not everything is good for you. You say, "I am allowed to do anything"—but not everything is beneficial. 24 Don't be concerned for your own good but for the good of others.

25 So you may eat any meat that is sold in the marketplace without raising questions of conscience. 26 For "the earth is the LORD's, and everything in it."*

27 If someone who isn't a believer asks you home for dinner, accept the invitation if you want to. Eat whatever is offered to you without raising questions of conscience. 28 (But suppose someone tells you, "This meat was offered to an idol." Don't eat it, out of consideration for the conscience of the one who told you. 29 It might not be a matter of conscience for you, but it is for the other person.) For why should my freedom be limited by what someone else thinks? 30 If I can thank God for the food and enjoy it, why should I be condemned for eating it?

31 So whether you eat or drink, or whatever you do, do it all for the glory of God. 32 Don't give offense to Jews or Gentiles* or the church of God. 33 I, too, try to please everyone in everything I do. I don't just do what is best for me; I do what is best for others so that many may be saved. 11:1 And you should imitate me, just as I imitate Christ.

INSTRUCTIONS FOR PUBLIC WORSHIP

11 2 I am so glad that you always keep me in your thoughts, and that you are following the teachings I passed on to you. 3 But there is one thing I want you to know: The head of every man is Christ, the head of woman is man, and the head of Christ is God.* 4 A man dishonors his head* if he covers his head while praying or prophesying. 5 But a woman dishonors her head* if she prays or prophesies without a covering on her head, for this is the same as shaving her head. 6 Yes, if she refuses to wear a head covering, she should cut off all her hair! But since it is shameful for a woman to have her hair cut or her head shaved, she should wear a covering.*

7 A man should not wear anything on his head when worshiping, for man is made in God's image and reflects God's glory. And woman reflects man's glory. 8 For the first man didn't come from woman, but the first woman came from man. 9 And man was not made

10:22 Deut 32:16, 21
10:23 1 Cor 6:12
10:24 Rom 15:1-2
10:25 Acts 10:15; 1 Cor 8:7
10:27 Luke 10:8
10:28 Rom 14:16
10:31 Col 3:17
10:32 Matt 5:29; Acts 24:16; Rom 14:13; 1 Cor 8:13
11:1 1 Cor 4:16
11:2 1 Cor 15:2-3; 2 Thes 2:15; 3:6
11:3 Gen 3:16; 1 Cor 3:23; Eph 5:23
11:7 Gen 1:26; 5:1; 9:6; Jas 3:9
11:8 Gen 2:21-23; 1 Tim 2:13

10:23 Greek *All things are lawful;* also in 10:23b. 10:26 Ps 24:1. 10:32 Greek *or Greeks.* 11:3 Or *to know: The source of every man is Christ, the source of woman is man, and the source of Christ is God.* Or *to know: Every man is responsible to Christ, a woman is responsible to her husband, and Christ is responsible to God.* 11:4 Or *dishonors Christ.* 11:5 Or *dishonors her husband.* 11:6 Or *should have long hair.*

10:23 Paul is again answering a common belief held by the Corinthian Christians. He repeats his insistence that Christian freedom should be used with an eye toward the good of other believers, not as a selfish assertion of freedom to do whatever someone wants.

10:25 Paul concludes his discussion concerning eating meat and idol sacrifices. Meat from the market may be bought and consumed without a need to research its origin. Even if that meat had been once sacrificed to an idol, there is no harm. However, if a weaker Christian (see note on 8:7) knows that the meat has been offered to an idol and shows concern, the proper response is not to eat it, but to desist for the sake of the weaker believer's conscience. Paul broadens this command in 10:31 to show he is really providing a principle to help guide decisions in all of life, not just the issue of eating meat.

11:1-3 Paul's main concern in this chapter is orderly worship. The first area that Paul needed to address was that of head coverings. The Corinthian church was enduring the clash of different cultural and religious traditions. Jewish women traditionally covered their heads during worship, whereas Corinthian women with a Greek background likely did not.

11:5-6 While there was not a cultural consensus in the Corinthian church regarding whether women should wear head coverings in church, there was a cultural consensus that it was shameful for a woman to have her head shaved. Here Paul was simply summarizing the common view at the time.

11:8-12 The theological basis Paul uses for his argument is the order of Creation. He views the order of Creation in Genesis 2 as having significance and creating some type of emphasis or priority within the church. He does not discuss the extent or limits of this, but discusses how it impacts the issue at hand, which is that women should cover their heads if they minister in the Corinthian church. However, lest this hierarchy be misinterpreted Paul hastens to add that it does not imply any difference in value between men and women, either in human societies or in the sight of God.

for woman, but woman was made for man. 10For this reason, and because the angels are
watching, a woman should wear a covering on her head to show she is under authority.*
11But among the Lord's people, women are not independent of men, and men are not
independent of women. 12For although the first woman came from man, every other man
was born from a woman, and everything comes from God.
13Judge for yourselves. Is it right for a woman to pray to God in public without covering
her head? 14Isn't it obvious that it's disgraceful for a man to have long hair? 15And isn't
long hair a woman's pride and joy? For it has been given to her as a covering. 16But if any-
one wants to argue about this, I simply say that we have no other custom than this, and
neither do God's other churches.

ORDER AT THE LORD'S SUPPER

17But in the following instructions, I cannot praise you. For it sounds as if more harm than
good is done when you meet together. 18First, I hear that there are divisions among you
when you meet as a church, and to some extent I believe it. 19But, of course, there must be
divisions among you so that you who have God's approval will be recognized!
20When you meet together, you are not really interested in the Lord's Supper. 21For some
of you hurry to eat your own meal without sharing with others. As a result, some go hungry
while others get drunk. 22What? Don't you have your own homes for eating and drinking?
Or do you really want to disgrace God's church and shame the poor? What am I supposed to
say? Do you want me to praise you? Well, I certainly will not praise you for this!
23For I pass on to you what I received from the Lord Himself. On the night when He was
betrayed, the Lord Jesus took some bread 24and gave thanks to God for it. Then He broke
it in pieces and said, "This is My body, which is given for you.* Do this to remember Me."
25In the same way, He took the cup of wine after supper, saying, "This cup is the new cov-
enant between God and His people—an agreement confirmed with My blood. Do this to
remember Me as often as you drink it." 26For every time you eat this bread and drink this
cup, you are announcing the Lord's death until He comes again.

11:12 Rom 11:36
11:16 1 Cor 7:17; 10:32
11:18 1 Cor 1:10-12; 3:3
11:19 1 Jn 2:19
11:21 2 Pet 2:13; Jude 1:12
11:22 1 Cor 10:32; Jas 2:6
11:23-25 *Matt 26:26-28; *Mark 14:22-24; *Luke 22:17-20
11:25 Luke 22:20; 1 Cor 10:16; 2 Cor 3:6
11:26 Luke 22:19

11:10 Greek *should have an authority on her head.* 11:24 Greek *which is for you;* other manuscripts read *which is broken for you.*

11:13-16 Paul equates a woman prophesying without a head covering to a woman having her head shaved. Why these two situations could be equated and why they were wrong is difficult for a modern reader to grasp, as they are viewed quite differently in our culture than they were in the first century. But in the culture of the churches of the first century, the equation was clear, and Paul encourages the Corinthian Christians to abide by this cultural consensus, not to cavalierly and unnecessarily cast it aside. Paul's principle is that, whenever possible, Christians should behave in a manner befitting their situation. The application of this principle in Corinth was that women should cover their heads in worship. The principle remains valid, although its application today may take a different form.

11:19 The interpretation of this verse is highly debated. Given that Paul had criticized divisions in chapter 1, what should a reader understand when he here seems to affirm them? There are three major interpretations. One is that Paul here is speaking sarcastically, mocking the Corinthians for their behavior and for the pride of wanting to be recognized. Another is that Paul recognizes these divisions as a symptom of God testing His people: The divisions are not good, and Got will approve those that resist such factionalism. A third interpretation is that Paul may be saying that those who are truly following the Lord will automatically be distinguished from those who do not.

11:20-22 Paul now makes clear the specific type of factionalism that he is critiquing, which is different from that of chapter 1. In chapter 11, the factionalism regards taking the Lord's Supper (Communion). The Lord's Supper in Corinth was celebrated with a full meal. Richer members of the congregation provided more, if not most, of the food, but instead of sharing with their poorer brothers and sisters, they hurried to eat their food first, even before the others arrived. Instead of a communal meal that celebrated the oneness of the church (see 1 Corinthians 10:17), they had turned the Lord's Supper into a cliquish affair, which demeaned the poorer members of the congregation and disgraced the church.

▶ CHURCH

11:23-26 Growing deeper. The Lord's Supper pictures the gospel for us. Through it we remember Christ's death, by which He rescued us from sin and from the wrath of God and restored us to fellowship with God. Yet Paul says that we not only remember Christ's death in the Lord's Supper, but we also proclaim the gospel as we celebrate the sacrament. For Paul, the Cross is central to Christian worship. We do not "grow past" the message of the gospel but instead grow deeper in it. Have you fallen into the idea that you understand the death of Jesus and now need to move on to advanced theology? Nothing could be further from the truth—advanced theology digs further and further into the implications of the basic gospel message. We never get past the gospel; we get deeper into it. (***See Church***> *Mission*> *Nurture*> *Developing maturity,* TopicGuide page A49.)

11:27 27So anyone who eats this bread or drinks this cup of the Lord unworthily is guilty of sin-
Heb 10:29 ning against* the body and blood of the Lord. 28That is why you should examine yourself
11:28 before eating the bread and drinking the cup. 29For if you eat the bread or drink the cup
2 Cor 13:5 without honoring the body of Christ,* you are eating and drinking God's judgment upon
11:31 1 Jn 1:9 yourself. 30That is why many of you are weak and sick and some have even died.
31 But if we would examine ourselves, we would not be judged by God in this way. 32Yet
11:32 Ps 94:12 when we are judged by the Lord, we are being disciplined so that we will not be con-
Heb 12:5-6 demned along with the world.
11:34 33So, my dear brothers and sisters,* when you gather for the Lord's Supper, wait for
1 Cor 4:19 each other. 34If you are really hungry, eat at home so you won't bring judgment upon
yourselves when you meet together. I'll give you instructions about the other matters after
I arrive.

SPIRITUAL GIFTS

12:2 Hab 2:18-19 **12** Now, dear brothers and sisters,* regarding your question about the special abili-
1 Thes 1:9 ties the Spirit gives us. I don't want you to misunderstand this. 2You know that
12:3 when you were still pagans, you were led astray and swept along in worshiping speech-
John 13:13 1 Jn 4:2-3 less idols. 3So I want you to know that no one speaking by the Spirit of God will curse
Jesus, and no one can say Jesus is Lord, except by the Holy Spirit.
12:4 Rom 12:6 4There are different kinds of spiritual gifts, but the same Spirit is the source of them all.
Eph 4:4 5There are different kinds of service, but we serve the same Lord. 6God works in different
Heb 2:4 ways, but it is the same God who does the work in all of us.
12:6 7A spiritual gift is given to each of us so we can help each other. 8To one person the
Eph 4:6 Spirit gives the ability to give wise advice*; to another the same Spirit gives a message of
12:7 1 Cor 14:26 special knowledge.* 9The same Spirit gives great faith to another, and to someone else the
Eph 4:12 one Spirit gives the gift of healing. 10He gives one person the power to perform miracles,
12:9 and another the ability to prophesy. He gives someone else the ability to discern whether
Matt 17:19-20 a message is from the Spirit of God or from another spirit. Still another person is given the

11:27 Or *is responsible for.* 11:29 Greek *the body;* other manuscripts read *the Lord's body.* 11:33 Greek *brothers.* 12:1 Greek *brothers.* 12:8a Or *gives a word of wisdom.* 12:8b Or *gives a word of knowledge.*

▶ WORSHIP

11:27-29 Preparing for the Lord's Supper. Paul indicates that self-examination before partaking of the Lord's Supper is essential. It is possible to eat of the Lord's Supper unworthily, and doing so is a sin, one that brings judgment. Do you prepare for the Lord's Supper at all? Make sure you know when your church will be celebrating the Lord's Supper and examine your heart beforehand—do not simply show up as if it is an ordinary day. Prepare by reflecting on the meaning of the sacrament, your repentance from sin, your love for God and others, and your desire for new obedience to Christ. (***See Worship****> NT> Our Role> Mind and Heart> Lord's supper to be taken in a worthy manner,* TopicGuide page A32.)

12:3 Paul mentions all three persons of the Trinity in 1 Corinthians. He mentions God the Father in 1:3 and 8:6. He mentions Jesus Christ throughout, specifically referring to Him as the Son in 1:9 and 15:28, and he mentions the Holy Spirit throughout as well (2:10, 12-14; 3:16; 6:11, 19; 12:3-13).

12:4-11 A spiritual gift is a special ability given to each Christian by God. A spiritual gift will often make use of someone's natural talents, though it need not do so. Regardless, it is particularly designed for service in the church. The Corinthians overemphasized the value of the gift of speaking in tongues, so Paul reminded them that it was the same Holy Spirit that gave all the different spiritual gifts to Christians.

▶ CHURCH

12:7 Gifted to serve. People have natural talents—musical, mathematical, athletic, etc.—whether they are Christians or not. But spiritual gifts are those given by God, through the Holy Spirit, that either augment old abilities or add new ones to believers for the good of the church. Your abilities in general, and particularly your spiritual gift, are given to you as a stewardship. You are charged to use them for God's glory by building up the church. What are your gifts—both your natural abilities and your spiritual gift? Where are you involved? Are you using your talents and gifts just to bless yourself, or are you using them to bless the rest of the church? (***See Church****> Role> Church Community> Using their gifts to build up the body,* TopicGuide page A49.)

12:8-10 Paul gives a list of some of the spiritual gifts that the Holy Spirit gives to Christians. This list is not exhaustive, but representative. Christians disagree over the continuity of these spiritual gifts. Some feel that a subset of the gifts (commonly called the "charismatic gifts," such as speaking in tongues and healing diseases) were given only as long as was necessary to authenticate the church and that these specific gifts ceased at the end of the apostolic age. Other Christians see no evidence of such a cessation and argue that all of these gifts continue today. Both groups believe that God continues to give gifts to every believer for the good of the church.

ability to speak in unknown languages,* while another is given the ability to interpret what
is being said. [11]It is the one and only Spirit who distributes all these gifts. He alone decides
which gift each person should have.

12:11 Rom 12:6-8; Eph 4:5-7

ONE BODY WITH MANY PARTS

[12]The human body has many parts, but the many parts make up one whole body. So it is
with the body of Christ. [13]Some of us are Jews, some are Gentiles,* some are slaves, and
some are free. But we have all been baptized into one body by one Spirit, and we all share
the same Spirit.*

[14]Yes, the body has many different parts, not just one part. [15]If the foot says, "I am not a
part of the body because I am not a hand," that does not make it any less a part of the
body. [16]And if the ear says, "I am not part of the body because I am not an eye," would that
make it any less a part of the body? [17]If the whole body were an eye, how would you
hear? Or if your whole body were an ear, how would you smell anything?

12:12 Rom 12:4-5; 1 Cor 10:17; 12:27
12:13 John 7:37-39; Gal 3:28; Eph 2:18; Col 3:11

[18]But our bodies have many parts, and God has put each part just where He wants it.
[19]How strange a body would be if it had only one part! [20]Yes, there are many parts, but
only one body. [21]The eye can never say to the hand, "I don't need you." The head can't
say to the feet, "I don't need you."

[22]In fact, some parts of the body that seem weakest and least important are actually the
most necessary. [23]And the parts we regard as less honorable are those we clothe with the

12:18 1 Cor 12:28

12:10 Or *in various tongues;* also in 12:28, 30. 12:13a Greek *some are Greeks.* 12:13b Greek *we were all given one Spirit to drink.*

12:12-25 Some believers thought themselves better than others because of how they were gifted by the Spirit. Paul speaks to these "spiritual" believers, helping them understand that every member of the body is gifted and every member is needed. First, he emphasizes again that all gifts come from the Holy Spirit, so they should unify the church, not divide it. Second, he compares the church to a human body. There are different parts of the body, but all of them are valuable, and the body only works correctly when all are performing their respective roles well. So it is with spiritual gifts—all believers are valuable and all deserve equal care and honor.

MY RESPONSE TO GOD

Connected with Others

1 CORINTHIANS 12:13

How do you feel when a coworker or classmate gets special attention? How do you feel when a friend at church is successful at evangelism or another church in town is growing? Are you happy? Are you jealous? Do you even care?

All believers are connected together by the Holy Spirit, just as the parts of your body are connected (1 Corinthians 12:13; Ephesians 4:4-7). If you stub your toe, your whole body responds to it–your hands grab your toe while you hop on your other foot–your lungs suck in air while your mouth shouts with pain! We have a connection to Christians around us and around the world. When they are happy, we should be happy with them and for them. When they are sad or hurting, we should share their sorrow and pain (Romans 12:15).

Our connection with other believers is so close that we are said to be "joined with Christ" (Romans 6:3; see also Romans 12:5). It is this spiritual union with Christ that links those who are in Christ (1 Corinthians 6:17). How do you manifest this union with other believers through Christ? Those of us who are joined through Christ can celebrate our diversity because our many differences point to the one thing we all have in common–Christ.

greatest care. So we carefully protect those parts that should not be seen, 24while the more
honorable parts do not require this special care. So God has put the body together such that
extra honor and care are given to those parts that have less dignity. 25This makes for har-
mony among the members, so that all the members care for each other. 26If one part suf-
fers, all the parts suffer with it, and if one part is honored, all the parts are glad.
27All of you together are Christ's body, and each of you is a part of it. 28Here are some of
the parts God has appointed for the church:

first are apostles,
second are prophets,
third are teachers,
then those who do miracles,
those who have the gift of healing,
those who can help others,
those who have the gift of leadership,
those who speak in unknown languages.

29Are we all apostles? Are we all prophets? Are we all teachers? Do we all have the
power to do miracles? 30Do we all have the gift of healing? Do we all have the ability to
speak in unknown languages? Do we all have the ability to interpret unknown languages?
Of course not! 31So you should earnestly desire the most helpful gifts.
But now let me show you a way of life that is best of all.

LOVE IS THE GREATEST

13 If I could speak all the languages of earth and of angels, but didn't love others, I
would only be a noisy gong or a clanging cymbal. 2If I had the gift of prophecy,
and if I understood all of God's secret plans and possessed all knowledge, and if I had such
faith that I could move mountains, but didn't love others, I would be nothing. 3If I gave
everything I have to the poor and even sacrificed my body, I could boast about it;* but if I
didn't love others, I would have gained nothing.
4Love is patient and kind. Love is not jealous or boastful or proud 5or rude. It does not
demand its own way. It is not irritable, and it keeps no record of being wronged. 6It does

12:27 Rom 12:5; Eph 1:23; 4:12; Col 1:18, 24
12:28 Rom 12:6-8; Eph 4:11-12
12:31 1 Cor 14:1, 39
13:1 1 Tim 1:5
13:2 Matt 17:20; 21:21; Mark 11:23; 1 Cor 12:9
13:3 Matt 6:2
13:4 1 Pet 4:8
13:5 1 Cor 10:24; Phil 2:4
13:6 2 Thes 2:12; 2 Jn 1:4; 3 Jn 1:3-4

13:3 Some manuscripts read *sacrificed my body to be burned.*

▸ADOPTION
12:25 Sympathetic suffering. Joy could very well be the dominant emotion of the Christian life (Psalm 126:5, 6; Isaiah 61:2, 3; Matthew 5:4; 1 Peter 4:13-14). But while the Christian life may be characterized by rejoicing, there is also pain. Paul indicates that if one Christian suffers, all others also do so, because we are part of a single body. For us to truly take Paul's words to heart, we must make an effort to know what is going on in the lives of other Christians and in the church around the world. We also need to be transparent with others so that they will know if we are suffering. Pray for suffering Christians in your congregation and around the world, and support them in tangible ways as well (see, for example, 1 Corinthians 16:1). Love those around you enough to suffer with them (Hebrews 13:3). (***See Adoption**> With Christ> Servants> Unified community of believers*, TopicGuide page A37.)

12:31 First, Paul makes clear that the Corinthians should desire the gifts that are most helpful to others, not the gifts that bring the most honor to themselves. But as wonderful as spiritual gifts are, they are not the pinnacle of the Christian life. No gift can be used effectively without love (1 Corinthians 13:1-3).

13:1 The central problem at Corinth was a lack of understanding and practice of biblical love. Paul's teaching on love sharply defines it against the selfish lusts of that age. The apostle John does the same but from a different perspective when he says, "God is love" (1 John 4:8), meaning that God Himself defines and embodies love. (Love is further defined in passages such as Leviticus 19:18; Deuteronomy 11:1; Nehemiah 9:17; Psalms 6:4; 36:5; 63:3; 119:64; Matthew 5:43-48; 22:36-40; John 3:16; 15:12-17; Galatians 5:14; Ephesians 3:14-21; 1 John 3:11–4:21.)

13:1-3 First Corinthians 13 is more than just beautiful poetry—it is the culmination of Paul's argument so far and a stinging rebuke to the Corinthian Christians. As Paul states what love is not, it becomes apparent that he is describing the Corinthian church: extremely talented and gifted, but rarely showing love. The Corinthians spoke in tongues (12:10) and prophesied (11:4-10), yet they showed little love for each other (see 11:17-34).

13:4-7 Paul now describes love, not by contrast (as he did in 13:1-3), but by listing its aspects. These terms show both emotion and action. Again, the Corinthian Christians had shown few of these characteristics. For example, they had not been patient or kind (11:33); they had been boastful and proud (5:6); and they kept record of wrongs (6:7).

not rejoice about injustice but rejoices whenever the truth wins out. 7Love never gives up,
never loses faith, is always hopeful, and endures through every circumstance.
8Prophecy and speaking in unknown languages* and special knowledge will become
useless. But love will last forever! 9Now our knowledge is partial and incomplete, and even
the gift of prophecy reveals only part of the whole picture! 10But when full understanding
comes, these partial things will become useless.
11When I was a child, I spoke and thought and reasoned as a child. But when I grew up, I
put away childish things. 12Now we see things imperfectly as in a cloudy mirror, but then
we will see everything with perfect clarity.* All that I know now is partial and incomplete,
but then I will know everything completely, just as God now knows me completely.
13Three things will last forever—faith, hope, and love—and the greatest of these is love.

TONGUES AND PROPHECY

14 Let love be your highest goal! But you should also desire the special abilities the
Spirit gives—especially the ability to prophesy. 2For if you have the ability to speak
in tongues,* you will be talking only to God, since people won't be able to understand you.
You will be speaking by the power of the Spirit, but it will all be mysterious. 3But one who
prophesies strengthens others, encourages them, and comforts them. 4A person who
speaks in tongues is strengthened personally, but one who speaks a word of prophecy
strengthens the entire church.
5I wish you could all speak in tongues, but even more I wish you could all prophesy. For
prophecy is greater than speaking in tongues, unless someone interprets what you are
saying so that the whole church will be strengthened.

13:7 Prov 10:12; 1 Pet 4:8
13:10 Phil 3:12
13:11 Ps 131:2
13:12 2 Cor 5:7; 1 Jn 3:2
13:13 Matt 22:37-40; Gal 5:5-6; 1 Thes 1:3; 1 Jn 4:16
14:1 Matt 22:37-40; Rom 12:6; Eph 5:2; Col 3:14; 1 Tim 1:5; Jas 2:8
14:2 Mark 16:17
14:3 Rom 14:19
14:5 Num 11:29

13:8 Or *in tongues.* 13:12 Greek *see face to face.* 14:2 Or *in unknown languages;* also in 14:4, 5, 13, 14, 18, 22, 26, 27, 28, 39.

▸ SPIRITUAL WARFARE
13:4-7 Example of love. Of the characteristics of mature love listed here—patient, kind, humble, noble, and the rest—which are most present in your love? Which are least present? One of many remarkable features of Jesus' love is that He loved God and God's people with a perfect, holy affection. He selflessly laid down His life to save sinners, even asking God the Father to forgive those who crucified Him (see Luke 23:34). We are told in 1 John 3:16 that we understand what love is by looking to the example of Christ. You can discover your weaknesses and build your strengths by following Jesus' example (Ephesians 5:2). Look to Christ and pray for a heart that loves God and His people more and more. (***See Spiritual Warfare**> Resisting Sin and Evil> Trusting God> Faithful Soldiers> Deny self,* TopicGuide page A46.)

13:8 Prophecy, speaking in tongues, and special knowledge were necessary when Paul wrote to the Corinthians because the end of their appointed time had not yet come. God's purpose for all three gifts was to build and expand the church, which God continued to do. Whether or not one believes that these specific three gifts continue today, God does continue building the church, so He continues giving spiritual gifts to believers. But at the end of their appointed time, these gifts will no longer be necessary because the building of the church will be complete. Love, however, will continue forever.

13:11-12 Paul illustrates his point by making an analogy to human development. Young children have not yet developed strong speaking and reasoning skills. Many of their statements and thoughts are correct, but very simple and obvious. Such a child's abilities are not bad, but simply incomplete. When the child grows to maturity, he or she will think and reason more strongly. Spiritual gifts, for all their wonder, are divine helps because we are spiritually little children; our understanding of spiritual things is cloudy, the equivalent of a young child's reasoning. When, at the end of time, we are able to understand spiritual things with full clarity, spiritual gifts will be unnecessary. However, love will remain.

13:12 Today's mirrors give an image that is very clear, but ancient mirrors were not so effective, as they were often nothing more than polished metal. The image they reflected was recognizable, but it lacked the clarity and detail of a modern mirror. Given the Corinthians' problem with pride in their own knowledge, Paul stresses the incompleteness of even his own knowledge in the present age as an example to them.

14:2 Speaking in tongues is supernatural speech in which the Christian speaks in a language which he or she does not ordinarily know. Speaking in tongues was first manifested in the early church at Pentecost (see Acts 2:8-11). Acts records other instances where a group of people, when receiving the Holy Spirit, spoke in tongues (Acts 10:46; 19:6). However, Acts also records cases where people received the Holy Spirit without any indication that they spoke in tongues, thereby showing that tongues was not the singular sign of having received the Holy Spirit (Acts 8:15-17; see also 1 Corinthians 12:30). Instead, the Bible teaches that the Spirit baptizes all believers when they become integrated into the body of Christ (the church; 1 Corinthians 12:13), and that the critical evidence of the work of the Holy Spirit is the fruit of the Spirit (see Galatians 5:22-23).

14:3-5 Paul does not condemn speaking in tongues—he even spoke in tongues himself (14:18)—but he encourages people to desire most the highest gift of prophecy. The gift of prophecy is difficult to define. Broadly, all those filled with the Spirit are empowered to declare the truths of God (Acts 2:11, 18; 1 Peter 2:9), but the Bible usually discriminates between gifts of prophecy and teaching (Ephesians 4:11). In the New Testament, prophecy ranges from encouragement (Acts 15:32) to prediction (Acts 11:27-28; 21:10-11). In a general sense, it is the Spirit-given gift that enables a believer to speak the words God wants at the right time, to the right person.

6 Dear brothers and sisters,* if I should come to you speaking in an unknown lan-
guage,* how would that help you? But if I bring you a revelation or some special knowl-
edge or prophecy or teaching, that will be helpful. 7 Even lifeless instruments like the flute
or the harp must play the notes clearly, or no one will recognize the melody. 8 And if
the bugler doesn't sound a clear call, how will the soldiers know they are being called
to battle?

9 It's the same for you. If you speak to people in words they don't understand, how will
they know what you are saying? You might as well be talking into empty space.

10 There are many different languages in the world, and every language has meaning.
11 But if I don't understand a language, I will be a foreigner to someone who speaks it, and
the one who speaks it will be a foreigner to me. 12 And the same is true for you. Since you
are so eager to have the special abilities the Spirit gives, seek those that will strengthen the
whole church.

13 So anyone who speaks in tongues should pray also for the ability to interpret what
has been said. 14 For if I pray in tongues, my spirit is praying, but I don't understand what I
am saying.

15 Well then, what shall I do? I will pray in the spirit,* and I will also pray in words I under-
stand. I will sing in the spirit, and I will also sing in words I understand. 16 For if you praise
God only in the spirit, how can those who don't understand you praise God along with you?
How can they join you in giving thanks when they don't understand what you are saying?
17 You will be giving thanks very well, but it won't strengthen the people who hear you.

18 I thank God that I speak in tongues more than any of you. 19 But in a church meeting I
would rather speak five understandable words to help others than ten thousand words in
an unknown language.

20 Dear brothers and sisters, don't be childish in your understanding of these things. Be
innocent as babies when it comes to evil, but be mature in understanding matters of this
kind. 21 It is written in the Scriptures*:

"I will speak to My own people
  through strange languages
  and through the lips of foreigners.
But even then, they will not listen to Me,"*
  says the LORD.

14:6 Rom 6:17; Eph 1:17
14:8 Num 10:9; Jer 4:19
14:12 Rom 14:19; 1 Cor 12:1
14:13 1 Cor 12:10
14:15 Eph 5:19; Col 3:16
14:16 1 Chr 16:36; Neh 8:6; Ps 106:48; Rev 5:14; 7:12
14:17 Rom 14:19
14:20 Eph 4:14; Heb 5:12
14:21 Deut 28:49; *Isa 28:11-12

14:6a Greek *brothers;* also in 14:20, 26, 39. **14:6b** Or *in tongues;* also in 14:19, 23. **14:15** Or *in the Spirit;* also in 14:15b, 16. **14:21a** Greek *in the law.* **14:21b** Isa 28:11-12.

14:7-8 Paul supports his argument for the superiority of prophecy with an analogy to musical instruments. Even with a musical instrument, which only has notes, not words, a tune must be discernible, or no one will know the meaning of what was played. If a bugle is used to summon troops into battle, but the bugler cannot play the tune clearly, the troops might instead think they have been called to their quarters, to lunch, or somewhere else. Confusion and disaster would result. Paul believes that clear communication is vital, and is more likely to occur through prophecy than through speaking in tongues.

▸ WORSHIP
14:14-16 Experiences in worship. Do not reject mystical experiences, but rather receive them as part of the Christian life. Yet these experiences, such as speaking in tongues, are not the peak of the Christian life and worship. We need to engage our minds, too. The Christian life cannot be solely intellectual and purely logical, but it also cannot be solely emotional, emphasizing the subjective. Healthy worship includes both spirit and truth, both mind and heart. Paul encourages us to pray and sing with both emotion and understanding. Most people lean toward one or the other, but Christian worship must include both. Which is your tendency? Be self-aware, and be certain to avoid neglecting either facet of worship. (***See Worship****> NT> Our Role> Mind and Heart> Worship in spirit and in truth because God is Spirit,* TopicGuide page A32.)

14:21-23 Paul quotes Isaiah 28:11-12 and applies it in a subtle way to speaking in tongues. In this portion of Isaiah's prophecy, God threatened that foreign armies would be His means of punishing Israel for rejecting the direction God gave through the prophets. Similarly, in the New Testament, foreign languages (speaking in tongues) served as a rebuke to unbelieving Israel, which had rejected Jesus the Messiah. Speaking in tongues was a supernatural way to rapidly spread the gospel to Gentiles and their many different languages, fulfilling the promise given to Abraham in Genesis 12:3 and 22:18 that God would even bless the Gentiles through him. Therefore, speaking in tongues was a sign to unbelieving Jews. Just as in Isaiah's time, however, even foreign tongues did not turn them back to God.

22So you see that speaking in tongues is a sign, not for believers, but for unbelievers.
Prophecy, however, is for the benefit of believers, not unbelievers. 23Even so, if unbeliev-
ers or people who don't understand these things come into your church meeting and hear
everyone speaking in an unknown language, they will think you are crazy. 24But if all of
you are prophesying, and unbelievers or people who don't understand these things come
into your meeting, they will be convicted of sin and judged by what you say. 25As they lis-
ten, their secret thoughts will be exposed, and they will fall to their knees and worship
God, declaring, "God is truly here among you."

A CALL TO ORDERLY WORSHIP

26Well, my brothers and sisters, let's summarize. When you meet together, one will sing,
another will teach, another will tell some special revelation God has given, one will speak
in tongues, and another will interpret what is said. But everything that is done must
strengthen all of you.

27No more than two or three should speak in tongues. They must speak one at a time,
and someone must interpret what they say. 28But if no one is present who can interpret,
they must be silent in your church meeting and speak in tongues to God privately.

29Let two or three people prophesy, and let the others evaluate what is said. 30But if
someone is prophesying and another person receives a revelation from the Lord, the one
who is speaking must stop. 31In this way, all who prophesy will have a turn to speak, one
after the other, so that everyone will learn and be encouraged. 32Remember that people
who prophesy are in control of their spirit and can take turns. 33For God is not a God of dis-
order but of peace, as in all the meetings of God's holy people.*

34Women should be silent during the church meetings. It is not proper for them to
speak. They should be submissive, just as the law says. 35If they have any questions,
they should ask their husbands at home, for it is improper for women to speak in church
meetings.*

36Or do you think God's word originated with you Corinthians? Are you the only ones to
whom it was given? 37If you claim to be a prophet or think you are spiritual, you should
recognize that what I am saying is a command from the Lord Himself. 38But if you do not
recognize this, you yourself will not be recognized.*

39So, my dear brothers and sisters, be eager to prophesy, and don't forbid speaking in
tongues. 40But be sure that everything is done properly and in order.

14:33 The phrase *as in all the meetings of God's holy people* could instead be joined to the beginning of 14:34. 14:35 Some manuscripts place verses 34-35 after 14:40. 14:38 Some manuscripts read *If you are ignorant of this, stay in your ignorance.*

14:22 1 Cor 14:1
14:23 Acts 2:13
14:24 John 16:8
14:25 Isa 45:14; Zech 8:23
14:26 Rom 14:19; 1 Cor 12:7-10; Eph 4:12; 5:19
14:27 1 Cor 14:2, 5, 13
14:29 1 Cor 12:10; 1 Thes 5:19-21
14:32 1 Jn 4:1
14:33 1 Cor 7:17
14:34 Gen 3:16; 1 Cor 11:3; Eph 5:22; Col 3:18; 1 Tim 2:11-12; Titus 2:5
14:37 2 Cor 10:7; 1 Jn 4:6
14:39 1 Cor 12:31; 1 Thes 5:20
14:40 1 Cor 14:33; Col 2:5

14:23 Unbelievers might misinterpret speaking in tongues if it were disorderly. If they came into the church's worship and everyone were speaking in tongues at once and without an interpreter, then they would simply conclude that Christians were insane. Peter had to correct a similar misinterpretation in Acts 2:13-18. For such unbelievers, prophecy would be more useful than speaking in tongues because it would be clearly understandable and would convict them of their sin and of the presence of God.

14:26-32 First Corinthians 14 contains one of few New Testament references to the content of worship. Paul's recitation of the Lord's Supper liturgy was "received from the Lord Himself" (1 Corinthians 11:23). Also Acts 2:43-46 speaks of the believers' commitment to the apostles' teaching, to fellowship, to the breaking of bread, and to regular prayer. The variations in the lists of the elements of worship show that they are not exhaustive descriptions of worship in the early church.

▸ CHURCH

14:26 Unity and worship. In worship, all gifts and abilities are to be used for edification in an orderly way. Believers should not refrain from using their gifts since this deprives the church of one of God's provisions for its growth. At the same time, believers should not disrupt worship by using their gifts to impress others. Our goal should be to edify the congregation and glorify God, not to show off our talents or satisfy our personal preferences concerning styles of music. Let godly character—not personal preferences or cultural idiosyncrasies—lead your church toward manifesting unity through worship. (***See Church****> Role> Preach> Topics> Proper use of spiritual gifts,* TopicGuide page A50.)

14:32 In the Old Testament, a prophet was not always in complete control of his faculties (1 Samuel 10:10; 19:20; Numbers 23). However, Paul teaches that under the New Covenant this has changed and that now prophets are in full control of their faculties. This control also extends to tongues and other spiritual experiences, as Paul gives regulations for how they are to be used and not used in the church (14:39).

THE RESURRECTION OF CHRIST

15 Let me now remind you, dear brothers and sisters,* of the Good News I preached
to you before. You welcomed it then, and you still stand firm in it. 2It is this Good
News that saves you if you continue to believe the message I told you—unless, of course,
you believed something that was never true in the first place.*
3I passed on to you what was most important and what had also been passed on to me.
Christ died for our sins, just as the Scriptures said. 4He was buried, and He was raised from
the dead on the third day, just as the Scriptures said. 5He was seen by Peter* and then by
the Twelve. 6After that, He was seen by more than 500 of His followers* at one time, most
of whom are still alive, though some have died. 7Then He was seen by James and later by
all the apostles. 8Last of all, as though I had been born at the wrong time, I also saw Him.
9For I am the least of all the apostles. In fact, I'm not even worthy to be called an apostle af-
ter the way I persecuted God's church.
10But whatever I am now, it is all because God poured out His special favor on me—and
not without results. For I have worked harder than any of the other apostles; yet it was not
I but God who was working through me by His grace. 11So it makes no difference whether
I preach or they preach, for we all preach the same message you have already believed.

THE RESURRECTION OF THE DEAD

12But tell me this—since we preach that Christ rose from the dead, why are some of you
saying there will be no resurrection of the dead? 13For if there is no resurrection of the
dead, then Christ has not been raised either. 14And if Christ has not been raised, then all our
preaching is useless, and your faith is useless. 15And we apostles would all be lying about
God—for we have said that God raised Christ from the grave. But that can't be true if there is
no resurrection of the dead. 16And if there is no resurrection of the dead, then Christ has not
been raised. 17And if Christ has not been raised, then your faith is useless and you are still
guilty of your sins. 18In that case, all who have died believing in Christ are lost! 19And if our
hope in Christ is only for this life, we are more to be pitied than anyone in the world.

15:3 Isa 53:5-9; Luke 24:25-27; 1 Pet 2:24
15:4 Ps 16:10; Hos 6:2; Jon 1:17; Luke 24:25-27; John 2:21-22; Acts 2:24-32
15:5 Matt 28:16-17; Mark 16:14; Luke 24:34, 36-43; John 20:19
15:7 Luke 24:33-37; Acts 1:3-4
15:8 Acts 9:3-6; 1 Cor 9:1; Gal 1:16
15:9 Acts 8:3; 2 Cor 12:11; Eph 3:8
15:10 2 Cor 6:1; 11:5, 23
15:12 Acts 17:32; 23:8; 2 Tim 2:18
15:15 Acts 2:24
15:17 Rom 4:25

15:1 Greek *brothers;* also in 15:31, 50, 58. 15:2 Or *unless you never believed it in the first place.* 15:5 Greek *Cephas.* 15:6 Greek *the brothers.*

14:34-35 These verses on women in worship come in the context of Paul's solutions to unity-destroying problems in the church. Paul is not commanding that women always be utterly silent in all church meetings, for he earlier (11:5, 13) regulated how women prophesied and prayed in public worship. Among the Greeks it was considered inappropriate for a woman to question a man or even speak in public, so it may be that Paul's command is similar to that from 11:13-16—encouraging the Corinthians not to antagonize their society unnecessarily. Christianity displayed a revolutionary view of women compared to its first century culture, for neither the Jews nor Greeks were willing to teach women, yet because of the honored position of women in Christianity (Galatians 3:28), Paul assumed that women would be learning and, to some extent, participating in worship services. But in this cultural situation, God made it clear that silence was better than causing a disruption in the church.

▸SALVATION

15:1-7 A simple gospel. The basic message of Christianity is not complicated—Jesus Christ died for our sins, just as the Bible says. He was buried, but on the third day He rose from the dead. That message is, as Paul says, "Good News," because it provides salvation from our sins and the sure hope of eternal life in a resurrected body. There is no need to add customs, denominational beliefs, or personal preference to the simple gospel message. And do not be dismissive of the gospel's simplicity; though you may be smart, or have attended church services all your life, perhaps you do not truly believe the gospel, or refuse to submit to it. Have you simply received Jesus as your Savior and Lord, accepting the benefits of what He did on your behalf? Do not wait; do so now. (***See Salvation*****> *Jesus' Work> Resurrection> Rose according to the Scriptures,* TopicGuide page A22.)

15:5-7 With this list of witnesses, Paul reminds the Corinthian believers that there is a historical basis for the Christian faith; Christianity is ultimately rooted in real events, not simply theories or beliefs. This is an essential foundation for the argument Paul will develop in the remainder of the chapter, which is that Christians can expect a bodily resurrection because Jesus Himself was, in fact, resurrected bodily.

15:12-20 Some in the Corinthian church were teaching that there would be no resurrection of the dead. Among first-century Jews, there were differing views concerning the dead. The Sadducees taught that there would be no resurrection, while the Pharisees taught otherwise. Such debates had apparently carried over into the Corinthian church. Paul responds by pointing out that Jesus had risen from the dead, so there was obviously a resurrection. Paul then expands the point to address the larger issue, noting that Christ's resurrection sets an expectation and pattern for all who follow Him.

[20]But in fact, Christ has been raised from the dead. He is the first of a great harvest of all
who have died.
[21]So you see, just as death came into the world through a man, now the resurrection
from the dead has begun through another Man. [22]Just as everyone dies because we all
belong to Adam, everyone who belongs to Christ will be given new life. [23]But there is an
order to this resurrection: Christ was raised as the first of the harvest; then all who belong
to Christ will be raised when He comes back.
[24]After that the end will come, when He will turn the Kingdom over to God the Father,
having destroyed every ruler and authority and power. [25]For Christ must reign until He
humbles all His enemies beneath His feet. [26]And the last enemy to be destroyed is death.
[27]For the Scriptures say, "God has put all things under His authority."* (Of course, when it
says "all things are under His authority," that does not include God Himself, who gave
Christ His authority.) [28]Then, when all things are under His authority, the Son will put Him-
self under God's authority, so that God, who gave His Son authority over all things, will be
utterly supreme over everything everywhere.
[29]If the dead will not be raised, what point is there in people being baptized for those
who are dead? Why do it unless the dead will someday rise again?
[30]And why should we ourselves risk our lives hour by hour? [31]For I swear, dear brothers
and sisters, that I face death daily. This is as certain as my pride in what Christ Jesus our
Lord has done in you. [32]And what value was there in fighting wild beasts—those people of
Ephesus*—if there will be no resurrection from the dead? And if there is no resurrection,
"Let's feast and drink, for tomorrow we die!"* [33]Don't be fooled by those who say such
things, for "bad company corrupts good character." [34]Think carefully about what is right,
and stop sinning. For to your shame I say that some of you don't know God at all.

THE RESURRECTION BODY

[35]But someone may ask, "How will the dead be raised? What kind of bodies will they
have?" [36]What a foolish question! When you put a seed into the ground, it doesn't grow
into a plant unless it dies first. [37]And what you put in the ground is not the plant that will
grow, but only a bare seed of wheat or whatever you are planting. [38]Then God gives it the
new body He wants it to have. A different plant grows from each kind of seed. [39]Similarly
there are different kinds of flesh—one kind for humans, another for animals, another for
birds, and another for fish.
[40]There are also bodies in the heavens and bodies on the earth. The glory of the heavenly

15:20 Col 1:18; 1 Pet 1:3; Rev 1:5
15:21 Rom 5:12, 18
15:23 1 Thes 4:16
15:24 Dan 2:44; 7:14
15:25 Ps 110:1; Isa 9:7; Matt 22:44
15:26 2 Tim 1:10; Rev 20:14; 21:4
15:27 Matt 28:18; Eph 1:22; Heb 2:8; 1 Pet 3:22
15:28 Phil 3:21
15:30 Rom 8:36; 2 Cor 11:26
15:31 2 Cor 4:10-11
15:32 Luke 12:19-21; 2 Cor 1:8
15:34 1 Cor 6:5; Eph 5:14
15:35 Ezek 37:3
15:36 John 12:24

15:27 Ps 8:6. 15:32a Greek *fighting wild beasts in Ephesus.* 15:32b Isa 22:13.

15:21-24 Paul's logic here is simple—all who have Adam as their father receive the inheritance that is due to all members of his race. But all who are relatives of Christ will receive the inheritance that Christ received and now offers to His children: "new life."

15:23-28 These verses are not in a strict chronological order. According to Acts 1:9, Jesus ascended into heaven after He appeared to the disciples and other believers following His resurrection. He currently reigns at the right hand of God the Father, and He is in the process of subduing all His enemies (15:25, 27). Paul teaches the Corinthians how to live in this interim period, one in which Jesus already reigns, but in which He has not yet completed humbling His enemies. Jesus' return will consummate that process (15:23), and He will then raise His people from the dead (15:23), destroy death (15:26), and present Himself to God the Father (15:28).

15:29 Little is known about this baptism for the dead, mentioned only here in the New Testament. The natural reading of the words indicates some form of baptism by substitute that was practiced in Corinth. Paul references this Corinthian practice to show the absurdity of their argument against the resurrection of the dead, but this reference doesn't confirm that he approved of it as a practice. The Greek text literally reads, "For what will they do, those who are baptized for the dead?" a phrasing that indicates Paul was not involved in the practice.

15:35-44 Paul anticipates a likely question: What will believers' resurrection bodies look like? Verses 40-44 make it clear that our resurrection bodies will be different from our current bodies; however, verses 36-39 indicate that our current bodies will not be entirely unrelated to our resurrection bodies. Paul uses the analogy of a seed to explain this relationship: A seed (an acorn, for example) often bears little or no physical resemblance to the plant that grows from it (an oak tree, for example). Accordingly, we can understand our current bodies to be seeds, which will be buried when we die, but transformed by God into our new bodies when He raises us from the dead.

bodies is different from the glory of the earthly bodies. 41 The sun has one kind of glory,
while the moon and stars each have another kind. And even the stars differ from each other
in their glory.
42 It is the same way with the resurrection of the dead. Our earthly bodies are planted
in the ground when we die, but they will be raised to live forever. 43 Our bodies are bur-
ied in brokenness, but they will be raised in glory. They are buried in weakness, but they
will be raised in strength. 44 They are buried as natural human bodies, but they will be
raised as spiritual bodies. For just as there are natural bodies, there are also spiritual
bodies.
45 The Scriptures tell us, "The first man, Adam, became a living person."* But the last
Adam—that is, Christ—is a life-giving Spirit. 46 What comes first is the natural body, then the
spiritual body comes later. 47 Adam, the first man, was made from the dust of the earth,
while Christ, the second man, came from heaven. 48 Earthly people are like the earthly
man, and heavenly people are like the heavenly man. 49 Just as we are now like the
earthly man, we will someday be like* the heavenly man.
50 What I am saying, dear brothers and sisters, is that our physical bodies cannot inherit
the Kingdom of God. These dying bodies cannot inherit what will last forever.
51 But let me reveal to you a wonderful secret. We will not all die, but we will all be trans-
formed! 52 It will happen in a moment, in the blink of an eye, when the last trumpet is
blown. For when the trumpet sounds, those who have died will be raised to live forever.
And we who are living will also be transformed. 53 For our dying bodies must be trans-
formed into bodies that will never die; our mortal bodies must be transformed into immor-
tal bodies.
54 Then, when our dying bodies have been transformed into bodies that will never die,*
this Scripture will be fulfilled:

> "Death is swallowed up in victory.*
> 55 O death, where is your victory?
> O death, where is your sting?*"

56 For sin is the sting that results in death, and the law gives sin its power. 57 But thank God!
He gives us victory over sin and death through our Lord Jesus Christ.
58 So, my dear brothers and sisters, be strong and immovable. Always work enthusiasti-
cally for the Lord, for you know that nothing you do for the Lord is ever useless.

15:42 Dan 12:2-3; Matt 13:43; 1 Cor 15:50
15:43 Phil 3:20-21; Col 3:4
15:45 *Gen 2:7; John 5:21; 6:63; Rom 8:2; 2 Cor 3:17
15:47 Gen 2:7; 3:19; John 3:13, 31
15:48 Phil 3:20-21
15:49 Gen 5:3; Rom 8:29
15:50 John 3:3, 5
15:51 2 Cor 5:2-4; Phil 3:21; 1 Thes 4:15-17
15:52 Matt 24:31
15:53 2 Cor 5:4
15:54 *Isa 25:8
15:55 *Hos 13:14
15:56 Rom 4:15; 5:12
15:57 Rom 8:37; 1 Jn 5:4
15:58 Rev 14:13

15:45 Gen 2:7. 15:49 Some manuscripts read *let us be like.* 15:54a Some manuscripts add *and our mortal bodies have been transformed into immortal bodies.* 15:54b Isa 25:8. 15:55 Hos 13:14 (Greek version).

15:45-49 Paul regularly makes use of the contrast between Adam, in whom all humans sinned, and Christ, the second Adam, in whom people are redeemed (see Romans 5:12-17; 1 Corinthians 15:21-23). Here he focuses on an implication of that contrast: the difference between our current bodies and our coming resurrection bodies. By referring to our resurrection bodies as "spiritual" (15:46), Paul does not mean that they will be incorporeal. Instead, they will be like Christ's body, fully able to live forever in the age to come. Christ is and will forever remain both God and man, fully (and physically) human and also fully God—two distinct natures in one body.

15:50-57 In another argument for the necessity of a resurrection, Paul points out that the deposit of all God's blessings for His people is so great that our fragile earthly bodies could not even contain all of them. A transformation of our bodies (2 Corinthians 5:1-10)—in which they will be resurrected and reconnected to our souls (Revelation 6:9-11)—will accompany the return of Christ, as John echoes in one of his final letters (1 John 3:2).

▸ PURPOSE

15:58 You can take it with you! The resurrection has a very practical application. Our continued human existence should make us enthusiastic about the Lord's work, for we know that the work we do for Him is neither worthless nor temporary (1 Corinthians 3:10-15). On the contrary, it is significant and will last forever—not only in God's perfect memory, but also in our own and in the memories of those whose lives we touched. Do you have trouble seeing purpose in what you do? Jesus offers you both a life and work of eternal purpose. He has gone before us to mark out good works (Ephesians 2:9-10) and promises to crown us with rewards (Matthew 25:29) as we participate in His grand plan of glory to God and goodness for His people. Go forth in His name, knowing that your resurrection guarantees that your life will be different—forever. (***See Purpose****> God's Means> God's Sovereignty> God's people are chosen for service,* TopicGuide page A52.)

THE COLLECTION FOR JERUSALEM

16 Now regarding your question about the money being collected for God's people in
Jerusalem. You should follow the same procedure I gave to the churches in Gala-
tia. 2On the first day of each week, you should each put aside a portion of the money you
have earned. Don't wait until I get there and then try to collect it all at once. 3When I come, I
will write letters of recommendation for the messengers you choose to deliver your gift to
Jerusalem. 4And if it seems appropriate for me to go along, they can travel with me.

PAUL'S FINAL INSTRUCTIONS

5I am coming to visit you after I have been to Macedonia,* for I am planning to travel
through Macedonia. 6Perhaps I will stay awhile with you, possibly all winter, and then you
can send me on my way to my next destination. 7This time I don't want to make just a
short visit and then go right on. I want to come and stay awhile, if the Lord will let me. 8In
the meantime, I will be staying here at Ephesus until the Festival of Pentecost. 9There is a
wide-open door for a great work here, although many oppose me.
10When Timothy comes, don't intimidate him. He is doing the Lord's work, just as I am.
11Don't let anyone treat him with contempt. Send him on his way with your blessing when
he returns to me. I expect him to come with the other believers.*
12Now about our brother Apollos—I urged him to visit you with the other believers, but
he was not willing to go right now. He will see you later when he has the opportunity.
13Be on guard. Stand firm in the faith. Be courageous.* Be strong. 14And do everything
with love.
15You know that Stephanas and his household were the first of the harvest of believers
in Greece,* and they are spending their lives in service to God's people. I urge you, dear
brothers and sisters,* 16to submit to them and others like them who serve with such devo-
tion. 17I am very glad that Stephanas, Fortunatus, and Achaicus have come here. They
have been providing the help you weren't here to give me. 18They have been a wonderful
encouragement to me, as they have been to you. You must show your appreciation to all
who serve so well.

16:5 *Macedonia* was in the northern region of Greece. 16:11 Greek *with the brothers;* also in 16:12. 16:13 Greek *Be men.* 16:15a Greek *in Achaia,* the southern region of the Greek peninsula. 16:15b Greek *brothers;* also in 16:20.

16:1 Acts 11:29; 24:17 Rom 15:25-26 2 Cor 8:9 Gal 2:10
16:2 Acts 20:7
16:3 2 Cor 3:1; 8:18-19
16:5 Acts 19:21 1 Cor 4:19
16:6 Rom 15:24 Titus 3:13
16:7 Acts 18:21
16:8 Acts 2:1; 18:19
16:9 Acts 14:27; 19:8-10 2 Cor 2:12
16:10 Acts 16:1
16:11 1 Tim 4:12
16:12 Acts 18:24 1 Cor 1:12
16:13 Eph 6:10 Phil 1:27; 4:1 1 Thes 3:8
16:14 1 Cor 14:1
16:15 1 Cor 1:16

16:1 The collection for the Christians in Jerusalem was for the support of financially poor Christians (see Romans 15:26). Jerusalem itself had little wealth during the first century and was highly dependent on financial support from Jews who lived outside Palestine. Additionally, Christians in Jerusalem were persecuted, so they would have been cut off from that support and were likely quite poor.

▸ ADOPTION
16:1-2 There is meaning in the mundane. It may initially seem anticlimactic, after the great discussions of spiritual gifts, love, worship, and the gospel, for Paul to close his letter with seemingly mundane issues such as the logistics of collecting an offering for the poor. However, God is pleased by faithfulness in life, not only in the big turning points but also in the moments of consistent, routine obedience and service. Do you serve "behind the scenes" in your church or fellowship? Your contribution is valuable and essential, and it is pleasing to God. Do it with all your heart—the routine is an opportunity to honor God. (***See Adoption***> *With Christ*> *Supernatural*> *The source for extraordinary living,* TopicGuide page A37.)

16:5 Macedonia was a Roman province in New Testament times. It included the northern region of Greece and the southern sections of present-day Albania, the former Yugoslavia, and present-day Bulgaria. The region served as a land trade route between Asia and the West. After incorporating Macedonia as a province, the Romans built the Via Egnatia, a paved road over 500 miles (804.5 kilometers) long, running from the Adriatic to the Aegean Sea. Paul would have traveled this road as he moved through the Macedonian cities, including Philippi and Thessalonica (Acts 16:11-12; 17:1), to whom Paul addressed the letters of Philippians and 1 and 2 Thessalonians.

16:12 Paul puts his teaching in 1:10-17 and 3:1-23 into action. In those chapters he had reminded the Corinthians that he and Apollos were partners in ministry and that neither of them sought his own glory, but God's alone. Now Paul demonstrates this by encouraging Apollos to go to Corinth, trusting God to use his associate in ministry to minister to his friends.

16:15-17 Stephanas was a Christian believer in Corinth, one of Paul's first converts in Greece. He and his family were some of the few Corinthian believers personally baptized by Paul. Fortunatus and Achaicus were members of the church at Corinth. The three of them visited Paul at Ephesus in Asia Minor. Their mission probably included bringing aid for Paul's personal needs and seeking his advice for resolving the problems in the Corinthian church. They likely carried the letter, which is mentioned in 7:1, from the church to Paul, and Paul likely sent the letter of 1 Corinthians back with them when they returned to Corinth.

16:19 Rom 16:5
16:20 Rom 16:16
16:21 Gal 6:11 Col 4:18 2 Thes 3:17 Phlm 1:19
16:22 Gal 1:8-9
16:23 Rom 16:20

PAUL'S FINAL GREETINGS

19 The churches here in the province of Asia* send greetings in the Lord, as do Aquila and
Priscilla* and all the others who gather in their home for church meetings. 20 All the broth-
ers and sisters here send greetings to you. Greet each other with Christian love.*

21 HERE IS MY GREETING IN MY OWN HANDWRITING—PAUL.

22 If anyone does not love the Lord, that person is cursed. Our Lord, come!*

23 May the grace of the Lord Jesus be with you.

24 My love to all of you in Christ Jesus.*

16:19a *Asia* was a Roman province in what is now western Turkey. **16:19b** Greek *Prisca.* **16:20** Greek *with a sacred kiss.* **16:22** From Aramaic, *Marana tha.* Some manuscripts read *Maran atha, "Our Lord has come."* **16:24** Some manuscripts add *Amen.*

16:19 Aquila and Priscilla were a Christian couple who were friends and possibly converts of the apostle Paul during his ministry at Corinth (Acts 18:1-3). Aquila was a Jew and a native of Pontus in Asia Minor. He had been expelled from Rome by the AD 49 edict of Claudius (Acts 18:2). From Rome, Aquila and Priscilla went to Corinth, where Paul (on his second missionary journey) met them. There they lived together and worked at the same trade of making tents. When Paul left Corinth, they accompanied him to Ephesus and were there when he wrote 1 Corinthians. They remained in Ephesus after Paul returned to Syria (Acts 18:18-19), and after such close association with Paul, they were able to instruct even the learned Apollos (Acts 18:23-26).

16:21-24 Paul had likely dictated the letter up to this point to a scribe or secretary (see 1 Corinthians 1:1). Now Paul takes the pen and writes the final portion of the letter in his own handwriting. Doing so would assure the Corinthians that this was a genuine letter, not a forgery.

▸ HOLINESS

16:22 Growing in love for the Lord. Do you love God? The Christian life is one of obedience, but we must offer this obedience with a grateful and loving heart, not a grudging one. Christ's yoke is easy and His burden is light (Matthew 11:30) because we follow Him with joy and love. There is much to learn in the study of 1 Corinthians, and there are several issues on which Christians have different opinions. But however much you study or learn about those issues, your study of this book must move you to love God and others more—otherwise it will be of no value: "If I understood all of God's secret plans and possessed all knowledge, and if I had such faith that I could move mountains, but didn't love others, I would be nothing" (1 Corinthians 13:2). (***See Holiness****> Maturing> Conformity to Christ> Following the Royal Law of love,* TopicGuide page A40.)

2 CORINTHIANS

PURPOSE

To establish the principles for authentic ministry and ministers in the life of the New Testament church.

Who is qualified to bring a message about Jesus? You may have run across some people who do not appear, by their words and actions, to be legitimate ministers. Some might be teaching or preaching for personal gain. Some do what they do without any real love for those they claim to serve. How can you determine a true minister from a false one?

Second Corinthians is, to a large degree, a defense of Paul's apostleship. There were some teachers who were stirring up trouble in the Corinthian community, most notably by raising questions about Paul's authority and integrity. This forced Paul to do what he would never ordinarily have done—write to the church and defend himself (2 Corinthians 11:1-15). As Paul made the case for his own calling, he laid the foundation for all legitimate ministry in the church. God's New Covenant plan—the gospel—is at the root of every genuine Christian ministry, and Paul recognized that his own apostleship was proven by the changed lives of the Corinthians (2 Corinthians 3:2-3), the character of his ministry (6:3-10; 7:2), his love for God's people (6:11-12; 7:3), his sacrificial suffering (11:23-33), and his working of miracles (12:12). From those, we can see general principles, further reinforced by Paul's other teachings (1 Timothy 3), to evaluate the authenticity of ministers today.

DISCOVER GOD IN 2 CORINTHIANS

Central to Paul's thinking in 2 Corinthians is the idea of the New Covenant, God's plan to bring blessing to His people. In the context of God's mission for redeeming His people, we see many facets of God's character:

The God Who Brings Comfort: Even though Paul has some strong words for the believers in Corinth, he begins this letter by reminding them that God is the One who comforts us in all the troubles we might encounter (1:3-7). No matter what the difficulty, God will bring us comfort and aid. This theme resurfaces later in the letter when Paul reminds the Corinthians that God supplies them with all that they need in whatever circumstance they might find themselves (9:6-15).

The Spirit Who Brings About Transformation: As Paul begins to discuss the New Covenant and what God is doing in the lives of those who have found life in Jesus, he highlights the Spirit's role in transforming us (3:1-18). For Paul, the Spirit is "the first installment" leading to our ultimate full renovation (1:22) as well as God's personal guarantee that we will one day experience the full fruit of redemption (5:5).

Jesus, Who Is the Heart of Our Message: Throughout this letter Paul returns to one of his favorite themes: Jesus. Although he doesn't spend long sections elaborating on his view of Jesus, everywhere you turn in the letter, you will find Paul referring to Jesus: Jesus is the subject of his preaching (1:19; 2:12; 4:5); Jesus is the One he seeks to represent in what he says and does (5:17-20); Jesus is the standard against which every thought is evaluated (10:5-6); and Jesus is the true object of devotion for all the saints (11:1-4).

GROWING THROUGH 2 CORINTHIANS

Not every Christian will have the same personal ministry that Paul had; Paul had the unique ministry of an apostle since he saw Jesus and was taught and specifically ordained by Him to be an apostle (Acts 1:20-26; 1 Corinthians 9:1; Galatians 1:11-18). Paul's writings do, however, provide general principles of ministry and principles of giving for all believers.

Principles of Ministry: Paul shows that legitimate ministry does not begin with people but is a work of the Holy Spirit (chapter 3). It is Christ-centered (chapter 4) and designed to increase the faith of those involved (chapter 5). Such a ministry is not easily swayed, not even by harsh suffering (chapter 6).

Principles of Giving: Mature stewardship of our finances is a response of joy, not guilt (8:1-4). It is preceded by and based on giving ourselves—everything we are and own—to the Lord (8:5-9). Godly giving is an act of unity, of participation in the life of the body of Christ. It is undergirded by God's graciousness, His blessings, and His magnificent gift of Jesus Christ to all who believe (9:6-11). Finally, giving is a way to glorify God, to lift up His name among the church and the world as the reason why we can be free from selfishness and free to give (9:12-13).

DISCOVERY VERSES

You see, we don't go around preaching about ourselves. We preach that Jesus Christ is Lord, and we ourselves are your servants for Jesus' sake. (2 CORINTHIANS 4:5)

We are Christ's ambassadors; God is making His appeal through us. We speak for Christ when we plead, "Come back to God!" For God made Christ, who never sinned, to be the offering for our sin, so that we could be made right with God through Christ. (2 CORINTHIANS 5:20-21)

You know the generous grace of our Lord Jesus Christ. Though He was rich, yet for your sakes He became poor, so that by His poverty He could make you rich. (2 CORINTHIANS 8:9)

2 CORINTHIANS FACTS

Author: Paul identifies himself as the author of this letter (1:1). Although Paul mentions Timothy, his companion and fellow worker at this time, it is not believed that Timothy had a part in writing this letter.

Written to: The church in Corinth was founded when Paul brought the gospel on one of his missionary journeys (Acts 18). Apparently, 2 Corinthians was actually the fourth letter Paul wrote to the Corinthians. In 1 Corinthians 5:9 there is a reference to a letter that (presumably) preceded 1 Corinthians. In 2 Corinthians 2:4, Paul speaks of a "sorrowful letter" that he had sent to them, which does not appear to be 1 Corinthians. Thus, 2 Corinthians is the fourth letter Paul wrote to this church that was close to his heart and facing some ongoing trouble.

Date of writing: In the closing chapter of 1 Corinthians, Paul let his readers know that he was in Ephesus and was intending to visit them after going through Macedonia (1 Corinthians 16:5-9). Based on what Acts 20 tells us about Paul's travels, 1 Corinthians was probably written in the spring of AD 55, and this letter followed several months later.

Setting: References in this letter (2:13 and 7:5) indicate that Paul was writing from Macedonia, in the northern part of the Grecian peninsula. He was writing to believers in Corinth, a city in the southern region of Greece.

OUTLINE

- **2 CORINTHIANS 1:1–2:11**—Paul's Personal Plans
- **2 CORINTHIANS 2:12–9:15**—God's New Plan
  - ***2 CORINTHIANS 2:12–3:18***—*The New Covenant Transforms Us*
  - ***2 CORINTHIANS 4:1–5:10***—*The New Covenant Gives Us Confidence in Living*
  - ***2 CORINTHIANS 5:11–6:13***—*The New Covenant Provides a Message of Reconciliation*
  - ***2 CORINTHIANS 6:14–9:15***—*The New Covenant Ushers In a New Way of Living*
- **2 CORINTHIANS 10:10–13:14**—Paul's Description of a Godly Minister

1:1 1 Cor 1:1; 2 Cor 1:19; Eph 1:1
1:2 Rom 1:7
1:3 Eph 1:3; 1 Pet 1:3
1:4 Isa 51:12; 66:13; 2 Cor 7:6
1:5 2 Cor 4:10; Phil 3:10; Col 1:24
1:6 2 Cor 4:15
1:9 Jer 17:5, 7
1:10 2 Tim 4:18; 2 Pet 2:9
1:11 Rom 15:30; 2 Cor 4:15; Phil 1:19
1:12 Acts 23:1; 1 Cor 1:17; 2 Cor 2:17; 4:15

GREETINGS FROM PAUL

1 This letter is from Paul, chosen by the will of God to be an apostle of Christ Jesus, and
from our brother Timothy.
I am writing to God's church in Corinth and to all of His holy people throughout Greece.*
2 May God our Father and the Lord Jesus Christ give you grace and peace.

GOD OFFERS COMFORT TO ALL

3 All praise to God, the Father of our Lord Jesus Christ. God is our merciful Father and the
source of all comfort. 4 He comforts us in all our troubles so that we can comfort others.
When they are troubled, we will be able to give them the same comfort God has given us.
5 For the more we suffer for Christ, the more God will shower us with His comfort through
Christ. 6 Even when we are weighed down with troubles, it is for your comfort and salva-
tion! For when we ourselves are comforted, we will certainly comfort you. Then you can
patiently endure the same things we suffer. 7 We are confident that as you share in our suf-
ferings, you will also share in the comfort God gives us.
8 We think you ought to know, dear brothers and sisters,* about the trouble we went
through in the province of Asia. We were crushed and overwhelmed beyond our ability to
endure, and we thought we would never live through it. 9 In fact, we expected to die. But as
a result, we stopped relying on ourselves and learned to rely only on God, who raises the
dead. 10 And He did rescue us from mortal danger, and He will rescue us again. We have
placed our confidence in Him, and He will continue to rescue us. 11 And you are helping us
by praying for us. Then many people will give thanks because God has graciously an-
swered so many prayers for our safety.

PAUL'S CHANGE OF PLANS

12 We can say with confidence and a clear conscience that we have lived with a God-given
holiness* and sincerity in all our dealings. We have depended on God's grace, not on our
own human wisdom. That is how we have conducted ourselves before the world, and es-
pecially toward you. 13 Our letters have been straightforward, and there is nothing written

1:1 Greek *Achaia*, the southern region of the Greek peninsula. 1:8 Greek *brothers*. 1:12 Some manuscripts read *honesty*.

1:1 Timothy was a convert from Paul's ministry and one of Paul's regular companions. For more information on Timothy, see the note on 1 Corinthians 4:17. Paul meant for this particular letter to be read not only in the Corinthian church but also in other churches throughout Greece. Its immediate context is the difficulties in the Corinthian church, but it also speaks to Christians in other situations.

▸ WORSHIP

1:3-7 Comforted to be a comforter. God comforts us in our troubles, especially when we suffer for Christ. It is easy to look instead to earthly things for comfort—money, alcohol, recreation, or something else—but those things are escapes, not true comfort. God is the only source of security that will never run dry. However, the gracious care we receive from God is not simply for our own benefit. God's comfort to us also gives us a responsibility—to comfort others. Do not simply receive God's comfort, but look for opportunities to comfort others just as God has comforted you. Is anyone in your community in the midst of troubles? Reach out to that person with the comfort and Good News of Jesus Christ. (***See Worship****> NT> Fellowship> Preserving> Comfort one another,* TopicGuide page A31.)

1:8 After the "painful visit" (see 2:1) that Paul had made to Corinth, he wrote to the Corinthians "in great anguish . . . and many tears" (2:4). That letter was written before 2 Corinthians (see 7:8-12), but has since been lost. Some time after that letter was written, a situation erupted that was so difficult that Paul expected he would die, most likely by being executed. This situation may have happened in Ephesus (see Acts 19:23-41; Romans 16:4), though the text of the letter only indicates that it was somewhere in Asia. Paul was not killed, but he learned a valuable lesson—that he could only rely on God, not his own strength or abilities. Paul had been so certain of death that he felt as if he himself had been raised from the dead.

1:10-11 Paul makes it clear to the Corinthians that prayer matters. Their prayers had made—and were making—a difference in the success of Paul's ministry and in his protection from crises such as he had just experienced. God is not constrained to act only in cases where believers pray, but doing so is His normal method, and it brings Him more glory because when He answers prayer, all those who had been praying give Him thanks and praise.

1:13 The Corinthians were completely capable of reading and understanding Paul's letters. They were not to read "between the lines," looking for a hidden or deeper meaning. Instead, Paul's letters to the Corinthians were plain and clear communication; the obvious meaning was the correct one. Paul did not intend this to mean that the Corinthians had already understood everything he sought to teach them, but he emphasized that they were capable of understanding everything in his letters by careful reading and application, and by hearts open to the Holy Spirit's illumination.

between the lines and nothing you can't understand. I hope someday you will fully under-
stand us, 14even if you don't understand us now. Then on the day when the Lord Jesus* re-
turns, you will be proud of us in the same way we are proud of you.
15Since I was so sure of your understanding and trust, I wanted to give you a double
blessing by visiting you twice—16first on my way to Macedonia and again when I returned
from Macedonia.* Then you could send me on my way to Judea.
17You may be asking why I changed my plan. Do you think I make my plans carelessly?
Do you think I am like people of the world who say "Yes" when they really mean "No"?
18As surely as God is faithful, my word to you does not waver between "Yes" and "No."
19For Jesus Christ, the Son of God, does not waver between "Yes" and "No." He is the One
whom Silas,* Timothy, and I preached to you, and as God's ultimate "Yes," He always does
what He says. 20For all of God's promises have been fulfilled in Christ with a resounding
"Yes!" And through Christ, our "Amen" (which means "Yes") ascends to God for His glory.
21It is God who enables us, along with you, to stand firm for Christ. He has commis-
sioned us, 22and He has identified us as His own by placing the Holy Spirit in our hearts as
the first installment that guarantees everything He has promised us.
23Now I call upon God as my witness that I am telling the truth. The reason I didn't return
to Corinth was to spare you from a severe rebuke. 24But that does not mean we want to
dominate you by telling you how to put your faith into practice. We want to work together
with you so you will be full of joy, for it is by your own faith that you stand firm.

2 So I decided that I would not bring you grief with another painful visit. 2For if I cause
you grief, who will make me glad? Certainly not someone I have grieved. 3That is
why I wrote to you as I did, so that when I do come, I won't be grieved by the very ones
who ought to give me the greatest joy. Surely you all know that my joy comes from your
being joyful. 4I wrote that letter in great anguish, with a troubled heart and many tears. I
didn't want to grieve you, but I wanted to let you know how much love I have for you.

FORGIVENESS FOR THE SINNER

5I am not overstating it when I say that the man who caused all the trouble hurt all of you
more than he hurt me. 6Most of you opposed him, and that was punishment enough.

1:14 2 Cor 5:12; Phil 2:16
1:15 Rom 1:11-13
1:16 Acts 19:21; 1 Cor 16:5-6
1:17 2 Cor 5:16
1:19 Acts 18:5; Heb 13:8
1:20 Rom 15:8-9; Rev 3:14
1:21 1 Jn 2:20, 27
1:22 2 Cor 5:5; Eph 1:13-14; 4:30
1:23 1 Cor 4:21
1:24 1 Cor 15:1
2:1 1 Cor 4:21; 2 Cor 12:21
2:2 2 Cor 7:8
2:4 2 Cor 2:9; 7:8, 12
2:5 1 Cor 5:1-2; 2 Cor 7:11

1:14 Some manuscripts read *our Lord Jesus*. 1:16 *Macedonia* was in the northern region of Greece. 1:19 Greek *Silvanus*.

1:15-17 Sometime after Paul had written 1 Corinthians and before he wrote his letter of anguish, he made a "painful visit" to Corinth (see 2:1). His original intent had been to stop at Corinth twice during his trip to Macedonia, once on the trip there and once on the return trip, possibly then receiving the collection mentioned in chapter 8 and going on to Jerusalem. However, Paul changed his plans and had not yet come again to Corinth. Some of his opponents argued this was a sign of carelessness. Paul responds (see 1:23) that he had changed his plans out of concern for the Corinthians' own good.

▸ HOLINESS
1:18-22 Living for God. When someone attacks you, what is the first thing that comes to your mind? Returning the insult? Paul doesn't directly answer his opponents' accusation of fickleness—he takes the opportunity to talk about the nature of God. He first notes that God is not fickle, and he grounds his own behavior in following the example of Jesus Christ. Following Christ's example is possible because Paul has been sealed with the Holy Spirit (1:22), a guarantee of all God's promises for sanctification. If you have received Jesus Christ as Lord and Savior, you have also been sealed, and you have the same promise: Your behavior can increasingly follow the model of the Lord Jesus Christ, just as Paul's did. Theology is not merely academic; what you believe about God determines how you live your Christian life. Consider how you can make your thoughts, words, and behavior God-centered. (***See Holiness***> *Disciplines*> *Of Engagement*> *Honesty,* TopicGuide page A42.)

1:23–2:4 Paul now adds detail concerning his previous letter and why he had not yet chosen to return to Corinth. Second Corinthians 7:8-12 also refers to this letter, but the letter itself has not been preserved. Had Paul visited the Corinthians again, it would have involved giving the church a severe rebuke. Instead, Paul chose to communicate by writing, feeling that a letter, though harsh, would be both gentler and more effective than a visit.

1:24 Paul models a collaborative view of discipleship for the Corinthians. Though he is their spiritual leader, he does not wish to simply give them orders about what they should do, nor does he wish to specify for them every detail of how they should live the Christian life. Instead, he wants discipleship to be a collaborative process, one in which he and they together work toward their growth in Christ. In Paul's view, Christian maturity for the Corinthians would not be mere obedience; it would be their ability to rightly apply the Word to their lives.

2:5 The text is not detailed enough to identify with certainty the man referenced in this verse. One theory is that this man had been a member of the Corinthian church who opposed Paul, possibly during Paul's painful visit. A second theory is

2:7 Gal 6:1 Eph 4:32 — [7]Now, however, it is time to forgive and comfort him. Otherwise he may be overcome by
discouragement. [8]So I urge you now to reaffirm your love for him.
[9]I wrote to you as I did to test you and see if you would fully comply with my instruc-
2:11 2 Cor 4:4 1 Pet 5:8 — tions. [10]When you forgive this man, I forgive him, too. And when I forgive whatever needs
to be forgiven, I do so with Christ's authority for your benefit, [11]so that Satan will not out-
2:12 Acts 14:27 2 Cor 4:3 — smart us. For we are familiar with his evil schemes.
[12]When I came to the city of Troas to preach the Good News of Christ, the Lord opened a
2:13 2 Cor 7:5-6 — door of opportunity for me. [13]But I had no peace of mind because my dear brother Titus
hadn't yet arrived with a report from you. So I said good-bye and went on to Macedonia to
find him.

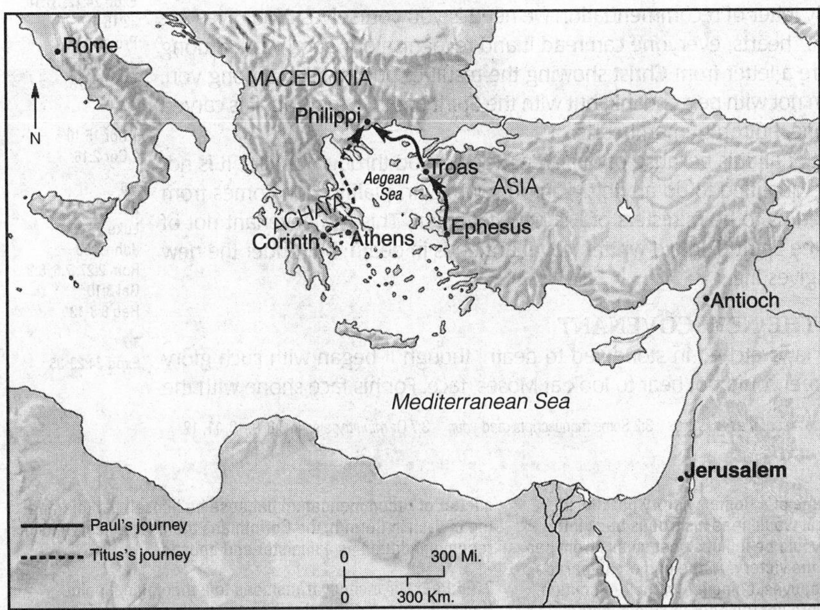

PAUL SEARCHES FOR TITUS
Paul had searched for Titus, hoping to meet him in Troas and receive news about the Corinthian church. When he did not find Titus in Troas, he went on to Macedonia (2:13), most likely to Philippi, where he found Titus.

that this man was an outsider to the Corinthian church but had nonetheless led an attack on Paul's authority. Still a third theory is that this is the man referenced in 1 Corinthians 5:3-5, who had been disciplined in response to Paul's instructions. Whichever theory one adopts, it is clear that the Corinthians had rejected this man. In response, he had repented, and, in line with the purpose of church discipline, Paul urged the Corinthian church to forgive and comfort him (Matthew 18:15-18; see also Deuteronomy 8:5; Hebrews 12:5-11; Revelation 3:19).

2:6-7 Paul indicates that the local church has authority to pronounce forgiveness and judgment (Matthew 18:19-20; Luke 24:47) on this man. The ultimate purpose of the church's judgments is to spur repentance in those who are judged. Once that repentance has been achieved, Paul indicates that the Christian course of action is to forgive and restore, not to continue punishment.

▸ CHURCH
2:10-11 Forgiveness is essential. We are to be forgiving, not vindictive, even in cases in which we have been called to participate in discipline by casting someone out of church fellowship. The goal of discipline should be the restoration of a sinner, and that must always be our hope and prayer. A lack of forgiveness is one of the devil's chief weapons—and not simply in cases of church discipline, but in all interpersonal relations. Are you harboring grudges against someone? Is there someone you need to forgive? If so, do it now. Do not let Satan confuse you by making you feel it is ever appropriate to harbor a grudge. (***See Church**> Role> Conflict> General Counsel> Forgive each other*, TopicGuide page A49.)

2:12-13 Before traveling into Macedonia, Paul had sent Titus to Corinth, probably with the letter of rebuke mentioned in 2:4. On the way to Macedonia, Paul stopped at Troas, which is a city in modern-day Turkey, on the shore of the Aegean Sea. The Lord opened opportunities for Paul to preach about Christ in Troas. Nonetheless, Paul was so concerned about the situation in Corinth that he could not rest in Troas without news of the Corinthians' reaction to his letter. He therefore left Troas, bypassing the open door of opportunity, and traveled on to Macedonia looking for Titus so that he could hear of the Corinthians' response.

2:13 Titus was one of Paul's converts who became an intimate and trusted associate in Paul's mission of spreading Christianity throughout the Mediterranean world. He was the recipient of the letter that bears his name, and he is also mentioned in Galatians and 2 Timothy. He was a companion of Paul and Barnabas on a visit to Jerusalem (see Galatians 2:3), and he probably accompanied Paul from that time on. Titus carried Paul's letter of rebuke and served as an ambassador from Paul to the Corinthian church, which was questioning his authority.

MINISTERS OF THE NEW COVENANT

14But thank God! He has made us His captives and continues to lead us along in Christ's tri-
umphal procession. Now He uses us to spread the knowledge of Christ everywhere, like a
sweet perfume. 15Our lives are a Christ-like fragrance rising up to God. But this fragrance is
perceived differently by those who are being saved and by those who are perishing. 16To
those who are perishing, we are a dreadful smell of death and doom. But to those who are
being saved, we are a life-giving perfume. And who is adequate for such a task as this?
17You see, we are not like the many hucksters* who preach for personal profit. We preach
the word of God with sincerity and with Christ's authority, knowing that God is watching us.

3 Are we beginning to praise ourselves again? Are we like others, who need to bring
you letters of recommendation, or who ask you to write such letters on their behalf?
Surely not! 2The only letter of recommendation we need is you yourselves. Your lives are
a letter written in our* hearts; everyone can read it and recognize our good work among
you. 3Clearly, you are a letter from Christ showing the result of our ministry among you.
This "letter" is written not with pen and ink, but with the Spirit of the living God. It is carved
not on tablets of stone, but on human hearts.
4We are confident of all this because of our great trust in God through Christ. 5It is not
that we think we are qualified to do anything on our own. Our qualification comes from
God. 6He has enabled us to be ministers of His new covenant. This is a covenant not of
written laws, but of the Spirit. The old written covenant ends in death; but under the new
covenant, the Spirit gives life.

THE GLORY OF THE NEW COVENANT

7The old way,* with laws etched in stone, led to death, though it began with such glory
that the people of Israel could not bear to look at Moses' face. For his face shone with the

2:15 1 Cor 1:18
2:16 Luke 2:34; 2 Cor 3:5-6
2:17 2 Cor 1:12; 12:19
3:1 Acts 18:27; 2 Cor 5:12; 10:12
3:2 1 Cor 9:2
3:3 Exod 24:12; 31:18; 32:15-16; Prov 3:3; Jer 31:33; Ezek 36:26
3:5 1 Cor 15:10; 2 Cor 2:16
3:6 Jer 31:31; Luke 22:20; John 6:63; Rom 2:27; 7:6; 8:2; Gal 3:10; Heb 8:8-13
3:7 Exod 34:29-35

2:17 Some manuscripts read *the rest of the hucksters.* 3:2 Some manuscripts read *your.* 3:7 Or *ministry;* also in 3:8, 9, 10, 11, 12.

2:14-16 Paul uses the image of a Roman victory parade, in which a victorious general would lead his troops back into their home city. The air would be full of sweet smells from perfumes used to celebrate the victory. At the end of the parade, however, marched the captives, being led to their execution. To them, the perfumes were not the odor of sweet victory, but the odor of impending death.

▸ PURPOSE
2:15-16 Do you smell something? Paul uses the dual nature of the fragrances of a Roman victory parade to illustrate how people respond to the Christian life. Preaching Christ and living for Him will both attract and repel. Some will react with joy, receiving the Good News of the gospel and becoming Christ's followers, but others will react with disapproval, spite, or even persecution because the Christian message reminds them of impending doom. Are you prepared to experience either reaction to your Christian witness? Ask the Holy Spirit to help you stand firm in your witness, regardless of the response. (***See Purpose**> God's Means> God's Sovereignty> God chooses some and leaves others in their rebellion,* TopicGuide page A52.)

2:17 Paul refutes the charge that he is a huckster, preaching only to get the Corinthians' money. On the contrary, he notes that he takes no money (see 11:7-10) and preaches as the captive of Christ.

3:1-2 It was common in the ancient world to bring a letter of recommendation, a statement by a recognized third party that the bearer of the letter should be received well and heeded. The Corinthians would be more likely to listen to a stranger's teaching if he bore such a letter with him. Paul reminds them that he, however, is no stranger to them. He does not need a letter of recommendation because he himself had planted the church in Corinth; the Corinthians themselves serve as his recommendation as a minister and apostle.

3:3-6 Paul surprisingly transitions to a theological point. Having just stated that the Corinthians' lives were his letter of recommendation, he contrasts this "letter" with typical letters of recommendation. The expected contrast would be between this living letter and a letter written in ink. Instead, Paul contrasts the letter of their hearts with a letter chiseled on stone. The letter on their hearts represents the New Covenant, as predicted in Ezekiel 11:19-20 and 36:26, in contrast to the letter of stone, which represents the Old Covenant (see Exodus 31:18).

▸ HOLINESS
3:4-5 Ministering by God's power. A constant temptation for Christians doing God's work is to do it in our own power, without reliance on Him. Whether in ministry-planning sessions or church staff meetings, theological concerns and walking by faith often take a backseat to pragmatic approaches to our decisions. But Paul, who was supremely gifted and talented for ministry (see chapters 10–11), did not view his abilities as a qualification for ministry; he believed his qualifications came only from the Lord. There is much to learn from business models, and we should use all our gifts in God's service, but we must not forget that ultimately it is God's power that makes ministry succeed, not our own skills or qualifications. (***See Holiness**> Changed by God> God Provides> Empowering us,* TopicGuide page A41.)

3:7-11 Is Paul saying that the Old Covenant was bad? At first glance, perhaps, it may seem he is, but look closer. The Old

glory of God, even though the brightness was already fading away. [8]Shouldn't we expect
3:9 far greater glory under the new way, now that the Holy Spirit is giving life? [9]If the old way,
Deut 27:26 which brings condemnation, was glorious, how much more glorious is the new way, which
Rom 1:17; 3:21 makes us right with God! [10]In fact, that first glory was not glorious at all compared with the
3:10-11 Exod 34:29-30 overwhelming glory of the new way. [11]So if the old way, which has been replaced, was
John 17:10, 22 glorious, how much more glorious is the new, which remains forever!
3:13 [12]Since this new way gives us such confidence, we can be very bold. [13]We are not like
Exod 34:33-35 Moses, who put a veil over his face so the people of Israel would not see the glory, even
3:14 though it was destined to fade away. [14]But the people's minds were hardened, and to this
Acts 13:15 Rom 11:7-8 day whenever the old covenant is being read, the same veil covers their minds so they
2 Cor 4:4 cannot understand the truth. And this veil can be removed only by believing in Christ.
3:16 [15]Yes, even today when they read Moses' writings, their hearts are covered with that veil,
Isa 25:7 Rom 11:23 and they do not understand.
[16]But whenever someone turns to the Lord, the veil is taken away. [17]For the Lord is the
3:17 Gal 4:6-7 Spirit, and wherever the Spirit of the Lord is, there is freedom. [18]So all of us who have had
3:18 that veil removed can see and reflect the glory of the Lord. And the Lord—who is the
Rom 8:29 2 Cor 4:4, 6 Spirit—makes us more and more like Him as we are changed into His glorious image.

4:2 2 Cor 2:17

TREASURE IN FRAGILE CLAY JARS

1 Thes 2:5 **4** Therefore, since God in His mercy has given us this new way,* we never give up.
4:3 [2]We reject all shameful deeds and underhanded methods. We don't try to trick
1 Cor 1:18 anyone or distort the word of God. We tell the truth before God, and all who are honest
2 Cor 3:14 know this.
4:4 [3]If the Good News we preach is hidden behind a veil, it is hidden only from people who
John 12:39-41 2 Cor 3:14 are perishing. [4]Satan, who is the god of this world, has blinded the minds of those who
Col 1:15 don't believe. They are unable to see the glorious light of the Good News. They don't
Heb 1:3 understand this message about the glory of Christ, who is the exact likeness of God.

4:1 Or *ministry.*

Covenant was from God and was His good gift to Israel, though it ultimately led to Israel's condemnation (see Romans 7:1-13; 9:30-33). Paul is clear that the Old Covenant was glorious (2 Corinthians 3:9) even while it led to death. If this is true, then the New Covenant, which leads to life, must be much more glorious. In fact, 3:10 indicates that the difference is so great that the Old Covenant can even be considered "not glorious" in comparison.

3:12-16 Paul is not saying that reading the Old Testament is bad or that doing so hardens a Christian. Instead, Paul makes it clear that he is referring to those who read the Old Testament without believing in Christ. Trying to understand Moses' writings (the Pentateuch) without believing in Christ is like trying to read them while looking through a piece of cloth—one will not be able to clearly make out what it is truly saying. Reading the law does harden the hearts of those who do not believe in Christ. In Paul's thought, believing in Jesus Christ is the only way to correctly understand the Old Covenant.

3:13 Paul heightens his argument about the relative glory of the Old and New Covenants by referring to the veil Moses put over his face after speaking with God (see Exodus 34:29-35). After receiving the Old Covenant, which Paul has already established is inferior to the New Covenant, Moses was literally radiating back God's glory to such an extent that the Israelites were frightened, and Moses put a veil over his face. But the glory of the New Covenant is still greater.

▸ GOD

3:17-18 Transforming Spirit. As Paul discusses the New Covenant, he highlights the Spirit's role in transforming us. When we turn to the Lord, we receive the Holy Spirit in our hearts, and the Spirit begins transforming our lives, making us more and more like Jesus Christ. Are you a Christian? If so, the Holy Spirit lives in you. You can leave your sins; you can be transformed. You do not need some additional power or some particular prayer. You simply need to cooperate with the Holy Spirit. And where the Holy Spirit is, there is freedom—we are free from sin's guilt; we are being made free from its power over our day-to-day lives; and we look forward to the day when we will be free from even its presence. (***See God> God's Names> Holy Spirit> Sanctifies,*** TopicGuide page A19.)

4:3 Paul answers questions some readers might ask: "What about those who hear the good news of Jesus Christ but do not embrace it? Is there a veil over the teaching of the New Covenant, too? Is the new covenant difficult to understand, just as Moses' was?" Continuing his metaphor from 3:12-16, Paul indicates that there in fact can be a veil over the New Covenant's teaching, but only for people who are perishing. This suggests that those who hear the gospel and never receive it will not be saved.

4:4 This verse teaches that conversion is a supernatural battle, and unbelievers have no ability to see the good news of the gospel. Paul explains this with an analogy: If the gospel is light (a common biblical motif for God), then unbelievers are blind. They cannot sense the light and therefore cannot respond to it. They cannot embrace it unless their blindness is first removed. People's minds are blinded by their own unbelief. Because of this, such people bear responsibility for their own rejection of the gospel, even though Satan is blinding them.

5You see, we don't go around preaching about ourselves. We preach that Jesus Christ is
Lord, and we ourselves are your servants for Jesus' sake. 6For God, who said, "Let there be
light in the darkness," has made this light shine in our hearts so we could know the glory
of God that is seen in the face of Jesus Christ.
7We now have this light shining in our hearts, but we ourselves are like fragile clay jars
containing this great treasure.* This makes it clear that our great power is from God, not
from ourselves.
8We are pressed on every side by troubles, but we are not crushed. We are perplexed,
but not driven to despair. 9We are hunted down, but never abandoned by God. We get
knocked down, but we are not destroyed. 10Through suffering, our bodies continue to
share in the death of Jesus so that the life of Jesus may also be seen in our bodies.

4:6 Gen 1:3; John 8:12; 12:46; Eph 5:8, 14; 1 Pet 2:9; 2 Pet 1:19
4:7 2 Cor 5:1; 2 Tim 2:20
4:8 2 Cor 7:5
4:9 Rom 8:35
4:10 Rom 8:17

4:7 Greek *We now have this treasure in clay jars.*

4:6 Paul compares becoming a Christian with Creation. In Genesis 1, God called for light out of total darkness and chaos, and there was light. An unbeliever is blind to the gospel, in darkness and chaos, but when God calls, the light of the gospel breaks through just as surely and powerfully as light appeared at Creation. God shines the light of the gospel into our hearts, and it allows us to see the glory of God in Jesus Christ, just as the light that shone at Creation was good, a reflection of the glory of the Creator. Conversion, then, is a recreation, where the chaos of sin is overcome by the light that God brings.

▸ WORSHIP
4:7-10 The strength of weakness. It can be frustrating to be physically limited, to become sick, to be vulnerable to persecution—or to be similarly prone to sin. Why does God send His glorious message through us, people who are so prone to weakness? Verse 7 says He does so to make it particularly obvious that it is God's power that does the work and that God's glory should result. Are you disabled? Are you sick? Is your body weak? Are you frustrated at your inabilities or even at your own sinfulness? Do not give up on ministry; God will use you. Do not think that sharing the gospel and discipling others should be left to those who look good by the world's standards. In fact, God may have you particularly marked out for great ministry, and the glory will be all His. (***See Worship****> NT> To the Father> God is to receive all praise and glory,* TopicGuide page A29.)

MY RESPONSE TO GOD

A New Creation

2 CORINTHIANS 5

A farmer once found a baby eagle and raised it with his chickens. The eagle learned to live as the chickens did, never attempting to fly. When a bird-watcher saw the eagle there, he bought it from the farmer and attempted to teach it to fly. But the eagle would only run around and flap its wings like a chicken. Finally, the man took the bird to a high mountain. "You are an eagle," he said. "You should fly." And he threw the bird off the side of the mountain. At first the eagle cried out in fear, but then it spread its wings and soared into the sky.

Perhaps that eagle sometimes flew over the old farmyard and missed the chickens. But it never returned to live like them, because now it knew what it meant to be an eagle.

In a similar way, many believers do not fully understand who they are in Christ. As a result, they miss the incredible blessings God has intended for His people. In a spiritual sense, they never learn to soar free above all creation.

What would it be like to see ourselves as our loving Father sees us? God says, "Anyone who belongs to Christ has become a new person. The old life is gone; a new life has begun!" (2 Corinthians 5:17). We can see ourselves as God does by exercising our faith as we read the Bible, believing what it says about God and what it says about us.

Isn't it time to stop listening to what others say about people—and start listening to God?

4:13 Ps 116:10
4:14 Acts 2:24; 1 Thes 2:19
4:15 2 Cor 1:3-6
4:16 Eph 3:16; Col 3:10
4:17 Rom 8:17-18; 1 Pet 1:6-7
4:18 Rom 8:24; 2 Cor 5:7
5:1 1 Cor 15:47; 2 Cor 4:7; 2 Pet 1:13-14
5:2 Rom 8:23; 1 Cor 15:53-54
5:4 1 Cor 15:53-54
5:5 Rom 8:23; 2 Cor 1:22; Eph 1:13-14
5:7 1 Cor 13:12
5:8 Phil 1:23

11 Yes, we live under constant danger of death because we serve Jesus, so that the life of
Jesus will be evident in our dying bodies. 12 So we live in the face of death, but this has re-
sulted in eternal life for you.
13 But we continue to preach because we have the same kind of faith the psalmist had
when he said, "I believed in God, so I spoke."* 14 We know that God, who raised the Lord
Jesus,* will also raise us with Jesus and present us to Himself together with you. 15 All of
this is for your benefit. And as God's grace reaches more and more people, there will be
great thanksgiving, and God will receive more and more glory.
16 That is why we never give up. Though our bodies are dying, our spirits are* being re-
newed every day. 17 For our present troubles are small and won't last very long. Yet they
produce for us a glory that vastly outweighs them and will last forever! 18 So we don't look
at the troubles we can see now; rather, we fix our gaze on things that cannot be seen. For
the things we see now will soon be gone, but the things we cannot see will last forever.

NEW BODIES

5 For we know that when this earthly tent we live in is taken down (that is, when we die
and leave this earthly body), we will have a house in heaven, an eternal body made for
us by God Himself and not by human hands. 2 We grow weary in our present bodies, and we
long to put on our heavenly bodies like new clothing. 3 For we will put on heavenly bodies;
we will not be spirits without bodies.* 4 While we live in these earthly bodies, we groan and
sigh, but it's not that we want to die and get rid of these bodies that clothe us. Rather, we
want to put on our new bodies so that these dying bodies will be swallowed up by life. 5 God
Himself has prepared us for this, and as a guarantee He has given us His Holy Spirit.
6 So we are always confident, even though we know that as long as we live in these bod-
ies we are not at home with the Lord. 7 For we live by believing and not by seeing. 8 Yes,

4:13 Ps 116:10. 4:14 Some manuscripts read *who raised Jesus.* 4:16 Greek *our inner being is.* 5:3 Greek *we will not be naked.*

4:11-12 Paul is speaking quite literally in these verses. He has been preaching in the face of death and at the risk of death, and his preaching has brought eternal life to the Corinthian Christians, as he had been the first to bring them good news of Jesus Christ. Further, Paul's life and preaching are a model and an example for his readers. He has sacrificed and lived in constant danger for the sake of bringing the gospel to those who have never heard it, to the Corinthians and beyond.

4:14 Paul is certain of a future bodily resurrection for himself and for the Corinthians. His certainty hinges on one fact: Jesus has risen from the dead (see 1 Thessalonians 4:14). Jesus is the firstborn of humanity, and He promises His followers that they will be with Him (see John 14:3). Just as Jesus died and was raised by the power of God, Paul and his Corinthian readers can expect to be raised, bodily, from the dead.

▸ BIBLE
4:16-18 An eternal perspective. Can you imagine doing what Paul did, preaching even at the risk of death? We have a natural desire to preserve our own lives and avoid pain. Nonetheless, Paul, who also had those desires, braved pain and the risk of death to preach the gospel. What made him able to do so? He had an eternal perspective. The things that are unseen and eternal motivated Paul, not the things of this world. What motivates you? If you will not preach or share the gospel, why not? Do the things of this world have a stronger hold on you than you would like to admit? Look around you—what do you have that is weighing you down or distracting you? Whatever it is, throw it away. Get rid of it. Don't let anything stop you from doing what is important—as defined by God—in this life. (***See Bible****> Power> Worldview> Offers God's perspective on issues,* TopicGuide page A12.)

5:1-4 Many ancient philosophers and religions argued that the physical world was inherently evil, and that it eventually would be removed. On the contrary, Paul tells the Corinthians, the Christian's destination does not involve an eternal separation of body and soul. Instead, the Christian looks forward to a new, perfect body, with only a temporary separation of body and soul (compare Revelation 6:9-11 and Revelation 20:5-6).

5:5 Paul views the Holy Spirit as the guarantee of the promise of a new body. The new body is yet to come, part of the promise of the new heavens and new earth in which God will dwell with His people (see 1 Thessalonians 4:16-17; Revelation 21:3-4). The Holy Spirit is a down payment on that future time, a piece of it given to believers now. As God, in the person of the Holy Spirit, is with the Corinthians now, they can have confidence that God will fully be with them in the future.

▸ GOD
5:6-8 God's promises give us confidence. Do you struggle with boldness as a Christian? Paul not only struggled with a difficult life (see 4:8-11), but he also struggled with the frustration of remaining sinful and remaining in his weak, earthly body. Yet even though the promise of having his new body and being at home with the Lord lay in the future, Paul was confident in the present. He could be confident in whatever his circumstances were because he knew that ultimate victory was already certain. If you follow Jesus Christ, you can have the same confidence. The Holy Spirit lives in you and God's promises are sure. Meditate on these promises and rest in the assurance of God's faithfulness to us. (***See God****> God's Attributes> True> God follows through on His promises,* TopicGuide page A18.)

we are fully confident, and we would rather be away from these earthly bodies, for then
we will be at home with the Lord. 9So whether we are here in this body or away from
this body, our goal is to please Him. 10For we must all stand before Christ to be judged. **5:10**
We will each receive whatever we deserve for the good or evil we have done in this Matt 16:27
earthly body. Acts 10:42

WE ARE GOD'S AMBASSADORS

11Because we understand our fearful responsibility to the Lord, we work hard to persuade **5:12**
others. God knows we are sincere, and I hope you know this, too. 12Are we commending 2 Cor 1:14; 3:1
ourselves to you again? No, we are giving you a reason to be proud of us,* so you can an-
swer those who brag about having a spectacular ministry rather than having a sincere
heart. 13If it seems we are crazy, it is to bring glory to God. And if we are in our right minds, **5:14**
it is for your benefit. 14Either way, Christ's love controls us.* Since we believe that Christ Rom 6:6-7
died for all, we also believe that we have all died to our old life.* 15He died for everyone so Gal 2:20 Col 3:3
that those who receive His new life will no longer live for themselves. Instead, they will live **5:15**
for Christ, who died and was raised for them. Rom 14:7-9
16So we have stopped evaluating others from a human point of view. At one time we **5:16**
thought of Christ merely from a human point of view. How differently we know Him now! 2 Cor 10:4
17This means that anyone who belongs to Christ has become a new person. The old life is **5:17** Isa 65:17
gone; a new life has begun! Gal 6:15 Rev 21:5

5:12 Some manuscripts read *proud of yourselves.* 5:14a Or *urges us on.* 5:14b Greek *Since One died for all, then all died.*

5:10 Christians are saved by grace and will not be punished for sin, but their lives and works will be judged to test its lasting value (1 Corinthians 3:10-15).

5:12 Paul answers comparisons that some people are making between themselves and him, saying they have spectacular ministries. In reply, Paul insists that a truly spectacular ministry is one marked by faithfulness and a sincere heart.

5:15 Christ's death has a universal benefit for all humanity. The message and mercy of God flowed forth from Christ's death in such a way that people from all over the world, whether saved or not, could partake of the common graces and benefits of God working through His people. Though Christ "died for everyone," this does not imply universal salvation, because in the very next clause Paul indicates that some people (and therefore not others) receive Christ's new life. Since, in this context, all for whom Christ suffered "died" as well, this likely refers to Christ's death being applied to all the church or the elect.

5:16 Paul corrects (by example) how the Corinthians evaluate other people. Evaluation from a human point of view includes appearance, success, wealth, power, and the like. Paul points out the fallacy of such measures by noting that Jesus Christ was not impressive based on those standards (see Isaiah 53:2-3), even though He was God Incarnate.

BECAUSE GOD IS JUST

He will always treat me fairly.

For we must all stand before Christ to be judged.
We will each receive whatever we deserve for the good or evil
we have done in this earthly body.

2 CORINTHIANS 5:10

FOR THE NEXT *GOD IS JUST* FEATURE SEE PAGE 2249.

5:18 [18]And all of this is a gift from God, who brought us back to Himself through Christ. And
Rom 5:10 God has given us this task of reconciling people to Him. [19]For God was in Christ, reconcil-
5:19 ing the world to Himself, no longer counting people's sins against them. And He gave us
Rom 3:24; 4:8 this wonderful message of reconciliation. [20]So we are Christ's ambassadors; God is mak-
5:20 Eph 6:20 ing His appeal through us. We speak for Christ when we plead, "Come back to God!" [21]For
5:21 God made Christ, who never sinned, to be the offering for our sin,* so that we could be
Gal 3:13 made right with God through Christ.
Heb 4:15; 7:26

1 Pet 2:22 **6** As God's partners,* we beg you not to accept this marvelous gift of God's kindness
6:1 1 Cor 3:9 and then ignore it. [2]For God says,

2 Cor 5:20 "At just the right time, I heard you.
On the day of salvation, I helped you."*

Indeed, the "right time" is now. Today is the day of salvation.

6:3
PAUL'S HARDSHIPS

1 Cor 8:9; 9:12 [3]We live in such a way that no one will stumble because of us, and no one will find fault with
6:4 our ministry. [4]In everything we do, we show that we are true ministers of God. We patiently
2 Cor 4:2 endure troubles and hardships and calamities of every kind. [5]We have been beaten, been put
6:5 2 Cor 11:23-27 in prison, faced angry mobs, worked to exhaustion, endured sleepless nights, and gone with-
6:6 out food. [6]We prove ourselves by our purity, our understanding, our patience, our kindness,
1 Tim 4:12 by the Holy Spirit within us,* and by our sincere love. [7]We faithfully preach the truth. God's
6:7 power is working in us. We use the weapons of righteousness in the right hand for attack and
1 Cor 2:4 2 Cor 10:4 the left hand for defense. [8]We serve God whether people honor us or despise us, whether
6:8 they slander us or praise us. We are honest, but they call us impostors. [9]We are ignored, even
Matt 27:63 though we are well known. We live close to death, but we are still alive. We have been beaten,
1 Cor 4:10, 13 but we have not been killed. [10]Our hearts ache, but we always have joy. We are poor, but we
6:9 Ps 118:18 give spiritual riches to others. We own nothing, and yet we have everything.
2 Cor 1:8-10; 4:10-11 [11]Oh, dear Corinthian friends! We have spoken honestly with you, and our hearts are

5:21 Or *to become sin itself.* 6:1 Or *As we work together.* 6:2 Isa 49:8 (Greek version). 6:6 Or *by our holiness of spirit.*

▸ MINISTRY
5:18–6:2 The message of reconciliation. Paul's appeal to the Corinthians is also his appeal to you. Have you been reconciled to God? Sinless Jesus took on your sin and died for you so that you could be declared right before God. Is this message of reconciliation permeating your life, or have you accepted it only to then ignore it (6:1)? If you have received salvation, you are one of Christ's ambassadors to the world. Are you a faithful ambassador? It's not so complicated—simply have significant, honest conversations with others and pray that God will turn that discussion toward Him and His Good News. (***See Ministry**> Great Commission> Reconcile> All believers have this ministry,* TopicGuide page A56.)

6:5 In the face of extreme trials, Paul and his coworkers responded with love and purity, the result of the Holy Spirit in them. (See Acts 14:19-20; 16:16-40; 17:5-9.)

6:7 Paul regularly uses military analogies in his letters (see, for example, 2 Corinthians 2:14-16; Ephesians 6:10-20), but here he begins to develop the idea that Christians do not fight physically. Instead, the weapon Christians use is righteousness. Righteousness is a weapon of both attack and defense. In place of a soldier's sword, which would be held in the right hand, righteousness serves to spread the gospel in the world, and in place of a soldier's shield, which would be held in the left hand, righteousness serves to counter the world's attacks against Christians.

▸ HOLINESS
6:8-10 Giving for the gospel. It's entirely possible that you have never, ever been persecuted for telling others about God—but that may be because you've been too afraid to tell anyone about your experience with God. Paul and his companions didn't just wonder what would happen if they told others about Jesus—they were shunned and slandered and beaten. Yet in the midst of their hardships, they had joy. Though they had almost no possessions, they felt as if they had everything. Instead of insisting on your own rights or comfort, be willing to step out of your comfort zone for the sake of sharing the gospel. How can you make contact with those who need to hear about Jesus and what He's doing in your life? Take the risk of rejection and reach out to the lost, hurting people around you. (***See Holiness**> Submission> Identifying with Christ> Suffering with Him,* TopicGuide page A40.)

6:11-13 Paul sums up his argument about the nature of his ministry to the Corinthians with an appeal. He is a coworker with God, using every means consistent with God's character to proclaim the message of salvation, and he is suffering everything imaginable to demonstrate the extent of God's love. Paul, then, has nothing against the Corinthians. If there was any strain in their relationship with him, it must be because of them.

open to you. 12 There is no lack of love on our part, but you have withheld your love from
us. 13 I am asking you to respond as if you were my own children. Open your hearts to us!

THE TEMPLE OF THE LIVING GOD

14 Don't team up with those who are unbelievers. How can righteousness be a partner with
wickedness? How can light live with darkness? 15 What harmony can there be between
Christ and the devil*? How can a believer be a partner with an unbeliever? 16 And what un-
ion can there be between God's temple and idols? For we are the temple of the living God.
As God said:

"I will live in them
and walk among them.
I will be their God,
and they will be My people.*

6:14 Eph 5:7, 11; 1 Jn 1:6
6:16 *Lev 26:12; *Jer 32:38; *Ezek 37:27

6:15 Greek *Beliar;* various other manuscripts render this proper name of the devil as *Belian, Beliab,* or *Belial.* 6:16 Lev 26:12; Ezek 37:27.

6:14-16 Paul digresses momentarily into a discussion of purity. Just as light and dark are opposites, so also there should be a contrast between believers and unbelievers. First Corinthians 5:10 indicates that Paul does not intend for the Corinthian Christians to avoid contact with unbelievers, but he does insist that they abstain from the unrighteousness of unbelievers.

▸ SPIRITUAL WARFARE
6:14 A careful connection. The Greek text literally reads, "Do not be unequally yoked with unbelievers." The image is that of two oxen plowing a field: One yoke is placed over both of them, and they work as a pair. They cannot go in opposite directions even if they wish to do so, because they are bound together. In a similar way, believers cannot avoid contact with unbelievers (1 Corinthians 5:10), but Paul commands us to avoid being bound to them. This has often been understood to mean that Christians should not enter into marriage with unbelievers, but could it apply more broadly, such as business contracts or other types of agreements? What commitments in your life have yoked you with unbelievers and made it impossible for you to follow Christ because of that relationship? Think carefully about your connections with the unconverted. (***See Spiritual Warfare*** *> Resisting Sin and Evil> Trusting God> Faithful Soldiers> Avoid entanglements,* TopicGuide page A46.)

6:16-18 Paul supports his point from the Old Testament. Phrases from Exodus 25:8; Leviticus 26:11-12; Isaiah 52:11; Ezekiel 37:27; and Hosea 1:10 merge into a single quotation, a style of argument familiar among Jewish writers. These quotations serve as a promise. Paul argues that Christians should not respond by binding themselves to unbelievers. Doing so will inevitably harm their own moral purity.

MY RESPONSE TO GOD

We Are God's Temple

2 CORINTHIANS 6:16

Although God is everywhere, He was present in the Temple in a unique way during the time of the Old Testament. Without that presence, the Temple was just another building.

The exciting news of the New Covenant is that now we are God's temple (1 Corinthians 3:16-17)—God's Spirit now manifests itself in our lives, makes us holy, and therefore, Paul reasoned, the Corinthians were to honor God with their temple-bodies by pursuing sexual purity and unity with one another. Their bodies were to be used as implements of worship.

Since God lives inside us through the Holy Spirit, we are empowered to overcome addictions, temptations, and sin. Without the Holy Spirit in us, the best we can do is cope with sin. But with God, we can stop coping and cooperating with sin, and start eradicating it. With the truth of the gospel and by the power of the Holy Spirit, we can overcome sin and the separation from God that it creates.

6:17 17 Therefore, come out from among unbelievers,
*Isa 52:11 Ezek 20:34 and separate yourselves from them, says the Lord.
Don't touch their filthy things,
and I will welcome you.*
6:18 18 And I will be your Father,
*2 Sam 7:8, 14 Isa 43:6 and you will be My sons and daughters,
Jer 31:9 says the Lord Almighty.*"

7:1 **7** Because we have these promises, dear friends, let us cleanse ourselves from every-
1 Pet 1:15-16 thing that can defile our body or spirit. And let us work toward complete holiness
7:2 2 Cor 6:12-13 because we fear God.
7:3 2 Please open your hearts to us. We have not done wrong to anyone, nor led anyone
2 Cor 6:11-12 astray, nor taken advantage of anyone. 3 I'm not saying this to condemn you. I said before
Phil 1:7 that you are in our hearts, and we live or die together with you. 4 I have the highest confi-
7:4 2 Cor 8:24 dence in you, and I take great pride in you. You have greatly encouraged me and made
me happy despite all our troubles.

PAUL'S JOY AT THE CHURCH'S REPENTANCE

7:5 5 When we arrived in Macedonia, there was no rest for us. We faced conflict from every di-
2 Cor 2:13; 4:8 rection, with battles on the outside and fear on the inside. 6 But God, who encourages
7:6 Isa 49:13 those who are discouraged, encouraged us by the arrival of Titus. 7 His presence was a joy,
2 Cor 1:3-4; 2:13 but so was the news he brought of the encouragement he received from you. When he
told us how much you long to see me, and how sorry you are for what happened, and how
loyal you are to me, I was filled with joy!
7:8 8 I am not sorry that I sent that severe letter to you, though I was sorry at first, for I know
2 Cor 2:2-4 it was painful to you for a little while. 9 Now I am glad I sent it, not because it hurt you, but
because the pain caused you to repent and change your ways. It was the kind of sorrow
7:10 God wants His people to have, so you were not harmed by us in any way. 10 For the kind of
Matt 27:3-5 sorrow God wants us to experience leads us away from sin and results in salvation.
There's no regret for that kind of sorrow. But worldly sorrow, which lacks repentance, re-
sults in spiritual death.
11 Just see what this godly sorrow produced in you! Such earnestness, such concern to
clear yourselves, such indignation, such alarm, such longing to see me, such zeal, and

6:17 Isa 52:11; Ezek 20:34 (Greek version). 6:18 2 Sam 7:14.

7:2-4 After the harsh challenge he had issued to the Corinthian church, Paul works for reconciliation. There were doubtless some hurt feelings and anger after his tearful letter, but Paul reassures the Corinthians of his love for them despite all the troubles between them. He reminds them of his good behavior toward them and points out that they have nothing substantial against him. He appeals to them in love and asks them to reconcile with him.

7:7 Paul had left Troas and continued to Macedonia (see 2:12-13), where he met Titus. Macedonia was a Roman province during New Testament times. Paul first brought the gospel to Macedonia during his second missionary journey, when he responded to a vision (see Acts 16:11–17:15). His work there centered in the cities of Philippi and Thessalonica, and he likely returned to one of those cities after leaving Macedonia (see note on 1 Corinthians 16:5). While there, Titus brought Paul the news that the Corinthian church had responded well to his letter, causing Paul to write 2 Corinthians.

▸ADOPTION
7:8-10 Godly sorrow versus worldly sorrow. Paul outlines two types of sorrow: godly sorrow and worldly sorrow. Both hurt, but they have different effects. Godly sorrow leads away from sin and toward repentance and goodness, while worldly sorrow has no repentance, bringing only spiritual death. Paul rejoices that, though painful, his letter of anguish resulted in godly sorrow among the Corinthians, leading them to repentance and earnest zeal for the Lord. What sorrows are happening in your life right now? Sorrow can lead you either to God or away from Him. Which is happening to you? Let your sorrow lead you to repentance and zeal for the Lord, rather than merely to self-pity. (***See Adoption*****>** ***With Christ> Children of God> God disciplines His children,*** TopicGuide page A36.)

7:11 Paul summarizes the report Titus had brought regarding the Corinthian church. In response to his letter of rebuke, they had been alarmed and eager to clear their name. Their actions showed that their hearts were inclined toward God and that their sorrow was godly, not worldly. Their response to Paul's challenge showed their allegiance to God.

such a readiness to punish wrong. You showed that you have done everything necessary
to make things right. 12My purpose, then, was not to write about who did the wrong or
who was wronged. I wrote to you so that in the sight of God you could see for yourselves
how loyal you are to us. 13We have been greatly encouraged by this.

In addition to our own encouragement, we were especially delighted to see how happy
Titus was about the way all of you welcomed Him and set his mind* at ease. 14I had told
him how proud I was of you—and you didn't disappoint me. I have always told you the
truth, and now my boasting to Titus has also proved true! 15Now he cares for you more
than ever when he remembers the way all of you obeyed him and welcomed him with
such fear and deep respect. 16I am very happy now because I have complete confidence
in you.

A CALL TO GENEROUS GIVING

8 Now I want you to know, dear brothers and sisters,* what God in His kindness has
done through the churches in Macedonia. 2They are being tested by many troubles,
and they are very poor. But they are also filled with abundant joy, which has overflowed in
rich generosity.

3For I can testify that they gave not only what they could afford, but far more. And they
did it of their own free will. 4They begged us again and again for the privilege of sharing in
the gift for the believers* in Jerusalem. 5They even did more than we had hoped, for their
first action was to give themselves to the Lord and to us, just as God wanted them to do.

6So we have urged Titus, who encouraged your giving in the first place, to return to you
and encourage you to finish this ministry of giving. 7Since you excel in so many ways—in
your faith, your gifted speakers, your knowledge, your enthusiasm, and your love from
us*—I want you to excel also in this gracious act of giving.

8I am not commanding you to do this. But I am testing how genuine your love is by
comparing it with the eagerness of the other churches.

9You know the generous grace of our Lord Jesus Christ. Though He was rich, yet for
your sakes He became poor, so that by His poverty He could make you rich.

7:12 1 Cor 5:1-2; 2 Cor 2:3, 9
7:13 2 Cor 2:13
7:15 Phil 2:12
7:16 2 Cor 2:3; 2 Thes 3:4; Phlm 1:21
8:1 Acts 16:9
8:2 2 Cor 9:11
8:4 Acts 24:17; Rom 15:26; 1 Cor 16:1, 3
8:6 2 Cor 12:13, 18
8:7 1 Cor 1:5; 16:1-2; 2 Cor 9:8
8:9 Matt 8:20; Phil 2:6-7

7:13 Greek *his spirit.* 8:1 Greek *brothers.* 8:4 Greek *for God's holy people.* 8:7 Some manuscripts read *your love for us.*

▸ BIBLE

7:15 The authority of a messenger. The Corinthians realized that Titus deserved to be not only welcomed but also obeyed. He was a messenger from Paul the apostle, and Paul's authority was behind his mission and his instructions to the church. The biblical texts play the same role for us today. They are not merely words or historical documents to be studied intellectually; they bear God's words, through the apostles, to us, and they have authority, just as Titus did. Do you recognize the Bible's authority in your life? Do you let the Scriptures correct your thoughts, words, and actions? How is the Bible calling you to a new life? (***See Bible**> Uniqueness> Authoritative> Demonstrates credibility,* TopicGuide page A10.)

▸ WORSHIP

8:3-5 God loves a cheerful giver. Though the Macedonians were enduring troubles of their own, they had given themselves completely to the Lord. Their financial giving followed their hearts. Unlike the Macedonians, many people give because of guilt. Such giving does not please God. Do you give to God's work and to the poor? Why or why not? What motivates your giving? First give yourself to the Lord (8:5). Focus on how God has saved and blessed you. Meditate on His gifts to you and the joy of following Christ. Then God will work deep joy into your life, and He will make it clear what amount (whether great or small) He calls for you to give. Give that amount, and you will be able to do it freely and joyfully, not out of guilt. (***See Worship**> NT> Offerings> Tithing and the heart,* TopicGuide page A31.)

8:4 Paul turns to the topic of the gift to the church in Jerusalem. Jerusalem was a poor city generally, and it had been further impoverished by famines in Judea in the AD 40s. The collection Paul was gathering was an act of both charity and unity between the Gentile churches Paul had planted and the predominantly Jewish church in Jerusalem. The Macedonians, though very poor, had given generously to the collection for those even less fortunate than themselves.

8:6 The Corinthians had, at Titus' instigation, previously begun a collection for the gift to Jerusalem. They had presumably discontinued this practice during the controversy with Paul. His frequent comments that he had taken nothing from them may be a response to accusations by Paul's opponents that he intended to make himself rich by his ministry. Having reestablished his credibility and reminded the Corinthians that his goals were ministry, not personal wealth, Paul now sends Titus to encourage a resumption of the collection.

8:6-9 By all accounts, the Corinthian church was a gifted and talented collection of believers. Paul lists some of their gifts and abilities: faith, eloquence, knowledge, enthusiasm, and love from himself. Verse 7 implicitly asks the Corinthian church a question: Will they add giving to the impressive list of things in which they excel? To do so would be to model their behavior after Christ, who, though He possessed infinitely more than they did, had become poor for their sakes.

8:10 10Here is my advice: It would be good for you to finish what you started a year ago. Last
2 Cor 9:2 year you were the first who wanted to give, and you were the first to begin doing it. 11Now
you should finish what you started. Let the eagerness you showed in the beginning be
8:12 matched now by your giving. Give in proportion to what you have. 12Whatever you give is
Prov 3:27-28 Mark 12:43-44 acceptable if you give it eagerly. And give according to what you have, not what you don't
2 Cor 9:7 have. 13Of course, I don't mean your giving should make life easy for others and hard for
8:14 yourselves. I only mean that there should be some equality. 14Right now you have plenty
Acts 4:34 and can help those who are in need. Later, they will have plenty and can share with you
2 Cor 9:12 8:15 when you need it. In this way, things will be equal. 15As the Scriptures say,

*Exod 16:18 "Those who gathered a lot had nothing left over,
and those who gathered only a little had enough."*

8:16
TITUS AND HIS COMPANIONS

2 Cor 2:14 16But thank God! He has given Titus the same enthusiasm for you that I have. 17Titus wel-
8:18 comed our request that he visit you again. In fact, he himself was very eager to go and see
2 Cor 12:18 you. 18We are also sending another brother with Titus. All the churches praise him as a
8:19 preacher of the Good News. 19He was appointed by the churches to accompany us as we take
Acts 14:23 1 Cor 16:3-4 the offering to Jerusalem*—a service that glorifies the Lord and shows our eagerness to help.
8:21 20We are traveling together to guard against any criticism for the way we are handling
Prov 3:4 this generous gift. 21We are careful to be honorable before the Lord, but we also want
Rom 12:17 everyone else to see that we are honorable.
22We are also sending with them another of our brothers who has proven himself many
times and has shown on many occasions how eager he is. He is now even more enthusias-
8:23 tic because of his great confidence in you. 23If anyone asks about Titus, say that he is my
Phil 2:25 partner who works with me to help you. And the brothers with him have been sent by the
8:24 churches,* and they bring honor to Christ. 24So show them your love, and prove to all the
2 Cor 7:4 churches that our boasting about you is justified.

THE COLLECTION FOR CHRISTIANS IN JERUSALEM

9:1 Acts 24:17 **9** I really don't need to write to you about this ministry of giving for the believers in Jerusa-
2 Cor 8:4, 20 lem.* 2For I know how eager you are to help, and I have been boasting to the churches in
9:2 Macedonia that you in Greece* were ready to send an offering a year ago. In fact, it was your
2 Cor 8:11-12, 19 enthusiasm that stirred up many of the Macedonian believers to begin giving.

8:15 Exod 16:18. 8:19 See 1 Cor 16:3-4. 8:23 Greek *are apostles of the churches.* 9:1 Greek *about the offering for God's holy people.* 9:2 Greek *in Achaia,* the southern region of the Greek peninsula. *Macedonia* was in the northern region of Greece.

8:10-11 Paul encourages the Corinthians to give in proportion to what they had, knowing that eagerness to give is what delights God. They need not promise more than they were able to give, but merely to resume the collection they had begun in the previous year.

▸ WORSHIP
8:12-14 Do you have plenty right now? Paul is not after a complete leveling of all economic distinctions within the church, but he is after a basic equality. Sacrificial Christian giving should ensure there are no poor among the covenant community (see Deuteronomy 15:4-11; Matthew 25:31-46). Verse 14 explains that Paul is calling for an equality of concern, where those with wealth, whether they are Corinthian Christians or Jerusalem Christians, care about others. Wealth, like any gift from God, is also a responsibility, and Paul encourages the Corinthians to use their wealth to provide for those who have needs. If you have plenty, are you giving to those who are poor? How might God be enabling you to care for others and to meet their needs? (***See Worship****> NT> Sacrificial Living> Enables us to help meet others' needs,* TopicGuide page A34.)

8:15 Paul argues that his principle of equality is supported by Scripture, quoting Exodus 16:18, where the Israelites began gathering manna in the wilderness. Though the Israelites gathered different amounts of manna, Exodus records that each gathered what he or she needed, and that when it was measured, no one had too much or too little. Similarly, Paul argues that the Corinthians should adequately supply their own needs, not starve themselves. Their objective, though, should be to use their surplus wealth for others, not simply to hoard their wealth.

8:18-23 These other brothers are not named because the Corinthians did not yet know them. Paul and his companions were exercising utmost prudence, traveling in a group with the offering for the Jerusalem church. By traveling together, they could assure that no one was alone with the offering money, which would avoid even the possibility of suspicion of their stewardship of the gift.

9:2 Paul has encouraged a friendly rivalry between the Macedonian believers and the Corinthian believers (see 8:8). Both wanted to do good works and support their poor brothers and sisters in Jerusalem.

3But I am sending these brothers to be sure you really are ready, as I have been telling
them, and that your money is all collected. I don't want to be wrong in my boasting about
you. 4We would be embarrassed—not to mention your own embarrassment—if some Mac-
edonian believers came with me and found that you weren't ready after all I had told
them! 5So I thought I should send these brothers ahead of me to make sure the gift you
promised is ready. But I want it to be a willing gift, not one given grudgingly.
6Remember this—a farmer who plants only a few seeds will get a small crop. But the one
who plants generously will get a generous crop. 7You must each decide in your heart how
much to give. And don't give reluctantly or in response to pressure. "For God loves a person
who gives cheerfully."* 8And God will generously provide all you need. Then you will always
have everything you need and plenty left over to share with others. 9As the Scriptures say,

"They share freely and give generously to the poor.
Their good deeds will be remembered forever."*

10For God is the One who provides seed for the farmer and then bread to eat. In the same
way, He will provide and increase your resources and then produce a great harvest of gen-
erosity* in you.
11Yes, you will be enriched in every way so that you can always be generous. And when
we take your gifts to those who need them, they will thank God. 12So two good things will
result from this ministry of giving—the needs of the believers in Jerusalem* will be met,
and they will joyfully express their thanks to God.
13As a result of your ministry, they will give glory to God. For your generosity to them
and to all believers will prove that you are obedient to the Good News of Christ. 14And
they will pray for you with deep affection because of the overflowing grace God has given
to you. 15Thank God for this gift* too wonderful for words!

9:3 1 Cor 16:2; 2 Cor 8:23
9:5 Phil 4:17
9:6 Prov 11:24-25; 22:9; Gal 6:7, 9
9:7 Exod 25:2; Deut 15:7-10; 2 Cor 8:12
9:8 Phil 4:19
9:9 *Ps 112:9
9:10 Isa 55:10; Hos 10:12
9:11 2 Cor 1:11; 4:15
9:12 2 Cor 8:14

9:7 See footnote on Prov 22:8. 9:9 Ps 112:9. 9:10 Greek *righteousness.* 9:12 Greek *of God's holy people.* 9:15 Greek *His gift.*

9:6 Paul transitions into a discussion of God's provision for those who give. Before making the point, he introduces it with an analogy to farming. Some of each year's crop is saved to serve as seed for the next year. If a farmer eats most of his current crop and saves very little, then he will plant few seeds the next year, and his next crop will be small. If, on the other hand, a farmer saves a generous amount of seeds and plants them, then his crop the next year will be abundant. Paul equates giving generously with the farmer who plants generously: God will provide a great harvest through that giving.

▸ HOLINESS

9:7-8 Having the faith to give. It can be scary to start giving, particularly if you do not have very much. Two principles can help. First, remember that you should give cheerfully and because God has led you to give, not in response to pressure. You are not obligated to give according to someone else's instruction, but according to God's conviction. Second, remember that God knows what you need and that He loves you and promises to provide for you. All gifts ultimately come from Him. Prove faithful with what God has given you, and trust that He loves you and will care for you. (***See Holiness****> Disciplines> Of Abstinence> Stewardship,* TopicGuide page A42.)

9:10 Paul understands that as one proves faithful with an opportunity God has given, He will often (though not always) increase that person's ability to give, providing more money, but also more opportunities to give. This is the same principle outlined in the parable of the talents (see Matthew 25:23), where faithfulness in small responsibilities is rewarded with greater responsibilities.

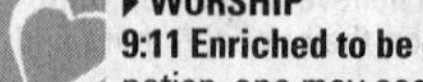

▸ WORSHIP

9:11 Enriched to be generous. Even in the richest nation, one may easily find the poor. Some are hard at work, while others are too ill to work and beg for food. So it is not surprising that Paul uses precious space in 2 Corinthians to speak of giving to the poor, starving Christians in Jerusalem. Paul is clear that wealth is a responsibility and that God looks for believers to cheerfully use the wealth God has given them for good. What do you do with your riches? Have you treated your wealth as if it were for your own good and pleasure? Perhaps you make excuses, withholding your money because the poor might not use it efficiently, or for any number of other reasons. But Jesus sacrificed His life, knowing that many would not receive His sacrifice rightly, yet nevertheless, He gave. What would it look like if you gave more like Jesus did? (***See Worship****> NT> Sacrificial Living> More blessed to give than to receive,* TopicGuide page A34.)

9:13 Paul tells the Corinthians that their generosity will prove their obedience. This does not mean that generosity will save them or that it will make them right with God. Instead, generosity is the result of the salvation they have already received, and it brings glory to the God who has saved them. Even the money that they give to the collection is only a return of what God has already given them (Psalms 24:1; 50:10).

9:15 The phrase "gift too wonderful for words" has both an immediate and a broader referent. First, it refers to 9:14, which mentions how God has given the Corinthians money so that they can give it to the Jerusalem church. Their gift will spark the Jerusalem Christians to pray for the Corinthians, thereby uniting the entire church. Second, because this verse summarizes Paul's argument in this section of the letter, the gift also points back to 8:9, the gift of the Lord Jesus Christ, who, though He was rich, became poor and by His poverty made us rich—a richness that is far more than economic.

10:1 1 Cor 2:3 2 Cor 10:10 · 10:2 1 Cor 4:21 · 10:4 Jer 1:10 Eph 6:13-17 · 10:5 Isa 2:11-12 1 Cor 1:19 · 10:6 2 Cor 2:9; 7:15 · 10:7 John 7:24 2 Cor 11:23 · 10:8 2 Cor 12:6; 13:10 · 10:10 1 Cor 1:17; 2:3 2 Cor 11:6 Gal 4:13-14 · 10:11 2 Cor 13:2, 10 · 10:12 2 Cor 3:1; 5:12 · 10:13 Rom 12:3 · 10:14 1 Cor 9:1 · 10:15 Rom 15:20 2 Thes 1:3 · 10:16 Acts 19:21

PAUL DEFENDS HIS AUTHORITY

10 Now I, Paul, appeal to you with the gentleness and kindness of Christ—though I re-
alize you think I am timid in person and bold only when I write from far away.
2Well, I am begging you now so that when I come I won't have to be bold with those who
think we act from human motives.

3We are human, but we don't wage war as humans do. 4*We use God's mighty weap-
ons, not worldly weapons, to knock down the strongholds of human reasoning and to de-
stroy false arguments. 5We destroy every proud obstacle that keeps people from knowing
God. We capture their rebellious thoughts and teach them to obey Christ. 6And after you
have become fully obedient, we will punish everyone who remains disobedient.

7Look at the obvious facts.* Those who say they belong to Christ must recognize that we
belong to Christ as much as they do. 8I may seem to be boasting too much about the au-
thority given to us by the Lord. But our authority builds you up; it doesn't tear you down.
So I will not be ashamed of using my authority.

9I'm not trying to frighten you by my letters. 10For some say, "Paul's letters are demand-
ing and forceful, but in person he is weak, and his speeches are worthless!" 11Those peo-
ple should realize that our actions when we arrive in person will be as forceful as what we
say in our letters from far away.

12Oh, don't worry; we wouldn't dare say that we are as wonderful as these other men
who tell you how important they are! But they are only comparing themselves with each
other, using themselves as the standard of measurement. How ignorant!

13We will not boast about things done outside our area of authority. We will boast only
about what has happened within the boundaries of the work God has given us, which in-
cludes our working with you. 14We are not reaching beyond these boundaries when we
claim authority over you, as if we had never visited you. For we were the first to travel all
the way to Corinth with the Good News of Christ.

15Nor do we boast and claim credit for the work someone else has done. Instead, we
hope that your faith will grow so that the boundaries of our work among you will be ex-
tended. 16Then we will be able to go and preach the Good News in other places far beyond

10:4 English translations divide verses 4 and 5 in various ways. 10:7 Or *You look at things only on the basis of appearance.*

10:1 Paul abruptly returns to a defense of his authority. Many theories have been advanced regarding the abruptness of the shift from chapters 1–9, which are fairly conciliatory, to chapters 10–13, which are quite aggressive. Among these many theories, two are the most plausible. First, some think Paul wrote chapters 1–9 immediately after receiving Titus's report and that he wrote chapters 10–13 later, as a separate letter. If this theory is correct, a later scribe combined the two letters, apparently removing the ending of the first letter and the introduction of the second. Second, others think Paul wrote chapters 1–9 after receiving Titus's report, but before he completed the letter he received news that the Corinthian church had returned to questioning his apostleship and authority. If this theory is correct, Paul simply picked up where he was writing, but with an abrupt change in tone.

10:1-2 Paul's kindness in person had been mischaracterized as timidity by his opponents. Further, verse 2 indicates he had been accused of acting from selfish motives, possibly regarding the collection. Paul was humble, and he preferred not to use his authority. Nonetheless, when necessary for the sake of the church, he would defend himself, and he does so for the remainder of this letter because the Corinthians were being misled by false apostles' attacks on his authority.

▸ ADOPTION
10:3-5 Welcome to the war. Christians are no strangers to war (2 Corinthians 6:7). But we do not fight our battles with physical weapons, though it is often tempting to do so. Paul shows us the way to use God's weapons to fight against His enemy—in this case, human arguments and poor logic that hinder people from the truth. In this portion of the letter, Paul aimed to defeat the arguments against his apostleship. However, Paul's point also applies to believers today. Do you see yourself as a soldier in a war? Do you understand that there are ideas and strategies in God's Word to show you how to be victorious? Think about how many around you have fallen because they ignored the realities of the spiritual and physical harm that come from sin. (***See Adoption*****>** *With Christ> Servants> Provided spiritual weapons,* TopicGuide page A37.)

10:8 Some may have thought Paul's appeal to authority was simply a power play, an attempt to enforce his will over them. But Paul makes it clear that his authority is for the Corinthians' good. He is neither selfish nor self-serving in his use of authority. Instead, he uses authority for others' good.

10:13-16 Paul reminds the Corinthians that he was the one who established the church in Corinth, not these interlopers who have claimed credit for the ministry among them. The credit, as far as it belongs to any human being, belongs to Paul, not these others. Further, Paul's work with the Corinthians was work that God had given him, so he is right to assert authority among them.

you, where no one else is working. Then there will be no question of our boasting about
work done in someone else's territory. [17]As the Scriptures say, "If you want to boast, boast
only about the LORD."*
[18]When people commend themselves, it doesn't count for much. The important thing is
for the Lord to commend them.

PAUL AND THE FALSE APOSTLES

11 I hope you will put up with a little more of my foolishness. Please bear with me.
[2]For I am jealous for you with the jealousy of God Himself. I promised you as a
pure bride* to one husband—Christ. [3]But I fear that somehow your pure and undivided de-
votion to Christ will be corrupted, just as Eve was deceived by the cunning ways of the ser-
pent. [4]You happily put up with whatever anyone tells you, even if they preach a different
Jesus than the One we preach, or a different kind of Spirit than the One you received, or a
different kind of gospel than the one you believed.
[5]But I don't consider myself inferior in any way to these "super apostles" who teach such
things. [6]I may be unskilled as a speaker, but I'm not lacking in knowledge. We have made
this clear to you in every possible way.
[7]Was I wrong when I humbled myself and honored you by preaching God's Good News
to you without expecting anything in return? [8]I "robbed" other churches by accepting their
contributions so I could serve you at no cost. [9]And when I was with you and didn't have
enough to live on, I did not become a financial burden to anyone. For the brothers who
came from Macedonia brought me all that I needed. I have never been a burden to you, and
I never will be. [10]As surely as the truth of Christ is in me, no one in all of Greece* will ever
stop me from boasting about this. [11]Why? Because I don't love you? God knows that I do.

10:17 *Jer 9:24; 1 Cor 1:31
10:18 Prov 27:2
11:1 2 Cor 5:13
11:2 Hos 2:19; Eph 5:26-27
11:3 Gen 3:1-6, 13; John 8:44; 1 Tim 2:14; Rev 12:9
11:4 Rom 8:15; Gal 1:6-8
11:5 2 Cor 12:11; Gal 2:6
11:6 1 Cor 1:17; Eph 3:4
11:7 1 Cor 9:12, 18; 2 Cor 12:13
11:9 2 Cor 12:13
11:11 2 Cor 7:3; 12:15

10:17 Jer 9:24. 11:2 Greek *a virgin.* 11:10 Greek *Achaia,* the southern region of the Greek peninsula.

▸ADOPTION
10:17-18 Glory to God. All of us have a natural, sinful tendency to focus on ourselves, to commend ourselves, and to brag. Paul's opponents had been doing exactly that, and Paul was clearly frustrated at being dragged into a contest of self-commendation with them. To protect the Corinthian church from these false apostles, he entered into such a debate (see chapter 11), but he first reminded his readers that self-commendation counts for nothing and that what is important is the Lord's approval. In what way are you commending yourself, whether in church, at work, or among your friends? Stop caring so much about what people think about you. Focus on gaining God's commendation, and let Him handle the rest. (***See Adoption***> *With Christ*> *Redemption*> *Humble self-estimation,* TopicGuide page A37.)

11:1 Paul's "foolishness" is his entering into a contest of comparison with his opponents, whom he mockingly calls "super apostles" in 11:5. This comparison of qualifications and boasting is foolish because it amounts to self-commendation before people, not devotion to God. Nonetheless, to protect the Corinthian church from these deceivers, Paul details his own qualifications and why he is superior to these others.

11:3 Paul compares the situation in Corinth to the fall of humanity in Genesis 3. In Genesis 3, Adam and Eve's full devotion to God was corrupted by the serpent's temptation. Similarly, the Corinthians' full devotion to Christ is in danger of corruption by these false apostles who had infiltrated the Corinthian church. The comparison equates the false apostles with Satan.

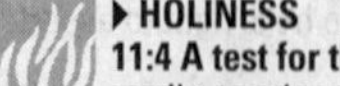
▸HOLINESS
11:4 A test for the teacher. Some people are far too easily convinced of a new idea or truth (Acts 17:11). Paul was shocked by how readily the Corinthians turned aside to every new doctrine presented to them. Instead of diligently keeping their doctrine pure, they happily listened to whatever anyone taught, even things that were clearly contrary to the gospel they believed, to Jesus, and to the Holy Spirit. How do you test the teaching you receive? It is common for people today to say, "I don't care about doctrine." Nothing could be more dangerous! You do not need to be abrasive or to look for minute flaws in your teachers, but be discerning enough to reject false teaching. Do not hesitate to ask questions of those who claim to be teachers. (***See Holiness***> *Law and Grace*> *Grace*> *True teachings,* TopicGuide page A42.)

11:5 Paul now sarcastically names the opponents who have sparked this portion of his letter. He calls them "super apostles," which was either their own self-designation or merely his sarcastic term for them. These were the interlopers who boasted about their own gifts and abilities and ministry success. Paul reminds the Corinthians that, while he may not speak as eloquently as these other men, he has knowledge that is far superior to the eloquent but empty words of the "super apostles."

11:7-12 Paul again reminds the Corinthians that he was never after their money, and he backs up his argument with facts. First, he never accepted any payment for preaching the gospel in Corinth. Second, his living expenses while in Corinth were paid by the gifts of other churches that supported his mission. Third, even when he ran out of funds, he did not become a financial burden in Corinth but instead was supplied by additional gifts from the Macedonian believers. The "super apostles" claimed that their work was just like Paul's, but they did not behave in the same way.

11:12 1 Cor 9:12
11:13 Rev 2:2
11:15 Phil 3:19
11:16 2 Cor 12:6
11:18 Phil 3:3-4
11:20 Gal 2:4; 4:9
11:21 2 Cor 10:10
11:22 Rom 11:1 Phil 3:5
11:23 Rom 8:36 1 Cor 15:10 2 Cor 6:4-5
11:24 Deut 25:3
11:25 Acts 14:19; 16:22; 27:41
11:26 Acts 9:23; 14:5; 20:3; 21:31 Gal 2:4
11:27 1 Cor 4:11 2 Cor 6:5
11:29 1 Cor 9:22
11:30 2 Cor 12:5
11:31 2 Cor 1:23
11:32-33 Acts 9:24-25

12But I will continue doing what I have always done. This will undercut those who are
looking for an opportunity to boast that their work is just like ours. 13These people are
false apostles. They are deceitful workers who disguise themselves as apostles of Christ.
14But I am not surprised! Even Satan disguises himself as an angel of light. 15So it is no
wonder that his servants also disguise themselves as servants of righteousness. In the end
they will get the punishment their wicked deeds deserve.

PAUL'S MANY TRIALS

16Again I say, don't think that I am a fool to talk like this. But even if you do, listen to me, as
you would to a foolish person, while I also boast a little. 17Such boasting is not from the
Lord, but I am acting like a fool. 18And since others boast about their human achieve-
ments, I will, too. 19After all, you think you are so wise, but you enjoy putting up with fools!
20You put up with it when someone enslaves you, takes everything you have, takes ad-
vantage of you, takes control of everything, and slaps you in the face. 21I'm ashamed to
say that we've been too "weak" to do that!

But whatever they dare to boast about—I'm talking like a fool again—I dare to boast
about it, too. 22Are they Hebrews? So am I. Are they Israelites? So am I. Are they descen-
dants of Abraham? So am I. 23Are they servants of Christ? I know I sound like a madman,
but I have served Him far more! I have worked harder, been put in prison more often, been
whipped times without number, and faced death again and again. 24Five different times
the Jewish leaders gave me thirty-nine lashes. 25Three times I was beaten with rods. Once
I was stoned. Three times I was shipwrecked. Once I spent a whole night and a day adrift at
sea. 26I have traveled on many long journeys. I have faced danger from rivers and from
robbers. I have faced danger from my own people, the Jews, as well as from the Gentiles. I
have faced danger in the cities, in the deserts, and on the seas. And I have faced danger
from men who claim to be believers but are not.* 27I have worked hard and long, enduring
many sleepless nights. I have been hungry and thirsty and have often gone without food. I
have shivered in the cold, without enough clothing to keep me warm.

28Then, besides all this, I have the daily burden of my concern for all the churches.
29Who is weak without my feeling that weakness? Who is led astray, and I do not burn
with anger?

30If I must boast, I would rather boast about the things that show how weak I am. 31God,
the Father of our Lord Jesus, who is worthy of eternal praise, knows I am not lying. 32When

11:26 Greek *from false brothers.*

11:13-15 Satan, who is a deceiver, can disguise himself, even appearing as an angel. If he can do so, Paul reasons, it is no surprise that his servants can disguise themselves as servants of righteousness. Paul's opposition, the "super apostles" pretend to be servants of the Lord, but, as he has already indicated in 11:3, they are actually servants of Satan.

11:16-21 Paul is for the sake of argument putting himself in the role of a fool. People will often allow a foolish person to prattle on, and they amusedly listen to the fool's words, though they know he or she does not speak sensibly. The Corinthians have been putting up with fools (by which Paul means the "super apostles") already, so Paul asks for the same hearing the Corinthians have given to them. Terming himself a fool allows Paul to simultaneously (and sarcastically) demand a hearing and also show how ridiculous it is for the Corinthians to listen to the "super apostles." Note Paul's clear sarcasm in 11:21 when he compares his behavior to that of his opponents.

11:22-29 Paul now begins a point-by-point comparison of his qualifications and the qualifications of his opponents. In all areas in which they may claim to be qualified for ministry, his life and experience have far surpassed them. Whether the claim is to Jewish background and education or to suffering for the gospel, Paul objectively has a stronger case for authority. Further, and unlike his opponents, Paul deeply cared for and identified with his congregations. He felt their weaknesses in himself and he burned with anger if any led them astray.

▸ WORSHIP

11:30 Standing up for yourself. Sometimes, even when we feel uncomfortable doing it, we have to stand up for ourselves. Paul takes a moment to remind the Corinthian readers of the limits of defending himself. If he has to boast, he would rather boast in the areas in which he is weak, for in those areas God's power is most clearly shown (see 1 Corinthians 1:18-31). As an example of his weakness, Paul notes his escape from Damascus: Hardly a victor, he was so helpless as to be lowered in a basket through a window in the city wall. Yes, you must occasionally stand up for yourself and those around you—but realize that this sort of defense has limits. Be quick to include your utter dependency on God and your gratitude for all that He has given you. (***See Worship***> *NT> Our Role> Mind and Heart> Glorify God in worship and all we do,* TopicGuide page A32.)

I was in Damascus, the governor under King Aretas kept guards at the city gates to catch
me. 33I had to be lowered in a basket through a window in the city wall to escape from him.

PAUL'S VISION AND HIS THORN IN THE FLESH

12 This boasting will do no good, but I must go on. I will reluctantly tell about visions 12:1
and revelations from the Lord. 2I* was caught up to the third heaven fourteen Gal 1:12
years ago. Whether I was in my body or out of my body, I don't know—only God knows.
3Yes, only God knows whether I was in my body or outside my body. But I do know 4that I 12:4
was caught up* to paradise and heard things so astounding that they cannot be expressed Luke 23:43
in words, things no human is allowed to tell. Rev 2:7
5That experience is worth boasting about, but I'm not going to do it. I will boast only 12:5 2 Cor 11:30
about my weaknesses. 6If I wanted to boast, I would be no fool in doing so, because I would 12:6
be telling the truth. But I won't do it, because I don't want anyone to give me credit beyond 2 Cor 10:8
what they can see in my life or hear in my message, 7even though I have received such 12:7
wonderful revelations from God. So to keep me from becoming proud, I was given a thorn Job 2:6
in my flesh, a messenger from Satan to torment me and keep me from becoming proud. 12:8 Matt 26:39, 44
8Three different times I begged the Lord to take it away. 9Each time He said, "My grace is 12:9
all you need. My power works best in weakness." So now I am glad to boast about my Phil 4:13
weaknesses, so that the power of Christ can work through me. 10That's why I take pleasure 12:10
in my weaknesses, and in the insults, hardships, persecutions, and troubles that I suffer for 2 Cor 6:4; 13:4
Christ. For when I am weak, then I am strong.

PAUL'S CONCERN FOR THE CORINTHIANS

12:11
11You have made me act like a fool—boasting like this.* You ought to be writing commen- 2 Cor 11:1, 5
dations for me, for I am not at all inferior to these "super apostles," even though I am noth- 12:12
ing at all. 12When I was with you, I certainly gave you proof that I am an apostle. For I Rom 15:19
patiently did many signs and wonders and miracles among you. 13The only thing I failed 12:13
to do, which I do in the other churches, was to become a financial burden to you. Please 1 Cor 9:12, 18 2 Cor 11:7
forgive me for this wrong!
14Now I am coming to you for the third time, and I will not be a burden to you. I don't 12:14
want what you have—I want you. After all, children don't provide for their parents. Rather, 1 Cor 4:14-15 2 Cor 13:1

12:2 Greek *I know a man in Christ who.* 12:3-4 Greek *But I know such a man, 4that he was caught up.* 12:11 Some manuscripts omit *boasting like this.*

12:2-4 Paul continues presenting his qualifications to the Corinthians. The Greek text begins, "I know a man in Christ who . . . ," but given the context of Paul's argument, it is reasonably clear that he is referring to himself. Paul's vision could simply have been in his mind, or he may have been transported into heaven. Regardless of which of these occurred, the point is clear: Paul's authority is validated because he has received visions and revelations directly from God, even seeing the inside of "the third heaven" or "paradise" or God's holy dwelling.

▶ SPIRITUAL WARFARE

12:6 Measuring our words. When we are right, it's tempting to go on and on—to keep clobbering our opponents with fact after fact, proof after proof, not for their own good, but because we like to sound smart. Instead of boasting more, even though his boasts would be true, Paul stops. He knows he has made his point, and that is enough. As you communicate in writing or face to face with people, learn to speak the truth clearly and succinctly—and then trust God for the results. Don't give in to the temptation to continue—for where there are too many words, there is often too much sin (Proverbs 10:19). (***See Spiritual Warfare***> *Resisting Sin and Evil> Trusting God> Faithful Soldiers> Control yourself,* TopicGuide page A46.)

12:7 There have been many theories about the identity of the thorn in Paul's flesh, including a physical problem and constant difficulties with his enemies. The text does not give enough information to be certain what the thorn was. All the text makes clear is that its particular function was to keep him humble in spite of all the qualifications and experiences he has just recounted.

12:12-13 Paul's ministry had not only been accompanied by the power of God through his preaching, but also through miracles. Paul now has listed accomplishments and qualifications of all kinds as he builds the case for his apostolic authority. He concludes his argument, ironically noting that the only qualification he does not have is that of having been a financial burden on the Corinthians.

12:14-15 Paul now indicates that he intends to visit Corinth for a third time. Like Paul's two previous visits, he will again place no financial burden upon them. Paul argues that he is like a parent to the Corinthians—he looks to support them, not to be supported by them. He seeks the Corinthians' allegiance and hearts, not their money.

parents provide for their children. 15I will gladly spend myself and all I have for you, even
though it seems that the more I love you, the less you love me.
16Some of you admit I was not a burden to you. But others still think I was sneaky and
took advantage of you by trickery. 17But how? Did any of the men I sent to you take ad-
vantage of you? 18When I urged Titus to visit you and sent our other brother with him, did
Titus take advantage of you? No! For we have the same spirit and walk in each other's
steps, doing things the same way.
19Perhaps you think we're saying these things just to defend ourselves. No, we tell you
this as Christ's servants, and with God as our witness. Everything we do, dear friends, is to
strengthen you. 20For I am afraid that when I come I won't like what I find, and you won't
like my response. I am afraid that I will find quarreling, jealousy, anger, selfishness, slan-
der, gossip, arrogance, and disorderly behavior. 21Yes, I am afraid that when I come again,
God will humble me in your presence. And I will be grieved because many of you have not
given up your old sins. You have not repented of your impurity, sexual immorality, and
eagerness for lustful pleasure.

12:15 2 Cor 11:11; Phil 2:17; 1 Thes 2:8
12:16 2 Cor 11:9
12:18 2 Cor 8:6, 16-18
12:19 Rom 9:1
12:20 1 Cor 4:21; 2 Cor 2:1-4
12:21 2 Cor 13:2

PAUL'S FINAL ADVICE

13 This is the third time I am coming to visit you (and as the Scriptures say, "The
facts of every case must be established by the testimony of two or three wit-
nesses"*). 2I have already warned those who had been sinning when I was there on my
second visit. Now I again warn them and all others, just as I did before, that next time I
will not spare them.
3I will give you all the proof you want that Christ speaks through me. Christ is not weak
when He deals with you; He is powerful among you. 4Although He was crucified in weak-
ness, He now lives by the power of God. We, too, are weak, just as Christ was, but when we
deal with you we will be alive with Him and will have God's power.
5Examine yourselves to see if your faith is genuine. Test yourselves. Surely you know
that Jesus Christ is among you*; if not, you have failed the test of genuine faith. 6As you test
yourselves, I hope you will recognize that we have not failed the test of apostolic authority.
7We pray to God that you will not do what is wrong by refusing our correction. I hope
we won't need to demonstrate our authority when we arrive. Do the right thing before we

13:1 *Deut 19:15; Matt 18:16; 2 Cor 12:14; 1 Tim 5:19
13:2 2 Cor 1:23; 12:21
13:3 Matt 10:20; 1 Cor 5:4
13:4 Rom 1:4; 6:4; Phil 2:7-8; 1 Pet 3:18
13:5 John 14:20; 17:23, 26; Rom 8:10; 1 Cor 11:28; Gal 4:19; Col 1:27

13:1 Deut 19:15. 13:5 Or *in you.*

12:16-18 Though Paul never took money from the Corinthians, some of his opponents argued that he had in fact taken advantage of them by some form of trickery, probably connected to the collection for the church in Jerusalem. Paul notes the complete lack of evidence for such an allegation. The collection for Jerusalem did not benefit him personally. Finally, when Titus and another brother had earlier visited regarding the collection (see 8:6), they also had the highest ethics in the matter.

12:19-21 Having disarmed all of the Corinthians' intellectual and authoritative arguments, Paul turns the conversation to focus on what he suspects is their real problem: their desire to remain in sin. Paul suspects that all the other arguments he has refuted are just smoke screens. He now challenges the Corinthians to look behind their embrace of the "super apostles" and ask why their teaching is so attractive to them.

13:1-2 Paul quotes Deuteronomy 19:15, in which Moses instructed the Jews that judgment can only follow the testimony of more than one witness. Paul's painful visit served as the first witness to their sin, and his current letter serves as a second witness. This indicates that his next visit will be for judgment, not more warnings.

▸ SALVATION

13:5 Put yourselves to the test. The Corinthians had tested Paul's apostolic authority, a test he had convincingly passed. Now Paul encourages them to test themselves regarding their faith. Do they know that Jesus is in them? If they do not know Jesus is in them, then they may not have genuine faith. On the other hand, if they are truly following Jesus, it should be apparent to them that Paul is also following faithfully. This is also a message to those who read Paul's letter today. How do you know your faith is genuine? Do you know that Jesus is in you? Do you rest on His grace alone for salvation? Do Paul's words ring true in your heart? If not, reevaluate your understanding of the gospel and be certain you truly understand it. (***See Salvation****> Receiving> Results> Assurance,* TopicGuide page A23.)

13:7-10 Perhaps the best indication of Paul's genuine concern for the Corinthians was his hope that he would not have to exercise his authority over them. Paul is not looking forward to punishing anyone. Indeed, he hopes he will not have to do so, even if that means his authority is never demonstrated. Some may then renew the charge that he is weak in person, but Paul is not bothered by such a possibility—he is happy to appear weak if it proves the Corinthians are, in fact, strong. Paul demonstrates loving, not selfish, authority.

come—even if that makes it look like we have failed to demonstrate our authority. 8For we
cannot oppose the truth, but must always stand for the truth. 9We are glad to seem weak if
it helps show that you are actually strong. We pray that you will become mature.
10I am writing this to you before I come, hoping that I won't need to deal severely with
you when I do come. For I want to use the authority the Lord has given me to strengthen
you, not to tear you down.

PAUL'S FINAL GREETINGS

11Dear brothers and sisters,* I close my letter with these last words: Be joyful. Grow to ma-
turity. Encourage each other. Live in harmony and peace. Then the God of love and peace
will be with you.
12Greet each other with Christian love.* 13All of God's people here send you their
greetings.
14*May the grace of the Lord Jesus Christ, the love of God, and the fellowship of the Holy
Spirit be with you all.

13:8 1 Cor 13:6
13:9 1 Cor 2:3; 4:10
13:10 2 Cor 10:8, 11
13:11 Rom 15:33; Phil 4:4
13:12 Rom 16:16; 1 Cor 16:20; 1 Pet 5:14
13:13 Rom 16:20; Phil 2:1

13:11 Greek *Brothers.* 13:12 Greek *with a sacred kiss.* 13:14 Some English translations include verse 13 as part of verse 12, and then verse 14 becomes verse 13.

▸ WORSHIP

13:9 Christians marked by selflessness. Are you willing to seem weak for the good of others? Are you willing to relinquish leadership if it provides a chance for another's faith to grow? Are you willing to take a supportive or less prominent role to advance the gospel? Paul is glad to appear weak if his doing so makes others strong. It is easy to live the Christian life saying that we seek the glory of God and the good of others, all the while actually seeking our own glory and good. Be willing instead to become weak for the good of others, just as Christ did for your sake. (***See Worship> NT> Fellowship> Preserving> Consider others more important,*** TopicGuide page A31.)

GALATIANS

PURPOSE

To demonstrate that believers are justified by faith in Christ because He was faithful, not because we keep the laws of the Old Covenant.

Can something be* too *good to be true? The message of the gospel of Jesus Christ is great Good News, yet the sad truth is that many think it must be too good to be true.

The believers in Galatia began their spiritual life as every Christian does—believing that they could offer God nothing but their need of His gift of salvation. But false teachers had begun to persuade them that their life with God should grow differently than it began—"grace through faith" seemed too good to be true. Paul writes to set them straight and bring them back to the simple truth that what had begun through the working of the Spirit would continue that way (3:1-5), and what had begun by faith in God's gracious promises would continue that way (3:24-29).

Paul penned Galatians to return Christians to the freedom that belongs to those who trust Jesus as their Savior. He also wrote it as a rebuke to those who add any additional requirements to those seeking entrance into the family of God (3:26–4:6). More than most New Testament documents, Galatians was written to a specific audience to confront a specific theological error. But it continues to resonate with believers of every age who desire to live life by dependence on God's promises, not through the merit of their own works.

DISCOVER GOD IN GALATIANS

Galatians is filled with the good news of the freedom in grace that belongs to us in Jesus. As Paul develops this concept, he highlights the following truths about God:

Father: Although in one sense, God, as Creator, is the Father of all people, there is a special sense in which He is Father of those who believe. Paul tells us that He adopts believers into His family (4:6-7), embracing us as His very own through what Jesus has done for us. Part of the gift of redemption (1:4) is an introduction into the family of God (3:26). Jesus taught us to pray to God as our Father (Matthew 6:5-13) and to trust His fatherly love (Matthew 6:25-34).

Redeemer: In ancient times, redemption carried the idea of buying someone out of slavery or indebtedness in order to make that person your own or set that person free. In this case, God is the One who redeems us and makes us His own (3:13; 4:5, 30). Paul saw himself as a man with an enormous spiritual debt, cast into debtor's prison, with no ability to work off his debt to God. But while he "stopped trying to meet all its requirements" (2:19) or "be made right with God by obeying [the law]" (3:21), he could trust in Christ, who "gave Himself for me" (2:20).

Covenant Maker: Crucial to Paul's train of thought in Galatians is the concept that God has made promises—He made a covenant agreement with Abraham (Genesis 12:1-3; 15:1-21;

17:1-14; Galatians 3:14-23). The blessings of that covenant ultimately fall on those who share the faith of Abraham (Romans 4:2), who lived prior to the establishment of the Mosaic law and knew God by faith, not by the works of the law—such as circumcision or prescribed offerings. Paul's reasoning in Galatians is based on his belief that God will be faithful to His promises that are based not on the Mosaic law, but on the free gift of faith from God to all who believe.

GROWING THROUGH GALATIANS

Paul addresses both the teachers and the recipients of the misguided teaching about grace and works. Paul makes it clear that every disciple needs to embrace and experience the following truths:

There Is Only One Gospel. The Good News of Jesus Christ is simple, powerful, and life changing, but some people struggle with its simplicity and graciousness. They add what they feel is missing to the message, creating something less than truly good news. Paul cautions about straying away from the simple message of the grace that is found in Jesus (1:6-9).

Even Leaders Need Correction. Peter, an apostle and close associate of Jesus, was a leader in the local church (Acts 2). But even Peter wasn't infallible; sometimes he sinned, too (Matthew 16:21-23). In Galatians, Paul recounts Peter's visit when he had to speak a word of correction to him (Galatians 2:11-21). Because even the most respected Christian leaders can sin, it is important for every Christian to know the foundational truths of the Christian faith. Every Christian should know the Word well enough to discern between truth and error (Matthew 18:15-20).

The Holy Spirit Is Necessary for Christian Living. The gospel is not another "self-help" program—it is a message of forgiveness of sin and adoption by God through Jesus Christ (Galatians 3:23–4:7). This new relationship leads to a Spirit-generated change of life (5:22-27). We don't experience this life through adherence to certain rules (3:23-29), but through a dependent relationship with the Spirit (2:17–3:9). The character qualities that flow from a Spirit-empowered Christian life are an expression of the Spirit revealing His presence in us (5:22-23).

DISCOVERY VERSES

Yet we know that a person is made right with God by faith in Jesus Christ, not by obeying the law. And we have believed in Christ Jesus, so that we might be made right with God because of our faith in Christ, not because we have obeyed the law. For no one will ever be made right with God by obeying the law. (GALATIANS 2:16)

It is no longer I who live, but Christ lives in me. So I live in this earthly body by trusting in the Son of God, who loved me and gave Himself for me. (GALATIANS 2:20)

And now that you belong to Christ, you are the true children of Abraham. You are his heirs, and God's promise to Abraham belongs to you. (GALATIANS 3:29)

Since we are living by the Spirit, let us follow the Spirit's leading in every part of our lives. (GALATIANS 5:25)

GALATIANS FACTS

Author: With a characteristic style, the letter to the Galatians is "classic Paul." He identified himself as the author in the opening of the letter (1:1), referred to himself later (5:2), and noted that he penned some of the closing words himself (6:11) as well as dictating the letter (Romans 16:22; 1 Corinthians 16:21; Colossians 4:18; 2 Thessalonians 3:17), which was his habit.

Written to: The term Galatia was used in Paul's day to refer to both a smaller region (defined ethnically) and a larger region (defined by Roman political boundaries). The smaller region was the central part of Asia Minor, while the larger region extended south to the Mediterranean Sea. Whichever region is in view, Paul is writing to relatively new Gentile believers in churches he had helped plant.

Date of writing: Because of the questions about which specific group of Galatians Paul is writing to, there is some uncertainty about the date of this letter. It was written after Paul's visit to Jerusalem (written as a past event in Galatians 2:1-11, also recorded in Acts 15). Given stylistic and topical similarities with Romans, it is possible it was written during Paul's stay in Corinth (Acts 20:2-3) in the winter of AD 57–58.

Setting: Paul most likely wrote from Corinth, a large Greek port 48 miles southwest of Athens.

OUTLINE

- **GALATIANS 1:1–2:21**—A Defense of Paul's Apostleship
- **GALATIANS 3:1–4:31**—A Defense of Justification by Faith Alone
- **GALATIANS 5:1–6:18**—A Defense of Christian Liberty

GREETINGS FROM PAUL

1 This letter is from Paul, an apostle. I was not appointed by any group of people or any
human authority, but by Jesus Christ Himself and by God the Father, who raised
Jesus from the dead.
2All the brothers and sisters* here join me in sending this letter to the churches of Galatia.
3May God our Father and the Lord Jesus Christ* give you grace and peace. 4Jesus gave
His life for our sins, just as God our Father planned, in order to rescue us from this evil
world in which we live. 5All glory to God forever and ever! Amen.

THERE IS ONLY ONE GOOD NEWS

6I am shocked that you are turning away so soon from God, who called you to Himself
through the loving mercy of Christ.* You are following a different way that pretends to be
the Good News 7but is not the Good News at all. You are being fooled by those who delib-
erately twist the truth concerning Christ.
8Let God's curse fall on anyone, including us or even an angel from heaven, who
preaches a different kind of Good News than the one we preached to you. 9I say again
what we have said before: If anyone preaches any other Good News than the one you
welcomed, let that person be cursed.
10Obviously, I'm not trying to win the approval of people, but of God. If pleasing people
were my goal, I would not be Christ's servant.

1:2 Greek *brothers;* also in 1:11. 1:3 Some manuscripts read *God the Father and our Lord Jesus Christ.* 1:6 Some manuscripts read *through loving mercy.*

1:1 Acts 20:24; Gal 1:11-12
1:3 Rom 1:7; Phil 1:2; Phlm 1:3
1:4 Rom 4:25; Gal 2:20; 1 Tim 2:6; Titus 2:14
1:5 Rom 11:36
1:6 2 Cor 11:4
1:7 Acts 15:1, 24; Gal 5:10
1:8 2 Cor 11:14
1:9 Deut 4:2; 12:32; 1 Cor 16:22; Rev 22:18
1:10 1 Thes 2:4

1:1-3 Paul opens his letter to the Galatians by identifying the sender and the recipient and providing a greeting, which was the Greek custom of his day. From the outset, Paul distinguishes himself as an apostle of Jesus Christ, an office that no human authority can grant. After His resurrection, Jesus Christ personally revealed Himself to Paul (Acts 9; 1 Corinthians 9:1; 15:3-8), appointed him to the office of apostle (1 Timothy 2:7; 2 Timothy 1:11), and authorized him to preach the Good News (Acts 9:15).

1:2 Paul received authority over the church from Jesus Christ (Colossians 1:23; Ephesians 2:20).

▸ SALVATION

1:3-5 Rescued to praise. Have you ever asked an unbeliever what they think it means to be a Christian? Some people may think it means going to church, following the teachings of Christ, or living a moral life. But how many people think that a Christian is someone who has been rescued by Jesus Christ? Paul explains that Jesus' death on the cross was a substitutionary sacrifice for our sins. Jesus rescued us from the penalty of our sin. God planned the work of salvation, and Christ accomplished salvation on our behalf. Praise God today for all that He has accomplished on your behalf through His Son—all glory belongs to Him! (***See Salvation***> *Receiving*> *When*> *Delivered or rescued,* TopicGuide page A22.)

1:6-7 Here is the first indication that there was a problem with the Christians in the province of Galatia. Shockingly, those who had once professed Jesus Christ as their Savior were now changing the definition of the Good News. The phrase "pretends to be" can be translated as "reverses." The apostle is saying that anything that reverses the gospel of grace invalidates the message.

1:8-9 The Good News must not be defined by one's own feelings or by anyone else other than God. All teachers or messengers of the truth, including Paul and the angels, are subject to God's definition of the Good News. Paul is very forceful in his statements against false teachers, even using the word "curse" two times for added emphasis. Those who twist the Good News will fall under God's wrath and judgment.

▸ SPIRITUAL WARFARE

1:10 Are you a God-pleaser? If you are devoted to living a life that is pleasing to God, you will be freed from a people-pleasing spirit. Far too many people live their lives trying to gain the approval of others at any cost, but this kind of attitude will keep you enslaved to fear and rob you of a godly confidence (Galatians 6:14-15). Paul's primary motivation for all he did was to please God (1 Thessalonians 2:4), which resulted in people glorifying God, not Paul, for his ministry (Galatians 1:23-24). Search your heart to see if you are motivated to act for human approval or for God's glory. Ask God to renew a desire in you to do what is right without concern for human approval. (***See Spiritual Warfare***> *Resisting Sin and Evil*> *Consequences*> *Of Obedience*> *Pleases God,* TopicGuide page A46.)

PAUL'S MESSAGE COMES FROM CHRIST

[11]Dear brothers and sisters, I want you to understand that the gospel message I preach is
not based on mere human reasoning. [12]I received my message from no human source,
and no one taught me. Instead, I received it by direct revelation from Jesus Christ.*
[13]You know what I was like when I followed the Jewish religion—how I violently perse-
cuted God's church. I did my best to destroy it. [14]I was far ahead of my fellow Jews in my
zeal for the traditions of my ancestors.
[15]But even before I was born, God chose me and called me by His marvelous grace.
Then it pleased Him [16]to reveal His Son to me* so that I would proclaim the Good News
about Jesus to the Gentiles.
When this happened, I did not rush out to consult with any human being.* [17]Nor did I go
up to Jerusalem to consult with those who were apostles before I was. Instead, I went away
into Arabia, and later I returned to the city of Damascus.
[18]Then three years later I went to Jerusalem to get to know Peter,* and I stayed with him
for fifteen days. [19]The only other apostle I met at that time was James, the Lord's brother.
[20]I declare before God that what I am writing to you is not a lie.
[21]After that visit I went north into the provinces of Syria and Cilicia. [22]And still the Chris-
tians in the churches in Judea didn't know me personally. [23]All they knew was that people
were saying, "The one who used to persecute us is now preaching the very faith he tried to
destroy!" [24]And they praised God because of me.

THE APOSTLES ACCEPT PAUL

2 Then fourteen years later I went back to Jerusalem again, this time with Barnabas;
and Titus came along, too. [2]I went there because God revealed to me that I should
go. While I was there I met privately with those considered to be leaders of the church and

1:11 1 Cor 15:1-3
1:12 1 Cor 2:10; Gal 1:1, 15-16; Eph 3:3
1:13 Acts 8:3; 9:21; 22:4-5; 26:4-11
1:14 Acts 22:3
1:15 Acts 9:15
1:16 Rom 1:17; 8:3, 10; Gal 2:9, 20; Col 1:27
1:18 Acts 9:22-23, 26-27
1:19 Matt 13:55; Acts 15:13; Gal 2:9, 12
1:23 Acts 9:20
2:1 Acts 15:2
2:2 Gal 1:6

1:12 Or *by the revelation of Jesus Christ.* 1:16a Or *in me.* 1:16b Greek *with flesh and blood.* 1:18 Greek *Cephas.*

1:17-18 Paul intentionally distinguishes himself from those who had perverted the Good News. The false teachers who came to the churches of Galatia may have originated in Jerusalem or somewhere in the province of Judea (Acts 15:1); they taught that belief in Christ was not sufficient for salvation—they also required circumcision and observance of the law of Moses (Galatians 5:12; 6:13).

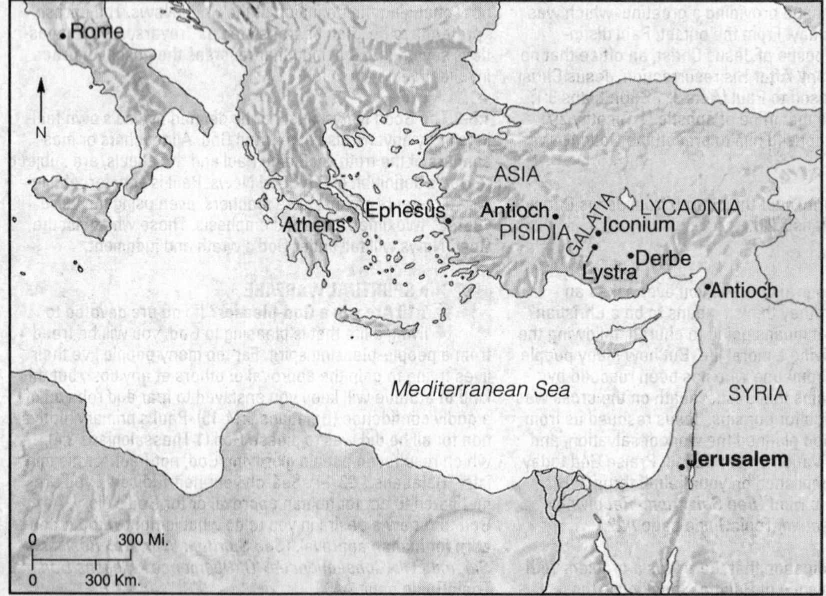

CITIES IN GALATIA
Paul visited several cities in Galatia on each of his three missionary journeys. On his first journey he went through Antioch in Pisidia, Iconium, Lystra, and Derbe, and then retraced his steps; on his second journey he went by land from Antioch of Syria through the four cities in Galatia; on his third journey he also went through those cities on the main route to Ephesus.

2:3 shared with them the message I had been preaching to the Gentiles. I wanted to make
Acts 16:3 sure that we were in agreement, for fear that all my efforts had been wasted and I was run-
2:4 ning the race for nothing. 3And they supported me and did not even demand that my
Gal 1:7; 5:1, 13 companion Titus be circumcised, though he was a Gentile.*
2:5 Gal 1:6; 2:14 4Even that question came up only because of some so-called Christians there—false
2:6 ones, really*—who were secretly brought in. They sneaked in to spy on us and take away
Deut 10:17 the freedom we have in Christ Jesus. They wanted to enslave us and force us to follow
Acts 10:34 Rom 2:11 their Jewish regulations. 5But we refused to give in to them for a single moment. We
2 Cor 12:11 wanted to preserve the truth of the gospel message for you.
2:7 6And the leaders of the church had nothing to add to what I was preaching. (By the way,
Acts 9:15; 22:21 their reputation as great leaders made no difference to me, for God has no favorites.) 7In-
1 Thes 2:4 stead, they saw that God had given me the responsibility of preaching the gospel to the
Gentiles, just as He had given Peter the responsibility of preaching to the Jews. 8For the
same God who worked through Peter as the apostle to the Jews also worked through me
as the apostle to the Gentiles.
2:9 9In fact, James, Peter,* and John, who were known as pillars of the church, recognized
Rom 1:5 the gift God had given me, and they accepted Barnabas and me as their co-workers. They
encouraged us to keep preaching to the Gentiles, while they continued their work with the
2:10 Jews. 10Their only suggestion was that we keep on helping the poor, which I have always
Acts 11:29-30; 24:17 been eager to do.

PAUL CONFRONTS PETER

11But when Peter came to Antioch, I had to oppose him to his face, for what he did was
2:12 very wrong. 12When he first arrived, he ate with the Gentile Christians, who were not cir-
Acts 11:2-3 cumcised. But afterward, when some friends of James came, Peter wouldn't eat with the
Gentiles anymore. He was afraid of criticism from these people who insisted on the neces-
sity of circumcision. 13As a result, other Jewish Christians followed Peter's hypocrisy, and
even Barnabas was led astray by their hypocrisy.
2:14 14When I saw that they were not following the truth of the gospel message, I said to Pe-
Acts 10:28 ter in front of all the others, "Since you, a Jew by birth, have discarded the Jewish laws and
2:15 are living like a Gentile, why are you now trying to make these Gentiles follow the Jewish
Phil 3:4-5 traditions?
2:16 15"You and I are Jews by birth, not 'sinners' like the Gentiles. 16Yet we know that a per-
Acts 15:10-11 Rom 1:17; 3:20, 28; 8:3 son is made right with God by faith in Jesus Christ, not by obeying the law. And we have
Gal 3:11 believed in Christ Jesus, so that we might be made right with God because of our faith in
Eph 2:8

2:3 Greek *a Greek.* 2:4 Greek *some false brothers.* 2:9 Greek *Cephas;* also in 2:11, 14.

2:3-5 Paul explains that he underwent a similar testing in one of his early trips to Jerusalem as the Galatian believers were now facing. Paul describes this account to encourage the Christians in Galatia to stand firm against the false teachers in their midst. Titus saw no need to be circumcised because his faith in Christ's salvation was sufficient to render him spiritually clean.

2:10 Recognizing that God indeed had called Paul to minister to the Gentile nations, the Christian church leaders asked Paul to remember the poor in Jerusalem. Paul was eager to minister to the poor, because God had not only called him to minister to the spiritual needs of people, but to meet their physical needs as well (Acts 24:17; Romans 15:26; 1 Corinthians 16:1-3; 2 Corinthians 8–9).

2:11-13 Fearing what others might say of him, Peter acted hypocritically by ceasing to eat with the Gentile believers. Previously, God had clearly revealed to Peter that the Good News of Jesus Christ was intended for the Gentiles as well as the Jews (Acts 10). The Lord had personally shown Peter that in Christ there was nothing unclean. Paul confronted Peter because Peter had allowed cultural differences and a desire to please people to dictate his decisions, rather than focusing on the unity generated by the Good News of Jesus Christ.

▶ HOLINESS

2:14 Sanctified by grace. The Good News of Jesus Christ is not just for unbelievers, but for Christians as well. The gospel teaches that nothing—nothing—you do can merit God's grace. What difference does this make? It means that the fight against sin is not waged on our willpower, our effort, or our theological prowess. It's a life we live empowered by God as we put our faith in Christ's efforts—His teachings, His atonement (Hebrews 2:17), and His constant intercession for us (Romans 8:34; Hebrews 7:25; 9:24; 1 John 2:1). So what do Christians do? Just what the Bible commands us—repent and believe, trusting that Jesus Christ will be faithful to complete the work He began in you (Hebrews 4:14; Philippians 1:6). Make your life one characterized by repenting and believing. (***See Holiness**> Law and Grace> Grace> The true gospel,* TopicGuide page A42.)

Christ, not because we have obeyed the law. For no one will ever be made right with God
by obeying the law."*
17But suppose we seek to be made right with God through faith in Christ and then we
are found guilty because we have abandoned the law. Would that mean Christ has led us
into sin? Absolutely not! 18Rather, I am a sinner if I rebuild the old system of law I already
tore down. 19For when I tried to keep the law, it condemned me. So I died to the law—I
stopped trying to meet all its requirements—so that I might live for God. 20My old self has
been crucified with Christ.* It is no longer I who live, but Christ lives in me. So I live in this
earthly body by trusting in the Son of God, who loved me and gave Himself for me. 21I do
not treat the grace of God as meaningless. For if keeping the law could make us right with
God, then there was no need for Christ to die.

2:19 Rom 6:10-14; 7:4 · 2 Cor 5:15
2:20 Rom 6:6; 8:37 · Gal 1:4 · 1 Tim 2:6 · Titus 2:14

THE LAW AND FAITH IN CHRIST

3 Oh, foolish Galatians! Who has cast an evil spell on you? For the meaning of Jesus
Christ's death was made as clear to you as if you had seen a picture of His death on
the cross. 2Let me ask you this one question: Did you receive the Holy Spirit by obeying
the law of Moses? Of course not! You received the Spirit because you believed the mes-
sage you heard about Christ. 3How foolish can you be? After starting your Christian lives in
the Spirit, why are you now trying to become perfect by your own human effort? 4Have
you experienced* so much for nothing? Surely it was not in vain, was it?
5I ask you again, does God give you the Holy Spirit and work miracles among you be-
cause you obey the law? Of course not! It is because you believe the message you heard
about Christ.
6In the same way, "Abraham believed God, and God counted him as righteous because
of his faith."* 7The real children of Abraham, then, are those who put their faith in God.

3:1 1 Cor 1:23 · Gal 5:7
3:2 Rom 10:17
3:3 Gal 4:9
3:4 2 Jn 1:8
3:5 1 Cor 12:10
3:6 *Gen 15:6 · Rom 4:3

2:16 Some translators hold that the quotation extends through verse 14; others through verse 16; and still others through verse 21. 2:20 Some English translations put this sentence in verse 19. 3:4 Or *Have you suffered.* 3:6 Gen 15:6.

▶ SALVATION

2:16 Justification by faith. Many heretical groups sound very Christian—if you ask them, they will readily tell you that they believe in God, Jesus, and the Holy Spirit. Upon further investigation, however, often you will find that they add additional requirements for salvation, such as baptism, membership in their special church, or even obedience to certain Old Testament laws. God continues to use signs such as baptism (Romans 6:3-5; Colossians 2:12) and the Lord's Supper (1 Corinthians 11:27-29) as symbols of our faith, but if we insist that such symbols are necessary for salvation, we invalidate the gospel (Galatians 1:7). Rely on nothing—nothing!—but Jesus Christ's work on your behalf for your own salvation. (***See Salvation**> Receiving> When> Justified/ declared innocent,* TopicGuide page A22.)

2:17 As Paul has already explained, the message of Jesus Christ frees believers from the necessity of keeping the Old Testament ceremonial and sacrificial laws. The Jews' argument was incorrect because it failed to recognize that the law cannot condemn those who are in Christ (John 3:18-19; Romans 8:1; Galatians 3:13).

2:20 When Paul says that he died with Christ on the cross, he means he died to his old self and desires when he came to faith in Christ. According to Paul's logic, when Christ was resurrected from the dead, Paul remained in the grave; this is why Paul can say that Christ alone lives in his body.

3:1-2 These believers at Galatia never personally saw Jesus Christ on the cross, but the preaching they heard from Paul and other church leaders provided a vivid depiction that Christ indeed was crucified on their behalf. The Holy Spirit came upon the Galatians as a testimony of their authentic belief in the message about Jesus Christ (John 3:5; Ephesians 4:30).

3:3-5 Some Galatians believed that though they had started their new life by believing in the Good News of Jesus Christ, they were to continue in their spiritual journey by following the law of Moses in order to maintain their salvation. But the reason that the Holy Spirit came to the believers in the first place was the same reason the Spirit continued to work in them—the Spirit initiated and sustained their belief in the message of the crucified Christ (Galatians 3:1). The Galatian believers did not understand that the message of the Good News called them to transfer to Jesus Christ all their trust in themselves.

▶ BIBLE

3:6-9 Saving Abraham, saving others. Paul believed that faith in the promises of God is not unique to the New Testament. In proving his case against the Jewish false teachers, Paul recalls Abraham's faith, which preceded the law of Moses, as a model for what it means to be called righteous (Genesis 15). It's not what time or place you are born in that determines whether you are a Christian—it's faith in God's promises of salvation. Perhaps you see people in other denominations that believe many different doctrines than you—do you wonder if they can be Christians? If they believe in the Good News of the promises of God, trusting in Christ alone for their salvation, then no matter how strange some of their other beliefs may be, they are just as saved as you are. Rather than judge them, celebrate the grace of God, who saves people—even those who may not have the same theology as you do. (***See Bible**> Unity> Christ> Christ in the promise to Abraham,* TopicGuide page A10.)

3:8 *Gen 12:3 Acts 3:25
3:10 *Deut 27:26 Jer 11:3
3:11 *Hab 2:4 Rom 1:17 Heb 10:38
3:12 *Lev 18:5 Rom 10:5
3:13 *Deut 21:23 Gal 4:5
3:14 Joel 2:28 Acts 2:33
3:15 Heb 9:17
3:16 *Gen 12:7; 13:15; 17:7; 24:7
3:17 Exod 12:40
3:18 Rom 4:14; 11:6
3:19 Exod 20:19 Deut 5:5 Acts 7:53 Heb 2:2
3:20 1 Tim 2:5
3:21 Rom 8:2-4
3:22 Rom 3:11-19; 11:32

[8]What's more, the Scriptures looked forward to this time when God would declare the Gentiles to be righteous because of their faith. God proclaimed this good news to Abraham long ago when He said, "All nations will be blessed through you."* [9]So all who put their faith in Christ share the same blessing Abraham received because of his faith.

[10]But those who depend on the law to make them right with God are under His curse, for the Scriptures say, "Cursed is everyone who does not observe and obey all the commands that are written in God's Book of the Law."* [11]So it is clear that no one can be made right with God by trying to keep the law. For the Scriptures say, "It is through faith that a righteous person has life."* [12]This way of faith is very different from the way of law, which says, "It is through obeying the law that a person has life."*

[13]But Christ has rescued us from the curse pronounced by the law. When He was hung on the cross, He took upon Himself the curse for our wrongdoing. For it is written in the Scriptures, "Cursed is everyone who is hung on a tree."* [14]Through Christ Jesus, God has blessed the Gentiles with the same blessing He promised to Abraham, so that we who are believers might receive the promised* Holy Spirit through faith.

THE LAW AND GOD'S PROMISE

[15]Dear brothers and sisters,* here's an example from everyday life. Just as no one can set aside or amend an irrevocable agreement, so it is in this case. [16]God gave the promises to Abraham and his child.* And notice that the Scripture doesn't say "to his children,*" as if it meant many descendants. Rather, it says "to His child"—and that, of course, means Christ. [17]This is what I am trying to say: The agreement God made with Abraham could not be canceled 430 years later when God gave the law to Moses. God would be breaking His promise. [18]For if the inheritance could be received by keeping the law, then it would not be the result of accepting God's promise. But God graciously gave it to Abraham as a promise.

[19]Why, then, was the law given? It was given alongside the promise to show people their sins. But the law was designed to last only until the coming of the child who was promised. God gave His law through angels to Moses, who was the mediator between God and the people. [20]Now a mediator is helpful if more than one party must reach an agreement. But God, who is one, did not use a mediator when He gave His promise to Abraham.

[21]Is there a conflict, then, between God's law and God's promises?* Absolutely not! If the law could give us new life, we could be made right with God by obeying it. [22]But the Scriptures declare that we are all prisoners of sin, so we receive God's promise of freedom only by believing in Jesus Christ.

3:8 Gen 12:3; 18:18; 22:18. 3:10 Deut 27:26. 3:11 Hab 2:4. 3:12 Lev 18:5. 3:13 Deut 21:23 (Greek version). 3:14 Some manuscripts read *the blessing of the.* 3:15 Greek *Brothers.* 3:16a Greek *seed;* also in 3:16c, 19. See notes on Gen 12:7 and 13:15. 3:16b Greek *seeds.* 3:21 Some manuscripts read *and the promises?*

3:10-12 Many of the Galatians had committed themselves to obeying the law for their salvation, but they failed to consider all that the law required. Paul clarified that it was impossible for anyone to avoid the curse that comes from disobeying the law of God (Deuteronomy 27:26), let alone keep it in such a way as to gain merit.

3:13-14 Paul explains to the Galatians that there is no escaping condemnation for violating the law—except through Jesus Christ. Paul does not mean that Jesus Christ became wicked, but rather that Jesus legally took on their guilt (Hebrews 4:15). Instead of becoming a curse, the Galatian believers could be considered perfect by trusting in Jesus Christ's death on the cross in their place (Romans 8:1).

▸ HOLINESS

3:19 Three purposes of the Law. Paul's concern about the misuse of the law in the lives of the believers in Galatia has led many to think that the law has no real authority in the life of the modern believer. But the law continues to help us today in at least three ways: 1) The law leads us to Christ by exposing our sin and teaching us of God's forgiveness found only in Christ (Romans 3:20; 4:15; 5:13; Galatians 3:19-24). 2) The law restrains evil in society by threatening judgment on violators (Deuteronomy 13:6-11; 19:16-21; Romans 13:3-4). 3) The law serves as a guide for godly behavior in everyday Christian living (Psalm 119:105; Matthew 5:17-19; Romans 3:31; 1 Corinthians 9:21). Do not ignore or reject God's law, but embrace it and rejoice in it (Psalm 119). (***See Holiness***> *Law and Grace*> *Law*> *A picture of God and His character,* TopicGuide page A41.)

GOD'S CHILDREN THROUGH FAITH

23Before the way of faith in Christ was available to us, we were placed under guard by the law. We were kept in protective custody, so to speak, until the way of faith was revealed.

24Let me put it another way. The law was our guardian until Christ came; it protected us until we could be made right with God through faith. 25And now that the way of faith has come, we no longer need the law as our guardian.

26For you are all children* of God through faith in Christ Jesus. 27And all who have been united with Christ in baptism have put on Christ, like putting on new clothes.* 28There is no longer Jew or Gentile,* slave or free, male and female. For you are all one in Christ Jesus. 29And now that you belong to Christ, you are the true children* of Abraham. You are his heirs, and God's promise to Abraham belongs to you.

4 Think of it this way. If a father dies and leaves an inheritance for his young children, those children are not much better off than slaves until they grow up, even though they actually own everything their father had. 2They have to obey their guardians until they reach whatever age their father set. 3And that's the way it was with us before Christ came. We were like children; we were slaves to the basic spiritual principles* of this world.

4But when the right time came, God sent His Son, born of a woman, subject to the law. 5God sent Him to buy freedom for us who were slaves to the law, so that He could adopt us as His very own children.* 6And because we* are His children, God has sent the Spirit of His Son into our hearts, prompting us to call out, "Abba, Father."* 7Now you are no longer a slave but God's own child.* And since you are His child, God has made you His heir.

PAUL'S CONCERN FOR THE GALATIANS

8Before you Gentiles knew God, you were slaves to so-called gods that do not even exist. 9So now that you know God (or should I say, now that God knows you), why do you want to go back again and become slaves once more to the weak and useless spiritual principles of this world? 10You are trying to earn favor with God by observing certain days or

3:26 Greek *sons.* 3:27 Greek *have put on Christ.* 3:28 Greek *Jew or Greek.* 3:29 Greek *seed.* 4:3 Or *powers;* also in 4:9. 4:5 Greek *sons;* also in 4:6. 4:6a Greek *you.* 4:6b *Abba* is an Aramaic term for "father." 4:7 Greek *son;* also in 4:7b.

3:24 Rom 10:4
3:27 Rom 6:3; 13:14
3:28 John 10:16; 17:21; 1 Cor 12:13; Eph 2:14-15; Col 3:11
3:29 Rom 8:17; Gal 3:16
4:3 Gal 3:23; Col 2:8, 20
4:4 Mark 1:15; John 1:14; Eph 1:10; Heb 2:14
4:5 Rom 8:15; Eph 1:5
4:6 Rom 8:15-16
4:7 Rom 8:17
4:8 2 Chr 13:9; Isa 37:19; Jer 2:11; 1 Cor 8:4-6; 1 Thes 1:9
4:9 Col 2:20
4:10 Rom 14:5; Col 2:16

3:27-29 There was no need for the Jews to force the Gentile believers in Galatia to become followers of Judaism. The Good News of Jesus Christ unites all kinds of people as the one true family of God. God shows no preferential treatment to one kind of person over another, for all who are clothed in Christ are considered as one in His eyes.

4:1-2 In the ancient world, the young heir of a fortune was not given immediate control of the estate. People were appointed to rule over both him and his possessions. But when he came of age, he could then enjoy all that he had previously legally possessed, but which had been beyond his personal control. Through this analogy Paul intended to convince the Galatians to come out of the guidance of the law into their full possession of everything Christ had for them.

4:4-5 When Christ came into the world, He was not separate from the law—He was subject to it. His obedience to the law and sacrifice upon the cross accomplished two things for God's people. First, Christ came into the world to remove the guilt and penalty of sin. Second, He adopts us into His family as sons and daughters. All this was possible because Christ's sacrifice fulfilled the ceremonial requirements of the law.

▸ ADOPTION

4:6-7 Sons, not slaves. Though at times Paul refers to himself as a slave to God (Romans 1:1; Philippians 1:1; Titus 1:1), here he uses the idea of slavery in a negative way to contrast the joy of adoption by God with the drudgery of slavery. A slave of Paul's time enjoyed very few rights, but those adopted by God enjoy all the liberties and privileges of being in God's family (Romans 8:17; John 1:12), including receiving His name (Jeremiah 14:9), His Spirit (Romans 8:15), unrestricted access to Him (Ephesians 3:12; Romans 5:2), and the right to call Him Father (Galatians 4:6). He protects us (Proverbs 14:26) and disciplines us (Hebrews 12:6), yet that discipline never threatens to disown us (Lamentations 3:31). And, as members of His family, we are now heirs of His best promises (Hebrews 6:12) and of everlasting salvation (1 Peter 1:3-4; Hebrews 1:14). In light of these blessings, why would we want to live like legalists, as if the rules of God were the best thing He could give us? What difference would it make in your thoughts, feelings, and actions if you truly believed God has adopted you? (***See Adoption*****>** *With Christ> Children of God> God's own children,* TopicGuide page A36.)

4:8-10 The Galatians could not hope to receive salvation by observing the rituals of the law of the Old Testament (Galatians 2:10-14). Paul compares the life of the person resting on the law for assurance of salvation to the life of an unsaved person. People who are not Christians rely on their own efforts to obtain salvation.

4:13 months or seasons or years. [11]I fear for you. Perhaps all my hard work with you was for
1 Cor 2:3 nothing. [12]Dear brothers and sisters,* I plead with you to live as I do in freedom from these
4:14 things, for I have become like you Gentiles—free from those laws.
Matt 10:40 You did not mistreat me when I first preached to you. [13]Surely you remember that I was
sick when I first brought you the Good News. [14]But even though my condition tempted
you to reject me, you did not despise me or turn me away. No, you took me in and cared
for me as though I were an angel from God or even Christ Jesus Himself. [15]Where is that
joyful and grateful spirit you felt then? I am sure you would have taken out your own eyes
4:16 and given them to me if it had been possible. [16]Have I now become your enemy because I
Amos 5:10 am telling you the truth?
4:17 [17]Those false teachers are so eager to win your favor, but their intentions are not good.
Gal 2:4, 12 They are trying to shut you off from me so that you will pay attention only to them. [18]If
someone is eager to do good things for you, that's all right; but let them do it all the time,
not just when I'm with you.
4:19 [19]Oh, my dear children! I feel as if I'm going through labor pains for you again, and they
Eph 4:13 will continue until Christ is fully developed in your lives. [20]I wish I were with you right now
so I could change my tone. But at this distance I don't know how else to help you.

ABRAHAM'S TWO CHILDREN

[21]Tell me, you who want to live under the law, do you know what the law actually says?
4:22 [22]The Scriptures say that Abraham had two sons, one from his slave wife and one from his
Gen 16:15; 21:2 freeborn wife.* [23]The son of the slave wife was born in a human attempt to bring about the
4:23 fulfillment of God's promise. But the son of the freeborn wife was born as God's own fulfill-
Rom 9:7-9 ment of His promise.
[24]These two women serve as an illustration of God's two covenants. The first woman,
Hagar, represents Mount Sinai where people received the law that enslaved them. [25]And
now Jerusalem is just like Mount Sinai in Arabia,* because she and her children live in
4:26 slavery to the law. [26]But the other woman, Sarah, represents the heavenly Jerusalem. She
Heb 12:22 is the free woman, and she is our mother. [27]As Isaiah said,
Rev 3:12; 21:2, 10

4:27 "Rejoice, O childless woman,
*Isa 54:1 you who have never given birth!
4:28 Break into a joyful shout,
Gal 3:29 you who have never been in labor!
4:29 For the desolate woman now has more children
Gen 21:9 than the woman who lives with her husband!"*
4:30

Gen 21:10 [28]And you, dear brothers and sisters, are children of the promise, just like Isaac. [29]But
John 8:35 you are now being persecuted by those who want you to keep the law, just as Ishmael, the
4:31 child born by human effort, persecuted Isaac, the child born by the power of the Spirit.
Gal 3:29 [30]But what do the Scriptures say about that? "Get rid of the slave and her son, for the son of
5:1
John 8:32, 36 the slave woman will not share the inheritance with the free woman's son."* [31]So, dear broth-
Acts 15:10
Gal 2:4 ers and sisters, we are not children of the slave woman; we are children of the free woman.

4:12 Greek *brothers;* also in 4:28, 31. 4:22 See Gen 16:15; 21:2-3. 4:25 Greek *And Hagar, which is Mount Sinai in Arabia, is now like Jerusalem;* other manuscripts read *And Mount Sinai in Arabia is now like Jerusalem.* 4:27 Isa 54:1. 4:30 Gen 21:10.

4:14-16 When Paul first came to the Galatians with his illness, they received him hospitably and listened to his preaching with joy. It appeared that after the false teachers, or Jewish legalists, had arrived, the believers in the region began to look at Paul as an adversary, rather than a dear friend who spoke the truth in love. Belief in a false doctrine had severed the relationship between the Galatians and Paul.

4:24-26 Paul brings his argument to a climax against the Galatians who had adopted the views of the false teachers. In an attempt to expose their error, the apostle compares the relationship of Sarah and Isaac to that of Hagar and Ishmael (Genesis 16:1-4; 18:10-14; 21:1-10). God had promised Abraham a child of the covenant (Galatians 4:28). Unfortunately, Abraham chose to rely on his own strength—rather than relying on a supernatural act in Sarah's womb for the fulfillment of God's promises. The followers of the false teachers were in essence children of Hagar, for they belonged to those who relied on human effort for salvation. By way of contrast, those who belonged to Christ belonged to Sarah, for they were born out of a gracious act by God.

FREEDOM IN CHRIST

5:2
5 So Christ has truly set us free. Now make sure that you stay free, and don't get tied up Acts 15:1
again in slavery to the law. 5:3
[2]Listen! I, Paul, tell you this: If you are counting on circumcision to make you right with Gal 3:10
God, then Christ will be of no benefit to you. [3]I'll say it again. If you are trying to find favor 5:5
with God by being circumcised, you must obey every regulation in the whole law of Rom 8:23-24
Moses. [4]For if you are trying to make yourselves right with God by keeping the law, you 5:6 1 Cor 7:19
have been cut off from Christ! You have fallen away from God's grace. 1 Thes 1:3
[5]But we who live by the Spirit eagerly wait to receive by faith the righteousness God 5:7
has promised to us. [6]For when we place our faith in Christ Jesus, there is no benefit in 1 Cor 9:24
being circumcised or being uncircumcised. What is important is faith expressing itself in 5:8
love. Rom 8:28
[7]You were running the race so well. Who has held you back from following the truth? [8]It 5:9
certainly isn't God, for He is the One who called you to freedom. [9]This false teaching is like 1 Cor 5:6
a little yeast that spreads through the whole batch of dough! [10]I am trusting the Lord to 5:10 Gal 1:7

5:2-4 Paul reverses the argument of the false teachers who said that unless the Galatians were circumcised they could not be saved (Acts 15:1, 5). Paul goes further by claiming that if they do become circumcised, then they will not be saved. They will invalidate their claims of salvation by trusting in the law, rather than in Christ. Paul is confident that they will see things his way and continue to trust in Christ, yet at the same time he warns them of the eternal consequences of not believing him.

5:5 Paul describes God's righteousness both as something that is credited to the account of the Christian at the moment they have faith in God's promise of salvation (3:6) and as something that yet awaits the believer in the future. Believers are to wait in such a way that the hope for a complete and final righteousness takes shape in their lives and forms the way they think and act today.

MY RESPONSE TO GOD

Following the Spirit

GALATIANS 5

Have you ever been lost in an unfamiliar city? Even with the best maps and directions, driving alone in new territory can make you nervous. Sometimes you feel alone in your spiritual journey, not sure which way to turn, or whom to ask for help. How can you find the path of holy thinking, feeling, and living without a guide?

Jesus knew His people needed a guide for living a holy life in a chaotic world, so He sent the Holy Spirit, who guides and comforts believers (John 14:16-17). We can struggle against the direction that the Holy Spirit provides (Ephesians 4:30), or we can submit to His purifying presence and experience the full blessing He intends for every believer.

So what is this guidance of the Spirit like? Paul contrasts following the Spirit with "doing what your sinful nature craves" (Galatians 5:16). He says, "Those who are controlled by the Holy Spirit think about things that please the Spirit" (Romans 8:5). "Since we are living by the Spirit," Paul writes, "let us follow the Spirit's leading in every part of our lives" (Galatians 5:25). Following the Spirit has an emotional impact as well, as it produces "a life of goodness and peace and joy" (Romans 14:17).

Everyone feels lost sometimes. But God has promised to supply believers with a constant companion, a Guide and Friend, who will help us on our journey. Earnestly pray for the guidance of the Holy Spirit to be made very real in your life.

keep you from believing false teachings. God will judge that person, whoever he is, who
has been confusing you.
5:11 11 Dear brothers and sisters,* if I were still preaching that you must be circumcised—as
1 Cor 1:23 some say I do—why am I still being persecuted? If I were no longer preaching salvation
through the cross of Christ, no one would be offended. 12 I just wish that those trouble-
makers who want to mutilate you by circumcision would mutilate themselves.*
5:13 13 For you have been called to live in freedom, my brothers and sisters. But don't use
1 Pet 2:16 your freedom to satisfy your sinful nature. Instead, use your freedom to serve one another
5:14 *Lev 19:18 in love. 14 For the whole law can be summed up in this one command: "Love your neigh-
Rom 13:9 bor as yourself."* 15 But if you are always biting and devouring one another, watch out!
Beware of destroying one another.

LIVING BY THE SPIRIT'S POWER

5:16 Rom 8:4-6 16 So I say, let the Holy Spirit guide your lives. Then you won't be doing what your sinful
5:17 nature craves. 17 The sinful nature wants to do evil, which is just the opposite of what the
Rom 7:15-23 Spirit wants. And the Spirit gives us desires that are the opposite of what the sinful nature
desires. These two forces are constantly fighting each other, so you are not free to carry
5:18 out your good intentions. 18 But when you are directed by the Spirit, you are not under ob-
Rom 6:14; 8:14 ligation to the law of Moses.
5:19-21 Rom 13:12-13 19 When you follow the desires of your sinful nature, the results are very clear: sexual
1 Cor 6:9-10 immorality, impurity, lustful pleasures, 20 idolatry, sorcery, hostility, quarreling, jealousy,
Eph 5:5 outbursts of anger, selfish ambition, dissension, division, 21 envy, drunkenness, wild par-
Rev 22:15 ties, and other sins like these. Let me tell you again, as I have before, that anyone living
that sort of life will not inherit the Kingdom of God.
5:22 22 But the Holy Spirit produces this kind of fruit in our lives: love, joy, peace, patience,
Eph 5:9 kindness, goodness, faithfulness, 23 gentleness, and self-control. There is no law against
5:24 Rom 6:6 these things!
Col 3:5 24 Those who belong to Christ Jesus have nailed the passions and desires of their sinful
5:25 nature to His cross and crucified them there. 25 Since we are living by the Spirit, let us fol-
Rom 8:4 Gal 5:16 low the Spirit's leading in every part of our lives. 26 Let us not become conceited, or pro-
5:26 voke one another, or be jealous of one another.
Phil 2:3

5:11 Greek *Brothers;* similarly in 5:13. 5:12 Or *castrate themselves,* or *cut themselves off from you;* Greek reads *cut themselves off.* 5:14 Lev 19:18.

▸ GOD

5:13-15 A misuse of freedom. The wonderful freedom we have to enjoy life in Christ can almost be intoxicating after years of the slavery of sin. It is for good reason that Paul warns against abusing our freedom in Christ. We can abuse this freedom by adopting an attitude such as, "I'll sin today and ask forgiveness tomorrow," or "I'm free in Christ to do this, so I'll do it regardless of whom it hurts!" Christ has not freed us so that we can harm others, but rather we are freed to live a life of righteousness (Romans 6:1-4) that helps, not hurts our neighbor (Romans 13:8-14). Don't abuse your freedom; instead, use it wisely, building up those around you. (***See God****> God's Attributes> True> True freedom comes from abiding in God's truth,* TopicGuide page A18.)

▸ SPIRITUAL WARFARE

5:16-18 Winning the spiritual war. There is only one way to claim victory in the Christian life: Live by the Spirit. The false teachers presented the Galatians with two ways they could live their lives: by observing the law or by indulging their sinful desires. But trying to live up to an impossible standard will never enable us to live right before God, because our sinful nature is more powerful than any human effort for good. Paul provides the Galatians (and us) with a third option: living by the Spirit. If you are struggling with a particular sin in your life, don't rely solely on your own strength to conquer it—you will lose every time. We must ask the Spirit to transform our heart to live righteously. The war will be won in time; meanwhile, rely on the Spirit for strength to succeed now. (***See Spiritual Warfare****> Resisting Sin and Evil> Standing Firm> Empowered to obey,* TopicGuide page A46.)

5:19-21 Paul contrasts the desires of the sinful nature with the desires produced by the Spirit. Paul lists the ways that the sinful nature manifests itself in a person's life. The person who succumbs to the sinful nature believes that he or she is at the center of the universe. Paul condemns this lifestyle and declares that such a person will not inherit eternal life.

5:22-26 Those who belong to Christ no longer live for themselves, but walk according to the leading of the Spirit. In time, the Spirit's work in a person's life produces fruit that is contrary to the works of the sinful nature. Those who are led by the Spirit are no longer under the administration of the law, but they are victorious over the deeds of the flesh. Paul exhorts the believers to join him in a life that is characterized by the fruit of the Spirit and a denial of fleshly desires.

WE HARVEST WHAT WE PLANT

6 Dear brothers and sisters, if another believer* is overcome by some sin, you who are
godly* should gently and humbly help that person back onto the right path. And be
careful not to fall into the same temptation yourself. 2 Share each other's burdens, and in
this way obey the law of Christ. 3 If you think you are too important to help someone, you
are only fooling yourself. You are not that important.
4 Pay careful attention to your own work, for then you will get the satisfaction of a job
well done, and you won't need to compare yourself to anyone else. 5 For we are each re-
sponsible for our own conduct.
6 Those who are taught the word of God should provide for their teachers, sharing all
good things with them.
7 Don't be misled—you cannot mock the justice of God. You will always harvest what
you plant. 8 Those who live only to satisfy their own sinful nature will harvest decay and
death from that sinful nature. But those who live to please the Spirit will harvest ever-
lasting life from the Spirit. 9 So let's not get tired of doing what is good. At just the right
time we will reap a harvest of blessing if we don't give up. 10 Therefore, whenever we have
the opportunity, we should do good to everyone—especially to those in the family of faith.

PAUL'S FINAL ADVICE

11 NOTICE WHAT LARGE LETTERS I USE AS I WRITE THESE CLOSING WORDS IN MY OWN HANDWRITING.
12 Those who are trying to force you to be circumcised want to look good to others. They
don't want to be persecuted for teaching that the cross of Christ alone can save. 13 And
even those who advocate circumcision don't keep the whole law themselves. They only
want you to be circumcised so they can boast about it and claim you as their disciples.
14 As for me, may I never boast about anything except the cross of our Lord Jesus Christ.
Because of that cross,* my interest in this world has been crucified, and the world's interest
in me has also died. 15 It doesn't matter whether we have been circumcised or not. What
counts is whether we have been transformed into a new creation. 16 May God's peace and
mercy be upon all who live by this principle; they are the new people of God.*
17 From now on, don't let anyone trouble me with these things. For I bear on my body
the scars that show I belong to Jesus.
18 Dear brothers and sisters,* may the grace of our Lord Jesus Christ be with your spirit.
Amen.

6:1 1 Cor 2:15; Jas 5:19-20; 1 Jn 5:16
6:2 Rom 15:1
6:3 Rom 12:3; 1 Cor 3:18
6:4 2 Cor 13:5
6:5 Rom 14:12
6:6 1 Cor 9:11, 14
6:7 1 Cor 6:9; 2 Cor 9:6
6:8 Job 4:8; Rom 8:13
6:9 2 Thes 3:13
6:10 Eph 2:19
6:11 1 Cor 16:21
6:13 Rom 2:25
6:14 Rom 6:2, 6; 1 Cor 2:2; Gal 2:20
6:15 1 Cor 7:19; 2 Cor 5:17; Gal 5:6
6:17 2 Cor 1:5; 4:10
6:18 Rom 16:20

6:1a Greek *Brothers, if a man.* 6:1b Greek *spiritual.* 6:14 Or *Because of Him.* 6:16 Greek *this principle, and upon the Israel of God.* 6:18 Greek *Brothers.*

▸ CHURCH

6:1 Principle of restoration. Are you your brother's keeper? Contrary to what many prefer to believe, the Bible does not permit you to sit back and idly allow a fellow Christian to ruin his or her life. Instead, we are to actively help to restore that person (Matthew 18:15-20). But take no prideful pleasure in confronting people with their faults (Matthew 7:1-5; 1 Peter 4:8; 1 Corinthians 13:5, 7); after all, you have problems of your own. Instead, confront erring brothers and sisters in a spirit of gentleness, recognizing that it is only by God's grace that you are kept from committing the same sin. How can you help others get back on the right track? (***See Church****> Mission> Nurture> Developing maturity,* TopicGuide page A49.)

6:2 Previously, Paul explained that the entire Old Testament law could be summarized in one single command: "Love your neighbor as yourself" (Galatians 5:13-15). "Share each other's burdens" is a logical extension of the care and concern that marks the believer.

6:5 At first, it might seem that verses two and five contradict each other. Verse two teaches that we are responsible to bear one another's burdens, but in verse five Paul teaches that each person is responsible for his or her own actions. Verses two and five work together as complementary truths in the Christian life: We are responsible to God for one another and for ourselves.

6:12-13 Paul presents three motivations behind the false teachers' attempt to enforce circumcision upon all those who belong to Christ: 1) They are consumed with outward appearance, rather than a changed heart. 2) They would rather change the meaning of the gospel than face persecution for Christ. 3) They want to be able to claim the followers of Christ as followers of their movement.

6:14-15 Paul clarifies that his security is not wrapped up in observing or failing to observe a particular practice, but rather his confidence is based on Christ's work of salvation and His promise to transform us into a new creation (2 Corinthians 5:17; Ephesians 4:24; Colossians 3:10-11; Revelation 21:5).

EPHESIANS

PURPOSE

To make clear the new position and practices of those who believe in Christ.

Like an heir who is unaware of his or her inheritance, some followers of Jesus don't realize the incredible blessings they have in Jesus Christ. Clarifying the new standing believers have before God because of Christ's work forms the heart of Paul's letter to the Ephesians.

In this letter, Paul lays out for all Christians—not just those in Ephesus—both what it is that Jesus has done for them and what difference it should make in the way Christians live. Unlike Paul's other letters, his letter to the Ephesians doesn't address particular problems being faced by a local church, nor is there any clear indication that Paul is responding to questions or issues raised by the recipients. Paul is writing to help believers throughout the Roman world understand just what Jesus did for them and what difference that makes in their lives—at church, at home, and at work (Ephesians 4; 5:22–6:9).

DISCOVER GOD IN EPHESIANS

Paul's letter to the Ephesians makes it clear that he is truly "Trinitarian." That is, Paul recognizes that God has revealed Himself in the Bible as one divine being that eternally exists in three persons. This understanding of God is reflected in the various ways Paul refers to God in this letter.

God the Father: As Paul writes about God, he gives us glimpses of the Father. We see Him as the One who bestows all blessings (1:3), has adopted us into His own family (1:5; 2:19) and is "over all" (4:6).

God the Son: Throughout this letter, Paul tells us about what Jesus Christ has done. Thus, we see the Son as the One who purchased our freedom from sin through His death (1:7), is the center of the Father's plan (1:9-10), is the real authority over the church (1:22-23), brings us near to God through His death (2:13), and loves the church as a husband loves his own wife (5:25).

God the Spirit: The Father bestows blessings through the work of the Son, which are mediated to every Christian by the Spirit of God. Paul describes the Spirit as the One who marks us out as God's own (1:13-14; 4:30), indwells those who believe (2:22), enables us to live as members of God's family (5:18), and empowers our battle prayers (6:18).

GROWING THROUGH EPHESIANS

Paul's letter describes the Christian's life as flowing from God and His eternal plan. This refreshing perspective is jarring to many self-centered approaches to Christian living. Step by step, Paul lays out a God-centered, God-initiated way of viewing our lives.

God's Plan Includes Us. God has chosen to pour out blessings on those who place their faith in Jesus (1:3-8) and He will bring everything under the authority of Jesus (1:10). This plan of God is not independent from our participation so Paul then prays for those he is writing to, that they would be granted genuine understanding of this plan (1:15-23). Our understanding might be limited by maturity and circumstances, but it is God's will that we believe, by faith, that He is busy accomplishing His eternal plan.

God Breaks Into the Lives of Individuals. Some have said, "God is a gentleman," but that's not how He appears in Ephesians. Without asking anyone's permission, He chose those He would redeem and make holy (1:4). He takes those who are spiritually dead, whose only spiritual activity is cooperating with Satan's plans (2:1-2) and makes them alive and sets them free by a gift of His grace (2:8-10). He takes those who were culturally alienated and puts them in a new family of faith (2:11–3:13). We can pray and share the gospel aggressively, knowing God can save and sanctify whomever He desires.

The Plan of God. In the lives of ordinary Christians, His plan practically works itself out. Living as this one new people (4:1-16), living as those spiritually alive (2:1; 4:17–6:9), and living as those who are participants in this grand work God is doing (6:10-20) is the proper response to a sovereign God's promises. The truth Paul shares with Christians he prays into their lives. The truth he prays into their lives is the truth he invites them to live out.

DISCOVERY VERSES

For we are God's masterpiece. He has created us anew in Christ Jesus, so we can do the good things He planned for us long ago. (EPHESIANS 2:10)

Therefore I, a prisoner for serving the Lord, beg you to lead a life worthy of your calling, for you have been called by God. Always be humble and gentle. Be patient with each other, making allowance for each other's faults because of your love. Make every effort to keep yourselves united in the Spirit, binding yourselves together with peace. (EPHESIANS 4:1-3)

EPHESIANS FACTS

Author: Paul (1:1), the apostle and church planter, penned this letter from house arrest in Rome as he awaited his hearing before Caesar (as recorded in Acts 28).

Written to: Although this letter was apparently written to the believers in the city of Ephesus, there are indications that Paul intended it to be widely circulated throughout the churches in Asia Minor. For example, the letter does not close with personal greetings, unlike Paul's letters to specific congregations with whom he was acquainted. Paul had spent three years in Ephesus (Acts 19) and dearly loved the church there (Acts 20:13-36), but this letter seems to have a broader audience. He appears to have his friends in Ephesus in mind, but he writes to the church at large.

Date of writing: As the book of Acts draws to a close, Paul is awaiting his hearing before Caesar. This would have been sometime around AD 60–62, late in the ministry of the apostle, after he had already been in prison awaiting trial. Ephesians is one of four letters (the others being Philippians, Colossians, and Philemon) that he wrote at that time (Ephesians 3:1; 4:1; 6:20).

Setting: The letter was written to believers in the city of Ephesus (Acts 18:19-21), a strategic city that functioned as a commercial center in ancient Asia Minor (modern Turkey). Prior to writing this letter, Paul lived in Ephesus for three years (Acts 18:23–19:41).

OUTLINE

- **EPHESIANS 1:1-14**—Praise of God's Plan
- **EPHESIANS 1:15-23**—Prayer for God's Power
- **EPHESIANS 1:24–3:13**—Position in Christ
- **EPHESIANS 3:14-21**—Prayer for the Church
- **EPHESIANS 4:1–6:24**—Practical Implications of Our Life in Christ

1:3 Eph 1:20; 2:6
1:4 2 Thes 2:13; 1 Pet 1:2, 20
1:5 Rom 8:15, 29
1:6 Rom 3:24; Col 1:13
1:7 1 Cor 6:20; Col 1:14; Heb 9:12; Rev 5:9
1:9 Rom 16:25; Eph 3:3, 9
1:10 Mark 1:15; Gal 4:4; Col 1:16, 20
1:11 Rom 8:28-29; Eph 3:11
1:12 Eph 1:6, 14
1:13 2 Cor 1:22; Eph 4:30; Col 1:5
1:14 Rom 8:23; 2 Cor 1:22; 5:5

GREETINGS FROM PAUL

1 This letter is from Paul, chosen by the will of God to be an apostle of Christ Jesus.
I am writing to God's holy people in Ephesus,* who are faithful followers of Christ Jesus.
2May God our Father and the Lord Jesus Christ give you grace and peace.

SPIRITUAL BLESSINGS

3All praise to God, the Father of our Lord Jesus Christ, who has blessed us with every spiri-
tual blessing in the heavenly realms because we are united with Christ. 4Even before He
made the world, God loved us and chose us in Christ to be holy and without fault in His
eyes. 5God decided in advance to adopt us into His own family by bringing us to Himself
through Jesus Christ. This is what He wanted to do, and it gave Him great pleasure. 6So we
praise God for the glorious grace He has poured out on us who belong to His dear Son.*
7He is so rich in kindness and grace that He purchased our freedom with the blood of His
Son and forgave our sins. 8He has showered His kindness on us, along with all wisdom
and understanding.

9God has now revealed to us His mysterious plan regarding Christ, a plan to fulfill His
own good pleasure. 10And this is the plan: At the right time He will bring everything to-
gether under the authority of Christ—everything in heaven and on earth. 11Furthermore,
because we are united with Christ, we have received an inheritance from God,* for He
chose us in advance, and He makes everything work out according to His plan.

12God's purpose was that we Jews who were the first to trust in Christ would bring praise
and glory to God. 13And now you Gentiles have also heard the truth, the Good News that
God saves you. And when you believed in Christ, He identified you as His own* by giving
you the Holy Spirit, whom He promised long ago. 14The Spirit is God's guarantee that He
will give us the inheritance He promised and that He has purchased us to be His own peo-
ple. He did this so we would praise and glorify Him.

1:1 The most ancient manuscripts do not include *in Ephesus.* 1:6 Greek *to us in the beloved.* 1:11 Or *we have become God's inheritance.* 1:13 Or *He put His seal on you.*

1:1 As in nearly all of his letters, Paul opens by affirming that he serves as an apostle in the service of Christ Jesus by God's choice. This idea of God's choice will have implications for all of the letter's recipients as it unfolds.

1:2 The first chapter of Ephesians unfolds a logical progression of Paul's thoughts about the grace of God. The benefits of God's grace are blessings in heaven (1:3) and the forgiveness of sin (1:7). The beginning of God's grace is His ancient decision (1:4-5). The purpose of His grace is our personal holiness (1:4) and our union with Christ (1:10). The great privilege of God's grace is the honor of adoption into His family (1:5). The price of God's grace is the very blood of Christ's sacrifice (1:7) and preaching is the means of His grace, leading to faith in Christ (1:12-13). The assurance that this grace is active in our life comes through the tangible presence of the Holy Spirit (1:13-14).

1:3 Paul uses a wordplay in this verse. In the original Greek, it says that we "bless" God, since He has "blessed" us. For us to bless God means we speak well of Him. For God to bless us means that He does good works to us.

▸ ADOPTION

1:3 What more could you ask for! Every journey, no matter the length, requires both appropriate planning and appropriate provisions. In order to reach the intended destination, the traveler needs to know how to get there and have what is necessary to reach the goal. Every follower of Jesus is on a journey; it began when we first came to faith in Christ and will culminate in our complete transformation into His glorious image. God has set the goal and laid out the plan in grace. How will you reach the destination? What provisions are available for this journey? Paul tells us that God has provided "every spiritual blessing" needed. Nothing is lacking; all has been provided for this great adventure. (***See Adoption****> With Christ> United with Christ> Provides blessings*, TopicGuide page A37.)

1:4 God chose believers in Jesus to be His own people (Romans 8:29-33; Colossians 3:12; 1 Thessalonians 1:4; Titus 1:1). This state of being "in Christ" is connected to God's choice (see 1 Corinthians 1:26-31). The idea of being united to Christ is variously stated and expanded throughout Paul's writings (Romans 7:4; 12:5; 1 Corinthians 1:30; 4:15; Galatians 3:27; Ephesians 2:10; 3:8) as well as by other authors in the New Testament (1 Peter 5:14; 1 John 2:27).

1:9 To speak of God's "mysterious plan" is not to say that He has been hiding something; He has been progressively revealing His intentions, and now, in and through Jesus Christ, the fullness of that plan can be known—that there is redemption through faith in Jesus.

1:13-14 Part of the blessings we receive through union with Christ is the gift of God's Spirit. Having made us His own, God sends His Spirit into our lives to "[identify us] as His own" and to "guarantee" the fullness of the blessings that will one day be ours when we are fully united to Christ in heaven.

PAUL'S PRAYER FOR SPIRITUAL WISDOM

15Ever since I first heard of your strong faith in the Lord Jesus and your love for God's peo-
ple everywhere,* 16I have not stopped thanking God for you. I pray for you constantly,
17asking God, the glorious Father of our Lord Jesus Christ, to give you spiritual wisdom*
and insight so that you might grow in your knowledge of God. 18I pray that your hearts will
be flooded with light so that you can understand the confident hope He has given to those
He called—His holy people who are His rich and glorious inheritance.*
19I also pray that you will understand the incredible greatness of God's power for us
who believe Him. This is the same mighty power 20that raised Christ from the dead and
seated Him in the place of honor at God's right hand in the heavenly realms. 21Now He is
far above any ruler or authority or power or leader or anything else—not only in this world
but also in the world to come. 22God has put all things under the authority of Christ and
has made Him head over all things for the benefit of the church. 23And the church is His
body; it is made full and complete by Christ, who fills all things everywhere with Himself.

1:16 Col 1:9
1:18 Acts 26:18; Eph 1:11; 4:4
1:19 Eph 3:7, 16; 6:10; Phil 3:21
1:21 Phil 2:9; Col 1:16; 2:10
1:22 Eph 4:15; Col 1:18; 2:19
1:23 Eph 3:19; 4:10; Col 1:19; 3:11

1:15 Some manuscripts read *your faithfulness to the Lord Jesus and to God's people everywhere.* 1:17 Or *to give you the Spirit of wisdom.* 1:18 Or *called, and the rich and glorious inheritance He has given to His holy people.*

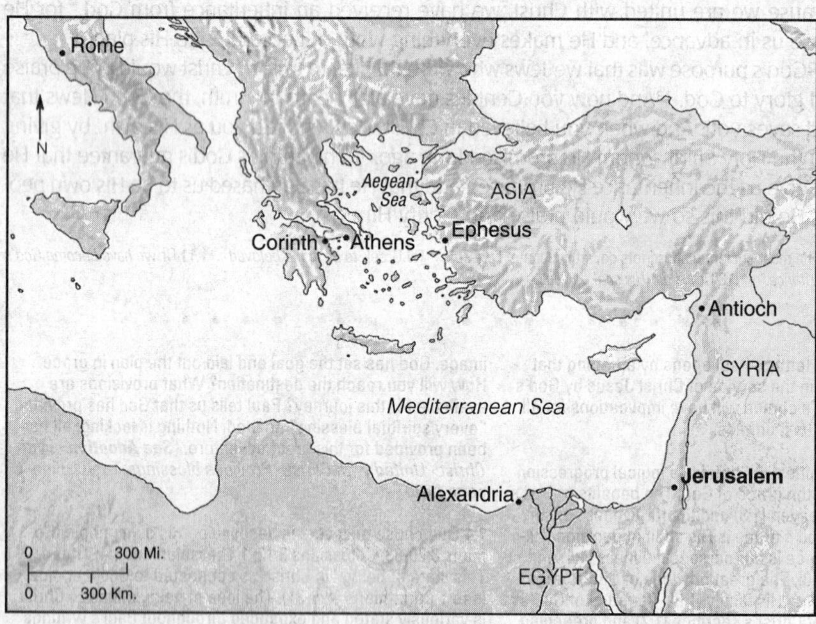

LOCATION OF EPHESUS
Ephesus was a strategic city, ranking in importance with Alexandria in Egypt and Antioch of Syria as a port. It lay on the most western edge of Asia Minor (modern-day Turkey), the most important port on the Aegean Sea on the main route from Rome to the east.

▸ WORSHIP

1:15-19 Intentional prayer. Prayer can occasionally degenerate into a social habit—like greeting people with "Good morning," or "How are you?" or responding "Fine, thank you" to the same no matter how bad you are actually feeling. Prayer should be more intentional, mindful of what we are saying and strategically planned to change our world according to His will. Paul's comments regarding his prayers can be a great model for us. Paul prays for fresh and profound spiritual experiences for those he knows. He invites God to do something supernatural in the lives of his friends. That's the kind of praying that makes a difference in a life! Since we all spend relatively little time in prayer, make your time count—plan your prayers and make sure they are big enough to match the size of God's abilities. (***See Worship> NT> Prayer> Examples> Paul> For Others> To grow in a spirit of wisdom and revelation,*** TopicGuide page A33.)

1:17 Paul does not pray that these Christians simply learn more "facts" about God. His prayer for their growth in spiritual wisdom and understanding and the "knowledge of God" is a prayer for an experiential grasp of the reality of life lived in relationship with this great God.

1:21-22 When Paul writes about "any ruler or authority or power or leader," he uses language that was commonly used to refer to spiritual beings, particularly those associated with the pagan religions of the day. Ephesus was a center for the worship of the Roman goddess Diana. Therefore, Christ's exaltation over all rival spiritual powers was a present reality for Paul's audience, not just a vague theory.

2:1 Eph 2:5; Col 2:13
2:2 Eph 5:6, 8; 6:12; Col 3:7
2:3 Gal 5:24; Col 3:6
2:5 Rom 5:6; 6:4; Eph 2:1; Col 2:13
2:6 Eph 1:3, 20; Col 2:12
2:8 John 4:10
2:9 Rom 3:28; 2 Tim 1:9; Titus 3:5

MADE ALIVE WITH CHRIST

2 Once you were dead because of your disobedience and your many sins. 2You used
to live in sin, just like the rest of the world, obeying the devil—the commander of the
powers in the unseen world.* He is the spirit at work in the hearts of those who refuse to
obey God. 3All of us used to live that way, following the passionate desires and inclina-
tions of our sinful nature. By our very nature we were subject to God's anger, just like
everyone else.
4But God is so rich in mercy, and He loved us so much, 5that even though we were dead
because of our sins, He gave us life when He raised Christ from the dead. (It is only by
God's grace that you have been saved!) 6For He raised us from the dead along with Christ
and seated us with Him in the heavenly realms because we are united with Christ Jesus.
7So God can point to us in all future ages as examples of the incredible wealth of His grace
and kindness toward us, as shown in all He has done for us who are united with Christ
Jesus.
8God saved you by His grace when you believed. And you can't take credit for this; it is a
gift from God. 9Salvation is not a reward for the good things we have done, so none of us
can boast about it. 10For we are God's masterpiece. He has created us anew in Christ Jesus,
so we can do the good things He planned for us long ago.

2:2 Greek *obeying the commander of the power of the air.*

2:1-3 Although Paul never identifies those who have come to know Jesus in faith as "sinners" (he always identifies them along the lines of "the chosen" or "holy people"), he doesn't want them to forget what they were rescued from by the grace of God and through the work of Christ Jesus.

2:3 For all the insistence on human "free will," Paul makes it clear that every human being is born with an evil nature that predisposes us to resist God and that giving in to that nature brings us under God's just judgment.

▸ GOD
2:4 An amazing juncture. What can turn someone's life around, bringing health and wholeness out of brokenness and disarray? Is it good luck? Fate? The right genes? Good parenting? Paul has described (2:1-3) what life was like for all of his readers, and it's not a pretty picture. His readers were spiritually bankrupt, enemies of God, and trapped in their own sin. What made the difference? Paul clearly states: "But God . . ." God acted in mercy, and that made all the difference in their lives, and God's mercy continues to deliver us today. In what ways do you need a "But God" moment in your life? (***See God***> *God's Attributes> Merciful> God's rich mercy gives believers new life in Christ,* TopicGuide page A17.)

2:8-9 The salvation we experience is not of ourselves—meaning we could not have conceived it. Second, it is not of works—meaning even if we could have conceived it we could never have achieved it. From start to finish, the life we enjoy with God is purely a gift.

2:10 All of salvation, even the good works and repentance that follow genuine belief, come from God.

BECAUSE GOD IS MERCIFUL

He forgives me of my sins when I sincerely confess them.

God is so rich in mercy, and He loved us so much, that even though we were dead because of our sins, He gave us life.

EPHESIANS 2:4-5

FOR THE NEXT *GOD IS MERCIFUL* FEATURE SEE PAGE 2190.

ONENESS AND PEACE IN CHRIST

11 Don't forget that you Gentiles used to be outsiders. You were called "uncircumcised hea-
thens" by the Jews, who were proud of their circumcision, even though it affected only
their bodies and not their hearts. 12 In those days you were living apart from Christ. You
were excluded from citizenship among the people of Israel, and you did not know the cov-
enant promises God had made to them. You lived in this world without God and without
hope. 13 But now you have been united with Christ Jesus. Once you were far away from
God, but now you have been brought near to Him through the blood of Christ.

14 For Christ Himself has brought peace to us. He united Jews and Gentiles into one peo-
ple when, in His own body on the cross, He broke down the wall of hostility that separated
us. 15 He did this by ending the system of law with its commandments and regulations. He
made peace between Jews and Gentiles by creating in Himself one new people from the
two groups. 16 Together as one body, Christ reconciled both groups to God by means of His
death on the cross, and our hostility toward each other was put to death.

17 He brought this Good News of peace to you Gentiles who were far away from Him,
and peace to the Jews who were near. 18 Now all of us can come to the Father through the
same Holy Spirit because of what Christ has done for us.

2:11 Col 2:11
2:12 Rom 9:4; 1 Thes 4:13
2:13 Col 1:20
2:14 1 Cor 12:13
2:15 2 Cor 5:17; Gal 3:28; Col 1:21-22; 2:14
2:16 Col 1:20
2:17 Isa 57:19; Zech 9:10
2:18 Eph 3:12; 4:4

2:11-13 Before Christ came, the world was divided into two groups of people: Jews and non-Jews (the Gentiles). God had identified the Jews as His own and gave promises through them for what He was going to do in the world. With the coming of Jesus, God began to unfold His ultimate plan to join the whole world together.

▸ ADOPTION
2:14-18 No grounds for separation. Competition seems to drive much of life. Whether it is two companies vying for customers, two athletes striving for a medal, or two people seeking the same person's favor, the "us versus them" mentality is everywhere. There is, however, one place where all such adversarial thinking is out of place: the church. Although historically religious animosity exists between Jew and Gentile, Paul writes that because of the work of Christ, all such divisions are removed. Because we approach the same Father through the same Spirit because of the work of the one Savior, we are all "on the same team." Embrace people of other denominations, and do what you can to demonstrate to a watching world that Jesus has united His church for one purpose—to glorify God and enjoy Him forever. (***See Adoption****> With Christ> United with Christ> One in/with Christ,* TopicGuide page A37.)

2:15 We learn from Jesus' own teaching in Matthew 5:17-19 that the Old Testament law was not abolished by the coming of the gospel. What Paul is saying here is that Jesus' life, death, and resurrection bridges the barrier between Jews and Gentiles that was part of the law (Exodus 12:43-48).

2:18 Paul strongly affirms the triune nature of God: We draw near to God the Father through God the Spirit because of the work of God the Son. Ephesians 1 demonstrates his assumption of the Trinity by his description of redemption coming through the Father (1:3), the Son (1:9-12), and the Holy Spirit (1:13-14). Paul saw no contradiction in the idea that God exists as a unified whole (1 Corinthians 8:6) and as a Trinity.

BECAUSE GOD
NEVER CHANGES

My future is secure and eternal.

For we are God's masterpiece. He has created us anew in Christ Jesus,
so we can do the good things He planned for us long ago.

EPHESIANS 2:10

FOR THE NEXT *GOD NEVER CHANGES* FEATURE SEE PAGE 2137.

2:19
A TEMPLE FOR THE LORD
Eph 2:12 19 So now you Gentiles are no longer strangers and foreigners. You are citizens along with
2:20 all of God's holy people. You are members of God's family. 20 Together, we are His house,
Ps 118:22 Isa 28:16 built on the foundation of the apostles and the prophets. And the cornerstone is Christ
Matt 16:18 Jesus Himself. 21 We are carefully joined together in Him, becoming a holy temple for the
Acts 4:11 1 Cor 3:11 Lord. 22 Through Him you Gentiles are also being made part of this dwelling where God
1 Pet 2:4-8 Rev 21:14 lives by His Spirit.

3:1
GOD'S MYSTERIOUS PLAN REVEALED
Eph 4:1 3 When I think of all this, I, Paul, a prisoner of Christ Jesus for the benefit of you
2 Tim 1:8 Gentiles* . . . 2 assuming, by the way, that you know God gave me the special respon-
3:3 Eph 1:9-10 sibility of extending His grace to you Gentiles. 3 As I briefly wrote earlier, God Himself re-
Col 1:26 vealed His mysterious plan to me. 4 As you read what I have written, you will understand
3:6 my insight into this plan regarding Christ. 5 God did not reveal it to previous generations,
Eph 2:14-16 but now by His Spirit He has revealed it to His holy apostles and prophets.
3:7 6 And this is God's plan: Both Gentiles and Jews who believe the Good News share
Rom 15:18 Col 1:23, 25 equally in the riches inherited by God's children. Both are part of the same body, and both
enjoy the promise of blessings because they belong to Christ Jesus.* 7 By God's grace and
3:8 1 Cor 15:9-10 mighty power, I have been given the privilege of serving Him by spreading this Good News.
3:9 8 Though I am the least deserving of all God's people, He graciously gave me the privi-
Rom 16:25 lege of telling the Gentiles about the endless treasures available to them in Christ. 9 I was
3:10 Rom 11:33 chosen to explain to everyone* this mysterious plan that God, the Creator of all things, had
1 Cor 2:7 kept secret from the beginning.
Eph 1:21; 6:12 10 God's purpose in all this was to use the church to display His wisdom in its rich variety
1 Pet 1:12 to all the unseen rulers and authorities in the heavenly places. 11 This was His eternal plan,
3:11 Eph 1:11 which He carried out through Christ Jesus our Lord.
12 Because of Christ and our faith in Him,* we can now come boldly and confidently into
3:12 Eph 2:18 God's presence. 13 So please don't lose heart because of my trials here. I am suffering for
Heb 4:16 you, so you should feel honored.
3:14

Phil 2:10
PAUL'S PRAYER FOR SPIRITUAL GROWTH
3:16 Phil 4:13, 19 14 When I think of all this, I fall to my knees and pray to the Father,* 15 the Creator of every-
Col 1:11 thing in heaven and on earth.* 16 I pray that from His glorious, unlimited resources He will
3:17 empower you with inner strength through His Spirit. 17 Then Christ will make His home in
John 14:23 Col 2:7 your hearts as you trust in Him. Your roots will grow down into God's love and keep you

3:1 Paul resumes this thought in verse 14: "When I think of all this, I fall to my knees and pray to the Father." 3:6 Or *because they are united with Christ Jesus.* 3:9 Some manuscripts omit *to everyone.* 3:12 Or *Because of Christ's faithfulness.* 3:14 Some manuscripts read *the Father of our Lord Jesus Christ.* 3:15 Or *from whom every family in heaven and on earth takes its name.*

2:22 Our God is an unlimited God; He dwells in the vastness of space and in the hearts of His people. However, the believing community is the "dwelling" where God lives through the active presence of the Spirit. Both the community and the individuals in the community exhibit manifestations of the presence of God (John 14:17; 1 Corinthians 3:16-17; 2 Corinthians 6:16).

3:3 By speaking about God's "mysterious plan," Paul is not referring to facts that are only known by God and himself. Paul is referring to a facet of God's redemptive work that had been previously unrevealed. God revealed this plan by the Spirit to the people of God (3:5).

3:8 Paul's description of himself throughout his writings has subtle differences, yet similar themes. (Compare 1 Corinthians 15:9 and 1 Timothy 1:15-16; also see 2 Corinthians 10–13.)

▸ WORSHIP

3:14-21 The need for growth. In His exchange with a woman in the city of Sychar, Jesus said, "If you only knew the gift God has for you and who you are speaking to, you would ask Me, and I would give you living water" (John 4:10). That's the case for all of us. We can ask God for what our souls need for growth, and Paul's prayer here is a great model of what to ask for. Notice that he is praying for those who already have a relationship with God through Christ. Also, notice the radical and wonderful things he prays for. He's asking God to work in the souls of believers to enrich their experience of Christ's life in them. He's asking for a work of the Spirit that would revitalize and enliven their grasp of God's love. All that is needed for growth in Christ is available, if only we would ask. (***See Worship***> *NT> Prayer> Examples> Paul> For Others> To be filled up to all the fullness of God,* TopicGuide page A33.)

strong. 18And may you have the power to understand, as all God's people should, how
wide, how long, how high, and how deep His love is. 19May you experience the love of
Christ, though it is too great to understand fully. Then you will be made complete with all
the fullness of life and power that comes from God.
20Now all glory to God, who is able, through His mighty power at work within us, to ac-
complish infinitely more than we might ask or think. 21Glory to Him in the church and in
Christ Jesus through all generations forever and ever! Amen.

UNITY IN THE BODY

4 Therefore I, a prisoner for serving the Lord, beg you to lead a life worthy of your call-
ing, for you have been called by God. 2Always be humble and gentle. Be patient with
each other, making allowance for each other's faults because of your love. 3Make every
effort to keep yourselves united in the Spirit, binding yourselves together with peace. 4For
there is one body and one Spirit, just as you have been called to one glorious hope for the
future. 5There is one Lord, one faith, one baptism, 6and one God and Father, who is over
all and in all and living through all.
7However, He has given each one of us a special gift* through the generosity of Christ.
8That is why the Scriptures say,

"When He ascended to the heights,
He led a crowd of captives
and gave gifts to His people."*

9Notice that it says "He ascended." This clearly means that Christ also descended to our
lowly world.* 10And the same One who descended is the One who ascended higher than
all the heavens, so that He might fill the entire universe with Himself.
11Now these are the gifts Christ gave to the church: the apostles, the prophets, the evan-
gelists, and the pastors and teachers. 12Their responsibility is to equip God's people to do
His work and build up the church, the body of Christ. 13This will continue until we all come
to such unity in our faith and knowledge of God's Son that we will be mature in the Lord,
measuring up to the full and complete standard of Christ.
14Then we will no longer be immature like children. We won't be tossed and blown
about by every wind of new teaching. We will not be influenced when people try to trick us
with lies so clever they sound like the truth. 15Instead, we will speak the truth in love, grow-

3:18 John 1:16; Col 2:9-10
3:19 Eph 1:23; Col 2:10
3:20 Eph 1:19-20; Col 1:29
4:1 Eph 3:1; Phil 1:7, 13
4:2 Col 3:12-13
4:4 Rom 12:5; 1 Cor 12:12-13; Eph 2:16, 18
4:5 1 Cor 8:6
4:6 Rom 11:36
4:7 Rom 12:3; 1 Cor 12:7
4:9 John 3:13; Acts 2:27; 1 Pet 3:18
4:12 1 Cor 12:27
4:13 Eph 1:23; Col 1:28
4:14 1 Cor 14:20; Eph 6:11
4:15 Eph 1:22

4:7 Greek *a grace.* 4:8 Ps 68:18. 4:9 Or *to the lowest parts of the earth.*

3:20-21 This blessing or benediction from Paul signals a transition from the first half of his letter, which is more theoretical, to the latter half, which is more practical. It might also show that the content of the first half of this letter is taken from an earlier letter that ended here, but the version God saw fit to include in Scripture was amended to include more concrete teachings on the Christian life.

4:1 This half of the letter is devoted to helping the reader live in the light of who God is and what He has done. The calling of God is significant only if the One doing the calling has the authority and the right to command and empower the one who is called.

4:4-6 Given the topic set in 2:11–3:11, Paul's repetition of "one" six times in these verses (and more in 4:10-11) cannot be overlooked as a coincidence. Paul wants his audience to recognize God's will for unity among His people. This cannot be manifested until they see themselves as "one" unit and not individual groups of people with their own claims and agendas.

4:8 Paul quotes from and summarizes the content of Psalm 68; specifically, that God, victorious over all powers, now gives strength and gifts to His people.

4:11-13 In some religious groups, the leaders are served by the status quo. This is not the case in Jesus' kingdom (see Mark 10:41-45). Here, the leaders are servants who Christ Jesus gives for the growth and good of the church.

▸ WORSHIP

4:11-16 Growing up healthy. Not everyone has a "green thumb"; some are more successful in raising plants and flowers than others. But when it comes right down to it, the process is not all that complex. With a little attention to the proper environment and the necessary ingredients for growth, most green things will grow. That's a great picture for what God is doing in every church; He is tending to the proper environment and the necessary ingredients for growth. As you find yourself loving others in a local church, and as you partake in the gifts God has given to the church, growth will follow. Make sure you and your family are "planted" in a place where you can grow: a church where love and relationships can prosper. (***See Worship****> NT> Prayer> Examples> Paul> For Others> To grow in spiritual maturity,* TopicGuide page A33.)

ing in every way more and more like Christ, who is the head of His body, the church. 16 He makes the whole body fit together perfectly. As each part does its own special work, it helps the other parts grow, so that the whole body is healthy and growing and full of love.

LIVING AS CHILDREN OF LIGHT

17 With the Lord's authority I say this: Live no longer as the Gentiles do, for they are hopelessly confused. 18 Their minds are full of darkness; they wander far from the life God gives because they have closed their minds and hardened their hearts against Him. 19 They have no sense of shame. They live for lustful pleasure and eagerly practice every kind of impurity.

20 But that isn't what you learned about Christ. 21 Since you have heard about Jesus and have learned the truth that comes from Him, 22 throw off your old sinful nature and your former way of life, which is corrupted by lust and deception. 23 Instead, let the Spirit renew your thoughts and attitudes. 24 Put on your new nature, created to be like God—truly righteous and holy.

25 So stop telling lies. Let us tell our neighbors the truth, for we are all parts of the same body. 26 And "don't sin by letting anger control you."* Don't let the sun go down while you are still angry, 27 for anger gives a foothold to the devil.

28 If you are a thief, quit stealing. Instead, use your hands for good hard work, and then give generously to others in need. 29 Don't use foul or abusive language. Let everything you say be good and helpful, so that your words will be an encouragement to those who hear them.

30 And do not bring sorrow to God's Holy Spirit by the way you live. Remember, He has identified you as His own,* guaranteeing that you will be saved on the day of redemption.

31 Get rid of all bitterness, rage, anger, harsh words, and slander, as well as all types of evil behavior. 32 Instead, be kind to each other, tenderhearted, forgiving one another, just as God through Christ has forgiven you.

LIVING IN THE LIGHT

5 Imitate God, therefore, in everything you do, because you are His dear children. 2 Live a life filled with love, following the example of Christ. He loved us* and offered Himself as a sacrifice for us, a pleasing aroma to God.

3 Let there be no sexual immorality, impurity, or greed among you. Such sins have no place among God's people. 4 Obscene stories, foolish talk, and coarse jokes—these are not for you. Instead, let there be thankfulness to God. 5 You can be sure that no immoral, impure, or greedy person will inherit the Kingdom of Christ and of God. For a greedy person is an idolater, worshiping the things of this world.

6 Don't be fooled by those who try to excuse these sins, for the anger of God will fall on all who disobey Him. 7 Don't participate in the things these people do. 8 For once you were

4:16 Col 2:19 **4:19** Rom 1:24; Col 3:5 **4:22** Rom 6:6; Col 3:5, 8-9; Jas 1:21 **4:23** Rom 12:2 **4:24** 2 Cor 5:17; Col 3:10 **4:25** Col 3:8-9 **4:28** 1 Thes 4:11 **4:29** Matt 12:36; Rom 14:19; Col 3:8 **4:30** Isa 63:10; Eph 1:13-14; 1 Thes 5:19 **4:31** Col 3:8; 1 Pet 2:1 **4:32** Col 3:12-13 **5:1** Matt 5:48 **5:3** Col 3:5 **5:5** 1 Cor 6:9-10 **5:6** Rom 1:18 **5:8** John 8:12; Eph 2:2

4:26 Ps 4:4. 4:30 Or *has put His seal on you.* 5:2 Some manuscripts read *loved you.*

▸ ADOPTION

4:22-24 Being what you are. Paul has already made it clear that this life we have in Christ is a gift (Ephesians 2:4-9). It's not the product of what we do; we don't earn life by living well. So what is the motivation to live right? The apostle puts it in simple terms: We are to live new kinds of lives because we already have a new kind of life! We don't live differently in order to obtain new life, but we live differently because the new life we have already received is flowing out from us. Rather than constantly wondering if you are good enough to do ministry or to pray effectively, start believing that God has already made you that way—and get to work! Move into the action that accompanies genuine belief. (***See Adoption> With Christ> New Nature,*** TopicGuide page A36.)

4:30 This verse explains that the Holy Spirit is a person who can be emotionally impacted by our unrepentant sin. The Holy Spirit is also an identifier, a seal showing all creation that God has put His mark on us and intends to redeem us completely. The Spirit also convicts of sin (John 16:8), comforts (John 14:16), and renews us (1 Corinthians 6:11). These activities point out the divinity and personal interest of the Holy Spirit in our redemption.

5:5 Paul is not reverting to saying that heaven can be gained by doing the right things or avoiding the wrong behavior. He is simply pointing out that those who don't have a relationship with God through Christ Jesus are characterized by certain behaviors and that those who truly have a relationship with God no longer live that way.

5:7-12 Through his command to not participate in "the things these people do" Paul encourages us to limit our relationships with unbelievers. Believers may have a degree of love and fellowship with unbelievers, but there are practical limits, such as marriage (2 Corinthians 6:15-17) and active involvement in their sinful behaviors.

full of darkness, but now you have light from the Lord. So live as people of light! [9]For this
light within you produces only what is good and right and true.
[10]Carefully determine what pleases the Lord. [11]Take no part in the worthless deeds of
evil and darkness; instead, expose them. [12]It is shameful even to talk about the things that
ungodly people do in secret. [13]But their evil intentions will be exposed when the light
shines on them, [14]for the light makes everything visible. This is why it is said,

"Awake, O sleeper,
rise up from the dead,
and Christ will give you light."

LIVING BY THE SPIRIT'S POWER

[15]So be careful how you live. Don't live like fools, but like those who are wise. [16]Make the
most of every opportunity in these evil days. [17]Don't act thoughtlessly, but understand
what the Lord wants you to do. [18]Don't be drunk with wine, because that will ruin your life.
Instead, be filled with the Holy Spirit, [19]singing psalms and hymns and spiritual songs
among yourselves, and making music to the Lord in your hearts. [20]And give thanks for
everything to God the Father in the name of our Lord Jesus Christ.

SPIRIT-GUIDED RELATIONSHIPS: WIVES AND HUSBANDS

[21]And further, submit to one another out of reverence for Christ.
[22]For wives, this means submit to your husbands as to the Lord. [23]For a husband is the head
of His wife as Christ is the head of the church. He is the Savior of His body, the church. [24]As the
church submits to Christ, so you wives should submit to your husbands in everything.
[25]For husbands, this means love your wives, just as Christ loved the church. He gave up
His life for her [26]to make her holy and clean, washed by the cleansing of God's word.* [27]He
did this to present her to Himself as a glorious church without a spot or wrinkle or any
other blemish. Instead, she will be holy and without fault. [28]In the same way, husbands
ought to love their wives as they love their own bodies. For a man who loves his wife actu-
ally shows love for himself. [29]No one hates his own body but feeds and cares for it, just as
Christ cares for the church. [30]And we are members of His body.
[31]As the Scriptures say, "A man leaves his father and mother and is joined to his wife,
and the two are united into one."* [32]This is a great mystery, but it is an illustration of the
way Christ and the church are one. [33]So again I say, each man must love his wife as he
loves himself, and the wife must respect her husband.

5:11 Rom 13:12
5:13 John 3:20-21
5:14 Isa 26:19; 51:17; 52:1; 60:1; John 5:25; Rom 13:11
5:16 Col 4:5
5:17 1 Thes 4:3
5:18 Prov 20:1; 23:31
5:19 Col 3:16
5:21 1 Pet 5:5
5:22 Gen 3:16
5:23 1 Cor 11:3
5:26 John 15:3; 17:17; Titus 3:5; Heb 10:22
5:27 Eph 1:4; Col 1:22
5:29 1 Cor 12:27
5:30 1 Cor 6:15; 12:27
5:31 *Gen 2:24; Matt 19:5
5:33 1 Pet 3:1-2, 5

5:26 Greek *washed by water with the word.* 5:31 Gen 2:24.

5:14 This quotation may be a portion of an early church liturgy. It also appears to be loosely based on Isaiah 26:19 and 60:1.

▸ HOLINESS
5:15-18 What does God want for you? What is God's will for you? What does He want you to do? These questions are critical for anyone who wants to live a life of holiness, a life pleasing to God. The Bible is filled with instructions to us on how to live out the will of God; the challenge is that those instructions are not always as specific as we may want. We know that He intends for us to work (2 Thessalonians 3:10-12), but how do we know which job to take? We know God approves of marriage, but how do we know to whom we should get married? One way to discern these details is to humbly yield to the Spirit of God (Romans 8:14; Galatians 5:18). This may be as subjective as heeding almost imperceptible nudges, or as objective as stopping our rebellious, Spirit-grieving sins (Ephesians 4:30-32). Both require a humble dependence on God and a willingness to receive His guidance through the illumination of His Word by His Spirit. With God at work, we can confidently move forward, knowing that we know everything we need to please Him. ***(See Holiness*** *> Submission> Yielding to Spirit> Power of the Spirit is for all,* TopicGuide page A41.)

5:19 Worship flows out of a life filled with the Spirit, seen in both corporate ("among yourselves") and private ("in your hearts") settings. Worship can take many forms, but the picture we see here is a creative, active, and thankful communication between God and man.

▸ CHURCH
5:21-33 Unity manifested at home. Though people get married all the time, true spiritual and physical union to another person is anything but natural. It can range anywhere from hard work to an impossible task! When Paul turns his attention to husbands and wives, he knows the challenges of human relationships. He knows that there is no better place to explain the implications of Spirit-filled living than in terms of the family. The unity to which God calls Jews and Gentiles is not substantially different from the unity He intends husbands and wives—both require a healthy dose of the supernatural work

6:1 Col 3:20
6:2-3 *Exod 20:12 *Deut 5:16 Matt 15:4
6:4 Col 3:21
6:5-7 //Col 3:22-23 Titus 2:9-10
6:8 Col 3:24-25
6:9 Job 31:13-14 Col 4:1
6:11 Rom 13:12 1 Thes 5:8
6:12 Eph 3:10
6:14 Isa 11:5; 59:17 1 Thes 5:8
6:15 Isa 52:7
6:16 1 Jn 5:4
6:17 Isa 59:17 1 Thes 5:8 Heb 4:12
6:18 Rom 8:26-27 Phil 4:6 Col 4:2-3

CHILDREN AND PARENTS

6 Children, obey your parents because you belong to the Lord,* for this is the right
thing to do. 2“Honor your father and mother.” This is the first commandment with a
promise: 3If you honor your father and mother, “things will go well for you, and you will
have a long life on the earth.”*
4Fathers, do not provoke your children to anger by the way you treat them. Rather,
bring them up with the discipline and instruction that comes from the Lord.

SLAVES AND MASTERS

5Slaves, obey your earthly masters with deep respect and fear. Serve them sincerely as
you would serve Christ. 6Try to please them all the time, not just when they are watching
you. As slaves of Christ, do the will of God with all your heart. 7Work with enthusiasm, as
though you were working for the Lord rather than for people. 8Remember that the Lord
will reward each one of us for the good we do, whether we are slaves or free.
9Masters, treat your slaves in the same way. Don't threaten them; remember, you both
have the same Master in heaven, and He has no favorites.

THE WHOLE ARMOR OF GOD

10A final word: Be strong in the Lord and in His mighty power. 11Put on all of God's armor so
that you will be able to stand firm against all strategies of the devil. 12For we* are not fighting
against flesh-and-blood enemies, but against evil rulers and authorities of the unseen world,
against mighty powers in this dark world, and against evil spirits in the heavenly places.
13Therefore, put on every piece of God's armor so you will be able to resist the enemy in
the time of evil. Then after the battle you will still be standing firm. 14Stand your ground,
putting on the belt of truth and the body armor of God's righteousness. 15For shoes, put on
the peace that comes from the Good News so that you will be fully prepared.* 16In addition
to all of these, hold up the shield of faith to stop the fiery arrows of the devil.* 17Put on sal-
vation as your helmet, and take the sword of the Spirit, which is the word of God.
18Pray in the Spirit at all times and on every occasion. Stay alert and be persistent in
your prayers for all believers everywhere.*

6:1 Or *Children, obey your parents who belong to the Lord;* some manuscripts read simply *Children, obey your parents.* 6:2-3 Exod 20:12; Deut 5:16. 6:12 Some manuscripts read *you.* 6:15 Or *For shoes, put on the readiness to preach the Good News of peace with God.* 6:16 Greek *the evil one.* 6:18 Greek *all of God's holy people.*

of the Spirit for success. If the commands of Ephesians 5:22-33 seem too difficult, then you are right—they are. But with God's Spirit at work in you and in those with whom God commands unity, you can and will see it happen. (***See Church**> Who> From every people> Together in unity,* TopicGuide page A48.)

6:1-3 Of the Ten Commandments, the second has a general promise of blessing, but it is the fifth ("honor your father and mother," Exodus 20:12) that has a specific promise of long, healthy life attached. Paul also demonstrates here that the law still has a role in the life of the believer—its promises may be applied to us, and its moral regulations are still in effect.

6:4 Fathers may ordinarily be in charge of the family, but they also bear grave responsibilities, as all do who are in authority.

6:11-12 The war the Christian is engaged in is not a culture war or a political fight; the war is spiritual, with direct applications to politics and culture and all of life. Christians fight to advance the cause of Christ in the world, not a limited political or sociological solution.

6:13-17 Much has been made of each of the individual pieces of armor listed here, but it is hard to be absolute in determining just how each metaphor is to be understood. Nevertheless, it is clear that all the armor is related to the truth of the gospel and its work in our lives. We cannot do ministry without God's empowerment, and we should not think ourselves so mighty that we don't need every bit of help God gives us.

▸ SPIRITUAL WARFARE

6:13-18 You'll only hold the ground you fight for. If you were living in a war zone, how would it change the way you went about life? If you knew that just stepping outside the walls of your house put you at risk of being shot, what would you do differently? There are some believers who live daily in the face of physical war, but all believers live daily in the face of spiritual warfare. We have a real enemy. He is opposed to our growth in Christ, and unless we fight defensively, we will lose ground. By getting a firm grasp on the truths of the gospel and giving ourselves to intentional and strategic prayer, we can hold the ground and advance. You are at war. Don't lose ground. Don't surrender. Don't make peace with the enemy of the gospel. Stand firm and let the enemy see that with God as your captain, you do not fear him or his threats. (***See Spiritual Warfare**> Resisting Sin and Evil> Putting On and Off> Putting On> The whole armor of God,* TopicGuide page A46.)

6:18 This spiritual battle is fought through regular communication with God. There is no effective battle against those who oppose God without constant prayer to our Commander.

[19]And pray for me, too. Ask God to give me the right words so I can boldly explain God's
mysterious plan that the Good News is for Jews and Gentiles alike.* [20]I am in chains now,
still preaching this message as God's ambassador. So pray that I will keep on speaking
boldly for Him, as I should.

FINAL GREETINGS

[21]To bring you up to date, Tychicus will give you a full report about what I am doing and
how I am getting along. He is a beloved brother and faithful helper in the Lord's work. [22]I
have sent him to you for this very purpose—to let you know how we are doing and to en-
courage you.

[23]Peace be with you, dear brothers and sisters,* and may God the Father and the Lord
Jesus Christ give you love with faithfulness. [24]May God's grace be eternally upon all who
love our Lord Jesus Christ.

6:19 Col 4:3-4
6:21 Acts 20:4; 2 Tim 4:12; Titus 3:12
6:22 Col 4:7-9
6:23 Gal 6:16; 2 Thes 3:16

6:19 Greek *explain the mystery of the Good News;* some manuscripts read simply *explain the mystery.* 6:23 Greek *brothers.*

6:19-20 Paul provides an example of how to pray "warfare" prayers when he asks the Christians in Ephesus to pray for God to grant him the right words to say when needed and to make him a bold witness.

6:20 An ambassador is one who is sent as a representative of one country to serve in a different country. As should be true of all Christians, Paul is an ambassador of the kingdom of God in the kingdom of this world.

MY RESPONSE TO GOD

Equipped for Battle

EPHESIANS 6

In Ephesians, Paul uses the metaphor of a Roman soldier's uniform to describe the ways God has prepared us for our daily adventure with Him. Each one of these tools of war has a purpose—can you imagine a soldier without a weapon? Or without protective gear? The phrase "all of God's armor" tells us that God has provided a complete uniform to prepare us for every situation Satan and his minions might throw at us. But without our sword, our armor would not be complete.

The only weapon in Paul's list that is dedicated to offensive purposes is the power of God's Word. As you come to know God better and live more fully in the power and presence of the Holy Spirit, some of your most intimate moments with Him will come when He speaks to you through His Word about your specific challenges. How could it be a chore or a bore to receive God's special message for you from His Word? As God draws us ever nearer to Himself, we will more clearly understand His will for our lives through Scripture; we can then wield God's Word like a sword, slicing through the lies in our own mind as well as the lies that come from those who oppose us.

PHILIPPIANS

PURPOSE

To present Jesus Christ as the center of life and the source of joy.

What keeps a friend and follower of Jesus going, even when life seems difficult? What allows a Christian to rise each day and face whatever comes without retreating, without regret? Paul's letter to the Philippians gives us a simple key: discovering the secret of heartfelt joy in Jesus.

Finding joy in Jesus isn't just a cliché—at least not to Paul. This mature apostle finds himself in less than enviable circumstances—he is in prison—and sends a letter off to a group of Christians he loves and who love him. He has received gifts from the Philippians, and he wants to thank them (4:18). They had heard that one of their own who was ministering to Paul was sick, and he wants to reassure them that he received their gift and is still safe (2:26-28). But, beyond that, he wants to share with them his own deep joy. There is nothing superficial here; he is writing from his heart. This letter gives us a glimpse into that heart—and the joyous passions that fill the soul of a mature believer.

DISCOVER GOD IN PHILIPPIANS

Paul's description of Jesus is a deep, mature look at the features of Christ's character and what difference those truths made in his life.

Servant: As Paul lays out his understanding of the Christian life, he rehearses for the Philippians what Jesus has done for God's people. And at the core of Paul's thoughts is the Incarnation—Jesus' departure from the glory of heaven and entrance into human life in order to redeem people from the consequences of their sin (2:5-8). This incredible work of love on our behalf shows clearly that Jesus is the God who serves us.

Power: A servant might be one who is weak and can only do the bidding of another, but this is not the case with Jesus. Woven throughout the letter are glimpses of the great power of God seen in Christ. In chapter 3, He is the One who will transform God's people from our humble, frail state to a glorified body like His own (3:21). In chapter 4, He is the power behind Paul's ability to endure any circumstance (4:13). Although the God we meet in Jesus is the God who serves us, He also wields—and gives—great power to accomplish His glorious ends.

GROWING THROUGH PHILIPPIANS

Believers today have much to gain from Paul's letter to the Philippians, which presents Jesus as the foundation for joyful Christian living.

The Center of Life: Paul declares that whether he lives or dies, life is really about Jesus (1:21). For Paul, Jesus is what really matters, and He is the reason for joy. You cannot begin to experience the fullness of joy God desires for you without making Jesus the center of your life.

The Example for Living: Paul calls all believers to look to Jesus as their model for living (2:5). Jesus not only gave His life for us, but He also lived His life as an example for us. Seeking to live and serve as Jesus did is the path to true joy.

Our Righteousness: As you follow the example of Jesus, you will find that you fall short, but you can be assured that you are still accepted by God because of Jesus' perfect sacrifice for us (3:7-10). Whatever good is in us is wholly the work of Jesus on our behalf.

Our Sustainer: Every day you face challenges in your walk with Christ, but don't despair; Jesus is more than enough, and He will supply your every need (4:11-13, 19). You can know true joy even in the midst of struggle, because you can be confident that Jesus will watch over you and provide for you.

DISCOVERY VERSES

For to me, living means living for Christ, and dying is even better. (PHILIPPIANS 1:21)

You must have the same attitude that Christ Jesus had. (PHILIPPIANS 2:5)

But we are citizens of heaven, where the Lord Jesus Christ lives. And we are eagerly waiting for Him to return as our Savior. (PHILIPPIANS 3:20)

PHILIPPIANS FACTS

Author: Paul, the apostle and church planter, penned this letter during house arrest in Rome as he awaited his hearing before Caesar (1:1, 12-30). Prior to this, Paul was prompted in a vision to preach the Good News in Philippi (Acts 16:11-40), and he returned there on at least two occasions to encourage the church (Acts 20:1-6; 2 Corinthians 2:13).

Written to: Founded in 360 BC, by 31 BC Philippi enjoyed the status of a Roman city. Due to the ranking military leaders and supporters of Rome who lived in this city, it was declared a "colony" and was given special privileges, such as exemption from taxes and the right to own and sell land. Its location on the famous Egnatian Way made the city a center of economy, trade, and military travel for the region. Philippi housed the first church Paul planted in Europe.

Date of writing: As the book of Acts draws to a close, we find Paul on his way to Rome to have the case against him heard in the court of the emperor himself. This would have been sometime around AD 60–62, late in the ministry of the apostle, after he had already been in prison (in various places) awaiting trial. He wrote this moving letter to his friends in Philippi during this time of waiting.

Setting: Paul wrote from Rome to thank the Philippians for sending him a gift and to assure them that he was being cared for by the church and by His Lord.

OUTLINE

- **PHILIPPIANS 1:1-30**—Jesus, Our Life
- **PHILIPPIANS 2:1-30**—Jesus, Our Model
- **PHILIPPIANS 3:1-21**—Jesus, Our Goal in Living
- **PHILIPPIANS 4:1-23**—Jesus, Our Sufficiency

GREETINGS FROM PAUL

1:1 **1** This letter is from Paul and Timothy, slaves of Christ Jesus.
Acts 16:1 2 Cor 1:1 I am writing to all of God's holy people in Philippi who belong to Christ Jesus, in-
Col 1:1 cluding the elders* and deacons.
Phlm 1:1 [2]May God our Father and the Lord Jesus Christ give you grace and peace.

PAUL'S THANKSGIVING AND PRAYER

1:2-3 [3]Every time I think of you, I give thanks to my God. [4]Whenever I pray, I make my requests
Rom 1:7-8 for all of you with joy, [5]for you have been my partners in spreading the Good News about
1:6 Christ from the time you first heard it until now. [6]And I am certain that God, who began the
1 Cor 1:8 good work within you, will continue His work until it is finally finished on the day when
Christ Jesus returns.
1:7 [7]So it is right that I should feel as I do about all of you, for you have a special place in my
2 Cor 7:3 heart. You share with me the special favor of God, both in my imprisonment and in de-
1:8 fending and confirming the truth of the Good News. [8]God knows how much I love you and
Rom 1:9 long for you with the tender compassion of Christ Jesus.
1:9 [9]I pray that your love will overflow more and more, and that you will keep on growing
1 Thes 3:12 in knowledge and understanding. [10]For I want you to understand what really matters, so
1:10 Rom 12:2 that you may live pure and blameless lives until the day of Christ's return. [11]May you al-
1 Cor 1:8 ways be filled with the fruit of your salvation—the righteous character produced in your
1:11 life by Jesus Christ*—for this will bring much glory and praise to God.
John 15:4

PAUL'S JOY THAT CHRIST IS PREACHED

1:12 [12]And I want you to know, my dear brothers and sisters,* that everything that has hap-
2 Tim 2:9 pened to me here has helped to spread the Good News. [13]For everyone here, including
1:13 the whole palace guard,* knows that I am in chains because of Christ. [14]And because of my
Acts 28:30-31 Eph 3:1; 4:1 imprisonment, most of the believers* here have gained confidence and boldly speak
1:14 God's message* without fear.
Phil 1:20 [15]It's true that some are preaching out of jealousy and rivalry. But others preach about
1:15 Christ with pure motives. [16]They preach because they love me, for they know I have been
Phil 2:3 appointed to defend the Good News. [17]Those others do not have pure motives as they
1:17 preach about Christ. They preach with selfish ambition, not sincerely, intending to make
Acts 21:33 my chains more painful to me. [18]But that doesn't matter. Whether their motives are false
or genuine, the message about Christ is being preached either way, so I rejoice. And I will
1:19 continue to rejoice. [19]For I know that as you pray for me and the Spirit of Jesus Christ helps
2 Cor 1:11 me, this will lead to my deliverance.

1:1 Or *overseers;* or *bishops.* 1:11 Greek *with the fruit of righteousness through Jesus Christ.* 1:12 Greek *brothers.*
1:13 Greek *including all the Praetorium.* 1:14a Greek *brothers in the Lord.* 1:14b Some manuscripts read *speak the message.*

1:3 God used Paul to bring the good news about Jesus to the city of Philippi (Acts 16:11-40). Those who had become followers of Jesus supported and encouraged Paul in his ministry.

▸ SALVATION

1:6 Hopeful rejoicing. Paul had genuine joy when he reflected on what was happening in the lives of his friends in Philippi. He was there to help them find life in Jesus, which gave him good reason for joy. But what if they didn't follow through? What if they didn't make it in the end? That might have turned Paul's joy sour. But Paul knew that Jesus Christ is an effective Redeemer; He accomplishes what He starts. And so Paul was certain that the work that Christ began in his friends in Philippi was a work that Christ would complete. Paul continuously pointed his friends' hearts and minds toward Jesus, encouraging them in their spiritual walk. We can serve our brothers and sisters in Christ in the same way! (***See Salvation****> Receiving> Results> Works> Saints should provoke each other to them,* TopicGuide page A23.)

1:7 Paul wrote this letter from prison in Rome, where he would later have to make a defense before the Roman authorities for the charges that had been brought against him (see Acts 28:17-31).

1:8-9 Paul prays that the genuine love the Philippians have for one another will keep on overflowing. But the love he prays for is not indiscriminate but one constrained by "knowledge" (a grasp of what is real and true) and "understanding" (an ability to discern).

1:15-17 Now that Paul's freedom to minister is restrained, some of those preaching the Good News are trying to steal a little of the spotlight for themselves in hopes of causing the apostle distress.

PAUL'S LIFE FOR CHRIST

[20]For I fully expect and hope that I will never be ashamed, but that I will continue to
be bold for Christ, as I have been in the past. And I trust that my life will bring honor
to Christ, whether I live or die. [21]For to me, living means living for Christ, and dying is
even better. [22]But if I live, I can do more fruitful work for Christ. So I really don't know
which is better. [23]I'm torn between two desires: I long to go and be with Christ, which
would be far better for me. [24]But for your sakes, it is better that I continue to live.
[25]Knowing this, I am convinced that I will remain alive so I can continue to help all of you
grow and experience the joy of your faith. [26]And when I come to you again, you will have
even more reason to take pride in Christ Jesus because of what He is doing through me.

LIVE AS CITIZENS OF HEAVEN

[27]Above all, you must live as citizens of heaven, conducting yourselves in a manner wor-
thy of the Good News about Christ. Then, whether I come and see you again or only hear
about you, I will know that you are standing together with one spirit and one purpose,
fighting together for the faith, which is the Good News. [28]Don't be intimidated in any way
by your enemies. This will be a sign to them that they are going to be destroyed, but that
you are going to be saved, even by God Himself. [29]For you have been given not only the
privilege of trusting in Christ but also the privilege of suffering for Him. [30]We are in this
struggle together. You have seen my struggle in the past, and you know that I am still in
the midst of it.

1:20 Rom 5:5; 14:8 1 Cor 6:20 Eph 6:19
1:21 Gal 2:20 Col 1:27
1:22 Rom 1:13
1:23 2 Cor 5:8 2 Tim 4:6
1:26 Phil 2:24
1:27 Eph 4:1 Phil 4:1-2
1:28 2 Tim 2:11 Heb 13:6
1:29 Matt 5:11-12 Acts 5:41
1:30 Acts 16:19-40 1 Thes 2:2

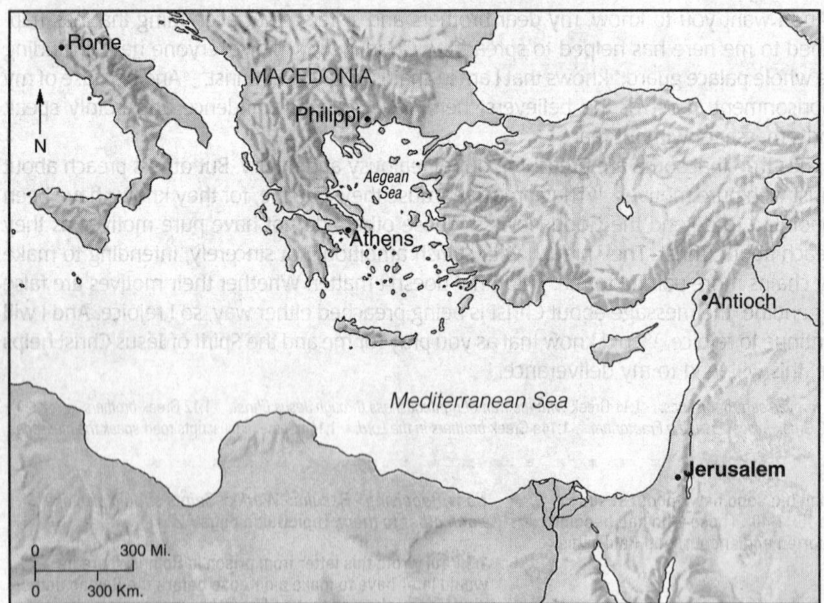

LOCATION OF PHILIPPI
Philippi sat on the Egnatian Way, the main transportation route in Macedonia, an extension of the Appian Way, which joined the eastern empire with Italy.

1:21 Paul literally says, "Life is Christ." Paul does not merely see his life as being lived *for* Christ; Paul's very life is all about Jesus. It is much like saying, "To live is to breathe"; this doesn't mean that life is lived for the purpose of breathing, but that breathing *is* living.

▸ ADOPTION
1:21 Captured by joy. No matter what happened to Paul, he kept his eyes on Jesus! Paul was chained to Roman soldiers, yet his longing was to personally encourage other saints and spread the gospel. Things weren't going the way Paul would have liked. But, in the midst of it, he had joy. How was that possible? When you have what you want most—even if you don't have other "lesser" wants—you have joy. Above all, Paul wanted Christ; for Paul, life was measured in terms of intimacy with Christ Jesus. So, wherever he was, whatever might have been happening, Paul found joy in Christ. You can find the same joy in your relationship with Jesus. Set your hope on Him, and He will bring you joy even in the midst of hardship. (***See Adoption> With Christ> Supernatural> A life of infinite joy,*** TopicGuide page A37.)

HAVE THE ATTITUDE OF CHRIST

2 Is there any encouragement from belonging to Christ? Any comfort from His love? Any fellowship together in the Spirit? Are your hearts tender and compassionate?
2 Then make me truly happy by agreeing wholeheartedly with each other, loving one another, and working together with one mind and purpose.
3 Don't be selfish; don't try to impress others. Be humble, thinking of others as better than
yourselves. 4 Don't look out only for your own interests, but take an interest in others, too.
5 You must have the same attitude that Christ Jesus had.

6 Though He was God,*
He did not think of equality with God
as something to cling to.
7 Instead, He gave up His divine privileges*;
He took the humble position of a slave*
and was born as a human being.
When He appeared in human form,*
8 He humbled Himself in obedience to God
and died a criminal's death on a cross.

9 Therefore, God elevated Him to the place of highest honor
and gave Him the name above all other names,
10 that at the name of Jesus every knee should bow,
in heaven and on earth and under the earth,
11 and every tongue confess that Jesus Christ is Lord,
to the glory of God the Father.

2:1 2 Cor 13:13; Col 3:12
2:2 1 Pet 3:8
2:3 Rom 12:10; Gal 5:26; 1 Pet 5:5
2:4 1 Cor 10:24
2:6 John 1:1-2; 5:18; 14:9-10; 17:5
2:7 John 1:14; Rom 8:3; 2 Cor 8:9; Gal 4:4
2:8 John 10:17-18; Heb 5:8; 12:2
2:9 Eph 1:20-21; Heb 1:3-4
2:10 Isa 45:23; Rom 14:11
2:11 John 13:13

2:6 Or *Being in the form of God.* 2:7a Greek *He emptied Himself.* 2:7b Or *the form of a slave.* 2:7c Some English translations put this phrase in verse 8.

▸ GOD

2:5-11 Growing into Him. Most people have role models—someone they look up to, someone they would like to "grow up to be like." For the Christian, the supreme role model is Jesus Christ Himself. Though He was truly God, Jesus chose to live like a man; though He was the true King, He chose to serve others like a slave. It wasn't an "act"; this is who Jesus is—a Servant-King. And that is why as we "grow up" in faith, we are to grow up to be like Jesus Christ. Adopt the attitude that Jesus had and put aside any privileges you may have that keep you from serving others. Obey God by looking for ways to show love to others. (***See God**> God's Attributes> Sovereign> God chose His people to become like Christ,* TopicGuide page A18.)

2:7 In "[giving] up His divine privileges" Christ did not cease to be divine or reduce any portion of His divine nature. The giving up came through addition, not subtraction; He didn't lose something (His divinity, for instance) as much as He added something—the role of a slave.

BECAUSE GOD NEVER CHANGES

My future is secure and eternal.

I am certain that God, who began the good work within you, will continue His work until it is finally finished on the day when Christ Jesus returns.

PHILIPPIANS 1:6

FOR THE NEXT *GOD NEVER CHANGES* FEATURE SEE PAGE 2221.

SHINE BRIGHTLY FOR CHRIST

[12]Dear friends, you always followed my instructions when I was with you. And now that I
am away, it is even more important. Work hard to show the results of your salvation,
obeying God with deep reverence and fear. [13]For God is working in you, giving you the
desire and the power to do what pleases Him.
[14]Do everything without complaining and arguing, [15]so that no one can criticize you.
Live clean, innocent lives as children of God, shining like bright lights in a world full of
crooked and perverse people. [16]Hold firmly to the word of life; then, on the day of Christ's
return, I will be proud that I did not run the race in vain and that my work was not useless.
[17]But I will rejoice even if I lose my life, pouring it out like a liquid offering to God,* just like
your faithful service is an offering to God. And I want all of you to share that joy. [18]Yes, you
should rejoice, and I will share your joy.

PAUL COMMENDS TIMOTHY

[19]If the Lord Jesus is willing, I hope to send Timothy to you soon for a visit. Then he can
cheer me up by telling me how you are getting along. [20]I have no one else like Timothy,
who genuinely cares about your welfare. [21]All the others care only for themselves and not
for what matters to Jesus Christ. [22]But you know how Timothy has proved himself. Like a
son with his father, he has served with me in preaching the Good News. [23]I hope to send
him to you just as soon as I find out what is going to happen to me here. [24]And I have con-
fidence from the Lord that I myself will come to see you soon.

PAUL COMMENDS EPAPHRODITUS

[25]Meanwhile, I thought I should send Epaphroditus back to you. He is a true brother, co-
worker, and fellow soldier. And he was your messenger to help me in my need. [26]I am
sending him because he has been longing to see you, and he was very distressed that you
heard he was ill. [27]And he certainly was ill; in fact, he almost died. But God had mercy on
him—and also on me, so that I would not have one sorrow after another.
[28]So I am all the more anxious to send him back to you, for I know you will be glad to
see him, and then I will not be so worried about you. [29]Welcome him with Christian love*
and with great joy, and give him the honor that people like him deserve. [30]For he risked
his life for the work of Christ, and he was at the point of death while doing for me what you
couldn't do from far away.

THE PRICELESS VALUE OF KNOWING CHRIST

3 Whatever happens, my dear brothers and sisters,* rejoice in the Lord. I never get tired
of telling you these things, and I do it to safeguard your faith.
[2]Watch out for those dogs, those people who do evil, those mutilators who say you
must be circumcised to be saved. [3]For we who worship by the Spirit of God* are the ones

2:13 Rom 8:28; 1 Cor 12:6; Heb 13:21
2:14 1 Cor 10:10
2:15 Matt 5:45; John 12:36; Eph 5:1
2:16 1 Thes 2:19
2:17 Rom 15:16; 2 Tim 4:6
2:20 1 Cor 16:10
2:21 1 Cor 10:24
2:22 1 Cor 4:17; 1 Tim 1:2
2:24 Phil 1:25-26
2:25 Phil 4:18
2:26 Phil 1:8
2:29 1 Cor 16:16, 18; 1 Tim 5:17
2:30 1 Cor 16:17
3:1 Phil 2:18; 4:4
3:2 Ps 22:16, 20; Rev 22:15
3:3 John 4:21-24; Rom 2:29; Gal 6:15; Col 2:11

2:17 Greek *I will rejoice even if I am to be poured out as a liquid offering.* 2:29 Greek *in the Lord.* 3:1 Greek *brothers;* also in 3:13, 17. 3:3 Some manuscripts read *worship God in spirit;* one early manuscript reads *worship in spirit.*

▸ HOLINESS

2:19-30 An attitude like Christ's. Paul has extended a call to the followers of Jesus: We are to think about life and relate to others the way Jesus did (2:3-11). But that call can seem to be out of reach. It's easy to think that Jesus could live that way "because He was God," but such a life is beyond us. Paul didn't see it that way. Notice what he said about Timothy and Epaphroditus. Timothy did not act out of selfishness. Epaphroditus considered the welfare of others more important than his own welfare. Paul was pointing out two men who were beginning to have the same attitude in their lives as Christ Jesus had (2:5). Evaluate your own actions. Are they self-centered or selfless? How would your Christian friends describe you in this area? Ask God to show you ways you can serve them better. (***See Holiness**> Maturing> Conformity to Christ> Christ's behavior,* TopicGuide page A40.)

2:25 Epaphroditus was apparently a member of the church of Philippi who communicated back and forth between the Philippian believers and Paul.

3:2 Some Jewish leaders were teaching that in addition to looking to Jesus as Savior, a Christian also needed to submit to the Old Testament instructions about circumcision. Paul opposes such ideas (see also Romans 2:25-29).

THE MOST GLORIOUS DEMOTION

HAVE YOU EVER EXPERIENCED A DEMOTION? That happened to James when the business he worked for ran into budget problems. Since James only had five years seniority, he was called into the department office and given an ultimatum: "Either take a clerical position or find another job."

James had few options. The job market in his area was tight, and he had a family to support. Even though it hurt his pride, he accepted the lower position. But he found the new job even harder to settle into than he expected. He had to work under supervisors who had once been his peers. Each day, he struggled to find satisfaction in a job he had come to dislike.

One day while James was reading his Bible, he came upon these verses:

> You must have the same attitude that Christ Jesus had. Though He was God, He did not think of equality with God as something to cling to. Instead, He gave up His divine privileges; He took the humble position of a slave and was born as a human being. When He appeared in human form, He humbled Himself in obedience to God and died a criminal's death on a cross. (Philippians 2:5-8)

This thought took James's breath away. Jesus also suffered a demotion—but one that He willingly accepted. He went from being the most honored in heaven where angels praised Him continuously to taking the place of a criminal on a cruel Roman cross—humiliated, rejected, and alone.

Suddenly, the pain James felt had new meaning. The pain didn't go away—Jesus' certainly didn't—but now James saw it from a different perspective. He began to understand more clearly the sacrifice Jesus, the Son of God, made for sinners. Why would the Son give up all His comfort, honor, and glory for people who would reject and crucify Him? To reveal God's saving love to a dying world.

Earthly sacrifice isn't the end of the story. James understood that it would be a path that would teach him more about being like Jesus, more about what it means to serve rather than lead.

We can honor the Son's sacrifice for us by being willing to make tough sacrifices to accomplish what we believe is right. Learning to accept that God allows suffering and sacrifice into our lives for His glory and our good is a step toward becoming more like our Master, the Lord Jesus Christ.

who are truly circumcised. We rely on what Christ Jesus has done for us. We put no confi-
dence in human effort, 4 though I could have confidence in my own effort if anyone could.
Indeed, if others have reason for confidence in their own efforts, I have even more!
5 I was circumcised when I was eight days old. I am a pure-blooded citizen of Israel and a
member of the tribe of Benjamin—a real Hebrew if there ever was one! I was a member of
the Pharisees, who demand the strictest obedience to the Jewish law. 6 I was so zealous
that I harshly persecuted the church. And as for righteousness, I obeyed the law without
fault.
7 I once thought these things were valuable, but now I consider them worthless because
of what Christ has done. 8 Yes, everything else is worthless when compared with the infi-
nite value of knowing Christ Jesus my Lord. For His sake I have discarded everything else,
counting it all as garbage, so that I could gain Christ 9 and become one with Him. I no lon-
ger count on my own righteousness through obeying the law; rather, I become righteous
through faith in Christ.* For God's way of making us right with Himself depends on faith. 10 I
want to know Christ and experience the mighty power that raised Him from the dead. I
want to suffer with Him, sharing in His death, 11 so that one way or another I will experi-
ence the resurrection from the dead!

PRESSING TOWARD THE GOAL

12 I don't mean to say that I have already achieved these things or that I have already
reached perfection. But I press on to possess that perfection for which Christ Jesus first pos-
sessed me. 13 No, dear brothers and sisters, I have not achieved it,* but I focus on this one
thing: Forgetting the past and looking forward to what lies ahead, 14 I press on to reach the
end of the race and receive the heavenly prize for which God, through Christ Jesus, is call-
ing us.
15 Let all who are spiritually mature agree on these things. If you disagree on some
point, I believe God will make it plain to you. 16 But we must hold on to the progress we
have already made.
17 Dear brothers and sisters, pattern your lives after mine, and learn from those who fol-
low our example. 18 For I have told you often before, and I say it again with tears in my
eyes, that there are many whose conduct shows they are really enemies of the cross of
Christ. 19 They are headed for destruction. Their god is their appetite, they brag about

3:5 Luke 1:59; 2:21; Acts 23:6; Rom 11:1; 2 Cor 11:22
3:6 Acts 8:3; 22:4; 26:9-11; Rom 10:5; Gal 1:13
3:8 John 17:3; Eph 4:13; 2 Pet 3:18
3:9 Rom 1:17; 3:21-22; Gal 2:16; 2 Pet 1:1
3:10 Rom 6:3-5; 8:17, 29; Gal 6:17
3:11 Acts 26:8; 1 Cor 15:23
3:12 Acts 9:5-6; 1 Tim 6:12, 19
3:13 Luke 9:62
3:14 1 Cor 9:24; 2 Tim 4:7-8; Heb 12:1
3:15 1 Cor 2:6
3:17 1 Cor 4:16; 1 Pet 5:3
3:18 Gal 6:12
3:19 Rom 8:5-6; 16:18

3:9 Or *through the faithfulness of Christ.* 3:13 Some manuscripts read *not yet achieved it.*

3:4-7 Paul reflects on his own Jewish heritage to refute those who are insisting that believers must also observe Jewish ritual practices. He highlights all the ways he could be considered righteous by virtue of his heritage and his observance of Jewish law, yet he insists that they are of no value because of what Christ has done to make His people righteous.

▸ SALVATION
3:7-9 Rules versus faith. Looking at all that he counted valuable in life before he came to know Jesus, Paul declares that everything pales in comparison to Jesus. Like a candle held up against the blazing sun, lesser desires fade in the presence of the greatest joy (Matthew 13:44). One of the things that Paul abandoned was depending on his own righteousness. He realized that his strength was worthless. Instead, he depended on faith in God. Are you following rules rather than living by faith? Make sure all your "rules" are based in your faith rather than on your own strength to keep them. (***See Salvation***> *Receiving> How> Faith in Christ,* TopicGuide page A22.)

3:9 The oneness that Paul speaks of with Christ is more than one in purpose or a united effort with Christ. He wants his life to be enveloped and caught up into Jesus Christ's life (Romans 6:3-5).

3:12 Although Paul is not yet all that Christ Jesus intends for him to be, he is certain he (and all the Philippians) will one day arrive at that destination (Philippians 1:6). His intent to "press on" is not a work to obtain as much as it is a joyous pursuit of what Jesus has already begun working out in his life.

▸ HOLINESS
3:12-14 Looking back. Have you ever watched a runner lose a lead because he looked back to see who was behind him? Those who win are always looking ahead—they have their eyes on the finish line. That's Paul's perspective on life. Christ has captured Paul's life and heart for *His* purposes. Christ has an end in mind for Paul—that Paul would become more like Christ. So like a good runner, Paul looks ahead to that. He is not distracted by what is behind him (in his past) or what may be alongside of him (in the trouble he may be facing). He leans forward, eyes on Christ, running to be all that Christ intends for him to be. How would you describe your Christian race? If your life isn't lived out at full speed for Jesus, commit yourself to "running harder." (***See Holiness***> *Submission> Trusting God> Faithfulness,* TopicGuide page A41.)

3:20 Eph 2:19; Col 3:1-3; Heb 12:22-23
3:21 Rom 8:29; 1 Cor 15:28, 43-53; Col 3:4
4:1 Phil 1:8
4:2 Phil 2:2
4:3 Exod 32:32-33; Ps 69:28; Rev 3:5; 13:8; 17:8; 20:12, 15; 21:27
4:4 Phil 3:1
4:5 Heb 10:37; Jas 5:8-9
4:6 Matt 6:25; 1 Pet 5:7
4:7 Isa 26:3; John 14:27

shameful things, and they think only about this life here on earth. 20But we are citizens of heaven, where the Lord Jesus Christ lives. And we are eagerly waiting for Him to return as our Savior. 21He will take our weak mortal bodies and change them into glorious bodies like His own, using the same power with which He will bring everything under His control.

4 Therefore, my dear brothers and sisters,* stay true to the Lord. I love you and long to see you, dear friends, for you are my joy and the crown I receive for my work.

WORDS OF ENCOURAGEMENT

2Now I appeal to Euodia and Syntyche. Please, because you belong to the Lord, settle your disagreement. 3And I ask you, my true partner,* to help these two women, for they worked hard with me in telling others the Good News. They worked along with Clement and the rest of my co-workers, whose names are written in the Book of Life.

4Always be full of joy in the Lord. I say it again—rejoice! 5Let everyone see that you are considerate in all you do. Remember, the Lord is coming soon.

6Don't worry about anything; instead, pray about everything. Tell God what you need, and thank Him for all He has done. 7Then you will experience God's peace, which exceeds anything we can understand. His peace will guard your hearts and minds as you live in Christ Jesus.

8And now, dear brothers and sisters, one final thing. Fix your thoughts on what is true, and honorable, and right, and pure, and lovely, and admirable. Think about things that

4:1 Greek *brothers;* also in 4:8. 4:3 Or *loyal Syzygus.*

3:20 Only a small minority of the people ruled by Rome were Roman citizens; the people of Philippi enjoyed that elite distinction. The city was, in a sense, a small outpost of Rome in the region of Macedonia, receiving the same privileges of the empire as Rome itself in 27 BC. Likewise, the Philippians (and all followers of Christ) are a small outpost of heaven where they were living.

4:2 Euodia and Syntyche were two women of some influence in the Philippian church who had been supporting and helping Paul, and who were now at odds with one another for reasons Paul did not mention.

▸ WORSHIP

4:6-7 Prayer brings peace. The life we are invited to enjoy as followers of Christ Jesus is not a matter of "positive thinking." Paul doesn't suggest that we will experience joy and peace by simply thinking nice thoughts. Instead, Paul calls believers to commit everything to God in prayer. Because our God knows our needs and because He will take care of us, we can take all our concerns to Him in prayer and leave our worries there. We can trade our concerns for peace. In what ways are you disobeying God by holding onto worry? Commit your worries to God and trust that He will take care of you. (***See Worship****> NT> Prayer> Instructions> Be anxious for nothing,* TopicGuide page A33.)

BECAUSE GOD IS
ALL POWERFUL

He can help me with anything.

For I can do everything through Christ, who gives me strength.

PHILIPPIANS 4:13

are excellent and worthy of praise. 9Keep putting into practice all you learned and re-
ceived from me—everything you heard from me and saw me doing. Then the God of
peace will be with you.

PAUL'S THANKS FOR THEIR GIFTS

10How I praise the Lord that you are concerned about me again. I know you have always
been concerned for me, but you didn't have the chance to help me. 11Not that I was ever
in need, for I have learned how to be content with whatever I have. 12I know how to live on
almost nothing or with everything. I have learned the secret of living in every situation,
whether it is with a full stomach or empty, with plenty or little. 13For I can do everything
through Christ,* who gives me strength. 14Even so, you have done well to share with me in
my present difficulty.

15As you know, you Philippians were the only ones who gave me financial help when I
first brought you the Good News and then traveled on from Macedonia. No other church
did this. 16Even when I was in Thessalonica you sent help more than once. 17I don't say this
because I want a gift from you. Rather, I want you to receive a reward for your kindness.

18At the moment I have all I need—and more! I am generously supplied with the gifts
you sent me with Epaphroditus. They are a sweet-smelling sacrifice that is acceptable and
pleasing to God. 19And this same God who takes care of me will supply all your needs
from His glorious riches, which have been given to us in Christ Jesus.

20Now all glory to God our Father forever and ever! Amen.

PAUL'S FINAL GREETINGS

21Give my greetings to each of God's holy people—all who belong to Christ Jesus. The
brothers who are with me send you their greetings. 22And all the rest of God's people send
you greetings, too, especially those in Caesar's household.

23May the grace of the Lord Jesus Christ be with your spirit.

4:9 Rom 15:33; 16:20; 1 Cor 14:33; 1 Thes 5:23
4:10 2 Cor 11:9
4:11 1 Tim 6:6
4:12 1 Cor 4:11; 2 Cor 11:9
4:13 2 Cor 12:9-10
4:14 Phil 1:7; Heb 10:33-34
4:15 2 Cor 11:8-9; Phil 1:5
4:16 Acts 17:1; 1 Thes 2:9
4:17 1 Cor 9:11
4:18 2 Cor 9:12; Phil 2:25
4:19 Ps 23:1; 2 Cor 9:8
4:20 Rom 11:36

4:13 Greek *through the One.*

4:9 Paul doesn't see himself as having reached perfection, but because there are poor models of what it means to be a follower of Jesus, he encourages the Philippians to follow the good example they have seen in him (3:12, 18-19).

▸ ADOPTION
4:11-13 Sustained by Jesus' power. Balance can bring enjoyment to life in many ways: We like when it is sunny, but not too hot; we like to be busy, but not stressed; we like company, but also some solitude. Such balance allows us to relax and gives us a sense that all is well. But some days do bring more of one thing than another, and we can quickly become concerned. How do we handle life when things are not going the way we want? Paul found the secret: Whatever he was facing, he was sustained not by externals that vary but by the constant supply of the life of Christ Jesus flowing into his own life. Being sustained by Jesus means walking daily—even moment by moment—in His Spirit. Will you make that choice today? (***See Adoption****> With Christ> Supernatural> A life of supernatural power,* TopicGuide page A37.)

COLOSSIANS

PURPOSE

To present Jesus as the final and full revelation of God.

Christians—the term was first used in Acts 11:26 to refer to believers in Antioch. The word refers to one who "belongs to Christ." For those early believers, it was critical to understand who this Christ was, and it should be for us as well.

In the city of Colosse some teachers were offering an alternative to what the apostles were teaching about Jesus. They were arguing that God Himself could not be known. Instead, He only revealed Himself through a hazy and somewhat vague series of "emanations." The further these emanations traveled from God, the easier they were to understand, but the less they revealed of God. Only by studying the teachings of those who understood these emanations could you gain knowledge of God. In a word, the false teachers were saying that Jesus was a good start, but if you really wanted to know God, you needed more.

Paul both resists and refutes such heresy in this letter. He affirms that Jesus is the final and full revelation of the true God. He insists that Jesus far surpasses any such emanations. He calls the Christians in Colosse and believers everywhere to see Jesus for who He really is—God united to human flesh.

DISCOVER GOD IN COLOSSIANS

Because of the concerns about the false teaching that has arisen in Colosse, a great deal of Paul's thought in this letter focuses on Jesus.

The Image of the Invisible God: Repeatedly in the first two chapters of this letter, Paul underscores the idea that Jesus Christ is the One who reveals God to us (1:15-19; 2:9-10). Paul uses very precise language to make his point: In Jesus Christ God has clothed Himself with human life. And, because of that, we can know God as we come to know Jesus.

The Guide for the Christian Life: In the latter half of this letter, Paul offers some very practical guidelines for living that are tied to Jesus Himself. Because Christians share their life with Jesus, their life should be different (2:20-23). The things that capture Jesus' attention should be the focus of their attention (3:1-4). The peace that Jesus Christ brings should impact every heart (3:15). The life and loves of Jesus Christ should be the guide for every relationship (3:16).

GROWING THROUGH COLOSSIANS

Paul provides his readers with a benchmark for measuring their life: Jesus Christ. All followers of Jesus can compare themselves to Jesus to assess how they are doing in their spiritual walk.

The Final and Complete Revelation: Paul goes to great lengths in his writings, but especially in Colossians, to present Jesus in all His power and authority (Colossians 1:15-29; 2:2, 9, 17;

see also 2 Corinthians 4:6 and Titus 2:13). You need not turn to someone else or some place else as a higher religious authority. Jesus, in His person and His work, reveals God fully. If Jesus is the final and complete revelation of God, we cannot take His words lightly. We cannot take our personal union with Him as insignificant, for it is through this union that God is finally and completely revealed in and to us (Colossians 2:10).

The Head of the Church: In his discussion of the glory of Jesus, Paul weaves insight into Jesus' role as the head and leader of the church (Colossians 1:18). Churches must have some kind of human leadership as well (1 Timothy 3:1-13), but those leaders ultimately represent God's authority (Exodus 18:19; 23:21; John 21:16-18; 2 Corinthians 8:23; 1 Timothy 3:1, 4-5) Do you see Jesus as the one who leads your church? Do His values and priorities govern the way your church uses its resources? Does His Word guide every step of your church?

The Source of Growth: Once we have come into life through Jesus Christ, we naturally ask, "What now? Where do I go from here?" Paul explains that we have to look no further—the same gracious Christ that saves us is the One we continue trusting and following (2:6-12)! We can never outgrow a humble, simple faith in Christ. What are you pursuing in your Christian life—new doctrines? New religious experiences? Make it your constant goal to grow more in faith in Jesus and in your dependence on Him.

DISCOVERY VERSES

For in Christ lives all the fullness of God in a human body. So you also are complete through your union with Christ, who is the head over every ruler and authority.

(COLOSSIANS 2:9-10)

For you died to this life, and your real life is hidden with Christ in God. And when Christ, who is your life, is revealed to the whole world, you will share in all His glory.

(COLOSSIANS 3:3-4)

COLOSSIANS FACTS

Author: Throughout this letter, Paul identifies himself as the author; he begins with personal greetings (1:1), refers to himself later (1:23), and closes the letter with a reference to the fact that he was signing the epistle in his own hand (4:18), to certify its origin.

Written to: Colosse was once a grand city, made commercially successful through exports of black wool. By the time of the New Testament, Colosse was surpassed by her neighboring cities, Laodicea and Hierapolis (4:13). It was nevertheless a significant place for the gospel to take root, for it was located near a busy road 100 miles east of the major city of Ephesus. The church there was struggling with a heresy that appears to be an early form of Gnosticism, given Paul's refutation in 2:8-23.

Date of writing: Clearly, Paul is writing this letter from prison (4:3, 10, 18). At the end of the letter, Paul mentions some of those who are with him, including Aristarchus, Mark, Epaphras, and Luke (4:10-14). The evidence indicates that Luke (Acts 28:14; 2 Timothy 4:11) and Aristarchus (Acts 27:2) were with Paul in Rome, one of the places he was imprisoned. Judging by the similar themes and personal greetings, Philemon and Ephesians were likely written around the same time as this book, AD 60–61.

Setting: Given the assumed dating of this letter, it is believed Paul wrote Colossians during his first imprisonment in Rome (Acts 28). The difficult conditions of Roman imprisonment were temporary and alleviated by the care of his friends (4:7-9; Ephesians 6:21; Philemon 1:10-12), who brought him supplies and news of the outside world (Philippians 4:18) and evidently supplied him with the money for a small residence, where he was kept under house arrest (Acts 28:30-31).

OUTLINE

- **COLOSSIANS 1:1-23**—Salutation and Paul's Prayer for the Colossians
- **COLOSSIANS 1:24–2:7**—Confirmation of Paul's Ministry to the Church
- **COLOSSIANS 2:8-23**—Exaltation of Jesus Christ over All Things
- **COLOSSIANS 3:1–4:6**—Exhortation to Holy Living
- **COLOSSIANS 1:15-23**—Authentication and Final Greetings

GREETINGS FROM PAUL

1:1 1 Cor 1:1 Eph 1:1

1 This letter is from Paul, chosen by the will of God to be an apostle of Christ Jesus, and
from our brother Timothy.

1:2 Rom 1:7

2 We are writing to God's holy people in the city of Colosse, who are faithful brothers
and sisters* in Christ.
May God our Father give you grace and peace.

PAUL'S THANKSGIVING AND PRAYER

1:4 Eph 1:15 · 1:5 Eph 1:13 1 Pet 1:4 · 1:6 Rom 1:13 · 1:7 Col 4:12 Phlm 1:23

3 We always pray for you, and we give thanks to God, the Father of our Lord Jesus Christ.
4 For we have heard of your faith in Christ Jesus and your love for all of God's people,
5 which come from your confident hope of what God has reserved for you in heaven. You
have had this expectation ever since you first heard the truth of the Good News.
6 This same Good News that came to you is going out all over the world. It is bearing fruit
everywhere by changing lives, just as it changed your lives from the day you first heard
and understood the truth about God's wonderful grace.
7 You learned about the Good News from Epaphras, our beloved co-worker. He is
Christ's faithful servant, and he is helping us on your behalf.* 8 He has told us about the
love for others that the Holy Spirit has given you.

1:2 Greek *faithful brothers.* 1:7 Or *he is ministering on your behalf;* some manuscripts read *he is ministering on our behalf.*

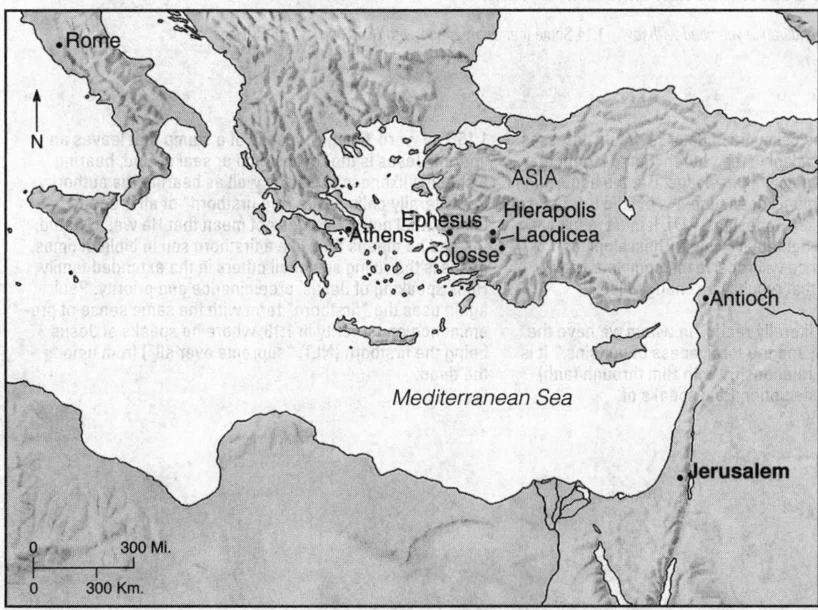

LOCATION OF COLOSSE
Paul had no doubt been through Laodicea on his third missionary journey, as it lay on the main route to Ephesus, but he had never been to Colosse. Though a large city with a significant population, Colosse was smaller and less important than the nearby cities of Laodicea and Hierapolis.

1:1 In Galatians, Paul identified himself as "an apostle" in response to a personal attack (Galatians 1:1), but here he identifies himself as a "chosen . . . apostle" because he is relatively unknown to the believers in Colosse.

1:5 When speaking of what the saints are looking forward to in heaven, Paul uses an expression that literally means "stored away for you," calling to mind various images from the ancient world, such as the inheritance of a child kept in a treasury or the storage of grain for later use.

▸ SALVATION
1:6 The blank stare. When you ask someone to do something and all you get in return is a blank stare, it is very likely that the person did not understand what you asked. There is a significant difference between something heard and something understood. And the only way to tell if people understand is if they respond appropriately. It is no different with the Good News about Jesus. Some people seem to have heard; they can tell you the facts about who Jesus is and what He did on the cross, but it doesn't seem to matter to them. They don't seem to "get it." But when the Colossian believers heard the Good News, it had a profound impact on their lives. Examine your life to see if God is producing spiritual fruit like joy, peace, and self-control. (***See Salvation****> Receiving> Results> Bear fruit of the Spirit,* TopicGuide page A23.)

[9]So we have not stopped praying for you since we first heard about you. We ask God to
give you complete knowledge of His will and to give you spiritual wisdom and under-
standing. [10]Then the way you live will always honor and please the Lord, and your lives
will produce every kind of good fruit. All the while, you will grow as you learn to know
God better and better.

[11]We also pray that you will be strengthened with all His glorious power so you will
have all the endurance and patience you need. May you be filled with joy,* [12]always
thanking the Father. He has enabled you to share in the inheritance that belongs to His
people, who live in the light. [13]For He has rescued us from the kingdom of darkness and
transferred us into the Kingdom of His dear Son, [14]who purchased our freedom* and for-
gave our sins.

CHRIST IS SUPREME

[15] Christ is the visible image of the invisible God.
He existed before anything was created and is supreme over all creation,*
[16] for through Him God created everything
in the heavenly realms and on earth.
He made the things we can see
and the things we can't see—
such as thrones, kingdoms, rulers, and authorities in the unseen world.
Everything was created through Him and for Him.

1:9 Eph 1:15-17
1:10 Eph 4:1; Phil 1:27; 1 Thes 2:12
1:11 Eph 3:16
1:12 Acts 26:18; Eph 5:20
1:13 Matt 3:17; Acts 26:18; Eph 1:6; 2:2; 6:12
1:14 Eph 1:7
1:15 John 1:1, 18; 14:9; 2 Cor 4:4; Heb 1:3; Rev 3:14
1:16 John 1:3; Heb 1:2

1:11 Or *all the patience and endurance you need with joy.* 1:14 Some manuscripts add *with His blood.* 1:15 Or *He is the firstborn of all creation.*

1:9-10 In his prayer for the believers in Colosse, Paul addresses a false teaching then prevalent in the church. Some taught that the greatest good was in gaining knowledge. But the acquisition of knowledge—even spiritual knowledge—is of little use unless it is applied to one's life (see Ephesians 1:17). It must result in a transformed attitude and righteous living (1 Thessalonians 1:6-7). Paul prays that his audience will receive the complete knowledge of God and His will that results in a changed life.

1:14 In Greek, this verse literally reads "*in whom* we have the purchase of our freedom and the forgiveness of our sins." It is as we are "in Christ" (in relationship with Him through faith) that we enter into this redemption Paul speaks of.

1:15 The word "image" speaks of a stamp that leaves an imprint; Jesus is the royal stamp or seal of God, bearing a specific likeness to God as well as bearing His authority. Paul literally calls Jesus "the firstborn" of all creation (see textual note). He does not mean that He was created. Instead he means that, like a firstborn son in biblical times, Jesus is the ruling son of all others in the extended family. He is speaking of Jesus' preeminence and priority. Paul again uses the "firstborn" term with the same sense of preeminence and priority in 1:18, where he speaks of Jesus being the firstborn (NLT, "supreme over all") from among the dead.

BECAUSE GOD IS SOVEREIGN

I will joyfully submit to His will.

Christ is the visible image of the invisible God. He existed before anything was created and is supreme over all creation. . . . Everything was created through Him and for Him.

COLOSSIANS 1:15-16

FOR THE NEXT *GOD IS SOVEREIGN* FEATURE SEE PAGE 2200.

17 He existed before anything else,
and He holds all creation together.
18 Christ is also the head of the church,
which is His body.
He is the beginning,
supreme over all who rise from the dead.*
So He is first in everything.
19 For God in all His fullness
was pleased to live in Christ,
20 and through Him God reconciled
everything to Himself.
He made peace with everything in heaven and on earth
by means of Christ's blood on the cross.

21 This includes you who were once far away from God. You were His enemies, sepa-
rated from Him by your evil thoughts and actions. 22 Yet now He has reconciled you to
Himself through the death of Christ in His physical body. As a result, He has brought you
into His own presence, and you are holy and blameless as you stand before Him without a
single fault.
23 But you must continue to believe this truth and stand firmly in it. Don't drift away from
the assurance you received when you heard the Good News. The Good News has been
preached all over the world, and I, Paul, have been appointed as God's servant to proclaim it.

PAUL'S WORK FOR THE CHURCH

24 I am glad when I suffer for you in my body, for I am participating in the sufferings of
Christ that continue for His body, the church. 25 God has given me the responsibility of
serving His church by proclaiming His entire message to you. 26 This message was kept se-
cret for centuries and generations past, but now it has been revealed to God's people.
27 For God wanted them to know that the riches and glory of Christ are for you Gentiles,
too. And this is the secret: Christ lives in you. This gives you assurance of sharing His glory.
28 So we tell others about Christ, warning everyone and teaching everyone with all the
wisdom God has given us. We want to present them to God, perfect* in their relationship
to Christ. 29 That's why I work and struggle so hard, depending on Christ's mighty power
that works within me.

1:17 John 1:1; 8:58
1:18 Acts 4:2; 26:23; Eph 1:22-23; Rev 1:5
1:19 Col 2:9
1:21 Rom 5:10; Eph 2:3, 12
1:22 Rom 7:4; Eph 1:4; 5:27
1:23 Eph 3:17; Col 1:5-6
1:24 Phil 2:17; 3:10; 2 Tim 1:8
1:25 Eph 3:2
1:26 Rom 16:25-26; Eph 3:3, 5, 9-10
1:27 Rom 8:10; Eph 3:9-11
1:28 Eph 4:13
1:29 Eph 1:19; 3:7; Phil 4:13

1:18 Or *the firstborn from the dead.* 1:28 Or *mature.*

▸ PURPOSE
1:17 God the Sustainer. Scientists tell us that life on planet Earth appears to exist rather precariously. If the Earth were a bit closer or a bit farther from the sun, life as we know it couldn't exist. If the fundamental properties of water were altered only slightly, life as we know it couldn't exist. For some, it seems that life on earth is simply one amazing "accident," but we know better. Life here is a gift from God. And life continues as a gift from Him. Paul tells us that Christ Jesus "holds all creation together." Today, your life is sustained by the grace and goodness and power of God. He upholds it all, and He is holding you up today. Praise the One who sustains your every heartbeat. (***See Purpose***> *God's Means> God's Sovereignty> God sustains His creation,* TopicGuide page A52.)

1:19 The false teachers in Colosse were teaching that God made Himself known through a whole variety of forms. Paul counters this by asserting that everything we need to know about God is found in Jesus alone. Paul is not saying that the Father lives in the Son (as if the Son is the incarnation of the Father). His point is that all that characterizes God as God ("His fullness") is fully at home in the person of Jesus.

1:28 The word "perfect" here could be translated "mature" (see textual note), or brought to the appropriate and complete end.

▸ MINISTRY
1:29–2:1 Service and suffering. Talk to a missionary or someone else involved in full-time Christian work and you will see that there is joy to be found in serving the cause of the kingdom. But did you know that effective ministry might also include agony? When Paul writes in 1:29 that he "work[s] and struggle[s] so hard" at what Christ has called him to do, he uses a word that is related to our English word *agony.* Although Paul is clear that the fruitfulness of ministry is dependent on what God does (1 Corinthians 3:6), he takes what he does very seriously. Do you? Would others say you agonize over what God has given you to do? If you don't, what will it take for you to become serious about what He has called you to do? (***See Ministry***> *Great Commission> Risk> Opposition and ill-treatment,* TopicGuide page A56.)

2 I want you to know how much I have agonized for you and for the church at Laodi-
cea, and for many other believers who have never met me personally. 2I want them
to be encouraged and knit together by strong ties of love. I want them to have complete
confidence that they understand God's mysterious plan, which is Christ Himself. 3In Him
lie hidden all the treasures of wisdom and knowledge.
4I am telling you this so no one will deceive you with well-crafted arguments. 5For
though I am far away from you, my heart is with you. And I rejoice that you are living as
you should and that your faith in Christ is strong.

FREEDOM FROM RULES AND NEW LIFE IN CHRIST

6And now, just as you accepted Christ Jesus as your Lord, you must continue to follow Him.
7Let your roots grow down into Him, and let your lives be built on Him. Then your faith will
grow strong in the truth you were taught, and you will overflow with thankfulness.
8Don't let anyone capture you with empty philosophies and high-sounding nonsense
that come from human thinking and from the spiritual powers* of this world, rather than
from Christ. 9For in Christ lives all the fullness of God in a human body.* 10So you also are
complete through your union with Christ, who is the head over every ruler and authority.
11When you came to Christ, you were "circumcised," but not by a physical procedure.
Christ performed a spiritual circumcision—the cutting away of your sinful nature.* 12For
you were buried with Christ when you were baptized. And with Him you were raised to
new life because you trusted the mighty power of God, who raised Christ from the dead.
13You were dead because of your sins and because your sinful nature was not yet cut
away. Then God made you alive with Christ, for He forgave all our sins. 14He canceled the

2:1 Col 4:12-13
2:2 Matt 11:25-27; Eph 1:18-19; Col 2:19
2:3 Isa 11:2; Rom 11:33; Eph 3:8, 19
2:5 1 Cor 5:3-4
2:7 Eph 3:17
2:8 Col 2:4; 1 Tim 6:20
2:9 John 1:14, 16; Col 1:19
2:10 Eph 1:21-22; 3:19
2:12 Rom 6:5; Eph 1:19-20; 2:6
2:13 Eph 2:1, 5
2:14 Eph 2:15; 1 Pet 2:24

2:8 Or *the spiritual principles;* also in 2:20. 2:9 Or *in Him dwells all the completeness of the Godhead bodily.* 2:11 Greek *the cutting away of the body of the flesh.*

2:2 As earlier in 1:27, the reference to "God's mysterious plan" does not imply that God is keeping something from people, but only that His plan to redeem people through Christ was not fully known in earlier ages but has now come to be understood.

2:3-4 Paul does not want the believers in Colosse to be deceived, so he reiterates that all the wisdom and knowledge about God that they need can be found in their relationship with Jesus Christ; they do not need what the false teachers are offering them.

▸ ADOPTION

2:6 Keeping in step with Him. According to the letter to the Hebrews, our life in faith depends on Jesus from start to finish (Hebrews 12:2). We begin by coming to trust Him, and in eternity, we will come to resemble Him in character (1 John 3:2). But what about the time "in between"? Paul tells us that we are to "continue to follow Him." Jesus is not just the starting point of our life or our final destination. Jesus also guides us through His Spirit, and He is our source of power and our comfort. You cannot begin life without Him. You won't finish apart from Him. Don't try living a single day without intimacy with Him. (***See Adoption****> With Christ> United with Christ> United to Christ,* TopicGuide page A37.)

▸ BIBLE

2:8-9 More than meets the eye. Most of us carry around a "picture" of Jesus in our head. Perhaps it is one that we adopted as children from stories and pictures in church or Sunday school. Maybe it is drawn from films we have seen or descriptions we have read about Jesus. Most of these pictures, however, fail to give us a clear glimpse of what's "inside" Jesus. Using the language of the false teachers against them, Paul says that the very essence of what makes God divine is fully present in the person of Jesus. If your image of Jesus doesn't reflect that, then you are not thinking of the Jesus we meet in the pages of Scripture! Get to know your Bible thoroughly. It may alter your "picture" of Jesus. (***See Bible****> Unity> Christ> Christ is the "God of Israel,"* TopicGuide page A10.)

2:11 In the Old Testament, God gave the practice of circumcision to Abraham (Genesis 17:10-14). It was confirmed before the nation of Israel left Egypt (Exodus 12:48-49). It was also given as part of the law of Moses (Leviticus 12:3). One of the rite's purposes was to mark a man as part of the covenant community of God's people. Paul is saying that what marks someone as belonging to God's people through Christ is not the outward, physical circumcision of skin, but a spiritual circumcision of our sinful nature.

2:12 Paul taught that no outward act—not even baptism—was a saving act; salvation is by grace through faith (Ephesians 2:8-9; Titus 3:5). But baptism does picture the death to an old life and the resurrection to new life that is found in Jesus. Baptism pictures the change that has already happened in a believer's life through faith.

▸ SALVATION

2:13-14 The cost for sins. When something bad happens, little children seem to have a knack for quickly declaring that they aren't at fault. With maturity comes a realization that we *are* often at fault and that we all have done something that justifies our being "blamed." We all have a long list of offenses we have committed against a holy God. Yet we are still invited into relationship with this God. So what happened to all those offenses? Did He forget? Did He overlook them? No. He took the list of charges against you and nailed them to the cross on which Jesus died and let Jesus pay the penalty for the wrong that you did. That is the heart of the Good News. Have you received this wonderful gift? (***See Salvation****> Receiving> When> Expiation/removal of sins,* TopicGuide page A23.)

record of the charges against us and took it away by nailing it to the cross. 15 In this way, He disarmed* the spiritual rulers and authorities. He shamed them publicly by His victory over them on the cross.

16 So don't let anyone condemn you for what you eat or drink, or for not celebrating certain holy days or new moon ceremonies or Sabbaths. 17 For these rules are only shadows of the reality yet to come. And Christ Himself is that reality. 18 Don't let anyone condemn you by insisting on pious self-denial or the worship of angels,* saying they have had visions about these things. Their sinful minds have made them proud, 19 and they are not connected to Christ, the head of the body. For He holds the whole body together with its joints and ligaments, and it grows as God nourishes it.

20 You have died with Christ, and He has set you free from the spiritual powers of this world. So why do you keep on following the rules of the world, such as, 21 "Don't handle! Don't taste! Don't touch!"? 22 Such rules are mere human teachings about things that deteriorate as we use them. 23 These rules may seem wise because they require strong devotion, pious self-denial, and severe bodily discipline. But they provide no help in conquering a person's evil desires.

LIVING THE NEW LIFE

3 Since you have been raised to new life with Christ, set your sights on the realities of heaven, where Christ sits in the place of honor at God's right hand. 2 Think about the things of heaven, not the things of earth. 3 For you died to this life, and your real life is hidden with Christ in God. 4 And when Christ, who is your* life, is revealed to the whole world, you will share in all His glory.

5 So put to death the sinful, earthly things lurking within you. Have nothing to do with sexual immorality, impurity, lust, and evil desires. Don't be greedy, for a greedy person is an idolater, worshiping the things of this world. 6 Because of these sins, the anger of God is coming.* 7 You used to do these things when your life was still part of this world. 8 But now is the time to get rid of anger, rage, malicious behavior, slander, and dirty language. 9 Don't lie to each other, for you have stripped off your old sinful nature and all its wicked deeds. 10 Put on your new nature, and be renewed as you learn to know your Creator and become like Him. 11 In this new life, it doesn't matter if you are a Jew or a Gentile,* circumcised or uncircumcised, barbaric, uncivilized,* slave, or free. Christ is all that matters, and He lives in all of us.

12 Since God chose you to be the holy people He loves, you must clothe yourselves with tenderhearted mercy, kindness, humility, gentleness, and patience. 13 Make allowance for each other's faults, and forgive anyone who offends you. Remember, the Lord forgave you, so you must forgive others. 14 Above all, clothe yourselves with love, which

2:15 John 12:31; 2 Cor 2:14; Eph 4:8
2:16 1 Chr 23:31; Rom 14:3, 5; Gal 4:10
2:19 Eph 1:22; 4:15-16
2:20 Rom 6:6; Gal 4:3, 9
2:22 Matt 15:9
2:23 1 Tim 4:3
3:1 Matt 6:33; Eph 2:6
3:2 Phil 3:19-20
3:3 Rom 6:2; 2 Cor 5:14
3:4 1 Cor 15:43
3:5 Rom 6:6; 8:13; Gal 5:19-21; Eph 4:19; 5:3, 5
3:8 Eph 4:25-31; 5:4
3:10 Rom 12:2; Eph 2:10; 4:24
3:11 Rom 10:12; Gal 3:28
3:12 Eph 4:2, 32
3:13 Eph 4:32; 5:2
3:14 Rom 13:8

2:15 Or *He stripped off.* 2:18 Or *or worshiping with angels.* 3:4 Some manuscripts read *our.* 3:6 Some manuscripts read *is coming on all who disobey Him.* 3:11a Greek *a Greek.* 3:11b Greek *Barbarian, Scythian.*

2:15 Paul refers to disarming wicked spiritual beings as in Ephesians 6:12.

2:16 The false teachers had insisted that the truly religious person abstain from certain foods, honor certain special holy days, and observe other traditions that were not rooted in faith in Christ (see also 2:20-21).

3:1 To "set your sights on the realities of heaven" means to continually keep your mind and heart oriented toward God's kingdom and not this world.

3:5 Since believers have died with Christ (3:3), Paul is not talking about dying again to the old way of life but seeing oneself as already dead to all the old ways. The old life should have no more power over the believer as physical life has over a corpse.

▸ GOD

3:8-14 Dressed and empowered. A police officer dresses a certain way, as do doctors and firemen. Those attending an important state function might also dress in a particular way, as is fitting for the event. Paul uses this metaphor of wearing what is fitting for the event to talk about how we should behave as believers. He reminds us that we have "stripped off" our sinful nature and deeds, and he calls us to "clothe" ourselves with behavior that pleases God. In a real sense, he is calling us to "dress appropriately" for living the Christian life. Don't live like you did before you came to know Jesus. That doesn't fit any more; it doesn't look good on you; it's not your style! Live out your new identity, empowered by the indwelling Holy Spirit. (***See God***> *Salvation> Holy Spirit> Strengthens us*, TopicGuide page A15.)

binds us all together in perfect harmony. 15And let the peace that comes from Christ rule
in your hearts. For as members of one body you are called to live in peace. And always
be thankful.
16Let the message about Christ, in all its richness, fill your lives. Teach and counsel each
other with all the wisdom He gives. Sing psalms and hymns and spiritual songs to God
with thankful hearts. 17And whatever you do or say, do it as a representative of the Lord
Jesus, giving thanks through Him to God the Father.

INSTRUCTIONS FOR CHRISTIAN HOUSEHOLDS

18Wives, submit to your husbands, as is fitting for those who belong to the Lord.
19Husbands, love your wives and never treat them harshly.
20Children, always obey your parents, for this pleases the Lord. 21Fathers, do not aggra-
vate your children, or they will become discouraged.
22Slaves, obey your earthly masters in everything you do. Try to please them all the
time, not just when they are watching you. Serve them sincerely because of your reverent
fear of the Lord. 23Work willingly at whatever you do, as though you were working for the
Lord rather than for people. 24Remember that the Lord will give you an inheritance as your
reward, and that the Master you are serving is Christ.* 25But if you do what is wrong, you
will be paid back for the wrong you have done. For God has no favorites.

4 Masters, be just and fair to your slaves. Remember that you also have a Master—
in heaven.

AN ENCOURAGEMENT FOR PRAYER

2Devote yourselves to prayer with an alert mind and a thankful heart. 3Pray for us, too, that
God will give us many opportunities to speak about His mysterious plan concerning Christ.
That is why I am here in chains. 4Pray that I will proclaim this message as clearly as I should.
5Live wisely among those who are not believers, and make the most of every opportu-
nity. 6Let your conversation be gracious and attractive* so that you will have the right re-
sponse for everyone.

PAUL'S FINAL INSTRUCTIONS AND GREETINGS

7Tychicus will give you a full report about how I am getting along. He is a beloved brother
and faithful helper who serves with me in the Lord's work. 8I have sent him to you for this

3:15 John 14:27 Eph 2:14-16 Phil 4:7
3:16 Rom 10:17 Eph 5:19
3:17 1 Cor 10:31 Eph 5:20
3:18 Eph 5:22
3:19 Eph 5:25 1 Pet 3:7
3:20 Eph 6:1
3:21-25 //Eph 6:4-8
3:25 Acts 10:34
4:1 Lev 25:43 Eph 6:9
4:2 Luke 18:1 Eph 6:18 1 Thes 5:17
4:4 Eph 6:20
4:5 Eph 5:15-16
4:6 Mark 9:50 Eph 4:29 1 Pet 3:15
4:7-8 Acts 20:4 Eph 6:21-22

3:24 Or *and serve Christ as your Master.* 4:6 Greek *and seasoned with salt.*

3:15 The peace that Christ gives should serve as the "umpire" in our lives. The presence or absence of Christ's peace can indicate how well we are living out this new life as we relate to one another.

▸ WORSHIP
3:16 Christ is speaking. For friends who haven't seen each other in a long time, a simple note or phone call can mean a lot. Friends long to hear from one another; it helps to keep the relationship alive. The same applies to friends of Jesus. When we pray, He hears from us. But how do we hear from Him? Here Paul highlights one of the most important ways: We are to speak Christ's words to one another, teaching and encouraging each other. And there, in that process, we can hear His voice to us. Are you listening? Are you letting Him speak through you? It is what friends would do. (***See Worship***> *NT> Teaching and Preaching> Exhortation to study Scripture,* TopicGuide page A34.)

3:18–4:1 In this section, Paul lays out some of the specifics of what it looks like to have the peace of Christ ruling and the word of Christ abiding in the hearts of believers as they relate to one another in certain specific relationships.

4:2 Paul's exhortation to the Colossians to "devote [themselves] to prayer" reflects the attitude of the church in Acts 2:42.

▸ WORSHIP
4:2-4 The importance of prayer. Prayer was a crucial practice in the ministry of Jesus and His disciples. On more than one occasion Jesus prayed all night (Luke 6:12), and Jesus' disciples specifically asked Him to teach them how to pray (Luke 11:1). Paul also considered prayer essential, and he called the Colossians to give themselves energetically to ongoing and regular prayer. He earnestly asked others to pray that he would be effective in ministry. How do you regard prayer? Do you pray as if it is essential to growth in faith and critical to effective ministry? Make prayer as important to you as it was to Paul. Set aside time each day to spend with God. (***See Worship***> *NT> Prayer> Instructions> Devote yourselves to prayer,* TopicGuide page A33.)

very purpose—to let you know how we are doing and to encourage you. [9]I am also send-
ing Onesimus, a faithful and beloved brother, one of your own people. He and Tychicus
will tell you everything that's happening here.
[10]Aristarchus, who is in prison with me, sends you his greetings, and so does Mark, Bar-
nabas's cousin. As you were instructed before, make Mark welcome if he comes your way.
[11]Jesus (the one we call Justus) also sends his greetings. These are the only Jewish believ-
ers among my co-workers; they are working with me here for the Kingdom of God. And
what a comfort they have been!
[12]Epaphras, a member of your own fellowship and a servant of Christ Jesus, sends you
his greetings. He always prays earnestly for you, asking God to make you strong and per-
fect, fully confident that you are following the whole will of God. [13]I can assure you that he
prays hard for you and also for the believers in Laodicea and Hierapolis.
[14]Luke, the beloved doctor, sends his greetings, and so does Demas. [15]Please give my
greetings to our brothers and sisters* at Laodicea, and to Nympha and the church that
meets in her house.
[16]After you have read this letter, pass it on to the church at Laodicea so they can read it,
too. And you should read the letter I wrote to them.
[17]And say to Archippus, "Be sure to carry out the ministry the Lord gave you."
[18]HERE IS MY GREETING IN MY OWN HANDWRITING—PAUL.
Remember my chains.
May God's grace be with you.

4:9 Phlm 1:10
4:10 Acts 12:12; 15:37; 19:29; 20:4; 27:2
4:12 Col 1:7; Phlm 1:23
4:13 Col 2:1
4:14 2 Tim 4:10-11; Phlm 1:24
4:15 Rom 16:5
4:16 1 Thes 5:27; 2 Thes 3:14
4:17 2 Tim 4:5; Phlm 1:2
4:18 1 Cor 16:21; 2 Thes 3:17

4:15 Greek *brothers.*

4:7 Tychicus was apparently the bearer of the letter that Paul sent to the Colossians and the letter he sent to the Ephesians (Ephesians 6:21).

4:9 Onesimus carried the letter to the Colossians along with Tychicus. Although a runaway slave (see Paul's letter to Philemon), Paul nevertheless holds Onesimus in high regard, and he encourages the Colossians to see him this way as well.

4:10 Aristarchus was originally from Thessalonica and traveled with Paul at times (Acts 19:29; 20:4; 27:2; Philemon 1:24). He was now in prison with Paul in Rome.

4:14 This is a reference to the same Luke who wrote the Gospel that bears his name. Paul also mentions him in 2 Timothy 4:11 and Philemon 1:24. Demas is also mentioned in that passage. Sadly, Demas later deserted Paul because he loved the things of the world more than the things of God (2 Timothy 4:10).

4:16 Some believe that the letter we know as Ephesians was actually a letter to various churches in the province of Asia where Ephesus was; in that case, the letter Paul refers to here would be the letter he wrote to the church in Laodicea (another city in the same general area).

4:18 Paul's remark about writing the greeting "in [his] own handwriting" is likely due to the rest of the letter being written by an amanuensis (a scribe), who wrote as Paul dictated the letter.

1 THESSALONIANS

PURPOSE

To present the reality of Jesus' return as grounds for encouragement and motivation to live responsibly in the midst of suffering.

How should you respond to suffering? What will help us endure hardships and answer antagonism toward the message of Jesus? Paul addresses these questions as he writes to the Christians in Thessalonica who were relatively young in the faith.

On his second missionary journey, Paul brought the news about Jesus to the city of Thessalonica (Acts 17:1-15). However, because of persecution from some Jewish leaders, he and his companions had to leave very soon after their arrival. Paul didn't get the chance to build as strong a foundation into the lives of the saints in Thessalonica as he would have liked, and the persecution he faced personally soon came to bear on this new congregation. How could Paul encourage a struggling church in the face of persecution? What could he tell them that would help them find their way through difficult times? In this letter, he offers simple, powerful encouragement in the face of difficulties by calling on the Thessalonians to realize God's plan for their future.

DISCOVER GOD IN 1 THESSALONIANS

Much of Paul's attention in this letter focuses on Jesus and His future physical return to the earth, but he also talks about other themes:

The One True God: In a cosmopolitan city like Thessalonica, you could readily encounter the worshipers of any number of gods, most of whom were from Greek or Roman sources. But the Christ revealed by Paul stood in stark contrast to the all-too-human pantheon of demigods of that time. In Thessalonians, Paul shows Jesus as the God who will rescue (1:10; 5:4-11), reward (2:19), renew (3:13), and resurrect all who trust in Him.

The Spirit who Empowers Ministry: Paul clearly affirms that it is the Spirit who empowers the preaching that brings conversion (1:4-6). But Paul also acknowledges the Spirit's work in the life of every believer, and to resist that work is to resist the Spirit (4:8). Paul also reminds his readers that it is the Spirit who speaks prophetically through the community (5:19-21), and they are to embrace that work of the Spirit as well.

Jesus who will Soon Return: A major focus is the return of Jesus. Each chapter ends with a reference to Jesus' physical return (1:10; 2:19-20; 3:13; 4:16-18; 5:23-24). It is the certainty of the promise of blessing and fulfillment that Jesus brings that forms the basis of Paul's exhortations in this letter.

GROWING THROUGH 1 THESSALONIANS

Paul affirms how the Thessalonian believers had become a model to saints in other places (1:7-9). With this in mind, journeying through this epistle can raise important questions for every disciple:

Am I living as a model for others? Not just in their own community, but also in the entire region around them, the Thessalonian believers had a reputation of faith, hope, and love (1:2-10). Paul commends them, saying that the way they were living is a true model and encouragement to others. Would Paul write the same about your life in Jesus? About the church you are a part of?

Am I responding to the word of God? Part of the reason for the tremendous growth in the lives of the Thessalonians must be attributed to the response they first made to the Good News (1:6; 2:13). They did not take a casual attitude toward the teaching of the Word; they embraced it as the life-giving message they needed. How might Paul assess your response to the teaching you hear from week to week? Are you responding to the messages you hear from the Word as if God Himself is speaking to you?

Am I standing strong even when the going gets tough? Paul not only notices how the Thessalonians are standing fast in spite of the persecution they are facing, but he prays that the Lord will continue to strengthen and sustain them (3:7-13). What do you do when the "going gets tough"? If someone challenges you about the faith or harasses you because of your commitment to Jesus, would Paul find you standing strong like the Thessalonians? Do you ask for God's strength to help you in such times?

Am I encouraging others with the truth of Jesus' return? Paul reminds the Thessalonians that, because Jesus is coming back, the future is certain, and their troubles will soon be over. He tells them to encourage one another with this truth (5:10-11). In spite of the challenges and obstacles of life, do you recognize that God is in control and that Jesus will soon return and make all things right? Do you encourage others with this truth? Or do you let the troubles of the moment overwhelm you and blind you to God's promises to His people?

DISCOVERY VERSES

So you received the message with joy from the Holy Spirit in spite of the severe suffering it brought you. In this way, you imitated both us and the Lord. As a result, you have become an example to all the believers in Greece—throughout both Macedonia and Achaia.

(1 THESSALONIANS 1:6-7)

We loved you so much that we shared with you not only God's Good News but our own lives, too.

(1 THESSALONIANS 2:8)

Now may the God of peace make you holy in every way, and may your whole spirit and soul and body be kept blameless until our Lord Jesus Christ comes again. God will make this happen, for He who calls you is faithful.

(1 THESSALONIANS 5:23-24)

1 THESSALONIANS FACTS

Author: As is common with his letters, Paul readily identifies himself right from the start (1:1). Later, he mentions himself by name again (2:18) in speaking of his desire to come and see the believers in Thessalonica, a church he helped plant (Acts 17:1-14).

Written to: Thessalonica was located on a major trade route that ran through the region going from the east to the west. It was a seaport and a major center for commerce and communication. The city's strategic location enabled the church there to become a very visible model for other churches in the region (1 Thessalonians 1:4-10)—for better or for worse.

Date of writing: Paul indicates that he is writing to the Thessalonians sometime after departing from them and after sending Timothy to them from Athens (1 Thessalonians 3:1-5; Acts 17:13-15). Timothy returned to Paul while he was in Corinth a short while later (Acts 18:1-5). Thus, based on the chronology we find in the book of Acts, this letter was one of Paul's earliest, being written sometime around AD 51.

Setting: Paul was on his second missionary journey and had stopped in Thessalonica to preach the Good News, but he was soon driven out because of persecution. Paul settled in Corinth to preach and teach for a while, and Timothy joined up with him there. It is from Corinth that Paul sent this letter to the Thessalonian congregation.

OUTLINE

▸ **1 THESSALONIANS 1:1-10**—The Thessalonians' Faith—Rooted in the Certainty of Jesus' Return

▸ **1 THESSALONIANS 2:1-20**—Paul's Ministry—Motivated by the Certainty of Jesus' Return

▸ **1 THESSALONIANS 3:1-13**—The Thessalonians' Endurance—Rooted in the Certainty of Jesus' Return

▸ **1 THESSALONIANS 4:1-18**—The Thessalonians' Lifestyle—Holy Living in Light of Jesus' Return

▸ **1 THESSALONIANS 5:1-28**—Paul's Perspective—the Sure Hope of Jesus' Return

GREETINGS FROM PAUL

1 This letter is from Paul, Silas,* and Timothy.
We are writing to the church in Thessalonica, to you who belong to God the Father
and the Lord Jesus Christ.
May God give you grace and peace.

THE FAITH OF THE THESSALONIAN BELIEVERS

[2]We always thank God for all of you and pray for you constantly. [3]As we pray to our God
and Father about you, we think of your faithful work, your loving deeds, and the enduring
hope you have because of our Lord Jesus Christ.
[4]We know, dear brothers and sisters,* that God loves you and has chosen you to be His
own people. [5]For when we brought you the Good News, it was not only with words but
also with power, for the Holy Spirit gave you full assurance* that what we said was true.
And you know of our concern for you from the way we lived when we were with you. [6]So
you received the message with joy from the Holy Spirit in spite of the severe suffering it
brought you. In this way, you imitated both us and the Lord. [7]As a result, you have be-
come an example to all the believers in Greece—throughout both Macedonia and Achaia.*
[8]And now the word of the Lord is ringing out from you to people everywhere, even be-
yond Macedonia and Achaia, for wherever we go we find people telling us about your
faith in God. We don't need to tell them about it, [9]for they keep talking about the wonder-
ful welcome you gave us and how you turned away from idols to serve the living and true
God. [10]And they speak of how you are looking forward to the coming of God's Son from
heaven—Jesus, whom God raised from the dead. He is the One who has rescued us from
the terrors of the coming judgment.

1:1 Acts 17:1; 2 Thes 1:1
1:2 Rom 1:8-10; Phil 1:3-4; Col 1:3; 2 Thes 1:11
1:3 1 Cor 13:13; Col 1:4-5; 2 Thes 1:11
1:4 Col 3:12; 2 Thes 2:13; 2 Pet 1:10
1:5 1 Cor 2:4-5; 4:20; 1 Thes 2:10; 2 Thes 3:7
1:6 Acts 17:1-9; 1 Cor 4:16
1:8 Rom 1:8; 2 Thes 3:1
1:9 Acts 14:15; 1 Cor 12:2
1:10 Phil 3:20; 1 Thes 5:9; Titus 2:13; Heb 9:28; Rev 1:7

1:1 Greek *Silvanus*, the Greek form of the name. 1:4 Greek *brothers*. 1:5 Or *with the power of the Holy Spirit, so you can have full assurance.* 1:7 *Macedonia* and *Achaia* were the northern and southern regions of Greece.

1:2-3 Paul expresses gratitude to God for three traits that he and others have observed in the Thessalonians: their faith, love, and hope, the three cardinal virtues Paul identifies in 1 Corinthians 13:13. The Thessalonians' faith and love were expressed in actions and deeds. Their "enduring hope" was centered on the return of Jesus Christ, which would bring an end to their troubles.

1:5 When Paul brought the gospel message to Thessalonica, he used words to proclaim it. But Paul's words and oratory were not the reason faith was kindled in the Thessalonians. It was the Spirit, not Paul, who convinced the Thessalonians to trust in Christ (1 Corinthians 2:23).

▸ **WORSHIP**

1:5 The messenger is the message. "Listen to the message, not the messenger." How often have you heard this statement used by teachers or preachers as a way to excuse their sin even while they continue their speaking ministry? Such people claim to know God, but they deny Him by their actions (Titus 1:16). There are also those, however, whose lives are an accurate reflection of the message they proclaim, and the apostle Paul was such a man. Here he boasts to the Thessalonians that they knew the way he lived when he was among them, and that they could testify that the message he taught was the message he lived out. Such integrity of life is God's intention not just for every preacher, but also for every Christian. (***See Worship****> NT> Teaching and Preaching> Preach the word in season and out,* TopicGuide page A34.)

1:6 Paul commends the Thessalonians for the joy that has marked their pilgrimage with Christ from the start. This joy was remarkable because the Thessalonians saw the affliction that the Jews brought on Paul and Silas for preaching the message (Acts 17:5-10), and it would not have been hard for them to guess that the wrath of the Jews also would fall on those who believed the gospel. Persecution did come, but these unhappy circumstances did not nullify the Thessalonian believers' joy, a sure sign of the Spirit's power working in them.

1:8 As Paul traveled, he found that reports about the faith and life of the Thessalonian believers had gone ahead of him. In an age of limited and very slow communication, reports about the vibrant faith of the Thessalonians had been "broadcast" throughout the Greek world and beyond.

PAUL REMEMBERS HIS VISIT

2 You yourselves know, dear brothers and sisters,* that our visit to you was not a fail-
ure. 2You know how badly we had been treated at Philippi just before we came to
you and how much we suffered there. Yet our God gave us the courage to declare His
Good News to you boldly, in spite of great opposition. 3So you can see we were not
preaching with any deceit or impure motives or trickery.

4For we speak as messengers approved by God to be entrusted with the Good News.
Our purpose is to please God, not people. He alone examines the motives of our hearts.
5Never once did we try to win you with flattery, as you well know. And God is our witness
that we were not pretending to be your friends just to get your money! 6As for human
praise, we have never sought it from you or anyone else.

7As apostles of Christ we certainly had a right to make some demands of you, but in-
stead we were like children* among you. Or we were like a mother feeding and caring for
her own children. 8We loved you so much that we shared with you not only God's Good
News but our own lives, too.

9Don't you remember, dear brothers and sisters, how hard we worked among you?
Night and day we toiled to earn a living so that we would not be a burden to any of you as
we preached God's Good News to you. 10You yourselves are our witnesses—and so is
God—that we were devout and honest and faultless toward all of you believers. 11And you
know that we treated each of you as a father treats his own children. 12We pleaded with
you, encouraged you, and urged you to live your lives in a way that God would consider
worthy. For He called you to share in His Kingdom and glory.

2:1 Greek *brothers;* also in 2:9, 14, 17. 2:7 Some manuscripts read *we were gentle.*

2:1 1 Thes 1:5, 9
2:2 Acts 16:22; 17:2; Phil 1:30
2:3 2 Cor 4:2; 2 Pet 1:16
2:4 Gal 1:10; 1 Tim 1:11
2:5 Acts 20:33
2:7 2 Tim 2:24
2:8 2 Cor 12:15
2:9 Acts 18:3; 2 Cor 11:9; 2 Thes 3:8
2:10 1 Thes 1:5
2:11 1 Cor 4:14
2:12 Eph 4:1; Col 1:10; 1 Pet 1:15

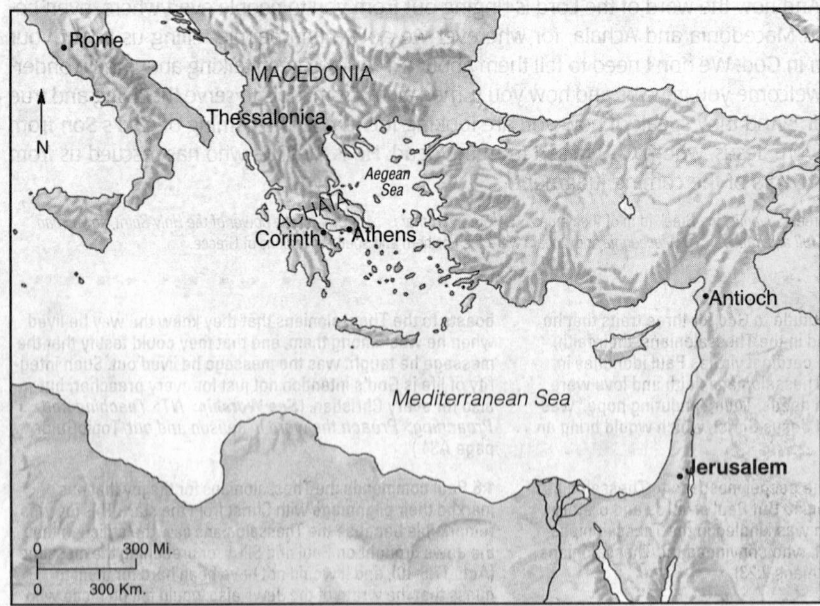

LOCATION OF THESSALONICA
Paul visited Thessalonica on his second and third missionary journeys. It was a seaport and trade center located on the Egnatian Way, a busy international highway. Paul probably wrote his two letters to the Thessalonians from Corinth.

2:2 Before coming to Thessalonica, Paul and his companions visited Philippi, where they endured persecution and were even put into jail for preaching the gospel (Acts 16). But God gave His servants courage to preach boldly. As a result, the gospel took hold with the conversions of Lydia, the jailer, and many in their households.

2:7 Paul had a right to make demands of the people to whom he preached—even financial ones—because, as he said in 1 Timothy 5:18, "Those who work deserve their pay." But Paul had a strong desire to set his ministry apart from those of others who were preaching the gospel from improper motives (2 Corinthians 11:8-13). For this reason, he worked hard to earn a living while he taught the people (1 Thessalonians 2:9; see also Acts 18:3).

2:13 13 Therefore, we never stop thanking God that when you received His message from us,
1 Thes 1:2; 2 Thes 2:13 you didn't think of our words as mere human ideas. You accepted what we said as the very
word of God—which, of course, it is. And this word continues to work in you who believe.
2:14 Acts 17:5 14 And then, dear brothers and sisters, you suffered persecution from your own country-
1 Thes 1:6 men. In this way, you imitated the believers in God's churches in Judea who, because of
2:15 their belief in Christ Jesus, suffered from their own people, the Jews. 15 For some of the
Luke 24:20; Acts 2:23; 7:52 Jews killed the prophets, and some even killed the Lord Jesus. Now they have persecuted
2:16 us, too. They fail to please God and work against all humanity 16 as they try to keep us
Matt 23:32-33 from preaching the Good News of salvation to the Gentiles. By doing this, they continue to
Acts 13:45, 50; 17:5; 20:3; 21:27; 24:9 pile up their sins. But the anger of God has caught up with them at last.

TIMOTHY'S GOOD REPORT ABOUT THE CHURCH

2:17 1 Cor 5:3; 1 Thes 3:10 17 Dear brothers and sisters, after we were separated from you for a little while (though our
2:18 Rom 1:13; 15:22 hearts never left you), we tried very hard to come back because of our intense longing to
see you again. 18 We wanted very much to come to you, and I, Paul, tried again and again,
2:19 Phil 2:16 but Satan prevented us. 19 After all, what gives us hope and joy, and what will be our proud
1 Thes 3:13; 2 Thes 1:4 reward and crown as we stand before our Lord Jesus when He returns? It is you! 20 Yes, you
Rev 1:7; 22:12 are our pride and joy.

2:20 2 Cor 1:14 **3** Finally, when we could stand it no longer, we decided to stay alone in Athens, 2 and
3:1 we sent Timothy to visit you. He is our brother and God's co-worker* in proclaiming
Acts 17:15 the Good News of Christ. We sent him to strengthen you, to encourage you in your faith,
3:2 Acts 16:1-3 3 and to keep you from being shaken by the troubles you were going through. But you
3:3 know that we are destined for such troubles. 4 Even while we were with you, we warned
2 Tim 3:12 you that troubles would soon come—and they did, as you well know. 5 That is why, when I
3:4 could bear it no longer, I sent Timothy to find out whether your faith was still strong. I was
1 Thes 2:14 afraid that the tempter had gotten the best of you and that our work had been useless.
3:5 Matt 4:3 6 But now Timothy has just returned, bringing us good news about your faith and love.
Phil 2:16 He reports that you always remember our visit with joy and that you want to see us as

3:6 Acts 18:5

3:2 Other manuscripts read *and God's servant;* still others read *and a co-worker,* or *and a servant and co-worker for God,* or *and God's servant and our co-worker.*

2:14-15 The Thessalonians were enduring persecution for believing the message of Christ. The initial Thessalonian converts were Jews, and the persecution they endured came from their fellow Jews (Acts 17:4-5). In this, the Thessalonian believers were experiencing the same enmity that the first Christians endured in Judea, indeed the same enmity that the Jewish leaders expressed toward Jesus Himself. But Paul traces this enmity back even further, to the persecutions directed at God's Old Testament messengers, the prophets. Jesus made the same connection (Matthew 5:11-12).

▸ SPIRITUAL WARFARE

2:18 Satan's influence. Most Christians fall into one of two categories when it comes to talking about the demonic: They give Satan either too much credit or too little credit. In the New Testament, Christ teaches that Satan has been bound (Matthew 12:23-31), which shows Satan's influence is diminished—but that influence will not be completely extinguished until Christ returns on the Day of Judgment to destroy the work of Satan (Revelation 20:10). In the meantime, Christians can expect to encounter Satan's schemes (2 Corinthians 2:11), but they are also able to resist them (1 Peter 5:8-9). Satan is real, but Christ is with you, and He is greater than Satan. Rejoice that Satan has no more authority over you than he does over your Master, Jesus. (***See Spiritual Warfare**> Resisting Sin and Evil> Resisting Temptation> How to Resist> By the help of God,* TopicGuide page A45.)

3:1 Timothy was a young man who became one of Paul's companions and helpers during the apostle's second missionary journey (Acts 16:1-3)—the journey that brought Paul to Thessalonica. Paul quickly came to esteem Timothy highly; he eventually referred to Timothy as his "beloved and faithful child in the Lord" (1 Corinthians 4:17). Since Paul was unable to return to visit the Thessalonians, he sent Timothy back to strengthen their faith during persecution and to bring back word to Paul about whether the church was standing firm (3:5). Paul is overjoyed by the good report Timothy brings (3:6-7).

▸ ADOPTION

3:3 The promise of suffering. When Paul says that Christians are "destined" for such persecutions, what does he mean? Many today think that once they come to Christ, He will take all their troubles and worries away. But this is not the truth of Scripture. God has designed His people for such hardships, for we are being made into the image of Christ, and that must include sharing in His suffering (Romans 8:17; Philippians 1:29). It is through persecution that God's people are refined in their faith and grow in perseverance, character, and hope (Romans 5:3-4). If you are in the midst of a trial or persecution, thank God for it. Through it, He is working to make you more like His Son, Jesus. (***See Adoption**> With Christ> Children of God> Children share suffering and glory,* TopicGuide page A36.)

much as we want to see you. 7So we have been greatly encouraged in the midst of our
troubles and suffering, dear brothers and sisters,* because you have remained strong in
your faith. 8It gives us new life to know that you are standing firm in the Lord.
9How we thank God for you! Because of you we have great joy as we enter God's pres-
ence. 10Night and day we pray earnestly for you, asking God to let us see you again to fill
the gaps in your faith.
11May God our Father and our Lord Jesus bring us to you very soon. 12And may the Lord
make your love for one another and for all people grow and overflow, just as our love for you
overflows. 13May He, as a result, make your hearts strong, blameless, and holy as you stand
before God our Father when our Lord Jesus comes again with all His holy people. Amen.

LIVE TO PLEASE GOD

4 Finally, dear brothers and sisters,* we urge you in the name of the Lord Jesus to live
in a way that pleases God, as we have taught you. You live this way already, and we
encourage you to do so even more. 2For you remember what we taught you by the au-
thority of the Lord Jesus.
3God's will is for you to be holy, so stay away from all sexual sin. 4Then each of you will
control his own body* and live in holiness and honor—5not in lustful passion like the pa-
gans who do not know God and His ways. 6Never harm or cheat a Christian brother in this
matter by violating his wife,* for the Lord avenges all such sins, as we have solemnly
warned you before. 7God has called us to live holy lives, not impure lives. 8Therefore, any-
one who refuses to live by these rules is not disobeying human teaching but is rejecting
God, who gives His Holy Spirit to you.
9But we don't need to write to you about the importance of loving each other,* for God
Himself has taught you to love one another. 10Indeed, you already show your love for all
the believers* throughout Macedonia. Even so, dear brothers and sisters, we urge you to
love them even more.
11Make it your goal to live a quiet life, minding your own business and working with
your hands, just as we instructed you before. 12Then people who are not Christians will re-
spect the way you live, and you will not need to depend on others.

THE HOPE OF THE RESURRECTION

13And now, dear brothers and sisters, we want you to know what will happen to the believ-
ers who have died* so you will not grieve like people who have no hope. 14For since we

3:7 2 Thes 1:4
3:8 1 Cor 16:13
3:10 1 Thes 2:16-17; 2 Tim 1:3
3:12 Phil 1:9
3:13 Zech 14:5; 1 Cor 1:8; 1 Thes 1:7, 10; 2:19
4:1 Eph 4:1; 2 Thes 3:6
4:3 Heb 10:10; 1 Pet 1:16
4:4 1 Cor 7:2
4:6 1 Cor 6:8
4:7 Lev 11:44; 2 Thes 2:13-14; 1 Pet 1:15
4:8 Rom 5:5; 1 Jn 3:24
4:9 Jer 31:33-34; John 6:45; 13:34; 1 Jn 2:20, 27
4:10 2 Thes 3:4
4:11 Eph 4:28; 2 Thes 3:10-12
4:13 Eph 2:12
4:14 Rom 14:9; 1 Cor 15:3-4, 12

3:7 Greek *brothers.* 4:1 Greek *brothers;* also in 4:10, 13. 4:4 Or *will know how to take a wife for himself;* or *will learn to live with his own wife;* Greek reads *will know how to possess his own vessel.* 4:6 Greek *Never harm or cheat a brother in this matter.* 4:9 Greek *about brotherly love.* 4:10 Greek *the brothers.* 4:13 Greek *those who have fallen asleep;* also in 4:14.

3:7-8 Hearing that the Thessalonian believers had remained faithful in their hardships encouraged Paul to remain faithful in his own trials (2 Corinthians 11:16–12:10). Paul characterizes this sense of encouragement as "new life."

▸ GOD
4:3-5 Clean living. Most people today disdain or ignore sexual purity. Even Christians sometimes indulge in immoral behavior, but God wants His people to live holy lives. Everything that is done and can be done is an opportunity to honor and glorify God, and that includes sexual behavior. God says there is a right way to relate to those to whom you are not married (that is, in holiness) and a wrong way (in lustful passions) (see also 1 Timothy 5:2). Do you relate to people of the opposite gender as sexual objects or possible conquests, or do you love them as brothers or sisters in Christ? Strive to conform your sexual behavior to God's standards. (***See God**> Relationship> God Enables> Relationship with God requires purity,* TopicGuide page A14.)

4:11-12 Paul's admonition that the Thessalonians lead "a quiet life" was not intended as a strategy for avoiding persecution. Rather, it was his prescription for earning the respect of unbelievers. By living in a humble way, the Thessalonian believers would give unbelievers no opportunities to reproach the church as a whole.

4:13-17 As the Thessalonians awaited the return of Christ, people began to die—which was not what they expected. This led them to ask what happens to believers who die before Christ returns. Paul elsewhere told believers that the spirits of dead Christians go to be with God (2 Corinthians 5:8), but here he assures the Thessalonians that their deceased loved ones will experience the triumphant return of Christ as surely as those who are alive when He comes.

believe that Jesus died and was raised to life again, we also believe that when Jesus re-
turns, God will bring back with Him the believers who have died.
15 We tell you this directly from the Lord: We who are still living when the Lord returns
will not meet Him ahead of those who have died.* 16 For the Lord Himself will come down
from heaven with a commanding shout, with the voice of the archangel, and with the
trumpet call of God. First, the Christians who have died* will rise from their graves. 17 Then,
together with them, we who are still alive and remain on the earth will be caught up in the
clouds to meet the Lord in the air. Then we will be with the Lord forever. 18 So encourage
each other with these words.

5 Now concerning how and when all this will happen, dear brothers and sisters,* we
don't really need to write you. 2 For you know quite well that the day of the Lord's re-
turn will come unexpectedly, like a thief in the night. 3 When people are saying, "Every-
thing is peaceful and secure," then disaster will fall on them as suddenly as a pregnant
woman's labor pains begin. And there will be no escape.
4 But you aren't in the dark about these things, dear brothers and sisters, and you
won't be surprised when the day of the Lord comes like a thief.* 5 For you are all children
of the light and of the day; we don't belong to darkness and night. 6 So be on your guard,
not asleep like the others. Stay alert and be clearheaded. 7 Night is the time when peo-
ple sleep and drinkers get drunk. 8 But let us who live in the light be clearheaded, pro-
tected by the armor of faith and love, and wearing as our helmet the confidence of our
salvation.
9 For God chose to save us through our Lord Jesus Christ, not to pour out His anger on us.
10 Christ died for us so that, whether we are dead or alive when He returns, we can live with
Him forever. 11 So encourage each other and build each other up, just as you are already
doing.

4:15 1 Cor 7:10, 25; 15:52
4:16 Matt 24:30; 1 Cor 15:52; 1 Thes 1:10; 2 Thes 1:7
4:17 Acts 1:9; Rev 11:12
5:2 Matt 24:42-44; Luke 12:39-40; 2 Pet 3:10
5:3 Jer 4:10; 6:14; Ezek 13:10; Matt 24:39; Luke 21:34-35
5:4 1 Jn 2:8
5:5 John 12:36; Eph 5:9
5:8 Isa 59:17; Eph 6:14, 17; 1 Pet 1:13
5:9 1 Thes 1:10; 2 Thes 2:13-14
5:10 Rom 14:8-9

4:15 Greek *those who have fallen asleep.* 4:16 Greek *the dead in Christ.* 5:1 Greek *brothers;* also in 5:4, 12, 14, 25, 26, 27. 5:4 Some manuscripts read *comes upon you as if you were thieves.*

4:14 Christ's resurrection broke the power of death, and Paul said that Christ was "the first of a great harvest" of dead saints who will be raised (1 Corinthians 15:20). He went on to say that "all who belong to Christ will be raised when he comes back" (1 Corinthians 15:23).

4:16 The sound of a trumpet was used to gather the entire congregation of God's people to Him at Sinai (Exodus 19:16). Trumpets were also used to rally God's armies (Joshua 6) and to call the people to worship (Leviticus 23:23-24). In the same way, a trumpet will be used to gather all of God's people at Christ's final return. At that time, the dead and the living alike will be gathered and will be with the Lord forever.

5:1-3 It seems likely that the Thessalonians had asked Paul to clarify the date and time of Christ's return, but Paul says they already know that no answer can be given. Jesus Himself said that even He did not know the precise time (Matthew 24:36), but He did say that believers, seeing certain signs, can judge when the time is close (Matthew 24:33). Unbelievers are blind to these signs, for which reason the return of Christ will be as surprising to them as a thief in the night or the onset of childbirth. The term *day of the Lord* is used extensively in the Bible as a synonym for a time of divine judgment.

▸ WORSHIP

5:2 Don't get too comfortable. A nice dinner can be spoiled if the guests don't arrive when expected. The Thessalonians got themselves into a bit of trouble because they expected Christ's imminent return; some of them apparently even quit their jobs to wait for His return (2 Thessalonians 3:6-10). Today, the opposite error is pervasive—most people act as if Christ will never return! Are you so content with worldly goods and with business and parenting that Christ's return and judgment of the world seem far off? There is a day, and a day that could be very soon, when people will have to give an account for all they have done (Matthew 25). Don't let anything take your eye off that coming day of rescue and judgment. (***See Worship****> NT> Christ's Kingship> Jesus shall return as king and judge,* TopicGuide page A30.)

5:5-8 Paul employs the popular biblical analogy of light and darkness to describe the two categories of people upon whom the day of the Lord will come. Believers are those God "called . . . out of the darkness into His wonderful light" (1 Peter 2:9). Having been born again from above, Christians are awake to spiritual realities. But unbelievers remain in spiritual darkness, where they are "asleep" to truths such as Christ's sure return.

PAUL'S FINAL ADVICE

12Dear brothers and sisters, honor those who are your leaders in the Lord's work. They
work hard among you and give you spiritual guidance. 13Show them great respect and
wholehearted love because of their work. And live peacefully with each other.
14Brothers and sisters, we urge you to warn those who are lazy. Encourage those who
are timid. Take tender care of those who are weak. Be patient with everyone.
15See that no one pays back evil for evil, but always try to do good to each other and to
all people.
16Always be joyful. 17Never stop praying. 18Be thankful in all circumstances, for this is
God's will for you who belong to Christ Jesus.
19Do not stifle the Holy Spirit. 20Do not scoff at prophecies, 21but test everything that is
said. Hold on to what is good. 22Stay away from every kind of evil.

PAUL'S FINAL GREETINGS

23Now may the God of peace make you holy in every way, and may your whole spirit and
soul and body be kept blameless until our Lord Jesus Christ comes again. 24God will make
this happen, for He who calls you is faithful.
25Dear brothers and sisters, pray for us.
26Greet all the brothers and sisters with Christian love.*
27I command you in the name of the Lord to read this letter to all the brothers and
sisters.
28May the grace of our Lord Jesus Christ be with you.

5:26 Greek *with a holy kiss.*

5:12 1 Tim 5:17
5:14 2 Thes 3:6-7, 11
5:15 Prov 20:22; Rom 12:17; 1 Pet 3:9
5:16 Phil 4:4
5:17 Luke 18:1
5:18 Eph 5:20
5:19 Eph 4:30
5:20 1 Cor 14:1, 39
5:21 1 Jn 4:1
5:23 Rom 15:33
5:24 1 Cor 1:9
5:27 Col 4:16

5:12-13 As the apostles went from city to city, they typically appointed elders to pastor the churches that they planted (Acts 14:23). Paul asked the people to give honor to those leaders and to support them in the Lord's work.

5:16-18 In a series of pithy admonitions, Paul stresses "God's will for you who belong to Christ Jesus." His first admonition is to "always be joyful," since Paul recognized that joy is a fruit of the Holy Spirit (Galatians 5:22-23) and is not dependent on circumstances.

5:21 When persecution drove Paul out of Thessalonica, he began to minister in Berea. The Jews to whom he preached listened to him eagerly and then "searched the Scriptures . . . to see if Paul and Silas were teaching the truth" (Acts 17:11). Paul here encourages this use of Scripture as the standard for judging all teaching.

5:27 Many of Paul's epistles are addressed to particular churches, and he intended his words to be communicated to every member. Here he commands that this letter be read aloud in the assembly of the Thessalonian saints.

2 THESSALONIANS

PURPOSE

To present the certain return of Jesus in the future as the motivation to continue in faith in the present.

How many doses of the truth do you need before it "takes"? Some medications don't become effective with just one dose. With most antibiotics you need to be on the medication for a little while before the effect is felt and you start to get better. You may need more than one dose. That image is helpful for understanding Paul's letters to the Thessalonians.

Paul brought the news about Jesus to the city of Thessalonica on his second missionary journey (Acts 17:1-15). Because of persecution from some Jewish leaders that arose, he and his companions had to leave after only a short while. As a result, this growing community didn't get the benefit of his extended teaching ministry, so he sent Timothy to check on the young church and bring back a report. That report prompted Paul to write 1 Thessalonians, in which the apostle sought to address some of the false teaching (particularly about the last days) that had arisen in the community there. Apparently, however, Paul needed to administer a second dose of solid teaching to these believers to counteract the false teaching they had heard. So, in much the same vein as 1 Thessalonians, Paul penned a second letter shortly after the first to remind the Thessalonians of the truths about Jesus' return in the future and how that truth should impact the way they live in the present.

DISCOVER GOD IN 2 THESSALONIANS

Although much of Paul's attention is on the return of Jesus, he also reminds us of some important insights about our great God.

God Who Is Just: The Thessalonians are facing persecution, and Paul reminds them that the God they serve is a just God who will rightly deal with their adversaries (1:5-10). The followers of Jesus do not have to worry about how things will turn out in the end; God will ensure that justice will be established and every wrong will be righted.

God Who Loves Us: With a pastor's tenderness for those who are suffering, Paul reminds the Thessalonians that their God loves them (2:13-16; 3:5). God's love is not merely a "warm feeling," it is active and personal. In love He chose the Thessalonians for the kind of life they now enjoy, and He intends for them to live in an ongoing experience of that love (3:5).

God Who Strengthens Us: Because the Thessalonians are facing difficulties, Paul reminds them that their God not only loves them but also will strengthen them and sustain them in everything (1:11-12; 2:16; 3:3). Likewise Paul recognizes that the Thessalonians, like all believers, long to live right in the sight of God. He reminds them that God Himself will work in and through them to bring to fulfillment all their desires for right living (1:11). Even the devil himself will not ultimately be able to frustrate what God intends to do in and through the followers of Jesus (3:3).

GROWING THROUGH 2 THESSALONIANS

Every Christian will face opposition from time to time, and sometimes it will be worse than others. By understanding the truths Paul offers in 2 Thessalonians, every Christian can be better prepared to face trouble and persecution.

God Will Grant Peace to Those Who Are Facing Trouble: Because God is always with us, we need not be overwhelmed by any trial that we face. Paul reminds us that God will provide peace of mind and heart (3:16). No matter how challenging the trial, God intends to provide a solid and stable peace for those who look to Him.

DISCOVERY VERSES

Now may our Lord Jesus Christ Himself and God our Father, who loved us and by His grace gave us eternal comfort and a wonderful hope, comfort you and strengthen you in every good thing you do and say.
(2 THESSALONIANS 2:16-17)

But the Lord is faithful; He will strengthen you and guard you from the evil one. (2 THESSALONIANS 3:3)

May the Lord lead your hearts into a full understanding and expression of the love of God and the patient endurance that comes from Christ.
(2 THESSALONIANS 3:5)

2 THESSALONIANS FACTS

Author: Paul is the author of this second letter to the church in Thessalonica (1:1; 3:17). He specifically refers to the time when he was among them (2:5) and helped plant their church (Acts 17:1-14).

Written to: Thessalonica was located on a major trade route that ran through the region going from the east to the west. It was a seaport and a major center for commerce and communication. As noted in the introduction to 1 Thessalonians, the city's strategic location made it possible for the church there to become a very visible model for other churches in the region (1 Thessalonians 1:4-10; 2 Thessalonians 1:4).

Date of writing: Paul indicates that he is writing to the Thessalonians sometime after departing from them and after sending Timothy to them from Athens (1 Thessalonians 3:1-5; Acts 17:13-15). A short while later Timothy joined Paul in Corinth (Acts 18:1-5). After the church received 1 Thessalonians, the report got back to Paul that there was still some misunderstanding that needed to be addressed, so he followed the first letter very soon after with 2 Thessalonians, writing sometime around AD 51–52.

Setting: Paul was on his second missionary journey and had stopped in Thessalonica to preach the Good News; he was quickly driven out by persecution. Paul settled in Corinth to preach and teach for a while, and Timothy joined him there. From Corinth Paul sent his first letter to the Thessalonian congregation. Shortly afterward, he sent this second letter to the community from the same location.

OUTLINE

- **2 THESSALONIANS 1:1-12**—Thanksgiving for a Secure and Certain Future
- **2 THESSALONIANS 2:1-17**—Encouragement to Rest in the Security of the Future
- **2 THESSALONIANS 3:1-18**—Exhortation to Live Faithfully in Light of the Future

1:1 1 Thes 1:1
1:2 Rom 1:7
1:3 1 Thes 1:2; 2 Thes 2:13

GREETINGS FROM PAUL

1 This letter is from Paul, Silas,* and Timothy.
We are writing to the church in Thessalonica, to you who belong to God our Father
and the Lord Jesus Christ.
2May God our Father* and the Lord Jesus Christ give you grace and peace.

1:5 Phil 1:28; 1 Thes 2:12
1:6 Rev 6:10
1:7 Matt 25:31; 1 Thes 4:16
1:8 Ps 79:6; Isa 66:15; Jer 10:25
1:9 Isa 2:10, 19, 21; 1 Thes 5:3; 2 Thes 2:8
1:10 John 17:10; 1 Thes 3:13

ENCOURAGEMENT DURING PERSECUTION

3Dear brothers and sisters,* we can't help but thank God for you, because your faith is
flourishing and your love for one another is growing. 4We proudly tell God's other
churches about your endurance and faithfulness in all the persecutions and hardships you
are suffering. 5And God will use this persecution to show His justice and to make you wor-
thy of His Kingdom, for which you are suffering. 6In His justice He will pay back those who
persecute you.
7And God will provide rest for you who are being persecuted and also for us when the
Lord Jesus appears from heaven. He will come with His mighty angels, 8in flaming fire,
bringing judgment on those who don't know God and on those who refuse to obey the
Good News of our Lord Jesus. 9They will be punished with eternal destruction, forever
separated from the Lord and from His glorious power. 10When He comes on that day, He
will receive glory from His holy people—praise from all who believe. And this includes you,
for you believed what we told you about Him.

1:1 Greek *Silvanus,* the Greek form of the name. 1:2 Some manuscripts read *God the Father.* 1:3 Greek *Brothers.*

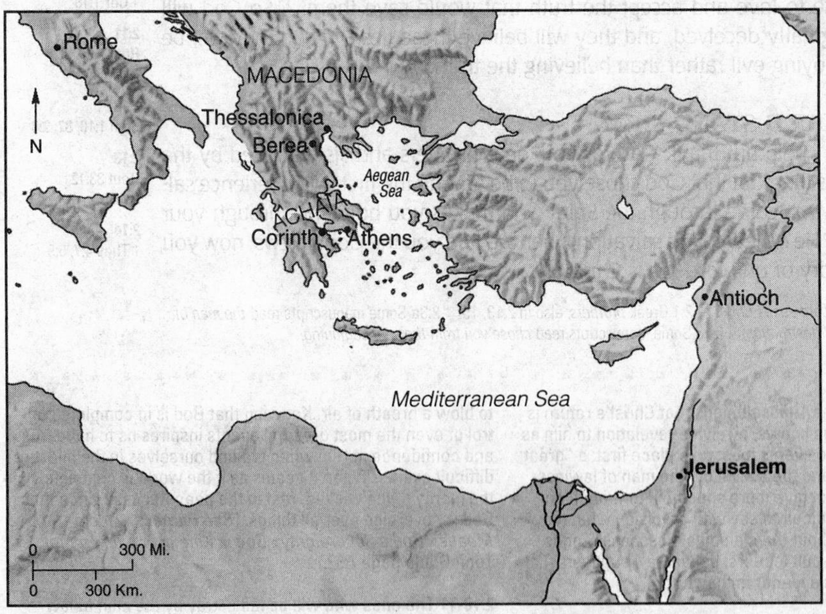

LOCATION OF THESSALONICA
After Paul visited Thessalonica on his second missionary journey, he went on to Berea, Athens, and Corinth (Acts 17–18). From Corinth, Paul wrote his two letters to the Thessalonian church.

1:5 By grace God purchased His people and brought them into His kingdom through the redemptive work of His Son (Colossians 1:13-14). But often He uses persecution to refine them, making them into faithful, trusting, and obedient citizens of the kingdom by encouraging them to depend on Him for mercy and grace.

▸ ADOPTION
1:9 A dreadful place to go. Now is the time to repent and believe the Good News, because once this life is over, there will be no second chances to receive eternal life. Those who refuse to repent and believe are destined for a place of eternal destruction. This place is often called hell or perdition, and it is a very real place (Matthew 5:29; 10:28). Though many today do not wish to believe in such a place, Scripture affirms it as the location where the wicked will be punished. Are there loved ones or friends in your life who might be facing eternity in hell? Reach out to them with the Good News of salvation through Christ. (*See Adoption> Without Christ> Separated from God> Facing second death,* TopicGuide page A36.)

11 So we keep on praying for you, asking our God to enable you to live a life worthy of
His call. May He give you the power to accomplish all the good things your faith prompts
you to do. 12 Then the name of our Lord Jesus will be honored because of the way you live,
and you will be honored along with Him. This is all made possible because of the grace of
our God and Lord, Jesus Christ.*

EVENTS PRIOR TO THE LORD'S SECOND COMING

2 Now, dear brothers and sisters,* let us clarify some things about the coming of our
Lord Jesus Christ and how we will be gathered to meet Him. 2 Don't be so easily
shaken or alarmed by those who say that the day of the Lord has already begun. Don't be-
lieve them, even if they claim to have had a spiritual vision, a revelation, or a letter suppos-
edly from us. 3 Don't be fooled by what they say. For that day will not come until there is a
great rebellion against God and the man of lawlessness* is revealed—the one who brings
destruction.* 4 He will exalt himself and defy everything that people call god and every ob-
ject of worship. He will even sit in the temple of God, claiming that he himself is God.

5 Don't you remember that I told you about all this when I was with you? 6 And you know
what is holding him back, for he can be revealed only when his time comes. 7 For this law-
lessness is already at work secretly, and it will remain secret until the one who is holding it
back steps out of the way. 8 Then the man of lawlessness will be revealed, but the Lord
Jesus will kill him with the breath of His mouth and destroy him by the splendor of His
coming.

9 This man will come to do the work of Satan with counterfeit power and signs and mira-
cles. 10 He will use every kind of evil deception to fool those on their way to destruction,
because they refuse to love and accept the truth that would save them. 11 So God will
cause them to be greatly deceived, and they will believe these lies. 12 Then they will be
condemned for enjoying evil rather than believing the truth.

BELIEVERS SHOULD STAND FIRM

13 As for us, we can't help but thank God for you, dear brothers and sisters loved by the
Lord. We are always thankful that God chose you to be among the first* to experience sal-
vation—a salvation that came through the Spirit who makes you holy and through your
belief in the truth. 14 He called you to salvation when we told you the Good News; now you
can share in the glory of our Lord Jesus Christ.

1:11 1 Thes 1:3
1:12 Isa 66:5; Mal 1:11
2:1 1 Thes 4:13-17
2:2 2 Thes 2:15; 3:17
2:3 1 Tim 4:1
2:4 Isa 14:13-14; 1 Cor 8:5
2:7 1 Jn 4:3
2:8 Job 4:9; Isa 11:4; Rev 19:15
2:9 Matt 24:24; Rev 13:13
2:10 1 Cor 1:18
2:11 Rom 1:24, 28; 2 Tim 4:4
2:12 Rom 1:18, 32; 2:8
2:13 Deut 33:12; Eph 1:4
2:14 1 Thes 4:7; 5:9

1:12 Or *of our God and our Lord Jesus Christ.* 2:1 Greek *brothers;* also in 2:13, 15. 2:3a Some manuscripts read *the man of sin.* 2:3b Greek *the son of destruction.* 2:13 Some manuscripts read *chose you from the very beginning.*

2:3-4 Paul can assure the Thessalonians that Christ's return is not imminent because he knows, by divine revelation to him as Christ's apostle, that two events must take place first: a "great rebellion against God" and the arrival of "the man of lawlessness." Scripture does not give more specific information on these events and it is difficult to say with precision what they might be. Speculation about the man of lawlessness ranges from political leaders to cult leaders, but verse 4 suggests that he will set himself up as a leader in the church.

▸ PURPOSE

2:7 The God who controls all things. When you see wickedness running rampant in the world, do you ever worry that those who follow God will be completely snuffed out? To some extent it is a mystery why God allows wicked people to prosper and oppress His people. Yet the Bible assures us that God uses them to accomplish His purposes (Isaiah 40:15; Daniel 7:25-27). The man of lawlessness (the antichrist) spoken about in these verses will be a dreadful person, yet he will be able to do only what God allows him to do. In the end, God will destroy him with as little effort as it takes to blow a breath of air. Knowing that God is in complete control of even the most dreadful events inspires us to have trust and confidence in Him when we find ourselves in the midst of difficult events. When it seems as if the world is completely at the mercy of the wicked, rest in the peaceful assurance that God is sovereign over all things. (***See Purpose****> God's Means> God's Sovereignty> God is King over every nation,* TopicGuide page A52.)

2:10-11 The ones who will be led astray by the man of lawlessness will be those who refuse to believe the Word of God. They will follow this man because they have chosen to reject God and His truth. Therefore, God in His sovereignty will cause them to believe the man of lawlessness and his lies.

2:15 The apostles were the authoritative teachers of the early church because they were eyewitnesses to Jesus and were specially chosen by Him as His disciples (see 1 John 1:1-4). The letters and other writings that the church accepted for the New Testament canon were those produced by apostles or by those writing under their auspices.

2:15 15With all these things in mind, dear brothers and sisters, stand firm and keep a strong
1 Cor 11:2; 16:13 grip on the teaching we passed on to you both in person and by letter.
2:16 16Now may our Lord Jesus Christ Himself and God our Father, who loved us and by His
John 3:16 grace gave us eternal comfort and a wonderful hope, 17comfort you and strengthen you in
2:17 1 Thes 3:2; 5:11 every good thing you do and say.

PAUL'S REQUEST FOR PRAYER

3:1 1 Thes 1:8; 5:25 **3** Finally, dear brothers and sisters,* we ask you to pray for us. Pray that the Lord's mes-
3:2 sage will spread rapidly and be honored wherever it goes, just as when it came to
Rom 15:31 you. 2Pray, too, that we will be rescued from wicked and evil people, for not everyone is a
3:3 believer. 3But the Lord is faithful; He will strengthen you and guard you from the evil one.*
1 Cor 1:9 4And we are confident in the Lord that you are doing and will continue to do the things we
3:4 commanded you. 5May the Lord lead your hearts into a full understanding and expression
1 Thes 4:10 of the love of God and the patient endurance that comes from Christ.

3:5 1 Chr 29:18

AN EXHORTATION TO PROPER LIVING

3:6 Rom 16:17 6And now, dear brothers and sisters, we give you this command in the name of our Lord
1 Cor 11:2 Jesus Christ: Stay away from all believers* who live idle lives and don't follow the tradition
3:8 they received* from us. 7For you know that you ought to imitate us. We were not idle
Acts 18:3 1 Thes 2:9 when we were with you. 8We never accepted food from anyone without paying for it. We
3:9 worked hard day and night so we would not be a burden to any of you. 9We certainly had
Matt 10:10 the right to ask you to feed us, but we wanted to give you an example to follow. 10Even
1 Cor 9:4, 6 while we were with you, we gave you this command: "Those unwilling to work will not get
3:10 to eat."
1 Thes 4:11 11Yet we hear that some of you are living idle lives, refusing to work and meddling in
3:11 1 Tim 5:13 other people's business. 12We command such people and urge them in the name of the
3:12 Lord Jesus Christ to settle down and work to earn their own living. 13As for the rest of you,
1 Thes 4:11 dear brothers and sisters, never get tired of doing good.
3:15 14Take note of those who refuse to obey what we say in this letter. Stay away from them
Gal 6:1 so they will be ashamed. 15Don't think of them as enemies, but warn them as you would a
1 Thes 5:14 brother or sister.*

PAUL'S FINAL GREETINGS

3:16 16Now may the Lord of peace Himself give you His peace at all times and in every situa-
Rom 15:33 tion. The Lord be with you all.
3:17 1 Cor 16:21 17HERE IS MY GREETING IN MY OWN HANDWRITING—PAUL. I DO THIS IN ALL MY LETTERS TO PROVE THEY ARE
Gal 6:11 FROM ME.
Col 4:18 18May the grace of our Lord Jesus Christ be with you all.
Phlm 1:19

3:1 Greek *brothers;* also in 3:6, 13. **3:3** Or *from evil.* **3:6a** Greek *from every brother.* **3:6b** Some manuscripts read *you received.* **3:15** Greek *as a brother.*

3:2 The apostles frequently asked believers to pray that God would restrain evil and otherwise help them in their work of sharing the gospel with other people (2 Corinthians 1:11; Ephesians 6:19; Colossians 4:3; Hebrews 13:18).

3:6-10 The problem of idleness among believers in Thessalonica, which Paul hinted at in his first letter (1 Thessalonians 4:11-12; 5:14), seems to have worsened. It is possible this idleness stemmed from an expectation that Christ's return was imminent, but Paul never explicitly makes this connection.

3:14 Paul commands the Thessalonians not to associate with those who do not follow the teaching of his letter (see also Matthew 18:15-17; 1 Corinthians 5:5, 9). Though this step may seem harsh, the goal is to bring these people to repentance and faith.

3:17 Paul typically dictated his letters to a scribe, who wrote his words down. But his letters usually contain a section or brief note, such as this one, that was written in Paul's own handwriting, thereby authenticating that the letter was truly from him (1 Corinthians 16:21; Colossians 4:18).

1 TIMOTHY

PURPOSE

To provide training to a young elder in the responsibilities of serving in the church.

So, who's in charge here? Without leadership of some kind, most enterprises ultimately grind to a halt. That is no less true with a local congregation of believers. Although it is true that the Lord Jesus is ultimately the head of the church, local congregations need local leadership in order to grow into maturity and health. But that local leadership is not so much "in charge" as "in service."

Paul wrote three "Pastoral Epistles"—letters that address the topics of growing in ministry and growing in the life of the church. Two letters were addressed to Timothy and one to Titus, and each is filled with practical advice about life and ministry.

Timothy was a young elder left by Paul to help guide the growth of the Ephesian church. The church in which Timothy was serving had the problems of any church—problems in worship (1 Timothy 2), problems in establishing mature leaders (1 Timothy 3), and problems regarding culture (1 Timothy 6:1-2). All of these problems combined to create a problem of disunity, which Paul had addressed in his letter to the Ephesians (see page 2123). The overarching problem Paul addresses in this letter is false teachers (1 Timothy 1:3-11). The way Paul coaches Timothy through that process has value for every Christian seeking to invest his or her life in a significant way in the cause of Christ. Whether you are an elder or a growing disciple, these letters provide real help to those who are committed to the church.

DISCOVER GOD IN 1 TIMOTHY

Tucked away in these comments to a young elder are some clear insights into the Lord of the church.

Jesus, the Savior: Even though Paul is a seasoned pastor and apostle, he still understands his own life in light of the grace that he found in Jesus as Savior (1:12-17); he is what he is because of Jesus' saving work. Paul understands the center of ministry to be the message about Jesus, who reconciles us to God (2:5-6; 4:10).

The Only True God: Confronted with the false teaching that is running rampant, Paul reaffirms to Timothy that there is only one true God (1:17). No others can claim our allegiance. God alone is the eternal and everlasting King, and we meet Him in and through Jesus (2:5; 6:14-16).

The Lord of the Church: Although there are, rightly, leaders in every local church, the church is not theirs. The church is God's. Paul affirms that the message of the church is God's message (1:11). Repeatedly, Paul identifies the church as God's church (3:5, 15).

GROWING THROUGH 1 TIMOTHY

Even if you do not have a role in the church like Timothy's or like those of the elders described in this letter, Paul offers good advice for growth in your spiritual life.

Do Not Neglect Your Spiritual Gift: Recognize what the Spirit has equipped you to do and look to be involved in a way that maximizes that gift.

Be Diligent in Serving: Prepare yourself to serve God fully in the ways you are gifted. A half-hearted effort will result in only a "half-way" ministry. Dive in with enthusiasm into what God intends for you to do.

Trust God for Growth: Maximize the effectiveness of your ministry. Don't hold back because you are not yet all you hope to be in ministry. God intends to mature you in the way you serve as you get involved in serving.

DISCOVERY VERSES

For there is only one God and one Mediator who can reconcile God and humanity—the man Christ Jesus. He gave His life to purchase freedom for everyone. This is the message God gave to the world at just the right time. (1 TIMOTHY 2:5-6)

Without question, this is the great mystery of our faith: Christ was revealed in a human body and vindicated by the Spirit. He was seen by angels and announced to the nations. He was believed in throughout the world and taken to heaven in glory. (1 TIMOTHY 3:16)

Fight the good fight for the true faith. Hold tightly to the eternal life to which God has called you, which you have confessed so well before many witnesses. (1 TIMOTHY 6:12)

1 TIMOTHY FACTS

Author: Paul addresses this somewhat personal letter to Timothy, whom he identifies as his "true son in the faith" (1:2). Paul's greeting and the entire tone of the letter indicate Paul is the author.

Written to: Timothy's father was Greek and his mother was Jewish (Acts 16:1). There is no mention in the Scriptures of his father's faith, but Paul does note that Timothy learned the Scriptures from his mother and grandmother (2 Timothy 1:5). Paul met Timothy in Lystra when Paul visited there (Acts 14:6; 16:1). He ultimately became Paul's protégé (1 Timothy 1:2; 2 Timothy 1:2; Philippians 2:22). It may well be that Paul was instrumental to Timothy's coming to faith in Jesus.

Date of writing: Acts 28 closes with Paul in prison. From what we read in the Pastoral Epistles (see Philippians 1:25-26; Philemon 1:22) it appears that Paul was released from that imprisonment and embarked on a fourth missionary journey (not recorded in Acts). He later endured a second imprisonment, which ended in martyrdom at the hands of Nero around AD 68. During Paul's fourth missionary journey, he left Timothy in a position of responsibility in the church in Ephesus, entrusting this growing congregation to Timothy's care (1 Timothy 1:3). Therefore, Paul likely wrote this first letter to Timothy earlier in his fourth journey, AD 62–64.

Setting: Paul had left Timothy behind in Ephesus while he went on to Macedonia on a fourth missionary journey (1 Timothy 1:3). Paul had spent three years in Ephesus (Acts 19:8-10; 20:31), but the church was still in need of some direction, so as he continued his ministry elsewhere, Paul wrote to Timothy back in Ephesus.

OUTLINE

- **1 TIMOTHY 1:1-20**—The Need to Encourage Good Leadership: to combat false teaching
- **1 TIMOTHY 2:1-15**—The Context for Developing Good Leadership: the local church
- **1 TIMOTHY 3:1-16**—Guidelines for Appointing Good Leadership: spiritual principles
- **1 TIMOTHY 4:1-16**—The Model of Good Leadership: sound life and teaching
- **1 TIMOTHY 5:1–6:2**—The Practice of Good Leadership: attentive care for others
- **1 TIMOTHY 6:3-21**—A Final Caution for Good Leadership: to live for God and not gain

GREETINGS FROM PAUL

1 This letter is from Paul, an apostle of Christ Jesus, appointed by the command of God
our Savior and Christ Jesus, who gives us hope.
2I am writing to Timothy, my true son in the faith.
May God the Father and Christ Jesus our Lord give you grace, mercy, and peace.

WARNINGS AGAINST FALSE TEACHINGS

3When I left for Macedonia, I urged you to stay there in Ephesus and stop those whose
teaching is contrary to the truth. 4Don't let them waste their time in endless discussion of
myths and spiritual pedigrees. These things only lead to meaningless speculations,* which
don't help people live a life of faith in God.*
5The purpose of my instruction is that all believers would be filled with love that comes
from a pure heart, a clear conscience, and genuine faith. 6But some people have missed
this whole point. They have turned away from these things and spend their time in mean-
ingless discussions. 7They want to be known as teachers of the law of Moses, but they
don't know what they are talking about, even though they speak so confidently.
8We know that the law is good when used correctly. 9For the law was not intended for
people who do what is right. It is for people who are lawless and rebellious, who are un-
godly and sinful, who consider nothing sacred and defile what is holy, who kill their father
or mother or commit other murders. 10The law is for people who are sexually immoral, or
who practice homosexuality, or are slave traders,* liars, promise breakers, or who do any-
thing else that contradicts the wholesome teaching 11that comes from the glorious Good
News entrusted to me by our blessed God.

PAUL'S GRATITUDE FOR GOD'S MERCY

12I thank Christ Jesus our Lord, who has given me strength to do His work. He considered
me trustworthy and appointed me to serve Him, 13even though I used to blaspheme the
name of Christ. In my insolence, I persecuted His people. But God had mercy on me be-
cause I did it in ignorance and unbelief. 14Oh, how generous and gracious our Lord was!
He filled me with the faith and love that come from Christ Jesus.
15This is a trustworthy saying, and everyone should accept it: "Christ Jesus came into the
world to save sinners"—and I am the worst of them all. 16But God had mercy on me so that
Christ Jesus could use me as a prime example of His great patience with even the worst sin-
ners. Then others will realize that they, too, can believe in Him and receive eternal life.

1:1 Col 1:27; Titus 1:3; 3:4
1:2 Acts 16:1; 1 Cor 4:17; 2 Tim 1:2; Titus 1:4
1:3 Acts 20:1; Gal 1:6-7; 1 Tim 6:3
1:4 1 Tim 4:7; Titus 3:9
1:5 Rom 13:10; Gal 5:14; 2 Tim 1:5
1:6 2 Tim 2:23; Titus 1:10
1:8 Rom 7:12, 16
1:9 Gal 3:19; 5:23
1:10 1 Tim 6:3; 2 Tim 4:3; Titus 1:9; 2:1
1:11 Gal 2:7
1:12 Acts 9:15; Gal 1:15-16; Phil 4:13
1:13 Luke 23:34; Acts 8:3; 26:9; 1 Cor 15:9
1:14 Rom 5:20; 2 Tim 1:13
1:15 Luke 15:2; 19:10; Rom 5:8

1:4a Greek *in myths and endless genealogies, which cause speculation.* 1:4b Greek *a stewardship of God in faith.* 1:10 Or *kidnappers.*

1:1-3 The apostle's reference to Timothy as his "true son in the faith" (see also Titus 1:4) does not mean that Timothy was converted under Paul's ministry—Timothy likely was already a Christian when the two met (see Acts 16:1-3; 2 Timothy 1:5). Paul was Timothy's mentor in Christian ministry, and Paul had enough confidence in Timothy to leave him in Ephesus to "stop those whose teaching is contrary to the truth." The responsibility of Christian leaders to teach sound doctrine is a major theme in the Pastoral Epistles (1 and 2 Timothy and Titus).

1:4-5 "Myths and spiritual pedigrees" (literally "genealogies") are references to Jewish and Greek extrabiblical religious stories. Telling stories from Jewish history that didn't really happen (see 1 Timothy 4:7; 2 Timothy 4:4; Titus 1:14) or emphasizing one's ancestry do nothing but "lead to meaningless speculations" and do not contribute at all to helping people "live a life of faith in God." Paul wanted Timothy to teach believers about "love," "a pure heart" (see 2 Timothy 2:22), "a clear conscience," and "genuine faith."

▸ SPIRITUAL WARFARE
1:15 One of the worst. How would you rate yourself on the sinfulness scale? Would you say you are very sinful, moderately sinful, or only a little sinful? As Paul considered what God had done in his life, he was filled with gratitude for the grace and generosity God had shown toward him, for he realized that he deserved only God's wrath. In sorrow over his previous way of life, he declared, "I am the worst" sinner of all. Of course, it is impossible for any person to know that he or she is the "worst" sinner among all human beings. The important thing is to realize that we all justly deserve God's wrath and displeasure. Do not minimize your sin; face it and admit it as Paul did, so that your gratitude for your salvation in Christ might be magnified. (***See Spiritual Warfare> Origin of Sin> Humanity's Fall> Spiritual> Sinful from birth,*** TopicGuide page A44.)

17All honor and glory to God forever and ever! He is the eternal King, the unseen One who
never dies; He alone is God. Amen.

TIMOTHY'S RESPONSIBILITY

18Timothy, my son, here are my instructions for you, based on the prophetic words spoken
about you earlier. May they help you fight well in the Lord's battles. 19Cling to your faith in
Christ, and keep your conscience clear. For some people have deliberately violated their
consciences; as a result, their faith has been shipwrecked. 20Hymenaeus and Alexander
are two examples. I threw them out and handed them over to Satan so they might learn
not to blaspheme God.

INSTRUCTIONS ABOUT WORSHIP

2 I urge you, first of all, to pray for all people. Ask God to help them; intercede on their
behalf, and give thanks for them. 2Pray this way for kings and all who are in authority
so that we can live peaceful and quiet lives marked by godliness and dignity. 3This is good
and pleases God our Savior, 4who wants everyone to be saved and to understand the
truth. 5For there is only one God and one Mediator who can reconcile God and humanity—
the man Christ Jesus. 6He gave His life to purchase freedom for everyone. This is the mes-
sage God gave to the world at just the right time. 7And I have been chosen as a preacher
and apostle to teach the Gentiles this message about faith and truth. I'm not exaggerat-
ing—just telling the truth.

8In every place of worship, I want men to pray with holy hands lifted up to God, free
from anger and controversy.

9And I want women to be modest in their appearance.* They should wear decent and
appropriate clothing and not draw attention to themselves by the way they fix their hair or
by wearing gold or pearls or expensive clothes. 10For women who claim to be devoted to
God should make themselves attractive by the good things they do.

11Women should learn quietly and submissively. 12I do not let women teach men or
have authority over them.* Let them listen quietly. 13For God made Adam first, and after-

1:17 Rom 16:27; 1 Tim 6:15
1:18 1 Tim 6:12
1:19 2 Tim 4:7
1:20 1 Cor 5:5; 2 Tim 2:17; 4:14
2:1 Eph 6:18; Phil 4:6
2:2 Rom 13:1
2:4 2 Tim 2:25
2:5 Rom 3:29-30
2:6 Gal 1:4; 2:20
2:7 Acts 9:15; 2 Tim 1:1
2:8 Pss 24:4; 63:4
2:9 1 Pet 3:3-5
2:11 1 Cor 14:34
2:12 Eph 5:22
2:13 Gen 1:27; 2:7, 22

2:9 Or *to pray in modest apparel.* 2:12 Or *teach men or usurp their authority.*

1:17-20 Several attributes of God are mentioned in verse 17. God is "eternal" and lives "forever and ever!" He is sovereign and reigns as "King." He is "unseen" (i.e., invisible), He "never dies" (i.e., immortal), and "He alone is God" (i.e., He is unique and transcendent over His creation). Based on who God is, Paul then encourages Timothy to remain faithful to Him and not to follow the example of those who violate their consciences and blaspheme God.

2:2-4 Scripture teaches Christians to submit to civil authorities (see also Matthew 22:17-21; Romans 13:1-7; 1 Peter 2:13-17) and to pray for them, from the most powerful to the least. Such prayer brings stability to society and allows Christians to "live peaceful and quiet lives" and to serve the Lord in "godliness and dignity" (2:2). The word "truth" in the Pastoral Epistles is often a synonym for the gospel (3:15; 4:3; 6:5; 2 Timothy 2:15; 3:7-8; Titus 1:1), as it is here. As used in these verses, truth does not mean only intellectual facts, but it does include them, since no one can be saved until he or she hears the facts of the gospel.

2:5-7 Scripture clearly teaches that faith in Jesus Christ is the only way of salvation for all people at all times, and this is nowhere more clearly taught than in 1 Timothy 2:5. The "one God" has provided only "one Mediator" between Himself and lost humanity.

▶ HOLINESS

2:9-10 Distracting appearances. How would you define "decent and appropriate clothing"? There are at least as many answers to that question as there are cultures in the world, but Paul offers guidance when he adds that women should not "draw attention to themselves by the way they fix their hair or by wearing gold or pearls or expensive clothes." Paul is not banning these things, but he implies that they should be practiced in a manner that does not invite undue attention. This is the essence of modesty, for women *and* men. Keep this principle in mind as you seek to present yourself in the best possible light before others. And remember that, regardless of external appearances, women (and men) make themselves attractive to God by "the good things they do." (***See Holiness> Maturing> Imitating God> His likeness,*** TopicGuide page A40.)

2:11-15 In the assembly, women are to submit to the leadership of the men by listening and learning "quietly and submissively" (compare 1 Corinthians 14:34-35). Verse 12 refers to the distinctive, authoritative activity by which the teacher presents God's Word and applies it. Thus, Paul forbids women to teach men and to hold positions of "authority over them." However, they are commanded to teach other women (compare Titus 2:4-5). The word "saved" in verse 15 makes sense if it refers to sanctification (compare 1 Timothy 4:16; Philippians 2:12), not justification. Christian women should recognize that childbearing can be a unique and important means of sanctification in their lives.

2:14 ward he made Eve. [14]And it was not Adam who was deceived by Satan. The woman was
Gen 3:1-6, 13 deceived, and sin was the result. [15]But women will be saved through childbearing,* as-
suming they continue to live in faith, love, holiness, and modesty.

3:1
LEADERS IN THE CHURCH

Acts 20:28 **3** This is a trustworthy saying: "If someone aspires to be an elder,* he desires an honor-
3:2-7 able position." [2]So an elder must be a man whose life is above reproach. He must be
Titus 1:6-9 faithful to his wife.* He must exercise self-control, live wisely, and have a good reputation.
He must enjoy having guests in his home, and he must be able to teach. [3]He must not be a
heavy drinker* or be violent. He must be gentle, not quarrelsome, and not love money.
[4]He must manage his own family well, having children who respect and obey him. [5]For if a
man cannot manage his own household, how can he take care of God's church?
[6]An elder must not be a new believer, because he might become proud, and the devil
3:7 would cause him to fall.* [7]Also, people outside the church must speak well of him so that
2 Cor 8:21 he will not be disgraced and fall into the devil's trap.
2 Tim 2:26
3:9 [8]In the same way, deacons must be well respected and have integrity. They must not be
1 Tim 1:19 heavy drinkers or dishonest with money. [9]They must be committed to the mystery of the
faith now revealed and must live with a clear conscience. [10]Before they are appointed as
deacons, let them be closely examined. If they pass the test, then let them serve as deacons.
[11]In the same way, their wives* must be respected and must not slander others. They
must exercise self-control and be faithful in everything they do.
[12]A deacon must be faithful to his wife, and he must manage his children and house-
hold well. [13]Those who do well as deacons will be rewarded with respect from others and
will have increased confidence in their faith in Christ Jesus.

THE TRUTHS OF OUR FAITH

3:15 [14]I am writing these things to you now, even though I hope to be with you soon, [15]so that
Matt 16:16-18 if I am delayed, you will know how people must conduct themselves in the household of
Eph 2:19-21 God. This is the church of the living God, which is the pillar and foundation of the truth.
3:16 [16]Without question, this is the great mystery of our faith*:
Isa 7:14
Matt 4:11 Christ* was revealed in a human body
John 1:14 and vindicated by the Spirit.*
Rom 1:3-4
Acts 1:9 He was seen by angels
1 Jn 4:2-3; 5:6 and announced to the nations.
He was believed in throughout the world
and taken to heaven in glory.

2:15 Or *will be saved by accepting their role as mothers,* or *will be saved by the birth of the Child.* **3:1** Or *an overseer,* or *a bishop;* also in 3:2, 6. **3:2** Or *must have only one wife,* or *must be married only once;* Greek reads *must be the husband of one wife;* also in 3:12. **3:3** Greek *must not drink too much wine;* similarly in 3:8. **3:6** Or *he might fall into the same judgment as the devil.* **3:11** Or *the women deacons.* The Greek word can be translated *women* or *wives.* **3:16a** Or *of godliness.* **3:16b** Greek *He who;* other manuscripts read *God.* **3:16c** Or *in His spirit.*

3:1-10, 12-13 Paul lists sixteen qualifications for those who seek to become elders in the church (3:2-7; compare Titus 1:6-9). The main qualification is that the prospective elder be "a man whose life is above reproach"; all the other qualifications describe this blameless lifestyle. Paul provides a list of nine qualifications for deacons, all of which are essentially mentioned among the sixteen for elders. Our word *deacon* comes directly from the Greek word *diakonos,* meaning "servant." The office of deacon is not a position of authority as is that of an elder. Although some deacons may teach, Paul does not list this as a qualification for their role as deacons.

3:11 The Greek word for "woman" also served as the term for "wife" in New Testament times, so there is a question here as to whether wives of deacons are in view or women who serve as deacons. A woman serving as a deacon likely would have been acceptable to Paul, since he made clear that the position was not one of authority. Paul previously called Phoebe a deacon (Romans 16:1).

3:16 This is a brief synopsis of Christian truth in the form of a hymn. A "mystery" (Greek, *musterion*) in the New Testament is a recently revealed secret, specifically the truths of the gospel, which were revealed by God in Christ to all who believe in Him (Ephesians 3:1-11). This ancient hymn gives the basic truths of the gospel in six poetic statements, or three groups of joined ideas, each one with Christ as the implied subject.

WARNINGS AGAINST FALSE TEACHERS

4 Now the Holy Spirit tells us clearly that in the last times some will turn away from the
true faith; they will follow deceptive spirits and teachings that come from demons.
2 These people are hypocrites and liars, and their consciences are dead.*
3 They will say it is wrong to be married and wrong to eat certain foods. But God created
those foods to be eaten with thanks by faithful people who know the truth. 4 Since every-
thing God created is good, we should not reject any of it but receive it with thanks. 5 For we
know it is made acceptable* by the word of God and prayer.

A GOOD SERVANT OF CHRIST JESUS

6 If you explain these things to the brothers and sisters,* Timothy, you will be a worthy ser-
vant of Christ Jesus, one who is nourished by the message of faith and the good teaching
you have followed. 7 Do not waste time arguing over godless ideas and old wives' tales. In-
stead, train yourself to be godly. 8 "Physical training is good, but training for godliness is
much better, promising benefits in this life and in the life to come." 9 This is a trustworthy
saying, and everyone should accept it. 10 This is why we work hard and continue to strug-
gle,* for our hope is in the living God, who is the Savior of all people and particularly of all
believers.
11 Teach these things and insist that everyone learn them. 12 Don't let anyone think less
of you because you are young. Be an example to all believers in what you say, in the way
you live, in your love, your faith, and your purity. 13 Until I get there, focus on reading the
Scriptures to the church, encouraging the believers, and teaching them.
14 Do not neglect the spiritual gift you received through the prophecy spoken over you
when the elders of the church laid their hands on you. 15 Give your complete attention to
these matters. Throw yourself into your tasks so that everyone will see your progress.
16 Keep a close watch on how you live and on your teaching. Stay true to what is right for
the sake of your own salvation and the salvation of those who hear you.

ADVICE ABOUT WIDOWS, ELDERS, AND SLAVES

5 Never speak harshly to an older man,* but appeal to him respectfully as you would to
your own father. Talk to younger men as you would to your own brothers. 2 Treat

4:1 John 16:13; 2 Tim 3:1; 2 Pet 3:3
4:2 Eph 4:19
4:3 Gen 9:3; Rom 14:6; 1 Cor 10:30-31
4:4 Gen 1:31; Acts 10:15
4:6 2 Tim 3:15
4:7 1 Tim 1:4; 2 Tim 2:16; Titus 1:14
4:8 1 Tim 6:6
4:9 1 Tim 1:15
4:10 1 Tim 2:3-4
4:11 1 Tim 5:7
4:12 Titus 2:15
4:13 1 Tim 3:14
4:14 Acts 6:6; 8:17; 2 Tim 1:6
5:1 Lev 19:32; Titus 2:2, 6

4:2 Greek *are seared.* 4:5 Or *made holy.* 4:6 Greek *brothers.* 4:10 Some manuscripts read *continue to suffer.*
5:1 Or *an elder.*

4:1-5 Paul warns Timothy not to be surprised if the church under his care experiences apostasy. Professing Christians often reject the truth to embrace demonic doctrines proclaimed by false teachers, who are "hypocrites and liars."

▸ GOD
4:7-8 Keep yourself spiritually fit. Do you have a spiritual workout routine? It is common for people to spend time training their bodies for various physical competitions or simply for the purpose of staying in shape, and Paul affirms here that this kind of training is "good." But a spiritual workout routine that trains a person for godliness is "much better," the apostle says, for it prepares the person for this life and life beyond the grave. Make time to read and study the Scriptures, to pray, to worship, to fellowship with other believers, and to share your faith with others. These disciplines, regularly practiced, will leave you spiritually fit, and you will then be a more productive citizen of the kingdom. (***See God*** *> Salvation> Holy Spirit> Strengthens us,* TopicGuide page A15.)

4:11-13 Timothy was "young," though not "a new believer" (see 3:6), since apparently he became a Christian during childhood (see 2 Timothy 1:5; 3:15). Despite his youth, Timothy was mature and had no need to be intimidated by older Christians in Ephesus who may have questioned his role and example as leader, particularly when his mentor, Paul, was not around.

▸ GOD
4:14-15 Put that gift to work! Like Timothy, each Christian has spiritual gifts that are to be used "so we can help each other" (1 Corinthians 12:7). Paul is emphatic that these gifts must not be put on the shelf. He tells Timothy, "Do not neglect the spiritual gift you received," but "give your complete attention" to its use and "throw yourself into your tasks." Are you aware of the abilities the Holy Spirit has bestowed on you? If not, spend time studying Romans 12:6-8, 1 Corinthians 12:4-11, Ephesians 4:11-13, and 1 Peter 4:10-11. Then seek godly counsel from believers who know you well. Finally, when you have identified your gift, use it "with all the strength and energy that God supplies" (1 Peter 4:11b) for the benefit of Christ's church. (***See God*** *> God's Names> Holy Spirit> Gives gifts,* TopicGuide page A19.)

▸ SALVATION
5:1-2 Treat believers as family members. The church of Jesus Christ is amazingly diverse, consisting of men and women, older and younger people, and so on. How can we know how to relate to each of these different people?

older women as you would your mother, and treat younger women with all purity as you would your own sisters.

3Take care of* any widow who has no one else to care for her. 4But if she has children or grandchildren, their first responsibility is to show godliness at home and repay their parents by taking care of them. This is something that pleases God.

5Now a true widow, a woman who is truly alone in this world, has placed her hope in God. She prays night and day, asking God for His help. 6But the widow who lives only for pleasure is spiritually dead even while she lives. 7Give these instructions to the church so that no one will be open to criticism.

8But those who won't care for their relatives, especially those in their own household, have denied the true faith. Such people are worse than unbelievers.

9A widow who is put on the list for support must be a woman who is at least sixty years old and was faithful to her husband.* 10She must be well respected by everyone because of the good she has done. Has she brought up her children well? Has she been kind to strangers and served other believers humbly?* Has she helped those who are in trouble? Has she always been ready to do good?

11The younger widows should not be on the list, because their physical desires will overpower their devotion to Christ and they will want to remarry. 12Then they would be guilty of breaking their previous pledge. 13And if they are on the list, they will learn to be lazy and will spend their time gossiping from house to house, meddling in other people's business and talking about things they shouldn't. 14So I advise these younger widows to marry again, have children, and take care of their own homes. Then the enemy will not be able to say anything against them. 15For I am afraid that some of them have already gone astray and now follow Satan.

16If a woman who is a believer has relatives who are widows, she must take care of them and not put the responsibility on the church. Then the church can care for the widows who are truly alone.

17Elders who do their work well should be respected and paid well,* especially those who work hard at both preaching and teaching. 18For the Scripture says, "You must not muzzle an ox to keep it from eating as it treads out the grain." And in another place, "Those who work deserve their pay!"*

5:4 Eph 6:2; 1 Tim 2:3
5:5 Luke 2:36-37; 1 Pet 3:5
5:6 Luke 15:24; Jas 5:5
5:10 Gen 18:3-5; Acts 9:36
5:13 2 Thes 3:11
5:14 1 Cor 7:9
5:15 1 Tim 1:19-20
5:17 Phil 2:29; 1 Thes 5:12
5:18 *Deut 25:4; Matt 10:10; *Luke 10:7; 1 Cor 9:9

5:3 Or *Honor.* 5:9 Greek *was the wife of one husband.* 5:10 Greek *and washed the feet of God's holy people?* 5:17 Greek *should be worthy of double honor.* 5:18 Deut 25:4; Luke 10:7.

For Paul, the controlling model for life in the church is the family. We should treat older men with the respect we would show our fathers. Likewise, older women are analogous to mothers, younger men to brothers, and younger women to sisters. These relationships should heavily influence all our behaviors in the church, but especially our speech. We should tailor our words and manner of speaking to match the person with whom we are conversing. When you interact with others in church this weekend, speak with respect that each person is due as your own relative. (***See Salvation****> Receiving> When> Member of God's family,* TopicGuide page A23.)

5:3-16 The law of Moses demanded that Israel take care of widows (Exodus 22:22; Deuteronomy 24:17), and Paul follows this precedent for widows in the church whose families cannot support them (5:3-4). The likelihood that "younger widows" would want to remarry precludes them from being added to the list of widows supported by the church (5:11-12). To keep them from being "lazy" and "gossiping," Paul recommends that young widows get married and stay at home to have children (5:13-14) lest Satan lead them astray with the lure of ungodly activities (5:15).

▸ CHURCH

5:17-18 Paying the pastor. What is your attitude toward your pastor? Do you respect him? The Scriptures clearly teach that we are to obey our spiritual leaders, for they have the monumental responsibility of watching over our souls (Hebrews 13:17). Such obedience is one kind of respect. But here in 1 Timothy, Paul declares that elders who are conscientious about their job should also be *paid* well. He then makes a distinction between elders in general and those who preach and teach. In most churches, only the pastor is paid because that is his life's work. That work, the care of our souls, is more beneficial to us than many services for which we pay much more money. Examine your heart attitude toward your pastor; if he is serving you well, show your respect by contributing generously to his support. (***See Church****> Role> Church Offices> Pastor-Teachers,* TopicGuide page A49.)

19Do not listen to an accusation against an elder unless it is confirmed by two or three
witnesses. 20Those who sin should be reprimanded in front of the whole church; this will
serve as a strong warning to others.
21I solemnly command you in the presence of God and Christ Jesus and the holy angels
to obey these instructions without taking sides or showing favoritism to anyone.
22Never be in a hurry about appointing a church leader.* Do not share in the sins of oth-
ers. Keep yourself pure.
23Don't drink only water. You ought to drink a little wine for the sake of your stomach
because you are sick so often.
24Remember, the sins of some people are obvious, leading them to certain judgment.
But there are others whose sins will not be revealed until later. 25In the same way, the
good deeds of some people are obvious. And the good deeds done in secret will someday
come to light.

6 All slaves should show full respect for their masters so they will not bring shame on
the name of God and His teaching. 2If the masters are believers, that is no excuse for
being disrespectful. Those slaves should work all the harder because their efforts are help-
ing other believers* who are well loved.

FALSE TEACHING AND TRUE RICHES

Teach these things, Timothy, and encourage everyone to obey them. 3Some people may
contradict our teaching, but these are the wholesome teachings of the Lord Jesus Christ.
These teachings promote a godly life. 4Anyone who teaches something different is arrogant
and lacks understanding. Such a person has an unhealthy desire to quibble over the mean-
ing of words. This stirs up arguments ending in jealousy, division, slander, and evil suspi-
cions. 5These people always cause trouble. Their minds are corrupt, and they have turned
their backs on the truth. To them, a show of godliness is just a way to become wealthy.
6Yet true godliness with contentment is itself great wealth. 7After all, we brought noth-
ing with us when we came into the world, and we can't take anything with us when we
leave it. 8So if we have enough food and clothing, let us be content.
9But people who long to be rich fall into temptation and are trapped by many foolish
and harmful desires that plunge them into ruin and destruction. 10For the love of money is

5:22 Greek *about the laying on of hands.* 6:2 Greek *brothers.*

5:19 Matt 18:16
5:20 Deut 13:11; Eph 5:11
5:21 1 Tim 6:13
5:22 1 Tim 4:14
5:23 1 Tim 3:8
5:24-25 Rev 14:13
6:1 Eph 6:5; Titus 2:9-10
6:2 Phlm 1:16
6:3 1 Tim 1:3, 10
6:4 2 Tim 2:14
6:5 2 Tim 3:8; 4:4; Titus 1:14
6:6 Phil 4:11-12; Heb 13:5
6:7 Eccl 5:15; Job 1:21
6:8 Prov 30:8; Heb 13:5
6:9 Prov 23:4; 28:22

5:19-20 The law of Moses called for at least "two or three witnesses" (see Deuteronomy 17:6; 19:15) to establish a case in court against someone, and Paul follows this precedent for charges against elders. If the accused elders are guilty, they "should be reprimanded in front of the whole church" to purify the church and to bring the guilty to repentance (see 1 Corinthians 5:3-8).

5:21-25 Paul gives Timothy practical instructions about a variety of subjects in these verses. Many have to do with understanding people. In closing this section, Paul reminds Timothy that some people expose their sins while others hide them, and conversely others do good things in the open and some in secret. Eventually, however, all secret sins will be judged, and God will bring all secret good deeds to light; compare 2 Timothy 4:1.

6:1-2 Paul addresses the proper attitudes of masters and slaves on two occasions (see Ephesians 6:5-9; Colossians 3:22–4:1), but he addresses only the latter here (compare 1 Peter 2:18-20). Paul may have been addressing a situation in which Christian slaves were arguing that they did not owe their masters obedience or loyalty in light of their freedom in Christ. But Paul says that slaves owe their masters "full respect" as a testimony about "God and His teaching" (6:1). Paul was not endorsing on slavery but was explaining how Christian slaves themselves should behave to win more to Christ. We can apply this principle today in how we conduct ourselves as Christ's ambassadors in our workplaces.

▸WORSHIP

6:6-10, 17-19 Craving contentment. Are you wealthy? Do you have a job that pays well? If so, rejoice! But be careful, too. Do not let love of your money or of the things it affords you breed runaway materialism in your heart. The better way, Paul says, is to be content with having enough, understanding that God gives us all that we need to enjoy when our hearts are fixed on Him. The love of money is fraught with danger; it can even lead a professing believer away from the faith. It is better for those who are wealthy to use their money to do good for others. Always remember, earthly treasures must remain on earth when we go on to heaven. Therefore, seek the true treasure that is above: your Lord Himself. (***See Worship***> *NT> Prohibitions> Wrong Objects> Money,* TopicGuide page A33.)

the root of all kinds of evil. And some people, craving money, have wandered from the true faith and pierced themselves with many sorrows.

6:11
PAUL'S FINAL INSTRUCTIONS

2 Tim 2:22 [11]But you, Timothy, are a man of God; so run from all these evil things. Pursue righteous-
6:12 1 Cor 9:25-26 ness and a godly life, along with faith, love, perseverance, and gentleness. [12]Fight the
2 Tim 4:7 good fight for the true faith. Hold tightly to the eternal life to which God has called you,
6:13 which you have confessed so well before many witnesses. [13]And I charge you before God,
John 18:33-37 who gives life to all, and before Christ Jesus, who gave a good testimony before Pontius Pi-
6:14 late, [14]that you obey this command without wavering. Then no one can find fault with you
1 Thes 3:13 from now until our Lord Jesus Christ comes again. [15]For at just the right time Christ will be
6:15 Deut 10:17 revealed from heaven by the blessed and only almighty God, the King of all kings and
1 Tim 1:17 Lord of all lords. [16]He alone can never die, and He lives in light so brilliant that no human
Rev 17:14 can approach Him. No human eye has ever seen Him, nor ever will. All honor and power
6:16 to Him forever! Amen.
Exod 33:20 Ps 104:2 [17]Teach those who are rich in this world not to be proud and not to trust in their money,
John 1:18; 5:26 which is so unreliable. Their trust should be in God, who richly gives us all we need for our
1 Tim 1:17 enjoyment. [18]Tell them to use their money to do good. They should be rich in good works
6:17 Luke 12:20 and generous to those in need, always being ready to share with others. [19]By doing this
6:19 they will be storing up their treasure as a good foundation for the future so that they may
Matt 6:20 experience true life.
1 Tim 6:12 [20]Timothy, guard what God has entrusted to you. Avoid godless, foolish discussions
6:20 with those who oppose you with their so-called knowledge. [21]Some people have wan-
2 Tim 1:14; 2:16 dered from the faith by following such foolishness.
6:21 2 Tim 2:18 May God's grace be with you all.

6:15-16 A sevenfold description of God the Father occurs in verses 15-16 (compare with a similar list in 1:17). Paul closes with a doxology of "honor and power" to his exalted God "forever! Amen."

6:17-21 Paul's final words to Timothy contain both a positive and negative instruction. He must "guard" his responsibilities as a servant of God, and he must avoid getting involved in "foolish discussions" that so often lead people astray (see note at 1:4-5). "May God's grace be with you all" was Paul's signature closing (see 2 Thessalonians 3:17-18, for instance). This statement or something similar can be found near or at the end of all 13 of his letters.

2 TIMOTHY

PURPOSE

To remind a young Christian leader how to endure testing and persevere until the end.

What would you write in your last letter to a dear friend? What advice about life would you share? When Paul writes 2 Timothy, his days are numbered. This letter is likely his final word to a dear friend and brother.

By the time Paul writes this letter to his protégé Timothy, the persecution of Christians under the Roman emperor has escalated. Fearing for their own safety, many who know of Paul and his condition are reluctant to be identified with him (2 Timothy 1:15). Paul now knows his death is imminent. And he has some final words to write to Timothy. He has no regrets but he is anticipating that Jesus will soon permit him to come home as he anticipates his martyrdom under Rome. He has made it clear on many occasions that he really has no one else like Timothy (Philippians 2:20), and so he wants to make sure he offers a few parting words to this dear friend and co-laborer (2 Timothy 1:3-4). Reflecting on his life of ministry and his impending death, Paul writes his last will and testament with regard to ministry.

What would a wise, experienced, and passionate follower of Jesus think about as his life draws to a close? What would he tell others about following after Jesus? We don't have to wonder, because in this letter to Timothy we get to listen in as Paul shares his final words with his friend and coworker.

DISCOVER GOD IN 2 TIMOTHY

As Paul reflects on life and ministry, he tells his close friend Timothy a great deal about Jesus.

Jesus Gives Grace: When Paul thinks of Jesus, he thinks of grace (1:8-10; 2:1; 4:17). Everywhere he turns, Paul sees and recognizes this grace, and it is woven throughout his life and his words.

Jesus Rescues from Trouble: Although Paul is anticipating that his earthly life will soon be over, he sees Jesus' hand protecting and guarding him throughout his life. As Paul looks back, he declares that Jesus saw him through his ministry (4:16-18) and his hardships (3:10-11), and now that his life is about to end, he has no regrets. Paul knows that Jesus will see him through this last trial as well (1:12-13).

Jesus Welcomes Us Home: Paul is confident that the Jesus he has walked with for so many years is waiting for him in heaven (1:9-12; 4:1, 6-8, 18). He has loved Jesus throughout his life, and he is expectant that he will see Him face to face very soon.

GROWING THROUGH 2 TIMOTHY

Although not all people are called to the same kind of personal ministry as Timothy, every disciple can learn from the principles found in this letter. Much of Paul's counsel to Timothy centers on the teachings found in other books of Scripture.

Secure the Message: Even in the early days of the church, there were those who sought to distort the gracious message of the gospel. So Paul reminds Timothy—and all who seek to live for Jesus—to guard the clear message of the Good News about Jesus (1:13-14; 2:8-10). Christians should be charitable concerning secondary issues, but vigilant in treasuring the essential truths of the Christian faith (1:8-10).

Study the Message: Paul reminds Timothy that the teachings of the Bible should always shape his faith and life, and he calls Timothy to ongoing and passionate study of the Scriptures (1:13; 3:14-17). Are you a casual reader of the Scriptures, or do you pore over them to find life? Those who are willing to dig for it find this life-giving truth in the Scriptures.

Suffer for the Message: Paul knows that faithful, courageous believers will experience troubles in this world, and those opposed to the Good News about Jesus will continue to fight against it (2:16-19; 3:1-9, 12-13; 4:3-5). Paul prepares Timothy and his church for the trials that lie ahead (3:1-9) and explains how to confront them (3:10-17)—with character and the Word of God.

Send the Message: Those who know the Good News of Jesus must be willing to teach it to others so that the message continues to spread (2:1-3, 14-15, 24-26; 4:3-5) and the church continues to grow and develop. Neither a desire for doctrinal purity nor fear of the suffering that frequently accompanies faithful Christian practice are adequate excuses to cease evangelism.

DISCOVERY VERSES

So never be ashamed to tell others about our Lord. And don't be ashamed of me, either, even though I'm in prison for Him. With the strength God gives you, be ready to suffer with me for the sake of the Good News. For God saved us and called us to live a holy life. He did this, not because we deserved it, but because that was His plan from before the beginning of time—to show us His grace through Christ Jesus. (2 TIMOTHY 1:8-9)

All Scripture is inspired by God and is useful to teach us what is true and to make us realize what is wrong in our lives. It corrects us when we are wrong and teaches us to do what is right. God uses it to prepare and equip His people to do every good work. (2 TIMOTHY 3:16-17)

2 TIMOTHY FACTS

Author: Paul clearly identifies himself as the author (1:1) of this warm letter he writes to one he considered his "dear son" (1 Timothy 1:2; also see 2 Timothy 1:2 and 2:1). The significant historical attestations to the authorship of this letter are the same as those for Paul's first letter to Timothy (see Introduction to 1 Timothy, page 2168).

Written to: Timothy's father was Greek and his mother was Jewish (Acts 16:1). There is no mention in the Scriptures of his father's faith, but Paul does note that Timothy learned the Scriptures from his mother and grandmother (2 Timothy 1:5). Paul met Timothy in Lystra when Paul visited there (Acts 14:6; 16:1), and he ultimately became Paul's protégé (1 Timothy 1:2; 2 Timothy 1:2; Philippians 2:22). It may well be that Paul was instrumental to Timothy's coming to faith in Jesus.

Date of writing: Acts 28 closes with Paul in prison. From what we read in the Pastoral Epistles (and from the testimony of early church writers) it appears that Paul was released from that imprisonment and embarked on a fourth missionary journey (not recorded in Acts). During this time, he left Timothy in a position of responsibility in the church in Ephesus, entrusting this growing congregation to Timothy's care. Paul wrote his first letter to Timothy during the time of his fourth missionary journey but was re-arrested. As Paul awaited trial (and, ultimately, execution) sometime during the reign of Nero around AD 66–67, he wrote this final letter to Timothy.

Setting: Paul had left Timothy behind in Ephesus while he went on to Macedonia on a fourth missionary journey (1 Timothy 1:3), but he was later rearrested and finds himself in prison in Rome again. Many years earlier Paul himself had been in Ephesus (Acts 19:8-10; 20:31) but rather than writing to the entire Ephesian church, Paul addresses this letter to Timothy, who had become so dear to him.

OUTLINE

- **2 TIMOTHY 1:1-18**—Guarding the Message of Truth Entrusted to You
- **2 TIMOTHY 2:1-26**—Passing on the Message of Truth
- **2 TIMOTHY 3:1-17**—Growing in the Message of Truth
- **2 TIMOTHY 4:1-22**—Freely Proclaiming the Message of Truth

1:1 John 5:24 Titus 1:1 1 Jn 5:10-11, 20

GREETINGS FROM PAUL

1 This letter is from Paul, chosen by the will of God to be an apostle of Christ Jesus. I
have been sent out to tell others about the life He has promised through faith in
Christ Jesus.

1:2 1 Tim 1:2

[2]I am writing to Timothy, my dear son.

1:3 Acts 23:1; 24:16 Rom 1:8-10

May God the Father and Christ Jesus our Lord give you grace, mercy, and peace.

ENCOURAGEMENT TO BE FAITHFUL

1:4 Acts 20:37 2 Tim 4:9

[3]Timothy, I thank God for you—the God I serve with a clear conscience, just as my ances-
tors did. Night and day I constantly remember you in my prayers. [4]I long to see you again,
for I remember your tears as we parted. And I will be filled with joy when we are together
again.

1:5 Acts 16:1

[5]I remember your genuine faith, for you share the faith that first filled your grand-
mother Lois and your mother, Eunice. And I know that same faith continues strong in you.
[6]This is why I remind you to fan into flames the spiritual gift God gave you when I laid my
hands on you. [7]For God has not given us a spirit of fear and timidity, but of power, love,
and self-discipline.

1:6 1 Tim 4:14 — 1:7 Rom 8:15 — 1:8 Rom 1:16 Eph 3:1 2 Tim 2:3

[8]So never be ashamed to tell others about our Lord. And don't be ashamed of me, ei-
ther, even though I'm in prison for Him. With the strength God gives you, be ready to
suffer with me for the sake of the Good News. [9]For God saved us and called us to live
a holy life. He did this, not because we deserved it, but because that was His plan from
before the beginning of time—to show us His grace through Christ Jesus. [10]And now
He has made all of this plain to us by the appearing of Christ Jesus, our Savior. He broke
the power of death and illuminated the way to life and immortality through the Good
News. [11]And God chose me to be a preacher, an apostle, and a teacher of this Good
News.

1:9 Rom 8:28; 11:14 Eph 2:8-9 Titus 3:5 — 1:10 1 Cor 15:54 — 1:11 1 Tim 2:7

1:2 Paul refers to Timothy as his "dear" (literally, "beloved") son. Timothy was not a literal son of Paul, but a very dear disciple (see Philippians 2:19-22).

1:4 Paul and Timothy's parting was heartbreaking for both of them; see Acts 20:37 as a possible description of their farewell.

1:6 Placing hands on someone while praying for that person is a sign of identification and partnership with the one being prayed for. The apostles first used this practice soon after Pentecost (Acts 6:6). In 1 Timothy 4:14, Paul first gave Timothy this charge. Now he is reminding Timothy to persevere.

▸ MINISTRY
1:6 Keeping the fire going. What happens in the lives of people when "ministry" is taking place? Is it coercive psychological influence? Are others just caught up with the minister's impressive skill? Paul says effective ministry is the result of the Spirit's work (1 Corinthians 3:5-7; 2 Corinthians 3:5-6), and effective ministers are those who are gifted by the Spirit (Romans 12:6; 1 Corinthians 12:7). Timothy was gifted by the Spirit (1 Timothy 4:14), but that didn't mean that ministry happened "automatically" through him. For Timothy to serve Jesus effectively, he had to intentionally give himself to his "giftedness." If he didn't, the "flame" of his ministry would wane. By purposefully serving, yielding to the Spirit, and strategically praying, Timothy could keep the fire burning and the ministry growing. How's your fire? Are you burning as bright as you could? (***See Ministry**> Great Commission> Witness> Witness in the power of the Holy Spirit,* TopicGuide page A56.)

1:8 Apparently Timothy had a gift of speaking or proclamation (1 Timothy 4:11-16), which explains why Paul encouraged him regarding this gift and urged him not to be ashamed to speak up about the Good News about Jesus.

12That is why I am suffering here in prison. But I am not ashamed of it, for I know the
One in whom I trust, and I am sure that He is able to guard what I have entrusted to Him*
until the day of His return.
13Hold on to the pattern of wholesome teaching you learned from me—a pattern shaped
by the faith and love that you have in Christ Jesus. 14Through the power of the Holy Spirit
who lives within us, carefully guard the precious truth that has been entrusted to you.
15As you know, everyone from the province of Asia has deserted me—even Phygelus
and Hermogenes.
16May the Lord show special kindness to Onesiphorus and all his family because he
often visited and encouraged me. He was never ashamed of me because I was in chains.
17When he came to Rome, he searched everywhere until he found me. 18May the Lord
show him special kindness on the day of Christ's return. And you know very well how
helpful he was in Ephesus.

A GOOD SOLDIER OF CHRIST JESUS

2 Timothy, my dear son, be strong through the grace that God gives you in Christ
Jesus. 2You have heard me teach things that have been confirmed by many reliable

1:12 Or *what has been entrusted to me.*

1:12 1 Tim 6:20
1:13 Rom 6:17; 1 Tim 1:14
1:14 Rom 8:9, 11, 16; Gal 4:6
1:15 2 Tim 4:10, 16
1:16 2 Tim 4:19
1:18 Heb 6:10
2:1 Eph 6:10
2:2 2 Tim 1:13

1:12 Paul is writing from prison, but he does not anticipate being released (see 4:6 and the introductory notes). Paul's comments regarding his confidence in God's ability to guard what he has entrusted to Him does not mean that Paul did not believe he would die before Christ's return. Rather, it means that he was confident that he was ultimately secure in God's hands, whether he lived or died (see 1 Timothy 6:20-21).

▸ SALVATION
1:12 Bank on it. Most people do some planning for their future, setting aside provisions to help prepare for the uncertainties of the days ahead. And it makes sense to place those provisions in the safest possible place; it wouldn't make sense to prepare and save for the future only to put what is saved in a risky place. That's true for our heavenly life as well. Have you made the kind of deposit that will ensure your "retirement" in heaven? Paul uses that kind of language in speaking of his own life. Like making an investment, Paul has placed his eternal future in Jesus' care. He's banking on Jesus' ability to guard and keep his life well into eternity. It's the kind of investment everyone should make. Have you planned ahead? (***See Salvation***> *Receiving> When> Eternal life,* TopicGuide page A23.)

2:1 The call to "be strong" is actually a call to be continually empowered with the strength Christ provides. It is not a call for Timothy to work up strength, but to avail himself of the strength Christ will provide by grace.

▸ MINISTRY
2:2 Worth passing on. Imagine walking through the woods and coming across a pond. Your thirst draws you to the water's edge, but then you notice the water is unfit to drink. There is nowhere for it to flow out of the pond, so the stagnant water has become contaminated and unhealthy. When the truth of the gospel first flows into your life, it brings transformation and life. But that truth is not supposed to just collect in your life; God intends for you to pass it on to others, just as Paul instructs Timothy. If that doesn't happen—if you are not involved in Jesus' call to "make disciples" (Matthew 28:18-20)—your spiritual life can end up no healthier than a stagnant pond. (***See Ministry***> *Great Commission> Make Disciples> Disciples are obligated to share Christ with others,* TopicGuide page A56.)

BECAUSE GOD IS FAITHFUL

I will trust Him to always keep His promises.

I know the One in whom I trust, and I am sure that He is able to guard what I have entrusted to Him until the day of His return.

2 TIMOTHY 1:12

FOR THE NEXT *GOD IS FAITHFUL* FEATURE SEE PAGE 2184.

witnesses. Now teach these truths to other trustworthy people who will be able to pass
them on to others.
2:3 [3]Endure suffering along with me, as a good soldier of Christ Jesus. [4]Soldiers don't get
2 Tim 1:8; 4:5 tied up in the affairs of civilian life, for then they cannot please the officer who enlisted
2:5 them. [5]And athletes cannot win the prize unless they follow the rules. [6]And hardworking
1 Cor 9:25 farmers should be the first to enjoy the fruit of their labor. [7]Think about what I am saying.
2:6 The Lord will help you understand all these things.
1 Cor 9:7, 10 [8]Always remember that Jesus Christ, a descendant of King David, was raised from the
2:8 Acts 2:24 dead. This is the Good News I preach. [9]And because I preach this Good News, I am suffer-
Rom 1:3 ing and have been chained like a criminal. But the word of God cannot be chained. [10]So I
2:9 am willing to endure anything if it will bring salvation and eternal glory in Christ Jesus to
Eph 3:1 those God has chosen.
Phil 1:12-14 [11]This is a trustworthy saying:

2:10 Col 1:24 If we die with Him,
2:11 we will also live with Him.
Rom 6:2-11 1 Thes 5:10 [12]If we endure hardship,
2:12 we will reign with Him.
Matt 10:33 If we deny Him,
Rom 8:17 1 Pet 4:13 He will deny us.
[13]If we are unfaithful,
2:13 Num 23:19 He remains faithful,
Rom 3:3 for He cannot deny who He is.
1 Cor 1:9

2:14 [14]Remind everyone about these things, and command them in God's presence to stop
1 Tim 1:4; 6:4 fighting over words. Such arguments are useless, and they can ruin those who hear them.
Titus 3:9

AN APPROVED WORKER

[15]Work hard so you can present yourself to God and receive His approval. Be a good
worker, one who does not need to be ashamed and who correctly explains the word of
2:17 truth. [16]Avoid worthless, foolish talk that only leads to more godless behavior. [17]This kind
1 Tim 1:20 of talk spreads like cancer, as in the case of Hymenaeus and Philetus. [18]They have left the
2:18 path of truth, claiming that the resurrection of the dead has already occurred; in this way,
1 Tim 1:19; 6:21 they have turned some people away from the faith.
2:19 [19]But God's truth stands firm like a foundation stone with this inscription: "The LORD
Num 16:5 Isa 52:11 knows those who are His," and "All who belong to the LORD must turn away from evil."*
John 10:14 [20]In a wealthy home some utensils are made of gold and silver, and some are made of
2:20 wood and clay. The expensive utensils are used for special occasions, and the cheap ones
Rom 9:21 are for everyday use. [21]If you keep yourself pure, you will be a special utensil for honor-
2:21 able use. Your life will be clean, and you will be ready for the Master to use you for every
2 Tim 3:17 good work.

2:19a Num 16:5. 2:19b See Isa 52:11.

2:11-13 In this portion of what appears to be an early hymn, Paul says that Jesus cannot deny Himself, meaning that He is unable to be anything less than who He is.

2:14 Paul is not opposed to a debate over legitimate issues, as is clear from his own personal ministry (see Acts 18:4). What he dislikes are arguments that don't advance the cause of Christ and end up merely being disputes about words rather than profitable discussions about the truth (see 2 Timothy 2:16, 23).

▸ BIBLE

2:15 Cutting it straight. Paul was a tentmaker by trade and often supported himself by this work (Acts 18:3). As he worked with the rough camel-hair cloth that was typically used for making a proper tent, he was careful to make the most of the pieces he had to work with, making straight cuts so sections could be easily and properly joined. That may be where he gets the imagery used here. The expression "correctly explains the word of truth" is literally translated "cuts it straight." Are you that careful when you read or teach the Bible? Do you pay close attention to what is before you to make sure you are not clipping out something important or curving around a difficult portion? The best tents are made with straight cuts; the best living is made when the Bible is read honestly and "cut straight." (***See Bible***> *Power*> *Convict*> *Cuts through deception,* TopicGuide page A11.)

[22]Run from anything that stimulates youthful lusts. Instead, pursue righteous living, **2:22**
faithfulness, love, and peace. Enjoy the companionship of those who call on the Lord with 1 Tim 6:11
pure hearts. **2:23**
[23]Again I say, don't get involved in foolish, ignorant arguments that only start fights. [24]A 1 Tim 4:7
servant of the Lord must not quarrel but must be kind to everyone, be able to teach, and **2:24** 1 Tim 3:2-3
be patient with difficult people. [25]Gently instruct those who oppose the truth. Perhaps God Titus 1:7
will change those people's hearts, and they will learn the truth. [26]Then they will come to **2:26**
their senses and escape from the devil's trap. For they have been held captive by him to 1 Tim 3:7
do whatever he wants.

THE DANGERS OF THE LAST DAYS

3 You should know this, Timothy, that in the last days there will be very difficult times. **3:1**
[2]For people will love only themselves and their money. They will be boastful and 1 Tim 4:1
proud, scoffing at God, disobedient to their parents, and ungrateful. They will consider Jude 1:18
nothing sacred. [3]They will be unloving and unforgiving; they will slander others and have **3:2-3**
no self-control. They will be cruel and hate what is good. [4]They will betray their friends, be Rom 1:29-31

2:22 Paul commands Timothy to run from what would lead him into sin and to "pursue" (literally, "chase after") what leads to right living before God.

3:1 According to Peter's first message, preached on Pentecost, the "last days" began with the outpouring of the Spirit and will continue until the second coming of Christ (see Acts 2:17-41). Paul anticipated a future final culmination of the work of Christ at the end of these "last days" (for example, see 2 Thessalonians 2:2), but he saw the signs of the "beginning of the end" even in his own days.

MY RESPONSE TO GOD

The Painful Promise

2 TIMOTHY 3:12

Some promises in the Bible are easy to hear and receive. Eternal life? Yes! Heavenly rewards? Sure! But the Bible also teaches that those who live godly lives will inevitably experience suffering and persecution. God gives a painful promise to His people when Paul says to Timothy, "Everyone who wants to live a godly life in Christ Jesus will suffer persecution" (2 Timothy 3:12). When Paul and Barnabas visited the believers in Lystra, Iconium, and Antioch of Pisidia, "they encouraged them to continue in the faith, reminding them that we must suffer many hardships to enter the Kingdom of God" (Acts 14:22).

The good news is that Jesus Himself promised, "Here on earth you will have many trials and sorrows. But take heart, because I have overcome the world" (John 16:33). We can rest assured that the world does not have the upper hand; Jesus has already defeated the powers of darkness, and He is in control.

Is this painful promise for every person who takes up his cross and follows Christ? Yes, all Christians should expect fiery trials. Suffering should not surprise us as if something strange were happening. We should rejoice instead, for God is making us partners with Christ in His suffering (Matthew 5:11-12; 2 Corinthians 4:10; Revelation 1:9)! This brief time of suffering is nothing compared to the eternal rewards Christ has for those who suffer according to God's will (2 Corinthians 4:17).

reckless, be puffed up with pride, and love pleasure rather than God. 5They will act reli-
gious, but they will reject the power that could make them godly. Stay away from people
like that!
3:6 6They are the kind who work their way into people's homes and win the confidence of*
Jude 1:4 vulnerable women who are burdened with the guilt of sin and controlled by various desires.
3:8 7(Such women are forever following new teachings, but they are never able to understand
1 Tim 6:5 the truth.) 8These teachers oppose the truth just as Jannes and Jambres opposed Moses.
They have depraved minds and a counterfeit faith. 9But they won't get away with this for
long. Someday everyone will recognize what fools they are, just as with Jannes and Jambres.

3:10

PAUL'S CHARGE TO TIMOTHY

1 Tim 4:6 10But you, Timothy, certainly know what I teach, and how I live, and what my purpose in
3:11 Ps 34:19 life is. You know my faith, my patience, my love, and my endurance. 11You know how
Acts 13:14, 50-51; much persecution and suffering I have endured. You know all about how I was persecuted
14:5, 19 in Antioch, Iconium, and Lystra—but the Lord rescued me from all of it. 12Yes, and every-
3:12 John 15:20 one who wants to live a godly life in Christ Jesus will suffer persecution. 13But evil people
Acts 14:22 and impostors will flourish. They will deceive others and will themselves be deceived.
3:14 14But you must remain faithful to the things you have been taught. You know they are
2 Tim 1:13; 2:2 true, for you know you can trust those who taught you. 15You have been taught the holy
3:15 Scriptures from childhood, and they have given you the wisdom to receive the salvation
John 5:39 that comes by trusting in Christ Jesus. 16All Scripture is inspired by God and is useful to
3:16 teach us what is true and to make us realize what is wrong in our lives. It corrects us when
Rom 15:4 2 Pet 1:20-21 we are wrong and teaches us to do what is right. 17God uses it to prepare and equip His
3:17 people to do every good work.
1 Tim 6:11 2 Tim 2:21

4:1 **4** I solemnly urge you in the presence of God and Christ Jesus, who will someday judge
Acts 10:42 the living and the dead when He appears to set up His Kingdom: 2Preach the word of
4:2 God. Be prepared, whether the time is favorable or not. Patiently correct, rebuke, and en-
1 Tim 5:20 courage your people with good teaching.
Titus 1:13 3For a time is coming when people will no longer listen to sound and wholesome teach-
4:3 ing. They will follow their own desires and will look for teachers who will tell them what-
2 Tim 3:1 ever their itching ears want to hear. 4They will reject the truth and chase after myths.
4:4 5But you should keep a clear mind in every situation. Don't be afraid of suffering for the
1 Tim 1:4 4:5 Lord. Work at telling others the Good News, and fully carry out the ministry God has given
2 Tim 1:8 you.

3:6 Greek *and take captive.*

3:8 According to Jewish tradition, Jannes and Jambres are the names of the Egyptian priests who opposed Moses during the time of the Exodus.

3:11 Paul's ministry in Antioch, Iconium, and Lystra is described in Acts (Acts 13:14, 45-50; 14:1-5, 6-20, respectively).

▸ MINISTRY

3:12 More than inconvenient. Life is sometimes filled with inconveniences. Essential tools break; unexpected delays upset plans. That's part of life. But when it comes to the ministry of the Kingdom, we should anticipate more than inconveniences. Jesus told His followers that they would face outright trouble (John 16:33). Paul reminds us that we have the "privilege" of suffering for Jesus' sake (Philippians 1:29). Paul, speaking from experience, lets us know that if we want to fully live out this life to which Jesus has called us, we will suffer persecution. The word He uses for "persecution" conveys the image of being hunted like a wild animal! To follow Jesus will be to swim against the flow; the world will hate us, and the devil will oppose us. So, recognize its coming . . . and get on living for the One who died for you! (***See Ministry***> *Great Commission> Risk> Opposition and ill-treatment,* TopicGuide page A56.)

▸ BIBLE

3:16-17 God-breathed words. Have you ever heard of anyone who was only half listening while their special someone made a proposal of marriage to them? Of course not. Such important words are carefully thought out and just as carefully received by both people involved. Yet how importantly do we regard God's words? He certainly feels every bit as strongly about you as that special someone, yet we often fail to pay attention to what He says. The Bible is God's very word to you; Paul tells us that it is "inspired" (literally, "breathed out by God"). Although God spoke these words through human authors, it was His message that was conveyed. Search His book with all diligence to learn all God has to say to you. (***See Bible***> *Uniqueness> Inspired> Divinely inspired,* TopicGuide page A10.)

6 As for me, my life has already been poured out as an offering to God. The time of my
death is near. 7 I have fought the good fight, I have finished the race, and I have remained
faithful. 8 And now the prize awaits me—the crown of righteousness, which the Lord, the
righteous Judge, will give me on the day of His return. And the prize is not just for me but
for all who eagerly look forward to His appearing.

PAUL'S FINAL WORDS

9 Timothy, please come as soon as you can. 10 Demas has deserted me because he loves
the things of this life and has gone to Thessalonica. Crescens has gone to Galatia, and Ti-
tus has gone to Dalmatia. 11 Only Luke is with me. Bring Mark with you when you come,
for he will be helpful to me in my ministry. 12 I sent Tychicus to Ephesus. 13 When you
come, be sure to bring the coat I left with Carpus at Troas. Also bring my books, and espe-
cially my papers.*

4:13 Greek *especially the parchments.*

4:6 Phil 2:17
4:7 1 Cor 9:24-27; Phil 3:12-14; 1 Tim 6:12
4:8 1 Cor 9:25; Phil 3:14; Col 1:5; Rev 2:10
4:10 Col 4:14; Phlm 1:24
4:11 Col 4:10, 14; Phlm 1:24

4:6 Unlike Paul's earlier "prison epistles" (see the introductions to Philippians and Colossians), Paul recognizes that he may not leave prison alive this time.

▸ ADOPTION

4:7-8 What are you running for? So many of us in Western society seem to be in a hurry all the time. Constantly on the run, we rush from one thing to another. But what are we running for? What are we chasing? What is at the end of the race? Money? Entertainment? Power? None of these were the prize Paul was running for. Instead, he raced for the only thing that ultimately matters: reward from his Master when his life was done. Take time today to evaluate your schedule and discern what you are ultimately running for. Consider reordering your priorities or perhaps even eliminating some of them in order to make your ultimate goal the approval of your Master and Savior, Jesus Christ. (***See Adoption****> In Heaven> Rewarded saints,* TopicGuide page A38.)

4:10 Demas is mentioned elsewhere only in Colossians 4:14, where he appears as a companion to Paul. Apparently, the others mentioned—Crescens and Titus—had not deserted Paul but had left him in order to undertake some further ministry elsewhere.

▸ CHURCH

4:11 Effective in ministry. Have you ever watched a small child trying to play catch? Try as he might, he can't seem to hold onto the ball when it comes to him. But with practice and encouragement, most children eventually learn to catch. Similarly, when we first begin to step out in ministry, we might be just as ineffective. Mark is a great case study of one who didn't seem to "catch well" spiritually. He messed up on an earlier trip with Paul and lost the chance to go on another trip (Acts 15:36-38). With the encouragement of Barnabas (Acts 15:39), however, Mark ends up writing one of the Gospels and becomes a significant help to Paul. The next time you see someone "bobble" a ministry opportunity, take some time to encourage him and help him grow in his responsibilities. (***See Church****> Role> Preach> Instructions> Equip the saints for the work of ministry,* TopicGuide page A50.)

4:13 The books (or possibly papyrus rolls) and the papers (probably prepared skins used in manuscript preparation) most likely included copies of the Old Testament books and perhaps some teachings of Jesus.

BECAUSE GOD IS FAITHFUL

I will trust Him to always keep His promises.

The Lord will deliver me from every evil attack and will bring me safely into His heavenly Kingdom.

2 TIMOTHY 4:18

FOR THE NEXT *GOD IS FAITHFUL* FEATURE SEE PAGE 2212

14 Alexander the coppersmith did me much harm, but the Lord will judge him for what he has done. 15 Be careful of him, for he fought against everything we said.

16 The first time I was brought before the judge, no one came with me. Everyone abandoned me. May it not be counted against them. 17 But the Lord stood with me and gave me strength so that I might preach the Good News in its entirety for all the Gentiles to hear. And He rescued me from certain death.* 18 Yes, and the Lord will deliver me from every evil attack and will bring me safely into His heavenly Kingdom. All glory to God forever and ever! Amen.

PAUL'S FINAL GREETINGS

19 Give my greetings to Priscilla and Aquila and those living in the household of Onesiphorus. 20 Erastus stayed at Corinth, and I left Trophimus sick at Miletus.

21 Do your best to get here before winter. Eubulus sends you greetings, and so do Pudens, Linus, Claudia, and all the brothers and sisters.*

22 May the Lord be with your spirit. And may His grace be with all of you.

4:17 Greek *from the mouth of a lion.* 4:21 Greek *brothers.*

4:14 1 Tim 1:20
4:16 Acts 7:60
4:17 Ps 22:21; Dan 6:22; Acts 9:15
4:18 Ps 121:7; Rom 11:36
4:19 Acts 18:2; 2 Tim 1:16
4:20 Acts 19:22; 20:4; Rom 16:23
4:22 Rom 16:20; Gal 6:18

4:17 Paul uses a proverbial expression to speak of his brush with death: He was rescued "from the mouth of a lion" (see NLT textual note). It is not clear whether he was referring literally to being thrown to the lions or only metaphorically to death.

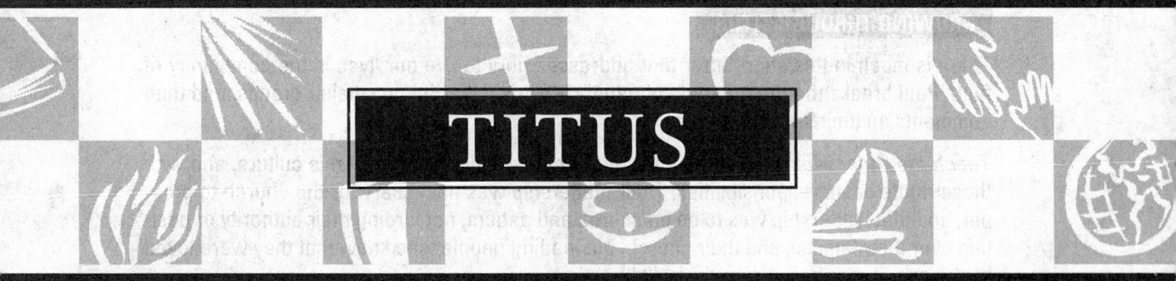

TITUS

PURPOSE

To help a young church leader organize the church in Crete by countering false teachings and encouraging holy living.

A good craftsman wants his apprentice to "learn the ropes." He wants him to understand the basics so that he will not only be able to help in the work but so that, one day, he might be able to work on his own in the same field. By the grace of God, Paul is a "craftsman" working in the kingdom; he has learned the essentials of the ministry and what it takes to be effective for Jesus' sake. Titus is a young church leader, growing in experience. This letter is part of Paul's attempt to help Titus "learn the ropes" so that his ministry might also be effective. Short though it is, it is filled with practical advice about critical components of living out the life of faith within the church community.

It cannot be determined with full certainty, but it could well be that the Good News was introduced to those on the island of Crete when Paul and Titus traveled there earlier (Acts 27:7-13). Now that Paul is on to other regions, he needs someone he trusts to help establish the community of faith on the island, and this letter provides some guidelines for Titus—both for his personal ministry and for the life of the church on the island. Paul's focus is on learning to do what is good (1:16; 2:7, 14; 3:1, 8, 14), not in an endeavor to earn salvation, but as an expression of life rooted in what God has done in saving those who have come to faith in Jesus.

DISCOVER GOD IN TITUS

Though Paul places a strong emphasis in this letter on doing what is good, he also sounds another important theme—salvation is God's work. Paul specifically refers to Jesus as Savior six times—half the total number of such references in all his letters combined. Paul sees the triune God at work in the Cretan believers' salvation.

God the Father as Savior: When Paul thinks of salvation, he thinks of the Father, who is the source of all saving work (1:1-3). Salvation is rooted in the grace and love of God the Father (2:10-11; 3:4).

God the Son as Savior: Paul recognizes that Jesus is both God and man, and He is also our God and Savior (1:4). Jesus entered the world to bring us salvation and will one day return and His glory will be revealed (2:13-14). He has made us right with God (3:5-6), and our salvation is founded on the work of Christ on our behalf.

God the Spirit as Savior: Although perhaps not as explicit as the references to the Father and the Son, Paul also states that the Spirit takes an active role in our salvation. All three persons of the Godhead are seen participating in this great work of grace and mercy and power (3:4-7). The Spirit brings renewal to our hearts and lives (3:5).

GROWING THROUGH TITUS

There is much in this short letter that addresses how to live our lives in the community of faith. Paul breaks the great variety of people in Titus' church into smaller groups, and then comments on their specific needs.

Teach the Older Men: Men were given more rights and privileges in this culture, and with those rights came responsibilities. Their leadership was necessary for the church to prosper, and that leadership was to be measured and patient, not lording their authority or position over their families and their church, but leading people who know that they were loved by the one given charge over them. (2:2)

Teach the Older Women: Men may have power, but in almost every society, women maintain great influence over every aspect of the family life. In this situation, Paul exhorts these influential women to love their husbands and children and teach others to do the same so that Christian families will not be out of phase with the words and message of the Christian church (2:5).

Teach the Young Men: Full of energy, full of passion, yet in need of self-control, the young men of Crete were no different from those today. Titus is given specific instructions to set a fine example for them, so that when they mature, they will be ready to assume leadership in the church and in their families and so that the false teachers will not be able to point to troubled youth as an example of weakness in the church (2:6-8).

Teach the Slaves: The slaves in the Roman world were not chattel slaves; they were either bondservants who had pledged themselves to service, or debt slaves who had been put into slavery through financial ruin. They had many rights in Roman society. Paul's message was that Titus should preach and teach and train them with the same Good News as their masters, for they were equal partners in God's work (Philemon 1:16). They could build up the church, or they could tear it down through their negative examples (Titus 2:9-10).

DISCOVERY VERSES

Everything is pure to those whose hearts are pure. But nothing is pure to those who are corrupt and unbelieving, because their minds and consciences are corrupted. (TITUS 1:15)

You yourself must be an example to them by doing good works of every kind. Let everything you do reflect the integrity and seriousness of your teaching. (TITUS 2:7)

He gave His life to free us from every kind of sin, to cleanse us, and to make us His very own people, totally committed to doing good deeds. (TITUS 2:14)

TITUS FACTS

Author: As with the other Pastoral Epistles (1 and 2 Timothy), Paul identifies himself as the author (1:1). See the introduction to 1 Timothy for more information.

Written to: Because of the language Paul uses in Titus 1:4, it is usually understood that Titus was a convert of Paul. After coming to faith in Jesus, Titus became a companion of Paul. He was with Paul at the Jerusalem Council (Galatians 2:1-3). He was probably also part of Paul's ministry in Ephesus and may have been sent to the church in Corinth for a time (2 Corinthians 2:12-13; 7:5-6; 8:6, 16-17). The last thing we know about this church planter and pastor is that during the time of Paul's final imprisonment, Titus was apparently ministering in Dalmatia (2 Timothy 4:10) in modern-day Bosnia and Croatia.

Date of writing: Acts 28 closes with Paul in prison, around AD 60. From what we read in the Pastoral Epistles (and from the testimony of early church writers), it appears that Paul most likely was released from that imprisonment and took a fourth missionary journey (one that is not recorded in Acts) around AD 63. During this time, Paul left Titus in a position of responsibility in the church in Crete and instructed him to appoint leaders in the local church who would be able to guide that congregation (Titus 1:5). This letter followed that visit, putting the letter between late AD 63 and 66, when Paul was rearrested.

Setting: On an earlier portion of Paul's last missionary journey (AD 63), he established Titus as the leader of the church. Timothy was left behind in Ephesus while Paul went on to Macedonia on the next leg of his fourth missionary journey (1 Timothy 1:3). Thus Titus was written as Paul traveled in and around Macedonia, which is in northern Greece.

OUTLINE

- ▸ **TITUS 1:1-16**—Instructions on Leadership in the Church
- ▸ **TITUS 2:1-15**—Instructions on a Holy Example
- ▸ **TITUS 3:1-15**—Instructions for a Holy Lifestyle

1:1 **GREETINGS FROM PAUL**

1 Tim 2:4 1 This letter is from Paul, a slave of God and an apostle of Jesus Christ. I have been sent
1:2 to proclaim faith to* those God has chosen and to teach them to know the truth that
2 Tim 1:1, 9 Titus 3:7 shows them how to live godly lives. 2 This truth gives them confidence that they have eter-
1:3 nal life, which God—who does not lie—promised them before the world began. 3 And now
1 Tim 1:1, 11 at just the right time He has revealed this message, which we announce to everyone. It is
Titus 2:10 by the command of God our Savior that I have been entrusted with this work for Him.
1:4 4 I am writing to Titus, my true son in the faith that we share.
2 Cor 2:13 2 Tim 4:10 May God the Father and Christ Jesus our Savior give you grace and peace.

1:5 Acts 14:23 **TITUS'S WORK IN CRETE**

1:6-9 5 I left you on the island of Crete so you could complete our work there and appoint elders in
//1 Tim 3:2-7 each town as I instructed you. 6 An elder must live a blameless life. He must be faithful to his
2 Tim 2:24-26 wife,* and his children must be believers who don't have a reputation for being wild or rebel-
1:7 lious. 7 For an elder* must live a blameless life. He must not be arrogant or quick-tempered;
1 Cor 4:1 he must not be a heavy drinker,* violent, or dishonest with money.

1:1 Or *to strengthen the faith of.* 1:6 Or *must have only one wife,* or *must be married only once;* Greek reads *must be the husband of one wife.* 1:7a Or *an overseer,* or *a bishop.* 1:7b Greek *must not drink too much wine.*

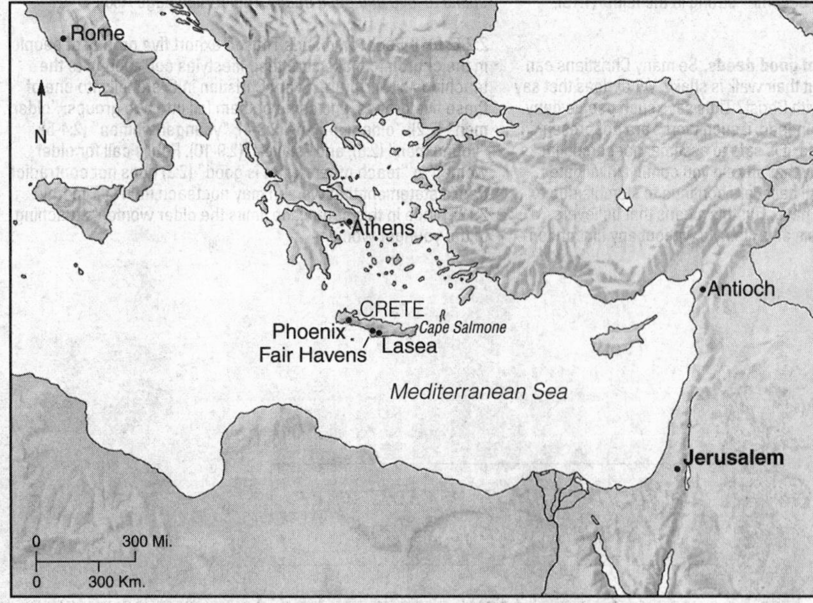

TITUS GOES TO CRETE
Tradition says that after Paul was released from prison in Rome (before his second and final Roman imprisonment), he and Titus traveled together for a while. They stopped in Crete, and when it was time for Paul to go, he left Titus behind to help the churches there.

1:5-9 Crete was a strong Roman province with a large Jewish population. It is probable that many of these Jews were already Christians before Paul and Titus arrived (see Acts 2:11), so their task was not only to plant more churches but also to help them grow through evangelism and teaching. The latter is mentioned several times in this letter (1:9, 11; 2:1, 7, 10). As Paul's "true son in the faith" (1:4), Titus was to "complete" their work in Crete, possibly a reference to evangelizing the rest of the island, and "appoint elders" in the churches that didn't yet have recognized leaders. Paul's list of qualifications for elders here is practically identical with the one in 1 Timothy 3:1-7.

[8]Rather, he must enjoy having guests in his home, and he must love what is good. He
must live wisely and be just. He must live a devout and disciplined life. [9]He must have a
strong belief in the trustworthy message he was taught; then he will be able to encourage
others with wholesome teaching and show those who oppose it where they are wrong.
[10]For there are many rebellious people who engage in useless talk and deceive others.
This is especially true of those who insist on circumcision for salvation. [11]They must be si-
lenced, because they are turning whole families away from the truth by their false teaching.
And they do it only for money. [12]Even one of their own men, a prophet from Crete, has said
about them, "The people of Crete are all liars, cruel animals, and lazy gluttons."* [13]This is
true. So reprimand them sternly to make them strong in the faith. [14]They must stop listen-
ing to Jewish myths and the commands of people who have turned away from the truth.
[15]Everything is pure to those whose hearts are pure. But nothing is pure to those who
are corrupt and unbelieving, because their minds and consciences are corrupted. [16]Such
people claim they know God, but they deny Him by the way they live. They are detestable
and disobedient, worthless for doing anything good.

1:9 1 Tim 1:10; 2 Tim 4:3; Titus 2:1
1:10 1 Tim 1:6
1:11 1 Tim 5:13
1:13 1 Tim 5:20
1:14 Col 2:22; 1 Tim 1:4; 4:7; 2 Tim 4:4
1:15 Matt 15:10-11; Rom 14:14-20
1:16 1 Jn 1:6; 2:4

PROMOTE RIGHT TEACHING

2 As for you, Titus, promote the kind of living that reflects wholesome teaching. [2]Teach
the older men to exercise self-control, to be worthy of respect, and to live wisely.
They must have sound faith and be filled with love and patience.

2:1 1 Tim 1:10; Titus 1:9

1:12 This quotation is from Epimenides of Knossos.

1:10-14 Paul quoted the eminent and highly regarded Cretan philosopher Epimenides (sixth century BC) to corroborate his charge that Cretans were "liars" (1:12), which prepared Titus for what he might be up against in the island churches. The Christians in the church who lived up to the Cretans' reputation for lying needed to be rebuked so they could become "strong in the faith" (1:13).

▸ CHURCH

1:16 A lifestyle of good deeds. So many Christians can "talk the talk," but their walk is shaky. What does that say about their relationship with Christ? Titus says such people deny God by the way they live. Indeed, if such works are not present in a professing Christian's life, it is safe to assume that person lacks true faith. This is not to say that any sin you commit invalidates your profession of faith. All believers continue to stumble due to the sinful nature they still have. But this means that believers should not be practicing sin as a lifestyle without any hint of conviction. By God's grace, there will be a discernible trajectory in our lives—our sinful deeds will grow fewer as the Spirit convicts us and helps us resist temptation, and our good works will grow in number. Does your lifestyle validate your profession or deny it? (***See Church****> Role> Preach> Topics> Disciple> Encourage the saints to love and good deeds,* TopicGuide page A50.)

2:2-6, 9-10 Paul commands Titus to exhort five groups of people in the church to make sure their lifestyles correspond to the teachings of Scripture. Every Christian in Crete fell into one of these five groups, and some of them fell into two groups: "older men" (2:2); "older women" (2:3-4); "younger women" (2:4-5); "young men" (2:6); and "slaves" (2:9-10). Paul's call for older women to "teach others what is good" (2:3) does not contradict Paul's statement that women may not teach men (1 Timothy 2:12), since in this context he limits the older women's teaching to the younger women.

BECAUSE GOD IS MERCIFUL

He forgives me of my sins when I sincerely confess them.

He saved us, not because of the righteous things we had done, but because of His mercy. . . . He generously poured out the Spirit upon us through Jesus Christ our Savior. Because of His grace He declared us righteous and gave us confidence that we will inherit eternal life. TITUS 3:5, 6-7

FOR THE NEXT *GOD IS MERCIFUL* FEATURE SEE PAGE 2205.

2:3 3 Similarly, teach the older women to live in a way that honors God. They must not slan-
1 Tim 3:8, 11 der others or be heavy drinkers.* Instead, they should teach others what is good. 4 These
2:5 older women must train the younger women to love their husbands and their children, 5 to
Eph 5:22 1 Tim 5:14 live wisely and be pure, to work in their homes,* to do good, and to be submissive to their
husbands. Then they will not bring shame on the word of God.
2:7 1 Tim 4:12 6 In the same way, encourage the young men to live wisely. 7 And you yourself must be an
1 Pet 5:3 example to them by doing good works of every kind. Let everything you do reflect the in-
2:9 tegrity and seriousness of your teaching. 8 Teach the truth so that your teaching can't be criti-
Eph 6:5 cized. Then those who oppose us will be ashamed and have nothing bad to say about us.
2:10 Titus 1:3; 3:4 9 Slaves must always obey their masters and do their best to please them. They must not
2:11 talk back 10 or steal, but must show themselves to be entirely trustworthy and good. Then
1 Tim 2:4 they will make the teaching about God our Savior attractive in every way.
2 Tim 1:9-10 11 For the grace of God has been revealed, bringing salvation to all people. 12 And we are
2:13 instructed to turn from godless living and sinful pleasures. We should live in this evil world
John 1:1; 20:28 Rom 9:5 with wisdom, righteousness, and devotion to God, 13 while we look forward with hope to
2:14 that wonderful day when the glory of our great God and Savior, Jesus Christ, will be re-
Eph 2:10 1 Pet 2:9 vealed. 14 He gave His life to free us from every kind of sin, to cleanse us, and to make us
1 Jn 1:7 His very own people, totally committed to doing good deeds.
2:15 15 You must teach these things and encourage the believers to do them. You have the
1 Tim 4:12 authority to correct them when necessary, so don't let anyone disregard what you say.

DO WHAT IS GOOD

3:1 Rom 13:1 **3** Remind the believers to submit to the government and its officers. They should be
1 Pet 2:13 obedient, always ready to do what is good. 2 They must not slander anyone and must
3:2 avoid quarreling. Instead, they should be gentle and show true humility to everyone.
Eph 4:31 3 Once we, too, were foolish and disobedient. We were misled and became slaves to
3:3 1 Cor 6:11 many lusts and pleasures. Our lives were full of evil and envy, and we hated each other.
Eph 5:8 4 But—"When God our Savior revealed His kindness and love, 5 He saved us, not because

2:3 Greek *be enslaved to much wine.* 2:5 Some manuscripts read *to care for their homes.*

2:7-8 In the midst of his instructions for various groups of people, Paul gives some personal instructions to Titus. The fact that these instructions follow Paul's exhortations for young men strongly suggests that Titus was a young man also (see also 1 Timothy 4:12).

2:11-15 God's grace, which is His unearned favor toward helpless humans, brings "salvation to all people" (2:11). This does not mean every person will be saved, but that Christ's death is valid and effective for people of all races and generations. The benefits of Christ's death on behalf of believers are fourfold: They receive freedom from sin, cleansing from sin, adoption into God's family, and the desire to do God's will. These truths are so important for all Christians that Titus—and every minister of the gospel in every age—"must teach these things" (2:15).

▸ GOD
2:12-13 Hope amid daily living. For Christians, living in this sinful world is a struggle. We are commanded to "turn from godless living and sinful pleasures" and to live "with wisdom, righteousness, and devotion to God." None of this is easy. Temptations assail us, unbelievers oppose us, and our faith grows weak. But one thing that sustains us is the sure prospect that Christ will come again. If we are still in this world at that point, Christ's return will mark the end of our struggle, for He will take us to be with Him and will complete the process of our sanctification. If you struggle daily to live out your Christian faith, take time to contemplate the glories that await Christ's return, and let that certain hope empower you to press on. Your struggle will not be forever! (***See God***> *God's Names> Holy Spirit> Fills with hope,* TopicGuide page A19.)

▸ ADOPTION
3:1-2 Gentle and humble toward all. How hard do you find it to go against the flow in our culture? Paul expected his readers to follow Christ first. Rather than disobeying duly appointed authorities, slandering others, and engaging in quarrels, believers are to be gentle and humble toward everyone. Could anything be more countercultural? How often is gentleness manifested in contemporary music, movies, television, highway traffic, business, and countless other areas? How often do human beings behave humbly toward one another in these spheres? These traits are exceedingly rare. Take a hard look at your behavior today. Do you display gentleness and humility in your dealings with non-Christians as well as your brothers and sisters in Christ? If not, pray that the Spirit will change you, and that you might show the world a better way. (***See Adoption***> *With Christ> Redemption> Humble self-estimation,* TopicGuide page A37.)

3:3-8 This is one of many passages in which Paul describes the corrupt condition of humanity since the fall of Adam and Eve (see Romans 1:18–3:18; 5:12-21; 1 Corinthians 6:9-10; Galatians 5:19-21; Ephesians 2:1-3; Colossians 1:21; 2:13; 3:5-9; 1 Timothy 1:9-10; 2 Timothy 3:2-5). Despite this flood of evil, God's kindness kept Him from immediately judging every person the first time they sinned, and His love motivated Him to provide salvation to lost sinners. God's provision of salvation is not based on a person's good works but on His "mercy" (3:5; see Ephesians 2:8-9).

of the righteous things we had done, but because of His mercy. He washed away our sins,
giving us a new birth and new life through the Holy Spirit.* 6He generously poured out the
Spirit upon us through Jesus Christ our Savior. 7Because of His grace He declared us righ-
teous and gave us confidence that we will inherit eternal life." 8This is a trustworthy say-
ing, and I want you to insist on these teachings so that all who trust in God will devote
themselves to doing good. These teachings are good and beneficial for everyone.
9Do not get involved in foolish discussions about spiritual pedigrees* or in quarrels and
fights about obedience to Jewish laws. These things are useless and a waste of time. 10If
people are causing divisions among you, give a first and second warning. After that, have
nothing more to do with them. 11For people like that have turned away from the truth, and
their own sins condemn them.

PAUL'S FINAL REMARKS AND GREETINGS

12I am planning to send either Artemas or Tychicus to you. As soon as one of them arrives,
do your best to meet me at Nicopolis, for I have decided to stay there for the winter. 13Do
everything you can to help Zenas the lawyer and Apollos with their trip. See that they are
given everything they need. 14Our people must learn to do good by meeting the urgent
needs of others; then they will not be unproductive.
15Everybody here sends greetings. Please give my greetings to the believers—all who
love us.
May God's grace be with you all.

3:6 Joel 2:28; Rom 5:5
3:7 Rom 3:24
3:8 Titus 2:14; 3:14
3:9 2 Tim 2:14, 16, 23
3:10 Matt 18:15-17; Rom 16:17
3:12 Acts 20:4; Eph 6:21-22; 2 Tim 4:9, 21
3:13 Acts 18:24
3:14 Eph 4:28; Titus 2:14; 3:8
3:15 Col 4:18

3:5 Greek *He saved us through the washing of regeneration and renewing of the Holy Spirit.* 3:9 Or *spiritual genealogies.*

3:9-11 Paul warned Titus against getting into arguments with those who wanted to introduce ideas and beliefs into the church that "are useless and a waste of time" (3:9; see 1 Timothy 1:4). Jesus said that those who continue to threaten the unity of the body should be excluded from the church after multiple warnings from the leadership and congregation (Matthew 18:15-17).

3:12-15 Paul decided to spend the winter months in Nicopolis, a good city for that purpose because it was located on the warm southwestern coast of Greece on the Adriatic Sea.

PHILEMON

PURPOSE

To provide a model of how the gospel can restore broken relationships.

How do you get past the wall? Someone offends us—whether intentionally or not—and we allow a wall to be built up against that person. Unless we deal with the problem and seek reconciliation, we might end up regarding someone we once considered a close friend as an enemy. Those who follow Jesus are supposed to live in love with one another, but too often we choose our own way and allow differences to come between us. Life in Paul's day was no different.

Onesimus was a runaway slave. Such a crime was punishable by death. Paul wanted to see Philemon reconciled with Onesimus because now everything had changed—Onesimus had become a Christian.

One of Paul's most personal letters, the intended purpose is to create a situation where Philemon would be moved, due to Paul's gentle prodding, to welcome back his runaway slave Onesimus as a brother in the Lord (1:17)—and not have him executed.

DISCOVER GOD IN PHILEMON

Paul paints a beautiful picture of Jesus' saving love for His sinful people.

The Substitute and Advocate: Onesimus is guilty of a capital crime (1:11, 18). But Paul shows us Christ in his example of interceding for Onesimus (1:10-17), laying aside his own privileges and becoming Onesimus' substitute by assuming his sin debt (1:8, 18-19). In this work of mediation, Paul is able to bring Onesimus to Philemon as a righteous man, ready to serve in his new relationship to his master. In this picture of grace, we are Onesimus; Jesus is our substitute (Matthew 20:28), and God now accepts us as His beloved (Acts 10:35; Hebrews 12:6), not His enemy.

GROWING THROUGH PHILEMON

One way to grow as a disciple through this book is to see how Paul attempts to reconcile Philemon to Onesimus.

A Work of Grace: Paul affirms the work of grace that God has done in Philemon's heart and life. Paul is not offering false flattery to Philemon (1:4-7); Philemon is a dear friend, and Paul is simply pointing out the genuine work of God he has seen in Onesimus's life. When seeking to reconcile with others, it is helpful to affirm what you see God doing in their lives already.

An Appeal to Love: Fostering reconciliation between those who are at odds with one another is hard work. The whole process becomes much easier, however, when you demonstrate your care for those you are seeking to aid. Clearly, Paul cares deeply for both Philemon and

Onesimus (1:4-7, 9-10, 16, 22). Paul's deep love for them draws these two men close enough so they can be reconciled, just as Christ's love for them has reconciled them to God (Ephesians 2:16; Colossians 1:20).

A Personal Sacrifice: It is clear that Onesimus has wronged Philemon. But Onesimus now has a new life; he is a new person because of Jesus. Paul sees this, yet he also knows that Philemon has suffered loss because of what Onesimus has done. To make amends, Paul steps in and gives of himself in order to promote the reconciliation. He is willing to accept the charges of any wrong that has been done to Philemon (1:17-19). Such personal involvement and investment can be a great help in smoothing out difficulties between those who need to be reconciled.

PHILEMON FACTS

DISCOVERY VERSES

Onesimus hasn't been of much use to you in the past, but now he is very useful to both of us. I am sending him back to you, and with him comes my own heart.

(PHILEMON 1:11-12)

Author: Paul wrote this short, personal letter (1:1, 9, 19) to a close friend of his.

Written to: In Paul's day, slavery was widely practiced (see Ephesians 6:5-9; Colossians 3:22–4:1; Titus 2:9-10). Philemon was a Christian who had slaves as part of his household. One of his slaves, Onesimus, had apparently stolen from him and run away (1:18). While he was still a fugitive slave, however, Onesimus met Paul, and he became a believer (1:10). Paul then wrote to Philemon to try to reconcile him with his runaway slave, who was now also a brother in the Lord.

Date of writing: Paul's reference to his imprisonment suggests that Paul was writing from house arrest in Rome (1:9-10; Acts 28:16-31). Paul had sent a letter to the Colossians by Tychicus and Onesimus (Colossians 4:7-9), and it appears that these messengers also delivered this letter to Philemon. This would place the writing of the letter around AD 60.

Setting: As was mentioned earlier, Paul is wrote this letter to Philemon from house arrest in Rome (Acts 28:16-31). From the indications in Paul's letters, Philemon was a believer living in Colosse (compare, for example, Colossians 4:9 with Philemon 1:2). For more details on Colosse, see the introduction to Colossians, page 2143.

OUTLINE

- **PHILEMON 1:1-7**—Paul's Prayer for Philemon for His Continued Growth
- **PHILEMON 1:8-21**—Paul's Plea to Philemon to Respond Well to Onesimus
- **PHILEMON 1:22-25**—Paul's Personal Request to Visit Philemon

GREETINGS FROM PAUL

1:1 This letter is from Paul, a prisoner for preaching the Good News about Christ Jesus, and
Eph 4:1 Phil 1:7 from our brother Timothy.
Phlm 1:9, 23 I am writing to Philemon, our beloved co-worker, [2]and to our sister Apphia, and to our
1:2 Rom 16:5 fellow soldier Archippus, and to the church that meets in your* house.
Phil 2:25 Col 4:17 [3]May God our Father and the Lord Jesus Christ give you grace and peace.

PAUL'S THANKSGIVING AND PRAYER

1:4 [4]I always thank my God when I pray for you, Philemon, [5]because I keep hearing about
Rom 1:8-9 your faith in the Lord Jesus and your love for all of God's people. [6]And I am praying that
1:6 you will put into action the generosity that comes from your faith as you understand and
Phil 1:9 experience all the good things we have in Christ. [7]Your love has given me much joy and
1:7 2 Cor 7:4, 13 comfort, my brother, for your kindness has often refreshed the hearts of God's people.

PAUL'S APPEAL FOR ONESIMUS

[8]That is why I am boldly asking a favor of you. I could demand it in the name of Christ be-
1:9 Eph 3:1; 4:1 cause it is the right thing for you to do. [9]But because of our love, I prefer simply to ask you.
Phil 1:7 Consider this as a request from me—Paul, an old man and now also a prisoner for the sake
of Christ Jesus.*
1:10 [10]I appeal to you to show kindness to my child, Onesimus. I became his father in the
1 Cor 4:14 Col 4:9 faith while here in prison. [11]Onesimus* hasn't been of much use to you in the past, but
now he is very useful to both of us. [12]I am sending him back to you, and with him comes
my own heart.
1:13 Phil 2:30 [13]I wanted to keep him here with me while I am in these chains for preaching the Good
1:14 News, and he would have helped me on your behalf. [14]But I didn't want to do anything
2 Cor 9:7 without your consent. I wanted you to help because you were willing, not because you
1 Pet 5:2 were forced. [15]It seems you lost Onesimus for a little while so that you could have him
1:15 Gen 45:5, 8 back forever. [16]He is no longer like a slave to you. He is more than a slave, for he is a be-
loved brother, especially to me. Now he will mean much more to you, both as a man and
1:16 Matt 23:8 as a brother in the Lord.
1 Cor 7:22 Eph 6:9 [17]So if you consider me your partner, welcome him as you would welcome me. [18]If he
1:17 has wronged you in any way or owes you anything, charge it to me. [19]I, Paul, write this
2 Cor 8:23 with my own hand: I will repay it. And I won't mention that you owe me your very soul!

1:19 1 Cor 16:21

2 Throughout this letter, *you* and *your* are singular except in verses 3, 22, and 25. 9 Or *a prisoner of Christ Jesus.*
11 *Onesimus* means "useful."

1:1-7 The terms of endearment Paul uses for the three members of this household—"our beloved co-worker," "our sister," and "our fellow soldier"—indicate a long and loving relationship between Paul and those receiving the letter. However, the main body of the letter is directed to Philemon.

▸ WORSHIP

1:6 The generosity of faith. Does your Christian faith make you generous? It certainly had that effect on the early believers. "They shared everything they had. . . . There were no needy people among them, because those who owned land or houses would sell them and bring the money to the apostles to give to those in need" (Acts 4:32, 34-35). Likewise, the churches of Macedonia "gave not only what they could afford, but far more" (2 Corinthians 8:3) for the believers in Jerusalem. When our hearts are truly changed by God's Spirit, our eyes are opened to see how generous God has been toward us, even when we did not deserve it. He calls us to be generous, too—generous in forgiving others, in bearing with their weaknesses, and in sharing our resources. Think about ways you can give of yourself to your brothers and sisters in the faith. (***See Worship***> *NT*> *Offerings*> *Christ's example of generosity,* TopicGuide page A31.)

1:8-14 Paul does not introduce himself as an apostle at the outset of this letter as he so often does in his epistles because he has no intention of exercising apostolic authority over Philemon. Paul asks Philemon for a "favor" (1:8) or "request" (1:9) instead of making a demand. He appeals to Philemon on the basis of their friendship and his old age, both of which are sure to soften any harsh feelings Philemon may have toward Onesimus, the runaway slave.

1:15-16 The word "seems" contains an allusion to God's providence in the case of Onesimus. A runaway slave was subject to punishment, but God's grace had intervened in Onesimus's life, and he is returning to his master. Paul sees God at work in this situation, and Philemon needs to see it, too. He lost Onesimus as a slave briefly, but he can receive him back again permanently—not just in this life but also in eternity.

[20]Yes, my brother, please do me this favor* for the Lord's sake. Give me this encourage-
ment in Christ.
[21]I am confident as I write this letter that you will do what I ask and even more! [22]One
more thing—please prepare a guest room for me, for I am hoping that God will answer
your prayers and let me return to you soon.

PAUL'S FINAL GREETINGS

[23]Epaphras, my fellow prisoner in Christ Jesus, sends you his greetings. [24]So do Mark, Aris-
tarchus, Demas, and Luke, my co-workers.
[25]May the grace of the Lord Jesus Christ be with your spirit.

20 Greek *onaimen,* a play on the name Onesimus.

1:22 Phil 1:25-26; 2:24

1:23 Col 1:7; 4:10

1:24 Acts 12:12; 19:29; 27:2; Col 4:10, 14; 2 Tim 4:10

1:25 Gal 6:18; 2 Tim 4:22

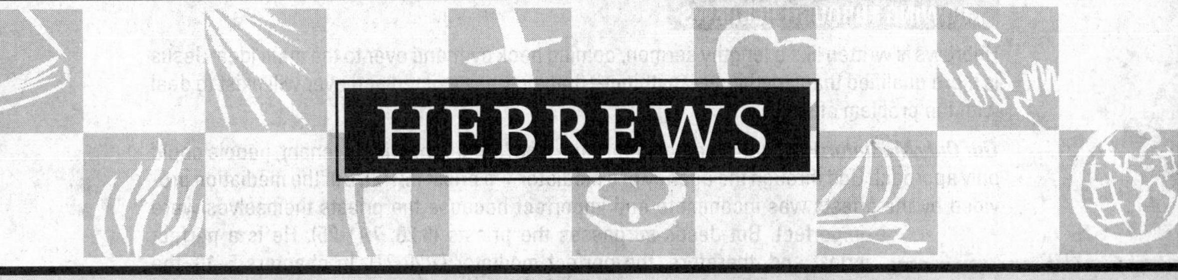

HEBREWS

PURPOSE

To encourage tenacious faith in Jesus Christ by presenting Him as the final solution for the problem of sin.

We live in a world where our faith in Christ is constantly challenged and other "gods" compete for our loyalty. The people for whom the book of Hebrews was written were no different. They were facing persecution for their faith, which they knew would end if they recanted from faith in Jesus Christ alone for salvation and returned to Judaism.

Like these early believers, we are easily tempted to fall away and trust in other things when facing persecution for our faith. But the writer of Hebrews proclaims that nothing is superior to the Lord Jesus Christ. All other people, gods, and traditions will fall short of satisfying us or saving us. This book calls on all who follow Christ to remain faithful and to persevere in following Him, for He surpasses all other gods, and He alone has achieved lasting and secure salvation for those who trust in Him.

DISCOVER GOD IN HEBREWS

Although God the Father is mentioned in the letter to the Hebrews (for example, in 1:5 and 2:11) and reference is made to the Spirit (for example, in 2:4; 9:14 and 10:15), the real focus of this letter is Jesus, who is God the Son, the second person of the Trinity.

Superior to Moses: For the Jewish people, Moses was the most outstanding "spokesman" for God, bringing a definitive and clear word from God. The book of Hebrews, however, presents Jesus as the preeminent spokesman for God. Moses was a faithful servant in God's house (3:2), but Jesus is the Son and the One who is in charge of "God's entire house" (3:6). So, if you want to hear what God has to say, listen to Jesus.

The Final Sacrifice for Sin: Every day, every month, every year, the Jewish people offered sacrifices to God for their sins. But those sacrifices only covered over the sin; they couldn't fully take it away (10:11-12). The book of Hebrews shows how Jesus offered Himself as the once-for-all sacrifice that resolved the problem of our sin. He has done, in His death on the cross, what no other sacrifice could ever do—put away sin (9:26-28). So, if you want to be freed from your sin, look to Jesus.

The Doorway to God: How can anyone come close to the Holy God? People have sought access to God since the dawn of time and done virtually everything under the sun to gain it. The book of Hebrews explains how Jesus Himself has made a way for us to enter the presence of the Holy God. Through Jesus' death (10:19-22) and His ongoing ministry of intercession (7:24-25), we can draw near to God. So, if you want to grow close to God, come to Jesus.

GROWING THROUGH HEBREWS

Hebrews is written like a lengthy sermon, coming back over and over to the main idea: Jesus is more qualified than anything—anything—that ever has existed and ever will exist to deal with the problem of sin.

Our Only Mediator: How can a person approach God? Under the Old Covenant, people could only approach God through the agency of a mediator—a priest (5:1-2). But the mediation provided by the priests was incomplete and imperfect because the priests themselves were imperfect. But Jesus surpasses the priests (6:20; 7:11-25). He is a perfect priest and, therefore, the perfect mediator (7:26-27). In chapters 5–10, the author shows us that Jesus has a role to play in our lives that makes Him superior to any other mediator or priest: He leads us into intimacy with God. Because of Jesus, we can draw near to God (10:19-22).

DISCOVERY VERSES

So then, since we have a great High Priest who has entered heaven, Jesus the Son of God, let us hold firmly to what we believe. This High Priest of ours understands our weaknesses, for He faced all of the same testings we do, yet He did not sin. So let us come boldly to the throne of our gracious God. There we will receive His mercy, and we will find grace to help us when we need it most. (HEBREWS 4:14-16)

Faith is the confidence that what we hope for will actually happen; it gives us assurance about things we cannot see. (HEBREWS 11:1)

Since we are receiving a Kingdom that is unshakable, let us be thankful and please God by worshiping Him with holy fear and awe. For our God is a devouring fire. (HEBREWS 12:28-29)

Our Foundation for Life: What does it mean to live in relationship with the holy God? It is one thing to know we can draw close to God because of Jesus; it is another thing to choose to follow Jesus into God's presence. Jesus leads us in the way to live. We can "run with endurance the race" God has set before us "by keeping our eyes on Jesus, the champion who initiates and perfects our faith" (12:1-2). In chapters 11–13, the author shows us the implications of life in this relationship of intimacy with God that Jesus has opened up for us. An intimate union with God produces in us a patient reliance on Him and a confidence that He will fulfill His promises.

Our Object and Example of Faith: When someone encourages you to live a godlier, trusting life, it's easy to avoid dealing with their words by pointing to their weaknesses and sins; if their advice is so great, then why are they still so sinful? But Jesus is the perfect person to trust in matters of faith because He alone was perfectly faithful to perform all that the Father required (Hebrews 2:17, 3:2, 6). So when the writer of Hebrews points to those who trusted and obeyed God (Hebrews 11–12), they too accomplished their spiritual heroics by faith in God—just like Jesus. No one will sustain a mature spiritual life or produce suitable spiritual fruit without learning to have simple faith in God's promises in Jesus Christ (Hebrews 6:12; 11:13, 17).

HEBREWS FACTS

Author: Since the earliest days of the church, Christians have debated about the unnamed author of this letter. The church fathers settled on Paul as its content demanded it be included in the collection of Old and New Testament books. However, in recent times, others have speculated that it was written by one of Paul's many coworkers, with Apollos (Acts 18:24, 27; 19:1; 1 Corinthians 1:12; 3:4-6, 22; Titus 3:13) being the most likely candidate. It is written in refined Greek, suggesting the author was a native Greek speaker. It also employs a distinct style of Old Testament interpretation that was characteristic of Alexandria, suggesting the author was affiliated with that city. Also, the writer sends greetings from the believers from Italy, suggesting that the author was writing to a congregation in Italy—or from Italy. While this still does not give us conclusive evidence regarding the author, it does set Apollos apart as the most probable candidate of whom we know.

Written to: Repeatedly throughout the letter, the author writes in such a way that indicates his readers were familiar with the Jewish sacrificial system. However, the greetings to those in Italy set the book apart from a letter written to those in Israel. Apparently, the recipients were believers in Jesus (3:1) and had been so for some time (5:12), so they were most likely Jewish Christians in Italy, having come to faith in Jesus after growing up under Judaism, perhaps under the ministry of the author (13:18-24).

Date of writing: With so little certainty about the author and audience, some speculation about the date is unavoidable. Clement of Rome quotes the book of Hebrews favorably in AD 95, so it must have been in circulation for some time prior to that. Its failure to mention the destruction of the Temple in Jerusalem in AD 70 (which ended the Old Covenant sacrificial system once and for all) is significant; indeed, the Temple seems to still be in working order (10:1-3, 11), so the book must have been written prior to AD 70. A young pastor mentored by Paul, Timothy, had not died (13:23) and had been released from prison, suggesting a date of the mid-60s.

Setting: The letter appears to be intended for Greek-reading believers from Jewish backgrounds living in Italy. They may have been Jews who converted, as the ancient title at the beginning of the oldest manuscripts reads "To Hebrews."

OUTLINE

- **HEBREWS 1:1–2:18**—Jesus, Superior to Prophets and Angels
- **HEBREWS 3:1–7:28**—Jesus, Superior to Moses and the Priesthood of Aaron
- **HEBREWS 8:1–10:18**—Jesus, Our High Priest and Perfect Sacrifice
- **HEBREWS 10:19–13:25**—Jesus, the Basis of Living and Persevering by Faith

JESUS CHRIST IS GOD'S SON

1 Long ago God spoke many times and in many ways to our ancestors through the
prophets. 2 And now in these final days, He has spoken to us through His Son. God
promised everything to the Son as an inheritance, and through the Son He created the
universe. 3 The Son radiates God's own glory and expresses the very character of God, and
He sustains everything by the mighty power of His command. When He had cleansed us
from our sins, He sat down in the place of honor at the right hand of the majestic God in
heaven. 4 This shows that the Son is far greater than the angels, just as the name God gave
Him is greater than their names.

THE SON IS GREATER THAN THE ANGELS

5 For God never said to any angel what He said to Jesus:

> "You are My Son.
> Today I have become Your Father.*"

1:5a Or *Today I reveal You as My Son.* Ps 2:7.

1:2 Ps 2:8, Matt 21:38, John 1:3, 1 Pet 1:20
1:3 Ps 110:1, Matt 22:44, Mark 16:19, John 14:9, 2 Cor 4:4, Col 1:15
1:4 Eph 1:21, Phil 2:9-10
1:5 *Ps 2:7, *2 Sam 7:14

1:1-2 Because the first readers of this letter were Jewish believers, the writer begins by reminding them of several commonly held beliefs. First, that God had used prophets in earlier times in Israel's history to communicate truth to His people. Prophets not only foretold the future (as we see in Daniel, Ezekiel, and other Old Testament books), but they also proclaimed the truth people needed to hear for that day (for example, Elijah, Elisha, Amos, and Hosea). The key phrase here is "and now." While prophets had been the messengers before, now we have heard from God's Son.

1:3 In striking terms, we are told here that God's Son is in fact God. In the Old Testament, God's glory was the ultimate manifestation of His being. For Jesus to reflect that glory and represent God exactly, He must be God, not a mere representative. Not only is He divine in His being, but we also see that by the power of His spoken word He upholds all of creation. This verse is one of the strongest affirmations of the divinity of Jesus that we find in the New Testament (along with John 1:1, 14 and Colossians 1:15).

▸ SALVATION

1:3 The stain we are unable to remove. Too many people do not understand the true problem of personal sin. They approach God as if they need a touch-up to remove superficial blemishes. But sin stains. No amount of scrubbing and working can remove it. All our efforts to do so are in vain (Isaiah 64:6). The writer of Hebrews speaks about Jesus' divine being, and then immediately applies that truth: Only He can deal with our sin (Hebrews 9:13, 14). Have you tired yet of trying to remove stains that only the Savior's work can remove? Trust His cleansing work alone. (***See Salvation****> Our Need> Sinful> Inability to save oneself,* TopicGuide page A22.)

1:4 In a very orderly fashion, the writer of Hebrews argues against each of the things that his readers have trusted in for security. The writer shows how Jesus is superior to each of these objects of faith. He begins with angels. In the first century, apparently many placed faith in the work of angels on their behalf. Throughout chapter 1, we are shown that while angels are servants of God, Jesus, God's Son, is far superior to them in power and position.

God also said,

"I will be His Father,
and He will be My Son."*

6And when He brought His firstborn Son into the world, God said,* 1:6 *Deut 32:43 *Ps 8:4

"Let all of God's angels worship Him."*

7Regarding the angels, He says, 1:7 *Ps 8:5

"He sends His angels like the winds,
His servants like flames of fire."*

8But to the Son He says, 1:8-9 *Ps 45:6-7

"Your throne, O God, endures forever and ever.
You rule with a scepter of justice.
9 You love justice and hate evil.
Therefore, O God, Your God has anointed You,
pouring out the oil of joy on You more than on anyone else."*

10He also says to the Son, 1:10-12 *Ps 102:25-27

"In the beginning, Lord, You laid the foundation of the earth
and made the heavens with Your hands.
11 They will perish, but You remain forever.
They will wear out like old clothing.
12 You will fold them up like a cloak
and discard them like old clothing.
But You are always the same;
You will live forever."*

1:5b 2 Sam 7:14. 1:6a Or *when He again brings His firstborn son into the world, God will say.* 1:6b Deut 32:43. 1:7 Ps 104:4 (Greek version). 1:8-9 Ps 45:6-7. 1:10-12 Ps 102:25-27.

1:8 By applying this quote from Psalm 45:6 to the Son, the writer is again making an explicit equation between Jesus the Son and God Himself. Together with 1:3, this is one of the clearest New Testament claims of Jesus' divine status—the Son is God forever.

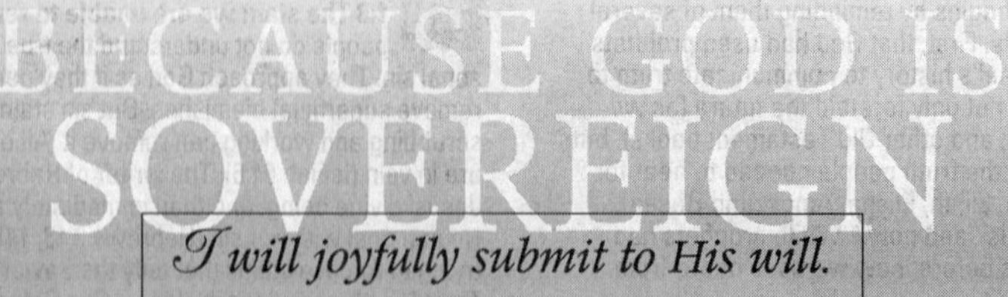

He sustains everything by the mighty power of His command.

HEBREWS 1:3

1:13 13 And God never said to any of the angels,
Ps 110:1
Matt 22:44 "Sit in the place of honor at My right hand
until I humble Your enemies,
making them a footstool under Your feet."*

1:14 14 Therefore, angels are only servants—spirits sent to care for people who will inherit salvation.
Pss 34:7; 91:11

A WARNING AGAINST DRIFTING AWAY

2 So we must listen very carefully to the truth we have heard, or we may drift away
2:2 from it. 2 For the message God delivered through angels has always stood firm, and
Deut 33:2 every violation of the law and every act of disobedience was punished. 3 So what makes
Acts 7:38, 53 us think we can escape if we ignore this great salvation that was first announced by the
Gal 3:19 Lord Jesus Himself and then delivered to us by those who heard Him speak? 4 And God
2:3 Heb 1:2; 10:29 confirmed the message by giving signs and wonders and various miracles and gifts of the
2:4 Holy Spirit whenever He chose.
Mark 16:20

JESUS, THE MAN

5 And furthermore, it is not angels who will control the future world we are talking about.
2:6-8 6 For in one place the Scriptures say,
Ps 8:4-6

"What are mere mortals that You should think about them,
or a son of man* that You should care for him?
7 Yet You made them only a little lower than the angels
and crowned them with glory and honor.*
2:8 8 You gave them authority over all things."*
1 Cor 15:27

Now when it says "all things," it means nothing is left out. But we have not yet seen all
2:9 Phil 2:6-9 things put under their authority. 9 What we do see is Jesus, who was given a position "a lit-
2:10 tle lower than the angels"; and because He suffered death for us, He is now "crowned with
Luke 13:32; 24:46 glory and honor." Yes, by God's grace, Jesus tasted death for everyone. 10 God, for whom
Rom 11:36
Heb 5:9 and through whom everything was made, chose to bring many children into glory. And it
2:11 was only right that He should make Jesus, through His suffering, a perfect leader, fit to
Matt 28:10 bring them into their salvation.
John 20:17
Rom 8:29 11 So now Jesus and the ones He makes holy have the same Father. That is why Jesus is
Heb 10:10; 13:12 not ashamed to call them His brothers and sisters.* 12 For He said to God,

2:12
*Ps 22:22 "I will proclaim Your name to My brothers and sisters.
I will praise You among Your assembled people."*

1:13 Ps 110:1. 2:6 Or *the Son of Man.* 2:7 Some manuscripts add *You gave them charge of everything You made.*
2:6-8 Ps 8:4-6 (Greek version). 2:11 Greek *brothers;* also in 2:12. 2:12 Ps 22:22.

1:13 The writer quotes here from Psalm 110, a favorite in Israel and the most frequently quoted psalm in both the New Testament and Hebrews. Comparing Jesus once again to angels, the writer points out that Jesus is a reigning power, given the place of honor and equality (the "right hand") with God, the great King of kings.

▶ BIBLE

2:1 Listen or drift away. "You deserve it!" "Just once won't hurt!" "There are exceptions to every rule." We hear messages like these all the time from the world around us. If we do not compare such statements with God's truth, it becomes easy to drift away. This verse in Hebrews warns us that even those who have heard truth and have been raised in truth can drift from it. Are there lies that you have listened to that are leading you to drift from the truth? Ask God to show you where you might be drifting. Seek to remain anchored to the truth of Scripture in all your ways. (***See Bible****> Power> Worldview> Means to know all truth,* TopicGuide page A12.)

2:4 God accompanied His work of redemption from Egypt with "signs and wonders," including the plagues in Egypt and the miracles in the wilderness. But here, the writer notes that signs and wonders also accompanied the redemption Christ accomplished. The deaf could hear, the lame could walk, the blind could see. Jesus and His apostles performed these signs.

2:9-10 This passage reveals that Jesus "tasted death" at least in some sense for the whole world. Yet, through Jesus' death, God would bring "many children into glory"—not all people. While Jesus' death was sufficient to save the whole world, God has made it *efficient* or effective to save a limited number (see also John 6:37, 44, 63-65; Ephesians 1:4-6; Romans 9:14-24).

13He also said,

"I will put My trust in Him,"
that is, "I and the children God has given Me."*

14Because God's children are human beings—made of flesh and blood—the Son also be-
came flesh and blood. For only as a human being could He die, and only by dying could
He break the power of the devil, who had* the power of death. 15Only in this way could He
set free all who have lived their lives as slaves to the fear of dying.

16We also know that the Son did not come to help angels; He came to help the descen-
dants of Abraham. 17Therefore, it was necessary for Him to be made in every respect like
us, His brothers and sisters,* so that He could be our merciful and faithful High Priest be-
fore God. Then He could offer a sacrifice that would take away the sins of the people.
18Since He Himself has gone through suffering and testing, He is able to help us when we
are being tested.

JESUS IS GREATER THAN MOSES

3 And so, dear brothers and sisters who belong to God and* are partners with those
called to heaven, think carefully about this Jesus whom we declare to be God's mes-
senger* and High Priest. 2For He was faithful to God, who appointed Him, just as Moses
served faithfully when he was entrusted with God's entire* house.

3But Jesus deserves far more glory than Moses, just as a person who builds a house de-
serves more praise than the house itself. 4For every house has a builder, but the One who
built everything is God.

5Moses was certainly faithful in God's house as a servant. His work was an illustration of
the truths God would reveal later. 6But Christ, as the Son, is in charge of God's entire
house. And we are God's house, if we keep our courage and remain confident in our hope
in Christ.*

7That is why the Holy Spirit says,

2:13 *Isa 8:17-18; John 17:11-12
2:14 John 1:14; Rom 8:3; 1 Cor 15:54-57; 2 Tim 1:10; 1 Jn 3:8
2:17 Phil 2:7; Heb 3:1; 4:15; 5:1; 1 Jn 2:2; 4:10
2:18 Heb 4:15; 5:2
3:1 Heb 2:17; 4:14
3:2 Num 12:7-8
3:3 2 Cor 3:7-11
3:5 Exod 14:31; Num 12:7
3:6 Eph 2:19-22; 1 Tim 3:15; 1 Pet 2:5
3:7-11 *Ps 95:7-11

2:13 Isa 8:17-18. 2:14 Or *has.* 2:17 Greek *like the brothers.* 3:1a Greek *And so, holy brothers who.* 3:1b Greek *God's apostle.* 3:2 Some manuscripts omit *entire.* 3:6 Some manuscripts add *faithful to the end.*

2:14 While chapter 1 focused on the divinity of Jesus as God's eternal Son, this chapter reveals the humanity of Jesus. Some people in the first century believed that God could not be "tainted" by taking on human form. But we see here that Jesus was indeed a man. He was not 50 percent God and 50 percent man. In a mystery impossible to fully grasp, the Scriptures affirm that Jesus was all God and all man, possessing a dual nature. The following verses tell us why it was necessary that He be completely human: to deliver other humans from the power of death.

2:16 The author says that Jesus came to help "the descendants of Abraham," which means that He came to help God's chosen children. Abraham was selected (in Genesis 12) from all people to be the father of a nation that God would bless. Abraham's descendants became the Hebrew nation (Exodus 1–2) through whom God brings all His chosen people into His family.

2:17 As people alienated from God by our sin, we need a priest, one who goes before God on our behalf. A priest represents the people before God, bringing sacrifices to pay for sin and offerings of thanksgiving. God gave extensive and exhaustive descriptions for the priests' qualifications and work in the books of Exodus, Leviticus, Numbers, and Deuteronomy.

▸ WORSHIP

2:18 Help in times of temptation. Jesus is unlike anyone who ever lived. He is God present in human form. As God, He is perfect and holy; as man, He has suffered temptation like us, so He is able to come to our aid. What do you turn to for strength when you are tempted? To a self-help book, an exercise routine, or a perfunctory prayer? Turn to the One who alone is truly able to help you. Turn to Jesus. He knows exactly what to do to help you. (***See Worship****> NT> To the Father> Worship of the Father combats temptation,* TopicGuide page A29.)

3:2 Though Abraham is considered the "father" of the Hebrew people, Moses was their great leader. God chose him in the book of Exodus to bring the people of Israel out of bondage in Egypt and into the Promised Land. The writer of Hebrews begins a crucial comparison between Moses and Jesus, demonstrating that Jesus deserves more glory.

3:5-6 Referring to Numbers 12:7, Moses is called a faithful servant *in* the house of God. But Jesus is declared to be the Son who exercises authority *over* the house of God. The writer continues his method of arguing from the lesser to the greater. All Jews would call Moses great, perhaps even the greatest. But Jesus is shown to be worthy of even more praise.

3:8 Exod 17:7 "Today when you hear His voice,
8 don't harden your hearts
as Israel did when they rebelled,
when they tested Me in the wilderness.
9 There your ancestors tested and tried My patience,
even though they saw My miracles for forty years.
10 So I was angry with them, and I said,
'Their hearts always turn away from Me.
3:11 They refuse to do what I tell them.'
Num 14:21-23 11 So in My anger I took an oath:
'They will never enter My place of rest.'"*

3:13 Eph 4:22 12 Be careful then, dear brothers and sisters.* Make sure that your own hearts are not evil
3:14 and unbelieving, turning you away from the living God. 13 You must warn each other
Heb 3:6 every day, while it is still "today," so that none of you will be deceived by sin and hardened
3:15 against God. 14 For if we are faithful to the end, trusting God just as firmly as when we first
*Ps 95:7-8 believed, we will share in all that belongs to Christ. 15 Remember what it says:

"Today when you hear His voice,
don't harden your hearts
3:16-18 Num 14:1-35 as Israel did when they rebelled."*

16 And who was it who rebelled against God, even though they heard His voice? Wasn't it
3:17 Num 14:29 the people Moses led out of Egypt? 17 And who made God angry for forty years? Wasn't it the
1 Cor 10:5 people who sinned, whose corpses lay in the wilderness? 18 And to whom was God speaking
3:18 when He took an oath that they would never enter His rest? Wasn't it the people who dis-
Num 14:22-23 obeyed Him? 19 So we see that because of their unbelief they were not able to enter His rest.

PROMISED REST FOR GOD'S PEOPLE

4:2 **4** God's promise of entering His rest still stands, so we ought to tremble with fear that
1 Thes 2:13 some of you might fail to experience it. 2 For this good news—that God has prepared
4:3 this rest—has been announced to us just as it was to them. But it did them no good be-
Ps 95:11 cause they didn't share the faith of those who listened to God. 3 For only we who believe
can enter His rest. As for the others, God said,

3:7-11 Ps 95:7-11. 3:12 Greek *brothers.* 3:15 Ps 95:7-8. 4:2 Some manuscripts read *they didn't combine what they heard with faith.*

3:8-9 These verses, drawn from the poetry of Psalm 95, refer back to a time during Israel's travels in the wilderness between Egypt and the Promised Land. Though the entire 40 years were a time of testing and rebellion, these verses probably refer specifically to an incident at a place called Rephidim in the Sinai Peninsula. Here, after the people complained of their thirst, Moses brought water from the rock, a miracle that validated his leadership over Israel.

▸ HOLINESS
3:12-13 A heart of repentance. Have you ever watched someone start out with excitement about her newfound faith, but then she slowly becomes entangled with sin again and eventually turns away from God? The hearts of people being led by God through the wilderness became evil and unbelieving—even while God was manifesting Himself in a cloud by day and a fire by night! When life is difficult, it can be hard for us to see God in the circumstances—unlike Israel's experience. We may be tempted to let sin deceive us and harden our hearts. Keep your heart soft through repentance and a loving relationship with God. Don't repeat the grave errors of our spiritual fathers, the people of Israel. (***See Holiness***> *Submission*> *Yielding to Spirit*> *Surrender your heart,* TopicGuide page A41.)

3:17-19 As Israel neared Canaan after leaving Mount Sinai, they refused to trust God and enter the land of promise, so God swore that the people would never enter the Promised Land at all. All but two people of adult age at that time would die in the desert over the next 38 years (Numbers 14:20-30). They never experienced the peace of settling down and enjoying what was promised to them.

▸ SALVATION
4:2 The key to the promise. Do you know people who say that they are going to heaven because their good deeds outweigh their bad deeds? Sadly, this is a widely held—but very mistaken—belief. Such people do not understand that heaven, the promised "rest" in Hebrews, is gained not by our work, but by grace through faith. Jesus said that everyone who believes in Him will never die (John 11:26). But to inherit that promise, one must believe. The Israelites in the wilderness did not believe the promise, so the promise did them no good. Are you trusting in the promise of Christ? He is the only hope for those who travel this earth, offering to bring us into God's promised rest in heaven. (***See Salvation***> *Receiving*> *How*> *Faith in Christ,* TopicGuide page A22.)

"In My anger I took an oath:
'They will never enter My place of rest,'"*

even though this rest has been ready since He made the world. 4We know it is ready be-
cause of the place in the Scriptures where it mentions the seventh day: "On the seventh
day God rested from all His work."* 5But in the other passage God said, "They will never
enter My place of rest."*
6So God's rest is there for people to enter, but those who first heard this good news
failed to enter because they disobeyed God. 7So God set another time for entering His rest,
and that time is today. God announced this through David much later in the words already
quoted:

"Today when you hear His voice,
don't harden your hearts."*

8Now if Joshua had succeeded in giving them this rest, God would not have spoken about
another day of rest still to come. 9So there is a special rest* still waiting for the people of
God. 10For all who have entered into God's rest have rested from their labors, just as God
did after creating the world. 11So let us do our best to enter that rest. But if we disobey
God, as the people of Israel did, we will fall.
12For the word of God is alive and powerful. It is sharper than the sharpest two-edged
sword, cutting between soul and spirit, between joint and marrow. It exposes our inner-
most thoughts and desires. 13Nothing in all creation is hidden from God. Everything is na-
ked and exposed before His eyes, and He is the One to whom we are accountable.

CHRIST IS OUR HIGH PRIEST

14So then, since we have a great High Priest who has entered heaven, Jesus the Son of
God, let us hold firmly to what we believe. 15This High Priest of ours understands our
weaknesses, for He faced all of the same testings we do, yet He did not sin. 16So let us
come boldly to the throne of our gracious God. There we will receive His mercy, and we
will find grace to help us when we need it most.

5 Every high priest is a man chosen to represent other people in their dealings with
God. He presents their gifts to God and offers sacrifices for their sins. 2And he is able
to deal gently with ignorant and wayward people because he himself is subject to the
same weaknesses. 3That is why he must offer sacrifices for his own sins as well as theirs.

4:3 Ps 95:11. 4:4 Gen 2:2. 4:5 Ps 95:11. 4:7 Ps 95:7-8. 4:9 Or *a Sabbath rest.*

4:4 *Gen 2:2
4:5 *Ps 95:11
4:6 Heb 3:18
4:7 *Ps 95:7-8
4:8 Josh 22:4
4:10 Gen 2:2; Rev 14:13
4:12 Isa 49:2; Jer 23:29; 1 Cor 14:24-25; Eph 6:17; 1 Pet 1:23
4:13 2 Chr 16:9; Ps 33:13-15
4:14 Heb 2:17; 3:1
4:15 2 Cor 5:21; Heb 2:17-18
4:16 Heb 7:19
5:1 Heb 2:17; 7:27; 8:3
5:2 Heb 2:17; 4:15
5:3 Lev 9:7; 16:6; Heb 7:27; 9:7

4:4 Genesis 1 says that God completed the work of creation in six days and rested on the seventh. This rest, symbolic of heaven, is a time and place where complete peace is found: peace with God, with other people, and with all creation.

4:7 David was the greatest king in Israel's history (see his story in 1 Samuel 16—1 Kings 2). The quote in this verse comes from Psalm 95. Though almost half of the psalms are directly attributed to David, this quote is drawn from a series of psalms (91–100) where no author is explicitly mentioned. However, it was common to refer to the entire body of the Psalms as being from David even though numerous other contributors are listed.

4:8 Joshua was the leader appointed by Moses to take the Israelites into the land, helping them conquer and settle it after their 40 years in the wilderness.

▸ SALVATION
4:16 A place of mercy and grace. "There's no such thing as a free lunch." While this proverb may be true in everyday life, it is not so with God. The writer of Hebrews makes sure his readers know that God's grace and mercy are there for the asking—all we have to do is declare our need. Our High Priest, Jesus, understands our plight and has access to the Father's presence, encouraging us to approach God's throne boldly. There we will receive mercy (release from deserved punishment) and grace (undeserved favor). Do you come boldly, admitting your deepest needs to God? Come without fear and admit your need for God's mercy and grace. (***See Salvation***> *Receiving> How> Submit to God's grace/special favor,* TopicGuide page A22.)

5:1 In the Old Testament, the priests were drawn from the family of Aaron (see 5:4), the brother of Moses, from the lineage of Levi. From this family of priests, one was selected through careful processes to represent the people as the high priest at certain times. Careful instructions were given concerning this high priest's personal appearance, clothing, and duties in order that his work of representing the people might be properly fulfilled (Leviticus 8–9).

5:4 4 And no one can become a high priest simply because he wants such an honor. He must
Exod 28:1 be called by God for this work, just as Aaron was. 5 That is why Christ did not honor Himself
5:5 *Ps 2:7 by assuming He could become High Priest. No, He was chosen by God, who said to Him,

Acts 13:33 "You are My Son.
Heb 1:5 Today I have become Your Father."*

5:6 *Ps 110:4 6 And in another passage God said to Him,

5:7 Ps 22:24 "You are a priest forever in the order of Melchizedek."*

Matt 26:38-46 7 While Jesus was here on earth, He offered prayers and pleadings, with a loud cry and
Mark 14:32-42 tears, to the One who could rescue Him from death. And God heard His prayers because of
Luke 22:39-46 His deep reverence for God. 8 Even though Jesus was God's Son, He learned obedience
5:8 Phil 2:8 from the things He suffered. 9 In this way, God qualified Him as a perfect High Priest, and
Heb 1:2 He became the source of eternal salvation for all those who obey Him. 10 And God desig-
5:9 nated Him to be a High Priest in the order of Melchizedek.
Isa 45:17

5:10 Ps 110:4

A CALL TO SPIRITUAL GROWTH

Heb 5:6 11 There is much more we would like to say about this, but it is difficult to explain, espe-
5:12 cially since you are spiritually dull and don't seem to listen. 12 You have been believers so
1 Cor 3:2 long now that you ought to be teaching others. Instead, you need someone to teach you
1 Pet 2:2 again the basic things about God's word.* You are like babies who need milk and cannot

5:5 Or *Today I reveal You as My Son.* Ps 2:7. 5:6 Ps 110:4. 5:12 Or *about the oracles of God.*

5:5-6 In verse 6, the writer mentions Melchizedek for the first time, the final element in the long list of comparisons he has made with Jesus. Melchizedek was a priest in Canaan who met Abraham (Genesis 14). It is clear from the story that Melchizedek was considered superior to Abraham, the father of the people of Israel.

5:7 Though Jesus was God, this verse reminds us again that He became a human being, and through His prayers and crying out to God, performed the work of a High Priest, going to God for the sake of people. The fact that God heard His prayers indicates that Jesus met the holy requirement of priesthood in God's eyes.

▸ WORSHIP

5:12 Advance with eagerness. Life is a constant journey in which it is impossible to stay in one place. We are either moving ahead toward growth and maturity, or we are falling back into immaturity. The writer of Hebrews recognized this, and he warned his readers of their failure to mature in Christ. Consider your own journey with Christ. Have you stayed too long in one place? Are you moving forward to new challenges, such as helping younger believers to grow? Ask God to spare you from the danger of regressing in your faith and to help you advance with eagerness. (***See Worship> NT> Prayer> Examples> Paul> For others> To grow in spiritual maturity***, TopicGuide page A33.)

BECAUSE GOD IS MERCIFUL

He forgives me of my sins when I sincerely confess them.

So let us come boldly to the throne of our gracious God.
There we will receive His mercy, and we will find grace
to help us when we need it most.

HEBREWS 4:16

FOR THE NEXT *GOD IS MERCIFUL* FEATURE SEE PAGE 2256.

eat solid food. 13For someone who lives on milk is still an infant and doesn't know how to
do what is right. 14Solid food is for those who are mature, who through training have the
skill to recognize the difference between right and wrong.

6 So let us stop going over the basic teachings about Christ again and again. Let us go
on instead and become mature in our understanding. Surely we don't need to start
again with the fundamental importance of repenting from evil deeds and placing our faith
in God. 2You don't need further instruction about baptisms, the laying on of hands, the
resurrection of the dead, and eternal judgment. 3And so, God willing, we will move for-
ward to further understanding.

4For it is impossible to bring back to repentance those who were once enlightened—
those who have experienced the good things of heaven and shared in the Holy Spirit,
5who have tasted the goodness of the word of God and the power of the age to come—
6and who then turn away from God. It is impossible to bring such people back to repen-
tance; by rejecting the Son of God, they themselves are nailing Him to the cross once
again and holding Him up to public shame.

7When the ground soaks up the falling rain and bears a good crop for the farmer, it has
God's blessing. 8But if a field bears thorns and thistles, it is useless. The farmer will soon
condemn that field and burn it.

9Dear friends, even though we are talking this way, we really don't believe it applies to
you. We are confident that you are meant for better things, things that come with salva-
tion. 10For God is not unjust. He will not forget how hard you have worked for Him and
how you have shown your love to Him by caring for other believers,* as you still do. 11Our
great desire is that you will keep on loving others as long as life lasts, in order to make cer-
tain that what you hope for will come true. 12Then you will not become spiritually dull and
indifferent. Instead, you will follow the example of those who are going to inherit God's
promises because of their faith and endurance.

GOD'S PROMISES BRING HOPE

13For example, there was God's promise to Abraham. Since there was no one greater to
swear by, God took an oath in His own name, saying:

14 "I will certainly bless you,
and I will multiply your descendants beyond number."*

5:13 1 Cor 14:20; Eph 4:14
5:14 Rom 16:19; 1 Cor 2:6
6:1 Phil 3:12-14; Heb 5:12; 9:14
6:2 Acts 2:4; 6:6; 17:18, 32
6:3 Acts 18:21
6:4 John 4:10; Eph 2:8; Heb 10:32
6:5 Ps 34:8; 1 Pet 2:3
6:6 Heb 10:26, 29; 2 Pet 2:21; 1 Jn 5:16
6:8 Gen 3:17-18
6:10 Matt 10:40, 42; 1 Thes 1:3
6:11 Heb 3:6; 10:22
6:12 Heb 10:36; 13:7
6:13 Gen 22:16
6:14 *Gen 22:17

6:10 Greek *for God's holy people.* 6:14 Gen 22:17.

6:4-6 Not everyone who attends church is truly a Christian, as Jesus illustrated in His parable of the wheat and weeds (Matthew 13:24-30). Eventually a person's actions will display the type and amount of spiritual fruit in his life. These "fake" believers are warned about the consequences of their actions. These verses imply that one may have spiritual experiences and partake of many of the blessings of the covenant community without truly being a Christian. Such people will face grave consequences for their rejection of the faith.

▸ **WORSHIP**

6:7-8 The sower and the soil. In words that remind us of Jesus' parable of the sower (see Matthew 13:1-13), the writer challenges readers to measure the nature of the soul's soil. Is your soul soft and receptive to the Word coming like rain (as mentioned in Isaiah 55:10-11), or have you developed a hard crusty surface where the truth of the Word runs off without sinking deep into your being? Ask God to break up any areas of hardness in your soul so that you may receive the Word and bear much spiritual fruit. (***See Worship****> NT> Christ's Kingship> Kingdom of God> The sower and soils,* TopicGuide page A30.)

▸ **HOLINESS**

6:12 The danger of spiritual apathy. If you have been a Christian for some years, you may be in danger! Sometimes we do what we do for so long that it becomes a rote exercise, lacking true affection or zeal. But our journey with Christ and His people must be marked by perseverance and patience over the long road. Examine your Christian disciplines to see if your heart has become dull toward God and His commands. If you sense indifference to the things of God setting in, seek some accountability with other believers to help you regain motivation to serve God and others out of love for Him. (***See Holiness****> Changed by God> God provides> Chastening us,* TopicGuide page A41.)

6:13-18 In Genesis 12 God promised Abraham that he would become a great nation and be a blessing to many throughout the earth. Then in Genesis 15:5-21 God repeated this promise (adding the promise of land). In the second promise, God swore an oath on His own death that He would fulfill the promise. Since God is eternally self-existent, it is impossible for Him to die, so the promise is absolutely secure.

6:15 15Then Abraham waited patiently, and he received what God had promised.
Gen 21:1-5 16Now when people take an oath, they call on someone greater than themselves to
6:16 hold them to it. And without any question that oath is binding. 17God also bound Himself
Exod 22:11 with an oath, so that those who received the promise could be perfectly sure that He
6:17 Ps 110:4 would never change His mind. 18So God has given both His promise and His oath. These
Heb 11:9 two things are unchangeable because it is impossible for God to lie. Therefore, we who
6:18 have fled to Him for refuge can have great confidence as we hold to the hope that lies be-
Num 23:19 fore us. 19This hope is a strong and trustworthy anchor for our souls. It leads us through
1 Sam 15:29 Titus 1:2 the curtain into God's inner sanctuary. 20Jesus has already gone in there for us. He has be-
Heb 3:6 come our eternal High Priest in the order of Melchizedek.

6:20 Ps 110:4 Heb 4:14; 5:6

MELCHIZEDEK IS GREATER THAN ABRAHAM

7:1-2 **7** This Melchizedek was king of the city of Salem and also a priest of God Most High.
Gen 14:17-20 When Abraham was returning home after winning a great battle against the kings,
7:3 Melchizedek met him and blessed him. 2Then Abraham took a tenth of all he had cap-
Ps 110:4 tured in battle and gave it to Melchizedek. The name Melchizedek means "king of justice,"
7:4 and king of Salem means "king of peace." 3There is no record of his father or mother or
Gen 14:20 any of his ancestors—no beginning or end to his life. He remains a priest forever, resem-
bling the Son of God.
7:5 4Consider then how great this Melchizedek was. Even Abraham, the great patriarch of
Num 18:21, 26 Israel, recognized this by giving him a tenth of what he had taken in battle. 5Now the law

6:18 God's oath to Abraham is secure not only because He is unable to die, but also because He is unable to lie. God is truth, and all He says and does manifests truth.

6:19 In the Old Testament Temple, a curtain hid the Most Holy Place from the people. Only the High Priest was allowed to enter, and only one day a year. This symbolized the separation that existed between a holy God and a sinful people. When Jesus died on the cross and paid for our sins, the Temple curtain was torn in two from top to bottom, symbolizing the open access believers have to God. God accepts us on the basis of Christ's purity and sacrifice.

7:3 The priests of Israel were chosen on the basis of their heritage. But Melchizedek appears in the story and disappears with no mention of his genealogy. His greatest characteristic was that he honored and worshiped God, and he is regarded as a priest on that basis alone. In the same way, Jesus, while not of a priestly line, functions as a priest for us forever.

7:4-6 Even from ancient days, the practice has existed of honoring someone greater by giving a portion of your harvest, your surplus, or in this case, the spoils of victory. All Israelites gave to the Levites at the Temple, showing their deference to them, and Abraham was greater than Levi, since Levi descended from him. But Melchizedek is shown to be even greater than Abraham, since Abraham gave gifts to him and received a blessing from him. The writer then shows that Jesus is even greater than Melchizedek and thus greater than the Levites and the priests.

BECAUSE GOD IS ABSOLUTE TRUTH

I will believe what He says and live accordingly.

It is impossible for God to lie. Therefore, we who have fled to Him for refuge can have great confidence as we hold to the hope that lies before us.

HEBREWS 6:18

of Moses required that the priests, who are descendants of Levi, must collect a tithe from the rest of the people of Israel,* who are also descendants of Abraham. 6But Melchizedek, who was not a descendant of Levi, collected a tenth from Abraham. And Melchizedek placed a blessing upon Abraham, the one who had already received the promises of God. 7And without question, the person who has the power to give a blessing is greater than the one who is blessed.

8The priests who collect tithes are men who die, so Melchizedek is greater than they are, because we are told that he lives on. 9In addition, we might even say that these Levites—the ones who collect the tithe—paid a tithe to Melchizedek when their ancestor Abraham paid a tithe to him. 10For although Levi wasn't born yet, the seed from which he came was in Abraham's body when Melchizedek collected the tithe from him.

11So if the priesthood of Levi, on which the law was based, could have achieved the perfection God intended, why did God need to establish a different priesthood, with a priest in the order of Melchizedek instead of the order of Levi and Aaron?*

12And if the priesthood is changed, the law must also be changed to permit it. 13For the priest we are talking about belongs to a different tribe, whose members have never served at the altar as priests. 14What I mean is, our Lord came from the tribe of Judah, and Moses never mentioned priests coming from that tribe.

JESUS IS LIKE MELCHIZEDEK

15This change has been made very clear since a different priest, who is like Melchizedek, has appeared. 16Jesus became a priest, not by meeting the physical requirement of belonging to the tribe of Levi, but by the power of a life that cannot be destroyed. 17And the psalmist pointed this out when he prophesied,

"You are a priest forever in the order of Melchizedek."*

18Yes, the old requirement about the priesthood was set aside because it was weak and useless. 19For the law never made anything perfect. But now we have confidence in a better hope, through which we draw near to God.

20This new system was established with a solemn oath. Aaron's descendants became priests without such an oath, 21but there was an oath regarding Jesus. For God said to Him,

"The LORD has taken an oath and will not break His vow:
'You are a priest forever.'"*

22Because of this oath, Jesus is the One who guarantees this better covenant with God.

23There were many priests under the old system, for death prevented them from remaining in office. 24But because Jesus lives forever, His priesthood lasts forever. 25Therefore He is able, once and forever, to save* those who come to God through Him. He lives forever to intercede with God on their behalf.

7:6 Rom 4:13
7:7 Gen 14:19
7:8 Heb 5:6; 6:20
7:11 Ps 110:4; Heb 5:6; 7:17
7:14 Gen 49:10; Isa 11:1; Matt 1:3; 2:6; Luke 3:33; Rom 1:3; Rev 5:5
7:17 *Ps 110:4; Heb 5:6; 6:20
7:18 Rom 8:3
7:19 Rom 3:20; Heb 9:9; 10:19-22
7:21 *Ps 110:4; Heb 5:6; 6:20; 7:17
7:22 Heb 8:6; 12:24
7:24 Isa 9:6-7; Rev 1:18
7:25 Rom 8:34; 1 Jn 2:1

7:5 Greek *from their brothers.* 7:11 Greek *the order of Aaron?* 7:17 Ps 110:4. 7:21 Ps 110:4. 7:25 Or *is able to save completely.*

7:12-15 The writer's careful argument deals with the perceived objection that Jesus cannot serve as priest since He was from the tribe of Judah. Only men from the tribe of Levi could serve in the Temple, and only those from the Levitical family of Aaron could be priests and high priests (7:14). Jesus could be High Priest because He is declared in Psalm 110 to be a priest in the order of Melchizedek, rather than Aaron. Melchizedek functioned as a priest to Abraham even though he was not even a descendant of Abraham. His credentials for his priestly position came from his spiritual relationship with God, not a physical heritage.

▸ GOD

7:19 Working out redemption. Are you frustrated with trying to keep Christian "rules"? Many Christians still live as if they must fulfill the Old Testament law in order to be right with God. But the law does not make us perfect. It condemns us by pointing out our sinfulness. Christ alone can release us from our slavery to sin and grant us new life (Romans 8:1-4). Are you trusting in your performance to get you to heaven? Instead, trust in the work of Christ alone to save you. Draw near to God through His work, not yours. (***See God**> Salvation> Son> Redeemed us from the curse of the law,* TopicGuide page A15.)

7:26 [26]He is the kind of high priest we need because He is holy and blameless, unstained by
2 Cor 5:21 Heb 4:14 sin. He has been set apart from sinners and has been given the highest place of honor in
heaven.* [27]Unlike those other high priests, He does not need to offer sacrifices every day.
7:27 Lev 9:7; 16:6, 11, 15 They did this for their own sins first and then for the sins of the people. But Jesus did this
Eph 5:2 once for all when He offered Himself as the sacrifice for the people's sins. [28]The law ap-
Heb 9:12 pointed high priests who were limited by human weakness. But after the law was given, God
7:28 Heb 2:10; 5:1-2 appointed His Son with an oath, and His Son has been made the perfect High Priest forever.

CHRIST IS OUR HIGH PRIEST

8:1 Heb 1:3; 2:17; 4:14; **8** Here is the main point: We have a High Priest who sat down in the place of honor be-
6:20; 7:26; 9:11 side the throne of the majestic God in heaven. [2]There He ministers in the heavenly
8:2 Tabernacle,* the true place of worship that was built by the Lord and not by human hands.
Heb 9:11 [3]And since every high priest is required to offer gifts and sacrifices, our High Priest must
8:3 make an offering, too. [4]If He were here on earth, He would not even be a priest, since there
Heb 5:1 already are priests who offer the gifts required by the law. [5]They serve in a system of wor-
8:5 *Exod 25:40; 26:30 ship that is only a copy, a shadow of the real one in heaven. For when Moses was getting
Col 2:17 ready to build the Tabernacle, God gave him this warning: "Be sure that you make every-
Heb 9:23 thing according to the pattern I have shown you here on the mountain."*
8:6 [6]But now Jesus, our High Priest, has been given a ministry that is far superior to the old
Heb 7:22; 9:15; 12:24 priesthood, for He is the One who mediates for us a far better covenant with God, based
on better promises.
8:7 Heb 7:11 [7]If the first covenant had been faultless, there would have been no need for a second
8:8-12 covenant to replace it. [8]But when God found fault with the people, He said:
*Jer 31:31-34 "The day is coming, says the LORD,
when I will make a new covenant
with the people of Israel and Judah.
[9] This covenant will not be like the one
I made with their ancestors
when I took them by the hand
and led them out of the land of Egypt.
They did not remain faithful to My covenant,
so I turned My back on them, says the LORD.
8:10 [10] But this is the new covenant I will make
Heb 10:16 with the people of Israel on that day,* says the LORD:

7:26 Or *has been exalted higher than the heavens.* 8:2 Or *tent;* also in 8:5. 8:5 Exod 25:40; 26:30. 8:10 Greek *after those days.*

7:26-27 These verses are the culmination of the writer's entire argument in the book. Jesus is superior to anything else we might trust in for salvation. He is holy and sinless, and He has been elevated to the highest place in heaven. He is the perfect Savior.

8:1 This "main point" of the epistle restates with almost the same words the point made in 1:3—we have in heaven One who has accomplished sacrificial work on our behalf. In chapter 1, however, the focus was on Jesus as God's Son; here the focus is on Jesus as High Priest. For the significance of our High Priest sitting down, see the note at Hebrews 10:11-13.

8:5 The writer makes a point that would have been difficult for his Jewish audience to accept: The Temple, and indeed the whole sacrificial priestly structure, is merely a "copy" and a "shadow." By its nature, a copy is less than the original, and a shadow is only cast by the substantial reality. While the Old Testament service of worship and sacrifice was better in God's sight than any other pagan worship, it remained a copy of the original. Now the real thing has come—Jesus Christ, who became the final sacrifice for sin.

8:6 Just as 8:1 can be compared to 1:3, so this verse can be compared to 1:4. The writer makes another difficult point for his Jewish audience: There is a better covenant based on better promises than those of the Old Testament.

▸ WORSHIP
8:10 Where is the law in your life? Obeying God does not come naturally. From the child who refuses to share to the man who indulges in sexually immorality, sin seems to pervade our entire nature. The Old Testament directed people to surround themselves with the law (see Deuteronomy 6:4-9) to set themselves apart from sin. For too many people, this became an external activity rather than an inward disposition of the heart. Those who have trusted in Christ have been freed from sin's power, and He has written God's law on our hearts—yet we must still choose to obey it. Ask God to give you an obedience that grows from His presence in you. (***See Worship****> NT> Teaching and Preaching> Law has a place in New Testament teaching,* TopicGuide page A34.)

I will put My laws in their minds,
and I will write them on their hearts.
I will be their God,
and they will be My people.
11 And they will not need to teach their neighbors,
nor will they need to teach their relatives,*
saying, 'You should know the LORD.'
For everyone, from the least to the greatest,
will know Me already.
12 And I will forgive their wickedness,
and I will never again remember their sins."*

13 When God speaks of a "new" covenant, it means He has made the first one obsolete. It is
now out of date and will soon disappear.

8:11 John 6:45
8:12 Heb 10:17
8:13 Heb 12:24

OLD RULES ABOUT WORSHIP

9 That first covenant between God and Israel had regulations for worship and a place
of worship here on earth. 2 There were two rooms in that Tabernacle.* In the first
room were a lampstand, a table, and sacred loaves of bread on the table. This room was
called the Holy Place. 3 Then there was a curtain, and behind the curtain was the second
room* called the Most Holy Place. 4 In that room were a gold incense altar and a wooden
chest called the Ark of the Covenant, which was covered with gold on all sides. Inside the
Ark were a gold jar containing manna, Aaron's staff that sprouted leaves, and the stone
tablets of the covenant. 5 Above the Ark were the cherubim of divine glory, whose wings
stretched out over the Ark's cover, the place of atonement. But we cannot explain these
things in detail now.

6 When these things were all in place, the priests regularly entered the first room* as they
performed their religious duties. 7 But only the high priest ever entered the Most Holy
Place, and only once a year. And he always offered blood for his own sins and for the sins
the people had committed in ignorance. 8 By these regulations the Holy Spirit revealed
that the entrance to the Most Holy Place was not freely open as long as the Tabernacle*
and the system it represented were still in use.

9 This is an illustration pointing to the present time. For the gifts and sacrifices that
the priests offer are not able to cleanse the consciences of the people who bring them. 10 For
that old system deals only with food and drink and various cleansing ceremonies—physical
regulations that were in effect only until a better system could be established.

9:1 Exod 25:8
9:2 Exod 25:23-40; 26:1-30 Lev 24:5
9:3 Exod 26:31-33
9:4 Exod 16:33; 25:10-16; 30:1-6 Num 17:8-10 Deut 10:3-5
9:5 Exod 25:17-22
9:6 Num 18:2-6
9:7 Exod 30:10 Lev 16:2, 14-15 Heb 5:2-3
9:8 John 14:6 Heb 10:19-20
9:9 Heb 5:1; 10:1-2
9:10 Lev 11:2, 25; 15:8 Num 6:3; 19:13

8:11 Greek *their brother.* 8:8-12 Jer 31:31-34. 9:2 Or *tent;* also in 9:11, 21. 9:3 Greek *second tent.* 9:6 Greek *first tent.* 9:8 Or *the first room;* Greek reads *the first tent.*

▸ GOD

8:12 Remembering and forgetting sin. Do your past sins weigh heavily on you? Do not let them pull you down any more! God has made it clear in this verse that He will not remember our sins any longer. The word "remember" does not refer to a thought process, but to a promise. Genesis 8:1 says, "God remembered Noah." That does not mean He had forgotten Noah and then Noah came to His mind. It means He was fulfilling His covenant promises to Noah. If we have trusted in Christ, God no longer holds our sin against us. He will not punish us as we deserve. Thank God for graciously forgiving your sins and remembering them no longer, and live in the freedom of your new life in Christ. (***See God**> God's Attributes> Forgiving> God is ready to forgive,* TopicGuide page A16.)

9:1-5 At this point the writer begins comparing the Old Covenant worship and sacrificial practices to the work of Christ. These verses briefly summarize the arrangement of the Tabernacle under the Old Covenant. Exodus 25 describes the features of the Holy Place in great detail.

9:4-5 Inside the Tabernacle, in the Holy Place, was a curtain leading to the Most Holy Place. This smaller room contained elements, including the Ark of the Covenant, which reminded Israel of God's covenant faithfulness in bringing them out of bondage into freedom and rest in the land. The Ark was where God's presence resided on earth (Ezekiel 9:3). It was so holy that no one could touch it without losing his life (see 1 Samuel 6:19; 2 Samuel 6:6-7).

▸ SPIRITUAL WARFARE

9:10 Unnecessary regulations. Many times Christians find it easy to supplant a vibrant walk with God with merely following rules. The Israelites were not exempt from

CHRIST IS THE PERFECT SACRIFICE

9:11 11 So Christ has now become the High Priest over all the good things that have come.* He
Heb 8:2; 10:1 has entered that greater, more perfect Tabernacle in heaven, which was not made by hu-
9:12 Heb 7:27 man hands and is not part of this created world. 12 With His own blood—not the blood of
9:13 goats and calves—He entered the Most Holy Place once for all time and secured our re-
Lev 16:3, 14-15 demption forever.
Num 19:9, 17 13 Under the old system, the blood of goats and bulls and the ashes of a young cow
9:14 could cleanse people's bodies from ceremonial impurity. 14 Just think how much more the
Heb 6:1 1 Pet 3:18 blood of Christ will purify our consciences from sinful deeds* so that we can worship the
1 Jn 1:7 living God. For by the power of the eternal Spirit, Christ offered Himself to God as a perfect
9:15 sacrifice for our sins. 15 That is why He is the One who mediates a new covenant between
1 Tim 2:5 Heb 7:22 God and people, so that all who are called can receive the eternal inheritance God has
promised them. For Christ died to set them free from the penalty of the sins they had com-
mitted under that first covenant.
16 Now when someone leaves a will,* it is necessary to prove that the person who made
it is dead.* 17 The will goes into effect only after the person's death. While the person who
9:18-19 Exod 24:6-8 made it is still alive, the will cannot be put into effect.
Lev 14:4 18 That is why even the first covenant was put into effect with the blood of an animal.
Num 19:6 19 For after Moses had read each of God's commandments to all the people, he took the
9:20 blood of calves and goats,* along with water, and sprinkled both the book of God's law
*Exod 24:8 Matt 26:28 and all the people, using hyssop branches and scarlet wool. 20 Then he said, "This blood
9:21 confirms the covenant God has made with you."* 21 And in the same way, he sprinkled
Lev 8:15, 19 blood on the Tabernacle and on everything used for worship. 22 In fact, according to the
9:22 law of Moses, nearly everything was purified with blood. For without the shedding of
Lev 17:11 blood, there is no forgiveness.
9:23 23 That is why the Tabernacle and everything in it, which were copies of things in
Heb 8:5 heaven, had to be purified by the blood of animals. But the real things in heaven had to be
9:24 Rom 8:34 purified with far better sacrifices than the blood of animals.
Heb 8:2; 9:12 24 For Christ did not enter into a holy place made with human hands, which was only a
1 Jn 2:1 copy of the true one in heaven. He entered into heaven itself to appear now before God

9:11 Some manuscripts read *that are about to come.* 9:14 Greek *from dead works.* 9:16a Or *covenant;* also in 9:17. 9:16b Or *Now when someone makes a covenant, it is necessary to ratify it with the death of a sacrifice.* 9:19 Some manuscripts omit *and goats.* 9:20 Exod 24:8.

this problem. Many of the hundreds of laws in the Old Covenant were meant to guide the people in their practice for a time. They were "external" activities—things like priestly dress, the kinds of animals brought for specific rituals, etc. But the people made the rules more important than the Ruler. Too often we Christians have also created external regulations and traditions that become like new laws. Examine your Christian life. Do you burden yourself with extra practices to gain the approval of others? Ask God to free you to worship Him in spirit and in truth. (***See Spiritual Warfare**> Resisting Sin and Evil> Putting On and Off> Taking Off> The yoke of legalism,* TopicGuide page A46.)

9:12 Jesus has gone into the true Temple—not a copy or shadow as mentioned in 8:5—and has offered a perfect and final sacrifice. Note the finality described here: "once for all time" and "forever." His sacrifice was completely and eternally acceptable to God. And the work it accomplished is also eternal.

▸ HOLINESS
9:14 Purified to worship. Do you ever wonder how people received salvation in the Old Testament? With all the rituals they practiced, did that make a difference? People were forgiven then just as today—by faith in God's promises to have mercy on those who repent. But now we can see clearly what they only saw partially—it is Christ's cleansing work, perfect and final, that makes all forgiveness possible. Under the Old and New Covenants, people were forgiven so they could "worship the living God" (9:14). God desires your worship and Jesus purifies you so that God is pleased when you worship. If you struggle to worship Him, look at your heart—have you confessed your sins? Are you living in sin? Ask for forgiveness and you'll recover your heart of worship for Him. (***See Holiness**> Submission> Delighting in God> Rejoicing in repentance,* TopicGuide page A40.)

9:15 The work of a priest was primarily to stand between God and the people—to mediate, to bring offerings to pay the price of sin. The Old Covenant made clear that God's holiness could not coexist with human sinfulness. But Christ's work allows us to inherit the benefits of the promise of salvation and to be freed from our just penalty for our sin. God's high standard, set forth in the Old Covenant, never changes.

on our behalf. 25And He did not enter heaven to offer Himself again and again, like the
high priest here on earth who enters the Most Holy Place year after year with the blood of
an animal. 26If that had been necessary, Christ would have had to die again and again,
ever since the world began. But now, once for all time, He has appeared at the end of the
age* to remove sin by His own death as a sacrifice.
27And just as each person is destined to die once and after that comes judgment, 28so
also Christ died once for all time as a sacrifice to take away the sins of many people. He
will come again, not to deal with our sins, but to bring salvation to all who are eagerly
waiting for Him.

9:25 Heb 9:7; 10:19
9:26 1 Cor 10:11; Heb 7:27; 1 Pet 3:18
9:27 Gen 3:19
9:28 Isa 53:12; Phil 3:20; Heb 7:27; 1 Pet 2:24

CHRIST'S SACRIFICE ONCE FOR ALL

10 The old system under the law of Moses was only a shadow, a dim preview of the
good things to come, not the good things themselves. The sacrifices under that
system were repeated again and again, year after year, but they were never able to pro-
vide perfect cleansing for those who came to worship. 2If they could have provided perfect
cleansing, the sacrifices would have stopped, for the worshipers would have been purified
once for all time, and their feelings of guilt would have disappeared.
3But instead, those sacrifices actually reminded them of their sins year after year. 4For it
is not possible for the blood of bulls and goats to take away sins. 5That is why, when
Christ* came into the world, He said to God,

"You did not want animal sacrifices or sin offerings.
But You have given Me a body to offer.
6 You were not pleased with burnt offerings
or other offerings for sin.
7 Then I said, 'Look, I have come to do Your will, O God—
as is written about Me in the Scriptures.'"*

10:1 Col 2:17; Heb 7:19; 8:5; 9:11
10:3 Lev 16:34; Heb 9:7
10:4 Lev 16:15, 21; Heb 9:13
10:5-7 *Ps 40:6-8

9:26 Greek *the ages.* 10:5 Greek *He;* also in 10:8. 10:5-7 Ps 40:6-8 (Greek version).

9:25-26 Unlike the constant offering of sacrifices that would have been so familiar to the writer's Jewish audience, Christ's work accomplished all that we need in one final offering.

10:1-4 The law of Moses includes the Ten Commandments in Exodus 20 as well as the hundreds of legal and ritual regulations found in the books of Leviticus, Numbers, and Deuteronomy. The writer makes it clear that these rituals, even when followed to the letter of the law, were not a final solution to the problem of sin and separation from God.

BECAUSE GOD IS FAITHFUL

I will trust Him to always keep His promises.

Let us hold tightly without wavering to the hope we affirm,
for God can be trusted to keep His promise.

HEBREWS 10:23

10:8 8First, Christ said, "You did not want animal sacrifices or sin offerings or burnt offerings or
*Ps 40:6 other offerings for sin, nor were You pleased with them" (though they are required by the
10:10 law of Moses). 9Then He said, "Look, I have come to do Your will." He cancels the first cov-
Eph 5:2 Heb 7:27; 9:12, 28 enant in order to put the second into effect. 10For God's will was for us to be made holy by
1 Pet 2:24 the sacrifice of the body of Jesus Christ, once for all time.
10:11 11Under the old covenant, the priest stands and ministers before the altar day after day,
Heb 5:1 offering the same sacrifices again and again, which can never take away sins. 12But our
10:12 High Priest offered Himself to God as a single sacrifice for sins, good for all time. Then He
Ps 110:1 Matt 22:44 sat down in the place of honor at God's right hand. 13There He waits until His enemies are
Col 3:1 humbled and made a footstool under His feet. 14For by that one offering He forever made
Heb 1:3 perfect those who are being made holy.
10:13 Ps 110:1 15And the Holy Spirit also testifies that this is so. For He says,

10:15 16 "This is the new covenant I will make
Heb 3:7 with My people on that day,* says the LORD:
I will put My laws in their hearts,
and I will write them on their minds."*

10:16-17 *Jer 31:33-34 17Then He says,

"I will never again remember
their sins and lawless deeds."*

10:19 18And when sins have been forgiven, there is no need to offer any more sacrifices.
Eph 3:12 Heb 4:16; 9:25

A CALL TO PERSEVERE

10:20 John 4:10, 14 19And so, dear brothers and sisters,* we can boldly enter heaven's Most Holy Place be-
Heb 6:19; 9:8 cause of the blood of Jesus. 20By His death,* Jesus opened a new and life-giving way
10:21 through the curtain into the Most Holy Place. 21And since we have a great High Priest who
Heb 2:17; 3:6 rules over God's house, 22let us go right into the presence of God with sincere hearts fully
10:22 trusting Him. For our guilty consciences have been sprinkled with Christ's blood to make
Ezek 36:25 Eph 5:26 us clean, and our bodies have been washed with pure water.
10:23 23Let us hold tightly without wavering to the hope we affirm, for God can be trusted to
1 Cor 1:9; 10:13 keep His promise. 24Let us think of ways to motivate one another to acts of love and good
Heb 3:6 works. 25And let us not neglect our meeting together, as some people do, but encourage
10:25 Acts 2:42 one another, especially now that the day of His return is drawing near.

Heb 3:13 10:16a Greek *after those days.* 10:16b Jer 31:33a. 10:17 Jer 31:34b. 10:19 Greek *brothers.* 10:20 Greek *Through His flesh.*

▶ WORSHIP

10:10, 14 Am I holy yet? When we receive Christ as Savior, we do not live sinless lives from that point on. We see marvelous changes as we begin to grow spiritually and learn the disciplines of a holy life. At the same time, we struggle with temptation and fall into sin. Paul lamented the sinful nature he still struggled with (Romans 7:21-25) but also gloried in the fact that Jesus can break the power of sin in us. Jesus' sacrifice gives us a sinless position before God. What a miraculous truth! If the temptations you experience discourage you, praise God that He sees you as perfect in Christ. (***See Worship****> NT> Our Role> Holiness> You shall be holy,* TopicGuide page A32.)

10:11-13 Under the Old Covenant the priest's work was never done; he remained standing always in God's presence mediating for the people. But Christ has finished the work and sat down. This profound action fulfills Psalm 110:1, where God invites His Messiah to sit at His side.

▶ HOLINESS

10:19-25 The gifts of God. Imagine that on your birthday you are given a pile of beautifully wrapped gifts. When the time comes, there is no question what to do with them: You open them! In these verses, the writer of Hebrews invites us to partake freely of God's best gifts. We are invited to enter His presence, to hold onto the hope we have inherited, to encourage one another, and to meet with believers faithfully and regularly. Do you partake of these gracious gifts from God, or do you ignore them? Do you regularly worship with God's people, sharing the hope of Christ and encouraging others? Do not cut yourself off from the remarkable gifts God has delivered to you. (***See Holiness****> Law and Grace> Grace> The gift of grace,* TopicGuide page A42.)

10:20 In the Old Testament Tabernacle and Temple, a curtain set off the Most Holy Place. Only the High Priest was allowed to enter, and then only once a year on the Day of Atonement. When Jesus died on the cross, the curtain was torn in two. This signified that in Christ, believers are invited into God's most holy presence to fellowship with Him.

[26]Dear friends, if we deliberately continue sinning after we have received knowledge of
the truth, there is no longer any sacrifice that will cover these sins. [27]There is only the terri-
ble expectation of God's judgment and the raging fire that will consume His enemies.
[28]For anyone who refused to obey the law of Moses was put to death without mercy on
the testimony of two or three witnesses. [29]Just think how much worse the punishment will
be for those who have trampled on the Son of God, and have treated the blood of the cov-
enant, which made us holy, as if it were common and unholy, and have insulted and dis-
dained the Holy Spirit who brings God's mercy to us. [30]For we know the One who said,

"I will take revenge.
I will pay them back."*

He also said,

"The LORD will judge His own people."*

[31]It is a terrible thing to fall into the hands of the living God.

10:26 Heb 6:4-8; 2 Pet 2:20
10:27 Isa 26:11
10:28 Deut 17:6
10:30 *Deut 32:35-36; Ps 135:14
10:31 2 Cor 5:11

10:30a Deut 32:35. **10:30b** Deut 32:36.

10:26-27 These verses, like the passage in Hebrews 6:4-6, must be understood in the context of the covenant community. The writer has noted that Christ's work is perfect and eternal, but he also warns those who take their standing in Christ for granted. Just as in ancient Israel there were some in the covenant community who did not believe the promise or inherit its blessings, there are some in the church who never truly embrace Christ's work on their behalf and claim His promises. Being born to Christian parents or baptized or raised in the church is no guarantee that one is a true believer.

MY RESPONSE TO GOD

Was Abraham a Christian?

HEBREWS 11

How were people saved in the Old Testament? Moses understood that Abram (later renamed Abraham) was saved by faith when he wrote, "And Abram believed the LORD, and the LORD counted him as righteous because of his faith" (Genesis 15:6). But faith in what? How could Abram be saved without knowing about Jesus, the cross, and a dozen other doctrines?

Old Testament saints certainly had less knowledge than those in New Testament times, but according to Genesis 15:6 and Hebrews 11, Abram knew enough to be saved even without the New Testament revelation. He knew that God had promised to bless him, he believed that promise, and he was justified on the basis of that belief. We don't know if Abraham understood the theological details about how salvation happens. We are told only that he believed God's great promises to him and his family.

God has always saved His people by the gift of His grace and through faith. Faith works like a rope—God lowers it down to His people, enabling us to firmly grasp it and hold on tight until we join Him in heaven. But what if Abraham let go of the rope? Speaking of those who trusted in God's promises through Christ, Jesus said, "I give them eternal life, and they will never perish. No one can snatch them away from Me, for My Father has given them to Me, and He is more powerful than anyone else. No one can snatch them from the Father's hand" (John 10:28-29; see also 10:6-16). Our grip on faith may loosen, but God's grip on us will not.

Abraham was saved by grace, through faith, and so he joined the vast host of Old Testament heroes who "did not receive what was promised, but they saw it all from a distance and welcomed it" (Hebrews 11:13).

10:33 1 Cor 4:9 1 Thes 2:14
10:34 Heb 13:3

32 Think back on those early days when you first learned about Christ.* Remember how
you remained faithful even though it meant terrible suffering. 33 Sometimes you were ex-
posed to public ridicule and were beaten, and sometimes you helped others who were
suffering the same things. 34 You suffered along with those who were thrown into jail, and
when all you owned was taken from you, you accepted it with joy. You knew there were
better things waiting for you that will last forever.

10:36 Heb 9:15

35 So do not throw away this confident trust in the Lord. Remember the great reward it
brings you! 36 Patient endurance is what you need now, so that you will continue to do
God's will. Then you will receive all that He has promised.

10:37-38 *Hab 2:3-4 Rom 1:17 Gal 3:11

37 "For in just a little while,
the Coming One will come and not delay.
38 And My righteous ones will live by faith.*
But I will take no pleasure in anyone who turns away."*

39 But we are not like those who turn away from God to their own destruction. We are the
faithful ones, whose souls will be saved.

11:1 Rom 8:24 Heb 3:6, 14

GREAT EXAMPLES OF FAITH

11 Faith is the confidence that what we hope for will actually happen; it gives us as-
surance about things we cannot see. 2 Through their faith, the people in days of old
earned a good reputation.

11:3 Gen 1:1-31 Ps 33:6, 9 John 1:3 Rom 1:19-20 Heb 1:2

3 By faith we understand that the entire universe was formed at God's command, that
what we now see did not come from anything that can be seen.

11:4 Gen 4:3-10

4 It was by faith that Abel brought a more acceptable offering to God than Cain did.
Abel's offering gave evidence that he was a righteous man, and God showed His approval
of his gifts. Although Abel is long dead, he still speaks to us by his example of faith.

11:5 Gen 5:22-24
11:6 Heb 7:19

5 It was by faith that Enoch was taken up to heaven without dying—"he disappeared, be-
cause God took him."* For before he was taken up, he was known as a person who pleased
God. 6 And it is impossible to please God without faith. Anyone who wants to come to Him
must believe that God exists and that He rewards those who sincerely seek Him.

11:7 Gen 6:13-22 Rom 3:22 1 Pet 3:20

7 It was by faith that Noah built a large boat to save his family from the flood. He obeyed
God, who warned him about things that had never happened before. By his faith Noah
condemned the rest of the world, and he received the righteousness that comes by faith.

10:32 Greek *when you were first enlightened.* 10:38 Or *My righteous ones will live by their faithfulness;* Greek reads *My righteous one will live by faith.* 10:37-38 Hab 2:3-4. 11:5 Gen 5:24.

▸ WORSHIP

10:33-34 Suffering with Christ's people. Right from the early days of the New Covenant, people have suffered for believing that Jesus is the final sacrifice and the perfect High Priest. In fact, suffering has often been the normal experience of believers. Even in the early years of the 21st century God's covenant people suffered in many places around the world. Has God presented you with the opportunity to suffer for what you believe? Just as important, have you taken the opportunity to stand with those who suffer? Find ways to contact them, send letters of encouragement. Pray for them (Acts 12:5). Help fund the organizations that specialize in aiding the persecuted church. Ask God to give you the faith to joyfully accept suffering for His name when the time comes. (***See Worship****> NT> Teaching and Preaching> Persecution for preaching the Word,* TopicGuide page A34.)

11:4 Abel was the second son of Adam and Eve (Genesis 4). He and his brother Cain brought sacrifices to God, but God accepted only Abel's offering. Angered by this, Cain killed his brother. Cain's problem began before he became jealous of his brother. He did not bring his offering by faith as Abel did. The disposition of Cain's heart from the beginning is the crucial factor.

▸ HOLINESS

11:6 The absolute necessity of faith. The people in Hebrews 11 were not always good people—Noah occasionally drank too much (Genesis 9:21), and Abraham lied about his wife (Genesis 12:13) to protect himself. But these sinners were not saved based on their perfect lives but by faith in God's promises. Faith is the foundation of hope (11:1), the way we understand creation (11:3), and the basis for worship (11:4). Are you striving to please God by doing or by believing? All your righteous acts will never make you right with God (Ephesians 2:8-9), and Christ's sacrifice provides all the approval you will ever need from Him. (***See Holiness****> Submission> Trusting God> Faithfulness,* TopicGuide page A41.)

8 It was by faith that Abraham obeyed when God called him to leave home and go to another land that God would give him as his inheritance. He went without knowing where he was going. 9 And even when he reached the land God promised him, he lived there by faith—for he was like a foreigner, living in tents. And so did Isaac and Jacob, who inherited the same promise. 10 Abraham was confidently looking forward to a city with eternal foundations, a city designed and built by God.

11 It was by faith that even Sarah was able to have a child, though she was barren and was too old. She believed* that God would keep His promise. 12 And so a whole nation came from this one man who was as good as dead—a nation with so many people that, like the stars in the sky and the sand on the seashore, there is no way to count them.

13 All these people died still believing what God had promised them. They did not receive what was promised, but they saw it all from a distance and welcomed it. They agreed that they were foreigners and nomads here on earth. 14 Obviously people who say such things are looking forward to a country they can call their own. 15 If they had longed for the country they came from, they could have gone back. 16 But they were looking for a better place, a heavenly homeland. That is why God is not ashamed to be called their God, for He has prepared a city for them.

17 It was by faith that Abraham offered Isaac as a sacrifice when God was testing him. Abraham, who had received God's promises, was ready to sacrifice his only son, Isaac, 18 even though God had told him, "Isaac is the son through whom your descendants will be counted."* 19 Abraham reasoned that if Isaac died, God was able to bring him back to life again. And in a sense, Abraham did receive his son back from the dead.

20 It was by faith that Isaac promised blessings for the future to his sons, Jacob and Esau.

21 It was by faith that Jacob, when he was old and dying, blessed each of Joseph's sons and bowed in worship as he leaned on his staff.

22 It was by faith that Joseph, when he was about to die, said confidently that the people of Israel would leave Egypt. He even commanded them to take his bones with them when they left.

23 It was by faith that Moses' parents hid him for three months when he was born. They saw that God had given them an unusual child, and they were not afraid to disobey the king's command.

24 It was by faith that Moses, when he grew up, refused to be called the son of Pharaoh's daughter. 25 He chose to share the oppression of God's people instead of enjoying the fleeting pleasures of sin. 26 He thought it was better to suffer for the sake of Christ than to own the treasures of Egypt, for he was looking ahead to his great reward. 27 It was by faith that Moses left the land of Egypt, not fearing the king's anger. He kept right on going

11:8 Gen 12:1-5 Acts 7:2-4
11:9 Gen 12:8
11:10 Heb 12:22 Rev 21:2
11:11 Gen 17:19; 21:1-3
11:12 Gen 15:5-6; 22:17 Rom 4:19
11:13 Gen 23:4 Matt 13:17 Heb 11:39
11:14 Heb 13:14
11:15 Gen 24:6-8
11:16 Gen 26:24 Exod 3:6, 15
11:17 Gen 22:1-10 Jas 2:21
11:19 Rom 4:21
11:20 Gen 27:27-29
11:21 Gen 47:31; 48:15-16
11:22 Gen 50:24-25 Exod 13:19
11:23 Exod 1:16, 22; 2:2
11:24 Exod 2:10-12
11:26 Heb 13:13
11:27 Exod 12:50-51

11:11 Or *It was by faith that he [Abraham] was able to have a child, even though Sarah was barren and he was too old. He believed.* 11:18 Gen 21:12.

11:8 Abraham is considered the father of the Hebrew nation. He followed God in true faith, and God made a covenant promise to him to bless the whole world through him. His story (Genesis 12–25) is so crucial that Abraham gets discussed more in this "Hall of Faith" (12 verses in this chapter) than any other biblical character.

11:17-19 Isaac was the promised son born to Abraham and his wife Sarah long after they even had hope of bearing a child (see Genesis 18 and 21). In a story that looks forward to the story of Jesus, Abraham was commanded to offer his only beloved son as a sacrifice to God (Genesis 22). God provided a ram as a substitute at the last moment, so it was as if Abraham received Isaac back from the dead.

11:21-22 Joseph was Jacob's favorite of his 12 sons of Jacob. Therefore, Jacob (who God renamed Israel) blessed him and gave to him the "double portion" normally reserved for the eldest. This double portion resulted in both of Joseph's two sons (Ephraim and Manasseh) receiving tribal land for their father Joseph.

11:23 Moses is considered the greatest leader of the Israelite people. Moses's leadership spans the final four books of the Pentateuch: Exodus, Leviticus, Numbers, and Deuteronomy. In the seven verses devoted to his story here, the phrase "by faith" appears five times. Moses's leadership was not based on strength but on faith in the strong God of Abraham, Isaac, and Jacob. God expanded the covenant promises made to Abraham into the great "Mosaic covenant," which is summed up in the Ten Commandments (Exodus 20 and Deuteronomy 5).

because he kept his eyes on the One who is invisible. 28It was by faith that Moses commanded the people of Israel to keep the Passover and to sprinkle blood on the doorposts so that the angel of death would not kill their firstborn sons.

29It was by faith that the people of Israel went right through the Red Sea as though they were on dry ground. But when the Egyptians tried to follow, they were all drowned.

30It was by faith that the people of Israel marched around Jericho for seven days, and the walls came crashing down.

31It was by faith that Rahab the prostitute was not destroyed with the people in her city who refused to obey God. For she had given a friendly welcome to the spies.

32How much more do I need to say? It would take too long to recount the stories of the faith of Gideon, Barak, Samson, Jephthah, David, Samuel, and all the prophets. 33By faith these people overthrew kingdoms, ruled with justice, and received what God had promised them. They shut the mouths of lions, 34quenched the flames of fire, and escaped death by the edge of the sword. Their weakness was turned to strength. They became strong in battle and put whole armies to flight. 35Women received their loved ones back again from death.

But others were tortured, refusing to turn from God in order to be set free. They placed their hope in a better life after the resurrection. 36Some were jeered at, and their backs were cut open with whips. Others were chained in prisons. 37Some died by stoning, some were sawed in half,* and others were killed with the sword. Some went about wearing skins of sheep and goats, destitute and oppressed and mistreated. 38They were too good for this world, wandering over deserts and mountains, hiding in caves and holes in the ground.

39All these people earned a good reputation because of their faith, yet none of them received all that God had promised. 40For God had something better in mind for us, so that they would not reach perfection without us.

GOD'S DISCIPLINE PROVES HIS LOVE

12 Therefore, since we are surrounded by such a huge crowd of witnesses to the life of faith, let us strip off every weight that slows us down, especially the sin that so easily trips us up. And let us run with endurance the race God has set before us. 2We do this by keeping our eyes on Jesus, the champion who initiates and perfects our faith.* Because of the joy* awaiting Him, He endured the cross, disregarding its shame. Now He is seated in the place of honor beside God's throne. 3Think of all the hostility He endured

11:37 Some manuscripts add *some were tested.* 12:2a Or *Jesus, the originator and perfecter of our faith.* 12:2b Or *Instead of the joy.*

11:28 Exod 12:21-30
11:29 Exod 14:21-31
11:30 Josh 6:12-21
11:31 Josh 2:11-12; 6:20-25; Jas 2:25
11:32 Judg 4–13; 1 Sam 1:20; 16:1, 13
11:33 1 Sam 17:34-36; Dan 6:1-27
11:34 2 Kgs 20:7; Dan 3:19-27
11:35 1 Kgs 17:17-24; 2 Kgs 4:25-37
11:36 Gen 39:20; Jer 20:2; 37:15
11:37 1 Kgs 19:10; 2 Chr 24:20-22
11:38 1 Kgs 18:4; 19:9
11:40 Rom 11:26; Rev 6:11
12:1 1 Cor 9:24; Phil 3:12-14
12:2 Ps 110:1; Phil 2:8-9; Heb 2:9-10; 1 Pet 1:11

11:31 Rahab knew God had given Israel the land and a blessing, so she sought to be included in that blessing. Though she was a prostitute (see Joshua 2:8-13) and was raised in pagan Jericho, she trusted in the God of Israel and so was saved. She even became part of the lineage of King David and the Messiah, Jesus (see Matthew 1:5). James 2:25 also points to her as an example of faith.

▸ CHURCH
11:40 Far better promises. It is profoundly important that as followers of Christ we recognize that we are connected to His body the church, visible and invisible. God is preparing a great future for His church. He has "something better in mind" for us even if we don't see the complete fulfillment in our lifetime. We are all building blocks in the magnificent spiritual temple He is building. Are you connected to God's people through membership in a church? The promises are inherited in community with Him and His people. God intends for us all to walk together. Be sure to find others with whom you can walk by faith. (***See Church****> Mission> Nurture> Fostering community,* TopicGuide page A49.)

▸ BIBLE
12:1 From God's view. Those who follow Christ are called to live not for this world, but for the One who created this world. But the world continually woos us with virtually limitless opportunities to be distracted from God and His kingdom. Such distractions slow us down on our journey and may even become sin that trips us up, causing us to stumble and fall. Ask God to open your eyes to allow you to see clearly those things in your life that belong to this world. If you see things threatening to entangle you in the race of faith, ask for strength to be set free to run with endurance. (***See Bible****> Power> Worldview> Offers God's perspective on issues,* TopicGuide page A12.)

12:3 The writer asks readers to think about the final suffering of Jesus. This suffering included arrest and beating, verbal mocking and abuse, scourging with a vicious whip, having a "crown" of thorns pressed onto his head, and finally being nailed hands and feet to wooden beams, hung in order to suffocate slowly. Of course, unseen, yet far more cruel was the spiritual suffering also caused by sinful people—Jesus bore the weight and penalty of human sin in His body on the cross (Mark 15; John 18–19).

from sinful people;* then you won't become weary and give up. 4After all, you have not yet given your lives in your struggle against sin.

5And have you forgotten the encouraging words God spoke to you as His children?* He said,

"My child,* don't make light of the LORD's discipline,
and don't give up when He corrects you.
6 For the LORD disciplines those He loves,
and He punishes each one He accepts as His child."*

7As you endure this divine discipline, remember that God is treating you as His own children. Who ever heard of a child who is never disciplined by its father? 8If God doesn't discipline you as He does all of His children, it means that you are illegitimate and are not really His children at all. 9Since we respected our earthly fathers who disciplined us, shouldn't we submit even more to the discipline of the Father of our spirits, and live forever?*

10For our earthly fathers disciplined us for a few years, doing the best they knew how. But God's discipline is always good for us, so that we might share in His holiness. 11No discipline is enjoyable while it is happening—it's painful! But afterward there will be a peaceful harvest of right living for those who are trained in this way.

12So take a new grip with your tired hands and strengthen your weak knees. 13Mark out a straight path for your feet so that those who are weak and lame will not fall but become strong.

A CALL TO LISTEN TO GOD

14Work at living in peace with everyone, and work at living a holy life, for those who are not holy will not see the Lord. 15Look after each other so that none of you fails to receive the grace of God. Watch out that no poisonous root of bitterness grows up to trouble you, corrupting many. 16Make sure that no one is immoral or godless like Esau, who traded his birthright as the firstborn son for a single meal. 17You know that afterward, when he wanted his father's blessing, he was rejected. It was too late for repentance, even though he begged with bitter tears.

18You have not come to a physical mountain,* to a place of flaming fire, darkness, gloom, and whirlwind, as the Israelites did at Mount Sinai. 19For they heard an awesome trumpet blast and a voice so terrible that they begged God to stop speaking. 20They staggered back under God's command: "If even an animal touches the mountain, it must be stoned to death."* 21Moses Himself was so frightened at the sight that he said, "I am terrified and trembling."*

12:4 Heb 10:32-34
12:5-6 *Prov 3:11-12
12:6 Rev 3:19
12:7 Deut 8:5; 2 Sam 7:14
12:8 1 Pet 5:9
12:9 Isa 38:16
12:10 2 Pet 1:4
12:11 Jas 3:17-18
12:12 Isa 35:3
12:13 Prov 4:26
12:14 Rom 14:19
12:15 Deut 29:17-18; Heb 4:1
12:16 Gen 25:29-34
12:17 Gen 27:30-40
12:18-19 Exod 19:16-22; 20:18-21; Deut 4:11-12; 5:22-27
12:20 *Exod 19:12-13
12:21 Deut 9:19

12:3 Some manuscripts read *Think of how people hurt themselves by opposing Him.* 12:5a Greek *sons;* also in 12:7, 8. 12:5b Greek *son;* also in 12:6, 7. 12:5-6 Prov 3:11-12 (Greek version). 12:9 Or *and really live?* 12:18 Greek *to something that can be touched.* 12:20 Exod 19:13. 12:21 Deut 9:19.

▸ ADOPTION
12:10 God's discipline for your good. Earthly fathers fail us. They may punish abusively. They may be too passive or maybe even be completely absent. But this passage reminds us that God is perfect, so His discipline is always right, good, and purposeful. God is holy, and He wants His children to look like Himself. In what ways has the heavenly Father brought the strong hand of sanctifying discipline upon your soul? How has it helped you look more like Jesus than when you first trusted in Him? (***See Adoption**> With Christ> Children of God> God disciplines His children,* TopicGuide page A36.)

12:16 Esau was the eldest son of Isaac and grandson of Abraham, to whom God gave the promises. For a bowl of stew Esau foolishly traded to Jacob his birthright as firstborn son. This event (found in Genesis 25:27-34 and 27:1-40) had monumental consequences, creating strife between their descendants for generations.

12:18 When God brought the tribes of Israel out of Egypt (in Exodus 12), they eventually came to Mount Sinai deep in the Sinai Peninsula (see Exodus 19). This mountain stands in a desolate and rugged area. When God wrapped the mountain in clouds, lightning, and winds, it became a fearful place as God proclaimed His law there to Moses.

AFTER WEEKS OF EXPERIENCING SYMPTOMS, a man went to the doctor. The doctor examined him carefully, and then called the patient's wife to speak to her alone in his office "Your husband is suffering from a rare form of anemia. Without treatment, he'll be dead in a few weeks. The good news is that it can be treated. You will need to fix him hearty, homemade meals for breakfast, lunch, and dinner and make him plenty of fresh bread and pies—these are the things that will give your husband the nourishment he needs to fight this disease.

"One more thing. His immune system is weak, so it's important that your home be kept spotless at all times. Do you have any questions?" The wife had none.

"Do you want to break the news, or shall I?" asked the doctor. "I will," the wife replied. She walked into the exam room. The husband, sensing the seriousness of his illness, asked her, "It's bad, isn't it?" She nodded, tears welling up in her eyes. With a sob, the wife blurted out, "The doctor says you're gonna die!"

Some people are just not interested in sacrifice. But Christ demonstrated a willingness to lay down everything—even His own life—for the sake of securing salvation for all who believe. The book of Hebrews is a showcase of the magnificence and grandeur of Christ's sacrifice for us.

While it took millions of sacrifices to sustain the Old Covenant, only one sacrifice was necessary to establish the New Covenant (Hebrews 8:7-13). Practically speaking, this means we should not attempt to atone for our sins through self-loathing or depression or any other punishment—Christ has, once and for all, willingly suffered for the sins of His people (Hebrews 10:8-10). Also, we have no need to mull over our sins repeatedly in our mind—Christ's one sacrifice gives us a clear conscience (Hebrews 9:9). But what if a Christian commits a sin that's perceived as particularly heinous—what then? Christ's one sacrifice is good for all times—whether we perceive our sins as small or great, there is no time or situation where Christ ceases to be your Savior and Mediator (Hebrews 10:12-13; 9:15).

But how do we know for sure this is true? Because Jesus ascended to heaven and sits in a place of authority (John 20:17; Acts 1:9; Ephesians 4:10). His efforts were successful and God crowned Him with glory in celebration of His great work of redemption (Hebrews 1:3, 6; 8:1). If Jesus' work of redemption weren't accomplished, then why would He be in heaven? Wouldn't He still be on earth, suffering for our sins? Jesus has succeeded. His one perfect sacrifice meets the greatest need of any person; we can now be reconciled with God by believing in His promises that He revealed in the perfect sacrifice of Christ.

22No, you have come to Mount Zion, to the city of the living God, the heavenly Jerusa-
lem, and to countless thousands of angels in a joyful gathering. 23You have come to the as-
sembly of God's firstborn children, whose names are written in heaven. You have come to
God Himself, who is the judge over all things. You have come to the spirits of the righteous
ones in heaven who have now been made perfect. 24You have come to Jesus, the One who
mediates the new covenant between God and people, and to the sprinkled blood, which
speaks of forgiveness instead of crying out for vengeance like the blood of Abel.

25Be careful that you do not refuse to listen to the One who is speaking. For if the people
of Israel did not escape when they refused to listen to Moses, the earthly messenger, we
will certainly not escape if we reject the One who speaks to us from heaven! 26When God
spoke from Mount Sinai His voice shook the earth, but now He makes another promise:
"Once again I will shake not only the earth but the heavens also."* 27This means that all of
creation will be shaken and removed, so that only unshakable things will remain.

28Since we are receiving a Kingdom that is unshakable, let us be thankful and please
God by worshiping Him with holy fear and awe. 29For our God is a devouring fire.

CONCLUDING WORDS

13 Keep on loving each other as brothers and sisters.* 2Don't forget to show hospital-
ity to strangers, for some who have done this have entertained angels without re-
alizing it! 3Remember those in prison, as if you were there yourself. Remember also those
being mistreated, as if you felt their pain in your own bodies.

4Give honor to marriage, and remain faithful to one another in marriage. God will surely
judge people who are immoral and those who commit adultery.

12:22 Gal 4:26; Rev 5:11; 21:2
12:23 Gen 18:25; Phil 3:12
12:24 Gen 4:10; Heb 9:19; 10:22
12:25 Heb 2:1-3; 10:28-29
12:26 Exod 19:18
12:27 2 Pet 3:10
12:29 Exod 24:17; Deut 4:24; 9:3; Isa 33:14
13:1 Rom 12:10
13:2 Gen 18:1-8; 19:1-3
13:3 Matt 25:36; Col 4:18; Heb 10:34
13:4 1 Cor 7:38

12:26 Hag 2:6. 13:1 Greek *Continue in brotherly love.*

12:22 Mount Zion is the primary hill on which the city of Jerusalem was built. Located in the central ridge in Israel, this place was strategic for safety. The city of Jerusalem has been used throughout Scripture as a symbol of God's heavenly dwelling. Contrasted with Sinai, Zion is a place of peace, not fear; redemption, not judgment; grace, not law; and the promise of life and satisfaction, not deprivation and death.

▶ WORSHIP

13:4-5 Marriage, money, and majesty. Almost like a preacher who is trying to fit his final points into too few minutes, the writer of Hebrews finishes his book with a flurry of commands and admonitions. But these two verses especially carry weighty commands. Marriage, especially in Western society in the 21st century, has been cheapened, even among God's people. Money often lies at the root of marital strife. And ultimately, not setting God above all things is the greatest weakness in our family life and our financial stewardship. Both family and money will find its proper place when we let God be God in our lives. (***See Worship***> *NT> Prohibitions> Wrong objects> Money,* TopicGuide page A33.)

BECAUSE GOD IS
EVER-PRESENT

He is always with me.

"I will never fail you. I will never abandon you."

HEBREWS 13:5

13:5 [5]Don't love money; be satisfied with what you have. For God has said,
Gen 28:15
Josh 1:5 "I will never fail you.
13:7 I will never abandon you."*
Heb 6:12 [6]So we can say with confidence,
13:8
Heb 1:12 "The LORD is my helper,
13:9 so I will have no fear.
Eph 4:14 What can mere people do to me?"*
Col 2:7, 16
13:11 [7]Remember your leaders who taught you the word of God. Think of all the good that
Lev 4:12, 21; 16:27 has come from their lives, and follow the example of their faith.
13:12 [8]Jesus Christ is the same yesterday, today, and forever. [9]So do not be attracted by
John 19:17 strange, new ideas. Your strength comes from God's grace, not from rules about food,
Heb 9:12 which don't help those who follow them.
13:13
Heb 11:26 [10]We have an altar from which the priests in the Tabernacle* have no right to eat. [11]Under
13:14 the old system, the high priest brought the blood of animals into the Holy Place as a sacrifice
Heb 11:10; 12:22 for sin, and the bodies of the animals were burned outside the camp. [12]So also Jesus suf-
13:15 fered and died outside the city gates to make His people holy by means of His own blood.
Hos 14:2 [13]So let us go out to Him, outside the camp, and bear the disgrace He bore. [14]For this world
1 Pet 2:5 is not our permanent home; we are looking forward to a home yet to come.
13:16
Phil 4:18 [15]Therefore, let us offer through Jesus a continual sacrifice of praise to God, proclaiming
13:17 our allegiance to His name. [16]And don't forget to do good and to share with those in need.
Isa 62:6 These are the sacrifices that please God.
Ezek 3:17 [17]Obey your spiritual leaders, and do what they say. Their work is to watch over your

13:5 Deut 31:6, 8. 13:6 Ps 118:6. 13:10 Or *tent.*

13:11-14 The burning of animals "outside the camp" refers to a purification ritual associated with the Day of Atonement during the time Israel traveled in the wilderness (see Leviticus 16:27). The Tabernacle stood at the center of the camp. People and things declared unclean were taken outside the camp. It may be that this passage in Hebrews calls followers of Christ to walk away from the prevailing religious Jewish worship and share in the shame of the cross by identifying with Christ, who also died "outside the city gates."

13:15 The New Covenant sacrifice does not involve the blood of animals but the praise of believing lips and hearts.

▸ CHURCH

13:17 Helping or hurting our leaders? As followers of Christ, we are called to obey and submit to God-given leaders. But many times believers are headstrong and stubborn, prone to be suspicious of a leader's decisions or motives. Bring joy to those who lead you. Find a way, even this week, to honor them for their spiritual investment in your soul. Ask God to direct you to a godly leader under whom you can learn and grow. (***See Church****> Role> Church Community> Submitting to one another,* TopicGuide page A49.)

BECAUSE GOD
NEVER CHANGES

My future is secure and eternal.

Jesus Christ is the same yesterday, today, and forever.

HEBREWS 13:8

FOR THE NEXT *GOD NEVER CHANGES* FEATURE SEE PAGE 2226.

souls, and they are accountable to God. Give them reason to do this with joy and not with
sorrow. That would certainly not be for your benefit.
[18]Pray for us, for our conscience is clear and we want to live honorably in everything we 13:18
do. [19]And especially pray that I will be able to come back to you soon. Acts 24:16

13:19 Phlm 1:22

[20] Now may the God of peace—
who brought up from the dead our Lord Jesus,
the great Shepherd of the sheep,
and ratified an eternal covenant with His blood—
[21] may He equip you with all you need
for doing His will.
May He produce in you,*
through the power of Jesus Christ,
every good thing that is pleasing to Him.
All glory to Him forever and ever! Amen.

13:20 Isa 55:3 Jer 32:40; 50:5 Ezek 37:26 Zech 9:11 John 10:11

13:21 Rom 11:36 Phil 2:13

[22]I urge you, dear brothers and sisters,* to pay attention to what I have written in this 13:22
brief exhortation. 1 Pet 5:12
[23]I want you to know that our brother Timothy has been released from jail. If he comes 13:23
here soon, I will bring him with me to see you. Acts 16:1
[24]Greet all your leaders and all the believers there.* The believers from Italy send you 13:24
their greetings. Heb 13:7, 17
[25]May God's grace be with you all.

13:25 Col 4:18 Titus 3:15

13:21 Some manuscripts read *in us.* 13:22 Greek *brothers.* 13:24 Greek *all of God's holy people.*

13:20-21 This benediction asks God to equip believers to do what pleases Him. This letter has repeatedly shown that it is faith that pleases Him. The writer also reminds his readers that such good works are only possible because Jesus has signed an eternal covenant with His own blood. The word "amen" comes from the Hebrew word for "truth." By saying "Amen," the believer is concurring that what has been said or written is true.

JAMES

PURPOSE

To show that the wise Christian pursues a life of faith revealed in personal holiness.

What difference does your faith make? That's not a question about eternity; the Bible is clear that those who put their faith in Jesus as Savior will one day enter into life forever in heaven. When James asks what difference faith makes to his readers, he is asking about what changes it evokes in their day-to-day lives.

As a pastor, James was concerned for those under his care. When persecution broke out against the church, many believers were scattered to other places. They were living as foreigners in strange new places, and life was sometimes difficult. James penned this letter to encourage these believers to continue in their faith, which would hopefully produce a visible difference to those around them regarding the way they thought and acted.

For the modern reader, James's book contains potent proverbs urging us to live a life of faith that will break down the barriers between hearing and doing (1:19-27), the rich and the poor (2:1-13; 5:1-6), faith and works (2:14-26), and words and reality (3:1–4:17).

DISCOVER GOD IN JAMES

When facing trials and difficulties, it is critical that we have a right view of God. James helps us by pointing out certain truths about Him.

God Gives Good Gifts: Whether we need wisdom in facing trials (1:5; 3:17), blessings in the midst of challenges (1:17), answers in response to prayer (4:2), grace to live rightly (4:6), or healing in times of physical trouble (5:13-16), James makes it clear that our God gives good things to those He loves. No matter what trial you might be facing, realize that God will provide what you need to endure.

God Never Changes: In the same verse in which James assures readers that our God is good and generous, he also makes it clear that our God never changes (1:17). God is full of compassion and mercy (5:11); He is unalterably good. Knowing that God never changes can give us courage to face whatever comes because we know that the One who has seen us through before will see us through again.

God Draws Near to Us: In the midst of tough times, it is good to know that God desires to draw near to us (4:8). We do not have to face our challenges alone; God will be near to us no matter what we are facing.

GROWING THROUGH JAMES

James's message is a blunt one; he knows life doesn't always seem to work out as we think it should. Part of growing as a disciple is learning how to face the tensions between our ideas of how the world ought to be and the way things really are.

Trials Mature Our Faith (1:2-4, 12; 5:11): While we are in the midst of a trial or difficulty, it is important to remember that God is using whatever you are facing to help you grow (Romans 8:38). The difficulties you face are not random events or purposeless circumstances (Job 37:15; Daniel 5:23). God is using all that comes into your life to promote faith in Him alone for your salvation.

When to Act and When to Wait (2:17; 4:7-10, 17; 5:7-12): The wise learn that faith does not always mean hasty action. Active, patient waiting on God can also reveal a heart fueled by faith (Psalm 62:1; Isaiah 64:4). Laziness may appear to be patience, but it is the very opposite of the watchful patience God calls all believers to embrace (Hebrews 6:12).

Calling Out for Help (1:5-6; 4:2-3; 5:14): The wise do not live in isolation, imagining themselves as being able to face the terrors and trials of life alone. They call on God, asking Him for wisdom and faith and whatever else His will requires us to have in various situations. James exhorts us all to call out to our church leaders and friends for help, who exist to care for (2:14-15) and pray for broken sinners and broken bodies (James 5:13-20).

DISCOVERY VERSES

Yes indeed, it is good when you obey the royal law as found in the Scriptures: "Love your neighbor as yourself." (JAMES 2:8)

So you see, faith by itself isn't enough. Unless it produces good deeds, it is dead and useless. (JAMES 2:17)

JAMES FACTS

Author: There are four men mentioned in the New Testament writings who share the name James and would be prominent enough to have written this letter. The first, the apostle named James, was martyred too early to have been the author (Acts 12:1-2). The other apostle named James, the son of Alphaeus (Mark 3:18; 15:40), and James the father of the apostle Judas (not Iscariot; Luke 6:16; Acts 1:13) were probably not widely known enough to be adequately identified as "James, a slave of God" (1:1). This leaves James "the Lord's brother" (Galatians 1:19), who was one of the leaders of the church in Jerusalem (Acts 12:17; 15:13; 21:18). Many have noted the similarities between this letter and the message given by James in Acts 15:13-21 as confirmation that the letter was written by James, the half-brother of Jesus.

Written to: The only direct indication given as to the recipients of this general letter is found in the opening reference to Jewish Christians spread throughout the Gentile nations. This is supported by the Jewish "flavor" of the letter, which is seen in James' use of a very Hebrew title for God in 5:4, his use of the word "synagogue" ("meeting," NLT) to refer to the meeting place in 2:2, and his casual references to Old Testament figures like Abraham, Job, and Elijah. Also, according to Acts 11:19, the Christians in Jerusalem (who were primarily Jewish believers) were scattered when persecution arose after Stephen's death, which fits with James's mention of the recipients being "scattered" (1:1). Thus, it is likely that James, a leader in the Jerusalem church, was writing to Jewish Christians who had been scattered throughout the Roman world after a time of persecution.

Date of writing: Because this letter makes no allusions to the meeting that Paul and James had in Jerusalem (Acts 15; sometime around AD 48), the letter could have been written before then. The Jewish Christians were scattered from Jerusalem sometime after the martyrdom of Stephen (Acts 7:57-60; 11:19; around AD 35). Thus, James must have written this in the late 30s or early 40s, making it one of the earliest epistles.

Setting: James was writing from Jerusalem, where he was serving as one of the leaders of the church, to Jewish Christians who had been dispersed throughout Israel, Phoenicia, Cyprus, and Antioch (Acts 11:19).

OUTLINE

- **JAMES 1:1-18**—Faith That Produces Wisdom
- **JAMES 1:19–4:12**—Faith That Produces Active Godliness
- **JAMES 4:13–5:6**—Faith That Produces Humble Dependence on God
- **JAMES 5:7-12**—Faith That Produces Patience
- **JAMES 5:1-20**—Faith That Produces Healing

GREETINGS FROM JAMES

1:1 **1** This letter is from James, a slave of God and of the Lord Jesus Christ.
1 Pet 1:1 I am writing to the "twelve tribes"—Jewish believers scattered abroad.
Greetings!

FAITH AND ENDURANCE

1:2 2Dear brothers and sisters,* when troubles come your way, consider it an opportunity for
1 Pet 1:6 great joy. 3For you know that when your faith is tested, your endurance has a chance to
1:3 grow. 4So let it grow, for when your endurance is fully developed, you will be perfect and
1 Pet 1:7 complete, needing nothing.
1:5 5If you need wisdom, ask our generous God, and He will give it to you. He will not re-
Prov 2:3-6 Matt 7:7 buke you for asking. 6But when you ask Him, be sure that your faith is in God alone. Do
1:6 not waver, for a person with divided loyalty is as unsettled as a wave of the sea that is
Matt 21:22 blown and tossed by the wind. 7Such people should not expect to receive anything from
Mark 11:24 the Lord. 8Their loyalty is divided between God and the world, and they are unstable in
everything they do.
9Believers who are* poor have something to boast about, for God has honored them.
1:10-11 10And those who are rich should boast that God has humbled them. They will fade away
Ps 102:4, 11 Isa 40:6-7 like a little flower in the field. 11The hot sun rises and the grass withers; the little flower
1 Pet 1:24 droops and falls, and its beauty fades away. In the same way, the rich will fade away with
1:12 all of their achievements.
1 Cor 9:25 2 Tim 4:8 12God blesses those who patiently endure testing and temptation. Afterward they will
Jas 5:11 Rev 2:10; 3:11 receive the crown of life that God has promised to those who love Him. 13And remember,

1:2 Greek *brothers;* also in 1:16, 19. 1:9 Greek *The brother who is.*

1:1 Although James is a half brother of Jesus (Galatians 1:19; Acts 12:17; 15:13-21; 21:18), he chooses to identify himself in a humble way—one who is in the service of God and the Lord Jesus Christ. (For additional information on James, see the introduction to this book.)

1:1 This letter was written to those who were "scattered" among the nations of the world. Persecution by Jewish leaders who opposed the message of Jesus' resurrection began driving Jewish Christians out of Jerusalem not long after Pentecost (Acts 8:1). Later persecution raised by Herod Agrippa (Acts 15:1ff) caused these Christians to spread even more widely.

▸ HOLINESS
1:5-8 Wisdom for the asking. Have you ever been out on a lake in a small boat when a storm blew in? The increasing winds can wrest control of the boat, and the waves can seem threateningly high. Sometimes that's how life feels when circumstances blast their way through our lives. But James promises that God will give us wisdom to handle our problems when we ask for it. He will show us how to grow in times of trouble through His Word (2 Timothy 3:16-17), through the encouragement of others (Hebrews 10:23-25), and through His Spirit's work in our heart (John 14:16; 16:13; Romans 8:26). Seek God's wisdom and build your life on the foundation of His truth. (***See Holiness***> *Submission> Trusting God> Overcoming,* TopicGuide page A40.)

1:9-10 Contrary to the way many people believed in his day, James affirms that God is not nearer to the wealthy. Echoing Jesus' own words, James says that both the poor and the rich have equal reason to be glad, since God is at work in each life (Ecclesiastes 5:19; Matthew 5:43-48; Mark 10:23-25; 12:42-44).

▸ SPIRITUAL WARFARE
1:13-15 Your sin or your God. Is God for you or not? He permits trials into your life. Sometimes those trials give rise to temptation. Does that mean God tempts us to sin? No! James makes it clear that trials come to help you grow in faith and endurance (see also 1 Corinthians 10:13), and temptations come from our own wrong desires. Instead, make the right choice. Follow God's lead. Do what His Word calls you to. Live holy in the power of the Spirit. (***See Spiritual Warfare***> *Resisting Sin and Evil> Resisting Temptation> What to Resist> We are to resist sinful urges,* TopicGuide page A45.)

when you are being tempted, do not say, "God is tempting me." God is never tempted to
do wrong,* and He never tempts anyone else. [14]Temptation comes from our own desires,
which entice us and drag us away. [15]These desires give birth to sinful actions. And when
sin is allowed to grow, it gives birth to death.
[16]So don't be misled, my dear brothers and sisters. [17]Whatever is good and perfect
comes down to us from God our Father, who created all the lights in the heavens.* He
never changes or casts a shifting shadow.* [18]He chose to give birth to us by giving us His
true word. And we, out of all creation, became His prized possession.*

LISTENING AND DOING

[19]Understand this, my dear brothers and sisters: You must all be quick to listen, slow to
speak, and slow to get angry. [20]Human anger* does not produce the righteousness* God
desires. [21]So get rid of all the filth and evil in your lives, and humbly accept the word God
has planted in your hearts, for it has the power to save your souls.
[22]But don't just listen to God's word. You must do what it says. Otherwise, you are only
fooling yourselves. [23]For if you listen to the word and don't obey, it is like glancing at your
face in a mirror. [24]You see yourself, walk away, and forget what you look like. [25]But if you
look carefully into the perfect law that sets you free, and if you do what it says and don't
forget what you heard, then God will bless you for doing it.
[26]If you claim to be religious but don't control your tongue, you are fooling yourself, and
your religion is worthless. [27]Pure and genuine religion in the sight of God the Father means
caring for orphans and widows in their distress and refusing to let the world corrupt you.

A WARNING AGAINST PREJUDICE

2 My dear brothers and sisters,* how can you claim to have faith in our glorious Lord
Jesus Christ if you favor some people over others?

1:14 Prov 19:3
1:16 1 Cor 6:9
1:17 Gen 1:16; Ps 136:7; Matt 7:11
1:18 John 1:13; 1 Pet 1:23
1:19 Prov 10:19; 15:1; Eccl 7:9
1:21 Eph 1:13; 4:22; Col 1:8; 1 Pet 2:1
1:22 Matt 7:21, 26; Rom 2:13
1:25 John 13:17; Rom 8:2; Gal 6:2; Jas 2:12; 1 Pet 2:16
1:27 Deut 14:29; Jas 4:4; 1 Jn 2:15-17
2:1 Prov 24:23; Acts 10:34; 1 Cor 2:8

1:13 Or *God should not be put to a test by evil people.* 1:17a Greek *from above, from the Father of lights.* 1:17b Some manuscripts read *He never changes, as a shifting shadow does.* 1:18 Greek *we became a kind of firstfruit of His creatures.* 1:20a Greek *A man's anger.* 1:20b Or *the justice.* 2:1 Greek *brothers;* also in 2:5, 14.

2:1 James's question ("How can you claim to have faith?") is not and accusation that his readers don't have faith; he is writing to Jewish believers (1:1) whom he considers to be his "brothers and sisters" in faith (1:2, 19). He is cautioning these Christians about making sure their behavior supports their faith.

FOR THE NEXT *GOD NEVER CHANGES* FEATURE SEE PAGE 2283.

BECAUSE GOD NEVER CHANGES

My future is secure and eternal.

Whatever is good and perfect comes down to us from God our Father,
who created all the lights in the heavens.
He never changes or casts a shifting shadow.

JAMES 1:17

2For example, suppose someone comes into your meeting* dressed in fancy clothes
and expensive jewelry, and another comes in who is poor and dressed in dirty clothes. 3If
you give special attention and a good seat to the rich person, but you say to the poor one,
"You can stand over there, or else sit on the floor"—well, 4doesn't this discrimination show
that your judgments are guided by evil motives?
5Listen to me, dear brothers and sisters. Hasn't God chosen the poor in this world to be
rich in faith? Aren't they the ones who will inherit the Kingdom He promised to those who
love Him? 6But you dishonor the poor! Isn't it the rich who oppress you and drag you into
court? 7Aren't they the ones who slander Jesus Christ, whose noble name* you bear?
8Yes indeed, it is good when you obey the royal law as found in the Scriptures: "Love
your neighbor as yourself."* 9But if you favor some people over others, you are commit-
ting a sin. You are guilty of breaking the law.
10For the person who keeps all of the laws except one is as guilty as a person who has
broken all of God's laws. 11For the same God who said, "You must not commit adultery,"
also said, "You must not murder."* So if you murder someone but do not commit adultery,
you have still broken the law.
12So whatever you say or whatever you do, remember that you will be judged by the
law that sets you free. 13There will be no mercy for those who have not shown mercy to
others. But if you have been merciful, God will be merciful when He judges you.

FAITH WITHOUT GOOD DEEDS IS DEAD

14What good is it, dear brothers and sisters, if you say you have faith but don't show it by
your actions? Can that kind of faith save anyone? 15Suppose you see a brother or sister who
has no food or clothing, 16and you say, "Good-bye and have a good day; stay warm and eat
well"—but then you don't give that person any food or clothing. What good does that do?
17So you see, faith by itself isn't enough. Unless it produces good deeds, it is dead and
useless.
18Now someone may argue, "Some people have faith; others have good deeds." But I
say, "How can you show me your faith if you don't have good deeds? I will show you my
faith by my good deeds."
19You say you have faith, for you believe that there is one God.* Good for you! Even the
demons believe this, and they tremble in terror. 20How foolish! Can't you see that faith
without good deeds is useless?
21Don't you remember that our ancestor Abraham was shown to be right with God by
his actions when he offered his son Isaac on the altar? 22You see, his faith and his actions

2:4 John 7:23-24
2:5 Luke 6:20; 1 Cor 1:26-28
2:7 Acts 11:26; 1 Pet 4:16
2:8 *Lev 19:18; Matt 7:12; Rom 13:8
2:10 Matt 5:19; Gal 5:3
2:11 *Exod 20:13-14; *Deut 5:17-18; Matt 19:18
2:12 Jas 1:25
2:13 Matt 18:32-35
2:15 Matt 25:35-36
2:16 1 Jn 3:17-18
2:17 Gal 5:6; Jas 2:20, 26
2:18 Matt 7:16-17; Rom 3:28
2:19 Deut 6:4; Matt 8:29
2:20 Gal 5:6; Jas 2:14, 17, 26
2:21 Gen 22:9, 12
2:22 Heb 11:17

2:2 Greek *your synagogue.* 2:7 Greek *slander the noble name.* 2:8 Lev 19:18. 2:11 Exod 20:13-14; Deut 5:17-18.
2:19 Some manuscripts read *that God is one;* see Deut 6:4.

▸ CHURCH

2:2-9 No favoritism. Are you glad that the church is made up of all kinds of people—rich, poor, married, single, young, old, dark skinned, light skinned? All share the same life in Jesus (Galatians 3:28; Ephesians 2:13-14; 4:15-16). Any time you divide up the church by giving *some* people preferential treatment, you are saying that the communion we share in Jesus does not fully include everyone. Favoritism is not simply a matter of personal preferences; James tells us such behavior is sin. Who have you been overlooking while preferring others? How can you make this right? (***See Church****> Role> Church Community> Loving one another,* TopicGuide page A49.)

2:4 James's warning against favoritism is reminiscent of Jesus' own words that a person cannot serve two masters (Matthew 6:24).

2:19 The demons "believe" only in the sense that they acknowledge what is true about God; they affirm reality (Mark 1:23-25, 34). However, such an affirmation doesn't bring them into a life-giving relationship with Him.

▸ HOLINESS

2:21-24 Go all the way. Where is your faith ultimately taking you? Some Christians see faith as merely a "ticket to heaven"—an entrance into eternal life. Faith in Christ certainly does give us eternal life (John 1:12; 3:16; 20:31), but that's not all it's about. Our faith—our constant dependence and reliance on God—is supposed to change us here and now and not just prepare us for eternity. Your faith will be "tested" so that it can grow (1:2-4) with the intended result that you will live differently. Abraham is an example of this. He trusted God, and as a result he grew in his dependence upon God. He truly acted "in faith." Go all the way. Complete your faith (2:22). Live differently today *because* you have a relationship with God. (***See Holiness****> Set Apart> Transforming> In the New Covenant,* TopicGuide page A40.)

worked together. His actions made his faith complete. 23And so it happened just as the Scriptures say: "Abraham believed God, and God counted him as righteous because of his faith."* He was even called the friend of God.* 24So you see, we are shown to be right with God by what we do, not by faith alone.

25Rahab the prostitute is another example. She was shown to be right with God by her actions when she hid those messengers and sent them safely away by a different road. 26Just as the body is dead without breath,* so also faith is dead without good works.

CONTROLLING THE TONGUE

3 Dear brothers and sisters,* not many of you should become teachers in the church, for we who teach will be judged more strictly. 2Indeed, we all make many mistakes. For if we could control our tongues, we would be perfect and could also control ourselves in every other way.

3We can make a large horse go wherever we want by means of a small bit in its mouth. 4And a small rudder makes a huge ship turn wherever the pilot chooses to go, even though the winds are strong. 5In the same way, the tongue is a small thing that makes grand speeches.

But a tiny spark can set a great forest on fire. 6And the tongue is a flame of fire. It is a whole world of wickedness, corrupting your entire body. It can set your whole life on fire, for it is set on fire by hell itself.*

7People can tame all kinds of animals, birds, reptiles, and fish, 8but no one can tame the tongue. It is restless and evil, full of deadly poison. 9Sometimes it praises our Lord and Father, and sometimes it curses those who have been made in the image of God. 10And so blessing and cursing come pouring out of the same mouth. Surely, my brothers and sisters, this is not right! 11Does a spring of water bubble out with both fresh water and bitter water? 12Does a fig tree produce olives, or a grapevine produce figs? No, and you can't draw fresh water from a salty spring.*

TRUE WISDOM COMES FROM GOD

13If you are wise and understand God's ways, prove it by living an honorable life, doing good works with the humility that comes from wisdom. 14But if you are bitterly jealous

2:23 *Gen 15:6 Isa 41:8 Rom 4:3-5
2:25 Josh 2:4, 6, 15 Heb 11:31
2:26 Gal 5:6 Jas 2:14, 17, 20
3:1 Rom 2:21 Jas 1:26
3:2 Jas 1:4, 26
3:3 Ps 32:9
3:5 Prov 26:20
3:6 Prov 16:27 Matt 12:36-37; 15:11, 18-19
3:8 Ps 140:3 Rom 3:13
3:9 Gen 1:26-27; 5:1 1 Cor 11:7
3:12 Matt 7:16
3:13 Jas 2:18
3:14 2 Cor 12:20

2:23a Gen 15:6. 2:23b See Isa 41:8. 2:26 Or *without spirit.* 3:1 Greek *brothers;* also in 3:10. 3:6 Or *for it will burn in hell* (Greek *Gehenna*). 3:12 Greek *from salt.*

2:24 Believers are not brought into right relationship with God through what they do (Ephesians 2:8-9; Titus 3:5), but a right relationship with God will be seen in how they live. In that sense believers are made right by their actions.

3:1 "Teacher" was a title of respect within the Jewish Christian community (Matthew 8:19; 19:16), and those who taught were held in honor in the church (Acts 13:1; Ephesians 4:11; 1 Timothy 5:17).

▸ HOLINESS
3:7-12 What's leaking out of you? Have you ever left some food in an unmarked container for a long time in the refrigerator, and it leaked out? Seeing all the mess will quickly remind you of what you had left there. In the same way, you can tell what's really going on in a person's heart by what leaks out through his or her mouth. It's a principle that Jesus Himself affirmed (Matthew 12:34). Your words betray whether your heart is filled with love and goodness or hate and evil. Since it's so hard to control your own tongue (3:1-2), why not ask for help? Ask God to reveal to you your difficult areas. Then confess your sin and ask Him to give you wisdom on how to deal with the problem and how to have more self-control. (***See Holiness***> *Maturing*> *Imitating God*> *His likeness,* TopicGuide page A40.)

3:12 James is using imagery very similar to that which Jesus used; He also spoke of only being able to find good fruit on trees that were truly good trees (Matthew 7:16-20). The fruit that is found on the tree is a true reflection of the character of the tree.

▸ BIBLE
3:13-17 Wise guy. What do you think a wise person looks like? A college professor? Some saffron-robed holy man? How can you tell what wisdom looks like? James says that it's really fairly simple: Wisdom leads to good works, mercy, and an honorable life. It's not a matter of what you wear but whether you know how to relate to others. It's not a matter of the job you may have but the character you possess. The wise person is the one who seeks to live according to God's design in relationship with Him and with others (Psalms 37:30; 111:10; Colossians 1:9-10). Adorn yourself with wisdom that leads to a godly life. (***See Bible***> *Power*> *Wisdom*> *The beginning of wisdom is obedience to Scripture,* TopicGuide page A11.)

and there is selfish ambition in your heart, don't cover up the truth with boasting and ly-
ing. 15 For jealousy and selfishness are not God's kind of wisdom. Such things are earthly,
unspiritual, and demonic. 16 For wherever there is jealousy and selfish ambition, there you
will find disorder and evil of every kind.
17 But the wisdom from above is first of all pure. It is also peace loving, gentle at all
times, and willing to yield to others. It is full of mercy and good deeds. It shows no favorit-
ism and is always sincere. 18 And those who are peacemakers will plant seeds of peace and
reap a harvest of righteousness.*

DRAWING CLOSE TO GOD

4 What is causing the quarrels and fights among you? Don't they come from the evil
desires at war within you? 2 You want what you don't have, so you scheme and kill to
get it. You are jealous of what others have, but you can't get it, so you fight and wage war
to take it away from them. Yet you don't have what you want because you don't ask God
for it. 3 And even when you ask, you don't get it because your motives are all wrong—you
want only what will give you pleasure.
4 You adulterers!* Don't you realize that friendship with the world makes you an enemy
of God? I say it again: If you want to be a friend of the world, you make yourself an enemy
of God. 5 What do you think the Scriptures mean when they say that the spirit God has
placed within us is filled with envy?* 6 But He gives us even more grace to stand against
such evil desires. As the Scriptures say,

"God opposes the proud
but favors the humble."*

7 So humble yourselves before God. Resist the devil, and he will flee from you. 8 Come close
to God, and God will come close to you. Wash your hands, you sinners; purify your hearts, for
your loyalty is divided between God and the world. 9 Let there be tears for what you have
done. Let there be sorrow and deep grief. Let there be sadness instead of laughter, and gloom
instead of joy. 10 Humble yourselves before the Lord, and He will lift you up in honor.

WARNING AGAINST JUDGING OTHERS

11 Don't speak evil against each other, dear brothers and sisters.* If you criticize and judge
each other, then you are criticizing and judging God's law. But your job is to obey the law, not
to judge whether it applies to you. 12 God alone, who gave the law, is the Judge. He alone has
the power to save or to destroy. So what right do you have to judge your neighbor?

3:16 1 Cor 3:3; Gal 5:20-21
3:17 Luke 6:36; Rom 12:9; Heb 12:11
3:18 Prov 11:18; Isa 32:17; Matt 5:9; Phil 1:11
4:2 1 Jn 3:15
4:3 1 Jn 3:22; 5:14
4:4 John 15:19; 1 Jn 2:15
4:5 1 Cor 6:19; 2 Cor 6:16
4:6 Matt 23:12; 1 Pet 5:5
4:7 Eph 6:12; 1 Pet 5:6-9
4:8 Ps 73:28; Isa 1:16; Zech 1:3; Mal 3:7
4:9 Luke 6:25
4:10 Job 5:11; 1 Pet 5:6
4:11 Matt 7:1; 2 Cor 12:20; 1 Pet 2:1
4:12 Matt 10:28; Rom 2:1; 14:4

3:18 Or *of good things,* or *of justice.* 4:4 Greek *You adulteresses!* 4:5 Or *that God longs jealously for the human spirit He has placed within us?* or *that the Holy Spirit, whom God has placed within us, opposes our envy?* 4:6 Prov 3:34 (Greek version). 4:11 Greek *brothers.*

▸WORSHIP

4:1-2 The sin we tolerate. Have you ever heard of an "adultery management class"? Have you ever seen a book for discovering healthy ways to express your murderous impulses? These ideas sound ludicrous because we clearly recognize these things as sin. But why don't we have the same disdain for anger? James has already told us that our anger never achieves God's ends (1:20). Paul tells us that our angry outbursts are expressions of our selfish nature (Galatians 5:19-21). Jesus even links anger with murder (Matthew 5:21-22). The next time you feel ready to vent your anger, don't. Confess your selfishness and ask God to open your eyes so you may see things His way. (***See Worship****> NT> Our Role> Holiness> Our hearts to be established in holiness,* TopicGuide page A32.)

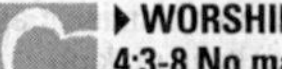

▸WORSHIP

4:3-8 No magic formula. God gives freely to those who ask (1:5). He invariably gives only what is good (1:17). So does that mean we can get whatever we want from God? No! Although it is true that God richly bestows blessings on His children, we can disqualify ourselves from receiving certain things. If you try to leverage God's goodness to simply satisfy your own selfish desires, you won't find Him a willing partner (4:3). So, when you ask of Him in prayer, make sure your request lines up with His will (1 John 5:14-15). Let Jesus' priorities guide your requests (John 16:23-24), and let His glory be the motive for your asking (John 15:7-8). (***See Worship****> NT> Prayer> Instructions> Pray earnestly,* TopicGuide page A33.)

4:4 James uses the expression "adulterers" to refer to those who lack faithfulness to live in right relationship with God. The image is frequent in the Old Testament, where God regards unfaithfulness by His people as spiritual adultery (Judges 2:16-17; 1 Chronicles 5:25; Jeremiah 2:18-37; Ezekiel 6:9).

WARNING ABOUT SELF-CONFIDENCE

13 Look here, you who say, "Today or tomorrow we are going to a certain town and will
stay there a year. We will do business there and make a profit." 14 How do you know what
your life will be like tomorrow? Your life is like the morning fog—it's here a little while,
then it's gone. 15 What you ought to say is, "If the Lord wants us to, we will live and do this
or that." 16 Otherwise you are boasting about your own plans, and all such boasting is evil.
17 Remember, it is sin to know what you ought to do and then not do it.

WARNING TO THE RICH

5 Look here, you rich people: Weep and groan with anguish because of all the terrible
troubles ahead of you. 2 Your wealth is rotting away, and your fine clothes are moth-
eaten rags. 3 Your gold and silver have become worthless. The very wealth you were
counting on will eat away your flesh like fire. This treasure you have accumulated will
stand as evidence against you on the day of judgment. 4 For listen! Hear the cries of the
field workers whom you have cheated of their pay. The wages you held back cry out
against you. The cries of those who harvest your fields have reached the ears of the LORD
of Heaven's Armies.
5 You have spent your years on earth in luxury, satisfying your every desire. You have
fattened yourselves for the day of slaughter. 6 You have condemned and killed innocent
people,* who do not resist you.*

PATIENCE AND ENDURANCE

7 Dear brothers and sisters,* be patient as you wait for the Lord's return. Consider the farm-
ers who patiently wait for the rains in the fall and in the spring. They eagerly look for the
valuable harvest to ripen. 8 You, too, must be patient. Take courage, for the coming of the
Lord is near.
9 Don't grumble about each other, brothers and sisters, or you will be judged. For look—
the Judge is standing at the door!
10 For examples of patience in suffering, dear brothers and sisters, look at the prophets
who spoke in the name of the Lord. 11 We give great honor to those who endure under suf-
fering. For instance, you know about Job, a man of great endurance. You can see how the
Lord was kind to him at the end, for the Lord is full of tenderness and mercy.
12 But most of all, my brothers and sisters, never take an oath, by heaven or earth or any-
thing else. Just say a simple yes or no, so that you will not sin and be condemned.

5:6a Or *killed the Righteous One.* 5:6b Or *Don't they resist you?* or *Doesn't God oppose you?* or *Aren't they now accusing you before God?* 5:7 Greek *brothers;* also in 5:9, 10, 12, 19.

4:13-14 Prov 27:1; Luke 12:18-20
4:15 Acts 18:21
4:16 1 Cor 5:6
4:17 Luke 12:47
5:1 Prov 11:4, 28; Isa 13:6
5:2 Matt 6:19
5:3 Ps 21:10
5:4 Lev 19:13; Deut 24:14-15; Isa 5:9
5:5 Jer 12:3; 25:34; Luke 16:19-23
5:7 Deut 11:14; Jer 5:24; Joel 2:23
5:8 Rom 13:11-12; Heb 10:37
5:9 Matt 24:33; 1 Cor 4:5; Jas 4:12
5:10 Matt 5:12
5:11 Job 1:20-22; 2:7-10; 42:10-17; Ps 103:8
5:12 Matt 5:34-37

5:1-6 James addresses those who are rich as a group, whether they are believers (1:10) or unbelievers (2:6). Both Jesus (Matthew 19:23-24) and Paul (1 Timothy 6:9-10, 17-19) highlight the significant challenge that those who are wealthy face in keeping their perspective right, trusting in God alone, and not trusting in their prosperity.

▸ WORSHIP
5:1-6 Materialism: a cancer of the soul. Is it sinful to be prosperous? Do you go to hell for having too much stuff? No, for God blessed many of His friends with material prosperity (Abraham, Genesis 13:1-4; and Job, Job 42:10-17). But there *is* a serious danger in wealth—the desire for "stuff" can get into your soul and eat away at your heart like a cancer (James 5:3; 1 Timothy 6:9-10). Without caution, material prosperity can draw your heart away from God (Matthew 6:24). How can you guard against this insidious cancer? (1) Be content with what you have (Philippians 4:11; Hebrews 13:5); (2) Hold your wealth loosely by giving freely (Luke 18:22-24; 1 Timothy 6:17-19); and (3) Don't put your confidence in what you have but in who has you in His grip (Luke 6:20-34; James 4:15-16). (***See Worship***> *NT> Offerings> Be faithful with riches,* TopicGuide page A31.)

5:7 The Lord is returning to earth to complete the establishment of His Kingdom (Joel 3:14-21; Matthew 24; Acts 2:9-11; Revelation 22:20).

5:11 In the account of his life, Job never discovered why he had to face the sufferings he did; however, he grew through the trials and endured patiently. This idea of growing through difficult times is a key theme in the book of James (1:2-6; 4:7-8).

5:12 Many people in James's day made an art of swearing oaths. They would find ways to affirm something with an oath, but by carefully wording the oath they could later dismiss it as nonbinding. Jesus addressed the same duplicity in making vows in Matthew 5:33-37.

THE POWER OF PRAYER

13 Are any of you suffering hardships? You should pray. Are any of you happy? You should
sing praises. 14 Are any of you sick? You should call for the elders of the church to come
and pray over you, anointing you with oil in the name of the Lord. 15 Such a prayer offered
in faith will heal the sick, and the Lord will make you well. And if you have committed any
sins, you will be forgiven.

16 Confess your sins to each other and pray for each other so that you may be healed.
The earnest prayer of a righteous person has great power and produces wonderful results.
17 Elijah was as human as we are, and yet when he prayed earnestly that no rain would fall,
none fell for three and a half years! 18 Then, when he prayed again, the sky sent down rain
and the earth began to yield its crops.

RESTORE WANDERING BELIEVERS

19 My dear brothers and sisters, if someone among you wanders away from the truth and
is brought back, 20 you can be sure that whoever brings the sinner back will save that per-
son from death and bring about the forgiveness of many sins.

5:13 Col 3:16
5:14 Mark 6:13
5:15 Mark 16:18; Jas 1:6
5:16 Matt 18:15-18; 1 Jn 1:9
5:17 1 Kgs 17:1-7; Luke 4:25
5:18 1 Kgs 18:42-45
5:19 Matt 18:15
5:20 Prov 10:12; 1 Pet 4:8

5:14-16 James links physical afflictions with sin, but that does not mean all illness is sin-related. Jesus' disciples erroneously thought that one blind man's affliction was due to some sin (John 9:2-3). Sometimes Jesus forgave someone's sin and physically healed that person with no explanation of whether there was a connection between the two or not (as in Mark 2:1-12). But there are times when some physical ailment does have a tie to some unforgiven sin (John 5:14; 1 Corinthians 11:30).

PURPOSE

To remind suffering believers of the glorious future God has for those who persevere in belief.

If you had the chance to speak to Christians spread around the globe, what message would you want them to hear?

Peter was an apostle and elder of the church (5:1) and a personal witness to Jesus' life and sufferings. He wrote this letter to address the needs of the church spread out throughout the world, which, at that time, was going through deep suffering. In this short letter Peter refers to God over three dozen times; that's about once every forty words! Peter believes that people who are struggling need to hear that God is making sure their suffering is not meaningless (1:3-4) and that it will be the gateway to the highest joy (1:8). Peter knows that his audience needs to see that Jesus suffered (2:24; 3:18) and is now in a place of honor—their suffering will be part of the way God will take them to a better place, where no one will ever hurt them again (5:10).

DISCOVER GOD IN 1 PETER

With all the references to God in Peter's first epistle, this letter becomes a rich field to mine for truths about the one true God:

The God of All Grace: Peter sees God as the One who gives abundant grace in every situation of life (5:10). Whether bringing us salvation (1:10; 3:7) or meeting our regular needs (1:2; 4:10), the God Peter points us toward freely offers us His richest blessings through His Son, Jesus Christ.

The God Who Keeps His Own: Peter, likely speaking from his own experiences, declares God's power to watch over those who are His (1:5; 5:6-7, 10-11). By His doing, we have been brought into life through Jesus' death and resurrection and will receive the full benefits of that salvation (1:3-5). Peter points us to the example of Jesus Himself who "left His case in the hands of God" (2:23), trusting God to bring Him through. And, like Jesus experienced, as we suffer and endure hardships, God Himself will "restore, support, and strengthen" us (5:10).

Jesus, Who Suffered to Bring Us Into Life: Peter was an eyewitness of the sufferings of Jesus (5:1); clearly that made an impression on him. That is evident in the way he speaks of Jesus' sufferings and the sufferings of believers. He calls his readers to remember that Jesus' blood makes us clean (1:2), that His death and resurrection gives us new life (1:3), that His painful suffering dealt with the problem of our sins (2:24-25), and that Jesus' death allows us to stand righteous before God (3:18). If all that can be accomplished through Christ, what might God accomplish through the suffering of His church?

GROWING THROUGH 1 PETER

What might aid us in our growth as disciples as we read and listen to Peter's words? One of Peter's most notable themes in this short but powerful letter is the grace of God.

The Foundation for Life: We enter into a wonderful relationship with God as a work of His free grace; it is by His doing, not our own works, that we have been given new life (1:3-4, 10-12). The full experience of this rich salvation that is yet to come is also a work of grace (1:13). You belong to God and enjoy a relationship with Him only because He extended mercy to you (2:9-10).

The Foundation for Ministry: Peter is diligent to call disciples to give themselves to a life of service; he wants us engage and participate in life with others in spreading the Kingdom of God. But he makes it clear that whatever we might do, we do it through the grace of God (4:10-11). Grace is not only useful for salvation, but it is also what we stand on as we proceed onward in mature ministry until the very end (5:12).

The Power to Endure: No other book in the New Testament focuses so much on the place of redemptive suffering in the life of the Christian and the necessity of enduring trials. This is not surprising as Peter is writing to those facing heavy persecution—their families, their friends, and entire churches were under attack. As he writes, he reminds us that we can and will make it through times of difficulties because of the strength God graciously provides (4:11; 5:10). Although you may suffer, God promises to strengthen His people to endure the testing of their faith.

DISCOVERY VERSES

Through Christ you have come to trust in God. And you have placed your faith and hope in God because He raised Christ from the dead and gave Him great glory. You were cleansed from your sins when you obeyed the truth, so now you must show sincere love to each other as brothers and sisters. Love each other deeply with all your heart. (1 PETER 1:21-22)

Dear friends, don't be surprised at the fiery trials you are going through, as if something strange were happening to you. Instead, be very glad—for these trials make you partners with Christ in His suffering, so that you will have the wonderful joy of seeing His glory when it is revealed to all the world. (1 PETER 4:12-13)

1 PETER FACTS

Author: In the opening of this letter, the author identifies himself as the apostle Peter (1:1). He sees himself as a fellow elder of the leaders he is addressing and an eyewitness to the sufferings of Jesus (5:1). These indications are supported by the author's manner of speaking, which suggests someone who knew Jesus intimately—and Peter was indeed part of the "band of brothers" that Jesus had drawn around Himself. Therefore it is quite certain that the author is Simon Peter, the close friend of Jesus and leader in the early church in Jerusalem.

Written to: Peter addresses this letter to Christians who, under Roman domination, are living scattered throughout the area that is modern Turkey (1:1-2). Because Peter makes reference to others who brought the Good News of Jesus to his readers, Peter is not writing to those whom he has personally evangelized (1:12). Instead he is writing to Christians he is aware of but with whom he, most likely, does not have close personal ties.

Date of writing: From references in the letter, it would seem that persecution was growing against the Christian community (1:5-7; 4:12-19). During Peter's time, the greatest persecution came through Emperor Nero. The "scattered" recipients likely spread out because of persecution. Most likely the letter was penned sometime in the early 60s.

Setting: Peter, in his closing, brings greetings from those who are "in Babylon." This aids us in determining where he is writing from, although there is some debate as to what Peter is referring to. There was a small town on the Euphrates in the first century called Babylon, and there was a Roman military outpost in Egypt by the same name, but there is little indication that Peter had been to either place. It is also unlikely that Peter, Silas, and Mark (1:1; 5:12-13) would all be located in either of those places. Instead, it is likely that Peter was using the term "Babylon" to symbolically refer to Rome, the corrupt capital of the Roman world (see also Revelation 17:9-10); and early church historians confirm this.

OUTLINE

- **1 PETER 1:1–2:12**—Salvation of the Believer
- **1 PETER 2:13–3:12**—Subjection of the Believer
- **1 PETER 3:13–5:14**—Suffering of the Believer

GREETINGS FROM PETER

1 This letter is from Peter, an apostle of Jesus Christ.
I am writing to God's chosen people who are living as foreigners in the provinces
of Pontus, Galatia, Cappadocia, Asia, and Bithynia.* [2]God the Father knew you and chose
you long ago, and His Spirit has made you holy. As a result, you have obeyed Him and
have been cleansed by the blood of Jesus Christ.
May God give you more and more grace and peace.

THE HOPE OF ETERNAL LIFE

[3]All praise to God, the Father of our Lord Jesus Christ. It is by His great mercy that we have
been born again, because God raised Jesus Christ from the dead. Now we live with great
expectation, [4]and we have a priceless inheritance—an inheritance that is kept in heaven
for you, pure and undefiled, beyond the reach of change and decay. [5]And through your
faith, God is protecting you by His power until you receive this salvation, which is ready to
be revealed on the last day for all to see.
[6]So be truly glad.* There is wonderful joy ahead, even though you have to endure many
trials for a little while. [7]These trials will show that your faith is genuine. It is being tested as
fire tests and purifies gold—though your faith is far more precious than mere gold. So
when your faith remains strong through many trials, it will bring you much praise and
glory and honor on the day when Jesus Christ is revealed to the whole world.
[8]You love Him even though you have never seen Him. Though you do not see Him
now, you trust Him; and you rejoice with a glorious, inexpressible joy. [9]The reward for
trusting Him will be the salvation of your souls.
[10]This salvation was something even the prophets wanted to know more about when

1:2 Rom 8:29; 2 Thes 2:13; Heb 12:24
1:3 2 Cor 1:3; Titus 3:5
1:4 Acts 20:32; Col 1:5, 12; 2 Tim 4:8
1:5 John 10:28; Phil 4:7; 2 Thes 2:13; 1 Pet 4:13
1:6 Rom 5:2; Jas 1:2; 1 Pet 4:12
1:7 Job 23:10; Prov 17:3; Isa 48:10; Jas 1:3
1:8 John 20:29; 2 Cor 5:7
1:9 Rom 6:22
1:10 Matt 13:17; 26:24

1:1 *Pontus, Galatia, Cappadocia, Asia,* and *Bithynia* were Roman provinces in what is now Turkey. 1:6 Or *So you are truly glad.*

ADOPTION

1:3 Born again. Christianity has some unique analogies. In this chapter, Peter twice describes the readers as "born again" (see also 1:23). New birth is a spiritual transformation brought about by God alone (John 1:12-13), through the resurrection of Jesus Christ, and by the power of the Holy Spirit (John 3:1-8). Everyone needs to be spiritually reborn because sin's presence in us causes spiritual death (Ephesians 2:4-5; Colossians 2:13). New birth from God begins an eternal life that is based on God's eternal word (1:23-25). Such a message is a source of hope for Peter's suffering audience (1:3-5), and a foundation for godly living and growth (2:1-3). Thank God that He has given us a new life, a new hope that goes beyond this earthly life. (***See Adoption**> With Christ> New Nature> Born again,* TopicGuide page A36.)

1:3-5 Peter begins the body of his letter by describing the eternal inheritance that God has secured for his readers. This inheritance is their hope. It cannot perish, and it results from their faith in God. The themes of persevering faith and hope in a final inheritance reappear throughout 1 Peter but are particularly evident in this chapter. In this way, Peter encourages his readers to look past their present trials to their future glory (1:6-8).

1:6-7 Peter writes to a group of believers who have had to face many different trials, including accusations of wrongdoing by unbelievers (2:12, 15; 3:16), scornful comments (4:4, 14), and suffering in various ways for doing right (2:19-20; 3:14, 17; 4:19). Peter encourages his readers that the trials, though difficult, both refine their faith and prove its true worth (James 1:2-4; Romans 5:3-4).

1:10-12 Since the readers' present sufferings might dim their hope in a future salvation, Peter affirms that the same message preached to them in the power of the Holy Spirit had been proclaimed long before by the same Spirit. The final salvation promised to God's people is not a new idea, but something Old Testament prophets wrote about (Luke 24:25-27; Daniel 12:12-13; Matthew 13:17). The prophets understood that this salvation would begin with the Messiah's sufferings (see note on 2:22-24; see also Isaiah 52:13–53:12) and climax in great glory (Acts 3:21; see also Isaiah 65:17-19).

they prophesied about this gracious salvation prepared for you. 11 They wondered what
time or situation the Spirit of Christ within them was talking about when He told them in
advance about Christ's suffering and His great glory afterward.

12 They were told that their messages were not for themselves, but for you. And now this
Good News has been announced to you by those who preached in the power of the Holy
Spirit sent from heaven. It is all so wonderful that even the angels are eagerly watching
these things happen.

A CALL TO HOLY LIVING

13 So think clearly and exercise self-control. Look forward to the gracious salvation that will
come to you when Jesus Christ is revealed to the world. 14 So you must live as God's obedi-
ent children. Don't slip back into your old ways of living to satisfy your own desires. You
didn't know any better then. 15 But now you must be holy in everything you do, just as God
who chose you is holy. 16 For the Scriptures say, "You must be holy because I am holy."*

17 And remember that the heavenly Father to whom you pray has no favorites. He will
judge or reward you according to what you do. So you must live in reverent fear of Him
during your time as "foreigners in the land." 18 For you know that God paid a ransom to

1:11 Ps 22; Isa 53; Luke 24:26; Acts 16:7; 2 Pet 1:21
1:12 Acts 2:2-4; Eph 3:10
1:13 1 Cor 1:7; 1 Thes 5:6
1:14 Rom 12:2; Eph 2:3; 4:17-18
1:15 2 Cor 7:1; 1 Thes 4:7; 1 Jn 3:3
1:17 Ps 89:26; Jer 3:19

1:16 Lev 11:44-45; 19:2; 20:7.

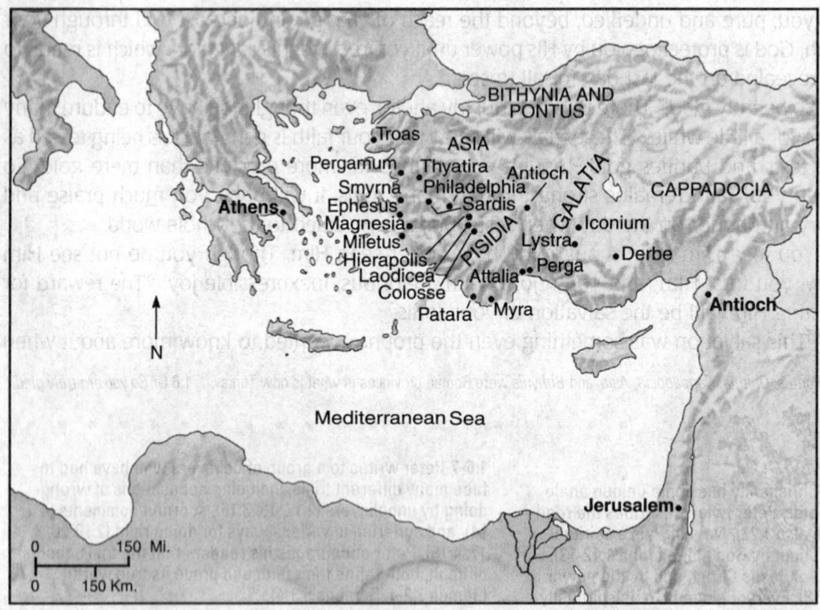

THE CHURCHES OF PETER'S LETTER
Peter addressed his letter to the churches located throughout Bithynia, Pontus, Asia, Galatia, and Cappadocia. Paul had evangelized many of these areas; other areas had churches that were begun by the Jews who were in Jerusalem on the day of Pentecost and heard Peter's powerful sermon (see Acts 2:9-11).

1:15-16 Peter's quotation of Leviticus 19:2 is his first direct citation of the Old Testament. Over 20 of the 105 verses in 1 Peter refer in some way to the Old Testament. Peter sees that the Old Testament speaks about both Jesus and the New Testament people of God. For example, the Old Testament calls believers to holiness (1:16; Leviticus 19:2), and the "word" from Isaiah is the New Testament gospel (1:24-25; Isaiah 40:6-8). Jesus is the Old Testament cornerstone (2:6-8; Isaiah 8:14; 28:16; Psalm 118:22), and the promised blessing from the Psalms applies to believers (3:10-12; Psalm 34:12-16). Peter recognized that across the Testaments there is one people of God with one grand story, the climax of which is Jesus.

▸ HOLINESS
1:15-16 God's holiness and ours. To be holy is to be separate or distinct in a moral sense. God is the essence of holiness because He is completely separate from all evil and impurity. Creatures around God's throne continually cry out, "Holy, holy, holy" (Isaiah 6:2-3; Revelation 4:8). God has always called His people to holiness (in this verse, Peter quotes a command from the time of Moses). Being holy means to live as Christ did, conforming to His image. Because holiness is impossible for us to achieve on our own, we must confess our sins to God and continually ask Him to help us live according to His word. Pray to God and ask Him to help you walk in His holiness. (***See Holiness**> Maturing> Conformity to Christ> Christ's likeness,* TopicGuide page A40.)

1:19 Exod 12:5 John 1:29 Heb 9:14
1:20 Acts 2:23 Eph 1:4
1:21 John 14:6 Rom 4:24
1:22 John 13:34 Rom 12:10
1:23 John 1:13; 3:3 Heb 4:12
1:24-25 *Isa 40:6-8
2:1 Eph 4:22, 31
2:2 1 Cor 3:2 Heb 5:12-13
2:3 *Ps 34:8
2:4 Ps 118:22 Isa 28:16 1 Pet 2:7

save you from the empty life you inherited from your ancestors. And the ransom He paid
was not mere gold or silver. 19 It was the precious blood of Christ, the sinless, spotless
Lamb of God. 20 God chose Him as your ransom long before the world began, but He has
now revealed Him to you in these last days.
21 Through Christ you have come to trust in God. And you have placed your faith and
hope in God because He raised Christ from the dead and gave Him great glory.
22 You were cleansed from your sins when you obeyed the truth, so now you must show
sincere love to each other as brothers and sisters.* Love each other deeply with all your
heart.*
23 For you have been born again, but not to a life that will quickly end. Your new life will
last forever because it comes from the eternal, living word of God. 24 As the Scriptures say,

"People are like grass;
their beauty is like a flower in the field.
The grass withers and the flower fades.
25 But the word of the Lord remains forever."*

And that word is the Good News that was preached to you.

2 So get rid of all evil behavior. Be done with all deceit, hypocrisy, jealousy, and all un-
kind speech. 2 Like newborn babies, you must crave pure spiritual milk so that you
will grow into a full experience of salvation. Cry out for this nourishment, 3 now that you
have had a taste of the Lord's kindness.

LIVING STONES FOR GOD'S HOUSE

4 You are coming to Christ, who is the living cornerstone of God's temple. He was rejected
by people, but He was chosen by God for great honor.

1:22a Greek *must have brotherly love.* 1:22b Some manuscripts read *with a pure heart.* 1:24-25 Isa 40:6-8.

2:4-6 The Old Testament Tabernacle (Exodus 25–29) and Temple (1 Kings 6–9) represented the presence of God and pointed to Jesus, who brought God's true presence (John 1:14; 2:19). Because God now reveals His presence in the church, Peter calls his readers a temple of God (1 Corinthians 3:16-17; 2 Corinthians 6:16; Ephesians 2:19-22). He quotes Isaiah 28:16, in which God promised to rebuild His rebellious people upon a foundation that had a firm and precious cornerstone. Jesus is that cornerstone, and God's people are now being reestablished as a spiritual temple, fulfilling the Old Testament promises of restoration.

BECAUSE GOD IS HOLY

I will devote myself to him in purity, worship and service.

But now you must be holy in everything you do, just as God who chose you is holy.

1 PETER 1:15

FOR THE NEXT *GOD IS HOLY* FEATURE SEE PAGE 2260.

[5]And you are living stones that God is building into His spiritual temple. What's more,
you are His holy priests.* Through the mediation of Jesus Christ, you offer spiritual sacri-
fices that please God. [6]As the Scriptures say,

"I am placing a cornerstone in Jerusalem,*
chosen for great honor,
and anyone who trusts in Him
will never be disgraced."*

[7]Yes, you who trust Him recognize the honor God has given Him. But for those who reject
Him,

"The stone that the builders rejected
has now become the cornerstone."*

[8]And,

"He is the stone that makes people stumble,
the rock that makes them fall."*

2:5 Exod 19:6; Isa 61:6; Eph 2:21-22; 1 Tim 3:15; Heb 13:15; Rev 1:6
2:6 *Isa 28:16; Rom 9:32-33; Eph 2:20
2:7 *Ps 118:22; Matt 21:42; Acts 4:11
2:8 *Isa 8:14; Luke 2:34; Rom 9:22

2:5 Greek *holy priesthood.* **2:6a** Greek *in Zion.* **2:6b** Isa 28:16 (Greek version). **2:7** Ps 118:22. **2:8** Isa 8:14.

MY RESPONSE TO GOD

What Is the Church Like?

1 PETER 2:9-10

Think about the last time you walked into a church. In your memory, look around. What do you see? What do you hear? What does the church look like?

The church is not identified as a building or as a ministry, but as a gathering of people that God has set apart, identified them as His own possession (Genesis 48:4; Deuteronomy 4:20; 1 Peter 2:9-10), called to worship Him (Deuteronomy 10:12; John 4:23; Revelation 22:3), and called them to be a witness to the world of His reality and purpose (Acts 14:17; 26:16; Revelation 6:9). From Adam and Eve (Genesis 4:26) to the body of Christ as we know it today, God's church has developed throughout the ages as a plant grows from a seed to a bud to a marvelous flower.

The Bible gives us a variety of images of the church that reveal to us what we should be and how we should act:

- As the bride of Christ (Jeremiah 2:23–3:25; Revelation 19:7; 21:2), we pursue purity and faithfulness to God.
- As a building or temple (2 Corinthians 5:1), we are a shelter and place for worship.
- As the body of Christ, which is Paul's favorite metaphor (Ephesians 1:22-23; 4:4, 15-16), we are connected to Jesus and each other, and He guides us.
- As the family of God (Hosea 11:1; Psalm 68:5; 103:13; Galatians 3:26–4:7), which is the most frequent image in the Scriptures, we are adopted into the Father's household, not as slaves, but as favored children.

Through these images we can see and rejoice in the great promises God has given His people, the church.

They stumble because they do not obey God's word, and so they meet the fate that was
planned for them.
9 But you are not like that, for you are a chosen people. You are royal priests,* a holy na-
tion, God's very own possession. As a result, you can show others the goodness of God, for
He called you out of the darkness into His wonderful light.

10 "Once you had no identity as a people;
now you are God's people.
Once you received no mercy;
now you have received God's mercy."*

11 Dear friends, I warn you as "temporary residents and foreigners" to keep away from
worldly desires that wage war against your very souls. 12 Be careful to live properly among
your unbelieving neighbors. Then even if they accuse you of doing wrong, they will see
your honorable behavior, and they will give honor to God when He judges the world.*

RESPECTING PEOPLE IN AUTHORITY

13 For the Lord's sake, respect all human authority—whether the king as head of state, 14 or
the officials he has appointed. For the king has sent them to punish those who do wrong
and to honor those who do right.
15 It is God's will that your honorable lives should silence those ignorant people who
make foolish accusations against you. 16 For you are free, yet you are God's slaves, so
don't use your freedom as an excuse to do evil. 17 Respect everyone, and love your Chris-
tian brothers and sisters.* Fear God, and respect the king.

SLAVES

18 You who are slaves must accept the authority of your masters with all respect.* Do what
they tell you—not only if they are kind and reasonable, but even if they are cruel. 19 For
God is pleased with you when you do what you know is right and patiently endure unfair
treatment. 20 Of course, you get no credit for being patient if you are beaten for doing
wrong. But if you suffer for doing good and endure it patiently, God is pleased with you.
21 For God called you to do good, even if it means suffering, just as Christ suffered* for
you. He is your example, and you must follow in His steps.

22 He never sinned,
nor ever deceived anyone.*

2:9 *Exod 19:5-6; Deut 7:6; 10:15; *Isa 43:20-21; Acts 26:18; 1 Pet 2:5; Rev 1:6
2:10 *Hos 1:6, 9; 2:23; Rom 9:25; 10:19
2:11 Rom 13:14; Gal 5:16; Jas 4:1
2:12 Phil 2:15; Titus 2:14
2:13-14 Rom 13:1-7; Titus 3:1
2:15 1 Pet 2:12; 3:17
2:16 Gal 5:13
2:17 Prov 24:21; Rom 12:10; 13:7
2:18 Eph 6:5; Jas 3:17
2:20 1 Pet 3:14, 17
2:21 Matt 16:24; Acts 14:22; 1 Pet 3:9, 18
2:22 *Isa 53:9; 2 Cor 5:21

2:9 Greek *a royal priesthood.* **2:10** Hos 1:6, 9; 2:23. **2:12** Or *on the day of visitation.* **2:17** Greek *love the brotherhood.* **2:18** Or *because you fear God.* **2:21** Some manuscripts read *died.* **2:22** Isa 53:9.

2:9 Peter expresses his readers' unique status as those chosen by God for special service. He draws the language "royal priests" and "holy nation" from Exodus 19:6. Priests were a consecrated group, set apart for special service. God's people are also distinct from other nations, and therefore holy. Peter's readers can face suffering in light of the fact that they belong to God and that He has transformed their identity and lifestyle.

▸ MINISTRY
2:11-12 In the world but not of the world. God calls His people both to set themselves apart from unbelievers and to reach out to them. Peter instructs his readers to live differently than their non-Christian neighbors, for believers are foreigners and aliens in this life (1 Peter 1:1, 17; see also Philippians 3:20; Hebrews 11:13-16; 13:14). At the same time, Peter does not expect his readers to abandon the unbelievers around them, for he knows that Christians serve as lights in the darkness (Matthew 5:14-16; Philippians 2:15). We must neither imitate those who live in the darkness, nor isolate our light from them. How can you make sure that the light of the gospel is shining brightly and clearly to those around you? (***See Ministry**> Transformation> Fill and subdue> Tearing down spiritual strongholds,* TopicGuide page A57.)

2:18-20 Some have accused Peter of supporting slavery because of his comments in these verses. These verses, however, do not condone slavery. Peter is simply addressing those under slavery and calling them to honor God in the midst of their unjust situation.

2:22-24 This passage explains the example that Jesus set for believers to follow (2:21). Jesus, though completely innocent, did not retaliate against the wrongs that people committed against Him but remained silent (Mark 15:3-5). Peter illustrates this point by quoting several verses from Isaiah 52:13–53:12. Though Peter directly addresses slaves in this section (2:18-25), verses 22-24 establish a paradigm for several groups who potentially face unjust treatment in their relationships. Besides slaves, Peter calls citizens (2:13), wives (3:1), husbands (3:7), and all Christians (3:8) to respect everyone despite potential mistreatment.

23 He did not retaliate when He was insulted,
nor threaten revenge when He suffered.
He left His case in the hands of God,
who always judges fairly.
24 He personally carried our sins
in His body on the cross
so that we can be dead to sin
and live for what is right.
By His wounds
you are healed.
25 Once you were like sheep
who wandered away.
But now you have turned to your Shepherd,
the Guardian of your souls.

2:23 Isa 53:7; 1 Pet 3:9
2:24 *Isa 53:4, 12
2:25 *Isa 53:6; Heb 13:20; 1 Pet 5:4

WIVES

3 In the same way, you wives must accept the authority of your husbands. Then, even
if some refuse to obey the Good News, your godly lives will speak to them without
any words. They will be won over 2 by observing your pure and reverent lives.
3 Don't be concerned about the outward beauty of fancy hairstyles, expensive jewelry,
or beautiful clothes. 4 You should clothe yourselves instead with the beauty that comes
from within, the unfading beauty of a gentle and quiet spirit, which is so precious to God.
5 This is how the holy women of old made themselves beautiful. They trusted God and ac-
cepted the authority of their husbands. 6 For instance, Sarah obeyed her husband, Abra-
ham, and called him her master. You are her daughters when you do what is right without
fear of what your husbands might do.

HUSBANDS

7 In the same way, you husbands must give honor to your wives. Treat your wife with under-
standing as you live together. She may be weaker than you are, but she is your equal part-
ner in God's gift of new life. Treat her as you should so your prayers will not be hindered.

3:1 1 Cor 7:16; 9:19; Eph 5:22; 1 Pet 2:18
3:3 Isa 3:18-23; 1 Tim 2:9
3:4 Rom 2:29
3:5 1 Tim 5:5
3:6 Gen 18:12
3:7 Eph 5:25; Col 3:19

▸ SPIRITUAL WARFARE

2:23 Two wrongs don't make a right. How did you respond the last time you were wronged? Bitterness and revenge are tremendous temptations for all who are treated unfairly. Nevertheless, this is not the way of Jesus (see note on 2:22-24). In verse 23, Peter explains that Jesus responded to abuse by entrusting Himself to God, the perfect judge. This encourages the readers of 1 Peter to act likewise when they are mistreated. We should not ignore situations in which we are wronged, but we should entrust them to God (Romans 12:17-21). Such faith allows us to act with appropriate wisdom and always in love (Matthew 5:43-47). (***See Spiritual Warfare***> *Resisting Sin and Evil> Resisting Temptation> What to Resist> We are to resist sinful urges,* TopicGuide page A45.)

3:1-7 Whenever the New Testament discusses marital roles in detail, it focuses on the wife's respect for her husband and the husband's love for his wife (Ephesians 5:22-33; Colossians 3:18-19). Submission and tender care are required without qualification. The wife should submit to the husband's authority regardless of his spiritual state and without fear. The husband should honor his wife and show all consideration for her. In this way, spouses fulfill Peter's command to gently love one another (3:8).

▸ HOLINESS

3:3-4 Beauty redefined. How do you define beauty? In a world that exalts external appearance many women are tempted to find security in physical beauty. Peter reminds them that a woman is not made beautiful by the intricacies of her hairstyle, her fashionable clothing, or her fine jewelry, for God sees below the surface. That does not mean, however, that Peter is prohibiting outward adornment or that women should not seek to make themselves physically beautiful, for their beauty is given by God and is a picture of the holiness of His people (Ezekiel 16:7-14; Revelation 21:2). Rather, Peter expresses the incomparable importance of the beauty within a woman's character (Proverbs 31:30). No amount of outward adornment will ever compare to the "unfading beauty of a gentle and quiet spirit, and trusting spirit, which is precious to God" (3:4-5). (***See Holiness***> *Disciplines> Of Abstinence> Resisting worldly influences,* TopicGuide page A42.)

3:7 When Peter says that wives are "weaker," most assume that he is referring to physical strength. Husbands are usually stronger than their wives. If so, then Peter admonishes husbands not to exert their wills over their wives, but rather to show understanding and consideration. Peter might also have meant that wives have the "weaker" role of submission to their husband's authority in marriage (3:1-6) and that husbands need to be understanding and considerate of their wives in this role. He might have had both views in mind. Regardless, Peter concludes his comments to husbands by pointing out that their wives share equally in their eternal inheritance (see also Galatians 3:28-29).

3:8 Rom 15:5 Eph 4:2, 32

ALL CHRISTIANS

8Finally, all of you should be of one mind. Sympathize with each other. Love each other as
brothers and sisters.* Be tenderhearted, and keep a humble attitude. 9Don't repay evil for
evil. Don't retaliate with insults when people insult you. Instead, pay them back with a
blessing. That is what God has called you to do, and He will bless you for it. 10For the Scrip-
tures say,

3:9 Matt 5:44 Rom 12:17 1 Thes 5:15 Heb 6:14

3:10-12 *Ps 34:12-16

"If you want to enjoy life
and see many happy days,
keep your tongue from speaking evil
and your lips from telling lies.
11 Turn away from evil and do good.
Search for peace, and work to maintain it.
12 The eyes of the Lord watch over those who do right,
and His ears are open to their prayers.
But the Lord turns His face
against those who do evil."*

3:13 Titus 2:14

SUFFERING FOR DOING GOOD

13Now, who will want to harm you if you are eager to do good? 14But even if you suffer for
doing what is right, God will reward you for it. So don't worry or be afraid of their threats.
15Instead, you must worship Christ as Lord of your life. And if someone asks about your

3:14-15 Isa 8:12-13

3:15 Col 4:6

3:8 Greek *Show brotherly love.* 3:10-12 Ps 34:12-16.

3:10-12 Quoting Psalm 34:12-16, Peter supports his assertion that refusing to retaliate against abuse will result in God's blessing (3:9). The psalm promises that the Lord will bless those who do right with good life and that He will hear their prayers. Peter obviously includes not just eternal blessings but also blessings in this lifetime, for he has already alluded to such examples (3:1-2, 7). He is urging readers, who are tempted to retaliate against injustice, that evil does not reap a blessing in this life or the next.

▸ MINISTRY

3:15-16 Active invitation. Starting a conversation about the Lord does not always require words. Peter expects unbelievers to ask his readers about their faith, because their lives should be different from unbelievers and ought to provoke their interest. Elsewhere, Peter instructs his readers to live carefully among unbelievers, for their actions will spark interest (4:4) and may even, by God's grace, win some over to the faith (2:12; 3:1-2). Though knowing how to articulate and defend what we believe is very important and necessary, it is often our actions that create conversations and give power to our words. (***See Ministry*** *> Great Commission> Description> People are invited to Christ,* TopicGuide page A56.)

BECAUSE
GOD IS RIGHTEOUS

I will live by His standards.

He personally carried our sins in His body on the cross
so that we can be dead to sin and live for what is right.

1 PETER 2:24

Christian hope, always be ready to explain it. 16 But do this in a gentle and respectful way.* Keep your conscience clear. Then if people speak against you, they will be ashamed when they see what a good life you live because you belong to Christ. 17 Remember, it is better to suffer for doing good, if that is what God wants, than to suffer for doing wrong!

18 Christ suffered* for our sins once for all time. He never sinned, but He died for sinners to bring you safely home to God. He suffered physical death, but He was raised to life in the Spirit.*

19 So He went and preached to the spirits in prison—20 those who disobeyed God long ago when God waited patiently while Noah was building his boat. Only eight people were saved from drowning in that terrible flood.* 21 And that water is a picture of baptism, which now saves you, not by removing dirt from your body, but as a response to God from* a clean conscience. It is effective because of the resurrection of Jesus Christ.

22 Now Christ has gone to heaven. He is seated in the place of honor next to God, and all the angels and authorities and powers accept His authority.

LIVING FOR GOD

4 So then, since Christ suffered physical pain, you must arm yourselves with the same attitude He had, and be ready to suffer, too. For if you have suffered physically for Christ, you have finished with sin.* 2 You won't spend the rest of your lives chasing your own desires, but you will be anxious to do the will of God. 3 You have had enough in the past of the evil things that godless people enjoy—their immorality and lust, their feasting and drunkenness and wild parties, and their terrible worship of idols.

4 Of course, your former friends are surprised when you no longer plunge into the flood of wild and destructive things they do. So they slander you. 5 But remember that they will have to face God, who will judge everyone, both the living and the dead. 6 That is why the Good News was preached to those who are now dead*—so although they were destined to die like all people,* they now live forever with God in the Spirit.*

7 The end of the world is coming soon. Therefore, be earnest and disciplined in your prayers. 8 Most important of all, continue to show deep love for each other, for love covers a multitude of sins. 9 Cheerfully share your home with those who need a meal or a place to stay.

3:16 Some English translations put this sentence in verse 15. 3:18a Some manuscripts read *died.* 3:18b Or *in spirit.* 3:20 Greek *saved through water.* 3:21 Or *as an appeal to God for.* 4:1 Or *For the one* [or *One*] *who has suffered physically has finished with sin.* 4:6a Greek *preached even to the dead.* 4:6b Or *so although people had judged them worthy of death.* 4:6c Or *in spirit.*

3:16 1 Pet 2:12
3:17 1 Pet 2:20; 4:15-16
3:18 Eph 2:18; Heb 9:26, 28; 1 Pet 2:21; 4:1
3:19 1 Pet 4:6
3:20 Gen 6:1–7:24
3:21 Heb 9:13; 10:22
3:22 Matt 28:18; Mark 16:19; Rom 8:38; Heb 1:4, 6; 4:14
4:1 Rom 6:7; Gal 2:20; Col 3:5; 1 Pet 2:21
4:2 Rom 6:2; 1 Pet 1:14
4:3 Rom 13:13; Eph 2:2
4:4 1 Pet 3:16
4:5 Acts 10:42
4:6 1 Pet 3:19
4:7 Rom 13:11-12
4:8 Prov 10:12; Jas 5:20; 1 Pet 1:22

3:19-20 Peter has already described the Spirit of Christ at work in the Old Testament prophets (1:11). Now he tells how Christ, through Noah, preached to the humans who were disobedient in Noah's day (Genesis 6:1-6)—but who, at the time Peter wrote, were imprisoned spirits awaiting final judgment (see also 2 Peter 2:9; see note on 4:6). Thus Peter encourages his readers, who—like Noah—must live righteously and proclaim God's word in a hostile environment.

3:21 The flood in Noah's day (3:19-20; Genesis 6–9) foreshadows baptism because its waters brought judgment (destroying the earth) and salvation (lifting Noah's boat to safety). Baptism, likewise, depicts God's judgment of sin through Christ's death and burial as well as God's salvation through Christ's resurrection. Baptism pictures our spiritual death, burial, and resurrection with Christ (Romans 6:3-4). Peter clarifies that baptism's bodily washing does not save us, but rather our response to God in recognition of the salvation we receive by faith.

4:1 Peter resumes his argument from 3:18. Christ, though innocent, suffered to the point of death. Similarly, the readers are to adopt a warlike mentality and "arm" themselves with the same attitude toward suffering. Peter adds that those who willingly suffer for Christ reveal that they have forsaken a sinful lifestyle and desire God's will above all else (4:2, 19). Those who choose to live according to evil human desires will either suffer as common criminals (4:15) or avoid suffering altogether.

4:6 The Greek text of verse 6 says that the gospel was "preached even to the dead," but the context suggests that Peter is talking about those who were alive at the time of the preaching but who are now dead. Peter's audience may have been concerned about deceased members of their Christian community. Peter clarifies for them that God is the judge not only of the living but also of the dead (4:5). Though their bodies have perished, being condemned because of sin (Genesis 2:7-17; Romans 5:12-18), they now live spiritually because of Christ.

4:7-9 Speculations about the end of the world were rampant in Peter's day. New Testament writers, however, never discuss the specific timing of Christ's return. They understood that God alone knows such details (Mark 13:32). Rather, they emphasize that the end could come at any time (Matthew 24:44; 1 Thessalonians 5:1-3); the end is "near" or "soon" (see Romans 13:11-12; James 5:9; Revelation 22:20). Peter urges that the impending judgment of God should motivate believers to obedience (2 Peter 3:11-13).

4:10 [10]God has given each of you a gift from His great variety of spiritual gifts. Use them well
Rom 12:6-8 to serve one another. [11]Do you have the gift of speaking? Then speak as though God Him-
4:11 self were speaking through you. Do you have the gift of helping others? Do it with all the
1 Cor 10:31 strength and energy that God supplies. Then everything you do will bring glory to God
4:12 1 Pet 1:6-7 through Jesus Christ. All glory and power to Him forever and ever! Amen.

4:13 Rom 8:17
SUFFERING FOR BEING A CHRISTIAN

2 Cor 1:5 [12]Dear friends, don't be surprised at the fiery trials you are going through, as if something
4:14 strange were happening to you. [13]Instead, be very glad—for these trials make you partners
Isa 11:2 Matt 5:11 with Christ in His suffering, so that you will have the wonderful joy of seeing His glory
John 15:21 when it is revealed to all the world.
4:15 [14]So be happy when you are insulted for being a Christian,* for then the glorious Spirit
1 Thes 4:11 of God* rests upon you.* [15]If you suffer, however, it must not be for murder, stealing, mak-
2 Thes 3:11 1 Tim 5:13 ing trouble, or prying into other people's affairs. [16]But it is no shame to suffer for being a
4:16 Christian. Praise God for the privilege of being called by His name! [17]For the time has
Acts 5:41 come for judgment, and it must begin with God's household. And if judgment begins with
4:17 us, what terrible fate awaits those who have never obeyed God's Good News? [18]And also,

Jer 25:29 2 Thes 1:8 "If the righteous are barely saved,
4:18 what will happen to godless sinners?"*

*Prov 11:31 [19]So if you are suffering in a manner that pleases God, keep on doing what is right, and
4:19 Ps 31:5 1 Pet 2:20 trust your lives to the God who created you, for He will never fail you.

5:1
ADVICE FOR ELDERS AND YOUNG MEN

5 And now, a word to you who are elders in the churches. I, too, am an elder and a wit-
Luke 24:48 Rev 1:9 ness to the sufferings of Christ. And I, too, will share in His glory when He is revealed

4:14a Greek *for the name of Christ.* **4:14b** Or *for the glory of God, which is His Spirit.* **4:14c** Some manuscripts add *On their part He is blasphemed, but on your part He is glorified.* **4:18** Prov 11:31 (Greek version).

▸ MINISTRY
4:10-11 To each his own. What is your part to play in the spiritual growth of the church? Whenever New Testament writers speak about spiritual gifts, they emphasize, first, that God has specially gifted each one of His people and, second, that all of the diverse gifts are given for the maturity of the community of faith (Romans 12:3-8; 1 Corinthians 12:1-31; 14:1-12; Ephesians 4:7-16). To this, Peter adds the call to serve others responsibly as stewards of God. Our spiritual gifts are not our own. God has given them to us so that our church communities will grow in Christ, and ultimately, so that God will receive praise in everything. (***See Ministry****> Great Commission> Make Disciples> Disciples strategically use knowledge, skills, and abilities,* TopicGuide page A56.)

4:13-14 Peter is not saying here that our earthly trials play any role in Christ's payment for sin. Jesus alone, being perfect, fulfilled that role (1 Peter 1:18-19; 2 Corinthians 5:21). Rather, Peter understands the close relationship between the sheep and the Shepherd and relates the suffering of Jesus' people to the Lord's own suffering (see also Acts 9:4-5; 2 Corinthians 1:5; Colossians 1:24). The world persecutes believers because it opposes Christ, with whom Christians identify themselves (John 15:20). Peter adds, however, that Christ's followers not only share in His suffering, but they share in His glory as well.

▸ ADOPTION
4:16 What's in a name? When someone claims to be "a Christian," he communicates more than he might realize. In Peter's day, people often described followers of a certain leader with a form of the leader's name. To be called a Christian is to be called by the name of Jesus Christ. God has always called His people by His own name (2 Chronicles 7:14; Isaiah 43:7; Acts 15:17; James 2:7). Such a calling indicates that they belong to Him completely and that He is pleased for them to represent Him in the world. We should derive great pleasure in being associated with the priceless name of Christ and proudly proclaim our association with Jesus. (***See Adoption****> With Christ> Children of God> Children chosen of God,* TopicGuide page A36.)

4:17-18 Peter seems to consider his readers' suffering as the beginning of God's final judgment of the world. Judgment here does not indicate condemnation but refers to an evaluation that could produce positive or negative results. God's judgment, in this sense, is like fire. In the form of present suffering, it proves and purifies Christians' faith (1 Peter 4:12; 1:6-7; Hebrews 12:4-11). Eventually, however, it will destroy everyone who does not follow Christ. A similar use of the imagery of fire that both refines and consumes is found in Malachi 3:1-3; 4:1.

▸ MINISTRY
5:1-4 Pressure, profit, and power. No one can enter spiritual leadership without facing tremendous temptation. Peter warns those who serve as elders to resist the lure of pressure, profit, and power. They should not serve under compulsion or out of greed, but rather willingly and eagerly. They should not abuse their authority, but rather serve as examples to those who follow. Peter presents the shepherd as a model for true servant leadership (2 Samuel 5:2; 1 Kings 22:17; Jeremiah 3:15; Acts 20:28). Good shepherds affectionately tend to every need of their flock with strength and tenderness. Those who lead well will ultimately be rewarded by the Great Shepherd Himself (see also John 10:1-16; Hebrews 13:20; Revelation 7:17). As you lead others, follow God's lead as your Great Shepherd. (***See Ministry****> Transformation> Fill and Subdue> Being salt and light in the world,* TopicGuide page A57.)

to the whole world. As a fellow elder, I appeal to you: 2Care for the flock that God has en-
trusted to you. Watch over it willingly, not grudgingly—not for what you will get out of it,
but because you are eager to serve God. 3Don't lord it over the people assigned to your
care, but lead them by your own good example. 4And when the Great Shepherd appears,
you will receive a crown of never-ending glory and honor.

5In the same way, you younger men must accept the authority of the elders. And all of
you, serve each other in humility, for

"God opposes the proud
but favors the humble."*

6So humble yourselves under the mighty power of God, and at the right time He will lift
you up in honor. 7Give all your worries and cares to God, for He cares about you.

8Stay alert! Watch out for your great enemy, the devil. He prowls around like a roaring
lion, looking for someone to devour. 9Stand firm against him, and be strong in your faith.
Remember that your Christian brothers and sisters* all over the world are going through
the same kind of suffering you are.

10In His kindness God called you to share in His eternal glory by means of Christ Jesus.
So after you have suffered a little while, He will restore, support, and strengthen you, and
He will place you on a firm foundation. 11All power to Him forever! Amen.

PETER'S FINAL GREETINGS

12I have written and sent this short letter to you with the help of Silas,* whom I commend
to you as a faithful brother. My purpose in writing is to encourage you and assure you that
what you are experiencing is truly part of God's grace for you. Stand firm in this grace.

13Your sister church here in Babylon* sends you greetings, and so does my son Mark.
14Greet each other with Christian love.*

Peace be with all of you who are in Christ.

5:2 John 21:16; Acts 20:28
5:3 2 Cor 1:24; Phil 3:17; Titus 2:7
5:4 1 Cor 9:25; Heb 13:20-21
5:5 Jas 4:6
5:6 Jas 4:10
5:7 Ps 55:22; Matt 6:25; Heb 13:5
5:8 Job 1:7; Jas 4:7
5:9 Eph 6:11-13; Jas 4:7
5:10 1 Thes 2:12; 2 Tim 2:10
5:12 Acts 15:22; Heb 13:22
5:13 Acts 12:12
5:14 Rom 16:16; Eph 6:23

5:5 Prov 3:34 (Greek version). 5:9 Greek *your brothers.* 5:12 Greek *Silvanus.* 5:13 Greek *The elect one in Babylon.* Babylon was probably symbolic for Rome. 5:14 Greek *with a kiss of love.*

5:5-9 This passage resembles James 4:6-10. Both passages quote Proverbs 3:34 and encourage their readers to resist the devil and humble themselves before God who exalts the humble. Since James probably wrote before Peter did, Peter may have used words and ideas from James's letter when he wrote his own. Peter was certainly aware of Paul's writing (2 Peter 3:15).

▸ SPIRITUAL WARFARE
5:8-9 On the prowl. The devil is no myth or product of human imagination. The Scriptures make clear that he exists and that he is the fiercest enemy of God's people. The Christian life is a battle against him and all the spiritual forces of darkness (Ephesians 6:10-17). Peter compares Satan to a roaring lion, roaming around in search of prey (Job 1:7). He implies in verse 9 that the suffering repeatedly mentioned in his letter is Satan's attack. In God's strength, Christians must resist or oppose the devil (James 4:7). We can do so with faith that we have already been freed from Satan's power (Ephesians 2:1-7; Colossians 1:13-14), that the power of Christ infinitely exceeds the devil's power (1 John 4:4), and that Christ will ultimately vanquish the enemy forever (Revelation 20:10). Don't be afraid of Satan. Confidently march forward in Christ's name, expecting to defeat the devil's ploys in the power of the Holy Spirit. (***See Spiritual Warfare**> Originator of Sin> Satan's Limits> Christians overcome him,* TopicGuide page A44.)

5:10 Peter begins his letter by praising God for giving believers a living hope, an imperishable inheritance, and a salvation that is soon to be revealed (1:3-5). Similarly, Peter often encourages his readers to look forward to God's final redemption and reward (1:7, 9, 13, 17, 21, 23; 3:14; 4:13; 5:1, 4). As he concludes the main section of the letter, Peter again highlights this confident expectation. Though suffering lasts for a brief time (1:6), God will replace it with glory that never ends (see 2 Corinthians 4:17).

5:12 Peter's purpose in writing is twofold: 1) to encourage, urge, and exhort his readers to stand firm in their faith and persevere in godliness despite many trials; 2) to testify to or affirm God's grace toward them in various ways. This grace supports Peter's call to obedience.

5:14 As he closes his letter, Peter instructs his readers to greet one another literally with a "kiss of love." The cultural practice of kissing cheeks took place regularly among family members and was a common greeting among friends as well (Luke 7:45; Acts 20:37). Paul similarly directs his readers to greet one another with a "holy kiss" (NLT, "Christian love"; Romans 16:16; 1 Corinthians 16:20; 2 Corinthians 13:12; 1 Thessalonians 5:26).

2 PETER

PURPOSE

To encourage a troubled church to remain steadfast in their faith in God.

Some new believers seem to grow quickly, maturing almost overnight into a stable believer. Others wobble like a newborn for years, stumbling about from place to place, from doctrine to doctrine, and show relatively little growth. What makes the difference? Peter believes that a key to spiritual growth is understanding the privileges (1:3-4) and responsibilities (1:5-11) of being connected to God through Christ.

Peter builds this letter to an internally troubled church on the foundational truth that God's mercies to His people through Christ are not only sufficient, but are able to sustain the believer through any trial. This church was troubled with trials from inside the church (false teachers; see 1:12–2:22), but Peter's advice applies in all situations—Christ is sufficient (1:3).

DISCOVER GOD IN 2 PETER

With so many unorthodox ideas about God being taught in this distressed church, Peter fills this small letter with an abundance of healthy ideas about God.

God the Father, from Whom All Blessings Flow: Jesus taught His followers to pray to the Father in His name (Luke 11:2; John 15:16). Peter echoes his Lord as he assures his friends that those who believe receive everything they need through God the Father, who has granted "great and precious promises" (1:2-4). While the blessings of God do not instantly solve every deficit of this sin-cursed world, the Father's blessing is exactly what His children need (2 Peter 1:17).

God the Spirit, Who Speaks through the Prophets: Rather than discard the works of the Old Testament, Peter emphasizes the authority of God's words spoken through the prophets. For Peter, the Spirit-inspired words of the past make sense of the present distress. The Spirit is the One behind true teachers, but the Spirit-less false teachers who plague the church will be swept away just as in the former days (Jeremiah 23; Ezekiel 13).

God the Son, Who Is Savior and Lord: It's tempting to want Jesus to simply be our Savior, keeping us from the just punishment for our sins without actually asking us to do anything. Peter understands this part of human nature and stresses over and over the need for diligence to obey God (1:5, 10, 3:14). Numerous times in this letter, Peter connects the roles of Jesus, who is both Lord and Savior (2 Peter 1:11; 2:20; 3:2; 3:18). God's people cannot separate these roles.

GROWING THROUGH 2 PETER

Every follower of Jesus recognizes the value of the Scriptures in his or her life. But Peter helps us understand, as growing disciples, a bit more about the nature and role of the Scriptures.

Truthful: Some people wonder whether we can know anything for certain about Jesus; Peter affirms that we can. He says that what he teaches and what he follows is not merely invented tales but is rooted in eyewitness experience (1:16-19). Although Peter doesn't specifically mention Scripture here, clearly it is consistent with Peter's argument to say that the teachings of the apostles as found in the Gospels and the Epistles are rooted in the truth about Jesus. You can meet the Jesus who lives forevermore in the pages of the Bible.

Word of God: How can we know what God has to say to us? How can we know what it takes to be in right relationship with Him? Peter affirms that the words of the Scriptures are not merely human words and reflections; instead, God, in the person of the Holy Spirit, guided the writers to record His own words to us (1:19-21). You can hear from God, through the Spirit, as you spend time reading the Bible.

Guiding: Many people are interested in the future. Where is life headed? What will happen as history draws to a close? Although Peter refrains from telling us all the details, he does let us know that we find instruction about God's plan for life on planet Earth through the prophets who spoke in the Scriptures (3:1-2). Although we may not end up learning everything we would like to know, we can learn what God has chosen to reveal to us about His plans for the end of the ages.

Understandable: Peter recognizes that some of the apostle Paul's comments are hard to understand (3:16). He does not say, however, that they are impossible to understand; he only cautions us against misinterpreting and distorting the Scriptures through ignorance and carelessness. As we approach the Scriptures with humility and diligence to study and understand it, we can be confident that God will make plain to us what He intends for us to know.

DISCOVERY VERSES

So, dear brothers and sisters, work hard to prove that you really are among those God has called and chosen. Do these things, and you will never fall away. Then God will give you a grand entrance into the eternal Kingdom of our Lord and Savior Jesus Christ. (2 PETER 1:10-11)

So you see, the Lord knows how to rescue godly people from their trials, even while keeping the wicked under punishment until the day of final judgment. (2 PETER 2:9)

2 PETER FACTS

Author: In this very personal letter, Peter identifies himself by his full name: "Simon Peter, a slave and apostle of Jesus Christ" (1:1). This is the same Peter we meet in the Gospels: the one who was with Jesus on the mount of transfiguration (1:16-18; see Matthew 17:1-13; Mark 9:1-13; Luke 9:28-36). However, Peter's authorship of this letter is among the most disputed of any in the Bible. It wasn't until late in the fourth century that it was universally accepted and included in the New Testament canon, finally gaining acceptance at the church council meetings at Hippo and at Carthage. The disagreement was over the stylistic differences between 1 and 2 Peter, and the similarities to the brief book of Jude (page 2273). However, the content of 2 Peter was never suspect, simply the authorship.

Written to: There is very little in this letter to inform us of whom Peter is addressing. If the reference in 3:1 is to the letter of 1 Peter, then this letter is apparently going to the same believers addressed in his first epistle—Christians scattered throughout the various provinces of the Roman world in what is now modern Turkey (1 Peter 1:1-2).

Date of writing: If, as noted, 3:1 refers to 1 Peter, then this letter was written after that one. It is believed that Peter was martyred in AD 67/68 so the letter comes before then. Toward the end of 2 Peter, Peter refers to the letters of Paul (3:15-16). We cannot be sure how many of Paul's letters Peter was aware of, but this must mean that Peter is writing this letter after Paul's writings began to be circulated. Recognizing this, and bearing in mind that Peter believes his death to be imminent (1:14), the writing of this letter was likely in the late 60s, shortly before his death.

Setting: The place of origin of this book is unknown, however Rome is the likeliest suggestion. First Peter was written from Rome (1 Peter 5:13) and early church history asserts that Peter was martyred there under Nero's harsh rule.

OUTLINE

GREETINGS FROM PETER

1 This letter is from Simon* Peter, a slave and apostle of Jesus Christ.
I am writing to you who share the same precious faith we have. This faith was
given to you because of the justice and fairness* of Jesus Christ, our God and Savior.
2May God give you more and more grace and peace as you grow in your knowledge of
God and Jesus our Lord.

GROWING IN FAITH

3By His divine power, God has given us everything we need for living a godly life. We have
received all of this by coming to know Him, the One who called us to Himself by means of
His marvelous glory and excellence. 4And because of His glory and excellence, He has
given us great and precious promises. These are the promises that enable you to share His
divine nature and escape the world's corruption caused by human desires.
5In view of all this, make every effort to respond to God's promises. Supplement your
faith with a generous provision of moral excellence, and moral excellence with knowl-
edge, 6and knowledge with self-control, and self-control with patient endurance, and pa-
tient endurance with godliness, 7and godliness with brotherly affection, and brotherly
affection with love for everyone.
8The more you grow like this, the more productive and useful you will be in your knowl-
edge of our Lord Jesus Christ. 9But those who fail to develop in this way are shortsighted
or blind, forgetting that they have been cleansed from their old sins.
10So, dear brothers and sisters,* work hard to prove that you really are among those
God has called and chosen. Do these things, and you will never fall away. 11Then God will
give you a grand entrance into the eternal Kingdom of our Lord and Savior Jesus Christ.

PAYING ATTENTION TO SCRIPTURE

12Therefore, I will always remind you about these things—even though you already know
them and are standing firm in the truth you have been taught. 13And it is only right that I
should keep on reminding you as long as I live.* 14For our Lord Jesus Christ has shown me

1:2 2 Pet 3:18; Jude 1:2
1:3 1 Pet 2:9
1:4 2 Cor 7:1; Jas 1:27
1:5 Col 2:3
1:6 Acts 24:25; 1 Cor 9:25; Gal 5:22
1:7 John 13:34-35; Rom 12:10; 1 Pet 1:22
1:8 John 15:2; Col 1:10; 2 Pet 1:2-3
1:9 Eph 5:26; 1 Jn 2:11
1:10 Rom 8:28; Jude 1:24
1:11 2 Tim 4:18; 2 Pet 3:18
1:12 1 Jn 2:21; Jude 1:5
1:13-14 John 13:36; 21:18-19; 2 Cor 5:1, 4

1:1a Greek *Symeon.* 1:1b Or *to you in the righteousness.* 1:10 Greek *brothers.* 1:13 Greek *as long as I am in this tent* [or *tabernacle*].

▸ HOLINESS

1:5-9 The journey and the destination. The Christian life is one of tension. While it is true, as Peter says, that we have been cleansed from our former sins, we have certainly not been perfected. That is why Peter calls those who know Christ to a life of ever-progressing growth. When Christ returns, God will perfect the work that He has begun in all of His people (Philippians 1:6). Until then, however, we continue on a difficult journey, always aware that the ultimate destination still lies ahead. If we expect perfection from ourselves in this life, we will thwart the plans God has for our growth. Submit yourself to the Holy Spirit and allow Him to make you continually more like Jesus. (***See Holiness****> Maturing> Obeying God's Word> Faithfulness is critical to obeying God's Word,* TopicGuide page A40.)

1:10 Good trees produce good fruit, and bad trees produce bad fruit (Matthew 7:18-20). As the readers of 2 Peter succeed in producing the good fruit described in verses 5-7, they prove, in a sense, that God has in fact called and chosen them. Their progress in godliness does not make their salvation more secure, for God chose His people before the foundation of the world (Ephesians 1:4-5). It does, however, give evidence of their true conversion.

1:14 As he wrote this letter, Peter knew that his death was near. When he says that Jesus had revealed this to him, Peter may be remembering an episode (recorded in the Gospel of John) in which Jesus told Peter that he would eventually be led away to his death (John 21:18-19). This revelation did not cause Peter to despair. Rather, it spurred him on to serve the church by reminding them to persevere in godliness (1:12-13).

that I must soon leave this earthly life,* 15so I will work hard to make sure you always re-
member these things after I am gone.
16For we were not making up clever stories when we told you about the powerful com-
ing of our Lord Jesus Christ. We saw His majestic splendor with our own eyes 17when He
received honor and glory from God the Father. The voice from the majestic glory of God
said to Him, "This is my dearly loved Son, who brings Me great joy."* 18We ourselves
heard that voice from heaven when we were with Him on the holy mountain.
19Because of that experience, we have even greater confidence in the message pro-
claimed by the prophets. You must pay close attention to what they wrote, for their words
are like a lamp shining in a dark place—until the Day dawns, and Christ the Morning Star
shines* in your hearts. 20Above all, you must realize that no prophecy in Scripture ever
came from the prophet's own understanding,* 21or from human initiative. No, those
prophets were moved by the Holy Spirit, and they spoke from God.

THE DANGER OF FALSE TEACHERS

2 But there were also false prophets in Israel, just as there will be false teachers among
you. They will cleverly teach destructive heresies and even deny the Master who
bought them. In this way, they will bring sudden destruction on themselves. 2Many will fol-
low their evil teaching and shameful immorality. And because of these teachers, the way of
truth will be slandered. 3In their greed they will make up clever lies to get hold of your
money. But God condemned them long ago, and their destruction will not be delayed.
4For God did not spare even the angels who sinned. He threw them into hell,* in gloomy
pits of darkness,* where they are being held until the day of judgment. 5And God did not
spare the ancient world—except for Noah and the seven others in his family. Noah warned

1:16-18 Matt 17:1-6; Mark 13:26; Luke 9:28-32
1:19 Ps 119:105; Luke 1:78; 2 Cor 4:6; 1 Pet 1:10-12; Rev 22:16
1:21 John 14:26; 1 Cor 2:13; 2 Tim 3:16
2:1 Deut 13:1-3; Matt 7:15; 1 Tim 4:1; Jude 1:4
2:2 Jude 1:4
2:3 Rom 16:18; 1 Thes 2:5
2:4 Gen 6:1-4; //Jude 1:6; Rev 20:1-2
2:5 Gen 6:5–8:18; 1 Pet 3:20; 2 Pet 3:6

1:14 Greek *I must soon put off my tent* [or *tabernacle*]. 1:17 Matt 17:5; Mark 9:7; Luke 9:35. 1:19 Or *rises.* 1:20 Or *is a matter of one's own interpretation.* 2:4a Greek *Tartarus.* 2:4b Some manuscripts read *in chains of gloom.*

1:16-19 When Peter mentions the power and coming of Christ, he refers not to the Lord's birth but rather to His return. The false teachers had apparently mocked the Lord's promise to return (3:3-10), so Peter provides evidence to refute their claims. One such piece of evidence is Peter's description of Jesus' Transfiguration, which occurred in the context of Jesus' assertions that He will return in glory (Matthew 16:27–17:2; Mark 8:38–9:2; Luke 9:26-29). In this event, Jesus led Peter, James, and John up a mountain and was transformed before their eyes, emanating pure radiance and splendor. During the event, God audibly declared His approval of Jesus, His beloved Son. Peter describes the episode to show that, unlike the deceitful false teachers (2:2-3, 13), his message is founded on the sacred Scriptures and reliable experience (1:16-19).

▸ BIBLE
1:19 Out with the old, in with the new? Since we no longer live under the Old Covenant (or Testament), why bother to read the Old Testament? This may have been a question on the minds of Peter's audience. Peter urges them to pay close attention to the writings of the Old Testament prophets. Peter himself made extensive use of the Old Testament in both of his New Testament letters (see study note on 1 Peter 1:15-16). The New Testament explains and expands the Old Testament's message; it does not replace it (Matthew 5:17-18). Both the Old and New Testaments are relevant and profitable for every generation (1 Corinthians 10:11; 2 Timothy 3:16). Are you spending time studying both the Old Testament and the New Testament? (***See Bible****> Unity> OT Points to NT> Fulfillment of Old Testament prophecy in the New Testament,* TopicGuide page A11.)

1:20-21 Verse 20 is extremely difficult to translate. It could mean that no one is free to say, without God's authority, that Scriptural prophecy must be understood in a certain way (see NLT textual note). A more likely interpretation of this verse is that the prophets of the Old Testament did not merely record their own ideas about what God was revealing to them; they were recording God's very revelation. The prophets spoke to their own situations in their own style, but the Holy Spirit ensured that every word they wrote was from God (2 Timothy 3:16; 1 Peter 1:10-12).

2:3-9 Peter shares three illustrations to reassure his readers that the wicked will not escape judgment and that the righteous will be preserved (see also Jude 1:6-7). For a discussion of the first illustration, see the study note on 2:4. The second illustration comes from Genesis 6–9. The Genesis account does not describe Noah's public preaching (see study note on 1 Peter 3:19-20), but the traditional Jewish writings of Peter's day mention it often. The third illustration, which recounts the dilemma of Lot with Sodom and Gomorrah, comes from Genesis 19:1-29. By sharing these accounts, Peter encourages his readers to trust that God will eventually condemn the false teachers and will protect the church from them until He does so.

2:4 Peter might have based this illustration on a common Jewish interpretation of Genesis 6:1-4 (see study note on Genesis 6:1-2), which suggested that angels, after committing perverse acts with human women, were cast down into dark dungeons to await their final judgment. Others suggest that Peter is referring to a heavenly rebellion of angels that occurred prior to the Fall of Adam, which might be alluded to in Isaiah 14:12-15 and Ezekiel 28:11-17. There is no way to know for sure, but we can be confident that Peter's account is accurate and take his point to heart that God does not leave the guilty unpunished.

2:6 the world of God's righteous judgment. So God protected Noah when He destroyed the
Gen 19:24 world of ungodly people with a vast flood. 6Later, God condemned the cities of Sodom
Matt 10:15 Rom 9:29 and Gomorrah and turned them into heaps of ashes. He made them an example of what
//Jude 1:7 will happen to ungodly people. 7But God also rescued Lot out of Sodom because he was a
2:7 righteous man who was sick of the shameful immorality of the wicked people around him.
Gen 19:1-16 2 Pet 3:17 8Yes, Lot was a righteous man who was tormented in his soul by the wickedness he saw
2:9 and heard day after day. 9So you see, the Lord knows how to rescue godly people from
//Jude 1:6 their trials, even while keeping the wicked under punishment until the day of final judg-
2:10 ment. 10He is especially hard on those who follow their own twisted sexual desire, and
2 Pet 3:3 who despise authority.
//Jude 1:7-8, 16, 18 These people are proud and arrogant, daring even to scoff at supernatural beings* with-
2:11 out so much as trembling. 11But the angels, who are far greater in power and strength, do
//Jude 1:9 not dare to bring from the Lord* a charge of blasphemy against those supernatural beings.
2:12 12These false teachers are like unthinking animals, creatures of instinct, born to be
//Jude 1:10 caught and destroyed. They scoff at things they do not understand, and like animals, they
2:13 will be destroyed. 13Their destruction is their reward for the harm they have done. They
Rom 13:13 1 Cor 11:20-21 love to indulge in evil pleasures in broad daylight. They are a disgrace and a stain among
//Jude 1:12 you. They delight in deception* even as they eat with you in your fellowship meals.
2:14 Eph 2:3 14They commit adultery with their eyes, and their desire for sin is never satisfied. They
2 Pet 2:18; 3:16 lure unstable people into sin, and they are well trained in greed. They live under God's

2:10 Greek *at glorious ones,* which are probably evil angels. 2:11 Other manuscripts read *to the Lord;* still others omit this phrase.
2:13 Some manuscripts read *in fellowship meals.*

2:10-11 Peter illustrates the extent of his opponents' arrogance by describing how they foolishly slander supernatural beings. The objects of the false teachers' rash talk cannot be angels, for Peter contrasts the discretion that angels show toward these beings with his opponents' flippancy of speech (see study note on Jude 1:9). Apparently, then, the false teachers regularly condemn demonic powers with arrogant boldness. Though demons are worthy of condemnation, Peter's opponents reveal their own conceit by scoffing at beings whose power is great and whose judgment belongs to the Lord alone (Acts 19:13-17).

▸ SPIRITUAL WARFARE

2:13-14 Harsh words for hedonists and heretics. Few would ever accuse Peter of lacking passion. Just as he boldly (though inappropriately) defended Jesus with a sword (John 18:10-11), so he boldly (and appropriately) defends his readers with his words. The false teachers of Peter's day actively seduced young believers (see also 2:18) and perverted the churches' meetings. Peter cared too much for the church to let these wicked teachers threaten its purity. We also have false teachers in the church today. Many distort God's word through television and radio broadcasts, in the teachings of cults, and even in our congregations. Always check everything you hear by the truth in God's word, and don't hesitate to correct those who are teaching in error. (***See Spiritual Warfare**> Originator of Sin> Satan's Strategies> Demons> Demons sow false doctrine,* TopicGuide page A45.)

BECAUSE GOD IS JUST

He will always treat me fairly.

The Lord knows how to rescue godly people from their trials, even while keeping the wicked under punishment until the day of final judgment.

2 PETER 2:9

curse. 15They have wandered off the right road and followed the footsteps of Balaam son
of Beor,* who loved to earn money by doing wrong. 16But Balaam was stopped from his
mad course when his donkey rebuked him with a human voice.
17These people are as useless as dried-up springs or as mist blown away by the wind.
They are doomed to blackest darkness. 18They brag about themselves with empty, foolish
boasting. With an appeal to twisted sexual desires, they lure back into sin those who have
barely escaped from a lifestyle of deception. 19They promise freedom, but they them-
selves are slaves of sin and corruption. For you are a slave to whatever controls you. 20And
when people escape from the wickedness of the world by knowing our Lord and Savior
Jesus Christ and then get tangled up and enslaved by sin again, they are worse off than
before. 21It would be better if they had never known the way to righteousness than to
know it and then reject the command they were given to live a holy life. 22They prove the
truth of this proverb: "A dog returns to its vomit."* And another says, "A washed pig returns
to the mud."

THE DAY OF THE LORD IS COMING

3 This is my second letter to you, dear friends, and in both of them I have tried to stimu-
late your wholesome thinking and refresh your memory. 2I want you to remember
what the holy prophets said long ago and what our Lord and Savior commanded through
your apostles.
3Most importantly, I want to remind you that in the last days scoffers will come, mock-
ing the truth and following their own desires. 4They will say, "What happened to the prom-
ise that Jesus is coming again? From before the times of our ancestors, everything has
remained the same since the world was first created."
5They deliberately forget that God made the heavens by the word of His command, and
He brought the earth out from the water and surrounded it with water. 6Then He used the
water to destroy the ancient world with a mighty flood. 7And by the same word, the pres-
ent heavens and earth have been stored up for fire. They are being kept for the day of
judgment, when ungodly people will be destroyed.
8But you must not forget this one thing, dear friends: A day is like a thousand years to
the Lord, and a thousand years is like a day. 9The Lord isn't really being slow about His

2:15 Some manuscripts read *Bosor*. 2:22 Prov 26:11.

2:15 Num 22:5-7, 17; Deut 23:5; //Jude 1:11; Rev 2:14
2:18 2 Pet 1:4; //Jude 1:16
2:19 John 8:34; Rom 6:16
2:20 Matt 12:45
2:21 Ezek 18:24; Heb 6:4; 10:26
3:2 //Jude 1:17
3:3 1 Tim 4:1; 2 Pet 2:10
3:4 Isa 5:19; Jer 17:15
3:5 Gen 1:6-9; Heb 11:3
3:6 Gen 7:11-21
3:7 Matt 10:15; 2 Thes 1:7
3:9 Hab 2:3; Rom 2:4; 1 Tim 2:4; Rev 2:21

▸ HOLINESS

2:19 Pick your master. The promise of freedom in one form or another has influenced countless numbers of people throughout history. Peter's opponents made bold promises of freedom but could never deliver on them. The false teachers apparently perverted Paul's teaching on the law (see study notes on 3:15-16 and Jude 1:4) and claimed that their spiritual freedom provided license to sin. Nothing could be further from Paul's doctrine (Romans 6; Galatians 5:13). Peter rightly points out that freedom from morality is not freedom at all; it is slavery to corruption. In contrast to the teachers, Peter calls himself a slave of Jesus Christ (1:1). Only in slavery to Christ and His righteousness do people find the freedom for which they long. Does your moral compass point toward freedom in Christ or toward slavery in licentiousness? (***See Holiness****> Disciplines> Of Abstinence> Resisting worldly influences,* TopicGuide page A42.)

2:20-22 Passages like this lead many to claim that true Christians can permanently fall away from Christ. But this is not what Peter is really saying (John 6:37-40; 10:27-29). Here he uses very strong language to describe the false teachers' former profession of the Christian faith. By turning away from the truth, however, and running back to a life of lavish sin, they prove that they never belonged to God (see study note on 1:10; see also Acts 20:28-30; 1 John 2:19). As Peter illustrates, washing a dirty animal does not change the animal's nature. Turning away is worse than having never embraced the gospel, for it makes true repentance much less likely (Hebrews 6:4-9).

3:1 The previous letter that Peter mentions here may have been 1 Peter, but this is not known for certain. Peter probably wrote other letters that are now lost. This is also the case with Paul (see 1 Corinthians 5:9; 2 Corinthians 7:8; Colossians 4:16). The most noticeable similarities between the two letters are 1 Peter 1:12-13, 15 and 2 Peter 1:13-21. Other than that, the situations that the two letters address do not share much in common.

3:5-7 The false teachers confidently claimed that Jesus would not return in judgment. After all, they alleged, God had not intervened in the world's affairs since Creation (3:4). But Peter responds that God clearly intervened in the world after the initial Creation (Genesis 1:1-10), and He also commanded the floodwaters that destroyed the earth in Noah's day (Genesis 6–8). By this same reliable and powerful word, Peter argues, God currently preserves the world for a judgment (this time, by fire; see Isaiah 66:15-16; Malachi 4:1; 2 Thessalonians 1:6-8) that the false teachers will soon be unable to deny.

3:10 promise, as some people think. No, He is being patient for your sake. He does not want
Matt 24:43-44 1 Thes 5:2 anyone to be destroyed, but wants everyone to repent. 10But the day of the Lord will come
Rev 3:3; 16:5 as unexpectedly as a thief. Then the heavens will pass away with a terrible noise, and the
3:12 very elements themselves will disappear in fire, and the earth and everything on it will be
Ps 50:3 found to deserve judgment.*
1 Cor 1:7 11Since everything around us is going to be destroyed like this, what holy and godly
3:13 Isa 60:21; 65:17; lives you should live, 12looking forward to the day of God and hurrying it along. On that
66:22 day, He will set the heavens on fire, and the elements will melt away in the flames. 13But
Rev 21:1, 27; 22:15 we are looking forward to the new heavens and new earth He has promised, a world filled
3:14 with God's righteousness.
1 Thes 3:13 1 Pet 1:7 14And so, dear friends, while you are waiting for these things to happen, make every ef-
3:15 fort to be found living peaceful lives that are pure and blameless in His sight.
Rom 2:4 15And remember, the Lord's patience gives people time to be saved. This is what our be-
Eph 3:3 Col 1:25-27 loved brother Paul also wrote to you with the wisdom God gave him—16speaking of these
things in all of his letters. Some of his comments are hard to understand, and those who
3:16 2 Pet 2:14 are ignorant and unstable have twisted his letters to mean something quite different, just
3:17 as they do with other parts of Scripture. And this will result in their destruction.

1 Cor 10:12 2 Pet 2:18

PETER'S FINAL WORDS

Rev 2:5 3:18 17I am warning you ahead of time, dear friends. Be on guard so that you will not be carried
Rom 11:36 away by the errors of these wicked people and lose your own secure footing. 18Rather,
2 Tim 4:18 you must grow in the grace and knowledge of our Lord and Savior Jesus Christ.
2 Pet 1:2, 11; 2:20 All glory to Him, both now and forever! Amen.

3:10 Other manuscripts read *will be burned up;* still others read *will be found destroyed.*

▸ HOLINESS
3:11 Living in light of the end. When a mother warns, "Daddy's coming home soon!" her children clean up the house in a hurry because they fear his displeasure. When time is limited and judgment is near, we tend to focus on getting prepared. In contrast to the false teachers who denied the judgment to come (see study note on 3:5-7) and pursued sinful pleasures (2:13-14), Peter describes the destruction of the world to spur his readers on to godly behavior. If everything will be destroyed through fire, then we should pursue those things that survive judgment and last eternally (Matthew 6:19-20; 1 Corinthians 3:12-15). Spend your precious hours striving for what will last beyond this life. (***See Holiness***> *Maturing> Obeying God's Word> Obedience to God's Word encourages our assurance of salvation,* TopicGuide page A40.)

3:13 Those who have believed in Christ will ultimately inhabit a re-created earth. Descriptions of the new heavens and earth, which were first given by the Old Testament prophets (Isaiah 65:17-25; 66:22), depict a renewal of the present universe (not a complete replacement of it, as some suppose). The new creation will resemble the one we now experience but will be altogether more glorious (Romans 8:19-22). Most importantly, righteousness will dwell there (Revelation 21:1-4, 22-27). Until that time, heaven is the place in which those who have died in Christ await the new creation.

▸ MINISTRY
3:15 While we're waiting. Jesus promises to come back soon (Revelation 22:20), but His people are still waiting. Peter explains why: God's patience provides time for more people to find salvation in Christ (Romans 2:4). Millions of people have believed in Christ since the time that Peter wrote this letter, and we must expend ourselves for the sake of all those who have yet to believe (2 Timothy 2:10). Though the pain and injustice of this world cause us to cry out for the Lord's return (Romans 8:22-24; Revelation 22:20), we nonetheless must make the most of the time we have left. How are you spending your time? (***See Ministry***> *Great Commission> Witness> Turn others from Satan to God,* TopicGuide page A56.)

3:15-16 The apostle Paul emphasized freedom from the law (Romans 3:28; 5:20; Galatians 5:1; 1 Corinthians 6:12), and Peter's opponents probably took such teaching out of context to promote their corrupt lifestyles (2 Peter 2:18-19). Others certainly accused Paul of teaching similar things (Romans 3:7-8). Peter affirms that Paul's writings never condone sinful behavior, and in a passing comment, Peter even equates the authority of Paul's letters with that of the Old Testament writings (3:2).

PURPOSE

To encourage believers toward a personal relationship with a God they can know.

The apostle John was uniquely identified as the disciple whom Jesus loved (John 13:23; 19:26; 20:2; 21:7, 20, 24). Though Jesus loved the other disciples, His relationship with John seemed to have a special warmth and intimacy that is not found in Jesus' relationships with the other disciples. Often Jesus would bring along John, Peter, and James, leaving the other disciples behind for some reason (e.g., Matthew 17:1-13; Mark 9:2-12; Luke 9:28-36). John shared life with Jesus in a way that few others did. This almost certainly had a profound impact on John's understanding of what life with Jesus is all about.

In this epistle, John writes a letter to Christians everywhere, and he speaks like a pastor sharing from his personal relationship with God. Simply put, it's all about love—loving God and loving others like God loves.

DISCOVER GOD IN 1 JOHN

With rich imagery and picturesque language, John gives us many glimpses into the God we have come to know:

God Is Light: When John speaks of God as "light," he is using a metaphor that tells us that our God is wholly characterized by truth (1:5-7). He always speaks and lives out of truth, and because we are invited into life with this God, we are to live "in the light" as well (1:6-8; 2:8-10).

God Is Love: For John, a primary character trait of God is love (4:10-19). This does not mean that God is merely a name for a universal concept of love but that God Himself embodies and lives out what love really is. And as we said about light, all those who share life with God should learn to walk in love (4:7-8).

God Is Known in the Son: The abstract qualities of light and love can make God seem difficult to understand. How do we come to know such a God? For John, the answer is clear: We know this God because He has made Himself known in the Incarnation—God the Son became human (1:1-4; 2:21-23; 4:1-3; 4:13-16; 5:10-12). To know Jesus is to know God. To live in Jesus is to live in God.

GROWING THROUGH 1 JOHN

In 1 John, we discover that knowing God demands a heartfelt response of obedience. Knowing God and His love doesn't simply mean a warm relationship with Him—intimacy with God means He takes an active interest in our lives. Living in intimacy with God means change for us.

Walk in the Light: Because of our relationship with the God of truth, we can live in honesty and truth before Him and before one another (1:5–2:2). What does this mean? It means that we have to be honest about what is really going on in our relationships with others and we have to be ready to confess our sins when God reveals them.

Walk in Love: Because the One who has brought us into life and adopted us as His own children is characterized by love, John encourages us to live out our "family resemblance." We are to walk in love (3:11-20; 4:16-21). Because we share the life that flows out of God, what flows out of our lives should resemble Him.

Walk Free from Sin: John knows us; he knows what our lives are like. When he writes, he writes to encourage us to live free from sin (2:1; 3:4-10). Because we have entered into a shared life with Jesus, John invites us to live like Jesus (2:6). Does this seem like an impossibly high calling? For many who have settled into contentment with their sin, such a call might indeed be impossible to answer. But John truly believes that because of what Jesus has done and through the power of the Spirit we can grow to live truly holy lives. But John urges us not to despair if we do sin; he in fact admits that we will sin (1:8). Jesus will keep on cleansing us as we confess our sins (1:9-2:2). Yet John doesn't want us to settle for a life of perpetual confession. He invites us to grow in grace and live in freedom from sin.

DISCOVERY VERSES

We proclaim to you the One who existed from the beginning, whom we have heard and seen. We saw Him with our own eyes and touched Him with our own hands. He is the Word of life. This One who is life itself was revealed to us, and we have seen Him. And now we testify and proclaim to you that He is the One who is eternal life. He was with the Father, and then He was revealed to us. (1 JOHN 1:1-2)

And this is what God has testified: He has given us eternal life, and this life is in His Son. Whoever has the Son has life; whoever does not have God's Son does not have life. (1 JOHN 5:11-12)

1 JOHN FACTS

Author: No specific mention is made in this letter regarding who wrote it; all we can tell from the writing itself is that it was written by an eyewitness of the life and ministry of Jesus (1:1-4). Many of the earliest church fathers attested that the author was John, the apostle and close associate of Jesus.

Written to: It is difficult to glean much from this letter regarding its recipients. From 1 John 2:12-14, 19; 3:1; and 5:13 we can infer that John intended for his letter to be widely circulated. Its form reinforces this supposition as 1 John is more like a sermon than a letter. But it has a unified message against a certain problem that was likely localized—the Gnostic heresy. The Gnostics taught that matter was evil and thus a divine being could not take on human form—so Jesus' incarnation was rejected. This led to a rejection of morality (since what they did with their bodies didn't matter) and an intellectualizing of their religion.

Date of writing: There is little in the text to inform us about when John wrote this letter, and there is little early historical data to guide us. John does not mention the bout of persecution that occurred at the end of the Roman Emperor Domitian's reign, so the book was likely written prior to AD 95.

Setting: John was likely in Ephesus when he wrote this letter. We learn from early church history that John spent most of his latter years in Ephesus. It may well be that he wrote from there to churches in the surrounding area.

OUTLINE

- **1 JOHN 1:1–2:29**—Walk in Light: the Reality of Life with God
- **1 JOHN 3:1-24**—Walk in Love: the Experience of Life with God
- **1 JOHN 4:1-21**—Walk in the Spirit: Discernment in Life with God
- **1 JOHN 5:1-21**—Walk in Faith: the Heart of Life with God

INTRODUCTION

1 We proclaim to you the One who existed from the beginning,* whom we have heard
and seen. We saw Him with our own eyes and touched Him with our own hands. He
is the Word of life. 2 This One who is life itself was revealed to us, and we have seen Him.
And now we testify and proclaim to you that He is the One who is eternal life. He was with
the Father, and then He was revealed to us. 3 We proclaim to you what we ourselves have
actually seen and heard so that you may have fellowship with us. And our fellowship is
with the Father and with His Son, Jesus Christ. 4 We are writing these things so that you
may fully share our joy.*

LIVING IN THE LIGHT

5 This is the message we heard from Jesus* and now declare to you: God is light, and there
is no darkness in Him at all. 6 So we are lying if we say we have fellowship with God but go
on living in spiritual darkness; we are not practicing the truth. 7 But if we are living in the
light, as God is in the light, then we have fellowship with each other, and the blood of
Jesus, His Son, cleanses us from all sin.
8 If we claim we have no sin, we are only fooling ourselves and not living in the truth.
9 But if we confess our sins to Him, He is faithful and just to forgive us our sins and to
cleanse us from all wickedness. 10 If we claim we have not sinned, we are calling God a liar
and showing that His word has no place in our hearts.

1:1 John 1:1, 4, 14; 1 Jn 4:14
1:2 John 1:1-4; 19:35; 20:30-31; 1 Jn 5:11, 13, 20
1:4 John 15:11; 16:24
1:5 John 1:9; 8:12; 1 Tim 6:16
1:6 John 3:19-21; 2 Cor 6:14; 1 Jn 2:4
1:7 Isa 2:5; Heb 9:14; Rev 1:5; 7:14
1:8 Prov 20:9
1:9 Ps 32:5; Prov 28:13; Heb 9:14

1:1 Greek *What was from the beginning.* 1:4 Or *so that our joy may be complete;* some manuscripts read *your joy.* 1:5 Greek *from Him.*

1:1 First John and the letter to the Hebrews are the only two letters in the New Testament whose authors do not identify themselves in any explicit way. It is widely accepted that the author of this letter is the apostle John, based on similarities in writing style and theological focus (compare John 1:1 with 1 John 1:1). Both have explicit purpose statements; John wrote his gospel "that you may continue to believe" (John 20:31), and this letter is written "that you may know you have eternal life" (1 John 5:13).

1:1-4 By speaking of the "Word of life," John identifies Jesus as God's self-revelation and the revelation of His purposes through the created order. The Word was the cause of creation (note the connection to "Then God said" throughout Genesis 1); the Word came through the prophets, and now the Word is a man, Jesus Christ.

1:1, 3 John is likely writing in response to an early version of Gnosticism, which was a heretical teaching that pitted the spirit against the flesh. Gnostics viewed the spirit as pure good and the body, or the material world, as pure evil. For the Gnostics, if Jesus was purely good, then He could not have been truly physical. John confidently affirms the physicality of Jesus—he and the other disciples saw, heard, and touched Him. John makes a concerted effort to tell his readers that they must believe in Jesus Christ, who is God in a human body.

▸ WORSHIP
1:3-4 Loving God and loving others. Have you ever known someone who lashes out at Christians for no good reason? John shows that there is a circular relationship between how we relate to God and how we relate to others. People who are hostile to God transfer their anger to His people and institutions. On the other hand, for us in the church, the ministry of other believers energizes our fellowship with God. John wants his readers to recognize this relationship between loving God and loving other Christians, so he repeats this theme throughout the letter (for instance, 4:20; 5:2). If you are struggling with your relationship with God, is it possible that your problem stems from a relational issue with another person (Matthew 5:24)? Remember the intimate connection John shows between those relationships. (***See Worship****> NT> Our Role> Obedience> Loving Jesus means keeping His commands,* TopicGuide page A32.)

1:5 Throughout this letter, John uses light and darkness, familiar philosophical concepts of John's day, to frame his attacks on Gnosticism. In a Christian worldview, John's use of light and darkness harkens back to Genesis 1, where darkness symbolized chaos and light represented goodness and order. Elsewhere Scripture uses light to refer to moral purity and darkness to refer to immorality (Isaiah 5:20; Romans 13:11-14; Ephesians 5:8-14). Also, in everyday experience the nature of light is to reveal our surroundings, whereas the nature of darkness is to conceal. Scripture uses this aspect of light in passages such as Psalm 119:105: "Your word is a lamp to guide my feet and a light for my path." The statement "God is light" is comprehensive, meaning that it is God's nature to reveal Himself and all reality.

▸ WORSHIP
1:8-10 Repenting of sin. How often does sin begin from incorrect beliefs about God and ourselves? Apparently some in John's flock claimed that they were no longer sinners, but John simply said those people make God a liar—a hefty indictment. Sin is an intrusive and pervasive cancer that has infested every part of who we are: mind, body, will, heart, spirit, soul—everything. Just as a cancer patient cannot by sheer force of will rid himself of his cancer, we can't remove the rancor of sin from our life. Instead, John says, we must confess our sins and repent, continually recognizing who we are in relation to who Jesus is. God's gradual cleansing confirms that we belong to Christ. When He returns, we will be free from sin forever. Until then, we repent and receive His gracious forgiveness. (***See Worship****> NT> Cleansing> God requires repentance from known sin,* TopicGuide page A30.)

2 My dear children, I am writing this to you so that you will not sin. But if anyone does
sin, we have an advocate who pleads our case before the Father. He is Jesus Christ,
the One who is truly righteous. [2]He Himself is the sacrifice that atones for our sins—and
not only our sins but the sins of all the world.
[3]And we can be sure that we know Him if we obey His commandments. [4]If someone
claims, "I know God," but doesn't obey God's commandments, that person is a liar and is
not living in the truth. [5]But those who obey God's word truly show how completely they
love Him. That is how we know we are living in Him. [6]Those who say they live in God
should live their lives as Jesus did.

A NEW COMMANDMENT

[7]Dear friends, I am not writing a new commandment for you; rather it is an old one you
have had from the very beginning. This old commandment—to love one another—is the
same message you heard before. [8]Yet it is also new. Jesus lived the truth of this command-
ment, and you also are living it. For the darkness is disappearing, and the true light is al-
ready shining.
[9]If anyone claims, "I am living in the light," but hates a Christian brother or sister,* that
person is still living in darkness. [10]Anyone who loves another brother or sister* is living in
the light and does not cause others to stumble. [11]But anyone who hates another brother
or sister is still living and walking in darkness. Such a person does not know the way to go,
having been blinded by the darkness.

[12]I am writing to you who are God's children
because your sins have been forgiven through Jesus.*
[13]I am writing to you who are mature in the faith*
because you know Christ, who existed from the beginning.

2:9 Greek *hates his brother;* similarly in 2:11. 2:10 Greek *loves his brother.* 2:12 Greek *through His name.* 2:13 Or *to you fathers;* also in 2:14.

2:1 Rom 8:34; 1 Tim 2:5; Heb 7:25; 9:24
2:2 John 1:29; Rom 3:25; Heb 2:17
2:5 John 14:21, 23; 1 Jn 3:24; 4:13; 5:2
2:6 Matt 11:29; John 13:15; 1 Pet 2:21
2:7 John 13:34; 1 Jn 2:24; 3:11
2:8 John 1:9; 13:34; Rom 13:12; Eph 5:8; 1 Thes 5:5
2:10 Ps 119:165; Rom 14:13
2:11 John 12:35; 2 Cor 4:4; 2 Pet 1:9
2:12 1 Cor 6:11
2:13 John 1:1; 16:33; 1 Jn 1:1; 4:4; 5:18

2:7-8 John calls the command "to love one another" both an old commandment and a new commandment. It is based on the law of Moses (Deuteronomy 6:5; Leviticus 19:18) but emphasized by Jesus (Luke 10:26-28) and His brother James (James 2:8). The command to love one another spans covenants and epochs because it is of the very essence of what it means to live as God does.

2:12-14 John assures his readers that he is condemning the false teachers, and he offers specific encouragement to three differing groups in the church: "you who are God's children," "you who are mature in the faith," and "you who are young in the faith." Grouping the believers in his flock according to maturity, John proceeds to affirm each group's growing faith and reiterate the source of their assurance and hope.

BECAUSE GOD IS MERCIFUL

He forgives me of my sins when I sincerely confess them.

If we confess our sins to Him, He is faithful and just to forgive us our sins and to cleanse us from all wickedness.

1 JOHN 1:9

I am writing to you who are young in the faith
 because you have won your battle with the evil one.
14 I have written to you who are God's children
 because you know the Father.
I have written to you who are mature in the faith
 because you know Christ, who existed from the beginning.
I have written to you who are young in the faith
 because you are strong.
God's word lives in your hearts,
 and you have won your battle with the evil one.

DO NOT LOVE THIS WORLD

15 Do not love this world nor the things it offers you, for when you love the world, you do
not have the love of the Father in you. 16 For the world offers only a craving for physical
pleasure, a craving for everything we see, and pride in our achievements and possessions.
These are not from the Father, but are from this world. 17 And this world is fading away,
along with everything that people crave. But anyone who does what pleases God will live
forever.

WARNING ABOUT ANTICHRISTS

18 Dear children, the last hour is here. You have heard that the Antichrist is coming, and al-
ready many such antichrists have appeared. From this we know that the last hour has
come. 19 These people left our churches, but they never really belonged with us; otherwise
they would have stayed with us. When they left, it proved that they did not belong with us.
20 But you are not like that, for the Holy One has given you His Spirit,* and all of you
know the truth. 21 So I am writing to you not because you don't know the truth but because
you know the difference between truth and lies. 22 And who is a liar? Anyone who says that
Jesus is not the Christ.* Anyone who denies the Father and the Son is an antichrist.*
23 Anyone who denies the Son doesn't have the Father, either. But anyone who acknowl-
edges the Son has the Father also.
24 So you must remain faithful to what you have been taught from the beginning. If you
do, you will remain in fellowship with the Son and with the Father. 25 And in this fellowship
we enjoy the eternal life He promised us.
26 I am writing these things to warn you about those who want to lead you astray. 27 But
you have received the Holy Spirit,* and He lives within you, so you don't need anyone to

2:14 John 1:1-2; Eph 6:10; 1 Jn 1:1; 1:10
2:15 Rom 12:2; Jas 4:4
2:16 Rom 13:14; Eph 2:3
2:17 Matt 7:21; 1 Cor 7:31
2:18 Matt 24:24
2:19 Acts 20:30; 1 Cor 11:19
2:20 1 Jn 2:27
2:22 1 Jn 4:3
2:23 John 8:19; 17:3; 1 Jn 4:15; 5:1
2:24 1 Jn 4:15; 5:1; 2 Jn 1:9
2:25 John 3:15; 6:40; 17:3
2:26 1 Jn 3:7
2:27 John 14:16, 26; 16:13; 1 Cor 2:10-12; 1 Jn 2:20

2:20 Greek *But you have an anointing from the Holy One.* 2:22a Or *not the Messiah.* 2:22b Or *the antichrist.* 2:27a Greek *the anointing from Him.*

2:15 The "world" John is condemning is God's creation in its sin-corrupted and unredeemed state. This encompasses all material things and all pride and cravings that distract us from God. John is not suggesting that we ought not love the people of the world, but that we should hate the kingdom and pursuits of the world. Throughout the letter, John refers to two realms: the world that has rejected God and the kingdom introduced in Jesus Christ.

2:18-20 According to John, false teachers will lure people away from Christ. The Bible calls these teachers antichrists. In the last days, a man called the Antichrist will arise and try to destroy God's people, the Jews. Daniel prophesied about this coming person (Daniel 9:27; 11:31; 12:11). John would later write about this man of evil when he penned Revelation (19:19-21). Also, as he says in 1 John 2:22, "Anyone who denies the Father and the Son is an antichrist" (compare Jesus' words in Matthew 12:30). These are forerunners to the antichrist figure who will complete the fulfillment of Daniel's prophecy in Daniel 11:31 and 12:11.

▸ BIBLE

2:24-25 What do you know? It has been fashionable—but untrue—to say that we only know what we experience—what we have tasted, touched, felt. This carries over into the Christian life when we say that we only know Jesus as we experience Him, but this gives an excuse for us to keep from learning about God from His people throughout history and in our own time. John assumes that we can truly know those things that we've been taught (2:20), and this leads to his expectation that we will "remain faithful to what [we] have been taught from the beginning" (2:24). Though sin affects how we think (Mark 12:30; 2 Corinthians 3:14; 4:4), that does not render Christians incapable of knowing and loving God truly. God reveals Himself as He is and has given us the Holy Spirit, so we can be certain that reliable knowledge and true love of God is possible for us. Trust God's revelation of Himself through His Word—never doubt it! (***See Bible*** > *Uniqueness> Flawless> God's Word abides forever,* TopicGuide page A10.)

teach you what is true. For the Spirit* teaches you everything you need to know, and what
He teaches is true—it is not a lie. So just as He has taught you, remain in fellowship with
Christ.

LIVING AS CHILDREN OF GOD

28 And now, dear children, remain in fellowship with Christ so that when He returns, you
will be full of courage and not shrink back from Him in shame.
29 Since we know that Christ is righteous, we also know that all who do what is right are
God's children.

3 See how very much our Father loves us, for He calls us His children, and that is what
we are! But the people who belong to this world don't recognize that we are God's
children because they don't know Him. 2 Dear friends, we are already God's children, but
He has not yet shown us what we will be like when Christ appears. But we do know that we
will be like Him, for we will see Him as He really is. 3 And all who have this eager expecta-
tion will keep themselves pure, just as He is pure.
4 Everyone who sins is breaking God's law, for all sin is contrary to the law of God. 5 And
you know that Jesus came to take away our sins, and there is no sin in Him. 6 Anyone who
continues to live in Him will not sin. But anyone who keeps on sinning does not know Him
or understand who He is.
7 Dear children, don't let anyone deceive you about this: When people do what is right, it
shows that they are righteous, even as Christ is righteous. 8 But when people keep on sin-
ning, it shows that they belong to the devil, who has been sinning since the beginning. But
the Son of God came to destroy the works of the devil. 9 Those who have been born into

2:28 Col 3:4; 1 Thes 2:19; 1 Jn 3:2, 21
2:29 1 Jn 3:7, 10; 4:7
3:1 John 1:12-13; 16:3; 17:26
3:2 Ps 17:15; John 17:24; Rom 8:19, 29; 2 Cor 3:18
3:3 2 Cor 7:1
3:4 Matt 7:23
3:5 Isa 53:1-12; John 1:29; 2 Cor 5:21
3:6 Rom 6:14
3:8 John 8:44
3:9 Jas 1:18; 1 Pet 1:3

2:27b Greek *the anointing.*

▸ WORSHIP
2:29–3:1 Children of God. Perhaps you've heard someone say, "We are all God's children." In some sense, they are right—we all exist because we are God's handiwork, created in His image (Revelation 4:11). But this connection is not enough to put us in a right relationship with God. In 2:29, John explicitly says that a child of God is one who does what is right according to Christ's righteousness, but this is not what *makes* a person a child of God. Instead, John joyfully proclaims that God Himself makes us His children. God offers us this relationship as we confess our sin and believe in Christ's sacrifice for us. (***See Worship****> NT> Cleansing> God requires repentance from known sin,* TopicGuide page A30.)

3:9 When John writes that believers do not "make a practice of sinning" or "keep on sinning," he is not saying that we no longer sin. Rather, he is saying that those who possess progressive habits that go unchallenged or unmitigated do not demonstrate their true nature in Christ. Because children of God live righteously, those who display no righteousness in their lives cannot be children of God. While Christians still sin, it is not an accepted habit for them, and their sin is followed by regular and sincere repentance.

BECAUSE GOD KNOWS EVERYTHING

I will go to Him with all my questions and concerns.

God is greater than our feelings, and He knows everything.

1 JOHN 3:20

God's family do not make a practice of sinning, because God's life* is in them. So they can't keep on sinning, because they are children of God. 10 So now we can tell who are children of God and who are children of the devil. Anyone who does not live righteously and does not love other believers* does not belong to God.

LOVE ONE ANOTHER

11 This is the message you have heard from the beginning: We should love one another. 12 We must not be like Cain, who belonged to the evil one and killed his brother. And why did he kill him? Because Cain had been doing what was evil, and his brother had been doing what was righteous. 13 So don't be surprised, dear brothers and sisters,* if the world hates you.

14 If we love our Christian brothers and sisters,* it proves that we have passed from death to life. But a person who has no love is still dead. 15 Anyone who hates another brother or sister* is really a murderer at heart. And you know that murderers don't have eternal life within them.

16 We know what real love is because Jesus gave up His life for us. So we also ought to give up our lives for our brothers and sisters. 17 If someone has enough money to live well and sees a brother or sister* in need but shows no compassion—how can God's love be in that person?

18 Dear children, let's not merely say that we love each other; let us show the truth by our actions. 19 Our actions will show that we belong to the truth, so we will be confident when we stand before God. 20 Even if we feel guilty, God is greater than our feelings, and He knows everything.

21 Dear friends, if we don't feel guilty, we can come to God with bold confidence. 22 And we will receive from Him whatever we ask because we obey Him and do the things that please Him.

23 And this is His commandment: We must believe in the name of His Son, Jesus Christ, and love one another, just as He commanded us. 24 Those who obey God's commandments remain in fellowship with Him, and He with them. And we know He lives in us because the Spirit He gave us lives in us.

DISCERNING FALSE PROPHETS

4 Dear friends, do not believe everyone who claims to speak by the Spirit. You must test them to see if the spirit they have comes from God. For there are many false prophets in the world. 2 This is how we know if they have the Spirit of God: If a person claiming to be a prophet* acknowledges that Jesus Christ came in a real body, that person has the Spirit of God. 3 But if someone claims to be a prophet and does not acknowledge

3:10 John 1:12-13
3:11 John 13:34; 15:12, 17
3:12 Gen 4:3-8
3:13 John 15:18; 17:14
3:14 John 5:24
3:15 Matt 5:21-22; John 8:44; Gal 5:20-21
3:16 John 13:1; 15:13; Phil 2:17; 1 Thes 2:8
3:17 Deut 15:7-8; Jas 2:15
3:18 Rom 12:9; Jas 1:22
3:19 John 18:37
3:20 John 21:17
3:21 Rom 5:1
3:22 Matt 7:7; John 8:29; 14:13
3:23 John 6:29; 13:34; 15:17
3:24 Rom 8:9
4:1 1 Thes 5:21
4:2 John 1:14; 1 Cor 12:3

3:9 Greek *because His seed.* 3:10 Greek *does not love his brother.* 3:13 Greek *brothers.* 3:14 Greek *the brothers;* similarly in 3:16. 3:15 Greek *hates his brother.* 3:17 Greek *sees his brother.* 4:2 Greek *If a spirit;* similarly in 4:3.

3:15-19 Loving one another shows that we have passed from death to life (3:14). But those who hate others are still in the same spiritual state as murderers: dead (see also Matthew 5:21-22). Likewise, the actions of unrepentant misers show they lack God's love.

▸ SPIRITUAL WARFARE

3:21 The disease of guilt. Are Christians still supposed to feel guilty when they sin? Sometimes we fail to distinguish between guilt and conviction. Guilt condemns, while conviction transforms (2 Samuel 12:1-26; Psalm 32:3-4; Hebrews 4:12-13; 12:10). Guilt impedes us from coming to God with confidence, as John points out here. When we bring self-condemnation for sin upon ourselves, we ignore the wrath that the Father poured onto Christ as He hung on the cross (Isaiah 53). We also ignore the unsurpassed power exhibited in Christ's resurrection as He displayed His incontestable victory over sin, death, and the devil. Because our relationship with God and our identity as His children are the result of Christ's effective work, guilt is a disease that has no place in the healthy Christian. It not only distracts us from who we are, but it distracts from who God is and what He has done in us. What guilt are you carrying around? Through repentance, get rid of it as soon as possible. (***See Spiritual Warfare***> *Resisting Sin and Evil> Consequences> Of Disobedience> Guilt,* TopicGuide page A46.)

4:2-3 In the early church, many people were claiming to speak messages given to them by the Spirit of God, but some of these were false teachers who denied the true humanity of Jesus. John says that those who are truly speaking by God's Spirit will acknowledge the humanity of Christ.

the truth about Jesus, that person is not from God. Such a person has the spirit of the Antichrist, which you heard is coming into the world and indeed is already here.

4But you belong to God, my dear children. You have already won a victory over those people, because the Spirit who lives in you is greater than the spirit who lives in the world. 5Those people belong to this world, so they speak from the world's viewpoint, and the world listens to them. 6But we belong to God, and those who know God listen to us. If they do not belong to God, they do not listen to us. That is how we know if someone has the Spirit of truth or the spirit of deception.

LOVING ONE ANOTHER

7Dear friends, let us continue to love one another, for love comes from God. Anyone who loves is a child of God and knows God. 8But anyone who does not love does not know God, for God is love.

9God showed how much He loved us by sending His one and only Son into the world so that we might have eternal life through Him. 10This is real love—not that we loved God, but that He loved us and sent His Son as a sacrifice to take away our sins.

11Dear friends, since God loved us that much, we surely ought to love each other. 12No one has ever seen God. But if we love each other, God lives in us, and His love is brought to full expression in us.

13And God has given us His Spirit as proof that we live in Him and He in us. 14Furthermore, we have seen with our own eyes and now testify that the Father sent His Son to be the Savior of the world. 15All who confess that Jesus is the Son of God have God living in them, and they live in God. 16We know how much God loves us, and we have put our trust in His love.

God is love, and all who live in love live in God, and God lives in them. 17And as we live in God, our love grows more perfect. So we will not be afraid on the day of judgment, but we can face Him with confidence because we live like Jesus here in this world.

4:4 John 12:31; Rom 8:31; 1 Jn 2:1
4:5 John 15:19; 17:14, 16
4:6 John 8:47; 14:17; 1 Cor 14:37; 1 Tim 4:1
4:7 1 Jn 2:29; 3:11
4:8 1 Jn 4:7, 16
4:9 John 3:16
4:10 Rom 5:8, 10; 1 Jn 2:2
4:11 Matt 18:33
4:12 John 1:18; 14:23; 1 Tim 6:16
4:13 Rom 8:9; 1 Jn 3:24
4:14 John 1:14; 3:17; 4:42; 1 Jn 2:2
4:15 John 6:69
4:17 1 Jn 2:5; 3:21

4:8 The incomparable magnitude and majesty of God's love leads John to equate God with love (see also 4:16). God is so loving that He personifies everything that love is in all its fullness.

▸ GOD

4:9-10 What is love? It's impossible to read John without asking, "What is love?" Is it a feeling? An action? A commitment? A way of believing and thinking? Yes—all of the above. But we can't glean the definition of love from our own lives because, as sinners, we cannot love perfectly. Love can only be properly defined according to who God is and what He has done. God's love for us defines and shapes our love for Him. God demonstrated His patient, passionate pursuit of us by sending His Son to be a sacrifice for us. He frees us from the hateful effects of sin, and we receive eternal life through Him—that's love at its best. Obviously, we can't match that kind of love perfectly, but as Christians we are called to imitate it. How can you better love family, friends, coworkers, neighbors, and strangers as God has loved you? (***See God***> *God's Attributes*> *Loving,* TopicGuide page A17.)

BECAUSE
GOD IS HOLY

I will devote myself to him in purity, worship and service.

If we love each other, God lives in us, and His love is brought to full expression in us.

1 JOHN 4:12

FOR THE NEXT *GOD IS HOLY* FEATURE SEE PAGE 2262.

GOD IS LOVE

MANY YEARS AGO, a popular song hit the charts that repeated the phrase "love, love, love" over 10 times. People yearn to be loved. How much do you think God loves you? Most of us can quote the verse, "God is love" (4:8), but what does that *really* mean to you? How does knowing that "God is love" affect your life? Does it change the nitty-gritty details of your day? One way to understand love is to see how God uses the word "love" in the Bible—both in describing God's love for us and in describing how we are to love others. Here are a few of the many passages about love:

- God's protective love—Psalm 91:14
- Spreading God's love—John 13:34
- Sacrificial love—John 15:13
- The fruit of love—Galatians 5:22-23
- Perfect love—1 John 4:17
- Love for God—Matthew 22:37
- Obedience and love—John 14:15
- God's love for us—1 John 4:19
- Christ's example of love—Ephesians 5:2
- The power of love—Romans 8:39

Notice that the same pattern is clear in all of them, regardless of the situation: God loves His people and expects us to spread His love to others in return. When we don't spread God's love, we become like a shutoff valve to the world, stopping the flow of God's love through us. Of course, spreading God's love is a difficult task. Not everyone will want to receive our love, and some will even outright reject us. In fact, loving others always makes us vulnerable, as the suffering and death of Jesus Christ made very clear.

But when we love others with God's love, He promises to be beside us. First John 4:16 says, "We know how much God loves us, and we have put our trust in His love. God is love, and all who live in love live in God, and God lives in them." Because Jesus, God's Son, gave us the greatest example of love through His sacrifice on the cross for our sins, we know what it really means to love others. Value people as Jesus values people. Speak with His gentleness. Act with His kindness. Forgive with His thoroughness. Love with His intensity.

18 Such love has no fear, because perfect love expels all fear. If we are afraid, it is for fear
of punishment, and this shows that we have not fully experienced His perfect love. 19 We
love each other* because He loved us first.

20 If someone says, "I love God," but hates a Christian brother or sister,* that person is a
liar; for if we don't love people we can see, how can we love God, whom we cannot see?
21 And He has given us this command: Those who love God must also love their Christian
brothers and sisters.*

FAITH IN THE SON OF GOD

5 Everyone who believes that Jesus is the Christ* has become a child of God. And
everyone who loves the Father loves His children, too. 2 We know we love God's chil-
dren if we love God and obey His commandments. 3 Loving God means keeping His com-
mandments, and His commandments are not burdensome. 4 For every child of God
defeats this evil world, and we achieve this victory through our faith. 5 And who can win
this battle against the world? Only those who believe that Jesus is the Son of God.

6 And Jesus Christ was revealed as God's Son by His baptism in water and by shedding
His blood on the cross*—not by water only, but by water and blood. And the Spirit, who is
truth, confirms it with His testimony. 7 So we have these three witnesses*—8 the Spirit, the
water, and the blood—and all three agree. 9 Since we believe human testimony, surely we
can believe the greater testimony that comes from God. And God has testified about His
Son. 10 All who believe in the Son of God know in their hearts that this testimony is true.

4:18 Rom 8:15
4:20 1 Jn 2:4; 3:17
4:21 Matt 5:43; 22:37-39
5:1 John 1:13; 3:3; 8:42
5:2 1 Jn 2:3
5:3 Deut 30:11; Matt 11:30; John 14:15
5:5 Rom 8:37
5:6 John 1:31-34; 14:7; 19:34-35
5:9 Matt 3:16-17; John 5:32-37; 8:17-18
5:10 John 3:33; Rom 8:16; Gal 4:6

4:19 Greek *We love.* Other manuscripts read *We love God;* still others read *We love Him.* 4:20 Greek *hates his brother.* 4:21 Greek *The one who loves God must also love his brother.* 5:1 Or *the Messiah.* 5:6 Greek *This is He who came by water and blood.* 5:7 A few very late manuscripts add *in heaven—the Father, the Word, and the Holy Spirit, and these three are one. And we have three witnesses on earth.*

4:18 The "perfect love" John refers to is not our love for God, but God's love for us. What John previously referred to as "real love" in 4:10, he calls "perfect love" here. Our intimate awareness of Christ's righteousness credited to us enables us to love one another.

5:1-3 John says that we *become* children of God through an act of faith in His Son, but *being* children of God means loving other children of God. We can't properly be called a Christian without loving other Christians (Matthew 22:37-40). Many of God's commands, in both the Old and the New Testaments, revolve around how this love is to play out in community with other believers (e.g., avoiding lies, sexual purity, not stealing). By keeping God's commandments, we show our love to others.

5:6-8 John so far has described Jesus as being both God and man; now he moves on to describe Jesus' mission on earth. God revealed His Son through two baptisms: one in the Jordan River with water to symbolize Christ's humanity (and declare His divinity) and one on Golgotha with blood to achieve our redemption. These baptisms confirmed that Jesus is the Son of God.

BECAUSE GOD IS HOLY

I will devote myself to him in purity, worship and service.

Keep away from anything that might take God's place in your hearts.

1 JOHN 5:21

FOR THE NEXT *GOD IS HOLY* FEATURE SEE PAGE 2287.

5:11 John 1:4
5:12 John 3:15-16, 36; 5:24; 14:6; 17:2-3
5:13 John 20:31
5:14 Matt 7:7; John 14:13; 15:7
5:16 Exod 23:21; Jer 7:16; 14:11; Matt 12:31; Heb 6:4-6; 10:26; Jas 5:15
5:18 John 10:28-29
5:19 John 17:15
5:20 Luke 24:45; John 1:1, 4; 17:3; Rom 9:5
5:21 1 Cor 10:14; 1 Thes 1:9

Those who don't believe this are actually calling God a liar because they don't believe what God has testified about His Son.

11 And this is what God has testified: He has given us eternal life, and this life is in His Son. 12 Whoever has the Son has life; whoever does not have God's Son does not have life.

CONCLUSION

13 I have written this to you who believe in the name of the Son of God, so that you may know you have eternal life. 14 And we are confident that He hears us whenever we ask for anything that pleases Him. 15 And since we know He hears us when we make our requests, we also know that He will give us what we ask for.

16 If you see a Christian brother or sister* sinning in a way that does not lead to death, you should pray, and God will give that person life. But there is a sin that leads to death, and I am not saying you should pray for those who commit it. 17 All wicked actions are sin, but not every sin leads to death.

18 We know that God's children do not make a practice of sinning, for God's Son holds them securely, and the evil one cannot touch them. 19 We know that we are children of God and that the world around us is under the control of the evil one.

20 And we know that the Son of God has come, and He has given us understanding so that we can know the true God.* And now we live in fellowship with the true God because we live in fellowship with His Son, Jesus Christ. He is the only true God, and He is eternal life.

21 Dear children, keep away from anything that might take God's place in your hearts.*

5:16 Greek *a brother.* 5:20 Greek *the One who is true.* 5:21 Greek *keep yourselves from idols.*

▸ GOD

5:10-11 Calling God a liar. Have you ever heard anyone call God a liar? Such an extreme act may seem rare, but in reality any person who rejects Jesus as Savior is doing just that. God has clearly testified concerning His Son's deity. If you've heard about the significance of Christ's life, death, and resurrection and still do not really believe it, ask God to continue revealing Himself to you and to send the Holy Spirit as an agent of change in your heart. If you have embraced these truths, be humbled by how amazing God is and how patient He was with you in your former unbelief. (***See God***> *God's Attributes> True> The Holy Spirit is characterized by truth in every way,* TopicGuide page A18.)

5:13 John now explicitly says what he has been implicitly writing about—that he wants his readers to *know* that they have eternal life. As he says in 2:24-25, we already enjoy eternal life now. Eternal life isn't some reward that we receive once we finish this life, but is something that God invites us into by giving us His Holy Spirit. We enter into fellowship with the Father and the Son through the Holy Spirit.

5:16 There has been much debate concerning what John means by "a sin that leads to death." Many have equated it with the unforgivable sin Jesus refers to in Matthew 12:21-32 while others have thought that John might mean open defiance toward and rejection of God's testimony concerning Himself. Still others believe it is a special case where the person dies while in deep moral or theological sin. Whatever the case, prayer is no longer required for that person as they are either apostate (Hebrews 6:4-6) or already experiencing judgment due to their passing from this life.

2 JOHN

PURPOSE

To demonstrate that true love and love for truth go together in the family of God.

During this time in history, churches were meeting in homes. Pastors were caring for congregations that were scattered around the area. Individual house churches often welcomed traveling teachers or evangelists, hoping to hear a word from the Lord or find encouragement in their lives with Jesus. God used many of these traveling ministers to spread the message of Jesus. But others took advantage of their status, gaining entrance into a local church to receive support while undermining the truth. They no doubt *claimed* to know Jesus, but what they taught and how they lived betrayed the truth: They didn't know the true God.

With a pastor's concern, John writes to advise a Christian woman and her family on how to respond when false teachers request hospitality. John's letter has a particularly important message for the church today as it is increasingly confronted with those who use religious language to ask for our money, but do not teach the core truths about Jesus.

DISCOVER GOD IN 2 JOHN

Cults and other false religions frequently attack the doctrine of the Incarnation—they know that if Jesus is not the God-man, then Christianity is little different from any other moralistic, monotheistic religion.

Jesus, Son of God and Son of Mary: This letter clearly states a recurring theme in John's writing, found in his Gospel and in his epistles: If anyone does not preach Jesus' full deity and full humanity, they are false teachers and are to be rejected (1:7-9).

GROWING THROUGH 2 JOHN

Every generation of Christians faces their own challenges to the truth. How should we respond to those who come claiming to know Jesus but appear to not "know the truth"?

Keep Loving: It might be easy to adopt a "fortress mentality" where we bar the doors and windows and refuse to welcome others who claim to know Jesus for fear of being misled. Indeed, we must guard against false teachers, and John affirms this. But John also tells us that we cannot let the fear of false teaching keep us from genuinely loving those who are genuine brothers and sisters in the family of God (1:4-6).

Be Discerning: Loving others does not mean that we must embrace any and all who come wanting to tell us about "the real Jesus." From John's day until the present, there are those who claim to know Jesus but who do not truly know Him. John instructs believers to be discerning about such people (1:7-11). This doesn't mean we should not have any relationship with those who don't know Jesus—otherwise we would have difficulty reaching them with the gospel. But John warns against welcoming, supporting, and encouraging those who teach false doctrine in the church.

2 JOHN FACTS

Author: John, the beloved disciple, identifies himself in this letter simply as "the elder" (1:1; "John" is not included in the original text). John's authorship of this letter is substantiated by its similarity to both 1 John and the Gospel of John in style, vocabulary, and content.

DISCOVERY VERSES

Love means doing what God has commanded us, and He has commanded us to love one another, just as you heard from the beginning. (2 JOHN 1:6)

Many deceivers have gone out into the world. They deny that Jesus Christ came in a real body. Such a person is a deceiver and an antichrist. (2 JOHN 1:7)

Written to: The recipient of this letter is "the chosen lady" (1:1). Some believe John used this expression to refer to a local church and its members ("her children"; verse 1). Others, however, regard the specific references to "your home" (1:10) and to talking with her "face to face" (1:12) as evidence that John is writing to a particular individual. In the book of Acts we encounter a woman named Lydia (Acts 16:11-15, 40) who opens her home to the spread of the kingdom. It is likely that John has someone like Lydia in mind as he writes. He writes to a woman he knows who hosts a local church in her home.

Date of writing: There is little indication in the text to inform us about when John wrote this letter. However, it is likely that it was written around the time that 1 John was written, as there are parallel concerns about Gnosticism and similar passages (compare 2 John 1:7 with 1 John 4:2-3). The emphasis of his "elder" status (1:1, see 3 John 1:1) has led many to suggest a later date for the letters of John: AD 85–95.

Setting: There is also little indication about where John or the "chosen lady" were when he wrote this letter. We do know from early church history that John spent most of his latter years in Ephesus. It may well be that he wrote from there.

OUTLINE

- **2 JOHN 1:1-3**—I Love You: John's Greeting
- **2 JOHN 1:4-6**—I Ask You: John's Request to Love
- **2 JOHN 1:7-11**—I Warn You: John's Call to Discernment
- **2 JOHN 1:12-13**—I Will See You: John's Plan to Visit

1:1 1 Pet 5:13; 1 Jn 3:18-19; 3 Jn 1:1
1:2 John 8:32; 14:17; 1 Jn 1:8; 3:18-19
1:3 1 Tim 1:2
1:4 3 Jn 1:3-4
1:5 John 13:34; 15:12; 1 Jn 2:7
1:6 John 14:15, 23-24; 1 Jn 2:5, 7; 4:7-12; 5:3
1:7 1 Tim 4:1-5; 2 Pet 2:1-3; 1 Jn 2:18, 26; 4:1-3
1:8 Matt 10:41-42; 1 Cor 3:8-9
1:9 John 8:31; 1 Jn 2:23
1:10 Rom 16:17; Eph 5:11
1:11 1 Tim 5:22
1:12 Num 12:8; 1 Jn 1:4; 3 Jn 1:13-14

GREETINGS

This letter is from John, the elder.*
I am writing to the chosen lady and to her children,* whom I love in the truth—as
does everyone else who knows the truth—2because the truth lives in us and will be with us
forever.
3Grace, mercy, and peace, which come from God the Father and from Jesus Christ—the
Son of the Father—will continue to be with us who live in truth and love.

LIVE IN THE TRUTH

4How happy I was to meet some of your children and find them living according to the
truth, just as the Father commanded.
5I am writing to remind you, dear friends,* that we should love one another. This is not a
new commandment, but one we have had from the beginning. 6Love means doing what
God has commanded us, and He has commanded us to love one another, just as you
heard from the beginning.
7I say this because many deceivers have gone out into the world. They deny that Jesus
Christ came* in a real body. Such a person is a deceiver and an antichrist. 8Watch out that
you do not lose what we* have worked so hard to achieve. Be diligent so that you receive
your full reward. 9Anyone who wanders away from this teaching has no relationship with
God. But anyone who remains in the teaching of Christ has a relationship with both the
Father and the Son.
10If anyone comes to your meeting and does not teach the truth about Christ, don't in-
vite that person into your home or give any kind of encouragement. 11Anyone who en-
courages such people becomes a partner in their evil work.

CONCLUSION

12I have much more to say to you, but I don't want to do it with paper and ink. For I hope to
visit you soon and talk with you face to face. Then our joy will be complete.
13Greetings from the children of your sister,* chosen by God.

1a Greek *From the elder.* 1b Or *the church God has chosen and its members.* 5 Greek *I urge you, lady.* 7 Or *will come.* 8 Some manuscripts read *you.* 13 Or *from the members of your sister church.*

1:1 While the writer simply identifies himself as "the elder," it is commonly accepted that John the apostle is the author. This self-identification sets the tone for the rest of the letter. In Greek, as in English, *elder* simply refers to an older man, but it was also used to refer to an official position of leadership within the church (see Philippians 1:1; 1 Timothy 3:1-7; Titus 1:6-9; James 5:14).

1:4 In 2 John we are given a brief summary of the same themes as in 1 John: the contrast between truth and error (compare 1 John 1:8–2:6; 5:6-12), between love and hatred (1 John 3:14-17; 4:7-21), and between the church and the world (1 John 2:12-17; 4:4-6). As was typical in letters like this, John expresses joy at good news he has received concerning his readers. But this also leads him to challenge their weaknesses as a community and to warn them against false prophets who were among them.

1:7 In Acts 20:29-30 Paul warns against false teachers, calling them "vicious wolves" (see also 2 Timothy 3:1-7; 4:3-4). John warns his flock against being led astray by "many deceivers." John is concerned that his dear brothers and sisters will deny that Jesus Christ was and is fully human. The deceivers might have been an early sect of Gnostics, who pitted matter, which they considered completely evil, against spirit, which they considered perfectly good. According to such antichrists, then, Christ could not be perfectly good and embodied in flesh and blood. Instead, they would have said that Christ only took on our flesh temporarily or only appeared to be human without truly being human.

▸ CHURCH

1:7-9 Misleading messages. People attend church for different reasons. Some come out of curiosity, and others because God is drawing them to Himself. "Some" believers among John's audience were living according to the truth (1:4), but "many deceivers" had wandered away from "this teaching." The deceivers may have formerly been members of the church that John was writing to, but they were eventually led astray by new, unscriptural ideas about God. We, too, must be careful not to allow our understanding of God to be shaped by ideas that contradict Scripture. John reminds his readers to obey the command that they heard in the beginning (1:6). Stay focused on the foundational truths of the Christian faith no matter how long you have been a Christian. When people come your way who advocate changes in basic Christian beliefs, do not hesitate to point out their error according to the Scriptures. (***See Church****> Role> Preach> Instructions> Prevent doctrinal error,* TopicGuide page A50.)

3 JOHN

PURPOSE

To encourage the church to show wisdom in their hospitality, especially toward ministers.

Ring! It's another phone call from someone wanting you to donate to a cause. Or perhaps it's an e-mail, or someone knocking on your door. In John's day, as in ours, ministers and ministries needed money. John gives advice to his dear friends—and to us—on how to decide who should be welcomed and who should be sent away.

As the Good News was first spreading, God used many traveling preachers and teachers and evangelists to spread the message of Jesus. But others often took advantage of this; false teachers would seek to gain entrance into a local church to receive support but were all the while undermining the truth. Every "local church" faced this abuse.

It is good to withhold support and encouragement from those who spread false teaching. But is there a danger in shutting the doors too tight and barring the windows a bit too firmly? John suggests to us that there is, indeed, a needed caution. We cannot turn away true followers of Jesus out of our concern for false teaching.

DISCOVER GOD IN 3 JOHN

All Christian charity is based on the goodness of God—He gives freely, to both good and bad people (Matthew 5:45), so that all may know Him as a merciful and gracious God.

God's Goodness: Although John does not state this explicitly, he clearly implies that God is known for His goodness. When John encourages Gaius to welcome those who are genuine brothers, he states that those who know God do what is good; those who do not do good do not know God (1:11). God Himself is good, so those who do good are showing their "family resemblance."

GROWING THROUGH 3 JOHN

Although this letter is short, it provides growing disciples with a few pointers about how to recognize those who are effective servants of the true God:

Walking in the Truth: True servants of God "walk" or live according to the truth found in Jesus, and this should be true for all believers (1:3-4).

Unconcerned about Glory: John points out that a local leader names Diotrephes is apparently not living the way Jesus would want. He wants recognition and status for himself (1:9-10). In John's eyes, this is something that marks him out as something less than a true servant of God.

Doing What Is Good: All too often we read in the news about someone claiming to be a minister of Jesus and living in deceit, either handling finances improperly or engaging in immoral behavior. John clearly says that such people are not true servants of God. Though they may be believers, they are not living as a true follower of God should live (1:11-12).

3 JOHN FACTS

Author: John, the beloved disciple, identifies himself in this letter simply as "the elder" (1:1, "John" is not included in the original text). He was persecuted for his faith in Jesus but never martyred, probably living into his 90s. Though some debate it, John's authorship of this letter is substantiated by its similarity to both 1 John and the Gospel of John in style, vocabulary, and content.

Written to: John is writing this letter to Gaius (1:1), apparently a leader in a local congregation. We have no clear indication as to where Gaius lived. His name is a common Roman name; perhaps he belongs to a church somewhere in the Roman province of Asia.

Date of writing: There is little indication in the text to inform us about when John wrote this letter. Outside of this text, there is little historical information that proves to be helpful. It is likely that it was written around the time that John wrote his first epistle: after writing his Gospel and before the time of his death. That would place it somewhere between AD 85 and 95.

Setting: There is little in the text to help us assess where John was when he wrote this letter. We do know from early church history that John spent most of his latter years in Ephesus. It may well be that he wrote from there.

DISCOVERY VERSES

Follow only what is good. Remember that those who do good prove that they are God's children, and those who do evil prove that they do not know God.

(3 JOHN 1:11)

OUTLINE

- **3 JOHN 1:1-8**—Encouraging Gaius: Continue to Love
- **3 JOHN 1:9-12**—Confronting Diotrephes: Stop Living Selfishly
- **3 JOHN 1:13-15**—Promising His Presence: I'll Visit You Soon

GREETINGS

This letter is from John, the elder.*
I am writing to Gaius, my dear friend, whom I love in the truth.
2Dear friend, I hope all is well with you and that you are as healthy in body as you are
strong in spirit. 3Some of the traveling teachers* recently returned and made me very
happy by telling me about your faithfulness and that you are living according to the truth.
4I could have no greater joy than to hear that my children are following the truth.

CARING FOR THE LORD'S WORKERS

5Dear friend, you are being faithful to God when you care for the traveling teachers who
pass through, even though they are strangers to you. 6They have told the church here of
your loving friendship. Please continue providing for such teachers in a manner that
pleases God. 7For they are traveling for the Lord,* and they accept nothing from people
who are not believers.* 8So we ourselves should support them so that we can be their part-
ners as they teach the truth.
9I wrote to the church about this, but Diotrephes, who loves to be the leader, refuses to
have anything to do with us. 10When I come, I will report some of the things he is doing
and the evil accusations he is making against us. Not only does he refuse to welcome the
traveling teachers, he also tells others not to help them. And when they do help, he puts
them out of the church.
11Dear friend, don't let this bad example influence you. Follow only what is good. Re-
member that those who do good prove that they are God's children, and those who do
evil prove that they do not know God.*
12Everyone speaks highly of Demetrius, as does the truth itself. We ourselves can say
the same for him, and you know we speak the truth.

CONCLUSION

13I have much more to say to you, but I don't want to write it with pen and ink. 14For I hope
to see you soon, and then we will talk face to face.
15*Peace be with you.
Your friends here send you their greetings. Please give my personal greetings to each of
our friends there.

1:1 2 Jn 1:1
1:3 2 Jn 1:4
1:4 1 Cor 4:15; Gal 4:19; 1 Jn 2:1
1:5 Rom 12:13; Heb 13:2; 1 Pet 4:10
1:6 Col 1:10; Titus 3:13
1:7 Matt 10:9-14; Mark 6:8-13; Luke 9:3-5; 10:4-11; Acts 20:33, 35
1:9 Matt 20:27
1:10 John 9:22, 34; 2 Jn 1:12; 3 Jn 1:5
1:11 Ps 34:14; 1 Jn 2:29; 3:6, 9-10
1:12 John 19:35; 21:24
1:13 Num 12:8; 2 Jn 1:12
1:14 2 Jn 1:12

1 Greek *From the elder.* 3 Greek *the brothers;* also in verses 5 and 10. 7a Greek *They went out on behalf of the Name.* 7b Greek *from Gentiles.* 11 Greek *they have not seen God.* 15 Some English translations combine verses 14 and 15 into verse 14.

1:1 While the writer simply identified himself as "the elder," it is commonly accepted that John the apostle is the author. Gaius is a common New Testament name, appearing in reference to multiple persons in Acts 19:29, Acts 20:4, Romans 16:23, and 1 Corinthians 1:14. We do not have enough evidence to identify which Gaius John was writing to, but we know that John deeply cared about the man. John refers to Gaius as his "dear friend" four times in this concise letter and describes him as one "whom I love in the truth."

1:3 The traveling teachers (literally, "brothers") mentioned here were itinerant missionaries who needed lodging as they went from town to town, and Gaius provided a home for them. The missionaries were probably John's source of information about Gaius, Diotrephes, and Demetrius. It becomes evident that John views an open house and an open heart as proof of faithfulness to God (see 1 John 3:17).

▸ CHURCH

1:5-6 Toward faithfulness. How does faith relate to life? John intimately links faithfulness in Gaius's life with the way he lived. He affirms Gaius's continuous practice of welcoming brothers who are strangers and admonishes him to continue to do so. We all grow weary of doing good and need God's people around us in order to continue in faithfulness. By providing for one another's needs we both imitate God and attest to His faithful provision to us before the world. How can you build up those around you and encourage them in faithfulness? (***See Church***> *What> Many Titles> Flock> A place for God's family,* TopicGuide page A48.)

1:9 The traveling teachers gave John a report concerning Diotrephes that was in great contrast with the report he received about Gaius and Demetrius (1:12). Whereas Gaius and Demetrius welcomed the missionaries with Christian love and warmth, Diotrephes went so far as to forbid other members in the church that he pastored from extending hospitality to them. These contrasting attitudes parallel the difference between those who know God and those who do not.

PURPOSE

To encourage Christians to passionately defend the truth about Jesus.

Do you realize that you are in a war? It's not a physical battle between two nations; it is a battle for truth—the truth about the Good News of Jesus Christ.

In this brief note, Jude uses vibrant and passionate language to warn his audience of the dangers of consorting with and believing those who teach lies about Jesus. The awful consequences of associating with those teaching heresy are too great for Jude to be overly concerned about being misinterpreted—he speaks boldly and concisely.

False teaching continues to this day. You may not think in terms of war or battle when it comes to the truth that you have come to know in Jesus, but make no mistake—there are forces arrayed against those truths you hold as precious. And whether you want to be or not, you are involved in that war. How will you fight? What is at stake? Bad teaching won't just go away if we ignore it; as in Jude's day, those who hold to truth must not surrender to those who hate it.

DISCOVER GOD IN JUDE

Through his call to resist false teaching, Jude affirms a powerful and encouraging truth about God:

God Is the One Who Keeps Us: False teaching and erroneous doctrine constantly bombard the church. How are we to stand against such an onslaught? Jude reminds us that we are kept safe and secure by the power and grace of God (1:1, 24-25). Though we are to resist false teaching, we do not need to fear for ourselves. God will keep us secure as we rest in Him.

GROWING THROUGH JUDE

Jude has helpful insights for those who fight the war for the truth about Jesus Christ:

Cling to True Doctrine: True faith is not merely what you personally *want* to believe; it is what the church has embraced as the foundational truths of the Christian life (2 Thessalonians 2:15; 2 Timothy 2:2; 3:14-17). Christianity has a set of uniting, corporately-affirmed beliefs that span the ages, and while the church is always reforming and seeking to become more faithful to God's truth, we must be equally committed to the ancient, universally affirmed beliefs of God's people.

Reject False Teachers: If false teachers are not in touch with the truth, then they are not in touch with God. That being the case, what drives them forward in their "ministry"? Jude tells us they are moved by their own desires, and not by the Spirit of God (1:20). Though false teachers may use language that mentions the Spirit, and though they may claim to be led by the Spirit, Jude says they do not have the Holy Spirit in them (1:19). Jude joins Jesus in warning us of all the dangers and doom of religious-sounding people who are devoid of the Holy Spirit (Matthew 25:31-46).

JUDE FACTS

Author: It is clear from the Gospel accounts that Jesus had brothers (technically, half-brothers, having the same mother but not the same father; Matthew 13:55; Mark 6:3). It is possible that some of Jesus' brothers were actually his step-brothers, who had been brought into the marriage by Joseph, who could have been a widower. Regardless of their status, one of those brothers was James, who penned the epistle that bears his name (see the introductory remarks on James, page 2223). The opening greeting in this epistle identifies the author as Jude, the brother of James and a slave of Jesus (1:1). For Jude to identify himself as the brother of James suggests that his brother was someone of reasonable note; this would make sense if he is referring to James, the brother of Jesus. Neither James nor Jude, however, seeks to capitalize on their family ties to Jesus. They are quite content to identify themselves as slaves of Jesus (James 1:1; Jude 1:1).

DISCOVERY VERSES

But you, dear friends, must build each other up in your most holy faith, pray in the power of the Holy Spirit, and await the mercy of our Lord Jesus Christ, who will bring you eternal life. In this way, you will keep yourselves safe in God's love. (JUDE 1:20-21)

Written to: Jude only gives us a very broad description of those to whom he is writing: "To all who have been called by God the Father" (1:1). Little else can be learned of the recipients.

Date of writing: There is no internal evidence citing a date, but there is one bit of evidence to guide the dating of Jude—the relationship of the book to 2 Peter, with whom Jude shares most of its themes and language. Second Peter likely preceded Jude, based on two points. First, 2 Peter anticipates coming false teachers—but Jude serves as the fulfillment of this (compare 2 Peter 2:1-2; 3:3 to Jude 1:4, 11-12, 17-18). Second, Jude quotes 2 Peter 3:3 and cites it as a quote from an apostle. If 2 Peter was written in the late 60s, then the date for Jude must be after that time but prior to the end of a normal lifespan of one of Jesus' brothers, which would place the book sometime between AD 70 and AD 90.

Setting: There are no real indicators, either in the text or in the early church fathers, to help us discern where Jude wrote from or exactly where his recipients resided.

OUTLINE

- **JUDE 1:1-19**—The Danger of False Teachers
- **JUDE 1:20-25**—A Call to Persevere

GREETINGS FROM JUDE

This letter is from Jude, a slave of Jesus Christ and a brother of James.

I am writing to all who have been called by God the Father, who loves you and keeps you safe in the care of Jesus Christ.*

2 May God give you more and more mercy, peace, and love.

THE DANGER OF FALSE TEACHERS

3 Dear friends, I had been eagerly planning to write to you about the salvation we all share. But now I find that I must write about something else, urging you to defend the faith that God has entrusted once for all time to His holy people. 4 I say this because some ungodly people have wormed their way into your churches, saying that God's marvelous grace allows us to live immoral lives. The condemnation of such people was recorded long ago, for they have denied our only Master and Lord, Jesus Christ.

5 So I want to remind you, though you already know these things, that Jesus* first rescued the nation of Israel from Egypt, but later He destroyed those who did not remain faithful. 6 And I remind you of the angels who did not stay within the limits of authority God gave them but left the place where they belonged. God has kept them securely chained in prisons of darkness, waiting for the great day of judgment. 7 And don't forget Sodom and Gomorrah and their neighboring towns, which were filled with immorality and every kind of sexual perversion. Those cities were destroyed by fire and serve as a warning of the eternal fire of God's judgment.

8 In the same way, these people—who claim authority from their dreams—live immoral lives, defy authority, and scoff at supernatural beings.* 9 But even Michael, one of the mightiest of the angels,* did not dare accuse the devil of blasphemy, but simply said, "The Lord rebuke you!" (This took place when Michael was arguing with the devil about Moses' body.) 10 But these people scoff at things they do not understand. Like unthinking animals, they do whatever their instincts tell them, and so they bring about their own destruction.

1:1 Matt 13:55; Rom 1:1, 6-7; Jas 1:1
1:2 2 Pet 1:2
1:3 1 Tim 6:12; Titus 1:4; 2 Pet 3:1-2
1:4 Gal 2:4; 2 Pet 2:1-2; 1 Jn 2:21
1:5 Exod 14:21-31; Num 14:29-37; Deut 2:15; 1 Cor 10:5-10
1:6 //2 Pet 2:4, 9
1:7 Gen 19:4-25; Matt 10:15; //2 Pet 2:6, 10
1:8 //2 Pet 2:10
1:9 Dan 10:13, 21; 12:1; Zech 3:2; //2 Pet 2:11; Rev 12:7
1:10 //2 Pet 2:12

1 Or *keeps you for Jesus Christ.* 5 As in the best manuscripts; various other manuscripts read *[the] Lord,* or *God,* or *Christ;* one reads *God Christ.* 8 Greek *at glorious ones,* which are probably evil angels. 9 Greek *Michael, the archangel.*

1:3 The presence of the corrupt teachers forced Jude to set aside his original purpose for writing and issue instead a call for his readers to contend for the faith (see note on 1:20-23). Jude most likely uses the term faith, as Paul often does, to describe the complete gospel message (Galatians 1:23; Philippians 1:27-28; 1 Timothy 3:9; 4:1, 6). When Jude says that this message was "entrusted" to God's people, he refers to the teaching that was delivered by the apostles (1 Corinthians 11:23; 15:3; see also 1:17), which was written down and became the New Testament. The message was given once for all, as Jude says, and cannot be added to or altered (Galatians 1:9; 2 Corinthians 11:4).

▸ GOD

1:4 Too much grace or not enough? Is it possible to overemphasize grace? Throughout history, many have used the free grace of God as an excuse to live ungodly lifestyles. Jude's opponents apparently taught that if God's grace in Christ had truly secured the forgiveness of sin, then they were free to engage in immorality. Some accuse such teaching of overemphasizing grace, but just the opposite is true. In Romans 6, Paul clarifies that such perverse ideas come not from overemphasizing grace, but rather from underemphasizing it. God's grace is so powerful that it not only frees us from the penalty of sin but also frees us from sin's dominating power. Those who live in sin reveal that they do not understand God's grace at all. (***See God****> Relationship> God's Desire> God's Covenants> Covenant of grace,* TopicGuide page A14.)

1:5-7 Jude is extremely confident of two things—that his opponents are corrupt and that the Lord will one day judge them for their corruption (1:4, 10). Using three illustrations, Jude assures his readers that God always punishes evil. He first cites the punishment of the Israelites who did not remain faithful after God rescued them from Egypt (Exodus 6–14; Numbers 32:10-13; Hebrews 3:12-19). Jude may symbolically attribute the people's deliverance to Jesus (see 1 Corinthians 10:4 for a similar attribution), but this is not certain (see NLT textual note). For a discussion of Jude's second illustration, see the note on 2 Peter 2:4. The third illustration comes from Genesis 19:1-25; the temporary fire at Sodom and Gomorrah points to God's eternal fire of judgment.

1:9 Jude condemns the scoffers' arrogant actions by alluding to a conflict between the archangel Michael and the devil. Michael's refusal to condemn Satan on his own authority contrasts with the scoffers' slandering of "supernatural beings" (1:8, either angels or demons). This incident does not appear in the Bible but was included in an ancient work known as the Assumption of Moses. Some have wondered whether a biblical writer could rely on a source outside the Bible for accurate information, but many nonbiblical writings contain true statements or stories. Paul quotes Jewish tradition (2 Timothy 3:8) and even pagan sources (Acts 17:28; 1 Corinthians 15:33; Titus 1:12). Ultimately, we trust that the Holy Spirit guided the biblical writers' judgment (2 Peter 1:20-21).

11 What sorrow awaits them! For they follow in the footsteps of Cain, who killed his
brother. Like Balaam, they deceive people for money. And like Korah, they perish in their
rebellion.
12 When these people eat with you in your fellowship meals commemorating the Lord's
love, they are like dangerous reefs that can shipwreck you.* They are like shameless shep-
herds who care only for themselves. They are like clouds blowing over the land without
giving any rain. They are like trees in autumn that are doubly dead, for they bear no fruit
and have been pulled up by the roots. 13 They are like wild waves of the sea, churning up
the foam of their shameful deeds. They are like wandering stars, doomed forever to black-
est darkness.
14 Enoch, who lived in the seventh generation after Adam, prophesied about these people.
He said, "Listen! The Lord is coming with countless thousands of His holy ones 15 to execute
judgment on the people of the world. He will convict every person of all the ungodly things
they have done and for all the insults that ungodly sinners have spoken against Him."*

1:11 Gen 4:3-8; Num 16:1-35; 22:7; 31:16; //2 Pet 2:15-16; 1 Jn 3:12; Rev 2:14
1:12 Ezek 34:8; Matt 15:13; 1 Cor 11:20-22
1:13 Isa 57:20; Phil 3:19
1:14 Gen 5:18-24; Deut 33:2; 1 Chr 1:1-3
1:15 2 Pet 2:6-9

12 Or *they are contaminants among you;* or *they are stains.* 14-15 The quotation comes from intertestamental literature: Enoch 1:9.

1:11 Jude finds his opponents' evil beliefs and lifestyles cause for concern, as they might entice his readers to embrace such things. Jude thus compares the false teachers to three Old Testament figures who were known in Jewish writings for their arrogance and for leading God's people astray. Adam's first son Cain murdered his brother and spoke arrogantly to God (Genesis 4:1-12; 1 John 3:11-12). Balaam led God's people into sin with his teaching (Numbers 25:1-3; 31:16; Revelation 2:14) and did so for profit (2 Peter 2:15-16). Korah led 250 leaders to rebel against the authority of Moses and Aaron and was consequently swallowed up by the earth (Numbers 16:1-3, 28-33). Likewise, the false teachers in Jude's day would not escape judgment.

1:14-15 Though the character Enoch appears in the Old Testament (Genesis 5:18-24), the quote that Jude mentions here does not. These words do appear, however, in a well-known Jewish writing called 1 Enoch, which was written shortly before Jude's time (not by the biblical figure himself) and was probably his source for this statement. Some find it strange that Jude refers to these words as prophecy, since 1 Enoch is not Scripture. This word, however, occasionally refers to statements of truth even from unbelievers (John 11:49-52; Titus 1:12).

MY RESPONSE TO GOD

Evaluating Our Enemy

JUDE 1

A young minister quietly said to Dr. Bill Bright one day: "I am afraid of Satan."

Dr. Bright replied, "You should be afraid of Satan–if you want to live your own life and do your own thing apart from God. But if you are willing to let Christ control your life, you have nothing to fear, because the Bible says, 'Greater is He that is in you than he that is in the world' (1 John 4:4)."

Satan was defeated two thousand years ago at the cross. Though he has great power to influence people, the Bible assures us that he has been dishonored (Genesis 3:14-15) and demoted (Luke 10:18; Jude 1:6) and that one day he will be utterly vanquished as a threat to God's people (Revelation 20:1-3; 2 Peter 2:4).

Since Jesus conquered Satan, we don't have to worry that he will conquer us. But the Bible does teach that we should give Satan some measure of respect–he remains a being of great power and evil intent (Jude 1:9). Thus, we do not face our foe arrogantly but in Christ's strength as we "put on all of God's armor so that [we] will be able to stand firm against all strategies of the devil" (Ephesians 6:11).

1:16 //2 Pet 2:10, 18; Jude 1:18
1:17 Heb 2:3; 2 Pet 3:2
1:18 //2 Pet 3:3; Jude 1:16
1:19 1 Cor 2:14-15
1:20 Eph 6:18; Col 2:7; 1 Thes 5:11
1:21 2 Tim 1:18; Titus 2:13; Heb 9:28
1:23 Amos 4:11; Zech 3:2-5; Rev 3:4
1:24 Rom 16:25; 2 Cor 4:14; Phil 1:10; 1 Thes 5:23

16These people are grumblers and complainers, living only to satisfy their desires. They
brag loudly about themselves, and they flatter others to get what they want.

A CALL TO REMAIN FAITHFUL

17But you, my dear friends, must remember what the apostles of our Lord Jesus Christ said.
18They told you that in the last times there would be scoffers whose purpose in life is to sat-
isfy their ungodly desires. 19These people are the ones who are creating divisions among
you. They follow their natural instincts because they do not have God's Spirit in them.

20But you, dear friends, must build each other up in your most holy faith, pray in the
power of the Holy Spirit,* 21and await the mercy of our Lord Jesus Christ, who will bring
you eternal life. In this way, you will keep yourselves safe in God's love.

22And you must show mercy to* those whose faith is wavering. 23Rescue others by
snatching them from the flames of judgment. Show mercy to still others,* but do so with
great caution, hating the sins that contaminate their lives.*

A PRAYER OF PRAISE

24Now all glory to God, who is able to keep you from falling away and will bring you with
great joy into His glorious presence without a single fault. 25All glory to Him who alone is
God, our Savior through Jesus Christ our Lord. All glory, majesty, power, and authority are
His before all time, and in the present, and beyond all time! Amen.

20 Greek *pray in the Holy Spirit.* **22** Some manuscripts read *must reprove.* **22-23a** Some manuscripts have only two categories of people: (1) those whose faith is wavering and therefore need to be snatched from the flames of judgment, and (2) those who need to be shown mercy. **23b** Greek *with fear, hating even the clothing stained by the flesh.*

MINISTRY

1:20-23 Search and rescue. In parts of the world where people tend to get lost (like large forests or snowy mountains), search and rescue teams save many lives. In the same way, Christians sometimes wander from the path of sound doctrine and holy living and need others to seek them out and rescue them from error. That's what Jude's letter is all about. He urges his readers to defend the faith (1:3) by avoiding his opponents' evil practices (1:17-19), building each other up (1:20-21), and pursuing those who have gone astray under the false teachers' influence (1:22-23). Jude's message calls all believers to show mercy to those who struggle and to make every effort to restore them (1:22-23). Do you seek this type of ministry in the life of someone you know? Ask God to help you become His search-and-rescue team member. (***See Ministry***> *Transformation> Fill and Subdue> Being salt and light in the world,* TopicGuide page A57.)

REVELATION

PURPOSE

To remind believers throughout all the ages that the Lord they follow is glorious and powerful and that all history is headed toward His designed end.

How will life on planet Earth play out? How far are we into God's future plan? What are the next events that must happen before Jesus Christ's physical return to earth? Since the days Jesus walked the earth, His followers have wrestled with such questions.

In the opening chapter of the book of Acts, Luke records for us the instructions Jesus gave His disciples after His resurrection and before the ascension (Acts 1:1-3). Because of some of the things He had told them, they wondered about the coming of the end—that is, they asked about the fulfillment of Old Testament prophecies about the end of human history and the establishment of God's eternal Kingdom on earth. They asked Jesus, "Lord, has the time come for you to free Israel and restore our kingdom?" (Acts 1:6).

Believers often turn to the book of Revelation in order to look for answers. But although it contains much information about the working out of God's plan for the end of time, ultimately it is as much about who Jesus is as it is about what is going to happen in the future. John's very first vision offers us a glimpse of Jesus in heavenly glory (1:9-19). John shares these visions, given by the grace of God in this one revelation, to encourage believers throughout all the ages that the Lord they follow is glorious and powerful and that He will ultimately reign victorious over all.

DISCOVER GOD IN REVELATION

The book of Revelation reveals God as exalted and powerful, master of history and mastered by nothing and no one.

The Triune God: If we were able to look into heaven, the very dwelling place of God, what would we see? John's accounts of his visions give us just that—a glimpse into heaven! One of the recurring thematic images in Revelation is the triune nature of God. In the opening greeting (1:4-5) we hear a word from the Father, the Son, and the Spirit. In chapter 14 an angel speaks of God (the Father), Jesus the Lord, and the Spirit (14:12-13). In the closing chapter we see the throne of God the Father, hear the words of Jesus, and are invited to respond by the Spirit (chapter 22). Throughout the book, God is clearly understood to exist in the three Persons of the Trinity.

The Almighty God: In many ways and through many images, this book makes it clear that God will ultimately have His way in the world. Numerous visions attest to God as the Almighty God (1:8; 4:8; 16:7; 21:22), and nothing can thwart the workings of His great plan for our redemption and for the renewal of the earth (7:10-12; 11:17; 15:3-4).

The Holy God: John speaks of a great chorus of angels and earthly saints that repeatedly cry out that God is holy (4:8; 15:3-4). He is altogether magnificent and perfect. There are none to compare to this great God.

The Coming King: With marvelous and encouraging focus on Jesus and His work, John's visions repeatedly declare that Jesus is not only returning to the earth to bring us our full redemption but also to rightly rule as King over all kings and Lord over all powers and authorities (11:15; 15:3-4; 17:14; 19:11-16).

The Righteous Judge: When the end of days comes, the entire world will be judged (14:7; 20:11-15). When Jesus returns, He will wage war with His enemies and will righteously judge those who have stood against Him (19:11-12). His judgment will be right, true, and just (16:7). Those who know Him as the Lamb slain for their sins, however, will enter into life forever (20:15; 21:22-27).

DISCOVERY VERSES

"You are worthy, O Lord our God, to receive glory and honor and power. For You created all things, and they exist because You created what You pleased." (REVELATION 4:11)

Then I heard again what sounded like the shout of a vast crowd or the roar of mighty ocean waves or the crash of loud thunder: "Praise the Lord! For the Lord our God, the Almighty, reigns. Let us be glad and rejoice, and let us give honor to Him. For the time has come for the wedding feast of the Lamb, and His bride has prepared herself. She has been given the finest of pure white linen to wear." For the fine linen represents the good deeds of God's holy people. (REVELATION 19:6-8)

GROWING THROUGH REVELATION

Before you read the account of John's visions, it might be helpful to know that throughout the years believers have understood these visions in different ways.

Idealists: This group sees the record of the visions as rendered more like poetry and less like prose. They believe all the images and all the visions offer us different glimpses or perspectives on the battle of good and evil—between God and those who oppose Him—that has been going on throughout human history and will culminate at Christ's return. These visions then give us a glimpse into the eternal activity of our great God. Amillennialists and postmillennialists are two groups that hold this position.

Futurists: This group finds in the Revelation a window on the events that surround the yet future coming of the Lord Jesus. The visions of John are taken as a literal chronological progression of events in the history of the world that continues into the future. They picture the end that God has in store and that He will bring to pass in days yet ahead. Premillennialists hold this position.

Fortunately, the blessing promised to those who read and give attention to the words John recorded (1:3) is not limited to those who adopt a particular interpretive approach. Believers throughout the ages have adopted many interpretive formulas to explain the mysteries of Revelation, but the goal is to stir hearts and minds to know and love the Savior who came for us and who is coming again.

REVELATION FACTS

Author: Four times—at the beginning and the end of this collection of visions—the author identifies himself as John (1:1, 4, 9; 22:8). Besides referring to himself as someone who is sharing in the suffering of those to whom he is writing and the reference to being on the isle of Patmos (1:9), there is little more to help us identify the writer. Although these few points do not definitively point us to John, the beloved disciple of Jesus and the author of one of the Gospels, they do fit what we know from history about John. It is unlikely that some other relatively unknown John would have identified himself this simply. The evidence thus points to John, who wrote the Gospel and the epistles bearing his name, and this view is supported by the testimony of church history.

Written to: John addresses this record of his visions to "the seven churches in the province of Asia" (1:4), which is located in modern day western Turkey. Jesus specifically names these same churches in John's visions (Revelation 2–3). The churches are situated roughly in a circle and are about 50 miles apart from each other.

Date of writing: From what we read in the book, it was written during a time of persecution. There were a number of Roman rulers who stirred up persecution against the church, and some would submit this time of persecution occurred before AD 70. However, most scholars date the book around AD 95, during the reign of the Roman emperor Domitian. John was exiled to the barren island of Patmos near the end of his life and during the reign of Domitian.

Setting: As noted, John is writing to churches spread throughout the region known as Asia. He writes from exile on the isle of Patmos, a small island in the Aegean Sea approximately 60 miles from the port city of Ephesus. At the time, it served as a Roman penal colony.

OUTLINE

- **REVELATION 1:1-19**—John's Vision of Jesus
- **REVELATION 2:1–3:22**—John's Visions Regarding the Seven Churches
- **REVELATION 4:1–22:21**—John's Visions of God's Glorious Salvation of His People and Victory over Satan

1:1 Dan 2:28-29, 45; John 12:49; 17:8; Rev 1:19; 5:7; 17:1; 22:6, 8, 16
1:2 Rev 1:9; 6:9
1:3 Rev 22:7, 10
1:4 Exod 3:14; Rev 1:8; 3:1; 4:5, 8; 5:6; 11:17; 16:5
1:5 Ps 89:27; Isa 40:2; Col 1:18; Rev 3:14; 19:11, 16
1:6 Exod 19:6; Isa 61:6; 1 Pet 2:5, 9

PROLOGUE

1 This is a revelation from* Jesus Christ, which God gave Him to show His servants the
events that must soon* take place. He sent an angel to present this revelation to His
servant John, 2 who faithfully reported everything he saw. This is his report of the word of
God and the testimony of Jesus Christ.
3 God blesses the one who reads the words of this prophecy to the church, and He
blesses all who listen to its message and obey what it says, for the time is near.

JOHN'S GREETING TO THE SEVEN CHURCHES

4 This letter is from John to the seven churches in the province of Asia.*
Grace and peace to you from the One who is, who always was, and who is still to come;
from the sevenfold Spirit* before His throne; 5 and from Jesus Christ. He is the faithful witness
to these things, the first to rise from the dead, and the ruler of all the kings of the world.
All glory to Him who loves us and has freed us from our sins by shedding His blood for
us. 6 He has made us a Kingdom of priests for God His Father. All glory and power to Him
forever and ever! Amen.

1:1a Or *of.* 1:1b Or *suddenly,* or *quickly.* 1:4a *Asia* was a Roman province in what is now western Turkey. 1:4b Greek *the seven spirits.*

1:1-3 These opening verses serve as an introduction to the book. The phrase rendered "revelation from Jesus Christ" could also be rendered "of Jesus." The word "revelation" speaks of an uncovering of something. Because so much of what follows gives us insight not simply into future events but into the person and work of Jesus, it may be best to understand the expression as "a manifestation of Jesus Christ."

1:1-3 John tells his readers that the events he touches on in this book are "near" and will happen soon. According to Peter in the book of Acts, the last days began during the opening days of the New Testament church (Acts 2:14-17). This means that God has already begun carrying out His end time plan for the earth. Thus, in John's day, and even more so today, we are in the "last hour" (1 John 2:18).

1:4 When John speaks of the churches in Asia, he is referring to a Roman province in what is now western Turkey. By speaking of the "sevenfold Spirit" (NLT textual note, "the seven Spirits"), John is referring to the one Holy Spirit in all His fullness. A similar sevenfold image denoting the presence and power of the Spirit is found in Zechariah 4:2-10. There also appears to be seven parallel sections in Revelation (1:1–3:22; 4:1–7:17; 8:1–11:19; 12:1–14:20; 15:1–16:21; 17:1–19:21; 20:1–21:27). These possibly cover the same period of history from the first coming of Christ to the second, but from different perspectives.

GOD

1:5-6 Very impressive! As we grow to know people, we can end up taking them for granted. We might overlook some of their most outstanding characteristics. Sadly, this can even happen in our relationship with Jesus. Here, John reminds us just how amazing our Savior Jesus really is. Jesus is the faithful witness who tells us the truth about God, He is the One who leads us into eternal life, He is the supreme sovereign Ruler over all other authorities, and He is the One who loved us enough to bring us out of slavery and into life through His own death on our behalf. Don't take Him for granted. Be rightly impressed with Him, keeping His perfect sacrifice for you in the front of your mind and heart. (***See God****> God's Names> Son> Glorification (through the Crucifixion and Resurrection),* TopicGuide page A19.)

7 Look! He comes with the clouds of heaven.
And everyone will see Him—
even those who pierced Him.
And all the nations of the world
will mourn for Him.
Yes! Amen!

8 "I am the Alpha and the Omega—the beginning and the end,"* says the Lord God. "I am
the One who is, who always was, and who is still to come—the Almighty One."

VISION OF THE SON OF MAN

9 I, John, am your brother and your partner in suffering and in God's Kingdom and in the
patient endurance to which Jesus calls us. I was exiled to the island of Patmos for preach-
ing the word of God and for my testimony about Jesus. 10 It was the Lord's Day, and I was
worshiping in the Spirit.* Suddenly, I heard behind me a loud voice like a trumpet blast.
11 It said, "Write in a book* everything you see, and send it to the seven churches in the cit-
ies of Ephesus, Smyrna, Pergamum, Thyatira, Sardis, Philadelphia, and Laodicea."

12 When I turned to see who was speaking to me, I saw seven gold lampstands. 13 And
standing in the middle of the lampstands was someone like the Son of Man.* He was
wearing a long robe with a gold sash across His chest. 14 His head and His hair were white
like wool, as white as snow. And His eyes were like flames of fire. 15 His feet were like pol-
ished bronze refined in a furnace, and His voice thundered like mighty ocean waves. 16 He
held seven stars in His right hand, and a sharp two-edged sword came from His mouth.
And His face was like the sun in all its brilliance.

1:8 Greek *I am the Alpha and the Omega,* referring to the first and last letters of the Greek alphabet. 1:10 Or *in spirit.* 1:11 Or *on a scroll.* 1:13 Or *like a son of man.* See Dan 7:13. "Son of Man" is a title Jesus used for Himself.

1:7 Dan 7:13; Zech 12:10; Matt 24:30; John 19:34, 37
1:8 Amos 3:13; 4:13; Rev 1:4; 4:8; 11:17; 21:6; 22:13
1:9 Phil 4:14; 2 Tim 2:12; Rev 1:1; 22:8
1:10 Rev 4:2; 21:10
1:11 Rev 1:2, 19; 2:1, 18, 24; 3:1, 7, 14
1:12 Zech 4:2
1:13 Dan 7:13; 10:5; Rev 14:14
1:14 Dan 7:9; 10:6; Rev 2:18; 19:12
1:15 Ezek 1:24; 43:2; Rev 14:2; 19:6
1:16 Isa 49:2

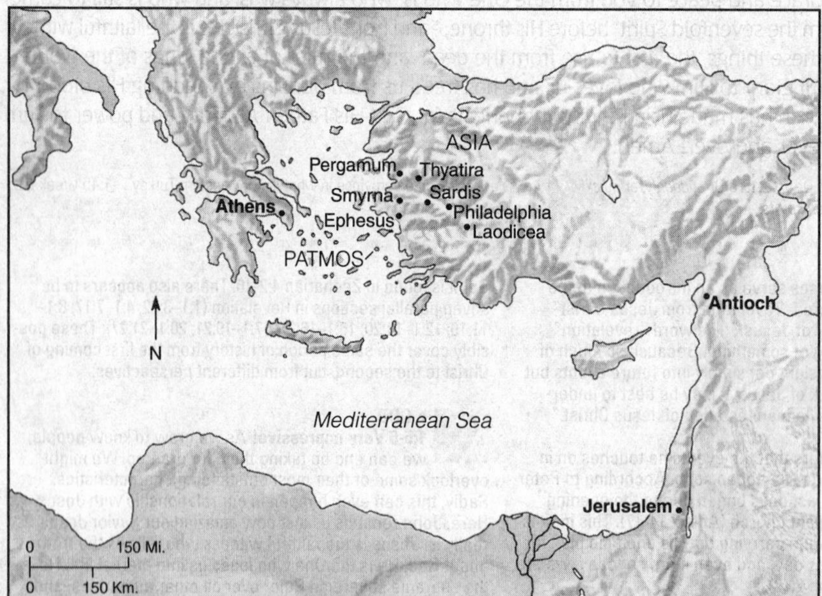

THE SEVEN CHURCHES
The seven churches were located on a major Roman road. A letter carrier would leave the island of Patmos (where John was exiled), arriving first at Ephesus. He would travel north to Smyrna and Pergamum, turn southeast to Thyatira, and continue on to Sardis, Philadelphia, and Laodicea—in the exact order in which the letters were dictated.

1:8 The Alpha and the Omega are the first and last letters of the Greek alphabet. By identifying Himself this way, the Lord demonstrates that He stands at the beginning and end of all history.

1:10 John was given visions that gave him insights into the life and ministry of Jesus as well as glimpses into the future outworking of God's great plan for the earth. See the comments on 1:1-3.

1:17 Isa 44:6; 48:12; Dan 8:18
1:18 Rev 2:8
1:19 Isa 48:6; Rev 1:1

17 When I saw Him, I fell at His feet as if I were dead. But He laid His right hand on me and said, "Don't be afraid! I am the First and the Last. 18 I am the living One. I died, but look—I am alive forever and ever! And I hold the keys of death and the grave.*

19 "Write down what you have seen—both the things that are now happening and the things that will happen.* 20 This is the meaning of the mystery of the seven stars you saw in My right hand and the seven gold lampstands: The seven stars are the angels* of the seven churches, and the seven lampstands are the seven churches.

2:1 Rev 1:12-16, 20; 3:1
2:2 2 Cor 11:13; 1 Jn 4:1; Rev 2:19
2:3 John 15:21
2:4 Jer 2:2; Matt 24:12
2:5 Rev 2:16, 22; 3:3, 19
2:6 Ps 139:21
2:7 Gen 2:8-9; 3:22-24; Ezek 31:8-9; Rev 22:2, 14

THE MESSAGE TO THE CHURCH IN EPHESUS

2 "Write this letter to the angel* of the church in Ephesus. This is the message from the One who holds the seven stars in His right hand, the One who walks among the seven gold lampstands:

2 "I know all the things you do. I have seen your hard work and your patient endurance. I know you don't tolerate evil people. You have examined the claims of those who say they are apostles but are not. You have discovered they are liars. 3 You have patiently suffered for Me without quitting.

4 "But I have this complaint against you. You don't love Me or each other as you did at first!* 5 Look how far you have fallen! Turn back to Me and do the works you did at first. If you don't repent, I will come and remove your lampstand from its place among the churches. 6 But this is in your favor: You hate the evil deeds of the Nicolaitans, just as I do.

7 "Anyone with ears to hear must listen to the Spirit and understand what He is saying to the churches. To everyone who is victorious I will give fruit from the tree of life in the paradise of God.

1:18 Greek *and Hades.* 1:19 Or *what you have seen and what they mean—the things that have already begun to happen.* 1:20 Or *the messengers.* 2:1 Or *the messenger;* also in 2:8, 12, 18. 2:4 Greek *You have lost your first love.*

2:1–3:22 After the initial vision, John is instructed to send a message to the seven principle churches in the Roman province of Asia. In each of the seven letters, Jesus addresses specifics about that particular church's situation, but the instructions He gives can speak to the situations in churches throughout the world during all times.

2:6 Little is known about the particular false teaching advanced by those called Nicolaitans. Apparently they sought to lead the Ephesian believers into some kind of compromise with those who opposed the things of God.

▸ GOD
2:7, 11, 17, 29 Listening to His voice. In his seven letters to the churches, John repeats one truth: We need the Spirit to help us hear and heed God's commands. We are weak in our own strength. Each of us must submit to the Spirit's conviction and obey the Spirit's instructions. That's part of the Spirit's role—to lead us (Romans 8:14). Submit yourself to the Holy Spirit's guidance, and seek to obey God in His strength. (***See God*> *God's Names*> *Holy Spirit*> *Leads,* TopicGuide page A19.)

BECAUSE GOD
NEVER CHANGES

My future is secure and eternal.

"I am the Alpha and the Omega—the beginning and the end," says the Lord God. "I am the One who is, who always was, and who is still to come—the Almighty One."

REVELATION 1:8

THE MESSAGE TO THE CHURCH IN SMYRNA

8"Write this letter to the angel of the church in Smyrna. This is the message from the One
who is the First and the Last, who was dead but is now alive:

9"I know about your suffering and your poverty—but you are rich! I know the
blasphemy of those opposing you. They say they are Jews, but they are not, because
their synagogue belongs to Satan. 10Don't be afraid of what you are about to suffer.
The devil will throw some of you into prison to test you. You will suffer for ten days.
But if you remain faithful even when facing death, I will give you the crown of life.

11"Anyone with ears to hear must listen to the Spirit and understand what He is
saying to the churches. Whoever is victorious will not be harmed by the second death.

2:8 Rev 1:11, 17-18
2:9 2 Cor 6:10; 11:14-15; Rev 3:9
2:10 Dan 1:12, 14; Jas 1:12; Rev 3:9; 17:14
2:11 Rev 2:7; 20:6, 14

THE MESSAGE TO THE CHURCH IN PERGAMUM

12"Write this letter to the angel of the church in Pergamum. This is the message from the
One with the sharp two-edged sword:

13"I know that you live in the city where Satan has his throne, yet you have remained
loyal to Me. You refused to deny Me even when Antipas, My faithful witness, was
martyred among you there in Satan's city.

14"But I have a few complaints against you. You tolerate some among you whose
teaching is like that of Balaam, who showed Balak how to trip up the people of Israel.
He taught them to sin by eating food offered to idols and by committing sexual sin.
15In a similar way, you have some Nicolaitans among you who follow the same
teaching. 16Repent of your sin, or I will come to you suddenly and fight against them
with the sword of My mouth.

17"Anyone with ears to hear must listen to the Spirit and understand what He is
saying to the churches. To everyone who is victorious I will give some of the manna
that has been hidden away in heaven. And I will give to each one a white stone, and
on the stone will be engraved a new name that no one understands except the one
who receives it.

2:12 Rev 1:16; 2:16
2:13 Rev 14:12
2:14 Num 31:16; 1 Cor 6:13; 2 Pet 2:15; Jude 1:11
2:15 Rev 2:6
2:16 2 Thes 2:8; Rev 1:16; 2:5; 22:7, 12, 20
2:17 Ps 78:24; Isa 62:2; 65:15; John 6:49-58; Rev 3:12; 19:12

THE MESSAGE TO THE CHURCH IN THYATIRA

18"Write this letter to the angel of the church in Thyatira. This is the message from the Son
of God, whose eyes are like flames of fire, whose feet are like polished bronze:

19"I know all the things you do. I have seen your love, your faith, your service, and
your patient endurance. And I can see your constant improvement in all these things.

20"But I have this complaint against you. You are permitting that woman—that
Jezebel who calls herself a prophet—to lead My servants astray. She teaches them to
commit sexual sin and to eat food offered to idols. 21I gave her time to repent, but
she does not want to turn away from her immorality.

22"Therefore, I will throw her on a bed of suffering,* and those who commit
adultery with her will suffer greatly unless they repent and turn away from her evil

2:18 Dan 10:6; Rev 1:14-15
2:19 Rev 2:2
2:20 1 Kgs 16:31; 2 Kgs 9:7, 22
2:21 Rev 9:20
2:22 Rev 17:2

2:22 Greek *a bed.*

2:12-13 The city of Pergamum was the site of Asia's longest-standing temple for emperor worship. It also had well-known temples devoted to Zeus, the chief Roman god, as well as temples for the worship of many other pagan gods. John called Pergamum a place where Satan "has his throne."

2:14-15 Balaam, mentioned in Numbers 25:1-9 and 31:16, attempted to draw Israel away from God and into idolatry and sexual sin. Apparently, whatever the teaching of the Nicolaitans was, it was being used to "trip up" the people of God in a similar way.

2:17 In the courts of law of John's day, a black stone was used to indicate condemnation and a white stone was used to indicate acquittal. The act of naming demonstrates one's ownership and authority over what is named. Therefore, when Jesus gives believers a new name, He is emphasizing that they are His and He will keep and guard them.

2:20 The label "Jezebel" invites comparisons to the Old Testament figure (1 Kings 16:31; 2 Kings 9:22) who attempted to replace the worship of God with the worship of idols.

deeds. 23I will strike her children dead. Then all the churches will know that I am the One who searches out the thoughts and intentions of every person. And I will give to each of you whatever you deserve.

24"But I also have a message for the rest of you in Thyatira who have not followed this false teaching ('deeper truths,' as they call them—depths of Satan, actually). I will ask nothing more of you 25except that you hold tightly to what you have until I come. 26To all who are victorious, who obey Me to the very end,

To them I will give authority over all the nations.
27 They will rule the nations with an iron rod
and smash them like clay pots.*

28They will have the same authority I received from My Father, and I will also give them the morning star!

29"Anyone with ears to hear must listen to the Spirit and understand what He is saying to the churches.

THE MESSAGE TO THE CHURCH IN SARDIS

3 "Write this letter to the angel* of the church in Sardis. This is the message from the One who has the sevenfold Spirit* of God and the seven stars:

"I know all the things you do, and that you have a reputation for being alive—but you are dead. 2Wake up! Strengthen what little remains, for even what is left is almost dead. I find that your actions do not meet the requirements of My God. 3Go back to what you heard and believed at first; hold to it firmly. Repent and turn to Me again. If you don't wake up, I will come to you suddenly, as unexpected as a thief.

4"Yet there are some in the church in Sardis who have not soiled their clothes with evil. They will walk with Me in white, for they are worthy. 5All who are victorious will be clothed in white. I will never erase their names from the Book of Life, but I will announce before My Father and His angels that they are Mine.

6"Anyone with ears to hear must listen to the Spirit and understand what He is saying to the churches.

THE MESSAGE TO THE CHURCH IN PHILADELPHIA

7"Write this letter to the angel of the church in Philadelphia.

This is the message from the One who is holy and true,
the One who has the key of David.
What He opens, no one can close;
and what He closes, no one can open:*

8"I know all the things you do, and I have opened a door for you that no one can close. You have little strength, yet you obeyed My word and did not deny Me. 9Look, I will force those who belong to Satan's synagogue—those liars who say they are Jews but are not—to come and bow down at your feet. They will acknowledge that you are the ones I love.

10"Because you have obeyed My command to persevere, I will protect you from

2:23 Prov 24:12; Jer 17:10; Matt 16:27; Luke 16:15; Rom 8:27
2:25 Rev 3:11
2:26-27 Ps 2:8-9; Matt 10:22; Rev 12:5
2:28 Rev 22:16
2:29 Rev 2:7
3:1 Rev 1:4, 11, 16; 3:8, 15
3:3 Matt 24:42-44; Luke 22:32; 1 Thes 5:2-6; 2 Pet 3:10; Rev 2:5; 16:15
3:4 Jude 1:23; Rev 3:5; 4:4; 6:11; 19:14
3:5 Exod 32:32-33; Ps 69:28; Matt 10:32; Luke 12:8; Rev 13:8; 17:8; 20:12
3:6 Rev 2:7
3:7 Job 12:14; Isa 22:22; Matt 16:19
3:8 Acts 14:27; Rev 2:13
3:9 Isa 43:4; 49:23; 2 Cor 11:14-15; Rev 2:9
3:10 2 Pet 2:9; Rev 2:10

2:26-27 Ps 2:8-9 (Greek Version). 3:1a Or *the messenger;* also in 3:7, 14. 3:1b Greek *the seven spirits.* 3:7 Isa 22:22.

3:5 There are repeated references to "the Book of Life" in the New Testament (Philippians 4:3; Revelation 13:8; 17:8; 20:12-15; 21:27). Names are found in this book that have been there from "before the world was made" (13:8; 17:8). The book is a list of those who belong to Jesus Christ through faith and are kept by His power; as He says, "I will announce before My Father . . . that they are Mine" (Revelation 3:5).

3:8 The image of an open door speaks of an opportunity, perhaps to extend the missionary endeavor of the church or simply to live right (see Acts 14:27; 1 Corinthians 16:9; 2 Corinthians 2:12).

the great time of testing that will come upon the whole world to test those who
belong to this world. 11I am coming soon.* Hold on to what you have, so that no one
will take away your crown. 12All who are victorious will become pillars in the Temple
of My God, and they will never have to leave it. And I will write on them the name of
My God, and they will be citizens in the city of My God—the new Jerusalem that
comes down from heaven from My God. And I will also write on them My new name.
13"Anyone with ears to hear must listen to the Spirit and understand what He is
saying to the churches.

THE MESSAGE TO THE CHURCH IN LAODICEA

14"Write this letter to the angel of the church in Laodicea. This is the message from the
One who is the Amen—the faithful and true witness, the beginning* of God's new creation:

15"I know all the things you do, that you are neither hot nor cold. I wish that you
were one or the other! 16But since you are like lukewarm water, neither hot nor cold,
I will spit you out of My mouth! 17You say, 'I am rich. I have everything I want. I don't
need a thing!' And you don't realize that you are wretched and miserable and poor
and blind and naked. 18So I advise you to buy gold from Me—gold that has been
purified by fire. Then you will be rich. Also buy white garments from Me so you will
not be shamed by your nakedness, and ointment for your eyes so you will be able to
see. 19I correct and discipline everyone I love. So be diligent and turn from your
indifference.
20"Look! I stand at the door and knock. If you hear My voice and open the door, I
will come in, and we will share a meal together as friends. 21Those who are victorious
will sit with Me on My throne, just as I was victorious and sat with My Father on His
throne.
22"Anyone with ears to hear must listen to the Spirit and understand what He is
saying to the churches."

WORSHIP IN HEAVEN

4 Then as I looked, I saw a door standing open in heaven, and the same voice I had
heard before spoke to me like a trumpet blast. The voice said, "Come up here, and I
will show you what must happen after this." 2And instantly I was in the Spirit,* and I saw a
throne in heaven and someone sitting on it. 3The One sitting on the throne was as brilliant

3:11 Or *suddenly*, or *quickly*. 3:14 Or *the ruler*, or *the source*. 4:2 Or *in spirit*.

3:11 Rev 2:25; 22:7, 12, 20
3:12 Ezek 48:35; Gal 4:26; Rev 21:2, 10
3:13 Rev 2:7
3:14 John 1:3; 2 Cor 1:20; Col 1:15-18; Rev 1:5
3:15 Rom 12:11
3:17 Hos 12:8; Zech 11:5; 1 Cor 4:8
3:18 1 Pet 1:7; Rev 3:4; 16:15
3:19 Prov 3:12; 1 Cor 11:32; Heb 12:6; Rev 2:5
3:20 John 14:23
3:21 Matt 19:28; Rev 5:5
3:22 Rev 2:7
4:1 Exod 19:20, 24; Ezek 1:1; Dan 2:28-29, 45
4:2 1 Kgs 22:19; Isa 6:1; Ezek 1:26-27
4:3 Ezek 1:26-28

3:11 The idea that Jesus is "coming soon" is found repeatedly in Revelation (2:16; 3:11; 22:7, 12, 20). It does not necessarily mean "in the next few seconds" but more like "at any time," and then things will move rapidly toward the final culmination.

3:15-16 Although Laodicea was a prominent and well-populated city, it did face a water problem: The water was brought through pipes from a distant source. Colosse, a nearby city, had water supplied by a mountain spring; their water was invigorating and cold. Hierapolis, another Roman city not far away, had hot springs. By the time water reached Laodicea, however, it was tepid. Thus, the followers of Jesus in Laodicea are described in terms with which they would readily identify.

3:18-19 This letter to the church at Laodicea draws upon some notable characteristics of the city. It was a wealthy city and was renowned for a local healing medicine for the eyes. It was also famous for its exports of expensive seamless garments made of glossy black wool.

▸ ADOPTION

3:20 At Jesus' table. In this letter, Jesus is speaking to those who already belong to Him. Though He has made new life available to them, they are choosing to live in their old ways. They think they're doing great; He tells them they are not. They think they have everything they need for their spiritual lives, but because they are not pursuing intimacy with Jesus, they really are living meager, lukewarm lives. They are not experiencing the warmth and delight of life with Jesus. Will they recognize that it is not enough to merely go through the motions of religious living? Will they admit that what they need more than anything else is personal intimacy with Jesus? Will they open the door, and step into that deeper intimacy? Will you? (***See Adoption***> *With Christ*> *Supernatural*> *An abundant life,* TopicGuide page A37.)

4:1-7 John's difficult, yet Spirit-guided task is to describe something that no one has ever seen. He has to use the language of "impression" since he has no specific words to describe what he sees. Notice, for example, phrases such as "the One sitting . . . was *as brilliant as* . . ." (4:3); "the glow . . . *like* a rainbow" (4:3); "the second *was like* . . ." (4:7).

4:4 Isa 24:23; Rev 11:16; 19:4
4:5 Exod 19:16; Ezek 1:13; Zech 4:2; Rev 1:4; 5:6
4:6-7 Ezek 1:5-22; 10:12, 14; Rev 15:7; 19:4
4:8 Isa 6:2; Ezek 1:18; 10:12; Amos 3:13
4:9 Dan 4:34; Rev 4:2; 5:1
4:10 Rev 4:4; 5:8, 14
4:11 Rev 10:6

as gemstones—like jasper and carnelian. And the glow of an emerald circled His throne
like a rainbow. 4Twenty-four thrones surrounded Him, and twenty-four elders sat on them.
They were all clothed in white and had gold crowns on their heads. 5From the throne
came flashes of lightning and the rumble of thunder. And in front of the throne were seven
torches with burning flames. This is the sevenfold Spirit* of God. 6In front of the throne was
a shiny sea of glass, sparkling like crystal.

In the center and around the throne were four living beings, each covered with eyes,
front and back. 7The first of these living beings was like a lion; the second was like an ox;
the third had a human face; and the fourth was like an eagle in flight. 8Each of these living
beings had six wings, and their wings were covered all over with eyes, inside and out. Day
after day and night after night they keep on saying,

"Holy, holy, holy is the Lord God, the Almighty—
the One who always was, who is, and who is still to come."

9Whenever the living beings give glory and honor and thanks to the One sitting on the
throne (the One who lives forever and ever), 10the twenty-four elders fall down and wor-
ship the One sitting on the throne (the One who lives forever and ever). And they lay their
crowns before the throne and say,

11 "You are worthy, O Lord our God,
to receive glory and honor and power.
For You created all things,
and they exist because You created what You pleased."

4:5 Greek *They are the seven spirits.*

4:6-8 The four "living beings" John describes are similar to the Old Testament descriptions of lofty angels who attend the throne of God (Ezekiel 1; 10; Isaiah 6). They likely refer to the four directions or the four major elements (earth, wind, fire, water), both symbolizing God's power over the entire world.

▸ WORSHIP
4:6-11 Constant worship. Will you play a harp in heaven? Probably not. Will you sit around on a cloud? Unlikely. Will you be bored? Definitely not! Here in the book of Revelation we get a glimpse into heaven, and the picture painted for us is quite unlike popular conceptions. Vibrant, participatory worship is the constant activity of heaven. In God's presence, in His glorious splendor, the inhabitants of heaven ceaselessly celebrate His greatness. As various facets of God's splendor come into focus, all heaven erupts in joyous celebration. All of heaven is forever caught up with and impressed with God. Start practicing for heaven today—learn to worship Him with every part of your life, every aspect of your being, every moment of your day. (*See Worship*> *NT*> *To the Father*> *God saves people in order to be worshiped and glorified,* TopicGuide page A29.)

BECAUSE
GOD IS HOLY

I will devote myself to him in purity, worship and service

"Holy, holy, holy is the Lord God, the Almighty—the One who always was, who is, and who is still to come."

REVELATION 4:8

THE LAMB OPENS THE SCROLL

5 Then I saw a scroll* in the right hand of the One who was sitting on the throne. There
was writing on the inside and the outside of the scroll, and it was sealed with seven
seals. 2 And I saw a strong angel, who shouted with a loud voice: "Who is worthy to break
the seals on this scroll and open it?" 3 But no one in heaven or on earth or under the earth
was able to open the scroll and read it.

4 Then I began to weep bitterly because no one was found worthy to open the scroll and
read it. 5 But one of the twenty-four elders said to me, "Stop weeping! Look, the Lion of the
tribe of Judah, the heir to David's throne,* has won the victory. He is worthy to open the
scroll and its seven seals."

6 Then I saw a Lamb that looked as if it had been slaughtered, but it was now standing
between the throne and the four living beings and among the twenty-four elders. He had
seven horns and seven eyes, which represent the sevenfold Spirit* of God that is sent out
into every part of the earth. 7 He stepped forward and took the scroll from the right hand of
the One sitting on the throne. 8 And when He took the scroll, the four living beings and the
twenty-four elders fell down before the Lamb. Each one had a harp, and they held gold
bowls filled with incense, which are the prayers of God's people. 9 And they sang a new
song with these words:

"You are worthy to take the scroll
 and break its seals and open it.
For You were slaughtered, and Your blood has ransomed people for God
 from every tribe and language and people and nation.
10 And You have caused them to become
 a Kingdom of priests for our God.
 And they will reign* on the earth."

11 Then I looked again, and I heard the voices of thousands and millions of angels around
the throne and of the living beings and the elders. 12 And they sang in a mighty chorus:

"Worthy is the Lamb who was slaughtered—
 to receive power and riches
and wisdom and strength
 and honor and glory and blessing."

13 And then I heard every creature in heaven and on earth and under the earth and in
the sea. They sang:

5:1 Isa 29:11; Ezek 2:9-10; Dan 12:4; Rev 5:7
5:2 Rev 10:1; 18:21
5:3 Phil 2:10
5:5 Gen 49:9; Isa 11:1, 10; Heb 7:14; Rev 22:16
5:6 Isa 53:7; Zech 4:10; John 1:29, 36; Rev 1:4; 4:5
5:7 Rev 5:1
5:8 Rev 4:4, 6; 8:3-4; 14:2; 15:2
5:9 Ps 144:9; Rev 14:3
5:10 Exod 19:6; 1 Pet 2:5-9; Rev 1:6; 20:4
5:11 Dan 7:10; Heb 12:22; Rev 4:4, 6
5:12 1 Chr 29:11; Isa 53:7; John 1:29, 36; Rev 4:11
5:13 Phil 2:10; Rev 4:11; 5:7

5:1 Or *book;* also in 5:2, 3, 4, 5, 7, 8, 9. 5:5 Greek *the root of David.* See Isa 11:10. 5:6 Greek *which are the seven spirits.* 5:10 Some manuscripts read *they are reigning.*

5:1 Unlike a book, a scroll is progressively unrolled in order to read it. God's plans are like that scroll. They are revealed as He opens the scroll of history. We cannot understand them ahead of time; we cannot see into the future. But we have great assurance that God is the One who holds it all together.

5:5-6 The image of the lion is used nowhere else in Scripture to speak of Jesus, but here the reference clearly is to Him. The references to the descendant of Judah and the heir to David's throne are ways of speaking of the Messiah, the Christ (see, for example, Genesis 49:9-10 and Isaiah 11:1-10). The lion image pictures the majesty and power of Jesus Christ as ruler. Jesus is also identified with the image of a lamb, picturing the sacrifice He would make for the sins of the world (Isaiah 53:1-7; John 1:29, 36; 1 Peter 1:19). Although slain (recalling His sacrifice), this lamb John sees is now alive (recalling His resurrection).

▸ WORSHIP

5:9-14 The goal of worship. If children are attentive and grateful, they thank their mom and dad for driving them here and there or for providing them special treats. But many times children fail to appreciate the sacrifices that their parents make for them. This happens in our relationship with Jesus as well. We fail to give Jesus the thanks for what He is doing in our lives. But in heaven, the focus is different. John describes all heaven joining in a chorus of praise to Jesus. He is the deserving One! Jesus is worshiped for giving His life so that we can have life. Let that grip your heart, as it does the hearts of all who dwell in heaven. (***See Worship****> NT> Christ's Supremacy> Christ willingly provided a sacrifice,* TopicGuide page A29.)

"Blessing and honor and glory and power
belong to the One sitting on the throne
and to the Lamb forever and ever."

14And the four living beings said, "Amen!" And the twenty-four elders fell down and
worshiped the Lamb.

THE LAMB BREAKS THE FIRST SIX SEALS

6 As I watched, the Lamb broke the first of the seven seals on the scroll.* Then I heard
one of the four living beings say with a voice like thunder, "Come!" 2I looked up and
saw a white horse standing there. Its rider carried a bow, and a crown was placed on his
head. He rode out to win many battles and gain the victory.
3When the Lamb broke the second seal, I heard the second living being say, "Come!"
4Then another horse appeared, a red one. Its rider was given a mighty sword and the au-
thority to take peace from the earth. And there was war and slaughter everywhere.
5When the Lamb broke the third seal, I heard the third living being say, "Come!" I
looked up and saw a black horse, and its rider was holding a pair of scales in his hand.
6And I heard a voice from among the four living beings say, "A loaf of wheat bread or three
loaves of barley will cost a day's pay.* And don't waste* the olive oil and wine."
7When the Lamb broke the fourth seal, I heard the fourth living being say, "Come!" 8I
looked up and saw a horse whose color was pale green. Its rider was named Death, and
his companion was the Grave.* These two were given authority over one-fourth of the
earth, to kill with the sword and famine and disease* and wild animals.
9When the Lamb broke the fifth seal, I saw under the altar the souls of all who had been
martyred for the word of God and for being faithful in their testimony. 10They shouted to
the Lord and said, "O Sovereign Lord, holy and true, how long before You judge the peo-
ple who belong to this world and avenge our blood for what they have done to us?"
11Then a white robe was given to each of them. And they were told to rest a little longer
until the full number of their brothers and sisters*—their fellow servants of Jesus who were
to be martyred—had joined them.
12I watched as the Lamb broke the sixth seal, and there was a great earthquake. The sun
became as dark as black cloth, and the moon became as red as blood. 13Then the stars of the
sky fell to the earth like green figs falling from a tree shaken by a strong wind. 14The sky was
rolled up like a scroll, and all of the mountains and islands were moved from their places.
15Then everyone—the kings of the earth, the rulers, the generals, the wealthy, the
powerful, and every slave and free person—all hid themselves in the caves and among
the rocks of the mountains. 16And they cried to the mountains and the rocks, "Fall on us

5:14 Rev 4:6, 9-10
6:1 Rev 5:1, 6
6:2 Zech 1:8; 6:1-3; Rev 14:14; 19:11-12
6:3 Rev 4:7
6:4 Zech 1:8; 6:2; Matt 10:34
6:5 Zech 6:2, 6-8; Rev 4:7
6:6-7 Rev 4:6-7
6:8 Jer 14:12; 15:2-3; Hos 13:14; Rev 1:18; 20:13
6:9 Exod 29:12; Lev 4:7
6:10 Ps 79:10; Zech 1:12; Luke 18:7; Rev 3:7, 10; 19:2
6:11 Heb 11:40
6:12 Joel 2:10; Matt 24:29; Rev 16:18
6:13 Isa 34:4
6:14 Ps 46:2; 2 Pet 3:10
6:15 Isa 2:10, 19, 21; Jer 4:29
6:16 Hos 10:8; Luke 23:30

6:1 Or *book.* 6:6a Greek *A choinix* [1 quart or 1 liter] *of wheat for a denarius, and 3 choinix of barley for a denarius.* A denarius was equivalent to a laborer's full day's wage. 6:6b Or *harm.* 6:8a Greek *was Hades.* 6:8b Greek *death.* 6:11 Greek *their brothers.*

6:1-8 The four riders pictured here have been called the "Four Horsemen of the Apocalypse" ("apocalypse" being another word for "revelation" or "showing"). They represent, respectively, conquest, war, famine, and death. Jesus said that these troubles will precede the cosmic cataclysm in which God will destroy the ruling powers of evil (Mark 13:6-8).

6:9-10 Although there is no ongoing sacrifice being offered in heaven, the image of the martyrs "under the altar" speaks of their safety and rich life that results from the sacrifice that was made on their behalf—the great sacrifice of the Lion and Lamb, Jesus. Their calling out for God's vengeance on those who had murdered them suggests that there will not be complete satisfaction in heaven until God is finished with His plan. Even in the perfection of heaven, there will remain a lack of resolution until God's cosmic work is complete. See Matthew 24:36 for an example of how heavenly beings remain ignorant of certain matters.

▸ SALVATION
6:16-17 Warn others about judgment. Those who know Jesus really do have good news to share with others. The bad news is that, because of sin, all people stand under the wrath of God (Romans 1:18; Ephesians 2:3). We deserve to suffer the full extent of His righteous anger. But the good news is that God has undertaken to bring those who believe in Jesus out from under His wrath and into forgiveness and life (Romans 5:9; 1 Thessalonians 5:9). The one who believes in Jesus has life and is free from judgment, but the one who does not believe remains under God's wrath (John 3:36). As we share the Good News with others, we must tell the whole story—including the fearsome coming judgment of God (2 Corinthians 5:11; Hebrews 10:30-31). Let everyone know the full story of what it means to be saved! (***See Salvation> Receiving> Results> Works> Redeemed from curse of the law,*** TopicGuide page A23.)

and hide us from the face of the One who sits on the throne and from the wrath of the
Lamb. 17For the great day of their wrath has come, and who is able to survive?"

GOD'S PEOPLE WILL BE PRESERVED

7 Then I saw four angels standing at the four corners of the earth, holding back the four
winds so they did not blow on the earth or the sea, or even on any tree. 2And I saw
another angel coming up from the east, carrying the seal of the living God. And he
shouted to those four angels, who had been given power to harm land and sea, 3"Wait!
Don't harm the land or the sea or the trees until we have placed the seal of God on the
foreheads of His servants."

4And I heard how many were marked with the seal of God—144,000 were sealed from
all the tribes of Israel:

5from Judah............12,000
from Reuben............12,000
from Gad............12,000
6from Asher............12,000
from Naphtali............12,000
from Manasseh............12,000
7from Simeon............12,000
from Levi............12,000
from Issachar............12,000
8from Zebulun............12,000
from Joseph............12,000
from Benjamin............12,000

PRAISE FROM THE GREAT CROWD

9After this I saw a vast crowd, too great to count, from every nation and tribe and people
and language, standing in front of the throne and before the Lamb. They were clothed in
white robes and held palm branches in their hands. 10And they were shouting with a
mighty shout,

"Salvation comes from our God who sits on the throne
and from the Lamb!"

11And all the angels were standing around the throne and around the elders and the
four living beings. And they fell before the throne with their faces to the ground and wor-
shiped God. 12They sang,

"Amen! Blessing and glory and wisdom
and thanksgiving and honor
and power and strength belong to our God
forever and ever! Amen."

13Then one of the twenty-four elders asked me, "Who are these who are clothed in
white? Where did they come from?"

6:17 Joel 2:11; Zeph 1:14-15; Mal 3:2
7:1 Jer 49:36; Ezek 37:9; Dan 7:2; Zech 6:5; Matt 24:31
7:2 Rev 9:4
7:3 Ezek 9:4, 6; Rev 6:6; 9:4; 14:1; 22:4
7:4 Rev 14:1, 3
7:9 Rev 3:5; 5:9
7:10 Rev 5:13; 12:10; 19:1; 22:3
7:11 Rev 4:4, 6, 10
7:12 Rev 5:12-14
7:13 Rev 6:11; 7:9

6:17 The day of God's wrath is coming upon the earth as declared by both the Old Testament prophets (Zephaniah 1:14-18) and the writers of the New Testament (Romans 2:5). As the inhabitants of earth realize that this final Day of Judgment draws near, they will rightly question, "Who is able to survive?" (See Nahum 1:6 and Malachi 3:2 for further discussion of God's judgment.)

7:1-10 Scholars have long argued about the identity of the 144,000. It most likely refers to all those that God intends to save throughout history. God is willing and able to preserve "His servants" in the midst of great difficulties, and He is gathering a "vast crowd" of people from every nation and tribe and people and language who will one day meet around His throne.

7:14 [14]And I said to him, "Sir, you are the one who knows."
Dan 12:1 Then he said to me, "These are the ones who died in* the great tribulation.* They have
Rev 6:11; 22:14 washed their robes in the blood of the Lamb and made them white.

7:15 [15] "That is why they stand in front of God's throne
Rev 4:9; 11:19; 22:3 and serve Him day and night in His Temple.
And He who sits on the throne
will give them shelter.
7:16 [16] They will never again be hungry or thirsty;
Isa 49:10 they will never be scorched by the heat of the sun.
7:17 [17] For the Lamb on the throne*
Ps 23:1-5; Isa 25:8; 49:10 will be their Shepherd.
John 10:11, 14 He will lead them to springs of life-giving water.
Rev 21:4, 6; 22:1 And God will wipe every tear from their eyes."

THE LAMB BREAKS THE SEVENTH SEAL

8:1 Rev 6:1-17 **8** When the Lamb broke the seventh seal on the scroll,* there was silence throughout
8:2 heaven for about half an hour. [2]I saw the seven angels who stand before God, and
Rev 9:1, 13; 11:15 they were given seven trumpets.
8:3 [3]Then another angel with a gold incense burner came and stood at the altar. And a
Exod 30:1-3 great amount of incense was given to him to mix with the prayers of God's people as an
Rev 9:13 offering on the gold altar before the throne. [4]The smoke of the incense, mixed with the
8:4 Ps 141:2 prayers of God's holy people, ascended up to God from the altar where the angel had
Rev 5:8; 8:3 poured them out. [5]Then the angel filled the incense burner with fire from the altar and
8:5 threw it down upon the earth; and thunder crashed, lightning flashed, and there was a ter-
Exod 19:16-19 rible earthquake.
Lev 16:12
Rev 4:5; 11:19; 16:18

THE FIRST FOUR TRUMPETS

[6]Then the seven angels with the seven trumpets prepared to blow their mighty blasts.
8:7 [7]The first angel blew his trumpet, and hail and fire mixed with blood were thrown down
Exod 9:23-25 on the earth. One-third of the earth was set on fire, one-third of the trees were burned, and
Ezek 38:22 all the green grass was burned.

7:14a Greek *who came out of.* **7:14b** Or *the great suffering.* **7:17** Greek *on the center of the throne.* **8:1** Or *book.*

7:14 Some identify the "great tribulation" as a period of distress on the earth just prior to the return of Christ (Matthew 24:21; Mark 13:19). But for John's readers—and for any who have lived throughout the time the church has been on the earth—tribulation is a part of life (Romans 5:3; 1 Thessalonians 1:6; 2 Thessalonians 1:4-5). Jesus will bring His people through the trials and tribulations of life in whatever age they occur.

▸ SALVATION

7:14-15 Wearing righteousness. Some special events require formal attire. To attend, you must wear what is appropriate. In one sense heaven is like that. No one can get in without the proper attire. And what is appropriate dress for heaven? Holiness. The problem is that people do not have such garments tucked away in their closet. Our own holiness is no better than "filthy rags" in God's sight (Isaiah 64:6). So what can we wear in the presence of God? Robes made white by the sacrifice of Jesus. Jesus removes our unrighteousness and clothes us with His own righteousness (Job 29:14; Isaiah 61:10). By relying on Jesus' sacrifice to save us, we joyfully wear the same Christ-cleansed robes as these tribulation-saints. (***See Salvation****> Receiving> When> Declared righteous,* TopicGuide page A23.)

▸ WORSHIP

8:3-4 Prayers that are heard in heaven. What do you do when life gets hard? Often we end up acting like the Israelites after they had been delivered from their bondage in Egypt. As they made their way toward the land God had promised them, they encountered hardships and complained (Exodus 14:11-12; 15:24; 16:1-2). But there is an alternative to complaining. As John watches the unfolding of God's plan, he notices that when troubles are stirring on the earth, the prayers of the people of God rise to heaven. In Hebrews 4:16 we are told that we can come in prayer before the throne of God and find the help we need. So ask for help from the One who longs to help you. It's a better choice than grumbling! (***See Worship****> NT> Prayer> Instructions> Be anxious for nothing,* TopicGuide page A33.)

8:6-12 The seven trumpets usher in seven plagues. Many believe that these plagues symbolize God's total judgment upon the earth. Others believe these plagues illustrate seven distinct events or periods of judgment in history. Even as these calamities are unleashed, God is still in control just as He was when He brought the plagues on Egypt during the time of the Exodus so many years earlier (Exodus 7–11).

8Then the second angel blew his trumpet, and a great mountain of fire was thrown into
the sea. One-third of the water in the sea became blood, 9one-third of all things living in
the sea died, and one-third of all the ships on the sea were destroyed.
10Then the third angel blew his trumpet, and a great star fell from the sky, burning like a
torch. It fell on one-third of the rivers and on the springs of water. 11The name of the star
was Bitterness.* It made one-third of the water bitter, and many people died from drinking
the bitter water.
12Then the fourth angel blew his trumpet, and one-third of the sun was struck, and one-
third of the moon, and one-third of the stars, and they became dark. And one-third of the
day was dark, and also one-third of the night.
13Then I looked, and I heard a single eagle crying loudly as it flew through the air, "Ter-
ror, terror, terror to all who belong to this world because of what will happen when the last
three angels blow their trumpets."

THE FIFTH TRUMPET BRINGS THE FIRST TERROR

9 Then the fifth angel blew his trumpet, and I saw a star that had fallen to earth from
the sky, and he was given the key to the shaft of the bottomless pit.* 2When he
opened it, smoke poured out as though from a huge furnace, and the sunlight and air
turned dark from the smoke.
3Then locusts came from the smoke and descended on the earth, and they were given
power to sting like scorpions. 4They were told not to harm the grass or plants or trees, but
only the people who did not have the seal of God on their foreheads. 5They were told not
to kill them but to torture them for five months with pain like the pain of a scorpion sting.
6In those days people will seek death but will not find it. They will long to die, but death
will flee from them!
7The locusts looked like horses prepared for battle. They had what looked like gold
crowns on their heads, and their faces looked like human faces. 8They had hair like
women's hair and teeth like the teeth of a lion. 9They wore armor made of iron, and their
wings roared like an army of chariots rushing into battle. 10They had tails that stung like
scorpions, and for five months they had the power to torment people. 11Their king is the
angel from the bottomless pit; his name in Hebrew is *Abaddon,* and in Greek, *Apollyon*—
the Destroyer.
12The first terror is past, but look, two more terrors are coming!

THE SIXTH TRUMPET BRINGS THE SECOND TERROR

13Then the sixth angel blew his trumpet, and I heard a voice speaking from the four horns
of the gold altar that stands in the presence of God. 14And the voice said to the sixth angel

8:8 Jer 51:25; Rev 16:3
8:9 Exod 7:20
8:10 Isa 14:12; Rev 6:13; 9:1; 16:4
8:11 Jer 9:15
8:12 Exod 10:21; Ezek 32:7-8; Rev 6:12-13
8:13 Rev 3:10; 9:12
9:1 Isa 14:12; Luke 8:31; 10:18
9:2 Gen 19:28; Exod 19:18; Joel 2:2, 10
9:3 Exod 10:12-15; Rev 9:5, 10
9:4 Ezek 9:4, 6
9:6 Job 3:21; Rev 6:16
9:7 Joel 2:4-5
9:8 Joel 1:6
9:9 Joel 2:5
9:11 Job 26:6; 28:22; Prov 15:11
9:13 Exod 30:1-3
9:14 Gen 15:18

8:11 Greek *Wormwood.* 9:1 Or *the abyss,* or *the underworld;* also in 9:11.

9:1 In chapter 8, the reference to a star appears to speak of an actual celestial body (8:10-11); here the star seems to represent an angelic being.

▸ GOD
9:1-5 God's sovereignty over calamity. Suffering can seem senseless. But the story of Job drives home the point that although Job didn't understand suffering, God was still in control and had a purpose for all that was occurring in Job's life—even the worst things. That idea permeates what is described in this section of Revelation. Although God wasn't punishing Job (not in the way He judges the nations of the world), still God is ultimately in control of all, even the harshest realities of this world. This is underscored when we read that God is the One who gives a key to the angel to loose this judgment, and the "locust" that are set free can only go as far as God permits them. Take comfort and have confidence in God. Our world is not out of control; it is in His control. (***See God**> God's Attributes> All-Powerful> God speaks and things happen,* TopicGuide page A16.)

9:3-10 In the Old Testament book of Joel (2:1-11), a swarm of locust foreshadows an invasion of a destroying army sent by God. The locust image here presents the same picture, except that this army is under the command of a fallen angel (although not out from under God's ultimate control; see Job 1:9-12).

9:14 Some Old Testament passages indicate that certain angels of God aid in controlling the affairs of nations (see Daniel 10:13-21). It may be that although the armies seen marching under the call of the sixth trumpet are human armies, they are still under God's ultimate control through the agency of His angels.

who held the trumpet, "Release the four angels who are bound at the great Euphrates
River." 15Then the four angels who had been prepared for this hour and day and month
and year were turned loose to kill one-third of all the people on earth. 16I heard the size of
their army, which was 200 million mounted troops.

17And in my vision, I saw the horses and the riders sitting on them. The riders wore ar-
mor that was fiery red and dark blue and yellow. The horses had heads like lions, and fire
and smoke and burning sulfur billowed from their mouths. 18One-third of all the people
on earth were killed by these three plagues—by the fire and smoke and burning sulfur that
came from the mouths of the horses. 19Their power was in their mouths and in their tails.
For their tails had heads like snakes, with the power to injure people.

20But the people who did not die in these plagues still refused to repent of their evil
deeds and turn to God. They continued to worship demons and idols made of gold, silver,
bronze, stone, and wood—idols that can neither see nor hear nor walk! 21And they did not
repent of their murders or their witchcraft or their sexual immorality or their thefts.

THE ANGEL AND THE SMALL SCROLL

10 Then I saw another mighty angel coming down from heaven, surrounded by a
cloud, with a rainbow over his head. His face shone like the sun, and his feet were
like pillars of fire. 2And in his hand was a small scroll* that had been opened. He stood with
his right foot on the sea and his left foot on the land. 3And he gave a great shout like the
roar of a lion. And when he shouted, the seven thunders answered.

4When the seven thunders spoke, I was about to write. But I heard a voice from heaven
saying, "Keep secret* what the seven thunders said, and do not write it down."

5Then the angel I saw standing on the sea and on the land raised his right hand toward
heaven. 6He swore an oath in the name of the One who lives forever and ever, who cre-
ated the heavens and everything in them, the earth and everything in it, and the sea and
everything in it. He said, "There will be no more delay. 7When the seventh angel blows his
trumpet, God's mysterious plan will be fulfilled. It will happen just as He announced it to
His servants the prophets."

8Then the voice from heaven spoke to me again: "Go and take the open scroll from the
hand of the angel who is standing on the sea and on the land."

9So I went to the angel and told him to give me the small scroll. "Yes, take it and eat it,"
he said. "It will be sweet as honey in your mouth, but it will turn sour in your stomach!"
10So I took the small scroll from the hand of the angel, and I ate it! It was sweet in my
mouth, but when I swallowed it, it turned sour in my stomach.

11Then I was told, "You must prophesy again about many peoples, nations, languages,
and kings."

10:2 Or *book;* also in 10:8, 9, 10. 10:4 Greek *Seal up.*

9:15 Rev 8:7-12; 9:18; 20:7
9:17 Job 41:10-12
9:20 Deut 4:28; 32:17; Ps 115:4-7; Dan 5:23; Mic 5:13; Acts 7:41; 1 Cor 10:19-20; Rev 2:21
9:21 Rev 16:9, 11, 21
10:1 Matt 17:2; Rev 1:15-16; 4:3; 5:2; 18:1
10:2 Rev 10:8
10:3 Ps 29:3-9; Rev 4:5
10:4 Dan 8:26; 12:4, 9; Rev 22:10
10:5 Deut 32:40; Dan 12:7
10:6 Gen 14:19, 22; Exod 20:11; Neh 9:6; Ps 146:6; Rev 4:11; 14:7; 16:17
10:7 Dan 9:6, 10; Amos 3:7; Rev 11:15
10:8 Rev 10:2
10:9 Jer 15:16; Ezek 2:8–3:3
10:11 Jer 1:9-10; 25:30; Rev 5:9

9:20-21 John describes people who "still refused to repent of their evil deeds" and "continued to worship . . . idols." John is making it clear that God's purpose in sending such trouble to the earth is to call people to repentance.

10:1 This mighty angel is not one of the seven (8:6) or, apparently, one of the four (9:14). Throughout Revelation, angels not only reveal portions of the God's plan, but they also participate directly in carrying out that plan.

▶ BIBLE
10:4 Only God knows. Some students of the Bible have approached the book of Revelation and other prophetic passages with the thought that, given enough time and study, they could understand the end-time plan of God. Such students assume that they have the capacity for fully understanding what God is going to do and that they have all the information necessary. Yet Jesus, in all His wisdom and understanding of Scripture, said He didn't understand some aspects of prophecy (Matthew 24:36; Mark 13:32). Likewise, in this passage, John is told not to record something regarding the end of time, keeping it secret from his readers. Biblical prophecy is often intentionally mysterious. God knows everything, but we only know what He reveals to us. We should trust in God's knowledge and let some mysteries and secrets remain so. (***See Bible*> *Unity*> *Kingdom of God*> *Kingdom is a mystery,* TopicGuide page A11.)

10:9-10 This vision of the scroll is similar to the experiences of Ezekiel (2:9–3:11). Ezekiel was given a scroll to eat that contained the words of the prophecies he was to proclaim. For both John and Ezekiel, the message of God is sweet because it is God's own word (Psalms 19:10; 119:103), but because the message is one of coming judgment, it also causes a bitter experience in the lives of those who receive the word.

THE TWO WITNESSES

11 Then I was given a measuring stick, and I was told, "Go and measure the Temple
of God and the altar, and count the number of worshipers. 2But do not measure
the outer courtyard, for it has been turned over to the nations. They will trample the holy
city for 42 months. 3And I will give power to My two witnesses, and they will be clothed in
burlap and will prophesy during those 1,260 days."

4These two prophets are the two olive trees and the two lampstands that stand before
the Lord of all the earth. 5If anyone tries to harm them, fire flashes from their mouths and
consumes their enemies. This is how anyone who tries to harm them must die. 6They have
power to shut the sky so that no rain will fall for as long as they prophesy. And they have
the power to turn the rivers and oceans into blood, and to strike the earth with every kind
of plague as often as they wish.

7When they complete their testimony, the beast that comes up out of the bottomless
pit* will declare war against them, and he will conquer them and kill them. 8And their bod-
ies will lie in the main street of Jerusalem,* the city that is figuratively called "Sodom" and
"Egypt," the city where their Lord was crucified. 9And for three and a half days, all peoples,
tribes, languages, and nations will stare at their bodies. No one will be allowed to bury
them. 10All the people who belong to this world will gloat over them and give presents to
each other to celebrate the death of the two prophets who had tormented them.

11But after three and a half days, God breathed life into them, and they stood up! Terror
struck all who were staring at them. 12Then a loud voice from heaven called to the two
prophets, "Come up here!" And they rose to heaven in a cloud as their enemies watched.

13At the same time there was a terrible earthquake that destroyed a tenth of the city.
Seven thousand people died in that earthquake, and everyone else was terrified and gave
glory to the God of heaven.

14The second terror is past, but look, the third terror is coming quickly.

THE SEVENTH TRUMPET BRINGS THE THIRD TERROR

15Then the seventh angel blew his trumpet, and there were loud voices shouting in heaven:

"The world has now become the Kingdom of our Lord and of His Christ,*
and He will reign forever and ever."

11:1 Ezek 40:3; Rev 21:15
11:2 Ezek 40:17-20; Luke 21:24; Rev 12:6; 13:5
11:3 Rev 2:13
11:4 Zech 4:3, 11, 14
11:5 2 Sam 22:9; 2 Kgs 1:10; Jer 5:14
11:6 Exod 7:17-20; 1 Kgs 17:1
11:7 Dan 7:21; Rev 13:1, 7
11:8 Isa 1:9-10
11:9 Ps 79:2-3
11:11 Ezek 37:5, 10
11:12 2 Kgs 2:11; Acts 1:9; Rev 4:1
11:13 Ezek 38:19-20; Rev 16:9, 11
11:15 Ps 10:16; Dan 2:44; 7:14, 27

11:7 Or *the abyss,* or *the underworld.* 11:8 Greek *the great city.* 11:15 Or *His Messiah.*

11:1-2 The image of the Temple here probably does not refer to the one that was standing (or had been standing shortly before) in Jerusalem in John's day, for its dimensions would have been already well known. The key to at least partially understanding it is in Ezekiel 40–42, which is an example of using architectural design to communicate idealized worship and theological truths about the object of our worship.

11:3-12 The two witnesses are reminiscent of key Old Testament figures. Their descriptions have similarities to Zechariah 4:1-14, which discusses leaders of the nation of Israel. The ministry ascribed to them resembles that of Elijah and Moses, who also are associated with the end of the ages in Malachi 4:4-6. Some believe this passage indicates an actual future reappearance of these two great prophets. Some see the witnesses as symbolic of the major divisions of the Old Testament—the Law (through Moses) and the Prophets (represented by Elijah), while others believe these witnesses represent faithful churches or people bearing witness to Christ (Luke 10:1). Many conclude that even in the midst of severe trials, God will provide for Himself a witness on the earth, and no matter what Satan plans, those witnesses will rise to judge those who have harmed them (1 Corinthians 6:2).

11:3 Periods of time are mentioned repeatedly in Revelation. Here, the time is 42 months (see also 13:5). The same length of time is referred to as 1,260 days (12:6), and it is probably the same as "time, times, and half a time," which is 3 1/2 years (12:14). In the book of Daniel (chapters 7 and 12) this period of time is associated with the culmination of God's plan. Some see this as a literal reference to a specific period of time; others would see it as a symbolical reference to a time of great distress. In either case, the references speak of a time of calamity that lasts for only a limited period of time.

▸ GOD
11:15-17 Sure victory. For John's readers, and for many in the world even today, life doesn't present a picture of ever-increasing peace and blessing and joy. If anything, life is getting more complicated, more chaotic. That is why John's visions are so very important. He tells us where the world is headed—sure victory for our Lord and Savior, Jesus. In spite of what things may look like at any given moment, God's plan has always been in place, and it will reach its culmination when Jesus fully exercises His rightful reign over all. It has already begun in the hearts of His people and His church. We are waiting for that glorious culmination. Manifest the joy of living under the rule of Christ to a watching world. (***See God***> *God's Attributes> Eternal> The Son's reign will have no end,* TopicGuide page A16.)

11:16 Rev 4:4, 10
11:17 Amos 3:13; 4:13 Rev 1:8; 19:6

16 The twenty-four elders sitting on their thrones before God fell with their faces to the ground and worshiped Him. 17 And they said,

> "We give thanks to You, Lord God, the Almighty,
> the One who is and who always was,
> for now You have assumed Your great power
> and have begun to reign.

11:18 Ps 2:1 Rev 10:7; 19:5; 20:12

> 18 The nations were filled with wrath,
> but now the time of Your wrath has come.
> It is time to judge the dead
> and reward Your servants the prophets,
> as well as Your holy people,
> and all who fear Your name,
> from the least to the greatest.
> It is time to destroy
> all who have caused destruction on the earth."

11:19 2 Chr 5:7 Rev 4:5; 15:5

19 Then, in heaven, the Temple of God was opened and the Ark of His covenant could be seen inside the Temple. Lightning flashed, thunder crashed and roared, and there was an earthquake and a terrible hailstorm.

12:2 Isa 26:17; 66:6-9 Mic 4:10
12:3 Dan 7:7, 24 Rev 13:1; 17:3, 7, 12, 16
12:4 Dan 8:10
12:5 Ps 2:9 Rev 2:27; 19:15
12:6 Rev 11:2; 13:5
12:7 Dan 10:13; 12:1 Jude 1:9 Rev 12:3
12:9 Gen 3:1 Zech 3:1-2 Matt 4:10 Luke 10:18 Rev 12:3; 20:2-10

THE WOMAN AND THE DRAGON

12 Then I witnessed in heaven an event of great significance. I saw a woman clothed with the sun, with the moon beneath her feet, and a crown of twelve stars on her head. 2 She was pregnant, and she cried out because of her labor pains and the agony of giving birth.

3 Then I witnessed in heaven another significant event. I saw a large red dragon with seven heads and ten horns, with seven crowns on his heads. 4 His tail swept away one-third of the stars in the sky, and he threw them to the earth. He stood in front of the woman as she was about to give birth, ready to devour her baby as soon as it was born.

5 She gave birth to a son who was to rule all nations with an iron rod. And her child was snatched away from the dragon and was caught up to God and to His throne. 6 And the woman fled into the wilderness, where God had prepared a place to care for her for 1,260 days.

7 Then there was war in heaven. Michael and his angels fought against the dragon and his angels. 8 And the dragon lost the battle, and he and his angels were forced out of heaven. 9 This great dragon—the ancient serpent called the devil, or Satan, the one deceiving the whole world—was thrown down to the earth with all his angels.

12:1 In this next section of Revelation, we are introduced to seven figures in a series of visions that picture a cosmic struggle waged in our world. In this vision, the children of the woman are those who "keep God's commandments and maintain their testimony for Jesus" (12:17). Although some see this woman as Mary, the mother of Jesus, this woman most likely refers to God's people, who have anticipated the coming of the Messiah throughout all history.

12:3 The dragon is a picture of Satan (12:9). He opposes not only Jesus (12:4-5), but all those who follow Jesus as well (12:17).

▸ SPIRITUAL WARFARE

12:3-11 Destruction is his goal. Many regard Satan as merely a myth; they don't think of him as a real enemy intent on our destruction. But Satan is very real. From the little glimpse that John gives us here, we can see that Satan is actively opposed to all that God is doing; He doesn't just idly watch. Also, Satan targets those who are followers of Jesus. He stirs up trouble for them and seeks to disturb their trust in Jesus. Those who follow Jesus can be sure of victory over Satan. However, it will only come through the power of the sacrifice that Jesus made on our behalf and our willingness to hold on to that—even in the face of death. Do not underestimate your enemy—he has destroyed the lives of many, even those who profess allegiance to Jesus (1 Peter 5:8; 1 John 3:8). (***See Spiritual Warfare*** > *Originator of Sin* > *Satan's Goals* > *Keep men from faith in God,* TopicGuide page A45.)

10Then I heard a loud voice shouting across the heavens,

"It has come at last—
  salvation and power
and the Kingdom of our God,
  and the authority of His Christ.*
For the accuser of our brothers and sisters*
  has been thrown down to earth—
the one who accuses them
  before our God day and night.
11 And they have defeated him by the blood of the Lamb
  and by their testimony.
And they did not love their lives so much
  that they were afraid to die.
12 Therefore, rejoice, O heavens!
  And you who live in the heavens, rejoice!
But terror will come on the earth and the sea,
  for the devil has come down to you in great anger,
  knowing that he has little time."

12:10 Job 1:9-11; Zech 3:1; Rev 7:10; 11:15
12:11 Rev 2:10; 6:9; 7:14; 15:2
12:12 Rev 8:13; 18:20

13When the dragon realized that he had been thrown down to the earth, he pursued the
woman who had given birth to the male child. 14But she was given two wings like those of
a great eagle so she could fly to the place prepared for her in the wilderness. There she
would be cared for and protected from the dragon* for a time, times, and half a time.
15Then the dragon tried to drown the woman with a flood of water that flowed from his
mouth. 16But the earth helped her by opening its mouth and swallowing the river that
gushed out from the mouth of the dragon. 17And the dragon was angry at the woman and
declared war against the rest of her children—all who keep God's commandments and
maintain their testimony for Jesus.
18Then the dragon took his stand* on the shore beside the sea.

12:14 Exod 19:4; Dan 7:25; 12:7; Rev 17:3, 18
12:17 Rev 1:2; 11:7; 13:7

THE BEAST OUT OF THE SEA

13 Then I saw a beast rising up out of the sea. It had seven heads and ten horns, with
ten crowns on its horns. And written on each head were names that blasphemed
God. 2This beast looked like a leopard, but it had the feet of a bear and the mouth of a
lion! And the dragon gave the beast his own power and throne and great authority.
3I saw that one of the heads of the beast seemed wounded beyond recovery—but the fa-
tal wound was healed! The whole world marveled at this miracle and gave allegiance to
the beast. 4They worshiped the dragon for giving the beast such power, and they also wor-
shiped the beast. "Who is as great as the beast?" they exclaimed. "Who is able to fight
against him?"

13:1 Dan 7:2-8; Rev 17:12
13:2 Dan 7:4-6; Rev 2:13; 12:3
13:3 2 Thes 2:9-12; Rev 17:8
13:4 Exod 15:11

12:10a Or *His Messiah.* 12:10b Greek *brothers.* 12:14 Greek *the serpent;* also in 12:15. See 12:9. 12:18 Greek *Then he took his stand;* some manuscripts read *Then I took my stand.* Some translations put this entire sentence into 13:1.

12:9 In this verse, John describes our enemy, Satan. Peter describes him as a roaring lion (1 Peter 5:8-9). Another description of Satan and his wiles is found in Job 1:6–2:7.

13:1-18 In this chapter we are introduced to two "beasts" that share in a common work (13:12). The first symbolizes a person with political and social power; the latter appears to be one with religious or spiritual power. Clearly, they are empowered by Satan, the great dragon (13:4). Together these beasts ultimately influence the whole world. They may represent past, present, and future world systems that are influenced by Satan and specific people that the original audience would have been able to identify.

13:7 The first beast takes his lead from Satan (12:17) and wages war against the followers of Jesus (13:7). His strategy is to demand worship (12:7-8). When the second beast arrives on the scene, he joins in the war, requiring all to submit to their authority or face retribution (12:17). Although followers of Jesus may lose their lives through remaining faithful to their Savior, they will find that such is the way to victory (12:11; see also 6:9-11).

5 Then the beast was allowed to speak great blasphemies against God. And he was
given authority to do whatever he wanted for forty-two months. 6 And he spoke terrible
words of blasphemy against God, slandering His name and His dwelling—that is, those
who dwell in heaven.* 7 And the beast was allowed to wage war against God's holy people
and to conquer them. And he was given authority to rule over every tribe and people and
language and nation. 8 And all the people who belong to this world worshiped the beast.
They are the ones whose names were not written in the Book of Life before the world was
made—the Book that belongs to the Lamb who was slaughtered.*

9 Anyone with ears to hear
should listen and understand.

10 Anyone who is destined for prison
will be taken to prison.
Anyone destined to die by the sword
will die by the sword.

This means that God's holy people must endure persecution patiently and remain faithful.

THE BEAST OUT OF THE EARTH

11 Then I saw another beast come up out of the earth. He had two horns like those of a
lamb, but he spoke with the voice of a dragon. 12 He exercised all the authority of the first
beast. And he required all the earth and its people to worship the first beast, whose fatal
wound had been healed. 13 He did astounding miracles, even making fire flash down to
earth from the sky while everyone was watching. 14 And with all the miracles he was al-
lowed to perform on behalf of the first beast, he deceived all the people who belong to this
world. He ordered the people to make a great statue of the first beast, who was fatally
wounded and then came back to life. 15 He was then permitted to give life to this statue so
that it could speak. Then the statue of the beast commanded that anyone refusing to wor-
ship it must die.
16 He required everyone—small and great, rich and poor, free and slave—to be given a
mark on the right hand or on the forehead. 17 And no one could buy or sell anything with-
out that mark, which was either the name of the beast or the number representing his
name. 18 Wisdom is needed here. Let the one with understanding solve the meaning of the
number of the beast, for it is the number of a man.* His number is 666.*

13:5 Dan 7:8, 11, 20, 25; 11:36; 2 Thes 2:4; Rev 11:2
13:6 Rev 12:12
13:7 Rev 5:9; 11:7
13:8 Dan 12:1
13:9 Rev 2:7
13:10 Jer 15:2; 43:11; Matt 26:52; Heb 6:12
13:11 Rev 13:1, 4
13:12 Rev 14:9-10; 19:20
13:13 1 Kgs 18:24-39; Matt 24:24; 2 Thes 2:9; Rev 19:20
13:14 2 Thes 2:9; Rev 12:9; 13:3, 12
13:15 Dan 3:3-6; Rev 20:4
13:16 Rev 14:9; 19:18
13:17 Rev 14:9, 11; 16:2; 19:20; 20:4
13:18 Rev 17:9

13:6 Some manuscripts read *and His dwelling and all who dwell in heaven.* 13:8 Or *not written in the Book of Life that belongs to the Lamb who was slaughtered before the world was made.* 13:18a Or *of humanity.* 13:18b Some manuscripts read *616.*

▸ SPIRITUAL WARFARE

13:8-10 The ending we all long for. If we could tell the future, we might find it easier to endure the challenges and heartache leading to a goal. Every student starting a class wants to know that she will pass. Every businessman launching a new initiative wants to know that his plan will turn a profit. Every couple considering marriage wishes for eyes to see what the future holds. The future John shows us in Revelation is not a pretty one: Life will be extremely hard. But, take heart; if you belong to Jesus, you are assured of ultimate victory. His claim on you stands from "before the world was made" (13:8). Although you may face hardship, you can endure, holding tightly to the One who holds you in His grip. (***See Spiritual Warfare**> Resisting Sin and Evil> Trusting God> God as Warrior> God's fight to final victory,* TopicGuide page A46.)

13:16-17 Signs on the hand and head held religious symbolism for Jews, with symbolic marks spoken of in Exodus 13:9 and more literal ones in Deuteronomy 6:8 and 11:18. In these cases, the hand and head seem to refer to a wholehearted commitment of mind and actions to God. To counter this, the beast commands that everyone must receive his mark.

13:18 Revelation was written to prepare God's people for a dramatic time of persecution from the Roman Empire. Using a common method of giving letters a numeric value, the Emperor Nero's name equals "666." Since Revelation was likely written after Nero's persecution, it may be that Nero's name was so associated with the religious persecution and the Roman Empire that "666" would have warned the readers that someone like Nero would come in the future, bringing great harm upon the church.

THE LAMB AND THE 144,000

14 Then I saw the Lamb standing on Mount Zion, and with Him were 144,000 who
had His name and His Father's name written on their foreheads. 2And I heard a
sound from heaven like the roar of mighty ocean waves or the rolling of loud thunder. It
was like the sound of many harpists playing together.
3This great choir sang a wonderful new song in front of the throne of God and before
the four living beings and the twenty-four elders. No one could learn this song except the
144,000 who had been redeemed from the earth. 4They have kept themselves as pure as
virgins,* following the Lamb wherever He goes. They have been purchased from among
the people on the earth as a special offering* to God and to the Lamb. 5They have told no
lies; they are without blame.

THE THREE ANGELS

6And I saw another angel flying through the sky, carrying the eternal Good News to pro-
claim to the people who belong to this world—to every nation, tribe, language, and people.
7"Fear God," he shouted. "Give glory to Him. For the time has come when He will sit as
judge. Worship Him who made the heavens, the earth, the sea, and all the springs of water."
8Then another angel followed him through the sky, shouting, "Babylon is fallen—that
great city is fallen—because she made all the nations of the world drink the wine of her
passionate immorality."
9Then a third angel followed them, shouting, "Anyone who worships the beast and his
statue or who accepts his mark on the forehead or on the hand 10must drink the wine of
God's anger. It has been poured full strength into God's cup of wrath. And they will be tor-
mented with fire and burning sulfur in the presence of the holy angels and the Lamb. 11The
smoke of their torment will rise forever and ever, and they will have no relief day or night,
for they have worshiped the beast and his statue and have accepted the mark of his name."
12This means that God's holy people must endure persecution patiently, obeying His
commands and maintaining their faith in Jesus.
13And I heard a voice from heaven saying, "Write this down: Blessed are those who die
in the Lord from now on. Yes, says the Spirit, they are blessed indeed, for they will rest
from their hard work; for their good deeds follow them!"

THE HARVEST OF THE EARTH

14Then I saw a white cloud, and seated on the cloud was someone like the Son of Man.*
He had a gold crown on His head and a sharp sickle in His hand.
15Then another angel came from the Temple and shouted to the one sitting on the cloud,
"Swing the sickle, for the time of harvest has come; the crop on earth is ripe." 16So the one
sitting on the cloud swung His sickle over the earth, and the whole earth was harvested.
17After that, another angel came from the Temple in heaven, and he also had a sharp
sickle. 18Then another angel, who had power to destroy with fire, came from the altar. He

14:1 Rev 3:12; 7:4
14:2 Rev 1:15; 19:6
14:3 Rev 4:4, 6
14:4 2 Cor 11:2; Rev 5:9; 7:17
14:5 Ps 32:2; Isa 53:9; Zeph 3:13; 1 Pet 2:22
14:6 Rev 5:9
14:7 Acts 4:24; Rev 15:4
14:8 Isa 21:9; Jer 51:8; Rev 16:19; 17:5; 18:2, 10
14:9 Rev 13:12-17
14:10 Ps 75:8; Isa 51:17, 22-23; Jer 25:15; Rev 16:19; 19:20; 20:10; 21:8
14:11 Isa 34:10; Rev 13:12-17
14:12 Rev 2:13; 12:17; 13:10
14:13 Heb 4:10
14:14 Dan 7:13; Rev 1:13
14:15 Joel 3:13; Matt 13:39-40; Mark 4:29
14:18 Joel 3:13; Rev 6:9; 14:15

14:4a Greek *They are virgins who have not defiled themselves with women.* 14:4b Greek *as firstfruits.* 14:14 Or *like a son of man.* See Dan 7:13. "Son of Man" is a title Jesus used for Himself.

14:1 In contrast to those who have "the mark . . . of the beast" (13:16-17), the 144,000 have the name of the Lamb written on them. It is not certain that the 144,000 here are identical with those mentioned in 7:4-8 (see the notes on 7:1-10). John is reminding readers again that no matter how hard things become, it is still possible to remain faithful to Jesus.

14:6-7 The vision of this angel flying through the sky with the gospel demonstrates the certainty that the message about Jesus will be preached to all the nations of the world (see Matthew 24:14).

14:8 This is the first of six mentions of "Babylon" in Revelation (see also 16:19; 17:5; 18:2, 10, 21). Those in John's day most likely would have thought of Rome, which was as much the capital of immorality and idolatry as the actual city of Babylon had been in the later part of the Old Testament. The city represents the center of earthly power that resists the work of God on earth.

14:14 The "Son of Man" was one of Jesus' favorite titles for Himself (for example, see Matthew 8:20; 9:6; 12:8). With roots in the Old Testament (Daniel 7:13-14), the title pictures one who is identified with humanity, but who also stands over all people.

shouted to the angel with the sharp sickle, "Swing your sickle now to gather the clusters of
grapes from the vines of the earth, for they are ripe for judgment." 19 So the angel swung
his sickle over the earth and loaded the grapes into the great winepress of God's wrath.
20 The grapes were trampled in the winepress outside the city, and blood flowed from the
winepress in a stream about 180 miles* long and as high as a horse's bridle.

THE SONG OF MOSES AND OF THE LAMB

15 Then I saw in heaven another marvelous event of great significance. Seven an-
gels were holding the seven last plagues, which would bring God's wrath to com-
pletion. 2 I saw before me what seemed to be a glass sea mixed with fire. And on it stood all
the people who had been victorious over the beast and his statue and the number repre-
senting his name. They were all holding harps that God had given them. 3 And they were
singing the song of Moses, the servant of God, and the song of the Lamb:

"Great and marvelous are Your works,
O Lord God, the Almighty.
Just and true are Your ways,
O King of the nations.*
4 Who will not fear You, Lord,
and glorify Your name?
For You alone are holy.
All nations will come and worship before You,
for Your righteous deeds have been revealed."

THE SEVEN BOWLS OF THE SEVEN PLAGUES

5 Then I looked and saw that the Temple in heaven, God's Tabernacle, was thrown wide
open. 6 The seven angels who were holding the seven plagues came out of the Temple.
They were clothed in spotless white linen* with gold sashes across their chests. 7 Then one
of the four living beings handed each of the seven angels a gold bowl filled with the wrath
of God, who lives forever and ever. 8 The Temple was filled with smoke from God's glory
and power. No one could enter the Temple until the seven angels had completed pouring
out the seven plagues.

16 Then I heard a mighty voice from the Temple say to the seven angels, "Go your
ways and pour out on the earth the seven bowls containing God's wrath."

14:19 Isa 63:2-6; Rev 19:15
14:20 Gen 49:11; Isa 63:3; Lam 1:15; Rev 19:15
15:1 Lev 26:21; Rev 15:6; 16:1; 21:9
15:2 Rev 4:6
15:3 Exod 15:1; Deut 32:1-4; Ps 145:17; Jer 10:7; Amos 3:13; 4:13; Rev 1:8; 4:8
15:4 Ps 86:9; Jer 10:6-7; Mal 1:11
15:5 Rev 11:19
15:6 Lev 26:21; Rev 1:13
15:7 Rev 4:6, 9
15:8 Exod 40:34; 1 Kgs 8:10-11; 2 Chr 5:13-14; Isa 6:4
16:1 Isa 66:6; Zeph 3:8; Rev 11:19; 15:1

14:20 Greek *1,600 stadia* [296 kilometers]. 15:3 Some manuscripts read *King of the ages.* 15:6 Other manuscripts read *white stone;* still others read *white [garments] made of linen.*

15:1 The last picture of the judgment coming upon the earth is seen in the angels with the seven gold bowls "filled with the wrath of God" (15:7). As the message of these bowls unfolds, we are given a picture of the culmination of God's judgment.

15:3 When God showed Himself as an awesome and powerful deliverer during the time of the Exodus, a victory song was sung under the direction of Moses offering praises to God (Exodus 15:1-19).

▸ GOD
15:3-4 No one else is close. As the end of history draws to its climax, the picture around the throne in Revelation is one of glorious celebration. Those gathered declare that there is none like God. He is just and absolutely right in all He does; He is true, faithful, and unerring; He is the Holy One, unlike any other being. Our God is unique and entirely worthy of all worship (Isaiah 46:9). Do not give the honor and respect that God alone deserves to anyone else. If you are tempted to let something in your life take His place (material possessions, money, children), readjust your focus and worship God, setting your heart on Him alone. (***See God> God's Nature> Unique> He alone is holy,*** TopicGuide page A15.)

15:8 Smoke has often been associated with the presence of God and His glory (Exodus 19:9, 16-18; Isaiah 6:4; Ezekiel 1:4). In this case the smoke was a barrier to warn others to stay clear of God's wrath about to be released, similar to the smoke that alternately protected Israel and threatened the pursuing Egyptians as the Israelites fled to the Promised Land (Exodus 13:21-22; 14:24).

16:1-10 In a brief account, the last cycle of God's judgment is pictured as the seven bowls of wrath are poured out on the earth. A number of these judgments are like the plagues that God sent upon Egypt: the sores (Exodus 9:8-12), the blood (Exodus 7:14-24), and the darkness (10:21-23). There also is a similarity between the pharaoh amassing his armies against the Israelites (Exodus 14) and those who fight against God amassing here.

2So the first angel left the Temple and poured out his bowl on the earth, and horrible,
malignant sores broke out on everyone who had the mark of the beast and who wor-
shiped his statue.
3Then the second angel poured out his bowl on the sea, and it became like the blood of
a corpse. And everything in the sea died.
4Then the third angel poured out his bowl on the rivers and springs, and they became
blood. 5And I heard the angel who had authority over all water saying,

"You are just, O Holy One, who is and who always was,
because You have sent these judgments.
6 Since they shed the blood
of Your holy people and Your prophets,
You have given them blood to drink.
It is their just reward."

7And I heard a voice from the altar,* saying,

"Yes, O Lord God, the Almighty,
Your judgments are true and just."

8Then the fourth angel poured out his bowl on the sun, causing it to scorch everyone
with its fire. 9Everyone was burned by this blast of heat, and they cursed the name of God,
who had control over all these plagues. They did not repent of their sins and turn to God
and give Him glory.
10Then the fifth angel poured out his bowl on the throne of the beast, and his kingdom was
plunged into darkness. His subjects ground their teeth in anguish, 11and they cursed the God
of heaven for their pains and sores. But they did not repent of their evil deeds and turn to God.
12Then the sixth angel poured out his bowl on the great Euphrates River, and it dried up
so that the kings from the east could march their armies toward the west without hin-
drance. 13And I saw three evil* spirits that looked like frogs leap from the mouths of the
dragon, the beast, and the false prophet. 14They are demonic spirits who work miracles
and go out to all the rulers of the world to gather them for battle against the Lord on that
great judgment day of God the Almighty.

15"Look, I will come as unexpectedly as a thief! Blessed are all who are watching for
Me, who keep their clothing ready so they will not have to walk around naked and
ashamed."

16And the demonic spirits gathered all the rulers and their armies to a place with the He-
brew name *Armageddon*.*
17Then the seventh angel poured out his bowl into the air. And a mighty shout came
from the throne in the Temple, saying, "It is finished!" 18Then the thunder crashed and
rolled, and lightning flashed. And a great earthquake struck—the worst since people were

16:2 Exod 9:9-11; Rev 8:7; 13:15-17
16:3 Exod 7:17-21; Rev 8:8-9
16:4 Exod 7:17-21; Ps 78:44; Rev 8:10
16:5 Rev 1:4, 8; 4:8; 11:17
16:6 Ps 79:3; Isa 49:26
16:7 Rev 1:8; 6:9; 14:18; 15:3; 19:2
16:8 Rev 6:12; 8:12
16:9 Rev 11:13
16:10 Exod 10:21; Isa 8:22; Rev 8:12; 9:2; 13:2
16:11 Rev 9:20-21
16:12 Isa 11:15-16; 44:27; Jer 50:38; 51:36; Rev 9:14
16:13 Rev 12:3; 13:1, 11-17
16:14 Rev 6:17; 17:14; 19:19
16:15 1 Thes 5:2; Rev 3:3, 18
16:16 Judg 5:19; 2 Kgs 9:27; 23:29; Zech 12:11
16:17 Isa 66:6; Rev 11:15; 21:6
16:18 Dan 12:1; Matt 24:21; Rev 4:5; 6:12

16:7 Greek *I heard the altar.* 16:13 Greek *unclean.* 16:16 Or *Harmagedon.*

▸ ADOPTION

16:6 Pray for the persecuted. All over the world, people suffer simply for being Christians. If you are in a place where you are not actively persecuted for your faith, you are an exception—geographically and historically. How should we respond to the suffering of fellow believers? Should we simply be grateful we aren't experiencing it? Do those who are suffering deserve it because of something they did wrong? No. The Bible instructs us to pray for those suffering for Christ (Hebrews 13:3). We can pray that they will be able to trust God, committing the suffering—and their very lives—to Him. Pray that they will follow in Christ's example (1 Peter 2:21-24) and that we will be faithful, too, when we experience difficulties for God's glory (Acts 14:22). (***See Adoption***> *With Christ*> *Children of God*> *Children share suffering and glory,* TopicGuide page A36.)

16:16 Armageddon may be a reference to the hill of the town of Meggido at the edge of the plain of Esdraelon. This area was a strategic military location, since it overlooked the great Jezreeel Valley and guarded the pass to the coastal plain. Israel won a significant battle there, remembered in the "Song of Deborah" (Judges 5). This is also the place where King Josiah lost his life when he attacked Pharaoh Neco of Egypt against God's will (2 Kings 23:29; 2 Chronicles 35:22).

16:19 placed on the earth. 19 The great city of Babylon split into three sections, and the cities of
Rev 14:8, 10 many nations fell into heaps of rubble. So God remembered all of Babylon's sins, and He
16:20 made her drink the cup that was filled with the wine of His fierce wrath. 20 And every island
Rev 6:14; 20:11 disappeared, and all the mountains were leveled. 21 There was a terrible hailstorm, and
16:21 Exod 9:23-25 hailstones weighing seventy-five pounds* fell from the sky onto the people below. They
Rev 11:19; 16:9, 11 cursed God because of the terrible plague of the hailstorm.

THE GREAT PROSTITUTE

17:1 Jer 51:13 **17** One of the seven angels who had poured out the seven bowls came over and
Rev 17:15; 19:2 spoke to me. "Come with me," he said, "and I will show you the judgment that is
17:2 going to come on the great prostitute, who rules over many waters. 2 The kings of the
Jer 51:7 Rev 14:8; 18:3 world have committed adultery with her, and the people who belong to this world have
17:3 been made drunk by the wine of her immorality."
Rev 1:10; 12:6; 13:1 3 So the angel took me in the Spirit* into the wilderness. There I saw a woman sitting on
a scarlet beast that had seven heads and ten horns, and blasphemies against God were
17:4 written all over it. 4 The woman wore purple and scarlet clothing and beautiful jewelry
Jer 51:7 made of gold and precious gems and pearls. In her hand she held a gold goblet full of ob-
Ezek 28:13 scenities and the impurities of her immorality. 5 A mysterious name was written on her
17:5 2 Thes 2:7 forehead: "Babylon the Great, Mother of All Prostitutes and Obscenities in the World." 6 I
Rev 17:2, 7 could see that she was drunk—drunk with the blood of God's holy people who were wit-
17:6 nesses for Jesus. I stared at her in complete amazement.
Rev 16:6; 18:24 7 "Why are you so amazed?" the angel asked. "I will tell you the mystery of this woman
17:8 and of the beast with seven heads and ten horns on which she sits. 8 The beast you saw
Dan 12:1 Rev 11:7; 13:1, 3 was once alive but isn't now. And yet he will soon come up out of the bottomless pit* and
go to eternal destruction. And the people who belong to this world, whose names were
not written in the Book of Life before the world was made, will be amazed at the reappear-
ance of this beast who had died.
17:9 Rev 13:18 9 "This calls for a mind with understanding: The seven heads of the beast represent the
seven hills where the woman rules. They also represent seven kings. 10 Five kings have al-
ready fallen, the sixth now reigns, and the seventh is yet to come, but his reign will be
brief.
11 "The scarlet beast that was, but is no longer, is the eighth king. He is like the other
17:12 Dan 7:20, 24 seven, and he, too, is headed for destruction. 12 The ten horns of the beast are ten kings
Rev 18:10, 17, 19 who have not yet risen to power. They will be appointed to their kingdoms for one brief
17:14 moment to reign with the beast. 13 They will all agree to give him their power and author-
Matt 22:14 1 Tim 6:15 ity. 14 Together they will go to war against the Lamb, but the Lamb will defeat them be-
Rev 16:14; 19:16 cause He is Lord of all lords and King of all kings. And His called and chosen and faithful
ones will be with Him."

16:21 Greek *1 talent* [34 kilograms]. 17:3 Or *in spirit.* 17:8 Or *the abyss,* or *the underworld.*

17:1-18 As noted in 14:8, Babylon represents the world's political and religious systems arrayed against God. Here we are given more details about this God-opposing power. The description fits well with corrupt Rome at the time of John. But ancient Rome likely does not exhaust the imagery here of what may one day be an overwhelming system that opposes the plans and people of God.

17:1 God often compares His relationship with His people to marriage, and when His people turned from Him He spoke of it as adultery (Jeremiah 3:8-9; 13:27; Ezekiel 23:37; Hosea 2:2). Babylon is pictured as a prostitute, one who would seek to lure people away from the worship of their spiritual "spouse."

17:3 In the tradition of Daniel's visions, the images of heads and horns often represent power and authority (Daniel 7).

▸ SALVATION

17:14 On the right side. Do you remember the feeling you experienced when your favorite team seemed headed for defeat and then pulled off a victory? That should be the image that rises in our hearts as we consider what is going on in this world. Jesus is the Lord over all lords and the King over all kings. He will demonstrate His reign over all His enemies. And as those who follow Him, we are on the winning side (2 Timothy 2:11-12; Matthew 16:24-27; Revelation 20:6). It's not too soon to start the celebration, so take time to make your day of worship a time of celebrating God's promised victory over sin, over Satan, and over everything else contrary to His will. (***See Salvation****> Receiving> How> Submit to God's grace/special favor,* TopicGuide page A22.)

[15]Then the angel said to me, "The waters where the prostitute is ruling represent
masses of people of every nation and language. [16]The scarlet beast and his ten horns all
hate the prostitute. They will strip her naked, eat her flesh, and burn her remains with fire.
[17]For God has put a plan into their minds, a plan that will carry out His purposes. They will
agree to give their authority to the scarlet beast, and so the words of God will be fulfilled.
[18]And this woman you saw in your vision represents the great city that rules over the kings
of the world."

17:15 Rev 13:7; 17:1
17:16 Lev 21:9; Ezek 16:37, 39; Rev 18:8, 19
17:17 Rev 10:7; 17:13
17:18 Rev 16:19

THE FALL OF BABYLON

18 After all this I saw another angel come down from heaven with great authority,
and the earth grew bright with His splendor. [2]He gave a mighty shout:

"Babylon is fallen—that great city is fallen!
She has become a home for demons.
She is a hideout for every foul* spirit,
a hideout for every foul vulture
and every foul and dreadful animal.*
[3] For all the nations have fallen*
because of the wine of her passionate immorality.
The kings of the world
have committed adultery with her.
Because of her desires for extravagant luxury,
the merchants of the world have grown rich."

[4]Then I heard another voice calling from heaven,

"Come away from her, My people.
Do not take part in her sins,
or you will be punished with her.
[5] For her sins are piled as high as heaven,
and God remembers her evil deeds.
[6] Do to her as she has done to others.
Double her penalty* for all her evil deeds.
She brewed a cup of terror for others,
so brew twice as much* for her.
[7] She glorified herself and lived in luxury,
so match it now with torment and sorrow.
She boasted in her heart,
'I am queen on my throne.

18:1 Ezek 43:2; Rev 10:1
18:2 Isa 13:19-22; 21:9; 34:10-11; Jer 50:39; Rev 14:8
18:3 Rev 17:2
18:4 Gen 19:15; Isa 48:20; 52:11; Jer 51:6, 9, 45; 2 Cor 6:17
18:5 Gen 18:20; Jer 51:9; Rev 16:19
18:6 Ps 137:8; Jer 50:15, 29; Rev 17:4
18:7 Isa 47:8

18:2a Greek *unclean;* also in each of the two following phrases. 18:2b Some manuscripts condense the last two lines to read *a hideout for every foul [unclean] and dreadful vulture.* 18:3 Some manuscripts read *have drunk.* 18:6a Or *Give her an equal penalty.* 18:6b Or *brew just as much.*

17:15-17 John's guide explicitly interprets this portion of John's vision. The prostitute's watery throne, ruling the bulk of the world's population, finds itself opposed by a consortium of rulers who attack and destroy her leadership. But even the infighting and betrayal of evil kingdoms against each other is under the sovereign command of God. Those who appear to be opposing God and all He is doing are ultimately not outside His control (Revelation 17:17; Isaiah 52:10).

18:1-24 This vision of the final destruction of Babylon echoes some of the imagery found in the Old Testament prophecies against Babylon (Jeremiah 50–51; Ezekiel 27; also see note at 14:8).

▸ ADOPTION

18:2 Celebrating their defeat. Normally it is considered dishonorable to rejoice in the downfall of others. Why then should angels in heaven and people of earth rejoice in the rout of Babylon? When Babylon is overthrown, then the enemies of God will be destroyed, the offense to His holiness will be removed, the snare for humanity will be done away with, and justice denied will become justice accomplished. That, not the actual pain and suffering of those who hate God, is grounds for rejoicing. This angelic rejoicing and our own holy happiness in God's victory are rooted in our joy over God's will being done on earth as it is in heaven (Matthew 6:10). Unashamedly rejoice as you see God's victory over sin in your life and in the lives of those around you. (***See Adoption**> With Christ> Servants> Defeated the evil world,* TopicGuide page A37.)

I am no helpless widow,
and I have no reason to mourn.'

18:8 Isa 47:9 Jer 50:31-34 Rev 17:16 8 Therefore, these plagues will overtake her in a single day—
death and mourning and famine.
She will be completely consumed by fire,
18:9 Ezek 26:16 Rev 17:2 for the Lord God who judges her is mighty."

9 And the kings of the world who committed adultery with her and enjoyed her great
18:10 Ezek 26:17 Rev 14:8 luxury will mourn for her as they see the smoke rising from her charred remains. 10 They
will stand at a distance, terrified by her great torment. They will cry out,

"How terrible, how terrible for you,
O Babylon, you great city!
In a single moment
God's judgment came on you."

18:11 Ezek 27:27, 36 Rev 18:3 11 The merchants of the world will weep and mourn for her, for there is no one left to
buy their goods. 12 She bought great quantities of gold, silver, jewels, and pearls; fine
18:12-13 Ezek 27:12-22 linen, purple, silk, and scarlet cloth; things made of fragrant thyine wood, ivory goods, and
objects made of expensive wood; and bronze, iron, and marble. 13 She also bought cinna-
mon, spice, incense, myrrh, frankincense, wine, olive oil, fine flour, wheat, cattle, sheep,
horses, chariots, and bodies—that is, human slaves.

14 "The fancy things you loved so much
are gone," they cry.
"All your luxuries and splendor
are gone forever,
never to be yours again."

18:15 Ezek 27:36 15 The merchants who became wealthy by selling her these things will stand at a dis-
tance, terrified by her great torment. They will weep and cry out,

18:16 Rev 17:4 16 "How terrible, how terrible for that great city!
She was clothed in finest purple and scarlet linens,
decked out with gold and precious stones and pearls!
18:17 Ezek 27:27-29 Rev 17:16 17 In a single moment
all the wealth of the city is gone!"

18:18 Ezek 27:32 Rev 13:4 And all the captains of the merchant ships and their passengers and sailors and crews
will stand at a distance. 18 They will cry out as they watch the smoke ascend, and they will
18:19 Ezek 27:30-34 say, "Where is there another city as great as this?" 19 And they will weep and throw dust on
their heads to show their grief. And they will cry out,

"How terrible, how terrible for that great city!
The shipowners became wealthy
by transporting her great wealth on the seas.
In a single moment it is all gone."

18:20 Jer 51:48 Rev 12:12; 19:2 20 Rejoice over her fate, O heaven
and people of God and apostles and prophets!
For at last God has judged her
for your sakes.

18:8 Whether the reference to a "single day" speaks of an actual twenty-four hour period is not certain. The point, however, is that Babylon's destruction will be sudden and swift.

18:21 Babylon's utter ruin is pictured in a boulder being cast into the sea—an irreversible and final act that ultimately leaves nothing behind but a memory.

[21]Then a mighty angel picked up a boulder the size of a huge millstone. He threw it into the ocean and shouted, 18:21 Jer 51:63-64

"Just like this, the great city Babylon
will be thrown down with violence
and will never be found again.
[22] The sound of harps, singers, flutes, and trumpets 18:22 Ezek 26:13
will never be heard in you again.
No craftsmen and no trades
will ever be found in you again.
The sound of the mill
will never be heard in you again.
[23] The light of a lamp 18:23 Jer 7:34; 16:9; 25:10 Nah 3:4
will never shine in you again.
The happy voices of brides and grooms
will never be heard in you again.
For your merchants were the greatest in the world,
and you deceived the nations with your sorceries.
[24] In your* streets flowed the blood of the prophets and of God's holy people 18:24 Jer 51:49 Matt 23:35-37 Rev 16:6; 17:6
and the blood of people slaughtered all over the world."

SONGS OF VICTORY IN HEAVEN

19 After this, I heard what sounded like a vast crowd in heaven shouting, 19:1 Rev 4:11; 7:10; 12:10

"Praise the LORD!*
Salvation and glory and power belong to our God.
[2] His judgments are true and just. 19:2 Rev 6:10; 16:7; 17:1
He has punished the great prostitute
who corrupted the earth with her immorality.
He has avenged the murder of His servants."

[3]And again their voices rang out: 19:3 Isa 34:10 Rev 14:11

"Praise the LORD!
The smoke from that city ascends forever and ever!"

[4]Then the twenty-four elders and the four living beings fell down and worshiped God, 19:4 Rev 4:4, 6, 10
who was sitting on the throne. They cried out, "Amen! Praise the LORD!"
[5]And from the throne came a voice that said, 19:5 Pss 115:13; 134:1; 135:1 Rev 11:18

"Praise our God,
all His servants,
all who fear Him,
from the least to the greatest."

[6]Then I heard again what sounded like the shout of a vast crowd or the roar of mighty 19:6 Rev 11:15
ocean waves or the crash of loud thunder:

"Praise the LORD!
For the Lord our God,* the Almighty, reigns.

18:24 Greek *her.* 19:1 Greek *Hallelujah;* also in 19:3, 4, 6. *Hallelujah* is the transliteration of a Hebrew term that means "Praise the LORD." 19:6 Some manuscripts read *the Lord God.*

19:6 The crowd in heaven rejoicing in the reign of God does not indicate that He has not controlled the events up until that point. As in 11:15-17, they rejoice at the manifestation of God's reign and the carrying out of His plan.

19:7-9 The imagery of a wedding and the accompanying feast pictures the intimacy and joy to be experienced by Jesus and His followers. The Old Testament occasionally pictures God as the bridegroom of Israel (Hosea 2:16; Isaiah 54:6; Ezekiel 16:8), and Jesus Himself is identified as the bridegroom of the believing community (2 Corinthians 11:2; Ephesians 5:25; John 3:29).

19:7 [7] Let us be glad and rejoice,
Matt 22:2; 25:10 Eph 5:32 and let us give honor to Him.
Rev 21:2, 9 For the time has come for the wedding feast of the Lamb,
19:8 and His bride has prepared herself.
Isa 61:10 [8] She has been given the finest of pure white linen to wear."
Rev 15:4, 6 For the fine linen represents the good deeds of God's holy people.
19:9 Luke 14:15 [9]And the angel said to me, "Write this: Blessed are those who are invited to the wedding
Rev 21:5; 22:6 feast of the Lamb." And he added, "These are true words that come from God."
19:10 Acts 10:25-26 [10]Then I fell down at his feet to worship him, but he said, "No, don't worship me. I am a
Rev 22:8-9 servant of God, just like you and your brothers and sisters* who testify about their faith in
Jesus. Worship only God. For the essence of prophecy is to give a clear witness for Jesus.*"

THE RIDER ON THE WHITE HORSE

19:11 Isa 11:4 [11] Then I saw heaven opened, and a white horse was standing there. Its rider was named
Rev 3:14 Faithful and True, for He judges fairly and wages a righteous war. [12]His eyes were like
19:12 flames of fire, and on His head were many crowns. A name was written on Him that no
Rev 1:14; 2:17 one understood except Himself. [13]He wore a robe dipped in blood, and His title was the
19:13 Isa 63:1-3 Word of God. [14]The armies of heaven, dressed in the finest of pure white linen, followed
John 1:1, 14 Him on white horses. [15]From His mouth came a sharp sword to strike down the nations.
1 Jn 1:1-2 He will rule them with an iron rod. He will release the fierce wrath of God, the Almighty,
19:14 Rev 3:4 like juice flowing from a winepress. [16]On His robe at His thigh* was written this title: King
of all kings and Lord of all lords.
19:15 Isa 11:4; 63:3 [17]Then I saw an angel standing in the sun, shouting to the vultures flying high in the
2 Thes 2:8 sky: "Come! Gather together for the great banquet God has prepared. [18]Come and eat the
Rev 2:27; 14:20 19:16 flesh of kings, generals, and strong warriors; of horses and their riders; and of all human-
Rev 17:14 ity, both free and slave, small and great."
19:17-18 [19]Then I saw the beast and the kings of the world and their armies gathered together to
Ezek 39:17-20 fight against the One sitting on the horse and His army. [20]And the beast was captured, and
19:19 with him the false prophet who did mighty miracles on behalf of the beast—miracles that
Rev 13:1; 16:14, 16 deceived all who had accepted the mark of the beast and who worshiped his statue. Both
19:20 the beast and his false prophet were thrown alive into the fiery lake of burning sulfur.
Isa 30:33 Dan 7:11 [21]Their entire army was killed by the sharp sword that came from the mouth of the One
Rev 13:12-16; 20:10, 14-15; 21:8 riding the white horse. And the vultures all gorged themselves on the dead bodies.

THE THOUSAND YEARS

20:1 Rev 1:18; 10:1 **20** Then I saw an angel coming down from heaven with the key to the bottomless
20:3 pit* and a heavy chain in his hand. [2]He seized the dragon—that old serpent, who
2 Pet 2:4 Jude 1:6 is the devil, Satan—and bound him in chains for a thousand years. [3]The angel threw him

19:10a Greek *brothers.* 19:10b Or *is the message confirmed by Jesus.* 19:16 Or *On His robe and thigh.* 20:1 Or *the abyss, or the underworld;* also in 20:3.

19:9-10 John mistakenly thought the angelic messenger was claiming to be God when he said, "These are true words that come from God." John humbly records his own error as a warning that even though he, too, had witnessed things seen by no human before or since, he was still a human being and unworthy of worship.

19:11-16 The rider on the white horse is none other than the Savior Jesus returning to bring to completion God's plan on earth and to vanquish His enemies. At the proper time He will return and show Himself to be the true and only sovereign, the King of kings and Lord of lords (1 Timothy 6:14-16).

19:17-21 The beasts and the forces of wickedness had been gathering together to begin this great cosmic conflict when Jesus Himself returns. John takes only five verses to describe this earth-altering war. When Jesus arrives on the scene, the victory is sure, swift, and decisive. It is no contest.

20:2 The "thousand years" mentioned here is often referred to as the "Millennium." Revelation 19 is the only time this concept of the Millennium is mentioned in the Bible. Depending on the approach one takes to the book of Revelation, it is understood as either literal or symbolic. Those who take it symbolically believe the beginning of the millennium began during the ministry of Christ (Luke 10:18) and continues today. Those who take it literally look for a future fulfillment. Regardless, the original audience understood that they could look forward to a temporary respite from the coming horrifying persecution.

into the bottomless pit, which he then shut and locked so Satan could not deceive the na-
tions anymore until the thousand years were finished. Afterward he must be released for a
little while.
4 Then I saw thrones, and the people sitting on them had been given the authority to
judge. And I saw the souls of those who had been beheaded for their testimony about
Jesus and for proclaiming the word of God. They had not worshiped the beast or his
statue, nor accepted his mark on their forehead or their hands. They all came to life again,
and they reigned with Christ for a thousand years.
5 This is the first resurrection. (The rest of the dead did not come back to life until the
thousand years had ended.) 6 Blessed and holy are those who share in the first resurrec-
tion. For them the second death holds no power, but they will be priests of God and of
Christ and will reign with him a thousand years.

THE DEFEAT OF SATAN

7 When the thousand years come to an end, Satan will be let out of his prison. 8 He will go
out to deceive the nations—called Gog and Magog—in every corner of the earth. He will
gather them together for battle—a mighty army, as numberless as sand along the sea-
shore. 9 And I saw them as they went up on the broad plain of the earth and surrounded
God's people and the beloved city. But fire from heaven came down on the attacking ar-
mies and consumed them.
10 Then the devil, who had deceived them, was thrown into the fiery lake of burning sul-
fur, joining the beast and the false prophet. There they will be tormented day and night
forever and ever.

THE FINAL JUDGMENT

11 And I saw a great white throne and the One sitting on it. The earth and sky fled from His
presence, but they found no place to hide. 12 I saw the dead, both great and small, standing
before God's throne. And the books were opened, including the Book of Life. And the
dead were judged according to what they had done, as recorded in the books. 13 The sea
gave up its dead, and death and the grave* gave up their dead. And all were judged ac-
cording to their deeds. 14 Then death and the grave were thrown into the lake of fire. This

20:4 Dan 7:9, 22, 27; Matt 19:28; Rev 13:12-16
20:5 Ezek 37:10; Luke 14:14
20:6 1 Pet 2:5, 9; Rev 1:6; 5:10; 20:14
20:7 Rev 20:2
20:8 Ezek 38:2; Rev 16:14
20:9 Ps 87:2; Ezek 38:22; 39:6
20:10 Rev 14:10; 19:20; 20:15
20:11-12 Dan 7:9-10; Matt 25:31-46
20:12 Exod 32:32; Ps 28:4; Dan 12:1; Phil 4:3; Rev 3:5; 21:27
20:13 Isa 26:19; Matt 16:27; John 5:28-29; Rev 1:18
20:14 1 Cor 15:26, 55; Rev 19:20

20:13 Greek *and Hades;* also in 20:14.

20:5 Some believe that the first resurrection refers to a spiritual resurrection and speaks of the regeneration of all those who have come to faith in Jesus. Others see it as a reference to a physical resurrection where only those who have life through Christ are raised.

20:8 The names Gog and Magog are drawn from Ezekiel 38–39 and represent the enemies who oppose God and His people.

▸ SPIRITUAL WARFARE
20:10 No fear of the enemy. Satan afflicts people in countless ways (1 Peter 5:8-9). He brings distress and calamity (Job 1–2). He endeavors to turn people's hearts away from the Savior (Ephesians 6:11-12). He seeks to blind the eyes of those who don't yet know Jesus (2 Corinthians 4:4). Should we live in fear of this enemy of our souls? No. Jesus has overthrown Satan and his power (Hebrews 2:14; 1 John 3:8), and we know his final end. Regardless of what Satan may attempt, he will not be able to escape his doom, and he will not win in the end. Through the power of the Holy Spirit, we can resist him now and find victory (Colossians 1:13; James 4:7; Revelation 12:10-11). Take confidence in knowing that your Savior has already defeated Satan and that your future is secure in Him. (***See Spiritual Warfare***> *Resisting Sin and Evil> Standing Firm> Empowered to do spiritual warfare,* TopicGuide page A46.)

▸ SALVATION
20:10 It's Who you know. Many people mistakenly think that entrance into heaven is granted on the basis of one's performance—that what they do will merit them acceptance before God. But it's not what you do that matters; it's who you know. Jesus said many will claim to do things in His name, but He will dismiss their claims because they never really knew Him (Matthew 7:22-23). To have life, one needs to have a genuine relationship with Jesus, the giver of life (John 3:16-18; 17:3; 1 John 5:11-12). We come to know Him by putting our ultimate trust and confidence in Jesus—resting in Him and relying on His work on the cross to solve the problem of our sins. Those who have trusted Jesus in this way are those whose names are in His book. That is the only way in. Is your name in His book? (***See Salvation***> *Receiving> How> Repent of/turn from sin,* TopicGuide page A22.)

20:11-15 Jesus Himself affirmed that one day there would be a day of reckoning (Matthew 25:31-46; John 5:22, 27). On that day He will overthrow His enemies, and they will stand in judgment before Him.

lake of fire is the second death. 15 And anyone whose name was not found recorded in the Book of Life was thrown into the lake of fire.

THE NEW JERUSALEM

21 Then I saw a new heaven and a new earth, for the old heaven and the old earth had disappeared. And the sea was also gone. 2 And I saw the holy city, the new Jerusalem, coming down from God out of heaven like a bride beautifully dressed for her husband.

3 I heard a loud shout from the throne, saying, "Look, God's home is now among His people! He will live with them, and they will be His people. God Himself will be with them.* 4 He will wipe every tear from their eyes, and there will be no more death or sorrow or crying or pain. All these things are gone forever."

5 And the One sitting on the throne said, "Look, I am making everything new!" And then He said to me, "Write this down, for what I tell you is trustworthy and true." 6 And He also said, "It is finished! I am the Alpha and the Omega—the Beginning and the End. To all who are thirsty I will give freely from the springs of the water of life. 7 All who are victorious will inherit all these blessings, and I will be their God, and they will be My children.

8 "But cowards, unbelievers, the corrupt, murderers, the immoral, those who practice witchcraft, idol worshipers, and all liars—their fate is in the fiery lake of burning sulfur. This is the second death."

9 Then one of the seven angels who held the seven bowls containing the seven last plagues came and said to me, "Come with me! I will show you the bride, the wife of the Lamb."

10 So he took me in the Spirit* to a great, high mountain, and he showed me the holy city, Jerusalem, descending out of heaven from God. 11 It shone with the glory of God and sparkled like a precious stone—like jasper as clear as crystal. 12 The city wall was broad and high, with twelve gates guarded by twelve angels. And the names of the twelve tribes of Israel were written on the gates. 13 There were three gates on each side—east, north,

20:15 Rev 3:5; 20:12
21:1 Isa 65:17; 66:22; 2 Pet 3:13
21:2 Isa 52:1; 61:10; Heb 11:10; 12:22; Rev 3:12
21:3 2 Chr 6:18; Ezek 37:27; Zech 2:10; 2 Cor 6:16
21:4 Isa 25:8; 35:10; 43:18; 65:19; Rev 7:17
21:6 Rev 1:8; 22:13
21:7 2 Sam 7:14; Rom 8:14; 2 Cor 6:16
21:8 Ps 5:6; 1 Cor 6:9; Eph 5:5; Rev 2:11; 22:15
21:10 Ezek 40:1-2; Rev 1:10; 17:3
21:11 Isa 60:1-2, 19; Ezek 43:2; Rev 4:3

21:3 Some manuscripts read *God Himself will be with them, their God.* 21:10 Or *in spirit.*

20:15 The Book of Life is mentioned seven times in the New Testament (Philippians 4:3; Revelation 3:5; 13:8; 17:8; 20:12, 15; 21:27; see the note on 3:5). From these various references, the book appears to refer to the names of those who have placed their faith in Jesus and, as such, are His people. Only those whose names are written there escape the judgment of the "second death"—eternal separation from God.

21:1 Various passages suggest that this new creation will be a transformation of the old world (Isaiah 65:17; 66:22; Romans 8:21-23). In this way, the coming change to creation parallels the transformation that will occur in our bodies at the time of the resurrection (1 Corinthians 15:35-57; 2 Corinthians 5:1-10).

21:1-5 Some believe that the new Jerusalem will be a literal city that will one day stand upon the earth; others think this vision symbolizes life after the return of Jesus. In any case, it is clear that God will make "everything new"; the whole old system of the world will pass away, and God will dwell in intimacy with His people in His renewed creation (Romans 8:18-30).

21:3 God long ago promised that He will one day dwell in an intimate, personal, and manifest way with His people (Ezekiel 37:27; Zechariah 2:10; 8:8). The word used here by John means, literally, "to pitch a tent" (like the Tabernacle in the Old Testament). John used the same word to speak of Jesus when He came to earth the first time (John 1:14). What Jesus began to do—dwell with His people—culminates in the world to come.

▸ SALVATION

21:5-11 Our glorious destination. Have you ever stood outside on a clear night with a full moon? It's amazing how much you can see in that light. But all that radiance and illumination is simply reflected light. The moon has no light of its own. Sunlight reflecting off the moon's surface causes the moon to glow. So it is with those of us who have life in Jesus. One day, we will be all that we were designed to be; we will be like Jesus in character (Romans 8:29). We will be, in the fullest sense, the children of God (1 John 3:2). And we will be filled with the glory of God (Revelation 21:11). But the glory that is seen in us will be a reflected glory. God Himself will illuminate us and the Lamb will be the light that is seen in us (21:23). Our responsibility now is to reflect the beauty of Jesus in our lives so that others can see Him. How do you reflect Christ's image to your neighbors? (***See Salvation**> Receiving> When> Glorified,* TopicGuide page A23.)

21:6 The reference to the "water of life" draws on a number of images from both the Old and the New Testaments that speak of life with God—a refreshing, everlasting, spiritual life (Jeremiah 2:13; John 4:10-11; 7:38).

21:10-27 In the Old Testament, Ezekiel used architectural description to communicate theological ideas about God and ideal worship of Him (Ezekiel 40–42), so it is likely that John is doing the same here. The center of all things is not the actual building but the glorious presence of God (1 Corinthians 2:9; 2 Corinthians 4:17).

south, and west. 14 The wall of the city had twelve foundation stones, and on them were
written the names of the twelve apostles of the Lamb.
15 The angel who talked to me held in his hand a gold measuring stick to measure the
city, its gates, and its wall. 16 When he measured it, he found it was a square, as wide as it
was long. In fact, its length and width and height were each 1,400 miles.* 17 Then he mea-
sured the walls and found them to be 216 feet thick* (according to the human standard
used by the angel).
18 The wall was made of jasper, and the city was pure gold, as clear as glass. 19 The wall
of the city was built on foundation stones inlaid with twelve precious stones:* the first was
jasper, the second sapphire, the third agate, the fourth emerald, 20 the fifth onyx, the sixth
carnelian, the seventh chrysolite, the eighth beryl, the ninth topaz, the tenth chrysoprase,
the eleventh jacinth, the twelfth amethyst.
21 The twelve gates were made of pearls—each gate from a single pearl! And the main
street was pure gold, as clear as glass.
22 I saw no temple in the city, for the Lord God Almighty and the Lamb are its temple.
23 And the city has no need of sun or moon, for the glory of God illuminates the city, and
the Lamb is its light. 24 The nations will walk in its light, and the kings of the world will enter
the city in all their glory. 25 Its gates will never be closed at the end of day because there is
no night there. 26 And all the nations will bring their glory and honor into the city.
27 Nothing evil* will be allowed to enter, nor anyone who practices shameful idolatry and
dishonesty—but only those whose names are written in the Lamb's Book of Life.

21:14 Eph 2:20; Heb 11:10
21:15 Ezek 40:3, 5; Rev 11:1
21:16-17 Ezek 48:16-17
21:19 Exod 28:17-20; Isa 54:11-12; Ezek 28:13
21:22 John 4:21-24; 17:21; Rev 1:8
21:23 Isa 60:19-20
21:24 Isa 60:3, 5
21:25 Isa 60:11; Zech 14:7
21:26 Ps 72:10-11
21:27 Isa 52:1

21:16 Greek *12,000 stadia* [2,220 kilometers]. 21:17 Greek *144 cubits* [65 meters]. 21:19 The identification of some of these gemstones is uncertain. 21:27 Or *ceremonially unclean.*

21:22-27 The new Jerusalem will be unique among all cities in history. The greatest characteristic of the city is that God will dwell in that place, and He will provide the light. Jesus said that He is the light of the world (John 9:5). Light exposes everything it touches. But in this city, God's light will not expose any sin or evil because none will exist there.

MY RESPONSE TO GOD

Making All Things New

REVELATION 21:5

Do you dislike your physical body? Are your emotions a bother, something you'd prefer to be without? If you answer, "Yes," then you might make a good Gnostic—but not a good Christian. Gnosticism is an ancient heresy still in circulation today that teaches that God doesn't care about what we do with our bodies—it's all about the ethereal, the ideal, and the spirit. But contrary to this New Age notion, God loves our bodies. After He created them, He announced that they, along with all creation, were excellent in every way (Genesis 1:31).

God is making the whole universe into something new (Romans 8:18-25), and that includes you! He has a plan not just for your interior, but for your body as well. The difference between Christians and the rest of the universe is that we are *in Christ.* Since we are already in Christ, the new creation has already begun inside of us. This new creation looks like an ordinary human on the outside, yet quietly and humbly contains the Gospel and the Holy Spirit. Inwardly, something is throbbing with a dynamic energy as a new being is created in the image of God's glorified Son.

God is making all things new (Revelation 21:5), and you are at the head of the line. All creation stands on tiptoes to see the mighty work God is doing to those who are in Christ.

22 Then the angel showed me a river with the water of life, clear as crystal, flowing
from the throne of God and of the Lamb. 2It flowed down the center of the main
street. On each side of the river grew a tree of life, bearing twelve crops of fruit,* with a
fresh crop each month. The leaves were used for medicine to heal the nations.
3No longer will there be a curse upon anything. For the throne of God and of the Lamb
will be there, and His servants will worship Him. 4And they will see His face, and His name
will be written on their foreheads. 5And there will be no night there—no need for lamps or
sun—for the Lord God will shine on them. And they will reign forever and ever.
6Then the angel said to me, "Everything you have heard and seen is trustworthy and
true. The Lord God, who inspires His prophets,* has sent His angel to tell His servants what
will happen soon.*"

JESUS IS COMING

7"Look, I am coming soon! Blessed are those who obey the words of prophecy
written in this book.*"

8I, John, am the one who heard and saw all these things. And when I heard and saw
them, I fell down to worship at the feet of the angel who showed them to me. 9But he said,
"No, don't worship me. I am a servant of God, just like you and your brothers the prophets,
as well as all who obey what is written in this book. Worship only God!"
10Then he instructed me, "Do not seal up the prophetic words in this book, for the time is
near. 11Let the one who is doing harm continue to do harm; let the one who is vile con-
tinue to be vile; let the one who is righteous continue to live righteously; let the one who is
holy continue to be holy."

12"Look, I am coming soon, bringing My reward with Me to repay all people
according to their deeds. 13I am the Alpha and the Omega, the First and the Last, the
Beginning and the End."

14Blessed are those who wash their robes. They will be permitted to enter through the
gates of the city and eat the fruit from the tree of life. 15Outside the city are the dogs—the
sorcerers, the sexually immoral, the murderers, the idol worshipers, and all who love to
live a lie.

16"I, Jesus, have sent My angel to give you this message for the churches. I am both
the source of David and the heir to His throne.* I am the bright morning star."

17The Spirit and the bride say, "Come." Let anyone who hears this say, "Come." Let
anyone who is thirsty come. Let anyone who desires drink freely from the water of life.
18And I solemnly declare to everyone who hears the words of prophecy written in this
book: If anyone adds anything to what is written here, God will add to that person the

22:1 Ezek 47:1; Joel 3:18; Zech 14:8; John 7:37-39
22:2 Gen 2:9; Ezek 47:12
22:3 Zech 14:11
22:4 Pss 17:15; 42:2; Matt 5:8
22:5 Isa 60:19-20; Dan 7:18, 27; Zech 14:7
22:6 Dan 2:28-29; Rev 1:1; 21:5
22:9 Rev 19:10
22:10 Rev 1:3
22:11 Dan 12:10
22:12 Matt 16:27; Rev 22:7
22:14 Gen 2:9; 3:22; Ezek 47:12
22:15 1 Cor 6:9-10; Gal 5:19-21
22:16 Num 24:17; Isa 11:1, 10; Matt 1:1; Rom 1:3
22:17 Isa 55:1; John 7:37-39
22:18 Deut 4:2; 12:32; Prov 30:6

22:2 Or *twelve kinds of fruit.* **22:6a** Or *The Lord, the God of the spirits of the prophets.* **22:6b** Or *suddenly,* or *quickly;* also in 22:7, 12, 20. **22:7** Or *scroll*; also in 22:9, 10, 18, 19. **22:16** Greek *I am the root and offspring of David.*

22:2 Here, the tree of life is not pictured as a single tree but as the common tree along the banks of the river flowing from the throne. In contrast to what happened in Eden when Adam was driven from the tree of life (Genesis 3:22-23), access is granted to all to come and drink.

22:4 Moses was not permitted to see the face of God (Exodus 33:20, 23), but Jesus promised that those who had found holiness in Him would, one day, see God's face (Matthew 5:8). It is a picture of free access and intimacy.

22:12 When Jesus Christ returns to the earth, He will judge the nations and reward His servants (2 Corinthians 5:10). The followers of Jesus do not have to fear condemnation from the Savior (John 5:24; Romans 8:1), but each will receive rewards according to his or her faithful service to Jesus.

22:17 The Holy Spirit and the church—the bride of Christ—both declare Jesus' invitation to a thirsty world. This portion of the mission of the bride is placed at the end of the book of Revelation not to instruct the church to evangelize after the events described have occurred, but to remind the church of its ongoing call to God's mission (Matthew 28:16-20).

plagues described in this book. 19And if anyone removes any of the words from this
book of prophecy, God will remove that person's share in the tree of life and in the holy
city that are described in this book.

20He who is the faithful witness to all these things says, "Yes, I am coming soon!"
Amen! Come, Lord Jesus!

21May the grace of the Lord Jesus be with God's holy people.*

22:19 Gen 2:9; 3:22 Ezek 47:12

22:20 1 Cor 16:22 Rev 3:11; 22:7, 12

22:21 Rom 16:20 2 Thes 3:18

22:21 Other manuscripts read *be with all;* still others read *be with all of God's holy people.* Some manuscripts add *Amen.*

22:20 Jesus' return is "coming soon." That means that at any moment the events described could have come upon the original audience (Revelation 1:1), just as they can come upon us.

▸ GOD

22:20 Look for His rescue. When we are in the midst of difficulties, it's easy to lose sight of hope. But the problems we encounter on our spiritual walk are not our final destination. Jesus invites all of us to join Him and His church and to share in the promises and privileges of being a child of God. But He does not wait for us to come to Him, for even at our best, we are never fit enough to stand before Him. He promises to come to us, to rescue us from the sins and selfishness that threaten even the heartiest of saints (Matthew 24:24). Look for His rescue daily, and eagerly wait for the final day of salvation for everyone who trusts in Him. (***See God****> Relationship> God Enables> Relationship with God requires a right heart,* TopicGuide page A14.)

Index to Discovery Articles on Character of God

Index to Our Response to God Articles

INDEX TO MAPS

Index to Charts

Four Spiritual Laws

By Bill Bright

Just as there are physical laws that govern the physical universe, so are there spiritual laws that govern your relationship with God.

LAW 1: GOD LOVES YOU AND OFFERS A WONDERFUL PLAN FOR YOUR LIFE.

GOD'S LOVE

"God loved the world so much that He gave His one and only Son, so that everyone who believes in Him will not perish but have eternal life" JOHN 3:16.

GOD'S PLAN

[Christ speaking] "I have come that they may have life, and that they may have it more abundantly" [that it might be full and meaningful] JOHN 10:10 NKJV.

Why is it that most people are not experiencing the abundant life? Because . . .

LAW 2: MAN IS SINFUL AND SEPARATED FROM GOD. THEREFORE, HE CANNOT KNOW AND EXPERIENCE GOD'S LOVE AND PLAN FOR HIS LIFE.

MAN IS SINFUL

"Everyone has sinned; we all fall short of God's glorious standard" ROMANS 3:23.

Man was created to have fellowship with God; but, because of his own stubborn self-will, he chose to go his own independent way and fellowship with God was broken. This self-will, characterized by an attitude of active rebellion or passive indifference, is an evidence of what the Bible calls sin.

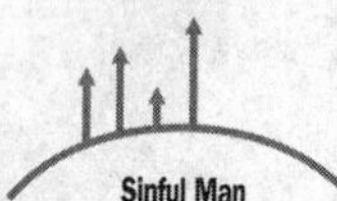

MAN IS SEPARATED

"The wages of sin is death" [spiritual separation from God] ROMANS 6:23.

This diagram illustrates that God is holy and man is sinful. A great gulf separates the two. The arrows illustrate that man is continually trying to reach God and the abundant life through his own efforts, such as a good life, philosophy, or religion—but he inevitably fails.

The third law explains the only way to bridge this gulf . . .

LAW 3: JESUS CHRIST IS GOD'S ONLY PROVISION FOR MAN'S SIN. THROUGH HIM YOU CAN KNOW AND EXPERIENCE GOD'S LOVE AND PLAN FOR YOUR LIFE.

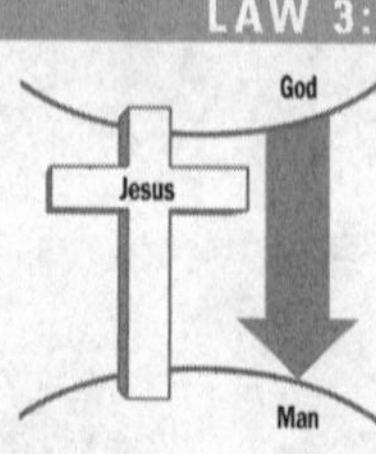

HE DIED IN OUR PLACE

"God showed His great love for us by sending Christ to die for us while we were still sinners" ROMANS 5:8.

HE IS THE ONLY WAY TO GOD

"Jesus told him, 'I am the way, the truth, and the life. No one can come to the Father except through Me'" JOHN 14:6.

This diagram illustrates that God has bridged the gulf that separates us from Him by sending His Son, Jesus Christ, to die on the cross in our place to pay the penalty for our sins.

It is not enough just to know these three laws . . .

LAW 4: WE MUST INDIVIDUALLY RECEIVE JESUS CHRIST AS SAVIOR AND LORD; THEN WE CAN KNOW AND EXPERIENCE GOD'S LOVE AND PLAN FOR OUR LIVES.

WE MUST RECEIVE CHRIST

"To all who believed Him and accepted Him, He gave the right to become children of God" JOHN 1:12.

WE RECEIVE CHRIST THROUGH FAITH

"God saved you by His grace when you believed. And you can't take credit for this; it is a gift from God. Salvation is not a reward for the good things we have done, so none of us can boast about it." EPHESIANS 2:8,9.

WHEN WE RECEIVE CHRIST, WE EXPERIENCE A NEW BIRTH

(READ JOHN 3:1–8.)

WE RECEIVE CHRIST THROUGH PERSONAL INVITATION

[Christ speaking] "Look! I stand at the door and knock. If you hear My voice and open the door, I will come in, and we will share a meal together as friends" REVELATION 3:20.

Receiving Christ involves turning to God from self (repentance) and trusting Christ to come into our lives to forgive our sins and to make us what He wants us to be. Just to agree intellectually that Jesus Christ is the Son of God and that He died on the cross for our sins is not enough. Nor is it enough to have an emotional experience. We receive Jesus Christ by faith, as an act of the will.

These two circles represent two kinds of lives:

Self-Directed Life

- S Self is on the throne
- † Christ is outside the life
- ● Interests are directed by self, often resulting in discord and frustration

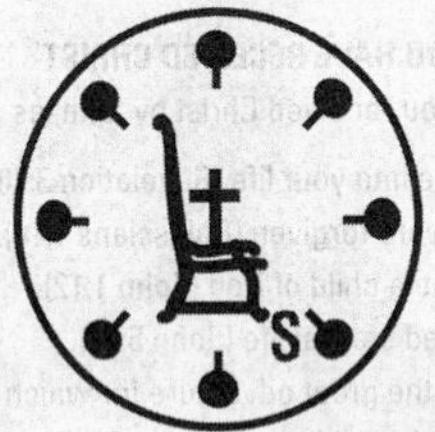

Christ-Directed Life

- † Christ is in the life and on the throne
- S Self is yielding to Christ, resulting in harmony with God's plan
- ● Interests are directed by Christ, resulting in harmony with God's plan

Which circle best represents your life?

Which circle would you like to have represent your life?

The following explains how you can receive Christ:

YOU CAN RECEIVE CHRIST RIGHT NOW BY FAITH THROUGH PRAYER (PRAYER IS TALKING WITH GOD)

God knows your heart and is not so concerned with your words as He is with the attitude of your heart. The following is a suggested prayer:

> *Lord Jesus, I need You. Thank You for dying on the cross for my sins. I open the door of my life and receive You as my Savior and Lord. Thank You for forgiving my sins and giving me eternal life. Take control of the throne of my life. Make me the kind of person You want me to be.*

Does this prayer express the desire of your heart?

If it does, I invite you to pray this prayer right now, and Christ will come into your life, as He promised.

HOW TO KNOW THAT CHRIST IS IN YOUR LIFE

Did you receive Christ into your life? According to His promise in Revelation 3:20, where is Christ right now in relation to you? Christ said that He would come into your life. Would He mislead you? On what authority do you know that God has answered your prayer? (The trustworthiness of God Himself and His Word.)

THE BIBLE PROMISES ETERNAL LIFE TO ALL WHO RECEIVE CHRIST

"He has given us eternal life, and this life is in His Son. Whoever has the Son has life; whoever does not have God's Son does not have life" 1 JOHN 5:11–12.

Thank God often that Christ is in your life and that He will never leave you HEBREWS 13:5.

You can know on the basis of His promise that Christ lives in you and that you have eternal life from the very moment you invite Him in. He will not deceive you.

An important reminder . . .

DO NOT DEPEND ON FEELINGS

The promise of God's Word, the Bible—not our feelings—is our authority. The Christian lives by faith (trust) in the trustworthiness of God Himself and His Word. This train diagram illustrates the relationship among fact (God and His Word), faith (our trust in God and His Word), and feeling (the result of our faith and obedience). (Read John 14:21.)

The train will run with or without the caboose. However, it would be useless to attempt to pull the train by the caboose. In the same way, as Christians we do not depend on feelings or emotions, but we place our faith (trust) in the trustworthiness of God and the promises of His Word.

NOW THAT YOU HAVE RECEIVED CHRIST

The moment you received Christ by faith, as an act of the will, many things happened, including the following:

- Christ came into your life (Revelation 3:20; Colossians 1:27).
- Your sins were forgiven (Colossians 1:14).
- You became a child of God (John 1:12).
- You received eternal life (John 5:24).
- You began the great adventure for which God created you (John 10:10).

Can you think of anything more wonderful that could happen to you than receiving Christ? Would you like to thank God in prayer right now for what He has done for you? By thanking God, you demonstrate your faith.

To enjoy your new life to the fullest . . .

SUGGESTIONS FOR CHRISTIAN GROWTH

Spiritual growth results from trusting Jesus Christ. A life of faith will enable you to trust God increasingly with every detail of your life, and to practice the following:

G Go to God in prayer daily (John 15:7).
R Read God's Word daily (Acts 17:11); begin with the Gospel of John.
O Obey God moment by moment (John 14:21).
W Witness for Christ by your life and words (Matthew 4:19; John 15:8).
T Trust God for every detail of your life (1 Peter 5:7).
H Holy Spirit—allow Him to control and empower your daily life and witness (Galatians 5:16, 17; Acts 1:8; Ephesians 5:18).

FELLOWSHIP IN A GOOD CHURCH

God's Word instructs us not to forsake "our meeting together" (Hebrews 10:25). If you do not belong to a church, do not wait to be invited. Take the initiative; call the pastor of a nearby church where Christ is honored and His Word is preached. Start this week, and make plans to attend regularly.

NLT Dictionary/Concordance

A

ABANDON, ABANDONED, ABANDONS (v)
to desert or forsake
Josh 1:5 . . . will not fail you or ***a*** *you.*
Josh 24:16 . . . We would never ***a*** *the* Lord
Ezra 9:9 . . . God did not ***a*** *us in our slavery.*
Neh 9:31 . . . completely or ***a*** *them forever.*
Ps 22:1 . . . why have You ***a-ed*** *me?*
Ps 37:25 . . . never seen the godly ***a-ed***
Ps 37:28 . . . He will never ***a*** *the godly.*
Prov 15:10 . . . Whoever ***a-s*** *the right path*
Matt 27:46 . . . why have You ***a-ed*** *me?*
John 16:1 . . . you won't ***a*** *your faith.*
Rom 1:24 . . . So God ***a-ed*** *them to do*
Rom 1:28 . . . ***a-ed*** *them to their foolish*
2 Cor 4:9 . . . down, but never ***a-ed*** *by God.*
Heb 13:5 . . . I will never ***a*** *you.*

ABASED (KJV)
Ezek 21:26 . . . mighty will be ***brought down.***
Matt 23:12 . . . themselves will be ***humbled***
Phil 4:12 . . . how to ***live on almost nothing***

ABIDE(TH), ABIDING (KJV)
Luke 2:8 . . . shepherds ***staying*** *in the fields*
John 12:46 . . . no longer ***remain*** *in the dark*
John 15:4 . . . be fruitful unless you ***remain***

ABOUND(ED) (KJV)
Prov 28:20 . . . person will ***get a rich reward***
Matt 24:12 . . . Sin will ***be rampant everywhere***
Rom 5:15 . . . ***even greater*** *is God's wonderful grace*
Rom 5:20 . . . grace ***became more abundant***
2 Cor 8:7 . . . ***excel*** *also in this gracious act*

ABUNDANCE (n)
great quantity, affluence; more than ample
Job 36:31 . . . giving them food in ***a.***
Ps 66:12 . . . a place of great ***a.***
Jer 31:14 . . . The priests will enjoy ***a,***
Matt 13:12 . . . have an ***a*** *of knowledge.*
Matt 25:29 . . . they will have an ***a.***
John 1:16 . . . From His ***a*** *we have all*

ABUSIVE (adj)
using harsh, insulting language; characterized by wrong or improper use or action
1 Cor 5:11 . . . worships idols, or is ***a,***
1 Cor 6:10 . . . drunkards, or are ***a,*** *or*
Eph 4:29 . . . use foul or ***a*** *language.*

ABYSS (KJV)
Luke 8:31 . . . to send them into the ***bottomless pit***
Rev 9:1-2 . . . the shaft of the ***bottomless pit***
Rev 9:11 . . . is the angel from the ***bottomless pit***

ACCEPT, ACCEPTED, ACCEPTS (v)
to receive willingly
Gen 4:4 . . . The Lord ***a-ed*** *Abel*
Gen 4:7 . . . be ***a-ed*** *if you do what is right.*
Deut 16:19 . . . Never ***a*** *a bribe, for bribes*
Job 42:8 . . . I will ***a*** *his prayer*
Job 42:9 . . . the Lord ***a-ed*** *Job's prayer.*
Eccl 5:18 . . . to ***a*** *their lot in life.*
Luke 4:24 . . . no prophet is ***a-ed*** *in his own*
Luke 10:16 . . . Anyone who ***a-s*** *your message*
John 1:12 . . . believed Him and ***a-ed*** *Him,*
John 17:8 . . . They ***a-ed*** *it and know that*
Rom 11:12 . . . when they finally ***a*** *it.*
Gal 2:9 . . . they ***a-ed*** *Barnabas and me*
Col 2:6 . . . just as you ***a-ed*** *Christ Jesus*
1 Tim 1:15 . . . everyone should ***a*** *it:*
1 Tim 4:9 . . . everyone should ***a*** *it.*
Jas 1:21 . . . ***a*** *the word God has planted*

ACCURSED (KJV)
Deut 21:23 . . . for anyone who is hung is ***cursed***
Josh 6:18 . . . things ***set apart for destruction***
1 Cor 12:3 . . . will ***curse*** *Jesus, and no one*
Gal 1:9 . . . let that person be ***cursed***

ACCUSE, ACCUSED, ACCUSES, ACCUSING (v)
to charge with fault or offense; blame
Job 22:4 . . . He ***a-s*** *you and brings judgment*
Ps 27:12 . . . For they ***a*** *me of things*
Dan 6:5 . . . finding grounds for ***a-ing*** *Daniel*
Luke 23:14 . . . ***a-ing*** *him of leading a revolt.*
John 5:45 . . . it isn't I who will ***a***
John 7:7 . . . because I ***a*** *it of doing evil.*
John 8:46 . . . can truthfully ***a*** *me of sin?*
Acts 18:13 . . . ***a-d*** *Paul of "persuading people to worship*
Rom 2:15 . . . and thoughts either ***a*** *them*
Rom 8:33 . . . Who dares ***a*** *us whom God*
Rev 12:10 . . . who ***a-s*** *them before our God*

ACKNOWLEDGE, ACKNOWLEDGES (v)
to express a gratitude of debt; to recognize as valid; to confess (wrongdoing)
Jer 3:13 . . . Only ***a*** *your guilt. Admit*
Matt 10:32 . . . Everyone who ***a-s*** *Me publicly*
Luke 12:8 . . . Son of Man will also ***a***
Rom 1:28 . . . thought it foolish to ***a*** *God,*
1 Jn 2:23 . . . anyone who ***a-s*** *the Son*
1 Jn 4:3 . . . and does not ***a*** *the truth*

ADD, ADDED (v)
to make or serve as an addition
Deut 4:2 . . . Do not ***a*** *to or subtract from*
Deut 12:32 . . . You must not ***a*** *anything to*
Prov 30:6 . . . Do not ***a*** *to His words,*
Eccl 3:14 . . . Nothing can be ***a-ed*** *to it*
Matt 6:27 . . . worries ***a*** *a single moment*
Luke 12:25 . . . worries ***a*** *a single moment*
Acts 2:47 . . . each day the Lord ***a-ed*** *to their*
Rev 22:18 . . . God will ***a*** *to that person*

ADMONISH(ED) (KJV)
Jer 42:19 . . . Don't forget this ***warning*** *I have*
Eccl 12:12 . . . give you ***some further advice***
Heb 8:5 . . . God ***gave*** *him this* ***warning***
2 Thes 3:15 . . . ***warn*** *them as you would*

ADMONITION (KJV)
1 Cor 10:11 . . . written down ***to warn us***
Eph 6:4 . . . ***instruction*** *that comes from the Lord*
Titus 3:10 . . . give a first and second ***warning***

ADOPT, ADOPTED (v)
to take another's child into one's own family
Rom 8:15 . . . when he ***a-ed*** *you as his own*
Rom 8:23 . . . full rights as his ***a-ed*** *children,*
Rom 9:4 . . . to be God's ***a-ed*** *children.*
Gal 4:5 . . . so that he could ***a*** *us as*
Eph 1:5 . . . decided in advance to ***a*** *us*

ADULTERY (n)
unlawful sexual relations between a married and an unmarried person; symbolic of idolatry
Exod 20:14 . . . You must not commit ***a.***
Deut 5:18 . . . You must not commit ***a.***
Prov 6:32 . . . who commits ***a*** *is an utter fool,*
Matt 5:27 . . . You must not commit ***a.***
Matt 19:18 . . . You must not commit ***a.***
Mark 10:11 . . . someone else commits ***a***
Luke 18:20 . . . You must not commit ***a.***
John 8:4 . . . caught in the act of ***a.***
1 Cor 6:9 . . . ***a,*** *or are male prostitutes,*

ADVICE (n)
recommendation regarding a decision or course of conduct; counsel
1 Kgs 12:8 . . . rejected the ***a*** *of*
2 Chr 10:8 . . . rejected the ***a*** *of*
Prov 12:5 . . . ***a*** *of the wicked is*
Prov 12:26 . . . godly give good ***a*** *to their*
Prov 15:22 . . . Plans go wrong for lack of ***a;***
Isa 44:25 . . . I cause the wise to give bad ***a,***
Rom 11:34 . . . enough to give him ***a?***

ADVOCATE (n)
one that pleads the cause of another; defender
Job 16:19 . . . My ***a*** *is there on high.*
John 14:16 . . . he will give you another ***A,***
John 14:26 . . . the Father sends the ***A***
John 15:26 . . . I will send you the ***A***—
John 16:7 . . . if I don't, the ***A*** *won't come.*
1 Jn 2:1 . . . an ***a*** *who pleads our case*

AFRAID (adj)
fearful or apprehensive about an unwanted or uncertain situation
Gen 3:10 . . . I was ***a*** *because I was naked.*
Gen 26:24 . . . Do not be ***a,*** *for I am*
Exod 3:6 . . . he was ***a*** *to look at God.*
Deut 1:21 . . . Don't be ***a!***
Deut 20:1 . . . your own, do not be ***a.***
Ps 23:4 . . . I will not be ***a,*** *for you are*
Isa 10:24 . . . do not be ***a*** *of the Assyrians*
Isa 41:10 . . . Don't be ***a,*** *for I am*
Isa 43:1 . . . Do not be ***a,*** *for I have*
Matt 8:26 . . . Why are you ***a?***
Matt 10:31 . . . So don't be ***a;***
Mark 5:36 . . . Don't be ***a.***
John 14:27 . . . don't be troubled or ***a.***
2 Tim 4:5 . . . Don't be ***a*** *of suffering*
1 Pet 3:14 . . . don't worry or be ***a***

ALCOHOL (n)
drink (as wine or beer) containing ethanol
Prov 20:1 . . . ***a*** *leads to brawls.*
Isa 5:22 . . . boast about all the ***a*** *they*

ALCOHOLIC (adj)
containing alcohol
Num 6:3 . . . give up wine and other ***a***

ALIEN (KJV)
Exod 18:3 . . . a ***foreigner*** *in a foreign land*
Job 19:15 . . . I am like a ***foreigner*** *to them*
Eph 2:12 . . . You were ***excluded from citizenship***

ALIENATED (KJV)
Ezek 48:14 . . . sold or traded or ***used by others***
Eph 4:18 . . . ***wander far from*** *the life God gives*

Col 1:21 . . . who were ***once far away from God***

ALIVE (adj)
animate, having life; active; aware
Gen 45:7 . . . keep you and your families ***a***
Ps 41:2 . . . them and keeps them ***a.***
Luke 24:23 . . . Jesus is ***a!***
Acts 1:3 . . . ways that He was actually ***a.***
Rom 6:11 . . . the power of sin and ***a*** *to God*
Rev 2:8 . . . who was dead but is now ***a:***

ALLELUIA (KJV)
*Rev 19:1 . . . shouting, "****Praise the Lord!***
*Rev 19:3 . . . voices rang out: "****Praise the Lord!***
Rev 19:4 . . . "Amen! ***Praise the Lord!"***
*Rev 19:6 . . . "****Praise the Lord!*** *For the Lord*

ALMIGHTY (n)
having absolute power over all; God
Gen 17:1 . . . I am El-Shaddai—'God ***A.'***
Exod 6:3 . . . as El-Shaddai—'God ***A'***—
Ruth 1:20 . . . ***A*** *has made life very bitter*
Job 6:14 . . . without any fear of the ***A.***
Job 33:4 . . . breath of the ***A*** *gives me life.*
Ps 91:1 . . . rest in the shadow of the ***A.***
Rev 4:8 . . . the ***A****—the one who always was,*
Rev 15:3 . . . O Lord God, the ***A.***
Rev 19:6 . . . our God, the ***A,*** *reigns.*

ALTAR, ALTARS (n)
high places of worship on which sacrifices are offered or incense is burned
Gen 8:20 . . . Noah built an ***a*** *to the LORD,*
Gen 12:7 . . . Abram built an ***a*** *there*
Gen 22:9 . . . Abraham built an ***a*** *and*
Gen 26:25 . . . Isaac built an ***a*** *there*
Exod 27:1 . . . construct a square ***a*** *7½ feet*
Exod 30:1 . . . make another ***a*** *of acacia*
Exod 37:25 . . . incense ***a*** *of acacia wood.*
Josh 8:30 . . . Joshua built an ***a*** *to the LORD,*
Josh 22:10 . . . a large and imposing ***a.***
1 Sam 7:17 . . . Samuel built an ***a*** *to the*
2 Chr 4:1 . . . made a bronze ***a*** *30 feet long,*
2 Chr 4:19 . . . Temple of God: the gold ***a;***
2 Chr 32:12 . . . only at the ***a*** *at the Temple*
2 Chr 33:16 . . . restored the ***a*** *of the LORD*
Ezra 3:2 . . . rebuilding the ***a*** *of the God*
Isa 6:6 . . . coal he had taken from the ***a***
Matt 5:23 . . . presenting a sacrifice at the ***a***
Acts 17:23 . . . your ***a-s*** *had this inscription*
Heb 13:10 . . . an ***a*** *from which the priests*
Rev 6:9 . . . I saw under the ***a*** *the souls*

AMBASSADOR, AMBASSADORS (n)
an authorized representative or messenger
2 Cor 5:20 . . . So we are Christ's ***a-s;***
Eph 6:20 . . . this message as God's ***a.***

AMBITION (n)
aspiration to achieve a particular goal, good or bad
Gal 5:20 . . . anger, selfish ***a,*** *dissension,*
Phil 1:17 . . . They preach with selfish ***a,***
Jas 3:14 . . . there is selfish ***a*** *in your heart,*

ANCESTOR, ANCESTORS (n)
one from whom a person is descended; forefather
Exod 3:15 . . . God of your ***a-s****—the God of*
Deut 19:14 . . . markers your ***a-s*** *set up*
Isa 9:7 . . . throne of His ***a*** *David for all eternity.*
Isa 43:27 . . . your first ***a*** *sinned against Me; all*
Mark 11:10 . . . Kingdom of our ***a*** *David!*
Luke 1:32 . . . the throne of his ***a*** *David.*
Rom 9:5 . . . Abraham, Isaac, and Jacob are their ***a-s,***
Gal 1:14 . . . for the traditions of my ***a-s.***
Heb 1:1 . . . to our ***a-s*** *through the prophets.*

ANGEL, ANGELS (n)
human or superhuman agent or messenger of God
Exod 23:20 . . . I am sending an ***a***
2 Sam 24:16 . . . and said to the death ***a,***
Ps 91:11 . . . will order His ***a-s*** *to protect*
Matt 4:6 . . . will order His ***a-s*** *to protect*
Matt 28:2 . . . an ***a*** *of the Lord came down*
Luke 1:26 . . . God sent the ***a*** *Gabriel*
Luke 2:9 . . . an ***a*** *of the Lord appeared*
Luke 20:36 . . . they will be like ***a-s.***
Acts 12:7 . . . The ***a*** *struck him on the side*
1 Cor 6:3 . . . we will judge ***a-s?***
2 Cor 11:14 . . . disguises himself as an ***a***
Gal 1:8 . . . or even an ***a*** *from heaven,*
Heb 1:6 . . . all of God's ***a-s*** *worship him.*
Heb 2:7 . . . a little lower than the ***a-s***
Heb 13:2 . . . entertained ***a-s*** *without*
1 Pet 1:12 . . . the ***a-s*** *are eagerly watching*
2 Pet 2:4 . . . even the ***a-s*** *who sinned.*
Jude 6 . . . I remind you of the ***a-s***

ANGER (n)
a strong feeling of displeasure
Exod 34:6 . . . slow to ***a*** *and filled with*
Num 14:18 . . . slow to ***a*** *and filled with*
Deut 9:19 . . . furious ***a*** *of the LORD,*
Deut 29:28 . . . In great ***a*** *and fury*
2 Kgs 22:13 . . . LORD's great ***a*** *is burning*
Ps 30:5 . . . His ***a*** *lasts only a moment,*
Ps 78:38 . . . Many times He held back His ***a***
Rom 1:18 . . . God shows His ***a*** *from heaven*
Rom 2:5 . . . a day of ***a*** *is coming,*
Eph 4:26 . . . by letting ***a*** *control you.*
1 Thes 5:9 . . . pour out His ***a*** *on us.*
Jas 1:20 . . . Human ***a*** *does not produce*
Rev 14:10 . . . the wine of God's ***a.***

ANGRY (adj)
feeling or showing anger; wrathful
Exod 32:11 . . . so ***a*** *with Your own people*
Neh 9:17 . . . merciful, slow to become ***a,***
Ps 103:8 . . . merciful, slow to get ***a***
Prov 22:24 . . . Don't befriend ***a*** *people*
Jon 4:2 . . . slow to get ***a*** *and filled*
Matt 5:22 . . . if you are even ***a*** *with*
Mark 10:14 . . . He was ***a*** *with His disciples.*
John 3:36 . . . under God's ***a*** *judgment.*
Acts 4:25 . . . Why were the nations so ***a?***
Jas 1:19 . . . to speak, and slow to get ***a.***

ANGUISH (n)
extreme pain, distress, or anxiety
Isa 53:11 . . . by his ***a,*** *he will be satisfied.*
Zeph 1:15 . . . of terrible distress and ***a,***
Matt 24:21 . . . greater ***a*** *than at any time*
Luke 16:24 . . . I am in ***a*** *in these flames.*
Rev 16:10 . . . ground their teeth in ***a,***

ANOINT, ANOINTED, ANOINTING (v)
to smear or rub with oil; used for healing or consecration to sacred duty; used for grooming or burial; figurative for divine appointment
see also ANOINTED ONE
Exod 30:26 . . . oil to ***a*** *the Tabernacle,*
Exod 30:30 . . . ***A*** *Aaron and his sons*
Lev 8:12 . . . ***a-ing*** *him and making him holy*
1 Sam 15:1 . . . told me to ***a*** *you as king*
2 Sam 23:1 . . . man ***a-ed*** *by the God of Jacob,*
Ps 23:5 . . . honor me by ***a-ing*** *my head*
Ps 92:10 . . . You have ***a-ed*** *me with*
Isa 61:1 . . . the LORD has ***a-ed*** *me*
Dan 9:24 . . . and to ***a*** *the Most Holy Place.*
Acts 10:38 . . . you know that God ***a-ed*** *Jesus*
Heb 1:9 . . . your God has ***a-ed*** *you,*
Jas 5:14 . . . pray over you, ***a-ing*** *you with oil*

ANOINTED ONE (n)
one chosen by divine election
1 Sam 2:10 . . . the strength of His ***a*** *one."*
1 Sam 26:9 . . . the LORD's ***a*** *one?*
Ps 132:17 . . . my ***a*** *one will be a light for*
Dan 9:25 . . . a ruler—the ***A*** *One—*
Isa 45:1 . . . says to Cyrus, His ***a*** *one,*

ANTICHRIST, ANTICHRISTS (n)
opponent of Christ; the personification of evil
1 Jn 2:18 . . . heard that the ***A*** *is coming,*
1 Jn 2:18 . . . many such ***a-s*** *have appeared.*
1 Jn 4:3 . . . has the spirit of the ***A,***
2 Jn 7 . . . deceiver and an ***a.***

ANXIETY, CARE(S) (KJV)
Ps 139:23 . . . and know my ***anxious thoughts***
Phil 4:6 . . . Don't ***worry*** *about anything*
1 Pet 5:7 . . . all your ***worries and cares*** *to God,*

APPEAR, APPEARED, APPEARING, APPEARS (v)
to come out of hiding and show up in public view; to make one's presence known
Gen 1:9 . . . so dry ground may ***a.***
Num 14:10 . . . presence of the LORD ***a-ed***
Deut 33:16 . . . ***a-ed*** *in the burning bush.*
Mal 3:2 . . . and face Him when He ***a-s?***
Matt 1:20 . . . angel of the Lord ***a-ed*** *to him*
Matt 24:30 . . . will ***a*** *in the heavens,*
Luke 2:9 . . . angel of the Lord ***a-ed*** *among*
Luke 16:15 . . . You like to ***a*** *righteous*
Phil 2:7 . . . When He ***a-ed*** *in human form,*
2 Thes 1:7 . . . the Lord Jesus ***a-s*** *from*
2 Tim 1:10 . . . by the ***a-ing*** *of Christ Jesus,*
2 Tim 4:1 . . . ***a-s*** *to set up His Kingdom:*
Heb 9:24 . . . ***a*** *now before God on our*
Heb 9:26 . . . He has ***a-ed*** *at the end of the age*
1 Pet 5:4 . . . when the Great Shepherd ***a-s,***
1 Jn 3:2 . . . will be like when Christ ***a-s.***

APPROVAL (n)
an act or instance of approving
Ps 90:17 . . . LORD our God show us his ***a***
John 6:27 . . . the seal of His ***a.***
Rom 14:4 . . . will receive His ***a.***
1 Cor 11:19 . . . you who have God's ***a***
2 Tim 2:15 . . . and receive His ***a.***
Heb 11:4 . . . God showed His ***a*** *of His gifts.*

ARCHANGEL, ARCHANGELS (n)
a leader and chief angel; biblically designated as Michael
Dan 12:1 . . . At that time Michael, the ***a***
Dan 10:13 . . . one of the ***a-s,*** *came to help me,*
1 Thes 4:16 . . . with the voice of the ***a,***

ARGUE, ARGUING (v)
to contend or disagree in words; to dispute
Job 13:8 . . . Will you ***a*** *God's case*
Job 40:2 . . . to ***a*** *with the Almighty?*
Prov 25:9 . . . When ***a-ing*** *with your neighbor,*
Isa 45:9 . . . those who ***a*** *with their Creator.*
Rom 14:1 . . . and don't ***a*** *with them*
1 Cor 11:16 . . . anyone wants to ***a***

ARM, ARMS (n)
upper limb of the body; extension or projection of; lineage; figurative of power or might
Num 11:23 . . . Has my ***a*** *lost its power?*
Deut 4:34 . . . a powerful ***a,*** *and terrifying*
Deut 7:19 . . . strong hand and powerful ***a***
Deut 33:27 . . . everlasting ***a-s*** *are under you.*
Ps 44:3 . . . it was not their own strong ***a***
Ps 98:1 . . . His holy ***a*** *has shown*
Isa 40:11 . . . carry the lambs in His ***a-s,***
Isa 65:2 . . . opened my ***a-s*** *to a rebellious*
Jer 27:5 . . . powerful ***a*** *I made the earth*
Mark 10:16 . . . took the children in His ***a-s***
1 Pet 4:1 . . . you must ***a*** *yourselves with*

ARMAGEDDON (n)
the gathering place for the final battle between God's forces and Satan's forces associated with Christ's second coming
Rev 16:16 . . . with the Hebrew name ***A.***

ARMOR (n)
weapons of war or self-defense; figurative of spiritual resources
Ps 91:4 . . . are your ***a*** *and protection.*
Isa 59:17 . . . righteousness as his body ***a***
Jer 46:4 . . . and prepare your ***a.***
Rom 13:12 . . . put on the shining ***a***
Eph 6:11 . . . Put on all of God's ***a***
Eph 6:13 . . . put on every piece of God's ***a***
1 Thes 5:8 . . . protected by the ***a*** *of faith*

ARMY, ARMIES (n)
large band of men organized and armed for war; any large multitude devoted to a cause
Ps 33:16 . . . best-equipped ***a*** *cannot save*
Ps 84:12 . . . LORD of Heaven's ***A-ies,***
Isa 6:3 . . . LORD of Heaven's ***A-ies!***
Isa 45:13 . . . LORD of Heaven's ***A-ies,***
Isa 51:15 . . . the LORD of Heaven's ***A-ies.***
Joel 2:2 . . . great and mighty ***a*** *appears.*
Joel 2:5 . . . like a mighty ***a*** *moving into*
Joel 2:11 . . . This is His mighty ***a,***
Hag 1:5 . . . LORD of Heaven's ***A-ies*** *says:*
Zech 8:6 . . . LORD of Heaven's ***A-ies*** *says:*
Rev 19:14 . . . The ***a-ies*** *of heaven,*
Rev 19:19 . . . the horse and His ***a.***

ASHAMED (v)
feeling shame, guilt, or disgrace
Ps 69:6 . . . be ***a*** *because of me,*
Jer 31:19 . . . I was thoroughly ***a*** *of all I did*
Jer 48:13 . . . were ***a*** *of their gold calf*
Mark 8:38 . . . If anyone is ***a*** *of Me*
Luke 9:26 . . . If anyone is ***a*** *of Me*
Rom 1:16 . . . I am not ***a*** *of this Good News*
2 Tim 1:8 . . . So never be ***a*** *to tell others*
2 Tim 2:15 . . . who does not need to be ***a***

ASLEEP (adj)
state of bodily rest; figurative for physical death or spiritual dullness
see also DIE, SLEEP
Judg 4:21 . . . Sisera fell ***a*** *from exhaustion,*
1 Kgs 18:27 . . . away on a trip, or is ***a*** *and*
Matt 9:24 . . . isn't dead; she's only ***a."***
Matt 26:40 . . . found them ***a.*** *He said to Peter,*
John 11:11 . . . Lazarus has fallen ***a,*** *but now I*
1 Thes 5:6 . . . be on your guard, not ***a*** *like*

ASTRAY (adv)
off the right path or route; in error, away from what is desirable or proper
Prov 20:1 . . . Those led ***a*** *by drink*
Isa 47:10 . . . 'knowledge' have led you ***a,***
Jer 50:6 . . . shepherds have led them ***a***
1 Jn 2:26 . . . who want to lead you ***a.***

ASTROLOGERS (n)
one who studies the stars and planets to foresee or foretell future events by their positions and aspects
Isa 47:13 . . . all your ***a,*** *those stargazers*
Dan 2:2 . . . enchanters, sorcerers, and ***a,***

ATHLETE, ATHLETES (n)
a person who is trained or skilled in exercises, sports, or games requiring physical strength, agility, or stamina
Ps 19:5 . . . like a great ***a*** *eager to run*
1 Cor 9:25 . . . All ***a-s*** *are disciplined*
1 Cor 9:27 . . . body like an ***a,*** *training it*
2 Tim 2:5 . . . ***a-s*** *cannot win the prize unless*

ATONEMENT (n)
reconciliation; reparation for an offense or injury; cleansing
see also FORGIVENESS
Exod 25:17 . . . cover—the place of ***a—***
Lev 23:27 . . . Day of ***A*** *on the tenth day*
2 Chr 29:24 . . . to make ***a*** *for the sins*
Prov 16:6 . . . faithfulness make ***a*** *for sin.*

ATTITUDE, ATTITUDES (n)
a mental position with regard to a fact or state; a feeling or emotion toward a fact or state
Eph 4:23 . . . your thoughts and ***a-s.***
Phil 2:5 . . . have the same ***a*** *that Christ*
1 Pet 3:8 . . . keep a humble ***a.***
1 Pet 4:1 . . . with the same ***a*** *He had,*

AUTHORITY, AUTHORITIES (n)
the right to govern; the freedom or ability to act
Matt 28:18 . . . been given all ***a*** *in heaven*
Luke 10:19 . . . have given you ***a*** *over*
John 5:22 . . . absolute ***a*** *to judge,*
Acts 1:7 . . . ***a*** *to set those dates and times,*
Rom 13:1 . . . submit to governing ***a-ies.***
Rom 13:1 . . . For all ***a*** *comes from God,*
Rom 13:2 . . . anyone who rebels against ***a***
Rom 13:3 . . . without fear of the ***a-ies?***
1 Cor 4:3 . . . by any human ***a.***
1 Cor 15:24 . . . ruler and ***a*** *and power.*
Eph 1:22 . . . things under the ***a*** *of Christ*
Eph 3:10 . . . all the unseen rulers and ***a-ies***
Eph 6:12 . . . against evil rulers and ***a-ies***
Col 2:10 . . . every ruler and ***a.***
Col 2:15 . . . the spiritual rulers and ***a-ies.***
1 Tim 2:2 . . . all who are in ***a*** *so that*
Titus 2:15 . . . You have the ***a*** *to correct*
1 Pet 2:18 . . . accept the ***a*** *of your masters*
1 Pet 3:1 . . . accept the ***a*** *of your husbands.*
1 Pet 3:22 . . . the angels and ***a-ies*** *and*
1 Pet 5:5 . . . accept the ***a*** *of the elders.*
Jude 6 . . . the limits of ***a*** *God gave them*

AVOID, AVOIDING (v)
to keep away from; to depart or withdraw from
Prov 4:24 . . . ***A*** *all perverse talk;*
Prov 14:16 . . . are cautious and ***a*** *danger;*
Prov 16:6 . . . By fearing the LORD, people ***a***
Prov 20:3 . . . ***A-ing*** *a fight is a mark*
Eccl 7:18 . . . fears God will ***a*** *both*
Rom 2:3 . . . think you can ***a*** *God's*

AWE (n)
an emotion variously combining dread, respect, and wonder that is inspired by authority or the sacred
see also FEAR, REVERENCE
1 Kgs 3:28 . . . people were in ***a*** *of the king,*
Ps 119:120 . . . I stand in ***a*** *of Your*
Luke 5:26 . . . with great wonder and ***a,***
Acts 2:43 . . . sense of ***a*** *came over them*
Heb 12:28 . . . holy fear and ***a.***

AWESOME (adj)
characterized by reverential fear; expressive of or inspiring awe
see also WONDERFUL
Exod 34:10 . . . the ***a*** *power I will display*
Deut 7:21 . . . a great and ***a*** *God.*
2 Sam 7:23 . . . You performed ***a*** *miracles*
Neh 1:5 . . . the great and ***a*** *God*
Job 10:16 . . . display Your ***a*** *power*
Ps 47:2 . . . Most High is ***a.***
Ps 65:5 . . . answer our prayers with ***a***
Ps 99:3 . . . Your great and ***a*** *name.*
Ps 106:22 . . . such ***a*** *deeds at the Red Sea.*
Ps 131:1 . . . too ***a*** *for me to grasp.*
Dan 9:4 . . . a great and ***a*** *God!*

B

BABY, BABIES (n)
infant child; youngest of a group; figurative of new or immature Christians
Exod 2:7 . . . women to nurse the ***b*** *for you?*
Luke 1:44 . . . ***b*** *in my womb jumped for*
Luke 2:12 . . . find a ***b*** *wrapped snugly*
Luke 2:16 . . . the ***b,*** *lying in the manger.*
Acts 7:19 . . . to abandon their newborn ***b-ies***
1 Cor 14:20 . . . Be innocent as ***b-ies*** *when*
1 Pet 2:2 . . . Like newborn ***b-ies,*** *you must*

BABYLON (n)
capital city of the Babylonian Empire; a city devoted to materialism and sensual pleasure; Biblical writers used as model of paganism and idolatry
Ps 137:1 . . . Beside the rivers of ***B,*** *we sat*
Jer 29:10 . . . will be in ***B*** *for seventy years.*
Jer 51:37 . . . ***B*** *will become a heap of ruins,*
*Rev 14:8 . . . shouting, "****B*** *is fallen—*

BAPTISM, BAPTISMS (n)
a Christian sacrament; a washing with water for cleansing from sin, linked with repentance and admission into the community of faith; figurative of an ordeal or initiation
Matt 3:16 . . . After His ***b,*** *as Jesus came up*
Luke 3:7 . . . crowds came to John for ***b,***
Acts 19:3 . . . what ***b*** *did you experience?*
Rom 6:3 . . . joined with Christ Jesus in ***b,***
Gal 3:27 . . . united with Christ in ***b***
Eph 4:5 . . . one Lord, one faith, one ***b,***
Heb 6:2 . . . further instruction about ***b-s,***
1 Pet 3:21 . . . that water is a picture of ***b,***

BEAST, BEASTS (n)
devilish creature(s) ravishing the earth during the Tribulation; animals, as distinguished from plants or humans; a contemptible person
Dan 7:3 . . . Then four huge ***b-s*** *came up*
Dan 7:6 . . . authority was given to this ***b.***
1 Cor 15:32 . . . fighting wild ***b-s—****those*
Rev 13:18 . . . number of the ***b,*** *for it is*
Rev 16:2 . . . had the mark of the ***b***
Rev 19:20 . . . accepted the mark of the ***b***

BEAUTY (n)
a particularly graceful, ornamental, or excellent quality; the quality in a person or thing that gives pleasure to the senses
2 Sam 11:2 . . . a woman of unusual ***b***
Ps 50:2 . . . the perfection of ***b,*** *God shines*
Prov 31:30 . . . and ***b*** *does not last;*
Isa 28:1 . . . but its glorious ***b*** *will fade*
Jas 1:11 . . . and its ***b*** *fades away.*
1 Pet 1:24 . . . their ***b*** *is like a flower*
1 Pet 3:4 . . . ***b*** *of a gentle and quiet spirit,*

BEGINNING (n)
the point at which something starts; the first part; the origin, source
Gen 1:1 . . . In the ***b*** *God created*
John 1:1 . . . In the ***b*** *the Word already*
Rom 16:25 . . . secret from the ***b*** *of time.*
1 Jn 1:1 . . . one who existed from the ***b,***
Rev 21:6 . . . the ***B*** *and the End.*
Rev 22:13 . . . the ***B*** *and the End.*

BELIEVE, BELIEVED, BELIEVES, BELIEVING (v)
to trust in; to hold a firm conviction about; to accept as true, genuine, or real
see also FAITH, TRUST
Gen 15:6 . . . Abram ***b-d*** *the LORD,*
Isa 53:1 . . . Who has ***b-d*** *our message?*
Mark 9:23 . . . is possible if a person ***b-s.***
Mark 9:24 . . . I do ***b,*** *but help me*
Luke 24:25 . . . You find it so hard to ***b***
John 1:7 . . . so that everyone might ***b***

John 1:12 . . . all who **b-d** Him and accepted
John 3:16 . . . so that everyone who **b-s** in Him
John 4:41 . . . hear His message and **b.**
John 5:38 . . . because you do not **b** Me—
John 7:39 . . . given to everyone **b-ing** in Him.
John 9:35 . . . asked, "Do you **b** in the Son
John 11:27 . . . **b-d** You are the Messiah,
John 11:40 . . . see God's glory if you **b?**
John 12:38 . . . who has **b-d** our message?
John 13:19 . . . you will **b** that I AM
John 14:11 . . . Or at least **b** because of the
John 17:21 . . . world will **b** You sent Me.
John 19:35 . . . so that you also can **b.**
John 20:29 . . . **b** because you have seen
Acts 10:43 . . . that everyone who **b-s** in Him
Acts 16:31 . . . **B** in the Lord Jesus and
Acts 19:4 . . . **b** in the one who would come
Acts 26:27 . . . do you **b** the prophets?
Acts 27:25 . . . For I **b** God.
Rom 1:16 . . . saving everyone who **b-s**—
Rom 3:22 . . . for everyone who **b-s,** no matter
Rom 3:25 . . . **b** that Jesus sacrificed His life,
Rom 10:9 . . . **b** in your heart that God
Rom 10:10 . . . For it is by **b-ing** in your heart
Rom 14:23 . . . anything you **b** is not right,
Rom 16:26 . . . they too might **b** and obey
1 Cor 1:21 . . . to save those who **b.**
2 Cor 5:7 . . . by **b-ing** and not by seeing.
Gal 3:2 . . . because you **b-d** the message
Eph 2:8 . . . His grace when you **b-d.**
Col 1:23 . . . continue to **b** this truth
1 Thes 4:14 . . . For since we **b** that Jesus
2 Thes 2:11 . . . and they will **b** these lies.
1 Tim 3:16 . . . He was **b-d** in throughout the
Heb 3:14 . . . firmly as when we first **b-d,**
Heb 11:6 . . . must **b** that God exists
Jas 2:19 . . . you **b** that there is one God.
1 Jn 3:23 . . . We must **b** in the name
1 Jn 4:1 . . . friends, do not **b** everyone
1 Jn 5:1 . . . Everyone who **b-s** that Jesus is
1 Jn 5:10 . . . All who **b** in the Son

BELONG, BELONGED, BELONGS (v)
to be the property of a person or thing
Lev 25:55 . . . people of Israel **b** to Me.
Lev 27:30 . . . **b-s** to the LORD and
Ps 22:28 . . . royal power **b-s** to the LORD.
John 8:47 . . . Anyone who **b-s** to God listens
John 15:19 . . . if you **b-ed** to it,
Rom 1:6 . . . called to **b** to Jesus
Rom 12:5 . . . we all **b** to each other.
2 Cor 10:7 . . . who say they **b** to Christ
Gal 5:24 . . . Those who **b** to Christ
1 Thes 5:5 . . . we don't **b** to darkness
2 Tim 2:19 . . . All who **b** to the LORD
1 Pet 3:16 . . . because you **b** to Christ.
1 Jn 4:6 . . . If they do not **b** to God,

BESTOWED (KJV)
Isa 63:7 . . . which he has **granted** according

BETHLEHEM (n)
a city about five miles south of Jerusalem in the hill country of Judah; the ancestral home of King David and the birthplace of Jesus Christ
Ruth 1:19 . . . When they came to **B,**
1 Sam 16:1 . . . go to **B.**
2 Sam 23:15 . . . the well by the gate in **B.**
Mic 5:2 . . . **B** Ephrathah, are only a small
Matt 2:1 . . . Jesus was born in **B** in Judea,
Matt 2:6 . . . you, O **B** in the land of Judah,

BETRAY, BETRAYED (v)
to turn your back on a friend; to deliver to an enemy by treachery; to lead astray, seduce
Num 5:6 . . . men or women—**b** the LORD
Deut 32:51 . . . both of you **b-ed** me
Jer 38:22 . . . They have **b-ed** and misled you.
Mal 2:10 . . . Then why do we **b** each other,
Matt 10:21 . . . A brother will **b** his brother
Matt 24:10 . . . and **b** and hate each other.
Matt 26:21 . . . one of you will **b** Me.
Matt 27:4 . . . for I have **b-ed** an innocent man.
Luke 6:16 . . . (who later **b-ed** Him).
John 18:5 . . . Judas, who **b-ed** Him,

BIRTH (n)
the emergence of a new individual from the body of its parent; beginning, start
Gen 25:24 . . . the time came to give **b,**
Ps 58:3 . . . even from **b** they have lied
Matt 24:8 . . . only the first of the **b** pains,
John 3:6 . . . Spirit gives **b** to spiritual life.
Titus 3:5 . . . giving us a new **b** and new life
Jas 1:15 . . . it gives **b** to death.

BIRTHRIGHT (KJV)
Gen 25:31 . . . trade me your **rights as the firstborn son**
1 Chr 5:1 . . . **birthright** was given to the sons
Heb 12:16 . . . his **birthright as the firstborn son**

BITTERNESS (n)
an intense or severe expression or feeling of pain, grief, or regret; exhibiting intense animosity
Prov 14:10 . . . Each heart knows its own **b,**
Prov 17:25 . . . **b** to the one who gave them
Rom 3:14 . . . full of cursing and **b.**
Eph 4:31 . . . Get rid of all **b,** rage,

BLAMELESS (adj)
characterized by being free from sin and fault
see also INTEGRITY, RIGHTEOUS
Gen 6:9 . . . only **b** person living on earth
Job 1:8 . . . **b**—a man of complete integrity.
Ps 18:23 . . . I am **b** before God;
Prov 13:6 . . . guards the path of the **b,**
Prov 29:10 . . . The bloodthirsty hate **b** people,
Phil 1:10 . . . live pure and **b** lives
Col 1:22 . . . and you are holy and **b**
1 Thes 5:23 . . . kept **b** until our Lord
Titus 1:6 . . . must live a **b** life.
2 Pet 3:14 . . . are pure and **b** in his sight.

BLASPHEME, BLASPHEMED, BLASPHEMES, BLASPHEMING (v)
to dishonor or revile God; to speak of or address with irreverence
Lev 24:11 . . . son of an Israelite woman **b-ed**
Lev 24:16 . . . Anyone who **b-s** the Name
Num 15:30 . . . have **b-ed** the LORD,
Isa 52:5 . . . My name is **b-ed** all day long.
Dan 11:36 . . . even **b-ing** the God of gods.
Mark 3:29 . . . anyone who **b-s** the Holy Spirit
Luke 12:10 . . . anyone who **b-s** the Holy Spirit
Acts 6:11 . . . We heard him **b** Moses,
Rom 2:24 . . . Gentiles **b** the name of God
1 Tim 1:13 . . . to **b** the name of Christ.
1 Tim 1:20 . . . learn not to **b** God.
Rev 13:1 . . . were names that **b-ed** God.

BLASPHEMY, BLASPHEMIES (n)
the words or actions that dishonor God; the act of insulting or showing contempt or lack of reverence for God
Neh 9:18 . . . They committed terrible **b-ies.**
Mark 3:28 . . . all sin and **b** can be forgiven,
Mark 14:64 . . . You have all heard His **b.**
John 10:33 . . . for any good work, but for **b!**
2 Pet 2:11 . . . a charge of **b** against those
Rev 13:5 . . . to speak great **b-ies** against God.
Rev 13:6 . . . words of **b** against God,
Rev 17:3 . . . and **b-ies** against God were

BLESS, BLESSED, BLESSES (v)
to confer prosperity or happiness upon; to honor in worship; to offer approval or encouragement; to bring pleasure or divine favor
Gen 1:22 . . . Then God **b-ed** them,
Gen 12:3 . . . I will **b** those who **b** you
Gen 22:18 . . . of the earth will be **b-ed**—
Ps 16:7 . . . I will **b** the LORD who guides
Prov 31:28 . . . Her children stand and **b**
Matt 5:3 . . . God **b-es** those who are poor
Matt 5:7 . . . God **b-es** those who are merciful,
Matt 5:9 . . . God **b-es** those who work for
Matt 5:11 . . . God **b-es** you when people mock
Acts 20:35 . . . **b-ed** to give than to receive.
Jas 1:12 . . . God **b-es** those who patiently
Rev 22:7 . . . **B-ed** are those who obey
Rev 22:14 . . . **B-ed** are those who wash their robes.

BLESSING, BLESSINGS (n)
happiness; praise; divine favor or heavenly reward; the antidote to cursings
Josh 8:34 . . . **b-s** and curses Moses
Prov 13:21 . . . **b-s** reward the righteous.
John 12:13 . . . **B-s** on the one who comes in
Acts 4:33 . . . God's great **b** was upon them
Acts 11:23 . . . evidence of God's **b,**
Rom 15:27 . . . spiritual **b-s** of the Good
Eph 3:6 . . . both enjoy the promise of **b-s**
Rev 7:12 . . . **B** and glory and wisdom

BLOOD (n)
fluid in the circulatory system; signifies human life; kinfolk; of animals, used in priestly sacrifices; of Christ, effective for the forgiveness of sins; on hands or head, symbolic of guilt
Exod 12:13 . . . When I see the **b,** I will pass
Deut 12:23 . . . But never eat the **b,**
Isa 1:11 . . . no pleasure from the **b** of bulls
Mark 14:24 . . . my **b,** which confirms the
John 6:53 . . . and drink his **b,** you cannot
Acts 15:20 . . . and from consuming **b.**
1 Cor 11:25 . . . confirmed with my **b.**
Eph 1:7 . . . with the **b** of His Son
Eph 2:13 . . . through the **b** of Christ.
Heb 9:7 . . . offered **b** for His own sins
Heb 9:20 . . . This **b** confirms the covenant
1 Pet 1:2 . . . cleansed by the **b** of Jesus
1 Pet 1:19 . . . the precious **b** of Christ,
1 Jn 1:7 . . . the **b** of Jesus, His Son, cleanses
Rev 1:5 . . . by shedding His **b** for us.
Rev 5:9 . . . your **b** has ransomed people
Rev 7:14 . . . in the **b** of the Lamb
Rev 12:11 . . . by the **b** of the Lamb
Rev 19:13 . . . He wore a robe dipped in **b,**

BOAST, BOASTED, BOASTING (v)
to puff oneself up in speech, brag
Isa 20:5 . . . and **b-ed** of their allies in Egypt!
Jer 9:23 . . . the wise **b** in their wisdom,
Rom 2:17 . . . **b** about your special
1 Cor 1:31 . . . **b, b** only about the Lord.
2 Cor 8:24 . . . our **b-ing** about you is justified.
2 Cor 10:13 . . . We will **b** only about
Gal 6:14 . . . **b** about anything except
Eph 2:9 . . . none of us can **b** about it.
Jas 1:9 . . . poor have something to **b** about,
Jas 4:16 . . . **b-ing** about your own plans,
2 Pet 2:18 . . . empty, foolish **b-ing.**

BODY, BODIES (n)
one's physical essence; a corpse; a group of people
Job 19:26 . . . in my **b** I will see God!
Ps 49:14 . . . Their **b-ies** will rot in the grave,
Isa 26:19 . . . their **b-ies** will rise again!
Matt 26:41 . . . willing, but the **b** is weak!
Mark 14:22 . . . Take it, for this is my **b.**
Rom 12:4 . . . our **b-ies** have many parts
1 Cor 6:15 . . . that your **b-ies** are actually
1 Cor 6:19 . . . that your **b** is the temple
1 Cor 6:20 . . . honor God with your **b.**

*1 Cor 11:24 . . . My **b**, which is given for*
*1 Cor 12:13 . . . into one **b** by one Spirit,*
*1 Cor 15:44 . . . as spiritual **b-ies**.*
*2 Cor 5:1 . . . eternal **b** made for us by God*
*2 Cor 5:2 . . . to put on our heavenly **b-ies***
*2 Cor 5:4 . . . so that these dying **b-ies** will*
*Eph 1:23 . . . the church is His **b**;*
*Eph 3:6 . . . Both are part of the same **b**,*
*Eph 5:28 . . . love their own **b-ies**.*
*Eph 5:30 . . . are members of His **b**.*
*Col 1:24 . . . for His **b**, the church.*

BOLD (adj)
fearless before danger; self-assured, confident; prominent
*2 Sam 7:27 . . . been **b** enough to pray*
*1 Chr 17:25 . . . been **b** enough to pray*
*Phil 1:20 . . . continue to be **b** for Christ,*

BOLDNESS (n)
fearlessness before danger; self-assurance; confidence; prominence
*Acts 4:13 . . . they saw the **b** of Peter*
*Acts 4:29 . . . give us, your servants, great **b***

BONE, BONES (n)
one of the hard parts of the skeleton
*Gen 2:23 . . . This one is **b** from my **b**,*
*Ezek 37:1 . . . a valley filled with **b-s**.*
*John 19:36 . . . Not one of His **b-s** will be*

BOOK, BOOKS (n)
a long written or printed literary composition; written records, register, or accounting
*Josh 1:8 . . . Study this **B** of Instruction*
*Ps 69:28 . . . names from the **B** of Life;*
*Ps 139:16 . . . recorded in Your **b**.*
*Eccl 12:12 . . . for writing **b-s** is endless,*
*Dan 7:10 . . . and the **b-s** were opened.*
*Dan 12:1 . . . name is written in the **b***
*John 21:25 . . . could not contain the **b-s***
*Phil 4:3 . . . are written in the **B** of Life.*
*Rev 3:5 . . . names from the **B** of Life,*
*Rev 20:12 . . . including the **B** of Life.*
*Rev 20:12 . . . as recorded in the **b-s**.*
*Rev 21:27 . . . in the Lamb's **B** of Life.*

BORN (v)
to give birth to or produce; to be productive; spiritually, to renew or confirm a commitment of faith
*Ps 51:5 . . . For I was **b** a sinner—*
*Eccl 3:2 . . . A time to be **b** and a time to die.*
*Isa 9:6 . . . For a child is **b** to us,*
*Luke 2:11 . . . the Lord—has been **b** today*
*John 3:3 . . . unless you are **b** again,*
*John 3:7 . . . You must be **b** again.*
*1 Pet 1:3 . . . we have been **b** again,*
*1 Pet 1:23 . . . you have been **b** again,*

BRANCH, BRANCHES (n)
limb of a (family) tree; part of a complex body (of knowledge); figurative of offspring and of disciples (of Christ and his disciples)
*Isa 4:2 . . . the **b** of the LORD will be beautiful*
*Dan 4:21 . . . nested in its **b-es**.*
*Zech 3:8 . . . bring my servant, the **B**.*
*John 15:2 . . . **b** of Mine that doesn't*
*John 15:4 . . . a **b** cannot produce fruit if*
*John 15:5 . . . You are the **b-es**.*
*Rom 11:20 . . . those **b-es** were broken off*
*Rom 11:21 . . . not spare the original **b-es**,*

BREAD (n)
basic staple in diet of ancient Israel; signifies livelihood
*Exod 23:15 . . . Festival of Unleavened **B**.*
*Prov 20:17 . . . Stolen **b** tastes sweet,*
*Mark 14:22 . . . Jesus took some **b** and blessed*
*Luke 4:3 . . . change this stone into a loaf of **b**.*
*Luke 9:13 . . . only five loaves of **b***
*John 6:48 . . . Yes, I am the **b** of life!*
*John 6:51 . . . I am the living **b***
*1 Cor 10:16 . . . when we break the **b**,*
*1 Cor 11:23 . . . the Lord Jesus took some **b***
*1 Cor 11:26 . . . eat this **b** and drink*

BREATH (n)
air inhaled and exhaled in breathing; a spoken sound, utterance; a slight indication, suggestion
*Gen 2:7 . . . He breathed the **b** of life*
*Exod 15:8 . . . At the blast of Your **b**,*
*Ps 18:15 . . . at the blast of Your **b**,*
*Ps 144:4 . . . we are like a **b** of air;*

BRIDE (n)
a woman just married or about to be married
*2 Cor 11:2 . . . as a pure **b** to one husband—*
*Rev 19:7 . . . **b** has prepared herself.*
*Rev 21:2 . . . like a **b** beautifully dressed*
*Rev 21:9 . . . the **b**, the wife of the Lamb.*
*Rev 22:17 . . . Spirit and the **b** say, "Come."*

BRIDEGROOM (n)
a man just married or about to be married
*Ps 19:5 . . . like a radiant **b** after*
*Matt 25:1 . . . and went to meet the **b**.*
*Matt 25:5 . . . When the **b** was delayed,*

BROTHER, BROTHERS (n)
male family members with the same parents; kinsmen in the extended family, church, or nation; co-workers in ministry; fellow believers, followers, or friends in Christ
*Ps 133:1 . . . **b-s** live together in harmony!*
*Prov 18:24 . . . friend sticks closer than a **b**.*
*Prov 27:10 . . . to ask your **b** for assistance.*
*Mark 3:33 . . . Who are My **b-s**?*
*Mark 10:29 . . . given up house or **b-s** or*
*John 7:5 . . . even His **b-s** didn't believe*
*Heb 2:11 . . . ashamed to call them His **b-s***
*Heb 13:1 . . . each other as **b-s** and sisters.*
*Jas 2:15 . . . you see a **b** or sister*
*Jas 4:11 . . . evil against each other, dear **b-s***
*1 Pet 1:22 . . . to each other as **b-s** and sisters.*
*1 Pet 3:8 . . . Love each other as **b-s** and*
*1 Jn 2:9 . . . a Christian **b** or sister,*
*1 Jn 3:16 . . . for our **b-s** and sisters.*
*1 Jn 3:17 . . . sees a **b** or sister in need*
*1 Jn 4:20 . . . hates a Christian **b** or sister,*
*1 Jn 4:21 . . . love their Christian **b-s** and*
*Rev 12:10 . . . the accuser of our **b-s** and*

BURDEN, BURDENS (n)
a (usually) heavy load to be borne—physically, emotionally, or spiritually
*Ps 38:4 . . . a **b** too heavy to bear.*
*Matt 11:28 . . . are weary and carry heavy **b-s**,*
*Matt 11:30 . . . the **b** I give you is light.*
*Acts 15:28 . . . to lay no greater **b** on you*
*2 Cor 11:9 . . . a financial **b** to anyone.*
*2 Cor 11:28 . . . the daily **b** of my concern*
*2 Cor 12:14 . . . I will not be a **b** to you.*
*Gal 6:2 . . . Share each other's **b-s**,*
*1 Thes 2:9 . . . so that we would not be a **b***
*2 Thes 3:8 . . . so we would not be a **b***

BURN, BURNED, BURNING (v)
to consume by fire; to be emotionally excited or agitated; to produce or undergo discomfort or pain
*Exod 27:20 . . . keep the lamps **b-ing***
*Lev 6:9 . . . must be kept **b-ing** all night.*
*Deut 7:5 . . . and **b** their idols.*
*Ps 79:5 . . . will your jealousy **b** like fire?*
*Isa 30:27 . . . from far away, **b-ing** with anger,*
*Jer 23:29 . . . Does not my word **b** like fire?*
*Rom 1:27 . . . **b-ed** with lust for each other.*
*1 Cor 7:9 . . . to marry than to **b** with lust.*

BURY, BURIED, BURIES (v)
to deposit (a dead body) in the earth or in a tomb; figurative of denying oneself and submitting to Christ
*Deut 34:6 . . . The LORD **b-ied** him*
*Ruth 1:17 . . . and there I will be **b-ied**.*
*Mark 6:29 . . . get His body and **b-ied** it in*
*Luke 9:60 . . . dead **b** their own dead!*
*Luke 23:30 . . . plead with the hills, '**B** us.'*
*Rom 6:4 . . . and were **b-ied** with Christ*
*1 Cor 15:4 . . . **b-ied**, and he was raised*
*Col 2:12 . . . For you were **b-ied** with Christ*

C

CALF (n)
the young of a domestic cow
*Exod 32:4 . . . it into the shape of a **c**.*
*Luke 15:23 . . . kill the **c** we have been*
*Acts 7:41 . . . made an idol shaped like a **c**,*

CALL, CALLED, CALLING, CALLS (v)
to make a request or demand; to designate or name
see also CHOSE, CHOSEN
*Gen 2:23 . . . She will be **c-ed** 'woman,'*
*1 Kgs 18:24 . . . **c** on the name of your god,*
*2 Kgs 5:11 . . . leprosy and **c** on the name*
*2 Chr 7:14 . . . who are **c-ed** by My name*
*Ps 147:4 . . . stars and **c-s** them all by name.*
*Isa 40:26 . . . **c-ing** each by its name.*
*Isa 45:3 . . . the one who **c-s** you by name.*
*Isa 56:7 . . . Temple will be **c-ed** a house of*
*Hos 11:1 . . . I **c-ed** My son out of Egypt.*
*Joel 2:32 . . . everyone who **c-s** on the name*
*Matt 2:15 . . . I **c-ed** my Son out of Egypt.*
*Matt 9:13 . . . I have come to **c** not those*
*Matt 22:14 . . . many are **c-ed**, but few are*
*Matt 22:43 . . . **c** the Messiah 'my Lord'?*
*Mark 2:17 . . . I have come to **c** not those*
*Mark 10:49 . . . Come on, He's **c-ing** you!*
*Luke 1:32 . . . **c-ed** the Son of the Most High.*
*Luke 23:15 . . . this man has done **c-s***
*Acts 2:21 . . . everyone who **c-s** on the name*
*Acts 2:39 . . . who have been **c-ed** by the Lord*
*Acts 9:14 . . . arrest everyone who **c-s** upon*
*Acts 22:16 . . . sins washed away by **c-ing** on*
*Rom 1:6 . . . **c-ed** to belong to Jesus*
*Rom 8:28 . . . **c-ed** according to His purpose*
*Rom 10:12 . . . to all who **c** on Him.*
*Rom 10:13 . . . Everyone who **c-s** on the*
*Rom 11:29 . . . **c** can never be withdrawn.*
*1 Cor 1:2 . . . who have been **c-ed** by God*
*1 Cor 1:2 . . . **c** on the name of our Lord*
*1 Cor 1:24 . . . those **c-ed** by God to salvation,*
*1 Cor 7:17 . . . when God first **c-ed** you.*
*Gal 1:6 . . . so soon from God, who **c-ed** you*
*Gal 5:13 . . . have been **c-ed** to live in freedom,*
*Eph 1:18 . . . to those He **c-ed**—His holy*
*Col 3:15 . . . you are **c-ed** to live in peace.*
*1 Thes 2:12 . . . **c-ed** you to share in His*
*1 Thes 4:7 . . . God has **c-ed** us to live holy*
*1 Thes 5:24 . . . He who **c-s** you is faithful.*
*2 Tim 2:22 . . . those who **c** on the Lord*
*Heb 9:15 . . . all who are **c-ed** can receive*
*1 Pet 2:9 . . . he **c-ed** you out of the darkness*
*1 Pet 3:9 . . . what God has **c-ed** you to do,*
*1 Pet 5:10 . . . God **c-ed** you to share in His*
*2 Pet 1:10 . . . are among those God has **c-ed***

CALVARY (KJV)
*Luke 23:33 . . . place called **The Skull**,*

CANDLESTICK(S) (KJV)
*Exod 25:31 . . . Make a **lampstand** of pure,*
*Dan 5:5 . . . palace, near the **lampstand**.*
*Matt 5:15 . . . a lamp is placed on a **stand***
*Heb 9:2 . . . a **lampstand**, a table, and sacred*
*Rev 1:12 . . . I saw seven gold **lampstands***

CAPSTONE, HEADSTONE (KJV)
*Ps 118:22 . . . become the **cornerstone***
*Zech 4:7 . . . the **final stone** of the Temple*
*Matt 21:42 . . . the **cornerstone.** This is the Lord's*
*Luke 20:17 . . . has now become the **cornerstone***

CARE, CARED, CARES, CARING (v)
to feel interest or concern; to attend to or provide for the needs, operation, or treatment of
*Deut 1:31 . . . LORD your God **c-d** for you*
*Ps 8:4 . . . mortals that You should **c***
*Ps 37:17 . . . LORD takes **c** of the godly.*
*Ps 65:9 . . . take **c** of the earth and*
*Ps 116:15 . . . **c-s** deeply when His loved ones*
*Ps 138:6 . . . is great, He **c-s** for the humble,*
*Prov 12:10 . . . godly **c** for their animals,*
*Prov 27:23 . . . heart into **c-ing** for your herds,*
*Isa 53:8 . . . No one **c-d** that He died without*
*Jer 23:2 . . . Instead of **c-ing** for My flock*
*Matt 6:30 . . . if God **c-s** so wonderfully for*
*Matt 25:36 . . . I was sick, and you **c-d** for Me.*
*Luke 10:34 . . . an inn, where he took **c** of*
*John 10:13 . . . really **c** about the sheep.*
*John 12:25 . . . who **c** nothing for their life*
*John 21:16 . . . Then take **c** of My sheep,*
*Eph 5:29 . . . just as Christ **c-s** for the church.*
*Phil 2:21 . . . others **c** only for themselves*
*1 Thes 2:7 . . . and **c-ing** for her own children.*
*1 Tim 5:14 . . . take **c** of their own homes.*
*1 Tim 5:16 . . . she must take **c** of them and*
*Heb 2:6 . . . that you should **c** for him?*
*1 Pet 5:2 . . . **C** for the flock that God*
*1 Pet 5:7 . . . and **c-s** to God, for He **c-s***

CAREFUL (adj)
marked by wary caution; meticulous
*Exod 34:12 . . . **c** never to make a treaty*
*Lev 18:4 . . . and be **c** to obey My decrees,*
*Lev 22:2 . . . be very **c** with the sacred gifts*
*Lev 26:3 . . . are **c** to obey My commands,*
*Deut 4:9 . . . But watch out! Be **c** never to*
*Deut 6:3 . . . and be **c** to obey.*
*Deut 8:1 . . . Be **c** to obey all the commands*
*Deut 12:1 . . . **c** to obey when you live in*
*Deut 12:28 . . . Be **c** to obey all My*
*Josh 1:7 . . . and very courageous. Be **c***
*Josh 23:11 . . . be very **c** to love the LORD*
*2 Kgs 21:8 . . . Israelites will be **c** to obey*
*1 Cor 8:9 . . . be **c** so that your freedom*
*1 Cor 10:12 . . . strong, be **c** not to fall.*
*Eph 5:15 . . . So be **c** how you live.*

CARNAL(LY) (KJV)
*Rom 7:14 . . . **all too human,** a slave to sin*
*Rom 8:6 . . . letting your **sinful nature** control*
*1 Cor 3:3 . . . still **controlled by your sinful nature***
*2 Cor 10:4 . . . not **worldly** weapons*

CARPENTER (n)
a worker who builds or repairs wooden structures or their structural parts
*Matt 13:55 . . . He's just the **c**'s son,*
*Mark 6:3 . . . He's just a **c**, the son of Mary*

CATTLE (n)
bovine animals on a farm or ranch
*Ps 50:10 . . . I own the **c** on a thousand*

CELEBRATE, CELEBRATED, CELEBRATING (v)
to perform (a sacrament or ceremony) publicly and with appropriate rites; to observe a notable occasion with festivities
*Exod 10:9 . . . join together in **c-ing** a festival*
*Exod 12:47 . . . Israel must **c** this Passover*
*Exod 13:5 . . . You must **c** this event in this*
*Exod 23:14 . . . **c** three festivals in My*
*Exod 34:18 . . . **c** the Festival of*
*Exod 34:22 . . . **c** the Festival of the Final*
*Num 9:2 . . . **c** the Passover at the*
*Deut 16:1 . . . your God, **c** the Passover*
*2 Sam 6:21 . . . so I **c** before the LORD.*
*2 Kgs 23:21 . . . **c** the Passover to the LORD*
*2 Chr 30:1 . . . to **c** the Passover.*
*2 Chr 30:13 . . . **c** the Festival of*
*2 Chr 30:23 . . . **c-d** joyfully for another week.*
*Neh 8:12 . . . to **c** with great joy*
*Esth 8:15 . . . people of Susa **c-d** the new*
*Esth 9:19 . . . villages **c** an annual festival*
*Esth 9:21 . . . to **c** an annual festival*
*Matt 25:21 . . . Let's **c** together!*
*Luke 15:23 . . . We must **c** with a feast,*
*Luke 15:32 . . . We had to **c** this happy day.*
*John 18:28 . . . to **c** the Passover.*
*Col 2:16 . . . for not **c-ing** certain holy days*
*Rev 11:10 . . . to **c** the death of the two prophets*

CELEBRATION, CELEBRATIONS (n)
a party or festival in honor of a religious ceremony or holiday; the observation of a notable occasion with festivities
*Num 9:3 . . . regulations concerning this **c.***
*2 Sam 6:12 . . . City of David with a great **c:***
*Esth 8:17 . . . had a great **c** and declared*
*Jer 31:13 . . . old and young—will join in the **c.***
*Joel 1:16 . . . No joyful **c-s** are held in the*
*Zech 8:19 . . . **c** for the people of Judah.*
*John 11:55 . . . for the Jewish Passover **c,***

CHARACTER (n)
moral excellence and firmness; main or essential nature
*Rom 5:4 . . . develops strength of **c,***
*1 Cor 15:33 . . . corrupts good **c.***
*Heb 1:3 . . . expresses the very **c** of God,*

CHARITY (KJV)
*1 Cor 8:1 . . . **love** that strengthens the church*
*1 Cor 13:1 . . . but didn't **love** others, I would*
*Col 3:14 . . . clothe yourselves with **love,** which*
*Tim 4:12 . . . in your **love,** your faith, and*
*2 Pet 1:7 . . . affection with **love** for everyone*

CHASTE (KJV)
*2 Cor 11:2 . . . as a **pure** bride to one husband—Christ*
*Titus 2:5 . . . to live wisely and be **pure***
*1 Pet 3:2 . . . **pure** and reverent lives*

CHASTEN(ED) (KJV)
*Ps 6:1 . . . or **discipline** me in Your rage*
*Prov 19:18 . . . **Discipline** Your children while*
*Heb 12:11 . . . No **discipline** is enjoyable while*
*1 Cor 11:32 . . . **being disciplined** so that we*
*Rev 3:19 . . . I correct and **discipline***

CHEAT, CHEATED, CHEATS (v)
to deprive of something valuable by deceit or fraud; to practice fraud or trickery
*Gen 31:7 . . . he has **c-ed** me, changing my*
*1 Sam 12:3 . . . Have I ever **c-ed** any of you?*
*1 Sam 12:4 . . . have never **c-ed** or oppressed*
*Amos 8:5 . . . get back to **c-ing** the helpless.*
*Mal 3:8 . . . You have **c-ed** me of the tithes*
*Mark 10:19 . . . You must not **c** anyone.*
*Mark 12:40 . . . they shamelessly **c** widows*
*1 Cor 5:10 . . . are greedy, or **c** people,*
*1 Cor 5:11 . . . is a drunkard, or **c-s** people.*
*1 Cor 6:7 . . . not let yourselves be **c-ed?***
*1 Cor 6:8 . . . who do wrong and **c** even*
*1 Cor 6:10 . . . abusive, or **c** people—*

CHILD, CHILDREN, CHILDREN (n)
an unborn or recently born person; a young person between infancy and youth, not yet of age; offspring or descendants
see also SON(S)
*Exod 20:5 . . . family is affected—even **c-ren***
*Deut 24:16 . . . sins of their **c-ren,** nor **c-ren***
*Deut 32:46 . . . as a command to your **c-ren***
*1 Kgs 3:26 . . . Give her the **c**—please do*
*Job 1:5 . . . Perhaps my **c-ren** have sinned*
*Ps 8:2 . . . You have taught **c-ren** and infants*
*Prov 20:7 . . . blessed are their **c-ren** who*
*Prov 23:13 . . . discipline your **c-ren.***
*Prov 29:15 . . . To discipline a **c** produces*
*Prov 31:28 . . . Her **c-ren** stand and bless her.*
*Isa 7:14 . . . The virgin will conceive a **c!***
*Isa 9:6 . . . For a **c** is born to us,*
*Isa 54:13 . . . I will teach all your **c-ren,***
*Mal 4:6 . . . the hearts of **c-ren** to their fathers.*
*Matt 1:23 . . . The virgin will conceive a **c!***
*Matt 5:9 . . . will be called the **c-ren** of God.*
*Matt 18:3 . . . and become like little **c-ren,***
*Mark 9:37 . . . welcomes a little **c** like this*
*Mark 10:14 . . . Let the **c-ren** come to me.*
*Mark 10:16 . . . he took the **c-ren** in His arms*
*Luke 1:42 . . . and Your **c** is blessed.*
*Luke 6:35 . . . as **c-ren** of the Most High,*
*Luke 18:15 . . . their little **c-ren** to Jesus*
*John 1:12 . . . to become **c-ren** of God.*
*John 12:36 . . . become **c-ren** of the light.*
*Acts 2:39 . . . to your **c-ren,** and even to the*
*Rom 9:26 . . . called '**c-ren** of the living God.'*
*1 Cor 13:11 . . . and reasoned as a **c.***
*Gal 3:26 . . . you are all **c-ren** of God*
*Eph 3:6 . . . riches inherited by God's **c-ren.***
*Eph 6:1 . . . **C-ren,** obey your parents*
*Eph 6:4 . . . do not provoke your **c-ren** to anger*
*Col 3:21 . . . do not aggravate your **c-ren,***
*1 Tim 3:4 . . . having **c-ren** who respect and*
*1 Tim 3:12 . . . manage his **c-ren** and*
*1 Tim 5:10 . . . brought up her **c-ren** well?*
*Heb 12:7 . . . treating you as His own **c-ren.***
*1 Jn 4:7 . . . Anyone who loves is a **c** of God*
*1 Jn 5:4 . . . every **c** of God defeats this evil*
*1 Jn 5:18 . . . God's **c-ren** do not make a*

CHILDLESS (adj)
a person characterized by lack of children; barren
*Ps 113:9 . . . He gives the **c** woman a family,*
*Isa 54:1 . . . Sing, O **c** woman, you who*
*Gal 4:27 . . . Rejoice, O **c** woman, you who*

CHILDLIKE (adj)
resembling, suggesting, or appropriate to a child; marked by innocence, trust, and ingenuousness
*Ps 116:6 . . . protects those of **c** faith;*
*Matt 11:25 . . . revealing them to the **c.***

CHOOSE, CHOOSES (v)
to decide; to have a preference for; to select freely and after consideration
see also CALL, CHOSE
*Deut 30:19 . . . Oh, that you would **c** life, so*
*Josh 24:15 . . . **c** today whom you will serve.*
*Eccl 10:2 . . . A wise person **c-s** the right road;*
*Jer 27:5 . . . things of mine to anyone I **c.***
*Dan 4:25 . . . gives them to anyone He **c-s.***
*John 15:16 . . . You didn't **c** me.*
*Rom 9:11 . . . God **c-s** people according to*
*Rom 9:18 . . . he **c-s** to harden the hearts of*

CHOSE, CHOSEN (v)
see also CALL, CHOOSE, CHOSEN
*Matt 22:14 . . . are called, but few are **c-n.***
*John 15:16 . . . You didn't choose me. I **c** you.*
*Rom 1:1 . . . **c-n** by God to be an apostle*
*Rom 8:29 . . . **c** them to become like his*
*1 Cor 1:1 . . . Paul, **c-n** by the will of God*
*1 Cor 1:27 . . . **c** things that are powerless*
*Eph 1:4 . . . loved us and **c** us in Christ*
*Eph 1:11 . . . God, for He **c** us in advance,*
*2 Thes 2:13 . . . thankful that God **c** you*
*1 Pet 1:15 . . . as God who **c** you is holy.*
*2 Pet 1:10 . . . God has called and **c-n.***

CHOSEN (adj)
selected or marked for special favor or privilege; elect
see also CALLED
*1 Chr 16:22 . . . Do not touch My **c** people,*
*Isa 41:8 . . . My **c** one, descended from Abraham*
*Mark 13:20 . . . for the sake of His **c** ones*
*Luke 23:35 . . . God's Messiah, the **C** One.*
*John 1:34 . . . that He is the **C** One of God.*
*1 Pet 1:1 . . . writing to God's **c** people*
*1 Pet 2:9 . . . for you are a **c** people.*

CHRISTIAN, CHRISTIANS (n)
one who professes belief in and follows the teachings of Jesus Christ; believer
*Acts 11:26 . . . believers were first called **C-s**.*
*Acts 26:28 . . . persuade me to become a **C***
*Gal 2:4 . . . some so-called **C-s***
*1 Thes 4:12 . . . people who are not **C-s***
*1 Pet 4:14 . . . insulted for being a **C**,*
*1 Pet 4:16 . . . to suffer for being a **C**.*
*1 Pet 5:9 . . . your **C** brothers and sisters*

CHURCH, CHURCHES (n)
"assembly" or "called ones"; the body of believers gathered to worship Jesus (not the building in which they meet)
*Matt 16:18 . . . this rock I will build My **c**,*
*Matt 18:17 . . . take your case to the **c**.*
*Acts 16:5 . . . the **c** were strengthened*
*Acts 20:28 . . . shepherd God's flock—His **c**,*
*1 Cor 15:9 . . . way I persecuted God's **c**.*
*Gal 1:13 . . . I violently persecuted God's **c**.*
*Eph 5:23 . . . Christ is the head of the **c**.*
*Col 1:18 . . . head of the **c**, which is His*
*Col 1:24 . . . continue for His body, the **c**.*
*2 Thes 1:4 . . . tell God's other **c** about your endurance*
*Rev 1:20 . . . angels of the seven **c**,*

CIRCUMCISE, CIRCUMCISED, CIRCUMCISING (v)
to cut off the foreskin of male children
*Gen 17:10 . . . male among you must be **c-ed**.*
*Gen 17:12 . . . **c-d** on the eighth day after his*
*Josh 5:3 . . . Joshua made flint knives and **c***
*John 7:23 . . . correct time for **c-ing** your son*
*Acts 21:21 . . . not to **c** their children*
*Rom 4:11 . . . even before he was **c-ed**.*
*1 Cor 7:19 . . . or not a man has been **c-ed**.*

CIRCUMCISION (n)
the condition of being circumcised; the ceremony signifying Israel's covenant with God; act symbolic of cleansing
*Rom 2:25 . . . **c** has value only if you obey*
*Rom 2:29 . . . true **c** is not merely*
*Gal 5:2 . . . If you are counting on **c** to make*

CITIZEN, CITIZENS (n)
a person owing allegiance to and deriving protection from a sovereign state
*Acts 22:28 . . . But I am a **c** by birth!*
*Eph 2:19 . . . You are **c-s** along with*
*Phil 3:20 . . . But we are **c-s** of heaven,*

CLAY (n)
an earthy material that is pliable when moist but hard when fired and is used for brick, tile, and pottery
*Isa 45:9 . . . Does the **c** dispute with the one*
*Isa 64:8 . . . **c**, and You are the potter.*
*Lam 4:2 . . . are now treated like pots of **c***
*Dan 2:33 . . . combination of iron and baked **c**.*
*Rom 9:21 . . . to use the same lump of **c***
*2 Cor 4:7 . . . **c** jars containing this great*
*2 Tim 2:20 . . . are made of wood and **c**.*

CLOSE, CLOSED, CLOSES (v)
to draw near; to contract, fold, swing, or slide so as to leave no opening
*Gen 7:16 . . . Then the LORD **c-d** the door*
*Ps 34:18 . . . is **c** to the brokenhearted;*
*Ps 148:14 . . . of Israel who are **c** to Him.*
*Prov 28:27 . . . who **c** their eyes to poverty*
*Isa 22:22 . . . no one will be able to **c** them;*
*Isa 40:11 . . . in His arms, holding them **c***
*Acts 28:27 . . . and they have **c-d** their eyes—*
*Rev 3:7 . . . what He **c-s**, no one can open.*
*Rev 21:25 . . . Its gates will never be **c-d***

COMFORT (n)
consolation in time of trouble or worry; solace
*Gen 24:67 . . . she was a special **c** to him*
*Job 10:20 . . . I may have a moment of **c***
*Ps 94:19 . . . Your **c** gave me renewed hope*
*Zech 10:2 . . . falsehoods that give no **c**.*
*2 Cor 1:5 . . . shower us with His **c***
*2 Cor 1:7 . . . share in the **c** God gives us.*
*Col 4:11 . . . And what a **c** they have been!*

COMFORT, COMFORTED, COMFORTS (v)
to give strength and hope to; to console
*Gen 37:35 . . . he refused to be **c-ed**.*
*Ruth 2:13 . . . You have **c-ed** me by speaking*
*Job 2:11 . . . traveled from their homes to **c***
*Job 42:11 . . . they consoled him and **c-ed** him*
*Ps 69:20 . . . one would turn and **c** me.*
*Ps 86:17 . . . O LORD, help and **c** me.*
*Ps 119:50 . . . it **c-s** me in all my troubles.*
*Ps 119:52 . . . O LORD, they **c** me.*
*Isa 40:1 . . . **C, c** My people,*
*Isa 49:13 . . . the LORD has **c-ed** His people*
*Isa 51:3 . . . The LORD will **c** Israel again*
*Isa 51:12 . . . I, am the one who **c-s** you.*
*Isa 51:19 . . . Who is left to **c** you?*
*Isa 52:9 . . . the LORD has **c-ed** His people.*
*Isa 61:1 . . . to **c** the brokenhearted*
*Isa 66:13 . . . as a mother **c-s** her child.*
*Lam 1:2 . . . there is no one left to **c** her.*
*Lam 1:17 . . . but no one **c-s** her.*
*Zech 1:17 . . . the LORD will again **c** Zion*
*Matt 5:4 . . . who mourn, for they will be **c-ed**.*
*1 Cor 14:3 . . . encourages them, and **c-s***
*2 Cor 1:4 . . . He **c-s** us in all our troubles*
*2 Cor 1:4 . . . so that we can **c** others.*
*2 Cor 1:6 . . . For when we ourselves are **c-ed**,*
*2 Cor 1:6 . . . we will certainly **c** you.*
*2 Cor 2:7 . . . forgive and **c** him.*

COMFORTER (KJV)
*John 14:16 . . . another **Advocate**, who will*
*John 14:26 . . . sends the **Advocate** as my*
*John 15:26 . . . the **Advocate**—the Spirit of*
*John 16:7 . . . if I don't, the **Advocate** won't*

COMMAND, COMMANDS (n)
an order given; religious instruction
see also COMMANDMENT
*Exod 20:6 . . . who love Me and obey My **c-s**.*
*Exod 24:12 . . . the instructions and **c-s***
*Lev 22:31 . . . keep all My **c-s***
*Num 15:39 . . . and obey all the **c-s***
*Deut 4:2 . . . or subtract from these **c-s***
*Deut 6:6 . . . wholeheartedly to these **c-s***
*Deut 7:9 . . . who love Him and obey His **c-s**.*
*Deut 8:1 . . . Be careful to obey all the **c-s***
*Deut 11:1 . . . decrees, regulations, and **c-s**.*
*Deut 11:27 . . . if you obey the **c-s** of the*
*Deut 28:1 . . . keep all His **c-s** that I am giving*
*Deut 32:46 . . . as a **c** to your children*
*Josh 1:9 . . . My **c**—be strong and*
*1 Kgs 8:58 . . . obey all the **c-s**, decrees,*
*1 Kgs 8:61 . . . obey His decrees and **c-s**,*
*1 Chr 28:7 . . . if he continues to obey My **c-s***
*Neh 1:5 . . . who love Him and obey His **c-s**,*
*Job 36:10 . . . **c-s** that they turn from evil.*
*Ps 33:9 . . . It appeared at His **c**.*
*Ps 78:7 . . . and obeying His **c-s**.*
*Ps 103:20 . . . listening for each of His **c-s**.*
*Ps 112:1 . . . and delight in obeying His **c-s**.*
*Ps 119:32 . . . I will pursue Your **c-s**,*
*Ps 119:47 . . . How I delight in Your **c-s**!*
*Ps 119:73 . . . the sense to follow Your **c-s**.*
*Ps 119:96 . . . Your **c-s** have no limit.*
*Ps 119:127 . . . I love Your **c-s** more than*
*Ps 119:143 . . . I find joy in Your **c-s**.*
*Ps 119:172 . . . all your **c-s** are right.*
*Ps 119:176 . . . I have not forgotten Your **c-s**.*
*Prov 3:1 . . . Store My **c-s** in your heart.*
*Prov 6:23 . . . For their **c** is a lamp*
*Eccl 12:13 . . . Fear God and obey His **c-s**,*
*Isa 48:18 . . . you had listened to My **c-s**!*
*Dan 9:4 . . . who love You and obey Your **c-s**.*
*Matt 28:20 . . . new disciples to obey all the **c-s***
*John 15:17 . . . My **c**: Love each other.*
*Acts 17:30 . . . He **c-s** everyone everywhere to*
*Rom 7:8 . . . sin used this **c** to arouse*
*Rom 7:9 . . . I learned the **c** not to covet,*
*Rom 7:12 . . . law itself is holy, and its **c-s** are*
*1 Cor 14:37 . . . saying is a **c** from the Lord*
*Gal 5:14 . . . summed up in this one **c**:*
*2 Thes 3:6 . . . we give you this **c***
*2 Pet 2:21 . . . reject the **c** they were given*

COMMAND, COMMANDED, COMMANDING (v)
to issue a charge or directive
*Gen 7:5 . . . everything as the LORD **c-ed***
*Exod 7:6 . . . did just as the LORD had **c-ed***
*Exod 19:7 . . . everything the LORD had **c-ed***
*Deut 6:1 . . . LORD your God **c-ed** me to teach*
*Deut 6:24 . . . our God **c-ed** us to obey*
*Deut 15:11 . . . why I am **c-ing** you to share*
*John 15:14 . . . my friends if you do what I **c**.*
*2 Tim 2:14 . . . **c** them in God's presence*
*2 Pet 3:2 . . . Savior **c-ed** through your*
*1 Jn 3:23 . . . just as He **c-ed** us.*
*2 Jn 4 . . . just as the Father **c-ed**.*

COMMANDMENT, COMMANDMENTS (n)
a gracious provision of God's law or covenant, obeyed as an act of love and devotion
see also COMMAND
*Exod 34:28 . . . Ten **C-s**—on the stone tablets.*
*Deut 4:13 . . . His covenant—the Ten **C-s***
*Deut 10:4 . . . LORD wrote the Ten **C-s** on*
*Ps 103:18 . . . of those who obey His **c-s**!*
*Ps 111:7 . . . all His **c-s** are trustworthy.*
*Ps 111:10 . . . who obey His **c-s** will grow*
*Ps 119:93 . . . I will never forget Your **c-s**,*
*Prov 19:16 . . . the **c-s** and keep your life;*
*Matt 5:19 . . . if you ignore the least **c***
*Matt 19:17 . . . eternal life, keep the **c-s**.*
*Matt 22:36 . . . the most important **c***
*Matt 22:38 . . . the first and greatest **c**.*
*Mark 10:19 . . . you know the **c-s**:*
*Mark 12:28 . . . **c-s**, which is the most*
*Luke 18:20 . . . you know the **c-s**:*
*John 13:34 . . . a new **c**: Love each other.*
*John 14:15 . . . If you love Me, obey My **c-s**.*
*Rom 13:9 . . . in this one **c**: "Love your*
*1 Cor 7:19 . . . is to keep God's **c-s**.*
*Eph 2:15 . . . law with its **c-s** and regulations.*
*Eph 6:2 . . . the first **c** with a promise:*
*Heb 9:19 . . . had read each of God's **c-s***
*1 Jn 2:3 . . . we know him if we obey His **c-s**.*
*1 Jn 3:24 . . . Those who obey God's **c-s***
*1 Jn 5:3 . . . God means keeping His **c-s**,*
*Rev 12:17 . . . who keep God's **c-s** and*

COMMIT, COMMITS, COMMITTED, COMMITTING (v)
to carry into action deliberately, perpetrate; to obligate or pledge oneself
*Deut 30:20 . . . **c-ting** yourself firmly to Him.*
*2 Chr 16:9 . . . hearts are fully **c-ted** to Him.*
*2 Chr 17:6 . . . deeply **c-ted** to the ways*
*Prov 6:32 . . . the man who **c-s** adultery*
*Prov 29:22 . . . a hot-tempered person **c-s***
*Matt 5:28 . . . has already **c-ted** adultery with*
*Matt 5:32 . . . causes her to **c** adultery.*
*Matt 19:9 . . . someone else **c-s** adultery—*
*Mark 10:11 . . . someone else **c-s** adultery*
*Mark 10:19 . . . You must not **c** adultery.*
*Luke 16:18 . . . from her husband **c-s** adultery.*
*Rom 13:9 . . . You must not **c** adultery.*
*Titus 2:14 . . . totally **c-ted** to doing good*
*Jas 2:11 . . . You must not **c** adultery,*
*Rev 18:3 . . . world have **c-ted** adultery with*
*Rev 18:9 . . . the world who **c-ted** adultery*

COMPASSION (n)
sympathy, usually granted because of unusual or distressing circumstances
*Exod 34:6 . . . The God of **c** and mercy!*
*Ps 51:1 . . . Because of Your great **c**,*
*Ps 86:15 . . . a God of **c** and mercy, slow to*
*Ps 145:9 . . . He showers **c** on all*
*Isa 49:13 . . . and will have **c** on them*
*Isa 63:15 . . . Your mercy and **c** now?*
*Lam 3:32 . . . brings grief, He also shows **c***
*Hos 2:19 . . . unfailing love and **c**.*
*Mic 7:19 . . . You will have **c** on us.*
*Zech 10:6 . . . because of my **c**.*
*Mark 1:41 . . . Moved with **c**, Jesus reached*
*Mark 6:34 . . . and He had **c** on them*
*Luke 15:20 . . . with love and **c**, He ran to*
*Rom 9:15 . . . show **c** to anyone I choose.*

COMPASSIONATE (adj)
having or showing compassion; sympathetic
*Ps 103:13 . . . tender and **c** to those who*
*Ps 112:4 . . . They are generous, **c**,*
*Ps 145:8 . . . is merciful and **c**, slow to*
*Joel 2:13 . . . He is merciful and **c**, slow to*
*Luke 6:36 . . . You must be **c**, just as Your*
*Phil 2:1 . . . Are your hearts tender and **c?***

COMPLAINED, COMPLAINING (v)
to express grief, pain, or discontent; to make a formal accusation or charge
*Exod 15:24 . . . the people **c** and turned*
*Num 14:2 . . . in the wilderness!" they **c**.*
*Num 14:29 . . . Because you **c** against Me,*
*John 6:43 . . . Jesus replied, "Stop **c-ing***
*Phil 2:14 . . . Do everything without **c-ing***

CONDEMN, CONDEMNED, CONDEMNING, CONDEMNS (v)
to declare guilty; to sentence or doom
*Job 15:6 . . . Your own mouth **c-s** you, not I.*
*Job 40:8 . . . my justice and **c** me just to*
*Ps 37:33 . . . or let the godly be **c-ed***
*Ps 102:20 . . . to release those **c-ed** to die.*
*Prov 12:2 . . . **c-s** those who plan wickedness.*
*Prov 17:15 . . . guilty and **c-ing** the innocent—*
*Isa 53:8 . . . Unjustly **c-ed**, he was led away.*
*Matt 12:7 . . . not have **c-ed** my innocent*
*Matt 12:37 . . . acquit you or **c** you.*
*Matt 12:41 . . . on judgment day and **c** it,*
*Matt 27:3 . . . Jesus had been **c-ed** to die,*
*Luke 11:31 . . . on judgment day and **c** it,*
*John 8:10 . . . even one of them **c** you?*
*Rom 2:1 . . . think you can **c** such people,*
*Rom 2:1 . . . you are **c-ing** yourself,*
*Rom 3:7 . . . how can God **c** me as a sinner*
*Rom 3:8 . . . deserve to be **c-ed**.*
*Rom 8:34 . . . Who then will **c** us? No one—*
*Rom 14:3 . . . foods must not **c** those who*
*Rom 14:13 . . . So let's stop **c-ing** each other.*
*1 Cor 4:9 . . . a victor's parade, **c-ed** to die.*
*2 Cor 7:3 . . . saying this to **c** you.*
*Col 2:16 . . . So don't let anyone **c** you*
*Jas 5:6 . . . You have **c-ed** and killed*
*Jas 5:12 . . . not sin and be **c-ed**.*

CONDEMNATION (n)
conviction of guilt; censure or blame
*Rom 5:9 . . . save us from God's **c**.*
*Rom 5:18 . . . Adam's one sin brings **c***
*Rom 7:13 . . . bring about my **c** to death.*
*Rom 8:1 . . . there is no **c** for those who*
*2 Cor 3:9 . . . which brings **c**, was glorious,*

CONFESS, CONFESSED, CONFESSES, CONFESSING (v)
to admit or acknowledge (sin or faith)
*1 Sam 7:6 . . . **c-ed** that they had sinned*
*Ezra 10:11 . . . So now **c** your sin to*
*Ps 32:3 . . . I refused to **c** my sin,*
*Ps 32:5 . . . Finally, I **c-ed** all my sins*
*Ps 38:18 . . . But I **c** my sins;*
*Ps 66:18 . . . If I had not **c-ed** the sin in my*
*Dan 9:4 . . . to the LORD my God and **c-ed:***
*Dan 9:20 . . . praying and **c-ing** my sin*
*Matt 18:15 . . . **c-es** it, you have won*
*Mark 1:5 . . . And when they **c-ed** their sins,*
*Rom 10:10 . . . it is by **c-ing** with your mouth*
*Rom 14:11 . . . every tongue will **c** and give*
*Phil 2:11 . . . and every tongue **c** that Jesus*
*1 Tim 6:12 . . . which you have **c-ed** so well*
*Jas 5:16 . . . **C** your sins to each other*
*1 Jn 1:9 . . . But if we **c** our sins to Him,*

CONFIDENCE (n)
faith or belief that one will act in a right, proper, or effective way; a feeling or consciousness of one's powers; a quality or state of being certain
*Ps 146:3 . . . Don't put your **c** in powerful*
*Isa 30:15 . . . In quietness and **c** is your*
*2 Cor 8:22 . . . of His great **c** in you.*
*Phil 1:14 . . . believers here have gained **c***
*Phil 2:24 . . . And I have **c** from the Lord*
*Phil 3:4 . . . I could have **c** in my own*
*Col 2:2 . . . want them to have complete **c***
*1 Thes 5:8 . . . as our helmet the **c** of our*
*Titus 1:2 . . . This truth gives them **c***
*Heb 11:1 . . . Faith is the **c** that what we*
*2 Pet 1:19 . . . we have even greater **c***
*1 Jn 4:17 . . . but we can face Him with **c***

CONFIDENT (adj)
full of conviction, certain; trustful
*Ps 27:13 . . . Yet I am **c** I will see the*
*Ps 57:7 . . . My heart is **c** in You, O God;*
*2 Cor 3:4 . . . We are **c** of all this*
*Eph 1:18 . . . can understand the **c** hope*
*Col 1:5 . . . **c** hope of what God has reserved*
*Col 4:12 . . . fully **c** that you are following*
*2 Thes 3:4 . . . And we are **c** in the Lord*
*Heb 3:6 . . . keep our courage and remain **c***

CONFLICT (n)
fight, battle, war
*Prov 13:10 . . . Pride leads to **c**;*
*Prov 17:1 . . . filled with feasting—and **c**.*
*Gal 3:21 . . . Is there a **c**, then, between*

CONSCIENCE, CONSCIENCES (n)
one's moral sensitivity or scruples
*2 Sam 24:10 . . . census, David's **c** began to*
*Acts 24:16 . . . maintain a clear **c** before God*
*Rom 14:2 . . . with a sensitive **c** will eat*
*1 Cor 8:7 . . . their weak **c-s** are violated.*
*1 Cor 8:10 . . . to violate their **c** by eating*
*1 Cor 10:25 . . . raising questions of **c**.*
*1 Tim 1:5 . . . a clear **c**, and genuine faith.*
*1 Tim 1:19 . . . and keep your **c** clear.*
*Titus 1:15 . . . minds and **c-s** are corrupted.*
*Heb 9:9 . . . are not able to cleanse the **c-s***
*Heb 9:14 . . . will purify our **c-s** from sinful*
*Heb 10:22 . . . guilty **c-s** have been sprinkled*
*Heb 13:18 . . . for our **c** is clear*
*1 Pet 3:16 . . . Keep your **c** clear.*
*1 Pet 3:21 . . . to God from a clean **c**.*

CONSECRATE, CONSECRATED (v)
to devote irrevocably to God by a solemn ceremony; to make or declare sacred
see also DEDICATE, DEVOTE
*Exod 40:9 . . . all its furnishings to **c** them*
*Lev 19:24 . . . the entire crop must be **c-d***
*2 Chr 29:31 . . . you have **c-d** yourselves*

CONTENT, CONTENTED (adj)
feeling or showing satisfaction with one's possessions, status, or situation; pleased
*Josh 7:7 . . . If only we had been **c***
*1 Kgs 4:20 . . . They were very **c-ed**,*
*Prov 13:25 . . . godly eat to their hearts' **c**,*
*Luke 3:14 . . . And be **c** with your pay.*
*Phil 4:11 . . . I have learned how to be **c***
*1 Tim 6:8 . . . food and clothing, let us be **c**.*

CONTROL, CONTROLS (v)
to exercise restraining or directing influence over; to rule
*Job 37:15 . . . know how God **c-s** the storm*
*Rom 6:12 . . . Do not let sin **c***
*Rom 8:6 . . . letting the Spirit **c** your mind*
*Rom 8:8 . . . still under the **c** of*
*1 Cor 7:9 . . . they can't **c** themselves,*
*1 Cor 7:37 . . . and he can **c** his passion,*
*2 Cor 5:14 . . . Christ's love **c-s** us.*
*Jas 1:26 . . . but don't **c** your tongue,*
*Jas 3:2 . . . could also **c** ourselves*
*2 Pet 2:19 . . . a slave to whatever **c-s** you.*

CONVICT, CONVICTED (v)
to find or prove guilty of an offense
*Prov 24:25 . . . for those who **c** the guilty;*
*John 7:51 . . . Is it legal to **c** a man*
*John 16:8 . . . he will **c** the world of*
*1 Cor 14:24 . . . they will be **c-ed** of sin*
*Jude 15 . . . He will **c** every person*

CONVINCE, CONVINCED, CONVINCING (v)
to persuade to a belief, consent, or course of action
*Exod 4:31 . . . people of Israel were **c-d***
*Job 6:26 . . . your words are **c-ing***
*Acts 18:4 . . . to **c** the Jews and Greeks*
*Rom 2:19 . . . are **c-d** that you are a guide*
*Rom 8:38 . . . I am **c-d** that nothing*
*Rom 14:14 . . . I know and am **c-d***
*Rom 15:14 . . . I am fully **c-d**,*
*Phil 1:25 . . . I am **c-d** that I will*

CORNERSTONE (n)
a stone forming a corner or angle in a wall; foundation
*Ps 118:22 . . . now become the **c**.*
*Mark 12:10 . . . now become the **c**.*
*Acts 4:11 . . . now become the **c**.*
*Eph 2:20 . . . And the **c** is Christ*
*1 Pet 2:7 . . . now become the **c**.*

CORRECT, CORRECTED, CORRECTING, CORRECTS (v)
to set right with remedies, revisions, or reforms
*Job 5:17 . . . joy of those **c-ed** by God!*
*Ps 141:5 . . . If they **c** me,*
*Prov 3:12 . . . For the LORD **c-s** those*
*Prov 9:8 . . . don't bother **c-ing** mockers;*
*Prov 19:25 . . . if you **c** the wise,*
*Jer 5:3 . . . refused to be **c-ed**.*
*Jer 10:24 . . . Do not **c** me in anger,*
*2 Tim 3:16 . . . It **c-s** us when we*

*2 Tim 4:2 . . . Patiently **c**, rebuke,*
*Titus 2:15 . . . the authority to **c** them*
*Heb 12:5 . . . give up when He **c-s** you.*

CORRECTION (n)
a rebuke or punishment; the action of making right
*Prov 10:17 . . . those who ignore **c***
*Prov 12:1 . . . it is stupid to hate **c**.*
*Prov 15:5 . . . learns from **c** is wise.*
*Prov 15:10 . . . whoever hates **c** will die.*
*Prov 15:32 . . . if you listen to **c**,*
*Zeph 3:2 . . . it refuses all **c**.*

CORRUPT (adj)
morally degenerate and perverted; depraved
*Gen 6:11 . . . the earth had become **c***
*Ps 14:1 . . . They are **c**,*
*Ps 14:3 . . . all have become **c**.*
*Prov 19:28 . . . A **c** witness*
*Luke 9:41 . . . faithless and **c** people,*

CORRUPT, CORRUPTED, CORRUPTS (v)
to change from good to bad, physically or morally
*Eccl 7:7 . . . and bribes **c** the heart.*
*1 Cor 15:33 . . . bad company **c-s** good*
*Jas 1:27 . . . let the world **c** you.*
*Titus 1:15 . . . and consciences are **c-ed**.*

COUNSEL (n)
advice; policy, plan, or action
*Ps 37:30 . . . godly offer good **c**;*
*Ps 73:24 . . . guide me with Your **c**,*
*Ps 107:11 . . . scorning the **c** of the*
*Prov 27:9 . . . The heartfelt **c** of a friend*
*1 Cor 7:40 . . . I am giving you **c***

COUNSEL (v)
to advise
*Col 3:16 . . . Teach and **c** each other*

COUNSELOR (n)
one who gives advice or wisdom
see also ADVOCATE, HOLY SPIRIT
*Isa 9:6 . . . Wonderful **C**, Mighty God,*

COUNTENANCE (KJV)
*Gen 4:6 . . . Why do you **look** so dejected*
*Num 6:26 . . . May the LORD **show you His favor***
*1 Sam 16:7 . . . Don't judge by his **appearance***
*Prov 15:13 . . . A glad heart makes a happy **face***
*Luke 9:29 . . . **appearance of his face** was transformed*

COURAGE (n)
mental or moral strength
*Judg 5:21 . . . March on with **c**, my soul!*
*2 Chr 15:8 . . . he took **c***
*Dan 11:25 . . . stir up his **c** and raise a*
*Mark 6:50 . . . Take **c**! I am here!*
*Acts 27:22 . . . But take **c**!*
*Heb 3:6 . . . if we keep our **c***
*Jas 5:8 . . . Take **c**, for the coming*
*1 Jn 2:28 . . . be full of **c** and not shrink*

COURAGEOUS (adj)
having or characterized by courage; brave
*Deut 31:6 . . . So be strong and **c**!*
*Josh 1:6 . . . Be strong and **c**,*
*2 Sam 10:12 . . . Be **c**!*
*2 Chr 32:7 . . . Be strong and **c**!*
*Ps 31:24 . . . be strong and **c**,*
*1 Cor 16:13 . . . Be **c**.*

COURT, COURTS (n)
a place for the administration of justice; an open space enclosed by buildings
*Ps 82:1 . . . presides over heaven's **c**;*
*Ps 84:10 . . . single day in Your **c-s***
*Ps 96:8 . . . come into His **c-s**.*
*Ps 100:4 . . . go into His **c-s***
*Prov 22:22 . . . exploit the needy in **c**.*
*Prov 25:8 . . . to go to **c**.*
*Isa 3:13 . . . takes his place in **c***
*Amos 5:15 . . . **c-s** into true halls of justice.*
*Zech 8:16 . . . verdicts in Your **c-s***
*Matt 5:25 . . . are on the way to **c***

COVENANT, COVENANTS (n)
a mutual agreement or contract (between persons, between nations, or between God and humanity) with conditions and consequences spelled out
see also PROMISE, VOW
*Gen 9:9 . . . hereby confirm my **c***
*Gen 17:2 . . . I will make a **c** with you,*
*Exod 19:5 . . . and keep My **c**,*
*Deut 4:13 . . . He proclaimed His **c**—*
*Judg 2:1 . . . never break My **c***
*1 Kgs 8:21 . . . which contains the **c***
*2 Kgs 23:2 . . . Book of the **C***
*2 Chr 6:14 . . . You keep Your **c***
*Neh 1:5 . . . keeps His **c** of unfailing love*
*Ps 105:8 . . . stands by His **c**—*
*Prov 2:17 . . . and ignores the **c***
*Isa 61:8 . . . an everlasting **c** with them.*
*Jer 31:31 . . . make a new **c** with the people*
*Hos 10:4 . . . make **c-s** they don't intend*
*Mal 3:1 . . . messenger of the **c**,*
*Mark 14:24 . . . confirms the **c***
*Luke 22:20 . . . new **c** between God and His*
*Rom 9:4 . . . He made **c-s** with them*
*1 Cor 11:25 . . . new **c** between God and His*
*2 Cor 3:6 . . . under the new **c**,*
*Heb 8:6 . . . a far better **c** with God,*
*Heb 9:15 . . . mediates a new **c** between*
*Heb 12:24 . . . the new **c** between God and*

COVET, COVETED, COVETING (v)
to inordinately desire unjust gain or another's property
see also DESIRE
*Exod 20:17 . . . not **c** your neighbor's wife,*
*Exod 34:24 . . . so no one will **c***
*Deut 7:25 . . . must not **c** the silver or gold*
*Acts 20:33 . . . **c-ed** anyone's silver or gold*
*Rom 7:7 . . . have known that **c-ing** is wrong*
*Rom 13:9 . . . You must not **c**.*

CREATE, CREATED, CREATING (v)
to bring into being; to form, make, or produce
*Gen 1:1 . . . God **c-d** the heavens*
*Gen 1:27 . . . male and female He **c-d** them;*
*Gen 6:7 . . . human race I have **c-d** from*
*Ps 51:10 . . . **C** in me a clean heart*
*Ps 104:30 . . . life is **c-d**, and You renew*
*Prov 8:22 . . . before He **c-d** anything else.*
*Isa 43:1 . . . the LORD who **c-d** you.*
*Isa 43:7 . . . I who **c-d** them.*
*Isa 45:8 . . . I, the LORD, **c-d** them.*
*Isa 54:16 . . . I have **c-d** the blacksmith*
*Isa 65:17 . . . I am **c-ing** new heavens and*
*John 1:3 . . . **c-d** everything through Him,*
*Rom 1:20 . . . since the world was **c-d**,*
*Rom 1:25 . . . served the things God **c-d***
*Rom 9:20 . . . the thing that was **c-d** say*
*Eph 2:10 . . . He has **c-d** us anew*
*Eph 2:15 . . . by **c-ing** in Himself*
*Eph 4:24 . . . **c-d** to be like God—*
*Col 1:16 . . . Everything was **c-d** through Him*
*1 Tim 4:3 . . . But God **c-d** those foods*
*Heb 1:2 . . . through the Son he **c-d***
*1 Pet 4:19 . . . to the God who **c-d** you,*
*Rev 4:11 . . . For you **c-d** all things,*
*Rev 10:6 . . . who **c-d** the heavens*

CREATION (n)
something that is created; the world; the act of bringing the world into existence
*Gen 2:3 . . . from all His work of **c**.*
*Mark 10:6 . . . from the beginning of **c**.*
*Rom 8:19 . . . For all **c** is waiting*
*Rom 8:39 . . . nothing in all **c** will ever*
*Gal 6:15 . . . into a new **c**.*
*Col 1:17 . . . holds all **c** together.*
*Heb 12:27 . . . all of **c** will be shaken*
*Jas 1:18 . . . we, out of all **c**,*
*Rev 3:14 . . . of God's new **c**:*

CREATOR (n)
maker; one who creates
see also MAKER
*Gen 14:19 . . . God Most High, **C** of heaven*
*Job 40:19 . . . only its **C** can threaten*
*Eccl 12:1 . . . to forget your **C**.*
*Isa 40:28 . . . the **C** of all the earth.*
*Isa 45:9 . . . argue with their **C**.*
*Isa 51:13 . . . the LORD, your **C**,*
*Jer 51:19 . . . He is the **C** of everything*
*Rom 1:25 . . . instead of the **C** himself,*
*Eph 3:9 . . . the **C** of all things,*
*Eph 3:15 . . . the **C** of everything*

CRITICISM (n)
a critical observation or remark; critique
*Prov 15:31 . . . listen to constructive **c**,*
*Prov 25:12 . . . valid **c** is like a gold*
*Prov 28:23 . . . people appreciate honest **c***
*Prov 29:1 . . . refuses to accept **c***
*2 Cor 8:20 . . . guard against any **c***

CRITICIZE, CRITICIZED, CRITICIZING(v)
to find fault with; to point out the faults of
*Job 34:29 . . . who can **c** Him?*
*Eccl 7:5 . . . be **c-d** by a wise person*
*Rom 14:16 . . . not be **c-d** for doing*
*Phil 2:15 . . . no one can **c** You.*
*Titus 2:8 . . . teaching can't be **c-d**.*
*Jas 4:11 . . . **c-ing** and judging God's law.*

CROSS (n)
an upright post used as an instrument of death in ancient times; the means by which atonement was made between God and humanity
*Mark 8:34 . . . take up your **c**,*
*Luke 9:23 . . . take up your **c** daily,*
*Acts 2:23 . . . you nailed Him to a **c***
*Acts 5:30 . . . hanging Him on a **c**.*
*1 Cor 1:18 . . . message of the **c** is*
*Gal 3:1 . . . death on the **c**.*
*Gal 6:12 . . . that the **c** of Christ alone*
*Phil 2:8 . . . criminal's death on a **c**.*
*Col 1:20 . . . Christ's blood on the **c**.*
*Heb 12:2 . . . He endured the **c**,*
*1 Pet 2:24 . . . His body on the **c***

CROWN, CROWNS (n)
top of the head; a cap or headdress worn by victors, priests, or royalty
*Prov 16:31 . . . Gray hair is a **c** of glory;*
*Song 3:11 . . . He wears the **c** his mother*
*Isa 61:3 . . . will give a **c** of beauty*
*Isa 62:3 . . . a splendid **c** in the hand*
*Zech 9:16 . . . like jewels in a **c**.*
*Matt 27:29 . . . thorn branches into a **c***
*Mark 15:17 . . . thorn branches into a **c***
*John 19:2 . . . wove a **c** of thorns*
*John 19:5 . . . wearing the **c** of thorns*
*Phil 4:1 . . . and the **c** I receive*
*1 Thes 2:19 . . . our proud reward and **c***
*Jas 1:12 . . . will receive the **c** of life*
*Rev 2:10 . . . will give you the **c** of life.*
*Rev 3:11 . . . take away your **c**.*
*Rev 4:4 . . . had gold **c-s** on their heads.*
*Rev 4:10 . . . lay their **c-s** before the throne*

*Rev 12:3 . . . with seven **c-s** on His heads.*
*Rev 14:14 . . . He had a gold **c** on His head*
*Rev 19:12 . . . on His head were many **c-s.***

CROWN, CROWNED, CROWNING, CROWNS (v)
to place a crown on the head of; to bless or adorn
*Ps 8:5 . . . and **c-ed** them with*
*Ps 149:4 . . . he **c-s** the humble*
*Prov 14:18 . . . are **c-ed** with knowledge.*
*Isa 51:11 . . . **c-ed** with everlasting joy.*
*Heb 2:7 . . . and **c-ed** them with*
*Heb 2:9 . . . **c-ed** with glory and honor.*

CRUCIFIXION (n)
the execution or death of a person on a cross
*Matt 23:34 . . . you will kill some by **c,***
*John 19:41 . . . The place of **c** was near*

CRUCIFY, CRUCIFIED (v)
to execute or nail to the cross; to put to death
*Matt 26:2 . . . handed over to be **c-ied.***
*Matt 27:22 . . . **C** Him!*
*Matt 27:44 . . . who were **c-ied** with Him*
*Mark 15:13 . . . **C** Him!*
*Mark 15:27 . . . revolutionaries were **c-ied***
*Mark 15:32 . . . who were **c-ied** with Jesus*
*Mark 16:6 . . . who was **c-ied.***
*Luke 23:21 . . . **C** Him! **C** Him!*
*Luke 23:23 . . . that Jesus be **c-ied,***
*Luke 23:33 . . . criminals were also **c-ied**—*
*Luke 24:20 . . . and they **c-ied** Him.*
*John 19:6 . . . **C** Him! **C** Him!*
*John 19:10 . . . to release You or **c** You?*
*John 19:20 . . . place where Jesus was **c-ied***
*John 19:32 . . . the two men **c-ied** with Jesus.*
*Acts 4:10 . . . the man You **c-ied***
*Rom 6:6 . . . were **c-ied** with Christ*
*1 Cor 1:13 . . . Was I, Paul, **c-ied** for you?*
*1 Cor 1:23 . . . preach that Christ was **c-ied,***
*1 Cor 2:8 . . . would not have **c-ied***
*2 Cor 13:4 . . . He was **c-ied** in weakness,*
*Gal 5:24 . . . and **c-ied** them there.*
*Rev 11:8 . . . where their Lord was **c-ied.***

CRY, CRIES (n)
entreaty, appeal; an inarticulate utterance of distress, rage, or pain
*Exod 2:23 . . . their **c** rose up to God.*
*Ps 5:2 . . . Listen to my **c** for help,*
*Ps 34:15 . . . open to their **c-ies** for help.*
*Ps 40:1 . . . and heard my **c.***
*Ps 142:6 . . . Hear my **c**, for I am*
*Prov 21:13 . . . to the **c-ies** of the poor*

CRY, CRIED (v)
to shout; to beg or beseech; to shed tears often noisily
*Exod 14:10 . . . They **c-ied** out to the LORD,*
*Josh 24:7 . . . When your ancestors **c-ied** out*
*Judg 3:9 . . . people of Israel **c-ied** out*
*Judg 4:3 . . . people of Israel **c-ied** out*
*Judg 6:6 . . . Then the Israelites **c-ied** out*
*Judg 10:12 . . . you **c-ied** out to Me*
*Ps 18:6 . . . in my distress I **c-ied** out*
*Eccl 3:4 . . . A time to **c** and a time*
*Lam 2:18 . . . **C** aloud before the LORD,*
*Hab 2:11 . . . walls **c** out against you,*

CURE (n)
recovery or relief from a disease; a complete or permanent solution
*Jer 30:15 . . . wound that has no **c?***
*Luke 8:43 . . . she could find no **c.***

CURE, CURED (v)
to restore to health, soundness, or normality
*Isa 30:26 . . . and **c** the wounds*
*Matt 11:5 . . . the lepers are **c-d,***
*John 5:10 . . . said to the man who was **c-d,***

CURSE (n)
a condemnation or judgment
*Num 5:23 . . . priest will write these **c-s***
*Josh 8:34 . . . blessings and **c-s** Moses had*
*Rom 8:20 . . . was subjected to God's **c.***
*Gal 3:10 . . . right with God are under His **c,***
*Gal 3:13 . . . the **c** for our wrongdoing.*
*Rev 22:3 . . . No longer will there be a **c***

CURSE, CURSES, CURSING (v)
to pronounce a sentence; to afflict; to call upon a supernatural power to bring injury upon; to utter profane language against
*Gen 8:21 . . . will never again **c** the ground*
*Gen 12:3 . . . **c** those who treat you*
*Prov 3:33 . . . **c-s** the house of the wicked,*
*Matt 5:22 . . . And if you **c** someone,*
*Rom 3:14 . . . full of **c-ing** and bitterness.*
*Rom 12:14 . . . Don't **c** them;*
*1 Cor 12:3 . . . will **c** Jesus, and no one*
*Jas 3:9 . . . and sometimes it **c-s** those who*
*Jas 3:10 . . . and **c-ing** come pouring out*

CURSED (adj)
being under or deserving a curse
*Gen 3:17 . . . the ground is **c** because*
*Deut 21:23 . . . anyone who is hung is **c***
*Deut 27:16 . . . **C** is anyone who dishonors*
*Deut 27:18 . . . **C** is anyone who leads*
*Deut 27:20 . . . **C** is anyone who has sexual*
*Deut 27:24 . . . **C** is anyone who attacks a*
*Deut 27:26 . . . **C** is anyone who does not*
*Prov 28:27 . . . poverty will be **c.***
*Gal 3:10 . . . **C** is everyone who does not*
*Gal 3:13 . . . **C** is everyone who is hung*

D

DANGER (n)
harm or damage
*Ps 57:1 . . . until the **d** passes by.*
*Prov 22:3 . . . prudent person foresees **d***
*Matt 5:22 . . . in **d** of being brought*
*Rom 8:35 . . . or in **d**, or threatened*
*2 Cor 1:10 . . . did rescue us from mortal **d,***
*2 Cor 11:26 . . . I have faced **d** from rivers*

DARK, DARKEST (adj)
devoid or partially devoid of light; wholly or partially black
*Exod 20:21 . . . approached the **d** cloud*
*Ps 23:4 . . . walk through the **d-est** valley,*
*Song 1:6 . . . because I am **d**—*
*Song 5:10 . . . My lover is **d** and dazzling,*
*Joel 2:31 . . . The sun will become **d,***
*Acts 2:20 . . . The sun will become **d,***
*2 Pet 1:19 . . . lamp shining in a **d** place—*

DAUGHTER, DAUGHTERS (n)
the female offspring or adopted offspring of parents
*Gen 19:36 . . . Lot's **d-s** became pregnant*
*Num 36:10 . . . The **d-s** of Zelophehad*
*Judg 11:40 . . . the fate of Jephthah's **d.***
*Esth 2:7 . . . raised her as his own **d.***
*Joel 2:28 . . . sons and **d-s** will prophesy.*
*Mark 5:34 . . . said to her, "**D**, your faith*
*Mark 7:29 . . . the demon has left your **d.***

DAY, DAYS (n)
the time of light between one night and the next; a specified time or period; a 24-hour time period
*Gen 1:5 . . . called the light "**d**" and the*
*Gen 2:2 . . . On the seventh **d** God had*
*Exod 16:30 . . . the seventh **d.***
*Lev 23:28 . . . it is the **D** of Atonement,*
*Josh 1:8 . . . Meditate on it **d** and night so*
*2 Kgs 7:9 . . . This is a **d** of good news,*
*Ps 23:6 . . . pursue me all the **d-s** of my life,*
*Ps 84:10 . . . A single **d** in Your*
*Ps 118:24 . . . This is the **d** the LORD has*
*Isa 13:9 . . . coming—the terrible **d** of his*
*Jer 46:10 . . . this is the **d** of the LORD,*
*Jer 50:31 . . . Your **d** of reckoning*
*Hos 3:5 . . . In the last **d-s**, they will*
*Joel 1:15 . . . How terrible that **d** will be!*
*Joel 2:31 . . . great and terrible **d** of the*
*Amos 5:20 . . . Yes, the **d** of the LORD*
*Zeph 1:14 . . . That terrible **d** of the*
*Zech 14:1 . . . Watch, for the **d** of the LORD*
*Zech 14:7 . . . be continuous **d!***
*Mal 4:5 . . . great and dreadful **d** of the*
*Matt 24:38 . . . In those **d-s** before the*
*Luke 11:3 . . . Give us each **d** the food we*
*Acts 2:17 . . . 'In the last **d-s**,' God says,*
*Rom 14:5 . . . some think one **d** is more holy*
*1 Cor 5:5 . . . be saved on the **d** the Lord*
*2 Cor 4:16 . . . renewed every **d.***
*1 Thes 5:2 . . . the **d** of the Lord's return*
*1 Thes 5:4 . . . surprised when the **d** of the*
*2 Thes 2:2 . . . say that the **d** of the Lord*
*2 Tim 3:1 . . . in the last **d-s** there will be*
*Heb 1:2 . . . now in these final **d-s**, He has*
*2 Pet 3:3 . . . in the last **d-s** scoffers will*
*2 Pet 3:10 . . . But the **d** of the Lord*
*Rev 16:14 . . . that great judgment **d** of God*

DEAD (n)
the state of being dead (physically or spiritually); (un)believers who have died
*Matt 8:22 . . . the spiritually **d** bury their*
*Luke 24:46 . . . rise from the **d** on the third*
*1 Cor 15:29 . . . If the **d** will not*
*Rev 20:12 . . . I saw the **d**, both great and*

DEAD (adj)
without (physical or spiritual) life; fatal; useless; unresponsive
*Rom 6:11 . . . be **d** to the power of sin*
*Eph 2:1 . . . Once you were **d** because of*
*Jas 2:17 . . . good deeds, it is **d** and useless.*
*1 Pet 2:24 . . . that we can be **d** to sin and*
*Rev 2:8 . . . Last, who was **d** but is now*

DEATH (n)
the cessation of (physical or spiritual) life; personification and consequence of evil
*Exod 21:12 . . . must be put to **d.***
*Ruth 1:17 . . . anything but **d** to separate*
*Prov 11:19 . . . evil people find **d.***
*Prov 14:12 . . . it ends in **d.***
*Prov 23:14 . . . save them from **d.***
*Isa 38:17 . . . have rescued me from **d***
*Acts 2:24 . . . for **d** could not keep him*
*Rom 5:12 . . . brought **d**, so **d** spread to*
*Rom 6:23 . . . the wages of sin is **d,***
*Rom 7:24 . . . dominated by sin and **d?***
*1 Cor 15:21 . . . see, just as **d** came into the*
*1 Cor 15:26 . . . enemy to be destroyed is **d.***
*2 Cor 3:6 . . . written covenant ends in **d;***
*Gal 3:1 . . . the meaning of Jesus Christ's **d***
*2 Tim 1:10 . . . power of **d** and illuminated*
*Heb 2:14 . . . the power of **d.***
*Heb 9:17 . . . after the person's **d.***
*1 Jn 5:16 . . . there is a sin that leads to **d,***
*Rev 2:11 . . . by the second **d.***
*Rev 20:6 . . . them the second **d** holds no*
*Rev 20:14 . . . is the second **d.***
*Rev 21:4 . . . be no more **d** or sorrow or*
*Rev 21:8 . . . This is the second **d.***

DEBAUCHERY (KJV)
*Rom 13:13 . . . promiscuity and **immoral living***
*2 Cor 12:21 . . . **eagerness for lustful pleasure***
*Gal 5:19 . . . impurity, **lustful pleasures***
*1 Pet 4:3 . . . their **immorality** and lust, their*

DEBT, DEBTS (n)
what is owing; sense of obligation
*Deut 15:1 . . . cancel the **d-s** of everyone*
*Deut 15:3 . . . This release from **d**, however,*
*Deut 15:9 . . . year for canceling **d-s** is close*
*1 Sam 22:2 . . . trouble or in **d** or who were*
*2 Kgs 4:7 . . . pay your **d-s**, and*
*Prov 22:26 . . . another person's **d** or put up*
*Neh 10:31 . . . will cancel all **d-s** owed to us.*
*Matt 18:25 . . . to pay the **d**.*
*Matt 18:27 . . . and forgave his **d**.*
*Matt 18:30 . . . in prison until the **d** could*
*Matt 18:32 . . . you that tremendous **d***
*Luke 7:42 . . . canceling their **d-s**.*
*Luke 7:43 . . . canceled the larger **d**.*

DECEIT (n)
fraud; trickery; lying
*Mark 7:22 . . . greed, wickedness, **d**, lustful*
*Acts 13:10 . . . of every sort of **d** and fraud,*
*1 Pet 2:1 . . . done with all **d**, hypocrisy,*

DECEITFUL (adj)
not honest; misleading, deceptive
*Isa 59:13 . . . planning our **d** lies.*
*2 Cor 11:13 . . . They are **d** workers who*

DECEIVE, DECEIVED, DECEIVES, DECEIVING (v)
to lead astray; to cause to accept as true what is false
*Gen 3:13 . . . "The serpent **d-d** me," she*
*Proverbs 10:31 . . . the tongue that **d-s** will be*
*Prov 14:8 . . . but fools **d** themselves.*
*Prov 26:24 . . . but they're **d-ing** you.*
*Matt 24:24 . . . so as to **d**, if possible, even*
*Mark 13:6 . . . They will **d** many.*
*Rom 7:11 . . . those commands and **d-d** me;*
*Rom 16:18 . . . they **d** innocent people.*
*Col 2:4 . . . so no one will **d** you with*
*1 Cor 3:18 . . . Stop **d-ing** yourselves.*
*2 Cor 11:3 . . . as Eve was **d-d** by the cunning*
*1 Tim 2:14 . . . The woman was **d-d**, and sin*
*2 Tim 3:13 . . . They will **d** others and will*
*2 Tim 3:13 . . . will themselves be **d-d**.*
*Heb 3:13 . . . you will be **d-d** by sin*
*Rev 20:3 . . . Satan could not **d** the nations*
*Rev 20:10 . . . devil, who had **d-d** them, was*

DECEPTION (n)
something that deceives; trick; the act of deceiving
*Isa 28:15 . . . refuge made of lies and **d**.*
*Dan 8:25 . . . He will be a master of **d***
*Rom 1:29 . . . quarreling, **d**, malicious*
*Eph 4:22 . . . corrupted by lust and **d**.*
*2 Thes 2:10 . . . kind of evil **d** to fool those*
*1 Jn 4:6 . . . truth or spirit of **d**.*

DECIDE, DECIDED, DECIDES (v)
to make a final choice or judgment about; to select as a course of action
*1 Sam 14:7 . . . whatever you **d**.*
*Job 14:5 . . . You have **d-d** the length of*
*Ps 75:7 . . . he **d-s** who will rise and*
*Rom 14:13 . . . **D** instead to live*
*Rom 14:22 . . . they have **d-d** is right.*
*1 Cor 2:2 . . . For I **d-d** that while I*
*1 Cor 6:2 . . . can't you **d** even these*
*1 Cor 12:11 . . . He alone **d-s** which gift*
*2 Cor 9:7 . . . You must each **d** in your heart*

DECISION, DECISIONS (n)
a determination arrived at after consideration; conclusion
*Joel 3:14 . . . waiting in the valley of **d**.*
*Mic 3:11 . . . You rulers make **d-s** based on*
*Rom 11:33 . . . to understand His **d-s** and His*

DEDICATE, DEDICATED (v)
to devote to the worship of a divine being; to set apart to a definite use
see also CONSECRATE, DEVOTE
*Exod 13:2 . . . **D** to Me every firstborn*
*Num 6:9 . . . the hair they have **d-d** will be*
*Num 6:18 . . . the hair that had been **d-d***
*Num 18:6 . . . a gift to you, **d-d** to the LORD*
*1 Kgs 8:63 . . . Israel **d-d** the Temple*
*Neh 3:1 . . . which they **d-d**, and the Tower*
*Luke 2:23 . . . he must be **d-d** to the LORD.*

DEED, DEEDS (n)
a signed instrument containing some legal transfer, bargain, or contract; a usually illustrious act or action; feat, exploit
*Ps 45:4 . . . perform awe-inspiring **d-s**!*
*Ps 66:3 . . . awesome are Your **d-s**!*
*Ps 71:24 . . . Your righteous **d-s** all day*
*Ps 88:12 . . . Your wonderful **d-s**?*
*Ps 96:3 . . . His glorious **d-s** among the*
*Ps 105:2 . . . His wonderful **d-s**.*
*Prov 31:31 . . . Let her **d-s** publicly declare*
*Isa 64:6 . . . our righteous **d-s**, they are*
*Jer 32:10 . . . and sealed the **d** of purchase*
*Matt 5:16 . . . let your good **d-s** shine out for*
*Rom 4:2 . . . If his good **d-s** had made him*
*2 Cor 9:9 . . . Their good **d-s** will be*
*Col 3:9 . . . all its wicked **d-s**.*
*Jas 2:18 . . . my faith by my good **d-s**.*
*Jas 2:20 . . . without good **d-s** is useless?*

DEFEND, DEFENDING, DEFENDS (v)
to maintain or support in the face of argument or hostile criticism; to drive danger or attack away from
*Deut 33:7 . . . strength to **d** their cause;*
*Ps 10:14 . . . You **d** the orphans.*
*Ps 34:7 . . . He surrounds and **d-s** all who*
*Ps 72:4 . . . Help Him to **d** the poor,*
*Ps 106:8 . . . saved them—to **d** the honor of*
*Phil 1:7 . . . and in **d-ing** and confirming the*
*Phil 1:16 . . . been appointed to **d** the Good*
*Jude 3 . . . urging you to **d** the faith*

DEFENDER (n)
one that guards and protects
*Ps 68:5 . . . the fatherless, **d** of widows—*
*Prov 22:23 . . . the LORD is their **d**.*
*Isa 51:22 . . . your God and **D**, says:*

DELIGHT, DELIGHTS (n)
source of great pleasure; joy
*Ps 36:8 . . . your river of **d-s**.*
*Ps 40:6 . . . You take no **d** in sacrifices*
*Ps 119:111 . . . they are My heart's **d**.*
*Prov 8:30 . . . I was His constant **d**,*
*Isa 58:13 . . . and speak of it with **d***
*Jer 15:16 . . . My joy and My heart's **d**,*
*Mal 3:12 . . . Your land will be such a **d**,*
*Mark 12:37 . . . to Him with great **d**.*

DELIGHT, DELIGHTED, DELIGHTING, DELIGHTS (v)
to enjoy
*Exod 4:14 . . . He will be **d-ed** to see you.*
*2 Sam 22:20 . . . because He **d-s** in me.*
*Ps 1:2 . . . But they **d** in the law of*
*Ps 18:19 . . . He rescued me because He **d-s***
*Ps 27:4 . . . **d-ing** in the LORD's*
*Ps 37:4 . . . Take **d** in the LORD,*
*Ps 119:70 . . . I **d** in Your instructions.*
*Prov 3:12 . . . a child in whom He **d-s**.*
*Prov 11:1 . . . He **d-s** in accurate weights.*
*Prov 11:20 . . . He **d-s** in those with integrity.*
*Song 8:10 . . . He is **d-ed** with what He sees.*
*Isa 11:3 . . . He will **d** in obeying*
*Isa 65:19 . . . and **d** in My people.*
*Isa 66:3 . . . **d-ing** in their detestable sins—*
*Jer 9:24 . . . I **d** in these things.*

DEMON-POSSESSED (adj)
characterized by the possession or control of demons
*Matt 4:24 . . . if they were **d** or epileptic*
*Matt 8:16 . . . That evening many **d** people*
*Matt 8:33 . . . happened to the **d** men.*
*Matt 9:32 . . . When they left, a **d** man who*
*Matt 12:22 . . . Then a **d** man, who was*
*Mark 1:32 . . . many sick and **d** people were*
*Mark 5:16 . . . about the **d** man and*
*Luke 8:36 . . . others how the **d** man had*

DENY, DENIED, DENIES (v)
to disavow or refuse to accept as true; to refuse to grant
*Exod 23:6 . . . you must not **d** justice to the*
*Deut 27:19 . . . is anyone who **d-ies** justice*
*Prov 30:9 . . . I may **d** you and say,*
*Matt 10:33 . . . everyone who **d-ies** Me*
*Matt 26:35 . . . I will never **d** You!*
*Matt 26:70 . . . But Peter **d-ied** it*
*Luke 12:9 . . . anyone who **d-ies** Me*
*Luke 22:34 . . . You will **d** three times*
*John 18:25 . . . He **d-ied** it, saying,*
*Acts 4:16 . . . We can't **d** that they*
*1 Tim 5:8 . . . have **d-ied** the true faith.*
*2 Tim 2:12 . . . **d** him, he will **d** us.*
*Titus 1:16 . . . **d** him by the way they live.*
*2 Pet 2:1 . . . and even **d** the Master who*
*1 Jn 2:22 . . . Anyone who **d-ies** the Father and*
*1 Jn 2:23 . . . Anyone who **d-ies** the Son*
*Jude 4 . . . they have **d-ied** our only Master*
*Rev 3:8 . . . and did not **d** Me.*

DESERT, DESERTS (n)
arid land with usually sparse vegetation
see also WILDERNESS
*Prov 21:19 . . . better to live alone in the **d***
*Isa 32:2 . . . like streams of water in the **d***
*Isa 43:20 . . . giving them water in the **d**.*
*2 Cor 11:26 . . . cities, in the **d-s**, and on the*

DESERVE, DESERVED, DESERVES (v)
to be worthy, fit, or suitable for some reward or requital; to merit
*Judg 9:16 . . . the honor he **d-s** for all He*
*2 Sam 12:5 . . . do such a thing **d-s** to die!*
*Neh 9:33 . . . gave us only what we **d-d**.*
*Ps 103:10 . . . with us, as we **d**.*
*Prov 14:14 . . . Backsliders get what they **d**;*
*Dan 9:18 . . . not because we **d** help,*
*Zech 1:6 . . . received what we **d-d** from the*
*Luke 7:4 . . . If anyone **d-s** your help,*
*Acts 26:31 . . . done anything to **d** death or*
*Rom 3:8 . . . who say such things **d** to be*
*Rom 11:9 . . . get what they **d**.*
*2 Cor 11:15 . . . their wicked deeds **d**.*
*1 Tim 5:18 . . . Those who work **d** their pay!*
*Heb 3:3 . . . But Jesus **d-s** far more*

DESIRE, DESIRES (n)
conscious impulse toward something that promises enjoyment or satisfaction in its attainment; longing, craving
*Job 17:11 . . . My heart's **d-s** are broken.*
*Ps 10:3 . . . brag about their evil **d-s**;*
*Ps 37:4 . . . give you your heart's **d-s**.*
*Ps 145:19 . . . He grants the **d-s** of those who*
*Mark 4:19 . . . wealth, and the **d** for other*
*Rom 1:26 . . . to their shameful **d-s**.*
*Rom 6:12 . . . not give in to sinful **d-s**.*
*Rom 7:5 . . . sinful **d-s** were at work*
*Rom 13:14 . . . indulge your evil **d-s**.*
*Gal 5:24 . . . the passions and **d-s** of their*
*Phil 2:13 . . . you the **d** and the power*
*Col 2:23 . . . a person's evil **d-s**.*
*Col 3:5 . . . lust, and evil **d-s**.*
*1 Tim 6:9 . . . and harmful **d-s** that plunge*
*2 Tim 4:3 . . . follow their own **d-s** and will*

*Jas 1:14 . . . from our own **d-s**, which entice*
*Jas 4:1 . . . from the evil **d-s** at war within*
*1 Pet 2:11 . . . from worldly **d-s** that wage*
*1 Pet 4:2 . . . chasing your own **d-s**,*
*2 Pet 2:10 . . . their own twisted sexual **d**,*
*2 Pet 2:18 . . . twisted sexual **d-s**, they lure*
*2 Pet 3:3 . . . following their own **d-s**.*
*Jude 18 . . . their ungodly **d-s**.*

DESPAIR (n)
utter loss of hope
*Ps 40:2 . . . out of the pit of **d**,*
*Ps 79:8 . . . on the brink of **d**.*
*Ps 130:1 . . . the depths of **d**, O LORD,*
*Isa 61:3 . . . praise instead of **d**.*
*2 Cor 4:8 . . . but not driven to **d**.*

DESPISE, DESPISED, DESPISES (n)
to scorn or regard as unworthy, sometimes with malice or outrage
*2 Sam 12:9 . . . you **d-d** the word of the LORD*
*Job 5:17 . . . Do not **d** the discipline*
*Job 9:21 . . . to me—I **d** my life.*
*Ps 22:6 . . . I am scorned and **d-d** by all!*
*Prov 1:7 . . . but fools **d** wisdom and*
*Prov 12:8 . . . a warped mind is **d-d**.*
*Prov 15:5 . . . Only a fool **d-s** a parent's*
*Prov 15:20 . . . foolish children **d** their*
*Prov 29:27 . . . The righteous **d** the unjust;*
*Prov 30:17 . . . and **d-s** a mother's*
*Isa 53:3 . . . He was **d-d**, and we did not*
*Mic 7:6 . . . For the son **d-s** his father.*
*Luke 16:13 . . . to one and **d** the other.*
*Gal 4:14 . . . you did not **d** me or*
*2 Pet 2:10 . . . and who **d** authority.*

DESTROY, DESTROYED, DESTROYING, DESTROYS (v)
to kill; to cause devastation or ruin
see also PERISH
*Gen 6:17 . . . that will **d** every living*
*Gen 9:11 . . . will a flood **d** the earth.*
*Num 32:15 . . . responsible for **d-ing** this*
*Deut 28:63 . . . find pleasure in **d-ing** you.*
*Josh 10:40 . . . He completely **d-ed** everyone*
*Prov 6:32 . . . fool, for he **d-s** himself.*
*Prov 10:21 . . . fools are **d-ed** by their lack*
*Prov 10:29 . . . but it **d-s** the wicked.*
*Prov 11:3 . . . dishonesty **d-s** treacherous*
*Prov 11:9 . . . the godless **d** their friends,*
*Prov 18:9 . . . as someone who **d-s** things.*
*Prov 18:24 . . . "friends" who **d** each other,*
*Prov 29:1 . . . will suddenly be **d-ed** beyond*
*Isa 11:4 . . . His mouth will **d** the wicked.*
*Dan 2:44 . . . will never be **d-ed** or conquered.*
*Jon 3:9 . . . fierce anger from **d-ing** us.*
*Jon 4:2 . . . turn back from **d-ing** people.*
*Matt 10:28 . . . God, who can **d** both soul*
*Luke 9:25 . . . but are yourself lost or **d-ed**?*
*John 10:10 . . . and kill and **d**.*
*Rom 2:12 . . . they will be **d-ed**, even though*
*1 Cor 3:17 . . . anyone who **d-s** this temple.*
*1 Cor 5:5 . . . nature will be **d-ed** and He*
*1 Cor 8:11 . . . died will be **d-ed**.*
*1 Cor 15:24 . . . **d-ed** every ruler and authority*
*1 Cor 15:26 . . . enemy to be **d-ed** is death.*
*2 Cor 4:9 . . . are not **d-ed**.*
*Gal 5:15 . . . Beware of **d-ing** one another.*
*Heb 7:16 . . . that cannot be **d-ed**.*
*2 Pet 2:12 . . . be caught and **d-ed**.*
*2 Pet 3:7 . . . people will be **d-ed**.*
*Jude 5 . . . but later He **d-ed** those who did*
*Rev 11:18 . . . It is time to **d** all who have*

DETERMINE, DETERMINED, DETERMINES (v)
to decide; to resolve
*Exod 28:30 . . . objects used to **d** the LORD's*
*Ezra 7:10 . . . because Ezra had **d-d** to study*
*Ps 17:3 . . . I am **d-d** not to sin in*
*Ps 119:30 . . . I have **d-d** to live by*
*Ps 119:112 . . . I am **d-d** to keep Your*
*Prov 4:23 . . . it **d-s** the course of your life.*
*Prov 16:9 . . . but the LORD **d-s** our steps.*
*Dan 1:8 . . . But Daniel was **d-d** not to*
*Dan 11:36 . . . what has been **d-d** will surely*
*Matt 12:34 . . . heart **d-s** what you say.*
*Luke 22:22 . . . it has been **d-d** that the Son of*
*Acts 4:28 . . . was **d-d** beforehand according*

DETEST, DETESTS (v)
to loathe; to denounce
*Prov 8:7 . . . the truth and **d** every kind of*
*Prov 12:22 . . . The LORD **d-s** lying lips,*
*Prov 15:8 . . . The LORD **d-s** the sacrifice*
*Prov 15:26 . . . The LORD **d-s** evil plans,*
*Prov 16:5 . . . The LORD **d-s** the proud;*
*Prov 17:15 . . . both are **d** to the LORD.*
*Prov 20:10 . . . the LORD **d-s** double*
*Prov 24:9 . . . everyone **d-s** a mocker.*

DETESTABLE, DETESTABLES (adj)
arousing or meriting intense dislike; abominable
*Lev 11:10 . . . They are **d** to You.*
*Prov 3:32 . . . wicked people are **d** to the*
*Prov 21:27 . . . an evil person is **d**,*
*Luke 16:15 . . . What this world honors is **d***

DEVOTE, DEVOTED (v)
to commit by a solemn act
see also CONSECRATE, DEDICATE
*2 Chr 31:4 . . . could **d** themselves fully*
*Acts 2:42 . . . the believers **d-d** themselves to*
*Col 4:2 . . . **D** yourselves to*

DEVOTED (adj)
characterized by loyalty and devotion
*1 Kgs 18:3 . . . (Obadiah was a **d** follower of*
*Ps 86:2 . . . for I am **d** to You.*
*Matt 6:24 . . . you will be **d** to one and*
*1 Tim 2:10 . . . claim to be **d** to God should*

DIE, DIED, DIES (v)
to pass from physical life; to cease from existence
see also PERISH
*Gen 2:17 . . . you are sure to **d**.*
*Gen 3:3 . . . if you do, you will **d**.*
*Esth 4:16 . . . If I must **d**, I must **d**.*
*Job 2:9 . . . Curse God and **d**.*
*Prov 5:23 . . . He will **d** for lack of*
*Prov 11:7 . . . When the wicked **d**, their*
*Prov 11:10 . . . when the wicked **d**.*
*Prov 23:13 . . . They won't **d** if you*
*Eccl 7:2 . . . After all, everyone **d-s**—so the*
*Isa 22:13 . . . drink, for tomorrow we **d**!*
*Isa 66:24 . . . that devour them will never **d**,*
*Jer 31:30 . . . All people will **d** for their*
*Matt 26:52 . . . will **d** by the sword.*
*Mark 9:48 . . . the maggots never **d** and the*
*Luke 16:22 . . . The rich man also **d-d** and*
*John 13:37 . . . I'm ready to **d** for You.*
*Rom 4:25 . . . handed over to **d** because of*
*Rom 5:6 . . . the right time and **d-d** for us*
*Rom 5:7 . . . be willing to **d** for a person*
*Rom 5:8 . . . by sending Christ to **d** for us*
*Rom 5:14 . . . Still, everyone **d-d**—from the*
*Rom 6:7 . . . For when we **d-d** with Christ we*
*Rom 6:10 . . . When He **d-d**, He **d** once*
*Rom 7:2 . . . But if He **d-s**, the laws of*
*Rom 7:6 . . . the law, for we **d-d** to it and*
*Rom 14:8 . . . whether we live or **d**, we*
*1 Cor 7:39 . . . If her husband **d-s**, she is free*
*1 Cor 9:15 . . . I would rather **d** than lose*
*1 Cor 15:6 . . . though some have **d-d**.*
*1 Cor 15:18 . . . all who have **d-d** believing in*
*1 Cor 15:22 . . . Just as everyone **d-s** because*
*1 Cor 15:32 . . . for tomorrow we **d**!*
*1 Cor 15:36 . . . plant unless it **d-s** first.*
*1 Cor 15:42 . . . in the ground when we **d**,*
*1 Cor 15:51 . . . will not all **d**, but we will*
*2 Cor 5:15 . . . for Christ, who **d-d** and was*
*Col 2:20 . . . You have **d-d** with Christ,*
*1 Thes 4:16 . . . who have **d-d** will rise from*
*1 Thes 5:10 . . . Christ **d-d** for us so*
*1 Tim 6:16 . . . He alone can never **d**,*
*2 Tim 2:11 . . . saying: If we **d** with Him,*
*Heb 9:27 . . . is destined to **d** once and*
*1 Pet 3:18 . . . sinned, but He **d-d** for sinners*

DILIGENT (adj)
characterized by steady, earnest, and energetic effort; painstaking
*Ezra 4:22 . . . Be **d**, and don't*
*Prov 12:27 . . . but the **d** make use of*

DISCERNMENT (n)
the quality of being able to grasp and comprehend what is obscure
*Ps 119:125 . . . Give **d** to me,*
*Prov 1:4 . . . knowledge and **d** to the young.*
*Prov 5:2 . . . you will show **d**, and your*
*Prov 8:12 . . . knowledge and **d**.*
*Prov 28:11 . . . a poor person with **d** can see*

DISCIPLE, DISCIPLES (n)
student or follower of some doctrine or teacher
*Matt 28:19 . . . go and make **d-s** of all the*
*Mark 16:20 . . . the **d-s** went everywhere and*
*Luke 6:13 . . . all of His **d-s** and chose twelve*
*Luke 14:26 . . . Otherwise, you cannot be My **d**.*
*Luke 14:33 . . . become My **d** without*
*John 6:66 . . . many of His **d-s** turned away*
*John 8:31 . . . are truly My **d-s** if you remain*
*John 13:5 . . . to wash the **d-s'** feet, drying*
*John 13:23 . . . The **d** Jesus loved*
*John 15:8 . . . are My true **d-s**.*
*John 19:26 . . . there beside the **d** he loved,*
*John 21:7 . . . Then the **d** Jesus loved*
*John 21:20 . . . the **d** Jesus loved—*

DISCIPLINE (n)
punishment; instruction
*Deut 11:2 . . . the **d** of the LORD*
*Prov 10:17 . . . People who accept **d** are on*
*Prov 13:1 . . . child accepts a parent's **d**;*
*Prov 13:24 . . . spare the rod of **d** hate their*
*Prov 15:32 . . . If you reject **d**, you only*
*Heb 12:5 . . . of the LORD's **d**, and don't*
*Heb 12:11 . . . No **d** is enjoyable*

DISCIPLINE, DISCIPLINED, DISCIPLINES (v)
to punish or correct with love; to exercise self-control
*Deut 8:5 . . . as a parent **d-s** a child,*
*Deut 8:5 . . . LORD your God **d-s** you for your*
*Ps 38:1 . . . in Your anger or **d** me in Your*
*Ps 39:11 . . . When You **d** us for our*
*Ps 119:67 . . . to wander off until You **d-d** me;*
*Ps 119:75 . . . You **d-d** me because I needed*
*Prov 15:10 . . . be severely **d-d**; whoever hates*
*Jer 30:11 . . . I will **d** You, but with*
*Jer 31:18 . . . saying, 'You **d-d** me severely,*
*1 Cor 9:25 . . . All athletes are **d-d** in their*
*1 Cor 9:27 . . . I **d** my body like*
*1 Cor 11:32 . . . we are being **d-d** so that we*
*Heb 12:6 . . . For the LORD **d-s** those he*
*Heb 12:7 . . . who is never **d-d** by its father?*
*Heb 12:9 . . . fathers who **d-d** us, shouldn't*
*1 Pet 4:7 . . . be earnest and **d-d** in your*

DISCOURAGED (v)
to dissuade or hinder; to deprive of courage or confidence
*Deut 31:8 . . . be afraid or **d**, for the LORD*
*2 Sam 11:25 . . . not to be **d**," David said.*
*1 Chr 28:20 . . . afraid or **d**, for the LORD*
*Isa 41:10 . . . Don't be **d**, for I am*
*2 Cor 7:6 . . . who are **d**, encouraged us by*
*Col 3:21 . . . will become **d**.*

DISCRIMINATION (n)
prejudiced outlook, action, or treatment
*Jas 2:4 . . . doesn't this **d** show that your*

DISEASE, DISEASES (n)
sickness, malady
*Exod 4:6 . . . a severe skin **d.***
*2 Chr 16:12 . . . a serious foot **d.***
*Ps 91:6 . . . not dread the **d** that stalks*
*Ps 103:3 . . . heals all my **d-s.***
*Matt 9:35 . . . every kind of **d** and illness.*
*Matt 10:1 . . . every kind of **d** and illness.*
*Luke 4:40 . . . matter what their **d-s** were,*

DISGRACE, DISGRACED (v)
to cause to lose favor or standing; to be a source of shame to
*Ps 25:3 . . . trusts in You will ever be **d-d,***
*Ps 37:19 . . . will not be **d-d** in hard times;*
*Prov 29:15 . . . but a mother is **d-d** by an*
*Matt 1:19 . . . did not want to **d** her*
*Rom 9:33 . . . in Him will never be **d-d.***
*Rom 10:11 . . . in Him will never be **d-d.***
*1 Tim 3:7 . . . will not be **d-d** and fall into*

DISHONEST (adj)
characterized by lack of truth, honesty, or trustworthiness
*Lev 19:35 . . . Do not use **d** standards when*
*Prov 20:23 . . . not pleased by **d** scales.*
*Luke 16:8 . . . to admire the **d** rascal for*
*Luke 16:10 . . . But if you are **d** in little*

DISHONESTY (n)
lack of honesty or integrity
*Jer 22:17 . . . eyes only for greed and **d!***
*Jer 23:14 . . . commit adultery and love **d.***
*Rom 3:7 . . . sinner if my **d** highlights His*
*Rev 21:27 . . . idolatry and **d**—but only*

DISHONOR, DISHONORED, DISHONORING, DISHONORS (v)
to degrade or bring shame upon
*Exod 21:17 . . . Anyone who **d-s** father or*
*Exod 22:28 . . . You must not **d** God or*
*Lev 20:19 . . . This would **d** a close*
*Deut 27:16 . . . is anyone who **d-s** father or*
*Ezra 4:14 . . . see the king **d-ed** in this way,*
*Lam 2:2 . . . **d-ing** the kingdom and its rulers.*
*John 8:49 . . . my Father—and you **d** Me.*
*Rom 2:23 . . . the law, but you **d** God by*
*1 Cor 11:4 . . . A man **d-s** his head if*
*1 Cor 11:5 . . . a woman **d-s** her head if*
*Jas 2:6 . . . But you **d** the poor!*

DISOBEY, DISOBEYED, DISOBEYING (v)
to fail to obey
*Judg 2:2 . . . But you **d-ed** My command.*
*1 Kgs 13:26 . . . man of God who **d-ed** the*
*2 Chr 24:20 . . . says: Why do you **d** the*
*Neh 9:29 . . . and obstinate and **d-ed** Your*
*Esth 3:3 . . . Why are you **d-ing** the king's*
*Dan 9:11 . . . Israel has **d-ed** Your instruction*
*Acts 7:53 . . . You deliberately **d-ed** God's law,*
*Rom 1:30 . . . and they **d** their parents.*
*Rom 5:19 . . . Because one person **d-ed** God,*
*Eph 5:6 . . . fall on all who **d** Him.*
*Heb 3:18 . . . the people who **d-ed** Him?*
*Heb 4:6 . . . enter because they **d-ed** God.*
*Heb 4:11 . . . But if we **d** God, as the*
*1 Pet 3:20 . . . those who **d-ed** God long ago*

DISTRESS (n)
a troubling or painful situation; a state of danger or desperate need
*Exod 3:7 . . . their cries of **d** because of*
*Job 36:16 . . . to a place free from **d.***
*Ps 18:6 . . . But in my **d** I cried out*
*Ps 118:5 . . . In my **d** I prayed to*
*Ps 143:11 . . . bring me out of this **d.***
*Jas 1:27 . . . and widows in their **d***

DIVISION, DIVISIONS (n)
act or process of dividing, separating, distributing; a portion, part, grouping, or distinction
*1 Cor 1:10 . . . there be no **d-s** in the church.*
*1 Cor 11:18 . . . that there are **d-s** among*
*Gal 5:20 . . . selfish ambition, dissension, **d,***
*Titus 3:10 . . . are causing **d-s** among you,*

DIVORCE (n)
the action or an instance of legally dissolving a marriage
*Deut 24:1 . . . a letter of **d,** hands it to*
*Mal 2:16 . . . "For I hate **d!**" says the*
*Matt 19:8 . . . Moses permitted **d** only as a*

DIVORCE, DIVORCED, DIVORCES (v)
to dissolve a marriage; to end a relationship
*Lev 21:7 . . . a woman who is **d-d** from her*
*Lev 21:14 . . . who is **d-d,** or a woman*
*Lev 22:13 . . . a widow or is **d-d** and has no*
*Num 30:9 . . . is a widow or is **d-d,** she must*
*Deut 22:19 . . . and he may never **d** her.*
*1 Chr 8:8 . . . After Shaharaim **d-d** his wives*
*Jer 3:1 . . . If a man **d-s** a woman and*
*Jer 3:8 . . . saw that I **d-d** faithless Israel*
*Matt 5:31 . . . A man can **d** his wife by*
*Matt 5:32 . . . a man who **d-s** his wife, unless*
*Matt 5:32 . . . who marries a **d-d** woman also*
*Mark 10:2 . . . be allowed to **d** his wife?*
*Mark 10:11 . . . Whoever **d-s** his wife and*
*Mark 10:12 . . . if a woman **d-s** her husband*
*Luke 16:18 . . . a man who **d-s** his wife and*
*Luke 16:18 . . . marries a woman **d-d** from*

DONKEY (n)
a domestic mammal smaller than the horse and having long ears
*Num 22:30 . . . same **d** you have ridden*
*Matt 21:5 . . . riding on a **d**—riding on a*
*2 Pet 2:16 . . . when his **d** rebuked him*

DOOR, DOORS (n)
a barrier by which an entry is closed and opened; a means of access or participation
*Ps 24:7 . . . Open up, ancient **d-s,** and let*
*Matt 7:7 . . . the **d** will be opened to you.*
*Luke 13:24 . . . enter the narrow **d** to God's*
*Acts 14:27 . . . had opened the **d** of faith to*
*1 Cor 16:9 . . . is a wide-open **d** for a great*
*2 Cor 2:12 . . . opened a **d** of opportunity*
*Rev 3:20 . . . stand at the **d** and knock.*

DOUBT, DOUBTS (n)
uncertainty of belief or opinion; lack of confidence; distrust
*Mark 11:23 . . . have no **d** in your heart.*
*Luke 24:38 . . . hearts filled with **d?***
*Rom 14:23 . . . if you have **d-s** about whether*

DOUBT (v)
to distrust; to be uncertain
*Matt 14:31 . . . Why did you **d** Me?*
*Matt 21:21 . . . faith and don't **d,** you*

DREAM, DREAMS (n)
a strongly desired goal or purpose; a series of thoughts, images, or emotions occurring during sleep
*Prov 13:12 . . . sick, but a **d** fulfilled is a*
*Prov 13:19 . . . pleasant to see **d-s** come true,*
*Eccl 5:3 . . . gives you restless **d-s;***

DREAM (v)
to have a dream
*Joel 2:28 . . . old men will **d** dreams,*
*Acts 2:17 . . . old men will **d** dreams.*

DRINK, DRINKING, DRINKS (v)
to swallow; to partake of alcoholic beverages
*1 Sam 1:13 . . . she had been **d-ing.***
*Isa 5:22 . . . who are heroes at **d-ing** wine*
*Isa 12:3 . . . you will **d** deeply from*
*Matt 26:27 . . . Each of you **d** from it,*
*Mark 16:18 . . . **d** anything poisonous,*
*John 4:13 . . . Anyone who **d-s** this water will*
*John 6:54 . . . My flesh and **d-s** My blood has*
*Rom 14:17 . . . we eat or **d,** but of living a*
*1 Cor 11:27 . . . this bread or **d-s** this cup of*
*Rev 14:10 . . . **d** the wine of God's anger.*
*Rev 22:17 . . . who desires **d** freely from*

DRINKER, DRINKERS (n)
a person who drinks alcoholic beverages
*1 Tim 3:3 . . . not be a heavy **d** or be violent.*
*1 Tim 3:8 . . . not be heavy **d-s** or dishonest*
*Titus 2:3 . . . or be heavy **d-s.***

DROWNED (v)
to suffocate by submersion especially in water
*Exod 15:4 . . . officers are **d** in the Red*
*Matt 18:6 . . . neck and be **d** in the depths*
*Heb 11:29 . . . they were all **d.***

DRUNK (adj)
having the faculties impaired by alcohol; intoxicated
*Acts 2:15 . . . These people are not **d,** as*

E

EAGLE, EAGLES (n)
any of various large diurnal birds of prey noted for their strength, size, keenness of vision, and powers of flight
*Deut 32:11 . . . Like an **e** that rouses her chicks*
*Isa 40:31 . . . on wings like **e-s.***
*Rev 4:7 . . . was like an **e** in flight.*
*Rev 12:14 . . . two wings like those of a great **e***

EAT, EATEN, EATING, EATS (v)
to ingest, chew, and swallow in turn
see also ATE
*Gen 2:16 . . . You may freely **e** the fruit*
*Gen 3:11 . . . Have you **e-en** from the tree*
*Deut 14:4 . . . the animals you may **e:***
*Isa 65:25 . . . The lion will **e** hay*
*Jer 31:29 . . . parents have **e-en** sour grapes,*
*Matt 26:26 . . . Take this and **e** it,*
*Luke 15:2 . . . sinful people—even **e-ing** with*
*John 6:52 . . . give us his flesh to **e?***
*John 6:54 . . . anyone who **e-s** My flesh and*
*Acts 10:13 . . . kill and **e** them.*
*Acts 10:14 . . . I have never **e-en** anything that*
*Rom 14:15 . . . Don't let your **e-ing** ruin*
*1 Cor 8:4 . . . So, what about **e-ing** meat that*
*1 Cor 8:10 . . . **e-ing** in the temple of an idol,*
*1 Cor 10:31 . . . So whether you **e** or drink,*
*1 Cor 11:26 . . . every time you **e** this bread*
*1 Cor 11:27 . . . anyone who **e-s** this bread or*

EDEN (n)
the garden where Adam and Eve first lived
*Gen 2:8 . . . a garden in **E** in the east,*
*Ezek 28:13 . . . in **E,** the garden of God.*

EDIFY, EDIFYING (KJV)
*1 Cor 10:23 . . . but not everything is **beneficial***
*1 Cor 14:5 . . . will be **strengthened***
*1 Cor 14:17 . . . it won't **strengthen** the people*
*Eph 4:12 . . . **build up** the church,*

ELECT (KJV)
*Isa 42:1 . . . My **chosen one,** who pleases Me*
*Matt 24:31 . . . gather His **chosen ones** from all*
*Rom 8:33 . . . **us whom God has chosen** for his*
*Col 3:12 . . . **chose** you to be the holy people*
*2 Tim 2:10 . . . Jesus to **those God has chosen***

ENCOURAGE, ENCOURAGED, ENCOURAGES, ENCOURAGING (v)
to inspire with courage, spirit, or hope; to spur on
Isa 41:7 . . . The carver ***e-s*** *the goldsmith,*
Acts 11:23 . . . and he ***e-d*** *the believers*
Acts 15:32 . . . at length to the believers, ***e-ing***
Acts 20:1 . . . sent for the believers and ***e-d***
Acts 28:15 . . . he was ***e-d*** *and thanked God.*
Rom 1:12 . . . I also want to be ***e-d*** *by yours.*
Rom 12:8 . . . your gift is to ***e*** *others,*
1 Cor 8:12 . . . against other believers by ***e-ing***
1 Cor 14:3 . . . strengthens others, ***e-s*** *them,*
2 Cor 7:6 . . . who ***e-s*** *those who are*
2 Cor 7:6 . . . ***e-d*** *us by the arrival of Titus.*
2 Cor 7:13 . . . have been greatly ***e-d*** *by this.*
Eph 6:22 . . . how we are doing and to ***e***
Col 4:8 . . . how we are doing and to ***e*** *you.*
1 Thes 2:12 . . . pleaded with you, ***e-d*** *you,*
1 Thes 3:2 . . . to strengthen you, to ***e*** *you*
1 Thes 3:7 . . . we have been greatly ***e-d*** *in the*
1 Thes 5:11 . . . So ***e*** *each other*
1 Thes 5:14 . . . ***E*** *those who are timid.*
Titus 1:9 . . . he will be able to ***e*** *others*
Heb 12:5 . . . you forgotten the ***e-ing*** *words*
1 Pet 5:12 . . . purpose in writing is to ***e*** *you*
2 Jn 11 . . . Anyone who ***e-s*** *such people*

ENCOURAGEMENT (n)
the act of encouraging; the state of being encouraged
Rom 15:5 . . . who gives this patience and ***e,***
1 Cor 16:18 . . . a wonderful ***e*** *to me,*
2 Cor 7:13 . . . In addition to our own ***e,***
Eph 4:29 . . . an ***e*** *to those who hear them.*
Phil 2:1 . . . any ***e*** *from belonging to Christ?*
Phlm 20 . . . Give me this ***e*** *in Christ.*

ENDURANCE (n)
the ability to withstand hardship or adversity
see also PERSEVERANCE
Rom 5:3 . . . they help us develop ***e.***
Col 1:11 . . . have all the ***e*** *and patience*
2 Thes 1:4 . . . your ***e*** *and faithfulness*
Heb 12:1 . . . let us run with ***e*** *the race*
Jas 1:3 . . . when your faith is tested, your ***e***
2 Pet 1:6 . . . self-control with patient ***e,***
Rev 1:9 . . . in the patient ***e*** *to which Jesus*

ENDURE, ENDURED, ENDURES, ENDURING (v)
to withstand, suffer, or persevere
see also PERSEVERE
Ps 89:2 . . . Your faithfulness is as ***e-ing*** *as*
Ps 136:1 . . . faithful love ***e-s*** *forever.*
Matt 10:22 . . . everyone who ***e-s*** *to the end*
Mark 13:13 . . . one who ***e-s*** *to the end*
1 Cor 13:7 . . . ***e-s*** *through every*
2 Cor 1:6 . . . Then you can patiently ***e***
2 Cor 6:4 . . . patiently ***e*** *troubles and*
2 Tim 2:3 . . . ***E*** *suffering along with me,*
2 Tim 2:12 . . . If we ***e*** *hardship,*
2 Tim 3:11 . . . suffering I have ***e-d.***
Heb 12:2 . . . He ***e-d*** *the cross,*
Heb 12:3 . . . hostility He ***e-d*** *from sinful*
Heb 12:7 . . . As you ***e*** *this divine discipline,*
Jas 1:12 . . . who patiently ***e*** *testing and*
Jas 5:11 . . . those who ***e*** *under suffering.*
1 Pet 2:19 . . . patiently ***e*** *unfair treatment.*
Rev 13:10 . . . must ***e*** *persecution patiently*

ENEMY, ENEMIES (n)
foe—personal, national, or spiritual
Ps 23:5 . . . the presence of my ***e-ies.***
Ps 62:7 . . . a rock where no ***e*** *can reach me.*
Prov 16:7 . . . even their ***e-ies*** *are at peace*
Prov 24:17 . . . rejoice when your ***e-ies*** *fall;*
Prov 25:21 . . . If your ***e-ies*** *are hungry,*
Prov 27:6 . . . than many kisses from an ***e.***
Isa 51:13 . . . fear the anger of your ***e-ies?***
Isa 59:18 . . . repay his ***e-ies*** *for their evil*
Matt 5:44 . . . love your ***e-ies!*** *Pray for those*
Luke 6:35 . . . Love your ***e-ies!*** *Do good to*
Luke 10:19 . . . over all the power of the ***e,***
Rom 5:10 . . . while we were still His ***e-ies,***
Rom 12:20 . . . If your ***e-ies*** *are hungry,*
1 Cor 15:25 . . . until He humbles all His ***e-ies***
1 Cor 15:26 . . . the last ***e*** *to be destroyed*
Phil 3:18 . . . they are really ***e-ies*** *of the cross*
Jas 4:4 . . . makes you an ***e*** *of God?*
1 Pet 5:8 . . . Watch out for your great ***e,***

ENTHRONED (v)
to seat ceremonially on a throne or in a place associated with power and authority
1 Sam 4:4 . . . who is ***e*** *between the cherubim.*
2 Kgs 19:15 . . . ***e*** *between the mighty*
1 Chr 13:6 . . . ***e*** *between the cherubim.*
Ps 22:3 . . . You are holy, ***e*** *on the praises*
Ps 113:5 . . . God, who is ***e*** *on high?*
Isa 37:16 . . . God of Israel, You are ***e***

ENVY (n)
discontent or resentment because of another's success, advantages, or superiority
see also JEALOUS(Y)
Mark 7:22 . . . lustful desires, ***e,*** *slander,*
Rom 1:29 . . . sin, greed, hate, ***e,*** *murder,*
Gal 5:21 . . . ***e,*** *drunkenness, wild parties,*
Titus 3:3 . . . full of evil and ***e,*** *and we hated*
Jas 4:5 . . . within us is filled with ***e?***

ENVY (v)
to feel or show envy; to begrudge
Prov 3:31 . . . Don't ***e*** *violent people*
Prov 24:1 . . . Don't ***e*** *evil people*

ESCAPE, ESCAPED, ESCAPING (v)
to avoid; to get free of or break away from
Ps 89:48 . . . can ***e*** *the power of the grave.*
Ps 139:7 . . . I can never ***e*** *from Your Spirit!*
Matt 23:33 . . . will you ***e*** *the judgment*
1 Cor 3:15 . . . barely ***e-ing*** *through a wall of*
Heb 2:3 . . . think we can ***e*** *if we ignore*
Heb 12:25 . . . we will certainly not ***e*** *if we*
2 Pet 2:18 . . . those who have barely ***e-d***
2 Pet 2:20 . . . ***e*** *from the wickedness*

ETERNAL (adj)
having infinite duration; valid or existing at all times
see also EVERLASTING, FOREVER
Gen 9:16 . . . will remember the ***e*** *covenant*
Exod 3:15 . . . My ***e*** *name, My name to*
Lev 24:8 . . . a requirement of the ***e***
Num 18:19 . . . an ***e*** *and unbreakable*
Ps 119:142 . . . Your justice is ***e,***
Jer 50:5 . . . with an ***e*** *covenant*
Dan 4:34 . . . and His kingdom is ***e.***
Dan 7:14 . . . His rule is ***e—***
Matt 18:8 . . . better to enter ***e*** *life with*
Matt 19:16 . . . must I do to have ***e*** *life?*
Matt 25:41 . . . into the ***e*** *fire*
Matt 25:46 . . . away into ***e*** *punishment,*
Mark 3:29 . . . a sin with ***e*** *consequences.*
Luke 10:25 . . . should I do to inherit ***e*** *life?*
Luke 18:18 . . . should I do to inherit ***e*** *life?*
John 3:15 . . . in Him will have ***e*** *life.*
John 3:16 . . . not perish but have ***e*** *life.*
John 3:36 . . . believes in God's Son has ***e***
John 5:29 . . . will rise to experience ***e*** *life,*
John 5:39 . . . you think they give you ***e*** *life.*
John 6:68 . . . the words that give ***e*** *life.*
John 12:50 . . . His commands lead to ***e*** *life;*
John 17:2 . . . He gives ***e*** *life*
Rom 1:20 . . . ***e*** *power and divine nature*
Rom 5:21 . . . resulting in ***e*** *life through*
Rom 6:23 . . . free gift of God is ***e*** *life*
Rom 9:5 . . . is worthy of ***e*** *praise! Amen.*
Rom 16:26 . . . the ***e*** *God has commanded,*
Eph 3:11 . . . This was His ***e*** *plan,*
2 Thes 1:9 . . . punished with ***e*** *destruction,*
1 Tim 6:12 . . . Hold tightly to the ***e*** *life*
Titus 3:7 . . . we will inherit ***e*** *life.*
Heb 5:9 . . . source of ***e*** *salvation*
Heb 9:15 . . . ***e*** *inheritance God has*
Heb 13:20 . . . an ***e*** *covenant with His blood—*
1 Pet 1:23 . . . from the ***e,*** *living word*
1 Pet 5:10 . . . to share in His ***e*** *glory*
1 Jn 1:2 . . . He is the one who is ***e*** *life.*
1 Jn 2:25 . . . we enjoy the ***e*** *life He*
1 Jn 5:20 . . . and He is ***e*** *life.*
Jude 7 . . . the ***e*** *fire of God's judgment.*
Jude 21 . . . who will bring you ***e*** *life.*

ETERNITY (n)
immortality; infinite time
Eccl 3:11 . . . has planted ***e*** *in the human*
Isa 57:15 . . . who lives in ***e,*** *the Holy One,*
John 12:25 . . . will keep it for ***e.***

EVERLASTING (adj)
continuing indefinitely
see also ETERNAL, FOREVER
Gen 17:7 . . . This is the ***e*** *covenant:*
Gen 48:4 . . . as an ***e*** *possession.*
2 Sam 23:5 . . . made an ***e*** *covenant with*
Ps 139:24 . . . lead me along the path of ***e*** *life.*
Isa 9:6 . . . God, ***E*** *Father, Prince of Peace.*
Isa 35:10 . . . crowned with ***e*** *joy.*
Isa 40:28 . . . The LORD *is the* ***e*** *God,*
Isa 54:8 . . . But with ***e*** *love*
Isa 55:3 . . . an ***e*** *covenant with You.*
Isa 60:19 . . . God will be Your ***e*** *light,*
Isa 60:20 . . . the LORD *will be Your* ***e*** *light.*
Isa 61:7 . . . and ***e*** *joy will be yours.*
Isa 61:8 . . . an ***e*** *covenant with them.*
Jer 10:10 . . . the living God and the ***e*** *King!*
Jer 31:3 . . . with an ***e*** *love.*
Ezek 16:60 . . . establish an ***e*** *covenant with*
Dan 4:34 . . . His rule is ***e,***
Dan 9:24 . . . to bring in ***e*** *righteousness,*
Dan 12:2 . . . to ***e*** *life and some to shame*
Gal 6:8 . . . will harvest ***e*** *life from the*

EVIL (adj)
bad, sinful, or morally reprehensible; of the Devil
Gen 6:5 . . . was consistently and totally ***e.***
Exod 32:22 . . . know how ***e*** *these people*
Ps 51:4 . . . what is ***e*** *in Your sight.*
Ps 140:8 . . . do not let ***e*** *people have their way.*
Prov 15:26 . . . The LORD *detests* ***e*** *plans,*
Matt 6:13 . . . rescue us from the ***e*** *one.*
Matt 12:45 . . . other spirits more ***e*** *than itself,*
Matt 15:19 . . . from the heart come ***e***
Mark 7:21 . . . heart, come ***e*** *thoughts,*
Luke 11:24 . . . When an ***e*** *spirit leaves*
John 17:15 . . . them safe from the ***e*** *one.*
Acts 19:13 . . . casting out ***e*** *spirits.*
Rom 2:9 . . . keeps on doing what is ***e—***
Rom 13:14 . . . ways to indulge your ***e*** *desires.*
1 Cor 5:13 . . . remove the ***e*** *person from*
Eph 5:16 . . . in these ***e*** *days.*
Col 3:5 . . . lust, and ***e*** *desires.*
2 Thes 3:3 . . . guard you from the ***e*** *one.*
1 Tim 6:4 . . . slander, and ***e*** *suspicions.*
2 Tim 3:13 . . . ***e*** *people and impostors*
1 Jn 2:13 . . . your battle with the ***e*** *one.*
1 Jn 3:12 . . . Cain, who belonged to the ***e*** *one*
1 Jn 5:18 . . . the ***e*** *one cannot touch*

EVIL (n)
something that brings sorrow, distress, or misfortune
Gen 2:9 . . . of the knowledge of good and ***e.***
Gen 3:5 . . . knowing both good and ***e.***
Judg 6:1 . . . The Israelites did ***e***
Ps 5:5 . . . for You hate all who do ***e.***
Ps 14:4 . . . Will those who do ***e*** *never learn?*

Ps 34:13 . . . *keep your tongue from speaking* ***e***
Ps 37:27 . . . *Turn from* ***e*** *and do good,*
Ps 45:7 . . . *You love justice and hate* ***e.***
Ps 53:4 . . . *Will those who do* ***e*** *never learn?*
Ps 92:15 . . . *There is no* ***e*** *in Him!*
Ps 101:4 . . . *and stay away from every* ***e.***
Ps 125:5 . . . *with those who do* ***e.***
Prov 6:18 . . . *a heart that plots* ***e,***
Prov 8:13 . . . *will hate* ***e.***
Prov 11:27 . . . *search for* ***e,*** *it will find you!*
Prov 13:6 . . . *but the* ***e*** *are misled by sin.*
Prov 17:13 . . . *repay good with* ***e, e*** *will*
Prov 20:30 . . . *cleanses away* ***e;*** *such*
Isa 5:20 . . . *those who say that* ***e*** *is good*
Isa 13:11 . . . *punish the world for its* ***e***
Jer 23:14 . . . *who are doing* ***e*** *so that*
Hab 1:13 . . . *cannot stand the sight of* ***e.***
Mal 3:15 . . . *those who do* ***e*** *get rich,*
Matt 5:45 . . . *to both the* ***e*** *and the good,*
Luke 13:27 . . . *all you who do* ***e.***
John 3:20 . . . *All who do* ***e*** *hate the light*
Rom 12:21 . . . *Don't let* ***e*** *conquer you,*
1 Cor 14:20 . . . *babies when it comes to* ***e,***
1 Thes 5:15 . . . *no one pays back* ***e*** *for* ***e,***
1 Thes 5:22 . . . *away from every kind of* ***e.***
1 Tim 6:10 . . . *the root of all kinds of* ***e.***
2 Tim 2:19 . . . *must turn away from* ***e.***
Heb 1:9 . . . *You love justice and hate* ***e.***
Jas 1:21 . . . *get rid of all the filth and* ***e***
Jas 3:8 . . . *It is restless and* ***e,***
1 Pet 2:16 . . . *as an excuse to do* ***e.***
1 Pet 3:9 . . . *Don't repay* ***e*** *for* ***e.***
1 Pet 3:11 . . . *Turn away from* ***e*** *and do*
3 Jn 11 . . . *those who do* ***e*** *prove that they*

EVILDOERS (n)
one who does evil
Ps 92:7 . . . *like weeds and* ***e*** *flourish,*
Ps 92:9 . . . *perish; all* ***e*** *will be scattered.*
Ps 94:16 . . . *will stand up for me against* ***e?***
Prov 21:15 . . . *it terrifies* ***e.***
Prov 24:19 . . . *Don't fret because of* ***e;***

EXALT, EXALTED, EXALTING, EXALTS (v)
to elevate; to glorify; to raise in rank or power
see also GLORIFY, HONOR
Exod 15:2 . . . *and I will* ***e*** *Him!*
2 Sam 22:47 . . . *of my salvation, be* ***e-ed!***
Neh 9:5 . . . *May it be* ***e-ed*** *above all blessing*
Job 36:7 . . . *with kings and* ***e-s*** *them forever.*
Ps 18:46 . . . *the God of my salvation be* ***e-ed!***
Ps 30:1 . . . *I will* ***e*** *you,* LORD,
Ps 92:8 . . . *O* LORD, *will be* ***e-ed*** *forever.*
Ps 97:9 . . . *you are* ***e-ed*** *far above all gods.*
Ps 107:32 . . . *Let them* ***e*** *Him publicly*
Ps 145:1 . . . *I will* ***e*** *You, my God and King,*
Dan 11:36 . . . *as he pleases,* ***e-ing*** *himself*
Luke 14:11 . . . *those who* ***e*** *themselves will*
Acts 2:33 . . . *is* ***e-ed*** *to the place of highest*
2 Thes 2:4 . . . *He will* ***e*** *Himself*

EXAMINE, EXAMINED, EXAMINES, EXAMINING (v)
to test the condition of; to inspect closely
1 Chr 29:17 . . . *You* ***e*** *our hearts*
Ps 11:4 . . . ***e-ing*** *every person on earth.*
Ps 11:5 . . . *The* LORD ***e-s*** *both*
Ps 17:3 . . . ***e-d*** *my heart in the night.*
Ps 139:1 . . . LORD, *You have* ***e-d*** *My heart*
Prov 5:21 . . . ***e-ing*** *every path he takes.*
Prov 21:2 . . . *the* LORD ***e-s*** *their heart.*
Jer 11:20 . . . *You* ***e*** *the deepest thoughts*
Jer 17:10 . . . *and* ***e*** *secret motives.*
Lam 3:40 . . . *let us test and* ***e*** *our ways.*
1 Cor 4:4 . . . *Lord Himself who will* ***e***
1 Cor 11:28 . . . *you should* ***e*** *yourself*
2 Cor 13:5 . . . ***E*** *yourselves to see*
1 Thes 2:4 . . . *He alone* ***e-s*** *the motives*

EXCUSE (n)
the apology or justification offered
John 15:22 . . . *they have no* ***e*** *for their sin.*
Rom 1:20 . . . *no* ***e*** *for not knowing God.*
Rom 2:1 . . . *and you have no* ***e!***
1 Pet 2:16 . . . *your freedom as an* ***e***

EXCUSE (v)
to overlook, justify, or make an apology for
Exod 34:7 . . . *But I do not* ***e*** *the guilty.*
Eph 5:6 . . . *those who try to* ***e*** *these sins,*

EXHORT(ATION) (KJV)
Rom 12:8 . . . *If your gift is to* ***encourage*** *others*
1 Thes 2:3 . . . *we were not* ***preaching*** *with any deceit*
Heb 3:13 . . . *You must* ***warn*** *each other every day*

EXPLAIN, EXPLAINED, EXPLAINS (v)
to make plain or understandable; to give the reason or cause
Gen 2:24 . . . *This* ***e-s*** *why a man leaves his*
Neh 8:8 . . . *and clearly* ***e-ed*** *the meaning*
Matt 19:5 . . . *This* ***e-s*** *why a man leaves his*
Acts 17:3 . . . *He* ***e-ed*** *the prophecies*
Acts 18:28 . . . ***e-ed*** *to them that Jesus was*
Eph 6:19 . . . ***e*** *God's mysterious plan*
2 Tim 2:15 . . . *who correctly* ***e-s*** *the word of*
1 Pet 3:15 . . . *always be ready to* ***e*** *it.*

EXTOL(LED) (KJV)
Ps 30:1 . . . *will* ***exalt*** *you,* LORD, *for you*
Ps 66:17 . . . *to him for help,* ***praising*** *him*
Ps 68:4 . . . ***Sing loud praises*** *to him who rides*
Isa 52:13 . . . *he will be* ***highly exalted***

F

FACE, FACED, FACING (v)
to confront; to be confronted by
Ps 112:8 . . . ***f*** *their foes triumphantly.*
Ps 116:6 . . . *I was* ***f-ing*** *death, and He saved*
2 Cor 6:5 . . . ***f-d*** *angry mobs,*

FAIL, FAILED, FAILS (v)
to disappoint; to fall short; to weaken; to miss performing an expected service; to be unsuccessful
Num 23:19 . . . *spoken and* ***f-ed*** *to act?*
Deut 31:6 . . . *He will neither* ***f*** *you*
Josh 23:14 . . . *Not a single one has* ***f-ed!***
1 Kgs 8:56 . . . *Not one word has* ***f-ed***
Ps 77:8 . . . *his promises permanently* ***f-ed?***
Luke 13:24 . . . *try to enter but will* ***f.***
Luke 22:32 . . . *faith should not* ***f.***
Rom 9:6 . . . *has God* ***f-ed*** *to fulfill his promise*
2 Cor 13:5 . . . *if not, you have* ***f-ed*** *the test*
2 Cor 13:6 . . . *we have not* ***f-ed*** *the test*
Heb 12:15 . . . *none of you* ***f-s*** *to receive*
Heb 13:5 . . . *I will never* ***f*** *you.*
1 Pet 4:19 . . . *He will never* ***f*** *you.*

FAINT (v)
to become weak or lose courage in body or spirit
Isa 40:31 . . . *will walk and not* ***f.***

FAIR (adj)
free from self-interest, prejudice, or favoritism; beautiful
Prov 1:3 . . . *do what is right, just, and* ***f.***
Song 2:13 . . . *away with me, my* ***f*** *one!*
Isa 11:4 . . . *make* ***f*** *decisions for the*
Rom 3:25 . . . *God was being* ***f*** *when He*
Rom 3:26 . . . *He Himself is* ***f*** *and just,*
Col 4:1 . . . *be just and* ***f*** *to your slaves.*

FAIRNESS (n)
the quality of being free from self-interest, prejudice, or favoritism
Ps 9:8 . . . *rule the nations with* ***f.***
Ps 98:9 . . . *and the nations with* ***f.***
Ps 99:4 . . . *you have established* ***f.***
Isa 9:7 . . . *will rule with* ***f*** *and justice*

FAITH (n)
reliance, loyalty, or complete trust in God; a system of religious beliefs
see also BELIEVE, TRUST
Exod 14:31 . . . *They put their* ***f*** *in the* LORD
Isa 7:9 . . . *Unless your* ***f*** *is firm,*
Matt 9:29 . . . *Because of your* ***f,*** *it will*
Matt 17:20 . . . ***f*** *even as small as a mustard*
Luke 7:50 . . . *Your* ***f*** *has saved you;*
Luke 8:48 . . . *your* ***f*** *has made you well.*
Luke 12:28 . . . *Why do you have so little* ***f?***
John 16:1 . . . *won't abandon your* ***f.***
Acts 6:5 . . . *full of* ***f*** *and the Holy Spirit*
Acts 14:9 . . . *he had* ***f*** *to be healed.*
Acts 24:24 . . . *told them about* ***f*** *in Christ*
Rom 1:12 . . . *to encourage you in your* ***f,***
Rom 1:17 . . . *from start to finish by* ***f.***
Rom 1:17 . . . *through* ***f*** *that a righteous*
Rom 3:28 . . . *right with God through* ***f***
Rom 4:5 . . . *because of their* ***f*** *in God*
Rom 4:12 . . . *same kind of* ***f*** *Abraham had*
Rom 5:1 . . . *made right in God's sight by* ***f,***
Rom 5:2 . . . *Because of our* ***f,*** *Christ has*
Rom 10:17 . . . *So* ***f*** *comes from hearing,*
1 Cor 12:9 . . . *gives great* ***f*** *to another,*
1 Cor 13:13 . . . ***f,*** *hope, and love—*
1 Cor 16:13 . . . *Stand firm in the* ***f.***
2 Cor 1:24 . . . *how to put your* ***f*** *into practice.*
Gal 3:11 . . . ***f*** *that a righteous person*
Gal 3:12 . . . *This way of* ***f*** *is very different*
Gal 3:14 . . . *Holy Spirit through* ***f.***
Gal 3:24 . . . *made right with God through* ***f.***
Gal 3:26 . . . *children of God through* ***f*** *in Christ*
Eph 4:5 . . . *one Lord, one* ***f,*** *one baptism,*
Eph 6:16 . . . *hold up the shield of* ***f***
Phil 3:9 . . . *righteous through* ***f*** *in Christ.*
Col 1:4 . . . *we have heard of your* ***f*** *in Christ*
1 Thes 3:5 . . . *whether your* ***f*** *was still strong.*
2 Thes 1:3 . . . *because your* ***f*** *is flourishing*
1 Tim 1:4 . . . *live a life of* ***f*** *in God.*
1 Tim 1:19 . . . *Cling to your* ***f*** *in Christ,*
1 Tim 6:12 . . . *good fight for the true* ***f.***
2 Tim 1:5 . . . *remember your genuine* ***f,***
Titus 1:1 . . . *have been sent to proclaim* ***f***
Titus 1:13 . . . *make them strong in the* ***f.***
Phlm 6 . . . *generosity that comes from your* ***f***
Heb 6:1 . . . *and placing our* ***f*** *in God.*
Heb 6:12 . . . *because of their* ***f*** *and endurance.*
Heb 10:38 . . . *will live by* ***f.***
Heb 12:2 . . . *perfects our* ***f.***
Jas 1:3 . . . *when your* ***f*** *is tested,*
Jas 2:14 . . . *Can that kind of* ***f*** *save anyone?*
Jas 2:17 . . . ***f*** *by itself isn't enough.*
Jas 2:20 . . . ***f*** *without good deeds*
Jas 2:22 . . . *made his* ***f*** *complete.*
Jas 2:24 . . . *not by* ***f*** *alone.*
Jas 2:26 . . . *so also* ***f*** *is dead*
Jas 5:15 . . . *prayer offered in* ***f*** *will heal*
1 Pet 1:21 . . . *you have placed your* ***f*** *and hope*
2 Pet 1:1 . . . *the same precious* ***f*** *we have.*

FAITHFUL (adj)
firm in adherence, utterly loyal
see also LOYAL, TRUSTWORTHY
Deut 7:9 . . . *He is the* ***f*** *God who keeps His*
1 Sam 2:9 . . . *will protect His* ***f*** *ones,*
1 Sam 20:14 . . . *me with the* ***f*** *love of the*
2 Sam 22:26 . . . *You show yourself* ***f;*** *to those*

1 Kgs 8:61 . . . You be completely ***f*** *to the*
1 Kgs 15:14 . . . remained completely ***f*** *to the*
2 Kgs 20:3 . . . have always been ***f*** *to You and*
Ps 18:25 . . . You show Yourself ***f;*** *to those*
Ps 71:22 . . . because You are ***f*** *to Your*
Ps 89:8 . . . You are entirely ***f.***
Ps 89:49 . . . with a ***f*** *pledge.*
Ps 143:1 . . . You are ***f*** *and righteous.*
Isa 38:3 . . . have always been ***f*** *to You and*
Hos 11:12 . . . God and is ***f*** *to the Holy One.*
Zech 8:3 . . . be called the ***F*** *City;*
Zech 8:8 . . . I will be ***f*** *and just toward*
Matt 24:45 . . . A ***f,*** *sensible*
Matt 25:21 . . . You have been ***f*** *in handling*
Matt 25:23 . . . My good and ***f*** *servant.*
Luke 12:42 . . . Lord replied, "A ***f,*** *sensible*
Luke 16:10 . . . If you are ***f*** *in little*
1 Cor 4:17 . . . My beloved and ***f*** *child in the*
2 Cor 1:18 . . . as God is ***f,*** *My word to you*
Eph 1:1 . . . who are ***f*** *followers of Christ*
Phil 2:17 . . . just like your ***f*** *service is*
Col 4:7 . . . brother and ***f*** *helper who*
Col 4:9 . . . Onesimus, a ***f*** *and beloved*
1 Thes 1:3 . . . we think of your ***f*** *work,*
1 Thes 5:24 . . . calls you is ***f.***
2 Thes 3:3 . . . But the Lord is ***f;*** *He will*
1 Tim 3:2 . . . He must be ***f*** *to his wife.*
1 Tim 3:11 . . . and be ***f*** *in everything they*
1 Tim 5:9 . . . old and was ***f*** *to her husband.*
2 Tim 4:7 . . . I have remained ***f.***
Heb 2:17 . . . merciful and ***f*** *High Priest*
Heb 3:2 . . . For he was ***f*** *to God, who*
Heb 8:9 . . . They did not remain ***f*** *to my*
Heb 13:4 . . . marriage, and remain ***f*** *to one*
1 Jn 1:9 . . . to Him, He is ***f*** *and just to*
Rev 1:5 . . . He is the ***f*** *witness to these*
Rev 2:10 . . . But if you remain ***f*** *even when*
Rev 3:14 . . . is the Amen—the ***f*** *and true*
Rev 17:14 . . . chosen and ***f*** *ones will be*

FAITHFULNESS (n)
the quality of steadfast loyalty or firm adherence to promises
Exod 34:6 . . . unfailing love and ***f.***
Ps 25:10 . . . with unfailing love and ***f***
Ps 36:5 . . . Your ***f*** *reaches beyond*
Ps 57:10 . . . Your ***f*** *reaches to the clouds.*
Ps 92:2 . . . Your ***f*** *in the evening,*
Ps 100:5 . . . ***f*** *continues to each*
Prov 14:22 . . . unfailing love and ***f.***
Prov 16:6 . . . love and ***f*** *make atonement*
Prov 20:28 . . . love and ***f*** *protect the king;*
Isa 38:18 . . . no longer hope in Your ***f.***
Lam 3:23 . . . Great is His ***f;***
Gal 5:22 . . . kindness, goodness, ***f,***
Eph 6:23 . . . give you love with ***f.***
2 Thes 1:4 . . . your endurance and ***f***
2 Tim 2:22 . . . pursue righteous living, ***f,***

FALL, FALLEN, FALLING (v)
to collapse; to drop down (wounded or dead); to become lower in degree or level; to come by assignment or inheritance; to descend; to stumble or stray (morally)
2 Sam 1:19 . . . the mighty heroes have ***f-en!***
Ps 37:24 . . . they will never ***f,***
Ps 69:9 . . . those who insult you have ***f-en*** *on*
Prov 10:8 . . . babbling fools ***f*** *flat on their*
Prov 24:17 . . . when your enemies ***f;***
Isa 14:12 . . . How you are ***f-en*** *from heaven,*
Matt 13:21 . . . They ***f*** *away as soon as*
Luke 10:18 . . . I saw Satan ***f*** *from heaven*
Rom 3:23 . . . we all ***f*** *short of*
Rom 14:13 . . . believer to stumble and ***f.***
Gal 5:4 . . . You have ***f-en*** *away from God's grace.*
2 Pet 1:10 . . . and you will never ***f*** *away.*
Jude 24 . . . able to keep you from ***f-ing*** *away*

FALSE (adj)
intentionally untrue; dishonest; misleading; unwise; faithless
Prov 12:17 . . . a ***f*** *witness tells lies.*
Isa 44:25 . . . I expose the ***f*** *prophets as*
Matt 24:11 . . . And many ***f*** *prophets will*
Mark 13:22 . . . For ***f*** *messiahs and* ***f***
2 Cor 11:13 . . . These people are ***f*** *apostles.*
Titus 1:11 . . . by their ***f*** *teaching.*
2 Pet 2:1 . . . were also ***f*** *prophets in Israel,*
1 Jn 4:1 . . . many ***f*** *prophets in the world.*
Rev 16:13 . . . and the ***f*** *prophet.*
Rev 19:20 . . . beast and his ***f*** *prophet were*
Rev 20:10 . . . the beast and the ***f*** *prophet.*

FAMILY, FAMILIES (n)
a household unit of related people, as in a clan
Josh 24:15 . . . my ***f,*** *we will serve the LORD.*
Ps 68:6 . . . God places the lonely in ***f-ies;***
Mark 3:25 . . . a ***f*** *splintered by feuding*
Luke 9:61 . . . let me say good-bye to my ***f.***
Luke 12:52 . . . ***f-ies*** *will be split apart,*
Gal 6:10 . . . to those in the ***f*** *of faith.*
Eph 2:19 . . . members of God's ***f.***
1 Tim 3:4 . . . manage his own ***f*** *well,*
Titus 1:11 . . . whole ***f-ies*** *away from the truth*
1 Jn 3:9 . . . who have been born into God's ***f***

FAST, FASTING (v)
to abstain from food
Ps 35:13 . . . denied myself by ***f-ing*** *for them,*
Joel 2:12 . . . Come with ***f-ing,*** *weeping,*
Matt 6:16 . . . when you ***f,*** *don't make it*
Acts 13:2 . . . worshiping the Lord and ***f-ing,***
Acts 14:23 . . . prayer and ***f-ing,*** *they turned*

FATHER, FATHERS (n)
male parent; ancestor(s); characteristic of a mentor or provider relationship; originator or creator
see also MOTHER, PARENT
Gen 2:24 . . . a man leaves his ***f*** *and mother*
Gen 17:4 . . . make you the ***f*** *of a multitude*
Exod 20:12 . . . Honor your ***f*** *and mother.*
Exod 21:15 . . . Anyone who strikes ***f*** *or*
2 Sam 7:14 . . . I will be his ***f,*** *and he*
Prov 10:1 . . . wise child brings joy to a ***f;***
Prov 23:22 . . . Listen to your ***f,***
Ezek 22:10 . . . sleep with their ***f-s'*** *wives*
Mal 4:6 . . . will turn the hearts of ***f-s***
Matt 10:37 . . . If you love your ***f*** *or mother*
Matt 15:4 . . . Honor your ***f*** *and mother,*
Matt 19:5 . . . a man leaves his ***f*** *and mother*
Matt 19:29 . . . or ***f*** *or mother or children*
Luke 1:17 . . . hearts of the ***f-s*** *to their*
Rom 4:11 . . . Abraham is the spiritual ***f***
Rom 4:16 . . . Abraham is the ***f*** *of all who*
Eph 5:31 . . . man leaves his ***f*** *and mother*
Eph 6:2 . . . Honor your ***f*** *and mother.*
Eph 6:4 . . . ***F-s,*** *do not provoke*
Col 3:21 . . . ***F-s,*** *do not aggravate*
Heb 12:7 . . . is never disciplined by its ***f?***
Heb 12:9 . . . earthly ***f-s*** *who disciplined*

FAVOR, FAVORS (n)
gracious kindness; approval from a superior; a special privilege or right granted or conceded
see also GRACE
Gen 6:8 . . . Noah found ***f*** *with the LORD.*
Exod 34:9 . . . if it is true that I have found ***f***
1 Sam 2:26 . . . and grew in ***f*** *with the LORD*
Prov 3:4 . . . you will find ***f*** *with both God*
Prov 18:22 . . . receives ***f*** *from the LORD.*
Prov 19:6 . . . Many seek ***f-s*** *from a ruler;*
Zech 11:7 . . . named one ***F*** *and the other*
Luke 1:30 . . . you have found ***f*** *with God!*
Luke 2:40 . . . and God's ***f*** *was on him.*
Luke 2:52 . . . and in ***f*** *with God*
Luke 4:19 . . . the time of the LORD's ***f***
Rom 11:7 . . . have not found the ***f*** *of God*
Phil 1:7 . . . with me the special ***f*** *of God,*

FEAR, FEARS (n)
dread or alarm in facing danger; profound reverence and awe
2 Sam 23:3 . . . who rules in the ***f*** *of God,*
Ps 2:11 . . . Serve the LORD with reverent ***f,***
Ps 34:4 . . . freed me from all my ***f-s.***
Prov 1:33 . . . untroubled by ***f*** *of harm.*
Heb 13:6 . . . will have no ***f.***

FEAR, FEARED, FEARING, FEARS (v)
to have reverential awe of God; to be afraid or apprehensive
Deut 6:13 . . . You must ***f*** *the LORD your*
Deut 8:6 . . . walking in His ways and ***f-ing***
Deut 13:4 . . . your God and ***f*** *Him alone.*
Deut 31:12 . . . learn to ***f*** *the LORD your God*
Josh 4:24 . . . might ***f*** *the LORD your God*
1 Sam 12:14 . . . if you ***f*** *and worship*
2 Chr 26:5 . . . taught him to ***f*** *God.*
Neh 5:15 . . . But because I ***f-ed*** *God,*
Neh 7:2 . . . a faithful man who ***f-ed*** *God*
Job 1:1 . . . He ***f-ed*** *God*
Job 1:8 . . . He ***f-s*** *God and stays away from*
Ps 34:7 . . . and defends all who ***f*** *Him.*
Ps 46:2 . . . not ***f*** *when earthquakes come*
Ps 61:5 . . . for those who ***f*** *your name.*
Ps 76:7 . . . You are greatly ***f-ed!***
Ps 103:17 . . . with those who ***f*** *Him.*
Ps 128:1 . . . joyful are those who ***f*** *the*
Prov 8:13 . . . All who ***f*** *the LORD will*
Prov 28:14 . . . those who ***f*** *to do wrong,*
Prov 31:30 . . . a woman who ***f-s*** *the LORD*
Isa 25:3 . . . nations will ***f*** *You.*
Jer 2:19 . . . your God and not to ***f*** *Him.*
Mal 3:16 . . . those who ***f-ed*** *the LORD spoke*
Mal 4:2 . . . for you who ***f*** *My name,*
2 Cor 7:1 . . . because we ***f*** *God.*
Rev 11:18 . . . and all who ***f*** *Your name,*

FEED, FEEDS (v)
to give food to; to eat; to provide something essential to the development, sustenance, maintenance, or operation of
Prov 15:14 . . . while the fool ***f-s*** *on trash.*
Prov 22:9 . . . because they ***f*** *the poor.*
Jer 50:19 . . . own land, to ***f*** *in the fields*
Matt 6:26 . . . your heavenly Father ***f-s*** *them.*
Matt 14:16 . . . you ***f*** *them.*
Matt 25:42 . . . and you didn't ***f*** *Me.*
John 6:57 . . . anyone who ***f-s*** *on Me will live*
John 21:15 . . . Then ***f*** *My lambs,*
John 21:17 . . . Then ***f*** *My sheep.*
Rom 12:20 . . . enemies are hungry, ***f*** *them.*

FEET (n)
see also FOOT
Ps 22:16 . . . pierced My hands and ***f.***
Ps 40:2 . . . He set My ***f*** *on solid ground*
Ps 73:2 . . . My ***f*** *were slipping,*
Ps 119:105 . . . a lamp to guide my ***f***
Isa 52:7 . . . are the ***f*** *of the messenger*
Matt 10:14 . . . shake its dust from your ***f***
Luke 24:39 . . . Look at My ***f.***
John 13:5 . . . began to wash the disciples' ***f,***
John 13:14 . . . wash each other's ***f.***
Rom 10:15 . . . beautiful are the ***f*** *of*
Rom 16:20 . . . crush Satan under Your ***f.***
1 Cor 15:25 . . . his enemies beneath His ***f.***
Heb 1:13 . . . a footstool under Your ***f.***
Heb 12:13 . . . a straight path for Your ***f***

FELLOWSHIP (n)
friendship; association; company; partnership
Gen 5:24 . . . walking in close ***f*** *with God.*
1 Cor 5:2 . . . remove this man from your ***f.***
2 Cor 13:14 . . . and the ***f*** *of the Holy Spirit*
1 Jn 1:3 . . . you may have ***f*** *with us.*

*1 Jn 1:3 . . . And our **f** is with the Father and*
*1 Jn 1:6 . . . we say we have **f** with God but*
*1 Jn 2:27 . . . remain in **f** with Christ.*

FIGHT, FIGHTING, FIGHTS (v)
to actively oppose or combat, as with weapons; to gain by struggle
*Exod 14:14 . . . LORD himself will **f** for you.*
*Josh 23:10 . . . the LORD your God **f-s** for you,*
*1 Sam 17:32 . . . I'll go **f** him!*
*1 Sam 25:28 . . . are **f-ing** the LORD's battles.*
*Neh 4:20 . . . our God will **f** for us!*
*Prov 28:25 . . . Greed causes **f-ing;***
*Ps 35:1 . . . **F** those who **f** against me.*
*Isa 49:25 . . . I will **f** those who **f** you,*
*1 Cor 15:32 . . . value was there in **f-ing** wild*
*Phil 1:27 . . . side by side, **f-ing** together for*
*1 Tim 6:12 . . . **F** the good fight*
*Jas 4:2 . . . so you **f** and wage war*

FILL, FILLED, FILLS (v)
to occupy the whole of; to supply fully; to spread through
*Gen 1:28 . . . **F** the earth and govern it.*
*Exod 34:6 . . . **f-ed** with unfailing love*
*1 Kgs 8:11 . . . presence of the LORD **f-ed** the*
*Ps 81:10 . . . and I will **f** it with good things.*
*Ps 107:9 . . . the thirsty and **f-s** the hungry*
*Ps 119:64 . . . unfailing love **f-s** the earth;*
*Ps 123:3 . . . have had our **f** of contempt.*
*Isa 6:3 . . . whole earth is **f-ed** with His glory!*
*Joel 2:13 . . . and **f-ed** with unfailing love.*
*Jon 4:2 . . . and **f-ed** with unfailing love.*
*Hag 2:7 . . . I will **f** this place with glory,*
*Luke 1:15 . . . be **f-ed** with the Holy Spirit,*
*Luke 1:41 . . . was **f-ed** with the Holy Spirit.*
*Luke 1:67 . . . **f-ed** with the Holy Spirit*
*Luke 2:40 . . . He was **f-ed** with wisdom,*
*Luke 24:49 . . . Holy Spirit comes and **f-s** you*
*Acts 2:4 . . . was **f-ed** with the Holy Spirit*
*Acts 2:28 . . . You will **f** me with the joy*
*Acts 4:8 . . . **f-ed** with the Holy Spirit,*
*Acts 4:31 . . . were all **f-ed** with the Holy Spirit.*
*Acts 9:17 . . . be **f-ed** with the Holy Spirit.*
*Acts 13:9 . . . was **f-ed** with the Holy Spirit,*
*Rom 5:5 . . . Holy Spirit to **f** our hearts*
*Rom 15:13 . . . **f** you completely with joy*
*Eph 1:23 . . . by Christ, who **f-s** all things*
*Eph 5:18 . . . be **f-ed** with the Holy Spirit,*
*Col 3:16 . . . in all its richness, **f** your lives.*

FIND, FINDS (v)
to attain or reach (a goal or conclusion); to discover by searching or effort; to experience
*1 Chr 28:9 . . . seek Him, you will **f** Him.*
*Job 23:3 . . . knew where to **f** God,*
*Prov 3:13 . . . the person who **f-s** wisdom,*
*Prov 8:17 . . . who search will surely **f** Me.*
*Prov 8:35 . . . For whoever **f-s** Me **f-s** life*
*Prov 11:27 . . . you will **f** favor;*
*Prov 31:10 . . . Who can **f** a virtuous and*
*Isa 55:6 . . . while you can **f** Him.*
*Jer 6:16 . . . will **f** rest for your souls.*
*Matt 7:7 . . . seeking, and you will **f**.*
*Matt 7:8 . . . Everyone who seeks, **f-s**.*
*Matt 10:39 . . . your life for Me, You will **f** it.*
*Luke 11:9 . . . and you will **f**.*
*Luke 11:10 . . . Everyone who seeks, **f-s**.*
*Luke 15:4 . . . that is lost until he **f-s** it?*
*Luke 15:8 . . . search carefully until she **f-s** it?*

FIRMAMENT (KJV)
*Gen 1:7 . . . this **space** to separate the waters*
*Ps 19:1 . . . The **skies** display his craftsmanship*
*Ezek 1:22 . . . a surface like the **sky**, glittering*
*Dan 12:3 . . . will shine as bright as the **sky***

FIRST (adj)
preceding all others in time, order, or importance
*Gen 1:5 . . . morning came, marking the **f** day.*
*Isa 44:6 . . . I am the **F** and the Last;*
*Isa 48:12 . . . God, the **F** and the Last.*
*Matt 22:38 . . . the **f** and greatest*
*Mark 9:35 . . . wants to be **f** must take last*
*Mark 13:10 . . . Good News must **f** be*
*Rom 1:16 . . . the Jew **f** and also the Gentile.*
*Rom 2:9 . . . the Jew **f** and also for the Gentile.*
*1 Cor 15:45 . . . The **f** man, Adam,*
*Eph 6:2 . . . the **f** commandment with a*
*1 Tim 2:13 . . . God made Adam **f**,*
*Heb 10:9 . . . He cancels the **f** covenant*
*1 Jn 4:19 . . . because He loved us **f**.*
*Rev 1:17 . . . I am the **F** and the Last.*
*Rev 22:13 . . . and the Omega, the **F** and the*

FIRSTBEGOTTEN (KJV)
*Heb 1:6 . . . His **firstborn Son** into the world*

FIRSTBORN (n)
eldest; the most prominent; the rightful heir
*Gen 25:34 . . . for his rights as the **f**.*
*Exod 11:5 . . . All the **f** sons will die*
*Exod 13:2 . . . every **f** among the Israelites.*
*Exod 34:19 . . . The **f** of every animal*
*Exod 34:20 . . . buy back every **f** son.*
*Ps 89:27 . . . I will make him my **f** son,*
*Mic 6:7 . . . sacrifice our **f** children to pay*
*Heb 1:6 . . . his **f** Son into the world,*
*Heb 12:23 . . . the assembly of God's **f***

FIRSTFRUITS (KJV)
*Exod 23:16 . . . the **first crops** of your harvest*
*Exod 23:19 . . . bring the **very best** of*
*Lev 2:14 . . . **first portion** of your harvest*
*Lev 23:10 . . . you harvest its **first crops**,*
*Num 28:26 . . . the **first** of your new grain*
*Rev 14:4 . . . as a **special offering** to God*

FISH, FISHING (n)
any of numerous cold-blooded aquatic vertebrates
*Jon 1:17 . . . had arranged for a great **f***
*Matt 12:40 . . . in the belly of the great **f***
*Luke 5:10 . . . you'll be **f-ing** for people!*
*Luke 9:13 . . . loaves of bread and two **f**,*
*John 6:9 . . . five barley loaves and two **f**.*

FISH, FISHED (v)
to attempt to catch fish
*Mark 1:16 . . . for they **f-ed** for a living.*
*Mark 1:17 . . . how to **f** for people!*

FISHERMEN
*Ezek 26:5 . . . a rock in the sea, a place for **f***

FISHERS (KJV)
*Isa 19:8 . . . **fishermen** will lament for lack of work*
*Jer 16:16 . . . **fishermen** who will catch*
*Matt 4:19 . . . show you **how to fish** for people*

FLOCK, FLOCKS (n)
a group of animals assembled or herded together; a group under the guidance of a leader
*Isa 40:11 . . . feed his **f** like a shepherd.*
*Jer 10:21 . . . and their **f-s** are scattered.*
*Jer 31:10 . . . as a shepherd does his **f**.*
*Zech 11:17 . . . who abandons the **f**!*
*Matt 26:31 . . . the **f** will be scattered.*
*Luke 2:8 . . . guarding their **f-s** of sheep.*
*Luke 12:32 . . . don't be afraid, little **f**.*
*John 10:16 . . . one **f** with one shepherd.*
*Acts 20:28 . . . shepherd God's **f**—*

FLOOD, FLOODS (n)
a rising and overflowing of a body of water; the destruction of the world by water during the time of Noah
*Gen 7:7 . . . the boat to escape the **f**—*
*Prov 27:4 . . . cruel, and wrath is like a **f**,*
*Matt 24:38 . . . In those days before the **f**,*
*Luke 6:49 . . . the **f-s** sweep down against*
*2 Pet 2:5 . . . ungodly people with a vast **f**.*

FOLLOW, FOLLOWED, FOLLOWING, FOLLOWS (v)
to pursue or run after; to imitate; to obey
*Deut 1:36 . . . because he has **f-ed** the LORD*
*Deut 5:32 . . . **f-ing** his instructions*
*Josh 14:14 . . . he wholeheartedly **f-ed** the*
*1 Kgs 3:3 . . . loved the LORD and **f-ed***
*2 Chr 10:14 . . . and **f-ed** the counsel*
*Prov 4:27 . . . feet from **f-ing** evil.*
*Prov 10:9 . . . those who **f** crooked paths*
*Isa 57:2 . . . For those who **f** godly paths*
*Isa 65:2 . . . But they **f** their own evil paths*
*Matt 4:20 . . . at once and **f-ed** Him.*
*Matt 7:24 . . . listens to My teaching and **f-s** it*
*Matt 8:19 . . . I will **f** you wherever you go.*
*Matt 8:22 . . . **F** Me now. Let the*
*Matt 9:9 . . . got up and **f-ed** Him.*
*Matt 16:24 . . . take up your cross, and **f***
*Matt 19:27 . . . given up everything to **f** You.*
*Matt 26:58 . . . Meanwhile, Peter **f-ed** Him*
*Mark 1:17 . . . Come, **f** Me, and I will show*
*Luke 9:23 . . . your cross daily, and **f** me.*
*Luke 17:23 . . . go out and **f** them.*
*Luke 18:43 . . . **f-ed** Jesus, praising God.*
*John 8:12 . . . If you **f** Me, you won't have to*
*John 10:4 . . . they **f** Him because they know*
*John 10:27 . . . know them, and they **f** Me.*
*John 12:26 . . . to be My disciple must **f** Me,*
*John 21:19 . . . Jesus told him, "**F** me."*
*1 Cor 1:12 . . . or "I **f** only Christ."*
*1 Cor 4:17 . . . of how I **f** Christ Jesus,*
*Gal 5:7 . . . held you back from **f-ing** the truth?*
*Gal 5:25 . . . **f** the Spirit's leading*
*Phil 2:12 . . . you always **f-ed** My instructions*
*Phil 3:17 . . . those who **f** our example.*
*2 Thes 3:6 . . . and don't **f** the tradition*
*1 Pet 2:21 . . . must **f** in His steps.*
*Rev 14:4 . . . pure as virgins, **f-ing** the Lamb*

FOLLY (KJV)
*Prov 14:18 . . . clothed with **foolishness***
*Prov 26:11 . . . so a fool repeats his **foolishness***
*Eccl 2:13 . . . Wisdom is better than **foolishness***
*Isa 9:17 . . . they all speak **foolishness***
*2 Tim 3:9 . . . will recognize what **fools** they are*

FOOL, FOOLS (n)
one deficient in intellectual, practical, or moral sense
*1 Sam 25:25 . . . He is a **f**, just as his name*
*Ps 14:1 . . . Only **f-s** say in their hearts,*
*Prov 6:32 . . . commits adultery is an utter **f**,*
*Prov 10:8 . . . babbling **f-s** fall flat on*
*Prov 10:23 . . . wrong is fun for a **f**,*
*Prov 17:7 . . . are not fitting for a **f**;*
*Prov 17:16 . . . to pay tuition to educate a **f**,*
*Prov 26:1 . . . associated with **f-s** than snow*
*Prov 26:7 . . . A proverb in the mouth of a **f***
*Prov 29:11 . . . **F-s** vent their anger,*
*Prov 29:20 . . . more hope for a **f** than for*
*Rom 1:22 . . . became utter **f-s**.*
*1 Cor 3:18 . . . need to become a **f** to be*
*2 Cor 11:21 . . . I'm talking like a **f** again—*
*Eph 5:15 . . . Don't live like **f-s**,*
*2 Tim 3:9 . . . will recognize what **f-s** they are,*

FOOLISH (adj)
lacking in sense, judgment, or discretion; irreverent
*Prov 26:4 . . . the **f** arguments of fools,*
*Prov 26:17 . . . else's argument is as **f***

*Rom 1:28 . . . abandoned them to their **f***
*1 Cor 1:18 . . . the cross is **f** to those who*
*1 Cor 1:27 . . . world considers **f** in order to*
*1 Cor 2:14 . . . It all sounds **f** to them*
*Eph 5:4 . . . Obscene stories, **f** talk,*
*1 Tim 6:20 . . . Avoid godless, **f** discussions*
*Titus 3:9 . . . not get involved in **f** discussions*

FOOT (n)
the end of the leg upon which an individual stands
see also FEET
*Josh 1:3 . . . Wherever you set **f**,*
*Matt 18:8 . . . with only one hand or one **f***
*Luke 4:11 . . . won't even hurt your **f***
*1 Cor 12:15 . . . If the **f** says,*
*Rev 10:2 . . . and His left **f** on the land.*

(FORE)FATHERS (KJV)
*Exod 10:6 . . . **ancestors** seen a plague like*
*Num 11:12 . . . swore to give their **ancestors***
*Jer 11:10 . . . the sins of their **f***
*Matt 23:32 . . . what your **ancestors** started*

FOREIGNER, FOREIGNERS (n)
nonresident, alien, or sojourner
see also STRANGER
*Exod 22:21 . . . not mistreat or oppress **f-s***
*Exod 23:9 . . . must not oppress **f-s**.*
*Lev 24:22 . . . and to the **f-s** living among you.*
*Neh 9:2 . . . separated themselves from all **f-s***
*Ps 119:19 . . . I am only a **f** in the land*
*Hos 7:8 . . . mingle with godless **f-s**,*
*Luke 17:18 . . . glory to God except this **f**?*
*1 Cor 14:11 . . . I will be a **f** to someone*
*Eph 2:19 . . . are no longer strangers and **f-s**.*
*1 Pet 1:1 . . . are living as **f-s** in the provinces*
*1 Pet 2:11 . . . temporary residents and **f-s***

FOREKNOW, FOREKNEW, FOREKNOWLEDGE (KJV)
*Acts 2:23 . . . God **knew what would happen***
*Rom 8:29 . . . God **knew** His people **in advance***
*Rom 11:2 . . . people whom He **chose from the very beginning***
*1 Pet 1:2 . . . Father **knew you and chose you** long ago*

FOREORDAINED (KJV)
*1 Pet 1:20 . . . **chose** him **as** your ransom long before*

FOREVER (adv)
for a limitless time; continually
see also ETERNAL, EVERLASTING
*Gen 3:22 . . . they will live **f**!*
*Gen 17:8 . . . be their possession **f**,*
*2 Sam 7:26 . . . name be honored **f***
*1 Chr 17:24 . . . be established and honored **f***
*1 Chr 29:10 . . . be praised **f** and ever!*
*Ezra 9:12 . . . prosperity to your children **f**.*
*Ps 9:7 . . . the LORD reigns **f**,*
*Ps 21:4 . . . of His life stretch on **f**.*
*Ps 28:9 . . . in Your arms **f**.*
*Ps 37:28 . . . keep them safe **f**,*
*Ps 61:8 . . . sing praises to Your name **f***
*Ps 73:26 . . . He is mine **f**.*
*Ps 79:13 . . . will thank You **f** and ever,*
*Ps 86:12 . . . glory to Your name **f**,*
*Ps 92:8 . . . will be exalted **f**.*
*Ps 100:5 . . . unfailing love continues **f**,*
*Ps 103:17 . . . the LORD remains **f** with*
*Ps 107:1 . . . faithful love endures **f**.*
*Ps 110:4 . . . are a priest **f***
*Ps 111:8 . . . They are **f** true,*
*Ps 112:9 . . . be remembered **f**.*
*Ps 119:152 . . . laws will last **f**.*
*Ps 146:6 . . . every promise **f**.*
*Isa 32:17 . . . and confidence **f**.*
*Isa 51:6 . . . but My salvation lasts **f**.*
*Isa 60:15 . . . make you beautiful **f**,*
*Isa 63:12 . . . making himself famous **f**?*
*Jer 25:5 . . . you and your ancestors **f**.*
*Dan 2:44 . . . and it will stand **f**.*
*Dan 4:3 . . . kingdom will last **f**, His rule*
*Dan 7:27 . . . kingdom will last **f**,*
*John 6:51 . . . eats this bread will live **f**;*
*1 Cor 13:8 . . . But love will last **f**!*
*1 Cor 13:13 . . . Three things will last **f**—*
*1 Cor 15:42 . . . will be raised to live **f**.*
*1 Cor 15:50 . . . inherit what will last **f**.*
*2 Cor 4:17 . . . and will last **f**!*
*2 Cor 4:18 . . . cannot see will last **f**.*
*1 Thes 4:17 . . . will be with the Lord **f**.*
*2 Thes 1:9 . . . destruction, **f** separated*
*Heb 5:6 . . . a priest **f** in the order*
*Heb 7:17 . . . a priest **f** in the order*
*Heb 7:24 . . . Jesus lives **f**,*
*Heb 9:12 . . . secured our redemption **f**.*
*Heb 13:8 . . . yesterday, today, and **f**.*
*1 Pet 1:25 . . . word of the Lord remains **f**.*
*1 Jn 2:17 . . . will live **f**.*
*Rev 22:5 . . . they will reign **f** and ever.*

FORGAVE (v)
see also FORGIVE
*Ps 78:38 . . . was merciful and **f** their sins*
*Luke 7:42 . . . so He kindly **f** them both,*
*Eph 1:7 . . . His Son and **f** our sins.*
*Col 1:14 . . . our freedom and **f** our sins.*
*Col 2:13 . . . with Christ, for He **f** all our*

FORGIVE, FORGIVEN, FORGIVES, FORGIVING (v)
to pardon or acquit of sins
see also FORGAVE
*Gen 50:17 . . . Please **f** your brothers*
*Exod 23:21 . . . He will not **f** your rebellion.*
*Exod 34:7 . . . I **f** iniquity, rebellion,*
*Exod 34:9 . . . but please **f** our iniquity and*
*Num 14:18 . . . **f-ing** every kind of sin*
*Num 14:19 . . . just as You have **f-n** them*
*1 Sam 3:14 . . . never be **f-n** by sacrifices*
*1 Kgs 8:34 . . . hear from heaven and **f***
*Ps 65:3 . . . by our sins, You **f** them all.*
*Ps 79:9 . . . Save us and **f** our sins*
*Ps 86:5 . . . so good, so ready to **f**,*
*Ps 103:3 . . . He **f-s** all my sins*
*Prov 17:9 . . . when a fault is **f-n**,*
*Isa 22:14 . . . you will never be **f-n** for this*
*Isa 38:17 . . . and **f-n** all my sins.*
*Isa 55:7 . . . for He will **f** generously.*
*Jer 31:34 . . . I will **f** their wickedness,*
*Dan 9:19 . . . O LORD, hear. O LORD, **f**.*
*Hos 14:2 . . . **F** all our sins and*
*Matt 6:12 . . . and **f** us our sins,*
*Matt 6:14 . . . If you **f** those who sin*
*Matt 6:15 . . . if you refuse to **f** others,*
*Matt 9:6 . . . authority on earth to **f** sins.*
*Matt 18:21 . . . how often should I **f***
*Matt 26:28 . . . to **f** the sins of many.*
*Mark 2:7 . . . Only God can **f** sins!*
*Mark 2:10 . . . authority on earth to **f** sins.*
*Mark 3:29 . . . will never be **f-n**.*
*Mark 11:25 . . . first **f** anyone you are*
*Mark 11:25 . . . will **f** your sins,*
*Luke 5:21 . . . Only God can **f** sins!*
*Luke 5:24 . . . authority on earth to **f** sins.*
*Luke 6:37 . . . **F** others, and you will be*
*Luke 7:47 . . . a person who is **f-n** little*
*Luke 7:49 . . . He goes around **f-ing** sins?*
*Luke 11:4 . . . **f** us our sins, as we*
*Luke 17:3 . . . if there is repentance, **f**.*
*Luke 17:4 . . . asks forgiveness, you must **f**.*
*Luke 23:34 . . . Father, **f** them,*
*John 20:23 . . . If you **f** anyone's sins,*
*Acts 5:31 . . . repent of their sins and be **f-n**.*
*Acts 8:22 . . . Perhaps He will **f** your evil*
*Rom 4:5 . . . faith in God who **f-s** sinners.*
*Rom 4:7 . . . whose disobedience is **f-n**,*
*2 Cor 2:7 . . . time to **f** and comfort*
*2 Cor 2:10 . . . When you **f** this man,*
*Col 3:13 . . . so you must **f** others.*
*Heb 8:12 . . . I will **f** their wickedness,*
*1 Jn 1:9 . . . is faithful and just to **f** us*

FORGIVENESS (n)
aquittal or pardon of sins
see also ATONEMENT, MERCY
*Neh 9:17 . . . you are a God of **f**,*
*Luke 24:47 . . . There is **f** of sins for all*
*Acts 13:38 . . . this man Jesus there is **f***
*Rom 5:15 . . . His gift of **f** to many*
*Heb 9:22 . . . of blood, there is no **f**.*
*Jas 5:20 . . . bring about the **f** of many sins.*

FORNICATION (KJV)
*Isa 23:17 . . . again **be a prostitute** to all kingdoms*
*Matt 19:9 . . . wife has been **unfaithful***
*1 Cor 6:18 . . . **sexual immorality** is a sin*
*1 Cor 5:1 . . . the **sexual immorality** going on*
*Jude 1:7 . . . which were filled with **immorality***

FORTRESS (n)
a fortified place; a place of security or survival
see also REFUGE
*2 Sam 22:2 . . . my **f**, and my savior;*
*Ps 27:1 . . . The LORD is my **f**,*
*Ps 71:3 . . . my rock and my **f**.*
*Ps 144:2 . . . and my **f**, my tower of safety,*
*Prov 18:10 . . . LORD is a strong **f**;*
*Zeph 3:6 . . . devastating their **f** walls and*

FOUNDATION (n)
basis upon which something is built, supported, or added to; substructure
*Prov 1:7 . . . Fear of the LORD is the **f***
*Prov 9:10 . . . the LORD is the **f** of wisdom.*
*Isa 28:16 . . . placing a **f** stone in Jerusalem,*
*Luke 6:49 . . . a house without a **f**.*
*Eph 2:20 . . . built on the **f** of the apostles*
*1 Tim 3:15 . . . pillar and **f** of the truth.*
*2 Tim 2:19 . . . stands firm like a **f** stone*
*Heb 1:10 . . . you laid the **f** of the earth*

FREE (adj)
not bound, confined, or detained by force; without restraint, inhibition, or cost; possessing the rights of citizenship
*John 8:32 . . . the truth will set you **f**.*
*John 8:36 . . . sets you **f**, you are truly **f**.*
*Rom 6:7 . . . we were set **f** from the power*
*Rom 6:18 . . . you are **f** from your slavery*
*Gal 3:28 . . . slave or **f**, male and female.*
*Jas 1:25 . . . the perfect law that sets you **f**,*
*1 Pet 2:16 . . . For you are **f**, yet*

FREE, FREED, FREES (v)
to relieve or rid of what restrains, confines, restricts, or embarrasses
*Ps 116:16 . . . **f-d** me from my chains.*
*Ps 146:7 . . . The LORD **f-s** the prisoners.*
*Isa 61:1 . . . prisoners will be **f-d**.*
*Rom 3:24 . . . He **f-d** us from the penalty*
*1 Cor 1:30 . . . and He **f-d** us from sin.*
*Rev 1:5 . . . and has **f-d** us from our sins*

FREEDOM (n)
liberation from slavery, restraint, or the power of another
*Ps 119:45 . . . I will walk in **f**, for I have*
*2 Cor 3:17 . . . the Lord is, there is **f**.*
*Gal 2:4 . . . take away the **f** we have in Christ*
*Gal 4:5 . . . sent Him to buy **f** for us*
*Gal 5:13 . . . don't use your **f** to satisfy*
*Eph 1:7 . . . purchased our **f** with the blood*
*1 Pet 2:16 . . . don't use your **f** as an excuse*

FRIEND, FRIENDS (n)
intimate associate; a favored companion
*Prov 16:28 . . . separates the best of **f-s.***
*Prov 17:9 . . . on it separates close **f-s.***
*Prov 20:6 . . . Many will say they are loyal **f-s,***
*Prov 27:6 . . . Wounds from a sincere **f** are*
*Prov 28:7 . . . those with wild **f-s** bring shame*
*Prov 29:5 . . . To flatter **f-s** is to lay a trap*
*Isa 41:8 . . . from Abraham my **f,***
*Zech 13:6 . . . was wounded at my **f-s'** house!*
*John 11:3 . . . Lord, Your dear **f** is very sick.*
*John 15:13 . . . one's life for one's **f-s.***
*John 15:14 . . . You are My **f-s** if you do*
*John 15:15 . . . Now you are My **f-s,***
*John 19:12 . . . You are no '**f** of Caesar.'*
*Jas 2:23 . . . even called the **f** of God.*
*Jas 4:4 . . . want to be a **f** of the world,*

FRIENDSHIP (n)
association of familiarity and companionship
*Prov 3:32 . . . he offers his **f** to the godly.*
*Rom 5:10 . . . since our **f** with God was*
*Jas 4:4 . . . you realize that **f** with the world*

FRUIT (n)
a product of plant growth; product or result
*Ps 1:3 . . . bearing **f** each season.*
*Isa 11:1 . . . new Branch bearing **f** from*
*Dan 4:12 . . . loaded with **f** for all to eat.*
*Matt 3:10 . . . not produce good **f** will be*
*Matt 7:20 . . . can identify a tree by its **f,***
*Matt 12:33 . . . is bad, its **f** will be bad.*
*John 15:2 . . . that doesn't produce **f,***
*John 15:16 . . . go and produce lasting **f,***
*Gal 5:22 . . . produces this kind of **f***
*Phil 1:11 . . . the **f** of your salvation—*
*2 Tim 2:6 . . . first to enjoy the **f***
*Rev 22:2 . . . bearing twelve crops of **f,***

FULFILL, FULFILLED, FULFILLS (v)
to complete or perform as promised; to measure up or satisfy
*Ps 57:2 . . . to God who will **f** His purpose*
*Dan 9:4 . . . You always **f** Your covenant*
*Matt 2:15 . . . This **f-ed** what the Lord had*
*Matt 2:23 . . . This **f-ed** what the prophets had*
*Matt 13:35 . . . This **f-ed** what God had spoken*
*Matt 27:9 . . . This **f-ed** the prophecy of*
*Luke 4:21 . . . has been **f-ed** this very day!*
*Luke 24:44 . . . in the Psalms must be **f-ed.***
*John 18:9 . . . this to **f** His own statement:*
*John 19:28 . . . and to **f** Scripture He said,*
*Acts 1:16 . . . Scriptures had to be **f-ed***
*Rom 3:31 . . . do we truly **f** the law.*
*Rom 13:8 . . . You will **f** the requirements*
*Rom 13:10 . . . love **f-s** the requirements*
*Eph 1:9 . . . plan to **f** His own good pleasure.*

FULLNESS (n)
the quality or state of containing all that is wanted, needed, or possible
*Eph 3:19 . . . with all the **f** of life and*
*Col 1:19 . . . God in all His **f** was pleased*
*Col 2:9 . . . lives all the **f** of God*

FURY (n)
wrath; fierceness; rage
*Exod 15:7 . . . You unleash Your blazing **f;***
*Deut 29:28 . . . In great anger and **f***
*Jer 32:37 . . . will scatter them in My **f.***

FUTURE (n)
time that is to come; what is going to happen
*Num 24:14 . . . do to your people in the **f.***
*Ps 31:15 . . . My **f** is in Your hands.*
*Ps 37:37 . . . a wonderful **f** awaits those*
*Isa 42:9 . . . tell you the **f** before it happens.*
*Isa 46:10 . . . can tell you the **f** before it*
*Jer 29:11 . . . to give you a **f** and a hope.*
*Jer 31:17 . . . There is hope for your **f,***

G

GALILEE (n)
a Roman province of Palestine during the time of Jesus
*Isa 9:1 . . . a time in the future when **G***
*Matt 4:15 . . . beyond the Jordan River, in **G***
*Matt 26:32 . . . I will go ahead of You to **G***
*Matt 28:10 . . . My brothers to leave for **G,***

GATE, GATES (n)
opening in a (city) wall or fence, consisting of a door and protected by defensive structures (as towers); the place of judicial decisions, town criers, and marketplace trade; entrance
*Esth 6:10 . . . sits at the **g** of the palace.*
*Ps 24:7 . . . Open up, ancient **g-s!***
*Ps 100:4 . . . Enter his **g-s** with thanksgiving;*
*Isa 62:10 . . . Go out through the **g-s!***
*Matt 7:13 . . . only through the narrow **g.***
*John 10:1 . . . going through the **g,***
*John 10:2 . . . who enters through the **g***
*John 10:7 . . . I am the **g** for the sheep.*
*Heb 13:12 . . . died outside the city **g-s***
*Rev 21:21 . . . **g-s** were made of pearls—*
*Rev 21:21 . . . each **g** from a single pearl!*

GENERATION, GENERATIONS (n)
the whole body of individuals born about the same time (=nation or racial group); the period of time during which those individuals lived (also, age or era); offspring
*Gen 17:7 . . . from generation to **g.***
*Exod 20:6 . . . love for a thousand **g-s***
*Num 32:13 . . . the entire **g** that sinned*
*Judg 2:10 . . . After that **g** died,*
*1 Chr 16:15 . . . to a thousand **g-s.***
*Ps 71:18 . . . Your power to this new **g,***
*Ps 100:5 . . . continues to each **g.***
*Ps 102:12 . . . endure to every **g.***
*Ps 102:18 . . . recorded for future **g-s,***
*Ps 105:8 . . . to a thousand **g-s.***
*Ps 119:90 . . . extends to every **g,***
*Ps 145:4 . . . Let each **g** tell its children*
*Ps 146:10 . . . throughout the **g-s.***
*Prov 27:24 . . . not be passed to the next **g.***
*Isa 41:4 . . . summoning each new **g***
*Lam 5:19 . . . from generation to **g.***
*Joel 1:3 . . . down from **g** to generation.*
*Matt 12:39 . . . Only an evil, adulterous **g***
*Mark 13:30 . . . this **g** will not pass*
*Luke 1:48 . . . all **g-s** will call Me blessed.*
*Luke 11:29 . . . This evil **g** keeps asking Me*
*Acts 2:40 . . . this crooked **g!***
*Eph 3:5 . . . did not reveal it to previous **g-s,***
*Eph 3:21 . . . through all **g-s** forever and ever!*

GENEROSITY (n)
the quality or fact of being magnanimous, kindly, or openhanded; abundance
*Acts 2:46 . . . meals with great joy and **g**—*
*2 Cor 9:10 . . . a great harvest of **g** in you.*
*Eph 4:7 . . . through the **g** of Christ.*
*Phlm 6 . . . put into action the **g** that*

GENEROUS (adj)
magnanimous, kindly; liberal in giving; abundant
*Deut 15:8 . . . Instead, be **g** and lend*
*Ps 37:26 . . . godly always give **g** loans to*
*2 Cor 9:6 . . . will get a **g** crop.*
*1 Tim 6:18 . . . **g** to those in need,*

GENTILE, GENTILES (n)
non-Jewish individuals or nations, often connoting heathens or pagans
see also NATION(S)
*Isa 49:6 . . . I will make you a light to the **G-s,***
*Luke 21:24 . . . period of the **G-s** comes*
*Acts 10:45 . . . out on the **G-s,** too.*
*Acts 14:27 . . . faith to the **G-s,** too.*
*Acts 15:14 . . . God first visited the **G-s***
*Acts 21:25 . . . As for the **G** believers,*
*Acts 28:28 . . . also been offered to the **G-s,***
*Rom 1:16 . . . and also the **G.***
*Rom 2:9 . . . and also for the **G.***
*Rom 3:9 . . . all people, whether Jews or **G-s,***
*Rom 3:29 . . . God of the **G-s?***
*Rom 10:12 . . . Jew and **G** are the same*
*Rom 11:11 . . . available to the **G-s.***
*Rom 15:9 . . . so that the **G-s** might give glory*
*Rom 15:27 . . . **G-s** received the spiritual*
*Gal 2:2 . . . preaching to the **G-s.***
*Gal 2:8 . . . apostle to the **G-s.***
*Gal 2:9 . . . keep preaching to the **G-s,***
*Gal 3:8 . . . God would declare the **G-s** to be*
*Gal 3:14 . . . blessed the **G-s** with the same*
*Gal 3:28 . . . no longer Jew or **G,** slave or*
*Eph 3:8 . . . the privilege of telling the **G-s***
*Col 3:11 . . . a Jew or a **G,** circumcised or*

GENTLENESS (n)
mildness of manners or disposition
*Gal 5:23 . . . **g,** and self-control.*
*Col 3:12 . . . kindness, humility, **g,** and*
*1 Tim 6:11 . . . perseverance, and **g.***

GETHSEMANE (n)
the garden where Jesus often went for prayer, rest, or fellowship; the site where Judas betrayed Jesus before the crucifixion
*Matt 26:36 . . . to the olive grove called **G,***
*Mark 14:32 . . . to the olive grove called **G,***

GIFT, GIFTS (n)
a present from people to people (often a bribe); a sacrifice from people to God; anything given voluntarily or at no cost; that which is given from God, enabling or empowering his people
*Prov 18:16 . . . Giving a **g** can open doors;*
*Matt 2:11 . . . and gave him **g-s** of gold,*
*Luke 11:13 . . . how to give good **g-s** to your*
*Rom 4:16 . . . given as a free **g.***
*Rom 5:15 . . . and God's gracious **g.***
*Rom 6:23 . . . free **g** of God is eternal*
*Rom 11:29 . . . For God's **g-s** and His call*
*1 Cor 12:4 . . . different kinds of spiritual **g-s,***
*1 Cor 12:7 . . . A spiritual **g** is given*
*1 Cor 12:31 . . . the most helpful **g-s.***
*2 Cor 9:5 . . . I want it to be a willing **g,***
*2 Cor 9:15 . . . Thank God for this **g***
*Gal 2:9 . . . recognized the **g** God had*
*Eph 2:8 . . . it is a **g** from God.*
*Eph 4:8 . . . and gave **g-s** to His people.*
*2 Tim 1:6 . . . the spiritual **g** God gave you*
*Heb 2:4 . . . **g-s** of the Holy Spirit*
*1 Pet 3:7 . . . equal partner in God's **g***
*1 Pet 4:10 . . . of spiritual **g-s.***

GIVE, GIVEN, GIVES, GIVING (v)
to grant, bestow, convey, offer, provide, or designate; to yield or produce; to suffer the loss of (life)
*Exod 30:15 . . . poor must not **g** less.*
*1 Sam 1:28 . . . **g-ing** him to the LORD,*
*Ps 112:9 . . . share freely and **g** generously*
*Ps 119:130 . . . your word **g-s** light,*
*Prov 21:26 . . . love to **g!***
*Prov 23:26 . . . O my son, **g** me your heart.*
*Isa 9:6 . . . a Son is **g-n** to us.*
*Matt 7:11 . . . heavenly Father **g** good gifts*
*Matt 16:19 . . . And I will **g** you the keys*
*Matt 22:30 . . . marry nor be **g-n** in marriage.*
*Mark 6:7 . . . two by two, **g-ing** them authority*
*Luke 11:13 . . . know how to **g** good gifts to*
*Luke 14:33 . . . My disciple without **g-ing** up*
*Luke 22:19 . . . body, which is **g-n** for you.*
*John 1:17 . . . the law was **g-n** through Moses,*
*John 5:21 . . . so the Son **g-s** life to anyone*

John 13:34 . . . So now I am **g-ing** you a new
John 14:27 . . . And the peace I **g** is a gift
Acts 5:32 . . . Spirit, who is **g-n** by God
Acts 14:3 . . . was true by **g-ing** them power to
Acts 15:8 . . . Gentiles by **g-ing** them the Holy
Acts 20:35 . . . is more blessed to **g** than to
Rom 2:7 . . . He will **g** eternal life
Rom 5:5 . . . because He has **g-n** us the Holy
Rom 8:32 . . . won't He also **g** us everything
Rom 10:12 . . . Lord, who **g-s** generously
Rom 12:8 . . . is giving, **g** generously.
Rom 14:12 . . . each of us will **g** a personal
1 Cor 9:17 . . . for God has **g-n** me this sacred
1 Cor 11:24 . . . body, which is **g-n** for you.
1 Cor 15:57 . . . thank God! He **g-s** us victory
2 Cor 3:6 . . . the Spirit **g-s** life.
2 Cor 8:6 . . . this ministry of **g-ing.**
2 Cor 9:7 . . . how much to **g.**
Eph 4:7 . . . However, He has **g-n** each one of
Eph 4:28 . . . and then **g** generously to
1 Thes 4:8 . . . rejecting God, who **g-s**
1 Tim 6:17 . . . God, who richly **g-s** us all we
1 Jn 4:13 . . . And God has **g-n** us his Spirit

GLAD (adj)
joyful or happy, often with shouts
Ps 16:9 . . . my heart is **g,** and I rejoice.
Ps 32:11 . . . LORD and be **g,** all you who
Ps 69:32 . . . at work and be **g.**
Ps 97:1 . . . coastlands be **g.**
Ps 104:15 . . . wine to make them **g,**
Ps 118:24 . . . will rejoice and be **g** in it.
Prov 10:8 . . . The wise are **g** to be
Prov 27:11 . . . make my heart **g.**
Isa 35:1 . . . and desert will be **g**
Zeph 3:14 . . . O Israel! Be **g** and rejoice
Matt 5:12 . . . Be very **g!**
John 11:15 . . . for your sakes, I'm **g** I wasn't
Acts 13:48 . . . they were very **g**
1 Cor 12:26 . . . the parts are **g.**
2 Cor 2:2 . . . will make me **g?**
Rev 19:7 . . . Let us be **g** and rejoice,

GLORIFY, GLORIFIED, GLORIFIES, GLORIFYING (v)
to bestow honor or praise (as in worship); to magnify
see also EXALT, HONOR
Ps 147:12 . . . **G** the LORD,
Isa 26:8 . . . desire is to **g** Your name.
Isa 42:12 . . . the whole world **g** the LORD;
Dan 4:37 . . . praise and **g** and honor the
Luke 2:20 . . . their flocks, **g-ing** and praising
John 8:50 . . . no wish to **g** Myself, God is
John 13:31 . . . God will be **g-ied**
John 17:1 . . . **G** Your Son so
John 21:19 . . . of death He would **g** God.
2 Cor 8:19 . . . a service that **g-ies** the Lord
Eph 1:14 . . . would praise and **g** Him.
Rev 15:4 . . . You, Lord, and **g** Your name?

GLORIOUS (adj)
possessing or deserving special honor; splendid or magnificent
Exod 15:6 . . . O LORD, is **g** in power.
Exod 33:18 . . . show me Your **g** presence.
Deut 32:3 . . . the LORD; how **g** is our God!
1 Chr 16:28 . . . the LORD is **g** and strong.
Neh 9:5 . . . prayed: "May Your **g** name be
Job 37:5 . . . God's voice is **g** in the
Ps 45:3 . . . You are so **g,** so majestic!
Ps 76:4 . . . You are **g** and more majestic
Ps 96:3 . . . Publish his **g** deeds among the
Ps 149:9 . . . This is the **g** privilege of
Isa 55:5 . . . of Israel, have made You **g.**
Isa 63:15 . . . from Your holy, **g** home,
Dan 8:9 . . . east and toward the **g** land of
Dan 11:45 . . . between the **g** holy mountain
Matt 19:28 . . . sits upon His **g** throne,
Acts 2:20 . . . that great and **g** day of the
Acts 7:2 . . . Our **g** God appeared to
Rom 1:23 . . . worshiping the **g,** ever-living
Rom 3:23 . . . of God's **g** standard.
Rom 8:21 . . . children in **g** freedom from
2 Cor 3:9 . . . how much more **g** is the new
2 Cor 3:10 . . . first glory was not **g** at all
2 Cor 3:18 . . . into His **g** image.
Eph 1:6 . . . God for the **g** grace He has
Eph 1:17 . . . asking God, the **g** Father of
Eph 3:16 . . . that from His **g,** unlimited
Eph 5:27 . . . himself as a **g** church without
Phil 3:21 . . . them into **g** bodies like His
Phil 4:19 . . . from His **g** riches, which have
Col 1:11 . . . with all His **g** power so you
Jas 2:1 . . . faith in our **g** Lord Jesus
1 Pet 1:8 . . . with a **g,** inexpressible joy.
1 Pet 4:14 . . . for then the **g** Spirit of God
Jude 24 . . . into His **g** presence without a

GLORY (n)
honor bestowed; splendor or magnificence; a distinguishing quality, asset, or attribute; eternity;
Exod 16:10 . . . awesome **g** of the LORD
Num 14:21 . . . filled with the LORD's **g,**
Josh 7:19 . . . My son, give **g** to the LORD,
1 Sam 4:21 . . . said, "Israel's **g** is gone."
Ps 8:5 . . . them with **g** and honor.
Ps 19:1 . . . proclaim the **g** of God.
Ps 29:1 . . . LORD for His **g** and strength.
Ps 44:8 . . . O God, we give **g** to You
Ps 57:11 . . . May Your **g** shine over all the
Ps 71:8 . . . I declare Your **g** all day
Ps 86:12 . . . I will give **g** to Your name
Ps 108:5 . . . May Your **g** shine over all the
Ps 145:12 . . . the majesty and **g** of Your
Prov 16:31 . . . is a crown of **g;** it is gained
Isa 6:3 . . . earth is filled with His **g!**
Isa 24:16 . . . songs that give **g** to the
Isa 35:2 . . . display His **g,** the splendor
Isa 42:8 . . . not give My **g** to anyone else,
Isa 48:11 . . . not share My **g** with idols!
Isa 66:11 . . . Drink deeply of her **g** even as an
Isa 66:19 . . . they will declare My **g** to the
Ezek 44:4 . . . saw that the **g** of the LORD
Matt 16:27 . . . angels in the **g** of His Father
Matt 25:31 . . . comes in His **g,** and all the
Mark 13:26 . . . great power and **g.**
Luke 2:14 . . . **G** to God in highest heaven,
Luke 9:26 . . . and in the **g** of the Father
Luke 9:32 . . . they saw Jesus' **g** and the two
Luke 21:27 . . . power and great **g.**
John 1:14 . . . have seen His **g,** the glory of
John 7:39 . . . not yet entered into His **g.**
John 11:40 . . . you would see God's **g** if
John 12:23 . . . enter into His **g.**
John 12:41 . . . the Messiah's **g.**
John 14:13 . . . the Son can bring **g** to the
John 16:14 . . . will bring Me **g** by telling
John 17:22 . . . given them the **g** you gave me,
Acts 3:13 . . . who has brought **g** to His
Rom 2:7 . . . seeking after the **g** and honor
Rom 2:10 . . . there will be **g** and honor and
Rom 3:7 . . . and brings Him more **g?**
Rom 4:20 . . . in this He brought **g** to God.
Rom 8:17 . . . heirs of God's **g.**
Rom 8:18 . . . compared to the **g** He will
Rom 8:30 . . . gave them His **g.**
Rom 9:4 . . . God revealed His **g** to them.
Rom 9:23 . . . riches of His **g** shine even
Rom 9:23 . . . in advance for **g.**
Rom 15:6 . . . giving praise and **g** to God,
Rom 15:9 . . . Gentiles might give **g** to God
Rom 16:27 . . . All **g** to the only
1 Cor 2:7 . . . for our ultimate **g** before the
1 Cor 10:31 . . . all for the **g** of God.
1 Cor 15:43 . . . will be raised in **g.**
2 Cor 1:20 . . . to God for His **g.**
2 Cor 3:7 . . . shone with the **g** of God, even
2 Cor 3:10 . . . In fact, that first **g** was not
2 Cor 4:4 . . . about the **g** of Christ, who is
2 Cor 4:17 . . . for us a **g** that vastly
Eph 1:12 . . . bring praise and **g** to God.
Phil 1:11 . . . will bring much **g** and praise
Phil 2:11 . . . is Lord, to the **g** of God the
Phil 4:20 . . . Now all **g** to God our
1 Thes 2:12 . . . Kingdom and **g.**
2 Thes 2:14 . . . share in the **g** of our Lord
1 Tim 1:17 . . . All honor and **g** to God
1 Tim 3:16 . . . to heaven in **g.**
2 Tim 4:18 . . . All **g** to God forever
Titus 2:13 . . . day when the **g** of our great God
Heb 1:3 . . . God's own **g** and expresses the
Heb 2:9 . . . crowned with **g** and honor.
Heb 3:3 . . . far more **g** than Moses, just
1 Pet 1:7 . . . much praise and **g** and honor
1 Pet 1:21 . . . gave Him great **g.**
1 Pet 5:4 . . . of never-ending **g** and honor.
2 Pet 1:3 . . . means of His marvelous **g** and
2 Pet 1:17 . . . from the majestic **g** of God
Jude 25 . . . All **g,** majesty, power,
Rev 4:9 . . . beings give **g** and honor and
Rev 4:11 . . . God, to receive **g** and honor
Rev 5:12 . . . honor and **g** and blessing.
Rev 5:13 . . . and honor and **g** and power
Rev 11:13 . . . terrified and gave **g** to the
Rev 16:9 . . . God and give him **g.**
Rev 21:11 . . . shone with the **g** of God and
Rev 21:23 . . . for the **g** of God
Rev 21:26 . . . will bring their **g** and honor

GOD-BREATHED (KJV)
2 Tim 3:16 . . . All Scripture is **inspired by God**

GODLINESS (n)
devotion to God; piety
see also RIGHTEOUSNESS
Prov 16:8 . . . Better to have little, with **g,**
1 Tim 4:8 . . . but training for **g** is much
1 Tim 5:4 . . . to show **g** at home
1 Tim 6:6 . . . Yet true **g** with contentment

GOLD (n)
a valuable yellow malleable metal especially used in coins and jewelry
1 Kgs 20:3 . . . Your silver and **g** are mine,
Ps 19:10 . . . more desirable than **g,**
Ps 119:127 . . . even the finest **g.**
Prov 3:14 . . . are better than **g.**
Matt 2:11 . . . gifts of **g,** frankincense,
Rev 3:18 . . . advise you to buy **g** from me—

GOLGOTHA (n)
a hill just outside Jerusalem; the place where Jesus was crucified
Matt 27:33 . . . a place called **G**
Mark 15:22 . . . a place called **G**
John 19:17 . . . (in Hebrew, **G**).

GOOD (n)
something that is excellent, profitable, or morally right; advancement of prosperity or well-being; something useful or beneficial
Gen 2:9 . . . the knowledge of **g** and evil.
Gen 3:22 . . . knowing both **g** and evil.
Gen 50:20 . . . God intended it all for **g.**
1 Sam 26:23 . . . reward for doing **g** and for
Ps 14:1 . . . not one of them does **g!**
Ps 53:3 . . . No one does **g,** not a single
Prov 3:27 . . . Do not withhold **g** from those
Prov 11:27 . . . If you search for **g,** you will
Prov 31:12 . . . She brings him **g,** not harm,
Isa 55:2 . . . does you no **g?**
Jer 13:23 . . . you start doing **g,** for you
Jer 32:39 . . . for their own **g** and for the
Matt 5:45 . . . evil and the **g,** and he sends
Rom 3:12 . . . No one does **g,** not a single

*Rom 8:28 . . . together for the **g** of those*
*Rom 13:4 . . . sent for your **g**.*
*1 Cor 10:24 . . . but for the **g** of others.*
*Gal 6:10 . . . we should do **g** to everyone—*
*Eph 2:10 . . . so we can do the **g** things He*
*Eph 6:8 . . . each one of us for the **g** we do,*
*1 Tim 5:10 . . . because of the **g** she has*
*Heb 13:16 . . . forget to do **g** and to share*
*1 Pet 2:20 . . . suffer for doing **g** and endure*
*1 Pet 3:17 . . . suffer for doing **g**, if that*

GOODNESS (n)
the beneficial quality of something; kindness
*Ps 145:7 . . . the story of Your wonderful **g**;*
*Isa 63:7 . . . in His great **g** to Israel,*
*Rom 14:17 . . . a life of **g** and peace and joy*
*Rom 15:14 . . . that You are full of **g**.*

GOSPEL (KJV)
*Mark 1:1 . . . the **Good News** about Jesus*
*Luke 4:18 . . . anointed me to bring **Good News***
*Rom 1:16 . . . not ashamed of this **Good News***
*Rom 10:15 . . . the feet of messengers who bring **good news***
*Gal 3:8 . . . God proclaimed this **good news** to*

GOSSIP (n)
rumor or report revealing personal or sensational facts about others
*Prov 16:28 . . . of strife; **g** separates the*
*Prov 26:20 . . . disappear when **g** stops.*
*2 Cor 12:20 . . . slander, **g**, arrogance,*

GOSSIP, GOSSIPING (v)
to relate rumors or reports about others
*Ps 15:3 . . . who refuse to **g** or harm their*
*1 Tim 5:13 . . . spend their time **g-ing***

GOVERNMENT (n)
the organization or agency through which a political unit exercises authority
*Isa 9:6 . . . The **g** will rest on His*
*Rom 13:6 . . . For **g** workers need*
*Titus 3:1 . . . to submit to the **g** and its*

GRACE (n)
God's free and unmerited favor toward sinful humanity
see also FAVOR
*Acts 6:8 . . . full of God's **g** and power,*
*Acts 14:3 . . . about the **g** of the Lord.*
*Acts 15:11 . . . by the undeserved **g** of the*
*Acts 20:32 . . . message of His **g** that is able*
*Rom 5:15 . . . is God's wonderful **g** and His*
*Rom 5:21 . . . now God's wonderful **g** rules*
*Rom 6:1 . . . of His wonderful **g**?*
*Rom 11:5 . . . of God's **g**—His undeserved*
*Rom 12:6 . . . In His **g**, God has*
*1 Cor 3:10 . . . Because of God's **g** to me,*
*1 Cor 16:23 . . . May the **g** of the Lord*
*2 Cor 4:15 . . . And as God's **g** reaches more*
*2 Cor 9:14 . . . of the overflowing **g** God has*
*Gal 1:15 . . . by His marvelous **g**.*
*Gal 2:21 . . . do not treat the **g** of God as*
*Gal 5:4 . . . away from God's **g**.*
*Eph 1:7 . . . in kindness and **g** that He*
*Eph 2:5 . . . only by God's **g** that you have*
*Eph 2:7 . . . wealth of His **g** and kindness*
*Eph 2:8 . . . saved you by His **g** when you*
*Eph 3:2 . . . of extending His **g** to you*
*Eph 3:7 . . . By God's **g** and mighty*
*Phil 4:23 . . . May the **g** of the Lord*
*2 Thes 1:12 . . . because of the **g** of our God*
*2 Thes 2:16 . . . and by His **g** gave us eternal*
*1 Tim 1:2 . . . Lord give you **g**, mercy,*
*2 Tim 1:9 . . . show us His **g** through Christ*
*2 Tim 2:1 . . . strong through the **g** that God*
*2 Tim 4:22 . . . And may His **g** be with all of*
*Titus 2:11 . . . For the **g** of God has*
*Titus 3:7 . . . Because of His **g** he declared*
*Titus 3:15 . . . May God's **g** be with you*
*Heb 4:16 . . . and we will find **g** to help us*
*Heb 12:15 . . . to receive the **g** of God.*
*Heb 13:9 . . . comes from God's **g**, not from*
*Heb 13:25 . . . May God's **g** be with you all.*
*Jas 4:6 . . . gives us even more **g** to stand*
*1 Pet 5:12 . . . Stand firm in this **g**.*
*2 Pet 3:18 . . . grow in the **g** and knowledge*
*Rev 22:21 . . . May the **g** of the Lord*

GRACIOUS (adj)
abounding in grace and kindness; merciful, compassionate
*2 Kgs 13:23 . . . the LORD was **g** and merciful*
*Ps 145:13 . . . He is **g** in all He*
*Prov 11:16 . . . A **g** woman gains*
*John 1:16 . . . received one **g** blessing after*
*2 Cor 8:7 . . . also in this **g** act of giving.*
*Col 4:6 . . . your conversation be **g** and*
*1 Tim 1:14 . . . and **g** our Lord*
*1 Pet 1:10 . . . about this **g** salvation*
*1 Pet 1:13 . . . to the **g** salvation that will*

GRAVE, GRAVES (n)
burial place; euphemism for Hades, hell, or Sheol
*Ps 5:9 . . . from an open **g**.*
*Ps 49:15 . . . power of the **g**.*
*John 5:28 . . . dead in their **g-s** will hear the*
*Acts 2:27 . . . rot in the **g**.*
*Rom 3:13 . . . from an open **g**.*
*Rev 20:13 . . . death and the **g** gave up their*

GREED (n)
a selfish and excessive desire for more of something (as money) than is needed
*Prov 15:27 . . . **G** brings grief*
*Rom 1:29 . . . of wickedness, sin, **g**, hate,*
*2 Pet 2:3 . . . In their **g** they will make up*
*2 Pet 2:14 . . . well trained in **g**.*

GREEDY (adj)
having or showing a selfish desire for wealth and possessions
*1 Sam 8:3 . . . for they were **g** for money.*
*Prov 1:19 . . . all who are **g** for money;*
*Prov 21:26 . . . people are always **g***
*1 Cor 6:10 . . . are thieves, or **g** people,*
*Eph 5:5 . . . For a **g** person is an*
*Col 3:5 . . . Don't be **g**, for a **g***

GRIEF (n)
deep and poignant distress due to bereavement; a cause of suffering
*Job 16:5 . . . take away your **g**.*
*Ps 10:14 . . . the trouble and **g** they cause.*
*Prov 10:1 . . . a foolish child brings **g** to a*
*Prov 15:27 . . . Greed brings **g** to the*
*John 16:20 . . . your **g** will suddenly turn*
*Rom 9:2 . . . sorrow and unending **g***

GRIEVE, GRIEVED (v)
to feel, show, or cause distress, vexation, sorrow, or regret
*Eccl 3:4 . . . A time to **g** and a time*
*Isa 63:10 . . . rebelled against Him and **g-d***
*Lam 3:20 . . . time, as I **g** over my loss.*
*1 Thes 4:13 . . . so you will not **g** like people*

GROW, GROWING, GROWS (v)
to become; to spring up and develop to maturity
*Isa 40:31 . . . run and not **g** weary.*
*1 Cor 3:6 . . . God who made it **g**.*
*Eph 4:16 . . . is healthy and **g-ing** and full of*
*Phil 1:25 . . . all of you **g** and experience*
*Col 2:19 . . . it **g-s** as God nourishes it.*
*2 Thes 1:3 . . . one another is **g-ing**.*
*Jas 1:15 . . . when sin is allowed to **g**,*
*2 Pet 3:18 . . . Rather, you must **g** in the*

GRUMBLE (v)
to mutter in discontent
*1 Cor 10:10 . . . And don't **g** as some*
*Jas 5:9 . . . Don't **g** about each other*

GUARD (adj)
defensively watchful; alert
*2 Pet 3:17 . . . Be on **g** so that you*

GUARD, GUARDING, GUARDS (v)
to protect by watchful attention; to watch over
see also KEEP
*Prov 4:23 . . . **G** your heart*
*Prov 7:2 . . . as you **g** your own eyes.*
*Prov 24:12 . . . He who **g-s** your soul knows*
*Luke 2:8 . . . fields nearby, **g-ing** their flocks*
*Phil 4:7 . . . His peace will **g** your hearts*
*2 Thes 3:3 . . . and **g** you from*

GUARDIAN (n)
one who has the care of the person or property of another
*Gen 4:9 . . . Am I my brother's **g**?*
*Gal 3:25 . . . the law as our **g**.*
*1 Pet 2:25 . . . your Shepherd, the **G** of your*

GUIDANCE (n)
direction or counsel provided by another person
*2 Chr 26:5 . . . as the king sought **g** from*
*Prov 24:6 . . . go to war without wise **g**;*
*Prov 29:18 . . . do not accept divine **g**,*

GUIDE, GUIDED, GUIDES, GUIDING (v)
to direct, supervise, or influence usually to a particular end
*Exod 13:21 . . . He **g-d** them during the*
*Exod 15:13 . . . In Your might, you **g** them*
*Deut 1:33 . . . **g-ing** you with a pillar of fire*
*Ps 16:7 . . . bless the LORD who **g-s** me;*
*Ps 23:3 . . . He **g-s** me along*
*Ps 32:8 . . . I will **g** You along*
*Ps 139:10 . . . Your hand will **g** me,*
*John 16:13 . . . He will **g** you into all*
*Gal 5:16 . . . let the Holy Spirit **g** your lives.*

GUILT (n)
the state or feeling of one who has committed an offense
*Job 6:29 . . . Stop assuming my **g**, for I*
*Ps 32:2 . . . the LORD has cleared of **g**,*
*Ps 38:4 . . . My **g** overwhelms me—*
*Ps 51:2 . . . Wash me clean from my **g**.*
*Isa 6:7 . . . Now your **g** is removed,*
*Dan 9:24 . . . atone for their **g**, to bring*

GUILTY (adj)
justly chargeable with wrongdoing
*Lev 19:17 . . . not be held **g** for their sin.*
*Rom 3:19 . . . entire world is **g** before God.*
*1 Cor 11:27 . . . **g** of sinning against*
*1 Jn 3:20 . . . if we feel **g**, God is greater*
*1 Jn 3:21 . . . we don't feel **g**, we can come*

H

HALLELUJAH (KJV)
*Rev 19:1 . . . shouting, "**Praise the Lord!***
*Rev 19:3 . . . voices rang out: "**Praise the Lord!***
*Rev 19:4 . . . "Amen! **Praise the Lord!"***
*Rev 19:6 . . . "**Praise the Lord!** For the Lord*

HALLOW(ED) (KJV)
*Exod 20:11 . . . the Sabbath day and **set it apart as holy***
*Lev 25:10 . . . **Set** this year **apart as holy***
*1 Kgs 9:3 . . . I have **set** this Temple **apart to be holy***
*Matt 6:9 . . . **may** Your name **be kept holy***

HAND, HANDS (n)
the end of the arm that serves as a grasping and handling tool for humans; symbolic of power
Gen 47:29 . . . Put your ***h*** *under my*
Exod 15:6 . . . Your right ***h,*** *O LORD,*
Exod 29:10 . . . will lay their ***h-s*** *on its head.*
Exod 33:22 . . . cover You with My ***h*** *until*
1 Kgs 13:4 . . . king's ***h*** *became paralyzed*
Ps 22:16 . . . have pierced my ***h-s*** *and feet.*
Ps 24:4 . . . Only those whose ***h-s*** *and hearts*
Ps 32:4 . . . Your ***h*** *of discipline*
Ps 44:3 . . . It was Your right ***h*** *and*
Ps 63:4 . . . lifting up my ***h-s*** *to You in prayer.*
Ps 75:8 . . . a cup in His ***h*** *that is full*
Ps 110:1 . . . at My right ***h*** *until I humble*
Ps 137:5 . . . let My right ***h*** *forget how to*
Ps 145:16 . . . You open Your ***h,*** *You satisfy*
Isa 40:12 . . . the oceans in His ***h?***
Isa 41:13 . . . by Your right ***h***—*I, the LORD*
Isa 55:12 . . . will clap their ***h-s!***
Isa 64:8 . . . formed by Your ***h.***
Dan 10:10 . . . Just then a ***h*** *touched me*
Matt 5:30 . . . And if your ***h***—*even your*
Matt 6:3 . . . don't let your left ***h*** *know what*
Matt 18:8 . . . with only one ***h*** *or one foot*
Matt 26:64 . . . at God's right ***h*** *and coming*
Mark 12:36 . . . at My right ***h*** *until I humble*
Acts 6:6 . . . they laid their ***h-s*** *on them.*
Acts 7:55 . . . at God's right ***h.***
Acts 8:18 . . . laid their ***h-s*** *on people,*
Acts 13:3 . . . men laid their ***h-s*** *on them and*
Acts 19:6 . . . Paul laid his ***h-s*** *on them,*
Acts 28:8 . . . and laying his ***h-s*** *on him,*
1 Thes 4:11 . . . working with your ***h-s,***
1 Tim 2:8 . . . pray with holy ***h-s*** *lifted up*
1 Tim 4:14 . . . church laid their ***h-s*** *on you.*
2 Tim 1:6 . . . when I laid my ***h-s*** *on you.*
Heb 1:13 . . . at My right ***h*** *until I humble*
Rev 13:16 . . . mark on the right ***h*** *or on the*

HAPPINESS (n)
a state of well-being and contentment; joy
Deut 24:5 . . . ***h*** *to the wife he has married.*
Job 7:7 . . . never again feel ***h.***
Job 9:25 . . . a glimpse of ***h.***
Ps 86:4 . . . Give me ***h,*** *O LORD,*
Ps 119:35 . . . that is where my ***h*** *is found.*
Eccl 8:15 . . . ***h*** *along with all the hard work*
Isa 65:18 . . . Jerusalem as a place of ***h.***
Luke 6:24 . . . you have your only ***h*** *now.*

HAPPY (adj)
expressing, reflecting, or suggestive of happiness
see also BLESSED
Deut 16:14 . . . festival will be a ***h*** *time*
Ps 113:9 . . . making her a ***h*** *mother.*
Prov 15:13 . . . A glad heart makes a ***h*** *face;*
Prov 15:15 . . . for the ***h*** *heart, life is*
Prov 23:25 . . . she who gave you birth be ***h.***
Eccl 9:7 . . . drink your wine with a ***h*** *heart,*
Zech 10:7 . . . will be made ***h*** *as if by wine.*
Rom 12:15 . . . Be ***h*** *with those who are* ***h,***
Phil 2:2 . . . make me truly ***h*** *by agreeing*
Jas 5:13 . . . Are any of you ***h?***

HARDEN, HARDENED (v)
to make callous or unfeeling
Exod 4:21 . . . But I will ***h*** *his heart*
Exod 10:20 . . . LORD ***h-ed*** *Pharaoh's heart*
Ps 95:8 . . . Don't ***h*** *your hearts as Israel did*
Isa 6:10 . . . ***H*** *the hearts of these people.*
Matt 13:15 . . . hearts of these people are ***h-ed,***
John 12:40 . . . and ***h-ed*** *their hearts*—
Eph 4:18 . . . their minds and ***h-ed*** *their hearts*
Heb 3:8 . . . don't ***h*** *your hearts as Israel did*

HARLOT (KJV)
Gen 38:15 . . . thought she was a ***prostitute***
Josh 2:1 . . . a ***prostitute*** *named Rahab*
Hos 4:15 . . . you, Israel, are a ***prostitute***
Matt 21:31 . . . and ***prostitutes*** *will get into the Kingdom*
Rev 17:5 . . . Mother of All ***Prostitutes*** *and*

HARMONY (n)
tranquility; agreement; unity
Zech 6:13 . . . will be perfect ***h*** *between His*
Rom 12:16 . . . Live in ***h*** *with each other.*
Rom 14:19 . . . aim for ***h*** *in the church*
Rom 15:5 . . . live in complete ***h*** *with each*
1 Cor 12:25 . . . This makes for ***h***
2 Cor 6:15 . . . What ***h*** *can there be*
2 Cor 13:11 . . . Live in ***h*** *and peace.*
Col 3:14 . . . together in perfect ***h.***

HARVEST, HARVESTS (n)
the time or fruit of reaping or gathering in a crop—physically or spiritually
Deut 16:15 . . . blesses you with bountiful ***h-s***
Matt 9:37 . . . The ***h*** *is great, but*
John 4:35 . . . fields are already ripe for ***h.***
1 Cor 15:23 . . . raised as the first of the ***h;***
2 Cor 9:10 . . . great ***h*** *of generosity*
Gal 6:9 . . . we will reap a ***h*** *of blessing*
Heb 12:11 . . . peaceful ***h*** *of right living*
Jas 3:18 . . . reap a ***h*** *of righteousness.*
Rev 14:15 . . . the time of ***h*** *has come;*

HARVEST, HARVESTS (v)
to gather in (a crop); to reap
Gen 8:22 . . . there will be planting and ***h,***
Job 4:8 . . . and cultivate evil will ***h***
Prov 10:5 . . . A wise youth ***h-s*** *in the summer,*
Gal 6:8 . . . sinful nature will ***h*** *decay and*

HATE, HATED, HATES, HATING (v)
to feel extreme enmity toward; to have a strong aversion to
Ps 45:7 . . . love justice and ***h*** *evil.*
Prov 1:22 . . . you fools ***h*** *knowledge?*
Prov 6:16 . . . six things the LORD ***h-s***—
Prov 13:5 . . . The godly ***h*** *lies;*
Prov 15:27 . . . those who ***h*** *bribes will live.*
Prov 26:28 . . . A lying tongue ***h-s*** *its victims,*
Prov 28:16 . . . but one who ***h-s*** *corruption*
Mal 2:16 . . . "For I ***h*** *divorce!"*
Matt 5:43 . . . and ***h*** *your enemy.*
Matt 24:9 . . . You will be ***h-d*** *all over the world*
Luke 6:22 . . . when people ***h*** *you*
John 3:20 . . . All who do evil ***h*** *the light*
John 15:18 . . . remember that it ***h-d*** *Me first.*
2 Tim 3:3 . . . be cruel and ***h*** *what is good.*
Heb 1:9 . . . You love justice and ***h*** *evil.*
1 Jn 2:9 . . . ***h-s*** *a Christian brother or sister,*
1 Jn 4:20 . . . ***h-s*** *a Christian brother or sister,*
Jude 23 . . . ***h-ing*** *the sins that contaminate*

HEAL, HEALED, HEALING, HEALS (v)
to mend, cure, make whole; to restore to health
Gen 20:17 . . . and God ***h-ed*** *Abimelech,*
Exod 15:26 . . . I am the LORD who ***h-s*** *you.*
Num 12:13 . . . I beg You, please ***h*** *her!*
Deut 32:39 . . . the one who wounds and ***h-s;***
2 Chr 30:20 . . . prayer and ***h-ed*** *the people.*
Job 5:18 . . . his hands also ***h.***
Ps 6:2 . . . ***H*** *me, LORD,*
Ps 103:3 . . . and ***h-s*** *all my diseases.*
Ps 107:20 . . . His word and ***h-ed*** *them,*
Prov 3:8 . . . you will have ***h-ing*** *for your body*
Prov 13:17 . . . messenger brings ***h-ing.***
Isa 6:10 . . . and turn to Me for ***h-ing.***
Isa 30:26 . . . LORD begins to ***h*** *His people*
Isa 57:18 . . . but I will ***h*** *them anyway!*
Isa 57:19 . . . the LORD, who ***h-s*** *them.*
Jer 8:18 . . . My grief is beyond ***h-ing;***
Jer 17:14 . . . O LORD, if you ***h*** *me, I will*
Jer 17:14 . . . I will be truly ***h-ed;***
Jer 30:13 . . . No medicine can ***h*** *you.*
Hos 6:1 . . . now He will ***h*** *us.*
Hos 7:1 . . . I want to ***h*** *Israel, but its*
Hos 14:4 . . . Then I will ***h*** *you of your*
Zech 11:16 . . . nor ***h*** *the injured,*
Mal 4:2 . . . with ***h-ing*** *in His wings.*
Matt 4:23 . . . And he ***h-ed*** *every kind*
Matt 8:7 . . . will come and ***h*** *him.*
Matt 8:16 . . . and He ***h-ed*** *all the sick.*
Matt 9:35 . . . He ***h-ed*** *every kind of disease*
Matt 10:8 . . . ***H*** *the sick, raise the*
Matt 15:30 . . . Jesus, and He ***h-ed*** *them all.*
Matt 17:16 . . . they couldn't ***h*** *him.*
Mark 1:34 . . . So Jesus ***h-ed*** *many people*
Mark 3:2 . . . If He ***h-ed*** *the man's*
Mark 3:10 . . . He had ***h-ed*** *many people*
Mark 5:28 . . . touch His robe, I will be ***h-ed.***
Mark 6:5 . . . sick people and ***h*** *them.*
Mark 6:13 . . . and ***h-ed*** *many sick*
Mark 6:56 . . . all who touched Him were ***h-ed.***
Mark 10:52 . . . your faith has ***h-ed*** *you.*
Luke 4:23 . . . Physician, ***h*** *yourself*
Luke 4:40 . . . His hand ***h-ed*** *every one.*
Luke 6:7 . . . If He ***h-ed*** *the man's*
Luke 8:50 . . . have faith, and she will be ***h-ed.***
Luke 10:9 . . . ***H*** *the sick, and tell them*
Luke 13:14 . . . indignant that Jesus had ***h-ed***
Luke 14:3 . . . ***h*** *people on the Sabbath*
Luke 14:4 . . . the sick man and ***h-ed*** *him*
Luke 17:19 . . . Your faith has ***h-ed*** *you.*
Luke 18:42 . . . Your faith has ***h-ed*** *you.*
Luke 22:51 . . . man's ear and ***h-ed*** *him.*
John 4:47 . . . to Capernaum to ***h*** *his son,*
John 7:23 . . . angry with Me for ***h-ing*** *a man*
John 12:40 . . . and have Me ***h*** *them.*
Acts 3:16 . . . this man was ***h-ed***—
Acts 4:9 . . . want to know how he was ***h-ed?***
Acts 4:14 . . . see the man who had been ***h-ed***
Acts 4:22 . . . sign—the ***h-ing*** *of a man*
Acts 8:7 . . . or lame were ***h-ed.***
Acts 9:34 . . . Jesus Christ ***h-s*** *you! Get up,*
Acts 10:38 . . . and ***h-ing*** *all who were*
Acts 28:8 . . . laying His hands on Him, He ***h-ed***
Acts 28:27 . . . cannot turn to me and let me ***h***
1 Cor 12:28 . . . the gift of ***h-ing,***
1 Cor 12:30 . . . have the gift of ***h-ing?***
Jas 5:16 . . . so that you may be ***h-ed.***
1 Pet 2:24 . . . By His wounds you are ***h-ed.***
Rev 13:3 . . . fatal wound was ***h-ed!***
Rev 13:12 . . . wound had been ***h-ed.***

HEALING (adj)
marked by restoring to original purity or integrity
Luke 6:19 . . . ***h*** *power went out from Him,*
Acts 4:30 . . . your hand with ***h*** *power;*

HEALTH (n)
the general condition of the body
Ps 38:3 . . . My ***h*** *is broken because of*
Ps 38:7 . . . and My ***h*** *is broken.*
Prov 15:30 . . . makes for good ***h.***
Isa 38:16 . . . You restore my ***h***
Jer 30:17 . . . I will give you back your ***h***

HEAR, HEARD, HEARING (v)
to perceive sound; to listen with attention; to be informed of; to take testimony from and make a legal decision
see also LISTEN
Gen 3:8 . . . and his wife ***h-d*** *the LORD God*
Exod 2:24 . . . God ***h-d*** *their groaning,*
Deut 1:16 . . . judges, 'You must ***h*** *the cases*
Josh 7:9 . . . people living in the land ***h***
1 Kgs 8:30 . . . May You ***h*** *the humble*
2 Chr 7:14 . . . I will ***h*** *from heaven and will*
Neh 1:11 . . . O LORD, please ***h*** *my prayer!*
Ps 5:1 . . . O LORD, ***h*** *me as I pray;*
Ps 89:1 . . . Young and old will ***h*** *of Your*
Isa 29:18 . . . the deaf will ***h*** *words read*
Isa 30:21 . . . own ears will ***h*** *him.*

Isa 40:28 . . . Have you never ***h-d?***
Isa 59:1 . . . too deaf to ***h*** *You call.*
Dan 10:12 . . . has been ***h-d*** *in heaven.*
Matt 5:21 . . . You have ***h-d*** *that our ancestors*
Matt 5:43 . . . You have ***h-d*** *the law*
Matt 11:5 . . . cured, the deaf ***h,*** *the dead*
Matt 13:14 . . . When you ***h*** *what I say,*
Mark 4:12 . . . When they ***h*** *what I say,*
Luke 7:22 . . . cured, the deaf ***h,*** *the dead*
John 8:26 . . . what I have ***h-d*** *from the one*
Acts 2:6 . . . When they ***h-d*** *the loud noise,*
Acts 13:7 . . . he wanted to ***h*** *the word of*
Rom 10:14 . . . how can they ***h*** *about Him*
Rom 10:17 . . . faith comes from ***h-ing,*** *that is,*
1 Cor 2:9 . . . no ear has ***h-d,*** *and no mind has*
1 Cor 12:17 . . . how would you ***h?***
Heb 3:7 . . . Today when you ***h*** *His voice,*
2 Jn 6 . . . just as you ***h-d*** *from the*
Rev 3:20 . . . If you ***h*** *My voice and*
Rev 22:8 . . . I, John, am the one who ***h-d***

HEART, HEARTS (n)
figuratively, the seat of emotions, thoughts, and intentions; personality, disposition; courage; love, affection; central or most vital part of something
Gen 6:6 . . . It broke His ***h.***
Exod 4:21 . . . will harden his ***h*** *so he*
Exod 35:21 . . . All whose ***h-s*** *were stirred*
Deut 6:5 . . . LORD your God with all your ***h,***
Deut 20:3 . . . Do not lose ***h*** *or panic*
Deut 28:65 . . . will cause your ***h*** *to tremble,*
Josh 22:5 . . . with all your ***h*** *and all your*
Josh 23:14 . . . Deep in your ***h-s*** *you know*
1 Sam 1:15 . . . pouring out my ***h***
1 Sam 10:9 . . . God gave him a new ***h,***
1 Sam 12:20 . . . the LORD with all your ***h,***
1 Sam 13:14 . . . a man after His own ***h.***
1 Sam 16:7 . . . but the LORD looks at the ***h.***
1 Kgs 8:48 . . . with their whole ***h*** *and soul*
1 Chr 22:19 . . . God with all your ***h*** *and soul.*
2 Chr 6:38 . . . with their whole ***h*** *and soul*
2 Chr 22:9 . . . sought the LORD with all his ***h.***
Job 4:5 . . . when trouble strikes, you lose ***h.***
Ps 9:1 . . . praise You, LORD, with all my ***h;***
Ps 14:1 . . . say in their ***h-s,*** *"There is no*
Ps 19:14 . . . meditation of my ***h***
Ps 24:4 . . . whose hands and ***h-s*** *are pure,*
Ps 36:1 . . . within their ***h-s.*** *They have no*
Ps 42:11 . . . Why is my ***h*** *so sad?*
Ps 51:10 . . . Create in me a clean ***h,*** *O God.*
Ps 57:7 . . . my ***h*** *is confident.*
Ps 73:7 . . . everything their ***h-s*** *could ever*
Ps 108:1 . . . with all my ***h!***
Ps 111:1 . . . thank the LORD with all my ***h***
Ps 119:2 . . . with all their ***h-s.***
Ps 119:11 . . . hidden Your word in my ***h,***
Ps 119:58 . . . With all my ***h*** *I want Your*
Ps 119:145 . . . I pray with all my ***h;***
Ps 139:23 . . . and know my ***h;*** *test me and*
Prov 3:3 . . . deep within your ***h.***
Prov 4:23 . . . Guard your ***h*** *above all else,*
Prov 13:12 . . . Hope deferred makes the ***h*** *sick,*
Prov 14:30 . . . A peaceful ***h*** *leads to a*
Prov 15:13 . . . a broken ***h*** *crushes the*
Prov 17:22 . . . A cheerful ***h*** *is good*
Prov 20:9 . . . have cleansed my ***h;*** *I am pure*
Prov 27:23 . . . and put your ***h*** *into caring*
Isa 1:5 . . . and your ***h*** *is sick.*
Isa 6:10 . . . Harden the ***h-s*** *of these people.*
Jer 3:15 . . . shepherds after My own ***h,***
Jer 3:22 . . . your wayward ***h-s.***
Jer 9:26 . . . have uncircumcised ***h-s.***
Jer 20:9 . . . burns in My ***h*** *like a fire.*
Ezek 44:7 . . . who have no ***h*** *for God.*
Joel 2:12 . . . Give Me your ***h-s.*** *Come with*
Matt 5:8 . . . those whose ***h-s*** *are pure,*
Matt 5:28 . . . adultery with her in his ***h.***
Matt 11:29 . . . I am humble and gentle at ***h,***
Matt 12:34 . . . whatever is in your ***h***
Matt 15:19 . . . For from the ***h*** *come evil*
Matt 22:37 . . . God with all your ***h,*** *all your*
Mark 11:23 . . . have no doubt in your ***h.***
Mark 12:30 . . . God with all your ***h,*** *all your*
Mark 12:33 . . . love him with all my ***h*** *and*
Luke 12:34 . . . desires of your ***h*** *will also*
Luke 24:38 . . . Why are your ***h-s*** *filled with*
John 5:38 . . . in your ***h-s,*** *because you do not*
Acts 1:24 . . . You know every ***h.*** *Show us*
Acts 8:21 . . . this, for your ***h*** *is not right*
Acts 15:8 . . . God knows people's ***h-s,*** *and he*
Acts 28:27 . . . hear, and their ***h-s*** *cannot*
Rom 2:15 . . . written in their ***h-s,*** *for their*
Rom 2:29 . . . changed ***h*** *seeks praise*
Rom 10:9 . . . believe in your ***h*** *that God*
2 Cor 7:2 . . . Please open your ***h-s*** *to us.*
2 Cor 9:7 . . . decide in your ***h*** *how much to*
Eph 1:18 . . . I pray that your ***h-s*** *will be*
Eph 3:13 . . . don't lose ***h*** *because of my*
Eph 5:19 . . . music to the Lord in your ***h-s.***
Eph 6:6 . . . of God with all your ***h.***
1 Tim 1:5 . . . comes from a pure ***h,*** *a clear*

HEAVEN, HEAVENS (n)
sky and stars above; God's dwelling place; abode of eternal bliss
Deut 30:12 . . . is not kept in ***h,*** *so distant*
Job 41:11 . . . Everything under ***h*** *is Mine.*
Ps 18:16 . . . down from ***h*** *and rescued me;*
Ps 71:19 . . . to the highest ***h-s.*** *You have*
Ps 108:4 . . . than the ***h-s.*** *Your faithfulness*
Matt 11:25 . . . Father, Lord of ***h*** *and earth,*
Matt 24:30 . . . appear in the ***h-s,*** *and there*
Rom 10:6 . . . go up to ***h'*** *(to bring Christ*
2 Cor 12:2 . . . to the third ***h*** *fourteen years*
Heb 9:24 . . . He entered into ***h*** *itself to*

HELL (n)
abode of the dead; place of punishment; personification of evil; lowest place one can go
Matt 5:22 . . . of the fires of ***h.***
Matt 16:18 . . . all the powers of ***h*** *will not*
Matt 23:33 . . . judgment of ***h?***
Mark 9:43 . . . fires of ***h*** *with two hands.*
Luke 12:5 . . . throw you into ***h.***
Jas 3:6 . . . on fire by ***h*** *itself.*
2 Pet 2:4 . . . threw them into ***h,*** *in gloomy*

HELMET (n)
any of various protective head coverings usually made of hard metal
Isa 59:17 . . . and placed the ***h*** *of salvation*
Eph 6:17 . . . salvation as your ***h,*** *and take*

HELP, HELPED, HELPING, HELPS (v)
to give assistance or support; to rescue or save
Exod 23:5 . . . Instead, stop and ***h.***
Deut 2:36 . . . our God also ***h-ed*** *us conquer*
1 Sam 7:12 . . . the LORD has ***h-ed*** *us!*
Ps 46:1 . . . always ready to ***h*** *in times of*
Ps 72:12 . . . He will ***h*** *the oppressed,*
Ps 145:14 . . . The LORD ***h-s*** *the fallen*
Prov 11:4 . . . Riches won't ***h*** *on the*
Prov 14:31 . . . their Maker, but ***h-ing*** *the poor*
Prov 19:17 . . . If you ***h*** *the poor,*
Isa 41:10 . . . strengthen you and ***h*** *you.*
Isa 44:10 . . . that cannot ***h*** *him one bit?*
Jer 51:9 . . . We would have ***h-ed*** *her if we*
Lam 4:16 . . . he no longer ***h-s*** *them.*
Mark 9:24 . . . but ***h*** *me overcome*
Acts 9:36 . . . for others and ***h-ing*** *the poor.*
Acts 16:9 . . . to Macedonia and ***h*** *us!*
Rom 12:13 . . . be ready to ***h*** *them.*
1 Cor 12:28 . . . those who can ***h*** *others,*
2 Cor 6:2 . . . salvation, I ***h-ed*** *you.*
Gal 6:1 . . . and humbly ***h*** *that person back*
1 Tim 5:10 . . . Has she ***h-ed*** *those who*
2 Tim 2:7 . . . Lord will ***h*** *you understand*
Heb 10:33 . . . you ***h-ed*** *others who*
1 Pet 4:11 . . . the gift of ***h-ing*** *others?*

HELPLESS (adj)
without any aid, comfort, protection, or chance of success
Ps 9:12 . . . cares for the ***h.*** *He does not*
Ps 10:12 . . . not ignore the ***h!***
Ps 34:2 . . . let all who are ***h*** *take heart.*
Ps 35:10 . . . Who else protects the ***h***
Amos 2:7 . . . They trample ***h*** *people in the*
Matt 9:36 . . . confused and ***h,*** *like sheep*
Rom 5:6 . . . were utterly ***h,*** *Christ came*

HOLINESS (n)
sanctity or purity
Exod 15:11 . . . glorious in ***h,*** *awesome in*
Deut 32:51 . . . to demonstrate My ***h*** *to the*
Ps 29:2 . . . the splendor of His ***h.***
Luke 1:75 . . . in ***h*** *and righteousness for*
1 Cor 7:14 . . . wife brings ***h*** *to her*
2 Cor 1:12 . . . a God-given ***h*** *and sincerity*
1 Thes 4:4 . . . and live in ***h*** *and honor—*
1 Tim 2:15 . . . faith, love, ***h,*** *and modesty.*
Heb 12:10 . . . share in His ***h.***

HOLY GHOST (KJV)
Matt 1:18 . . . the power of the ***Holy Spirit***
Matt 3:11 . . . baptize you with the ***Holy Spirit***
Matt 28:19 . . . and the Son and the ***Holy Spirit***
Luke 3:22 . . . ***Holy Spirit,*** *in bodily form,*
1 Jn 5:7-8 . . . three witnesses—the ***Spirit***

HOLY SPIRIT (KJV)
Luke 11:13 . . . give the ***Holy Spirit*** *to those*
Eph 1:13 . . . ***Holy Spirit,*** *whom He promised*
Eph 4:30 . . . bring sorrow to God's ***Holy Spirit***
1 Thes 4:8 . . . who gives His ***Holy Spirit*** *to you*

HOLY (adj)
consecrated or set aside for sacred use (as opposed to pagan or common use); standing apart from sin and evil; characteristic of God, especially the third person of the Trinity
see also PURE
Gen 2:3 . . . and declared it ***h,*** *because it*
Exod 3:5 . . . are standing on ***h*** *ground.*
Exod 19:6 . . . priests, My ***h*** *nation.*
Exod 26:33 . . . separate the ***H*** *Place*
Exod 29:37 . . . be absolutely ***h,***
Exod 30:10 . . . LORD's most ***h*** *altar.*
Exod 31:13 . . . the LORD, who makes you ***h.***
Lev 11:45 . . . you must be ***h*** *because I am*
Lev 19:8 . . . for defiling what is ***h*** *to the*
Lev 20:7 . . . set yourselves apart to be ***h,***
Lev 20:26 . . . You must be ***h*** *because I,*
Lev 21:12 . . . for he has been made ***h*** *by the*
Lev 22:32 . . . the LORD who makes you ***h.***
Lev 27:9 . . . to the LORD will be considered ***h.***
Deut 5:12 . . . by keeping it ***h,*** *as the LORD*
Josh 5:15 . . . where you are standing is ***h.***
Josh 24:19 . . . He is a ***h*** *and jealous God.*
1 Chr 16:35 . . . we can thank Your ***h*** *name and*
Neh 11:1 . . . in Jerusalem, the ***h*** *city.*
Ps 22:3 . . . Yet You are ***h,*** *enthroned on*
Ps 30:4 . . . Praise His ***h*** *name.*
Ps 99:3 . . . Your name is ***h!***
Ps 105:3 . . . Exult in His ***h*** *name; rejoice,*
Ps 111:9 . . . What a ***h,*** *awe-inspiring name*
Prov 9:10 . . . of the ***H*** *One results in good*
Isa 6:3 . . . to each other, ***"H,*** *holy, holy*
Isa 40:25 . . . My equal?" asks the ***H*** *One.*
Isa 54:5 . . . your Redeemer, the ***H*** *One of*
Isa 66:20 . . . them to My ***h*** *mountain in*
Dan 7:18 . . . But in the end, the ***h*** *people*
Dan 9:24 . . . anoint the Most ***H*** *Place.*
Zech 14:5 . . . and all His ***h*** *ones with Him.*
Matt 24:15 . . . in the ***H*** *Place.*
Mark 1:24 . . . —the ***H*** *One sent from*

*Luke 1:35 . . . baby to be born will be **h**,*
*Luke 1:49 . . . Mighty One is **h**, and He has*
*Luke 4:34 . . . You are—the **H** One sent from*
*Luke 11:2 . . . Your name be kept **h**. May Your*
*John 6:69 . . . You are the **H** One of God.*
*John 17:17 . . . Make them **h** by your*
*Acts 13:35 . . . not allow Your **H** One to rot*
*Rom 7:12 . . . the law itself is **h**, and its*
*Rom 14:5 . . . day is more **h** than another*
*Rom 15:16 . . . made **h** by the **H** Spirit.*
*1 Cor 1:2 . . . be His own **h** people.*
*1 Cor 1:30 . . . made us pure and **h**,*
*1 Cor 3:17 . . . God's temple is **h**, and you*
*1 Cor 6:11 . . . you were made **h**; you were*
*1 Cor 7:14 . . . children would not be **h**, but*
*2 Cor 5:5 . . . given us His **H** Spirit.*
*Eph 1:4 . . . in Christ to be **h** and without*
*Eph 2:21 . . . becoming a **h** temple for*
*Eph 4:24 . . . righteous and **h**.*
*Eph 5:26 . . . to make her **h** and clean,*
*Col 1:22 . . . and you are **h** and blameless*
*1 Thes 3:13 . . . blameless, and **h** as you stand*
*1 Thes 4:7 . . . called us to live **h** lives, not*
*1 Thes 5:23 . . . make you **h** in every*
*2 Thes 1:10 . . . from His **h** people—praise*
*1 Tim 2:8 . . . to pray with **h** hands lifted*
*2 Tim 1:9 . . . called us to live a **h** life.*
*2 Tim 3:15 . . . taught the **h** Scriptures from*
*Heb 2:11 . . . ones He makes **h** have the same*
*Heb 10:14 . . . those who are being made **h**.*
*Heb 10:19 . . . heaven's Most **H** Place*
*Heb 10:29 . . . which made us **h**, as if it*
*Heb 13:12 . . . make His people **h** by means of*
*1 Pet 1:16 . . . You must be **h** because I am*
*1 Pet 2:5 . . . are His **h** priests.*
*1 Pet 2:9 . . . priests, a **h** nation, God's*
*1 Pet 3:5 . . . is how the **h** women of old*
*2 Pet 1:18 . . . on the **h** mountain.*
*2 Pet 2:21 . . . to live a **h** life.*
*2 Pet 3:11 . . . like this, what **h** and godly*
*Rev 3:7 . . . one who is **h** and true,*
*Rev 4:8 . . . on saying, "Holy, **h**, holy is*
*Rev 15:4 . . . You alone are **h**. All nations*
*Rev 20:6 . . . Blessed and **h** are those who*
*Rev 22:11 . . . continue to be **h**.*

HOMOSEXUALITY (n)
erotic activity with another of the same sex
*1 Cor 6:9 . . . prostitutes, or practice **h**,*
*1 Tim 1:10 . . . or who practice **h**, or are*

HONEST (adj)
truthful; genuine; reputable; marked by integrity
*Exod 18:21 . . . some capable, **h** men*
*2 Kgs 12:15 . . . were **h** and trustworthy*
*Ps 37:37 . . . those who are **h** and good,*
*Prov 12:17 . . . An **h** witness tells*
*Prov 28:6 . . . Better to be poor and **h** than*
*Jer 5:1 . . . find even one just and **h** person,*
*Matt 22:16 . . . We know how **h** You are.*
*1 Thes 2:10 . . . devout and **h** and faultless*

HONESTY (n)
fairness and straightforwardness of conduct; sincerity
*Ps 51:6 . . . But You desire **h** from the*
*Prov 11:5 . . . are directed by **h**; the wicked*
*Jer 5:3 . . . searching for **h**. You struck*

HONOR, HONORS (n)
having a renowned reputation or social standing; physical or spiritual blessing (from God); a showing of merited respect
*Ps 8:5 . . . crowned them with glory and **h**.*
*Ps 104:1 . . . are robed with **h** and majesty.*
*Prov 3:35 . . . The wise inherit **h**, but fools*
*Prov 15:33 . . . humility precedes **h**.*
*Prov 25:27 . . . not good to seek **h-s***
*Isa 53:12 . . . I will give Him the **h-s** of a*
*Isa 55:13 . . . will bring great **h** to the*
*Luke 14:8 . . . don't sit in the seat of **h**.*
*Eph 1:20 . . . the place of **h** at God's right*
*Heb 13:4 . . . Give **h** to marriage,*
*1 Pet 2:6 . . . chosen for great **h**, and*
*1 Pet 2:12 . . . they will give **h** to God when*
*1 Pet 3:7 . . . husbands must give **h** to*
*2 Pet 1:17 . . . when He received **h** and glory*
*Rev 4:9 . . . give glory and **h** and thanks*
*Rev 19:7 . . . and let us give **h** to Him.*

HONOR, HONORED, HONORING, HONORS (v)
of God, to reverence his majesty; of man, to respect or esteem; to confer honor upon
*Exod 20:12 . . . **H** your father and mother.*
*1 Kgs 8:43 . . . Temple I have built **h-s***
*Neh 1:11 . . . who delight in **h-ing** You.*
*Ps 29:1 . . . **H** the LORD, you*
*Ps 45:11 . . . **h** Him, for He is your LORD.*
*Ps 46:10 . . . I will be **h-ed** by every nation.*
*Ps 47:9 . . . He is highly **h-ed** everywhere.*
*Prov 14:31 . . . helping the poor **h-s** Him.*
*Isa 66:5 . . . the LORD be **h-ed**!*
*Matt 15:4 . . . God says, '**H** your father and*
*Mark 6:4 . . . A prophet is **h-ed** everywhere*
*Luke 16:15 . . . What this world **h-s***
*John 5:23 . . . that everyone will **h** the Son,*
*John 12:26 . . . the Father will **h** anyone who*
*Rom 12:10 . . . delight in **h-ing** each other.*
*Rom 13:3 . . . and they will **h** you.*
*1 Cor 6:20 . . . So you must **h** God with your*
*1 Cor 12:26 . . . if one part is **h-ed**, all the*
*Eph 6:2 . . . **H** your father and mother*
*Col 1:10 . . . the way you live will always **h***
*1 Thes 5:12 . . . and sisters, **h** those who are*
*2 Thes 1:12 . . . be **h-ed** along with Him.*
*Titus 2:3 . . . a way that **h-s** God.*

HOPE, HOPES (n)
confident trust with the expectation of fulfillment
*1 Sam 9:20 . . . focus of all Israel's **h-s**.*
*Job 31:16 . . . crushed the **h-s** of widows?*
*Ps 10:17 . . . LORD, You know the **h-s** of the*
*Ps 42:5 . . . I will put my **h** in God!*
*Ps 112:10 . . . slink away, their **h-s** thwarted.*
*Ps 119:49 . . . to me; it is my only **h**.*
*Ps 119:74 . . . I have put my **h** in Your word.*
*Prov 10:24 . . . the **h-s** of the godly will be*
*Prov 13:12 . . . **H** deferred makes the heart*
*Zech 9:12 . . . prisoners who still have **h**!*
*Rom 5:4 . . . our confident **h** of salvation.*
*Rom 8:20 . . . curse. But with eager **h**,*
*Rom 12:12 . . . Rejoice in our confident **h**.*
*Rom 15:4 . . . give us **h** and encouragement*
*Rom 15:13 . . . God, the source of **h**, will*
*1 Cor 13:13 . . . faith, **h**, and love—*
*1 Cor 15:19 . . . And if our **h** in Christ is*
*Eph 2:12 . . . without God and without **h**.*
*1 Thes 1:3 . . . and the enduring **h** you have*
*1 Tim 4:10 . . . struggle, for our **h** is in the*
*Heb 10:23 . . . wavering to the **h** we affirm,*
*1 Pet 3:15 . . . about your Christian **h**,*

HORSE (n)
a large solid-hoofed herbivorous mammal often used for working or riding
*Zech 1:8 . . . on a red **h** that was standing*
*Rev 6:2 . . . saw a white **h** standing there.*
*Rev 6:4 . . . Then another **h** appeared,*
*Rev 6:5 . . . saw a black **h**, and its rider*
*Rev 6:8 . . . and saw a **h** whose color was*
*Rev 19:11 . . . and a white **h** was standing*

HOSANNA (KJV)
*Matt 21:9 . . . **Praise God** in highest heaven!*
*Matt 21:15 . . . **Praise God** for the Son of David*
*Mark 11:9 . . . **Praise God**! Blessings on the One*
*Mark 11:10 . . . **Praise God** in highest heaven*
*John 12:13 . . . **Praise God**! Blessings on the*

HOSPITALITY (n)
generous and cordial treatment, reception, or disposition
*Matt 25:38 . . . and show you **h**?*
*Luke 10:7 . . . Don't hesitate to accept **h**,*
*Rom 12:13 . . . be eager to practice **h**.*

HOSTILITY (n)
deep-seated ill will; enmity
*Gen 3:15 . . . I will cause **h** between you*
*Lev 26:28 . . . I will give full vent to My **h**.*
*Gal 5:20 . . . sorcery, **h**, quarreling,*
*Eph 2:14 . . . the wall of **h** that separated*
*Eph 2:16 . . . our **h** toward each other was*
*Heb 12:3 . . . of all the **h** He endured from*

HUMAN (adj)
of, relating to, or characteristic of men and women collectively; mortal; finite
*Gen 1:26 . . . Let us make **h** beings in our*
*Gen 3:22 . . . Look, the **h** beings have*
*Gen 9:6 . . . If anyone takes a **h** life,*
*Ps 9:20 . . . they are merely **h**.*
*Ps 33:13 . . . sees the whole **h** race.*
*Ps 89:47 . . . futile this **h** existence!*
*John 1:14 . . . So the Word became **h***
*John 2:24 . . . because He knew **h** nature.*
*John 8:15 . . . judge Me by **h** standards,*
*Rom 6:19 . . . weakness of your **h** nature,*
*1 Cor 2:5 . . . trust not in **h** wisdom but in*
*1 Cor 2:13 . . . come from **h** wisdom.*
*2 Cor 3:3 . . . of stone, but on **h** hearts.*
*2 Cor 10:3 . . . We are **h**, but we*
*Gal 3:3 . . . by your own **h** effort?*
*Col 2:9 . . . of God in a **h** body.*
*1 Thes 2:13 . . . words as mere **h** ideas.*
*Heb 7:28 . . . limited by **h** weakness.*
*2 Pet 1:21 . . . or from **h** initiative.*

HUMBLE (adj)
not proud or haughty; can imply lower social or economic status; meek or gentle
*Num 12:3 . . . Moses was very **h**—*
*Ps 138:6 . . . cares for the **h**, but He keeps*
*Ps 149:4 . . . He crowns the **h** with victory.*
*Zech 9:9 . . . yet He is **h**, riding on a*
*Matt 5:5 . . . those who are **h**,*
*Matt 11:29 . . . I am **h** and gentle at*
*Matt 21:5 . . . He is **h**, riding on a*
*Eph 4:2 . . . Always be **h** and gentle.*
*Phil 2:3 . . . Be **h**, thinking of*
*Jas 4:6 . . . but favors the **h**.*
*1 Pet 3:8 . . . and keep a **h** attitude.*

HUMBLE, HUMBLED, HUMBLES (v)
to not think too highly of oneself; to bring low or prostrate
*Isa 26:5 . . . He **h-s** the proud and*
*Luke 14:11 . . . themselves will be **h-d**,*
*Luke 18:14 . . . will be **h-d**, and those who*
*2 Cor 11:7 . . . wrong when I **h-d** Myself*
*Phil 2:8 . . . He **h-d** Himself in obedience*
*Jas 1:10 . . . that God has **h-d** them.*
*Jas 4:10 . . . **H** yourselves before the Lord,*
*1 Pet 5:6 . . . So **h** yourselves under*

HUMILIATE, HUMILIATED (v)
to shame or mortify
*Deut 21:14 . . . for you have **h-ed** her.*
*2 Sam 22:28 . . . watch the proud and **h** them*
*Ps 18:27 . . . but you **h** the proud*

HUMILITY (n)
show of submission or meekness; quality or state of being humble
*Prov 11:2 . . . but with **h** comes wisdom.*
*Prov 15:33 . . . **h** precedes honor.*
*Prov 22:4 . . . True **h** and fear*

*Col 3:12 . . . kindness, **h,** gentleness,*
*Jas 3:13 . . . works with the **h** that comes*
*1 Pet 5:5 . . . each other in **h,** for "God*

HUNGRY (adj)
feeling a strong desire for food; a craving for anything
*Prov 25:21 . . . If your enemies are **h,***
*Matt 15:32 . . . to send them away **h,***
*Matt 25:35 . . . For I was **h,** and you fed Me.*
*Luke 1:53 . . . He has filled the **h** with good*
*Luke 6:21 . . . you who are **h** now, for you*
*John 6:35 . . . never be **h** again.*
*Rom 8:35 . . . or are persecuted, or **h,** or*
*Rom 12:20 . . . enemies are **h,** feed them.*
*Rev 7:16 . . . never again be **h** or thirsty;*

HUSBAND, HUSBANDS (n)
male partner in a marriage; head of family; protector and provider; figurative of Christ
*Ruth 1:11 . . . could grow up to be your **h-s?***
*Prov 12:4 . . . is a crown for her **h,***
*Prov 31:28 . . . Her **h** praises her:*
*Jer 3:20 . . . wife who leaves her **h.***
*Rom 7:2 . . . binds her to her **h** as long as*
*1 Cor 7:3 . . . The **h** should fulfill*
*1 Cor 7:10 . . . not leave her **h.***
*1 Cor 7:39 . . . is bound to her **h** as long as*
*2 Cor 11:2 . . . bride to one **h**—Christ.*
*Gal 4:27 . . . lives with her **h!***
*Eph 5:22 . . . means submit your **h-s** as to the*
*Eph 5:23 . . . For a **h** is the head*
*Eph 5:25 . . . For **h-s,** this means*
*Eph 5:28 . . . the same way, **h-s** ought to love*
*Col 3:18 . . . submit to your **h-s,** as is*
*Col 3:19 . . . **H-s,** love your*
*1 Tim 5:9 . . . faithful to her **h.***
*Titus 2:4 . . . to love their **h-s** and their*
*1 Pet 3:1 . . . accept the authority of your **h-s.***
*1 Pet 3:7 . . . the same way, you **h-s** must give*

HYPOCRITE, HYPOCRITES (n)
a person who portrays a false appearance of religion; a person who acts in contradiction to his or her stated beliefs; pretender
*Matt 6:16 . . . make it obvious, as the **h-s***
*Matt 7:5 . . . **H!** First get rid of the log*
*Matt 23:13 . . . and you Pharisees. **H-s!***
*Luke 6:42 . . . the log in your own eye? **H!***
*Luke 13:15 . . . Lord replied, "You **h-s!***
*1 Tim 4:2 . . . These people are **h-s** and liars,*

I

IDOL, IDOLS (n)
a representation or symbol of a false god
*Exod 20:4 . . . make for yourself an **i***
*Deut 27:15 . . . who carves or casts an **i***
*1 Sam 15:23 . . . as bad as worshiping **i-s.***
*Isa 40:19 . . . Can He be compared to an **i***
*Isa 44:9 . . . who worship **i-s** don't know*
*Isa 44:15 . . . makes an **i** and bows down*
*Isa 44:17 . . . and makes his god: a carved **i!***
*Isa 44:19 . . . who made the **i** never stops to*
*Hab 2:18 . . . What good is an **i** carved*
*Acts 15:20 . . . eating food offered to **i-s,***
*Rom 1:23 . . . worshiped **i-s** made to look*
*1 Cor 6:9 . . . or who worship **i-s,** or commit*
*1 Cor 8:1 . . . has been offered to **i-s.***
*1 Cor 8:4 . . . an **i** is not really a god*
*Rev 2:14 . . . sin by eating food offered to **i-s***

IDOLATRY (n)
the worship of a physical object as a god; immoderate attachment or devotion to something
*Gal 5:20 . . . pleasures, **i,** sorcery,*

IMAGE (n)
a God-given likeness or reflection; a tangible or visible representation
*Gen 1:26 . . . make human beings in our **i,***
*Gen 1:27 . . . human beings in His own **i.***
*Gen 9:6 . . . made human beings in His own **i.***
*Col 1:15 . . . Christ is the visible **i** of the*
*Jas 3:9 . . . have been made in the **i** of God.*

IMMORAL (adj)
characterized by conflicting with traditionally (biblically) held moral principles; sinful or impure
*Prov 2:16 . . . save you from the **i** woman,*
*Prov 6:24 . . . keep you from the **i** woman,*
*Prov 22:14 . . . an **i** woman is a dangerous*
*Luke 7:37 . . . a certain **i** woman from*
*Rom 13:13 . . . promiscuity and **i** living,*
*Eph 5:5 . . . be sure that no **i,** impure,*
*1 Tim 1:10 . . . people who are sexually **i,***
*Jude 4 . . . grace allows us to live **i** lives.*
*Rev 22:15 . . . the sorcerers, the sexually **i,***

IMMORALITY (n)
the quality or state of being immoral; an immoral act or practice
*Matt 15:19 . . . all sexual **i,** theft, lying,*
*Acts 15:29 . . . animals, and from sexual **i.***
*1 Cor 6:13 . . . made for sexual **i.***
*1 Cor 6:18 . . . **i** is a sin against*
*1 Cor 7:2 . . . there is so much sexual **i,***
*Gal 5:19 . . . very clear: sexual **i,** impurity,*
*2 Pet 2:7 . . . who was sick of the shameful **i***
*Jude 7 . . . towns, which were filled with **i***

IMPARTIAL (adj)
not partial or biased; treating all equally
*Deut 1:17 . . . and **i** in your judgments.*
*Matt 22:16 . . . **i** and don't play favorites.*

IMPOSSIBLE (adj)
incapable of being or occurring
*Zech 8:6 . . . All this may seem **i** to you now,*
*Luke 1:37 . . . For nothing is **i** with God.*
*Heb 6:4 . . . it is **i** to bring back*
*Heb 11:6 . . . it is **i** to please God*

INDULGE, INDULGED, INDULGES (v)
to take unrestrained pleasure in
*Rom 1:26 . . . **i-d** in sex with each other.*
*Rom 13:14 . . . ways to **i** your evil desires.*
*1 Cor 5:9 . . . people who **i** in sexual sin.*
*1 Cor 5:11 . . . claims to be a believer yet **i-s***

INFANTS (n)
a child in the first period of (physical or spiritual) life
*Ps 8:2 . . . and **i** to tell of Your strength,*
*Matt 21:16 . . . and **i** to give You praise.*
*1 Cor 3:1 . . . were **i** in the Christian life.*

INHERITANCE (n)
the acquisition of a possession, condition, or trait from past generations; something that is or may be inherited
*Ps 16:6 . . . What a wonderful **i!***
*Ps 33:12 . . . people He has chosen as His **i.***
*Ps 61:5 . . . an **i** reserved for those who fear*
*Gal 4:30 . . . will not share the **i***
*Eph 1:14 . . . give us the **i** He promised*
*Col 3:24 . . . give you an **i** as your reward,*
*Heb 9:15 . . . receive the eternal **i** God has*

INIQUITY, INIQUITIES (KJV)
*Ps 51:9 . . . Remove the stain of my **guilt***
*Isa 6:7 . . . your **guilt** is removed,*
*Isa 53:6 . . . the LORD laid on Him the **sins** of us*
*1 Cor 13:6 . . . not rejoice about **injustice***
*Rev 18:5 . . . God remembers her **evil deeds***

INNOCENCE (n)
freedom from guilt or sin through being unacquainted with evil; blamelessness
*Gen 20:5 . . . I acted in complete **i!***
*2 Sam 22:25 . . . He has seen my **i.***
*Hos 8:5 . . . will you be incapable of **i?***

INNOCENT (adj)
regarded as righteous; free from guilt or sin; unaware or ignorant
*Job 13:18 . . . I will be proved **i.***
*Job 34:5 . . . Job also said, 'I am **i,***
*Ps 7:8 . . . for I am **i,** O Most High!*
*Ps 26:1 . . . Declare me **i,** O LORD, for I*
*Ps 143:2 . . . no one is **i** before You.*
*Matt 27:4 . . . I have betrayed an **i** man.*
*Matt 27:24 . . . I am **i** of this man's blood.*
*Rom 16:18 . . . they deceive **i** people.*

INSIGHT (n)
the power or act of seeing into a situation; discernment
*Ps 19:8 . . . are clear, giving **i** for living.*
*Prov 7:4 . . . make **i** a beloved member*
*Eph 1:17 . . . and **i** so that you might grow*

INSPIRED (adj)
to influence, move, or guide by divine influence
*2 Tim 3:16 . . . All Scripture is **i** by God*

INSTRUCT, INSTRUCTED, INSTRUCTS (v)
to provide with authoritative information or advice; to teach, train, or direct
*Exod 4:12 . . . I will **i** you in what to say.*
*Deut 2:1 . . . just as the LORD had **i-ed** me,*
*Deut 4:36 . . . so He could **i** you.*
*Josh 11:9 . . . chariots, as the LORD had **i-ed.***
*Josh 11:23 . . . as the LORD had **i-ed** Moses.*
*Ps 105:22 . . . He could **i** the king's aides*
*Prov 9:9 . . . **I** the wise, and they will be even*
*Prov 10:8 . . . The wise are glad to be **i-ed,***
*Prov 21:11 . . . if You **i** the wise,*
*Acts 8:31 . . . unless someone **i-s** me?*
*2 Tim 2:25 . . . Gently **i** those who oppose*
*Titus 2:12 . . . **i-ed** to turn from godless living*

INSTRUCTION, INSTRUCTIONS (n)
a command or principle intended especially as a general rule of action; an order; directions; the action, practice, or profession of teaching
see also LAW(S), COMMANDMENT(S)
*Exod 34:32 . . . Moses gave them all the **i-s***
*Deut 31:11 . . . you must read this Book of **I***
*Josh 1:7 . . . Be careful to obey all the **i-s***
*Josh 1:8 . . . Study this Book of **I***
*Ps 19:7 . . . The **i-s** of the LORD are perfect,*
*Ps 40:8 . . . your **i-s** are written on my heart.*
*Ps 119:97 . . . Oh, how I love your **i-s!***
*Prov 4:13 . . . Take hold of my **i-s;***
*Prov 7:2 . . . Guard my **i-s** as you guard*
*Prov 8:33 . . . Listen to my **i** and be wise.*
*Prov 23:12 . . . Commit yourself to **i;***
*Isa 40:14 . . . need **i** about what is good?*
*Jer 31:33 . . . put my **i-s** deep within*
*Zech 7:12 . . . they could not hear the **i-s***
*1 Tim 1:5 . . . purpose of my **i** is that all*
*1 Tim 1:18 . . . here are my **i-s** for you,*

INTEGRITY (n)
honesty; without compromise or corruption
*Job 2:3 . . . a man of complete **i.***
*Job 2:9 . . . still trying to maintain your **i?***
*Job 27:5 . . . I will defend my **i** until I die.*
*Ps 25:21 . . . May **i** and honesty protect me,*
*Ps 26:11 . . . I live with **i.** So redeem*
*Ps 111:8 . . . faithfully and with **i.***
*Ps 119:1 . . . Joyful are people of **i,***
*Prov 2:7 . . . shield to those who walk with **i.***

*Prov 10:9 . . . People with **i** walk safely,*
*Titus 2:7 . . . you do reflect the **i***

INVISIBLE (adj)
hidden; imperceptible
*Rom 1:20 . . . see His **i** qualities—*
*Col 1:15 . . . visible image of the **i** God.*
*Heb 11:27 . . . his eyes on the one who is **i.***

ISRAEL
1. The United Kingdom of Israel, including all twelve tribes, as ruled by Saul, David, and Solomon.
2. The Northern Kingdom of Israel, including the ten northern tribes, in contrast to Judah (Southern Kingdom) (*see* 2 Sam 19:41-43).

*Exod 3:9 . . . cry of the people of **I** has*
*Exod 12:37 . . . **I** left Rameses and started for*
*Exod 16:1 . . . **I** set out from Elim*
*Exod 28:29 . . . **I** on the sacred chestpiece*
*Exod 31:16 . . . **I** must keep the Sabbath day*
*Exod 39:42 . . . **I** followed all of the LORD's*
*Lev 25:55 . . . the people of **I** belong to Me.*
*Num 6:23 . . . **I** with this special blessing:*
*Num 9:17 . . . **I** would break camp and follow it.*
*Num 20:22 . . . community of **I** left Kadesh*
*Num 27:12 . . . I have given the people of **I.***
*Num 35:10 . . . instructions to the people of **I.***
*Deut 10:12 . . . **I,** what does the LORD your God*
*Josh 21:3 . . . **I** gave the Levites the following*
*Judg 17:6 . . . In those days **I** had no king;*
*1 Sam 3:20 . . . And all **I,** from Dan*
*1 Sam 4:21 . . . said, "**I**'s glory is gone."*
*1 Sam 15:26 . . . rejected you as king of **I.***
*1 Sam 18:16 . . . all **I** and Judah loved David*
*2 Sam 14:25 . . . most handsome man in all **I.***
*1 Kgs 1:35 . . . appointed him to be ruler over **I***
*1 Kgs 12:1 . . . **I** had gathered to make him king.*
*1 Kgs 19:18 . . . I will preserve 7,000 others in **I***
*2 Kgs 17:24 . . . replacing the people of **I.***
*1 Chr 11:4 . . . David and all **I** went to Jerusalem*
*1 Chr 21:1 . . . Satan rose up against **I***
*2 Chr 9:8 . . . Because God loves **I***
*Ps 73:1 . . . Truly God is good to **I,***
*Ps 98:3 . . . to love and be faithful to **I.***
*Isa 44:6 . . . says—**I**'s King and Redeemer,*
*Isa 44:21 . . . you are my servant, O **I.***
*Jer 2:3 . . . In those days **I** was holy*
*Jer 31:2 . . . I will give rest to the people of **I.***
*Jer 31:9 . . . For I am **I**'s father,*
*Jer 31:31 . . . new covenant with the people of **I***
*Ezek 3:17 . . . as a watchman for **I.***
*Hos 1:10 . . . **I**'s people will be like the sands*
*Hos 3:1 . . . LORD still loves **I,** even though*
*Amos 4:12 . . . in judgment, you people of **I!***
*Amos 8:2 . . . Like this fruit, **I** is ripe*
*Mic 5:2 . . . a ruler of **I** will come from you,*
*Mal 1:5 . . . far beyond **I**'s borders!*
*Matt 2:6 . . . the shepherd for My people **I.***
*Matt 10:6 . . . people of **I**—God's lost sheep.*
*Matt 15:24 . . . lost sheep—the people of **I.***
*Mark 12:29 . . . Listen, O **I!***
*Acts 1:6 . . . has the time come for You to free **I***
*Acts 9:15 . . . as well as to the people of **I.***
*Rom 9:4 . . . **I,** chosen to be God's adopted*
*Rom 9:6 . . . **I** are truly members of God's*
*Rom 9:27 . . . **I** are as numerous as the sand*
*Rom 9:31 . . . **I,** who tried so hard to get right*
*Rom 10:1 . . . the people of **I** to be saved.*
*Rom 11:7 . . . **I** have not found the favor of God*
*Rom 11:26 . . . And so all **I** will be saved.*
*Eph 2:12 . . . citizenship among the people of **I,***
*Heb 8:8 . . . new covenant with the people of **I***
*Rev 7:4 . . . sealed from all the tribes of **I:***
*Rev 21:12 . . . **I** were written on the gates.*

J

JEALOUSY (n)
a jealous feeling, disposition, or attitude
*Prov 27:4 . . . but **j** is even more dangerous.*
*Rom 10:19 . . . I will rouse Your **j***
*Rom 13:13 . . . or in quarreling and **j.***
*1 Cor 10:22 . . . dare to rouse the Lord's **j?***
*2 Cor 11:2 . . . you with the **j** of God*
*Gal 5:20 . . . **j,** outbursts of anger,*
*1 Tim 6:4 . . . arguments ending in **j,***
*1 Pet 2:1 . . . with all deceit, hypocrisy, **j,***

JEHOVAH (KJV)
*Exod 6:3 . . . did not reveal My name, **Yahweh,** to*
*Ps 83:18 . . . You alone are called **the LORD***
*Isa 12:2 . . . The LORD **God** is my strength and*
*Isa 26:4 . . . the LORD **God** is the eternal Rock*

JERICHO (n)
a city in the plain of the Jordan Valley at the foot of the ascent to the Judean mountains
*Num 22:1 . . . across from **J.***
*Josh 3:16 . . . near the town of **J.***
*Josh 5:10 . . . at Gilgal on the plains of **J,***
*Luke 10:30 . . . trip from Jerusalem to **J,***
*Heb 11:30 . . . around **J** for seven days,*

JERUSALEM (n)
sacred city and well-known capital of Palestine during Bible times
*Judg 1:8 . . . Judah attacked **J** and captured it,*
*2 Sam 5:5 . . . **J** he reigned over all Israel*
*2 Sam 11:1 . . . David stayed behind in **J.***
*1 Kgs 14:25 . . . Egypt came up and attacked **J.***
*2 Kgs 19:31 . . . will spread out from **J,***
*2 Kgs 21:12 . . . I will bring such disaster on **J***
*2 Kgs 25:9 . . . and all the houses of **J.***
*1 Chr 21:16 . . . reaching out over **J.***
*2 Chr 3:1 . . . the Temple of the LORD in **J***
*2 Chr 9:1 . . . she came to **J** to test him*
*2 Chr 36:19 . . . tore down the walls of **J,***
*Ezra 2:1 . . . but now they returned to **J***
*Ezra 6:12 . . . God who has chosen the city of **J***
*Ezra 9:9 . . . a protective wall in Judah and **J.***
*Neh 1:3 . . . The wall of **J** has been torn*
*Neh 12:43 . . . joy of the people of **J** could be*
*Ps 9:11 . . . the LORD who reigns in **J.***
*Ps 51:18 . . . rebuild the walls of **J.***
*Ps 87:2 . . . He loves the city of **J** more than*
*Ps 122:6 . . . Pray for peace in **J.***
*Ps 128:5 . . . May you see **J** prosper*
*Ps 137:3 . . . Sing us one of those songs of **J!***
*Ps 137:5 . . . If I forget You, O **J,***
*Ps 147:2 . . . The LORD is rebuilding **J***
*Ps 147:12 . . . Glorify the LORD, O **J!***
*Isa 1:1 . . . saw concerning Judah and **J.***
*Isa 3:1 . . . take away from **J** and Judah*
*Isa 4:3 . . . who survive the destruction of **J***
*Isa 27:13 . . . return to **J** to worship the LORD*
*Isa 51:11 . . . They will enter **J** singing,*
*Isa 52:8 . . . they see the LORD returning to **J.***
*Isa 62:7 . . . he makes **J** the pride of the earth.*
*Jer 39:1 . . . came with His army to besiege **J.***
*Jer 51:50 . . . think about Your home in **J.***
*Dan 6:10 . . . windows open toward **J.***
*Dan 9:2 . . . **J** must lie desolate for seventy*
*Dan 9:12 . . . such a disaster as happened in **J.***
*Dan 9:25 . . . the command is given to rebuild **J***
*Joel 3:16 . . . from Zion and thunder from **J,***
*Amos 2:5 . . . fortresses of **J** will be destroyed.*
*Zeph 3:16 . . . the announcement to **J** will be,*
*Zech 1:17 . . . Zion and choose **J** as His own.*
*Zech 2:4 . . . **J** will someday be so full*
*Zech 8:8 . . . home again to live safely in **J.***
*Zech 8:22 . . . nations will come to **J** to seek*
*Zech 9:10 . . . and the warhorses from **J.***
*Zech 12:10 . . . and on the people of **J.***
*Zech 14:8 . . . waters will flow out from **J,***
*Matt 20:18 . . . going up to **J,** where the Son*
*Matt 21:10 . . . city of **J** was in an uproar*
*Mark 10:33 . . . going up to **J,** where the Son*
*Luke 2:22 . . . parents took Him to **J***
*Luke 4:9 . . . Then the devil took Him to **J,***
*Luke 9:31 . . . about to be fulfilled in **J.***
*Luke 21:20 . . . you see **J** surrounded*
*Luke 24:47 . . . all the nations, beginning in **J:***
*Acts 1:8 . . . about me everywhere—in **J,***
*Acts 6:7 . . . believers greatly increased in **J,***
*Acts 20:22 . . . bound by the Spirit to go to **J.***
*Acts 23:11 . . . a witness to Me here in **J,***
*Rom 9:33 . . . I am placing a stone in **J***
*Rom 11:26 . . . who rescues will come from **J,***
*Gal 4:25 . . . **J** is just like Mount Sinai*
*Gal 4:26 . . . Sarah, represents the heavenly **J.***
*Heb 12:22 . . . of the living God, the heavenly **J,***
*Rev 21:10 . . . He showed me the holy city, **J,***

JOIN, JOINED, JOINS (v)
to put or bring into close association or relationship; to take part in a collective activity
*Ps 26:5 . . . I refuse to **j** in with the wicked.*
*Dan 11:34 . . . who **j** them will not be sincere.*
*Zech 2:11 . . . will **j** themselves to the LORD*
*Matt 19:6 . . . what God has **j-ed** together.*
*Mark 10:9 . . . what God has **j-ed** together.*
*Rom 6:3 . . . **j-ed** with Christ Jesus in baptism,*
*Rom 8:16 . . . his Spirit **j-s** with our spirit*
*Rom 15:30 . . . **j** in my struggle by praying*
*1 Cor 6:16 . . . if a man **j-s** himself to*
*Eph 2:21 . . . carefully **j-ed** together in him,*

JOY, JOYS (n)
the emotion evoked by well-being, success, or good fortune
*Deut 16:15 . . . be a time of great **j** for all.*
*1 Sam 18:6 . . . danced for **j** with tambourines*
*Neh 8:10 . . . **j** of the LORD is your strength!*
*Neh 8:17 . . . they were all filled with great **j!***
*Esth 9:22 . . . and their mourning into **j.***
*Ps 2:12 . . . **j** for all who take refuge in Him!*
*Ps 9:2 . . . filled with **j** because of You.*
*Ps 19:8 . . . are right, bringing **j** to the heart.*
*Ps 21:1 . . . He shouts with **j***
*Ps 28:7 . . . my heart is filled with **j.***
*Ps 30:11 . . . and clothed me with **j,***
*Ps 32:2 . . . what **j** for those whose record*
*Ps 42:4 . . . singing for **j** and giving thanks*
*Ps 45:7 . . . pouring out the oil of **j** on you*
*Ps 51:12 . . . to Me the **j** of Your salvation,*
*Ps 65:8 . . . You inspire shouts of **j.***
*Ps 65:13 . . . They all shout and sing for **j!***
*Ps 71:23 . . . I will shout for **j** and sing*
*Ps 92:4 . . . I sing for **j** because of what*
*Ps 98:4 . . . in praise and sing for **j!***
*Ps 126:2 . . . with laughter, and we sang for **j.***
*Ps 132:9 . . . loyal servants sing for **j.***
*Ps 132:16 . . . servants will sing for **j.***
*Ps 145:7 . . . with **j** about your righteousness.*
*Prov 10:1 . . . A wise child brings **j***
*Prov 15:20 . . . Sensible children bring **j** to*
*Prov 23:25 . . . your father and mother **j!***
*Isa 12:6 . . . Jerusalem shout His praise with **j!***
*Isa 26:19 . . . will rise up and sing for **j!***
*Isa 35:10 . . . crowned with everlasting **j.***
*Isa 49:13 . . . Sing for **j,** O heavens!*
*Isa 51:11 . . . filled with **j** and gladness.*
*Isa 52:8 . . . watchmen shout and sing with **j,***
*Isa 56:7 . . . fill them with **j** in My house*
*Isa 61:7 . . . everlasting **j** will be yours.*
*Isa 65:14 . . . My servants will sing for **j,** but*
*Jer 31:13 . . . young women will dance for **j,***
*Jer 31:13 . . . turn their mourning into **j.***
*Matt 2:10 . . . they were filled with **j!***
*Matt 28:8 . . . but also filled with great **j,***
*Mark 1:11 . . . Son, and You bring Me great **j.***

Luke 1:44 . . . in my womb jumped for **j**.
Luke 10:21 . . . with the **j** of the Holy Spirit,
Luke 24:41 . . . filled with **j** and wonder.
John 15:11 . . . you will be filled with My **j**.
John 16:20 . . . turn to wonderful **j**.
John 16:24 . . . and you will have abundant **j**.
John 20:20 . . . with **j** when they saw the Lord!
Acts 2:28 . . . You will fill me with the **j**
Acts 2:46 . . . their meals with great **j**
Acts 11:23 . . . filled with **j**
Acts 13:52 . . . believers were filled with **j**
Rom 14:17 . . . and **j** in the Holy Spirit.
2 Cor 1:24 . . . so you will be full of **j**,
2 Cor 7:7 . . . I was filled with **j**!
Gal 5:22 . . . fruit in our lives: love, **j**, peace,
Phil 1:4 . . . requests for all of you with **j**,
Phil 1:25 . . . and experience the **j** of your faith.
Phil 4:1 . . . you are my **j** and the crown I
1 Thes 1:6 . . . received the message with **j**
1 Thes 2:19 . . . what gives us hope and **j**,
1 Thes 2:20 . . . Yes, you are our pride and **j**.
1 Thes 3:9 . . . we have great **j**
2 Tim 1:4 . . . with **j** when we are together
Heb 10:34 . . . you accepted it with **j**.
Heb 13:17 . . . reason to do this with **j**
Jas 1:2 . . . it an opportunity for great **j**.
1 Pet 1:8 . . . a glorious, inexpressible **j**.
1 Jn 1:4 . . . you may fully share our **j**.

JUDAH
The Southern Kingdom of Judah, including the tribes of Judah and Benjamin, in contrast to Israel (Northern Kingdom) (*see* 2 Sam 12:8).

JUDEA (n)
the Greco-Roman name for the land of Judah
Matt 2:1 . . . was born in Bethlehem in **J**,
Matt 24:16 . . . in **J** must flee to the hills.
Luke 3:1 . . . Pilate was governor over **J**;
Acts 1:8 . . . throughout **J**, in Samaria,
Acts 9:31 . . . had peace throughout **J**,
1 Thes 2:14 . . . in God's churches in **J**

JUDGE, JUDGES (n)
a public official authorized to decide issues brought before a court; one of a cycle of charismatic deliverers of ancient Israel
Deut 17:12 . . . to reject the verdict of the **j**
Judg 2:16 . . . LORD raised up **j-s** to rescue
Judg 2:18 . . . the LORD raised up a **j**
1 Sam 7:6 . . . Samuel became Israel's **j**.)
1 Sam 7:15 . . . continued as Israel's **j**
Ps 50:6 . . . God himself will be the **j**.
Isa 33:22 . . . the LORD is our **j**, our lawgiver,
Acts 7:35 . . . you a ruler and **j** over us?
Acts 10:42 . . . **j** of all—the living and
Rev 14:7 . . . He will sit as **j**.

JUDGE, JUDGED, JUDGES, JUDGING (v)
to form an evaluation of; to decide as a judge; to govern or rule; to punish or condemn; to form a negative opinion about
1 Sam 16:7 . . . Don't **j** by his appearance or
1 Sam 24:12 . . . the LORD **j** between us.
2 Chr 19:7 . . . **j** with integrity, for the LORD
Ps 7:8 . . . The LORD **j-s** the nations.
Ps 9:4 . . . For you have **j-d** in my favor;
Ps 9:8 . . . He will **j** the world
Ps 82:8 . . . Rise up, O God, and **j** the earth,
Ps 96:10 . . . He will **j** all peoples fairly.
Ps 96:13 . . . He will **j** the world with justice,
Prov 16:10 . . . He must never **j** unfairly.
Prov 29:14 . . . If a king **j-s** the poor fairly,
Isa 11:3 . . . He will not **j** by appearance
Isa 66:16 . . . He will **j** the earth,
Matt 7:1 . . . Do not **j** others, and you
Matt 16:27 . . . will **j** all people according
Matt 19:28 . . . twelve thrones, **j-ing** the twelve
John 3:18 . . . already been **j-d** for not believing
John 5:22 . . . the Father **j-s** no one.
John 5:22 . . . absolute authority to **j**,
John 5:27 . . . authority to **j** everyone
John 5:30 . . . I **j** as God tells me.
John 12:31 . . . time for **j-ing** this world
John 12:47 . . . not **j** those who hear me
Acts 17:31 . . . He has set a day for **j-ing**
Rom 2:16 . . . Jesus, will **j** everyone's secret
Rom 3:6 . . . be qualified to **j** the world?
1 Cor 6:2 . . . we believers will **j** the world?
1 Cor 11:31 . . . ourselves, we would not be **j-d**
2 Cor 5:10 . . . all stand before Christ to be **j-d**.
2 Tim 4:1 . . . Jesus, who will someday **j**
Heb 10:30 . . . The LORD will **j** His own
Heb 13:4 . . . **j** people who are immoral
Jas 2:13 . . . God will be merciful when He **j-s**
Jas 3:1 . . . we who teach will be **j-d** more
Jas 4:11 . . . criticizing and **j-ing** God's law.
Jas 4:12 . . . So what right do you have to **j**
1 Pet 1:17 . . . He will **j** or reward you
1 Pet 2:23 . . . God, who always **j-s** fairly.
Rev 19:11 . . . **j-s** fairly and wages a righteous
Rev 20:4 . . . given the authority to **j**.
Rev 20:12 . . . the dead were **j-d** according to

JUDGMENT, JUDGMENTS (n)
a ruling or moral decision by a ruler (often God), a judge, or an individual; the process of forming an opinion or evalution by discerning and comparing;
see also JUSTICE
Deut 1:17 . . . impartial in Your **j-s**.
1 Sam 3:13 . . . warned him that **j** is coming
Ps 1:5 . . . be condemned at the time of **j**.
Ps 37:13 . . . He sees their day of **j** coming.
Ps 51:4 . . . Your **j** against me is just.
Prov 4:1 . . . Pay attention and learn good **j**,
Prov 4:7 . . . else you do, develop good **j**.
Prov 9:10 . . . results in good **j**.
Isa 3:14 . . . comes forward to pronounce **j**
Jer 11:20 . . . You make righteous **j-s**,
Jer 25:31 . . . His cry of **j** will reach
Dan 9:11 . . . curses and **j-s** written in
Hos 6:5 . . . with **j-s** as inescapable as light.
Joel 3:12 . . . LORD, will sit to pronounce **j**
Matt 5:21 . . . murder, you are subject to **j**.
Matt 11:24 . . . will be better off on **j** day
Matt 12:36 . . . on **j** day for every idle word
Matt 12:41 . . . this generation on **j** day
John 5:30 . . . **j** is just, because I carry out
John 8:16 . . . if I did, my **j** would be correct
John 16:8 . . . and of the coming **j**.
Acts 24:25 . . . coming day of **j**,
1 Cor 4:3 . . . I don't even trust my own **j**
1 Cor 4:5 . . . don't make **j-s** about anyone
1 Cor 11:29 . . . eating and drinking God's **j**
2 Thes 1:8 . . . **j** on those who don't know
Heb 9:27 . . . and after that comes **j**,
1 Pet 4:17 . . . And if **j** begins with us,
2 Pet 2:9 . . . until the day of final **j**.
2 Pet 3:7 . . . being kept for the day of **j**,
Jude 6 . . . waiting for the great day of **j**.
Rev 16:7 . . . Your **j-s** are true and just.

JUST (adj)
conforming to a standard of correctness; faithful to the original design; honest, fair, upright
see also RIGHT, RIGHTEOUS
Gen 18:19 . . . by doing what is right and **j**.
Deut 32:4 . . . Everything He does is **j**
2 Sam 8:15 . . . did what was **j** and right
Neh 9:13 . . . and instructions that were **j**,
Job 37:23 . . . He is **j** and righteous,
Ps 33:5 . . . He loves whatever is **j** and good;
Ps 92:15 . . . The LORD is **j**! He is
Ps 119:121 . . . I have done what is **j**
Prov 1:3 . . . do what is right, **j**, and fair.
Prov 2:9 . . . will understand what is right, **j**,
Prov 12:5 . . . The plans of the godly are **j**;
Isa 16:5 . . . He will always do what is **j**
Isa 59:8 . . . or what it means to be **j**
Jer 22:3 . . . Be fair-minded and **j**.
Ezek 18:5 . . . and does what is **j** and right.
Dan 4:37 . . . All His acts are **j** and true,
Matt 5:45 . . . rain on the **j** and the unjust
1 Cor 11:1 . . . imitate me, **j** as I imitate
1 Jn 1:9 . . . He is faithful and **j** to forgive
Rev 15:3 . . . **J** and true are Your ways,
Rev 16:5 . . . You are **j**, O Holy One,
Rev 16:7 . . . your judgments are true and **j**.
Rev 19:2 . . . His judgments are true and **j**.

JUSTICE (n)
the administration of law that determines what is right, based on principles of equity and correctness, and rewards accordingly; the quality of being just, impartial, or fair
see also JUDGMENT, RIGHTEOUSNESS
Exod 23:2 . . . by the crowd to twist **j**.
Lev 19:15 . . . Do not twist **j** in legal matters
Deut 16:19 . . . never twist **j**
Deut 32:36 . . . LORD will give **j** to His
1 Sam 8:3 . . . accepted bribes and perverted **j**.
1 Kgs 3:11 . . . governing My people with **j**
1 Kgs 7:7 . . . Hall of **J**, where he sat to hear
2 Chr 9:8 . . . so you can rule with **j**
Job 8:3 . . . Does God twist **j**?
Job 19:7 . . . I protest, but there is no **j**.
Job 31:6 . . . weigh me on the scales of **j**,
Job 34:17 . . . God govern if He hated **j**?
Ps 9:8 . . . He will judge the world with **j**
Ps 10:18 . . . You will bring **j** to the orphans
Ps 36:6 . . . Your **j** like the ocean depths.
Ps 45:4 . . . defending truth, humility, and **j**.
Ps 45:7 . . . You love **j** and hate evil.
Ps 72:1 . . . Give Your love of **j** to the king,
Ps 82:3 . . . Give **j** to the poor
Ps 96:13 . . . He will judge the world with **j**,
Ps 98:9 . . . **j**, and the nations with fairness.
Ps 99:4 . . . You have acted with **j**
Ps 103:6 . . . **j** to all who are treated
Ps 146:7 . . . He gives **j** to the oppressed
Prov 16:12 . . . His rule is built on **j**.
Prov 19:28 . . . makes a mockery of **j**;
Prov 29:26 . . . but **j** comes from the LORD.
Prov 31:9 . . . and see that they get **j**.
Isa 1:17 . . . Seek **j**. Help the oppressed.
Isa 1:27 . . . Zion will be restored by **j**;
Isa 5:16 . . . will be exalted by His **j**.
Isa 10:2 . . . They deprive the poor of **j**
Isa 28:17 . . . with the measuring line of **j**
Isa 33:5 . . . make Jerusalem His home of **j**
Isa 42:1 . . . He will bring **j** to the nations.
Isa 51:4 . . . My **j** will become a light
Isa 59:9 . . . there is no **j** among us,
Isa 59:14 . . . **j** is nowhere to be found.
Isa 61:8 . . . I, the LORD, love **j**.
Jer 4:2 . . . you could do so with truth, **j**,
Jer 9:24 . . . who brings **j** and righteousness
Jer 21:12 . . . Give **j** each morning
Jer 30:11 . . . discipline you, but with **j**;
Lam 3:36 . . . if they twist **j** in the courts—
Hos 2:19 . . . righteousness and **j**,
Amos 5:7 . . . You twist **j**, making it a bitter
Amos 5:15 . . . courts into true halls of **j**.
Amos 6:12 . . . when you turn **j** into poison
Mic 3:8 . . . I am filled with **j** and strength
Hab 1:4 . . . there is no **j** in the courts.
Zeph 3:5 . . . Day by day He hands down **j**,
Mal 2:17 . . . Where is the God of **j**?
Matt 5:6 . . . who hunger and thirst for **j**,
Matt 12:18 . . . proclaim **j** to the nations.
Matt 23:23 . . . aspects of the law—**j**,
Luke 11:42 . . . ignore **j** and the love of God.

Luke 18:3 . . . Give me **j** in this dispute
Acts 8:33 . . . was humiliated and received no **j.**
Acts 17:31 . . . **j** by the man
Rom 2:2 . . . God, in His **j,** will punish
2 Thes 1:5 . . . persecution to show His **j**
2 Thes 1:6 . . . In His **j** He will pay back
Heb 1:8 . . . You rule with a scepter of **j.**
Heb 7:2 . . . Melchizedek means "king of **j,**"
Heb 11:33 . . . ruled with **j,**

JUSTIFY, JUSTIFIED (v)
to prove to be just, right, or reasonable; to acquit or absolve
see also RIGHT, RIGHTEOUS
Luke 10:29 . . . wanted to **j** his actions,
Luke 18:14 . . . returned home **j-ied**
2 Cor 8:24 . . . boasting about You is **j-ied.**

K

KEEP, KEEPING, KEEPS, KEPT (v)
to be faithful to; to have in control; to refrain from granting, giving, or allowing; to cause to remain in a given place, situation, or condition; to refrain from revealing; to maintain or preserve
see also GUARD, OBEY, PROTECT
Exod 12:42 . . . the LORD **k-pt** His promise
Exod 20:8 . . . Sabbath day by **k-ing** it holy.
Exod 31:13 . . . Be careful to **k** My Sabbath
Deut 5:12 . . . Sabbath day by **k-ing** it holy,
Deut 7:8 . . . **k-ing** the oath He had sworn
Deut 7:9 . . . God who **k-s** His covenant for a
Deut 7:12 . . . your God will **k** His covenant
2 Chr 6:14 . . . You **k** Your covenant
2 Chr 34:31 . . . to obey the LORD by **k-ing**
Neh 1:5 . . . God who **k-s** His covenant of
Ps 15:4 . . . **k** their promises even when
Ps 116:14 . . . I will **k** My promises to
Ps 119:100 . . . **k-pt** Your commandments.
Ps 121:7 . . . The LORD **k-s** you from
Ps 130:3 . . . LORD, if You **k-pt** a record of
Ps 146:6 . . . He **k-s** every promise
Prov 10:19 . . . and **k** your mouth
Prov 15:3 . . . **k-ing** his eye on
Prov 21:23 . . . your tongue and **k**
Eccl 3:6 . . . A time to **k** and a time to
John 17:6 . . . and they have **k-pt** Your word.
Acts 2:24 . . . death could not **k** Him in its
Rom 10:3 . . . by trying to **k** the law.
Rom 14:22 . . . **k** it between yourself
1 Cor 1:8 . . . He will **k** you strong
1 Cor 7:19 . . . **k** God's commandments.
1 Cor 13:5 . . . it **k-s** no record
Eph 4:3 . . . effort to **k** yourselves united
1 Tim 5:22 . . . **K** yourself pure.
2 Tim 4:5 . . . But you should **k** a clear mind
Heb 11:27 . . . going because he **k-pt** his eyes
Jas 2:10 . . . the person who **k-s** all of the
1 Pet 1:4 . . . **k-pt** in heaven for you, pure and
1 Jn 5:3 . . . means **k-ing** His commandments,
Jude 21 . . . **k** yourselves safe in God's love.
Rev 12:17 . . . **k** God's commandments

KILL, KILLED, KILLING, KILLS (v)
to take or deprive of life
Gen 4:8 . . . Abel, and **k-ed** him.
Exod 2:12 . . . Moses **k-ed** the Egyptian
Exod 21:12 . . . assaults and **k-s** another
Lev 24:21 . . . but whoever **k-s** another person
2 Sam 2:26 . . . always be **k-ing** each other?
Neh 9:26 . . . they **k-ed** Your prophets
Job 13:15 . . . God might **k** me, but I
Ps 44:22 . . . for Your sake we are **k-ed**
Prov 6:17 . . . hands that **k** the innocent,
Eccl 3:3 . . . A time to **k** and a time to
Matt 10:28 . . . who want to **k** your body;
Matt 16:21 . . . He would be **k-ed,**
Mark 10:34 . . . flog him with a whip, and **k**
Luke 11:48 . . . They **k-ed** the prophets,
Acts 3:15 . . . You **k-ed** the author
Rom 8:36 . . . For Your sake we are **k-ed**
1 Tim 1:9 . . . who **k** their father or mother
1 Jn 3:12 . . . evil one and **k-ed** his brother.

KIND (adj)
affectionate, loving; of a sympathetic or helping nature; gentle
Luke 6:35 . . . for He is **k** to those who are
1 Cor 13:4 . . . is patient and **k.** Love is not
Eph 4:32 . . . Instead, be **k** to each other,
2 Tim 2:24 . . . but must be **k** to everyone,

KINDNESS (n)
a kind deed; affection; the quality or state of being kind
Ps 106:7 . . . His many acts of **k** to them.
Rom 2:4 . . . His **k** is intended to turn you
Rom 3:24 . . . with undeserved **k,** declares
Rom 12:8 . . . gift for showing **k** to others,
2 Cor 6:1 . . . marvelous gift of God's **k**
2 Cor 8:1 . . . God in his **k** has done through
2 Cor 10:1 . . . gentleness and **k** of Christ—
Gal 5:22 . . . peace, patience, **k,** goodness,
Eph 2:7 . . . His grace and **k** toward us,
Col 3:12 . . . mercy, **k,** humility,
Titus 3:4 . . . revealed His **k** and love,
1 Pet 2:3 . . . a taste of the Lord's **k.**

KINGDOM (n)
rule or realm; dominion of a king
Exod 19:6 . . . will be My **k** of priests,
1 Kgs 11:31 . . . to tear the **k** from the hand
1 Chr 28:7 . . . make His **k** last forever.
Ps 145:11 . . . glory of Your **k;**
Matt 3:2 . . . for the **K** of Heaven is near.
Matt 5:10 . . . right, for the **K** of Heaven is
Matt 6:10 . . . May your **K** come soon.
Matt 7:21 . . . will enter the **K** of Heaven.
Matt 8:12 . . . for whom the **K** was prepared—
Matt 13:11 . . . secrets of the **K** of Heaven,
Matt 13:38 . . . people of the **K.** The weeds
Matt 13:45 . . . Again, the **K** of Heaven is
Matt 18:4 . . . greatest in the **K** of Heaven.
Matt 19:12 . . . sake of the **K** of Heaven.
Matt 19:23 . . . to enter the **K** of Heaven.
Matt 20:1 . . . For the **K** of Heaven is
Matt 23:13 . . . shut the door of the **K** of Heaven
Matt 25:34 . . . inherit the **K** prepared for
Mark 3:24 . . . A **k** divided by
Mark 9:1 . . . they see the **K** of God arrive
Mark 10:15 . . . doesn't receive the **K** of God
Mark 10:24 . . . to enter the **K** of God.
Mark 13:8 . . . and **k** against **k.**
Luke 7:28 . . . the least person in the **K** of God
Luke 9:60 . . . preach about the **K** of God.
Luke 10:11 . . . know this—the **K** of God is
Luke 11:20 . . . the **K** of God has arrived
Luke 12:31 . . . Seek the **K** of God
Luke 13:18 . . . What is the **K** of God like?
Luke 17:20 . . . When will the **K** of God
Luke 21:10 . . . and **k** against **k.**
Luke 22:16 . . . fulfilled in the **K** of God.
Luke 23:42 . . . come into Your **K.**
John 3:3 . . . you cannot see the **K** of God.
John 18:36 . . . But My **K** is not of
Acts 28:23 . . . testified about the **K** of God
1 Cor 6:10 . . . will inherit the **K** of God.
1 Cor 15:24 . . . will turn the **K** over to God
Gal 5:21 . . . will not inherit the **K** of God.
Eph 5:5 . . . will inherit the **K** of Christ
Col 4:11 . . . with me here for the **K** of God.
1 Thes 2:12 . . . to share in His **K** and glory.
2 Thes 1:5 . . . worthy of His **K,** for which
2 Tim 4:18 . . . His heavenly **K.** All glory to
Heb 12:28 . . . we are receiving a **K** that is
Jas 2:5 . . . inherit the **K** He promised to
Rev 1:6 . . . made us a **K** of priests for
Rev 5:10 . . . to become a **K** of priests for
Rev 11:15 . . . now become the **K** of our Lord
Rev 12:10 . . . power and the **K** of our God,

KISS, KISSES (n)
a greeting or caress with the lips; an expression of affection
Prov 27:6 . . . better than many **k-es** from an
Song 7:9 . . . May your **k-es** be as
Mark 14:45 . . . and gave Him the **k.**
Luke 22:48 . . . the Son of Man with a **k?**

KNEEL, KNELT (v)
to bend the knee; to fall or rest on the knees; usually a gesture of submission, defeat, or reverence
2 Chr 6:13 . . . then he **k-lt** in front of
Ps 95:6 . . . Let us **k** before the LORD
Dan 6:10 . . . went home and **k-lt** down
Matt 8:2 . . . approached Him and **k-lt**
Matt 9:18 . . . came and **k-lt** before Him.
Matt 17:14 . . . came and **k-lt** before Jesus
Matt 27:29 . . . **k-lt** before Him in mockery
Luke 22:41 . . . stone's throw, and **k-lt** down
Acts 20:36 . . . speaking, He **k-lt** and prayed
Acts 21:5 . . . There we **k-lt,** prayed,

KNOCK, KNOCKING, KNOCKS (v)
to strike sharply
Matt 7:7 . . . Keep on **k-ing,** and the door
Matt 7:8 . . . to everyone who **k-s,** the door
Luke 11:9 . . . Keep on **k-ing,** and the door
Rev 3:20 . . . I stand at the door and **k.**

KNOW, KNOWN, KNOWS (v)
to be intimately familiar with; to discern, recognize, regard, acknowledge, pay heed to, approve, learn
Exod 6:7 . . . Then you will **k** that I am the
Deut 18:21 . . . How will we **k** whether or not
Deut 29:29 . . . God has secrets **k-n** to no one.
Job 19:25 . . . for me, I **k** that my Redeemer
Ps 9:10 . . . Those who **k** Your name trust
Ps 46:10 . . . Be still, and **k** that I am
Ps 94:10 . . . doesn't he also **k** what You
Ps 94:11 . . . The LORD **k-s** people's thoughts;
Ps 103:14 . . . For He **k-s** how weak we are;
Ps 119:168 . . . You **k** everything I do.
Ps 139:2 . . . You **k** when I sit
Ps 139:23 . . . O God, and **k** my heart;
Jer 31:34 . . . will **k** Me already,
Dan 11:32 . . . the people who **k** their God
Matt 6:3 . . . don't let your left hand **k** what
Matt 11:27 . . . and no one truly **k-s** the Father
Mark 12:24 . . . you don't **k** the Scriptures,
Luke 13:25 . . . will reply, 'I don't **k** you
Luke 16:15 . . . but God **k-s** your hearts.
Luke 23:34 . . . they don't **k** what they are
John 3:11 . . . you what we **k** and have seen,
John 6:69 . . . we **k** You are the Holy One
John 7:28 . . . Yes, you **k** Me, and you
John 8:32 . . . And you will **k** the truth,
John 10:4 . . . because they **k** His voice.
John 10:27 . . . I **k** them, and they follow
John 14:7 . . . If you had really **k-n** Me,
John 16:30 . . . we understand that You **k**
John 17:23 . . . the world will **k** that You sent
Acts 1:24 . . . O Lord, You **k** every heart.
Rom 1:19 . . . They **k** the truth
Rom 12:16 . . . And don't think you **k** it all!
Rom 16:26 . . . this message is made **k-n** to all
1 Cor 2:11 . . . no one can **k** God's thoughts
1 Cor 13:12 . . . All that I **k** now is partial
2 Cor 4:6 . . . so we could **k** the glory of
Phil 3:10 . . . I want to **k** Christ and
Col 1:10 . . . you learn to **k** God better and
2 Thes 1:8 . . . on those who don't **k** God
2 Tim 1:12 . . . I **k** the one in whom I trust,
2 Tim 2:19 . . . The LORD **k-s** those who are

*Jas 4:17 . . . it is sin to **k** what you ought*
*1 Pet 2:19 . . . do what you **k** is right and*
*1 Jn 2:3 . . . we can be sure that we **k** Him*
*1 Jn 2:4 . . . claims, "I **k** God," but*
*1 Jn 2:29 . . . Since we **k** that Christ*
*1 Jn 3:1 . . . they don't **k** Him.*
*1 Jn 3:24 . . . And we **k** He lives in us*
*1 Jn 4:6 . . . is how we **k** if someone has*
*1 Jn 4:7 . . . is a child of God and **k-s** God.*
*1 Jn 4:8 . . . does not **k** God, for God*
*1 Jn 5:13 . . . that you may **k** you have eternal*
*1 Jn 5:15 . . . And since we **k** He hears us*
*1 Jn 5:20 . . . And we **k** that the Son of*
*Rev 3:15 . . . I **k** all the things you do,*

KNOWLEDGE (n)
the fact or condition of being aware of something, of having information, or of being learned; information, wisdom
*Gen 2:9 . . . the tree of the **k** of good and*
*Gen 2:17 . . . the tree of the **k** of good and*
*Prov 1:7 . . . foundation of true **k**, but fools*
*Prov 2:6 . . . From his mouth come **k** and*
*Prov 3:20 . . . By his **k** the deep*
*Prov 8:10 . . . **k** rather than pure gold.*
*Prov 14:6 . . . **k** comes easily to those with*
*Prov 18:15 . . . Their ears are open for **k**.*
*Isa 11:2 . . . the Spirit of **k** and the fear*
*Luke 11:52 . . . the key to **k***
*Rom 2:20 . . . gives you complete **k***
*1 Cor 12:8 . . . gives a message of special **k**.*
*1 Cor 13:2 . . . and possessed all **k**,*
*1 Cor 13:9 . . . Now our **k** is partial*
*2 Cor 2:14 . . . to spread the **k** of Christ*
*Eph 1:17 . . . grow in your **k** of God.*
*Eph 4:13 . . . our faith and **k** of God's Son*
*Phil 1:9 . . . will keep on growing in **k** and*
*Col 1:9 . . . to give you complete **k** of His*
*Col 2:3 . . . treasures of wisdom and **k**.*
*Heb 10:26 . . . we have received **k** of the*
*2 Pet 1:5 . . . and moral excellence with **k**,*
*2 Pet 1:8 . . . **k** of our Lord Jesus Christ.*
*2 Pet 3:18 . . . the grace and **k** of our Lord*

L

LAID (v)
see also LAY
*Isa 53:6 . . . Yet the LORD **l** on him the*
*Acts 6:6 . . . as they **l** their hands on them.*
*Acts 8:18 . . . the apostles **l** their hands on*
*1 Tim 4:14 . . . elders of the church **l** their*
*2 Tim 1:6 . . . when I **l** my hands on*

LAMB, LAMBS (n)
a young sheep that is less than one year old
*Exod 12:21 . . . pick out a **l** or young goat*
*Isa 53:7 . . . He was led like a **l** to the*
*Mark 14:12 . . . the Passover **l** is sacrificed,*
*John 1:29 . . . and said, "Look! The **L** of God*
*John 21:15 . . . "Then feed My **l-s**," Jesus*
*Luke 10:3 . . . out as **l-s** among wolves.*
*Acts 8:32 . . . And as a **l** is silent before*
*1 Pet 1:19 . . . sinless, spotless **L** of God.*
*Rev 5:6 . . . Then I saw a **L** that looked as*
*Rev 5:12 . . . Worthy is the **L** who was*
*Rev 7:14 . . . robes in the blood of the **L***
*Rev 15:3 . . . the song of the **L**:*
*Rev 17:14 . . . to war against the **L**, but the*
*Rev 19:9 . . . to the wedding feast of the **L**.*
*Rev 21:23 . . . and the **L** is its light.*

LAME (adj)
having a disabled body part as to impair freedom of movement
*Isa 33:23 . . . Even the **l** will take*
*Isa 35:6 . . . The **l** will leap like a*
*Matt 11:5 . . . blind see, the **l** walk,*
*Matt 15:31 . . . the **l** were walking,*
*Luke 14:21 . . . the blind, and the **l**.*
*Heb 12:13 . . . weak and **l** will not fall*

LAMP, LAMPS (n)
a source of intellectual or spiritual illumination; any of various devices for producing light
*2 Sam 22:29 . . . O LORD, You are my **l**.*
*Ps 18:28 . . . You light a **l** for me.*
*Ps 119:105 . . . Your word is a **l** to guide my*
*Prov 6:23 . . . For their command is a **l***
*Prov 31:18 . . . her **l** burns late*
*Matt 6:22 . . . Your eye is a **l** that*
*Matt 25:1 . . . who took their **l-s***
*Matt 25:7 . . . got up and prepared their **l-s**.*
*Luke 8:16 . . . No one lights a **l** and then*
*Luke 12:35 . . . and keep your **l-s** burning,*
*Rev 22:5 . . . no need for **l-s** or sun—for the*

LAMPSTAND, LAMPSTANDS (n)
a support that holds a lamp
*Exod 25:31 . . . Make the entire **l** and its*
*2 Chr 4:7 . . . cast ten gold **l-s** according to*
*Zech 4:2 . . . a solid gold **l** with a bowl of*
*Zech 4:11 . . . on each side of the **l**,*
*Heb 9:2 . . . In the first room were a **l**,*
*Rev 1:12 . . . I saw seven gold **l-s**.*
*Rev 1:20 . . . the seven gold **l-s**:*
*Rev 2:5 . . . and remove Your **l** from its*

LANGUAGE, LANGUAGES (n)
audible, meaningful sound; dialect or manner of speech peculiar to a certain people; a special language gift given by the Holy Spirit
see also TONGUE(S)
*Gen 11:9 . . . the people with different **l-s**.*
*Isa 28:11 . . . speak a strange **l**!*
*Mark 16:17 . . . they will speak in new **l-s**.*
*Acts 2:4 . . . speaking in other **l-s**, as the*
*1 Cor 12:28 . . . speak in unknown **l-s**.*
*1 Cor 12:30 . . . to interpret unknown **l-s**?*
*1 Cor 13:8 . . . in unknown **l-s** and special*
*1 Cor 14:19 . . . in an unknown **l**.*
*Eph 4:29 . . . or abusive **l**. Let everything*
*Col 3:8 . . . slander, and dirty **l**.*
*Rev 5:9 . . . every tribe and **l** and people*
*Rev 7:9 . . . and tribe and people and **l**,*
*Rev 14:6 . . . nation, tribe, **l**, and people.*

LASCIVIOUSNESS (KJV)
*Mark 7:22 . . . deceit, **lustful desires**, envy,*
*2 Cor 12:21 . . . and **eagerness for lustful pleasure***
*Gal 5:19 . . . impurity, **lustful pleasures***
*Eph 4:19 . . . They live for **lustful pleasure***
*1 Pet 4:3 . . . their immorality and **lust**,*

LAST, LASTING (adj)
following all the rest; being the only remaining; belonging to the final stage; of or relating to being continuous in time; existing or continuing a long while
*Prov 10:25 . . . have a **l-ing** foundation.*
*Isa 41:4 . . . First and the **L**. I alone*
*Isa 44:6 . . . First and the **L**; there is no*
*Isa 48:12 . . . God, the First and the **L**.*
*John 15:16 . . . to go and produce **l-ing** fruit,*
*Acts 2:17 . . . 'In the **l** days,' God says,*
*1 Cor 15:26 . . . And the **l** enemy to be*
*1 Cor 15:52 . . . **l** trumpet is blown.*
*2 Tim 3:1 . . . that in the **l** days there will*
*2 Pet 3:3 . . . that in the **l** days scoffers*
*Jude 18 . . . you that in the **l** times there*
*Rev 1:17 . . . I am the First and the **L**.*
*Rev 22:13 . . . the Omega, the First and the **L**,*

LAUGH, LAUGHED, LAUGHS (v)
to show mirth or joy or to despise or mock something with a chuckle or explosive vocal sound
*Gen 17:17 . . . **l-ed** to himself in disbelief.*
*Gen 18:12 . . . So she **l-ed** silently to herself*
*Ps 2:4 . . . the one who rules in heaven **l-s**.*
*Ps 37:13 . . . the LORD just **l-s**, for he sees*
*Ps 59:8 . . . But LORD, you **l** at them.*
*Prov 31:25 . . . and she **l-s** without fear of the*
*Eccl 3:4 . . . and a time to **l**. A time to*
*Luke 6:21 . . . for in due time you will **l**.*
*Luke 6:25 . . . awaits you who **l** now,*

LAW, LAWS (n)
words of Moses; a binding decree; a universal principle; governing authority
see also COMMANDMENT(S), INSTRUCTION(S), REGULATIONS, TEACHING(S)
*2 Chr 17:9 . . . the Book of the **L***
*Ps 1:2 . . . delight in the **l** of the LORD,*
*Ps 93:5 . . . Your royal **l-s** cannot be*
*Ps 119:14 . . . rejoiced in Your **l-s** as much as*
*Ps 119:36 . . . for Your **l-s** rather than a love*
*Ps 119:125 . . . I will understand Your **l-s**.*
*Ps 119:152 . . . days that Your **l-s** will last*
*Matt 5:17 . . . to abolish the **l** of Moses or*
*Matt 5:19 . . . who obeys God's **l-s***
*Matt 22:40 . . . The entire **l** and all the*
*Matt 23:23 . . . of the **l**—justice, mercy,*
*Mark 7:8 . . . ignore God's **l** and substitute*
*Luke 11:52 . . . experts in religious **l**!*
*Luke 23:56 . . . they rested as required by the **l**.*
*Luke 24:44 . . . written about me in the **l***
*John 1:17 . . . For the **l** was given*
*Rom 2:12 . . . be judged by that **l** when they*
*Rom 2:15 . . . that God's **l** is written in*
*Rom 2:20 . . . that God's **l** gives you*
*Rom 2:25 . . . if you don't obey God's **l**,*
*Rom 3:19 . . . Obviously, the **l** applies to*
*Rom 3:21 . . . requirements of the **l**, as was*
*Rom 3:28 . . . not by obeying the **l**.*
*Rom 4:13 . . . his obedience to God's **l**,*
*Rom 4:16 . . . according to the **l** of Moses,*
*Rom 5:13 . . . was not yet any **l** to break.*
*Rom 6:15 . . . has set us free from the **l**,*
*Rom 7:4 . . . power of the **l** when you died*
*Rom 7:5 . . . the **l** aroused these evil desires*
*Rom 7:8 . . . If there were no **l**, sin would*
*Rom 7:12 . . . But still, the **l** itself is*
*Rom 7:22 . . . I love God's **l** with all my*
*Rom 7:25 . . . I really want to obey God's **l**,*
*Rom 8:3 . . . did what the **l** could not do.*
*Rom 8:4 . . . requirement of the **l** would be*
*Rom 8:7 . . . did obey God's **l-s**, and it*
*Rom 9:4 . . . gave them His **l**. He gave them*
*Rom 9:31 . . . with God by keeping the **l**,*
*Rom 10:4 . . . for which the **l** was given.*
*Rom 13:10 . . . requirements of God's **l**.*
*1 Cor 9:9 . . . For the **l** of Moses*
*1 Cor 9:21 . . . I obey the **l** of Christ.*
*2 Cor 3:6 . . . not of written **l-s**, but of the*
*Gal 2:16 . . . by obeying the **l**. And we have*
*Gal 2:19 . . . So I died to the **l**—I stopped*
*Gal 3:2 . . . by obeying the **l** of Moses?*
*Gal 3:5 . . . because you obey the **l**?*
*Gal 3:11 . . . by trying to keep the **l**.*
*Gal 3:19 . . . But the **l** was designed*
*Gal 3:21 . . . If the **l** could give us*
*Gal 3:23 . . . placed under guard by the **l**.*
*Gal 4:21 . . . live under the **l**, do you know*
*Gal 5:3 . . . in the whole **l** of Moses.*
*Gal 5:14 . . . the whole **l** can be summed*
*Gal 6:2 . . . this way obey the **l** of Christ.*
*Eph 2:15 . . . the system of **l** with its*
*Phil 3:6 . . . I obeyed the **l** without fault.*
*1 Tim 1:8 . . . know that the **l** is good when*
*Heb 10:1 . . . under the **l** of Moses*
*Jas 1:25 . . . into the perfect **l** that sets*
*Jas 2:8 . . . obey the royal **l** as found in*
*Jas 2:10 . . . all of the **l-s** except one is as*

LAWLESSNESS (n)
the quality or state of not being restrained or controlled by law
*2 Thes 2:3 . . . the man of **l** is revealed—*
*2 Thes 2:7 . . . For this **l** is already*
*2 Thes 2:8 . . . Then the man of **l** will be*

LAY, LAYING (v)
to put or set down
see also LAID
*Exod 29:10 . . . his sons will **l** their hands*
*Lev 1:4 . . . **L** your hand on*
*Lev 4:15 . . . must then **l** their hands on*
*Num 8:10 . . . of Israel must **l** their hands*
*Num 27:18 . . . in him, and **l** your hands on*
*Acts 8:19 . . . so that when I **l** my hands on*
*Heb 6:2 . . . the **l-ing** on of hands,*
*Rev 4:10 . . . And they **l** their crowns*

LAZINESS (n)
a disinclination to activity or exertion
*Prov 31:27 . . . suffers nothing from **l**.*
*Ezek 16:49 . . . gluttony, and **l**, while the*

LAZY (adj)
disinclined to activity or exertion; not energetic or vigorous
*Prov 12:27 . . . **L** people don't*
*Prov 20:4 . . . Those too **l** to plow in the*
*Rom 12:11 . . . Never be **l**, but work*
*1 Tim 5:13 . . . they will learn to be **l***
*Titus 1:12 . . . animals, and **l** gluttons.*

LEAD, LEADING, LEADS (v)
to guide by direction or example; to go at the head of; to result in
see also LED
*Deut 27:18 . . . anyone who **l-s** a blind person*
*Deut 31:2 . . . no longer able to **l** you.*
*Josh 1:6 . . . one who will **l** these people*
*2 Chr 1:10 . . . knowledge to **l** them*
*Ps 25:9 . . . He **l-s** the humble in*
*Ps 73:24 . . . with Your counsel, **l-ing** me to a*
*Prov 6:22 . . . counsel will **l** you.*
*Prov 14:30 . . . A peaceful heart **l-s** to a*
Prov 19:23 . . . Fear of the LORD ***l-s** to life,*
*Isa 11:6 . . . little child will **l** them all.*
*Matt 15:14 . . . are blind guides **l-ing** the blind,*
*John 10:3 . . . by name and **l-s** them out.*
*Rom 6:16 . . . to sin, which **l-s** to death,*
*Rom 6:22 . . . things that **l** to holiness and*
*1 Tim 5:24 . . . **l-ing** them to certain judgment.*
*Rev 7:17 . . . He will **l** them to*

LEADER, LEADERS (n)
a person who has commanding authority or influence; chief among others
*1 Sam 13:14 . . . to be the **l** of His people,*
*Prov 17:26 . . . to flog **l-s** for being honest.*
*Jer 51:46 . . . **l-s** fight against each other.*
*Matt 20:26 . . . a **l** among you must be*
*Mark 10:43 . . . a **l** among you must be*
*Luke 22:26 . . . **l** should be like a servant.*
*3 Jn 9 . . . to be the **l**, refuses to have*
*Acts 13:27 . . . Jerusalem and their **l-s** did not*
*1 Thes 5:12 . . . who are your **l-s** in the Lord's*
*Heb 13:7 . . . Remember your **l-s** who taught*
*Heb 13:17 . . . Obey your spiritual **l-s**, and do*

LEARN, LEARNED, LEARNS (v)
to come to know or realize; to acquire knowledge, skill, or behavioral tendency
*Deut 4:10 . . . Then they will **l** to fear Me*
*Deut 5:1 . . . so you may **l** them and obey*
*Prov 9:9 . . . and they will **l** even more.*
*Prov 18:15 . . . are always ready to **l**.*
*Isa 1:17 . . . **L** to do good.*
*Isa 26:9 . . . will people **l** what is right.*
*Isa 29:13 . . . but man-made rules **l-ed** by rote.*
*Matt 2:7 . . . and he **l-ed** from them the time*
*John 6:45 . . . listens to the Father and **l-s***
*Phil 4:9 . . . all you **l-ed** and received from*
*Phil 4:11 . . . for I have **l-ed** how to be content*
*Col 1:10 . . . grow as you **l** to know God*
*1 Tim 2:11 . . . Women should **l** quietly and*
*2 Tim 1:13 . . . teaching you **l-ed** from me—*
*Heb 5:8 . . . he **l-ed** obedience from the things*

LEAVEN (KJV)
*Exod 12:20 . . . anything made with **yeast***
*Exod 13:7 . . . any **yeast** at all found within*
*Matt 13:33 . . . of Heaven is like the **yeast***
*Matt 16:6 . . . the **yeast** of the Pharisees*
*1 Cor 5:6 . . . this sin is like a little **yeast***

LED (v)
see also LEAD
*Ps 68:18 . . . the heights, You **l** a crowd of*
*Isa 53:7 . . . He was **l** like a lamb*
*Jer 11:19 . . . like a lamb being **l** to the*
*Luke 4:1 . . . He was **l** by the Spirit*
*Acts 8:32 . . . He was **l** like a sheep*
*Rom 8:14 . . . all who are **l** by the Spirit*
*Eph 4:8 . . . the heights, He **l** a crowd of*

LEFT (adj)
of, relating to, situated on, or being the side of the body in which the heart is mostly located
*Matt 6:3 . . . don't let your **l** hand know*

LEFT (n)
the location or direction of the left side
*Josh 1:7 . . . or to the **l**. Then you will be*
*Josh 23:6 . . . either to the right or to the **l**.*
*Isa 30:21 . . . to the right or to the **l**.*
*Matt 25:33 . . . and the goats at His **l**.*
*Matt 25:41 . . . those on the **l** and say, 'Away*

LEGION (n)
a very large number; multitude
*Mark 5:9 . . . My name is **L**, because there*

LEPERS (n)
one who suffers from a severe contagious skin and nerve disease
*Matt 11:5 . . . lame walk, the **l** are cured,*
*Luke 17:12 . . . ten **l** stood at a distance,*

LEPROSY (n)
a chronic infectious disease affecting the skin and peripheral nerves which causes loss of sensation, paralysis, and deformities
*Num 12:10 . . . as white as snow from **l**.*
*2 Kgs 5:1 . . . he suffered from **l**.*
*2 Kgs 7:3 . . . four men with **l** sitting at*
*2 Chr 26:21 . . . King Uzziah had **l** until the*

LIAR, LIARS (n)
a person who deceives by telling untruths or falsehoods
*Ps 63:11 . . . while **l-s** will be silenced.*
*Ps 116:11 . . . These people are all **l-s!***
*Prov 17:4 . . . **l-s** pay close attention to*
*Prov 29:12 . . . pays attention to **l-s**, all his*
*Prov 30:6 . . . expose you as a **l**.*
*Isa 57:4 . . . of sinners and **l-s!***
*Rom 3:4 . . . everyone else is a **l**, God is true.*
*1 Tim 1:10 . . . are slave traders, **l-s**, promise*
*Titus 1:12 . . . are all **l-s**, cruel animals,*
*1 Jn 1:10 . . . calling God a **l** and showing*
*1 Jn 2:4 . . . that person is a **l** and is not*
*1 Jn 4:20 . . . that person is a **l**; for if we*
*1 Jn 5:10 . . . calling God a **l** because they*
*Rev 3:9 . . . synagogue—those **l-s** who say*
*Rev 21:8 . . . and all **l-s**—their fate is in*

LIE, LIES (n)
an untrue or inaccurate statement; something that misleads or deceives
*Ps 7:14 . . . give birth to **l-s**.*
*Ps 24:4 . . . and never tell **l-s**.*
*Ps 34:13 . . . lips from telling **l-s!***
*Prov 12:17 . . . a false witness tells **l-s**.*
*Prov 30:8 . . . never to tell a **l**.*
*John 8:44 . . . the father of **l-s**.*
*Rom 1:25 . . . about God for a **l**.*
*Rom 3:13 . . . filled with **l-s**.*
*Eph 4:14 . . . to trick us with **l-s** so clever*
*Eph 4:25 . . . So stop telling **l-s**.*
*2 Thes 2:11 . . . they will believe these **l-s**.*
*1 Pet 3:10 . . . and your lips from telling **l-s**.*
*2 Pet 2:3 . . . make up clever **l-s** to get hold*
*1 Jn 2:21 . . . between truth and **l-s**.*
*Rev 14:5 . . . They have told no **l-s;***

LIE, LIED, LIES (v)
to make an untrue statement with intent to deceive; to create a false or misleading impression
see also LYING
*Lev 6:3 . . . lost property and **l** about it,*
*Job 31:5 . . . Have I **l-d** to anyone or*
*Ps 58:3 . . . even from birth they have **l-d***
*Ps 89:35 . . . in My holiness I cannot **l**:*
*Prov 24:28 . . . don't **l** about them.*
*Prov 26:19 . . . who **l-s** to a friend*
*Jer 7:9 . . . commit adultery, **l**, and burn*
*Matt 5:11 . . . persecute you and **l***
*Col 3:9 . . . Don't **l** to each other,*
*Titus 1:2 . . . God—who does not **l***

LIFE (n)
the quality that distinguishes a vital and functional being from a dead body; period from birth to death; a way or manner of living; spiritual existence transcending death; salvation
*Gen 2:7 . . . He breathed the breath of **l***
*Gen 2:9 . . . the tree of **l** and the tree of*
*Gen 9:5 . . . who takes another person's **l**.*
*Deut 19:21 . . . be life for **l**, eye for eye,*
*Deut 30:19 . . . choice between **l** and death,*
*Ps 23:6 . . . the days of my **l**, and I will*
*Ps 69:28 . . . the Book of **L**; don't let them*
*Ps 91:16 . . . with a long **l** and give them*
*Ps 139:24 . . . the path of everlasting **l**.*
*Prov 3:2 . . . your **l** will be satisfying.*
*Prov 6:26 . . . will cost you your **l**.*
*Prov 15:4 . . . Gentle words are a tree of **l**;*
*Prov 21:21 . . . will find **l**, righteousness,*
*Prov 28:16 . . . will have a long **l**.*
*Lam 3:58 . . . You have redeemed my **l**.*
*Matt 7:14 . . . But the gateway to **l** is very*
*Matt 18:8 . . . to enter eternal **l** with only*
*Matt 20:28 . . . and to give His **l** as a ransom*
*Mark 8:35 . . . to hang on to your **l**,*
*Mark 10:45 . . . and to give His **l** as a ransom*
*Luke 6:9 . . . a day to save **l** or to destroy*
*Luke 9:24 . . . give up your **l** for my sake,*
*Luke 12:25 . . . single moment to your **l**?*
*John 1:4 . . . The Word gave **l** to everything*
*John 3:15 . . . will have eternal **l**.*
*John 5:24 . . . passed from death into **l**.*
*John 5:39 . . . they give you eternal **l**.*
*John 6:35 . . . I am the bread of **l**.*
*John 6:47 . . . who believes has eternal **l**.*
*John 6:68 . . . the words that give eternal **l**.*
*John 10:10 . . . a rich and satisfying **l**.*
*John 10:15 . . . So I sacrifice My **l** for the*
*John 14:6 . . . the truth, and the **l**.*
*John 20:31 . . . you will have **l** by the power*
*Rom 1:17 . . . a righteous person has **l**.*
*Rom 5:10 . . . be saved through the **l** of His*
*Rom 5:18 . . . God and new **l** for everyone.*
*Rom 5:21 . . . in eternal **l** through Jesus*
*Rom 6:13 . . . now you have new **l**.*
*Rom 6:23 . . . is eternal **l** through Christ*
*Rom 8:38 . . . death nor **l**, neither angels*
*2 Cor 3:6 . . . the Spirit gives **l**.*
*2 Cor 4:10 . . . so that the **l** of Jesus may*

*Gal 3:21 . . . give us new **l**, we could be*
*Gal 6:8 . . . harvest everlasting **l** from*
*Eph 2:5 . . . He gave us **l** when He raised*
*Eph 4:1 . . . to lead a **l** worthy of Your*
*Phil 2:16 . . . Hold firmly to the word of **l**;*
*Phil 4:3 . . . written in the Book of **L**.*
*1 Tim 6:19 . . . may experience true **l**.*
*2 Tim 1:9 . . . called us to live a holy **l**.*
*Titus 3:5 . . . new **l** through the Holy Spirit.*
*Jas 1:12 . . . the crown of **l** that God has*
*1 Pet 3:7 . . . God's gift of new **l**.*
*1 Jn 1:1 . . . He is the Word of **l**.*
*1 Jn 3:14 . . . have passed from death to **l**.*
*1 Jn 3:16 . . . gave up His **l** for us.*
*Rev 3:5 . . . their names from the Book of **L**,*
*Rev 22:1 . . . with the water of **l**, clear as*
*Rev 22:2 . . . a tree of **l**, bearing twelve*
*Rev 22:14 . . . eat the fruit from the tree of **l**.*
*Rev 22:17 . . . from the water of **l**.*
*Rev 22:19 . . . in the tree of **l** and in the*

LIFT, LIFTED, LIFTING, LIFTS (v)
to raise from a lower to a higher position; to raise in rank or condition
*Lev 23:11 . . . the priest will **l** it up*
*1 Sam 2:7 . . . some down and **l-s** others up.*
*Neh 8:6 . . . Amen!" as they **l-ed** their hands.*
*Ps 28:2 . . . I **l** my hands toward Your holy*
*Ps 63:4 . . . **l-ing** up my hands to You in prayer.*
*Ps 89:13 . . . Your right hand is **l-ed** high in*
*Ps 113:7 . . . He **l-s** the poor from the dust*
*Ps 123:1 . . . I **l** my eyes to*
*Ps 134:2 . . . **L** up holy hands*
*Lam 1:9 . . . no one to **l** her out.*
*Lam 3:41 . . . Let us **l** our hearts and*
*John 3:14 . . . Son of Man must be **l-ed** up,*
*John 8:28 . . . When You have **l-ed** up the Son*
*John 12:32 . . . And when I am **l-ed** up*
*1 Tim 2:8 . . . with holy hands **l-ed** up to God,*
*Jas 4:10 . . . he will **l** you up in honor.*
*1 Pet 5:6 . . . he will **l** you up in honor.*

LIGHT, LIGHTS (n)
daylight; brightness; illumination; celestial body; spiritual enlightenment; exposure to the truth and justice
*Gen 1:3 . . . "Let there be **l**," and there*
*Gen 1:14 . . . God said, "Let great **l-s** appear*
*Exod 13:21 . . . and He provided **l** at night*
*Job 38:19 . . . Where does **l** come from,*
*Ps 27:1 . . . The Lord is my **l** and my*
*Ps 56:13 . . . in your life-giving **l**.*
*Ps 119:105 . . . my feet and a **l** for my path.*
*Ps 132:17 . . . will be a **l** for My people.*
*Ps 139:12 . . . Darkness and **l** are the*
*Isa 2:5 . . . us walk in the **l** of the Lord!*
*Isa 42:6 . . . You will be a **l** to guide the*
*Isa 45:7 . . . I create the **l** and make the*
*Isa 49:6 . . . make you a **l** to the Gentiles,*
*Matt 5:14 . . . You are the **l** of the world—*
*Luke 2:32 . . . He is a **l** to reveal God to*
*Luke 11:33 . . . its **l** can be seen by all*
*John 1:4 . . . life brought **l** to everyone.*
*John 1:9 . . . who is the true **l**, who gives*
*John 3:20 . . . All who do evil hate the **l***
*John 3:21 . . . come to the **l** so others can*
*John 8:12 . . . I am the **l** of the world.*
*John 9:5 . . . I am the **l** of the world.*
*John 12:46 . . . I have come as a **l** to shine*
*Acts 13:47 . . . made you a **l** to the Gentiles,*
*2 Cor 4:6 . . . said, "Let there be **l** in the*
*2 Cor 6:14 . . . can **l** live with darkness?*
*2 Cor 11:14 . . . as an angel of **l**.*
*Eph 1:18 . . . be flooded with **l** so that you*
*Eph 5:8 . . . live as people of **l**!*
*Phil 2:15 . . . like bright **l-s** in a world*
*1 Thes 5:5 . . . children of the **l** and of the*
*1 Tim 6:16 . . . he lives in **l** so brilliant*
*1 Pet 2:9 . . . into His wonderful **l**.*
*1 Jn 1:5 . . . God is **l**, and there is*
*1 Jn 1:7 . . . living in the **l**, as God is in*
*1 Jn 2:9 . . . I am living in the **l**,*
*Rev 21:23 . . . city, and the Lamb is its **l**.*

LIGHT, LIGHTS (v)
to brighten; to ignite something
*Ps 18:28 . . . The Lord, my God, **l-s** up my*
*Luke 8:16 . . . No one **l-s** a lamp and*

LION, LIONS (n)
a wild beast with a threatening roar; symbolic of a strong and fierce enemy
*Isa 65:25 . . . The **l** will eat hay like a cow.*
*Dan 6:7 . . . thrown into the den of **l-s**.*
*Dan 7:4 . . . was like a **l** with eagles'*
*1 Pet 5:8 . . . like a roaring **l**, looking for*
*Rev 5:5 . . . Look, the **L** of the tribe of*

LISTEN, LISTENED, LISTENING (v)
to hear something with thoughtful attention
see also HEAR
*Deut 6:4 . . . **L**, O Israel! The Lord*
*Deut 18:15 . . . You must **l** to him.*
*1 Sam 3:9 . . . Lord, your servant is **l-ing**.*
*Neh 8:3 . . . All the people **l-ed** closely to*
*Ps 95:7 . . . If only you would **l** to His voice*
*Prov 12:15 . . . but the wise **l** to others.*
*Prov 18:13 . . . Spouting off before **l-ing** to the*
*Isa 6:9 . . . to this people, '**L** carefully,*
*Dan 9:6 . . . We have refused to **l** to Your*
*Mark 9:7 . . . dearly loved Son. **L** to Him.*
*Luke 10:39 . . . the Lord's feet, **l-ing** to*
*Luke 16:31 . . . If they won't **l** to Moses and*
*John 10:27 . . . My sheep **l** to My*
*John 15:20 . . . And if they had **l-ed** to Me,*
*Rom 2:13 . . . For merely **l-ing** to the law*
*1 Tim 2:12 . . . Let them **l** quietly.*
*Jas 1:19 . . . be quick to **l**, slow to speak,*
*1 Jn 4:6 . . . they do not **l** to us.*
*Rev 1:3 . . . he blesses all who **l** to its*
*Rev 2:7 . . . to hear must **l** to the Spirit*

LOAN, LOANS (n)
money lent at interest
*Deut 15:2 . . . must cancel the **l-s** they have*
*Deut 15:9 . . . refuse someone a **l***
*Deut 24:6 . . . as security for a **l**, for the*
*Ps 37:26 . . . give generous **l-s** to others,*

LOANED (v)
to lend
*Luke 7:41 . . . A man **l** money to two*

LOAVES (n)
*Mark 6:41 . . . took the five **l** and two fish,*
*Mark 8:6 . . . took the seven **l**, thanked God*
*Luke 11:5 . . . to borrow three **l** of bread.*

LOCUSTS (n)
a short-horned grasshopper
*Exod 10:4 . . . a swarm of **l** on your country.*
*Joel 2:25 . . . and the cutting **l**. It was I*
*Matt 3:4 . . . he ate **l** and wild honey.*
*Rev 9:3 . . . Then **l** came from*

LOG (n)
a usually bulky piece or length of a tree
*Matt 7:3 . . . you have a **l** in your own?*
*Luke 6:41 . . . you have a **l** in your own?*

LONGSUFFERING (KJV)
*Exod 34:6 . . . I am **slow to anger** and filled with*
*Num 14:18 . . . The Lord is **slow to anger***
*Ps 86:15 . . . mercy, **slow to get angry***
*Gal 5:22 . . . love, joy, peace, **patience**, kindness*
*Eph 4:2 . . . Be **patient** with each other*

LOOK, LOOKED, LOOKING, LOOKS (v)
to direct the eyes; to examine; to see; to make sure or take care (that something is done); to regard with contempt; to seem; to search
*Gen 19:17 . . . And don't **l** back or*
*Gen 19:26 . . . But Lot's wife **l-ed** back as she*
*Exod 3:6 . . . was afraid to **l** at God.*
*1 Sam 6:19 . . . because they **l-ed** into the Ark*
*1 Sam 16:7 . . . the Lord **l-s** at the heart.*
*Ps 34:5 . . . Those who **l** to him for*
*Ps 113:6 . . . He stoops to **l** down on heaven*
*Ps 123:2 . . . We keep **l-ing** to the Lord*
*Isa 65:1 . . . but no one was **l-ing** for Me.*
*Dan 10:5 . . . I **l-ed** up and saw a man*
*Zech 12:10 . . . They will **l** on Me*
*Matt 5:28 . . . who even **l-s** at a woman*
*Mark 16:6 . . . You are **l-ing** for Jesus*
*Luke 9:62 . . . plow and then **l-s** back is not*
*Luke 22:61 . . . Lord turned and **l-ed** at Peter.*
*John 4:23 . . . The Father is **l-ing** for those*
*John 17:1 . . . Jesus **l-ed** up to heaven*
*Rom 14:10 . . . Why do you **l** down*
*Phil 2:4 . . . Don't **l** out only*
*Hab 3:6 . . . When He **l-s**, the nations*
*Heb 11:16 . . . But they were **l-ing** for a better*
*Jas 1:25 . . . But if you **l** carefully into*
*2 Pet 3:12 . . . **l-ing** forward to the day of God*
*Rev 5:6 . . . I saw a Lamb that **l-ed** as if it*

LOVE, LOVED, LOVING (adj)
of or relating to a strong affection for another; affectionate, painstaking
*Ps 88:18 . . . my companions and **l-d** ones.*
*Ps 127:2 . . . gives rest to His **l-d** ones.*
*Ezek 33:32 . . . who sings **l** songs with a*
*Mark 1:11 . . . are my dearly **l-d** Son, and you*
*Mark 9:7 . . . is my dearly **l-d** Son.*
*1 Thes 1:3 . . . work, your **l-ing** deeds, and the*

LOVE (n)
the ultimate expression of God's loyalty, purity, and mercy extended toward his people—to be reflected in human relationships of brotherly concern, marital fidelity, and adoration of God; a beloved person
*Gen 32:10 . . . unfailing **l** and faithfulness*
*Exod 20:6 . . . unfailing **l** for a thousand*
*Exod 34:6 . . . filled with unfailing **l** and*
*Num 14:18 . . . with unfailing **l**, forgiving*
*Deut 7:9 . . . his unfailing **l** on those who*
*Deut 10:15 . . . the objects of His **l**.*
*Deut 10:18 . . . He shows **l** to the*
*Deut 10:19 . . . must show **l** to foreigners,*
*1 Sam 18:1 . . . bond of **l** between them,*
*1 Kgs 8:23 . . . and show unfailing **l** to all*
*1 Kgs 10:9 . . . Lord's eternal **l** for Israel,*
*1 Chr 16:41 . . . for "His faithful **l** endures*
*2 Chr 20:21 . . . His faithful **l** endures forever!*
*Ezra 3:11 . . . His faithful **l** for Israel*
*Job 37:13 . . . to show His unfailing **l**.*
*Ps 6:4 . . . because of Your unfailing **l**.*
*Ps 13:5 . . . I trust in Your unfailing **l**.*
*Ps 23:6 . . . and unfailing **l** will pursue*
*Ps 33:18 . . . those who rely on His unfailing **l**.*
*Ps 36:5 . . . Your unfailing **l**, O Lord, is*
*Ps 36:10 . . . Pour out Your unfailing **l** on*
*Ps 51:1 . . . Your unfailing **l**. Because of*
*Ps 59:10 . . . In His unfailing **l**, my God*
*Ps 62:12 . . . unfailing **l**, O Lord, is Yours.*
*Ps 66:20 . . . His unfailing **l** from me.*
*Ps 100:5 . . . His unfailing **l** continues*
*Ps 101:1 . . . sing of Your **l** and justice,*
*Ps 103:4 . . . crowns me with **l** and tender*
*Ps 103:17 . . . But the **l** of the Lord*
*Ps 106:1 . . . His faithful **l** endures*
*Ps 119:41 . . . give me Your unfailing **l**,*
*Ps 119:76 . . . let Your unfailing **l** comfort me,*
*Ps 119:124 . . . deal with me in unfailing **l**,*

*Ps 130:7 . . . with the LORD there is unfailing **l**.*
*Prov 21:21 . . . and unfailing **l** will find*
*Prov 27:5 . . . better than hidden **l**!*
*Isa 55:3 . . . the unfailing **l** I promised to*
*Isa 63:7 . . . LORD's unfailing **l**.*
*Isa 63:9 . . . In His **l** and mercy He*
*Jer 31:3 . . . with an everlasting **l**.*
*Jer 33:11 . . . His faithful **l** endures*
*Lam 3:22 . . . The faithful **l** of the*
*Lam 3:32 . . . the greatness of His unfailing **l**.*
*Hos 2:19 . . . and justice, unfailing **l** and*
*Hos 2:23 . . . I will show **l** to those I*
*Hos 6:6 . . . want you to show **l**, not offer*
*Hos 11:4 . . . My ropes of kindness and **l**.*
*Hos 12:6 . . . Act with **l** and justice,*
*Zeph 3:17 . . . With His **l**, He will*
*Mark 10:21 . . . Jesus felt genuine **l** for him.*
*John 5:42 . . . have God's **l** within you.*
*John 15:9 . . . Remain in My **l**.*
*John 15:13 . . . is no greater **l** than to lay*
*John 17:26 . . . Then Your **l** for Me will*
*Rom 5:5 . . . fill our hearts with His **l**.*
*Rom 5:8 . . . showed His great **l** for us by*
*Rom 8:35 . . . us from Christ's **l**?*
*Rom 8:39 . . . us from the **l** of God that is*
*Rom 13:10 . . . **L** does no wrong*
*1 Cor 4:21 . . . I come with **l** and a gentle*
*1 Cor 8:1 . . . it is **l** that strengthens the*
*1 Cor 13:13 . . . faith, hope, and **l**—and the*
*1 Cor 13:13 . . . greatest of these is **l**.*
*2 Cor 2:8 . . . to reaffirm your **l** for Him.*
*2 Cor 5:14 . . . Either way, Christ's **l** controls*
*Gal 5:22 . . . **l**, joy, peace,*
*Eph 3:18 . . . how deep His **l** is.*
*Eph 4:15 . . . the truth in **l**, growing in*
*Eph 5:2 . . . filled with **l**, following the*
*Col 2:2 . . . strong ties of **l**.*
*1 Thes 3:6 . . . your faith and **l**.*
*1 Thes 3:12 . . . the Lord make your **l** for one*
*2 Thes 3:5 . . . expression of the **l** of God*
*1 Tim 1:5 . . . be filled with **l** that comes*
*1 Tim 2:15 . . . in faith, **l**, holiness,*
*1 Tim 4:12 . . . live, in your **l**, your faith,*
*1 Tim 6:10 . . . For the **l** of money is the*
*1 Tim 6:11 . . . with faith, **l**, perseverance,*
*2 Tim 1:7 . . . but of power, **l**, and*
*2 Tim 1:13 . . . the faith and **l** that you have*
*Heb 10:24 . . . to acts of **l** and good works.*
*1 Pet 4:8 . . . for **l** covers a multitude*
*1 Jn 3:14 . . . who has no **l** is still dead.*
*1 Jn 3:16 . . . know what real **l** is because*
*1 Jn 4:7 . . . for **l** comes from God.*
*1 Jn 4:8 . . . for God is **l**.*
*1 Jn 4:16 . . . put our trust in His **l**.*
*1 Jn 4:16 . . . God is **l**, and all who*
*1 Jn 4:18 . . . because perfect **l** expels all*
*Jude 21 . . . safe in God's **l**.*

LOVE, LOVED, LOVES, LOVING (v)
to hold dear; to feel a lover's passion, devotion, or tenderness for; to feel affection or experience desire; to like or desire actively
*Gen 29:32 . . . my husband will **l** me.*
*Exod 21:5 . . . may declare, 'I **l** my master,*
*Lev 19:34 . . . as you **l** yourself.*
*Deut 4:37 . . . Because He **l-d** your ancestors,*
*Deut 6:5 . . . And you must **l** the LORD your*
*Deut 7:8 . . . that the LORD **l-s** you, and He*
*Deut 11:13 . . . and if you **l** the LORD your*
*Deut 13:3 . . . if you truly **l** Him with all*
*Deut 15:16 . . . because He **l-s** you and*
*Deut 30:6 . . . that you will **l** Him with all*
*Deut 30:20 . . . this choice by **l-ing** the LORD*
*Deut 30:20 . . . And if you **l** and obey the*
*Josh 23:11 . . . be very careful to **l** the LORD*
*2 Sam 12:24 . . . The LORD **l-d** the child*
*1 Kgs 3:3 . . . Solomon **l-d** the LORD and*
*2 Chr 2:11 . . . the LORD **l-s** His people*
*Neh 1:5 . . . with those who **l** Him and obey*
*Ps 11:7 . . . righteous LORD **l-s** justice.*
*Ps 26:8 . . . I **l** Your sanctuary,*
*Ps 40:16 . . . those who **l** Your salvation*
*Ps 70:4 . . . those who **l** Your salvation*
*Ps 78:68 . . . Mount Zion, which He **l-d**.*
*Ps 89:33 . . . I will never stop **l-ing** Him nor*
*Ps 97:10 . . . You who **l** the LORD,*
*Ps 119:119 . . . no wonder I **l** to obey Your*
*Ps 119:127 . . . Truly, I **l** Your commands more*
*Ps 145:20 . . . all those who **l** Him, but He*
*Ps 146:8 . . . The LORD **l-s** the godly.*
*Prov 3:12 . . . corrects those He **l-s**, just as*
*Prov 8:36 . . . All who hate me **l** death.*
*Prov 12:1 . . . you must **l** discipline; it is*
*Prov 19:8 . . . wisdom is to **l** oneself;*
*Prov 21:17 . . . Those who **l** pleasure*
*Eccl 3:8 . . . A time to **l** and a time*
*Eccl 9:9 . . . the woman you **l** through all*
*Isa 56:6 . . . serve Him and **l** His name, who*
*Isa 61:8 . . . I, the LORD, **l** justice.*
*Jer 2:2 . . . long ago, how You **l-d** me and*
*Jer 8:2 . . . My people have **l-d**, served,*
*Hos 2:1 . . . The ones I **l**.*
*Hos 2:23 . . . to those I called 'Not **l-d**.'*
*Hos 11:1 . . . was a child, I **l-d** Him, and I*
*Amos 5:15 . . . Hate evil and **l** what is good;*
*Mic 6:8 . . . is right, to **l** mercy, and to*
*Mal 1:2 . . . "I have always **l-d** you," says*
*Matt 5:43 . . . that says, '**L** your neighbor'*
*Matt 5:44 . . . But I say, **l** your enemies!*
*Matt 5:46 . . . If you **l** only those*
*Matt 6:24 . . . hate one and **l** the other;*
*Matt 10:37 . . . If you **l** your father or*
*Matt 19:19 . . . **L** your neighbor*
*Matt 22:37 . . . You must **l** the LORD Your*
*Mark 12:6 . . . His son whom He **l-d** dearly.*
*Mark 12:30 . . . And you must **l** the LORD your*
*Mark 12:33 . . . it is important to **l** Him with*
*Mark 12:33 . . . and to **l** my neighbor as*
*Luke 6:27 . . . I say, **l** your enemies!*
*Luke 6:32 . . . If you **l** only those who*
*Luke 10:27 . . . You must **l** the LORD Your*
*John 3:16 . . . For God **l-d** the world so*
*John 3:35 . . . The Father **l-s** His Son*
*John 5:20 . . . For the Father **l-s** the Son and*
*John 13:1 . . . He had **l-d** His disciples during*
*John 13:34 . . . **L** each other.*
*John 13:34 . . . as I have **l-d** you, you should*
*John 14:21 . . . are the ones who **l** Me.*
*John 14:28 . . . If you really **l-d** Me, you would*
*John 17:24 . . . gave Me because you **l-d** Me*
*John 19:26 . . . beside the disciple he **l-d**,*
*John 20:2 . . . one whom Jesus **l-d**.*
*John 21:15 . . . do you **l** Me more than*
*Rom 8:28 . . . of those who **l** God and are*
*Rom 8:37 . . . through Christ, who **l-d** us.*
*Rom 9:25 . . . And I will **l** those whom I did*
*Rom 12:10 . . . **L** each other*
*1 Cor 2:9 . . . for those who **l** Him.*
*1 Cor 13:2 . . . but didn't **l** others, I would*
*1 Cor 16:22 . . . anyone does not **l** the Lord,*
*2 Cor 9:7 . . . For God **l-s** a person*
*Gal 2:20 . . . Son of God, who **l-d** Me and gave*
*Eph 1:4 . . . God **l-d** us and chose us*
*Eph 5:25 . . . this means **l** your wives, just*
*Eph 5:25 . . . just as Christ **l-d** the church.*
*Eph 5:28 . . . their wives as they **l** their own*
*Eph 5:28 . . . a man who **l-s** his wife actually*
*Eph 5:33 . . . love his wife as he **l-s** himself,*
*1 Thes 1:4 . . . God **l-s** you and has chosen*
*1 Thes 4:10 . . . urge you to **l** them even more.*
*2 Thes 2:10 . . . they refuse to **l** and accept*
*2 Thes 2:16 . . . our Father, who **l-d** us and by*
*Titus 1:8 . . . and he must **l** what is good.*
*Titus 2:4 . . . women to **l** their husbands and*
*Heb 12:6 . . . disciplines those He **l-s**,*
*Heb 13:5 . . . Don't **l** money;*
*Jas 2:5 . . . to those who **l** Him?*
*1 Pet 3:8 . . . **L** each other*
*1 Jn 2:10 . . . Anyone who **l-s** another brother*
*1 Jn 3:1 . . . how very much our Father **l-s** us,*
*1 Jn 4:9 . . . how much He **l-d** us by sending*
*1 Jn 4:10 . . . not that we **l-d** God, but that*
*1 Jn 4:11 . . . since God **l-d** us that much,*
*1 Jn 4:11 . . . surely ought to **l** each other.*
*1 Jn 4:19 . . . We **l** each other*
*1 Jn 4:19 . . . because He **l-d** us first.*
*1 Jn 4:20 . . . how can we **l** God, whom we*
*Rev 1:5 . . . glory to Him who **l-s** us and has*
*Rev 3:9 . . . you are the ones I **l**.*
*Rev 3:19 . . . discipline everyone I **l**.*

LOVINGKINDNESS (KJV)
*Ps 25:6 . . . **unfailing love**, which You have*
*Ps 40:11 . . . Let Your **unfailing love** and*
*Ps 63:3 . . . Your **unfailing love** is better than life*
*Ps 143:8 . . . Your **unfailing love** each morning*
*Isa 63:7 . . . His **mercy and love***

LOYAL (adj)
unswerving in allegiance; faithful
see also *FAITHFUL, TRUSTWORTHY*
*1 Sam 26:23 . . . and for being **l**,*
*2 Sam 2:6 . . . May the LORD be **l** to you in*
*1 Chr 12:33 . . . and completely **l** to David.*
*Ps 31:23 . . . those who are **l** to Him,*
*Ps 51:10 . . . Renew a **l** spirit within*
*Prov 17:17 . . . A friend is always **l**, and a*
*Prov 20:6 . . . say they are **l** friends,*

LUST, LUSTS (n)
usually intense or unbridled sexual desire; an intense longing
*1 Cor 7:9 . . . than to burn with **l**.*
*Eph 4:22 . . . corrupted by **l** and deception.*
*Col 3:5 . . . immorality, impurity, **l**, and*
*2 Tim 2:22 . . . stimulates youthful **l-s**.*
*Titus 3:3 . . . to many **l-s** and pleasures.*

LUST, LUSTED (v)
to have an intense (sexual) desire or need
*Prov 6:25 . . . Don't **l** for her*
*Ezek 23:5 . . . Then Oholah **l-ed** after other*

LUSTFUL (adj)
excited by lust; lecherous
*Mark 7:22 . . . deceit, **l** desires, envy,*
*Gal 5:19 . . . impurity, **l** pleasures,*
*Eph 4:19 . . . They live for **l** pleasure and*

LYING (adj)
marked by or containing falsehoods; false
*Prov 6:17 . . . haughty eyes, a **l** tongue,*
*Prov 12:22 . . . The LORD detests **l** lips,*
*Prov 21:6 . . . Wealth created by a **l** tongue*
*Prov 26:28 . . . A **l** tongue hates*

LYING (v)
see also *LIE*
*Mic 6:12 . . . are so used to **l** that their*
*Matt 15:19 . . . immorality, theft, **l**, and*
*Matt 28:6 . . . see where his body was **l**.*
*Acts 5:4 . . . You weren't **l** to us but*
*1 Cor 15:15 . . . would all be **l** about God—*

M

MAGICIANS (n)
one skilled in extraordinary power or influence seemingly from a supernatural source; sorcerer
*Exod 7:11 . . . Egyptian **m** did the same*
*Dan 2:2 . . . called in his **m**, enchanters,*

MAJESTIC (adj)
having or exhibiting majesty; grand, stately
*Ps 8:1 . . . your **m** name fills the earth!*

Ps 29:4 . . . the voice of the LORD *is* ***m.***
Ps 145:5 . . . I will meditate on Your ***m,***
Isa 53:2 . . . nothing beautiful or ***m*** *about*
Heb 1:3 . . . hand of the ***m*** *God in heaven.*
Heb 8:1 . . . the throne of the ***m*** *God*
2 Pet 1:16 . . . saw his ***m*** *splendor with our*
2 Pet 1:17 . . . from the ***m*** *glory of God*

MAKER (n)
one that makes; God
see also CREATOR
Ps 95:6 . . . before the LORD *our* ***m,***
Ps 149:2 . . . Israel, rejoice in your ***M.***
Prov 17:5 . . . mock the poor insult their ***M;***
Isa 45:9 . . . clay pot argue with its ***m?***
Hos 8:14 . . . Israel has forgotten its ***M***

MAMMON (KJV)
Matt 6:24 . . . serve both God and ***money***
Luke 16:9 . . . your ***worldly resources*** *to benefit*
Luke 16:11 . . . untrustworthy about ***worldly wealth,***

MAN (n)
an adult male human; individual, person
Gen 2:7 . . . the ***m*** *from the dust*
Gen 2:15 . . . the ***m*** *in the Garden*
Gen 2:18 . . . for the ***m*** *to be alone.*
*Gen 2:23 . . . she was taken from '****m.****'*
Gen 2:25 . . . ***m*** *and his wife were both*
Gen 3:9 . . . God called to the ***m,*** *"Where*
Isa 53:3 . . . rejected—a ***m*** *of sorrows,*
1 Cor 11:3 . . . of every ***m*** *is Christ,*
1 Cor 11:3 . . . the head of woman is ***m,***
1 Cor 15:45 . . . The first ***m,*** *Adam,*
Eph 5:31 . . . A ***m*** *leaves his father and*
1 Tim 2:5 . . . the ***m*** *Christ Jesus.*

MANAGE, MANAGING (v)
to handle or direct with a degree of skill
Luke 12:42 . . . of ***m-ing*** *his other household*
1 Tim 3:4 . . . ***m*** *his own family well,*
1 Tim 3:12 . . . he must ***m*** *his children*

MANAGER (n)
a person who conducts business or household affairs
Luke 16:1 . . . had a ***m*** *handling his affairs.*
1 Cor 4:2 . . . as a ***m*** *must be faithful.*

MANGER (n)
a trough or open box in a stable designed to hold feed for livestock
Luke 2:7 . . . cloth and laid him in a ***m,***
Luke 2:12 . . . strips of cloth, lying in a ***m.***

MANNA (n)
in Hebrew, the word means "What is it?"; miraculous supply of food given to Israel in the wilderness; symbolic of spiritual nourishment
Exod 16:31 . . . Israelites called the food ***m.***
Deut 8:16 . . . He fed you with ***m*** *in the*
John 6:49 . . . Your ancestors ate ***m*** *in the*
Rev 2:17 . . . some of the ***m*** *that has been*

MARRIAGE (n)
the state of being lawfully united to a person of the opposite sex as husband or wife; an act of marrying
Matt 22:30 . . . marry nor be given in ***m.***
Rom 7:2 . . . laws of ***m*** *no longer apply*
1 Cor 7:14 . . . brings holiness to her ***m,***
1 Cor 7:27 . . . do not seek to end the ***m.***
Heb 13:4 . . . Give honor to ***m,*** *and remain*

MARRY, MARRIED, MARRIES, MARRYING (v)
to take a spouse according to law or custom
Exod 21:10 . . . who has ***m-ied*** *a slave wife*
Deut 24:4 . . . first husband may not ***m*** *her*
Deut 24:5 . . . newly ***m-ied*** *man must not be*
Deut 25:5 . . . husband's brother should ***m***
Ezra 10:10 . . . By ***m-ing*** *pagan women,*
Hos 1:2 . . . Go and ***m*** *a prostitute, so that*
Matt 1:18 . . . to be ***m-ied*** *to Joseph.*
Matt 19:9 . . . divorces his wife and ***m-ies***
Matt 22:30 . . . will neither ***m*** *nor be given*
Mark 12:23 . . . all seven were ***m-ied*** *to her.*
Luke 16:18 . . . his wife and ***m-ies*** *someone*
Rom 7:2 . . . when a woman ***m-ies,*** *the law*
1 Cor 7:9 . . . better to ***m*** *than to burn*
1 Cor 7:28 . . . if you do get ***m-ied,*** *it is not*
1 Cor 7:33 . . . a ***m-ied*** *man has to think*
1 Tim 5:14 . . . these younger widows to ***m***

MASTER, MASTERS (n)
one in authority or leadership; employer; teacher; lord or Lord
Jer 3:14 . . . the LORD*, "for I am your* ***m.***
Matt 10:24 . . . are not greater than their ***m.***
Luke 16:13 . . . No one can serve two ***m-s.***
Rom 6:14 . . . Sin is no longer your ***m,***
Eph 6:5 . . . obey your earthly ***m-s*** *with deep*
Col 3:22 . . . Slaves, obey your earthly ***m-s***
1 Tim 6:1 . . . full respect for their ***m-s***
1 Tim 6:2 . . . If the ***m-s*** *are believers,*
2 Tim 2:21 . . . ready for the ***M*** *to use you*
Titus 2:9 . . . always obey their ***m-s*** *and do*
1 Pet 2:18 . . . the authority of your ***m-s***
2 Pet 2:1 . . . deny the ***M*** *who bought them.*
Jude 4 . . . denied our only ***M*** *and Lord,*

MEASURE, MEASURED, MEASURING (v)
to gauge or regulate the specific dimensions of; to have a specified measurement; to regulate by a standard
Ps 145:3 . . . No one can ***m*** *His greatness.*
Isa 40:28 . . . No one can ***m*** *the depths*
Jer 31:37 . . . heavens cannot be ***m-d*** *and the*
Ezek 45:3 . . . area, ***m*** *out a portion of land*
Dan 5:27 . . . balances and have not ***m-d*** *up.*
Zech 2:2 . . . I am going to ***m*** *Jerusalem,*
Luke 12:15 . . . Life is not ***m-d*** *by how much*
Eph 4:13 . . . mature in the Lord, ***m-ing*** *up*
Rev 11:1 . . . Go and ***m*** *the Temple*

MEDIATE, MEDIATES (v)
to act as an intermediary agent in bringing, effecting, or communicating; to interpose
Job 16:21 . . . to ***m*** *between God and me,*
Isa 2:4 . . . LORD *will* ***m*** *between nations*
Heb 8:6 . . . the one who ***m-s*** *for us a far*
Heb 9:15 . . . who ***m-s*** *a new covenant*
Heb 12:24 . . . Jesus, the one who ***m-s***

MEDIATOR (n)
one who mediates
Job 9:33 . . . If only there were a ***m*** *between*
1 Tim 2:5 . . . one God and one ***M*** *who can*

MEDICINE (n)
a substance or preparation used in treating disease; something that affects well-being
Prov 17:22 . . . A cheerful heart is good ***m,***
Jer 8:22 . . . Is there no ***m*** *in Gilead?*
Rev 22:2 . . . The leaves were used for ***m***

MEDITATE, MEDITATING (v)
to contemplate, reflect, or ponder
see also THINK
Gen 24:63 . . . walking and ***m-ing*** *in the fields,*
Ps 1:2 . . . LORD*,* ***m-ing*** *on it day and night.*
Ps 48:9 . . . O God, we ***m*** *on Your unfailing*
Ps 63:6 . . . ***m-ing*** *on You through the night.*
Ps 119:23 . . . but I will ***m*** *on Your decrees.*
Ps 119:27 . . . ***m*** *on Your wonderful deeds.*
Ps 119:48 . . . I ***m*** *on Your decrees.*
Ps 145:5 . . . I will ***m*** *on Your majestic,*

MEDITATION (n)
the act or process of meditating
Ps 19:14 . . . words of my mouth and the ***m***

MERCIFUL (adj)
compassionate; forgiving
Deut 4:31 . . . your God is a ***m*** *God;*
Ps 78:38 . . . Yet He was ***m*** *and forgave*
Dan 4:27 . . . and be ***m*** *to the poor.*
Dan 9:9 . . . our God is ***m*** *and forgiving,*
Matt 5:7 . . . God blesses those who are ***m,***
Luke 1:54 . . . and remembered to be ***m.***
Heb 2:17 . . . ***m*** *and faithful High Priest*
Jas 2:13 . . . God will be ***m*** *when he judges*

MERCY, MERCIES (n)
a blessing that is an act of divine favor or compassion; withholding of the punishment or judgment our sins deserve
see also COMPASSION, FORGIVENESS
Exod 34:6 . . . God of compassion and ***m!***
2 Sam 24:14 . . . for His ***m*** *is great.*
Neh 9:27 . . . In Your great ***m,*** *You sent*
Job 41:3 . . . beg You for ***m*** *or implore*
Ps 28:6 . . . He has heard my cry for ***m.***
Ps 103:4 . . . me with love and tender ***m-ies.***
Ps 119:77 . . . with Your tender ***m-ies*** *so I*
Ps 119:156 . . . how great is Your ***m;***
Isa 14:1 . . . LORD *will have* ***m*** *on*
Isa 49:10 . . . LORD *in His* ***m*** *will lead*
Isa 60:10 . . . I will now have ***m*** *on you*
Lam 3:22 . . . His ***m-ies*** *never cease.*
Dan 9:18 . . . because of Your ***m.***
Jon 2:8 . . . their backs on all God's ***m-ies.***
Mic 6:8 . . . do what is right, to love ***m,***
Matt 5:7 . . . for they will be shown ***m.***
Matt 9:13 . . . I want you to show ***m,***
Matt 18:33 . . . just as I had ***m*** *on you?*
Matt 23:23 . . . law—justice, ***m,*** *and faith.*
Rom 9:15 . . . I will show ***m*** *to anyone*
Rom 9:18 . . . God chooses to show ***m***
Rom 11:32 . . . have ***m*** *on everyone.*
2 Cor 4:1 . . . God in His ***m*** *has given us*
Gal 1:6 . . . through the loving ***m*** *of Christ.*
Eph 2:4 . . . But God is so rich in ***m,*** *and*
1 Tim 1:13 . . . But God had ***m*** *on me*
Titus 3:5 . . . but because of His ***m.***
Heb 4:16 . . . we will receive His ***m,***
Heb 10:29 . . . who brings God's ***m*** *to us.*
Jas 2:13 . . . will be no ***m*** *for those*
Jas 3:17 . . . It is full of ***m*** *and good*
1 Pet 1:3 . . . by His great ***m*** *that we*
Jude 22 . . . show ***m*** *to those whose faith*

MIGHTY, MIGHTIER, MIGHTIEST (adj)
powerful; great or imposing in size or extent
Gen 49:24 . . . hands of the ***M*** *One of Jacob,*
Deut 10:17 . . . God, the ***m*** *and awesome*
Deut 34:12 . . . With ***m*** *power, Moses*
2 Sam 23:8 . . . David's ***m-iest*** *warriors.*
2 Chr 20:6 . . . You are powerful and ***m;***
Neh 9:32 . . . and ***m*** *and awesome God,*
Job 9:4 . . . For God is so wise and so ***m.***
Job 36:5 . . . He is ***m*** *in both power and*
Ps 24:8 . . . LORD*, strong and* ***m;***
Ps 47:5 . . . ascended with a ***m*** *shout.*
Ps 50:1 . . . LORD*, the* ***M*** *One, is God,*
Ps 71:16 . . . I will praise Your ***m*** *deeds,*
Ps 77:12 . . . thinking about Your ***m*** *works.*
Ps 89:27 . . . son, the ***m-iest*** *king on earth.*
Ps 93:4 . . . But ***m-ier*** *than the violent raging*
Ps 93:4 . . . LORD *above is* ***m-ier*** *than these!*
Ps 95:4 . . . and the ***m-iest*** *mountains.*
Ps 145:4 . . . children of Your ***m*** *acts;*
Ps 145:12 . . . will tell about Your ***m*** *deeds*
Ps 150:2 . . . Praise Him for His ***m*** *works;*
Prov 24:5 . . . wise are ***m-ier*** *than the strong,*
Isa 9:6 . . . Wonderful Counselor, ***M*** *God,*
Isa 60:16 . . . your Redeemer, the ***M*** *One of*
Zeph 3:17 . . . He is a ***m*** *savior.*
Eph 1:19 . . . This is the same ***m*** *power*
Eph 6:10 . . . in the Lord and in His ***m***

*Heb 1:3 . . . sustains everything by the **m***
*1 Pet 5:6 . . . yourselves under the **m***
*Jude 9 . . . Michael, one of the **m-iest** of the angels,*

MIND, MINDS (n)
the part of humans that engages in conscious thinking, feeling, and decision making; in the Bible, mind is akin to the heart, not the brain
*Num 23:19 . . . He does not change His **m.***
*1 Sam 15:29 . . . nor will He change His **m,***
*Mark 12:30 . . . all your soul, all your **m,***
*Luke 24:45 . . . opened their **m-s***
*Acts 4:32 . . . were united in heart and **m.***
*Rom 8:6 . . . Spirit control your **m***
*1 Cor 1:10 . . . be of one **m,** united in*
*1 Cor 2:9 . . . heard, and no **m** has imagined*
*Col 2:18 . . . sinful **m-s** have made them*
*2 Cor 4:4 . . . has blinded the **m-s** of those*
*2 Tim 4:5 . . . clear **m** in every situation.*
*Heb 8:10 . . . I will put my laws in their **m-s,***
*Heb 10:16 . . . I will write them on their **m-s.***

MIRACLE, MIRACLES (n)
an extraordinary event manifesting divine intervention in human affairs
*Exod 3:20 . . . performing all kinds of **m-s***
*Exod 7:9 . . . demand, 'Show me a **m.**'*
*Deut 13:1 . . . they promise you signs or **m-s,***
*Job 9:10 . . . He performs countless **m-s.***
*Ps 105:5 . . . he has performed, His **m-s,***
*Ps 106:2 . . . the glorious **m-s** of the LORD?*
*Jer 32:19 . . . and do great and mighty **m-s.***
*Matt 7:22 . . . and performed many **m-s***
*Matt 13:54 . . . and the power to do **m-s?***
*Mark 6:2 . . . power to perform such **m-s?***
*Mark 9:39 . . . No one who performs a **m***
*Luke 19:37 . . . wonderful **m-s** they had seen.*
*Luke 23:8 . . . to see Him perform a **m.***
*John 7:21 . . . I did one **m** on the Sabbath,*
*Acts 2:22 . . . by doing powerful **m-s,***
*Acts 8:13 . . . **m-s** Philip performed.*
*Acts 19:11 . . . to perform unusual **m-s.***
*1 Cor 12:28 . . . those who do **m-s,** those who*
*2 Cor 12:12 . . . and **m-s** among you.*
*Gal 3:5 . . . Spirit and work **m-s** among you*
*Heb 2:4 . . . and various **m-s** and gifts of*

MONEY (n)
officially coined or stamped metal or paper currency
see also POSSESSIONS, RICHES, TREASURE(S), WEALTH
*2 Chr 24:10 . . . gladly brought their **m** and*
*Eccl 5:10 . . . who love **m** will never have*
*Matt 6:24 . . . serve both God and **m.***
*Luke 3:14 . . . Don't extort **m** or make false*
*1 Tim 3:3 . . . and not love **m.***
*1 Tim 6:10 . . . love of **m** is the root of all*
*1 Tim 6:17 . . . and not to trust in their **m,***
*1 Jn 3:17 . . . If someone has enough **m***

MORNING (n)
the time from sunrise to noon
*Gen 1:5 . . . evening passed and **m** came,*
*Ps 5:3 . . . Listen to My voice in the **m,***
*Lam 3:23 . . . mercies begin afresh each **m.***

MORTAL (adj)
subject to death
*Gen 6:3 . . . for they are only **m** flesh.*
*Rom 8:11 . . . will give life to your **m** bodies*
*1 Cor 15:53 . . . our **m** bodies must be*

MOTHER (n)
a female parent; a woman in authority
see also PARENT
*Gen 2:24 . . . a man leaves his father and **m***
*Gen 3:20 . . . she would be the **m** of all who*
*Exod 20:12 . . . Honor your father and **m.***
*Deut 21:18 . . . not obey his father or **m,***
*Judg 5:7 . . . Deborah arose as a **m***
*Prov 10:1 . . . brings grief to a **m.***
*Prov 23:22 . . . don't despise your **m***
*Isa 66:13 . . . as a **m** comforts her child.*
*Matt 10:35 . . . a daughter against her **m,***
*Matt 10:37 . . . father or **m** more than You*
*Matt 12:48 . . . Who is My **m?***
*Mark 10:19 . . . Honor your father and **m.***
*John 19:27 . . . disciple, "Here is Your **m.**"*
*Eph 5:31 . . . A man leaves his father and **m***
*Eph 6:2 . . . Honor your father and **m.***

MOTIVES (n)
something (as a need or desire) that causes a person to act
*1 Chr 29:17 . . . all this with good **m,***
*Ps 26:2 . . . Test my **m** and my heart.*
*Prov 16:2 . . . LORD examines their **m.***
*Jer 17:10 . . . hearts and examine secret **m.***
*1 Cor 4:5 . . . will reveal our private **m.***
*Phil 1:18 . . . Whether their **m** are false or*
*1 Thes 2:3 . . . with any deceit or impure **m***
*1 Thes 2:4 . . . He alone examines the **m** of*
*Jas 4:3 . . . because your **m** are all wrong—*

MOUNTAIN, MOUNTAINS (n)
a landmass that projects conspicuously above its surroundings and is higher than a hill
*Exod 24:18 . . . on the **m** forty days*
*Deut 5:4 . . . At the **m** the LORD*
*Ps 36:6 . . . is like the mighty **m-s,***
*Ps 121:1 . . . I look up to the **m-s**—*
*Isa 14:13 . . . preside on the **m** of the gods*
*Matt 17:20 . . . say to this **m,** 'Move*
*Mark 9:2 . . . led them up a high **m***
*Mark 9:9 . . . went back down the **m,***
*Luke 23:30 . . . beg the **m-s,** 'Fall on us,'*
*1 Cor 13:2 . . . faith that I could move **m-s,***
*2 Pet 1:18 . . . with him on the holy **m.***
*Rev 6:16 . . . they cried to the **m-s** and*

MOURN (v)
to feel or express grief or sorrow
*Zech 12:10 . . . have pierced and **m***
*Matt 5:4 . . . God blesses those who **m,***

MOURNING (n)
the act of sorrowing; a period of time during which signs of grief are shown
*Gen 50:11 . . . watched them **m***
*Ps 30:11 . . . my clothes of **m** and clothed*
*Isa 60:20 . . . Your days of **m** will come to*
*Isa 61:3 . . . instead of **m,** festive praise*
*Jer 31:13 . . . I will turn their **m** into joy.*
*Zech 8:19 . . . times of **m** you have kept*

MOUTH, MOUTHS (n)
the natural opening through which food passes into the body of an animal; voice, speech
*Ps 10:7 . . . Their **m-s** are full of cursing,*
*Ps 19:14 . . . words of my **m** and*
*Prov 13:3 . . . opening your **m** can ruin*
*Isa 51:16 . . . have put My words in your **m***
*Isa 53:7 . . . he did not open his **m.***
*Isa 59:3 . . . and your **m** spews corruption.*
*Jer 31:29 . . . their children's **m-s** pucker*
*Matt 4:4 . . . word that comes from the **m***
*Rom 3:14 . . . Their **m-s** are full of cursing*
*Rom 10:9 . . . **m** that Jesus is Lord*
*Rev 2:16 . . . with the sword of My **m.***

MOVE, MOVED, MOVES, MOVING (v)
to change the place or position of; to go from one place to another in continuous motion; to carry on one's life or activities in a specified environment; to stir the emotions or passions of; to prompt to the doing of something
*Exod 35:21 . . . and whose spirits were **m-d***
*Deut 19:14 . . . steal anyone's land by **m-ing***
*Deut 23:14 . . . LORD your God **m-s** around*
*Prov 4:15 . . . Turn away and keep **m-ing.***
*Prov 23:10 . . . cheat your neighbor by **m-ing***
*Isa 54:10 . . . For the mountains may **m***
*Acts 17:28 . . . For in him we live and **m***
*1 Cor 13:2 . . . faith that I could **m***
*2 Pet 1:21 . . . were **m-d** by the Holy Spirit,*

MURDER, MURDERED, MURDERS (v)
to kill (a human being) unlawfully and with premeditated malice
*Gen 9:5 . . . **m-s** a fellow human must die.*
*Exod 20:13 . . . You must not **m.***
*Deut 5:17 . . . You must not **m.***
*Matt 23:31 . . . those who **m-ed** the prophets.*
*Acts 7:52 . . . whom you betrayed and **m-ed.***
*Rom 13:9 . . . You must not **m.***
*Jas 2:11 . . . You must not **m.***

MURDERER, MURDERERS (n)
one who commits the crime of murder
*Num 35:16 . . . **m** must be executed.*
*Ps 5:6 . . . LORD detests **m-s** and deceivers.*
*Ps 26:9 . . . condemn me along with **m-s.***
*Ps 59:2 . . . save me from these **m-s.***
*Ezek 18:10 . . . a robber or **m** and refuses*
*1 Jn 3:15 . . . brother or sister is really a **m***
*Rev 21:8 . . . the corrupt, **m-s,** the immoral,*
*Rev 22:15 . . . the sexually immoral, the **m-s,***

MUSIC (n)
vocal, instrumental, or mechanical sounds having rhythm, melody, or harmony
*Judg 5:3 . . . I will make **m** to the LORD,*
*1 Chr 6:31 . . . lead the **m** at the house of*
*Neh 12:27 . . . and with the **m** of cymbals,*
*Ps 45:8 . . . the **m** of strings entertains*
*Amos 5:23 . . . to the **m** of Your harps.*
*Eph 5:19 . . . and making **m** to the Lord*

MYSTERY, MYSTERIES (n)
something not understood or beyond understanding; a religious truth that one can know only by revelation and cannot fully understand
see also SECRET(S)
*Dan 4:9 . . . and that no **m** is too great*
*Rom 11:25 . . . to understand this **m,***
*1 Cor 2:7 . . . speak of is the **m** of God—*
*1 Cor 4:1 . . . explaining God's **m-ies.***
*1 Tim 3:9 . . . to the **m** of the faith*
*1 Tim 3:16 . . . the great **m** of our faith:*
*Rev 1:20 . . . the **m** of the seven stars*
*Rev 17:7 . . . tell you the **m** of this woman*

N

NAIL, NAILED, NAILING (v)
to fasten with or as if with a nail
*Matt 27:35 . . . they had **n-ed** Him to the cross,*
*Mark 15:24 . . . soldiers **n-ed** Him to the cross.*
*Acts 2:23 . . . you **n-ed** Him to a cross*
*Col 2:14 . . . away by **n-ing** it to the cross.*
*Heb 6:6 . . . are **n-ing** Him to the cross*

NATION, NATIONS (n)
group of people defined by geography or ethnicity
see also GENTILE(S), PEOPLES
*Gen 12:2 . . . I will make you into a great **n.***
*Gen 17:4 . . . father of a multitude of **n-s!***
*Gen 17:16 . . . the mother of many **n-s.***
*Gen 25:23 . . . will become two **n-s.***
*Gen 28:3 . . . multiply and become many **n-s!***
*Exod 19:6 . . . of priests, My holy **n.***
*Deut 15:6 . . . You will rule many **n-s,** but*
*Deut 28:10 . . . the **n-s** of the world will see*
*Ps 2:8 . . . you the **n-s** as your inheritance,*
*Ps 22:28 . . . He rules all the **n-s.***
*Ps 46:10 . . . I will be honored by every **n.***
*Ps 66:7 . . . every movement of the **n-s;***
*Ps 68:30 . . . Scatter the **n-s** that delight in*

Ps 87:6 . . . the LORD registers the **n-s,**
Ps 99:2 . . . exalted above all the **n-s.**
Ps 113:4 . . . LORD is high above the **n-s;**
Prov 14:34 . . . Godliness makes a **n** great,
Isa 11:10 . . . The **n-s** will rally to Him,
Isa 34:1 . . . listen, O **n-s** of the earth.
Isa 40:15 . . . for all the **n-s** of the world
Isa 42:1 . . . He will bring justice to the **n-s.**
Isa 52:15 . . . And He will startle many **n-s.**
Isa 56:7 . . . a house of prayer for all **n-s.**
Isa 60:12 . . . the **n-s** that refuse to serve
Isa 66:8 . . . Has a **n** ever been born in a
Ezek 37:22 . . . divided into two **n-s** or into two
Joel 3:2 . . . My people among the **n-s,**
Amos 9:12 . . . the **n-s** I have called to be Mine.
Mic 4:3 . . . disputes between strong **n-s**
Mic 5:7 . . . will take their place among the **n-s.**
Zeph 3:8 . . . stand and accuse these evil **n-s.**
Hag 2:7 . . . I will shake all the **n-s,**
Zech 8:13 . . . Among the other **n-s,** Judah and
Zech 12:2 . . . makes the nearby **n-s** stagger
Matt 12:18 . . . proclaim justice to the **n-s.**
Matt 24:14 . . . so that all **n-s** will hear it;
Matt 28:19 . . . make disciples of all the **n-s,**
Mark 11:17 . . . house of prayer for all **n-s,**
Acts 4:25 . . . Why were the **n-s** so angry?
Gal 3:8 . . . All **n-s** will be blessed through
1 Pet 2:9 . . . royal priests, a holy **n,**
Rev 5:9 . . . and language and people and **n.**
Rev 14:6 . . . to every **n,** tribe, language,
Rev 21:24 . . . The **n-s** will walk in its light,
Rev 22:2 . . . for medicine to heal the **n-s.**

NATURE (n)
inherent character or essence; given by God at birth
Rom 1:20 . . . eternal power and divine **n.**
Rom 8:4 . . . follow our sinful **n**
Rom 8:7 . . . For the sinful **n** is always
Gal 5:19 . . . the desires of your sinful **n,**
Gal 5:24 . . . desires of their sinful **n** to
2 Pet 1:4 . . . share His divine **n** and escape

NEED, NEEDS (n)
a condition requiring supply or relief; poverty; obligation; a lack of something requisite, desirable, or useful
1 Kgs 8:59 . . . according to each day's **n-s.**
Ps 79:8 . . . compassion quickly meet our **n-s,**
Ps 112:9 . . . give generously to those in **n.**
Prov 11:26 . . . who sells in time of **n.**
Prov 30:8 . . . just enough to satisfy my **n-s.**
Matt 6:2 . . . give to someone in **n,**
Acts 2:45 . . . the money with those in **n.**
Acts 20:35 . . . You can help those in **n** by
Rom 12:13 . . . God's people are in **n,**
1 Cor 7:3 . . . fulfill his wife's sexual **n-s,**
Eph 4:28 . . . give generously to others in **n.**
Phil 4:19 . . . will supply all your **n-s** from His
Titus 3:14 . . . by meeting the urgent **n-s**

NEED, NEEDED, NEEDING (v)
to require; to be necessary; to be in want
Ps 34:9 . . . fear Him will have all they **n.**
Ps 119:75 . . . disciplined me because I **n-ed** it.
Phil 4:6 . . . Tell God what you **n,** and
Heb 4:16 . . . grace to help us when we **n** it
Jas 1:4 . . . complete, **n-ing** nothing.
Jas 1:5 . . . If you **n** wisdom, ask our

NEIGHBOR, NEIGHBORS (n)
one living or located near another; fellow man
Lev 19:18 . . . but love your **n** as yourself.
Ps 15:3 . . . to gossip or harm their **n-s**
Prov 24:28 . . . your **n-s** without cause;
Prov 27:10 . . . better to go to a **n** than
Jer 31:34 . . . not need to teach their **n-s,**
Mark 12:31 . . . Love your **n** as yourself.
Luke 10:29 . . . And who is my **n?**
Rom 13:8 . . . If you love your **n,** you will
Gal 5:14 . . . Love your **n** as yourself.
Eph 4:25 . . . Let us tell our **n-s** the truth,
Heb 8:11 . . . not need to teach their **n-s,**
Jas 2:8 . . . Love your **n** as yourself.

NEW (adj)
fresh; original; different than before; unfamiliar
Ps 98:1 . . . Sing a **n** song to the LORD,
Jer 31:31 . . . I will make a **n** covenant with
Ezek 36:26 . . . I will give you a **n** heart,
Mark 16:17 . . . will speak in **n** languages.
Luke 22:20 . . . cup is the **n** covenant
Rom 6:4 . . . we also may live **n** lives.
Rom 12:2 . . . you into a **n** person
1 Cor 11:25 . . . cup is the **n** covenant
2 Cor 3:6 . . . but under the **n** covenant,
2 Cor 5:17 . . . is gone; a **n** life has begun!
Gal 6:15 . . . into a **n** creation.
Eph 4:24 . . . Put on your **n** nature,
Col 3:10 . . . Put on your **n** nature,
Heb 8:8 . . . when I will make a **n** covenant
Heb 9:15 . . . mediates a **n** covenant
Heb 12:24 . . . the **n** covenant
2 Pet 3:13 . . . new heavens and **n** earth he
Rev 2:17 . . . a **n** name that no one
Rev 21:1 . . . **n** heaven and a **n** earth,

NEWS (n)
a report of recent events; "Good News" = the Gospel of Jesus Christ
Isa 40:9 . . . of good **n,** shout from the
Matt 4:23 . . . the Good **N** about
Mark 1:15 . . . sins and believe the Good **N!**
Luke 4:43 . . . I must preach the Good **N**
Acts 13:32 . . . to bring you this Good **N.**
Acts 14:21 . . . preaching the Good **N**
Rom 1:16 . . . not ashamed of this Good **N**
Rom 10:17 . . . the Good **N** about Christ.
Rom 15:16 . . . I bring you the Good **N**
Rom 16:25 . . . just as my Good **N** says.
1 Cor 1:17 . . . to preach the Good **N**—
1 Cor 9:12 . . . an obstacle to the Good **N**
1 Cor 9:16 . . . preach the Good **N!**
1 Cor 9:23 . . . to spread the Good **N**
1 Cor 15:1 . . . the Good **N** I preached
2 Cor 4:4 . . . glorious light of the Good **N.**
2 Cor 9:13 . . . obedient to the Good **N**
2 Cor 11:7 . . . preaching God's Good **N**
Gal 1:7 . . . is not the Good **N** at all.
Eph 6:15 . . . comes from the Good **N**
Phil 1:27 . . . worthy of the Good **N**
Col 1:5 . . . heard the truth of the Good **N.**
Col 1:23 . . . Good **N** has been preached
1 Thes 2:4 . . . entrusted with the Good **N.**
2 Thes 1:8 . . . obey the Good **N** of our Lord
2 Tim 1:10 . . . through the Good **N.**
2 Tim 4:5 . . . telling others the Good **N,**
Rev 14:6 . . . the eternal Good **N**

NIGHT, NIGHTS (n)
period of darkness between sunset and sunrise; figurative of suffering and sorrow or the reign of sin and immorality
Gen 1:16 . . . smaller one to govern the **n.**
Exod 13:21 . . . provided light at **n**
Job 35:10 . . . who gives songs in the **n?**
Ps 1:2 . . . meditating on it day and **n.**
Ps 19:2 . . . **n** after **n** they make him
Ps 77:6 . . . my **n-s** were filled with joyful
Jon 1:17 . . . fish for three days and three **n-s.**
Matt 4:2 . . . forty days and forty **n-s** he fasted
Matt 12:40 . . . for three days and three **n-s.**
Luke 2:8 . . . That **n** there were shepherds
2 Cor 6:5 . . . endured sleepless **n-s,** and gone
1 Thes 5:2 . . . like a thief in the **n.**
1 Thes 5:5 . . . belong to darkness and **n.**
Rev 21:25 . . . there is no **n** there.

O

OATH (n)
an appeal to God to witness the truth of some statement
Ps 95:11 . . . in my anger I took an **o:**
Ps 110:4 . . . LORD has taken an **o**
Ezek 20:42 . . . I promised with a solemn **o**
Heb 6:16 . . . people take an **o,** they call
Heb 7:20 . . . established with a solemn **o.**
Heb 7:21 . . . was an **o** regarding Jesus.
Jas 5:12 . . . never take an **o,** by heaven

OBEDIENCE (n)
an act or instance of obeying; the quality or state of being obedient
Judg 2:17 . . . who had walked in **o** to the
1 Sam 15:22 . . . **O** is better than sacrifice,
Phil 2:8 . . . he humbled himself in **o** to God
Heb 5:8 . . . learned **o** from the things he

OBEY, OBEYED, OBEYING, OBEYS (v)
to follow the commands or guidance of; to conform to or comply with
see also KEEP
Gen 22:18 . . . because you have **o-ed** Me.
Exod 20:6 . . . love Me and **o** My commands.
Lev 18:4 . . . be careful to **o** My decrees,
Lev 25:18 . . . decrees and **o** My regulations.
Deut 4:2 . . . Just **o** the commands of the
Deut 5:27 . . . we will listen and **o.**
Deut 6:17 . . . diligently **o** the commands of
Deut 6:25 . . . when we **o** all the commands
Deut 11:1 . . . and **o** all His requirements,
Deut 11:22 . . . Be careful to **o** all these
Deut 13:4 . . . **O** His commands, listen to his
Deut 26:16 . . . to **o** them wholeheartedly.
Deut 28:1 . . . If you fully **o** the LORD
Deut 30:2 . . . if you **o** with all your heart
Deut 30:12 . . . so we can hear it and **o?**
Deut 30:20 . . . love and **o** the LORD,
Josh 1:7 . . . to **o** all the instructions Moses
Josh 22:5 . . . all His ways, **o** His commands,
1 Sam 7:3 . . . to **o** only the LORD;
1 Kgs 8:61 . . . May you always **o** His decrees
2 Kgs 17:13 . . . **O** My commands and
2 Kgs 18:6 . . . **o-ed** all the commands
2 Kgs 23:3 . . . pledged to **o** the LORD
Neh 1:5 . . . love Him and **o** His commands,
Job 36:11 . . . they listen and **o** God,
Ps 111:10 . . . All who **o** his commandments
Ps 119:17 . . . I may live and **o** Your word.
Ps 119:129 . . . No wonder I **o** them!
Eccl 8:2 . . . **O** the king since you vowed
Eccl 12:13 . . . and **o** His commands,
Isa 11:3 . . . delight in **o-ing** the LORD.
Jer 32:33 . . . not receive instruction or **o.**
Jer 42:6 . . . For if we **o** Him, everything
Jer 43:4 . . . refused to **o** the LORD's
Dan 9:4 . . . love You and **o** Your commands.
Dan 9:10 . . . We have not **o-ed** the LORD
Jon 3:3 . . . This time Jonah **o-ed** the LORD's
Mic 5:15 . . . nations that refuse to **o** Me.
Matt 5:19 . . . anyone who **o-s** God's laws
Matt 8:27 . . . the winds and waves **o** Him!
Matt 19:20 . . . **o-ed** all these commandments,
Matt 28:20 . . . to **o** all the commands
Luke 8:21 . . . hear God's word and **o** it.
John 3:36 . . . who doesn't **o** the Son
John 8:51 . . . anyone who **o-s** My teaching
John 14:15 . . . **o** My commandments.
Acts 4:19 . . . to **o** You rather than him?
Acts 5:29 . . . We must **o** God rather than
Rom 1:5 . . . believe and **o** Him,
Rom 2:27 . . . possess God's law but don't **o**
Rom 3:28 . . . and not by **o-ing** the law.
Rom 6:16 . . . of whatever you choose to **o?**
Rom 6:17 . . . wholeheartedly **o** this
Rom 15:31 . . . in Judea who refuse to **o** God.

*2 Cor 10:5 . . . teach them to **o** Christ.*
*Gal 2:16 . . . Christ, not by **o-ing** the law.*
*Gal 3:2 . . . by **o-ing** the law of Moses?*
*Gal 3:10 . . . and **o** all the commands*
*Eph 2:2 . . . who refuse to **o** God.*
*Eph 6:1 . . . Children, **o** your parents*
*Eph 6:5 . . . Slaves, **o** your earthly masters*
*2 Thes 3:14 . . . who refuse to **o** what we*
*1 Tim 3:4 . . . who respect and **o** him.*
*Titus 2:9 . . . Slaves must always **o** their*
*Heb 11:8 . . . that Abraham **o-ed** when God*
*Heb 11:31 . . . who refused to **o** God.*
*Jas 2:8 . . . good when you **o** the royal law*
*1 Pet 1:2 . . . you have **o-ed** Him and have*
*1 Pet 1:22 . . . when you **o-ed** the truth,*
*1 Pet 2:8 . . . they do not **o** God's word,*
*1 Jn 3:22 . . . because we **o** Him and do*
*Rev 22:7 . . . Blessed are those who **o** the*

OFFERING, OFFERINGS (n)
a sacrifice ceremonially offered as a part of worship; a contribution to the support of a church
*Gen 22:8 . . . a sheep for the burnt **o**,*
*1 Sam 13:9 . . . Bring me the burnt **o***
*1 Sam 15:22 . . . burnt **o-s** and sacrifices*
*Ps 40:6 . . . no delight in sacrifices or **o-s**.*
*Ps 141:2 . . . hands as an evening **o**.*
*Isa 53:10 . . . his life is made an **o** for sin,*
*Hos 6:6 . . . more than I want burnt **o-s**.*
*Mal 3:8 . . . cheated Me of the tithes and **o-s***
*Mark 12:33 . . . all of the burnt **o-s***
*Rom 15:26 . . . taken up an **o** for the poor*
*Phil 2:17 . . . faithful service is an **o***
*Heb 10:5 . . . animal sacrifices or sin **o-s**.*
*Heb 10:14 . . . that one **o** He forever made*
*Heb 11:4 . . . Abel's **o** gave evidence that he*

OIL (n)
a liquid substance produced from olives used in biblical times for lamp fuel, anointing, trade, and dressing wounds; often symbolic of the Holy Spirit
*Exod 29:7 . . . anointing **o** over his head.*
*Exod 30:25 . . . to make a holy anointing **o**.*
*1 Sam 10:1 . . . **o** and poured it over Saul's*
*1 Sam 16:13 . . . **o** he had brought and*
*Ps 23:5 . . . anointing my head with **o**.*
*Ps 133:2 . . . as precious as the anointing **o***
*Heb 1:9 . . . pouring out the **o** of joy*

OPPOSE, OPPOSED, OPPOSES (v)
to set onself against or opposite someone or something; to resist
*Exod 23:22 . . . **o** those who **o** you.*
*Ps 8:2 . . . enemies and all who **o** You.*
*Ps 35:1 . . . **o** those who **o** me.*
*Acts 26:11 . . . was so violently **o-d** to them*
*Gal 2:11 . . . I had to **o** him to his face,*
*1 Tim 6:20 . . . with those who **o***
*2 Tim 2:25 . . . instruct those who **o***
*Titus 1:9 . . . show those who **o** it*
*Titus 2:8 . . . who **o** us will be ashamed*
*Jas 4:6 . . . God **o-s** the proud but favors*
*1 Pet 5:5 . . . God **o-s** the proud but favors*

OPPRESS, OPPRESSED, OPPRESSES, OPPRESSING (v)
to crush or burden by abuse of power or authority
*Exod 22:21 . . . not mistreat or **o** foreigners*
*Ps 9:9 . . . a shelter for the **o-ed**, a refuge*
*Ps 14:6 . . . frustrate the plans of the **o-ed**,*
*Ps 82:3 . . . uphold the rights of the **o-ed** and*
*Ps 146:7 . . . He gives justice to the **o-ed***
*Prov 22:16 . . . gets ahead by **o-ing** the poor*
*Prov 28:16 . . . no understanding will **o***
*Prov 31:5 . . . not give justice to the **o-ed**.*
*Isa 1:17 . . . Seek justice. Help the **o-ed**.*
*Isa 3:5 . . . People will **o** each other—*
*Isa 58:3 . . . you keep **o-ing** your workers.*
*Ezek 18:12 . . . **o-es** the poor and helpless,*
*Dan 7:25 . . . defy the Most High and **o** the*
*Amos 2:7 . . . shove the **o-ed** out of the way.*
*Amos 5:12 . . . **o** good people by taking*
*Zech 7:10 . . . Do not **o** widows, orphans,*
*Luke 4:18 . . . that the **o-ed** will be set free,*
*Jas 2:6 . . . the rich who **o** you and drag*

ORPHAN, ORPHANS (n)
a child deprived by death of one or usually both parents
*Exod 22:22 . . . not exploit a widow or an **o**.*
*Deut 10:18 . . . **o-s** and widows receive*
*Deut 24:17 . . . among you and to **o-s**,*
*Deut 24:19 . . . **o-s**, and widows.*
*Ps 10:14 . . . trust in You. You defend the **o-s**.*
*Ps 82:3 . . . justice to the poor and the **o**;*
*Prov 23:10 . . . the land of defenseless **o-s**.*
*John 14:18 . . . will not abandon you as **o-s**—*
*Jas 1:27 . . . caring for **o-s** and widows in*

OVERSEER(S) (KJV)
*2 Chr 2:18 . . . and 3,600 as **foremen***
*Neh 11:22 . . . **chief officer** of the Levites*
*Prov 6:7 . . . or **governor** or ruler to make them*
*Acts 20:28 . . . appointed you as **elders***
*1 Tim 3:1 . . . an **elder** must be a man whose*
*1 Pet 2:25 . . . Shepherd, the **Guardian** of your*

OX, OXEN (n)
a domestic bovine mammal
*Deut 25:4 . . . not muzzle an **o** to keep it*
*1 Kgs 7:25 . . . base of twelve bronze **o-en**,*
*1 Kgs 19:20 . . . Elisha left the **o-en***
*Isa 1:3 . . . **o** knows its owner, and a*
*Ezek 1:10 . . . the face of an **o** on the left*
*1 Cor 9:9 . . . not muzzle an **o** to keep it*
*1 Tim 5:18 . . . not muzzle an **o** to keep it*
*Rev 4:7 . . . the second was like an **o**;*

P

PAGAN, PAGANS (n)
a follower of a false god or a heathen religion; one who delights in sensual pleasures and material goods
*Ps 106:35 . . . they mingled among the **p-s***
*Isa 2:6 . . . have made alliances with **p-s**.*
*Matt 5:47 . . . Even **p-s** do that.*
*Matt 18:17 . . . treat that person as a **p***
*1 Cor 5:1 . . . something that even **p-s** don't*
*1 Cor 12:2 . . . when you were still **p-s**, you*

PAIN, PAINS (n)
physical, mental, or emotional suffering; the spasms of childbirth
*Job 6:10 . . . Despite the **p**, I have not*
*Ps 73:14 . . . every morning brings me **p**.*
*Jer 4:19 . . . my heart—I writhe in **p**!*
*Matt 24:8 . . . only the first of the birth **p-s**,*
*John 16:21 . . . suffering the **p-s** of labor.*
*Rom 8:22 . . . in the **p-s** of childbirth*
*Gal 4:19 . . . going through labor **p-s** for you*
*1 Thes 5:3 . . . woman's labor **p-s** begin.*
*Heb 13:3 . . . as if you felt their **p** in your*
*Rev 21:4 . . . death or sorrow or crying or **p**.*

PAINFUL (adj)
feeling or giving pain
*Gen 5:29 . . . the **p** labor of farming*
*Prov 17:21 . . . **p** to be the parent of a fool;*
*2 Cor 2:1 . . . grief with another **p** visit.*
*Heb 12:11 . . . while it is happening—it's **p**!*

PARABLE, PARABLES (n)
a brief narrative story told with earthly analogies to illustrate a spiritual truth
*Ps 78:2 . . . I will speak to you in a **p**.*
*Matt 13:35 . . . I will speak to you in **p-s**.*
*Luke 8:10 . . . I use **p-s** to teach the*

PARDON, PARDONED (v)
to allow (an offense) to pass without punishment; to forgive
*Num 14:19 . . . **p** the sins of this people,*
*Deut 29:20 . . . LORD will never **p** such*
*2 Kgs 5:18 . . . may the LORD **p** me*
*2 Chr 30:18 . . . LORD, who is good, **p***
*Isa 40:2 . . . gone and her sins are **p-ed**.*
*Jer 5:7 . . . How can I **p** you?*
*Joel 3:21 . . . I will **p** My people's crimes,*
*Joel 3:21 . . . which I have not yet **p-ed**;*

PARENT, PARENTS (n)
one that produces and cares for offspring
see also FATHER, MOTHER
*Exod 20:5 . . . I lay the sins of the **p-s** upon*
*Prov 13:1 . . . child accepts a **p's** discipline;*
*Jer 31:29 . . . **p-s** have eaten sour grapes,*
*Ezek 18:19 . . . child pay for the **p's** sins?*
*Matt 10:21 . . . will rebel against their **p-s***
*Rom 1:30 . . . and they disobey their **p-s**.*
*Eph 6:1 . . . Children, obey your **p-s***
*Col 3:20 . . . always obey your **p-s**,*

PARTNER, PARTNERS (n)
a person with whom one shares an intimate relationship; one associated with another especially in action
*Mal 2:14 . . . she remained your faithful **p**,*
*2 Cor 6:14 . . . can righteousness be a **p***
*Phil 1:5 . . . **p-s** in spreading the Good*
*1 Pet 3:7 . . . but she is your equal **p** in*
*1 Pet 4:13 . . . trials make you **p-s** with*
*3 Jn 8 . . . be their **p-s** as they teach*
*Rev 1:9 . . . your **p** in suffering and in God's*

PASSION, PASSIONS (n)
intense, driving, or overmastering feeling or conviction; ardent affection; sexual desire
*Isa 59:17 . . . himself in a cloak of divine **p**.*
*Zech 8:2 . . . with **p** for Jerusalem!*
*1 Cor 7:37 . . . he can control his **p**, he does*
*Gal 5:24 . . . Jesus have nailed the **p-s***
*1 Thes 4:5 . . . lustful **p** like the pagans*

PASSOVER (n)
a festival that commemorated the Hebrew departure from Egypt in haste
*Num 9:2 . . . celebrate the **P***
*Deut 16:1 . . . celebrate the **P** each year*
*Ezra 6:19 . . . returned exiles celebrated **P**.*
*Mark 14:12 . . . **P** lamb is sacrificed,*
*Heb 11:28 . . . to keep the **P** and to sprinkle*

PATH, PATHS (n)
course, route; a way of life, conduct, or thought
*1 Kgs 8:36 . . . follow the right **p**,*
*Ps 23:3 . . . He guides me along right **p-s**,*
*Ps 27:11 . . . Lead me along the right **p**,*
*Prov 2:13 . . . to walk down dark **p-s**.*
*Prov 3:6 . . . show you which **p** to take.*
*Prov 5:21 . . . examining every **p** he takes.*
*Prov 8:20 . . . in **p-s** of justice.*
*Prov 14:12 . . . a **p** before each person that*
*Isa 48:17 . . . leads you along the **p-s***
*Hos 14:9 . . . **p-s** of the LORD are true*
*2 Tim 2:18 . . . have left the **p** of truth,*
*Heb 12:13 . . . Mark out a straight **p***

PATIENCE (n)
the power or capacity to endure without complaint something difficult or disagreeable; forbearance, longsuffering
*Rom 15:5 . . . May God, who gives this **p***
*Gal 5:22 . . . joy, peace, **p**, kindness,*
*Col 1:11 . . . endurance and **p** you need.*
*Col 3:12 . . . humility, gentleness, and **p**.*
*2 Tim 3:10 . . . my faith, my **p**, my love,*

*Titus 2:2 . . . and be filled with love and **p**.*
*Jas 5:10 . . . examples of **p** in suffering,*
*2 Pet 3:15 . . . Lord's **p** gives people time*

PAY (n)
something paid for a purpose and especially as a salary or wage
*1 Tim 5:18 . . . who work deserve their **p**!*

PAY, PAYS (v)
to suffer the consequences of an act; to requite according to what is deserved; to make due return to for services or goods rendered
*Exod 22:3 . . . A thief who is caught must **p***
*Deut 32:35 . . . I will **p** them back.*
*Ps 137:8 . . . Happy is the one who **p-s** you*
*Matt 22:17 . . . to **p** taxes to Caesar or not?*
*Rom 12:19 . . . I will **p** them back,*
*1 Thes 5:15 . . . no one **p-s** back evil*
*2 Thes 1:6 . . . he will **p** back those who*

PEACE (n)
a state of tranquility or quiet; a pact or agreement to end hostilities between those who have been at war or in a state of enmity; harmony in personal relations, especially with God; a state of security or order within a community; freedom from disquieting or oppressive thoughts or emotions
*Exod 20:24 . . . and **p** offerings, your sheep*
*Lev 26:6 . . . I will give you **p** in the land,*
*Num 6:26 . . . His favor and give You his **p**.*
*Deut 20:10 . . . offer its people terms for **p**.*
*1 Sam 7:14 . . . there was **p** between Israel*
*1 Kgs 5:4 . . . God has given me **p** on every*
*1 Chr 22:9 . . . a son who will be a man of **p**.*
*2 Chr 14:7 . . . has given us **p** on every side.*
*Job 3:26 . . . I have no **p**, no quietness.*
*Job 25:2 . . . He enforces **p** in the heavens.*
*Ps 34:14 . . . Search for **p**, and work to*
*Ps 37:37 . . . awaits those who love **p**.*
*Ps 120:7 . . . I search for **p**;*
*Ps 147:14 . . . He sends **p** across your nation*
*Prov 12:20 . . . hearts that are planning **p**!*
*Eccl 3:8 . . . for war and a time for **p**.*
*Isa 9:6 . . . Everlasting Father, Prince of **P**.*
*Isa 32:17 . . . righteousness will bring **p**.*
*Isa 48:22 . . . there is no **p** for the wicked,*
*Isa 52:7 . . . good news of **p** and salvation,*
*Jer 6:14 . . . They give assurances of **p** when*
*Jer 46:27 . . . return to a life of **p** and quiet,*
*Ezek 34:25 . . . I will make a covenant of **p***
*Zech 8:19 . . . So love truth and **p**.*
*Matt 5:9 . . . blesses those who work for **p**,*
*Mark 9:50 . . . live in **p** with each other.*
*Luke 1:79 . . . guide us to the path of **p**.*
*John 16:33 . . . you may have **p** in Me.*
*Rom 5:1 . . . by faith, we have **p** with God*
*Rom 8:6 . . . your mind leads to life and **p**.*
*1 Cor 14:33 . . . God of disorder but of **p**,*
*Gal 5:22 . . . love, joy, **p**, patience,*
*Eph 2:14 . . . Christ Himself has brought **p***
*Eph 2:15 . . . made **p** between Jews and*
*Eph 2:17 . . . Good News of **p** to you Gentiles*
*Eph 6:15 . . . put on the **p** that comes from*
*Phil 4:7 . . . experience God's **p**,*
*1 Thes 5:23 . . . God of **p** make you holy*
*2 Thes 3:16 . . . Lord of **p** Himself give you*
*2 Tim 2:22 . . . faithfulness, love, and **p**.*
*Heb 13:20 . . . the God of **p**—who brought*
*Jas 3:17 . . . It is also **p** loving, gentle*
*1 Pet 3:11 . . . Search for **p**, and work to*

PEACEMAKER, PEACEMAKERS (n)
one who makes peace especially by reconciling parties at variance
*Acts 7:26 . . . He tried to be a **p**.*
*Jas 3:18 . . . **p-s** will plant seeds of peace*

PENTECOST (n)
a Jewish feast celebrated on the 50th day after the Feast of Unleavened Bread; the day God sent the Holy Spirit after Christ's resurrection
*Acts 2:1 . . . the day of **P** all the believers*
*Acts 20:16 . . . in time for the Festival of **P**.*
*1 Cor 16:8 . . . until the Festival of **P**.*

PEOPLE, PEOPLES (n)
human beings making up a group or assembly or linked by a common interest; clan or nation; humanity
see also NATION(S)
*Exod 5:1 . . . says: Let my **p** go*
*Exod 8:23 . . . between my **p** and your people.*
*Exod 19:5 . . . among all the **p-s** on earth;*
*Exod 19:8 . . . all the **p** responded together,*
*Exod 33:13 . . . nation is your very own **p**.*
*Lev 26:12 . . . and you will be My **p**.*
*Num 14:11 . . . How long will these **p***
*Deut 7:6 . . . you are a holy **p**, who belong*
*Deut 14:1 . . . are the **p** of the* LORD
*Deut 32:9 . . . For the **p** of Israel belong*
*Deut 33:29 . . . **p** saved by the* LORD*?*
*Ruth 1:16 . . . Your **p** will be My people,*
*2 Chr 7:20 . . . uproot the **p** from this land*
*Neh 1:10 . . . The **p** You rescued by Your*
*Neh 8:1 . . . the **p** assembled with a unified*
*Ps 8:4 . . . what are **p** that You should think*
*Ps 33:12 . . . whose **p** He has chosen*
*Ps 53:6 . . . When God restores His **p**,*
*Ps 94:14 . . . will not reject His **p**;*
*Ps 96:10 . . . He will judge all **p-s** fairly.*
*Ps 135:14 . . . will give justice to His **p***
*Isa 2:2 . . . **p** from all over the world*
*Isa 6:10 . . . Harden the hearts of these **p**.*
*Isa 40:1 . . . Comfort, comfort My **p**,*
Isa 49:13 . . . LORD *has comforted His **p***
*Isa 52:6 . . . I will reveal my name to My **p**,*
*Isa 53:8 . . . for the rebellion of My **p**.*
*Isa 55:4 . . . My power among the **p-s**.*
*Jer 2:11 . . . Yet My **p** have exchanged their*
*Jer 2:32 . . . My **p** have forgotten Me,*
*Jer 7:16 . . . Pray no more for these **p**,*
*Jer 32:27 . . . of all the **p-s** of the world.*
*Dan 8:24 . . . and devastate the holy **p**.*
*Dan 9:24 . . . decreed for Your **p***
*Hos 1:10 . . . You are not My **p**,*
*Hos 2:23 . . . Now you are My **p**.*
*Mic 4:1 . . . **p** from all over the world*
Mic 4:3 . . . LORD *will mediate between **p-s***
*Matt 4:19 . . . show you how to fish for **p**!*
*Mark 7:7 . . . **p** honor Me with their lips,*
*Mark 8:27 . . . Who do **p** say I am?*
*Luke 1:68 . . . visited and redeemed His **p**.*
*John 11:50 . . . should die for the **p***
*John 18:14 . . . should die for the **p**.*
*Rom 9:25 . . . Those who were not My **p**,*
*Rom 11:1 . . . **p**, the nation of Israel?*
*2 Cor 6:16 . . . and they will be My **p**.*
*Gal 6:16 . . . they are the new **p** of God.*
*Eph 1:14 . . . purchased us to be His own **p**.*
*Eph 1:18 . . . He called—His holy **p***
*Eph 2:15 . . . creating in Himself one new **p***
*Eph 4:8 . . . and gave gifts to His **p**.*
*2 Tim 2:2 . . . trustworthy **p** who will*
*2 Tim 3:17 . . . and equip His **p** to do every*
*Titus 2:11 . . . bringing salvation to all **p**.*
*Titus 2:14 . . . make us His very own **p**,*
*Heb 4:9 . . . waiting for the **p** of God.*
*1 Pet 2:9 . . . for you are a chosen **p**.*
*1 Pet 2:10 . . . now you are God's **p**.*
*Rev 5:8 . . . prayers of God's **p**.*
*Rev 10:11 . . . again about many **p-s**,*
*Rev 18:4 . . . from her, My **p**.*
*Rev 19:8 . . . of God's holy **p**.*
*Rev 21:3 . . . God's home is now among His **p**!*

PERFECT (adj)
being entirely without fault or defect; corresponding to an ideal standard or abstract concept; mature, pure, complete
*Deut 32:4 . . . the Rock; His deeds are **p**.*
Ps 19:7 . . . instructions of the LORD *are **p**,*
*Ps 119:138 . . . laws are **p** and completely*
*Matt 5:48 . . . you are to be **p**, even as*
*John 17:23 . . . experience such **p** unity*
*Gal 3:3 . . . become **p** by your*
*Col 4:12 . . . God to make you strong and **p**,*
*Heb 2:10 . . . suffering, a **p** leader,*
*Heb 5:9 . . . as a **p** High Priest,*
*Heb 7:19 . . . law never made anything **p**.*
*Heb 9:11 . . . greater, more **p** Tabernacle*
*Heb 9:14 . . . as a **p** sacrifice for our sins.*
*Heb 10:14 . . . He forever made **p** those*
*Heb 12:23 . . . who have now been made **p**.*
*Jas 1:25 . . . look carefully into the **p** law*
*1 Jn 4:18 . . . because **p** love expels all fear.*

PERISH, PERISHING (v)
to become destroyed or ruined physically or spiritually; to die
see also DESTROY, DIE
*Ps 102:26 . . . They will **p**, but You remain*
*John 3:16 . . . believes in Him will not **p** but*
*John 10:28 . . . they will never **p**.*
*2 Cor 2:15 . . . by those who are **p-ing**.*
*2 Cor 4:3 . . . from people who are **p-ing**.*
*Jude 11 . . . they **p** in their rebellion.*

PERSECUTE, PERSECUTED, PERSECUTING (v)
to harass or punish in a manner designed to injure, grieve, or afflict; to cause to suffer because of belief
*Ps 140:12 . . . help those they **p**;*
*Matt 5:10 . . . blesses those who are **p-d***
*Matt 5:11 . . . when people mock you and **p***
*Matt 5:12 . . . prophets were **p-d***
*Matt 5:44 . . . Pray for those who **p** you!*
*Matt 13:21 . . . **p-d** for believing God's*
*John 15:20 . . . they **p-d** Me, naturally*
*John 15:20 . . . they will **p** you.*
*Acts 9:4 . . . Why are you **p-ing** me?*
*Rom 8:35 . . . or are **p-d**, or hungry,*
*Rom 12:14 . . . Bless those who **p** you.*
*1 Cor 15:9 . . . the way I **p-d** God's church.*
*2 Thes 1:7 . . . for you who are being **p-d***

PERSECUTION, PERSECUTIONS (n)
the condition of being persecuted, harassed, or annoyed
*Mark 10:30 . . . along with **p**.*
*2 Cor 12:10 . . . insults, hardships, **p-s**,*
*2 Thes 1:4 . . . all the **p-s** and hardships*
*2 Thes 1:5 . . . God will use this **p** to show*
*2 Tim 3:11 . . . You know how much **p** and*
*2 Tim 3:12 . . . in Christ Jesus will suffer **p**.*
*Rev 13:10 . . . must endure **p** patiently*

PERSEVERANCE (n)
enduring hardships with patience; steadfastness
see also ENDURANCE
*1 Tim 6:11 . . . along with faith, love, **p**, and*

PERSEVERE (v)
to persist in a state, enterprise, or undertaking in spite of counterinfluences, opposition, or discouragement
see also ENDURE
*Rev 3:10 . . . obeyed My command to **p**,*

PHARISEE, PHARISEES (n)
a religious and political party in Palestine in New Testament times known for strict observance of rites and ceremonies of the

written law and for insistence on the validity of their own oral traditions concerning the law
*Matt 5:20 . . . **P-s**, you will never enter*
*Matt 16:6 . . . of the yeast of the **P-s***
*Matt 23:13 . . . and you **P-s**. Hypocrites!*
*John 3:1 . . . religious leader who was a **P**.*
*Acts 23:6 . . . **P**, as were my ancestors!*

PHYSICAL (adj)
having material existence; of or relating to the body
*John 1:13 . . . reborn—not with a **p** birth*
*Col 1:22 . . . of Christ in His **p** body.*
*1 Tim 4:8 . . . **P** training is good, but*
*1 Tim 5:11 . . . **p** desires will overpower*
*1 John 2:16 . . . a craving for **p** pleasure*

PIERCE, PIERCED (v)
to make a hold through; to stab
*Exod 21:6 . . . and publicly **p** his ear*
*Ps 22:16 . . . have **p-d** my hands and feet.*
*Zech 12:10 . . . me whom they have **p-d***
*Luke 2:35 . . . sword will **p** your very soul.*
*John 19:37 . . . look on the one they **p-d**.*
*Rev 1:7 . . . even those who **p-d** Him.*

PILGRIM(S) (KJV)
*Heb 11:13 . . . **nomads** here on earth*
*1 Pet 2:11 . . . as "temporary residents and **foreigners**"*

PILLAR, PILLARS (n)
a column or shaft standing alone as a monument or supporting a superstructure; miraculous cloud by day and fire by night; memorial pile of stones; a supporting, integral, or upstanding member of a group
*Gen 19:26 . . . she turned into a **p** of salt.*
*Exod 13:21 . . . night with a **p** of fire.*
*Exod 24:4 . . . set up twelve **p-s**, one for*
*Deut 1:33 . . . by night and a **p** of cloud by*
*Judg 16:26 . . . my hands against the **p-s***
*Gal 2:9 . . . known as **p-s** of the church,*
*1 Tim 3:15 . . . **p** and foundation of*
*Rev 3:12 . . . victorious will become **p-s***

PLAGUE, PLAGUES (n)
a disastrous evil, affliction, or epidemic of infectious disease, issued by God in judgment
*2 Chr 6:28 . . . or a **p** or crop disease*
*Luke 21:11 . . . will be famines and **p-s***
*Rev 21:9 . . . the seven last **p-s** came*
*Rev 22:18 . . . add to that person the **p-s***

PLAN, PLANS (n)
a detailed formulation of a program of action; goal, aim
see also PURPOSE
*Ps 2:1 . . . waste their time with futile **p-s?***
*Ps 33:10 . . . frustrates the **p-s** of the*
*Ps 40:5 . . . **p-s** for us are too numerous*
*Isa 30:1 . . . You make **p-s** that are contrary*
*Isa 32:6 . . . and make evil **p-s**.*
*Acts 2:23 . . . His prearranged **p** was carried*
*Acts 4:25 . . . waste their time with futile **p-s?***
*Acts 7:44 . . . according to the **p** God had*
*Rom 16:25 . . . **p** kept secret from*
*Eph 3:9 . . . this mysterious **p** that God,*
*Eph 3:11 . . . This was His eternal **p**,*
*2 Tim 1:9 . . . **p** from before the beginning*

PLAN, PLANNED, PLANNING (v)
to devise or project the realization or achievement of
*Prov 12:20 . . . hearts that are **p-ning** peace!*
*Isa 25:1 . . . You **p-ned** them long ago,*
*Jer 23:20 . . . has finished all He has **p-ned**.*
*Eph 2:10 . . . do the good things He **p-ned***

PLANT, PLANTED, PLANTING, PLANTS (v)
to put or set (seeds or plants) in the ground for growth; to establish or settle
*Gen 2:8 . . . the LORD God **p-ed** a garden*
*Gen 8:22 . . . there will be **p-ing** and harvest,*
*Ps 1:3 . . . like trees **p-ed** along the riverbank,*
*Ps 126:5 . . . who **p** in tears will harvest*
*Prov 22:8 . . . who **p** injustice will harvest*
*Prov 31:16 . . . earnings she **p-s** a vineyard.*
*Hos 10:12 . . . **P** the good seeds*
*Amos 9:15 . . . I will firmly **p** them there*
*Matt 6:26 . . . They don't **p** or harvest or*
*Matt 13:3 . . . A farmer went out to **p** some*
*Matt 13:18 . . . about the farmer **p-ing***
*1 Cor 3:6 . . . **p-ed** the seed in your hearts,*
*1 Cor 3:7 . . . who does the **p-ing**,*
*1 Cor 9:7 . . . What farmer **p-s** a vineyard*
*1 Cor 15:42 . . . earthly bodies are **p-ed***
*2 Cor 9:6 . . . a farmer who **p-s** only a few*
*Jas 1:21 . . . accept the word God has **p-ed***
*Jas 3:18 . . . will **p** seeds of peace*

PLEASE, PLEASED, PLEASES (v)
to make glad; to satisfy; to like or wish; to be the will or pleasure of
*Deut 12:25 . . . doing what **p-s** the LORD.*
*Ps 135:6 . . . The LORD does whatever **p-s***
*Prov 16:7 . . . people's lives **p** the LORD,*
*Isa 42:1 . . . My chosen one, who **p-s** Me.*
*Matt 12:18 . . . My Beloved, who **p-s** Me.*
*Luke 2:14 . . . those with whom God is **p-d**.*
*Luke 10:21 . . . Yes, Father, it **p-d** You to do*
*John 8:29 . . . I always do what **p-s** Him.*
*Rom 8:8 . . . sinful nature can never **p** God.*
*Rom 14:18 . . . this attitude, you will **p** God,*
*2 Cor 5:9 . . . our goal is to **p** Him.*
*Gal 6:8 . . . live to **p** the Spirit will harvest*
*Eph 5:10 . . . determine what **p-s** the*
*Phil 2:13 . . . power to do what **p-s** Him.*
*Col 1:10 . . . always honor and **p** the Lord,*
*Col 1:19 . . . God in all His fullness was **p-d***
*1 Thes 2:4 . . . Our purpose is to **p** God,*
*1 Thes 2:15 . . . They fail to **p** God*
*1 Tim 2:3 . . . is good and **p-s** God our*
*1 Tim 5:4 . . . is something that **p-s** God.*
*Heb 10:6 . . . not **p-d** with burnt offerings*
*Heb 11:6 . . . to **p** God without faith.*
*Heb 13:16 . . . sacrifices that **p** God.*
*1 Pet 2:19 . . . God is **p-d** with you when*
*1 Jn 2:17 . . . does what **p-s** God will live*
*Rev 4:11 . . . you created what you **p-d**.*

PLEASURE, PLEASURES (n)
desire, inclination; a source of delight or joy; sensual gratification
*Ps 5:4 . . . you take no **p** in wickedness;*
*Ps 16:3 . . . I take **p** in them!*
*Ps 16:11 . . . the **p-s** of living with You*
*Isa 1:11 . . . I get no **p** from the blood of*
*Luke 8:14 . . . cares and riches and **p-s***
*Eph 1:9 . . . a plan to fulfill His own good **p**.*
*1 Tim 5:6 . . . widow who lives only for **p***
*2 Tim 3:4 . . . and love **p** rather than God.*
*Titus 2:12 . . . living and sinful **p-s**.*
*Titus 3:3 . . . slaves to many lusts and **p-s**.*
*Heb 11:25 . . . the fleeting **p-s** of sin.*
*Jas 4:3 . . . want only what will give you **p**.*

PLOWSHARES (n)
a part of a plow that cuts the furrow
*Isa 2:4 . . . will hammer their swords into **p***
*Joel 3:10 . . . Hammer your **p** into swords*
*Mic 4:3 . . . hammer their swords into **p***

POOR (adj)
characterized by poverty or insufficient resources; humble
*Lev 19:10 . . . Leave them for the **p***
*Deut 15:4 . . . should be no **p** among you,*
*Deut 15:11 . . . some in the land who are **p**.*
*Deut 24:12 . . . If your neighbor is **p***
*1 Sam 2:7 . . . The LORD makes some **p***
*Job 5:16 . . . at last the **p** have hope,*
*Ps 35:10 . . . protects the helpless and **p***
*Ps 41:1 . . . those who are kind to the **p!***
*Ps 82:3 . . . Give justice to the **p** and the*
*Prov 10:4 . . . Lazy people are soon **p;***
*Prov 13:7 . . . Some who are **p** pretend*
*Prov 14:21 . . . those who help the **p**.*
*Prov 17:5 . . . mock the **p** insult*
*Prov 21:13 . . . cries of the **p** will be ignored*
*Prov 22:2 . . . rich and **p** have this*
*Prov 22:22 . . . Don't rob the **p** just because*
*Prov 28:27 . . . Whoever gives to the **p** will*
*Prov 31:20 . . . helping hand to the **p***
*Isa 3:14 . . . things stolen from the **p**.*
*Isa 14:30 . . . I will feed the **p** in my pasture;*
*Isa 32:7 . . . They lie to convict the **p**,*
*Isa 61:1 . . . to bring good news to the **p**.*
*Jer 22:16 . . . help to the **p** and needy,*
*Amos 4:1 . . . who oppress the **p** and crush*
*Amos 5:11 . . . trample the **p**, stealing their*
*Zech 7:10 . . . foreigners, and the **p**.*
*Matt 11:5 . . . is being preached to the **p**.*
*Matt 19:21 . . . and give the money to the **p**,*
*Mark 12:42 . . . Then a **p** widow came and*
*Mark 14:7 . . . You will always have the **p***
*Luke 4:18 . . . to bring Good News to the **p**.*
*Luke 14:13 . . . Instead, invite the **p**, the*
*John 12:8 . . . You will always have the **p***
*Rom 15:26 . . . an offering for the **p** among*
*2 Cor 8:9 . . . for your sakes He became **p**,*
*Jas 2:2 . . . another comes in who is **p***
*Jas 2:6 . . . you dishonor the **p!***

POSSESS, POSSESSED (v)
to seize, gain, or take (control of); to own
*Ps 37:11 . . . The lowly will **p** the land*
*Ps 37:29 . . . The godly will **p** the land*
*John 7:20 . . . You're demon **p-ed!***
*John 8:48 . . . you were **p-ed** by a demon?*
*John 8:52 . . . you are **p-ed** by a demon.*
*John 10:20 . . . He's demon **p-ed** and out*
*John 10:21 . . . like a man **p-ed** by a demon!*
*Phil 3:12 . . . press on to **p** that perfection*

POSSESSION, POSSESSIONS (n)
something owned, occupied, or controlled
see also INHERITANCE, RICHES, TREASURE(S), WEALTH
*Exod 6:8 . . . as your very own **p**.*
*Deut 4:20 . . . and His special **p**,*
*Deut 32:9 . . . is His special **p**.*
*Zech 2:12 . . . the LORD's special **p***
*Matt 19:21 . . . sell all your **p-s** and*
*Mark 10:22 . . . for he had many **p-s**.*
*1 Pet 2:9 . . . God's very own **p**.*

POTTER (n)
one that makes pottery
*Isa 29:16 . . . **p** who made me is stupid"?*
*Isa 64:8 . . . the clay, and You are the **p**.*
*Zech 11:13 . . . threw them to the **p***

POUR, POURED, POURING, POURS (v)
to move or come continuously; to supply or produce freely
*Ps 42:8 . . . LORD **p-s** his unfailing love*
*Ps 45:7 . . . **p-ing** out the oil of joy on*
*Isa 32:15 . . . Spirit is **p-ed** out on us*
*Isa 44:3 . . . I will **p** out My Spirit*
*Ezek 39:29 . . . I will **p** out My Spirit*
*Joel 2:28 . . . I will **p** out My Spirit*
*Zech 12:10 . . . I will **p** out a spirit of*
*Mal 3:10 . . . I will **p** out a blessing*
*Luke 22:20 . . . blood, which is **p-ed** out*
*Acts 2:17 . . . I will **p** out My Spirit*

*Acts 2:33 . . . the Holy Spirit to **p** out*
*Acts 10:45 . . . Holy Spirit had been **p-ed***
*Eph 1:6 . . . grace He has **p-ed** out on us*
*Phil 2:17 . . . **p-ing** it out like a liquid*
*Titus 3:6 . . . generously **p-ed** out the Spirit*

POVERTY (n)
the state of one who lacks money or material possessions
*Prov 6:11 . . . **p** will pounce on you like*
*Prov 13:18 . . . end in **p** and disgrace;*
*Prov 21:5 . . . hasty shortcuts lead to **p.***
*Prov 24:34 . . . **p** will pounce on you like*
*Prov 31:7 . . . drink to forget their **p***
*2 Cor 8:9 . . . by his **p** he could make you*
*Rev 2:9 . . . your suffering and your **p**—*

POWER, POWERS (n)
ability to act or produce an effect; possession of control, authority, or influence over others; physical might; mental or moral efficacy; a controlling group
see also STRENGTH
*Exod 15:6 . . . LORD, is glorious in **p.***
*Deut 8:18 . . . one who gives you **p** to be*
*Ps 89:7 . . . angelic **p-s** stand in awe of God.*
*Isa 40:26 . . . great **p** and incomparable*
*Jer 9:23 . . . the powerful boast in their **p,***
*Mic 3:8 . . . I am filled with **p**—*
*Matt 16:18 . . . all the **p-s** of hell will not*
*Matt 22:29 . . . don't know the **p** of God.*
*Luke 1:35 . . . the **p** of the Most High will*
*Luke 4:14 . . . the Holy Spirit's **p.***
*Luke 9:1 . . . gave them **p** and authority*
*Luke 10:19 . . . over all the **p** of the enemy,*
*Luke 11:20 . . . demons by the **p** of God,*
*Acts 1:8 . . . receive **p** when the Holy Spirit*
*Rom 1:16 . . . the **p** of God at work,*
*Rom 1:20 . . . his eternal **p** and divine*
*Rom 6:9 . . . Death no longer has any **p** over*
*Rom 7:23 . . . another **p** within me that is*
*Rom 8:38 . . . not even the **p-s** of hell can*
*Rom 15:13 . . . the **p** of the Holy Spirit.*
*1 Cor 1:18 . . . is the very **p** of God.*
*1 Cor 6:14 . . . from the dead by His **p,***
*1 Cor 15:24 . . . ruler and authority and **p.***
*2 Cor 4:7 . . . our great **p** is from God,*
*2 Cor 13:4 . . . now lives by the **p** of God.*
*Eph 6:10 . . . Lord and in His mighty **p.***
*Phil 3:10 . . . and experience the mighty **p***
*Col 1:11 . . . with all His glorious **p***
*Col 1:29 . . . depending on Christ's mighty **p***
*1 Thes 1:5 . . . words but also with **p,***
*2 Tim 1:7 . . . but of **p,** love, and*
*2 Tim 3:5 . . . reject the **p** that could make*
*Heb 2:14 . . . break the **p** of the devil,*
*Jas 5:16 . . . righteous person has great **p***
*1 Pet 1:5 . . . is protecting you by His **p***
*1 Pet 3:22 . . . **p-s** accept His authority.*
*1 Pet 4:11 . . . All glory and **p** to Him*
*2 Pet 1:3 . . . **p,** God has given us everything*
*Jude 25 . . . majesty, **p,** and authority are his*
*Rev 4:11 . . . receive glory and honor and **p.***
*Rev 5:12 . . . receive **p** and riches and*
*Rev 19:1 . . . glory and **p** belong to our God.*
*Rev 20:6 . . . the second death holds no **p,***

PRAISE, PRAISES (n)
worship; commendation; value, merit
*Deut 26:19 . . . **p,** honor, and renown.*
*2 Sam 22:4 . . . LORD, who is worthy of **p,***
*2 Chr 29:30 . . . So they offered joyous **p***
*Ps 7:17 . . . I will sing **p** to the name*
*Ps 18:49 . . . I will sing **p-s** to Your name.*
*Ps 34:1 . . . will constantly speak His **p-s.***
*Ps 81:1 . . . Sing **p-s** to God,*
*Ps 108:1 . . . Your **p-s** with all my heart!*
*Ps 145:3 . . . He is most worthy of **p!***
*Ps 149:6 . . . Let the **p-s** of God be in*
*John 12:43 . . . loved human **p** more than*
*Rom 2:29 . . . heart seeks **p** from God,*
*Rom 15:9 . . . will sing **p-s** to Your name.*
*1 Thes 2:6 . . . As for human **p,***
*2 Thes 1:10 . . . His holy people—**p** from all*
*Jas 5:13 . . . You should sing **p-s.***

PRAISE, PRAISED, PRAISES, PRAISING (v)
to worship, commend, or give honor to
*Exod 15:2 . . . and I will **p** Him—*
*1 Chr 16:35 . . . name and rejoice and **p** You.*
*2 Chr 5:13 . . . together in unison to **p** and*
*2 Chr 20:21 . . . **p-ing** Him for His holy*
*Neh 9:5 . . . Stand up and **p** the LORD*
*Ps 9:1 . . . I will **p** You, LORD,*
*Ps 12:8 . . . evil is **p-d** throughout the land.*
*Ps 34:1 . . . I will **p** the LORD*
*Ps 42:5 . . . I will **p** Him again—*
*Ps 45:17 . . . nations will **p** You forever*
*Ps 51:15 . . . my mouth may **p** You.*
*Ps 63:3 . . . how I **p** You!*
*Ps 71:8 . . . why I can never stop **p-ing** You;*
*Ps 71:14 . . . I will **p** You more and*
*Ps 74:21 . . . and needy **p** Your name.*
*Ps 89:5 . . . angels will **p** You for Your*
*Ps 96:2 . . . LORD; **p** His name.*
*Ps 102:18 . . . not yet born will **p** the*
*Ps 104:1 . . . all that I am **p** the*
*Ps 115:18 . . . But we can **p** the LORD*
*Ps 135:20 . . . LORD, **p** the LORD!*
*Ps 144:1 . . . **P** the LORD, who is*
*Ps 148:13 . . . Let them all **p** the name*
*Ps 150:2 . . . **p** His unequaled greatness!*
*Prov 27:2 . . . Let someone else **p** you,*
*Prov 27:21 . . . person is tested by being **p-d.***
*Isa 63:7 . . . I will **p** the LORD*
*Dan 2:19 . . . Daniel **p-d** the God of heaven.*
*Dan 2:20 . . . He said, "**P** the name*
*Dan 4:34 . . . **p-d** and worshiped the Most High*
*Matt 5:16 . . . will **p** your heavenly Father.*
*Mark 11:9 . . . were shouting, "**P** God!*
*Luke 1:46 . . . how my soul **p-s** the Lord.*
*Luke 2:13 . . . armies of heaven—**p-ing** God*
*Luke 2:20 . . . glorifying and **p-ing** God for all*
*Luke 19:37 . . . **p-ing** God for all the wonderful*
*Luke 18:43 . . . all who saw it **p-d** God, too.*
*Acts 2:47 . . . all the while **p-ing** God*
*Acts 10:46 . . . in tongues and **p-ing** God*
*1 Cor 14:16 . . . if you **p** God only in*
*Gal 1:24 . . . they **p-d** God because of me.*
*Eph 1:6 . . . we **p** God for the glorious*
*Jas 3:9 . . . Sometimes it **p-s** our Lord*
*Rev 19:1 . . . heaven shouting, "**P** the LORD!*

PRAY, PRAYED, PRAYING, PRAYS (v)
to address God with adoration, confession, supplication, or thanksgiving; to intercede
*Gen 24:45 . . . I had finished **p-ing** in my*
*1 Sam 1:12 . . . she was **p-ing** to the LORD,*
*2 Chr 7:14 . . . humble themselves and **p** and*
*2 Chr 30:18 . . . King Hezekiah **p-ed** for*
*Neh 4:9 . . . we **p-ed** to our God and*
*Job 42:8 . . . servant Job will **p** for you,*
*Job 42:10 . . . When Job **p-ed** for his friends,*
*Ps 5:2 . . . I **p** to no one but You.*
*Ps 32:6 . . . all the godly **p** to You*
*Ps 34:6 . . . In my desperation I **p-ed,***
*Dan 6:10 . . . He **p-ed** three times a day,*
*Dan 9:4 . . . I **p-ed** to the LORD*
*Jon 2:1 . . . Jonah **p-ed** to the LORD*
*Matt 6:5 . . . When you **p,** don't be like*
*Matt 26:39 . . . face to the ground, **p-ing,***
*Mark 11:24 . . . you can **p** for anything,*
*Mark 11:25 . . . when you are **p-ing,** first*
*Luke 3:21 . . . **p-ing,** the heavens opened,*
*Luke 9:29 . . . he was **p-ing,** the appearance*
*Luke 11:1 . . . teach us to **p,***
*Luke 22:41 . . . and knelt down and **p-ed,***
*John 17:20 . . . I am **p-ing** not only for these*
*Acts 6:6 . . . apostles, who **p-ed** for them*
*Acts 9:11 . . . He is **p-ing** to Me right now.*
*Acts 16:25 . . . Paul and Silas were **p-ing***
*Romans 8:26 . . . the Holy Spirit **p-s** for us*
*Rom 12:12 . . . and keep on **p-ing.***
*Rom 15:30 . . . join in my struggle by **p-ing***
*1 Cor 14:14 . . . For if I **p** in tongues,*
*1 Cor 14:14 . . . my spirit is **p-ing,***
*2 Cor 13:9 . . . We **p** that you will become*
*Eph 1:18 . . . I **p** that your hearts will be*
*Eph 3:16 . . . I **p** that from His glorious,*
*Phil 4:6 . . . instead, **p** about everything.*
*1 Thes 1:3 . . . As we **p** to our God and*
*1 Thes 5:17 . . . Never stop **p-ing.***
*2 Thes 1:11 . . . we keep on **p-ing** for you,*
*1 Tim 2:8 . . . to **p** with holy hands*
*Jas 5:13 . . . You should **p.***
*Jas 5:16 . . . **p** for each other so that*
*Jude 20 . . . **p** in the power of the Holy*

PRAYER, PRAYERS (n)
conversation with God—in praise, thanksgiving, or intercession
*2 Chr 30:27 . . . God heard their **p** from*
*Ps 4:1 . . . mercy on me and hear my **p.***
*Ps 17:1 . . . Pay attention to my **p,***
*Ps 20:5 . . . LORD answer all your **p-s.***
*Ps 86:6 . . . Listen closely to my **p,***
*Prov 15:8 . . . in the **p-s** of the upright.*
*Isa 1:15 . . . Though you offer many **p-s,***
*Isa 56:7 . . . will be called a house of **p***
*Matt 11:25 . . . Jesus prayed this **p:***
*John 17:9 . . . My **p** is not for the world,*
*Acts 1:14 . . . were constantly united in **p,***
*Acts 4:31 . . . After this **p,** the meeting*
*Acts 6:4 . . . can spend our time in **p***
*Acts 10:31 . . . your **p** has been heard,*
*Acts 13:3 . . . So after more fasting and **p,***
*Eph 6:18 . . . persistent in your **p-s** for all*
*Col 4:2 . . . Devote yourselves to **p** with an*
*1 Pet 3:7 . . . your **p-s** will not be hindered.*
*1 Pet 3:12 . . . ears are open to their **p-s.***
*Rev 5:8 . . . are the **p-s** of God's people.*

PREACH, PREACHED, PREACHES, PREACHING (v)
to deliver a sermon; to exhort an idea or course of action
see also PROCLAIM, TEACH
*Luke 9:6 . . . **p-ing** the Good News and*
*Luke 9:60 . . . go and **p** about the Kingdom*
*Acts 5:42 . . . teach and **p** this message:*
*Acts 9:20 . . . he began **p-ing** about Jesus*
*Acts 16:10 . . . to **p** the Good News*
*Acts 18:5 . . . all his time **p-ing** the word.*
*Rom 1:15 . . . to **p** the Good News.*
*1 Cor 2:4 . . . my message and my **p-ing***
*1 Cor 9:27 . . . I fear that after **p-ing** to*
*1 Cor 15:1 . . . Good News I **p-ed** to you*
*2 Cor 4:5 . . . We **p** that Jesus Christ is Lord,*
*2 Cor 11:4 . . . Jesus than the one we **p,***
*Gal 1:8 . . . **p-es** a different kind of Good*
*Gal 1:8 . . . than the one we **p-ed** to you.*
*Gal 1:9 . . . **p-es** any other Good News*
*Gal 5:11 . . . I were no longer **p-ing** salvation*
*Phil 1:18 . . . Christ is being **p-ed** either way,*
*Col 1:23 . . . Good News has been **p-ed** all*
*1 Tim 5:17 . . . work hard at both **p-ing** and*
*2 Tim 4:17 . . . might **p** the Good News*
*1 Pet 1:25 . . . Good News that was **p-ed** to*
*1 Pet 3:19 . . . went and **p-ed** to the spirits*

PRECEPTS (KJV)
*Ps 119:15 . . . study Your **commandments** and*
*Ps 119:159 . . . how I love Your **commandments,***

*Mark 10:5 . . . this **commandment** only as a*
*Heb 9:19 . . . each of God's **commandments***

PREDICTED (v)
to declare or indicate in advance; to foretell
*Isa 43:12 . . . First I **p** your rescue,*
*John 12:38 . . . the prophet had **p:***
*Acts 7:52 . . . **p** the coming of*

PREDICTIONS (n)
something that is predicted; forecast
*Isa 44:26 . . . I carry out the **p** of my*
*Jer 28:9 . . . Only when his **p** come true*

PREPARE, PREPARED (v)
to make ready beforehand for some purpose, use, or activity; to get ready
*Exod 23:20 . . . to the place I have **p-d** for*
*Ps 23:5 . . . You **p** a feast for me*
*Zeph 1:7 . . . Lord has **p-d** His people*
*Mal 3:1 . . . he will **p** the way before me.*
*Matt 25:34 . . . inherit the Kingdom **p-d***
*John 14:2 . . . I am going to **p** a place*
*1 Cor 2:9 . . . has **p-d** for those who love*
*2 Cor 5:5 . . . God Himself has **p-d** us for*
*2 Tim 4:2 . . . the word of God. Be **p-d,***

PRESBYTERY (KJV)
*1 Tim 4:14 . . . **elders of the church** laid their hands on*

PRESENT (adj)
being in view or at hand; now existing or in progress
*Lev 16:2 . . . I myself am **p** in the cloud*
*1 Cor 7:26 . . . Because of the **p** crisis,*

PRESENT, PRESENTED, PRESENTING (v)
to give or bestow formally
*Gen 28:22 . . . I will **p** to God a tenth*
*Matt 5:23 . . . you are **p-ing** a sacrifice*
*Rom 3:25 . . . **p-ed** Jesus as the sacrifice*
*Rom 15:19 . . . fully **p-ed** the Good News*
*Eph 5:27 . . . did this to **p** her to Himself*
*2 Tim 2:15 . . . Work hard so you can **p***

PRESERVE, PRESERVES (v)
to keep safe from injury, harm, or destruction
see also SAVE
*Gen 45:5 . . . ahead of you to **p** your lives.*
*Deut 33:12 . . . **p-s** them from every harm.*
*1 Kgs 19:18 . . . I will **p** 7,000 others*
*Jer 10:12 . . . He **p-s** it by His wisdom.*

PRETEND, PRETENDED (v)
to give a false appearance of being, possessing, or performing
*1 Sam 21:13 . . . So he **p-ed** to be insane,*
*Zech 13:4 . . . No one will **p** to be a prophet*
*Rom 12:9 . . . Don't just **p** to love*

PRICE (n)
the quantity of one thing that is exchanged or demanded in barter or sale for another
*Job 28:18 . . . **p** of wisdom is far above*
*1 Cor 6:20 . . . bought you with a high **p.***

PRIDE (n)
inordinate self-esteem or conceit; disdainful behavior or treatment of others
*Ps 101:5 . . . will not endure conceit and **p.***
*Prov 6:3 . . . Now swallow your **p;***
*Prov 8:13 . . . I hate **p** and arrogance,*
*Mark 7:22 . . . envy, slander, **p,***
*1 Jn 2:16 . . . **p** in our achievements and*

PRIEST, PRIESTS (n)
one authorized to perform the sacred rites of sacrifice and worship; a mediator between God and humans
*Exod 19:6 . . . will be my kingdom of **p-s,***
*Ps 110:4 . . . You are a **p** forever*
*Mal 1:6 . . . Armies says to the **p-s:***
*Heb 4:14 . . . since we have a great High **P***
*Heb 5:6 . . . You are a **p** forever*
*Heb 6:20 . . . our eternal High **P***
*Heb 8:1 . . . a High **P** who sat down*
*1 Pet 2:5 . . . you are His holy **p-s.***
*1 Pet 2:9 . . . You are royal **p-s,***
*Rev 5:10 . . . Kingdom of **p-s** for our God.*
*Rev 20:6 . . . but they will be **p-s** of God*

PRISON, PRISONS (n)
a state of confinement or captivity; jail
*Ps 142:7 . . . Bring me out of **p***
*Isa 42:7 . . . will free the captives from **p,***
*Matt 25:36 . . . I was in **p,** and you visited*
*2 Cor 11:23 . . . been put in **p** more often,*
*Heb 11:36 . . . were chained in **p-s.***
*Heb 13:3 . . . Remember those in **p,***
*1 Pet 3:19 . . . preached to the spirits in **p**—*
*Jude 6 . . . chained in **p-s** of darkness,*
*Rev 20:7 . . . Satan will be let out of his **p.***

PRISONER, PRISONERS (n)
a person deprived of liberty and kept under involuntary restraint, confinement, or custody
*Ps 79:11 . . . to the moaning of the **p-s.***
*Ps 146:7 . . . The Lord frees the **p-s.***
*Zech 9:12 . . . you **p-s** who still have hope!*
*Gal 3:22 . . . we are all **p-s** of sin,*
*Eph 3:1 . . . I, Paul, a **p** of Christ Jesus*

PRIZE (n)
something offered or striven for in competitions or in contests
*1 Cor 9:24 . . . one person gets the **p?***
*1 Cor 9:25 . . . we do it for an eternal **p.***
*Phil 3:14 . . . heavenly **p** for which God,*
*2 Tim 2:5 . . . cannot win the **p** unless*
*2 Tim 4:8 . . . **p** awaits me—the crown*

PROCLAIM, PROCLAIMING, PROCLAIMS (v)
to declare publicly
see also PREACH
*Lev 25:10 . . . a time to **p** freedom*
*Deut 32:3 . . . I will **p** the name of*
*1 Chr 16:8 . . . and **p** His greatness.*
*Ps 2:7 . . . king **p-s** the Lord's decree:*
*Ps 50:6 . . . heavens **p** His justice,*
*Ps 97:6 . . . heavens **p** His righteousness;*
*Ps 145:4 . . . let them **p** Your power.*
*Isa 61:1 . . . to **p** that captives will be*
*Acts 28:31 . . . **p-ing** the Kingdom of God*
*Col 1:25 . . . **p-ing** His entire message to you.*
*1 Thes 3:2 . . . in **p-ing** the Good News*
*Titus 1:1 . . . I have been sent to **p** faith*
*1 Jn 1:1 . . . **p** to you the One who existed*

PRODUCE, PRODUCES (v)
to yield, make, or manufacture
*Prov 3:9 . . . best part of everything you **p.***
*Isa 55:11 . . . and it always **p-s** fruit.*
*Matt 7:18 . . . good tree can't **p** bad fruit,*
*Luke 3:9 . . . tree that does not **p** good fruit*
*John 15:8 . . . When you **p** much fruit,*
*John 15:16 . . . to go and **p** lasting fruit,*
*Rom 7:4 . . . **p** a harvest of good deeds*
*Eph 5:9 . . . light within you **p-s** only what*
*Col 1:10 . . . lives will **p** every kind of good*
*Jas 2:17 . . . Unless it **p-s** good deeds, it is*

PROMISE, PROMISES (n)
a declaration that one will do or refrain from doing something specified
see also COVENANT, VOW
*2 Sam 7:25 . . . a **p** that will last forever.*
*Neh 5:13 . . . If you fail to keep your **p,***
*Ps 91:4 . . . faithful **p-s** are your armor*
*Ps 116:14 . . . keep my **p-s** to the Lord*
*Ps 145:13 . . . Lord always keeps His **p-s;***
*Ps 146:6 . . . He keeps every **p** forever.*
*Rom 4:20 . . . in believing God's **p.***
*Rom 9:4 . . . receiving His wonderful **p-s.***
*Rom 15:4 . . . patiently for God's **p-s** to be*
*2 Cor 1:20 . . . **p-s** have been fulfilled*
*2 Cor 7:1 . . . Because we have these **p-s,***
*Eph 2:12 . . . covenant **p-s** God had made*
*Heb 6:13 . . . God's **p** to Abraham.*
*Heb 8:6 . . . based on better **p-s.***
*Heb 10:23 . . . be trusted to keep His **p.***
*Heb 11:11 . . . that God would keep His **p.***
*2 Pet 3:4 . . . **p** that Jesus is coming again?*
*2 Pet 3:9 . . . being slow about His **p,***

PROMISE, PROMISED, PROMISES, PROMISING (v)
to pledge to do, bring about, or provide
*Exod 3:17 . . . I have **p-d** to rescue you*
*Deut 15:6 . . . bless you as He has **p-d.***
*Josh 23:15 . . . the good things He **p-d,***
*Luke 24:49 . . . as my Father **p-d.***
*Acts 1:4 . . . sends you the gift He **p-d,***
*Rom 4:21 . . . able to do whatever He **p-s.***
*Gal 3:14 . . . blessing He **p-d** to Abraham,*
*1 Tim 4:8 . . . **p-ing** benefits in this life*
*Titus 1:2 . . . God—who does not lie—**p-d***
*Heb 10:36 . . . receive all that He has **p-d.***
*Jas 1:12 . . . of life that God has **p-d***
*Jas 2:5 . . . inherit the Kingdom He **p-d***
*2 Pet 3:13 . . . new earth He has **p-d,***
*1 Jn 2:25 . . . eternal life He **p-d** us.*

PROPHECY, PROPHECIES (n)
the spoken or written word from God; to forthtell (consoling or corrective material) and foretell (predicative material)
*Matt 13:14 . . . fulfills the **p** of Isaiah*
*Acts 13:29 . . . all that the **p-ies** said about*
*Acts 17:3 . . . the **p-ies** and proved that the Messiah*
*Acts 21:9 . . . who had the gift of **p.***
*Acts 21:10 . . . who also had the gift of **p,***
*1 Cor 13:2 . . . If I had the gift of **p,***
*1 Cor 13:9 . . . gift of **p** reveals only part*
*1 Cor 14:6 . . . knowledge or **p** or teaching,*
*Rev 22:18 . . . words of **p** written in*

PROPHESY, PROPHESIED, PROPHESIES, PROPHESYING (v)
to issue a prophecy
*Num 11:25 . . . upon them, they **p-ied.***
*1 Sam 19:24 . . . day and all night, **p-ing** in*
*Isa 42:9 . . . Everything I **p-ied** has come true,*
*Joel 2:28 . . . sons and daughters will **p.***
*Matt 7:22 . . . We **p-ied** in Your name and*
*Acts 2:17 . . . sons and daughters will **p.***
*Acts 19:6 . . . in other tongues and **p-ied.***
*Rom 12:6 . . . the ability to **p,***
*1 Cor 11:4 . . . his head while praying or **p-ing.***
*1 Cor 12:10 . . . the ability to **p.***
*1 Cor 14:1 . . . the ability to **p.***
*1 Cor 14:3 . . . one who **p-ies** strengthens*
*1 Cor 14:39 . . . be eager to **p,***

PROPHET, PROPHETS (n)
an interpreter of the times and of people's hearts; one who issues divinely inspired revelations
*Exod 7:1 . . . Aaron, will be your **p.***
*Exod 15:20 . . . Miriam the **p,** Aaron's*
*Deut 13:1 . . . there are **p-s** among you*
*Deut 18:18 . . . I will raise up a **p** like you*
*1 Sam 9:9 . . . **p-s** used to be called seers.*
*1 Kgs 18:36 . . . Elijah the **p** walked up to*
*2 Kgs 5:8 . . . a true **p** here in Israel.*
*2 Kgs 6:12 . . . Elisha, the **p** in Israel,*
*Isa 44:26 . . . the predictions of My **p-s!***
*Hos 9:7 . . . you say, "The **p-s** are crazy*

*Amos 7:14 . . . I'm not a professional **p,***
*Hab 1:1 . . . that the **p** Habakkuk received*
*Zech 7:12 . . . through the earlier **p-s.***
*Mal 4:5 . . . the **p** Elijah before the great*
*Matt 5:17 . . . or the writings of the **p-s.***
*Matt 7:12 . . . in the law and the **p-s.***
*Matt 10:41 . . . the same reward as a **p.***
*Matt 11:9 . . . Yes, and He is more than a **p.***
*Matt 12:39 . . . sign of the **p** Jonah.*
*Matt 23:37 . . . the city that kills the **p-s***
*Matt 26:56 . . . fulfill the words of the **p-s***
*Luke 4:24 . . . no **p** is accepted in his own*
*Luke 7:16 . . . A mighty **p** has risen*
*Luke 11:49 . . . will send **p-s** and apostles*
*Luke 24:19 . . . **p** who did powerful*
*Luke 24:25 . . . all that the **p-s** wrote in*
*Luke 24:44 . . . law of Moses and the **p-s***
*John 1:21 . . . you the **P** we are expecting?*
*Acts 7:37 . . . a **P** like me from among your*
*Acts 10:43 . . . all the **p-s** testified about,*
*Acts 13:1 . . . Among the **p-s** and teachers*
*Rom 1:2 . . . long ago through His **p-s***
*Rom 3:21 . . . Moses and the **p-s** long ago.*
*Rom 11:3 . . . they have killed Your **p-s***
*1 Cor 12:28 . . . second are **p-s,** third are*
*1 Cor 14:37 . . . If you claim to be a **p** or*
*Eph 2:20 . . . of the apostles and the **p-s.***
*Eph 3:5 . . . to His holy apostles and **p-s.***
*Eph 4:11 . . . the apostles, the **p-s,** the*
*1 Pet 1:10 . . . the **p-s** wanted to know*
*2 Pet 1:19 . . . proclaimed by the **p-s.***
*2 Pet 1:21 . . . those **p-s** were moved by*
*2 Pet 3:2 . . . what the holy **p-s** said long*
*Rev 11:10 . . . death of the two **p-s** who*
*Rev 18:20 . . . God and apostles and **p-s!***

PROPITIATION (KJV)
*Rom 3:25 . . . Jesus as the **sacrifice** for sin*
*1 Jn 2:2 . . . the **sacrifice that atones***
*1 Jn 4:10 . . . a **sacrifice to take away** our sins*

PROSPER, PROSPERS (v)
to achieve economic success; to become strong and flourishing
*Deut 28:63 . . . pleasure in causing you to **p***
*Ps 37:3 . . . safely in the land and **p.***
*Ps 73:3 . . . **p** despite their wickedness.*
*Prov 16:20 . . . listen to instruction will **p;***
*Prov 17:9 . . . Love **p-s** when a fault is forgiven,*
*Prov 19:8 . . . cherish understanding will **p.***
*Isa 53:10 . . . LORD's good plan will **p***
*Isa 55:11 . . . it will **p** everywhere I send it.*
*Dan 4:27 . . . then you will continue to **p.***

PROSPERITY (n)
the condition of being successful or thriving
*Gen 41:29 . . . will be a period of great **p***
*Deut 28:11 . . . LORD will give you **p***
*Deut 30:15 . . . life and death, between **p***
*1 Sam 25:6 . . . Peace and **p** to you,*
*Ps 41:2 . . . He gives them **p** in the land*
*Prov 21:5 . . . and hard work lead to **p,***
*Prov 28:25 . . . trusting the LORD leads to **p.***
*Jer 33:6 . . . give it **p** and true peace.*
*Mic 4:4 . . . will live in peace and **p,***

PROSPEROUS (adj)
marked by success or economic well-being; flourishing
*Deut 5:33 . . . live long and **p** lives*
*Ps 30:6 . . . When I was **p,** I said,*
*Ps 34:12 . . . a life that is long and **p?***
*Ps 128:2 . . . How joyful and **p** you will be!*
*Ps 132:15 . . . bless this city and make it **p;***
*Jer 12:1 . . . Why are the wicked so **p?***

PROTECT, PROTECTED, PROTECTING, PROTECTS (v)
to cover or shield from exposure, injury, damage, or destruction; to defend
see also KEEP
*Gen 15:1 . . . for I will **p** you,*
*Num 6:24 . . . bless you and **p** you.*
*Josh 6:17 . . . for she **p-ed** our spies.*
*1 Sam 2:9 . . . He will **p** His faithful ones,*
*Ps 23:4 . . . Your staff **p** and comfort me.*
*Ps 27:1 . . . fortress, **p-ing** me from danger,*
*Ps 41:2 . . . LORD **p-s** them and keeps*
*Ps 116:6 . . . LORD **p-s** those of childlike*
*Ps 127:1 . . . Unless the LORD **p-s** a city,*
*Ps 145:20 . . . LORD **p-s** all those who love*
*Ps 146:9 . . . LORD **p-s** the foreigners*
*Prov 2:8 . . . **p-s** those who are faithful*
*Isa 31:5 . . . like a bird **p-ing** its nest.*
*Isa 57:1 . . . God is **p-ing** them from the evil*
*John 17:11 . . . now **p** them by the power of*
*Acts 26:22 . . . But God has **p-ed** me*
*Gal 3:24 . . . **p-ed** us until we could be*
*1 Pet 1:5 . . . God is **p-ing** you by His power*
*Rev 3:10 . . . I will **p** you from the great*

PROTECTION (n)
the act of protecting; the state of being protected
see also REFUGE
*2 Sam 22:3 . . . my rock, in whom I find **p.***
*2 Sam 22:31 . . . look to Him for **p.***
*Ps 5:11 . . . Spread Your **p** over them,*
*Ps 31:2 . . . Be my rock of **p,***
*Ps 71:1 . . . I have come to You for **p;***
*Ps 91:4 . . . promises are your armor and **p.***
*Prov 19:23 . . . security and **p** from harm.*

PROUD (adj)
having or displaying excessive self-esteem
*Ps 5:5 . . . **p** may not stand in Your presence,*
*Prov 16:5 . . . LORD detests the **p;***
*Prov 21:4 . . . Haughty eyes, a **p** heart,*
*Dan 4:37 . . . he is able to humble the **p.***
*Rom 1:30 . . . haters of God, insolent, **p,***
*1 Cor 13:4 . . . not jealous or boastful or **p***
*1 Tim 3:6 . . . he might become **p,***
*1 Tim 6:17 . . . rich in this world not to be **p***
*2 Tim 3:2 . . . They will be boastful and **p,***
*Jas 4:6 . . . God opposes the **p** but favors*
*1 Pet 5:5 . . . God opposes the **p** but favors*

PROVIDE, PROVIDED, PROVIDES (v)
to furnish or supply, implying foresight in making provision for the future
*Gen 22:8 . . . God will **p** a sheep*
*Gen 22:14 . . . means "the LORD will **p**"*
*Ps 68:10 . . . O God, You **p-d** for Your needy*
*Isa 4:5 . . . the LORD will **p** shade*
*Jer 5:28 . . . refuse to **p** justice to orphans*
*Ezek 18:7 . . . and **p-s** clothes for the needy.*
*2 Cor 9:8 . . . God will generously **p** all you*
*2 Cor 9:10 . . . he will **p** and increase your*

PUBLICAN(S) (KJV)
*Matt 5:46 . . . Even **corrupt tax collectors** do*
*Matt 9:10 . . . along with many **tax collectors***
*Matt 10:3 . . . Matthew (the **tax collector**),*
*Luke 5:30 . . . eat and drink with **such scum?***
*Luke 18:11 . . . not like that **tax collector***

PUNISH, PUNISHED, PUNISHES, PUNISHING (v)
to impose a penalty to fit the crime: from corrective measures (fines or scolding) and corporal punishment (spanking or whipping) to capital punishment and eternal damnation
*Gen 15:14 . . . But I will **p** the nation*
*1 Kgs 8:32 . . . **P** the guilty as they deserve.*
*Prov 11:21 . . . people will surely be **p-ed,***
*Jer 25:14 . . . I will **p** them in proportion*
*Lam 3:39 . . . when we are **p-ed** for our sins?*
*Mark 12:40 . . . will be more severely **p-ed.***
*Acts 7:7 . . . But I will **p** the nation*
*Rom 2:2 . . . God, in His justice, will **p***
*Rom 13:4 . . . they have the power to **p** you.*
*Rom 13:4 . . . the very purpose of **p-ing***
*2 Thes 1:9 . . . **p-ed** with eternal destruction,*
*Heb 2:2 . . . act of disobedience was **p-ed.***
*Heb 12:6 . . . He **p-es** each one He accepts*
*1 Pet 2:14 . . . sent them to **p** those who*
*Rev 19:2 . . . has **p-ed** the great prostitute*

PUNISHMENT (n)
suffering, pain, or loss that serves as retribution
*Isa 53:4 . . . troubles were a **p** from God,*
*Jer 2:19 . . . will bring its own **p.***
*Jer 4:18 . . . This **p** is bitter, piercing*
*Hos 5:9 . . . On your day of **p,** you will*
*Matt 25:46 . . . will go away into eternal **p,***
*Rom 13:5 . . . not only to avoid **p,** but also*
*2 Pet 2:9 . . . keeping the wicked under **p***

PURCHASE, PURCHASED (v)
to gain or acquire; to buy
see also REDEEM
*Acts 20:28 . . . **p-d** with His own blood—*
*Eph 1:7 . . . **p-d** our freedom with the*
*Eph 1:14 . . . **p-d** us to be His own people.*
*Col 1:14 . . . who **p-d** our freedom*
*1 Tim 2:6 . . . gave His life to **p** freedom*
*Rev 14:4 . . . have been **p-d** from among*

PURE (adj)
free of contamination or impurities; ritually clean; guileless; faultless; guiltless; chaste
see also HOLY
*Ps 19:9 . . . Reverence for the LORD is **p,***
*Prov 20:9 . . . I am **p** and free*
*Matt 5:8 . . . those whose hearts are **p,***
*1 Cor 1:30 . . . He made us **p** and holy,*
*Phil 4:8 . . . right, and **p,** and lovely,*
*1 Tim 5:22 . . . Keep yourself **p.***
*2 Tim 2:21 . . . If you keep yourself **p,***
*Titus 1:15 . . . Everything is **p** to those*
*Titus 2:5 . . . to live wisely and be **p,***
*Jas 1:27 . . . **P** and genuine religion*
*1 Pet 3:2 . . . your **p** and reverent*
*2 Pet 3:14 . . . are **p** and blameless*
*1 Jn 3:3 . . . will keep themselves **p,** just as*

PURIFY, PURIFIED (v)
to make pure or remove (physical or moral) blemishes; to make ritually clean
*Exod 30:10 . . . offering made to **p** the people*
*Exod 30:15 . . . given to the LORD to **p***
*Num 25:13 . . . **p-ied** the people of Israel,*
*1 Chr 15:12 . . . You must **p** yourselves and*
*2 Chr 30:17 . . . had not **p-ied** themselves,*
*Neh 12:30 . . . Levites first **p-ied** themselves;*
*Isa 52:11 . . . and **p** yourselves,*
*John 15:3 . . . pruned and **p-ied** by the*
*Heb 9:14 . . . Christ will **p** our consciences*
*Heb 9:22 . . . everything was **p-ied** with blood.*
*Jas 4:8 . . . you sinners; **p** your hearts,*

PURITY (n)
the quality or state of being pure
*Job 14:4 . . . Who can bring **p** out of an*
*Ps 86:11 . . . Grant me **p** of heart,*
*2 Cor 6:6 . . . by our **p,** our understanding,*
*1 Tim 4:12 . . . love, your faith, and your **p.***
*1 Tim 5:2 . . . younger women with all **p***

PURPOSE, PURPOSES (n)
something set up as an object or end to be attained; resolution, determination
see also PLAN
*Exod 9:16 . . . I have spared you for a **p**—*
*Prov 19:21 . . . the LORD's **p** will prevail.*
*Rom 8:28 . . . according to His **p** for them.*

Rom 9:11 . . . according to His own **p-s;**
Rom 9:17 . . . for the very **p** of displaying
1 Cor 3:8 . . . with the same **p.**
1 Cor 9:26 . . . I run with **p** in every step.
Phil 2:2 . . . together with one mind and **p.**

PURSUE, PURSUES (v)
to follow in order to overtake, capture, kill, or defeat; to seek
Ps 23:6 . . . unfailing love will **p** me
Ps 119:32 . . . I will **p** Your commands,
Prov 15:9 . . . those who **p** godliness.
Prov 21:21 . . . Whoever **p-s** righteousness
1 Tim 6:11 . . . **P** righteousness and a godly
2 Tim 2:22 . . . Instead, **p** righteous living,

Q

QUARREL, QUARRELS (n)
a usually verbal conflict between antagonists
Prov 10:12 . . . Hatred stirs up **q-s,**
Prov 17:14 . . . Starting a **q** is like opening
Prov 26:20 . . . **q-s** disappear when gossip
Prov 30:33 . . . anger causes **q-s.**
Titus 3:9 . . . **q-s** and fights about
Jas 4:1 . . . causing the **q-s** and fights

QUARREL, QUARRELING (v)
to find fault; to contend or dispute actively
Prov 17:19 . . . Anyone who loves to **q** loves
Prov 20:3 . . . fools insist on **q-ing.**
Rom 13:13 . . . or in **q-ing** and jealousy.
1 Cor 3:3 . . . and **q** with each other.
2 Cor 12:20 . . . will find **q-ing,** jealousy,

QUIET (adj)
calm; gentle; peaceful, still; free from noise
Prov 11:12 . . . a sensible person keeps **q.**
Eccl 3:7 . . . A time to be **q** and a time
Eccl 9:17 . . . to hear the **q** words of a wise
Luke 19:40 . . . If they kept **q,** the stones
1 Thes 4:11 . . . to live a **q** life,
1 Tim 2:2 . . . peaceful and **q** lives marked

R

RABBI (n)
a title of honor and respect given by the Jews to a teacher of the Law
Matt 23:8 . . . anyone call you **'R,'**
John 3:2 . . . **"R,"** he said, "we all know

RACE (n)
an athletic contest; an ethnic classification
Ps 19:5 . . . athlete eager to run the **r.**
Eccl 9:11 . . . doesn't always win the **r,**
Dan 7:14 . . . people of every **r** and nation
1 Cor 9:24 . . . that in a **r** everyone runs,
Gal 2:2 . . . running the **r** for nothing.
Gal 5:7 . . . were running the **r** so well.
2 Tim 4:7 . . . I have finished the **r,**
Heb 12:1 . . . run with endurance the **r** God

RADIANT (adj)
vividly bright and shining; marked by or expressive of love, confidence, or happiness
Exod 34:29 . . . face had become **r** because
Ps 34:5 . . . help will be **r** with joy;
Ps 80:1 . . . display Your **r** glory

RAISE, RAISED (v)
to recall from death
see also RESURRECTION
Luke 7:22 . . . the dead are **r-d** to life,
John 6:39 . . . that I should **r** them up
Acts 2:32 . . . God **r-d** Jesus from the dead,
Acts 24:15 . . . that He will **r** both the
Rom 1:4 . . . He was **r-d** from the dead
Rom 6:5 . . . we will also be **r-d** to life
Rom 10:9 . . . God **r-d** Him from the dead,
1 Cor 15:4 . . . He was **r-d** from the dead
Phil 3:10 . . . mighty power that **r-d** Him
1 Thes 4:14 . . . died and was **r-d** to life
1 Pet 1:3 . . . because God **r-d** Jesus Christ

RAM, RAMS (n)
a male sheep
Gen 22:13 . . . he took the **r** and sacrificed
1 Sam 15:22 . . . offering the fat of **r-s.**
Dan 8:3 . . . I saw a **r** with two long
Mic 6:7 . . . him thousands of **r-s** and ten

RANSOM (n)
price paid or demanded to release someone or something from captivity
Matt 20:28 . . . His life as a **r** for many.
Mark 10:45 . . . His life as a **r** for many.
1 Pet 1:18 . . . that God paid a **r** to save

READ, READING, READS (v)
to receive and interpret letters or symbols by sight; to utter aloud the printed or written words of
Deut 17:19 . . . with him and **r** it daily
Josh 8:34 . . . Joshua then **r** to them
2 Kgs 23:2 . . . There the king **r** to them
Acts 8:28 . . . carriage, he was **r-ing** aloud
2 Cor 3:2 . . . everyone can **r** it and
1 Tim 4:13 . . . focus on **r-ing** the Scriptures
Rev 1:3 . . . the one who **r-s** the words of

REAP
see also HARVEST
Gal 6:9 . . . we will **reap** a harvest of blessing if
Jas 3:18 . . . **reap** a harvest of righteousness.

REAPERS (KJV)
Ruth 2:3 . . . gather grain behind the **harvesters**
2 Kgs 4:18 . . . working with the **harvesters**
Matt 13:30 . . . the **harvesters** to sort out
Matt 13:39 . . . the **harvesters** are the angels

REBEL, REBELLED, REBELLING, REBELS (v)
to oppose or disobey one in authority or control
Num 14:9 . . . Do not **r** against the
Num 27:14 . . . of Israel **r-led,** you failed to
1 Sam 12:14 . . . if you do not **r** against the
Ps 78:56 . . . testing and **r-ling** against God
Isa 63:10 . . . But they **r-led** against Him
Matt 10:21 . . . children will **r** against their
Rom 13:2 . . . So anyone who **r-s** against

REBELLION (n)
opposition to one in authority or dominance; defiance
Exod 34:7 . . . forgive iniquity, **r,** and sin.
Ps 32:5 . . . I will confess my **r** to the
Ps 39:8 . . . Rescue me from my **r.**
Ps 51:3 . . . I recognize my **r;** it haunts
Isa 53:5 . . . was pierced for our **r,**
Isa 53:8 . . . for the **r** of My people.
Dan 9:24 . . . to finish their **r,** to put an
2 Thes 2:3 . . . is a great **r** against God

REBELS (n)
one who rebels or participates in a rebellion
Ps 51:13 . . . will teach Your ways to **r,**
Isa 53:12 . . . He was counted among the **r.**
Luke 22:37 . . . was counted among the **r.**
Rom 11:30 . . . Gentiles were **r** against God,
Rom 11:31 . . . they are the **r,** and God's

RECEIVE, RECEIVED, RECEIVES (v)
to acquire or take possession of; to welcome
Matt 7:8 . . . For everyone who asks, **r-s.**
Matt 19:17 . . . you want to **r** eternal life,
John 20:22 . . . said, "**R** the Holy Spirit.
Acts 1:8 . . . But you will **r** power when the
Acts 2:38 . . . Then you will **r** the gift of
Acts 8:17 . . . they **r-d** the Holy Spirit.
Acts 10:47 . . . they have **r-d** the Holy
Acts 19:2 . . . Did you **r** the Holy Spirit
Rom 8:15 . . . Instead, you **r-d** God's Spirit
1 Tim 1:16 . . . in Him and **r** eternal life.
Rev 4:11 . . . our God, to **r** glory and honor

RECONCILE, RECONCILED, RECONCILING (v)
to restore to friendship or harmony, especially between God and human beings
2 Cor 5:18 . . . task of **r-ing** people to Him.
Eph 2:16 . . . Christ **r-d** both groups to God
Col 1:20 . . . God **r-d** everything to Himself.
Col 1:22 . . . now He has **r-d** you to Himself

RECONCILIATION (n)
the action of reconciling; the state of being reconciled
Prov 14:9 . . . acknowledge it and seek **r.**
2 Cor 5:19 . . . this wonderful message of **r.**

RED (adj)
of the color red
Exod 15:4 . . . are drowned in the **R** Sea.
Ps 106:9 . . . He commanded the **R** Sea to
Isa 1:18 . . . they are **r** like crimson,

REDEEM, REDEEMED, REDEEMS (v)
to buy back; to save by payment of a ransom; to free from the consequences of sin
see also PURCHASE, RANSOM, RESCUE
Exod 6:6 . . . I will **r** you with a powerful
2 Sam 7:23 . . . have you **r-ed** from slavery
Ps 34:22 . . . the LORD will **r** those
Ps 49:15 . . . God will **r** my life.
Ps 74:2 . . . the tribe You **r-ed** as Your own
Ps 103:4 . . . He **r-s** me from death and
Ps 107:2 . . . Has the LORD **r-ed** you?
Ps 130:8 . . . He himself will **r** Israel from
Isa 35:9 . . . Only the **r-ed** will walk
Isa 63:9 . . . love and mercy He **r-ed** them.
Hos 7:13 . . . I wanted to **r** them, but they

REDEEMER (n)
one who frees or delivers another from difficulty, danger, or bondage, usually by the payment of a ransom price
Ruth 3:9 . . . for you are my family **r.**
Ruth 4:14 . . . has now provided a **r** for
Job 19:25 . . . I know that my **R** lives,
Ps 19:14 . . . LORD, my rock and my **r.**
Prov 23:11 . . . For their **R** is strong;
Isa 44:6 . . . Israel's King and **R,** the LORD
Isa 48:17 . . . your **R,** the Holy One of Israel:
Isa 59:20 . . . The **R** will come to Jerusalem

REDEMPTION (n)
the act, process, or an instance of redeeming
Ps 130:7 . . . love. His **r** overflows.
Eph 4:30 . . . be saved on the day of **r.**
Heb 9:12 . . . and secured our **r** forever.

REFUGE (n)
shelter or protection from danger or distress
see also FORTRESS, PROTECTION, SHELTER
Deut 33:27 . . . eternal God is your **r,**
2 Sam 22:3 . . . He is my **r,** my savior,
Ps 2:12 . . . for all who take **r** in Him!
Ps 5:11 . . . But let all who take **r** in You
Ps 17:7 . . . those who seek **r** from their
Ps 34:8 . . . those who take **r** in Him!
Ps 46:1 . . . God is our **r** and strength,
Ps 91:2 . . . He alone is my **r,** my place

REGENERATION (KJV)
Matt 19:28 . . . world is **made new** and the Son
Titus 3:5 . . . giving us a **new birth** and new life

REGULATIONS (n)
an authoritative rule dealing with details or procedure
see also LAW(S)
Exod 21:1 . . . These are the **r** you must

*Deut 33:10 . . . They teach Your **r** to Jacob;*
*Ps 119:30 . . . determined to live by Your **r.***
*Ps 119:43 . . . for Your **r** are my only hope.*
*Ps 119:120 . . . I stand in awe of Your **r.***
*Ps 119:164 . . . because all Your **r** are just.*
*Ps 119:175 . . . and may Your **r** help me.*

REIGN, REIGNED, REIGNING, REIGNS (v)
to possess or exercise sovereign power; to rule
*Exod 15:18 . . . The LORD will **r** forever*
*Ps 9:7 . . . But the LORD **r-s** forever,*
*Ps 29:10 . . . LORD **r-s** as king forever.*
*Ps 96:10 . . . The LORD **r-s!***
*Ps 146:10 . . . The LORD will **r** forever.*
*Isa 52:7 . . . that the God of Israel **r-s!***
*1 Cor 4:8 . . . then we would be **r-ing** with You.*
*1 Cor 15:25 . . . For Christ must **r** until He*
*Rev 5:10 . . . And they will **r** on the earth.*
*Rev 11:15 . . . and He will **r** forever*
*Rev 19:6 . . . our God, the Almighty, **r-s.***
*Rev 20:4 . . . again, and they **r-ed** with Christ*
*Rev 22:5 . . . And they will **r** forever*

REJECT, REJECTED, REJECTING (v)
to refuse to accept, consider, submit to, or take for some purpose, or use; to refuse to hear, receive, or admit
*1 Sam 8:7 . . . Me they are **r-ing,** not you.*
*Ps 51:17 . . . not **r** a broken and repentant*
*Ps 118:22 . . . stone that the builders **r-ed***
*Prov 3:11 . . . My child, don't **r** the LORD's*
*Mal 1:3 . . . but I **r-ed** his brother,*
*Matt 21:42 . . . stone that the builders **r-ed***
*Luke 10:16 . . . who **r-s** Me is **r-ing** God,*
*John 6:37 . . . I will never **r** them.*
*John 12:48 . . . But all who **r** Me and My*
*Rom 9:13 . . . loved Jacob, but I **r-ed** Esau.*
*1 Thes 4:8 . . . teaching but is **r-ing** God,*
*1 Tim 4:4 . . . we should not **r** any of it*
*2 Tim 3:5 . . . but they will **r** the power*
*Heb 6:6 . . . by **r-ing** the Son of God, they*
*1 Pet 2:4 . . . He was **r-ed** by people,*
*1 Pet 2:7 . . . stone that the builders **r-ed***

REJOICE, REJOICED, REJOICES, REJOICING (v)
to feel joy or great delight; to gladden
*1 Chr 16:31 . . . glad, and the earth **r!***
*1 Chr 29:17 . . . **r** when you find integrity*
*Esth 8:17 . . . decree arrived, the Jews **r-d***
*Ps 5:11 . . . who take refuge in You **r;***
*Ps 13:5 . . . I will **r** because You*
*Ps 35:9 . . . I will **r** in the LORD.*
*Ps 48:2 . . . the whole earth **r-s** to see it!*
*Ps 58:10 . . . The godly will **r** when they*
*Ps 66:6 . . . There we **r-d** in Him.*
*Ps 68:4 . . . LORD—**r** in His presence!*
*Ps 119:14 . . . I have **r-d** in Your laws*
*Ps 119:162 . . . I **r** in Your word like one*
*Prov 8:31 . . . I **r-d** with the human family!*
*Prov 17:5 . . . who **r** at the misfortune*
*Prov 29:2 . . . in authority, the people **r.***
*Isa 9:3 . . . and its people will **r.***
*Isa 35:1 . . . wasteland will **r** and blossom*
*Isa 62:5 . . . **r** over you as a bridegroom **r-s***
*Jer 51:48 . . . the heavens and earth will **r,***
*Lam 4:21 . . . Are you **r-ing** in the land*
*Hab 1:15 . . . while they **r** and celebrate?*
*Zeph 3:17 . . . He will **r** over you*
*Zech 2:10 . . . Shout and **r,** O beautiful*
*Luke 1:14 . . . and many will **r** at His birth,*
*Luke 1:47 . . . How my spirit **r-s** in God my*
*Luke 1:58 . . . everyone **r-d** with her.*
*Luke 10:20 . . . But don't **r** because evil*
*Luke 13:17 . . . but all the people **r-d** at the*
*Acts 5:41 . . . high council **r-ing** that God*
*Acts 16:34 . . . his entire household **r-d***
*1 Cor 13:6 . . . **r** about injustice but **r-s***
*Phil 2:18 . . . you should **r,** and I will*
*Phil 3:1 . . . and sisters, **r** in the Lord.*
*Phil 4:4 . . . I say it again—**r!***
*Col 2:5 . . . I **r** that you are living as*
*Rev 19:7 . . . Let us be glad and **r,** and*

RELIGION, RELIGIONS (n)
a personal set or institutionalized system of religious attitudes, beliefs, and practices; the service and worship of God or the supernatural
*Matt 6:7 . . . as people of other **r-s** do.*
*Acts 25:19 . . . something about their **r** and*
*Acts 26:5 . . . the strictest sect of our **r.***
*Gal 1:13 . . . I followed the Jewish **r**—*
*Jas 1:26 . . . and your **r** is worthless.*

REMAIN, REMAINED, REMAINS (v)
to stay in the same place or with the same person or group; to continue unchanged
*2 Kgs 18:6 . . . He **r-ed** faithful to the LORD*
*John 15:7 . . . But if you **r** in Me and My*
*John 15:9 . . . loved Me. **R** in My love.*
*Rom 11:5 . . . of Israel have **r-ed** faithful*
*2 Tim 2:13 . . . unfaithful, He **r-s** faithful,*
*2 Tim 3:14 . . . But you must **r** faithful*
*2 Tim 4:7 . . . and I have **r-ed** faithful.*
*Heb 7:3 . . . He **r-s** a priest forever,*
*Heb 10:32 . . . how you **r-ed** faithful even*
*Heb 13:4 . . . and **r** faithful to one another*
*1 Pet 1:25 . . . word of the Lord **r-s***
*1 Jn 2:27 . . . **r** in fellowship with Christ.*

REMEMBER, REMEMBERED, REMEMBERING, REMEMBERS (v)
to bring to mind or think of again; to keep in mind for attention or consideration; to retain in the memory
*Gen 9:15 . . . I will **r** My covenant with*
*Exod 2:24 . . . **r-ed** His covenant promise*
*1 Chr 16:12 . . . **R** the wonders He has*
*Ps 49:13 . . . though they are **r-ed** as being*
*Ps 103:14 . . . He **r-s** we are only dust.*
*Ps 106:45 . . . **r-ed** his covenant with them*
*Ps 111:5 . . . He always **r-s** His covenant.*
*Ps 136:23 . . . He **r-ed** us in our weakness.*
*Jer 31:34 . . . never again **r** their sins.*
*Jer 32:20 . . . things still **r-ed** to this day!*
*Hab 3:2 . . . in your anger, **r** your mercy.*
*Matt 26:13 . . . will be **r-ed** and discussed.*
*Luke 1:72 . . . **r-ing** His sacred covenant—*
*Luke 22:19 . . . Do this to **r** Me.*
*1 Cor 11:24 . . . Do this to **r** Me.*
*2 Tim 2:8 . . . Always **r** that Jesus*
*Heb 8:12 . . . never again **r** their sins.*
*2 Pet 1:15 . . . you always **r** these things*

REMISSION (KJV)
*Acts 10:43 . . . sins **forgiven** through His name*
*Rom 3:25 . . . fair when He **held back and did not punish***
*Matt 26:28 . . . as a sacrifice **to forgive***
*Heb 9:22 . . . of blood, there is no **forgiveness***

REMNANT (n)
a usually small part, member, or trace remaining; the few people left who gathered together after God scattered them into exile
*Ezra 9:8 . . . few of us to survive as a **r.***
*Isa 6:13 . . . a tenth—a **r**—survive,*
*Isa 11:11 . . . to bring back the **r** of His*
*Jer 23:3 . . . gather together the **r** of My*
*Zech 8:12 . . . will cause the **r** in Judah*

RENEW, RENEWED, RENEWS (v)
to restore to freshness, vigor, or perfection; to make new spiritually
*Ps 23:3 . . . He **r-s** my strength.*
*Ps 51:10 . . . **R** a loyal spirit within me.*
*Isa 57:10 . . . Desire gave you **r-ed** strength,*
*Eph 4:23 . . . let the Spirit **r** your thoughts*
*Col 3:10 . . . be **r-ed** as you learn to know*

RENOWN (KJV)
*Gen 6:4 . . . the **heroes** and famous warriors*
*Isa 14:20 . . . will never again **receive honor***
*Ezek 16:14 . . . **fame** soon spread*
*Ezek 39:13 . . . a **glorious victory** for Israel*

REPAY, REPAYS (v)
to give or inflict in return or requital; to pay back (money)
*Ps 62:12 . . . Surely you **r** all people*
*Prov 17:13 . . . If you **r** good with evil,*
*Prov 19:17 . . . and he will **r** you!*
*Jer 51:6 . . . he will **r** her in full.*
*Jer 51:56 . . . he always **r-s** in full.*
*Luke 6:34 . . . to those who can **r** you,*
*Luke 7:42 . . . neither of them could **r** him,*
*1 Tim 5:4 . . . **r** their parents by taking*
*1 Pet 3:9 . . . Don't **r** evil for evil.*

REPENT, REPENTED, REPENTING, REPENTS (v)
to turn from sin and change one's heart and behavior; to feel regret and contrition
*Matt 3:2 . . . **R** of your sins and turn*
*Matt 3:8 . . . that you have **r-ed** of your sins*
*Matt 4:17 . . . began to preach, "**R** of your*
*Matt 11:21 . . . people would have **r-ed** of*
*Luke 3:8 . . . that you have **r-ed** of your sins*
*Luke 15:7 . . . lost sinner who **r-s** and returns*
*Luke 15:10 . . . when even one sinner **r-s.***
*Acts 2:38 . . . you must **r** of your sins,*
*Acts 17:30 . . . everywhere to **r** of their sins*
*Acts 20:21 . . . necessity of **r-ing** from sin*
*Heb 6:1 . . . importance of **r-ing** from evil*
*2 Pet 3:9 . . . but wants everyone to **r.***
*Rev 2:5 . . . If you don't **r,** I will come*

REPENTANCE (n)
a turning away from sin, disobedience, or rebellion, and a turning back to God
*1 Kgs 8:47 . . . to you in **r** and pray,*
*Job 42:6 . . . dust and ashes to show my **r.***
*Luke 17:3 . . . if there is **r,** forgive.*
*2 Cor 7:10 . . . sorrow, which lacks **r,***

REPUTATION (n)
overall quality or character as seen or judged by people in general
*Ps 109:21 . . . the sake of your own **r!***
*Prov 3:4 . . . you will earn a good **r.***
*Prov 22:1 . . . Choose a good **r** over great*
*Eccl 7:1 . . . A good **r** is more valuable*
*1 Tim 3:2 . . . wisely, and have a good **r.***
*Heb 11:39 . . . good **r** because of their*

RESCUE, RESCUED, RESCUES, RESCUING (v)
to save or deliver
see also REDEEM, SAVE
*2 Kgs 13:5 . . . someone to **r** the Israelites*
*Ps 9:14 . . . rejoice that you have **r-d** me.*
*Ps 17:7 . . . mighty power you **r** those who*
*Ps 22:8 . . . let the LORD **r** him!*
*Ps 31:2 . . . listen to me; **r** me quickly.*
*Ps 37:39 . . . The LORD **r-s** the godly;*
*Ps 37:40 . . . LORD helps them, **r-ing** them*
*Ps 68:20 . . . The Sovereign LORD **r-s** us*
*Ps 72:12 . . . He will **r** the poor when*
*Ps 145:19 . . . cries for help and **r-s** them.*
*Prov 11:8 . . . godly are **r-d** from trouble,*
*Isa 56:1 . . . coming soon to **r** you and*
*Dan 6:27 . . . He **r-s** and saves His people;*
*Zech 8:7 . . . that I will **r** My people from*
*Matt 6:13 . . . but **r** us from the evil one.*
*Rom 11:26 . . . The one who **r-s** will come*
*2 Cor 1:10 . . . And he did **r** us from mortal*
*Gal 1:4 . . . in order to **r** us from this*

Gal 3:13 . . . But Christ has ***r-d*** *us from the*
Col 1:13 . . . For he has ***r-d*** *us from the*
1 Thes 1:10 . . . the one who has ***r-d*** *us*
2 Pet 2:9 . . . knows how to ***r*** *godly people*

RESIST (v)
to withstand the force or effect of; to counteract or defeat
Dan 11:32 . . . will be strong and will ***r*** *him.*
Matt 5:39 . . . do not ***r*** *an evil person!*
Jas 4:7 . . . ***R*** *the devil, and he will flee*

RESPECT (n)
a high or special regard; esteem
see also AWE, REVERENCE
Prov 11:16 . . . A gracious woman gains ***r,***
Mal 1:6 . . . the honor and ***r*** *I deserve?*
Titus 2:2 . . . be worthy of ***r,*** *and to live*

RESPECT, RESPECTED (v)
to consider worthy of high regard; to esteem
Eph 5:33 . . . the wife must ***r*** *her husband.*
1 Tim 3:4 . . . children who ***r*** *and obey him.*
1 Tim 3:8 . . . deacons must be well ***r-ed***
1 Tim 3:11 . . . their wives must be ***r-ed***
1 Tim 5:17 . . . work well should be ***r-ed***
1 Pet 2:17 . . . Fear God, and ***r*** *the king.*

RESPONSIBLE (adj)
marked by or involving responsibility or accountability; liable to be called to account as the primary cause, motive, or agent
Exod 32:34 . . . hold them ***r*** *for their sins.*
Num 1:53 . . . The Levites are ***r*** *to stand*
Ezek 33:6 . . . he is ***r*** *for their captivity.*
Jon 1:14 . . . And don't hold us ***r*** *for his*
Gal 6:5 . . . For we are each ***r*** *for our own*

REST (n)
freedom from activity or labor; peace of mind or spirit; repose, sleep
see also SABBATH
Exod 31:15 . . . day of complete ***r,*** *a holy*
Exod 33:14 . . . and I will give you ***r***—
Ps 23:2 . . . He lets me ***r*** *in green*
Ps 91:1 . . . Most High will find ***r*** *in the*
Ps 127:2 . . . for God gives ***r*** *to His loved*
Jer 6:16 . . . you will find ***r*** *for your*
Matt 11:28 . . . and I will give you ***r.***
2 Thes 1:7 . . . God will provide ***r*** *for you*
Heb 4:3 . . . even though this ***r*** *has been*
Heb 4:9 . . . a special ***r*** *still waiting*
Heb 4:10 . . . who have entered into God's ***r***

REST, RESTED, RESTING, RESTS (v)
to sit or lie on; to cease from action or motion; to take relief or respite
Gen 2:2 . . . of creation, so he ***r-ed*** *from all*
Ps 16:9 . . . My body ***r-s*** *in safety.*
Isa 11:2 . . . Spirit of the LORD *will* ***r***
Isa 30:15 . . . and ***r-ing*** *in Me will you*
John 1:32 . . . from heaven and ***r-ing*** *upon*
Heb 4:4 . . . seventh day God ***r-ed*** *from all*
Rev 14:13 . . . will ***r*** *from their hard work;*

RESTORE, RESTORED, RESTORES, RESTORING (v)
to give back, return; to renew
Ps 14:7 . . . When the LORD ***r-s*** *his people,*
Ps 30:2 . . . and you ***r-d*** *my health.*
Isa 58:11 . . . are dry and ***r-ing*** *your strength.*
Jer 30:3 . . . when I will ***r*** *the fortunes of*
Jer 30:18 . . . from captivity and ***r*** *their*
Jer 31:18 . . . Turn me again to You and ***r***
Hos 6:2 . . . a short time He will ***r*** *us,*
Nah 2:2 . . . but He will ***r*** *its splendor.*
Rom 5:10 . . . friendship with God was ***r-d***
1 Pet 5:10 . . . He will ***r,*** *support,*

RESURRECTION (n)
the state of one risen from the dead; the rising again to life of all the human dead before the final judgment
see also RAISE, RISE
Matt 27:53 . . . cemetery after Jesus' ***r,***
Mark 12:23 . . . will she be in the ***r?***
Luke 20:36 . . . children of the ***r.***
John 11:25 . . . I am the ***r*** *and the life.*
Acts 1:22 . . . as a witness of Jesus' ***r.***
Acts 2:31 . . . speaking of the Messiah's ***r.***
Acts 4:2 . . . there is a ***r*** *of the dead.*
Acts 4:33 . . . powerfully to the ***r*** *of*
Acts 17:32 . . . Paul speak about the ***r*** *of*
1 Cor 15:13 . . . if there is no ***r*** *of the*
1 Cor 15:42 . . . way with the ***r*** *of the dead.*
Phil 3:11 . . . experience the ***r*** *from the*
2 Tim 2:18 . . . claiming that the ***r*** *of the*
Heb 6:2 . . . of hands, the ***r*** *of the dead,*
Heb 11:35 . . . a better life after the ***r.***
1 Pet 3:21 . . . because of the ***r*** *of Jesus*
Rev 20:5 . . . This is the first ***r.***

REVEAL, REVEALED (v)
to make known through divine inspiration; to make (something secret or hidden) publicly or generally known; to display
Exod 6:3 . . . did not ***r*** *my name, Yahweh,*
Deut 29:29 . . . all that He has ***r-ed*** *to us,*
Isa 40:5 . . . the LORD *will be* ***r-ed,***
Isa 53:1 . . . the LORD ***r-ed*** *His powerful*
Matt 10:26 . . . is covered will be ***r-ed,***
Matt 11:27 . . . Son chooses to ***r*** *Him.*
Luke 2:32 . . . He is a light to ***r*** *God*
John 12:38 . . . the LORD ***r-ed*** *His powerful*
John 14:21 . . . love them and ***r*** *Myself*
John 17:6 . . . I have ***r-ed*** *you to the*
Rom 8:18 . . . glory He will ***r*** *to us*
Rom 16:25 . . . Christ has ***r-ed*** *His plan*
1 Cor 2:10 . . . that God ***r-ed*** *these things*
Gal 1:16 . . . to ***r*** *his Son to me so that*
Gal 2:2 . . . because God ***r-ed*** *to me*
Eph 3:3 . . . Himself ***r-ed*** *His mysterious*
Col 1:26 . . . it has been ***r-ed*** *to God's*
2 Thes 2:3 . . . man of lawlessness is ***r-ed***
Titus 2:13 . . . Christ, will be ***r-ed.***
Heb 9:8 . . . the Holy Spirit ***r-ed*** *that*
1 Pet 1:7 . . . when Jesus Christ is ***r-ed***

REVELRY (n)
noisy partying or merrymaking
Exod 32:6 . . . they indulged in pagan ***r.***
1 Cor 10:7 . . . they indulged in pagan ***r.***

REVENGE (n)
an act or instance of retaliating in order to get even
Lev 19:18 . . . Do not seek ***r*** *or bear*
Num 31:3 . . . war of ***r*** *against Midian.*
Deut 32:35 . . . I will take ***r;*** *I will*
Josh 20:3 . . . relatives seeking ***r*** *for*
Judg 20:10 . . . will take ***r*** *on Gibeah*
Isa 34:8 . . . day of the LORD*'s* ***r,***
Heb 10:30 . . . I will take ***r.*** *I will*

REVERENCE (n)
profound, adoring, awed respect
see also AWE, FEAR, RESPECT
Lev 19:30 . . . of rest, and show ***r*** *toward*
Job 15:4 . . . fear of God, no ***r*** *for Him?*
Job 37:24 . . . who are wise show Him ***r.***
Eph 5:21 . . . another out of ***r*** *for Christ.*
Heb 5:7 . . . of his deep ***r*** *for God.*

REWARD, REWARDS (n)
something that is given in return for good or evil done or received or that is offered or given for some service or attainment
Gen 15:1 . . . and your ***r*** *will be*
1 Sam 26:23 . . . gives his own ***r*** *for doing*
Prov 12:14 . . . and hard work brings ***r-s.***
Isa 49:4 . . . I will trust God for my ***r.***
Matt 5:12 . . . For a great ***r*** *awaits you*
Matt 6:5 . . . all the ***r*** *they will ever*
Luke 6:23 . . . For a great ***r*** *awaits you*
Luke 6:35 . . . your ***r*** *from heaven will*
Phil 4:17 . . . you to receive a ***r*** *for your*
1 Thes 2:19 . . . be our proud ***r*** *and crown*
Heb 10:35 . . . the great ***r*** *it brings you!*
1 Pet 1:9 . . . The ***r*** *for trusting him*

REWARD, REWARDED, REWARDS (v)
to give a reward to or for; to recompense
2 Sam 22:21 . . . The LORD ***r-ed*** *me for*
Prov 13:21 . . . while blessings ***r*** *the*
Prov 25:22 . . . the LORD *will* ***r*** *you.*
Jer 31:16 . . . for I will ***r*** *you," says*
Matt 6:18 . . . sees everything, will ***r*** *you.*
Luke 12:37 . . . for His return will be ***r-ed.***
Luke 14:14 . . . God will ***r*** *you for*
1 Cor 3:8 . . . both will be ***r-ed*** *for their*
Eph 6:8 . . . the Lord will ***r*** *each one*
1 Tim 3:13 . . . will be ***r-ed*** *with respect*
Heb 11:6 . . . that He ***r-s*** *those who*
Rev 11:18 . . . the dead and ***r*** *Your servants*

RICH (adj)
having abundant possessions and especially material wealth
Job 34:19 . . . no more attention to the ***r***
Ps 49:16 . . . the wicked grow ***r*** *and*
Prov 10:4 . . . poor; hard workers get ***r.***
Prov 11:18 . . . Evil people get ***r*** *for*
Prov 13:7 . . . are poor pretend to be ***r;***
Prov 21:17 . . . and luxury will never be ***r.***
Prov 22:2 . . . The ***r*** *and poor have this*
Prov 23:4 . . . yourself out trying to get ***r.***
Prov 28:6 . . . than to be dishonest and ***r.***
Prov 28:22 . . . Greedy people try to get ***r***
Eccl 5:12 . . . But the ***r*** *seldom get a*
Isa 53:9 . . . put in a ***r*** *man's grave.*
Matt 19:23 . . . hard for a ***r*** *person to enter*
Luke 1:53 . . . and sent the ***r*** *away with*
Luke 6:24 . . . you who are ***r,*** *for you have*
Luke 16:1 . . . was a certain ***r*** *man who had*
Luke 21:1 . . . watched the ***r*** *people*
2 Cor 8:9 . . . Though he was ***r,*** *yet for your*
1 Tim 6:9 . . . who long to be ***r*** *fall into*
1 Tim 6:17 . . . who are ***r*** *in this world*
Jas 1:10 . . . those who are ***r*** *should boast*
Jas 2:3 . . . seat to the ***r*** *person, but you*
Jas 5:1 . . . Look here, you ***r*** *people:*

RICHES (n)
things that make one rich; wealth
see also MONEY, POSSESSIONS, TREASURE(S), WEALTH
2 Chr 1:11 . . . ask for wealth, ***r,*** *fame,*
Ps 49:6 . . . wealth and boast of great ***r.***
Prov 27:24 . . . for ***r*** *don't last forever,*
Eccl 5:13 . . . Hoarding ***r*** *harms the*
Jer 9:23 . . . rich boast in their ***r.***
Luke 8:14 . . . cares and ***r*** *and pleasures*
Rom 11:33 . . . great are God's ***r*** *and*
2 Cor 6:10 . . . give spiritual ***r*** *to others.*
Col 1:27 . . . know that the ***r*** *and glory*

RIGHT (adj)
being in accordance with what is good, just, or proper; being in a correct or proper state; located opposite of left; acting or judging in accordance with truth or fact
see also JUST, JUSTIFY, RIGHTEOUS, UPRIGHT
Gen 4:7 . . . do what is ***r,*** *then watch out!*
Gen 18:19 . . . by doing what is ***r*** *and just.*
Exod 15:26 . . . do what is ***r*** *in His sight,*
Num 25:13 . . . making them ***r*** *with Me.*
Deut 6:18 . . . Do what is ***r*** *and good*
Deut 25:1 . . . that one is ***r*** *and the other*
Josh 1:7 . . . either to the ***r*** *or to the*

Judg 17:6 . . . whatever seemed **r** in their
1 Sam 12:23 . . . what is good and **r.**
1 Kgs 3:9 . . . difference between **r** and
2 Chr 12:6 . . . The LORD is **r** in doing
Ps 19:8 . . . LORD are **r,** bringing joy
Ps 24:5 . . . have a **r** relationship with
Ps 25:8 . . . does what is **r;** he shows the
Ps 37:30 . . . they teach **r** from wrong.
Ps 64:10 . . . do what is **r** will praise him.
Ps 71:2 . . . do what is **r.** Turn your ear
Ps 84:11 . . . from those who do what is **r.**
Ps 97:11 . . . on those whose hearts are **r.**
Ps 106:3 . . . and always do what is **r.**
Ps 119:144 . . . laws are always **r;** help me
Prov 1:3 . . . do what is **r,** just, and fair.
Prov 2:13 . . . men turn from the **r** way
Prov 14:2 . . . who follow the **r** path
Prov 14:12 . . . person that seems **r,** but
Prov 15:21 . . . stays on the **r** path.
Prov 15:23 . . . to say the **r** thing at the
Prov 18:17 . . . in court sounds **r**—until
Eccl 8:5 . . . and a way to do what is **r,**
Eccl 9:11 . . . being in the **r** place at the
Isa 7:15 . . . choose what is **r** and reject
Isa 16:5 . . . be eager to do what is **r.**
Isa 26:7 . . . who does what is **r,** and you
Jer 23:5 . . . is just and **r** throughout the
Ezek 18:5 . . . and does what is just and **r.**
Ezek 18:21 . . . and do what is just and **r,**
Hos 14:9 . . . are true and **r,** and righteous
Mic 3:1 . . . to know **r** from wrong,
Mic 6:8 . . . do what is **r,** to love mercy,
Zeph 2:3 . . . to do what is **r** and to live
Matt 6:3 . . . hand know what your **r** hand is
Matt 22:44 . . . of honor at My **r** hand until
Acts 2:34 . . . the place of honor at My **r** hand
Acts 7:55 . . . honor at God's **r** hand.
Acts 13:39 . . . is declared **r** with God—
Rom 1:17 . . . God makes us **r** in His sight.
Rom 2:13 . . . doesn't make us **r** with God.
Rom 3:4 . . . will be proved **r** in what you
Rom 3:20 . . . ever be made **r** with God by
Rom 3:22 . . . We are made **r** with God by
Rom 3:28 . . . So we are made **r** with God
Rom 3:30 . . . makes people **r** with Himself
Rom 4:13 . . . but on a **r** relationship with
Rom 4:25 . . . life to make us **r** with God.
Rom 5:1 . . . we have been made **r** in God's
Rom 5:16 . . . being made **r** with God,
Rom 6:13 . . . to do what is **r** for the glory
Rom 8:10 . . . have been made **r** with God.
Rom 8:30 . . . given them **r** standing,
Rom 9:30 . . . they were made **r** with God.
Rom 10:3 . . . way of getting **r** with God by
Rom 10:10 . . . you are made **r** with God,
1 Cor 6:11 . . . you were made **r** with God
2 Cor 3:9 . . . which makes us **r** with God!
2 Cor 5:21 . . . be made **r** with God
Gal 2:16 . . . person is made **r** with God by
Gal 2:17 . . . to be made **r** with God through
Gal 2:21 . . . law could make us **r** with God,
Gal 3:11 . . . can be made **r** with God by
Gal 3:21 . . . could be made **r** with God by
Gal 3:24 . . . could be made **r** with God
Gal 5:4 . . . to make yourselves **r** with God
Eph 5:9 . . . what is good and **r** and true.
Phil 4:8 . . . honorable, and **r,** and pure,
2 Tim 3:16 . . . teaches us to do what is **r.**
Heb 2:10 . . . it was only **r** that he should
Heb 12:11 . . . harvest of **r** living for those
Jas 2:24 . . . are shown to be **r** with God by
1 Jn 2:29 . . . who do what is **r** are God's

RIGHTEOUS (adj)
acting in accord with divine or moral law; free from guilt or sin; morally right or justifiable
see also JUST, JUSTIFY, RIGHT, UPRIGHT
Gen 6:9 . . . Noah was a **r** man, the only
Gen 15:6 . . . counted him as **r** because of
Gen 18:23 . . . sweep away both the **r** and
Ps 7:8 . . . Declare me **r,** O LORD, for
Ps 17:15 . . . Because I am **r,** I will see
Ps 106:31 . . . regarded as a **r** man ever
Ps 119:7 . . . I learn your **r** regulations,
Ps 119:137 . . . O LORD, You are **r,**
Ps 145:17 . . . The LORD is **r** in everything
Prov 4:18 . . . The way of the **r** is like the
Prov 9:9 . . . Teach the **r,** and they
Prov 29:6 . . . but the **r** escape, shouting
Isa 26:2 . . . to all who are **r;** allow the
Isa 42:21 . . . Because He is **r,** the LORD
Isa 64:6 . . . we display our **r** deeds,
Jer 11:20 . . . You make **r** judgments, and
Jer 23:5 . . . raise up a **r** descendant from
Ezek 3:20 . . . None of their **r** acts will be
Amos 5:24 . . . river of **r** living.
Hab 2:4 . . . But the **r** will live
Mal 3:18 . . . between the **r** and the wicked,
Matt 9:13 . . . think they are **r,** but those
Matt 13:43 . . . Then the **r** will shine
Matt 25:37 . . . Then these **r** ones will
Luke 1:6 . . . and Elizabeth were **r** in God's
Luke 16:15 . . . like to appear **r** in public,
Rom 1:17 . . . faith that a **r** person has
Rom 3:5 . . . people see how **r** God is.
Rom 3:10 . . . No one is **r**—not even one.
Rom 4:3 . . . counted him as **r** because of
Rom 4:6 . . . who are declared **r** without
Rom 4:22 . . . God counted him as **r.**
Rom 6:19 . . . be slaves to **r** living so that
Gal 3:6 . . . counted him as **r** because of
Eph 4:24 . . . like God—truly **r** and holy.
Phil 1:11 . . . salvation—the **r** character
2 Tim 2:22 . . . Instead, pursue **r** living,
Titus 3:7 . . . He declared us **r** and gave us
Jas 2:23 . . . counted him as **r** because of
Jas 5:16 . . . prayer of a **r** person has
1 Jn 2:1 . . . the one who is truly **r.**
1 Jn 3:7 . . . that they are **r,** even as

RIGHTEOUSNESS (n)
the state or quality of being righteous
see also GODLINESS, JUSTICE
Ps 36:6 . . . Your **r** is like the mighty
Ps 71:15 . . . tell everyone about Your **r.**
Ps 85:10 . . . **R** and peace have kissed!
Ps 98:2 . . . has revealed His **r** to every
Ps 111:3 . . . His **r** never fails.
Prov 21:21 . . . Whoever pursues **r** and
Isa 11:5 . . . He will wear **r** like a belt
Isa 42:6 . . . you to demonstrate My **r.**
Isa 45:8 . . . so salvation and **r** can sprout
Isa 56:1 . . . to display My **r** among you.
Isa 59:17 . . . He put on **r** as his body
Jer 9:24 . . . brings justice and **r** to the
Jer 23:6 . . . LORD Is Our **R.**
Hos 10:12 . . . come and shower **r** upon
Mic 7:9 . . . and I will see His **r.**
Mal 4:2 . . . the Sun of **R** will rise
Matt 5:20 . . . unless your **r** is better
John 16:8 . . . and of God's **r,** and of the
Acts 24:25 . . . about **r** and self-control
Rom 3:26 . . . to demonstrate His **r,** for He
Rom 5:18 . . . one act of **r** brings a right
2 Cor 6:7 . . . the weapons of **r** in the
Eph 6:14 . . . the body armor of God's **r.**
Phil 3:6 . . . And as for **r,** I obeyed the
2 Tim 4:8 . . . the crown of **r,** which
Heb 11:7 . . . he received the **r** that comes
Jas 3:18 . . . and reap a harvest of **r.**
2 Pet 3:13 . . . filled with God's **r.**

RISE, RISEN, RISES (v)
to ascend or extend above other objects; to return from death; to assume an upright position
see also RESURRECTION
Num 24:17 . . . A star will **r** from Jacob;
Isa 26:19 . . . bodies will **r** again!
Mal 4:2 . . . of Righteousness will **r** with
Matt 22:30 . . . when the dead **r,** they will
Matt 27:63 . . . I will **r** from the dead.
Matt 28:6 . . . He is **r-n** from the dead,
Mark 8:31 . . . later He would **r** from the
Mark 16:6 . . . He is **r-n** from the dead!
Luke 18:33 . . . day He will **r** again.
Luke 24:34 . . . The Lord has really **r-n!**
John 5:29 . . . and they will **r** again.
John 11:24 . . . when everyone else **r-s,** at
John 20:9 . . . said Jesus must **r** from the
Acts 17:3 . . . must suffer and **r** from the
1 Thes 4:16 . . . have died will **r** from

ROCK (n)
a stone; a cliff; foundation, support; refuge
Exod 17:6 . . . Moses struck the **r** as he was
Num 20:8 . . . speak to the **r** over there,
Deut 32:13 . . . honey from the **r** and olive
2 Sam 22:2 . . . LORD is my **r,** my
Ps 18:2 . . . God is my **r,** in whom I
Ps 19:14 . . . LORD, my **r** and my redeemer.
Ps 61:2 . . . to the towering **r** of safety,
Ps 62:7 . . . my refuge, a **r** where no enemy
Ps 92:15 . . . He is my **r!**
Isa 26:4 . . . GOD is the eternal **R.**
Matt 7:24 . . . builds a house on solid **r.**
Matt 16:18 . . . upon this **r** I will build
Rom 9:33 . . . stumble, a **r** that makes them
1 Cor 10:4 . . . and that **r** was Christ.
1 Pet 2:8 . . . stumble, the **r** that makes

ROD, RODS (n)
a straight, slender stick used as a walking stick, a club or weapon, a shepherd's crook, a paddling stick, a royal scepter, or a measuring stick; figurative of divine authority
see also STAFF
2 Sam 7:14 . . . him with the **r,** like any
Ps 2:9 . . . will break them with an iron **r**
Ps 23:4 . . . Your **r** and Your staff
Prov 13:24 . . . spare the **r** of discipline
2 Cor 11:25 . . . times I was beaten with **r-s.**
Rev 2:27 . . . the nations with an iron **r**
Rev 12:5 . . . rule all nations with an iron **r.**
Rev 19:15 . . . rule them with an iron **r.**

ROOT, ROOTS (n)
the usually underground part of a plant body; something that is an origin or source (as of a condition or quality)
Isa 11:1 . . . bearing fruit from the old **r.**
Isa 53:2 . . . green shoot, like a **r** in dry
Matt 3:10 . . . to sever the **r-s** of the trees.
Matt 13:21 . . . don't have deep **r-s,** they
Eph 3:17 . . . Your **r-s** will grow down
1 Tim 6:10 . . . money is the **r** of all kinds
Jude 12 . . . have been pulled up by the **r-s.**

RUIN, RUINED, RUINING, RUINS (v)
to damage irreparably; to subject to frustration, failure, or disaster
Prov 19:3 . . . People **r** their lives by
Prov 19:18 . . . you will **r** their lives.
Prov 22:23 . . . He will **r** anyone who **r-s**
Isa 3:14 . . . You have **r-ed** Israel,
Matt 9:17 . . . the wine and **r-ing** the skins.
2 Tim 2:14 . . . they can **r** those who hear

RULE, RULES (n)
a prescribed guide for conduct or action
Isa 29:13 . . . but man-made **r-s** learned by
2 Tim 2:5 . . . unless they follow the **r-s.**
Heb 13:9 . . . not from **r-s** about food,

RULE, RULED, RULES (v)
to exert control, direction, or influence on; to exercise authority or power over
*Gen 3:16 . . . but he will **r** over you.*
*Ps 2:4 . . . But the One who **r-s** in heaven*
*Ps 11:4 . . . LORD still **r-s** from heaven.*
*Ps 55:19 . . . God, who has **r-d** forever,*
*Ps 66:7 . . . great power He **r-s** forever.*
*Ps 89:9 . . . You **r** the oceans.*
*Ps 103:19 . . . there He **r-s** over everything.*
*Prov 17:2 . . . wise servant will **r** over the*
*Isa 9:7 . . . He will **r** with fairness*
*Isa 40:10 . . . He will **r** with a powerful*
*Jer 23:5 . . . a King who **r-s** with wisdom.*
*Zech 6:13 . . . honor and will **r** as king*
*Rom 5:21 . . . as sin **r-d** over all people*
*Rom 15:12 . . . come, and He will **r** over*
*Col 3:15 . . . comes from Christ **r** in your*
*Rev 19:15 . . . He will **r** them with*

RULER, RULERS (n)
person with authority; tribal chief; prince or king; city magistrate; powerful spiritual beings; God himself
*Judg 8:22 . . . to Gideon, "Be our **r!***
*1 Sam 10:1 . . . to be the **r** over Israel,*
*Prov 19:6 . . . favors from a **r;** everyone is*
*Prov 23:1 . . . with a **r,** pay attention to*
*Jer 30:21 . . . have their own **r** again,*
*Dan 7:27 . . . all **r-s** will serve and obey Him.*
*Dan 9:25 . . . until a **r**—the Anointed One—*
*Mic 5:2 . . . a **r** of Israel will come from*
*Matt 2:6 . . . for a **r** will come from*
*Matt 20:25 . . . that the **r-s** in this world*
*John 12:31 . . . when Satan, the **r** of this*
*1 Cor 2:6 . . . or to the **r-s** of this world,*
*Eph 1:21 . . . far above any **r** or authority*
*Eph 3:10 . . . the unseen **r-s** and authorities*
*Eph 6:12 . . . but against evil **r-s** and*
*Col 1:16 . . . as thrones, kingdoms, **r-s,** and*
*Col 2:15 . . . disarmed the spiritual **r-s** and*
*Rev 1:5 . . . and the **r** of all the kings*

RUN, RUNNING (v)
to go faster than a walk; to flee
*Ps 19:5 . . . athlete eager to **r** the race.*
*Prov 4:12 . . . when you **r,** you won't*
*Isa 40:31 . . . will **r** and not grow weary.*
*1 Cor 9:26 . . . So I **r** with purpose in*
*Gal 2:2 . . . and I was **r-ning** the race for*
*Gal 5:7 . . . You were **r-ning** the race so*
*Phil 2:16 . . . that I did not **r** the race in*
*1 Tim 6:11 . . . so **r** from all these evil*
*2 Tim 2:22 . . . **R** from anything that*
*Heb 12:1 . . . let us **r** with endurance*

RUST (n)
the reddish brittle coating formed on iron
*Matt 6:19 . . . them and **r** destroys them,*

S

SABAOTH (KJV)
*Rom 9:29 . . . Lord of **Heaven's Armies** had not*
*Jas 5:4 . . . the Lord of **Heaven's Armies***

SABBATH, SABBATHS (n)
cessation of activity; a holy day set aside to honor God through rest and worship
see also REST
*Exod 20:8 . . . to observe the **S** day by*
*Exod 31:14 . . . must keep the **S** day, for it*
*Lev 25:2 . . . must observe a **S** rest before*
*Deut 5:12 . . . Observe the **S** day by*
*2 Chr 2:4 . . . morning and evening, on the **S-s,***
*Isa 56:2 . . . who honor My **S** days of rest*
*Isa 56:6 . . . do not desecrate the **S** day*
*Isa 58:13 . . . Honor the **S** in everything*
*Matt 12:1 . . . some grainfields on the **S.***
*Luke 13:10 . . . One **S** day as Jesus was*
*Col 2:16 . . . or new moon ceremonies or **S-s.***

SACRIFICE, SACRIFICES (n)
worship or atonement offering; something given up or lost
*Exod 12:27 . . . It is the Passover **s** to the*
*1 Sam 15:22 . . . Obedience is better than **s,***
*Ps 40:6 . . . no delight in **s-s** or offerings.*
*Ps 51:16 . . . do not desire a **s,** or I would*
*Ps 51:17 . . . The **s** You desire is*
*Ps 107:22 . . . offer **s-s** of thanksgiving*
*Prov 15:8 . . . LORD detests the **s** of*
*Hos 6:6 . . . to show love, not offer **s-s.***
*Matt 9:13 . . . to show mercy, not offer **s-s.***
*Rom 3:25 . . . Jesus as the **s** for sin.*
*Rom 8:3 . . . Son as a **s** for our sins.*
*Rom 12:1 . . . a living and holy **s**—the*
*Eph 5:2 . . . Himself as a **s** for us,*
*Heb 5:3 . . . He must offer **s-s** for His own*
*Heb 7:27 . . . need to offer **s-s** every day.*
*Heb 9:28 . . . time as a **s** to take away*
*Heb 10:5 . . . did not want animal **s-s** or sin*
*Heb 10:10 . . . holy by the **s** of the body of*
*Heb 13:15 . . . Jesus a continual **s** of praise*
*Heb 13:16 . . . These are the **s-s** that please*
*1 Pet 2:5 . . . offer spiritual **s-s** that please*
*1 Jn 2:2 . . . Himself is the **s** that atones*
*1 Jn 4:10 . . . His Son as a **s** to take away*

SACRIFICE, SACRIFICED, SACRIFICES (v)
to suffer loss of, give up, renounce, injure, kill, or destroy, especially for an ideal, belief, or end
*Gen 22:2 . . . Go and **s** him as a*
*John 10:11 . . . good shepherd **s-s** his life*
*John 10:15 . . . I **s** My life for the sheep.*
*1 Cor 5:7 . . . Lamb, has been **s-d** for us.*
*1 Cor 13:3 . . . poor and even **s-d** my body,*

SAFE (adj)
free from harm or risk; secure from threat of danger, harm, or loss
*Deut 29:19 . . . I am **s,** even though I am*
*1 Sam 30:23 . . . has kept us **s** and helped*
*Ps 4:8 . . . O LORD, will keep me **s.***
*Ps 28:8 . . . He is a **s** fortress for His*
*Prov 2:11 . . . will keep you **s.***
*Prov 4:26 . . . stay on the **s** path.*
*Prov 18:10 . . . godly run to him and are **s.***
*Prov 28:26 . . . who walks in wisdom is **s.***
*John 17:15 . . . keep them **s** from the evil*

SAFETY (n)
the condition of being safe from undergoing or causing hurt, injury, or loss
*Deut 33:12 . . . and live in **s** beside Him.*
*2 Sam 23:5 . . . ensure my **s** and success.*
*Ps 16:9 . . . My body rests in **s.***
*Ps 59:16 . . . my refuge, a place of **s***
*Prov 11:14 . . . is **s** in having many advisers.*
*Prov 29:25 . . . trusting the LORD means **s.***
*Hos 2:18 . . . live unafraid in peace and **s.***

SAINTS (KJV)
*Ps 34:9 . . . you His **godly people,** for*
*Ps 97:10 . . . the lives of His **godly people***
*Dan 7:18 . . . the **holy people** of the Most High*
*Rom 8:27 . . . Spirit pleads for **us believers** in*
*1 Cor 6:2 . . . **we believers** will judge the world*

SALVATION (n)
deliverance from the power and effects of sin, danger, or difficulty by God's intervention
see also SAVE
*2 Sam 22:47 . . . Rock of my **s,** be exalted!*
*2 Chr 6:41 . . . be clothed with **s;** may your*
*Ps 18:46 . . . God of my **s** be exalted!*
*Ps 27:1 . . . light and my **s**—so why should*
*Ps 40:16 . . . love your **s** repeatedly shout,*
*Ps 51:12 . . . joy of Your **s,** and make me*
*Ps 62:2 . . . rock and my **s,** my fortress*
*Ps 69:13 . . . my prayer with Your sure **s.***
*Ps 74:12 . . . ages past, bringing **s** to*
*Ps 85:4 . . . us again, O God of our **s.***
*Ps 89:26 . . . and the Rock of my **s.***
*Ps 91:16 . . . long life and give them My **s.***
*Ps 95:1 . . . joyfully to the Rock of our **s.***
*Isa 25:9 . . . rejoice in the **s** He brings!*
*Isa 26:18 . . . We have not given **s** to the*
*Isa 33:6 . . . rich store of **s,** wisdom,*
*Isa 45:8 . . . wide so **s** and righteousness*
*Isa 45:22 . . . the world look to Me for **s!***
*Isa 49:6 . . . will bring My **s** to the ends*
*Isa 51:6 . . . but My **s** lasts forever.*
*Isa 52:7 . . . of peace and **s,** the news that*
*Isa 59:17 . . . the helmet of **s** on His head.*
*Isa 62:1 . . . dawn, and her **s** blazes like*
*Lam 3:26 . . . wait quietly for **s** from the*
*Jon 2:9 . . . For my **s** comes from the*
*Luke 1:77 . . . to find **s** through forgiveness*
*Luke 2:30 . . . I have seen Your **s,***
*Luke 3:6 . . . will see the **s** sent from*
*Luke 21:28 . . . up, for Your **s** is near!*
*John 4:22 . . . Him, for **s** comes through the*
*Acts 13:26 . . . this message of **s** has been*
*Acts 13:47 . . . Gentiles, to bring **s** to the*
*Acts 28:28 . . . know that this **s** from God*
*Rom 11:11 . . . so God made **s** available to*
*Rom 13:11 . . . for our **s** is nearer now*
*2 Cor 6:2 . . . the day of **s,** I helped you.*
*2 Cor 7:10 . . . from sin and results in **s.***
*Eph 6:17 . . . Put on **s** as your helmet,*
*Phil 2:12 . . . show the results of your **s,***
*2 Thes 2:13 . . . to experience **s**—a **s***
*Titus 2:11 . . . bringing **s** to all people.*
*Heb 2:3 . . . if we ignore this great **s** that*
*Heb 5:9 . . . source of eternal **s** for all*
*Heb 9:28 . . . but to bring **s** to all who*
*1 Pet 1:9 . . . will be the **s** of your souls.*
*1 Pet 1:13 . . . to the gracious **s** that will*
*1 Pet 2:2 . . . into a full experience of **s.***
*Rev 7:10 . . . a mighty shout, "**S** comes from*

SAMARITAN (n)
a native or inhabitant of Samaria
*Luke 10:33 . . . a despised **S** came along,*
*Luke 17:16 . . . man was a **S.***
*John 4:5 . . . he came to the **S** village of*
*John 4:7 . . . a **S** woman came to draw*

SANCTIFY, SANCTIFIED (KJV)
*Gen 2:3 . . . and **declared it holy***
*Exod 31:13 . . . I am the LORD, who **makes you holy***
*Deut 5:12 . . . Sabbath day by **keeping it holy***
*John 17:19 . . . give Myself as a **holy sacrifice***
*Heb 10:10 . . . for us to **be made holy** by*

SANCTUARY (n)
a holy place set apart for worship of God or refuge from danger
see also TABERNACLE, TEMPLE
*Exod 25:8 . . . build Me a holy **s** so I can*
*Lev 19:30 . . . show reverence toward My **s.***
*Ps 27:5 . . . He will hide me in His **s.***
*Ps 63:2 . . . You in Your **s** and gazed upon*
*Ps 68:35 . . . God is awesome in His **s.***
*Ps 150:1 . . . Praise God in His **s;** praise*
*Heb 6:19 . . . curtain into God's inner **s.***

SANDAL, SANDALS (n)
a shoe consisting of a sole strapped to the foot
*Exod 3:5 . . . Take off your **s-s,** for you are*
*Exod 12:11 . . . wear your **s-s,** and carry*
*Deut 25:9 . . . elders, pull his **s** from his*
*Josh 5:15 . . . Take off your **s-s,** for the*

Ruth 4:7 . . . to remove his ***s*** *and hand it*
Matt 3:11 . . . His slave and carry His ***s-s.***

SANG (v)
see also SING
Exod 15:1 . . . people of Israel ***s*** *this*
Exod 15:21 . . . And Miriam ***s*** *this song:*
Num 21:17 . . . the Israelites ***s*** *this song:*
Judg 5:1 . . . son of Abinoam ***s*** *this song:*
2 Sam 22:1 . . . David ***s*** *this song to*
Ezra 3:11 . . . and thanks, they ***s*** *this song*
Job 38:7 . . . morning stars ***s*** *together and*
Ps 106:12 . . . Then they ***s*** *His praise.*
Matt 26:30 . . . Then they ***s*** *a hymn*
Rev 5:9 . . . And they ***s*** *a new song*
Rev 5:13 . . . They ***s:*** *"Blessing and*
Rev 14:3 . . . great choir ***s*** *a wonderful*

SAVE, SAVED, SAVES, SAVING (v)
to rescue or deliver from danger or harm; to deliver from sin; to preserve or guard from injury, destruction, or loss; to maintain or preserve
see also PRESERVE, RESCUE, SALVATION
2 Sam 22:3 . . . the power that ***s-s*** *me,*
1 Chr 16:23 . . . good news that He ***s-s.***
Ps 7:10 . . . is my shield, ***s-ing*** *those whose*
Ps 18:48 . . . You ***s*** *me from violent*
Ps 22:8 . . . let the Lord ***s*** *him!*
Ps 25:5 . . . You are the God who ***s-s*** *me.*
Ps 33:16 . . . army cannot ***s*** *a king, nor*
Ps 34:6 . . . Lord *listened; He* ***s-d*** *me*
Ps 44:6 . . . not count on my sword to ***s***
Ps 68:20 . . . Our God is a God who ***s-s!***
Ps 109:31 . . . the needy, ready to ***s*** *them*
Ps 116:6 . . . death, and He ***s-d*** *me.*
Prov 2:16 . . . Wisdom will ***s*** *you from*
Prov 10:2 . . . right living can ***s*** *your*
Isa 25:9 . . . trusted in Him, and He ***s-d*** *us!*
Isa 30:15 . . . resting in Me will you be ***s-d.***
Isa 35:4 . . . He is coming to ***s*** *you.*
Isa 59:1 . . . arm is not too weak to ***s***
Isa 63:1 . . . who has the power to ***s!***
Jer 4:14 . . . your heart that you may be ***s-d.***
Jer 17:14 . . . if You ***s*** *me, I will*
Jer 51:9 . . . nothing can ***s*** *her now.*
Dan 3:17 . . . we serve is able to ***s*** *us.*
Joel 2:32 . . . name of the Lord *will be* ***s-d,***
Mic 7:7 . . . wait confidently for God to ***s***
Zeph 1:18 . . . gold will not ***s*** *you*
Matt 1:21 . . . he will ***s*** *His people*
Matt 16:25 . . . My sake, you will ***s*** *it.*
Matt 24:13 . . . to the end will be ***s-d.***
Luke 17:33 . . . life go, you will ***s*** *it.*
Luke 19:10 . . . seek and ***s*** *those who are*
John 10:9 . . . in through Me will be ***s-d.***
John 12:47 . . . I have come to ***s*** *the world*
Acts 2:21 . . . name of the Lord *will be* ***s-d.***
Acts 4:12 . . . by which we must be ***s-d.***
Acts 15:11 . . . we are all ***s-d*** *the same way,*
Acts 16:30 . . . what must I do to be ***s-d?***
Rom 1:16 . . . God at work, ***s-ing*** *everyone*
Rom 5:9 . . . He will certainly ***s*** *us from*
Rom 10:9 . . . the dead, you will be ***s-d.***
Rom 10:13 . . . of the Lord *will be* ***s-d.***
1 Cor 1:18 . . . we who are being ***s-d*** *know*
1 Cor 5:5 . . . himself will be ***s-d*** *on the*
1 Cor 7:16 . . . wives might be ***s-d*** *because*
1 Cor 10:33 . . . so that many may be ***s-d.***
1 Cor 15:2 . . . this Good News that ***s-s***
Eph 1:13 . . . Good News that God ***s-s*** *you.*
1 Thes 5:9 . . . God chose to ***s*** *us through*
1 Tim 1:15 . . . the world to ***s*** *sinners*
1 Tim 2:4 . . . wants everyone to be ***s-d*** *and*
1 Tim 2:15 . . . women will be ***s-d*** *through*
2 Tim 1:9 . . . For God ***s-d*** *us and called*
Titus 3:5 . . . He ***s-d*** *us, not because of the*
Heb 7:25 . . . and forever, to ***s*** *those who*
Jas 5:20 . . . sinner back will ***s*** *that person*
2 Pet 3:15 . . . gives people time to be ***s-d.***

SAVING (adj)
of or relating to delivering or rescuing
Ps 40:10 . . . faithfulness and ***s*** *power.*
Ps 67:2 . . . the earth, Your ***s*** *power*
Ps 69:29 . . . God, by Your ***s*** *power.*
Ps 71:15 . . . proclaim Your ***s*** *power,*
Ps 98:1 . . . has shown His ***s*** *power!*

SAVIOR (n)
one who delivers from trouble, sin, or judgment
2 Sam 22:2 . . . my fortress, and My ***s;***
Ps 38:22 . . . help me, O Lord *my* ***s.***
Ps 40:17 . . . You are my helper and my ***s.***
Ps 106:21 . . . They forgot God, their ***s,***
Isa 43:11 . . . and there is no other ***S.***
Isa 45:21 . . . a righteous God and ***S.***
Isa 49:26 . . . the Lord, *am your* ***S*** *and*
Isa 62:11 . . . Look, your ***S*** *is coming.*
Jer 14:8 . . . Hope of Israel, our ***S*** *in*
Hos 13:4 . . . for there is no other ***s.***
Zeph 3:17 . . . He is a mighty ***s.***
Luke 1:47 . . . rejoices in God my ***S!***
Luke 1:69 . . . He has sent us a mighty ***S***
John 4:42 . . . He is indeed the ***S*** *of the*
Acts 5:31 . . . right hand as Prince and ***S.***
Acts 13:23 . . . God's promised ***S*** *of Israel!*
Eph 5:23 . . . He is the ***S*** *of His body,*
1 Tim 2:3 . . . good and pleases God our ***S,***
1 Tim 4:10 . . . who is the ***S*** *of all people*
Titus 2:10 . . . about God our ***S*** *attractive*
Titus 3:4 . . . When God our ***S*** *revealed His*
2 Pet 3:2 . . . Lord and ***S*** *commanded*
1 Jn 4:14 . . . Son to be the ***S*** *of the world.*

SCAPEGOAT (n)
a goat upon whose head are symbolically placed the sins of the people, after which he is sent into the wilderness on the Day of Atonement
Lev 16:10 . . . other goat, the ***s*** *chosen by*

SCARLET (adj)
of the color of any various bright reds
Josh 2:21 . . . leaving the ***s*** *rope hanging*
Isa 1:18 . . . sins are like ***s,*** *I will make*
Matt 27:28 . . . and put a ***s*** *robe on Him.*

SCATTER, SCATTERED (v)
to separate and go in various directions; to disperse
Deut 4:27 . . . the Lord *will* ***s*** *you*
Neh 1:8 . . . to Me, I will ***s*** *you among*
Isa 11:12 . . . will gather the ***s-ed*** *people*
Jer 9:16 . . . I will ***s*** *them around*
Jer 30:11 . . . where I have ***s-ed*** *you, but I*
Jer 31:10 . . . Lord, *who* ***s-ed*** *His people,*
Ezek 34:21 . . . flock until You ***s-ed*** *them to*
Zech 2:6 . . . for I have ***s-ed*** *you to the four*
Zech 10:9 . . . Though I have ***s-ed*** *them like*
Zech 13:7 . . . sheep will be ***s-ed,*** *and I will*
Matt 26:31 . . . of the flock will be ***s-ed.***
John 11:52 . . . children of God ***s-ed*** *around*
Acts 8:4 . . . who were ***s-ed*** *preached the Good*
Jas 1:1 . . . Jewish believers ***s-ed*** *abroad.*

SCEPTER (n)
the official staff of a ruler, symbolizing his authority and power
Gen 49:10 . . . The ***s*** *will not depart from*
Num 24:17 . . . a ***s*** *will emerge from Israel.*
Heb 1:8 . . . rule with a ***s*** *of justice.*

SCOFF, SCOFFING (v)
to show contempt by derisive acts or language; to mock
Lam 2:15 . . . They ***s*** *and insult*
Ps 123:4 . . . fill of the ***s-ing*** *of the proud*
1 Thes 5:20 . . . Do not ***s*** *at prophecies,*
2 Pet 2:12 . . . They ***s*** *at things they do not*
Jude 8 . . . defy authority, and ***s*** *at*

SCORN (n)
open dislike, disrespect, or derision often mixed with indignation
Ps 109:25 . . . they shake their heads in ***s.***
Isa 51:7 . . . not be afraid of people's ***s,***

SCRIPTURE, SCRIPTURES (n)
the Law; the writings of Moses; the entire collection of sacred books
Matt 21:16 . . . you ever read the ***S-s?***
Matt 22:29 . . . you don't know the ***S-s,***
Luke 24:27 . . . from all the ***S-s*** *the things*
Luke 24:45 . . . to understand the ***S-s.***
John 2:22 . . . believed both the ***S-s*** *and*
John 5:39 . . . You search the ***S-s*** *because*
John 7:42 . . . the ***S-s*** *clearly state that*
John 10:35 . . . know that the ***S-s*** *cannot*
Acts 8:32 . . . The passage of ***S*** *he had*
1 Cor 4:6 . . . quoted from the ***S-s,*** *you won't*
1 Tim 4:13 . . . focus on reading the ***S-s*** *to*
2 Tim 3:16 . . . All ***S*** *is inspired by God*
Heb 10:7 . . . written about Me in the ***S-s.***
2 Pet 1:20 . . . no prophecy in ***S*** *ever came*
2 Pet 3:16 . . . do with other parts of ***S.***

SCROLL (n)
a roll (as of papyrus, leather, or parchment) for writing a document
Isa 34:4 . . . disappear like a rolled-up ***s.***
Ezek 3:1 . . . giving you—eat this ***s!***
Rev 6:14 . . . sky was rolled up like a ***s,***
Rev 10:8 . . . take the open ***s*** *from the hand*

SEA, SEAS (n)
a great body of salt water that covers much of the earth
Exod 14:16 . . . middle of the ***s*** *on dry*
Deut 30:13 . . . not kept beyond the ***s,***
1 Kgs 7:23 . . . rim to rim, called the ***S.***
Job 11:9 . . . and wider than the ***s.***
Ps 93:4 . . . violent raging of the ***s-s,***
Ps 95:5 . . . The ***s*** *belongs to Him,*
Eccl 11:1 . . . your grain across the ***s-s,***
Isa 57:20 . . . like the restless ***s,*** *which*
Jon 1:4 . . . wind over the ***s,*** *causing a*
Hab 2:14 . . . waters fill the ***s,*** *the earth*
Matt 18:6 . . . in the depths of the ***s.***
Jas 1:6 . . . wave of the ***s*** *that is blown*
Jude 13 . . . waves of the ***s,*** *churning up*
Rev 10:2 . . . right foot on the ***s*** *and*
Rev 13:1 . . . rising up out of the ***s.***
Rev 20:13 . . . The ***s*** *gave up its dead,*
Rev 21:1 . . . And the ***s*** *was also gone.*

SEARCH, SEARCHES (v)
to investigate or examine thoroughly in an effort to find or verify something
Ps 34:14 . . . ***S*** *for peace, and work*
Ps 139:23 . . . ***S*** *me, O God, and know*
Eccl 3:6 . . . A time to ***s*** *and a time to*
Jer 17:10 . . . I, the Lord, ***s*** *all hearts*
1 Cor 2:10 . . . Spirit ***s-es*** *out everything*
1 Pet 3:11 . . . ***S*** *for peace, and work*

SEATED (v)
to put into a sitting position; to take one's seat or place
Matt 26:64 . . . Son of Man ***s*** *in the place*
Luke 22:69 . . . of Man will be ***s*** *in the place*
Eph 1:20 . . . the dead and ***s*** *Him in the*
Eph 2:6 . . . with Christ and ***s*** *us with Him*
Heb 12:2 . . . Now He is ***s*** *in the place of*
Rev 14:14 . . . a white cloud, and ***s*** *on the*

SECRET (adj)
kept from knowledge or view; hidden
Ps 90:8 . . . before You—our ***s*** *sins—*
Jer 23:24 . . . from me in a ***s*** *place?*

*Matt 10:26 . . . all that is **s** will be*
*Rom 2:16 . . . judge everyone's **s** life.*
*Rom 16:25 . . . a plan kept **s** from the*
*1 Cor 13:2 . . . all of God's **s** plans*
*1 Cor 14:25 . . . their **s** thoughts will be*
*Col 1:26 . . . was kept **s** for centuries and*

SECRET, SECRETS (n)
something kept hidden or unexplained; something kept from the knowledge of others or shared only confidentially with a few
see also MYSTERY
*Deut 29:29 . . . God has **s-s** known to no*
*Judg 16:15 . . . don't share your **s-s** with*
*Ps 44:21 . . . He knows the **s-s** of every*
*Prov 11:13 . . . goes around telling **s-s,***
*Dan 2:28 . . . heaven who reveals **s-s**, and*
*Dan 2:29 . . . who reveals **s-s** has shown*
*Mark 4:11 . . . to understand the **s***
*Mark 4:22 . . . and every **s** will be brought*
*Luke 8:10 . . . to understand the **s-s** of*
*1 Cor 15:51 . . . reveal to you a wonderful **s.***
*Phil 4:12 . . . have learned the **s** of living*
*Col 1:27 . . . the **s:** Christ lives in you.*

SEE, SEEING, SEES (v)
to perceive by the eye; to understand or recognize; to come to know
*Ps 34:8 . . . Taste and **s** that the*
*Ps 36:2 . . . they cannot **s** how wicked*
*Ps 90:8 . . . sins—and You **s** them*
*Ps 119:82 . . . straining to **s** Your promises*
*Prov 5:21 . . . For the LORD **s-s** clearly*
*Prov 13:19 . . . pleasant to **s** dreams come*
*Eccl 3:11 . . . people cannot **s** the whole*
*Matt 6:18 . . . Father, who **s-s** everything,*
*John 12:45 . . . you are **s-ing** the one who*
*Rom 1:20 . . . can clearly **s** His invisible*
*Rom 7:13 . . . So we can **s** how terrible sin*
*1 Cor 13:12 . . . we will **s** everything with*
*2 Cor 4:18 . . . things we cannot **s** will last*
*2 Cor 5:7 . . . by believing and not by **s-ing.***
*2 Cor 8:21 . . . everyone else to **s** that we*
*Phil 4:5 . . . Let everyone **s** that you are*
*Col 1:16 . . . things we can't **s**—such as*
*Rev 1:7 . . . everyone will **s** Him—even*

SEED, SEEDS (n)
the grains of plants used for sowing
*Gen 1:11 . . . These **s-s** will then produce*
*Prov 11:30 . . . The **s-s** of good deeds*
*Matt 13:3 . . . went out to plant some **s-s.***
*Matt 13:31 . . . like a mustard **s** planted in*
*Matt 17:20 . . . as a mustard **s**, you could say*
*Mark 4:15 . . . The **s** that fell on*
*Luke 8:12 . . . The **s-s** that fell on*
*1 Cor 3:6 . . . I planted the **s** in your*
*2 Cor 9:6 . . . few **s-s** will get a small*
*2 Cor 9:10 . . . one who provides **s** for the*

SEEK, SEEKING, SEEKS (v)
to go in search of; to ask for; to try to acquire or gain
*2 Chr 7:14 . . . pray and **s** My face and*
*2 Chr 15:2 . . . Whenever you **s** Him,*
*Prov 3:6 . . . **S** His will in all you do,*
*Prov 25:27 . . . not good to **s** honors*
*Prov 29:26 . . . Many **s** the ruler's favor,*
*Isa 55:6 . . . **S** the LORD while you can*
*Hos 10:12 . . . time to **s** the LORD,*
*Zeph 2:3 . . . **S** the LORD, all who are*
*Matt 6:33 . . . **S** the Kingdom of God above*
*Matt 7:7 . . . Keep on **s-ing**, and you*
*Matt 7:8 . . . Everyone who **s-s**, finds.*
*Luke 12:31 . . . **S** the Kingdom of God*
*Luke 19:10 . . . Son of Man came to **s** and*
*Rom 3:11 . . . no one is **s-ing** God.*
*1 Cor 7:27 . . . have a wife, do not **s** to get*
*Heb 11:6 . . . those who sincerely **s** Him.*

SELF-CONTROL (n)
restraint exercised over one's own impulses, emotions, or desires
*Prov 5:23 . . . He will die for lack of **s;***
*Prov 16:32 . . . better to have **s** than to*
*Acts 24:25 . . . righteousness and **s** and the*
*Gal 5:23 . . . gentleness, and **s.** There is no*
*1 Tim 3:2 . . . must exercise **s**, live wisely,*
*1 Tim 3:11 . . . They must exercise **s** and be*
*Titus 2:2 . . . older men to exercise **s,***
*1 Pet 1:13 . . . think clearly and exercise **s.***
*2 Pet 1:6 . . . and knowledge with **s**, and*

SELFISH (adj)
seeking or concentrating on one's own advantage, pleasure, or well-being without regard for others
*Matt 16:24 . . . turn from your **s** ways,*
*Luke 9:23 . . . turn from your **s** ways,*
*Gal 5:20 . . . of anger, **s** ambition,*
*Phil 1:17 . . . They preach with **s** ambition,*
*Jas 3:14 . . . and there is **s** ambition in*
*Jas 3:16 . . . is jealousy and **s** ambition,*

SEND, SENDING (v)
to direct, order, or request to go
see also SENT
*Isa 6:8 . . . Here I am. **S** me.*
*Isa 55:11 . . . with My word. I **s** it out,*
*Mal 3:1 . . . I am **s-ing** My messenger,*
*Matt 9:38 . . . ask Him to **s** more workers*
*Mark 1:2 . . . I am **s-ing** My messenger*
*1 Cor 1:17 . . . For Christ didn't **s** me to*

SENSE (n)
sound and prudent judgment based on a simple perception of the situation or facts; intelligence
*Prov 3:21 . . . common **s** and discernment.*
*Prov 8:14 . . . Common **s** and success*
*Prov 12:11 . . . chases fantasies has no **s.***
*Prov 15:21 . . . brings joy to those with no **s;***
*Prov 18:1 . . . they lash out at common **s.***
*Prov 24:30 . . . of one with no common **s.***

SENT (v)
see also SEND
*Exod 3:14 . . . I AM has **s** me*
*Matt 10:40 . . . the Father who **s** me.*
*Luke 10:16 . . . God, who **s** me.*
*John 3:17 . . . God **s** His Son into the*
*John 20:21 . . . As the Father has **s** Me, so*
*Rom 8:3 . . . He **s** His own Son in a*
*Rom 10:15 . . . them without being **s?***
*Gal 4:4 . . . time came, God **s** his Son,*

SEPARATE, SEPARATED, SEPARATES (v)
to set or keep apart; to sort
*Prov 17:9 . . . on it **s-s** close friends.*
*Matt 25:32 . . . a shepherd **s-s** the sheep*
*Rom 8:35 . . . Can anything ever **s** us*
*Eph 2:14 . . . of hostility that **s-d** us.*
*Col 1:21 . . . His enemies, **s-d** from Him*

SERAPHIM (n)
6-winged angels standing in the presence of God
*Isa 6:2 . . . were mighty **s**, each having*
*Isa 6:6 . . . Then one of the **s** flew to me*

SERPENT (n)
a snake or crawling reptile often associated with temptation, sin, and evil; Satan
*Gen 3:1 . . . The **s** was the shrewdest of*
*Isa 27:1 . . . **s**, the coiling, writhing **s.***
*2 Cor 11:3 . . . the cunning ways of the **s.***
*Rev 12:9 . . . the ancient **s** called the devil,*
*Rev 20:2 . . . that old **s**, who is the devil,*

SERVANT, SERVANTS (n)
one who performs tasks under the direction of another
see also SLAVE(S)
*Exod 14:31 . . . LORD and in His **s** Moses.*
*Lev 25:55 . . . They are My **s-s**, whom I*
*1 Sam 3:10 . . . Speak, Your **s** is listening.*
*2 Kgs 17:13 . . . My **s-s** the prophets.*
*Job 1:8 . . . Have you noticed My **s** Job?*
*Ps 19:13 . . . Keep Your **s** from deliberate*
*Ps 31:16 . . . your favor shine on Your **s.***
*Ps 89:3 . . . with David, My chosen **s.***
*Ps 104:4 . . . flames of fire are Your **s-s.***
*Prov 14:35 . . . king rejoices in wise **s-s***
*Prov 17:2 . . . A wise **s** will rule*
*Prov 22:7 . . . so the borrower is **s** to the*
*Prov 31:15 . . . work for her **s** girls.*
*Eccl 7:21 . . . may hear your **s** curse you.*
*Eccl 10:7 . . . seen **s-s** riding horseback*
*Isa 53:11 . . . My righteous **s** will make it*
*Isa 65:8 . . . I still have true **s-s** there.*
*Zech 3:8 . . . to bring My **s**, the Branch.*
*Mal 1:6 . . . father, and a **s** respects his*
*Matt 20:26 . . . among you must be your **s,***
*Matt 24:45 . . . faithful, sensible **s** is one*
*Luke 1:48 . . . of his lowly **s** girl, and*
*Luke 17:10 . . . We are unworthy **s-s** who*
*Luke 22:26 . . . leader should be like a **s.***
*John 12:26 . . . because My **s-s** must be*
*Rom 13:4 . . . authorities are God's **s-s,***
*1 Cor 3:5 . . . are only God's **s-s** through*
*Col 1:23 . . . God's **s** to proclaim it.*
*1 Tim 4:6 . . . be a worthy **s** of Christ*
*Heb 1:7 . . . His **s-s** like flames of fire.*
*Heb 1:14 . . . angels are only **s-s**—spirits*

SERVE, SERVED, SERVES, SERVING (v)
to meet the needs of and subject one's will to that of another
*Deut 10:12 . . . love Him and **s** Him with*
*Deut 11:13 . . . your God and **s** Him with*
*Deut 28:47 . . . If you do not **s** the LORD*
*Deut 30:17 . . . drawn away to **s** and*
*Josh 24:15 . . . family, we will **s** the LORD.*
*2 Chr 12:8 . . . between **s-ing** Me and*
*Ps 34:22 . . . redeem those who **s** Him.*
*Ps 101:6 . . . be allowed to **s** Me.*
*Ps 103:21 . . . of angels who **s** Him and do*
*Isa 38:3 . . . have **s-d** You single-mindedly*
*Dan 3:17 . . . the God whom we **s** is able to*
*Matt 4:10 . . . your God and **s** only Him.*
*Matt 6:24 . . . No one can **s** two masters.*
*Matt 20:28 . . . not to be **s-d** but to **s***
*Luke 22:27 . . . among you as one who **s-s.***
*John 12:2 . . . Martha **s-d**, and Lazarus was*
*John 12:26 . . . honor anyone who **s-s** Me.*
*Acts 17:25 . . . hands can't **s** His needs—*
*Rom 1:25 . . . worshiped and **s-d** the things*
*Rom 12:7 . . . your gift is **s-ing** others, **s***
*Rom 12:11 . . . work hard and **s** the Lord*
*Rom 13:6 . . . They are **s-ing** God in what*
*Rom 14:18 . . . If you **s** Christ with*
*Rom 16:18 . . . people are not **s-ing** Christ*
*1 Cor 16:18 . . . to all who **s** so well.*
*Gal 5:13 . . . your freedom to **s** one another*
*Col 3:24 . . . Master you are **s-ing** Christ.*
*1 Tim 5:10 . . . kind to strangers and **s-d** other*
*1 Pet 5:5 . . . all of you, **s** each other in*

SEVEN (adj)
of or relating to the number 7
*Josh 6:4 . . . around the town **s** times, with*
*Prov 6:16 . . . LORD hates—no, **s** things*
*Prov 24:16 . . . godly may trip **s** times,*
*Isa 4:1 . . . so few men will be left that **s***
*Luke 11:26 . . . spirit finds **s** other spirits*
*Rev 1:4 . . . John to the **s** churches in the*
*Rev 6:1 . . . first of the **s** seals on the*

Rev 8:2 . . . were given ***s*** *trumpets.*
Rev 10:4 . . . what the ***s*** *thunders said,*
Rev 15:7 . . . handed each of the ***s*** *angels*

SEXUAL (adj)
of, relating to, or associated with sex or the sexes; having or involving sex
Exod 22:19 . . . who has ***s*** *relations with*
Lev 18:6 . . . never have ***s*** *relations with*
Num 25:1 . . . by having ***s*** *relations with*
Matt 1:25 . . . did not have ***s*** *relations with*
Matt 15:19 . . . adultery, all ***s*** *immorality,*
Acts 15:20 . . . to idols, from ***s*** *immorality,*
1 Cor 5:1 . . . about the ***s*** *immorality going*
1 Cor 5:11 . . . yet indulges in ***s sin***
1 Cor 6:9 . . . who indulge in ***s*** *sin, or who*
1 Cor 6:18 . . . Run from ***s*** *sin! No other*
1 Cor 10:8 . . . not engage in ***s*** *immorality*
2 Cor 12:21 . . . impurity, ***s*** *immorality,*
Eph 5:3 . . . be no ***s*** *immorality, impurity,*
Col 3:5 . . . nothing to do with ***s*** *immorality,*
1 Thes 4:3 . . . stay away from all ***s sin***
2 Pet 2:10 . . . own twisted ***s*** *desire, and*
2 Pet 2:18 . . . to twisted ***s*** *desires,*
Rev 2:14 . . . and by committing ***s*** *sin.*
Rev 2:20 . . . teaches them to commit ***s*** *sin*

SHADOW, SHADOWS (n)
shelter from danger or observation; an imperfect and faint representation; partial darkness or obscurity within a part of space
Ps 17:8 . . . me in the ***s*** *of Your wings.*
Ps 36:7 . . . shelter in the ***s*** *of Your*
Ps 39:6 . . . are merely moving ***s-s,*** *and*
Ps 91:1 . . . find rest in the ***s*** *of the*
Col 2:17 . . . these rules are only ***s-s*** *of*
Heb 8:5 . . . only a copy, a ***s*** *of the real*
Heb 10:1 . . . was only a ***s,*** *a dim preview*

SHAME (n)
a condition or feeling of humiliating disgrace or disrepute; something that brings censure and reproach
Lev 19:12 . . . Do not bring ***s*** *on the name*
Ps 34:5 . . . no shadow of ***s*** *will darken*
Prov 28:7 . . . wild friends bring ***s*** *to*
Dan 12:2 . . . some to ***s*** *and everlasting*
Titus 2:5 . . . not bring ***s*** *on the word*
Heb 6:6 . . . holding him up to public ***s.***
1 Jn 2:28 . . . shrink back from Him in ***s.***

SHAMEFUL (adj)
bringing shame
Prov 18:13 . . . facts is both ***s*** *and foolish.*
Hab 2:15 . . . over their ***s*** *nakedness.*
Rom 1:24 . . . do whatever ***s*** *things their*
Rom 1:27 . . . Men did ***s*** *things with*
2 Cor 4:2 . . . We reject all ***s*** *deeds*
2 Pet 2:2 . . . teaching and ***s*** *immorality.*

SHARE (n)
a portion belonging to or due to
Deut 10:9 . . . Levites have no ***s*** *of property*
2 Kgs 2:9 . . . inherit a double ***s*** *of Your*
Matt 21:34 . . . to collect his ***s*** *of the crop.*
Rev 22:19 . . . remove that person's ***s*** *in*

SHARE, SHARED, SHARING (v)
to grant or give a share in; to partake of, use, experience, occupy, or enjoy with others; to have in common
Gen 21:10 . . . to ***s*** *the inheritance*
1 Sam 30:24 . . . We ***s*** *and* ***s*** *alike—*
Ps 41:9 . . . the one who ***s-d*** *my food,*
Luke 3:11 . . . If you have food, ***s*** *it with*
Acts 2:42 . . . fellowship, and to ***s-ing*** *in*
Acts 2:45 . . . possessions and ***s-d*** *the*
Rom 8:17 . . . we must also ***s*** *his suffering.*
Rom 11:31 . . . they, too, will ***s*** *in God's*
1 Cor 10:16 . . . aren't we ***s-ing*** *in the blood*
1 Cor 12:13 . . . we all ***s*** *the same Spirit.*
2 Cor 1:7 . . . as you ***s*** *in our sufferings,*
2 Cor 9:8 . . . left over to ***s*** *with others.*
Gal 4:30 . . . will not ***s*** *the inheritance*
Gal 6:6 . . . teachers, ***s-ing*** *all good things*
Phil 3:10 . . . suffer with Him, ***s-ing*** *in His*
Col 1:12 . . . has enabled you to ***s*** *in the*
1 Thes 2:8 . . . much that we ***s-d*** *with you*
2 Thes 2:14 . . . you can ***s*** *in the glory*
1 Tim 6:18 . . . ready to ***s*** *with others.*
Heb 6:4 . . . and ***s-d*** *in the Holy Spirit,*
Heb 12:10 . . . we might ***s*** *in His holiness.*
Heb 13:16 . . . to ***s*** *with those in need.*
Rev 3:20 . . . and we will ***s*** *a meal together*

SHEEP (n)
a small domesticated animal, representing wealth and livelihood for many Israelites; figurative of God's people
Gen 22:8 . . . God will provide a ***s*** *for*
Num 27:17 . . . not be like ***s*** *without a*
Deut 17:1 . . . defective cattle, ***s,*** *or*
1 Sam 15:14 . . . bleating of ***s*** *and goats*
Ps 44:22 . . . being slaughtered like ***s.***
Ps 78:52 . . . people like a flock of ***s,***
Ps 100:3 . . . We are His people, the ***s***
Ps 119:176 . . . wandered away like a lost ***s;***
Isa 53:7 . . . as a ***s*** *is silent before*
Jer 50:6 . . . people have been lost ***s.***
Matt 7:15 . . . disguised as harmless ***s*** *but*
Matt 9:36 . . . like ***s*** *without a shepherd.*
Matt 10:16 . . . you out as ***s*** *among wolves.*
Matt 12:11 . . . a ***s*** *that fell into a well*
Matt 25:32 . . . separates the ***s*** *from the*
John 10:3 . . . calls His own ***s*** *by name*
John 10:7 . . . I am the gate for the ***s.***
John 10:15 . . . sacrifice My life for the ***s.***
John 21:17 . . . Then feed My ***s.***
1 Pet 2:25 . . . were like ***s*** *who wandered*

SHELTER, SHELTERS (n)
something that covers or affords protection
see also REFUGE
Lev 23:34 . . . the Festival of ***S-s*** *on the*
Deut 16:16 . . . the Festival of ***S-s.***
Ps 9:9 . . . LORD is a ***s*** *for the*
Ps 31:20 . . . hide them in the ***s*** *of Your*
Ps 36:7 . . . All humanity finds ***s*** *in the*
Ps 61:4 . . . safe beneath the ***s*** *of Your*
Isa 4:6 . . . will be a ***s*** *from daytime heat*
Isa 32:2 . . . be like a ***s*** *from the wind*
Isa 58:7 . . . give ***s*** *to the homeless.*
Zech 14:16 . . . the Festival of ***S-s.***

SHEPHERD, SHEPHERDS (n)
a person who tends sheep; figurative of political and religious leaders, especially those who care for God's people
Gen 48:15 . . . has been my ***s*** *all my life,*
Gen 49:24 . . . by the ***S,*** *the Rock of Israel.*
Num 27:17 . . . be like sheep without a ***s.***
2 Sam 7:7 . . . tribal leaders, the ***s-s*** *of My*
1 Kgs 22:17 . . . like sheep without a ***s.***
Ps 23:1 . . . The LORD is my ***s;***
Ps 28:9 . . . Lead them like a ***s,*** *and*
Isa 40:11 . . . feed His flock like a ***s.***
Jer 23:1 . . . My people—the ***s-s*** *of My*
Jer 31:10 . . . as a ***s*** *does his flock.*
Ezek 34:5 . . . scattered without a ***s,*** *and*
Ezek 34:8 . . . you were My ***s-s,*** *you didn't*
Ezek 34:12 . . . like a ***s*** *looking for his*
Zech 11:9 . . . won't be your ***s*** *any longer.*
Zech 13:7 . . . Strike down the ***s,*** *and*
Matt 2:6 . . . will be the ***s*** *for My people*
Matt 9:36 . . . like sheep without a ***s.***
Matt 26:31 . . . God will strike the ***S,***
John 10:11 . . . I am the good ***s.***
Acts 20:28 . . . Feed and ***s*** *God's flock—*
Heb 13:20 . . . Jesus, the great ***S*** *of the*
Jude 12 . . . are like shameless ***s-s*** *who care*
Rev 7:17 . . . will be their ***S.*** *He will lead*

SHIELD (n)
a broad piece of defensive armor carried on the arm; one that protects or defends
2 Sam 22:3 . . . He is my ***s,*** *the power that*
2 Sam 22:36 . . . given me Your ***s*** *of victory;*
Ps 3:3 . . . LORD, are a ***s*** *around me;*
Ps 5:12 . . . them with Your ***s*** *of love.*
Ps 7:10 . . . God is my ***s,*** *saving those*
Ps 18:2 . . . He is my ***s,*** *the power that*
Ps 28:7 . . . LORD is my strength and ***s.***
Ps 33:20 . . . is our help and our ***s.***
Ps 35:2 . . . armor, and take up Your ***s.***
Ps 84:11 . . . God is our sun and our ***s.***
Ps 119:114 . . . are my refuge and my ***s;***
Ps 144:2 . . . He is my ***s,*** *and I take refuge*
Prov 2:7 . . . He is a ***s*** *to those who walk*
Eph 6:16 . . . hold up the ***s*** *of faith*

SHINE, SHINES, SHINING (v)
to emit rays of light; to be eminent, conspicuous, or distinguished; to have a bright, glowing appearance
Ps 37:6 . . . of Your cause will ***s*** *like*
Ps 50:2 . . . God ***s-s*** *in glorious radiance.*
Ps 112:4 . . . Light ***s-s*** *in the darkness for*
Ps 118:27 . . . LORD is God, ***s-ing*** *upon us.*
Isa 60:1 . . . Let your light ***s*** *for all*
Ezek 1:27 . . . like a burning flame, ***s-ing***
Dan 2:31 . . . you a huge, ***s-ing*** *statue of a*
Dan 12:3 . . . righteousness will ***s*** *like*
Matt 13:43 . . . the righteous will ***s*** *like*
John 1:5 . . . The light ***s-s*** *in the darkness,*
Rom 13:12 . . . put on the ***s-ing*** *armor of*
2 Cor 4:6 . . . has made this light ***s*** *in*
Phil 2:15 . . . of God, ***s-ing*** *like bright lights*

SHOULDERS (n)
the place on the human body where the arm is joined to the trunk
Isa 9:6 . . . government will rest on His ***s.***
Luke 15:5 . . . carry it home on His ***s.***

SHOUT, SHOUTED, SHOUTING (v)
to utter a loud cry or in a loud voice
Job 38:7 . . . all the angels ***s-ed*** *for joy?*
Ps 95:1 . . . Let us ***s*** *joyfully to*
Ps 100:1 . . . ***S*** *with joy to the LORD,*
Isa 12:6 . . . people of Jerusalem ***s*** *His*
Isa 40:3 . . . someone ***s-ing,*** *"Clear the way*
Isa 40:9 . . . news, ***s*** *from the mountaintops!*
Isa 42:2 . . . He will not ***s*** *or raise His*
Zech 9:9 . . . people of Zion! ***S*** *in triumph,*
Matt 3:3 . . . a voice ***s-ing*** *in the wilderness,*
Matt 10:27 . . . ***s*** *from the housetops for all*

SHOW, SHOWED, SHOWN, SHOWS (v)
to cause or permit to be seen; to point out; to reveal or demonstrate; to bestow
Exod 33:18 . . . Then ***s*** *me Your glorious*
2 Sam 22:26 . . . To the faithful You ***s***
Neh 9:19 . . . pillar of fire ***s-ed*** *them the*
Ps 4:6 . . . Who will ***s*** *us better times?*
Ps 16:11 . . . You will ***s*** *me the way*
Ps 119:132 . . . Come and ***s*** *me Your*
Prov 3:6 . . . He will ***s*** *you which path*
Prov 24:23 . . . wrong to ***s*** *favoritism*
Eccl 9:1 . . . God will ***s*** *them favor.*
Isa 30:18 . . . so He can ***s*** *you His love*
Hos 6:6 . . . I want you to ***s*** *love, not*
Zech 7:9 . . . Judge fairly, and ***s*** *mercy*
Luke 24:40 . . . ***s-ed*** *them His hands and His*
Acts 2:28 . . . You have ***s-n*** *me the way*
Acts 10:34 . . . that God ***s-s*** *no favoritism.*
Rom 3:20 . . . The law simply ***s-s*** *us how*
Rom 3:21 . . . But now God has ***s-n*** *us a way*
Rom 5:8 . . . God ***s-ed*** *His great love for us*
Rom 9:22 . . . the right to ***s*** *His anger*

*Eph 2:7 . . . as **s-n** in all He has done*
*Jas 2:18 . . . I will **s** you my faith*
*1 Jn 4:9 . . . God **s-ed** how much He loved*

SICK (adj)
affected with disease or ill health; lacking vigor
*Ps 41:3 . . . when they are **s** and restores*
*Prov 13:12 . . . deferred makes the heart **s,***
*Matt 9:12 . . . need a doctor—**s** people do.*
*Matt 10:8 . . . Heal the **s,** raise the dead,*
*Matt 25:36 . . . I was **s,** and you cared for*
*Mark 3:10 . . . all the **s** people eagerly*
*1 Cor 11:30 . . . many of you are weak and **s***
*Jas 5:14 . . . Are any of you **s?***

SICKNESS, SICKNESSES (n)
a disordered, weakened, or unsound condition; illness
*Matt 4:24 . . . whatever their **s** or disease,*
*Matt 8:17 . . . He took our **s-es** and removed*

SIGN, SIGNS (n)
something indicating the presence or existence of something else; something material or external that stands for or signifies something spiritual
*Gen 9:12 . . . you a **s** of My covenant*
*Gen 17:11 . . . your foreskin as a **s** of*
*Ps 105:27 . . . performed miraculous **s-s***
*Isa 55:13 . . . be an everlasting **s** of*
*Dan 6:27 . . . He performs miraculous **s-s** and*
*Matt 12:38 . . . a miraculous **s** to prove*
*Matt 24:3 . . . What **s** will signal your*
*Matt 24:30 . . . the **s** that the Son of Man*
*Mark 16:17 . . . These miraculous **s-s** will*
*Luke 11:29 . . . them is the **s** of Jonah.*
*John 3:2 . . . Your miraculous **s-s** are*
*John 20:30 . . . do many other miraculous **s-s***
*1 Cor 14:22 . . . in tongues is a **s,** not for*
*2 Cor 12:12 . . . did many **s-s** and wonders*
*2 Thes 2:9 . . . counterfeit power and **s-s***

SILENT (adj)
mute, speechless; still
*Ps 30:12 . . . praises to You and not be **s.***
*Isa 53:7 . . . as a sheep is **s** before the*
*Isa 62:1 . . . Jerusalem, I cannot remain **s.***
*Hab 2:20 . . . the earth be **s** before Him.*
*Acts 8:32 . . . And as a lamb is **s** before*
*Acts 18:9 . . . Speak out! Don't be **s!***
*1 Cor 14:34 . . . Women should be **s** during*

SILVER (n)
a silvery-white metal valued next to gold, capable of a high polish; coin made of silver
*Ps 66:10 . . . have purified us like **s.***
*Prov 3:14 . . . is more profitable than **s,***
*Prov 8:10 . . . instruction rather than **s,***
*Prov 22:1 . . . is better than **s** or gold.*
*Isa 48:10 . . . but not as **s** is refined.*
*Zech 11:12 . . . wages thirty pieces of **s.***
*Zech 13:9 . . . refine them like **s** and*
*Matt 25:15 . . . two bags of **s** to another,*
*Matt 26:15 . . . gave him thirty pieces of **s.***
*Luke 7:41 . . . 500 pieces of **s** to one*
*Acts 3:6 . . . don't have any **s** or gold*
*1 Cor 3:12 . . . materials—gold, **s,** jewels,*

SIN, SINS (n)
moral evil; transgression of or rebellion against God's laws
*Gen 4:7 . . . **S** is crouching at the door,*
*Lev 5:5 . . . ways, you must confess your **s.***
*Num 32:23 . . . be sure that your **s** will find*
*Deut 24:16 . . . to death for the **s-s** of their*
*Ps 19:13 . . . servant from deliberate **s-s!***
*Ps 32:1 . . . whose **s** is put out of sight!*
*Ps 38:18 . . . I confess my **s-s;** I am deeply*
*Ps 51:1 . . . blot out the stain of my **s-s.***
*Ps 51:2 . . . Purify me from my **s.***
*Ps 65:3 . . . we are overwhelmed by our **s-s,***
*Ps 79:9 . . . Save us and forgive our **s-s***
*Ps 103:12 . . . removed our **s-s** as far from*
*Prov 5:22 . . . held captive by his own **s-s;***
*Prov 10:19 . . . Too much talk leads to **s.***
*Prov 14:21 . . . **s** to belittle one's neighbor;*
*Prov 17:19 . . . who loves to quarrel loves **s;***
*Prov 28:13 . . . who conceal their **s-s** will*
*Prov 29:22 . . . commits all kinds of **s.***
*Isa 1:18 . . . your **s-s** are like scarlet,*
*Isa 53:6 . . . laid on Him the **s-s** of us all.*
*Isa 59:2 . . . Because of your **s-s,** He has*
*Jer 31:30 . . . die for their own **s-s**—*
*Jer 31:34 . . . again remember their **s-s.***
*Ezek 18:19 . . . pay for the parent's **s-s?***
*Matt 1:21 . . . save His people from their **s-s.***
*Matt 6:12 . . . forgive us our **s-s,** as we*
*Matt 26:28 . . . to forgive the **s-s** of many.*
*Mark 3:29 . . . This is a **s** with eternal*
*Luke 5:24 . . . on earth to forgive **s-s.***
*John 1:29 . . . takes away the **s** of the world!*
*John 20:23 . . . forgive anyone's **s-s,** they*
*Acts 2:38 . . . repent of your **s-s,** turn to*
*Rom 4:25 . . . because of our **s-s,** and He*
*Rom 6:2 . . . we have died to **s,** how can*
*Rom 6:11 . . . the power of **s** and alive to*
*Rom 6:23 . . . the wages of **s** is death,*
*Rom 7:7 . . . law that showed me my **s.***
*Rom 7:25 . . . nature I am a slave to **s.***
*1 Cor 6:18 . . . is a **s** against your own body.*
*1 Cor 15:3 . . . died for our **s-s,** just as*
*1 Cor 15:56 . . . the law gives **s** its power.*
*Gal 1:4 . . . gave His life for our **s-s,** just*
*Gal 6:1 . . . believer is overcome by some **s,***
*Eph 2:5 . . . were dead because of our **s-s,***
*1 Tim 5:22 . . . share in the **s-s** of others.*
*Heb 2:17 . . . would take away the **s-s** of*
*Heb 9:28 . . . to take away the **s-s** of many*
*Heb 10:12 . . . sacrifice for **s-s,** good for*
*Heb 12:1 . . . the **s** that so easily trips*
*Jas 1:15 . . . when **s** is allowed to grow,*
*Jas 4:17 . . . is **s** to know what you ought*
*Jas 5:16 . . . Confess your **s-s** to each other*
*1 Pet 2:24 . . . carried our **s-s** in His body*
*1 Pet 3:18 . . . suffered for our **s-s** once for*
*1 Jn 1:8 . . . claim we have no **s,** we are*
*1 Jn 1:9 . . . to forgive us our **s-s** and to*
*1 Jn 2:1 . . . if anyone does **s,** we have*
*1 Jn 3:5 . . . take away our **s-s,** and*
*1 Jn 3:5 . . . there is no **s** in Him.*
*1 Jn 5:16 . . . a **s** that leads to death,*
*Rev 1:5 . . . from our **s-s** by shedding His*

SIN, SINNED, SINNING, SINS (v)
to commit an offense or fault against God; to break God's law
*Exod 20:20 . . . will keep you from **s-ning!***
*2 Sam 12:13 . . . I have **s-ned** against the*
*2 Chr 6:37 . . . We have **s-ned,** done evil,*
*Job 1:5 . . . my children have **s-ned***
*Ps 51:4 . . . and You alone, have I **s-ned;***
*Ps 119:11 . . . I might not **s** against You.*
*Jer 14:20 . . . all have **s-ned** against You.*
*Dan 9:5 . . . have **s-ned** and done wrong.*
*Mark 9:43 . . . causes you to **s,** cut it off.*
*Luke 15:18 . . . I have **s-ned** against both*
*Luke 17:3 . . . another believer **s-s,** rebuke*
*John 8:7 . . . who has never **s-ned** throw*
*John 8:11 . . . Go and **s** no more.*
*Rom 1:30 . . . invent new ways of **s-ning,***
*Rom 3:23 . . . everyone has **s-ned;** we all*
*Rom 5:12 . . . When Adam **s-ned, s** entered*
*Rom 14:23 . . . is not right, you are **s-ning.***
*1 Cor 15:34 . . . is right, and stop **s-ning.***
*Heb 4:15 . . . we do, yet He did not **s.***
*Heb 10:26 . . . deliberately continue **s-ning***
*1 Pet 2:22 . . . He never **s-ned,** nor ever*
*1 Jn 1:10 . . . we have not **s-ned,** we are*
*1 Jn 3:6 . . . who keeps on **s-ning** does not*
*1 Jn 5:18 . . . not make a practice of **s-ning,***

SINFUL (adj)
tainted with, marked by, or full of sin; wicked
*Lev 5:1 . . . is **s** to refuse to testify,*
*1 Sam 15:23 . . . is as **s** as witchcraft,*
*Luke 11:13 . . . So if you **s** people know*
*Rom 5:20 . . . could see how **s** they were.*
*Rom 7:5 . . . harvest of **s** deeds, resulting*
*Rom 7:18 . . . is, in my **s** nature.*
*Rom 7:25 . . . because of my **s** nature I am*
*Rom 8:4 . . . follow our **s** nature but*
*Rom 8:13 . . . deeds of your **s** nature,*
*Gal 5:13 . . . to satisfy your **s** nature.*
*Col 2:11 . . . away of your **s** nature.*

SING (v)
to produce musical tones by means of the voice
*Exod 15:1 . . . I will **s** to the LORD,*
*Ps 5:11 . . . let them **s** joyful praises*
*Ps 13:6 . . . I will **s** to the LORD*
*Ps 47:6 . . . to our King, **s** praises!*
*Ps 51:14 . . . I will joyfully **s** of*
*Ps 63:7 . . . my helper, I **s** for joy*
*Ps 69:30 . . . praise God's name with **s-ing,***
*Ps 89:1 . . . I will **s** of the*
*Ps 95:1 . . . let us **s** to the LORD!*
*Ps 96:1 . . . **S** a new song to the LORD!*
*Ps 98:4 . . . praise and **s** for joy!*
*Ps 100:2 . . . Come before Him, **s-ing** with*
*Ps 101:1 . . . I will **s** of Your love*
*Ps 108:1 . . . can **s** Your praises with all*
*Ps 147:1 . . . How good to **s** praises to*
*Isa 35:10 . . . enter Jerusalem **s-ing***
*Jer 16:9 . . . to the happy **s-ing** and laughter*
*Acts 16:25 . . . praying and **s-ing** hymns*
*1 Cor 14:15 . . . I will also **s** in words*
*1 Cor 14:26 . . . one will **s,** another will*
*Col 3:16 . . . **S** psalms and hymns and*
*Rev 15:3 . . . And they were **s-ing** the song*

SINNER, SINNERS (n)
those guilty of sin
*Ps 51:5 . . . I was born a **s**—yes,*
*Prov 1:10 . . . if **s-s** entice you, turn*
*Prov 23:17 . . . Don't envy **s-s,** but*
*Eccl 9:18 . . . one **s** can destroy much that*
*Isa 59:12 . . . we know what **s-s** we are.*
*Isa 64:5 . . . We are constant **s-s;** how*
*Matt 9:13 . . . who know they are **s-s.***
*Luke 5:8 . . . I'm too much of a **s** to be*
*Luke 15:7 . . . over one lost **s** who repents*
*Luke 18:13 . . . to me, for I am a **s.***
*Rom 4:5 . . . faith in God who forgives **s-s.***
*Rom 5:6 . . . time and died for us **s-s.***
*1 Tim 1:15 . . . into the world to save **s-s***
*Jas 5:20 . . . whoever brings the **s** back*
*1 Pet 3:18 . . . he died for **s-s** to bring*

SLANDER (n)
the utterance of false charges or misrepresentations which defame and damage another's reputation
*Matt 15:19 . . . theft, lying, and **s.***
*Mark 7:22 . . . desires, envy, **s,** pride,*
*2 Cor 12:20 . . . selfishness, **s,** gossip,*
*Eph 4:31 . . . harsh words, and **s,** as*
*Col 3:8 . . . malicious behavior, **s,***

SLANDER, SLANDERED, SLANDERING (v)
to utter slander; to malign or defame
*Prov 10:18 . . . **s-ing** others makes you a*
*1 Tim 3:11 . . . must not **s** others.*
*2 Tim 3:3 . . . they will **s** others*
*Titus 2:3 . . . They must not **s** others*
*Titus 3:2 . . . They must not **s** anyone*
*2 Pet 2:2 . . . way of truth will be **s-ed.***

SLAUGHTER (n)
the butchering of livestock for market or sacrifice
Isa 53:7 . . . led like a lamb to the ***s.***
Jer 11:19 . . . lamb being led to the ***s.***
Acts 8:32 . . . led like a sheep to the ***s.***

SLAUGHTER, SLAUGHTERED (v)
to discredit, defeat, or demolish completely; to kill in a bloody or violent manner
Hos 6:5 . . . to ***s*** *you with my words,*
Rev 5:6 . . . looked as if it had been ***s-ed,***
Rev 5:12 . . . Lamb who was ***s-ed****—to receive*

SLAVE, SLAVES (n)
a person bound in servitude; one who has lost his liberty and has no rights
see also SERVANT(S)
Matt 20:27 . . . must become Your ***s.***
John 8:34 . . . who sins is a ***s*** *of sin.*
John 15:15 . . . longer call you ***s-s,*** *because*
Rom 1:1 . . . is from Paul, a ***s*** *of Christ*
Rom 6:6 . . . are no longer ***s-s*** *to sin.*
Rom 6:16 . . . you become the ***s*** *of whatever*
Rom 6:22 . . . and have become ***s-s*** *of God.*
Rom 7:23 . . . makes me a ***s*** *to the sin*
1 Cor 6:12 . . . not become a ***s*** *to anything.*
1 Cor 9:19 . . . have become a ***s*** *to all*
1 Cor 12:13 . . . some are ***s-s,*** *and some*
Gal 3:28 . . . Jew or Gentile, ***s*** *or free,*
Gal 4:7 . . . no longer a ***s*** *but God's own*
Gal 4:8 . . . you were ***s-s*** *to so-called gods*
Gal 4:30 . . . rid of the ***s*** *and her son,*
Eph 6:5 . . . ***S-s,*** *obey your earthly masters*
Phil 2:7 . . . position of a ***s*** *and was born*
Col 3:11 . . . barbaric, uncivilized, ***s,*** *or*
Col 4:1 . . . be just and fair to your ***s-s.***
1 Tim 1:10 . . . or are ***s*** *traders, liars,*
Titus 3:3 . . . became ***s-s*** *to many lusts*
Phlm 16 . . . no longer like a ***s*** *to you.*
2 Pet 2:19 . . . For you are a ***s*** *to whatever*

SLAVERY (n)
submission to a dominating influence; the practice of slaveholding
Exod 2:23 . . . under their burden of ***s.***
Rom 6:19 . . . the illustration of ***s*** *to help*

SLEEP (n)
natural or induced state of rest; a state of lazy inactivity
Gen 2:21 . . . man to fall into a deep ***s.***
Gen 15:12 . . . Abram fell into a deep ***s,***
Prov 20:13 . . . If you love ***s,*** *you will*
Prov 23:21 . . . too much ***s*** *clothes them*
Rom 11:8 . . . has put them into a deep ***s.***

SLEEP, SLEEPING, SLEEPS (v)
to rest in a state of natural unconsciousness
Gen 28:11 . . . against and lay down to ***s.***
Ps 4:8 . . . peace I will lie down and ***s,***
Ps 121:4 . . . Israel never slumbers or ***s-s.***
Prov 6:9 . . . how long will you ***s?***
Eccl 5:12 . . . who work hard ***s*** *well,*
Mark 13:36 . . . find you ***s-ing*** *when He*

SLOTHFUL(NESS) (KJV)
Prov 15:19 . . . a ***lazy*** *person's way is blocked*
Prov 21:25 . . . the ***lazy*** *will come to ruin, for*
Eccl 10:18 . . . ***Laziness*** *leads to a sagging roof*
Rom 12:11 . . . Never be ***lazy,*** *but work hard*
Heb 6:12 . . . ***spiritually dull and indifferent***

SLUGGARD (KJV)
Prov 6:6 . . . a lesson from the ants, you ***lazybones***
Prov 10:26 . . . ***Lazy people*** *irritate their employers*
Prov 13:4 . . . ***Lazy people*** *want much but*
Prov 20:4 . . . ***Those too lazy*** *to plow*
Prov 26:16 . . . ***Lazy people*** *consider themselves smarter*

SMILE (v)
to bestow approval
Num 6:25 . . . May the LORD ***s*** *on you and*
Ps 4:6 . . . Let Your face ***s*** *on us,* LORD.
Ps 67:1 . . . May His face ***s*** *with favor on*

SMOKE (n)
the gaseous products of burning materials
Exod 19:18 . . . The ***s*** *billowed into the sky*
Isa 6:4 . . . building was filled with ***s.***
Joel 2:30 . . . and fire and columns of ***s.***
Acts 2:19 . . . and fire and clouds of ***s.***
Rev 9:2 . . . air turned dark from the ***s.***
Rev 15:8 . . . filled with ***s*** *from God's*

SNAKE, SNAKES (n)
any of numerous limbless scaled reptiles; a worthless or treacherous person
Num 21:8 . . . replica of a poisonous ***s*** *and*
Prov 23:32 . . . it bites like a poisonous ***s;***
Matt 10:16 . . . shrewd as ***s-s*** *and harmless*
Luke 3:7 . . . You brood of ***s-s!*** *Who warned*
John 3:14 . . . lifted up the bronze ***s*** *on a*
Rom 3:13 . . . ***S*** *venom drips from their*

SNOW (n)
precipitation in the form of small white ice crystals
Prov 25:13 . . . refresh like ***s*** *in summer.*
Isa 1:18 . . . will make them as white as ***s.***
Dan 7:9 . . . clothing was as white as ***s,***

SODOM (n)
a city at the southern end of the Dead Sea destroyed because of its wickedness
Gen 13:12 . . . to a place near ***S*** *and settled*
Gen 19:24 . . . the sky on ***S*** *and Gomorrah.*
Isa 1:9 . . . have been wiped out like ***S,***
Luke 10:12 . . . you, even wicked ***S*** *will be*
Rom 9:29 . . . have been wiped out like ***S,***
*Rev 11:8 . . . figuratively called "****S****"*

SON, SONS (n)
a parent's male child or descendant further removed; spiritual heir (of Christ)
see also CHILD(REN)
Gen 17:19 . . . birth to a ***s*** *for you.*
Gen 21:10 . . . slave-woman and her ***s.***
Gen 22:2 . . . Take your ***s,*** *your only*
Ruth 4:15 . . . better to you than seven ***s-s!***
Ps 2:7 . . . You are my ***s.*** *Today I have*
Isa 7:14 . . . birth to a ***s*** *and will call*
Dan 7:13 . . . I saw someone like a ***s*** *of man*
Hos 11:1 . . . I called My ***s*** *out of Egypt.*
Joel 2:28 . . . ***s-s*** *and daughters will*
Matt 1:21 . . . will have a ***s,*** *and you are*
Matt 13:55 . . . the carpenter's ***s,*** *and we*
Luke 2:7 . . . first child, a ***s.*** *She wrapped*
Luke 15:20 . . . ran to his ***s,*** *embraced him,*
2 Cor 6:18 . . . be my ***s-s*** *and daughters,*
Gal 4:30 . . . slave and her ***s,*** *for the son*

SONG, SONGS (n)
a short musical composition of words and music; the act of singing
Exod 15:2 . . . my strength and my ***s;***
Job 35:10 . . . who gives ***s-s*** *in the night?*
Ps 40:3 . . . given me a new ***s*** *to sing,*
Ps 63:5 . . . praise You with ***s-s*** *of joy.*
Ps 96:1 . . . Sing a new ***s*** *to the* LORD!
Ps 119:54 . . . theme of My ***s-s*** *wherever*
Ps 137:3 . . . of those ***s-s*** *of Jerusalem!*
Ps 149:1 . . . Sing to the LORD *a new* ***s.***
Isa 49:13 . . . Burst into ***s,*** *O mountains!*
Isa 55:12 . . . and hills will burst into ***s,***
Rev 5:9 . . . they sang a new ***s*** *with these*
Rev 15:3 . . . God, and the ***s*** *of the Lamb:*

SORCERER, SORCERERS (n)
a person who practices sorcery
Exodus 7:11 . . . his own wise men and ***s-s,***
Acts 8:9 . . . a ***s*** *there for many years,*
Acts 13:6 . . . a Jewish ***s,*** *a false prophet*
Rev 22:15 . . . the dogs—the ***s,*** *the sexually*

SORCERY (n)
the use of power gained from the assistance or control of evil spirits, especially for divining
Gal 5:20 . . . idolatry, ***s,*** *hostility, quarreling,*

SORROW, SORROWS (n)
deep distress, sadness, or regret
Ps 116:3 . . . I saw only trouble and ***s.***
Isa 65:14 . . . will cry in ***s*** *and despair.*
Jer 31:12 . . . all their ***s-s*** *will be gone.*
Ezek 34:2 . . . What ***s*** *awaits you*
Amos 5:18 . . . What ***s*** *awaits you*
Matt 18:7 . . . What ***s*** *awaits the*
Matt 23:13 . . . What ***s*** *awaits you*
Luke 11:46 . . . what ***s*** *also awaits*
Rom 9:2 . . . with bitter ***s*** *and unending*
2 Cor 7:10 . . . the kind of ***s*** *God wants*
Eph 4:30 . . . do not bring ***s*** *to God's Holy*
1 Tim 6:10 . . . themselves with many ***s-s.***
Heb 13:17 . . . with joy and not with ***s.***
Jude 11 . . . What ***s*** *awaits them!*
Rev 21:4 . . . more death or ***s*** *or crying*

SOUL, SOULS (n)
the inner life of a human being, the seat of emotions, and the center of human personality
Deut 6:5 . . . heart, all your ***s,*** *and all*
Deut 28:65 . . . fail, and your ***s*** *to despair.*
Deut 30:6 . . . your heart and ***s*** *and so you*
Josh 22:5 . . . all your heart and all your ***s.***
2 Kgs 23:25 . . . heart and ***s*** *and strength,*
Prov 3:22 . . . for they will refresh your ***s.***
Prov 16:24 . . . sweet to the ***s*** *and healthy*
Jer 6:16 . . . you will find rest for your ***s-s.***
Matt 10:28 . . . can destroy both ***s*** *and body*
Matt 11:29 . . . you will find rest for your ***s-s.***
Matt 22:37 . . . all your heart, all your ***s,***
Mark 8:37 . . . worth more than your ***s?***
Mark 12:30 . . . heart, all your ***s,*** *all your*
Luke 16:23 . . . his ***s*** *went to the place of*
Luke 21:19 . . . firm, you will win your ***s-s.***
John 12:27 . . . my ***s*** *is deeply troubled.*
Heb 4:12 . . . cutting between ***s*** *and spirit,*

SOW(ED), SOWING (KJV)
Lev 25:3 . . . you may ***plant*** *your fields*
Ps 126:5 . . . Those who ***plant*** *in tears*
Matt 13:4 . . . As he ***scattered*** *them across*
Luke 12:24 . . . the ravens. They don't ***plant*** *or*
Luke 19:21 . . . crops you didn't ***plant***

SOWER (KJV)
Isa 55:10 . . . producing seed for the ***farmer*** *and*
Jer 50:16 . . . all ***those who plant crops***
Matt 13:18 . . . parable about the ***farmer planting seeds***
2 Cor 9:10 . . . provides seed for the ***farmer***

SPANK (n)
to strike especially on the buttocks with the open hand
Prov 23:13 . . . won't die if you ***s*** *them.*

SPARE, SPARED, SPARES (v)
to hold back from destroying, punishing, or harming; to have left over or as margin; to relieve of the necessity of doing or undergoing something
Esth 7:3 . . . lives of My people will be ***s-d.***
Prov 13:24 . . . Those who ***s*** *the rod of*
Isa 54:2 . . . your home, and ***s*** *no expense!*
Mal 3:17 . . . as a father ***s-s*** *an obedient*
Rom 8:32 . . . did not ***s*** *even His own Son*
Rom 11:21 . . . if God did not ***s*** *the original*
2 Pet 2:4 . . . God did not ***s*** *even the angels*
2 Pet 2:5 . . . And God did not ***s*** *the ancient*

SPEAK, SPEAKING, SPEAKS (v)
to express thoughts, opinions, or feelings orally; to talk
*Deut 18:22 . . . If the prophet **s-s** in the*
*Ps 15:3 . . . or **s** evil of their friends.*
*Ps 78:2 . . . will **s** to you in a parable.*
*Isa 3:8 . . . because they **s** out against*
*Isa 32:4 . . . stammer will **s** out plainly.*
*Matt 12:34 . . . men like you **s** what is good*
*Matt 15:18 . . . the words you **s** come from*
*Acts 2:11 . . . hear these people **s-ing** in our*
*1 Cor 14:2 . . . ability to **s** in tongues,*
*1 Cor 14:19 . . . I would rather **s** five*
*1 Pet 3:16 . . . if people **s** against you,*

SPEECH (n)
the communication or expression of thoughts in spoken words
*Prov 16:23 . . . a wise mind comes wise **s;***
*Prov 22:11 . . . gracious **s** will have the king*
*Prov 25:15 . . . soft **s** can break bones.*
*Zeph 3:9 . . . I will purify the **s** of all*
*1 Cor 1:17 . . . not with clever **s,** for*

SPEND, SPENT (v)
to use up or pay out; to exhaust or wear out
*Prov 21:20 . . . but fools **s** whatever they*
*Isa 55:2 . . . Why **s** your money on food that*
*Mark 5:26 . . . she had **s-t** everything she had*
*2 Cor 12:15 . . . I will gladly **s** myself*

SPIRIT, SPIRITS (n)
"wind" or "breath"; a supernatural being; an attitude, mood, or disposition; an evil presence that can possess or influence a person; invisible, nonmaterial part of humans (as opposed to body or flesh)
*Deut 34:9 . . . full of the **s** of wisdom,*
*1 Sam 16:14 . . . a tormenting **s** that filled*
*2 Kgs 2:9 . . . double share of Your **s** and*
*Ps 31:5 . . . I entrust my **s** into Your*
*Ps 34:18 . . . those whose **s-s** are crushed.*
*Ps 51:10 . . . Renew a loyal **s** within me.*
*Ps 51:17 . . . You desire is a broken **s.***
*Ezek 11:19 . . . put a new **s** within them.*
*Mark 5:12 . . . pigs," the **s-s** begged.*
*2 Cor 5:3 . . . not be **s-s** without bodies.*
*Eph 6:12 . . . and against evil **s-s** in the*
*2 Tim 1:7 . . . not given us a **s** of fear*
*1 Pet 3:4 . . . gentle and quiet **s,** which*

SPIRITUAL (adj)
having to do with the spirit, usually God's Spirit
*Jon 4:11 . . . living in **s** darkness, not*
*Rom 7:14 . . . for it is **s** and good.*
*1 Cor 2:14 . . . who are **s** can understand*
*1 Cor 14:37 . . . think you are **s,** you should*
*1 Cor 15:44 . . . there are also **s** bodies.*
*Eph 5:19 . . . and hymns and **s** songs among*
*1 Pet 2:5 . . . you offer **s** sacrifices that*

SPLENDOR (n)
great brightness or luster; magnificence
*2 Chr 20:21 . . . Him for His holy **s.***
*Ps 29:2 . . . the LORD in the **s** of*
*Ps 145:5 . . . majestic, glorious **s** and*
*Prov 20:29 . . . experience is the **s** of*
*Isa 33:17 . . . see the king in all his **s,***
*Hab 3:3 . . . brilliant **s** fills the heavens,*

STAFF (n)
a long stick used for walking or a weapon, often a symbol of authority and protection
see also ROD
*Gen 49:10 . . . nor the ruler's **s** from his*
*Exod 7:12 . . . then Aaron's **s** swallowed up*
*Num 17:6 . . . Aaron, brought Moses a **s.***
*2 Kgs 4:29 . . . travel; take my **s** and go!*
*Ps 23:4 . . . Your rod and Your **s** protect*

STAND, STANDING, STANDS (v)
to remain stationary; to remain erect; to maintain one's position; to endure successfully
see also STOOD
*Exod 3:5 . . . you are **s-ing** on holy ground.*
*Josh 5:15 . . . where you are **s-ing** is holy.*
*Josh 10:12 . . . Let the sun **s** still*
*2 Chr 20:17 . . . then **s** still and*
*Ps 24:3 . . . Who may **s** in His holy*
*Ps 33:11 . . . LORD's plans **s** firm*
*Ps 76:7 . . . Who can **s** before You*
*Ps 119:89 . . . word, O LORD, **s-s** firm*
*Prov 12:7 . . . family of the godly **s-s** firm.*
*Isa 40:8 . . . word of our God **s-s** forever.*
*Mal 3:2 . . . be able to **s** and face Him*
*Luke 6:48 . . . the house, it **s-s** firm because*
*Rom 14:10 . . . all **s** before the judgment*
*1 Cor 10:12 . . . think you are **s-ing** strong,*
*1 Cor 10:13 . . . to be more than you can **s.***
*2 Cor 5:10 . . . we must all **s** before Christ*
*Eph 6:14 . . . **S** your ground, putting on the*
*Phil 1:27 . . . that you are **s-ing** side by side,*
*2 Tim 2:19 . . . But God's truth **s-s** firm like*
*1 Pet 5:9 . . . **S** firm against him, and*
*Rev 3:20 . . . I **s** at the door and knock.*

STANDING (n)
a position or condition
*Rom 8:33 . . . us right **s** with himself.*

STAR, STARS (n)
a natural luminous body visible in the sky especially at night; sometimes symbolic for angels
*Gen 1:16 . . . He also made the **s-s.***
*Num 24:17 . . . A **s** will rise from Jacob;*
*Job 38:7 . . . morning **s-s** sang together*
*Isa 14:12 . . . O shining **s,** son of the*
*Dan 12:3 . . . shine like the **s-s** forever.*
*Matt 2:2 . . . We saw his **s** as it rose,*
*2 Pet 1:19 . . . the Morning **S** shines in*
*Rev 2:28 . . . also give them the morning **s!***
*Rev 22:16 . . . I am the bright morning **s.***

STATUTES (KJV)
*Exod 15:26 . . . keeping all His **decrees***
*Deut 4:40 . . . If you obey all the **decrees** and*
*1 Kgs 3:14 . . . **decrees** and My commands*
*Ps 19:8 . . . The **commandments** of the LORD*
*Ps 119:112 . . . to keep Your **decrees***

STEDFAST (KJV)
*Ps 78:37 . . . They did not **keep** His covenant*
*1 Cor 15:58 . . . be **strong** and immovable.*
*Heb 3:14 . . . if we are **faithful** to the end,*
*1 Pet 5:9 . . . and be **strong** in your faith*

STEAL, STEALING, STEALS (v)
to take the property of another wrongfully
*Exod 20:15 . . . You must not **s.***
*Lev 19:11 . . . Do not **s.***
*Deut 5:19 . . . You must not **s.***
*Prov 28:24 . . . who **s-s** from his father*
*Matt 19:18 . . . You must not **s.***
*Matt 27:64 . . . coming and **s-ing** His body*
*Rom 13:9 . . . You must not **s.***
*Eph 4:28 . . . If you are a thief, quit **s-ing.***
*1 Pet 4:15 . . . not be for murder, **s-ing,***

STIFFNECKED (KJV)
*Exod 32:9 . . . how **stubborn and rebellious***
*Exod 34:9 . . . **stubborn and rebellious** people*
*Deut 10:16 . . . stop being **stubborn***
*2 Chr 30:8 . . . not be **stubborn,** as they were,*
*Acts 7:51 . . . You **stubborn** people! You are*

STIFFHEARTED (KJV)
*Ezek 2:4 . . . stubborn and **hard-hearted***

STILL (adj)
devoid of or abstaining from motion; quiet, calm
*Ps 46:10 . . . Be **s,** and know that I am*
*Isa 57:20 . . . never **s** but continually*
*Mark 4:39 . . . Silence! Be **s!***

STING (n)
a wound or pain caused by or as if by stinging
*1 Cor 15:55 . . . where is your **s?***

STONE (adj)
of, relating to, or made of stone
*Deut 4:13 . . . he wrote on two **s** tablets.*

STONE, STONES (n)
hardened mineral or rock; figurative of Christ or of hardened hearts
*Exod 28:10 . . . Six names will be on each **s,***
*Josh 4:3 . . . Take twelve **s-s** from the very*
*1 Sam 17:40 . . . picked up five smooth **s-s***
*Ps 91:12 . . . even hurt your foot on a **s.***
*Ps 118:22 . . . **s** that the builders rejected*
*Isa 8:14 . . . a **s** that makes people stumble,*
*Isa 28:16 . . . a foundation **s** in Jerusalem,*
*Isa 50:7 . . . face like a **s,** determined to*
*Jer 51:26 . . . Even your **s-s** will never again*
*Matt 3:9 . . . Abraham from these very **s-s.***
*Matt 7:9 . . . give them a **s** instead?*
*Matt 21:42 . . . **s** that the builders rejected*
*Matt 24:2 . . . Not one **s** will be left*
*Mark 16:3 . . . roll away the **s** for us from*
*Luke 4:3 . . . change this **s** into a loaf of*
*John 8:7 . . . sinned throw the first **s!***
*1 Pet 2:5 . . . you are living **s-s** that God*

STOOD (v)
see also STAND
*Josh 10:13 . . . So the sun **s** still and*
*2 Tim 4:17 . . . But the Lord **s** with me*

STOP, STOPS (v)
to cease activity or operation; to pause or hesitate; to restrain or prevent
*Job 37:14 . . . **S** and consider the wonderful*
*Prov 15:18 . . . cool-tempered person **s-s***
*Jer 7:5 . . . only if you **s** your evil*
*Jer 32:40 . . . I will never **s** doing good*
*Lam 3:49 . . . flow endlessly; they will not **s***
*Dan 4:35 . . . No one can **s** him or say to*
*Matt 19:14 . . . come to Me. Don't **s** them!*
*Eph 6:16 . . . shield of faith to **s** the*

STORE, STORED (v)
to lay away; to accumulate
*Matt 6:19 . . . Don't **s** up treasures*
*Matt 6:26 . . . plant or harvest or **s** food*
*Luke 2:51 . . . And His mother **s-d** all these*

STORM (n)
a heavy fall of rain, snow, or hail sometimes accompanied by thunder and lightning; a disturbed or agitated state
see also WHIRLWIND
*Ps 50:3 . . . and a great **s** rages around*
*Ps 55:8 . . . from this wild **s** of hatred.*
*Ps 107:29 . . . He calmed the **s** to a whisper*
*Luke 8:24 . . . **s** stopped and all was calm!*

STRANGER, STRANGERS (n)
a person who is unknown or with whom one is unacquainted
see also FOREIGNER(S)
*Job 31:32 . . . turned away a **s** but have*
*Matt 25:35 . . . I was a **s,** and you invited*
*John 10:5 . . . They won't follow a **s;***
*1 Tim 5:10 . . . been kind to **s-s** and served*
*Heb 13:2 . . . to show hospitality to **s-s,** for*

STRAYED (v)
to wander
*Isa 53:6 . . . like sheep, have **s** away.*
*Ezek 34:16 . . . lost ones who **s** away, and*

STRENGTH (n)
capacity for exertion or endurance; support; the power of a person or of God, measured variously in terms of wealth, wisdom, military might, or physical prowess
*Exod 15:2 . . . LORD is my **s** and my*
*Deut 6:5 . . . your soul, and all your **s.***
*2 Kgs 23:25 . . . his heart and soul and **s,***
*1 Chr 16:11 . . . LORD and for His **s;***
*Neh 8:10 . . . of the LORD is your **s!***
*Ps 23:3 . . . He renews my **s.** He guides me*
*Ps 28:7 . . . LORD is my **s** and shield.*
*Ps 33:16 . . . nor is great **s** enough to save*
*Ps 46:1 . . . God is our refuge and **s,***
*Ps 59:17 . . . O my **S,** to You I sing*
*Ps 65:6 . . . armed yourself with mighty **s.***
*Ps 84:5 . . . for those whose **s** comes from*
*Ps 139:10 . . . Your **s** will support me.*
*Isa 31:1 . . . depending on the **s** of human*
*Isa 40:26 . . . power and incomparable **s,***
*Jer 27:5 . . . With my great **s** and powerful*
*Mic 5:4 . . . with the LORD's **s,** in*
*Hab 3:19 . . . LORD is my **s!***
*Zech 4:6 . . . nor by **s,** but by my Spirit,*
*Mark 12:30 . . . your mind, and all your **s.***
*1 Cor 1:25 . . . the greatest of human **s.***
*Phil 4:13 . . . Christ, who gives me **s.***
*Heb 11:34 . . . weakness was turned to **s.***
*Heb 13:9 . . . Your **s** comes from God's*

STRENGTHEN, STRENGTHENED, STRENGTHENS (v)
to make or become stronger
*2 Chr 16:9 . . . in order to **s** those whose*
*Isa 41:10 . . . I will **s** you and help you.*
*1 Cor 8:1 . . . is love that **s-s** the church.*
*1 Cor 14:4 . . . in tongues is **s-ed** personally,*
*1 Cor 14:4 . . . word of prophecy **s-s** the entire*
*1 Cor 14:5 . . . whole church will be **s-ed.***
*1 Cor 14:12 . . . seek those that will **s** the*
*1 Cor 14:17 . . . but it won't **s** the people*
*1 Cor 14:26 . . . is done must **s** all of you.*
*2 Cor 13:10 . . . has given me to **s** you, not*
*Heb 12:12 . . . tired hands and **s** your weak*
*1 Pet 5:10 . . . support, and **s** you, and He*

STRONG, STRONGER, STRONGEST (adj)
having or marked by great physical power, moral or intellectual power, or great resources (as of wealth or talent); firm
*Exod 6:1 . . . force of my **s** hand, He*
*Deut 5:15 . . . you out with His **s** hand*
*Deut 7:8 . . . with such a **s** hand from Your*
*Deut 31:6 . . . So be **s** and courageous!*
*Josh 1:6 . . . Be **s** and courageous,*
*Judg 16:5 . . . makes him so **s** and how he*
*2 Sam 22:33 . . . God is my **s** fortress, and*
*1 Kgs 8:42 . . . and Your **s** hand and Your*
*1 Chr 28:20 . . . Be **s** and courageous, and*
*Ezra 10:4 . . . so be **s** and take action.*
*Ps 24:8 . . . The LORD, **s** and mighty;*
*Ps 96:7 . . . LORD is glorious and **s.***
*Prov 18:10 . . . LORD is a **s** fortress;*
*Prov 24:5 . . . wise are mightier than the **s,***
*Prov 30:25 . . . Ants—they aren't **s,** but*
*Prov 31:17 . . . She is energetic and **s,** a*
*Eccl 9:11 . . . **s-est** warrior doesn't always win*
*Isa 35:4 . . . Be **s,** and do not fear,*
*Jer 50:34 . . . one who redeems them is **s.***
*Zeph 1:14 . . . when even **s** men will cry*
*Luke 1:80 . . . and became **s** in spirit.*
*Luke 2:40 . . . grew up healthy and **s.***
*Luke 11:22 . . . someone even **s-er** attacks and*
*1 Cor 1:8 . . . keep you **s** to the end*
*1 Cor 1:25 . . . God's weakness is **s-er** than*
*1 Cor 16:13 . . . Be courageous. Be **s.***
*Eph 6:10 . . . final word: Be **s** in the Lord*
*1 Thes 3:13 . . . your hearts **s,** blameless,*
*2 Tim 2:1 . . . dear son, be **s** through the*

STRUGGLE (n)
strife; a violent effort or exertion
*Rom 15:30 . . . to join in my **s** by praying*
*Heb 12:4 . . . lives in your **s** against sin.*

STRUGGLE (v)
to proceed with difficulty or with great effort; to make strenuous or violent efforts in the face of difficulties or opposition
*Gen 3:17 . . . will **s** to scratch a living*
*Col 1:29 . . . why I work and **s** so hard,*
*1 Tim 4:10 . . . and continue to **s,** for our*

STUBBORN (adj)
unreasonably or perversely unyielding
*Exod 33:5 . . . You are a **s** and rebellious*
*Exod 34:9 . . . this is a **s** and rebellious*
*Lev 26:41 . . . at last their **s** hearts will*
*Deut 10:16 . . . hearts and stop being **s.***
*2 Chr 36:13 . . . a hard and **s** man, refusing*
*Ps 78:8 . . . ancestors—**s,** rebellious,*
*Prov 28:14 . . . the **s** are headed for serious*
*Ezek 36:26 . . . out your stony, **s** heart and*
*Rom 2:5 . . . because you are **s** and refuse*

STUDY (v)
to read in detail, especially with the intention of learning
*Josh 1:8 . . . **S** this Book of Instruction*
*Ezra 7:10 . . . had determined to **s** and obey*
*2 Tim 2:15 . . . **Work hard** so you can present*

STUMBLE, STUMBLES, STUMBLING (v)
to trip or walk unsteadily; to fall into sin or waywardness
*Lev 19:14 . . . or cause the blind to **s.***
*Ps 37:24 . . . Though they **s,** they will*
*Ps 66:9 . . . He keeps our feet from **s-ing.***
*Ps 119:165 . . . great peace and do not **s.***
*Ps 121:3 . . . He will not let you **s;***
*Prov 3:23 . . . and your feet will not **s.***
*Prov 24:17 . . . don't be happy when they **s.***
*Isa 8:14 . . . stone that makes people **s,***
*Jer 13:16 . . . causing you to **s** and fall*
*Hos 14:9 . . . paths sinners **s** and fall.*
*Mal 2:8 . . . caused many to **s** into sin.*
*Matthew 21:44 . . . Anyone who **s-s** over that*
*John 11:10 . . . is danger of **s-ing** because*
*Rom 9:33 . . . that makes people **s,***
*Rom 14:13 . . . believer to **s** and fall.*
*Rom 14:20 . . . makes another person **s.***
*1 Cor 8:9 . . . weaker conscience to **s.***
*2 Cor 6:3 . . . no one will **s** because of us,*
*1 Jn 2:10 . . . does not cause others to **s.***

SUBMISSIVE (adj)
submitting to others
*1 Cor 14:34 . . . They should be **s,** just*
*Titus 2:5 . . . be **s** to their husbands.*

SUBMIT, SUBMITS (v)
to yield to authority or be accountable to another—God, society, or fellow believers
*Ps 2:12 . . . **S** to God's royal Son,*
*Rom 13:1 . . . Everyone must **s** to governing*
*Rom 13:5 . . . So you must **s** to them, not*
*Eph 5:21 . . . **s** to one another out of*
*Eph 5:24 . . . As the church **s-s** to Christ,*
*Col 3:18 . . . Wives, **s** to your husbands,*
*Heb 12:9 . . . shouldn't we **s** even more*

SUCCEED (v)
to turn out well; to attain a desired end
*Gen 39:23 . . . everything he did to **s.***
*Josh 1:8 . . . prosper and **s** in all you*
*1 Sam 2:9 . . . No one will **s** by strength*
*1 Sam 18:14 . . . continued to **s** in*
*2 Chr 20:20 . . . prophets, and you will **s.***
*Ps 20:4 . . . and make all your plans **s.***
*Prov 11:10 . . . celebrates when the godly **s;***
*Prov 13:13 . . . respect a command will **s.***
*Prov 16:3 . . . and your plans will **s.***
*Prov 20:18 . . . Plans **s** through good*
*Prov 28:12 . . . When the godly **s,** everyone*
*Eccl 10:10 . . . wisdom; it helps you **s.***

SUCCESS (n)
the attainment of wealth, favor, or eminence; favorable or desired outcome
*1 Chr 12:18 . . . and **s** to all who help*
*2 Chr 26:5 . . . LORD, God gave him **s.***
*Prov 15:22 . . . many advisers bring **s.***

SUCCESSFUL (adj)
resulting or terminating in success; gaining or having gained success
*Deut 8:18 . . . gives you power to be **s,***
*Deut 30:9 . . . make you **s** in everything*
*1 Kgs 2:3 . . . that you will be **s** in all*
*2 Kgs 18:7 . . . Hezekiah was **s** in*
*1 Chr 22:13 . . . For you will be **s** if you*
*2 Chr 31:21 . . . result, he was very **s.***
*Ps 90:17 . . . and make our efforts **s.***
*Prov 1:3 . . . disciplined and **s** lives,*
*Eccl 9:11 . . . don't always lead **s** lives.*

SUFFER, SUFFERED, SUFFERING, SUFFERS (v)
to endure death, pain, distress, or loss
*Job 36:15 . . . rescues those who **s.***
*Mark 8:31 . . . Son of Man must **s** many*
*Luke 24:26 . . . would have to **s** all these*
*Luke 24:46 . . . Messiah would **s** and die*
*Rom 8:18 . . . Yet what we **s** now is nothing*
*1 Cor 12:26 . . . If one part **s-s,** all the parts*
*2 Cor 1:5 . . . the more we **s** for Christ,*
*2 Cor 12:10 . . . troubles that I **s** for Christ.*
*Phil 3:10 . . . I want to **s** with Him, sharing*
*2 Thes 1:4 . . . and hardships you are **s-ing.***
*Heb 11:26 . . . better to **s** for the sake*
*1 Pet 2:21 . . . just as Christ **s-ed** for you.*
*1 Pet 4:1 . . . since Christ **s-ed** physical pain,*
*1 Pet 4:16 . . . is no shame to **s** for being*
*1 Pet 5:10 . . . So after you have **s-ed** a little*
*Rev 2:3 . . . You have patiently **s-ed** for me*

SUFFERING, SUFFERINGS (n)
the state or experience of one that suffers; pain, distress
*Deut 16:3 . . . the bread of **s**—so that*
*Job 36:15 . . . means of their **s,** He rescues*
*Ps 119:71 . . . My **s** was good for me,*
*Isa 48:10 . . . you in the furnace of **s.***
*Isa 49:13 . . . on them in their **s.***
*Lam 1:12 . . . if there is any **s** like mine,*
*Luke 22:15 . . . You before my **s** begins.*
*2 Cor 1:7 . . . as You share in our **s-s,** You*
*Phil 1:29 . . . the privilege of **s** for Him.*
*Col 1:24 . . . participating in the **s-s** of*
*2 Tim 2:3 . . . Endure **s** along with me,*
*2 Tim 4:5 . . . afraid of **s** for the Lord.*
*Heb 2:10 . . . through His **s,** a perfect*
*Heb 2:18 . . . gone through **s** and testing,*
*1 Pet 1:11 . . . about Christ's **s** and His*
*1 Pet 4:13 . . . Christ in His **s,** so that*

SUSTAINS (v)
to keep up or prolong
*Heb 1:3 . . . God, and he **s** everything by*

SWADDLED, SWADDLING (KJV)
*Ezek 16:4 . . . salt, and **wrapped in cloth***
*Luke 2:7 . . . wrapped Him **snugly in strips of cloth***
*Luke 2:12 . . . a baby **wrapped snugly***

SWALLOW, SWALLOWED (v)
to take through the mouth and esophagus into the stomach; to envelop or absorb
*Isa 25:8 . . . He will **s** up death*
*Jon 1:17 . . . a great fish to **s** Jonah.*
*Hab 1:13 . . . while the wicked **s** up people*
*Matt 23:24 . . . a gnat, but you **s** a camel!*
*1 Cor 15:54 . . . fulfilled: "Death is **s-ed** up*
*2 Cor 5:4 . . . bodies will be **s-ed** up by life.*

SWORD, SWORDS (n)
a handheld weapon with a long blade; figurative of war or persecution by government, also of God's word in spiritual warfare
*Gen 3:24 . . . a flaming **s** that flashed*
*Deut 32:41 . . . My flashing **s** and begin*
*1 Sam 17:45 . . . come to me with **s**, spear,*
*1 Sam 31:4 . . . Take your **s** and kill me*
*2 Sam 12:10 . . . live by the **s** because you*
*1 Kgs 20:11 . . . putting on his **s** for battle*
*Ps 44:6 . . . not count on my **s** to save me.*
*Ps 45:3 . . . Put on Your **s**, O mighty*
*Ps 64:3 . . . their tongues like **s-s** and aim*
*Joel 3:10 . . . plowshares into **s-s** and your*
*Amos 9:4 . . . I will command the **s** to kill*
*Mic 4:3 . . . will hammer their **s-s** into*
*Matt 10:34 . . . not to bring peace, but a **s**.*
*Matt 26:52 . . . who use the **s** will die by*
*Luke 2:35 . . . a **s** will pierce your very*
*Eph 6:17 . . . take the **s** of the Spirit,*
*Heb 4:12 . . . sharpest two-edged **s**, cutting*
*Rev 1:16 . . . sharp two-edged **s** came*
*Rev 19:15 . . . came a sharp **s** to strike*

SYNAGOGUE (n)
the house of worship and communal center of a Jewish congregation
*Luke 4:16 . . . to the **s** on the Sabbath*
*Acts 17:2 . . . he went to the **s** service,*

T

TABERNACLE (n)
portable shrine or tent designated for the worship of God; metaphor for God dwelling among his people
see also SANCTUARY, TEMPLE
*Exod 27:21 . . . stand in the **T**, in front of*
*Exod 40:2 . . . Set up the **T** on the first*
*Exod 40:34 . . . cloud covered the **T**, and*
*Exod 40:34 . . . of the LORD filled the **T**.*
*Num 3:29 . . . area south of the **T** for their*
*Heb 8:5 . . . to build the **T**, God gave him*
*Heb 9:11 . . . more perfect **T** in heaven,*
*Heb 9:21 . . . blood on the **T** and on*
*Rev 15:5 . . . heaven, God's **T**, was thrown*

TABLETS (n)
a flat slab or plaque suited for or bearing an inscription
*Exod 31:18 . . . two stone **t** inscribed with*
*Deut 10:5 . . . and placed the **t** in the Ark*
*2 Cor 3:3 . . . carved not on **t** of stone,*

TAME (v)
to reduce from a wild to a domestic state; to harness
*Jas 3:7 . . . People can **t** all kinds of*
*Jas 3:8 . . . no one can **t** the tongue.*

TASTE (n)
the act of tasting; a sample experience
*Prov 24:13 . . . honeycomb is sweet to the **t**.*
*1 Pet 2:3 . . . a **t** of the Lord's kindness.*

TASTE, TASTED, TASTES (v)
to become acquainted with by experience; to ascertain the flavor of by taking a little into the mouth
*Ps 34:8 . . . **T** and see that the LORD*
*Prov 9:17 . . . eaten in secret **t-s** the best!*
*Song 2:3 . . . and **t** his delicious fruit.*
*Ezek 3:3 . . . I ate it, it **t-d** as sweet as*
*Col 2:21 . . . Don't handle! Don't **t**!*

TAX, TAXES (n)
a charge usually of money imposed by authority on persons or property for public purposes
*Matt 11:19 . . . a friend of **t** collectors*
*Matt 17:24 . . . teacher pay the Temple **t**?*
*Matt 22:17 . . . right to pay **t-es** to Caesar*
*Rom 13:7 . . . Pay your **t-es** and*

TEACH, TEACHES, TEACHING (v)
to cause to know something; to instruct by precept, example, or experience
see also INSTRUCT, PREACH, TRAIN
*Lev 10:11 . . . you must **t** the Israelites*
*Deut 6:1 . . . commanded me to **t** you.*
*2 Chr 17:9 . . . of Judah, **t-ing** the people.*
*Job 21:22 . . . who can **t** a lesson to God,*
*Ps 37:30 . . . they **t** right from wrong.*
*Ps 51:13 . . . Then I will **t** Your ways*
*Prov 15:33 . . . the LORD **t-es** wisdom;*
*Isa 2:3 . . . He will **t** us His ways,*
*Matt 5:19 . . . obeys God's laws and **t-es***
*Matt 11:29 . . . Let Me **t** You, because*
*Matt 15:9 . . . they **t** man-made ideas*
*Matt 22:16 . . . You **t** the way of God*
*Matt 28:20 . . . **T** these new disciples to*
*Mark 10:1 . . . as usual He was **t-ing** them.*
*Luke 11:1 . . . Lord, **t** us to pray,*
*Luke 12:12 . . . Holy Spirit will **t** you*
*John 14:26 . . . He will **t** you everything*
*Acts 6:4 . . . in prayer and **t-ing** the word.*
*Rom 15:4 . . . Scriptures long ago to **t***
*Rom 15:14 . . . you can **t** each other all*
*1 Cor 2:16 . . . knows enough to **t** him?*
*1 Cor 14:26 . . . another will **t**, another*
*1 Tim 2:12 . . . do not let women **t** men*
*1 Tim 3:2 . . . he must be able to **t**.*
*2 Tim 3:16 . . . is useful to **t** us what*
*2 Tim 3:16 . . . **t-es** us to do what is right.*
*Titus 2:15 . . . You must **t** these things*
*Heb 5:12 . . . you ought to be **t-ing** others.*
*1 Jn 2:27 . . . need anyone to **t** you what*

TEACHER, TEACHERS (n)
one that teaches
*Job 36:22 . . . Who is a **t** like Him?*
*Prov 5:13 . . . didn't I listen to my **t-s**?*
*Eccl 1:1 . . . words of the **T**, King David's*
*Matt 10:24 . . . not greater than their **t**,*
*Matt 23:10 . . . only one **t**, the Messiah.*
*Luke 6:40 . . . will become like the **t**.*
*Luke 20:46 . . . these **t-s** of religious law!*
*John 13:14 . . . Lord and **T**, have washed*
*Rom 12:7 . . . If you are a **t**, teach well.*
*1 Cor 12:28 . . . third are **t-s**, then those*
*Gal 6:6 . . . should provide for their **t-s**,*
*Eph 4:11 . . . and the pastors and **t-s**.*
*2 Tim 4:3 . . . look for **t-s** who will tell*
*Jas 3:1 . . . of you should become **t-s***
*3 Jn 10 . . . the traveling **t-s**, he also*

TEACHING, TEACHINGS (n)
something taught; doctrine
see also INSTRUCTION(S), LAW(S)
*Isa 8:20 . . . to God's instructions and **t-s**!*
*Luke 6:47 . . . listens to My **t**, and then*
*John 7:17 . . . whether My **t** is from God*
*John 8:31 . . . remain faithful to My **t-s**.*
*Acts 2:42 . . . themselves to the apostles' **t**,*
*Eph 4:14 . . . about by every wind of new **t**.*
*1 Thes 4:8 . . . not disobeying human **t** but*
*2 Thes 2:15 . . . grip on the **t** we passed on*
*1 Tim 1:3 . . . those whose **t** is contrary to*
*1 Tim 1:10 . . . contradicts the wholesome **t***
*1 Tim 4:6 . . . and the good **t** you have*
*1 Tim 4:16 . . . how you live and on your **t**.*
*1 Tim 6:3 . . . people may contradict our **t**,*
*2 Tim 4:2 . . . Your people with good **t**.*
*Titus 1:9 . . . with wholesome **t** and show*
*Titus 3:8 . . . insist on these **t-s** so that*
*Heb 6:1 . . . stop going over the basic **t-s***

TEAR, TEARS (n)
a drop of clear saline fluid secreted from the eye
*Job 16:20 . . . I pour out my **t-s** to God.*
*Isa 25:8 . . . will wipe away all **t-s**.*
*Rev 7:17 . . . will wipe every **t** from their*
*Rev 21:4 . . . will wipe every **t** from their*

TEMPER (n)
calmness of mind; proneness to anger
*Ps 37:8 . . . Do not lose your **t**—it only*
*Prov 14:29 . . . **t** shows great foolishness.*
*Prov 19:11 . . . people control their **t**;*
*Eccl 7:9 . . . Control your **t**, for anger*

TEMPLE, TEMPLES (n)
first built in Solomon's reign as a permanent worship center, which was destroyed then rebuilt under Herod's reign; figurative of the human body and of Christ
see also SANCTUARY, TABERNACLE
*1 Kgs 6:1 . . . to construct the **T** of the*
*1 Kgs 8:10 . . . cloud filled the **T** of the*
*1 Chr 29:16 . . . to build a **T** to honor Your*
*2 Chr 36:19 . . . his army burned the **T***
*Ps 27:4 . . . meditating in His **T**.*
*Isa 6:1 . . . train of his robe filled the **T**.*
*Jer 7:8 . . . suffer because the **T** is here.*
*Joel 3:18 . . . forth from the LORD's **T**,*
*Hab 2:20 . . . LORD is in His holy **T**.*
*Hag 2:18 . . . of the LORD's **T** began.*
*Matt 12:6 . . . is even greater than the **T**!*
*Matt 26:61 . . . able to destroy the **T** of God*
*Matt 27:51 . . . sanctuary of the **T** was torn*
*Luke 21:5 . . . stonework of the **T** and the*
*John 2:14 . . . the **T** area He saw merchants*
*Acts 5:20 . . . Go to the **T** and give the*
*Acts 17:24 . . . live in man-made **t-s**,*
*1 Cor 3:16 . . . together are the **t** of God*
*1 Cor 6:19 . . . body is the **t** of the Holy*
*Eph 2:21 . . . becoming a holy **t** for the*
*1 Pet 2:5 . . . building into His spiritual **t**.*
*Rev 21:22 . . . and the Lamb are its **t**.*

TEMPT, TEMPTED, TEMPTING (v)
to entice to do wrong by promise of pleasure or gain; to test
*Isa 13:17 . . . They cannot be **t-ed** by silver*
*Matt 4:1 . . . wilderness to be **t-ed** there by*
*Luke 4:2 . . . where He was **t-ed** by the devil*
*Luke 4:13 . . . finished **t-ing** Jesus, He left*
*1 Cor 7:5 . . . be able to **t** you because*
*1 Cor 10:13 . . . When you are **t-ed**, He will*
*Jas 1:13 . . . you are being **t-ed**, do not say,*
*Jas 1:13 . . . God is never **t-ed** to do wrong,*

TEMPTATION, TEMPTATIONS (n)
a cause or occasion of enticement
*Matt 6:13 . . . don't let us yield to **t**,*
*Matt 18:7 . . . **T-s** are inevitable, but what*
*Matt 26:41 . . . will not give in to **t**.*
*Luke 8:13 . . . fall away when they face **t**.*
*1 Cor 10:13 . . . The **t-s** in your life are*
*1 Cor 10:13 . . . not allow the **t** to be*
*Gal 6:1 . . . fall into the same **t** yourself.*
*1 Tim 6:9 . . . to be rich fall into **t** and*
*Jas 1:12 . . . endure testing and **t**.*

TENTH (n)
one-tenth of any property or produce
see also TITHE
*Gen 14:20 . . . gave Melchizedek a **t** of all*
*Heb 7:2 . . . Abraham took a **t** of all he*

TERRIBLE (adj)
extremely bad; terrifying
*Jer 8:6 . . . What a **t** thing I have done*
*Zeph 1:15 . . . a day of **t** distress and*
*Heb 10:31 . . . It is a **t** thing to fall into*

TERRIFY, TERRIFIED, TERRIFIES (v)
to scare, deter, or intimidate; to fill with terror
*Deut 2:25 . . . the earth **t-ied** because of you.*
*Deut 28:67 . . . you will be **t-ied** by the awful*
*1 Sam 12:18 . . . were **t-ied** of the LORD*
*Prov 21:15 . . . but it **t-ies** evildoers.*
*Isa 13:8 . . . and people are **t-ied.** Pangs of*
*Zeph 2:11 . . . The LORD will **t** them*
*Matt 14:26 . . . on the water, they were **t-ied.***
*Matt 17:6 . . . disciples were **t-ied** and fell*
*Matt 27:54 . . . the crucifixion were **t-ied***
*Mark 4:41 . . . disciples were absolutely **t-ied.***
*Luke 21:26 . . . will be **t-ied** at what they*

TERRIFYING (adj)
causing terror or apprehension
*Deut 4:34 . . . powerful arm, and **t** acts?*
*Deut 34:12 . . . Moses performed **t** acts in the*
*Judg 13:6 . . . of God's angels, **t** to see.*

TERROR, TERRORS (n)
a state of intense fear; a frightening aspect
*Deut 7:19 . . . Remember the great **t-s** the*
*Job 9:34 . . . no longer live in **t** of His*
*Ps 53:5 . . . will grip them, **t** like they*
*Ps 91:5 . . . afraid of the **t-s** of the night,*
*Prov 22:8 . . . their reign of **t** will come to*
*Isa 51:17 . . . the cup of **t**, tipping out its*
*Mic 7:17 . . . trembling in **t** at His*
*Luke 9:34 . . . them, and **t** gripped them*
*Acts 7:32 . . . Moses shook with **t** and did*

TEST, TESTINGS, TESTS (n)
a critical examination, observation, or evaluation
see also TRIAL(S), TROUBLE(S)
*Deut 29:3 . . . all the great **t-s** of strength,*
*1 Cor 10:9 . . . should we put Christ to the **t**,*
*1 Tim 3:10 . . . If they pass the **t**, then let*
*Heb 4:15 . . . of the same **t-ings** we do, yet*

TEST, TESTED, TESTING, TESTS (v)
to put to test or proof
*Gen 22:1 . . . God **t-ed** Abraham's faith.*
*Deut 6:16 . . . You must not **t** the LORD your*
*Judg 3:1 . . . land to **t** those Israelites*
*1 Kgs 10:1 . . . she came to **t** him with hard*
*Job 23:10 . . . when He **t-s** me, I will come*
*Ps 17:3 . . . You have **t-ed** my thoughts*
*Ps 66:10 . . . You have **t-ed** us,*
*Ps 78:18 . . . They stubbornly **t-ed** God in*
*Ps 106:14 . . . ran wild, **t-ing** God's patience*
*Ps 139:23 . . . **t** me and know my anxious*
*Prov 17:3 . . . the LORD **t-s** the heart.*
*Luke 4:12 . . . You must not **t** the LORD your*
*Acts 5:9 . . . of conspiring to **t** the Spirit*
*1 Thes 5:21 . . . but **t** everything that is said.*
*Heb 2:18 . . . suffering and **t-ing,** He is able*
*Heb 2:18 . . . us when we are being **t-ed.***
*Heb 3:8 . . . they **t-ed** Me in the wilderness.*
*Heb 11:17 . . . when God was **t-ing** Him.*
*Jas 1:3 . . . when your faith is **t-ed,** your*
*Jas 1:12 . . . who patiently endure **t-ing** and*
*1 Pet 1:7 . . . It is being **t-ed** as fire tests*
*1 Jn 4:1 . . . You must **t** them to see if*
*Rev 2:10 . . . you into prison to **t** you.*
*Rev 3:10 . . . great time of **t-ing** that will*

TESTIFY, TESTIFIED, TESTIFIES, TESTIFYING (v)
to make a statement based on personal knowledge or belief; to give evidence or proof
*Exod 20:16 . . . must not **t** falsely against*
*Deut 5:20 . . . must not **t** falsely against*
*Prov 24:28 . . . Don't **t** against your*
*Luke 18:20 . . . You must not **t** falsely.*
*John 1:34 . . . Jesus, so I **t** that He is*
*John 5:32 . . . else is also **t-ing** about me,*
*John 15:26 . . . Father and will **t** all about*
*John 18:37 . . . the world to **t** to the truth.*
*John 21:24 . . . one who **t-ies** to these events*
*Acts 4:33 . . . The apostles **t-ied** powerfully*
*Acts 10:43 . . . the prophets **t-ied** about,*
*1 Jn 4:14 . . . own eyes and now **t** that the*

TESTIMONY (n)
the evidence given by a witness
see also TESTIFY
*Num 35:30 . . . to death on the **t** of only*
*John 1:7 . . . might believe because of his **t**.*
*1 Tim 6:13 . . . gave a good **t** before Pontius*
*1 Jn 5:9 . . . Since we believe human **t**,*
*Rev 12:11 . . . of the Lamb and by their **t**.*

THANK, THANKING (v)
to express gratitude to; to acknowledge God's goodness
*Ps 35:18 . . . Then I will **t** you in front*
*Ps 79:13 . . . pasture, will **t** you forever*
*Ps 145:10 . . . works will **t** you, LORD,*
*Isa 12:4 . . . sing: "**T** the LORD!*
*1 Cor 10:30 . . . If I can **t** God for the food*
*Phil 4:6 . . . and **t** Him for all He has done.*
*1 Thes 2:13 . . . we never stop **t-ing** God*
*1 Thes 3:9 . . . How we **t** God for you!*

THANKFUL (adj)
conscious of benefit received; expressive of thanks
*Col 3:15 . . . And always be **t**.*
*Col 3:16 . . . to God with **t** hearts.*
*1 Thes 5:18 . . . Be **t** in all circumstances,*
*Heb 12:28 . . . let us be **t** and please God by*

THANKS (n)
kindly or grateful thoughts; gratitude
*1 Chr 16:4 . . . to give **t**, and to praise*
*Ps 30:12 . . . I will give You **t** forever!*
*Ps 107:1 . . . Give **t** to the LORD,*
*Rom 1:21 . . . as God or even give Him **t**.*
*1 Cor 11:24 . . . gave **t** to God for it.*
*Phil 1:3 . . . of you, I give **t** to my God.*
*1 Tim 2:1 . . . behalf, and give **t** for them.*
*1 Tim 4:3 . . . be eaten with **t** by faithful*
*Rev 4:9 . . . and honor and **t** to the one*

THANKSGIVING (n)
a prayer expressing gratitude; a public acknowledgment or celebration of God's goodness
*Ps 26:7 . . . singing a song of **t** and telling*
*Ps 28:7 . . . I burst out in songs of **t**.*
*Ps 100:4 . . . Enter His gates with **t**; go*
*Isa 51:3 . . . Songs of **t** will fill the air.*

THIEF, THIEVES (n)
one that steals, especially stealthily or secretly
*Prov 6:30 . . . might be found for a **t***
*Prov 29:24 . . . If you assist a **t**, you only*
*Jer 7:11 . . . has become a den of **t-ves?***
*Matt 6:19 . . . where **t-ves** break in and steal.*
*Luke 19:46 . . . turned it into a den of **t-ves.***
*John 10:1 . . . surely be a **t** and a robber!*
*John 10:8 . . . me were **t-ves** and robbers.*
*1 Cor 6:10 . . . or are **t-ves,** or greedy people,*
*1 Thes 5:2 . . . unexpectedly, like a **t** in the*
*Rev 16:15 . . . as unexpectedly as a **t!***

THINK, THINKING, THINKS (v)
to reflect, ponder, or remember; to subject to the processes of logical thought; to have as an opinion; to conceive or reason
see also MEDITATE, THOUGHT
*1 Sam 12:24 . . . **T** of all the wonderful*
*2 Chr 19:6 . . . Always **t** carefully before*
*Ps 8:4 . . . You should **t** about them,*
*Ps 63:6 . . . I lie awake **t-ing** of You,*
*Ps 77:12 . . . I cannot stop **t-ing** about Your*
*Ps 119:97 . . . I **t** about them all day long.*
*Ps 119:148 . . . the night, **t-ing** about Your*
*Prov 13:16 . . . Wise people **t** before they*
*Prov 15:28 . . . godly **t-s** carefully before*
*Prov 21:29 . . . the virtuous **t** before they*
*Prov 23:7 . . . are always **t-ing** about how*
*Prov 29:20 . . . who speaks without **t-ing.***
*Isa 44:18 . . . are shut, and they cannot **t**.*
*Matt 22:42 . . . What do you **t** about the*
*Rom 11:20 . . . So don't **t** highly of*
*Phil 1:3 . . . Every time I **t** of you, I give*
*Phil 2:3 . . . Be humble, **t-ing** of others as*
*Phil 3:19 . . . they **t** only about this life*
*Heb 10:24 . . . Let us **t** of ways to motivate*
*1 Pet 1:13 . . . So **t** clearly and exercise*

THIRST (v)
to crave vehemently and urgently
*Ps 42:2 . . . I **t** for God, the living God.*
*Matt 5:6 . . . who hunger and **t** for justice,*

THIRSTY (adj)
feeling a desire for liquids; having a strong desire
*Ps 107:9 . . . he satisfies the **t** and fills*
*Prov 25:21 . . . If they are **t**, give them*
*Isa 55:1 . . . Is anyone **t?** Come and drink—*
*Matt 25:35 . . . I was **t**, and you gave*
*John 4:14 . . . will never be **t** again.*
*Rom 12:20 . . . If they are **t**, give them*
*2 Cor 11:27 . . . been hungry and **t** and*
*Rev 7:16 . . . never again be hungry or **t**;*
*Rev 22:17 . . . Let anyone who is **t** come.*

THORN, THORNS (n)
a woody plant bearing sharp impeding prickles or spines; something that causes distress or irritation
*Gen 3:18 . . . It will grow **t-s** and thistles*
*Num 33:55 . . . in your eyes and **t-s** in your*
*Matt 13:7 . . . seeds fell among **t-s** that*
*Matt 27:29 . . . wove **t** branches into a*
*2 Cor 12:7 . . . I was given a **t** in my flesh,*
*Heb 6:8 . . . a field bears **t-s** and thistles,*

THOUGHT, THOUGHTS (n)
the action or process of thinking; a developed intention or plan; recollection, remembrance
*Ps 77:12 . . . They are constantly in my **t-s.***
*Ps 92:5 . . . And how deep are Your **t-s.***
*Ps 94:11 . . . LORD knows people's **t-s;***
*Ps 104:34 . . . May all my **t-s** be pleasing*
*Ps 139:23 . . . and know my anxious **t-s.***
*Ps 142:4 . . . no one gives me a passing **t!***
*Isa 26:3 . . . whose **t-s** are fixed on You!*
*Isa 55:8 . . . My **t-s** are nothing like Your*
*Matt 9:4 . . . you have such evil **t-s** in your*
*Matt 15:19 . . . heart come evil **t-s,** murder,*
*1 Cor 14:25 . . . their secret **t-s** will be*
*Eph 4:23 . . . renew your **t-s** and attitudes.*
*Rev 2:23 . . . searches out the **t-s** and*

THRONE, THRONES (n)
seat of power for a king or deity; symbolic of royal authority and the king's role as a judge
*Deut 17:18 . . . he sits on the **t** as king,*
*2 Sam 7:16 . . . and your **t** will be secure*
*1 Chr 17:12 . . . will secure his **t** forever.*
*Job 36:7 . . . sets them on **t-s** with kings*
*Ps 45:6 . . . Your **t**, O God, endures*
*Ps 47:8 . . . nations, sitting on His holy **t**.*
*Ps 89:14 . . . are the foundation of Your **t**.*
*Ps 99:1 . . . He sits on His **t** between the*
*Ps 102:12 . . . sit on Your **t** forever.*
*Ps 103:19 . . . has made the heavens His **t**;*
*Isa 6:1 . . . He was sitting on a lofty **t**,*
*Isa 66:1 . . . Heaven is My **t**, and the*
*Dan 7:9 . . . on a fiery **t** with wheels*

Matt 19:28 . . . upon His glorious ***t****, you who*
Matt 19:28 . . . sit on twelve ***t-s****, judging*
Acts 7:49 . . . Heaven is My ***t****, and the*
Rom 15:12 . . . heir to David's ***t*** *will come,*
Col 1:16 . . . such as ***t-s****, kingdoms, rulers,*
Heb 12:2 . . . place of honor beside God's ***t.***
Rev 3:21 . . . sat with My Father on His ***t.***
Rev 4:2 . . . and I saw a ***t*** *in heaven*
Rev 4:4 . . . Twenty-four ***t-s*** *surrounded*
Rev 5:5 . . . heir to David's ***t****, has won*
Rev 20:11 . . . a great white ***t*** *and the*
Rev 22:3 . . . the ***t*** *of God and of the Lamb*

TIME, TIMES (n)
occasion; an opportune or suitable moment; an appointed, fixed, or customary moment or hour for something to happen, begin, or end; duration; conditions at present or at some specified period; added or accumulated quantities or instances
Esth 4:14 . . . keep quiet at a ***t*** *like this,*
Ps 9:9 . . . a refuge in ***t-s*** *of trouble.*
Ps 62:8 . . . trust in Him at all ***t-s.***
Eccl 3:1 . . . a ***t*** *for every activity under*
Eccl 7:14 . . . when hard ***t-s*** *strike,*
Eccl 8:5 . . . wise will find a ***t*** *and a way*
Dan 12:7 . . . times, and half a ***t.***
Hos 10:12 . . . for now is the ***t*** *to seek the*
Amos 5:13 . . . shut, for it is an evil ***t.***
Matt 16:3 . . . interpret the signs of the ***t-s!***
Matt 18:21 . . . sins against me? Seven ***t-s?***
Luke 12:40 . . . ready all the ***t****, for the Son*
John 4:53 . . . was the very ***t*** *Jesus had told*
John 12:23 . . . the ***t*** *has come for the Son*
Acts 1:7 . . . those dates and ***t-s****, and they*
Acts 18:5 . . . spent all his ***t*** *preaching*
1 Cor 7:29 . . . The ***t*** *that remains is very*
2 Cor 6:2 . . . the "right ***t****" is now.*
Gal 6:9 . . . just the right ***t*** *we will reap*
2 Tim 1:9 . . . the beginning of ***t****—to show*
Heb 9:28 . . . once for all ***t*** *as a sacrifice*
Heb 10:12 . . . for sins, good for all ***t.***
1 Pet 4:17 . . . For the ***t*** *has come for*
Rev 12:14 . . . for a time, ***t-s****, and half a*

TIRED (adj)
drained of strength and energy
Exod 17:12 . . . became so ***t*** *he could no*
Isa 35:3 . . . those who have ***t*** *hands,*
Gal 6:9 . . . let's not get ***t*** *of doing what*
2 Thes 3:13 . . . never get ***t*** *of doing good.*
Heb 12:12 . . . new grip with your ***t*** *hands*

TITHE, TITHES (n)
one-tenth of any property or produce
see also TENTH
Num 18:21 . . . give them the ***t-s*** *from the*
Deut 12:17 . . . neither the ***t*** *of your grain*
2 Chr 31:12 . . . brought all the ***t-s*** *and*
Amos 4:4 . . . bring your ***t-s*** *every three*
Mal 3:8 . . . of the ***t-s*** *and offerings due*
Mal 3:10 . . . Bring all the ***t-s*** *into the*

TITHE (v)
to pay or give a tenth of as an offering to God
Matt 23:23 . . . You should ***t****, yes,*
Luke 11:42 . . . you are careful to ***t*** *even the*

TOMORROW (n)
the day after the present; the future
Prov 27:1 . . . Don't brag about ***t****, since you*
Isa 22:13 . . . and drink, for ***t*** *we die!*
Rom 8:38 . . . our worries about ***t****—not even*

TONGUE, TONGUES (n)
part of the mouth that enables speech; dialect or language of a people; a special gift of speech given by the Holy Spirit
see also LANGUAGE(S)
Ps 5:9 . . . Their ***t-s*** *are filled*
Ps 34:13 . . . keep your ***t*** *from speaking*
Ps 39:1 . . . I will hold my ***t*** *when*
Ps 45:1 . . . king, for my ***t*** *is like*
Ps 78:36 . . . lied to him with their ***t-s.***
Ps 119:172 . . . Let my ***t*** *sing about*
Ps 137:6 . . . May my ***t*** *stick to the*
Prov 13:3 . . . who control their ***t*** *will have*
Prov 15:4 . . . a deceitful ***t*** *crushes the*
Prov 17:20 . . . the lying ***t*** *tumbles into*
Prov 21:23 . . . Watch your ***t*** *and keep*
Luke 16:24 . . . in water and cool my ***t.***
Acts 2:3 . . . like flames or ***t-s*** *of fire*
Acts 10:46 . . . speaking in ***t-s*** *and praising*
Acts 19:6 . . . in other ***t-s*** *and prophesied.*
Rom 14:11 . . . Me, and every ***t*** *will confess*
1 Cor 14:2 . . . to speak in ***t-s****, you will*
1 Cor 14:4 . . . speaks in ***t-s*** *is strengthened*
1 Cor 14:5 . . . speak in ***t-s****, but even more*
1 Cor 14:13 . . . speaks in ***t-s*** *should pray*
1 Cor 14:18 . . . I speak in ***t-s*** *more than*
1 Cor 14:27 . . . three should speak in ***t-s.***
1 Cor 14:39 . . . forbid speaking in ***t-s.***
Phil 2:11 . . . and every ***t*** *confess that*
Jas 3:2 . . . if we could control our ***t-s****, we*
Jas 3:5 . . . same way, the ***t*** *is a small*

TORTURED (v)
to punish or coerce by inflicting excruciating pain
Matt 18:34 . . . prison to be ***t*** *until he*
Heb 11:35 . . . others were ***t****, refusing to*

TOUCH, TOUCHED, TOUCHES (v)
to reach out or come in contact with; to lay hands upon; to have an influence upon
Gen 3:3 . . . must not eat it or even ***t*** *it;*
Exod 19:12 . . . or even ***t*** *its boundaries.*
Exod 19:12 . . . Anyone who ***t-es*** *the mountain*
Isa 6:7 . . . this coal has ***t-ed*** *your lips.*
Matt 9:21 . . . If I can just ***t*** *His robe,*
Matt 14:36 . . . who ***t-ed*** *Him were healed.*
Luke 8:45 . . . "Who ***t-ed*** *Me?" Jesus asked.*
Luke 18:15 . . . so He could ***t*** *and bless*
Luke 24:39 . . . ***T*** *Me and make sure that*
2 Cor 6:17 . . . Don't ***t*** *their filthy things,*
Col 2:21 . . . Don't taste! Don't ***t!****"?*
1 Jn 1:1 . . . ***t-ed*** *Him with our own hands.*
1 Jn 5:18 . . . evil one cannot ***t*** *them.*

TRADE, TRADED (v)
to give one thing in exchange for another
Gen 25:31 . . . Jacob replied, "but ***t*** *me your*
Ps 106:20 . . . They ***t-d*** *their glorious God*
Rom 1:25 . . . They ***t-d*** *the truth about God*

TRADITION, TRADITIONS (n)
an inherited, customary, or established pattern of thought, action, or behavior
Matt 15:6 . . . for the sake of your own ***t.***
Mark 7:5 . . . disciples follow our age-old ***t?***
Mark 7:8 . . . law and substitute your own ***t.***
Mark 7:13 . . . to hand down your own ***t.***
Gal 1:14 . . . in my zeal for the ***t-s*** *of my*

TRAIN, TRAINED (v)
to form by or undergo instruction, discipline, or drill
see also TEACH
Isa 2:4 . . . against nation, nor ***t*** *for war*
Luke 6:40 . . . who is fully ***t-ed*** *will become*
John 7:15 . . . when he hasn't been ***t-ed?***
Acts 22:3 . . . I was carefully ***t-ed*** *in our*
1 Tim 4:7 . . . ***t*** *yourself to be godly.*
Titus 2:4 . . . women must ***t*** *the younger*
Heb 12:11 . . . those who are ***t-ed*** *in this way.*

TRAMPLE, TRAMPLED (v)
to crush, injure, or destroy by or as if by treading
Ps 60:12 . . . for He will ***t*** *down our foes.*
Ps 91:13 . . . You will ***t*** *upon lions*
Amos 5:11 . . . You ***t*** *the poor,*
Amos 8:4 . . . rob the poor and ***t*** *down the*
Mic 4:13 . . . so You can ***t*** *many nations to*
Mic 7:19 . . . You will ***t*** *our sins under*
Matt 7:6 . . . They will ***t*** *the pearls,*
Luke 21:24 . . . Jerusalem will be ***t-d*** *down*
Heb 10:29 . . . who have ***t-d*** *on the Son*
Rev 14:20 . . . The grapes were ***t-d*** *in the*

TRANSFIGURED (KJV)
Matt 17:2 . . . Jesus' appearance was ***transformed***
Mark 9:2 . . . Jesus' appearance was ***transformed***

TRANSFORM, TRANSFORMED (v)
to change the outward appearance of; to change in character or condition
Matt 17:2 . . . appearance was ***t-ed*** *so that*
Rom 12:2 . . . let God ***t*** *you into a new*
1 Cor 15:51 . . . but we will all be ***t-ed!***

TRANSGRESSED, TRANSGRESSION (KJV)
Josh 7:11 . . . and ***broken*** *My covenant*
1 Chr 5:25 . . . tribes were ***unfaithful***
1 Chr 10:13 . . . because he was ***unfaithful***
Rom 4:15 . . . to avoid ***breaking*** *the law*
1 John 3:4 . . . all sin is ***contrary to*** *the law*

TRAP, TRAPS (n)
something by which one is caught or stopped unawares; a position or situation from which it is difficult or impossible to escape; a device for taking game or other animals
Deut 7:25 . . . will become a ***t*** *to you,*
Deut 12:30 . . . fall into the ***t*** *of following*
Ps 91:3 . . . you from every ***t*** *and protect*
Prov 1:17 . . . a bird sees a ***t*** *being set,*
Prov 3:26 . . . foot from being caught in a ***t.***
Prov 28:10 . . . into their own ***t****, but the*
Prov 29:5 . . . is to lay a ***t*** *for their feet.*
Prov 29:25 . . . a dangerous ***t****, but trusting*
Isa 8:14 . . . he will be a ***t*** *and a snare.*
Isa 24:17 . . . Terror and ***t-s*** *and snares will*
Matt 16:23 . . . are a dangerous ***t*** *to me.*
Rom 11:9 . . . a snare, a ***t*** *that makes them*
1 Tim 3:7 . . . into the devil's ***t.***
2 Tim 2:26 . . . from the devil's ***t.***

TRAP, TRAPPED, TRAPS (v)
to catch or take in or as if in a trap
Ps 7:15 . . . a deep pit to ***t*** *others, then*
Ps 9:16 . . . wicked are ***t-ped*** *by their own*
Prov 6:2 . . . if you have ***t-ped*** *yourself by*
Prov 12:13 . . . wicked are ***t-ped*** *by their*
Prov 18:7 . . . they ***t*** *themselves with*
Matt 22:15 . . . to plot how to ***t*** *Jesus into*
1 Cor 3:19 . . . He ***t-s*** *the wise in the snare*
1 Tim 6:9 . . . temptation and are ***t-ped*** *by*

TREASURE, TREASURES (n)
wealth or a collection of precious things; something of great value
Exod 19:5 . . . My own special ***t*** *from*
Deut 7:6 . . . to be His own special ***t.***
1 Chr 29:3 . . . my own private ***t-s*** *of gold*
Ps 119:111 . . . Your laws are my ***t****; they*
Ps 135:4 . . . Israel for His own special ***t.***
Prov 2:4 . . . seek them like hidden ***t-s.***
Prov 18:22 . . . finds a wife finds a ***t,***
Song 4:10 . . . delights me, my ***t****, my bride.*
Isa 10:3 . . . Where will your ***t-s*** *be safe?*
Hag 2:7 . . . the ***t-s*** *of all the nations*
Mal 3:17 . . . they will be My own special ***t.***
Matt 6:19 . . . Don't store up ***t-s*** *here on*
Matt 6:21 . . . Wherever your ***t*** *is, there the*
Matt 13:44 . . . Heaven is like a ***t*** *that a man*
Luke 12:33 . . . will store up ***t*** *for you in*
2 Cor 4:7 . . . jars containing this great ***t.***

*Eph 3:8 . . . the endless **t-s** available to*
*Col 2:3 . . . hidden all the **t-s** of wisdom*
*1 Tim 6:19 . . . storing up their **t** as a good*
*Heb 11:26 . . . to own the **t-s** of Egypt, for*

TREASURE, TREASURED (v)
to hold or keep as precious
*Job 23:12 . . . but have **t-d** His words more*
*Prov 2:1 . . . I say, and **t** My commands.*
*Prov 7:1 . . . always **t** My commands.*
*Prov 10:14 . . . Wise people **t** knowledge,*

TREASURY (n)
a place in which stores of wealth are kept
*Deut 28:12 . . . time from his rich **t** in the*
*Luke 6:45 . . . things from the **t** of a good*

TREE, TREES (n)
woody perennial plants, many of which produce crops; highly treasured natural resource; often linked with worship of pagan gods; symbolic of a growing believer
*Gen 2:9 . . . He placed the **t** of life and*
*Deut 21:23 . . . from the **t** overnight.*
*Judg 9:8 . . . the **t-s** decided to elect*
*2 Sam 18:9 . . . got caught in the **t**.*
*1 Kgs 14:23 . . . and under every green **t**.*
*Ps 1:3 . . . They are like **t-s** planted along*
*Ps 52:8 . . . like an olive **t**, thriving in*
*Ps 92:12 . . . like palm **t-s** and grow*
*Ps 96:12 . . . Let the **t-s** of the forest*
*Prov 3:18 . . . Wisdom is a **t** of life to*
*Prov 11:30 . . . deeds become a **t** of life;*
*Isa 55:12 . . . and the **t-s** of the field*
*Isa 65:22 . . . people will live as long as **t-s**,*
*Jer 17:8 . . . They are like **t-s** planted along*
*Dan 4:10 . . . saw a large **t** in the middle*
*Mic 4:4 . . . and fig **t-s**, for there will be*
*Matt 3:10 . . . sever the roots of the **t-s**.*
*Matt 3:10 . . . every **t** that does not produce*
*Matt 12:33 . . . **t** is identified by its fruit.*
*Mark 8:24 . . . look like **t-s** walking*
*Luke 19:4 . . . a sycamore-fig **t** beside the*
*Rom 11:24 . . . cut from a wild olive **t**.*
*Gal 3:13 . . . everyone who is hung on a **t**.*
*Jas 3:12 . . . Does a fig **t** produce olives,*
*Jude 12 . . . They are like **t-s** in autumn*
*Rev 22:2 . . . the river grew a **t** of life,*
*Rev 22:14 . . . the fruit from the **t** of life.*
*Rev 22:19 . . . share in the **t** of life and*

TREMBLE, TREMBLED, TREMBLES, TREMBLING (v)
to be affected with great fear or anxiety; to shake involuntarily
*Exod 15:14 . . . hear and **t**; anguish grips*
*Exod 19:16 . . . horn, and all the people **t-d**.*
*Exod 20:18 . . . a distance, **t-ing** with fear.*
*2 Sam 22:8 . . . the earth quaked and **t-d**.*
*1 Chr 16:30 . . . all the earth **t** before Him.*
*Ps 2:11 . . . fear, and rejoice with **t-ing**.*
*Ps 97:4 . . . The earth sees and **t-s**.*
*Ps 102:15 . . . the earth will **t** before His*
*Ps 104:32 . . . The earth **t-s** at His glance;*
*Isa 66:2 . . . contrite hearts, who **t** at My*
*Jer 10:10 . . . whole earth **t-s** at His anger.*
*Dan 10:10 . . . and lifted me, still **t-ing**,*
*Joel 2:1 . . . Let everyone **t** in fear*
*Nah 1:5 . . . hills melt away; the earth **t-s**,*
*Hab 3:6 . . . the nations **t**. He shatters*
*Heb 4:1 . . . we ought to **t** with fear that*
*Heb 12:21 . . . I am terrified and **t-ing**.*

TRESPASS(ES) (KJV)
*Lev 19:21 . . . a ram as a **guilt** offering*
*2 Chr 24:18 . . . Because of this **sin**, divine*
*Matt 18:15 . . . believer **sins** against You,*
*Matt 6:15 . . . Father will not forgive your **sins***
*Eph 2:1 . . . because of your **disobedience***

TRIAL, TRIALS (n)
a legal proceeding based in court; a test of faith, patience, or stamina through subjection to suffering or temptation
see also TEMPTATION(S), TEST(S), TROUBLE(S)
*Job 42:11 . . . all the **t-s** the LORD had*
*Ps 26:2 . . . Put me on **t**, LORD,*
*Ps 37:33 . . . when they are put on **t**.*
*Ps 143:2 . . . Don't put your servant on **t**,*
*Mark 13:11 . . . and stand **t**, don't worry in*
*Luke 22:28 . . . with me in my time of **t**.*
*John 16:33 . . . have many **t-s** and sorrows.*
*Rom 5:3 . . . into problems and **t-s**, for we*
*1 Pet 1:7 . . . through many **t-s**, it will*
*1 Pet 4:12 . . . the fiery **t-s** you are going*
*2 Pet 2:9 . . . from their **t-s**, even while*

TRICKERY (n)
deception
*Isa 29:21 . . . those who use **t** to pervert*
*2 Cor 12:16 . . . advantage of you by **t**.*

TROUBLE, TROUBLES (n)
a state, condition, or cause of distress, annoyance, difficulty, or inconvenience
see also TEST(S), TRIAL(S)
*Gen 41:51 . . . made me forget all my **t-s***
*Josh 7:25 . . . have you brought **t** on us?*
*2 Chr 15:4 . . . they were in **t** and turned*
*Job 5:7 . . . are born for **t** as readily as*
*Ps 7:14 . . . they are pregnant with **t***
*Ps 9:9 . . . a refuge in times of **t**.*
*Ps 10:14 . . . you see the **t** and grief*
*Ps 22:11 . . . from me, for **t** is near,*
*Ps 27:5 . . . me there when **t-s** come;*
*Ps 32:7 . . . You protect me from **t**.*
*Ps 34:17 . . . them from all their **t-s**.*
*Ps 37:39 . . . their fortress in times of **t**.*
*Ps 40:12 . . . For **t-s** surround me—*
*Ps 41:1 . . . them when they are in **t**.*
*Ps 46:1 . . . ready to help in times of **t**.*
*Ps 49:5 . . . I fear when **t** comes, when*
*Ps 50:15 . . . when you are in **t**, and I will*
*Ps 54:7 . . . have rescued me from my **t-s***
*Ps 55:3 . . . They bring **t** on me*
*Ps 66:14 . . . I was in deep **t**.*
*Ps 81:7 . . . cried to me in **t**, and*
*Ps 86:7 . . . whenever I'm in **t**, and*
*Ps 91:15 . . . I will be with them in **t**.*
*Ps 107:6 . . . they cried in their **t**,*
*Ps 107:41 . . . rescues the poor from **t***
*Ps 116:3 . . . I saw only **t** and sorrow.*
*Ps 120:1 . . . took my **t-s** to the LORD;*
*Ps 138:7 . . . I am surrounded by **t-s**, You*
*Prov 6:14 . . . they constantly stir up **t**.*
*Prov 10:10 . . . who wink at wrong cause **t**,*
*Prov 11:8 . . . godly are rescued from **t**,*
*Prov 11:29 . . . Those who bring **t** on their*
*Prov 12:13 . . . the godly escape such **t**.*
*Prov 12:21 . . . wicked have their fill of **t**.*
*Prov 13:20 . . . with fools and get in **t**.*
*Prov 25:19 . . . in times of **t** is like chewing*
*Eccl 4:10 . . . falls alone is in real **t**.*
*Isa 38:14 . . . I am in **t**, LORD. Help me!*
*Isa 53:4 . . . And we thought his **t-s** were*
*Isa 58:10 . . . and help those in **t**.*
*Hos 5:15 . . . as soon as **t** comes, they*
*Nah 1:7 . . . strong refuge when **t** comes.*
*Matt 6:34 . . . Today's **t** is enough*
*Rom 8:35 . . . if we have **t** or calamity,*
*1 Cor 7:28 . . . at this time will have **t-s**,*
*2 Cor 4:17 . . . our present **t-s** are small*
*2 Cor 6:4 . . . We patiently endure **t-s** and*
*2 Cor 7:4 . . . me happy despite all our **t-s**.*
*2 Cor 8:2 . . . being tested by many **t-s**,*
*1 Thes 3:3 . . . shaken by the **t-s** you were*
*1 Tim 6:5 . . . These people always cause **t**.*
*Jas 1:2 . . . when **t-s** come your way,*
*Jas 5:1 . . . all the terrible **t-s** ahead*

TRUE (adj)
fully realized or fulfilled; accurate; properly so called; steadfast, loyal, honest, and just; ideal, essential; being in accordance with the actual state of affairs; legitimate, rightful
*Num 11:23 . . . My word comes **t**!*
*Deut 18:22 . . . does not happen or come **t**,*
*Josh 23:14 . . . your God has come **t**.*
*1 Sam 9:6 . . . everything He says comes **t**.*
*1 Kgs 10:6 . . . and wisdom is **t**!*
*2 Chr 15:3 . . . without the **t** God,*
*Ps 7:10 . . . hearts are **t** and right.*
*Ps 19:9 . . . laws of the LORD are **t**;*
*Ps 119:142 . . . instructions are perfectly **t**.*
*Ps 119:151 . . . Your commands are **t**.*
*Isa 45:19 . . . speak only what is **t** and*
*Jer 10:10 . . . is the only **t** God.*
*Jer 26:15 . . . it is absolutely **t** that*
*Jer 28:9 . . . when His predictions come **t***
*Luke 16:11 . . . the **t** riches of heaven?*
*Luke 18:31 . . . Son of Man will come **t**.*
*John 1:9 . . . one who is the **t** light,*
*John 3:33 . . . can affirm that God is **t**.*
*John 4:23 . . . **t** worshipers will worship*
*John 6:32 . . . offers you the **t** bread*
*John 6:55 . . . my flesh is **t** food, and*
*John 7:28 . . . one who sent Me is **t**,*
*John 15:1 . . . I am the **t** grapevine,*
*John 17:3 . . . know You, the only **t** God,*
*Rom 3:4 . . . else is a liar, God is **t**.*
*Rom 15:8 . . . God is **t** to the promises*
*Eph 5:9 . . . is good and right and **t**.*
*Phil 4:1 . . . stay **t** to the Lord.*
*Phil 4:8 . . . thoughts on what is **t**,*
*Jas 1:18 . . . giving us His **t** word.*
*1 Jn 2:8 . . . the **t** light is already*
*1 Jn 2:27 . . . to teach you what is **t**.*
*1 Jn 5:20 . . . He is the only **t** God,*
*Rev 19:9 . . . These are **t** words that come*
*Rev 22:6 . . . seen is trustworthy and **t**.*

TRUMPET, TRUMPETS (n)
a wind instrument made of metal or an animal horn used to rally troops on the battlefield or by priests during sacrifices
*Isa 27:13 . . . the great **t** will sound.*
*Matt 24:31 . . . blast of a **t**, and they will*
*1 Cor 15:52 . . . when the last **t** is blown.*
*1 Thes 4:16 . . . with the **t** call of God.*
*Rev 8:2 . . . they were given seven **t-s**.*
*Rev 8:7 . . . angel blew his **t**, and hail*
*Rev 18:22 . . . flutes, and **t-s** will never*

TRUST (n)
assured reliance on the character, ability, strength, or truth of someone or something; hope
see also BELIEVE, FAITH
*Job 31:24 . . . Have I put my **t** in money*
*Ps 40:3 . . . put their **t** in the LORD.*
*Ps 56:3 . . . I will put my **t** in You.*
*Isa 2:22 . . . Don't put your **t** in mere*
*Jer 13:25 . . . putting your **t** in false*
*Jer 17:5 . . . who put their **t** in mere*
*John 12:46 . . . who put their **t** in me*
*Heb 2:13 . . . will put my **t** in Him,*
*1 Jn 4:16 . . . have put our **t** in His love.*

TRUST, TRUSTED, TRUSTING, TRUSTS (v)
to place confidence or depend; to commit or place in one's care or keeping; to rely on the truthfulness or accuracy of
see also BELIEVE, FAITH
*Gen 39:8 . . . My master **t-s** me with everything*
*Deut 1:32 . . . refused to **t** the LORD*
*Deut 28:52 . . . walls you **t-ed** to protect*

2 Kgs 18:5 . . . Hezekiah **t-ed** in the
2 Kgs 18:19 . . . What are you **t-ing** in that
1 Chr 5:20 . . . because they **t-ed** in Him.
2 Chr 13:18 . . . they **t-ed** in the LORD,
Job 4:18 . . . God does not **t** His own angels
Job 15:31 . . . fool themselves by **t-ing** in
Ps 13:5 . . . I **t** in Your unfailing love.
Ps 21:7 . . . the king **t-s** in the LORD.
Ps 25:2 . . . I **t** in You, my God!
Ps 25:3 . . . No one who **t-s** in You will ever
Ps 31:14 . . . I am **t-ing** You, O LORD,
Ps 33:4 . . . we can **t** everything He
Ps 37:3 . . . **T** in the LORD and do
Ps 41:9 . . . the one I **t-ed** completely,
Ps 44:6 . . . I do not **t** in my bow;
Ps 55:23 . . . but I am **t-ing** You to save
Ps 62:8 . . . O my people, **t** in Him at
Ps 71:5 . . . I've **t-ed** You, O LORD,
Ps 84:12 . . . for those who **t** in You.
Ps 86:2 . . . serve You and **t** You.
Ps 112:7 . . . confidently **t** the LORD
Ps 115:8 . . . as are all who **t** in them.
Ps 118:8 . . . LORD than to **t** in
Ps 119:42 . . . for I **t** in Your word.
Prov 3:5 . . . **T** in the LORD with
Prov 21:22 . . . fortress in which they **t**.
Prov 28:25 . . . **t-ing** the LORD leads to
Prov 28:26 . . . who **t** their own insight
Prov 29:25 . . . **t-ing** the LORD means safety.
Prov 31:11 . . . Her husband can **t** her,
Isa 12:2 . . . I will **t** in Him and
Isa 25:9 . . . We **t-ed** in Him, and He saved
Isa 26:3 . . . peace all who **t** in you,
Isa 31:1 . . . for help, **t-ing** their horses,
Isa 40:31 . . . who **t** in the LORD
Jer 7:14 . . . this Temple that you **t** in
Jer 12:6 . . . Do not **t** them, no matter
Jer 48:7 . . . Because you have **t-ed** in your
Dan 3:28 . . . His servants who **t-ed** in Him.
Dan 6:23 . . . for he had **t-ed** in his God.
Nah 1:7 . . . to those who **t** in Him.
Hab 2:4 . . . They **t** in themselves,
Hab 2:18 . . . foolish to **t** in your own
Matt 18:6 . . . little ones who **t-s** in Me to
John 2:24 . . . Jesus didn't **t** them,
John 12:44 . . . you are **t-ing** not only Me,
John 14:1 . . . in God, and **t** also in Me.
Rom 9:32 . . . instead of by **t-ing** in Him.
Rom 9:33 . . . But anyone who **t-s** in Him will
Rom 10:11 . . . Anyone who **t-s** in Him will
Rom 15:13 . . . peace because you **t** in
1 Cor 2:5 . . . so you would **t** not in
1 Cor 7:25 . . . wisdom that can be **t-ed**,
Eph 3:17 . . . hearts as you **t** in Him.
Phil 1:29 . . . the privilege of **t-ing** in Christ
Col 2:12 . . . because you **t-ed** the mighty
1 Tim 6:17 . . . not to **t** in their money,
2 Tim 1:12 . . . the One in whom I **t**,
2 Tim 3:15 . . . that comes by **t-ing** in Christ
Heb 10:22 . . . hearts fully **t-ing** Him.
Heb 10:23 . . . God can be **t-ed** to keep His
1 Pet 1:9 . . . reward for **t-ing** Him will be
1 Pet 2:6 . . . anyone who **t-s** in Him will
1 Pet 2:7 . . . you who **t** Him recognize

TRUSTWORTHY (adj)
worthy of confidence; dependable
see also FAITHFUL, LOYAL
2 Kgs 22:7 . . . honest and **t** men.
Ps 19:7 . . . of the LORD are **t**,
Ps 119:86 . . . All Your commands are **t**.
Ps 119:138 . . . perfect and completely **t**.
Prov 11:13 . . . those who are **t** can keep
Dan 6:4 . . . responsible, and completely **t**.
Titus 2:10 . . . to be entirely **t** and good.
Heb 6:19 . . . a strong and **t** anchor

TRUTH, TRUTHS (n)
the property (as of a statement) of being in accord with fact or reality (natural and spiritual); sincerity in action, character, and utterance
Ps 15:2 . . . speaking the **t** from sincere
Ps 25:5 . . . Lead me by Your **t** and teach
Ps 26:3 . . . lived according to Your **t**.
Ps 43:3 . . . light and Your **t**; let them
Ps 45:4 . . . defending **t**, humility, and
Ps 86:11 . . . live according to Your **t**!
Ps 119:160 . . . essence of Your words is **t**;
Prov 8:7 . . . for I speak the **t** and detest
Prov 12:17 . . . honest witness tells the **t**;
Prov 12:22 . . . in those who tell the **t**.
Prov 23:23 . . . Get the **t** and never sell
Isa 45:23 . . . I have spoken the **t**,
Isa 59:15 . . . Yes, **t** is gone,
Jer 4:2 . . . do so with **t**, justice,
Jer 9:3 . . . to stand up for the **t**.
Dan 10:21 . . . written in the Book of **T**.
Dan 11:2 . . . I will reveal the **t** to you.
Amos 5:10 . . . people who tell the **t**!
Zech 8:16 . . . Tell the **t** to each other.
Zech 8:19 . . . So love **t** and peace.
Luke 1:4 . . . can be certain of the **t**
John 4:23 . . . Father in spirit and in **t**.
John 7:18 . . . Him speaks **t**, not lies.
John 8:32 . . . the **t** will set you free.
John 8:44 . . . there is no **t** in him.
John 14:6 . . . way, the **t**, and the life.
John 14:17 . . . who leads into all **t**.
John 15:26 . . . Advocate—the Spirit of **t**.
John 16:13 . . . the Spirit of **t** comes,
John 17:17 . . . Your word, which is **t**.
John 18:37 . . . to testify to the **t**.
Acts 20:30 . . . distort the **t** in order
Acts 21:34 . . . find out the **t** in all
Acts 24:8 . . . can find out the **t** of our
Rom 1:18 . . . who suppress the **t** by their
Rom 1:25 . . . They traded the **t** about God
Rom 2:8 . . . to obey the **t** and instead
Rom 2:20 . . . complete knowledge and **t**.
1 Cor 2:13 . . . to explain spiritual **t-s**.
2 Cor 6:7 . . . We faithfully preach the **t**.
2 Cor 13:8 . . . always stand for the **t**.
Gal 2:5 . . . wanted to preserve the **t**
Gal 5:7 . . . back from following the **t**?
Eph 1:13 . . . also heard the **t**, the Good
Eph 4:15 . . . will speak the **t** in love,
Eph 6:14 . . . the belt of **t** and the body
2 Thes 2:10 . . . **t** that would save them.
2 Thes 2:12 . . . rather than believing the **t**.
1 Tim 2:4 . . . and to understand the **t**.
1 Tim 3:15 . . . and foundation of the **t**.
1 Tim 4:3 . . . people who know the **t**.
1 Tim 6:5 . . . their backs on the **t**.
2 Tim 2:15 . . . explains the word of **t**.
2 Tim 3:7 . . . able to understand the **t**.
Titus 1:14 . . . turned away from the **t**.
Heb 10:26 . . . received knowledge of the **t**,
Jas 3:14 . . . don't cover up the **t** with
Jas 5:19 . . . wanders away from the **t**
1 Pet 1:22 . . . you obeyed the **t**, so now
2 Pet 1:12 . . . standing firm in the **t**
2 Pet 2:2 . . . the way of **t** will be
1 Jn 1:8 . . . and not living in the **t**.
1 Jn 2:20 . . . all of you know the **t**.
1 Jn 3:19 . . . belong to the **t**, so we
1 Jn 4:6 . . . Spirit of **t** or the spirit
1 Jn 5:6 . . . Spirit, who is **t**, confirms
2 Jn 2 . . . because the **t** lives
2 Jn 3 . . . who live in **t** and love.
3 Jn 3 . . . living according to the **t**.
3 Jn 8 . . . partners as they teach the **t**.

TURN, TURNED, TURNING, TURNS (v)
to convert or change allegiance; to return or change direction; to face toward or away; to divert one's attention from; to become or transform; to shape or bend
Deut 28:14 . . . You must not **t** away from
Deut 30:10 . . . if you **t** to the LORD
1 Kgs 11:4 . . . old age, they **t-ed** his heart
2 Chr 7:14 . . . seek My face and **t** from
2 Chr 34:33 . . . they did not **t** away from
Esth 9:22 . . . sorrow was **t-ed** into gladness
Ps 14:3 . . . no, all have **t-ed** away; all
Ps 30:11 . . . You have **t-ed** my mourning
Ps 40:1 . . . and he **t-ed** to me and
Ps 119:59 . . . I **t-ed** to follow Your
Ps 119:102 . . . I haven't **t-ed** away from
Prov 3:7 . . . fear the LORD and **t** away
Prov 28:13 . . . confess and **t** from them,
Isa 17:7 . . . Creator and **t** their eyes to
Isa 54:8 . . . anger I **t-ed** my face away
Isa 55:7 . . . Let them **t** to the LORD
Isa 59:2 . . . He has **t-ed** away and will
Jer 14:7 . . . We have **t-ed** away from You
Jer 31:13 . . . I will **t** their mourning into
Jer 31:19 . . . I **t-ed** away from God,
Lam 3:40 . . . Let us **t** back to the LORD.
Mal 4:6 . . . preaching will **t** the hearts
Matt 3:8 . . . your sins and **t-ed** to God.
Matt 18:3 . . . truth, unless you **t** from your
Mark 4:12 . . . Otherwise, they will **t** to Me
Mark 8:34 . . . must **t** from your selfish
Luke 1:17 . . . He will **t** the hearts of
Luke 22:32 . . . you have repented and **t-ed**
John 12:40 . . . and they cannot **t** to Me
John 16:20 . . . will suddenly **t** to wonderful
Acts 3:19 . . . of your sins and **t** to God,
Acts 7:42 . . . Then God **t-ed** away from them
Acts 26:18 . . . so they may **t** from darkness
Rom 1:26 . . . Even the women **t-ed** against
Rom 2:4 . . . to **t** you from your sin?
Rom 3:12 . . . All have **t-ed** away;
Gal 1:6 . . . that you are **t-ing** away so
2 Tim 2:19 . . . LORD must **t** away from
Titus 2:12 . . . instructed to **t** from godless
Heb 10:38 . . . in anyone who **t-s** away.
1 Pet 2:25 . . . But now you have **t-ed** to

TWELVE (adj)
of or relating to the number 12
Gen 35:22 . . . names of the **t** sons of Jacob:
Gen 49:28 . . . These are the **t** tribes of
Matt 10:1 . . . Jesus called his **t** disciples
Luke 9:17 . . . picked up **t** baskets of
Rev 21:12 . . . names of the **t** tribes of
Rev 21:14 . . . names of the **t** apostles of
Rev 21:21 . . . The **t** gates were made of

U

UNBELIEF (n)
incredulity or skepticism in matters of religious truth
Matt 13:58 . . . there because of their **u**.
Mark 6:6 . . . He was amazed at their **u**.
Mark 9:24 . . . help me overcome my **u**!
Mark 16:14 . . . them for their stubborn **u**
Rom 11:23 . . . Israel turn from their **u**,
1 Tim 1:13 . . . it in ignorance and **u**.
Heb 3:19 . . . because of their **u** they

UNBELIEVER, UNBELIEVERS (n)
one who does not believe; a non-Christian
Matt 6:32 . . . dominate the thoughts of **u-s**,
Luke 12:30 . . . the thoughts of **u-s** all over
1 Cor 6:6 . . . right in front of **u-s**!
1 Cor 14:22 . . . for believers, but for **u-s**.
2 Cor 6:15 . . . a partner with an **u**?

1 Tim 5:8 . . . *people are worse than* ***u-s.***
Rev 21:8 . . . *But cowards,* ***u-s,*** *the corrupt,*

UNCLEAN (adj)
morally or spiritually impure; prohibited by ritual law for use or contact
Lev 10:10 . . . *is ceremonially* ***u*** *and what is*
Lev 11:4 . . . *it is ceremonially* ***u*** *for you.*
Lev 17:15 . . . *remain ceremonially* ***u*** *until*
Lev 27:11 . . . *vow involves an* ***u*** *animal—*
Isa 52:11 . . . *everything you touch is* ***u.***
Acts 10:14 . . . *have declared impure and* ***u.***
Acts 10:15 . . . *not call something* ***u*** *if God*

UNDERSTAND (v)
to grasp the meaning or reasonableness of; to be thoroughly familiar with
Job 5:9 . . . *things too marvelous to* ***u.***
Job 36:26 . . . *is greater than we can* ***u.***
Ps 73:16 . . . *tried to* ***u*** *why the wicked*
Ps 119:27 . . . *Help me* ***u*** *the meaning of*
Ps 119:125 . . . *then I will* ***u*** *Your laws.*
Ps 119:130 . . . *so even the simple can* ***u.***
Prov 2:5 . . . *will* ***u*** *what it means to fear*
Prov 2:9 . . . *you will* ***u*** *what is right,*
Prov 28:5 . . . *the* L*ORD* ***u*** *completely.*
Prov 30:18 . . . *things that I don't* ***u:***
Eccl 7:25 . . . *and to* ***u*** *the reason*
Isa 6:9 . . . *carefully, but do not* ***u.***
Isa 40:21 . . . *you heard? Don't you* ***u?***
Jer 9:24 . . . *truly know Me and* ***u*** *that*
Hos 14:9 . . . *who are wise* ***u*** *these things.*
Matt 13:11 . . . *permitted to* ***u*** *the secrets*
Matt 13:23 . . . *truly hear and* ***u*** *God's*
Luke 19:42 . . . *people would* ***u*** *the way*
Luke 24:45 . . . *minds to* ***u*** *the Scriptures.*
Acts 8:30 . . . *Do you* ***u*** *what you are*
Rom 7:15 . . . *I don't really* ***u*** *myself,*
Rom 15:21 . . . *never heard of Him will* ***u.***
1 Cor 2:14 . . . *and they can't* ***u*** *it,*
1 Cor 14:14 . . . *but I don't* ***u*** *what I am*
2 Cor 3:14 . . . *they cannot* ***u*** *the truth.*
Gal 1:11 . . . *you to* ***u*** *that the gospel*
Eph 1:18 . . . *you can* ***u*** *the confident*
Eph 5:17 . . . *thoughtlessly, but* ***u*** *what*
Phil 1:10 . . . *want you to* ***u*** *what really*
Phil 4:7 . . . *exceeds anything we can* ***u.***
Col 2:2 . . . *that they* ***u*** *God's mysterious*
1 Tim 2:4 . . . *saved and to* ***u*** *the truth.*
2 Tim 2:7 . . . *will help you* ***u*** *all these*
Heb 11:3 . . . *By faith we* ***u*** *that the entire*
2 Pet 3:16 . . . *are hard to* ***u,*** *and those*

UNITED (v)
to become one or as if one; in one accord or spirit
Gen 2:24 . . . *the two are* ***u*** *into one.*
Mark 10:8 . . . *the two are* ***u*** *into one.*
Rom 6:5 . . . *we have been* ***u*** *with Him*
Rom 7:4 . . . *now you are* ***u*** *with the One*
1 Cor 6:16 . . . *The two are* ***u*** *into One.*
Eph 4:3 . . . *to keep yourselves* ***u*** *in the*

UNITY (n)
the quality or state of oneness or harmony
John 17:23 . . . *perfect* ***u*** *that the world*
Eph 4:13 . . . *come to such* ***u*** *in our faith*

UPRIGHT (adj)
marked by strong moral integrity
see also RIGHT, RIGHTEOUS
Deut 32:4 . . . *how just and* ***u*** *He is!*
Prov 3:33 . . . *blesses the home of the* ***u.***
Prov 15:8 . . . *in the prayers of the* ***u.***

USEFUL (adj)
serviceable for an end or purpose
2 Tim 3:16 . . . *inspired by God and is* ***u*** *to*
2 Pet 1:8 . . . *productive and* ***u*** *you will be*

USELESS (adj)
having or being of no use; ineffectual, inept
Acts 26:14 . . . *It is* ***u*** *for you to fight*
1 Cor 13:8 . . . *knowledge will become* ***u.***
1 Cor 15:14 . . . ***u,*** *and your faith is* ***u.***
1 Cor 15:58 . . . *do for the Lord is ever* ***u.***
2 Tim 2:14 . . . *Such arguments are* ***u,*** *and*
Titus 1:10 . . . *who engage in* ***u*** *talk and*
Heb 7:18 . . . *because it was weak and* ***u.***

V

VALLEY, VALLEYS (n)
a depression in the earth's surface between ranges of mountains, hills, or other uplands
Ps 23:4 . . . *through the darkest* ***v,*** *I will*
Song 2:1 . . . *lily of the* ***v.***
Isa 40:4 . . . *Fill in the* ***v-s,*** *and level*
Joel 3:14 . . . *waiting in the* ***v*** *of decision.*
Luke 3:5 . . . *The* ***v-s*** *will be filled, and*

VALUABLE (adj)
having desirable or esteemed characteristics or qualities; of great use or service
Job 28:17 . . . *Wisdom is more* ***v*** *than gold*
Ps 119:72 . . . *instructions are more* ***v***
Prov 8:11 . . . *is far more* ***v*** *than rubies.*
Prov 20:15 . . . *words are more* ***v*** *than*
Matt 10:31 . . . *you are more* ***v*** *to God than*
Luke 12:24 . . . *are far more* ***v*** *to Him than*
Phil 3:7 . . . *these things were* ***v,*** *but now*

VALUE (n)
monetary worth of something; relative worth, utility, or importance
Matt 13:46 . . . *a pearl of great* ***v,*** *he sold*
1 Cor 3:13 . . . *a person's work has any* ***v.***
Phil 3:8 . . . *the infinite* ***v*** *of knowing*

VENGEANCE (n)
punishment inflicted in retaliation for an injury or offense
1 Sam 25:26 . . . *taking* ***v*** *into your own*
1 Sam 25:33 . . . *carrying out* ***v*** *with My*
Ps 94:1 . . . *O* L*ORD, the God of* ***v,***
Isa 66:6 . . . *the* L*ORD taking* ***v*** *against*
Luke 21:22 . . . *be days of God's* ***v,*** *and the*

VICTORY, VICTORIES (n)
the overcoming of an enemy, antagonist, or struggle
Exod 15:2 . . . *He has given me* ***v.***
2 Sam 22:51 . . . *You give great* ***v-ies*** *to Your*
Ps 18:50 . . . *You give great* ***v-ies*** *to Your*
Ps 20:5 . . . *we hear of Your* ***v*** *and*
Ps 21:1 . . . *because You give him* ***v.***
Ps 35:3 . . . *I will give you* ***v!***
Ps 44:4 . . . *You command* ***v-ies*** *for Israel.*
Ps 45:4 . . . *majesty, ride out to* ***v,***
Ps 48:10 . . . *right hand is filled with* ***v.***
Ps 62:1 . . . *for my* ***v*** *comes from Him.*
Ps 98:3 . . . *have seen the* ***v*** *of our God.*
Ps 118:14 . . . *He has given me* ***v.***
Ps 149:4 . . . *crowns the humble with* ***v.***
Isa 12:2 . . . *He has given me* ***v.***
Isa 52:10 . . . *see the* ***v*** *of our God.*
Rom 8:37 . . . *overwhelming* ***v*** *is ours*
1 Cor 15:54 . . . *Death is swallowed up in* ***v.***
Col 2:15 . . . *publicly by His* ***v*** *over them*
Rev 5:5 . . . *David's throne, has won the* ***v.***

VINEYARD (n)
a plantation of grapevines
1 Kgs 21:1 . . . *who owned a* ***v*** *in Jezreel*
Prov 31:16 . . . *earnings she plants a* ***v.***
Song 1:6 . . . *for myself—my own* ***v.***
Isa 5:1 . . . *beloved had a* ***v*** *on a rich*
1 Cor 9:7 . . . *farmer plants a* ***v*** *and*

VIOLATE, VIOLATED, VIOLATES, VIOLATING (v)
to do harm to the person or especially the chastity of; to fail to show proper respect for; to break or disregard
Lev 18:7 . . . *Do not* ***v*** *your father*
Lev 18:8 . . . *for this would* ***v*** *your father.*
Lev 18:10 . . . *this would* ***v*** *yourself.*
Lev 18:14 . . . *Do not* ***v*** *your uncle,*
Lev 18:16 . . . *this would* ***v*** *your brother.*
Lev 20:11 . . . *If a man* ***v-s*** *his father by*
Lev 20:20 . . . *he has* ***v-d*** *his uncle.*
Lev 20:21 . . . *He has* ***v-d*** *his brother, and*
Num 15:30 . . . *who brazenly* ***v*** *the* L*ORD's*
Deut 22:30 . . . *for this would* ***v*** *his father.*
Deut 27:20 . . . *for he has* ***v-d*** *his father.*
Isa 24:5 . . . *instructions,* ***v-d*** *His laws,*
Mal 2:10 . . . *each other,* ***v-ing*** *the covenant of*

VIOLENCE (n)
exertion of physical force so as to injure or abuse
Gen 6:11 . . . *and was filled with* ***v.***
Ps 12:5 . . . *I have seen* ***v*** *done to the*
Ps 72:14 . . . *them from oppression and* ***v,***
Isa 60:18 . . . ***V*** *will disappear from your*
Jon 3:8 . . . *and stop all their* ***v.***
Mic 2:2 . . . *take it by fraud and* ***v.***

VOICE (n)
verbal communication by human and divine means
Isa 40:3 . . . *the* ***v*** *of someone shouting,*
Mark 1:3 . . . *He is a* ***v*** *shouting in the*
John 10:3 . . . *sheep recognize His* ***v*** *and*
John 12:28 . . . *a* ***v*** *spoke from heaven,*
Rev 3:20 . . . *If you hear My* ***v*** *and open*

VOW, VOWS (n)
a binding promise or pledge
see also COVENANT, PROMISE
Num 6:2 . . . *the special* ***v*** *of a Nazirite,*
Judg 11:30 . . . *Jephthah made a* ***v*** *to the*
Ps 110:4 . . . *and will not break His* ***v:***
Matt 5:34 . . . *do not make any* ***v-s!***
Heb 7:21 . . . *and will not break His* ***v:***

VOWED (v)
to promise solemnly
Eccl 8:2 . . . *since you* ***v*** *to God that*
Mark 7:11 . . . *For I have* ***v*** *to give to*

W

WAGE, WAGES (n)
payment for labor or services; compensation
Hag 1:6 . . . *Your* ***w-s*** *disappear as though*
Zech 11:12 . . . *give me my* ***w-s,*** *whatever*
Mal 3:5 . . . *cheat employees of their* ***w-s,***
Matt 20:2 . . . *the normal daily* ***w*** *and*
Rom 4:4 . . . *their* ***w-s*** *are not a gift,*
Rom 6:23 . . . *For the* ***w-s*** *of sin is death,*

WAIT, WAITED, WAITING (v)
to look forward expectantly; to stay in place in expectation of
Ps 40:1 . . . *I* ***w-ed*** *patiently for the* L*ORD*
Ps 62:5 . . . *that I am* ***w*** *quietly before*
Ps 69:3 . . . ***w-ing*** *for my God to help me.*
Isa 30:18 . . . *Blessed are those who* ***w*** *for*
Mic 7:7 . . . *I* ***w*** *confidently for God to*
Hab 3:16 . . . *I will* ***w*** *quietly for the*
Luke 12:37 . . . *who are ready and* ***w-ing***
Rom 8:19 . . . *all creation is* ***w-ing*** *eagerly*
Rom 8:23 . . . *We, too,* ***w*** *with eager hope*
Heb 9:28 . . . *are eagerly* ***w-ing*** *for Him.*

WALK, WALKED, WALKING (v)
to roam, traverse, or advance by steps; to pursue a course of action or way of life
Gen 3:8 . . . *God* ***w-ing*** *about in the garden.*

*Lev 26:12 . . . I will **w** among you;*
*Deut 11:22 . . . your God by **w-ing** in His ways*
*Deut 26:17 . . . promised to **w** in His ways,*
*Josh 22:5 . . . God, **w** in all His ways,*
*Ps 23:4 . . . when I **w** through the*
*Ps 89:15 . . . they will **w** in the light*
*Prov 4:12 . . . When you **w**, you won't*
*Prov 6:22 . . . When you **w**, their counsel*
*Isa 2:3 . . . we will **w** in His paths.*
*Isa 40:31 . . . They will **w** and not*
*Isa 43:2 . . . When you **w** through the*
*Jer 6:16 . . . godly way, and **w** in it.*
*Dan 3:25 . . . **w-ing** around in the fire*
*Amos 3:3 . . . two people **w** together*
*Mic 6:8 . . . to **w** humbly with your God.*
*Mal 2:6 . . . they **w-ed** with me, living good*
*Matt 14:29 . . . boat and **w-ed** on the water*
*Mark 2:9 . . . pick up your mat, and **w***
*John 8:12 . . . have to **w** in darkness,*

WANDER, WANDERED, WANDERS (v)
to follow a winding course; to stray
*Num 32:13 . . . them **w** in the wilderness*
*Ps 119:10 . . . don't let me **w** from Your*
*Ps 119:67 . . . I used to **w** off until You*
*Ps 119:176 . . . I have **w-ed** away like a*
*Matt 18:12 . . . one of them **w-s** away*
*Eph 4:18 . . . they **w** far from the life God*
*1 Tim 6:10 . . . have **w-ed** from the true*
*Jas 5:19 . . . someone among you **w-s***
*1 Pet 2:25 . . . like sheep who **w-ed** away.*
*2 Pet 2:15 . . . They have **w-ed** off the*

WAR, WARS (n)
armed conflict with an opposing military force; a state of hostility, conflict, or antagonism
*Josh 11:23 . . . finally had rest from **w**.*
*Ps 46:9 . . . He causes **w-s** to end*
*Ps 68:30 . . . nations that delight in **w**.*
*Ps 120:7 . . . peace, they want **w**!*
*Ps 144:1 . . . He trains my hands for **w***
*Isa 2:4 . . . nor train for **w** anymore.*
*2 Cor 10:3 . . . we don't wage **w** as humans*
*1 Pet 2:11 . . . that wage **w** against your*
*Rev 12:7 . . . Then there was **w** in heaven.*
*Rev 19:11 . . . and wages a righteous **w**.*

WARN, WARNED, WARNING (v)
to give notice to beforehand especially of danger or evil; to counsel
*Gen 2:16 . . . God **w-ed** him, "You may freely*
*Gen 31:24 . . . told him, "I'm **w-ing** you—*
*Gen 31:29 . . . to me last night and **w-ed** me,*
*Exod 19:21 . . . down and **w** the people*
*Num 16:40 . . . This would **w** the Israelites*
*1 Sam 8:9 . . . but solemnly **w** them about*
*1 Kgs 2:42 . . . LORD and **w** you not to*
*2 Kgs 17:13 . . . and seers to **w** both Israel*
*2 Chr 19:10 . . . must **w** them not to sin*
*Ezek 3:18 . . . If I **w** the wicked,*
*Ezek 33:3 . . . the alarm to **w** the people.*
*Luke 16:28 . . . I want him to **w** them so*
*Matt 16:6 . . . "Watch out!" Jesus **w-ed** them.*
*Acts 4:17 . . . must **w** them not to speak*
*1 Cor 4:14 . . . to **w** you as My beloved*
*1 Cor 10:11 . . . written down to **w** us who*
*Col 1:28 . . . **w-ing** everyone and teaching*
*1 Thes 4:6 . . . solemnly **w-ed** you before.*
*1 Thes 5:14 . . . urge you to **w** those who*
*2 Thes 3:15 . . . but **w** them as you would*
*Heb 3:13 . . . You must **w** each other*

WARNING, WARNINGS (n)
something that warns or serves to warn; the act of warning
*Ps 19:11 . . . They are a **w** to Your servant,*
*Ps 81:8 . . . while I give you stern **w-s**.*
*Jer 6:8 . . . Listen to this **w**, Jerusalem,*
*Jer 42:19 . . . Don't forget this **w** I have*
*Zeph 3:7 . . . they will listen to My **w-s**.*
*1 Cor 10:6 . . . happened as a **w** to us,*
*1 Tim 5:20 . . . as a strong **w** to others.*
*Titus 3:10 . . . give a first and second **w**.*

WARRIOR, WARRIORS (n)
a man engaged or experienced in warfare
*Gen 6:4 . . . and famous **w-s** of ancient*
*Exod 15:3 . . . LORD is a **w**; Yahweh*
*Josh 1:14 . . . strong **w-s**, fully armed,*
*1 Chr 28:3 . . . for you are a **w** and*
*Ps 45:3 . . . Your sword, O mighty **w**!*
*Jer 20:11 . . . beside me like a great **w**.*

WASH, WASHED (v)
to cleanse—of physical, ceremonial, or spiritual significance
*Ps 51:7 . . . **w** me, and I will be whiter*
*John 13:5 . . . He began to **w** the disciples'*
*John 13:10 . . . does not need to **w**, except*
*Acts 22:16 . . . Have your sins **w-ed** away*
*Eph 5:26 . . . holy and clean, **w-ed** by the*
*Titus 3:5 . . . He **w-ed** away our sins,*
*Heb 10:22 . . . bodies have been **w-ed***
*Jas 4:8 . . . **W** your hands, you sinners;*
*2 Pet 2:22 . . . **w-ed** pig returns to the mud.*
*Rev 7:14 . . . They have **w-ed** their robes in*
*Rev 22:14 . . . those who **w** their robes.*

WASTE, WASTED (v)
to spend or use carelessly or inefficiently
*Ps 127:1 . . . work of the builders is **w-d**.*
*Prov 29:3 . . . prostitutes, his wealth is **w-d**.*
*Prov 31:3 . . . do not **w** your strength*
*Luke 15:13 . . . there he **w-d** all his money*
*John 6:12 . . . so that nothing is **w-d**.*
*Gal 2:2 . . . all my efforts had been **w-d***

WATCH, WATCHES, WATCHING (v)
to diligently wait or keep guard; to observe closely
*Judg 18:6 . . . the LORD is **w-ing** over*
*Job 14:16 . . . my steps, instead of **w-ing***
*Job 34:21 . . . God **w-es** how people live;*
*Ps 1:6 . . . For the LORD **w-es** over the*
*Ps 17:11 . . . and surround me, **w-ing** for*
*Ps 61:7 . . . faithfulness **w** over him.*
*Ps 121:3 . . . one who **w-es** over you will*
*Prov 2:11 . . . Wise choices will **w** over*
*Prov 31:27 . . . carefully **w-es** everything*
*Eccl 11:4 . . . If they **w** every cloud,*
*Jer 24:6 . . . I will **w** over and care for*
*Jer 31:10 . . . gather them and **w** over*
*Acts 1:9 . . . while they were **w-ing**, and*
*Eph 6:6 . . . just when they are **w-ing** you.*
*Heb 13:17 . . . is to **w** over your souls,*
*1 Pet 1:12 . . . eagerly **w-ing** these things*
*1 Pet 3:12 . . . eyes of the Lord **w** over*

WATER, WATERS (n)
precious resource for drink and irrigation, usually associated with blessing; a body of water
*Exod 7:20 . . . struck the **w** of the Nile.*
*Exod 17:1 . . . there was no **w** there for*
*Num 20:2 . . . was no **w** for the people*
*2 Sam 23:15 . . . good **w** from the well*
*Ps 42:1 . . . streams of **w**, so I long*
*Prov 25:21 . . . give them **w** to drink.*
*Song 8:7 . . . Many **w-s** cannot quench*
*Isa 11:9 . . . for as the **w-s** fill the sea,*
*Isa 32:2 . . . like streams of **w** in the*
*Isa 43:2 . . . through deep **w-s**, I will be*
*Isa 49:10 . . . lead them beside cool **w-s**.*
*Jer 17:8 . . . reach deep into the **w**.*
*Jon 2:3 . . . The mighty **w-s** engulfed me;*
*Hab 2:14 . . . For as the **w-s** fill the sea,*
*Zech 14:8 . . . life-giving **w-s** will flow*
*Matt 14:25 . . . them, walking on the **w**.*
*John 3:5 . . . born of **w** and the Spirit.*
*John 4:10 . . . would give you living **w**.*
*John 7:38 . . . Rivers of living **w** will*
*1 Jn 5:6 . . . His baptism in **w** and by*
*Rev 7:17 . . . springs of life-giving **w**.*
*Rev 21:6 . . . springs of the **w** of life.*

WAY, WAYS (n)
characteristic, regular, or habitual manner or mode of being, behaving, or happening; manner or method of doing or happening; a course of action; route
*Exod 33:13 . . . let me know your **w-s***
*Deut 26:17 . . . to walk in His **w-s**, and*
*Deut 30:16 . . . by walking in His **w-s**.*
*Josh 22:5 . . . walk in all His **w-s**, obey*
*2 Sam 22:31 . . . God's **w** is perfect.*
*Ps 77:13 . . . O God, Your **w-s** are holy.*
*Ps 86:11 . . . Teach me Your **w-s**, O LORD,*
*Prov 2:9 . . . find the right **w** to go.*
*Prov 4:11 . . . teach you wisdom's **w-s***
*Eccl 8:6 . . . and a **w** for everything,*
*Isa 2:3 . . . teach us His **w-s**, and we will*
*Isa 40:3 . . . Clear the **w** through the*
*Jer 6:16 . . . old, godly **w**, and walk in*
*Mic 4:2 . . . teach us His **w-s**, and we will*
*Mal 3:1 . . . prepare the **w** before me.*
*Matt 3:3 . . . Prepare the **w** for the*
*Matt 3:8 . . . Prove by the **w** you live*
*Luke 7:27 . . . prepare your **w** before you.*
*John 14:6 . . . I am the **w**, the truth,*
*Acts 9:2 . . . followers of the **W** he*
*Acts 24:14 . . . I follow the **W**, which*
*Rom 1:30 . . . invent new **w-s** of sinning,*
*1 Cor 10:13 . . . will show you a **w** out*
*1 Cor 12:31 . . . show you a **w** of life*
*Col 1:10 . . . Then the **w** you live will*
*Heb 10:20 . . . and life-giving **w** through*

WEAK, WEAKER, WEAKEST (adj)
lacking strength; not able to withstand temptation or persuasion
*Ps 72:13 . . . pity for the **w** and the*
*Ps 103:14 . . . He knows how **w** we are;*
*Isa 59:1 . . . arm is not too **w** to save*
*Matt 12:20 . . . will not crush the **w-est** reed*
*Matt 26:41 . . . but the body is **w**!*
*Rom 14:1 . . . who are **w** in faith,*
*1 Cor 9:22 . . . bring the **w** to Christ.*
*1 Cor 8:9 . . . others with a **w-er** conscience*
*1 Cor 11:30 . . . many of you are **w** and*
*1 Cor 12:22 . . . of the body that seem **w-est***
*2 Cor 12:10 . . . For when I am **w**, then*
*1 Thes 5:14 . . . care of those who are **w**.*

WEAKNESS, WEAKNESSES (n)
the quality or state of being weak
*Ps 136:23 . . . He remembered us in our **w**.*
*Isa 53:4 . . . it was our **w-es** He carried;*
*Rom 8:3 . . . the **w** of our sinful nature.*
*Rom 8:26 . . . Spirit helps us in our **w**.*
*1 Cor 1:25 . . . God's **w** is stronger than*
*1 Cor 2:3 . . . I came to you in **w**—timid*
*2 Cor 12:5 . . . boast only about my **w-es**.*
*2 Cor 12:10 . . . take pleasure in my **w-es**,*
*2 Cor 13:4 . . . He was crucified in **w**,*
*Heb 5:2 . . . is subject to the same **w-es**.*

WEALTH (n)
abundance of valuable material possessions or resources
see also MONEY, POSSESSIONS, RICHES, TREASURE(S)
*2 Chr 1:11 . . . not ask for **w**, riches,*
*Job 36:18 . . . you may be seduced by **w**.*
*Ps 39:6 . . . We heap up **w**, not knowing*
*Ps 62:10 . . . if your **w** increases, don't*
*Prov 3:9 . . . the LORD with your **w***
*Prov 10:2 . . . Tainted **w** has no lasting*
*Prov 13:11 . . . **w** from hard work grows*
*Prov 21:20 . . . wise have **w** and luxury,*

Prov 29:3 . . . prostitutes, his **w** *is wasted.*
Eccl 4:8 . . . gain as much **w** *as he can.*
Luke 19:8 . . . give half my **w** *to the poor,*
Eph 2:7 . . . of the incredible **w** *of his*
1 Tim 6:6 . . . contentment is itself great **w.**
Jas 5:3 . . . The very **w** *you were counting*

WEALTHY (adj)
characterized by abundance
Prov 11:24 . . . freely and become more **w;**
Eccl 2:26 . . . sinner becomes **w,** *God takes*
1 Cor 1:26 . . . or **w** *when God called you.*

WEARY (adj)
exhausted in strength, endurance, or vigor
Isa 40:31 . . . They will run and not grow **w.**
Isa 50:4 . . . know how to comfort the **w.**
Matt 11:28 . . . you who are **w** *and carry*
2 Cor 5:2 . . . We grow **w** *in our present*
Heb 12:3 . . . won't become **w** *and give up.*

WEDDING, WEDDINGS (n)
a marriage ceremony usually with its accompanying festivities
Matt 11:17 . . . We played **w** *songs, and*
Matt 22:11 . . . the proper clothes for a **w.**
Matt 24:38 . . . parties and **w-s** *right up*
Rev 19:7 . . . for the **w** *feast of the Lamb,*

WEEP, WEEPING (v)
to cry aloud, often linked with prayer and repentance
2 Sam 1:26 . . . How I **w** *for you,*
Ps 126:6 . . . They **w** *as they go to*
Jer 31:15 . . . deep anguish and bitter **w-ing.**
Jer 31:16 . . . Do not **w** *any longer,*
Jer 50:4 . . . will come **w-ing** *and seeking*
*Matt 2:18 . . . heard in Ramah—***w-ing** *and*
Matt 8:12 . . . will be **w-ing** *and gnashing*
Luke 6:21 . . . blesses you who **w** *now,*
Luke 22:62 . . . the courtyard, **w-ing** *bitterly.*
Luke 23:28 . . . don't **w** *for Me, but* **w**
Rom 12:15 . . . and **w** *with those who* **w.**

WHEAT (n)
a cereal grain that yields a fine white flour
Matt 3:12 . . . gathering the **w** *into his barn*
Matt 13:25 . . . among the **w,** *then slipped*
Mark 4:28 . . . the heads of **w** *are formed,*
Luke 22:31 . . . sift each of you like **w.**
John 12:24 . . . a kernel of **w** *is planted in*

WHIRLWIND (n)
a small rotating windstorm, sometimes violent and destructive
see also STORM
2 Kgs 2:1 . . . to heaven in a **w,**
Job 38:1 . . . answered Job from the **w:**
Hos 8:7 . . . and will harvest the **w.**
Nah 1:3 . . . in the **w** *and the storm.*

WHISPER (n)
a minor or softer reflection of the original noise; hint, trace
1 Kgs 19:12 . . . sound of a gentle **w.**
Job 26:14 . . . merely a **w** *of His power.*
Ps 107:29 . . . calmed the storm to a **w**

WHITE, WHITER (adj)
free from color; of the color white
Ps 51:7 . . . I will be **w-r** *than snow.*
Isa 1:18 . . . make them as **w** *as snow.*
Dan 7:9 . . . clothing was as **w** *as snow,*
Matt 28:3 . . . clothing was as **w** *as snow.*
Rev 1:14 . . . like wool, as **w** *as snow.*
Rev 6:2 . . . saw a **w** *horse standing*
Rev 19:11 . . . a **w** *horse was standing*
Rev 20:11 . . . saw a great **w** *throne*

WHITE (n)
the absence of color
Rev 3:4 . . . will walk with Me in **w,**
Rev 7:13 . . . who are clothed in **w?**

WHOLE (adj)
entire; complete, unmodified; undivided
1 Sam 1:28 . . . LORD *his* **w** *life.*
1 Sam 17:46 . . . the **w** *world will know*
1 Chr 28:9 . . . Him with your **w** *heart*
Ps 72:19 . . . Let the **w** *earth be filled*
Ps 103:1 . . . with my **w** *heart, I will*
Prov 4:22 . . . healing to their **w** *body.*
Eccl 12:13 . . . That's the **w** *story.*
Isa 6:3 . . . The **w** *earth is filled*
Isa 14:26 . . . plan for the **w** *earth,*
Dan 2:35 . . . covered the **w** *earth.*
Zeph 1:18 . . . For the **w** *land will be*
Matt 6:22 . . . eye is good, your **w** *body*
Matt 16:26 . . . gain the **w** *world but lose*
Matt 24:14 . . . throughout the **w** *world,*
John 21:25 . . . I suppose the **w** *world*
Acts 17:26 . . . throughout the **w** *earth.*
1 Cor 12:17 . . . Or if your **w** *body were*
Gal 5:3 . . . regulation in the **w** *law of*

WHORE (KJV)
Lev 21:7 . . . marry a woman ***defiled by prostitution***
Deut 23:18 . . . from the earnings of a ***prostitute***
Prov 23:27 . . . A ***prostitute*** *is a dangerous trap*
Hosea 4:14 . . . sinning with ***whores***
Rev 17:1 . . . ***prostitute,*** *who rules over*

WICKED (adj)
morally very bad
Gen 13:13 . . . area were extremely **w** *and*
2 Sam 22:27 . . . but to the **w** *You show*
Ps 1:1 . . . the advice of the **w,** *or stand*
Ps 7:9 . . . those who are **w,** *and defend*
Ps 10:13 . . . Why do the **w** *get away with*
Ps 12:8 . . . though the **w** *strut about,*
Ps 14:6 . . . The **w** *frustrate the plans*
Ps 18:26 . . . but to the **w** *You show*
Ps 37:1 . . . worry about the **w** *or envy*
Ps 82:2 . . . by favoring the **w?**
Ps 101:8 . . . ferret out the **w** *and free*
Ps 139:19 . . . you would destroy the **w!**
Ps 146:9 . . . the plans of the **w.**
Prov 4:14 . . . Don't do as the **w** *do,*
Prov 9:7 . . . who corrects the **w** *will*
Prov 10:7 . . . name of a **w** *person rots*
Prov 10:28 . . . expectations of the **w** *come*
Prov 11:10 . . . joy when the **w** *die.*
Prov 12:5 . . . of the **w** *is treacherous.*
Prov 26:23 . . . may hide a **w** *heart, just*
Prov 29:7 . . . the **w** *don't care at all.*
Isa 5:23 . . . to let the **w** *go free,*
Isa 11:4 . . . mouth will destroy the **w.**
Isa 26:10 . . . the **w** *keep doing wrong*
Isa 48:22 . . . no peace for the **w,**
Jer 35:15 . . . Turn from your **w** *ways,*
Ezek 18:21 . . . But if **w** *people turn away*
Ezek 21:25 . . . you corrupt and **w** *prince*
Ezek 33:8 . . . that some **w** *people are sure*
Hos 10:9 . . . not right that the **w** *men of*
Jon 1:2 . . . I have seen how **w** *its people*
Mal 4:1 . . . arrogant and the **w** *will be*
Luke 6:35 . . . who are unthankful and **w.**
1 Jn 5:17 . . . All **w** *actions are sin,*

WICKEDNESS (n)
the quality or state of being wicked; something wicked
Lev 16:21 . . . it all the **w,** *rebellion,*
Lev 19:29 . . . with prostitution and **w.**
Deut 9:4 . . . because of the **w** *of the other*
Ps 73:3 . . . them prosper despite their **w.**
Jer 3:2 . . . your prostitution and your **w.**
Jer 14:16 . . . out their own **w** *on them.*
Jer 14:20 . . . we confess our **w** *and that*
Ezek 33:19 . . . turn from their **w** *and do*
Luke 11:39 . . . of greed and **w!**
Rom 1:18 . . . the truth by their **w.**
Rom 1:29 . . . every kind of **w,** *sin, greed,*
Rom 2:8 . . . and instead live lives of **w.**
2 Cor 6:14 . . . be a partner with **w?**
Heb 8:12 . . . I will forgive their **w,**

WIDOW, WIDOWS (n)
a woman whose husband has died
Deut 10:18 . . . orphans and **w-s** *receive*
Ps 68:5 . . . defender of **w-s***—this is God,*
Ps 146:9 . . . for the orphans and **w-s,** *but*
Isa 1:17 . . . Fight for the rights of **w-s.**
Luke 21:2 . . . Then a poor **w** *came by and*
Acts 6:1 . . . that their **w-s** *were being*
1 Cor 7:8 . . . aren't married and to **w-s***—*
1 Tim 5:3 . . . Take care of any **w** *who*
1 Tim 5:16 . . . care for the **w-s** *who are*
Jas 1:27 . . . for orphans and **w-s** *in their*

WIFE (n)
the female partner in a marriage
see also WIVES
Gen 2:24 . . . and is joined to his **w,**
Gen 19:26 . . . But Lot's **w** *looked back*
Exod 20:17 . . . covet your neighbor's **w,**
Lev 20:10 . . . his neighbor's **w,** *both*
Deut 5:21 . . . not covet your neighbor's **w.**
Deut 24:5 . . . happiness to the **w** *he has*
Prov 5:18 . . . Rejoice in the **w** *of your*
Prov 12:4 . . . A worthy **w** *is a crown*
Prov 18:22 . . . man who finds a **w**
Prov 19:13 . . . a quarrelsome **w** *is as*
Prov 21:9 . . . a quarrelsome **w** *in a*
Prov 31:10 . . . a virtuous and capable **w?**
Mal 2:14 . . . vows you and your **w** *made*
Matt 1:20 . . . to take Mary as your **w.**
Matt 19:3 . . . to divorce his **w** *for just*
Luke 17:32 . . . happened to Lot's **w!**
Luke 18:29 . . . up house or **w** *or brothers*
1 Cor 7:2 . . . should have his own **w,**
1 Cor 7:15 . . . the husband or **w** *who isn't*
1 Cor 7:33 . . . and how to please his **w.**
Eph 5:23 . . . head of his **w** *as Christ*
Eph 5:33 . . . love his **w** *as he loves*
1 Tim 3:12 . . . be faithful to his **w,**
Titus 1:6 . . . be faithful to his **w,**
1 Pet 3:7 . . . Treat your **w** *with*
Rev 21:9 . . . bride, the **w** *of the Lamb.*

WILDERNESS (n)
any desolate, barren, or unpopulated area, usually linked with danger
see also DESERT
Num 16:13 . . . kill us here in this **w,**
Num 26:65 . . . all die in the **w.**
Num 32:13 . . . wander in the **w** *for forty*
Deut 8:16 . . . manna in the **w,** *a food*
Deut 29:5 . . . led you through the **w,**
Ps 78:19 . . . give us food in the **w.**
Ps 78:52 . . . safely through the **w.**
Isa 32:15 . . . **w** *will become a fertile*
Isa 35:6 . . . will gush forth in the **w,**
Matt 3:3 . . . the **w,** *'Prepare the way*
Luke 5:16 . . . withdrew to the **w** *for*
Rev 12:6 . . . fled into the **w,** *where God*

WILL (n)
desire, wish
Ps 40:8 . . . in doing Your **w,** *my God,*
Ps 143:10 . . . me to do Your **w,** *for You*
Prov 3:6 . . . Seek His **w** *in all you do,*
Matt 6:10 . . . May Your **w** *be done on*
Matt 7:21 . . . who actually do the **w**
Matt 12:50 . . . does the **w** *of My Father*
Matt 18:14 . . . heavenly Father's **w** *that*
Matt 26:39 . . . want Your **w** *to be done,*
Matt 26:42 . . . I drink it, Your **w** *be done.*

*John 5:30 . . . carry out the **w** of the one*
*John 6:38 . . . heaven to do the **w** of God*
*1 Thes 5:18 . . . this is God's **w** for you*
*Heb 10:7 . . . come to do Your **w**, O God—*
*Heb 13:21 . . . need for doing His **w**.*
*1 Pet 4:2 . . . to do the **w** of God.*

WINE (n)
the fermented juice of grapes, linked positively with blessings and negatively with strong drink
*Ps 104:15 . . . **w** to make them glad,*
*Prov 31:6 . . . and **w** for those in bitter*
*Song 1:2 . . . love is sweeter than **w**.*
*Isa 28:7 . . . who reel with **w** and stagger*
*Mark 15:36 . . . with sour **w**, holding it*
*John 2:3 . . . The **w** supply ran out*
*Rom 14:21 . . . to eat meat or drink **w***
*Eph 5:18 . . . Don't be drunk with **w**,*
*1 Tim 5:23 . . . drink a little **w** for*
*Rev 16:19 . . . was filled with the **w***

WINEBIBBER(S) (KJV)
*Prov 23:20 . . . Do not carouse with **drunkards***
*Matt 11:19 . . . glutton and a **drunkard**, and*
*Luke 7:34 . . . glutton and a **drunkard**, and*

WINESKINS (n)
a bag made from the skin of an animal that holds wine
*Matt 9:17 . . . stored in new **w** so that*
*Luke 5:37 . . . new wine into old **w**.*

WISDOM (n)
knowledge, insight, judgment
*Gen 3:6 . . . she wanted the **w** it would*
*1 Kgs 4:29 . . . gave Solomon very great **w***
*1 Kgs 10:24 . . . to hear the **w** God had*
*2 Chr 1:10 . . . Give me the **w** and*
*Job 11:6 . . . **w**, for true **w** is not*
*Job 42:3 . . . that questions my **w** with such*
*Ps 51:6 . . . teaching me **w** even there.*
*Prov 2:6 . . . the LORD grants **w**!*
*Prov 3:13 . . . the person who finds **w**,*
*Prov 8:11 . . . **w** is far more valuable*
*Prov 11:2 . . . with humility comes **w**.*
*Prov 16:16 . . . better to get **w** than gold,*
*Prov 23:23 . . . also get **w**, discipline,*
*Prov 29:3 . . . man who loves **w** brings joy*
*Eccl 10:10 . . . the value of **w**; it helps*
*Isa 11:2 . . . on him—the Spirit of **w***
*Isa 50:4 . . . me His words of **w**, so that*
*Luke 2:52 . . . Jesus grew in **w** and in*
*Acts 6:3 . . . full of the Spirit and **w**.*
*1 Cor 1:21 . . . him through human **w**, he*
*Eph 1:17 . . . you spiritual **w** and insight*
*Col 2:3 . . . treasures of **w** and knowledge.*
*Col 3:16 . . . with all the **w** He gives.*
*2 Tim 3:15 . . . given you the **w** to receive*
*Titus 2:12 . . . world with **w**, righteousness,*
*Jas 1:5 . . . If you need **w**, ask our*
*Rev 5:12 . . . riches and **w** and strength*

WISE, WISER, WISEST (adj)
marked by deep understanding, keen discernment, and a capacity for sound judgment
*1 Kgs 3:12 . . . you a **w** and understanding*
*Job 9:4 . . . God is so **w** and so mighty.*
*Ps 14:2 . . . anyone is truly **w**, if anyone*
*Ps 19:7 . . . are trustworthy, making **w** the*
*Ps 119:100 . . . I am even **w-r** than my*
*Prov 4:7 . . . wisdom is the **w-st** thing*
*Prov 9:8 . . . correct the **w**, and they*
*Prov 10:1 . . . A **w** child brings joy to*
*Prov 11:30 . . . a **w** person wins friends.*
*Prov 12:16 . . . a **w** person stays calm*
*Prov 12:18 . . . of the **w** bring healing.*
*Prov 13:1 . . . A **w** child accepts a parent's*
*Prov 13:10 . . . who take advice are **w**.*
*Prov 13:20 . . . Walk with the **w** and*
*Prov 15:5 . . . learns from correction is **w**.*
*Prov 16:23 . . . From a **w** mind comes **w***
*Prov 18:4 . . . wisdom flows from the **w***
*Prov 19:25 . . . they will be all the **w-r**.*
*Prov 24:5 . . . **w** are mightier than the*
*Prov 28:7 . . . who obey the law are **w**;*
*Eccl 8:5 . . . who are **w** will find a time*
*Eccl 9:17 . . . quiet words of a **w** person*
*Matt 2:1 . . . some **w** men from eastern*
*Matt 11:25 . . . who think themselves **w***
*Matt 25:2 . . . foolish, and five were **w**.*
*Rom 3:11 . . . No one is truly **w**; no one*
*1 Cor 1:19 . . . wisdom of the **w** and*
*1 Cor 1:25 . . . plan of God is **w-r** than*
*1 Cor 12:8 . . . ability to give **w** advice;*
*Jas 3:13 . . . If you are **w** and understand*

WITCHCRAFT (n)
the use of sorcery or magic
*Lev 19:26 . . . practice fortune-telling or **w**.*
*Deut 18:10 . . . omens, or engage in **w**,*
*Rev 21:8 . . . those who practice **w**, idol*

WITNESS, WITNESSES (n)
a person who gives testimony; one asked to be present at a transaction so as to be able to testify to its having taken place
*Deut 19:15 . . . of two or three **w-es**.*
*Prov 19:5 . . . A false **w** will not go*
*Prov 21:28 . . . but a credible **w** will be*
*Matt 18:16 . . . by two or three **w-es**.*
*John 1:8 . . . simply a **w** to tell about*
*Acts 1:8 . . . will be My **w-es**, telling people*
*1 Tim 5:19 . . . by two or three **w-es**.*
*1 Jn 5:7 . . . we have these three **w-es**—*

WIVES (n)
see also WIFE
*Eph 5:22 . . . For **w**, this means submit*
*Eph 5:25 . . . this means love your **w**,*
*1 Pet 3:1 . . . way, you **w** must accept*

WOE (KJV)
*Isa 6:5 . . . **It's all over!** I am doomed*
*Matt 18:7 . . . **What sorrow awaits** the world*
*Matt 23:13 . . . **What sorrow awaits** you*
*1 Cor 9:16 . . . **How terrible** for me if I didn't*
*Rev 8:13 . . . **Terror, terror, terror** to all who*

WOMAN (n)
an adult female person
*Gen 2:22 . . . God made a **w** from the rib,*
*Gen 3:6 . . . The **w** was convinced.*
*Gen 3:12 . . . It was the **w** You gave me*
*Gen 3:16 . . . he said to the **w**, "I will*
*Exod 3:22 . . . Every Israelite **w** will ask*
*Lev 12:2 . . . If a **w** becomes pregnant*
*Lev 15:19 . . . a **w** has her menstrual*
*Lev 15:25 . . . a **w** has a flow of blood*
*Num 5:29 . . . If a **w** goes astray and defiles*
*Judg 4:9 . . . be at the hands of a **w**.*
*Judg 16:4 . . . love with a **w** named Delilah,*
*Ruth 3:11 . . . knows you are a virtuous **w**.*
*2 Sam 11:2 . . . he noticed a **w** of unusual*
*2 Sam 20:16 . . . But a wise **w** in the town*
*Prov 11:16 . . . A gracious **w** gains respect,*
*Prov 11:22 . . . A beautiful **w** who lacks*
*Prov 14:1 . . . A wise **w** builds her*
*Prov 30:19 . . . how a man loves a **w**.*
*Prov 30:23 . . . a bitter **w** who finally gets*
*Prov 31:30 . . . **w** who fears the LORD*
*Matt 5:28 . . . looks at a **w** with lust*
*Matt 9:20 . . . Just then a **w** who had*
*Matt 26:7 . . . was eating, a **w** came in*
*Mark 7:25 . . . Right away a **w** who had*
*Luke 7:39 . . . what kind of **w** is touching*
*John 4:7 . . . Soon a Samaritan **w** came to*
*John 8:3 . . . Pharisees brought a **w** who*
*Rom 7:2 . . . when a **w** marries, the law*
*1 Cor 7:2 . . . and each **w** should have*
*1 Cor 7:34 . . . a married **w** has to think*
*1 Cor 11:3 . . . the head of **w** is man, and*
*1 Cor 11:6 . . . shameful for a **w** to have*
*1 Cor 11:13 . . . it right for a **w** to pray*
*Gal 4:4 . . . born of a **w**, subject to the*
*Gal 4:31 . . . are children of the free **w**.*
*Rev 12:1 . . . I saw a **w** clothed with the*
*Rev 12:13 . . . he pursued the **w** who had*
*Rev 17:3 . . . There I saw a **w** sitting on a*

WOMB (n)
uterus
*Ps 139:13 . . . together in my mother's **w**.*
*Prov 31:2 . . . O son of my **w**, O son*
*Jer 1:5 . . . you in your mother's **w**.*
*Luke 1:44 . . . baby in my **w** jumped for joy.*
*John 3:4 . . . into his mother's **w** and be*

WONDERFUL (adj)
marked by a marvelous, amazing, or extraordinary quality
*1 Chr 16:9 . . . about his **w** deeds.*
*Job 37:14 . . . consider the **w** miracles*
*Ps 16:6 . . . What a **w** inheritance!*
*Ps 17:7 . . . unfailing love in **w** ways.*
*Ps 71:17 . . . about the **w** things you*
*Ps 72:18 . . . does such **w** things.*
*Ps 75:1 . . . tell of Your **w** deeds.*
*Ps 105:2 . . . about His **w** deeds.*
*Ps 118:23 . . . it is **w** to see.*
*Ps 119:18 . . . to see the **w** truths in*
*Ps 119:27 . . . meditate on Your **w** deeds.*
*Ps 119:129 . . . Your laws are **w**.*
*Ps 139:6 . . . knowledge is too **w** for*
*Ps 145:5 . . . and Your **w** miracles.*
*Eccl 11:9 . . . Young people, it's **w** to be*
*Isa 9:6 . . . be called: **W** Counselor,*
*Isa 12:5 . . . He has done **w** things.*
*Isa 25:1 . . . You do such **w** things!*
*Matt 21:15 . . . saw these **w** miracles*
*Matt 21:42 . . . and it is **w** to see.*
*Luke 13:17 . . . rejoiced at the **w** things*
*Acts 2:11 . . . about the **w** things God has*
*Acts 20:24 . . . News about the **w** grace of*
*2 Cor 10:12 . . . we are as **w** as these*
*Titus 2:13 . . . hope to that **w** day when*

WORD, WORDS (n)
something that is said; special revelation from God; commands
*Deut 8:3 . . . live by every **w** that comes*
*Deut 11:18 . . . to these **w-s** of mine. Tie*
*Job 38:2 . . . with such ignorant **w-s**?*
*Ps 19:3 . . . speak without a sound or **w**;*
*Ps 52:4 . . . others with your **w-s**, you liar!*
*Ps 119:9 . . . pure? By obeying your **w**.*
*Ps 119:11 . . . hidden Your **w** in my heart,*
*Ps 119:103 . . . How sweet Your **w-s** taste*
*Ps 119:160 . . . essence of Your **w-s** is*
*Ps 119:162 . . . I rejoice in Your **w** like*
*Prov 12:19 . . . Truthful **w-s** stand the test*
*Prov 12:25 . . . an encouraging **w** cheers*
*Prov 16:24 . . . Kind **w-s** are like honey—*
*Prov 17:27 . . . wise person uses few **w-s**;*
*Prov 26:23 . . . Smooth **w-s** may hide a*
*Isa 40:21 . . . deaf to the **w-s** of God—*
*Jer 15:16 . . . Your **w-s**, I devoured*
*Jer 23:29 . . . Does not My **w** burn like*
*Amos 8:13 . . . for the LORD's **w**.*
*Matt 4:4 . . . but by every **w** that comes*
*Matt 15:6 . . . you cancel the **w** of God*
*Matt 24:35 . . . **w-s** will never disappear.*
*John 1:1 . . . the beginning the **W** already*
*John 6:68 . . . the **w-s** that give eternal life.*
*John 15:7 . . . and My **w-s** remain in you,*
*John 17:17 . . . teach them Your **w**, which*
*Rom 10:18 . . . the **w-s** to all the world.*
*1 Cor 2:1 . . . use lofty **w-s** and impressive*
*1 Cor 2:13 . . . do not use **w-s** that come*
*1 Cor 14:9 . . . to people in **w-s** they don't*

1 Cor 14:19 . . . than ten thousand **w-s** in
2 Cor 2:17 . . . We preach the **w** of God
2 Cor 4:2 . . . or distort the **w** of God.
Eph 6:17 . . . which is the **w** of God.
Phil 2:16 . . . firmly to the **w** of life;
2 Tim 2:15 . . . explains the **w** of truth.
Titus 2:5 . . . shame on the **w** of God.
Heb 4:12 . . . For the **w** of God is
Heb 5:12 . . . things about God's **w.**
Jas 1:22 . . . listen to God's **w.**
1 Pet 1:23 . . . eternal, living **w** of God.
1 Pet 2:8 . . . not obey God's **w,** and so
1 Pet 3:1 . . . to them without any **w-s.**
2 Pet 3:5 . . . the heavens by the **w** of
Rev 19:13 . . . title was the **W** of God.
Rev 22:19 . . . of the **w-s** from this book

WORK, WORKS (n)
one's occupation; physical or creative effort
see also DEEDS
Gen 2:2 . . . finished his **w** of creation,
Exod 20:9 . . . week for your ordinary **w,**
Deut 5:13 . . . week for your ordinary **w,**
Ps 77:12 . . . about your mighty **w-s.**
Ps 107:24 . . . impressive **w-s** on the
Ps 127:1 . . . **w** of the builders is wasted.
Ps 150:2 . . . Praise him for his mighty **w-s;**
Prov 21:5 . . . planning and hard **w** lead
Eccl 2:19 . . . my skill and hard **w** under
Eccl 5:19 . . . To enjoy your **w** and accept
John 4:34 . . . and from finishing his **w.**
John 5:36 . . . Father gave me these **w-s** to
John 10:32 . . . have done many good **w-s.**
Acts 13:2 . . . for the special **w** to which
Acts 20:24 . . . finishing the **w** assigned
Rom 4:5 . . . not because of their **w,** but
1 Cor 3:5 . . . the **w** the Lord gave us.
Gal 6:4 . . . attention to your own **w,** for
Eph 4:12 . . . people to do his **w** and build
Eph 4:16 . . . part does its own special **w,**
Eph 4:28 . . . your hands for good hard **w,**
Phil 1:6 . . . began the good **w** within you,
1 Tim 6:18 . . . rich in good **w-s** and
2 Tim 3:17 . . . people to do every good **w.**
Heb 10:24 . . . acts of love and good **w-s.**
Jas 2:26 . . . faith is dead without good **w-s.**
Rev 15:3 . . . marvelous are your **w-s,** O

WORK, WORKED, WORKING (v)
to exert oneself physically or mentally
Prov 13:4 . . . but those who **w** hard will
Eccl 5:12 . . . who **w** hard sleep well,
Matt 6:28 . . . They don't **w** or make their
Matt 12:30 . . . anyone who isn't **w-ing** with
Luke 10:7 . . . who **w** deserve their pay.
Luke 13:24 . . . **W** hard to enter the narrow
Rom 4:6 . . . righteous without **w-ing** for
Rom 8:28 . . . to **w** together for the good
Rom 12:11 . . . Never be lazy, but **w** hard
1 Cor 15:10 . . . I have **w-ed** harder than
1 Cor 15:58 . . . Always **w** enthusiastically
2 Cor 11:27 . . . I have **w-ed** hard and
Eph 6:7 . . . you were **w-ing** for the Lord
1 Thes 4:11 . . . and **w-ing** with your hands,
2 Thes 3:10 . . . unwilling to **w** will not
1 Tim 5:18 . . . Those who **w** deserve their
1 Tim 6:2 . . . slaves should **w** all the harder
Heb 6:10 . . . how hard you have **w-ed** for
2 Pet 1:10 . . . **w** hard to prove that you

WORLD (n)
the earth and its inhabitants; the human race; the current age and its value system
Ps 33:9 . . . he spoke, the **w** began!
Ps 50:12 . . . for all the **w** is mine
Ps 96:13 . . . judge the **w** with justice,
Isa 13:11 . . . will punish the **w** for its
Matt 16:26 . . . you gain the whole **w** but
John 1:29 . . . away the sin of the **w!**
John 3:16 . . . God loved the **w** so much
John 8:12 . . . I am the light of the **w.**
John 13:35 . . . prove to the **w** that you
John 16:33 . . . I have overcome the **w.**
John 17:5 . . . shared before the **w** began.
John 17:14 . . . And the **w** hates them
John 18:36 . . . Kingdom is not of this **w.**
Rom 3:19 . . . the entire **w** is guilty
1 Cor 1:27 . . . things the **w** considers
1 Cor 2:7 . . . glory before the **w** began.
1 Cor 3:1 . . . you belonged to this **w** or
1 Cor 3:19 . . . of this **w** is foolishness
1 Cor 6:2 . . . to judge the **w,** can't you
2 Cor 5:19 . . . reconciling the **w** to himself,
Eph 2:12 . . . lived in this **w** without God
Eph 4:9 . . . also descended to our lowly **w.**
Phil 2:15 . . . lights in a **w** full of crooked
Titus 1:2 . . . them before the **w** began.
Heb 9:26 . . . ever since the **w** began.
Jas 2:5 . . . poor in this **w** to be rich
Jas 4:4 . . . a friend of the **w,** you make
1 Jn 2:2 . . . the sins of all the **w.**
1 Jn 2:15 . . . Do not love this **w** nor
1 Jn 5:4 . . . defeats this evil **w,** and

WORRY, WORRIES (n)
mental distress or agitation resulting from concern; anxiety
Prov 12:25 . . . **W** weighs a person down;
Matt 6:27 . . . Can all your **w-ies** add a single
Luke 21:34 . . . and by the **w-ies** of this life.
1 Pet 5:7 . . . Give all your **w-ies** and cares

WORRY, WORRIED, WORRYING (v)
to feel or experience concern or anxiety
Deut 20:8 . . . anyone here afraid or **w-ied?**
Ps 37:1 . . . Don't **w** about the wicked
Isa 7:4 . . . Tell him to stop **w-ing.**
Matt 6:25 . . . I tell you not to **w** about
Matt 10:19 . . . don't **w** about how to
Luke 6:41 . . . And why **w** about a speck in
Acts 27:33 . . . You have been so **w-ied** that
Phil 4:6 . . . Don't **w** about anything;

WORSHIP, WORSHIPED, WORSHIPING, WORSHIPS (v)
to regard with great extravagant respect, honor, or devotion
Gen 12:8 . . . and he **w-ed** the LORD.
Gen 13:4 . . . and there he **w-ed** the LORD
Gen 21:33 . . . and there he **w-ed** the LORD,
Gen 26:25 . . . altar there and **w-ed** the LORD.
Deut 12:30 . . . and **w-ing** their gods.
2 Kgs 17:36 . . . But **w** only the LORD,
Ps 29:2 . . . **W** the LORD in the splendor
Ps 95:6 . . . Come, let us **w** and bow down.
Ps 105:3 . . . rejoice, you who **w** the LORD.
Isa 44:19 . . . bow down to **w** a piece of
Jer 16:11 . . . **w-ed** other gods and served
Dan 3:28 . . . die rather than serve or **w** any
Hos 9:1 . . . like prostitutes, **w-ing** other
Hos 9:10 . . . as vile as the god they **w-ed.**
Hos 13:1 . . . Ephraim sinned by **w-ing** Baal
Zeph 3:9 . . . everyone can **w** the LORD
Zech 14:17 . . . to Jerusalem to **w** the King,
Matt 2:2 . . . we have come to **w** Him.
Matt 4:9 . . . kneel down and **w** Me.
Matt 15:25 . . . But she came and **w-ed** Him,
Matt 28:9 . . . grasped his feet, and **w-ed** Him.
Luke 23:47 . . . he **w-ed** God and said,
John 4:24 . . . **w** in spirit and in truth.
1 Cor 5:11 . . . is greedy, or **w-s** idols,
Heb 9:14 . . . we can **w** the living God.

WORTHY (adj)
having sufficient merit or importance; estimable, honorable
Gen 32:10 . . . I am not **w** of all the
Prov 12:4 . . . A **w** wife is a crown
Matt 8:8 . . . Lord, I am not **w** to have
Matt 10:37 . . . are not **w** of being mine;
Matt 22:8 . . . I invited aren't **w** of the
Luke 15:19 . . . I am no longer **w** of being
1 Cor 15:9 . . . I'm not even **w** to be called
Eph 4:1 . . . lead a life **w** of your calling,
Phil 1:27 . . . a manner **w** of the Good News
Rev 5:5 . . . He is **w** to open the scroll

WRATH (n)
extreme displeasure, anger, or hostility; God's response to sin
Isa 13:13 . . . Armies displays His **w** in
Nah 1:2 . . . filled with vengeance and **w.**
Rev 6:16 . . . and from the **w** of the Lamb.
Rev 16:19 . . . the wine of His fierce **w.**

WRITE, WRITING (v)
to inscribe or engrave; to record
see also WRITTEN
Deut 10:2 . . . I will **w** on the tablets
Prov 3:3 . . . **W** them deep within your
Prov 7:3 . . . **W** them deep within your
Eccl 12:12 . . . for **w-ing** books is endless,
Jer 31:33 . . . I will **w** them on their hearts.
1 Tim 3:14 . . . I am **w-ing** these things to
Heb 8:10 . . . I will **w** them on their hearts.
Rev 3:12 . . . I will **w** on them the name of

WRITTEN (v)
see also WRITE
Deut 28:58 . . . that are **w** in this book,
Josh 1:8 . . . to obey everything **w** in it.
Isa 49:16 . . . See, I have **w** your name
Dan 12:1 . . . whose name is **w** in the book
Mal 3:16 . . . scroll of remembrance was **w**
Luke 24:44 . . . everything **w** about Me in
John 20:31 . . . these are **w** so that you
John 21:25 . . . the books that would be **w.**
Rom 2:15 . . . law is **w** in their hearts,
1 Cor 10:11 . . . They were **w** down to warn
Heb 12:23 . . . names are **w** in heaven.
Rev 21:27 . . . whose names are **w** in the

WRONG (n)
an injurious, unfair, or unjust act; something wrong, immoral, or unethical
Exod 23:2 . . . the crowd in doing **w.**
Deut 32:4 . . . faithful God who does no **w;**
Job 34:10 . . . The Almighty can do no **w.**
Ps 141:9 . . . snares of those who do **w.**
Isa 53:9 . . . done no **w** and had never
Rom 13:10 . . . Love does no **w** to others,
Rom 16:19 . . . to stay innocent of any **w.**
1 Cor 6:9 . . . those who do **w** will not
Jas 1:13 . . . God is never tempted to do **w,**
1 Pet 3:17 . . . to suffer for doing **w!**

WRONGED (v)
to injure or harm; to malign or discredit
Num 5:7 . . . to the person who was **w.**
Isa 42:3 . . . to all who have been **w.**
1 Cor 13:5 . . . keeps no record of being **w.**

YEAR, YEARS (n)
the period of about 365 days; a period having special significance; a measure of age or duration
Gen 1:14 . . . the seasons, days, and **y-s.**
Exod 12:40 . . . lived in Egypt for 430 **y-s.**
Exod 16:35 . . . manna for forty **y-s** until
Exod 34:23 . . . Three times each **y** every
Lev 16:34 . . . the LORD once each **y.**
Lev 25:11 . . . During that **y** you must
Job 36:26 . . . His **y-s** cannot be counted.
Ps 90:4 . . . a thousand **y-s** are as a
Luke 3:23 . . . about thirty **y-s** old when
Heb 10:1 . . . again and again, **y** after **y,**

*Heb 10:3 . . . of their sins **y** after **y**.*
*2 Pet 3:8 . . . like a thousand **y-s** to the*
*Rev 20:2 . . . in chains for a thousand **y-s**.*

YOUNG, YOUNGER (adj)
being in the first or an early stage of life, growth, or development
*2 Chr 10:14 . . . counsel of his **y-er** advisers.*
*Ps 119:9 . . . How can a **y** person stay pure?*
*Prov 20:29 . . . The glory of the **y** is their*
*Joel 2:28 . . . your **y** men will see visions.*
*Acts 2:17 . . . Your **y** men will see visions,*
*Acts 7:58 . . . feet of a **y** man named Saul.*
*1 Tim 5:1 . . . Talk to **y-er** men as you*
*Titus 2:4 . . . must train the **y-er** women to*
*Titus 2:6 . . . encourage the **y** men to live*
*1 Pet 5:5 . . . same way, you **y-er** men must*
*1 Jn 2:13 . . . you who are **y** in the faith*

Z

ZEAL (n)
eagerness and ardent interest in pursuit of something
*Num 25:13 . . . in his **z** for Me, his God,*
*Rom 10:2 . . . but it is misdirected **z**.*

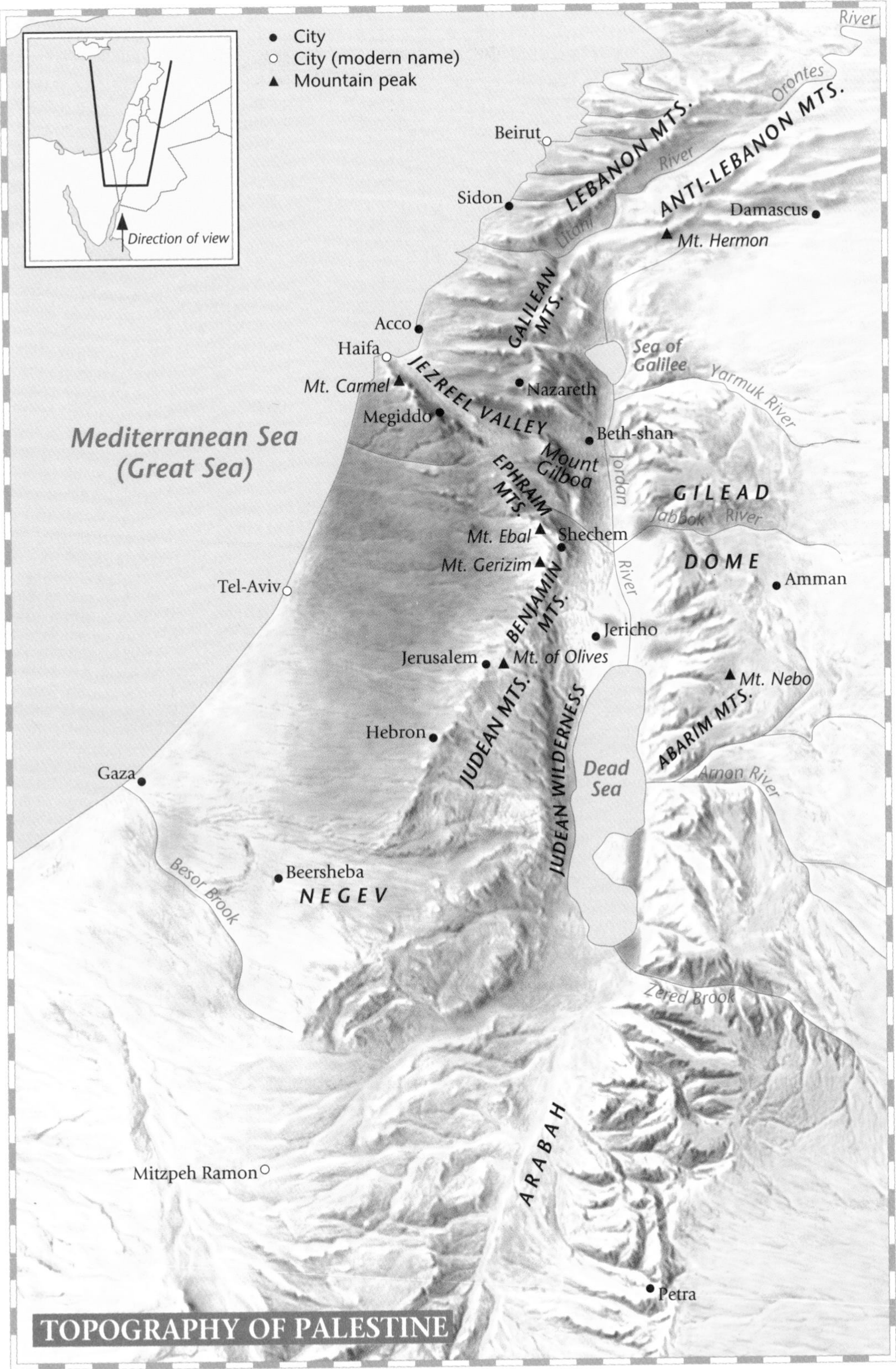
City
City (modern name)
Mountain peak
Direction of view
River
Orontes
LEBANON MTS.
ANTI-LEBANON MTS.
Beirut
River
Sidon
Litani
Damascus
Mt. Hermon
GALILEAN MTS.
Acco
Haifa
Sea of Galilee
Yarmuk River
Mt. Carmel
JEZREEL VALLEY
Nazareth
Megiddo
Beth-shan
Mediterranean Sea (Great Sea)
Mount Gilboa
EPHRAIM MTS.
Jordan
GILEAD
Jabbok River
Mt. Ebal
Shechem
Mt. Gerizim
DOME
River
Amman
Tel-Aviv
BENJAMIN MTS.
Jericho
Jerusalem
Mt. of Olives
Mt. Nebo
JUDEAN WILDERNESS
ABARIM MTS.
Hebron
JUDEAN MTS.
Dead Sea
Gaza
Arnon River
Besor Brook
Beersheba
NEGEV
Zered Brook
ARABAH
Mitzpeh Ramon
Petra
TOPOGRAPHY OF PALESTINE

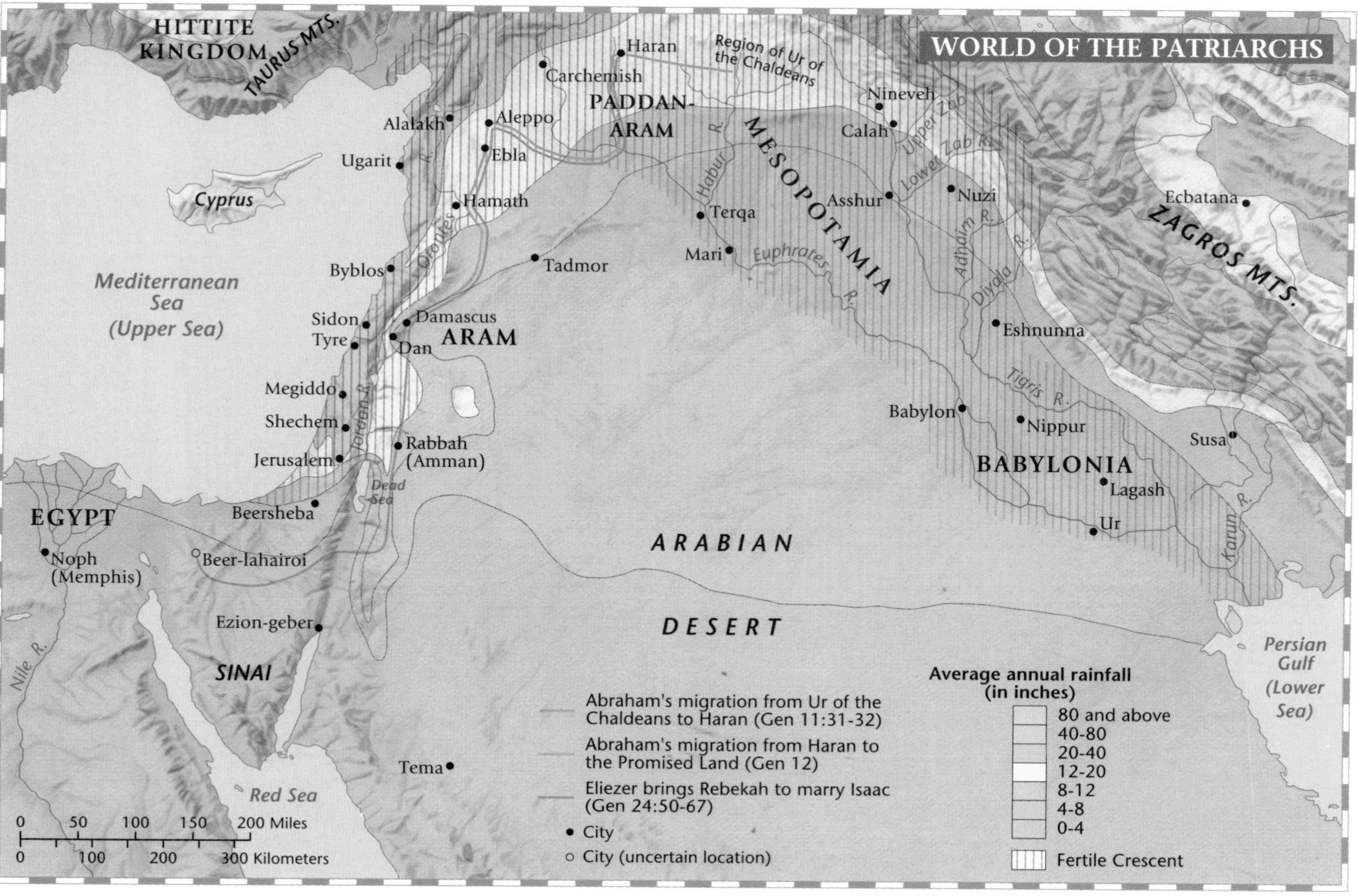

WORLD OF THE PATRIARCHS
HITTITE KINGDOM
TAURUS MTS.
Haran
Region of Ur of the Chaldeans
Carchemish
PADDAN-ARAM
Nineveh
Calah
Upper Zab R.
Lower Zab R.
Alalakh
Aleppo
Ebla
Ugarit
Cyprus
Hamath
Orontes R.
MESOPOTAMIA
Habur R.
Asshur
Nuzi
Terqa
Mari
Euphrates R.
Adhaim R.
Diyala R.
Ecbatana
ZAGROS MTS.
Byblos
Tadmor
Mediterranean Sea (Upper Sea)
Sidon
Tyre
Damascus
Dan
ARAM
Eshnunna
Megiddo
Jordan R.
Shechem
Rabbah (Amman)
Jerusalem
Dead Sea
Tigris R.
Babylon
Nippur
Susa
BABYLONIA
Lagash
Ur
Karun R.
EGYPT
Beersheba
Noph (Memphis)
Beer-lahairoi
ARABIAN
DESERT
Ezion-geber
SINAI
Nile R.
Tema
Red Sea
Persian Gulf (Lower Sea)
Abraham's migration from Ur of the Chaldeans to Haran (Gen 11:31-32)
Abraham's migration from Haran to the Promised Land (Gen 12)
Eliezer brings Rebekah to marry Isaac (Gen 24:50-67)
City
City (uncertain location)
Average annual rainfall (in inches)
80 and above
40-80
20-40
12-20
8-12
4-8
0-4
Fertile Crescent
0 50 100 150 200 Miles
0 100 200 300 Kilometers

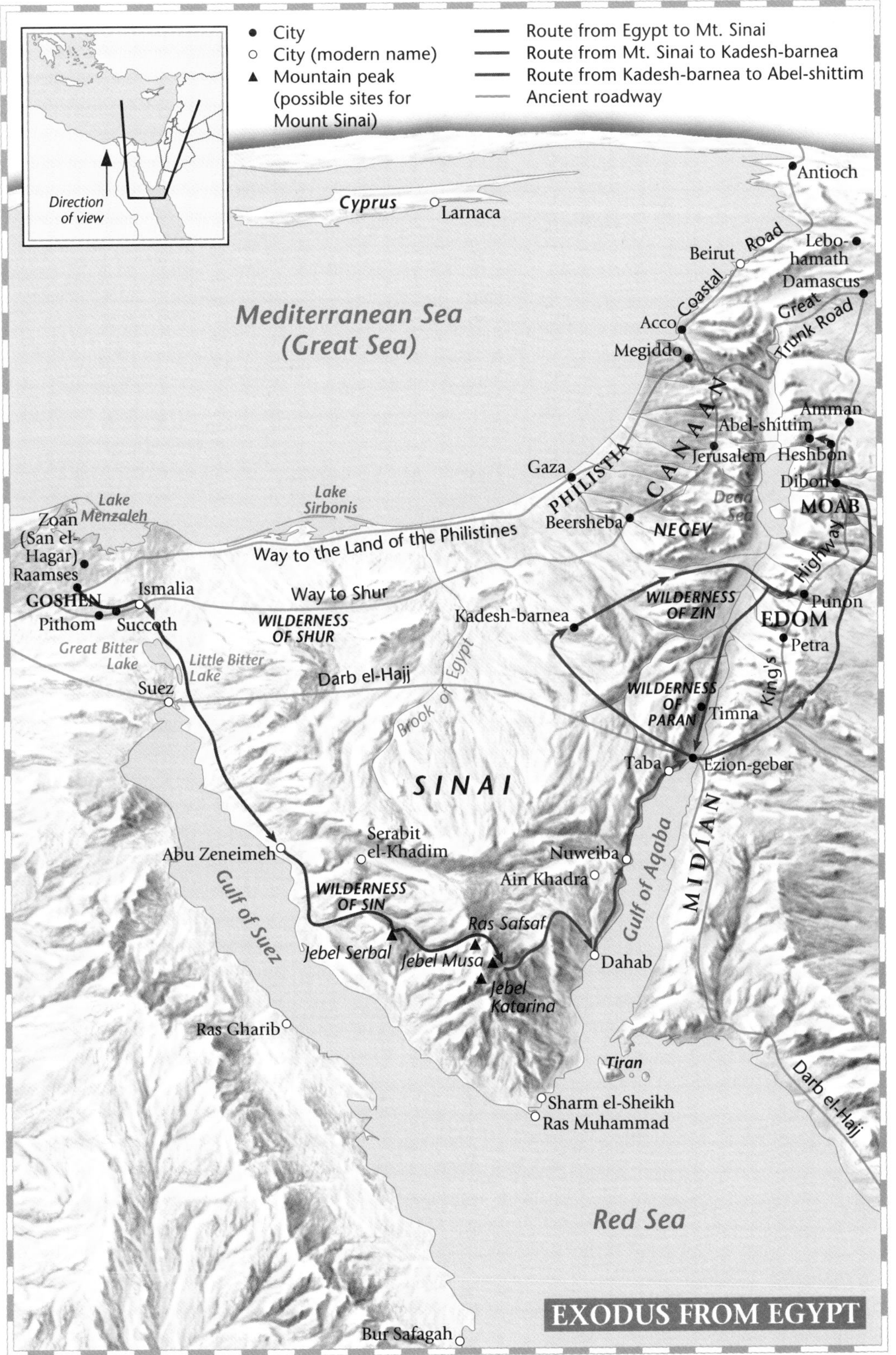

City
City (modern name)
Mountain peak (possible sites for Mount Sinai)
Route from Egypt to Mt. Sinai
Route from Mt. Sinai to Kadesh-barnea
Route from Kadesh-barnea to Abel-shittim
Ancient roadway
Direction of view
Mediterranean Sea (Great Sea)
Cyprus
Larnaca
Antioch
Beirut
Coastal Road
Lebo-hamath
Damascus
Great Trunk Road
Acco
Megiddo
CANAAN
Abel-shittim
Amman
Jerusalem
Heshbon
Gaza
PHILISTIA
Dibon
Dead Sea
MOAB
Beersheba
NEGEV
Lake Menzaleh
Lake Sirbonis
Zoan (San el-Hagar)
Raamses
Way to the Land of the Philistines
Highway
GOSHEN
Ismalia
Way to Shur
WILDERNESS OF ZIN
Punon
Pithom
Succoth
WILDERNESS OF SHUR
Kadesh-barnea
EDOM
Petra
Great Bitter Lake
Little Bitter Lake
Darb el-Hajj
Brook of Egypt
King's
Suez
WILDERNESS OF PARAN
Timna
Taba
Ezion-geber
SINAI
MIDIAN
Serabit el-Khadim
Abu Zeneimeh
Nuweiba
Gulf of Aqaba
Ain Khadra
Gulf of Suez
WILDERNESS OF SIN
Ras Safsaf
Jebel Serbal
Jebel Musa
Dahab
Jebel Katarina
Ras Gharib
Tiran
Darb el-Hajj
Sharm el-Sheikh
Ras Muhammad
Red Sea
EXODUS FROM EGYPT
Bur Safagah

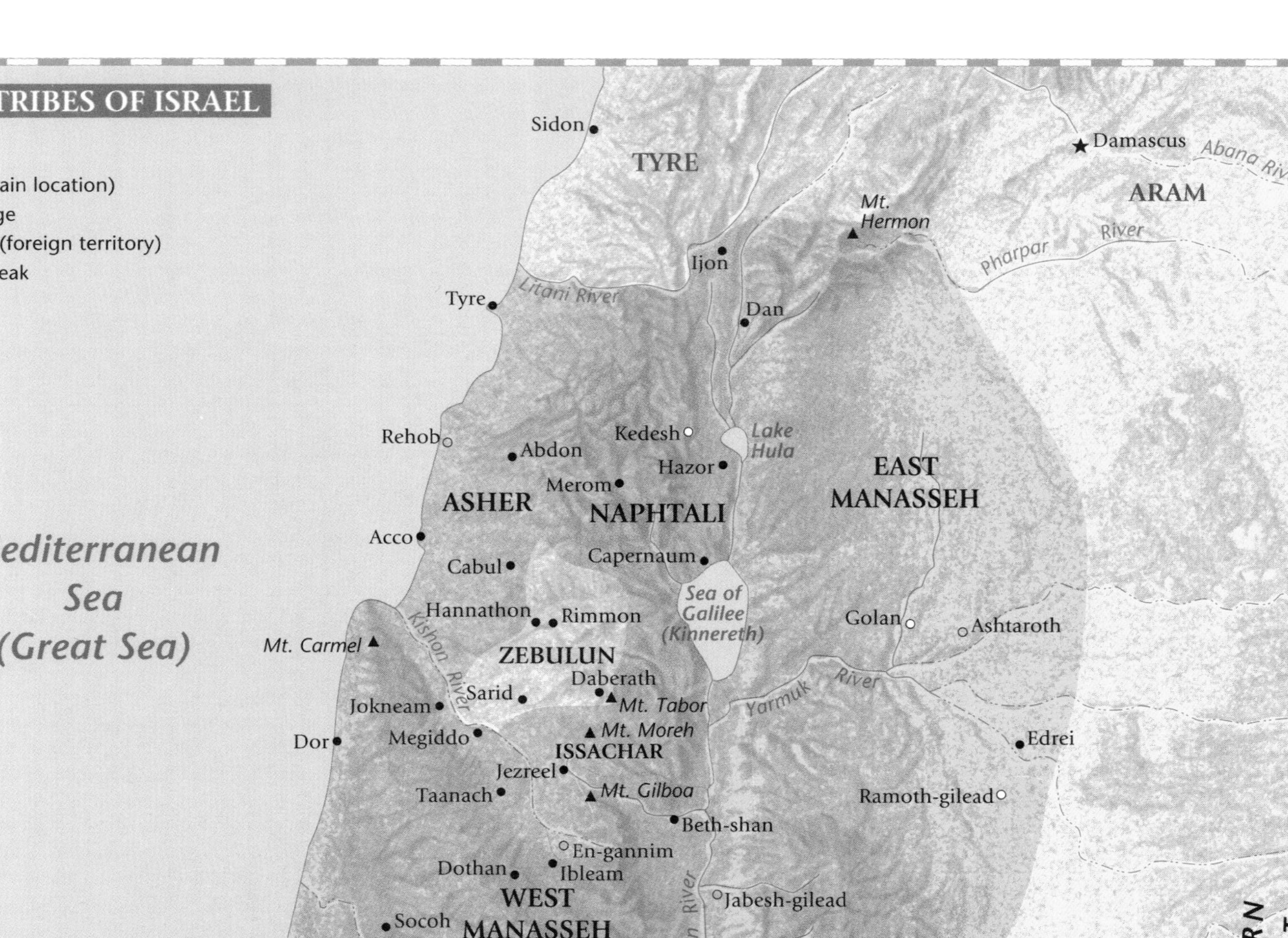
TWELVE TRIBES OF ISRAEL
City
City (uncertain location)
City of refuge
Capital city (foreign territory)
Mountain peak
Mediterranean Sea (Great Sea)
Sidon
TYRE
Damascus
Abana River
ARAM
Mt. Hermon
Pharpar River
Ijon
Tyre
Litani River
Dan
Rehob
Kedesh
Lake Hula
Abdon
Hazor
EAST MANASSEH
Merom
ASHER
NAPHTALI
Acco
Capernaum
Cabul
Sea of Galilee (Kinnereth)
Hannathon
Rimmon
Golan
Ashtaroth
Mt. Carmel
Kishon River
ZEBULUN
Daberath
Yarmuk River
Sarid
Mt. Tabor
Jokneam
Mt. Moreh
Dor
Megiddo
ISSACHAR
Edrei
Jezreel
Taanach
Mt. Gilboa
Ramoth-gilead
Beth-shan
En-gannim
Dothan
Ibleam
Jordan River
WEST MANASSEH
Jabesh-gilead
Socoh
Tirzah
Samaria
Mt. Ebal
Mt. Gerizim
Succoth
Penuel
Mahanaim

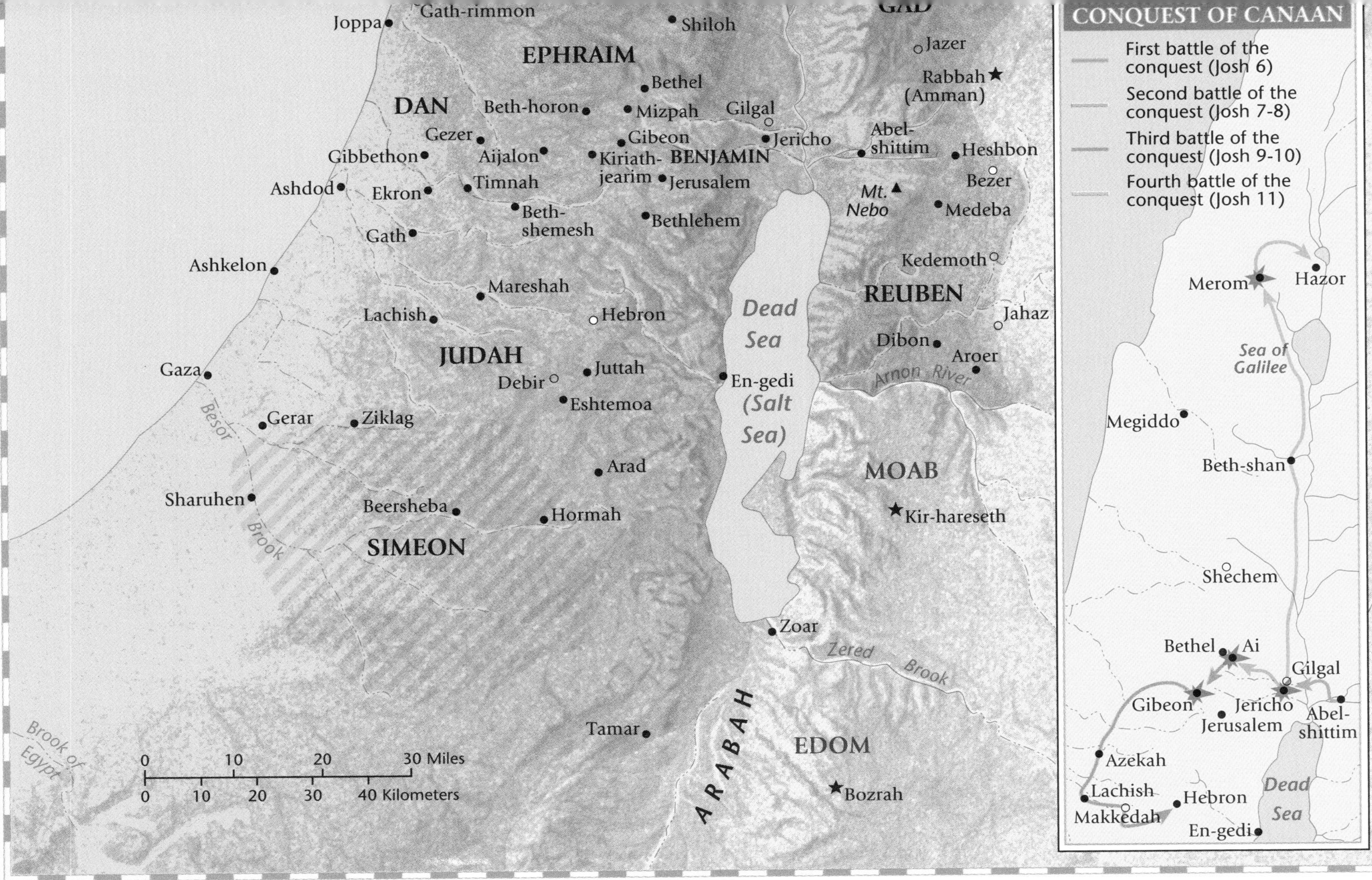

CONQUEST OF CANAAN
First battle of the conquest (Josh 6)
Second battle of the conquest (Josh 7-8)
Third battle of the conquest (Josh 9-10)
Fourth battle of the conquest (Josh 11)
Merom
Hazor
Sea of Galilee
Megiddo
Beth-shan
Shechem
Bethel
Ai
Gilgal
Gibeon
Jericho
Jerusalem
Abel-shittim
Azekah
Lachish
Hebron
Makkedah
Dead Sea
En-gedi
Joppa
Gath-rimmon
Shiloh
GAD
EPHRAIM
Jazer
Rabbah (Amman)
DAN
Bethel
Beth-horon
Mizpah
Gilgal
Gezer
Gibeon
Jericho
Abel-shittim
Heshbon
Gibbethon
Aijalon
Kiriath-jearim
BENJAMIN
Bezer
Ashdod
Ekron
Timnah
Jerusalem
Mt. Nebo
Medeba
Beth-shemesh
Bethlehem
Gath
Ashkelon
Kedemoth
REUBEN
Mareshah
Lachish
Hebron
Dead Sea
Jahaz
Dibon
Aroer
Gaza
JUDAH
Juttah
En-gedi
(Salt Sea)
Arnon River
Debir
Eshtemoa
Besor
Gerar
Ziklag
Arad
MOAB
Sharuhen
Beersheba
Hormah
Kir-hareseth
Brook
SIMEON
Zoar
Zered
Brook
ARABAH
Tamar
EDOM
Brook of Egypt
0 10 20 30 Miles
0 10 20 30 40 Kilometers
Bozrah

0 40 Miles
0 40 Kilometers
Aleppo
YAMHAD
Euphrates R.
Tiphsah
Cyprus
Hamath
HAMATH
Arvad
Tadmor
Byblos
Lebo-hamath
PHOENICIA
Mediterranean Sea (Great Sea)
Damascus
ARAM
Tyre
Dan
Hazor
Sea of Galilee (Kinnereth)
Dor
Megiddo
Jordan R.
Shechem
AMMON
Joppa
Gezer
Rabbah (Amman)
PHILISTIA
Gaza
Jerusalem
Dead Sea (Salt Sea)
MOAB
Raphia
Beersheba
AMALEK
Petra
EDOM
Kadesh-barnea
Ezion-geber
EASTERN DESERT
Kingdom of Saul
Kingdom of David
Kingdom of Solomon
Gulf of Aqaba
SINAI
UNITED KINGDOM
0 25 50 Miles
0 25 50 Kilometers
AMURRU
Great Trunk Road
Hamath
HAMATH
Mediterranean Sea (Great Sea)
Arvad
Qatna
Kadesh
Orontes R.
Coastal Road
PHOENICIA
Byblos
Sadad
Lebo-hamath
Berothai
Sidon
Damascus
Litani R.
Tyre
Dan
Kedesh
ARAM
Hazor
Acco
Sea of Galilee (Kinnereth)
Dor
Ashtaroth
Megiddo
Ramoth-gilead
Salecah
Beth-shan
Jordan R.
Jabbok R.
Shechem
Joppa
ISRAEL
Rabbah (Amman)
Gezer
Gibeah
AMMON
Ashdod
Jerusalem
Medeba
Gath
Dead Sea (Salt Sea)
Lachish
Aroer
Gaza
Hebron
Highway
Trunk
Raphia
JUDAH
MOAB
Beersheba
Kir-hareseth (Kir-moab)
Great
PHILISTIA
NEGEV
Brook of Egypt
King's
Kadesh-barnea
Bozrah
Petra
EDOM
Territory periodically contested by Edom and Judah
WILDERNESS OF ZIN
EASTERN DESERT
Ezion-geber
Gulf of Aqaba
SINAI
DIVIDED KINGDOM

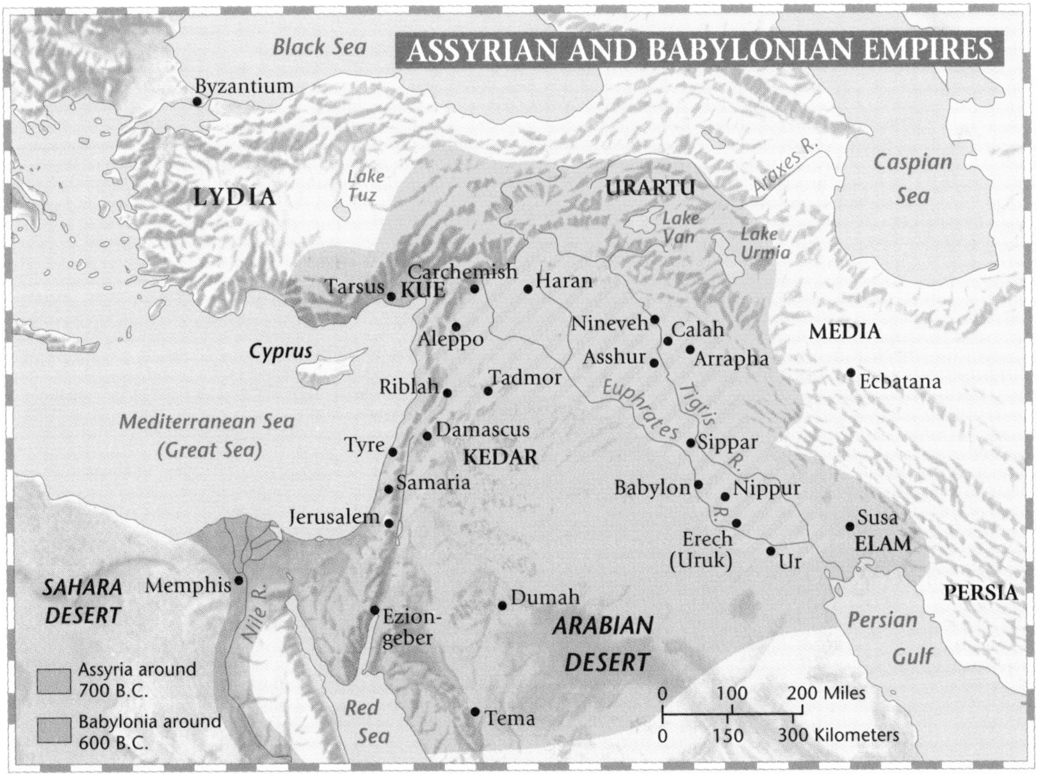

ASSYRIAN AND BABYLONIAN EMPIRES
Black Sea
Byzantium
LYDIA
Lake Tuz
URARTU
Araxes R.
Caspian Sea
Lake Van
Lake Urmia
Carchemish
Tarsus
KUE
Haran
Nineveh
Calah
Aleppo
MEDIA
Cyprus
Asshur
Arrapha
Riblah
Tadmor
Ecbatana
Euphrates
Tigris R.
Mediterranean Sea
(Great Sea)
Damascus
Tyre
KEDAR
Sippar
Samaria
Babylon
Nippur
Jerusalem
R.
Susa
Erech
(Uruk)
ELAM
Ur
SAHARA DESERT
Memphis
PERSIA
Nile R.
Dumah
Ezion-geber
ARABIAN DESERT
Persian Gulf
Assyria around 700 B.C.
Babylonia around 600 B.C.
Red Sea
Tema
0 100 200 Miles
0 150 300 Kilometers

GREEK EMPIRE
Danube R.
MACEDONIA
Black Sea
CAUCASUS MTS.
Caspian Sea
Sinope
Pella
THRACE
Araxes R.
Lake Tuz
ARMENIA
Athens
ASIA
Lake Van
HELLAS
Lake Urmia
Ephesus
Sparta
Carchemish
Tarsus
Haran
Aleppo
Gaugamela
Euphrates R.
Crete
Cyprus
Arbela
MEDIA
Tadmor
Tigris R.
Ecbatana
Mediterranean Sea
(Great Sea)
Damascus
Opis
Cyrene
Tyre
BABYLONIA
Babylon
LIBYA
Alexandria
Jerusalem
NABATEA
Susa
Erech
(Uruk)
Ur
EGYPT
Ezion-geber
Memphis
Extent of Alexandrian empire
SAHARA DESERT
Nile R.
ARABIAN DESERT
Ptolemaic realm
Persian Gulf
Seleucid realm
Red Sea
Antigonid realm
0 200 400 Miles
Minor Hellenistic provinces
Thebes
0 250 500 Kilometers

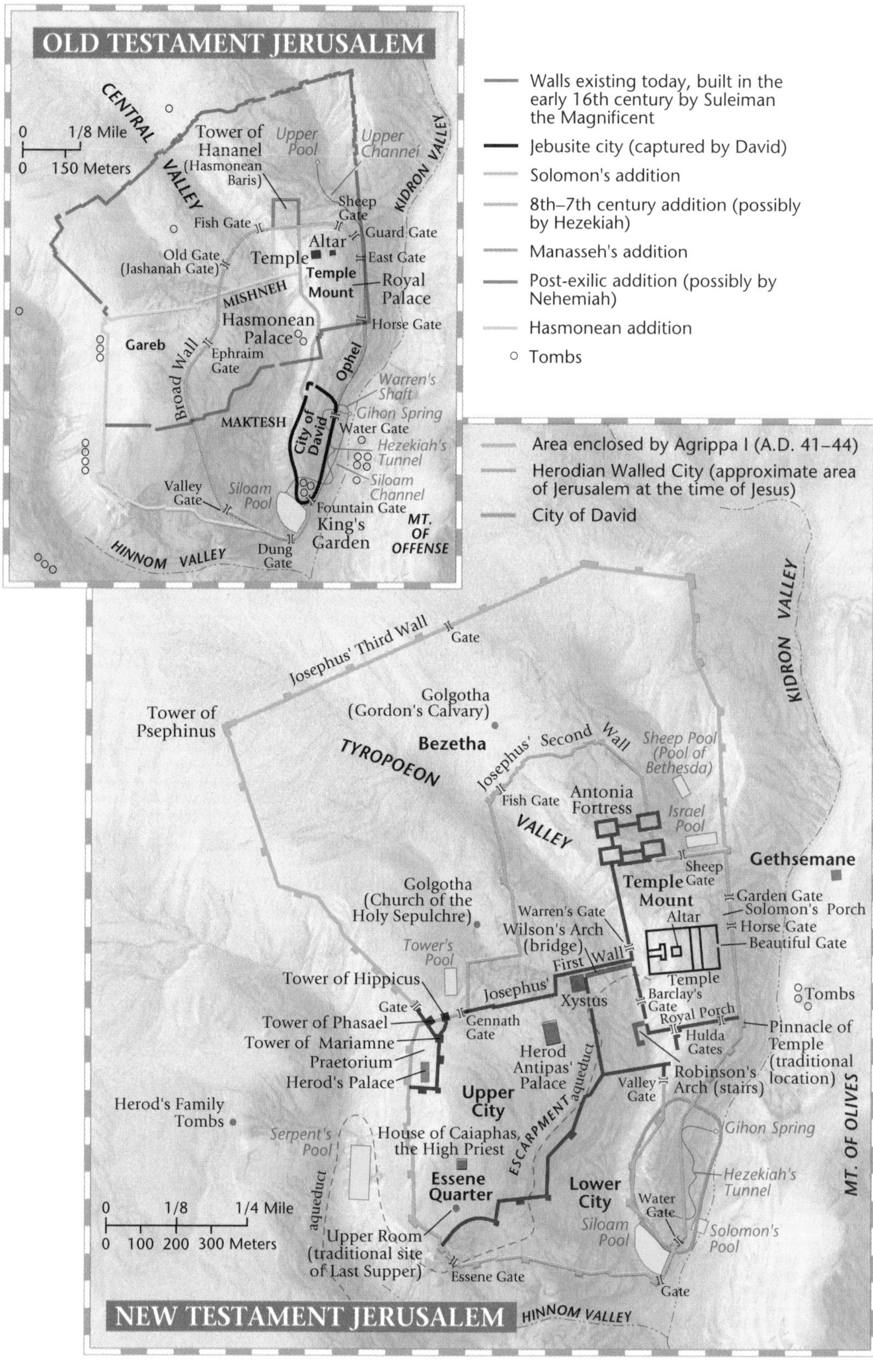

OLD TESTAMENT JERUSALEM
Walls existing today, built in the early 16th century by Suleiman the Magnificent
Jebusite city (captured by David)
Solomon's addition
8th–7th century addition (possibly by Hezekiah)
Manasseh's addition
Post-exilic addition (possibly by Nehemiah)
Hasmonean addition
Tombs
0 1/8 Mile
0 150 Meters
CENTRAL VALLEY
KIDRON VALLEY
Tower of Hananel (Hasmonean Baris)
Upper Pool
Upper Channel
Sheep Gate
Fish Gate
Guard Gate
Altar
Old Gate (Jashanah Gate)
Temple
East Gate
Temple Mount
Royal Palace
MISHNEH
Hasmonean Palace
Horse Gate
Gareb
Broad Wall
Ephraim Gate
Ophel
Warren's Shaft
Gihon Spring
City of David
MAKTESH
Water Gate
Hezekiah's Tunnel
Siloam Channel
Valley Gate
Siloam Pool
Fountain Gate
King's Garden
MT. OF OFFENSE
HINNOM VALLEY
Dung Gate
Area enclosed by Agrippa I (A.D. 41–44)
Herodian Walled City (approximate area of Jerusalem at the time of Jesus)
City of David
KIDRON VALLEY
Josephus' Third Wall
Gate
Golgotha (Gordon's Calvary)
Tower of Psephinus
Bezetha
TYROPOEON
Josephus' Second Wall
Sheep Pool (Pool of Bethesda)
Fish Gate
Antonia Fortress
VALLEY
Israel Pool
Gethsemane
Sheep Gate
Temple Mount
Golgotha (Church of the Holy Sepulchre)
Garden Gate
Warren's Gate
Altar
Solomon's Porch
Wilson's Arch (bridge)
Horse Gate
Beautiful Gate
Tower's Pool
First Wall
Tower of Hippicus
Josephus'
Temple
Xystus
Barclay's Gate
Tombs
Gate
Royal Porch
Tower of Phasael
Gennath Gate
Pinnacle of Temple (traditional location)
Tower of Mariamne
Hulda Gates
Praetorium
Herod Antipas' Palace
Herod's Palace
Robinson's Arch (stairs)
Valley Gate
Upper City
Herod's Family Tombs
ESCARPMENT aqueduct
Gihon Spring
MT. OF OLIVES
Serpent's Pool
House of Caiaphas, the High Priest
Hezekiah's Tunnel
Essene Quarter
Lower City
0 1/8 1/4 Mile
Water Gate
aqueduct
Siloam Pool
Solomon's Pool
0 100 200 300 Meters
Upper Room (traditional site of Last Supper)
Essene Gate
Gate
NEW TESTAMENT JERUSALEM
HINNOM VALLEY

ROMAN DIVISION OF PALESTINE
0 10 20 30 Miles
0 10 20 30 40 Kilometers
Mediterranean Sea (Great Sea)
PHOENICIA
ABILENE
Abila
Abana
Sidon
ITUREA
Mt. Hermon
Damascus
SYRIA
Pharpar R.
Road
Litani R.
Coastal
Tyre
Caesarea Philippi
Cadasa (Kedesh)
GAULANITIS
TRACHONITIS
Raphana
Lake Hula
Mt. Meron
Thella
GALILEE
Ptolemais (Acco)
Korazin
Capernaum
Bethsaida
Gennesaret
Gergesa
Magdala
Sea of Galilee (Kinnereth)
Mt. Carmel
Tiberias
Hippus
BATANEA
Mt. Tabor
Gebae
Kishon R.
Yarmuk R.
Abila
Dora
Nain
Gadara
Edrei
AURANITIS
Caesarea
DECAPOLIS
Pella
Dothan
Scythopolis (Beth-shan)
Dion
SAMARIA
Gerasa
Great Trunk Road
Sebaste (Samaria)
Mt. Ebal
Sychar
Amathus
Jabbok R.
Mt. Gerizim
Yarkon R.
Antipatris (Aphek)
Alexandrium
Jordan R.
Joppa
PEREA
Lydda (Lod)
Ephraim
Philadelphia (Amman)
Bethel
Tyrus
Jericho
Abila
Azotus (Ashdod)
Jamnia
Jerusalem
Cyprus
Esbus (Heshbon)
Mt. of Olives
Bethany
Medeba
Hyrcania
Bethlehem
Herodium
Ascalon
JUDEA
Marisa
Machaerus
NABATEA
Hebron
Adora
Dead Sea (Salt Sea)
En-gedi
Gaza
Arnon R.
King's Highway
Raphia
Besor Brook
Arad
Masada
Beersheba
IDUMEA
Malatha
Division of Herod's Kingdom to his three sons
Territory of Archelaus
Territory of Herod Antipas
Territory of Philip
Territory of the Proconsul of Syria
City
Decapolis city
Herodian fortress
Decapolis city (uncertain location)
Mountain peak
Extent of Herod the Great's kingdom

MINISTRY OF JESUS

Chronologically speaking, it is not possible to sequentially arrange the events in the life of Christ in any definitive way; none of the New Testament gospels follows an overtly chronological pattern. Accordingly, the arrangement here follows a geographic order, basically proceeding from north to south on the map. Because the gospel of Matthew most frequently contains information cited here, and because it is the most geographically particularistic gospel, synoptic passages are keyed to the book of Matthew, except where they are unattested there or where more pertinent information about the event cited is available in another gospel.

A. *Region of Tyre:* Gentile woman's daughter healed (Mt 15:21-28)

B. *Caesarea Philippi:* Peter's great declaration (Mt 16:13-20)

C. *Mt. Meron/Mt. Tabor/Mt. Hermon:* (1) possible location of Transfiguration (Mt 17:1-13); (2) demon-possessed boy healed nearby (Mt 17:14-21)

D. *Cana of Galilee:* (1) water changed to wine (Jn 2:1-11); (2) Capernaum official's son healed (Jn 4:46-54)

E. *Gennesaret:* (1) possible location of feeding of multitudes (Mt 14:13-21; 15:32-39); (2) many healings (Mk 6:53-56)

F. *Area of Korazin:* (1) judgment pronounced on the cities of Korazin, Bethsaida, and Capernaum (Mt 11:20-24); (2) possible area of Sermon on the Mount (Mt 5–7)

G. *Capernaum:* (1) catch of fish (Lk 5:1-11); (2) evil spirit cast out (Mk 1:21-28); (3) Sermon on the Mount (Mt 5–7); (4) Peter's mother-in-law healed (Mt 8:5-13); (5) Roman officer's servant healed (Mt 8:5-13); (6) paralyzed man healed (Mk 2:1-12); (7) woman with a hemorrhage healed (Mk 5:25-34); (8) Jairus's daughter raised (Lk 8:40-56); (9) two blind men healed (Mt 9:27-31); (10) a mute, demon-possessed man healed (Mt 9:32-34); (11) the twelve apostles sent out (Mt 10:1-15); (12) man with deformed hand healed (Mt 12:9-13); (13) another demon-possessed man healed (Mt 12:22-37); (14) Temple tax provided (Mt 17:24-27); (15) Bread of Life discourse (Jn 6:22-59)

H. *Bethsaida:* (1) possible location of feeding of multitudes (Mt 14:13-21; 15:32-39); (2) blind man healed (Mk 8:22-26)

I. *Sea of Galilee near Bethsaida:* walking on water (Mt 14:22-33)

J. *Sea of Galilee:* storm quieted (Mt 8:23-27)

K. *Gergesa/Gadara:* possible location of casting out demons, which enter pigs; the pigs then rush down a steep bank and drown (Lk 8:26-39)

L. *Nazareth:* (1) childhood home (Mt 2:19-23); (2) rejected by townspeople (Lk 4:16-30)

M. *Nain:* widow's son raised (Lk 7:11-17)

N. *Region of Galilee:* (1) leper cleansed (Mk 1:40-45); (2) post-resurrection appearances to the disciples (Mt 28:16-20)

O. *Region of Ten Towns:* many healings (Mt 15:29-31; Mk 7:31-37)

P. *Region between Galilee and Samaria:* (1) refused entry into village (Lk 9:51-56); (2) ten lepers healed (Lk 17:11-19)

Q. *Sychar:* woman at the well of Samaria (Jn 4:1-42)

R. *Ephraim:* enters into seclusion with the disciples (Jn 11:54)

S. *Region of Perea:* (1) teaching on marriage (Mt 19:1-12); (2) possible location of healing of woman with infirmity (Lk 13:10-13); (3) possible location of healing of man with swollen limbs (Lk 14:1-6); (4) possible location of the rich young ruler (Lk 18:18-30)

T. *Jericho:* (1) Bartimaeus healed (Mk 10:46-52); (2) Zacchaeus converted (Lk 19:1-10)

U. *Bethany:* (1) Lazarus raised (Jn 11:1-44); (2) anointing of Mary (Jn 12:1-11)

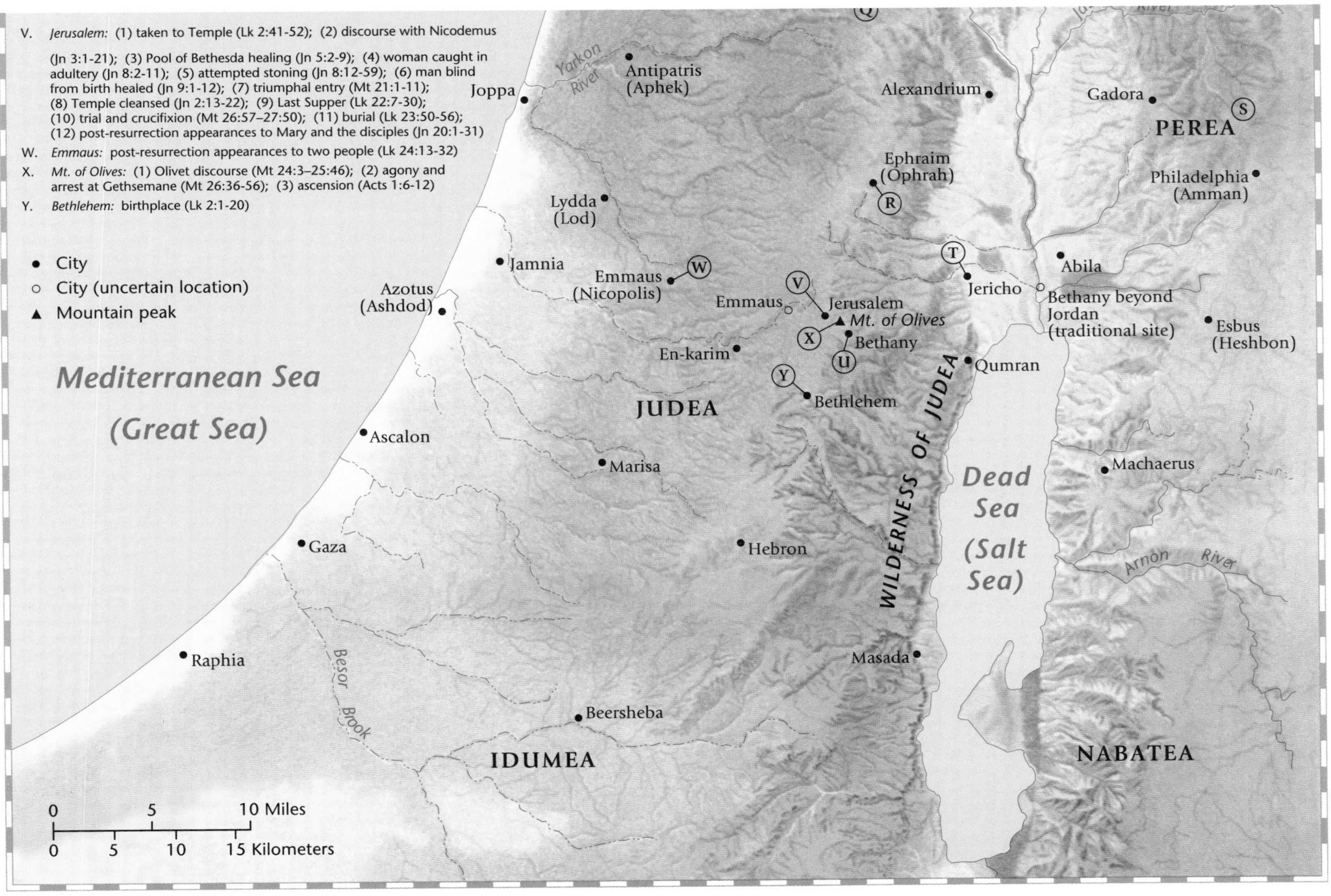

V. Jerusalem: (1) taken to Temple (Lk 2:41-52); (2) discourse with Nicodemus (Jn 3:1-21); (3) Pool of Bethesda healing (Jn 5:2-9); (4) woman caught in adultery (Jn 8:2-11); (5) attempted stoning (Jn 8:12-59); (6) man blind from birth healed (Jn 9:1-12); (7) triumphal entry (Mt 21:1-11); (8) Temple cleansed (Jn 2:13-22); (9) Last Supper (Lk 22:7-30); (10) trial and crucifixion (Mt 26:57–27:50); (11) burial (Lk 23:50-56); (12) post-resurrection appearances to Mary and the disciples (Jn 20:1-31)
W. Emmaus: post-resurrection appearances to two people (Lk 24:13-32)
X. Mt. of Olives: (1) Olivet discourse (Mt 24:3–25:46); (2) agony and arrest at Gethsemane (Mt 26:36-56); (3) ascension (Acts 1:6-12)
Y. Bethlehem: birthplace (Lk 2:1-20)
City
City (uncertain location)
Mountain peak
Mediterranean Sea
(Great Sea)
Joppa
Yarkon River
Antipatris (Aphek)
Alexandrium
Gadora
PEREA
Ephraim (Ophrah)
Philadelphia (Amman)
Lydda (Lod)
Jamnia
Emmaus (Nicopolis)
Emmaus
Jerusalem
Mt. of Olives
Bethany
Jericho
Abila
Bethany beyond Jordan (traditional site)
Esbus (Heshbon)
Azotus (Ashdod)
En-karim
Qumran
Bethlehem
JUDEA
WILDERNESS OF JUDEA
Ascalon
Marisa
Dead Sea (Salt Sea)
Machaerus
Gaza
Hebron
Arnon River
Raphia
Besor Brook
Masada
Beersheba
IDUMEA
NABATEA
0 5 10 Miles
0 5 10 15 Kilometers

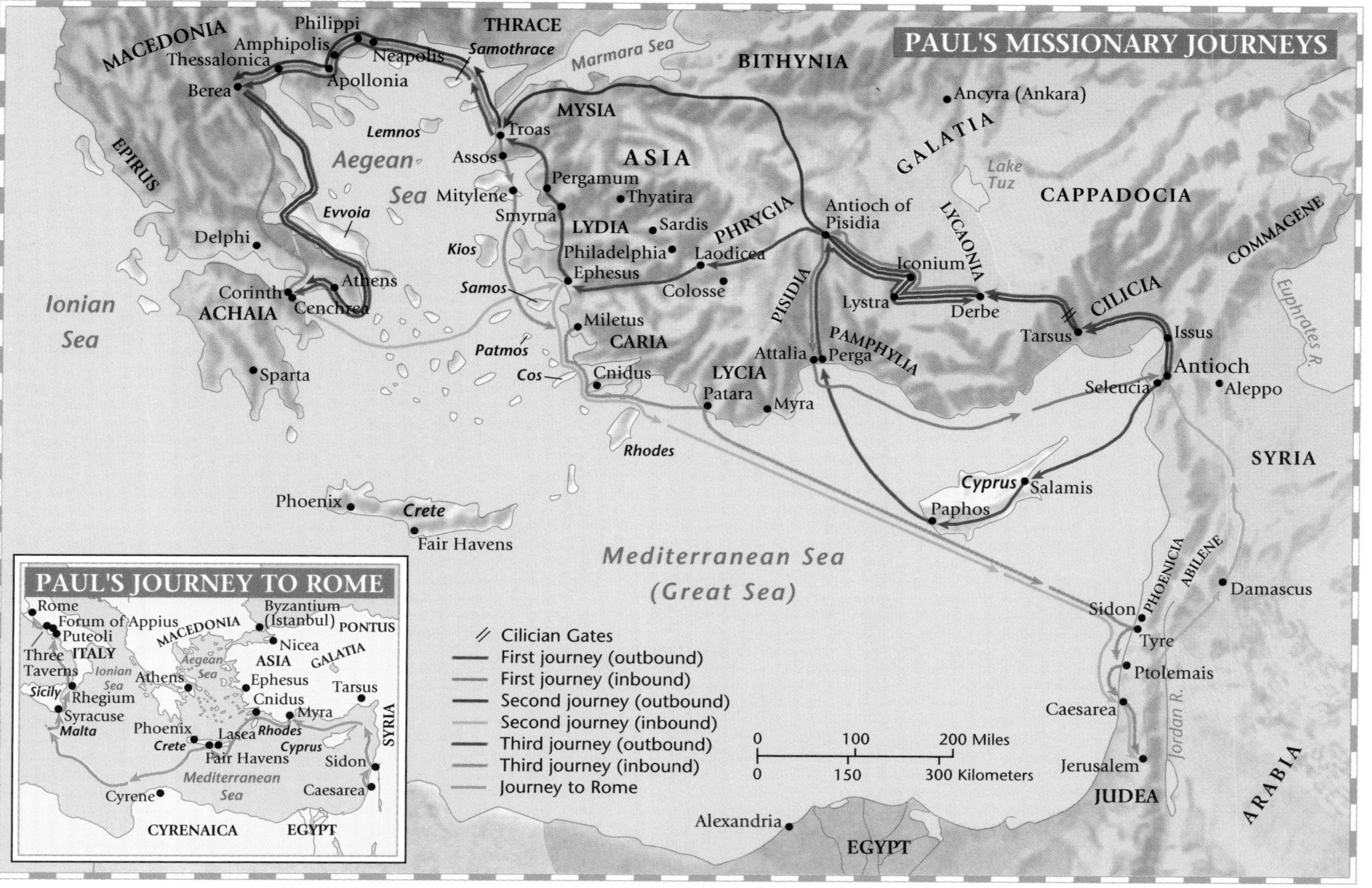
PAUL'S MISSIONARY JOURNEYS
MACEDONIA
THRACE
Samothrace
Marmara Sea
BITHYNIA
Ancyra (Ankara)
Philippi
Amphipolis
Thessalonica
Neapolis
Apollonia
Berea
MYSIA
Troas
Lemnos
EPIRUS
Aegean Sea
Assos
ASIA
GALATIA
Lake Tuz
CAPPADOCIA
Pergamum
Mitylene
Thyatira
Smyrna
LYDIA
Sardis
Evvoia
Delphi
PHRYGIA
Antioch of Pisidia
LYCAONIA
COMMAGENE
Philadelphia
Laodicea
Kios
Ephesus
Iconium
Samos
Colosse
Corinth
Athens
Cenchrea
ACHAIA
Ionian Sea
Lystra
Derbe
PISIDIA
CILICIA
Miletus
CARIA
Euphrates R.
Tarsus
Issus
Patmos
PAMPHYLIA
Attalia
Perga
Sparta
Cos
Cnidus
LYCIA
Antioch
Seleucia
Aleppo
Patara
Myra
Rhodes
SYRIA
Cyprus
Salamis
Phoenix
Crete
Paphos
Fair Havens
Mediterranean Sea
(Great Sea)
PHOENICIA
ABILENE
Damascus
Sidon
Tyre
Ptolemais
Caesarea
Jordan R.
Jerusalem
JUDEA
ARABIA
Alexandria
EGYPT
// Cilician Gates
First journey (outbound)
First journey (inbound)
Second journey (outbound)
Second journey (inbound)
Third journey (outbound)
Third journey (inbound)
Journey to Rome
0 100 200 Miles
0 150 300 Kilometers
PAUL'S JOURNEY TO ROME
Rome
Forum of Appius
Puteoli
Three Taverns
ITALY
Ionian Sea
Sicily
Rhegium
Syracuse
Malta
MACEDONIA
Aegean Sea
Athens
Byzantium (Istanbul)
PONTUS
Nicea
ASIA
GALATIA
Ephesus
Tarsus
Cnidus
Myra
Phoenix
Crete
Lasea
Rhodes
Cyprus
Fair Havens
SYRIA
Sidon
Mediterranean Sea
Caesarea
Cyrene
CYRENAICA
EGYPT

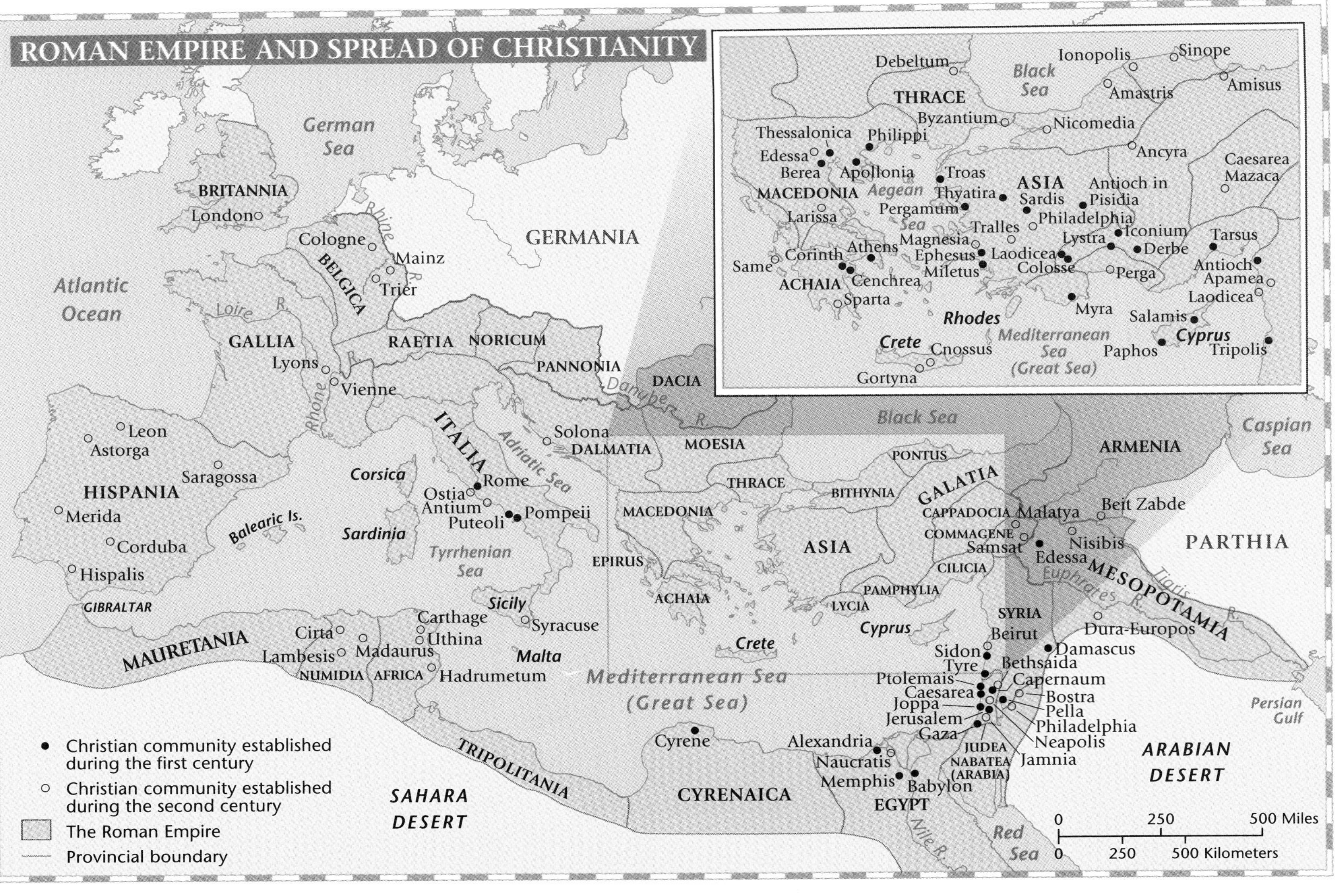

ROMAN EMPIRE AND SPREAD OF CHRISTIANITY
German Sea
BRITANNIA
London
Atlantic Ocean
Loire R.
GALLIA
Lyons
Vienne
Rhone R.
Cologne
BELGICA
Rhine R.
Mainz
Trier
GERMANIA
RAETIA
NORICUM
PANNONIA
Danube R.
DACIA
Leon
Astorga
Saragossa
HISPANIA
Merida
Corduba
Hispalis
GIBRALTAR
Balearic Is.
Corsica
Sardinia
ITALIA
Rome
Ostia
Antium
Puteoli
Pompeii
Adriatic Sea
Tyrrhenian Sea
Solona
DALMATIA
MOESIA
Black Sea
PONTUS
THRACE
BITHYNIA
GALATIA
CAPPADOCIA
Malatya
COMMAGENE
Samsat
Edessa
Nisibis
Beit Zabde
ARMENIA
Caspian Sea
PARTHIA
MACEDONIA
EPIRUS
ACHAIA
ASIA
CILICIA
PAMPHYLIA
LYCIA
Cyprus
Crete
Sicily
Syracuse
Malta
Carthage
Uthina
Hadrumetum
Cirta
Madaurus
Lambesis
NUMIDIA
AFRICA
MAURETANIA
Mediterranean Sea (Great Sea)
Cyrene
TRIPOLITANIA
CYRENAICA
SAHARA DESERT
Alexandria
Naucratis
Memphis
Babylon
EGYPT
Nile R.
Red Sea
SYRIA
Beirut
Sidon
Tyre
Ptolemais
Caesarea
Joppa
Jerusalem
Gaza
JUDEA
NABATEA (ARABIA)
Damascus
Bethsaida
Capernaum
Bostra
Pella
Philadelphia
Neapolis
Jamnia
MESOPOTAMIA
Euphrates R.
Tigris R.
Dura-Europos
Persian Gulf
ARABIAN DESERT
Debeltum
THRACE
Byzantium
Black Sea
Ionopolis
Sinope
Amastris
Amisus
Nicomedia
Ancyra
Caesarea Mazaca
Thessalonica
Philippi
Edessa
Berea
Apollonia
MACEDONIA
Aegean Sea
Larissa
Troas
Thyatira
Pergamum
ASIA
Sardis
Antioch in Pisidia
Philadelphia
Tralles
Magnesia
Ephesus
Miletus
Laodicea
Colosse
Lystra
Iconium
Derbe
Perga
Tarsus
Antioch
Apamea
Laodicea
Same
Corinth
Athens
Cenchrea
ACHAIA
Sparta
Rhodes
Myra
Salamis
Cyprus
Paphos
Tripolis
Crete
Cnossus
Gortyna
Mediterranean Sea (Great Sea)
Christian community established during the first century
Christian community established during the second century
The Roman Empire
Provincial boundary
0 250 500 Miles
0 250 500 Kilometers

TIMELINE OF BIBLICAL EVENTS

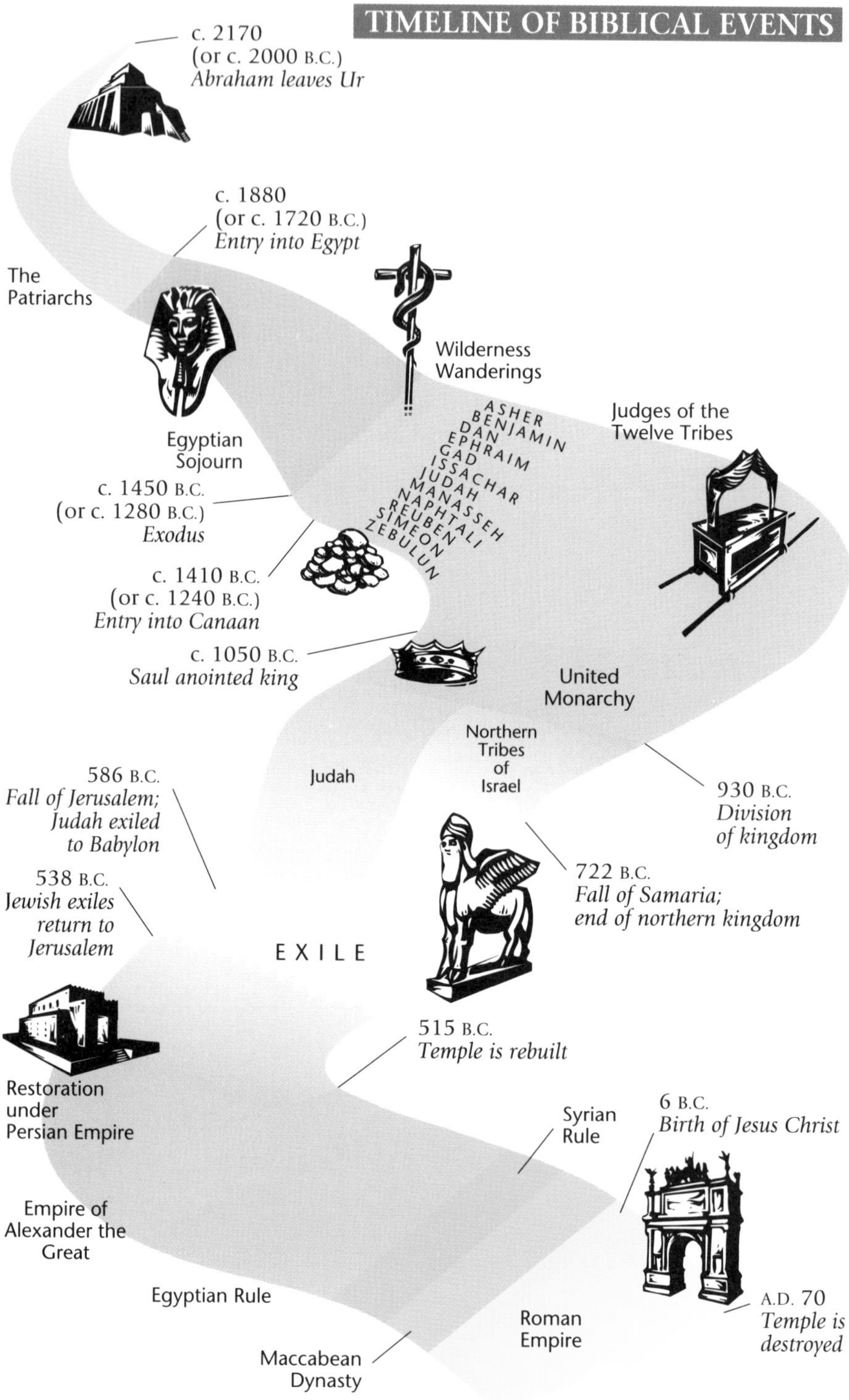

c. 2170
(or c. 2000 B.C.)
Abraham leaves Ur

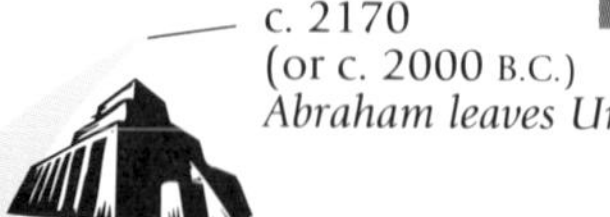

The Patriarchs

c. 1880
(or c. 1720 B.C.)
Entry into Egypt

Egyptian Sojourn

c. 1450 B.C.
(or c. 1280 B.C.)
Exodus

Wilderness Wanderings

c. 1410 B.C.
(or c. 1240 B.C.)
Entry into Canaan

ASHER
BENJAMIN
DAN
EPHRAIM
GAD
ISSACHAR
JUDAH
MANASSEH
NAPHTALI
REUBEN
SIMEON
ZEBULUN

Judges of the Twelve Tribes

c. 1050 B.C.
Saul anointed king

United Monarchy

930 B.C.
Division of kingdom

Judah

Northern Tribes of Israel

722 B.C.
Fall of Samaria; end of northern kingdom

586 B.C.
Fall of Jerusalem; Judah exiled to Babylon

EXILE

538 B.C.
Jewish exiles return to Jerusalem

Restoration under Persian Empire

515 B.C.
Temple is rebuilt

Empire of Alexander the Great

Egyptian Rule

Syrian Rule

Maccabean Dynasty

Roman Empire

6 B.C.
Birth of Jesus Christ

A.D. 70
Temple is destroyed

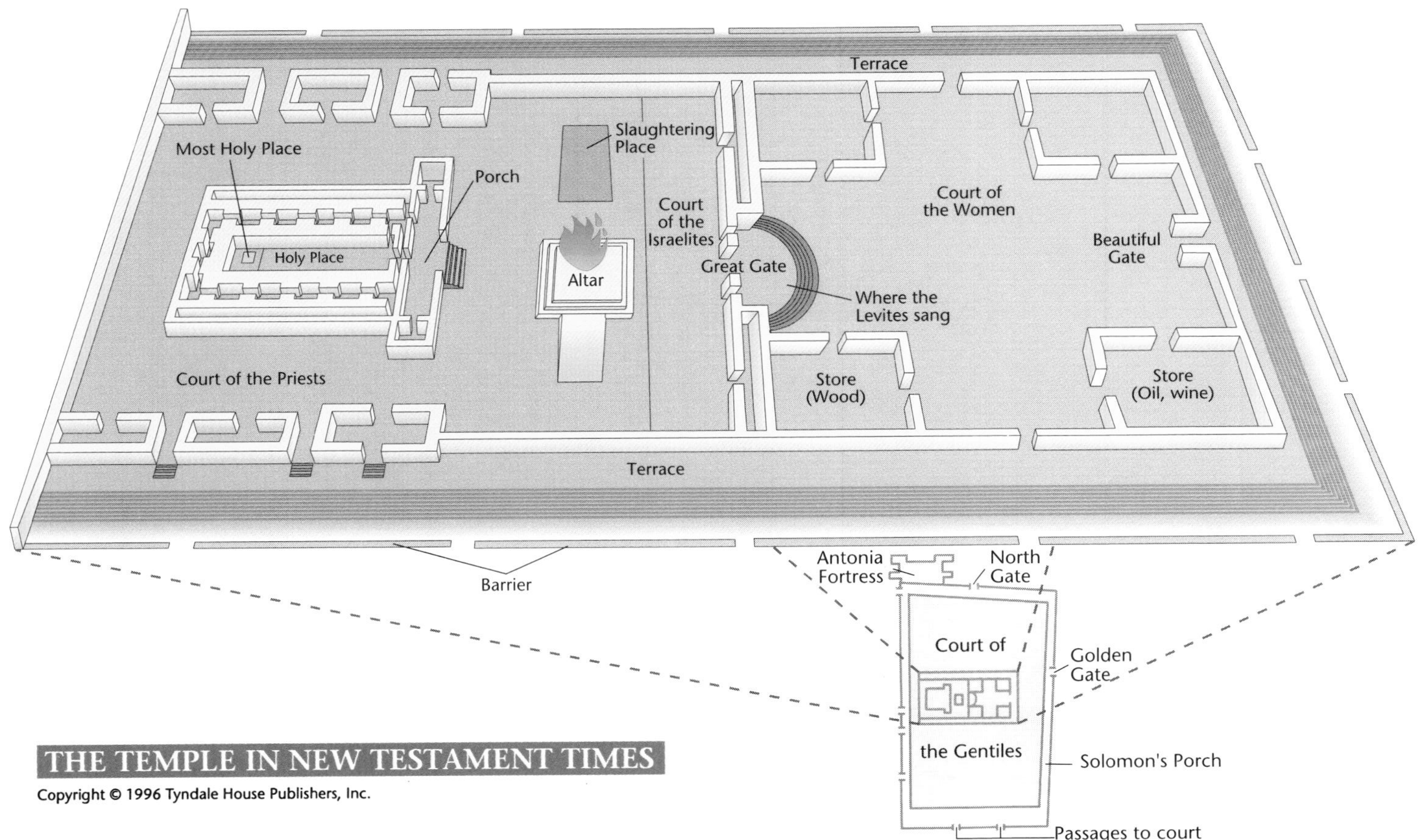

THE TEMPLE IN NEW TESTAMENT TIMES

Note the comparative size of Israel to the state of Florida